
Manufactured in the United States of America

Published by Beckett Media LP, an Apprise Media Company

Beckett Media LP
15850 Dallas Parkway
Dallas, TX 75248
(972) 991-6657
www.beckett.com

Apprise Media LLC
450 Park Avenue
New York, NY 10022
(212) 751-3182
www.apprisemedia.com

First Printing
ISBN 1-930692-38-2

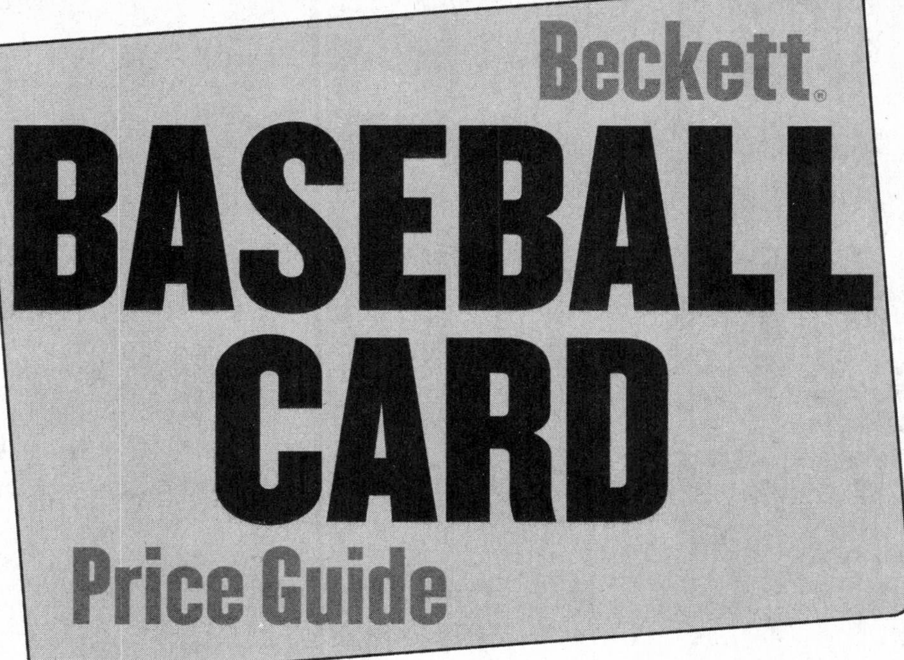

Number 27

Founder & Advisor: Dr. James Beckett III

Edited By
Rich Klein & Grant Sandground
with the staff of
BECKETT BASEBALL

Beckett Media LP - Dallas, Texas

CONTENTS

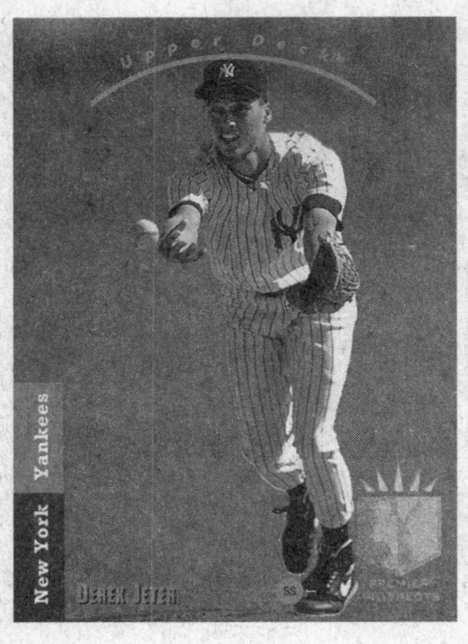
Upper Deck
New York Yankees
Derek Jeter
SS

topps®

topps®

PLAYERS
©MLBPA

THE CYBER SIDE OF THE HOBBY

How the Internet can help your collection

By David Lee and Hugh Murphy

No matter if you just bought your first pack of cards or just sealed the deal on your 100th trade, the Internet has something to offer you and your collection. Every year, more and more collectors are using the vast resources of the Internet to buy, sell, trade or to just get updated on hobby happenings.

The Internet as a whole isn't really a collecting tool as much as it is a collecting toolbox filled with various devices that can be used by any type of hobbyist. Whether you're looking for information, searching for a rare card or wanting to complete that set you've been building for over a year, the Internet can help.

Below are various websites and online tools that are readily available to help you in your collecting endeavors.

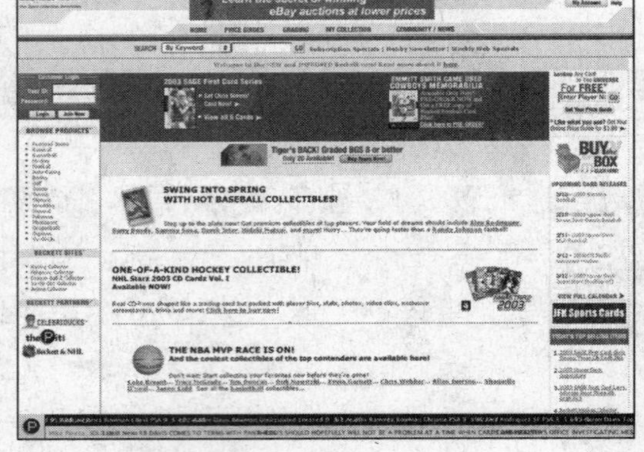

www.beckett.com home page

Your Sports Collectibles Marketplace

The One-Stop Shop

Need a card or collectible?

Pay a visit to Beckett.com - quite simply the largest full service cyber sports collectibles shop in the world.

At Beckett.com, you'll find the industry's largest and most varied inventory of sports collectibles (more than 16.8 million at time of publication) available at fixed prices. Plus, collectors gain instant access to card pricing information, product checklists, the latest hobby news, card grading information and much more.

Convenient and easy to use, Beckett.com is perfectly suited for both novice and veteran collectors. The site offers all of the tools needed to make informed buying decisions along with the assurances of a seamless collectibles purchase.

BUY IT

Manufacturers, distributors and respected dealers from around the country join with Beckett.com to offer single cards, boxes, autographed memorabilia, bobblehead dolls and many more collectibles exclusive to Beckett. Collectors can easily find what they are looking for, searching by sport, team, player or product category.

More importantly, collectors can enjoy the security of buying from someone they know and someone they trust. The Beckett.com name provides that.

Every day, the Beckett.com home page features exclusive

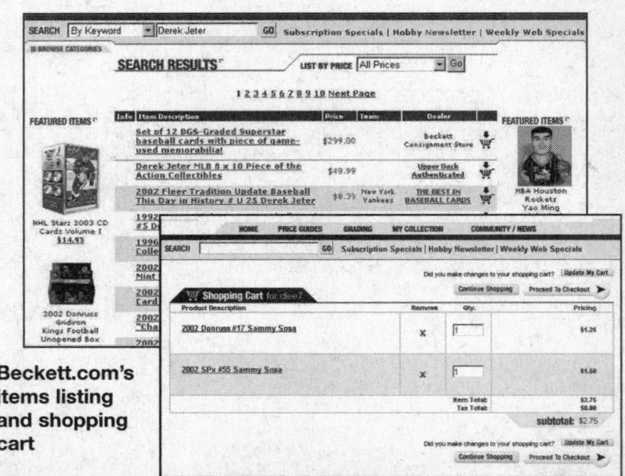

Beckett.com's items listing and shopping cart

products for sale of the hottest players in the hobby. Collectors can find special graded cards with memorabilia swatches, unique graded card packages featuring hot players, as well as limited-edition collectible products.

More than 150 individual dealers offer their inventory of sports collectibles via Beckett.com. Collectors can browse the product inventory of specific dealers and instantly purchase multiple items using the site's easy-to-use and convenient shopping cart checkout method.

Collectors looking for that last card to complete a set are likely to find it on Beckett.com. Check out each dealer's personalized webpage and search for items solely from his or her inventory. With this method, multiple items can be shipped together.

At this writing, more than 10 million baseball collectibles are available for purchase at Beckett.com. Baseball collectors can find cards, photos, autographed memorabilia and more of top players like Barry Bonds (more than 32,000 items), Alex Rodriguez (27,975), Derek Jeter (22,917) and Ichiro Suzuki (10,086).

Beckett products such as annual price guide books, subscriptions and back issues of the monthly and quarterly Beckett Plus magazines are also available on the site.

READ ALL ABOUT IT

Beckett.com is a sports collector's community consisting of nearly 2 million registered members. Becoming a registered member is easy – and, best of all, it's free.

You'll find box breakdowns, new product release information, player hot lists and other updated hobby news.

Each week, the Beckett Hobby Newsletter is sent straight to your e-mailbox. Stay in touch with market happenings and the latest news by subscribing, and take advantage of the many special and exclusive offers that accompany the full-color graphics newsletter.

beckett.com message boards

Beckett.com's Community/News area features more helpful information that every collector can use. A card release calendar lets you know when to expect each product release from major manufacturers.

You can find MLB, NFL, NBA and NHL team addresses and contact information. Card company addresses, phone numbers and links to their websites are also readily available for your reference. Also, a glossary of card collecting hobby terms and answers to frequently asked questions are included.

The Message Boards at Beckett.com allow you to communicate with other collectors. You can talk cards, post your want lists to find other collectors willing to trade with you, or just converse about current hobby happenings.

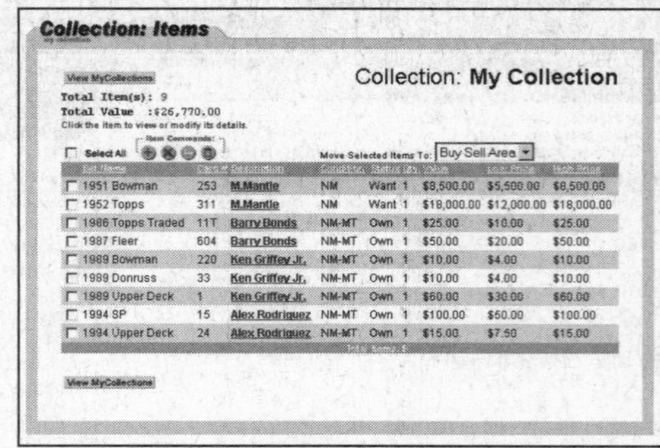

Create your own My Collection online.

ORGANIZE IT

Beckett.com offers the most powerful way for collectors to organize and keep track of their card collections – the free online My Collections card management tool.

With My Collections, collectors get seamless integration with a variety of Beckett.com services. You can:

- Organize your collection with just a few clicks.
- Price your collection with optional integrated Online Price Guide coverage ($3.99 per month).
- Offer your cards for sale directly from your online collections.
- Quickly search out and add cards to your collection that are offered for sale by other collectors.
- Choose to receive instant e-mail notices of cards on your personal want list.
- Account for the cards in your collection from purchase to pricing to selling.

PRICE IT

Beckett.com's Online Price Guides (OPGs) are fully integrated with the My Collections suite of online software. This means you can price, track and manage your collection, and buy and sell with other collectors, all in one place.

The OPGs allow you to search by player, card number and set name and year. Cards pulled in an OPG search can be sorted by year, price or description. This allows you to, for instance, see a certain player's highest or lowest priced cards.

New Release Pricing is included every week, plus seven different prices on every single card listed. Included with a subscription to an OPG is a complete searchable checklist of every card and every set for the particular sport.

A free single card lookup on the Beckett.com home page provides just a taste of what you get with a subscription to an OPG.

As a bonus to Beckett magazine subscribers, new release pricing is made available before it appears in print.

VALUE IT

Beckett and eBay launched the Beckett.com Sports Card Value Guide – a landmark resource for sports card buyers and sellers.

For the first time, the Beckett.com Value Guide has made eBay marketplace data available to the public in one

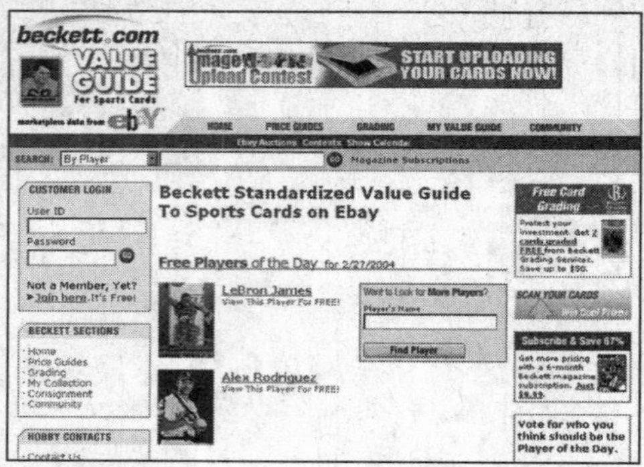

centralized location. Beckett's industry-standard card identification and pricing analysis provides buyers and sellers with an easy-to-use reference. In addition, customers can employ the software to automatically list their cards on eBay directly from the Beckett.com Value Guide.

Customers can access the Beckett.com Value Guide at http://valueguide.beckett.com. With a free daily trial, buyers and sellers can experience the benefits of the Beckett.com Value Guide with a featured player and card set of the day. For a minimal fee, customers can find current and historical sports card pricing, accurate card descriptions and cumulative auction results for every card actively traded on eBay.

GRADE IT

Beckett Grading Services (BGS) is the leading innovator in third-party sports card grading. That fact is especially evident when it comes to the hobby's first, completely online-based grading technology and services.

In addition to BGS, Beckett Vintage Grading (BVG) is available for pre-1981 cards, which takes into the consideration the technology of the time before a final grade is made.

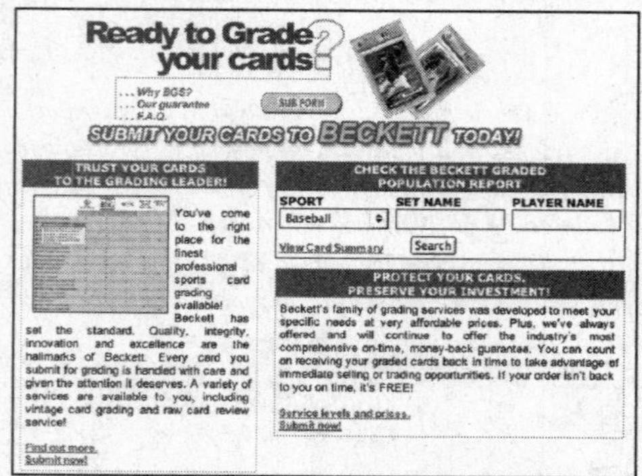

Yet another grading service Beckett provides is Beckett Collectors Club Grading (BCCG). BCCG is a high-volume grading service intended to provide collectors with an attractive and affordable alternative to other graded card products. A simplified 10-point grading scale is used.

At Beckett.com, collectors can find loads of information and the services provided for BGS, BVG and BCCG. Find out how to submit cards and what to expect when you get your cards graded.

Beckett.com's online offerings include:

- Electronic Submissions – Submit your card list electronically and print out a packing list to send along with your cards.
- Grading Standards – Learn about the grading scale and what parts of the card are graded to make up the card's "subgrades."
- Order Status Check – Know where your card is in the grading process via our online Order Status Check.
- E-mail Notification – You get an e-mail notification when your order is received and when it's on its way back to you. This includes links for tracking your card shipment and for accessing information about your card grades.
- Graded Card Lookup – Grade breakdowns, searches by set and by player name are available. This can be helpful when you are looking to buy a certain card graded by BGS. Type in the serial number of the graded card in question to see if BGS graded it.
- Online Population Report – Find out how many of a particular card have been graded by BGS and what grades were attained. Easily searchable.
- Show Listings – Find a listing of all sports card shows around the country at which BGS appears for on-site grading.

AUTHENTICATE IT

The most trusted name in the sports collectibles hobby is now the most trusted name in memorabilia authentication. Beckett Authentic is an autograph and merchandise verification service. The Beckett seal certifies authenticity to avoid questions of counterfeits and questionable autograph practices.

Beckett Authentic began by authenticating collectibles of NBA rookie sensation Carmelo Anthony. Such items as game-worn Denver Nuggets road and home jerseys, shoes, headbands and a wide range of other memorabilia are available at Beckett.com.

In addition to authenticating Carmelo Anthony memorabilia, Beckett Authentic partnered with Ole Miss star quarterback Eli Manning, a top pick in the 2004 NFL Draft. Limited-edition signed items like mini-helmets, photos and NFL footballs can be purchased at Beckett.com.

Card Company Websites

All of the major card companies have websites. Donruss/Playoff, Fleer, Topps and Upper Deck all offer information such as product previews, checklists, special products and background information on their companies. Each site is a little different from the other as each card company offers various products and services.

DONRUSS/PLAYOFF

The important thing to remember about Donruss/Playoff is that the company produces Playoff, Donruss and Score products. So, each "division" has its own web address.

All three sites feature a lot of product preview information. With most sets, collectors can view a mock-up of certain base cards and scheduled inserts. If available, insertion rates will be given for certain cards.

- The sites also have many checklists available for current

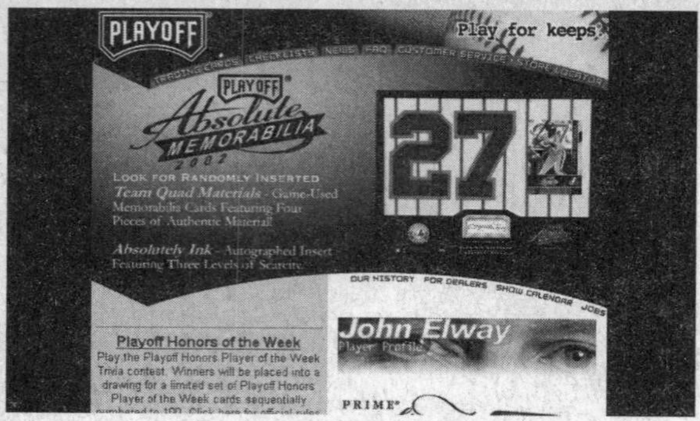

Address: www.playoffinc.com, www.donruss.com, www.scoreonline.net

and past products. Checking these out can answer a lot of questions you may have on the number of cards in a particular set or, for instance, the number of rookies.

- As most sites do, Donruss/Playoff has a Frequently Asked Questions (FAQ) section along with links to contact the company.

FLEER

In addition to previews of upcoming products and card release calendars, the Fleer Collectibles section offers products such as licensed collectible trucks, planes and other unique items. These products can be purchased at the Fleer Store at www.fleercollectiblesstore.com.

- Fleer's Bullpen offers a free membership that gives collectors access to online forums where they can discuss topics on various sports and entertainment cards. There is a "Collector Stories" section in which members can write about their lucky pulls or great boxes. Members also get access to updated news and announcements. There is also a Fleer card search where members can search by player and pull up virtually any Fleer card a particular player ever appeared on.

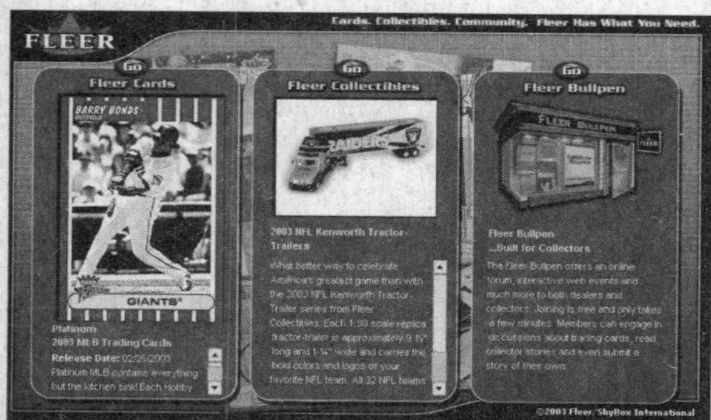

Address: www.fleer.com

TOPPS

Topps produces many other non-sports card products but the Sports Collectibles section on their home page is not hard to find. In that section, when a particular sport is chosen, a list of Topps brands will appear such as Bowman, Topps Gallery and Stadium Club. Selecting a brand will bring up the latest information on each sport with that particular brand.

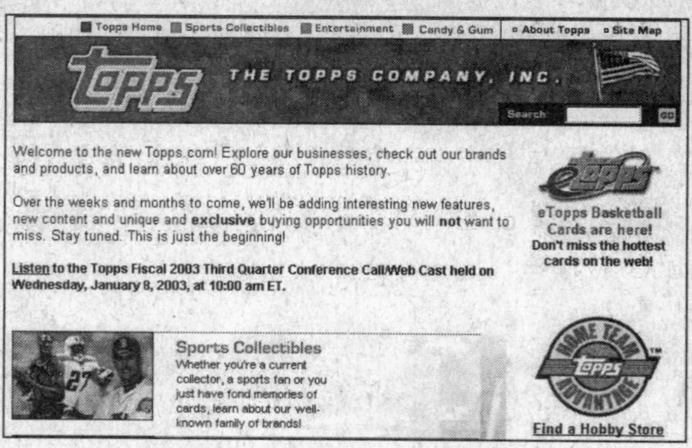

Address: www.topps.com

- Perhaps the most unique feature of topps.com is the Topps Vault (also accessible at www.thetoppsvault.com). This section offers unique items such as original concept art for cards and uncut proof sheets. Currently, all the items are sold on eBay. The original paintings for the Topps Gallery cards have been sold via the Topps Vault.

UPPER DECK

In addition to detailed product information, Upper Deck offers a slew of products through Upper Deck Authenticated. These can be purchased at the Upper Deck Store at www.upperdeckstore.com. Perhaps you have seen advertisement cards in packs that feature discounts at the Upper Deck Store. Items for purchase include autographed photos, baseballs, jerseys and even bobblehead dolls.

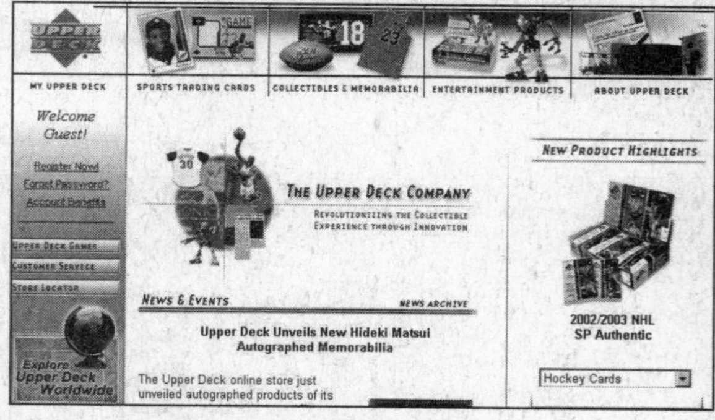

Address: www.upperdeck.com

- With Upper Deck's e/card inserts, collectors who have pulled the inserts can go to the site and see if their card evolves into an upgrade card, such as an autographed or game-used memorabilia card. Once the card's information is entered, it remains part of a collector's digital portfolio and could evolve at a later time.
- Upper Deck's online redemption program is also available on the site. The key to the program is a hidden serial number on the redemption card that customers enter in to redeem their cards.

Online Auctions

Online auctions can offer a tremendous amount of quality collectibles that your local hobby shop may not have. Auctions allow collectors to pre-buy boxes from

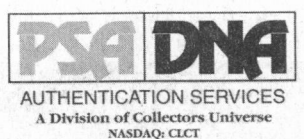

dealers across the country. This can help those collectors looking to snag a few boxes before a possible rise in price. Likewise, dealers can lock up sales before their orders arrive.

The important thing to remember when buying items via online auctions is to know what you're buying and whom you are buying from. In other words, be careful and do your homework before you buy. If you do that, you should be fine and you'll add a very handy tool to your collecting methods. Below you will find information on three of the top auction sites on the Web.

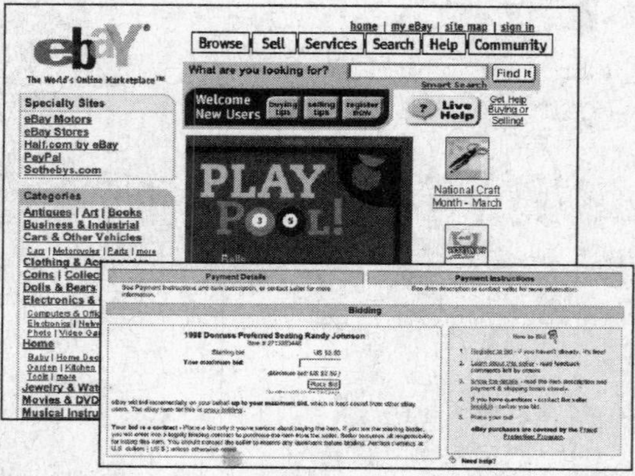

WWW.EBAY.COM

Even if you have never bought a single card via the Internet, you've no doubt heard of eBay. This auction site has an enormous selection of just about any type sports collectible you can think of. Items include rare cards, memorabilia and autographs as well as tons of current product releases.

BUYING ON EBAY

Anyone can buy or sell on eBay – anyone at least 18 years old with an e-mail address, that is. All you need to do is register (it's free) and get your eBay user ID. Sellers consist of collectors and dealers from around the world. Some dealers run part of their businesses on eBay, using it to reach customers from across the globe.

Being an online auction, the buyer decides most of the prices (some items have a set price). The best way to explain how an auction works is to take a walk through one. So, lets go buy a hypothetical Randy Johnson card.

Step 1: Once we are on eBay, we can search for "Randy Johnson" from the home page. There are more detailed ways to perform searches on the site but we will stick with the simple basics here. Our search pulls up pages of items with "Randy Johnson" in the listings.

Step 2: We scroll through the listings and find a card we like. We see that the "current price" is $5, there have been three bids on the card and the auction closes in two days and three hours. What does this mean? This is where we decide how much we are willing to pay for the card. Let's say we want to pay no more than $15. So, we will enter in a maximum bid of $15. Now, that does not mean that we will pay that much after the auction ends.

Step 3: We really don't have to do anything in this step because the site runs the auction automatically and the price increases in increments. If someone else bids on the Randy Johnson card we are bidding on and his or her bid is lower than ours, we will still be the high bidders. For example, if Joe Shmoe bids $12 on the same card we are bidding on (remember, our maximum bid is $15 and the maximum bids are not viewable) we would still be the high bidders. The current price would most likely be $12.50, given a 50-cent increment increase. Still, all we have to do is sit back and wait for the auction to end. We do not have to bid again. This type of bidding is called "proxy bidding."

Step 4: If we are still the high bidders after the auction closes we can purchase the card from the seller for the closing price. Let's say the seller contacts us, giving us the final price including the shipping cost. We now pay the seller (this can be done via many methods). Once the seller receives the payment, he or she sends the item to us. We now have our Randy Johnson card to add to our collection.

This may raise the question of dependability. Most online auctions and stores now utilize some sort of feedback rating. Every person buying or selling on eBay has a feedback rating which is the sum of all positive, negative and neutral comments. These are left by eBayers who complete transactions with each other.

Feedback plays a big role in online collecting, especially for new collectors just starting to use an online auction as a collecting tool. It gives collectors a sense of comfort knowing that they've purchased an item from a reputable and experienced seller.

SELLING ON EBAY

EBay is a great way to reach both dealers and collectors who might be looking to buy some of the collectibles you want to sell.

Listing items for sale is quite simple once you know the details and descriptions you want to include when listing the items. There are a variety of options sellers can chose but the main steps include typing in an item name and description (more details and tips on this later), selecting the proper category, setting the starting price and setting the duration of the auction. After this is done and your item is up for sale, the bidding begins. All you have to do is wait until the auction ends and contact the high bidder to request payment.

WWW.MASTRONET.COM

MastroNet is among the most well-known, high-ticket auction houses on the Internet. The site handles auctions for organizations, dealers and individuals. Items such as complete vintage card sets, autographed vintage baseballs and occasional game-used equipment can be found on

Other online auctions to visit

www.auctions.yahoo.com
www.americanmemorabilia.com
www.ccsauction.com
www.sportsauction.com

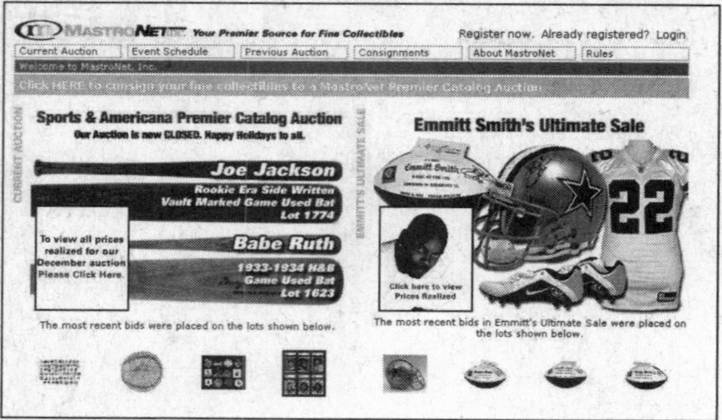

MastroNet. Most of the items are available for bidding for about one month and all include detailed descriptions.

If you're looking for rare collectibles and don't mind paying top dollar for them, give this site a look.

WWW.LELANDS.COM

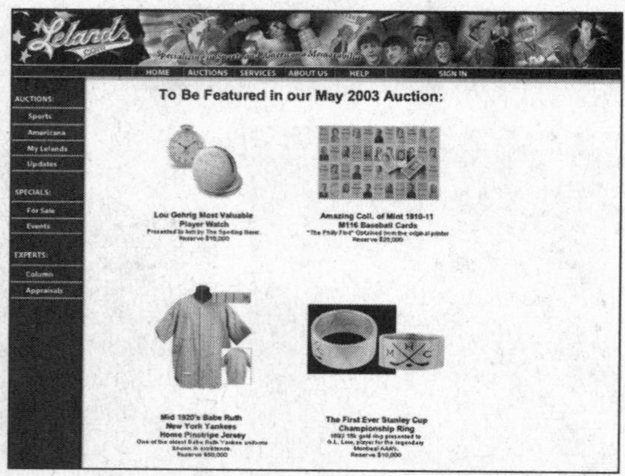

Lelands specializes in vintage sports and Americana memorabilia. The site has sold over $25 million of collectibles in its existence and has occasionally held auctions for various charitably organizations. There are numerous sports categories to choose from. Some items are categorized by player name, sport, team name or the type of collectible.

As far as sports collectibles go, Lelands is a cross between eBay and MastroNet. Collectors will find vintage cards (many of them being graded cards), autographed memorabilia and novelty sports items.

Some of the highlights of Lelands include game-worn and game-used equipment from athletes of many sports.

Online Tips

It always helps to know the tips and tricks of navigating online stores and auctions. Knowing how and where to use them can lead you to some great buys or help find that obscure card you've been looking for. Here are a few easy hints to get you started.

SEARCH TRICKS

When selling cards in online auctions, most sellers include the year of the card in the listings. Some will put, for example "2003" and some will put "03" or perhaps both. In order to maximize your search, you'll want to pull up all variations. Let's say you're searching for 2003 Roger Clemens cards. Go to the online site and in the search box, type the following: (2003, 03) Roger Clemens. This will pull up all listings with combinations of 2003 and/or 03 and Roger Clemens. This also works when different sellers use various types of listings for the same item. For example, some sellers may use the words "Upper Deck" and others may use the "UD" abbreviation. Just separate the two variations, whatever they may be, with a comma, one space after the comma and enclose them in parentheses.

Basic Search: roger clemens auto* | In titles & descriptions | Search | Refine Search

Matching Categories: Items matching your search were found in: Sports (66) – Autographs (44), Trading Cards (19), Memorabilia (2); Movies & Television (3) – Memorabilia (3); Sothebys.com (1) – Collectibles & Memorabilia (1)

Display: Gifts view, Completed items, Gallery view, Items near me, PayPal items

All Categories — Save this search

68 items found for roger clemens auto*

Sort by items: ending first | newly listed | lowest priced | highest priced

Picture	Item Title	Price	Bids	Time Left
	Blue Jays Roger Clemens Autographed Card	$4.99	-	29m
	Yankees Roger Clemens Autographed Card	$11.75	5	42m
	Roger Clemens Autographed Red Sox Yearbook	$41.00	12	2h 11m
	ROGER CLEMENS SIGNED AUTO 8X10 PIC SIGNING	$34.99 $39.99 Buy It Now	-	4h 48m
	ROGER CLEMENS AUTOGRAPHED 8X10 PHOTO W/COA	$21.95 $27.00 Buy It Now	-	7h 19m
	02 HERITAGE ROGER CLEMENS AUTO *SP* BV 150	$44.00	3	8h 41m
	Roger Clemens Auto 2001 All-Star Baseball	$149.99	7	8h 43m

This eBay search for Roger Clemens autographed (Roger Clemens auto*) items brought up listings that included the words "autograph" "autographed" and "auto."

Another secret is the asterisk (*) tip. The perfect use for this is when you're searching for autographed cards. Many sellers either will list these cards as one or a combination of the following: "autograph" "autographed" "auto" or "autos." Again, in order to maximize your search, you want to pull up all of these variations. So, the trick to this is to type in "auto" with an asterisk directly at the end: auto*. This will pull up all listings with words that have an "auto" prefix. This means that any listing that contains a word beginning with "auto" will be pulled up in your search. Try it out and see what you find.

IMAGING

When selling items via the Internet, using images is always a plus. As they say, image is everything. Many collectors are concerned with a card's condition, especially if it's an older card. Good images of the front and back of a card can better show the condition of the surface, corners, edges and potential buyers can get a better view of the card's centering.

Scanners are good for capturing flat images such as cards or photos, and digital cameras are good for three-dimensional items such as autographed balls. Most auction sites have picture services in which images can be uploaded. Naturally, it's always a plus for a potential buyer to actually see the item.

SORT IT OUT

Many times collectors know exactly what they're looking for and have no trouble finding multiple listings for the same item. Some auction sites and online stores allow you to sort by price, item name (or title) and, if it's an online auction, the ending date. This can help in many ways.

Sorting by price allows you to separate the items you can afford and the ones you can't. It helps to have all of the items together that are in your price range.

If you are looking for a particular item in an online auction that is ending soon, sort the items by ending date. This will group those items ending soon and those that have been newly listed.

COLLECTING 101

New to collecting? These fundamentals will help you better understand the hobby.

Getting Started

There are so many sets out there. What should I buy?

There's no single right answer to that question – the response varies from person to person. What we can suggest is that you build a collection that makes you happy. Maybe it's complete sets, Rookie Cards, your favorite team or star, etc. Whatever it is, base your purchases on what you'd like to own, not on what its value might be potentially. If you're looking for an investment vehicle, you face the chance of disappointment, but if you're buying something you like, price fluctuations just won't matter.

What year is my card?

The easiest way to determine the year of your card is to look at the statistics on the back. The year of issue typically is the one following the last season for which stats are listed. For example, if you have a Barry Bonds card that has stats up to 1997, your card almost certainly was issued in 1998. If that card doesn't have any stats on the card back, things can get a bit trickier. Many cards carry a copyright date on them, but this can be confusing. Many cards will carry a copyright date from the year before they are issued, depending on when the bulk of the design work was done for the card.

'92	Pirates	140	473	109	147	34	103	39	.456	.624	.311
'93	Giants	159	539	129	181	46	123	29	.458	.677	.336
'94	Giants	112	391	89	122	37	81	29	.426	.647	.312
'95	Giants	144	506	109	149	33	104	31	.431	.577	.294
'96	Giants	158	517	122	159	42	129	40	.461	.615	.308
'97	Giants	159	532	123	155	40	101	37	.446	.585	.291
Career Totals		1742	6069	1244	1750	374	1094	417	.408	.551	.288

DONRUSS

MAJOR LEAGUE BASEBALL TRADEMARKS AND COPYRIGHTS ARE USED WITH PERMISSION OF MAJOR LEAGUE BASEBALL PROPERTIES, INC. OFFICIAL LICENSEE OF MLBPA. ©1998 DONRUSS TRADING CARD CO. PRODUCT OF USA

The back of this 1998 Barry Bonds Donruss Elite card includes stats up to 1997. This indicates that the card is a 1998 issue, as does the copyright date at the bottom of the card back.

What condition is my card?

Without seeing the actual card, no one can determine its condition. The condition is derived from a set of guidelines that has evolved over the years using terminology often borrowed from other established hobbies. Along with the player featured and the set's scarcity, condition is one of the top three factors that determine a card's value.

What's a Rookie Card?

A Rookie Card is a player's first appearance on a regular issue card from one of the major card companies. Some of these companies are Donruss/Playoff, Fleer, Pacific, Topps and Upper Deck. In many cases, a player appears on a card before he ever plays in the major leagues. You will often see Rookie Card abbreviated in the Price Guide or the magazine as RC.

Why are Rookie Cards such a big deal?

Many hobbyists are interested in collecting a Rookie Card simply because it's a player's first mainstream card. This additional demand makes them more valuable than, say, a third-year card.

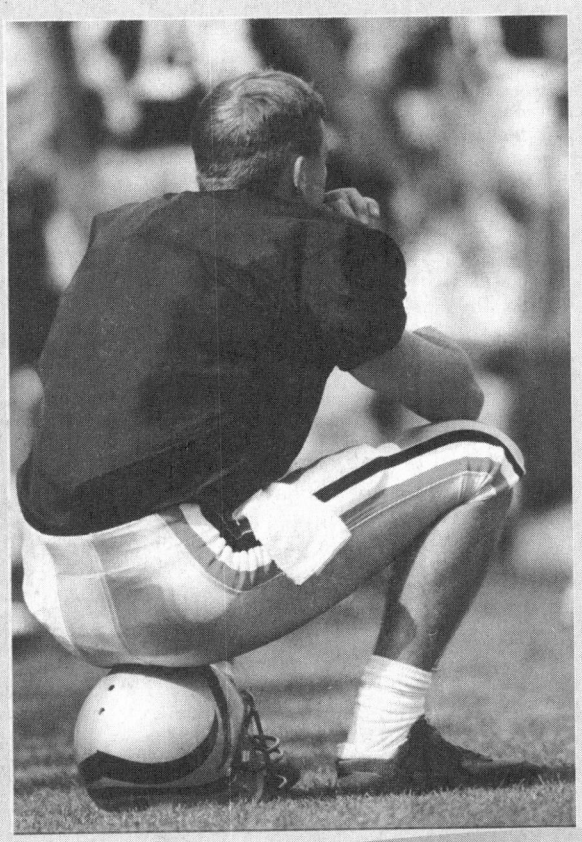

So what's an XRC?

That term was created to recognize an early card from a player that appeared in a non-traditional set. Some card sets are issued in an uncommon way - for example, through the mail only - while others might be printed through a limited license. For a card to be a true RC, it must be issued in a fully-licensed mainstream set.

What Does SP mean?

SP is an abbreviation for Short Print. That means that the card company intentionally chose to print fewer copies of a given card than others in the set. This is done to create additional demand for these singles, and to add a challenge to building a particular set.

I've found errors, such as misspellings, incorrect birth dates and erroneous statistics, on some of my cards. Are they rare? Are they more valuable?

Ninety-nine times out of 100, the answer to that question is NO. The only time an error adds value to a card is if the company stops the presses and creates a corrected version of the card. Because of the expense, that almost never happens anymore, thereby ensuring that error cards rarely have additional value. However, this has happened and some collectors have put a premium on certain error cards throughout the years. Throughout the Price Guide you will run across the abbreviations for error cards (ERR), corrected cards (COR), which are versions of error cards that were fixed by the manufacturer, and uncorrected error cards (UER), which are error cards not corrected by the manufacturer.

This 1986 Barry Bonds Topps Traded XRC #11T is one of the best know XRCs in the hobby.

The 1990 Frank Thomas Topps RC #414A (left) is one of the better-known error cards, missing Thomas' name on the front. The corrected version (right) does include his name and is listed as card #414B.

Using the Price Guide

How do I find my card in the Price Guide?

It may seem hard at first, but it's quite easy. This annual publication lists the sets alphabetically, then the years for the sets in chronological order. Main sets are listed first, followed by any inserts that were included in that product. So, grab a card that you want to look up, find the set name in the Price Guide, locate the year of your card, and then find your card's number in the price listing.

How do I use multipliers?

For parallel sets, there are, for example, multipliers for stars, young stars and rookies. The stars multiplier is used for established professional players with a consistent hobby presence. The young stars multiplier is used for a small group of elite prospects in their second or third year of trading cards. The rookie multiplier is used for parallels of Rookie Cards.

Once you've figured out the correct multiplier to use, locate the value of the player's card within the basic issue set listing (that's easy to do because parallel cards share the same card number as basic issue cards). If the multiplier provided is 8X to 20X BASIC CARDS and the basic card you've located is listed at $1 in the MINT column, your parallel card is valued at $8-$20. Keep in mind that multipliers are to be used only with the MINT column price of the accompanying basic issue card.

2000 Fleer Glossy

The 2000 Fleer Glossy set was released in early December, 2000 and features a 500-card base set. Please note that you only receive 455 of the 500 total cards that make up this set per sealed factory set. Card 451-500 are short-printed and are inserted into sets at five per factory sealed set. Cards 451-500 are serial numbered to 1000.

	MINT	NRMT
COMPLETE SET (500)	900.00	400.00
COMP.FACT.SET (455)	80.00	36.00
COMMON CARD (1-450)	.30	.14
*STARS 1-450: .75X TO 2X BASIC		
*YNG.STARS 1-450: .75X TO 2X BASIC		
*ROOKIES 1-450: .75X TO 2X BASIC		
COMMON (451-500)	10.00	4.50
451 Carlos Casimiro RC	10.00	4.50
452 Adam Melhuse RC	10.00	4.50
453 Adam Bernero RC	10.00	4.50
454 Dusty Allen RC	10.00	4.50
455 Chan Perry RC	10.00	4.50
456 Damian Rolls RC	10.00	4.50
457 Josh Phelps RC	25.00	11.00
458 Barry Zito	40.00	18.00
459 Hector Ortiz RC	10.00	4.50
460 Juan Pierre RC	25.00	11.00
461 Jose Ortiz RC	60.00	27.00
462 Chad Zerbe RC	10.00	4.50
463 Julio Zuleta RC	10.00	4.50
464 Eric Byrnes	10.00	4.50
465 Wilf. Rodriguez RC	10.00	4.50
466 Wascar Serrano RC	12.00	5.50
467 Aaron McNeal RC	10.00	4.50
468 Paul Rigdon RC	10.00	4.50
469 John Snyder RC	10.00	4.50
470 J.C. Romero RC	10.00	4.50
471 Talmadge Nunnari RC	10.00	4.50

Where do you get your prices?

The prices reflected in Beckett Price Guides are derived from reported secondary market sales and common asking prices of cards. We take many segments of the market into account, such as retail card shop prices, card shows, print ads,

mail-order catalogs and online auctions. These prices reflect national trends, but variations in demand may make certain cards more or less affordable in your hometown.

Inserts, Parallels and Graded Cards

What's an insert card?

This term applies to any card that comes in a pack that is not part of the main set. Traditionally, insert cards are printed in shorter quantities than regular cards, and therefore tend to sell for higher prices.

What's a parallel?

A parallel is a special insert card that features the same photo and design elements as a regular card, but adds additional distinguishing such features as background color, die-cutting, foil elements or serial numbering. Parallels typically are scarcer than regular cards, and therefore are more expensive. To determine the value of a parallel card, look for the multipliers that are listed under the title of the appropriate set.

The basic 1998 Jeff Bagwell Leaf #149 (left) was traditionally cut while the Fractal Diamond Axis parallel features a die-cut design.

What's the difference between Tiffany cards/glossy cards and regular cards?

Topps Tiffany or Fleer Glossy are examples of upgraded parallels to base issue sets that are issued directly to the hobby. They typically were released in factory set form, not in packs, with each card featuring a high gloss or heavy UV glossy coating on the card's front surface. Since these sets are considered parallels to the base sets, they usually don't have cards marked as RCs. However, these rookie players quite often sell at premium prices over their base set counterparts due to the smaller print run associated with Tiffany or Glossy sets.

What is a premium swatch?

First of all, swatch is the term used to describe the piece of jersey, bat, base, etc. that is applied to a memorabilia card. A piece is considered to be a premium swatch when it possesses a unique quality, such as two or more colors, seams, stitches and so on. As most swatches tend to be one color, the premium swatches are more in demand, and thus often command premiums. Cards intended to display premium swatches do NOT earn a premium over the listed price.

This 2002 Upper Deck Ultimate Collection Patch Card Double features two premium swatches. Notice the stitching from the patches.

What does Graded Card mean? Why are Graded Cards more expensive than regular cards?

The term applies to a card that has been submitted to an independent service for certification of condition and preservation within a sealed holder. Professional grading services are growing in popularity because a card's grade is a huge factor in its secondary market value. Although not all Graded Cards earn a premium on the secondary market, those rare cards that receive high grades often do sell for prices significantly above book values for raw, or ungraded, cards. That's because cards in Gem Mint or Pristine condition are quite scarce, and therefore, quite desirable. The demand for these cards exceeds the supply, which leads to higher prices. For more information on grading go to www.beckett.com/grading.

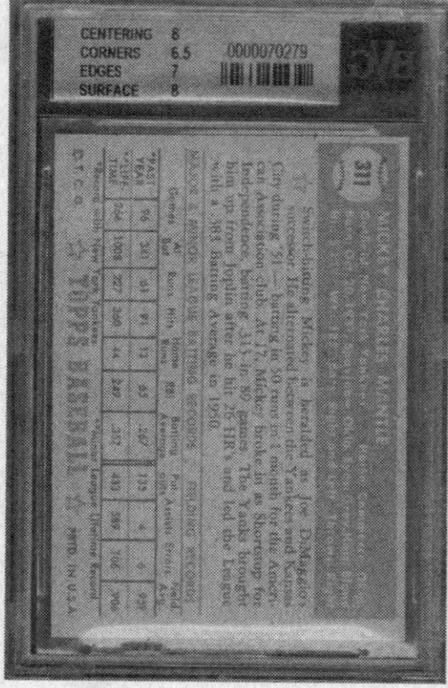

A 1952 Topps Mickey Mantle graded a Near Mint 7 by Beckett Vintage Grading. The back of the grading slab (right) shows the individual grades for the four grading categories: Centering, Corners, Edges and Surface.

Kevin Savage Cards Is Buying!!!

Kevin Savage Cards needs your card collection. As our business continues to grow, we need to buy more cards, memorabilia, autographs, large collections, hoards, accumulations, old sports magazines, game used equipment, and card shop closeouts.

We will travel to purchase significant collections!

When it is time to raise some cash - Give us a call on our toll free line at (866)861-2330. Ask for Kevin Savage or Pat Blandford. You will be treated with respect and confidentiality. We have been in the sportscard business for over 20 years - and our staff has over 90 years of collective industry experience. No collection is too large - so when it is time to sell - please give us a call!

Remember to make the call
Toll Free (866) 861-2330
Ph: (419) 861-2330
Fax: (419) 865-8685

email: ksavagecards@mindspring.com
Visit us and check out our current auctions at

www.KevinSavageCards.com

Kevin Savage Cards

3509 Briarfield Blvd., Maumee, Ohio 43537

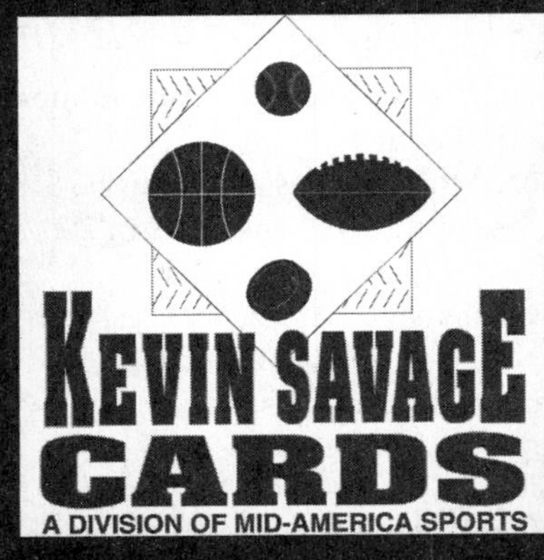

ebay ID: ksavagecards

COUNTERFEITS

Buyer Beware: What You Need to Know About Counterfeit Cards

Most anything of value has been counterfeited at some point. The sports card marketplace is no exception. To the untrained eye, a solid fake can be deceptive enough to change hands multiple times before anyone notices.

In particular, as online purchases have overwhelmingly become the largest source of transactions, it is even easier to be taken in by a counterfeit. More and more cards are bought sight unseen (often online), with blurry or miniscule scans, or even with switched scans (when legitimate cards are pictured but the actual cards received are fakes). This only increases the odds that any given collector may become a victim.

Usually, matching the card up against a known legitimate card will clearly identify the imposter, but how many collectors carry around a stack of samples? If another sample is unavailable, a common card from the same set will often be just as helpful.

If you receive a card and have doubts as to its legitimacy, it is best to take the cards to other reputable dealers or collectors to garner their opinions. If you are still not satisfied, or prefer a more definitive answer right away, send the card to a professional grading service. If the card is returned ungraded, be sure to save any paperwork you receive and keep the card in the original holder it was returned in, in case you choose to pursue legal action.

While it can be difficult to retrieve your money from the seller, it is not impossible. If the seller was an innocent victim as well, he or she may be more willing to work with you. If the seller is the counterfeiter, or working in conjunction with them, you may be out of luck. Pursue the matter with the site the purchase was made on, and consider filing fraud charges with appropriate agencies. In some instances, the card manufacturers themselves have stepped in to pursue those counterfeiting their cards.

– Mark Anderson

Feds Crack Down on Counterfeit Ring

So, just how big of a problem has counterfeiting become over the past few years? Big enough for a major FBI operation.

In February of 2002, the FBI, in affiliation with the U.S. Attorney's Office in San Diego, Calif., announced some eye-opening news in conjunction with Operation Bullpen, their investigation of fraudulent sports memorabilia that's still functioning today.

The case, which previously had dealt mainly with forged autographs, discovered a new twist: counterfeit Rookie Cards.

For two years, a ring had been producing thousands of counterfeits of Mark McGwire, Tony Gwynn, Dan Marino and John Elway, the authorities reported. According to Gregory Vega, U.S. Attorney for the Southern District of California, the fakes were made at a printing company in the Los Angeles suburb of Gardena in a highly sophisticated operation.

"It is virtually impossible to distinguish the counterfeit trading cards from legitimate trading cards," Vega stated.

Six people pleaded guilty to various federal charges in connection with the counterfeit ring, including Vincent Ferrucio, owner of the printing business.

Authorities said that the cards were sold at sports card shows in San Francisco and Miami, and that fake Rookie Cards of Sammy Sosa were printed but did not reach the market.

Federal agents seized a total of about 50,000 cards. They estimate that 10,000 to 50,000 were sold at the two shows, and possibly other shows as well, and some of the cards are now circulating within the hobby. At card shows, the fake cards sold for about $100 each and were then resold for several hundred dollars, according to the FBI.

Ironically, agents could only tell the difference between the fakes and originals due to the higher quality of the counterfeits, which can sell for $1,000 or more. The counterfeits are of slightly higher quality because of better printing technology now available.

Federal authorities began investigating the counterfeit trading cards as part of Operation Bullpen, a sweeping, nationwide probe of fake autographs and memorabilia that has resulted in over 30 convictions and the seizure of more than $11 million in cash and property.

Topps, which produced the originals of all but the Sosa card, assisted federal agents in the San Diego case in 2002 to detect the fake cards.

"This case does serve to remind consumers to deal with reputable dealers and remember the old saying that if something appears too good to be true, it usually is," says William O'Connor, a Topps vice president at the time of the investigation.

How to Spot the Not

The key areas of concern on any counterfeit card

WEIGHT

Weight is one of the easiest factors to consider, but the problem here is that few collectors have access to a fine digital scale, which is the best equipment for this. Any scale that weighs to the hundredth of a gram will suffice. The majority of counterfeits weigh either significantly more or less than a real card, as it is impossible to perfectly duplicate the card stock used. Weigh several samples from the real set, as some sets naturally fluctuate greatly. Anything more than a tenth of a gram variance on most sets should raise a red flag. Size is not usually an issue, but there are a number of fakes that measure too long or too short.

DOT PATTERN

Another major area of concern is the dot pattern. Anyone who deals in high-end Rookie Cards, vintage material or other high-ticket items should invest in a quality loupe. The choices are numerous, but we suggest a 16X doublet. It is small, but has a reasonably large field of vision, and costs just a third of a triplet loupe. Using this loupe, examine any of the printing areas, but primarily the black inked portions and the text.

On the genuine sample, search for areas that are printed in solid ink. Search for small print dots on a counterfeit. Usually, fake cards are re-screened, which results in a blurry appearance. Copying a card on a photocopier will typically leave this kind of pattern. This process uses small dots to create the card, but depending on the counterfeiters, some will re-screen the entire card while others do a more professional job of re-screening only the photo, and rebuilding the other design elements from scratch.

PHOTO SHARPNESS AND FEEL

While weight and dot pattern are the major areas of identification for most counterfeits, there are a handful of other tricks. Photos are usually blurred or faded or just show less contrast. Color ink may appear either far brighter than usual, or on the opposite end of the spectrum – far too dull. Minute areas of text typically blur together into an unreadable mess.

The counterfeit card may display a different "feel" – either too thick or thin, too cleanly or roughly cut, or even slightly "rubbery."

Printing on most counterfeits is comprised of print dots, as shown in the example above, as opposed to solid lines on original cards.

RULES OF THUMB

It is difficult to create a simple catch-all rule to weed out counterfeits. As each one is discovered, a new one pops up soon thereafter. A poorly faked card might be re-counterfeited later, removing the elements that easily marked it as an imitation.

As always, the best rule is to be very careful, especially if the deal seems far too good to be true, or if you are dealing with any high-end cards. However, even low-dollar cards have been counterfeited over the years. If in doubt, find another sample of the card to compare it to, but if the same card is not available, a common card from the same set will often be just as helpful.

The Most Common Baseball Counterfeits and How to Spot Them

By Beckett Grading Staff

We've talked about the general telltale signs of counterfeits and how to distinguish a phony from the real deal. Now we're going to take a look at some of the most commonly counterfeited baseball cards currently on the market.

Remember, education is the key to avoid being ripped off. Most of the red flags on the cards we will discuss over the next few pages can be applied to many other counterfeited cards from the same era. Some cards are easier to detect than others. What follows are a few working examples of identifying phony issues.

1980 Rickey Henderson Topps RC #482

He's been on seven different Major League Baseball teams and harbors an interesting reputation, to say the least. But nobody can deny the statistics Rickey Henderson has put up over the last two-plus decades. He's reached the 3,000 hits mark, is the stolen base king, and now holds the all-time runs scored record.

With these numbers, it is no surprise that his 1980 Topps RC has been counterfeited. These have been known to exist for many years; however, a fresh stock has popped up in large quantities. What follows are some hints to keep in mind when trying to detect a counterfeit.

Mass quantities of this fake were being sold on an online auction (we're

talking 100 copies at a time) in early 2000. It's an awful counterfeit if you look close.

For collectors familiar with the 1980 Topps set, just physically picking up and holding the fake is enough to clue a person in that something is amiss. The counterfeit is quite thick, and weighs much more than a standard card (2.26 grams compared to 1.70-1.80 grams).

The next easiest spot to check is any of the black print, especially black borders and text. On a genuine card, all of this printing should be solid black ink, but the counterfeits will be composed entirely of small black print dots, leaving the overall appearance very fuzzy or blurry. Using a loupe of 6X to 16X is the easiest method of spotting this, but it is apparent even to the naked eye. On the Henderson RC, the green background of the "A's" logo displays small print dots, while the genuine item is a solid green. The photograph itself is blurred more than usual.

Looking at the back of the card, the light areas appear nearly brown on the fake version, but the original color should be closer to a very light blue-gray. The © logo should be solid and unbroken, but our sample fake card shows the circle surrounding this copyright logo as being broken.

With 1,403 stolen bases after the 2002 season, Henderson is the King of baseball thefts. Collectors are warned to not fall prey to other thieves attempting to dupe fans into buying counterfeit Henderson RCs.

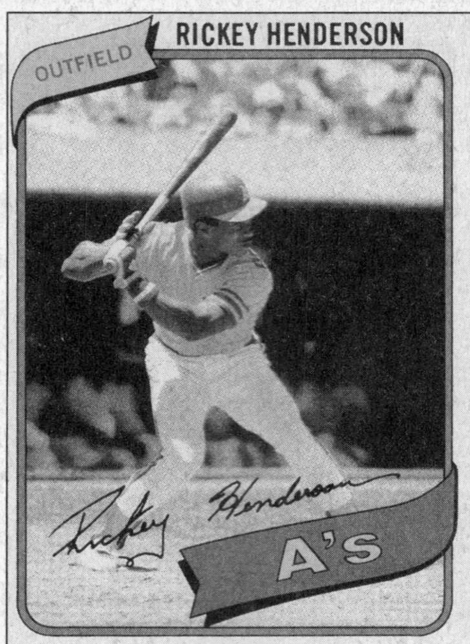

On the counterfeit pictured above, the print dots cause a fuzzy appearance to the name, whereas the genuine card below is crisp with solid ink.

TWO RIPKEN RIP-OFFS

1982 Donruss RC #405

It's not his best rookie-year card; it's not even his second-best. Yet the 1982 Donruss Cal Ripken Jr. Rookie Card has become a recent target for counterfeiters.

Perhaps because it is less of a high-visibility card than Cal's 1982 Topps or Topps Traded issues, the Donruss is still a popular item as it offers a very affordable RC of a future first-ballot Hall-of-Famer.

Although there are numerous problems with this counterfeit, one thing the culprits did get right is the weight – this is right on for '82 Donruss, in the range of 1.70 to 1.73 grams.

Beyond that, one close look at the upper right area of a common sample card from the 1982 Donruss set is all it takes to note that this Ripken is bad.

The logos and text are the first spots to check, and it's all about size on this one. The Orioles logo uses a circle that is too thin, as is the text and the red stitching on the baseball. Ripken's name and position are in the wrong font – too tall and skinny compared to an original. The registration is off-kilter a bit, and the card stock is a brighter white.

In the upper right corner of the card, the black lines in the "d" of the Donruss logo are far too thin, while the "Donruss" text and year " '82" are too large as shown in the

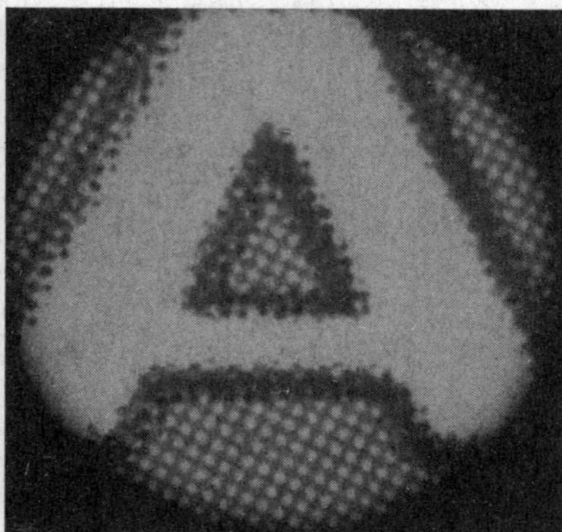

Areas of black text are one of the first giveaways of a counterfeit. On the 1980 Topps Rickey Henderson fake above, the letters in Henderson's name are comprised of numerous dots, as opposed to the solid black ink of an original. The "A's" logo on the fake Henderson shows a green and white dot pattern to create the background, but on a real issue, the green background is solid. Note the broken circle surrounding the © logo on the back of the Henderson counterfeit.

The counterfeit 1982 Donruss Cal Ripken Jr. card is shown above left, while the real card above right.

close-up scan. Notice the fake on the left, with the thin black lines and fat logo, and the real card on the right.

On the back of the card, the blue tint is far too light, closer to a baby blue than the dark blue of a genuine card. The black text also appears much darker than usual.

The reasons why forgers have targeted Ripken's 1982 Donruss remain foggy. Cal collectors with a watchful eye should be able to steer clear of this counterfeit, however, and knowing what to look for is half the battle.

1982 Topps RC #21

The Donruss RC is a newer counterfeit than Ripken's 1982 Topps RC, which has two variations we will examine.

Ripken's Topps RC (Orioles Future Stars) has always been a popular item. Of this issue, there are two known counterfeits. The first, oldest, and most common is the blank back variation. This card was printed with borders on the back, but no text, and was often passed off as some sort of test issue. Obviously, a quick peek at the back of your card will tell you whether you have a counterfeit or not.

A cousin to the blank back, the Type II version has added the back printing, and is more recent. Other than the corrected back text, the card is very similar to the blank back fake. The key area to examine on this version is a flaw that it shares with the front of the blank back. The black borders around the three player photos on the front of the card feature black print dots as opposed to the solid black lines of a legitimate issue. The text of the players' names on some cards will also appear washed out.

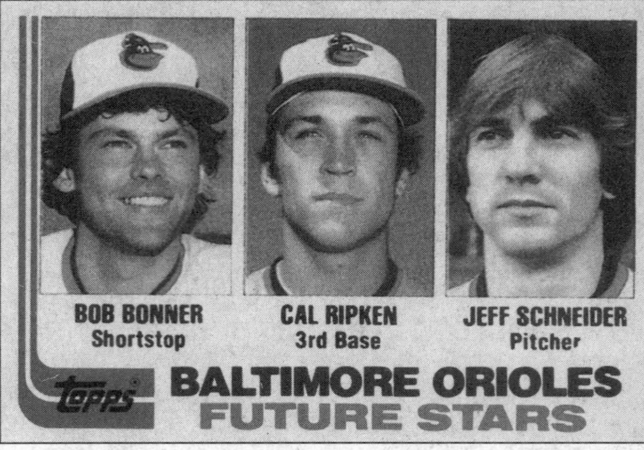

Note the print dot pattern of the black borders (below), typical of both counterfeit versions.

To date, the only major league Ripken RC not counterfeited is the 1982 Fleer. The Topps, Topps Traded, and Donruss issues all have met the hand of the counterfeiters, as well as some minor league issues. With the Iron Man's place in baseball history well cemented, his top issues will

The blank back counterfeit (above), and the Type II fake with the added text (below).

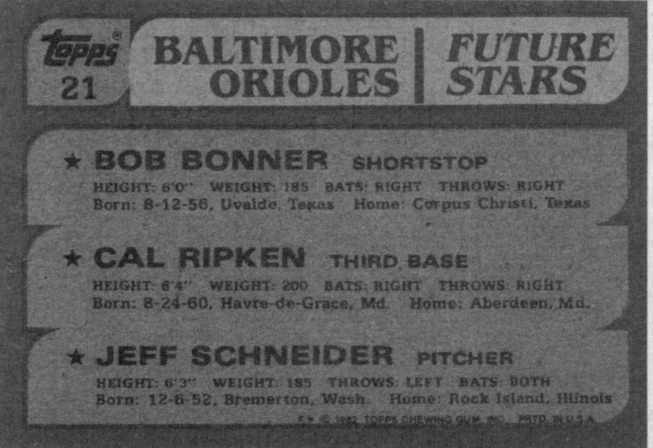

always remain a target for unscrupulous forgers, so keep a sharp lookout to avoid being burned.

1968 Nolan Ryan Topps RC #177

As arguably the greatest pitcher of all time, Nolan Ryan is a frequent target of counterfeiters.

Numerous examples of his 1970s and even 1980s cards have been illegally reproduced. Not surprisingly, however, it is his 1968 Topps Rookie Card #177, shared with Jerry Koosman, which has been the most commonly faked. One of a handful of different versions of imposter Ryan RCs, this particular incarnation is one of the most deceptive fakes out there.

Standard printing traits normally found on counterfeits have been attended to very well on this card. Dot patterns within text and areas of dark ink are generally correct, with only one minor exception – the tan, cross-hatch pattern in the background.

Note the difference in the cross-hatch pattern between the fake card above (top) and the real one (bottom).

Using a high-powered loupe, examine the white areas within the weaving. On an original card, these areas are clean and free of any dots, but on the fake there will be a small amount of tiny, scattered red print dots within the white areas. When magnified, the weaved pattern becomes an indistinct jumble of dots, whereas the correct version continues to show clean, white patches.

Aside from this, the other warning signs of this counterfeit are its lighter card stock (1.60 grams compared to 1.92 grams on a genuine card), and overall "oily" appearance. Particularly on the back, the card looks and feels slightly greasy, with the normally white areas appearing gray due to the oiliness. On the front of the card, the cross-hatch pattern is much lighter and indistinct, while the normally purple circle surrounding the Mets logo appears nearly dark blue on the fake.

counterfeit

genuine

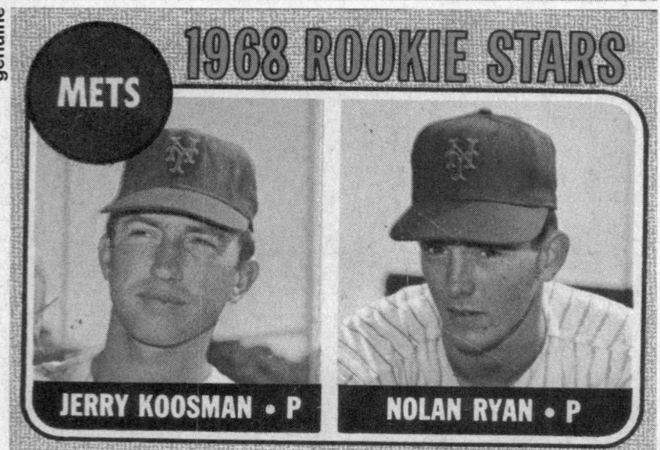

1969 Reggie Jackson Topps RC #260

Here is one of the more easily identifiable fakes that has circulated in the baseball card hobby.

Reggie Jackson, appropriately nicknamed "Mr. October" for his past post-season prowess, is one of baseball's true legends and remains a fan favorite even some 15 years removed from playing the game.

Twice named the World Series MVP, Reggie is unfortunately also a favorite of forgers.

However, a fake 1969 Topps Reggie Jackson RC can easily be spotted by a handful of indicators, several of which are similar in nature to the Rickey Henderson RC examined earlier.

First, the weight of the Jackson card is far less than a normal sample (1.42 grams compared to 1.98). Secondly, the surface is too glossy and waxy, and the photo is too light.

Looking at the black lines around the border, or the black lines bordering the word "Athletics," these will be composed of small print dots. A normal card would consist of solid black ink. The yellow ink itself will be dotted with small white print dots, but it actually should be solid yellow ink, as well.

Note the print dot pattern in the black ink areas, resulting in an overall fuzzy appearance.

On the back, the black text appears ragged and thinner, and the color is far brighter. In addition, the © logo is a bit clearer on the original card.

As long as Reggie Jackson remains a hero in the hearts of baseball fans, his cards – especially this high dollar 1969 Topps rookie – will stay on the counterfeit market. By developing a discerning eye and applying a bit of

The black border on the fake Jackson RC is composed of small print dots.

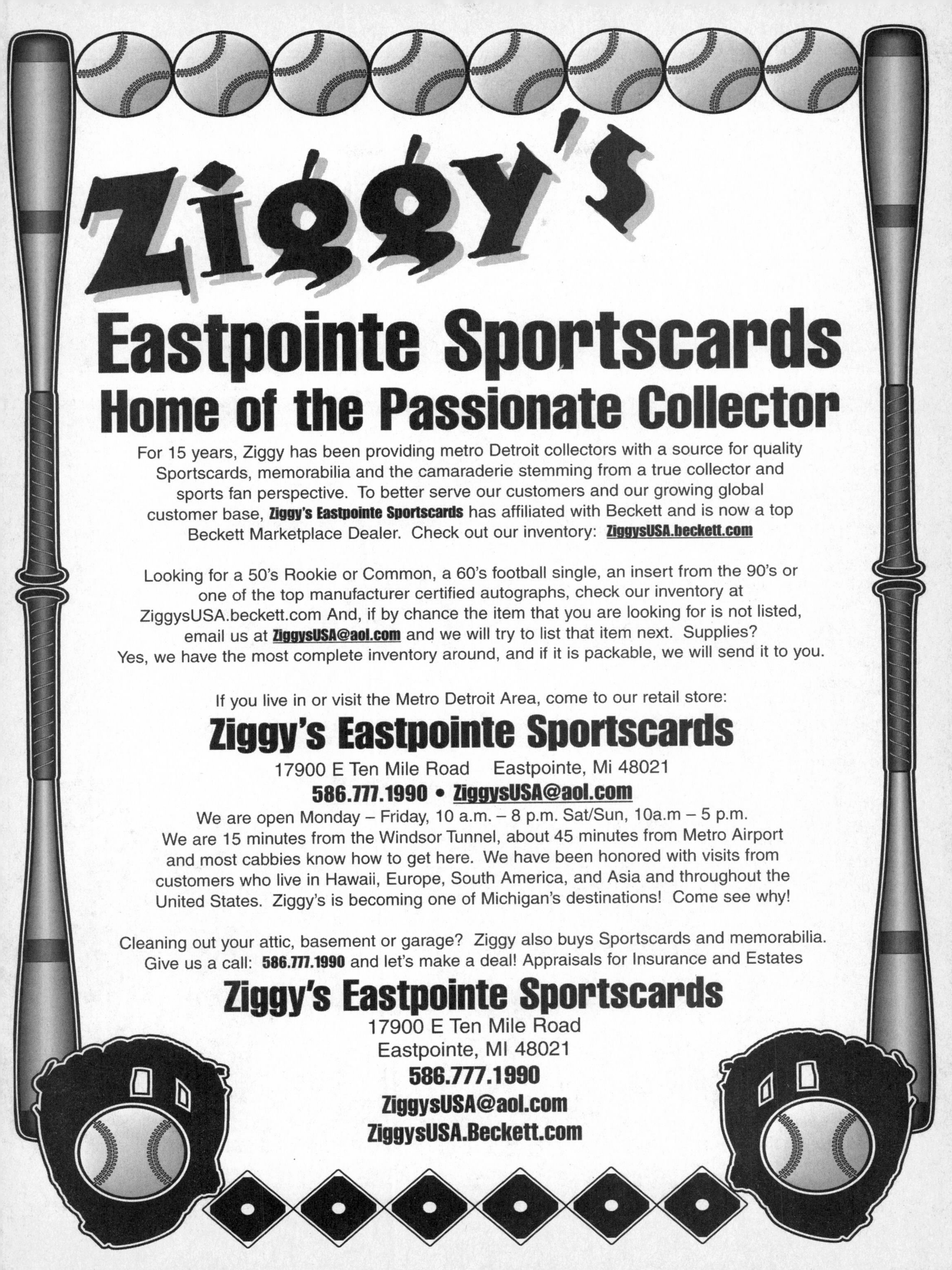
Ziggy's
Eastpointe Sportscards
Home of the Passionate Collector
For 15 years, Ziggy has been providing metro Detroit collectors with a source for quality Sportscards, memorabilia and the camaraderie stemming from a true collector and sports fan perspective. To better serve our customers and our growing global customer base, Ziggy's Eastpointe Sportscards has affiliated with Beckett and is now a top Beckett Marketplace Dealer. Check out our inventory: ZiggysUSA.beckett.com
Looking for a 50's Rookie or Common, a 60's football single, an insert from the 90's or one of the top manufacturer certified autographs, check our inventory at ZiggysUSA.beckett.com And, if by chance the item that you are looking for is not listed, email us at ZiggysUSA@aol.com and we will try to list that item next. Supplies? Yes, we have the most complete inventory around, and if it is packable, we will send it to you.
If you live in or visit the Metro Detroit Area, come to our retail store:
Ziggy's Eastpointe Sportscards
17900 E Ten Mile Road Eastpointe, Mi 48021
586.777.1990 • ZiggysUSA@aol.com
We are open Monday – Friday, 10 a.m. – 8 p.m. Sat/Sun, 10a.m – 5 p.m.
We are 15 minutes from the Windsor Tunnel, about 45 minutes from Metro Airport and most cabbies know how to get here. We have been honored with visits from customers who live in Hawaii, Europe, South America, and Asia and throughout the United States. Ziggy's is becoming one of Michigan's destinations! Come see why!
Cleaning out your attic, basement or garage? Ziggy also buys Sportscards and memorabilia. Give us a call: 586.777.1990 and let's make a deal! Appraisals for Insurance and Estates
Ziggy's Eastpointe Sportscards
17900 E Ten Mile Road
Eastpointe, MI 48021
586.777.1990
ZiggysUSA@aol.com
ZiggysUSA.Beckett.com

knowledge, however, collectors should be able to steer clear of the fakes.

1985 Mark McGwire Topps RC #401

Along with Michael Jordan's 1986-87 Fleer RC, the 1985 Topps Mark McGwire RC is probably the most commonly counterfeited sports card today. Even before hitting the record-setting 70 homers, Big Mac fakes were prevalent, but afterwards, the card attracted the attention of even more unscrupulous printers.

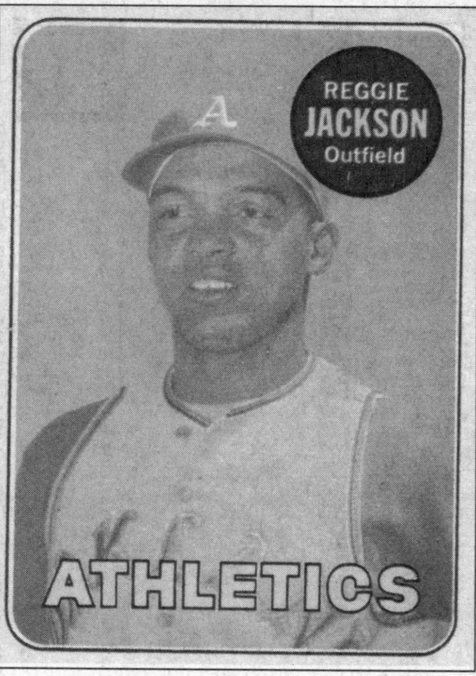

Giving a run-down of every characteristic of each of the fakes is possible, but not necessary. Instead, we will focus on a handful of key areas. By looking closely at each of these areas on a McGwire, it is possible to generally narrow down the fake examples with great accuracy.

First up is the most recent series of the straight-line versions. On a real McGwire, the outer black borders on the front of the card may look straight at first glance, but closer inspection under magnification reveals very small breaks along the edges of the ink, as well as slightly rounded corners. On the counterfeits, these lines are more solid, and the junctions come to a perfect 90-degree point. Held next to a legitimate card, this subtle difference is more noticeable.

A second area of the card is also too neatly printed. The letter "E" in "1984 United States Baseball Team" is printed in a font that leaves each angle perfectly formed into the same 90-degree point as the borders. A real card uses a more rounded font with no sharp points.

The final area to examine involves the bleachers over McGwire's right shoulder, next to his bat. At least two different counterfeits exist in which the photo was re-screened poorly. While the bleachers should have print dots in them, a quick glance at the fake reveals a crosshatch pattern. The alternating dark and light "squares" leave the impression of a checkerboard design. One of the versions of this fake also tends to feature too much yellow ink around McGwire's eyes, resulting in an eerie photo.

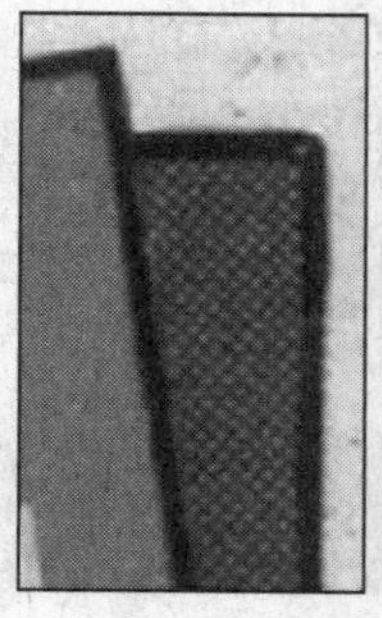

Left: the slightly rounded genuine card. Right: the fake with the perfect 90-degree points.

Using these critical areas to focus on, and comparing the card to a known legitimate version (or even a common card from the same set) can end up saving the savvy collector the time, trouble, and cost of purchasing a worthless counterfeit.

The "E" of a real card has rounded edges. The scan on the right is fake.

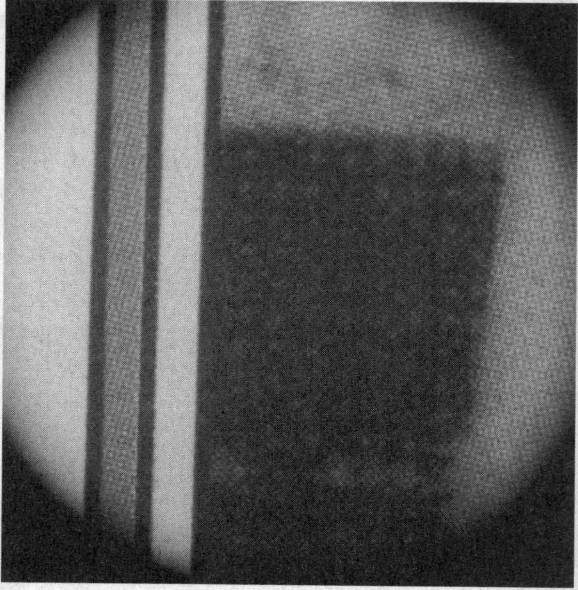

Examine the area of the bleachers behind McGwire's bat. The fake, as illustrated above, displays a cross-hatch or checkerboard pattern that is not found on the legitimate issue.

How To Use This Book

Isn't it great? Every year this book gets better with all the new sets coming out. But even more exciting is that every year there are more options in collecting the cards we love so much. This edition has been enhanced and expanded from the previous edition. The cards you collect who appears on them, what they look like, where they are from, and (most important to most of you) what their current values are are enumerated within. Many of the features contained in the other Beckett Price Guides have been incorporated into this volume since condition grading, terminology, and many other aspects of collecting are common to the card hobby in general. We hope you find the book both interesting and useful in your collecting pursuits.

The Beckett Guide has been successful where other attempts have failed because it is complete, current, and valid. This Price Guide contains not just one, but two prices by condition for all the baseball cards listed. The prices were added to the card lists just prior to printing and reflect not the author's opinions or desires but the going retail prices for each card, based on the marketplace (sports memorabilia conventions and shows, sports card shops, hobby papers, current mail-order catalogs, auction results, and other firsthand reportings of actually realized prices).

What is the best price guide available on the market today? Of course, card sellers prefer the price guide with the highest prices, while card buyers naturally prefer the one with the lowest prices. Accuracy, however, is the true test. Use the price guide trusted by more collectors and dealers than all the others combined. Look for the Beckett® name. We wound't put our name on anything we wouldn't stake our reputation on. Not the lowest and not the highest but the most accurate, with integrity.

To facilitate your use of this book, read the complete introductory section on the following pages before going to the pricing pages. Every collectible field has its own terminology; we've tried to capture most of these terms and definitions in our glossary. Please read carefully the section on grading and the condition of your cards, as you cannot determine which price column is appropriate for a given card without first knowing its condition.

Introduction

Welcome To The World Of Baseball Cards.

Welcome to the exciting world of baseball card collecting, America's fastest-growing avocation. You have made a good choice in buying this book, since it will open up to you the entire panorama of this field in the simplest, most concise way.

The growth of *Beckett Baseball*, *Beckett Basketball*, *Beckett Football*, *Beckett Hockey*, and *Beckett Racing* is an indication of the unprecedented popularity of sports cards. Founded in 1984 by Dr. James Beckett, *Beckett Baseball* contains the most extensive and accepted monthly price guide, collectible glossy superstar covers, colorful feature articles, "Short Prints," Convention Calendar, tips for beginners, "Readers Write" letters to and responses from the editor, information on errors and varieties, autograph collecting tips and profiles of the sport's Hottest stars. Published every month, BBCM is the hobby's largest paid circulation periodical. The other five magazines were built on the success of BBC.

So collecting baseball cards while still pursued as a hobby with youthful exuberance by kids in the neighborhood has also taken on the trappings of an industry, with thousands of full- and part-time card dealers, as well as vendors of supplies, clubs and conventions. In fact, each year since 1980 thousands of hobbyists have assembled for a National Sports Collectors Convention, at which hundreds of dealers have displayed their wares, seminars have been conducted, autographs penned by sports notables, and millions of cards changed hands. The Beckett Guide is the best annual guide available to the exciting world of baseball cards. Read it and use it. May your enjoyment and your card collection increase in the coming months and years.

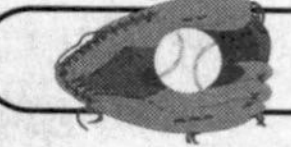
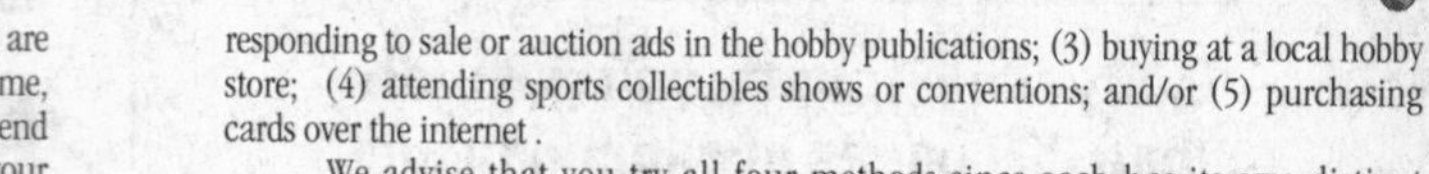

How To Collect

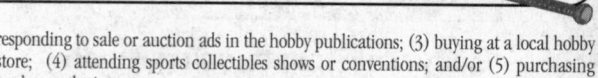

Each collection is personal and reflects the individuality of its owner. There are no set rules on how to collect cards. Since card collecting is a hobby or leisure pastime, what you collect, how much you collect, and how much time and money you spend collecting are entirely up to you. The funds you have available for collecting and your own personal taste should determine how you collect. Information and ideas presented here are intended to help you get the most enjoyment from this hobby.

It is impossible to collect every card ever produced. Therefore, beginners as well as intermediate and advanced collectors usually specialize in some way. One of the reasons this hobby is popular is that individual collectors can define and tailor their collecting methods to match their own tastes. To give you some ideas of the various approaches to collecting, we will list some of the more popular areas of specialization.

Many collectors select complete sets from particular years. For example, they may concentrate on assembling complete sets from all the years since their birth or since they became avid sports fans. They may try to collect a card for every player during that specified period of time.

Many others wish to acquire only certain players. Usually such players are the superstars of the sport, but occasionally collectors will specialize in all the cards of players who attended a particular college or came from a certain town. Some collectors are only interested in the first cards or Rookie Cards of certain players. A handy guide for collectors interested in pursuing the hobby this way is the Beckett Baseball Card Alphabetical Checklist.

Another fun way to collect cards is by team. Most fans have a favorite team, and it is natural for that loyalty to be translated into a desire for cards of the players on that favorite team. For most of the recent years, team sets (all the cards from a given team for that year) are readily available at a reasonable price. The Sport Americana Team Baseball Card Checklist will open up this field to the collector.

Obtaining Cards

Several avenues are open to card collectors. Cards still can be purchased in the traditional way: by the pack at the local candy, grocery, drug or major discount stores.

But there are also thousands of card shops across the country that specialize in selling cards individually or by the pack, box, or set. Another alternative is the thousands of card shows held each month around the country, which feature anywhere from eight to 800 tables of sports cards and memorabilia for sale.

For many years, it has been possible to purchase complete sets of baseball cards through mail-order advertisers found in traditional sports media publications, such as The Sporting News, Baseball Digest, Street & Smith yearbooks, and others. These sets also are advertised in the card collecting periodicals. Many collectors will begin by subscribing to at least one of the hobby periodicals, all with good up-to-date information. In fact, subscription offers can be found in the advertising section of this book.

Most serious card collectors obtain old (and new) cards from one or more of several main sources: (1) trading or buying from other collectors or dealers; (2) responding to sale or auction ads in the hobby publications; (3) buying at a local hobby store; (4) attending sports collectibles shows or conventions; and/or (5) purchasing cards over the internet .

We advise that you try all four methods since each has its own distinct advantages: (1) trading is a great way to make new friends; (2) hobby periodicals help you keep up with what's going on in the hobby (including when and where the conventions are happening); (3) stores provide the opportunity to enjoy personalized service and consider a great diversity of material in a relaxed sports-oriented atmosphere; (4) shows allow you to choose from multiple dealers and thousands of cards under one roof in a competitive situation; and (5) the internet allows one to purchase cards in a convenient manner from almost anywhere in the world.

Preserving Your Cards

Cards are fragile. They must be handled properly in order to retain their value. Careless handling can easily result in creased or bent cards. It is, however, not recommended that tweezers or tongs be used to pick up your cards since such utensils might mar or indent card surfaces and thus reduce those cards' conditions and values.

In general, your cards should be handled directly as little as possible. This is sometimes easier to say than to do.

Although there are still many who use custom boxes, storage trays, or even shoe boxes, plastic sheets are the preferred method of many collectors for storing cards.

A collection stored in plastic pages in a three-ring album allows you to view your collection at any time without the need to touch the card itself. Cards can also be kept in single holders (of various types and thickness) designed for the enjoyment of each card individually.

For a large collection, some collectors may use a combination of the above methods. When purchasing plastic sheets for your cards, be sure that you find the pocket size that fits the cards snugly. Don't put your 1951 Bowman in a sheet designed to fit 1981 Topps.

Most hobby and collectibles shops and virtually all collectors' conventions will have these plastic pages available in quantity for the various sizes offered, or you can purchase them directly from the advertisers in this book.

Also, remember that pocket size isn't the only factor to consider when looking for plastic sheets. Other factors such as safety, economy, appearance, availability, or personal preference also may indicate which types of sheets a collector may want to buy.

Damp, sunny and/or hot conditions no, this is not a weather forecast are three elements to avoid in extremes if you are interested in preserving your collection. Too much (or too little) humidity can cause the gradual deterioration of a card. Direct, bright sun (or fluorescent light) over time will bleach out the color of a card. Extreme heat accelerates the decomposition of the card. On the other hand, many cards have lasted more than 75 years without much scientific intervention. So be cautious, even if the above factors typically present a problem only when present in the extreme. It never hurts to be prudent.

Collecting vs. Investing

Collecting individual players and collecting complete sets are both popular vehicles for investment and speculation.

Most investors and speculators stock up on complete sets or on quantities of players they think have good investment potential.

There is obviously no guarantee in this book, or anywhere else for that matter, that cards will outperform the stock market or other investment alternatives in the future. After all, baseball cards do not pay quarterly dividends and cards cannot be sold at their "current values" as easily as stocks or bonds.

Nevertheless, investors have noticed a favorable long-term trend in the past performance of baseball and other sports collectibles, and certain cards and sets have outperformed just about any other investment in some years.

Many hobbyists maintain that the best investment is and always will be the building of a collection, which traditionally has held up better than outright speculation.

Some of the obvious questions are: Which cards? When to buy? When to sell? The best investment you can make is in your own education.

The more you know about your collection and the hobby, the more informed the decisions you will be able to make. We're not selling investment tips. We're selling information about the current value of baseball cards. It's up to you to use that information to your best advantage.

Terminology

Each hobby has its own language to describe its area of interest. The nomenclature traditionally used for trading cards is derived from the American Card Catalog, published in 1960 by Nostalgia Press. That catalog, written by Jefferson Burdick (who is called the "Father of Card Collecting" for his pioneering work), uses letter and number designations for each separate set of cards. The letter used in the ACC designation refers to the generic type of card. While both sport and non-sport issues are classified in the ACC, we shall confine ourselves to the sport issues. The following list defines the letters and their meanings as used by the American Card Catalog.

(none) or N - 19th Century U.S. Tobacco
B - Blankets
D - Bakery Inserts Including Bread
E - Early Candy and Gum
F - Food Inserts
H - Advertising
M - Periodicals
PC - Postcards
R - Candy and Gum since 1930 Following the letter prefix and an optional hyphen are one-, two-, or three-digit numbers,
R(-)999. These typically represent the company or entity issuing the cards. In several cases, the ACC number is extended by an additional hyphen and another one- or two-digit numerical suffix. For example, the 1957 Topps regular-series baseball card issue carries an ACC designation of
R414-11. The "R" indicates a Candy or Gum card produced since 1930. The "414" is the ACC designation for Topps Chewing Gum baseball card issues, and the "11" is the ACC designation for the 1957 regular issue **(Topps' eleventh baseball set)**. Like other traditional methods of identification, this system provides order to the process of cataloging cards; however, most serious collectors learn the ACC designation of the popular sets by repetition and familiarity, rather than by attempting to "figure out" what they might or should be. From 1948 forward, collectors and dealers commonly refer to all sets by their year, maker, type of issue, and any other distinguishing characteristic. For example, such a characteristic could be an unusual issue or one of several regular issues put out by a specific maker in a single year. Regional issues are usually referred to by year, maker, and sometimes by title or theme of the set.

Glossary/Legend

Our glossary defines terms used in the card collecting hobby and in this book. Many of these terms are also common to other types of sports memorabilia collecting. Some terms may have several meanings depending on use and context.

ACETATE—A transparent plastic.
AS— All-Star card. A card portraying an All-Star Player of the previous year that says "All-Star" on its face.
ATG-All-Time Great card.
ATL-All-Time Leaders card.
AU(TO)—Autographed card.
AW—Award Winner
BB—Building Blocks
BC—Bonus card.
BF—Bright Futures
BL—Blue letters.
BNR—Banner Season
BOX CARD—Card issued on a box (e.g., 1987 Topps Box Bottoms).
BRICK—A group of 50 or more cards having common characteristics that is intended to be bought, sold, or traded as a unit.
CABINETS—Popular and highly valuable photographs on thick card stock produced in the 19th and early 20th century.
CC—Curtain Call
CG—Cornerstones of the Game
CHECKLIST—A list of the cards contained in a particular set. The list is always in numerical order if the cards are numbered. Some unnumbered sets are artificially numbered in alphabetical order, by team and alphabetically within the team, or by uniform number for convenience.
CL—Checklist card. A card that lists in order the cards and players in the set or series. Older checklist cards in Mint condition that have not been marked are very desirable and command premiums.
CP—Changing Places
CO—Coach.
COMM—Commissioner.
COMMON CARD—The typical card of any set; it has no premium value accruing from subject matter, numerical scarcity, popular demand, or anomaly.
CONVENTION—A gathering of dealers and collectors at a single location for the purpose of buying, selling, and trading sports memorabilia items. Conventions are open to the public and sometimes feature autograph guests, door prizes, contests, seminars, etc. They are frequently referred to simply as "shows."
COOP—Cooperstown.
COR—Corrected card.
CT—Cooperstown
CY—Cy Young Award.
DD—Decade of Dominance
DEALER—A person who engages in buying, selling, and trading sports collectibles or supplies. A dealer may also be a collector, but as a dealer, his main goal is to earn a profit.
DIE-CUT—A card with part of its stock partially cut, allowing one or more parts to be folded or removed. After removal or appropriate folding, the remaining part of the card can frequently be made to stand up.
DK—Diamond King.
DL—Division Leaders.
DP—Double Print (a card that was printed in double the quantity compared to the other cards in the same series) or a Draft Pick card.
DT—Dream Team
DUFEX—A method of card manufacturing technology patented by Pinnacle Brands, Inc. It involves a refractive quality to a card with a foil coating.
ERA—Earned Run Average.
ERR—Error card. A card with erroneous information, spelling, or depiction on either side of the card. Most errors are not corrected by the producing card company.
FC—Fan Club
FDP—First or First-Round Draft Pick.
FF—Future Foundation
FOIL—Foil embossed stamp on card.
FOLD—Foldout.
FP—Franchise Player
Fran—Franchise
FS—Father/son card.
FS—Future Star
FUN—Fun cards.
FY—First Year
GL—Green letters.
GLOSS—A card with luster; a shiny finish as in a card with UV coating.
GO—could not find on page 202
HG—Heroes of the Game
HIGH NUMBER—The cards in the last series of numbers in a year in which such higher-numbered cards were printed or distributed in significantly lesser amounts than the lower-numbered cards. The high-number designation refers to a scarcity of the high-numbered cards. Not all years have high numbers in terms of this

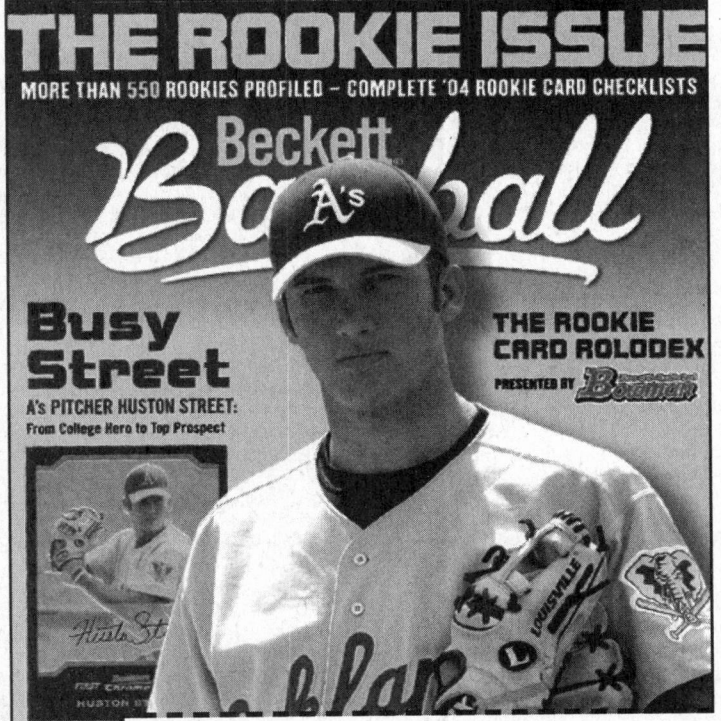

definition.
HL—Highlight card.
HOF—Hall of Fame, or a card that portrays a Hall of Famer (HOFer).
HOLOGRAM—A three-dimensional photographic image.
HH—Hometown Heroes
HOR—Horizontal pose on card as opposed to the standard vertical orientation found on most cards.
IA—In Action card.
IF—Infielder.
INSERT—A card of a different type or any other sports collectible (typically a poster or sticker) contained and sold in the same package along with a card or cards of a major set. An insert card is either unnumbered or not numbered in the same sequence as the major set. Sometimes the inserts are randomly distributed and are not found in every pack.
INTERACTIVE—A concept that involves collector participation.
IRT—International Road Trip
ISSUE—Synonymous with set, but usually used in conjunction with a manufaturer, e.g., a Topps issue.
JSY—means Jersey
KM—K-Men
LHP—Left-handed pitcher.
LL—League Leaders or large letters on card.
LUM—Lumberjack
MAJOR SET—A set produced by a national manufacturer of cards containing a large number of cards. Usually 100 or more different cards constitute a major set.
MB—Master Blasters
MEM—Memorial card. For example, the 1990 Donruss and Topps Bart Giamatti cards.
METALLIC—A glossy design method that enhances card features.
MG—Manager.
MI—Maximum Impact
MINI—A small card; for example, a 1975 Topps card of identical design but smaller dimensions than the regular Topps issue of 1975.
ML—Major League.
MM—Memorable Moments
MULTI-PLAYER CARD—A single card depicting two or more players (but not a team card).
MVP—Most Valuable Player.
NAU—No autograph on card.
NG—Next Game
NH—No-Hitter.
NNOF—No name on front.
NOF—Name on front.
NOTCHING—The grooving of the card, usually caused by fingernails, rubber bands, or bumping card edges against other objects.
NT—Now and Then
NV—Novato
OF—Outfield or Outfielder.
OLY—Olympics Card.
P—Pitcher or Pitching pose.
P1—First Printing.
P2—Second Printing.
P3—Third Printing.
PACKS—A means by which cards are issued in terms of pack type (wax, cello, foil, rack, etc.) and channel of distribution (hobby, retail, etc.).
PARALLEL— A card that is similar in design to its counterpart from a basic set but offers a distinguishing quality.
PF—Profiles.
PG—Postseason Glory
PLASTIC SHEET—A clear, plastic page that is punched for insertion into a binder (with standard three-ring spacing) containing pockets for displaying cards. Many different styles of sheets exist with pockets of varying sizes to hold the many differing card formats. Also called a display sheet or storage sheet.
PP—Power Passion
PLATINUM—A metallic element used in the process of creating a glossy card.
PR—Printed name on back.
PREMIUM—A card, sometimes on photographic stock, that is purchased or obtained in conjunction with, or redemption for, another card or product. The premium is not packaged in the same unit as the primary item.
PRES—President.
PRISMATIC/PRISM—A glossy or bright design that refracts or disperses light.
PS—Pace Setters
PT—Power Tools
PUZZLE CARD—A card whose back contains a part of a picture which, when joined correctly with other puzzle cards, forms the completed picture.
PUZZLE PIECE—A die-cut piece designed to interlock with similar pieces (e.g., early 1980s Donruss).
PVC—Polyvinyl chloride, a substance used to make many of the popular card display protective sheets. Non-PVC sheets are considered preferable for long-term storage of cards by many.
RARE—A card or series of cards of very limited availability. Unfortunately, "rare" is a subjective term frequently used indiscriminately to hype value. "Rare" cards are harder to obtain than "scarce" cards.
RB—Record Breaker.
RC—Rookie Card
REDEMPTION—A program established by multiple card manufacturers that allows collectors to mail in a special card (usually a random insert) in return for special cards, sets, or other prizes not available through conventional channels.
REFRACTORS—A card that features a design element that enhances (distorts) its color/appearance through deflecting light.
REV NEG—Reversed or flopped photo side of the card. This is a major type of error card, but only some are corrected.
RHP—Right-handed pitcher.
RHW—Rookie Home Whites
RIF—Rifleman
RPM—Rookie Premiere Materials
RR—Rated Rookie
ROO—Rookie
ROY—Rookie of the Year.
RP—Relief pitcher.
RTC—Rookie True Colors
SA—Super Action card.
SASE—Self-Addressed, Stamped Envelope.
SB—Scrapbook
SB—Stolen Bases.
SCARCE—A card or series of cards of limited availability. This subjective term is sometimes used indiscriminately to hype value. "Scarce" cards are not as difficult to obtain as "rare" cards.
SCR—Script name on back.
SD—San Diego Padres.
SEMI-HIGH—A card from the next-to-last series of a sequentially issued set. It has more value than an average card and generally less value than a high number. A card is not called a semi-high unless the next-to-last series in which it exists has an additional premium attached to it.
SERIES—The entire set of cards issued by a particular producer in a particular year; e.g., the 1971 Topps series. Also, within a particular set, series can refer to a group of (consecutively numbered) cards printed at the same time, e.g., the first series of the 1957 Topps issue (#1 through #88).
SET—One each of the entire run of cards of the same type produced by a particular manufacturer during a single year. In other words, if you have a complete set of 1976 Topps then you have every card from #1 up to and including #660; i.e., all the different cards that were produced.
SF—Starflics.
SH—Season Highlight
SHEEN—Brightness or luster emitted by card.
SKIP-NUMBERED—A set that has many unissued card numbers between the lowest number in the set and the highest number in the set, e.g., the 1948 Leaf baseball set contains 98 cards skip-numbered from #1 to #168. A major set in which a few numbers were not printed is not considered to be skip-numbered.
SP—Single or Short Print (a card that was printed in lesser quantity compared to the other cards in the same series; see also DP and TP).
SPECIAL CARD—A card that portrays something other than a single player or team, for example, a card that portrays the previous year's statistical leaders or the results from the previous year's World Series.
SS—Shortstop.
STANDARD SIZE—Most modern sports cards measure 2—1/2 by 3-1/2 inches. Exceptions are noted in card descriptions throughout this book.
STAR CARD—A card that portrays a player of some repute, usually determined by his ability; but, sometimes referring to sheer popularity.
STOCK—The cardboard or paper on which the card is printed.
SUPERIMPOSED—To be affixed on top of something; i.e., a player photo over a solid background.
SUPERSTAR CARD—A card that portrays a superstar, e.g., a Hall of Famer or player with strong Hall of Fame potential.
TC—Team Checklist.
TEAM CARD—A card that depicts an entire team.
THREE-DIMENSIONAL (3D)—A visual image that provides an illusion of depth and perspective.
TOPICAL—A subset or group of cards that have a common theme (e.g., MVP award winners).
TP—Triple Print (a card that was printed in triple the quantity compared to the other cards in the same series).
TR—Trade reference on card.
TRANSPARENT—Clear, see-through.
UDCA—Upper Deck Classic Alumni.
UER—Uncorrected Error.
UMP—Umpire.
USA—Team USA.
UV—Ultraviolet, a glossy coating used in producing cards.
VAR—Variation card. One of two or more cards from the same series with

the same number (or player with identical pose if the series is unnumbered) differing from one another by some aspect, the different feature stemming from the printing or stock of the card. This can be caused when the manufacturer of the cards notices an error in one or more of the cards, makes the changes, and then resumes the print run. In this case there will be two versions or variations of the same card. Sometimes one of the variations is relatively scarce.

VERT—Vertical pose on card.

WAS—Washington National League (1974 Topps).

WC—What's the Call?

WL—White letters on front.

WS—World Series card.

YL—Yellow letters on front

YT—Yellow team name on front.

*****—to denote multi-sport sets.

Understanding Card Values

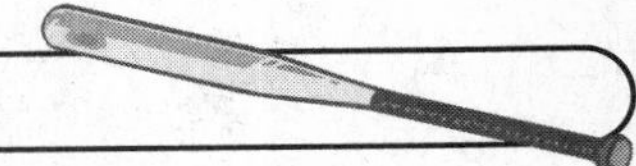

Determining Value

Why are some cards more valuable than others? Obviously, the economic laws of supply and demand are applicable to card collecting just as they are to any other field where a commodity is bought, sold or traded in a free, unregulated market.

Supply (the number of cards available on the market) is less than the total number of cards originally produced since attrition diminishes that original quantity. Each year a percentage of cards is typically thrown away, destroyed or otherwise lost to collectors. This percentage is much, much smaller today than it was in the past because more and more people have become increasingly aware of the value of their cards.

For those who collect only Mint condition cards, the supply of older cards can be quite small indeed. Until recently, collectors were not so conscious of the need to preserve the condition of their cards. For this reason, it is difficult to know exactly how many 1953 Topps are currently available, Mint or otherwise. It is generally accepted that there are fewer 1953 Topps available than 1963, 1973 or 1983 Topps cards. If demand were equal for each of these sets, the law of supply and demand would increase the price for the least available sets. Demand, however, is never equal for all sets, so price correlations can be complicated. The demand for a card is influenced by many factors. These include: (1) the age of the card; (2) the number of cards printed; (3) the player(s) portrayed on the card; (4) the attractiveness and popularity of the set; and (5) the physical condition of the card.

In general, (1) the older the card, (2) the fewer the number of the cards printed, (3) the more famous, popular and talented the player, (4) the more attractive and popular the set, and (5) the better the condition of the card, the higher the value of the card will be. There are exceptions to all but one of these factors: the condition of the card. Given two cards similar in all respects except condition, the one in the best condition will always be valued higher.

While those guidelines help to establish the value of a card, the countless exceptions and peculiarities make any simple, direct mathematical formula to determine card values impossible.

Regional Variation

Since the market varies from region to region, card prices of local players may be higher. This is known as a regional premium. How significant the premium is and if there is any premium at all depends on the local popularity of the team and the player.

The largest regional premiums usually do not apply to superstars, who often are so well-known nationwide that the prices of their key cards are too high for local dealers to realize a premium.

Lesser stars often command the strongest premiums. Their popularity is concentrated in their home region, creating local demand that greatly exceeds overall demand.

Regional premiums can apply to popular retired players and sometimes can be found in the areas where the players grew up or starred in college.

A regional discount is the converse of a regional premium. Regional discounts occur when a player has been so popular in his region for so long that local collectors and dealers have accumulated quantities of his key cards. The abundant supply may make the cards available in that area at the lowest prices anywhere.

Set Prices

A somewhat paradoxical situation exists in the price of a complete set vs. the combined cost of the individual cards in the set. In nearly every case, the sum of the prices for the individual cards is higher than the cost for the complete set. This is prevalent especially in the cards of the last few years. The reasons for this apparent anomaly stem from the habits of collectors and from the carrying costs to dealers. Today, each card in a set normally is produced in the same quantity as all other cards in its set.

Many collectors pick up only stars, superstars and particular teams. As a result, the dealer is left with a shortage of certain player cards and an abundance of others. He therefore incurs an expense in simply "carrying" these less desirable cards in stock. On the other hand, if he sells a complete set, he gets rid of large numbers of cards at one time. For this reason, he generally is willing to receive less money for a complete set. By doing this, he recovers all of his costs and also makes a profit.

The disparity between the price of the complete set and the sum of the individual cards also has been influenced by the fact that some of the major manufacturers now are pre-collating card sets. Since "pulling" individual cards from the sets involves a specific type of labor (and cost), the singles or star card market is not affected significantly by pre-collation.

Set prices also do not include rare card varieties, unless specifically stated. Of course, the prices for sets do include one example of each type for the given set, but this is the least expensive variety.

Scarce Series

Scarce series occur because cards issued before 1974 were made available to the public each year in several series of finite numbers of cards, rather than all cards of the set being available for purchase at one time. At some point during the year, usually toward the end of the baseball season, interest in current year baseball cards waned. Consequently, the manufacturers produced smaller numbers of these later-series cards.

Nearly all nationwide issues from post-World War II manufacturers (1948 to 1973) exhibit these series variations. In the past, Topps, for example, may have issued series consisting of many different numbers of cards, including 55, 66, 80, 88 and others. Recently, Topps has settled on what is now its standard sheet size of 132 cards, six of which comprise its 792-card set.

While the number of cards within a given series is usually the same as the number of cards on one printed sheet, this is not always the case. For example, Bowman used 36 cards on its standard printed sheets, but in 1948 substituted 12 cards during later print runs of that year's baseball cards. Twelve of the cards from the initial sheet of 36 cards were removed and replaced by 12 different cards giving, in effect, a first series of 36 cards and a second series of 12 new cards. This replacement produced a scarcity of 24 cards the 12 cards removed from the original sheet and the 12 new cards added to the sheet. A full sheet of 1948 Bowman cards (second printing) shows that card numbers 37 through 48 have replaced 12 of the cards on the first printing sheet.

The Topps Company also has created scarcities and/or excesses of certain cards in many of its sets. Topps, however, has most frequently gone the other direction by double printing some of the cards. Double printing causes an abundance of cards of the players who are on the same sheet more than one time. During the years from 1978 to 1981, Topps double printed 66 cards out of their large 726-card set. The Topps practice of double printing cards in earlier years is the most logical explanation for the known scarcities of particular cards in some of these Topps sets.

From 1988 through 1990, Donruss short printed and double printed certain cards in its major sets. Ostensibly this was because of its addition of bonus team MVP cards in its regular-issue wax packs.

We are always looking for information or photographs of printing sheets of cards for research. Each year, we try to update the hobby's knowledge of distribution anomalies. Please let us know at the address in this book if you have first-hand knowledge that would be helpful in this pursuit.

Grading Your Cards

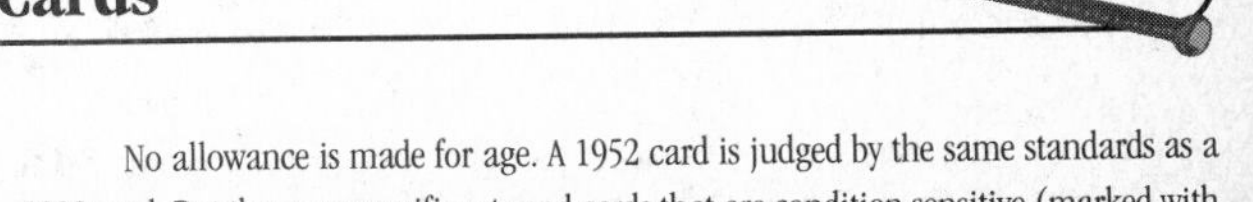

Each hobby has its own grading terminology stamps, coins, comic books, record collecting, etc. Collectors of sports cards are no exception. The one invariable criterion for determining the value of a card is its condition: The better the condition of the card, the more valuable it is. Condition grading, however, is subjective. Individual card dealers and collectors differ in the strictness of their grading, but the stated condition of a card should be determined without regard to whether it is being bought or sold.

No allowance is made for age. A 1952 card is judged by the same standards as a 1992 card. But there are specific sets and cards that are condition sensitive (marked with "!" in the Price Guide) because of their border color, consistently poor centering, etc. Such cards and sets sometimes command premiums above the listed percentages in Mint condition.

Centering

Slightly Off-centered

Off-centered

Well-centered

Badly Off-centered

Miscut

Condition Guide

Centering

Current centering terminology uses numbers representing the percentage of border on either side of the main design. Obviously, centering is diminished in importance for borderless cards such as Stadium Club.

Slightly Off-Center (60/40): A slightly off-center card is one that, upon close inspection, is found to have one border bigger than the opposite border. This degree once was offensive to only purists, but now some hobbyists try to avoid cards that are anything other than perfectly centered.

Off-Center (70/30): An off-center card has one border that is noticeably more than twice as wide as the opposite border.

Badly Off-Center (80/20 or worse): A badly off-center card has virtually no border on one side of the card.

Miscut: A miscut card actually shows part of the adjacent card in its larger border and consequently a corresponding amount of its card is cut off.

Corner Wear

Corner wear is the most scrutinized grading criteria in the hobby. These are the major categories of corner wear:

- **Corner with a slight touch of wear**: The corner still is sharp, but there is a slight touch of wear showing. On a dark-bordered card, this shows as a dot of white.
- **Fuzzy corner**: The corner still comes to a point, but the point has just begun to fray. A slightly "dinged" corner is considered the same as a fuzzy corner.
- **Slightly rounded corner:** The fraying of the corner has increased to where there is only a hint of a point. Mild layering may be evident. A "dinged" corner is considered the same as a slightly rounded corner.
- **Rounded corner**: The point is completely gone. Some layering is noticeable.
- **Badly rounded corner**: The corner is completely round and rough. Severe layering is evident.

Creases

A third common defect is the crease. The degree of creasing in a card is difficult to show in a drawing or picture. On giving the specific condition of an expensive card for sale, the seller should note any creases additionally. Creases can be categorized as to severity according to the following scale:

Light Crease: A light crease is a crease that is barely noticeable upon close inspection. In fact, when cards are in plastic sheets or holders, a light crease may not be seen (until the card is taken out of the holder). A light crease on the front is much more serious than a light crease on the card back only.

Medium Crease: A medium crease is noticeable when held and studied at arm's length by the naked eye, but does not overly detract from the appearance of the card. It is an obvious crease, but not one that breaks the picture surface of the card.

Heavy Crease: A heavy crease is one that has torn or broken through the card's picture surface, e.g., puts a tear in the photo surface.

Alterations

Deceptive Trimming: This occurs when someone alters the card in order (1) to shave off edge wear, (2) to improve the sharpness of the corners, or (3) to improve centering obviously their objective is to falsely increase the perceived value of the card to an unsuspecting buyer. The shrinkage usually is evident only if the trimmed card is compared to an adjacent full-sized card or if the trimmed card is itself measured.

Obvious Trimming: Obvious trimming is noticeable and unfortunate. It is usually performed by non-collectors who give no thought to the present or future value of their cards.

Deceptively Retouched Borders: This occurs when the borders (especially on those cards with dark borders) are touched up on the edges and corners with magic marker or crayons of appropriate color in order to make the card appear Mint.

Categorization of Defects - Miscellaneous Flaws

The following are common minor flaws that, depending on severity, lower a card's condition by one to four grades and often render it no better than Excellent-Mint: bubbles (lumps in surface), gum and wax stains, diamond cutting (slanted borders), notching, off-centered backs, paper wrinkles, scratched-off cartoons or puzzles on back, rubber band marks, scratches, surface impressions and warping.

The following are common serious flaws that, depending on severity, lower a card's condition at least four grades and often render it no better than Good: chemical or sun fading, erasure marks, mildew, miscutting (severe off-centering), holes, bleached or re-touched borders, tape marks, tears, trimming, water or coffee stains and writing.

Grades

Mint (Mt) - A card with no flaws or wear. The card has four perfect corners, 60/40 or better centering from top to bottom and from left to right, original gloss, smooth edges and original color borders. A Mint card does not have print spots, color or focus imperfections.

Near Mint-Mint (NrMt-Mt) - A card with one minor flaw. Any one of the following would lower a Mint card to Near Mint-Mint: one corner with a slight touch of wear, barely noticeable print spots, color or focus imperfections. The card must have 60/40 or better centering in both directions, original gloss, smooth edges and original color borders.

Near Mint (NrMt) - A card with one minor flaw. Any one of the following would lower a Mint card to Near Mint: one fuzzy corner or two to four corners with slight touches of wear, 70/30 to 60/40 centering, slightly rough edges, minor print spots, color or focus imperfections. The card must have original gloss and original color borders.

Excellent-Mint (ExMt) - A card with two or three fuzzy, but not rounded, corners and centering no worse than 80/20. The card may have no more than two of the following: slightly rough edges, very slightly discolored borders, minor print spots, color or focus imperfections. The card must have original gloss.

Excellent (Ex) - A card with four fuzzy but definitely not rounded corners and centering no worse than 80/20. The card may have a small amount of original gloss lost, rough edges, slightly discolored borders and minor print spots, color or focus imperfections.

Very Good (Vg) - A card that has been handled but not abused: slightly rounded corners with slight layering, slight notching on edges, a significant amount of gloss lost from the surface but no scuffing and moderate discoloration of borders. The card may have a few light creases.

Good (G), Fair (F), Poor (P) - A well-worn, mishandled or abused card: badly rounded and layered corners, scuffing, most or all original gloss missing, seriously discolored borders, moderate or heavy creases, and one or more serious flaws. The grade of Good, Fair or Poor depends on the severity of wear and flaws. Good, Fair and Poor cards generally are used only as fillers.

The most widely used grades are defined above. Obviously, many cards will not perfectly fit one of the definitions.

Therefore, categories between the major grades known as in-between grades are used, such as Good to Very Good (G-Vg), Very Good to Excellent (VgEx), and Excellent-Mint to Near Mint (ExMt-NrMt). Such grades indicate a card with all qualities of the lower category but with at least a few qualities of the higher category.

Beckett Baseball Card Price Guide lists each card and set in two grades, with the middle grade valued at about 40-45% of the top grade.

The value of cards that fall between the listed columns can also be calculated using a percentage of the top grade. For example, a card that falls between the top and middle grades (Ex, ExMt or NrMt in most cases) will generally be valued at anywhere from 50% to 90% of the top grade.

Similarly, a card that falls between the middle and bottom grades (G-Vg, Vg or VgEx in most cases) will generally be valued at anywhere from 20% to 40% of the top grade.

There are also cases where cards are in better condition than the top grade or worse than the bottom grade. Cards that grade worse than the lowest grade are generally valued at 5-10% of the top grade.

When a card exceeds the top grade by one such as NrMt-Mt when the top grade is NrMt, or Mint when the top grade is NrMt-Mt a premium of up to 50% is possible, with 10-20% the usual norm.

When a card exceeds the top grade by two such as Mint when the top grade is NrMt, or NrMt-Mt when the top grade is ExMt a premium of 25-50% is the usual norm. But certain condition sensitive cards or sets, particularly those from the pre-war era, can bring premiums of up to 100% or even more.

Unopened packs, boxes and factory-collated sets are considered Mint in their unknown (and presumed perfect) state. Once opened, however, each card can be graded (and valued) in its own right by taking into account any defects that may be present in spite of the fact that the card has never been handled.

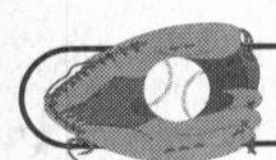

Corner Wear

The partial cards shown below have been photographed at 300%. This was done in order to magnify each card's corner wear to such a degree that differences could be shown on a printed page.

The 1962 Topps Hank Aaron card has a slightly rounded corner. Note that there is definite corner wear evident by the fraying and that the corner no longer sports a sharp point.

The 1962 Topps Gil Hodges card has corner wear; it is slightly better than the Aaron card above. Nevertheless, some collectors might classify this Hodges corner as slightly rounded.

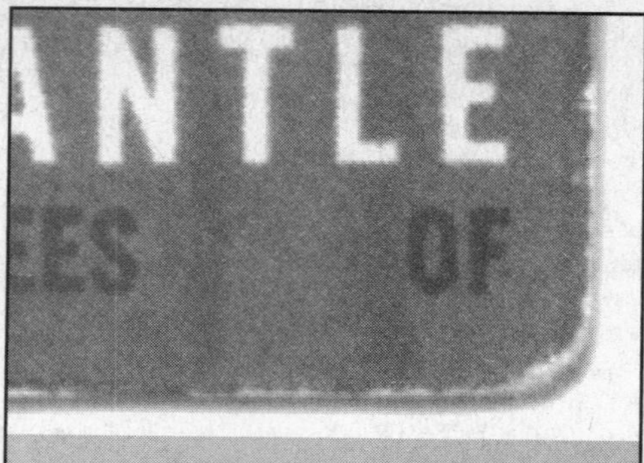

The 1962 Topps Hank Aaron card has a slightly rounded corner. Note that there is definite corner wear evident by the fraying and that the corner no longer sports a sharp point.

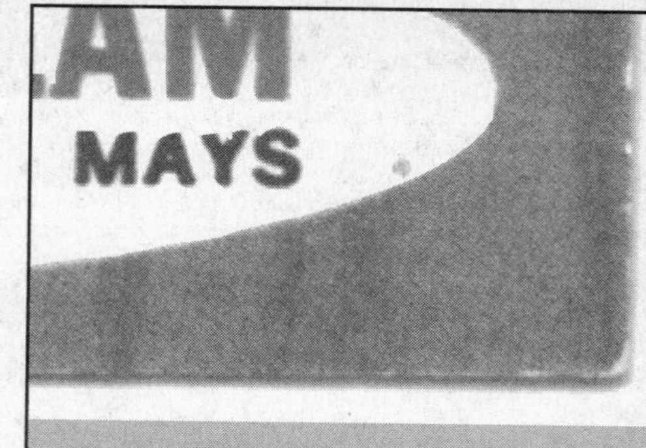

The 1962 Topps Gil Hodges card has corner wear; it is slightly better than the Aaron card above. Nevertheless, some collectors might classify this Hodges corner as slightly rounded.

The 1962 Topps Don Mossi card has very slight corner wear such that it might be called a fuzzy corner. A close look at the original card shows the corner is not perfect, but almost. However, note that corner wear is somewhat academic on this card. As you can plainly see, the heavy crease going across his name breaks through the photo surface.

Selling Your Cards

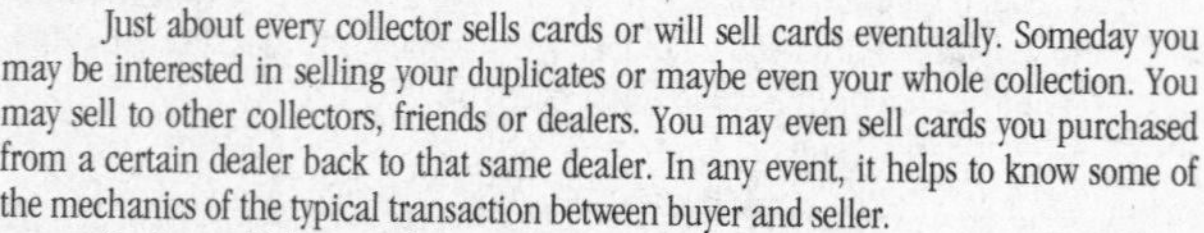

Just about every collector sells cards or will sell cards eventually. Someday you may be interested in selling your duplicates or maybe even your whole collection. You may sell to other collectors, friends or dealers. You may even sell cards you purchased from a certain dealer back to that same dealer. In any event, it helps to know some of the mechanics of the typical transaction between buyer and seller.

Dealers will buy cards in order to resell them to other collectors who are interested in the cards. Dealers will always pay a higher percentage for items that (in their opinion) can be resold quickly, and a much lower percentage for those items that are perceived as having low demand and hence are slow moving. In either case, dealers must buy at a price that allows for the expense of doing business and a margin for profit.

If you have cards for sale, the best advice we can give is that you get several offers for your cards either from card shops or at a card show and take the best offer, all things considered. Note, the "best" offer may not be the one for the highest amount. And remember, if a dealer really wants your cards, he won't let you get away without making his best competitive offer. Another alternative is to place your cards in an auction as one or several lots.

Many people think nothing of going into a department store and paying $15 for an item of clothing for which the store paid $5. But if you were selling your $15 card to a dealer and he offered you $5 for it, you might consider his mark-up unreasonable. To complete the analogy: Most department stores (and card dealers) that consistently pay $10 for $15 items eventually go out of business. An exception is when the dealer has lined up a willing buyer for the item(s) you are attempting to sell, or if the cards are so Hot that it's likely he'll likely have to hold the cards for just a short period of time.

In those cases, an offer of up to 75 percent of book value still will allow the dealer to make a reasonable profit considering the short time he will need to hold the merchandise. In general, however, most cards and collections will bring offers in the range of 25 to 50 percent of retail price. Also consider that most material from the last five to 10 years is plentiful. If that's what you're selling, don't be surprised if your best offer is well below that range.

Interesting Notes

The first card numerically of an issue is the single card most likely to obtain excessive wear.

Consequently, you typically will find the price on the #1 card (in NrMt or Mint condition) somewhat higher than might otherwise be the case.

Similarly, but to a lesser extent (because normally the less important, reverse side of the card is the one exposed), the last card numerically in an issue also is prone to abnormal wear. This extra wear and tear occurs because the first and last cards are exposed to the elements (human element included) more than any of the other cards. They are generally end cards in any brick formations, rubber bandings, stackings on wet surfaces and like activities.

Sports cards have no intrinsic value. The value of a card, like the value of other collectibles, can be determined only by you and your enjoyment in viewing and possessing these cardboard treasures.

Remember, the buyer ultimately determines the price of each baseball card. You are the determining price factor because you have the ability to say "No" to the price of any card by not exchanging your hard-earned money for a given issue. When the cost of a trading card exceeds the enjoyment you will receive from it, your answer should be "No." We assess and report the prices. You set them!

We are always interested in receiving the price input of collectors and dealers. We happily credit major contributors. We welcome your opinions, since your contributions assist us in ensuring a better guide each year. If you would like to join our survey list for the next editions of this book and others authored by Dr. Beckett, please send your name and address to Dr. James Beckett, 15850 Dallas Parkway, Dallas, TX 75248.

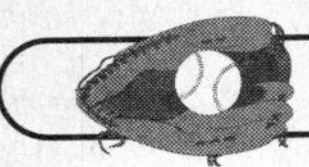
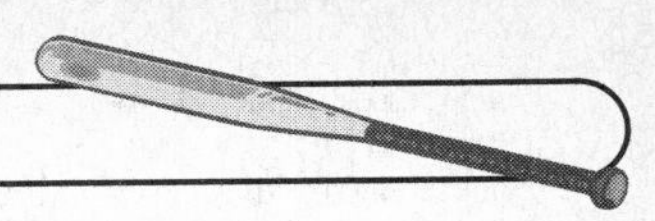

History of Baseball Cards

Today's version of the baseball card, with its colorful and oftentimes high-tech front and back, is a far cry from its earliest predecessors. The issue remains cloudy as to which was the very first baseball card ever produced, but the institution of baseball cards dates from the latter half of the 19th century, more than 100 years ago. Early issues, generally printed on heavy cardboard, were of poor quality, with photographs, drawings, and printing far short of today's standards.

Goodwin & Co., of New York, makers of Gypsy Queen, Old Judge, and other cigarette brands, is considered by many to be the first issuer of baseball and other sports cards. Its issues, predominantly sized 1-1/2 by 2-1/2 inches, generally consisted of photographs of baseball players, boxers, wrestlers, and other subjects mounted on stiff cardboard. More than 2,000 different photos of baseball players alone have been identified. These "Old Judges" a collective name commonly used for the Goodwin & Co. cards, were issued from 1886 to 1890 and are treasured parts of many collections today.

Among the other cigarette companies that issued baseball cards still attracting attention today are Allen & Ginter, D. Buchner & Co. (Gold Coin Chewing Tobacco), and P. H. Mayo & Brother. Cards from the first two companies bear colored line drawings, while the Mayos are sepia photographs on black cardboard. In addition to the small-size cards from this era, several tobacco companies issued cabinet-size baseball cards. These "cabinets" were considerably larger than the small cards, usually about 4-1/4 by 6-1/2 inches, and were printed on heavy stock. Goodwin & Co.'s Old Judge cabinets and the National Tobacco Works' "Newsboy" baseball photos are two that remain popular today.

By 1895, the American Tobacco Company began to dominate its competition. They discontinued baseball card inserts in their cigarette packages (actually slide boxes in those days). The lack of competition in the cigarette market had made these inserts unnecessary. This marked the end of the first era of baseball cards. At the dawn of the 20th century, few baseball cards were being issued. But once again, it was the cigarette companies, particularly, the American Tobacco Company, followed to a lesser extent by the candy and gum makers that revived the practice of including baseball cards with their products. The bulk of these cards, identified in the American Card Catalog (designated hereafter as ACC) as T or E cards for 20th century "Tobacco" or "Early Candy and Gum" issues, respectively, were released from 1909 to 1915.

This romantic and popular era of baseball card collecting produced many desirable items. The most outstanding is the fabled T-206 Honus Wagner card. Other perennial favorites among collectors are the T-206 Eddie Plank card, and the T-206 Magee error card. The former was once the second most valuable card and only recently relinquished that position to a more distinctive and aesthetically pleasing Napoleon Lajoie card from the 1933–34 Goudey Gum series. The latter misspells the player's name as "Magie" the most famous and most valuable blooper card.

The ingenuity and distinctiveness of this era has yet to be surpassed. Highlights include:

- The T-202 Hassan triple-folders, one of the best looking and the most distinctive cards ever issued;
- The durable T-201 Mecca double-folders, one of the first sets with players' records on the reverse;
- The T-3 Turkey Reds, the hobby's most popular cabinet card;
- The E-145 Cracker Jacks, the only major set containing Federal League player cards; and
- The T-204 Ramlys, with their distinctive black-and-white oval photos and ornate gold borders.

These are but a few of the varieties issued during this period.

Increasing Popularity

While the American Tobacco Company dominated the field, several other tobacco companies, as well as clothing manufacturers, newspapers and periodicals, game makers, and companies whose identities remain anonymous, also issued cards during this period. In fact, the Collins-McCarthy Candy Company, makers of Zeenuts Pacific Coast League baseball cards, issued cards yearly from 1911 to 1938. Its record for continuous annual card production has been exceeded only by the Topps Chewing Gum Company. The era of the tobacco card issues closed with the onset of World War I, with the exception of the Red Man chewing tobacco sets produced from 1952 to 1955.

The next flurry of card issues broke out in the roaring and prosperous 1920s, the era of the E card. The caramel companies (National Caramel, American Caramel, York Caramel) were the leading distributors of these E cards. In addition, the strip card, a continuos strip with several cards divided by dotted lines or other sectioning features, flourished during this time. While the E cards and the strip cards generally are considered less imaginative than the T cards or the recent candy and gum issues, they still are pursued by many advanced collectors.

Another significant event of the 1920s was the introduction of the arcade card. Taking its designation from its issuer, the Exhibit Supply Company of Chicago, it is usually known as the "Exhibit" card. Once a trademark of the penny arcades, amusement parks, and county fairs across the country, Exhibit machines dispensed nearly postcard-size photos on thick stock for one penny. These picture cards bore likenesses of a favorite cowboy, actor, actress, or baseball player. Exhibit Supply and its associated companies produced baseball cards during a longer time span, although discontinuous, than any other manufacturer. Its first cards appeared in 1921, while its last issue was in 1966. In 1979, the Exhibit Supply Company was bought and somewhat revived by a collector/dealer who has since reprinted Exhibit photos of the past.

If the T card period, from 1909 to 1915, can be designated the "Golden Age" of baseball card collecting, then perhaps the "Silver Age" commenced with the introduction of the Big League Gum series of 239 cards in 1933 (a 240th card was added in 1934). These are the forerunners of today's baseball gum cards, and the Goudey Gum Company of Boston is responsible for their success. This era spanned the period from the Depression days of 1933 to America's formal involvement in World War II in 1941.

Goudey's attractive designs, with full-color line drawings on thick card stock, greatly influenced other cards being issued at that time. As a result, the most attractive and popular vintage cards in history were produced in this "Silver Age." The 1933 Goudey Big League Gum series also owes its popularity to the more than 40 Hall of Fame players in the set. These include four cards of Babe Ruth and two of Lou Gehrig. Goudey's reign continued in 1934, when it issued a 96-card set in color, together with the single remaining card from the 1933 series, #106, the Napoleon Lajoie card.

In addition to Goudey, several other bubblegum manufacturers issued baseball cards during this era. DeLong Gum Company issued an extremely attractive set in 1933. National Chicle Company's 192-card "Batter-Up" series of 1934–1936 became the largest die-cut set in card history. In addition, that company offered the popular "Diamond Stars" series during the same period. Other popular sets included the "Tattoo Orbit" set of 60 color cards issued in 1933 and Gum Products' 75-card "Double Play" set, featuring sepia depictions of two players per card.

In 1939, Gum Inc., which later became Bowman Gum, replaced Goudey Gum as the leading baseball card producer. In 1939 and the following year, it issued two important sets of black-and-white cards. In 1939, its "Play Ball America" set consisted of 162 cards. The larger, 240-card "Play Ball" set of 1940 still is considered by many to be the most attractive black-and-white cards ever produced. That firm introduced its only color set in 1941, consisting of 72 cards titled "Play Ball Sports Hall of Fame." Many of these were colored repeats of poses from the black-and-white 1940 series.

In addition to regular gum cards, many manufacturers distributed premium issues during the 1930s. These premiums were printed on paper or photographic stock, rather than card stock. They were much larger than the regular cards and were sold for a penny across the counter with gum (which was packaged separately from the premium). They often were redeemed at the store or through the mail in exchange for the wrappers of previously purchased gum cards, like proof-of-purchase box-top premiums today. The gum premiums are scarcer than the card issues of the 1930s and in most cases no manufacturer's name is present.

World War II brought an end to this popular era of card collecting when paper and rubber shortages curtailed the production of bubblegum baseball cards. They were resurrected again in 1948 by the Bowman Gum Company (the direct descendent of Gum Inc.). This marked the beginning of the modern era of card collecting.

In 1948, Bowman Gum issued a 48-card set in black and white consisting of one card and one slab of gum in every 1-cent pack. That same year, the Leaf Gum Company also issued a set of cards. Although rather poor in quality, these cards were issued in color. A squabble over the rights to use players' pictures developed between Bowman and Leaf. Eventually Leaf dropped out of the card market, but not before it had left a lasting heritage to the hobby by issuing some of the rarest cards now in existence. Leaf's baseball card series of 1948–49 contained 98 cards, skip numbered to #168 (not all numbers were printed). Of these 98 cards, 49 are relatively plentiful; the other 49, however, are rare and quite valuable.

Bowman continued its production of cards in 1949 with a color series of 240 cards. Because there are many scarce "high numbers," this series remains the most difficult Bowman regular issue to complete. Although the set was printed in color and commands great interest due to its scarcity, it is considered aesthetically inferior to the Goudey and National Chicle issues of the 1930s. In addition to the regular issue of 1949, Bowman also produced a set of 36 Pacific Coast League players. While this was not a regular issue, it still is prized by collectors. In fact, it has become the most valuable Bowman series.

In 1950 (representing Bowman's one-year monopoly of the baseball card market), the company began a string of top-quality cards that continued until its demise in 1955. The 1950 series was itself something of an oddity because the low numbers, rather than the traditional high numbers, were the more difficult cards to obtain.

The year 1951 marked the beginning of the most competitive and perhaps the highest quality period of baseball card production. In that year, Topps Chewing Gum Company of Brooklyn entered the market. Topps' 1951 series consisted of two sets of 52 cards each, one set with red backs and the other with blue backs. In addition, Topps also issued 31 insert cards, three of which remain the rarest Topps cards ("Current All-Stars" Konstanty, Roberts, and Stanky). The 1951 Topps cards were unattractive and paled in comparison to the 1951 Bowman issues. They were successful, however, and Topps has continued to produce cards ever since.

Intensified Competition

Topps issued a larger and more attractive card set in 1952. This larger size became standard for the next five years. (Bowman followed with larger-size baseball cards in 1953.) This 1952 Topps set has become, like the 1933 Goudey series and the T-206 white border series, the classic set of its era. The 407-card set is a collector's dream of scarcities, rarities, errors, and variations. It also contains the first Topps issues of Mickey Mantle and Willie Mays.

As with Bowman and Leaf in the late 1940s, competition over player rights arose.

Ensuing court battles occurred between Topps and Bowman. The market split due to stiff competition, and in January 1956, Topps bought out Bowman. (Topps, using the Bowman name, resurrected Bowman as a label in 1989.) Topps remained essentially unchallenged as the primary producer of baseball cards through 1980. So, the story of major baseball card sets from 1956 through 1980 is by and large the story of Topps' issues. Notable exceptions include the small sets produced by Fleer Gum in 1959, 1960, 1961, and 1963, and the Kellogg's Cereal and Hostess Cakes baseball cards issued to promote their products.

A court decision in 1980 paved the way for two other large gum companies to enter (or reenter, in Fleer's case) the baseball card arena. Fleer, which had last made photo cards in 1963, and the Donruss Company (then a division of General Mills) secured rights to produce baseball cards of current players, thus breaking Topps' monopoly. Each company issued major card sets in 1981 with bubblegum products.

Then a higher court decision in that year overturned the lower court ruling against Topps. It appeared that Topps had regained its sole position as a producer of baseball cards. Undaunted by the revocation ruling, Fleer and Donruss continued to issue cards in 1982 but without bubblegum or any other edible product. Fleer issued its current player baseball cards with "team logo stickers," while Donruss issued its cards with a piece of a baseball jigsaw puzzle.

Sharing the Pie

Since 1981, these three major baseball card producers all have thrived, sharing relatively equal recognition. Each has steadily increased its involvement in terms of numbers of issues per year. To the delight of collectors, their competition has generated novel, and in some cases exceptional, issues of current Major League Baseball players. Collectors also eagerly accepted the debut efforts of Score (1988) and Upper Deck (1989). These five companies were about to embark on a wild ride through the 1990s.

Upper Deck's successful entry into the market turned out to be very important. The company's card stock, photography, packaging, and marketing gave baseball cards a new standard for quality and began the "premium card" trend that continues today. The second premium baseball card set to be issued was the 1990 Leaf set, named for and issued by the parent company of Donruss. To gauge the significance of the premium card trend, one need only note that two of the most valuable post-1986 regular-issue cards in the hobby are the 1989 Upper Deck Ken Griffey Jr. and 1990 Leaf Frank Thomas Rookie Cards.

The impressive debut of Leaf in 1990 was followed by Studio, Ultra, and Stadium Club in 1991. Of those, Stadium Club with its dramatic borderless photo, un-coated card fronts made the biggest impact. In 1992, Bowman and Pinnacle joined the premium fray. In 1992, Donruss and Fleer abandoned the traditional 50-cent pack market and instead produced premium sets comparable to (and presumably designed to compete against) Upper Deck's set. Those moves, combined with the almost instantaneous spread of premium cards to the other major team sports cards, serve as strong indicators that premium cards were here to stay. Bowman had been a lower-level product from 1989 to 1991.

In 1993, Fleer, Topps, and Upper Deck produced the first "super premium" cards with Flair, Finest, and SP, respectively. The success of all three products was an indication the baseball card market was headed toward even higher price levels, and that turned out to be the case in 1994 with the introduction of Bowman's Best (a Topps hybrid of prospect-oriented Bowman and the superpremium Finest) and Leaf Limited. Other 1994 debuts included Upper Deck's entry-level Collector's Choice and Pinnacle's hobby-only Select.

Overall, inserts continued to dominate the hobby scene. Specifically, the parallel chase cards introduced in 1992 with Topps Gold became the latest major hobby trend. Topps Gold was followed by 1993 Finest Refractors (at the time the scarcest insert ever produced and still a landmark set) and the one-per-box Stadium Club First Day Issue.

Of course, the biggest on-field news of 1994 was the owner-provoked players' strike that halted the season prematurely. While the baseball card hobby suffered noticeably from the strike, there was no catastrophic market crash as some had feared. However, the strike drasticly slowed down a market that was both strong and growing and contributed to a serious hobby contraction that continues to this day.

By 1995, parallel insert sets were commonplace and had taken on a new complexion: the most popular ones were those that had announced (or at least suspected) print runs of 500 or less, such as Finest Refractors and Select Artist's Proofs.

This trend continued in 1996, with several parallel inserts that were printed in quantities of 250 or less, such as Finest Gold Refractors, Fleer Circa Rave, Studio Silver Press Proofs, and three of the six Select Certified parallels. It could be argued that the high price tags on these extremely limited parallel cards (many exceeded the $1,000 plateau) were driving many single-player collectors to frustration, and even completely out of the hobby. At the same time, average pack prices soared while average number of cards per pack dropped, making the baseball card hobby increasingly expensive.

On the positive side, two trends from 1996 clearly brought in new collectors: Topps' Mickey Mantle retrospective inserts in both series of Topps and Stadium Club and Leaf's Signature Series, which included one certified autograph per pack. While the Mantle craze following his passing seemed to be a short-term phenomenon, the inclusion of autographs in packs seemed to have more long-term significance.

In 1997 the print runs in selected sets got even lower. Both Fleer/SkyBox and Pinnacle brands issued cards of which only one exists.

The growth in popularity of autographs also continued. Many products had autographed cards in their packs. A very positive trend was a return to basics. Many collectors bought Rookie Cards, as they understood that concept, and worked on finishing sets.

There was also an increase in international players collecting. Hideo Nomo was incredibly popular in Japan while Chan Ho Park was in demand in Korea. This bodes well for an international growth in the hobby.

Clearly, 1998 was a year of rebirth and growth for the hobby. The big boost came from the home run chase being conducted by Mark McGwire and Sammy Sosa, as well as the continued brilliance of stalwarts like Ken Griffey Jr. and Roger Clemens. The baseball card hobby received a great deal of positive publicity from the renewed interest in the game.

Rookie Cards of the key players of 1998 made significant gains in value as the hobby once again turned to Rookie Cards as the collectible of choice. Also, cards professionally graded by companies such as PSA and SGC were becoming more heavily traded in both older and newer material.

In addition, the Internet and various services such as eBay contributed to the strong growth in collecting interest over the year.

There were downsides in 1998, though. Pinnacle Brands folded, leaving a legacy of innovation and promotions not seen by other companies. In addition, there still was the problem of collectors being frustrated by the extremely short printed cards of their favorite players, making set completion almost impossible.

During 1998, Pacific received a full baseball license and added many innovations to the card market. Their 1998 OnLine set is the most comprehensive set issued in the last five years and many veteran collectors applauded Pacific's continuing attempts to get as many players as possible into their sets.

In the last couple of years, card companies have been printing specific subsets (usually young players or Rookie Cards) in shorter supply than the regular cards. This is not in every set, but in many sets produced since 1998.

In 1999, many of the trends of the last couple of years continued to gain strength. Buying, selling, and trading cards over the Internet became a dominant factor in the secondary market. Beckett Publications began its own Marketplace, offering the collectors a chance to search across inventory from many of the finest dealers nationwide in one comprehensive online database; eBay continued to flourish, while many other parties began to reap the benefits of the burgeoning online auction market. The Barry Halper collection was auctioned off; bringing many museum quality items to the market and giving the older memorabilia market a significant boost as many treasures were made available to collectors.

Also, the boom in Internet trading created a perfect fit for professionally graded cards, as buyers and sellers traded cards sight unseen with the confidence established by a third-party grader.

From a field of almost a dozen contenders, three companies emerged in 1999 to dominate the field of professional grading, BGS (Beckett Grading Services), PSA (Professional Sports Authenticator), and SGC (Sportscard Guaranty L.L.C.). In 1999 these companies made dramatic expansions in onsite grading and submissions at card shows throughout the nation. In response to the widespread acceptance of graded cards, the line of monthly Beckett Price Guides each added a separate section within the price guide area for professionally graded cards.

Similar to 1998, four licensed manufacturers (Fleer/SkyBox, Pacific, Topps, and Upper Deck) produced slightly more than fifty different products for 1999.

Perhaps the biggest hit of the 1999 card season was created by Topps. Card #220 within the basic issue first series 1999 Topps brand featured Home Run King Mark McGwire in 70 variations, one for each homer he slugged in 1998, and many collectors went after the whole set. Continuing a legacy as strong as the Yankees, the basic Topps issue was one of the most popular sets released in 1999.

Closely trailing the Topps McGwire promotion was Upper Deck's dynamic A Piece of History bat card promotion. The card that kicked off the frenzy was the Babe Ruth A Piece of History distributed in 1999 Upper Deck series 1 packs. Upper Deck actually purchased a cracked game-used Babe Ruth bat for $24,000 and proceeded to cut it up into approximately 350-400 chips of wood to create the now famous Ruth bat card. The card instantly created polar opposites of opinion among hobbyists. Traditional collectors howled at the sacrilegious act of destroying such a historic piece of memorabilia while more open-minded collectors jumped at the opportunity to chase such an important card. The Ruth card was followed up by the cross-brand "500 Club bat card promotion, whereby UD produced bat cards from every major league ballplayer who hit 500 or more home runs in their career (except for Mark McGwire, who hit his 500th in the midst of the 1999 season and promptly stated that he did not support Upper Deck's promotion).

More memorabilia cards than ever were offered to collectors in 1999 as Fleer/SkyBox kicked up their efforts to match the standards set by Upper Deck in previous years. Batting gloves, hats, and shoes joined the typical bats and jerseys as pieces of game-used equipment to be featured on trading cards. Sets like E-X Century Authen-Kicks and Fleer Mystique Feel the Game typified the new offerings.

Topps only dabbled with memorabilia cards in 1999, but continued to offer some of the hottest autographed inserts, highlighted by the Topps Stars Rookie Reprint Autographs and the Topps Nolan Ryan Autographs.

Pacific made a clear decision to steer free of memorabilia and autograph inserts, instead focusing on offering collectors a wide selection of beautifully designed insert and parallel cards. Those themes worked beautifully with their established presence for making comprehensive sets, providing collectors with the necessary challenge to pursue regional stars and a favorite team in addition to the typical superstars.

An astounding total of 264 players made their first appearance on a major league licensed trading card in 1999. What may go down as the deepest class of Rookie Cards of all time features a cornucopia of talented youngsters led by Rick Ankiel, Josh Beckett, Pat Burrell, Josh Hamilton, Eric Munson, Corey Patterson, and Alfonso Soriano.

As in years past, Topps continued to provide collectors with a fistful of Rookie Cards within their Bowman, Bowman Chrome and Bowman's Best brands. In a trend established in 1998 by Fleer when they released their Fleer Update set (fueled largely by a J. D. Drew Rookie Card), hobbyists enjoyed a bevy of late-season sets chock full of RC's. Fleer/SkyBox made an all out effort by stuffing more than 100 Rookie Cards into their 1999 Fleer Update set. Topps produced their first boxed Traded set since 1994. Each 1999 Topps Traded set contained 1 of 75 different cards autographed by a rookie prospect. Considering how much wider the selection of Rookie Cards became in 1999, it's amazing to see that so few of these RC's were serial numbered. When one looks at the success established with serial numbered Rookie Cards in the basketball and football card markets with brands like SP Authentic and SPx Finite, one can only scratch his head when realizing that Fleer Mystique was the only brand to offer baseball collectors serial numbered RC's. Thus, it's not surprising to see that despite having 25 different Rookie Cards issued in 1999, Pat Burrell's Fleer Mystique RC (#'d of 2,999) had been established as his "best" RC by year's end.

Youngsters weren't the only players in the limelight in 1999 as retired stars and Hall of Famers were featured on more cards than any other year in the 1990s. Upper Deck's Century Legends brand, featuring the top 50 active and top 50 retired players of the decade as chosen by the Sporting News was a runaway hit.

Perhaps the most popular insert set of the year, outpacing all of the dazzling high-dollar memorabilia cards, was Topps Gallery Heritage. Utilizing the design and painting style of artist Gerry Dvorak from the classic 1953 Topps set, these modern masterpieces proved that insert cards can still be a hot commodity in the secondary market, albeit assuming they're well conceived and well made, an unfortunate rarity these days.

The spate of basic issue sets with short-printed subsets continued across many brands in 1999. In reaction to many frustrated dealers and collectors struggling to complete these sets, Fleer/SkyBox created dual versions of each prospect card for the 1999 SkyBox Premium set, an action shot was short-printed and a posed shot was seeded at the same rate as other basic issue cards. The idea was well received by collectors but enjoyed a surprisingly short-lived period of active trading in the secondary market.

The year 2000 was marked by several major developments that would continue shaping the future of our hobby. First off, Pacific decided to forfeit their baseball card license on January 1st, 2000, in an effort to more sharply focus their production expenditures into football and hockey.

In a separate development, Wizards of the Coast (primarily known for their non-sport gaming cards) was granted a license to produce baseball trading cards and debuted their MLB Showdown brand. The cards proved to be quite successful in that they were collected as a set by veteran collectors and played as a game by children (and some adults) both inside and outside of the typical collecting community.

By year's end, Fleer fazed out their SkyBox and Flair brand names in an effort to take full advantage of the historic significance and brand recognition of their flagship Fleer sets issued sporadically during the late 1950s–1970s and consistently from 1981 to the present.

Almost sixty brands of MLB-licensed cards, issued by five manufacturers were produced in 2000. In addition, Just Minors and Team Best produced a variety of attractive minor league products. Most shop owners continued to generate their income primarily through the sales of packs and boxes of new product, and, as in years past, they had to make careful decisions as to what to keep in stock for customers and what to pass up in fear of a low sell through.

Vintage (or retro-themed) sets dominated the market highlighted by Fleer Greats of the Game, Upper Deck Yankees Legends, and the run of 3,000 hit club and Joe DiMaggio game-used cards issued by Fleer and Upper Deck. In 2001, Topps Heritage (mimicking the style of the classic '52 Topps cards), Upper Deck Vintage (in an homage to '63 Topps baseball), and the return of Topps Archives (after a six-year hiatus) added fuel to the fire.

Using the vintage-theme to tap into a base of wealthy consumers, Upper Deck rolled out their line of Master Collection products (which debuted in basketball a year prior with a Michael Jordan set). Both the Yankees Master Collection and Brooklyn Dodgers Master Collection sets carried initial SRP's of $4,000 or more, marking the most expensive "factory set" of all-time. Each of these sets was serial numbered (500 Yankees and 250 Dodgers), came in a stylish wood box and contained an assortment of game-used and autograph cards from legends of days gone by.

Game-used memorabilia cards became more abundant in all products to the point where a few early 2001 releases (2001 Pacific Private Stock and 2001 SP Game Bat Edition both carrying SRP's in the $15–$20 range) included them at a rate of one per pack. Both products enjoyed a dynamic sell through and proved to be very popular in the secondary market. The result, however, on the secondary market values of game-used memorabilia cards has been dramatic. An Alex Rodriguez or Ken Griffey Jr. game bat or game jersey card that sold for $200+ in 1999 could be had for as little as $25-$50 in early 2001.

Patch cards (a swatch of jersey that contains part of a multi-colored patch) really caught on by year's end as the market formalized premium values on these cards. Upper Deck was the first to create separate "super-premium" jersey Patch inserts within 2000 Upper Deck 1 and 2000 Upper Deck Game Jersey Edition (aka series 2). Pacific followed suit with their Game Gear patch subset within the invincible brand.

By early 2001, Major League Baseball Properties had gotten involved with the trading card autograph and memorabilia programs. From 2001 on, all MLB-licensed trading cards produced by the manufacturers that involved an autograph or game-used memorabilia item had to have the procurement of the item witnessed by a representative of Andersen Consulting, a firm hired by MLB to oversee this historic program. Never before had consumers been provided such an effort by the league and manufacturers to be offered autographed or game-used memorabilia trading cards of such authentic provenance.

Short-printed subset cards, a trend started in 1999, continued to be a common element in most basic sets. The trend, however, evolved to the point where these short prints were now being serial numbered, autographed by the player or incorporating an element of game-used material onto the card. The result was higher values on the key singles, but lower odds of actually finding a good RC in a pack. By year's end, a general sentiment of frustration over not being able to pull good Rookie Cards from a box was beginning to be heard more and more often from collectors.

Rookie Cards incorporating game-used material debuted at year's end in 2000 Black Diamond Rookie Edition. Also, Rookie Cards signed by the player, introduced within the basketball and football card markets in 1999 (with Upper Deck's SPx brand), made their baseball debut in 2000 SPx. Serial-numbered Rookie Cards grew in total usage, but shrank in print run numbers as production figures reached an all-time low of 999 copies for a basic issue RC within the 2000 Pacific Omega set.

Year-end boxed sets, a trend brought back from a four year hiatus by Fleer in 1998 with their Fleer Update set, continued to expand as Topps issued their Bowman Draft Picks and Bowman Chrome Draft Picks sets to cap the now single-series accompanying standard Bowman and Bowman Chrome products.

Fleer broke new ground by blending a 1980s "old-school" concept with some postmodern angles in their 2000 Fleer Glossy boxed set. Harkening back to the run of Glossy parallel factory sets produced from 1987 to 1989, the 2000 Fleer Glossy set included a parallel version of the complete 400-card basic 2000 Fleer set. In addition, 50 new cards (card #'s 401–450, each serial numbered to 1,000 copies) featuring a selection of prospects and rookies were created. Each Glossy factory set contained 5 of the 50 new cards, making it a real challenge to complete the Glossy set.

In a first of its kind for the baseball market, Upper Deck issued a product in December 2000 called Rookie Update that incorporated new cards for three separate popular brands (SP Authentic, SPx, and UD Pros and Prospects) into each pack of cards.

Upper Deck came to terms with Major League Baseball for a license to produce cards featuring members of past and present Team USA squads (bringing back a run of cards last seen seven years ago in 1993 Topps Traded). That allowed Upper Deck the opportunity to radically expand their production of "true" Rookie Cards in year-end 2000 products, adding a spate of cards featuring heroes from the Olympics in Sydney, Australia, like Ben Sheets. Not surprisingly, the number of prospects making their Rookie Card debut in 2000 sets jumped from about 280 players in 1999 to slightly more than 350 players in 2000.

The influence of sports card dealers and collectors from the Far East (and most noticeably Japan) continued to grow in 2000 as stateside buying approached frenzied levels over scarce Hideo Nomo and Kazuhiro Sasaki cards. A much-traveled starter these days, Nomo's first-ever certified autograph card (issued within the Fleer Mystique Fresh Ink insert set) was the hottest card in the hobby for two months (initially trading for as much as $600–$800).

Not all trends were met with success this year. In particular, low-end products geared towards the youth audience (like 2000 Impact by Fleer) were roundly ignored. The hobby still faces a tough road ahead to keep new waves of collectors involved from generation to generation. Part of the Catch-22 with creating affordable brands catered to youths is that the same customers are most interested in the high-end, expensive material.

Also, Upper Deck's PowerDeck product faced an indifferent audience for a second year in a row, as collectors and even general sports enthusiasts outside the hobby failed to get excited over the CD-ROM cards. More success was met by UD's e-Card insert program, whereby collectors who pulled an e-Card from a pack of UD cards had to go to UD's website and check the serial number printed on the card to see if it could evolve into an autograph, game jersey, or game jersey autograph exchange.

The Internet continued to have profound ramifications on shaping the destiny of sports card collecting. By 2000, nearly every dealer (and hard-core collector) was buying or selling cards to some degree in on-line auctions. Auction sales had become so prolific, that they were now having a strong effect on the secondary market sales levels of trading cards in arenas entirely outside of cyberspace, like shops, shows, and mail order.

The eBay site continued to dominate the online auction action, introducing what appears to be a popular "Buy It Now" option to their already established auction format. The Pit.com opened in mid-year with their concept of buying and selling a portfolio of professionally graded sports cards through their Web site. The concept is based almost exactly upon the methodology used for buying and selling stocks through a brokerage house, with daily ebbs and flows in posted buy and sell prices on your inventory.

Beckett.com made radical improvements to their Marketplace search engines and expanded their inventory of sports cards to the point where they were providing both a wider and a deeper selection of trading cards than any site on the Internet. In addition, a company-wide effort to provide daily news content on their site (coupled with a weekly newsletter sent to over 400,000 collectors) began at year's end, and the hobby has reaped the benefits ever since.

As the 2001 season approached, hobbyists waited with bated breath for seven-time Japanese batting champ Ichiro Suzuki to make his debut in the Seattle Mariner's outfield. And what a stunning debut it was. Ichiro led the league in hitting, led the Mariners to their best record ever, and walked off with the A.L. Rookie of the Year and

Most Valuable Player awards. Upper Deck obtained the exclusive rights to produce his autograph cards and they hit a grand slam in midsummer by releasing his SPx Rookie Card, featuring a game jersey swatch and a cut signature autograph. In a year studded with notable cards this one was likely the most memorable.

In the National League, 37-year-old San Francisco Giants superstar Barry Bonds captivated the nation by bashing a jaw-dropping 73 home runs, shattering Mark McGwire's 1998 single-season home run record.

Cardinals' rookie Albert Pujols emerged out of the low minor leagues to become an instant hobby superstar and walk away with N.L. Rookie of the Year honors.

The year 2001 was a tumultuous one for sports cards. Topps started the year off with a bang by celebrating their 50th anniversary producing baseball cards. Pacific forfeited its license to make baseball cards after an eight-year run to focus on football and hockey cards. Playoff, a company based out of Grand Prairie, Texas, that had earned its stripes producing football cards in the late 1990s, purchased the rights to the much-hallowed Donruss corporate name and became a formal MLB licensee in the spring of 2001. Their entrance into the baseball card market heralded the return of benchmark brands like Donruss, Donruss Signature and Leaf.

Competition was fiercer than ever amongst the four primary licensees (Donruss-Playoff, Fleer, Topps, and Upper Deck) as they cranked out almost 80 different products over the course of 2001.

Of all these, likely the most historically important product, Upper Deck Prospect Premieres, was widely overlooked upon release. In a bold move, Upper Deck created a set of 102 prospects, none of which had played a day in the majors. Each player was pictured, however, in the major league uniforms of their parent ballclubs and signed to individual contracts. Because no active major leaguers were featured, Upper Deck did not have to include licensing rights from the MLB Players Association, though they did get licensing from Major League Properties. The industry had never seen a major release featuring active ballplayers marketed to the mainstream audience that lacked licensing from the MLBPA. Because of its lack of historical predecessors and a mixed reception from collectors, the cards were tagged by Beckett Baseball Card Monthly as XRC's (or Extended Rookie Cards), a term that had not been used since 1989.

UD's Prospect Premieres was the first major effort by a manufacturer to level the playing field between Topps and everyone else in that Topps has exclusive rights from the MLBPA to include minor leaguers in their basic brands.

Rookie Cards continued to fascinate collectors, especially in a year with talents like Ichiro, Mark Prior and Albert Pujols. The number of players featured on Rookie Cards in 2001 ballooned to an almost absurd figure of 505.

Exchange cards became more prevalent than ever, as manufacturers expanded their use from autograph cards that didn't get returned in time for pack out to slots within basic sets left open in brands released early in the year to fill in with late-season rookie call-ups.

Certified autograph cards remained a huge player in how brands were structured, but the quality of the players suffered greatly as autograph fees continued to spiral out of control. Signatures from superstars like Barry Bonds and Derek Jeter were now being featured on cards with miniscule print runs of 25 or 50 copies while unknown (and often aging and marginal) prospects signed their serial-numbered Rookies Cards by the hundred count.

More serial-numbered Rookie Cards were produced than ever before, but the quantities produced kept sinking lower and lower as companies tried to create secondary market value by simply limiting supply, a dangerous move to say the least. Donruss-Playoff produced the scarcest Rookie Cards of the year, a handful of Game Base cards (including Ichiro) each serial #'d to a scant 100 copies, within their Leaf Limited set.

After a six-month delay, Topps released their much awaited e-Topps program, a product sold entirely on their Web site whereby trading is conducted in a similar fashion to the buying and selling of stocks, in September. The product was met with a reasonable amount of excitement but has struggled to find its place in the market since that point in time.

Several products incorporated non-card memorabilia such as signed caps, bobbing head dolls, and signed baseballs with mixed results.

Memorabilia cards continued to over-saturate the market as the number of cards featuring various bits and pieces of balls, bases, bats, jerseys, pants, shoes, seats, and whatever else could be dreamt up continued to be offered to consumers. To battle consumer apathy, companies often started to offer combination memorabilia cards featuring notable teammates or several pieces of equipment from a notable star.

Retro-themed cards continued to grow in popularity, and some of the innovations seen in these sets were remarkable. Of particular note was Upper Deck's SP Legendary Cuts Autographs set, featuring 84 deceased players. The set required UD to purchase more than 3,300 autograph cuts, which were then incorporated into a windowpane card design. The result was the first certified autograph cards for legends like Roger Maris, Satchell Paige, and Jackie Robinson. Also, Topps Tribute released at year's end and carrying a hefty $40 per pack suggested retail was widely hailed as one of the most beautiful retro-themed cards ever designed, with their crystal-board fronts encasing full-color, razor-sharp photos.

Pack prices continued to escalate, but surprisingly, the public did not balk as long as they delivered value. The most notable high-end product to hit the market in 2001 was Upper Deck Ultimate Collection with a suggested retail of $100 per pack.

September 11th, 2001, is a day that will go down as one of the most devastating in the history of the United States of America. The game of baseball and the hobby of collecting sports cards were rightfully cast aside as the nation mourned the tragic loss of lives in New York, Pennsylvania, and Washington, D.C. America's economy tumbled as airline traveling ground to a near halt and threats of anthrax crippled the mail system. An economy threatening to slip into recession at the beginning of the year dove headlong into it. The sports card market, along with many other industries, felt the hit for several months. Slowly, Americans looked to move past the grief and the sports card industry, steeped in American nostalgia, provided an ideal retreat for many.

The Arizona Diamondbacks beat the New York Yankees in one of the dramatic World Series ever played . . . a much-needed diversion for a grief-stricken nation and a calling card for the dramatic power and glory of our National Pastime.

2002 was a relatively quiet one for baseball cards. Dodger's rookie pitcher Kazuhisa Ishii got off to a blazing first half start and his cards carried many releases through to the All-Star break. Ishii stumbled badly in the second half and no notable rookies were in place to pick up market interest. Cubs hurler Mark Prior created a stir, and his 2001 Rookie Cards were red hot at mid-season. For the second straight season, Barry Bonds was the most dominant star in our sport. His early cards continued to outpace all others in volume trading and professional grading submissions.

The number of players featured on Rookie Cards (or Extended Rookie Cards) reached an all-time high of 524 in 2002 as the manufacturers continued to push the envelope toward more immediate coverage of the current year draft. Though few collectors took notice at the time of release, Upper Deck's incorporation of collegiate Team USA athletes into several year-end brands may take hold and grow into a more prominent position in our industry for collegiate ballplayers. The results of these trends, however, are cards that feature a lot of talented youngsters whom most collectors, unfortunately, have never heard of and won't see in a major league uniform for several years. Brewers second baseman Rickie Weeks, the #2 overall selection in the 2003 MLB draft, was the first Team USA player to reap immediate dividends for Upper Deck as his key early cards surged in value as the draft approached.

In 2002 Topps was the exclusive manufacturer with the licensing rights to produce Rookie Cards for Twins catching prospect Joe Mauer – the #1 overall selection from the 202 MLB draft. Though his cards traded moderately well upon release, it would be over a year later that his name started to show up on the Beckett Baseball Collector Hot List.

To make up for the void in excitement generated by rookies and prospects upon release, the manufacturers made some interesting innovations in product distribution and brand development. In general, base sets got noticeably bigger (including Upper Deck's 1,182 card 40-Man brand and Topps 990-card Topps Total brand). In addition, brands like Topps 206, Leaf Rookies and Stars, and Fleer Fall Classics started to incorporate variations of the base cards directly into the basic issue set (different images, switched out teams, etc.).

One of the bigger surprise hits of the year was the aforementioned Topps 206 brand, of which borrowed design elements and set composition from the legendary T-206 tobacco set. Other brands continued to successfully mine from cards and eras long since passed.

Rookie Cards maintained their status as primary drivers for box sales, exemplified by the incendiary late season release of Bowman Draft and Bowman Chrome Draft (released together in an intermingled pack).

Donruss continued to push the creative envelope by incorporating 8 ½" by 11" framed signature pieces directly into boxes of their Playoff Absolute brand. After a four-year hiatus, Fleer brought back their eponymous "Fleer" name brand with a 540-card set. Donruss introduced their wildly successful Diamond Kings brand, of which featured a 150-card painted set. Fleer's Box Score brand was also a popular debut utilizing a unique box-inside-a-box distribution concept. Popular brands like SP Legendary Cuts, Leaf Certified, Topps Heritage, and Topps Tribute all received warm welcomes for their follow-ups to their successes achieved the prior year.

By 2003 the nation was still struggling to dig out of recession and the sport of baseball narrowly averted a season-ending strike that could have seriously injured the baseball card industry. For the third straight season, the top prospect to have a significant impact on the industry hailed from Japan, slugger Hideki Matsui. Coming off a 50 home run campaign in the Nippon league, Matsui assumed duties as the New York Yankees left fielder and no other first year player was watched more closely. Though he produced 106 RBI's, Matsui lost the A.L. Rookie of the Year award to Kansas City Royals shortstop Angel Berroa in a controversial vote. The influx of talented players from Japan's Nippon League continued in the 2003 off-season as the New York Mets picked up 7-time All-Star shortstop Kazuo Matsui.

Donruss-Playoff had a big year in 2003 highlighted by Leaf Certified, Leaf Limited and Timeless Treasures. Leaf Certified was arguably the product of the year, sporting some of the most beautiful game used and autograph cards ever created within the run of Mirror parallels. Timeless Treasures established an all-time high for suggested retail price per pack at $150 a pop. The product was consumed with relish as collectors were rewarded with a wide array of attractive cards sporting miniscule print runs.

The Grand Prairie, TX based manufacturer continued to establish themselves as market leaders in high-end, game used cards at year's end by purchasing a 1925 Babe Ruth game worn jersey for $264,000.

Donruss-Playoff also made waves in the world of certified autographs by inking superstars Hideo Nomo and Mike Piazza to autograph contracts. Both players had signed very few cards prior to the D/P contract and their newly signed releases were hot commodities at $300-$1000 per throughout the 2003 release season.

Despite garnering high praise from dealers and collectors alike for providing exciting products with strong value throughout 2003, some industry experts fear D/P's aggressive redefining of set structure and content may result in short term gains and potential long-term damage to the industry. By year's end the secondary market was saturated with variation upon variation of Donruss-Playoff autograph and game used cards with print runs of 25 or fewer copies. In addition, their recently released 2004 Diamond Kings brand has shaken up the secondary market for "1 of 1" cards. By creating an unheard of 79 parallel versions to the base set, the product development team at D/P managed to mass-produce more than 3,500 true 1 of 1's of which were reported as hitting at a rate of three per sealed hobby case. Three years ago, a signed card with a print run of 25 copies and a true 1 of 1 parallel were regarded as truly rare commodities. By 2004, however, these items are being met with caution by some and apathy by others. It remains to be seen how Donruss-Playoff will continue to generate the excitement established within many of their 2003 brands – but their talented product development staff will likely have some interesting cards to pick up the slack.

2003 was a quiet year for Fleer that ended in widely circulated rumors that the company was for sale. By early 2004, however, the company was reported to be moving forward with an aggressive campaign to reestablish themselves as a force to be reckoned with in the baseball card market by rejuvenating autograph and game used content and returning from an almost year-long hiatus from advertising.

With the proven success of brands like Timeless Treasures in 2003, the manufacturers continue to push the envelope for high end packs this year. Upper Deck sent shockwaves through the basketball card market by releasing UD Exquisite at $500 per pack. That figure makes the $200 per pack SP Game Patch baseball product seem modest by comparison but the product nonetheless established a new all-time high for SRP's in the baseball card market.

The potentially rich trend of incorporating notable figures from outside the sporting world into trading card sets continued to quietly gain steam in early 2003 with the inclusion of certified autograph cards featuring actors Jason Alexander and John Goodman within Upper Deck's Yankees Legends brand. In November, within packs 2004 Topps series one baseball, Topps included a certified autograph card for every U.S. President from George Washington to George W. Bush in their ground-breaking American Treasures Autograph Relics insert set. In December, Upper Deck quickly followed suit with their Presidential Signature Cuts within their SP Legendary Cuts brand. These cards had a profound effect upon the super high-end market redefining the limits of what could be marketed within a pack of trading cards.

By early 2004, Donruss-Playoff had announced their Fans of the Game insert featuring James Gandolfini (made famous for his Emmy-winning turn as mob boss Tony Soprano on HBO). In addition to Gandolfini, D/P announced intentions to incorporate up to 75 additional entertainment celebrities of whom have connections to America's Pastime.

The 2003 Postseason was one for the ages with the long-suffering Red Sox and Cubs in the mix alongside the New York Yankees and Barry Bonds' San Francisco Giants. An unfortunate chap by the name of Steve Bartman gained infamy as the unfortunate scapegoat for the Cubs demise. Josh Beckett gained notoriety alongside a gritty Ivan Rodriguez as the Florida Marlins snuck up on everyone to beat the Yankees in the World Series.

Marlins rookie hurler Dontrelle Willis, with a colorful delivery that reminded many of Vida Blue and Luis Tiant, dominated the Beckett Baseball Collector Hot List for much of the Summer. Tampa Bay D-Rays prospect Delmon Young and Rickie Weeks picked up the slack for Willis as the year came to a close. Albert Pujols and Mark Prior assumed superstar status in the hobby by the end of the '03 season. Pujol's 2001 Bowman Chrome Rookie Card (of which only 500 serial #'d signed copies were produced) moved up to the $1,000 mark and Prior's 2001 Ultimate Collection RC (250 serial #'d signed copies produced) was a hot ticket at $600.

Barry Bonds shook up the baseball world in the off-season by opting out of his MLB Player's Association contract in an effort to single-handedly monetize his run towards Hank Aaron's All-Time record of 755 home runs. Rumors of steroid usage dogged Bonds throughout the off-season (and to a lesser degree had fans questioning how clean Mark McGwire and Sammy Sosa were in 1998 when they both broke Roger Maris's single-season home run record). All that news was overshadowed when Alex Rodriguez was signed to become the New York Yankees third baseman (after the Red Sox failed to consummate a deal with the Rangers only one month prior).

By 2003 the baseball card market resumed its place at the forefront of the card-collecting hobby, outpacing football, basketball, hockey, golf, and motor sports in volume dollars. In fact, industry experts had estimates of baseball card sales accounting for as much as 60% of total sports card sales as 2004 approached. As the hobby of collecting basebll cards moves towards the 21st century, we face a market that is blessed with bold creativity and superlative quality and also challenged with the need to reach new consumers both in mass retail and in cyberspace to continue its growth.

The most important new concept of 2004 was the allowance for all the card companies to use any player drafted in the current year in one of their products. However, some of the luster was taken off that development as those players (except for those signed by Topps) were not allowed to wear liscenced uniforms.

Finding Out More

The above has been a thumbnail sketch of card collecting from its inception in the 1880s to the present. It is difficult to tell the whole story in just a few pages - there are several other good sources of information. Serious collectors should subscribe to at least one of the excellent hobby periodicals. We also suggest that collectors visit their local card shop(s) and also attend a sports collectibles show in their area. Card collecting is still a young and informal hobby. You can learn more about it in either place. After all, smart dealers realize that spending a few minutes teaching beginners about the hobby often pays off in the long run.

Additional Reading

Each year Beckett Publications produces comprehensive annual price guides for these sports: Beckett Almanac of Baseball Cards and Collectibles, Beckett Basketball Card Price Guide, Beckett Football Card Price Guide, Beckett Hockey Card Price Guide, Beckett Racing Price Guide and a line of Beckett Alphabetical Checklists Books have been released as well. The aim of these annual guides is to provide information and accurate pricing on a wide array of sports cards, ranging from main issues by the major card manufacturers to various regional, promotional, and food issues. Also alphabetical checklist books are published to assist the collector in identifying all the cards of any particular player. The seasoned collector will find these tools valuable sources of information that will enable him to pursue his hobby interests.

In addition, abridged editions of the Beckett Price Guides have been published for each of these major sports as part of the House of Collectibles series: The Official Price Guide to Baseball Cards, The Official Price Guide to Football Cards, The Official Price Guide to Basketball Cards. Published in a convenient mass-market paperback format, these price guides provide information and accurate pricing on all the main issues by the major card manufacturers.

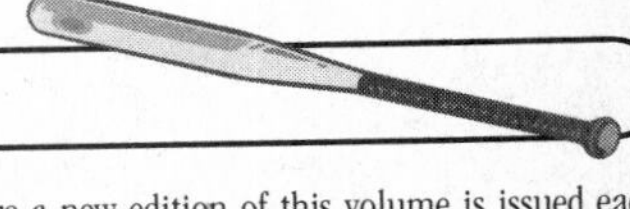

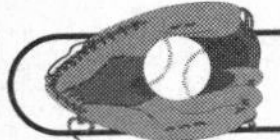

Advertising

Within this Price Guide you will find advertisements for sports memorabilia material, mail order, and retail sports collectibles establishments. All advertisements were accepted in good faith based on the reputation of the advertiser; however, neither the author, the publisher, the distributors, nor the other advertisers in this Price Guide accept any responsibility for any particular advertiser not complying with the terms of his or her ad.Readers also should be aware that prices in advertisements are subject to change over the annual period before a new edition of this volume is issued each spring. When replying to an advertisement late in the baseball year, the reader should take this into account, and contact the dealer by phone or in writing for up-to-date price information. Should you come into contact with any of the advertisers in this guide as a result of their advertisement herein, please mention this source as your contact.

Prices in this Guide

Prices found in this guide reflect current retail rates just prior to the printing of this book. They do not reflect the FOR SALE prices of the author, the publisher, the distributors, the advertisers, or any card dealers associated with this guide. No one is obligated in any way to buy, sell or trade his or her cards based on these prices. The price listings were compiled by the author from actual buy/sell transactions at sports conventions, sports card shops, buy/sell advertisements in the hobby papers, for sale prices from dealer catalogs and price lists, and discussions with leading hobbyists in the U.S. and Canada. All prices are in U.S. dollars.

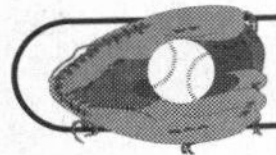

Acknowledgments

A great deal of diligence, hard work, and dedicated effort went into this year's volume. However, the high standards to which we hold ourselves could not have been met without the expert input and generous amount of time contributed by many people. Our sincere thanks are extended to each and every one of you.

A complete list of these invaluable contributors appears after the Price Guide section.

2001 Absolute Memorabilia

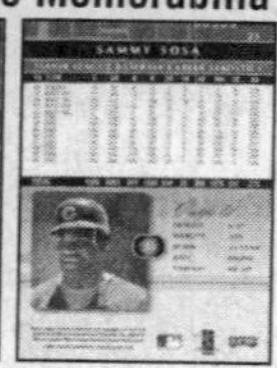

The 2001 Playoff Absolute Memorabilia set was issued in one series totally 200 cards. The set features color action player photos highlighted on metalized film board with the 50 rookie cards infused with a swatch of game-worn/used bat and jersey. The following cards were available via mail exchange cards (of which expired on June 1st, 2003): 151 - Bud Smith, 154 - Josh Beckett, 161 Ben Sheets, 164 - Carlos Garcia, 169 - Donaldo Mendez, 171 Jackson Melian, 173 Adrian Hernandez, 186 - C.C. Sabathia, 188 - Adam Pettyjohn, 193 - Alfonso Soriano, 196 - Billy Sylvester and 200 - Matt White.

	Nm-Mt	Ex-Mt
COMP.SET w/o SP's (150)	40.00	12.00
COMMON CARD (1-150)	.75	.23
COMMON RPM (151-200)	10.00	3.00
1 Alex Rodriguez	3.00	.90
2 Barry Bonds	5.00	1.50
3 Cal Ripken	6.00	1.80
4 Chipper Jones	2.00	.60
5 Derek Jeter	5.00	1.50
6 Troy Glaus	.75	.23
7 Frank Thomas	2.00	.60
8 Greg Maddux	3.00	.90
9 Ivan Rodriguez	2.00	.60
10 Jeff Bagwell	1.25	.35
11 Ryan Dempster	.75	.23
12 Todd Helton	1.25	.35
13 Ken Griffey Jr.	3.00	.90
14 Manny Ramirez	1.25	.35
15 Mark McGwire	5.00	1.50
16 Mike Piazza	3.00	.90
17 Nomar Garciaparra	3.00	.90
18 Pedro Martinez	2.00	.60
19 Randy Johnson	2.00	.60
20 Rick Ankiel	.75	.23
21 Rickey Henderson	2.00	.60
22 Roger Clemens	4.00	1.20
23 Sammy Sosa	3.00	.90
24 Tony Gwynn	2.50	.75
25 Vladimir Guerrero	2.00	.60
26 Kazuhiro Sasaki	.75	.23
27 Roberto Alomar	1.25	.35
28 Barry Zito	1.25	.35
29 Pat Burrell	.75	.23
30 Harold Baines	.75	.23
31 Carlos Delgado	.75	.23
32 J.D. Drew	.75	.23
33 Jim Edmonds	.75	.23
34 Darin Erstad	.75	.23
35 Jason Giambi	.75	.23
36 Tom Glavine	1.25	.35
37 Juan Gonzalez	1.25	.35
38 Mark Grace	1.25	.35
39 Shawn Green	.75	.23
40 Tim Hudson	.75	.23
41 Andruw Jones	.75	.23
42 David Justice	.75	.23
43 Jeff Kent	.75	.23
44 Barry Larkin	1.25	.35
45 Rafael Furcal	.75	.23
46 Mike Mussina	1.25	.35
47 Hideo Nomo	2.00	.60
48 Rafael Palmeiro	1.25	.35
49 Adam Piatt	.75	.23
50 Scott Rolen	2.00	.60
51 Gary Sheffield	.75	.23
52 Bernie Williams	1.25	.35
53 Bob Abreu	.75	.23
54 Edgardo Alfonzo	.75	.23
55 Edgar Renteria	.75	.23
56 Phil Nevin	.75	.23
57 Craig Biggio	1.25	.35
58 Andres Galarraga	.75	.23
59 Edgar Martinez	1.25	.35
60 Fred McGriff	1.25	.35
61 Magglio Ordonez	.75	.23
62 Jim Thome	2.00	.60
63 Matt Williams	.75	.23
64 Kerry Wood	2.00	.60
65 Moises Alou	.75	.23
66 Brady Anderson	.75	.23
67 Garret Anderson	.75	.23
68 Russell Branyan	.75	.23
69 Tony Batista	.75	.23
70 Vernon Wells	.75	.23
71 Carlos Beltran	1.25	.35
72 Adrian Beltre	1.25	.35
73 Kris Benson	.75	.23
74 Lance Berkman	.75	.23
75 Kevin Brown	.75	.23
76 Dee Brown	.75	.23
77 Jeromy Burnitz	.75	.23
78 Timo Perez	.75	.23
79 Sean Casey	.75	.23
80 Luis Castillo	.75	.23
81 Eric Chavez	.75	.23
82 Jeff Cirillo	.75	.23
83 Bartolo Colon	.75	.23
84 David Cone	.75	.23
85 Freddy Garcia	.75	.23
86 Johnny Damon	1.25	.35
87 Ray Durham	.75	.23
88 Jermaine Dye	.75	.23
89 Juan Encarnacion	.75	.23
90 Terrence Long	.75	.23
91 Carl Everett	.75	.23
92 Steve Finley	.75	.23
93 Cliff Floyd	.75	.23
94 Brad Fullmer	.75	.23
95 Brian Giles	.75	.23
96 Luis Gonzalez	.75	.23
97 Rusty Greer	.75	.23
98 Jeffrey Hammonds	.75	.23
99 Mike Hampton	.75	.23
100 Orlando Hernandez	.75	.23
101 Richard Hidalgo	.75	.23
102 Geoff Jenkins	.75	.23
103 Jacque Jones	.75	.23
104 Brian Jordan	.75	.23
105 Gabe Kapler	.75	.23
106 Eric Karros	.75	.23
107 Jason Kendall	.75	.23
108 Adam Kennedy	.75	.23
109 Deion Sanders	1.25	.35
110 Ryan Klesko	.75	.23
111 Chuck Knoblauch	.75	.23
112 Paul Konerko	.75	.23
113 Carlos Lee	.75	.23
114 Kenny Lofton	.75	.23
115 Javy Lopez	.75	.23
116 Tino Martinez	1.25	.35
117 Ruben Mateo	.75	.23
118 Kevin Millwood	.75	.23
119 Jimmy Rollins	.75	.23
120 Raul Mondesi	.75	.23
121 Trot Nixon	.75	.23
122 John Olerud	.75	.23
123 Paul O' Neill	1.25	.35
124 Chan Ho Park	.75	.23
125 Andy Pettitte	1.25	.35
126 Jorge Posada	1.25	.35
127 Mark Quinn	.75	.23
128 Aramis Ramirez	.75	.23
129 Mariano Rivera	1.25	.35
130 Tim Salmon	1.25	.35
131 Curt Schilling	.75	.23
132 Richie Sexson	.75	.23
133 John Smoltz	1.25	.35
134 J.T. Snow	.75	.23
135 Jay Payton	.75	.23
136 Shannon Stewart	.75	.23
137 B.J. Surhoff	.75	.23
138 Mike Sweeney	.75	.23
139 Fernando Tatis	.75	.23
140 Miguel Tejada	.75	.23
141 Jason Varitek	1.25	.35
142 Greg Vaughn	.75	.23
143 Mo Vaughn	.75	.23
144 Robin Ventura	.75	.23
145 Jose Vidro	.75	.23
146 Omar Vizquel	1.25	.35
147 Larry Walker	1.25	.35
148 David Wells	.75	.23
149 Rondell White	.75	.23
150 Preston Wilson	.75	.23
151 Bud Smith RPM RC	10.00	3.00
152 C. Aldridge RPM RC	10.00	3.00
153 W.Caceres RPM RC	10.00	3.00
154 Josh Beckett RPM	10.00	3.00
155 W.Betemit RPM RC	10.00	3.00
156 J.Michaels RPM RC	10.00	3.00
157 Albert Pujols RPM RC	100.00	30.00
158 A.Torres RPM RC	10.00	3.00
159 Jack Wilson RPM RC	15.00	4.50
160 Alex Escobar RPM	10.00	3.00
161 Ben Sheets RPM	12.00	3.60
162 R.Soriano RPM RC	12.00	3.60
163 Nate Frese RPM RC	10.00	3.00
164 C. Garcia RPM EXCH	10.00	3.00
165 B.Larson RPM RC	10.00	3.00
166 A.Gomez RPM RC	10.00	3.00
167 Jason Hart RPM	10.00	3.00
168 Nick Johnson RPM	10.00	3.00
169 Donaldo Mendez RPM	10.00	3.00
170 C. Parker RPM RC	10.00	3.00
171 Jackson Melian RPM	10.00	3.00
172 Jack Cust RPM	10.00	3.00
173 Adrian Hernandez RPM	10.00	3.00
174 Joe Crede RPM	10.00	3.00
175 Jose Mieses RPM RC	10.00	3.00
176 Roy Oswalt RPM	12.00	3.60
177 Eric Munson RPM	10.00	3.00
178 Xavier Nady RPM	10.00	3.00
179 H. Ramirez RPM RC	12.00	3.60
180 Abraham Nunez RPM	10.00	3.00
181 Jose Ortiz RPM	10.00	3.00
182 J. Owens RPM RC	10.00	3.00
183 C. Vargas RPM RC	10.00	3.00
184 Marcus Giles RPM	10.00	3.00
185 Aubrey Huff RPM	10.00	3.00
186 C.C. Sabathia RPM	10.00	3.00
187 Adam Dunn RPM	12.00	3.60
188 Adam Pettyjohn RPM	10.00	3.00
189 El. Guzman RPM RC	10.00	3.00
190 Jay Gibbons RPM RC	12.00	3.60
191 Wilkin Ruan RPM RC	10.00	3.00
192 T. Shinjo RPM RC	12.00	3.60
193 Alfonso Soriano RPM	12.00	3.60
194 Corey Patterson RPM	10.00	3.00
195 Ichiro Suzuki RPM RC	80.00	24.00
196 Billy Sylvester RPM	10.00	3.00
197 Juan Uribe RPM RC	12.00	3.60
198 J. Estrada RPM RC	12.00	3.60
199 C. Valderrama RPM RC	10.00	3.00
200 Matt White RPM	10.00	3.00

2001 Absolute Memorabilia Ball Hoggs

Randomly inserted in packs, this 46 card set features color action player photos with swatches of game-used baseballs embedded in the cards. Each card was sequentially numbered and the print runs are listed after the players' names in the checklist below. The first 25 of each card are spotlighted with a holo-foil stamp and labeled "Boss Hoggs." Exchange cards were seeded into packs for the following players: Jeff Bagwell, Darin Erstad, Chipper Jones, Magglio Ordonez, Cal Ripken and Alex Rodriguez. The deadline to redeem the cards was June 1st, 2003.

	Nm-Mt	Ex-Mt
BH1 Vladimir Guerrero/75	25.00	7.50
BH2 Troy Glaus/75	15.00	4.50
BH3 Tony Gwynn/75	25.00	7.50
BH4 Cal Ripken/175	50.00	15.00
BH5 Todd Helton/75	25.00	7.50
BH6 Jacque Jones/125	15.00	4.50
BH7 Shawn Green/100	15.00	4.50
BH8 Ichiro Suzuki/50	120.00	36.00
BH9 Scott Rolen/100	25.00	7.50
BH10 Roger Clemens/75	25.00	7.50
BH11 Ken Griffey Jr./25		
BH14 Sammy Sosa/75	25.00	7.50
BH15 J.D. Drew/50	15.00	4.50
BH16 Barry Bonds/75	40.00	12.00
BH17 Pat Burrell/75	15.00	4.50
BH18 Mark McGwire/75	80.00	24.00
BH19 Mike Piazza/50	25.00	7.50
BH20 Magglio Ordonez/125	15.00	4.50
BH21 Miguel Tejada/75	15.00	4.50
BH22 Albert Pujols/75	150.00	45.00
BH23 Derek Jeter/50	50.00	15.00
BH24 Johnny Damon/125	25.00	7.50
BH25 Mike Sweeney/75	15.00	4.50
BH26 Ben Grieve/125	15.00	4.50
BH27 Jeff Kent/75	15.00	4.50
BH28 Andres Galarraga/75	15.00	4.50
BH29 Richie Sexson/25		
BH30 J.Encarnacion/125	15.00	4.50
BH31 Ruben Mateo/75	15.00	4.50
BH33 Manny Ramirez/75	25.00	7.50
BH35 Ivan Rodriguez/75	25.00	7.50
BH36 D. Erstad/125 EXCH	15.00	4.50
BH37 Carlos Delgado/100	15.00	4.50
BH38 J. Bagwell/125 EXCH	25.00	7.50
BH39 Jermaine Dye/75	15.00	4.50
BH40 Jose Ortiz/50	15.00	4.50
BH41 Gary Sheffield/75	15.00	4.50
BH42 Eric Chavez/125	15.00	4.50
BH43 Mark Grace/75	25.00	7.50
BH44 Rafael Palmeiro/125	25.00	7.50
BH45 Tsuyoshi Shinjo/75	25.00	7.50
BH46 Terrence Long/75	15.00	4.50
BH47 Carlos Delgado/25		
BH48 Frank Thomas/75	25.00	7.50
BH49 C. Jones/25 EXCH		
BH50 Jason Giambi/75	15.00	4.50

2001 Absolute Memorabilia Boss Hoggs

Randomly inserted in packs, this 50-card set is a parallel version of the regular insert set with a holo-foil stamp and labeled "Boss Hoggs." Each card features a patch of a game-used baseball. This set is the first 25 of each card printed in the regular insert set. The following cards are autographed: 1/2/3/5/10/22/32/34/41/49. Exchange cards (with a redemption deadline of June 1st, 2003) were issued in packs for Jeff Bagwell, Darin Erstad, Chipper Jones, Magglio Ordonez, Cal Ripken and Alex Rodriguez. The Chipper and A-Rod cards were intended to be redeemed for autograph cards, the others were all for non-autographed cards.

	Nm-Mt	Ex-Mt
AU CL: 1-3/5/10/22/32/34/41/49		

2001 Absolute Memorabilia Home Opener Souvenirs

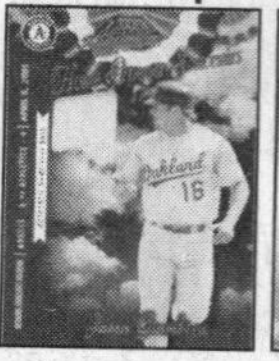

Randomly inserted in packs at the rate of one per box, this 50-card set features color photos of top performers showcased on conventional board with foil featuring a swatch of an authentic game-used base embedded in the cards. Only 400 serially numbered sets were produced.

	Nm-Mt	Ex-Mt
OD1 Barry Bonds	25.00	7.50
OD2 Cal Ripken	40.00	12.00
OD3 Pedro Martinez	10.00	3.00
OD4 Troy Glaus	8.00	2.40
OD5 Frank Thomas	10.00	3.00
OD6 Alex Rodriguez	15.00	4.50
OD7 Ivan Rodriguez	10.00	3.00
OD8 Jeff Bagwell	10.00	3.00
OD9 Mark McGwire	40.00	12.00
OD10 Todd Helton	10.00	3.00
OD11 Gary Sheffield	8.00	2.40
OD12 Manny Ramirez	10.00	3.00
OD13 Mike Piazza	15.00	4.50
OD14 Sammy Sosa	15.00	4.50
OD15 Preston Wilson	8.00	2.40
OD16 Tony Gwynn	15.00	4.50
OD17 Vladimir Guerrero	10.00	3.00
OD18 Carlos Delgado	8.00	2.40
OD19 Roberto Alomar	10.00	3.00
OD20 Todd Helton	10.00	3.00
OD21 Albert Pujols UER Base shows a DiamondBacks logo Dbacks did not play Cards opening day	50.00	15.00
OD22 Jason Giambi	8.00	2.40
OD23 Sammy Sosa	15.00	4.50
OD24 Ken Griffey Jr.	15.00	4.50
OD25 Darin Erstad	8.00	2.40
OD26 Mark McGwire	40.00	12.00
OD27 Carlos Delgado	8.00	2.40
OD28 Juan Gonzalez	10.00	3.00
OD29 Mike Sweeney	8.00	2.40
OD30 Alex Rodriguez	15.00	4.50
OD31 Roger Clemens	15.00	4.50
OD32 Tsuyoshi Shinjo	10.00	3.00
OD33 Ben Grieve	8.00	2.40
OD34 Jeff Kent	8.00	2.40
OD35 Vladimir Guerrero	10.00	3.00
OD36 Shawn Green	8.00	2.40
OD37 Rafael Palmeiro	10.00	3.00
OD38 Tony Gwynn	15.00	4.50
OD39 Scott Rolen	10.00	3.00
OD40 Ken Griffey Jr.	15.00	4.50
OD41 Albert Pujols	50.00	15.00
OD42 Barry Bonds	25.00	7.50
OD43 Mark Grace	10.00	3.00
OD44 Bernie Williams	10.00	3.00
OD45 Frank Thomas	10.00	3.00
OD46 Jermaine Dye	8.00	2.40
OD47 Mike Piazza	15.00	4.50
OD48 Chipper Jones	10.00	3.00
OD49 Richie Sexson	8.00	2.40
OD50 Magglio Ordonez	8.00	2.40

2001 Absolute Memorabilia Home Opener Souvenirs Autographs

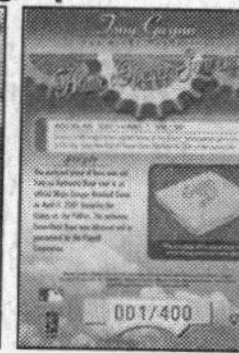

Randomly inserted in packs, this ten-card set features autographed action color photos of top players with a swatch of a game-used baseball and/or base embedded in the card. Only 25 serially numbered sets were produced but the cards are actually serial numbered out of 400 (whereby the first 25 of each card were signed by players participating in this program). No pricing is provided due to market scarcity. Exchange cards, with a redemption deadline of June 1st, 2003, were seeded into packs for Troy Glaus, Cal Ripken and Alex Rodriguez.

	Nm-Mt	Ex-Mt
OD2 Cal Ripken		
OD4 Troy Glaus		
OD6 Alex Rodriguez		
OD16 Tony Gwynn		
OD17 Vladimir Guerrero		
OD19 Roberto Alomar		
OD21 Albert Pujols		
OD28 Juan Gonzalez		
OD31 Roger Clemens		
OD37 Rafael Palmeiro		

2001 Absolute Memorabilia Home Opener Souvenirs Double

Randomly inserted in packs, this 50-card set is parallel to the regular insert set with two swatches of game-used bases embedded in the card. Only 200 serially numbered sets were produced.

Nm-Mt Ex-Mt

*DOUBLE: .6X TO 1.5X BASIC SOUV..

2001 Absolute Memorabilia Home Opener Souvenirs Triple

Randomly inserted in packs, this 50-card set is parallel to the regular insert set with three swatches of game-used bases embedded in the card. Only 75 serially numbered sets were produced.

Nm-Mt Ex-Mt

*TRIPLE: 1.25X TO 3X BASIC SOUV...

2001 Absolute Memorabilia Signing Bonus Baseballs

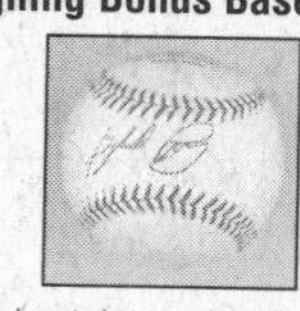

Randomly inserted one per box, this set features baseballs signed by a select group of stellar performers. The players' names are listed below in alphabetical order with the sequential numbering of the quantity signed following the names.

	Nm-Mt	Ex-Mt
1 Al Oliver/500	25.00	7.50
2 Andre Dawson/550	25.00	7.50
3 Barry Bonds/25		
4 Bill Madlock/524	25.00	7.50
5 Bill Mazeroski/25		
6 Billy Williams/325	25.00	7.50
7 Bob Feller/550	25.00	7.50
8 Bob Gibson/25		
9 Bobby Doerr/300	30.00	9.00
10 Bobby Richardson/500	30.00	9.00
11 Boog Powell/500	40.00	12.00
12 Brian Jordan/25		
13 Bucky Dent/500	25.00	7.50
14 Charles Johnson/25		
15 Chipper Jones/25		
16 Clete Boyer/500	25.00	7.50
17 Dale Murphy/25		
18 Dave Concepcion/500	25.00	7.50
19 Dave Kingman/500	25.00	7.50
20 Don Larsen/200	50.00	15.00
21 Don Newcombe/500	25.00	7.50
22 Don Zimmer/500	25.00	7.50
23 Duke Snider/25		
24 Earl Weaver/300	30.00	9.00
25 Enos Slaughter/525	30.00	9.00
26 Fergie Jenkins/1000	25.00	7.50
27 Frank Howard/500	25.00	7.50
28 Frank Robinson/25		
29 Frank Thomas/25		
30 Gary Carter/200	25.00	7.50
31 Gaylord Perry/1000	25.00	7.50
32 George Foster/500	25.00	7.50
33 George Kell/300	30.00	9.00
34 Goose Gossage/500	25.00	7.50
35 Greg Maddux/25		
36 Hank Aaron/25		
37 Hank Bauer/500	30.00	9.00
38 Harmon Killebrew/200	80.00	24.00
39 Henry Rodriguez/400	25.00	7.50
40 Herb Score/500	25.00	7.50
41 Hoyt Wilhelm/500	25.00	7.50
42 J.D. Drew/25		
43 Javy Lopez/25		
44 Jim Edmonds/25		
45 Jim Palmer/500	25.00	7.50
46 Joe Pepitone/500	25.00	7.50
47 Johnny Bench/25		
48 Johnny Podres/500	30.00	9.00
49 Juan Marichal/485	25.00	7.50
50 Kirby Puckett/25		
51 Larry Doby/300	40.00	12.00
52 Lou Brock/25		
53 Luis Tiant/500	25.00	7.50
54 Magglio Ordonez/200	25.00	7.50
55 Manny Ramirez/25		
56 Maury Wills/500	30.00	9.00
57 Mike Schmidt/25		
58 Minnie Minoso/1000	25.00	7.50
59 Monte Irvin/500	30.00	9.00
60 Moose Skowron/500	30.00	9.00
61 Nolan Ryan/25		
62 Ozzie Smith/25		
63 Phil Rizzuto/25		
64 Ralph Kiner/100	50.00	15.00
65 Randy Johnson/25		
66 Red Schoendienst/500	30.00	9.00
67 Reggie Jackson/25		
68 Rickey Henderson/25		
69 Robin Roberts/500	30.00	9.00
70 Roger Clemens/25		
71 Rollie Fingers/575	25.00	7.50
72 Ryne Sandberg/25		
73 Sean Casey/25		
74 Stan Musial/25		
75 Steve Carlton/25		
76 Steve Garvey/1000	25.00	7.50
77 Todd Helton/25		
78 Tom Glavine/25		
79 Tom Seaver/25		
80 Tommy John/1000	25.00	7.50
81 Tony Gwynn/25		
82 Tony Perez/400	25.00	7.50
83 Wade Boggs/25		
84 Warren Spahn/500	80.00	24.00
85 Whitey Ford/25		
86 Willie Mays/25		
87 Willie McCovey/25		
88 Willie Stargell/25		
89 Yogi Berra/25		

2001 Absolute Memorabilia Tools of the Trade

Randomly inserted in packs, this 50-card set features action color player images with game-worn/used jerseys, batting gloves, bats, and hats embedded in the cards. The cards with swatches of batting gloves were serially numbered to 50, with hats to 100, and with jerseys to 300. Exchange cards with a redemption deadline of June 1st, 2003 were seeded into packs for the following cards: Roberto Alomar Bat, Roberto Alomar Glove, Jeff Bagwell Bat, Darin Erstad Bat, Troy Glaus Bat, Troy Glaus Hat, Troy Glaus Jsy, Tom Glavine Hat, Shawn Green Bat, Tony Gwynn Glove, David Justice Bat, Greg Maddux Hat, Kazuhiro Sasaki Jsy and Larry Walker Jsy.

	Nm-Mt	Ex-Mt
TT1 Vladimir Guerrero Jsy	15.00	4.50
TT2 Troy Glaus Jsy	10.00	3.00
TT3 Tony Gwynn Jsy	25.00	7.50
TT4 Todd Helton Jsy	15.00	4.50
TT5 Scott Rolen Jsy	15.00	4.50
TT6 Roger Clemens Jsy	40.00	12.00
TT7 Pedro Martinez Jsy	15.00	4.50
TT8 Richie Sexson Jsy	10.00	3.00
TT9 Magglio Ordonez Jsy	10.00	3.00
TT10 Ben Grieve Jsy	10.00	3.00
TT11 Jeff Bagwell Jsy	15.00	4.50
TT12 Edgar Martinez Jsy	15.00	4.50
TT13 Greg Maddux Jsy	25.00	7.50
TT14 Larry Walker Jsy	15.00	4.50
TT15 Frank Thomas Jsy	15.00	4.50
TT16 Edgardo Alfonzo Jsy	10.00	3.00
TT17 Cal Ripken Jsy	50.00	15.00
TT18 Jose Vidro Jsy	10.00	3.00
TT19 Andruw Jones Jsy	10.00	3.00
TT20 K. Sasaki Jsy EXCH	10.00	3.00
TT21 Barry Bonds Bat	80.00	24.00
TT22 Juan Gonzalez Bat	40.00	12.00
TT23 Andruw Jones Bat	25.00	7.50
TT24 Cal Ripken Bat	100.00	30.00
TT25 Greg Maddux Bat	40.00	12.00
TT26 Manny Ramirez Bat	40.00	12.00
TT27 Roberto Alomar Bat	40.00	12.00
TT28 S. Green Bat EXCH	25.00	7.50
TT29 Edgardo Alfonzo Bat	25.00	7.50
TT30 Rafael Palmeiro Bat	40.00	12.00
TT31 Hideo Nomo Bat	150.00	45.00
TT32 A. Galarraga Bat	25.00	7.50
TT33 Todd Helton Bat	40.00	12.00
TT34 Darin Erstad Bat	25.00	7.50
TT35 Ivan Rodriguez Bat	40.00	12.00
TT36 Sean Casey Bat	25.00	7.50
TT37 V. Guerrero Bat	40.00	12.00
TT38 David Justice Bat	25.00	7.50

TT39 Troy Glaus Bat 25.00 7.50
TT40 Jeff Bagwell Bat
TT41 Barry Bonds Glove 150.00 45.00
TT42 Cal Ripken Glove 200.00 60.00
TT43 Rob Alomar Glove 40.00 12.00
TT44 Sean Casey Glove 40.00 12.00
TT45 Tony Gwynn Glove
TT46 Bernie Williams Hat 40.00 12.00
TT47 Barry Zito Hat 40.00 12.00
TT48 Greg Maddux Hat
TT49 Tom Glavine Hat 40.00 12.00
TT50 Troy Glaus Hat 25.00 7.50

2001 Absolute Memorabilia Tools of the Trade Autographs

Randomly inserted in packs, this 10-card set is an autographed partial parallel version of the regular insert set. Only 25 serially numbered sets were produced. Due to market scarcity, no pricing is provided. An exchange card with a redemption deadline of June 1st, 2003 was placed into packs for the Troy Glaus Bat card.

Nm-Mt Ex-Mt
TT1 Vladimir Guerrero Jsy
TT3 Tony Gwynn Jsy
TT5 Scott Rolen Jsy
TT6 Roger Clemens Jsy
TT17 Cal Ripken Bat
TT22 Juan Gonzalez Bat
TT32 Andres Galarraga Bat
TT33 Todd Helton Bat
TT35 Ivan Rodriguez Bat
TT39 Troy Glaus Bat

2002 Absolute Memorabilia

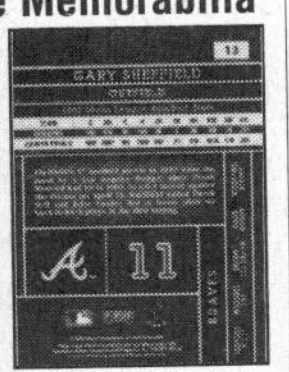

This 200 card standard-size set was issued in August, 2002. The set was released in a big box which contained two nine pack mini-boxes as well as a "Signing Bonus" framed piece. The first 150 cards of this set featured veterans while the final cards feature rookies and prospects with a stated print run of 1000 serial numbered sets.

Nm-Mt Ex-Mt
COMP.SET w/o SP's (150) 40.00 12.00
COMMON CARD (1-150) .75 .23
COMMON CARD (151-200) 5.00 1.50
1 David Eckstein .75 .23
2 Darin Erstad .75 .23
3 Troy Glaus .75 .23
4 Garret Anderson .75 .23
5 Tim Salmon 1.25 .35
6 Curt Schilling .75 .23
7 Randy Johnson 2.00 .60
8 Luis Gonzalez .75 .23
9 Mark Grace 1.25 .35
10 Tom Glavine 1.25 .35
11 Greg Maddux 3.00 .90
12 Chipper Jones 2.00 .60
13 Gary Sheffield .75 .23
14 John Smoltz 1.25 .35
15 Andruw Jones .75 .23
16 Wilson Betemit .75 .23
17 Tony Batista .75 .23
18 Javier Vazquez .75 .23
19 Scott Erickson .75 .23
20 Josh Towers .75 .23
21 Pedro Martinez 2.00 .60
22 Johnny Damon Sox 2.00 .60
23 Manny Ramirez 1.25 .35
24 Rickey Henderson 2.00 .60
25 Trot Nixon .75 .23
26 Nomar Garciaparra 3.00 .90
27 Juan Cruz .75 .23
28 Kerry Wood 2.00 .60
29 Fred McGriff 1.25 .35
30 Moises Alou .75 .23
31 Sammy Sosa 3.00 .90
32 Corey Patterson .75 .23
33 Mark Buehrle .75 .23
34 Keith Foulke .75 .23
35 Frank Thomas 2.00 .60
36 Kenny Lofton .75 .23
37 Magglio Ordonez .75 .23
38 Barry Larkin 1.25 .35
39 Ken Griffey Jr. 3.00 .90
40 Adam Dunn 1.25 .35
41 Juan Encarnacion .75 .23
42 Sean Casey .75 .23
43 Bartolo Colon .75 .23
44 C.C. Sabathia .75 .23
45 Travis Fryman .75 .23
46 Jim Thome 2.00 .60
47 Omar Vizquel 1.25 .35
48 Ellis Burks .75 .23
49 Russell Branyan .75 .23
50 Mike Hampton .75 .23
51 Todd Helton 1.25 .35
52 Jose Ortiz .75 .23
53 Juan Uribe .75 .23
54 Juan Pierre .75 .23
55 Larry Walker 1.25 .35
56 Mike Rivera .75 .23
57 Robert Fick .75 .23
58 Bobby Higginson .75 .23
59 Josh Beckett .75 .23
60 Richard Hidalgo .75 .23
61 Cliff Floyd .75 .23
62 Mike Lowell .75 .23
63 Roy Oswalt .75 .23
64 Morgan Ensberg .75 .23
65 Jeff Bagwell 1.25 .35
66 Craig Biggio 1.25 .35
67 Lance Berkman .75 .23
68 Carlos Beltran 1.25 .35
69 Mike Sweeney .75 .23
70 Neifi Perez .75 .23
71 Kevin Brown .75 .23
72 Hideo Nomo 2.00 .60
73 Paul Lo Duca .75 .23
74 Adrian Beltre 1.25 .35
75 Shawn Green .75 .23
76 Eric Karros .75 .23
77 Brad Radke .75 .23
78 Corey Koskie .75 .23
79 Doug Mientkiewicz .75 .23
80 Torii Hunter .75 .23
81 Jacque Jones .75 .23
82 Ben Sheets .75 .23
83 Richie Sexson .75 .23
84 Geoff Jenkins .75 .23
85 Tony Armas Jr. .75 .23
86 Michael Barrett .75 .23
87 Jose Vidro .75 .23
88 Vladimir Guerrero 2.00 .60
89 Roger Clemens 4.00 1.20
90 Derek Jeter 5.00 1.50
91 Bernie Williams 1.25 .35
92 Jason Giambi .75 .23
93 Jorge Posada 1.25 .35
94 Mike Mussina 1.25 .35
95 Andy Pettitte 1.25 .35
96 Nick Johnson .75 .23
97 Alfonso Soriano 1.25 .35
98 Shawn Estes .75 .23
99 Al Leiter .75 .23
100 Mike Piazza 3.00 .90
101 Roberto Alomar 1.25 .35
102 Mo Vaughn .75 .23
103 Jeromy Burnitz .75 .23
104 Tim Hudson .75 .23
105 Barry Zito .75 .23
106 Mark Mulder .75 .23
107 Eric Chavez .75 .23
108 Miguel Tejada .75 .23
109 Carlos Pena .75 .23
110 Jermaine Dye .75 .23
111 Mike Lieberthal .75 .23
112 Scott Rolen 2.00 .60
113 Pat Burrell .75 .23
114 Brandon Duckworth .75 .23
115 Bobby Abreu .75 .23
116 Jason Kendall .75 .23
117 Aramis Ramirez .75 .23
118 Brian Giles .75 .23
119 Pokey Reese .75 .23
120 Phil Nevin .75 .23
121 Ryan Klesko .75 .23
122 Jeremy Giambi .75 .23
123 Trevor Hoffman .75 .23
124 Barry Bonds 5.00 1.50
125 Rich Aurilia .75 .23
126 Jeff Kent .75 .23
127 Tsuyoshi Shinjo .75 .23
128 Ichiro Suzuki 3.00 .90
129 Edgar Martinez 1.25 .35
130 Freddy Garcia .75 .23
131 Bret Boone .75 .23
132 Matt Morris .75 .23
133 Tino Martinez 1.25 .35
134 Albert Pujols 4.00 1.20
135 J.D. Drew .75 .23
136 Jim Edmonds .75 .23
137 Gabe Kapler .75 .23
138 Paul Wilson .75 .23
139 Ben Grieve .75 .23
140 Wade Miller .75 .23
141 Chan Ho Park .75 .23
142 Alex Rodriguez 3.00 .90
143 Rafael Palmeiro 1.25 .35
144 Juan Gonzalez 1.25 .35
145 Ivan Rodriguez 2.00 .60
146 Carlos Delgado .75 .23
147 Jose Cruz Jr. .75 .23
148 Shannon Stewart .75 .23
149 Raul Mondesi .75 .23
150 Vernon Wells .75 .23
151 So Taguchi RP RC 8.00 2.40
152 Kazuhisa Ishii RP RC 10.00 3.00
153 Hank Blalock RP 8.00 2.40
154 Sean Burroughs RP 5.00 1.50
155 Geronimo Gil RP 5.00 1.50
156 Jon Rauch RP 5.00 1.50
157 Fernando Rodney RP 5.00 1.50
158 Miguel Asencio RP RC 5.00 1.50
159 Franklyn German RP RC 5.00 1.50
160 Luis Ugueto RP RC 5.00 1.50
161 Jorge Sosa RP RC 5.00 1.50
162 Felix Escalona RP RC 5.00 1.50
163 Colby Lewis RP 5.00 1.50
164 Mark Teixeira RP 8.00 2.40
165 Mark Prior RP 12.00 3.60
166 Francis Beltran RP RC 5.00 1.50
167 Joe Thurston RP 5.00 1.50
168 Earl Snyder RP RC 8.00 2.40
169 Takahito Nomura RP RC 5.00 1.50
170 Bill Hall RP 5.00 1.50
171 Marlon Byrd RP 5.00 1.50
172 Dave Williams RP 5.00 1.50
173 Yorvit Torrealba RP 5.00 1.50
174 Brandon Backe RP RC 8.00 2.40
175 Jorge De La Rosa RP RC 5.00 1.50
176 Brian Mallette RP RC 5.00 1.50
177 Rodrigo Rosario RP RC 5.00 1.50
178 Anderson Machado RP RC 5.00 1.50
179 Jorge Padilla RP RC 5.00 1.50
180 Allan Simpson RP RC 5.00 1.50
181 Doug Devore RP RC 5.00 1.50
182 Steve Bechler RP RC 5.00 1.50
183 Raul Chavez RP RC 5.00 1.50
184 Tom Shearn RP RC 5.00 1.50
185 Ben Howard RP RC 5.00 1.50
186 Chris Baker RP RC 5.00 1.50
187 Travis Hughes RP RC 5.00 1.50
188 Kevin Mench RP 5.00 1.50
189 Drew Henson RP 5.00 1.50
190 Mike Moriarty RP RC 5.00 1.50
191 Corey Thurman RP RC 5.00 1.50
192 Bobby Hill RP 5.00 1.50
193 Steve Kent RP RC 5.00 1.50
194 Satoru Komiyama RP RC 5.00 1.50
195 Jason Lane RP 5.00 1.50
196 Angel Berroa RP 5.00 1.50
197 Brandon Puffer RP RC 5.00 1.50
198 Brian Fitzgerald RP RC 5.00 1.50
199 Rene Reyes RP RC 5.00 1.50
200 Hee Seop Choi RP 5.00 1.50
NNO Mark Prior Promo

2002 Absolute Memorabilia Spectrum

Randomly inserted into packs, this is a parallel to the basic set. The veteran cards (1-150) were issued to a stated print run of 100 serial numbered sets while the rookies and prospects were issued to a stated print run of 50 serial numbered sets.

Nm-Mt Ex-Mt
*SPECTRUM 1-150: 2.5X TO 6X BASIC
72 Hideo Nomo 12.00 3.60
151 So Taguchi RP 15.00 4.50
152 Kazuhisa Ishii RP 40.00 12.00
153 Hank Blalock RP 25.00 7.50
154 Sean Burroughs RP 10.00 3.00
155 Geronimo Gil RP 10.00 3.00
156 Jon Rauch RP 10.00 3.00
157 Fernando Rodney RP 10.00 3.00
158 Miguel Asencio RP 10.00 3.00
159 Franklyn German RP 10.00 3.00
160 Luis Ugueto RP 10.00 3.00
161 Jorge Sosa RP 10.00 3.00
162 Felix Escalona RP 10.00 3.00
163 Colby Lewis RP 10.00 3.00
164 Mark Teixeira RP 15.00 4.50
165 Mark Prior RP 25.00 7.50
166 Francis Beltran RP 10.00 3.00
167 Joe Thurston RP 10.00 3.00
168 Earl Snyder RP 15.00 4.50
169 Takahito Nomura RP 25.00 7.50
170 Bill Hall RP 10.00 3.00
171 Marlon Byrd RP 10.00 3.00
172 Dave Williams RP 10.00 3.00
173 Yorvit Torrealba RP 10.00 3.00
174 Brandon Backe RP 25.00 7.50
175 Jorge De La Rosa RP 15.00 4.50
176 Brian Mallette RP 10.00 3.00
177 Rodrigo Rosario RP 10.00 3.00
178 Anderson Machado RP 10.00 3.00
179 Jorge Padilla RP 10.00 3.00
180 Allan Simpson RP 10.00 3.00
181 Doug Devore RP 10.00 3.00
182 Steve Bechler RP 10.00 3.00
183 Raul Chavez RP 10.00 3.00
184 Tom Shearn RP 10.00 3.00
185 Ben Howard RP 10.00 3.00
186 Chris Baker RP 10.00 3.00
187 Travis Hughes RP 10.00 3.00
188 Kevin Mench RP 10.00 3.00
189 Drew Henson RP 10.00 3.00
190 Mike Moriarty RP 10.00 3.00
191 Corey Thurman RP 10.00 3.00
192 Bobby Hill RP 10.00 3.00
193 Steve Kent RP 10.00 3.00
194 Satoru Komiyama RP 10.00 3.00
195 Jason Lane RP 10.00 3.00
196 Angel Berroa RP 10.00 3.00
197 Brandon Puffer RP 10.00 3.00
198 Brian Fitzgerald RP 10.00 3.00
199 Rene Reyes RP 10.00 3.00
200 Hee Seop Choi RP 10.00 3.00

2002 Absolute Memorabilia Absolutely Ink

Inserted into packs at stated odds of one in 22 hobby and one in 36 retail, these 59 cards feature a mix of active player and retired superstars who signed cards for this set. Many players were printed to shorter supply and we have notated that information next to their name in our checklist. Cards with a stated print run of 50 or fewer are not priced due to market scarcity.

Nm-Mt Ex-Mt
GOLD RANDOM INSERTS IN PACKS
GOLD PRINT RUN 25 SERIAL #'d SETS
NO GOLD PRICING DUE TO SCARCITY
1 Adrian Beltre 25.00 7.50
2 Alex Rodriguez SP/50 120.00 36.00
3 Ben Sheets 15.00 4.50
4 Bernie Williams SP/25
5 Bobby Doerr 15.00 4.50
6 Blaine Neal 10.00 3.00
7 Carlos Beltran 40.00 12.00
8 Carlos Pena 10.00 3.00
10 Corey Patterson SP/150 15.00 4.50
11 Curt Schilling SP/15
12 Dave Parker 15.00 4.50
13 David Justice SP/65 25.00 7.50
14 Don Mattingly SP/75 80.00 24.00
15 Duaner Sanchez 10.00 3.00
16 Eric Chavez SP/100 15.00 4.50
17 Freddy Garcia SP/200 15.00 4.50
18 Gary Carter SP/150 15.00 4.50
19 Gary Sheffield SP/25
20 George Brett SP/25
21 Greg Maddux SP/25
22 Ivan Rodriguez SP/50 50.00 15.00
23 J.D. Drew SP/100 25.00 7.50
24 Jack Cust 10.00 3.00
25 Jason Michaels 10.00 3.00
26 Jermaine Dye SP/125 15.00 4.50
27 Jim Palmer SP/150 15.00 4.50
28 Jose Vidro 10.00 3.00
29 Josh Towers 10.00 3.00
30 Kerry Wood SP/50 50.00 15.00
31 Kirby Puckett SP/50 80.00 24.00
32 Luis Gonzalez SP/75 25.00 7.50
33 Luis Rivera 10.00 3.00
34 Manny Ramirez SP/50 50.00 15.00
35 Marcus Giles 15.00 4.50
36 Mark Prior SP/100 50.00 15.00
37 Mark Teixeira SP/100 25.00 7.50
38 Marlon Byrd SP/250 15.00 4.50
39 Matt Ginter 10.00 3.00
40 Moises Alou SP/150 15.00 4.50
41 Nate Frese 10.00 3.00
42 Nick Johnson 10.00 3.00
43 Nomar Garciaparra SP/15
44 Pablo Ozuna 10.00 3.00
45 Paul Lo Duca SP/200 15.00 4.50
46 Richie Sexson 15.00 4.50
47 Roberto Alomar SP/100 25.00 7.50
48 Roy Oswalt SP/300 15.00 4.50
49 Ryan Klesko SP/75 25.00 7.50
50 Sean Casey SP/125 15.00 4.50
51 Shannon Stewart 15.00 4.50
52 So Taguchi 15.00 4.50
53 Terrence Long 10.00 3.00
54 Timo Perez 10.00 3.00
55 Todd Helton SP/25
56 Tony Gwynn SP/50 80.00 24.00
57 Troy Glaus SP/300 15.00 4.50
58 Vladimir Guerrero SP/225 40.00 12.00
59 Wade Miller 10.00 3.00
60 Wilson Betemit 10.00 3.00

2002 Absolute Memorabilia Absolutely Ink Numbers

This is a parallel to the Absolutely Ink insert set. Each card can be identified as they were issued to that player's print uniform number. If a player signed 25 or fewer or these cards, there is no pricing due to market scarcity.

Nm-Mt Ex-Mt
1 Adrian Beltre/29 50.00 15.00
2 Alex Rodriguez/3
3 Ben Sheets/15
5 Bobby Doerr/1
7 Carlos Beltran/15
8 Carlos Pena/15
10 Corey Patterson/20
12 Dave Parker/39 25.00 7.50
13 David Justice/23
14 Don Mattingly/23
16 Eric Chavez/3
17 Freddy Garcia/34 30.00 9.00
18 Gary Carter/8
19 Gary Sheffield/10
20 George Brett/5
21 Greg Maddux/31 100.00 30.00
22 Ivan Rodriguez/7
23 J.D. Drew/7
24 Jack Cust/67 15.00 4.50
25 Jason Michaels/22
26 Jermaine Dye/24
27 Jim Palmer/22
28 Jose Vidro/3
29 Josh Towers/35 20.00 6.00
30 Kerry Wood/34 60.00 18.00
31 Kirby Puckett/34 100.00 30.00
32 Luis Gonzalez/20
33 Luis Rivera/60 15.00 4.50
34 Manny Ramirez/24
35 Marcus Giles/22
36 Mark Prior/22
40 Moises Alou/18
42 Nick Johnson/36 20.00 6.00
43 Nomar Garciaparra/5
44 Pablo Ozuna/3
45 Paul Lo Duca/16
46 Richie Sexson/11
47 Roberto Alomar/12
48 Roy Oswalt/44 25.00 7.50
49 Ryan Klesko/30 30.00 9.00
50 Sean Casey/21
51 Shannon Stewart/24
52 So Taguchi/99 25.00 7.50
53 Terrence Long/12
54 Timo Perez/6
56 Tony Gwynn/19
57 Troy Glaus/25
58 Vladimir Guerrero/27 60.00 18.00
59 Wade Miller/52 15.00 4.50
60 Wilson Betemit/24

2002 Absolute Memorabilia Signing Bonus

Inserted into "full" boxes at one per box and with a SRP of $40 per frame, these 313 items was highlighted by a signature of the featured player. These frame have all different stated print runs and we have notated that information in our checklist next to their names. Frames with a print run of 25 or less are not priced due to market scarcity.

Nm-Mt Ex-Mt
1 Bob Abreu Gray-N/53 40.00 12.00
2 Bob Abreu Stripe-N/53 40.00 12.00
3 Grover Alexander Gray/1
4 Rob Alomar Gray-N/12
5 Rob Alomar Gray-N/100 40.00 12.00
6 Rob Alomar Stripe-N/100 40.00 12.00
7 Moises Alou Blue-L/250 25.00 7.50
8 Moises Alou Blue-N/18
9 Moises Alou Gray-N/18
10 Moises Alou Stripe-L/250 25.00 7.50
11 Moises Alou Stripe-N/18
12 Jeff Bagwell Gray-N/5
13 Jeff Bagwell Red-N/5
14 Jeff Bagwell Stripe-N/5
15 Jeff Bagwell White-N/5
16 Carlos Beltran Black-N/15
17 Carlos Beltran Blue-N/50 60.00 18.00
18 Carlos Beltran Gray-N/50 60.00 18.00
19 Carlos Beltran White-N/15
20 Adrian Beltre Blue-N/150 30.00 9.00
21 Adrian Beltre Gray-N/150 30.00 9.00
22 Adrian Beltre White-N/29 80.00 24.00
23 Lance Berkman Gray-N/17
24 Lance Berkman Red-N/17
25 Lance Berkman Stripe-N/17
26 Lance Berkman White-N/17
27 Angel Berroa Black-N/100 20.00 6.00
28 Angel Berroa Blue-N/100 20.00 6.00
29 Angel Berroa Gray-N/50 25.00 7.50
30 Angel Berroa White-N/4
31 Wilson Betemit Gray-N/250 15.00 4.50
32 Wilson Betemit White-N/250 15.00 4.50
33 Craig Biggio Gray-N/7
34 Craig Biggio Red-N/7
35 Craig Biggio Stripe-N/7
36 Craig Biggio White-N/7
37 Hank Blalock Gray-N/12
38 Hank Blalock Gray-N/50 60.00 18.00
39 Hank Blalock White-N/100 50.00 15.00
40 George Brett Blue-N/5
41 George Brett Gray-N/5
42 George Brett White-N/5
43 Lou Brock Gray-N/100 40.00 12.00
44 Lou Brock White-N/200 30.00 9.00
45 Kevin Brown Blue-N/27 50.00 15.00
46 Kevin Brown Gray-N/150 25.00 7.50
47 Kevin Brown White-N/100 30.00 9.00
48 Mark Buehrle Black-N/200 25.00 7.50
49 Mark Buehrle Gray-N/200 25.00 7.50
50 Mark Buehrle Stripe-N/56 40.00 12.00
51 Sean Burroughs Blue-N/21
52 Sean Burroughs Gray-N/21
53 Sean Burroughs White-N/21
54 Marlon Byrd Gray-N/61 25.00 7.50
55 Marlon Byrd Stripe-N/61 25.00 7.50
56 Steve Carlton Gray-N/100 40.00 12.00
57 Steve Carlton Stripe-N/150 30.00 9.00
58 Sean Casey Gray-N/21
59 Sean Casey Stripe-L/100 30.00 9.00
60 Sean Casey Stripe-N/21
61 Eric Chavez Gray-N/25
62 Eric Chavez Green-N/3
63 Eric Chavez White-N/28 50.00 15.00
64 Roger Clemens Gray-N/10
65 Roger Clemens Stripe-N/10
66 Ty Cobb Gray/6
67 Eddie Collins Gray/1
68 Juan Cruz Blue-L/51 25.00 7.50
69 Juan Cruz Blue-N/51 25.00 7.50
70 Juan Cruz Gray-N/51 25.00 7.50
71 Juan Cruz Stripe-L/51 25.00 7.50
72 Juan Cruz Stripe-N/51 25.00 7.50
73 J.D. Drew Gray-N/100 40.00 12.00
74 J.D. Drew White-N/7
75 Bran Duckworth Gray-N/56 25.00 7.50
76 B.Duckworth Stripe-N/150 15.00 4.50
77 Adam Dunn Gray-N/10
78 Adam Dunn Stripe-L/10
79 Adam Dunn Stripe-N/44 60.00 18.00
80 Jermaine Dye Gray-N/250 25.00 7.50
81 Jermaine Dye Green-N/100 30.00 9.00
82 Jermaine Dye White-N/100 30.00 9.00
83 Morg Ensberg Gray-N/100 20.00 6.00
84 Morg Ensberg Red-N/100 20.00 6.00
85 Morg Ensberg Stripe-N/100 20.00 6.00
86 Morg Ensberg White-N/100 20.00 6.00
87 Darin Erstad Gray-N/5
88 Darin Erstad White-N/17
89 Cliff Floyd Gray-N/200 25.00 7.50
90 Cliff Floyd Stripe-N/200 25.00 7.50
91 Jimmie Foxx Gray/1
92 Freddy Garcia Blue-N/34 50.00 15.00
93 Freddy Garcia Gray-N/34 50.00 15.00
94 Freddy Garcia White-N/125 25.00 7.50
95 Nomar Garciaparra Gray-N/5
96 Nomar Garciaparra White-N/5
97 Troy Glaus Gray-N/50 40.00 12.00
98 Troy Glaus White-N/100 30.00 9.00
99 Tom Glavine Gray-N/25
100 Tom Glavine White-N/200 50.00 15.00
101 Luis Gonzalez Black-N/20
102 Luis Gonzalez Gray-N/125 25.00 7.50
103 Luis Gonzalez Purple-N/125 25.00 7.50
104 Luis Gonzalez Stripe-N/125 25.00 7.50
105 Hank Greenberg Gray/1
106 Vlad Guerrero Gray-N/27 120.00 36.00
107 V.Guerrero Stripe-N/150 80.00 24.00
108 Tony Gwynn Blue-N/19
109 Tony Gwynn Gray-N/19
110 Tony Gwynn White-N/19
111 Rich Hidalgo Gray-N/100 20.00 6.00
112 Rich Hidalgo Red-N/135 15.00 4.50
113 Rich Hidalgo Stripe-N/15
114 Rich Hidalgo White-N/150 15.00 4.50
115 Rogers Hornsby Gray/1
116 Tim Hudson Gray-N/50 60.00 18.00
117 Tim Hudson Green-N/100 40.00 12.00
118 Tim Hudson White-N/15
119 Kazuhisa Ishii Blue-N/17
120 Kazuhisa Ishii Gray-N/17
121 Kazuhisa Ishii White-N/17
122 Reg Jackson Gray-N/44 80.00 24.00
123 Reg Jackson Stripe-N/44 100.00 30.00
124 Nick Johnson Gray-N/200 25.00 7.50
125 Nick Johnson Stripe-N/200 25.00 7.50
126 Walter Johnson Gray/4
127 Andruw Jones Gray-N/75 40.00 12.00

128 Andruw Jones White-N/25
129 Chipper Jones Gray-N/10
130 Chipper Jones White-N/10
131 Al Kaline Gray-N/6
132 Al Kaline White-L/250 .... 50.00 15.00
133 Al Kaline White-N/6
134 Gabe Kapler Blue-N/125 ..... 15.00 4.50
135 Gabe Kapler Gray-N/18
136 Gabe Kapler White-N/175 .. 15.00 4.50
137 Ryan Klesko Blue-N/30 ...... 50.00 15.00
138 Ryan Klesko Gray-N/30 ...... 50.00 15.00
139 Ryan Klesko White-N/30 .... 50.00 15.00
140 Nap Lajoie Gray/1
141 Jason Lane Gray-N/100 ..... 20.00 6.00
142 Jason Lane Red-N/100 ..... 20.00 6.00
143 Jason Lane Stripe-N/100 ... 20.00 6.00
144 Jason Lane White-N/100 .... 20.00 6.00
145 Barry Larkin Gray-N/50 ...... 60.00 18.00
146 Barry Larkin Stripe-L/100 .. 40.00 12.00
147 Barry Larkin Stripe-N/11
148 Paul LoDuca Blue-N/16
149 Paul LoDuca Gray-N/16
150 Paul LoDuca White-N/16 ... 40.00 12.00
151 Fred Lynn Gray-N/250 ...... 25.00 7.50
152 Fred Lynn White-N/150 ...... 25.00 7.50
153 Connie Mack Gray/2
154 Greg Maddux Gray-N/31 .. 200.00 60.00
155 Greg Maddux White-N/31 200.00 60.00
156 Roger Maris Gray/3
157 Edgar Martinez Blue-N/150 50.00 15.00
158 Edgar Martinez Gray-N/150 50.00 15.00
159 Edgar Martinez White-N/11
160 Pedro Martinez Gray-N/5
161 P.Martinez White-N/45 ..... 120.00 36.00
162 Don Mattingly Gray-N/100 150.00 45.00
163 D.Mattingly Stripe-N/100 . 150.00 45.00
164 Will McCovey Gray-N/190 .. 30.00 9.00
165 Will McCovey White-N/250 30.00 9.00
166 Wade Miller Gray-N/150 .... 15.00 4.50
167 Wade Miller Stripe-N/250 .. 15.00 4.50
168 Wade Miller Red-N/52 .... 25.00 7.50
169 Wade Miller White-N/52 ..... 25.00 7.50
170 Paul Molitor Blue-N/75 ...... 60.00 18.00
171 Paul Molitor Gray-N/100 .... 40.00 12.00
172 Paul Molitor White-N/125 .. 60.00 18.00
173 Mark Mulder Gray-N/20
174 Mark Mulder Green-N/20
175 Mark Mulder White-N/40 ... 40.00 12.00
176 Mike Mussina Gray-N/5
177 Mike Mussina Stripe-N/5
178 Jose Ortiz Gray-N/125 ...... 15.00 4.50
179 Jose Ortiz Purple-N/125 .... 15.00 4.50
180 Jose Ortiz Stripe-L/125 ..... 15.00 4.50
181 Jose Ortiz Stripe-N/125 ..... 15.00 4.50
182 Roy Oswalt Gray-N/44 .... 40.00 12.00
183 Roy Oswalt Red-N/44 .... 40.00 12.00
184 Roy Oswalt Stripe-N/100 ... 30.00 9.00
185 Roy Oswalt White-N/100 ... 30.00 9.00
186 Mel Ott Gray/3
187 Rafael Palmeiro Blue-N/25
188 Rafael Palmeiro Gray-N/25
189 Rafael Palmeiro White-N/25
190 Jim Palmer Gray-N/250 ...... 25.00 7.50
191 Jim Palmer White-N/150 .... 25.00 7.50
192 Dave Parker Black-N/150 ... 30.00 9.00
193 Dave Parker White-N/150 .. 30.00 9.00
194 Cor Patterson Blue-L/250 .. 25.00 7.50
195 Cor Patterson Blue-N/20
196 Cor Patterson Gray-N/250 .. 25.00 7.50
197 Cor Patterson Stripe-L/250 25.00 7.50
198 Cor Patterson Stripe-N/250 25.00 7.50
199 Carlos Pena Gray-N/19
200 Carlos Pena Green-N/250 .. 15.00 4.50
201 Carlos Pena White-N/150 ... 15.00 4.50
202 Tony Perez Gray-N/24
203 Tony Perez Stripe-L/250 .... 25.00 7.50
204 Tony Perez Stripe-N/24
205 Juan Pierre Gray-N/75 ...... 40.00 12.00
206 Juan Pierre Purple-N/75 .... 25.00 7.50
207 Juan Pierre White-L/75 ...... 25.00 7.50
208 Juan Pierre White-N/75 ...... 25.00 7.50
209 Mark Prior Blue-L/75 .... 100.00 30.00
210 Mark Prior Blue-N/125 ...... 80.00 24.00
211 Mark Prior Gray-N/75 .... 100.00 30.00
212 Mark Prior Stripe-L/50 ..... 120.00 36.00
213 Mark Prior Stripe-N/22
214 Kirby Puckett Blue-N/34 ... 100.00 30.00
215 Kirby Puckett Gray-N/34
216 Kirby Puckett Stripe-N/34 100.00 30.00
217 Albert Pujols Gray-N/5
218 Albert Pujols White-N/100 200.00 60.00
219 Aram Ramirez Black-N/125 25.00 7.50
220 Aram Ramirez Gray-N/50 ... 40.00 12.00
221 Aram Ramirez White-N/16
222 Manny Ramirez Gray-N/24
223 Manny Ramirez White-N/5
224 Phil Rizzuto Gray-N/250 ..... 80.00 24.00
225 Phil Rizzuto Stripe-N/10
226 B.Robinson Gray-N/250 ..... 30.00 9.00
227 B.Robinson White-N/150 ... 80.00 24.00
227A Brooks Robinson ERR White-N/150
Card says in print it was signed by Jim Palmer
228 Jackie Robinson Gray/3
229 Alex Rodriguez Blue-N/3
230 Alex Rodriguez Gray-N/15
231 Alex Rodriguez White-N/15
232 Ivan Rodriguez Blue-N/7
233 Ivan Rodriguez Gray-N/7
234 Ivan Rodriguez White-N/7
235 Scott Rolen Gray-N/17
236 Scott Rolen Stripe-N/17
237 Babe Ruth Gray/8
238 N.Ryan Angel Gray-N/30 .. 250.00 75.00
239 N.Ryan Angel White-N/30 250.00 75.00
240 N.Ryan Astro Gray-N/34 .. 250.00 75.00
241 N.Ryan Astro White-N/34 250.00 75.00
242 N.Ryan Rgr Blue-N/34 ...... 250.00 75.00
243 N.Ryan Rgr Gray-N/34 ..... 250.00 75.00
244 N.Ryan Rgr White-N/34 ... 250.00 75.00
245 C.C. Sabathia Blue-N/15
246 C.C. Sabathia Gray-N/10
247 C.C. Sabathia White-N/10
248 Ryne Sandberg Blue-L/50 150.00 45.00
249 Ryne Sandberg Blue-N/23
250 Ryne Sandberg Gray-N/23
251 R.Sandberg Stripe-L/50 ... 150.00 45.00
252 Ryne Sandberg Stripe-N/23
253 Curt Schilling Black-N/10
254 Curt Schilling Gray-N/10
255 Curt Schilling Purple-N/10
256 Curt Schilling Stripe-N/5
257 Mike Schmidt Gray-N/100 120.00 36.00
258 M.Schmidt Stripe-N/100 .. 120.00 36.00
259 Richie Sexson Blue-N/100 . 30.00 9.00
260 Richie Sexson Gray-N/100 . 30.00 9.00
261 Richie Sexson White-N/100 30.00 9.00
262 Ben Sheets Blue-N/150 ...... 25.00 7.50
263 Ben Sheets Gray-N/100 ..... 30.00 9.00
264 Ben Sheets White-N/100 .... 30.00 9.00
265 Gary Sheffield Gray-N/11
266 Gary Sheffield White-N/11
267 George Sisler Gray/3
268 Alfonso Soriano Gray-N/12
269 A.Soriano Stripe-N/100 ...... 60.00 18.00
270 Tris Speaker Gray/1
271 Shan Stewart Blue-N/150 ... 25.00 7.50
272 Shan Stewart Gray-N/100 .. 20.00 6.00
273 Shan Stewart White-N/24
274 Mike Sweeney Black-N/100 30.00 9.00
275 Mike Sweeney Blue-N/100 . 30.00 9.00
276 Mike Sweeney Gray-N/100. 30.00 9.00
277 Mike Sweeney White-N/100 30.00 9.00
278 So Taguchi Gray-N/99 .... 50.00 15.00
279 So Taguchi White-N/99 ...... 50.00 15.00
280 Mark Teixeira Blue-N/100 ... 40.00 12.00
281 Mark Teixeira Gray-N/23
282 Mark Teixeira White-N/100 40.00 12.00
283 Miguel Tejada Gray-N/50 .... 40.00 12.00
284 Miguel Tejada Green-N/4
285 Miguel Tejada White-N/40 .. 40.00 12.00
286 Frank Thomas Black-N/35 150.00 45.00
287 Frank Thomas Gray-N/10
288 Frank Thomas White-N/10
289 Juan Uribe Gray-N/25
290 Juan Uribe Purple-N/25
291 Juan Uribe White-L/4
292 Juan Uribe White-N/4
293 Jav Vazquez Gray-N/125 .... 25.00 7.50
294 Jav Vazquez Stripe-N/125 .. 25.00 7.50
295 Jose Vidro Gray-N/150 ...... 15.00 4.50
296 Jose Vidro Stripe-N/150 .... 15.00 4.50
297 Honus Wagner Gray/11
298 Bernie Williams Gray-N/15
299 Bernie Williams Stripe-N/15
300 Ted Williams Gray/1
301 Hack Wilson Gray/1
302 Dave Winfield Gray-N/25
303 Dave Winfield Stripe-N/25
304 Kerry Wood Blue-L/34 ..... 100.00 30.00
305 Kerry Wood Blue-N/34 ..... 100.00 30.00
306 Kerry Wood Gray-N/34 .... 100.00 30.00
307 Kerry Wood Stripe-L/34 ... 100.00 30.00
308 Kerry Wood Stripe-N/34 .. 100.00 30.00
309 Cy Young Gray/2
310 Barry Zito Gray-N/25
311 Barry Zito Green-N/25
312 Barry Zito White-N/50 .... 60.00 18.00

2002 Absolute Memorabilia Team Quads

Inserted into hobby packs at a stated rate of one in 18, these cards feature four players from 20 of the 30 different major league teams.

Nm-Mt Ex-Mt
*GOLD: .75X TO 2X BASIC QUADS
*SPECTRUM: .6X TO 1.5X BASIC QUADS
SPECTRUM ODDS 1:36 HOBBY
1 Troy Glaus 5.00 1.50
Darin Erstad
Garret Anderson
Troy Percival
2 Curt Schilling 5.00 1.50
Randy Johnson
Luis Gonzalez
Mark Grace
3 Chipper Jones 8.00 2.40
Andruw Jones
Greg Maddux
Tom Glavine
4 Nomar Garciaparra 8.00 2.40
Manny Ramirez
Trot Nixon
Pedro Martinez
5 Kerry Wood 8.00 2.40
Sammy Sosa
Fred McGriff
Moises Alou
6 Frank Thomas 5.00 1.50
Magglio Ordonez
Mark Buehrle
Kenny Lofton
7 Ken Griffey Jr. 8.00 2.40
Barry Larkin
Adam Dunn
Sean Casey
8 C.C Sabathia 5.00 1.50
Jim Thome
Bartolo Colon
Russell Branyan
9 Todd Helton 5.00 1.50
Larry Walker
Juan Pierre
Mike Hampton
10 Jeff Bagwell 5.00 1.50
Craig Biggio
Lance Berkman
Richard Hidalgo
11 Shawn Green 5.00 1.50
Adrian Beltre
Hideo Nomo
Paul Lo Duca
12 Mike Piazza 8.00 2.40
Roberto Alomar
Mo Vaughn
Roger Cedeno
13 Roger Clemens 12.00 3.60
Derek Jeter
Jason Giambi
Mike Mussina
14 Barry Zito 5.00 1.50
Tim Hudson
Eric Chavez
Miguel Tejada
15 Pat Burrell 5.00 1.50
Scott Rolen
Bobby Abreu
Marlon Byrd
16 Bernie Williams 5.00 1.50
Jorge Posada
Alfonso Soriano
Andy Pettitte
17 Barry Bonds 10.00 3.00
Rich Aurilia
Tsuyoshi Shinjo
Jeff Kent
18 Ichiro Suzuki 8.00 2.40
Kazuhiro Sasaki
Bret Boone
Edgar Martinez
19 Albert Pujols 10.00 3.00
J.D. Drew
Jim Edmonds
Tino Martinez
20 Alex Rodriguez 8.00 2.40
Ivan Rodriguez
Juan Gonzalez
Rafael Palmeiro

2002 Absolute Memorabilia Team Quads Materials

Randomly inserted into packs, these 19 cards parallel the Team Quads insert set. Each card be identified by both the four pieces of memorabilia on the card as well as having a stated print run of 100 serial numbered sets. Please note that card number 7 does not exist.

Nm-Mt Ex-Mt
GOLD PRINT RUN 25 SERIAL #'d SETS
NO GOLD PRICING DUE TO SCARCITY
1 Troy Glaus Jsy 25.00 7.50
Darin Erstad Jsy
Garret Anderson Jsy
Troy Percival Jsy
2 Curt Schilling Jsy 40.00 12.00
Randy Johnson Jsy
Luis Gonzalez Jsy
Mark Grace Jsy
3 Chipper Jones Jsy 50.00 15.00
Andruw Jones Jsy
Greg Maddux Jsy
Tom Glavine Jsy
4 Nomar Garciaparra Jsy 50.00 15.00
Manny Ramirez Jsy
Pedro Martinez Jsy
Trot Nixon Bat
5 Kerry Wood Base 40.00 12.00
Sammy Sosa Base
Fred McGriff Base
Moises Alou Base
6 Frank Thomas Jsy 40.00 12.00
Magglio Ordonez Jsy
Mark Buehrle Jsy
Kenny Lofton Bat
7 Does Not Exist
8 C.C Sabathia Jsy 40.00 12.00
Jim Thome Jsy
Bartolo Colon Jsy
Russell Branyan Jsy
9 Todd Helton Jsy 40.00 12.00
Larry Walker Jsy
Juan Pierre Jsy
Mike Hampton Jsy
10 Jeff Bagwell Jsy 40.00 12.00
Craig Biggio Jsy
Lance Berkman Jsy
Richard Hidalgo Pants
11 Shawn Green Jsy 60.00 18.00
Adrian Beltre Jsy
Hideo Nomo Jsy
Paul Lo Duca Jsy
12 Mike Piazza Jsy 40.00 12.00
Roberto Alomar Shoe
Mo Vaughn Bat
Roger Cedeno Bat
13 Roger Clemens Base 80.00 24.00
Derek Jeter Ball
Jason Giambi Ball
Mike Mussina Ball
14 Barry Zito Jsy 25.00 7.50
Tim Hudson Jsy
Eric Chavez Bat
Miguel Tejada Jsy
15 Pat Burrell Jsy 40.00 12.00
Scott Rolen Jsy
Bobby Abreu Jsy
Marlon Byrd Jsy
16 Bernie Williams Jsy 40.00 12.00
Jorge Posada Jsy
Alfonso Soriano Bat
Andy Pettitte Jsy
17 Barry Bonds Ball 50.00 15.00
Rich Aurilia Base
Tsuyoshi Shinjo Base
Jeff Kent Base
18 Ichiro Deck 80.00 24.00
Kazuhiro Sasaki Deck
Edgar Martinez Base
Bret Boone Base
19 Albert Pujols Ball 60.00 18.00
J.D. Drew Base
Jim Edmonds Base
Tino Martinez Base
20 Alex Rodriguez Jsy 40.00 12.00
Ivan Rodriguez Jsy
Juan Gonzalez Jsy
Rafael Palmeiro Jsy

2002 Absolute Memorabilia Team Tandems

Inserted into hobby packs at stated odds of one in 12 hobby and one in 36 retail packs, these 40 cards feature two stars who are also teammates.

Nm-Mt Ex-Mt
*GOLD: .75X TO 2X BASIC TANDEMS
GOLD ODDS 1:72 HOBBY, 1:216 RETAIL
*SPECTRUM: .6X TO 1.5X BASIC TANDEMS
SPECTRUM ODDS 1:36 HOBBY
1 Troy Glaus .... 3.00 .90
Darin Erstad
2 Curt Schilling 5.00 1.50
Randy Johnson
3 Chipper Jones 5.00 1.50
Andruw Jones
4 Greg Maddux 8.00 2.40
Tom Glavine
5 Nomar Garciaparra 8.00 2.40
Manny Ramirez
6 Pedro Martinez 5.00 1.50
Trot Nixon
7 Kerry Wood 8.00 2.40
Sammy Sosa
8 Frank Thomas 5.00 1.50
Magglio Ordonez
9 Ken Griffey Jr. 8.00 2.40
Barry Larkin
10 C.C Sabathia 5.00 1.50
Jim Thome
11 Todd Helton .... 3.00 .90
Larry Walker
12 Bobby Higginson .... 3.00 .90
Shane Halter
13 Cliff Floyd .... 3.00 .90
Brad Penny
14 Jeff Bagwell .... 3.00 .90
Craig Biggio
15 Shawn Green .... 3.00 .90
Adrian Beltre
16 Ben Sheets .... 3.00 .90
Richie Sexson
17 Vladimir Guerrero 5.00 1.50
Jose Vidro
18 Mike Piazza 8.00 2.40
Roberto Alomar
19 Roger Clemens 10.00 3.00
Mike Mussina
20 Derek Jeter 12.00 3.60
Jason Giambi
21 Barry Zito .... 3.00 .90
Tim Hudson
22 Eric Chavez .... 3.00 .90
Miguel Tejada
23 Pat Burrell 5.00 1.50
Scott Rolen
24 Brian Giles .... 3.00 .90
Aramis Ramirez
25 Ryan Klesko .... 3.00 .90
Phil Nevin
26 Barry Bonds 10.00 3.00
Rich Aurilia
27 Ichiro Suzuki 8.00 2.40
Kazuhiro Sasaki
28 Albert Pujols 10.00 3.00
J.D. Drew
29 Alex Rodriguez 8.00 2.40
Ivan Rodriguez
30 Carlos Delgado .... 3.00 .90
Shannon Stewart
31 Mo Vaughn .... 3.00 .90
Roger Cedeno
32 Carlos Beltran .... 3.00 .90
Mike Sweeney
33 Edgar Martinez .... 3.00 .90
Bret Boone
34 Juan Gonzalez .... 3.00 .90
Rafael Palmeiro
35 Johnny Damon 5.00 1.50
Rickey Henderson
36 Sean Casey .... 3.00 .90
Adam Dunn
37 Jeff Kent .... 3.00 .90
Tsuyoshi Shinjo
38 Lance Berkman .... 3.00 .90
Richard Hidalgo
39 So Taguchi .... 3.00 .90
Tino Martinez
40 Hideo Nomo 8.00 2.40
Kazuhisa Ishii

2002 Absolute Memorabilia Team Tandems Materials

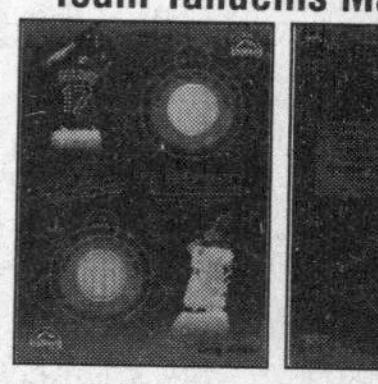

Inserted into hobby packs at a stated rate of one in 33 hobby and one in 164 retail, these 40 cards form a complete parallel to the Team Tandem insert set. These cards feature two pieces of memorabilia on each card. According to the manufacturer a few cards were printed in shorter supply and we have notated the announced print runs next to the card in our checklist. It was believed shortly after release that card 27 was not produced. Copies of the card eventually did surface but it's generally accepted to be one of the shortest cards in the set though a specific print run has never been divulged.

Nm-Mt Ex-Mt
1 Troy Glaus Jsy 10.00 3.00
Darin Erstad Bat
2 Curt Schilling Jsy 15.00 4.50
Randy Johnson Jsy
3 Chipper Jones Bat 15.00 4.50
Andruw Jones Bat
4 Greg Maddux Jsy 25.00 7.50
Tom Glavine Jsy
5 Nomar Garciaparra Bat 25.00 7.50
Manny Ramirez Bat SP/200
6 Pedro Martinez Jsy 20.00 6.00
Trot Nixon Bat SP/200
7 Kerry Wood Base 20.00 6.00
Sammy Sosa Base SP/250
8 Frank Thomas Bat 15.00 4.50
Magglio Ordonez Bat
9 Ken Griffey Jr. Base 15.00 4.50
Barry Larkin Base
10 C.C Sabathia Jsy 20.00 6.00
Jim Thome Bat SP/225
11 Todd Helton Bat 15.00 4.50
Larry Walker Bat
12 Bobby Higginson Bat 10.00 3.00
Shane Halter Bat
13 Cliff Floyd Bat 10.00 3.00
Brad Penny Jsy
14 Jeff Bagwell Bat 15.00 4.50
Craig Biggio Bat
15 Shawn Green Bat 15.00 4.50
Adrian Beltre Bat
16 Ben Sheets Jsy 10.00 3.00
Richie Sexson Bat
17 Vladimir Guerrero Bat 15.00 4.50
Jose Vidro Bat
18 Mike Piazza Bat 20.00 6.00
Roberto Alomar Bat SP/250
19 Roger Clemens Fld Glv 100.00 30.00
Mike Mussina Fld Glv SP/50
20 Derek Jeter Base 30.00 9.00
Jason Giambi Base SP/200
21 Barry Zito Jsy 15.00 4.50
Tim Hudson Shoe SP/200
22 Eric Chavez Bat 15.00 4.50
Miguel Tejada Bat SP/200
23 Pat Burrell Bat 15.00 4.50
Scott Rolen Bat
24 Brian Giles Bat 10.00 3.00
Aramis Ramirez Bat
25 Ryan Klesko Bat 15.00 4.50
Phil Nevin Jsy SP/250
26 Barry Bonds Base 20.00 6.00
Rich Aurilia Base
27 Ichiro Suzuki Deck
Kazuhiro Sasaki Deck SP
28 Albert Pujols Base 20.00 6.00
J.D. Drew Base SP/150
29 Alex Rodriguez Bat 20.00 6.00
Ivan Rodriguez Bat
30 Carlos Delgado Bat 10.00 3.00
Shannon Stewart Bat
31 Mo Vaughn Bat 10.00 3.00
Roger Cedeno Bat
32 Carlos Beltran Bat 15.00 4.50
Mike Sweeney Bat
33 Edgar Martinez Bat 15.00 4.50
Bret Boone Bat
34 Juan Gonzalez Bat 15.00 4.50
Rafael Palmeiro Bat
35 Johnny Damon Bat 15.00 4.50
Rickey Henderson Bat
36 Sean Casey Bat 20.00 6.00
Adam Dunn Shoe SP/100
37 Jeff Kent Bat 15.00 4.50
Tsuyoshi Shinjo Bat SP/250
38 Lance Berkman Bat 10.00 3.00
Richard Hidalgo Bat
39 So Taguchi Bat 20.00 6.00
Tino Martinez Bat SP/100
40 Hideo Nomo Jsy 60.00 18.00
Kazuhisa Ishii Jsy SP/50

2002 Absolute Memorabilia Team Tandems Materials Gold

Randomly inserted into packs, this is a parallel to the Team Tandem insert set. Each card has gold foil and was issued to a stated print run of 50 serial numbered sets.

Nm-Mt Ex-Mt
1 Troy Glaus Jsy 25.00 7.50
Darin Erstad Jsy
2 Curt Schilling Jsy 40.00 12.00
Randy Johnson Jsy
3 Chipper Jones Jsy 40.00 12.00
Andruw Jones Jsy
4 Greg Maddux Jsy 60.00 18.00
Tom Glavine Jsy
5 Nomar Garciaparra Jsy 50.00 15.00
Manny Ramirez Jsy
6 Pedro Martinez Jsy 40.00 12.00
Trot Nixon Bat
7 Kerry Wood Base 40.00 12.00
Sammy Sosa Ball
8 Frank Thomas Jsy 40.00 12.00
Magglio Ordonez Jsy
9 Ken Griffey Jr. Base 40.00 12.00
Barry Larkin Base
10 C.C Sabathia Jsy 40.00 12.00
Jim Thome Jsy
11 Todd Helton Jsy 40.00 12.00
Larry Walker Jsy
12 Bobby Higginson Bat 25.00 7.50
Shane Halter Bat
13 Cliff Floyd Jsy 25.00 7.50
Brad Penny Jsy
14 Jeff Bagwell Jsy 40.00 12.00
Craig Biggio Jsy

15 Shawn Green Jsy 40.00 12.00
Adrian Beltre Jsy
16 Ben Sheets Jsy 25.00 7.50
Richie Sexson Jsy
17 Vladimir Guerrero Jsy 40.00 12.00
Jose Vidro Jsy
18 Mike Piazza Jsy 40.00 12.00
Roberto Alomar Shoe
19 Roger Clemens Jsy 120.00 36.00
Mike Mussina Shoe
20 Derek Jeter Ball 60.00 18.00
Jason Giambi Ball
21 Barry Zito Jsy 30.00 9.00
Tim Hudson Jsy
22 Eric Chavez Bat 30.00 9.00
Miguel Tejada Jsy
23 Pat Burrell Jsy 40.00 12.00
Scott Rolen Jsy
24 Brian Giles Jsy 25.00 7.50
Aramis Ramirez Jsy
25 Ryan Klesko Fld Glv 30.00 9.00
Phil Nevin Jsy
26 Barry Bonds Ball 50.00 15.00
Rich Aurilia Base
27 Ichiro Suzuki Ball 100.00 30.00
Kazuhiro Sasaki Deck
28 Albert Pujols Ball 40.00 12.00
J.D. Drew Base
29 Alex Rodriguez Jsy 50.00 15.00
Ivan Rodriguez Jsy
30 Carlos Delgado Jsy 25.00 7.50
Shannon Stewart Jsy
31 Mo Vaughn Bat 25.00 7.50
Roger Cedeno Bat
32 Carlos Beltran Jsy 40.00 12.00
Mike Sweeney Jsy
33 Edgar Martinez Jsy 40.00 12.00
Bret Boone Jsy
34 Juan Gonzalez Jsy 40.00 12.00
Rafael Palmeiro Jsy
35 Johnny Damon Bat 40.00 12.00
Rickey Henderson Bat
36 Sean Casey Jsy 30.00 9.00
Adam Dunn Hat
37 Jeff Kent Jsy 30.00 9.00
Tsuyoshi Shinjo Bat
38 Lance Berkman Jsy 25.00 7.50
Richard Hidalgo Pants
39 So Taguchi Jsy 30.00 9.00
Tino Martinez Bat
40 Hideo Nomo Jsy ....
Kazuhisa Ishii Jsy

2002 Absolute Memorabilia Tools of the Trade

Issued in hobby packs at stated odds of one in nine hobby and one in 24 retail, these 95 cards feature many of the leading players in the game.

Nm-Mt Ex-Mt
*GOLD: .75X TO 2X BASIC TOOLS .....
GOLD ODDS 1:45 HOBBY, 1:144 RETAIL
1 Mike Mussina 4.00 1.20
2 Rickey Henderson 6.00 1.80
3 Raul Mondesi .... 2.50 .75
4 Nomar Garciaparra 10.00 3.00
5 Randy Johnson 6.00 1.80
6 Roger Clemens 12.00 3.60
7 Shawn Green .... 2.50 .75
8 Todd Helton 4.00 1.20
9 Aramis Ramirez .... 2.50 .75
10 Barry Larkin 4.00 1.20
11 Byung-Hyun Kim .... 2.50 .75
12 C.C. Sabathia .... 2.50 .75
13 Curt Schilling .... 2.50 .75
14 Darin Erstad .... 2.50 .75
15 Eric Karros .... 2.50 .75
16 Freddy Garcia .... 2.50 .75
17 Greg Maddux 10.00 3.00
18 Jason Kendall .... 2.50 .75
19 Jim Thome 6.00 1.80
20 Juan Gonzalez 4.00 1.20
21 Kazuhiro Sasaki .... 2.50 .75
22 Kerry Wood 6.00 1.80
23 Luis Gonzalez .... 2.50 .75
24 Mark Mulder .... 2.50 .75
25 Rich Aurilia .... 2.50 .75
26 Ray Durham .... 2.50 .75
27 Ben Grieve .... 2.50 .75
28 Bret Boone .... 2.50 .75
29 Edgar Martinez 4.00 1.20
30 Ivan Rodriguez 6.00 1.80
31 Jorge Posada 4.00 1.20
32 Mike Piazza 10.00 3.00
33 Pat Burrell .... 2.50 .75
34 Robin Ventura .... 2.50 .75
35 Trot Nixon .... 2.50 .75
36 Adrian Beltre 4.00 1.20
37 Bernie Williams 4.00 1.20
38 Bobby Abreu .... 2.50 .75
39 Carlos Delgado .... 2.50 .75
40 Craig Biggio 4.00 1.20
41 Garret Anderson .... 2.50 .75
42 Jermaine Dye .... 2.50 .75
43 Johnny Damon Sox 6.00 1.80
44 Tim Salmon 4.00 1.20
45 Tino Martinez 4.00 1.20
46 Fred McGriff 4.00 1.20
47 Gary Sheffield .... 2.50 .75
48 Adam Dunn 4.00 1.20
49 Joe Mays .... 2.50 .75
50 Kenny Lofton .... 2.50 .75
51 Josh Beckett .... 2.50 .75
52 Bud Smith .... 2.50 .75
53 Johnny Estrada .... 2.50 .75
54 Charles Johnson .... 2.50 .75
55 Craig Wilson .... 2.50 .75
56 Terrence Long .... 2.50 .75
57 Andy Pettitte 4.00 1.20
58 Brian Giles .... 2.50 .75
59 Juan Pierre .... 2.50 .75
60 Cliff Floyd .... 2.50 .75
61 Ivan Rodriguez 6.00 1.80
62 Andruw Jones .... 2.50 .75
63 Lance Berkman .... 2.50 .75
64 Mark Buehrle .... 2.50 .75
65 Miguel Tejada .... 2.50 .75
66 Wade Miller .... 2.50 .75
67 Johnny Estrada .... 2.50 .75
68 Tsuyoshi Shinjo .... 2.50 .75
69 Scott Rolen 6.00 1.80
70 Roberto Alomar 4.00 1.20
71 Mark Grace 4.00 1.20
72 Larry Walker 4.00 1.20
73 Jim Edmonds .... 2.50 .75
74 Jeff Kent .... 2.50 .75
75 Frank Thomas 6.00 1.80
76 Carlos Beltran 4.00 1.20
77 Barry Zito .... 2.50 .75
78 Alex Rodriguez 10.00 3.00
79 Troy Glaus .... 2.50 .75
80 Ryan Klesko .... 2.50 .75
81 Tom Glavine 4.00 1.20
82 Ben Sheets .... 2.50 .75
83 Manny Ramirez 4.00 1.20
84 Shannon Stewart .... 2.50 .75
85 Vladimir Guerrero 6.00 1.80
86 Chipper Jones 6.00 1.80
87 Jeff Bagwell 4.00 1.20
88 Richie Sexson .... 2.50 .75
89 Sean Casey .... 2.50 .75
90 Tim Hudson .... 2.50 .75
91 J.D. Drew .... 2.50 .75
92 Ivan Rodriguez 6.00 1.80
93 Magglio Ordonez .... 2.50 .75
94 John Buck .... 2.50 .75
95 Paul Lo Duca .... 2.50 .75

2002 Absolute Memorabilia Tools of the Trade Materials

Randomly inserted into packs, this is a parallel to the Tools of the Trade insert set. Each card features a game worn piece(or pieces) of the featued player. Cards in this set were printed to all sorts of different print runs which we have notated.

Nm-Mt Ex-Mt
1-32 PRINT RUN 300 SERIAL #'d SETS
33-47 PRINT RUN 250 SERIAL #'d SETS
48-55 PRINT RUN 150 SERIAL #'d SETS
56-61 PRINT RUN 125 SERIAL #'d SETS
62-66 PRINT RUN 50 SERIAL #'d SETS
67 PRINT RUN 100 SERIAL #'d CARDS
68-82 PRINT RUN 200 SERIAL #'d SETS
83-87 PRINT RUN 75 SERIAL #'d SETS
88-95 PRINT RUN 50 SERIAL #'d SETS
1 Mike Mussina Jsy 10.00 3.00
2 Rickey Henderson Jsy 10.00 3.00
3 Raul Mondesi Jsy 8.00 2.40
4 Nomar Garciaparra Jsy 15.00 4.50
5 Randy Johnson Jsy 10.00 3.00
6 Roger Clemens Jsy 15.00 4.50
7 Shawn Green Jsy 8.00 2.40
8 Todd Helton Jsy 10.00 3.00
9 Aramis Ramirez Jsy 8.00 2.40
10 Barry Larkin Jsy 10.00 3.00
11 Byung-Hyun Kim Jsy 10.00 3.00
12 C.C. Sabathia Jsy 8.00 2.40
13 Curt Schilling Jsy 8.00 2.40
14 Darin Erstad Jsy 8.00 2.40
15 Eric Karros Jsy 8.00 2.40
16 Freddy Garcia Jsy 8.00 2.40
17 Greg Maddux Jsy 15.00 4.50
18 Jason Kendall Jsy 8.00 2.40
19 Jim Thome Jsy 10.00 3.00
20 Juan Gonzalez Jsy 10.00 3.00
21 Kazuhiro Sasaki Jsy 8.00 2.40
22 Kerry Wood Jsy 10.00 3.00
23 Luis Gonzalez Jsy 8.00 2.40
24 Mark Mulder Jsy 8.00 2.40
25 Rich Aurilia Jsy 8.00 2.40
26 Ray Durham Jsy 8.00 2.40
27 Ben Grieve Jsy 8.00 2.40
28 Bret Boone Jsy 8.00 2.40
29 Edgar Martinez Jsy 10.00 3.00
30 Ivan Rodriguez Jsy 10.00 3.00
31 Jorge Posada Jsy 10.00 3.00
32 Mike Piazza Jsy 15.00 4.50
33 Pat Burrell Bat 8.00 2.40
34 Robin Ventura Bat 8.00 2.40
35 Trot Nixon Bat 8.00 2.40
36 Adrian Beltre Bat 10.00 3.00
37 Bernie Williams Bat 10.00 3.00
38 Bobby Abreu Bat 8.00 2.40
39 Carlos Delgado Bat 8.00 2.40
40 Craig Biggio Bat 10.00 3.00
41 Garret Anderson Bat 8.00 2.40
42 Jermaine Dye Bat 8.00 2.40
43 Johnny Damon Sox Bat 10.00 3.00
44 Tim Salmon Bat 10.00 3.00
45 Tino Martinez Bat 10.00 3.00
46 Fred McGriff Bat 10.00 3.00
47 Gary Sheffield Bat 8.00 2.40
48 Adam Dunn Shoe 15.00 4.50
49 Joe Mays Shoe 10.00 3.00
50 Kenny Lofton Shoe 10.00 3.00
51 Josh Beckett Shoe 10.00 3.00
52 Bud Smith Shoe 10.00 3.00
53 Johnny Estrada Shin 10.00 3.00
54 Charles Johnson Shin 10.00 3.00
55 Craig Wilson Shin 15.00 4.50
56 Terrence Long Fld Glv 10.00 3.00
57 Andy Pettitte Fld Glv 15.00 4.50
58 Brian Giles Fld Glv 10.00 3.00
59 Juan Pierre Fld Glv 10.00 3.00
60 Cliff Floyd Fld Glv 10.00 3.00
61 Ivan Rodriguez Fld Glv 25.00 7.50
62 Andruw Jones Hat 15.00 4.50
63 Lance Berkman Hat 15.00 4.50
64 Mark Buehrle Hat 15.00 4.50
65 Miguel Tejada Hat 15.00 4.50
66 Wade Miller Hat 15.00 4.50
67 Johnny Estrada Mask 10.00 3.00
68 Tsuyoshi Shinjo Bat-Shoe 15.00 4.50
69 Scott Rolen Jsy-Bat 20.00 6.00
70 Roberto Alomar Bat-Shoe 20.00 6.00
71 Mark Grace Jsy-Fld Glv 15.00 4.50
72 Larry Walker Jsy-Bat 20.00 6.00
73 Jim Edmonds Jsy-Bat 15.00 4.50
74 Jeff Kent Jsy-Bat 15.00 4.50
75 Frank Thomas Jsy-Bat 20.00 6.00
76 Carlos Beltran Jsy-Bat 20.00 6.00
77 Barry Zito Jsy-Shoe 15.00 4.50
78 Alex Rodriguez Jsy-Bat 25.00 7.50
79 Troy Glaus Jsy-Jsy 15.00 4.50
80 Ryan Klesko Bat-Fld Glv 15.00 4.50
81 Tom Glavine Jsy-Shoe 20.00 6.00
82 Ben Sheets Jsy-Bat 15.00 4.50
83 Manny Ramirez 40.00 12.00
Jsy-Fld Glv-Shoe
84 Shannon Stewart Jsy-Bat-Hat 20.00 6.00
85 Vladimir Guerrero 50.00 15.00
Jsy-Bat-Fld Glv
86 Chipper Jones Jsy-Bat-Fld Glv 50.00 15.00
87 Jeff Bagwell Jsy-Bat-Hat 40.00 12.00
88 Richie Sexson 40.00 12.00
Jsy-Bat-Shoe-Btg Glv
89 Sean Casey Jsy-Bat-Shoe-Hat 40.00 12.00
90 Tim Hudson 40.00 12.00
Jsy-Hat-Shoe-Fld Glv
91 J.D. Drew Jsy-Bat-Hat-Shoe 40.00 12.00
92 Ivan Rodriguez 60.00 18.00
Glv-Chest-Jsy-Mask
93 Magglio Ordonez 40.00 12.00
Jsy-Shoe-Hat-Btg Glv
94 John Buck Glv-Chest-Shin-Mask 25.00 7.50
95 Paul Lo Duca 40.00 12.00
Jsy-Chest-Shin-Mask

2003 Absolute Memorabilia

This 208-card set was issued in two separate series. The primary Absolute Memorabilia product - containing cards 1-200 from the basic set - was released in July, 2003. The cards were issued in six card packs with an approximate SRP of $7.50 which came 18 packs to a box and 16 boxes to a case. The first 150 cards feature veterans while the final 50 cards feature a mix of rookies and veterans. Those cards were issued to a stated print run of 1500 serial numbered sets. Cards 201-208 were randomly seeded into packs of DLP Rookies and Traded issued in December, 2003. Each card was serial-numbered to 1000 copies.

MINT NRMT
COMP.LO SET w/o SP's (150) .. 40.00 18.00
COMMON CARD (1-150) .... .75 .35
COMMON CARD (151-208) 4.00 1.80
1 Nomar Garciaparra 3.00 1.35
2 Barry Bonds 5.00 2.20
3 Greg Maddux 3.00 1.35
4 Roger Clemens 4.00 1.80
5 Derek Jeter 5.00 2.20
6 Alex Rodriguez 3.00 1.35
7 Chipper Jones .... 2.00 .90
8 Sammy Sosa 3.00 1.35
9 Alfonso Soriano .... 1.25 .55
10 Albert Pujols 4.00 1.80
11 Adam Dunn .... 1.25 .55
12 Tom Glavine .... 1.25 .55
13 Pedro Martinez .... 2.00 .90
14 Jim Thome .... 2.00 .90
15 Hideo Nomo .... 2.00 .90
16 Roberto Alomar .... 1.25 .55
17 Barry Zito .... .75 .35
18 Troy Glaus .... .75 .35
19 Kerry Wood .... 2.00 .90
20 Magglio Ordonez .... .75 .35
21 Todd Helton .... 1.25 .55
22 Craig Biggio .... 1.25 .55
23 Roy Oswalt .... .75 .35
24 Torii Hunter .... .75 .35
25 Miguel Tejada .... .75 .35
26 Tsuyoshi Shinjo .... .75 .35
27 Scott Rolen .... 2.00 .90
28 Rafael Palmeiro .... 1.25 .55
29 Victor Martinez .... 1.25 .55
30 Hank Blalock .... 1.25 .55
31 Jason Lane .... .75 .35
32 Junior Spivey .... .75 .35
33 Gary Sheffield .... .75 .35
34 Corey Patterson .... .75 .35
35 Corky Miller .... .75 .35
36 Brian Tallet .... .75 .35
37 Cliff Lee .... .75 .35
38 Jason Jennings .... .75 .35
39 Kirk Saarloos .... .75 .35
40 Wade Miller .... .75 .35
41 Angel Berroa .... .75 .35
42 Mike Sweeney .... .75 .35
43 Paul Lo Duca .... .75 .35
44 A.J. Pierzynski .... .75 .35
45 Drew Henson .... .75 .35
46 Eric Chavez .... .75 .35
47 Tim Hudson .... .75 .35
48 Aramis Ramirez .... .75 .35
49 Jack Wilson .... .75 .35
50 Ryan Klesko .... .75 .35
51 Antonio Perez .... .75 .35
52 Dewon Brazelton .... .75 .35
53 Mark Teixeira .... .75 .35
54 Eric Hinske .... .75 .35
55 Freddy Sanchez .... .75 .35
56 Mike Rivera .... .75 .35
57 Alfredo Amezaga .... .75 .35
58 Cliff Floyd .... .75 .35
59 Brandon Larson .... .75 .35
60 Richard Hidalgo .... .75 .35
61 Cesar Izturis .... .75 .35
62 Richie Sexson .... .75 .35
63 Michael Cuddyer .... .75 .35
64 Javier Vazquez .... .75 .35
65 Brandon Claussen .... .75 .35
66 Carlos Rivera .... .75 .35
67 Vernon Wells .... .75 .35
68 Kenny Lofton .... .75 .35
69 Aubrey Huff .... .75 .35
70 Adam LaRoche .... .75 .35
71 Jeff Baker .... .75 .35
72 Jose Castillo .... .75 .35
73 Joe Borchard .... .75 .35
74 Walter Young .... .75 .35
75 Jose Morban .... .75 .35
76 Vinnie Chulk .... .75 .35
77 Christian Parker .... .75 .35
78 Mike Piazza 3.00 1.35
79 Ichiro Suzuki 3.00 1.35
80 Kazuhisa Ishii .... .75 .35
81 Rickey Henderson .... 2.00 .90
82 Ken Griffey Jr. 3.00 1.35
83 Jason Giambi .... .75 .35
84 Randy Johnson .... 2.00 .90
85 Curt Schilling .... .75 .35
86 Manny Ramirez .... 1.25 .55
87 Barry Larkin .... 1.25 .55
88 Jeff Bagwell .... 1.25 .55
89 Vladimir Guerrero .... 2.00 .90
90 Mike Mussina .... 1.25 .55
91 Juan Gonzalez .... 1.25 .55
92 Andruw Jones .... .75 .35
93 Frank Thomas .... 2.00 .90
94 Sean Casey .... .75 .35
95 Josh Beckett .... .75 .35
96 Lance Berkman .... .75 .35
97 Shawn Green .... .75 .35
98 Bernie Williams .... 1.25 .55
99 Pat Burrell .... .75 .35
100 Edgar Martinez .... 1.25 .55
101 Ivan Rodriguez .... 2.00 .90
102 Jeremy Guthrie .... .75 .35
103 Alexis Rios .... 1.25 .55
104 Nic Jackson .... .75 .35
105 Jason Anderson .... .75 .35
106 Travis Chapman .... .75 .35
107 Mac Suzuki .... .75 .35
108 Toby Hall .... .75 .35
109 Mark Prior .... 2.00 .90
110 So Taguchi .... .75 .35
111 Marlon Byrd .... .75 .35
112 Garret Anderson .... .75 .35
113 Luis Gonzalez .... .75 .35
114 Jay Gibbons .... .75 .35
115 Mark Buehrle .... .75 .35
116 Wily Mo Pena .... .75 .35
117 C.C. Sabathia .... .75 .35
118 Ricardo Rodriguez .... .75 .35
119 Robert Fick .... .75 .35
120 Rodrigo Rosario .... .75 .35
121 Alexis Gomez .... .75 .35
122 Carlos Beltran .... 1.25 .55
123 Joe Thurston .... .75 .35
124 Ben Sheets .... .75 .35
125 Jose Vidro .... .75 .35
126 Nick Johnson .... .75 .35
127 Mark Mulder .... .75 .35
128 Bobby Abreu .... .75 .35
129 Brian Giles .... .75 .35
130 Brian Lawrence .... .75 .35
131 Jeff Kent .... .75 .35
132 Chris Snelling .... .75 .35
133 Kevin Mench .... .75 .35
134 Carlos Delgado .... .75 .35
135 Orlando Hudson .... .75 .35
136 Juan Cruz .... .75 .35
137 Jim Edmonds .... .75 .35
138 Geronimo Gil .... .75 .35
139 Joe Crede .... .75 .35
140 Wilson Valdez .... .75 .35
141 Runelvys Hernandez .... .75 .35
142 Nick Neugebauer .... .75 .35
143 Takahito Nomura .... .75 .35
144 Andres Galarraga .... .75 .35
145 Mark Grace .... 1.25 .55
146 Brandon Duckworth .... .75 .35
147 Oliver Perez .... .75 .35
148 Xavier Nady .... .75 .35
149 Rafael Soriano .... .75 .35
150 Ben Kozlowski .... .75 .35
151 Pr. Redman ROO RC 4.00 1.80
152 Craig Brazell ROO RC 5.00 2.20
153 Nook Logan ROO RC 4.00 1.80
154 Greg Aquino ROO RC 4.00 1.80
155 Matt Kata ROO RC 5.00 2.20
156 Ian Ferguson ROO RC 4.00 1.80
157 C.Wang ROO RC 5.00 2.20
158 Beau Kemp ROO RC 4.00 1.80
159 Alej. Machado ROO RC 4.00 1.80
160 Mi. Hessman ROO RC 4.00 1.80
161 Fran. Rosario ROO RC 4.00 1.80
162 Pedro Liriano ROO 4.00 1.80
163 Rich Fischer ROO RC 4.00 1.80
164 Franklin Perez ROO RC 4.00 1.80
165 Oscar Villarreal ROO RC 4.00 1.80
166 Arnie Munoz ROO RC 4.00 1.80
167 Tim Olson ROO RC 5.00 2.20
168 Jose Contreras ROO RC 5.00 2.20
169 Fran. Cruceta ROO RC 4.00 1.80
170 Jer. Bonderman ROO RC 5.00 2.20
171 Jeremy Griffiths ROO RC 5.00 2.20
172 John Webb ROO 4.00 1.80
173 Phil Seibel ROO RC 4.00 1.80
174 Aaron Looper ROO RC 4.00 1.80
175 Brian Stokes ROO RC 4.00 1.80
176 G.Quiroz ROO RC 5.00 2.20
177 Fern. Cabrera ROO RC 4.00 1.80
178 Josh Hall ROO RC 5.00 2.20
179 D. Markwell ROO RC 4.00 1.80
180 Andrew Brown ROO RC 5.00 2.20
181 Doug Waechter ROO RC 5.00 2.20
182 Felix Sanchez ROO RC 4.00 1.80
183 Gerardo Garcia ROO 4.00 1.80
184 Matt Bruback ROO RC 4.00 1.80
185 Mi. Hernandez ROO RC 4.00 1.80
186 Rett Johnson ROO RC 5.00 2.20
187 Ryan Cameron ROO RC 4.00 1.80
188 Rob Hammock ROO RC 5.00 2.20
189 Clint Barmes ROO RC 5.00 2.20
190 Brandon Webb ROO RC 5.00 2.20
191 Jon Leicester ROO RC 4.00 1.80
192 Shane Bazzell ROO RC 4.00 1.80
193 Joe Valentine ROO RC 4.00 1.80
194 Josh Stewart ROO RC 4.00 1.80
195 Pete LaForest ROO RC 5.00 2.20
196 Shane Victorino ROO RC 4.00 1.80
197 Terrmel Sledge ROO RC 5.00 2.20
198 Lew Ford ROO RC 5.00 2.20
199 T.Wellemeyer ROO RC 5.00 2.20
200 Hideki Matsui ROO RC 10.00 4.50
201 Adam Loewen ROO RC 5.00 2.20
202 Ramon Nivar ROO RC 5.00 2.20
203 Dan Haren ROO RC 5.00 2.20
204 Dontrelle Willis ROO 5.00 2.20
205 Chad Gaudin ROO RC 4.00 1.80
206 Rickie Weeks ROO RC 8.00 3.60
207 Ryan Wagner ROO RC 5.00 2.20
208 Delmon Young ROO RC 10.00 4.50

2003 Absolute Memorabilia Spectrum

MINT NRMT
*SPECTRUM 1-150: 2.5X TO 6X BASIC
*SPECTRUM 151-208: .6X TO 1.5X BASIC
1-200 RANDOM INSERTS IN PACKS
201-208 RANDOM IN DLP R/T PACKS
STATED PRINT RUN 100 SERIAL #'d SETS
190 Brandon Webb ROO 8.00 3.60
200 Hideki Matsui ROO 15.00 6.75
201 Adam Loewen ROO 8.00 3.60
206 Rickie Weeks ROO 12.00 5.50
208 Delmon Young ROO 15.00 6.75

2003 Absolute Memorabilia Absolutely Ink

Inserted at a stated rate of one in 552, these 40 cards feature authentic autographs from a mix of established major leaguers and some of the best prospects. Due to market scarcity, no pricing is provided for these cards.

MINT NRMT
STATED ODDS 1:552...........................
NO PRICING DUE TO SCARCITY ....
1 Vladimir Guerrero ....
2 Adam Dunn ....
3 Roy Oswalt ....
4 Victor Martinez ....
5 Edgar Martinez ....
6 Eric Hinske ....
7 Adam Johnson ....
8 Jose Vidro ....
9 Jeff Baker ....
10 Jeremy Guthrie ....
11 Wily Mo Pena ....
12 Toby Hall ....
13 Bobby Abreu ....
14 Fernando Rodney ....
15 Doug Nickle ....
16 Rodrigo Rosario ....
17 Brandon Claussen ....
18 Jermaine Dye ....
19 Rafael Soriano ....
20 Dee Brown ....
21 Donaldo Mendez ....
22 Mark Prior ....
23 Joe Borchard ....
24 Brian Lawrence ....
25 Nick Neugebauer ....
26 Doug Davis ....
27 Tim Hudson ....
28 Christian Parker ....
29 Barry Larkin ....
30 Drew Henson ....
31 Mike Maroth ....
32 Corey Patterson ....
33 Jeremy Giambi ....
34 Cliff Bartosh ....
35 Tom Glavine ....
36 Mark Teixeira ....
37 Jack Wilson ....
38 Roberto Alomar ....
39 Barry Zito ....
40 Troy Glaus ....

2003 Absolute Memorabilia Absolutely Ink Blue

MINT NRMT
RANDOM INSERTS IN PACKS
PRINT RUNS B/WN 10-25 COPIES PER
NO PRICING DUE TO SCARCITY ....
1 Vladimir Guerrero/25 ....
2 Adam Dunn/10 ....
3 Roy Oswalt/25 ....
4 Victor Martinez/10 ....
5 Edgar Martinez/25 ....
6 Eric Hinske/25 ....
7 Adam Johnson/15 ....
8 Jose Vidro/25 ....
9 Jeff Baker/25 ....
10 Jeremy Guthrie/25 ....
11 Wily Mo Pena/15 ....
12 Toby Hall/15 ....
13 Bobby Abreu/25 ....
14 Fernando Rodney/15 ....
15 Doug Nickle/15 ....
16 Rodrigo Rosario/25 ....

17 Brandon Claussen/15
18 Jermaine Dye/25
19 Rafael Soriano/15
20 Dee Brown/15
21 Donaldo Mendez/15
22 Mark Prior/10
23 Joe Borchard/10
24 Brian Lawrence/15
25 Nick Neugebauer/15
26 Doug Davis/15
27 Tim Hudson/10
28 Christian Parker/15
29 Barry Larkin/10
30 Drew Henson/10
31 Mike Maroth/15
32 Corey Patterson/10
33 Jeremy Giambi/25
34 Cliff Bartosh/15
35 Tom Glavine/10
36 Mark Teixeira/10
37 Jack Wilson/15
38 Roberto Alomar/10
39 Barry Zito/10
40 Troy Glaus/10

2003 Absolute Memorabilia Absolutely Ink Gold

MINT NRMT
RANDOM INSERTS IN PACKS
PRINT RUNS B/WN 5-10 COPIES PER
NO PRICING DUE TO SCARCITY
1 Vladimir Guerrero/10
2 Adam Dunn/5
3 Roy Oswalt/10
4 Victor Martinez/5
5 Edgar Martinez/10
6 Eric Hinske/10
7 Adam Johnson/10
8 Jose Vidro/10
9 Jeff Baker/10
10 Jeremy Guthrie/10
11 Wily Mo Pena/10
12 Toby Hall/10
13 Bobby Abreu/10
14 Fernando Rodney/10
15 Doug Nickle/10
16 Rodrigo Rosario/10
17 Brandon Claussen/10
18 Jermaine Dye/10
19 Rafael Soriano/10
20 Dee Brown/10
21 Donaldo Mendez/10
22 Mark Prior/5
23 Joe Borchard/5
24 Brian Lawrence/10
25 Nick Neugebauer/10
26 Doug Davis/10
27 Tim Hudson/5
28 Christian Parker/10
29 Barry Larkin/5
30 Drew Henson/5
31 Mike Maroth/10
32 Corey Patterson/5
33 Jeremy Giambi/10
34 Cliff Bartosh/10
35 Tom Glavine/5
36 Mark Teixeira/5
37 Jack Wilson/10
38 Roberto Alomar/5
39 Barry Zito/5
40 Troy Glaus/5

2003 Absolute Memorabilia Glass Plaques

Inserted at the stated rate of one per sealed box, these 273 cards feature etched-glass collectibles with an autograph and/or a piece of game-used memorabilia. We have identified what comes with the card along with the stated print run in our checklist. Please note that for plaques with stated print runs of 25 or fewer no pricing is provided due to market scarcity.

MINT NRMT
1 Roberto Alomar AU/25
2 Roberto Alomar AU-Jsy/25
3 Roberto Alomar Bat-Jsy/100 60.00 27.00
4 Roberto Alomar Jsy/150 50.00 22.00
5 Jeff Bagwell AU/15
6 Jeff Bagwell AU-Jsy/10
7 Jeff Bagwell Bat-Jsy/100 60.00 27.00
8 Jeff Bagwell Jsy/150
9 Ernie Banks AU/15
10 Ernie Banks AU-Jsy/10
11 Ernie Banks Bat-Jsy/25
12 Ernie Banks Jsy/150 50.00 22.00
13 Lance Berkman AU/25
14 Lance Berkman AU-Jsy/25
15 Lance Berkman Bat-Jsy/100 50.00 22.00
16 Lance Berkman Jsy/150 40.00 18.00
17 Yogi Berra AU/25
18 Yogi Berra AU-Jsy/25
19 Yogi Berra Bat-Jsy/150
20 Yogi Berra Jsy/150
21 Barry Bonds Ball-Base/50 120.00 55.00
22 Barry Bonds Ball-Base/100 100.00 45.00
23 Barry Bonds Base/200 80.00 36.00
24 George Brett AU/15
25 George Brett AU-Jsy/10
26 George Brett Bat-Jsy/50 200.00 90.00
27 George Brett Jsy/200 80.00 36.00
28 Pat Burrell AU/25
29 Pat Burrell AU-Jsy/25
30 Pat Burrell Bat-Jsy/100 50.00 22.00
31 Pat Burrell Jsy/150 40.00 18.00
32 Steve Carlton AU/50 100.00 45.00
33 Steve Carlton AU-Jsy/25
34 Steve Carlton Bat-Jsy/100
35 Steve Carlton Jsy/150 40.00 18.00
36 R.Clemens Sox AU/15
37 R.Clemens Sox AU-Jsy/25
38 R.Clemens Sox Fld Glv-Jsy/50 200.00 90.00
39 R.Clemens Sox Jsy/150 80.00 36.00
40 R.Clemens Yanks AU/15
41 R.Clemens Yanks AU-Jsy/10
42 Clemens Yanks Glv-Jsy/50. 200.00 90.00
43 R.Clemens Yanks Jsy/200 80.00 36.00
44 Roberto Clemente Bat-Jsy/50
45 Roberto Clemente Bat-Jsy/150
46 Roberto Clemente Jsy/200
47 Jose Contreras AU/25
48 Jose Contreras AU-Jsy/25
49 Jose Contreras Jsy-Jsy/100
50 Jose Contreras Jsy/150
51 Adam Dunn AU/25
52 Adam Dunn AU-Jsy/25
53 Adam Dunn Bat-Jsy/100 60.00 27.00
54 Adam Dunn Jsy/150 50.00 22.00
55 Bob Feller AU/50 60.00 27.00
56 Bob Feller AU-Jsy/25
57 Bob Feller Jsy-Jsy/50 60.00 27.00
58 Bob Feller Jsy/100 40.00 18.00
59 N.Garciaparra Bat-Jsy/100 80.00 36.00
60 N.Garciaparra Jsy/200 60.00 27.00
61 Jason Giambi Bat-Jsy/100 50.00 22.00
62 Jason Giambi Jsy/150 40.00 18.00
63 Troy Glaus AU/25
64 Troy Glaus AU-Jsy/25
65 Troy Glaus Bat-Jsy/100
66 Troy Glaus Jsy/150 40.00 18.00
67 Juan Gonzalez AU/15
68 Juan Gonzalez AU-Jsy/10
69 Juan Gonzalez Bat-Jsy/100
70 Juan Gonzalez Jsy/150
71 Luis Gonzalez AU/25
72 Luis Gonzalez AU-Jsy/25
73 Luis Gonzalez Bat-Jsy/100 50.00 22.00
74 Luis Gonzalez Jsy/150 40.00 18.00
75 Mark Grace AU/50 120.00 55.00
76 Mark Grace AU-Jsy/25
77 Mark Grace Bat-Jsy/100
78 Mark Grace Jsy/150 50.00 22.00
79 Shawn Green AU/15
80 Shawn Green AU-Jsy/10
81 Shawn Green Bat-Jsy/100 50.00 22.00
82 Shawn Green Jsy/150 40.00 18.00
83 Ken Griffey Jr. Ball-Base/50
84 Ken Griffey Jr. Ball-Base/100
85 Ken Griffey Jr. Base/200
86 Vladimir Guerrero AU/25
87 Vladimir Guerrero AU-Jsy/25
88 Vladimir Guerrero Bat-Jsy/100 60.00 27.00
89 Vladimir Guerrero Jsy/150
90 Tony Gwynn AU/15
91 Tony Gwynn AU-Jsy/10
92 Tony Gwynn Bat-Jsy/150
93 Tony Gwynn Jsy/200
94 Todd Helton AU/25
95 Todd Helton AU-Jsy/25
96 Todd Helton Bat-Jsy/100
97 Todd Helton Jsy/150
98 R.Henderson AU/15
99 R.Henderson AU-Jsy/10
100 R.Henderson Bat-Jsy/100 60.00 27.00
101 R.Henderson Jsy/200 50.00 22.00
102 Tim Hudson AU/50 100.00 45.00
103 Tim Hudson AU-Jsy/25
104 Tim Hudson Hat-Jsy/100 50.00 22.00
105 Tim Hudson Jsy/150 40.00 18.00
106 Torii Hunter AU/50 80.00 36.00
107 Torii Hunter AU-Jsy/25
108 Torii Hunter Hat-Jsy/100 50.00 22.00
109 Torii Hunter Jsy/150
110 Kazuhisa Ishii AU/15
111 Kazuhisa Ishii AU-Jsy/10
112 Kazuhisa Ishii Bat-Jsy/100 50.00 22.00
113 Kazuhisa Ishii Jsy/200 40.00 18.00
114 Derek Jeter Ball-Base/50
115 Derek Jeter Ball-Base/150
116 Derek Jeter Base/200
117 Randy Johnson AU/15
118 Randy Johnson AU-Jsy/10
119 Randy Johnson Bat -Jsy/100 60.00 27.00
120 Randy Johnson Jsy/150 50.00 22.00
121 Andruw Jones AU/25
122 Andruw Jones AU-Jsy/25
123 Andruw Jones Bat-Jsy/100
124 Andruw Jones Jsy/150 40.00 18.00
125 Chipper Jones AU/15
126 Chipper Jones AU-Jsy/10
127 Chipper Jones Bat-Jsy/100 60.00 27.00
128 Chipper Jones Jsy/150 50.00 22.00
129 Al Kaline AU/50
130 Al Kaline AU-Jsy/25
131 Al Kaline Bat-Jsy/100 60.00 27.00
132 Al Kaline Jsy/150 50.00 22.00
133 Barry Larkin AU/50 100.00 45.00
134 Barry Larkin AU-Jsy/25
135 Barry Larkin Bat-Jsy/100 60.00 27.00
136 Barry Larkin Jsy/150 50.00 22.00
137 Greg Maddux AU/15
138 Greg Maddux AU-Jsy/10
139 Greg Maddux Bat -Jsy/100 60.00 27.00
140 Greg Maddux Jsy/200 50.00 22.00
141 Pedro Martinez AU/10
142 Pedro Martinez AU-Jsy/10
143 Pedro Martinez Bat-Jsy/100 60.00 27.00
144 Pedro Martinez Jsy/150 50.00 22.00
145 H.Matsui Ball-Base/50 100.00 45.00
146 H.Matsui Ball-Base/150 60.00 27.00
147 H.Matsui Base/200 40.00 18.00
148 Don Mattingly AU/25
149 Don Mattingly AU-Jsy/25
150 Don Mattingly Bat-Jsy/100
151 Don Mattingly Jsy/200
152 Mark Mulder AU/50 80.00 36.00
153 Mark Mulder AU-Jsy/25
154 Mark Mulder Jsy/150 40.00 18.00
155 Mark Mulder AU-Jsy/100 50.00 22.00
156 Stan Musial AU/15
157 Stan Musial AU-Jsy/10
158 Stan Musial Bat-Jsy/150
159 Stan Musial Jsy/200
160 Hideo Nomo AU/15
161 Hideo Nomo AU-Jsy/10
162 Hideo Nomo Bat-Jsy/50 120.00 55.00
163 Hideo Nomo Bat-Jsy/100 60.00 27.00
164 Hideo Nomo Jsy/200 50.00 22.00
165 Maggio Ordonez AU/50 80.00 36.00
166 Maggio Ordonez AU-Jsy/25
167 M.Ordonez Bat-Jsy/100 50.00 22.00
168 Magglio Ordonez Jsy/150 40.00 18.00
169 Roy Oswalt AU/50 80.00 36.00
170 Roy Oswalt AU-Jsy/25
171 Roy Oswalt Bat-Jsy/100 50.00 22.00
172 Roy Oswalt Jsy/150 40.00 18.00
173 Rafael Palmeiro AU/25
174 Rafael Palmeiro AU-Jsy/25
175 Rafael Palmeiro Bat-Jsy/100 60.00 27.00
176 Rafael Palmeiro Jsy/150 50.00 22.00
177 Mike Piazza AU/15
178 Mike Piazza AU-Jsy/10
179 Mike Piazza Bat-Jsy/50 100.00 45.00
180 Mike Piazza Bat-Jsy/100 60.00 27.00
181 Mike Piazza Jsy/200 50.00 22.00
182 Mark Prior AU/25
183 Mark Prior AU-Jsy/25
184 Mark Prior Bat-Jsy/100 60.00 27.00
185 Mark Prior Jsy/150 50.00 22.00
186 Albert Pujols AU/25
187 Albert Pujols AU-Jsy/25
188 Albert Pujols Bat-Jsy/150 100.00 45.00
189 Albert Pujols Jsy/150 80.00 36.00
190 Manny Ramirez AU/15
191 Manny Ramirez AU-Jsy 10
192 Manny Ramirez Bat-Jsy/100 60.00 27.00
193 Manny Ramirez Jsy/150 50.00 22.00
194 Cal Ripken AU/15
195 Cal Ripken AU-Jsy/10
196 Cal Ripken Bat-Jsy/150 120.00 55.00
197 Cal Ripken Jsy/200 100.00 45.00
198 Frank Robinson AU/50 100.00 45.00
199 Frank Robinson AU-Jsy/25
200 Frank Robinson Bat-Jsy/100 60.00 27.00
201 Frank Robinson Jsy/150 50.00 22.00
202 Alex Rodriguez AU/15
203 Alex Rodriguez AU-Jsy/25
204 Alex Rodriguez Bat-Jsy/100
205 Alex Rodriguez Jsy/200
206 N.Ryan Angels AU/15
207 N.Ryan Angels AU-Jsy 25
208 N.Ryan Angels Jacket-Jsy/150
209 N.Ryan Angels Jsy/200 100.00 45.00
210 N.Ryan Astros AU/15
211 N.Ryan Astros AU-Jsy/25
212 N.Ryan Astros Fld Glv-Jsy/25
213 N.Ryan Astros Jsy/200 100.00 45.00
214 N.Ryan Astros Jsy-Jsy/100 120.00 55.00
215 N.Ryan Rgr AU/15
216 N.Ryan Rgr AU-Jsy/10
217 N.Ryan Rgr Fld Glv-Jsy/25
218 N.Ryan Rgr Jsy/200 100.00 45.00
219 N.Ryan Rgr Jsy-Jsy/100 120.00 55.00
220 R.Sandberg AU/15
221 R.Sandberg AU-Jsy/10
222 R.Sandberg Bat-Jsy G/50 150.00 70.00
223 R.Sandberg Bat-Jsy S/50 150.00 70.00
224 R.Sandberg Jsy/200 80.00 36.00
225 Curt Schilling AU/25
226 Curt Schilling AU-Jsy/25
227 Curt Schilling Fld Glv-Jsy/50
228 Curt Schilling Jsy/150 40.00 18.00
229 Mike Schmidt AU/25
230 Mike Schmidt AU-Jsy/25
231 Mike Schmidt Bat-Jsy/100 100.00 45.00
232 Mike Schmidt Jsy/200 80.00 36.00
233 Ozzie Smith AU/15
234 Ozzie Smith AU-Jsy/10
235 Ozzie Smith Bat-Jsy/100 100.00 45.00
236 Ozzie Smith Jsy/150 80.00 36.00
237 A.Soriano AU/15
238 A.Soriano AU-Jsy/10
239 A.Soriano Bat-Jsy/150 60.00 27.00
240 A.Soriano Jsy/150 50.00 22.00
241 Sammy Sosa Bat-Jsy/150 80.00 36.00
242 Sammy Sosa Jsy/200 60.00 27.00
243 Junior Spivey AU/50
244 Junior Spivey AU-Jsy/25
245 Junior Spivey Bat-Jsy/100 50.00 22.00
246 Junior Spivey Jsy/150 40.00 18.00
247 I.Suzuki Ball-Base/50 120.00 55.00
248 I.Suzuki Ball-Base/150 100.00 45.00
249 I.Suzuki Base/200 60.00 27.00
250 Mark Teixeira AU/50
251 Mark Teixeira AU-Jsy/25
252 Mark Teixeira Bat-Jsy/100 50.00 22.00
253 Mark Teixeira Jsy/150 40.00 18.00
254 Miguel Tejada AU/50 80.00 36.00
255 Miguel Tejada AU-Jsy/25
256 Miguel Tejada Bat-Jsy/100 50.00 22.00
257 Miguel Tejada Jsy/150 40.00 18.00
258 Frank Thomas AU/25
259 Frank Thomas AU-Jsy/25
260 Frank Thomas Bat-Jsy/100 60.00 27.00
261 Frank Thomas Jsy/150 50.00 22.00
262 Bernie Williams AU/15
263 Bernie Williams AU-Jsy/10
264 Bernie Williams Bat-Jsy/100 60.00 27.00
265 Bernie Williams Jsy/150 50.00 22.00
266 Kerry Wood AU/50 100.00 45.00
267 Kerry Wood AU-Jsy/25
268 Kerry Wood Bat-Jsy/100 60.00 27.00
269 Kerry Wood Jsy/150 50.00 22.00
270 Barry Zito AU/50 80.00 36.00
271 Barry Zito AU-Jsy/25
272 Barry Zito Hat-Jsy/100 50.00 22.00
273 Barry Zito Jsy/150 40.00 18.00

2003 Absolute Memorabilia Portraits Promos

MINT NRMT
STATED ODDS ONE PER BOX
1 Vladimir Guerrero 2.50 1.10
2 Luis Gonzalez 1.00 .45
3 Andruw Jones 1.00 .45
4 Manny Ramirez 1.50 .70
5 Derek Jeter 6.00 2.70
6 Eric Hinske 1.00 .45
7 Curt Schilling 1.00 .45
8 Adam Dunn 1.50 .70
9 Jason Jennings 1.00 .45
10 Mike Piazza 4.00 1.80
11 Jason Giambi 1.00 .45
12 Jeff Bagwell 1.50 .70
13 Rickey Henderson 2.50 1.10
14 Randy Johnson 2.50 1.10
15 Roger Clemens 5.00 2.20
16 Troy Glaus 1.00 .45
17 Hideo Nomo 2.50 1.10
18 Joe Borchard 1.00 .45
19 Torii Hunter 1.00 .45
20 Lance Berkman 1.00 .45
21 Todd Helton 1.50 .70
22 Mike Mussina 1.00 .45
23 Vernon Wells 1.00 .45
24 Pat Burrell 1.00 .45
25 Ichiro Suzuki 4.00 1.80
26 Shawn Green 1.00 .45
27 Frank Thomas 2.50 1.10
28 Barry Zito 1.00 .45
29 Barry Bonds 6.00 2.70
30 Ken Griffey Jr. 4.00 1.80
31 Albert Pujols 5.00 2.20
32 Roberto Alomar 1.50 .70
33 Barry Larkin 1.50 .70
34 Tony Gwynn 3.00 1.35
35 Chipper Jones 2.50 1.10
36 Pedro Martinez 2.50 1.10
37 Juan Gonzalez 1.50 .70
38 Greg Maddux 4.00 1.80
39 Tim Hudson 1.00 .45
40 Sammy Sosa 4.00 1.80
41 Victor Martinez 1.50 .70
42 Mark Buehrle 1.00 .45
43 Austin Kearns 1.00 .45
44 Kerry Wood 2.50 1.10
45 Nomar Garciaparra 4.00 1.80
46 Alfonso Soriano 1.50 .70
47 Mark Prior 2.50 1.10
48 Richie Sexson 1.00 .45
49 Mark Teixeira 1.00 .45
50 Craig Biggio 1.00 .45
51 Rafael Palmeiro 1.50 .70
52 Carlos Beltran 1.50 .70
53 Bernie Williams 1.50 .70
54 Eric Chavez 1.00 .45
55 Paul Konerko 1.00 .45
56 Nolan Ryan 6.00 2.70
57 Mark Mulder 1.00 .45
58 Miguel Tejada 1.00 .45
59 Roy Oswalt 1.00 .45
60 Jim Edmonds 1.00 .45
61 Ryan Klesko 1.00 .45
62 Cal Ripken 8.00 3.60
63 Josh Beckett 1.00 .45
64 Kazuhisa Ishii 1.00 .45
65 Alex Rodriguez 4.00 1.80
66 Mike Sweeney 1.00 .45
67 C.C. Sabathia 1.00 .45
68 Jose Vidro 1.00 .45
69 Magglio Ordonez 1.00 .45
70 Carlos Delgado 1.00 .45
71 Jorge Posada 1.50 .70
72 Bobby Abreu 1.00 .45

2003 Absolute Memorabilia Rookie Materials Jersey Number

Randomly inserted into packs, these 15 cards feature not only game-worn jersey swatches but were printed to a stated print run which matched the player's jersey number. For cards with a print run of 25 or fewer, no pricing is provided due to market scarcity.

MINT NRMT
RANDOM INSERTS IN PACKS
PRINT RUNS B/WN 5-51 COPIES PER
NO PRICING ON QTY OF 25 OR LESS
1 Stan Musial Jsy/6
2 Yogi Berra Jsy/35 50.00 22.00
3 Vladimir Guerrero Jsy/27 50.00 22.00
4 Randy Johnson Jsy/51 50.00 22.00
5 Andruw Jones Jsy/25
6 Jeff Kent Jsy/11
7 Nomar Garciaparra Jsy/5
8 Hideo Nomo Jsy/16
9 Ivan Rodriguez Jsy/7
10 Alfonso Soriano Jsy/33 50.00 22.00
11 Scott Rolen Jsy/17
12 Juan Gonzalez Jsy/19
13 Rafael Palmeiro Bat/25
14 Mike Schmidt Bat/20
15 Cal Ripken Bat/8

2003 Absolute Memorabilia Rookie Materials Season

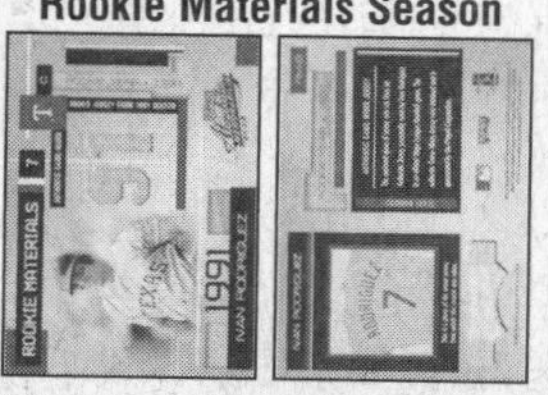

Randomly inserted into packs, these 15 cards feature not only game-worn jersey swatches but were printed to a stated print run which matched the player's debut season.

MINT NRMT
RANDOM INSERTS IN PACKS
PRINT RUNS B/WN 42-101 COPIES PER
1 Stan Musial Jsy/42 120.00 55.00
2 Yogi Berra Jsy/47 60.00 27.00
3 Vladimir Guerrero Jsy/97 25.00 11.00
4 Randy Johnson Jsy/89 25.00 11.00
5 Andruw Jones Jsy/96 15.00 6.75
6 Jeff Kent Jsy/92 15.00 6.75
8 Hideo Nomo Jsy/95 40.00 18.00
9 Ivan Rodriguez Jsy/91 25.00 11.00
10 Alfonso Soriano Jsy/101 25.00 11.00
11 Scott Rolen Jsy/96 25.00 11.00
12 Juan Gonzalez Jsy/89 25.00 11.00
13 Rafael Palmeiro Bat/86 25.00 11.00
14 Mike Schmidt Bat/73 60.00 27.00
15 Cal Ripken Bat/82 80.00 36.00

2003 Absolute Memorabilia Signing Bonus

Randomly inserted into packs, these 10 cards feature authentic autographs of baseball legends. Each of these cards were issued to a stated print run of 15 serial numbered sets and no pricing is provided due to market scarcity.

MINT NRMT
STATED PRINT RUN 15 SERIAL #'d SETS
BLUE PRINT RUN 10 SERIAL #'d SETS
GOLD PRINT RUN 5 SERIAL #'d SETS
RANDOM INSERTS IN PACKS
NO PRICING DUE TO SCARCITY
1 Nolan Ryan
2 Cal Ripken
3 Don Mattingly
4 Kirby Puckett
5 Tony Gwynn
6 Ozzie Smith
7 Mike Schmidt
8 Reggie Jackson
9 Yogi Berra
10 Stan Musial

2003 Absolute Memorabilia Spectrum Signatures

Randomly inserted into packs, these cards not only parallel the basic Playoff Absolute Memorabilia set but also were signed by the featured player. Cards 201-208 were randomly seeded into packs of DLP Rookies and Traded. Quantities of each card range from 5-304 copies per. Please note that we have put the stated print run next to the player's name in our checklist. If 25 or fewer of a card was signed, there is no pricing due to market scarcity.

MINT NRMT
3 Greg Maddux/10
4 Roger Clemens/15
6 Alex Rodriguez/15
7 Chipper Jones/10
9 Alfonso Soriano/15
10 Albert Pujols/10
11 Adam Dunn/15
12 Tom Glavine/25
13 Pedro Martinez/5
14 Jim Thome/10
15 Hideo Nomo/5
16 Roberto Alomar/15
17 Barry Zito/25
18 Troy Glaus/10
19 Kerry Wood/15
20 Magglio Ordonez/25
21 Todd Helton/10
22 Craig Biggio/10
23 Roy Oswalt/25
24 Torii Hunter/25
25 Miguel Tejada/25
27 Scott Rolen/10
28 Rafael Palmeiro/10
29 Victor Martinez/100 40.00 18.00
30 Hank Blalock/50 40.00 18.00
31 Jason Lane/50
32 Junior Spivey/50 15.00 6.75
33 Gary Sheffield/10
34 Corey Patterson/50 25.00 11.00
35 Corky Miller/100
36 Brian Tallet/100
37 Cliff Lee/100
38 Jason Jennings/100
39 Kirk Saarloos/100
40 Wade Miller/50 15.00 6.75
41 Angel Berroa/100 15.00 6.75
42 Mike Sweeney/50 25.00 11.00
43 Paul Lo Duca/50 25.00 11.00
44 A.J. Pierzynski/100 25.00 11.00
45 Drew Henson/50 40.00 18.00
46 Eric Chavez/10
47 Tim Hudson/50 40.00 18.00
48 Aramis Ramirez/10
49 Jack Wilson/25
50 Ryan Klesko/25

Antonio Perez/25....................
2 Dewon Brazelton/50............ 15.00 6.75
Mark Teixeira/50 .... 40.00 18.00
Eric Hinske/100.................. 15.00 6.75
Freddy Sanchez/100............ 15.00 6.75
Mike Rivera/25....................
Alfredo Amezaga/100.......... 15.00 6.75
Cliff Floyd/25....................
Brandon Larson/100 ....
Richard Hidalgo/100 .... 15.00 6.75
Cesar Izturis/25....................
2 Richie Sexson/25 ....
3 Michael Cuddyer/100.......... 15.00 6.75
Javier Vazquez/25 ....
5 Brandon Claussen/25...............
5 Carlos Rivera/100 ....
7 Vernon Wells/25...............
3 Kenny Lofton/50 .... 40.00 18.00
9 Aubrey Huff/100................ 25.00 11.00
Adam LaRoche/100 .... 15.00 6.75
1 Jeff Baker/100.................. 15.00 6.75
2 Jose Castillo/100 .... 15.00 6.75
3 Joe Borchard/100 .... 15.00 6.75
4 Walter Young/100 .... 15.00 6.75
5 Jose Morban/100...............
6 Vinnie Chulk/100................ 15.00 6.75
7 Christian Parker/25 ....
8 Mike Piazza/5 ....
0 Kazuhisa Ishii/25...............
1 Rickey Henderson/5...............
5 Curt Schilling/10 ....
6 Manny Ramirez/10...............
7 Barry Larkin/50 .... 80.00 36.00
8 Jeff Bagwell/5 ....
9 Vladimir Guerrero/50 .... 50.00 22.00
0 Mike Mussina/10...............
1 Juan Gonzalez/5...............
2 Andruw Jones/25...............
4 Sean Casey/10 ....
5 Josh Beckett/100 .... 40.00 18.00
6 Lance Berkman/25 ....
7 Shawn Green/25 ....
8 Bernie Williams/10...............
9 Pat Burrell/10...............
00 Edgar Martinez/50............. 50.00 22.00
01 Ivan Rodriguez/5...............
02 Jeremy Guthrie/100 .... 15.00 6.75
03 Alexis Rios/100.................. 40.00 18.00
04 Nic Jackson/100 .... 15.00 6.75
05 Jason Anderson/100...............
06 Travis Chapman/100 .... 15.00 6.75
07 Mac Suzuki/304 .... 25.00 11.00
08 Toby Hall/25...............
09 Mark Prior/50.................... 80.00 36.00
10 So Taguchi/25 ....
11 Marlon Byrd/100................ 15.00 6.75
12 Garret Anderson/10...............
13 Luis Gonzalez/10...............
14 Jay Gibbons/100................ 15.00 6.75
15 Mark Buehrle/25 ....
16 Wily Mo Pena/25...............
17 C.C. Sabathia/25 ....
18 Ricardo Rodriguez/100 ...... 15.00 6.75
19 Robert Fick/100 .... 15.00 6.75
120 Rodrigo Rosario/25...............
121 Alexis Gomez/100 .... 15.00 6.75
122 Carlos Beltran/25 ....
123 Joe Thurston/100...............
124 Ben Sheets/50................... 25.00 11.00
125 Jose Vidro/25...............
126 Nick Johnson/50................ 15.00 6.75
127 Mark Mulder/50 .... 25.00 11.00
128 Bobby Abreu/25 ....
129 Brian Giles/10 ....
130 Brian Lawrence/25...............
132 Chris Snelling/100 .... 15.00 6.75
133 Kevin Mench/100............... 15.00 6.75
135 Orlando Hudson/50............ 15.00 6.75
136 Juan Cruz/100...............
138 Geronimo Gil/25...............
139 Joe Crede/100.................... 15.00 6.75
140 Wilson Valdez/25 ....
141 Runelvys Hernandez/100 ... 15.00 6.75
142 Nick Neugebauer/25...............
143 Takahito Nomura/47........... 25.00 11.00
144 Andres Galarraga/25 ....
145 Mark Grace/25 ....
146 Brandon Duckworth/25...............
147 Oliver Perez/50.................. 25.00 11.00
148 Xavier Nady/100................ 15.00 6.75
149 Rafael Soriano/25 ....
150 Ben Kozlowski/100............ 15.00 6.75
151 Prentice Redman ROO/250 10.00 4.50
152 Craig Brazell ROO/250 .... 15.00 6.75
153 Nook Logan ROO/250........ 10.00 4.50
154 Greg Aquino ROO/250 .... 10.00 4.50
155 Matt Kata ROO/250............ 15.00 6.75
156 Ian Ferguson ROO/250 ...... 10.00 4.50
157 Chien Wang ROO/250........ 25.00 11.00
158 Beau Kemp ROO/250......... 10.00 4.50
159 Alej Machado ROO/250...... 10.00 4.50
160 Mike Hessman ROO/250.... 10.00 4.50
161 Franc Rosario ROO/250 ..... 10.00 4.50
162 Pedro Liriano ROO/250...... 10.00 4.50
163 Rich Fischer ROO/250 .... 10.00 4.50
164 Franklin Perez ROO/250...............
165 Oscar Villarreal ROO/250... 10.00 4.50
166 Arnie Munoz ROO/250....... 10.00 4.50
167 Tim Olson ROO/250........... 15.00 6.75
168 Jose Contreras ROO/250 ... 25.00 11.00
169 Franc Cruceta ROO/250 ..... 10.00 4.50
170 J.Bonderman ROO/250...... 15.00 6.75
171 Jeremy Griffiths ROO/250.. 15.00 6.75
172 John Webb ROO/250 ....
173 Phil Seibel ROO/250 ....
174 Aaron Looper ROO/250 ..... 10.00 4.50
175 Brian Stokes ROO/250....... 10.00 4.50
176 Guillermo Quiroz ROO/250 15.00 6.75
177 Fernando Cabrera ROO/250 10.00 4.50
178 Josh Hall ROO/250 .... 15.00 6.75
179 Diego Markwell ROO/250... 10.00 4.50
180 Andrew Brown ROO/250.... 15.00 6.75
181 Doug Waechter ROO/250... 15.00 6.75
182 Felix Sanchez ROO/250...... 10.00 4.50
183 Gerardo Garcia ROO/250 ....
184 Matt Bruback ROO/250...... 10.00 4.50
185 Michel Hernandez ROO/250...............
186 Rett Johnson ROO/250...... 15.00 6.75
187 Ryan Cameron ROO/250.... 10.00 4.50
188 Rob Hammock ROO/250 ... 15.00 6.75
189 Clint Barmes ROO/250....... 15.00 6.75
190 Brandon Webb ROO/250.... 20.00 9.00
191 Jon Leicester ROO/250...... 10.00 4.50
192 Shane Bazzell ROO/250 ..... 10.00 4.50
193 Joe Valentine ROO/250...... 10.00 4.50
194 Josh Stewart ROO/250 ....
195 Pete LaForest ROO/250 ..... 15.00 6.75
196 Shane Victorino ROO/250.. 10.00 4.50
197 Terrmel Sledge ROO/250 ... 15.00 6.75
198 Lew Ford ROO/250 .... 20.00 9.00
199 Todd Wellemeyer ROO/250 15.00 6.75
201 Adam Loewen ROO/100..... 25.00 11.00
202 Ramon Nivar ROO/100 ...... 20.00 9.00
203 Dan Haren ROO/100 .... 20.00 9.00
204 Dontrelle Willis ROO/25...............
205 Chad Gaudin ROO/50......... 15.00 6.75
206 Rickie Weeks ROO/25...............
207 Ryan Wagner ROO/100...... 15.00 6.75
208 Delmon Young ROO/25...............

2003 Absolute Memorabilia Team Tandems

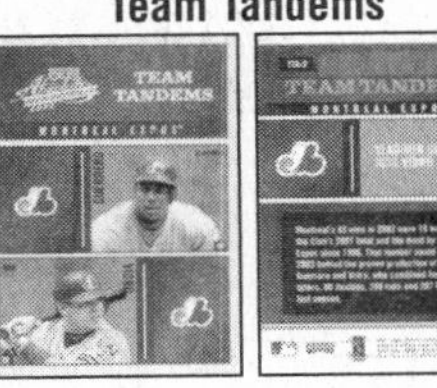

MINT NRMT
STATED ODDS 1:48...............
*SPECTRUM: 1.25X TO 3X BASIC......
SPECTRUM RANDOM INSERTS IN PACKS
SPECTRUM PRINT RUN 100 #'d SETS
1 Sammy Sosa........................ 8.00 3.60
Mark Prior
2 Vladimir Guerrero 5.00 2.20
Jose Vidro
3 Bernie Williams..................... 5.00 2.20
Alfonso Soriano
4 Mike Sweeney........................ 5.00 2.20
Carlos Beltran
5 Magglio Ordonez..................... 3.00 1.35
Paul Konerko
6 Adam Dunn............................ 5.00 2.20
Austin Kearns
7 Randy Johnson....................... 5.00 2.20
Curt Schilling
8 Hideo Nomo........................... 5.00 2.20
Kazuhisa Ishii
9 Pat Burrell............................. 3.00 1.35
Bobby Abreu
10 Todd Helton 5.00 2.20
Larry Walker

2003 Absolute Memorabilia Team Tandems Materials

MINT NRMT
1-7/10 PRINT RUN 100 SERIAL #'d SETS
8-9 PRINT RUN 40 SERIAL #'d SETS.
SPECTRUM 1-7/10 PRINT RUN 25 #'d SETS
SPECTRUM 8-9 PRINT RUN 10 #'d SETS
NO SPECTRUM PRICING DUE TO SCARCITY
RANDOM INSERTS IN PACKS ....
ALL FEATURE DUAL JERSEY SWATCHES
1 Sammy Sosa........................ 30.00 13.50
Mark Prior
2 Vladimir Guerrero 25.00 11.00
Jose Vidro
3 Bernie Williams..................... 25.00 11.00
Alfonso Soriano
4 Mike Sweeney........................ 25.00 11.00
Carlos Beltran
5 Magglio Ordonez..................... 15.00 6.75
Paul Konerko
6 Adam Dunn............................ 25.00 11.00
Austin Kearns
7 Randy Johnson....................... 25.00 11.00
Curt Schilling
8 Hideo Nomo........................... 80.00 36.00
Kazuhisa Ishii/40
9 Pat Burrell............................. 25.00 11.00
Bobby Abreu/40
10 Todd Helton 25.00 11.00
Larry Walker

2003 Absolute Memorabilia Team Trios

MINT NRMT
STATED ODDS 1:88...............
*SPECTRUM: 1X TO 2.5X BASIC........
SPECTRUM RANDOM INSERTS IN PACKS
SPECTRUM PRINT RUN 50 SERIAL #'d SETS
1 Greg Maddux 15.00 6.75
Chipper Jones
Andruw Jones
2 Sammy Sosa........................ 12.00 5.50
Mark Prior
Kerry Wood
3 Pedro Martinez...................... 15.00 6.75
Nomar Garciaparra
Manny Ramirez
4 Jason Giambi........................ 15.00 6.75
Alfonso Soriano
Roger Clemens
5 Alex Rodriguez...................... 15.00 6.75
Rafael Palmeiro
Mark Teixeira
6 Mike Piazza 15.00 6.75
Roberto Alomar
Tsuyoshi Shinjo
7 Jeff Bagwell 10.00 4.50
Craig Biggio
Lance Berkman
8 Troy Glaus............................ 10.00 4.50
Garret Anderson
Troy Percival
9 Miguel Tejada........................ 10.00 4.50
Eric Chavez
Barry Zito
10 Luis Gonzalez...................... 10.00 4.50
Randy Johnson
Curt Schilling

2003 Absolute Memorabilia Team Trios Materials

MINT NRMT
1-2/4-5/7/9-10 PRINT RUN 100 #'d SETS
3/6/8 PRINT RUNS B/WN 40-50 COPIES PER
SPECTRUM 1-2/4-5/7/9-10 PRINT 25 #'d SETS
SPECTRUM 3/6/8 PRINT RUN 10 #'d SETS
NO SPECTRUM PRICING DUE TO SCARCITY
RANDOM INSERTS IN PACKS ....
ALL FEATURE THREE JERSEY SWATCHES
1 Greg Maddux 40.00 18.00
Chipper Jones
Andruw Jones
2 Sammy Sosa........................ 40.00 18.00
Mark Prior
Kerry Wood
3 Pedro Martinez...................... 80.00 36.00
Nomar Garciaparra
Manny Ramirez/50
4 Jason Giambi........................ 50.00 22.00
Alfonso Soriano
Roger Clemens
5 Alex Rodriguez...................... 40.00 18.00
Rafael Palmeiro
Mark Teixeira
6 Mike Piazza 60.00 27.00
Roberto Alomar
Tsuyoshi Shinjo/40
7 Jeff Bagwell 40.00 18.00
Craig Biggio
Lance Berkman
8 Troy Glaus............................ 40.00 18.00
Garret Anderson
Troy Percival/40
9 Miguel Tejada........................ 40.00 18.00
Eric Chavez
Barry Zito
10 Luis Gonzalez...................... 40.00 18.00
Randy Johnson
Curt Schilling

2003 Absolute Memorabilia Tools of the Trade

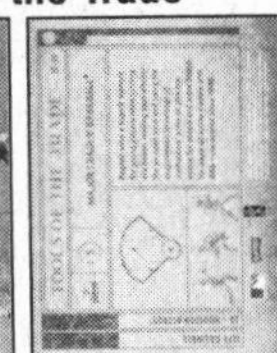

MINT NRMT
STATED ODDS 1:5...............
*SPECTRUM: 1X TO 2.5X BASIC........
SPECTRUM RANDOM INSERTS IN PACKS
SPECTRUM PRINT RUN 100 #'d SETS
1 Sammy Sosa......................... 6.00 2.70
2 Nomar Garciaparra................. 6.00 2.70
3 Andruw Jones....................... 1.50 .70
4 Troy Glaus............................ 1.50 .70
5 Greg Maddux 6.00 2.70
6 Rickey Henderson.................. 4.00 1.80
7 Alex Rodriguez...................... 6.00 2.70
8 Manny Ramirez..................... 2.50 1.10
9 Lance Berkman .... 1.50 .70
10 Roger Clemens 8.00 3.60
11 Ivan Rodriguez..................... 4.00 1.80
12 Kazuhisa Ishii....................... 1.50 .70
13 Alfonso Soriano 2.50 1.10
14 Austin Kearns....................... 1.50 .70
15 Mike Piazza 6.00 2.70
16 Curt Schilling .... 1.50 .70
17 Jeff Bagwell 2.50 1.10
18 Todd Helton 2.50 1.10
19 Randy Johnson..................... 4.00 1.80
20 Vladimir Guerrero 4.00 1.80
21 Kerry Wood.......................... 4.00 1.80
22 Rafael Palmeiro.................... 2.50 1.10
23 Roy Oswalt........................... 1.50 .70
24 Chipper Jones...................... 4.00 1.80
25 Pat Burrell............................ 1.50 .70
26 Jason Giambi .... 1.50 .70
27 Pedro Martinez.................... 4.00 1.80
28 Roberto Alomar 2.50 1.10
29 Shawn Green 2.50 1.10
30 Adam Dunn.......................... 2.50 1.10
31 Juan Gonzalez..................... 2.50 1.10
32 Mark Prior............................ 4.00 1.80
33 Hideo Nomo......................... 4.00 1.80
34 Torii Hunter......................... 1.50 .70
35 Mark Teixeira....................... 1.50 .70
36 Craig Biggio 2.50 1.10
37 Rafael Palmeiro.................... 2.50 1.10
38 Jeff Bagwell 2.50 1.10
39 Albert Pujols 8.00 3.60
40 Richie Sexson .... 1.50 .70
41 Alex Rodriguez..................... 6.00 2.70
42 Carlos Delgado.................... 1.50 .70
43 Frank Thomas 4.00 1.80
44 Sammy Sosa........................ 6.00 2.70
45 Marlon Byrd .... 1.50 .70
46 Mark Prior............................ 4.00 1.80
47 Adrian Beltre 2.50 1.10
48 Tom Glavine 2.50 1.10
49 So Taguchi .... 1.50 .70
50 Jeff Bagwell 2.50 1.10
51 Mike Sweeney...................... 1.50 .70
52 Luis Gonzalez....................... 1.50 .70
53 Chipper Jones...................... 4.00 1.80
54 Jason Giambi .... 1.50 .70
55 Miguel Tejada....................... 1.50 .70
56 Todd Helton 2.50 1.10
57 Andruw Jones .... 1.50 .70
58 Mike Piazza 6.00 2.70
59 Manny Ramirez.................... 2.50 1.10
60 Randy Johnson.................... 4.00 1.80
61 Carlos Beltran 2.50 1.10
62 Victor Martinez..................... 2.50 1.10
63 Orlando Hudson................... 1.50 .70
64 Jeff Kent............................... 1.50 .70
65 Greg Maddux 6.00 2.70
66 Garret Anderson................... 1.50 .70
67 Joe Thurston........................ 1.50 .70
68 Mark Teixeira....................... 1.50 .70
69 Kazuhisa Ishii....................... 1.50 .70
70 Austin Kearns....................... 1.50 .70
71 Pat Burrell............................ 1.50 .70
72 Joe Borchard........................ 1.50 .70
73 Josh Phelps .... 1.50 .70
74 Travis Hafner........................ 1.50 .70
75 So Taguchi .... 1.50 .70
76 Victor Martinez..................... 2.50 1.10
77 Paul Lo Duca .... 1.50 .70
78 Bernie Williams.................... 2.50 1.10
79 Josh Phelps .... 1.50 .70
80 Marlon Byrd .... 1.50 .70
81 Manny Ramirez.................... 2.50 1.10
82 Jason Giambi .... 1.50 .70
83 Jeff Bagwell 2.50 1.10
84 Sammy Sosa........................ 6.00 2.70
85 Josh Phelps .... 1.50 .70
86 Tim Hudson .... 1.50 .70
87 Randy Johnson.................... 4.00 1.80
88 Troy Glaus............................ 1.50 .70
89 Joe Thurston........................ 1.50 .70
90 Miguel Tejada....................... 1.50 .70
91 Adam Dunn.......................... 2.50 1.10
92 Magglio Ordonez.................. 1.50 .70
93 Mike Sweeney...................... 1.50 .70
94 Andruw Jones .... 1.50 .70
95 Carlos Beltran 2.50 1.10
96 Joe Borchard........................ 1.50 .70
97 Austin Kearns....................... 1.50 .70
98 Richie Sexson .... 1.50 .70
99 Mark Prior............................ 4.00 1.80
100 Mark Teixeira..................... 1.50 .70
101 Ryan Klesko .... 1.50 .70
102 Jason Jennings.................. 1.50 .70
103 Travis Hafner..................... 1.50 .70
104 Mark Buehrle .... 1.50 .70
105 Eric Hinske......................... 1.50 .70
106 Rafael Palmeiro.................. 2.50 1.10
107 Roy Oswalt......................... 1.50 .70
108 Kerry Wood........................ 4.00 1.80
109 Brian Giles .... 1.50 .70
110 Ivan Rodriguez................... 4.00 1.80

2003 Absolute Memorabilia Tools of the Trade Materials

MINT NRMT
1-74 PRINT RUNS B/WN 40-250 COPIES PER
75-90 PRINT RUNS B/WN 50-125 COPIES PER
....
91-97 PRINT RUN 100 SERIAL #'d SETS
98-104 PRINT RUN 50 SERIAL #'d SETS
105-110 PRINT RUN 50 SERIAL #'d SETS
RANDOM INSERTS IN PACKS ....
1 Sammy Sosa Jsy/250........... 15.00 6.75
2 Nomar Garciaparra Jsy/250 ... 15.00 6.75
3 Andruw Jones Jsy/250 .... 8.00 3.60
4 Troy Glaus Jsy/250 .... 8.00 3.60
5 Greg Maddux Jsy/250........... 10.00 4.50
6 Rickey Henderson Jsy/40 ...... 25.00 11.00
7 Alex Rodriguez Jsy/250 .... 15.00 6.75
8 Manny Ramirez Jsy/250 .... 10.00 4.50
9 Lance Berkman Jsy/250.......... 8.00 3.60
10 Roger Clemens Jsy/250....... 15.00 6.75
11 Ivan Rodriguez Jsy/250 .... 10.00 4.50
12 Kazuhisa Ishii Jsy/40 .... 15.00 6.75
13 Alfonso Soriano Jsy/250...... 10.00 4.50
14 Austin Kearns Jsy/250.......... 8.00 3.60
15 Mike Piazza Jsy/250............ 10.00 4.50
16 Curt Schilling Jsy/250.......... 8.00 3.60
17 Jeff Bagwell Jsy/250............ 10.00 4.50
18 Todd Helton Jsy/250............ 10.00 4.50
19 Randy Johnson Jsy/250 ...... 10.00 4.50
20 Vladimir Guerrero Jsy/250... 10.00 4.50
21 Kerry Wood Jsy/250 .... 10.00 4.50
22 Rafael Palmeiro Jsy/250 ...... 10.00 4.50
23 Roy Oswalt Jsy/250 .... 8.00 3.60
24 Chipper Jones Jsy/250 .... 10.00 4.50
25 Pat Burrell Jsy/40 .... 15.00 6.75
26 Jason Giambi Jsy/250 .... 8.00 3.60
27 Pedro Martinez Jsy/250 .... 10.00 4.50
28 Roberto Alomar Jsy/40........ 25.00 11.00
29 Shawn Green Jsy/250............ 8.00 3.60
30 Adam Dunn Jsy/250 .... 10.00 4.50
31 Juan Gonzalez Jsy/40 .... 25.00 11.00
32 Mark Prior Jsy/250 .... 10.00 4.50
33 Hideo Nomo Jsy/250 .... 15.00 6.75
34 Torii Hunter Jsy/250 .... 8.00 3.60
35 Mark Teixeira Jsy/250............ 8.00 3.60
36 Craig Biggio Pants/250 .... 10.00 4.50
37 Rafael Palmeiro Pants/250... 10.00 4.50
38 Jeff Bagwell Pants/250 .... 10.00 4.50
39 Albert Pujols Jsy/200........... 15.00 6.75
40 Richie Sexson Pants/250....... 8.00 3.60
41 Alex Rodriguez Bat/250 .... 15.00 6.75
42 Carlos Delgado Bat/250 .... 8.00 3.60
43 Frank Thomas Bat/75........... 15.00 6.75
44 Sammy Sosa Bat/250 .... 15.00 6.75
45 Marlon Byrd Bat/250.............. 8.00 3.60
46 Mark Prior Bat/250 .... 10.00 4.50
47 Adrian Beltre Bat/250........... 10.00 4.50
48 Tom Glavine Bat/250............ 10.00 4.50
49 So Taguchi Bat/250................ 8.00 3.60
50 Jeff Bagwell Bat/250 .... 10.00 4.50
51 Mike Sweeney Bat/250........... 8.00 3.60
52 Luis Gonzalez Bat/250 .... 8.00 3.60
53 Chipper Jones Bat/100......... 15.00 6.75
54 Jason Giambi Bat/250............ 8.00 3.60
55 Miguel Tejada Bat/250............ 8.00 3.60
56 Todd Helton Bat/250 .... 10.00 4.50
57 Andruw Jones Bat/250........... 8.00 3.60
58 Mike Piazza Bat/250............. 10.00 4.50
59 Manny Ramirez Bat/250....... 10.00 4.50
60 Randy Johnson Bat/250....... 10.00 4.50
61 Carlos Beltran Bat/250 .... 10.00 4.50
62 Victor Martinez Bat/250 .... 10.00 4.50
63 Orlando Hudson Bat/250 .... 8.00 3.60
64 Jeff Kent Bat/250 .... 8.00 3.60
65 Greg Maddux Bat/250.......... 10.00 4.50
66 Garret Anderson Bat/150 .... 8.00 3.60
67 Joe Thurston Bat/250 .... 8.00 3.60
68 Mark Teixeira Bat/250 .... 8.00 3.60
69 Kazuhisa Ishii Bat/250 .... 8.00 3.60
70 Austin Kearns Bat/250 .... 8.00 3.60
71 Pat Burrell Bat/100.............. 10.00 4.50
72 Joe Borchard Bat/250 .... 8.00 3.60
73 Josh Phelps Bat/250............... 8.00 3.60
74 Travis Hafner Bat/250 .... 8.00 3.60
75 So Taguchi Shoe/125.......... 10.00 4.50
76 Victor Martinez Fld Glv/125 . 15.00 6.75
77 Paul Lo Duca Shoe/125 .... 10.00 4.50
78 Bernie Williams Shoe/125.... 15.00 6.75
79 Josh Phelps Shoe/125......... 10.00 4.50
80 Marlon Byrd Fld Glv/125...... 10.00 4.50
81 Manny Ramirez Hat/100 ...... 15.00 6.75
82 Jason Giambi Hat/125 .... 8.00 3.60
83 Jeff Bagwell Hat/50...............
84 Sammy Sosa Shoe/125 .... 25.00 11.00
85 Josh Phelps Hat/125............ 10.00 4.50
86 Tim Hudson Hat/125............ 10.00 4.50
87 Randy Johnson Hat/125 ....
88 Troy Glaus Btg Glv/125........ 10.00 4.50
89 Joe Thurston Fld Glv/125..... 10.00 4.50
90 Miguel Tejada Hat/125 .... 10.00 4.50
91 Adam Dunn Btg Glv-Fld Glv/100 25.00 11.00
92 Magglio Ordonez Btg Glv-Hat 15.00 6.75
93 Mike Sweeney Btg Glv-Fld Glv 15.00 6.75
94 Andruw Jones Btg-Glv-Hat .. 15.00 6.75
95 Carlos Beltran Hat-Shoe....... 25.00 11.00
96 Joe Borchard Fld Glv-Shoe .. 15.00 6.75
97 Austin Kearns Hat-Shoe....... 15.00 6.75
98 Richie Sexson 25.00 11.00
Btg Glv-Fld Glv-Hat
99 Mark Prior............................ 40.00 18.00
Fld Glv-Hat-Shoe
100 Mark Teixeira...................... 25.00 11.00
Fld Glv-Hat-Shoe
101 Ryan Klesko 25.00 11.00
Btg Glv-Hat-Shoe
102 Jason Jennings...............
Btg Glv-Hat-Shoe
103 Travis Hafner....................... 25.00 11.00
Btg Glv-Fld Glv-Shoe
104 Mark Buehrle 25.00 11.00
Btg Glv-Fld Glv-Hat
105 Eric Hinske.......................... 25.00 11.00
Btg Glv-Fld Glv-Hat-Shoe
106 Rafael Palmeiro.................... 60.00 27.00
Btg Glv-Fld Glv-Hat-Shoe
107 Roy Oswalt.......................... 40.00 18.00
Btg Glv-Fld Glv-Hat-Shoe
108 Kerry Wood.......................... 60.00 27.00
Btg Glv-Fld Glv-Hat-Shoe
109 Brian Giles 40.00 18.00
Btg Glv-Fld Glv-Hat-Shoe
110 Ivan Rodriguez.................... 60.00 27.00
Btg Glv-Fld Glv-Hat-Shoe

2003 Absolute Memorabilia Tools of the Trade Materials Spectrum

MINT NRMT
*SPECTRUM p/r 40-50: 1.25X TO 3X BASIC
PRINT RUNS B/WN 10-50 COPIES PER
NO PRICING ON QTY OF 25 OR LESS

2003 Absolute Memorabilia Total Bases

MINT NRMT
STATED ODDS 1:16
1 Albert Pujols 8.00 3.60
2 Nomar Garciaparra 6.00 2.70
3 Jason Giambi 1.50 .70
4 Miguel Tejada 1.50 .70
5 Rafael Palmeiro 2.50 1.10
6 Sammy Sosa 6.00 2.70
7 Pat Burrell 1.50 .70
8 Lance Berkman 1.50 .70
9 Bernie Williams 2.50 1.10
10 Jim Thome 4.00 1.80
11 Carlos Beltran 2.50 1.10
12 Eric Chavez 1.50 .70
13 Alex Rodriguez 6.00 2.70
14 Magglio Ordonez 1.50 .70
15 Brian Giles 1.50 .70
16 Alfonso Soriano 2.50 1.10
17 Shawn Green 1.50 .70
18 Vladimir Guerrero 4.00 1.80
19 Garret Anderson 1.50 .70
20 Todd Helton 2.50 1.10
21 Barry Bonds 10.00 4.50
22 Jeff Kent 1.50 .70
23 Torii Hunter 1.50 .70
24 Ichiro Suzuki 6.00 2.70
25 Derek Jeter 10.00 4.50
26 Chipper Jones 4.00 1.80
27 Jeff Bagwell 2.50 1.10
28 Mike Piazza 6.00 2.70
29 Rickey Henderson 4.00 1.80
30 Ken Griffey Jr. 6.00 2.70

2003 Absolute Memorabilia Total Bases Materials 1B

MINT NRMT
RANDOM INSERTS IN PACKS
PRINT RUNS B/WN 28-165 COPIES PER
1 Albert Pujols/109 20.00 9.00
2 Nomar Garciaparra/112 20.00 9.00
3 Jason Giambi/100 10.00 4.50
4 Miguel Tejada/140 10.00 4.50
5 Rafael Palmeiro/58 25.00 11.00
6 Sammy Sosa/90 20.00 9.00
7 Pat Burrell/87 10.00 4.50
8 Lance Berkman/90 10.00 4.50
9 Bernie Williams/146 10.00 4.50
10 Jim Thome/73 15.00 6.75
11 Carlos Beltran/94 15.00 6.75
12 Eric Chavez/93 10.00 4.50
13 Alex Rodriguez/101 20.00 9.00
14 Magglio Ordonez/103 10.00 4.50
15 Brian Giles/68 10.00 4.50
16 Alfonso Soriano/117 15.00 6.75
17 Shawn Green/92 10.00 4.50
18 Vladimir Guerrero/128 10.00 4.50
19 Garret Anderson/107 10.00 4.50
20 Todd Helton/109 15.00 6.75
21 Barry Bonds/70 30.00 13.50
22 Jeff Kent/114 10.00 4.50
23 Torii Hunter/92 10.00 4.50
24 Ichiro Suzuki/165 40.00 18.00
25 Derek Jeter/147 40.00 18.00
26 Chipper Jones/117 15.00 6.75
27 Jeff Bagwell/100 15.00 6.75
28 Mike Piazza/76
29 Rickey Henderson/28 40.00 18.00
30 Ken Griffey Jr./36

2003 Absolute Memorabilia Total Bases Materials 2B

MINT NRMT
RANDOM INSERTS IN PACKS
PRINT RUNS B/WN 6-56 COPIES PER
NO PRICING ON QTY OF 25 OR LESS
1 Albert Pujols/40 50.00 22.00
2 Nomar Garciaparra/56 40.00 18.00
3 Jason Giambi/34
4 Miguel Tejada/30
5 Rafael Palmeiro/34
6 Sammy Sosa/19
7 Pat Burrell/39 15.00 6.75
8 Lance Berkman/35 25.00 11.00
9 Bernie Williams/37
10 Jim Thome/19
11 Carlos Beltran/44 25.00 11.00
12 Eric Chavez/31
13 Alex Rodriguez/27 80.00 36.00
14 Magglio Ordonez/47 15.00 6.75
15 Brian Giles/37
16 Alfonso Soriano/51 25.00 11.00
17 Shawn Green/31 25.00 11.00
18 Vladimir Guerrero/37 25.00 11.00
19 Garret Anderson/56 15.00 6.75
20 Todd Helton/39 25.00 11.00
21 Barry Bonds/31 60.00 27.00
22 Jeff Kent/42 15.00 6.75
23 Torii Hunter/37 15.00 6.75
24 Ichiro Suzuki/37
25 Derek Jeter/26 80.00 36.00
26 Chipper Jones/35 40.00 18.00
27 Jeff Bagwell/33 40.00 18.00
28 Mike Piazza/23
29 Rickey Henderson/6
30 Ken Griffey Jr./8

2003 Absolute Memorabilia Total Bases Materials 3B

MINT NRMT
RANDOM INSERTS IN PACKS
PRINT RUNS B/WN 1-8 COPIES PER
NO PRICING DUE TO SCARCITY

2003 Absolute Memorabilia Total Bases Materials HR

MINT NRMT
RANDOM INSERTS IN PACKS
PRINT RUNS B/WN 5-57 COPIES PER
NO PRICING ON QTY OF 25 OR LESS
1 Albert Pujols/34 60.00 27.00
2 Nomar Garciaparra/24
3 Jason Giambi/41 15.00 6.75
4 Miguel Tejada/34 25.00 11.00
5 Rafael Palmeiro/43 25.00 11.00
6 Sammy Sosa/49
7 Pat Burrell/37 15.00 6.75
8 Lance Berkman/42 15.00 6.75
9 Bernie Williams/19
10 Jim Thome/52 25.00 11.00
11 Carlos Beltran/29
12 Eric Chavez/34 25.00 11.00
13 Alex Rodriguez/57 40.00 18.00
14 Magglio Ordonez/38 15.00 6.75
15 Brian Giles/38 15.00 6.75
16 Alfonso Soriano/39 25.00 11.00
17 Shawn Green/42 15.00 6.75
18 Vladimir Guerrero/39 25.00 11.00
19 Garret Anderson/29 25.00 11.00
20 Todd Helton/30
21 Barry Bonds/46 50.00 22.00
22 Jeff Kent/37 15.00 6.75
23 Torii Hunter/29 25.00 11.00
24 Ichiro Suzuki/8
25 Derek Jeter/18
26 Chipper Jones 26 40.00 18.00
27 Jeff Bagwell/31 40.00 18.00
28 Mike Piazza/33 50.00 22.00
29 Rickey Henderson/5
30 Ken Griffey Jr./8

2004 Absolute Memorabilia

Nm-Mt Ex-Mt
COMMON ACTIVE (1-200) 2.00 .60
COMMON RETIRED (1-200) 2.00 .60
1-200 PRINT RUN 1349 SERIAL #'d SETS
COMMON CARD (201-250) 4.00 1.20
COMMON AU (201-250) 8.00 2.40
201-250 RANDOM INSERTS IN PACKS
201-250 NON AU PRINT RUNS 1000 #'d PER
201-250 AU PRINTS B/WN 500-700 #'d PER
1 Troy Glaus 2.00 .60
2 Garret Anderson 2.00 .60
3 Tim Salmon 2.00 .60
4 Bartolo Colon 2.00 .60
5 Troy Percival 2.00 .60
6 Nolan Ryan Angels 8.00 2.40
7 Vladimir Guerrero 3.00 .90
8 Richie Sexson 2.00 .60
9 Shea Hillenbrand 2.00 .60
10 Luis Gonzalez 2.00 .60
11 Brandon Webb 2.00 .60
12 Randy Johnson 3.00 .90
13 Robby Hammock 2.00 .60
14 Edgar Gonzalez 2.00 .60
15 Roberto Alomar 2.00 .60
16 Andruw Jones 2.00 .60
17 Chipper Jones 3.00 .90
18 Dale Murphy 2.00 .60
19 Rafael Furcal 2.00 .60
20 J.D. Drew 2.00 .60
21 Bubba Nelson 2.00 .60
22 Julio Franco 2.00 .60
23 Adam LaRoche 2.00 .60
24 Michael Hessman 2.00 .60
25 Warren Spahn 2.00 .60
26 Jay Gibbons 2.00 .60
27 Cal Ripken 12.00 3.60
28 Miguel Tejada 2.00 .60
29 Adam Loewen 2.00 .60
30 Rafael Palmeiro 2.00 .60
31 Javy Lopez 2.00 .60
32 Luis Matos 2.00 .60
33 Jason Varitek 2.00 .60
34 Carl Yastrzemski 5.00 1.50
35 Manny Ramirez 2.00 .60
36 Trot Nixon 2.00 .60
37 Curt Schilling 3.00 .90
38 Pedro Martinez 3.00 .90
39 Nomar Garciaparra 5.00 1.50
40 Luis Tiant 2.00 .60
41 Kevin Youkilis 2.00 .60
42 Michel Hernandez 2.00 .60
43 Sammy Sosa 5.00 1.50
44 Greg Maddux 5.00 1.50
45 Kerry Wood 3.00 .90
46 Mark Prior 3.00 .90
47 Ernie Banks 3.00 .90
48 Aramis Ramirez 2.00 .60
49 Brendan Harris 2.00 .60
50 Todd Wellemeyer 2.00 .60
51 Frank Thomas 3.00 .90
52 Magglio Ordonez 2.00 .60
53 Carlos Lee 2.00 .60
54 Joe Crede 2.00 .60
55 Joe Borchard 2.00 .60
56 Mark Buehrle 2.00 .60
57 Sean Casey 2.00 .60
58 Adam Dunn 2.00 .60
59 Austin Kearns 2.00 .60
60 Ken Griffey Jr. 5.00 1.50
61 Barry Larkin 2.00 .60
62 Ryan Wagner 2.00 .60
63 Jody Gerut 2.00 .60
64 Jeremy Guthrie 2.00 .60
65 Travis Hafner 2.00 .60
66 Brian Tallet 2.00 .60
67 Todd Helton 2.00 .60
68 Preston Wilson 2.00 .60
69 Jeff Baker 2.00 .60
70 Clint Barmes 2.00 .60
71 Joe Kennedy 2.00 .60
72 Jack Morris 2.00 .60
73 George Kell 2.00 .60
74 Preston Larrison 2.00 .60
75 Dmitri Young 2.00 .60
76 Ivan Rodriguez 3.00 .90
77 Dontrelle Willis 2.00 .60
78 Josh Beckett 2.00 .60
79 Miguel Cabrera 2.00 .60
80 Mike Lowell 2.00 .60
81 Luis Castillo 2.00 .60
82 Juan Pierre 2.00 .60
83 Jeff Bagwell 2.00 .60
84 Jeff Kent 2.00 .60
85 Craig Biggio 2.00 .60
86 Lance Berkman 2.00 .60
87 Andy Pettitte 2.00 .60
88 Roy Oswalt 2.00 .60
89 Chris Burke 2.00 .60
90 Jason Lane 2.00 .60
91 Roger Clemens 6.00 1.80
92 Mike Sweeney 2.00 .60
93 Carlos Beltran 2.00 .60
94 Angel Berroa 2.00 .60
95 Juan Gonzalez 2.00 .60
96 Ken Harvey 2.00 .60
97 Byron Gettis 2.00 .60
98 Alexis Gomez 2.00 .60
99 Ian Ferguson 2.00 .60
100 Duke Snider 2.00 .60
101 Shawn Green 2.00 .60
102 Hideo Nomo 3.00 .90
103 Kazuhisa Ishii 2.00 .60
104 Edwin Jackson 2.00 .60
105 Fred McGriff 2.00 .60
106 Hong-Chih Kou 2.00 .60
107 Don Sutton 2.00 .60
108 Rickey Henderson 3.00 .90
109 Cesar Izturis 2.00 .60
110 Robin Ventura 2.00 .60
111 Paul Lo Duca 2.00 .60
112 Rickie Weeks 2.00 .60
113 Scott Podsednik 2.00 .60
114 Junior Spivey 2.00 .60
115 Lyle Overbay 2.00 .60
116 Tony Oliva 2.00 .60
117 Jacque Jones 2.00 .60
118 Shannon Stewart 2.00 .60
119 Torii Hunter 2.00 .60
120 Johan Santana 2.00 .60
121 J.D. Durbin 2.00 .60
122 Jason Kubel 2.00 .60
123 Michael Cuddyer 2.00 .60
124 Nick Johnson 2.00 .60
125 Jose Vidro 2.00 .60
126 Orlando Cabrera 2.00 .60
127 Zach Day 2.00 .60
128 Mike Piazza 5.00 1.50
129 Tom Glavine 2.00 .60
130 Jae Weong Seo 2.00 .60
131 Gary Carter 2.00 .60
132 Phil Seibel 2.00 .60
133 Edwin Almonte 2.00 .60
134 Aaron Boone 2.00 .60
135 Kenny Lofton 2.00 .60
136 Don Mattingly 6.00 1.80
137 Jason Giambi 2.00 .60
138 Alex Rodriguez Yanks 5.00 1.50
139 Jorge Posada 2.00 .60
140 Bernie Williams 2.00 .60
141 Hideki Matsui 5.00 1.50
142 Mike Mussina 2.00 .60
143 Mariano Rivera 2.00 .60
144 Gary Sheffield 2.00 .60
145 Derek Jeter 6.00 1.80
146 Chien-Ming Wang 2.00 .60
147 Javier Vazquez 2.00 .60
148 Jose Contreras 2.00 .60
149 Whitey Ford 2.00 .60
150 Kevin Brown 2.00 .60
151 Eric Chavez 2.00 .60
152 Barry Zito 2.00 .60
153 Mark Mulder 2.00 .60
154 Tim Hudson 2.00 .60
155 Rich Harden 2.00 .60
156 Eric Byrnes 2.00 .60
157 Jim Thome 3.00 .90
158 Bobby Abreu 2.00 .60
159 Marlon Byrd 2.00 .60
160 Lenny Dykstra 2.00 .60
161 Steve Carlton 2.00 .60
162 Ryan Howard 2.00 .60
163 Bobby Hill 2.00 .60
164 Jose Castillo 2.00 .60
165 Jay Payton 2.00 .60
166 Ryan Klesko 2.00 .60
167 Brian Giles 2.00 .60
168 Henri Stanley 2.00 .60
169 Jason Schmidt 2.00 .60
170 Jerome Williams 2.00 .60
171 J.T. Snow 2.00 .60
172 Bret Boone 2.00 .60
173 Edgar Martinez 2.00 .60
174 Ichiro Suzuki 5.00 1.50
175 Jamie Moyer 2.00 .60
176 Rich Aurilia 2.00 .60
177 Chris Snelling 2.00 .60
178 Scott Rolen 3.00 .90
179 Albert Pujols 6.00 1.80
180 Jim Edmonds 2.00 .60
181 Stan Musial 5.00 1.50
182 Dan Haren 2.00 .60
183 Red Schoendienst 2.00 .60
184 Aubrey Huff 2.00 .60
185 Delmon Young 2.00 .60
186 Rocco Baldelli 2.00 .60
187 Dewon Brazelton 2.00 .60
188 Mark Teixeira 2.00 .60
189 Hank Blalock 2.00 .60
190 Nolan Ryan Rgr 8.00 2.40
191 Alfonso Soriano 2.00 .60
192 Michael Young 2.00 .60
193 Vernon Wells 2.00 .60
194 Roy Halladay 2.00 .60
195 Carlos Delgado 2.00 .60
196 Dustin McGowan 2.00 .60
197 Josh Phelps 2.00 .60
198 Alexis Rios 2.00 .60
199 Eric Hinske 2.00 .60
200 Josh Towers 2.00 .60
201 Kazuo Matsui/1000 RC 8.00 2.40
202 Fernando Nieve AU/500 RC 8.00 2.40
203 Mike Rouse/1000 RC 4.00 1.20
204 Dennis Sarfate AU/500 RC 8.00 2.40
205 Josh Labandeira AU/500 RC 8.00 2.40
206 Chris Oxspring AU/500 RC 10.00 3.00
207 Alfredo Simon/1000 RC 4.00 1.20
208 Cory Sullivan AU/500 RC 8.00 2.40
209 Ruddy Yan AU/500 8.00 2.40
210 Jason Bartlett AU/500 RC 10.00 3.00
211 Akinori Otsuka/1000 RC 4.00 1.20
212 Lincoln Holdzkom/1000 RC 4.00 1.20
213 Justin Leone/1000 RC 5.00 1.50
214 Jorge Sequea AU/500 RC 8.00 2.40
215 John Gall/1000 RC 5.00 1.50
216 Jerome Gamble/1000 RC 4.00 1.20
217 Tim Bittner AU/500 RC 8.00 2.40
218 Ronny Cedeno AU/500 RC 8.00 2.40
219 Justin Hampson/1000 RC 4.00 1.20
220 Ryan Wing AU/500 RC 8.00 2.40
221 Mariano Gomez AU/500 RC 8.00 2.40
222 Carlos Vasquez/1000 RC 4.00 1.20
223 Casey Daigle AU/500 RC 8.00 2.40
224 Renyel Pinto AU/500 RC 10.00 3.00
225 Chris Shelton AU/500 RC 10.00 3.00
226 Mike Gosling AU/700 RC 8.00 2.40
227 Aarom Baldiris AU/700 RC 10.00 3.00
228 Ramon Ramirez AU/700 RC 8.00 2.40
229 Roberto Novoa AU/500 RC 10.00 3.00
230 Sean Henn AU/500 RC 8.00 2.40
231 Jamie Brown AU/500 RC 8.00 2.40
232 Nick Regilio AU/500 RC 8.00 2.40
233 Dave Crouthers AU/700 RC 8.00 2.40
234 Greg Dobbs AU/500 RC 8.00 2.40
235 Angel Chavez AU/500 RC 8.00 2.40
236 Willy Taveras AU/500 RC 10.00 3.00
237 Justin Knoedler AU/500 RC 8.00 2.40
238 Ian Snell AU/700 RC 10.00 3.00
239 Jason Frasor AU/500 RC 8.00 2.40
240 Jerry Gil AU/500 RC 8.00 2.40
241 Carlos Hines AU/500 RC 8.00 2.40
242 Ivan Ochoa AU/500 RC 8.00 2.40
243 Jose Capellan AU/700 RC 20.00 6.00
244 Onil Joseph AU/700 RC 8.00 2.40
245 Hector Gimenez AU/700 RC 8.00 2.40
246 Shawn Hill AU/700 RC 8.00 2.40
247 Freddy Guzman AU/700 RC 8.00 2.40
248 Graham Koonce AU/500 8.00 2.40
249 Ronald Belisario AU/500 RC 8.00 2.40
250 Merkin Valdez AU/700 RC 10.00 3.00

2004 Absolute Memorabilia Retail

Nm-Mt Ex-Mt
*RETAIL 1-200 : .1X TO .25X BASIC
1-200 ISSUED IN RETAIL PACKS
RETAIL CARDS ARE NOT SERIAL #'d.

2004 Absolute Memorabilia Spectrum Gold

Nm-Mt Ex-Mt
*GOLD 1-200: 1.5X TO 4X BASIC ACTIVE
*GOLD 1-200: 1.5X TO 4X BASIC RETIRED
*GOLD 201-250: .6X TO 1.5X BASIC
*GOLD 201-250: .3X TO .8X BASIC AU
RANDOM INSERTS IN PACKS
STATED PRINT RUN 50 SERIAL #'d SETS

2004 Absolute Memorabilia Spectrum Platinum

Nm-Mt Ex-Mt
RANDOM INSERTS IN PACKS
STATED PRINT RUN 1 SERIAL #'d SET
NO PRICING DUE TO SCARCITY

2004 Absolute Memorabilia Spectrum Silver

Nm-Mt Ex-Mt
*SILVER 1-200: 1X TO 2.5X BASIC ACTIVE
*SILVER 1-200: 1X TO 2.5X BASIC RETIRED
*SILVER 201-250: .4X TO 1X BASIC
*SILVER 201-250: .2X TO .5X BASIC AU
RANDOM INSERTS IN PACKS
STATED PRINT RUN 100 SERIAL #'d SETS

2004 Absolute Memorabilia Signature Spectrum Gold

Nm-Mt Ex-Mt
RANDOM INSERTS IN PACKS
PRINT RUNS B/WN 1-100 COPIES PER
NO PRICING ON QTY OF 10 OR LESS
1 Troy Glaus/15 40.00 12.00
2 Garret Anderson/100 15.00 4.50
6 Nolan Ryan Angels/10
7 Vladimir Guerrero/25 60.00 18.00
8 Richie Sexson/15 40.00 12.00
9 Shea Hillenbrand/100 10.00 3.00
11 Brandon Webb/100 10.00 3.00
12 Randy Johnson/1
15 Roberto Alomar/25 50.00 15.00
16 Andruw Jones/5
17 Chipper Jones/5
18 Dale Murphy/100 25.00 7.50
19 Rafael Furcal/100 15.00 4.50
22 Julio Franco/25 30.00 9.00
23 Adam LaRoche/100 10.00 3.00
25 Warren Spahn/5
26 Jay Gibbons/100 10.00 3.00
27 Cal Ripken/1
29 Adam Loewen/100 10.00 3.00
30 Rafael Palmeiro/1
32 Luis Matos/50 12.00 3.60
33 Jason Varitek/25 60.00 18.00
34 Carl Yastrzemski/1
35 Manny Ramirez/1
36 Trot Nixon/100 15.00 4.50
37 Curt Schilling/1
40 Luis Tiant/50 20.00 6.00
41 Kevin Youkilis/25 30.00 9.00
43 Sammy Sosa/5
45 Kerry Wood/25 60.00 18.00
46 Mark Prior/100 60.00 18.00
47 Ernie Banks/100 50.00 15.00
48 Aramis Ramirez/5
51 Frank Thomas/5
52 Magglio Ordonez/100 15.00 4.50
53 Carlos Lee/100 15.00 4.50
54 Joe Crede/50 12.00 3.60
56 Mark Buehrle/10
57 Sean Casey/1
58 Adam Dunn/5
59 Austin Kearns/100 15.00 4.50
61 Barry Larkin/25 50.00 15.00
62 Ryan Wagner/50 12.00 3.60
63 Jody Gerut/100 15.00 4.50
64 Jeremy Guthrie/25 20.00 6.00
65 Travis Hafner/25 20.00 6.00
67 Todd Helton/5
68 Preston Wilson/100 15.00 4.50
69 Jeff Baker/25 20.00 6.00
72 Jack Morris/100
73 George Kell/100 15.00 4.50
77 Dontrelle Willis/10
78 Josh Beckett/5
79 Miguel Cabrera/100 25.00 7.50
80 Mike Lowell/1
81 Luis Castillo/25 20.00 6.00
83 Jeff Bagwell/25 80.00 24.00
85 Craig Biggio/5
86 Lance Berkman/5
87 Andy Pettitte/25 60.00 18.00
88 Roy Oswalt/10
93 Carlos Beltran/100 40.00 12.00
94 Angel Berroa/100 10.00 3.00
95 Juan Gonzalez/10
100 Duke Snider/100 25.00 7.50
101 Shawn Green/1
102 Hideo Nomo/1
103 Kazuhisa Ishii/5
104 Edwin Jackson/50 20.00 6.00
105 Fred McGriff/1
106 Hong-Chih Kou/25 30.00 9.00
107 Don Sutton/25 30.00 9.00
108 Rickey Henderson/5
110 Robin Ventura/10
111 Paul Lo Duca/5
112 Rickie Weeks/24 30.00 9.00
113 Scott Podsednik/100 15.00 4.50
114 Junior Spivey/10
115 Lyle Overbay/10
116 Tony Oliva/50 20.00 6.00
117 Jacque Jones/100 15.00 4.50
118 Shannon Stewart/5
119 Torii Hunter/100 15.00 4.50
120 Johan Santana/10
124 Nick Johnson/5
125 Jose Vidro/10
126 Orlando Cabrera/10
128 Mike Piazza/1
130 Jae Weong Seo/100 15.00 4.50
131 Gary Carter/100 15.00 4.50
136 Don Mattingly/100 60.00 18.00
138 Alex Rodriguez/1
139 Jorge Posada/25 50.00 15.00
140 Bernie Williams/5
142 Mike Mussina/1
143 Mariano Rivera/1
144 Gary Sheffield/25 50.00 15.00
146 Chien-Ming Wang/25 50.00 15.00
147 Javier Vazquez/5
148 Jose Contreras/5
149 Whitey Ford/5
151 Eric Chavez/1
152 Barry Zito/1
153 Mark Mulder/100 15.00 4.50
154 Tim Hudson/5
155 Rich Harden/50 20.00 6.00
158 Bobby Abreu/5
159 Marlon Byrd/100 10.00 3.00
160 Lenny Dykstra/100 15.00 4.50
161 Steve Carlton/50 30.00 9.00
164 Jose Castillo/50 12.00 3.60
165 Jay Payton/100 10.00 3.00
166 Ryan Klesko/5
170 Jerome Williams/50 30.00 9.00
171 J.T. Snow/10
173 Edgar Martinez/5
175 Jamie Moyer/5
176 Rich Aurilia/5
178 Scott Rolen/50 50.00 15.00
179 Albert Pujols/1
180 Jim Edmonds/10
181 Stan Musial/100 60.00 18.00
182 Dan Haren/25 20.00 6.00
183 Red Schoendienst/100 15.00 4.50
184 Aubrey Huff/100 15.00 4.50
185 Delmon Young/100 25.00 7.50
186 Rocco Baldelli/5
187 Dewon Brazelton/25 20.00 6.00
188 Mark Teixeira/50 30.00 9.00
189 Hank Blalock/25 30.00 9.00
190 Nolan Ryan Rgr/10
192 Michael Young/100 25.00 7.50
193 Vernon Wells/10
194 Roy Halladay/25 20.00 6.00
197 Josh Phelps/5
198 Alexis Rios/50 20.00 6.00
199 Eric Hinske/1
202 Fernando Nieve/100 10.00 3.00
205 Josh Labandeira/100 10.00 3.00
206 Chris Oxspring/100 15.00 4.50
208 Cory Sullivan/100 10.00 3.00
209 Ruddy Yan/100 10.00 3.00
210 Jason Bartlett/100 15.00 4.50
212 Lincoln Holdzkom/100 15.00 4.50
213 Justin Leone/100 15.00 4.50
214 Jorge Sequea/100 10.00 3.00
217 Tim Bittner/100 10.00 3.00
219 Justin Hampson/100 10.00 3.00

0 Ryan Wing/100 10.00 3.00
1 Mariano Gomez/100 10.00 3.00
2 Carlos Vasquez/100 15.00 4.50
4 Renyel Pinto/100 15.00 4.50
5 Chris Shelton/100 20.00 6.00
6 Mike Gosling/10
7 Aarom Baldiris/10
8 Ramon Ramirez/10
0 Sean Henn/100 10.00 3.00
2 Nick Regilio/100 10.00 3.00
3 Dave Crouthers/10
4 Greg Dobbs/50 15.00 4.50
5 Angel Chavez/100 10.00 3.00
8 Ian Snell/10
2 Ivan Ochoa/100 10.00 3.00
3 Jose Capellan/10
4 Onil Joseph/10
5 Hector Gimenez/10
6 Shawn Hill/10
7 Freddy Guzman/10
8 Graham Koonce/100 10.00 3.00
0 Merkin Valdez/10

2004 Absolute Memorabilia Signature Spectrum Platinum

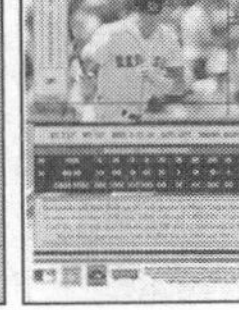

Nm-Mt Ex-Mt
ANDOM INSERTS IN PACKS
TATED PRINT RUN 1 SERIAL #'d SET
O PRICING DUE TO SCARCITY

2004 Absolute Memorabilia Signature Spectrum Silver

Nm-Mt Ex-Mt
ANDOM INSERTS IN PACKS
RINT RUNS B/WN 1-250 COPIES PER
O PRICING ON QTY OF 14 OR LESS
Troy Glaus/34 30.00 9.00
Garret Anderson/100 15.00 4.50
Nolan Ryan Angels/25 150.00 45.00
Vladimir Guerrero/100 40.00 12.00
Richie Sexson/34 30.00 9.00
Shea Hillenbrand/100 10.00 3.00
1 Brandon Webb/100 10.00 3.00
2 Randy Johnson/1
3 Robby Hammock/250 10.00 3.00
4 Edgar Gonzalez/100 10.00 3.00
5 Roberto Alomar/32 50.00 15.00
6 Andruw Jones/50 20.00 6.00
7 Chipper Jones/10
8 Dale Murphy/100 25.00 7.50
9 Rafael Furcal/100 15.00 4.50
21 Bubba Nelson/250 10.00 3.00
22 Julio Franco/100 15.00 4.50
23 Adam LaRoche/100 10.00 3.00
24 Michael Hessman/250 10.00 3.00
25 Warren Spahn/10
26 Jay Gibbons/100 10.00 3.00
27 Cal Ripken/5
29 Adam Loewen/100 10.00 3.00
30 Rafael Palmeiro/5
32 Luis Matos/100 10.00 3.00
33 Jason Varitek/50 50.00 15.00
34 Carl Yastrzemski/5
35 Manny Ramirez/5
36 Trot Nixon/100 15.00 4.50
37 Curt Schilling/5
40 Luis Tiant/100 15.00 4.50
41 Kevin Youkilis/25 30.00 9.00
42 Michael Hernandez/190 10.00 3.00
43 Sammy Sosa/21 150.00 45.00
45 Kerry Wood/50 50.00 15.00
46 Mark Prior/100 60.00 18.00
47 Ernie Banks/100 50.00 15.00
48 Aramis Ramirez/50 20.00 6.00
49 Brendan Harris/250 10.00 3.00
50 Todd Wellemeyer/250 10.00 3.00
51 Frank Thomas/50 50.00 15.00
52 Magglio Ordonez/100 15.00 4.50
53 Carlos Lee/100 15.00 4.50
54 Joe Crede/100 10.00 3.00
55 Joe Borchard/250 10.00 3.00
56 Mark Buehrle/10
57 Sean Casey/50 20.00 6.00
58 Adam Dunn/100 25.00 7.50
59 Austin Kearns/100 15.00 4.50
61 Barry Larkin/50 30.00 9.00
62 Ryan Wagner/100 10.00 3.00
63 Jody Gerut/100 15.00 4.50
64 Jeremy Guthrie/50 12.00 3.60
65 Travis Hafner/50 12.00 3.60
66 Brian Tallet/250 10.00 3.00
67 Todd Helton/10
68 Preston Wilson/100 15.00 4.50
69 Jeff Baker/50 12.00 3.60
70 Clint Barmes/250 10.00 3.00
71 Joe Kennedy/250 10.00 3.00
72 Jack Morris/96
73 George Kell/100 15.00 4.50
74 Preston Larrison/250 10.00 3.00
77 Dontrelle Willis/100 15.00 4.50
78 Josh Beckett/25 50.00 15.00
79 Miguel Cabrera/100 25.00 7.50
80 Mike Lowell/25 30.00 9.00
81 Luis Castillo/50 12.00 3.60
83 Jeff Bagwell/50 60.00 18.00
85 Craig Biggio/50 20.00 6.00
86 Lance Berkman/25 50.00 15.00
87 Andy Pettitte/25 60.00 18.00
88 Roy Oswalt/25 30.00 9.00
89 Chris Burke/250 10.00 3.00
90 Jason Lane/231 10.00 3.00
93 Carlos Beltran/100 40.00 12.00
94 Angel Berroa/100 10.00 3.00
95 Juan Gonzalez/25 50.00 15.00
96 Ken Harvey/200 15.00 4.50
97 Byron Gettis/250 10.00 3.00
98 Alexis Gomez/250 10.00 3.00
99 Ian Ferguson/104 10.00 3.00
100 Duke Snider/100 25.00 7.50
101 Shawn Green/1
102 Hideo Nomo/1
103 Kazuhisa Ishii/25 50.00 15.00
104 Edwin Jackson/100 15.00 4.50
105 Fred McGriff/50 60.00 18.00
106 Hong-Chih Kou/50 20.00 6.00
107 Don Sutton/100 15.00 4.50
108 Rickey Henderson/10
109 Cesar Izturis/101 10.00 3.00
110 Robin Ventura/25 30.00 9.00
111 Paul Lo Duca/50 20.00 6.00
112 Rickie Weeks/21 30.00 9.00
113 Scott Podsednik/100 15.00 4.50
114 Junior Spivey/89 10.00 3.00
115 Lyle Overbay/89 15.00 4.50
116 Tony Oliva/72 15.00 4.50
117 Jacque Jones/100 15.00 4.50
118 Shannon Stewart/100 15.00 4.50
119 Torii Hunter/100 15.00 4.50
120 Johan Santana/50 50.00 15.00
121 J.D. Durbin/250 10.00 3.00
122 Jason Kubel/250 15.00 4.50
123 Michael Cuddyer/225 10.00 3.00
124 Nick Johnson/25 20.00 6.00
125 Jose Vidro/25 20.00 6.00
126 Orlando Cabrera/25 30.00 9.00
127 Zach Day/100 10.00 3.00
128 Mike Piazza/5
130 Jae Weong Seo/100 15.00 4.50
131 Gary Carter/100 15.00 4.50
132 Phil Seibel/177 10.00 3.00
133 Edwin Almonte/250 10.00 3.00
136 Don Mattingly/100 60.00 18.00
138 Alex Rodriguez/1
139 Jorge Posada/50 30.00 9.00
140 Bernie Williams/10
142 Mike Mussina/1
143 Mariano Rivera/5
144 Gary Sheffield/100 25.00 7.50
146 Chien-Ming Wang/50 30.00 9.00
147 Javier Vazquez/25 30.00 9.00
148 Jose Contreras/25 30.00 9.00
149 Whitey Ford/50 30.00 9.00
151 Eric Chavez/50 20.00 6.00
152 Barry Zito/1
153 Mark Mulder/100 15.00 4.50
154 Tim Hudson/50 20.00 6.00
155 Rich Harden/100 15.00 4.50
156 Eric Byrnes/250 15.00 4.50
158 Bobby Abreu/10
159 Marlon Byrd/100 10.00 3.00
160 Lenny Dykstra/100 15.00 4.50
161 Steve Carlton/100 25.00 7.50
162 Ryan Howard/250 15.00 4.50
163 Bobby Hill/250 10.00 3.00
164 Jose Castillo/100 10.00 3.00
165 Jay Payton/100 10.00 3.00
168 Henri Stanley/112 10.00 3.00
170 Jerome Williams/100 25.00 7.50
171 J.T. Snow/89 15.00 4.50
173 Edgar Martinez/50 30.00 9.00
175 Jamie Moyer/19 40.00 12.00
176 Rich Aurilia/25 20.00 6.00
177 Chris Snelling/177 10.00 3.00
178 Scott Rolen/100 40.00 12.00
179 Albert Pujols/5
180 Jim Edmonds/50 30.00 9.00
181 Stan Musial/100 60.00 18.00
182 Dan Haren/200 10.00 3.00
183 Red Schoendienst/100 15.00 4.50
184 Aubrey Huff/100 15.00 4.50
185 Delmon Young/100 25.00 7.50
186 Rocco Baldelli/50 20.00 6.00
187 Dewon Brazelton/50 12.00 3.60
188 Mark Teixeira/100 25.00 7.50
189 Hank Blalock/50 20.00 6.00
190 Nolan Ryan Rgr/25 150.00 45.00
192 Michael Young/100 25.00 7.50
193 Vernon Wells/14
194 Roy Halladay/50 12.00 3.60
196 Dustin McGowan/250 10.00 3.00
197 Josh Phelps/25 20.00 6.00
198 Alexis Rios/100 15.00 4.50
199 Eric Hinske/5
200 Josh Towers/158 10.00 3.00
202 Fernando Nieve/250 10.00 3.00
203 Mike Rouse/100 10.00 3.00
204 Dennis Sarfate/100 10.00 3.00
205 Josh Labandeira/250 10.00 3.00
206 Chris Oxspring/250 15.00 4.50
207 Alfredo Simon/100 10.00 3.00
208 Cory Sullivan/250 10.00 3.00
209 Ruddy Yan/250 10.00 3.00
210 Jason Bartlett/250 15.00 4.50
211 Akinori Otsuka/100 40.00 12.00
212 Lincoln Holdzkom/250 10.00 3.00
213 Justin Leone/250 15.00 4.50
214 Jorge Sequea/250 10.00 3.00
215 John Gall/50 20.00 6.00
217 Tim Bittner/250 10.00 3.00
219 Justin Hampson/250 10.00 3.00
220 Ryan Wing/250 10.00 3.00
221 Mariano Gomez/250 10.00 3.00
222 Carlos Vasquez/250 15.00 4.50
223 Casey Daigle/150 10.00 3.00
224 Renyel Pinto/250 15.00 4.50
225 Chris Shelton/250 15.00 4.50
229 Roberto Novoa/225 15.00 4.50
230 Sean Henn/250 10.00 3.00
231 Jamie Brown/200 10.00 3.00
232 Nick Regilio/250 10.00 3.00
234 Greg Dobbs/250 10.00 3.00
235 Angel Chavez/250 10.00 3.00
236 Willy Taveras/225 15.00 4.50
237 Justin Knoedler/225 10.00 3.00
239 Jason Frasor/225 10.00 3.00
240 Jerry Gil/225 10.00 3.00
241 Carlos Hines/225 10.00 3.00
242 Ivan Ochoa/250 10.00 3.00
248 Graham Koonce/250 10.00 3.00
249 Ronald Belisario/225 10.00 3.00

2004 Absolute Memorabilia Absolutely Ink

Nm-Mt Ex-Mt
PRINT RUNS B/WN 1-100 COPIES PER
NO PRICING ON QTY OF 10 OR LESS
*SPECTRUM p/r 25: .75X TO 2Xp/r 100
*SPECTRUM p/r 25: .6X TO 1.5X p/r 50
*SPECTRUM p/r 25: .5X TO 1.2X p/r 25
SPECTRUM PRINTS B/WN 1-25 COPIES PER
NO SPECT.PRICING ON QTY OF 10 OR LESS
RANDOM INSERTS IN PACKS
1 Adam Dunn/100 25.00 7.50
2 Al Kaline/100 50.00 15.00
3 Alan Trammell/100 15.00 4.50
4 Albert Pujols/5
5 Alex Rodriguez Rgr/1
6 Andre Dawson Cubs/100 15.00 4.50
7 Andre Dawson Expos/100 15.00 4.50
8 Andruw Jones/50 20.00 6.00
9 Angel Berroa/50 12.00 3.60
10 Aramis Ramirez/50 20.00 6.00
11 Aubrey Huff/100 15.00 4.50
12 Austin Kearns/100 15.00 4.50
13 Barry Larkin/50 30.00 9.00
14 Barry Zito/5
15 Bernie Williams/5
16 Bert Blyleven/100 15.00 4.50
17 Billy Williams/100 15.00 4.50
18 Bo Jackson/5
19 Bob Feller/100 25.00 7.50
20 Bob Gibson/25 50.00 15.00
21 Bobby Doerr/100 15.00 4.50
22 Brandon Webb/100 10.00 3.00
23 Brett Myers/50 12.00 3.60
24 Brooks Robinson/100 25.00 7.50
25 Cal Ripken/5
26 Carl Yastrzemski/5
27 Carlos Beltran/100 40.00 12.00
28 Carlos Lee/100 15.00 4.50
29 Carlton Fisk/10
30 Chipper Jones/5
31 Craig Biggio/50 20.00 6.00
32 Curt Schilling/5
33 Dale Murphy/100 25.00 7.50
34 Darryl Strawberry/100 15.00 4.50
35 Dave Concepcion/50 20.00 6.00
36 Dave Parker/50 20.00 6.00
37 Deion Sanders/10
38 Don Mattingly/100 60.00 18.00
39 Dontrelle Willis/100 15.00 4.50
40 Duke Snider/100 25.00 7.50
41 Dwight Gooden/100 15.00 4.50
42 Edgar Martinez/50 30.00 9.00
43 Eric Chavez/50 20.00 6.00
44 Ernie Banks/100 50.00 15.00
45 Fergie Jenkins/100 15.00 4.50
46 Frank Robinson/100 25.00 7.50
47 Frank Thomas/25 60.00 18.00
48 Fred Lynn/50 12.00 3.60
49 Fred McGriff/25 80.00 24.00
50 Garret Anderson/100 15.00 4.50
51 Gary Carter Expos/100 15.00 4.50
52 Gary Carter Mets/100 15.00 4.50
53 Gary Sheffield/50 30.00 9.00
54 Gaylord Perry/100 15.00 4.50
55 George Brett/5
57 Hank Blalock/100 15.00 4.50
58 Harold Baines/50 20.00 6.00
59 Hideo Nomo/1
62 Jacque Jones/100 15.00 4.50
63 Jae Weong Seo/100 15.00 4.50
64 Jamie Moyer/25 30.00 9.00
65 Jason Varitek/50 50.00 15.00
66 Jay Gibbons/50 12.00 3.60
67 Jim Edmonds/25 50.00 15.00
68 Jim Palmer/100 25.00 7.50
69 Jim Rice/50 20.00 6.00
70 Joe Carter/5
71 Johan Santana/50 50.00 15.00
72 Jorge Posada/50 30.00 9.00
73 Josh Beckett/25 50.00 15.00
74 Juan Gonzalez/25 50.00 15.00
75 Keith Hernandez/100 15.00 4.50
76 Kirby Puckett/25 60.00 18.00
77 Luis Tiant/100 15.00 4.50
78 Magglio Ordonez/100 15.00 4.50
79 Manny Ramirez/1
80 Mariano Rivera/1
81 Mark Grace/25 60.00 18.00
82 Mark Mulder/100 15.00 4.50
83 Mark Prior/100 60.00 18.00
84 Mark Teixeira/100 25.00 7.50
85 Marty Marion/100 15.00 4.50
86 Mike Lowell/25 30.00 9.00
87 Mike Mussina/1
88 Mike Piazza/5
89 Nick Johnson/10
90 Nolan Ryan/25 150.00 45.00
91 Orel Hershiser/100 40.00 12.00
92 Orlando Cepeda/100 15.00 4.50
95 Paul O'Neill/5
96 Pedro Martinez/1
97 Phil Niekro/100 15.00 4.50
98 Rafael Palmeiro/5
99 Ralph Kiner/100 25.00 7.50
100 Randy Johnson/5
101 Red Schoendienst/100 15.00 4.50
102 Rickey Henderson/10
103 Robin Roberts/50 20.00 6.00
104 Robin Ventura/100 15.00 4.50
105 Robin Yount/5
106 Rocco Baldelli/25 30.00 9.00
108 Ryne Sandberg/10
109 Sammy Sosa/21 150.00 45.00
110 Sean Casey/23 30.00 9.00
111 Shannon Stewart/50 12.00 3.60
112 Shawn Green/10
113 Stan Musial/100 60.00 18.00
114 Steve Carlton/50 30.00 9.00
115 Steve Garvey/100 15.00 4.50
116 Todd Helton/10
117 Tommy John/100 15.00 4.50
118 Tony Gwynn/25 80.00 24.00
119 Tony Oliva/100 15.00 4.50
120 Torii Hunter/100 15.00 4.50
121 Trot Nixon/100 20.00 6.00
122 Troy Glaus/50 20.00 6.00
123 Vernon Wells/25 30.00 9.00
124 Vladimir Guerrero/100 40.00 12.00
125 Will Clark/100 40.00 12.00

2004 Absolute Memorabilia Absolutely Ink Material

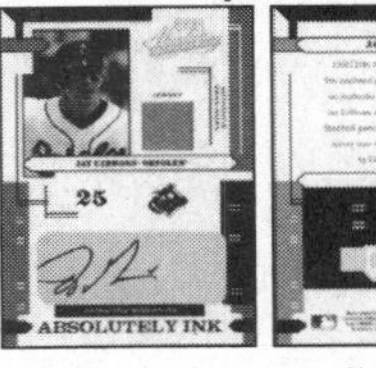

Nm-Mt Ex-Mt
PRINT RUNS B/WN 5-100 COPIES PER
NO PRICING ON QTY OF 14 OR LESS
*PRIME p/r 25: .5X TO 1.2X BASIC p/r 25
PRIME PRINT RUNS B/WN 1-25 COPIES PER
NO PRIME PRICING ON QTY OF 5 OR LESS
RANDOM INSERTS IN PACKS
ADD 20% FOR NOTATED AUTOGRAPHS
1 Adam Dunn Jsy/100 30.00 9.00
2 Al Kaline Pants/50 60.00 18.00
3 Alan Trammell Jsy/100 30.00 9.00
4 Albert Pujols Jsy/5
5 Alex Rodriguez Rgr Jsy/5
6 Andre Dawson Cubs Jsy/100 20.00 6.00
7 Andre Dawson Expos Jsy/100 20.00 6.00
8 Andruw Jones Jsy/10
9 Angel Berroa Jsy/100 15.00 4.50
11 Aubrey Huff Jsy/100 20.00 6.00
12 Austin Kearns Jsy/100 20.00 6.00
13 Barry Larkin Jsy/10
14 Barry Zito Jsy/5
15 Bernie Williams Jsy/5
16 Bert Blyleven Jsy/100 20.00 6.00
17 Billy Williams Jsy/100 30.00 9.00
18 Bo Jackson Jsy/10
19 Bob Feller Jsy/100 30.00 9.00
20 Bob Gibson Jsy/7
21 Bobby Doerr Jsy/100 20.00 6.00
22 Brandon Webb Jsy/50 15.00 4.50
23 Brett Myers Jsy/100 15.00 4.50
24 Brooks Robinson Jsy/100 30.00 9.00
25 Cal Ripken Jsy/5
26 Carl Yastrzemski Jsy/5
27 Carlos Beltran Jsy/100 50.00 15.00
28 Carlos Lee Jsy/100 20.00 6.00
29 Carlton Fisk Jsy/5
30 Chipper Jones Jsy/5
31 Craig Biggio Jsy/10
32 Curt Schilling Jsy/5
33 Dale Murphy Jsy/100 30.00 9.00
34 Darryl Strawberry Jsy/100 20.00 6.00
35 Dave Concepcion Jsy/50 25.00 7.50
36 Dave Parker Jsy/100 20.00 6.00
37 Deion Sanders Jsy/7
38 Don Mattingly Jsy/50 100.00 30.00
39 Dontrelle Willis Jsy/20 30.00 9.00
41 Dwight Gooden Jsy/60 25.00 7.50
42 Edgar Martinez Jsy/100 50.00 15.00
43 Eric Chavez Jsy/10
44 Ernie Banks Jsy/50 60.00 18.00
45 Fergie Jenkins Pants/100 20.00 6.00
46 Frank Robinson Jsy/50 40.00 12.00
47 Frank Thomas Jsy/5
48 Fred Lynn Jsy/100 15.00 4.50
49 Fred McGriff Jsy/20 80.00 24.00
50 Garret Anderson Jsy/100 20.00 6.00
51 Gary Carter Expos Jsy/100 20.00 6.00
52 Gary Carter Mets Jacket/100 20.00 6.00
53 Gary Sheffield Jsy/100 30.00 9.00
54 Gaylord Perry Jsy/100 20.00 6.00
55 George Brett Jsy/5
57 Hank Blalock Jsy/100 20.00 6.00
58 Harold Baines Jsy/100 20.00 6.00
59 Hideo Nomo Jsy/5
62 Jacque Jones Jsy/5
63 Jae Weong Seo Jsy/100 15.00 4.50
64 Jamie Moyer Jsy/100 20.00 6.00
65 Jason Varitek Jsy/100 50.00 15.00
66 Jay Gibbons Jsy/100 15.00 4.50
67 Jim Edmonds Jsy/5
68 Jim Palmer Jsy/100 30.00 9.00
69 Jim Rice Jsy/100 20.00 6.00
70 Joe Carter Jsy/50 25.00 7.50
71 Johan Santana Jsy/100 50.00 15.00
72 Jorge Posada Jsy/15 60.00 18.00
73 Josh Beckett Jsy/5
74 Juan Gonzalez Jsy/10
75 Keith Hernandez Jsy/100 20.00 6.00
76 Kirby Puckett Jsy/5
77 Luis Tiant Jsy/100 20.00 6.00
78 Magglio Ordonez Jsy/10
79 Manny Ramirez Jsy/5
80 Mariano Rivera Jsy/14
81 Mark Grace Jsy/10
82 Mark Mulder Jsy/20 30.00 9.00
83 Mark Prior Jsy/5
84 Mark Teixeira Jsy/10
85 Marty Marion Jsy/100 20.00 6.00
86 Mike Lowell Jsy/60 25.00 7.50
87 Mike Mussina Jsy/5
88 Mike Piazza Jsy/5
89 Nick Johnson Jsy/5
90 Nolan Ryan Jsy/10
92 Orlando Cepeda Bat/65 25.00 7.50
95 Paul O'Neill Bat/10
96 Pedro Martinez Jsy/5
97 Phil Niekro Jsy/25 30.00 9.00
98 Rafael Palmeiro Jsy/5
99 Ralph Kiner Bat/100 30.00 9.00
100 Randy Johnson Jsy/5
101 Red Schoendienst Jsy/60 25.00 7.50
102 Rickey Henderson Jsy/5
103 Robin Roberts Hat/50 25.00 7.50
104 Robin Ventura Jsy/65 40.00 12.00
105 Robin Yount Jsy/5
106 Rocco Baldelli Jsy/10
108 Ryne Sandberg Jsy/5
109 Sammy Sosa Jsy/10
110 Sean Casey Jsy/75 20.00 6.00
111 Shannon Stewart Jsy/100 15.00 4.50
112 Shawn Green Jsy/5
113 Stan Musial Jsy/5
114 Steve Carlton Jsy/50 40.00 12.00
115 Steve Garvey Bat/100 30.00 9.00
116 Todd Helton Jsy/5
117 Tommy John Jsy/100 20.00 6.00
118 Tony Gwynn Jsy/5
119 Tony Oliva Jsy/100 20.00 6.00
120 Torii Hunter Jsy/50 25.00 7.50
121 Trot Nixon Jsy/100 20.00 6.00
122 Troy Glaus Jsy/10
123 Vernon Wells Jsy/10
124 Vladimir Guerrero Jsy/55 60.00 18.00
125 Will Clark Jsy/100 50.00 15.00

2004 Absolute Memorabilia Absolutely Ink Combo Material

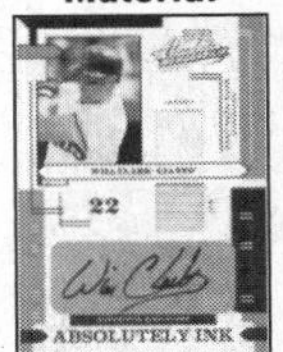

Nm-Mt Ex-Mt
*COMBO p/r 100: .5X TO 1.2X p/r 100
*COMBO p/r 50-65: .6X TO 1.5X p/r 75-100
*COMBO p/r 50-65: .5X TO 1.2X p/r 50-65
*COMBO p/r 25: .75X TO 2X p/r 100
PRINT RUNS B/WN 1-100 COPIES PER
NO PRICING ON QTY OF 10 OR LESS
PRIME PRINT RUNS B/WN 1-5 COPIES PER
NO PRIME PRICING DUE TO SCARCITY
RANDOM INSERTS IN PACKS
43 E.Chavez Bat-Jsy/15 40.00 12.00
74 J.Gonzalez Bat-Jsy/15 60.00 18.00

2004 Absolute Memorabilia Absolutely Ink Triple Material

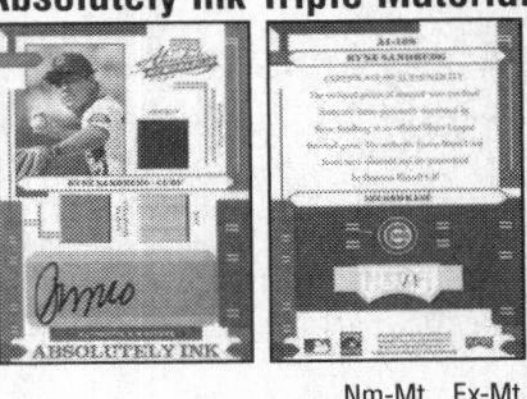

Nm-Mt Ex-Mt
RANDOM INSERTS IN PACKS
PRINT RUNS B/WN 1-10 COPIES PER
PRIME PRINT RUNS B/WN 1-5 COPIES PER
RANDOM INSERTS IN PACKS
NO PRICING DUE TO SCARCITY

2004 Absolute Memorabilia Fans of the Game

Nm-Mt Ex-Mt
RANDOM INSERTS IN RETAIL PACKS
251 Landon Donovan 2.00 .60
252 Jennie Finch 5.00 1.50
253 Bonnie Blair 2.00 .60
254 Dan Jansen 2.00 .60
255 Kerri Strug 3.00 .90

2004 Absolute Memorabilia Fans of the Game Autographs

Nm-Mt Ex-Mt
RANDOM INSERTS IN RETAIL PACKS

251 Landon Donovan 40.00 12.00
252 Jennie Finch 150.00 45.00
253 Bonnie Blair 40.00 12.00
254 Dan Jansen 30.00 9.00
255 Kerri Strug 50.00 15.00

2004 Absolute Memorabilia Marks of Fame

Nm-Mt Ex-Mt
STATED PRINT RUN 100 SERIAL #'d SETS
*SPECTRUM: .75X TO 2X BASIC
SPECTRUM PRINT RUN 25 SERIAL #'d SETS
RANDOM INSERTS IN PACKS
1 Nolan Ryan 20.00 6.00
2 Ernie Banks 8.00 2.40
3 Bob Feller 5.00 1.50
4 Duke Snider 8.00 2.40
5 Sammy Sosa 12.00 3.60
6 Whitey Ford 8.00 2.40
7 Steve Carlton 5.00 1.50
8 Tony Gwynn 10.00 3.00
9 Jim Bunning 5.00 1.50
10 Stan Musial 12.00 3.60
11 Cal Ripken 40.00 12.00
12 George Brett 20.00 6.00
13 Gary Carter 5.00 1.50
14 Jim Palmer 5.00 1.50
15 Gaylord Perry 5.00 1.50

2004 Absolute Memorabilia Marks of Fame Signature

Nm-Mt Ex-Mt
PRINT RUNS B/WN 10-100 COPIES PER
NO PRICING ON QTY OF 10 OR LESS
*SPECTRUM p/r 25: .6X TO 1.5X p/r 100
*SPECTRUM p/r 25: .5X TO 1.2X p/r 50
SPECTRUM PRINTS B/WN 1-25 COPIES PER
NO SPECT.PRICING ON QTY OF 10 OR LESS
RANDOM INSERTS IN PACKS
1 Nolan Ryan/50 150.00 45.00
2 Ernie Banks/100 50.00 15.00
3 Bob Feller/100 25.00 7.50
4 Duke Snider/100 25.00 7.50
5 Sammy Sosa/21 150.00 45.00
6 Whitey Ford/25 50.00 15.00
7 Steve Carlton/100 25.00 7.50
8 Tony Gwynn/25 80.00 24.00
9 Jim Bunning/100 25.00 7.50
10 Stan Musial/50 60.00 18.00
11 Cal Ripken/10
12 George Brett/25 120.00 36.00
13 Gary Carter/100 15.00 4.50
14 Jim Palmer/50 20.00 6.00
15 Gaylord Perry/100 15.00 4.50

2004 Absolute Memorabilia Signature Club

Nm-Mt Ex-Mt
RANDOM INSERTS IN PACKS
PRINT RUNS B/WN 5-50 COPIES PER
NO PRICING ON QTY OF 5 OR LESS
1 Sammy Sosa Bat/5
2 Gary Sheffield Bat/50 40.00 12.00
3 Vladimir Guerrero Bat/5
4 Will Clark Bat/50 60.00 18.00
5 Ernie Banks Bat/50 60.00 18.00

2004 Absolute Memorabilia Signature Material

Nm-Mt Ex-Mt
PRINT RUNS B/WN 25-50 COPIES PER
PRIME PRINT RUN 5 SERIAL #'d SETS
NO PRIME PRICING DUE TO SCARCITY
*COMBO: .5X TO 1.2X BASIC
COMBO PRINTS B/WN 25-50 COPIES PER
COMBO PRIME PRINT 5 SERIAL #'d SETS
NO COMBO PRIME PRICE DUE SCARCITY
RANDOM INSERTS IN PACKS
2 Gary Carter Jsy/50 25.00 7.50
3 Dale Murphy Jsy/50 40.00 12.00
4 Don Mattingly Jsy/25 120.00 36.00
5 Stan Musial Jsy/25 120.00 36.00

2004 Absolute Memorabilia Team Quad

Nm-Mt Ex-Mt
STATED PRINT RUN 100 SERIAL #'d SETS
*SPECTRUM: 1X TO 2.5X BASIC
SPECTRUM PRINT RUN 25 SERIAL #'d SETS
RANDOM INSERTS IN PACKS
1 Craig Biggio 8.00 2.40
Lance Berkman
Jeff Kent
Jeff Bagwell
2 Nomar Garciaparra 12.00 3.60
Manny Ramirez
Pedro Martinez
Trot Nixon
3 Paul Konerko 8.00 2.40
Carlos Lee
Magglio Ordonez
Frank Thomas
4 John Smoltz 8.00 2.40
Chipper Jones
Andruw Jones
Rafael Furcal
5 Garret Anderson 5.00 1.50
Troy Percival
Troy Glaus
Darin Erstad
6 Steve Finley 8.00 2.40
Brandon Webb
Randy Johnson
Luis Gonzalez
7 Paul Lo Duca 8.00 2.40
Hideo Nomo
Shawn Green
Kazuhisa Ishii
8 Larry Walker 8.00 2.40
Todd Helton
Jason Jennings
Preston Wilson
9 A.J. Burnett 5.00 1.50
Dontrelle Willis
Brad Penny
Josh Beckett
10 Jose Reyes 12.00 3.60
Jae Weong Seo
Tom Glavine
Mike Piazza
11 Bernie Williams 20.00 6.00
Derek Jeter
Jason Giambi
Alfonso Soriano
12 Rich Harden 5.00 1.50
Tim Hudson
Barry Zito
Mark Mulder
13 Kevin Millwood 8.00 2.40
Marlon Byrd
Jim Thome
Bobby Abreu
14 Edgar Renteria 15.00 4.50
Jim Edmonds
Albert Pujols
Scott Rolen
15 Roger Clemens 15.00 4.50
Andy Pettitte
Wade Miller
Roy Oswalt

2004 Absolute Memorabilia Team Quad Material

Nm-Mt Ex-Mt
STATED PRINT RUN 100 SERIAL #'d SETS
PRIME PRINT RUN 5 SERIAL #'d SETS
NO PRIME PRICING DUE TO SCARCITY
RANDOM INSERTS IN PACKS
ALL HAVE 4 JSY SWATCHES UNLESS NOTED
CARD 15 IS BAT-BAT-JSY-JSY
1 Jeff Kent 25.00 7.50
Lance Berkman
Craig Biggio
Jeff Bagwell
2 Nomar Garciaparra 40.00 12.00
Manny Ramirez
Pedro Martinez
Trot Nixon
3 Paul Konerko 25.00 7.50
Carlos Lee
Magglio Ordonez
Frank Thomas
4 John Smoltz 25.00 7.50
Chipper Jones
Andruw Jones
Rafael Furcal
5 Garret Anderson 15.00 4.50
Troy Percival
Troy Glaus
Darin Erstad
6 Steve Finley 25.00 7.50
Brandon Webb
Randy Johnson
Luis Gonzalez
7 Paul Lo Duca 25.00 7.50
Hideo Nomo
Shawn Green
Kazuhisa Ishii
8 Larry Walker 25.00 7.50
Todd Helton
Jason Jennings
Preston Wilson
9 A.J. Burnett 15.00 4.50
Dontrelle Willis
Brad Penny
Josh Beckett
10 Jose Reyes 25.00 7.50
Jae Weong Seo
Tom Glavine
Mike Piazza
11 Bernie Williams 40.00 12.00
Derek Jeter
Jason Giambi
Alfonso Soriano
12 Rich Harden 15.00 4.50
Tim Hudson
Barry Zito
Mark Mulder
13 Kevin Millwood 25.00 7.50
Marlon Byrd
Jim Thome
Bobby Abreu
14 Edgar Renteria 40.00 12.00
Jim Edmonds
Albert Pujols
Scott Rolen
15 Roger Clemens Bat 40.00 12.00
Andy Pettitte Bat
Wade Miller Jsy
Roy Oswalt Jsy

2004 Absolute Memorabilia Team Tandem

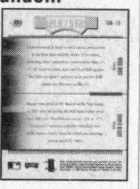

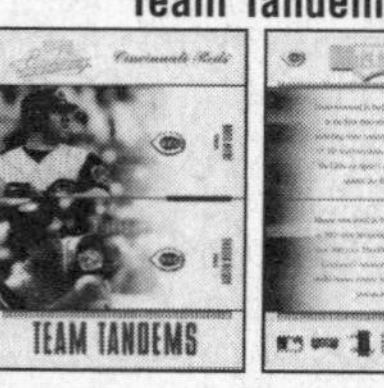

Nm-Mt Ex-Mt
STATED PRINT RUN 250 SERIAL #'d SETS
*SPECTRUM: 2X TO 5X BASIC
SPECTRUM PRINT RUN 25 SERIAL #'d SETS
RANDOM INSERTS IN PACKS
1 Vladimir Guerrero 4.00 1.20
Reggie Jackson
2 Dale Murphy 4.00 1.20
Chipper Jones
3 Gary Carter 5.00 1.50
Mike Piazza
4 Miguel Tejada 12.00 3.60
Cal Ripken
5 Gary Sheffield 6.00 1.80
Derek Jeter
6 Curt Schilling 4.00 1.20
Pedro Martinez
7 Roger Clemens 6.00 1.80
Andy Pettitte
8 Mike Sweeney 8.00 2.40
George Brett
9 Kazuhisa Ishii 4.00 1.20
Hideo Nomo
10 Austin Kearns 4.00 1.20
Adam Dunn
11 Miguel Cabrera 4.00 1.20
Dontrelle Willis
12 Don Mattingly 8.00 2.40
Derek Jeter
13 Barry Zito 2.50 .75
Eric Chavez
14 Jim Thome 6.00 1.80
Mike Schmidt
15 Albert Pujols 6.00 1.80
Stan Musial
16 Nolan Ryan 10.00 3.00
Alex Rodriguez
17 Kerry Wood 4.00 1.20
Mark Prior
18 Rafael Palmeiro 4.00 1.20
Jay Gibbons
19 Nomar Garciaparra 5.00 1.50
Manny Ramirez
20 Ivan Rodriguez 5.00 1.50
Mike Piazza

2004 Absolute Memorabilia Team Tandem Material

Nm-Mt Ex-Mt
STATED PRINT RUN 250 SERIAL #'d SETS
PRIME PRINT RUN 5 SERIAL #'d SETS
NO PRIME PRICING DUE TO SCARCITY
RANDOM INSERTS IN PACKS
1 Reggie Jackson Bat 10.00 3.00
Vladimir Guerrero Bat
2 Chipper Jones Jsy 10.00 3.00
Dale Murphy Jsy
3 Gary Carter Jsy 10.00 3.00
Mike Piazza Jsy
4 Miguel Tejada Bat 25.00 7.50
Cal Ripken Bat
5 Derek Jeter Bat 25.00 7.50
Gary Sheffield Bat
6 Curt Schilling Bat 10.00 3.00
Pedro Martinez Bat
7 Roger Clemens Bat 15.00 4.50
Andy Pettitte Bat
8 Mike Sweeney Jsy 15.00 4.50
George Brett Jsy
9 Kazuhisa Ishii Jsy 10.00 3.00
Hideo Nomo Jsy
10 Austin Kearns Jsy 10.00 3.00
Adam Dunn Jsy
11 Dontrelle Willis Jsy 10.00 3.00
Miguel Cabrera Jsy
12 Don Mattingly Jsy 40.00 12.00
Derek Jeter Jsy
13 Barry Zito Jsy 8.00 2.40
Eric Chavez Jsy
14 Jim Thome Jsy 20.00 6.00
Mike Schmidt Jsy
15 Albert Pujols Jsy 40.00 12.00
Stan Musial Jsy
16 Nolan Ryan Jsy 30.00 9.00
Alex Rodriguez Jsy
17 Mark Prior Jsy 15.00 4.50
Kerry Wood Jsy
18 Rafael Palmeiro Jsy 10.00 3.00
Jay Gibbons Jsy
19 Nomar Garciaparra Jsy 15.00 4.50
Manny Ramirez Jsy
20 Ivan Rodriguez Jsy 10.00 3.00
Mike Piazza Jsy

2004 Absolute Memorabilia Team Trio

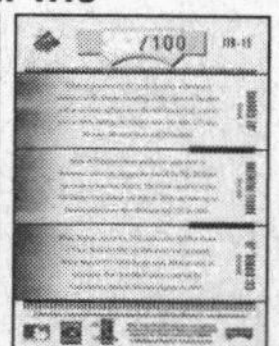

Nm-Mt Ex-Mt
STATED PRINT RUN 100 SERIAL #'d SETS
*SPECTRUM: 1X TO 2.5X BASIC
SPECTRUM PRINT RUN 25 SERIAL #'d SETS
RANDOM INSERTS IN PACKS
1 Kerry Wood 15.00 4.50
Mark Prior
Sammy Sosa
2 Hank Blalock 12.00 3.60
Mark Teixeira
Alex Rodriguez
3 Vernon Wells 5.00 1.50
Roy Halladay
Carlos Delgado
4 Mike Mussina 8.00 2.40
Jorge Posada
Mariano Rivera
5 Shannon Stewart 5.00 1.50
Torii Hunter
Jacque Jones
6 Carlos Beltran 8.00 2.40
Mike Sweeney
Angel Berroa
7 Dontrelle Willis 8.00 2.40
Miguel Cabrera
Josh Beckett
8 Jeff Bagwell 8.00 2.40
Craig Biggio
Lance Berkman
9 Nomar Garciaparra 12.00 3.60
Pedro Martinez
Manny Ramirez
10 Shawn Green 8.00 2.40
Kazuhisa Ishii
Hideo Nomo
11 Mark Mulder 5.00 1.50
Barry Zito
Tim Hudson
12 Jim Edmonds 15.00 4.50
Scott Rolen
Albert Pujols
13 Cal Ripken 25.00 7.50
Jay Gibbons
Rafael Palmeiro
14 Sammy Sosa 15.00 4.50
Mark Grace
Ryne Sandberg
15 Nolan Ryan 25.00 7.50
Roger Clemens
Randy Johnson

2004 Absolute Memorabilia Team Trio Material

Nm-Mt Ex-Mt
STATED PRINT RUN 100 SERIAL #'d SETS
CARD 15 PRINT RUN 25 SERIAL #'d CARDS
PRIME PRINT RUN 5 SERIAL #'d SETS
NO PRIME PRICING DUE TO SCARCITY
RANDOM INSERTS IN PACKS
ALL HAVE 3 JSY SWATCHES UNLESS NOTED
CARD 15 HAS 4 FIELD GLOVE SWATCHES
1 Sammy Sosa 40.00 12.00
Mark Prior
Kerry Wood
2 Hank Blalock 15.00 4.50
Mark Teixeira
Alex Rodriguez
3 Vernon Wells 10.00 3.00
Roy Halladay
Carlos Delgado
4 Mike Mussina 30.00 9.00
Jorge Posada
Mariano Rivera
5 Shannon Stewart 10.00 3.00
Jacque Jones
Torii Hunter
6 Carlos Beltran 15.00 4.50
Mike Sweeney
Angel Berroa
7 Dontrelle Willis 15.00 4.50
Miguel Cabrera
Josh Beckett
8 Jeff Bagwell 15.00 4.50
Craig Biggio
Lance Berkman
9 Nomar Garciaparra 25.00 7.50
Pedro Martinez
Manny Ramirez
10 Shawn Green 15.00 4.50
Kazuhisa Ishii
Hideo Nomo
11 Mark Mulder 10.00 3.00
Barry Zito
Tim Hudson
12 Jim Edmonds 25.00 7.50
Scott Rolen
Albert Pujols
13 Cal Ripken 50.00 15.00
Jay Gibbons
Rafael Palmeiro
14 Sammy Sosa 40.00 12.00
Mark Grace
Ryne Sandberg
15 Roger Clemens 100.00 30.00
Nolan Ryan
Randy Johnson/25

2004 Absolute Memorabilia Tools of the Trade Blue

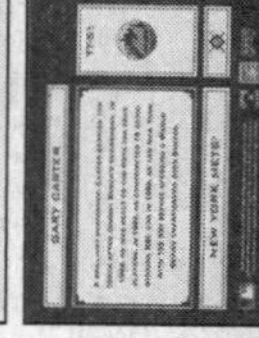

Nm-Mt Ex-Mt
STATED PRINT RUN 250 SERIAL #'d SETS
BLACK PRINT RUN 1 SERIAL #'d SET
NO BLACK PRICING DUE TO SCARCITY
BLACK SPECTRUM PRINT RUN 1 #'d SET
NO BLACK SPEC.PRICING DUE SCARCITY
*BLUE SPEC: .75X TO 2X BASIC
BLUE SPECTRUM PRINT RUN 125 #'d SETS
*GREEN: .6X TO 1.5X BASIC
GREEN PRINT RUN 150 SERIAL #'d SETS
*GREEN SPEC: 1.5X TO 4X BASIC
GREEN SPECTRUM PRINT RUN 50 #'d SETS
*RED: .5X TO 1.2X BASIC
RED PRINT RUN 200 SERIAL #'d SETS
*RED SPECTRUM: 1X TO 2.5X BASIC
RED SPECTRUM PRINT RUN 100 #'d SETS
RANDOM INSERTS IN PACKS
1 Adam Dunn H 4.00 1.20
2 Adam Dunn A 4.00 1.20
3 Alan Trammell 2.50 .75
4 Albert Pujols H 6.00 1.80
5 Albert Pujols A 6.00 1.80
6 Alex Rodriguez M's 5.00 1.50
7 Alex Rodriguez Rgr H 5.00 1.50
8 Alex Rodriguez Rgr Alt 5.00 1.50
9 Alfonso Soriano 4.00 1.20
10 Andre Dawson 2.50 .75
11 Andruw Jones H 2.50 .75
12 Andruw Jones A 2.50 .75
13 Andy Pettitte H 4.00 1.20
14 Andy Pettitte A 4.00 1.20
15 Angel Berroa 2.50 .75
16 Aubrey Huff 2.50 .75
17 Austin Kearns 2.50 .75
18 Barry Zito Alt 2.50 .75
19 Barry Zito A 2.50 .75
20 Bernie Williams 4.00 1.20
21 Bobby Abreu 2.50 .75
22 Brandon Webb 2.50 .75
23 Cal Ripken H 12.00 3.60
24 Cal Ripken A 12.00 3.60
25 Cal Ripken Alt 12.00 3.60
26 Carlos Beltran 4.00 1.20
27 Carlos Delgado H 2.50 .75
28 Carlos Delgado A 2.50 .75
29 Carlos Lee 2.50 .75
30 Chipper Jones H 4.00 1.20
31 Chipper Jones A 4.00 1.20
32 Craig Biggio H 2.50 .75
33 Craig Biggio A 2.50 .75
34 Curt Schilling D'backs 2.50 .75
35 Curt Schilling Phils 2.50 .75
36 Dale Murphy H 4.00 1.20
37 Dale Murphy A 4.00 1.20
38 Darryl Strawberry 2.50 .75
39 Derek Jeter H 6.00 1.80
40 Derek Jeter A 6.00 1.80
41 Don Mattingly H 8.00 2.40
42 Don Mattingly A 8.00 2.40
43 Dontrelle Willis H 2.50 .75
44 Dontrelle Willis A 2.50 .75
45 Dwight Gooden 2.50 .75
46 Edgar Martinez 4.00 1.20
47 Eric Chavez 2.50 .75
48 Frank Thomas A 4.00 1.20
49 Frank Thomas Alt 4.00 1.20
50 Garret Anderson 2.50 .75
51 Gary Carter 2.50 .75
52 Gary Sheffield 2.50 .75

53 George Brett H 8.00 2.40
54 George Brett A 8.00 2.40
55 Greg Maddux 5.00 1.50
56 Hank Blalock 2.50 .75
57 Hideo Nomo 4.00 1.20
58 Ivan Rodriguez Marlins 4.00 1.20
59 Ivan Rodriguez Rgr 4.00 1.20
60 Jacque Jones 2.50 .75
61 Jae Weong Seo 2.50 .75
62 Jason Giambi Yanks 2.50 .75
63 Jason Giambi A's 2.50 .75
64 Javy Lopez 2.50 .75
65 Jay Gibbons 2.50 .75
66 Jeff Bagwell A 4.00 1.20
67 Jeff Bagwell Alt 4.00 1.20
68 Jeff Kent 2.50 .75
69 Jim Edmonds 2.50 .75
70 Jim Thome 4.00 1.20
71 Jorge Posada 4.00 1.20
72 Jose Canseco 4.00 1.20
73 Jose Reyes 2.50 .75
74 Josh Beckett 2.50 .75
75 Juan Gonzalez 4.00 1.20
76 Kazuhisa Ishii 2.50 .75
77 Kerry Wood H 4.00 1.20
78 Kerry Wood Alt 4.00 1.20
79 Kirby Puckett 4.00 1.20
80 Lance Berkman 2.50 .75
81 Lou Brock 4.00 1.20
82 Luis Castillo 2.50 .75
83 Luis Gonzalez 2.50 .75
84 Magglio Ordonez 2.50 .75
85 Manny Ramirez Sox 4.00 1.20
86 Manny Ramirez Indians 4.00 1.20
87 Marcus Giles 2.50 .75
88 Mark Grace 4.00 1.20
89 Mark Mulder 2.50 .75
90 Mark Prior H 4.00 1.20
91 Mark Prior A 4.00 1.20
92 Mark Teixeira 2.50 .75
93 Marlon Byrd 2.50 .75
94 Miguel Cabrera 4.00 1.20
95 Miguel Tejada 2.50 .75
96 Mike Lowell 2.50 .75
97 Mike Mussina O's 4.00 1.20
98 Mike Mussina Yanks 4.00 1.20
99 Mike Piazza Marlins 5.00 1.50
100 Mike Piazza Dodgers 5.00 1.50
101 Mike Piazza Mets 5.00 1.50
102 Mike Schmidt H 6.00 1.80
103 Mike Schmidt A 6.00 1.80
104 Mike Sweeney 2.50 .75
105 Nick Johnson 2.50 .75
106 Nolan Ryan Angels 10.00 3.00
107 Nolan Ryan Astros 10.00 3.00
108 Nolan Ryan Rangers 10.00 3.00
109 Nomar Garciaparra H 5.00 1.50
110 Nomar Garciaparra A 5.00 1.50
111 Pat Burrell 2.50 .75
112 Paul Lo Duca 2.50 .75
113 Pedro Martinez Sox 4.00 1.20
114 Pedro Martinez Expos 4.00 1.20
115 Preston Wilson 2.50 .75
116 Rafael Palmeiro O's 4.00 1.20
117 Rafael Palmeiro Rgr 4.00 1.20
118 Randy Johnson D'backs 4.00 1.20
119 Randy Johnson M's 4.00 1.20
120 Richie Sexson 2.50 .75
121 Rickey Henderson A's 4.00 1.20
122 Rickey Henderson Padres 4.00 1.20
123 Rickey Henderson M's 4.00 1.20
124 Roberto Alomar 4.00 1.20
125 Rocco Baldelli 2.50 .75
126 Rod Carew 4.00 1.20
127 Roger Clemens Sox 6.00 1.80
128 Roger Clemens Yanks 6.00 1.80
129 Roy Halladay 2.50 .75
130 Roy Oswalt 2.50 .75
131 Ryne Sandberg 6.00 1.80
132 Sammy Sosa H 5.00 1.50
133 Sammy Sosa A 5.00 1.50
134 Sammy Sosa Sox 5.00 1.50
135 Scott Rolen 4.00 1.20
136 Shawn Green 2.50 .75
137 Steve Carlton 4.00 1.20
138 Tim Hudson 2.50 .75
139 Todd Helton H 4.00 1.20
140 Todd Helton A 4.00 1.20
141 Tom Glavine Braves 4.00 1.20
142 Tom Glavine Mets 4.00 1.20
143 Tony Gwynn A 5.00 1.50
144 Tony Gwynn Alt 5.00 1.50
145 Torii Hunter 2.50 .75
146 Trot Nixon 2.50 .75
147 Troy Glaus 2.50 .75
148 Vernon Wells 2.50 .75
149 Vladimir Guerrero 4.00 1.20
150 Will Clark 4.00 1.20

2004 Absolute Memorabilia Tools of the Trade Signature Blue Spectrum

Nm-Mt Ex-Mt
PRINT RUNS B/WN 1-100 COPIES PER
NO PRICING ON QTY OF 10 OR LESS
BLACK PRINT RUN 1 SERIAL #'d SET
NO BLACK PRICING DUE TO SCARCITY
GREEN PRINT RUN B/WN 1-10 COPIES PER
NO GREEN PRICING DUE TO SCARCITY
*RED p/r 50: .5X TO 1.2X BLUE p/r 100
*RED p/r 25: .6X TO 1.5X BLUE p/r 100
*RED p/r 23-25: .5X TO 1.2X BLUE p/r 50
*RED p/r 25: .4X TO 1X BLUE p/r 25..
RED PRINT RUNS B/WN 1-50 COPIES PER
NO RED PRICING ON QTY OF 11 OR LESS
RANDOM INSERTS IN PACKS
1 Adam Dunn H/10
2 Adam Dunn A/10
3 Alan Trammell/100 15.00 4.50
4 Albert Pujols H/1
5 Albert Pujols A/1
10 Andre Dawson/100 15.00 4.50
11 Andruw Jones H/1
12 Andruw Jones A/1
13 Andy Pettitte H/1
14 Andy Pettitte A/1
15 Angel Berroa/100 10.00 3.00
16 Aubrey Huff/100 15.00 4.50
17 Austin Kearns/100 15.00 4.50
18 Barry Zito Alt/1
19 Barry Zito A/1
20 Bernie Williams/1
22 Brandon Webb/100 10.00 3.00
23 Cal Ripken H/8
24 Cal Ripken A/8
25 Cal Ripken Alt/8
26 Carlos Beltran/100 40.00 12.00
29 Carlos Lee/100 15.00 4.50
30 Chipper Jones H/10
31 Chipper Jones A/10
32 Craig Biggio H/1
33 Craig Biggio A/1
34 Curt Schilling D'backs/1
35 Curt Schilling Phils/1
36 Dale Murphy H/50 40.00 12.00
37 Dale Murphy A/50 40.00 12.00
38 Darryl Strawberry/50 25.00 7.50
41 Don Mattingly H/50 80.00 24.00
42 Don Mattingly A/50 80.00 24.00
43 Dontrelle Willis H/25 30.00 9.00
44 Dontrelle Willis A/25 30.00 9.00
45 Dwight Gooden/50 25.00 7.50
46 Edgar Martinez/25 50.00 15.00
47 Eric Chavez/1
48 Frank Thomas A/25 60.00 18.00
49 Frank Thomas Alt/25 60.00 18.00
50 Garret Anderson/100 15.00 4.50
51 Gary Carter/100 15.00 4.50
52 Gary Sheffield/10
53 George Brett H/5
54 George Brett A/5
56 Hank Blalock/10
57 Hideo Nomo/1
60 Jacque Jones/50 25.00 7.50
61 Jae Weong Seo/25 30.00 9.00
65 Jay Gibbons/50 15.00 4.50
66 Jeff Bagwell A/5
67 Jeff Bagwell Alt/5
69 Jim Edmonds/25 50.00 15.00
71 Jorge Posada/25 50.00 15.00
73 Jose Reyes/25 30.00 9.00
74 Josh Beckett/5
75 Juan Gonzalez/20 50.00 15.00
76 Kazuhisa Ishii/5
77 Kerry Wood H/25 60.00 18.00
78 Kerry Wood Alt/25 60.00 18.00
79 Kirby Puckett/10
80 Lance Berkman/10
81 Lou Brock/10 25.00 7.50
82 Luis Castillo/10
84 Magglio Ordonez/50 25.00 7.50
85 Manny Ramirez Sox/1
86 Manny Ramirez Indians/1
87 Marcus Giles/50 25.00 7.50
88 Mark Grace/25 50.00 15.00
89 Mark Mulder/100 15.00 4.50
90 Mark Prior H/50 80.00 24.00
91 Mark Prior A/50 80.00 24.00
92 Mark Teixeira/50 40.00 12.00
93 Marlon Byrd/50 15.00 4.50
94 Miguel Cabrera/100 25.00 7.50
96 Mike Lowell/1
99 Mike Piazza Marlins/5
100 Mike Piazza Dodgers/5
101 Mike Piazza Mets/5
102 Mike Schmidt H/25 100.00 30.00
103 Mike Schmidt A/25 100.00 30.00
105 Nick Johnson/1
106 Nolan Ryan Angels/25 150.00 45.00
107 Nolan Ryan Astros/25 150.00 45.00
108 Nolan Ryan Rangers/25 150.00 45.00
112 Paul Lo Duca/50 25.00 7.50
115 Preston Wilson/100 15.00 4.50
116 Rafael Palmeiro O's/1
117 Rafael Palmeiro Rgr/1
118 Randy Johnson D'backs/1
119 Randy Johnson M's/1
121 Rickey Henderson A's/10
122 Rickey Henderson Padres/5
123 Rickey Henderson M's/5
124 Roberto Alomar/10
125 Rocco Baldelli/10
126 Rod Carew/10
129 Roy Halladay/25 20.00 6.00
130 Roy Oswalt/25 30.00 9.00
131 Ryne Sandberg/5
132 Sammy Sosa H/5
133 Sammy Sosa A/5
134 Sammy Sosa Sox/5
135 Scott Rolen/50 50.00 15.00
136 Shawn Green/1
137 Steve Carlton/50 40.00 12.00
138 Tim Hudson/10
139 Todd Helton H/1
140 Todd Helton A/1
141 Tom Glavine Braves/10
142 Tom Glavine Mets/10
143 Tony Gwynn A/25 80.00 24.00
144 Tony Gwynn Alt/25 80.00 24.00
145 Torii Hunter/50 25.00 7.50
146 Trot Nixon/25 30.00 9.00
147 Troy Glaus/1
148 Vernon Wells/10
149 Vladimir Guerrero/25 60.00 18.00
150 Will Clark/50 50.00 15.00

2004 Absolute Memorabilia Tools of the Trade Material Combo

Nm-Mt Ex-Mt
PRINT RUNS B/WN 25-250 COPIES PER
SINGLE PRINT RUNS B/WN 1-5 COPIES PER
NO SINGLE PRICING DUE TO SCARCITY
SINGLE PS PRINT RUN 1 SERIAL #'d SET

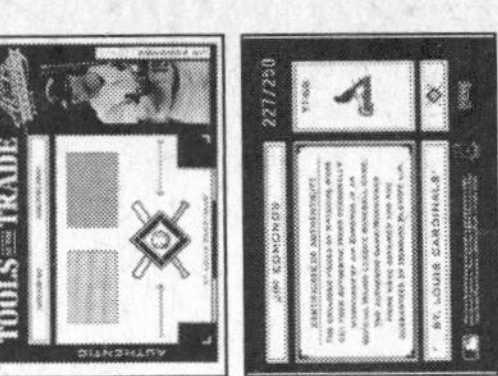

NO SINGLE PS PRICING DUE TO SCARCITY
*COMBO PS p/r 25: 1.5X TO 4X COM.p/r 250
*COMBO PS p/r 25: 1X TO 2.5X COM.p/r 100
COMBO PS PRINT RUNS B/WN 1-25 PER
NO COMBO PS PRICING ON 10 OR LESS
*TRIO p/r 100: .6X TO 1.5X COMBO p/r 250
*TRIO p/r 100: .5X TO 1.2X COMBO p/r 100
*TRIO p/r 50: 1X TO 2.5X COMBO p/r 250
*TRIO p/r 50: .6X TO 1.5X COMBO p/r 100
*TRIO p/r 25: 1.5X TO 4X COMBO p/r 250
*TRIO p/r 25: .75X TO 2X COMBO p/r 100
TRIO PRINT RUNS B/WN 5-100 COPIES PER
NO TRIO PRICING ON QTY OF 10 OR LESS
TRIO PS PRINT RUNS B/WN 1-10 PER
NO TRIO PS PRICING DUE TO SCARCITY
*QUAD p/r 50: 1.5X TO 4X COMBO p/r 250
*QUAD p/r 50: 1.25X TO 3X COMBO p/r 100
*QUAD p/r 50: .6X TO 1.5X COMBO p/r 25
*QUAD p/r 25: 2X TO 5X COMBO p/r 250
*QUAD p/r 25: 1X TO 2.5X COMBO p/r 100
QUAD PRINT RUNS B/WN 1-50 COPIES PER
NO QUAD PRICING ON QTY OF 10 OR LESS
QUAD PS PRINT RUNS B/WN 1-10 PER
NO QUAD PS PRICING DUE TO SCARCITY
*FIVE p/r 25: 2.5X TO 6X COMBO p/r 250
*FIVE p/r 25: 2X TO 5X COMBO p/r 100
*FIVE p/r 25: .75X TO 2X COMBO p/r 25
FIVE PRINT RUNS B/WN 10-25 COPIES PER
NO FIVE PRICING ON QTY OF 10 OR LESS
FIVE PS PRINT RUNS B/WN 1-5 COPIES PER
NO FIVE PS PRICING DUE TO SCARCITY
*SIX p/r 25: 3X TO 8X COMBO p/r 250
*SIX p/r 25: 2.5X TO 6X COMBO p/r 100
SIX PRINT RUNS B/WN 5-25 COPIES PER
NO SIX PRICING ON QTY OF 5 OR LESS
SIX PS PRINT RUNS B/WN 1-5 COPIES PER
NO SIX PS PRICING DUE TO SCARCITY
RANDOM INSERTS IN PACKS
1 A.Dunn H Bat-Jsy/250 8.00 2.40
2 A.Dunn A Bat-Jsy/250 8.00 2.40
3 A.Trammell Bat-Jsy/250 6.00 1.80
4 A.Pujols H Bat-Jsy/250 20.00 6.00
5 A.Pujols A Bat-Jsy/250 20.00 6.00
6 A.Rod M's Bat-Jsy/250 10.00 3.00
7 A.Rod Rgr H Bat-Jsy/250 10.00 3.00
8 A.Rod Rgr Alt Bat-Jsy/250 10.00 3.00
9 A.Soriano Bat-Jsy/100 10.00 3.00
10 A.Dawson Bat-Jsy/250 6.00 1.80
11 A.Jones H Bat-Jsy/100 8.00 2.40
12 A.Jones A Bat-Jsy/250 6.00 1.80
13 A.Pettitte H Bat-Jsy/100 10.00 3.00
14 A.Pettitte A Bat-Jsy/100 10.00 3.00
15 A.Berroa Bat-Jsy/250 5.00 1.50
16 A.Huff Bat-Jsy/250 6.00 1.80
17 A.Kearns Bat-Jsy/250 6.00 1.80
18 B.Zito Alt Bat-Jsy/250 6.00 1.80
19 B.Zito A Bat-Jsy/250 6.00 1.80
20 B.Williams Bat-Jsy/250 8.00 2.40
21 B.Abreu Bat-Jsy/250 6.00 1.80
22 B.Webb Bat-Jsy/250 5.00 1.50
23 C.Ripken H Bat-Jsy/250 30.00 9.00
24 C.Ripken A Bat-Jsy/250 30.00 9.00
25 C.Ripken Alt Bat-Jsy/250 30.00 9.00
26 C.Beltran Bat-Jsy/250 8.00 2.40
27 C.Delgado H Bat-Jsy/250 6.00 1.80
28 C.Delgado A Bat-Jsy/250 6.00 1.80
29 C.Lee Bat-Jsy/250 6.00 1.80
30 C.Jones H Bat-Jsy/250 10.00 3.00
31 C.Jones A Bat-Jsy/250 10.00 3.00
32 C.Biggio H Bat-Jsy/250 6.00 1.80
33 C.Biggio A Bat-Jsy/100 8.00 2.40
34 C.Schill D'backs Bat-Jsy/250 6.00 1.80
35 C.Schill Phils Bat-Jsy/250 6.00 1.80
36 D.Murphy H Bat-Jsy/250 8.00 2.40
37 D.Murphy A Bat-Jsy/100 10.00 3.00
38 D.Strawberry Bat-Jsy/250 6.00 1.80
39 D.Jeter H Bat-Jsy/100 40.00 12.00
40 D.Jeter A Bat-Jsy/100 40.00 12.00
41 D.Mattingly H Bat-Jsy/100 25.00 7.50
42 D.Mattingly A Bat-Jsy/100 25.00 7.50
43 D.Willis H Bat-Jsy/250 6.00 1.80
44 D.Willis A Bat-Jsy/250 6.00 1.80
45 D.Gooden Bat-Jsy/250 6.00 1.80
46 E.Martinez Bat-Jsy/250 8.00 2.40
47 E.Chavez Bat-Jsy/250 6.00 1.80
48 F.Thomas A Bat-Jsy/250 10.00 3.00
49 F.Thomas Alt Bat-Jsy/250 10.00 3.00
50 G.Anderson Bat-Jsy/250 6.00 1.80
51 G.Carter Bat-Jsy/250 6.00 1.80
52 G.Sheffield Bat-Jsy/250 6.00 1.80
53 G.Brett H Bat-Jsy/250 20.00 6.00
54 G.Brett A Bat-Jsy/250 20.00 6.00
55 G.Maddux Bat-Jsy/250 12.00 3.60
56 H.Blalock Bat-Jsy/250 6.00 1.80
57 H.Nomo Bat-Jsy/250 12.00 3.60
58 I.Rod Marlins Bat-Jsy/250 10.00 3.00
59 I.Rod Rgr Bat-Jsy/250 10.00 3.00
60 J.Jones Bat-Jsy/250 6.00 1.80
62 J.Giambi Yanks Bat-Jsy/250 6.00 1.80
63 J.Giambi A's Bat-Jsy/250 6.00 1.80
64 J.Lopez Bat-Jsy/250 6.00 1.80
65 J.Gibbons Bat-Jsy/250 5.00 1.50
66 J.Bagwell A Bat-Jsy/250 8.00 2.40
67 J.Bagwell Alt Bat-Jsy/250 8.00 2.40
68 J.Kent Bat-Jsy/250 6.00 1.80
69 J.Edmonds Bat-Jsy/250 6.00 1.80
70 J.Thome Bat-Jsy/250 10.00 3.00
71 J.Posada Bat-Jsy/250 8.00 2.40
72 J.Canseco Bat-Jsy/250 10.00 3.00
73 J.Reyes Bat-Jsy/250 6.00 1.80
74 J.Beckett Bat-Jsy/250 6.00 1.80
75 J.Gonzalez Bat-Jsy/250 10.00 3.00
76 K.Ishii Bat-Jsy/250 6.00 1.80
77 K.Wood H Bat-Jsy/250 10.00 3.00
78 K.Wood Alt Bat-Jsy/250 10.00 3.00
79 K.Puckett Bat-Jsy/250 15.00 4.50
80 L.Berkman Bat-Jsy/250 6.00 1.80
81 L.Brock Bat-Jsy/250 8.00 2.40
82 L.Castillo Bat-Jsy/250 5.00 1.50
83 L.Gonzalez Bat-Jsy/250 6.00 1.80
84 M.Ordonez Bat-Jsy/250 6.00 1.80
85 M.Ramirez Sox Bat-Jsy/250 8.00 2.40
86 M.Ram Indians Bat-Jsy/250 8.00 2.40
87 M.Giles Bat-Jsy/25 15.00 4.50
88 M.Grace Bat-Jsy/250 8.00 2.40
89 M.Mulder Bat-Jsy/250 6.00 1.80
90 M.Prior H Bat-Jsy/100 10.00 3.00
91 M.Prior A Bat-Jsy/100 10.00 3.00
92 M.Teixeira Bat-Jsy/250 6.00 1.80
93 M.Byrd Bat-Jsy/250 5.00 1.50
94 M.Cabrera Bat-Jsy/250 8.00 2.40
95 M.Tejada Bat-Jsy/250 6.00 1.80
96 M.Lowell Bat-Jsy/250 6.00 1.80
97 M.Muss O's Jsy-Pants/250 8.00 2.40
98 M.Muss Yanks Jsy-Jsy/250 8.00 2.40
99 M.Piazza Marlins Bat-Jsy/250 12.00 3.60
100 M.Piaz Dodgers Bat-Jsy/250 12.00 3.60
101 M.Piazza Mets Bat-Jsy/250 12.00 3.60
102 M.Schmidt H Bat-Jsy/100 20.00 6.00
103 M.Schmidt A Bat-Jsy/100 20.00 6.00
104 M.Sweeney Bat-Jsy/250 6.00 1.80
105 N.Johnson Bat-Jsy/250 5.00 1.50
106 N.Ryan Angels Jkt-Jsy/250 25.00 7.50
107 N.Ryan Astros Jkt-Jsy/250 25.00 7.50
108 N.Ryan Rgr Jsy-Pants/250 25.00 7.50
109 N.Garciaparra H Bat-Jsy/250 12.00 3.60
110 N.Garciaparra A Bat-Jsy/250 12.00 3.60
111 P.Burrell Bat-Jsy/250 6.00 1.80
112 P.Lo Duca Bat-Jsy/250 6.00 1.80
113 P.Martinez Sox Bat-Jsy/250 10.00 3.00
114 P.Mart Expos Bat-Jsy/250 10.00 3.00
115 P.Wilson Bat-Jsy/250 6.00 1.80
116 R.Palmeiro O's Bat-Jsy/250 8.00 2.40
117 R.Palmeiro Rgr Bat-Jsy/250 8.00 2.40
118 R.John D'backs Bat-Jsy/250 10.00 3.00
119 R.Johnson M's Bat-Jsy/250 10.00 3.00
120 R.Sexson Bat-Jsy/250 6.00 1.80
121 R.Hend A's Bat-Jsy/250 10.00 3.00
122 R.Hend Padres Bat-Jsy/250 10.00 3.00
123 R.Hend M's Bat-Jsy/250 10.00 3.00
124 R.Alomar Bat-Jsy/250 8.00 2.40
125 R.Baldelli Bat-Jsy/250 6.00 1.80
126 R.Carew Bat-Jsy/250 8.00 2.40
127 R.Clemens Sox Bat-Jsy/250 15.00 4.50
128 R.Clem Yanks Bat-Jsy/250 15.00 4.50
129 R.Halladay Jsy-Jsy/250 5.00 1.50
130 R.Oswalt Bat-Jsy/250 6.00 1.80
131 R.Sandberg Bat-Jsy/250 15.00 4.50
132 S.Sosa H Bat-Jsy/250 12.00 3.60
133 S.Sosa A Bat-Jsy/250 12.00 3.60
134 S.Sosa Sox Bat-Jsy/250 12.00 3.60
135 S.Rolen Bat-Jsy/250 10.00 3.00
136 S.Green Bat-Jsy/250 6.00 1.80
137 S.Carlton Bat-Jsy/250 6.00 1.80
138 T.Hudson Bat-Jsy/250 6.00 1.80
139 T.Helton H Bat-Jsy/250 8.00 2.40
140 T.Helton A Bat-Jsy/250 8.00 2.40
141 T.Glav Braves Bat-Jsy/250 8.00 2.40
142 T.Glav Mets Bat-Jsy/250 8.00 2.40
143 T.Gwynn A Bat-Jsy/250 15.00 4.50
144 T.Gwynn Alt Bat-Jsy/250 15.00 4.50
145 T.Hunter Bat-Jsy/250 6.00 1.80
146 T.Nixon Bat-Jsy/250 6.00 1.80
147 T.Glaus Bat-Jsy/250 6.00 1.80
148 V.Wells Bat-Jsy/250 6.00 1.80
149 V.Guerrero Bat-Jsy/250 10.00 3.00
150 W.Clark Bat-Jsy/250 10.00 3.00

2004 Absolute Memorabilia Tools of the Trade Material Signature Single

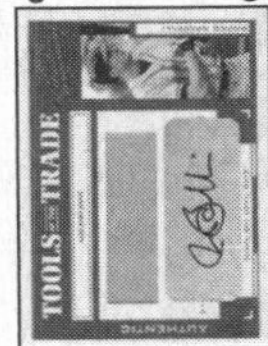

Nm-Mt Ex-Mt
PRINT RUNS B/WN 1-50 COPIES PER
NO PRICING ON QTY OF 11 OR LESS
SINGLE PS PRINT RUNS B/WN 1-5 PER
NO SINGLE PS PRICING DUE TO SCARCITY
*COMBO p/r 25: .5X TO 1.2X SINGLE p/r 50
COMBO PRINT RUNS B/WN 1-25 PER
NO COMBO PRICES ON QTY OF 10 OR LESS
COMBO PS PRINT RUNS B/WN 1-5 PER
NO COMBO PS PRICING DUE TO SCARCITY
TRIO PRINT RUNS B/WN 1-10 COPIES PER
NO TRIO PRICING DUE TO SCARCITY
TRIO PS PRINT RUNS B/WN 1-5 PER
NO TRIO PS PRICING DUE TO SCARCITY
QUAD PRINT RUNS B/WN 1-10 COPIES PER
NO QUAD PRICING DUE TO SCARCITY
QUAD PS PRINT RUNS B/WN 1-5 PER
NO QUAD PS PRICING DUE TO SCARCITY
RANDOM INSERTS IN PACKS
1 Adam Dunn H Jsy/25 50.00 15.00
2 Adam Dunn A Jsy/25 50.00 15.00
3 Alan Trammell Jsy/25 50.00 15.00
4 Albert Pujols H Jsy/5
5 Albert Pujols A Jsy/5
6 Alex Rodriguez M's Jsy/5
7 Alex Rodriguez Rgr H Jsy/5
8 Alex Rodriguez Rgr Alt Jsy/5
10 Andre Dawson Jsy/25 30.00 9.00
11 Andruw Jones H Jsy/5
12 Andruw Jones A Jsy/5
15 Angel Berroa Jsy/50 15.00 4.50
16 Aubrey Huff Jsy/1
17 Austin Kearns Jsy/28 30.00 9.00
18 Barry Zito Alt Jsy/1
19 Barry Zito A Jsy/1
20 Bernie Williams Jsy/5
21 Bobby Abreu Jsy/25 30.00 9.00
22 Brandon Webb Jsy/25 25.00 7.50
23 Cal Ripken H Jsy/8
24 Cal Ripken A Pants/8
25 Cal Ripken Alt Jsy/8
26 Carlos Beltran Jsy/15 100.00 30.00
29 Carlos Lee Jsy/25 30.00 9.00
30 Chipper Jones H Jsy/10
31 Chipper Jones A Jsy/10
32 Craig Biggio H Jsy/7
33 Craig Biggio A Jsy/7
34 Curt Schilling D'backs Jsy/1
35 Curt Schilling Phils Jsy/1
36 Dale Murphy H Jsy/25 50.00 15.00
37 Dale Murphy A Jsy/25 50.00 15.00
38 Darryl Strawberry Jsy/39 25.00 7.50
41 Don Mattingly H Jsy/5
42 Don Mattingly A Jsy/5
43 Dontrelle Willis H Jsy/25 30.00 9.00
44 Dontrelle Willis A Jsy/25 30.00 9.00
45 Dwight Gooden Jsy/16 40.00 12.00
46 Edgar Martinez Jsy/11
47 Eric Chavez Jsy/3
48 Frank Thomas A Jsy/5
49 Frank Thomas Alt Jsy/5
50 Garret Anderson Jsy/16 40.00 12.00
51 Gary Carter Jsy/8
52 Gary Sheffield Jsy/11
53 George Brett H Jsy/5
54 George Brett A Jsy/5
55 Greg Maddux Jsy/11
56 Hank Blalock Jsy/9
57 Hideo Nomo Jsy/1
60 Jacque Jones Jsy/1
61 Jae Weong Seo Jsy/25 25.00 7.50
65 Jay Gibbons Jsy/5
66 Jeff Bagwell A Jsy/5
67 Jeff Bagwell Alt Jsy/5
69 Jim Edmonds Jsy/5
71 Jorge Posada Jsy/20 50.00 15.00
72 Jose Canseco Jsy/5
74 Josh Beckett Jsy/21 50.00 15.00
75 Juan Gonzalez Jsy/5
76 Kazuhisa Ishii Jsy/5
79 Kirby Puckett Jsy/5
80 Lance Berkman Jsy/5
81 Lou Brock Jsy/5
82 Luis Castillo Jsy/25 25.00 7.50
84 Magglio Ordonez Jsy/5
85 Manny Ramirez Sox Jsy/5
86 Manny Ramirez Indians Jsy/5
88 Mark Grace Jsy/5
89 Mark Mulder Jsy/20 30.00 9.00
90 Mark Prior H Jsy/10
91 Mark Prior A Jsy/10
92 Mark Teixeira Jsy/10
93 Marlon Byrd Jsy/29 25.00 7.50
94 Miguel Cabrera Jsy/20 50.00 15.00
96 Mike Lowell Jsy/19 40.00 12.00
97 Mike Mussina O's Jsy/5
98 Mike Mussina Yanks Jsy/5
99 Mike Piazza Marlins Jsy/1
100 Mike Piazza Dodgers Jsy/1
101 Mike Piazza Mets Jsy/1
106 Nolan Ryan Angels Jsy/5
107 Nolan Ryan Astros Jsy/5
108 Nolan Ryan Rgr Jsy/5
112 Paul Lo Duca Jsy/50 25.00 7.50
113 Pedro Martinez Sox Jsy/1
114 Pedro Martinez Expos Jsy/1
115 Preston Wilson Jsy/44 25.00 7.50
116 Rafael Palmeiro O's Jsy/5
117 Rafael Palmeiro Rgr Jsy/5
118 Randy Johnson D'backs Jsy/1
119 Randy Johnson M's Jsy/1
120 Richie Sexson Jsy/11
125 Rocco Baldelli Jsy/25 30.00 9.00
126 Rod Carew Jsy/10
129 Roy Halladay Jsy/32 25.00 7.50
130 Roy Oswalt Jsy/10
131 Ryne Sandberg Jsy/5
132 Sammy Sosa H Jsy/1
133 Sammy Sosa A Jsy/1
134 Sammy Sosa Sox Jsy/1
137 Steve Carlton Jsy/25 50.00 15.00
138 Tim Hudson Jsy/5
139 Todd Helton H Jsy/5
140 Todd Helton A Jsy/5
141 Tom Glavine Braves Jsy/5
142 Tom Glavine Mets Jsy/5
143 Tony Gwynn A Jsy/10
144 Tony Gwynn Alt Jsy/10
145 Torii Hunter Jsy/25 30.00 9.00
146 Trot Nixon Jsy/25 30.00 9.00
147 Troy Glaus Jsy/5
148 Vernon Wells Jsy/10
149 Vladimir Guerrero Jsy/5
150 Will Clark Jsy/10

1959 Bazooka

The 23 full-color, unnumbered cards comprising the 1959 Bazooka set were cut from the bottom of the boxes of gum marketed nationally that year by Topps. Bazooka was the brand name which Topps had been using to sell its one cent bubblegum; this year Topps decided to distribute 25 pieces of Bazooka gum in a box. The cards themselves measure 2 13/16" by 4 15/16". Only nine cards were originally issued; 14 more were added to the set at a later date (these are marked with SP in the checklist). The latter are less plentiful and hence more valuable than the original nine. All the cards are blank backed and the catalog designation is R414-15. The prices below are for the cards cut from the box; complete boxes intact would be worth about 50 percent more.

NM Ex
COMPLETE SET (23) 7000.00 3500.00
COMMON CARD (1-23) 50.00 25.00
COMMON CARD SP 200.00 100.00
1 Hank Aaron 500.00 250.00
2 Richie Ashburn SP 400.00 200.00

3 Ernie Banks SP 600.00 300.00
4 Ken Boyer SP 300.00 150.00
5 Orlando Cepeda 200.00 100.00
6 Bob Cerv SP 200.00 100.00
7 Rocky Colavito SP 400.00 200.00
8 Del Crandall 50.00 25.00
9 Jim Davenport 50.00 25.00
10 Don Drysdale SP 500.00 250.00
11 Nellie Fox SP 400.00 200.00
12 Jackie Jensen SP 300.00 150.00
13 Harvey Kuenn SP 250.00 125.00
14 Mickey Mantle 1500.00 750.00
15 Willie Mays 600.00 300.00
16 Bill Mazeroski 200.00 100.00
17 Roy McMillan 50.00 25.00
18 Billy Pierce SP 250.00 125.00
19 Roy Sievers SP 200.00 100.00
20 Duke Snider SP 800.00 400.00
21 Gus Triandos SP 200.00 100.00
22 Bob Turley 100.00 50.00
23 Vic Wertz SP 200.00 100.00

1960 Bazooka

In 1960, Topps introduced a 36-card baseball player set in three card panels on the bottom of Bazooka gum boxes. The cards measure 1 13/16" by 2 3/4" and the panels measure 2 3/4" by 5 1/2". The cards carried full color pictures and were numbered at the bottom underneath the team position. The checklist below contains prices for individual cards. Complete panels of three would have a 50 percent more than the sum of the indiviudal cards (prices) on the panel and complete boxes would command a premium of another 50 percent above those prices.

NM Ex
COMPLETE INDIV.SET 1000.00 400.00
1 Ernie Banks 50.00 20.00
2 Bud Daley 12.00 4.80
3 Wally Moon 12.00 4.80
4 Hank Aaron 100.00 40.00
5 Milt Pappas 12.00 4.80
6 Dick Stuart 12.00 4.80
7 Roberto Clemente 200.00 80.00
8 Yogi Berra 70.00 28.00
9 Ken Boyer 15.00 6.00
10 Orlando Cepeda 30.00 12.00
11 Gus Triandos 12.00 4.80
12 Frank Malzone 12.00 4.80
13 Willie Mays 120.00 47.50
14 Camilo Pascual 12.00 4.80
15 Bob Cerv 12.00 4.80
16 Vic Power 12.00 4.80
17 Larry Sherry 12.00 4.80
18 Al Kaline 50.00 20.00
19 Warren Spahn 50.00 20.00
20 Harmon Killebrew 50.00 20.00
21 Jackie Jensen 15.00 6.00
22 Luis Aparicio 30.00 12.00
23 Gil Hodges 30.00 12.00
24 Richie Ashburn 40.00 16.00
25 Nellie Fox 40.00 16.00
26 Robin Roberts 40.00 16.00
27 Joe Cunningham 12.00 4.80
28 Early Wynn 30.00 12.00
29 Frank Robinson 50.00 20.00
30 Rocky Colavito 30.00 12.00
31 Mickey Mantle 300.00 120.00
32 Glen Hobbie 12.00 4.80
33 Roy McMillan 12.00 4.80
34 Harvey Kuenn 12.00 4.80
35 Johnny Antonelli 12.00 4.80
36 Del Crandall 12.00 4.80

1961 Bazooka

The 36 card set issued by Bazooka in 1961 follows the format established in 1960; three full color, numbered cards to each panel found on a Bazooka gum box. The individual cards measure 1 13/16" by 2 3/4" whereas the panels measure 2 3/4" by 5 1/2". The cards of 1960 and 1961 are similar in design but are easily distinguished from one another by their numbers. Complete panels of three would have a value of 40 percent more than the sum of the individual cards (prices) on the panel and complete boxes would command a premium of another 40 percent above those prices.

NM Ex
COMPLETE INDIV. SET 800.00 325.00
1 Art Mahaffey 12.00 4.80
2 Mickey Mantle 300.00 120.00
3 Ron Santo 15.00 6.00
4 Bud Daley 12.00 4.80
5 Roger Maris 70.00 28.00
6 Eddie Yost 12.00 4.80
7 Minnie Minoso 15.00 6.00
8 Dick Groat 12.00 4.80
9 Frank Malzone 12.00 4.80
10 Dick Donovan 12.00 4.80
11 Eddie Mathews 50.00 20.00
12 Jim Lemon 12.00 4.80
13 Chuck Estrada 12.00 4.80
14 Ken Boyer 15.00 6.00
15 Harvey Kuenn 12.00 4.80
16 Ernie Broglio 12.00 4.80
17 Rocky Colavito 30.00 12.00
18 Ted Kluszewski 30.00 12.00
19 Ernie Banks 50.00 20.00
20 Al Kaline 50.00 20.00
21 Ed Bailey 12.00 4.80
22 Jim Perry 12.00 4.80
23 Willie Mays 100.00 40.00
24 Bill Mazeroski 30.00 12.00
25 Gus Triandos 12.00 4.80
26 Don Drysdale 40.00 16.00
27 Frank Herrera 12.00 4.80
28 Earl Battey 12.00 4.80
29 Warren Spahn 50.00 20.00
30 Gene Woodling 12.00 4.80
31 Frank Robinson 50.00 20.00
32 Pete Runnels 12.00 4.80
33 Woodie Held 12.00 4.80
34 Norm Larker 12.00 4.80
35 Luis Aparicio 30.00 12.00
36 Bill Tuttle 12.00 4.80

1962 Bazooka

The 1962 Bazooka set of 45 full color, blank backed, unnumbered cards was issued in panels of three on Bazooka bubble gum. The individual cards measure 1 13/16" by 2 3/4" whereas the panels measure 2 3/4" by 5 1/2". The cards below are numbered by panel alphabetically based on the last name of the player pictured on the far left card of the panel. The cards with SP in the checklist below are more difficult to obtain. Complete panels would have a value of 40 percent more than the sum of the individual cards (prices) on the panel and complete boxes would command a premium of another 40 percent above those prices.

NM Ex
COMPLETE INDIV. SET 3000.00 1200.00
COMMON CARD (1-45) 12.00 4.80
COMMON SP 70.00 28.00
1 Bob Allison SP 70.00 28.00
2 Eddie Mathews SP 500.00 200.00
3 Vada Pinson SP 100.00 40.00
4 Earl Battey 12.00 4.80
5 Warren Spahn 50.00 20.00
6 Lee Thomas 12.00 4.80
7 Orlando Cepeda 30.00 12.00
8 Woodie Held 12.00 4.80
9 Bob Aspromonte 12.00 4.80
10 Dick Howser 12.00 4.80
11 Roberto Clemente 200.00 80.00
12 Al Kaline 50.00 20.00
13 Joe Jay 12.00 4.80
14 Roger Maris 70.00 28.00
15 Frank Howard 15.00 6.00
16 Sandy Koufax 70.00 28.00
17 Jim Gentile 12.00 4.80
18 Johnny Callison 12.00 4.80
19 Jim Landis 12.00 4.80
20 Ken Boyer 15.00 6.00
21 Chuck Schilling 12.00 4.80
22 Art Mahaffey 12.00 4.80
23 Mickey Mantle 275.00 110.00
24 Dick Stuart 12.00 4.80
25 Ken McBride 12.00 4.80
26 Frank Robinson 50.00 20.00
27 Gil Hodges 40.00 16.00
28 Milt Pappas 12.00 4.80
29 Hank Aaron 100.00 40.00
30 Luis Aparicio 30.00 12.00
31 Johnny Romano SP 70.00 28.00
32 Ernie Banks SP 500.00 200.00
33 Norm Siebern SP 70.00 28.00
34 Ron Santo 20.00 8.00
35 Norm Cash 15.00 6.00
36 Jim Piersall 15.00 6.00
37 Don Schwall 12.00 4.80
38 Willie Mays 110.00 45.00
39 Norm Larker 12.00 4.80
40 Bill White 15.00 6.00
41 Whitey Ford 50.00 20.00
42 Rocky Colavito 30.00 12.00
43 Don Zimmer SP 100.00 40.00
44 Harmon Killebrew SP 500.00 200.00
45 Gene Woodling SP 70.00 28.00

1963 Bazooka

The 1963 Bazooka set of 36 full color, blank backed numbered cards was issued on Bazooka bubble gum boxes. This year marked a change in format from previous Bazooka issues with a smaller sized card being issued. The individual cards measure 1 9/16" by 2 1/2" whereas the panels measure 2 1/2" by 4 11/16". The card features a white strip with the player's name printed in black on the card. The number appears in the white border on the bottom of the card. Three cards were issued per panel. Complete panels of three would have a value of 15 percent more than the sum of the individual cards (prices) on the panel and complete boxes would command a premium of another 30 percent above those prices.

NM Ex
COMPLETE INDIV.SET 800.00 325.00
1 Mickey Mantle 200.00 80.00
2 Bob Rodgers 8.00 3.20
3 Ernie Banks 50.00 20.00
4 Norm Siebern 8.00 3.20
5 Warren Spahn 40.00 16.00
6 Bill Mazeroski 20.00 8.00
7 Harmon Killebrew 40.00 16.00
8 Dick Farrell 8.00 3.20
9 Hank Aaron 80.00 32.00
10 Dick Donovan 8.00 3.20
11 Jim Gentile 8.00 3.20
12 Willie Mays 80.00 32.00
13 Camilo Pascual 8.00 3.20
14 Roberto Clemente 100.00 40.00
15 Johnny Callison 8.00 3.20
16 Carl Yastrzemski 40.00 16.00
17 Don Drysdale 30.00 12.00
18 Johnny Romano 8.00 3.20
19 Al Jackson 8.00 3.20
20 Ralph Terry 8.00 3.20
21 Bill Monbouquette 8.00 3.20
22 Orlando Cepeda 20.00 8.00
23 Stan Musial 50.00 20.00
24 Floyd Robinson 8.00 3.20
25 Chuck Hinton 8.00 3.20
26 Bob Purkey 8.00 3.20
27 Ken Hubbs 10.00 4.00
28 Bill White 10.00 4.00
29 Ray Herbert 8.00 3.20
30 Brooks Robinson 50.00 20.00
31 Frank Robinson 50.00 20.00
32 Lee Thomas 8.00 3.20
33 Rocky Colavito 20.00 8.00
34 Al Kaline 50.00 20.00
35 Art Mahaffey 8.00 3.20
36 Tommy Davis 8.00 3.20

1963 Bazooka ATG

The 1963 Bazooka All Time Greats set contains 41 black and white numbered cards issued as inserts in boxes of Bazooka Bubble gum. The cards feature bust shots with gold trim and measure 1 9/16" by 2 1/2". The backs are yellow with black print containing vital information and a biography of the player. Many of the players are pictured not as they looked during their playing careers but as they looked many years after their playing days were through. The cards also exist in a scarcer variety with silver trim instead of gold; the silver trim variety cards are worth approximately double the prices listed below. Cards are numbered on the back.

NM Ex
COMPLETE SET (41) 350.00 140.00
1 Joe Tinker 6.00 2.40
2 Harry Heilmann 6.00 2.40
3 Jack Chesbro 4.00 1.60
4 Christy Mathewson 15.00 6.00
5 Herb Pennock 6.00 2.40
6 Cy Young 10.00 4.00
7 Ed Walsh 6.00 2.40
8 Nap Lajoie 10.00 4.00
9 Eddie Plank 6.00 2.40
10 Honus Wagner 20.00 8.00
11 Chief Bender 6.00 2.40
12 Walter Johnson 15.00 6.00
13 Mordecai Brown 6.00 2.40
14 Rabbit Maranville 6.00 2.40
15 Lou Gehrig 50.00 20.00
16 Ban Johnson 4.00 1.60
17 Babe Ruth 80.00 32.00
18 Connie Mack 6.00 2.40
19 Hank Greenberg 6.00 2.40
20 John McGraw 6.00 2.40
21 Johnny Evers 6.00 2.40
22 Al Simmons 6.00 2.40
23 Jimmy Collins 6.00 2.40
24 Tris Speaker 8.00 3.20
25 Frank Chance 6.00 2.40
26 Fred Clarke 6.00 2.40
27 Wilbert Robinson 6.00 2.40
28 Dazzy Vance 6.00 2.40
29 Pete Alexander 8.00 3.20
30 Judge Landis 6.00 2.40
31 Willie Keeler 6.00 2.40
32 Rogers Hornsby 10.00 4.00
33 Hugh Duffy 6.00 2.40
34 Mickey Cochrane 6.00 2.40
35 Ty Cobb 50.00 20.00
36 Mel Ott 10.00 4.00
37 Clark Griffith 6.00 2.40
38 Ted Lyons 6.00 2.40
39 Cap Anson 6.00 2.40
40 Bill Dickey 6.00 2.40
41 Eddie Collins 6.00 2.40

1964 Bazooka

The 1964 Bazooka set of 36 full color, blank backed, numbered cards were issued in panels of three on the backs of Bazooka bubble gum boxes. The individual cards measure 1 9/16" by 2 1/2" whereas the panels measure 2 1/2" by 4 11/16". Many players who were in the 1963 set have the same number in this set; however, the pictures are different. Complete panels of three would have a value of 15 percent more than the sum of the individual cards (prices) on the panel and complete boxes would command a premium of another 40 percent above those prices.

NM Ex
COMPLETE INDIV. SET 800.00 325.00
1 Mickey Mantle 200.00 80.00
2 Dick Groat 8.00 3.20
3 Steve Barber 8.00 3.20
4 Ken McBride 8.00 3.20
5 Warren Spahn 40.00 16.00
6 Bob Friend 8.00 3.20
7 Harmon Killebrew 40.00 16.00
8 Dick Farrell 8.00 3.20
9 Hank Aaron 80.00 32.00
10 Rich Rollins 8.00 3.20
11 Jim Gentile 8.00 3.20
12 Willie Mays 80.00 32.00
13 Camilo Pascual 8.00 3.20
14 Roberto Clemente 100.00 40.00
15 Johnny Callison 8.00 3.20
16 Carl Yastrzemski 50.00 20.00
17 Billy Williams 20.00 8.00
18 Johnny Romano 8.00 3.20
19 Jim Maloney 8.00 3.20
20 Norm Cash 10.00 4.00
21 Willie McCovey 20.00 8.00
22 Jim Fregosi 8.00 3.20
23 George Altman 8.00 3.20
24 Floyd Robinson 8.00 3.20
25 Chuck Hinton 8.00 3.20
26 Ron Hunt 8.00 3.20
27 Gary Peters 8.00 3.20
28 Dick Ellsworth 8.00 3.20
29 Elston Howard 10.00 4.00
30 Brooks Robinson 50.00 20.00
31 Frank Robinson 50.00 20.00
32 Sandy Koufax 70.00 28.00
33 Rocky Colavito 20.00 8.00
34 Al Kaline 50.00 20.00
35 Ken Boyer 10.00 4.00
36 Tommy Davis 8.00 3.20

1964 Bazooka Stamps

Many of the 100 color portraits of baseball players featured in this 1964 Topps stamp series show players without caps. Each small stamp is 1" by 1 1/2". The subject's name, team and position are found in a colored rectangle beneath the picture area. Each sheet is numbered in the upper left hand corner outside the picture area. The sheet number is given after the player's name in the checklist below with the prefix S. The stamps were issued in sheets of 10 but an album to hold this particular set has not yet been seen.

NM Ex
COMPLETE SET (100) 450.00 180.00
1 Ed Charles 1.00 .40
2 Vada Pinson 2.00 .80
3 Jimmy Hall 1.00 .40
4 Milt Pappas 1.50 .60
5 Dick Ellsworth 1.00 .40
6 Frank Malzone 1.50 .60
7 Max Alvis 1.00 .40
8 Pete Ward 1.00 .40
9 Tony Taylor 1.50 .60
10 Bill White 2.50 1.00
11 Don Zimmer 2.00 .80
12 Bobby Richardson 5.00 2.00
13 Larry Jackson 1.00 .40
14 Norm Siebern 1.00 .40
15 Frank Robinson 15.00 6.00
16 Bob Aspromonte 1.00 .40
17 Al McBean 1.00 .40
18 Floyd Robinson 1.00 .40
19 Bill Monbouquette 1.00 .40
20 Willie Mays 40.00 16.00
21 Brooks Robinson S3 20.00 8.00
22 Joe Pepitone S3 2.50 1.00
23 Carl Yastrzemski S3 20.00 8.00
24 Don Lock S3 1.00 .40
25 Ernie Banks S3 20.00 8.00
26 Dave Nicholson S3 1.00 .40
27 Roberto Clemente S3 50.00 20.00
28 Curt Flood S3 2.50 1.00
29 Woody Held S3 1.00 .40
30 Jesse Gonder S3 1.00 .40
31 Juan Pizarro 1.00 .40
32 Jim Maloney S4 1.50 .60
33 Ron Santo 2.50 1.00
34 Harmon Killebrew 10.00 4.00
35 Ed Roebuck S4 1.00 .40
36 Boog Powell 2.50 1.00
37 Jim Grant S4 1.00 .40
38 Hank Aguirre S4 1.00 .40
39 Juan Marichal 10.00 4.00
40 Bill Mazeroski 3.00 1.20
41 Dick Radatz S5 1.00 .40
42 Albie Pearson S5 1.00 .40
43 Tommy Harper S5 1.50 .60
44 Carl Willey S5 1.00 .40
45 Jim Bouton 2.50 1.00
46 Ron Perranoski S5 1.00 .40
47 Chuck Hinton S5 1.00 .40
48 John Romano S5 1.00 .40
49 Norm Cash 2.50 1.00
50 Orlando Cepeda 5.00 2.00
51 Dick Stuart S6 1.00 .40
52 Rich Rollins S6 1.00 .40
53 Mickey Mantle S6 80.00 32.00
54 Steve Barber S6 1.00 .40
55 Jim O'Toole S6 1.00 .40
56 Gary Peters S6 1.00 .40
57 Warren Spahn S6 12.00 4.80
58 Tony Gonzalez S6 1.00 .40
59 Joe Torre S6 2.50 1.00
60 Jim Fregosi S6 2.00 .80
61 Ken Boyer 2.50 1.00
62 Felipe Alou 1.50 .60
63 Jim Davenport S7 1.00 .40
64 Tommy Davis 2.00 .80
65 Rocky Colavito 4.00 1.60
66 Bob Friend S7 1.50 .60
67 Billy Moran S7 1.00 .40
68 Bill Freehan 2.00 .80
69 George Altman S7 1.00 .40
70 Ken Johnson S7 1.00 .40
71 Earl Battey S8 1.00 .40
72 Elston Howard 2.50 1.00
73 Billy Williams 10.00 4.00
74 Claude Osteen 1.50 .60
75 Jim Gentile 1.50 .60
76 Donn Clendenon 1.50 .60
77 Ernie Broglio 1.00 .40
78 Hal Woodeshick 1.00 .40
79 Don Drysdale 10.00 4.00
80 John Callison 1.50 .60
81 Dick Groat 1.50 .60
82 Moe Drabowsky 1.00 .40
83 Frank Howard 1.50 .60
84 Hank Aaron 40.00 16.00
85 Al Jackson 1.00 .40
86 Jerry Lumpe 1.00 .40
87 Wayne Causey 1.00 .40
88 Rusty Staub 2.50 1.00
89 Ken McBride 1.00 .40
90 Jack Baldschun 1.00 .40
91 Sandy Koufax S10 25.00 10.00
92 Camilo Pascual S10 1.00 .40
93 Ron Hunt S10 1.00 .40
94 Willie McCovey S10 12.00 4.80
95 Al Kaline S10 15.00 6.00
96 Ray Culp S10 1.00 .40
97 Ed Mathews S10 12.00 4.80
98 Dick Farrell S10 1.00 .40
99 Lee Thomas S10 1.50 .60
100 Vic Davalillo S10 1.00 .40

1965 Bazooka

The 1965 Bazooka set of 36 full color, blank backed, numbered cards was issued in panels of three on the backs of Bazooka bubble gum boxes. The individual cards measure 1 9/16" by 2 1/2" whereas the panels measure 2 1/2" by 4 11/16". As in the previous two years some of the players have the same numbers on their cards; however all pictures are different from the previous two years. Complete panels of three would have a value of 15 percent more than the sum of the individual cards (prices) on the panel and complete boxes would command a premium of another 40 percent above those prices.

NM Ex
COMPLETE INDIV. SET 800.00 325.00
1 Mickey Mantle 200.00 80.00
2 Larry Jackson 8.00 3.20
3 Chuck Hinton 8.00 3.20
4 Tony Oliva 15.00 6.00
5 Dean Chance 8.00 3.20
6 Jim O'Toole 8.00 3.20
7 Harmon Killebrew 30.00 12.00
8 Pete Ward 8.00 3.20
9 Hank Aaron 80.00 32.00
10 Dick Radatz 8.00 3.20
11 Boog Powell 10.00 4.00
12 Willie Mays 80.00 32.00
13 Bob Veale 8.00 3.20
14 Roberto Clemente 100.00 40.00
15 Johnny Callison 8.00 3.20
16 Joe Torre 15.00 6.00
17 Billy Williams 25.00 10.00
18 Bob Chance 8.00 3.20
19 Bob Aspromonte 8.00 3.20
20 Joe Christopher 8.00 3.20
21 Jim Bunning 20.00 8.00
22 Jim Fregosi 8.00 3.20
23 Bob Gibson 30.00 12.00
24 Juan Marichal 30.00 12.00
25 Dave Wickersham 8.00 3.20
26 Ron Hunt 8.00 3.20
27 Gary Peters 8.00 3.20
28 Ron Santo 15.00 6.00
29 Elston Howard 10.00 4.00
30 Brooks Robinson 40.00 16.00
31 Frank Robinson 40.00 16.00
32 Sandy Koufax 50.00 20.00
33 Rocky Colavito 20.00 8.00
34 Al Kaline 40.00 16.00
35 Ken Boyer 10.00 4.00
36 Tommy Davis 8.00 3.20

1966 Bazooka

The 1966 Bazooka set of 48 full color, blank backed, numbered cards was issued in panels of three on the backs of Bazooka bubble gum boxes. The individual cardsd measure 1 9/16" by 2 1/2" whereas the complete panels measure 2 1/2" by 4 11/16". The set is distinguishable from the previous years by mention of "48 card set" at the bottom of the card. Complete panels of three would have a value of 15 percent more than the sum of the individual cards (prices) on the panel and complete boxes would command a premium of another 40 percent above those prices.

	NM	Ex
COMPLETE INDIV. SET	800.00	325.00
1 Sandy Koufax	50.00	20.00
2 Willie Horton	8.00	3.20
3 Frank Howard	10.00	4.00
4 Richie Allen	10.00	4.00
5 Mel Stottlemyre	10.00	4.00
6 Tony Conigliaro	12.00	4.80
7 Mickey Mantle	200.00	80.00
8 Leon Wagner	8.00	3.20
9 Ed Kranepool	8.00	3.20
10 Juan Marichal	25.00	10.00
11 Harmon Killebrew	25.00	10.00
12 Johnny Callison	8.00	3.20
13 Roy McMillan	8.00	3.20
14 Willie McCovey	25.00	10.00
15 Rocky Colavito	15.00	6.00
16 Willie Mays	80.00	32.00
17 Sam McDowell	8.00	3.20
18 Vern Law	8.00	3.20
19 Jim Fregosi	8.00	3.20
20 Ron Fairly	8.00	3.20
21 Bob Gibson	25.00	10.00
22 Carl Yastrzemski	30.00	12.00
23 Bill White	10.00	4.00
24 Bob Aspromonte	8.00	3.20
25 Dean Chance	8.00	3.20
26 Roberto Clemente	100.00	40.00
27 Tony Cloninger	8.00	3.20
28 Curt Blefary	8.00	3.20
29 Milt Pappas	8.00	3.20
30 Hank Aaron	80.00	32.00
31 Jim Bunning	15.00	6.00
32 Frank Robinson	30.00	12.00
33 Bill Skowron	10.00	4.00
34 Brooks Robinson	30.00	12.00
35 Jim Wynn	8.00	3.20
36 Joe Torre	12.00	4.80
37 Jim Grant	8.00	3.20
38 Pete Rose	60.00	24.00
39 Ron Santo	12.00	4.80
40 Tom Tresh	10.00	4.00
41 Tony Oliva	12.00	4.80
42 Don Drysdale	25.00	10.00
43 Pete Richert	8.00	3.20
44 Bert Campaneris	8.00	3.20
45 Jim Maloney	8.00	3.20
46 Al Kaline	30.00	12.00
47 Eddie Fisher	8.00	3.20
48 Billy Williams	20.00	8.00

1967 Bazooka

The 1967 Bazooka set of 48 full color, blank backed, numbered cards was issued in panels of three on the backs of Bazooka bubble gum boxes. The individual cards measure 1 9/16" by 2 1/2" whereas the complete panels measure 2 1/2" by 4 11/16". This set is virtually identical to the 1966 set with the exception of ten new cards as replacements for ten 1966 cards. The remaining 38 cards are identical in pose and number. The replacement cards are listed in the checklist below with an asterisk. Complete panels of three would have a value of 15 percent more than the sum of the individual cards (prices) on the panel and complete boxes would command a premium of another 40 percent above those prices.

	NM	Ex
COMPLETE INDIV. SET	800.00	325.00
1 Rick Reichardt	8.00	3.20
2 Tommie Agee	8.00	3.20
3 Frank Howard	10.00	4.00
4 Richie Allen	10.00	4.00
5 Mel Stottlemyre	10.00	4.00
6 Tony Conigliaro	12.00	4.80
7 Mickey Mantle	200.00	80.00
8 Leon Wagner	8.00	3.20
9 Gary Peters	8.00	3.20
10 Juan Marichal	25.00	10.00
11 Harmon Killebrew	25.00	10.00
12 Johnny Callison	8.00	3.20
13 Denny McLain	12.00	4.80
14 Willie McCovey	25.00	10.00
15 Rocky Colavito	15.00	6.00
16 Willie Mays	80.00	32.00
17 Sam McDowell	8.00	3.20
18 Jim Kaat	12.00	4.80
19 Jim Fregosi	8.00	3.20
20 Ron Fairly	8.00	3.20
21 Bob Gibson	25.00	10.00
22 Carl Yastrzemski	30.00	12.00
23 Bill White	10.00	4.00
24 Bob Aspromonte	8.00	3.20
25 Dean Chance	8.00	3.20
26 Roberto Clemente	100.00	40.00
27 Tony Cloninger	8.00	3.20
28 Curt Blefary	8.00	3.20
29 Phil Regan	8.00	3.20
30 Hank Aaron	80.00	32.00
31 Jim Bunning	15.00	6.00
32 Frank Robinson	30.00	12.00
33 Ken Boyer	10.00	4.00
34 Brooks Robinson	30.00	12.00
35 Jim Wynn	8.00	3.20
36 Joe Torre	12.00	4.80
37 Tommy Davis	8.00	3.20
38 Pete Rose	60.00	24.00
39 Ron Santo	12.00	4.80
40 Tom Tresh	10.00	4.00
41 Tony Oliva	12.00	4.80
42 Don Drysdale	25.00	10.00
43 Pete Richert	8.00	3.20
44 Bert Campaneris	8.00	3.20
45 Jim Maloney	8.00	3.20
46 Al Kaline	30.00	12.00
47 Matty Alou	8.00	3.20
48 Billy Williams	20.00	8.00

1968 Bazooka

The 1968 Bazooka Tipps from the Topps is a set of 15 numbered boxes (measuring 5 1/2" by 6 1/4" when detached). each containing on the back panel (measuring 3" by 6 1/4") a baseball playing tip from a star, and on the side panels four mini cards, two per side, in full color, measuring 1 1/4" by 3 1/8". Although the set contains a total of 60 of these small cards, 4 are repeated; therefore there are only 56 different small cards. Some collectors cut the panels into individual card; however most collectors retain entire panels or boxes. The prices in the checklist therfore reflect only the values of the complete boxes.

	NM	Ex
COMPLETE BOX SET	1000.00	400.00
COMMON BOX	50.00	20.00
COMMON INDIV. PLAYER	3.00	1.20
1 Maury Wills: Bunting Al Kaline Paul Casanova Clete Boyer Tom Seaver	120.00	47.50
2 C.Yastrzemski: Batting Jim Hunter Bill Freehan Matty Alou Jim Lefebvre	80.00	32.00
3 B.Campaneris: Stealing Tim McCarver Bob Veale Frank Robinson Bobby Knoop	50.00	20.00
4 Maury Wills: Sliding Ken Holtzman Jose Azcue Tony Conigliaro Bill White	50.00	20.00
5 J.Javier: Double Play Juan Marichal Rico Petrocelli Joe Pepitone Hank Aaron	120.00	47.50
6 O.Cepeda: 1st Base Ron Santo Don Drysdale Pete Rose Tommie Agee	80.00	32.00
7 B.Mazeroski: 2nd Base John Roseboro Jim Bunning Frank Howard George Scott	50.00	20.00
8 B.Robinson: 3rd Base Tony Gonzalez Jim McGlothlin Wille Horton Harmon Killebrew	60.00	24.00
9 Jim Fregosi: Shortstop Max Alvis Bob Gibson Tony Oliva Vada Pinson	50.00	20.00
10 Joe Torre: Catching Dean Chance Fergie Jenkins Tommy Davis Rick Monday	50.00	20.00
11 Jim Lonborg: Pitching Joel Horlen Jim Wynn Curt Flood Mickey Mantle	200.00	80.00
12 Mike McCormick: Fielding Pitcher Don Mincher Tony Perez Roberto Clemente Al Downing	50.00	20.00
13 F.Crosetti: Coaching Rod Carew Don Wilson Ron Swoboda Willie McCovey	50.00	20.00
14 Willie Mays: Outfield Richie Allen Gary Peters Billy Williams Rusty Staub	120.00	47.50
15 L.Brock: Base Running Tommie Agee Pete Rose Ron Santo Don Drysdale	120.00	47.50

1969-70 Bazooka

The 1969-70 Bazooka Baseball Extra News set contains 12 complete panels, each comprising a large action shot of a significant event in baseball history and four small cards, comparable to those in the Tipps from the Topps set of 1968, of Hall of Famers. Although some collectors cut the panels into individual cards (measuring 3" by 6 1/4" or 1 1/4" by 3 1/8"), most collectors retain the entire panel, or box (measuring 5 1/2" by 6 1/4"). The prices in the checklist below reflect the value for the entire box, as these cards are more widely seen and collected as complete panels or boxes.

	NM	Ex
COMPLETE PANEL SET	400.00	160.00
COMMON PANEL (1-12)	30.00	12.00
COMMON INDIV. PLAYER	.50	.20
1 No-Hit Duel by Fred Toney Hippo Vaughn: Ty Cobb Willie Keeler Mordecai Brown Eddie Plank	40.00	16.00
2 Alexander Conquers Yankees: Al Simmons Ban Johnson Walter Johnson Rogers Hornsby	30.00	12.00
3 Yanks' Lazzeri Sets AL Record: Christy Mathewson Chief Bender Grover Alexander Cy Young	30.00	12.00
4 Homerun Almost Hit Out of Stadium: Lou Gehrig Hugh Duffy Tris Speaker Joe Tinker	40.00	16.00
5 Four Consecutive Homers by Lou: John McGraw Frank Chance Babe Ruth Mickey Cochrane	100.00	40.00
6 No-Hit Game by Walter Johnson: Cy Young Walter Johnson Johnny Evers John McGraw	30.00	12.00
7 Twelve RBIs by Jim Bottomley: Johnny Evers Eddie Collins Lou Gehrig Ty Cobb	50.00	20.00
8 Ty Cobb Ties Record: Honus Wagner Mickey Cochrane Eddie Collins Mel Ott	40.00	16.00
9 Babe Ruth Hits Three Homers in Game: Cap Anson Tris Speaker Jack Chesbro Al Simmons	50.00	20.00
10 Babe Ruth Calls Shot in Series Game: Rabbit Maranville Ed Walsh Nap Lajoie Connie Mack	50.00	20.00
11 Babe Ruth's 60th Homer Sets New Record: Joe Tinker Nap Lajoie Mel Ott Frank Chance	50.00	20.00
12 Double Shutout by Ed Reulbach: Rogers Hornsby Rabbit Maranville Christy Mathewson Honus Wagner	30.00	12.00

1971 Bazooka Numbered Test

This was supposedly a test issue which was different from the more common unnumbered set and much more difficult to find. There are 48 cards (16 panels) in this numbered set whereas the unnumbered set had only 12 panels or 36 individual cards. Individual cards measure approximately 2" by 2 5/8" whereas the panels measure 2 5/8" by 5 15/16". Complete panels of three would have a value of 10 percent more than the sum of the individual cards (prices) on the panel and complete boxes would command a premium of another 30 percent above those prices.

	NM	Ex
COMPLETE SET (48)	650.00	250.00
1 Tim McCarver	6.00	2.40
2 Frank Robinson	30.00	12.00
3 Bill Mazeroski	20.00	8.00
4 Willie McCovey	20.00	8.00
5 Carl Yastrzemski	30.00	12.00
6 Clyde Wright	4.00	1.60
7 Jim Merritt	4.00	1.60
8 Luis Aparicio	20.00	8.00
9 Bobby Murcer	6.00	2.40
10 Rico Petrocelli	4.00	1.60
11 Sam McDowell	4.00	1.60
12 Clarence Gaston	4.00	1.60
13 Fergie Jenkins	20.00	8.00
14 Al Kaline	30.00	12.00
15 Ken Harrelson	4.00	1.60
16 Tommie Agee	4.00	1.60
17 Harmon Killebrew	20.00	8.00
18 Reggie Jackson	50.00	20.00
19 Juan Marichal	20.00	8.00
20 Frank Howard	6.00	2.40
21 Bill Melton	4.00	1.60
22 Brooks Robinson	30.00	12.00
23 Hank Aaron	50.00	20.00
24 Larry Dierker	4.00	1.60
25 Jim Fregosi	4.00	1.60
26 Billy Williams	20.00	8.00
27 Dave McNally	4.00	1.60
28 Rico Carty	4.00	1.60
29 Johnny Bench	40.00	16.00
30 Tommy Harper	4.00	1.60
31 Bert Campaneris	4.00	1.60
32 Pete Rose	50.00	20.00
33 Orlando Cepeda	20.00	8.00
34 Maury Wills	6.00	2.40
35 Tom Seaver	40.00	16.00
36 Tony Oliva	15.00	6.00
37 Bill Freehan	4.00	1.60
38 Roberto Clemente	90.00	36.00
39 Claude Osteen	4.00	1.60
40 Rusty Staub	6.00	2.40
41 Bob Gibson	20.00	8.00
42 Amos Otis	4.00	1.60
43 Jim Wynn	6.00	2.40
44 Rich Allen	15.00	6.00
45 Tony Conigliaro	15.00	6.00
46 Randy Hundley	4.00	1.60
47 Willie Mays	50.00	20.00
48 Jim Hunter	20.00	8.00

1971 Bazooka Unnumbered

The 1971 Bazooka set of 36 full-color, unnumbered cards was issued in 12 panels of three cards each on the backs of boxes containing one cent Bazooka bubble gum. Individual cards measure approximately 2" by 2 5/8" whereas the panels measure 2 5/8" by 5 15/16". The panels are numbered in the checklist alphabetically by the player's last name on the left most card of the panel. Complete panels of three would have a value of 10 percent more than the sum of the individual cards (prices) on the panel and complete boxes would command a premium of another 30 percent above those prices.

	NM	Ex
COMPLETE INDIV.SET	300.00	120.00
1 Tommie Agee	3.00	1.20
2 Harmon Killebrew	15.00	6.00
3 Reggie Jackson	30.00	12.00
4 Bert Campaneris	3.00	1.20
5 Pete Rose	30.00	12.00
6 Orlando Cepeda	15.00	6.00
7 Rico Carty	3.00	1.20
8 Johnny Bench	25.00	10.00
9 Tommy Harper	3.00	1.20
10 Bill Freehan	3.00	1.20
11 Roberto Clemente	60.00	24.00
12 Claude Osteen	3.00	1.20
13 Jim Fregosi	3.00	1.20
14 Billy Williams	15.00	6.00
15 Dave McNally	3.00	1.20
16 Randy Hundley	3.00	1.20
17 Willie Mays	35.00	14.00
18 Jim Hunter	15.00	6.00
19 Juan Marichal	15.00	6.00
20 Frank Howard	5.00	2.00
21 Bill Melton	3.00	1.20
22 Willie McCovey	15.00	6.00
23 Carl Yastrzemski	20.00	8.00
24 Clyde Wright	3.00	1.20
25 Jim Merritt	3.00	1.20
26 Luis Aparicio	15.00	6.00
27 Bobby Murcer	5.00	2.00
28 Rico Petrocelli	3.00	1.20
29 Sam McDowell	3.00	1.20
30 Clarence Gaston	3.00	1.20
31 Brooks Robinson	20.00	8.00
32 Hank Aaron	30.00	12.00
33 Larry Dierker	3.00	1.20
34 Rusty Staub	5.00	2.00
35 Bob Gibson	15.00	6.00
36 Amos Otis	3.00	1.20

1988 Bazooka

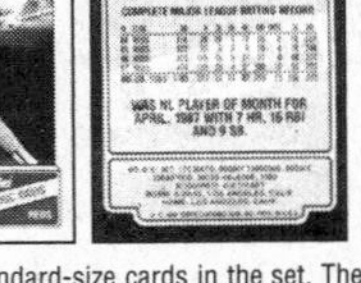

There are 22 standard-size cards in the set. The cards have extra thick white borders. Card backs are printed in blue and red on white card stock. Some sets can also be found with gray backs; these gray backs carry no additional value premium. Cards are numbered on the back; they were numbered by Topps alphabetically. The word "Bazooka" only appears faintly as background for the statistics on the back of the card. Cards were available inside specially marked boxes of Bazooka gum retailing between 59 cents and 99 cents. The emphasis in the player selection for this set is on young stars of baseball.

	Nm-Mt	Ex-Mt
COMPLETE SET (22)	8.00	3.20
1 George Bell	.10	.04
2 Wade Boggs	.75	.30
3 Jose Canseco	.75	.30
4 Roger Clemens	1.25	.50
5 Vince Coleman	.10	.04
6 Eric Davis	.25	.10
7 Tony Fernandez	.10	.04
8 Dwight Gooden	.25	.10
9 Tony Gwynn	1.25	.50
11 Don Mattingly	1.25	.50
13 Mark McGwire	2.00	.80
14 Kirby Puckett	.75	.30
15 Tim Raines	.25	.10
16 Dave Righetti	.10	.04
17 Cal Ripken	2.50	1.00
18 Juan Samuel	.10	.04
19 Ryne Sandberg	.75	.30
20 Benito Santiago	.25	.10
21 Darryl Strawberry	.25	.10
22 Todd Worrell	.10	.04

1989 Bazooka

The 1989 Bazooka Shining Stars set contains 22 standard-size cards. The fronts have white borders and a large yellow stripe; the vertically oriented backs are pink, red and white and have career stats. The cards were inserted one per box of Bazooka Gum. The set is sequenced in alphabetical order.

	Nm-Mt	Ex-Mt
COMPLETE SET (22)	5.00	2.00
1 Tim Belcher	.10	.04
2 Damon Berryhill	.10	.04
3 Wade Boggs	1.00	.40
4 Jay Buhner	.25	.10
5 Jose Canseco	1.00	.40
6 Vince Coleman	.10	.04
7 Cecil Espy	.10	.04
8 Dave Gallagher	.10	.04
9 Ron Gant	.25	.10
10 Kirk Gibson	.25	.10
11 Paul Gibson	.10	.04
12 Mark Grace	1.00	.40
13 Tony Gwynn	1.25	.50
14 Rickey Henderson	1.25	.50
15 Orel Hershiser	.25	.10
16 Gregg Jefferies	.10	.04
17 Ricky Jordan	.10	.04
18 Chris Sabo	.10	.04
19 Gary Sheffield	1.25	.50
20 Darryl Strawberry	.25	.10
21 Frank Viola	.10	.04
22 Walt Weiss	.10	.04

1990 Bazooka

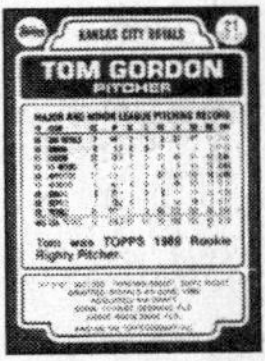

The 1990 Bazooka Shining Stars set contains 22 standard-size cards with a mix of award winners, league leaders, and young stars. This set was issued by Topps using the Bazooka name. Card backs were printed in blue and red on white card stock. The word "Bazooka" appears faintly as background for the statistics on the back of the card as well as appearing prominently on the front of each card.

	Nm-Mt	Ex-Mt
COMPLETE SET (22)	6.00	1.80
1 Kevin Mitchell	.10	.03
2 Robin Yount	.75	.23
3 Mark Davis	.10	.03
4 Bret Saberhagen	.25	.07
5 Fred McGriff	.50	.15
6 Tony Gwynn	1.50	.45
7 Kirby Puckett	.75	.23
8 Vince Coleman	.10	.03
9 Rickey Henderson	1.25	.35
10 Ben McDonald	.10	.03
11 Gregg Olson	.10	.03
12 Todd Zeile	.25	.07
13 Carlos Martinez	.10	.03
14 Gregg Jefferies	.10	.03
15 Craig Worthington	.10	.03
16 Gary Sheffield	1.00	.30
17 Greg Briley	.10	.03
18 Ken Griffey Jr.	2.50	.75
19 Jerome Walton	.10	.03
20 Bob Geren	.10	.03
21 Tom Gordon	.10	.03
22 Jim Abbott	.25	.07

1991 Bazooka

The 1991 Bazooka Shining Stars set contains 22 standard-size cards featuring league leaders and rookie sensations. The set was produced by Topps for Bazooka. One card was inserted in each box of Bazooka Bubble Gum. The fronts are similar to the Topps regular issue, only that the "Shining Star" emblem appears at the card top and the Bazooka logo overlays the lower right corner of the picture. In a blue and red design on white card stock, the backs have statistics and biography.

	Nm-Mt	Ex-Mt
COMPLETE SET (22)	6.00	1.80
1 Barry Bonds	2.00	.60
2 Rickey Henderson	1.25	.35
3 Bob Welch	.10	.03
4 Doug Drabek	.10	.03
5 Alex Fernandez	.10	.03
6 Jose Offerman	.10	.03
7 Frank Thomas	1.00	.30
8 Cecil Fielder	.25	.07
9 Ryne Sandberg	1.00	.30
10 George Brett	1.00	.30
11 Willie McGee	.25	.07
12 Vince Coleman	.10	.03
13 Hal Morris	.10	.03
14 Delino DeShields	.10	.03
15 Robin Ventura	.50	.15
16 Jeff Huson	.10	.03
17 Felix Jose	.10	.03
18 Dave Justice	.50	.15
19 Larry Walker	.75	.23
20 Sandy Alomar Jr.	.25	.07
21 Kevin Appier	.10	.03
22 Scott Radinsky	.10	.03

1993 Bazooka Team USA

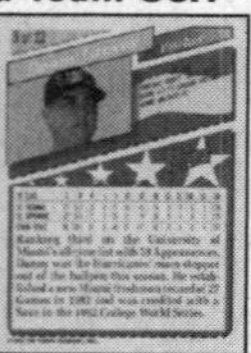

Originally available only in a special Bazooka collector's box, these 22 standard-size cards were produced by Topps and feature the 1993 Team USA players. The card design is similar to that of the '93 Topps series. The white-bordered fronts feature posed color player photos. The player's name appears in a blue stripe near the bottom; the Bazooka logo appears at the upper right. The colorful white-bordered backs carry a color head shot, biography, statistics, and career highlights. The cards are numbered on the back as "X of 22." Todd Helton has a very early card in this set. The full box this set came in also contained 50 pieces of Bazooka gum.

	Nm-Mt	Ex-Mt
COMP.FACT. SET (22)	100.00	30.00
1 Terry Harvey	.10	.03
2 Dante Powell	.10	.03
3 Andy Barkett	.10	.03
4 Steve Reich	.10	.03
5 Charlie Nelson	.10	.03
6 Todd Walker	6.00	1.80
7 Dustin Hermanson	1.50	.45
8 Pat Clougherty	.10	.03
9 Danny Graves	5.00	1.50
10 Paul Wilson	1.00	.30
11 Todd Helton	80.00	24.00
12 Russ Johnson	.25	.07
13 Darren Grass	.10	.03
14 A.J. Hinch	.25	.07
15 Mark Merila	.10	.03
16 John Powell	.10	.03
17 Bob Scafa	.10	.03
18 Matt Beaumont	.10	.03
19 Todd Dunn	.10	.03
20 Mike Martin	.10	.03
21 Carlton Loewer	.50	.15
22 Bret Wagner	.10	.03

1995 Bazooka

This 132-card standard-size set was issued by Topps. For the previous 35 years, Topps had used the Bazooka label to issue various cards, but this was the first time a mainstream set was issued in pack form. The five-card packs, with a suggested retail price of 50 cents, included an info card as well as a piece of bubble gum. The fronts have an action photo surrounded by white borders. The "Bazooka" label is in the upper left corner, while the player's name and team are on the bottom of the card. The player's position is identified on the right. The backs have a game as well as his previous season and career stats. There are no Rookie Cards in this set. Factory sets included five Red Hot inserts.

	Nm-Mt	Ex-Mt
COMPLETE SET (132)	10.00	3.00
COMP.FACT.SET (137)	10.00	3.00
1 Greg Maddux	.75	.23
2 Cal Ripken Jr.	1.50	.45
3 Lee Smith	.20	.06
4 Sammy Sosa	.75	.23
5 Jason Bere	.10	.03
6 David Justice	.20	.06
7 Kevin Mitchell	.10	.03
8 Ozzie Guillen	.10	.03
9 Roger Clemens	1.00	.30
10 Mike Mussina	.30	.09
11 Sandy Alomar Jr.	.10	.03
12 Cecil Fielder	.20	.06
13 Dennis Martinez	.20	.06
14 Randy Myers	.20	.06
15 Jay Buhner	.20	.06
16 Ivan Rodriguez	.50	.15
17 Mo Vaughn	.20	.06
18 Ryan Klesko	.20	.06
19 Chuck Finley	.20	.06
20 Barry Bonds	1.25	.35
21 Dennis Eckersley	.20	.06
22 Kenny Lofton	.20	.06
23 Rafael Palmeiro	.30	.09
24 Mike Stanley	.10	.03
25 Gregg Jefferies	.10	.03
26 Robin Ventura	.20	.06
27 Mark McGwire	1.25	.35
28 Ozzie Smith	.75	.23
29 Troy Neel	.10	.03
30 Tony Gwynn	.60	.18
31 Ken Griffey Jr.	.75	.23
32 Will Clark	.50	.15
33 Craig Biggio	.30	.09
34 Shawon Dunston	.10	.03
35 Wilson Alvarez	.10	.03
36 Bobby Bonilla	.20	.06
37 Marquis Grissom	.20	.06
38 Ben McDonald	.10	.03
39 Delino DeShields	.10	.03
40 Barry Larkin	.30	.09
41 John Olerud	.20	.06
42 Jose Canseco	.50	.15
43 Greg Vaughn	.10	.03
44 Gary Sheffield	.20	.06
45 Paul O'Neill	.30	.09
46 Bob Hamelin	.10	.03
47 Don Mattingly	1.25	.35
48 John Franco	.20	.06
49 Bret Boone	.20	.06
50 Rick Aguilera	.20	.06
51 Tim Wallach	.10	.03
52 Roberto Kelly	.10	.03
53 Danny Tartabull	.10	.03
54 Randy Johnson	.50	.15
55 Greg McMichael	.10	.03
56 Bip Roberts	.10	.03
57 David Cone	.20	.06
58 Raul Mondesi	.20	.06
59 Travis Fryman	.20	.06
60 Jeff Conine	.20	.06
61 Jeff Bagwell	.30	.09
62 Rickey Henderson	.50	.15
63 Fred McGriff	.30	.09
64 Matt Williams	.20	.06
65 Rick Wilkins	.10	.03
66 Eric Karros	.20	.06
67 Mel Rojas	.10	.03
68 Juan Gonzalez	.30	.09
69 Chuck Carr	.10	.03
70 Moises Alou	.20	.06
71 Mark Grace	.30	.09
72 Alex Fernandez	.10	.03
73 Rod Beck	.10	.03
74 Ray Lankford	.10	.03
75 Dean Palmer	.20	.06
76 Joe Carter	.20	.06
77 Mike Piazza	.75	.23
78 Eddie Murray	.50	.15
79 Dave Nilsson	.10	.03
80 Brett Butler	.20	.06
81 Roberto Alomar	.30	.09
82 Jeff Kent	.20	.06
83 Andres Galarraga	.20	.06
84 Brady Anderson	.20	.06
85 Jimmy Key	.20	.06
86 Bret Saberhagen	.20	.06
87 Chili Davis	.20	.06
88 Jose Rijo	.10	.03
89 Wade Boggs	.30	.09
90 Len Dykstra	.20	.06
91 Steve Howe	.10	.03
92 Hal Morris	.10	.03
93 Larry Walker	.30	.09
94 Jeff Montgomery	.10	.03
95 Wil Cordero	.10	.03
96 Jay Bell	.20	.06
97 Tom Glavine	.30	.09
98 Chris Hoiles	.10	.03
99 Steve Avery	.10	.03
100 Ruben Sierra	.10	.03
101 Mickey Tettleton	.10	.03
102 Paul Molitor	.30	.09
103 Carlos Baerga	.10	.03
104 Walt Weiss	.10	.03
105 Darren Daulton	.20	.06
106 Jack McDowell	.10	.03
107 Doug Drabek	.10	.03
108 Mark Langston	.10	.03
109 Manny Ramirez	.30	.09
110 Kevin Appier	.20	.06
111 Andy Benes	.10	.03
112 Chuck Knoblauch	.20	.06
113 Kirby Puckett	.50	.15
114 Dante Bichette	.20	.06
115 Deion Sanders	.30	.09
116 Albert Belle	.20	.06
117 Todd Zeile	.20	.06
118 Devon White	.20	.06
119 Tim Salmon	.30	.09
120 Frank Thomas	.50	.15
121 John Wetteland	.20	.06
122 James Mouton	.10	.03
123 Javier Lopez	.20	.06
124 Carlos Delgado	.20	.06
125 Cliff Floyd	.20	.06
126 Alex Gonzalez	.10	.03
127 Billy Ashley	.10	.03
128 Rondell White	.20	.06
129 Rico Brogna	.10	.03
130 Melvin Nieves	.10	.03
131 Jose Oliva	.10	.03
132 J.R. Phillips	.10	.03

1995 Bazooka Red Hot

This 22-card standard-size set, featuring some of the most popular players, is similar to the regular issue. Differences between these cards and the regular issue include the photo being shaded in a red background, the position is also in red and the player's name is stamped in gold foil. The backs are numbered with an "RH" prefix.

	Nm-Mt	Ex-Mt
COMPLETE SET (22)	20.00	6.00
RH1 Greg Maddux	1.50	.45
RH2 Cal Ripken Jr.	3.00	.90
RH3 Barry Bonds	2.50	.75
RH4 Kenny Lofton	.40	.12
RH5 Mike Stanley	.40	.12
RH6 Tony Gwynn	1.25	.35
RH7 Ken Griffey Jr.	1.50	.45
RH8 Barry Larkin	.50	.15
RH9 Jose Canseco	.75	.23
RH10 Paul O'Neill	.50	.15
RH11 Randy Johnson	.75	.23
RH12 David Cone	.40	.12
RH13 Jeff Bagwell	.50	.15
RH14 Matt Williams	.40	.12
RH15 Mike Piazza	1.50	.45
RH16 Roberto Alomar	.50	.15
RH17 Jimmy Key	.40	.12
RH18 Wade Boggs	.50	.15
RH19 Paul Molitor	.50	.15
RH20 Carlos Baerga	.40	.12
RH21 Albert Belle	.40	.12
RH22 Frank Thomas	.75	.23

1996 Bazooka

The 1996 Bazooka standard-size set was issued in one series totalling 132 cards. The five-card packs retailed for $.50 each. The set contains baseball's best rookies, rising stars and veterans. The card fronts feature an exciting full-color photo of the player. The back of each card contains one of five different Bazooka Joe characters, along with the Bazooka Ball flipping game, the player's biographical data and 1995 career statistics. Additionally, every card contains a Funny Fortune, which predicts the fate of each player on a particular date. Packs contain five cards plus one chunk of Bazooka gum. Finally, each factory set also included a reprint of Mickey Mantle's 1959 Bazooka card.

	Nm-Mt	Ex-Mt
COMP.FACT.SET (133)	12.00	3.60
COMPLETE SET (132)	10.00	3.00
1 Ken Griffey, Jr.	.75	.23
2 J.T. Snow	.20	.06
3 Rondell White	.20	.06
4 Reggie Sanders	.20	.06
5 Jeff Montgomery	.20	.06
6 Mike Stanley	.20	.06
7 Bernie Williams	.30	.09
8 Mike Piazza	.75	.23
9 Brian L.Hunter	.20	.06
10 Len Dykstra	.20	.06
11 Ray Lankford	.20	.06
12 Kenny Lofton	.20	.06
13 Robin Ventura	.20	.06
14 Devon White	.20	.06
15 Cal Ripken	1.50	.45
16 Heathcliff Slocumb	.20	.06
17 Ryan Klesko	.20	.06
18 Terry Steinbach	.20	.06
19 Travis Fryman	.20	.06
20 Sammy Sosa	.75	.23
21 Jim Thome	.50	.15
22 Kenny Rogers	.20	.06
23 Don Mattingly	1.25	.35
24 Kirby Puckett	.50	.15
25 Matt Williams	.20	.06
26 Larry Walker	.30	.09
27 Tim Wakefield	.20	.06
28 Greg Vaughn	.20	.06
29 Denny Neagle	.20	.06
30 Ken Caminiti	.20	.06
31 Garret Anderson	.20	.06
32 Brady Anderson	.20	.06
33 Carlos Baerga	.20	.06
34 Wade Boggs	.30	.09
35 Roberto Alomar	.30	.09
36 Eric Karros	.20	.06
37 Jay Buhner	.20	.06
38 Dante Bichette	.20	.06
39 Darren Daulton	.20	.06
40 Jeff Bagwell	.30	.09
41 Jay Bell	.20	.06
42 Dennis Eckersley	.20	.06
43 Will Clark	.50	.15
44 Tom Glavine	.30	.09
45 Rick Aguilera	.20	.06
46 Kevin Seitzer	.20	.06
47 Bret Boone	.20	.06
48 Mark Grace	.30	.09
49 Ray Durham	.20	.06
50 Rico Brogna	.20	.06
51 Kevin Appier	.20	.06
52 Moises Alou	.20	.06
53 Jeff Conine	.20	.06
54 Marty Cordova	.20	.06
55 Jose Mesa	.20	.06
56 Rod Beck	.20	.06
57 Marquis Grissom	.20	.06
58 David Cone	.20	.06
59 Albert Belle	.20	.06
60 Lee Smith	.20	.06
61 Frank Thomas	.50	.15
62 Roger Clemens	1.00	.30
63 Bobby Bonilla	.20	.06
64 Paul Molitor	.30	.09
65 Chuck Knoblauch	.20	.06
66 Steve Finley	.20	.06
67 Craig Biggio	.30	.09
68 Ramon Martinez	.20	.06
69 Jason Isringhausen	.20	.06
70 Mark Wohlers	.20	.06
71 Vinny Castilla	.20	.06
72 Ron Gant	.20	.06
73 Juan Gonzalez	.30	.09
74 Mark McGwire	1.25	.35
75 Jeff King	.20	.06
76 Pedro Martinez	.50	.15
77 Chad Curtis	.20	.06
78 John Olerud	.20	.06
79 Greg Maddux	.75	.23
80 Derek Jeter	1.25	.35
81 Mike Mussina	.30	.09
82 Gregg Jefferies	.20	.06
83 Jim Edmonds	.20	.06
84 Carlos Perez	.20	.06
85 Mo Vaughn	.20	.06
86 Todd Hundley	.20	.06
87 Roberto Hernandez	.20	.06
88 Derek Bell	.20	.06
89 Andres Galarraga	.20	.06
90 Brian McRae	.20	.06
91 Joe Carter	.20	.06
92 Orlando Merced	.20	.06
93 Cecil Fielder	.20	.06
94 Dean Palmer	.20	.06
95 Randy Johnson	.50	.15
96 Chipper Jones	.50	.15
97 Barry Larkin	.30	.09
98 Hideo Nomo	.50	.15
99 Gary Gaetti	.20	.06
100 Edgar Martinez	.30	.09
101 John Wetteland	.20	.06
102 Rafael Palmeiro	.30	.09
103 Chuck Finley	.20	.06
104 Ivan Rodriguez	.50	.15
105 Shawn Green	.20	.06
106 Manny Ramirez	.30	.09
107 Lance Johnson	.20	.06
108 Jose Canseco	.50	.15
109 Fred McGriff	.30	.09
110 David Segui	.20	.06
111 Tim Salmon	.30	.09
112 Hal Morris	.20	.06
113 Tino Martinez	.30	.09
114 Bret Saberhagen	.20	.06
115 Brian Jordan	.20	.06
116 David Justice	.20	.06
117 Jack McDowell	.20	.06
118 Barry Bonds	1.25	.35
119 Mark Langston	.20	.06
120 John Valentin	.20	.06
121 Raul Mondesi	.20	.06
122 Quilvio Veras	.20	.06
123 Randy Myers	.20	.06
124 Tony Gwynn	.60	.18
125 Johnny Damon	.30	.09
126 Doug Drabek	.20	.06
127 Bill Pulsipher	.20	.06
128 Paul O'Neill	.30	.09
129 Rickey Henderson	.50	.15
130 Deion Sanders	.30	.09
131 Orel Hershiser	.20	.06
132 Gary Sheffield	.20	.06
NNO Mickey Mantle 1959 Bazooka	10.00	3.00

2003 Bazooka

This 280 card set was released in March, 2003. The set was isssued in eight card packs that had an $2 SRP. These packs came 24 packs to a box and 10 boxes to a case. The Bazooka Joe card (number 7) was issued in a basic version as well as feauturing a logo of all the major league teams. In addition, 20 cards from the set featured a fascimile signature of the featured player as well as a colorized Bazooka logo. These regular and special logo cards of those player were printed to the same quantity.

	Nm-Mt	Ex-Mt
COMP.SET w/LOGO's (330)	80.00	24.00
COMPLETE SET (310)	60.00	18.00
COMP.SET w/o JOE's (280)	50.00	15.00
COMMON CARD (1-280)	.40	.12
COMMON ROOKIE	.40	.12
COMMON LOGO	.40	.12
1 Luis Castillo	.40	.12
2 Randy Winn	.40	.12
3 Orlando Hudson	.40	.12
3A Orlando Hudson Logo	.40	.12
4 Fernando Vina	.40	.12
5 Pat Burrell	.40	.12
6 Brad Wilkerson	.40	.12
7 Bazooka Joe	.40	.12
7AN Bazooka Joe Angels	.40	.12
7AS Bazooka Joe A's	.40	.12
7AT Bazooka Joe Astros	.40	.12
7BL Bazooka Joe Blue Jays	.40	.12
7BR Bazooka Joe Braves	.40	.12
7BW Bazooka Joe Brewers	.40	.12
7CA Bazooka Joe Cardinals	.40	.12
7CU Bazooka Joe Cubs	.40	.12
7DE Bazooka Joe Devil Rays	.40	.12
7DI Bazooka Joe Diamondbacks	.40	.12
7DO Bazooka Joe Dodgers	.40	.12
7EX Bazooka Joe Expos	.40	.12
7GI Bazooka Joe Giants	.40	.12
7IN Bazooka Joe Indians	.40	.12
7MA Bazooka Joe Mariners	.40	.12
7ME Bazooka Joe Mets	.40	.12
7MR Bazooka Joe Marlins	.40	.12
7OR Bazooka Joe Orioles	.40	.12
7PA Bazooka Joe Padres	.40	.12
7PH Bazooka Joe Phillies	.40	.12
7PI Bazooka Joe Pirates	.40	.12
7RA Bazooka Joe Rangers	.40	.12
7RC Bazooka Joe Rockies	.40	.12
7RD Bazooka Joe Reds	.40	.12
7RS Bazooka Joe Red Sox	.40	.12
7RY Bazooka Joe Royals	.40	.12
7TI Bazooka Joe Tigers	.40	.12
7TW Bazooka Joe Twins	.40	.12
7WS Bazooka Joe White Sox	.40	.12
7YA Bazooka Joe Yankees	.40	.12
8 Javy Lopez	.40	.12
9 Juan Pierre	.40	.12
10 Hideo Nomo	1.00	.30
11 Barry Larkin	.60	.18
12 Alfonso Soriano	.60	.18
12A Alfonso Soriano Logo	.60	.18
13 Rodrigo Lopez	.40	.12
14 Mark Ellis	.40	.12
15 Tim Salmon	.60	.18
16 Garret Anderson	.40	.12
16A Garret Anderson Logo	.40	.12
17 Aaron Boone	.40	.12
18 Jason Kendall	.40	.12
19 Hee Seop Choi	.40	.12
20 Jorge Posada	.60	.18
21 Sammy Sosa	1.50	.45
22 Mark Prior	1.00	.30
22A Mark Prior Logo	1.00	.30
23 Mark Teixeira	.40	.12
24 Manny Ramirez	.60	.18
25 Jim Thome	1.00	.30
26 A.J. Pierzynski	.40	.12
27 Scott Rolen	1.00	.30
28 Austin Kearns	.40	.12
29 Bret Boone	.40	.12
30 Ken Griffey Jr.	1.50	.45
31 Greg Maddux	1.50	.45
32 Derek Lowe	.40	.12
33 David Wells	.40	.12
34 A.J. Burnett	.40	.12
35 Randall Simon	.40	.12
36 Nick Johnson	.40	.12
37 Junior Spivey	.40	.12
38 Eric Gagne	1.00	.30
39 Darin Erstad	.40	.12
40 Marty Cordova	.40	.12
41 Brett Myers	.40	.12
42 Mo Vaughn	.40	.12
43 Randy Wolf	.40	.12
44 Vicente Padilla	.40	.12
45 Elmer Dessens	.40	.12
46 Jason Simontacchi	.40	.12
47 John Mabry	.40	.12
48 Torii Hunter	.40	.12
48A Torii Hunter Logo	.40	.12
49 Lyle Overbay	.40	.12
50 Kirk Saarloos	.40	.12
51 Bernie Williams	.60	.18
52 Wade Miller	.40	.12
53 Bobby Abreu	.40	.12
54 Wilson Betemit	.40	.12
55 Edwin Almonte	.40	.12
56 Jarrod Washburn	.40	.12
57 Drew Henson	.40	.12
58 Tony Batista	.40	.12
59 Juan Rivera	.40	.12
60 Larry Walker	.60	.18
61 Brandon Phillips	.40	.12
62 Franklyn German	.40	.12
63 Victor Martinez	.60	.18
63A Victor Martinez Logo	.60	.18
64 Moises Alou	.40	.12
65 Nomar Garciaparra	1.50	.45
66 Willie Harris	.40	.12
67 Sean Casey	.40	.12
68 Omar Vizquel	.60	.18
69 Robert Fick	.40	.12
70 Curt Schilling	.40	.12
70A Curt Schilling Logo	.40	.12
71 Adam Kennedy	.40	.12
72 Scott Hairston	.40	.12
73 Jimmy Journell	.40	.12
74 Rafael Furcal	.40	.12
75 Barry Zito	.40	.12
76 Ed Rogers	.40	.12
77 Cliff Floyd	.40	.12
78 Matt Clement	.40	.12
79 Mike Lowell	.40	.12
80 Randy Johnson	1.00	.30
81 Craig Biggio	.60	.18
82 Carlos Beltran	.60	.18
83 Paul Lo Duca	.40	.12
84 Jose Vidro	.40	.12
85 Gary Sheffield	.40	.12
86 Jacque Jones	.40	.12
87 Corey Hart	.40	.12
88 Roberto Alomar	.60	.18
89 Robin Ventura	.40	.12
90 Pedro Martinez	1.00	.30
91 Scott Hatteberg	.40	.12
92 Marlon Byrd	.40	.12
93 Pokey Reese	.40	.12
94 Sean Burroughs	.40	.12
95 Magglio Ordonez	.40	.12
96 Mariano Rivera	.60	.18
97 John Olerud	.40	.12
98 Edgar Renteria	.40	.12
99 Ben Grieve	.40	.12
100 Barry Bonds	2.50	.75
100A Barry Bonds Logo	2.50	.75
101 Ivan Rodriguez	1.00	.30
102 Josh Phelps	.40	.12
103 Nobuaki Yoshida RC	.50	.15
103A Nobuaki Yoshida Logo	.50	.15
104 Roy Halladay	.40	.12
105 Mark Buehrle	.40	.12
106 Chan Ho Park	.40	.12
107 Joe Kennedy	.40	.12
108 Shin-Soo Choo	.40	.12

08A Shin-Soo Choo Logo .40 .12
09 Ryan Jensen .40 .12
10 Todd Helton .60 .18
11 Chris Duncan RC .50 .15
12 Taggert Bozied .40 .12
13 Sean Burnett .40 .12
14 Mike Lieberthal .40 .12
15 Josh Beckett .40 .12
16 Andy Pettitte .60 .18
17 Jose Reyes .40 .12
17A Jose Reyes Logo .40 .12
18 Bartolo Colon .40 .12
19 Justin Morneau .60 .18
20 Lance Berkman .40 .12
21 Mike Wodnicki RC .50 .15
22 Craig Brazell RC .75 .23
22A Craig Brazell Logo .75 .23
23 Troy Glaus .40 .12
24 John Smoltz .60 .18
25 Mike Sweeney .40 .12
26 Jay Gibbons .40 .12
27 Kerry Wood 1.00 .30
28 Ellis Burks .40 .12
29 Carlos Pena .40 .12
30 Shawn Green .40 .12
31 Jason Stokes .60 .18
31A Jason Stokes Logo .60 .18
32 Raul Ibanez .40 .12
33 Francisco Rodriguez .40 .12
33A Francisco Rodriguez Logo .40 .12
34 Adrian Beltre .60 .18
35 Richie Sexson .40 .12
36 Paul Byrd .40 .12
37 Bobby Kielty .40 .12
38 Dewon Brazelton .40 .12
39 Jeremy Griffiths RC .75 .23
40 Vladimir Guerrero 1.00 .30
40A Vladimir Guerrero Logo 1.00 .30
41 Jake Peavy .40 .12
42 Bryan Bullington RC 1.25 .35
43 Orlando Cabrera .40 .12
44 Scott Erickson .40 .12
45 Doug Mientkiewicz .40 .12
46 Derrek Lee .40 .12
47 Daryl Clark RC .75 .23
48 Trevor Hoffman .40 .12
49 Gabe Gross .40 .12
50 Roger Clemens 2.00 .60
51 Khalil Greene 2.00 .60
51A Khalil Greene Logo 2.00 .60
52 Cory Doyne RC .50 .15
153 Brandon Roberson RC .50 .15
154 Josh Fogg .40 .12
155 Eric Chavez .40 .12
156 Kris Benson .40 .12
157 Billy Koch .40 .12
158 Jermaine Dye .40 .12
159 Kip Bouknight RC .75 .23
160 Brian Giles .40 .12
161 Justin Huber .40 .12
162 Mike Restovich .40 .12
163 Brandon Webb RC 1.00 .30
164 Odalis Perez .40 .12
165 Phil Nevin .40 .12
166 Dontrelle Willis .60 .18
167 Aaron Heilman .40 .12
168 Dustin Moseley RC .75 .23
169 Rylan Reed RC .50 .15
170 Miguel Tejada .40 .12
171 Nic Jackson .40 .12
172 Anthony Webster RC .75 .23
173 Jorge Julio .40 .12
174 Kevin Millwood .40 .12
175 Brian Jordan .40 .12
176 Terry Tiffee RC .75 .23
177 Dallas McPherson 1.00 .30
178 Freddy Garcia .40 .12
179 Jaime Moyer .40 .12
180 Rafael Palmeiro .60 .18
181 Mike O'Keefe RC .50 .15
182 Kevin Youkilis RC 1.50 .45
183 Kip Wells .40 .12
184 Joe Mauer 1.00 .30
185 Edgar Martinez .60 .18
186 Jamie Bubela RC .50 .15
187 Jose Hernandez .40 .12
188 Josh Hamilton .40 .12
189 Matt Diaz RC .75 .23
190 Chipper Jones 1.00 .30
191 Kevin Mench .40 .12
192 Joey Gomes RC .50 .15
193 Shannon Stewart .40 .12
194 David Eckstein .40 .12
195 Mike Piazza 1.50 .45
196 Damian Moss .40 .12
197 Mike Fontenot .40 .12
198 Shea Hillenbrand .40 .12
199 Evel Bastida-Martinez RC .50 .15
200 Jason Giambi .40 .12
201 Aron Weston RC .50 .15
202 Frank Thomas 1.00 .30
203 Carlos Lee .40 .12
204 C.C. Sabathia .40 .12
205 Jim Edmonds .40 .12
206 Jemel Spearman RC .50 .15
207 Jason Jennings .40 .12
208 Jeremy Bonderman RC .75 .23
209 Preston Wilson .40 .12
210 Eric Hinske .40 .12
210A Eric Hinske Logo .40 .12
211 Will Smith .40 .12
212 Matthew Hagen RC .75 .23
213 Joe Randa .40 .12
214 James Loney .40 .12
215 Carlos Delgado .40 .12
216 Chris Kroski RC .50 .15
217 Cristian Guzman .40 .12
218 Tomo Ohka .40 .12
219 Al Leiter .40 .12
220 Adam Dunn .60 .18
221 Raul Mondesi .40 .12
222 Donald Hood RC .75 .23
223 Mark Mulder .40 .12
224 Mike Williams .40 .12
225 Ryan Klesko .40 .12
226 Rich Aurilia .40 .12
227 Chris Snelling .40 .12
228 Gary Schneidmiller RC .50 .15
229 Ichiro Suzuki 1.50 .45
229A Ichiro Suzuki Logo 1.50 .45
230 Luis Gonzalez .40 .12
231 Rocco Baldelli .40 .12
232 Callix Crabbe RC .75 .23
233 Adrian Gonzalez .40 .12
234 Corey Koskie .40 .12
235 Tom Glavine .60 .18
236 Kevin Beavers RC .50 .15
237 Frank Catalanotto .40 .12
238 Kevin Cash .40 .12
239 Nick Trzesniak RC .50 .15
240 Paul Konerko .40 .12
241 Jose Cruz Jr. .40 .12
242 Hank Blalock .60 .18
243 J.D. Drew .40 .12
244 Kazuhiro Sasaki .40 .12
245 Jeff Bagwell .60 .18
246 Jason Schmidt .40 .12
247 Xavier Nady .40 .12
248 Aramis Ramirez .40 .12
249 Jimmy Rollins .40 .12
250 Alex Rodriguez 1.50 .45
250A Alex Rodriguez Logo 1.50 .45
251 Terrence Long .40 .12
252 Derek Jeter 2.50 .75
253 Edgardo Alfonzo .40 .12
254 Toby Hall .40 .12
255 Kazuhisa Ishii .40 .12
256 Brad Nelson .40 .12
257 Kevin Brown .40 .12
258 Roy Oswalt .40 .12
259 Mike Cameron .40 .12
260 Juan Gonzalez .60 .18
261 Dmitri Young .40 .12
262 Jose Jimenez .40 .12
263 Wily Mo Pena .40 .12
264 Joe Borchard .40 .12
265 Mike Mussina .60 .18
266 Fred McGriff .60 .18
267 Johnny Damon 1.00 .30
268 Joel Pineiro .40 .12
269 Andruw Jones .40 .12
270 Tim Hudson .40 .12
271 Chad Tracy .40 .12
272 Brad Fullmer .40 .12
273 Boof Bonser .40 .12
274 Clint Nageotte .40 .12
275 Jeff Kent .40 .12
276 Tino Martinez .60 .18
277 Matt Morris .40 .12
278 Jonny Gomes .40 .12
279 Benito Santiago .40 .12
280 Albert Pujols 2.00 .60
280A Albert Pujols Logo 2.00 .60

2003 Bazooka Minis

Issued at a stated rate of one per pack, this is a complete parallel of the Bazooka set. All the cards were issued in this parallel set including all 31 Bazooka Joe cards as well as the 20 logo variation cards. These cards measure approximately 2 1/4" by 3 1/8"/

Nm-Mt Ex-Mt
*MINIS: .75X TO 2X BASIC
*MINIS JOE'S: .75X TO 2X BASIC JOE'S
*MINIS LOGO'S: .75X TO 2X BASIC LOGO'S
*MINI'S RC'S: .75X TO 2X BASIC RC'S

2003 Bazooka Silver

Issued at a stated rate of almost one per pack, this is a complete parallel to the Bazooka set. These cards can be identified by their silver borders. Again, all the Bazooka Joe varieties as well as the logo cards were issued in a silver version.

Nm-Mt Ex-Mt
*SILVER: .75X TO 2X BASIC
*SILVER JOE'S: .75X TO 2X BASIC JOE'S
*SILVER LOGO'S: .75X TO 2X BASIC LOGO'S
*SILVER RC'S: .75X TO 2X BASIC

2003 Bazooka 4 on 1 Sticker

Inserted at a stated rate of one in four hobby and one in 6 retail packs, these 55 sticker cards feature four players on the front

Nm-Mt Ex-Mt
1 Mark Prior 2.00 .60
Roy Oswalt
Jarrod Washburn
Barry Zito
2 Troy Glaus 1.00 .30
Shea Hillenbrand
Eric Chavez
Eric Hinske
3 Orlando Hudson 1.25 .35
Alfonso Soriano
Roberto Alomar
Jose Vidro
4 Nomar Garciaparra 5.00 1.50
Derek Jeter
Miguel Tejada
Alex Rodriguez
5 Jason Giambi 2.00 .60
Jim Thome
Todd Helton
Rafael Palmeiro
6 Mike Williams 1.25 .35
Trevor Hoffman
Billy Koch
John Smoltz
7 Jorge Posada 3.00 .90
Mike Piazza
A.J. Pierzynski
Ivan Rodriguez
8 Vladimir Guerrero 2.00 .60
Jim Edmonds
Manny Ramirez
Brad Wilkerson
9 Shawn Green 3.00 .90
Sammy Sosa
Torri Hunter
Larry Walker
10 Bernie Williams 3.00 .90
Ken Griffey Jr.
Ichiro Suzuki
Adam Dunn
11 John Olerud 1.00 .30
Mike Lieberthal
Terrence Long
Drew Henson
12 Edgar Martinez 1.25 .35
Bret Boone
Mo Vaughn
Robert Fick
13 Randy Johnson 4.00 1.20
Roger Clemens
Pedro Martinez
Greg Maddux
14 Curt Schilling 2.00 .60
Tim Hudson
Tom Glavine
Kerry Wood
15 Paul Konerko 2.00 .60
Mike Sweeney
Cristian Guzman
Scott Rolen
16 Josh Phelps 1.25 .35
Brandon Phillips
Hee Seop Choi
Hank Blalock
17 Benito Santiago 1.25 .35
Barry Larkin
Gary Sheffield
Carlos Delgado
18 Juan Rivera 1.00 .30
Jose Reyes
Sean Burroughs
Carlos Pena
19 Tony Batista 1.25 .35
Tim Salmon
Jeff Bagwell
Raul Ibanez
20 Edgardo Alfonzo 1.00 .30
Nic Jackson
Luis Castillo
David Eckstein
21 David Wells 1.00 .30
Ryan Klesko
Phil Nevin
Jeff Kent
22 Derek Lowe 1.00 .30
Vicente Padilla
Kevin Millwood
Joel Pineiro
23 Fernando Vina 1.00 .30
Darin Erstad
Jimmy Rollins
Doug Mientkiewicz
24 Joe Mauer 2.00 .60
Justin Huber
Jason Stokes
Chad Tracy
25 Austin Kearns 1.25 .35
Junior Spivey
Brett Myers
Victor Martinez
26 Khalil Greene 4.00 1.20
Gabe Gross
Kevin Cash
James Loney
27 Albert Pujols 4.00 1.20
Mark Buehrle
Chipper Jones
Lance Berkman
28 Adam Kennedy 2.00 .60
Craig Biggio
Johnny Damon
Randy Winn
29 Brian Giles 1.00 .30
J.D. Drew
Marlon Byrd
Joe Borchard
30 Al Leiter 1.25 .35
Mike Mussina
Bartolo Colon
Freddy Garcia
31 Jason Kendall 1.00 .30
Richie Sexson
Mike Lowell
Paul LoDuca
32 Pat Burrell 1.00 .30
Garret Anderson
Cliff Floyd
Andruw Jones
33 Xavier Nady 1.25 .35
Bobby Abreu
Taggert Bozied
Adrian Beltre
34 Rocco Baldelli 1.00 .30
Dontrelle Willis
Chris Snelling
Mark Teixeira
35 Willie Harris 1.00 .30
Nick Johnson
Jason Jennings
Kazuhisa Ishii
36 Mark Mulder 1.00 .30
Sean Burnett
Paul Byrd
Josh Beckett
37 Corey Koskie 1.25 .35
Aramis Ramirez
Tino Martinez
Moises Alou
38 Jose Cruz Jr. 1.00 .30
Roy Halladay
Dewon Brazelton
Jonny Gomes
39 Odalis Perez 1.00 .30
Kevin Brown
Matt Clement
Randy Wolf
40 Eric Gagne 2.00 .60
Jose Jimenez
Franklyn German
Edwin Almonte
41 Luis Gonzalez 1.25 .35
Shannon Stewart
Brian Jordan
Juan Gonzalez
42 Toby Hall 1.00 .30
Joe Kennedy
Javier Lopez
Damian Moss
43 Magglio Ordonez 1.00 .30
Carlos Lee
Randall Simon
Dmitri Young
44 Sean Casey 1.00 .30
Aaron Boone
Jacque Jones
Michael Restovich
45 Adrian Gonzalez 2.00 .60
Corey Hart
Fred McGriff
Frank Thomas
46 C.C. Sabathia 1.25 .35
Omar Vizquel
Andy Pettitte
Robin Ventura
47 Jason Schmidt 1.00 .30
Ellis Burks
Joe Randa
Kris Benson
48 Mike Cameron 1.00 .30
Pokey Reese
Jermaine Dye
Preston Wilson
49 Chan Ho Park 2.00 .60
Kazuhiro Sasaki
Tomo Ohka
Hideo Nomo
50 Jason Simontacchi 1.00 .30
Kip Wells
Matt Morris
Rodrigo Lopez
51 Dallas McPherson 1.50 .45
Josh Hamilton
Jeremy Bonderman
Aaron Heilman
52 Nobuaki Yoshida 2.50 .75
Chris Duncan
Craig Brazell
Bryan Bullington
53 Daryl Clark 2.00 .60
Brandon Webb
Dustin Moseley
Mike O'Keefe
54 Kevin Youkilis 3.00 .90
Jaime Bubela
Matt Diaz
Joey Gomes
55 Chris Kroski 1.00 .30
Donald Hood
Gary Schneidmiller
Callix Crabbe

2003 Bazooka Blasts Relics

Issued at different odds depending on what group the player belonged to, these 35 cards feature a game-used bat chip of the featured player.

Nm-Mt Ex-Mt
GROUP A STATED ODDS 1:1666
GROUP B STATED ODDS 1:306
GROUP C STATED ODDS 1:197
GROUP D STATED ODDS 1:95
GROUP E STATED ODDS 1:52
GROUP F STATED ODDS 1:76
GROUP G STATED ODDS 1:326
GROUP H STATED ODDS 1:48
PARALLEL 25 ODDS 1:524
PARALLEL 25 PRINT RUN 25 #'d SETS
NO PARALLEL 25 PRICING DUE TO SCARCITY
AG Andres Galarraga C 8.00 2.40
ANR Aramis Ramirez E 8.00 2.40
AR Alex Rodriguez F 15.00 4.50
AS Alfonso Soriano D 10.00 3.00
BB Barry Bonds F 20.00 6.00
BW Bernie Williams D 10.00 3.00
CD Carlos Delgado D 8.00 2.40
CI Cesar Izturis B 10.00 3.00
CJ Chipper Jones E 10.00 3.00
DE Darin Erstad F 8.00 2.40
DH Drew Henson H 8.00 2.40
EM Edgar Martinez D 10.00 3.00
GS Gary Sheffield H 8.00 2.40
IR Ivan Rodriguez G 10.00 3.00
JD Johnny Damon H 10.00 3.00
JDD J.D. Drew B 10.00 3.00
JP Jorge Posada D 10.00 3.00
LB Lance Berkman E 8.00 2.40
LG Luis Gonzalez B 10.00 3.00
MP Mike Piazza H 15.00 4.50
MR Manny Ramirez F 10.00 3.00
MS Mike Sweeney C 8.00 2.40
NJ Nick Johnson B 10.00 3.00
PL Paul Lo Duca A 10.00 3.00
RA Roberto Alomar E 10.00 3.00
RH Rickey Henderson H 10.00 3.00
RK Ryan Klesko E 8.00 2.40
RM Raul Mondesi C 8.00 2.40
RP Rafael Palmeiro E 10.00 3.00
RV Robin Ventura F 8.00 2.40
SG Shawn Green D 8.00 2.40
TG Tony Gwynn H 15.00 4.50
TM Tino Martinez E 10.00 3.00
TS Tsuyoshi Shinjo E 8.00 2.40
WB Wilson Betemit E 8.00 2.40

2003 Bazooka Comics

Issued at a stated rate of one in four, these 24 comics, drawn in the style of the old Bazooka

Joe comics, feature some of the leading players in the game.

Nm-Mt Ex-Mt
COMPLETE SET (24) 25.00 7.50
1 Albert Pujols 2.50 .75
2 Alex Rodriguez 2.00 .60
3 Alfonso Soriano 1.00 .30
4 Barry Zito 1.00 .30
5 Chipper Jones 1.25 .35
6 Derek Jeter 3.00 .90
7 Greg Maddux 2.00 .60
8 Ichiro Suzuki 2.00 .60
9 Jason Giambi 1.00 .30
10 Jim Thome 1.25 .35
11 John Smoltz 1.00 .30
12 Mike Piazza 2.00 .60
13 Randy Johnson 1.25 .35
14 Roger Clemens 2.50 .75
15 Sammy Sosa 2.00 .60
16 Shawn Green 1.00 .30
17 Pedro Martinez 1.25 .35
18 Manny Ramirez 1.00 .30
19 Torii Hunter 1.00 .30
20 Ivan Rodriguez 1.25 .35
21 Miguel Tejada 1.00 .30
22 Troy Glaus 1.00 .30
23 Ken Griffey Jr. 2.00 .60
24 Nomar Garciaparra 2.00 .60

2003 Bazooka Piece of Americana Relics

These 30 cards, which feature game-work uniform swatches were issued at different odds depending on which group the card belonged to.

Nm-Mt Ex-Mt
GROUP A STATED ODDS 1:1666
GROUP B STATED ODDS 1:611
GROUP C STATED ODDS 1:226
GROUP D STATED ODDS 1:118
GROUP E STATED ODDS 1:36
GROUP F STATED ODDS 1:73
GROUP G STATED ODDS 1:190
PARALLEL 25 ODDS 1:611
PARALLEL 25 PRINT RUN 25 #'d SETS
NO PARALLEL 25 PRICING DUE TO SCARCITY
AD Adam Dunn G 10.00 3.00
AH Aubrey Huff F 8.00 2.40
AJ Andruw Jones E 8.00 2.40
AL Al Leiter D 8.00 2.40
BB Bret Boone E 8.00 2.40
CB Craig Biggio E 10.00 3.00
CD Carlos Delgado E 8.00 2.40
CG Cristian Guzman E 8.00 2.40
CJ Chipper Jones E 10.00 3.00
CS Curt Schilling D 8.00 2.40
DB Dewon Brazelton F 8.00 2.40
FT Frank Thomas F 10.00 3.00
IR Ivan Rodriguez D 10.00 3.00
JB Jeff Bagwell A 15.00 4.50
JE Jim Edmonds E 8.00 2.40
JK Jeff Kent D 8.00 2.40
LW Larry Walker D 10.00 3.00
MM Mike Mussina C 10.00 3.00
MO Magglio Ordonez E 8.00 2.40
MP Mike Piazza E 15.00 4.50
NG Nomar Garciaparra B 20.00 6.00
PA Albert Pujols E 15.00 4.50
PL Paul Lo Duca B 10.00 3.00
PW Preston Wilson C 8.00 2.40
RF Rafael Furcal C 8.00 2.40
RP Rafael Palmeiro E 10.00 3.00
SG Shawn Green E 8.00 2.40
TG Tony Gwynn G 15.00 4.50
TH Todd Helton E 10.00 3.00
THA Toby Hall F 8.00 2.40

2003 Bazooka Stand-Ups

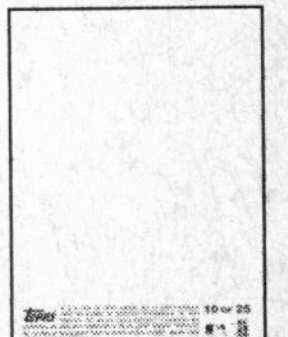

Issued at a stated rate of one in eight hobby and one in 24 retail, this 25 card set features a design similar to the 1964 Topps Stand-Up set.

Nm-Mt Ex-Mt
1 Albert Pujols 6.00 1.80
2 Alfonso Soriano 2.00 .60
3 Ichiro Suzuki 5.00 1.50
4 Sammy Sosa 5.00 1.50
5 Randy Johnson 3.00 .90
6 Barry Bonds 8.00 2.40
7 Vladimir Guerrero 3.00 .90
8 Nomar Garciaparra 5.00 1.50

9 Alex Rodriguez 5.00 1.50
10 Troy Glaus 2.00 .60
11 Barry Zito 2.00 .60
12 Derek Jeter 8.00 2.40
13 Lance Berkman 2.00 .60
14 Larry Walker 2.00 .60
15 Adam Dunn 2.00 .60
16 Shawn Green 2.00 .60
17 Curt Schilling 2.00 .60
18 Todd Helton 2.00 .60
19 Pedro Martinez 3.00 .90
20 Pat Burrell 2.00 .60
21 Miguel Tejada 2.00 .60
22 Manny Ramirez 2.00 .60
23 Mike Piazza 5.00 1.50
24 Jim Thome 3.00 .90
25 Jason Giambi 2.00 .60

2003 Bazooka Stand-Ups Red

Issued as an unperforated card on top of each Bazooka box, these four cards feature some of the leading players. These cards can be differentiated from the regular stand-ups as they have a red border.

Nm-Mt Ex-Mt
COMPLETE SET (4) 8.00 2.40
1 Barry Bonds 4.00 1.20
2 Albert Pujols 3.00 .90
3 Jim Thome 1.50 .45
4 Barry Zito 1.50 .45

2004 Bazooka

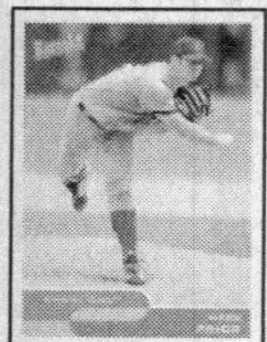

This 300 card set was released in March, 2004. This was issued in eight-card hobby and retail packs with an $2 SRP which came 24 packs to a box and 10 boxes to a case. Cards numbered 1-270 feature veterans while cards 271-300 are all Rookie Cards. It is also important to note that there were 30 variation cards issued as part of this set; each of these variations were produced in the same quantity as their counterpart and thus there is no scarcity and a set is considered complete at 330 cards.

Nm-Mt Ex-Mt
COMPLETE SET (330) 60.00 18.00
COMMON CARD (1-270) .40 .12
COMMON CARD (271-300) .30 .09
1 Bobby Abreu .40 .12
2 Jesse Foppert .40 .12
3 Shea Hillenbrand .40 .12
4 Jose Lima .40 .12
5 Manny Ramirez .60 .18
6 Denny Neagle .40 .12
7 Frank Thomas 1.00 .30
8 A.J. Burnett .40 .12
9 Carl Everett .40 .12
10A Scott Podsednik Blue Jsy .40 .12
10B Scott Podsednik White Jsy .40 .12
11 Travis Lee .40 .12
12 Mike Mussina .60 .18
13 Runelvys Hernandez .40 .12
14 Shannon Stewart .40 .12
15 Miguel Cabrera .60 .18
16 Edgardo Alfonzo .40 .12
17 Victor Zambrano .40 .12
18 Rafael Furcal .40 .12
19 Eric Hinske .40 .12
20 Paul Lo Duca .40 .12
21 Phil Nevin .40 .12
22 Aramis Ramirez .40 .12
23 Jim Thome 1.00 .30
24 Jeromy Burnitz .40 .12
25A Mark Prior Glove Chest 1.00 .30
25B Mark Prior Glove Face 1.00 .30
26 Ramon Hernandez .40 .12
27 Cliff Lee .40 .12
28 Greg Myers .40 .12
29 Robert Fick .40 .12
30 Mike Sweeney .40 .12
31 Carlos Zambrano .40 .12
32 Roberto Alomar .60 .18
33 Orlando Cabrera .40 .12
34 Orlando Hudson .40 .12
35A Nomar Garciaparra Batting 1.50 .45
35B Nomar Garciaparra Fielding 1.50 .45
36 Esteban Loaiza .40 .12
37 Laynce Nix .40 .12
38 Joe Randa .40 .12
39 Juan Uribe .40 .12
40 Pat Burrell .40 .12
41 Steve Finley .40 .12
42 Livan Hernandez .40 .12
43 Al Leiter .40 .12
44 Brett Myers .40 .12
45 Jody Gerut .40 .12
46 Mark Teixeira .40 .12
47 Barry Zito .40 .12
48 Moises Alou .40 .12
49 Mike Cameron .40 .12
50A Albert Pujols One Hand 2.00 .60
50B Albert Pujols Two Hands 2.00 .60
51 Tim Hudson .40 .12
52 Kenny Lofton .40 .12
53 Trot Nixon .40 .12
54 Tim Redding .40 .12
55 Marlon Byrd .40 .12
56 Javier Vazquez .40 .12
57 Sean Burroughs .40 .12
58 Cliff Floyd .40 .12
59 Juan Rivera .40 .12
60 Mike Lieberthal .40 .12
61 Xavier Nady .40 .12
62 Brad Radke .40 .12
63 Miguel Tejada .40 .12
64A Ichiro Suzuki Running 1.50 .45
64B Ichiro Suzuki Throwing 1.50 .45
65 Garret Anderson .40 .12
66 Sean Casey .40 .12
67A Jason Giambi Fielding .40 .12
67B Jason Giambi Hitting .40 .12
68 Aubrey Huff .40 .12
69 Javy Lopez .40 .12
70 Hideo Nomo 1.00 .30
71 Mark Redman .40 .12
72 Jose Vidro .40 .12
73 Rich Aurilia .40 .12
74 Luis Castillo .40 .12
75 Jay Gibbons .40 .12
76 Torii Hunter .40 .12
77 Derek Lowe .40 .12
78 Wes Obermueller .40 .12
79 Edgar Renteria .40 .12
80 Jeff Bagwell .60 .18
81 Fernando Vina .40 .12
82 Frank Catalanotto .40 .12
83 Marcus Giles .40 .12
84 Raul Ibanez .40 .12
85 Mike Lowell .40 .12
86 Tomo Ohka .40 .12
87A Jose Reyes w/Bat .40 .12
87B Jose Reyes w/o Bat .40 .12
88 Omar Vizquel .60 .18
89 Shawn Chacon .40 .12
90 Rocco Baldelli .40 .12
91A Brian Giles w/Bat .40 .12
91B Brian Giles w/o Bat .40 .12
92 Kazuhisa Ishii .40 .12
93 Greg Maddux 1.50 .45
94 John Olerud .40 .12
95 Eric Chavez .40 .12
96 Doug Waechter .40 .12
97 Tony Batista .40 .12
98 Jeriome Robertson .40 .12
99 Troy Glaus .40 .12
100A Eric Gagne Hand Out 1.00 .30
100B Eric Gagne Hand Up 1.00 .30
101A Pedro Martinez Leg Down 1.00 .30
101B Pedro Martinez Leg Up 1.00 .30
102 Magglio Ordonez .40 .12
103A Alex Rodriguez w/Bat 1.50 .45
103B Alex Rodriguez w/o Bat 1.50 .45
104 Jason Bay .40 .12
105 Larry Walker .60 .18
106 Matt Clement .40 .12
107 Tom Glavine .60 .18
108 Geoff Jenkins .40 .12
109 Victor Martinez .40 .12
110 David Ortiz 1.00 .30
111 Ivan Rodriguez 1.00 .30
112 Jarrod Washburn .40 .12
113 Josh Beckett .40 .12
114 Bartolo Colon .40 .12
115 Juan Gonzalez .60 .18
116A Derek Jeter Fielding 2.00 .60
116B Derek Jeter Hitting 2.00 .60
117 Edgar Martinez .60 .18
118 Ramon Ortiz .40 .12
119 Scott Rolen 1.00 .30
120A Brandon Webb w/Ball .40 .12
120B Brandon Webb w/o Ball .40 .12
121 Carlos Beltran .60 .18
122 Jose Contreras .40 .12
123 Luis Gonzalez .40 .12
124 Jason Johnson .40 .12
125 Luis Matos .40 .12
126 Russ Ortiz .40 .12
127 Damian Rolls .40 .12
128 David Wells .40 .12
129 Adrian Beltre .60 .18
130 Shawn Green .40 .12
131 Nate Cornejo .40 .12
132 Nick Johnson .40 .12
133 Joe Mays .40 .12
134 Roy Oswalt .40 .12
135 C.C. Sabathia .40 .12
136A Vernon Wells Fielding .40 .12
136B Vernon Wells Hitting .40 .12
137 Kris Benson .40 .12
138 Carl Crawford .40 .12
139A Ken Griffey Jr. Fielding 1.50 .45
139B Ken Griffey Jr. Hitting 1.50 .45
140A Randy Johnson Black Jsy 1.00 .30
140B Randy Johnson White Jsy 1.00 .30
141 Fred McGriff .60 .18
142 Vicente Padilla .40 .12
143 Tim Salmon .60 .18
144 Kip Wells .40 .12
145 Lance Berkman .40 .12
146 Jose Cruz Jr. .40 .12
147 Marquis Grissom .40 .12
148 Jacque Jones .40 .12
149 Gil Meche .40 .12
150A Vladimir Guerrero Fielding 1.00 .30
150B Vladimir Guerrero Hitting 1.00 .30
151 Reggie Sanders .40 .12
152 Ty Wigginton .40 .12
153 Angel Berroa .40 .12
154 Johnny Damon 1.00 .30
155 Rafael Palmeiro .60 .18
156A Chipper Jones w/Bat 1.00 .30
156B Chipper Jones w/o Bat 1.00 .30
157 Kevin Millar .40 .12
158 Corey Patterson .40 .12
159A Johan Santana Both Feet .60 .18
159B Johan Santana One Foot .60 .18
160 Bernie Williams .60 .18
161 Craig Biggio .60 .18
162A Carlos Delgado Blue Jsy .40 .12
162B Carlos Delgado White Jsy .40 .12
163 Aaron Guiel .40 .12
164 Wade Miller .40 .12
165 Andruw Jones .40 .12
166 Jay Payton .40 .12
167 Benito Santiago .40 .12
168 Woody Williams .40 .12
169 Casey Blake .40 .12
170 Adam Dunn .60 .18
171 Jose Guillen .40 .12
172 Brian Jordan .40 .12
173 Kevin Millwood .40 .12
174 Carlos Pena .40 .12
175 Curt Schilling 1.00 .30
176 Jerome Williams .40 .12
177A Hank Blalock Grey Jsy .40 .12
177B Hank Blalock White Jsy .40 .12
178 Erubiel Durazo .40 .12
179 Cristian Guzman .40 .12
180 Austin Kearns .40 .12
181 Raul Mondesi .40 .12
182 Andy Pettitte .60 .18
183 Jason Schmidt .40 .12
184 Jeremy Bonderman .40 .12
185A Dontrelle Willis w/Ball .40 .12
185B Dontrelle Willis w/o Ball .40 .12
186 Ray Durham .40 .12
187 Jerry Hairston Jr. .40 .12
188 Jason Kendall .40 .12
189 Melvin Mora .40 .12
190 Jeff Kent .40 .12
191 Jae Weong Seo .40 .12
192 Jack Wilson .40 .12
193 Cesar Izturis .40 .12
194 Jermaine Dye .40 .12
195A Roy Halladay w/Ball .40 .12
195B Roy Halladay w/o Ball .40 .12
196 Jason Phillips .40 .12
197 Matt Morris .40 .12
198A Mike Piazza Fielding 1.50 .45
198B Mike Piazza Running 1.50 .45
199 Richie Sexson .40 .12
200 Alfonso Soriano .60 .18
201 Mark Mulder .40 .12
202 David Eckstein .40 .12
203 Mike Hampton .40 .12
204 Ryan Klesko .40 .12
205 Damian Moss .40 .12
206 Juan Pierre .40 .12
207 Ben Sheets .40 .12
208 Randy Winn .40 .12
209 Bret Boone .40 .12
210 Jim Edmonds .40 .12
211 Rich Harden .40 .12
212 Paul Konerko .40 .12
213 Jamie Moyer .40 .12
214 A.J. Pierzynski .40 .12
215 Gary Sheffield .40 .12
216 Randy Wolf .40 .12
217 Kevin Brown .40 .12
218 Morgan Ensberg .40 .12
219 Bo Hart .40 .12
220 Bill Mueller .40 .12
221 Corey Koskie .40 .12
222 Joel Pineiro .40 .12
223 Preston Wilson .40 .12
224 Aaron Boone .40 .12
225 Kerry Wood 1.00 .30
226 Darin Erstad .40 .12
227 Wes Helms .40 .12
228 Brian Lawrence .40 .12
229 Mark Buehrle .40 .12
230A Sammy Sosa w/Ball 1.50 .45
230B Sammy Sosa w/Bat 1.50 .45
231 Sidney Ponson .40 .12
232 Dmitri Young .40 .12
233 Ellis Burks .40 .12
234 Kelvim Escobar .40 .12
235 Todd Helton .60 .18
236 Matt Lawton .40 .12
237 Eric Munson .40 .12
238 Jorge Posada .60 .18
239 Mariano Rivera .60 .18
240 Michael Young .40 .12
241 Ramon Nivar .40 .12
242 Edwin Jackson .40 .12
243 Felix Pie .40 .12
244 Joe Mauer .60 .18
245 Grady Sizemore .40 .12
246 Bobby Jenks .40 .12
247 Chad Billingsley .40 .12
248 Casey Kotchman .40 .12
249 Bobby Crosby .60 .18
250 Khalil Greene 1.00 .30
251 Danny Garcia .40 .12
252 Nick Markakis .40 .12
253 Bernie Castro .40 .12
254 Aaron Hill .40 .12
255 Josh Barfield .40 .12
256 Ryan Wagner .40 .12
257 Ryan Harvey .40 .12
258 Jimmy Gobble .40 .12
259 Ryan Madson .40 .12
260 Zack Greinke .40 .12
261 Rene Reyes .40 .12
262 Eric Duncan .40 .12
263 Chris Lubanski .40 .12
264 Jeff Mathis .40 .12
265 Rickie Weeks .40 .12
266 Justin Morneau .40 .12
267 Brian Snyder .40 .12
268 Neal Cotts .40 .12
269 Joe Borchard .40 .12
270 Larry Bigbie .40 .12
271 Marcus McBeth FY RC .30 .09
272 Tydus Meadows FY RC .30 .09
273 Zach Miner FY RC .50 .15
274A A.Lerew w/Ball FY RC .75 .23
274B A.Lerew w/o Ball FY RC .75 .23
275A Y.Molina w/Bat FY RC 1.00 .30
275B Y.Molina w/o Bat FY RC 1.00 .30
276A Jon Knott w/Bat FY RC .40 .12
276B Jon Knott w/o Bat FY RC .40 .12
277 Matthew Moses FY RC 1.00 .30
278 Sung Jung FY RC .30 .09
279 Mike Gosling FY RC .30 .09
280 David Murphy FY RC 1.00 .30
281 Tim Frend FY RC .40 .12
282 Casey Myers FY RC .30 .09
283 Brayan Pena FY RC .40 .12
284 Omar Falcon FY RC .30 .09
285 Blake Hawksworth FY RC .50 .15
286 Jesse Roman FY RC .30 .09
287 Kyle Davies FY RC .75 .23
288 Matt Creighton FY RC .40 .12
289 Rodney Choy Foo FY RC .30 .09
290 Kyle Sleeth FY RC 1.00 .30
291 Carlos Quentin FY RC 2.00 .60
292 Khalid Ballouli FY RC .30 .09
293A Tim Stauffer w/Ball FY RC .75 .23
293B Tim Stauffer w/o Ball FY RC .75 .23
294 Craig Ansman FY RC .40 .12
295 Dioner Navarro FY RC 1.25 .35
296A Josh Labandeira w/Ball FY RC .40 .12
296B Josh Labandeira w/o Ball FY RC .40 .12
297 Jeffrey Allison FY RC .50 .15
298 Anthony Acevedo FY RC .40 .12
299 Brad Sullivan FY RC .50 .15
300 Conor Jackson FY RC 2.00 .60

2004 Bazooka Red Border Chunks

Nm-Mt Ex-Mt
*CHUNKS 1-270: .75X TO 2X BASIC
*CHUNKS 271-300: .75X TO 2X BASIC
ONE PER PACK

2004 Bazooka Minis

Nm-Mt Ex-Mt
*MINIS 1-270: .75X TO 2X BASIC
*MINIS 271-300: .75X TO 2X BASIC
ONE PER PACK

2004 Bazooka 4 on 1 Sticker

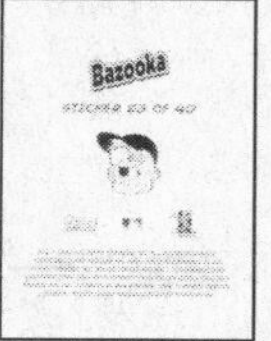

Nm-Mt Ex-Mt
STATED ODDS 1:4 H, 1:6 R
1 Rich Harden 1.00 .30
Dontrelle Willis
Jerome Williams
Brandon Webb
2 Eric Duncan 4.00 1.20
Derek Jeter
Alfonso Soriano
Jason Giambi
3 Grady Sizemore 3.00 .90
Rocco Baldelli
Ichiro Suzuki
Vladimir Guerrero
4 Roy Halladay 2.00 .60
Pedro Martinez
Curt Schilling
Brett Myers
5 Alex Rodriguez 3.00 .90
Angel Berroa
Jose Reyes
Khalil Greene
6 Kerry Wood 2.00 .60
Adam Dunn
Jeff Kent
Scott Rolen
7 Miguel Cabrera 1.25 .35
Scott Podsednik
Bo Hart
Mark Teixeira
8 Rickie Weeks 4.00 1.20
Josh Barfield
Albert Pujols
Vernon Wells
9 Torii Hunter 3.00 .90
Garret Anderson
Bobby Abreu
Ken Griffey Jr.
10 Jay Gibbons 3.00 .90
Chipper Jones
Mike Piazza
Mike Sweeney
11 David Ortiz 2.00 .60
Nick Johnson
Carlos Delgado
Frank Thomas
12 Todd Helton 1.25 .35
Jose Vidro
Mike Lowell
Miguel Tejada
13 Randy Wolf 2.00 .60
Mark Mulder
Johan Santana
Randy Johnson
14 Bret Boone 1.00 .30
Aubrey Huff
Eric Chavez
Javy Lopez
15 Jason Schmidt 2.00 .60
Roy Oswalt
Joel Pineiro
Mark Prior
16 Kevin Millwood 1.25 .35
Andy Pettitte
Matt Morris
Tim Hudson
17 Javier Vazquez 1.25 .35
Esteban Loaiza
Orlando Cabrera
Roberto Alomar
18 Al Leiter 1.00 .30
David Wells
Mike Hampton
Jarrod Washburn
19 Paul Lo Duca 1.00 .30
Mike Lieberthal
Brian Giles
Andruw Jones
20 Magglio Ordonez 1.25 .35
Corey Patterson
Aaron Boone
Jeff Bagwell
21 Troy Glaus 1.25 .35
Edgar Martinez
Manny Ramirez
Raul Ibanez
22 Sammy Sosa 3.00 .90
Barry Zito
Bartolo Colon
Austin Kearns
23 Jim Edmonds 1.00 .30
Gary Sheffield
Preston Wilson
Shawn Green
24 Bernie Williams 1.00 .30
Juan Pierre
Josh Beckett
Mike Mussina
25 Ramon Hernandez 1.00 .30
Jason Kendall
Jason Phillips
A.J. Pierzynski
26 Pat Burrell 1.00 .30
Laynce Nix
Mike Cameron
Cliff Floyd
27 Eric Gagne 2.00 .60
Carl Crawford
Jose Guillen
Steve Finley
28 Ellis Burks 1.00 .30
Livan Hernandez
Derek Lowe
Kazuhisa Ishii
29 Jorge Posada 2.00 .60
Jeff Mathis
Victor Martinez
Ivan Rodriguez
30 Jim Thome 3.00 .90
Marcus Giles
Nomar Garciaparra
Hank Blalock
31 Edgar Renteria 1.25 .35
Bobby Crosby
Neal Cotts
Russ Ortiz
32 Zack Greinke 1.00 .30
Cristian Guzman
Cesar Izturis
Kevin Brown
33 Bobby Jenks 1.00 .30
Ramon Nivar
Richie Sexson
Ryan Klesko
34 Omar Vizquel 1.25 .35
Carlos Pena
Rafael Furcal
Gil Meche
35 Kenny Lofton 1.25 .35
Tim Salmon
Marquis Grissom
Craig Biggio
36 Kyle Davies 2.00 .60
Anthony Lerew
Brayan Pena
Sung Jung
37 Rodney Choy Foo 2.00 .60
Craig Ansman
David Murphy
Matthew Moses
38 Carlos Quentin 5.00 1.50
Dioner Navarro
Marcus McBeth
Josh Labandeira
39 Kyle Sleeth 5.00 1.50
Conor Jackson
Brad Sullivan
Jeffrey Allison
40 Yadier Molina 2.50 .75
Jon Knott
Blake Hawksworth
Tim Stauffer

2004 Bazooka Adventures Relics

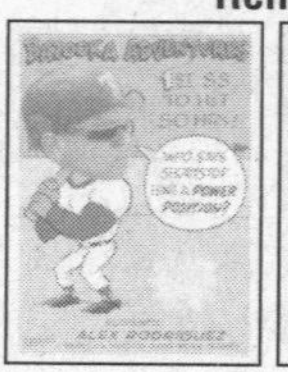

Nm-Mt Ex-Mt
GROUP A ODDS 1:134 H, 1:187 R
GROUP B ODDS 1:207 H, 1:289 R
GROUP C ODDS 1:74 H, 1:104 R
GROUP D ODDS 1:57 H, 1:80 R
GROUP E ODDS 1:86 H, 1:119 R
OVERALL PARALLEL 25 ODDS 1:94
PARALLEL 25 PRINT RUN 25 #'d SETS
NO PARALLEL 25 PRICING DUE TO SCARCITY
AD1 Adam Dunn Stripe Jsy A 10.00 3.00
AD2 Adam Dunn Grey Jsy A 10.00 3.00
AJ Andruw Jones Jsy D 8.00 2.40
AP Albert Pujols Uni D 20.00 6.00
AR1 Alex Rodriguez Blue Jsy E 10.00 3.00
AR2 Alex Rodriguez White Jsy D 10.00 3.00
AS Alfonso Soriano Uni C 10.00 3.00
BG Ben Grieve Jsy A 8.00 2.40
BP Brad Penny Jsy A 8.00 2.40
BW Bernie Williams Jsy B 10.00 3.00
BZ Barry Zito Jsy B 8.00 2.40
CB Craig Biggio Uni A 10.00 3.00
CE Carl Everett Uni D 8.00 2.40
CF Cliff Floyd Jsy B 8.00 2.40
CG Cristian Guzman Jsy C 8.00 2.40
CJ Chipper Jones Jsy D 10.00 3.00
CS Curt Schilling Jsy A 10.00 3.00
DW Dontrelle Willis Uni D 8.00 2.40
EA Edgardo Alfonzo Uni D 8.00 2.40
EC Eric Chavez Uni A 8.00 2.40
GJ Geoff Jenkins Jsy E 8.00 2.40
GM Greg Maddux Jsy D 15.00 4.50
HN Hideo Nomo Jsy C 10.00 3.00
JB Jeff Bagwell Uni A 10.00 3.00
JDG Jeremy Giambi Jsy E 8.00 2.40
JG Jason Giambi Jsy D 8.00 2.40
JK Jason Kendall Jsy B 8.00 2.40
JO John Olerud Jsy E 8.00 2.40

T Jim Thome Jsy C 10.00 3.00
W Jarrod Washburn Uni C 8.00 2.40
KB Kevin Brown Jsy A 8.00 2.40
KM Kevin Millwood Jsy E 8.00 2.40
KW Kerry Wood Jsy A 10.00 3.00
.B Lance Berkman Jsy D 8.00 2.40
.C Luis Castillo Jsy D 8.00 2.40
.G Luis Gonzalez Uni A 8.00 2.40
.W Larry Walker Jsy A 10.00 3.00
MB Marlon Byrd Jsy C 8.00 2.40
MCM Mike Mussina Uni C 10.00 3.00
ML Mike Lowell Jsy D 8.00 2.40
MM Mark Mulder Uni A 8.00 2.40
MP1 M.Piazza 2nd Most Jsy C 15.00 4.50
MP2 M.Piazza 10 Straight Jsy D 15.00 4.50
MR Manny Ramirez Uni C 10.00 3.00
MT Miguel Tejada Uni E 8.00 2.40
MV Mo Vaughn Jsy A 8.00 2.40
NG Nomar Garciaparra Uni C 15.00 4.50
PB Pat Burrell Jsy E 8.00 2.40
PK Paul Konerko Jsy B 8.00 2.40
PL Paul Lo Duca Jsy C 8.00 2.40
PW Preston Wilson Jsy E 8.00 2.40
RJ Randy Johnson Jsy C 10.00 3.00
RP1 R.Palmeiro 500th HR Jsy D 10.00 3.00
RP2 R.Palmeiro 9 Straight Jsy D 10.00 3.00
SC Sean Casey Jsy D 8.00 2.40
SG Shawn Green Jsy C 8.00 2.40
TAH1 T.Hudson Most Wins Jsy B 8.00 2.40
TAH2 T.Hudson 3rd Best Uni D 8.00 2.40
TEG Troy Glaus Uni A 8.00 2.40
TG Tom Glavine Jsy A 10.00 3.00
TH Toby Hall Jsy A 8.00 2.40
TJS Tim Salmon Uni B 10.00 3.00
VG Vladimir Guerrero Jsy C 10.00 3.00

2004 Bazooka Blasts Bat Relics

	Nm-Mt	Ex-Mt
GROUP A ODDS 1:62 H, 1:86 R		
GROUP B ODDS 1:29 H, 1:40 R		
OVERALL PARALLEL 25 ODDS 1:94		
PARALLEL 25 PRINT RUN 25 #'d SETS		
NO PARALLEL 25 PRICING DUE TO SCARCITY		
AD Adam Dunn A	10.00	3.00
AG Adrian Gonzalez B	8.00	2.40
AH Aubrey Huff A	8.00	2.40
AJG Andres Galarraga A	8.00	2.40
ANR Aramis Ramirez B	8.00	2.40
AP Albert Pujols B	20.00	6.00
AR Alex Rodriguez B	10.00	3.00
AS Alfonso Soriano A	10.00	3.00
BB Bret Boone B	8.00	2.40
BF Brad Fullmer A	8.00	2.40
BW Bernie Williams A	10.00	3.00
CB Craig Biggio A	10.00	3.00
CC Carl Crawford A	8.00	2.40
CE Carl Everett B	8.00	2.40
CG Cristian Guzman A	8.00	2.40
CB Carlos Beltran A	10.00	3.00
CJ Chipper Jones B	10.00	3.00
CL Carlos Lee A	8.00	2.40
CP Corey Patterson A	8.00	2.40
DM Doug Mientkiewicz A	8.00	2.40
EM Edgar Martinez B	10.00	3.00
FM Fred McGriff A	10.00	3.00
FT Frank Thomas B	10.00	3.00
GS Gary Sheffield B	8.00	2.40
HB Hank Blalock A	8.00	2.40
IR Ivan Rodriguez B	10.00	3.00
JG Juan Gonzalez B	10.00	3.00
JB Jeff Bagwell A	10.00	3.00
JG Jason Giambi A	8.00	2.40
JB Jeromy Burnitz A	8.00	2.40
JO John Olerud A	8.00	2.40
JP Jorge Posada A	10.00	3.00
JR Juan Rivera B	8.00	2.40
LB Lance Berkman B	8.00	2.40
LG Luis Gonzalez A	8.00	2.40
LW Larry Walker B	10.00	3.00
MA Moises Alou A	8.00	2.40
MAT Michael Tucker A	8.00	2.40
MCT Mark Teixeira A	8.00	2.40
MG Marquis Grissom B	8.00	2.40
ML Matt Lawton B	8.00	2.40
MO Magglio Ordonez B	8.00	2.40
MP Mike Piazza A	15.00	4.50
MR Manny Ramirez B	10.00	3.00
MT Miguel Tejada A	8.00	2.40
MV Mo Vaughn B	8.00	2.40
NG Nomar Garciaparra A	15.00	4.50
NH Nathan Haynes B	8.00	2.40
OV Omar Vizquel B	10.00	3.00
PK Paul Konerko A	8.00	2.40
PL Paul Lo Duca A	8.00	2.40
RA Roberto Alomar B	10.00	3.00
RB Rocco Baldelli A	8.00	2.40
RF Rafael Furcal B	8.00	2.40
RP Rafael Palmeiro B	10.00	3.00
RS Ruben Sierra B	8.00	2.40
SA Rich Aurilia B	8.00	2.40
RW Rondell White B	8.00	2.40
SB Sean Burroughs B	8.00	2.40
SG Shawn Green B	8.00	2.40
SR Scott Rolen A	10.00	3.00
SS Shannon Stewart A	8.00	2.40
ST So Taguchi B	8.00	2.40
TB Tony Batista B	8.00	2.40
TG Troy Glaus A	8.00	2.40
TH Torii Hunter A	8.00	2.40
TJS Tim Salmon A	10.00	3.00
TKH Todd Helton B	10.00	3.00
TM Tino Martinez A	10.00	3.00
VG Vladimir Guerrero B	10.00	3.00
VW Vernon Wells A	8.00	2.40

2004 Bazooka Comics

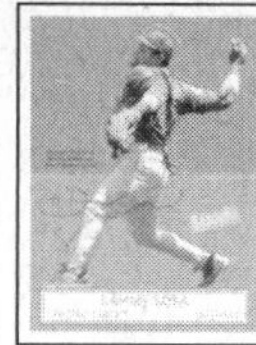

	Nm-Mt	Ex-Mt
COMPLETE SET (24)	25.00	7.50
STATED ODDS 1:4		
BC1 Garret Anderson	1.00	.30
BC2 Jeff Bagwell	1.00	.30
BC3 Hank Blalock	1.00	.30
BC4 Roy Halladay	1.00	.30
BC5 Dontrelle Willis	1.00	.30
BC6 Roger Clemens	2.50	.75
BC7 Carlos Delgado	1.00	.30
BC8 Rafael Furcal	1.00	.30
BC9 Eric Gagne	1.25	.35
BC10 Nomar Garciaparra	2.00	.60
BC11 Derek Jeter	2.50	.75
BC12 Esteban Loaiza	1.00	.30
BC13 Kevin Millwood	1.00	.30
BC14 Bill Mueller	1.00	.30
BC15 Rafael Palmeiro	1.00	.30
BC16 Albert Pujols	2.50	.75
BC17 Jose Reyes	1.00	.30
BC18 Alex Rodriguez	2.00	.60
BC19 Alfonso Soriano	1.00	.30
BC20 Sammy Sosa	2.00	.60
BC21 Ichiro Suzuki	2.00	.60
BC22 Frank Thomas	1.25	.35
BC23 Brad Wilkerson	1.00	.30
BC24 Roy Oswalt	1.00	.30

Pete Munro
Kirk Saarloos
Brad Lidge
Octavio Dotel
Billy Wagner

2004 Bazooka One-Liners Relics

	Nm-Mt	Ex-Mt
GROUP A ODDS 1:62 H, 1:86 R		
GROUP B ODDS 1:98 H, 1:136 R		
OVERALL PARALLEL 25 ODDS 1:94		
PARALLEL 25 PRINT RUN 25 #'d SETS		
NO PARALLEL 25 PRICING DUE TO SCARCITY		
AD Andre Dawson Bat A	10.00	3.00
BB Bert Blyleven Jsy A	10.00	3.00
BC Bert Campaneris Jsy A	10.00	3.00
BM Bill Madlock Bat A	10.00	3.00
BS Bret Saberhagen Jsy A	10.00	3.00
CS Chris Sabo Bat A	10.00	3.00
CY Carl Yastrzemski Uni A	30.00	9.00
DA Dick Allen Bat A	10.00	3.00
DE Dennis Eckersley Jsy A	10.00	3.00
DJ1 David Justice Bat A	10.00	3.00
DJ2 David Justice Uni A	10.00	3.00
DM Dale Murphy Bat A	15.00	4.50
DP Dave Parker Jsy A	10.00	3.00
DW Dwight Gooden Jsy A	10.00	3.00
EM Eddie Murray Uni A	25.00	7.50
FR Frank Robinson Uni A	10.00	3.00
GB George Brett Jsy B	25.00	7.50
GC Gary Carter Bat A	10.00	3.00
GP Gaylord Perry Uni A	10.00	3.00
HK Harmon Killebrew Jsy A	30.00	9.00
JB Johnny Bench Bat B	15.00	4.50
JC Jose Canseco Bat B	15.00	4.50
JCA Joe Carter Jsy A	10.00	3.00
JK Jerry Koosman Jsy A	10.00	3.00
JM Joe Morgan Jsy A	10.00	3.00
KG1 Kirk Gibson Bat A	10.00	3.00
KG2 Kirk Gibson Jsy A	10.00	3.00
KH Keith Hernandez Bat B	10.00	3.00
KP1 Kirby Puckett Bat B	15.00	4.50
KP2 Kirby Puckett Jsy B	15.00	4.50
MS Mike Schmidt Jsy B	20.00	6.00
NR Nolan Ryan Jsy A	60.00	18.00
OC Orlando Cepeda Bat A	10.00	3.00
PN Phil Niekro Uni A	10.00	3.00
RC Rod Carew Bat B	15.00	4.50
RD Ron Darling Jsy A	10.00	3.00
RJ Reggie Jackson Jsy A	15.00	4.50
RS Red Schoendienst Bat B	10.00	3.00
RSA Ron Santo Bat A	15.00	4.50
RY Robin Yount Bat A	15.00	4.50
TM Tug McGraw Jsy A	15.00	4.50
TS Tom Seaver Uni A	15.00	4.50
WB1 Wade Boggs Bat B	15.00	4.50
WB2 Wade Boggs Jsy B	15.00	4.50
WM Willie Mays Uni A	60.00	18.00
WMC Willie McGee Bat A	15.00	4.50
WS Willie Stargell Bat A	15.00	4.50

2004 Bazooka Stand-Ups

	Nm-Mt	Ex-Mt
STATED ODDS 1:8 H, 1:24 R		
1 Jose Reyes	2.00	.60
2 Jim Thome	3.00	.90
3 Roy Halladay	2.00	.60
4 Jason Giambi	3.00	.90
5 Dontrelle Willis	2.00	.60
6 Mike Piazza	5.00	1.50
7 Chipper Jones	3.00	.90
8 Mark Prior	3.00	.90

9 Todd Helton	2.00	.60
10 Miguel Cabrera	2.00	.60
11 Derek Jeter	6.00	1.80
12 Nomar Garciaparra	5.00	1.50
13 Alex Rodriguez	5.00	1.50
14 Miguel Tejada	2.00	.60
15 Carlos Delgado	2.00	.60
16 Pedro Martinez	3.00	.90
17 Sammy Sosa	5.00	1.50
18 Ichiro Suzuki	5.00	1.50
19 Vladimir Guerrero	3.00	.90
20 Alfonso Soriano	2.00	.60
21 Eric Chavez	2.00	.60
22 Albert Pujols	6.00	1.80
23 Ivan Rodriguez	3.00	.90
24 Vernon Wells	2.00	.60
25 Eric Gagne	3.00	.90

2004 Bazooka Tattoos

	Nm-Mt	Ex-Mt
STATED ODDS 1:4 H, 1:6 R		
AD Adam Dunn	1.50	.45
AJ Andruw Jones	1.00	.30
AP Albert Pujols	5.00	1.50
AR Alex Rodriguez	4.00	1.20
AS Alfonso Soriano	1.50	.45
BAZ Bazooka Logo	1.00	.30
BP Brad Penny	1.00	.30
BW Bernie Williams	1.50	.45
BZ Barry Zito	1.00	.30
CB Craig Biggio	1.50	.45
CF Cliff Floyd	1.00	.30
CG Cristian Guzman	1.00	.30
CJ Chipper Jones	2.50	.75
CS Curt Schilling	2.50	.75
DW Dontrelle Willis	1.00	.30
EC Eric Chavez	1.00	.30
GJ Geoff Jenkins	1.00	.30
GM Greg Maddux	4.00	1.20
HN Hideo Nomo	2.50	.75
JB Jeff Bagwell	1.50	.45
JG Jason Giambi	1.00	.30
JK Jason Kendall	1.00	.30
JO John Olerud	1.00	.30
JT Jim Thome	2.50	.75
JW Jarrod Washburn	1.00	.30
KB Kevin Brown	1.00	.30
KM Kevin Millwood	1.00	.30
KW Kerry Wood	2.50	.75
LB Lance Berkman	1.00	.30
LC Luis Castillo	1.00	.30
LG Luis Gonzalez	1.00	.30
LW Larry Walker	1.50	.45
MB Marlon Byrd	1.00	.30
MCM Mike Mussina	1.50	.45
ML Mike Lowell	1.00	.30
MM Mark Mulder	1.00	.30
MP Mike Piazza	4.00	1.20
MR Manny Ramirez	1.50	.45
MT Miguel Tejada	1.00	.30
NG Nomar Garciaparra	4.00	1.20
PB Pat Burrell	1.00	.30
PK Paul Konerko	1.00	.30
PL Paul Lo Duca	1.00	.30
PW Preston Wilson	1.00	.30
RJ Randy Johnson	2.50	.75
RP Rafael Palmeiro	1.50	.45
SC Sean Casey	1.00	.30
SG Shawn Green	1.00	.30
TAH Tim Hudson	1.00	.30
TEG Troy Glaus	1.00	.30
TG Tom Glavine	1.50	.45
TH Toby Hall	1.00	.30
TJS Tim Salmon	1.50	.45
TOP Topps Logo	1.00	.30
VG Vladimir Guerrero	2.50	.75

1948 Bowman

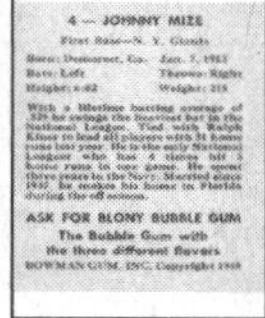

The 48-card Bowman set of 1948 was the first major set of the post-war period. Each 2 1/16" by 2 1/2" card had a black and white photo of a current player, with his biographical information printed in black ink on a gray back. Due to the printing process and the 36-card sheet size upon which Bowman was then printing, the 12 cards marked with an SP in the checklist are scarcer numerically, as they were removed from the printing sheet in order to make room for the 12 high numbers (37-48). Cards were issued in one-card penny packs. Many cards are found with over-printed, transposed, or blank backs. The set features the Rookie Cards of Hall of Famers Yogi Berra, Ralph Kiner, Stan Musial, Red Schoendienst, and Warren Spahn. Half of the cards in the set feature New York players (Yankees or Giants).

	NM	Ex
COMPLETE SET (48)	3600.00	1800.00
COMMON CARD (1-36)	20.00	10.00
COMMON CARD (37-48)	30.00	15.00
WRAPPER (5-CENT)	700.00	350.00
WRAPPER (1-CENT)		
1 Bob Elliott RC	125.00	19.00
2 Ewell Blackwell RC	60.00	30.00
3 Ralph Kiner RC	150.00	75.00
4 Johnny Mize RC	125.00	60.00
5 Bob Feller RC	250.00	125.00
6 Yogi Berra RC	500.00	250.00
7 Pete Reiser SP	125.00	60.00
8 Phil Rizzuto SP RC	350.00	180.00
9 Walker Cooper RC	20.00	10.00
10 Buddy Rosar	20.00	10.00
11 Johnny Lindell	25.00	12.50
12 Johnny Sain RC	80.00	40.00
13 Willard Marshall SP	40.00	20.00
14 Allie Reynolds RC	60.00	30.00
15 Eddie Joost	20.00	10.00
16 Jack Lohrke SP	40.00	20.00
17 Enos Slaughter RC	100.00	50.00
18 Warren Spahn RC	300.00	150.00
19 Tommy Henrich	60.00	30.00
20 Buddy Kerr SP	40.00	20.00
21 Ferris Fain RC	40.00	20.00
22 Floyd Bevens SP RC	50.00	25.00
23 Larry Jansen RC	25.00	12.50
24 Dutch Leonard SP	40.00	20.00
25 Barney McCosky	20.00	10.00
26 Frank Shea SP RC	50.00	25.00
27 Sid Gordon RC	25.00	12.50
28 Emil Verban SP	40.00	20.00
29 Joe Page SP RC	80.00	40.00
30 W.Lockman SP RC	50.00	25.00
31 Bill McCahan	20.00	10.00
32 Bill Rigney RC	20.00	10.00
33 Bill Johnson	25.00	12.50
34 Sheldon Jones SP	40.00	20.00
35 Snuffy Stirnweiss RC	40.00	20.00
36 Stan Musial RC	800.00	400.00
37 Clint Hartung RC	30.00	15.00
38 Red Schoendienst RC	200.00	100.00
39 Augie Galan	30.00	15.00
40 Marty Marion RC	80.00	40.00
41 Rex Barney RC	60.00	30.00
42 Ray Poat	30.00	15.00
43 Bruce Edwards	40.00	20.00
44 Johnny Wyrostek	30.00	15.00
45 Hank Sauer RC	60.00	30.00
46 Herman Wehmeier	30.00	15.00
47 Bobby Thomson RC	100.00	50.00
48 Dave Koslo RC	80.00	19.50

1949 Bowman

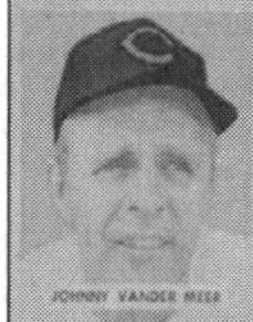

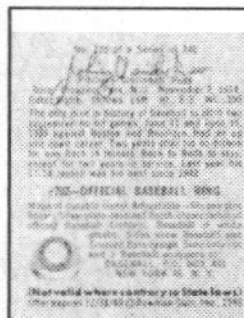

The cards in this 240-card set measure approximately 2 1/16" by 2 1/2". In 1949 Bowman took an intermediate step between black and white and full color with this set of tinted photos on colored backgrounds. Collectors should note the series price variations, which reflect some inconsistencies in the printing process. There are four major varieties in name printing, which are noted in the checklist below: NOF: name on front; NNOF: no name on front; PR: printed name on back; and SCR: script name on back. Cards were issued in five card nickel packs. These variations resulted when Bowman used twelve of the lower numbers to fill out the last press sheet of 36 cards, adding to numbers 217-240. Cards 1-3 and 5-73 can be found with either gray or white backs. Certain cards have been seen with a "gray" or "slate" background on the front. These cards are a result of a color printing error and are rarely seen on the secondary market so no value is established for them. Not all numbers are known to exist in this fashion. However, within the numbers between 75 and 107, slightly more of these cards have appeared on the market. Within the high numbers series (145-240), these cards have been seen but the appearance of these cards are very rare. Other cards are known to be extant with double printed backs. The set features the Rookie Cards of Hall of Famers Roy Campanella, Bob Lemon, Robin Roberts, Duke Snider, and Early Wynn as well as Rookie Cards of Richie Ashburn and Gil Hodges.

	NM	Ex
COMP. MASTER SET (252)	16000.00	8000.00
COMPLETE SET (240)	15000.00	7500.00
COMMON CARD (1-144)	15.00	7.50
COMMON (145-240)	50.00	25.00
WRAPPER (1-CENT,Rd,Wh,Bl)		
WRAP.(5-CENT,GREEN)	250.00	125.00
WRAP.(5-CENT,BLUE)	200.00	100.00
1 Vern Bickford RC	125.00	25.00
2 Whitey Lockman	40.00	20.00
3 Bob Porterfield	15.00	7.50
4A Jerry Priddy NNOF	15.00	7.50
4B Jerry Priddy NOF	50.00	25.00
5 Hank Sauer	40.00	20.00
6 Phil Cavarretta	40.00	20.00
7 Joe Dobson	15.00	7.50
8 Murry Dickson	15.00	7.50
9 Ferris Fain	40.00	20.00
10 Ted Gray	15.00	7.50
11 Lou Boudreau	80.00	40.00
12 Cass Michaels	15.00	7.50
13 Bob Chesnes	15.00	7.50
14 Curt Simmons RC	40.00	20.00
15 Ned Garver	15.00	7.50
16 Al Kozar	15.00	7.50
17 Earl Torgeson	15.00	7.50
18 Bobby Thomson	40.00	20.00
19 Bobby Brown RC	60.00	30.00
20 Gene Hermanski	15.00	7.50
21 Frank Baumholtz	25.00	12.50
22 Peanuts Lowrey	15.00	7.50
23 Bobby Doerr	80.00	40.00
24 Stan Musial	600.00	300.00
25 Carl Scheib	15.00	7.50
26 George Kell RC	80.00	40.00
27 Bob Feller	300.00	150.00
28 Don Kolloway	15.00	7.50
29 Ralph Kiner	125.00	60.00
30 Andy Seminick	40.00	20.00
31 Dick Kokos	15.00	7.50
32 Eddie Yost RC	60.00	30.00
33 Warren Spahn	200.00	100.00
34 Dave Koslo	15.00	7.50
35 Vic Raschi RC	60.00	30.00
36 Pee Wee Reese	200.00	100.00
37 Johnny Wyrostek	15.00	7.50
38 Emil Verban	15.00	7.50
39 Billy Goodman	25.00	12.50
40 George Munger	15.00	7.50
41 Lou Brissie	15.00	7.50
42 Hoot Evers	15.00	7.50
43 Dale Mitchell RC	40.00	20.00
44 Dave Philley	15.00	7.50
45 Wally Westlake	15.00	7.50
46 Robin Roberts RC	250.00	125.00
47 Johnny Sain	60.00	30.00
48 Willard Marshall	15.00	7.50
49 Frank Shea	25.00	12.50
50 Jackie Robinson RC	1200.00	600.00
51 Herman Wehmeier	15.00	7.50
52 Johnny Schmitz	15.00	7.50
53 Jack Kramer	15.00	7.50
54 Marty Marion	60.00	30.00
55 Eddie Joost	15.00	7.50
56 Pat Mullin	15.00	7.50
57 Gene Bearden	40.00	20.00
58 Bob Elliott	40.00	20.00
59 Jack Lohrke	15.00	7.50
60 Yogi Berra	300.00	150.00
61 Rex Barney	40.00	20.00
62 Grady Hatton	15.00	7.50
63 Andy Pafko	40.00	20.00
64 Dom DiMaggio	60.00	30.00
65 Enos Slaughter	80.00	40.00
66 Elmer Valo	15.00	7.50
67 Alvin Dark RC	40.00	20.00
68 Sheldon Jones	15.00	7.50
69 Tommy Henrich	40.00	20.00
70 Carl Furillo RC	125.00	60.00
71 Vern Stephens	15.00	7.50
72 Tommy Holmes	40.00	20.00
73 Billy Cox RC	40.00	20.00
74 Tom McBride	15.00	7.50
75 Eddie Mayo	15.00	7.50
76 Bill Nicholson RC	25.00	12.50
77 Ernie Bonham	15.00	7.50
78A Sam Zoldak NNOF	15.00	7.50
78B Sam Zoldak NOF	50.00	25.00
79 Ron Northey	15.00	7.50
80 Bill McCahan	15.00	7.50
81 Virgil Stallcup	15.00	7.50
82 Joe Page	60.00	30.00
83A Bob Scheffing NNOF	15.00	7.50
83B Bob Scheffing NOF	50.00	25.00
84 Roy Campanella RC	800.00	400.00
85A Johnny Mize NNOF	100.00	50.00
85B Johnny Mize NOF	150.00	75.00
86 Johnny Pesky	60.00	30.00
87 Randy Gumpert	15.00	7.50
88A Bill Salkeld NNOF	15.00	7.50
88B Bill Salkeld NOF	50.00	25.00
89 Mizell Platt	15.00	7.50
90 Gil Coan	15.00	7.50
91 Dick Wakefield	15.00	7.50
92 Willie Jones	40.00	20.00
93 Ed Stevens	15.00	7.50
94 Mickey Vernon RC	40.00	20.00
95 Howie Pollet RC	15.00	7.50
96 Taft Wright	15.00	7.50
97 Danny Litwhiler	15.00	7.50
98A Phil Rizzuto NNOF	200.00	100.00
98B Phil Rizzuto NOF	250.00	125.00
99 Frank Gustine	15.00	7.50
100 Gil Hodges RC	250.00	125.00
101 Sid Gordon	15.00	7.50
102 Stan Spence	15.00	7.50
103 Joe Tipton	15.00	7.50
104 Eddie Stanky RC	40.00	20.00
105 Bill Kennedy	15.00	7.50
106 Jake Early	15.00	7.50
107 Eddie Lake	15.00	7.50
108 Ken Heintzelman	15.00	7.50
109A Ed Fitzgerald SCR	15.00	7.50
109B Ed Fitzgerald PR	60.00	30.00
110 Early Wynn RC	150.00	75.00
111 Red Schoendienst	100.00	50.00
112 Sam Chapman	40.00	20.00
113 Ray LaManno	15.00	7.50
114 Allie Reynolds	60.00	30.00
115 Dutch Leonard	15.00	7.50
116 Joe Hatton	15.00	7.50
117 Walker Cooper	15.00	7.50
118 Sam Mele	15.00	7.50
119 Floyd Baker	15.00	7.50
120 Cliff Fannin	15.00	7.50
121 Mark Christman	15.00	7.50
122 George Vico	15.00	7.50
123 Johnny Blatnick	15.00	7.50
124A D.Murtaugh SCR RC	50.00	25.00
124B D.Murtaugh PR RC	60.00	30.00
125 Ken Keltner	25.00	12.50
126A Al Brazle SCR	15.00	7.50
126B Al Brazle PR	60.00	30.00
127A Hank Majeski SCR	15.00	7.50
127B Hank Majeski PR	60.00	30.00
128 Johnny VanderMeer	60.00	30.00
129 Bill Johnson	40.00	20.00
130 Harry Walker	15.00	7.50
131 Paul Lehner	15.00	7.50
132A Al Evans SCR	15.00	7.50
132B Al Evans PR	60.00	30.00
133 Aaron Robinson	15.00	7.50
134 Hank Borowy	15.00	7.50

135 Stan Rojek 15.00 7.50
136 Hank Edwards 15.00 7.50
137 Ted Wilks 15.00 7.50
138 Buddy Rosar 15.00 7.50
139 Hank Arft 15.00 7.50
140 Ray Scarborough 15.00 7.50
141 Tony Lupien 15.00 7.50
142 Eddie Waitkus RC 40.00 20.00
143A B.Dillinger RC SCR 25.00 12.50
143B Bob Dillinger RC PR 60.00 30.00
144 Mickey Haefner 15.00 7.50
145 Sylvester Donnelly 50.00 25.00
146 Mike McCormick 50.00 25.00
147 Bert Singleton 50.00 25.00
148 Bob Swift 50.00 25.00
149 Roy Partee 50.00 25.00
150 Allie Clark 50.00 25.00
151 Mickey Harris 50.00 25.00
152 Clarence Maddern 50.00 25.00
153 Phil Masi 50.00 25.00
154 Clint Hartung 60.00 30.00
155 Mickey Guerra 50.00 25.00
156 Al Zarilla 50.00 25.00
157 Walt Masterson 50.00 25.00
158 Harry Brecheen 60.00 30.00
159 Glen Moulder 50.00 25.00
160 Jim Blackburn 50.00 25.00
161 Jocko Thompson 50.00 25.00
162 Preacher Roe RC 125.00 60.00
163 Clyde McCullough 50.00 25.00
164 Vic Wertz RC 80.00 40.00
165 Snuffy Stirnweiss 80.00 40.00
166 Mike Tresh 50.00 25.00
167 Babe Martin 50.00 25.00
168 Doyle Lade 50.00 25.00
169 Jeff Heath 60.00 30.00
170 Bill Rigney 60.00 30.00
171 Dick Fowler 50.00 25.00
172 Eddie Pellagrini 50.00 25.00
173 Eddie Stewart 50.00 25.00
174 Terry Moore RC 80.00 40.00
175 Luke Appling 125.00 60.00
176 Ken Raffensberger 50.00 25.00
177 Stan Lopata 60.00 30.00
178 Tom Brown 60.00 30.00
179 Hugh Casey 80.00 40.00
180 Connie Berry 50.00 25.00
181 Gus Niarhos 50.00 25.00
182 Hal Peck 50.00 25.00
183 Lou Stringer 50.00 25.00
184 Bob Chipman 50.00 25.00
185 Pete Reiser 80.00 40.00
186 Buddy Kerr 50.00 25.00
187 Phil Marchildon 50.00 25.00
188 Karl Drews 50.00 25.00
189 Earl Wooten 50.00 25.00
190 Jim Hearn 50.00 25.00
191 Joe Haynes 50.00 25.00
192 Harry Gumbert 50.00 25.00
193 Ken Trinkle 50.00 25.00
194 Ralph Branca RC 100.00 50.00
195 Eddie Bockman 50.00 25.00
196 Fred Hutchinson 60.00 30.00
197 Johnny Lindell 60.00 30.00
198 Steve Gromek 50.00 25.00
199 Tex Hughson 50.00 25.00
200 Jess Dobernic 50.00 25.00
201 Sibby Sisti 50.00 25.00
202 Larry Jansen 60.00 30.00
203 Barney McCosky 50.00 25.00
204 Bob Savage 50.00 25.00
205 Dick Sisler 60.00 30.00
206 Bruce Edwards 50.00 25.00
207 Johnny Hopp 50.00 25.00
208 Dizzy Trout 60.00 30.00
209 Charlie Keller 80.00 40.00
210 Joe Gordon 80.00 40.00
211 Boo Ferriss 50.00 25.00
212 Ralph Hamner 50.00 25.00
213 Red Barrett 50.00 25.00
214 Richie Ashburn RC 600.00 300.00
215 Kirby Higbe 50.00 25.00
216 Schoolboy Rowe 60.00 30.00
217 Marino Pieretti 50.00 25.00
218 Dick Kryhoski 50.00 25.00
219 Virgil Fire Trucks 60.00 30.00
220 Johnny McCarthy 50.00 25.00
NY Giants Cap but listed as Sioux City MG
221 Bob Muncrief 50.00 25.00
222 Alex Kellner 50.00 25.00
223 Bobby Hofman 50.00 25.00
224 Satchell Paige RC 1500.00 750.00
225 Jerry Coleman RC 80.00 40.00
226 Duke Snider RC 1000.00 500.00
227 Fritz Ostermueller 50.00 25.00
228 Jackie Mayo 50.00 25.00
229 Ed Lopat RC 125.00 60.00
230 Augie Galan 60.00 30.00
231 Earl Johnson 50.00 25.00
232 George McQuinn 60.00 30.00
233 Larry Doby RC 200.00 100.00
234 Rip Sewell 50.00 25.00
235 Jim Russell 50.00 25.00
236 Fred Sanford 50.00 25.00
237 Monte Kennedy 50.00 25.00
238 Bob Lemon RC 200.00 100.00
239 Frank McCormick 50.00 25.00
240 Babe Young UER 100.00 25.00
(Photo actually Bobby Young)

1950 Bowman

The cards in this 252-card set measure approximately 2 1/16" by 2 1/2". This set, marketed in 1950 by Bowman, represented a major improvement in terms of quality over their previous efforts. Each card was a beautifully colored line drawing developed from a simple photograph. The first 72 cards are the scarcest in the set, while the final 72 cards may be found with or without the copyright line. This was the only Bowman sports set to carry the famous "5-Star" logo. Cards were issued in five-card nickel packs. Key rookies in this set are Hank Bauer, Don Newcombe, and Al Rosen.

NM Ex
COMPLETE SET (252) 8500.00 4200.00
COMMON CARD (1-72) 50.00 25.00
COMMON CARD (73-252) 15.00 7.50
WRAPPER (1-cent) 250.00 125.00
WRAPPER (5-cent) 250.00 125.00
1 Mel Parnell RC 150.00 30.00
2 Vern Stephens 60.00 30.00
3 Dom DiMaggio 80.00 40.00
4 Gus Zernial RC 60.00 30.00
5 Bob Kuzava 50.00 25.00
6 Bob Feller 300.00 150.00
7 Jim Hegan 60.00 30.00
8 George Kell 80.00 40.00
9 Vic Wertz 60.00 30.00
10 Tommy Henrich 80.00 40.00
11 Phil Rizzuto 300.00 150.00
12 Joe Page 80.00 40.00
13 Ferris Fain 60.00 30.00
14 Alex Kellner 50.00 25.00
15 Al Kozar 50.00 25.00
16 Roy Sievers RC 80.00 40.00
17 Sid Hudson 50.00 25.00
18 Eddie Robinson 50.00 25.00
19 Warren Spahn 300.00 150.00
20 Bob Elliott 60.00 30.00
21 Pee Wee Reese 300.00 150.00
22 Jackie Robinson 1200.00 600.00
23 Don Newcombe RC 150.00 75.00
24 Johnny Schmitz 50.00 25.00
25 Hank Sauer 60.00 30.00
26 Grady Hatton 50.00 25.00
27 Herman Wehmeier 50.00 25.00
28 Bobby Thomson 80.00 40.00
29 Eddie Stanky 60.00 30.00
30 Eddie Waitkus 60.00 30.00
31 Del Ennis 80.00 40.00
32 Robin Roberts 150.00 75.00
33 Ralph Kiner 100.00 50.00
34 Murry Dickson 50.00 25.00
35 Enos Slaughter 100.00 50.00
36 Eddie Kazak 60.00 30.00
37 Luke Appling 80.00 40.00
38 Bill Wight 50.00 25.00
39 Larry Doby 100.00 50.00
40 Bob Lemon 80.00 40.00
41 Hoot Evers 50.00 25.00
42 Art Houtteman 50.00 25.00
43 Bobby Doerr 80.00 40.00
44 Joe Dobson 50.00 25.00
45 Al Zarilla 50.00 25.00
46 Yogi Berra 400.00 200.00
47 Jerry Coleman 80.00 40.00
48 Lou Brissie 50.00 25.00
49 Elmer Valo 50.00 25.00
50 Dick Kokos 50.00 25.00
51 Ned Garver 60.00 30.00
52 Sam Mele 50.00 25.00
53 Clyde Vollmer 50.00 25.00
54 Gil Coan 50.00 25.00
55 Buddy Kerr 50.00 25.00
56 Del Crandall RC 60.00 30.00
57 Vern Bickford 50.00 25.00
58 Carl Furillo 80.00 40.00
59 Ralph Branca 80.00 40.00
60 Andy Pafko 60.00 30.00
61 Bob Rush 50.00 25.00
62 Ted Kluszewski 125.00 60.00
63 Ewell Blackwell 60.00 30.00
64 Alvin Dark 60.00 30.00
65 Dave Koslo 50.00 25.00
66 Larry Jansen 60.00 30.00
67 Willie Jones 60.00 30.00
68 Curt Simmons 60.00 30.00
69 Wally Westlake 50.00 25.00
70 Bob Chesnes 50.00 25.00
71 Red Schoendienst 80.00 40.00
72 Howie Pollet 50.00 25.00
73 Willard Marshall 15.00 7.50
74 Johnny Antonelli RC 60.00 30.00
75 Roy Campanella 300.00 150.00
76 Rex Barney 40.00 20.00
77 Duke Snider 300.00 150.00
78 Mickey Owen 25.00 12.50
79 Johnny VanderMeer 40.00 20.00
80 Howard Fox 15.00 7.50
81 Ron Northey 15.00 7.50
82 Whitey Lockman 25.00 12.50
83 Sheldon Jones 15.00 7.50
84 Richie Ashburn 125.00 60.00
85 Ken Heintzelman 15.00 7.50
86 Stan Rojek 15.00 7.50
87 Bill Werle 15.00 7.50
88 Marty Marion 40.00 20.00
89 George Munger 15.00 7.50
90 Harry Brecheen 40.00 20.00
91 Cass Michaels 15.00 7.50
92 Hank Majeski 15.00 7.50
93 Gene Bearden 40.00 20.00
94 Lou Boudreau 60.00 30.00
95 Aaron Robinson 15.00 7.50
96 Virgil Trucks 25.00 12.50
97 Maurice McDermott RC 15.00 7.50
98 Ted Williams 1000.00 500.00
99 Billy Goodman 25.00 12.50
100 Vic Raschi 60.00 30.00
101 Bobby Brown 60.00 30.00
102 Billy Johnson 25.00 12.50
103 Eddie Joost 15.00 7.50
104 Sam Chapman 15.00 7.50
105 Bob Dillinger 15.00 7.50
106 Cliff Fannin 15.00 7.50
107 Sam Dente 15.00 7.50
108 Ray Scarborough 15.00 7.50
109 Sid Gordon 15.00 7.50
110 Tommy Holmes 25.00 12.50
111 Walker Cooper 15.00 7.50
112 Gil Hodges 125.00 60.00
113 Gene Hermanski 15.00 7.50
114 Wayne Terwilliger RC 15.00 7.50
115 Roy Smalley 15.00 7.50
116 Virgil Stallcup 15.00 7.50
117 Bill Rigney 15.00 7.50
118 Clint Hartung 15.00 7.50
119 Dick Sisler 25.00 12.50
120 John Thompson 15.00 7.50
121 Andy Seminick 25.00 12.50
122 Johnny Hopp 25.00 12.50
123 Dino Restelli 15.00 7.50
124 Clyde McCullough 15.00 7.50
125 Del Rice 15.00 7.50
126 Al Brazle 15.00 7.50
127 Dave Philley 15.00 7.50
128 Phil Masi 15.00 7.50
129 Joe Gordon 25.00 12.50
130 Dale Mitchell 25.00 12.50
131 Steve Gromek 15.00 7.50
132 Mickey Vernon 25.00 12.50
133 Don Kolloway 15.00 7.50
134 Paul Trout 15.00 7.50
135 Pat Mullin 15.00 7.50
136 Buddy Rosar 15.00 7.50
137 Johnny Pesky 25.00 12.50
138 Allie Reynolds 60.00 30.00
139 Johnny Mize 80.00 40.00
140 Pete Suder 15.00 7.50
141 Joe Coleman 25.00 12.50
142 Sherman Lollar RC 40.00 20.00
143 Eddie Stewart 15.00 7.50
144 Al Evans 15.00 7.50
145 Jack Graham 15.00 7.50
146 Floyd Baker 15.00 7.50
147 Mike Garcia RC 40.00 20.00
148 Early Wynn 80.00 40.00
149 Bob Swift 15.00 7.50
150 George Vico 15.00 7.50
151 Fred Hutchinson 25.00 12.50
152 Ellis Kinder RC 15.00 7.50
153 Walt Masterson 15.00 7.50
154 Gus Niarhos 15.00 7.50
155 Frank Shea 25.00 12.50
156 Fred Sanford 25.00 12.50
157 Mike Guerra 15.00 7.50
158 Paul Lehner 15.00 7.50
159 Joe Tipton 15.00 7.50
160 Mickey Harris 15.00 7.50
161 Sherry Robertson 15.00 7.50
162 Eddie Yost 25.00 12.50
163 Earl Torgeson 15.00 7.50
164 Sibby Sisti 15.00 7.50
165 Bruce Edwards 15.00 7.50
166 Joe Hatton 15.00 7.50
167 Preacher Roe 60.00 30.00
168 Bob Scheffing 15.00 7.50
169 Hank Edwards 15.00 7.50
170 Dutch Leonard 15.00 7.50
171 Harry Gumbert 15.00 7.50
172 Peanuts Lowrey 15.00 7.50
173 Lloyd Merriman 15.00 7.50
174 Hank Thompson RC 40.00 20.00
175 Monte Kennedy 15.00 7.50
176 Sylvester Donnelly 15.00 7.50
177 Hank Borowy 15.00 7.50
178 Ed Fitzgerald 15.00 7.50
179 Chuck Diering 15.00 7.50
180 Harry Walker 25.00 12.50
181 Marino Pieretti 15.00 7.50
182 Sam Zoldak 15.00 7.50
183 Mickey Haefner 15.00 7.50
184 Randy Gumpert 15.00 7.50
185 Howie Judson 15.00 7.50
186 Ken Keltner 25.00 12.50
187 Lou Stringer 15.00 7.50
188 Earl Johnson 15.00 7.50
189 Owen Friend 15.00 7.50
190 Ken Wood 15.00 7.50
191 Dick Starr 15.00 7.50
192 Bob Chipman 15.00 7.50
193 Pete Reiser 40.00 20.00
194 Billy Cox 60.00 30.00
195 Phil Cavarretta 40.00 20.00
196 Doyle Lade 15.00 7.50
197 Johnny Wyrostek 15.00 7.50
198 Danny Litwhiler 15.00 7.50
199 Jack Kramer 15.00 7.50
200 Kirby Higbe 25.00 12.50
201 Pete Castiglione 15.00 7.50
202 Cliff Chambers 15.00 7.50
203 Danny Murtaugh 25.00 12.50
204 Granny Hamner RC 40.00 20.00
205 Mike Goliat 15.00 7.50
206 Stan Lopata 25.00 12.50
207 Max Lanier 15.00 7.50
208 Jim Hearn 15.00 7.50
209 Johnny Lindell 15.00 7.50
210 Ted Gray 15.00 7.50
211 Charlie Keller 40.00 20.00
212 Jerry Priddy 15.00 7.50
213 Carl Scheib 15.00 7.50
214 Dick Fowler 15.00 7.50
215 Ed Lopat 60.00 30.00
216 Bob Porterfield 25.00 12.50
217 Casey Stengel MG 125.00 60.00
218 Cliff Mapes RC 25.00 12.50
219 Hank Bauer RC 100.00 50.00
220 Leo Durocher MG 60.00 30.00
221 Don Mueller RC 60.00 30.00
222 Bobby Morgan 15.00 7.50
223 Jim Russell 15.00 7.50
224 Jack Banta 15.00 7.50
225 Eddie Sawyer MG 25.00 12.50
226 Jim Konstanty RC 60.00 30.00
227 Bob Miller 25.00 12.50
228 Bill Nicholson 25.00 12.50
229 Frank Frisch MG 60.00 30.00
230 Bill Serena 15.00 7.50
231 Preston Ward 15.00 7.50
232 Al Rosen RC 60.00 30.00
233 Allie Clark 15.00 7.50
234 Bobby Shantz RC 60.00 30.00
235 Harold Gilbert 15.00 7.50
236 Bob Cain 15.00 7.50
237 Bill Salkeld 15.00 7.50
238 Nippy Jones 15.00 7.50
239 Bill Howerton 15.00 7.50
240 Eddie Lake 15.00 7.50
241 Neil Berry 15.00 7.50
242 Dick Kryhoski 15.00 7.50
243 Johnny Groth 15.00 7.50
244 Dale Coogan 15.00 7.50
245 Al Papai 15.00 7.50
246 Walt Dropo RC 40.00 20.00
247 Irv Noren RC 25.00 12.50
248 Sam Jethroe RC 60.00 30.00
249 Snuffy Stirnweiss 25.00 12.50
250 Ray Coleman 15.00 7.50
251 Les Moss 15.00 7.50
252 Billy DeMars RC 60.00 16.50

1951 Bowman

The cards in this 324-card set measure approximately 2 1/16" by 3 1/8". Many of the obverses of the cards appearing in the 1951 Bowman set are enlargements of those appearing in the previous year. The high number series (253-324) is highly valued and contains the true "Rookie" cards of Mickey Mantle and Willie Mays. Card number 195 depicts Paul Richards in caricature. George Kell's card (number 46) incorrectly lists him as being in the "1941" Bowman series. Cards were issued either in one card penny packs which came 120 to a box or in six-card nickel packs which came 24 to a box. Player names are found printed in a panel on the front of the card. These cards were supposedly also sold in sheets in variety stores in the Philadelphia area.

NM Ex
COMPLETE SET (324) 20000.00 10000.00
COMMON CARD (1-252) 20.00 10.00
COMMON (253-324) 50.00 25.00
WRAPPER (1-cent) 200.00 100.00
WRAPPER (5-cent) 250.00 125.00
1 Whitey Ford RC 2000.00 500.00
2 Yogi Berra 400.00 200.00
3 Robin Roberts 80.00 40.00
4 Del Ennis 25.00 12.50
5 Dale Mitchell 25.00 12.50
6 Don Newcombe 60.00 30.00
7 Gil Hodges 125.00 60.00
8 Paul Lehner 20.00 10.00
9 Sam Chapman 20.00 10.00
10 Red Schoendienst 60.00 30.00
11 George Munger 20.00 10.00
12 Hank Majeski 20.00 10.00
13 Eddie Stanky 25.00 12.50
14 Alvin Dark 40.00 20.00
15 Johnny Pesky 25.00 12.50
16 Maurice McDermott 20.00 10.00
17 Pete Castiglione 20.00 10.00
18 Gil Coan 20.00 10.00
19 Sid Gordon 20.00 10.00
20 Del Crandall UER 25.00 12.50
(Misspelled Crandell on card)
21 Snuffy Stirnweiss 25.00 12.50
wearing St.L.Browns hat
22 Hank Sauer 25.00 12.50
23 Hoot Evers 20.00 10.00
24 Ewell Blackwell 40.00 20.00
25 Vic Raschi 60.00 30.00
26 Phil Rizzuto 125.00 60.00
27 Jim Konstanty 25.00 12.50
28 Eddie Waitkus 20.00 10.00
29 Allie Clark 20.00 10.00
30 Bob Feller 125.00 60.00
31 Roy Campanella 300.00 150.00
32 Duke Snider 250.00 125.00
33 Bob Hooper 20.00 10.00
34 Marty Marion 40.00 20.00
35 Al Zarilla 20.00 10.00
36 Joe Dobson 20.00 10.00
37 Whitey Lockman 40.00 20.00
38 Al Evans 20.00 10.00
39 Ray Scarborough 20.00 10.00
40 Gus Bell RC 60.00 30.00
41 Eddie Yost 25.00 12.50
42 Vern Bickford 20.00 10.00
43 Billy DeMars 20.00 10.00
44 Roy Smalley 20.00 10.00
45 Art Houtteman 20.00 10.00
46 George Kell 1941 UER 60.00 30.00
47 Grady Hatton 20.00 10.00
48 Ken Raffensberger 20.00 10.00
49 Jerry Coleman 25.00 12.50
50 Johnny Mize 80.00 40.00
51 Andy Seminick 20.00 10.00
52 Dick Sisler 40.00 20.00
53 Bob Lemon 60.00 30.00
54 Ray Boone RC 40.00 20.00
55 Gene Hermanski 20.00 10.00
56 Ralph Branca 60.00 30.00
57 Alex Kellner 20.00 10.00
58 Enos Slaughter 60.00 30.00
59 Randy Gumpert 20.00 10.00
60 Chico Carrasquel RC 60.00 30.00
61 Jim Hearn 20.00 10.00
62 Lou Boudreau 60.00 30.00
63 Bob Dillinger 20.00 10.00
64 Bill Werle 20.00 10.00
65 Mickey Vernon 40.00 20.00
66 Bob Elliott 25.00 12.50
67 Roy Sievers 25.00 12.50
68 Dick Kokos 20.00 10.00
69 Johnny Schmitz 20.00 10.00
70 Ron Northey 20.00 10.00
71 Jerry Priddy 20.00 10.00
72 Lloyd Merriman 20.00 10.00
73 Tommy Byrne 20.00 10.00
74 Billy Johnson 25.00 12.50
75 Russ Meyer RC 25.00 12.50
76 Stan Lopata 25.00 12.50
77 Mike Goliat 25.00 12.50
78 Early Wynn 60.00 30.00
79 Jim Hegan 25.00 12.50
80 Pee Wee Reese 200.00 100.00
81 Carl Furillo 60.00 30.00
82 Joe Tipton 20.00 10.00
83 Carl Scheib 20.00 10.00
84 Barney McCosky 20.00 10.00
85 Eddie Kazak 20.00 10.00
86 Harry Brecheen 25.00 12.50
87 Floyd Baker 20.00 10.00
88 Eddie Robinson 20.00 10.00
89 Hank Thompson 25.00 12.50
90 Dave Koslo 20.00 10.00
91 Clyde Vollmer 20.00 10.00
92 Vern Stephens 25.00 12.50
93 Danny O'Connell 20.00 10.00
94 Clyde McCullough 20.00 10.00
95 Sherry Robertson 20.00 10.00
96 Sandy Consuegra 20.00 10.00
97 Bob Kuzava 20.00 10.00
98 Willard Marshall 20.00 10.00
99 Earl Torgeson 20.00 10.00
100 Sherm Lollar 25.00 12.50
101 Owen Friend 20.00 10.00
102 Dutch Leonard 20.00 10.00
103 Andy Pafko 40.00 20.00
104 Virgil Trucks 25.00 12.50
105 Don Kolloway 20.00 10.00
106 Pat Mullin 20.00 10.00
107 Johnny Wyrostek 20.00 10.00
108 Virgil Stallcup 20.00 10.00
109 Allie Reynolds 60.00 30.00
110 Bobby Brown 40.00 20.00
111 Curt Simmons 25.00 12.50
112 Willie Jones 20.00 10.00
113 Bill Nicholson 20.00 10.00
114 Sam Zoldak 20.00 10.00
Pictured in Indians uniform
115 Steve Gromek 20.00 10.00
116 Bruce Edwards 20.00 10.00
117 Eddie Miksis 20.00 10.00
118 Preacher Roe 60.00 30.00
119 Eddie Joost 20.00 10.00
120 Joe Coleman 25.00 12.50
121 Gerry Staley 20.00 10.00
122 Joe Garagiola RC 100.00 50.00
123 Howie Judson 20.00 10.00
124 Gus Niarhos 20.00 10.00
125 Bill Rigney 25.00 12.50
126 Bobby Thomson 60.00 30.00
127 Sal Maglie RC 60.00 30.00
128 Ellis Kinder 20.00 10.00
129 Matt Batts 20.00 10.00
130 Tom Saffell 20.00 10.00
131 Cliff Chambers 20.00 10.00
132 Cass Michaels 20.00 10.00
133 Sam Dente 20.00 10.00
134 Warren Spahn 125.00 60.00
135 Walker Cooper 20.00 10.00
136 Ray Coleman 20.00 10.00
137 Dick Starr 20.00 10.00
138 Phil Cavarretta 25.00 12.50
139 Doyle Lade 20.00 10.00
140 Eddie Lake 20.00 10.00
141 Fred Hutchinson 25.00 12.50
142 Aaron Robinson 20.00 10.00
143 Ted Kluszewski 80.00 40.00
144 Herman Wehmeier 20.00 10.00
145 Fred Sanford 25.00 12.50
146 Johnny Hopp 25.00 12.50
147 Ken Heintzelman 20.00 10.00
148 Granny Hamner 20.00 10.00
149 Bubba Church 20.00 10.00
150 Mike Garcia 25.00 12.50
151 Larry Doby 60.00 30.00
152 Cal Abrams 20.00 10.00
153 Rex Barney 25.00 12.50
154 Pete Suder 20.00 10.00
155 Lou Brissie 20.00 10.00
156 Del Rice 20.00 10.00
157 Al Brazle 20.00 10.00
158 Chuck Diering 20.00 10.00
159 Eddie Stewart 20.00 10.00
160 Phil Masi 20.00 10.00
161 Wes Westrum RC 20.00 10.00
162 Larry Jansen 25.00 12.50
163 Monte Kennedy 20.00 10.00
164 Bill Wight 20.00 10.00
165 Ted Williams UER 800.00 400.00
Wrong birthdate
166 Stan Rojek 20.00 10.00
Pictured in Pirates uniform
167 Murry Dickson 20.00 10.00
168 Sam Mele 20.00 10.00
169 Sid Hudson 20.00 10.00
170 Sibby Sisti 20.00 10.00
171 Buddy Kerr 20.00 10.00
172 Ned Garver 20.00 10.00
173 Hank Arft 20.00 10.00
174 Mickey Owen 25.00 12.50
175 Wayne Terwilliger 20.00 10.00
176 Vic Wertz 40.00 20.00
177 Charlie Keller 25.00 12.50
178 Ted Gray 20.00 10.00
179 Danny Litwhiler 20.00 10.00
180 Howie Fox 20.00 10.00
181 Casey Stengel MG 80.00 40.00
182 Tom Ferrick 20.00 10.00
183 Hank Bauer 60.00 30.00
184 Eddie Sawyer MG 40.00 20.00
185 Jimmy Bloodworth 20.00 10.00
186 Richie Ashburn 100.00 50.00
187 Al Rosen 40.00 20.00
188 Bobby Avila RC 25.00 12.50
189 Erv Palica 20.00 10.00
190 Joe Hatten 20.00 10.00
191 Billy Hitchcock 20.00 10.00
192 Hank Wyse 20.00 10.00
193 Ted Wilks 20.00 10.00
194 Peanuts Lowrey 20.00 10.00
195 Paul Richards MG 25.00 12.50
(Caricature)
196 Billy Pierce RC 60.00 30.00
197 Bob Cain 20.00 10.00
198 Monte Irvin RC 100.00 50.00
199 Sheldon Jones 20.00 10.00
200 Jack Kramer 20.00 10.00
Pictured in NY Giants uniform
201 Steve O'Neill MG 20.00 10.00
202 Mike Guerra 20.00 10.00
203 Vernon Law RC 60.00 30.00
204 Vic Lombardi 20.00 10.00
205 Mickey Grasso 20.00 10.00
206 Conrado Marrero 20.00 10.00
207 Billy Southworth MG 20.00 10.00
208 Blix Donnelly 20.00 10.00

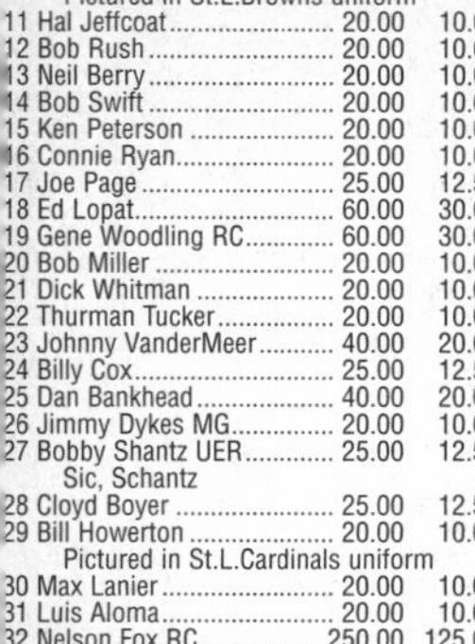

09 Ken Wood 20.00 10.00
10 Les Moss 20.00 10.00
Pictured in St.L.Browns uniform
11 Hal Jeffcoat 20.00 10.00
12 Bob Rush 20.00 10.00
13 Neil Berry 20.00 10.00
14 Bob Swift 20.00 10.00
15 Ken Peterson 20.00 10.00
16 Connie Ryan 20.00 10.00
17 Joe Page 25.00 12.50
18 Ed Lopat 60.00 30.00
19 Gene Woodling RC 60.00 30.00
20 Bob Miller 20.00 10.00
21 Dick Whitman 20.00 10.00
22 Thurman Tucker 20.00 10.00
23 Johnny VanderMeer 40.00 20.00
24 Billy Cox 25.00 12.50
25 Dan Bankhead 40.00 20.00
26 Jimmy Dykes MG 20.00 10.00
27 Bobby Shantz UER 25.00 12.50
Sic, Schantz
28 Cloyd Boyer 25.00 12.50
29 Bill Howerton 20.00 10.00
Pictured in St.L.Cardinals uniform
30 Max Lanier 20.00 10.00
31 Luis Aloma 20.00 10.00
32 Nelson Fox RC 250.00 125.00
33 Leo Durocher MG 60.00 30.00
34 Clint Hartung 25.00 12.50
35 Jack Lohrke 20.00 10.00
36 Buddy Rosar 20.00 10.00
37 Billy Goodman 25.00 12.50
38 Pete Reiser 40.00 20.00
39 Bill MacDonald 20.00 10.00
40 Joe Haynes 20.00 10.00
41 Irv Noren 25.00 12.50
42 Sam Jethroe 25.00 12.50
43 Johnny Antonelli 25.00 12.50
44 Cliff Fannin 20.00 10.00
45 John Berardino RC 60.00 30.00
46 Bill Serena 20.00 10.00
47 Bob Ramazzotti 20.00 10.00
48 Johnny Klippstein 20.00 10.00
49 Johnny Groth 20.00 10.00
50 Hank Borowy 20.00 10.00
51 Willard Ramsdell 20.00 10.00
52 Dixie Howell 20.00 10.00
53 Mickey Mantle RC 8000.00 4200.00
54 Jackie Jensen RC 100.00 50.00
55 Milo Candini 50.00 25.00
56 Ken Silvestri 50.00 25.00
57 Birdie Tebbetts RC 60.00 30.00
58 Luke Easter RC 60.00 30.00
59 Chuck Dressen MG 60.00 30.00
60 Carl Erskine RC 100.00 50.00
61 Wally Moses 60.00 30.00
62 Gus Zernial 60.00 30.00
63 Howie Pollet 60.00 30.00
Pictured in Cardinals uniform
64 Don Richmond 50.00 25.00
65 Steve Bilko 50.00 25.00
66 Harry Dorish 50.00 25.00
67 Ken Holcombe 50.00 25.00
68 Don Mueller 60.00 30.00
69 Ray Noble 50.00 25.00
70 Willard Nixon 50.00 25.00
71 Tommy Wright 50.00 25.00
72 Billy Meyer MG 50.00 25.00
73 Danny Murtaugh 60.00 30.00
74 George Metkovich 50.00 25.00
75 Bucky Harris MG 80.00 40.00
76 Frank Quinn 50.00 25.00
77 Roy Hartsfield 50.00 25.00
78 Norman Roy 50.00 25.00
79 Jim Delsing 50.00 25.00
80 Frank Overmire 50.00 25.00
Pictured in Browns uniform
81 Al Widmar 50.00 25.00
82 Frank Frisch MG 100.00 50.00
83 Walt Dubiel 50.00 25.00
84 Gene Bearden 60.00 30.00
85 Johnny Lipon 50.00 25.00
86 Bob Usher 50.00 25.00
87 Jim Blackburn 50.00 25.00
88 Bobby Adams 50.00 25.00
89 Cliff Mapes 60.00 30.00
90 Bill Dickey CO 100.00 50.00
91 Tommy Henrich CO 80.00 40.00
92 Eddie Pellagrini 50.00 25.00
93 Ken Johnson 50.00 25.00
94 Jocko Thompson 50.00 25.00
95 Al Lopez MG 125.00 60.00
96 Bob Kennedy 60.00 30.00
97 Dave Philley 50.00 25.00
98 Joe Astroth 50.00 25.00
99 Clyde King 50.00 25.00
00 Hal Rice 50.00 25.00
01 Tommy Glaviano 50.00 25.00
02 Jim Busby 50.00 25.00
03 Marv Rotblatt 50.00 25.00
04 Al Gettel 50.00 25.00
05 Willie Mays RC 2500.00 1500.00
06 Jim Piersall RC 125.00 60.00
07 Walt Masterson 50.00 25.00
08 Ted Beard 50.00 25.00
09 Mel Queen 50.00 25.00
10 Erv Dusak 50.00 25.00
11 Mickey Harris 50.00 25.00
12 Gene Mauch RC 60.00 30.00
13 Ray Mueller 50.00 25.00
14 Johnny Sain 80.00 40.00
15 Zack Taylor MG 50.00 25.00
16 Duane Pillette 50.00 25.00
17 Smoky Burgess RC 80.00 40.00
18 Warren Hacker 50.00 25.00
19 Red Rolfe MG 60.00 30.00
20 Hal White 50.00 25.00
21 Earl Johnson 50.00 25.00
22 Luke Sewell MG 60.00 30.00
23 Joe Adcock RC 80.00 40.00
24 Johnny Pramesa RC 125.00 38.00

1952 Bowman

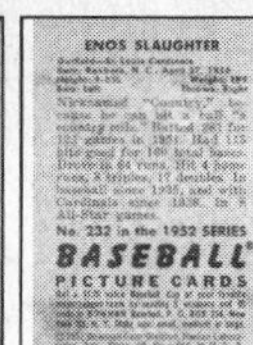

he cards in this 252-card set measure approxi- ately 2 1/16" by 3 1/8". While the Bowman set 1952 retained the card size introduced in 951, it employed a modification of color tones om the two preceding years. The cards also ppeared with a facsimile autograph on the front and, for the first time since 1949, premium advertising on the back. The 1952 set was apparently sold in sheets as well as in gum packs. Artwork for 15 cards that were never issued was discovered in the early 1980s. Cards were issued in one card penny packs or five card nickel packs. The five cent packs came 24 to a box. Notable Rookie Cards in this set are Lew Burdette, Gil McDougald, and Minnie Minoso.

NM Ex
COMPLETE SET (252) 8500.00 4200.00
COMMON CARD (1-216) 15.00 6.75
COMMON (217-252) 60.00 30.00
WRAPPER (1-cent) 200.00 100.00
WRAPPER (5-cent) 100.00 50.00
1 Yogi Berra 600.00 220.00
2 Bobby Thomson 40.00 20.00
3 Fred Hutchinson 25.00 12.50
4 Robin Roberts 80.00 40.00
5 Minnie Minoso RC 125.00 60.00
6 Virgil Stallcup 15.00 7.50
7 Mike Garcia 25.00 12.50
8 Pee Wee Reese 150.00 75.00
9 Vern Stephens 25.00 12.50
10 Bob Hooper 15.00 7.50
11 Ralph Kiner 60.00 30.00
12 Max Surkont 15.00 7.50
13 Cliff Mapes 15.00 7.50
14 Cliff Chambers 15.00 7.50
15 Sam Mele 15.00 7.50
16 Turk Lown 15.00 7.50
17 Ed Lopat 40.00 20.00
18 Don Mueller 25.00 12.50
19 Bob Cain 15.00 7.50
20 Willie Jones 15.00 7.50
21 Nellie Fox 100.00 50.00
22 Willard Ramsdell 15.00 7.50
23 Bob Lemon 60.00 30.00
24 Carl Furillo 40.00 20.00
25 Mickey McDermott 15.00 7.50
26 Eddie Joost 15.00 7.50
27 Joe Garagiola 40.00 20.00
28 Roy Hartsfield 15.00 7.50
29 Ned Garver 15.00 7.50
30 Red Schoendienst 60.00 30.00
31 Eddie Yost 25.00 12.50
32 Eddie Miksis 15.00 7.50
33 Gil McDougald RC 80.00 40.00
34 Alvin Dark 25.00 12.50
35 Granny Hamner 15.00 7.50
36 Cass Michaels 15.00 7.50
37 Vic Raschi 25.00 12.50
38 Whitey Lockman 25.00 12.50
39 Vic Wertz 25.00 12.50
40 Bubba Church 15.00 7.50
41 Chico Carrasquel 25.00 12.50
42 Johnny Wyrostek 15.00 7.50
43 Bob Feller 150.00 75.00
44 Roy Campanella 250.00 125.00
45 Johnny Pesky 25.00 12.50
46 Carl Scheib 15.00 7.50
47 Pete Castiglione 15.00 7.50
48 Vern Bickford 15.00 7.50
49 Jim Hearn 15.00 7.50
50 Gerry Staley 15.00 7.50
51 Gil Coan 15.00 7.50
52 Phil Rizzuto 150.00 75.00
53 Richie Ashburn 125.00 60.00
54 Billy Pierce 25.00 12.50
55 Ken Raffensberger 15.00 7.50
56 Clyde King 25.00 12.50
57 Clyde Vollmer 15.00 7.50
58 Hank Majeski 15.00 7.50
59 Murry Dickson 15.00 7.50
60 Sid Gordon 15.00 7.50
61 Tommy Byrne 15.00 7.50
62 Joe Presko 15.00 7.50
63 Irv Noren 15.00 7.50
64 Roy Smalley 15.00 7.50
65 Hank Bauer 40.00 20.00
66 Sal Maglie 25.00 12.50
67 Johnny Groth 15.00 7.50
68 Jim Busby 15.00 7.50
69 Joe Adcock 25.00 12.50
70 Carl Erskine 40.00 20.00
71 Vernon Law 25.00 12.50
72 Earl Torgeson 15.00 7.50
73 Jerry Coleman 25.00 12.50
74 Wes Westrum 25.00 12.50
75 George Kell 60.00 30.00
76 Del Ennis 25.00 12.50
77 Eddie Robinson 15.00 7.50
78 Lloyd Merriman 15.00 7.50
79 Lou Brissie 15.00 7.50
80 Gil Hodges 100.00 50.00
81 Billy Goodman 15.00 7.50
82 Gus Zernial 15.00 7.50
83 Howie Pollet 15.00 7.50
84 Sam Jethroe 15.00 7.50
85 Marty Marion CO 25.00 12.50
86 Cal Abrams 15.00 7.50
87 Mickey Vernon 25.00 12.50
88 Bruce Edwards 15.00 7.50
89 Billy Hitchcock 15.00 7.50
90 Larry Jansen 25.00 12.50
91 Don Kolloway 15.00 7.50
92 Eddie Waitkus 25.00 12.50
93 Paul Richards MG 25.00 12.50
94 Luke Sewell MG 25.00 12.50
95 Luke Easter 25.00 12.50
96 Ralph Branca 25.00 12.50
97 Willard Marshall 15.00 7.50
98 Jimmy Dykes MG 25.00 12.50
99 Clyde McCullough 15.00 7.50
100 Sibby Sisti 15.00 7.50
101 Mickey Mantle 2500.00 1250.00
102 Peanuts Lowrey 15.00 7.50
103 Joe Haynes 15.00 7.50
104 Hal Jeffcoat 15.00 7.50
105 Bobby Brown 25.00 12.50
106 Randy Gumpert 15.00 7.50
107 Del Rice 15.00 7.50
108 George Metkovich 15.00 7.50
109 Tom Morgan 15.00 7.50
110 Max Lanier 15.00 7.50
111 Hoot Evers 15.00 7.50
112 Smoky Burgess 25.00 12.50
113 Al Zarilla 15.00 7.50
114 Frank Hiller 15.00 7.50
115 Larry Doby 60.00 30.00
116 Duke Snider 200.00 100.00
117 Bill Wight 15.00 7.50
118 Ray Murray 15.00 7.50
119 Bill Howerton 15.00 7.50
120 Chet Nichols 15.00 7.50
121 Al Corwin 15.00 7.50
122 Billy Johnson 15.00 7.50
123 Sid Hudson 15.00 7.50
124 Birdie Tebbetts 15.00 7.50
125 Howie Fox 15.00 7.50
126 Phil Cavarretta 25.00 12.50
127 Dick Sisler 15.00 7.50
128 Don Newcombe 60.00 30.00
129 Gus Niarhos 15.00 7.50
130 Allie Clark 15.00 7.50
131 Bob Swift 15.00 7.50
132 Dave Cole 15.00 7.50
133 Dick Kryhoski 15.00 7.50
134 Al Brazle 15.00 7.50
135 Mickey Harris 15.00 7.50
136 Gene Hermanski 15.00 7.50
137 Stan Rojek 15.00 7.50
138 Ted Wilks 15.00 7.50
139 Jerry Priddy 15.00 7.50
140 Ray Scarborough 15.00 7.50
141 Hank Edwards 15.00 7.50
142 Early Wynn 60.00 30.00
143 Sandy Consuegra 15.00 7.50
144 Joe Hatton 15.00 7.50
145 Johnny Mize 60.00 30.00
146 Leo Durocher MG 60.00 30.00
147 Marlin Stuart 15.00 7.50
148 Ken Heintzelman 15.00 7.50
149 Howie Judson 15.00 7.50
150 Herman Wehmeier 15.00 7.50
151 Al Rosen 25.00 12.50
152 Billy Cox 25.00 12.50
153 Fred Hatfield 15.00 7.50
154 Ferris Fain 25.00 12.50
155 Billy Meyer MG 15.00 7.50
156 Warren Spahn 125.00 60.00
157 Jim Delsing 15.00 7.50
158 Bucky Harris MG 40.00 20.00
159 Dutch Leonard 15.00 7.50
160 Eddie Stanky 25.00 12.50
161 Jackie Jensen 40.00 20.00
162 Monte Irvin 60.00 30.00
163 Johnny Lipon 15.00 7.50
164 Connie Ryan 15.00 7.50
165 Saul Rogovin 15.00 7.50
166 Bobby Adams 15.00 7.50
167 Bobby Avila 25.00 12.50
168 Preacher Roe 25.00 12.50
169 Walt Dropo 25.00 12.50
170 Joe Astroth 15.00 7.50
171 Mel Queen 15.00 7.50
172 Ebba St.Claire 15.00 7.50
173 Gene Bearden 15.00 7.50
174 Mickey Grasso 15.00 7.50
175 Randy Jackson 15.00 7.50
176 Harry Brecheen 25.00 12.50
177 Gene Woodling 25.00 12.50
178 Dave Williams RC 25.00 12.50
179 Pete Suder 15.00 7.50
180 Ed Fitzgerald 15.00 7.50
181 Joe Collins RC 25.00 12.50
182 Dave Koslo 15.00 7.50
183 Pat Mullin 15.00 7.50
184 Curt Simmons 25.00 12.50
185 Eddie Stewart 15.00 7.50
186 Frank Smith 15.00 7.50
187 Jim Hegan 25.00 12.50
188 Chuck Dressen MG 25.00 12.50
189 Jimmy Piersall 25.00 12.50
190 Dick Fowler 15.00 7.50
191 Bob Friend RC 40.00 20.00
192 John Cusick 15.00 7.50
193 Bobby Young 15.00 7.50
194 Bob Porterfield 15.00 7.50
195 Frank Baumholtz 15.00 7.50
196 Stan Musial 500.00 300.00
197 Charlie Silvera RC 15.00 7.50
198 Chuck Diering 15.00 7.50
199 Ted Gray 15.00 7.50
200 Ken Silvestri 15.00 7.50
201 Ray Coleman 15.00 7.50
202 Harry Perkowski 15.00 7.50
203 Steve Gromek 15.00 7.50
204 Andy Pafko 25.00 12.50
205 Walt Masterson 15.00 7.50
206 Elmer Valo 15.00 7.50
207 George Strickland 15.00 7.50
208 Walker Cooper 15.00 7.50
209 Dick Littlefield 15.00 7.50
210 Archie Wilson 15.00 7.50
211 Paul Minner 15.00 7.50
212 Solly Hemus RC 15.00 7.50
213 Monte Kennedy 15.00 7.50
214 Ray Boone 15.00 7.50
215 Sheldon Jones 15.00 7.50
216 Matt Batts 15.00 7.50
217 Casey Stengel MG 150.00 75.00
218 Willie Mays 1500.00 750.00
219 Neil Berry 60.00 30.00
220 Russ Meyer 60.00 30.00
221 Lou Kretlow 60.00 30.00
222 Dixie Howell 60.00 30.00
223 Harry Simpson 60.00 30.00
224 Johnny Schmitz 60.00 30.00
225 Del Wilber 60.00 30.00
226 Alex Kellner 60.00 30.00
227 Clyde Sukeforth CO 60.00 30.00
228 Bob Chipman 60.00 30.00
229 Hank Arft 60.00 30.00
230 Frank Shea 60.00 30.00
231 Dee Fondy 60.00 30.00
232 Enos Slaughter 100.00 50.00
233 Bob Kuzava 60.00 30.00
234 Fred Fitzsimmons CO 60.00 30.00
235 Steve Souchock 60.00 30.00
236 Tommy Brown 60.00 30.00
237 Sherm Lollar 60.00 30.00
238 Roy McMillan RC 60.00 30.00
239 Dale Mitchell 60.00 30.00
240 Billy Loes RC 60.00 30.00
241 Mel Parnell 60.00 30.00
242 Everett Kell 60.00 30.00
243 George Munger 60.00 30.00
244 Lew Burdette RC 80.00 40.00
245 George Schmees 60.00 30.00
246 Jerry Snyder 60.00 30.00
247 Johnny Pramesa 60.00 30.00
248 Bill Werle 60.00 30.00
Full name in signature
248A Bill Werle 60.00 30.00
Signature on front has no W
249 Hank Thompson 60.00 30.00
250 Ike Delock 60.00 30.00
251 Jack Lohrke 60.00 30.00
252 Frank Crosetti CO 125.00 31.00

1953 Bowman B/W

The cards in this 64-card set measure approximately 2 1/2" by 3 3/4". Some collectors believe that the high cost of producing the 1953 color series forced Bowman to issue this set in black and white, since the two sets are identical in design except for the element of color. This set was also produced in fewer numbers than its color counterpart, and is popular among collectors for the challenge involved in completing it and the lack of short prints. Cards were issued in five-card nickel packs. There are no key Rookie Cards in this set. Recently, a variation of the Hal Bevan card (number 43) was discovered, that card exists with him being born in either 1930 or 1950. The 1950 version is much more difficult.

NM Ex
COMPLETE SET (64) 3000.00 1500.00
WRAPPER (1-CENT) 350.00 180.00
1 Gus Bell 125.00 25.00
2 Willard Nixon 40.00 20.00
3 Bill Rigney 40.00 20.00
4 Pat Mullin 40.00 20.00
5 Dee Fondy 40.00 20.00
6 Ray Murray 40.00 20.00
7 Andy Seminick 40.00 20.00
8 Pete Suder 40.00 20.00
9 Walt Masterson 40.00 20.00
10 Dick Sisler 60.00 30.00
11 Dick Gernert 40.00 20.00
12 Randy Jackson 40.00 20.00
13 Joe Tipton 40.00 20.00
14 Bill Nicholson 60.00 30.00
15 Johnny Mize 125.00 60.00
16 Stu Miller RC 60.00 30.00
17 Virgil Trucks 60.00 30.00
18 Billy Hoeft 40.00 20.00
19 Paul LaPalme 40.00 20.00
20 Eddie Robinson 40.00 20.00
21 Clarence Podbielan 40.00 20.00
22 Matt Batts 40.00 20.00
23 Wilmer Mizell 60.00 30.00
24 Del Wilber 40.00 20.00
25 Johnny Sain 80.00 40.00
26 Preacher Roe 80.00 40.00
27 Bob Lemon 175.00 90.00
28 Hoyt Wilhelm 125.00 60.00
29 Sid Hudson 40.00 20.00
30 Walker Cooper 40.00 20.00
31 Gene Woodling 80.00 40.00
32 Rocky Bridges 40.00 20.00
33 Bob Kuzava 40.00 20.00
34 Ebba St.Claire 40.00 20.00
35 Johnny Wyrostek 40.00 20.00
36 Jimmy Piersall 80.00 40.00
37 Hal Jeffcoat 40.00 20.00
38 Dave Cole 40.00 20.00
39 Casey Stengel MG 350.00 180.00
40 Larry Jansen 60.00 30.00
41 Bob Ramazzotti 40.00 20.00
42 Howie Judson 40.00 20.00
43 Hal Bevan ERR 40.00 20.00
Born in 1950
43A Hal Bevan COR
Born in 1930
44 Jim Delsing 40.00 20.00
45 Irv Noren 60.00 30.00
46 Bucky Harris MG 80.00 40.00
47 Jack Lohrke 40.00 20.00
48 Steve Ridzik 40.00 20.00
49 Floyd Baker 40.00 20.00
50 Dutch Leonard 40.00 20.00
51 Lou Burdette 80.00 40.00
52 Ralph Branca 80.00 40.00
53 Morrie Martin 40.00 20.00
54 Bill Miller 40.00 20.00
55 Don Johnson 40.00 20.00
56 Roy Smalley 40.00 20.00
57 Andy Pafko 60.00 30.00
58 Jim Konstanty 60.00 30.00
59 Duane Pillette 40.00 20.00
60 Billy Cox 80.00 40.00
61 Tom Gorman 40.00 20.00
62 Keith Thomas 40.00 20.00
63 Steve Gromek 40.00 20.00
64 Andy Hansen 80.00 26.00

1953 Bowman Color

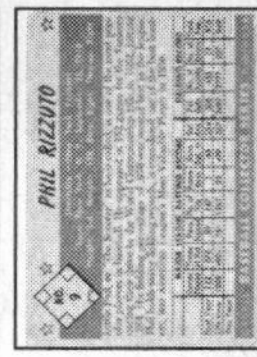

The cards in this 160-card set measure approximately 2 1/2" by 3 3/4". The 1953 Bowman Color set, considered by many to be the best looking set of the modern era, contains Kodachrome photographs with no names or facsimile autographs on the face. Cards were issued in five-card nickel packs in a 24 pack box with each pack having gum in it. The entire low number run were also printed in three card strips; it is believed that these three card strips in numerical order were box toppers to retailers. The box features an endorsement from Joe DiMaggio. Numbers 113 to 160 are somewhat more difficult to obtain, with numbers 113 to 128 being the most difficult. There are two cards of Al Corwin (126 and 149). There are no key Rookie Cards in this set.

NM Ex
COMPLETE SET (160) 15000.00 7500.00
COMMON CARD (1-112) 40.00 20.00
COMMON (113-128) 80.00 40.00
COMMON (129-160) 75.00 38.00
WRAPPER (1-cent) 400.00 200.00
WRAPPER (5-CENT) 300.00 150.00
1 Dave Williams 175.00 35.00
2 Vic Wertz 50.00 25.00
3 Sam Jethroe 50.00 25.00
4 Art Houtteman 40.00 20.00
5 Sid Gordon 40.00 20.00
6 Joe Ginsberg 40.00 20.00
7 Harry Chiti 40.00 20.00
8 Al Rosen 50.00 25.00
9 Phil Rizzuto 225.00 110.00
10 Richie Ashburn 150.00 75.00
11 Bobby Shantz 50.00 25.00
12 Carl Erskine 60.00 30.00
13 Gus Zernial 50.00 25.00
14 Billy Loes 50.00 25.00
15 Jim Busby 40.00 20.00
16 Bob Friend 50.00 25.00
17 Gerry Staley 40.00 20.00
18 Nellie Fox 150.00 75.00
19 Alvin Dark 50.00 25.00
20 Don Lenhardt 40.00 20.00
21 Joe Garagiola 60.00 30.00
22 Bob Porterfield 40.00 20.00
23 Herman Wehmeier 40.00 20.00
24 Jackie Jensen 60.00 30.00
25 Hoot Evers 40.00 20.00
26 Roy McMillan 50.00 25.00
27 Vic Raschi 60.00 30.00
28 Smoky Burgess 50.00 25.00
29 Bobby Avila 50.00 25.00
30 Phil Cavarretta 50.00 25.00
31 Jimmy Dykes MG 50.00 25.00
32 Stan Musial 600.00 400.00
33 Pee Wee Reese 1000.00 500.00
34 Gil Coan 40.00 20.00
35 Maurice McDermott 40.00 20.00
36 Minnie Minoso 80.00 40.00
37 Jim Wilson 40.00 20.00
38 Harry Byrd 40.00 20.00
39 Paul Richards MG 50.00 25.00
40 Larry Doby 100.00 50.00
41 Sammy White 40.00 20.00
42 Tommy Brown 40.00 20.00
43 Mike Garcia 50.00 25.00
44 Yogi Berra 800.00 400.00
Hank Bauer
Mickey Mantle
45 Walt Dropo 50.00 25.00
46 Roy Campanella 350.00 180.00
47 Ned Garver 40.00 20.00
48 Hank Sauer 50.00 25.00
49 Eddie Stanky MG 50.00 25.00
50 Lou Kretlow 40.00 20.00
51 Monte Irvin 80.00 40.00
52 Marty Marion MG 50.00 25.00
53 Del Rice 40.00 20.00
54 Chico Carrasquel 40.00 20.00
55 Leo Durocher MG 80.00 40.00
56 Bob Cain 40.00 20.00
57 Lou Boudreau MG 80.00 40.00
58 Willard Marshall 40.00 20.00
59 Mickey Mantle 2000.00 1000.00
60 Granny Hamner 40.00 20.00
61 George Kell 80.00 40.00
62 Ted Kluszewski 100.00 50.00
63 Gil McDougald 80.00 40.00
64 Curt Simmons 50.00 25.00
65 Robin Roberts 125.00 60.00
66 Mel Parnell 50.00 25.00
67 Mel Clark 40.00 20.00
68 Allie Reynolds 60.00 30.00
69 Charlie Grimm MG 50.00 25.00
70 Clint Courtney 40.00 20.00
71 Paul Minner 40.00 20.00
72 Ted Gray 40.00 20.00
73 Billy Pierce 50.00 25.00
74 Don Mueller 50.00 25.00
75 Saul Rogovin 40.00 20.00
76 Jim Hearn 40.00 20.00
77 Mickey Grasso 40.00 20.00
78 Carl Furillo 60.00 30.00
79 Ray Boone 50.00 25.00
80 Ralph Kiner 100.00 50.00
81 Enos Slaughter 100.00 50.00
82 Joe Astroth 40.00 20.00
83 Jack Daniels 40.00 20.00
84 Hank Bauer 60.00 30.00
85 Solly Hemus 40.00 20.00
86 Harry Simpson 40.00 20.00
87 Harry Perkowski 40.00 20.00
88 Joe Dobson 40.00 20.00
89 Sandy Consuegra 40.00 20.00
90 Joe Nuxhall 50.00 25.00
91 Steve Souchock 40.00 20.00
92 Gil Hodges 300.00 150.00
93 Phil Rizzuto and 300.00 150.00
Billy Martin
94 Bob Addis 40.00 20.00

95 Wally Moses CO 50.00 25.00
96 Sal Maglie 50.00 25.00
97 Eddie Mathews 350.00 180.00
98 Hector Rodriguez 40.00 20.00
99 Warren Spahn 350.00 180.00
100 Bill Wight 40.00 20.00
101 Red Schoendienst 80.00 40.00
102 Jim Hegan 50.00 25.00
103 Del Ennis 50.00 25.00
104 Luke Easter 50.00 25.00
105 Eddie Joost 40.00 20.00
106 Ken Raffensberger 40.00 20.00
107 Alex Kellner 40.00 20.00
108 Bobby Adams 40.00 20.00
109 Ken Wood 40.00 20.00
110 Bob Rush 40.00 20.00
111 Jim Dyck 40.00 20.00
112 Toby Atwell 40.00 20.00
113 Karl Drews 80.00 40.00
114 Bob Feller 500.00 250.00
115 Cloyd Boyer 80.00 40.00
116 Eddie Yost 100.00 50.00
117 Duke Snider 600.00 300.00
118 Billy Martin 400.00 200.00
119 Dale Mitchell 100.00 50.00
120 Marlin Stuart 80.00 40.00
121 Yogi Berra 800.00 400.00
122 Bill Serena 80.00 40.00
123 Johnny Lipon 80.00 40.00
124 Charlie Dressen MG 100.00 50.00
125 Fred Hatfield 80.00 40.00
126 Al Corwin 80.00 40.00
127 Dick Kryhoski 80.00 40.00
128 Whitey Lockman 100.00 50.00
129 Russ Meyer 75.00 38.00
130 Cass Michaels 75.00 38.00
131 Connie Ryan 75.00 38.00
132 Fred Hutchinson 90.00 45.00
133 Willie Jones 75.00 38.00
134 Johnny Pesky 90.00 45.00
135 Bobby Morgan 75.00 38.00
136 Jim Brideweser 75.00 38.00
137 Sam Dente 75.00 38.00
138 Bubba Church 75.00 38.00
139 Pete Runnels 90.00 45.00
140 Al Brazle 75.00 38.00
141 Frank Shea 75.00 38.00
142 Larry Miggins 75.00 38.00
143 Al Lopez MG 110.00 55.00
144 Warren Hacker 75.00 38.00
145 George Shuba 90.00 45.00
146 Early Wynn 200.00 100.00
147 Clem Koshorek 75.00 38.00
148 Billy Goodman 90.00 45.00
149 Al Corwin 75.00 38.00
150 Carl Scheib 75.00 38.00
151 Joe Adcock 110.00 55.00
152 Clyde Vollmer 75.00 38.00
153 Whitey Ford 800.00 400.00
154 Turk Lown 75.00 38.00
155 Allie Clark 75.00 38.00
156 Max Surkont 75.00 38.00
157 Sherm Lollar 90.00 45.00
158 Howard Fox 75.00 38.00
159 Mickey Vernon UER 90.00 45.00
(Photo actually Floyd Baker)
160 Cal Abrams 500.00 170.00

1954 Bowman

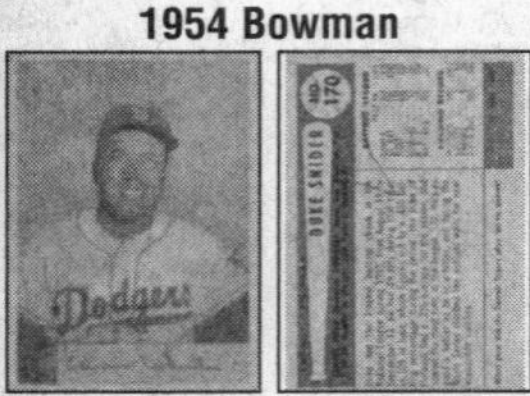

The cards in this 224-card set measure approximately 2 1/2" by 3 3/4". The set was distributed in two separate series: 1-128 in first series and 129-224 in second series. A contractual problem apparently resulted in the deletion of the number 66 Ted Williams card from this Bowman set, thereby creating a scarcity that is highly valued among collectors. The set price below does NOT include number 66 Williams but does include number 66 Jim Piersall, the apparent replacement for Williams in spite of the fact that Piersall was already number 210 to appear later in the set. Many errors in players' statistics exist (and some were corrected) while a few players' names were printed on the front, instead of appearing as a facsimile autograph. Most of these differences are so minor that there is no price differential for either card. The cards which changes were made on are numbers 12, 22,25,26,35,38,41,43,47,53,61,67,80,81,82,85, 93,94,99,103,105,124,138,139, 140,145,153,156,174,179,185,212,216 and 217. The set was issued in seven-card nickel packs and one-card penny packs. The penny packs were issued 120 to a box while the nickel packs were issued 24 to a box. The notable Rookie Cards in this set are Harvey Kuenn and Don Larsen.

	NM	Ex
COMPLETE SET (224)	4000.00	2000.00
WRAP.(1-CENT, DATED)	150.00	75.00
WRAP.(1-CENT, UNDATED)	200.00	100.00
WRAP.(5-CENT, DATED)	150.00	75.00
WRAP.(5-CENT, UNDATED)	60.00	30.00

1 Phil Rizzuto 175.00 52.50
2 Jackie Jensen 30.00 15.00
3 Marion Fricano 12.00 6.00
4 Bob Hooper 12.00 6.00
5 Billy Hunter 12.00 6.00
6 Nellie Fox 80.00 40.00
7 Walt Dropo 20.00 10.00
8 Jim Busby 12.00 6.00
9 Dave Williams 12.00 6.00
10 Carl Erskine 20.00 10.00
11 Sid Gordon 12.00 6.00
12 Roy McMillan 20.00 10.00
13 Paul Minner 12.00 6.00
14 Gerry Staley 12.00 6.00
15 Richie Ashburn 80.00 40.00
16 Jim Wilson 12.00 6.00
17 Tom Gorman 12.00 6.00
18 Hoot Evers 12.00 6.00
19 Bobby Shantz 20.00 10.00
20 Art Houtteman 12.00 6.00
21 Vic Wertz 20.00 10.00
22 Sam Mele 12.00 6.00
23 Harvey Kuenn RC 30.00 15.00
24 Bob Porterfield 12.00 6.00
25 Wes Westrum 20.00 10.00
26 Billy Cox 20.00 10.00
27 Dick Cole 12.00 6.00
28 Jim Greengrass 12.00 6.00
29 Johnny Klippstein 12.00 6.00
30 Del Rice 12.00 6.00
31 Smoky Burgess 20.00 10.00
32 Del Crandall 20.00 10.00
33A Vic Raschi 20.00 10.00
(No mention of trade on back)
33B Vic Raschi 30.00 15.00
(Traded to St.Louis)
34 Sammy White 12.00 6.00
35 Eddie Joost 12.00 6.00
36 George Strickland 12.00 6.00
37 Dick Kokos 12.00 6.00
38 Minnie Minoso 30.00 15.00
39 Ned Garver 12.00 6.00
40 Gil Coan 12.00 6.00
41 Alvin Dark 20.00 10.00
42 Billy Loes 20.00 10.00
43 Bob Friend 20.00 10.00
44 Harry Perkowski 12.00 6.00
45 Ralph Kiner 50.00 25.00
46 Rip Repulski 12.00 6.00
47 Granny Hamner 12.00 6.00
48 Jack Dittmer 12.00 6.00
49 Harry Byrd 12.00 6.00
50 George Kell 50.00 25.00
51 Alex Kellner 12.00 6.00
52 Joe Ginsberg 12.00 6.00
53 Don Lenhardt 12.00 6.00
54 Chico Carrasquel 12.00 6.00
55 Jim Delsing 12.00 6.00
56 Maurice McDermott 12.00 6.00
57 Hoyt Wilhelm 50.00 25.00
58 Pee Wee Reese 80.00 40.00
59 Bob Schultz 12.00 6.00
60 Fred Baczewski 12.00 6.00
61 Eddie Miksis 12.00 6.00
62 Enos Slaughter 50.00 25.00
63 Earl Torgeson 12.00 6.00
64 Eddie Mathews 80.00 40.00
65 Mickey Mantle 1500.00 750.00
66A Ted Williams 3000.00 1500.00
66B Jimmy Piersall 80.00 40.00
67 Carl Scheib 12.00 6.00
68 Bobby Avila 20.00 10.00
69 Clint Courtney 12.00 6.00
70 Willard Marshall 12.00 6.00
71 Ted Gray 12.00 6.00
72 Eddie Yost 20.00 10.00
73 Don Mueller 20.00 10.00
74 Jim Gilliam 30.00 15.00
75 Max Surkont 12.00 6.00
76 Joe Nuxhall 20.00 10.00
77 Bob Rush 12.00 6.00
78 Sal Yvars 12.00 6.00
79 Curt Simmons 20.00 10.00
80 Johnny Logan 12.00 6.00
81 Jerry Coleman 20.00 10.00
82 Billy Goodman 20.00 10.00
83 Ray Murray 12.00 6.00
84 Larry Doby 50.00 25.00
85 Jim Dyck 12.00 6.00
86 Harry Dorish 12.00 6.00
87 Don Lund 12.00 6.00
88 Tom Umphlett 12.00 6.00
89 Willie Mays 500.00 250.00
90 Roy Campanella 150.00 75.00
91 Cal Abrams 12.00 6.00
92 Ken Raffensberger 12.00 6.00
93 Bill Serena 12.00 6.00
94 Solly Hemus 12.00 6.00
95 Robin Roberts 50.00 25.00
96 Joe Adcock 20.00 10.00
97 Gil McDougald 20.00 10.00
98 Ellis Kinder 12.00 6.00
99 Pete Suder 12.00 6.00
100 Mike Garcia 20.00 10.00
101 Don Larsen RC 80.00 40.00
102 Billy Pierce 20.00 10.00
103 Steve Souchock 12.00 6.00
104 Frank Shea 12.00 6.00
105 Sal Maglie 20.00 10.00
106 Clem Labine 20.00 10.00
107 Paul LaPalme 12.00 6.00
108 Bobby Adams 12.00 6.00
109 Roy Smalley 12.00 6.00
110 Red Schoendienst 50.00 25.00
111 Murry Dickson 12.00 6.00
112 Andy Pafko 20.00 10.00
113 Allie Reynolds 20.00 10.00
114 Willard Nixon 12.00 6.00
115 Don Bollweg 12.00 6.00
116 Luke Easter 20.00 10.00
117 Dick Kryhoski 12.00 6.00
118 Bob Boyd 12.00 6.00
119 Fred Hatfield 12.00 6.00
120 Mel Hoderlein 12.00 6.00
121 Ray Katt 12.00 6.00
122 Carl Furillo 30.00 15.00
123 Toby Atwell 12.00 6.00
124 Gus Bell 20.00 10.00
125 Warren Hacker 12.00 6.00
126 Cliff Chambers 12.00 6.00
127 Del Ennis 20.00 10.00
128 Ebba St.Claire 12.00 6.00
129 Hank Bauer 30.00 15.00
130 Milt Bolling 12.00 6.00
131 Joe Astroth 12.00 6.00
132 Bob Feller 80.00 40.00
133 Duane Pillette 12.00 6.00
134 Luis Aloma 12.00 6.00
135 Johnny Pesky 20.00 10.00
136 Clyde Vollmer 12.00 6.00
137 Al Corwin 12.00 6.00
138 Gil Hodges 80.00 40.00
139 Preston Ward 12.00 6.00
140 Saul Rogovin 12.00 6.00
141 Joe Garagiola 30.00 15.00
142 Al Brazle 12.00 6.00
143 Willie Jones 12.00 6.00
144 Ernie Johnson RC 30.00 15.00
145 Billy Martin 80.00 40.00
146 Dick Gernert 12.00 6.00
147 Joe DeMaestri 12.00 6.00
148 Dale Mitchell 20.00 10.00
149 Bob Young 12.00 6.00
150 Cass Michaels 12.00 6.00
151 Pat Mullin 12.00 6.00
152 Mickey Vernon 20.00 10.00
153 Whitey Lockman 20.00 10.00
154 Don Newcombe 30.00 15.00
155 Frank Thomas RC 20.00 10.00
156 Rocky Bridges 12.00 6.00
157 Turk Lown 12.00 6.00
158 Stu Miller 20.00 10.00
159 Johnny Lindell 12.00 6.00
160 Danny O'Connell 12.00 6.00
161 Yogi Berra 175.00 90.00
162 Ted Lepcio 12.00 6.00
163A Dave Philley 20.00 10.00
(No mention of trade on back)
163B Dave Philley 30.00 15.00
(Traded to Cleveland)
164 Early Wynn 50.00 25.00
165 Johnny Groth 12.00 6.00
166 Sandy Consuegra 12.00 6.00
167 Billy Hoeft 12.00 6.00
168 Ed Fitzgerald 12.00 6.00
169 Larry Jansen 20.00 10.00
170 Duke Snider 175.00 90.00
171 Carlos Bernier 12.00 6.00
172 Andy Seminick 12.00 6.00
173 Dee Fondy 12.00 6.00
174 Pete Castiglione 12.00 6.00
175 Mel Clark 12.00 6.00
176 Vern Bickford 12.00 6.00
177 Whitey Ford 100.00 50.00
178 Del Wilber 12.00 6.00
179 Morrie Martin 12.00 6.00
180 Joe Tipton 12.00 6.00
181 Les Moss 12.00 6.00
182 Sherm Lollar 20.00 10.00
183 Matt Batts 12.00 6.00
184 Mickey Grasso 12.00 6.00
185 Daryl Spencer 12.00 6.00
186 Russ Meyer 12.00 6.00
187 Vern Law 20.00 10.00
188 Frank Smith 12.00 6.00
189 Randy Jackson 12.00 6.00
190 Joe Presko 12.00 6.00
191 Karl Drews 12.00 6.00
192 Lou Burdette 20.00 10.00
193 Eddie Robinson 12.00 6.00
194 Sid Hudson 12.00 6.00
195 Bob Cain 12.00 6.00
196 Bob Lemon 50.00 25.00
197 Lou Kretlow 12.00 6.00
198 Virgil Trucks 12.00 6.00
199 Steve Gromek 12.00 6.00
200 Conrado Marrero 12.00 6.00
201 Bobby Thomson 30.00 15.00
202 George Shuba 20.00 10.00
203 Vic Janowicz 20.00 10.00
204 Jack Collum 12.00 6.00
205 Hal Jeffcoat 12.00 6.00
206 Steve Bilko 12.00 6.00
207 Stan Lopata 12.00 6.00
208 Johnny Antonelli 20.00 10.00
209 Gene Woodling 12.00 6.00
210 Jimmy Piersall 30.00 15.00
211 Al Robertson 12.00 6.00
212 Owen Friend 12.00 6.00
213 Dick Littlefield 12.00 6.00
214 Ferris Fain 20.00 10.00
215 Johnny Bucha 12.00 6.00
216 Jerry Snyder 12.00 6.00
217 Hank Thompson 20.00 10.00
218 Preacher Roe 20.00 10.00
219 Hal Rice 12.00 6.00
220 Hobie Landrith 12.00 6.00
221 Frank Baumholtz 12.00 6.00
222 Memo Luna 12.00 6.00
223 Steve Ridzik 12.00 6.00
224 Bill Bruton 50.00 12.50

1955 Bowman

The cards in this 320-card set measure approximately 2 1/2" by 3 3/4". The Bowman set of 1955 is known as the "TV set" because each player photograph is cleverly shown within a television set design. The set contains umpire cards, some transposed pictures (e.g., Johnsons and Bollings), an incorrect spelling for Harvey Kuenn, and a traded line for Palica (all of which are noted in the checklist below). Some three-card advertising strips exist, the backs of these panels contain advertising for Bowman products. Print advertisments for these cards featured Willie Mays along with publicizing the great value in nine cards for a nickel. Advertising panels seen include Nellie Fox/Carl Furillo/Carl Erskine; Hank Aaron/Johnny Logan/Eddie Miksis; Bob Rush/Ray Katt/Willie Mays; Steve Gromek/Milt Bolling/Vern Stephens, Russ Kemmemer/ Hal Jeffcoat/Dee Fondy and a Bob Darnell/Early Wynn/Pee Wee Reese. Cards were issued either in nine-card nickel packs or one card penny packs. Cello packs containing approximately 20 cards have also been seen, albeit on a very limited basis. The notable Rookie Cards in this set are Elston Howard and Don Zimmer. Hall of Fame umpires pictured in the set are Al Barlick, Jocko Conlon and Cal Hubbard. Undated five cent wrappers are also known to exist for this set.

	NM	Ex
COMPLETE SET (320)	5000.00	2500.00
COMMON CARD (1-96)	12.00	6.00
COMMON CARD (97-224)	10.00	5.00
COMMON (225-320)	15.00	7.50
COMMON UMP. 225-320	30.00	15.00
WRAPPER (1-CENT)	60.00	30.00
WRAPPER (5-CENT)	60.00	30.00

1 Hoyt Wilhelm 100.00 22.00
2 Alvin Dark 15.00 7.50
3 Joe Coleman 15.00 7.50
4 Eddie Waitkus 15.00 7.50
5 Jim Robertson 12.00 6.00
6 Pete Suder 12.00 6.00
7 Gene Baker 12.00 6.00
8 Warren Hacker 12.00 6.00
9 Gil McDougald 20.00 10.00
10 Phil Rizzuto 125.00 60.00
11 Bill Bruton 15.00 7.50
12 Andy Pafko 15.00 7.50
13 Clyde Vollmer 12.00 6.00
14 Gus Keriazakos 12.00 6.00
15 Frank Sullivan 12.00 6.00
16 Jimmy Piersall 20.00 10.00
17 Del Ennis 15.00 7.50
18 Stan Lopata 12.00 6.00
19 Bobby Avila 15.00 7.50
20 Al Smith 15.00 7.50
21 Don Hoak 12.00 6.00
22 Roy Campanella 125.00 60.00
23 Al Kaline 150.00 75.00
24 Al Aber 12.00 6.00
25 Minnie Minoso 30.00 15.00
26 Virgil Trucks 15.00 7.50
27 Preston Ward 12.00 6.00
28 Dick Cole 12.00 6.00
29 Red Schoendienst 30.00 15.00
30 Bill Sarni 12.00 6.00
31 Johnny Temple RC 15.00 7.50
32 Wally Post 15.00 7.50
33 Nellie Fox 50.00 25.00
34 Clint Courtney 12.00 6.00
35 Bill Tuttle 12.00 6.00
36 Wayne Belardi 12.00 6.00
37 Pee Wee Reese 100.00 50.00
38 Early Wynn 30.00 15.00
39 Bob Darnell 15.00 7.50
40 Vic Wertz 15.00 7.50
41 Mel Clark 12.00 6.00
42 Bob Greenwood 12.00 6.00
43 Bob Buhl 15.00 7.50
44 Danny O'Connell 12.00 6.00
45 Tom Umphlett 12.00 6.00
46 Mickey Vernon 15.00 7.50
47 Sammy White 12.00 6.00
48A Milt Bolling ERR 20.00 10.00
(Name on back is Frank Bolling)
48B Milt Bolling COR 20.00 10.00
49 Jim Greengrass 12.00 6.00
50 Hobie Landrith 12.00 6.00
51 Elvin Tappe 12.00 6.00
52 Hal Rice 12.00 6.00
53 Alex Kellner 12.00 6.00
54 Don Bollweg 12.00 6.00
55 Cal Abrams 12.00 6.00
56 Billy Cox 15.00 7.50
57 Bob Friend 15.00 7.50
58 Frank Thomas 15.00 7.50
59 Whitey Ford 100.00 50.00
60 Enos Slaughter 30.00 15.00
61 Paul LaPalme 12.00 6.00
62 Royce Lint 12.00 6.00
63 Irv Noren 15.00 7.50
64 Curt Simmons 15.00 7.50
65 Don Zimmer RC 20.00 10.00
66 George Shuba 20.00 10.00
67 Don Larsen 20.00 10.00
68 Elston Howard RC 80.00 40.00
69 Billy Hunter 12.00 6.00
70 Lou Burdette 20.00 10.00
71 Dave Jolly 12.00 6.00
72 Chet Nichols 12.00 6.00
73 Eddie Yost 15.00 7.50
74 Jerry Snyder 12.00 6.00
75 Brooks Lawrence RC 12.00 6.00
76 Tom Poholsky 12.00 6.00
77 Jim McDonald 12.00 6.00
78 Gil Coan 12.00 6.00
79 Willie Miranda 12.00 6.00
80 Lou Limmer 12.00 6.00
81 Bobby Morgan 12.00 6.00
82 Lee Walls 12.00 6.00
83 Max Surkont 12.00 6.00
84 George Freese 12.00 6.00
85 Cass Michaels 12.00 6.00
86 Ted Gray 12.00 6.00
87 Randy Jackson 12.00 6.00
88 Steve Bilko 12.00 6.00
89 Lou Boudreau MG 30.00 15.00
90 Art Ditmar 12.00 6.00
91 Dick Marlowe 12.00 6.00
92 George Zuverink 12.00 6.00
93 Andy Seminick 12.00 6.00
94 Hank Thompson 15.00 7.50
95 Sal Maglie 15.00 7.50
96 Ray Narleski RC 12.00 6.00
97 Johnny Podres 30.00 15.00
98 Jim Gilliam 20.00 10.00
99 Jerry Coleman 15.00 7.50
100 Tom Morgan 10.00 5.00
101A Don Johnson ERR 20.00 10.00
(Photo actually Ernie Johnson)
101B Don Johnson COR 20.00 10.00
102 Bobby Thomson 15.00 7.50
103 Eddie Mathews 80.00 40.00
104 Bob Porterfield 10.00 5.00
105 Johnny Schmitz 10.00 5.00
106 Del Rice 10.00 5.00
107 Solly Hemus 10.00 5.00
108 Lou Kretlow 10.00 5.00
109 Vern Stephens 15.00 7.50
110 Bob Miller 10.00 5.00
111 Steve Ridzik 10.00 5.00
112 Granny Hamner 10.00 5.00
113 Bob Hall 10.00 5.00
114 Vic Janowicz 15.00 7.50
115 Roger Bowman 10.00 5.00
116 Sandy Consuegra 10.00 5.00
117 Johnny Groth 10.00 5.00
118 Bobby Adams 10.00 5.00
119 Joe Astroth 10.00 5.00
120 Ed Burtschy 10.00 5.00
121 Rufus Crawford 10.00 5.00
122 Al Corwin 10.00 5.00
123 Marv Grissom 10.00 5.00
124 Johnny Antonelli 15.00 7.50
125 Paul Giel 15.00 7.50
126 Billy Goodman 15.00 7.50
127 Hank Majeski 10.00 5.00
128 Mike Garcia 15.00 7.50
129 Hal Naragon 10.00 5.00
130 Richie Ashburn 50.00 25.00
131 Willard Marshall 10.00 5.00
132A Harvey Kueen ERR 50.00 25.00
(Sic& Kuenn)
132B Harvey Kuenn COR 30.00 15.00
133 Charles King 10.00 5.00
134 Bob Feller 80.00 40.00
135 Lloyd Merriman 10.00 5.00
136 Rocky Bridges 10.00 5.00
137 Bob Talbot 10.00 5.00
138 Davey Williams 15.00 7.50
139 Shantz Brothers 15.00 7.50
Wilmer Shantz
Bobby Shantz
140 Bobby Shantz 15.00 7.50
141 Wes Westrum 15.00 7.50
142 Rudy Regalado 10.00 5.00
143 Don Newcombe 30.00 15.00
144 Art Houtteman 10.00 5.00
145 Bob Nieman 10.00 5.00
146 Don Liddle 10.00 5.00
147 Sam Mele 10.00 5.00
148 Bob Chakales 10.00 5.00
149 Cloyd Boyer 10.00 5.00
150 Billy Klaus 10.00 5.00
151 Jim Brideweser 10.00 5.00
152 Johnny Klippstein 10.00 5.00
153 Eddie Robinson 10.00 5.00
154 Frank Lary RC 15.00 7.50
155 Gerry Staley 10.00 5.00
156 Jim Hughes 15.00 7.50
157A Ernie Johnson ERR 20.00 10.00
(Photo actually Don Johnson)
157B Ernie Johnson COR 20.00 10.00
158 Gil Hodges 50.00 25.00
159 Harry Byrd 10.00 5.00
160 Bill Skowron 20.00 10.00
161 Matt Batts 10.00 5.00
162 Charlie Maxwell 10.00 5.00
163 Sid Gordon 15.00 7.50
164 Toby Atwell 10.00 5.00
165 Maurice McDermott 10.00 5.00
166 Jim Busby 10.00 5.00
167 Bob Grim RC 20.00 10.00
168 Yogi Berra 125.00 60.00
169 Carl Furillo 30.00 15.00
170 Carl Erskine 20.00 10.00
171 Robin Roberts 50.00 25.00
172 Willie Jones 10.00 5.00
173 Chico Carrasquel 10.00 5.00
174 Sherm Lollar 15.00 7.50
175 Wilmer Shantz 10.00 5.00
176 Joe DeMaestri 10.00 5.00
177 Willard Nixon 10.00 5.00
178 Tom Brewer 10.00 5.00
179 Hank Aaron 250.00 125.00
180 Johnny Logan 15.00 7.50
181 Eddie Miksis 10.00 5.00
182 Bob Rush 10.00 5.00
183 Ray Katt 10.00 5.00
184 Willie Mays 250.00 125.00
185 Vic Raschi 10.00 5.00
186 Alex Grammas 10.00 5.00
187 Fred Hatfield 10.00 5.00
188 Ned Garver 10.00 5.00
189 Jack Collum 10.00 5.00
190 Fred Baczewski 10.00 5.00
191 Bob Lemon 30.00 15.00
192 George Strickland 10.00 5.00
193 Howie Judson 10.00 5.00
194 Joe Nuxhall 15.00 7.50
195A Erv Palica 15.00 7.50
(Without trade)
195B Erv Palica 40.00 20.00
(With trade)
196 Russ Meyer 15.00 7.50
197 Ralph Kiner 30.00 15.00
198 Dave Pope 10.00 5.00
199 Vern Law 15.00 7.50
200 Dick Littlefield 10.00 5.00
201 Allie Reynolds 20.00 10.00
202 Mickey Mantle UER 800.00 400.00
Birthdate listed as 10/30/31
Should be 10/20/31
203 Steve Gromek 10.00 5.00
204A Frank Bolling ERR 20.00 10.00
(Name on back is Milt Bolling)
204B Frank Bolling COR 20.00 10.00
205 Rip Repulski 10.00 5.00
206 Ralph Beard 10.00 5.00
207 Frank Shea 10.00 5.00
208 Ed Fitzgerald 10.00 5.00
209 Smoky Burgess 15.00 7.50
210 Earl Torgeson 10.00 5.00
211 Sonny Dixon 10.00 5.00
212 Jack Dittmer 10.00 5.00
213 George Kell 30.00 15.00
214 Billy Pierce 15.00 7.50
215 Bob Kuzava 10.00 5.00
216 Preacher Roe 20.00 10.00
217 Del Crandall 15.00 7.50
218 Joe Adcock 15.00 7.50
219 Whitey Lockman 15.00 7.50
220 Jim Hearn 10.00 5.00
221 Hector Brown 10.00 5.00
222 Russ Kemmerer 10.00 5.00
223 Hal Jeffcoat 10.00 5.00
224 Dee Fondy 10.00 5.00
225 Paul Richards MG 15.00 7.50
226 Bill McKinley UMP RC 30.00 15.00

27 Frank Baumholtz 15.00 7.50
28 John Phillips 15.00 7.50
29 Jim Brosnan RC 20.00 10.00
30 Al Brazle 15.00 7.50
31 Jim Konstanty 20.00 10.00
32 Birdie Tebbetts MG 20.00 10.00
33 Bill Serena 15.00 7.50
34 Dick Bartell CO 20.00 10.00
35 Joe Paparella UMP RC 30.00 15.00
36 Murry Dickson 15.00 7.50
37 Johnny Wyrostek 15.00 7.50
38 Eddie Stanky MG 20.00 10.00
39 Edwin Rommel UMP 40.00 20.00
40 Billy Loes 20.00 10.00
41 Johnny Pesky CO 20.00 10.00
42 Ernie Banks 350.00 180.00
43 Gus Bell 20.00 10.00
44 Duane Pillette 15.00 7.50
45 Bill Miller 15.00 7.50
46 Hank Bauer 30.00 15.00
47 Dutch Leonard CO 15.00 7.50
48 Harry Dorish 15.00 7.50
49 Billy Gardner RC 20.00 10.00
50 Larry Napp UMP RC 30.00 15.00
51 Stan Jok 15.00 7.50
52 Roy Smalley 15.00 7.50
53 Jim Wilson 15.00 7.50
54 Bennett Flowers 15.00 7.50
55 Pete Runnels 20.00 10.00
56 Owen Friend 15.00 7.50
57 Tom Alston 15.00 7.50
58 John Stevens UMP RC 30.00 15.00
59 Don Mossi RC 30.00 15.00
60 Edwin Hurley UMP RC 30.00 15.00
61 Walt Moryn 20.00 10.00
62 Jim Lemon 15.00 7.50
63 Eddie Joost 15.00 7.50
64 Bill Henry 15.00 7.50
65 Albert Barlick UMP RC 80.00 40.00
66 Mike Fornieles 15.00 7.50
67 Jim Honochick UMP RC 80.00 40.00
68 Roy Lee Hawes 15.00 7.50
69 Joe Amalfitano RC 20.00 10.00
70 Chico Fernandez 20.00 10.00
71 Bob Hooper 15.00 7.50
72 John Flaherty UMP RC 30.00 15.00
73 Bubba Church 15.00 7.50
74 Jim Delsing 15.00 7.50
75 William Grieve UMP RC 30.00 15.00
76 Ike Delock 15.00 7.50
77 Ed Runge UMP RC 30.00 15.00
78 Charlie Neal RC 40.00 20.00
79 Hank Soar UMP RC 40.00 20.00
80 Clyde McCullough 15.00 7.50
81 Charles Berry UMP 40.00 20.00
82 Phil Cavarretta 20.00 10.00
83 Nestor Chylak UMP RC 80.00 40.00
84 Bill Jackowski UMP RC 30.00 15.00
85 Walt Dropo 20.00 10.00
86 Frank Secory UMP RC 30.00 15.00
87 Ron Mrozinski 15.00 7.50
88 Dick Smith 15.00 7.50
89 Arthur Gore UMP RC 30.00 15.00
90 Hershell Freeman 15.00 7.50
91 Frank Dascoli UMP RC 30.00 15.00
92 Marv Blaylock 15.00 7.50
93 Thomas Gorman UMP RC 40.00 20.00
94 Wally Moses CO 15.00 7.50
95 Lee Ballanfant UMP RC 30.00 15.00
96 Bill Virdon RC 30.00 15.00
97 Dusty Boggess UMP RC 30.00 15.00
98 Charlie Grimm MG 20.00 10.00
99 Lon Warneke UMP 40.00 20.00
00 Tommy Byrne 20.00 10.00
01 William Engeln UMP RC 30.00 15.00
02 Frank Malzone RC 30.00 15.00
03 Jocko Conlan UMP 80.00 40.00
04 Harry Chiti 15.00 7.50
05 Frank Umont UMP RC 30.00 15.00
06 Bob Cerv 20.00 10.00
07 Babe Pinelli UMP 40.00 20.00
08 Al Lopez MG 50.00 25.00
09 Hal Dixon UMP RC 30.00 15.00
10 Ken Lehman 15.00 7.50
11 Lawrence Goetz UMP RC 30.00 15.00
12 Bill Wight 15.00 7.50
13 Augie Donatelli UMP RC 50.00 25.00
14 Dale Mitchell 20.00 10.00
15 Cal Hubbard UMP RC 80.00 40.00
16 Marion Fricano 15.00 7.50
17 W. Summers UMP 20.00 10.00
18 Sid Hudson 15.00 7.50
19 Al Schroll 15.00 7.50
20 George Susce RC 50.00 10.00

1989 Bowman

he 1989 Bowman set, produced by Topps, con- ins 484 slightly oversized cards (measuring 2 /2" by 3 3/4"). The cards were released in mid- eason 1989 in wax, rack, cello and factory set rmats. The fronts have white-bordered color hotos with facsimile autographs and small owman logos. The backs feature charts detail- g 1988 player performances vs. each team. he cards are ordered alphabetically according teams in the AL and NL. Cards 258-261 form father/son subset. Rookie Cards in this set clude Sandy Alomar Jr., Steve Finley, Ken riffey Jr., Tino Martinez, Gary Sheffield, John moltz and Robin Ventura.

Nm-Mt Ex-Mt
OMPLETE SET (484) 25.00 10.00
OMP.FACT.SET (484) 25.00 10.00
Oswald Peraza .05 .02
Brian Holton .10 .04
Jose Bautista RC .10 .04
Pete Harnisch RC .25 .10
5 Dave Schmidt .05 .02
6 Gregg Olson RC .25 .10
7 Jeff Ballard .05 .02
8 Bob Melvin .05 .02
9 Cal Ripken .75 .30
10 Randy Milligan .05 .02
11 Juan Bell RC .10 .04
12 Billy Ripken .05 .02
13 Jim Traber .05 .02
14 Pete Stanicek .05 .02
15 Steve Finley RC .50 .20
16 Larry Sheets .05 .02
17 Phil Bradley .05 .02
18 Brady Anderson RC .40 .16
19 Lee Smith .10 .04
20 Tom Fischer .05 .02
21 Mike Boddicker .05 .02
22 Rob Murphy .05 .02
23 Wes Gardner .05 .02
24 John Dopson .05 .02
25 Bob Stanley .05 .02
26 Roger Clemens .50 .20
27 Rich Gedman .05 .02
28 Marty Barrett .05 .02
29 Luis Rivera .05 .02
30 Jody Reed .05 .02
31 Nick Esasky .05 .02
32 Wade Boggs .15 .06
33 Jim Rice .10 .04
34 Mike Greenwell .05 .02
35 Dwight Evans .10 .04
36 Ellis Burks .10 .04
37 Chuck Finley .10 .04
38 Kirk McCaskill .05 .02
39 Jim Abbott RC* .50 .20
40 Bryan Harvey RC * .25 .10
41 Bert Blyleven .10 .04
42 Mike Witt .05 .02
43 Bob McClure .05 .02
44 Bill Schroeder .05 .02
45 Lance Parrish .10 .04
46 Dick Schofield .05 .02
47 Wally Joyner .10 .04
48 Jack Howell .05 .02
49 Johnny Ray .05 .02
50 Chili Davis .10 .04
51 Tony Armas .10 .04
52 Claudell Washington .05 .02
53 Brian Downing .10 .04
54 Devon White .10 .04
55 Bobby Thigpen .05 .02
56 Bill Long .05 .02
57 Jerry Reuss .05 .02
58 Shawn Hillegas .05 .02
59 Melido Perez .05 .02
60 Jeff Bittiger .05 .02
61 Jack McDowell .10 .04
62 Carlton Fisk .15 .06
63 Steve Lyons .05 .02
64 Ozzie Guillen .05 .02
65 Robin Ventura RC .75 .30
66 Fred Manrique .05 .02
67 Dan Pasqua .05 .02
68 Ivan Calderon .05 .02
69 Ron Kittle .05 .02
70 Daryl Boston .05 .02
71 Dave Gallagher .05 .02
72 Harold Baines .10 .04
73 Charles Nagy RC .25 .10
74 John Farrell .05 .02
75 Kevin Wickander .05 .02
76 Greg Swindell .05 .02
77 Mike Walker .05 .02
78 Doug Jones .05 .02
79 Rich Yett .05 .02
80 Tom Candiotti .05 .02
81 Jesse Orosco .05 .02
82 Bud Black .05 .02
83 Andy Allanson .05 .02
84 Pete O'Brien .05 .02
85 Jerry Browne .05 .02
86 Brook Jacoby .05 .02
87 Mark Lewis RC .25 .10
88 Luis Aguayo .05 .02
89 Cory Snyder .05 .02
90 Oddibe McDowell .05 .02
91 Joe Carter .10 .04
92 Frank Tanana .05 .02
93 Jack Morris .10 .04
94 Doyle Alexander .05 .02
95 Steve Searcy .05 .02
96 Randy Bockus .05 .02
97 Jeff M. Robinson .05 .02
98 Mike Henneman .05 .02
99 Paul Gibson .05 .02
100 Frank Williams .05 .02
101 Matt Nokes .05 .02
102 Rico Brogna RC UER .40 .16
(Misspelled Ricco on card back)
103 Lou Whitaker .10 .04
104 Al Pedrique .05 .02
105 Alan Trammell .10 .04
106 Chris Brown .05 .02
107 Pat Sheridan .05 .02
108 Chet Lemon .10 .04
109 Keith Moreland .05 .02
110 Mel Stottlemyre Jr. .05 .02
111 Bret Saberhagen .10 .04
112 Floyd Bannister .05 .02
113 Jeff Montgomery .05 .02
114 Steve Farr .05 .02
115 Tom Gordon UER .40 .16
(Front shows autograph of Don Gordon)
116 Charlie Leibrandt .05 .02
117 Mark Gubicza .05 .02
118 Mike Macfarlane RC .25 .10
119 Bob Boone .10 .04
120 Kurt Stillwell .05 .02
121 George Brett .60 .24
122 Frank White .10 .04
123 Kevin Seitzer .05 .02
124 Willie Wilson .10 .04
125 Pat Tabler .05 .02
126 Bo Jackson .25 .10
127 Hugh Walker RC .10 .04
128 Danny Tartabull .05 .02
129 Teddy Higuera .05 .02
130 Don August .05 .02
131 Juan Nieves .05 .02
132 Mike Birkbeck .05 .02
133 Dan Plesac .05 .02
134 Chris Bosio .05 .02
135 Bill Wegman .05 .02
136 Chuck Crim .05 .02
137 B.J. Surhoff .10 .04
138 Joey Meyer .05 .02
139 Dale Sveum .05 .02
140 Paul Molitor .15 .06
141 Jim Gantner .05 .02
142 Gary Sheffield RC 1.50 .60
143 Greg Brock .05 .02
144 Robin Yount .40 .16
145 Glenn Braggs .05 .02
146 Rob Deer .05 .02
147 Fred Toliver .05 .02
148 Jeff Reardon .10 .04
149 Allan Anderson .05 .02
150 Frank Viola .10 .04
151 Shane Rawley .05 .02
152 Juan Berenguer .05 .02
153 Johnny Ard .05 .02
154 Tim Laudner .05 .02
155 Brian Harper .05 .02
156 Al Newman .05 .02
157 Kent Hrbek .10 .04
158 Gary Gaetti .10 .04
159 Wally Backman .05 .02
160 Gene Larkin .05 .02
161 Greg Gagne .05 .02
162 Kirby Puckett .25 .10
163 Dan Gladden .05 .02
164 Randy Bush .05 .02
165 Dave LaPoint .05 .02
166 Andy Hawkins .05 .02
167 Dave Righetti .10 .04
168 Lance McCullers .05 .02
169 Jimmy Jones .05 .02
170 Al Leiter .25 .10
171 John Candelaria .05 .02
172 Don Slaught .05 .02
173 Jamie Quirk .05 .02
174 Rafael Santana .05 .02
175 Mike Pagliarulo .05 .02
176 Don Mattingly .60 .24
177 Ken Phelps .05 .02
178 Steve Sax .05 .02
179 Dave Winfield .10 .04
180 Stan Jefferson .05 .02
181 Rickey Henderson .25 .10
182 Bob Brower .05 .02
183 Roberto Kelly .05 .02
184 Curt Young .05 .02
185 Gene Nelson .05 .02
186 Bob Welch .10 .04
187 Rick Honeycutt .05 .02
188 Dave Stewart .10 .04
189 Mike Moore .05 .02
190 Dennis Eckersley .15 .06
191 Eric Plunk .05 .02
192 Storm Davis .05 .02
193 Terry Steinbach .10 .04
194 Ron Hassey .05 .02
195 Stan Royer RC .10 .04
196 Walt Weiss .10 .04
197 Mark McGwire 1.00 .40
198 Carney Lansford .10 .04
199 Glenn Hubbard .05 .02
200 Dave Henderson .05 .02
201 Jose Canseco .25 .10
202 Dave Parker .10 .04
203 Scott Bankhead .05 .02
204 Tom Niedenfuer .05 .02
205 Mark Langston .05 .02
206 Erik Hanson RC .25 .10
207 Mike Jackson .05 .02
208 Dave Valle .05 .02
209 Scott Bradley .05 .02
210 Harold Reynolds .10 .04
211 Tino Martinez RC .75 .30
212 Rich Renteria .05 .02
213 Rey Quinones .05 .02
214 Jim Presley .05 .02
215 Alvin Davis .05 .02
216 Edgar Martinez .25 .10
217 Darnell Coles .05 .02
218 Jeffrey Leonard .05 .02
219 Jay Buhner .10 .04
220 Ken Griffey Jr. RC 8.00 3.20
221 Drew Hall .05 .02
222 Bobby Witt .05 .02
223 Jamie Moyer .10 .04
224 Charlie Hough .10 .04
225 Nolan Ryan 1.00 .40
226 Jeff Russell .05 .02
227 Jim Sundberg .10 .04
228 Julio Franco .10 .04
229 Buddy Bell .10 .04
230 Scott Fletcher .05 .02
231 Jeff Kunkel .05 .02
232 Steve Buechele .05 .02
233 Monty Fariss .05 .02
234 Rick Leach .05 .02
235 Ruben Sierra .05 .02
236 Cecil Espy .05 .02
237 Rafael Palmeiro .25 .10
238 Pete Incaviglia .05 .02
239 Dave Stieb .10 .04
240 Jeff Musselman .05 .02
241 Mike Flanagan .05 .02
242 Todd Stottlemyre .05 .02
243 Jimmy Key .10 .04
244 Tony Castillo RC .10 .04
245 Alex Sanchez .05 .02
246 Tom Henke .05 .02
247 John Cerutti .05 .02
248 Ernie Whitt .05 .02
249 Bob Brenly .05 .02
250 Rance Mulliniks .05 .02
251 Kelly Gruber .05 .02
252 Ed Sprague RC .25 .10
253 Fred McGriff .15 .06
254 Tony Fernandez .05 .02
255 Tom Lawless .05 .02
256 George Bell .10 .04
257 Jesse Barfield .10 .04
258 Roberto Alomar .15 .06
Sandy Alomar
259 Ken Griffey Jr. 1.00 .40
Ken Griffey Sr.
260 Cal Ripken Jr. .25 .10
Cal Ripken Sr.
261 Mel Stottlemyre Jr. .05 .02
Mel Stottlemyre Sr.
262 Zane Smith .05 .02
263 Charlie Puleo .05 .02
264 Derek Lilliquist RC .10 .04
265 Paul Assenmacher .05 .02
266 John Smoltz RC 1.00 .40
267 Tom Glavine .25 .10
268 Steve Avery RC .25 .10
269 Pete Smith .05 .02
270 Jody Davis .05 .02
271 Bruce Benedict .05 .02
272 Andres Thomas .05 .02
273 Gerald Perry .05 .02
274 Ron Gant .10 .04
275 Darrell Evans .10 .04
276 Dale Murphy .15 .06
277 Dion James .05 .02
278 Lonnie Smith .05 .02
279 Geronimo Berroa .05 .02
280 Steve Wilson RC .10 .04
281 Rick Sutcliffe .10 .04
282 Kevin Coffman .05 .02
283 Mitch Williams .05 .02
284 Greg Maddux .50 .20
285 Paul Kilgus .05 .02
286 Mike Harkey RC .10 .04
287 Lloyd McClendon .05 .02
288 Damon Berryhill .05 .02
289 Ty Griffin .05 .02
290 Ryne Sandberg .40 .16
291 Mark Grace .25 .10
292 Curt Wilkerson .05 .02
293 Vance Law .05 .02
294 Shawon Dunston .05 .02
295 Jerome Walton RC .25 .10
296 Mitch Webster .05 .02
297 Dwight Smith RC .25 .10
298 Andre Dawson .10 .04
299 Jeff Sellers .05 .02
300 Jose Rijo .10 .04
301 John Franco .10 .04
302 Rick Mahler .05 .02
303 Ron Robinson .05 .02
304 Danny Jackson .05 .02
305 Rob Dibble RC .50 .20
306 Tom Browning .05 .02
307 Bo Diaz .05 .02
308 Manny Trillo .05 .02
309 Chris Sabo RC * .40 .16
310 Ron Oester .05 .02
311 Barry Larkin .15 .06
312 Todd Benzinger .05 .02
313 Paul O'Neill .15 .06
314 Kal Daniels .05 .02
315 Joel Youngblood .05 .02
316 Eric Davis .10 .04
317 Dave Smith .05 .02
318 Mark Portugal .05 .02
319 Brian Meyer .05 .02
320 Jim Deshaies .05 .02
321 Juan Agosto .05 .02
322 Mike Scott .10 .04
323 Rick Rhoden .05 .02
324 Jim Clancy .05 .02
325 Larry Andersen .05 .02
326 Alex Trevino .05 .02
327 Alan Ashby .05 .02
328 Craig Reynolds .05 .02
329 Bill Doran .05 .02
330 Rafael Ramirez .05 .02
331 Glenn Davis .05 .02
332 Willie Ansley RC .10 .04
333 Gerald Young .05 .02
334 Cameron Drew .05 .02
335 Jay Howell .05 .02
336 Tim Belcher .10 .04
337 Fernando Valenzuela .10 .04
338 Ricky Horton .05 .02
339 Tim Leary .05 .02
340 Bill Bene .05 .02
341 Orel Hershiser .10 .04
342 Mike Scioscia .10 .04
343 Rick Dempsey .05 .02
344 Willie Randolph .10 .04
345 Alfredo Griffin .05 .02
346 Eddie Murray .25 .10
347 Mickey Hatcher .05 .02
348 Mike Sharperson .05 .02
349 John Shelby .05 .02
350 Mike Marshall .05 .02
351 Kirk Gibson .10 .04
352 Mike Davis .05 .02
353 Bryn Smith .05 .02
354 Pascual Perez .05 .02
355 Kevin Gross .05 .02
356 Andy McGaffigan .05 .02
357 Brian Holman RC .10 .04
358 Dave Wainhouse RC .10 .04
359 Dennis Martinez .10 .04
360 Tim Burke .05 .02
361 Nelson Santovenia .05 .02
362 Tim Wallach .05 .02
363 Spike Owen .05 .02
364 Rex Hudler .05 .02
365 Andres Galarraga .10 .04
366 Otis Nixon .05 .02
367 Hubie Brooks .05 .02
368 Mike Aldrete .05 .02
369 Tim Raines .10 .04
370 Dave Martinez .05 .02
371 Bob Ojeda .05 .02
372 Ron Darling .10 .04
373 Wally Whitehurst RC .10 .04
374 Randy Myers .10 .04
375 David Cone .10 .04
376 Dwight Gooden .10 .04
377 Sid Fernandez .05 .02
378 Dave Proctor .05 .02
379 Gary Carter .10 .04
380 Keith Miller .05 .02
381 Gregg Jefferies .05 .02
382 Tim Teufel .05 .02
383 Kevin Elster .05 .02
384 Dave Magadan .05 .02
385 Keith Hernandez .10 .04
386 Mookie Wilson .10 .04
387 Darryl Strawberry .10 .04
388 Kevin McReynolds .05 .02
389 Mark Carreon .05 .02
390 Jeff Parrett .05 .02
391 Mike Maddux .05 .02
392 Don Carman .05 .02
393 Bruce Ruffin .05 .02
394 Ken Howell .05 .02
395 Steve Bedrosian .05 .02
396 Floyd Youmans .05 .02
397 Larry McWilliams .05 .02
398 Pat Combs RC * .10 .04
399 Steve Lake .05 .02
400 Dickie Thon .05 .02
401 Ricky Jordan RC * .25 .10
402 Mike Schmidt .50 .20
403 Tom Herr .05 .02
404 Chris James .05 .02
405 Juan Samuel .05 .02
406 Von Hayes .05 .02
407 Ron Jones .10 .04
408 Curt Ford .05 .02
409 Bob Walk .05 .02
410 Jeff D. Robinson .05 .02
411 Jim Gott .05 .02
412 Scott Medvin .05 .02
413 John Smiley .05 .02
414 Bob Kipper .05 .02
415 Brian Fisher .05 .02
416 Doug Drabek .05 .02
417 Mike LaValliere .05 .02
418 Ken Oberkfell .05 .02
419 Sid Bream .05 .02
420 Austin Manahan .05 .02
421 Jose Lind .05 .02
422 Bobby Bonilla .10 .04
423 Glenn Wilson .05 .02
424 Andy Van Slyke .10 .04
425 Gary Redus .05 .02
426 Barry Bonds 1.25 .50
427 Don Heinkel .05 .02
428 Ken Dayley .05 .02
429 Todd Worrell .05 .02
430 Brad DuVall .05 .02
431 Jose DeLeon .05 .02
432 Joe Magrane .05 .02
433 John Ericks .05 .02
434 Frank DiPino .05 .02
435 Tony Pena .05 .02
436 Ozzie Smith .40 .16
437 Terry Pendleton .10 .04
438 Jose Oquendo .05 .02
439 Tim Jones .05 .02
440 Pedro Guerrero .10 .04
441 Milt Thompson .05 .02
442 Willie McGee .10 .04
443 Vince Coleman .05 .02
444 Tom Brunansky .05 .02
445 Walt Terrell .05 .02
446 Eric Show .05 .02
447 Mark Davis .05 .02
448 Andy Benes RC .40 .16
449 Ed Whitson .05 .02
450 Dennis Rasmussen .05 .02
451 Bruce Hurst .05 .02
452 Pat Clements .05 .02
453 Benito Santiago .10 .04
454 Sandy Alomar Jr. RC .40 .16
455 Garry Templeton .10 .04
456 Jack Clark .10 .04
457 Tim Flannery .05 .02
458 Roberto Alomar .25 .10
459 Carmelo Martinez .05 .02
460 John Kruk .10 .04
461 Tony Gwynn .30 .12
462 Jerald Clark RC .10 .04
463 Don Robinson .05 .02
464 Craig Lefferts .05 .02
465 Kelly Downs .05 .02
466 Rick Reuschel .10 .04
467 Scott Garrelts .05 .02
468 Wil Tejada .05 .02
469 Kirt Manwaring .05 .02
470 Terry Kennedy .05 .02
471 Jose Uribe .05 .02
472 Royce Clayton RC .40 .16
473 Robby Thompson .05 .02
474 Kevin Mitchell .10 .04
475 Ernie Riles .05 .02
476 Will Clark .25 .10
477 Donell Nixon .05 .02
478 Candy Maldonado .05 .02
479 Tracy Jones .05 .02
480 Brett Butler .10 .04
481 Checklist 1-121 .05 .02
482 Checklist 122-242 .05 .02
483 Checklist 243-363 .05 .02
484 Checklist 364-484 .05 .02

1989 Bowman Tiffany

This is a parallel to the regular 1989 Bowman set. This set was issued with a glossy front and white-stock backs, thus joining other sets known in the Topps family as "Tiffany" sets. The set measure 2 1/2" by 3 3/4" and was issued in factory set form only. In addition to the 484 regular cards, the 11 Reprint inserts were also included in the factory set. Reportedly, only 6,000 factory sets were printed.

Nm-Mt Ex-Mt
COMP.FACT.SET (495) 250.00 100.00
*STARS: 8X TO 20X BASIC CARDS
*ROOKIES: 8X TO 20X BASIC CARDS

1989 Bowman Reprint Inserts

The 1989 Bowman Reprint Inserts set contains 11 cards measuring approximately 2 1/2" by 3 3/4". The fronts depict reproduced actual size "classic" Bowman cards, which are noted as reprints. The backs are devoted to a sweepstakes entry form. One of these reprint cards was included in each 1989 Bowman wax pack thus making these "reprints" quite easy to find. Since the cards are unnumbered, they are ordered below in alphabetical order by player's name and year within player.

Nm-Mt Ex-Mt
*TIFFANY: 10X TO 20X HI COLUMN
ONE TIFF.REP.SET PER TIFF.FACT.SET
1 Richie Ashburn 49 .40 .16
2 Yogi Berra 48 .25 .10
3 Whitey Ford 51 .40 .16
4 Gil Hodges 49 .50 .20
5 Mickey Mantle 51 1.00 .40
6 Mickey Mantle 53 1.00 .40
7 Willie Mays 51 .50 .20
8 Satchel Paige 49 .50 .20
9 Jackie Robinson 50 .50 .20
10 Duke Snider 49 .25 .10
11 Ted Williams 54 .50 .20

1990 Bowman

The 1990 Bowman set (produced by Topps) consists of 528 standard-size cards. The cards were issued in wax packs and factory sets. Each wax pack contained one of 11 different 1950's retro art cards. Unlike most sets, player selection focused primarily on rookies instead of proven major leaguers. The cards feature a white border with the player's photo inside and the Bowman logo on top. The card numbering is in team order with the teams themselves being ordered alphabetically within each league. Notable Rookie Cards include Moises Alou, Travis Fryman, Juan Gonzalez, Chuck Knoblauch, Ray Lankford, Sammy Sosa, Frank Thomas, Mo Vaughn, Larry Walker, and Bernie Williams.

Nm-Mt Ex-Mt
COMPLETE SET (528) 25.00 7.50
COMP.FACT.SET (528) 25.00 7.50
1 Tommy Greene RC .10 .03
2 Tom Glavine .15 .04
3 Andy Nezelek .05 .02
4 Mike Stanton RC .25 .07
5 Rick Luecken .05 .02
6 Kent Mercker RC .25 .07
7 Derek Lilliquist .05 .02
8 Charlie Leibrandt .05 .02
9 Steve Avery .05 .02
10 John Smoltz .25 .07
11 Mark Lemke .05 .02
12 Lonnie Smith .05 .02
13 Oddibe McDowell .05 .02
14 Tyler Houston RC .25 .07
15 Jeff Blauser .05 .02
16 Ernie Whitt .05 .02
17 Alexis Infante .05 .02
18 Jim Presley .05 .02
19 Dale Murphy .25 .07
20 Nick Esasky .05 .02
21 Rick Sutcliffe .10 .03
22 Mike Bielecki .05 .02
23 Steve Wilson .05 .02
24 Kevin Blankenship .05 .02
25 Mitch Williams .05 .02
26 Dean Wilkins .05 .02
27 Greg Maddux .40 .12
28 Mike Harkey .05 .02
29 Mark Grace .15 .04
30 Ryne Sandberg .40 .12
31 Greg Smith .05 .02
32 Dwight Smith .05 .02
33 Damon Berryhill .05 .02
34 E.Cunningham UER RC .10 .03
(Errant * by the word "in")
35 Jerome Walton .05 .02
36 Lloyd McClendon .05 .02
37 Ty Griffin .05 .02
38 Shawon Dunston .05 .02
39 Andre Dawson .10 .03
40 Luis Salazar .05 .02
41 Tim Layana .05 .02
42 Rob Dibble .10 .03
43 Tom Browning .05 .02
44 Danny Jackson .05 .02
45 Jose Rijo .05 .02
46 Scott Scudder .05 .02
47 Randy Myers UER .10 .03
(Career ERA .274& should be 2.74)
48 Brian Lane RC .10 .03
49 Paul O'Neill .15 .04
50 Barry Larkin .15 .04
51 Reggie Jefferson RC .25 .07
52 Jeff Branson RC** .10 .03
53 Chris Sabo .05 .02
54 Joe Oliver .05 .02
55 Todd Benzinger .05 .02
56 Rolando Roomes .05 .02
57 Hal Morris .05 .02
58 Eric Davis .10 .03
59 Scott Bryant .05 .02
60 Ken Griffey Sr. .10 .03
61 Darryl Kile RC 1.00 .30
62 Dave Smith .05 .02
63 Mark Portugal .05 .02
64 Jeff Juden RC .10 .03
65 Bill Gullickson .05 .02
66 Danny Darwin .05 .02
67 Larry Andersen .05 .02
68 Jose Cano .05 .02
69 Dan Schatzeder .05 .02
70 Jim Deshaies .05 .02
71 Mike Scott .05 .02
72 Gerald Young .05 .02
73 Ken Caminiti .10 .03
74 Ken Oberkfell .05 .02
75 Dave Rohde .05 .02
76 Bill Doran .05 .02
77 Andujar Cedeno RC .10 .03
78 Craig Biggio .15 .04
79 Karl Rhodes RC .25 .07
80 Glenn Davis .05 .02
81 Eric Anthony RC .10 .03
82 John Wetteland .25 .07
83 Jay Howell .05 .02
84 Orel Hershiser .10 .03
85 Tim Belcher .05 .02
86 Kiki Jones .05 .02
87 Mike Hartley .05 .02
88 Ramon Martinez .05 .02
89 Mike Scioscia .05 .02
90 Willie Randolph .10 .03
91 Juan Samuel .05 .02
92 Jose Offerman RC .25 .07
93 Dave Hansen RC .25 .07
94 Jeff Hamilton .05 .02
95 Alfredo Griffin .05 .02
96 Tom Goodwin RC .25 .07
97 Kirk Gibson .10 .03
98 Jose Vizcaino RC .25 .07
99 Kal Daniels .05 .02
100 Hubie Brooks .05 .02
101 Eddie Murray .25 .07
102 Dennis Boyd .05 .02
103 Tim Burke .05 .02
104 Bill Sampen .05 .02
105 Brett Gideon .05 .02
106 Mark Gardner RC .10 .03
107 Howard Farmer .05 .02
108 Mel Rojas RC .10 .03
109 Kevin Gross .05 .02
110 Dave Schmidt .05 .02
111 Dennis Martinez .10 .03
112 Jerry Goff .05 .02
113 Andres Galarraga .10 .03
114 Tim Wallach .05 .02
115 Marquis Grissom RC .50 .15
116 Spike Owen .05 .02
117 Larry Walker RC 1.50 .45
118 Tim Raines .10 .03
119 Delino DeShields RC .25 .07
120 Tom Foley .05 .02
121 Dave Martinez .05 .02
122 Frank Viola UER .05 .02
(Career ERA .384 should be 3.84)
123 Julio Valera RC .05 .02
124 Alejandro Pena .05 .02
125 David Cone .10 .03
126 Dwight Gooden .10 .03
127 Kevin D. Brown .05 .02
128 John Franco .10 .03
129 Terry Bross .05 .02
130 Blaine Beatty .05 .02
131 Sid Fernandez .05 .02
132 Mike Marshall .05 .02
133 Howard Johnson .05 .02
134 Jaime Roseboro .05 .02
135 Alan Zinter RC .10 .03
136 Keith Miller .05 .02
137 Kevin Elster .05 .02
138 Kevin McReynolds .05 .02
139 Barry Lyons .05 .02
140 Gregg Jefferies .10 .03
141 Darryl Strawberry .10 .03
142 Todd Hundley RC .25 .07
143 Scott Service .05 .02
144 Chuck Malone .05 .02
145 Steve Ontiveros .05 .02
146 Roger McDowell .05 .02
147 Ken Howell .05 .02
148 Pat Combs .05 .02
149 Jeff Parrett .05 .02
150 Chuck McElroy RC .10 .03
151 Jason Grimsley RC .10 .03
152 Len Dykstra .10 .03
153 M.Morandini RC .25 .07
154 John Kruk .10 .03
155 Dickie Thon .05 .02
156 Ricky Jordan .05 .02
157 Jeff Jackson RC .10 .03
158 Darren Daulton .10 .03
159 Tom Herr .05 .02
160 Von Hayes .05 .02
161 Dave Hollins RC .25 .07
162 Carmelo Martinez .05 .02
163 Bob Walk .05 .02
164 Doug Drabek .05 .02
165 Walt Terrell .05 .02
166 Bill Landrum .05 .02
167 Scott Ruskin .05 .02
168 Bob Patterson .05 .02
169 Bobby Bonilla .10 .03
170 Jose Lind .05 .02
171 Andy Van Slyke .10 .03
172 Mike LaValliere .05 .02
173 Willie Greene RC .10 .03
174 Jay Bell .10 .03
175 Sid Bream .05 .02
176 Tom Prince .05 .02
177 Wally Backman .05 .02
178 Moises Alou RC .75 .23
179 Steve Carter .05 .02
180 Gary Redus .05 .02
181 Barry Bonds .60 .18
182 Don Slaught UER .05 .02
(Card back shows headings for a pitcher)
183 Joe Magrane .05 .02
184 Bryn Smith .05 .02
185 Todd Worrell .05 .02
186 Jose DeLeon .05 .02
187 Frank DiPino .05 .02
188 John Tudor .05 .02
189 Howard Hilton .05 .02
190 John Ericks .05 .02
191 Ken Dayley .05 .02
192 Ray Lankford RC .25 .07
193 Todd Zeile .10 .03
194 Willie McGee .10 .03
195 Ozzie Smith .40 .12
196 Milt Thompson .05 .02
197 Terry Pendleton .10 .03
198 Vince Coleman .05 .02
199 Paul Coleman RC .10 .03
200 Jose Oquendo .05 .02
201 Pedro Guerrero .05 .02
202 Tom Brunansky .05 .02
203 Roger Smithberg .05 .02
204 Eddie Whitson .05 .02
205 Dennis Rasmussen .05 .02
206 Craig Lefferts .05 .02
207 Andy Benes .10 .03
208 Bruce Hurst .05 .02
209 Eric Show .05 .02
210 Rafael Valdez .05 .02
211 Joey Cora .10 .03
212 Thomas Howard .05 .02
213 Rob Nelson .05 .02
214 Jack Clark .10 .03
215 Garry Templeton .05 .02
216 Fred Lynn .05 .02
217 Tony Gwynn .30 .09
218 Benito Santiago .10 .03
219 Mike Pagliarulo .05 .02
220 Joe Carter .10 .03
221 Roberto Alomar .15 .04
222 Bip Roberts .05 .02
223 Rick Reuschel .05 .02
224 Russ Swan .05 .02
225 Eric Gunderson .05 .02
226 Steve Bedrosian .05 .02
227 Mike Remlinger .05 .02
228 Scott Garrelts .05 .02
229 Ernie Camacho .05 .02
230 Andres Santana RC .10 .03
231 Will Clark .25 .07
232 Kevin Mitchell .05 .02
233 Robby Thompson .05 .02
234 Bill Bathe .05 .02
235 Tony Perezchica .05 .02
236 Gary Carter .10 .03
237 Brett Butler .10 .03
238 Matt Williams .10 .03
239 Earnie Riles .05 .02
240 Kevin Bass .05 .02
241 Terry Kennedy .05 .02
242 Steve Hosey RC .10 .03
243 Ben McDonald RC .25 .07
244 Jeff Ballard .05 .02
245 Joe Price .05 .02
246 Curt Schilling 1.00 .30
247 Pete Harnisch .05 .02
248 Mark Williamson .05 .02
249 Gregg Olson .10 .03
250 Chris Myers .05 .02
251 David Segui RC ERR .25 .07
(Missing vital stats at top of card back under name)
251B David Segui COR RC .25 .07
252 Joe Orsulak .05 .02
253 Craig Worthington .05 .02
254 Mickey Tettleton .05 .02
255 Cal Ripken .75 .23
256 Bill Ripken .05 .02
257 Randy Milligan .05 .02
258 Brady Anderson .10 .03
259 Chris Hoiles RC UER .25 .07
Baltimore is spelled Baltimore
260 Mike Devereaux .05 .02
261 Phil Bradley .05 .02
262 Leo Gomez RC .10 .03
263 Lee Smith .10 .03
264 Mike Rochford .05 .02
265 Jeff Reardon .10 .03
266 Wes Gardner .05 .02
267 Mike Boddicker .05 .02
268 Roger Clemens .50 .15
269 Rob Murphy .05 .02
270 Mickey Pina .05 .02
271 Tony Pena .05 .02
272 Jody Reed .05 .02
273 Kevin Romine .05 .02
274 Mike Greenwell .05 .02
275 Maurice Vaughn RC 1.00 .30
276 Danny Heep .05 .02
277 Scott Cooper RC .10 .03
278 Greg Blosser RC .10 .03
279 Dwight Evans UER .10 .03
(* by "1990 Team Breakdown")
280 Ellis Burks .15 .04
281 Wade Boggs .15 .04
282 Marty Barrett .05 .02
283 Kirk McCaskill .05 .02
284 Mark Langston .05 .02
285 Bert Blyleven .10 .03
286 Mike Fetters RC .25 .07
287 Kyle Abbott .05 .02
288 Jim Abbott .15 .04
289 Chuck Finley .10 .03
290 Gary DiSarcina RC .25 .07
291 Dick Schofield .05 .02
292 Devon White .10 .03
293 Bobby Rose .05 .02
294 Brian Downing .05 .02
295 Lance Parrish .05 .02
296 Jack Howell .05 .02
297 Claudell Washington .05 .02
298 John Orton RC .10 .03
299 Wally Joyner .10 .03
300 Lee Stevens .05 .02
301 Chili Davis .10 .03
302 Johnny Ray .05 .02
303 Greg Hibbard RC .10 .03
304 Eric King .05 .02
305 Jack McDowell .05 .02
306 Bobby Thigpen .05 .02
307 Adam Peterson .05 .02
308 Scott Radinsky RC .25 .07
309 Wayne Edwards .05 .02
310 Melido Perez .05 .02
311 Robin Ventura .25 .07
312 Sammy Sosa RC 8.00 2.40
313 Dan Pasqua .05 .02
314 Carlton Fisk .15 .04
315 Ozzie Guillen .05 .02
316 Ivan Calderon .05 .02
317 Daryl Boston .05 .02
318 Craig Grebeck RC .25 .07
319 Scott Fletcher .05 .02
320 Frank Thomas RC 2.00 .60
321 Steve Lyons .05 .02
322 Carlos Martinez .05 .02
323 Joe Skalski .05 .02
324 Tom Candiotti .05 .02
325 Greg Swindell .05 .02
326 Steve Olin RC .25 .07
327 Kevin Wickander .05 .02
328 Doug Jones .05 .02
329 Jeff Shaw .05 .02
330 Kevin Bearse .05 .02
331 Dion James .05 .02
332 Jerry Browne .05 .02
333 Joey Belle .25 .07
334 Felix Fermin .05 .02
335 Candy Maldonado .05 .02
336 Cory Snyder .05 .02
337 Sandy Alomar Jr. .10 .03
338 Mark Lewis .05 .02
339 Carlos Baerga RC .25 .07
340 Chris James .05 .02
341 Brook Jacoby .05 .02
342 Keith Hernandez .10 .03
343 Frank Tanana .05 .02
344 Scott Aldred .05 .02
345 Mike Henneman .05 .02
346 Steve Wapnick .05 .02
347 Greg Gohr RC .10 .03
348 Eric Stone .05 .02
349 Brian DuBois .05 .02
350 Kevin Ritz .05 .02
351 Rico Brogna .25 .07
352 Mike Heath .05 .02
353 Alan Trammell .10 .03
354 Chet Lemon .05 .02
355 Dave Bergman .05 .02
356 Lou Whitaker .10 .03
357 Cecil Fielder UER .10 .03
* by 1990 Team Breakdown
358 Milt Cuyler RC .10 .03
359 Tony Phillips .05 .02
360 Travis Fryman RC .50 .15
361 Ed Romero .05 .02
362 Lloyd Moseby .05 .02
363 Mark Gubicza .05 .02
364 Bret Saberhagen .10 .03
365 Tom Gordon .10 .03
366 Steve Farr .05 .02
367 Kevin Appier .10 .03
368 Storm Davis .05 .02
369 Mark Davis .05 .02
370 Jeff Montgomery .10 .03
371 Frank White .10 .03
372 Brent Mayne RC .25 .07
373 Bob Boone .10 .03
374 Jim Eisenreich .05 .02
375 Danny Tartabull .05 .02
376 Kurt Stillwell .05 .02
377 Bill Pecota .05 .02
378 Bo Jackson .25 .07
379 Bob Hamelin RC .25 .07
380 Kevin Seitzer .05 .02
381 Rey Palacios .05 .02
382 George Brett .60 .18
383 Gerald Perry .05 .02
384 Teddy Higuera .05 .02
385 Tom Filer .05 .02
386 Dan Plesac .05 .02
387 Cal Eldred RC .25 .07
388 Jaime Navarro .05 .02
389 Chris Bosio .05 .02
390 Randy Veres .05 .02
391 Gary Sheffield .25 .07
392 George Canale .05 .02
393 B.J. Surhoff .10 .03
394 Tim McIntosh .05 .02
395 Greg Brock .05 .02
396 Greg Vaughn .05 .02
397 Darryl Hamilton .05 .02
398 Dave Parker .10 .03
399 Paul Molitor .15 .04
400 Jim Gantner .05 .02
401 Rob Deer .05 .02
402 Billy Spiers .05 .02
403 Glenn Braggs .05 .02
404 Robin Yount .40 .12
405 Rick Aguilera .10 .03
406 Johnny Ard .05 .02
407 Kevin Tapani RC .25 .07
408 Park Pittman .05 .02
409 Allan Anderson .05 .02
410 Juan Berenguer .05 .02
411 Willie Banks RC .10 .03
412 Rich Yett .05 .02
413 Dave West .05 .02
414 Greg Gagne .05 .02
415 Chuck Knoblauch RC .50 .15
416 Randy Bush .05 .02
417 Gary Gaetti .10 .03
418 Kent Hrbek .10 .03
419 Al Newman .05 .02
420 Danny Gladden .05 .02
421 Paul Sorrento RC .25 .07
422 Derek Parks RC .10 .03
423 Scott Leius RC .10 .03
424 Kirby Puckett .25 .07
425 Willie Smith .05 .02
426 Dave Righetti .05 .02
427 Jeff D. Robinson .05 .02
428 Alan Mills RC .10 .03
429 Tim Leary .05 .02
430 Pascual Perez .05 .02
431 Alvaro Espinoza .05 .02
432 Dave Winfield .10 .03
433 Jesse Barfield .05 .02
434 Randy Velarde .05 .02
435 Rick Cerone .05 .02
436 Steve Balboni .05 .02
437 Mel Hall .05 .02
438 Bob Geren .05 .02
439 Bernie Williams RC 1.50 .45
440 Kevin Maas RC .25 .07
441 Mike Blowers RC .10 .03
442 Steve Sax .05 .02
443 Don Mattingly .60 .18
444 Roberto Kelly .05 .02
445 Mike Moore .05 .02
446 Reggie Harris RC .10 .03
447 Scott Sanderson .05 .02
448 Dave Otto .05 .02
449 Dave Stewart .10 .03
450 Rick Honeycutt .05 .02
451 Dennis Eckersley .10 .03
452 Carney Lansford .10 .03
453 Scott Hemond RC .10 .03
454 Mark McGwire .60 .18
455 Felix Jose .05 .02
456 Terry Steinbach .05 .02
457 Rickey Henderson .25 .07
458 Dave Henderson .05 .02
459 Mike Gallego .05 .02
460 Jose Canseco .25 .07
461 Walt Weiss .05 .02
462 Ken Phelps .05 .02
463 Darren Lewis RC .10 .03
464 Ron Hassey .05 .02
465 Roger Salkeld RC .10 .03
466 Scott Bankhead .05 .02
467 Keith Comstock .05 .02
468 Randy Johnson .50 .12
469 Erik Hanson .05 .02
470 Mike Schooler .05 .02
471 Gary Eave .05 .02
472 Jeffrey Leonard .05 .02
473 Dave Valle .05 .02
474 Omar Vizquel .25 .07
475 Pete O'Brien .05 .02
476 Henry Cotto .05 .02
477 Jay Buhner .10 .03
478 Harold Reynolds .10 .03
479 Alvin Davis .05 .02
480 Darnell Coles .05 .02
481 Ken Griffey Jr. .75 .23
482 Greg Briley .05 .02
483 Scott Bradley .05 .02
484 Tino Martinez .25 .07
485 Jeff Russell .05 .02
486 Nolan Ryan 1.00 .30
487 Robb Nen RC .50 .15
488 Kevin Brown .10 .03
489 Brian Bohanon RC .10 .03
490 Ruben Sierra .05 .02
491 Pete Incaviglia .05 .02
492 Juan Gonzalez RC 2.00 .60
493 Steve Buechele .05 .02
494 Scott Coolbaugh .05 .02
495 Geno Petralli .05 .02
496 Rafael Palmeiro .15 .04
497 Julio Franco .10 .03
498 Gary Pettis .05 .02
499 Donald Harris .05 .02
500 Monty Fariss .05 .02
501 Harold Baines .10 .03
502 Cecil Espy .05 .02
503 Jack Daugherty .05 .02
504 Willie Blair RC .10 .03
505 Dave Stieb .10 .03
506 Tom Henke .05 .02
507 John Cerutti .05 .02
508 Paul Kilgus .05 .02
509 Jimmy Key .10 .03
510 John Olerud RC 1.00 .30
511 Ed Sprague .10 .03
512 Manuel Lee .05 .02
513 Fred McGriff .25 .07
514 Glenallen Hill .05 .02
515 George Bell .05 .02
516 Mookie Wilson .10 .03
517 Luis Sojo RC .25 .07
518 Nelson Liriano .05 .02
519 Kelly Gruber .05 .02
520 Greg Myers .05 .02
521 Pat Borders .05 .02
522 Junior Felix .05 .02
523 Eddie Zosky RC .10 .03
524 Tony Fernandez .05 .02
525 Checklist 1-132 UER .05 .02
(No copyright mark on the back)
526 Checklist 133-264 .05 .02
527 Checklist 265-396 .05 .02
528 Checklist 397-528 .05 .02

1990 Bowman Tiffany

These 528 standard-size cards were issued as a factory set by Topps. These cards parallel the regular Bowman issue except they have glossy fronts and a very easy to read white stock back. In addition to the 528 basic cards, the 11 insert art cards were also included in the factory set. According to published reports at the time, approximately 3,000 of these sets were produced.

Nm-Mt Ex-Mt
COMP.FACT.SET (539) 250.00 75.00
*STARS: 8X TO 20X BASIC CARDS
*ROOKIES: 5X TO 12X BASIC CARDS

1990 Bowman Art Inserts

These standard-size cards were included as an insert in every 1990 Bowman pack. This set, which consists of 11 superstars, depicts drawings by Craig Pursley with the backs being descriptions of the 1990 Bowman sweepstakes. We have checklisted the set alphabetically by player. All the cards in this set can be found with either one asterisk or two on the back.

Nm-Mt Ex-Mt
COMPLETE SET (11) 2.00 .60
*TIFFANY: 8X TO 20X BASIC ART INSERT
ONE TIFF.REP.SET PER TIFF.FACT.SET
1 Will Clark .25 .07
2 Mark Davis .05 .01

3 Dwight Gooden .10 .03
4 Bo Jackson .25 .07
5 Don Mattingly .60 .18
6 Kevin Mitchell .05 .01
7 Gregg Olson .10 .03
8 Nolan Ryan 1.00 .30
9 Bret Saberhagen .10 .03
10 Jerome Walton .05 .01
11 Robin Yount .40 .12

1991 Bowman

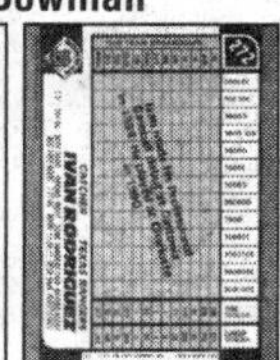

This single-series 704-card standard-size set marked the third straight year that Topps issued a set weighted towards prospects using the Bowman name. Cards were issued in wax packs and factory sets. The cards share a design very similar to the 1990 Bowman set with white borders enframing a color photo. The player name, however, is more prominent than in the previous year set. The cards are arranged in team order by division as follows: AL East, AL West, NL East, and NL West. Subsets include Rod Carew Tribute (1-5), Minor League MVP's (180-185/693-698), AL Silver Sluggers (367-375), NL Silver Sluggers (376-384) and checklists (699-704). Rookie Cards in this set include Jeff Bagwell, Jeromy Burnitz, Carl Everett, Chipper Jones, Eric Karros, Ryan Klesko, Kenny Lofton, Javier Lopez, Raul Mondesi, Mike Mussina, Ivan "Pudge" Rodriguez, Tim Salmon, Jim Thome, and Rondell White. There are two instances of misnumbering in the set; Ken Griffey (should be 255) and Ken Griffey Jr. are both numbered 246 and Donovan Osborne (should be 406) and Thomson/Branca share number 410.

Nm-Mt Ex-Mt
COMPLETE SET (704) 40.00 12.00
COMP.FACT.SET (704) 40.00 12.00
1 Rod Carew I .15 .04
2 Rod Carew II .15 .04
3 Rod Carew III .15 .04
4 Rod Carew IV .15 .04
5 Rod Carew V .15 .04
6 Willie Fraser .05 .02
7 John Olerud .10 .03
8 William Suero .05 .02
9 Roberto Alomar .15 .04
10 Todd Stottlemyre .05 .02
11 Joe Carter .10 .03
12 Steve Karsay RC .50 .15
13 Mark Whiten .05 .02
14 Pat Borders .05 .02
15 Mike Timlin RC .75 .23
16 Tom Henke .05 .02
17 Eddie Zosky .05 .02
18 Kelly Gruber .05 .02
19 Jimmy Key .10 .03
20 Jerry Schunk .05 .02
21 Manuel Lee .05 .02
22 Dave Stieb .05 .02
23 Pat Hentgen RC .50 .15
24 Glenallen Hill .05 .02
25 Rene Gonzales .05 .02
26 Ed Sprague .05 .02
27 Ken Dayley .05 .02
28 Pat Tabler .05 .02
29 Denis Boucher RC .15 .04
30 Devon White .10 .03
31 Dante Bichette .10 .03
32 Paul Molitor .15 .04
33 Greg Vaughn .05 .02
34 Dan Plesac .05 .02
35 Chris George RC .15 .04
36 Tim McIntosh .05 .02
37 Franklin Stubbs .05 .02
38 Bo Dodson RC .15 .04
39 Ron Robinson .05 .02
40 Ed Nunez .05 .02
41 Greg Brock .05 .02
42 Jaime Navarro .05 .02
43 Chris Bosio .05 .02
44 B.J. Surhoff .10 .03
45 Chris Johnson .05 .02
46 Willie Randolph .10 .03
47 Narciso Elvira .05 .02
48 Jim Gantner .05 .02
49 Kevin Brown .05 .02
50 Julio Machado .05 .02
51 Chuck Crim .05 .02
52 Gary Sheffield .10 .03
53 Angel Miranda RC .15 .04
54 Ted Higuera .05 .02
55 Robin Yount .40 .12
56 Cal Eldred .05 .02
57 Sandy Alomar Jr. .05 .02
58 Greg Swindell .05 .02
59 Brook Jacoby .05 .02
60 Efrain Valdez .05 .02
61 Ever Magallanes .05 .02
62 Tom Candiotti .05 .02
63 Eric King .05 .02
64 Alex Cole .05 .02
65 Charles Nagy .05 .02
66 Mitch Webster .05 .02
67 Chris James .05 .02
68 Jim Thome RC 5.00 1.50
69 Carlos Baerga .05 .02
70 Mark Lewis .05 .02
71 Jerry Browne .05 .02
72 Jesse Orosco .05 .02
73 Mike Huff .05 .02
74 Jose Escobar .05 .02
75 Jeff Manto .05 .02
76 Turner Ward RC .15 .04
77 Doug Jones .05 .02
78 Bruce Egloff .05 .02
79 Tim Costo RC .15 .04
80 Beau Allred .05 .02
81 Albert Belle .10 .03
82 John Farrell .05 .02
83 Glenn Davis .05 .02
84 Joe Orsulak .05 .02
85 Mark Williamson .05 .02
86 Ben McDonald .05 .02
87 Billy Ripken .05 .02
88 Leo Gomez UER .05 .02
Baltimore is spelled Balitmore
89 Bob Melvin .05 .02
90 Jeff M. Robinson .05 .02
91 Jose Mesa .05 .02
92 Gregg Olson .05 .02
93 Mike Devereaux .05 .02
94 Luis Mercedes RC .15 .04
95 Arthur Rhodes RC .50 .15
96 Juan Bell .05 .02
97 Mike Mussina RC 2.50 .75
98 Jeff Ballard .05 .02
99 Chris Hoiles .05 .02
100 Brady Anderson .10 .03
101 Bob Milacki .05 .02
102 David Segui .05 .02
103 Dwight Evans .10 .03
104 Cal Ripken .75 .23
105 Mike Linskey .05 .02
106 Jeff Tackett RC .15 .04
107 Jeff Reardon .10 .03
108 Dana Kiecker .05 .02
109 Ellis Burks .10 .03
110 Dave Owen .05 .02
111 Danny Darwin .05 .02
112 Mo Vaughn .10 .03
113 Jeff McNeely RC .15 .04
114 Tom Bolton .05 .02
115 Greg Blosser .05 .02
116 Mike Greenwell .05 .02
117 Phil Plantier RC .15 .04
118 Roger Clemens .50 .15
119 John Marzano .05 .02
120 Jody Reed .05 .02
121 Scott Taylor RC .15 .04
122 Jack Clark .10 .03
123 Derek Livernois .05 .02
124 Tony Pena .05 .02
125 Tom Brunansky .05 .02
126 Carlos Quintana .05 .02
127 Tim Naehring .05 .02
128 Matt Young .05 .02
129 Wade Boggs .15 .04
130 Kevin Morton .05 .02
131 Pete Incaviglia .05 .02
132 Rob Deer .05 .02
133 Bill Gullickson .05 .02
134 Rico Brogna .05 .02
135 Lloyd Moseby .05 .02
136 Cecil Fielder .10 .03
137 Tony Phillips .05 .02
138 Mark Leiter RC .15 .04
139 John Cerutti .05 .02
140 Mickey Tettleton .05 .02
141 Milt Cuyler .05 .02
142 Greg Gohr .05 .02
143 Tony Bernazard .05 .02
144 Dan Gakeler .05 .02
145 Travis Fryman .10 .03
146 Dan Petry .05 .02
147 Scott Aldred .05 .02
148 John DeSilva .05 .02
149 Rusty Meacham RC .15 .04
150 Lou Whitaker .10 .03
151 Dave Haas .05 .02
152 Luis de los Santos .05 .02
153 Ivan Cruz .05 .02
154 Alan Trammell .10 .03
155 Pat Kelly RC .05 .02
156 Carl Everett RC .75 .23
157 Greg Cadaret .05 .02
158 Kevin Maas .05 .02
159 Jeff Johnson .05 .02
160 Willie Smith .05 .02
161 Gerald Williams RC .50 .15
162 Mike Humphreys RC .15 .04
163 Alvaro Espinoza .05 .02
164 Matt Nokes .05 .02
165 Wade Taylor .05 .02
166 Roberto Kelly .05 .02
167 John Habyan .05 .02
168 Steve Farr .05 .02
169 Jesse Barfield .05 .02
170 Steve Sax .05 .02
171 Jim Leyritz .05 .02
172 Robert Eenhoorn RC .15 .04
173 Bernie Williams .25 .07
174 Scott Lusader .05 .02
175 Torey Lovullo .05 .02
176 Chuck Cary .05 .02
177 Scott Sanderson .05 .02
178 Don Mattingly .60 .18
179 Mel Hall .05 .02
180 Juan Gonzalez .15 .04
181 Hensley Meulens .05 .02
182 Jose Offerman .05 .02
183 Jeff Bagwell RC 2.00 .60
184 Jeff Conine RC .75 .23
185 Henry Rodriguez RC .50 .15
186 Jimmie Reese CO .10 .03
187 Kyle Abbott .05 .02
188 Lance Parrish .10 .03
189 Rafael Montalvo .05 .02
190 Floyd Bannister .05 .02
191 Dick Schofield .05 .02
192 Scott Lewis .05 .02
193 Jeff D. Robinson .05 .02
194 Kent Anderson .05 .02
195 Wally Joyner .10 .03
196 Chuck Finley .10 .03
197 Luis Sojo .05 .02
198 Jeff Richardson .05 .02
199 Dave Parker .10 .03
200 Jim Abbott .15 .04
201 Junior Felix .05 .02
202 Mark Langston .05 .02
203 Tim Salmon RC 2.00 .60
204 Cliff Young .05 .02
205 Scott Bailes .05 .02
206 Bobby Rose .05 .02
207 Gary Gaetti .10 .03
208 Ruben Amaro RC .15 .04
209 Luis Polonia .05 .02
210 Dave Winfield .10 .03
211 Bryan Harvey .05 .02
212 Mike Moore .05 .02
213 Rickey Henderson .25 .07
214 Steve Chitren .05 .02
215 Bob Welch .05 .02
216 Terry Steinbach .05 .02
217 Earnest Riles .05 .02
218 Todd Van Poppel RC .50 .15
219 Mike Gallego .05 .02
220 Curt Young .05 .02
221 Todd Burns .05 .02
222 Vance Law .05 .02
223 Eric Show .05 .02
224 Don Peters .05 .02
225 Dave Stewart .10 .03
226 Dave Henderson .05 .02
227 Jose Canseco .25 .07
228 Walt Weiss .05 .02
229 Dann Howitt .05 .02
230 Willie Wilson .05 .02
231 Harold Baines .10 .03
232 Scott Hemond .05 .02
233 Joe Slusarski .05 .02
234 Mark McGwire .60 .18
235 K.Dressendorfer RC .15 .04
236 Craig Paquette RC .50 .15
237 Dennis Eckersley .10 .03
238 Dana Allison .05 .02
239 Scott Bradley .05 .02
240 Brian Holman .05 .02
241 Mike Schooler .05 .02
242 Rich DeLucia .05 .02
243 Edgar Martinez .15 .04
244 Henry Cotto .05 .02
245 Omar Vizquel .15 .04
246 Ken Griffey Jr. .50 .15
(See also 255)
247 Jay Buhner .10 .03
248 Bill Krueger .05 .02
249 Dave Fleming RC .15 .04
250 Patrick Lennon .05 .02
251 Dave Valle .05 .02
252 Harold Reynolds .10 .03
253 Randy Johnson .30 .09
254 Scott Bankhead .05 .02
255 Ken Griffey Sr. UER .05 .02
(Card number is 246)
256 Greg Briley .05 .02
257 Tino Martinez .15 .04
258 Alvin Davis .05 .02
259 Pete O'Brien .05 .02
260 Erik Hanson .05 .02
261 Bret Boone RC 3.00 .90
262 Roger Salkeld .05 .02
263 Dave Burba RC .50 .15
264 Kerry Woodson RC .15 .04
265 Julio Franco .10 .03
266 Dan Peltier RC .15 .04
267 Jeff Russell .05 .02
268 Steve Buechele .05 .02
269 Donald Harris .05 .02
270 Robb Nen .15 .04
271 Rich Gossage .10 .03
272 Ivan Rodriguez RC 2.50 .75
273 Jeff Huson .05 .02
274 Kevin Brown .10 .03
275 Dan Smith RC .15 .04
276 Gary Pettis .05 .02
277 Jack Daugherty .05 .02
278 Mike Jeffcoat .05 .02
279 Brad Arnsberg .05 .02
280 Nolan Ryan 1.00 .30
281 Eric McCray .05 .02
282 Scott Chiamparino .10 .03
283 Ruben Sierra .05 .02
284 Geno Petralli .05 .02
285 Monty Fariss .05 .02
286 Rafael Palmeiro .15 .04
287 Bobby Witt .05 .02
288 Dean Palmer UER .10 .03
Photo is Dan Peltier
289 Tony Scruggs .05 .02
290 Kenny Rogers .10 .03
291 Bret Saberhagen .10 .03
292 Brian McRae RC .50 .15
293 Storm Davis .05 .02
294 Danny Tartabull .05 .02
295 David Howard .05 .02
296 Mike Boddicker .05 .02
297 Joel Johnston RC .15 .04
298 Tim Spehr .05 .02
299 Hector Wagner .05 .02
300 George Brett .60 .18
301 Mike Macfarlane .05 .02
302 Kirk Gibson .10 .03
303 Harvey Pulliam RC .15 .04
304 Jim Eisenreich .05 .02
305 Kevin Seitzer .05 .02
306 Mark Davis .05 .02
307 Kurt Stillwell .05 .02
308 Jeff Montgomery .05 .02
309 Kevin Appier .10 .03
310 Bob Hamelin .05 .02
311 Tom Gordon .05 .02
312 Kerwin Moore RC .15 .04
313 Hugh Walker .05 .02
314 Terry Shumpert .05 .02
315 Warren Cromartie .05 .02
316 Gary Thurman .05 .02
317 Steve Bedrosian .05 .02
318 Danny Gladden .05 .02
319 Jack Morris .10 .03
320 Kirby Puckett .25 .07
321 Kent Hrbek .10 .03
322 Kevin Tapani .05 .02
323 Denny Neagle RC .50 .15
324 Rich Garces RC .15 .04
325 Larry Casian .05 .02
326 Shane Mack .05 .02
327 Allan Anderson .05 .02
328 Junior Ortiz .05 .02
329 Paul Abbott RC .15 .04
330 Chuck Knoblauch .50 .15
331 Chili Davis .10 .03
332 Todd Ritchie RC .50 .15
333 Brian Harper .05 .02
334 Rick Aguilera .10 .03
335 Scott Erickson .05 .02
336 Pedro Munoz RC .15 .04
337 Scott Leius .05 .02
338 Greg Gagne .05 .02
339 Mike Pagliarulo .05 .02
340 Terry Leach .05 .02
341 Willie Banks .05 .02
342 Bobby Thigpen .05 .02
343 R.Hernandez RC .50 .15
344 Melido Perez .05 .02
345 Carlton Fisk .15 .04
346 Norberto Martin .05 .02
347 Johnny Ruffin RC .15 .04
348 Jeff Carter .05 .02
349 Lance Johnson .05 .02
350 Sammy Sosa .50 .15
351 Alex Fernandez .05 .02
352 Jack McDowell .05 .02
353 Bob Wickman RC .15 .04
354 Wilson Alvarez .05 .02
355 Charlie Hough .10 .03
356 Ozzie Guillen .05 .02
357 Cory Snyder .05 .02
358 Robin Ventura .10 .03
359 Scott Fletcher .05 .02
360 Cesar Bernhardt .05 .02
361 Dan Pasqua .05 .02
362 Tim Raines .10 .03
363 Brian Drahman .05 .02
364 Wayne Edwards .05 .02
365 Scott Radinsky .05 .02
366 Frank Thomas .25 .07
367 Cecil Fielder SLUG .05 .02
368 Julio Franco SLUG .05 .02
369 Kelly Gruber SLUG .05 .02
370 Alan Trammell SLUG .10 .03
371 R.Henderson SLUG .15 .04
372 Jose Canseco SLUG .10 .03
373 Ellis Burks SLUG .05 .02
374 Lance Parrish SLUG .05 .02
375 Dave Parker SLUG .05 .02
376 Eddie Murray SLUG .15 .04
377 Ryne Sandberg SLUG .25 .07
378 Matt Williams SLUG .05 .02
379 Barry Larkin SLUG .10 .03
380 Barry Bonds SLUG .30 .09
381 Bobby Bonilla SLUG .05 .02
382 D.Strawberry SLUG .05 .02
383 Benny Santiago SLUG .05 .02
384 Don Robinson SLUG .05 .02
385 Paul Coleman .05 .02
386 Milt Thompson .05 .02
387 Lee Smith .10 .03
388 Ray Lankford .05 .02
389 Tom Pagnozzi .05 .02
390 Ken Hill .05 .02
391 Jamie Moyer .10 .03
392 Greg Carmona .05 .02
393 John Ericks .05 .02
394 Bob Tewksbury .05 .02
395 Jose Oquendo .05 .02
396 Rheal Cormier RC .15 .04
397 Mike Milchin .05 .02
398 Ozzie Smith .40 .12
399 Aaron Holbert RC .15 .04
400 Jose DeLeon .05 .02
401 Felix Jose .05 .02
402 Juan Agosto .05 .02
403 Pedro Guerrero .10 .03
404 Todd Zeile .05 .02
405 Gerald Perry .05 .02
406 D.Osborne UER RC .15 .04
Card number is 410
407 Bryn Smith .05 .02
408 Bernard Gilkey .05 .02
409 Rex Hudler .05 .02
410 Bobby Thomson .25 .07
Ralph Branca
Shot Heard Round the World
See also 406
411 Lance Dickson RC .15 .04
412 Danny Jackson .05 .02
413 Jerome Walton .05 .02
414 Sean Cheetham .05 .02
415 Joe Girardi .05 .02
416 Ryne Sandberg .40 .12
417 Mike Harkey .05 .02
418 George Bell .05 .02
419 Rick Wilkins RC .15 .04
420 Earl Cunningham .05 .02
421 H.Slocumb RC .15 .04
422 Mike Bielecki .05 .02
423 Jessie Hollins RC .15 .04
424 Shawon Dunston .05 .02
425 Dave Smith .05 .02
426 Greg Maddux .40 .12
427 Jose Vizcaino .05 .02
428 Luis Salazar .05 .02
429 Andre Dawson .10 .03
430 Rick Sutcliffe .10 .03
431 Paul Assenmacher .05 .02
432 Erik Pappas .05 .02
433 Mark Grace .15 .04
434 Dennis Martinez .10 .03
435 Marquis Grissom .10 .03
436 Wil Cordero RC .50 .15
437 Tim Wallach .05 .02
438 Brian Barnes RC .15 .04
439 Barry Jones .05 .02
440 Ivan Calderon .05 .02
441 Stan Spencer .05 .02
442 Larry Walker .25 .07
443 Chris Haney RC .15 .04
444 Hector Rivera .05 .02
445 Delino DeShields .10 .03
446 Andres Galarraga .10 .03
447 Gilberto Reyes .05 .02
448 Willie Greene .05 .02
449 Greg Colbrunn RC .50 .15
450 Rondell White RC .75 .23
451 Steve Frey .05 .02
452 Shane Andrews RC .15 .04
453 Mike Fitzgerald .05 .02
454 Spike Owen .05 .02
455 Dave Martinez .05 .02
456 Dennis Boyd .05 .02
457 Eric Bullock .05 .02
458 Reid Cornelius RC .15 .04
459 Chris Nabholz .05 .02
460 David Cone .10 .03
461 Hubie Brooks .05 .02
462 Sid Fernandez .05 .02
463 Doug Simons .05 .02
464 Howard Johnson .05 .02
465 Chris Donnels .05 .02
466 Anthony Young RC .15 .04
467 Todd Hundley .05 .02
468 Rick Cerone .05 .02
469 Kevin Elster .05 .02
470 Wally Whitehurst .05 .02
471 Vince Coleman .05 .02
472 Dwight Gooden .10 .03
473 Charlie O'Brien .05 .02
474 Jeromy Burnitz RC 1.00 .30
475 John Franco .10 .03
476 Daryl Boston .05 .02
477 Frank Viola .10 .03
478 D.J. Dozier .05 .02
479 Kevin McReynolds .05 .02
480 Tom Herr .05 .02
481 Gregg Jefferies .05 .02
482 Pete Schourek RC .15 .04
483 Ron Darling .05 .02
484 Dave Magadan .05 .02
485 Andy Ashby RC .50 .15
486 Dale Murphy .25 .07
487 Von Hayes .05 .02
488 Kim Batiste RC .15 .04
489 Tony Longmire RC .15 .04
490 Wally Backman .05 .02
491 Jeff Jackson .05 .02
492 Mickey Morandini .05 .02
493 Darrel Akerfelds .05 .02
494 Ricky Jordan .05 .02
495 Randy Ready .05 .02
496 Darrin Fletcher .05 .02
497 Chuck Malone .05 .02
498 Pat Combs .05 .02
499 Dickie Thon .05 .02
500 Roger McDowell .05 .02
501 Len Dykstra .10 .03
502 Joe Boever .05 .02
503 John Kruk .10 .03
504 Terry Mulholland .05 .02
505 Wes Chamberlain RC .15 .04
506 Mike Lieberthal RC .75 .23
507 Darren Daulton .10 .03
508 Charlie Hayes .05 .02
509 John Smiley .05 .02
510 Gary Varsho .05 .02
511 Curt Wilkerson .05 .02
512 Orlando Merced RC .15 .04
513 Barry Bonds .60 .18
514 Mike LaValliere .05 .02
515 Doug Drabek .05 .02
516 Gary Redus .05 .02
517 W.Pennyfeather RC .15 .04
518 Randy Tomlin RC .05 .02
519 Mike Zimmerman RC .15 .04
520 Jeff King .05 .02
521 Kurt Miller RC .15 .04
522 Jay Bell .10 .03
523 Bill Landrum .05 .02
524 Zane Smith .05 .02
525 Bobby Bonilla .10 .03
526 Bob Walk .05 .02
527 Austin Manahan .05 .02
528 Joe Ausanio .05 .02
529 Andy Van Slyke .10 .03
530 Jose Lind .05 .02
531 Carlos Garcia RC .15 .04
532 Don Slaught .05 .02
533 Gen.Colin Powell .50 .15
534 Frank Bolick RC .15 .04
535 Gary Scott .05 .02
536 Nikco Riesgo .05 .02
537 Reggie Sanders RC .75 .23
538 Tim Howard RC .15 .04
539 Ryan Bowen RC .15 .04
540 Eric Anthony .05 .02
541 Jim Deshaies .05 .02
542 Tom Nevers RC .15 .04
543 Ken Caminiti .10 .03
544 Karl Rhodes .05 .02
545 Xavier Hernandez .05 .02
546 Mike Scott .05 .02
547 Jeff Juden .05 .02
548 Darryl Kile .10 .03
549 Willie Ansley .05 .02
550 Luis Gonzalez RC 1.00 .30
551 Mike Simms .05 .02
552 Mark Portugal .05 .02
553 Jimmy Jones .05 .02
554 Jim Clancy .05 .02
555 Pete Harnisch .05 .02
556 Craig Biggio .15 .04
557 Eric Yelding .05 .02
558 Dave Rohde .05 .02
559 Casey Candaele .05 .02
560 Curt Schilling .25 .07
561 Steve Finley .10 .03
562 Javier Ortiz .05 .02
563 Andujar Cedeno .05 .02
564 Rafael Ramirez .05 .02
565 Kenny Lofton RC 1.00 .30
566 Steve Avery .05 .02
567 Lonnie Smith .05 .02
568 Kent Mercker .05 .02
569 Chipper Jones RC 4.00 1.20
570 Terry Pendleton .10 .03
571 Otis Nixon .05 .02
572 Juan Berenguer .05 .02
573 Charlie Leibrandt .05 .02
574 David Justice .10 .03
575 Keith Mitchell RC .15 .04
576 Tom Glavine .15 .04
577 Greg Olson .05 .02
578 Rafael Belliard .05 .02
579 Ben Rivera RC .15 .04
580 John Smoltz .15 .04
581 Tyler Houston .05 .02
582 Mark Wohlers RC .50 .15
583 Ron Gant .10 .03
584 Ramon Caraballo RC .15 .04
585 Sid Bream .05 .02
586 Jeff Treadway .05 .02
587 Javy Lopez RC 3.00 .90
588 Deion Sanders .15 .04
589 Mike Heath .05 .02
590 Ryan Klesko RC 1.00 .30
591 Bob Ojeda .05 .02

592 Alfredo Griffin .05 .02
593 Raul Mondesi RC .75 .23
594 Greg Smith .05 .02
595 Orel Hershiser .10 .03
596 Juan Samuel .05 .02
597 Brett Butler .10 .03
598 Gary Carter .10 .03
599 Stan Javier .05 .02
600 Kal Daniels .05 .02
601 Jamie McAndrew RC .15 .04
602 Mike Sharperson .05 .02
603 Jay Howell .05 .02
604 Eric Karros RC .75 .23
605 Tim Belcher .05 .02
606 Dan Opperman .05 .02
607 Lenny Harris .05 .02
608 Tom Goodwin .05 .02
609 Darryl Strawberry .10 .03
610 Ramon Martinez .05 .02
611 Kevin Gross .05 .02
612 Zakary Shinall .05 .02
613 Mike Scioscia .05 .02
614 Eddie Murray .25 .07
615 Ronnie Walden RC .15 .04
616 Will Clark .25 .07
617 Adam Hyzdu RC .50 .15
618 Matt Williams .10 .03
619 Don Robinson .05 .02
620 Jeff Brantley .05 .02
621 Greg Litton .05 .02
622 Steve Decker .05 .02
623 Robby Thompson .05 .02
624 Mark Leonard .05 .02
625 Kevin Bass .05 .02
626 Scott Garrelts .05 .02
627 Jose Uribe .05 .02
628 Eric Gunderson .05 .02
629 Steve Hosey .05 .02
630 Trevor Wilson .05 .02
631 Terry Kennedy .05 .02
632 Dave Righetti .10 .03
633 Kelly Downs .05 .02
634 Johnny Ard .05 .02
635 E.Christopherson RC .15 .04
636 Kevin Mitchell .05 .02
637 John Burkett .05 .02
638 Kevin Rogers RC .15 .04
639 Bud Black .05 .02
640 Willie McGee .10 .03
641 Royce Clayton .05 .02
642 Tony Fernandez .05 .02
643 Ricky Bones RC .15 .04
644 Thomas Howard .05 .02
645 Dave Staton RC .15 .04
646 Jim Presley .05 .02
647 Tony Gwynn .30 .09
648 Marty Barrett .05 .02
649 Scott Coolbaugh .05 .02
650 Craig Lefferts .05 .02
651 Eddie Whitson .05 .02
652 Oscar Azocar .05 .02
653 Wes Gardner .05 .02
654 Bip Roberts .05 .02
655 Robbie Beckett RC .15 .04
656 Benito Santiago .10 .03
657 Greg W.Harris .05 .02
658 Jerald Clark .05 .02
659 Fred McGriff .15 .04
660 Larry Andersen .05 .02
661 Bruce Hurst .05 .02
662 Steve Martin UER RC .15 .04
Card said he pitched at Waterloo
He's an outfielder
663 Rafael Valdez .05 .02
664 Paul Faries .05 .02
665 Andy Benes .05 .02
666 Randy Myers .05 .02
667 Rob Dibble .10 .03
668 Glenn Sutko .05 .02
669 Glenn Braggs .05 .02
670 Billy Hatcher .05 .02
671 Joe Oliver .05 .02
672 Freddie Benavides RC .15 .04
673 Barry Larkin .15 .04
674 Chris Sabo .05 .02
675 Mariano Duncan .05 .02
676 Chris Jones RC .05 .02
677 Gino Minutelli .05 .02
678 Reggie Jefferson .05 .02
679 Jack Armstrong .05 .02
680 Chris Hammond .05 .02
681 Jose Rijo .05 .02
682 Bill Doran .05 .02
683 Terry Lee .05 .02
684 Tom Browning .05 .02
685 Paul O'Neill .15 .04
686 Eric Davis .10 .03
687 Dan Wilson RC .50 .15
688 Ted Power .05 .02
689 Tim Layana .05 .02
690 Norm Charlton .05 .02
691 Hal Morris .05 .02
692 Rickey Henderson .15 .04
693 Sam Militello RC .15 .04
694 Matt Mieske RC .15 .04
695 Paul Russo RC .15 .04
696 Domingo Mota MVP .05 .02
697 Todd Guggiana RC .15 .04
698 Marc Newfield RC .15 .04
699 Checklist 1-122 .05 .02
700 Checklist 123-244 .05 .02
701 Checklist 245-366 .05 .02
702 Checklist 367-471 .05 .02
703 Checklist 472-593 .05 .02
704 Checklist 594-704 .05 .02

1992 Bowman

This 705-card standard-size set was issued in one comprehensive series. Unlike the previous Bowman issues, the 1992 set was radically upgraded to slick stock with gold foil subset cards in an attempt to reposition the brand as a premium level product. It initially stumbled out of the gate, but its superior selection of prospects enabled it to eventually gain acceptance in the hobby and now stands as one of the more important issues of the 1990's. Cards were distributed in plastic wrap packs, retail jumbo packs and special 80-card retail carton packs. Card fronts feature posed and action color player photos on a UV-coated white card face. . Forty-five foil cards inserted at a stated rate of one per wax pack and two per jumbo (23 regular cards) pack. These foil cards feature past and present Team USA players and minor league POY Award winners. Each foil card has an extremely slight variation in that the photos are cropped differently. There is no additional value to either version. Some of the regular and special cards picture prospects in civilian clothing who were still in the farm system. Rookie Cards in this set include Garret Anderson, Carlos Delgado, Mike Hampton, Brian Jordan, Mike Piazza, Manny Ramirez and Mariano Rivera.

Nm-Mt Ex-Mt
COMPLETE SET (705) 150.00 45.00
1 Ivan Rodriguez 1.25 .35
2 Kirk McCaskill .50 .15
3 Scott Livingstone .50 .15
4 Salomon Torres RC .50 .15
5 Carlos Hernandez .50 .15
6 Dave Hollins .50 .15
7 Scott Fletcher .50 .15
8 Jorge Fabregas RC .50 .15
9 Andujar Cedeno .50 .15
10 Howard Johnson .50 .15
11 Trevor Hoffman RC 5.00 1.50
12 Roberto Kelly .50 .15
13 Gregg Jefferies .50 .15
14 Marquis Grissom .50 .15
15 Mike Ignasiak .50 .15
16 Jack Morris .50 .15
17 William Pennyfeather .50 .15
18 Todd Stottlemyre .50 .15
19 Chito Martinez .50 .15
20 Roberto Alomar .75 .23
21 Sam Militello .50 .15
22 Hector Fajardo RC .50 .15
23 Paul Quantrill RC .50 .15
24 Chuck Knoblauch .50 .15
25 Reggie Jefferson .50 .15
26 Jeremy McGarity RC .50 .15
27 Jerome Walton .50 .15
28 Chipper Jones 8.00 2.40
29 Brian Barber RC .50 .15
30 Ron Darling .50 .15
31 Roberto Petagine RC .50 .15
32 Chuck Finley .50 .15
33 Edgar Martinez .75 .23
34 Napoleon Robinson .50 .15
35 Andy Van Slyke .50 .15
36 Bobby Thigpen .50 .15
37 Travis Fryman .50 .15
38 Eric Christopherson .50 .15
39 Terry Mulholland .50 .15
40 Darryl Strawberry .50 .15
41 Manny Alexander RC .50 .15
42 Tracy Sanders RC .50 .15
43 Pete Incaviglia .50 .15
44 Kim Batiste .50 .15
45 Frank Rodriguez .50 .15
46 Greg Swindell .50 .15
47 Delino DeShields .50 .15
48 John Ericks .50 .15
49 Franklin Stubbs .50 .15
50 Tony Gwynn 1.50 .45
51 Clifton Garrett RC .50 .15
52 Mike Gardella .50 .15
53 Scott Erickson .50 .15
54 Gary Caraballo RC .50 .15
55 Jose Oliva RC .50 .15
56 Brook Fordyce .50 .15
57 Mark Whiten .50 .15
58 Joe Slusarski .50 .15
59 J.R. Phillips RC .50 .15
60 Barry Bonds 3.00 .90
61 Bob Milacki .50 .15
62 Keith Mitchell .50 .15
63 Angel Miranda .50 .15
64 Raul Mondesi .50 .15
65 Brian Koelling RC .50 .15
66 Brian McRae .50 .15
67 John Patterson RC .50 .15
68 John Wetteland .50 .15
69 Wilson Alvarez .50 .15
70 Wade Boggs .75 .23
71 Darryl Ratliff RC .50 .15
72 Jeff Jackson .50 .15
73 Jeremy Hernandez RC .50 .15
74 Darryl Hamilton .50 .15
75 Rafael Belliard .50 .15
76 Rick Trlicek RC .50 .15
77 Felipe Crespo RC .50 .15
78 Carney Lansford .50 .15
79 Ryan Long RC .50 .15
80 Kirby Puckett 1.25 .35
81 Earl Cunningham .50 .15
82 Pedro Martinez 10.00 3.00
83 Scott Hatteberg RC 1.00 .30
84 Juan Gonzalez UER .75 .23
(65 doubles vs. Tigers)
85 Robert Nutting RC .50 .15
86 Pokey Reese RC 2.00 .60
87 Dave Silvestri .50 .15
88 Scott Ruffcorn RC .50 .15
89 Rick Aguilera .50 .15
90 Cecil Fielder .50 .15
91 Kirk Dressendorfer .50 .15
92 Jerry DiPoto RC .50 .15
93 Mike Felder .50 .15
94 Craig Paquette .50 .15
95 Elvin Paulino RC .50 .15
96 Donovan Osborne .50 .15
97 Hubie Brooks .50 .15
98 Derek Lowe RC 5.00 1.50
99 David Zancanaro .50 .15
100 Ken Griffey Jr. 2.00 .60
101 Todd Hundley .50 .15
102 Mike Trombley RC .50 .15
103 Ricky Gutierrez RC 1.00 .30
104 Braulio Castillo .50 .15
105 Craig Lefferts .50 .15
106 Rick Sutcliffe .50 .15
107 Dean Palmer .50 .15
108 Henry Rodriguez .50 .15
109 Mark Clark RC 1.00 .30
110 Kenny Lofton .75 .23
111 Mark Carreon .50 .15
112 J.T. Bruett .50 .15
113 Gerald Williams .50 .15
114 Frank Thomas 1.25 .35
115 Kevin Reimer .50 .15
116 Sammy Sosa 2.00 .60
117 Mickey Tettleton .50 .15
118 Reggie Sanders .50 .15
119 Trevor Wilson .50 .15
120 Cliff Brantley .50 .15
121 Spike Owen .50 .15
122 Jeff Montgomery .50 .15
123 Alex Sutherland .50 .15
124 Brien Taylor RC 1.00 .30
125 Brian Williams RC .50 .15
126 Kevin Seitzer .50 .15
127 Carlos Delgado RC 15.00 4.50
128 Gary Scott .50 .15
129 Scott Cooper .50 .15
130 Domingo Jean RC .50 .15
131 Pat Mahomes RC 1.00 .30
132 Mike Boddicker .50 .15
133 Roberto Hernandez .50 .15
134 Dave Valle .50 .15
135 Kurt Stillwell .50 .15
136 Brad Pennington RC .50 .15
137 Jermaine Swinton RC .50 .15
138 Ryan Hawblitzel RC .50 .15
139 Tito Navarro RC .50 .15
140 Sandy Alomar Jr. .50 .15
141 Todd Benzinger .50 .15
142 Danny Jackson .50 .15
143 Melvin Nieves RC .50 .15
144 Jim Campanis .50 .15
145 Luis Gonzalez .50 .15
146 D.Doorneweerd RC .50 .15
147 Charlie Hayes .50 .15
148 Greg Maddux 2.00 .60
149 Brian Harper .50 .15
150 Brent Miller RC .50 .15
151 Shawn Estes RC 1.00 .30
152 Mike Williams RC 1.00 .30
153 Charlie Hough .50 .15
154 Randy Myers .50 .15
155 Kevin Young RC 1.00 .30
156 Rick Wilkins .50 .15
157 Terry Shumpert .50 .15
158 Steve Karsay .50 .15
159 Gary DiSarcina .50 .15
160 Deion Sanders .75 .23
161 Tom Browning .50 .15
162 Dickie Thon .50 .15
163 Luis Mercedes .50 .15
164 Riccardo Ingram .50 .15
165 Tavo Alvarez RC .50 .15
166 Rickey Henderson 1.25 .35
167 Jaime Navarro .50 .15
168 Billy Ashley RC .50 .15
169 Phil Dauphin RC .50 .15
170 Ivan Cruz .50 .15
171 Harold Baines .50 .15
172 Bryan Harvey .50 .15
173 Alex Cole .50 .15
174 Curtis Shaw RC .50 .15
175 Matt Williams .50 .15
176 Felix Jose .50 .15
177 Sam Horn .50 .15
178 Randy Johnson 1.25 .35
179 Ivan Calderon .50 .15
180 Steve Avery .50 .15
181 William Suero .50 .15
182 Bill Swift .50 .15
183 Howard Battle RC .50 .15
184 Ruben Amaro .50 .15
185 Jim Abbott .75 .23
186 Mike Fitzgerald .50 .15
187 Bruce Hurst .50 .15
188 Jeff Juden .50 .15
189 Jeromy Burnitz .50 .15
190 Dave Burba .50 .15
191 Kevin Brown .50 .15
192 Patrick Lennon .50 .15
193 Jeff McNeely .50 .15
194 Wil Cordero .50 .15
195 Chili Davis .50 .15
196 Milt Cuyler .50 .15
197 Von Hayes .50 .15
198 Todd Revenig RC .50 .15
199 Joel Johnston .50 .15
200 Jeff Bagwell 1.25 .35
201 Alex Fernandez .50 .15
202 Todd Jones RC 1.00 .30
203 Charles Nagy .50 .15
204 Tim Raines .50 .15
205 Kevin Maas .50 .15
206 Julio Franco .50 .15
207 Randy Velarde .50 .15
208 Lance Johnson .50 .15
209 Scott Leius .50 .15
210 Derek Lee .50 .15
211 Joe Sondrini RC .50 .15
212 Royce Clayton .50 .15
213 Chris George .50 .15
214 Gary Sheffield .50 .15
215 Mark Gubicza .50 .15
216 Mike Moore .50 .15
217 Rick Huisman RC .50 .15
218 Jeff Russell .50 .15
219 D.J. Dozier .50 .15
220 Dave Martinez .50 .15
221 Alan Newman RC .50 .15
222 Nolan Ryan 4.00 1.20
223 Teddy Higuera .50 .15
224 Damon Buford RC .50 .15
225 Ruben Sierra .50 .15
226 Tom Nevers .50 .15
227 Tommy Greene .50 .15
228 Nigel Wilson RC .50 .15
229 John DeSilva .50 .15
230 Bobby Witt .50 .15
231 Greg Cadaret .50 .15
232 John Vander Wal RC 1.00 .30
233 Jack Clark .50 .15
234 Bill Doran .50 .15
235 Bobby Bonilla .50 .15
236 Steve Olin .50 .15
237 Derek Bell .50 .15
238 David Cone .50 .15
239 Victor Cole .50 .15
240 Rod Bolton RC .50 .15
241 Tom Pagnozzi .50 .15
242 Rob Dibble .50 .15
243 Michael Carter RC .50 .15
244 Don Peters .50 .15
245 Mike LaValliere .50 .15
246 Joe Perona RC .50 .15
247 Mitch Williams .50 .15
248 Jay Buhner .50 .15
249 Andy Benes .50 .15
250 Alex Ochoa RC 1.00 .30
251 Greg Blosser .50 .15
252 Jack Armstrong .50 .15
253 Juan Samuel .50 .15
254 Terry Pendleton .50 .15
255 Ramon Martinez .50 .15
256 Rico Brogna .50 .15
257 John Smiley .50 .15
258 Carl Everett .50 .15
259 Tim Salmon 1.25 .35
260 Will Clark 1.25 .35
261 Ugueth Urbina RC 1.00 .30
262 Jason Wood RC .50 .15
263 Dave Magadan .50 .15
264 Dante Bichette .50 .15
265 Jose DeLeon .50 .15
266 Mike Neill RC 1.00 .30
267 Paul O'Neill .75 .23
268 Anthony Young .50 .15
269 Greg W. Harris .50 .15
270 Todd Van Poppel .50 .15
271 Pedro Castellano RC .50 .15
272 Tony Phillips .50 .15
273 Mike Gallego .50 .15
274 Steve Cooke RC .50 .15
275 Robin Ventura .50 .15
276 Kevin Mitchell .50 .15
277 Doug Linton RC .50 .15
278 Robert Eenhoorn .50 .15
279 Gabe White RC .50 .15
280 Dave Stewart .50 .15
281 Mo Sanford .50 .15
282 Greg Perschke .50 .15
283 Kevin Flora RC .50 .15
284 Jeff Williams RC 1.00 .30
285 Keith Miller .50 .15
286 Andy Ashby .50 .15
287 Doug Dascenzo .50 .15
288 Eric Karros .50 .15
289 Glenn Murray RC .50 .15
290 Troy Percival RC 3.00 .90
291 Orlando Merced .50 .15
292 Peter Hoy .50 .15
293 Tony Fernandez .50 .15
294 Juan Guzman .50 .15
295 Jesse Barfield .50 .15
296 Sid Fernandez .50 .15
297 Scott Cepicky .50 .15
298 Garret Anderson RC 8.00 2.40
299 Cal Eldred .50 .15
300 Ryne Sandberg 2.50 .75
301 Jim Gantner .50 .15
302 Mariano Rivera RC 10.00 3.00
303 Ron Lockett RC .50 .15
304 Jose Offerman .50 .15
305 Dennis Martinez .50 .15
306 Luis Ortiz RC .50 .15
307 David Howard .50 .15
308 Russ Springer RC 1.00 .30
309 Chris Howard .50 .15
310 Kyle Abbott .50 .15
311 Aaron Sele RC 2.00 .60
312 David Justice .50 .15
313 Pete O'Brien .50 .15
314 Greg Hansell RC .50 .15
315 Dave Winfield .50 .15
316 Lance Dickson .50 .15
317 Eric King .50 .15
318 Vaughn Eshelman RC .50 .15
319 Tim Belcher .50 .15
320 Andres Galarraga .50 .15
321 Scott Bullett RC .50 .15
322 Doug Strange .50 .15
323 Jerald Clark .50 .15
324 Dave Righetti .50 .15
325 Greg Hibbard .50 .15
326 Eric Hillman RC .50 .15
327 Shane Reynolds RC 1.00 .30
328 Chris Hammond .50 .15
329 Albert Belle .50 .15
330 Rich Becker RC .50 .15
331 Eddie Williams RC .50 .15
332 Donald Harris .50 .15
333 Dave Smith .50 .15
334 Steve Fireovid .50 .15
335 Steve Buechele .50 .15
336 Mike Schooler .50 .15
337 Kevin McReynolds .50 .15
338 Hensley Meulens .50 .15
339 Benji Gil RC 1.00 .30
340 Don Mattingly 3.00 .90
341 Alvin Davis .50 .15
342 Alan Mills .50 .15
343 Kelly Downs .50 .15
344 Leo Gomez .50 .15
345 Tarrik Brock RC .50 .15
346 Ryan Turner RC .50 .15
347 John Smoltz .75 .23
348 Bill Sampen .50 .15
349 Paul Byrd RC 1.00 .30
350 Mike Bordick .50 .15
351 Jose Lind .50 .15
352 David Wells .50 .15
353 Barry Larkin .75 .23
354 Bruce Ruffin .50 .15
355 Luis Rivera .50 .15
356 Sid Bream .50 .15
357 Julian Vasquez RC .50 .15
358 Jason Bere RC 1.00 .30
359 Ben McDonald .50 .15
360 Scott Stahoviak RC .50 .15
361 Kirt Manwaring .50 .15
362 Jeff Johnson .50 .15
363 Rob Deer .50 .15
364 Tony Pena .50 .15
365 Melido Perez .50 .15
366 Clay Parker .50 .15
367 Dale Sveum .50 .15
368 Mike Scioscia .50 .15
369 Roger Salkeld .50 .15
370 Mike Stanley .50 .15
371 Jack McDowell .50 .15
372 Tim Wallach .50 .15
373 Billy Ripken .50 .15
374 Mike Christopher .50 .15
375 Paul Molitor .75 .23
376 Dave Stieb .50 .15
377 Pedro Guerrero .50 .15
378 Russ Swan .50 .15
379 Bob Ojeda .50 .15
380 Donn Pall .50 .15
381 Eddie Zosky .50 .15
382 Darnell Coles .50 .15
383 Tom Smith RC .50 .15
384 Mark McGwire 3.00 .90
385 Gary Carter .50 .15
386 Rich Amaral RC .50 .15
387 Alan Embree RC 4.00 1.20
388 Jonathan Hurst RC .50 .15
389 Bobby Jones RC 1.00 .30
390 Rico Rossy .50 .15
391 Dan Smith .50 .15
392 Terry Steinbach .50 .15
393 Jon Farrell RC .50 .15
394 Dave Anderson .50 .15
395 Benny Santiago .50 .15
396 Mark Wohlers .50 .15
397 Mo Vaughn .50 .15
398 Randy Kramer .50 .15
399 John Jaha RC 1.00 .30
400 Cal Ripken 4.00 1.20
401 Ryan Bowen .50 .15
402 Tim McIntosh .50 .15
403 Bernard Gilkey .50 .15
404 Junior Felix .50 .15
405 Cris Colon RC .50 .15
406 Marc Newfield .50 .15
407 Bernie Williams .75 .23
408 Jay Howell .50 .15
409 Zane Smith .50 .15
410 Jeff Shaw .50 .15
411 Kerry Woodson .50 .15
412 Wes Chamberlain .50 .15
413 Dave Mlicki RC 1.00 .30
414 Benny Distefano .50 .15
415 Kevin Rogers .50 .15
416 Tim Naehring .50 .15
417 Clemente Nunez RC .50 .15
418 Luis Sojo .50 .15
419 Kevin Ritz .50 .15
420 Omar Olivares .50 .15
421 Manuel Lee .50 .15
422 Julio Valera .50 .15
423 Omar Vizquel .75 .23
424 Darren Burton RC .50 .15
425 Mel Hall .50 .15
426 Dennis Powell .50 .15
427 Lee Stevens .50 .15
428 Glenn Davis .50 .15
429 Willie Greene .50 .15
430 Kevin Wickander .50 .15
431 Dennis Eckersley .50 .15
432 Joe Orsulak .50 .15
433 Eddie Murray 1.25 .35
434 Matt Stairs RC 1.00 .30
435 Wally Joyner .50 .15
436 Rondell White .50 .15
437 Rob Maurer .50 .15
438 Joe Redfield .50 .15
439 Mark Lewis .50 .15
440 Darren Daulton .50 .15
441 Mike Henneman .50 .15
442 John Cangelosi .50 .15
443 Vince Moore RC .50 .15
444 John Wehner .50 .15
445 Kent Hrbek .50 .15
446 Mark McLemore .50 .15
447 Bill Wegman .50 .15
448 Robby Thompson .50 .15
449 Mark Anthony RC .50 .15
450 Archi Cianfrocco RC .50 .15
451 Johnny Ruffin .50 .15
452 Javy Lopez 2.50 .75
453 Greg Gohr .50 .15
454 Tim Scott .50 .15
455 Stan Belinda .50 .15
456 Darrin Jackson .50 .15
457 Chris Gardner .50 .15
458 Esteban Beltre .50 .15
459 Phil Plantier .50 .15
460 Jim Thome 8.00 2.40
461 Mike Piazza RC 40.00 12.00
462 Matt Sinatro .50 .15
463 Scott Servais .50 .15
464 Brian Jordan RC 2.00 .60
465 Doug Drabek .50 .15
466 Carl Willis .50 .15
467 Bret Barberie .50 .15
468 Hal Morris .50 .15
469 Steve Sax .50 .15
470 Jerry Willard .50 .15
471 Dan Wilson .50 .15
472 Chris Hoiles .50 .15
473 Rheal Cormier .50 .15
474 John Morris .50 .15
475 Jeff Reardon .50 .15
476 Mark Leiter .50 .15
477 Tom Gordon .50 .15
478 Kent Bottenfield RC 1.00 .30
479 Gene Larkin .50 .15
480 Dwight Gooden .50 .15
481 B.J. Surhoff .50 .15
482 Andy Stankiewicz .50 .15
483 Tino Martinez .75 .23
484 Craig Biggio .75 .23
485 Denny Neagle .50 .15
486 Rusty Meacham .50 .15
487 Kal Daniels .50 .15
488 Dave Henderson .50 .15
489 Tim Costo .50 .15
490 Doug Davis .50 .15

491 Frank Viola .50 .15
492 Cory Snyder .50 .15
493 Chris Martin .50 .15
494 Dion James .50 .15
495 Randy Tomlin .50 .15
496 Greg Vaughn .50 .15
497 Dennis Cook .50 .15
498 Rosario Rodriguez .50 .15
499 Dave Staton .50 .15
500 George Brett 3.00 .90
501 Brian Barnes .50 .15
502 Butch Henry RC .50 .15
503 Harold Reynolds .50 .15
504 David Nied RC .50 .15
505 Lee Smith .50 .15
506 Steve Chitren .50 .15
507 Ken Hill .50 .15
508 Robbie Beckett .50 .15
509 Troy Afenir .50 .15
510 Kelly Gruber .50 .15
511 Bret Boone 1.25 .35
512 Jeff Branson .50 .15
513 Mike Jackson .50 .15
514 Pete Harnisch .50 .15
515 Chad Kreuter .50 .15
516 Joe Vitko RC .50 .15
517 Orel Hershiser .50 .15
518 John Doherty RC .50 .15
519 Jay Bell .50 .15
520 Mark Langston .50 .15
521 Dann Howitt .50 .15
522 Bobby Reed RC .50 .15
523 Bobby Munoz RC .50 .15
524 Todd Ritchie .50 .15
525 Bip Roberts .50 .15
526 Pat Listach RC 1.00 .30
527 Scott Brosius RC 2.00 .60
528 John Roper RC .50 .15
529 Phil Hiatt RC .50 .15
530 Denny Walling .50 .15
531 Carlos Baerga .50 .15
532 Manny Ramirez RC 25.00 7.50
533 Pat Clements UER .50 .15
(Mistakenly numbered 553)
534 Ron Gant .50 .15
535 Pat Kelly .50 .15
536 Bill Spiers .50 .15
537 Darren Reed .50 .15
538 Ken Caminiti .50 .15
539 Butch Huskey RC .50 .15
540 Matt Nokes .50 .15
541 John Kruk .50 .15
542 John Jaha FOIL .50 .15
543 Justin Thompson RC .50 .15
544 Steve Hosey .50 .15
545 Joe Kmak .50 .15
546 John Franco .50 .15
547 Devon White .50 .15
548 E.Hansen FOIL RC .50 .15
549 Ryan Klesko 1.25 .35
550 Danny Tartabull .50 .15
551 Frank Thomas FOIL 1.25 .35
552 Kevin Tapani .50 .15
553 Willie Banks .50 .15
(See also 533)
554 B.J. Wallace RC FOIL .50 .15
555 Orlando Miller RC .50 .15
556 Mark Smith RC .50 .15
557 Tim Wallach FOIL .50 .15
558 Bill Gullickson .50 .15
559 Derek Bell FOIL .50 .15
560 Joe Randa FOIL RC 1.00 .30
561 Frank Seminara RC .50 .15
562 Mark Gardner .50 .15
563 Rick Greene RC FOIL .50 .15
564 Gary Gaetti .50 .15
565 Ozzie Guillen .50 .15
566 Charles Nagy FOIL .50 .15
567 Mike Milchin .50 .15
568 Ben Shelton RC .50 .15
569 Chris Roberts FOIL .50 .15
570 Ellis Burks .50 .15
571 Scott Scudder .50 .15
572 Jim Abbott FOIL .75 .23
573 Joe Carter .50 .15
574 Steve Finley .50 .15
575 Jim Olander FOIL .50 .15
576 Carlos Garcia .50 .15
577 Gregg Olson .50 .15
578 Greg Swindell FOIL .50 .15
579 Matt Williams FOIL .50 .15
580 Mark Grace .75 .23
581 Howard House FOIL RC .50 .15
582 Luis Polonia .50 .15
583 Erik Hanson .50 .15
584 Salomon Torres FOIL .50 .15
585 Carlton Fisk .75 .23
586 Bret Saberhagen .50 .15
587 C.McConnell FOIL RC .50 .15
588 Jimmy Key .50 .15
589 Mike Macfarlane .50 .15
590 Barry Bonds FOIL 3.00 .90
591 Jamie McAndrew .50 .15
592 Shane Mack .50 .15
593 Kerwin Moore .50 .15
594 Joe Oliver .50 .15
595 Chris Sabo .50 .15
596 Alex Gonzalez RC 2.00 .60
597 Brett Butler .50 .15
598 Mark Hutton RC .50 .15
599 Andy Benes FOIL .50 .15
600 Jose Canseco 1.25 .35
601 Darryl Kile .50 .15
602 Matt Stairs FOIL .50 .15
603 R.Butler RC FOIL .50 .15
604 Willie McGee .50 .15
605 Jack McDowell FOIL .50 .15
606 Tom Candiotti .50 .15
607 Ed Martel RC .50 .15
608 Matt Mieske FOIL .50 .15
609 Darrin Fletcher .50 .15
610 Rafael Palmeiro .75 .23
611 Bill Swift FOIL .50 .15
612 Mike Mussina 1.25 .35
613 Vince Coleman .50 .15
614 Scott Cepicky COR .50 .15
614A S.Cepicky FOIL UER .50 .15
Bats: LEFLT
615 Mike Greenwell .50 .15
616 Kevin McGehee RC .50 .15
617 J.Hammonds FOIL .50 .15
618 Scott Taylor .50 .15
619 Dave Otto .50 .15
620 Mark McGwire FOIL 3.00 .90
621 Kevin Tatar RC .50 .15
622 Steve Farr .50 .15
623 Ryan Klesko FOIL .50 .15
624 Dave Fleming .50 .15
625 Andre Dawson .50 .15
626 Tino Martinez FOIL .75 .23
627 Chad Curtis RC 1.00 .30
628 Mickey Morandini .50 .15
629 Gregg Olson FOIL .50 .15
630 Lou Whitaker .50 .15
631 Arthur Rhodes .50 .15
632 Brandon Wilson RC .50 .15
633 Lance Jennings RC .50 .15
634 Allen Watson RC .50 .15
635 Len Dykstra .50 .15
636 Joe Girardi .50 .15
637 K.Hernandez RC FOIL .50 .15
638 Mike Hampton RC 2.00 .60
639 Al Osuna .50 .15
640 Kevin Appier .50 .15
641 Rick Helling FOIL .50 .15
642 Jody Reed .50 .15
643 Ray Lankford .50 .15
644 John Olerud .50 .15
645 Paul Molitor FOIL .75 .23
646 Pat Borders .50 .15
647 Mike Morgan .50 .15
648 Larry Walker .75 .23
649 P.Castellano FOIL .50 .15
650 Fred McGriff .75 .23
651 Walt Weiss .50 .15
652 C.Murray RC FOIL 1.00 .30
653 Dave Nilsson .50 .15
654 Greg Pirkl RC .50 .15
655 Robin Ventura FOIL .50 .15
656 Mark Portugal .50 .15
657 Roger McDowell .50 .15
658 Rick Hirtensteiner FOIL RC .50 .15
659 Glenallen Hill .50 .15
660 Greg Gagne .50 .15
661 Charles Johnson FOIL .50 .15
662 Brian Hunter .50 .15
663 Mark Lemke .50 .15
664 Tim Belcher FOIL .50 .15
665 Rich DeLucia .50 .15
666 Bob Walk .50 .15
667 Joe Carter FOIL .50 .15
668 Jose Guzman .50 .15
669 Otis Nixon .50 .15
670 Phil Nevin FOIL .75 .23
671 Eric Davis .50 .15
672 Damion Easley RC 1.00 .30
673 Will Clark FOIL 1.25 .35
674 Mark Kiefer RC .50 .15
675 Ozzie Smith 2.00 .60
676 Manny Ramirez FOIL 5.00 1.50
677 Gregg Olson .50 .15
678 Cliff Floyd RC 2.00 .60
679 Duane Singleton RC .50 .15
680 Jose Rijo .50 .15
681 Willie Randolph .50 .15
682 M.Tucker FOIL RC 2.00 .60
683 Darren Lewis .50 .15
684 Dale Murphy 1.25 .35
685 Mike Pagliarulo .50 .15
686 Paul Miller RC .50 .15
687 Mike Robertson RC .50 .15
688 Mike Devereaux .50 .15
689 Pedro Astacio RC 1.00 .30
690 Alan Trammell .50 .15
691 Roger Clemens 2.50 .75
692 Bud Black .50 .15
693 Turk Wendell RC 1.00 .30
694 Barry Larkin FOIL .75 .23
695 Todd Zeile .50 .15
696 Pat Hentgen .50 .15
697 Eddie Taubensee RC 1.00 .30
698 G.Velasquez RC .50 .15
699 Tom Glavine .75 .23
700 Robin Yount 2.00 .60
701 Checklist 1-141 .50 .15
702 Checklist 142-282 .50 .15
703 Checklist 283-423 .50 .15
704 Checklist 424-564 .50 .15
705 Checklist 565-705 .50 .15

1993 Bowman

This 708-card standard-size set (produced by Topps) was issued in one series and features one of the more comprehensive selection of prospects and rookies available that year. Cards were distributed in 14-card plastic wrapped packs and jumbo packs. Each 14-card pack contained one silver foil bordered subset card. The basic issue card fronts feature white-bordered color action player photos. The 48 foil subset cards (339-374 and 693-704) feature sixteen 1992 MVPs of the Minor Leagues, top prospects and a few father/son combinations. Rookie Cards in this set include James Baldwin, Roger Cedeno, Derek Jeter, Jason Kendall, Andy Pettitte, Jose Vidro and Preston Wilson.

Nm-Mt Ex-Mt
COMPLETE SET (708) 50.00 15.00
1 Glenn Davis .15 .04
2 Hector Roa RC .15 .04
3 Ken Ryan RC .25 .07
4 Derek Wallace RC .25 .07
5 Jorge Fabregas .15 .04
6 Joe Oliver .15 .04
7 Brandon Wilson .15 .04
8 Mark Thompson RC .25 .07
9 Tracy Sanders .15 .04
10 Rich Renteria .15 .04
11 Lou Whitaker .30 .09
12 Brian L. Hunter RC .50 .15
13 Joe Vitiello .15 .04
14 Eric Karros .30 .09
15 Joe Kmak .15 .04
16 Tavo Alvarez .15 .04
17 Steve Dunn RC .25 .07
18 Tony Fernandez .15 .04
19 Melido Perez .15 .04
20 Mike Lieberthal .30 .09
21 Terry Steinbach .15 .04
22 Stan Belinda .15 .04
23 Jay Buhner .30 .09
24 Allen Watson .15 .04
25 Daryl Henderson RC .25 .07
26 Ray McDavid RC .25 .07
27 Shawn Green 1.00 .30
28 Bud Black .15 .04
29 Sherman Obando RC .25 .07
30 Mike Hostetler RC .25 .07
31 Nate Minchey RC .25 .07
32 Randy Myers .15 .04
33 Brian Grebeck .15 .04
34 John Roper .15 .04
35 Larry Thomas .15 .04
36 Alex Cole .15 .04
37 Tom Kramer RC .25 .07
38 Matt Whisenant RC .25 .07
39 Chris Gomez RC .50 .15
40 Luis Gonzalez .30 .09
41 Kevin Appier .30 .09
42 Omar Daal RC .50 .15
43 Duane Singleton .15 .04
44 Bill Risley .15 .04
45 Pat Meares RC .50 .15
46 Butch Huskey .15 .04
47 Bobby Munoz .15 .04
48 Juan Bell .15 .04
49 Scott Lydy RC .25 .07
50 Dennis Moeller .15 .04
51 Marc Newfield .15 .04
52 Tripp Cromer RC .25 .07
53 Kurt Miller .15 .04
54 Jim Pena .15 .04
55 Juan Guzman .15 .04
56 Matt Williams .30 .09
57 Harold Reynolds .30 .09
58 Donnie Elliott RC .25 .07
59 Jon Shave RC .25 .07
60 Kevin Roberson RC .25 .07
61 Hilly Hathaway RC .25 .07
62 Jose Rijo .15 .04
63 Kerry Taylor RC .15 .04
64 Ryan Hawblitzel .15 .04
65 Glenallen Hill .15 .04
66 Ramon Martinez RC .25 .07
67 Travis Fryman .30 .09
68 Tom Nevers .15 .04
69 Phil Hiatt .15 .04
70 Tim Wallach .15 .04
71 B.J. Surhoff .30 .09
72 Rondell White .30 .09
73 Denny Hocking RC .50 .15
74 Mike Oquist RC .25 .07
75 Paul O'Neill .50 .15
76 Willie Banks .15 .04
77 Bob Welch .15 .04
78 Jose Sandoval RC .25 .07
79 Bill Haselman .15 .04
80 Rheal Cormier .15 .04
81 Dean Palmer .30 .09
82 Pat Gomez RC .25 .07
83 Steve Karsay .15 .04
84 Carl Hanselman RC .25 .07
85 T.R. Lewis RC .25 .07
86 Chipper Jones .75 .23
87 Scott Hatteberg .15 .04
88 Greg Hibbard .15 .04
89 Lance Painter RC .25 .07
90 Chad Mottola RC .50 .15
91 Jason Bere .15 .04
92 Dante Bichette .30 .09
93 Sandy Alomar Jr. .15 .04
94 Carl Everett .30 .09
95 Danny Bautista RC 1.00 .30
96 Steve Finley .30 .09
97 David Cone .30 .09
98 Todd Hollandsworth .15 .04
99 Matt Mieske .15 .04
100 Larry Walker .50 .15
101 Shane Mack .15 .04
102 Aaron Ledesma RC .25 .07
103 Andy Pettitte RC 8.00 2.40
104 Kevin Stocker .15 .04
105 Mike Mohler RC .25 .07
106 Tony Menendez .15 .04
107 Derek Lowe .75 .23
108 Basil Shabazz .15 .04
109 Dan Smith .15 .04
110 Scott Sanders RC .50 .15
111 Todd Stottlemyre .15 .04
112 Benji Simonton RC .25 .07
113 Rick Sutcliffe .30 .09
114 Lee Heath RC .25 .07
115 Jeff Russell .15 .04
116 Dave Stevens RC .25 .07
117 Mark Holzemer RC .25 .07
118 Tim Belcher .15 .04
119 Bobby Thigpen .15 .04
120 Roger Bailey RC .25 .07
121 Tony Mitchell RC .25 .07
122 Junior Felix .15 .04
123 Rich Robertson RC .25 .07
124 Andy Cook RC .25 .07
125 Brian Bevil RC .25 .07
126 Darryl Strawberry .30 .09
127 Cal Eldred .15 .04
128 Cliff Floyd .30 .09
129 Alan Newman .15 .04
130 Howard Johnson .15 .04
131 Jim Abbott .50 .15
132 Chad McConnell .15 .04
133 Miguel Jimenez RC .25 .07
134 Brett Backlund RC .25 .07
135 John Cummings RC .25 .07
136 Brian Barber .15 .04
137 Rafael Palmeiro .50 .15
138 Tim Worrell RC .25 .07
139 Jose Pett RC .25 .07
140 Barry Bonds 2.00 .60
141 Damon Buford .15 .04
142 Jeff Blauser .15 .04
143 Frankie Rodriguez .15 .04
144 Mike Morgan .15 .04
145 Gary DiSarcina .15 .04
146 Pokey Reese .15 .04
147 Johnny Ruffin .15 .04
148 David Nied .15 .04
149 Charles Nagy .15 .04
150 Mike Myers RC .25 .07
151 Kenny Carlyle RC .25 .07
152 Eric Anthony .15 .04
153 Jose Lind .15 .04
154 Pedro Martinez 1.50 .45
155 Mark Kiefer .15 .04
156 Tim Laker RC .25 .07
157 Pat Mahomes .15 .04
158 Bobby Bonilla .30 .09
159 Domingo Jean .15 .04
160 Darren Daulton .30 .09
161 Mark McGwire 2.00 .60
162 Jason Kendall RC 1.50 .45
163 Desi Relaford .15 .04
164 Ozzie Canseco .15 .04
165 Rick Helling .15 .04
166 Steve Pegues RC .25 .07
167 Paul Molitor .50 .15
168 Larry Carter RC .25 .07
169 Arthur Rhodes .15 .04
170 Damon Hollins RC .50 .15
171 Frank Viola .30 .09
172 Steve Trachsel RC .50 .15
173 J.T. Snow RC 1.00 .30
174 Keith Gordon RC .25 .07
175 Carlton Fisk .50 .15
176 Jason Bates RC .25 .07
177 Mike Crosby RC .25 .07
178 Benny Santiago .30 .09
179 Mike Moore .15 .04
180 Jeff Juden .15 .04
181 Darren Burton .15 .04
182 Todd Williams RC .50 .15
183 John Jaha .15 .04
184 Mike Lansing RC .50 .15
185 Pedro Grifol RC .25 .07
186 Vince Coleman .15 .04
187 Pat Kelly .15 .04
188 Clemente Alvarez RC .25 .07
189 Ron Darling .15 .04
190 Orlando Merced .15 .04
191 Chris Bosio .15 .04
192 Steve Dixon RC .25 .07
193 Doug Dascenzo .15 .04
194 Ray Holbert RC .25 .07
195 Howard Battle .15 .04
196 Willie McGee .30 .09
197 John O'Donoghue RC .25 .07
198 Steve Avery .15 .04
199 Greg Blosser .15 .04
200 Ryne Sandberg 1.25 .35
201 Joe Grahe .15 .04
202 Dan Wilson .30 .09
203 Domingo Martinez RC .25 .07
204 Andres Galarraga .30 .09
205 Jamie Taylor RC .25 .07
206 Darrell Whitmore RC .25 .07
207 Ben Blomdahl RC .25 .07
208 Doug Drabek .15 .04
209 Keith Miller .15 .04
210 Billy Ashley .15 .04
211 Mike Farrell RC .25 .07
212 John Wetteland .30 .09
213 Randy Tomlin .15 .04
214 Sid Fernandez .15 .04
215 Quilvio Veras RC .50 .15
216 Dave Hollins .15 .04
217 Mike Neill .15 .04
218 Andy Van Slyke .30 .09
219 Bret Boone .50 .15
220 Tom Pagnozzi .15 .04
221 Mike Welch RC .25 .07
222 Frank Seminara .15 .04
223 Ron Villone .15 .04
224 D.J. Thielen RC .25 .07
225 Cal Ripken 2.50 .75
226 Pedro Borbon Jr. RC .25 .07
227 Carlos Quintana .15 .04
228 Tommy Shields .15 .04
229 Tim Salmon .50 .15
230 John Smiley .15 .04
231 Ellis Burks .30 .09
232 Pedro Castellano .15 .04
233 Paul Byrd .15 .04
234 Bryan Harvey .15 .04
235 Scott Livingstone .15 .04
236 James Mouton RC .25 .07
237 Joe Randa .30 .09
238 Pedro Astacio .15 .04
239 Darryl Hamilton .15 .04
240 Joey Eischen RC .25 .07
241 Edgar Herrera RC .25 .07
242 Dwight Gooden .30 .09
243 Sam Militello .15 .04
244 Ron Blazier RC .25 .07
245 Ruben Sierra .15 .04
246 Al Martin .15 .04
247 Mike Felder .15 .04
248 Bob Tewksbury .15 .04
249 Craig Lefferts .15 .04
250 Luis Lopez RC .25 .07
251 Devon White .30 .09
252 Will Clark .75 .23
253 Mark Smith .15 .04
254 Terry Pendleton .30 .09
255 Aaron Sele .15 .04
256 Jose Viera RC .25 .07
257 Damion Easley .15 .04
258 Rod Lofton RC .25 .07
259 Chris Snopek RC .25 .07
260 Q.McCracken RC .50 .15
261 Mike Matthews RC .25 .07
262 Hector Carrasco RC .25 .07
263 Rick Greene .15 .04
264 Chris Holt RC .50 .15
265 George Brett 2.00 .60
266 Rick Gorecki RC .25 .07
267 Francisco Gamez RC .25 .07
268 Marquis Grissom .30 .09
269 Kevin Tapani UER .15 .04
(Misspelled Tapan
on card front)
270 Ryan Thompson .15 .04
271 Gerald Williams .15 .04
272 Paul Fletcher RC .25 .07
273 Lance Blankenship .15 .04
274 Marty Neff RC .25 .07
275 Shawn Estes .15 .04
276 Rene Arocha RC .50 .15
277 Scott Eyre RC .25 .07
278 Phil Plantier .15 .04
279 Paul Spoljaric RC .25 .07
280 Chris Gambs .15 .04
281 Harold Baines .30 .09
282 Jose Oliva .15 .04
283 Matt Whiteside RC .25 .07
284 Brant Brown RC .50 .15
285 Russ Springer .15 .04
286 Chris Sabo .15 .04
287 Ozzie Guillen .15 .04
288 Marcus Moore RC .25 .07
289 Chad Ogea .15 .04
290 Walt Weiss .15 .04
291 Brian Edmondson .15 .04
292 Jimmy Gonzalez .15 .04
293 Danny Miceli RC .50 .15
294 Jose Offerman .15 .04
295 Greg Vaughn .15 .04
296 Frank Bolick .15 .04
297 Mike Maksudian RC .25 .07
298 John Franco .30 .09
299 Danny Tartabull .15 .04
300 Len Dykstra .30 .09
301 Bobby Witt .15 .04
302 Trey Beamon RC .25 .07
303 Tino Martinez .50 .15
304 Aaron Holbert .15 .04
305 Juan Gonzalez .50 .15
306 Billy Hall RC .25 .07
307 Duane Ward .15 .04
308 Rod Beck .15 .04
309 Jose Mercedes RC .25 .07
310 Otis Nixon .15 .04
311 Gettys Glaze RC .25 .07
312 Candy Maldonado .15 .04
313 Chad Curtis .15 .04
314 Tim Costo .15 .04
315 Mike Robertson .15 .04
316 Nigel Wilson .15 .04
317 Greg McMichael RC .50 .15
318 Scott Pose RC .25 .07
319 Ivan Cruz .15 .04
320 Greg Swindell .15 .04
321 Kevin McReynolds .15 .04
322 Tom Candiotti .15 .04
323 Rob Wishnevski RC .25 .07
324 Ken Hill .15 .04
325 Kirby Puckett .75 .23
326 Tim Bogar RC .25 .07
327 Mariano Rivera 1.00 .30
328 Mitch Williams .15 .04
329 Craig Paquette .15 .04
330 Jay Bell .30 .09
331 Jose Martinez RC .25 .07
332 Rob Deer .15 .04
333 Brook Fordyce .15 .04
334 Matt Nokes .15 .04
335 Derek Lee .15 .04
336 Paul Ellis RC .25 .07
337 Desi Wilson RC .25 .07
338 Roberto Alomar .50 .15
339 Jim Tatum FOIL RC .25 .07
340 J.T. Snow FOIL 1.00 .30
341 Tim Salmon FOIL .50 .15
342 Russ Davis FOIL RC .50 .15
343 Javy Lopez FOIL .50 .15
344 Troy O'Leary FOIL RC .50 .15
345 M.Cordova FOIL RC .50 .15
346 Bubba Smith RC FOIL .25 .07
347 Chipper Jones FOIL .75 .23
348 Jessie Hollins FOIL .15 .04
349 Willie Greene FOIL .15 .04
350 Mark Thompson FOIL .15 .04
351 Nigel Wilson FOIL .15 .04
352 Todd Jones FOIL .15 .04
353 Raul Mondesi FOIL .30 .09
354 Cliff Floyd FOIL .30 .09
355 Bobby Jones FOIL .30 .09
356 Kevin Stocker FOIL .15 .04
357 M.Cummings FOIL .15 .04
358 Allen Watson FOIL .15 .04
359 Ray McDavid FOIL .15 .04
360 Steve Hosey FOIL .15 .04
361 B.Pennington FOIL .15 .04
362 F.Rodriguez FOIL .15 .04
363 Troy Percival FOIL .50 .15
364 Jason Bere FOIL .15 .04
365 Manny Ramirez FOIL .75 .23
366 J.Thompson FOIL .15 .04
367 Joe Vitiello FOIL .15 .04
368 Tyrone Hill FOIL .15 .04
369 David McCarty FOIL .15 .04
370 Brien Taylor FOIL .15 .04
371 T.Van Poppel FOIL .15 .04
372 Marc Newfield FOIL .15 .04
373 T.Lowery RC FOIL .50 .15
374 Alex Gonzalez FOIL .15 .04
375 Ken Griffey Jr. 1.25 .35
376 Donovan Osborne .15 .04
377 Ritchie Moody RC .25 .07
378 Shane Andrews .15 .04
379 Carlos Delgado .75 .23
380 Bill Swift .15 .04
381 Leo Gomez .15 .04
382 Ron Gant .30 .09
383 Scott Fletcher .15 .04
384 Matt Walbeck RC .50 .15
385 Chuck Finley .30 .09
386 Kevin Mitchell .15 .04
387 Wilson Alvarez UER .15 .04
(Misspelled Alverez
on card front)
388 John Burke RC .25 .07
389 Alan Embree .75 .23
390 Trevor Hoffman .30 .09
391 Alan Trammell .30 .09
392 Todd Jones .15 .04
393 Felix Jose .15 .04
394 Orel Hershiser .30 .09
395 Pat Listach .15 .04

396 Gabe White .15 .04
397 Dan Serafini RC .25 .07
398 Todd Hundley .15 .04
399 Wade Boggs .50 .15
400 Tyler Green .15 .04
401 Mike Bordick .15 .04
402 Scott Bullett .15 .04
403 LaGrande Russell RC .25 .07
404 Ray Lankford .15 .04
405 Nolan Ryan 3.00 .90
406 Robbie Beckett .15 .04
407 Brent Bowers RC .25 .07
408 Adell Davenport RC .25 .07
409 Brady Anderson .30 .09
410 Tom Glavine .50 .15
411 Doug Hecker RC .25 .07
412 Jose Guzman .15 .04
413 Luis Polonia .15 .04
414 Brian Williams .15 .04
415 Bo Jackson .75 .23
416 Eric Young .15 .04
417 Kenny Lofton .30 .09
418 Orestes Destrade .15 .04
419 Tony Phillips .15 .04
420 Jeff Bagwell .50 .15
421 Mark Gardner .15 .04
422 Brett Butler .30 .09
423 Graeme Lloyd RC .50 .15
424 Delino DeShields .15 .04
425 Scott Erickson .15 .04
426 Jeff Kent .75 .23
427 Jimmy Key .30 .09
428 Mickey Morandini .15 .04
429 Marcos Armas RC .25 .07
430 Don Slaught .15 .04
431 Randy Johnson .75 .23
432 Omar Olivares .15 .04
433 Charlie Leibrandt .15 .04
434 Kurt Stillwell .15 .04
435 Scott Brow RC .25 .07
436 Robby Thompson .15 .04
437 Ben McDonald .15 .04
438 Deion Sanders .50 .15
439 Tony Pena .15 .04
440 Mark Grace .50 .15
441 Eduardo Perez .15 .04
442 Tim Pugh RC .25 .07
443 Scott Ruffcorn .15 .04
444 Jay Gainer RC .25 .07
445 Albert Belle .30 .09
446 Bret Barberie .15 .04
447 Justin Mashore .15 .04
448 Pete Harnisch .15 .04
449 Greg Gagne .15 .04
450 Eric Davis .30 .09
451 Dave Mlicki .15 .04
452 Moises Alou .30 .09
453 Rick Aguilera .15 .04
454 Eddie Murray .75 .23
455 Bob Wickman .15 .04
456 Wes Chamberlain .15 .04
457 Brent Gates .15 .04
458 Paul Wagner .15 .04
459 Mike Hampton .30 .09
460 Ozzie Smith 1.25 .35
461 Tom Henke .15 .04
462 Ricky Gutierrez .15 .04
463 Jack Morris .30 .09
464 Joel Chimelis .15 .04
465 Gregg Olson .15 .04
466 Javy Lopez .50 .15
467 Scott Cooper .15 .04
468 Willie Wilson .15 .04
469 Mark Langston .15 .04
470 Barry Larkin .50 .15
471 Rod Bolton .15 .04
472 Freddie Benavides .15 .04
473 Ken Ramos RC .25 .07
474 Chuck Carr .15 .04
475 Cecil Fielder .30 .09
476 Eddie Taubensee .15 .04
477 Chris Eddy RC .25 .07
478 Greg Hansell .15 .04
479 Kevin Reimer .15 .04
480 Dennis Martinez .30 .09
481 Chuck Knoblauch .30 .09
482 Mike Draper .15 .04
483 Spike Owen .15 .04
484 Terry Mulholland .15 .04
485 Dennis Eckersley .30 .09
486 Blas Minor .15 .04
487 Dave Fleming .15 .04
488 Dan Cholowsky .15 .04
489 Ivan Rodriguez .75 .23
490 Gary Sheffield .30 .09
491 Ed Sprague .15 .04
492 Steve Hosey .15 .04
493 Jimmy Haynes RC .50 .15
494 John Smoltz .50 .15
495 Andre Dawson .30 .09
496 Rey Sanchez .15 .04
497 Ty Van Burkleo .15 .04
498 Bobby Ayala RC .25 .07
499 Tim Raines .30 .09
500 Charlie Hayes .15 .04
501 Paul Sorrento .15 .04
502 Richie Lewis RC .25 .07
503 Jason Pfaff RC .25 .07
504 Ken Caminiti .30 .09
505 Mike Macfarlane .15 .04
506 Jody Reed .15 .04
507 Bobby Hughes RC .25 .07
508 Wil Cordero .15 .04
509 George Tsamis RC .25 .07
510 Bret Saberhagen .30 .09
511 Derek Jeter RC 15.00 4.50
512 Gene Schall .15 .04
513 Curtis Shaw .15 .04
514 Steve Cooke .15 .04
515 Edgar Martinez .50 .15
516 Mike Milchin .15 .04
517 Billy Ripken .15 .04
518 Andy Benes .15 .04
519 Juan de la Rosa RC .25 .07
520 John Burkett .15 .04
521 Alex Ochoa .15 .04
522 Tony Tarasco RC .50 .15
523 Luis Ortiz .15 .04
524 Rick Wilkins .15 .04
525 Chris Turner RC .25 .07
526 Rob Dibble .30 .09
527 Jack McDowell .15 .04
528 Daryl Boston .15 .04
529 Bill Wertz RC .25 .07
530 Charlie Hough .30 .09
531 Sean Bergman .15 .04
532 Doug Jones .15 .04
533 Jeff Montgomery .15 .04
534 Roger Cedeno RC .50 .15
535 Robin Yount 1.25 .35
536 Mo Vaughn .30 .09
537 Brian Harper .15 .04
538 Juan Castillo RC .15 .04
539 Steve Farr .15 .04
540 John Kruk .30 .09
541 Troy Neel .15 .04
542 Danny Clyburn RC .25 .07
543 Jim Converse RC .25 .07
544 Gregg Jefferies .15 .04
545 Jose Canseco .75 .23
546 Julio Bruno RC .25 .07
547 Rob Butler .15 .04
548 Royce Clayton .15 .04
549 Chris Hoiles .15 .04
550 Greg Maddux 1.25 .35
551 Joe Ciccarella RC .25 .07
552 Ozzie Timmons .15 .04
553 Chili Davis .30 .09
554 Brian Koelling .15 .04
555 Frank Thomas .75 .23
556 Vinny Castilla .30 .09
557 Reggie Jefferson .15 .04
558 Rob Natal .15 .04
559 Mike Henneman .15 .04
560 Craig Biggio .50 .15
561 Billy Brewer .15 .04
562 Dan Melendez .15 .04
563 Kenny Felder RC .25 .07
564 Miguel Batista RC 1.00 .30
565 Dave Winfield .30 .09
566 Al Shirley .15 .04
567 Robert Eenhoorn .15 .04
568 Mike Williams .15 .04
569 Tanyon Sturtze RC .50 .15
570 Tim Wakefield .75 .23
571 Greg Pirkl .15 .04
572 Sean Lowe RC .25 .07
573 Terry Burrows RC .25 .07
574 Kevin Higgins .15 .04
575 Joe Carter .30 .09
576 Kevin Rogers .15 .04
577 Manny Alexander .15 .04
578 David Justice .30 .09
579 Brian Conroy RC .25 .07
580 Jessie Hollins .15 .04
581 Ron Watson RC .25 .07
582 Bip Roberts .15 .04
583 Tom Urbani RC .25 .07
584 Jason Hutchins RC .25 .07
585 Carlos Baerga .15 .04
586 Jeff Mutis .15 .04
587 Justin Thompson .15 .04
588 Orlando Miller .15 .04
589 Brian McRae .15 .04
590 Ramon Martinez .15 .04
591 Dave Nilsson .15 .04
592 Jose Vidro RC 1.50 .45
593 Rich Becker .15 .04
594 Preston Wilson RC 1.50 .45
595 Don Mattingly 2.00 .60
596 Tony Longmire .15 .04
597 Kevin Seitzer .15 .04
598 Midre Cummings RC .25 .07
599 Omar Vizquel .50 .15
600 Lee Smith .30 .09
601 David Hulse RC .25 .07
602 Darrell Sherman RC .25 .07
603 Alex Gonzalez .15 .04
604 Geronimo Pena .15 .04
605 Mike Devereaux .15 .04
606 S.Hitchcock RC .50 .15
607 Mike Greenwell .15 .04
608 Steve Buechele .15 .04
609 Troy Percival .50 .15
610 Roberto Kelly .15 .04
611 James Baldwin RC .50 .15
612 Jerald Clark .15 .04
613 Albie Lopez RC .50 .15
614 Dave Magadan .15 .04
615 Mickey Tettleton .15 .04
616 Sean Runyan RC .25 .07
617 Bob Hamelin .15 .04
618 Raul Mondesi .30 .09
619 Tyrone Hill .15 .04
620 Darrin Fletcher .15 .04
621 Mike Trombley .15 .04
622 Jeromy Burnitz .30 .09
623 Bernie Williams .50 .15
624 Mike Farmer RC .25 .07
625 Rickey Henderson .75 .23
626 Carlos Garcia .15 .04
627 Jeff Darwin RC .25 .07
628 Todd Zeile .15 .04
629 Benji Gil .15 .04
630 Tony Gwynn 1.00 .30
631 Aaron Small RC .25 .07
632 Joe Rosselli RC .25 .07
633 Mike Mussina .50 .15
634 Ryan Klesko .30 .09
635 Roger Clemens 1.50 .45
636 Sammy Sosa 1.25 .35
637 Orlando Palmeiro RC .25 .07
638 Willie Greene .15 .04
639 George Bell .15 .04
640 Garvin Alston RC .25 .07
641 Pete Janicki RC .25 .07
642 Chris Sheff RC .25 .07
643 Felipe Lira RC .25 .07
644 Roberto Petagine .15 .04
645 Wally Joyner .30 .09
646 Mike Piazza 2.00 .60
647 Jaime Navarro .15 .04
648 Jeff Hartsock .15 .04
649 David McCarty .15 .04
650 Bobby Jones .30 .09
651 Mark Hutton .15 .04
652 Kyle Abbott .15 .04
653 Steve Cox RC .50 .15
654 Jeff King .15 .04
655 Norm Charlton .15 .04
656 Mike Gulan RC .25 .07
657 Julio Franco .30 .09
658 C.Cairncross RC .25 .07
659 John Olerud .30 .09
660 Salomon Torres .15 .04
661 Brad Pennington .15 .04
662 Melvin Nieves .15 .04
663 Ivan Calderon .15 .04
664 Turk Wendell .15 .04
665 Chris Pritchett .15 .04
666 Reggie Sanders .30 .09
667 Robin Ventura .30 .09
668 Joe Girardi .15 .04
669 Manny Ramirez .75 .23
670 Jeff Conine .30 .09
671 Greg Gohr .15 .04
672 Andujar Cedeno .15 .04
673 Les Norman RC .25 .07
674 Mike James RC .25 .07
675 Marshall Boze RC .25 .07
676 B.J. Wallace .15 .04
677 Kent Hrbek .30 .09
678 Jack Voigt RC .25 .07
679 Brien Taylor .15 .04
680 Curt Schilling .30 .09
681 Todd Van Poppel .15 .04
682 Kevin Young .30 .09
683 Tommy Adams .15 .04
684 Bernard Gilkey .15 .04
685 Kevin Brown .30 .09
686 Fred McGriff .50 .15
687 Pat Borders .15 .04
688 Kirt Manwaring .15 .04
689 Sid Bream .15 .04
690 John Valentin .15 .04
691 Steve Olsen RC .25 .07
692 Roberto Mejia RC .25 .07
693 Carlos Delgado FOIL .75 .23
694 S.Gibralter FOIL RC .25 .07
695 Gary Mota FOIL RC .25 .07
696 Jose Malave FOIL RC .25 .07
697 Larry Sutton FOIL RC .25 .07
698 Dan Frye FOIL RC .25 .07
699 Tim Clark FOIL RC .25 .07
700 Brian Rupp FOIL RC .25 .07
701 Felipe Alou FOIL .30 .09
Moises Alou
702 Barry Bonds FOIL .75 .23
Bobby Bonds
703 Ken Griffey Sr. FOIL .75 .23
Ken Griffey Jr.
704 Brian McRae FOIL .15 .04
Hal McRae
705 Checklist 1 .15 .04
706 Checklist 2 .15 .04
707 Checklist 3 .15 .04
708 Checklist 4 .15 .04

1994 Bowman Previews

This 10-card standard-size set served as a preview to the 1994 Bowman set. The cards were randomly inserted one in every 24 1994 Stadium Club second series pack. The backs are identical to the basic issue with a horizontal layout containing a player photo, text and statistics.

	Nm-Mt	Ex-Mt
COMPLETE SET (10)	25.00	7.50
1 Frank Thomas	5.00	1.50
2 Mike Piazza	10.00	3.00
3 Albert Belle	2.00	.60
4 Javier Lopez	2.00	.60
5 Cliff Floyd	2.00	.60
6 Alex Gonzalez	1.25	.35
7 Ricky Bottalico	2.00	.60
8 Tony Clark	2.00	.60
9 Mac Suzuki	2.00	.60
10 James Mouton Foil	1.25	.35

1994 Bowman

The 1994 Bowman set consists of 682 standard-size, full-bleed cards primarily distributed in plastic wrap packs and jumbo packs. There are 52 Foil cards (337-388) that include a number of top young stars and prospects. These foil cards were issued one per foil pack and two per jumbo. Rookie Cards of note include Edgardo Alfonzo, Tony Clark, Jermaine Dye, Brad Fullmer, Richard Hidalgo, Derrek Lee, Chan Ho Park, Jorge Posada and Edgar Renteria.

	Nm-Mt	Ex-Mt
COMPLETE SET (682)	60.00	18.00

1 Joe Carter .40 .12
2 Marcus Moore .25 .07
3 Doug Creek RC .50 .15
4 Pedro Martinez 1.00 .30
5 Ken Griffey Jr. 1.50 .45
6 Greg Swindell .25 .07
7 J.J. Johnson .25 .07
8 Homer Bush RC 1.00 .30
9 Arquimedez Pozo RC .50 .15
10 Bryan Harvey .25 .07
11 J.T. Snow .40 .12
12 Alan Benes RC 1.00 .30
13 Chad Kreuter .25 .07
14 Eric Karros .40 .12
15 Frank Thomas 1.00 .30
16 Bret Saberhagen .40 .12
17 Terrell Lowery .25 .07
18 Rod Bolton .25 .07
19 Harold Baines .40 .12
20 Matt Walbeck .25 .07
21 Tom Glavine .60 .18
22 Todd Jones .25 .07
23 Alberto Castillo RC .50 .15
24 Ruben Sierra .25 .07
25 Don Mattingly 2.50 .75
26 Mike Morgan .25 .07
27 Jim Musselwhite RC .50 .15
28 Matt Brunson RC .50 .15
29 A.Meinershagen RC .50 .15
30 Joe Girardi .25 .07
31 Shane Halter .25 .07
32 Jose Paniagua RC 1.00 .30
33 Paul Perkins RC .50 .15
34 John Hudek RC .50 .15
35 Frank Viola .40 .12
36 David Lamb RC .50 .15
37 Marshall Boze .25 .07
38 Jorge Posada RC 10.00 3.00
39 Brian Anderson RC 1.00 .30
40 Mark Whiten .25 .07
41 Sean Bergman .25 .07
42 Jose Parra RC .50 .15
43 Mike Robertson .25 .07
44 Pete Walker RC .50 .15
45 Juan Gonzalez .60 .18
46 Cleveland Ladell RC .50 .15
47 Mark Smith .25 .07
48 Kevin Jarvis UER .50 .15
(team listed as Yankees on back)
49 Amaury Telemaco RC .50 .15
50 Andy Van Slyke .40 .12
51 Rikkert Faneyte RC .50 .15
52 Curtis Shaw .25 .07
53 Matt Drews RC .50 .15
54 Wilson Alvarez .25 .07
55 Manny Ramirez .60 .18
56 Bobby Munoz .25 .07
57 Ed Sprague .25 .07
58 Jamey Wright RC 1.00 .30
59 Jeff Montgomery .25 .07
60 Kirk Rueter .40 .12
61 Edgar Martinez .60 .18
62 Luis Gonzalez .40 .12
63 Tim Vanegmond RC .50 .15
64 Bip Roberts .25 .07
65 John Jaha .25 .07
66 Chuck Carr .25 .07
67 Chuck Finley .40 .12
68 Aaron Holbert .25 .07
69 Cecil Fielder .40 .12
70 Tom Engle RC .50 .15
71 Ron Karkovice .25 .07
72 Joe Orsulak .25 .07
73 Duff Brumley RC .50 .15
74 Craig Clayton RC .50 .15
75 Cal Ripken 3.00 .90
76 Brad Fulmer RC 1.50 .45
77 Tony Tarasco .25 .07
78 Terry Farrar RC .50 .15
79 Matt Williams .40 .12
80 Rickey Henderson 1.00 .30
81 Terry Mulholland .25 .07
82 Sammy Sosa 1.50 .45
83 Paul Sorrento .25 .07
84 Pete Incaviglia .25 .07
85 Darren Hall RC .50 .15
86 Scott Klingenbeck .25 .07
87 Dario Perez RC .50 .15
88 Ugueth Urbina .25 .07
89 Dave Vanhof RC .50 .15
90 Domingo Jean .25 .07
91 Otis Nixon .25 .07
92 Andres Berumen .25 .07
93 Jose Valentin .25 .07
94 Edgar Renteria RC 10.00 2.40
95 Chris Turner .25 .07
96 Ray Lankford .25 .07
97 Danny Bautista .25 .07
98 Chan Ho Park RC 1.50 .45
99 Glenn DiSarcina RC .50 .15
100 Butch Huskey .25 .07
101 Ivan Rodriguez 1.00 .30
102 Johnny Ruffin .25 .07
103 Alex Ochoa .25 .07
104 Torii Hunter RC 10.00 3.00
105 Ryan Klesko .40 .12
106 Jay Bell .40 .12
107 Kurt Peltzer RC .50 .15
108 Miguel Jimenez .25 .07
109 Russ Davis .25 .07
110 Derek Wallace .25 .07
111 Keith Lockhart RC 1.00 .30
112 Mike Lieberthal .40 .12
113 Dave Stewart .40 .12
114 Tom Schmidt .25 .07
115 Brian McRae .25 .07
116 Moises Alou .40 .12
117 Dave Fleming .25 .07
118 Jeff Bagwell .60 .18
119 Luis Ortiz .25 .07
120 Tony Gwynn 1.25 .35
121 Jaime Navarro .25 .07
122 Benito Santiago .40 .12
123 Darrell Whitmore .25 .07
124 John Mabry RC 1.00 .30
125 Mickey Tettleton .25 .07
126 Tom Candiotti .25 .07
127 Tim Raines .40 .12
128 Bobby Bonilla .40 .12
129 John Dettmer .25 .07
130 Hector Carrasco .25 .07
131 Chris Hoiles .25 .07
132 Rick Aguilera .25 .07
133 David Justice .40 .12
134 Esteban Loaiza RC 1.50 .45
135 Barry Bonds 2.50 .75
136 Bob Welch .25 .07
137 Mike Stanley .25 .07
138 Roberto Hernandez .25 .07
139 Sandy Alomar Jr. .25 .07
140 Darren Daulton .40 .12
141 Angel Martinez RC .50 .15
142 Howard Johnson .25 .07
143 Bob Hamelin UER .25 .07
(name and card number colors don't match)
144 J.J. Thobe RC .50 .15
145 Roger Salkeld .25 .07
146 Orlando Miller .25 .07
147 Dmitri Young .40 .12
148 Tim Hyers RC .50 .15
149 Mark Loretta RC 5.00 1.50
150 Chris Hammond .25 .07
151 Joel Moore RC .50 .15
152 Todd Zeile .25 .07
153 Wil Cordero .25 .07
154 Chris Smith .25 .07
155 James Baldwin .25 .07
156 Edgardo Alfonzo RC 1.50 .45
157 Kym Ashworth RC .50 .15
158 Paul Bako RC .50 .15
159 Rick Krivda RC .50 .15
160 Pat Mahomes .25 .07
161 Damon Hollins .40 .12
162 Felix Martinez RC .50 .15
163 Jason Myers RC .50 .15
164 Izzy Molina RC .50 .15
165 Brien Taylor .25 .07
166 Kevin Orie RC .50 .15
167 Casey Whitten RC .50 .15
168 Tony Longmire .25 .07
169 John Olerud .40 .12
170 Mark Thompson .25 .07
171 Jorge Fabregas .25 .07
172 John Wetteland .40 .12
173 Dan Wilson .25 .07
174 Doug Drabek .25 .07
175 Jeff McNeely .25 .07
176 Melvin Nieves .25 .07
177 Doug Glanville RC 1.00 .30
178 Javier De La Hoya RC .50 .15
179 Chad Curtis .25 .07
180 Brian Barber .25 .07
181 Mike Henneman .25 .07
182 Jose Offerman .25 .07
183 Robert Ellis RC .50 .15
184 John Franco .40 .12
185 Benji Gil .25 .07
186 Hal Morris .25 .07
187 Chris Sabo .25 .07
188 Blaise Ilsley RC .50 .15
189 Steve Avery .25 .07
190 Rick White RC .50 .15
191 Rod Beck .25 .07
192 Mark McGwire UER 2.50 .75
(No card number on back)
193 Jim Abbott .60 .18
194 Randy Myers .25 .07
195 Kenny Lofton .40 .12
196 Mariano Duncan .25 .07
197 Lee Daniels RC .50 .15
198 Armando Reynoso .25 .07
199 Joe Randa .40 .12
200 Cliff Floyd .40 .12
201 Tim Harkrider RC .50 .15
202 Kevin Gallaher RC .50 .15
203 Scott Cooper .25 .07
204 Phil Stidham RC .50 .15
205 Jeff D'Amico RC 1.00 .30
206 Matt Whisenant .25 .07
207 De Shawn Warren .25 .07
208 Rene Arocha .25 .07
209 Tony Clark RC 1.00 .30
210 Jason Jacome RC .50 .15
211 Scott Christman RC .50 .15
212 Bill Pulsipher .40 .12
213 Dean Palmer .40 .12
214 Chad Mottola .25 .07
215 Manny Alexander .25 .07
216 Rich Becker .25 .07
217 Andre King RC .50 .15
218 Carlos Garcia .25 .07
219 Ron Pezzoni RC .50 .15
220 Steve Karsay .25 .07
221 Jose Musset RC .50 .15
222 Karl Rhodes .25 .07
223 Frank Cimorelli RC .50 .15
224 Kevin Jordan RC .50 .15
225 Duane Ward .25 .07
226 John Burke .25 .07
227 Mike Macfarlane .25 .07
228 Mike Lansing .25 .07
229 Chuck Knoblauch .40 .12
230 Ken Caminiti .40 .12
231 Gar Finnvold RC .50 .15
232 Derrek Lee RC 2.50 .75
233 Brady Anderson .40 .12
234 Vic Darensbourg RC .50 .15
235 Mark Langston .25 .07
236 T.J. Mathews RC .50 .15
237 Lou Whitaker .40 .12
238 Roger Cedeno .25 .07
239 Alex Fernandez .25 .07
240 Ryan Thompson .25 .07
241 Kerry Lacy RC .50 .15
242 Reggie Sanders .25 .07
243 Brad Pennington .25 .07
244 Bryan Eversgerd RC .50 .15
245 Greg Maddux 1.50 .45
246 Jason Kendall .40 .12
247 J.R. Phillips .25 .07
248 Bobby Witt .25 .07
249 Paul O'Neill .60 .18
250 Ryne Sandberg 1.50 .45
251 Charles Nagy .25 .07
252 Kevin Stocker .25 .07
253 Shawn Green 1.00 .30
254 Charlie Hayes .25 .07
255 Donnie Elliott .25 .07
256 Rob Fitzpatrick RC .50 .15
257 Tim Davis .25 .07
258 James Mouton .25 .07
259 Mike Greenwell .25 .07
260 Ray McDavid .25 .07
261 Mike Kelly .25 .07
262 Andy Larkin RC .50 .15
263 Marquis Riley UER .25 .07
(No card number on back)
264 Bob Tewksbury .25 .07
265 Brian Edmondson .25 .07
266 Eduardo Lantigua RC .50 .15
267 Brandon Wilson .25 .07
268 Mike Welch .25 .07
269 Tom Henke .25 .07
270 Pokey Reese .25 .07
271 Greg Zaun RC 1.00 .30
272 Todd Ritchie .25 .07
273 Javier Lopez .40 .12
274 Kevin Young .25 .07
275 Kirt Manwaring .25 .07
276 Bill Taylor RC .25 .07
277 Robert Eenhoorn .25 .07
278 Jessie Hollins .25 .07
279 Julian Tavarez RC 1.00 .30
280 Gene Schall .25 .07

1 Paul Molitor .60 .18
2 Neifi Perez RC 1.00 .30
3 Greg Gagne .25 .07
4 Marquis Grissom .40 .12
5 Randy Johnson 1.00 .30
6 Pete Harnisch .25 .07
7 Joel Bennett RC .50 .15
8 Derek Bell .25 .07
9 Darryl Hamilton .25 .07
0 Gary Sheffield .40 .12
1 Eduardo Perez .25 .07
2 Basil Shabazz .25 .07
3 Eric Davis .40 .12
4 Pedro Astacio .25 .07
5 Robin Ventura .40 .12
6 Jeff Kent .40 .12
7 Rick Helling .25 .07
8 Joe Oliver .25 .07
9 Lee Smith .40 .12
0 Dave Winfield .40 .12
1 Deion Sanders .60 .18
2 R.Manzanillo RC .50 .15
3 Mark Portugal .25 .07
4 Brent Gates .25 .07
5 Wade Boggs .60 .18
6 Rick Wilkins .25 .07
7 Carlos Baerga .25 .07
8 Curt Schilling .40 .12
9 Shannon Stewart 1.00 .30
0 Darren Holmes .25 .07
1 Robert Toth RC .50 .15
2 Gabe White .25 .07
3 Mac Suzuki RC 1.00 .30
4 Alvin Morman RC .50 .15
5 Mo Vaughn .40 .12
6 Bryce Florie RC .50 .15
7 Gabby Martinez RC .50 .15
8 Carl Everett .40 .12
9 Kerwin Moore .25 .07
0 Tom Pagnozzi .25 .07
1 Chris Gomez .25 .07
2 Todd Williams .25 .07
3 Pat Hentgen .25 .07
4 Kirk Presley RC .50 .15
5 Kevin Brown .40 .12
6 J.Isringhausen RC 2.50 .75
7 Rick Forney RC .50 .15
8 Carlos Pulido RC .50 .15
9 Terrell Wade RC .50 .15
0 Al Martin .25 .07
1 Dan Carlson RC .50 .15
2 Mark Acre RC .50 .15
3 Sterling Hitchcock .25 .07
4 Jon Ratliff RC .50 .15
5 Alex Ramirez RC .50 .15
6 Phil Geisler RC .25 .07
7 E.Zambrano FOIL RC .50 .15
8 Jim Thome FOIL 1.00 .30
9 James Mouton FOIL .25 .07
0 Cliff Floyd FOIL .40 .12
1 Carlos Delgado FOIL .60 .18
2 R.Petagine FOIL .25 .07
3 Tim Clark FOIL .25 .07
4 Bubba Smith FOIL .25 .07
5 Randy Curtis FOIL RC .50 .15
6 Joe Biasucci FOIL RC .50 .15
7 D.J. Boston FOIL RC .50 .15
8 R.Rivera FOIL RC .50 .15
9 Bryan Link FOIL RC .50 .15
0 Mike Bell FOIL RC .50 .15
1 M.Watson FOIL RC .50 .15
2 Jason Myers FOIL .25 .07
3 Chipper Jones FOIL 1.00 .30
4 B.Kieschnick FOIL .25 .07
5 Pokey Reese FOIL .25 .07
6 John Burke FOIL .25 .07
7 Kurt Miller FOIL .25 .07
8 Orlando Miller FOIL .25 .07
9 T.Hollandsworth FOIL .25 .07
0 Rondell White FOIL .40 .12
1 Bill Pulsipher FOIL .40 .12
2 Tyler Green FOIL .25 .07
3 M.Cummings FOIL .25 .07
4 Brian Barber FOIL .25 .07
5 Melvin Nieves FOIL .25 .07
6 Salomon Torres FOIL .25 .07
7 Alex Ochoa FOIL .25 .07
8 F.Rodriguez FOIL .25 .07
9 Brian Anderson FOIL .40 .12
0 James Baldwin FOIL .25 .07
1 Manny Ramirez FOIL .60 .18
2 J.Thompson FOIL .25 .07
3 Johnny Damon FOIL 1.00 .30
4 Jeff D'Amico FOIL 1.00 .30
5 Rich Becker FOIL .25 .07
6 Derek Jeter FOIL 3.00 .90
7 Steve Karsay FOIL .25 .07
8 Mac Suzuki FOIL .40 .12
9 Benji Gil FOIL .25 .07
80 Alex Gonzalez FOIL .25 .07
81 Jason Bere FOIL .25 .07
82 Brett Butler FOIL .40 .12
83 Jeff Conine FOIL .40 .12
84 Darren Daulton FOIL .40 .12
85 Jeff Kent FOIL .40 .12
86 Don Mattingly FOIL 2.50 .75
87 Mike Piazza FOIL 2.00 .60
88 Ryne Sandberg FOIL 1.50 .45
89 Rich Amaral .25 .07
90 Craig Biggio .60 .18
91 Jeff Suppan RC 1.00 .30
92 Andy Benes .25 .07
93 Cal Eldred .25 .07
94 Jeff Conine .40 .12
95 Tim Salmon .60 .18
96 Ray Suplee RC .50 .15
97 Tony Phillips .25 .07
98 Ramon Martinez .25 .07
99 Julio Franco .40 .12
00 Dwight Gooden .40 .12
01 Kevin Lomon RC .50 .15
02 Jose Rijo .25 .07
03 Mike Devereaux .25 .07
04 Mike Zolecki RC .50 .15
05 Fred McGriff .60 .18
06 Danny Clyburn .25 .07
07 Robby Thompson .25 .07
08 Terry Steinbach .25 .07
09 Luis Polonia .25 .07
10 Mark Grace .60 .18
411 Albert Belle .40 .12
412 John Kruk .40 .12
413 Scott Spiezio RC 1.00 .30
414 Ellis Burks UER .40 .12
(Name spelled Elkis on front)
415 Joe Vitiello .25 .07
416 Tim Costo .25 .07
417 Marc Newfield .25 .07
418 Oscar Henriquez RC .50 .15
419 Matt Perisho RC .50 .15
420 Julio Bruno .25 .07
421 Kenny Felder .25 .07
422 Tyler Green .25 .07
423 Jim Edmonds 1.00 .30
424 Ozzie Smith 1.50 .45
425 Rick Greene .25 .07
426 Todd Hollandsworth .25 .07
427 Eddie Pearson RC .50 .15
428 Quilvio Veras .25 .07
429 Kenny Rogers .40 .12
430 Willie Greene .25 .07
431 Vaughn Eshelman .25 .07
432 Pat Meares .25 .07
433 Jermaine Dye RC 1.50 .45
434 Steve Cooke .25 .07
435 Bill Swift .25 .07
436 Fausto Cruz RC .50 .15
437 Mark Hutton .25 .07
438 B.Kieschnick RC 1.00 .30
439 Yorkis Perez .25 .07
440 Len Dykstra .40 .12
441 Pat Borders .25 .07
442 Doug Walls RC .50 .15
443 Wally Joyner .40 .12
444 Ken Hill .25 .07
445 Eric Anthony .25 .07
446 Mitch Williams .25 .07
447 Cory Bailey RC .50 .15
448 Dave Staton .25 .07
449 Greg Vaughn .25 .07
450 Dave Magadan .25 .07
451 Chili Davis .40 .12
452 Gerald Santos RC .50 .15
453 Joe Perona .25 .07
454 Delino DeShields .25 .07
455 Jack McDowell .25 .07
456 Todd Hundley .25 .07
457 Ritchie Moody .25 .07
458 Bret Boone .40 .12
459 Ben McDonald .25 .07
460 Kirby Puckett 1.00 .30
461 Gregg Olson .25 .07
462 Rich Aude RC .50 .15
463 John Burkett .25 .07
464 Troy Neel .25 .07
465 Jimmy Key .40 .12
466 Ozzie Timmons .25 .07
467 Eddie Murray 1.00 .30
468 Mark Tranberg RC .50 .15
469 Alex Gonzalez .25 .07
470 David Nied .25 .07
471 Barry Larkin .60 .18
472 Brian Looney RC .50 .15
473 Shawn Estes .25 .07
474 A.J. Sager RC .50 .15
475 Roger Clemens 2.00 .60
476 Vince Moore .25 .07
477 Scott Karl RC .50 .15
478 Kurt Miller .25 .07
479 Garret Anderson 1.00 .30
480 Allen Watson .25 .07
481 Jose Lima RC 2.50 .75
482 Rick Gorecki .25 .07
483 Jimmy Hurst RC .50 .15
484 Preston Wilson .40 .12
485 Will Clark 1.00 .30
486 Mike Ferry RC .50 .15
487 Curtis Goodwin RC .50 .15
488 Mike Myers .25 .07
489 Chipper Jones 1.00 .30
490 Jeff King .25 .07
491 W.VanLandingham RC .50 .15
492 Carlos Reyes RC .50 .15
493 Andy Pettitte 1.00 .30
494 Brant Brown .25 .07
495 Daron Kirkreit .25 .07
496 Ricky Bottalico RC 1.00 .30
497 Devon White .40 .12
498 Jason Johnson RC .50 .15
499 Vince Coleman .25 .07
500 Larry Walker .60 .18
501 Bobby Ayala .25 .07
502 Steve Finley .40 .12
503 Scott Fletcher .25 .07
504 Brad Ausmus .25 .07
505 Scott Talanoa RC .50 .15
506 Orestes Destrade .25 .07
507 Gary DiSarcina .25 .07
508 Willie Smith RC .50 .15
509 Alan Trammell .40 .12
510 Mike Piazza 2.00 .60
511 Ozzie Guillen .25 .07
512 Jeromy Burnitz .40 .12
513 Darren Oliver RC 1.00 .30
514 Kevin Mitchell .25 .07
515 Rafael Palmeiro .60 .18
516 David McCarty .25 .07
517 Jeff Blauser .25 .07
518 Trey Beamon .25 .07
519 Royce Clayton .25 .07
520 Dennis Eckersley .40 .12
521 Bernie Williams .60 .18
522 Steve Buechele .25 .07
523 Dennis Martinez .40 .12
524 Dave Hollins .25 .07
525 Joey Hamilton .25 .07
526 Andres Galarraga .40 .12
527 Jeff Granger .25 .07
528 Joey Eischen .25 .07
529 Desi Relaford .25 .07
530 Roberto Petagine .25 .07
531 Andre Dawson .40 .12
532 Ray Holbert .25 .07
533 Duane Singleton .25 .07
534 Kurt Abbott RC 1.00 .30
535 Bo Jackson 1.00 .30
536 Gregg Jefferies .25 .07
537 David Mysel .25 .07
538 Raul Mondesi .40 .12
539 Chris Snopek .25 .07
540 Brook Fordyce .25 .07
541 Ron Frazier RC .50 .15
542 Brian Koelling .25 .07
543 Jimmy Haynes .25 .07
544 Marty Cordova .25 .07
545 Jason Green RC .50 .15
546 Orlando Merced .25 .07
547 Lou Pote RC .50 .15
548 Todd Van Poppel .25 .07
549 Pat Kelly .25 .07
550 Turk Wendell .25 .07
551 Herbert Perry RC 1.00 .30
552 Ryan Karp RC .50 .15
553 Juan Guzman .25 .07
554 Bryan Rekar RC .50 .15
555 Kevin Appier .40 .12
556 Chris Schwab RC .50 .15
557 Jay Buhner .40 .12
558 Andujar Cedeno .25 .07
559 Ryan McGuire RC .50 .15
560 Ricky Gutierrez .25 .07
561 Keith Kimsey RC .50 .15
562 Tim Clark .25 .07
563 Damion Easley .25 .07
564 Clint Davis RC .50 .15
565 Mike Moore .25 .07
566 Orel Hershiser .40 .12
567 Jason Bere .25 .07
568 Kevin McReynolds .25 .07
569 Leland Macon RC .50 .15
570 John Courtright RC .50 .15
571 Sid Fernandez .25 .07
572 Chad Roper .25 .07
573 Terry Pendleton .40 .12
574 Danny Miceli .25 .07
575 Joe Rosselli .25 .07
576 Mike Bordick .25 .07
577 Danny Tartabull .25 .07
578 Jose Guzman .25 .07
579 Omar Vizquel .60 .18
580 Tommy Greene .25 .07
581 Paul Spoljaric .25 .07
582 Walt Weiss .25 .07
583 Oscar Jimenez RC .50 .15
584 Rod Henderson .25 .07
585 Derek Lowe .60 .18
586 Richard Hidalgo RC 1.50 .45
587 Shayne Bennett RC .50 .15
588 Tim Belk RC .50 .15
589 Matt Mieske .25 .07
590 Nigel Wilson .25 .07
591 Jeff Knox RC .50 .15
592 Bernard Gilkey .25 .07
593 David Cone .40 .12
594 Paul LoDuca RC 8.00 2.40
595 Scott Ruffcorn .25 .07
596 Chris Roberts .25 .07
597 Oscar Munoz RC .50 .15
598 Scott Sullivan RC .50 .15
599 Matt Jarvis RC .50 .15
600 Jose Canseco 1.00 .30
601 Tony Graffanino RC 1.00 .30
602 Don Slaught .25 .07
603 Brett King RC .50 .15
604 Jose Herrera RC .50 .15
605 Melido Perez .25 .07
606 Mike Hubbard RC .50 .15
607 Chad Ogea .25 .07
608 Wayne Gomes RC 1.00 .30
609 Roberto Alomar .60 .18
610 Angel Echevarria RC .50 .15
611 Jose Lind .25 .07
612 Darrin Fletcher .25 .07
613 Chris Bosio .25 .07
614 Darryl Kile .40 .12
615 Frankie Rodriguez .25 .07
616 Phil Plantier .25 .07
617 Pat Listach .25 .07
618 Charlie Hough .40 .12
619 Ryan Hancock RC .50 .15
620 Darrel Deak RC .50 .15
621 Travis Fryman .40 .12
622 Brett Butler .40 .12
623 Lance Johnson .25 .07
624 Pete Smith .25 .07
625 James Hurst RC .50 .15
626 Roberto Kelly .25 .07
627 Mike Mussina .60 .18
628 Kevin Tapani .25 .07
629 John Smoltz .60 .18
630 Midre Cummings .25 .07
631 Salomon Torres .25 .07
632 Willie Adams .25 .07
633 Derek Jeter 3.00 .90
634 Steve Trachsel .25 .07
635 Albie Lopez .25 .07
636 Jason Moler .25 .07
637 Carlos Delgado .60 .18
638 Roberto Mejia .25 .07
639 Darren Burton .25 .07
640 B.J. Wallace .25 .07
641 Brad Clontz RC .50 .15
642 Billy Wagner RC 2.50 .75
643 Aaron Sele .25 .07
644 Cameron Cairncross .25 .07
645 Brian Harper .25 .07
646 Marc Valdes UER .25 .07
(No card number on back)
647 Mark Ratekin .25 .07
648 Terry Bradshaw RC .50 .15
649 Justin Thompson .25 .07
650 Mike Busch RC .50 .15
651 Joe Hall RC .50 .15
652 Bobby Jones .25 .07
653 Kelly Stinnett RC 1.00 .30
654 Rod Steph RC .50 .15
655 Jay Powell RC 1.00 .30
656 K.Garagozzo RC UER .50 .15
No card number on back
657 Todd Dunn .25 .07
658 Charles Peterson RC .50 .15
659 Darren Lewis .25 .07
660 John Wasdin RC .50 .15
661 Tate Seefried RC .50 .15
662 Hector Trinidad RC .50 .15
663 John Carter RC .25 .07
664 Larry Mitchell .25 .07
665 David Catlett RC .50 .15
666 Dante Bichette .40 .12
667 Felix Jose .25 .07
668 Rondell White .40 .12
669 Tino Martinez .60 .18
670 Brian L. Hunter .25 .07
671 Jose Malave .25 .07
672 Archi Cianfrocco .25 .07
673 Mike Matheny RC 5.00 1.50
674 Bret Barberie .25 .07
675 Andrew Lorraine RC .50 .15
676 Brian Jordan .40 .12
677 Tim Belcher .25 .07
678 Antonio Osuna RC .50 .15
679 Checklist .25 .07
680 Checklist .25 .07
681 Checklist .25 .07
682 Checklist .25 .07

1995 Bowman

Cards from this 439-card standard-size prospect-oriented set were primarily issued in plastic wrapped packs and jumbo packs. Card fronts feature white borders enframing full color photos. The left border is a reversed negative of the photo. The set includes 54 silver foil subset cards (221-274). The foil subset, largely comprising of minor league stars, have embossed borders and are found one per pack and two per jumbo pack. Rookie Cards of note include Bob Abreu, Bartolo Colon, Vladmir Guerrero, Andruw Jones, Hideo Nomo and Scott Rolen.

	Nm-Mt	Ex-Mt
COMPLETE SET (439)	150.00	45.00
1 Billy Wagner	.50	.15
2 Chris Widger	.25	.07
3 Brent Bowers	.25	.07
4 Bob Abreu RC	6.00	1.80
5 Lou Collier RC	1.00	.30
6 Juan Acevedo RC	.50	.15
7 Jason Kelley RC	.50	.15
8 Brian Sackinsky	.25	.07
9 Scott Christman	.25	.07
10 Damon Hollins	.25	.07
11 Willis Otanez RC	.50	.15
12 Jason Ryan RC	.50	.15
13 Jason Giambi	.75	.23
14 Andy Taulbee RC	.50	.15
15 Mark Thompson	.25	.07
16 Hugo Pivaral RC	.50	.15
17 Brien Taylor	.25	.07
18 Antonio Osuna	.25	.07
19 Edgardo Alfonzo	.50	.15
20 Carl Everett	.50	.15
21 Matt Drews	.25	.07
22 Bartolo Colon RC	3.00	.90
23 Andruw Jones RC	20.00	6.00
24 Robert Person RC	1.00	.30
25 Derrek Lee	.50	.15
26 John Ambrose RC	.50	.15
27 Eric Knowles RC	.50	.15
28 Chris Roberts	.25	.07
29 Don Wengert	.25	.07
30 Marcus Jensen RC	1.00	.30
31 Brian Barber	.25	.07
32 Kevin Brown C	.50	.15
33 Benji Gil	.25	.07
34 Mike Hubbard	.25	.07
35 Bart Evans RC	.50	.15
36 Enrique Wilson RC	.50	.15
37 Brian Buchanan RC	1.00	.30
38 Ken Ray RC	.50	.15
39 Micah Franklin RC	.50	.15
40 Ricky Otero RC	.50	.15
41 Jason Kendall	.50	.15
42 Jimmy Hurst	.25	.07
43 Jerry Wolak RC	.50	.15
44 Jayson Peterson RC	.50	.15
45 Allen Battle RC	.50	.15
46 Scott Stahoviak	.25	.07
47 Steve Schrenk RC	.50	.15
48 Travis Miller RC	.50	.15
49 Eddie Rios RC	.50	.15
50 Mike Hampton	.50	.15
51 Chad Frontera RC	.50	.15
52 Tom Evans	.25	.07
53 C.J. Nitkowski	.25	.07
54 Clay Caruthers RC	.50	.15
55 Shannon Stewart	.50	.15
56 Jorge Posada	1.25	.35
57 Aaron Holbert	.25	.07
58 Harry Berrios RC	.50	.15
59 Steve Rodriguez	.25	.07
60 Shane Andrews	.25	.07
61 Will Cunnane RC	.50	.15
62 Richard Hidalgo	.25	.07
63 Bill Selby RC	.50	.15
64 Jay Cranford RC	.50	.15
65 Jeff Suppan	.25	.07
66 Curtis Goodwin	.25	.07
67 John Thomson RC	1.00	.30
68 Justin Thompson	.25	.07
69 Troy Percival	.50	.15
70 Matt Wagner RC	.50	.15
71 Terry Bradshaw	.25	.07
72 Greg Hansell	.25	.07
73 John Burke	.25	.07
74 Jeff D'Amico	.25	.07
75 Ernie Young	.25	.07
76 Jason Bates	.25	.07
77 Chris Stynes	.25	.07
78 Cade Gaspar RC	.50	.15
79 Melvin Nieves	.25	.07
80 Rick Gorecki	.25	.07
81 Felix Rodriguez RC	1.00	.30
82 Ryan Hancock	.25	.07
83 Chris Carpenter RC	2.00	.60
84 Ray McDavid	.25	.07
85 Chris Wimmer	.25	.07
86 Doug Glanville	.25	.07
87 DeShawn Warren	.25	.07
88 Damian Moss RC	1.00	.30
89 Rafael Orellano RC	.50	.15
90 Vladimir Guerrero RC	50.00	15.00
91 Raul Casanova RC	.50	.15
92 Karim Garcia RC	1.00	.30
93 Bryce Florie	.25	.07
94 Kevin Orie	.25	.07
95 Ryan Nye RC	.50	.15
96 Matt Sachse RC	.50	.15
97 Ivan Arteaga RC	.50	.15
98 Glenn Murray	.25	.07
99 Stacy Hollins RC	.50	.15
100 Jim Pittsley	.25	.07
101 Craig Mattson RC	.50	.15
102 Neifi Perez	.25	.07
103 Keith Williams	.25	.07
104 Roger Cedeno	.25	.07
105 Tony Terry RC	.50	.15
106 Jose Malave	.25	.07
107 Joe Rosselli	.25	.07
108 Kevin Jordan	.25	.07
109 Sid Roberson RC	.50	.15
110 Alan Embree	.25	.07
111 Terrell Wade	.25	.07
112 Bob Wolcott	.25	.07
113 Carlos Perez RC	1.00	.30
114 Mike Bovee RC	.50	.15
115 Tommy Davis RC	.50	.15
116 Jeremey Kendall RC	.50	.15
117 Rich Aude	.25	.07
118 Rick Huisman	.25	.07
119 Tim Belk	.25	.07
120 Edgar Renteria	1.25	.23
121 Calvin Maduro RC	.50	.15
122 Jerry Martin RC	.50	.15
123 Ramon Fermin RC	.50	.15
124 Kimera Bartee RC	.50	.15
125 Mark Farris	.25	.07
126 Frank Rodriguez	.25	.07
127 Bobby Higginson RC	2.00	.60
128 Bret Wagner	.25	.07
129 Edwin Diaz RC	.50	.15
130 Jimmy Haynes	.25	.07
131 Chris Weinke RC	1.00	.30
132 Damian Jackson RC	1.00	.30
133 Felix Martinez	.25	.07
134 Edwin Hurtado RC	.50	.15
135 Matt Raleigh RC	.50	.15
136 Paul Wilson	.25	.07
137 Ron Villone	.25	.07
138 E.Stuckenschneider RC	.50	.15
139 Tate Seefried	.25	.07
140 Rey Ordonez RC	2.00	.60
141 Eddie Pearson	.25	.07
142 Kevin Gallaher	.25	.07
143 Torii Hunter	.75	.23
144 Daron Kirkreit	.25	.07
145 Craig Wilson	.25	.07
146 Ugueth Urbina	.25	.07
147 Chris Snopek	.25	.07
148 Kym Ashworth	.25	.07
149 Wayne Gomes	.25	.07
150 Mark Loretta	.50	.15
151 Ramon Morel RC	.50	.15
152 Trot Nixon	.50	.15
153 Desi Relaford	.25	.07
154 Scott Sullivan	.25	.07
155 Marc Barcelo	.25	.07
156 Willie Adams	.25	.07
157 Derrick Gibson RC	.50	.15
158 Brian Meadows RC	.50	.15
159 Julian Tavarez	.25	.07
160 Bryan Rekar	.25	.07
161 Steve Gibralter	.25	.07
162 Esteban Loaiza	.25	.07
163 John Wasdin	.25	.07
164 Kirk Presley	.25	.07
165 Mariano Rivera	.75	.23
166 Andy Larkin	.25	.07
167 Sean Whiteside RC	.50	.15
168 Matt Apana RC	.50	.15
169 Shawn Senior RC	.50	.15
170 Scott Gentile	.25	.07
171 Quilvio Veras	.25	.07
172 Eli Marrero RC	1.50	.45
173 Mendy Lopez RC	.50	.15
174 Homer Bush	.25	.07
175 Brian Stephenson RC	.50	.15
176 Jon Nunnally	.25	.07
177 Jose Herrera	.25	.07
178 Corey Avrard RC	.50	.15
179 David Bell	.25	.07
180 Jason Isringhausen	.50	.15
181 Jamey Wright	.25	.07
182 Lonell Roberts RC	.25	.07
183 Marty Cordova	.25	.07
184 Amaury Telemaco	.25	.07
185 John Mabry	.25	.07
186 Andrew Vessel RC	.50	.15
187 Jim Cole RC	.50	.15
188 Marquis Riley	.25	.07
189 Todd Dunn	.25	.07
190 John Carter	.25	.07
191 Donnie Sadler RC	1.00	.30
192 Mike Bell	.25	.07
193 Chris Cumberland RC	.50	.15
194 Jason Schmidt	1.25	.35
195 Matt Brunson	.25	.07
196 James Baldwin	.25	.07
197 Bill Simas RC	.50	.15
198 Gus Gandarillas	.25	.07
199 Mac Suzuki	.25	.07
200 Rick Holifield RC	.50	.15
201 Fernando Lunar RC	.50	.15
202 Kevin Jarvis	.25	.07
203 Everett Stull	.25	.07
204 Steve Wojciechowski	.25	.07
205 Shawn Estes	.25	.07
206 Jermaine Dye	.50	.15
207 Marc Kroon	.25	.07
208 Peter Munro RC	1.00	.30
209 Pat Watkins	.25	.07
210 Matt Smith	.25	.07
211 Joe Vitiello	.25	.07
212 Gerald Witasick Jr.	.25	.07
213 Freddy A. Garcia RC	.50	.15
214 Glenn Dishman RC	.50	.15
215 Jay Canizaro RC	.50	.15
216 Angel Martinez	.25	.07

217 Yamil Benitez RC .50 .15
218 Fausto Macey RC .50 .15
219 Eric Owens .25 .07
220 Checklist .25 .07
221 D.Hosey FOIL RC .50 .15
222 B.Woodall FOIL RC .50 .15
223 Billy Ashley FOIL .25 .07
224 M.Grudzielanek FOIL RC 1.00 .30
225 M.Johnson FOIL RC 1.00 .30
226 Tim Unroe FOIL RC .50 .15
227 Todd Greene FOIL .25 .07
228 Larry Sutton FOIL .25 .07
229 Derek Jeter FOIL 4.00 1.20
230 Sal Fasano FOIL RC .50 .15
231 Ruben Rivera FOIL .25 .07
232 Chris Truby FOIL RC .50 .15
233 John Donati FOIL .25 .07
234 D.Conner FOIL RC .50 .15
235 Sergio Nunez FOIL RC .50 .15
236 Ray Brown FOIL RC .50 .15
237 Juan Melo FOIL RC .50 .15
238 Hideo Nomo FOIL RC 5.00 1.50
239 Jamie Bluma RC FOIL .50 .15
240 Jay Payton FOIL RC 2.00 .60
241 Paul Konerko FOIL 1.00 .30
242 Scott Elarton FOIL RC 1.00 .30
243 Jeff Abbott FOIL RC 1.00 .30
244 Jim Brower FOIL RC .50 .15
245 Geoff Blum FOIL RC 1.00 .30
246 Aaron Boone FOIL RC 2.00 .60
247 J.R. Phillips FOIL .25 .07
248 Alex Ochoa FOIL .25 .07
249 N.Garciaparra FOIL 8.00 2.40
250 Garret Anderson FOIL .50 .15
251 Ray Durham FOIL .50 .15
252 Paul Shuey FOIL .25 .07
253 Tony Clark FOIL .25 .07
254 Johnny Damon FOIL .75 .23
255 Duane Singleton FOIL .25 .07
256 LaTroy Hawkins FOIL .25 .07
257 Andy Pettitte FOIL .75 .23
258 Ben Grieve FOIL .50 .15
259 Marc Newfield FOIL .25 .07
260 Terrell Lowery FOIL .25 .07
261 Shawn Green FOIL .50 .15
262 Chipper Jones FOIL 1.25 .35
263 B.Kieschnick FOIL .25 .07
264 Pokey Reese FOIL .25 .07
265 Doug Million FOIL .25 .07
266 Marc Valdes FOIL .25 .07
267 Brian L.Hunter FOIL .25 .07
268 T.Hollandsworth FOIL .25 .07
269 Rod Henderson FOIL .25 .07
270 Bill Pulsipher FOIL .25 .07
271 Scott Rolen FOIL RC 25.00 7.50
272 Trey Beamon FOIL .25 .07
273 Alan Benes FOIL .25 .07
274 D.Hermanson FOIL .25 .07
275 Ricky Bottalico .25 .07
276 Albert Belle .50 .15
277 Deion Sanders .75 .23
278 Matt Williams .50 .15
279 Jeff Bagwell .75 .23
280 Kirby Puckett 1.25 .35
281 Dave Hollins .25 .07
282 Don Mattingly 3.00 .90
283 Joey Hamilton .25 .07
284 Bobby Bonilla .50 .15
285 Moises Alou .50 .15
286 Tom Glavine .75 .23
287 Brett Butler .50 .15
288 Chris Hoiles .25 .07
289 Kenny Rogers .50 .15
290 Larry Walker .75 .23
291 Tim Raines .50 .15
292 Kevin Appier .50 .15
293 Roger Clemens 2.50 .75
294 Chuck Carr .25 .07
295 Randy Myers .25 .07
296 Dave Nilsson .25 .07
297 Joe Carter .50 .15
298 Chuck Finley .50 .15
299 Ray Lankford .25 .07
300 Roberto Kelly .25 .07
301 Jon Lieber .25 .07
302 Travis Fryman .50 .15
303 Mark McGwire 3.00 .90
304 Tony Gwynn 1.50 .45
305 Kenny Lofton .50 .15
306 Mark Whiten .25 .07
307 Doug Drabek .25 .07
308 Terry Steinbach .25 .07
309 Ryan Klesko .50 .15
310 Mike Piazza 2.00 .60
311 Ben McDonald .25 .07
312 Reggie Sanders .25 .07
313 Alex Fernandez .25 .07
314 Aaron Sele .25 .07
315 Gregg Jefferies .25 .07
316 Rickey Henderson 1.25 .35
317 Brian Anderson .25 .07
318 Jose Valentin .25 .07
319 Rod Beck .25 .07
320 Marquis Grissom .50 .15
321 Ken Griffey Jr. 2.00 .60
322 Bret Saberhagen .50 .15
323 Juan Gonzalez .75 .23
324 Paul Molitor .75 .23
325 Gary Sheffield .50 .15
326 Darren Daulton .50 .15
327 Bill Swift .25 .07
328 Brian McRae .25 .07
329 Robin Ventura .50 .15
330 Lee Smith .50 .15
331 Fred McGriff .75 .23
332 Delino DeShields .25 .07
333 Edgar Martinez .75 .23
334 Mike Mussina .75 .23
335 Orlando Merced .25 .07
336 Carlos Baerga .25 .07
337 Wil Cordero .25 .07
338 Tom Pagnozzi .25 .07
339 Pat Hentgen .25 .07
340 Chad Curtis .25 .07
341 Darren Lewis .25 .07
342 Jeff Kent .50 .15
343 Bip Roberts .25 .07
344 Ivan Rodriguez 1.25 .35
345 Jeff Montgomery .25 .07
346 Hal Morris .25 .07
347 Danny Tartabull .25 .07
348 Raul Mondesi .50 .15
349 Ken Hill .25 .07
350 Pedro Martinez 1.25 .35
351 Frank Thomas 1.25 .35
352 Manny Ramirez .75 .23
353 Tim Salmon .75 .23
354 W. VanLandingham .25 .07
355 Andres Galarraga .50 .15
356 Paul O'Neill .75 .23
357 Brady Anderson .50 .15
358 Ramon Martinez .25 .07
359 John Olerud .50 .15
360 Ruben Sierra .25 .07
361 Cal Eldred .25 .07
362 Jay Buhner .50 .15
363 Jay Bell .50 .15
364 Wally Joyner .50 .15
365 Chuck Knoblauch .50 .15
366 Len Dykstra .50 .15
367 John Wetteland .50 .15
368 Roberto Alomar .75 .23
369 Craig Biggio .75 .23
370 Ozzie Smith 2.00 .60
371 Terry Pendleton .50 .15
372 Sammy Sosa 2.00 .60
373 Carlos Garcia .25 .07
374 Jose Rijo .25 .07
375 Chris Gomez .25 .07
376 Barry Bonds 3.00 .90
377 Steve Avery .25 .07
378 Rick Wilkins .25 .07
379 Pete Harnisch .25 .07
380 Dean Palmer .50 .15
381 Bob Hamelin .25 .07
382 Jason Bere .25 .07
383 Jimmy Key .50 .15
384 Dante Bichette .50 .15
385 Rafael Palmeiro .75 .23
386 David Justice .50 .15
387 Chili Davis .50 .15
388 Mike Greenwell .25 .07
389 Todd Zeile .25 .07
390 Jeff Conine .50 .15
391 Rick Aguilera .25 .07
392 Eddie Murray 1.25 .35
393 Mike Stanley .25 .07
394 Cliff Floyd UER .50 .15
(numbered 294)
395 Randy Johnson 1.25 .35
396 David Nied .25 .07
397 Devon White .50 .15
398 Royce Clayton .25 .07
399 Andy Benes .25 .07
400 John Hudek .25 .07
401 Bobby Jones .25 .07
402 Eric Karros .50 .15
403 Will Clark 1.25 .35
404 Mark Langston .25 .07
405 Kevin Brown .50 .15
406 Greg Maddux 2.00 .60
407 David Cone .50 .15
408 Wade Boggs .75 .23
409 Steve Trachsel .25 .07
410 Greg Vaughn .25 .07
411 Mo Vaughn .50 .15
412 Wilson Alvarez .25 .07
413 Cal Ripken 4.00 1.20
414 Rico Brogna .25 .07
415 Barry Larkin .75 .23
416 Cecil Fielder .50 .15
417 Jose Canseco 1.25 .35
418 Jack McDowell .25 .07
419 Mike Lieberthal .50 .15
420 Andrew Lorraine .25 .07
421 Rich Becker .25 .07
422 Tony Phillips .25 .07
423 Scott Ruffcorn .25 .07
424 Jeff Granger .25 .07
425 Greg Pirkl .25 .07
426 Dennis Eckersley .50 .15
427 Jose Lima .25 .07
428 Russ Davis .25 .07
429 Armando Benitez .50 .15
430 Alex Gonzalez .25 .07
431 Carlos Delgado .50 .15
432 Chan Ho Park .50 .15
433 Mickey Tettleton .25 .07
434 Dave Winfield .50 .15
435 John Burkett .25 .07
436 Orlando Miller .25 .07
437 Rondell White .50 .15
438 Jose Oliva .25 .07
439 Checklist .25 .07

1995 Bowman Gold Foil

Numbered 221-274, this 54-card standard-size set is the gold insert parallel version of the silver foil subset found in the basic issue. The odds of finding a gold foil version are one in six packs.

Nm-Mt Ex-Mt
COMPLETE SET (54) 150.00 45.00
*STARS: .6X TO 1.5X BASIC CARDS..
*ROOKIES: .5X TO 1.2X BASIC.

1996 Bowman

The 1996 Bowman set was issued in one series totalling 385 cards. The 11-card packs retailed for $2.50 each. The fronts feature color action player photos in a tan-checkered frame with the player's name printed in silver foil at the bottom. The backs carry another color player photo with player information, 1995 and career player statistics. Each pack contained 10 regular issue cards plus either one foil parallel or an insert card. In a special promotional program, Topps offered collector's a $100 guarantee on complete sets. To get the guarantee, collectors had to mail in a Guaranteed Value Certificate request form, found in packs, along with a $5 processing and registration fee before the December 31st, 1996 deadline. Collectors would then receive a $100 Guaranteed Value Certificate, of which they could mail back to Topps between August 31st, 1999 and December 31st, 1999, along with their complete set, to receive $100. A reprint version of the 1952 Bowman Mickey Mantle card was randomly inserted into packs. Rookie Cards in this set include Russell Branyan, Mike Cameron, Luis Castillo, Ryan Dempster, Livan Hernandez, Geoff Jenkins, Ben Petrick and Mike Sweeney

Nm-Mt Ex-Mt
COMPLETE SET (385) 60.00 18.00
1 Cal Ripken 2.50 .75
2 Ray Durham .30 .09
3 Ivan Rodriguez .75 .23
4 Fred McGriff .50 .15
5 Hideo Nomo .75 .23
6 Troy Percival .30 .09
7 Moises Alou .30 .09
8 Mike Stanley .30 .09
9 Jay Buhner .30 .09
10 Shawn Green .30 .09
11 Ryan Klesko .30 .09
12 Andres Galarraga .30 .09
13 Dean Palmer .30 .09
14 Jeff Conine .30 .09
15 Brian L.Hunter .30 .09
16 J.T. Snow .30 .09
17 Larry Walker .50 .15
18 Barry Larkin .50 .15
19 Alex Gonzalez .30 .09
20 Edgar Martinez .50 .15
21 Mo Vaughn .30 .09
22 Mark McGwire 2.00 .60
23 Jose Canseco .75 .23
24 Jack McDowell .30 .09
25 Dante Bichette .30 .09
26 Wade Boggs .50 .15
27 Mike Piazza 1.25 .35
28 Ray Lankford .30 .09
29 Craig Biggio .50 .15
30 Rafael Palmeiro .50 .15
31 Ron Gant .30 .09
32 Javy Lopez .30 .09
33 Brian Jordan .30 .09
34 Paul O'Neill .50 .15
35 Mark Grace .50 .15
36 Matt Williams .30 .09
37 Pedro Martinez UER .75 .23
Wrong birthdate
38 Rickey Henderson .75 .23
39 Bobby Bonilla .30 .09
40 Todd Hollandsworth .30 .09
41 Jim Thome .75 .23
42 Gary Sheffield .75 .23
43 Tim Salmon .50 .15
44 Gregg Jefferies .30 .09
45 Roberto Alomar .50 .15
46 Carlos Baerga .30 .09
47 Mark Grudzielanek .30 .09
48 Randy Johnson .75 .23
49 Tino Martinez .50 .15
50 Robin Ventura .30 .09
51 Ryne Sandberg 1.25 .35
52 Jay Bell .30 .09
53 Jason Schmidt .50 .15
54 Frank Thomas .75 .23
55 Kenny Lofton .30 .09
56 Ariel Prieto .30 .09
57 David Cone .30 .09
58 Reggie Sanders .30 .09
59 Michael Tucker .30 .09
60 Vinny Castilla .30 .09
61 Len Dykstra .30 .09
62 Todd Hundley .30 .09
63 Brian McRae .30 .09
64 Dennis Eckersley .30 .09
65 Rondell White .30 .09
66 Eric Karros .30 .09
67 Greg Maddux 1.25 .35
68 Kevin Appier .30 .09
69 Eddie Murray .75 .23
70 John Olerud .30 .09
71 Tony Gwynn 1.00 .30
72 David Justice .30 .09
73 Ken Caminiti .30 .09
74 Terry Steinbach .30 .09
75 Alan Benes .30 .09
76 Chipper Jones .75 .23
77 Jeff Bagwell .50 .15
78 Barry Bonds 2.00 .60
79 Ken Griffey Jr. 1.50 .45
80 Roger Cedeno .30 .09
81 Joe Carter .30 .09
82 Henry Rodriguez .30 .09
83 Jason Isringhausen .30 .09
84 Chuck Knoblauch .30 .09
85 Manny Ramirez .50 .15
86 Tom Glavine .50 .15
87 Jeffrey Hammonds .30 .09
88 Paul Molitor .50 .15
89 Roger Clemens 1.50 .45
90 Greg Vaughn .30 .09
91 Marty Cordova .30 .09
92 Albert Belle .30 .09
93 Mike Mussina .50 .15
94 Garret Anderson .30 .09
95 Juan Gonzalez .50 .15
96 John Valentin .30 .09
97 Jason Giambi .30 .09
98 Kirby Puckett .75 .23
99 Jim Edmonds .30 .09
100 Cecil Fielder .30 .09
101 Mike Aldrete .30 .09
102 Marquis Grissom .30 .09
103 Derek Bell .30 .09
104 Raul Mondesi .30 .09
105 Sammy Sosa 1.25 .35
106 Travis Fryman .30 .09
107 Rico Brogna .30 .09
108 Will Clark .75 .23
109 Bernie Williams .50 .15
110 Brady Anderson .30 .09
111 Torii Hunter .30 .09
112 Derek Jeter 2.00 .60
113 Mike Kusiewicz RC .50 .15
114 Scott Rolen .75 .23
115 Ramon Castro .30 .09
116 Jose Guillen RC 3.00 .90
117 Wade Walker RC .50 .15
118 Shawn Senior .30 .09
119 Onan Masaoka RC .75 .23
120 Marlon Anderson RC 1.25 .35
121 Katsuhiro Maeda RC .75 .23
122 G.Stephenson RC .75 .23
123 Butch Huskey .30 .09
124 D'Angelo Jimenez RC 1.25 .35
125 Tony Mounce RC .50 .15
126 Jay Canizaro .30 .09
127 Juan Melo .30 .09
128 Steve Gibralter .30 .09
129 Freddy Garcia .30 .09
130 Julio Santana UER .30 .09
Card has him born in 1993
131 Richard Hidalgo .30 .09
132 Jermaine Dye .30 .09
133 Willie Adams .30 .09
134 Everett Stull .30 .09
135 Ramon Morel .30 .09
136 Chan Ho Park .30 .09
137 Jamey Wright .30 .09
138 Luis R.Garcia RC .50 .15
139 Dan Serafini .30 .09
140 Ryan Dempster RC 1.25 .35
141 Tate Seefried .30 .09
142 Jimmy Hurst .30 .09
143 Travis Miller .30 .09
144 Curtis Goodwin .30 .09
145 Rocky Coppinger RC .50 .15
146 Enrique Wilson .30 .09
147 Jaime Bluma .30 .09
148 Andrew Vessel .30 .09
149 Damian Moss .30 .09
150 Shawn Gallagher RC .50 .15
151 Pat Watkins .30 .09
152 Jose Paniagua .30 .09
153 Danny Graves .30 .09
154 Bryon Gainey RC .50 .15
155 Steve Soderstrom .30 .09
156 Cliff Brumbaugh RC .50 .15
157 Eugene Kingsale RC .75 .23
158 Lou Collier .30 .09
159 Todd Walker .30 .09
160 Kris Detmers RC .50 .15
161 Josh Booty RC .75 .23
162 Greg Whiteman RC .50 .15
163 Damian Jackson .30 .09
164 Tony Clark .30 .09
165 Jeff D'Amico .30 .09
166 Johnny Damon .50 .15
167 Rafael Orellano .30 .09
168 Ruben Rivera .30 .09
169 Alex Ochoa .30 .09
170 Jay Powell .30 .09
171 Tom Evans .30 .09
172 Ron Villone .30 .09
173 Shawn Estes .30 .09
174 John Wasdin .30 .09
175 Bill Simas .30 .09
176 Kevin Brown .30 .09
177 Shannon Stewart .30 .09
178 Todd Greene .30 .09
179 Bob Wolcott .30 .09
180 Chris Snopek .30 .09
181 Nomar Garciaparra 1.50 .45
182 Cameron Smith RC .50 .15
183 Matt Drews .30 .09
184 Jimmy Haynes .30 .09
185 Chris Carpenter .30 .09
186 Desi Relaford .30 .09
187 Ben Grieve .30 .09
188 Mike Bell .30 .09
189 Luis Castillo RC 2.00 .60
190 Ugueth Urbina .30 .09
191 Paul Wilson .30 .09
192 Andruw Jones .75 .23
193 Wayne Gomes .30 .09
194 Craig Counsell RC 1.25 .35
195 Jim Cole .30 .09
196 Brooks Kieschnick .30 .09
197 Trey Beamon .30 .09
198 Marino Santana RC .50 .15
199 Bob Abreu .30 .09
200 Pokey Reese .30 .09
201 Dante Powell .30 .09
202 George Arias .30 .09
203 Jorge Velandia RC .50 .15
204 George Lombard RC .50 .15
205 Byron Browne RC .50 .15
206 John Frascatore .30 .09
207 Terry Adams .30 .09
208 Wilson Delgado RC .50 .15
209 Billy McMillon .30 .09
210 Jeff Abbott .30 .09
211 Trot Nixon .30 .09
212 Amaury Telemaco .30 .09
213 Scott Sullivan .30 .09
214 Justin Thompson .30 .09
215 Decomba Conner .30 .09
216 Ryan McGuire .30 .09
217 Matt Luke .30 .09
218 Doug Million .30 .09
219 Jason Dickson RC .50 .15
220 Ramon Hernandez RC 1.25 .35
221 Mark Bellhorn RC 4.00 1.20
222 Eric Ludwick RC .50 .15
223 Luke Wilcox RC .50 .15
224 Marty Malloy RC .50 .15
225 Gary Coffee RC .50 .15
226 Wendell Magee RC .50 .15
227 Brett Tomko RC .75 .23
228 Derek Lowe .30 .09
229 Jose Rosado RC .50 .15
230 Steve Bourgeois RC .50 .15
231 Neil Weber RC .50 .15
232 Jeff Ware .30 .09
233 Edwin Diaz .30 .09
234 Greg Norton .30 .09
235 Aaron Boone .30 .09
236 Jeff Suppan .30 .09
237 Bret Wagner .30 .09
238 Elieser Marrero .30 .09
239 Will Cunnane .30 .09
240 Brian Barkley RC .50 .15
241 Jay Payton .30 .09
242 Marcus Jensen .30 .09
243 Ryan Nye .30 .09
244 Chad Mottola .30 .09
245 Scott McClain RC .50 .15
246 Jessie Ibarra RC .50 .15
247 Mike Darr RC .75 .23
248 Bobby Estalella RC .75 .23
249 Michael Barrett .30 .09
250 Jamie Lopiccolo RC .50 .15
251 Shane Spencer RC 1.25 .35
252 Ben Petrick RC .50 .15
253 Jason Bell RC .50 .15
254 Arnold Gooch RC .50 .15
255 T.J. Mathews .30 .09
256 Jason Ryan .30 .09
257 Pat Cline RC .50 .15
258 Rafael Carmona RC .50 .15
259 Carl Pavano RC 10.00 1.20
260 Ben Davis .30 .09
261 Matt Lawton RC 1.25 .35
262 Kevin Sefcik RC .50 .15
263 Chris Fussell RC .50 .15
264 Mike Cameron RC 2.00 .60
265 Marty Janzen RC .50 .15
266 Livan Hernandez RC 1.25 .35
267 Raul Ibanez RC 1.25 .35
268 Juan Encarnacion .30 .09
269 David Yocum RC .50 .15
270 Jonathan Johnson RC .50 .15
271 Reggie Taylor .30 .09
272 Danny Buxbaum RC .50 .15
273 Jacob Cruz .30 .09
274 Bobby Morris RC .50 .15
275 Andy Fox RC .50 .15
276 Greg Keagle .30 .09
277 Charles Peterson .30 .09
278 Derrek Lee .50 .15
279 Bryant Nelson RC .50 .15
280 Antone Williamson .30 .09
281 Scott Elarton .30 .09
282 Shad Williams RC .50 .15
283 Rich Hunter RC .50 .15
284 Chris Sheff .30 .09
285 Derrick Gibson .30 .09
286 Felix Rodriguez .30 .09
287 Brian Banks RC .50 .15
288 Jason McDonald .30 .09
289 Glendon Rusch RC .75 .23
290 Gary Rath .30 .09
291 Peter Munro .30 .09
292 Tom Fordham .30 .09
293 Jason Kendall .30 .09
294 Russ Johnson .30 .09
295 Joe Long .30 .09
296 Robert Smith RC .75 .23
297 Jarrod Washburn RC 1.25 .35
298 Dave Coggin RC .50 .15
299 Jeff Yoder RC .50 .15
300 Jed Hansen RC .50 .15
301 Matt Morris RC 3.00 .90
302 Josh Bishop RC .50 .15
303 Dustin Hermanson .30 .09
304 Mike Gulan .30 .09
305 Felipe Crespo .30 .09
306 Quinton McCracken .30 .09
307 Jim Bonnici RC .50 .15
308 Sal Fasano .30 .09
309 Gabe Alvarez RC .50 .15
310 Heath Murray RC .50 .15
311 Javier Valentin RC .50 .15
312 Bartolo Colon .30 .09
313 Olmedo Saenz .30 .09
314 Norm Hutchins RC .50 .15
315 Chris Holt .30 .09
316 David Doster RC .50 .15
317 Robert Person .30 .09
318 Donne Wall RC .30 .09
319 Adam Riggs RC .50 .15
320 Homer Bush .30 .09
321 Brad Rigby RC .50 .15
322 Lou Merloni RC .75 .23
323 Neifi Perez .30 .09
324 Chris Cumberland .30 .09
325 Alvie Shepherd RC .50 .15
326 Jarrod Patterson RC .50 .15
327 Ray Ricken RC .50 .15
328 Danny Klassen RC .50 .15
329 David Miller RC .50 .15
330 Chad Alexander RC .50 .15
331 Matt Beaumont .30 .09
332 Damon Hollins .30 .09
333 Todd Dunn .30 .09
334 Mike Sweeney RC 3.00 .90
335 Richie Sexson .30 .09
336 Billy Wagner .30 .09
337 Ron Wright RC .50 .15
338 Paul Konerko .30 .09
339 Tommy Phelps RC .50 .15
340 Karim Garcia .30 .09
341 Mike Grace RC .50 .15
342 Russell Branyan RC .75 .23
343 Randy Winn RC 1.25 .35
344 A.J. Pierzynski RC 2.00 .60
345 Mike Busby RC .50 .15
346 Matt Beech RC .50 .15
347 Jose Cepeda RC .50 .15
348 Brian Stephenson .30 .09
349 Rey Ordonez .30 .09
350 Rich Aurilla RC 1.25 .35
351 Edgard Velazquez RC .50 .15
352 Raul Casanova .30 .09
353 Carlos Guillen RC 4.00 1.20
354 Bruce Aven RC .50 .15
355 Ryan Jones RC .50 .15
356 Derek Aucoin RC .50 .15
357 Brian Rose RC .50 .15
358 Richard Almanzar RC .50 .15
359 Fletcher Bates RC .50 .15
360 Russ Ortiz RC 3.00 .90
361 Wilton Guerrero RC .75 .23
362 Geoff Jenkins RC 2.00 .60
363 Pete Janicki .30 .09
364 Yamil Benitez .30 .09
365 Aaron Holbert .30 .09
366 Tim Belk .30 .09
367 Terrell Wade .30 .09
368 Terrence Long .30 .09
369 Brad Fullmer .30 .09
370 Matt Wagner .30 .09

1 Craig Wilson RC .50 .15
2 Mark Loretta .30 .09
3 Eric Owens .30 .09
4 Vladimir Guerrero 1.50 .45
5 Tommy Davis .30 .09
6 Donnie Sadler .30 .09
7 Edgar Renteria .30 .09
8 Todd Helton 1.50 .45
9 Ralph Milliard RC .50 .15
0 Darin Blood RC .50 .15
1 Shayne Bennett .30 .09
2 Mark Redman .30 .09
3 Felix Martinez .30 .09
4 Sean Watkins RC .50 .15
5 Oscar Henriquez .30 .09
0 Mickey Mantle 5.00 1.50
1952 Bowman Reprint
0 Checklists .30 .09

1996 Bowman Foil

ese parallel foil cards were seeded at an proximate rate of one per pack. Packs that did t contain a Foil card had a Bowman's Best eview or Minor League Player of the Year ert card instead. The striking silver foil card nts differ them from the base 1996 Bowman rds.

Nm-Mt Ex-Mt
MPLETE SET (385) 300.00 90.00
TARS: 1X TO 2.5X BASIC CARDS...
OOKIES: 1.25X TO 2.5X BASIC CARDS

996 Bowman Minor League POY

ndomly inserted in packs at a rate of one in , this 15-card set features top minor league ospects for Player of the Year Candidates. The nts carry a color player photo with red-and-ver foil printing. The backs display player ormation including his career bests.

Nm-Mt Ex-Mt
MPLETE SET (15) 25.00 7.50
Andruw Jones 2.00 .60
Derrick Gibson .75 .23
Bob Abreu .75 .23
Todd Walker .75 .23
Jamey Wright .75 .23
Wes Helms 1.25 .35
Karim Garcia .75 .23
Bartolo Colon .75 .23
Alex Ochoa .75 .23
Mike Sweeney 3.00 .90
Ruben Rivera .75 .23
Gabe Alvarez .50 .15
Billy Wagner .75 .23
Vladimir Guerrero 4.00 1.20
Edgard Velazquez .50 .15

1997 Bowman

e 1997 Bowman set was issued in two series eries one numbers 1-221, series two numbers 2-441) and was distributed in 10 card packs th a suggested retail price of $2.50. The 441-rd set features color photos of 300 top ospects with silver and blue foil stamping and 0 veteran stars designated by silver and red il stamping. An unannounced Hideki Irabu red ordered card (number 441) was also included series two packs. Players that were featured r the first time on a Bowman card also carried blue foil "1st Bowman Card" logo on the card ont. Topps offered collectors a $125 guarantee complete sets. To get the guarantee, collec-rs had to mail in the Guaranteed Certificate equest Form which was found in every three cks of either series along with a $5 registra-on and processing fee. To redeem the guaran-e, collectors had to send a complete set of owman regular cards (441 cards in both series) ong with the certificate to Topps between ugust 31 and December 31 in the year 2000. ookie Cards in this set include Adrian Beltre, is Benson, Eric Chavez, Jose Cruz Jr, Travis e, Aramis Ramirez, Miguel Tejada and Kerry ood. Please note that cards 155 and 158 don't ist. Calvin "Pokey" Reese and George Arias are oth numbered 156 (Reese is an uncorrected ror - should be numbered 155). Chris arpenter and Eric Milton are both numbered 59 (Carpenter is an uncorrected error - should e numbered 158).

Nm-Mt Ex-Mt
OMPLETE SET (441) 50.00 15.00
OMP. SERIES 1 (221) 25.00 7.50
OMP. SERIES 2 (220) 25.00 7.50
Derek Jeter 2.00 .60
Edgar Renteria .30 .09
Chipper Jones .75 .23
Hideo Nomo .75 .23
Tim Salmon .50 .15
Jason Giambi .30 .09
Robin Ventura .30 .09
8 Tony Clark .30 .09
9 Barry Larkin .50 .15
10 Paul Molitor .50 .15
11 Bernard Gilkey .30 .09
12 Jack McDowell .30 .09
13 Andy Benes .30 .09
14 Ryan Klesko .30 .09
15 Mark McGwire 2.00 .60
16 Ken Griffey Jr. 1.25 .35
17 Robb Nen .30 .09
18 Cal Ripken 2.50 .75
19 John Valentin .30 .09
20 Ricky Bottalico .30 .09
21 Mike Lansing .30 .09
22 Ryne Sandberg 1.25 .35
23 Carlos Delgado .30 .09
24 Craig Biggio .50 .15
25 Eric Karros .30 .09
26 Kevin Appier .30 .09
27 Mariano Rivera .50 .15
28 Vinny Castilla .30 .09
29 Juan Gonzalez .50 .15
30 Al Martin .30 .09
31 Jeff Cirillo .30 .09
32 Eddie Murray .75 .23
33 Ray Lankford .30 .09
34 Manny Ramirez .50 .15
35 Roberto Alomar .50 .15
36 Will Clark .75 .23
37 Chuck Knoblauch .30 .09
38 Harold Baines .30 .09
39 Trevor Hoffman .30 .09
40 Edgar Martinez .50 .15
41 Geronimo Berroa .30 .09
42 Rey Ordonez .30 .09
43 Mike Stanley .30 .09
44 Mike Mussina .50 .15
45 Kevin Brown .30 .09
46 Dennis Eckersley .30 .09
47 Henry Rodriguez .30 .09
48 Tino Martinez .50 .15
49 Eric Young .30 .09
50 Bret Boone .30 .09
51 Raul Mondesi .30 .09
52 Sammy Sosa 1.25 .35
53 John Smoltz .50 .15
54 Billy Wagner .30 .09
55 Jeff D'Amico .30 .09
56 Ken Caminiti .30 .09
57 Jason Kendall .30 .09
58 Wade Boggs .50 .15
59 Andres Galarraga .30 .09
60 Jeff Brantley .30 .09
61 Mel Rojas .30 .09
62 Brian L. Hunter .30 .09
63 Bobby Bonilla .30 .09
64 Roger Clemens 1.50 .45
65 Jeff Kent .30 .09
66 Matt Williams .30 .09
67 Albert Belle .30 .09
68 Jeff King .30 .09
69 John Wetteland .30 .09
70 Deion Sanders .50 .15
71 Bubba Trammell RC .50 .15
72 Felix Heredia RC .50 .15
73 Billy Koch RC .75 .23
74 Sidney Ponson RC .75 .23
75 Ricky Ledee RC .50 .15
76 Brett Tomko .30 .09
77 Braden Looper RC .50 .15
78 Damian Jackson .30 .09
79 Jason Dickson .30 .09
80 Chad Green RC .50 .15
81 R.A. Dickey RC .50 .15
82 Jeff Liefer .30 .09
83 Matt Wagner .30 .09
84 Richard Hidalgo .30 .09
85 Adam Riggs .30 .09
86 Robert Smith .30 .09
87 Chad Hermansen RC .50 .15
88 Felix Martinez .30 .09
89 J.J. Johnson .30 .09
90 Todd Dunwoody .30 .09
91 Katsuhiro Maeda .30 .09
92 Darin Erstad .30 .09
93 Elieser Marrero .30 .09
94 Bartolo Colon .30 .09
95 Chris Fussell .30 .09
96 Ugueth Urbina .30 .09
97 Josh Paul RC .50 .15
98 Jaime Bluma .30 .09
99 Seth Greisinger RC .50 .15
100 Jose Cruz Jr. RC .75 .23
101 Todd Dunn .30 .09
102 Joe Young RC .50 .15
103 Jonathan Johnson .30 .09
104 Justin Towle RC .50 .15
105 Brian Rose .30 .09
106 Jose Guillen .30 .09
107 Andruw Jones .30 .09
108 Mark Kotsay RC 1.00 .30
109 Wilton Guerrero .30 .09
110 Jacob Cruz .30 .09
111 Mike Sweeney .30 .09
112 Julio Mosquera .30 .09
113 Matt Morris .30 .09
114 Wendell Magee .30 .09
115 John Thomson .30 .09
116 Javier Valentin .30 .09
117 Tom Fordham .30 .09
118 Ruben Rivera .30 .09
119 Mike Drumright RC .50 .15
120 Chris Holt .30 .09
121 Sean Maloney .30 .09
122 Michael Barrett .30 .09
123 Tony Saunders RC .50 .15
124 Kevin Brown C .30 .09
125 Richard Almanzar .30 .09
126 Mark Redman .30 .09
127 Anthony Sanders RC .50 .15
128 Jeff Abbott .30 .09
129 Eugene Kingsale .30 .09
130 Paul Konerko .30 .09
131 Randall Simon RC .50 .15
132 Andy Larkin .30 .09
133 Rafael Medina .30 .09
134 Mendy Lopez .30 .09
135 Freddy Adrian Garcia .30 .09
136 Karim Garcia .30 .09
137 Larry Rodriguez RC .50 .15
138 Carlos Guillen .30 .09
139 Aaron Boone .30 .09
140 Donnie Sadler .30 .09
141 Brooks Kieschnick .30 .09
142 Scott Spiezio .30 .09
143 Everett Stull .30 .09
144 Enrique Wilson .30 .09
145 Milton Bradley RC 2.50 .75
146 Kevin Orie .30 .09
147 Derek Wallace .30 .09
148 Russ Johnson .30 .09
149 Joe Lagarde RC .50 .15
150 Luis Castillo .30 .09
151 Jay Payton .30 .09
152 Joe Long .30 .09
153 Livan Hernandez .30 .09
154 Vladimir Nunez RC .50 .15
155 Pokey Reese UER .30 .09
Card actually numbered 156
156 George Arias .30 .09
157 Homer Bush .30 .09
158 Chris Carpenter UER .30 .09
Card numbered 159
159 Eric Milton RC 1.00 .30
160 Richie Sexson .30 .09
161 Carl Pavano 1.00 .09
162 Chris Gissell RC .50 .15
163 Mac Suzuki .30 .09
164 Pat Cline .30 .09
165 Ron Wright .30 .09
166 Dante Powell .30 .09
167 Mark Bellhorn .30 .09
168 George Lombard .30 .09
169 Pee Wee Lopez RC .50 .15
170 Paul Wilder RC .50 .15
171 Brad Fullmer .30 .09
172 Willie Martinez RC .50 .15
173 Dario Veras RC .50 .15
174 Dave Coggin .30 .09
175 Kris Benson RC 1.00 .30
176 Torii Hunter .30 .09
177 D.T. Cromer .30 .09
178 Nelson Figueroa RC .50 .15
179 Hiram Bocachica RC .50 .15
180 Shane Monahan .30 .09
181 Jimmy Anderson RC .50 .15
182 Juan Melo .30 .09
183 Pablo Ortega RC .50 .15
184 Calvin Pickering RC .75 .23
185 Reggie Taylor .30 .09
186 Jeff Farnsworth RC .50 .15
187 Terrence Long .30 .09
188 Geoff Jenkins .30 .09
189 Steve Rain RC .50 .15
190 Nerio Rodriguez RC .50 .15
191 Derrick Gibson .30 .09
192 Darin Blood .30 .09
193 Ben Davis .30 .09
194 Adrian Beltre RC 5.00 1.50
195 Damian Sapp RC UER .50 .15
196 Kerry Wood RC 8.00 2.40
197 Nate Rolison RC .50 .15
198 Fernando Tatis RC .50 .15
199 Brad Penny RC 2.00 .60
200 Jake Westbrook RC 1.00 .30
201 Edwin Diaz .30 .09
202 Joe Fontenot RC .50 .15
203 Matt Halloran RC .50 .15
204 Blake Stein RC .50 .15
205 Onan Masaoka .30 .09
206 Ben Petrick .30 .09
207 Matt Clement RC 1.00 .30
208 Todd Greene .30 .09
209 Ray Ricken .30 .09
210 Eric Chavez RC 3.00 .90
211 Edgard Velazquez .30 .09
212 Bruce Chen RC .50 .15
213 Danny Patterson .30 .09
214 Jeff Yoder .30 .09
215 Luis Ordaz RC .50 .15
216 Chris Widger .30 .09
217 Jason Brester .30 .09
218 Carlton Loewer .30 .09
219 Chris Reitsma RC .50 .15
220 Neifi Perez .30 .09
221 Hideki Irabu RC .50 .15
222 Ellis Burks .30 .09
223 Pedro Martinez UER .75 .23
Wrong birthdate
224 Kenny Lofton .30 .09
225 Randy Johnson .75 .23
226 Terry Steinbach .30 .09
227 Bernie Williams .50 .15
228 Dean Palmer .30 .09
229 Alan Benes .30 .09
230 Marquis Grissom .30 .09
231 Gary Sheffield .30 .09
232 Curt Schilling .50 .15
233 Reggie Sanders .30 .09
234 Bobby Higginson .30 .09
235 Moises Alou .30 .09
236 Tom Glavine .50 .15
237 Mark Grace .50 .15
238 Ramon Martinez .30 .09
239 Rafael Palmeiro .50 .15
240 John Olerud .30 .09
241 Dante Bichette .30 .09
242 Greg Vaughn .30 .09
243 Jeff Bagwell .50 .15
244 Barry Bonds 2.00 .60
245 Pat Hentgen .30 .09
246 Jim Thome .75 .23
247 J.Allensworth .30 .09
248 Andy Pettitte .50 .15
249 Jay Bell .30 .09
250 John Jaha .30 .09
251 Jim Edmonds .30 .09
252 Ron Gant .30 .09
253 David Cone .30 .09
254 Jose Canseco .75 .23
255 Jay Buhner .30 .09
256 Greg Maddux 1.25 .35
257 Brian McRae .30 .09
258 Lance Johnson .30 .09
259 Travis Fryman .30 .09
260 Paul O'Neill .50 .15
261 Ivan Rodriguez .75 .23
262 Gregg Jefferies .30 .09
263 Fred McGriff .50 .15
264 Derek Bell .30 .09
265 Jeff Conine .30 .09
266 Mike Piazza 1.25 .35
267 Mark Grudzielanek .30 .09
268 Brady Anderson .30 .09
269 Marty Cordova .30 .09
270 Ray Durham .30 .09
271 Joe Carter .30 .09
272 Brian Jordan .30 .09
273 David Justice .30 .09
274 Tony Gwynn 1.00 .30
275 Larry Walker .50 .15
276 Cecil Fielder .30 .09
277 Mo Vaughn .30 .09
278 Alex Fernandez .30 .09
279 Michael Tucker .30 .09
280 Jose Valentin .30 .09
281 Sandy Alomar Jr. .30 .09
282 Todd Hollandsworth .30 .09
283 Rico Brogna .30 .09
284 Rusty Greer .30 .09
285 Roberto Hernandez .30 .09
286 Hal Morris .30 .09
287 Johnny Damon .50 .15
288 Todd Hundley .30 .09
289 Rondell White .30 .09
290 Frank Thomas .75 .23
291 Don Denbow RC .50 .15
292 Derrek Lee .30 .09
293 Todd Walker .30 .09
294 Scott Rolen .75 .23
295 Wes Helms .30 .09
296 Bob Abreu .30 .09
297 John Patterson RC .75 .23
298 Alex Gonzalez RC .75 .23
299 Grant Roberts RC .50 .15
300 Jeff Suppan .30 .09
301 Luke Wilcox .30 .09
302 Marlon Anderson .30 .09
303 Ray Brown .30 .09
304 Mike Caruso RC .50 .15
305 Sam Marsonek RC .50 .15
306 Brady Raggio RC .50 .15
307 Kevin McGlinchy RC .50 .15
308 Roy Halladay RC 1.00 .30
309 Jeremi Gonzalez RC .50 .15
310 Aramis Ramirez RC 2.50 .75
311 Dee Brown RC .50 .15
312 Justin Thompson .30 .09
313 Jay Tessmer RC .50 .15
314 Mike Johnson RC .50 .15
315 Danny Clyburn .30 .09
316 Bruce Aven .30 .09
317 Keith Foulke RC 4.00 1.20
318 Jimmy Osting RC .50 .15
319 Val.De Los Santos RC .50 .15
320 Shannon Stewart .30 .09
321 Willie Adams .30 .09
322 Larry Barnes RC .50 .15
323 Mark Johnson RC .50 .15
324 Chris Stowers RC .50 .15
325 Brandon Reed .30 .09
326 Randy Winn .30 .09
327 Steve Chavez RC .50 .15
328 Nomar Garciaparra 1.25 .35
329 Jacque Jones RC 1.00 .30
330 Chris Clemons .30 .09
331 Todd Helton .75 .23
332 Ryan Brannan RC .50 .15
333 Alex Sanchez RC .75 .23
334 Arnold Gooch .30 .09
335 Russell Branyan .30 .09
336 Daryle Ward .50 .15
337 John LeRoy RC .50 .15
338 Steve Cox .30 .09
339 Kevin Witt .30 .09
340 Norm Hutchins .30 .09
341 Gabby Martinez .30 .09
342 Kris Detmers .30 .09
343 Mike Villano RC .50 .15
344 Preston Wilson .30 .09
345 James Manias RC .50 .15
346 Deivi Cruz RC .50 .15
347 Donzell McDonald RC .50 .15
348 Rod Myers RC .50 .15
349 Shawn Chacon RC .75 .23
350 Elvin Hernandez RC .50 .15
351 Orlando Cabrera RC 1.50 .60
352 Brian Banks .30 .09
353 Robbie Bell .50 .15
354 Brad Rigby .30 .09
355 Scott Elarton .30 .09
356 Kevin Sweeney RC .50 .15
357 Steve Soderstrom .30 .09
358 Ryan Nye .30 .09
359 Marlon Allen RC .50 .15
360 Donny Leon RC .50 .15
361 Garrett Neubart RC .50 .15
362 Abraham Nunez RC .50 .15
363 Adam Eaton RC .50 .15
364 Octavio Dotel RC .50 .15
365 Dean Crow RC .50 .15
366 Jason Baker RC .50 .15
367 Sean Casey 1.00 .30
368 Joe Lawrence RC .50 .15
369 Adam Johnson RC .50 .15
370 S.Schoeneweis RC .50 .15
371 Gerald Witasick Jr. .30 .09
372 Ronnie Belliard RC .75 .23
373 Russ Ortiz .30 .09
374 Robert Stratton RC .50 .15
375 Bobby Estalella .30 .09
376 Corey Lee RC .50 .15
377 Carlos Beltran 3.00 .90
378 Mike Cameron .30 .09
379 Scott Randall RC .50 .15
380 Corey Erickson RC .50 .15
381 Jay Canizaro .30 .09
382 Kerry Robinson RC .50 .15
383 Todd Noel RC .50 .15
384 A.J. Zapp RC .50 .15
385 Jarrod Washburn .30 .09
386 Ben Grieve .30 .09
387 Javier Vazquez RC 1.25 .35
388 Tony Graffanino .30 .09
389 Travis Lee RC .50 .15
390 DaRond Stovall .30 .09
391 Dennis Reyes RC .50 .15
392 Danny Buxbaum .30 .09
393 Marc Lewis RC .50 .15
394 Kelvim Escobar RC .75 .23
395 Danny Klassen .30 .09
396 Ken Cloude RC .50 .15
397 Gabe Alvarez .30 .09
398 Jaret Wright RC 1.50 .30
399 Raul Casanova .30 .09
400 Clayton Bruner RC .50 .15
401 Jason Marquis RC 1.00 .30
402 Marc Kroon .30 .09
403 Jamey Wright .30 .09
404 Matt Snyder RC .50 .15
405 Josh Garrett RC .50 .15
406 Juan Encarnacion .30 .09
407 Heath Murray .30 .09
408 Brett Herbison RC .50 .15
409 Brent Butler RC .50 .15
410 Danny Peoples RC .50 .15
411 Miguel Tejada RC 4.00 1.20
412 Damian Moss .30 .09
413 Jim Pittsley .30 .09
414 Dmitri Young .30 .09
415 Glendon Rusch .30 .09
416 Vladimir Guerrero .75 .23
417 Cole Liniak RC .50 .15
418 R.Hernandez UER .30 .09
Card back says 1st Bowman card is
1997, he had a 1996 Bowman
419 Cliff Politte RC .50 .15
420 Mel Rosario RC .50 .15
421 Jorge Carrion RC .50 .15
422 John Barnes RC .50 .15
423 Chris Stowe RC .50 .15
424 Vernon Wells RC 2.00 .60
425 Brett Caradonna RC .50 .15
426 Scott Hodges RC .50 .15
427 Jon Garland RC .75 .23
428 Nathan Haynes RC .50 .15
429 Geoff Goetz RC .50 .15
430 Adam Kennedy RC .75 .23
431 T.J. Tucker RC .50 .15
432 Aaron Akin RC .50 .15
433 Jayson Werth RC 1.00 .30
434 Glenn Davis RC .50 .15
435 Mark Mangum RC .50 .15
436 Troy Cameron RC .50 .15
437 J.J. Davis RC .50 .15
438 Lance Berkman RC 5.00 1.50
439 Jason Standridge RC .50 .15
440 Jason Dellaero RC .50 .15
441 Hideki Irabu .50 .15

1997 Bowman International

Inserted one in every pack, this 441-card set is parallel to the regular Bowman set. The difference is found in the flag in the background of each card that tells in what country the pictured player was born.

Nm-Mt Ex-Mt
COMPLETE SET (441) 160.00 47.50
COMP.SERIES 1 (221) 80.00 24.00
COMP.SERIES 2 (220) 80.00 24.00
*STARS: 1X TO 2.5X BASIC CARDS...
*ROOKIES: .5X TO 1.2X BASIC CARDS

1997 Bowman 1998 ROY Favorites

Randomly inserted in 1997 Bowman Series two packs at the rate of one in 12, this 15-card set features color photos of prospective 1998 Rookie of the Year candidates.

Nm-Mt Ex-Mt
COMPLETE SET (15) 15.00 4.50
ROY1 Jeff Abbott 1.00 .30
ROY2 Karim Garcia 1.00 .30
ROY3 Todd Helton 2.50 .75
ROY4 Richard Hidalgo 1.00 .30
ROY5 Geoff Jenkins 1.00 .30
ROY6 Russ Johnson 1.00 .30
ROY7 Paul Konerko 1.00 .30
ROY8 Mark Kotsay 1.25 .35
ROY9 Ricky Ledee .60 .18
ROY10 Travis Lee .60 .18
ROY11 Derrek Lee 1.00 .30
ROY12 Elieser Marrero 1.00 .30
ROY13 Juan Melo 1.00 .30
ROY14 Brian Rose 1.00 .30
ROY15 Fernando Tatis .60 .18

1997 Bowman Certified Blue Ink Autographs

Randomly inserted in first and second series packs at a rate of one in 96 and ANCO packs at one in 115, this 90-card set features color player photos of top prospects with blue ink autographs and printed on sturdy 16 pt. card stock with the Topps Certified Autograph Issue Stamp. The Derek Jeter blue ink and green ink versions are seeded in every 1,928 packs.

Nm-Mt Ex-Mt
*BLACK INK: .5X TO 1.2X BLUE INK..
BLACK STATED ODDS 1:503, ANCO 1:600
*GOLD INK: 1X TO 2.5X BLUE INK.....
GOLD: STATED ODDS 1:1509, ANCO 1:1795

Card	Nm-Mt	Ex-Mt
*GREEN JETER: SAME VALUE AS BLUE INK		
D.JETER BLUE SER.1 ODDS 1:1928		
D.JETER GREEN SER.2 ODDS 1:1928		
CA1 Jeff Abbott	10.00	3.00
CA2 Bob Abreu	15.00	4.50
CA3 Willie Adams	10.00	3.00
CA4 Brian Banks	10.00	3.00
CA5 Kris Benson	25.00	7.50
CA6 Darin Blood	10.00	3.00
CA7 Jaime Bluma	10.00	3.00
CA8 Kevin L. Brown	10.00	3.00
CA9 Ray Brown	10.00	3.00
CA10 Homer Bush	10.00	3.00
CA11 Mike Cameron	15.00	4.50
CA12 Jay Canizaro	10.00	3.00
CA13 Luis Castillo	15.00	4.50
CA14 Dave Coggin	10.00	3.00
CA15 Bartolo Colon	15.00	4.50
CA16 Rocky Coppinger	10.00	3.00
CA17 Jacob Cruz	10.00	3.00
CA18 Jose Cruz Jr.	20.00	6.00
CA19 Jeff D'Amico	10.00	3.00
CA20 Ben Davis	10.00	3.00
CA21 Mike Drumright	10.00	3.00
CA22 Scott Elarton	10.00	3.00
CA23 Darin Erstad	15.00	4.50
CA24 Bobby Estalella	10.00	3.00
CA25 Joe Fontenot	10.00	3.00
CA26 Tom Fordham	10.00	3.00
CA27 Brad Fullmer	10.00	3.00
CA28 Chris Fussell	10.00	3.00
CA29 Karim Garcia	10.00	3.00
CA30 Kris Detmers	10.00	3.00
CA31 Todd Greene	10.00	3.00
CA32 Ben Grieve	10.00	3.00
CA33 Vladimir Guerrero	50.00	15.00
CA34 Jose Guillen	15.00	4.50
CA35 Roy Halladay	25.00	7.50
CA36 Wes Helms	10.00	3.00
CA37 Chad Hermansen	15.00	4.50
CA38 Richard Hidalgo	10.00	3.00
CA39 Todd Hollandsworth	10.00	3.00
CA40 Damian Jackson	10.00	3.00
CA41 Derek Jeter	120.00	36.00
CA42 Andruw Jones	25.00	7.50
CA43 Brooks Kieschnick	10.00	3.00
CA44 Eugene Kingsale	10.00	3.00
CA45 Paul Konerko	15.00	4.50
CA46 Marc Kroon	10.00	3.00
CA47 Derrek Lee	15.00	4.50
CA48 Travis Lee	15.00	4.50
CA49 Terrence Long	10.00	3.00
CA50 Curt Lyons	10.00	3.00
CA51 Eli Marrero	10.00	3.00
CA52 Rafael Medina	10.00	3.00
CA53 Juan Melo	10.00	3.00
CA54 Shane Monahan	10.00	3.00
CA55 Julio Mosquera	10.00	3.00
CA56 Heath Murray	10.00	3.00
CA57 Ryan Nye	10.00	3.00
CA58 Kevin Orie	10.00	3.00
CA59 Russ Ortiz	15.00	4.50
CA60 Carl Pavano	40.00	7.50
CA61 Jay Payton	10.00	3.00
CA62 Neifi Perez	10.00	3.00
CA63 Sidney Ponson	20.00	6.00
CA64 Pokey Reese	15.00	4.50
CA65 Ray Ricken	10.00	3.00
CA66 Brad Rigby	10.00	3.00
CA67 Adam Riggs	10.00	3.00
CA68 Ruben Rivera	10.00	3.00
CA69 J.J. Johnson	10.00	3.00
CA70 Scott Rolen	40.00	12.00
CA71 Tony Saunders	10.00	3.00
CA72 Donnie Sadler	10.00	3.00
CA73 Richie Sexson	15.00	4.50
CA74 Scott Spiezio	10.00	3.00
CA75 Everett Stull	10.00	3.00
CA76 Mike Sweeney	15.00	4.50
CA77 Fernando Tatis	15.00	4.50
CA78 Miguel Tejada	60.00	18.00
CA79 Justin Thompson	10.00	3.00
CA80 Justin Towle	10.00	3.00
CA81 Billy Wagner	25.00	7.50
CA82 Todd Walker	15.00	4.50
CA83 Luke Wilcox	10.00	3.00
CA84 Paul Wilder	10.00	3.00
CA85 Enrique Wilson	10.00	3.00
CA86 Kerry Wood	150.00	45.00
CA87 Jamey Wright	10.00	3.00
CA88 Ron Wright	10.00	3.00
CA89 Dmitri Young	15.00	4.50
CA90 Nelson Figueroa	10.00	3.00

1997 Bowman International Best

Randomly inserted in series two packs at the rate of one in 12, this 20-card set features color photos of both prospects and veterans from far and wide who have made an impact on the game.

Card	Nm-Mt	Ex-Mt
COMPLETE SET (20)	50.00	15.00
*ATOMIC: 1.5X TO 4X BASIC INT.BEST		
ATOMIC SER.2 STATED ODDS 1:96		
*REFRACTORS: .75X TO 2X BASIC INT.BEST		
REFRACTOR SER.2 STATED ODDS 1:48		
BBI1 Frank Thomas	3.00	.90
BBI2 Ken Griffey Jr.	5.00	1.50
BBI3 Juan Gonzalez	2.00	.60
BBI4 Bernie Williams	2.00	.60
BBI5 Hideo Nomo	3.00	.90
BBI6 Sammy Sosa	5.00	1.50
BBI7 Larry Walker	2.00	.60
BBI8 Vinny Castilla	1.25	.35
BBI9 Mariano Rivera	2.00	.60
BBI10 Rafael Palmeiro	2.00	.60
BBI11 Nomar Garciaparra	5.00	1.50
BBI12 Todd Walker	1.25	.35
BBI13 Andruw Jones	1.25	.35
BBI14 Vladimir Guerrero	3.00	.90
BBI15 Ruben Rivera	1.25	.35
BBI16 Bob Abreu	1.25	.35
BBI17 Karim Garcia	1.25	.35
BBI18 Katsuhiro Maeda	1.25	.35
BBI19 Jose Cruz Jr.	2.00	.60
BBI20 Damian Moss	1.25	.35

1997 Bowman Scout's Honor Roll

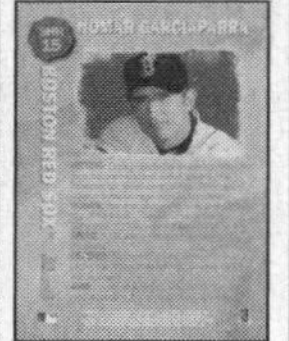

Randomly inserted in first series packs at a rate of one in 12, this 15-card set features color photos of top prospects and rookies printed on double-etched foil cards.

Card	Nm-Mt	Ex-Mt
COMPLETE SET (15)	25.00	7.50
1 Dmitri Young	.75	.23
2 Bob Abreu	.75	.23
3 Vladimir Guerrero	2.00	.60
4 Paul Konerko	.75	.23
5 Kevin Orie	.75	.23
6 Todd Walker	.75	.23
7 Ben Grieve	.75	.23
8 Darin Erstad	.75	.23
9 Derrek Lee	.75	.23
10 Jose Cruz Jr.	.75	.23
11 Scott Rolen	2.00	.60
12 Travis Lee	.75	.23
13 Andruw Jones	.75	.23
14 Wilton Guerrero	.75	.23
15 Nomar Garciaparra	3.00	.90

1998 Bowman Previews

Randomly inserted in Stadium Club first series hobby and retail packs at the rate of one in 12 and first series Home Team Advantage packs at a rate of one in four, this 10-card set is a sneak preview of the Bowman series and features color photos of top players. The cards are numbered with a BP prefix on the backs.

Card	Nm-Mt	Ex-Mt
COMPLETE SET (10)	25.00	7.50
BP1 Nomar Garciaparra	4.00	1.20
BP2 Scott Rolen	2.50	.75
BP3 Ken Griffey Jr.	4.00	1.20
BP4 Frank Thomas	2.50	.75
BP5 Larry Walker	1.50	.45
BP6 Mike Piazza	4.00	1.20
BP7 Chipper Jones	2.50	.75
BP8 Tino Martinez	1.50	.45
BP9 Mark McGwire	6.00	1.80
BP10 Barry Bonds	6.00	1.80

1998 Bowman Prospect Previews

Randomly seeded in Stadium Club second series hobby and retail packs at a rate of one in twelve and second series Home Team Advantage packs at a rate of one in four, this ten card set previewed the upcoming 1998 Bowman brand, featuring a selection of top youngsters expected to make an impact in 1998.

Card	Nm-Mt	Ex-Mt
COMPLETE SET (10)	10.00	3.00
BP1 Ben Grieve	1.00	.30
BP2 Brad Fullmer	1.00	.30
BP3 Ryan Anderson	1.25	.35
BP4 Mark Kotsay	1.00	.30
BP5 Bobby Estalella	1.00	.30
BP6 Juan Encarnacion	1.00	.30
BP7 Todd Helton	1.50	.45
BP8 Mike Lowell	4.00	1.20
BP9 A.J. Hinch	1.00	.30
BP10 Richard Hidalgo	1.00	.30

1998 Bowman

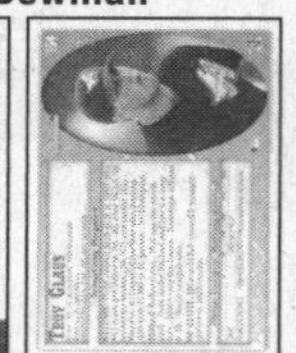

The complete 1998 Bowman set was distributed amongst two series with a total of 441 cards. The 10-card packs retailed for $2.50 each. Series one contains 221 cards while series two contains 220 cards. Each player's facsimile signature taken from the contract they signed with Topps is also on the left border. Players new to Bowman are marked with the new Bowman Rookie Card stamp. Notable Rookie Cards include Ryan Anderson, Jack Cust, Troy Glaus, Orlando Hernandez, Gabe Kapler, Ruben Mateo, Kevin Millwood and Magglio Ordonez. The 1991 BBM (Major Japanese Card set) cards of Shigetoshi Hasegawa, Hideki Irabu and Hideo Nomo (All of which are considered Japanese Rookie Cards) were randomly inserted into these packs.

Card	Nm-Mt	Ex-Mt
COMPLETE SET (441)	50.00	15.00
COMP. SERIES 1 (221)	25.00	7.50
COMP. SERIES 2 (220)	25.00	7.50
1 Nomar Garciaparra	1.25	.35
2 Scott Rolen	.75	.23
3 Andy Pettitte	.50	.15
4 Ivan Rodriguez	.75	.23
5 Mark McGwire	2.00	.60
6 Jason Dickson	.30	.09
7 Jose Cruz Jr.	.30	.09
8 Jeff Kent	.30	.09
9 Mike Mussina	.50	.15
10 Jason Kendall	.30	.09
11 Brett Tomko	.30	.09
12 Jeff King	.30	.09
13 Brad Radke	.30	.09
14 Robin Ventura	.30	.09
15 Jeff Bagwell	.50	.15
16 Greg Maddux	1.25	.35
17 John Jaha	.30	.09
18 Mike Piazza	1.25	.35
19 Edgar Martinez	.50	.15
20 David Justice	.30	.09
21 Todd Hundley	.30	.09
22 Tony Gwynn	1.00	.30
23 Larry Walker	.50	.15
24 Bernie Williams	.50	.15
25 Edgar Renteria	.30	.09
26 Rafael Palmeiro	.50	.15
27 Tim Salmon	.50	.15
28 Matt Morris	.30	.09
29 Shawn Estes	.30	.09
30 Vladimir Guerrero	.75	.23
31 Fernando Tatis	.30	.09
32 Justin Thompson	.30	.09
33 Ken Griffey Jr.	1.25	.35
34 Edgardo Alfonzo	.30	.09
35 Mo Vaughn	.30	.09
36 Marty Cordova	.30	.09
37 Craig Biggio	.50	.15
38 Roger Clemens	1.50	.45
39 Mark Grace	.50	.15
40 Ken Caminiti	.30	.09
41 Tony Womack	.30	.09
42 Albert Belle	.30	.09
43 Tino Martinez	.50	.15
44 Sandy Alomar Jr.	.30	.09
45 Jeff Cirillo	.30	.09
46 Jason Giambi	.30	.09
47 Darin Erstad	.30	.09
48 Livan Hernandez	.30	.09
49 Mark Grudzielanek	.30	.09
50 Sammy Sosa	1.25	.35
51 Curt Schilling	.30	.09
52 Brian Hunter	.30	.09
53 Neifi Perez	.30	.09
54 Todd Walker	.30	.09
55 Jose Guillen	.30	.09
56 Jim Thome	.75	.23
57 Tom Glavine	.50	.15
58 Todd Greene	.30	.09
59 Rondell White	.30	.09
60 Roberto Alomar	.50	.15
61 Tony Clark	.30	.09
62 Vinny Castilla	.30	.09
63 Barry Larkin	.50	.15
64 Hideki Irabu	.30	.09
65 Johnny Damon	.50	.15
66 Juan Gonzalez	.50	.15
67 John Olerud	.30	.09
68 Gary Sheffield	.30	.09
69 Raul Mondesi	.30	.09
70 Chipper Jones	.75	.23
71 David Ortiz	1.00	.30
72 Warren Morris RC	.30	.09
73 Alex Gonzalez	.30	.09
74 Nick Bierbrodt	.30	.09
75 Roy Halladay	.30	.09
76 Danny Buxbaum	.30	.09
77 Adam Kennedy	.30	.09
78 Jared Sandberg	.30	.09
79 Michael Barrett	.30	.09
80 Gil Meche	.30	.09
81 Jayson Werth	.30	.09
82 Abraham Nunez	.30	.09
83 Ben Petrick	.30	.09
84 Brett Caradonna	.30	.09
85 Mike Lowell RC	1.50	.45
86 Clayton Bruner	.30	.09
87 John Curtice RC	.40	.12
88 Bobby Estalella	.30	.09
89 Juan Melo	.30	.09
90 Arnold Gooch	.30	.09
91 Kevin Millwood RC	.75	.23
92 Richie Sexson	.30	.09
93 Orlando Cabrera	.30	.09
94 Pat Cline	.30	.09
95 Anthony Sanders	.30	.09
96 Russ Johnson	.30	.09
97 Ben Grieve	.30	.09
98 Kevin McGlinchy	.30	.09
99 Paul Wilder	.30	.09
100 Russ Ortiz	.30	.09
101 Ryan Jackson RC	.30	.09
102 Heath Murray	.30	.09
103 Brian Rose	.30	.09
104 R.Radmanovich RC	.30	.09
105 Ricky Ledee	.30	.09
106 Jeff Wallace RC	.30	.09
107 Ryan Minor RC	.30	.09
108 Dennis Reyes	.30	.09
109 James Manias	.30	.09
110 Chris Carpenter	.30	.09
111 Daryle Ward	.30	.09
112 Vernon Wells	.30	.09
113 Chad Green	.30	.09
114 Mike Stoner RC	.30	.09
115 Brad Fullmer	.30	.09
116 Adam Eaton	.30	.09
117 Jeff Liefer	.30	.09
118 Corey Koskie RC	1.00	.30
119 Todd Helton	.50	.15
120 Jaime Jones RC	.30	.09
121 Mel Rosario	.30	.09
122 Geoff Goetz	.30	.09
123 Adrian Beltre	.75	.23
124 Jason Dellaero	.30	.09
125 Gabe Kapler RC	.50	.15
126 Scott Schoeneweis	.30	.09
127 Ryan Brannan	.30	.09
128 Aaron Akin	.30	.09
129 Ryan Anderson RC	.40	.12
130 Brad Penny	.30	.09
131 Bruce Chen	.30	.09
132 Eli Marrero	.30	.09
133 Eric Chavez	.30	.09
134 Troy Glaus RC	2.00	.60
135 Troy Cameron	.30	.09
136 Brian Sikorski RC	.30	.09
137 Mike Kinkade RC	.30	.09
138 Braden Looper	.30	.09
139 Mark Mangum	.30	.09
140 Danny Peoples	.30	.09
141 J.J. Davis	.30	.09
142 Ben Davis	.30	.09
143 Jacque Jones	.30	.09
144 Derrick Gibson	.30	.09
145 Bronson Arroyo	.75	.23
146 L.De Los Santos RC UER	.30	.09
has hitting stat line instead of pitching		
147 Jeff Abbott	.30	.09
148 Mike Cuddyer RC	.50	.15
149 Jason Romano	.30	.09
150 Shane Monahan	.30	.09
151 Ntema Ndungidi RC	.30	.09
152 Alex Sanchez	.30	.09
153 Jack Cust RC	.40	.12
154 Brent Butler	.30	.09
155 Ramon Hernandez	.30	.09
156 Norm Hutchins	.30	.09
157 Jason Marquis	.30	.09
158 Jacob Cruz	.30	.09
159 Rob Burger RC	.30	.09
160 Dave Coggin	.30	.09
161 Preston Wilson	.30	.09
162 Jason Fitzgerald RC	.30	.09
163 Dan Serafini	.30	.09
164 Peter Munro	.30	.09
165 Trot Nixon	.30	.09
166 Homer Bush	.30	.09
167 Dermal Brown	.30	.09
168 Chad Hermansen	.30	.09
169 Julio Moreno RC	.30	.09
170 John Roskos RC	.30	.09
171 Grant Roberts	.30	.09
172 Ken Cloude	.30	.09
173 Jason Brester	.30	.09
174 Jason Conti	.30	.09
175 Jon Garland	.30	.09
176 Robbie Bell	.30	.09
177 Nathan Haynes	.30	.09
178 Ramon Ortiz RC	.50	.15
179 Shannon Stewart	.30	.09
180 Pablo Ortega	.30	.09
181 Jimmy Rollins RC	.75	.23
182 Sean Casey	.30	.09
183 Ted Lilly RC	.50	.15
184 Chris Enochs RC	.30	.09
185 M.Ordonez RC UER	2.50	.75
Front photo is Mario Valdez		
186 Mike Drumright	.30	.09
187 Aaron Boone	.30	.09
188 Matt Clement	.30	.09
189 Todd Dunwoody	.30	.09
190 Larry Rodriguez	.30	.09
191 Todd Noel	.30	.09
192 Geoff Jenkins	.30	.09
193 George Lombard	.30	.09
194 Lance Berkman	.50	.15
195 Marcus McCain	.30	.09
196 Ryan McGuire	.30	.09
197 Jhensy Sandoval	.30	.09
198 Corey Lee	.30	.09
199 Mario Valdez	.30	.09
200 Robert Fick RC	.40	.12
201 Donnie Sadler	.30	.09
202 Marc Kroon	.30	.09
203 David Miller	.30	.09
204 Jarrod Washburn	.30	.09
205 Miguel Tejada	.30	.09
206 Raul Ibanez	.30	.09
207 John Patterson	.30	.09
208 Calvin Pickering	.30	.09
209 Felix Martinez	.30	.09
210 Mark Redman	.30	.09
211 Scott Elarton	.30	.09
212 Jose Amado RC	.30	.09
213 Kerry Wood	.75	.23
214 Dante Powell	.30	.09
215 Aramis Ramirez	.30	.09
216 A.J. Hinch	.30	.09
217 Dustin Carr RC	.30	.09
218 Mark Kotsay	.30	.09
219 Jason Standridge	.30	.09
220 Luis Ordaz	.30	.09
221 O.Hernandez RC	.75	.23
222 Cal Ripken	2.50	.75
223 Paul Molitor	.50	.15
224 Derek Jeter	2.00	.60
225 Barry Bonds	2.00	.60
226 Jim Edmonds	.30	.09
227 John Smoltz	.50	.15
228 Eric Karros	.30	.09
229 Ray Lankford	.30	.09
230 Rey Ordonez	.30	.09
231 Kenny Lofton	.30	.09
232 Alex Rodriguez	1.25	.35
233 Dante Bichette	.30	.09
234 Pedro Martinez	.75	.23
235 Carlos Delgado	.30	.09
236 Rod Beck	.30	.09
237 Matt Williams	.30	.09
238 Charles Johnson	.30	.09
239 Rico Brogna	.30	.09
240 Frank Thomas	.75	.23
241 Paul O'Neill	.50	.15
242 Jaret Wright	.30	.09
243 Brant Brown	.30	.09
244 Ryan Klesko	.30	.09
245 Chuck Finley	.30	.09
246 Derek Bell	.30	.09
247 Delino DeShields	.30	.09
248 Chan Ho Park	.30	.09
249 Wade Boggs	.50	.15
250 Jay Buhner	.30	.09
251 Butch Huskey	.30	.09
252 Steve Finley	.30	.09
253 Will Clark	.75	.23
254 John Valentin	.30	.09
255 Bobby Higginson	.30	.09
256 Darryl Strawberry	.30	.09
257 Randy Johnson	.75	.23
258 Al Martin	.30	.09
259 Travis Fryman	.30	.09
260 Fred McGriff	.50	.15
261 Jose Valentin	.30	.09
262 Andruw Jones	.30	.09
263 Kenny Rogers	.30	.09
264 Moises Alou	.30	.09
265 Denny Neagle	.30	.09
266 Ugueth Urbina	.30	.09
267 Derrek Lee	.30	.09
268 Ellis Burks	.30	.09
269 Mariano Rivera	.50	.15
270 Dean Palmer	.30	.09
271 Eddie Taubensee	.30	.09
272 Brady Anderson	.30	.09
273 Brian Giles	.30	.09
274 Quinton McCracken	.30	.09
275 Henry Rodriguez	.30	.09
276 Andres Galarraga	.30	.09
277 Jose Canseco	.75	.23
278 David Segui	.30	.09
279 Bret Saberhagen	.30	.09
280 Kevin Brown	.50	.15
281 Chuck Knoblauch	.30	.09
282 Jeromy Burnitz	.30	.09
283 Jay Bell	.30	.09
284 Manny Ramirez	.50	.15
285 Rick Helling	.30	.09
286 Francisco Cordova	.30	.09
287 Bob Abreu	.30	.09
288 J.T. Snow	.30	.09
289 Hideo Nomo	.75	.23
290 Brian Jordan	.30	.09
291 Javy Lopez	.30	.09
292 Travis Lee	.30	.09
293 Russell Branyan	.30	.09
294 Paul Konerko	.30	.09
295 Masato Yoshii RC	.50	.15
296 Kris Benson	.30	.09
297 Juan Encarnacion	.30	.09
298 Eric Milton	.30	.09
299 Mike Caruso	.30	.09
300 R.Aramboles RC	.40	.12
301 Bobby Smith	.30	.09
302 Billy Koch	.30	.09
303 Richard Hidalgo	.30	.09
304 Justin Baughman RC	.30	.09
305 Chris Gissell	.30	.09
306 Donnie Bridges RC	.30	.09
307 Nelson Lara RC	.30	.09
308 Randy Wolf RC	.50	.15
309 Jason LaRue RC	.40	.12
310 Jason Gooding RC	.30	.09
311 Edgard Clemente	.30	.09
312 Andrew Vessel	.30	.09
313 Chris Reitsma	.30	.09
314 Jesus Sanchez RC	.30	.09
315 Buddy Carlyle RC	.30	.09
316 Randy Winn	.30	.09
317 Luis Rivera RC	.30	.09
318 Marcus Thames RC	.50	.15
319 A.J. Pierzynski	.30	.09
320 Scott Randall	.30	.09
321 Damian Sapp	.30	.09
322 Ed Yarnall RC	.30	.09
323 Luke Allen RC	.40	.12
324 J.D. Smart	.30	.09
325 Willie Martinez	.30	.09
326 Alex Ramirez	.30	.09
327 Eric DuBose RC	.40	.12
328 Kevin Witt	.30	.09
329 Dan McKinley RC	.30	.09
330 Cliff Politte	.30	.09
331 Vladimir Nunez	.30	.09
332 John Halama RC	.30	.09
333 Nerio Rodriguez	.30	.09
334 Desi Relaford	.30	.09
335 Robinson Checo	.30	.09
336 John Nicholson	.50	.15
337 Tom LaRosa RC	.30	.09
338 Kevin Nicholson RC	.30	.09
339 Javier Vazquez	.30	.09
340 A.J. Zapp	.30	.09
341 Tom Evans	.30	.09
342 Kerry Robinson	.30	.09
343 Gabe Gonzalez RC	.30	.09
344 Ralph Milliard	.30	.09
345 Enrique Wilson	.30	.09
346 Elvin Hernandez	.30	.09
347 Mike Lincoln RC	.30	.09
348 Cesar King RC	.30	.09
349 Cristian Guzman RC	.50	.15
350 Donzell McDonald	.30	.09
351 Jim Parque RC	.30	.09
352 Mike Saipe RC	.30	.09
353 Carlos Febles RC	.40	.12
354 Dernell Stenson RC	.40	.12
355 Mark Osborne RC	.30	.09
356 Odalis Perez RC	.75	.23
357 Jason Dewey RC	.30	.09
358 Joe Fontenot	.30	.09
359 Jason Grilli RC	.30	.09
360 Kevin Haverbusch RC	.30	.09
361 Jay Yennaco RC	.30	.09
362 Brian Buchanan	.30	.09
363 John Barnes	.30	.09
364 Chris Fussell	.30	.09
365 Kevin Gibbs RC	.30	.09
366 Joe Lawrence	.30	.09
367 DaRond Stovall	.30	.09
368 Brian Fuentes RC	.30	.09
369 Jimmy Anderson	.30	.09
370 Lariel Gonzalez RC	.30	.09
371 Scott Williamson RC	.40	.12
372 Milton Bradley	.30	.09
373 Jason Halper RC	.30	.09
374 Brent Billingsley RC	.30	.09
375 Joe DePastino RC	.30	.09
376 Jake Westbrook	.30	.09
377 Octavio Dotel	.30	.09
378 Jason Williams RC	.30	.09
379 Julio Ramirez RC	.30	.09
380 Seth Greisinger	.30	.09
381 Mike Judd RC	.30	.09
382 Ben Ford RC	.30	.09
383 Tom Bennett RC	.30	.09
384 Adam Butler RC	.30	.09
385 Wade Miller RC	.50	.15
386 Kyle Peterson RC	.30	.09
387 Tommy Peterman RC	.30	.09

8 Onan Masaoka .30 .09
9 Jason Rakers RC .30 .09
0 Rafael Medina .30 .09
1 Luis Lopez RC .30 .09
2 Jeff Yoder .30 .09
3 Vance Wilson RC .30 .09
4 F.Seguignol RC .30 .09
5 Ron Wright .30 .09
6 Ruben Mateo RC .40 .12
7 Steve Lomasney RC .40 .12
8 Damian Jackson .30 .09
9 Mike Jerzembeck RC .30 .09
0 Luis Rivas RC .75 .23
1 Kevin Burford RC .30 .09
2 Glenn Davis .30 .09
3 Robert Luce RC .30 .09
4 Cole Liniak .30 .09
5 Matt LeCroy RC .40 .12
6 Jeremy Giambi RC .40 .12
7 Shawn Chacon .30 .09
8 Dewayne Wise RC .30 .09
9 Steve Woodard .30 .09
0 F.Cordero RC .50 .15
1 Damon Minor RC .30 .09
2 Lou Collier .30 .09
3 Justin Towle .30 .09
4 Juan LeBron .30 .09
5 Michael Coleman .30 .09
6 Felix Rodriguez .30 .09
7 Paul Ah Yat RC .30 .09
8 Kevin Barker RC .30 .09
9 Brian Meadows .30 .09
0 Darnell McDonald RC .30 .09
1 Matt Kinney RC .40 .12
2 Mike Vavrek RC .30 .09
3 Courtney Duncan RC .30 .09
4 Kevin Millar RC 3.00 .90
5 Ruben Rivera .30 .09
6 Steve Shoemaker RC .30 .09
7 Dan Reichert RC .30 .09
8 Carlos Lee RC .75 .23
9 Rod Barajas .50 .15
0 Pablo Ozuna RC .40 .12
1 Todd Belitz RC .30 .09
2 Sidney Ponson .30 .09
3 Steve Carver RC .30 .09
4 Esteban Yan RC .40 .12
5 Cedrick Bowers .30 .09
6 Marlon Anderson .30 .09
7 Carl Pavano .30 .09
8 Jae Weong Seo RC .50 .15
9 Jose Taveras RC .30 .09
0 Matt Anderson RC .40 .12
1 Darron Ingram RC .30 .09
0 S.Hasegawa '91 BBM 10.00 3.00
0 H.Irabu '91 BBM 10.00 3.00
0 H.Nomo '91 BBM 25.00 7.50

1998 Bowman Golden Anniversary

ndomly inserted in first series packs at a rate one in 237 and second series packs at a rate one in 194, this 441-card set is a parallel to Bowman base set. The set celebrates wman's 50th birthday. Each card is highlight- by gold-stamped facsimile autographs stead of silver foil on the basic cards) and are quentially numbered to 50.

Nm-Mt Ex-Mt
TARS: 12.5X TO 30X BASIC CARDS
OOKIES: 10X TO 20X BASIC CARDS
4 Kevin Millar 25.00 7.50

1998 Bowman International

erted one per pack, this 441-card set is a par- l to the Bowman base set. The set allows col- tors to see where their favorite players were rn and learn the vitals on each of them as nslated in the player's home language.

Nm-Mt Ex-Mt
MPLETE SET (441) 150.00 45.00
MP. SERIES 1 (221) 75.00 22.00
MP. SERIES 2 (220) 75.00 22.00
TARS: 1.25X TO 3X BASIC CARDS.
OOKIES: .6X TO 1.5X BASIC CARDS

1998 Bowman 1999 ROY Favorites

ndomly inserted in second series packs at a e of one in 12, this 10-card insert features or action photography on borderless, double- hed foil cards. The players featured on these ds were among the leading early candidates the 1999 ROY award.

Nm-Mt Ex-Mt
MPLETE SET (10) 20.00 6.00
Y1 Adrian Beltre 3.00 .90
Y2 Troy Glaus 4.00 1.20
Y3 Chad Hermansen 1.25 .35
Y4 Matt Clement 1.25 .35
Y5 Eric Chavez 1.25 .35
Y6 Kris Benson 1.25 .35
Y7 Richie Sexson 1.25 .35
Y8 Randy Wolf 2.00 .60
Y9 Ryan Minor 1.25 .35
Y10 Alex Gonzalez 1.25 .35

998 Bowman Certified Blue Autographs

ndomly inserted in first series packs at a rate one in 149 and second series packs at a rate one in 122.

Nm-Mt Ex-Mt
*GOLD FOIL: 1.5X TO 4X BLUE AU'S.
SER.1 GOLD FOIL STATED ODDS 1:2976
SER.2 GOLD FOIL STATED ODDS 1:2445
*SILVER FOIL: .75X TO 2X BLUE AU'S
SER.1 SILVER FOIL STATED ODDS 1:992
SER.2 SILVER FOIL STATED ODDS 1:815
1 Adrian Beltre 40.00 12.00
2 Brad Fullmer 10.00 3.00
3 Ricky Ledee 10.00 3.00
4 David Ortiz 40.00 12.00
5 Fernando Tatis 10.00 3.00
6 Kerry Wood 60.00 18.00
7 Mel Rosario 10.00 3.00
8 Cole Liniak 10.00 3.00
9 A.J. Hinch 10.00 3.00
10 Jhensy Sandoval 10.00 3.00
11 Jose Cruz Jr. 10.00 3.00
12 Richard Hidalgo 10.00 3.00
13 Geoff Jenkins 15.00 4.50
14 Carl Pavano 25.00 4.50
15 Richie Sexson 15.00 4.50
16 Tony Womack 10.00 3.00
17 Scott Rolen 40.00 12.00
18 Ryan Minor 10.00 3.00
19 Eli Marrero 10.00 3.00
20 Jason Marquis 15.00 4.50
21 Mike Lowell 20.00 6.00
22 Todd Helton 25.00 7.50
23 Chad Green 10.00 3.00
24 Scott Elarton 10.00 3.00
25 Russell Branyan 10.00 3.00
26 Mike Drumright 10.00 3.00
27 Ben Grieve 10.00 3.00
28 Jacque Jones 15.00 4.50
29 Jared Sandberg 10.00 3.00
30 Grant Roberts 10.00 3.00
31 Mike Stoner 10.00 3.00
32 Brian Rose 10.00 3.00
33 Randy Winn 10.00 3.00
34 Justin Towle 10.00 3.00
35 Anthony Sanders 10.00 3.00
36 Rafael Medina 10.00 3.00
37 Corey Lee 10.00 3.00
38 Mike Kinkade 15.00 4.50
39 Norm Hutchins 10.00 3.00
40 Jason Brester 10.00 3.00
41 Ben Davis 10.00 3.00
42 Nomar Garciaparra 120.00 36.00
43 Jeff Liefer 10.00 3.00
44 Eric Milton 10.00 3.00
45 Preston Wilson 15.00 4.50
46 Miguel Tejada 15.00 4.50
47 Luis Ordaz 10.00 3.00
48 Travis Lee 10.00 3.00
49 Kris Benson 10.00 3.00
50 Jacob Cruz 10.00 3.00
51 Dermal Brown 10.00 3.00
52 Marc Kroon 10.00 3.00
53 Chad Hermansen 10.00 3.00
54 Roy Halladay 10.00 3.00
55 Eric Chavez 15.00 4.50
56 Jason Conti 10.00 3.00
57 Juan Encarnacion 10.00 3.00
58 Paul Wilder 10.00 3.00
59 Aramis Ramirez 15.00 4.50
60 Cliff Politte 10.00 3.00
61 Todd Dunwoody 10.00 3.00
62 Paul Konerko 15.00 4.50
63 Shane Monahan 10.00 3.00
64 Alex Sanchez 10.00 3.00
65 Jeff Abbott 10.00 3.00
66 John Patterson 10.00 3.00
67 Peter Munro 10.00 3.00
68 Jarrod Washburn 10.00 3.00
69 Derrek Lee 15.00 4.50
70 Ramon Hernandez 10.00 3.00

1998 Bowman Minor League MVP's

Randomly inserted in second series packs at a rate of one in 12, this 11-card insert features former Minor League MVP award winners in color action photography.

Nm-Mt Ex-Mt
COMPLETE SET (11) 25.00 7.50
MVP1 Jeff Bagwell 1.50 .45
MVP2 Andres Galarraga 1.00 .30
MVP3 Juan Gonzalez 1.50 .45
MVP4 Tony Gwynn 3.00 .90
MVP5 Vladimir Guerrero 2.50 .75
MVP6 Derek Jeter 6.00 1.80
MVP7 Andruw Jones 1.00 .30
MVP8 Tino Martinez 1.50 .45
MVP9 Manny Ramirez 1.50 .45
MVP10 Gary Sheffield 1.00 .30
MVP11 Jim Thome 2.50 .75

1998 Bowman Scout's Choice

Randomly inserted in first series packs at a rate of one in 12, this borderless 21-card set is an insert featuring leading minor league prospects.

Nm-Mt Ex-Mt
COMPLETE SET (21) 25.00 7.50
SC1 Paul Konerko 2.00 .60
SC2 Richard Hidalgo 2.00 .60
SC3 Mark Kotsay 2.00 .60
SC4 Ben Grieve 2.00 .60
SC5 Chad Hermansen 2.00 .60
SC6 Matt Clement 2.00 .60
SC7 Brad Fullmer 2.00 .60
SC8 Eli Marrero 2.00 .60
SC9 Kerry Wood 5.00 1.50
SC10 Adrian Beltre 5.00 1.50
SC11 Ricky Ledee 2.00 .60
SC12 Travis Lee 2.00 .60
SC13 Abraham Nunez 2.00 .60
SC14 Brian Rose 2.00 .60
SC15 Dermal Brown 2.00 .60
SC16 Juan Encarnacion 2.00 .60
SC17 Aramis Ramirez 2.00 .60
SC18 Todd Helton 3.00 .90
SC19 Kris Benson 2.00 .60
SC20 Russell Branyan 2.00 .60
SC21 Mike Stoner 2.00 .60

1999 Bowman

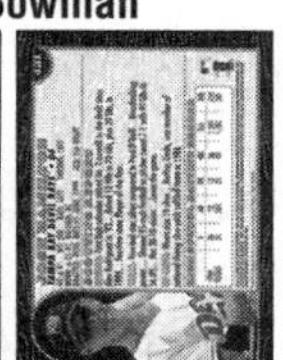

The 1999 Bowman set was issued in two series and was distributed in 10 card packs with a suggested retail price of $3.00. The 440-card set featured the newest faces and potential talent that would carry Major League Baseball into the next millennium. This set features 300 top prospects and 140 veterans. Prospect cards are designated with a silver and blue design while the veteran cards are shown with a silver and red design. Prospects making their debut on a Bowman card each featured a "Bowman Rookie Card" stamp on front. Notable Rookie Cards include Pat Burrell, Sean Burroughs, Adam Dunn, Rafael Furcal, Tim Hudson, Nick Johnson, Austin Kearns, Corey Patterson, Wily Mo Pena, Adam Piatt and Alfonso Soriano.

Nm-Mt Ex-Mt
COMPLETE SET (440) 80.00 24.00
COMP. SERIES 1 (220) 30.00 9.00
COMP. SERIES 2 (220) 50.00 15.00
1 Ben Grieve .30 .09
2 Kerry Wood .75 .23
3 Ruben Rivera .30 .09
4 Sandy Alomar Jr. .30 .09
5 Cal Ripken 2.50 .75
6 Mark McGwire 2.00 .60
7 Vladimir Guerrero .75 .23
8 Moises Alou .30 .09
9 Jim Edmonds .30 .09
10 Greg Maddux 1.25 .35
11 Gary Sheffield .30 .09
12 John Valentin .30 .09
13 Chuck Knoblauch .30 .09
14 Tony Clark .30 .09
15 Rusty Greer .30 .09
16 Al Leiter .30 .09
17 Travis Lee .30 .09
18 Jose Cruz Jr. .30 .09
19 Pedro Martinez .75 .23
20 Paul O'Neill .50 .15
21 Todd Walker .30 .09
22 Vinny Castilla .30 .09
23 Barry Larkin .50 .15
24 Curt Schilling .30 .09
25 Jason Kendall .30 .09
26 Scott Erickson .30 .09
27 Andres Galarraga .30 .09
28 Jeff Shaw .30 .09
29 John Olerud .30 .09
30 Orlando Hernandez .30 .09
31 Larry Walker .50 .15
32 Andruw Jones .30 .09
33 Jeff Cirillo .30 .09
34 Barry Bonds 2.00 .60
35 Manny Ramirez .50 .15
36 Mark Kotsay .30 .09
37 Ivan Rodriguez .75 .23
38 Jeff King .30 .09
39 Brian Hunter .30 .09
40 Ray Durham .30 .09
41 Bernie Williams .50 .15
42 Darin Erstad .30 .09
43 Chipper Jones .75 .23
44 Pat Hentgen .30 .09
45 Eric Young .30 .09
46 Jaret Wright .30 .09
47 Juan Guzman .30 .09
48 Jorge Posada .50 .15
49 Bobby Higginson .30 .09
50 Jose Guillen .30 .09
51 Trevor Hoffman .30 .09
52 Ken Griffey Jr. 1.25 .35
53 David Justice .30 .09
54 Matt Williams .30 .09
55 Eric Karros .30 .09
56 Derek Bell .30 .09
57 Ray Lankford .30 .09
58 Mariano Rivera .50 .15
59 Brett Tomko .30 .09
60 Mike Mussina .50 .15
61 Kenny Lofton .30 .09
62 Chuck Finley .30 .09
63 Alex Gonzalez .30 .09
64 Mark Grace .50 .15
65 Raul Mondesi .30 .09
66 David Cone .30 .09
67 Brad Fullmer .30 .09
68 Andy Benes .30 .09
69 John Smoltz .50 .15
70 Shane Reynolds .30 .09
71 Bruce Chen .30 .09
72 Adam Kennedy .30 .09
73 Jack Cust .30 .09
74 Matt Clement .30 .09
75 Derrick Gibson .30 .09
76 Darnell McDonald .30 .09
77 Adam Everett RC .50 .15
78 Ricardo Aramboles .30 .09
79 Mark Quinn RC .40 .12
80 Jason Rakers .30 .09
81 Seth Etherton RC .30 .09
82 Jeff Urban RC .40 .12
83 Manny Aybar .30 .09
84 Mike Nannini RC .30 .09
85 Onan Masaoka .30 .09
86 Rod Barajas .30 .09
87 Mike Frank .30 .09
88 Scott Randall .30 .09
89 Justin Bowles RC .30 .09
90 Chris Haas .30 .09
91 Arturo McDowell RC .30 .09
92 Matt Belisle RC .30 .35
93 Scott Elarton .30 .09
94 Vernon Wells .30 .09
95 Pat Cline .30 .09
96 Ryan Anderson .30 .09
97 Kevin Barker .30 .09
98 Ruben Mateo .30 .09
99 Robert Fick .30 .09
100 Corey Koskie .30 .09
101 Ricky Ledee .30 .09
102 Rick Elder RC .40 .12
103 Jack Cressend RC .30 .09
104 Joe Lawrence .30 .09
105 Mike Lincoln .30 .09
106 Kit Pellow RC .30 .09
107 Matt Burch RC .40 .12
108 Cole Liniak .30 .09
109 Jason Dewey .30 .09
110 Cesar King .30 .09
111 Julio Ramirez .30 .09
112 Jake Westbrook .30 .09
113 Eric Valent RC .40 .12
114 Roosevelt Brown RC .30 .09
115 Choo Freeman RC .40 .12
116 Juan Melo .30 .09
117 Jason Grilli .30 .09
118 Jared Sandberg .30 .09
119 Glenn Davis .30 .09
120 David Riske RC .30 .09
121 Jacque Jones .30 .09
122 Corey Lee .30 .09
123 Michael Barrett .30 .09
124 Lariel Gonzalez .30 .09
125 Mitch Meluskey .30 .09
126 Freddy Adrian Garcia .30 .09
127 Tony Torcato RC .40 .12
128 Jeff Liefer .30 .09
129 Ntema Ndungidi .30 .09
130 Andy Brown RC .30 .09
131 Ryan Mills RC .30 .09
132 Andy Abad RC .30 .09
133 Carlos Febles .30 .09
134 Jason Tyner RC .30 .09
135 Mark Osborne .30 .09
136 Phil Norton RC .30 .09
137 Nathan Haynes .30 .09
138 Roy Halladay .30 .09
139 Juan Encarnacion .30 .09
140 Brad Penny .30 .09
141 Grant Roberts .30 .09
142 Aramis Ramirez .30 .09
143 Cristian Guzman .30 .09
144 Mamon Tucker RC .30 .09
145 Ryan Bradley .30 .09
146 Brian Simmons .30 .09
147 Dan Reichert .30 .09
148 Russ Branyan .30 .09
149 Victor Valencia RC .30 .09
150 Scott Schoeneweis .30 .09
151 Sean Spencer RC .30 .09
152 Odalis Perez .30 .09
153 Joe Fontenot .30 .09
154 Milton Bradley .30 1.30
155 Josh McKinley RC .40 .12
156 Terrence Long .30 .09
157 Danny Klassen .30 .09
158 Paul Hoover RC .40 .12
159 Ron Belliard .30 .09
160 Armando Rios .30 .09
161 Ramon Hernandez .30 .09
162 Jason Conti .30 .09
163 Chad Hermansen .30 .09
164 Jason Standridge .30 .09
165 Jason Dellaero .30 .09
166 John Curtice .30 .09
167 Clayton Andrews RC .30 .09
168 Jeremy Giambi .30 .09
169 Alex Ramirez .30 .09
170 Gabe Molina RC .30 .09
171 M.Encarnacion RC .30 .09
172 Mike Zywica RC .30 .09
173 Chip Ambres RC .30 .09
174 Trot Nixon .30 .09
175 Pat Burrell RC 2.50 .75
176 Jeff Yoder .30 .09
177 Chris Jones RC .30 .09
178 Kevin Witt .30 .09
179 Keith Luuloa RC .30 .09
180 Billy Koch .30 .09
181 Damaso Marte RC .30 .09
182 Ryan Glynn RC .30 .09
183 Calvin Pickering .30 .09
184 Michael Cuddyer .30 .09
185 Nick Johnson RC .75 .23
186 D.Mientkiewicz RC .75 .23
187 Nate Cornejo RC .50 .15
188 Octavio Dotel .30 .09
189 Wes Helms .30 .09
190 Nelson Lara .30 .09
191 Chuck Abbott RC .30 .09
192 Tony Armas Jr. .30 .09
193 Gil Meche .30 .09
194 Ben Petrick .30 .09
195 Chris George RC .40 .12
196 Scott Hunter RC .30 .09
197 Ryan Brannan .30 .09
198 Amaury Garcia RC .40 .12
199 Chris Gissell .30 .09
200 Austin Kearns RC 2.50 .75
201 Alex Gonzalez .30 .09
202 Wade Miller .30 .09
203 Scott Williamson .30 .09
204 Chris Enochs .30 .09
205 Fernando Seguignol .30 .09
206 Marlon Anderson .30 .09
207 Todd Sears RC .40 .12
208 Nate Bump RC .30 .09
209 J.M. Gold RC .30 .09
210 Matt LeCroy .30 .09
211 Alex Hernandez .30 .09
212 Luis Rivera .30 .09
213 Troy Cameron .30 .09
214 Alex Escobar RC .40 .12
215 Jason LaRue .30 .09
216 Kyle Peterson .30 .09
217 Brent Butler .30 .09
218 Dernell Stenson .30 .09
219 Adrian Beltre .50 .15
220 Daryle Ward .30 .09
221 Jim Thome .75 .23
222 Cliff Floyd .30 .09
223 Rickey Henderson .75 .23
224 Garret Anderson .30 .09
225 Ken Caminiti .30 .09
226 Bret Boone .30 .09
227 Jeromy Burnitz .30 .09
228 Steve Finley .30 .09
229 Miguel Tejada .30 .09
230 Greg Vaughn .30 .09
231 Jose Offerman .30 .09
232 Andy Ashby .30 .09
233 Albert Belle .30 .09
234 Fernando Tatis .30 .09
235 Todd Helton .50 .15
236 Sean Casey .30 .09
237 Brian Giles .30 .09
238 Andy Pettitte .50 .15
239 Fred McGriff .50 .15
240 Roberto Alomar .50 .15
241 Edgar Martinez .50 .15
242 Lee Stevens .30 .09
243 Shawn Green .30 .09
244 Ryan Klesko .30 .09
245 Sammy Sosa 1.25 .35
246 Todd Hundley .30 .09
247 Shannon Stewart .30 .09
248 Randy Johnson .75 .23
249 Rondell White .30 .09
250 Mike Piazza 1.25 .35
251 Craig Biggio .50 .15
252 David Wells .30 .09
253 Brian Jordan .30 .09
254 Edgar Renteria .30 .09
255 Bartolo Colon .30 .09
256 Frank Thomas .75 .23
257 Will Clark .75 .23
258 Dean Palmer .30 .09
259 Dmitri Young .30 .09
260 Scott Rolen .75 .23
261 Jeff Kent .30 .09
262 Dante Bichette .30 .09
263 Nomar Garciaparra 1.25 .35
264 Tony Gwynn 1.00 .30
265 Alex Rodriguez 1.25 .35
266 Jose Canseco .75 .23
267 Jason Giambi .30 .09
268 Jeff Bagwell .50 .15
269 Carlos Delgado .30 .09
270 Tom Glavine .50 .15
271 Eric Davis .30 .09
272 Edgardo Alfonzo .30 .09
273 Tim Salmon .50 .15
274 Johnny Damon .50 .15
275 Rafael Palmeiro .50 .15
276 Denny Neagle .30 .09
277 Neifi Perez .30 .09
278 Roger Clemens 1.50 .45
279 Brant Brown .30 .09
280 Kevin Brown .50 .15
281 Jay Bell .30 .09
282 Jay Buhner .30 .09
283 Matt Lawton .30 .09
284 Robin Ventura .30 .09
285 Juan Gonzalez .50 .15
286 Mo Vaughn .30 .09
287 Kevin Millwood .30 .09
288 Tino Martinez .50 .15
289 Justin Thompson .30 .09
290 Derek Jeter 2.00 .60
291 Ben Davis .30 .09
292 Mike Lowell .30 .09
293 Calvin Murray .30 .09
294 Micah Bowie RC .30 .09
295 Lance Berkman .30 .09
296 Jason Marquis .30 .09
297 Chad Green .30 .09
298 Dee Brown .30 .09
299 Jerry Hairston Jr. .30 .09
300 Gabe Kapler .30 .09
301 Brent Stentz RC .40 .12
302 Scott Mullen RC .30 .09
303 Brandon Reed .30 .09
304 Shea Hillenbrand RC .75 .23
305 J.D. Closser RC .50 .15
306 Gary Matthews Jr. .30 .09
307 Toby Hall RC .40 .12
308 Jason Phillips RC .30 .09
309 Jose Macias RC .30 .09
310 Jung Bong RC .40 .12
311 Ramon Soler RC .30 .09
312 Kelly Dransfeldt RC .30 .09
313 Carl. E. Hernandez RC .40 .12
314 Kevin Haverbusch .30 .09
315 Aaron Myette RC .30 .09
316 Chad Harville RC .30 .09
317 Kyle Farnsworth RC .40 .12
318 Gookie Dawkins RC .40 .12
319 Willie Martinez .30 .09

320 Carlos Lee .30 .09
321 Carlos Pena RC .50 .15
322 Peter Bergeron RC .40 .12
323 A.J. Burnett RC .75 .23
324 Bucky Jacobsen RC 4.00 1.20
325 Mo Bruce RC .30 .09
326 Reggie Taylor .30 .09
327 Jackie Rexrode .30 .09
328 Alvin Morrow RC .30 .09
329 Carlos Beltran .50 .15
330 Eric Chavez .30 .09
331 John Patterson .30 .09
332 Jayson Werth .30 .09
333 Richie Sexson .30 .09
334 Randy Wolf .30 .09
335 Eli Marrero .30 .09
336 Paul LoDuca .30 .09
337 J.D Smart .30 .09
338 Ryan Minor .30 .09
339 Kris Benson .30 .09
340 George Lombard .30 .09
341 Troy Glaus .30 .09
342 Eddie Yarnall .30 .09
343 Kip Wells RC .50 .15
344 C.C. Sabathia RC 1.00 .30
345 Sean Burroughs RC 1.25 .35
346 Felipe Lopez RC .40 .12
347 Ryan Rupe RC .30 .09
348 Orber Moreno RC .30 .09
349 Rafael Roque RC .30 .09
350 Alfonso Soriano RC 5.00 1.50
351 Pablo Ozuna .30 .09
352 Corey Patterson RC 2.00 .60
353 Braden Looper .30 .09
354 Robbie Bell .30 .09
355 Mark Mulder RC 2.00 .45
356 Angel Pena .30 .09
357 Kevin McGlinchy .30 .09
358 M.Restovich RC .40 .12
359 Eric DuBose .30 .09
360 Geoff Jenkins .30 .09
361 Mark Harriger RC .30 .09
362 Junior Herndon RC .40 .12
363 Tim Raines Jr. RC .40 .12
364 Rafael Furcal RC 1.00 .30
365 Marcus Giles RC 1.00 .30
366 Ted Lilly .30 .09
367 Jorge Toca RC .40 .12
368 David Kelton RC .40 .12
369 Adam Dunn RC 4.00 1.20
370 Guillermo Mota RC .30 .09
371 Brett Laxton RC .30 .09
372 Travis Harper RC .40 .12
373 Tom Davey RC .30 .09
374 Darren Blakely RC .30 .09
375 Tim Hudson RC 2.00 .60
376 Jason Romano .30 .09
377 Dan Reichert .30 .09
378 Julio Lugo RC .40 .12
379 Jose Garcia RC .30 .09
380 Erubiel Durazo RC .50 .15
381 Jose Jimenez .30 .09
382 Chris Fussell .30 .09
383 Steve Lomasney .30 .09
384 Juan Pena RC .40 .12
385 Allen Levrault RC .30 .09
386 Juan Rivera RC .40 .12
387 Steve Colyer RC .40 .12
388 Joe Nathan RC .75 .23
389 Ron Walker RC .30 .09
390 Nick Bierbrodt .30 .09
391 Luke Prokopec RC .30 .09
392 Dave Roberts RC .50 .15
393 Mike Darr .30 .09
394 Abraham Nunez RC .40 .12
395 G.Chiaramonte RC .30 .09
396 J.Van Buren RC .30 .09
397 Mike Kusiewicz .30 .09
398 Matt Wise RC .30 .09
399 Joe McEwing RC .40 .12
400 Matt Holliday RC .75 .23
401 Willi Mo Pena RC 2.00 .60
402 Ruben Quevedo RC .30 .09
403 Rob Ryan RC .30 .09
404 Freddy Garcia RC .75 .23
405 Kevin Eberwein RC .30 .09
406 Jesus Colome RC .30 .09
407 Chris Singleton .30 .09
408 Bubba Crosby RC .50 .15
409 Jesus Cordero RC .40 .12
410 Donny Leon .30 .09
411 G.Tomlinson RC .40 .12
412 Jeff Winchester RC .30 .09
413 Adam Piatt RC .40 .12
414 Robert Stratton .30 .09
415 T.J. Tucker .30 .09
416 Ryan Langerhans RC .30 .09
417 A.Shumaker RC .30 .09
418 Matt Miller RC .30 .09
419 Doug Clark RC .30 .09
420 Kory DeHaan RC .30 .09
421 David Eckstein RC .50 .15
422 Brian Cooper RC .30 .09
423 Brady Clark RC .30 .09
424 Chris Magruder RC .40 .12
425 Bobby Seay RC .30 .09
426 Aubrey Huff RC 1.00 .30
427 Mike Jerzembeck .30 .09
428 Matt Blank RC .40 .12
429 Benny Agbayani RC .40 .12
430 Kevin Beirne RC .40 .12
431 Josh Hamilton RC .50 .15
432 Josh Girdley RC .30 .09
433 Kyle Snyder RC .30 .09
434 Mike Paradis RC .30 .09
435 Jason Jennings RC .50 .15
436 David Walling RC .30 .09
437 Omar Ortiz RC .40 .12
438 Jay Gehrke RC .40 .12
439 Casey Burns RC .40 .12
440 Carl Crawford RC 1.50 .45

1999 Bowman Gold

Randomly inserted in first series packs at a rate of one in 111 and second series packs at a rate of one in 59, this 440-card set is a parallel to the Bowman base set. The set features facsimile autographs printed in gold foil with gold border designs. Each card is serial numbered to 99 on the back.

Nm-Mt Ex-Mt
*STARS: 10X TO 25X BASIC CARDS..
*ROOKIES: 4X TO 10X BASIC CARDS

1999 Bowman International

Inserted one per pack, this 440-card set is a parallel to the Bowman base set. Card fronts contain each player's nationality with a background photograph of a landmark native to his homeland. Card backs contain vital information which are translated into the player's home language giving the collector insight into the player's background. Card fronts are printed on a distinctive foil board.

	Nm-Mt	Ex-Mt
COMPLETE SET (440)	200.00	60.00
COMP.SERIES 1 (220)	80.00	24.00
COMP.SERIES 2 (220)	120.00	36.00

*STARS: 1X TO 2.5X BASIC CARDS...
*ROOKIES: .6X TO 1.5X BASIC CARDS

1999 Bowman Autographs

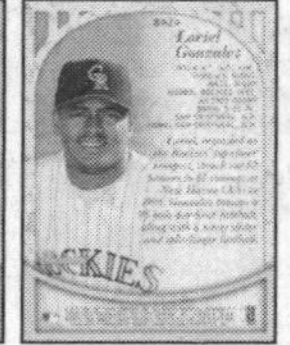

This set contains a selection of top young prospects, all of whom participated by signing their cards in blue ink. Card rarity is differentiated by either a blue, silver or gold foil Topps Certified Autograph Issue Stamp. The insert rates for Blue are at a rate of one in 162; Silver one in 485 and Gold one in 1,194.

	Nm-Mt	Ex-Mt
BA1 Ruben Mateo B	10.00	3.00
BA2 Troy Glaus G	25.00	7.50
BA3 Ben Davis G	15.00	4.50
BA4 Jayson Werth B	10.00	3.00
BA5 Jerry Hairston Jr. S	10.00	1.50
BA6 Darnell McDonald B	10.00	3.00
BA7 Calvin Pickering S	15.00	4.50
BA8 Ryan Minor S	15.00	4.50
BA9 Alex Escobar B	15.00	4.50
BA10 Grant Roberts B	10.00	3.00
BA11 Carlos Guillen B	15.00	4.50
BA12 Ryan Anderson S	15.00	4.50
BA13 Gil Meche S	15.00	4.50
BA14 Russell Branyan S	15.00	4.50
BA15 Alex Ramirez S	15.00	4.50
BA16 Jason Rakers S	15.00	4.50
BA17 Eddie Yarnall B	15.00	4.50
BA18 Freddy Garcia B	20.00	6.00
BA19 Jason Conti B	10.00	3.00
BA20 Corey Koskie B	15.00	4.50
BA21 Roosevelt Brown B	10.00	3.00
BA22 Willie Martinez B	10.00	3.00
BA23 Mike Jerzembeck B	10.00	3.00
BA24 Lariel Gonzalez B	10.00	3.00
BA25 F.Seguignol B	10.00	3.00
BA26 Robert Fick S	15.00	4.50
BA27 J.D. Smart B	10.00	3.00
BA28 Ryan Mills B	10.00	3.00
BA29 Chad Hermansen G	15.00	4.50
BA30 Jason Grilli B	10.00	3.00
BA31 Michael Cuddyer B	10.00	3.00
BA32 Jacque Jones S	25.00	7.50
BA33 Reggie Taylor B	10.00	3.00
BA34 Richie Sexson G	25.00	7.50
BA35 Michael Barrett B	10.00	3.00
BA36 Paul LoDuca B	15.00	4.50
BA37 Adrian Beltre G	40.00	12.00
BA38 Peter Bergeron B	15.00	4.50
BA39 Joe Fontenot B	10.00	3.00
BA40 Randy Wolf B	15.00	4.50
BA41 Nick Johnson B	25.00	7.50
BA42 Ryan Bradley B	10.00	3.00
BA43 Mike Lowell S	25.00	7.50
BA44 Ricky Ledee G	10.00	2.00
BA45 Mike Lincoln S	15.00	4.50
BA46 Jeremy Giambi B	10.00	3.00
BA47 Dermal Brown S	15.00	4.50
BA48 Derrick Gibson B	10.00	3.00
BA49 Scott Randall B	10.00	3.00
BA50 Ben Petrick S	15.00	4.50
BA51 Jason LaRue B	10.00	3.00
BA52 Cole Liniak B	10.00	3.00
BA53 John Curtice B	10.00	3.00
BA54 Jackie Rexrode B	10.00	3.00
BA55 John Patterson B	10.00	3.00
BA56 Brad Penny S	25.00	7.50
BA57 Jared Sandberg B	10.00	3.00
BA58 Kerry Wood G	40.00	12.00
BA59 Eli Marrero S	15.00	4.50
BA60 Jason Marquis B	15.00	4.50
BA61 George Lombard S	15.00	4.50
BA62 Bruce Chen S	15.00	4.50
BA63 Kevin Witt S	15.00	4.50
BA64 Vernon Wells B	15.00	4.50
BA65 Billy Koch B	15.00	4.50
BA66 Roy Halladay G	15.00	4.50
BA67 Nathan Haynes B	15.00	4.50
BA68 Ben Grieve G	15.00	4.50
BA69 Eric Chavez G	25.00	7.50
BA70 Lance Berkman S	40.00	12.00

1999 Bowman 2000 ROY Favorites

Randomly inserted in second series packs at a rate of one in twelve, this 10-card insert set features borderless, double-etched foil cards and feature players that had serious potential to win the 2000 Rookie of the Year award.

	Nm-Mt	Ex-Mt
COMPLETE SET (10)	10.00	3.00
ROY1 Ryan Anderson	.50	.15
ROY2 Pat Burrell	1.25	.35
ROY3 A.J. Burnett	.75	.23
ROY4 Ruben Mateo	.50	.15
ROY5 Alex Escobar	.50	.15
ROY6 Pablo Ozuna	.50	.15
ROY7 Mark Mulder	2.00	.45
ROY8 Corey Patterson	2.00	.45
ROY9 George Lombard	.50	.15
ROY10 Nick Johnson	.75	.23

1999 Bowman Early Risers

Randomly inserted in second series packs at a rate of one in twelve, this 11-card insert set features current superstars who have already won a ROY award and who continue to prove their worth on the diamond.

	Nm-Mt	Ex-Mt
COMPLETE SET (11)	25.00	7.50
ER1 Mike Piazza	2.50	.75
ER2 Cal Ripken	5.00	1.50
ER3 Jeff Bagwell	1.00	.30
ER4 Ben Grieve	.60	.18
ER5 Kerry Wood	1.50	.45
ER6 Mark McGwire	4.00	1.20
ER7 Nomar Garciaparra	2.50	.75
ER8 Derek Jeter	4.00	1.20
ER9 Scott Rolen	1.50	.45
ER10 Jose Canseco	1.50	.45
ER11 Raul Mondesi	.60	.18

1999 Bowman Late Bloomers

Randomly inserted in first series packs at a rate of one in twelve, this 10-card insert set features late round picks from previous drafts. Players featured include Mike Piazza and Jim Thome.

	Nm-Mt	Ex-Mt
COMPLETE SET (10)	8.00	2.40
LB1 Mike Piazza	2.50	.75
LB2 Jim Thome	1.50	.45
LB3 Larry Walker	1.00	.30
LB4 Vinny Castilla	.60	.18
LB5 Andy Pettitte	1.00	.30
LB6 Jim Edmonds	.60	.18
LB7 Kenny Lofton	.60	.18
LB8 John Smoltz	1.00	.30
LB9 Mark Grace	1.00	.30
LB10 Trevor Hoffman	.60	.18

1999 Bowman Scout's Choice

Randomly inserted in first series packs at a rate of one in twelve, this 21-card insert set features a selection of gifted prospects.

	Nm-Mt	Ex-Mt
COMPLETE SET (21)	20.00	6.00
SC1 Ruben Mateo	1.00	.30
SC2 Ryan Anderson	1.00	.30
SC3 Pat Burrell	1.50	.45
SC4 Troy Glaus	1.00	.30
SC5 Eric Chavez	1.00	.30
SC6 Adrian Beltre	1.50	.45
SC7 Bruce Chen	1.00	.30
SC8 Carlos Beltran	1.50	.45
SC9 Alex Gonzalez	1.00	.30
SC10 Carlos Lee	1.00	.30
SC11 George Lombard	1.00	.30
SC12 Matt Clement	1.00	.30
SC13 Calvin Pickering	1.00	.30
SC14 Marlon Anderson	1.00	.30
SC15 Chad Hermansen	1.00	.30
SC16 Russell Branyan	1.00	.30
SC17 Jeremy Giambi	1.00	.30
SC18 Ricky Ledee	1.00	.30
SC19 John Patterson	1.00	.30
SC20 Roy Halladay	1.00	.30
SC21 Michael Barrett	1.00	.30

2000 Bowman

The 2000 Bowman product was released in May, 2000 as a 440-card set. The set features 140 veteran players and 300 rookies and prospects. Each pack contained 10 cards and carried a suggested retail price of $3.00. Rookie Cards

include Rick Asadoorian, Bobby Bradley, Kevin Mench, Nick Neugebauer, Ben Sheets and Barry Zito.

	Nm-Mt	Ex-Mt
COMPLETE SET (440)	60.00	18.00
1 Vladimir Guerrero	.75	.23
2 Chipper Jones	.75	.23
3 Todd Walker	.30	.09
4 Barry Larkin	.50	.15
5 Bernie Williams	.50	.15
6 Todd Helton	.50	.15
7 Jermaine Dye	.30	.09
8 Brian Giles	.30	.09
9 Freddy Garcia	.30	.09
10 Greg Vaughn	.30	.09
11 Alex Gonzalez	.30	.09
12 Luis Gonzalez	.30	.09
13 Ron Belliard	.30	.09
14 Ben Grieve	.30	.09
15 Carlos Delgado	.30	.09
16 Brian Jordan	.30	.09
17 Fernando Tatis	.30	.09
18 Ryan Rupe	.30	.09
19 Miguel Tejada	.30	.09
20 Mark Grace	.50	.15
21 Kenny Lofton	.30	.09
22 Eric Karros	.30	.09
23 Cliff Floyd	.30	.09
24 John Halama	.30	.09
25 Cristian Guzman	.30	.09
26 Scott Williamson	.30	.09
27 Mike Lieberthal	.30	.09
28 Tim Hudson	.30	.09
29 Warren Morris	.30	.09
30 Pedro Martinez	.75	.23
31 John Smoltz	.50	.15
32 Ray Durham	.30	.09
33 Chad Allen	.30	.09
34 Tony Clark	.30	.09
35 Tino Martinez	.50	.15
36 J.T. Snow	.30	.09
37 Kevin Brown	.30	.09
38 Bartolo Colon	.30	.09
39 Rey Ordonez	.30	.09
40 Jeff Bagwell	.50	.15
41 Ivan Rodriguez	.75	.23
42 Eric Chavez	.30	.09
43 Eric Milton	.30	.09
44 Jose Canseco	.75	.23
45 Shawn Green	.30	.09
46 Rich Aurilia	.30	.09
47 Roberto Alomar	.50	.15
48 Brian Daubach	.30	.09
49 Magglio Ordonez	.30	.09
50 Derek Jeter	2.00	.60
51 Kris Benson	.30	.09
52 Albert Belle	.30	.09
53 Rondell White	.30	.09
54 Justin Thompson	.30	.09
55 Nomar Garciaparra	1.25	.35
56 Chuck Finley	.30	.09
57 Omar Vizquel	.50	.15
58 Luis Castillo	.30	.09
59 Richard Hidalgo	.30	.09
60 Barry Bonds	2.00	.60
61 Craig Biggio	.50	.15
62 Doug Glanville	.30	.09
63 Gabe Kapler	.30	.09
64 Johnny Damon	.50	.15
65 Pokey Reese	.30	.09
66 Andy Pettitte	.50	.15
67 B.J. Surhoff	.30	.09
68 Richie Sexson	.30	.09
69 Javy Lopez	.30	.09
70 Raul Mondesi	.30	.09
71 Darin Erstad	.30	.09
72 Kevin Millwood	.30	.09
73 Ricky Ledee	.30	.09
74 John Olerud	.30	.09
75 Sean Casey	.30	.09
76 Carlos Febles	.30	.09
77 Paul O'Neill	.50	.15
78 Bob Abreu	.30	.09
79 Neifi Perez	.30	.09
80 Tony Gwynn	1.00	.30
81 Russ Ortiz	.30	.09
82 Matt Williams	.30	.09
83 Chris Carpenter	.30	.09
84 Roger Cedeno	.30	.09
85 Tim Salmon	.50	.15
86 Billy Koch	.30	.09
87 Jeromy Burnitz	.30	.09
88 Edgardo Alfonzo	.30	.09
89 Jay Bell	.30	.09
90 Manny Ramirez	.50	.15
91 Frank Thomas	.75	.23
92 Mike Mussina	.50	.15
93 J.D. Drew	.30	.09
94 Adrian Beltre	.50	.15
95 Alex Rodriguez	1.25	.35
96 Larry Walker	.50	.15
97 Juan Encarnacion	.30	.09
98 Mike Sweeney	.30	.09
99 Rusty Greer	.30	.09
100 Randy Johnson	.75	.23
101 Jose Vidro	.30	.09
102 Preston Wilson	.30	.09
103 Greg Maddux	1.25	.35
104 Jason Giambi	.75	.23
105 Cal Ripken	2.50	.75
106 Carlos Beltran	.50	.15
107 Vinny Castilla	.30	.09
108 Mariano Rivera	.50	.15
109 Mo Vaughn	.30	.09
110 Rafael Palmeiro	.50	.15
111 Shannon Stewart	.30	.09
112 Mike Hampton	.30	.09
113 Joe Nathan	.30	.09
114 Ben Davis	.30	.09
115 Andruw Jones	.30	.09
116 Robin Ventura	.30	.09
117 Damion Easley	.30	.09
118 Jeff Cirillo	.30	.09
119 Kerry Wood	.75	.23
120 Scott Rolen	.75	.23
121 Sammy Sosa	1.25	.35
122 Ken Griffey Jr.	1.25	.35
123 Shane Reynolds	.30	.09
124 Troy Glaus	.30	.09
125 Tom Glavine	.50	.15
126 Michael Barrett	.30	.09
127 Al Leiter	.30	.09
128 Jason Kendall	.30	.09
129 Roger Clemens	1.50	.45
130 Juan Gonzalez	.50	.15
131 Corey Koskie	.30	.09
132 Curt Schilling	.30	.09
133 Mike Piazza	1.25	.35
134 Gary Sheffield	.30	.09
135 Jim Thome	.75	.23
136 Orlando Hernandez	.30	.09
137 Ray Lankford	.30	.09
138 Geoff Jenkins	.30	.09
139 Jose Lima	.30	.09
140 Mark McGwire	2.00	.60
141 Adam Piatt	.30	.09
142 Pat Manning RC	.30	.09
143 Marcos Castillo RC	.30	.09
144 Lesli Brea RC	.30	.09
145 Humberto Cota RC	.40	.12
146 Ben Petrick	.30	.09
147 Kip Wells	.30	.09
148 Wily Pena	.30	.09
149 Chris Wakeland RC	.30	.09
150 Brad Baker RC	.40	.12
151 Robbie Morrison RC	.30	.09
152 Reggie Taylor	.30	.09
153 Matt Ginter RC	.40	.12
154 Peter Bergeron	.30	.09
155 Roosevelt Brown	.30	.09
156 Matt Cepicky RC	.30	.09
157 Ramon Castro	.30	.09
158 Brad Baisley RC	.30	.09
159 Jeff Goldbach RC	.30	.09
160 Mitch Meluskey	.30	.09
161 Chad Harville	.30	.09
162 Brian Cooper	.30	.09
163 Marcus Giles	.30	.09
164 Jim Morris	.75	.23
165 Geoff Goetz	.30	.09
166 Bobby Bradley RC	.40	.12
167 Rob Bell	.30	.09
168 Joe Crede	.30	.09
169 Michael Restovich	.30	.09
170 Quincy Foster RC	.30	.09
171 Enrique Cruz RC	.30	.09
172 Mark Quinn	.30	.09
173 Nick Johnson	.30	.09
174 Jeff Liefer	.30	.09
175 Kevin Mench RC	.75	.23
176 Steve Lomasney	.30	.09
177 Jayson Werth	.30	.09
178 Tim Drew	.30	.09
179 Chip Ambres	.30	.09
180 Ryan Anderson	.30	.09
181 Matt Blank	.30	.09
182 G.Chiaramonte	.30	.09
183 Corey Myers RC	.40	.12
184 Jeff Yoder	.30	.09
185 Craig Dingman RC	.30	.09
186 Jon Hamilton RC	.30	.09
187 Toby Hall	.30	.09
188 Russell Branyan	.30	.09
189 Brian Falkenborg RC	.30	.09
190 Aaron Harang RC	.40	.12
191 Juan Pena	.30	.09
192 Travis Thompson RC	.30	.09
193 Alfonso Soriano	.75	.23
194 Alejandro Diaz RC	.30	.09
195 Carlos Pena	.30	.09
196 Kevin Nicholson	.30	.09
197 Mo Bruce	.30	.09
198 C.C. Sabathia	.30	.09
199 Carl Crawford	.30	.09
200 Rafael Furcal	.30	.09
201 Andrew Beinbrink RC	.30	.09
202 Jimmy Osting	.30	.09
203 Aaron McNeal RC	.40	.12
204 Brett Laxton	.30	.09
205 Chris George	.30	.09
206 Felipe Lopez	.30	.09
207 Ben Sheets RC	2.00	.60
208 Mike Meyers RC	.40	.12
209 Jason Conti	.30	.09
210 Milton Bradley	.30	.09
211 Chris Mears RC	.30	.09
212 Carlos Hernandez RC	.50	.15
213 Jason Romano	.30	.09
214 Geofrey Tomlinson	.30	.09
215 Jimmy Rollins	.30	.09
216 Pablo Ozuna	.30	.09
217 Steve Cox	.30	.09
218 Terrence Long	.30	.09
219 Jeff DaVanon RC	.40	.12
220 Rick Ankiel	.30	.09
221 Jason Standridge	.30	.09
222 Tony Armas Jr.	.30	.09
223 Jason Tyner	.30	.09
224 Ramon Ortiz	.30	.09
225 Daryle Ward	.30	.09
226 Enger Veras RC	.30	.09
227 Chris Jones	.30	.09
228 Eric Cammack RC	.30	.09
229 Ruben Mateo	.30	.09
230 Ken Harvey RC	.75	.23
231 Jake Westbrook	.30	.09
232 Rob Purvis RC	.30	.09
233 Choo Freeman	.30	.09
234 Aramis Ramirez	.30	.09
235 A.J. Burnett	.30	.09
236 Kevin Barker	.30	.09
237 Chance Caple RC	.30	.09
238 Jarrod Washburn	.30	.09
239 Lance Berkman	.30	.09
240 Michael Wenner RC	.30	.09
241 Alex Sanchez	.30	.09
242 Pat Daneker	.30	.09

243 Grant Roberts .30 .09
244 Mark Ellis RC .40 .12
245 Donny Leon .30 .09
246 David Eckstein .30 .09
247 Dicky Gonzalez RC .30 .09
248 John Patterson .30 .09
249 Chad Green .30 .09
250 Scot Shields RC .30 .09
251 Troy Cameron .30 .09
252 Jose Molina .30 .09
253 Rob Pugmire RC .30 .09
254 Rick Elder .30 .09
255 Sean Burroughs .30 .09
256 Josh Kalinowski RC .30 .09
257 Matt LeCroy .30 .09
258 Alex Graman RC .30 .09
259 Tomo Ohka RC .40 .12
260 Brady Clark .30 .09
261 Rico Washington RC .30 .09
262 Gary Matthews Jr. .30 .09
263 Matt Wise .30 .09
264 Keith Reed RC .40 .12
265 Santiago Ramirez RC .30 .09
266 Ben Broussard RC .75 .23
267 Ryan Langerhans .30 .09
268 Juan Rivera .30 .09
269 Shawn Gallagher .30 .09
270 Jorge Toca .30 .09
271 Brad Lidge .30 .09
272 Leoncio Estrella RC .30 .09
273 Ruben Quevedo .30 .09
274 Jack Cust .30 .09
275 T.J. Tucker .30 .09
276 Mike Colangelo .30 .09
277 Brian Schneider .30 .09
278 Calvin Murray .30 .09
279 Josh Girdley .30 .09
280 Mike Paradis .30 .09
281 Chad Hermansen .30 .09
282 Ty Howington RC .40 .12
283 Aaron Myette .30 .09
284 D'Angelo Jimenez .30 .09
285 Dernell Stenson .30 .09
286 Jerry Hairston Jr. .30 .09
287 Gary Majewski RC .50 .15
288 Derrin Ebert .30 .09
289 Steve Fish RC .30 .09
290 Carlos E. Hernandez .30 .09
291 Allen Levrault .30 .09
292 Sean McNally RC .30 .09
293 Randey Dorame RC .30 .09
294 Wes Anderson RC .40 .12
295 B.J. Ryan .30 .09
296 Alan Webb RC .30 .09
297 Brandon Inge RC .40 .12
298 David Walling .30 .09
299 Sun Woo Kim RC .40 .12
300 Pat Burrell .30 .09
301 Rick Guttormson RC .30 .09
302 Gil Meche .30 .09
303 Carlos Zambrano RC 3.00 .90
304 Eric Byrnes UER RC .75 .23
Bo Porter pictured
305 Robb Quinlan RC .75 .23
306 Jackie Rexrode .30 .09
307 Nate Bump .30 .09
308 Sean DePaula RC .30 .09
309 Matt Riley .30 .09
310 Ryan Minor .30 .09
311 J.J. Davis .30 .09
312 Randy Wolf .30 .09
313 Jason Jennings .30 .09
314 Scott Seabol RC .30 .09
315 Doug Davis .30 .09
316 Todd Moser RC .30 .09
317 Rob Ryan .30 .09
318 Bubba Crosby .30 .09
319 Ryan Knox RC 1.25 .35
320 Mario Encarnacion .30 .09
321 F.Rodriguez RC 2.00 .60
322 Michael Cuddyer .30 .09
323 Ed Yarnall .30 .09
324 Cesar Saba RC .30 .09
325 Gookie Dawkins .30 .09
326 Alex Escobar .30 .09
327 Julio Zuleta RC .30 .09
328 Josh Hamilton .30 .09
329 Nick Neugebauer RC .40 .12
330 Matt Belisle .30 .09
331 Kurt Ainsworth RC .40 .12
332 Tim Raines Jr. .30 .09
333 Eric Munson .30 .09
334 Donzell McDonald .30 .09
335 Larry Bigbie RC .75 .23
336 Matt Watson RC .30 .09
337 Aubrey Huff .30 .09
338 Julio Ramirez .30 .09
339 Jason Grabowski RC .40 .12
340 Jon Garland .30 .09
341 Austin Kearns .50 .15
342 Josh Pressley RC .30 .09
343 Miguel Olivo RC .50 .15
344 Julio Lugo .30 .09
345 Roberto Vaz .30 .09
346 Ramon Soler .30 .09
347 Brandon Phillips RC .50 .15
348 Vince Faison RC .30 .09
349 Mike Venafro .30 .09
350 Rick Asadoorian RC .40 .12
351 B.J. Garbe RC .30 .09
352 Dan Reichert .30 .09
353 Jason Stumm RC .30 .09
354 Ruben Salazar RC .30 .09
355 Francisco Cordero .30 .09
356 Juan Guzman RC .30 .09
357 Mike Bacsik RC .30 .09
358 Jared Sandberg .30 .09
359 Rod Barajas .30 .09
360 Junior Brignac RC .30 .09
361 J.M. Gold .30 .09
362 Octavio Dotel .30 .09
363 David Kelton .30 .09
364 Scott Morgan .30 .09
365 Wascar Serrano RC .30 .09
366 Wilton Veras .30 .09
367 Eugene Kingsale .30 .09
368 Ted Lilly .30 .09
369 George Lombard .30 .09
370 Chris Haas .30 .09
371 Wilton Pena RC .30 .09
372 Vernon Wells .30 .09
373 Jason Royer RC .30 .09
374 Jeff Heaverlo RC .30 .09
375 Calvin Pickering .30 .09
376 Mike Lamb RC .40 .12
377 Kyle Snyder .30 .09
378 Javier Cardona RC .30 .09
379 Aaron Rowand RC 1.25 .35
380 Dee Brown .30 .09
381 Brett Myers RC .50 .15
382 Abraham Nunez .30 .09
383 Eric Valent .30 .09
384 Jody Gerut RC .75 .23
385 Adam Dunn .75 .23
386 Jay Gehrke .30 .09
387 Omar Ortiz .30 .09
388 Darnell McDonald .30 .09
389 Tony Schrager RC .30 .09
390 J.D. Closser .30 .09
391 Ben Christensen RC .30 .09
392 Adam Kennedy .30 .09
393 Nick Green RC .75 .23
394 Ramon Hernandez .30 .09
395 Roy Oswalt RC 2.50 .75
396 Andy Tracy RC .30 .09
397 Eric Gagne 1.25 .35
398 Michael Tejera RC .30 .09
399 Adam Everett .30 .09
400 Corey Patterson .30 .09
401 Gary Knotts RC .30 .09
402 Ryan Christianson RC .40 .12
403 Eric Ireland RC .30 .09
404 Andrew Good RC .30 .09
405 Brad Penny .30 .09
406 Jason LaRue .30 .09
407 Kit Pellow .30 .09
408 Kevin Beirne .30 .09
409 Kelly Dransfeldt .30 .09
410 Jason Grilli .30 .09
411 Scott Downs RC .30 .09
412 Jesus Colome .30 .09
413 John Sneed RC .30 .09
414 Tony McKnight .30 .09
415 Luis Rivera .30 .09
416 Adam Eaton .30 .09
417 Mike MacDougal RC .40 .12
418 Mike Nannini .30 .09
419 Barry Zito RC 2.00 .60
420 DeWayne Wise .30 .09
421 Jason Dellaero .30 .09
422 Chad Moeller .30 .09
423 Jason Marquis .30 .09
424 Tim Redding RC .40 .12
425 Mark Mulder .30 .09
426 Josh Paul .30 .09
427 Chris Enochs .30 .09
428 W.Rodriguez RC .30 .09
429 Kevin Witt .30 .09
430 Scott Sobkowiak RC .30 .09
431 McKay Christensen .30 .09
432 Jung Bong .30 .09
433 Keith Evans RC .30 .09
434 Garry Maddox Jr. RC .30 .09
435 Ramon Santiago RC .40 .12
436 Alex Cora .30 .09
437 Carlos Lee .30 .09
438 Jason Repko RC .40 .12
439 Matt Burch .30 .09
440 Shawn Sonnier RC .30 .09

2000 Bowman Gold

Randomly inserted into hobby/retail packs at one in 64, this 440-card insert is a complete parallel of the Bowman base set. Each card features a gold facsimile autograph that runs down the right side of the card. Each card in the set is also individually serial numbered to 99.

Nm-Mt Ex-Mt
*STARS: 10X TO 25X BASIC CARDS..
*ROOKIES: 5X TO 12X BASIC CARDS

2000 Bowman Retro/Future

Randomly inserted into hobby/retail packs at one per pack, this 440-card insert is a complete parallel of the Bowman base set. Each card features a television border similar to that of the classic 1955 Bowman set.

Nm-Mt Ex-Mt
COMPLETE SET (440) 200.00 60.00
*STARS: 1X TO 2.5X BASIC CARDS...
*ROOKIES: .6X TO 1.5X BASIC CARDS

2000 Bowman Autographs

Randomly inserted into packs, this 40-card insert features autographed cards from young players like Corey Patterson, Ruben Mateo, and Alfonso Soriano. Please note that this is a three tiered autographed set. Cards that are marked with a "B" are part of the Blue Tier (1:144 HOB/RET, 1:69 HTC). Cards marked with an "S" are part of the Silver Tier (1:312 HOB/RET, 1:148 HTC), and cards marked with a "G" are part of the Gold Tier (1:1604 HOB/RET, 1:762 HTC).

Nm-Mt Ex-Mt
AD Adam Dunn B 25.00 7.50
AH Aubrey Huff B 10.00 3.00
AK Austin Kearns B 15.00 4.50
AP Adam Piatt S 15.00 4.50
AS Alfonso Soriano S 40.00 12.00
BP Ben Petrick G 25.00 7.50
BS Ben Sheets B 40.00 12.00
BWP Brad Penny B 10.00 3.00
CA Chip Ambres B 10.00 3.00
CB Carlos Beltran G 40.00 12.00
CF Choo Freeman B 10.00 3.00
CP Corey Patterson S 20.00 6.00
DB Dee Brown S 15.00 4.50
DK David Kelton B 10.00 3.00
EV Eric Valent B 10.00 3.00
EY Ed Yarnall S 15.00 4.50
JC Jack Cust S 15.00 4.50
JDC J.D. Closser B 10.00 3.00
JDD J.D. Drew G 40.00 12.00
JJ Jason Jennings B 10.00 3.00
JR Jason Romano B 10.00 3.00
JV Jose Vidro S 15.00 4.50
JZ Julio Zuleta B 10.00 3.00
KJW Kevin Witt S 15.00 4.50
KLW Kerry Wood S 30.00 9.00
LB Lance Berkman S 25.00 7.50
MC Michael Cuddyer S 15.00 4.50
MJR Mike Restovich B 10.00 3.00
MM Mike Meyers B 10.00 3.00
MQ Mark Quinn S 15.00 4.50
MR Matt Riley S 20.00 6.00
NJ Nick Johnson S 20.00 6.00
RA Rick Ankiel G 25.00 7.50
RF Rafael Furcal S 20.00 6.00
RM Ruben Mateo G 25.00 7.50
SB Sean Burroughs S 20.00 6.00
SC Steve Cox B 10.00 3.00
SD Scott Downs S 15.00 4.50
SW Scott Williamson G 25.00 7.50
VW Vernon Wells G 25.00 7.50

2000 Bowman Early Indications

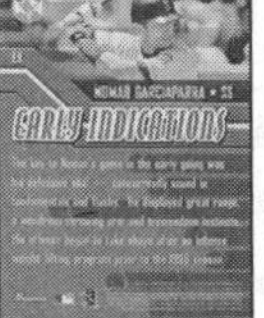

Randomly inserted into hobby/retail packs at one in 24, this 10-card insert features players that put up big numbers early on in their careers. Card backs carry an "E" prefix.

Nm-Mt Ex-Mt
COMPLETE SET (10) 50.00 15.00
E1 Nomar Garciaparra 5.00 1.50
E2 Cal Ripken 10.00 3.00
E3 Derek Jeter 8.00 2.40
E4 Mark McGwire 8.00 2.40
E5 Alex Rodriguez 5.00 1.50
E6 Chipper Jones 3.00 .90
E7 Todd Helton 2.00 .60
E8 Vladimir Guerrero 3.00 .90
E9 Mike Piazza 5.00 1.50
E10 Jose Canseco 3.00 .90

2000 Bowman Major Power

Randomly inserted into hobby/retail packs at one in 24, this 10-card insert features the major league's top sluggers. Card backs carry a "MP" prefix.

Nm-Mt Ex-Mt
COMPLETE SET (10) 50.00 15.00
MP1 Mark McGwire 8.00 2.40
MP2 Chipper Jones 3.00 .90
MP3 Alex Rodriguez 5.00 1.50
MP4 Sammy Sosa 5.00 1.50
MP5 Rafael Palmeiro 2.00 .60
MP6 Ken Griffey Jr. 5.00 1.50
MP7 Nomar Garciaparra 5.00 1.50
MP8 Barry Bonds 8.00 2.40
MP9 Derek Jeter 8.00 2.40
MP10 Jeff Bagwell 2.00 .60

2000 Bowman Tool Time

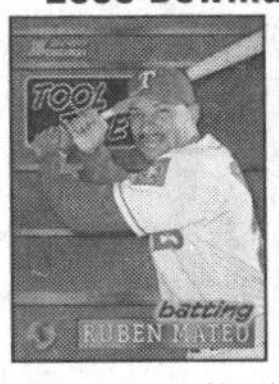

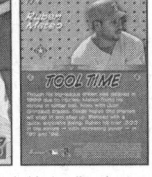

Randomly inserted into hobby/retail packs at one in eight, this 20-card insert grades the major league's top prospects on their batting, power, speed, arm strength, and defensive skills. Card backs carry a "TT" prefix.

Nm-Mt Ex-Mt
COMPLETE SET (20) 20.00 6.00
TT1 Pat Burrell 1.00 .30
TT2 Aaron Rowand 2.00 .60
TT3 Chris Wakeland 1.00 .30
TT4 Ruben Mateo 1.00 .30
TT5 Pat Burrell 1.00 .30
TT6 Adam Piatt 1.00 .30
TT7 Nick Johnson 1.00 .30
TT8 Jack Cust 1.00 .30
TT9 Rafael Furcal 1.00 .30
TT10 Julio Ramirez 1.00 .30
TT11 Gookie Dawkins 1.00 .30
TT12 Corey Patterson 1.00 .30
TT13 Ruben Mateo 1.00 .30
TT14 Jason Dellaero 1.00 .30
TT15 Sean Burroughs 1.00 .30
TT16 Ryan Langerhans 1.00 .30
TT17 D'Angelo Jimenez 1.00 .30
TT18 Corey Patterson 1.00 .30
TT19 Troy Cameron 1.00 .30
TT20 Michael Cuddyer 1.00 .30

2000 Bowman Draft Picks

The 2000 Bowman Draft Picks set was released in November, 2000 as a 110-card set. Each factory set was initially distributed in a tight, clear cello wrap and contained the 110-card set plus one of 60 different autographs. Topps announced that due to the unavailability of certain players previously scheduled to sign autographs, a small quantity (less than ten percent) of autographed cards from the 2000 Topps Baseball Rookies/Traded set were be included into its 2000 Bowman Baseball Draft Picks set. Rookie Cards include Chin-Feng Chen, Adrian Gonzalez, Kazuhiro Sasaki, Grady Sizemore and Chin-Hui Tsao.

Nm-Mt Ex-Mt
COMP.FACT.SET (111) 40.00 12.00
COMPLETE SET (110) 25.00 7.50
1 Pat Burrell .30 .09
2 Rafael Furcal .30 .09
3 Grant Roberts .30 .09
4 Barry Zito 1.50 .45
5 Julio Zuleta .30 .09
6 Mark Mulder .30 .09
7 Rob Bell .30 .09
8 Adam Piatt .30 .09
9 Mike Lamb .50 .15
10 Pablo Ozuna .30 .09
11 Jason Tyner .30 .09
12 Jason Marquis .30 .09
13 Eric Munson .30 .09
14 Seth Etherton .30 .09
15 Milton Bradley .30 .09
16 Nick Green .75 .23
17 Chin-Feng Chen RC .75 .23
18 Matt Boone RC .30 .09
19 Kevin Gregg RC .40 .12
20 Eddy Garabito RC .30 .09
21 Aaron Capista RC .30 .09
22 Esteban German RC .30 .09
23 Derek Thompson RC .30 .09
24 Phil Merrell RC .30 .09
25 Brian O'Connor RC .30 .09
26 Yamid Haad .30 .09
27 Hector Mercado RC .30 .09
28 Jason Woolf RC .30 .09
29 Eddy Furniss RC .30 .09
30 Cha Sueng Baek RC .30 .09
31 Colby Lewis RC .40 .12
32 Pasqual Coco RC .30 .09
33 Jorge Cantu RC .50 .15
34 Erasmo Ramirez RC .30 .09
35 Bobby Kielty RC .40 .12
36 Joaquin Benoit RC .40 .12
37 Brian Esposito RC .30 .09
38 Michael Wenner .30 .09
39 Juan Rincon RC .30 .09
40 Yorvit Torrealba RC .30 .09
41 Chad Durham RC .30 .09
42 Jim Mann RC .30 .09
43 Shane Loux RC .30 .09
44 Luis Rivas .30 .09
45 Ken Chenard RC .30 .09
46 Mike Lockwood RC .30 .09
47 Yovanny Lara RC .30 .09
48 Bubba Carpenter RC .30 .09
49 Ryan Dittfurth RC .30 .09
50 John Stephens RC .40 .12
51 Pedro Feliz RC .75 .23
52 Kenny Kelly RC .40 .12
53 Neil Jenkins RC .30 .09
54 Mike Glendenning RC .30 .09
55 Bo Porter .30 .09
56 Eric Byrnes .75 .23
57 Tony Alvarez RC .30 .09
58 Kazuhiro Sasaki RC .75 .23
59 Chad Durbin RC .30 .09
60 Mike Bynum RC .30 .09
61 Travis Wilson RC .30 .09
62 Jose Leon RC .30 .09
63 Ryan Vogelsong RC .40 .12
64 Geraldo Guzman RC .30 .09
65 Craig Anderson RC .30 .09
66 Carlos Silva RC .50 .15
67 Brad Thomas RC .30 .09
68 Chin-Hui Tsao RC .75 .23
69 Mark Buehrle RC 1.25 .35
70 Juan Salas RC .30 .09
71 Denny Abreu RC .30 .09
72 Keith McDonald RC .30 .09
73 Chris Richard RC .30 .09
74 Tomas De la Rosa RC .30 .09
75 Vicente Padilla RC .40 .12
76 Justin Brunette RC .30 .09
77 Scott Linebrink RC .30 .09
78 Jeff Sparks RC .30 .09
79 Tike Redman RC .50 .15
80 John Lackey RC .75 .23
81 Joe Strong RC .30 .09
82 Brian Tollberg RC .30 .09
83 Steve Sisco RC .30 .09
84 Chris Clapinski RC .30 .09
85 Augie Ojeda RC .30 .09
86 Adrian Gonzalez RC 1.25 .35
87 Mike Stodolka RC .30 .09
88 Adam Johnson RC .40 .12
89 Matt Wheatland RC .30 .09
90 Corey Smith RC .40 .12
91 Rocco Baldelli RC 4.00 1.20
92 Keith Bucktrot RC .30 .09
93 Adam Wainwright RC .75 .23
94 Blaine Boyer RC .30 .09
95 Aaron Herr RC .40 .12
96 Scott Thorman RC .50 .15
97 Bryan Digby RC .40 .12
98 Josh Shortslef RC .30 .09
99 Sean Smith RC .40 .12
100 Alex Cruz RC .30 .09
101 Marc Love RC .30 .09
102 Kevin Lee RC .30 .09
103 Victor Ramos RC .40 .12
104 Jason Kaanoi RC .30 .09
105 Luis Escobar RC .30 .09
106 Tripper Johnson RC .40 .12
107 Phil Dumatrait RC .40 .12
108 Bryan Edwards RC .30 .09
109 Grady Sizemore RC 8.00 2.40
110 Thomas Mitchell RC .30 .09

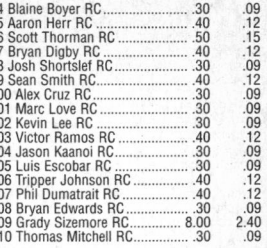

2000 Bowman Draft Picks Autographs

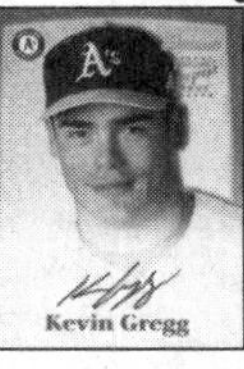

Inserted into 2000 Bowman Draft Pick sets at one per set, this 55-card insert features autographed cards of some of the hottest prospects in baseball. Card backs carry a "BDPA" prefix. Please note that cards BDPA16, BDPA32, BDPA34, BDPA45, BDPA56 do not exist.

Nm-Mt Ex-Mt
BDPA1 Pat Burrell 15.00 4.50
BDPA2 Rafael Furcal 15.00 4.50
BDPA3 Grant Roberts 10.00 3.00
BDPA4 Barry Zito 40.00 12.00
BDPA5 Julio Zuleta 10.00 3.00
BDPA6 Mark Mulder 15.00 4.50
BDPA7 Rob Bell 10.00 3.00
BDPA8 Adam Piatt 10.00 3.00
BDPA9 Mike Lamb 10.00 3.00
BDPA10 Pablo Ozuna 10.00 3.00
BDPA11 Jason Tyner 10.00 3.00
BDPA12 Jason Marquis 15.00 4.50
BDPA13 Eric Munson 10.00 3.00
BDPA14 Seth Etherton 10.00 3.00
BDPA15 Milton Bradley 15.00 4.50
BDPA16 Does Not Exist
BDPA17 Michael Wenner 10.00 3.00
BDPA18 M.Glendenning 10.00 3.00
BDPA19 Tony Alvarez 10.00 3.00
BDPA20 Adrian Gonzalez 25.00 7.50
BDPA21 Corey Smith 10.00 3.00
BDPA22 Matt Wheatland 10.00 3.00
BDPA23 Adam Johnson 10.00 3.00
BDPA24 Mike Stodolka 10.00 3.00
BDPA25 Rocco Baldelli 60.00 18.00
BDPA26 Juan Rincon 10.00 3.00
BDPA27 Chad Durbin 10.00 3.00
BDPA28 Yorvit Torrealba 10.00 3.00
BDPA29 Nick Green 25.00 7.50
BDPA30 Derek Thompson 10.00 3.00
BDPA31 John Lackey 20.00 6.00
BDPA32 Does Not Exist
BDPA33 Kevin Gregg 10.00 3.00
BDPA34 Does Not Exist
BDPA35 Denny Abreu 10.00 3.00
BDPA36 Brian Tollberg 10.00 3.00
BDPA37 Yamid Haad 10.00 3.00
BDPA38 Grady Sizemore 80.00 24.00
BDPA39 Carlos Silva 15.00 4.50
BDPA40 Jorge Cantu 15.00 4.50
BDPA41 Bobby Kielty 10.00 3.00
BDPA42 Scott Thorman 10.00 3.00
BDPA43 Juan Salas 10.00 3.00
BDPA44 Phil Dumatrait 10.00 3.00
BDPA45 Does Not Exist
BDPA46 Mike Lockwood 10.00 3.00
BDPA47 Yovanny Lara 10.00 3.00
BDPA48 Tripper Johnson 10.00 3.00
BDPA49 Colby Lewis 10.00 3.00
BDPA50 Neil Jenkins 10.00 3.00
BDPA51 Keith Bucktrot 10.00 3.00
BDPA52 Eric Byrnes 20.00 6.00
BDPA53 Aaron Herr 10.00 3.00
BDPA54 Erasmo Ramirez 10.00 3.00
BDPA55 Chris Richard 10.00 3.00
BDPA56 Does Not Exist
BDPA57 Mike Bynum 10.00 3.00
BDPA58 Brian Esposito 10.00 3.00
BDPA59 Chris Clapinski 10.00 3.00
BDPA60 Augie Ojeda 10.00 3.00

2001 Bowman

Issued in one series, this 440 card set features a mix of 140 veteran cards along with 300 cards of young players. The cards were issued in either 10-card retail or hobby packs or 21-card hobby collector packs. The 10 card packs had an SRP of $3 while the jumbo packs had an SRP of $6. The 10 card packs were inserted 24 packs to a box and 12 boxes to a case. The 21 card packs were inserted 12 packs per box and eight boxes per case. An exchange card with a redemption deadline of May 31st, 2002, good for a signed Sean Burroughs baseball, was randomly seeded into packs at a miniscule rate of 1:30,432. Only eighty exchange cards were produced. In addition, a special card featuring game-used jersey swatches of A.L. and N.L. Rookie of the Year winners Kazuhiro Sasaki and Rafael Furcal was randomly seeded into packs at the following rates; hobby 1:2,202 and Home Team Advantage 1:1,045.

Nm-Mt Ex-Mt
COMPLETE SET (440) 100.00 30.00
COMMON CARD (1-440) .30 .09
COMMON RC .30 .09
1 Jason Giambi .30 .09
2 Rafael Furcal .30 .09
3 Rick Ankiel .30 .09
4 Freddy Garcia .30 .09
5 Magglio Ordonez .30 .09
6 Bernie Williams .50 .15
7 Kenny Lofton .30 .09
8 Al Leiter .30 .09
9 Albert Belle .30 .09
10 Craig Biggio .50 .15
11 Mark Mulder .30 .09
12 Carlos Delgado .30 .09
13 Darin Erstad .30 .09
14 Richie Sexson .30 .09
15 Randy Johnson .75 .23
16 Greg Maddux 1.25 .35
17 Cliff Floyd .30 .09
18 Mark Buehrle .30 .09
19 Chris Singleton .30 .09
20 Orlando Hernandez .30 .09
21 Javier Vazquez .30 .09
22 Jeff Kent .30 .09
23 Jim Thome .75 .23
24 John Olerud .30 .09
25 Jason Kendall .30 .09
26 Scott Rolen .75 .23
27 Tony Gwynn 1.00 .30
28 Edgardo Alfonzo .30 .09
29 Pokey Reese .30 .09
30 Todd Helton .50 .15
31 Mark Quinn .30 .09
32 Dan Tosca RC .40 .12
33 Dean Palmer .30 .09
34 Jacque Jones .30 .09
35 Ray Durham .30 .09
36 Rafael Palmeiro .50 .15
37 Carl Everett .30 .09
38 Ryan Dempster .30 .09
39 Randy Wolf .30 .09
40 Vladimir Guerrero .75 .23
41 Livan Hernandez .30 .09
42 Mo Vaughn .30 .09
43 Shannon Stewart .30 .09
44 Preston Wilson .30 .09
45 Jose Vidro .30 .09
46 Fred McGriff .50 .15
47 Kevin Brown .30 .09
48 Peter Bergeron .30 .09
49 Miguel Tejada .30 .09
50 Chipper Jones .75 .23
51 Edgar Martinez .50 .15
52 Tony Batista .30 .09
53 Jorge Posada .50 .15
54 Ricky Ledee .30 .09
55 Sammy Sosa 1.25 .35
56 Steve Cox .30 .09
57 Tony Armas Jr. .30 .09
58 Gary Sheffield .30 .09
59 Bartolo Colon .30 .09
60 Pat Burrell .30 .09
61 Jay Payton .30 .09
62 Sean Casey .30 .09
63 Larry Walker .50 .15
64 Mike Mussina .50 .15
65 Nomar Garciaparra 1.25 .35
66 Darren Dreifort .30 .09
67 Richard Hidalgo .30 .09
68 Troy Glaus .30 .09
69 Ben Grieve .30 .09
70 Jim Edmonds .30 .09
71 Raul Mondesi .30 .09
72 Andruw Jones .30 .09
73 Luis Castillo .30 .09
74 Mike Sweeney .30 .09
75 Derek Jeter 2.00 .60
76 Ruben Mateo .30 .09
77 Carlos Lee .30 .09
78 Cristian Guzman .30 .09
79 Mike Hampton .30 .09
80 J.D. Drew .30 .09
81 Matt Lawton .30 .09
82 Moises Alou .30 .09
83 Terrence Long .30 .09
84 Geoff Jenkins .30 .09
85 Manny Ramirez .50 .15
86 Johnny Damon .50 .15
87 Barry Larkin .50 .15
88 Pedro Martinez .75 .23
89 Juan Gonzalez .50 .15
90 Roger Clemens 1.50 .45
91 Carlos Beltran .50 .15
92 Brad Radke .30 .09
93 Orlando Cabrera .30 .09
94 Roberto Alomar .50 .15
95 Barry Bonds 2.00 .60
96 Tim Hudson .30 .09
97 Tom Glavine .50 .15
98 Jeromy Burnitz .30 .09
99 Adrian Beltre .50 .15
100 Mike Piazza 1.25 .35
101 Kerry Wood .75 .23
102 Steve Finley .30 .09
103 Alex Cora .30 .09
104 Bob Abreu .30 .09
105 Neifi Perez .30 .09
106 Mark Redman .30 .09
107 Paul Konerko .30 .09
108 Jermaine Dye .30 .09
109 Brian Giles .30 .09
110 Ivan Rodriguez .75 .23
111 Vinny Castilla .30 .09
112 Adam Kennedy .30 .09
113 Eric Chavez .30 .09
114 Billy Koch .30 .09
115 Shawn Green .30 .09
116 Matt Williams .30 .09
117 Greg Vaughn .30 .09
118 Gabe Kapler .30 .09
119 Jeff Cirillo .30 .09
120 Frank Thomas .75 .23
121 David Justice .30 .09
122 Cal Ripken 2.50 .75
123 Rich Aurilia .30 .09
124 Curt Schilling .50 .15
125 Barry Zito .50 .15
126 Brian Jordan .30 .09
127 Chan Ho Park .30 .09
128 J.T. Snow .30 .09
129 Kazuhiro Sasaki .30 .09
130 Alex Rodriguez 1.25 .35
131 Mariano Rivera .50 .15
132 Eric Milton .30 .09
133 Andy Pettitte .50 .15
134 Scott Elarton .30 .09
135 Ken Griffey Jr. 1.25 .35
136 Bengie Molina .30 .09
137 Jeff Bagwell .50 .15
138 Kevin Millwood .30 .09
139 Tino Martinez .50 .15
140 Mark McGwire 2.00 .60
141 Larry Barnes .30 .09
142 John Buck RC .50 .15
143 Freddie Bynum RC .40 .12
144 Abraham Nunez .30 .09
145 Felix Diaz RC .40 .12
146 Horacio Estrada .30 .09
147 Ben Diggins .30 .09
148 Tsuyoshi Shinjo RC .50 .15
149 Rocco Baldelli .50 .15
150 Rod Barajas .30 .09
151 Luis Terrero .30 .09
152 Milton Bradley .30 .09
153 Kurt Ainsworth .30 .09
154 Russell Branyan .30 .09
155 Ryan Anderson .30 .09
156 Mitch Jones RC .40 .12
157 Chip Ambres .30 .09
158 Steve Bennett RC .30 .09
159 Ivanon Coffie .30 .09
160 Sean Burroughs .30 .09
161 Keith Bucktrot .30 .09
162 Tony Alvarez .30 .09
163 Joaquin Benoit .30 .09
164 Rick Asadoorian .30 .09
165 Ben Broussard .30 .09
166 Ryan Madson RC .75 .23
167 Dee Brown .30 .09
168 Sergio Contreras RC .40 .12
169 John Barnes .30 .09
170 Ben Washburn RC .40 .12
171 Erick Almonte RC .40 .12
172 Shawn Fagan RC .30 .09
173 Gary Johnson RC .40 .12
174 Brady Clark .30 .09
175 Grant Roberts .30 .09
176 Tony Torcato .30 .09
177 Ramon Castro .30 .09
178 Esteban German .30 .09
179 Joe Hamer RC .40 .12
180 Nick Neugebauer .30 .09
181 Dernell Stenson .30 .09
182 Yhency Brazoban RC .75 .23
183 Aaron Myette .30 .09
184 Juan Sosa .30 .09
185 Brandon Inge .30 .09
186 Domingo Guante RC .40 .12
187 Adrian Brown .30 .09
188 Deivi Mendez RC .40 .12
189 Luis Matos .30 .09
190 Pedro Liriano RC .40 .12
191 Donnie Bridges .30 .09
192 Alex Cintron .30 .09
193 Jace Brewer .30 .09
194 Ron Davenport RC .40 .12
195 Jason Belcher RC .40 .12
196 Adrian Hernandez RC .30 .09
197 Bobby Kielty .30 .09
198 Reggie Griggs RC .40 .12
199 R. Abercrombie RC .40 .12
200 Troy Farnsworth RC .40 .12
201 Matt Belisle .30 .09
202 Miguel Villilo RC .30 .09
203 Adam Everett .30 .09
204 John Lackey .30 .09
205 Pasqual Coco .30 .09
206 Adam Wainwright .30 .09
207 Matt White RC .40 .12
208 Chin-Feng Chen .30 .09
209 Jeff Andra RC .40 .12
210 Willie Bloomquist .30 .09
211 Wes Anderson .30 .09
212 Enrique Cruz .30 .09
213 Jerry Hairston Jr. .30 .09
214 Mike Bynum .30 .09
215 Brian Hitchcox RC .40 .12
216 Ryan Christianson .30 .09
217 J.J. Davis .30 .09
218 Jovanny Cedeno .30 .09
219 Elvin Nina .30 .09
220 Alex Graman .30 .09
221 Arturo McDowell .30 .09
222 Deivis Santos RC .40 .12
223 Jody Gerut .30 .09
224 Sun Woo Kim .30 .09
225 Jimmy Rollins .30 .09
226 Ntema Ndungidi .30 .09
227 Ruben Salazar .30 .09
228 Josh Girdley .30 .09
229 Carl Crawford .30 .09
230 Luis Montanez RC .40 .12
231 Ramon Carvajal RC .40 .12
232 Matt Riley .30 .09
233 Ben Davis .30 .09
234 Jason Grabowski .30 .09
235 Chris George .30 .09
236 Hank Blalock RC 8.00 2.40
237 Roy Oswalt .50 .15
238 Eric Reynolds RC .40 .12
239 Brian Cole .30 .09
240 Denny Bautista RC .75 .23
241 Hector Garcia RC .40 .12
242 Joe Thurston RC .40 .12
243 Brad Cresse .30 .09
244 Corey Patterson .30 .09
245 Brett Evert RC .40 .12
246 Elpidio Guzman RC .40 .12
247 Vernon Wells .30 .09
248 Roberto Miniel RC .40 .12
249 Brian Bass RC .40 .12
250 Mark Burnett RC .40 .12
251 Juan Silvestre .30 .09
252 Pablo Ozuna .30 .09
253 Jayson Werth .30 .09
254 Russ Jacobson .30 .09
255 Chad Hermansen .30 .09
256 Travis Hafner RC 1.50 .45
257 Brad Baker .30 .09
258 Gookie Dawkins .30 .09
259 Michael Cuddyer .30 .09
260 Mark Buehrle .30 .09
261 Ricardo Aramboles .30 .09
262 Esix Snead RC .40 .12
263 Wilson Betemit RC .40 .12
264 Albert Pujols RC 50.00 15.00
265 Joe Lawrence .30 .09
266 Ramon Ortiz .30 .09
267 Ben Sheets .50 .15
268 Luke Lockwood RC .40 .12
269 Toby Hall .30 .09
270 Jack Cust .30 .09
271 Pedro Feliz UER .30 .09
No facsimile signature on card
272 Noel Devarez RC .40 .12
273 Josh Beckett .30 .09
274 Alex Escobar .30 .09
275 Doug Gredvig RC .40 .12
276 Marcus Giles .30 .09
277 Jon Rauch .30 .09
278 Brian Schmitt RC .40 .12
279 Seung Song RC .50 .15
280 Kevin Mench .30 .09
281 Adam Eaton .30 .09
282 Shawn Sonnier .30 .09
283 Andy Van Hekken RC .40 .12
284 Aaron Rowand .30 .09
285 Tony Blanco RC .75 .23
286 Ryan Kohlmeier .30 .09
287 C.C. Sabathia .30 .09
288 Bubba Crosby .30 .09
289 Josh Hamilton .30 .09
290 Dee Haynes RC .40 .12
291 Jason Marquis .30 .09
292 Julio Zuleta .30 .09
293 Carlos Hernandez .30 .09
294 Matt Lecroy .30 .09
295 Andy Beal RC .40 .12
296 Carlos Pena .30 .09
297 Reggie Taylor .30 .09
298 Bob Keppel RC .50 .15
299 Miguel Cabrera UER 1.50 .45
Photo is Manuel Esquivia
300 Ryan Franklin .30 .09
301 Brandon Phillips .30 .09
302 Victor Hall RC .40 .12
303 Tony Pena Jr. .30 .09
304 Jim Journell RC .40 .12
305 Cristian Guerrero .30 .09
306 Miguel Olivo .30 .09
307 Jin Ho Cho .30 .09
308 Choo Freeman .30 .09
309 Danny Borrell RC .40 .12
310 Doug Mientkiewicz .30 .09
311 Aaron Herr .30 .09
312 Keith Ginter .30 .09
313 Felipe Lopez .30 .09
314 Jeff Goldbach .30 .09
315 Travis Harper .30 .09
316 Paul LoDuca .30 .09
317 Joe Torres .30 .09
318 Eric Byrnes .30 .09
319 George Lombard .30 .09
320 Dave Krynzel .30 .09
321 Ben Christensen .30 .09
322 Aubrey Huff .30 .09
323 Lyle Overbay .30 .09
324 Sean McGowan .30 .09
325 Jeff Heaverlo .30 .09
326 Timo Perez .30 .09
327 Octavio Martinez RC .40 .12
328 Vince Faison .30 .09
329 David Parrish RC .40 .12
330 Bobby Bradley .30 .09
331 Jason Miller RC .40 .12
332 Corey Spencer RC .40 .12
333 Craig House .30 .09
334 Maxim St. Pierre RC .40 .12
335 Adam Johnson .30 .09
336 Joe Crede .30 .09
337 Greg Nash RC .40 .12
338 Chad Durbin .30 .09
339 Pat Magness RC .40 .12
340 Matt Wheatland .30 .09
341 Julio Lugo .30 .09
342 Grady Sizemore .75 .23
343 Adrian Gonzalez .30 .09
344 Tim Raines Jr. .30 .09
345 Ranier Olmedo RC .40 .12
346 Phil Dumatrait .30 .09
347 Brandon Mims RC .40 .12
348 Jason Jennings .30 .09
349 Phil Wilson RC .40 .12
350 Jason Hart .30 .09
351 Cesar Izturis .30 .09
352 Matt Butler RC .40 .12
353 David Kelton .30 .09
354 Luke Prokopec .30 .09
355 Corey Smith .30 .09
356 Joel Pineiro .75 .23
357 Ken Chenard .30 .09
358 Keith Reed .30 .09
359 David Walling .30 .09
360 Alexis Gomez RC .40 .12
361 Justin Morneau RC 8.00 2.40
362 Josh Fogg RC .40 .12
363 J.R. House .30 .09
364 Andy Tracy .30 .09
365 Kenny Kelly .30 .09
366 Aaron McNeal .30 .09
367 Nick Johnson .30 .09
368 Brian Esposito .30 .09
369 Charles Frazier RC .40 .12
370 Scott Heard .30 .09
371 Pat Strange .30 .09
372 Mike Meyers .30 .09
373 Ryan Ludwick RC .40 .12
374 Brad Wilkerson .30 .09
375 Allen Levrault .30 .09
376 Seth McClung RC .40 .12
377 Joe Nathan .30 .09
378 Rafael Soriano RC .50 .15
379 Chris Richard .30 .09
380 Jared Sandberg .30 .09
381 Tike Redman .30 .09
382 Adam Dunn UER .50 .15
Card lists him as a pitcher
383 Jared Abruzzo RC .40 .12
384 Jason Richardson RC .40 .12
385 Matt Holliday .30 .09
386 Darwin Cubillan RC .40 .12
387 Mike Nannini .30 .09
388 Blake Williams RC .40 .12
389 V. Pascucci RC .40 .12
390 Jon Garland .30 .09
391 Josh Pressley .30 .09
392 Jose Ortiz .30 .09
393 Ryan Hannaman RC .40 .12
394 Steve Smyth RC .40 .12
395 John Patterson .30 .09
396 Chad Petty RC .40 .12
397 Jake Peavy RC 2.00 .60
UER last name misspelled Peavey
398 Onix Mercado RC .40 .12
399 Jason Romano .30 .09
400 Luis Torres RC .40 .12
401 Casey Fossum RC .40 .12
402 Eduardo Figueroa RC .40 .12
403 Bryan Barnowski RC .40 .12
404 Tim Redding .30 .09
405 Jason Standridge .30 .09
406 Marvin Seale RC .40 .12
407 Todd Moser .30 .09
408 Alex Gordon .30 .09
409 Steve Smitherman RC .50 .15
410 Ben Petrick .30 .09
411 Eric Munson .30 .09
412 Luis Rivas .30 .09
413 Matt Ginter .30 .09
414 Alfonso Soriano .50 .15
415 Rafael Boitel RC .40 .12
416 Dany Morban RC .40 .12
417 Justin Woodrow RC .40 .12
418 Wilfredo Rodriguez .30 .09
419 Derrick Van Dusen RC .40 .12
420 Josh Spoerl RC .40 .12
421 Juan Pierre .30 .09
422 J.C. Romero .30 .09
423 Ed Rogers RC .40 .12
424 Tomo Ohka .30 .09
425 Ben Hendrickson RC .50 .15
426 Carlos Zambrano .50 .15
427 Brett Myers .30 .09
428 Scott Seabol .30 .09
429 Thomas Mitchell .30 .09
430 Jose Reyes RC 2.50 .75
431 Kip Wells .30 .09
432 Donzell McDonald .30 .09
433 Adam Pettyjohn RC .40 .12
434 Austin Kearns .30 .09
435 Rico Washington .30 .09
436 Doug Nickle RC .30 .09
437 Steve Lomasney .30 .09
438 Jason Jones RC .40 .12
439 Bobby Seay .30 .09
440 Justin Wayne RC .40 .12
ROYR Kazuhiro Sasaki 25.00 7.50
Rafael Furcal ROY Jsy
NNO Sean Burroughs Ball/80 40.00 12.00

2001 Bowman Gold

Inserted one per pack, these 440 cards are a parallel to the basic Bowman set.

Nm-Mt Ex-Mt
*STARS: 1.25X TO 3X BASIC CARDS
*ROOKIES: 1X TO 2.5X BASIC CARDS

2001 Bowman Autographs

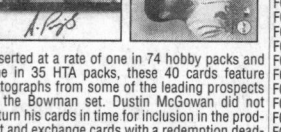

Inserted at a rate of one in 74 hobby packs and one in 35 HTA packs, these 40 cards feature autographs from some of the leading prospects in the Bowman set. Dustin McGowan did not return his cards in time for inclusion in the product and exchange cards with a redemption deadline of April 30th, 2003 were seeded into packs in their place.

Nm-Mt Ex-Mt
BA-AE Alex Escobar 10.00 3.00
BA-AG Adrian Gonzalez 10.00 3.00
BA-AJ Adam Johnson 10.00 3.00
BA-AP Albert Pujols 350.00 105.00
BA-ADP Adam Piatt 10.00 3.00
BA-AJG Alex Graman 10.00 3.00
BA-AKG Alex Gordon 10.00 3.00
BA-BB Brian Barnowski 10.00 3.00
BA-BD Ben Diggins 10.00 3.00
BA-BS Ben Sheets 15.00 4.50
BA-BW Brad Wilkerson 10.00 3.00
BA-BZ Barry Zito 15.00 4.50
BA-CG Cristian Guerrero 10.00 3.00
BA-DK Dave Krynzel 10.00 3.00
BA-DM D. McGowan EXCH 15.00 4.50
BA-DWK David Kelton 10.00 3.00
BA-FB Freddie Bynum 10.00 3.00
BA-JB Jason Botts 25.00 7.50
BA-JD Jose Diaz 10.00 3.00
BA-JH Josh Hamilton 10.00 3.00
BA-JM Justin Morneau 60.00 18.00
BA-JP Josh Pressley 10.00 3.00
BA-JRH J.R. House 10.00 3.00
BA-JWH Jason Hart 10.00 3.00
BA-KM Kevin Mench 10.00 3.00
BA-LM Luis Montanez 10.00 3.00
BA-LO Lyle Overbay 10.00 3.00
BA-MV Miguel Villilo 10.00 3.00
BA-ND Noel Devarez 10.00 3.00
BA-PL Pedro Liriano 10.00 3.00
BA-RF Rafael Furcal 10.00 3.00
BA-RJ Russ Jacobson 10.00 3.00
BA-SB Sean Burroughs 10.00 3.00
BA-SM S. McGowan EXCH 10.00 3.00
BA-SS Shawn Sonnier 10.00 3.00
BA-SU Sixto Urena 10.00 3.00
BA-SDS Steve Smyth 10.00 3.00
BA-TH Travis Hafner 25.00 7.50
BA-TJ Tripper Johnson 10.00 3.00
BA-WB Wilson Betemit 10.00 3.00

2001 Bowman AutoProofs

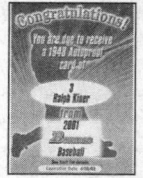

Inserted at a rate of 1 in 18,239 hobby packs and 1 in 8,306 HTA packs; these 10 cards feature players signing their actual Bowman Rookie Cards. Each player signed 25 cards for this promotion. Hank Bauer, Pat Burrell, Carlos Delgado, Chipper Jones, Ralph Kiner, Gil McDougald, and Ivan Rodriguez did not return their cards in time for inclusion in this product and exchange cards with a redemption deadline of April 30th, 2003 were seeded in to packs in their place.

Nm-Mt Ex-Mt
1 Hank Bauer 50
2 Pat Burrell 99
3 Carlos Delgado 92
4 Carl Erskine 51
5 Rafael Furcal 99
6 Chipper Jones 91
7 Ralph Kiner 48
8 Don Larsen 54
9 Gil McDougald 52
10 Ivan Rodriguez EXCH

2001 Bowman Futures Game Relics

Inserted at overall odds of one in 82 hobby packs and one in 39 HTA packs, these 34 cards feature relics used by the featured players in the futures game. These cards were inserted at different ratios and our checklist provides that information as to what group each insert belongs to.

Nm-Mt Ex-Mt
FGRAE Alex Escobar A 10.00 3.00
FGRAM Aaron Myette B 10.00 3.00
FGRBB Bobby Bradley B 10.00 3.00
FGRBP Ben Petrick C 10.00 3.00
FGRBS Ben Sheets B 15.00 4.50
FGRBW Brad Wilkerson C 10.00 3.00
FGRBZ Barry Zito B 15.00 4.50
FGRCA Craig Anderson B 10.00 3.00
FGRCC Chin-Feng Chen A 40.00 12.00
FGRCG Chris George D 10.00 3.00
FGRCH C. Hernandez D 10.00 3.00
FGRCP Corey Patterson A 10.00 3.00
FGRCP Carlos Pena A 10.00 3.00
FGRCT Chin-Hui Tsao D 15.00 4.50
FGREM Eric Munson A 10.00 3.00
FGRFL Felipe Lopez A 10.00 3.00
FGRGR Grant Roberts D 10.00 3.00
FGRJC Jack Cust A 10.00 3.00
FGRJH Josh Hamilton A 10.00 3.00
FGRJR Jason Romano C 10.00 3.00
FGRJZ Julio Zuleta A 10.00 3.00
FGRKA Kurt Ainsworth B 10.00 3.00
FGRMB Mike Bynum D 10.00 3.00
FGRMG Marcus Giles A 10.00 3.00
FGRNN N. Ndungidi A 10.00 3.00
FGRRA Ryan Anderson B 10.00 3.00
FGRRC Ramon Castro C 10.00 3.00
FGRRD R. Dorame D 10.00 3.00
FGRRO Ramon Ortiz D 10.00 3.00
FGRSK Sun Woo Kim D 10.00 3.00
FGRTD Travis Dawkins C 10.00 3.00
FGRTO Tomokazu Ohka B 10.00 3.00
FGRTW Travis Wilson A 10.00 3.00
FGRVW Vernon Wells C 10.00 3.00

2001 Bowman Multiple Game Relics

Issued at overall odds of one in 1,476 hobby packs and one in 701 HTA packs, these cards have three different pieces of memorabilia on them. These cards feature a piece of a jersey, helmet and a base fragment.

Nm-Mt Ex-Mt
MGR-AE Alex Escobar B 25.00 7.50
MGR-BP Ben Petrick A 25.00 7.50
MGR-BW B. Wilkerson B 25.00 7.50

MGR-CC C. Chen A 150.00 45.00
MGR-CP Carlos Pena A 25.00 7.50
MGR-EM Eric Munson B 25.00 7.50
MGR-FL Felipe Lopez A 25.00 7.50
MGR-JC Jack Cust A 25.00 7.50
MGR-JH Josh Hamilton B 25.00 7.50
MGR-JR Jason Romano A 25.00 7.50
MGR-JZ Julio Zuleta A 25.00 7.50
MGR-MG Marcus Giles A 30.00 9.00
MGR-NN N. Ndungidi A 25.00 7.50
MGR-RC Ramon Castro A 25.00 7.50
MGR-TD Travis Dawkins A 25.00 7.50
MGR-TW Travis Wilson A 25.00 7.50
MGR-VW Vernon Wells A 30.00 9.00
MGR-DCP C. Patterson B 30.00 9.00

2001 Bowman Multiple Game Relics Autograph

Inserted in packs at a rate of one in 18,259 Hobby and one in 8,306 HTA packs, these five cards feature not only three pieces of memorabilia from the featured players but also included an authentic signature.

Nm-Mt Ex-Mt
AMGR-AE Alex Escobar
AMGR-BW Brad Wilkerson
AMGR-CP Corey Patterson
AMGR-EM Eric Munson
AMGR-JH Josh Hamilton

2001 Bowman Rookie Reprints

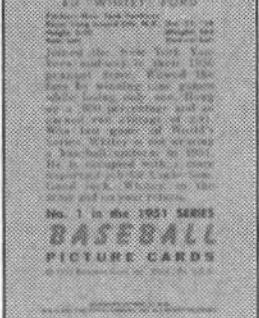

Inserted at a rate of one in 12, these 25 cards feature reprint cards of various stars who made their debut between 1948 and 1955.

Nm-Mt Ex-Mt
COMPLETE SET (25) 60.00 18.00
1 Yogi Berra 5.00 1.50
2 Ralph Kiner 3.00 .90
3 Stan Musial 10.00 3.00
4 Warren Spahn 3.00 .90
5 Roy Campanella 5.00 1.50
6 Bob Lemon 3.00 .90
7 Robin Roberts 3.00 .90
8 Duke Snider 3.00 .90
9 Early Wynn 3.00 .90
10 Richie Ashburn 3.00 .90
11 Gil Hodges 5.00 1.50
12 Hank Bauer 3.00 .90
13 Don Newcombe 3.00 .90
14 Al Rosen 3.00 .90
15 Willie Mays 12.00 3.60
16 Joe Garagiola 3.00 .90
17 Whitey Ford 3.00 .90
18 Lew Burdette 3.00 .90
19 Gil McDougald 3.00 .90
20 Minnie Minoso 3.00 .90
21 Eddie Mathews 5.00 1.50
22 Harvey Kuenn 3.00 .90
23 Don Larsen 3.00 .90
24 Elston Howard 3.00 .90
25 Don Zimmer 3.00 .90

2001 Bowman Rookie Reprints Autographs

Inserted at a rate of one in 2,467 hobby packs and one in 1,162 HTA packs, these 10 cards feature the players signing their rookie reprint cards. Duke Snider did not return his card in time for inclusion in packs. His card was redeemable until April 30, 2003. Please note that card number 7 does not exist.

Nm-Mt Ex-Mt
1 Yogi Berra 80.00 24.00
2 Willie Mays 200.00 60.00
3 Stan Musial 120.00 36.00
4 Duke Snider EXCH 40.00 12.00
5 Warren Spahn 60.00 18.00
6 Ralph Kiner 25.00 7.50
7 Does Not Exist
8 Don Larsen 40.00 12.00
9 Don Zimmer 25.00 7.50
10 Minnie Minoso 25.00 7.50

2001 Bowman Rookie Reprints Relic Bat

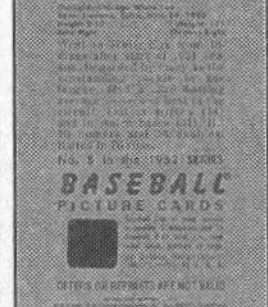

Issued at a rate of one in 1,954 hobby packs and one in 928 HTA packs, these five cards feature not only the rookie reprint of these players but also a piece of a bat they used during their career.

Nm-Mt Ex-Mt
1 Willie Mays 80.00 24.00
2 Duke Snider 25.00 7.50
3 Minnie Minoso 15.00 4.50
4 Hank Bauer 15.00 4.50
5 Gil McDougald 15.00 4.50

2001 Bowman Rookie Reprints Relic Bat Autographs

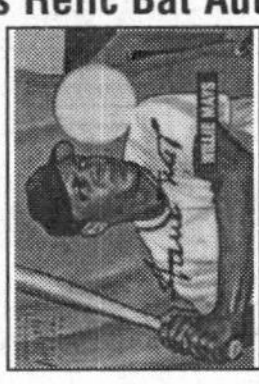

Issued at a rate of one in 18,259 hobby packs and one in 8,306 HTA packs, these five cards feature not only the rookie reprint of these players but also a piece of a bat they used during their career as well as an authentic autograph.

Nm-Mt Ex-Mt
1 Willie Mays
2 Duke Snider
3 Minnie Minoso
4 Hank Bauer
5 Gil McDougald

2001 Bowman Draft Picks

Issued as a 112-card factory set with a SRP of $45.99, these sets feature 100 cards of young players along with an autograph and relic card in each box. Twelve sets were included in each case. Cards BDP51 and BDP71 featuring Alex Herrera and Brad Thomas are uncorrected errors in that the card backs were switched for each player.

Nm-Mt Ex-Mt
COMP.FACT.SET (112) 30.00 9.00
COMPLETE SET (110) 25.00 7.50
BDP1 Alfredo Amezaga RC .40 .12
BDP2 Andrew Good .30 .09
BDP3 Kelly Johnson RC .40 .12
BDP4 Larry Bigbie .30 .09
BDP5 Matt Thompson RC .40 .12
BDP6 Wilton Chavez RC .40 .12
BDP7 Joe Borchard RC .75 .23
BDP8 David Espinosa .30 .09
BDP9 Zach Day RC .40 .12
BDP10 Brad Hawpe RC 2.00 .60
BDP11 Nate Cornejo .30 .09
BDP12 Matt Cooper RC .40 .12
BDP13 Brad Lidge .30 .09
BDP14 Angel Berroa RC .75 .23
BDP15 L. Matthews RC .40 .12
BDP16 Jose Garcia .30 .09
BDP17 Grant Balfour RC .30 .09
BDP18 Ron Chiavacci RC .30 .09
BDP19 Jae Seo .30 .09
BDP20 Juan Rivera .30 .09
BDP21 D'Angelo Jimenez .30 .09
BDP22 Juan A.Pena RC .40 .12
BDP23 Marlon Byrd RC 1.00 .30
BDP24 Sean Burnett .30 .09
BDP25 Josh Pearce RC .40 .12
BDP26 B. Duckworth RC .40 .12
BDP27 Jack Taschner RC .40 .12
BDP28 Marcus Thames .30 .09
BDP29 Brent Abernathy .30 .09
BDP30 David Elder RC .40 .12
BDP31 Scott Cassidy RC .40 .12
BDP32 D. Tankersley RC .40 .12
BDP33 Denny Stark .30 .09
BDP34 Dave Williams RC .40 .12
BDP35 Boof Bonser RC .40 .12
BDP36 Kris Foster RC .30 .09
BDP37 Luis Garcia RC .40 .12
BDP38 Shawn Chacon .30 .09
BDP39 Mike Rivera RC .40 .12
BDP40 Will Smith RC .40 .12
BDP41 M. Ensberg RC .75 .23
BDP42 Ken Harvey .30 .09
BDP43 R. Rodriguez RC .40 .12
BDP44 Jose Mieses RC .40 .12
BDP45 Luis Maza RC .40 .12
BDP46 Julio Perez RC .40 .12
BDP47 Dustan Mohr RC .40 .12
BDP48 Randy Flores RC .30 .09
BDP49 Covelli Crisp RC 1.50 .45
BDP50 Kevin Reese RC .40 .12
BDP51 Brad Thomas UER .30 .09
Card back is BDP71 Alex Herrera
BDP52 Xavier Nady .30 .09
BDP53 Ryan Vogelsong .30 .09
BDP54 Carlos Silva .30 .09
BDP55 Dan Wright .30 .09
BDP56 Brent Butler .30 .09
BDP57 Brandon Knight RC .30 .09
BDP58 Brian Reith RC .40 .12
BDP59 M. Valenzuela RC .40 .12
BDP60 Bobby Hill RC .50 .15
BDP61 Rich Rundles RC .40 .12
BDP62 Rick Elder .30 .09
BDP63 J.D. Closser .30 .09
BDP64 Scot Shields .30 .09
BDP65 Miguel Olivo .30 .09
BDP66 Stubby Clapp RC .30 .09
BDP67 J. Williams RC 2.50 .75
BDP68 Jason Lane RC .40 .12
BDP69 Chase Utley RC 4.00 1.20
BDP70 Erik Bedard RC .40 .12
BDP71 A. Herrera UER RC .30 .09
Card back is BDP51 Brad Thomas
BDP72 Juan Cruz RC .40 .12
BDP73 Billy Martin RC .40 .12
BDP74 Ronnie Merrill RC .40 .12
BDP75 Jason Kinchen RC .40 .12
BDP76 Wilkin Ruan RC .40 .12
BDP77 Cody Ransom RC .30 .09
BDP78 Bud Smith RC .40 .12
BDP79 Wily Mo Pena .30 .09
BDP80 Jeff Nettles RC .40 .12
BDP81 Jamal Strong RC .40 .12
BDP82 Bill Ortega RC .40 .12
BDP83 Mike Bell .30 .09
BDP84 Ichiro Suzuki RC 10.00 3.00
BDP85 F. Rodney RC .40 .12
BDP86 Chris Smith RC .40 .12
BDP87 J.VanBenschoten RC 1.50 .45
BDP88 Bobby Crosby RC 10.00 3.00
BDP89 Kenny Baugh RC .40 .12
BDP90 Jake Gautreau RC .40 .12
BDP91 Gabe Gross RC .50 .15
BDP92 Kris Honel RC 1.50 .45
BDP93 Dan Denham RC .40 .12
BDP94 Aaron Heilman RC .40 .12
BDP95 Irvin Guzman RC 4.00 1.20
BDP96 Mike Jones RC .50 .15
BDP97 J. Griffin RC .40 .12
BDP98 Macay McBride RC .40 .12
BDP99 J. Rheinecker RC .40 .12
BDP100 B. Sardinha RC .75 .23
BDP101 J. Weintraub RC .40 .12
BDP102 J.D. Martin RC .40 .12
BDP103 Jayson Nix RC .75 .23
BDP104 Noah Lowry RC 2.50 .75
BDP105 Richard Lewis RC 1.50 .45
BDP106 B. Hennessey RC .75 .23
BDP107 Jeff Mathis RC 2.00 .60
BDP108 Jon Skaggs RC .40 .12
BDP109 Justin Pope RC .40 .12
BDP110 Josh Burrus RC .40 .12

2001 Bowman Draft Picks Autographs

Inserted one per Bowman draft pick factory set, these 37 cards feature autographs of some of the leading players from the Bowman Draft Pick set.

Nm-Mt Ex-Mt
BDPAAA A. Amezaga 10.00 3.00
BDPAAC Alex Cintron 10.00 3.00
BDPAAE Adam Everett 10.00 3.00
BDPAAF Alex Fernandez 10.00 3.00
BDPAAG Alexis Gomez 10.00 3.00
BDPAAH Aaron Herr 10.00 3.00
BDPAAK Austin Kearns 15.00 4.50
BDPABB Bobby Bradley 10.00 3.00
BDPABH Beau Hale 10.00 3.00
BDPABP Brandon Phillips 10.00 3.00
BDPABS Bud Smith 10.00 3.00
BDPACG C. Guerrero 10.00 3.00
BDPACI Cesar Izturis 15.00 4.50
BDPACP Christian Parra 10.00 3.00
BDPAER Ed Rogers 10.00 3.00
BDPAFL Felipe Lopez 10.00 3.00
BDPAGA Garrett Atkins 25.00 7.50
BDPAGJ Gary Johnson 10.00 3.00
BDPAJA Jared Abruzzo 10.00 3.00
BDPAJK Joe Kennedy 15.00 4.50
BDPAJL John Lackey 15.00 4.50
BDPAJP Joel Pineiro 25.00 7.50
BDPAJT Joe Torres 10.00 3.00
BDPANJ Nick Johnson 15.00 4.50
BDPANR Nick Regilio 10.00 3.00
BDPARC Ryan Church 20.00 6.00
BDPARD Ryan Dittfurth 10.00 3.00
BDPARL Ryan Ludwick 10.00 3.00
BDPARO Roy Oswalt 20.00 6.00
BDPASH Scott Heard 10.00 3.00
BDPASS Scott Seabol 10.00 3.00
BDPATO Tomo Ohka 15.00 4.50
BDPAANC A. Cameron 10.00 3.00
BDPABJS Brian Specht 10.00 3.00
BDPAJMW Justin Wayne 10.00 3.00
BDPARMM Ryan Madson 15.00 4.50
BDPAROC R. Carvajal 10.00 3.00

2001 Bowman Draft Picks Futures Game Relics

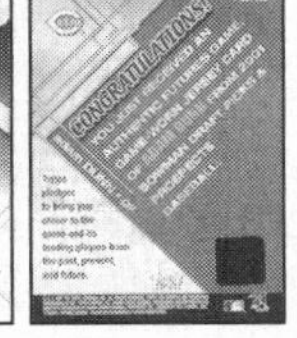

Inserted one per factory set, these 26 cards feature relics from the futures game.

Nm-Mt Ex-Mt
FGRAA Alfredo Amezaga 8.00 2.40
FGRAD Adam Dunn 10.00 3.00
FGRAG Adrian Gonzalez 8.00 2.40
FGRAH Alex Herrera 8.00 2.40
FGRBM Brett Myers 8.00 2.40
FGRCD Cody Ransom 8.00 2.40
FGRCG Chris George 8.00 2.40
FGRCH Carlos Hernandez 8.00 2.40
FGRCU Chase Utley 25.00 7.50
FGREB Erik Bedard 8.00 2.40
FGRGB Grant Balfour 8.00 2.40
FGRHB Hank Blalock 25.00 7.50
FGRJB Joe Borchard 10.00 3.00
FGRJC Juan Cruz 8.00 2.40
FGRJP Josh Pearce 8.00 2.40
FGRJR Juan Rivera 8.00 2.40
FGRJAP Juan A.Pena 8.00 2.40
FGRLG Luis Garcia 8.00 2.40
FGRMC Miguel Cabrera 15.00 4.50
FGRMR Mike Rivera 8.00 2.40
FGRRR R. Rodriguez 8.00 2.40
FGRSC Scott Chiasson 8.00 2.40
FGRSS Seung Song 10.00 3.00
FGRTB Toby Hall 8.00 2.40
FGRWB Wilson Betemit 8.00 2.40
FGRWP Wily Mo Pena 8.00 2.40

2001 Bowman Draft Picks Relics

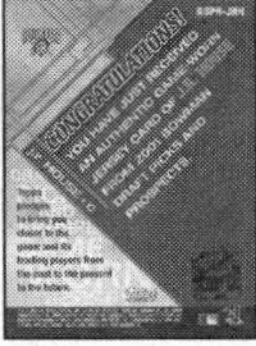

Inserted one per factory set, these six cards feature relics from some of the most popular prospects in the Bowman Draft Pick set.

Nm-Mt Ex-Mt
BDPRCI Cesar Izturis 10.00 3.00
BDPRGJ Gary Johnson 10.00 3.00
BDPRNR Nick Regilio 10.00 3.00
BDPRRC Ryan Church 15.00 4.50
BDPRBJS Brian Specht 10.00 3.00
BDPRJRH J.R. House 10.00 3.00

2002 Bowman

This 440 card set was issued in May, 2002. It was issued in 10 card packs which were packed 24 packs to a box and 12 boxes per case. These packs had an SRP of $3 per pack. The first 110 cards of this set featured veterans while the rest of the set featured rookies and prospects.

Nm-Mt Ex-Mt
COMPLETE SET (440) 80.00 24.00
COMMON CARD (1-110) .30 .09
COMMON CARD (111-440) .30 .09
1 Adam Dunn .50 .15
2 Derek Jeter 2.00 .60
3 Alex Rodriguez 1.25 .35
4 Miguel Tejada .30 .09
5 Nomar Garciaparra 1.25 .35
6 Toby Hall .30 .09
7 Brandon Duckworth .30 .09
8 Paul LoDuca .30 .09
9 Brian Giles .30 .09
10 C.C. Sabathia .30 .09
11 Curt Schilling .30 .09
12 Tsuyoshi Shinjo .30 .09
13 Ramon Hernandez .30 .09
14 Jose Cruz Jr. .30 .09
15 Albert Pujols 1.50 .45
16 Joe Mays .30 .09
17 Javy Lopez .30 .09
18 J.T. Snow .30 .09
19 David Segui .30 .09
20 Jorge Posada .50 .15
21 Doug Mientkiewicz .30 .09
22 Jerry Hairston Jr. .30 .09
23 Bernie Williams .50 .15
24 Mike Sweeney .30 .09
25 Jason Giambi .30 .09
26 Ryan Dempster .30 .09
27 Ryan Klesko .30 .09
28 Mark Quinn .30 .09
29 Jeff Kent .30 .09
30 Eric Chavez .30 .09
31 Adrian Beltre .50 .15
32 Andruw Jones .30 .09
33 Alfonso Soriano .50 .15
34 Aramis Ramirez .30 .09
35 Greg Maddux 1.25 .35
36 Andy Pettitte .50 .15
37 Bartolo Colon .30 .09
38 Ben Sheets .30 .09
39 Bobby Higginson .30 .09
40 Ivan Rodriguez .75 .23
41 Brad Penny .30 .09
42 Carlos Lee .30 .09
43 Damion Easley .30 .09
44 Preston Wilson .30 .09
45 Jeff Bagwell .50 .15
46 Eric Milton .30 .09
47 Rafael Palmeiro .50 .15
48 Gary Sheffield .30 .09
49 J.D. Drew .30 .09
50 Jim Thome .75 .23
51 Ichiro Suzuki 1.25 .35
52 Bud Smith .30 .09
53 Chan Ho Park .30 .09
54 D'Angelo Jimenez .30 .09
55 Ken Griffey Jr. 1.25 .35
56 Wade Miller .30 .09
57 Vladimir Guerrero .75 .23
58 Troy Glaus .30 .09
59 Shawn Green .30 .09
60 Kerry Wood .75 .23
61 Jack Wilson .30 .09
62 Kevin Brown .30 .09
63 Marcus Giles .30 .09
64 Pat Burrell .30 .09
65 Larry Walker .50 .15
66 Sammy Sosa 1.25 .35
67 Raul Mondesi .30 .09
68 Tim Hudson .30 .09
69 Lance Berkman .30 .09
70 Mike Mussina .50 .15
71 Barry Zito .30 .09
72 Jimmy Rollins .30 .09
73 Barry Bonds 2.00 .60
74 Craig Biggio .50 .15
75 Todd Helton .50 .15
76 Roger Clemens 1.50 .45
77 Frank Catalanotto .30 .09
78 Josh Towers .30 .09
79 Roy Oswalt .30 .09
80 Chipper Jones .75 .23
81 Cristian Guzman .30 .09
82 Darin Erstad .30 .09
83 Freddy Garcia .30 .09
84 Jason Tyner .30 .09
85 Carlos Delgado .30 .09
86 Jon Lieber .30 .09
87 Juan Pierre .30 .09
88 Matt Morris .30 .09
89 Phil Nevin .30 .09
90 Jim Edmonds .30 .09
91 Magglio Ordonez .30 .09
92 Mike Hampton .30 .09
93 Rafael Furcal .30 .09
94 Richie Sexson .30 .09
95 Luis Gonzalez .30 .09
96 Scott Rolen .75 .23
97 Tim Redding .30 .09
98 Moises Alou .30 .09
99 Jose Vidro .30 .09
100 Mike Piazza 1.25 .35
101 Pedro Martinez UER .75 .23
Career strikeout total incorrect
102 Geoff Jenkins .30 .09
103 Johnny Damon Sox .75 .23
104 Mike Cameron .30 .09
105 Randy Johnson .75 .23
106 David Eckstein .30 .09
107 Javier Vazquez .30 .09
108 Mark Mulder .30 .09
109 Robert Fick .30 .09
110 Roberto Alomar .50 .15
111 Wilson Betemit .30 .09
112 Chris Tritle RC .40 .12
113 Ed Rogers .30 .09
114 Juan Pena .30 .09
115 Josh Beckett .40 .12
116 Juan Cruz .30 .09
117 Noochie Varner RC .40 .12
118 Taylor Buchholz RC .40 .12
119 Mike Rivera .30 .09
120 Hank Blalock 1.00 .30
121 Hansel Izquierdo RC .40 .12
122 Orlando Hudson .30 .09
123 Bill Hall .30 .09
124 Jose Reyes .60 .18
125 Juan Rivera .30 .09
126 Eric Valent .30 .09
127 Scotty Layfield RC .40 .12
128 Austin Kearns .40 .12
129 Nic Jackson RC .40 .12
130 Chris Baker RC .40 .12
131 Chad Qualls RC .40 .12
132 Marcus Thames .30 .09
133 Nathan Haynes .30 .09
134 Brett Evert .30 .09
135 Joe Borchard .30 .09
136 Ryan Christianson .30 .09
137 Josh Hamilton .30 .09
138 Corey Patterson .40 .12
139 Travis Wilson .30 .09
140 Alex Escobar .30 .09
141 Alexis Gomez .30 .09
142 Nick Johnson .30 .09
143 Kenny Kelly .30 .09
144 Marlon Byrd .30 .09
145 Kory DeHaan .30 .09
146 Matt Belisle .30 .09
147 Carlos Hernandez .30 .09
148 Sean Burroughs .40 .12
149 Angel Berroa .30 .09
150 Aubrey Huff .40 .12
151 Travis Hafner .40 .12
152 Brandon Berger .30 .09
153 David Krynzel .30 .09
154 Ruben Salazar .30 .09
155 J.R. House .30 .09
156 Juan Silvestre .30 .09
157 Dewon Brazelton .30 .09
158 Jayson Werth .30 .09
159 Larry Barnes .30 .09
160 Elvis Pena .30 .09
161 Ruben Gotay RC .40 .12
162 Tommy Marx RC .40 .12
163 John Suomi RC .40 .12
164 Javier Colina .30 .09
165 Greg Sain RC .50 .15
166 Robert Cosby RC .40 .12
167 Angel Pagan RC .40 .12
168 Ralph Santana RC .40 .12
169 Joe Orloski RC .40 .12
170 Shayne Wright RC .40 .12
171 Jay Caligiuri RC .40 .12
172 Greg Montalbano RC .40 .12
173 Rich Harden RC 4.00 1.20
174 Rich Thompson RC .40 .12
175 Fred Bastardo RC .40 .12
176 Alejandro Giron RC .40 .12
177 Jesus Medrano RC .40 .12
178 Kevin Deaton RC .40 .12
179 Mike Rosamond RC .40 .12
180 Jon Guzman RC .40 .12
181 Gerard Oakes RC .40 .12
182 Francisco Liriano RC .50 .15
183 Matt Allegra RC .40 .12
184 Mike Snyder RC .40 .12
185 James Shanks RC .40 .12

186 Anderson Hernandez RC........ .40 .12
187 Dan Trumble RC.................... .40 .12
188 Luis DePaula RC .... .40 .12
189 Randall Shelley RC................ .40 .12
190 Richard Lane RC.................... .40 .12
191 Antwon Rollins RC................ .40 .12
192 Ryan Bukvich RC .... .40 .12
193 Derrick Lewis .... .30 .09
194 Eric Miller RC........................ .40 .12
195 Justin Schuda RC .... .40 .12
196 Brian West RC........................ .40 .12
197 Adam Roller RC .... .40 .12
198 Neal Frendling RC .... .40 .12
199 Jeremy Hill RC........................ .40 .12
200 James Barrett RC.................... .40 .12
201 Brett Kay RC .... .40 .12
202 Ryan Mottl RC .... .40 .12
203 Brad Nelson RC .... 1.25 .35
204 Juan M. Gonzalez RC............ .40 .12
205 Curtis Legendre RC................ .40 .12
206 Ronald Acuna RC.................... .40 .12
207 Chris Flinn RC........................ .40 .12
208 Nick Alvarez RC .... .40 .12
209 Jason Ellison RC...................... .40 .12
210 Blake McGinley RC.................. .40 .12
211 Dan Phillips RC .... .40 .12
212 Demetrius Heath RC .... .40 .12
213 Eric Bruntlett RC .... .40 .12
214 Joe Jiannetti RC...................... .40 .12
215 Mike Hill RC .... .40 .12
216 Ricardo Cordova RC .... .40 .12
217 Mark Hamilton RC .... .40 .12
218 David Mattox RC...................... .40 .12
219 Jose Morban RC .... .40 .12
220 Scott Wiggins RC.................... .30 .09
221 Steve Green .... .30 .09
222 Brian Rogers............................ .30 .09
223 Chin-Hui Tsao .... .40 .12
224 Kenny Baugh............................ .30 .09
225 Nate Teut.................................. .30 .09
226 Josh Wilson RC .... .40 .12
227 Christian Parker .... .30 .09
228 Tim Raines Jr............................ .30 .09
229 Anastacio Martinez RC........... .40 .12
230 Richard Lewis .... .40 .12
231 Tim Kalita RC .... .40 .12
232 Edwin Almonte RC .... .40 .12
233 Hee-Seop Choi .... .30 .09
234 Ty Howington............................ .30 .09
235 Victor Alvarez RC .... .40 .12
236 Morgan Ensberg .... .40 .12
237 Jeff Austin RC.......................... .40 .12
238 Luis Terrero.............................. .30 .09
239 Adam Wainwright .... .30 .09
240 Clint Weibl RC.......................... .30 .09
241 Eric Cyr .... .30 .09
242 Marlyn Tisdale RC.................... .40 .12
243 John VanBenschoten .... .30 .09
244 Ryan Raburn RC .... .40 .12
245 Miguel Cabrera.................... 1.50 .45
246 Jung Bong .... .30 .09
247 Raul Chavez RC .... .30 .09
248 Erik Bedard .... .30 .09
249 Chris Snelling RC.................... .40 .12
250 Joe Rogers RC.......................... .40 .12
251 Nate Field RC .... .40 .12
252 Matt Herges RC .... .30 .09
253 Matt Childers RC...................... .40 .12
254 Erick Almonte............................ .30 .09
255 Nick Neugebauer...................... .30 .09
256 Ron Calloway RC...................... .40 .12
257 Seung Song .... .30 .09
258 Brandon Phillips........................ .30 .09
259 Cole Barthel RC........................ .40 .12
260 Jason Lane................................ .30 .09
261 Jae Seo .... .30 .09
262 Randy Flores............................ .30 .09
263 Scott Chiasson.......................... .30 .09
264 Chase Utley .... .60 .18
265 Tony Alvarez.............................. .30 .09
266 Ben Howard RC .... .40 .12
267 Nelson Castro RC...................... .40 .12
268 Mark Lukasiewicz RC.............. .30 .09
269 Eric Glaser RC.......................... .40 .12
270 Rob Henkel RC.......................... .40 .12
271 Jose Valverde RC...................... .50 .15
272 Ricardo Rodriguez .... .30 .09
273 Chris Smith................................ .30 .09
274 Mark Prior.............................. 2.00 .60
275 Miguel Olivo.............................. .30 .09
276 Ben Broussard .... .30 .09
277 Zach Sorensen.......................... .30 .09
278 Brian Mallette RC .... .30 .09
279 Brad Wilkerson .... .30 .09
280 Carl Crawford............................ .40 .12
281 Chone Figgins RC .... .75 .23
282 Jimmy Alvarez RC.................... .40 .12
283 Gavin Floyd RC .... 2.50 .75
284 Josh Bonifay RC .... .40 .12
285 Garrett Guzman RC.................. .40 .12
286 Blake Williams .... .30 .09
287 Matt Holliday............................ .30 .09
288 Ryan Madson............................ .30 .09
289 Luis Torres................................ .30 .09
290 Jeff Verplancke RC.................. .40 .12
291 Nate Espy RC............................ .40 .12
292 Jeff Lincoln RC .... .40 .12
293 Ryan Snare RC.......................... .40 .12
294 Jose Ortiz.................................. .30 .09
295 Eric Munson.............................. .30 .09
296 Denny Bautista.......................... .30 .09
297 Willy Aybar................................ .30 .09
298 Kelly Johnson .... .30 .09
299 Justin Morneau .... 1.00 .30
300 Derrick Van Dusen .... .30 .09
301 Chad Petty .... .40 .12
302 Mike Restovich .... .30 .09
303 Shawn Fagan .... .30 .09
304 Yurendell DeCaster RC............ .40 .12
305 Justin Wayne .... .30 .09
306 Mike Peeples RC...................... .30 .09
307 Joel Guzman.............................. .60 .18
308 Ryan Vogelsong........................ .30 .09
309 Jorge Padilla RC .... .40 .12
310 Grady Sizemore .... .40 .12
311 Joe Jester RC............................ .40 .12
312 Jim Journell.............................. .30 .09
313 Bobby Seay................................ .30 .09
314 Ryan Church RC .... 1.00 .30
315 Grant Balfour .... .30 .09
316 Mitch Jones .... .30 .09
317 Travis Foley RC .... .40 .12
318 Bobby Crosby .... 1.00 .30
319 Adrian Gonzalez .... .40 .12
320 Ronnie Merrill .... .30 .09
321 Joel Pineiro.............................. .40 .12
322 John-Ford Griffin .... .30 .09
323 Brian Forystek RC .... .40 .12
324 Sean Douglass.......................... .30 .09
325 Manny Delcarmen RC .... .40 .12
326 Donnie Bridges .... .30 .09
327 Jim Kavourias RC .... .40 .12
328 Gabe Gross................................ .30 .09
329 Jon Rauch.................................. .30 .09
330 Bill Ortega .... .30 .09
331 Joey Hammond RC.................. .40 .12
332 Ramon Moreta RC .... .40 .12
333 Ron Davenport.......................... .30 .09
334 Brett Myers .... .30 .09
335 Carlos Pena.............................. .30 .09
336 Ezequiel Astacio RC .... .40 .12
337 Edwin Yan RC .... .40 .12
338 Josh Girdley.............................. .30 .09
339 Shaun Boyd .... .30 .09
340 Juan Rincon.............................. .30 .09
341 Chris Duffy RC .... .40 .12
342 Jason Kinchen .... .30 .09
343 Brad Thomas .... .30 .09
344 David Kelton.............................. .30 .09
345 Rafael Soriano .... .30 .09
346 Colin Young RC........................ .40 .12
347 Eric Byrnes................................ .30 .09
348 Chris Narveson RC .... .50 .15
349 John Rheinecker .... .30 .09
350 Mike Wilson RC .... .40 .12
351 Justin Sherrod RC .... .40 .12
352 Deivi Mendez .... .30 .09
353 Wily Mo Pena............................ .40 .12
354 Brett Roneberg RC.................. .40 .12
355 Trey Lunsford RC.................... .40 .12
356 Jimmy Gobble RC.................... .75 .23
357 Brent Butler.............................. .30 .09
358 Aaron Heilman .... .30 .09
359 Wilkin Ruan .... .30 .09
360 Brian Wolfe RC .... .40 .12
361 Cody Ransom............................ .30 .09
362 Koyie Hill.................................. .30 .09
363 Scott Cassidy............................ .30 .09
364 Tony Fontana RC...................... .40 .12
365 Mark Teixeira............................ .60 .18
366 Doug Sessions RC.................... .40 .12
367 Victor Hall .... .30 .09
368 Josh Cisneros RC .... .40 .12
369 Kevin Mench .... .30 .09
370 Tike Redman .... .30 .09
371 Jeff Heaverlo............................ .30 .09
372 Carlos Brackley RC .... .40 .12
373 Brad Hawpe .... .30 .09
374 Jesus Colome .... .30 .09
375 David Espinosa .... .30 .09
376 Jesse Foppert RC.................. 1.00 .30
377 Ross Peeples RC .... .40 .12
378 Alex Requena RC .... .40 .12
379 Joe Mauer RC 5.00 1.50
380 Carlos Silva.............................. .30 .09
381 David Wright RC 10.00 3.00
382 Craig Kuzmic RC...................... .40 .12
383 Pete Zamora RC...................... .40 .12
384 Matt Parker RC .... .40 .12
385 Keith Ginter.............................. .30 .09
386 Gary Cates Jr. .... .40 .12
387 Justin Reid RC.......................... .40 .12
388 Jake Mauer RC.......................... .40 .12
389 Dennis Tankersley.................... .30 .09
390 Josh Barfield RC .... 1.50 .45
391 Luis Maza.................................. .30 .09
392 Henry Pichardo RC .... .40 .12
393 Michael Floyd RC .... .40 .12
394 Clint Nageotte RC.................. 1.00 .30
395 Raymond Cabrera RC .... .40 .12
396 Mauricio Lara RC .... .40 .12
397 Alejandro Cadena RC.............. .40 .12
398 Jonny Gomes RC .... .75 .23
399 Jason Bulger RC .... .40 .12
400 Bobby Jenks RC........................ .75 .23
401 David Gil RC.............................. .40 .12
402 Joel Crump RC.......................... .40 .12
403 Kazuhisa Ishii RC .... 1.25 .35
404 So Taguchi RC .... 1.25 .35
405 Ryan Doumit RC .... .50 .15
406 Macay McBride .... .30 .09
407 Brandon Claussen.................... .30 .09
408 Chin-Feng Chen .... .40 .12
409 Josh Phelps .... .30 .09
410 Freddie Money RC .... .50 .15
411 Cliff Bartosh RC .... .40 .12
412 Josh Pearce .... .30 .09
413 Lyle Overbay .... .40 .12
414 Ryan Anderson .... .30 .09
415 Terrance Hill RC .... .40 .12
416 John Rodriguez RC.................. .40 .12
417 Richard Stahl .... .30 .09
418 Brian Specht .... .30 .09
419 Chris Latham RC...................... .30 .09
420 Carlos Cabrera RC .... .40 .12
421 Jose Bautista RC...................... .50 .15
422 Kevin Frederick RC.................. .40 .12
423 Jerome Williams .... .60 .18
424 Napoleon Calzado RC.............. .40 .12
425 Benito Baez .... .30 .09
426 Xavier Nady.............................. .30 .09
427 Jason Botts RC .... .75 .23
428 Steve Bechler RC .... .40 .12
429 Reed Johnson RC .... .50 .15
430 Mark Outlaw RC........................ .40 .12
431 Billy Sylvester .... .30 .09
432 Luke Lockwood.......................... .30 .09
433 Jake Peavy .... .40 .12
434 Alfredo Amezaga...................... .30 .09
435 Aaron Cook RC .... .40 .12
436 Josh Shaffer RC........................ .40 .12
437 Dan Wright................................ .30 .09
438 Ryan Gripp RC .... .40 .12
439 Alex Herrera.............................. .30 .09
440 Jason Bay RC........................ 2.50 .75

2002 Bowman Gold

Inserted one per pack, this is a parallel to the 2002 Bowman set. These cards can be differentiated by the Bowman logo and the facsimile signature in gold foil stamping.

Nm-Mt Ex-Mt
*RED 1-110: 1.25X TO 3X BASIC ....
*BLUE 111-440: .75X TO 2X BASIC ...
*BLUE ROOKIES 111-440: .75X TO 2X BASIC

2002 Bowman Autographs

Inserted in packs at overall odds of one in 40 hobby packs, one in 24 HTA packs and one in 53 retail packs, this 45 card set featued autographs of leading rookies and prospects.

Nm-Mt Ex-Mt
GROUP A 1:67 H, 1:39 HTA, 1:89 R ...
GROUP B 1:129 H, 1:74 HTA, 1:170 R
GROUP C 1:881 H, 1:507 HTA, 1:1165 R
GROUP D 1:1558 H, 1:896 HTA, 1:2060 R
GROUP E 1:1685 H, 1:968 HTA, 1:2238 R
OVERALL ODDS 1:40 H, 1:24 HTA, 1:53 R
ONE ADD'L AUTO PER SEALED HTA BOX
BA-AA Alfredo Amezaga A 10.00 3.00
BA-AH Aubrey Huff A................ 15.00 4.50
BA-BA Brandon Claussen A 10.00 3.00
BA-BC Ben Christensen A 10.00 3.00
BA-BD Brian Cardwell A............ 10.00 3.00
BA-BBC Boof Bonser A 10.00 3.00
BA-BJC Brian Specht C 10.00 3.00
BA-BSS Bud Smith B 10.00 3.00
BA-CK Charles Kegley A............ 10.00 3.00
BA-CR Cody Ransom B............. 10.00 3.00
BA-CS Chris Smith B 10.00 3.00
BA-CT Chris Tritle B 10.00 3.00
BA-CU Chase Utley A 25.00 7.50
BA-DV Domingo Valdez A 10.00 3.00
BA-DW Dan Wright B................ 10.00 3.00
BA-GA Garrett Atkins A 15.00 4.50
BA-GJ Gary Johnson C 10.00 3.00
BA-HB Hank Blalock B 25.00 7.50
BA-JB Josh Beckett B 25.00 7.50
BA-JD Jeff Davanon A.............. 10.00 3.00
BA-JL Jason Lane A................. 10.00 3.00
BA-JP Juan Pena A.................. 10.00 3.00
BA-JS Juan Silvestre A 10.00 3.00
BA-JAB Jason Botts B.............. 15.00 4.50
BA-JLW Jerome Williams A 15.00 4.50
BA-KG Keith Ginter B 10.00 3.00
BA-LB Larry Bigbie A................ 15.00 4.50
BA-MB Marlon Byrd B............... 10.00 3.00
BA-MC Matt Cooper A.............. 10.00 3.00
BA-MD Manny Delcarmen A 10.00 3.00
BA-ME Morgan Ensberg A 15.00 4.50
BA-MP Mark Prior B 60.00 18.00
BA-NJ Nick Johnson B.............. 15.00 4.50
BA-NN Nick Neugebauer E........ 10.00 3.00
BA-NV Noochie Varner B 10.00 3.00
BA-RF Randy Flores D 10.00 3.00
BA-RF Ryan Franklin B............. 10.00 3.00
BA-RH Ryan Hannaman A......... 10.00 3.00
BA-RO Roy Oswalt B................ 15.00 4.50
BA-RV Ryan Vogelsong B 10.00 3.00
BA-TB Tony Blanco A............... 10.00 3.00
BA-TH Toby Hall B 10.00 3.00
BA-TS Terrmel Sledge B........... 15.00 4.50
BA-WB Wilson Betemit B.......... 10.00 3.00
BA-WS Will Smith A 10.00 3.00

2002 Bowman Futures Game Autograph Relics

Inserted at overall odds of one in 196 hobby packs, one in 113 HTA packs and one in 259 retail packs for jersey cards and one in 126 HTA packs for base cards, these cards feature pieces of memorabilia and the player's autograph from the 2001 Futures Game.

Nm-Mt Ex-Mt
GROUP A JSY 1:2193 H, 1:1262 HTA, 1:2898 R
GROUP B JSY 1:1599 H, 1:923 HTA, 1:2125 R
GROUP C JSY 1:522 H, 1:301 HTA, 1:688 R
GROUP D JSY 1:1533 H, 1:882 HTA, 1:2028 R
GROUP E JSY 1:1425 H, 1:822 HTA, 1:1882 R
GROUP F JSY 1:1316 H, 1:759 HTA, 1:1738 R
CH Carlos Hernandez Jsy B 25.00 7.50
CP Carlos Pena Jsy D 25.00 7.50
DT Dennis Tankersley Jsy E 25.00 7.50
JRH J.R. House Jsy C.............. 25.00 7.50
JW Jerome Williams Jsy F........ 30.00 9.00
NJ Nick Johnson Jsy C............. 25.00 7.50
RL Ryan Ludwick Jsy C 25.00 7.50
TH Toby Hall Base.................... 25.00 7.50
WB Wilson Betemit Jsy A 25.00 7.50

2002 Bowman Game Used Relics

Inserted at an overall stated odd of one in 74 hobby packs, one in 43 HTA packs and one in 99 retail packs, these 26 cards features some of the leading prospects from the set along a piece of game-used memorabilia.

Nm-Mt Ex-Mt
GROUP A BAT 1:3236 H, 1:1866 HTA, 1:4331 R
GROUP B BAT 1:1472 H, 1:849 HTA, 1:1949 R
GROUP C BAT 1:1647 H, 1:948 HTA, 1:2180 R

GROUP D BAT 1:894 H, 1:515 HTA, 1:1180 R
GROUP E BAT 1:375 H, 1:216 HTA, 1:496 R
GROUP F BAT 1:1042 H, 1:601 HTA, 1:1381 R
GROUP G BAT 1:939 H, 1:541 HTA, 1:1237 R
OVERALL BAT 1:135 H, 1:78 HTA, 1:179 R
GROUP A JSY 1:2085 H,1:1202 HTA,1:2762 R
GROUP B JSY 1:1916 H, 1:528 HTA, 1:1213 R
GROUP C JSY 1:223 H, 1:129 HTA, 1:295 R
OVERALL JSY 1:165 H, 1:95 HTA, 1:219 R
BR-AB Angel Berroa Bat B 10.00 3.00
BR-AC Antoine Cameron Bat C . 10.00 3.00
BR-AE Adam Everett Bat E.......... 8.00 2.40
BR-AF Alex Fernandez Bat B 10.00 3.00
BR-AF Alex Fernandez Jsy C 8.00 2.40
BR-AG Alexis Gomez Bat A 10.00 3.00
BR-AK Austin Kearns Bat E......... 8.00 2.40
BR-ALC Alex Cintron Bat E 8.00 2.40
BR-CG Cristian Guerrero Bat E ... 8.00 2.40
BR-CI Cesar Izturis Bat D........... 8.00 2.40
BR-CP Corey Patterson Bat B ... 15.00 4.50
BR-CY Colin Young Jsy C 8.00 2.40
BR-DJ D'Angelo Jimenez Bat C 10.00 3.00
BR-FJ Forrest Johnson Bat G 8.00 2.40
BR-GA Garrett Atkins Bat F 10.00 3.00
BR-JA Jared Abruzzo Bat D 8.00 2.40
BR-JA Jared Abruzzo Jsy C 8.00 2.40
BR-JL Jason Lane Jsy B 8.00 2.40
BR-JS Jamal Strong Jsy A.......... 8.00 2.40
BR-NC Nate Cornejo Jsy C.......... 8.00 2.40
BR-NN Nick Neugebauer Jsy C ... 8.00 2.40
BR-RC Ryan Church Bat D........ 10.00 3.00
BR-RD Ryan Dittfurth Jsy C........ 8.00 2.40
BR-RM Ryan Madson Bat E......... 8.00 2.40
BR-RS Ruben Salazar Bat A...... 10.00 3.00
BR-RST Richard Stahl Jsy B....... 8.00 2.40

2002 Bowman Draft

This 165 card set was issued in December, 2002. These cards were issued in seven card packs which came 24 packs to a box and 10 boxes to a case. Each pack contained four regular Bowman Draft Pick Cards, two Bowman Chrome Draft cards and one Bowman gold card.

Nm-Mt Ex-Mt
COMPLETE SET (165)............... 40.00 12.00
BDP1 Clint Everts RC.................. 1.50 .45
BDP2 Fred Lewis RC...................... .40 .12
BDP3 Jon Broxton RC.................... .75 .23
BDP4 Jason Anderson RC .... .40 .12
BDP5 Mike Eusebio RC.................. .40 .12
BDP6 Zack Greinke RC .... 3.00 .90
BDP7 Joe Blanton RC .... 1.50 .45
BDP8 Sergio Santos RC.............. 2.00 .60
BDP9 Jason Cooper RC .... .50 .15
BDP10 Delwyn Young RC .... 1.25 .35
BDP11 Jeremy Hermida RC........ 2.00 .60
BDP12 Dan Ortmeier RC................ .75 .23
BDP13 Kevin Jepsen RC .... 1.00 .30
BDP14 Russ Adams RC.............. 1.00 .30
BDP15 Mike Nixon RC.................... .40 .12
BDP16 Nick Swisher RC .... 2.50 .75
BDP17 Cole Hamels RC............. 4.00 1.20
BDP18 Brian Dopirak RC .... 3.00 .90
BDP19 James Loney RC............ 2.00 .60
BDP20 Denard Span RC .... .40 .12
BDP21 Billy Petrick RC .... .40 .12
BDP22 Jared Doyle RC .... .40 .12
BDP23 Jeff Francoeur RC .... 3.00 .90
BDP24 Nick Bourgeois RC.............. .40 .12
BDP25 Matt Cain RC.................. 2.50 .75
BDP26 John McCurdy RC............... .40 .12
BDP27 Mark Kiger RC..................... .40 .12
BDP28 Bill Murphy RC.................... .50 .15
BDP29 Matt Craig RC .... .50 .15
BDP30 Mike Megrew RC............. 1.00 .30
BDP31 Ben Crockett RC.................. .40 .12
BDP32 Luke Hagerty RC .... .40 .12
BDP33 Matt Whitney RC................. .50 .15
BDP34 Dan Meyer RC................ 1.00 .30
BDP35 Jeremy Brown RC .... .75 .23
BDP36 Doug Johnson RC................ .40 .12
BDP37 Steve Obenchain RC .... .40 .12
BDP38 Matt Clanton RC.................. .40 .12
BDP39 Mark Teahen RC............. 1.50 .45
BDP40 Tom Carrow RC.................... .40 .12
BDP41 Micah Schilling RC.............. .40 .12
BDP42 Blair Johnson RC................ .40 .12
BDP43 Jason Pridie RC .... 1.00 .30
BDP44 Joey Votto RC .... 1.25 .35
BDP45 Taber Lee RC....................... .40 .12
BDP46 Adam Peterson RC............... .40 .12
BDP47 Adam Donachie RC.............. .40 .12
BDP48 Josh Murray RC................... .40 .12
BDP49 Brent Clevlen RC .... 1.00 .30
BDP50 Chad Pleiness RC................ .40 .12
BDP51 Zach Hammes RC .... .40 .12
BDP52 Chris Snyder RC .... .75 .23
BDP53 Chris Smith RC .... .40 .12
BDP54 Justin Maureau RC .... .40 .12
BDP55 David Bush RC................ 1.00 .30
BDP56 Tim Gilhooly RC.................. .40 .12
BDP57 Blair Barbier RC .... .40 .12
BDP58 Zach Segovia RC.................. .50 .15
BDP59 Jeremy Reed RC .... 3.00 .90
BDP60 Matt Pender RC................... .40 .12
BDP61 Eric Thomas RC .... .40 .12
BDP62 Justin Jones RC .... 1.25 .35
BDP63 Brian Slocum RC.................. .40 .12
BDP64 Larry Broadway RC......... 1.00 .30
BDP65 Bo Flowers RC .... .40 .12
BDP66 Scott White RC .... .40 .12
BDP67 Steve Stanley RC................. .40 .12
BDP68 Alex Merricks RC .... .40 .12
BDP69 Josh Womack RC................. .40 .12
BDP70 Dave Jensen RC .... .40 .12
BDP71 Curtis Granderson RC ..... 1.50 .45
BDP72 Pat Osborn RC .... .40 .12
BDP73 Nic Carter RC .... .40 .12
BDP74 Mitch Talbot RC .... .40 .12
BDP75 Don Murphy RC .... .40 .12
BDP76 Val Majewski RC .... 1.25 .35
BDP77 Javy Rodriguez RC............. .40 .12
BDP78 Fernando Pacheco RC....... .40 .12
BDP79 Steve Russell RC................. .40 .12
BDP80 Jon Slack RC....................... .40 .12
BDP81 John Baker RC .... .40 .12
BDP82 Aaron Coonrod RC.............. .40 .12
BDP83 Josh Johnson RC................ .40 .12
BDP84 Jake Blalock RC .... 1.50 .45
BDP85 Alex Hart RC .... .75 .23
BDP86 Wes Bankston RC .... 1.25 .35
BDP87 Josh Rupe RC .... .40 .12
BDP88 Dan Cevette RC .... .40 .12
BDP89 Kiel Fisher RC .... .50 .15
BDP90 Alan Rick RC........................ .40 .12
BDP91 Charlie Morton RC .... .40 .12
BDP92 Chad Spann RC.................... .75 .23
BDP93 Kyle Boyer RC...................... .40 .12
BDP94 Bob Malek RC...................... .40 .12
BDP95 Ryan Rodriguez RC.............. .40 .12
BDP96 Jordan Renz RC .... .40 .12
BDP97 Randy Frye RC..................... .40 .12
BDP98 Rich Hill RC......................... .40 .12
BDP99 B.J. Upton RC 8.00 2.40
BDP100 Dan Christensen RC.......... .40 .12
BDP101 Casey Kotchman RC ..... 3.00 .90
BDP102 Eric Good RC .... .30 .09
BDP103 Mike Fontenot RC .... .40 .12
BDP104 John Webb RC................... .40 .12
BDP105 Jason Dubois RC .... 1.25 .35
BDP106 Ryan Kibler RC.................. .40 .12
BDP107 Jhohny Peralta RC .... 1.25 .35
BDP108 Kirk Saarloos RC............... .40 .12
BDP109 Rhett Parrott RC .... .40 .12
BDP110 Jason Grove RC .... .40 .12
BDP111 Colt Griffin RC.................. .50 .15
BDP112 Dallas McPherson RC ... 6.00 1.80
BDP113 Oliver Perez RC............. 3.00 .90
BDP114 Mar. McDougall RC .... .40 .12
BDP115 Mike Wood RC .... .40 .12
BDP116 Scott Hairston RC .... 1.50 .45
BDP117 Jason Simontacchi RC..... .40 .12
BDP118 Taggert Bozied RC............ .75 .23
BDP119 Shelley Duncan RC .... .40 .12
BDP120 Dontrelle Willis RC........ 3.00 .90
BDP121 Sean Burnett .... .30 .09
BDP122 Aaron Cook .... .30 .09
BDP123 Brett Evert......................... .30 .09
BDP124 Jimmy Journell .... .30 .09
BDP125 Brett Myers .... .30 .09
BDP126 Brad Baker .... .30 .09
BDP127 Billy Traber RC .... 1.00 .30
BDP128 Adam Wainwright .... .30 .09
BDP129 Jason Young RC .... .40 .12
BDP130 John Buck.......................... .30 .09
BDP131 Kevin Cash RC .... .40 .12
BDP132 Jason Stokes RC........... 3.00 .90
BDP133 Drew Henson .... .30 .09
BDP134 Chad Tracy RC .... 1.50 .45
BDP135 Orlando Hudson................. .30 .09
BDP136 Brandon Phillips................ .30 .09
BDP137 Joe Borchard...................... .30 .09
BDP138 Marlon Byrd .... .30 .09
BDP139 Carl Crawford.................... .30 .09
BDP140 Michael Restovich............. .30 .09
BDP141 Corey Hart RC .... 1.25 .35
BDP142 Edwin Almonte................... .30 .09
BDP143 Francis Beltran RC .... .40 .12
BDP144 Jorge De La Rosa RC....... .40 .12
BDP145 Gerardo Garcia RC .... .40 .12
BDP146 Franklyn German RC .... .40 .12
BDP147 Francisco Liriano............... .50 .15
BDP148 Francisco Rodriguez .... .30 .09
BDP149 Ricardo Rodriguez .... .30 .09
BDP150 Seung Song .... .30 .09
BDP151 John Stephens................... .30 .09
BDP152 Justin Huber RC................ .75 .23
BDP153 Victor Martinez.................. .75 .23
BDP154 Hee Seop Choi .... .30 .09
BDP155 Justin Morneau .... .75 .23
BDP156 Miguel Cabrera............. 1.25 .35
BDP157 Victor Diaz RC.............. 1.50 .45
BDP158 Jose Reyes......................... .50 .15
BDP159 Omar Infante .... .30 .09
BDP160 Angel Berroa .... .30 .09
BDP161 Tony Alvarez...................... .30 .09
BDP162 Shin Soo Choo RC .... 1.25 .35
BDP163 Wily Mo Pena.................... .30 .09
BDP164 Andres Torres.................... .30 .09
BDP165 Jose Lopez RC .... 3.00 .90

2002 Bowman Draft Gold

Issued one per pack, this is a parallel to the Bowman Draft Set. These cards have the player's fascimile autograph set off in gold foil.

Nm-Mt Ex-Mt
*GOLD: 1.25X TO 3X BASIC ....
*GOLD RC'S: .6X TO 1.5X BASIC ....

2002 Bowman Draft Fabric of the Future Relics

Inserted at a stated rate of one in 55, these 28 cards feature prospects from the 2002 All-Star Futures Game who are very close to be major leaguers. All of these cards have a game-worn jersey relic piece on them.

Nm-Mt Ex-Mt
AB Angel Berroa........................... 8.00 2.40
AT Andres Torres 8.00 2.40
AW Adam Wainwright................... 8.00 2.40
BM Brett Myers............................. 8.00 2.40
BT Billy Traber............................. 8.00 2.40

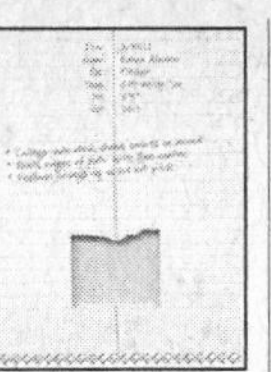

CC Carl Crawford 10.00 3.00
CH Corey Hart 10.00 3.00
CT Chad Tracy 10.00 3.00
DH Drew Henson 10.00 3.00
EA Edwin Almonte 8.00 2.40
FB Francis Beltran 8.00 2.40
FG Franklyn German 8.00 2.40
FL Francisco Liriano 8.00 2.40
GG Gerardo Garcia 8.00 2.40
HC Hee Seop Choi 8.00 2.40
JH Justin Huber 8.00 2.40
JK Josh Karp 8.00 2.40
JL Jose Lopez 12.00 3.60
JR Jorge De La Rosa 8.00 2.40
JS1 Jason Stokes 10.00 3.00
JS2 John Stephens 8.00 2.40
KC Kevin Cash 8.00 2.40
MR Michael Restovich 8.00 2.40
SB Sean Burnett 8.00 2.40
SC Shin Soo Choo 10.00 3.00
TA Tony Alvarez 8.00 2.40
VD Victor Diaz 15.00 4.50
WP Wily Mo Pena 10.00 3.00

2002 Bowman Draft Freshman Fiber

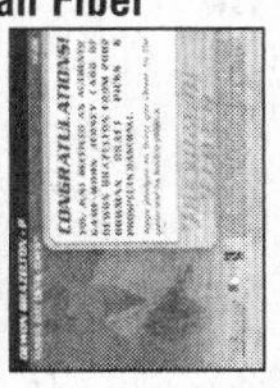

Issued at a stated rate of one in 605 for the bat cards and one in 45 for the jersey cards, these 13 cards feature some of the leading young players in the game along with a game-worn piece.

Nm-Mt Ex-Mt
AH Aubrey Huff Jsy 5.00 1.50
AK Austin Kearns Bat 8.00 2.40
BA Brent Abernathy Jsy 5.00 1.50
BD Dewon Brazelton Jsy 5.00 1.50
JH Josh Hamilton Jsy 5.00 1.50
JK Joe Kennedy Jsy 5.00 1.50
JS Jared Sandberg Jsy 5.00 1.50
JV John VanBenschoten Jsy 5.00 1.50
JWS Jason Standridge Jsy 5.00 1.50
MB Marlon Byrd Bat 8.00 2.40
MT Mark Teixeira Bat 10.00 3.00
NB Nick Bierbrodt Jsy 5.00 1.50
TH Toby Hall Jsy 5.00 1.50

2002 Bowman Draft Signs of the Future

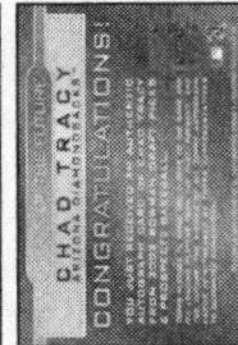

Inserted at different odds depending on what group the player belonged to, these 21 cards feature authentic autographs of the featured player.

Nm-Mt Ex-Mt
GROUP A ODDS 1:100
GROUP B ODDS 1:110
GROUP C ODDS 1:1028
GROUP D ODDS 1:1103
GROUP E ODDS 1:386
GROUP F ODDS 1:2807
BI Brandon Inge E 10.00 3.00
BK Bob Keppel C 10.00 3.00
BP Brandon Phillips B 10.00 3.00
BS Bud Smith E 10.00 3.00
CP Christian Parra D 10.00 3.00
CT Chad Tracy A 20.00 6.00
DD Dan Denham A 10.00 3.00
EB Erik Bedard A 10.00 3.00
JEM Justin Morneau B 20.00 6.00
JM Jake Mauer B 10.00 3.00
JR Juan Rivera B 10.00 3.00
JW Jerome Williams F 15.00 4.50
KH Kris Honel A 10.00 3.00
LB Larry Bigbie E 10.00 3.00
LN Lance Niekro A 10.00 3.00
ME Morgan Ensberg E 10.00 3.00
MF Mike Fontenot A 15.00 4.50
MJ Mitch Jones A 10.00 3.00
NJ Nic Jackson B 10.00 3.00
TB Taylor Buchholz B 10.00 3.00
TL Todd Linden B 15.00 4.50

2003 Bowman

This 330 card set was released in May, 2003. These cards were mixed between veteran cards with red borders on the bottom (1-155) and rookie/prospect cards with blue on the bottom (156-330). This set was issued in 10 card packs which came 24 packs to a box and 12 boxes to a case with an $3 SRP per pack. A special card was inserted featured game-used relics of the two 2002 Major League Rookie of the Years.

Nm-Mt Ex-Mt
COMPLETE SET (330) 80.00 24.00
COMMON CARD (1-155) .30 .09
COMMON CARD (156-330) .30 .09
1 Garret Anderson .30 .09
2 Derek Jeter 2.00 .60
3 Gary Sheffield .30 .09
4 Matt Morris .30 .09
5 Derek Lowe .30 .09
6 Andy Van Hekken .30 .09
7 Sammy Sosa 1.25 .35
8 Ken Griffey Jr. 1.25 .35
9 Omar Vizquel .50 .15
10 Jorge Posada .50 .15
11 Lance Berkman .30 .09
12 Mike Sweeney .30 .09
13 Adrian Beltre .50 .15
14 Richie Sexson .30 .09
15 A.J. Pierzynski .30 .09
16 Bartolo Colon .30 .09
17 Mike Mussina .50 .15
18 Paul Byrd .30 .09
19 Bobby Abreu .30 .09
20 Miguel Tejada .30 .09
21 Aramis Ramirez .30 .09
22 Edgardo Alfonzo .30 .09
23 Edgar Martinez .50 .15
24 Albert Pujols 1.50 .45
25 Carl Crawford .30 .09
26 Eric Hinske .30 .09
27 Tim Salmon .50 .15
28 Luis Gonzalez .30 .09
29 Jay Gibbons .30 .09
30 John Smoltz .50 .15
31 Tim Wakefield .30 .09
32 Mark Prior .75 .23
33 Magglio Ordonez .30 .09
34 Adam Dunn .50 .15
35 Larry Walker .50 .15
36 Luis Castillo .30 .09
37 Wade Miller .30 .09
38 Carlos Beltran .50 .15
39 Odalis Perez .30 .09
40 Alex Sanchez .30 .09
41 Torii Hunter .30 .09
42 Cliff Floyd .30 .09
43 Andy Pettitte .50 .15
44 Francisco Rodriguez .30 .09
45 Eric Chavez .30 .09
46 Kevin Millwood .30 .09
47 Dennis Tankersley .30 .09
48 Hideo Nomo .75 .23
49 Freddy Garcia .30 .09
50 Randy Johnson .75 .23
51 Aubrey Huff .30 .09
52 Carlos Delgado .30 .09
53 Troy Glaus .30 .09
54 Junior Spivey .30 .09
55 Mike Hampton .30 .09
56 Sidney Ponson .30 .09
57 Aaron Boone .30 .09
58 Kerry Wood .75 .23
59 Runelvys Hernandez .30 .09
60 Nomar Garciaparra 1.25 .35
61 Todd Helton .50 .15
62 Mike Lowell .30 .09
63 Roy Oswalt .30 .09
64 Raul Ibanez .30 .09
65 Brian Jordan .30 .09
66 Geoff Jenkins .30 .09
67 Jermaine Dye .30 .09
68 Tom Glavine .50 .15
69 Bernie Williams .50 .15
70 Vladimir Guerrero .75 .23
71 Mark Mulder .30 .09
72 Jimmy Rollins .30 .09
73 Oliver Perez .30 .09
74 Rich Aurilia .30 .09
75 Joel Pineiro .30 .09
76 J.D. Drew .30 .09
77 Ivan Rodriguez .75 .23
78 Josh Phelps .30 .09
79 Darin Erstad .30 .09
80 Curt Schilling .30 .09
81 Paul Lo Duca .30 .09
82 Marty Cordova .30 .09
83 Manny Ramirez .50 .15
84 Bobby Hill .30 .09
85 Paul Konerko .30 .09
86 Austin Kearns .50 .15
87 Jason Jennings .30 .09
88 Brad Penny .30 .09
89 Jeff Bagwell .50 .15
90 Shawn Green .30 .09
91 Jason Schmidt .30 .09
92 Doug Mientkiewicz .30 .09
93 Jose Vidro .30 .09
94 Bret Boone .30 .09
95 Jason Giambi .30 .09
96 Barry Zito .30 .09
97 Roy Halladay .30 .09
98 Pat Burrell .30 .09
99 Sean Burroughs .30 .09
100 Barry Bonds 2.00 .60
101 Kazuhiro Sasaki .30 .09
102 Fernando Vina .30 .09
103 Chan Ho Park .30 .09
104 Andruw Jones .30 .09
105 Adam Kennedy .30 .09
106 Shea Hillenbrand .30 .09
107 Greg Maddux 1.25 .35
108 Jim Edmonds .30 .09
109 Pedro Martinez .75 .23
110 Moises Alou .30 .09
111 Jeff Weaver .30 .09
112 C.C. Sabathia .30 .09
113 Robert Fick .30 .09
114 A.J. Burnett .30 .09
115 Jeff Kent .30 .09
116 Kevin Brown .30 .09
117 Rafael Furcal .30 .09
118 Cristian Guzman .30 .09
119 Brad Wilkerson .30 .09
120 Mike Piazza 1.25 .35
121 Alfonso Soriano .50 .15
122 Mark Ellis .30 .09
123 Vicente Padilla .30 .09
124 Eric Gagne .75 .23
125 Ryan Klesko .30 .09
126 Ichiro Suzuki 1.25 .35
127 Tony Batista .30 .09
128 Roberto Alomar .50 .15
129 Alex Rodriguez 1.25 .35
130 Jim Thome .75 .23
131 Jarrod Washburn .30 .09
132 Orlando Hudson .30 .09
133 Chipper Jones .75 .23
134 Rodrigo Lopez .30 .09
135 Johnny Damon .75 .23
136 Matt Clement .30 .09
137 Frank Thomas .75 .23
138 Ellis Burks .30 .09
139 Carlos Pena .30 .09
140 Josh Beckett .30 .09
141 Joe Randa .30 .09
142 Brian Giles .30 .09
143 Kazuhisa Ishii .30 .09
144 Corey Koskie .30 .09
145 Orlando Cabrera .30 .09
146 Mark Buehrle .30 .09
147 Roger Clemens 1.50 .45
148 Tim Hudson .30 .09
149 Randy Wolf UER .30 .09
resume says AL leaders; he pitches in NL
150 Josh Fogg .30 .09
151 Phil Nevin .30 .09
152 John Olerud .30 .09
153 Scott Rolen .75 .23
154 Joe Kennedy .30 .09
155 Rafael Palmeiro .50 .15
156 Chad Hutchinson .30 .09
157 Quincy Carter XRC .50 .15
158 Hee Seop Choi .30 .09
159 Joe Borchard .30 .09
160 Brandon Phillips .30 .09
161 Wily Mo Pena .30 .09
162 Victor Martinez .50 .15
163 Jason Stokes .50 .15
164 Ken Harvey .30 .09
165 Juan Rivera .30 .09
166 Jose Contreras RC 1.00 .30
167 Dan Haren RC .75 .23
168 Michel Hernandez RC .40 .12
169 Eider Torres RC .40 .12
170 Chris De La Cruz RC .40 .12
171 Ramon Nivar-Martinez RC .75 .23
172 Mike Adams RC .40 .12
173 Justin Arneson RC .40 .12
174 Jamie Athas RC .40 .12
175 Dwaine Bacon RC .40 .12
176 Clint Barmes RC .50 .15
177 B.J. Barns RC .40 .12
178 Tyler Johnson RC .40 .12
179 Bobby Basham RC .50 .15
180 T.J. Bohn RC .40 .12
181 J.D. Durbin RC .75 .23
182 Brandon Bowe RC .40 .12
183 Craig Brazell RC .50 .15
184 Dusty Brown RC .40 .12
185 Brian Bruney RC .50 .15
186 Greg Bruso RC .40 .12
187 Jaime Bubela RC .40 .12
188 Bryan Bullington RC 1.25 .35
189 Brian Burgamy RC .40 .12
190 Eny Cabreja RC .40 .12
191 Daniel Cabrera RC 1.00 .30
192 Ryan Cameron RC .40 .12
193 Lance Caraccioli RC .40 .12
194 David Cash RC .40 .12
195 Bernie Castro RC .40 .12
196 Ismael Castro RC .50 .15
197 Daryl Clark RC .50 .15
198 Jeff Clark RC .40 .12
199 Chris Colton RC .40 .12
200 Dexter Cooper RC .40 .12
201 Callix Crabbe RC .50 .15
202 Chien-Ming Wang RC 1.00 .30
203 Eric Crozier RC .50 .15
204 Nook Logan RC .50 .15
205 David DeJesus RC .50 .15
206 Matt DeMarco RC .40 .12
207 Chris Duncan RC .40 .12
208 Eric Eckenstahler .30 .09
209 Willie Eyre RC .40 .12
210 Evel Bastida-Martinez RC .40 .12
211 Chris Fallon RC .40 .12
212 Mike Flannery RC .40 .12
213 Mike O'Keefe RC .40 .12
214 Ben Francisco RC .50 .15
215 Kason Gabbard RC .40 .12
216 Mike Gallo RC .40 .12
217 Jairo Garcia RC .75 .23
218 Angel Garcia RC .40 .12
219 Michael Garciaparra RC .75 .23
220 Joey Gomes RC .40 .12
221 Dusty Gomon RC .50 .15
222 Bryan Grace RC .40 .12
223 Tyson Graham RC .40 .12
224 Henry Guerrero RC .40 .12
225 Franklin Gutierrez RC 2.00 .60
226 Carlos Guzman RC .50 .15
227 Matthew Hagen RC .75 .23
228 Josh Hall RC .50 .15
229 Rob Hammock RC .50 .15
230 Brendan Harris RC .50 .15
231 Gary Harris RC .40 .12
232 Clay Hensley RC .40 .12
233 Michael Hinckley RC 1.00 .30
234 Luis Hodge RC .40 .12
235 Donnie Hood RC .50 .15
236 Travis Ishikawa RC .40 .12
237 Edwin Jackson RC 2.50 .75
238 Ardley Jansen RC .50 .15
239 Ferenc Jongejan RC .40 .12
240 Matt Kata RC .75 .23
241 Kazuhiro Takeoka RC .40 .12
242 Beau Kemp RC .40 .12
243 Il Kim RC .40 .12
244 Brennan King RC .40 .12
245 Chris Kroski RC .40 .12
246 Jason Kubel RC 2.00 .60
247 Pete LaForest RC .50 .15
248 Wil Ledezma RC .50 .15
249 Jeremy Bonderman RC .75 .23
250 Gonzalo Lopez RC .40 .12
251 Brian Luderer RC .40 .12
252 Ruddy Lugo RC .40 .12
253 Wayne Lydon RC .40 .12
254 Mark Malaska RC .40 .12
255 Andy Marte RC 2.50 .75
256 Tyler Martin RC .40 .12
257 Branden Florence RC .40 .12
258 Aneudis Mateo RC .40 .12
259 Derell McCall RC .40 .12
260 Brian McCann RC .75 .23
261 Mike McNutt RC .40 .12
262 Jacabo Meque RC .40 .12
263 Derek Michaelis RC .40 .12
264 Aaron Miles RC 1.00 .30
265 Jose Morales RC .40 .12
266 Dustin Moseley RC .50 .15
267 Adrian Myers RC .40 .12
268 Dan Neil RC .40 .12
269 Jon Nelson RC .50 .15
270 Mike Neu RC .40 .12
271 Leigh Neuage RC .40 .12
272 Wes O'Brien RC .40 .12
273 Trent Oeltjen RC .50 .15
274 Tim Olson RC .50 .15
275 David Pahucki RC .40 .12
276 Nathan Panther RC .75 .23
277 Arnie Munoz RC .40 .12
278 Dave Pember RC .40 .12
279 Jason Perry RC .75 .23
280 Matthew Peterson RC .40 .12
281 Ryan Shealy RC .75 .23
282 Jorge Piedra RC .50 .15
283 Simon Pond RC .75 .23
284 Aaron Rakers RC .40 .12
285 Hanley Ramirez RC 2.00 .60
286 Manuel Ramirez RC .50 .15
287 Kevin Randel RC .40 .12
288 Darrell Rasner RC .40 .12
289 Prentice Redman RC .40 .12
290 Eric Reed RC .75 .23
291 Wilton Reynolds RC .50 .15
292 Eric Riggs RC .50 .15
293 Carlos Rijo RC .40 .12
294 Rajai Davis RC .50 .15
295 Aron Weston RC .40 .12
296 Arturo Rivas RC .40 .12
297 Kyle Roat RC .40 .12
298 Bubba Nelson RC .50 .15
299 Levi Robinson RC .40 .12
300 Ray Sadler RC .40 .12
301 Gary Schneidmiller RC .40 .12
302 Jon Schuerholz RC .40 .12
303 Corey Shafer RC .50 .15
304 Brian Shackelford RC .40 .12
305 Bill Simon RC .40 .12
306 Haj Turay RC .50 .15
307 Sean Smith RC .50 .15
308 Ryan Spataro RC .40 .12
309 Jemel Spearman RC .40 .12
310 Keith Stamler RC .40 .12
311 Luke Steidlmayer RC .40 .12
312 Adam Stern RC .40 .12
313 Jay Sitzman RC .40 .12
314 Thomari Story-Harden RC .50 .15
315 Terry Tiffee RC .75 .23
316 Nick Trzesniak RC .40 .12
317 Denny Tussen RC .40 .12
318 Scott Tyler RC .50 .15
319 Shane Victorino RC .40 .12
320 Doug Waechter RC .50 .15
321 Brandon Watson RC .40 .12
322 Todd Wellemeyer RC .50 .15
323 Eli Whiteside RC .40 .12
324 Josh Willingham RC .50 .15
325 Travis Wong RC .50 .15
326 Brian Wright RC .40 .12
327 Kevin Youkilis RC 1.50 .45
328 Andy Sisco RC 1.00 .30
329 Dustin Yount RC .50 .15
330 Andrew Dominique RC .40 .12
NNO Eric Hinske Bat 15.00 4.50
Jason Jennings Jsy
ROY Relic

2003 Bowman Gold

Nm-Mt Ex-Mt
COMPLETE SET (330) 150.00 45.00
*RED 1-155: 1.25X TO 3X BASIC
*BLUE 156-330: 1.25X TO 3X BASIC
*BLUE ROOKIES: .75X TO 2X BASIC
ONE PER PACK

2003 Bowman Uncirculated Metallic Gold

These cards were originally issued as exchange cards in the silver packs which were inserted one per hobby box. In addition, these exchange cards were seeded into retail packs at a stated rate of one in 49. These cards could be mailed into the Pit.Com for redemption for a hermetically sealed card. Please note that the original stated print run for these cards are 230 sets. These cards could be redeemed until April 30th, 2004.

Nm-Mt Ex-Mt
NNO Exchange Card

2003 Bowman Uncirculated Silver

These cards were issued at a stated rate of one per silver pack, which were inserted one per sealed hobby box. This is a parallel set to the basic Bowman set and each card was issued in already sealed holder. Please note that each card was issued to a stated print run of 250 serial numbered sets. In addition, a few cards were issued as redemption cards for the entire Uncirculated Silver set. These cards could be redeemed until April 30th, 2004.

Nm-Mt Ex-Mt
*UNC.SILVER 1-155: 5X TO 12X BASIC
*UNC.SILVER 156-330: 5X TO 12X BASIC
*UNC.SILVER ROOKIES: 2.5X TO 6X BASIC
NNO Set Exchange Card

2003 Bowman Future Fiber Bats

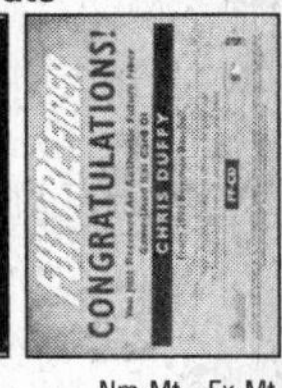

Nm-Mt Ex-Mt
GROUP A ODDS 1:96 H, 1:34 HTA, 1:196 R
GROUP B ODDS 1:393 H, 1:140 HTA, 1:803 R
AG Adrian Gonzalez A 8.00 2.40
AH Aubrey Huff A 8.00 2.40
AK Austin Kearns A 8.00 2.40
BS Bud Smith B 8.00 2.40
CD Chris Duffy B 8.00 2.40
CK Casey Kotchman A 10.00 3.00
DH Drew Henson A 8.00 2.40
DW David Wright A 25.00 7.50
ES Esix Snead A 8.00 2.40
EY Edwin Yan B 8.00 2.40
FS Freddy Sanchez A 8.00 2.40
HB Hank Blalock A 10.00 3.00
JB Jason Botts A 8.00 2.40
JDM Jake Mauer A 8.00 2.40
JG Jason Grove A 8.00 2.40
JH Josh Hamilton A 8.00 2.40
JM Joe Mauer A 20.00 6.00
JW Justin Wayne B 8.00 2.40
KC Kevin Cash B 8.00 2.40
KD Kory DeHaan A 8.00 2.40
MR Michael Restovich A 8.00 2.40
NH Nathan Haynes A 8.00 2.40
PF Pedro Feliz A 8.00 2.40
RB Rocco Baldelli B 8.00 2.40
RJ Reed Johnson A 8.00 2.40
RK Ryan Langerhans A 8.00 2.40
RS Randall Shelley A 8.00 2.40
SB Sean Burroughs A 8.00 2.40
ST So Taguchi A 8.00 2.40
TW Travis Wilson A 8.00 2.40
WB Wilson Betemit A 8.00 2.40
WR Wilkin Ruan B 8.00 2.40
XN Xavier Nady A 8.00 2.40

2003 Bowman Futures Game Base Autograph

Nm-Mt Ex-Mt
STATED ODDS 1:141 HTA
JR Jose Reyes 25.00 7.50

2003 Bowman Futures Game Gear Jersey Relics

Nm-Mt Ex-Mt
STATED ODDS 1:26 H, 1:9 HTA, 1:52 R
AC Aaron Cook 8.00 2.40
AW Adam Wainwright 8.00 2.40
BB Brad Baker 8.00 2.40
BE Brett Evert 8.00 2.40
BH Bill Hall 8.00 2.40
BM Brett Myers 8.00 2.40
BP Brandon Phillips 8.00 2.40
BT Billy Traber 8.00 2.40
CC Carl Crawford 8.00 2.40
CH Corey Hart 8.00 2.40
CT Chad Tracy 8.00 2.40
DH Drew Henson 8.00 2.40
EA Edwin Almonte 8.00 2.40
FB Francis Beltran 8.00 2.40
FL Francisco Liriano 8.00 2.40
FR Francisco Rodriguez 8.00 2.40
GG Gerardo Garcia 8.00 2.40
HC Hee Seop Choi 8.00 2.40
JB John Buck 8.00 2.40
JDR Jorge De La Rosa 8.00 2.40
JEB Joe Borchard 8.00 2.40
JH Justin Huber 8.00 2.40
JJ Jimmy Journell 8.00 2.40
JK Josh Karp 8.00 2.40
JL Jose Lopez 10.00 3.00
JM Justin Morneau 10.00 3.00
JMS John Stephens 8.00 2.40
JR Jose Reyes 8.00 2.40
JS Jason Stokes 10.00 3.00
JY Jason Young 8.00 2.40
KC Kevin Cash 8.00 2.40
LO Lyle Overbay 8.00 2.40

MB Marlon Byrd 8.00 2.40
MC Miguel Cabrera 10.00 3.00
MR Michael Restovich 8.00 2.40
OH Orlando Hudson 8.00 2.40
OI Omar Infante 8.00 2.40
RD Ryan Dittfurth 8.00 2.40
RR Ricardo Rodriguez 8.00 2.40
SB Sean Burnett 8.00 2.40
SC Shin Soo Choo 8.00 2.40
SS Seung Song 8.00 2.40
TA Tony Alvarez 8.00 2.40
VD Victor Diaz 8.00 2.40
VM Victor Martinez 10.00 3.00
WP Wily Mo Pena 8.00 2.40

2003 Bowman Signs of the Future

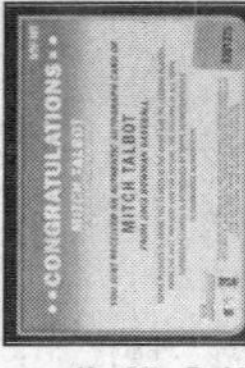

Nm-Mt Ex-Mt
GROUP A ODDS 1:39 H, 1:13 HTA, 1:79 R
GROUP B ODDS 1:183 H, 1:65 HTA, 1:374 R
GROUP C ODDS 1:2288 H,1:816 HTA,1:4720 R
*RED INK: 1.25X TO 3X GROUP A
*RED INK: 1.25X TO 3X GROUP B
*RED INK: .75X TO 2X GROUP C
RED INK ODDS 1:687 H, 1:245 HTA, 1:1402 R
AV Andy Van Hekken A 8.00 2.40
BB Bryan Bullington A 15.00 4.50
BJ Bobby Jenks B 8.00 2.40
BK Ben Kozlowski A 8.00 2.40
BL Brandon League B 8.00 2.40
BS Brian Slocum A 8.00 2.40
CH Cole Hamels A 25.00 7.50
CJH Corey Hart A 10.00 3.00
CMH Chad Hutchinson C 15.00 4.50
CP Chris Piersoll B 8.00 2.40
DG Doug Gredvig A 8.00 2.40
DHM Dustin McGowan A 10.00 3.00
DL Donald Levinski A 8.00 2.40
DS Doug Sessions B 8.00 2.40
FL Fred Lewis A 8.00 2.40
FS Freddy Sanchez B 8.00 2.40
HR Hanley Ramirez A 20.00 6.00
JA Jason Arnold B 8.00 2.40
JB John Buck A 8.00 2.40
JC Jesus Cota B 8.00 2.40
JG Jason Grove B 8.00 2.40
JGU Jeremy Guthrie A 8.00 2.40
JL James Loney A 8.00 2.40
JOG Jonny Gomes B 8.00 2.40
JR Jose Reyes A 10.00 3.00
JRH Joel Hanrahan A 10.00 3.00
JSC Jason St. Clair B 8.00 2.40
KG Khalil Greene A 40.00 12.00
KH Koyie Hill B 8.00 2.40
MT Mitch Talbot A 8.00 2.40
NC Nelson Castro B 8.00 2.40
OV Oscar Villareal A 8.00 2.40
PR Prentice Redman A 8.00 2.40
QC Quincy Carter C 20.00 6.00
RC Ryan Church B 8.00 2.40
RS Ryan Snare B 8.00 2.40
TL Todd Linden B 8.00 2.40
VM Val Majewski A 10.00 3.00
ZG Zack Greinke A 15.00 4.50
ZS Zach Segovia A 8.00 2.40

2003 Bowman Signs of the Future Dual

Nm-Mt Ex-Mt
STAT.ODDS 1:9220 H,1:3264 HTA,1:20,390 R
CH Quincy Carter 100.00 30.00
Chad Hutchinson

2003 Bowman Draft

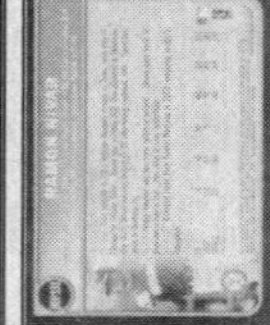

This 165-card standard-size set was released in December, 2003. The set was issued in 10 card packs with a $2.99 SRP which came 24 packs to a box and 10 boxes to a case. Please note that each Draft pack included 2 Chrome cards.

MINT NRMT
COMPLETE SET (165) 40.00 18.00
1 Dontrelle Willis .50 .23
2 Freddy Sanchez .30 .14
3 Miguel Cabrera .75 .35
4 Ryan Ludwick .30 .14
5 Ty Wigginton .30 .14
6 Mark Teixeira .30 .14
7 Trey Hodges .30 .14
8 Laynce Nix .30 .14
9 Antonio Perez .30 .14
10 Jody Gerut .30 .14
11 Jae Weong Seo .30 .14
12 Erick Almonte .30 .14
13 Lyle Overbay .30 .14
14 Billy Traber .30 .14
15 Andres Torres .30 .14
16 Jose Valverde .30 .14
17 Aaron Heilman .30 .14
18 Brandon Larson .30 .14
19 Jung Bong .30 .14
20 Jesse Foppert .30 .14
21 Angel Berroa .30 .14
22 Jeff DaVanon .30 .14
23 Kurt Ainsworth .30 .14
24 Brandon Claussen .30 .14
25 Xavier Nady .30 .14
26 Travis Hafner .30 .14
27 Jerome Williams .30 .14
28 Jose Reyes .30 .14
29 Sergio Mitre RC .50 .23
30 Bo Hart RC .50 .23
31 Adam Miller RC 1.50 .70
32 Brian Finch RC .40 .18
33 Taylor Mattingly RC 1.25 .55
34 Daric Barton RC 2.50 1.10
35 Chris Ray RC .50 .23
36 Jarrod Saltalamacchia RC .75 .35
37 Dennis Dove RC .50 .23
38 James Houser RC .50 .23
39 Clint King RC .75 .35
40 Lou Palmisano RC 1.25 .55
41 Dan Moore RC .40 .18
42 Craig Stansberry RC .50 .23
43 Jo Jo Reyes RC .50 .23
44 Jake Stevens RC 1.25 .55
45 Tom Gorzelanny RC .75 .35
46 Brian Marshall RC .40 .18
47 Scott Beerer RC .40 .18
48 Javi Herrera RC .50 .23
49 Steve LeRud RC .75 .35
50 Josh Banks RC 1.00 .45
51 Jon Papelbon RC .40 .18
52 Juan Valdes RC .50 .23
53 Beau Vaughan RC .50 .23
54 Matt Chico RC 1.00 .45
55 Todd Jennings RC .50 .23
56 Anthony Gwynn RC 1.25 .55
57 Matt Harrison RC .75 .35
58 Aaron Marsden RC .50 .23
59 Casey Abrams RC .40 .18
60 Cory Stuart RC .40 .18
61 Mike Wagner RC .40 .18
62 Jordan Pratt RC .50 .23
63 Andre Randolph RC .50 .23
64 Blake Balkcom RC .50 .23
65 Josh Muecke RC .40 .18
66 Jamie D'Antona RC 1.50 .70
67 Cole Seifrig RC .75 .35
68 Josh Anderson RC 1.00 .45
69 Matt Lorenzo RC .50 .23
70 Nate Spears RC .75 .35
71 Chris Goodman RC .40 .18
72 Brian McFall RC .75 .35
73 Billy Hogan RC .50 .23
74 Jamie Romak RC .50 .23
75 Jeff Cook RC .50 .23
76 Brooks McNiven RC .40 .18
77 Xavier Paul RC 1.50 .70
78 Bob Zimmermann RC .40 .18
79 Mickey Hall RC .50 .23
80 Shaun Marcum RC .40 .18
81 Matt Nachreiner RC .50 .23
82 Chris Kinsey RC .40 .18
83 Jonathan Fulton RC .50 .23
84 Edgardo Baez RC .50 .23
85 Robert Valido RC .75 .35
86 Kenny Lewis RC .50 .23
87 Trent Peterson RC .40 .18
88 Johnny Woodard RC .50 .23
89 Wes Littleton RC .50 .23
90 Sean Rodriguez RC 1.25 .55
91 Kyle Pearson RC .40 .18
92 Josh Rainwater RC .50 .23
93 Travis Schlichting RC .50 .23
94 Tim Battle RC .50 .23
95 Aaron Hill RC 1.00 .45
96 Bob McCrory RC .40 .18
97 Rick Guarno RC .40 .18
98 Brandon Yarbrough RC .40 .18
99 Peter Stonard RC .40 .18
100 Darin Downs RC .50 .23
101 Matt Bruback RC .30 .14
102 Danny Garcia RC .40 .18
103 Cory Stewart RC .40 .18
104 Ferdin Tejeda RC .40 .18
105 Kade Johnson RC .40 .18
106 Andrew Brown RC .50 .23
107 Aquilino Lopez RC .40 .18
108 Stephen Randolph RC .40 .18
109 Dave Matranga RC .40 .18
110 Dustin McGowan RC .75 .35
111 Juan Camacho RC .40 .18
112 Cliff Lee .30 .14
113 Jeff Duncan RC .50 .23
114 C.J. Wilson .30 .14
115 Brandon Roberson RC .40 .18
116 David Corrente RC .40 .18
117 Kevin Beavers RC .40 .18
118 Anthony Webster RC .50 .23
119 Oscar Villarreal RC .40 .18
120 Hong-Chih Kuo RC .75 .35
121 Josh Barfield .30 .14
122 Denny Bautista .30 .14
123 Chris Burke RC .75 .35
124 Robinson Cano RC 1.00 .45
125 Jose Castillo .30 .14
126 Neal Cotts .30 .14
127 Jorge De La Rosa .30 .14
128 J.D. Durbin .75 .35
129 Edwin Encarnacion .30 .14
130 Gavin Floyd .30 .14
131 Alexis Gomez .30 .14
132 Edgar Gonzalez RC .40 .18
133 Khalil Greene 1.50 .70
134 Zack Greinke .30 .14
135 Franklin Gutierrez .75 .35
136 Rich Harden .50 .23
137 J.J. Hardy RC 1.50 .70
138 Ryan Howard RC 3.00 1.35
139 Justin Huber .30 .14
140 David Kelton .30 .14
141 Dave Krynzel .30 .14
142 Pete LaForest .50 .23
143 Adam LaRoche .30 .14
144 Preston Larrison RC .50 .23
145 John Maine RC 1.50 .70
146 Andy Marte 1.25 .55
147 Jeff Mathis .30 .14
148 Joe Mauer UER .75 .35
Card has playing for New Haven
149 Clint Nageotte .30 .14
150 Chris Narveson .30 .14
151 Ramon Nivar .75 .35
152 Felix Pie RC 2.00 .90
153 Guillermo Quiroz RC .75 .35
154 Rene Reyes .30 .14
155 Royce Ring .30 .14
156 Alexis Rios .50 .23
157 Grady Sizemore .30 .14
158 Stephen Smitherman .30 .14
159 Seung Song .30 .14
160 Scott Thorman .30 .14
161 Chad Tracy .30 .14
162 Chin-Hui Tsao .30 .14
163 John VanBenschoten .30 .14
164 Kevin Youkilis 1.50 .70
165 Chien-Ming Wang 1.00 .45

2003 Bowman Draft Gold

MINT NRMT
COMPLETE SET (165) 100.00 45.00
*GOLD: 1.25X TO 3X BASIC
*GOLD RC'S: 6X TO 1.5X BASIC
*GOLD RC YR: .6X TO 1.5X BASIC
ONE PER PACK

2003 Bowman Draft Fabric of the Future Jersey Relics

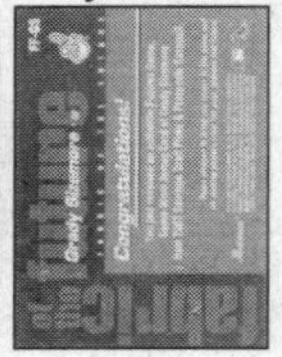

MINT NRMT
GROUP A ODDS 1:721 H, 1:720 R
GROUP B ODDS 1:315 H/R
GROUP C ODDS 1:98 H/R
GROUP D ODDS 1:81 H, 1:82 R
GROUP E ODDS 1:263 H/R
GROUP F ODDS 1:241 H, 1:240 R
AL Adam LaRoche D 5.00 2.20
AM Andy Marte D 15.00 6.75
CN Chris Narveson C 5.00 2.20
EG Edgar Gonzalez D 5.00 2.20
FG Franklin Gutierrez C 8.00 3.60
FP Felix Pie A 10.00 4.50
GF Gavin Floyd E 8.00 3.60
GS Grady Sizemore D 8.00 3.60
JB Josh Barfield B 8.00 3.60
JD J.D. Durbin D 8.00 3.60
JH Justin Huber D 5.00 2.20
JM Joe Mauer C 15.00 6.75
JSM Jeff Mathis B 8.00 3.60
KG Khalil Greene D 20.00 9.00
RC Robinson Cano C 8.00 3.60
RH Rich Harden C 10.00 4.50
RJH Ryan Howard F 15.00 6.75
RR Rene Reyes E 5.00 2.20
RRR Royce Ring F 5.00 2.20
ZG Zack Greinke C 10.00 4.50

2003 Bowman Draft Prospect Premiums Relics

MINT NRMT
GROUP A ODDS 1:216 H/R
GROUP B ODDS 1:470 H, 1:469 R
AK Austin Kearns Jsy B 5.00 2.20
BH Brendan Harris Bat A 8.00 3.60
BM Brett Myers Jsy B 5.00 2.20
CC Carl Crawford Bat A 8.00 3.60
CS Chris Snelling Bat A 8.00 3.60
CU Chase Utley Bat A 8.00 3.60
HB Hank Blalock Bat A 10.00 4.50
JM Justin Morneau Bat A 10.00 4.50
JT Joe Thurston Bat A 8.00 3.60
NH Nathan Haynes Bat A 8.00 3.60
RB Rocco Baldelli Bat A 8.00 3.60
TH Travis Hafner Bat A 8.00 3.60

2003 Bowman Draft Signs of the Future

MINT NRMT
GROUP A ODDS 1:385 H, 1:720 R
GROUP B ODDS 1:491 H, 1:491 R
GROUP C ODDS 1:2160 H, 1:12,185 R
AT Andres Torres A 10.00 4.50
CS Cory Stewart B 10.00 4.50
DT Dennis Tankersley A 10.00 4.50
JA Jason Arnold B 10.00 4.50
ZG Zack Greinke C 20.00 9.00

2004 Bowman

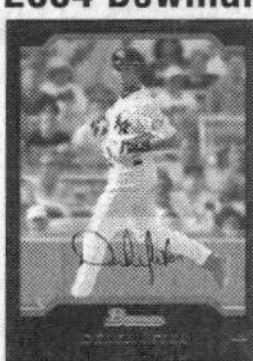

This 330-card set was released in May, 2004. The set was issued in hobby, retail and HTA versions. The hobby version was 10 card packs with an $3 SRP which came 24 packs to a box and 12 boxes to a case. The HTA version had 21 card packs with an $6 SRP which came 12 packs to a box and eight boxes to a case. Meanwhile the Retail version consisted of seven card packs with an $3 SRP which came 24 packs to a box and 12 boxes to a case. Cards numbered 1 through 144 feature veterans while cards card 145 through 165 feature prospects and cards numbered 166 through 330 feature Rookie Cards. Please note that there is a special card featuring memorabilia pieces from 2003 ROY's Dontrelle Willis and Angel Berroa which we have notated at the end of our checklist.

Nm-Mt Ex-Mt
COMPLETE SET (330) 80.00 24.00
ROY ODDS 1:829 H, 1:284 HTA, 1:1632 R
1 Garret Anderson .30 .09
2 Larry Walker .50 .15
3 Derek Jeter 1.50 .45
4 Curt Schilling .75 .23
5 Carlos Zambrano .30 .09
6 Shawn Green .30 .09
7 Manny Ramirez .50 .15
8 Randy Johnson .75 .23
9 Jeremy Bonderman .30 .09
10 Alfonso Soriano .50 .15
11 Scott Rolen .75 .23
12 Kerry Wood .75 .23
13 Eric Gagne .75 .23
14 Ryan Klesko .30 .09
15 Kevin Millar .30 .09
16 Ty Wigginton .30 .09
17 David Ortiz .75 .23
18 Luis Castillo .30 .09
19 Bernie Williams .50 .15
20 Edgar Renteria .30 .09
21 Matt Kata .30 .09
22 Bartolo Colon .30 .09
23 Derrek Lee .30 .09
24 Gary Sheffield .30 .09
25 Nomar Garciaparra 1.25 .35
26 Kevin Millwood .30 .09
27 Corey Patterson .30 .09
28 Carlos Beltran .50 .15
29 Mike Lieberthal .30 .09
30 Troy Glaus .30 .09
31 Preston Wilson .30 .09
32 Jorge Posada .50 .15
33 Bo Hart .30 .09
34 Mark Prior .75 .23
35 Hideo Nomo .75 .23
36 Jason Kendall .30 .09
37 Roger Clemens 1.50 .45
38 Dmitri Young .30 .09
39 Jason Giambi .30 .09
40 Jim Edmonds .30 .09
41 Ryan Ludwick .30 .09
42 Brandon Webb .30 .09
43 Todd Helton .50 .15
44 Jacque Jones .30 .09
45 Jamie Moyer .30 .09
46 Tim Salmon .50 .15
47 Kelvim Escobar .30 .09
48 Tony Batista .30 .09
49 Nick Johnson .30 .09
50 Jim Thome .75 .23
51 Casey Blake .30 .09
52 Trot Nixon .30 .09
53 Luis Gonzalez .30 .09
54 Dontrelle Willis .30 .09
55 Mike Mussina .50 .15
56 Carl Crawford .30 .09
57 Mark Buehrle .30 .09
58 Scott Podsednik .30 .09
59 Brian Giles .30 .09
60 Rafael Furcal .30 .09
61 Miguel Cabrera .50 .15
62 Rich Harden .30 .09
63 Mark Teixeira .30 .09
64 Frank Thomas .75 .23
65 Johan Santana .50 .15
66 Jason Schmidt .30 .09
67 Aramis Ramirez .30 .09
68 Jose Reyes .30 .09
69 Magglio Ordonez .30 .09
70 Mike Sweeney .30 .09
71 Eric Chavez .30 .09
72 Rocco Baldelli .30 .09
73 Sammy Sosa 1.25 .35
74 Javy Lopez .30 .09
75 Roy Oswalt .30 .09
76 Raul Ibanez .30 .09
77 Ivan Rodriguez .75 .23
78 Jerome Williams .30 .09
79 Carlos Lee .30 .09
80 Geoff Jenkins .30 .09
81 Sean Burroughs .30 .09
82 Marcus Giles .30 .09
83 Mike Lowell .30 .09
84 Barry Zito .30 .09
85 Aubrey Huff .30 .09
86 Esteban Loaiza .30 .09
87 Torii Hunter .30 .09
88 Phil Nevin .30 .09
89 Andruw Jones .30 .09
90 Josh Beckett .30 .09
91 Mark Mulder .30 .09
92 Hank Blalock .30 .09
93 Jason Phillips .30 .09
94 Russ Ortiz .30 .09
95 Juan Pierre .30 .09
96 Tom Glavine .50 .15
97 Gil Meche .30 .09
98 Ramon Ortiz .30 .09
99 Richie Sexson .30 .09
100 Albert Pujols 1.50 .45
101 Javier Vazquez .30 .09
102 Johnny Damon .75 .23
103 Alex Rodriguez Yanks 1.25 .35
104 Omar Vizquel .50 .15
105 Chipper Jones .75 .23
106 Lance Berkman .30 .09
107 Tim Hudson .30 .09
108 Carlos Delgado .30 .09
109 Austin Kearns .30 .09
110 Orlando Cabrera .30 .09
111 Edgar Martinez .50 .15
112 Melvin Mora .30 .09
113 Jeff Bagwell .50 .15
114 Marlon Byrd .30 .09
115 Vernon Wells .30 .09
116 C.C. Sabathia .30 .09
117 Cliff Floyd .30 .09
118 Ichiro Suzuki 1.25 .35
119 Miguel Olivo .30 .09
120 Mike Piazza 1.25 .35
121 Adam Dunn .50 .15
122 Paul Lo Duca .30 .09
123 Brett Myers .30 .09
124 Michael Young .30 .09
125 Sidney Ponson .30 .09
126 Greg Maddux 1.25 .35
127 Vladimir Guerrero .75 .23
128 Miguel Tejada .30 .09
129 Andy Pettitte .50 .15
130 Rafael Palmeiro .50 .15
131 Ken Griffey Jr. 1.25 .35
132 Shannon Stewart .30 .09
133 Joel Pineiro .30 .09
134 Luis Matos .30 .09
135 Jeff Kent .30 .09
136 Randy Wolf .30 .09
137 Chris Woodward .30 .09
138 Jody Gerut .30 .09
139 Jose Vidro .30 .09
140 Bret Boone .30 .09
141 Bill Mueller .30 .09
142 Angel Berroa .30 .09
143 Bobby Abreu .30 .09
144 Roy Halladay .30 .09
145 Delmon Young .50 .15
146 Jonny Gomes .30 .09
147 Rickie Weeks .30 .09
148 Edwin Jackson .30 .09
149 Neal Cotts .30 .09
150 Jason Bay .30 .09
151 Khalil Greene .75 .23
152 Joe Mauer .50 .15
153 Bobby Jenks .30 .09
154 Chin-Feng Chen .30 .09
155 Chien-Ming Wang .30 .09
156 Mickey Hall .30 .09
157 James Houser .30 .09
158 Jay Sborz .30 .09
159 Jonathan Fulton .30 .09
160 Steven Lerud .30 .09
161 Grady Sizemore .30 .09
162 Felix Pie .30 .09
163 Dustin McGowan .30 .09
164 Chris Lubanski .30 .09
165 Tom Gorzelanny .30 .09
166 Rudy Guillen FY RC 1.00 .30
167 Bobby Brownlie FY RC .75 .23
168 Conor Jackson FY RC 2.00 .60
169 Matt Moses FY RC 1.00 .30
170 Ervin Santana FY RC 1.25 .35
171 Merkin Valdez FY RC 1.00 .30
172 Erick Aybar FY RC 1.25 .35
173 Brad Sullivan FY RC .50 .15
174 David Aardsma FY RC .40 .12
175 Brad Snyder FY RC 1.00 .30
176 Alberto Callaspo FY RC .75 .23
177 Brandon Medders FY RC .30 .09
178 Zach Miner FY RC .50 .15
179 Charlie Zink FY RC .30 .09
180 Adam Greenberg FY RC .50 .15
181 Kevin Howard FY RC .50 .15
182 Wanell Severino FY RC .30 .09
183 Kevin Kouzmanoff FY RC .75 .23
184 Joel Zumaya FY RC .75 .23
185 Skip Schumaker FY RC .40 .12
186 Nic Ungs FY RC .40 .12
187 Todd Self FY RC .40 .12
188 Brian Steffek FY RC .30 .09
189 Brock Peterson FY RC .40 .12
190 Greg Thissen FY RC .40 .12
191 Frank Brooks FY RC .30 .09
192 Estee Harris FY RC .40 .12
193 Chris Mabeus FY RC .40 .12
194 Dan Giese FY RC .40 .12
195 Jared Wells FY RC .30 .09
196 Carlos Sosa FY RC .40 .12
197 Bobby Madritsch FY .75 .23
198 Calvin Hayes FY RC .50 .15
199 Omar Quintanilla FY RC 1.00 .30
200 Chris O'Riordan FY RC .40 .12
201 Tim Hutting FY RC .30 .09
202 Carlos Quentin FY RC 2.00 .60
203 Brayan Pena FY RC .40 .12
204 Jeff Salazar FY RC 1.00 .30
205 David Murphy FY RC 1.00 .30
206 Alberto Garcia FY RC .50 .15
207 Ramon Ramirez FY RC .40 .12
208 Luis Bolivar FY RC .50 .15
209 Rodney Choy Foo FY RC .30 .09
210 Kyle Sleeth FY RC 1.00 .30
211 Anthony Acevedo FY RC .40 .12
212 Chad Santos FY RC .40 .12
213 Jason Frasor FY RC .40 .12
214 Jesse Roman FY RC .30 .09
215 James Tomlin FY RC .40 .12
216 Josh Labandeira FY RC .40 .12

7 Joaquin Arias FY RC .40 .12
8 Don Sutton FY UER RC 1.00 .30
Nick Swisher pictured
9 Danny Gonzalez FY RC .30 .09
0 Javier Guzman FY RC .50 .15
1 Anthony Lerew FY RC .75 .23
2 Jon Knott FY RC .40 .12
3 Jesse English FY RC .40 .12
4 Felix Hernandez FY RC 3.00 .90
5 Travis Hanson FY RC .40 .12
6 Jesse Floyd FY RC .40 .12
7 Nick Gorneault FY RC .50 .15
8 Craig Ansman FY RC .40 .12
9 Wardell Starling FY RC .40 .12
0 Carl Loadenthal FY RC .50 .15
1 Dave Crouthers FY RC .30 .09
2 Harvey Garcia FY RC .30 .09
3 Casey Kopitzke FY RC .30 .09
4 Ricky Nolasco FY RC .40 .12
5 Miguel Perez FY RC .40 .12
6 Ryan Mulhern FY RC .30 .09
7 Chris Aguila FY RC .40 .12
8 Brooks Conrad FY RC .50 .15
9 Damaso Espino FY RC .30 .09
0 Jeremy Milons FY RC .40 .12
1 Luke Hughes FY RC .30 .09
2 Kory Casto FY RC .40 .12
3 Jose Valdez FY RC .40 .12
4 J.T. Stotts FY RC .30 .09
5 Lee Gwaltney FY RC .30 .09
6 Yoann Torrealba FY RC .30 .09
7 Omar Falcon FY RC .40 .12
8 Jon Coutlangus FY RC .30 .09
9 George Sherrill FY RC .40 .12
0 John Santor FY RC .30 .09
1 Tony Richie FY RC .40 .12
2 Kevin Richardson FY RC .30 .09
3 Tim Bittner FY RC .40 .12
4 Dustin Nippert FY RC 1.25 .35
5 Jose Capellan FY RC 1.50 .45
6 Donald Levinski FY RC .30 .09
7 Jerome Gamble FY RC .30 .09
8 Jeff Keppinger FY RC .75 .23
9 Jason Szuminski FY RC .30 .09
0 Akinori Otsuka FY RC .40 .12
1 Ryan Budde FY RC .40 .12
2 Shingo Takatsu FY RC 1.00 .30
3 Jeff Allison FY RC .50 .15
4 Hector Gimenez FY RC .30 .09
5 Tim Frend FY RC .40 .12
6 Tom Farmer FY RC .30 .09
7 Shawn Hill FY RC .40 .12
8 Lastings Milledge FY RC 2.00 .60
9 Scott Proctor FY RC .50 .15
0 Jorge Mejia FY RC .40 .12
1 Terry Jones FY RC .50 .15
2 Zach Duke FY RC 1.50 .45
3 Tim Stauffer FY RC .75 .23
4 Luke Anderson FY RC .30 .09
5 Hunter Brown FY RC .30 .09
6 Matt Lemanczyk FY RC .40 .12
7 Fernando Cortez FY RC .30 .09
8 Vince Perkins FY RC .50 .15
9 Tommy Murphy FY RC .40 .12
0 Mike Gosling FY RC .30 .09
1 Paul Bacot FY RC .50 .15
2 Matt Capps FY RC .40 .12
3 Juan Gutierrez FY RC .40 .12
4 Teodoro Encarnacion FY RC .50 .15
5 Juan Cedeno FY RC .40 .12
6 Matt Creighton FY RC .40 .12
7 Ryan Hankins FY RC .30 .09
8 Leo Nunez FY RC .40 .12
9 Dave Wallace FY RC .40 .12
0 Rob Tejeda FY RC .30 .09
1 Lincoln Holdzkom FY RC .40 .12
2 Jason Hirsh FY RC .40 .12
3 Tydus Meadows FY RC .40 .12
4 Khalid Ballouli FY RC .30 .09
5 Benji DeQuin FY RC .30 .09
6 Tyler Davidson FY RC 1.50 .45
7 Brant Colamarino FY RC .75 .23
8 Marcus McBeth FY RC .30 .09
9 Brad Eldred FY RC 1.25 .35
0 David Pauley FY RC .30 .09
1 Yadier Molina FY RC 1.00 .30
2 Chris Shelton FY RC .75 .23
3 Travis Blackley FY RC .50 .15
4 Jon DeVries FY RC .40 .12
5 Sheldon Fulse FY RC .30 .09
6 Vito Chiaravalloti FY RC .75 .23
7 Warner Madrigal FY RC .75 .23
8 Reid Gorecki FY RC .40 .12
9 Sung Jung FY RC .30 .09
0 Pete Shier FY RC .30 .09
1 Michael Mooney FY RC .40 .12
2 Kenny Perez FY RC .40 .12
3 Michael Mallory FY RC .40 .12
4 Ben Himes FY RC .30 .09
5 Ivan Ochoa FY RC .40 .12
6 Donald Kelly FY RC .40 .12
7 Logan Kensing FY RC .40 .12
8 Kevin Davidson FY RC .30 .09
9 Brian Pilkington FY RC .40 .12
0 Alex Romero FY RC .40 .12
1 Chad Chop FY RC .40 .12
2 Dioner Navarro FY RC 1.25 .35
3 Casey Myers FY RC .30 .09
4 Mike Rouse FY RC .40 .12
5 Sergio Silva FY RC .30 .09
6 J.J. Furmaniak FY RC .75 .23
7 Brad Vericker FY RC .40 .12
8 Blake Hawksworth FY RC .50 .15
9 Brock Jacobsen FY RC .30 .09
0 Alec Zumwalt FY RC .30 .09
V Angel Berroa Bat 15.00 4.50
Dontrelle Willis Jsy ROY

2004 Bowman 1st Edition

Nm-Mt Ex-Mt
MPLETE SET (330)
ST EDITION 1-165: .75X TO 2X BASIC
ST EDITION 166-330: .75X TO 2X BASIC
SUED IN FIRST EDITION PACKS

2004 Bowman Gold

Nm-Mt Ex-Mt
MPLETE SET (330) 150.00 45.00
OLD 1-165: 1.25X TO 3X BASIC
*GOLD 166-330: 1X TO 2.5X BASIC
ONE PER HOBBY PACK
ONE PER HTA PACK
ONE PER RETAIL PACK

2004 Bowman Uncirculated Gold

Nm-Mt Ex-Mt
ONE EXCH.CARD PER SILVER PACK
ONE SILVER PACK PER SEALED HOBBY BOX
ONE SILVER PACK PER SEALED HTA BOX
STATED ODDS 1:44 RETAIL
STATED PRINT RUN 210 SETS
SEE WWW.THEPIT.COM FOR PRICING
NNO Exchange Card 5.00 1.50

2004 Bowman Uncirculated Silver

Nm-Mt Ex-Mt
*UNC.SILVER 1-165: 5X TO 12X BASIC
*UNC.SILVER 166-330: 3X TO 8X BASIC
ONE PER SILVER PACK
ONE SILVER PACK PER SEALED HOBBY BOX
ONE SILVER PACK PER SEALED HTA BOX
SET EXCH.CARD ODDS 1:9159 H, 1:3718 HTA
STATED PRINT RUN 245 SERIAL #'d SETS
1ST 100 SETS PRINTED HELD FOR EXCH.
LAST 145 SETS PRINTED DIST.IN BOXES
EXCHANGE DEADLINE 05/31/06
NNO Set Exchange Card/100 500.00 150.00

2004 Bowman Autographs

Nm-Mt Ex-Mt
STATED ODDS 1:72 H, 1:24 HTA, 1:139 R
RED INK ODDS 1:1466 H,1:501 HTA,1:2901 R
RED INK PRINT RUN 25 SETS
RED INK ARE NOT SERIAL-NUMBERED
RED INK PRINT RUN PROVIDED BY TOPPS
NO RED INK PRICING DUE TO SCARCITY
161 Grady Sizemore 10.00 3.00
162 Felix Pie 10.00 3.00
163 Dustin McGowan 8.00 2.40
164 Chris Lubanski 10.00 3.00
165 Tom Gorzelanny 8.00 2.40
166 Rudy Guillen 10.00 3.00
167 Bobby Brownlie 10.00 3.00
168 Conor Jackson 25.00 7.50
169 Matt Moses 12.00 3.60
170 Ervin Santana 15.00 4.50
171 Merkin Valdez 10.00 3.00
172 Erick Aybar 15.00 4.50
173 Brad Sullivan 10.00 3.00
174 David Aardsma 8.00 2.40
175 Brad Snyder 10.00 3.00

2004 Bowman Relics

Nm-Mt Ex-Mt
GROUP A 1:346 H, 1:118 HTA, 1:1685 R
GROUP B 1:133 H, 1:44 HTA, 1:269 R
HS JSY MEANS HIGH SCHOOL JERSEY
154 Chin-Feng Chen Jsy B 15.00 4.50
155 Chien-Ming Wang Uni B 15.00 4.50
156 Mickey Hall HS Jsy B 8.00 2.40
157 James Houser HS Jsy A 8.00 2.40
158 Jay Sborz HS Jsy B 8.00 2.40
159 Jonathan Fulton HS Jsy B 8.00 2.40
160 Steve Lerud HS Jsy A 8.00 2.40
164 Chris Lubanski HS Jsy B 8.00 2.40
192 Estee Harris HS Jsy A 8.00 2.40
221 Anthony Lerew Jsy B 8.00 2.40

2004 Bowman Base of the Future Autograph

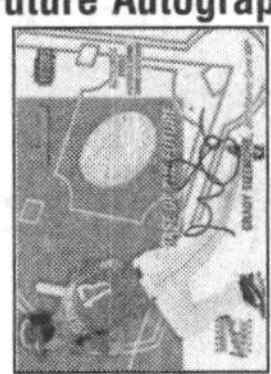

Nm-Mt Ex-Mt
STATED ODDS 1:110 HTA
RED INK ODDS 1:5112 HTA
RED INK PRINT RUN 25 SERIAL #'d CARDS
NO RED INK PRICING DUE TO SCARCITY
GS Grady Sizemore 25.00 7.50

2004 Bowman Futures Game Gear Jersey Relics

Nm-Mt Ex-Mt
GROUP A 1:167 H, 1:58 HTA, 1:333 R
GROUP B 1:71 H, 1:23 HTA, 1:148 R
GROUP C 1:181 H, 1:63 HTA, 1:362 R

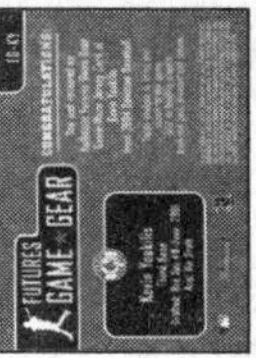

GROUP D 1:173 H, 1:59 HTA, 1:341 R
GROUP E 1:145 H, 1:70 HTA, 1:318 R
AR Alexis Rios A 8.00 2.40
CB Chris Burke B 8.00 2.40
CN Clint Nageotte B 8.00 2.40
CT Chad Tracy B 8.00 2.40
CW Chien-Ming Wang C 15.00 4.50
DB Denny Bautista D 8.00 2.40
DBK Dave Krynzel B 8.00 2.40
DK David Kelton E 8.00 2.40
EE Edwin Encarnacion A 8.00 2.40
EJ Edwin Jackson C 8.00 2.40
ES Ervin Santana D 10.00 3.00
GQ Guillermo Quiroz A 8.00 2.40
JC Jose Castillo E 8.00 2.40
JD Jorge De La Rosa C 8.00 2.40
JH J.J. Hardy A 8.00 2.40
JM John Maine B 8.00 2.40
JV John VanBenschoten B 8.00 2.40
KY Kevin Youkilis E 8.00 2.40
MV Merkin Valdez E 8.00 2.40
NC Neal Cotts D 8.00 2.40
PL Pete LaForest B 8.00 2.40
PWL Preston Larrison B 8.00 2.40
RN Ramon Nivar A 8.00 2.40
SH Shawn Hill D 8.00 2.40
SJS Seung Song B 8.00 2.40
SS Stephen Smitherman B 8.00 2.40
ST Scott Thorman C 8.00 2.40
TB Travis Blackley B 8.00 2.40

2004 Bowman Signs of the Future

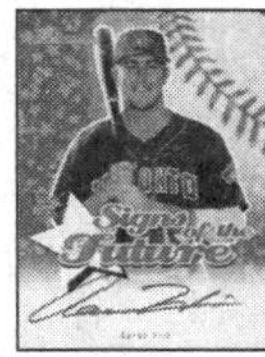

Nm-Mt Ex-Mt
GROUP A 1:75 H, 1:25 HTA, 1:147 R
GROUP B 1:847 H, 1:289 HTA, 1:1675 R
GROUP C 1:582 H, 1:198 HTA, 1:1148 R
GROUP D 1:315 H, 1:105 HTA, 1:605 R
RED INK ODDS 1:1466 H,1:501 HTA,1:2901 R
RED INK PRINT RUN 25 SETS
RED INK CARDS ARE NOT SERIAL #'d
RED INK PRINT RUN PROVIDED BY TOPPS
NO RED INK PRICING DUE TO SCARCITY
AH Aaron Hill A 8.00 2.40
BC Brent Clevlen A 10.00 3.00
BF Brian Finch D 10.00 3.00
BM Brandon Medders A 8.00 2.40
BS Brian Snyder D 10.00 3.00
BW Brandon Wood B 8.00 2.40
CS Corey Shafer A 8.00 2.40
DS Denard Span A 8.00 2.40
ED Eric Duncan D 15.00 4.50
GS Grady Sizemore D 15.00 4.50
IC Ismael Castro A 8.00 2.40
JB Justin Backsmeyer D 10.00 3.00
JH James Houser A 8.00 2.40
JV Joey Votto A 10.00 3.00
MM Matt Murton D 10.00 3.00
NM Nick Markakis C 10.00 3.00
RH Ryan Harvey C 10.00 3.00
TJ Tyler Johnson A 8.00 2.40
TL Todd Linden A 8.00 2.40

2004 Bowman Draft

Nm-Mt Ex-Mt
COMPLETE SET (165) 40.00 12.00
COMMON CARD (1-165) .30 .09
COMMON RC (1-165) .30 .09
COMMON RC YR .30 .09
PLATES ODDS 1:559 HOBBY
PLATES PRINT RUN 1 SERIAL #'d SET
BLACK-CYAN-MAGENTA-YELLOW EXIST
NO PLATES PRICING DUE TO SCARCITY
1 Lyle Overbay .30 .09
2 Dave Newhan .30 .09
3 J.R. House .30 .09
4 Chad Tracy .30 .09
5 Humberto Quintero .30 .09
6 Dave Bush .30 .09
7 Scott Hairston .30 .09
8 Mike Wood .30 .09
9 Alexis Rios .30 .09
10 Sean Burnett .30 .09
11 Wilson Valdez .30 .09
12 Lew Ford .30 .09
13 Freddy Thon RC .40 .12
14 Zack Greinke .30 .09
15 Bucky Jacobsen .30 .09
16 Kevin Youkilis .30 .09
17 Grady Sizemore .30 .09
18 Denny Bautista .30 .09
19 David DeJesus .30 .09
20 Casey Kotchman .75 .23
21 David Kelton .30 .09
22 Charles Thomas RC .50 .15
23 Kazuhito Tadano RC .50 .15
24 Justin Leone RC .50 .15
25 Eduardo Villacis RC .40 .12
26 Brian Dallimore RC .30 .09
27 Nick Green .30 .09
28 Sam McConnell RC .40 .12
29 Brad Halsey RC .50 .15
30 Roman Colon RC .30 .09
31 Josh Fields RC 1.50 .45
32 Cody Bunkelman RC .50 .15
33 Jay Rainville RC 1.00 .30
34 Richie Robnett RC 1.00 .30
35 Jon Poterson RC 1.00 .30
36 Huston Street RC 1.00 .30
37 Erick San Pedro RC .40 .12
38 Cory Dunlap RC 1.25 .35
39 Kurt Suzuki RC 1.25 .35
40 Anthony Swarzak RC .50 .15
41 Ian Desmond RC .50 .15
42 Chris Covington RC .50 .15
43 Christian Garcia RC .75 .23
44 Gaby Hernandez RC .75 .23
45 Steven Register RC .50 .15
46 Eduardo Morlan RC .50 .15
47 Collin Balester RC .50 .15
48 Nathan Phillips RC .50 .15
49 Dan Schwartzbauer RC .50 .15
50 Rafael Gonzalez RC .50 .15
51 K.C. Herren RC .75 .23
52 William Susdorf RC .40 .12
53 Rob Johnson RC .40 .12
54 Louis Marson RC .75 .23
55 Joe Koshansky RC .40 .12
56 Jamar Walton RC 1.50 .45
57 Mark Lowe RC .40 .12
58 Matt Macri RC .75 .23
59 Donny Lucy RC .40 .12
60 Mike Ferris RC .50 .15
61 Mike Nickeas RC .50 .15
62 Eric Hurley RC .75 .23
63 Scott Elbert RC 1.00 .30
64 Blake DeWitt RC 2.00 .60
65 Danny Putnam RC .75 .23
66 J.P. Howell RC .75 .23
67 John Wiggins RC .40 .12
68 Justin Orenduff RC .75 .23
69 Ray Liotta RC .50 .15
70 Billy Buckner RC .50 .15
71 Eric Campbell RC 1.25 .35
72 Olin Wick RC .40 .12
73 Sean Gamble RC .50 .15
74 Seth Smith RC 1.25 .35
75 Wade Davis RC .50 .15
76 Joe Jacobitz RC .40 .12
77 J.A. Happ RC .75 .23
78 Eric Ridener RC .40 .12
79 Matt Tuiasosopo RC 3.00 .90
80 Brad Bergesen RC .50 .15
81 Javy Guerra RC .50 .15
82 Buck Shaw RC .75 .23
83 Paul Janish RC .50 .15
84 Sean Kazmar RC .50 .15
85 Josh Johnson RC .50 .15
86 Angel Salome RC .50 .15
87 Jordan Parraz RC .50 .15
88 Kelvin Vazquez RC .40 .12
89 Grant Hansen RC .40 .12
90 Matt Fox RC .75 .23
91 Trevor Plouffe RC 1.25 .35
92 Wes Whisler RC .50 .15
93 Curtis Thigpen RC .75 .23
94 Donnie Smith RC .40 .12
95 Luis Rivera RC .50 .15
96 Jesse Hoover RC .50 .15
97 Jason Vargas RC .75 .23
98 Clary Carlsen RC .40 .12
99 Mark Robinson RC .40 .12
100 J.C. Holt RC .75 .23
101 Chad Blackwell RC .50 .15
102 Daryl Jones RC .75 .23
103 Jonathan Tierce RC .40 .12
104 Patrick Bryant RC .40 .12
105 Eddie Prasch RC .50 .15
106 Mitch Einertson RC 2.50 .75
107 Kyle Waldrop RC 1.00 .30
108 Jeff Marquez RC .75 .23
109 Zach Jackson RC .50 .15
110 Josh Wahpepah RC .40 .12
111 Adam Lind RC .75 .23
112 Kyle Bloom RC .50 .15
113 Ben Harrison RC .50 .15
114 Taylor Tankersley RC 1.00 .30
115 Steven Jackson RC .40 .12
116 David Purcey RC .75 .23
117 Jacob McGee RC .50 .15
118 Lucas Harrell RC .40 .12
119 Brandon Allen RC .75 .23
120 Van Pope RC .50 .15
121 Jeff Francis .30 .09
122 Joe Blanton .50 .15
123 Wil Ledezma .30 .09
124 Bryan Bullington .30 .09
125 Jairo Garcia .30 .09
126 Matt Cain .30 .09
127 Arnie Munoz .30 .09
128 Clint Everts .30 .09
129 Jesus Cota .30 .09
130 Gavin Floyd .30 .09
131 Edwin Encarnacion .30 .09
132 Koyie Hill .30 .09
133 Ruben Gotay .30 .09
134 Jeff Mathis .30 .09
135 Andy Marte .30 .09
136 Dallas McPherson .50 .15
137 Justin Morneau .50 .15
138 Rickie Weeks .30 .09
139 Joel Guzman .50 .15
140 Shin Soo Choo .30 .09
141 Yusmeiro Petit RC 2.00 .60
142 Jorge Cortes RC .40 .12
143 Val Majewski .30 .09
144 Felix Pie .30 .09
145 Aaron Hill .30 .09
146 Jose Capellan .75 .23
147 Dioner Navarro .50 .15
148 Fausto Carmona RC .75 .23
149 Robinzon Diaz RC .40 .12
150 Felix Hernandez 1.25 .35
151 Andres Blanco RC .40 .12
152 Jason Kubel .30 .09
153 Willy Taveras RC .50 .15
154 Merkin Valdez .50 .15
155 Robinson Cano .30 .09
156 Bill Murphy .30 .09
157 Chris Burke .30 .09
158 Kyle Sleeth .50 .15
159 B.J. Upton .50 .15
160 Tim Stauffer .50 .15
161 David Wright .75 .23
162 Conor Jackson .75 .23
163 Brad Thompson RC .50 .15
164 Delmon Young .50 .15
165 Jeremy Reed .30 .09

2004 Bowman Draft Gold

Nm-Mt Ex-Mt
COMPLETE SET (165) 80.00 24.00
*GOLD RC's: .6X TO 1.5X BASIC
*GOLD RC YR: .6X TO 1.5X BASIC
ONE PER PACK

2004 Bowman Draft Red

Nm-Mt Ex-Mt
STATED ODDS 1:4471 HOBBY
STATED PRINT RUN 1 SERIAL #'d SET
NO PRICING DUE TO SCARCITY

2004 Bowman Draft AFLAC Exchange Cards

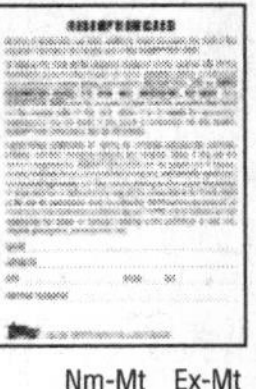

Nm-Mt Ex-Mt
ONE AFLAC PER BOX
RED PRINT RUN 1 CARD
PRINT RUN PROVIDED BY TOPPS
EXCHANGE DEADLINE 06/15/05
NO RED PRICING DUE TO SCARCITY
1 Base Set 10.00 3.00
2 Red Set/1

2004 Bowman Draft Futures Game Jersey Relics

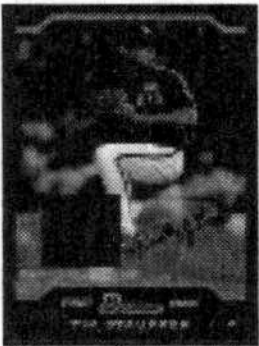
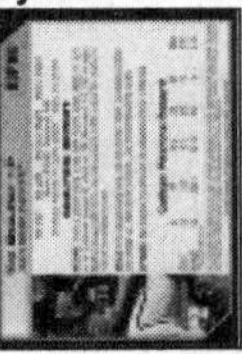

Nm-Mt Ex-Mt
STATED ODDS 1:31 HOBBY, 1:30 RETAIL
146 Jose Capellan 8.00 2.40
147 Dioner Navarro 8.00 2.40
148 Fausto Carmona 8.00 2.40
149 Robinzon Diaz 5.00 1.50
150 Felix Hernandez 10.00 3.00
151 Andres Blanco 5.00 1.50
152 Jason Kubel 5.00 1.50
153 Willy Taveras 8.00 2.40
154 Merkin Valdez 8.00 2.40
155 Robinson Cano 5.00 1.50
156 Bill Murphy 5.00 1.50
157 Chris Burke 5.00 1.50
158 Kyle Sleeth 8.00 2.40
159 B.J. Upton 8.00 2.40
160 Tim Stauffer 8.00 2.40
161 David Wright 15.00 4.50
162 Conor Jackson 8.00 2.40
163 Brad Thompson 8.00 2.40
164 Delmon Young 8.00 2.40
165 Jeremy Reed 8.00 2.40

2004 Bowman Draft Blue Chips Autographs

Nm-Mt Ex-Mt
STATED ODDS 1:136 H, 1:136 R
SEE '03 TOPPS BLUE CHIPS FOR PRICING

2004 Bowman Draft Prospect Premiums Relics

Nm-Mt Ex-Mt
GROUP A ODDS 1:145 H, 1:153 R
GROUP B ODDS 1:387 H, 1:411 R
AB Angel Berroa Bat A 5.00 1.50
BU B.J. Upton Bat B 8.00 2.40
CJ Conor Jackson Bat B 8.00 2.40
CQ Carlos Quentin Bat B 8.00 2.40
DN Dioner Navarro Bat A 8.00 2.40
DY Delmon Young Bat A 8.00 2.40
EJ Edwin Jackson Jsy A 5.00 1.50

JR Jeremy Reed Bat A 8.00 2.40
KC Kevin Cash Bat B 5.00 1.50
LM Lastings Milledge Bat A 10.00 3.00
NS Nick Swisher Bat B 10.00 2.40
RH Ryan Harvey Bat A 8.00 2.40

2004 Bowman Draft Signs of the Future

Nm-Mt Ex-Mt
GROUP A ODDS 1:127 H, 1:127 R
GROUP B ODDS 1:509 H, 1:511 R
EXCHANGE DEADLINE 11/30/05
AL Adam Loewen A 10.00 3.00
CC Chad Cordero B 10.00 3.00
JH James Houser B 10.00 3.00
PM Paul Maholm A EXCH 10.00 3.00
TP Tyler Pelland A 10.00 3.00
TT Terry Tiffee A 10.00 3.00

1997 Bowman Chrome

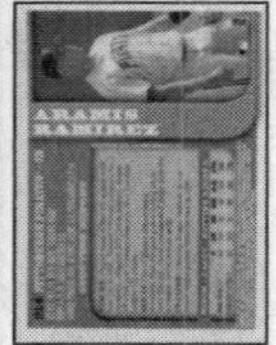

The 1997 Bowman Chrome set was issued in one series totalling 300 cards and was distributed in four-card packs with a suggested retail price of $3.00. The cards parallel the 1997 Bowman brand and the 300 card set represents a selection of top cards taken from the 441-card 1997 Bowman set. The product was released in the Winter, after the end of the 1997 season. The fronts feature color action player photos printed on dazzling chromium stock. The backs carry player information. Rookie Cards in this set include Adrian Beltre, Kris Benson, Lance Berkman, Kris Benson, Eric Chavez, Jose Cruz Jr., Travis Lee, Aramis Ramirez, Miguel Tejada, Vernon Wells and Kerry Wood.

Nm-Mt Ex-Mt
COMPLETE SET (300) 180.00 55.00
1 Derek Jeter 3.00 .90
2 Chipper Jones 1.25 .35
3 Hideo Nomo 1.25 .35
4 Tim Salmon .75 .23
5 Robin Ventura .50 .15
6 Tony Clark .50 .15
7 Barry Larkin .75 .23
8 Paul Molitor .75 .23
9 Andy Benes .50 .15
10 Ryan Klesko .50 .15
11 Mark McGwire 3.00 .90
12 Ken Griffey Jr. 2.00 .60
13 Robb Nen .50 .15
14 Cal Ripken 4.00 1.20
15 John Valentin .50 .15
16 Ricky Bottalico .50 .15
17 Mike Lansing .50 .15
18 Ryne Sandberg 2.00 .60
19 Carlos Delgado .50 .15
20 Craig Biggio .75 .23
21 Eric Karros .50 .15
22 Kevin Appier .50 .15
23 Mariano Rivera .75 .23
24 Vinny Castilla .50 .15
25 Juan Gonzalez .75 .23
26 Al Martin .50 .15
27 Jeff Cirillo .50 .15
28 Ray Lankford .50 .15
29 Manny Ramirez .75 .23
30 Roberto Alomar .75 .23
31 Will Clark 1.25 .35
32 Chuck Knoblauch .50 .15
33 Harold Baines .50 .15
34 Edgar Martinez .75 .23
35 Mike Mussina .75 .23
36 Kevin Brown .50 .15
37 Dennis Eckersley .50 .15
38 Tino Martinez .75 .23
39 Raul Mondesi .50 .15
40 Sammy Sosa 2.00 .60
41 John Smoltz .75 .23
42 Billy Wagner .50 .15
43 Ken Caminiti .50 .15
44 Wade Boggs .75 .23
45 Andres Galarraga .50 .15
46 Roger Clemens 2.50 .75
47 Matt Williams .50 .15
48 Albert Belle .50 .15
49 Jeff King .50 .15
50 John Wetteland .50 .15
51 Deion Sanders .75 .23
52 Ellis Burks .50 .15
53 Pedro Martinez 1.25 .35
54 Kenny Lofton .50 .15
55 Randy Johnson 1.25 .35
56 Bernie Williams .75 .23
57 Marquis Grissom .50 .15
58 Gary Sheffield .50 .15
59 Curt Schilling .50 .15
60 Reggie Sanders .50 .15
61 Bobby Higginson .50 .15
62 Moises Alou .50 .15
63 Tom Glavine .75 .23
64 Mark Grace .75 .23
65 Rafael Palmeiro .75 .23
66 John Olerud .50 .15
67 Dante Bichette .50 .15
68 Jeff Bagwell .75 .23
69 Barry Bonds 3.00 .90
70 Pat Hentgen .50 .15
71 Jim Thome 1.25 .35
72 Andy Pettitte .75 .23
73 Jay Bell .50 .15
74 Jim Edmonds .50 .15
75 Ron Gant .50 .15
76 David Cone .50 .15
77 Jose Canseco 1.25 .35
78 Jay Buhner .50 .15
79 Greg Maddux 2.00 .60
80 Lance Johnson .50 .15
81 Travis Fryman .50 .15
82 Paul O'Neill .75 .23
83 Ivan Rodriguez 1.25 .35
84 Fred McGriff .75 .23
85 Mike Piazza 2.00 .60
86 Brady Anderson .50 .15
87 Marty Cordova .50 .15
88 Joe Carter .50 .15
89 Brian Jordan .50 .15
90 David Justice .50 .15
91 Tony Gwynn 1.50 .45
92 Larry Walker .75 .23
93 Mo Vaughn .50 .15
94 Sandy Alomar Jr. .50 .15
95 Rusty Greer .50 .15
96 Roberto Hernandez .50 .15
97 Hal Morris .50 .15
98 Todd Hundley .50 .15
99 Rondell White .50 .15
100 Frank Thomas 1.25 .35
101 Bubba Trammell RC 1.50 .45
102 Sidney Ponson RC 2.50 .75
103 Ricky Ledee RC 1.50 .45
104 Brett Tomko .50 .15
105 Braden Looper RC 1.00 .30
106 Jason Dickson .50 .15
107 Chad Green RC 1.00 .30
108 R.A. Dickey RC 1.00 .30
109 Jeff Liefer .50 .15
110 Richard Hidalgo .50 .15
111 Chad Hermansen RC 1.50 .45
112 Felix Martinez .50 .15
113 J.J. Johnson .50 .15
114 Todd Dunwoody .50 .15
115 Katsuhiro Maeda .50 .15
116 Darin Erstad .50 .15
117 Elieser Marrero .50 .15
118 Bartolo Colon .50 .15
119 Ugueth Urbina .50 .15
120 Jaime Bluma .50 .15
121 Seth Greisinger RC 1.00 .30
122 Jose Cruz Jr. RC 2.50 .75
123 Todd Dunn .50 .15
124 Justin Towle RC 1.00 .30
125 Brian Rose .50 .15
126 Jose Guillen .50 .15
127 Andruw Jones .50 .15
128 Mark Kotsay RC 4.00 1.20
129 Wilton Guerrero .50 .15
130 Jacob Cruz .50 .15
131 Mike Sweeney .50 .15
132 Matt Morris .50 .15
133 John Thomson .50 .15
134 Javier Valentin .50 .15
135 Mike Drumright RC 1.00 .30
136 Michael Barrett .50 .15
137 Tony Saunders RC 1.00 .30
138 Kevin Brown .50 .15
139 Anthony Sanders RC 1.00 .30
140 Jeff Abbott .50 .15
141 Eugene Kingsale .50 .15
142 Paul Konerko .50 .15
143 Randall Simon RC 1.50 .45
144 Freddy Adrian Garcia .50 .15
145 Karim Garcia .50 .15
146 Carlos Guillen .50 .15
147 Aaron Boone .50 .15
148 Donnie Sadler .50 .15
149 Brooks Kieschnick .50 .15
150 Scott Spiezio .50 .15
151 Kevin Orie .50 .15
152 Russ Johnson .50 .15
153 Livan Hernandez .50 .15
154 Vladimir Nunez RC 1.00 .30
155 Pokey Reese .50 .15
156 Chris Carpenter .50 .15
157 Eric Milton RC 4.00 1.20
158 Richie Sexson .50 .15
159 Carl Pavano 1.50 .45
160 Pat Cline .50 .15
161 Ron Wright .50 .15
162 Dante Powell .50 .15
163 Mark Bellhorn .50 .15
164 George Lombard .50 .15
165 Paul Wilder RC 1.00 .30
166 Brad Fullmer .50 .15
167 Kris Benson RC 4.00 1.20
168 Torii Hunter .50 .15
169 D.T. Cromer RC 1.00 .30
170 Nelson Figueroa RC 1.00 .30
171 Hiram Bocachica RC 1.50 .45
172 Shane Monahan .50 .15
173 Juan Melo .50 .15
174 Calvin Pickering RC 2.50 .75
175 Reggie Taylor .50 .15
176 Geoff Jenkins .50 .15
177 Steve Rain RC 1.00 .30
178 Nerio Rodriguez RC 1.00 .30
179 Derrick Gibson .50 .15
180 Darin Blood .50 .15
181 Ben Davis .50 .15
182 Adrian Beltre RC 20.00 6.00
183 Kerry Wood RC 30.00 9.00
184 Nate Rolison RC 1.00 .30
185 Fernando Tatis RC 1.50 .45
186 Jake Westbrook RC 4.00 1.20
187 Edwin Diaz .50 .15
188 Joe Fontenot RC 1.00 .30
189 Matt Halloran RC 1.00 .30
190 Matt Clement RC 4.00 1.20
191 Todd Greene .50 .15
192 Eric Chavez RC 12.00 3.60
193 Edgard Velazquez .50 .15
194 Bruce Chen RC 1.50 .45
195 Jason Brester .50 .15
196 Chris Reitsma RC 1.50 .45
197 Neifi Perez .50 .15
198 Hideki Irabu RC 1.50 .45
199 Don Denbow RC 1.00 .30
200 Derrek Lee .50 .15
201 Todd Walker .50 .15
202 Scott Rolen 1.25 .35
203 Wes Helms .50 .15
204 Bob Abreu .50 .15
205 John Patterson RC 2.50 .75
206 Alex Gonzalez RC 2.50 .75
207 Grant Roberts RC 1.50 .45
208 Jeff Suppan .50 .15
209 Luke Wilcox .50 .15
210 Marlon Anderson .50 .15
211 Mike Caruso RC 1.00 .30
212 Roy Halladay RC 4.00 1.20
213 Jeremi Gonzalez RC 1.00 .30
214 Aramis Ramirez RC 10.00 3.00
215 Dee Brown RC 1.50 .45
216 Justin Thompson .50 .15
217 Danny Clyburn .50 .15
218 Bruce Aven .50 .15
219 Keith Foulke RC 5.00 1.50
220 Shannon Stewart .50 .15
221 Larry Barnes RC 1.00 .30
222 Mark Johnson RC 1.00 .30
223 Randy Winn .50 .15
224 Nomar Garciaparra 2.00 .60
225 Jacque Jones RC 4.00 1.20
226 Chris Clemons .50 .15
227 Todd Helton 1.25 .35
228 Ryan Brannan RC 1.00 .30
229 Alex Sanchez RC 2.50 .75
230 Russell Branyan .50 .15
231 Daryle Ward 1.00 .30
232 Kevin Witt .50 .15
233 Gabby Martinez .50 .15
234 Preston Wilson .50 .15
235 Donzell McDonald RC 1.00 .30
236 Orlando Cabrera RC 4.00 1.50
237 Brian Banks .50 .15
238 Robbie Bell 1.00 .30
239 Brad Rigby .50 .15
240 Scott Elarton .50 .15
241 Donny Leon RC 1.00 .30
242 Abraham Nunez RC 1.00 .30
243 Adam Eaton RC 1.50 .45
244 Octavio Dotel RC 1.50 .45
245 Sean Casey 4.00 1.20
246 Joe Lawrence RC 1.00 .30
247 Adam Johnson RC 1.00 .30
248 Ronnie Belliard RC 2.50 .75
249 Bobby Estalella .50 .15
250 Corey Lee RC 1.00 .30
251 Mike Cameron .50 .15
252 Kerry Robinson RC 1.00 .30
253 A.J. Zapp RC 1.00 .30
254 Jarrod Washburn .50 .15
255 Ben Grieve .50 .15
256 Javier Vazquez RC 5.00 1.50
257 Travis Lee RC 1.50 .45
258 Dennis Reyes RC 1.00 .30
259 Danny Buxbaum .50 .15
260 Kelvim Escobar RC 2.50 .75
261 Danny Klassen .50 .15
262 Ken Cloude RC 1.50 .45
263 Gabe Alvarez .50 .15
264 Clayton Bruner RC 1.00 .30
265 Jason Marquis RC 4.00 1.20
266 Jamey Wright .50 .15
267 Matt Snyder RC 1.00 .30
268 Josh Garrett RC 1.00 .30
269 Juan Encarnacion .50 .15
270 Heath Murray .50 .15
271 Brent Butler RC 1.50 .45
272 Danny Peoples RC 1.00 .30
273 Miguel Tejada RC 15.00 4.50
274 Jim Pittsley .50 .15
275 Dmitri Young .50 .15
276 Vladimir Guerrero 1.25 .35
277 Cole Liniak RC 1.00 .30
278 Ramon Hernandez .50 .15
279 Cliff Politte RC 1.00 .30
280 Mel Rosario RC 1.00 .30
281 Jorge Carrion RC 1.00 .30
282 John Barnes RC 1.00 .30
283 Chris Stowe RC 1.00 .30
284 Vernon Wells RC 8.00 2.40
285 Brett Caradonna RC 1.00 .30
286 Scott Hodges RC 1.00 .30
287 Jon Garland RC 2.50 .75
288 Nathan Haynes RC 1.50 .45
289 Geoff Goetz RC 1.00 .30
290 Adam Kennedy RC 2.50 .75
291 T.J. Tucker RC 1.00 .30
292 Aaron Akin RC 1.00 .30
293 Jayson Werth RC 4.00 1.20
294 Glenn Davis RC 1.00 .30
295 Mark Mangum RC 1.00 .30
296 Troy Cameron RC 1.00 .30
297 J.J. Davis RC 1.50 .45
298 Lance Berkman RC 20.00 6.00
299 Jason Standridge RC 1.50 .45
300 Jason Dellaero RC 1.00 .30

1997 Bowman Chrome International

Randomly inserted in packs at the rate of one in four, this 300-card set is parallel to the base set and is distinguished by the flag on the background of each card front identifying the country where that player was born.

Nm-Mt Ex-Mt
*STARS: 1.25X TO 3X BASIC CARDS.
*ROOKIES: .4X TO 1X BASIC CARDS.

1997 Bowman Chrome International Refractors

Randomly inserted in packs at the rate of one in 24, this 300-card set is a parallel version of the Bowman Chrome International set and is similar in design. The difference is found in the refractive quality of the card front.

Nm-Mt Ex-Mt
*STARS: 6X TO 15X BASIC CARDS
*ROOKIES: 2X TO 5X BASIC CARDS

1997 Bowman Chrome Refractors

Randomly inserted in packs at the rate of one in 12, this 300-card set is parallel to the base set and is similar in design. The difference can be found in the refractive quality of the cards fronts.

Nm-Mt Ex-Mt
*STARS: 3X TO 8X BASIC CARDS
*ROOKIES: 1.5X TO 4X BASIC CARDS

1997 Bowman Chrome 1998 ROY Favorites

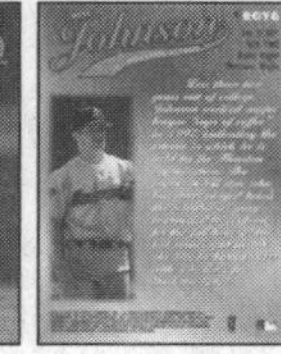

Randomly inserted in packs at the rate of one in 24, cards from this 15-card set features color action photos of 1998 Rookie of the Year prospective candidtates printed on chromium cards.

Nm-Mt Ex-Mt
COMPLETE SET (15) 25.00 7.50
*REFRACTORS: .75X TO 2X BASIC ROY
REFRACTOR STATED ODDS 1:72
ROY1 Jeff Abbott 1.50 .45
ROY2 Karim Garcia 1.50 .45
ROY3 Todd Helton 4.00 1.20
ROY4 Richard Hidalgo 1.50 .45
ROY5 Geoff Jenkins 1.50 .45
ROY6 Russ Johnson 1.50 .45
ROY7 Paul Konerko 1.50 .45
ROY8 Mark Kotsay 2.50 .75
ROY9 Ricky Ledee 1.00 .30
ROY10 Travis Lee 1.00 .30
ROY11 Derrek Lee 1.50 .45
ROY12 Elieser Marrero 1.50 .45
ROY13 Juan Melo 1.50 .45
ROY14 Brian Rose 1.50 .45
ROY15 Fernando Tatis 1.00 .30

1997 Bowman Chrome Scout's Honor Roll

Randomly inserted in packs at a rate of one in 12, this 15-card set features color photos of top prospects and rookies printed on chromium cards. The backs carry player information.

Nm-Mt Ex-Mt
COMPLETE SET (15) 30.00 9.00
*REF: .75X TO 2X BASIC CHR.HONOR
REFRACTOR STATED ODDS 1:36
SHR1 Dmitri Young 1.25 .35
SHR2 Bob Abreu 1.25 .35
SHR3 Vladimir Guerrero 3.00 .90
SHR4 Paul Konerko 1.25 .35
SHR5 Kevin Orie 1.25 .35
SHR6 Todd Walker 1.25 .35
SHR7 Ben Grieve 1.25 .35
SHR8 Darin Erstad 1.25 .35
SHR9 Derrek Lee 1.25 .35
SHR10 Jose Cruz Jr. 1.25 .35
SHR11 Scott Rolen 3.00 .90
SHR12 Travis Lee 1.25 .35
SHR13 Andruw Jones 1.25 .35
SHR14 Wilton Guerrero 1.25 .35
SHR15 Nomar Garciaparra 5.00 1.50

1998 Bowman Chrome

The 1998 Bowman Chrome set was issued in two separate series with a total of 441 cards. The four-card packs retailed for $3.00 each. These cards are parallel to the regular Bowman set but with a premium Chrome finish. Unlike the 1997 brand, the 1998 issue parallels the entire Bowman brand. Rookie Cards include Ryan Anderson, Jack Cust, Troy Glaus, Orlando Hernandez, Gabe Kapler, Carlos Lee, Ruben Mateo, Kevin Millwood, Magglio Ordonez and Jimmy Rollins.

Nm-Mt Ex-Mt
COMPLETE SET (441) 160.00 47.50
COMP. SERIES 1 (221) 80.00 24.00
COMP. SERIES 2 (220) 80.00 24.00
1 Nomar Garciaparra 2.00 .60
2 Scott Rolen 1.25 .35
3 Andy Pettitte .75 .23
4 Ivan Rodriguez 1.25 .35
5 Mark McGwire 3.00 .90
6 Jason Dickson .50 .15
7 Jose Cruz Jr. .50 .15
8 Jeff Kent .50 .15
9 Mike Mussina .75 .23
10 Jason Kendall .50 .15
11 Brett Tomko .50 .15
12 Jeff King .50 .15
13 Brad Radke .50 .15
14 Robin Ventura .50 .15
15 Jeff Bagwell .75 .23
16 Greg Maddux 2.00 .60
17 John Jaha .50 .15
18 Mike Piazza 2.00 .60
19 Edgar Martinez .75 .23
20 David Justice .50 .15
21 Todd Hundley .50 .15
22 Tony Gwynn 1.50 .45
23 Larry Walker .75 .23
24 Bernie Williams .75 .23
25 Edgar Renteria .50 .15
26 Rafael Palmeiro .75 .23
27 Tim Salmon .75 .23
28 Matt Morris .50 .15
29 Shawn Estes .50 .15
30 Vladimir Guerrero 1.25 .35
31 Fernando Tatis .50 .15
32 Justin Thompson .50 .15
33 Ken Griffey Jr. 2.00 .60
34 Edgardo Alfonzo .50 .15
35 Mo Vaughn .50 .15
36 Marty Cordova .50 .15
37 Craig Biggio .75 .23
38 Roger Clemens 2.50 .75
39 Mark Grace .75 .23
40 Ken Caminiti .50 .15
41 Tony Womack .50 .15
42 Albert Belle .50 .15
43 Tino Martinez .75 .23
44 Sandy Alomar Jr. .50 .15
45 Jeff Cirillo .50 .15
46 Jason Giambi .50 .15
47 Darin Erstad .50 .15
48 Livan Hernandez .50 .15
49 Mark Grudzielanek .50 .15
50 Sammy Sosa 2.00 .60
51 Curt Schilling .50 .15
52 Brian Hunter .50 .15
53 Neifi Perez .50 .15
54 Todd Walker .50 .15
55 Jose Guillen .50 .15
56 Jim Thome 1.25 .35
57 Tom Glavine .75 .23
58 Todd Greene .50 .15
59 Rondell White .50 .15
60 Roberto Alomar .75 .23
61 Tony Clark .50 .15
62 Vinny Castilla .50 .15
63 Barry Larkin .75 .23
64 Hideki Irabu .50 .15
65 Johnny Damon .75 .23
66 Juan Gonzalez .75 .23
67 John Olerud .50 .15
68 Gary Sheffield .50 .15
69 Raul Mondesi .50 .15
70 Chipper Jones 1.25 .35
71 David Ortiz 4.00 1.20
72 Warren Morris RC 1.00 .30
73 Alex Gonzalez .50 .15
74 Nick Bierbrodt .50 .15
75 Roy Halladay .50 .15
76 Danny Buxbaum .50 .15
77 Adam Kennedy .50 .15
78 Jared Sandberg .50 .15
79 Michael Barrett .50 .15
80 Gil Meche 1.00 .30
81 Jayson Werth .50 .15
82 Abraham Nunez .50 .15
83 Ben Petrick .50 .15
84 Brett Caradonna .50 .15
85 Mike Lowell RC 8.00 2.40
86 Clay Bruner .50 .15
87 John Curtice RC 1.50 .45
88 Bobby Estalella .50 .15
89 Juan Melo .50 .15
90 Arnold Gooch .50 .15
91 Kevin Millwood RC 4.00 1.20
92 Richie Sexson .50 .15
93 Orlando Cabrera .50 .15
94 Pat Cline .50 .15
95 Anthony Sanders .50 .15
96 Russ Johnson .50 .15
97 Ben Grieve .50 .15
98 Kevin McGlinchy .50 .15
99 Paul Wilder .50 .15
100 Russ Ortiz .50 .15
101 Ryan Jackson RC 1.00 .30
102 Heath Murray .50 .15
103 Brian Rose .50 .15
104 R.Radmanovich RC 1.00 .30
105 Ricky Ledee .50 .15
106 Jeff Wallace RC 1.00 .30
107 Ryan Minor RC 1.00 .30
108 Dennis Reyes .50 .15
109 James Manias .50 .15
110 Chris Carpenter .50 .15
111 Daryle Ward .50 .15
112 Vernon Wells .50 .15
113 Chad Green .50 .15
114 Mike Stoner RC 1.00 .30
115 Brad Fullmer .50 .15
116 Adam Eaton .50 .15
117 Jeff Liefer .50 .15
118 Corey Koskie RC 5.00 1.50
119 Todd Helton .75 .23
120 Jaime Jones RC 1.00 .30
121 Mel Rosario .50 .15
122 Geoff Goetz .50 .15
123 Adrian Beltre 1.25 .35
124 Jason Dellaero .50 .15
125 Gabe Kapler RC 2.50 .75
126 Scott Schoeneweis .50 .15
127 Ryan Brannan .50 .15
128 Aaron Akin .50 .15
129 Ryan Anderson RC 1.50 .45
130 Brad Penny .50 .15
131 Bruce Chen .50 .15
132 Eli Marrero .50 .15
133 Eric Chavez .50 .15
134 Troy Glaus RC 10.00 3.00
135 Troy Cameron .50 .15
136 Brian Sikorski RC 1.00 .30
137 Mike Kinkade RC 1.00 .30
138 Braden Looper .50 .15
139 Mark Mangum .50 .15

0 Danny Peoples .50 .15
1 J.J. Davis .50 .15
2 Ben Davis .50 .15
3 Jacque Jones .50 .15
4 Derrick Gibson .50 .15
5 Bronson Arroyo 4.00 1.20
6 L.De Los Santos RC 1.00 .30
7 Jeff Abbott .50 .15
8 Mike Cuddyer RC 2.50 .75
9 Jason Romano .50 .15
0 Shane Monahan .50 .15
1 Ntema Ndungidi RC 1.00 .30
2 Alex Sanchez .50 .15
3 Jack Cust RC 1.50 .45
4 Brent Butler .50 .15
5 Ramon Hernandez .50 .15
6 Norm Hutchins .50 .15
7 Jason Marquis .50 .15
8 Jacob Cruz .50 .15
9 Rob Burger RC 1.00 .30
0 Dave Coggin .50 .15
1 Preston Wilson .50 .15
2 Jason Fitzgerald RC 1.00 .30
3 Dan Serafini .50 .15
4 Pete Munro .50 .15
5 Trot Nixon .50 .15
6 Homer Bush .50 .15
7 Dermal Brown .50 .15
8 Chad Hermansen .50 .15
9 Julio Moreno RC 1.00 .30
0 John Roskos RC 1.00 .30
1 Grant Roberts .50 .15
2 Ken Cloude .50 .15
3 Jason Brester .50 .15
4 Jason Conti .50 .15
5 Jon Garland .50 .15
6 Robbie Bell .50 .15
7 Nathan Haynes .50 .15
8 Ramon Ortiz RC 2.50 .75
9 Shannon Stewart .50 .15
0 Pablo Ortega .50 .15
1 Jimmy Rollins RC 4.00 1.20
2 Sean Casey .50 .15
3 Ted Lilly RC 2.50 .75
4 Chris Enochs RC 1.00 .30
5 M.Ordonez RC UER 10.00 3.00
Front photo is Mario Valdez
6 Mike Drumright .50 .15
7 Aaron Boone .50 .15
8 Matt Clement .50 .15
9 Todd Dunwoody .50 .15
0 Larry Rodriguez .50 .15
1 Todd Noel .50 .15
2 Geoff Jenkins .50 .15
3 George Lombard .50 .15
4 Lance Berkman .75 .23
5 Marcus McCain .50 .15
6 Ryan McGuire .50 .15
7 Jhensy Sandoval .50 .15
8 Corey Lee .50 .15
9 Mario Valdez .50 .15
0 Robert Fick RC 1.50 .45
1 Donnie Sadler .50 .15
2 Marc Kroon .50 .15
3 David Miller .50 .15
4 Jarrod Washburn .50 .15
5 Miguel Tejada .50 .15
6 Raul Ibanez .50 .15
7 John Patterson .50 .15
8 Calvin Pickering .50 .15
9 Felix Martinez .50 .15
0 Mark Redman .50 .15
1 Scott Elarton .50 .15
2 Jose Amado RC 1.00 .30
3 Kerry Wood 1.25 .35
4 Dante Powell .50 .15
5 Aramis Ramirez .50 .15
6 A.J. Hinch .50 .15
7 Dustin Carr RC 1.00 .30
8 Mark Kotsay .50 .15
9 Jason Standridge .50 .15
0 Luis Ordaz .50 .15
1 O.Hernandez RC 4.00 1.20
2 Cal Ripken 4.00 1.20
3 Paul Molitor .75 .23
4 Derek Jeter 3.00 .90
5 Barry Bonds 3.00 .90
6 Jim Edmonds .50 .15
7 John Smoltz .75 .23
8 Eric Karros .50 .15
9 Ray Lankford .50 .15
0 Rey Ordonez .50 .15
1 Kenny Lofton .50 .15
2 Alex Rodriguez 2.00 .60
3 Dante Bichette .50 .15
4 Pedro Martinez 1.25 .35
5 Carlos Delgado .50 .15
6 Rod Beck .50 .15
7 Matt Williams .50 .15
8 Charles Johnson .50 .15
9 Rico Brogna .50 .15
0 Frank Thomas 1.25 .35
1 Paul O'Neill .75 .23
2 Jaret Wright .50 .15
3 Brant Brown .50 .15
4 Ryan Klesko .50 .15
5 Chuck Finley .50 .15
6 Derek Bell .50 .15
7 Delino DeShields .50 .15
8 Chan Ho Park .50 .15
9 Wade Boggs .75 .23
0 Jay Buhner .50 .15
1 Butch Huskey .50 .15
2 Steve Finley .50 .15
3 Will Clark 1.25 .35
4 John Valentin .50 .15
5 Bobby Higginson .50 .15
6 Darryl Strawberry .50 .15
7 Randy Johnson 1.25 .35
8 Al Martin .50 .15
9 Travis Fryman .50 .15
0 Fred McGriff .75 .23
1 Jose Valentin .50 .15
2 Andruw Jones .50 .15
3 Kenny Rogers .50 .15
4 Moises Alou .50 .15
5 Denny Neagle .50 .15
6 Ugueth Urbina .50 .15
7 Derrek Lee .50 .15
8 Ellis Burks .50 .15
269 Mariano Rivera .75 .23
270 Dean Palmer .50 .15
271 Eddie Taubensee .50 .15
272 Brady Anderson .50 .15
273 Brian Giles .50 .15
274 Quinton McCracken .50 .15
275 Henry Rodriguez .50 .15
276 Andres Galarraga .50 .15
277 Jose Canseco 1.25 .35
278 David Segui .50 .15
279 Bret Saberhagen .50 .15
280 Kevin Brown .75 .23
281 Chuck Knoblauch .50 .15
282 Jeromy Burnitz .50 .15
283 Jay Bell .50 .15
284 Manny Ramirez .75 .23
285 Rick Helling .50 .15
286 Francisco Cordova .50 .15
287 Bob Abreu .50 .15
288 J.T. Snow .50 .15
289 Hideo Nomo 1.25 .35
290 Brian Jordan .50 .15
291 Javy Lopez .50 .15
292 Travis Lee .50 .15
293 Russell Branyan .50 .15
294 Paul Konerko .50 .15
295 Masato Yoshii RC 2.50 .75
296 Kris Benson .50 .15
297 Juan Encarnacion .50 .15
298 Eric Milton .50 .15
299 Mike Caruso .50 .15
300 R. Aramboles RC 1.50 .45
301 Bobby Smith .50 .15
302 Billy Koch .50 .15
303 Richard Hidalgo .50 .15
304 Justin Baughman RC 1.00 .30
305 Chris Gissell .50 .15
306 Donnie Bridges RC 1.00 .30
307 Nelson Lara RC 1.00 .30
308 Randy Wolf RC 2.50 .75
309 Jason LaRue RC 1.50 .45
310 Jason Gooding RC 1.00 .30
311 Edgard Clemente .50 .15
312 Andrew Vessel .50 .15
313 Chris Reitsma .50 .15
314 Jesus Sanchez RC 1.00 .30
315 Buddy Carlyle RC 1.00 .30
316 Randy Winn .50 .15
317 Luis Rivera RC 1.00 .30
318 Marcus Thames RC 2.50 .75
319 A.J. Pierzynski .50 .15
320 Scott Randall .50 .15
321 Damian Sapp .50 .15
322 Ed Yarnall RC 1.00 .30
323 Luke Allen RC 1.50 .45
324 J.D. Smart .50 .15
325 Willie Martinez .50 .15
326 Alex Ramirez .50 .15
327 Eric DuBose RC 1.50 .45
328 Kevin Witt .50 .15
329 Dan McKinley RC 1.00 .30
330 Cliff Politte .50 .15
331 Vladimir Nunez .50 .15
332 John Halama RC 1.00 .30
333 Nerio Rodriguez .50 .15
334 Desi Relaford .50 .15
335 Robinson Checo .50 .15
336 John Nicholson .75 .23
337 Tom LaRosa RC 1.00 .30
338 Kevin Nicholson RC 1.00 .30
339 Javier Vazquez .50 .15
340 A.J. Zapp .50 .15
341 Tom Evans .50 .15
342 Kerry Robinson .50 .15
343 Gabe Gonzalez RC 1.00 .30
344 Ralph Milliard .50 .15
345 Enrique Wilson .50 .15
346 Elvin Hernandez .50 .15
347 Mike Lincoln RC 1.00 .30
348 Cesar King RC 1.00 .30
349 Cristian Guzman RC 2.50 .75
350 Donzell McDonald .50 .15
351 Jim Parque RC 1.00 .30
352 Mike Saipe RC 1.00 .30
353 Carlos Febles RC 1.50 .45
354 Dernell Stenson RC 1.50 .45
355 Mark Osborne RC 1.00 .30
356 Odalis Perez RC 4.00 1.20
357 Jason Dewey RC 1.00 .30
358 Joe Fontenot .50 .15
359 Jason Grilli RC 1.00 .30
360 Kevin Haverbusch RC 1.00 .30
361 Jay Yennaco RC 1.00 .30
362 Brian Buchanan .50 .15
363 John Barnes .50 .15
364 Chris Fussell .50 .15
365 Kevin Gibbs RC 1.00 .30
366 Joe Lawrence .50 .15
367 DaRond Stovall .50 .15
368 Brian Fuentes RC 1.00 .30
369 Jimmy Anderson .50 .15
370 Lariel Gonzalez RC 1.00 .30
371 Scott Williamson RC 1.50 .45
372 Milton Bradley .50 .15
373 Jason Halper RC 1.00 .30
374 Brent Billingsley RC 1.00 .30
375 Joe DePastino RC 1.00 .30
376 Jake Westbrook .50 .15
377 Octavio Dotel .50 .15
378 Jason Williams RC 1.00 .30
379 Julio Ramirez RC 1.00 .30
380 Seth Greisinger .50 .15
381 Mike Judd RC 1.00 .30
382 Ben Ford RC 1.00 .30
383 Tom Bennett RC 1.00 .30
384 Adam Butler RC 1.00 .30
385 Wade Miller RC 2.50 .75
386 Kyle Peterson RC 1.00 .30
387 Tommy Peterman RC 1.00 .30
388 Onan Masaoka .50 .15
389 Jason Rakers RC 1.00 .30
390 Rafael Medina .50 .15
391 Luis Lopez RC 1.00 .30
392 Jeff Yoder .50 .15
393 Vance Wilson RC 1.00 .30
394 F. Seguignol RC 1.00 .30
395 Ron Wright .50 .15
396 Ruben Mateo RC 1.50 .45
397 Steve Lomasney RC 1.50 .45
398 Damian Jackson .50 .15
399 Mike Jerzembeck RC 1.00 .30
400 Luis Rivas RC 4.00 1.20
401 Kevin Burford RC 1.00 .30
402 Glenn Davis .50 .15
403 Robert Luce RC 1.00 .30
404 Cole Liniak .50 .15
405 Matt LeCroy RC 1.50 .45
406 Jeremy Giambi RC 1.50 .45
407 Shawn Chacon .50 .15
408 Dewayne Wise RC 1.00 .30
409 Steve Woodard .50 .15
410 F.Cordero RC 2.50 .75
411 Damon Minor RC 1.00 .30
412 Lou Collier .50 .15
413 Justin Towle .50 .15
414 Juan LeBron .50 .15
415 Michael Coleman .50 .15
416 Felix Rodriguez .50 .15
417 Paul Ah Yat RC 1.00 .30
418 Kevin Barker RC 1.00 .30
419 Brian Meadows .50 .15
420 Darnell McDonald RC 1.00 .30
421 Matt Kinney RC 1.50 .45
422 Mike Vavrek RC 1.00 .30
423 Courtney Duncan RC 1.00 .30
424 Kevin Millar RC 5.00 1.50
425 Ruben Rivera .50 .15
426 Steve Shoemaker RC 1.00 .30
427 Dan Reichert RC 1.00 .30
428 Carlos Lee RC 4.00 1.20
429 Rod Barajas 2.50 .75
430 Pablo Ozuna RC 1.50 .45
431 Todd Belitz RC 1.00 .30
432 Sidney Ponson .50 .15
433 Steve Carver RC 1.00 .30
434 Esteban Yan RC 1.50 .45
435 Cedrick Bowers .50 .15
436 Marlon Anderson .50 .15
437 Carl Pavano .75 .15
438 Jae Weong Seo RC 2.50 .75
439 Jose Taveras RC 1.00 .30
440 Matt Anderson RC 1.50 .45
441 Darron Ingram RC 1.00 .30

1998 Bowman Chrome Golden Anniversary

Randomly inserted in first series packs at a rate of one in 164 and second series packs at a rate of one in 133, this 441-card set is a parallel to the Bowman Chrome base set. The set is sequentially numbered to 50 and is highlighted by gold facsimile signatures.

Nm-Mt Ex-Mt
*STARS: 6X TO 15X BASIC CARDS
*ROOKIES: 3X TO 8X BASIC CARDS
GOLD.ANN.REF.SER.1 ODDS 1:1279
GOLD.ANN.REF.SER.2 ODDS 1:1022
GOLD.ANN.REF.PRINT RUN 5 SERIAL #'d SETS
GOLD.ANN.REF.NOT PRICED DUE TO SCARCITY

1998 Bowman Chrome International

Randomly inserted in packs at a rate of one in four, this 441-card set is a parallel to the Bowman Chrome base set. These cards are differentiated by maps of the player's hometown area in the background of each card front.

Nm-Mt Ex-Mt
COMPLETE SET (441) 700.00 210.00
COMP. SERIES 1 (221) 400.00 120.00
COMP. SERIES 2 (220) 300.00 90.00
*STARS: 1.5X TO 4X BASIC CARDS
*ROOKIES: .4X TO 1X BASIC CARDS.

1998 Bowman Chrome International Refractors

Randomly inserted in packs at a rate of one in 24, this 441-card set is a parallel to the Bowman Chrome base set. These cards are differentiated by maps of the player's hometown area in the background of each card front.

Nm-Mt Ex-Mt
*STARS: 5X TO 12X BASIC CARDS
*ROOKIES: 2X TO 5X BASIC CARDS

1998 Bowman Chrome Refractors

Randomly inserted in packs at a rate of one in 12, this 441-card set is a parallel of the Bowman Chrome base set. The refractive quality of the card fronts differentiate themselves from basic issue cards.

Nm-Mt Ex-Mt
*STARS: 3X TO 8X BASIC CARDS
*ROOKIES: 1.5X TO 4X BASIC CARDS

1998 Bowman Chrome Reprints

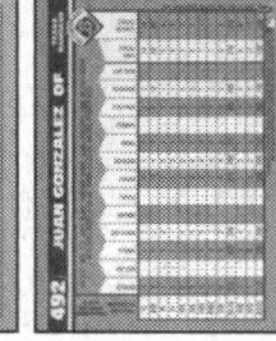

Randomly inserted in first and second packs at a rate of one in 12, these cards are replicas of classic Bowman Rookie Cards from 1948-1955 and 1989-present. Odd numbered cards (1, 3, 5 etc) were distributed in first series packs and even numbered cards in second series packs. The upgraded Chrome silver-colored stock gives them a striking appearance and makes them easy to differentiate from the originals.

Nm-Mt Ex-Mt
COMPLETE SET (50) 160.00 47.50
COMPLETE SERIES 1 (25) 80.00 24.00
COMPLETE SERIES 2 (25) 80.00 24.00
*REFRACTORS: 1X TO 2.5X BASIC REPRINTS
REFRACTOR STATED ODDS 1:36
1 Yogi Berra 4.00 1.20
2 Jackie Robinson 4.00 1.20
3 Don Newcombe 1.50 .45
4 Satchell Paige 4.00 1.20
5 Willie Mays 10.00 3.00
6 Gil McDougald 1.50 .45
7 Don Larsen 1.50 .45
8 Elston Howard 2.50 .75
9 Robin Ventura 1.50 .45
10 Brady Anderson 1.50 .45
11 Gary Sheffield 1.50 .45
12 Tino Martinez 2.50 .75
13 Ken Griffey Jr. 6.00 1.80
14 John Smoltz 2.50 .75
15 Sandy Alomar Jr. 1.00 .30
16 Larry Walker 2.50 .75
17 Todd Hundley 1.00 .30
18 Mo Vaughn 1.50 .45
19 Sammy Sosa 6.00 1.80
20 Frank Thomas 4.00 1.20
21 Chuck Knoblauch 1.50 .45
22 Bernie Williams 2.50 .75
23 Juan Gonzalez 2.50 .75
24 Mike Mussina 2.50 .75
25 Jeff Bagwell 2.50 .75
26 Tim Salmon 2.50 .75
27 Ivan Rodriguez 4.00 1.20
28 Kenny Lofton 1.50 .45
29 Chipper Jones 4.00 1.20
30 Javy Lopez 1.50 .45
31 Ryan Klesko 1.50 .45
32 Raul Mondesi 1.50 .45
33 Jim Thome 4.00 1.20
34 Carlos Delgado 1.50 .45
35 Mike Piazza 6.00 1.80
36 Manny Ramirez 2.50 .75
37 Andy Pettitte 2.50 .75
38 Derek Jeter 10.00 3.00
39 Brad Fullmer 1.00 .30
40 Richard Hidalgo 1.00 .30
41 Tony Clark 1.00 .30
42 Andruw Jones 1.50 .45
43 Vladimir Guerrero 4.00 1.20
44 Nomar Garciaparra 6.00 1.80
45 Paul Konerko 1.50 .45
46 Ben Grieve 1.00 .30
47 Hideo Nomo 4.00 1.20
48 Scott Rolen 4.00 1.20
49 Jose Guillen 1.50 .45
50 Livan Hernandez 1.00 .30

1999 Bowman Chrome

The 1999 Bowman Chrome set was issued in two distinct series and were distributed in four card packs with a suggested retail price of $3.00. The set contains 440 regular cards printed on brilliant chromium 18-pt. Stock. Within the set are 300 top prospects that are designated with silver and blue foil. Each player's facsimile rookie signature are featured on these cards. There are also 140 vereran stars designated with a red and silver foil stamp. The backs contain information on each player's rookie and most recent season, career statistics and a scouting report from early league days Rookie Cards include Pat Burrell, Adam Dunn, Rafael Furcal, Freddy Garcia, Tim Hudson, Nick Johnson, Austin Kearns, Willy Mo Pena, Adam Piatt, Corey Patterson and Alfonso Soriano.

Nm-Mt Ex-Mt
COMPLETE SET (440) 230.00 70.00
COMP. SERIES 1 (220) 80.00 24.00
COMP. SERIES 2 (220) 150.00 45.00
1 Ben Grieve .50 .15
2 Kerry Wood 1.25 .35
3 Ruben Rivera .50 .15
4 Sandy Alomar Jr. .50 .15
5 Cal Ripken 4.00 1.20
6 Mark McGwire 3.00 .90
7 Vladimir Guerrero 1.25 .35
8 Moises Alou .50 .15
9 Jim Edmonds .50 .15
10 Greg Maddux 2.00 .60
11 Gary Sheffield .50 .15
12 John Valentin .50 .15
13 Chuck Knoblauch .50 .15
14 Tony Clark .50 .15
15 Rusty Greer .50 .15
16 Al Leiter .50 .15
17 Travis Lee .50 .15
18 Jose Cruz Jr. .50 .15
19 Pedro Martinez 1.25 .35
20 Paul O'Neill .75 .23
21 Todd Walker .50 .15
22 Vinny Castilla .50 .15
23 Barry Larkin .75 .23
24 Curt Schilling .50 .15
25 Jason Kendall .50 .15
26 Scott Erickson .50 .15
27 Andres Galarraga .50 .15
28 Jeff Shaw .50 .15
29 John Olerud .50 .15
30 Orlando Hernandez .50 .15
31 Larry Walker .75 .23
32 Andruw Jones .50 .15
33 Jeff Cirillo .50 .15
34 Barry Bonds 3.00 .90
35 Manny Ramirez .75 .23
36 Mark Kotsay .50 .15
37 Ivan Rodriguez 1.25 .35
38 Jeff King .50 .15
39 Brian Hunter .50 .15
40 Ray Durham .50 .15
41 Bernie Williams .75 .23
42 Darin Erstad .50 .15
43 Chipper Jones 1.25 .35
44 Pat Hentgen .50 .15
45 Eric Young .50 .15
46 Jaret Wright .50 .15
47 Juan Guzman .50 .15
48 Jorge Posada .75 .23
49 Bobby Higginson .50 .15
50 Jose Guillen .50 .15
51 Trevor Hoffman .50 .15
52 Ken Griffey Jr. 2.00 .60
53 David Justice .50 .15
54 Matt Williams .50 .15
55 Eric Karros .50 .15
56 Derek Bell .50 .15
57 Ray Lankford .50 .15
58 Mariano Rivera .75 .23
59 Brett Tomko .50 .15
60 Mike Mussina .75 .23
61 Kenny Lofton .50 .15
62 Chuck Finley .50 .15
63 Alex Gonzalez .50 .15
64 Mark Grace .75 .23
65 Raul Mondesi .50 .15
66 David Cone .50 .15
67 Brad Fullmer .50 .15
68 Andy Benes .50 .15
69 John Smoltz .75 .23
70 Shane Reynolds .50 .15
71 Bruce Chen .50 .15
72 Adam Kennedy .50 .15
73 Jack Cust .50 .15
74 Matt Clement .50 .15
75 Derrick Gibson .50 .15
76 Darnell McDonald .50 .15
77 Adam Everett RC 2.50 .75
78 Ricardo Aramboles .50 .15
79 Mark Quinn RC 1.50 .45
80 Jason Rakers .50 .15
81 Seth Etherton RC 1.00 .30
82 Jeff Urban RC 1.00 .30
83 Manny Aybar .50 .15
84 Mike Nannini RC 1.00 .30
85 Onan Masaoka .50 .15
86 Rod Barajas .50 .15
87 Mike Frank .50 .15
88 Scott Randall .50 .15
89 Justin Bowles RC 1.00 .30
90 Chris Haas .50 .15
91 Arturo McDowell RC 1.00 .30
92 Matt Belisle RC 1.00 .30
93 Scott Elarton .50 .15
94 Vernon Wells .50 .15
95 Pat Cline .50 .15
96 Ryan Anderson .50 .15
97 Kevin Barker .50 .15
98 Ruben Mateo .50 .15
99 Robert Fick .50 .15
100 Corey Koskie .50 .15
101 Ricky Ledee .50 .15
102 Rick Elder RC 1.50 .45
103 Jack Cressend RC 1.00 .30
104 Joe Lawrence .50 .15
105 Mike Lincoln .50 .15
106 Kit Pellow RC 1.00 .30
107 Matt Burch RC 1.00 .30
108 Cole Liniak .50 .15
109 Jason Dewey .50 .15
110 Cesar King .50 .15
111 Julio Ramirez .50 .15
112 Jake Westbrook .50 .15
113 Eric Valent RC 1.50 .45
114 Roosevelt Brown RC 1.00 .30
115 Choo Freeman RC 1.50 .45
116 Juan Melo .50 .15
117 Jason Grilli .50 .15
118 Jared Sandberg .50 .15
119 Glenn Davis .50 .15
120 David Riske RC 1.00 .30
121 Jacque Jones .50 .15
122 Corey Lee .50 .15
123 Michael Barrett .50 .15
124 Lariel Gonzalez .50 .15
125 Mitch Meluskey .50 .15
126 Freddy Adrian Garcia .50 .15
127 Tony Torcato RC 1.50 .45
128 Jeff Liefer .50 .15
129 Ntema Ndungidi .50 .15
130 Andy Brown RC 1.00 .30
131 Ryan Mills RC 1.00 .30
132 Andy Abad RC 1.00 .30
133 Carlos Febles .50 .15
134 Jason Tyner RC 1.00 .30
135 Mark Osborne .50 .15
136 Phil Norton RC 1.00 .30
137 Nathan Haynes .50 .15
138 Roy Halladay .50 .15
139 Juan Encarnacion .50 .15
140 Brad Penny .50 .15
141 Grant Roberts .50 .15
142 Aramis Ramirez .50 .15
143 Cristian Guzman .50 .15
144 Mamon Tucker RC 1.00 .30
145 Ryan Bradley .50 .15
146 Brian Simmons .50 .15
147 Dan Reichert .50 .15
148 Russell Branyan .50 .15
149 Victor Valencia RC 1.00 .30
150 Scott Schoeneweis .50 .15
151 Sean Spencer RC 1.00 .30
152 Odalis Perez .50 .15
153 Joe Fontenot .50 .15
154 Milton Bradley .50 .15
155 Josh McKinley RC 1.50 .45
156 Terrence Long .50 .15
157 Danny Klassen .50 .15
158 Paul Hoover RC 1.00 .30
159 Ron Belliard .50 .15
160 Armando Rios .50 .15
161 Ramon Hernandez .50 .15
162 Jason Conti .50 .15
163 Chad Hermansen .50 .15
164 Jason Standridge .50 .15
165 Jason Dellaero .50 .15
166 John Curtice .50 .15
167 Clayton Andrews RC 1.00 .30
168 Jeremy Giambi .50 .15
169 Alex Ramirez .50 .15
170 Gabe Molina RC 1.00 .30

171 M.Encarnacion RC 1.00 .30
172 Mike Zywica RC 1.00 .30
173 Chip Ambres RC 1.00 .30
174 Trot Nixon .50 .15
175 Pat Burrell RC 8.00 2.40
176 Jeff Yoder .50 .15
177 Chris Jones RC 1.00 .30
178 Kevin Witt .50 .15
179 Keith Luuloa RC 1.00 .30
180 Billy Koch .50 .15
181 Damaso Marte RC 1.00 .30
182 Ryan Glynn RC 1.00 .30
183 Calvin Pickering .50 .15
184 Michael Cuddyer .50 .15
185 Nick Johnson RC 4.00 1.20
186 D.Mientkiewicz RC 4.00 1.20
187 Nate Cornejo RC 1.50 .45
188 Octavio Dotel .50 .15
189 Wes Helms .50 .15
190 Nelson Lara .50 .15
191 Chuck Abbott RC 1.00 .30
192 Tony Armas Jr. .50 .15
193 Gil Meche .50 .15
194 Ben Petrick .50 .15
195 Chris George RC 1.50 .45
196 Scott Hunter RC 1.00 .30
197 Ryan Brannan .50 .15
198 Amaury Garcia RC 1.00 .30
199 Chris Gissell .50 .15
200 Austin Kearns RC 12.00 3.60
201 Alex Gonzalez .50 .15
202 Wade Miller .50 .15
203 Scott Williamson .50 .15
204 Chris Enochs .50 .15
205 Fernando Seguignol .50 .15
206 Marlon Anderson .50 .15
207 Todd Sears RC 1.50 .45
208 Nate Bump RC 1.00 .30
209 J.M. Gold RC 1.00 .30
210 Matt LeCroy .50 .15
211 Alex Hernandez .50 .15
212 Luis Rivera .50 .15
213 Troy Cameron .50 .15
214 Alex Escobar RC 1.50 .45
215 Jason LaRue .50 .15
216 Kyle Peterson .50 .15
217 Brent Butler .50 .15
218 Dernell Stenson .50 .15
219 Adrian Beltre .75 .23
220 Daryle Ward .50 .15
221 Jim Thome 1.25 .35
222 Cliff Floyd .50 .15
223 Rickey Henderson 1.25 .35
224 Garret Anderson .50 .15
225 Ken Caminiti .50 .15
226 Bret Boone .50 .15
227 Jeromy Burnitz .50 .15
228 Steve Finley .50 .15
229 Miguel Tejada .50 .15
230 Greg Vaughn .50 .15
231 Jose Offerman .50 .15
232 Andy Ashby .50 .15
233 Albert Belle .50 .15
234 Fernando Tatis .50 .15
235 Todd Helton .75 .23
236 Sean Casey .50 .15
237 Brian Giles .50 .15
238 Andy Pettitte .75 .23
239 Fred McGriff .75 .23
240 Roberto Alomar .75 .23
241 Edgar Martinez .75 .23
242 Lee Stevens .50 .15
243 Shawn Green .50 .15
244 Ryan Klesko .50 .15
245 Sammy Sosa 2.00 .60
246 Todd Hundley .50 .15
247 Shannon Stewart .50 .15
248 Randy Johnson 1.25 .35
249 Rondell White .50 .15
250 Mike Piazza 2.00 .60
251 Craig Biggio .75 .23
252 David Wells .50 .15
253 Brian Jordan .50 .15
254 Edgar Renteria .50 .15
255 Bartolo Colon .50 .15
256 Frank Thomas 1.25 .35
257 Will Clark 1.25 .35
258 Dean Palmer .50 .15
259 Dmitri Young .50 .15
260 Scott Rolen 1.25 .35
261 Jeff Kent .50 .15
262 Dante Bichette .50 .15
263 Nomar Garciaparra 2.00 .60
264 Tony Gwynn 1.50 .45
265 Alex Rodriguez 2.00 .60
266 Jose Canseco 1.25 .35
267 Jason Giambi .50 .15
268 Jeff Bagwell .75 .23
269 Carlos Delgado .50 .15
270 Tom Glavine .75 .23
271 Eric Davis .50 .15
272 Edgardo Alfonzo .50 .15
273 Tim Salmon .75 .23
274 Johnny Damon .75 .23
275 Rafael Palmeiro .75 .23
276 Denny Neagle .50 .15
277 Neifi Perez .50 .15
278 Roger Clemens 2.50 .75
279 Brant Brown .50 .15
280 Kevin Brown .75 .23
281 Jay Bell .50 .15
282 Jay Buhner .50 .15
283 Matt Lawton .50 .15
284 Robin Ventura .50 .15
285 Juan Gonzalez .75 .23
286 Mo Vaughn .50 .15
287 Kevin Millwood .50 .15
288 Tino Martinez .75 .23
289 Justin Thompson .50 .15
290 Derek Jeter 3.00 .90
291 Ben Davis .50 .15
292 Mike Lowell .50 .15
293 Calvin Murray .50 .15
294 Micah Bowie RC 1.00 .30
295 Lance Berkman .50 .15
296 Jason Marquis .50 .15
297 Chad Green .50 .15
298 Dee Brown .50 .15
299 Jerry Hairston Jr. .50 .15
300 Gabe Kapler .50 .15
301 Brent Stentz RC 1.00 .30
302 Scott Mullen RC 1.00 .30
303 Brandon Reed .50 .15
304 Shea Hillenbrand RC 4.00 1.20
305 J.D. Closser RC 2.50 .75
306 Gary Matthews Jr. .50 .15
307 Toby Hall RC 1.50 .45
308 Jason Phillips RC 1.50 .45
309 Jose Macias RC 1.00 .30
310 Jung Bong RC 1.50 .45
311 Ramon Soler RC 1.00 .30
312 Kelly Dransfeldt RC 1.00 .30
313 Carlos E. Hernandez RC 1.50 .45
314 Kevin Haverbusch .50 .15
315 Aaron Myette RC 1.00 .30
316 Chad Harville RC 1.00 .30
317 Kyle Farnsworth RC 1.50 .45
318 Gookie Dawkins RC 1.50 .45
319 Willie Martinez .50 .15
320 Carlos Lee .50 .15
321 Carlos Pena RC 2.50 .75
322 Peter Bergeron RC 1.50 .45
323 A.J. Burnett RC 4.00 1.20
324 Bucky Jacobsen RC 8.00 2.40
325 Mo Bruce RC 1.00 .30
326 Reggie Taylor .50 .15
327 Jackie Rexrode .50 .15
328 Alvin Morrow RC 1.00 .30
329 Carlos Beltran .75 .23
330 Eric Chavez .50 .15
331 John Patterson .50 .15
332 Jayson Werth .50 .15
333 Richie Sexson .50 .15
334 Randy Wolf .50 .15
335 Eli Marrero .50 .15
336 Paul LoDuca .50 .15
337 J.D Smart .50 .15
338 Ryan Minor .50 .15
339 Kris Benson .50 .15
340 George Lombard .50 .15
341 Troy Glaus .50 .15
342 Eddie Yarnall .50 .15
343 Kip Wells RC 2.50 .75
344 C.C. Sabathia RC 5.00 1.50
345 Sean Burroughs RC 6.00 1.80
346 Felipe Lopez RC 1.50 .45
347 Ryan Rupe RC 1.00 .30
348 Orber Moreno RC 1.00 .30
349 Rafael Roque RC 1.00 .30
350 Alfonso Soriano RC 25.00 7.50
351 Pablo Ozuna .50 .15
352 Corey Patterson RC 10.00 3.00
353 Braden Looper .50 .15
354 Robbie Bell .50 .15
355 Mark Mulder RC 10.00 2.40
356 Angel Pena .50 .15
357 Kevin McGlinchy .50 .15
358 M.Restovich RC 1.50 .45
359 Eric DuBose .50 .15
360 Geoff Jenkins .50 .15
361 Mark Harriger RC 1.00 .30
362 Junior Herndon RC 1.50 .45
363 Tim Raines Jr. RC 1.50 .45
364 Rafael Furcal RC 5.00 1.50
365 Marcus Giles RC 5.00 1.50
366 Ted Lilly .50 .15
367 Jorge Toca RC 1.50 .45
368 David Kelton RC 1.50 .45
369 Adam Dunn RC 20.00 6.00
370 Guillermo Mota RC 1.00 .30
371 Brett Laxton RC 1.00 .30
372 Travis Harper RC 1.00 .30
373 Tom Davey RC 1.00 .30
374 Darren Blakely RC 1.00 .30
375 Tim Hudson RC 10.00 3.00
376 Jason Romano .50 .15
377 Dan Reichert .50 .15
378 Julio Lugo RC 1.50 .45
379 Jose Garcia RC 1.00 .30
380 Erubiel Durazo RC 2.50 .75
381 Jose Jimenez .50 .15
382 Chris Fussell .50 .15
383 Steve Lomasney .50 .15
384 Juan Pena RC 1.00 .30
385 Allen Levrault RC 1.00 .30
386 Juan Rivera RC 1.50 .45
387 Steve Colyer RC 1.50 .45
388 Joe Nathan RC 4.00 1.20
389 Ron Walker RC 1.00 .30
390 Nick Bierbrodt .50 .15
391 Luke Prokopec RC 1.00 .30
392 Dave Roberts RC 2.50 .75
393 Mike Darr .50 .15
394 Abraham Nunez RC 1.50 .45
395 G.Chiaramonte RC 1.00 .30
396 J.Van Buren RC 1.00 .30
397 Mike Kusiewicz .50 .15
398 Matt Wise RC 1.00 .30
399 Joe McEwing RC 1.50 .45
400 Matt Holliday RC 4.00 1.20
401 Willi Mo Pena RC 10.00 3.00
402 Ruben Quevedo RC 1.00 .30
403 Rob Ryan RC 1.00 .30
404 Freddy Garcia RC 4.00 1.20
405 Kevin Eberwein RC 1.00 .30
406 Jesus Colome RC 1.00 .30
407 Chris Singleton .50 .15
408 Bubba Crosby RC 2.50 .75
409 Jesus Cordero RC 1.50 .45
410 Donny Leon .50 .15
411 G.Tomlinson RC 1.00 .30
412 Jeff Winchester RC 1.00 .30
413 Adam Piatt RC 1.50 .45
414 Robert Stratton .50 .15
415 T.J. Tucker .50 .15
416 Ryan Langerhans RC 1.00 .30
417 A.Shumaker RC 1.00 .30
418 Matt Miller RC 1.00 .30
419 Doug Clark RC 1.00 .30
420 Kory DeHaan RC 1.00 .30
421 David Eckstein RC 2.50 .75
422 Brian Cooper RC 1.00 .30
423 Brady Clark RC 1.00 .30
424 Chris Magruder RC 1.00 .30
425 Bobby Seay RC 1.00 .30
426 Aubrey Huff RC 5.00 1.50
427 Mike Jerzembeck .50 .15
428 Matt Blank RC 1.00 .30
429 Benny Agbayani RC 1.00 .30
430 Kevin Beirne RC 1.50 .45
431 Josh Hamilton RC 2.50 .75
432 Josh Girdley RC 1.00 .30
433 Kyle Snyder RC 1.00 .30
434 Mike Paradis RC 1.00 .30
435 Jason Jennings RC 2.50 .75
436 David Walling RC 1.00 .30
437 Omar Ortiz RC 1.00 .30
438 Jay Gehrke RC 1.50 .45
439 Casey Burns RC 1.00 .30
440 Carl Crawford RC 8.00 2.40

1999 Bowman Chrome Gold

Randomly inserted in first series packs a rate of one in twelve , and second series packs at one in 24, this 440-card set is highlighted by gold facsimile signatures and borders and is a parallel to the 1999 Bowman Chrome base set.

Nm-Mt Ex-Mt
*SER.1 STARS: 2.5X TO 6X BASIC CARDS
*SER.1 ROOKIES: .75X TO 2X BASIC.
*SER.2 STARS: 3X TO 8X BASIC CARDS
*SER.2 ROOKIES: 1X TO 2.5X BASIC.

1999 Bowman Chrome Gold Refractors

Randomly inserted in first series packs at a rate of one in 305 and second series packs at a rate of one in 200, this 440-card set is a parallel insert to the Bowman Chrome base set. Gold foil fascimile signatures and refractive chrome fronts highlight the design. In addition, only 25 serial numbered sets were printed.

Nm-Mt Ex-Mt
*STARS: 20X TO 50X BASIC CARDS..

1999 Bowman Chrome International

Randomly inserted in first series packs at a rate of one in four, and second series packs at a rate of one in 12, this 440-card set is a parallel insert to the Bowman Chrome Base set. Metallic foil fronts and backgrounds taken from notable scenes of the featured players hometown highlight the design.

Nm-Mt Ex-Mt
COMPLETE SET (440) 900.00 275.00
COMP. SERIES 1 (220) 300.00 90.00
COMP. SERIES 2 (220) 600.00 180.00
*SER.1 STARS: 1.25X TO 3X BASIC CARDS
*SER.1 ROOKIES: .4X TO 1X BASIC...
*SER.2 STARS: 2X TO 5X BASIC CARDS
*SER.2 ROOKIES: .5X TO 1.2X BASIC

1999 Bowman Chrome International Refractors

Randomly inserted in first series packs at a rate of one in 76 and second series packs at a rate of one in 50, this 440-card set is a refractive parallel insert to the Bowman Chrome International set. Only 100 serial numbered sets were printed.

Nm-Mt Ex-Mt
*STARS: 8X TO 20X BASIC CARDS....
*ROOKIES: 2.5X TO 6X BASIC...

1999 Bowman Chrome Refractors

Randomly inserted at a rate of one in twelve, this 440-card set is a refractive parallel insert to the Bowman Chrome base set. The refractive sheen of each card highlights the design.

Nm-Mt Ex-Mt
*STARS: 4X TO 10X BASIC CARDS....
*ROOKIES: 1.5X TO 4X BASIC...

1999 Bowman Chrome 2000 ROY Favorites

Randomly inserted in second series packs at a rate of one in 20, this 10-card insert set features borderless, double-etched foil cards and feature players that had potential to win Rookie of the Year honors for the 2000 seasons.

Nm-Mt Ex-Mt
COMPLETE SET (10) 20.00 6.00
*REF: .75X TO 2X BASIC CHR.2000 ROY
REFRACTOR SER.2 STATED ODDS 1:100
ROY1 Ryan Anderson 1.00 .30
ROY2 Pat Burrell 2.00 .60
ROY3 A.J. Burnett 1.50 .45
ROY4 Ruben Mateo 1.00 .30
ROY5 Alex Escobar 1.00 .30
ROY6 Pablo Ozuna 1.00 .30
ROY7 Mark Mulder 2.50 .60
ROY8 Corey Patterson 2.50 .75
ROY9 George Lombard 1.00 .30
ROY10 Nick Johnson 1.50 .45

1999 Bowman Chrome Diamond Aces

Randomly inserted in first series packs at the rate of one in 21, this 18-card set features nine emerging stars such as Pat Burrell and Troy Glaus as well as nine proven veterans including Derek Jeter and Ken Griffey Jr.

Nm-Mt Ex-Mt
COMPLETE SET (18) 80.00 24.00
*REF: .75X TO 2X BASIC CHR.ACES 4.00 1.20
REFRACTOR SER.1 ODDS 1:84
DA1 Troy Glaus 1.50 .45
DA2 Eric Chavez 1.50 .45
DA3 Fernando Seguignol 1.50 .45

DA4 Ryan Anderson 1.50 .45
DA5 Ruben Mateo 1.50 .45
DA6 Carlos Beltran 2.50 .75
DA7 Adrian Beltre 2.50 .75
DA8 Bruce Chen 1.50 .45
DA9 Pat Burrell 4.00 1.20
DA10 Mike Piazza 6.00 1.80
DA11 Ken Griffey Jr. 6.00 1.80
DA12 Chipper Jones 4.00 1.20
DA13 Derek Jeter 10.00 3.00
DA14 Mark McGwire 10.00 3.00
DA15 Nomar Garciaparra 6.00 1.80
DA16 Sammy Sosa 6.00 1.80
DA17 Juan Gonzalez 2.50 .75
DA18 Alex Rodriguez 6.00 1.80

1999 Bowman Chrome Impact

Randomly inserted in second series packs at the rate of one in 15, this 15-card insert set features 20 players separated into three distinct categories; Early Impact, Initial Impact and Lasting Impact.

Nm-Mt Ex-Mt
COMPLETE SET (20) 80.00 24.00
*REF 1-10: .75X TO 2X BASIC IMPACT
*REF 11-20: .75X TO 2X BASIC IMPACT
REFRACTOR SER.2 STATED ODDS 1:75
I1 Alfonso Soriano 6.00 1.80
I2 Pat Burrell 2.50 .75
I3 Ruben Mateo 1.25 .35
I4 A.J. Burnett 1.25 .35
I5 Corey Patterson 3.00 .90
I6 Daryle Ward 1.25 .35
I7 Eric Chavez 1.25 .35
I8 Troy Glaus 1.25 .35
I9 Sean Casey 1.25 .35
I10 Joe McEwing .50 .15
I11 Gabe Kapler 1.25 .35
I12 Michael Barrett 1.25 .35
I13 Sammy Sosa 5.00 1.50
I14 Alex Rodriguez 5.00 1.50
I15 Mark McGwire 8.00 2.40
I16 Derek Jeter 8.00 2.40
I17 Nomar Garciaparra 5.00 1.50
I18 Mike Piazza 5.00 1.50
I19 Chipper Jones 3.00 .90
I20 Ken Griffey Jr. 5.00 1.50

1999 Bowman Chrome Scout's Choice

Randomly inserted in first series packs at the rate of one in twelve, this 21-card insert set features borderless, double-etched foil cards showcase a selection of the game's top young prospects.

Nm-Mt Ex-Mt
COMPLETE SET (21) 25.00 7.50
*REFRACTORS: .75X TO 2X BASIC SCOUT'S
REFRACTOR SER.1 ODDS 1:48
SC1 Ruben Mateo 1.50 .45
SC2 Ryan Anderson 1.50 .45
SC3 Pat Burrell 2.50 .75
SC4 Troy Glaus 1.50 .45
SC5 Eric Chavez 1.50 .45
SC6 Adrian Beltre 2.50 .75
SC7 Bruce Chen 1.50 .45
SC8 Carlos Beltran 2.50 .75
SC9 Alex Gonzalez 1.50 .45
SC10 Carlos Lee 1.50 .45
SC11 George Lombard 1.50 .45
SC12 Matt Clement 1.50 .45
SC13 Calvin Pickering 1.50 .45
SC14 Marlon Anderson 1.50 .45
SC15 Chad Hermansen 1.50 .45
SC16 Russell Branyan 1.50 .45
SC17 Jeremy Giambi 1.50 .45
SC18 Ricky Ledee 1.50 .45
SC19 John Patterson 1.50 .45
SC20 Roy Halladay 1.50 .45
SC21 Michael Barrett 1.50 .45

2000 Bowman Chrome

The 2000 Bowman Chrome product was released in late July, 2000 as a 440-card set that featured 140 veteran players (1-140), and 300 rookies and prospects (141-440). Each pack contained four cards, and carried a suggested retail price of $3.00. Rookie Cards include Rick

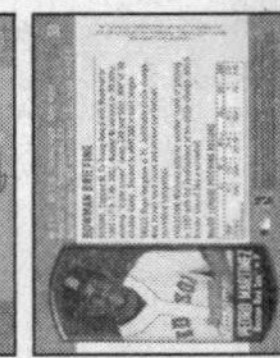

Asadoorian, Bobby Bradley, Kevin Mench, Be Sheets and Barry Zito. In addition, Topps desi nated five prospects as Bowman Chrome "excl sives" whereby their only appearance in a Top brand for the year 2000 would be in this se Jason Hart and Chin-Hui Tsao highlight th selection of Bowman Chrome exclusive Rook Cards.

Nm-Mt Ex-Mt
COMPLETE SET (440) 120.00 36.0
1 Vladimir Guerrero 1.25 .3
2 Chipper Jones 1.25 .3
3 Todd Walker .50 .1
4 Barry Larkin .75 .2
5 Bernie Williams .75 .2
6 Todd Helton .75 .2
7 Jermaine Dye .50 .1
8 Brian Giles .50 .1
9 Freddy Garcia .50 .1
10 Greg Vaughn .50 .1
11 Alex Gonzalez .50 .1
12 Luis Gonzalez .50 .1
13 Ron Belliard .50 .1
14 Ben Grieve .50 .1
15 Carlos Delgado .50 .1
16 Brian Jordan .50 .1
17 Fernando Tatis .50 .1
18 Ryan Rupe .50 .1
19 Miguel Tejada .50 .1
20 Mark Grace .75 .2
21 Kenny Lofton .50 .1
22 Eric Karros .50 .1
23 Cliff Floyd .50 .1
24 John Halama .50 .1
25 Cristian Guzman .50 .1
26 Scott Williamson .50 .1
27 Mike Lieberthal .50 .1
28 Tim Hudson .50 .1
29 Warren Morris .50 .1
30 Pedro Martinez 1.25 .3
31 John Smoltz .75 .2
32 Ray Durham .50 .1
33 Chad Allen .50 .1
34 Tony Clark .50 .1
35 Tino Martinez .75 .2
36 J.T. Snow .50 .1
37 Kevin Brown .75 .2
38 Bartolo Colon .50 .1
39 Rey Ordonez .50 .1
40 Jeff Bagwell .75 .2
41 Ivan Rodriguez 1.25 .3
42 Eric Chavez .50 .1
43 Eric Milton .50 .1
44 Jose Canseco 1.25 .3
45 Shawn Green .50 .1
46 Rich Aurilia .50 .1
47 Roberto Alomar .75 .2
48 Brian Daubach .50 .1
49 Magglio Ordonez .50 .1
50 Derek Jeter 3.00 .9
51 Kris Benson .50 .1
52 Albert Belle .50 .1
53 Rondell White .50 .1
54 Justin Thompson .50 .1
55 Nomar Garciaparra 2.00 .6
56 Chuck Finley .50 .1
57 Omar Vizquel .75 .2
58 Luis Castillo .50 .1
59 Richard Hidalgo .50 .1
60 Barry Bonds 3.00 .9
61 Craig Biggio .75 .2
62 Doug Glanville .50 .1
63 Gabe Kapler .50 .1
64 Johnny Damon .75 .2
65 Pokey Reese .50 .1
66 Andy Pettitte .75 .2
67 B.J. Surhoff .50 .1
68 Richie Sexson .50 .1
69 Javy Lopez .50 .1
70 Raul Mondesi .50 .1
71 Darin Erstad .50 .1
72 Kevin Millwood .50 .1
73 Ricky Ledee .50 .1
74 John Olerud .50 .1
75 Sean Casey .50 .1
76 Carlos Febles .50 .1
77 Paul O'Neill .75 .2
78 Bob Abreu .50 .1
79 Neifi Perez .50 .1
80 Tony Gwynn 1.50 .4
81 Russ Ortiz .50 .1
82 Matt Williams .50 .1
83 Chris Carpenter .50 .1
84 Roger Cedeno .50 .1
85 Tim Salmon .75 .2
86 Billy Koch .50 .1
87 Jeromy Burnitz .50 .1
88 Edgardo Alfonzo .50 .1
89 Jay Bell .50 .1
90 Manny Ramirez .75 .2
91 Frank Thomas 1.25 .3
92 Mike Mussina .75 .2
93 J.D. Drew .50 .1
94 Adrian Beltre .75 .2
95 Alex Rodriguez 2.00 .6
96 Larry Walker .75 .2
97 Juan Encarnacion .50 .1
98 Mike Sweeney .50 .1
99 Rusty Greer .50 .1
100 Randy Johnson 1.25 .3
101 Jose Vidro .50 .1
102 Preston Wilson .50 .1
103 Greg Maddux 2.00 .6
104 Jason Giambi .50 .1
105 Cal Ripken 4.00 1.2
106 Carlos Beltran .75 .2
107 Vinny Castilla .50 .1

108 Mariano Rivera .75 .23
109 Mo Vaughn .50 .15
110 Rafael Palmeiro .75 .23
111 Shannon Stewart .50 .15
112 Mike Hampton .50 .15
113 Joe Nathan .50 .15
114 Ben Davis .50 .15
115 Andruw Jones .50 .15
116 Robin Ventura .50 .15
117 Damion Easley .50 .15
118 Jeff Cirillo .50 .15
119 Kerry Wood 1.25 .35
120 Scott Rolen 1.25 .35
121 Sammy Sosa 2.00 .60
122 Ken Griffey Jr. 2.00 .60
123 Shane Reynolds .50 .15
124 Troy Glaus .50 .15
125 Tom Glavine .75 .23
126 Michael Barrett .50 .15
127 Al Leiter .50 .15
128 Jason Kendall .50 .15
129 Roger Clemens 2.50 .75
130 Juan Gonzalez .75 .23
131 Corey Koskie .50 .15
132 Curt Schilling .50 .15
133 Mike Piazza 2.00 .60
134 Gary Sheffield .50 .15
135 Jim Thome 1.25 .35
136 Orlando Hernandez .50 .15
137 Ray Lankford .50 .15
138 Geoff Jenkins .50 .15
139 Jose Lima .50 .15
140 Mark McGwire 3.00 .90
141 Adam Piatt .50 .15
142 Pat Manning RC .75 .23
143 Marcos Castillo RC .75 .23
144 Lesli Brea RC .75 .23
145 Humberto Cota RC 1.25 .35
146 Ben Petrick .50 .15
147 Kip Wells .50 .15
148 Wily Pena .50 .15
149 Chris Wakeland RC .75 .23
150 Brad Baker RC 1.25 .35
151 Robbie Morrison RC .75 .23
152 Reggie Taylor .50 .15
153 Matt Ginter RC 1.25 .35
154 Peter Bergeron .50 .15
155 Roosevelt Brown .50 .15
156 Matt Cepicky RC .75 .23
157 Ramon Castro .50 .15
158 Brad Baisley RC .75 .23
159 Jason Hart RC .75 .23
160 Mitch Meluskey .50 .15
161 Chad Harville .50 .15
162 Brian Cooper .50 .15
163 Marcus Giles .50 .15
164 Jim Morris 1.25 .35
165 Geoff Goetz .50 .15
166 Bobby Bradley RC 1.25 .35
167 Rob Bell .50 .15
168 Joe Crede .50 .15
169 Michael Restovich .50 .15
170 Quincy Foster RC .75 .23
171 Enrique Cruz RC .75 .23
172 Mark Quinn .50 .15
173 Nick Johnson .50 .15
174 Jeff Liefer .50 .15
175 Kevin Mench RC 3.00 .90
176 Steve Lomasney .50 .15
177 Jayson Werth .50 .15
178 Tim Drew .50 .15
179 Chip Ambres .50 .15
180 Ryan Anderson .50 .15
181 Matt Blank .50 .15
182 G. Chiaramonte .50 .15
183 Corey Myers RC 1.25 .35
184 Jeff Yoder .50 .15
185 Craig Dingman RC .75 .23
186 Jon Hamilton RC .75 .23
187 Toby Hall .50 .15
188 Russell Branyan .50 .15
189 Brian Falkenborg RC .75 .23
190 Aaron Harang RC 1.25 .35
191 Juan Pena .50 .15
192 Chin-Hui Tsao RC 3.00 .90
193 Alfonso Soriano 1.25 .35
194 Alejandro Diaz RC .75 .23
195 Carlos Pena .50 .15
196 Kevin Nicholson .50 .15
197 Mo Bruce .50 .15
198 C.C. Sabathia .50 .15
199 Carl Crawford .50 .15
200 Rafael Furcal .50 .15
201 Andrew Beinbrink RC .75 .23
202 Jimmy Osting .50 .15
203 Aaron McNeal RC 1.25 .35
204 Brett Laxton .50 .15
205 Chris George .50 .15
206 Felipe Lopez .50 .15
207 Ben Sheets RC 8.00 2.40
208 Mike Meyers RC 1.25 .35
209 Jason Conti .50 .15
210 Milton Bradley .50 .15
211 Chris Mears RC .75 .23
212 Carlos Hernandez RC 1.25 .35
213 Jason Romano .50 .15
214 Geofrey Tomlinson .50 .15
215 Jimmy Rollins .50 .15
216 Pablo Ozuna .50 .15
217 Steve Cox .50 .15
218 Terrence Long .50 .15
219 Jeff DaVanon RC 1.25 .35
220 Rick Ankiel .50 .15
221 Jason Standridge .50 .15
222 Tony Armas Jr. .50 .15
223 Jason Tyner .50 .15
224 Ramon Ortiz .50 .15
225 Daryle Ward .50 .15
226 Enger Veras RC .75 .23
227 Chris Jones .50 .15
228 Eric Cammack RC .75 .23
229 Ruben Mateo .50 .15
230 Ken Harvey RC 3.00 .90
231 Jake Westbrook .50 .15
232 Rob Purvis RC .75 .23
233 Choo Freeman .50 .15
234 Aramis Ramirez .50 .15
235 A.J. Burnett .50 .15
236 Kevin Barker .50 .15
237 Chance Caple RC .75 .23
238 Jarrod Washburn .50 .15
239 Lance Berkman .50 .15
240 Michael Wenner RC .75 .23
241 Alex Sanchez .50 .15
242 Pat Daneker .50 .15
243 Grant Roberts .50 .15
244 Mark Ellis RC 1.25 .35
245 Donny Leon .50 .15
246 David Eckstein .50 .15
247 Dicky Gonzalez RC .75 .23
248 John Patterson .50 .15
249 Chad Green .50 .15
250 Scot Shields RC .75 .23
251 Troy Cameron .50 .15
252 Jose Molina .50 .15
253 Rob Pugmire RC .75 .23
254 Rick Elder .50 .15
255 Sean Burroughs .50 .15
256 Josh Kalinowski RC .75 .23
257 Matt LeCroy .50 .15
258 Alex Graman RC .75 .23
259 Juan Silvestre RC .75 .23
260 Brady Clark .50 .15
261 Rico Washington RC .75 .23
262 Gary Matthews Jr. .50 .15
263 Matt Wise .50 .15
264 Keith Reed RC 1.25 .35
265 Santiago Ramirez RC .75 .23
266 Ben Broussard RC 3.00 .90
267 Ryan Langerhans .50 .15
268 Juan Rivera .50 .15
269 Shawn Gallagher .50 .15
270 Jorge Toca .50 .15
271 Brad Lidge .50 .15
272 Leoncio Estrella RC .75 .23
273 Ruben Quevedo .50 .15
274 Jack Cust .50 .15
275 T.J. Tucker .50 .15
276 Mike Colangelo .50 .15
277 Brian Schneider .50 .15
278 Calvin Murray .50 .15
279 Josh Girdley .50 .15
280 Mike Paradis .50 .15
281 Chad Hermansen .50 .15
282 Ty Howington RC 1.25 .35
283 Aaron Myette .50 .15
284 D'Angelo Jimenez .50 .15
285 Dernell Stenson .50 .15
286 Jerry Hairston Jr. .50 .15
287 Gary Majewski RC 2.00 .60
288 Derrin Ebert .50 .15
289 Steve Fish RC .75 .23
290 Carlos E. Hernandez .50 .15
291 Allen Levrault .50 .15
292 Sean McNally RC .75 .23
293 Randey Dorame RC .75 .23
294 Wes Anderson RC 1.25 .35
295 B.J. Ryan .50 .15
296 Alan Webb RC .75 .23
297 Brandon Inge RC 1.25 .35
298 David Walling .50 .15
299 Sun Woo Kim RC 1.25 .35
300 Pat Burrell .50 .15
301 Rick Guttormson RC .75 .23
302 Gil Meche .50 .15
303 Carlos Zambrano RC 12.00 3.60
304 Eric Byrnes UER RC 3.00 .90
Bo Porter pictured
305 Robb Quinlan RC 3.00 .90
306 Jackie Rexrode .50 .15
307 Nate Bump .50 .15
308 Sean DePaula RC .75 .23
309 Matt Riley .50 .15
310 Ryan Minor .50 .15
311 J.J. Davis .50 .15
312 Randy Wolf .50 .15
313 Jason Jennings .50 .15
314 Scott Seabol RC .75 .23
315 Doug Davis .50 .15
316 Todd Moser RC .75 .23
317 Rob Ryan .50 .15
318 Bubba Crosby .50 .15
319 Lyle Overbay RC 5.00 1.50
320 Mario Encarnacion .50 .15
321 F.Rodriguez RC 8.00 2.40
322 Michael Cuddyer .50 .15
323 Ed Yarnall .50 .15
324 Cesar Saba RC .75 .23
325 Gookie Dawkins .50 .15
326 Alex Escobar .50 .15
327 Julio Zuleta RC .75 .23
328 Josh Hamilton .50 .15
329 Carlos Urquiola RC .75 .23
330 Matt Belisle .50 .15
331 Kurt Ainsworth RC 1.25 .35
332 Tim Raines Jr. .50 .15
333 Eric Munson .50 .15
334 Donzell McDonald .50 .15
335 Larry Bigbie RC 3.00 .90
336 Matt Watson RC .75 .23
337 Aubrey Huff .50 .15
338 Julio Ramirez .50 .15
339 Jason Grabowski RC 1.25 .35
340 Jon Garland .50 .15
341 Austin Kearns .50 .15
342 Josh Pressley RC .75 .23
343 Miguel Olivo RC 2.00 .60
344 Julio Lugo .50 .15
345 Roberto Vaz .50 .15
346 Ramon Soler .50 .15
347 Brandon Phillips RC 2.00 .60
348 Vince Faison RC .75 .23
349 Mike Venafro .50 .15
350 Rick Asadoorian RC 1.25 .35
351 B.J. Garbe RC .75 .23
352 Dan Reichert .50 .15
353 Jason Stumm RC .75 .23
354 Ruben Salazar RC .75 .23
355 Francisco Cordero .50 .15
356 Juan Guzman RC .75 .23
357 Mike Bacsik RC .75 .23
358 Jared Sandberg .50 .15
359 Rod Barajas .50 .15
360 Junior Brignac RC .75 .23
361 J.M. Gold .50 .15
362 Octavio Dotel .50 .15
363 David Kelton .50 .15
364 Scott Morgan .50 .15
365 Wascar Serrano RC .75 .23
366 Wilton Veras .50 .15
367 Eugene Kingsale .50 .15
368 Ted Lilly .50 .15
369 George Lombard .50 .15
370 Chris Haas .50 .15
371 Wilton Pena RC .75 .23
372 Vernon Wells .50 .15
373 Keith Ginter RC .75 .23
374 Jeff Heaverlo RC .75 .23
375 Calvin Pickering .50 .15
376 Mike Lamb RC 1.25 .35
377 Kyle Snyder .50 .15
378 Javier Cardona RC .75 .23
379 Aaron Rowand RC 5.00 1.50
380 Dee Brown .50 .15
381 Brett Myers RC 2.00 .60
382 Abraham Nunez .50 .15
383 Eric Valent .50 .15
384 Jody Gerut RC 3.00 .90
385 Adam Dunn 1.25 .35
386 Jay Gehrke .50 .15
387 Omar Ortiz .50 .15
388 Darnell McDonald .50 .15
389 Tony Schrager RC .75 .23
390 J.D. Closser .50 .15
391 Ben Christensen RC .75 .23
392 Adam Kennedy .50 .15
393 Nick Green RC 3.00 .90
394 Ramon Hernandez .50 .15
395 Roy Oswalt RC 10.00 3.00
396 Andy Tracy RC .75 .23
397 Eric Gagne 2.00 .60
398 Michael Tejera RC .75 .23
399 Adam Everett .50 .15
400 Corey Patterson .50 .15
401 Gary Knotts RC .75 .23
402 Ryan Christianson RC 1.25 .35
403 Eric Ireland RC .75 .23
404 Andrew Good RC .75 .23
405 Brad Penny .50 .15
406 Jason LaRue .50 .15
407 Kit Pellow .50 .15
408 Kevin Beirne .50 .15
409 Kelly Dransfeldt .50 .15
410 Jason Grilli .50 .15
411 Scott Downs RC .75 .23
412 Jesus Colome .50 .15
413 John Sneed RC .75 .23
414 Tony McKnight .50 .15
415 Luis Rivera .50 .15
416 Adam Eaton .50 .15
417 Mike MacDougal RC 1.25 .35
418 Mike Nannini .50 .15
419 Barry Zito RC 8.00 2.40
420 DeWayne Wise .50 .15
421 Jason Dellaero .50 .15
422 Chad Moeller .50 .15
423 Jason Marquis .50 .15
424 Tim Redding RC 1.25 .35
425 Mark Mulder .50 .15
426 Josh Paul .50 .15
427 Chris Enochs .50 .15
428 W.Rodriguez RC .75 .23
429 Kevin Witt .50 .15
430 Scott Sobkowiak RC .75 .23
431 McKay Christensen .50 .15
432 Jung Bong .50 .15
433 Keith Evans RC .75 .23
434 Garry Maddox Jr. RC .75 .23
435 Ramon Santiago RC 1.25 .35
436 Alex Cora .50 .15
437 Carlos Lee .50 .15
438 Jason Repko RC 1.25 .35
439 Matt Burch .50 .15
440 Shawn Sonnier RC .75 .23

2000 Bowman Chrome Oversize

Inserted into hobby boxes as a chip-topper at one per box, this eight-card oversized set features some of the Major Leagues most promising young players.

Nm-Mt Ex-Mt
COMPLETE SET (8) 15.00 4.50
1 Pat Burrell 1.25 .35
2 Josh Hamilton 1.25 .35
3 Rafael Furcal .50 .15
4 Corey Patterson .75 .23
5 A.J. Burnett .75 .23
6 Eric Munson .75 .23
7 Nick Johnson .50 .15
8 Alfonso Soriano .50 .15

2000 Bowman Chrome Refractors

Randomly inserted into packs at one in 12, this 440-card insert is a complete parallel of the Bowman Chrome base set. This parallel was produced using Topps' refractor technology.

Nm-Mt Ex-Mt
*STARS: 3X TO 8X BASIC CARDS
*ROOKIES: 2X TO 5X BASIC CARDS

2000 Bowman Chrome Retro/Future

Randomly inserted into hobby/retail packs at one in six, this 440-card insert is a complete parallel of the Bowman Chrome base set. Each card features a television border similar to that of the 1955 Bowman set.

Nm-Mt Ex-Mt
*STARS: 1.5X TO 4X BASIC CARDS
*ROOKIES: .5X TO 1.2X BASIC CARDS

2000 Bowman Chrome Retro/Future Refractors

Randomly inserted into hobby/retail packs at one in 60, this 440-card insert is a complete parallel of the Bowman Chrome base set. Each card features a television border similar to that of the 1955 Bowman set. These cards were produced using Topps' refractor technology.

Nm-Mt Ex-Mt
*STARS: 6X TO 15X BASIC CARDS
*ROOKIES: 4X TO 10X BASIC CARDS

2000 Bowman Chrome Bidding for the Call

Randomly inserted into packs at one in 16, this 15-card insert features players that are looking to break into the Major Leagues during the 2000 season. Card backs carry a "BC" prefix. It's worth noting that top prospect Chin-Feng Chen's very first MLB-licensed card was included in this set.

Nm-Mt Ex-Mt
COMPLETE SET (15) 30.00 9.00
*REFFRACTORS: 1.25X TO 3X BASIC BID
REFRACTOR STATED ODDS 1:160
BC1 Adam Piatt 1.00 .30
BC2 Pat Burrell 1.00 .30
BC3 Mark Mulder 1.00 .30
BC4 Nick Johnson 1.00 .30
BC5 Alfonso Soriano 2.00 .60
BC6 Chin-Feng Chen 2.00 .60
BC7 Scott Sobkowiak 1.00 .30
BC8 Corey Patterson 1.00 .30
BC9 Jack Cust 1.00 .30
BC10 Sean Burroughs 1.00 .30
BC11 Josh Hamilton 1.00 .30
BC12 Corey Myers 1.00 .30
BC13 Eric Munson 1.00 .30
BC14 Wes Anderson 1.50 .45
BC15 Lyle Overbay 2.00 .60

2000 Bowman Chrome Meteoric Rise

Randomly inserted into packs at one in 24, this 10-card insert features players that have risen to the occasion during their careers. Card backs carry a "MR" prefix.

Nm-Mt Ex-Mt
COMPLETE SET (10) 50.00 15.00
*REF: 1.25X TO 3X BASIC METEORIC
REFRACTOR STATED ODDS 1:240
MR1 Nomar Garciaparra 5.00 1.50
MR2 Mark McGwire 8.00 2.40
MR3 Ken Griffey Jr. 5.00 1.50
MR4 Chipper Jones 3.00 .90
MR5 Manny Ramirez 2.00 .60
MR6 Mike Piazza 5.00 1.50
MR7 Cal Ripken 10.00 3.00
MR8 Ivan Rodriguez 3.00 .90
MR9 Greg Maddux 5.00 1.50
MR10 Randy Johnson 3.00 .90

2000 Bowman Chrome Rookie Class 2000

Randomly inserted into packs at one in 24, this 10-card insert features players that made their Major League debuts in 2000. Card backs carry a "RC" prefix.

Nm-Mt Ex-Mt
COMPLETE SET (10) 20.00 6.00
*REF: 1.25X TO 3X BASIC ROOKIE CLASS
REFRACTOR STATED ODDS 1:240
RC1 Pat Burrell 1.50 .45
RC2 Rick Ankiel 1.50 .45
RC3 Ruben Mateo 1.50 .45
RC4 Vernon Wells 1.50 .45
RC5 Mark Mulder 1.50 .45
RC6 A.J. Burnett 1.50 .45
RC7 Chad Hermansen 1.50 .45
RC8 Corey Patterson 1.50 .45
RC9 Rafael Furcal 1.50 .45
RC10 Mike Lamb 1.50 .45

2000 Bowman Chrome Teen Idols

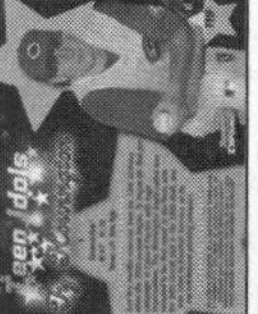

Randomly inserted into packs at one in 16, this 15-card insert set features Major League players that either made it to the majors as teenagers or are top current prospects who are still in their teens in 2000. Card backs carry a "TI" prefix.

Nm-Mt Ex-Mt
COMPLETE SET (15) 50.00 15.00
*SINGLES: 1X TO 2.5X BASIC CARDS
*REFRACTORS: 1.25X TO 3X BASIC TEEN
REFRACTOR STATED ODDS 1:160
TI1 Alex Rodriguez 6.00 1.80
TI2 Andruw Jones 1.50 .45
TI3 Juan Gonzalez 2.50 .75
TI4 Ivan Rodriguez 4.00 1.20
TI5 Ken Griffey Jr. 6.00 1.80
TI6 Bobby Bradley 1.50 .45
TI7 Brett Myers 2.00 .60
TI8 C.C. Sabathia 1.50 .45
TI9 Ty Howington 1.50 .45
TI10 Brandon Phillips 2.00 .60
TI11 Rick Asadoorian 1.50 .45
TI12 Wily Mo Pena 1.50 .45
TI13 Sean Burroughs 1.50 .45
TI14 Josh Hamilton 1.50 .45
TI15 Rafael Furcal 1.50 .45

2000 Bowman Chrome Draft Picks

The 2000 Bowman Chrome Draft Picks and Prospects set was released in December, 2000 as a 110-card parallel of the 2000 Bowman Draft Picks set. This product was distributed only in factory set form. Each set features Topps' Chrome technology. A limited selection of prospects were switched out from the Bowman checklist and are featured exclusively in this Bowman Chrome set. The most notable of these players include Timo Perez and Jon Rauch. Other notable Rookie Cards include Chin-Feng Chen and Adrian Gonzalez.

Nm-Mt Ex-Mt
COMP.FACT.SET (110) 50.00 15.00
1 Pat Burrell .50 .15
2 Rafael Furcal .50 .15
3 Grant Roberts .50 .15
4 Barry Zito 4.00 1.20
5 Julio Zuleta .50 .15
6 Mark Mulder .50 .15
7 Rob Bell .50 .15
8 Adam Piatt .50 .15
9 Mike Lamb .75 .23
10 Pablo Ozuna .50 .15
11 Jason Tyner .50 .15
12 Jason Marquis .50 .15
13 Eric Munson .50 .15
14 Seth Etherton .50 .15
15 Milton Bradley .50 .15
16 Nick Green 1.25 .35
17 Chin-Feng Chen RC 2.50 .75
18 Matt Boone RC .50 .15
19 Kevin Gregg RC 1.00 .30
20 Eddy Garabito RC .50 .15
21 Aaron Capista RC .50 .15
22 Esteban German RC .50 .15
23 Derek Thompson RC .50 .15
24 Phil Merrell RC .50 .15
25 Brian O'Connor RC .50 .15
26 Yamid Haad .50 .15
27 Hector Mercado RC .50 .15
28 Jason Woolf RC .50 .15
29 Eddy Furniss RC .50 .15
30 Cha Sueng Baek RC .50 .15
31 Colby Lewis RC 1.00 .30
32 Pasqual Coco RC .50 .15
33 Jorge Cantu RC 1.50 .45
34 Erasmo Ramirez RC .50 .15
35 Bobby Kielty RC 1.00 .30
36 Joaquin Benoit RC 1.00 .30
37 Brian Esposito RC .50 .15
38 Michael Wenner .50 .15
39 Juan Rincon RC .50 .15
40 Yorvit Torrealba RC .50 .15
41 Chad Durham RC .50 .15
42 Jim Mann RC .50 .15
43 Shane Loux RC .50 .15
44 Luis Rivas .50 .15
45 Ken Chenard RC .50 .15
46 Mike Lockwood RC .50 .15
47 Yovanny Lara RC .50 .15
48 Bubba Carpenter RC .50 .15
49 Ryan Dittfurth RC .50 .15
50 John Stephens RC 1.00 .30
51 Pedro Feliz RC 2.50 .75
52 Kenny Kelly RC 1.00 .30
53 Neil Jenkins RC .50 .15
54 Mike Glendenning RC .50 .15
55 Bo Porter .50 .15
56 Eric Byrnes 1.25 .35
57 Tony Alvarez RC .50 .15
58 Kazuhiro Sasaki RC 2.50 .75
59 Chad Durbin RC .50 .15
60 Mike Bynum RC .50 .15
61 Travis Wilson RC .50 .15
62 Jose Leon RC .50 .15
63 Ryan Vogelsong RC 1.00 .30
64 Geraldo Guzman RC .50 .15
65 Craig Anderson RC .50 .15
66 Carlos Silva RC 1.50 .45
67 Brad Thomas RC .50 .15
68 Chin-Hui Tsao 1.25 .35
69 Mark Buehrle RC 4.00 1.20
70 Juan Salas RC .50 .15
71 Denny Abreu RC .50 .15
72 Keith McDonald RC .50 .15
73 Chris Richard RC .50 .15
74 Tomas De la Rosa RC .50 .15
75 Vicente Padilla RC 1.00 .30
76 Justin Brunette RC .50 .15
77 Scott Linebrink RC .50 .15

78 Jeff Sparks RC .50 .15
79 Tike Redman RC 1.50 .45
80 John Lackey RC 2.50 .75
81 Joe Strong RC .50 .15
82 Brian Tollberg RC .50 .15
83 Steve Sisco RC .50 .15
84 Chris Clapinski RC .50 .15
85 Augie Ojeda RC .50 .15
86 Adrian Gonzalez RC 4.00 1.20
87 Mike Stodolka RC .50 .15
88 Adam Johnson RC 1.00 .30
89 Matt Wheatland RC .50 .15
90 Corey Smith RC 1.00 .30
91 Rocco Baldelli RC 12.00 3.60
92 Keith Bucktrot RC .50 .15
93 Adam Wainwright RC 2.50 .75
94 Blaine Boyer RC .50 .15
95 Aaron Herr RC 1.00 .30
96 Scott Thorman RC 1.00 .30
97 Bryan Digby RC 1.00 .30
98 Josh Shortslef RC .50 .15
99 Sean Smith RC 1.00 .30
100 Alex Cruz RC .50 .15
101 Marc Love RC .50 .15
102 Kevin Lee RC .50 .15
103 Timo Perez RC 1.00 .30
104 Alex Cabrera RC 1.00 .30
105 Shane Heams RC .50 .15
106 Tripper Johnson RC 1.00 .30
107 Brent Abernathy RC .50 .15
108 John Cotton RC .50 .15
109 Brad Wilkerson RC 1.50 .45
110 Jon Rauch RC 1.00 .30

2001 Bowman Chrome

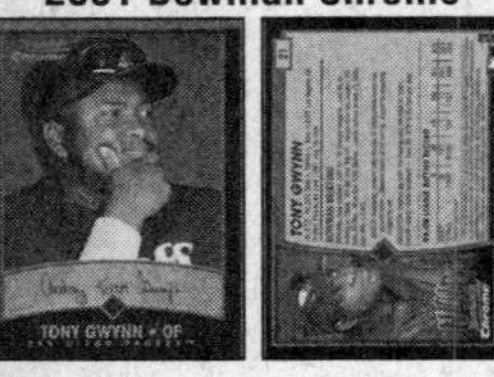

The 2001 Bowman Chrome set was distributed in four-card packs with a suggested retail price of $3.99. This 352-card set consists of 110 leading hitters and pitchers (1-110), 110 rising young stars (201-310), 110 top rookies including 20 not found in the regular Bowman set (111-200, 311-330), 20 autographed rookie refractor cards (331-350) each serial numbered to 500 copies and two Ichiro Suzuki Rookie Cards (351) in available in English and Japanese text variations. Both Ichiro cards were only available via mail redemption whereby exchange cards were seeded into packs. In addition, an exchange card was seeded into packs for the Albert Pujols signed Rookie Card. The deadline to send these cards in was June 30th, 2003.

Nm-Mt Ex-Mt
COMP.SET w/o SP's (220) 50.00 15.00
COMMON (1-110/201-310) .50 .15
COMMON (111-200/311-330) 5.00 1.50
COMMON (331-350) 30.00 9.00
1 Jason Giambi .50 .15
2 Rafael Furcal .50 .15
3 Bernie Williams .75 .23
4 Kenny Lofton .50 .15
5 Al Leiter .50 .15
6 Albert Belle .50 .15
7 Craig Biggio .75 .23
8 Mark Mulder .50 .15
9 Carlos Delgado .50 .15
10 Darin Erstad .50 .15
11 Richie Sexson .50 .15
12 Randy Johnson 1.25 .35
13 Greg Maddux 2.00 .60
14 Orlando Hernandez .50 .15
15 Javier Vazquez .50 .15
16 Jeff Kent .50 .15
17 Jim Thome 1.25 .35
18 John Olerud .50 .15
19 Jason Kendall .50 .15
20 Scott Rolen 1.25 .35
21 Tony Gwynn 1.50 .45
22 Edgardo Alfonzo .50 .15
23 Pokey Reese .50 .15
24 Todd Helton .75 .23
25 Mark Quinn .50 .15
26 Dean Palmer .50 .15
27 Ray Durham .50 .15
28 Rafael Palmeiro .75 .23
29 Carl Everett .50 .15
30 Vladimir Guerrero 1.25 .35
31 Livan Hernandez .50 .15
32 Preston Wilson .50 .15
33 Jose Vidro .50 .15
34 Fred McGriff .75 .23
35 Kevin Brown .50 .15
36 Miguel Tejada .50 .15
37 Chipper Jones 1.25 .35
38 Edgar Martinez .75 .23
39 Tony Batista .50 .15
40 Jorge Posada .75 .23
41 Sammy Sosa 2.00 .60
42 Gary Sheffield .50 .15
43 Bartolo Colon .50 .15
44 Pat Burrell .50 .15
45 Jay Payton .50 .15
46 Mike Mussina .75 .23
47 Nomar Garciaparra 2.00 .60
48 Darren Dreifort .50 .15
49 Richard Hidalgo .50 .15
50 Troy Glaus .50 .15
51 Ben Grieve .50 .15
52 Jim Edmonds .50 .15
53 Raul Mondesi .50 .15
54 Andruw Jones .50 .15
55 Mike Sweeney .50 .15
56 Derek Jeter 3.00 .90
57 Ruben Mateo .50 .15
58 Cristian Guzman .50 .15
59 Mike Hampton .50 .15
60 J.D. Drew .50 .15
61 Matt Lawton .50 .15
62 Moises Alou .50 .15
63 Terrence Long .50 .15
64 Geoff Jenkins .50 .15
65 Manny Ramirez .75 .23
66 Johnny Damon .75 .23
67 Pedro Martinez 1.25 .35
68 Juan Gonzalez .75 .23
69 Roger Clemens 2.50 .75
70 Carlos Beltran .75 .23
71 Roberto Alomar .75 .23
72 Barry Bonds 3.00 .90
73 Tim Hudson .50 .15
74 Tom Glavine .75 .23
75 Jeromy Burnitz .50 .15
76 Adrian Beltre .75 .23
77 Mike Piazza 2.00 .60
78 Kerry Wood 1.25 .35
79 Steve Finley .50 .15
80 Bob Abreu .50 .15
81 Neifi Perez .50 .15
82 Mark Redman .50 .15
83 Paul Konerko .50 .15
84 Jermaine Dye .50 .15
85 Brian Giles .50 .15
86 Ivan Rodriguez 1.25 .35
87 Adam Kennedy .50 .15
88 Eric Chavez .50 .15
89 Billy Koch .50 .15
90 Shawn Green .50 .15
91 Matt Williams .50 .15
92 Greg Vaughn .50 .15
93 Jeff Cirillo .50 .15
94 Frank Thomas 1.25 .35
95 David Justice .50 .15
96 Cal Ripken 4.00 1.20
97 Curt Schilling .50 .15
98 Barry Zito .75 .23
99 Brian Jordan .50 .15
100 Chan Ho Park .50 .15
101 J.T. Snow .50 .15
102 Kazuhiro Sasaki .50 .15
103 Alex Rodriguez 2.00 .60
104 Mariano Rivera .75 .23
105 Eric Milton .50 .15
106 Andy Pettitte .75 .23
107 Ken Griffey Jr. 2.00 .60
108 Bengie Molina .50 .15
109 Jeff Bagwell .75 .23
110 Mark McGwire 3.00 .90
111 Dan Tosca RC 8.00 2.40
112 Sergio Contreras RC 8.00 2.40
113 Mitch Jones RC 8.00 2.40
114 Ramon Carvajal RC 8.00 2.40
115 Ryan Madson RC 10.00 3.00
116 Hank Blalock RC 70.00 21.00
117 Ben Washburn RC 8.00 2.40
118 Erick Almonte RC 8.00 2.40
119 Shawn Fagan RC 8.00 2.40
120 Gary Johnson RC 8.00 2.40
121 Brett Evert RC 8.00 2.40
122 Joe Hamer RC 8.00 2.40
123 Yhency Brazoban RC 10.00 3.00
124 Domingo Guante RC 8.00 2.40
125 Deivi Mendez RC 8.00 2.40
126 Adrian Hernandez RC 8.00 2.40
127 R. Abercrombie RC 8.00 2.40
128 Steve Bennett RC 5.00 1.50
129 Matt White RC 8.00 2.40
130 Brian Hitchcox RC 5.00 1.50
131 Deivis Santos RC 8.00 2.40
132 Luis Montanez RC 8.00 2.40
133 Eric Reynolds RC 5.00 1.50
134 Denny Bautista RC 10.00 3.00
135 Hector Garcia RC 8.00 2.40
136 Joe Thurston RC 8.00 2.40
137 Tsuyoshi Shinjo RC 10.00 3.00
138 Elpidio Guzman RC 8.00 2.40
139 Brian Bass RC 8.00 2.40
140 Mark Burnett RC 8.00 2.40
141 Russ Jacobson UER 5.00 1.50
Last name misspelled Jacobsen on front
142 Travis Hafner RC 20.00 6.00
143 Wilson Betemit RC 8.00 2.40
144 Luke Lockwood RC 8.00 2.40
145 Noel Devarez RC 8.00 2.40
146 Doug Gredvig RC 8.00 2.40
147 Seung Song RC 10.00 3.00
148 Andy Van Hekken RC 8.00 2.40
149 Ryan Kohlmeier 5.00 1.50
150 Dee Haynes RC 8.00 2.40
151 Jim Journell RC 8.00 2.40
152 Chad Petty RC 8.00 2.40
153 Danny Borrell RC 8.00 2.40
154 Dave Krynzel 5.00 1.50
155 Octavio Martinez RC 8.00 2.40
156 David Parrish RC 8.00 2.40
157 Jason Miller RC 8.00 2.40
158 Corey Spencer RC 5.00 1.50
159 Maxim St. Pierre RC 8.00 2.40
160 Pat Magness RC 8.00 2.40
161 Ranier Olmedo RC 8.00 2.40
162 Brandon Mims RC 8.00 2.40
163 Phil Wilson RC 8.00 2.40
164 Jose Reyes RC 50.00 15.00
165 Matt Butler RC 8.00 2.40
166 Joel Pineiro 8.00 2.40
167 Ken Chenard 5.00 1.50
168 Alexis Gomez RC 8.00 2.40
169 Justin Morneau RC 60.00 18.00
170 Josh Fogg RC 8.00 2.40
171 Charles Frazier RC 8.00 2.40
172 Ryan Ludwick RC 8.00 2.40
173 Seth McClung RC 8.00 2.40
174 Justin Wayne RC 8.00 2.40
175 Rafael Soriano RC 10.00 3.00
176 Jared Abruzzo RC 8.00 2.40
177 Jason Richardson RC 8.00 2.40
178 Darwin Cubillan RC 5.00 1.50
179 Blake Williams RC 8.00 2.40
180 V. Pascucci RC 8.00 2.40
181 Ryan Hannaman RC 8.00 2.40
182 Steve Smyth RC 8.00 2.40
183 Jake Peavy RC 30.00 9.00
184 Onix Mercado RC 8.00 2.40
185 Luis Torres RC 8.00 2.40
186 Casey Fossum RC 8.00 2.40
187 Eduardo Figueroa RC 8.00 2.40
188 Bryan Barnowski RC 8.00 2.40
189 Jason Standridge 5.00 1.50
190 Marvin Seale RC 8.00 2.40
191 Steve Smitherman RC 10.00 3.00
192 Rafael Boitel RC 8.00 2.40
193 Dany Morban RC 8.00 2.40
194 Justin Woodrow RC 8.00 2.40
195 Ed Rogers RC 8.00 2.40
196 Ben Hendrickson RC 10.00 3.00
197 Thomas Mitchell 5.00 1.50
198 Adam Pettyjohn RC 8.00 2.40
199 Doug Nickle RC 5.00 1.50
200 Jason Jones RC 8.00 2.40
201 Larry Barnes .50 .15
202 Ben Diggins .50 .15
203 Dee Brown .50 .15
204 Rocco Baldelli .75 .23
205 Luis Terrero .50 .15
206 Milton Bradley .50 .15
207 Kurt Ainsworth .50 .15
208 Sean Burroughs .50 .15
209 Rick Asadoorian .50 .15
210 Ramon Castro .50 .15
211 Nick Neugebauer .50 .15
212 Aaron Myette .50 .15
213 Luis Matos .50 .15
214 Donnie Bridges .50 .15
215 Alex Cintron .50 .15
216 Bobby Kielty .50 .15
217 Matt Belisle .50 .15
218 Adam Everett .50 .15
219 John Lackey .50 .15
220 Adam Wainwright .50 .15
221 Jerry Hairston Jr. .50 .15
222 Mike Bynum .50 .15
223 Ryan Christianson .50 .15
224 J.J. Davis .50 .15
225 Alex Graman .50 .15
226 Abraham Nunez .50 .15
227 Sun Woo Kim .50 .15
228 Jimmy Rollins .50 .15
229 Ruben Salazar .50 .15
230 Josh Girdley .50 .15
231 Carl Crawford .50 .15
232 Ben Davis .50 .15
233 Jason Grabowski .50 .15
234 Chris George .50 .15
235 Roy Oswalt .75 .23
236 Brian Cole .50 .15
237 Corey Patterson .50 .15
238 Vernon Wells .50 .15
239 Brad Baker .50 .15
240 Gookie Dawkins .50 .15
241 Michael Cuddyer .50 .15
242 Ricardo Aramboles .50 .15
243 Ben Sheets .75 .23
244 Toby Hall .50 .15
245 Jack Cust .50 .15
246 Pedro Feliz .50 .15
247 Josh Beckett .50 .15
248 Alex Escobar .50 .15
249 Marcus Giles .50 .15
250 Jon Rauch .50 .15
251 Kevin Mench .50 .15
252 Shawn Sonnier .50 .15
253 Aaron Rowand .50 .15
254 C.C. Sabathia .50 .15
255 Bubba Crosby .50 .15
256 Josh Hamilton .50 .15
257 Carlos Hernandez .50 .15
258 Carlos Pena .50 .15
259 Miguel Cabrera 4.00 1.20
260 Brandon Phillips .50 .15
261 Tony Pena Jr. .50 .15
262 Cristian Guerrero .50 .15
263 Jin Ho Cho .50 .15
264 Aaron Herr .50 .15
265 Keith Ginter .50 .15
266 Felipe Lopez .50 .15
267 Travis Harper .50 .15
268 Joe Torres .50 .15
269 Eric Byrnes .50 .15
270 Ben Christensen .50 .15
271 Aubrey Huff .50 .15
272 Lyle Overbay .50 .15
273 Vince Faison .50 .15
274 Bobby Bradley .50 .15
275 Joe Crede .50 .15
276 Matt Wheatland .50 .15
277 Grady Sizemore 1.25 .35
278 Adrian Gonzalez .50 .15
279 Tim Raines Jr. .50 .15
280 Phil Dumatrait .50 .15
281 Jason Hart .50 .15
282 David Kelton .50 .15
283 David Walling .50 .15
284 J.R. House .50 .15
285 Kenny Kelly .50 .15
286 Aaron McNeal .50 .15
287 Nick Johnson .50 .15
288 Scott Heard .50 .15
289 Brad Wilkerson .50 .15
290 Allen Levrault .50 .15
291 Chris Richard .50 .15
292 Jared Sandberg .50 .15
293 Tike Redman .50 .15
294 Adam Dunn .75 .23
295 Josh Pressley .50 .15
296 Jose Ortiz .50 .15
297 Jason Romano .50 .15
298 Tim Redding .50 .15
299 Alex Gordon .50 .15
300 Ben Petrick .50 .15
301 Eric Munson .50 .15
302 Luis Rivas .50 .15
303 Matt Ginter .50 .15
304 Alfonso Soriano .75 .23
305 Wilfredo Rodriguez .50 .15
306 Brett Myers .50 .15
307 Scott Seabol .50 .15
308 Tony Alvarez .50 .15
309 Donzell McDonald .50 .15
310 Austin Kearns .50 .15
311 Will Ohman RC 8.00 2.40
312 Ryan Soules RC 5.00 1.50
313 Cody Ross RC 8.00 2.40
314 Bill Whitecotton RC 8.00 2.40
315 Mike Burns RC 8.00 2.40
316 Manuel Acosta RC 8.00 2.40
317 Lance Niekro RC 8.00 2.40
318 Travis Thompson RC 8.00 2.40
319 Zach Sorensen RC 8.00 2.40
320 Austin Evans RC 5.00 1.50
321 Brad Stiles RC 8.00 2.40
322 Joe Kennedy RC 10.00 3.00
323 Luke Martin RC 8.00 2.40
324 Juan Diaz RC 8.00 2.40
325 Pat Hallmark RC 5.00 1.50
326 Christian Parker RC 5.00 1.50
327 Ronny Corona RC 8.00 2.40
328 Jermaine Clark RC 5.00 1.50
329 Scott Dunn RC 8.00 2.40
330 Scott Chiasson RC 8.00 2.40
331 Greg Nash AU RC 30.00 9.00
332 Brad Cresse AU 30.00 9.00
333 John Buck AU RC 50.00 15.00
334 Freddie Bynum AU RC 30.00 9.00
335 Felix Diaz AU RC 30.00 9.00
336 Jason Belcher AU RC 30.00 9.00
337 T.Farnsworth AU RC 30.00 9.00
338 Roberto Miniel AU RC 30.00 9.00
339 Esix Snead AU RC 30.00 9.00
340 Albert Pujols AU RC 1200.00 350.00
341 Jeff Andra AU RC 30.00 9.00
342 Victor Hall AU RC 30.00 9.00
343 Pedro Liriano AU RC 30.00 9.00
344 Andy Beal AU RC 30.00 9.00
345 Bob Keppel AU RC 50.00 15.00
346 Brian Schmitt AU RC 30.00 9.00
347 Ron Davenport AU RC 200.00 60.00
348 Tony Blanco AU RC 80.00 24.00
349 Reggie Griggs AU RC 30.00 9.00
350 D. Van Dusen AU RC 30.00 9.00
351A I. Suzuki English RC 80.00 24.00
351B I. Suzuki Japan RC 80.00 24.00

2001 Bowman Chrome Gold Refractors

Randomly inserted in packs at the rate of one in 47, this 330-card set is a parallel version of the base set with a distinctive gold refractive quality. Only 99 serially numbered sets were produced. Exchange cards with a redemption deadline of June 30th, 2003 for two separate Ichiro Suzuki issues were seeded into packs. One of the features English text on the card back with 50 copies produced and the other features Japanese text on the card back with 49 copies produced. Both cards were serial-numbered together resulting in an intermingled print run of 99 copies with English cards featuring odd serial-numbering (i.e. 1/99, 3/99, 5/99 etc.) and Japanese cards featuring even serial-numbering (i.e. 2/99, 4/99, 6/99 etc.).

Nm-Mt Ex-Mt
*STARS: 8X TO 20X BASIC CARDS
*ROOKIES: 1.5X TO 4X BASIC CARDS
ICHIRO JAPAN PRINT RUN 49 #'d CARDS
ICHIRO ENGLISH ARE EVEN SERIAL #'d
ICHIRO ENGLISH ARE ODD SERIAL #'d
NNO-A Ichiro Suzuki 350.00 105.00
English/50 EXCH
NNO-B Ichiro Suzuki 350.00 105.00
Japan/49 EXCH

2001 Bowman Chrome X-Fractors

Randomly inserted in packs at the rate of one in 23, this 330-card set is a parallel version of the base set highlighted by a distinct background pattern. Exchange cards with a redemption deadline of June 30th, 2003 for two separate Ichiro Suzuki issues (English text and Japanese text) were randomly seeded into packs.

Nm-Mt Ex-Mt
*STARS: 4X TO 10X BASIC CARDS
*ROOKIES: .75X TO 2X BASIC CARDS

2001 Bowman Chrome Futures Game Relics

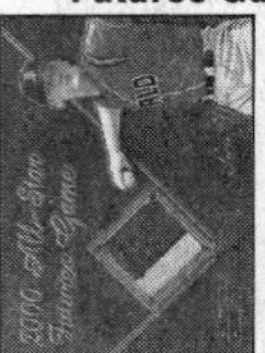

Randomly inserted in packs at the rate of one in 460, this 30-card set features color photos of players who participated in the 2000 Futures Game in Atlanta with pieces of game-worn uniform numbers and letters embedded in the cards.

Nm-Mt Ex-Mt
FGR-AE Alex Escobar 8.00 2.40
FGR-AM Aaron Myette 8.00 2.40
FGR-BB Bobby Bradley 8.00 2.40
FGR-BP Ben Petrick 8.00 2.40
FGR-BS Ben Sheets 15.00 4.50
FGR-BW Brad Wilkerson 8.00 2.40
FGR-BZ Barry Zito 15.00 4.50
FGR-CA Craig Anderson 8.00 2.40
FGR-CC Chin-Feng Chen 50.00 15.00
FGR-CG Chris George 8.00 2.40
FGR-CH Carlos Hernandez 10.00 3.00
FGR-CP Carlos Pena 8.00 2.40
FGR-CT Chin-Hui Tsao 25.00 7.50
FGR-EM Eric Munson 8.00 2.40
FGR-FL Felipe Lopez 8.00 2.40
FGR-JC Jack Cust 8.00 2.40
FGR-JH Josh Hamilton 8.00 2.40
FGR-JR Jason Romano 8.00 2.40
FGR-JZ Julio Zuleta 8.00 2.40
FGR-KA Kurt Ainsworth 8.00 2.40
FGR-MB Mike Bynum 8.00 2.40
FGR-MG Marcus Giles 10.00 3.00
FGR-NN Ntema Ndungidi 8.00 2.40
FGR-RA Ryan Anderson 8.00 2.40
FGR-RC Ramon Castro 8.00 2.40
FGR-RD Randey Dorame 8.00 2.40
FGR-SK Sun Woo Kim 8.00 2.40
FGR-TO Tomo Ohka 8.00 2.40
FGR-TW Travis Wilson 8.00 2.40
FGR-DCP Corey Patterson 10.00 3.00

2001 Bowman Chrome Rookie Reprints

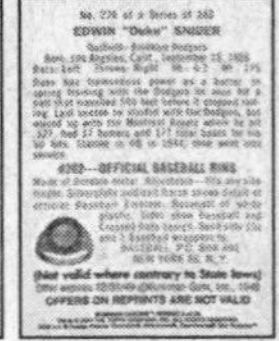

Randomly inserted in packs at the rate of one in 12, this 25-card set features reprints of classic 1948-1955 Bowman rookies printed on polished Chrome finishes.

Nm-Mt Ex-Mt
COMPLETE SET (25) 50.00 15.00
*REFRACTORS: .75X TO 2X BASIC REPRINT
REFRACTOR STATED ODDS 1:203
REF.PRINT RUN 299 SERIAL #'d SETS
1 Yogi Berra 8.00 2.40
2 Ralph Kiner 4.00 1.20
3 Stan Musial 12.00 3.60
4 Warren Spahn 4.00 1.20
5 Roy Campanella 8.00 2.40
6 Bob Lemon 4.00 1.20
7 Robin Roberts 4.00 1.20
8 Duke Snider 4.00 1.20
9 Early Wynn 4.00 1.20
10 Richie Ashburn 4.00 1.20
11 Gil Hodges 6.00 1.80
12 Hank Bauer 4.00 1.20
13 Don Newcombe 4.00 1.20
14 Al Rosen 4.00 1.20
15 Willie Mays 15.00 4.50
16 Joe Garagiola 4.00 1.20
17 Whitey Ford 4.00 1.20
18 Lew Burdette 4.00 1.20
19 Gil McDougald 4.00 1.20
20 Minnie Minoso 4.00 1.20
21 Eddie Mathews 6.00 1.80
22 Harvey Kuenn 4.00 1.20
23 Don Larsen 4.00 1.20
24 Elston Howard 4.00 1.20
25 Don Zimmer 4.00 1.20

2001 Bowman Chrome Rookie Reprints Relics

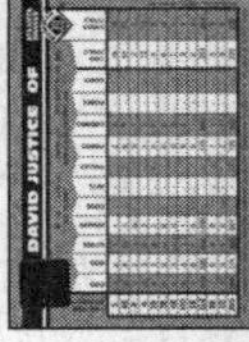

This six-card insert set features color player photos with pieces of their Rookie Season game-worn jerseys or game-used bats embedded in the cards. The insertion rate for the Mike Piazza Bat card is one in 3674 and one in 244 for the jersey cards. Three cards are Bowman Rookie card reprints and three cards are re-created "cards that never were."

Nm-Mt Ex-Mt
1 David Justice Jsy 10.00 3.00
2 Richie Sexson Jsy 10.00 3.00
3 Sean Casey Jsy 10.00 3.00
4 Mike Piazza Bat 40.00 12.00
5 Carlos Delgado Jsy 10.00 3.00
6 Chipper Jones Jsy 15.00 4.50

2002 Bowman Chrome

This 405 card set was issued in July, 2002. It was issued in four card packs with an SRP of $4 which were packed 18 packs to a box and 12 boxes to a case. The first 110 card of the set featured veteran players. The next grouping of cards (111-383) featured a mix of rookies and prospect cards. The then final grouping (384-405) featured signed rookie cards. Both So Taguchi and Kazuhisa Ishii were also printed without autographs on their cards. An exchange was inserted into packs for Jake Mauer's autographed RC. The exchange card was intended to be card number 388 in the checklist but the actual Mauer autograph mailed out to collectors was card number 324. Thus, this set actually has two cards numbered 324 (the Jake Mauer autograph and a basic-issue Ben Broussard card) and no number 388.

Nm-Mt Ex-Mt
COMP.RED SET (110) 40.00 12.00
COMP.BLUE w/o SP's (110) 40.00 12.00
COMMON RED (1-110) .50 .15
COMMON BLUE (111-383) .75 .23
COMMON AU (324B/384-405) 10.00 3.00
324B/384-405 GROUP A AUTO ODDS 1:28
403-404 GROUP B AUTO ODDS 1:1290
324B/384-405 OVERALL AUTO ODDS 1:27
1 Adam Dunn .75 .23
2 Derek Jeter 3.00 .90
3 Alex Rodriguez 2.00 .60
4 Miguel Tejada .50 .15
5 Nomar Garciaparra 2.00 .60
6 Toby Hall .50 .15

7 Brandon Duckworth .50 .15
8 Paul LoDuca .50 .15
9 Brian Giles .50 .15
10 C.C. Sabathia .50 .15
11 Curt Schilling .50 .15
12 Tsuyoshi Shinjo .50 .15
13 Ramon Hernandez .50 .15
14 Jose Cruz Jr. .50 .15
15 Albert Pujols 2.50 .75
16 Joe Mays .50 .15
17 Javy Lopez .50 .15
18 J.T. Snow .50 .15
19 David Segui .50 .15
20 Jorge Posada .75 .23
21 Doug Mientkiewicz .50 .15
22 Jerry Hairston Jr. .50 .15
23 Bernie Williams .75 .23
24 Mike Sweeney .50 .15
25 Jason Giambi .50 .15
26 Ryan Dempster .50 .15
27 Ryan Klesko .50 .15
28 Mark Quinn .50 .15
29 Jeff Kent .50 .15
30 Eric Chavez .50 .15
31 Adrian Beltre .75 .23
32 Andruw Jones .50 .15
33 Alfonso Soriano .75 .23
34 Aramis Ramirez .50 .15
35 Greg Maddux 2.00 .60
36 Andy Pettitte .75 .23
37 Bartolo Colon .50 .15
38 Ben Sheets .50 .15
39 Bobby Higginson .50 .15
40 Ivan Rodriguez 1.25 .35
41 Brad Penny .50 .15
42 Carlos Lee .50 .15
43 Damion Easley .50 .15
44 Preston Wilson .50 .15
45 Jeff Bagwell .75 .23
46 Eric Milton .50 .15
47 Rafael Palmeiro .75 .23
48 Gary Sheffield .50 .15
49 J.D. Drew .50 .15
50 Jim Thome 1.25 .35
51 Ichiro Suzuki 2.00 .60
52 Bud Smith .50 .15
53 Chan Ho Park .50 .15
54 D'Angelo Jimenez .50 .15
55 Ken Griffey Jr. 2.00 .60
56 Wade Miller .50 .15
57 Vladimir Guerrero 1.25 .35
58 Troy Glaus .50 .15
59 Shawn Green .50 .15
60 Kerry Wood 1.25 .35
61 Jack Wilson .50 .15
62 Kevin Brown .50 .15
63 Marcus Giles .50 .15
64 Pat Burrell .50 .15
65 Larry Walker .75 .23
66 Sammy Sosa 2.00 .60
67 Raul Mondesi .50 .15
68 Tim Hudson .50 .15
69 Lance Berkman .50 .15
70 Mike Mussina .75 .23
71 Barry Zito .50 .15
72 Jimmy Rollins .50 .15
73 Barry Bonds 3.00 .90
74 Craig Biggio .75 .23
75 Todd Helton .75 .23
76 Roger Clemens 2.50 .75
77 Frank Catalanotto .50 .15
78 Josh Towers .50 .15
79 Roy Oswalt .50 .15
80 Chipper Jones 1.25 .35
81 Cristian Guzman .50 .15
82 Darin Erstad .50 .15
83 Freddy Garcia .50 .15
84 Jason Tyner .50 .15
85 Carlos Delgado .50 .15
86 Jon Lieber .50 .15
87 Juan Pierre .50 .15
88 Matt Morris .50 .15
89 Phil Nevin .50 .15
90 Jim Edmonds .50 .15
91 Magglio Ordonez .50 .15
92 Mike Hampton .50 .15
93 Rafael Furcal .50 .15
94 Richie Sexson .50 .15
95 Luis Gonzalez .50 .15
96 Scott Rolen 1.25 .35
97 Tim Redding .50 .15
98 Moises Alou .50 .15
99 Jose Vidro .50 .15
100 Mike Piazza 2.00 .60
101 Pedro Martinez 1.25 .35
102 Geoff Jenkins .50 .15
103 Johnny Damon Sox 1.25 .35
104 Mike Cameron .50 .15
105 Randy Johnson 1.25 .35
106 David Eckstein .50 .15
107 Javier Vazquez .50 .15
108 Mark Mulder .50 .15
109 Robert Fick .50 .15
110 Roberto Alomar .75 .23
111 Wilson Betemit .75 .23
112 Chris Tritle SP RC 5.00 1.50
113 Ed Rogers .75 .23
114 Juan Pena .75 .23
115 Josh Beckett 1.25 .35
116 Juan Cruz .75 .23
117 Noochie Varner SP RC 5.00 1.50
118 Blake Williams .75 .23
119 Mike Rivera .75 .23
120 Hank Blalock 3.00 .90
121 Hansel Izquierdo SP RC 5.00 1.50
122 Orlando Hudson .75 .23
123 Bill Hall SP 5.00 1.50
124 Jose Reyes 2.00 .60
125 Juan Rivera .75 .23
126 Eric Valent .75 .23
127 Scotty Layfield SP RC 5.00 1.50
128 Austin Kearns 1.25 .35
129 Nic Jackson SP RC 5.00 1.50
130 Scott Chiasson .75 .23
131 Chad Qualls SP RC 5.00 1.50
132 Marcus Thames .75 .23
133 Nathan Haynes .75 .23
134 Joe Borchard .75 .23
135 Josh Hamilton .75 .23
136 Corey Patterson 1.25 .35
137 Travis Wilson .75 .23
138 Alex Escobar .75 .23
139 Alexis Gomez .75 .23
140 Nick Johnson .75 .23
141 Marlon Byrd .75 .23
142 Kory DeHaan .75 .23
143 Carlos Hernandez .75 .23
144 Sean Burroughs 1.25 .35
145 Angel Berroa .75 .23
146 Aubrey Huff 1.25 .35
147 Travis Hafner 1.25 .35
148 Brandon Berger .75 .23
149 J.R. House .75 .23
150 Dewon Brazelton .75 .23
151 Jayson Werth .75 .23
152 Larry Barnes .75 .23
153 Ruben Gotay SP RC 5.00 1.50
154 Tommy Marx SP RC 5.00 1.50
155 John Suomi SP RC 5.00 1.50
156 Javier Colina SP 5.00 1.50
157 Greg Sain SP RC 8.00 2.40
158 Robert Cosby SP RC 5.00 1.50
159 Angel Pagan SP RC 5.00 1.50
160 Ralph Santana RC 1.25 .35
161 Joe Orloski RC 1.25 .35
162 Shayne Wright SP RC 5.00 1.50
163 Jay Caligiuri SP RC 5.00 1.50
164 Greg Montalbano SP RC 5.00 1.50
165 Rich Harden SP RC 30.00 9.00
166 Rich Thompson SP RC 5.00 1.50
167 Fred Bastardo SP RC 5.00 1.50
168 Alejandro Giron SP RC 5.00 1.50
169 Jesus Medrano SP RC 5.00 1.50
170 Kevin Deaton SP RC 5.00 1.50
171 Mike Rosamond RC 1.25 .35
172 Jon Guzman SP RC 5.00 1.50
173 Gerard Oakes SP RC 5.00 1.50
174 Francisco Liriano SP RC 8.00 2.40
175 Matt Allegra SP RC 5.00 1.50
176 Mike Snyder SP RC 5.00 1.50
177 James Shanks SP RC 5.00 1.50
178 And. Hernandez SP RC 5.00 1.50
179 Dan Trumble SP RC 5.00 1.50
180 Luis DePaula SP RC 5.00 1.50
181 Randall Shelley SP RC 5.00 1.50
182 Richard Lane SP RC 5.00 1.50
183 Antwon Rollins SP RC 5.00 1.50
184 Ryan Bukvich SP RC 5.00 1.50
185 Derrick Lewis SP 5.00 1.50
186 Eric Miller SP RC 5.00 1.50
187 Justin Schuda SP RC 5.00 1.50
188 Brian West SP RC 5.00 1.50
189 Brad Wilkerson .75 .23
190 Neal Frendling SP RC 5.00 1.50
191 Jeremy Hill SP RC 5.00 1.50
192 James Barrett SP RC 5.00 1.50
193 Brett Kay SP RC 5.00 1.50
194 Ryan Mottl SP RC 5.00 1.50
195 Brad Nelson SP RC 15.00 4.50
196 Juan M. Gonzalez SP RC 5.00 1.50
197 Curtis Legendre SP RC 5.00 1.50
198 Ronald Acuna SP RC 5.00 1.50
199 Chris Flinn SP RC 5.00 1.50
200 Nick Alvarez SP RC 5.00 1.50
201 Jason Ellison SP RC 5.00 1.50
202 Blake McGinley SP RC 5.00 1.50
203 Dan Phillips SP RC 5.00 1.50
204 Demetrius Heath SP RC 5.00 1.50
205 Eric Bruntlett SP RC 5.00 1.50
206 Joe Jiannetti SP RC 5.00 1.50
207 Mike Hill SP RC 5.00 1.50
208 Ricardo Cordova SP RC 5.00 1.50
209 Mark Hamilton SP RC 5.00 1.50
210 David Mattox SP RC 5.00 1.50
211 Jose Morban SP RC 5.00 1.50
212 Scott Wiggins SP RC 5.00 1.50
213 Steve Green .75 .23
214 Brian Rogers SP 5.00 1.50
215 Kenny Baugh .75 .23
216 Anastacio Martinez SP RC 5.00 1.50
217 Richard Lewis 1.25 .35
218 Tim Kalita SP RC 5.00 1.50
219 Edwin Almonte SP RC 5.00 1.50
220 Hee Seop Choi .75 .23
221 Ty Howington .75 .23
222 Victor Alvarez SP RC 5.00 1.50
223 Morgan Ensberg 1.25 .35
224 Jeff Austin SP RC 5.00 1.50
225 Clint Weibl SP RC 5.00 1.50
226 Eric Cyr .75 .23
227 Marlyn Tisdale SP RC 5.00 1.50
228 John VanBenschoten .75 .23
229 David Krynzel .75 .23
230 Raul Chavez SP RC 5.00 1.50
231 Brett Evert .75 .23
232 Joe Rogers SP RC 5.00 1.50
233 Adam Wainwright .75 .23
234 Matt Herges RC .75 .23
235 Matt Childers SP RC 5.00 1.50
236 Nick Neugebauer .75 .23
237 Carl Crawford 1.25 .35
238 Seung Song .75 .23
239 Randy Flores .75 .23
240 Jason Lane .75 .23
241 Chase Utley 2.00 .60
242 Ben Howard SP RC 5.00 1.50
243 Eric Glaser SP RC 5.00 1.50
244 Josh Wilson RC 1.25 .35
245 Jose Valverde SP RC 8.00 2.40
246 Chris Smith .75 .23
247 Mark Prior 8.00 2.40
248 Brian Mallette SP RC 5.00 1.50
249 Chone Figgins SP RC 10.00 3.00
250 Jimmy Alvarez SP RC 5.00 1.50
251 Luis Terrero .75 .23
252 Josh Bonifay SP RC 5.00 1.50
253 Garrett Guzman SP RC 5.00 1.50
254 Jeff Verplancke SP RC 5.00 1.50
255 Nate Espy SP RC 5.00 1.50
256 Jeff Lincoln SP RC 5.00 1.50
257 Ryan Snare SP RC 5.00 1.50
258 Jose Ortiz .75 .23
259 Denny Bautista .75 .23
260 Willy Aybar .75 .23
261 Kelly Johnson .75 .23
262 Shawn Fagan .75 .23
263 Yurendell DeCaster SP RC 5.00 1.50
264 Mike Peeples SP RC 5.00 1.50
265 Joel Guzman 2.00 .60
266 Ryan Vogelsong .75 .23
267 Jorge Padilla SP RC 5.00 1.50
268 Joe Jester SP RC 5.00 1.50
269 Ryan Church SP RC 10.00 3.00
270 Mitch Jones .75 .23
271 Travis Foley SP RC 5.00 1.50
272 Bobby Crosby 5.00 1.50
273 Adrian Gonzalez 1.25 .35
274 Ronnie Merrill .75 .23
275 Joel Pineiro 1.25 .35
276 John-Ford Griffin .75 .23
277 Brian Forystek SP RC 5.00 1.50
278 Sean Douglass .75 .23
279 Manny Delcarmen SP RC 5.00 1.50
280 Jim Kavourias SP RC 5.00 1.50
281 Gabe Gross .75 .23
282 Bill Ortega .75 .23
283 Joey Hammond SP RC 5.00 1.50
284 Brett Myers .75 .23
285 Carlos Pena .75 .23
286 Ezequiel Astacio SP RC 5.00 1.50
287 Edwin Yan SP RC 5.00 1.50
288 Chris Duffy SP RC 5.00 1.50
289 Jason Kinchen .75 .23
290 Rafael Soriano .75 .23
291 Colin Young RC 5.00 1.50
292 Eric Byrnes .75 .23
293 Chris Narveson SP RC 8.00 2.40
294 John Rheinecker .75 .23
295 Mike Wilson SP RC 5.00 1.50
296 Justin Sherrod SP RC 5.00 1.50
297 Deivi Mendez .75 .23
298 Wily Mo Pena 1.25 .35
299 Brett Roneberg SP RC 5.00 1.50
300 Trey Lunsford SP RC 5.00 1.50
301 Christian Parker .75 .23
302 Brent Butler .75 .23
303 Aaron Heilman .75 .23
304 Wilkin Ruan .75 .23
305 Kenny Kelly .75 .23
306 Cody Ransom .75 .23
307 Koyie Hill SP 5.00 1.50
308 Tony Fontana SP RC 5.00 1.50
309 Mark Teixeira 2.00 .60
310 Doug Sessions SP RC 5.00 1.50
311 Josh Cisneros SP RC 5.00 1.50
312 Carlos Brackley SP RC 5.00 1.50
313 Tim Raines Jr. .75 .23
314 Ross Peeples SP RC 5.00 1.50
315 Alex Requena SP RC 5.00 1.50
316 Chin-Hui Tsao 1.25 .35
317 Tony Alvarez .75 .23
318 Craig Kuzmic SP RC 5.00 1.50
319 Pete Zamora SP RC 5.00 1.50
320 Matt Parker SP RC 5.00 1.50
321 Keith Ginter .75 .23
322 Gary Cates Jr. SP RC 5.00 1.50
323 Matt Belisle .75 .23
324A Ben Broussard .75 .23
324B Ja.Mauer AU A RC EXCH UER 10.00 3.00
Card was mistakenly numbered as 324
325 Dennis Tankersley .75 .23
326 Juan Silvestre .75 .23
327 Henry Pichardo SP RC 5.00 1.50
328 Michael Floyd SP RC 5.00 1.50
329 Clint Nageotte SP RC 12.00 3.60
330 Raymond Cabrera SP RC 5.00 1.50
331 Mauricio Lara SP RC 5.00 1.50
332 Alejandro Cadena SP RC 5.00 1.50
333 Jonny Gomes SP RC 10.00 3.00
334 Jason Bulger SP RC 5.00 1.50
335 Nate Teut .75 .23
336 David Gil SP RC 5.00 1.50
337 Joel Crump SP RC 5.00 1.50
338 Brandon Phillips .75 .23
339 Macay McBride .75 .23
340 Brandon Claussen 5.00 1.50
341 Josh Phelps .75 .23
342 Freddie Money SP RC 5.00 1.50
343 Cliff Bartosh SP RC 5.00 1.50
344 Terrance Hill SP RC 5.00 1.50
345 John Rodriguez SP RC 5.00 1.50
346 Chris Latham SP RC 5.00 1.50
347 Carlos Cabrera SP RC 5.00 1.50
348 Jose Bautista SP RC 8.00 2.40
349 Kevin Frederick SP RC 5.00 1.50
350 Jerome Williams 2.00 .60
351 Napoleon Calzado SP RC 5.00 1.50
352 Benito Baez SP 5.00 1.50
353 Xavier Nady .75 .23
354 Jason Botts SP RC 10.00 3.00
355 Steve Bechler SP RC 5.00 1.50
356 Reed Johnson SP RC 8.00 2.40
357 Mark Outlaw SP RC 5.00 1.50
358 Jake Peavy 1.25 .35
359 Josh Shaffer SP RC 5.00 1.50
360 Dan Wright SP 5.00 1.50
361 Ryan Gripp SP RC 5.00 1.50
362 Nelson Castro SP RC 5.00 1.50
363 Jason Bay SP RC 20.00 6.00
364 Franklyn German SP RC 5.00 1.50
365 Corwin Malone SP RC 5.00 1.50
366 Kelly Ramos SP RC 5.00 1.50
367 John Ennis SP RC 5.00 1.50
368 George Perez SP 5.00 1.50
369 Rene Reyes SP RC 5.00 1.50
370 Rolando Viera SP RC 5.00 1.50
371 Earl Snyder SP RC 8.00 2.40
372 Kyle Kane SP RC 5.00 1.50
373 Mario Ramos SP RC 5.00 1.50
374 Tyler Yates SP RC 8.00 2.40
375 Jason Young SP RC 5.00 1.50
376 Chris Bootcheck SP RC 5.00 1.50
377 Jesus Cota SP RC 5.00 1.50
378 Corky Miller SP 5.00 1.50
379 Matt Erickson SP RC 5.00 1.50
380 Justin Huber SP RC 10.00 3.00
381 Felix Escalona SP RC 5.00 1.50
382 Kevin Cash SP RC 5.00 1.50
383 J.J. Putz SP RC 5.00 1.50
384 Chris Snelling AU A RC 10.00 3.00
385 David Wright AU A RC 120.00 36.00
386 Brian Wolfe AU A RC 10.00 3.00
387 Justin Reid AU A RC 10.00 3.00
388 Ryan Raburn AU A RC 10.00 3.00
389 Josh Barfield AU A RC 30.00 9.00
390 Joe Mauer AU A RC 100.00 30.00
391 Bobby Jenks AU A RC 15.00 4.50
392 Rob Henkel AU A RC 10.00 3.00
393 Jimmy Gobble AU A RC 15.00 4.50
395 Jesse Foppert AU A RC 20.00 6.00
396 Gavin Floyd AU A RC 50.00 15.00
397 Nate Field AU A RC 10.00 3.00
398 Ryan Doumit AU A RC 15.00 4.50
399 Ron Calloway AU A RC 10.00 3.00
400 Taylor Buchholz AU A RC 10.00 3.00
401 Adam Roller AU A RC 10.00 3.00
402 Cole Barthel AU A RC 10.00 3.00
403 Kazuhisa Ishii SP RC 10.00 3.00
403 Kazuhisa Ishii AU B 60.00 18.00
404 So Taguchi SP RC 8.00 2.40
404 So Taguchi AU B 40.00 12.00
405 Chris Baker AU A RC 10.00 3.00

2002 Bowman Chrome Facsimile Autograph Variations

This 20 card partial parallel to the Bowman Chrome set were issued in this special version with a facsimile autograph as part of the card. These cards were not originally expected to be issued and caused some confusion in the secondary market upon the product's release.

Nm-Mt Ex-Mt
118 Taylor Buchholz
130 Chris Baker
189 Adam Roller
229 Ryan Raburn
231 Chris Snelling
233 Nate Field
237 Ron Calloway
239 Cole Barthel
244 Rob Henkel
251 Gavin Floyd
301 Jimmy Gobble
305 Brian Wolfe
313 Jesse Foppert
316 Joe Mauer
317 David Wright
323 Justin Reid
324 Jake Mauer
326 Josh Barfield
335 Bobby Jenks
338 Ryan Doumit

2002 Bowman Chrome Gold Refractors

This is a complete parallel set to the Bowman Chrome set. These cards were issued in several different tiers but it is important to note that most of these cards have a stated print run of 50 sets. The Ishii and Taguchi autograph cards have a stated print run of 10 sets.

Nm-Mt Ex-Mt
*GOLD REF RED: 5X TO 12X BASIC
*GOLD REF BLUE: 4X TO 10X BASIC
*GOLD REF BLUE SP: 2X TO 5X BASIC
*GOLD REF AU: 1.5X TO 4X BASIC
384-405 GROUP A AUTO ODDS 1:879
403-404 GROUP B AUTO ODDS 1:59,616
324B/384-405 OVERALL AUTO ODDS 1:866
1-383/403-404 PRINT 50 SERIAL #'d SETS
324B/384-405 GROUP A AU PRINT 50 SETS
403-404 GROUP B AU PRINT RUN 10 SETS
403 Kazuhisa Ishii 50.00 15.00
403 Kazuhisa Ishii AU B
404 So Taguchi 40.00 12.00
404 So Taguchi AU B

2002 Bowman Chrome Refractors

This is a complete parallel set to the Bowman Chrome set. These cards were issued in several different tiers but it is important to note that most of these cards have a stated print run of 500 sets. The Ishii and Taguchi autograph cards have a stated print run of 100 sets.

Nm-Mt Ex-Mt
*REF RED: 1.5X TO 4X BASIC
*REF BLUE: 1X TO 2.5X BASIC
*REF BLUE SP: .6X TO 1.5X BASIC
*REF AU: .5X TO 1.2X BASIC AU'S
324B/384-405 GROUP A AUTO ODDS 1:88
403-404 GROUP B AUTO ODDS 1:4392
324B/384-405 OVERALL AUTO ODDS 1:86
1-383/403-404 PRINT 500 SERIAL #'d SETS
324B/384-405 GROUP A PRINT RUN 500 SETS
403-404 GROUP B PRINT RUN 100 SETS
403 Kazuhisa Ishii 15.00 4.50
403 Kazuhisa Ishii AU B 100.00 30.00
404 So Taguchi 12.00 3.60
404 So Taguchi AU B 60.00 18.00

2002 Bowman Chrome X-Fractors

This is a complete parallel set to the Bowman Chrome set. These cards were issued in several different tiers but it is important to note that most of these cards have a stated print run of 250 sets. The Ishii and Taguchi autograph cards have a stated print run of 50 sets.

Nm-Mt Ex-Mt
*XFRACT RED: 3X TO 8X BASIC
*XFRACT BLUE: 1.5X TO 4X BASIC
*XFRACT BLUE SP: .75X TO 2X BASIC
*XFRACT AU: .75X TO 2X BASIC
324B/384-405 GROUP A AUTO ODDS 1:176
403-404 GROUP B AUTO ODDS 1:9072
324B/384-405 OVERALL AUTO ODDS 1:173
1-383/403-404 PRINT 250 SERIAL #'d SETS
324B/384-405 GROUP A PRINT RUN 250 SETS
403-404 GROUP B PRINT RUN 50 SETS
403 Kazuhisa Ishii 20.00 6.00
403 Kazuhisa Ishii AU B 120.00 36.00
404 So Taguchi 15.00 4.50
404 So Taguchi AU B 80.00 24.00

2002 Bowman Chrome Reprints

Isssued at stated odds of one in six, these 20 cards feature reprint cards of players who have made their debut since Bowman was reintroduced as a major brand in 1989.

Nm-Mt Ex-Mt
COMPLETE SET (20) 25.00 7.50
*BLACK REF: .6X TO 1.5X BASIC REPRINTS
BLACK REFRACTOR ODDS 1:18
BCR-AJ Andruw Jones 95 2.00 .60
BCR-BC Bartolo Colon 95 2.00 .60
BCR-BW Bernie Williams 90 2.00 .60
BCR-CD Carlos Delgado 92 2.00 .60
BCR-CJ Chipper Jones 91 2.50 .75
BCR-DJ Derek Jeter 93 8.00 2.40
BCR-FT Frank Thomas 90 2.50 .75
BCR-GS Gary Sheffield 89 2.00 .60
BCR-IR Ivan Rodriguez 91 2.50 .75
BCR-JB Jeff Bagwell 91 2.00 .60
BCR-JG Juan Gonzalez 90 2.00 .60
BCR-JK Jason Kendall 93 2.00 .60
BCR-JP Jorge Posada 94 2.00 .60
BCR-KG Ken Griffey Jr. 89 5.00 1.50
BCR-LG Luis Gonzalez 91 2.00 .60
BCR-LW Larry Walker 90 2.00 .60
BCR-MP Mike Piazza 92 5.00 1.50
BCR-MS Mike Sweeney 96 2.00 .60
BCR-SR Scott Rolen 95 2.50 .75
BCR-VG Vladimir Guerrero 95 2.50 .75

2002 Bowman Chrome Draft

Inserted one per pack, this is a parallel to the Bowman Draft Pick set. Each of these cards uses the Topps "Chrome" technology and these cards were inserted two per bowman draft pack. Cards numbered 166 through 175 are not parallels to the regular Bowman cards and they feature autographs of the players. Those ten cards were issued at a stated rate of one in 45 Bowman Draft packs.

Nm-Mt Ex-Mt
COMPLETE SET (175) 300.00 90.00
COMP.SET w/o AU's (165) 175.00 52.50
COMMON CARD (1-165) .40 .12
COMMON CARD (166-175) 10.00 3.00
1 Clint Everts RC 5.00 1.50
2 Fred Lewis RC 1.00 .30
3 Jon Broxton RC 2.50 .75
4 Jason Anderson RC 1.00 .30
5 Mike Eusebio RC 1.00 .30
6 Zack Greinke RC 10.00 3.00
7 Joe Blanton RC 5.00 1.50
8 Sergio Santos RC 6.00 1.80
9 Jason Cooper RC 1.50 .45
10 Delwyn Young RC 4.00 1.20
11 Jeremy Hermida RC 6.00 1.80
12 Dan Ortmeier RC 2.50 .75
13 Kevin Jepsen RC 3.00 .90
14 Russ Adams RC 3.00 .90
15 Mike Nixon RC 1.00 .30
16 Nick Swisher RC 8.00 2.40
17 Cole Hamels RC 12.00 3.60
18 Brian Dopirak RC 10.00 3.00
19 James Loney RC 6.00 1.80
20 Denard Span RC 1.00 .30
21 Billy Petrick RC 1.00 .30
22 Jared Doyle RC 1.00 .30
23 Jeff Francoeur RC 15.00 4.50
24 Nick Bourgeois RC 1.00 .30
25 Matt Cain RC 8.00 2.40
26 John McCurdy RC 1.00 .30
27 Mark Kiger RC 1.00 .30
28 Bill Murphy RC 1.50 .45
29 Matt Craig RC 1.50 .45
30 Mike Megrew RC 3.00 .90
31 Ben Crockett RC 1.00 .30
32 Luke Hagerty RC 1.00 .30
33 Matt Whitney RC 1.50 .45
34 Dan Meyer RC 3.00 .90
35 Jeremy Brown RC 2.50 .75
36 Doug Johnson RC 1.00 .30
37 Steve Obenchain RC 1.00 .30
38 Matt Clanton RC 1.00 .30
39 Mark Teahen RC 5.00 1.50
40 Tom Carrow RC 1.00 .30
41 Micah Schilling RC 1.00 .30
42 Blair Johnson RC 1.00 .30
43 Jason Pridie RC 3.00 .90
44 Joey Votto RC 4.00 1.20
45 Taber Lee RC 1.00 .30
46 Adam Peterson RC 1.00 .30
47 Adam Donachie RC 1.00 .30
48 Josh Murray RC 1.00 .30
49 Brent Clevlen RC 3.00 .90
50 Chad Pleiness RC 1.00 .30
51 Zach Hammes RC 1.00 .30
52 Chris Snyder RC 2.50 .75
53 Chris Smith RC 1.00 .30

54 Justin Maureau RC 1.00 .30
55 David Bush RC 3.00 .90
56 Tim Gilhooly RC 1.00 .30
57 Blair Barbier RC 1.00 .30
58 Zach Segovia RC 1.50 .45
59 Jeremy Reed RC 10.00 3.00
60 Matt Pender RC 1.00 .30
61 Eric Thomas RC 1.00 .30
62 Justin Jones RC 4.00 1.20
63 Brian Slocum RC 1.00 .30
64 Larry Broadway RC 3.00 .90
65 Bo Flowers RC 1.00 .30
66 Scott White RC 1.00 .30
67 Steve Stanley RC 1.00 .30
68 Alex Merricks RC 1.00 .30
69 Josh Womack RC 1.00 .30
70 Dave Jensen RC 1.00 .30
71 Curtis Granderson RC 5.00 1.50
72 Pat Osborn RC 1.00 .30
73 Nic Carter RC 1.00 .30
74 Mitch Talbot RC 1.00 .30
75 Don Murphy RC 1.00 .30
76 Val Majewski RC 4.00 1.20
77 Javy Rodriguez RC 1.00 .30
78 Fernando Pacheco RC 1.00 .30
79 Steve Russell RC 1.00 .30
80 Jon Slack RC 1.00 .30
81 John Baker RC 1.00 .30
82 Aaron Coonrod RC 1.00 .30
83 Josh Johnson RC 1.00 .30
84 Jake Blalock RC 5.00 1.50
85 Alex Hart RC 2.50 .75
86 Wes Bankston RC 4.00 1.20
87 Josh Rupe RC 1.00 .30
88 Dan Cevette RC 1.00 .30
89 Kiel Fisher RC 1.50 .45
90 Alan Rick RC 1.00 .30
91 Charlie Morton RC 1.00 .30
92 Chad Spann RC 2.50 .75
93 Kyle Boyer RC 1.00 .30
94 Bob Malek RC 1.00 .30
95 Ryan Rodriguez RC 1.00 .30
96 Jordan Renz RC 1.00 .30
97 Randy Frye RC 1.00 .30
98 Rich Hill RC 1.00 .30
99 B.J. Upton RC 25.00 7.50
100 Dan Christensen RC 1.00 .30
101 Casey Kotchman RC 10.00 3.00
102 Eric Good RC 1.00 .30
103 Mike Fontenot RC 1.00 .30
104 John Webb RC 1.00 .30
105 Jason Dubois RC 4.00 1.20
106 Ryan Kibler RC 1.00 .30
107 Jhohny Peralta RC 4.00 1.20
108 Kirk Saarloos RC 1.00 .30
109 Rhett Parrott RC 1.00 .30
110 Jason Grove RC 1.00 .30
111 Colt Griffin RC 1.50 .45
112 Dallas McPherson RC 20.00 6.00
113 Oliver Perez RC 10.00 3.00
114 Marshall McDougall RC 1.00 .30
115 Mike Wood RC 2.00 .60
116 Scott Hairston RC 5.00 1.50
117 Jason Simontacchi RC 1.00 .30
118 Taggert Bozied RC 2.50 .75
119 Shelley Duncan RC 1.00 .30
120 Dontrelle Willis RC 10.00 3.00
121 Sean Burnett .40 .12
122 Aaron Cook .60 .18
123 Brett Evert .40 .12
124 Jimmy Journell .40 .12
125 Brett Myers .40 .12
126 Brad Baker .40 .12
127 Billy Traber RC 2.50 .75
128 Adam Wainwright .40 .12
129 Jason Young 1.00 .30
130 John Buck .40 .12
131 Kevin Cash 1.00 .30
132 Jason Stokes RC 10.00 3.00
133 Drew Henson .60 .18
134 Chad Tracy RC 5.00 1.50
135 Orlando Hudson .40 .12
136 Brandon Phillips .40 .12
137 Joe Borchard .40 .12
138 Marlon Byrd .40 .12
139 Carl Crawford .60 .18
140 Michael Restovich .40 .12
141 Corey Hart RC 4.00 1.20
142 Edwin Almonte .60 .18
143 Francis Beltran RC 1.00 .30
144 Jorge De La Rosa RC 1.00 .30
145 Gerardo Garcia RC 1.00 .30
146 Franklyn German RC 1.00 .30
147 Francisco Liriano .60 .18
148 Francisco Rodriguez .60 .18
149 Ricardo Rodriguez .40 .12
150 Seung Song .40 .12
151 John Stephens .40 .12
152 Justin Huber RC 2.50 .75
153 Victor Martinez 1.50 .45
154 Hee Seop Choi .40 .12
155 Justin Morneau 1.50 .45
156 Miguel Cabrera 2.50 .75
157 Victor Diaz RC 5.00 1.50
158 Jose Reyes 1.00 .30
159 Omar Infante .40 .12
160 Angel Berroa .40 .12
161 Tony Alvarez .40 .12
162 Shin Soo Choo RC 4.00 1.20
163 Wily Mo Pena .60 .18
164 Andres Torres .40 .12
165 Jose Lopez RC 10.00 3.00
166 Scott Moore AU RC 15.00 4.50
167 Chris Gruler AU RC 15.00 4.50
168 Joe Saunders AU RC 10.00 3.00
169 Jeff Francis AU RC 40.00 12.00
170 Royce Ring AU RC 15.00 4.50
171 Greg Miller AU RC 30.00 9.00
172 Brandon Weeden AU RC 10.00 3.00
173 Drew Meyer AU RC 10.00 3.00
174 Khalil Greene AU RC 80.00 24.00
175 Mark Schramek AU RC 15.00 4.50

2002 Bowman Chrome Draft Gold Refractors

Issued at a stated rate of one in 67 Bowman Draft packs, these cards are gold refractors of the Bowman Chrome Draft set. Those cards have a stated print run of 50 serial numbered sets. Cards numbered 166 through 175, which are autographed were issued at a stated rate of one in 1546 Bowman Draft cards and there is no pricing provided on these cards due to market scarcity.

Nm-Mt Ex-Mt
*GOLD REF 1-165: 8X TO 20X BASIC
*GOLD REF RC 1-165: 7.5X TO 15X BASIC
1-165 ODDS 1:67 BOWMAN DRAFT...
166-175 AU ODDS 1:1546 BOWMAN DRAFT
1-165 PRINT RUN 50 SERIAL #'d SETS
166-175 ARE NOT SERIAL-NUMBERED
166-175 NO PRICING DUE TO SCARCITY

2002 Bowman Chrome Draft Refractors

Issued at a stated rate of one in 11 Bowman Draft packs, these cards are refractor parallels of the Bowman Chrome Draft set. Those cards have a stated print run of 300 serial numbered sets. Cards numbered 166 through 175, which are autographed were issued at a stated rate of one in 154 Bowman Draft packs.

Nm-Mt Ex-Mt
*REFRACTOR 1-165: 2.5X TO 6X BASIC
*REFRACTOR RC 1-165: 2X TO 5X BASIC
*REFRACTOR 166-175: .5X TO 1.2X BASIC

2002 Bowman Chrome Draft X-Fractors

Issued at a stated rate of one in 22 Bowman Draft packs, these cards are x-fractor parallels of the Bowman Chrome Draft set. Those cards have a stated print run of 150 serial numbered sets. Cards numbered 166 through 175, which are autographed were issued at a stated rate of one in 309 Bowman Draft packs.

Nm-Mt Ex-Mt
*X-FRACTOR 1-165: 3X TO 8X BASIC
*X-FRACTOR RC 1-165: 3X TO 6X BASIC
*X-FRACTOR 166-175: .75X TO 1.5X BASIC

2003 Bowman Chrome

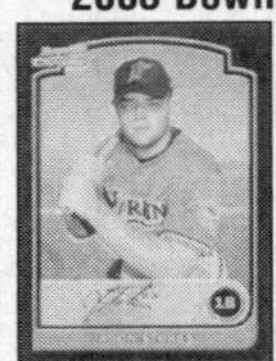

This 351 card set was released in July, 2003. The set was issued in four-card packs with an $4 SRP which came 18 to a box and 12 boxes to a case. Cards numbered 1 through 165 feature veteran players while cards 166 through 330 feature rookie players. Cards numbered 331 through 350 feature autograph cards of Rookie Cards. Each of those cards, with the exception of Jose Contreras (number 332) was issued to a stated print run of 1700 sets and were seeded at a stated rate of one in 26. The Contreras card was issued to a stated print run of 340 cards and was issued at a stated rate of one in 3,3351 packs. The final card of the set features baseball legend Willie Mays. That card was issued as a box-loader and an authentic autograph on that card was also randomly inserted into packs. The autograph card was inserted at a stated rate of one in 384 box loader packs and was issued to a stated print run of 150 sets. Bryan Bullington did not return his cards in time for pack out and those cards could be redeemed until July 31, 2005.

MINT NRMT
COMPLETE SET (351) 500.00 220.00
COMP.SET w/o AU's (331) 150.00 70.00
COMMON CARD (1-165) .50 .23
COMMON CARD (166-330) .50 .23
COMMON RC (156-330) 1.00 .45
COMP.SET w/o AU'S INCLUDES 351 MAYS
MAYS AU IS NOT PART OF 351-CARD SET
1 Garret Anderson .50 .23
2 Derek Jeter 3.00 1.35
3 Gary Sheffield .50 .23
4 Matt Morris .50 .23
5 Derek Lowe .50 .23
6 Andy Van Hekken .50 .23
7 Sammy Sosa 2.00 .90
8 Ken Griffey Jr. 2.00 .90
9 Omar Vizquel .75 .35
10 Jorge Posada .75 .35
11 Lance Berkman .50 .23
12 Mike Sweeney .50 .23
13 Adrian Beltre .75 .35
14 Richie Sexson .50 .23
15 A.J. Pierzynski .50 .23
16 Bartolo Colon .50 .23
17 Mike Mussina .75 .35
18 Paul Byrd .50 .23
19 Bobby Abreu .50 .23
20 Miguel Tejada .50 .23
21 Aramis Ramirez .50 .23
22 Edgardo Alfonzo .50 .23
23 Edgar Martinez .75 .35
24 Albert Pujols 2.50 1.10
25 Carl Crawford .50 .23
26 Eric Hinske .50 .23
27 Tim Salmon .75 .35
28 Luis Gonzalez .50 .23
29 Jay Gibbons .50 .23
30 John Smoltz .50 .23
31 Tim Wakefield .50 .23
32 Mark Prior 1.25 .55
33 Magglio Ordonez .50 .23
34 Adam Dunn .75 .35
35 Larry Walker .75 .35
36 Luis Castillo .50 .23
37 Wade Miller .50 .23
38 Carlos Beltran .75 .35
39 Odalis Perez .50 .23
40 Alex Sanchez .50 .23
41 Torii Hunter .50 .23
42 Cliff Floyd .50 .23
43 Andy Pettitte .75 .35
44 Francisco Rodriguez .50 .23
45 Eric Chavez .50 .23
46 Kevin Millwood .50 .23
47 Dennis Tankersley .50 .23
48 Hideo Nomo 1.25 .55
49 Freddy Garcia .50 .23
50 Randy Johnson 1.25 .55
51 Aubrey Huff .50 .23
52 Carlos Delgado .50 .23
53 Troy Glaus .50 .23
54 Junior Spivey .50 .23
55 Mike Hampton .50 .23
56 Sidney Ponson .50 .23
57 Aaron Boone .50 .23
58 Kerry Wood 1.25 .55
59 Willie Harris .50 .23
60 Nomar Garciaparra 2.00 .90
61 Todd Helton .75 .35
62 Mike Lowell .50 .23
63 Roy Oswalt .50 .23
64 Raul Ibanez .50 .23
65 Brian Jordan .50 .23
66 Geoff Jenkins .50 .23
67 Jermaine Dye .50 .23
68 Tom Glavine .75 .35
69 Bernie Williams .75 .35
70 Vladimir Guerrero 1.25 .55
71 Mark Mulder .50 .23
72 Jimmy Rollins .50 .23
73 Oliver Perez .50 .23
74 Rich Aurilia .50 .23
75 Joel Pineiro .50 .23
76 J.D. Drew .50 .23
77 Ivan Rodriguez 1.25 .55
78 Josh Phelps .50 .23
79 Darin Erstad .50 .23
80 Curt Schilling .50 .23
81 Paul Lo Duca .50 .23
82 Marty Cordova .50 .23
83 Manny Ramirez .75 .35
84 Bobby Hill .50 .23
85 Paul Konerko .50 .23
86 Austin Kearns .50 .23
87 Jason Jennings .50 .23
88 Brad Penny .50 .23
89 Jeff Bagwell .75 .35
90 Shawn Green .50 .23
91 Jason Schmidt .50 .23
92 Doug Mientkiewicz .50 .23
93 Jose Vidro .50 .23
94 Bret Boone .50 .23
95 Jason Giambi .50 .23
96 Barry Zito .50 .23
97 Roy Halladay .50 .23
98 Pat Burrell .50 .23
99 Sean Burroughs .50 .23
100 Barry Bonds 3.00 1.35
101 Kazuhiro Sasaki .50 .23
102 Fernando Vina .50 .23
103 Chan Ho Park .50 .23
104 Andruw Jones .50 .23
105 Adam Kennedy .50 .23
106 Shea Hillenbrand .50 .23
107 Greg Maddux 2.00 .90
108 Jim Edmonds .50 .23
109 Pedro Martinez 1.25 .55
110 Moises Alou .50 .23
111 Jeff Weaver .50 .23
112 C.C. Sabathia .50 .23
113 Robert Fick .50 .23
114 A.J. Burnett .50 .23
115 Jeff Kent .50 .23
116 Kevin Brown .50 .23
117 Rafael Furcal .50 .23
118 Cristian Guzman .50 .23
119 Brad Wilkerson .50 .23
120 Mike Piazza 2.00 .90
121 Alfonso Soriano .75 .35
122 Mark Ellis .50 .23
123 Vicente Padilla .50 .23
124 Eric Gagne 1.25 .55
125 Ryan Klesko .50 .23
126 Ichiro Suzuki 2.00 .90
127 Tony Batista .50 .23
128 Roberto Alomar .75 .35
129 Alex Rodriguez 2.00 .90
130 Jim Thome 1.25 .55
131 Jarrod Washburn .50 .23
132 Orlando Hudson .50 .23
133 Chipper Jones 1.25 .55
134 Rodrigo Lopez .50 .23
135 Johnny Damon 1.25 .55
136 Matt Clement .50 .23
137 Frank Thomas 1.25 .55
138 Ellis Burks .50 .23
139 Carlos Pena .50 .23
140 Josh Beckett .50 .23
141 Joe Randa .50 .23
142 Brian Giles .50 .23
143 Kazuhisa Ishii .50 .23
144 Corey Koskie .50 .23
145 Orlando Cabrera .50 .23
146 Mark Buehrle .50 .23
147 Roger Clemens 2.50 1.10
148 Tim Hudson .50 .23
149 Randy Wolf .50 .23
150 Josh Fogg .50 .23
151 Phil Nevin .50 .23
152 John Olerud .50 .23
153 Scott Rolen 1.25 .55
154 Joe Kennedy .50 .23
155 Rafael Palmeiro .75 .35
156 Chad Hutchinson .50 .23
157 Quincy Carter XRC 2.00 .90
158 Hee Seop Choi .50 .23
159 Joe Borchard .50 .23
160 Brandon Phillips .50 .23
161 Wily Mo Pena .50 .23
162 Victor Martinez .75 .35
163 Jason Stokes .75 .35
164 Ken Harvey .50 .23
165 Juan Rivera .50 .23
166 Joe Valentine RC 1.50 .70
167 Dan Haren RC 3.00 1.35
168 Michel Hernandez RC 1.50 .70
169 Eider Torres RC 1.50 .70
170 Chris De La Cruz RC 1.50 .70
171 Ramon Nivar-Martinez RC 3.00 1.35
172 Mike Adams RC 1.50 .70
173 Justin Arneson RC 1.50 .70
174 Jamie Athas RC 1.50 .70
175 Dwaine Bacon RC 1.50 .70
176 Clint Barmes RC 2.00 .90
177 B.J. Barns RC 1.50 .70
178 Tyler Johnson RC 1.50 .70
179 Brandon Webb RC 4.00 1.80
180 T.J. Bohn RC 1.50 .70
181 Ozzie Chavez RC 1.50 .70
182 Brandon Bowe RC 1.50 .70
183 Craig Brazell RC 2.00 .90
184 Dusty Brown RC 1.50 .70
185 Brian Bruney RC 2.00 .90
186 Greg Bruso RC 1.50 .70
187 Jaime Bubela RC 1.50 .70
188 Matt Diaz RC 2.00 .90
189 Brian Burgamy RC 1.50 .70
190 Eny Cabreja RC 1.50 .70
191 Daniel Cabrera RC 4.00 1.80
192 Ryan Cameron RC 1.50 .70
193 Lance Caraccioli RC 1.50 .70
194 David Cash RC 1.50 .70
195 Bernie Castro RC 1.50 .70
196 Ismael Castro RC 2.00 .90
197 Cory Doyne RC 1.50 .70
198 Jeff Clark RC 1.50 .70
199 Chris Colton RC 1.50 .70
200 Dexter Cooper RC 1.50 .70
201 Callix Crabbe RC 2.00 .90
202 Chien-Ming Wang RC 4.00 1.80
203 Eric Crozier RC 2.00 .90
204 Nook Logan RC 1.50 .70
205 David DeJesus RC 2.00 .90
206 Matt DeMarco RC 1.50 .70
207 Chris Duncan RC 1.50 .70
208 Eric Eckenstahler .50 .23
209 Willie Eyre RC 1.50 .70
210 Evel Bastida-Martinez RC 1.50 .70
211 Chris Fallon RC 1.50 .70
212 Mike Flannery RC 1.50 .70
213 Mike O'Keefe RC 1.50 .70
214 Lew Ford RC 5.00 2.20
215 Kason Gabbard RC 1.50 .70
216 Mike Gallo RC 1.50 .70
217 Jairo Garcia RC 3.00 1.35
218 Angel Garcia RC 2.00 .90
219 Michael Garciaparra RC 3.00 1.35
220 Jeremy Griffiths RC 2.00 .90
221 Dusty Gomon RC 2.00 .90
222 Bryan Grace RC 1.50 .70
223 Tyson Graham RC 1.50 .70
224 Henry Guerrero RC 1.50 .70
225 Franklin Gutierrez RC 8.00 3.60
226 Carlos Guzman RC 2.00 .90
227 Matthew Hagen RC 3.00 1.35
228 Josh Hall RC 2.00 .90
229 Rob Hammock RC 2.00 .90
230 Brendan Harris RC 2.00 .90
231 Gary Harris RC 1.50 .70
232 Clay Hensley RC 1.50 .70
233 Michael Hinckley RC 4.00 1.80
234 Luis Hodge RC 1.50 .70
235 Donnie Hood RC 2.00 .90
236 Matt Hensley RC 1.50 .70
237 Edwin Jackson RC 10.00 4.50
238 Ardley Jansen RC 2.00 .90
239 Ferenc Jongejan RC 1.50 .70
240 Matt Kata RC 3.00 1.35
241 Kazuhiro Takeoka RC 1.50 .70
242 Charlie Manning RC 1.50 .70
243 Il Kim RC 1.50 .70
244 Brennan King RC 1.50 .70
245 Chris Kroski RC 1.50 .70
246 David Martinez RC 1.50 .70
247 Pete LaForest RC 2.00 .90
248 Wil Ledezma RC 2.00 .90
249 Jeremy Bonderman RC 3.00 1.35
250 Gonzalo Lopez RC 1.50 .70
251 Brian Luderer RC 1.50 .70
252 Ruddy Lugo RC 1.50 .70
253 Wayne Lydon RC 1.50 .70
254 Mark Malaska RC 1.50 .70
255 Andy Marte RC 10.00 4.50
256 Tyler Martin RC 1.50 .70
257 Branden Florence RC 1.50 .70
258 Aneudis Mateo RC 1.50 .70
259 Derell McCall RC 1.50 .70
260 Elizardo Ramirez RC 3.00 1.35
261 Mike McNutt RC 1.50 .70
262 Jacobo Meque RC 1.50 .70
263 Derek Michaelis RC 1.50 .70
264 Aaron Miles RC 4.00 1.80
265 Jose Morales RC 1.50 .70
266 Dustin Moseley RC 2.00 .90
267 Adrian Myers RC 1.50 .70
268 Dan Neil RC 1.50 .70
269 Jon Nelson RC 2.00 .90
270 Mike Neu RC 1.50 .70
271 Leigh Neuage RC 1.50 .70
272 Wes O'Brien RC 1.50 .70
273 Trent Oeltjen RC 2.00 .90
274 Tim Olson RC 2.00 .90
275 David Pahucki RC 1.50 .70
276 Nathan Panther RC 3.00 1.35
277 Arnie Munoz RC 1.50 .70
278 Dave Pember RC 1.50 .70
279 Jason Perry RC 3.00 1.35
280 Matthew Peterson RC 1.50 .70
281 Greg Aquino RC 1.50 .70
282 Jorge Piedra RC 2.00 .90
283 Simon Pond RC 3.00 1.35
284 Aaron Rakers RC 1.50 .70
285 Felix Sanchez RC 1.50 .70
286 Manuel Ramirez RC 2.00 .90
287 Kevin Randel RC 1.50 .70
288 Kelly Shoppach RC 4.00 1.80
289 Prentice Redman RC 1.50 .70
290 Eric Reed RC 3.00 1.35
291 Wilton Reynolds RC 2.00 .90
292 Eric Riggs RC 2.00 .90
293 Carlos Rijo RC 1.50 .70
294 Tyler Adamczyk RC 1.50 .70
295 Jon-Mark Sprowl RC 3.00 1.35
296 Arturo Rivas RC 1.50 .70
297 Kyle Roat RC 1.50 .70
298 Bubba Nelson RC .75 .35
299 Levi Robinson RC 1.50 .70
300 Ray Sadler RC 1.50 .70
301 Rylan Reed RC 1.50 .70
302 Jon Schuerholz RC 1.50 .70
303 Nobuaki Yoshida RC 1.50 .70
304 Brian Shackelford RC 1.50 .70
305 Bill Simon RC 1.50 .70
306 Haj Turay RC 2.00 .90
307 Sean Smith RC 2.00 .90
308 Ryan Spataro RC 1.50 .70
309 Jemel Spearman RC 1.50 .70
310 Keith Stamler RC 1.50 .70
311 Luke Steidlmayer RC 1.50 .70
312 Adam Stern RC 1.50 .70
313 Jay Sitzman RC 1.50 .70
314 Mike Wodnicki RC 1.50 .70
315 Terry Tiffee RC 3.00 1.35
316 Nick Trzesniak RC 1.50 .70
317 Denny Tussen RC 1.50 .70
318 Scott Tyler RC 2.00 .90
319 Shane Victorino RC 1.50 .70
320 Doug Waechter RC 2.00 .90
321 Brandon Watson RC 1.50 .70
322 Todd Wellemeyer RC 2.00 .90
323 Eli Whiteside RC 1.50 .70
324 Josh Willingham RC 2.00 .90
325 Travis Wong RC 2.00 .90
326 Brian Wright RC 1.50 .70
327 Felix Pie RC 8.00 3.60
328 Andy Sisco RC 4.00 1.80
329 Dustin Yount RC 2.00 .90
330 Andrew Dominique RC 1.50 .70
331 Brian McCann AU A RC 20.00 9.00
332 Jose Contreras AU B RC 200.00 90.00
333 Corey Shafer AU A RC 20.00 9.00
334 Hanley Ramirez AU A RC 50.00 22.00
335 Ryan Shealy AU A RC 20.00 9.00
336 Kevin Youkilis AU A RC 40.00 18.00
337 Jason Kubel AU A RC 50.00 22.00
338 Aron Weston AU A RC 15.00 6.75
338B Rajai Davis AU A ERR
339 J.D. Durbin AU A RC 20.00 9.00
340 G. Schneidmiller AU A RC 15.00 6.75
341 Travis Ishikawa AU A RC 15.00 6.75
342 Ben Francisco AU A RC 20.00 9.00
343 Bobby Basham AU A RC 20.00 9.00
344 Joey Gomes AU A RC 15.00 6.75
345 Beau Kemp AU A RC 15.00 6.75
346 T.Story-Harden AU A RC 15.00 6.75
347 Daryl Clark AU A RC 20.00 9.00
348 B.Bullington AU A RC EXCH 25.00 11.00
349 Rajai Davis AU A RC 20.00 9.00
350 Darrell Rasner AU A RC 15.00 6.75
351 Willie Mays 2.00 .90
351AU Willie Mays AU 300.00 135.00

2003 Bowman Chrome Blue Refractors

These cards were issued at a stated rate of one per box loader pack. Each of those packs contained an exchange card for an uncirculated card of which had to be redeemed from ThePit.Com by November, 30, 2005.

MINT NRMT
*BLUE: 1.5X TO 4X BASIC
NNO Exchange Card 8.00 3.60

2003 Bowman Chrome Gold Refractors

This is a full parallel to the 2003 Bowman Chrome set. Cards 1-330 were issued at a stated rate of one per box loader pack. The cards 331-350 were inserted at much tougher odds. Cards 331-350 (except for number 332) were issued at a stated rate of one in 1202 hobby packs and were issued to a stated print run of 50 sets. Card number 332 was issued at a stated rate of one in 177,606 hobby packs and was issued to a stated rate of 10 sets. The Willie Mays card (number 351) was issued at a stated rate of one in 116 box loader packs. There were also cards inserted for a complete set of these randomly inserted in packs at a stated rate of one in 78,936 packs. That exchange card was issued to a stated print run on 10 sets and those cards could be redeemed until November 30, 2005.

MINT NRMT
*GOLD REF 1-155: 3X TO 8X BASIC
*GOLD REF 156-330: 3X TO 8X BASIC
*GOLD REF RC'S 156-330: 2X TO 5X BASIC
1-330 ODDS ONE PER BOX LOADER PACK
1-330 PRINT RUN 170 SERIAL #'d SETS
*GOLD REF AU A 331/333-350: 1.5X TO 3X
NNO Set Exchange Card

2003 Bowman Chrome Refractors

This is a complete parallel to the regular Bowman Chrome set. Cards numbered 1-330 were issued at a stated rate of one in four hobby packs. Cards numbers 331-350 (with the exception of number 332) were issued at a stated rate of one in 92 packs. Those cards were issued to a stated print run of 500 sets. Card number 332 was issued at a stated rate of one in 11,479 packs and was issued to a stated print run of 100 sets. Card number 351 featuring Willie Mays was issued at a stated rate of one in 12 box loader packs.

MINT NRMT
*REF 1-155: 1.5X TO 4X BASIC
*REF 156-330: 2X TO 5X BASIC
*REF 156-330 RC'S: 1X TO 2.5X BASIC
*REF AU A 331/333-350: .5X TO 1.2X BASIC
*REF.MAYS: 2X TO 5X BASIC

2003 Bowman Chrome X-Fractors

This is a complete parallel to the basic Bowman Chrome set. Cards numbered 1-330 were issued at a stated rate of one in nine hobby packs. Cards numbered 331-350 (with the exception of number 332) were issued at a stated rate of one in 199 hobby packs and were issued to a stated print run of 250 sets. The Jose Contreras Card (number 332) was issued at a stated rate of one in 22,959 sets and was issued to a stated print run of 50 sets. The Willie Mays card (number 351) was issued at a stated rate of one in 58 box loader packs.

MINT NRMT
*X-FR 1-155: 2.5X TO 6X BASIC
*X-FR 156-330: 2.5X TO 6X BASIC
*X-FR RC'S 156-330: 1.25X TO 3X BASIC
*X-FR AU A 331/333-350: .6X TO 1.5X BASIC
*X-FR MAYS: 4X TO 10X BASIC

2003 Bowman Chrome Draft

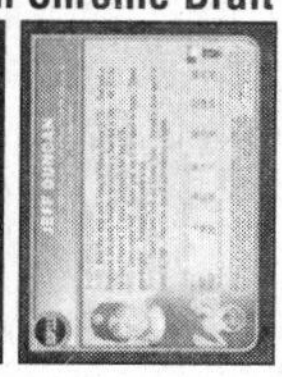

This 176-card set was inserted as part of the 2003 Bowman Draft Packs. Each pack contained 2 Bowman Chrome Cards numbered between 1-165. In addition, cards numbered 166 through 176 were inserted at a stated rate of one in 41 packs. Each of those cards can be easily identifed as they were autographed. Please note that these cards were issued as a mix of live and exchange cards with a deadline for redeeming the exchange cards of November 30, 2005.

MINT NRMT
COMPLETE SET (176) 350.00 160.00
COMP.SET w/o AU's (165) 100.00 45.00
COMMON CARD (1-165) .40 .18
1-165 TWO PER BOWMAN DRAFT PACK
COMMON CARD (166-176) 15.00 6.75
166-176 STATED ODDS 1:41 H/R
168-176 ARE ALL PARTIAL LIVE/EXCH DIST.
168-176 EXCH.DEADLINE 11/30/05
LUBANSKI EXCH IS AN SP BY 1000 COPIES
1 Dontrelle Willis 1.00 .45
2 Freddy Sanchez .40 .18
3 Miguel Cabrera 1.50 .70
4 Ryan Ludwick .40 .18
5 Ty Wigginton .40 .18
6 Mark Teixeira .60 .25
7 Trey Hodges .40 .18
8 Laynce Nix .60 .25
9 Antonio Perez .40 .18
10 Jody Gerut .40 .18
11 Jae Weong Seo .40 .18
12 Erick Almonte .40 .18
13 Lyle Overbay .60 .25
14 Billy Traber .40 .18
15 Andres Torres .40 .18
16 Jose Valverde .40 .18
17 Aaron Heilman .40 .18
18 Brandon Larson .40 .18
19 Jung Bong .40 .18
20 Jesse Foppert .60 .25
21 Angel Berroa .40 .18
22 Jeff DaVanon .40 .18
23 Kurt Ainsworth .40 .18
24 Brandon Claussen .40 .18
25 Xavier Nady .40 .18
26 Travis Hafner .60 .25
27 Jerome Williams .60 .25
28 Jose Reyes .60 .25
29 Sergio Mitre RC 1.50 .70
30 Bo Hart RC 1.50 .70
31 Adam Miller RC 5.00 2.20
32 Brian Finch RC 1.00 .45
33 Taylor Mattingly RC 4.00 1.80
34 Daric Barton RC 8.00 3.60
35 Chris Ray RC 1.50 .70
36 Jarrod Saltalamacchia RC 2.50 1.10
37 Dennis Dove RC 1.50 .70
38 James Houser RC 1.50 .70
39 Clint King RC 2.50 1.10
40 Lou Palmisano RC 4.00 1.80
41 Dan Moore RC 1.00 .45
42 Craig Stansberry RC 1.50 .70
43 Jo Jo Reyes RC 1.50 .70
44 Jake Stevens RC 4.00 1.80
45 Tom Gorzelanny RC 2.50 1.10
46 Brian Marshall RC 1.00 .45
47 Scott Beerer RC 1.00 .45
48 Javi Herrera RC 1.50 .70
49 Steve LeRud RC 2.50 1.10
50 Josh Banks RC 3.00 1.35
51 Jon Papelbon RC 1.00 .45
52 Juan Valdes RC 1.50 .70
53 Beau Vaughan RC 1.50 .70
54 Matt Chico RC 3.00 1.35
55 Todd Jennings RC 1.50 .70
56 Anthony Gwynn RC 4.00 1.80
57 Matt Harrison RC 2.50 1.10
58 Aaron Marsden RC 1.50 .70
59 Casey Abrams RC 1.00 .45
60 Cory Stuart RC 1.00 .45
61 Mike Wagner RC 1.00 .45
62 Jordan Pratt RC 1.50 .70
63 Andre Randolph RC 1.50 .70
64 Blake Balkcom RC 1.50 .70
65 Josh Muecke RC 1.00 .45
66 Jamie D'Antona RC 4.00 1.80
67 Cole Seifrig RC 2.50 1.10
68 Josh Anderson RC 3.00 1.35
69 Matt Lorenzo RC 1.50 .70
70 Nate Spears RC 2.50 1.10
71 Chris Goodman RC 1.00 .45
72 Brian McFall RC 2.50 1.10
73 Billy Hogan RC 1.50 .70
74 Jamie Romak RC 1.50 .70
75 Jeff Cook RC 1.50 .70
76 Brooks McNiven RC 1.00 .45
77 Xavier Paul RC 5.00 2.20
78 Bob Zimmerman RC 1.00 .45
79 Mickey Hall RC 1.50 .70
80 Shaun Marcum RC 1.00 .45
81 Matt Nachreiner RC 1.50 .70
82 Chris Kinsey RC 1.00 .45
83 Jonathan Fulton RC 1.50 .70
84 Edgardo Baez RC 1.50 .70
85 Robert Valido RC 2.50 1.10
86 Kenny Lewis RC 1.50 .70
87 Trent Peterson RC 1.00 .45
88 Johnny Woodard RC 1.50 .70
89 Wes Littleton RC 1.50 .70
90 Sean Rodriguez RC 4.00 1.80
91 Kyle Pearson RC 1.00 .45
92 Josh Rainwater RC 1.50 .70
93 Travis Schlichting RC 1.50 .70
94 Tim Battle RC 1.50 .70
95 Aaron Hill RC 3.00 1.35
96 Bob McCrory RC 1.00 .45
97 Rick Guarno RC 1.50 .70
98 Brandon Yarbrough RC 1.00 .45
99 Peter Stonard RC 1.00 .45
100 Darin Downs RC 1.50 .70
101 Matt Bruback RC 1.00 .45
102 Danny Garcia RC 1.00 .45
103 Cory Stewart RC 1.00 .45
104 Ferdin Tejeda RC 1.00 .45
105 Kade Johnson RC 1.00 .45
106 Andrew Brown RC 1.50 .70
107 Aquilino Lopez RC 1.00 .45
108 Stephen Randolph RC 1.00 .45
109 Dave Matranga RC 1.00 .45
110 Dustin McGowan RC 2.50 1.10
111 Juan Camacho RC 1.00 .45
112 Cliff Lee .40 .18
113 Jeff Duncan RC 1.50 .70
114 C.J. Wilson .40 .18
115 Brandon Roberson RC 1.00 .45
116 David Corrente RC 1.00 .45
117 Kevin Beavers RC 1.00 .45
118 Anthony Webster RC 1.50 .70
119 Oscar Villarreal RC 1.00 .45
120 Hong-Chih Kuo RC 2.50 1.10
121 Josh Barfield .60 .25
122 Denny Bautista .40 .18
123 Chris Burke RC 2.50 1.10
124 Robinson Cano RC 3.00 1.35
125 Jose Castillo .40 .18
126 Neal Cotts .60 .25
127 Jorge De La Rosa .40 .18
128 J.D. Durbin 1.50 .70
129 Edwin Encarnacion .40 .18
130 Gavin Floyd .60 .25
131 Alexis Gomez .40 .18
132 Edgar Gonzalez RC 1.00 .45
133 Khalil Greene 3.00 1.35
134 Zack Greinke 1.00 .45
135 Franklin Gutierrez 2.50 1.10
136 Rich Harden 1.00 .45
137 J.J. Hardy RC 5.00 2.20
138 Ryan Howard RC 10.00 4.50
139 Justin Huber .40 .18
140 David Kelton .40 .18
141 Dave Krynzel .40 .18
142 Pete LaForest 1.00 .45
143 Adam LaRoche .40 .18
144 Preston Larrison RC 1.00 .45
145 John Maine RC 5.00 2.20
146 Andy Marte 5.00 2.20
147 Jeff Mathis .60 .25
148 Joe Mauer 1.50 .70
149 Clint Nageotte .60 .25
150 Chris Narveson .40 .18
151 Ramon Nivar 1.50 .70
152 Felix Pie 3.00 1.35
153 Guillermo Quiroz RC 2.50 1.10
154 Rene Reyes .40 .18
155 Royce Ring .40 .18
156 Alexis Rios 2.00 .90
157 Grady Sizemore .60 .25
158 Stephen Smitherman .40 .18
159 Seung Song .40 .18
160 Scott Thorman .40 .18
161 Chad Tracy .60 .25
162 Chin-Hui Tsao .60 .25
163 John VanBenschoten .40 .18
164 Kevin Youkilis 3.00 1.35
165 Chien-Ming Wang 2.00 .90
166 Chris Lubanski AU SP RC 40.00 18.00
167 Ryan Harvey AU RC 30.00 13.50
168 Matt Murton AU RC 15.00 6.75
169 Jay Sborz AU RC 15.00 6.75
170 Brandon Wood AU RC 20.00 9.00
171 Nick Markakis AU RC 20.00 9.00
172 Rickie Weeks AU RC 50.00 22.00
173 Eric Duncan AU RC 25.00 11.00
174 Chad Billingsley AU RC 25.00 11.00
175 Ryan Wagner AU RC 20.00 9.00
176 Delmon Young AU RC 60.00 27.00

2003 Bowman Chrome Draft Gold Refractors

MINT NRMT
*GOLD REF 1-165: 8X TO 20X BASIC
*GOLD REF RC 1-165: 10X TO 20X BASIC
*GOLD REF RC YR 1-165: 7.5X TO 15X BASIC
1-165 ODDS 1:98 BOWMAN DRAFT HOBBY
166-176 AU ODDS 1:1479 BOW.DRAFT HOBBY
1-165 PRINT RUN 50 SERIAL #'d SETS
166-176 AU PRINT RUN 50 SETS
166-176 AU PRINT RUN PROVIDED BY TOPPS
166-176 AU'S ARE NOT SERIAL-NUMBERED
GOLD.REF ARE HOBBY-ONLY DISTRIBUTION

2003 Bowman Chrome Draft Refractors

MINT NRMT
*REFRACTOR 1-165: 1.5X TO 4X BASIC
*REFRACTOR RC 1-165: 1.25X TO 3X BASIC
*REFRACTOR RC YR 1-165: 1.5X TO 4X BASIC
*REFRACTOR AU 166-176: .6X TO 1.5X BASIC
1-165 ODDS 1:11 BOWMAN DRAFT H/R
166-176 AU ODDS 1:196 BOW.DRAFT HOBBY
166-176 AU ODDS 1:197 BOW.DRAFT RETAIL
166-176 AU PRINT RUN 500 SETS
166-176 AU PRINT RUN PROVIDED BY TOPPS
166-176 AU'S ARE NOT SERIAL-NUMBERED

2003 Bowman Chrome Draft X-Fractors

MINT NRMT
*X-FRACTOR 1-165: 3X TO 8X BASIC
*X-FRACTOR RC 1-165: 2.5X TO 6X BASIC
*X-FRACTOR RC YR 1-165: 2.5X TO 6X BASIC
*X-FRACTOR AU 166-176: .75X TO 2X BASIC
1-165 ODDS 1:50 BOWMAN DRAFT HOBBY
1-165 ODDS 1:52 BOWMAN DRAFT RETAIL
166-176 AU ODDS 1:393 BOW.DRAFT HOBBY
166-176 AU ODDS 1:394 BOW.DRAFT RETAIL
1-165 PRINT RUN 130 SERIAL #'d SETS
166-176 AU PRINT RUN 250 SETS
166-176 AU PRINT RUN PROVIDED BY TOPPS
166-176 AU'S ARE NOT SERIAL-NUMBERED

2004 Bowman Chrome

This 350-card set was released in August, 2004. The set was issued in four card packs with an $4 SRP which came 18 packs and 12 boxes to a case. The first 144 cards feature veterans while cards numbered 145 through 165 feature leading prospects. Cards numbered 166 through 350 are all Rookie Cards with the last 20 cards of the set being autographed. The Autographed cards (331-350) were inserted at a stated rate of one in 25 with a stated print run of 2000 sets. The Bobby Brownlie cards were issued as exchange cards with a stated expiry date of August 31, 2006.

Nm-Mt Ex-Mt
COMPLETE SET (350) 500.00 150.00
COMP.SET w/o AU's (330) 150.00 45.00
COMMON CARD (1-150) .50 .15
COMMON CARD (151-165) .50 .15
COMMON AUTO (331-350) 15.00 4.50
331-350 AU'S ARE NOT SERIAL-NUMBERED
331-350 PRINT RUN PROVIDED BY TOPPS
1 Garret Anderson .50 .15
2 Larry Walker .75 .23
3 Derek Jeter 2.50 .75
4 Curt Schilling 1.25 .35
5 Carlos Zambrano .50 .15
6 Shawn Green .50 .15
7 Manny Ramirez .75 .23
8 Randy Johnson 1.25 .35
9 Jeremy Bonderman .50 .15
10 Alfonso Soriano .75 .23
11 Scott Rolen 1.25 .35
12 Kerry Wood 1.25 .35
13 Eric Gagne 1.25 .35
14 Ryan Klesko .50 .15
15 Kevin Millar .50 .15
16 Ty Wigginton .50 .15
17 David Ortiz 1.25 .35
18 Luis Castillo .50 .15
19 Bernie Williams .75 .23
20 Edgar Renteria .50 .15
21 Matt Kata .50 .15
22 Bartolo Colon .50 .15
23 Derrek Lee .50 .15
24 Gary Sheffield .50 .15
25 Nomar Garciaparra 2.00 .60
26 Kevin Millwood .50 .15
27 Corey Patterson .50 .15
28 Carlos Beltran .75 .23
29 Mike Lieberthal .50 .15
30 Troy Glaus .50 .15
31 Preston Wilson .50 .15
32 Jorge Posada .75 .23
33 Bo Hart .50 .15
34 Mark Prior 1.25 .35
35 Hideo Nomo 1.25 .35
36 Jason Kendall .50 .15
37 Roger Clemens 2.50 .75
38 Dmitri Young .50 .15
39 Jason Giambi .50 .15
40 Jim Edmonds .50 .15
41 Ryan Ludwick .50 .15
42 Brandon Webb .50 .15
43 Todd Helton .75 .23
44 Jacque Jones .50 .15
45 Jamie Moyer .50 .15
46 Tim Salmon .75 .23
47 Kelvim Escobar .50 .15
48 Tony Batista .50 .15
49 Nick Johnson .50 .15
50 Jim Thome 1.25 .35
51 Casey Blake .50 .15
52 Trot Nixon .50 .15
53 Luis Gonzalez .50 .15
54 Dontrelle Willis .50 .15
55 Mike Mussina .75 .23
56 Carl Crawford .50 .15
57 Mark Buehrle .50 .15
58 Scott Podsednik .50 .15
59 Brian Giles .50 .15
60 Rafael Furcal .50 .15
61 Miguel Cabrera .75 .23
62 Rich Harden .50 .15
63 Mark Teixeira .50 .15
64 Frank Thomas 1.25 .35
65 Johan Santana .75 .23
66 Jason Schmidt .50 .15
67 Aramis Ramirez .50 .15
68 Jose Reyes .50 .15
69 Magglio Ordonez .50 .15
70 Mike Sweeney .50 .15
71 Eric Chavez .50 .15
72 Rocco Baldelli .50 .15
73 Sammy Sosa 2.00 .60
74 Javy Lopez .50 .15
75 Roy Oswalt .50 .15
76 Raul Ibanez .50 .15
77 Ivan Rodriguez 1.25 .35
78 Jerome Williams .50 .15
79 Carlos Lee .50 .15
80 Geoff Jenkins .50 .15
81 Sean Burroughs .50 .15
82 Marcus Giles .50 .15
83 Mike Lowell .50 .15
84 Barry Zito .50 .15
85 Aubrey Huff .50 .15
86 Esteban Loaiza .50 .15
87 Torii Hunter .50 .15
88 Phil Nevin .50 .15
89 Andruw Jones .50 .15
90 Josh Beckett .50 .15
91 Mark Mulder .50 .15
92 Hank Blalock .50 .15
93 Jason Phillips .50 .15
94 Russ Ortiz .50 .15
95 Juan Pierre .50 .15
96 Tom Glavine .75 .23
97 Gil Meche .50 .15
98 Ramon Ortiz .50 .15
99 Richie Sexson .50 .15
100 Albert Pujols 2.50 .75
101 Javier Vazquez .50 .15
102 Johnny Damon 1.25 .35
103 Alex Rodriguez 2.00 .60
104 Omar Vizquel .75 .23
105 Chipper Jones 1.25 .35
106 Lance Berkman .50 .15
107 Tim Hudson .50 .15
108 Carlos Delgado .50 .15
109 Austin Kearns .50 .15
110 Orlando Cabrera .50 .15
111 Edgar Martinez .75 .23
112 Melvin Mora .50 .15
113 Jeff Bagwell .75 .23
114 Marlon Byrd .50 .15
115 Vernon Wells .50 .15
116 C.C. Sabathia .50 .15
117 Cliff Floyd .50 .15
118 Ichiro Suzuki 2.00 .60
119 Miguel Olivo .50 .15
120 Mike Piazza 2.00 .60
121 Adam Dunn .75 .23
122 Paul Lo Duca .50 .15
123 Brett Myers .50 .15
124 Michael Young .50 .15
125 Sidney Ponson .50 .15
126 Greg Maddux 2.00 .60
127 Vladimir Guerrero 1.25 .35
128 Miguel Tejada .50 .15
129 Andy Pettitte .75 .23
130 Rafael Palmeiro .75 .23
131 Ken Griffey Jr. 2.00 .60
132 Shannon Stewart .50 .15
133 Joel Pineiro .50 .15
134 Luis Matos .50 .15
135 Jeff Kent .50 .15
136 Randy Wolf .50 .15
137 Chris Woodward .50 .15
138 Jody Gerut .50 .15
139 Jose Vidro .50 .15
140 Bret Boone .50 .15
141 Bill Mueller .50 .15
142 Angel Berroa .50 .15
143 Bobby Abreu .50 .15
144 Roy Halladay .50 .15
145 Delmon Young .75 .23
146 Jonny Gomes .50 .15
147 Rickie Weeks .50 .15
148 Edwin Jackson .50 .15
149 Neal Cotts .50 .15
150 Jason Bay .50 .15
151 Khalil Greene 1.50 .45
152 Joe Mauer 1.00 .30
153 Bobby Jenks .50 .15
154 Chin-Feng Chen .50 .15
155 Chien-Ming Wang .60 .18
156 Mickey Hall .50 .15
157 James Houser .50 .15
158 Jay Sborz .50 .15
159 Jonathan Fulton .50 .15
160 Steven Lerud .50 .15
161 Grady Sizemore .60 .18
162 Felix Pie 1.50 .45
163 Dustin McGowan .50 .15
164 Chris Lubanski .60 .18
165 Tom Gorzelanny .50 .15
166 Rudy Guillen RC 4.00 1.20
167 Aarom Baldiris RC 2.00 .60
168 Conor Jackson RC 8.00 2.40
169 Matt Moses RC 4.00 1.20
170 Ervin Santana RC 5.00 1.50
171 Merkin Valdez RC 4.00 1.20
172 Erick Aybar RC 5.00 1.50
173 Brad Sullivan RC 2.00 .60
174 Joey Gathright RC 4.00 1.20
175 Brad Snyder RC 4.00 1.20
176 Alberto Callaspo RC 3.00 .90
177 Brandon Medders RC 1.00 .30
178 Zach Miner RC 2.00 .60
179 Charlie Zink RC 1.00 .30
180 Adam Greenberg RC 2.00 .60
181 Kevin Howard RC 2.00 .60
182 Wanell Severino RC 1.00 .30
183 Chin-Lung Hu RC 4.00 1.20
184 Joel Zumaya RC 3.00 .90
185 Skip Schumaker RC 1.50 .45
186 Nic Ungs RC 1.50 .45
187 Todd Self RC 1.50 .45
188 Brian Steffek RC 1.00 .30
189 Brock Peterson RC 1.50 .45
190 Greg Thissen RC 1.00 .30
191 Frank Brooks RC 1.00 .30
192 Scott Olsen RC 5.00 1.50
193 Chris Mabeus RC 1.50 .45
194 Dan Giese RC 1.50 .45
195 Jared Wells RC 1.00 .30
196 Carlos Sosa RC 1.00 .30
197 Bobby Madritsch 3.00 .90
198 Calvin Hayes RC 2.00 .60
199 Omar Quintanilla RC 4.00 1.20
200 Chris O'Riordan RC 1.00 .30
201 Tim Hutting RC 1.00 .30
202 Carlos Quentin RC 8.00 2.40
203 Brayan Pena RC 1.50 .45
204 Jeff Salazar RC 4.00 1.20
205 David Murphy RC 4.00 1.20
206 Alberto Garcia RC 2.00 .60
207 Ramon Ramirez RC 1.50 .45
208 Luis Bolivar RC 1.50 .45
209 Rodney Choy Foo RC 1.00 .30
210 Fausto Carmona RC 3.00 .90
211 Anthony Acevedo RC 1.50 .45
212 Chad Santos RC 1.50 .45
213 Jason Frasor RC 1.50 .45
214 Jesse Roman RC 1.00 .30
215 James Tomlin RC 1.50 .45
216 Josh Labandeira RC 1.50 .45
217 Ryan Meaux RC 1.50 .45
218 Don Sutton RC 4.00 1.20
219 Danny Gonzalez RC 1.00 .30
220 Javier Guzman RC 2.00 .60
221 Anthony Lerew RC 3.00 .90
222 Jon Connolly RC 4.00 1.20
223 Jesse English RC 1.50 .45
224 Hector Made RC 3.00 .90
225 Travis Hanson RC 1.50 .45
226 Jesse Floyd RC 1.50 .45
227 Nick Gorneault RC 2.00 .60
228 Craig Ansman RC 1.50 .45
229 Paul McAnulty RC 3.00 .90
230 Carl Loadenthal RC 2.00 .60
231 Dave Crouthers RC 1.00 .30
232 Harvey Garcia RC 1.00 .30
233 Casey Kopitzke RC 1.00 .30
234 Ricky Nolasco RC 1.50 .45
235 Miguel Perez RC 1.50 .45
236 Ryan Mulhern RC 1.00 .30
237 Chris Aguila RC 1.50 .45
238 Brooks Conrad RC 2.00 .60
239 Damaso Espino RC 1.00 .30
240 Jereme Milons RC 1.50 .45
241 Luke Hughes RC 1.00 .30
242 Kory Casto RC 1.50 .45
243 Jose Valdez RC 1.50 .45
244 J.T. Stotts RC 1.00 .30
245 Lee Gwaltney RC 1.00 .30
246 Yoann Torrealba RC 1.00 .30
247 Omar Falcon RC 1.50 .45
248 Jon Coutlangus RC 1.00 .30
249 George Sherrill RC 1.50 .45
250 John Santor RC 1.00 .30
251 Tony Richie RC 1.50 .45
252 Kevin Richardson RC 1.00 .30
253 Tim Bittner RC 1.50 .45
254 Chris Saenz RC 1.00 .30
255 Jose Capellan RC 6.00 1.80
256 Donald Levinski RC 1.00 .30
257 Jerome Gamble RC 1.00 .30
258 Jeff Keppinger RC 3.00 .90
259 Jason Szuminski RC 1.00 .30
260 Akinori Otsuka RC 1.50 .45
261 Ryan Budde RC 1.50 .45
262 Marland Williams RC 2.00 .60
263 Jeff Allison RC 2.00 .60
264 Hector Gimenez RC 1.00 .30
265 Tim Frend RC 1.50 .45
266 Tom Farmer RC 1.00 .30
267 Shawn Hill RC 1.50 .45
268 Mike Huggins RC 1.50 .45
269 Scott Proctor RC 2.00 .60
270 Jorge Mejia RC 1.50 .45
271 Terry Jones RC 2.00 .60
272 Zach Duke RC 6.00 1.80
273 Jesse Crain RC 3.00 .90
274 Luke Anderson RC 1.00 .30
275 Hunter Brown RC 1.00 .30
276 Matt Lemanczyk RC 1.50 .45
277 Fernando Cortez RC 1.00 .30
278 Vince Perkins RC 2.00 .60
279 Tommy Murphy RC 1.50 .45
280 Mike Gosling RC 1.00 .30
281 Paul Bacot RC 2.00 .60
282 Matt Capps RC 1.50 .45
283 Juan Gutierrez RC 1.50 .45
284 Teodoro Encarnacion RC 2.00 .60
285 Chad Bentz RC 1.50 .45
286 Kazuo Matsui RC 5.00 1.50
287 Ryan Hankins RC 1.00 .30
288 Leo Nunez RC 1.50 .45
289 Dave Wallace RC 1.50 .45
290 Rob Tejeda RC 1.00 .30
291 Paul Maholm RC 3.00 .90
292 Casey Daigle RC 1.50 .45
293 Tydus Meadows RC 1.00 .30
294 Khalid Ballouli RC 1.00 .30
295 Benji DeQuin RC 1.00 .30
296 Tyler Davidson RC 2.00 .60
297 Brant Colamarino RC 3.00 .90
298 Marcus McBeth RC 1.00 .30
299 Brad Eldred RC 5.00 1.50
300 David Pauley RC 1.00 .30
301 Yadier Molina RC 4.00 1.20
302 Chris Shelton RC 3.00 .90
303 Nyjer Morgan RC 1.00 .30
304 Jon DeVries RC 1.50 .45
305 Sheldon Fulse RC 1.00 .30
306 Vito Chiaravalloti RC 3.00 .90
307 Warner Madrigal RC 3.00 .90
308 Reid Gorecki RC 1.50 .45
309 Sung Jung RC 1.00 .30
310 Pete Shier RC 1.00 .30
311 Michael Mooney RC 1.50 .45
312 Kenny Perez RC 1.50 .45
313 Michael Mallory RC 1.50 .45
314 Ben Himes RC 1.00 .30
315 Ivan Ochoa RC 1.50 .45
316 Donald Kelly RC 1.50 .45
317 Tom Mastny RC 1.50 .45
318 Kevin Davidson RC 1.00 .30
319 Brian Pilkington RC 1.50 .45
320 Alex Romero RC 1.50 .45
321 Chad Chop RC 1.50 .45
322 Kody Kirkland RC 3.00 .90
323 Casey Myers RC 1.00 .30
324 Mike Rouse RC 1.50 .45
325 Sergio Silva RC 1.00 .30
326 J.J. Furmaniak RC 3.00 .90
327 Brad Vericker RC 1.50 .45
328 Blake Hawksworth RC 2.00 .60
329 Brock Jacobsen RC 1.00 .30
330 Alec Zumwalt RC 1.00 .30
331 Wardell Starling AU RC 15.00 4.50
332 Estee Harris AU RC 15.00 4.50
333 Kyle Sleeth AU RC 25.00 7.50
334 Dioner Navarro AU RC 25.00 7.50
335 Logan Kensing AU RC 15.00 4.50
336 Travis Blackley AU RC 20.00 6.00
337 Lincoln Holdzkom AU RC 15.00 4.50
338 Jason Hirsh AU RC 15.00 4.50
339 Juan Cedeno AU RC 15.00 4.50
340 Matt Creighton AU RC 15.00 4.50
341 Tim Stauffer AU RC 20.00 6.00
342 Shingo Takatsu AU RC 25.00 7.50
343 Lastings Milledge AU RC 40.00 12.00
344 Dustin Nippert AU RC 15.00 4.50
345 Felix Hernandez AU RC 50.00 15.00

346 Joaquin Arias AU RC 15.00 4.50
347 Kevin Kouzmanoff AU RC .. 20.00 6.00
348 B.Brownlie AU RC EXCH 20.00 6.00
349 David Aardsma AU RC 15.00 4.50
350 Jon Knott AU RC 15.00 4.50

2004 Bowman Chrome Blue Refractors

Nm-Mt Ex-Mt
*BLUE REF 166-330: 1.25X TO 3X BASIC
EXCH.CARDS AVAIL VIA PIT.COM WEBSITE
ONE EXCH.CARD PER BOX-LOADER PACK
ONE BOX-LOADER PACK PER HOBBY BOX
STATED PRINT RUN 290 SETS..........
EXCHANGE DEADLINE 05/31/06.........
NNO Exchange Card............. 8.00 2.40

2004 Bowman Chrome Gold Refractors

Nm-Mt Ex-Mt
*GOLD REF 1-150: 5X TO 12X BASIC
*GOLD REF 151-165: 8X TO 20X BASIC
*GOLD REF 166-330: 7.5X TO 15X BASIC
1-330 STATED ODDS 1:4 HOBBY ....
1-330 PRINT RUN 50 SERIAL #'d SETS
*GOLD REF 331-350: 2X TO 4X BASIC
331-350 AU ODDS 1:1003 HOBBY .....
331-350 AU STATED PRINT RUN 50 SETS
331-350 AU'S ARE NOT SERIAL-NUMBERED
331-350 PRINT RUN PROVIDED BY TOPPS
EXCHANGE DEADLINE 08/31/06.........

2004 Bowman Chrome Refractors

Nm-Mt Ex-Mt
*REF 1-150: 1.5X TO 4X BASIC..........
*REF 151-165: 2X TO 5X BASIC..........
*REF 166-330: 1X TO 2.5X BASIC..........
1-330 STATED ODDS 1:4 HOBBY ....
*REF AU 331-350: .5X TO 1.2X BASIC
331-350 AU ODDS 1:100 HOBBY ....
331-350 AU PRINT RUN 500 SETS ....
331-350 AU'S ARE NOT SERIAL-NUMBERED
331-350 PRINT RUN PROVIDED BY TOPPS
EXCHANGE DEADLINE 08/31/06.........

2004 Bowman Chrome X-Fractors

Nm-Mt Ex-Mt
*X-FR 1-150: 3X TO 8X BASIC ....
*X-FR 151-165: 4X TO 10X BASIC ....
*X-FR 166-330: 2X TO 5X BASIC ....
1-330 ODDS ONE PER BOX LOADER PACK
ONE BOX LOADER PACK PER HOBY BOX
INSTANT WIN 1-330 ODDS 1:103,968 H
1-330 PRINT RUN 172 SERIAL #'d SETS
SETS 1-10 AVAIL.VIA INSTANT WIN CARD
SETS 11-172 ISSUED IN BOX-LOADER PACKS
*X-FR AU 331-350: .6X TO 1.5X BASIC
331-350 AU ODDS 1:200 HOBBY ....
331-350 AU STATED PRINT RUN 250 SETS
331-350 AU'S ARE NOT SERIAL-NUMBERED
331-350 PRINT RUNS PROVIDED BY TOPPS
EXCHANGE DEADLINE 08/31/06.........
NNO Complete 1-330 Instant Win/10..

2004 Bowman Chrome Stars of the Future

Nm-Mt Ex-Mt
STATED ODDS 1:600 HOBBY...........
STATED PRINT RUN 500 SETS...........
CARDS ARE NOT SERIAL-NUMBERED
PRINT RUN INFO PROVIDED BY TOPPS
REFRACTORS RANDOM INSERTS IN PACKS
NO REFRACTOR PRICING DUE TO SCARCITY
EXCHANGE DEADLINE 08/31/06.........
LHC Chris Lubanski 50.00 15.00
Ryan Harvey
Chad Cordero EXCH
MHD Nick Markakis 50.00 15.00
Aaron Hill
Eric Duncan
YSS Delmon Young.................. 80.00 24.00
Kyle Sleeth
Tim Stauffer

2004 Bowman Chrome Draft

Nm-Mt Ex-Mt
COMP.SET w/o SP's (165)....... 100.00 30.00
COMMON CARD (1-165) .... .40 .12
COMMON RC .... 1.00 .30
COMMON RC YR .... .40 .12
1-165 TWO PER BOWMAN DRAFT PACK
166-175 ODDS 1:60 BOWMAN DRAFT HOBBY
166-175 ODDS 1:60 BOWMAN DRAFT RETAIL
166-175 STATED PRINT RUN 1695 SETS
166-175 ARE NOT SERIAL-NUMBERED
166-175 PRINT RUN PROVIDED BY TOPPS
PLATES 1-165 ODDS 1:559 HOBBY ...
PLATES 166-175 ODDS 1:18,354 HOBBY
PLATES PRINT RUN 1 SERIAL #'d SET
BLACK-CYAN-MAGENTA-YELLOW EXIST
NO PLATES PRICING DUE TO SCARCITY
1 Lyle Overbay .... .60 .18
2 David Newhan........................ .40 .12
3 J.R. House .... .40 .12
4 Chad Tracy............................ .40 .12
5 Humberto Quintero .... .40 .12
6 Dave Bush............................. .40 .12
7 Scott Hairston........................ .40 .12
8 Mike Wood............................ .40 .12
9 Alexis Rios .... .60 .18
10 Sean Burnett .... .40 .12
11 Wilson Valdez .... .40 .12
12 Lew Ford.............................. .60 .18
13 Freddy Thon RC .... 1.00 .30
14 Zack Greinke .... .60 .18
15 Bucky Jacobsen .... 1.00 .30
16 Kevin Youkilis...................... .60 .18
17 Grady Sizemore .... .60 .18
18 Denny Bautista..................... .40 .12
19 David DeJesus .... .40 .12
20 Casey Kotchman .... 1.50 .45
21 David Kelton........................ .40 .12
22 Charles Thomas RC .... 1.50 .45
23 Kazuhito Tadano RC .... 1.50 .45
24 Justin Leone RC.................. 1.50 .45
25 Eduardo Villacis RC .... 1.00 .30
26 Brian Dallimore RC .... 1.00 .30
27 Nick Green .... .40 .12
28 Sam McConnell RC .... 1.00 .30
29 Brad Halsey RC .... 1.50 .45
30 Roman Colon RC .... 1.00 .30
31 Josh Fields RC..................... 5.00 1.50
32 Cody Bunkelman RC .... 1.50 .45
33 Jay Rainville RC .... 3.00 .90
34 Richie Robnett RC .... 3.00 .90
35 Jon Poterson RC.................. 3.00 .90
36 Huston Street RC .... 3.00 .90
37 Erick San Pedro RC .... 1.00 .30
38 Cory Dunlap RC 4.00 1.20
39 Kurt Suzuki RC..................... 4.00 1.20
40 Anthony Swarzak RC .... 1.50 .45
41 Ian Desmond RC.................. 1.50 .45
42 Chris Covington RC .... 1.50 .45
43 Christian Garcia RC............. 2.50 .75
44 Gaby Hernandez RC............ 2.50 .75
45 Steven Register RC............. 1.50 .45
46 Eduardo Morlan RC.............. 1.50 .45
47 Collin Balester RC................ 1.50 .45
48 Nathan Phillips RC............... 1.50 .45
49 Dan Schwartzbauer RC........ 1.50 .45
50 Rafael Gonzalez RC............. 1.50 .45
51 K.C. Herren RC..................... 2.50 .75
52 William Susdorf RC.............. 1.00 .30
53 Rob Johnson RC................... 1.00 .30
54 Louis Marson RC.................. 2.50 .75
55 Joe Koshansky RC............... 1.00 .30
56 Jamar Walton RC................. 5.00 1.50
57 Mark Lowe RC...................... 1.00 .30
58 Matt Macri RC...................... 2.50 .75
59 Donny Lucy RC..................... 1.00 .30
60 Mike Ferris RC...................... 1.50 .45
61 Mike Nickeas RC.................. 1.50 .45
62 Eric Hurley RC...................... 2.50 .75
63 Scott Elbert RC.................... 3.00 .90
64 Blake DeWitt RC.................. 6.00 1.80
65 Danny Putnam RC................ 2.50 .75
66 J.P. Howell RC...................... 2.50 .75
67 John Wiggins RC.................. 1.00 .30
68 Justin Orenduff RC .... 2.50 .75
69 Ray Liotta RC....................... 1.50 .45
70 Billy Buckner RC.................. 1.50 .45
71 Eric Campbell RC 4.00 1.20
72 Olin Wick RC........................ 1.00 .30
73 Sean Gamble RC.................. 1.50 .45
74 Seth Smith RC...................... 4.00 1.20
75 Wade Davis RC..................... 1.50 .45
76 Joe Jacobitz RC................... 1.00 .30
77 J.A. Happ RC........................ 2.50 .75
78 Eric Ridener RC .... 1.00 .30
79 Matt Tuiasosopo RC............. 10.00 3.00
80 Brad Bergesen RC................ 1.50 .45
81 Javy Guerra RC.................... 1.50 .45
82 Buck Shaw RC...................... 2.50 .75
83 Paul Janish RC..................... 1.50 .45
84 Sean Kazmar RC................... 1.50 .45
85 Josh Johnson RC.................. 1.50 .45
86 Angel Salome RC.................. 1.50 .45
87 Jordan Parraz RC.................. 1.50 .45
88 Kelvin Vazquez RC................ 1.00 .30
89 Grant Hansen RC.................. 1.00 .30
90 Matt Fox RC.......................... 2.50 .75
91 Trevor Plouffe RC................. 4.00 1.20
92 Wes Whisler RC.................... 1.50 .45
93 Curtis Thigpen RC................ 2.50 .75
94 Donnie Smith RC................... 1.00 .30
95 Luis Rivera RC...................... 1.50 .45
96 Jesse Hoover RC .... 1.50 .45
97 Jason Vargas RC................... 2.50 .75
98 Clary Carlsen RC.................. 1.00 .30
99 Mark Robinson RC................ 1.00 .30
100 J.C. Holt RC....................... 2.50 .75
101 Chad Blackwell RC.............. 1.50 .45
102 Daryl Jones RC .... 2.50 .75
103 Jonathan Tierce RC............. 1.00 .30
104 Patrick Bryant RC................ 1.00 .30
105 Eddie Prasch RC.................. 1.50 .45
106 Mitch Einertson RC............. 8.00 2.40
107 Kyle Waldrop RC.................. 3.00 .90
108 Jeff Marquez RC.................. 2.50 .75
109 Zach Jackson RC................. 1.50 .45
110 Josh Wahpepah RC............. 1.00 .30
111 Adam Lind RC...................... 2.50 .75
112 Kyle Bloom RC..................... 1.50 .45
113 Ben Harrison RC.................. 1.50 .45
114 Taylor Tankersley RC.......... 3.00 .90
115 Steven Jackson RC.............. 1.00 .30
116 David Purcey RC.................. 2.50 .75
117 Jacob McGee RC.................. 1.50 .45
118 Lucas Harrell RC.................. 1.00 .30
119 Brandon Allen RC................. 2.50 .75
120 Van Pope RC........................ 1.50 .45
121 Jeff Francis .... .60 .18
122 Joe Blanton.......................... 1.00 .30
123 Wil Ledezma .... .40 .12
124 Bryan Bullington .... .60 .18
125 Jairo Garcia.......................... .60 .18
126 Matt Cain .... .60 .18
127 Arnie Munoz......................... .40 .12
128 Clint Everts.......................... .40 .12
129 Jesus Cota .... .40 .12
130 Gavin Floyd .... .60 .18
131 Edwin Encarnacion............... .40 .12
132 Koyie Hill.............................. .40 .12
133 Ruben Gotay .... .40 .12
134 Jeff Mathis .... .40 .12
135 Andy Marte .... .60 .18
136 Dallas McPherson................ 1.00 .30
137 Justin Morneau................... 1.00 .30
138 Rickie Weeks....................... .60 .18
139 Joel Guzman .... 1.00 .30
140 Shin Soo Choo..................... .40 .12
141 Yusmeiro Petit RC............... 6.00 1.80
142 Jorge Cortes RC.................. 1.00 .30
143 Val Majewski .... .40 .12
144 Felix Pie .... .60 .18
145 Aaron Hill .... .40 .12
146 Jose Capellan...................... 1.50 .45
147 Dioner Navarro.................... 1.00 .30
148 Fausto Carmona................... 1.00 .30
149 Robinzon Diaz RC .... 1.00 .30
150 Felix Hernandez.................. 4.00 1.20
151 Andres Blanco RC............... 1.00 .30
152 Jason Kubel .... .60 .18
153 Willy Taveras RC................. 1.50 .45
154 Merkin Valdez .... .40 .12
155 Robinson Cano .... .60 .18
156 Bill Murphy .... .40 .12
157 Chris Burke .... .40 .12
158 Kyle Sleeth .... 1.00 .30
159 B.J. Upton............................ 1.00 .30
160 Tim Stauffer .... 1.00 .30
161 David Wright........................ 1.50 .45
162 Conor Jackson..................... 2.50 .75
163 Brad Thompson RC .... 1.50 .45
164 Delmon Young...................... 1.00 .30
165 Jeremy Reed .... .60 .18
166 Matt Bush AU RC............... 40.00 12.00
167 Mark Rogers AU RC........... 30.00 9.00
168 Thomas Diamond AU RC.. 25.00 7.50
169 Greg Golson AU RC.......... 25.00 7.50
170 Homer Bailey AU RC......... 30.00 9.00
171 Chris Lambert AU RC........ 20.00 6.00
172 Neil Walker AU RC............ 20.00 6.00
173 Bill Bray AU RC 15.00 4.50
174 Phillip Hughes AU RC........ 20.00 6.00
175 Gio Gonzalez AU RC......... 20.00 6.00

2004 Bowman Chrome Draft Gold Refractors

Nm-Mt Ex-Mt
*GOLD REF 1-165: 8X TO 20X BASIC
*GOLD REF RC 1-165: 8X TO 20X BASIC
*GOLD REF RC YR 1-165: 6X TO 15X BASIC
1-165 ODDS 1:119 BOWMAN DRAFT HOBBY
1-165 ODDS 1:205 BOWMAN DRAFT RETAIL
1-165 PRINT RUN 50 SERIAL #'d SETS
*GOLD REF 166-175: 4X TO 8X BASIC
166-175 AU ODDS 1:2045 BOW.DRAFT HOB
166-175 AU ODDS 1:2055 BOW.DRAFT RET
166-175 STATED PRINT RUN 50 SETS
166-175 ARE NOT SERIAL-NUMBERED
166-175 PRINT RUN PROVIDED BY TOPPS
31 Josh Fields.................... 150.00 45.00
64 Blake DeWitt 120.00 36.00
79 Matt Tuiasosopo 200.00 60.00
106 Mitch Einertson............ 200.00 60.00
141 Yusmeiro Petit 120.00 36.00
166 Matt Bush AU............... 300.00 90.00
167 Mark Rogers AU 250.00 75.00
168 Thomas Diamond AU..... 200.00 60.00
169 Greg Golson AU 200.00 60.00
170 Homer Bailey AU........... 250.00 75.00

2004 Bowman Chrome Draft Red Refractors

Nm-Mt Ex-Mt
STATED ODDS 1:4471 BOW.DRAFT HOBBY
STATED PRINT RUN 1 SERIAL #'d SET
NO PRICING DUE TO SCARCITY ....

2004 Bowman Chrome Draft Refractors

Nm-Mt Ex-Mt
*REF 1-165: 8X TO 20X BASIC..........
*REF RC 1-165: 1.25X TO 3X BASIC..
*REF RC YR 1-165: 1.5X TO 4X BASIC
1-165 ODDS 1:11 BOWMAN DRAFT HOBBY
1-165 ODDS 1:11 BOWMAN DRAFT RETAIL
*REF AU 166-175: .6X TO 1.5X BASIC
166-175 AU ODDS BOW.DRAFT 1:204 HOB
166-175 AU ODDS BOW.DRAFT 1:204 RET
166-175 STATED PRINT RUN 500 SETS
166-175 ARE NOT SERIAL-NUMBERED
166-175 PRINT RUN PROVIDED BY TOPPS

2004 Bowman Chrome Draft X-fractors

Nm-Mt Ex-Mt
*XF 1-165: 3X TO 8X BASIC ....
*XF RC 1-165: 2.5X TO 6X BASIC ......
*XF RC YR 1-165: 2.5X TO 6X BASIC
1-165 ODDS 1:48 BOWMAN DRAFT HOBBY
1-165 ODDS 1:80 BOWMAN DRAFT HOBBY
1-165 PRINT RUN 125 SERIAL #'d SETS
*XF AU 166-175: .75X TO 2X BASIC ..
166-175 AU ODDS 1:407 BOW.DRAFT HOB
166-175 AU ODDS 1:407 BOW.DRAFT RET
166-175 STATED PRINT RUN 250 SETS
166-175 ARE NOT SERIAL-NUMBERED
166-175 PRINT RUN PROVIDED BY TOPPS
79 Matt Tuiasosopo 60.00 18.00
106 Mitch Einertson............. 50.00 15.00
166 Matt Bush AU............... 100.00 30.00
167 Mark Rogers AU 60.00 18.00
168 Thomas Diamond AU....... 50.00 15.00
169 Greg Golson AU 50.00 15.00
170 Homer Bailey AU............ 60.00 18.00

2004 Bowman Chrome Draft AFLAC Exchange Cards

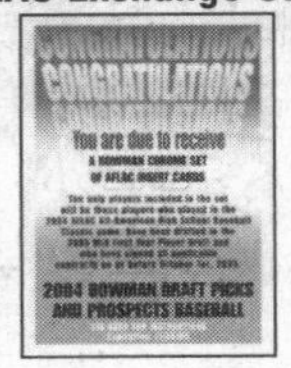

Nm-Mt Ex-Mt
ONE AFLAC PER BOWMAN DRAFT BOX
REFRACTOR EXCH.PRINT RUN 550 CARDS
X-FRACTOR EXCH.PRINT RUN 125 CARDS
GOLD REF.EXCH.PRINT RUN 50 CARDS
RED REF.EXCH.PRINT RUN 1 CARD....
PRINT RUNS PROVIDED BY TOPPS....
NO RED PRICING DUE TO SCARCITY
1 Basic Set........................... 40.00 12.00
2 Refractors Set/550.............. 120.00 36.00
3 X-Fractors Set/125.............. 200.00 60.00
4 Gold Refractors Set/50 .... 600.00 180.00
5 Red Set/1..............................

2001 Bowman Heritage

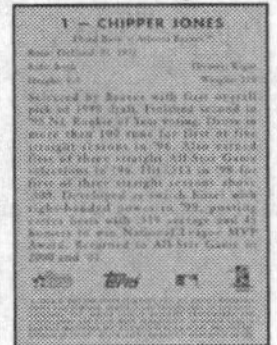

This 440-card product was issued in 10 card packs, along with a slab of gum, with an SRP of $3 per pack. The packs were issued 16 to a box with 24 boxes to a case. Cards numbered 331-440 were inserted at a rate of one every two packs.

Nm-Mt Ex-Mt
COMPLETE SET (440).............. 250.00 75.00
COMP.SET w/o SP's (330)........ 50.00 15.00
COMMON CARD (1-330) .... .40 .12
COMMON RC (1-330) .... .50 .15
COMMON (331-440).................. 2.00 .60
1 Chipper Jones...................... 1.00 .30
2 Pete Harnisch........................ .40 .12
3 Brian Giles .... .75 .23
4 J.T. Snow .... .75 .23
5 Bartolo Colon .... .75 .23
6 Jorge Posada .... .60 .18
7 Shawn Green .... .75 .23
8 Derek Jeter........................... 2.50 .75
9 Benito Santiago...................... .75 .23
10 Ramon Hernandez .... .40 .12
11 Bernie Williams .... .60 .18
12 Greg Maddux .... 1.50 .45
13 Barry Bonds .... 2.50 .75
14 Roger Clemens .... 2.00 .60
15 Miguel Tejada........................ .75 .23
16 Pedro Feliz .... .40 .12
17 Jim Edmonds......................... .75 .23
18 Tom Glavine .... .60 .18
19 David Justice .... .75 .23
20 Rich Aurilia .... .40 .12
21 Jason Giambi .... .75 .23
22 Orlando Hernandez .... .40 .12
23 Shawn Estes .... .40 .12
24 Nelson Figueroa..................... .40 .12
25 Terrence Long........................ .40 .12
26 Mike Mussina......................... .60 .18
27 Eric Davis............................... .75 .23
28 Jimmy Rollins .... .75 .23
29 Andy Pettitte .... .60 .18
30 Shawon Dunston .... .40 .12
31 Tim Hudson .... .75 .23
32 Jeff Kent................................. .75 .23
33 Scott Brosius .... .75 .23
34 Livan Hernandez .... .40 .12
35 Alfonso Soriano .... .60 .18
36 Mark McGwire .... 2.50 .75
37 Russ Ortiz .... .75 .23
38 Fernando Vina......................... .40 .12
39 Ken Griffey Jr. .... 1.50 .45
40 Edgar Renteria .... .75 .23
41 Kevin Brown............................ .75 .23
42 Robb Nen................................ .75 .23
43 Paul LoDuca............................ .75 .23
44 Bobby Abreu .... .75 .23
45 Adam Dunn .... .60 .18
46 Osvaldo Fernandez .... .40 .12
47 Marvin Benard .... .40 .12
48 Mark Gardner........................... .40 .12
49 Alex Rodriguez .... 1.50 .45
50 Preston Wilson .... .75 .23
51 Roberto Alomar .... .60 .18
52 Ben Davis.................................. .40 .12
53 Derek Bell.................................. .40 .12
54 Ken Caminiti.............................. .75 .23
55 Barry Zito .... .60 .18
56 Scott Rolen .... 1.00 .30
57 Geoff Jenkins .... .75 .23
58 Mike Cameron........................... .75 .23
59 Ben Grieve .... .40 .12
60 Chuck Knoblauch .... .75 .23
61 Matt Lawton.............................. .40 .12
62 Chan Ho Park............................ .75 .23
63 Lance Berkman .... .75 .23
64 Carlos Beltran .... .60 .18
65 Dean Palmer .... .75 .23
66 Alex Gonzalez .... .40 .12
67 Larry Walker .... .60 .18
68 Magglio Ordonez....................... .75 .23
69 Ellis Burks................................. .75 .23
70 Mark Mulder .... .75 .23
71 Randy Johnson .... 1.00 .30
72 John Smoltz.............................. .60 .18
73 Jerry Hairston Jr. .... .40 .12
74 Pedro Martinez......................... 1.00 .30
75 Fred McGriff.............................. .60 .18
76 Sean Casey .... .75 .23
77 C.C. Sabathia .... .75 .23
78 Todd Helton .... .60 .18
79 Brad Penny .... .40 .12
80 Mike Sweeney............................ .75 .23
81 Billy Wagner............................... .75 .23
82 Mark Buehrle .... .75 .23
83 Cristian Guzman......................... .40 .12
84 Jose Vidro................................... .40 .12
85 Pat Burrell................................... .75 .23
86 Jermaine Dye.............................. .75 .23
87 Brandon Inge .... .40 .12
88 David Wells................................. .75 .23
89 Mike Piazza .... 1.50 .45
90 Jose Cabrera................................ .40 .12
91 Cliff Floyd.................................... .75 .23
92 Matt Morris.................................. .75 .23
93 Raul Mondesi .... .75 .23
94 Joe Kennedy RC........................... .75 .23
95 Jack Wilson RC.......................... 2.00 .60
96 Andruw Jones .... .75 .23
97 Mariano Rivera .... .60 .18
98 Mike Hampton .... .75 .23
99 Roger Cedeno .... .40 .12
100 Jose Cruz .... .40 .12
101 Mike Lowell .... .75 .23
102 Pedro Astacio............................ .40 .12
103 Joe Mays .... .40 .12
104 John Franco .... .75 .23
105 Tim Redding .... .40 .12
106 Sandy Alomar Jr. .... .40 .12
107 Bret Boone................................. .75 .23
108 Josh Towers RC.......................... .50 .15
109 Matt Stairs .... .40 .12
110 Chris Truby .... .40 .12
111 Jeff Suppan................................ .40 .12
112 J.C. Romero................................ .40 .12
113 Felipe Lopez .... .40 .12
114 Ben Sheets .... .60 .18
115 Frank Thomas........................... 1.00 .30
116 A.J. Burnett .... .40 .12
117 Tony Clark................................... .40 .12
118 Mac Suzuki .... .40 .12
119 Brad Radke .... .75 .23
120 Jeff Shaw .... .40 .12
121 Nick Neugebauer.......................... .40 .12
122 Kenny Lofton .... .75 .23
123 Jacque Jones .... .75 .23
124 Brent Mayne.................................. .40 .12
125 Carlos Hernandez.......................... .40 .12
126 Shane Spencer............................... .40 .12
127 John Lackey................................... .40 .12
128 Sterling Hitchcock.......................... .40 .12
129 Darren Dreifort............................... .40 .12
130 Rusty Greer..................................... .75 .23
131 Michael Cuddyer .... .40 .12
132 Tyler Houston.................................. .40 .12
133 Chin-Feng Chen .... .75 .23
134 Ken Harvey .... .40 .12
135 Marquis Grissom .... .75 .23
136 Russell Branyan .... .40 .12
137 Eric Karros....................................... .75 .23
138 Josh Beckett .... .75 .23
139 Todd Zeile .... .75 .23
140 Corey Koskie..................................... .75 .23
141 Steve Sparks...................................... .40 .12
142 Bobby Seay.. .40 .12
143 Tim Raines Jr. .... .40 .12
144 Julio Zuleta .... .40 .12
145 Jose Lima .... .40 .12
146 Dante Bichette..................................... .75 .23
147 Randy Keisler....................................... .40 .12
148 Brent Butler.. .40 .12
149 Antonio Alfonseca .... .40 .12
150 Bryan Rekar .... .40 .12
151 Jeffrey Hammonds................................. .40 .12
152 Larry Bigbie .... .40 .12
153 Blake Stein... .40 .12
154 Robin Ventura .... .75 .23
155 Rondell White .... .75 .23
156 Juan Silvestre .... .40 .12
157 Marcus Thames .... .40 .12
158 Sidney Ponson.. .40 .12
159 Juan A. Pena RC....................................... .50 .15
160 C.J. Nitkowski... .40 .12
161 Adam Everett .... .40 .12
162 Eric Munson... .40 .12
163 Jason Isringhausen.................................... .40 .12
164 Brad Fullmer .... .40 .12
165 Miguel Olivo.. .40 .12
166 Fernando Tatis.. .40 .12
167 Freddy Garcia.. .75 .23
168 Tom Goodwin... .40 .12
169 Armando Benitez... .75 .23
170 Paul Konerko .... .75 .23
171 Jeff Cirillo.. .40 .12
172 Shane Reynolds... .40 .12
173 Kevin Tapani.. .40 .12
174 Joe Crede.. .40 .12
175 Omar Infante RC .... 2.00 .60
176 Jake Peavy RC .... 3.00 .90
177 Corey Patterson .... .75 .23
178 Mike Penney RC.. .50 .15
179 Jeromy Burnitz.. .75 .23
180 David Segui.. .40 .12
181 Marcus Giles .... .75 .23
182 Paul O'Neill .... .60 .18
183 John Olerud .... .75 .23
184 Andy Benes... .40 .12
185 Brad Cresse .... .40 .12
186 Ricky Ledee .... .40 .12
187 Allen Levrault UER .... .40 .12
Last name misspelled Leverault
188 Royce Clayton.. .40 .12
189 Kelly Johnson RC.. .50 .15
190 Quilvio Veras.. .40 .12
191 Mike Williams .... .40 .12
192 Jason Lane RC.. .50 .15
193 Rick Helling... .40 .12
194 Tim Wakefield .... .75 .23
195 James Baldwin... .40 .12
196 Cody Ransom RC... .50 .15
197 Bobby Kielty .... .40 .12
198 Bobby Jones .... .40 .12
199 Steve Cox... .40 .12
200 Jamal Strong RC .... .50 .15
201 Steve Lomasney.. .40 .12
202 Brian Cardwell RC .... .50 .15
203 Mike Matheny .... .75 .23

204 Jeff Randazzo RC .50 .15
205 Aubrey Huff .75 .23
206 Chuck Finley .75 .23
207 Denny Bautista RC 1.25 .35
208 Terry Mulholland .40 .12
209 Rey Ordonez .40 .12
210 Keith Surkont RC .50 .15
211 Orlando Cabrera .75 .23
212 Juan Encarnacion .40 .12
213 Dustin Hermanson .40 .12
214 Luis Rivas .40 .12
215 Mark Quinn .40 .12
216 Randy Velarde .40 .12
217 Billy Koch .40 .12
218 Ryan Rupe .40 .12
219 Keith Ginter .40 .12
220 Woody Williams .40 .12
221 Ryan Franklin .40 .12
222 Aaron Myette .40 .12
223 Joe Borchard RC 1.25 .35
224 Nate Cornejo .40 .12
225 Julian Tavarez .40 .12
226 Kevin Millwood .75 .23
227 Travis Hafner RC 2.50 .75
228 Charles Nagy .40 .12
229 Mike Lieberthal .75 .23
230 Jeff Nelson .40 .12
231 Ryan Dempster .40 .12
232 Andres Galarraga .75 .23
233 Chad Durbin .40 .12
234 Timo Perez .40 .12
235 Troy O'Leary .40 .12
236 Kevin Young .40 .12
237 Gabe Kapler .40 .12
238 Juan Cruz RC .50 .15
239 Masato Yoshii .40 .12
240 Aramis Ramirez .75 .23
241 Matt Cooper RC .50 .15
242 Randy Flores RC .50 .15
243 Rafael Furcal .75 .23
244 David Eckstein .40 .12
245 Matt Clement .40 .12
246 Craig Biggio .60 .18
247 Rick Reed .40 .12
248 Jose Macias .40 .12
249 Alex Escobar .40 .12
250 Roberto Hernandez .40 .12
251 Andy Ashby .40 .12
252 Tony Armas Jr. .40 .12
253 Jamie Moyer .75 .23
254 Jason Tyner .40 .12
255 Charles Kegley RC .50 .15
256 Jeff Conine .75 .23
257 Francisco Cordova .40 .12
258 Ted Lilly .40 .12
259 Joe Randa .40 .12
260 Jeff D'Amico .40 .12
261 Albie Lopez .40 .12
262 Kevin Appier .75 .23
263 Richard Hidalgo .40 .12
264 Omar Daal .40 .12
265 Ricky Gutierrez .40 .12
266 John Rocker .40 .12
267 Ray Lankford .40 .12
268 Beau Hale RC .50 .15
269 Tony Blanco RC 1.25 .35
270 Derrek Lee UER .75 .23
First name misspelled Derrick
271 Jamey Wright .40 .12
272 Alex Gordon .40 .12
273 Jeff Weaver .40 .12
274 Jaret Wright .40 .12
275 Jose Hernandez .40 .12
276 Bruce Chen .40 .12
277 Todd Hollandsworth .40 .12
278 Wade Miller .40 .12
279 Luke Prokopec .40 .12
280 Rafael Soriano RC .75 .23
281 Damion Easley .40 .12
282 Darren Oliver .40 .12
283 B. Duckworth RC .50 .15
284 Aaron Herr .40 .12
285 Ray Durham .75 .23
286 Wilmy Caceras RC .50 .15
287 Ugueth Urbina .40 .12
288 Scott Seabol .40 .12
289 Lance Niekro RC .50 .15
290 Trot Nixon .75 .23
291 Adam Kennedy .40 .12
292 Brian Schmitt RC .50 .15
293 Grant Roberts .40 .12
294 Benny Agbayani .40 .12
295 Travis Lee .40 .12
296 Erick Almonte RC .50 .15
297 Jim Thome 1.00 .30
298 Eric Young .40 .12
299 Dan Denham RC .50 .15
300 Boof Bonser RC .50 .15
301 Denny Neagle .40 .12
302 Kenny Rogers .75 .23
303 J.D. Closser .40 .12
304 Chase Utley RC 5.00 1.50
305 Rey Sanchez .40 .12
306 Sean McGowan .40 .12
307 Justin Pope RC .50 .15
308 Torii Hunter .75 .23
309 B.J. Surhoff .75 .23
310 Aaron Heilman RC .50 .15
311 Gabe Gross RC .75 .23
312 Lee Stevens .40 .12
313 Todd Hundley .40 .12
314 Macay McBride RC .50 .15
315 Edgar Martinez .60 .18
316 Omar Vizquel .60 .18
317 Reggie Sanders .40 .12
318 John-Ford Griffin RC .50 .15
319 Tim Salmon UER .75 .23
Photo is Troy Glaus
320 Pokey Reese .40 .12
321 Jay Payton .40 .12
322 Doug Glanville .40 .12
323 Greg Vaughn .40 .12
324 Ruben Sierra .40 .12
325 Kip Wells .40 .12
326 Carl Everett .75 .23
327 Garret Anderson .75 .23
328 Jay Bell .75 .23
329 Barry Larkin .60 .18
330 Jeff Mathis RC 2.50 .75
331 Adrian Gonzalez SP 2.00 .60
332 Juan Rivera SP 2.00 .60
333 Tony Alvarez SP 2.00 .60
334 Xavier Nady SP 2.00 .60
335 Josh Hamilton SP 2.00 .60
336 Will Smith SP RC 2.00 .60
337 Israel Alcantara SP 2.00 .60
338 Chris George SP 2.00 .60
339 Sean Burroughs SP 2.00 .60
340 Jack Cust SP 2.00 .60
341 Henry Mateo SP RC 2.00 .60
342 Carlos Pena SP 2.00 .60
343 J.R. House SP 2.00 .60
344 Carlos Silva SP 2.00 .60
345 Mike Rivera SP RC 2.00 .60
346 Adam Johnson SP 2.00 .60
347 Scott Heard SP 2.00 .60
348 Alex Cintron SP 2.00 .60
349 Miguel Cabrera SP 8.00 2.40
350 Nick Johnson SP 2.00 .60
351 Albert Pujols SP RC 50.00 15.00
352 Ichiro Suzuki SP RC 40.00 12.00
353 Carlos Delgado SP 2.00 .60
354 Troy Glaus SP 2.00 .60
355 Sammy Sosa SP 5.00 1.50
356 Ivan Rodriguez SP 3.00 .90
357 Vladimir Guerrero SP 3.00 .90
358 Manny Ramirez SP 3.00 .90
359 Luis Gonzalez SP 2.00 .60
360 Roy Oswalt SP 3.00 .90
361 Moises Alou SP 2.00 .60
362 Juan Gonzalez SP 3.00 .90
363 Tony Gwynn SP 4.00 1.20
364 Hideo Nomo SP 3.00 .90
365 T. Shinjo SP RC 2.00 .60
366 Kazuhiro Sasaki SP 2.00 .60
367 Cal Ripken SP 10.00 3.00
368 Rafael Palmeiro SP 3.00 .90
369 J.D. Drew SP 2.00 .60
370 Doug Mientkiewicz SP 2.00 .60
371 Jeff Bagwell SP 3.00 .90
372 Darin Erstad SP 2.00 .60
373 Tom Gordon SP 2.00 .60
374 Ben Petrick SP 2.00 .60
375 Eric Milton SP 2.00 .60
376 N. Garciaparra SP 5.00 1.50
377 Julio Lugo SP 2.00 .60
378 Tino Martinez SP 3.00 .90
379 Javier Vazquez SP 2.00 .60
380 Jeremy Giambi SP 2.00 .60
381 Marty Cordova SP 2.00 .60
382 Adrian Beltre SP 3.00 .90
383 John Burkett SP 2.00 .60
384 Aaron Boone SP 2.00 .60
385 Eric Chavez SP 2.00 .60
386 Curt Schilling SP 2.00 .60
387 Cory Lidle UER 2.00 .60
First name misspelled Corey
388 Jason Schmidt SP 2.00 .60
389 Johnny Damon SP 3.00 .90
390 Steve Finley SP 2.00 .60
391 Edgardo Alfonzo SP 2.00 .60
392 Jose Valentin SP 2.00 .60
393 Jose Canseco SP 3.00 .90
394 Ryan Klesko SP 2.00 .60
395 David Cone SP 2.00 .60
396 Jason Kendall UER 2.00 .60
Last name misspelled Kendell
397 Placido Polanco SP 2.00 .60
398 Glendon Rusch SP 2.00 .60
399 Aaron Sele SP 2.00 .60
400 D'Angelo Jimenez SP 2.00 .60
401 Mark Grace SP 3.00 .90
402 Al Leiter SP 2.00 .60
403 Brian Jordan SP 2.00 .60
404 Phil Nevin SP 2.00 .60
405 Brent Abernathy SP 2.00 .60
406 Kerry Wood SP 3.00 .90
407 Alex Gonzalez SP 2.00 .60
408 Robert Fick SP 2.00 .60
409 Dmitri Young UER 2.00 .60
First name misspelled Dimitri
410 Wes Helms SP 2.00 .60
411 Trevor Hoffman SP 2.00 .60
412 Rickey Henderson SP 3.00 .90
413 Bobby Higginson SP 2.00 .60
414 Gary Sheffield SP 2.00 .60
415 Darryl Kile SP 2.00 .60
416 Richie Sexson SP 2.00 .60
417 F. Menechino SP RC 2.00 .60
418 Javy Lopez SP 2.00 .60
419 Carlos Lee SP 2.00 .60
420 Jon Lieber SP 2.00 .60
421 Hank Blalock SP RC 15.00 4.50
422 Marlon Byrd SP RC 1.25 .35
423 Jason Kinchen SP RC 2.00 .60
424 M. Ensberg SP RC 2.00 .60
425 Greg Nash SP RC 2.00 .60
426 D. Tankersley SP RC 2.00 .60
427 Nate Murphy SP RC 2.00 .60
428 Chris Smith SP RC 2.00 .60
429 Jake Gautreau SP RC 2.00 .60
430 J. VanBenschoten SP RC 5.00 1.50
431 T.Thompson SP RC 2.00 .60
432 O.Hudson SP RC 2.00 .60
433 J.Williams SP RC 10.00 3.00
434 Kevin Reese SP RC 2.00 .60
435 Ed Rogers SP RC 2.00 .60
436 Ryan Jamison SP RC 2.00 .60
437 A. Pettyjohn SP RC 2.00 .60
438 Hee Seop Choi SP RC 2.00 .60
439 J. Morneau SP RC 15.00 4.50
440 Mitch Jones SP RC 2.00 .60

2001 Bowman Heritage Chrome

Inserted at a rate of one in 12 packs, the first 110 cards of this set are featured in this partial parallel set. Please see the multipliers to assess the values for the individual cards.

Nm-Mt Ex-Mt
*CHROME STARS: 4X TO 10X BASIC CARDS
*CHROME RC'S: 2.5X TO 6X BASIC CARDS

2001 Bowman Heritage 1948 Reprints

Issued one per two packs, these 13 cards feature reprints of the featured players 1948 Bowman card.

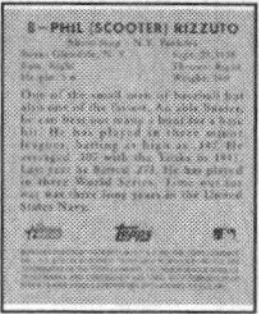

Nm-Mt Ex-Mt
COMPLETE SET (13) 10.00 3.00
1 Ralph Kiner 1.00 .30
2 Johnny Mize 1.00 .30
3 Bobby Thomson 1.00 .30
4 Yogi Berra 1.50 .45
5 Phil Rizzuto 1.25 .35
6 Bob Feller 1.00 .30
7 Enos Slaughter 1.00 .30
8 Stan Musial 2.00 .60
9 Hank Sauer 1.00 .30
10 Ferris Fain 1.00 .30
11 Red Schoendienst 1.00 .30
12 Allie Reynolds UER 1.00 .30
Original Card number is incorrect
13 Johnny Sain 1.00 .30

2001 Bowman Heritage 1948 Reprints Autographs

Inserted at an overall rate of one in 1,523 these two cards have autographs from the feature players on their 1948 reprint cards.

Nm-Mt Ex-Mt
1 Warren Spahn 1 60.00 18.00
2 Bob Feller 2 50.00 15.00

2001 Bowman Heritage 1948 Reprints Relics

Issued at an overall odds of one in 53, these 12 cards feature relic cards from the featured players. The cards featuring pieces of actual seats were inserted at a rate of one in 291 while the odds for bats were one in 2,113 and the odds for jerseys were one in 2,905.

Nm-Mt Ex-Mt
BHM-BF Bob Feller Seat A 15.00 4.50
BHM-BT Bobby Thomson Seat C 15.00 4.50
BHM-ES Enos Slaughter Seat C 15.00 4.50
BHM-FF Ferris Fain Seat A 15.00 4.50
BHM-HS Hank Sauer Seat A 15.00 4.50
BHM-JM Johnny Mize Seat C 20.00 6.00
BHM-PR Phil Rizzuto Seat B 20.00 6.00
BHM-RK Ralph Kiner Seat B 15.00 4.50
BHM-RS R.Schoendienst Bat 15.00 4.50
BHM-SM1 Stan Musial Seat C 30.00 9.00
BHM-YB1 Yogi Berra Seat B 25.00 7.50
BHM-YB2 Yogi Berra Jsy 40.00 12.00

2001 Bowman Heritage Autographs

Inserted at overall odds of one in 358, these three cards feature active players who signed cards for the Bowman Heritage set.

Nm-Mt Ex-Mt
HAAR Alex Rodriguez B 100.00 30.00
HABB Barry Bonds A 250.00 75.00
HARC Roger Clemens A 100.00 30.00

2002 Bowman Heritage

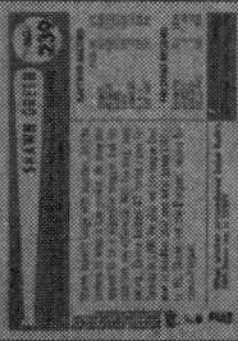

This 440 card standard-size, designed in the style of the 1954 Bowman set, was released in August, 2002. The 10-card packs had an SRP of $3 per pack and were issued 24 packs to a box and 16 boxes to a case. 110 cards were issued in shorter supply than the rest of the set and we have notated that information next to the player's name in our checklist. There were two versions of card number 66 which paid tribute to the Ted Williams/Jim Piersall numbering issue in the original 1954 Bowman set.

Nm-Mt Ex-Mt
COMP.SET w/o SP's (324) 50.00 15.00
COMMON CARD (1-439) .40 .12
COMMON SP 2.00 .60
1 Brent Abernathy .40 .12
2 Jermaine Dye .40 .12
3 James Shanks RC .40 .12
4 Chris Flinn RC .40 .12
5 Mike Peeples SP RC 2.00 .60
6 Gary Sheffield .40 .12
7 Livan Hernandez SP 2.00 .60
8 Jeff Austin RC .40 .12
9 Jeremy Giambi .40 .12
10 Adam Roller RC .40 .12
11 Sandy Alomar Jr. SP 2.00 .60
12 Matt Williams SP 2.00 .60
13 Hee Seop Choi .40 .12
14 Jose Offerman .40 .12
15 Robin Ventura .40 .12
16 Craig Biggio .60 .18
17 David Wells .40 .12
18 Rob Henkel RC .40 .12
19 Edgar Martinez .60 .18
20 Matt Morris SP 2.00 .60
21 Jose Valentin .40 .12
22 Barry Bonds 2.50 .75
23 Justin Schuda RC .40 .12
24 Josh Phelps .40 .12
25 John Rodriguez RC .40 .12
26 Angel Pagan RC .40 .12
27 Aramis Ramirez .40 .12
28 Jack Wilson .40 .12
29 Roger Clemens 2.00 .60
30 Kazuhisa Ishii RC 1.25 .35
31 Carlos Beltran .60 .18
32 Drew Henson SP 2.00 .60
33 Kevin Young SP 2.00 .60
34 Juan Cruz SP 2.00 .60
35 Curtis Legendre RC .40 .12
36 Jose Morban RC .40 .12
37 Ricardo Cordova SP RC 2.00 .60
38 Adam Everett .40 .12
39 Mark Prior 2.00 .60
40 Jose Bautista RC .50 .15
41 Travis Foley RC .40 .12
42 Kerry Wood 1.00 .30
43 B.J. Surhoff .40 .12
44 Moises Alou .40 .12
45 Joey Hammond .40 .12
46 Eric Bruntlett RC .40 .12
47 Carlos Guillen .40 .12
48 Joe Crede .40 .12
49 Dan Phillips RC .40 .12
50 Jason LaRue .40 .12
51 Javy Lopez .40 .12
52 Larry Bigbie SP 2.00 .60
53 Chris Baker RC .40 .12
54 Marty Cordova .40 .12
55 C.C. Sabathia .40 .12
56 Mike Piazza 1.50 .45
57 Brian Giles .40 .12
58 Mike Bordick SP 2.00 .60
59 Tyler Houston SP 2.00 .60
60 Gabe Kapler .40 .12
61 Ben Broussard .40 .12
62 Steve Finley SP 2.00 .60
63 Koyie Hill .40 .12
64 Jeff D'Amico .40 .12
65 Edwin Almonte RC .40 .12
66 Pedro Martinez 1.00 .30
66B Nomar Garciaparra 66 1.50 .45
67 Travis Fryman SP 2.00 .60
68 Brady Clark SP 2.00 .60
69 Reed Johnson SP RC 3.00 .90
70 Mark Grace SP 3.00 .90
71 Tony Batista SP 2.00 .60
72 Roy Oswalt .40 .12
73 Pat Burrell SP 2.00 .60
74 Dennis Tankersley .40 .12
75 Ramon Ortiz .40 .12
76 Neal Frendling SP RC 2.00 .60
77 Omar Vizquel SP 3.00 .90
78 Hideo Nomo 1.00 .30
79 Orlando Hernandez SP 2.00 .60
80 Andy Pettitte .60 .18
81 Cole Barthel RC .40 .12
82 Bret Boone .40 .12
83 Alfonso Soriano .60 .18
84 Brandon Duckworth .40 .12
85 Ben Grieve .40 .12
86 Mike Rosamond SP RC 2.00 .60
87 Luke Prokopec .40 .12
88 Chone Figgins RC .75 .23
89 Rick Ankiel SP 2.00 .60
90 David Eckstein .40 .12
91 Corey Koskie .40 .12
92 David Justice .40 .12
93 Jimmy Alvarez RC .40 .12
94 Jason Schmidt .40 .12
95 Reggie Sanders .40 .12
96 Victor Alvarez RC .40 .12
97 Brett Roneberg RC .40 .12
98 D'Angelo Jimenez .40 .12
99 Hank Blalock 1.00 .30
100 Juan Rivera .40 .12
101 Mark Buehrle SP 2.00 .60
102 Juan Uribe .40 .12
103 Royce Clayton SP 2.00 .60
104 Brett Kay RC .40 .12
105 John Olerud .40 .12
106 Richie Sexson .40 .12
107 Chipper Jones 1.00 .30
108 Adam Dunn .60 .18
109 Tim Salmon SP 3.00 .90
110 Eric Karros .40 .12
111 Jose Vidro .40 .12
112 Jerry Hairston Jr. .40 .12
113 Anastacio Martinez RC .40 .12
114 Robert Fick SP 2.00 .60
115 Randy Johnson 1.00 .30
116 Trot Nixon SP 2.00 .60
117 Nick Bierbrodt SP 2.00 .60
118 Jim Edmonds .40 .12
119 Rafael Palmeiro .60 .18
120 Jose Macias .40 .12
121 Josh Beckett .40 .12
122 Sean Douglass .40 .12
123 Jeff Kent .40 .12
124 Tim Redding .40 .12
125 Xavier Nady .40 .12
126 Carl Everett .40 .12
127 Joe Randa .40 .12
128 Luke Hudson SP 2.00 .60
129 Eric Miller RC .40 .12
130 Melvin Mora .40 .12
131 Adrian Gonzalez .40 .12
132 Larry Walker SP 3.00 .90
133 Nic Jackson SP RC 2.00 .60
134 Mike Lowell SP 2.00 .60
135 Jim Thome 1.00 .30
136 Eric Milton .40 .12
137 Rich Thompson SP RC 2.00 .60
138 Placido Polanco SP 2.00 .60
139 Juan Pierre .40 .12
140 David Segui .40 .12
141 Chuck Finley .40 .12
142 Felipe Lopez .40 .12
143 Toby Hall .40 .12
144 Fred Bastardo RC .40 .12
145 Troy Glaus .60 .18
146 Todd Helton .60 .18
147 Ruben Gotay SP RC 2.00 .60
148 Darin Erstad .40 .12
149 Ryan Gripp SP RC 2.00 .60
150 Orlando Cabrera .40 .12
151 Jason Young RC .40 .12
152 Sterling Hitchcock SP 2.00 .60
153 Miguel Tejada .40 .12
154 Al Leiter .40 .12
155 Taylor Buchholz RC .40 .12
156 Juan M. Gonzalez RC .40 .12
157 Damion Easley .40 .12
158 Jimmy Gobble RC .75 .23
159 Dennis Ulacia SP RC 2.00 .60
160 Shane Reynolds SP 2.00 .60
161 Javier Colina .40 .12
162 Frank Thomas 1.00 .30
163 Chuck Knoblauch .40 .12
164 Sean Burroughs .40 .12
165 Greg Maddux 1.50 .45
166 Jason Ellison RC .40 .12
167 Tony Womack .40 .12
168 Randall Shelley SP RC 2.00 .60
169 Jason Marquis .40 .12
170 Brian Jordan .40 .12
171 Vicente Padilla .40 .12
172 Barry Zito .40 .12
173 Matt Allegra SP RC 2.00 .60
174 Ralph Santana SP RC 2.00 .60
175 Carlos Lee .40 .12
176 Richard Hidalgo SP 2.00 .60
177 Kevin Deaton RC .40 .12
178 Juan Encarnacion .40 .12
179 Mark Quinn .40 .12
180 Rafael Furcal .40 .12
181 Garret Anderson UER .40 .12
Photo is Chone Figgins
182 David Wright RC 10.00 3.00
183 Jose Reyes .60 .18
184 Mario Ramos SP RC 2.00 .60
185 J.D. Drew .60 .18
186 Juan Gonzalez .60 .18
187 Nick Neugebauer .40 .12
188 Alejandro Giron RC .40 .12
189 John Burkett .40 .12
190 Ben Sheets .40 .12
191 Vinny Castilla SP 2.00 .60
192 Cory Lidle .40 .12
193 Fernando Vina .40 .12
194 Russell Branyan SP 2.00 .60
195 Ben Davis .40 .12
196 Angel Berroa .40 .12
197 Alex Gonzalez .40 .12
198 Jared Sandberg .40 .12
199 Travis Lee SP 2.00 .60
200 Luis DePaula SP 2.00 .60
201 Ramon Hernandez SP 2.00 .60
202 Brandon Inge .40 .12
203 Aubrey Huff .40 .12
204 Mike Rivera .40 .12
205 Brad Nelson RC 1.25 .35
206 Colt Griffin SP RC 3.00 .90
207 Joel Pineiro .40 .12
208 Adam Pettyjohn .40 .12
209 Mark Redman .40 .12
210 Roberto Alomar SP 3.00 .90
211 Denny Neagle .40 .12
212 Adam Kennedy .40 .12
213 Jason Arnold SP RC 5.00 1.50
214 Jamie Moyer .40 .12
215 Aaron Boone .40 .12
216 Doug Glanville .40 .12
217 Nick Johnson SP 2.00 .60
218 Mike Cameron SP 2.00 .60
219 Tim Wakefield SP 2.00 .60
220 Todd Stottlemyre SP 2.00 .60
221 Mo Vaughn SP 2.00 .60
222 Vladimir Guerrero 1.00 .30
223 Bill Ortega .40 .12
224 Kevin Brown .40 .12
225 Peter Bergeron SP 2.00 .60
226 Shannon Stewart SP 2.00 .60
227 Eric Chavez .40 .12
228 Clint Weibl RC .40 .12
229 Todd Hollandsworth SP 2.00 .60
230 Jeff Bagwell .60 .18
231 Chad Qualls RC .40 .12
232 Ben Howard RC .40 .12
233 Rondell White SP 2.00 .60
234 Fred McGriff .60 .18
235 Steve Cox SP 2.00 .60
236 Chris Tritle RC .40 .12
237 Eric Valent .40 .12
238 Joe Mauer RC 5.00 1.50

239 Shawn Green .40 .12
240 Jimmy Rollins .40 .12
241 Edgar Renteria .40 .12
242 Edwin Yan RC .40 .12
243 Noochie Varner RC .40 .12
244 Kris Benson SP 2.00 .60
245 Mike Hampton .40 .12
246 So Taguchi RC .50 .15
247 Sammy Sosa 1.50 .45
248 Terrence Long .40 .12
249 Jason Bay RC 2.50 .75
250 Kevin Millar SP 2.00 .60
251 Albert Pujols 2.00 .60
252 Chris Latham RC .40 .12
253 Eric Byrnes .40 .12
254 Napoleon Calzado SP RC 2.00 .60
255 Bobby Higginson .40 .12
256 Ben Molina .40 .12
257 Torii Hunter SP 2.00 .60
258 Jason Giambi .40 .12
259 Bartolo Colon .40 .12
260 Benito Baez .40 .12
261 Ichiro Suzuki 1.50 .45
262 Mike Sweeney .40 .12
263 Brian West RC .40 .12
264 Brad Penny .40 .12
265 Kevin Millwood SP 2.00 .60
266 Orlando Hudson .40 .12
267 Doug Mientkiewicz .40 .12
268 Luis Gonzalez SP 2.00 .60
269 Jay Caligiuri RC .40 .12
270 Nate Cornejo SP 2.00 .60
271 Lee Stevens .40 .12
272 Eric Hinske .40 .12
273 Antwon Rollins RC .40 .12
274 Bobby Jenks RC .75 .23
275 Joe Mays .40 .12
276 Josh Shaffer RC .40 .12
277 Jonny Gomes RC .75 .23
278 Bernie Williams .60 .18
279 Ed Rogers .40 .12
280 Carlos Delgado .40 .12
281 Raul Mondesi SP 2.00 .60
282 Jose Ortiz .40 .12
283 Cesar Izturis .40 .12
284 Ryan Dempster SP 2.00 .60
285 Brian Daubach .40 .12
286 Hansel Izquierdo RC .40 .12
287 Mike Lieberthal SP 2.00 .60
288 Marcus Thames .40 .12
289 Nomar Garciaparra 1.50 .45
290 Brad Fullmer .40 .12
291 Tino Martinez .60 .18
292 James Barrett RC .40 .12
293 Jacque Jones .40 .12
294 Nick Alvarez SP RC 2.00 .60
295 Jason Grove SP RC 2.00 .60
296 Mike Wilson SP RC 2.00 .60
297 J.T. Snow .40 .12
298 Cliff Floyd .40 .12
299 Todd Hundley SP 2.00 .60
300 Tony Clark SP 2.00 .60
301 Demetrius Heath RC .40 .12
302 Morgan Ensberg .40 .12
303 Cristian Guzman .40 .12
304 Frank Catalanotto .40 .12
305 Jeff Weaver .40 .12
306 Tim Hudson .40 .12
307 Scott Wiggins SP RC 2.00 .60
308 Shea Hillenbrand SP 2.00 .60
309 Todd Walker SP 2.00 .60
310 Tsuyoshi Shinjo .40 .12
311 Adrian Beltre .60 .18
312 Craig Kuzmic RC .40 .12
313 Paul Konerko .40 .12
314 Scott Hairston RC 1.50 .45
315 Chan Ho Park .40 .12
316 Jorge Posada .60 .18
317 Chris Snelling RC .40 .12
318 Keith Foulke .40 .12
319 John Smoltz .60 .18
320 Ryan Church SP RC 5.00 1.50
321 Mike Mussina .60 .18
322 Tony Armas Jr. SP 2.00 .60
323 Craig Counsell .40 .12
324 Marcus Giles .40 .12
325 Greg Vaughn .40 .12
326 Curt Schilling .40 .12
327 Jeromy Burnitz .40 .12
328 Eric Byrnes .40 .12
329 Johnny Damon Sox 1.00 .30
330 Michael Floyd SP RC 2.00 .60
331 Edgardo Alfonzo .40 .12
332 Jeremy Hill RC .40 .12
333 Josh Bonifay RC .40 .12
334 Byung-Hyun Kim .40 .12
335 Keith Ginter .40 .12
336 Ronald Acuna SP RC 2.00 .60
337 Mike Hill SP RC 2.00 .60
338 Sean Casey .40 .12
339 Matt Anderson SP 2.00 .60
340 Dan Wright .40 .12
341 Ben Petrick .40 .12
342 Mike Sirotka SP 2.00 .60
343 Alex Rodriguez 1.50 .45
344 Einar Diaz .40 .12
345 Derek Jeter 2.50 .75
346 Jeff Conine .40 .12
347 Ray Durham SP 2.00 .60
348 Wilson Betemit SP 2.00 .60
349 Jeffrey Hammonds .40 .12
350 Dan Trumble RC .40 .12
351 Phil Nevin SP 2.00 .60
352 A.J. Burnett .40 .12
353 Bill Mueller .40 .12
354 Charles Nagy .40 .12
355 Rusty Greer SP 2.00 .60
356 Jason Botts RC .75 .23
357 Magglio Ordonez .40 .12
358 Kevin Appier .40 .12
359 Brad Radke .40 .12
360 Chris George .40 .12
361 Chris Piersoll RC .40 .12
362 Ivan Rodriguez 1.00 .30
363 Jim Kavourias RC .40 .12
364 Rick Helling SP 2.00 .60
365 Dean Palmer .40 .12
366 Rich Aurilia SP 2.00 .60
367 Ryan Vogelsong .40 .12
368 Matt Lawton .40 .12
369 Wade Miller .40 .12
370 Dustin Hermanson .40 .12
371 Craig Wilson .40 .12
372 Todd Zeile SP 2.00 .60
373 Jon Guzman RC .40 .12
374 Ellis Burks .40 .12
375 Robert Cosby SP RC 2.00 .60
376 Jason Kendall .40 .12
377 Scott Rolen SP 5.00 1.50
378 Andruw Jones .40 .12
379 Greg Sain RC .50 .15
380 Paul LoDuca .40 .12
381 Scotty Layfield RC .40 .12
382 Tomo Ohka .40 .12
383 Garrett Guzman RC .40 .12
384 Jack Cust SP 2.00 .60
385 Shayne Wright RC .40 .12
386 Derrek Lee .40 .12
387 Jesus Medrano RC .40 .12
388 Javier Vazquez .40 .12
389 Preston Wilson SP 2.00 .60
390 Gavin Floyd RC 2.50 .75
391 Sidney Ponson SP 2.00 .60
392 Jose Hernandez .40 .12
393 Scott Erickson SP 2.00 .60
394 Jose Valverde RC .50 .15
395 Mark Hamilton SP RC 2.00 .60
396 Brad Cresse .40 .12
397 Danny Bautista .40 .12
398 Ray Lankford SP 2.00 .60
399 Miguel Batista SP 2.00 .60
400 Brent Butler .40 .12
401 Manny Delcarmen SP RC 2.00 .60
402 Kyle Farnsworth SP 2.00 .60
403 Freddy Garcia .40 .12
404 Joe Jiannetti RC .40 .12
405 Josh Barfield RC 1.50 .45
406 Corey Patterson .40 .12
407 Josh Towers .40 .12
408 Carlos Pena .40 .12
409 Jeff Cirillo .40 .12
410 Jon Lieber .40 .12
411 Woody Williams SP 2.00 .60
412 Richard Lane SP RC 2.00 .60
413 Alex Gonzalez .40 .12
414 Wilkin Ruan .40 .12
415 Geoff Jenkins .40 .12
416 Carlos Hernandez .40 .12
417 Matt Clement SP 2.00 .60
418 Jose Cruz Jr. .40 .12
419 Jake Mauer RC .40 .12
420 Matt Childers RC .40 .12
421 Tom Glavine SP 3.00 .90
422 Ken Griffey Jr. 1.50 .45
423 Anderson Hernandez RC .40 .12
424 John Suomi RC .40 .12
425 Doug Sessions RC .40 .12
426 Jaret Wright .40 .12
427 Rolando Viera SP RC 2.00 .60
428 Aaron Sele .40 .12
429 Dmitri Young .40 .12
430 Ryan Klesko .40 .12
431 Kevin Tapani SP 2.00 .60
432 Joe Kennedy .40 .12
433 Austin Kearns .40 .12
434 Roger Cedeno SP 2.00 .60
435 Lance Berkman .40 .12
436 Frank Menechino .40 .12
437 Brett Myers .40 .12
438 Bob Abreu .40 .12
439 Shawn Estes SP 2.00 .60

2002 Bowman Heritage Black Box

Issued at stated odds of one in two packs, these 55 cards form a partial parallel of the Bowman Heritage set. These cards can be notated by the players "signature" being placed in a black box.

Nm-Mt Ex-Mt
13 Hee Seop Choi .75 .23
22 Barry Bonds 5.00 1.50
23 Justin Schuda .60 .18
27 Aramis Ramirez .75 .23
30 Kazuhisa Ishii 2.00 .60
39 Mark Prior 4.00 1.20
41 Travis Foley .60 .18
56 Mike Piazza 3.00 .90
66 Nomar Garciaparra 2.00 .60
72 Roy Oswalt .75 .23
96 Victor Alvarez .60 .18
99 Hank Blalock 2.00 .60
107 Chipper Jones 2.00 .60
108 Adam Dunn 1.25 .35
120 Jose Macias .75 .23
121 Josh Beckett .75 .23
139 Juan Pierre .75 .23
143 Toby Hall .75 .23
145 Troy Glaus .75 .23
146 Todd Helton 1.25 .35
153 Miguel Tejada .75 .23
167 Tony Womack .75 .23
170 Rafael Furcal .75 .23
182 David Wright 15.00 4.50
185 J.D. Drew .75 .23
222 Vladimir Guerrero 2.00 .60
227 Eric Chavez .75 .23
238 Joe Mauer 8.00 2.40
240 Jimmy Rollins .75 .23
246 So Taguchi .75 .23
247 Sammy Sosa 3.00 .90
251 Albert Pujols 4.00 1.20
258 Jason Giambi .75 .23
261 Ichiro Suzuki 3.00 .90
266 Orlando Hudson .75 .23
269 Jay Caligiuri .60 .18
274 Bobby Jenks 1.25 .35
275 Joe Mays .75 .23
277 Jonny Gomes 1.25 .35
310 Tsuyoshi Shinjo .75 .23
314 Scott Hairston 2.50 .75
316 Jorge Posada 1.25 .35
317 Chris Snelling .60 .18
335 Keith Ginter .75 .23
343 Alex Rodriguez 3.00 .90
345 Derek Jeter 5.00 1.50
352 Ivan Rodriguez 2.00 .60
390 Gavin Floyd 4.00 1.20
396 Brad Cresse .75 .23
405 Josh Barfield 2.50 .75
414 Wilkin Ruan .75 .23
416 Carlos Hernandez .75 .23
418 Jose Cruz Jr. .75 .23
422 Ken Griffey Jr. 3.00 .90
433 Austin Kearns .75 .23

2002 Bowman Heritage Chrome Refractors

Issued at stated odds of one in 16, these 110 cards partially parallel the regular Bowman Heritage set. Please note that although the numbering is different, the cards are the same as the regular cards except for the Chrome technology used. These cards were issued to a stated print run of 350 serial numbered sets.

Nm-Mt Ex-Mt
*CHROME: 4X TO 10X BASIC CARDS
*CHROME SP's: .75X TO 2X BASIC SP'S
*CHROME RC's: 3X TO 8X BASIC RC'S

2002 Bowman Heritage Gold Chrome Refractors

Issued at stated odds of one in 32, these 110 cards partially parallel the regular Bowman Heritage set. Please note that although the numbering is different, the cards are the same as the regular cards except for the Chrome technology used. Each card was issued to a stated print run of 175 serial numbered sets.

Nm-Mt Ex-Mt
*GOLD: 6X TO 15X BASIC CARDS
*GOLD SP'S: 1.25X TO 3X BASIC SP'S
*GOLD RC'S: 5X TO 12X BASIC RC'S

2002 Bowman Heritage 1954 Reprints

Issued at stated odds of one in 12, these 20 cards feature reprinted versions of the featured player 1954 Bowman card.

Nm-Mt Ex-Mt
COMPLETE SET (20) 50.00 15.00
BHR-AR Allie Reynolds 2.00 .60
BHR-BF Bob Feller 2.00 .60
BHR-CL Clem Labine 2.00 .60
BHR-DC Del Crandall 2.00 .60
BHR-DL Don Larsen 2.00 .60
BHR-DM Don Mueller 2.00 .60
BHR-DS Duke Snider 5.00 1.50
BHR-DW Dave Williams 2.00 .60
BHR-ES Enos Slaughter 2.00 .60
BHR-GM Gil McDougald 2.00 .60
BHR-HW Hoyt Wilhelm 2.00 .60
BHR-JL Johnny Logan 2.00 .60
BHR-JP Jim Piersall 2.00 .60
BHR-NF Nellie Fox 3.00 .90
BHR-PR Phil Rizzuto 3.00 .90
BHR-RA Richie Ashburn 3.00 .90
BHR-WF Whitey Ford 3.00 .90
BHR-WM Willie Mays 10.00 3.00
BHR-WW Wes Westrum 2.00 .60
BHR-YB Yogi Berra 5.00 1.50

2002 Bowman Heritage 1954 Reprints Autographs

Inserted at stated odds of one in 126, these six cards have autographs of the featured player on their 1954 Reprint card.

Nm-Mt Ex-Mt
*SPEC.ED: 1.25X TO 3X BASIC AUTOS
SPEC.ED STATED ODDS 1:1910
SPEC.ED. PRINT RUN 54 SERIAL #'d SETS
BHRA-CL Clem Labine 25.00 7.50
BHRA-DC Del Crandall 25.00 7.50
BHRA-DM Don Mueller 15.00 4.50
BHRA-DW Dave Williams 15.00 4.50
BHRA-JL Johnny Logan 25.00 7.50
BHRA-YB Yogi Berra 50.00 15.00

2002 Bowman Heritage Autographs

Issued at overall stated odds of one in 45, these 13 cards feature players signing copies of their Bowman Heritage card. Please note that these cards were issued in three different groups with differing odds and we have noted which players belong to which group in our checklist.

Nm-Mt Ex-Mt
GROUP A STATED ODDS 1:620
GROUP B STATED ODDS 1:89
GROUP C STATED ODDS 1:103
OVERALL STATED ODDS 1:45
BHA-AP Albert Pujols A 150.00 45.00
BHA-CI Cesar Izturis B 10.00 3.00
BHA-DH Drew Henson B 20.00 6.00
BHA-HB Hank Blalock C 25.00 7.50
BHA-JM Joe Mauer C 50.00 15.00
BHA-JR Juan Rivera C 15.00 4.50
BHA-KG Keith Ginter B 10.00 3.00
BHA-KI Kazuhisa Ishii A 40.00 12.00
BHA-LB Lance Berkman B 20.00 6.00
BHA-MP Mark Prior B 80.00 24.00
BHA-PL Paul LoDuca C 15.00 4.50
BHA-RO Roy Oswalt B 15.00 4.50
BHA-TH Toby Hall B 10.00 3.00

2002 Bowman Heritage Relics

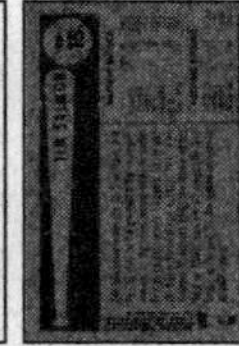

Inserted in packs at overall stated odds of one in 47 for Jersey cards and one in 75 for Uniform cards, these 26 cards feature game-worn swatches on them. Many cards belong to different groups and we have noted that information next to their name in our checklist.

Nm-Mt Ex-Mt
GROUP A JSY ODDS 1:1910
GROUP B JSY ODDS 1:1551
GROUP C JSY ODDS 1:138
GROUP D JSY ODDS 1:207
GROUP E JSY ODDS 1:165
GROUP F JSY ODDS 1:2072
GROUP G JSY ODDS 1:653
GROUP A UNI ODDS 1:1551
GROUP B UNI ODDS 1:855
GROUP C UNI ODDS 1:124
GROUP D UNI ODDS 1:284
BH-AP Albert Pujols Uni C 20.00 6.00
BH-BB Barry Bonds Uni D 25.00 7.50
BH-CD Carlos Delgado Jsy G 10.00 3.00
BH-CJ Chipper Jones Jsy C 15.00 4.50
BH-DE Darin Erstad Uni C 10.00 3.00
BH-EA Edgardo Alfonzo Jsy C 10.00 3.00
BH-EC Eric Chavez Jsy C 10.00 3.00
BH-EM Edgar Martinez Jsy C 15.00 4.50
BH-FT Frank Thomas Jsy F 15.00 4.50
BH-GM Greg Maddux Jsy C 15.00 4.50
BH-IR Ivan Rodriguez Uni B 15.00 4.50
BH-JB Josh Beckett Jsy E 10.00 3.00
BH-JE Jim Edmonds Jsy D 10.00 3.00
BH-JS John Smoltz Jsy C 15.00 4.50
BH-JT Jim Thome Jsy E 15.00 4.50
BH-KS Kazuhiro Sasaki Jsy C 10.00 3.00
BH-LW Larry Walker Jsy C 15.00 4.50
BH-MP Mike Piazza Uni A 15.00 4.50
BH-MR Mariano Rivera Uni C 15.00 4.50
BH-NG Nomar Garciaparra Jsy A 20.00 6.00
BH-PK Paul Konerko Jsy E 10.00 3.00
BH-PW Preston Wilson Jsy B 10.00 3.00
BH-SR Scott Rolen Jsy C 15.00 4.50
BH-TG Tony Gwynn Jsy D 15.00 4.50
BH-TH Todd Helton Jsy D 15.00 4.50
BH-TS Tim Salmon Uni C 15.00 4.50

2003 Bowman Heritage

This 300-card standard-size set was released in December, 2003. The set was issued in four-card packs with an $3 SRP which came 24 packs to a box and 10 boxes to a case. This set was designed in the style of what the 1956 Bowman set would have been if that set had been issued. Cards numbered 161 through 170 feature players who debuted in the 2003 season and each of those players have a double image. Cards numbered 171-180 featured retired greats and those cards were issued in three styles: Regular design, Double Image and Knothole Design, Cards number 180 through 300 are all Rookie Cards and all those cards are issued in the knothole design.

MINT NRMT
COMPLETE SET (300) 100.00 45.00
1 Jorge Posada .60 .25
2 Todd Helton .60 .25
3 Marcus Giles .40 .18
4 Eric Chavez .40 .18
5 Edgar Martinez .60 .25
6 Luis Gonzalez .40 .18
7 Corey Patterson .40 .18
8 Preston Wilson .40 .18
9 Ryan Klesko .40 .18
10 Randy Johnson 1.00 .45
11 Jose Guillen .40 .18
12 Carlos Lee .40 .18
13 Steve Finley .40 .18
14 A.J. Pierzynski .40 .18
15 Troy Glaus .40 .18
16 Darin Erstad .40 .18
17 Moises Alou .40 .18
18 Torii Hunter .40 .18
19 Marlon Byrd .40 .18
20 Mark Prior 1.00 .45
21 Shannon Stewart .40 .18
22 Craig Biggio .60 .25
23 Johnny Damon 1.00 .45
24 Robert Fick .40 .18
25 Jason Giambi .40 .18
26 Fernando Vina .40 .18
27 Aubrey Huff .40 .18
28 Benito Santiago .40 .18
29 Jay Gibbons .40 .18
30 Ken Griffey Jr. 1.50 .70
31 Rocco Baldelli .40 .18
32 Pat Burrell .40 .18
33 A.J. Burnett .40 .18
34 Omar Vizquel .60 .25
35 Greg Maddux 1.50 .70
36 Cliff Floyd .40 .18
37 C.C. Sabathia .40 .18
38 Geoff Jenkins .40 .18
39 Ty Wigginton .40 .18
40 Jeff Kent .40 .18
41 Orlando Hudson .40 .18
42 Edgardo Alfonzo .40 .18
43 Greg Myers .40 .18
44 Melvin Mora .40 .18
45 Sammy Sosa 1.50 .70
46 Russ Ortiz .40 .18
47 Josh Beckett .40 .18
48 David Wells .40 .18
49 Woody Williams .40 .18
50 Alex Rodriguez 1.50 .70
51 Randy Wolf .40 .18
52 Carlos Beltran .60 .25
53 Austin Kearns .40 .18
54 Trot Nixon .40 .18
55 Ivan Rodriguez 1.00 .45
56 Shea Hillenbrand .40 .18
57 Roberto Alomar .60 .25
58 John Olerud .40 .18
59 Michael Young .60 .25
60 Garret Anderson .40 .18
61 Mike Lieberthal .40 .18
62 Adam Dunn .60 .25
63 Raul Ibanez .40 .18
64 Kenny Lofton .40 .18
65 Ichiro Suzuki 1.50 .70
66 Jarrod Washburn .40 .18
67 Shawn Chacon .40 .18
68 Alex Gonzalez .40 .18
69 Roy Halladay .40 .18
70 Vladimir Guerrero 1.00 .45
71 Hee Seop Choi .40 .18
72 Jody Gerut .40 .18
73 Ray Durham .40 .18
74 Mark Teixeira .40 .18
75 Hank Blalock .60 .25
76 Jerry Hairston Jr. .40 .18
77 Erubiel Durazo .40 .18
78 Frank Catalanotto .40 .18
79 Jacque Jones .40 .18
80 Bobby Abreu .40 .18
81 Mike Hampton .40 .18
82 Zach Day .40 .18
83 Jimmy Rollins .40 .18
84 Joel Pineiro .40 .18
85 Brett Myers .40 .18
86 Frank Thomas 1.00 .45
87 Aramis Ramirez .40 .18
88 Paul Lo Duca .40 .18
89 Dmitri Young .40 .18
90 Brian Giles .40 .18
91 Jose Cruz Jr. .40 .18
92 Derek Lowe .40 .18
93 Mark Buehrle .40 .18
94 Wade Miller .40 .18
95 Derek Jeter 2.50 1.10
96 Bret Boone .40 .18
97 Tony Batista .40 .18
98 Sean Casey .40 .18
99 Eric Hinske .40 .18
100 Albert Pujols 2.00 .90
101 Runelvys Hernandez .40 .18
102 Vernon Wells .40 .18
103 Kerry Wood 1.00 .45
104 Lance Berkman .40 .18
105 Alfonso Soriano .60 .25
106 Bill Mueller .40 .18
107 Bartolo Colon .40 .18
108 Andy Pettitte .60 .25
109 Rafael Furcal .40 .18
110 Dontrelle Willis .60 .25
111 Carl Crawford .40 .18
112 Scott Rolen 1.00 .45
113 Chipper Jones 1.00 .45
114 Magglio Ordonez .40 .18
115 Bernie Williams .60 .25
116 Roy Oswalt .40 .18
117 Kevin Brown .40 .18
118 Cristian Guzman .40 .18
119 Kazuhisa Ishii .40 .18
120 Larry Walker .60 .25
121 Miguel Tejada .40 .18
122 Manny Ramirez .60 .25
123 Mike Mussina .60 .25
124 Mike Lowell .40 .18
125 Scott Podsednik .40 .18
126 Aaron Boone .40 .18
127 Carlos Delgado .40 .18
128 Jose Vidro .40 .18
129 Brad Radke .40 .18
130 Rafael Palmeiro .60 .25
131 Mark Mulder .40 .18
132 Jason Schmidt .40 .18
133 Gary Sheffield .40 .18
134 Richie Sexson .40 .18
135 Barry Zito .40 .18
136 Tom Glavine .60 .25
137 Jim Edmonds .40 .18
138 Andruw Jones .40 .18
139 Pedro Martinez 1.00 .45
140 Curt Schilling .40 .18
141 Phil Nevin .40 .18
142 Nomar Garciaparra 1.50 .70
143 Vicente Padilla .40 .18
144 Kevin Millwood .40 .18
145 Shawn Green .40 .18
146 Jeff Bagwell .60 .25
147 Hideo Nomo 1.00 .45
148 Fred McGriff .60 .25
149 Matt Morris .40 .18

50 Roger Clemens 2.00 .90
51 Jerome Williams .40 .18
52 Orlando Cabrera .40 .18
53 Tim Hudson .40 .18
54 Mike Sweeney .40 .18
55 Jim Thome 1.00 .45
56 Rich Aurilia .40 .18
57 Mike Piazza 1.50 .70
58 Edgar Renteria .40 .18
59 Javy Lopez .40 .18
60 Jamie Moyer .40 .18
61 Miguel Cabrera DI 1.00 .45
62 Adam Loewen DI RC 1.25 .55
63 Jose Reyes DI .40 .18
64 Zack Greinke DI .60 .25
65 Gavin Floyd DI .40 .18
66 Jeremy Guthrie DI .40 .18
67 Victor Martinez DI .60 .25
68 Rich Harden DI .60 .25
69 Joe Mauer DI 1.00 .45
70 Khalil Greene DI 2.00 .90
71A Willie Mays 2.00 .90
71B Willie Mays DI 2.00 .90
71C Willie Mays KN 2.00 .90
72A Phil Rizzuto .60 .25
72B Phil Rizzuto DI .60 .25
72C Phil Rizzuto KN .60 .25
73A Al Kaline 1.00 .45
73B Al Kaline DI 1.00 .45
73C Al Kaline KN 1.00 .45
74A Warren Spahn .60 .25
74B Warren Spahn DI .60 .25
74C Warren Spahn KN .60 .25
75A Jimmy Piersall .40 .18
75B Jimmy Piersall DI .40 .18
75C Jimmy Piersall KN .40 .18
76A Luis Aparicio .40 .18
76B Luis Aparicio DI .40 .18
76C Luis Aparicio KN .40 .18
77A Whitey Ford .60 .25
77B Whitey Ford DI .60 .25
77C Whitey Ford KN .60 .25
78A Harmon Killebrew 1.00 .45
78B Harmon Killebrew DI 1.00 .45
78C Harmon Killebrew KN 1.00 .45
79A Duke Snider .60 .25
79B Duke Snider DI .60 .25
79C Duke Snider KN .60 .25
80A Roberto Clemente 2.50 1.10
80B Roberto Clemente DI 2.50 1.10
80C Roberto Clemente KN 2.50 1.10
81 David Martinez KN RC .40 .18
82 Felix Pie KN RC 2.50 1.10
83 Kevin Correia KN RC .40 .18
84 Brandon Webb KN RC 1.25 .55
85 Matt Diaz KN RC .60 .25
86 Lew Ford KN RC 1.50 .70
87 Jeremy Griffiths KN RC .60 .25
88 Matt Hensley KN RC .40 .18
89 Danny Garcia KN RC .40 .18
90 Elizardo Ramirez KN RC 1.00 .45
91 Greg Aquino KN RC .40 .18
92 Felix Sanchez KN RC .40 .18
93 Kelly Shoppach KN RC 1.25 .55
94 Bubba Nelson KN RC .60 .25
95 Mike O'Keefe KN RC .40 .18
96 Hanley Ramirez KN RC 2.50 1.10
97 Todd Wellemeyer KN RC .60 .25
98 Dustin Moseley KN RC .60 .25
99 Eric Crozier KN RC .60 .25
00 Ryan Shealy KN RC 1.00 .45
01 Jeremy Bonderman KN RC 1.00 .45
02 Bo Hart KN RC .60 .25
03 Dusty Brown KN RC .40 .18
04 Rob Hammock KN RC .60 .25
05 Jorge Piedra KN RC .60 .25
06 Jason Kubel KN RC 2.50 1.10
07 Stephen Randolph KN RC .40 .18
08 Andy Sisco KN RC 1.25 .55
09 Matt Kata KN RC 1.00 .45
10 Robinson Cano KN RC 1.00 .45
11 Ben Francisco KN RC .60 .25
12 Arnie Munoz KN RC .40 .18
13 Ozzie Chavez KN RC .40 .18
14 Beau Kemp KN RC .40 .18
15 Travis Wong KN RC .60 .25
16 Brian McCann KN RC 1.00 .45
17 Aquilino Lopez KN RC .40 .18
18 Bobby Basham KN RC .60 .25
19 Tim Olson KN RC .60 .25
20 Nathan Panther KN RC 1.00 .45
21 Wil Ledezma KN RC .60 .25
22 Josh Willingham KN RC .60 .25
23 David Cash KN RC .40 .18
24 Oscar Villarreal KN RC .40 .18
25 Jeff Duncan KN RC .60 .25
26 Dan Haren KN RC 1.00 .45
27 Michel Hernandez KN RC .40 .18
28 Matt Murton KN RC .40 .18
29 Clay Hensley KN RC .40 .18
30 Tyler Johnson KN RC .40 .18
31 Tyler Martin KN RC .40 .18
32 J.D. Durbin KN RC 1.00 .45
33 Shane Victorino KN RC .40 .18
34 Rajai Davis KN RC .60 .25
35 Chien-Ming Wang KN RC 1.25 .55
36 Travis Ishikawa KN RC .40 .18
37 Eric Eckenstahler KN .40 .18
38 Dustin McGowan KN RC 1.00 .45
39 Prentice Redman KN RC .40 .18
40 Haj Turay KN RC .60 .25
41 Matt DeMarco KN RC .40 .18
42 Lou Palmisano KN RC 1.50 .70
43 Eric Reed KN RC .40 .18
44 Willie Eyre KN RC .40 .18
45 Ferdin Tejeda KN RC .40 .18
46 Michael Garciaparra KN RC 1.00 .45
47 Michael Hinckley KN RC 1.25 .55
48 Branden Florence KN RC .40 .18
49 Trent Oeltjen KN RC .60 .25
50 Mike Neu KN RC .40 .18
51 Chris Lubanski KN RC 2.00 .90
52 Brandon Wood KN RC 1.25 .55
53 Delmon Young KN RC 4.00 1.80
54 Matt Harrison KN RC 1.00 .45
55 Chad Billingsley KN RC 1.50 .70
56 Josh Anderson KN RC 1.25 .55
57 Brian McFall KN RC 1.00 .45
58 Ryan Wagner KN RC .60 .25
59 Billy Hogan KN RC .60 .25
260 Nate Spears KN RC 1.00 .45
261 Ryan Harvey KN RC 2.00 .90
262 Wes Littleton KN RC .60 .25
263 Xavier Paul KN RC 2.00 .90
264 Sean Rodriguez KN RC 1.25 .55
265 Brian Finch KN RC .40 .18
266 Josh Rainwater KN RC .60 .25
267 Brian Snyder KN RC .60 .25
268 Eric Duncan KN RC 1.50 .70
269 Rickie Weeks KN RC 3.00 1.35
270 Tim Battle KN RC .60 .25
271 Scott Beerer KN RC .40 .18
272 Aaron Hill KN RC 1.25 .55
273 Casey Abrams KN RC .40 .18
274 Jonathan Fulton KN RC .60 .25
275 Todd Jennings KN RC .60 .25
276 Jordan Pratt KN RC .60 .25
277 Tom Gorzelanny KN RC 1.00 .45
278 Matt Lorenzo KN RC .60 .25
279 Jarrod Saltalamacchia KN RC 1.00 .45
280 Mike Wagner KN RC .40 .18

2003 Bowman Heritage Autographs

MINT NRMT
STATED ODDS 1:1014
EXCHANGE DEADLINE 12/31/05
253 Delmon Young KN EXCH 50.00 22.00

2003 Bowman Heritage Box Toppers

MINT NRMT
COMPLETE SET (8) 25.00 11.00
*BOX TOPPER: .4X TO 1X BASIC
ONE PER SEALED BOX

2003 Bowman Heritage Facsimile Signature

MINT NRMT
*FACSIMILE 161-170: 1X TO 2.5X BASIC
*FACSIMILE 171A-180C: 1X TO 2.5X BASIC
*FACSIMILE 181-280: .6X TO 1.5X BASIC
ONE PER PACK

2003 Bowman Heritage Gold Rainbow

MINT NRMT
STATED ODDS 1:4178
STATED PRINT RUN 1 SERIAL #'d SET
NO PRICING DUE TO SCARCITY

2003 Bowman Heritage Rainbow

MINT NRMT
COMPLETE SET (100) 80.00 36.00
*RAINBOW: .4X TO 1X BASIC
ONE PER PACK

2003 Bowman Heritage Diamond Cuts Relics

MINT NRMT
BAT ODDS 1:133
JSY GROUP A ODDS 1:28
JSY GROUP B ODDS 1:936
JSY GROUP C ODDS 1:626
UNI ODDS 1:35
GOLD STATED ODDS 1:8193
GOLD PRINT RUN 1 SERIAL #'d SET.
NO GOLD PRICING DUE TO SCARCITY
*RED BAT: .6X TO 1.5X BASIC BAT
*RED JSY: 1X TO 2.5X BASIC JSY
*RED UNI: 1X TO 2.5X BASIC UNI
RED STATED ODDS 1:143
RED PRINT RUN 56 SERIAL #'d SETS
AJ Andruw Jones Jsy A 8.00 3.60
AK Austin Kearns Jsy A 8.00 3.60
AP Albert Pujols Bat 25.00 11.00
AR1 Alex Rodriguez Bat 15.00 6.75
AR2 Alex Rodriguez Jsy A 10.00 4.50
AS Alfonso Soriano Bat 15.00 6.75
BB Bret Boone Jsy A 8.00 3.60
BM Brett Myers Jsy A 8.00 3.60
BW Bernie Williams Uni 10.00 4.50
BZ Barry Zito Uni 8.00 3.60
CB Craig Biggio Uni 10.00 4.50
CF Cliff Floyd Uni 8.00 3.60
CG Cristian Guzman Jsy A 8.00 3.60
CJ1 Chipper Jones Bat 15.00 6.75
CJ2 Chipper Jones Jsy A 10.00 4.50
EC Eric Chavez Uni 8.00 3.60
GS Gary Sheffield Uni 8.00 3.60
HB Hank Blalock Bat 15.00 6.75
HN Hideo Nomo Jsy A 10.00 4.50
JA Jeremy Affeldt Uni 8.00 3.60
JB Jeff Bagwell Jsy A 10.00 4.50
JE Jim Edmonds Uni 8.00 3.60
JG Jason Giambi Uni 8.00 3.60
JJ Jason Jennings Jsy A 8.00 3.60
JL Javy Lopez Jsy A 8.00 3.60
JLP Josh Phelps Jsy C 8.00 3.60
JR Jose Reyes Jsy A 8.00 3.60
JV Javier Vazquez Jsy A 8.00 3.60
JW Jarrod Washburn Uni 8.00 3.60
KI Kazuhiro Sasaki Jsy A 8.00 3.60
KM Kevin Millwood Jsy A 8.00 3.60
KW Kerry Wood Uni 10.00 4.50
MA Moises Alou Jsy C 8.00 3.60
MG Mark Grace Jsy B 10.00 4.50
ML Mike Lowell Jsy A 8.00 3.60
MM Mark Mulder Uni 8.00 3.60
MS Mike Sweeney Jsy A 8.00 3.60
MT Miguel Tejada Uni 8.00 3.60
PL Paul Lo Duca Jsy A 8.00 3.60
PM Pedro Martinez Jsy A 10.00 4.50
RC Roberto Clemente Bat 80.00 36.00
RH Rickey Henderson Bat 15.00 6.75
RP1 Rafael Palmeiro Bat 15.00 6.75
RP2 Rafael Palmeiro Uni 10.00 4.50
SR1 Scott Rolen Bat 15.00 6.75
SR2 Scott Rolen Uni 10.00 4.50
SS1 Sammy Sosa Bat 15.00 6.75
SS2 Sammy Sosa Jsy A 10.00 4.50
TA Tony Armas Jr. Jsy A 8.00 3.60
TG Troy Glaus Uni 8.00 3.60
TH Todd Helton Jsy A 10.00 4.50
THA Tim Hudson Uni 8.00 3.60
TW Ty Wigginton Uni 8.00 3.60
VG Vladimir Guerrero Bat 15.00 6.75
VW Vernon Wells Jsy A 8.00 3.60

2003 Bowman Heritage Olbermann Autograph

MINT NRMT
STATED ODDS 1:1421
KOA Keith Olbermann 80.00 36.00

2003 Bowman Heritage Signs of Greatness

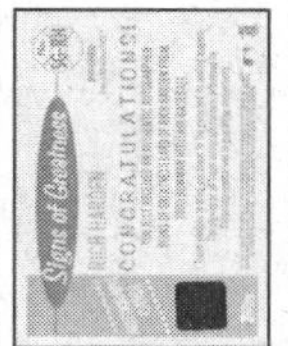

MINT NRMT
STATED ODDS 1:30
RED INK STATED ODDS 1:32,141
RED INK PRINT RUN 1 SERIAL #'d SET
NO RED INK PRICING DUE TO SCARCITY
BF Brian Finch 10.00 4.50
BS Brian Snyder 10.00 4.50
CB Chad Billingsley 15.00 6.75
DW Dontrelle Willis 20.00 9.00
FP Felix Pie 15.00 6.75
JD Jeff Duncan 10.00 4.50
KY Kevin Youkilis 20.00 9.00
MM Matt Murton 10.00 4.50
RC Robinson Cano 15.00 6.75
RH Rich Harden 20.00 9.00
RW Rickie Weeks 25.00 11.00
TG Tom Gorzelanny 10.00 4.50

2003 Bowman Heritage Topps Blue Chips Autographs

MINT NRMT
GROUP A ODDS 1:709
GROUP B ODDS 1:142
SEE 03 TEAM TOPPS BLUE CHIP FOR PRICES

1994 Bowman's Best

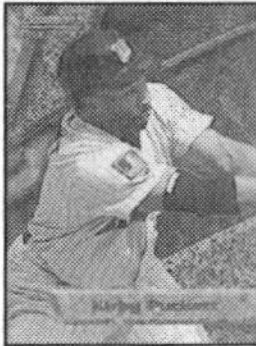

This 200-card standard-size set (produced by Topps) consists of 90 veteran stars, 90 rookies and prospects and 20 Mirror Image cards. The veteran cards have red fronts and are designated 1R-90R. The rookies and prospects cards have blue fronts and are designated 1B-90B. The Mirror Image cards feature a veteran star and a prospect matched by position in a horizontal design. These cards are numbered 91-110. Subsets featured are Super Vet (1R-6R), Super Rookie (82R-90R), and Blue Chip (1B-11B). Rookie Cards include Edgardo Alfonzo, Tony Clark, Brad Fullmer, Chan Ho Park, Jorge Posada and Edgar Renteria.

Nm-Mt Ex-Mt
COMPLETE SET (200) 40.00 12.00
B1 Chipper Jones 1.25 .35
B2 Derek Jeter 4.00 1.20
B3 Bill Pulsipher .50 .15
B4 James Baldwin .25 .07
B5 Brooks Kieschnick RC 1.00 .30
B6 Justin Thompson .25 .07
B7 Midre Cummings .25 .07
B8 Joey Hamilton .25 .07
B9 Pokey Reese .25 .07
B10 Brian Barber .25 .07
B11 John Burke .25 .07
B12 DeShawn Warren .25 .07
B13 Edgardo Alfonzo RC 1.50 .45
B14 Eddie Pearson RC .50 .15
B15 Jimmy Haynes .25 .07
B16 Danny Bautista .25 .07
B17 Roger Cedeno .25 .07
B18 Jon Lieber .25 .07
B19 Billy Wagner RC 2.50 .75
B20 Tate Seefried RC .50 .15
B21 Chad Mottola .25 .07
B22 Jose Malave .25 .07
B23 Terrell Wade RC .50 .15
B24 Shane Andrews .25 .07
B25 Chan Ho Park RC 1.50 .45
B26 Kirk Presley RC .50 .15
B27 Robbie Beckett .25 .07
B28 Orlando Miller .25 .07
B29 Jorge Posada RC 10.00 3.00
B30 Frankie Rodriguez .25 .07
B31 Brian L. Hunter .25 .07
B32 Billy Ashley .25 .07
B33 Rondell White .50 .15
B34 John Roper .25 .07
B35 Marc Valdes .25 .07
B36 Scott Ruffcorn .25 .07
B37 Rod Henderson .25 .07
B38 Curtis Goodwin RC .50 .15
B39 Russ Davis .25 .07
B40 Rick Gorecki .25 .07
B41 Johnny Damon 1.25 .35
B42 Roberto Petagine .25 .07
B43 Chris Snopek .25 .07
B44 Mark Acre RC .50 .15
B45 Todd Hollandsworth .25 .07
B46 Shawn Green 1.25 .35
B47 John Carter RC .50 .15
B48 Jim Pittsley RC .50 .15
B49 John Wasdin RC .50 .15
B50 D.J. Boston RC .50 .15
B51 Tim Clark .25 .07
B52 Alex Ochoa .25 .07
B53 Chad Roper .25 .07
B54 Mike Kelly .25 .07
B55 Brad Fullmer RC 1.50 .45
B56 Carl Everett .50 .15
B57 Tim Belk RC .50 .15
B58 Jimmy Hurst RC .50 .15
B59 Mac Suzuki RC 1.00 .30
B60 Mike Moore .25 .07
B61 Alan Benes RC .50 .15
B62 Tony Clark RC 1.00 .30
B63 Edgar Renteria RC 10.00 2.40
B64 Trey Beamon .25 .07
B65 LaTroy Hawkins RC 1.50 .45
B66 Wayne Gomes RC 1.00 .30
B67 Ray McDavid .25 .07
B68 John Dettmer .25 .07
B69 Willie Greene .25 .07
B70 Dave Stevens .25 .07
B71 Kevin Orie RC .50 .15
B72 Chad Ogea .25 .07
B73 Ben Van Ryn RC .50 .15
B74 Kym Ashworth RC .50 .15
B75 Dmitri Young .50 .15
B76 Herbert Perry RC 1.00 .30
B77 Joey Eischen .25 .07
B78 Arquimedez Pozo RC .50 .15
B79 Ugueth Urbina .25 .07
B80 Keith Williams RC .50 .15
B81 John Frascatore RC .50 .15
B82 Garey Ingram RC .50 .15
B83 Aaron Small .25 .07
B84 Olmedo Saenz RC .50 .15
B85 Jesus Tavarez RC .50 .15
B86 Jose Silva RC 1.00 .30
B87 Jay Witasick RC .50 .15
B88 Jay Maldonado RC .50 .15
B89 Keith Heberling RC .50 .15
B90 Rusty Greer RC 1.50 .45
R1 Paul Molitor .75 .23
R2 Eddie Murray 1.25 .35
R3 Ozzie Smith 2.00 .60
R4 Rickey Henderson 1.25 .35
R5 Lee Smith .50 .15
R6 Dave Winfield .50 .15
R7 Roberto Alomar .75 .23
R8 Matt Williams .50 .15
R9 Mark Grace .75 .23
R10 Lance Johnson .25 .07
R11 Darren Daulton .50 .15
R12 Tom Glavine .75 .23
R13 Gary Sheffield .50 .15
R14 Rod Beck .25 .07
R15 Fred McGriff .75 .23
R16 Joe Carter .50 .15
R17 Dante Bichette .50 .15
R18 Danny Tartabull .25 .07
R19 Juan Gonzalez .75 .23
R20 Steve Avery .25 .07
R21 John Wetteland .50 .15
R22 Ben McDonald .25 .07
R23 Jack McDowell .25 .07
R24 Jose Canseco 1.25 .35
R25 Tim Salmon .75 .23
R26 Wilson Alvarez .25 .07
R27 Gregg Jefferies .25 .07
R28 John Burkett .25 .07
R29 Greg Vaughn .25 .07
R30 Robin Ventura .50 .15
R31 Paul O'Neill .75 .23
R32 Cecil Fielder .50 .15
R33 Kevin Mitchell .25 .07
R34 Jeff Conine .50 .15
R35 Carlos Baerga .25 .07
R36 Greg Maddux 2.00 .60
R37 Roger Clemens 2.50 .75
R38 Deion Sanders .75 .23
R39 Delino DeShields .25 .07
R40 Ken Griffey Jr. 2.00 .60
R41 Albert Belle .50 .15
R42 Wade Boggs .75 .23
R43 Andres Galarraga .50 .15
R44 Aaron Sele .25 .07
R45 Don Mattingly 3.00 .90
R46 David Cone .50 .15
R47 Len Dykstra .50 .15
R48 Brett Butler .50 .15
R49 Bill Swift .25 .07
R50 Bobby Bonilla .50 .15
R51 Rafael Palmeiro .75 .23
R52 Moises Alou .50 .15
R53 Jeff Bagwell .75 .23
R54 Mike Mussina .75 .23
R55 Frank Thomas 1.25 .35
R56 Jose Rijo .25 .07
R57 Ruben Sierra .25 .07
R58 Randy Myers .25 .07
R59 Barry Bonds 3.00 .90
R60 Jimmy Key .50 .15
R61 Travis Fryman .50 .15
R62 John Olerud .50 .15
R63 David Justice .50 .15
R64 Ray Lankford .25 .07
R65 Bob Tewksbury .25 .07
R66 Chuck Carr .25 .07
R67 Jay Buhner .50 .15
R68 Kenny Lofton .50 .15
R69 Marquis Grissom .50 .15
R70 Sammy Sosa 2.00 .60
R71 Cal Ripken 4.00 1.20
R72 Ellis Burks .50 .15
R73 Jeff Montgomery .25 .07
R74 Julio Franco .50 .15
R75 Kirby Puckett 1.25 .35
R76 Larry Walker .75 .23
R77 Andy Van Slyke .50 .15
R78 Tony Gwynn 1.50 .45
R79 Will Clark 1.25 .35
R80 Mo Vaughn .50 .15
R81 Mike Piazza 2.50 .75
R82 James Mouton .25 .07
R83 Carlos Delgado .75 .23
R84 Ryan Klesko .50 .15
R85 Javier Lopez .50 .15
R86 Raul Mondesi .50 .15
R87 Cliff Floyd .50 .15
R88 Manny Ramirez .75 .23
R89 Hector Carrasco .25 .07
R90 Jeff Granger .25 .07
X91 Frank Thomas .75 .23
Dmitri Young
X92 Fred McGriff .50 .15
Brooks Kieschnick
X93 Matt Williams .25 .07
Shane Andrews
X94 Cal Ripken 2.00 .60
Kevin Orie
X95 Barry Larkin 2.00 .60
Derek Jeter
X96 Ken Griffey Jr. 1.00 .30
Johnny Damon
X97 Barry Bonds 1.50 .45
Rondell White
X98 Albert Belle .50 .15
Jimmy Hurst
X99 Raul Mondesi .50 .15
Ruben Rivera RC
X100 Roger Clemens 1.25 .35
Scott Ruffcorn
X101 Greg Maddux 1.25 .35
John Wasdin
X102 Tim Salmon .75 .23
Chad Mottola
X103 Carlos Baerga .25 .07
Arquimedez Pozo
X104 Mike Piazza 1.25 .35
Bobby Hughes
X105 Carlos Delgado .75 .23
Melvin Nieves
X106 Javier Lopez 2.50 .75
Jorge Posada
X107 Manny Ramirez .75 .23
Jose Malave
X108 Travis Fryman .75 .23
Chipper Jones
X109 Steve Avery .25 .07
Bill Pulsipher
X110 John Olerud 1.25 .35
Shawn Green

1994 Bowman's Best Refractors

This 200-card standard-size set is a parallel to the basic Bowman's Best issue. The cards were randomly inserted in packs at a rate of one in nine packs. The only difference is the refractive coating on front that allows for a brighter, shinier appearance.

Nm-Mt Ex-Mt
*RED STARS: 4X TO 10X BASIC CARDS
*BLUE STARS: 4X TO 10X BASIC CARDS
*BLUE ROOKIES: 1.5X TO 4X BASIC..
*MIRROR IMAGE STARS: 2X TO 5X BASIC
B63 Edgar Renteria 50.00 9.00

1995 Bowman's Best

This 195 card standard-size set (produced by Topps) consists of 90 veteran stars, 90 rookies and prospects and 15 dual player Mirror Image cards. The packs contain seven cards and the suggested retail price was $5. The veteran cards have red fronts and are designated R1-R90. Cards of rookies and prospects have blue fronts and are designated B1-B90. The Mirror Image cards feature a veteran star and a prospect matched by position in a horizontal design. These cards are numbered X1-X15. Rookie Cards include Bob Abreu, Bartolo Colon, Scott Elarton, Juan Encarnacion, Vladimir Guerrero, Andruw Jones, Hideo Nomo, Rey Ordonez, Scott Rolen and Richie Sexson.

Nm-Mt Ex-Mt
COMPLETE SET (195)............ 250.00 75.00
COMMON CARD (B1-R90)........... .50 .15
COMMON CARD (X1-X15)........... .50 .15
B1 Derek Jeter........................ 3.00 .90
B2 Vladimir Guerrero RC 80.00 24.00
B3 Bob Abreu RC................... 10.00 3.00
B4 Chan Ho Park........................ .50 .15
B5 Paul Wilson........................... .50 .15
B6 Chad Ogea............................. .50 .15
B7 Andruw Jones RC.............. 40.00 12.00
B8 Brian Barber.......................... .50 .15
B9 Andy Larkin............................ .50 .15
B10 Richie Sexson RC............. 10.00 3.00
B11 Everett Stull.......................... .50 .15
B12 Brooks Kieschnick................ .50 .15
B13 Matt Murray............................ .50 .15
B14 John Wasdin........................... .50 .15
B15 Shannon Stewart.................... .50 .15
B16 Luis Ortiz................................ .50 .15
B17 Marc Kroon............................. .50 .15
B18 Todd Greene........................... .50 .15
B19 Juan Acevedo RC................ 1.00 .30
B20 Tony Clark.............................. .50 .15
B21 Jermaine Dye.......................... .50 .15
B22 Derrek Lee.............................. .50 .15
B23 Pat Watkins............................ .50 .15
B24 Pokey Reese........................... .50 .15
B25 Ben Grieve.............................. .50 .15
B26 Julio Santana RC.................... .50 .15
B27 Felix Rodriguez RC.............. 2.00 .60
B28 Paul Konerko......................... 2.00 .60
B29 Nomar Garciaparra 8.00 2.40
B30 Pat Ahearne............................ .50 .15
B31 Jason Schmidt...................... 1.25 .35
B32 Billy Wagner........................... .50 .15
B33 Rey Ordonez RC.................. 3.00 .90
B34 Curtis Goodwin...................... .50 .15
B35 Sergio Nunez RC.................. 1.00 .30
B36 Tim Belk.................................. .50 .15
B37 Scott Elarton RC.................. 2.00 .60
B38 Jason Isringhausen .... .50 .15
B39 Trot Nixon............................... .50 .15
B40 Sid Roberson RC.................. 1.00 .30
B41 Ron Villone............................. .50 .15
B42 Ruben Rivera.......................... .50 .15
B43 Rick Huisman.......................... .50 .15
B44 Todd Hollandsworth............... .50 .15
B45 Johnny Damon......................... .75 .23
B46 Garret Anderson..................... .50 .15
B47 Jeff D'Amico.......................... .50 .15
B48 Dustin Hermanson................. .50 .15
B49 Juan Encarnacion RC.......... 3.00 .90
B50 Andy Pettitte.......................... .75 .23
B51 Chris Stynes.......................... .50 .15
B52 Troy Percival.......................... .50 .15
B53 LaTroy Hawkins..................... .50 .15
B54 Roger Cedeno........................ .50 .15
B55 Alan Benes............................. .50 .15
B56 Karim Garcia RC.................. 2.00 .60
B57 Andrew Lorraine..................... .50 .15
B58 Gary Rath RC........................ 1.00 .30
B59 Bret Wagner........................... .50 .15
B60 Jeff Suppan............................ .50 .15
B61 Bill Pulsipher......................... .50 .15
B62 Jay Payton RC...................... 3.00 .90
B63 Alex Ochoa............................. .50 .15
B64 Ugueth Urbina........................ .50 .15
B65 Armando Benitez.................... .50 .15
B66 George Arias.......................... .50 .15
B67 Raul Casanova RC................ 1.00 .30
B68 Matt Drews.............................. .50 .15
B69 Jimmy Haynes........................ .50 .15
B70 Jimmy Hurst........................... .50 .15
B71 C.J. Nitkowski........................ .50 .15
B72 Tommy Davis RC.................. 1.00 .30
B73 Bartolo Colon RC................. 5.00 1.50
B74 Chris Carpenter RC.............. 3.00 .90
B75 Trey Beamon.......................... .50 .15
B76 Bryan Rekar............................ .50 .15
B77 James Baldwin....................... .50 .15
B78 Marc Valdes............................ .50 .15
B79 Tom Fordham RC.................. 1.00 .30
B80 Marc Newfield......................... .50 .15
B81 Angel Martinez....................... .50 .15
B82 Brian L. Hunter..................... .50 .15
B83 Jose Herrera........................... .50 .15
B84 Glenn Dishman RC............... 1.00 .30
B85 Jacob Cruz RC...................... 2.00 .60
B86 Paul Shuey.............................. .50 .15
B87 Scott Rolen RC.................. 40.00 12.00
B88 Doug Million........................... .50 .15
B89 Desi Relaford......................... .50 .15
B90 Michael Tucker...................... .50 .15
R1 Randy Johnson..................... 1.25 .35
R2 Joe Carter................................ .50 .15
R3 Chili Davis.............................. .50 .15
R4 Moises Alou............................ .50 .15
R5 Gary Sheffield........................ .50 .15
R6 Kevin Appier........................... .50 .15
R7 Denny Neagle......................... .50 .15
R8 Ruben Sierra.......................... .50 .15
R9 Darren Daulton....................... .50 .15
R10 Cal Ripken........................... 4.00 1.20
R11 Bobby Bonilla........................ .50 .15
R12 Manny Ramirez...................... .75 .23
R13 Barry Bonds........................ 3.00 .90
R14 Eric Karros............................ .50 .15
R15 Greg Maddux........................ 2.00 .60
R16 Jeff Bagwell........................... .75 .23
R17 Paul Molitor............................ .75 .23
R18 Ray Lankford.......................... .50 .15
R19 Mark Grace............................ .75 .23
R20 Kenny Lofton.......................... .50 .15
R21 Tony Gwynn........................ 1.50 .45
R22 Will Clark............................. 1.25 .35
R23 Roger Clemens.................... 2.50 .75
R24 Dante Bichette........................ .50 .15
R25 Barry Larkin............................ .75 .23
R26 Wade Boggs........................... .75 .23
R27 Kirby Puckett....................... 1.25 .35
R28 Cecil Fielder........................... .50 .15
R29 Jose Canseco...................... 1.25 .35
R30 Juan Gonzalez....................... .75 .23
R31 David Cone............................ .50 .15
R32 Craig Biggio........................... .75 .23
R33 Tim Salmon............................ .75 .23
R34 David Justice......................... .50 .15
R35 Sammy Sosa....................... 2.00 .60
R36 Mike Piazza......................... 2.00 .60
R37 Carlos Baerga........................ .50 .15
R38 Jeff Conine............................ .50 .15
R39 Rafael Palmeiro..................... .75 .23
R40 Bret Saberhagen.................... .50 .15
R41 Len Dykstra........................... .50 .15
R42 Mo Vaughn............................. .50 .15
R43 Wally Joyner......................... .50 .15
R44 Chuck Knoblauch.................. .50 .15
R45 Robin Ventura........................ .50 .15
R46 Don Mattingly...................... 3.00 .90
R47 Dave Hollins.......................... .50 .15
R48 Andy Benes........................... .50 .15
R49 Ken Griffey Jr...................... 2.00 .60
R50 Albert Belle........................... .50 .15
R51 Matt Williams........................ .50 .15
R52 Rondell White........................ .50 .15
R53 Raul Mondesi........................ .50 .15
R54 Brian Jordan......................... .50 .15
R55 Greg Vaughn......................... .50 .15
R56 Fred McGriff.......................... .75 .23
R57 Roberto Alomar..................... .75 .23
R58 Dennis Eckersley................. .50 .15
R59 Lee Smith............................... .50 .15
R60 Eddie Murray...................... 1.25 .35
R61 Kenny Rogers....................... .50 .15
R62 Ron Gant................................ .50 .15
R63 Larry Walker.......................... .75 .23
R64 Chad Curtis........................... .50 .15
R65 Frank Thomas.................... 1.25 .35
R66 Paul O'Neill........................... .75 .23
R67 Kevin Seitzer........................ .50 .15
R68 Marquis Grissom.................. .50 .15
R69 Mark McGwire.................... 4.00 1.20
R70 Travis Fryman....................... .50 .15
R71 Andres Galarraga................. .50 .15
R72 Carlos Perez RC................. 2.00 .60
R73 Tyler Green........................... .50 .15
R74 Marty Cordova...................... .50 .15
R75 Shawn Green........................ .50 .15
R76 Vaughn Eshelman................ .50 .15
R77 John Mabry........................... .50 .15
R78 Jason Bates.......................... .50 .15
R79 Jon Nunnally......................... .50 .15
R80 Ray Durham........................... .50 .15
R81 Edgardo Alfonzo................... .50 .15
R82 Esteban Loaiza.................... .50 .15
R83 Hideo Nomo RC............... 10.00 3.00
R84 Orlando Miller....................... .50 .15
R85 Alex Gonzalez...................... .50 .15
R86 M.Grudzielanek RC........... 2.00 .60
R87 Julian Tavarez..................... .50 .15
R88 Benji Gil................................ .50 .15
R89 Quilvio Veras....................... .50 .15
R90 Ricky Bottalico.................... .50 .15
X1 Ben Davis RC.................... 1.50 .45
Ivan Rodriguez
X2 Mark Redman RC............... 1.50 .45
Manny Ramirez
X3 Reggie Taylor RC............... 1.50 .45
Deion Sanders
X4 Ryan Jaroncyk RC................ .50 .15
Shawn Green
X5 Juan LeBron RC................. 5.00 1.50
Juan Gonzalez UER
Card pictures Carlos Beltran instead of Juan LeBron.
X6 Tony McKnight RC................ .50 .15
Craig Biggio
X7 Michael Barrett RC............ 1.50 .45
Travis Fryman
X8 Corey Jenkins RC................ .50 .15
Mo Vaughn
X9 Ruben Rivera...................... 1.25 .35
Frank Thomas
X10 Curtis Goodwin.................... .50 .15
Kenny Lofton
X11 Brian L. Hunter.................... .75 .23
Tony Gwynn
X12 Todd Greene..................... 1.25 .35
Ken Griffey Jr.
X13 Karim Garcia....................... .50 .15
Matt Williams
X14 Billy Wagner........................ .75 .23
Randy Johnson
X15 Pat Watkins......................... .75 .23
Jeff Bagwell

1995 Bowman's Best Refractors

Randomly inserted at a rate of one in six packs, this set is a parallel to the basic Bowman's Best issue. As far as the refractive qualities, the final 15 Mirror Image cards (X1-X15) are considered diffractors which reflects light in a different manner than the typical refractor. Unlike the 180 red and blue Refractors, the Mirror Image Diffractors are seeded into packs at a rate of 1:12. The veteran red refractor cards have been seen with or without the word refractor on the back. These cards without the refractor markings are valued at the same price as the regular refractors.

Nm-Mt Ex-Mt
*STARS: 4X TO 10X BASIC CARDS....
*RCs: 1.5X TO 4X BASIC CARDS.......
*MIRROR IMAGE: 1.25X TO 3X BASIC CARDS

1996 Bowman's Best Previews

Printed with Finest technology, this 30-card set features the hottest 15 top prospects and 15 veterans and was randomly inserted in 1996 Bowman packs at the rate of one in 12. The fronts display a color action player photo. The backs carry player information.

Nm-Mt Ex-Mt
COMPLETE SET (30)................ 60.00 18.00
*REFRACTORS: .5X TO 1.2X BASIC PREVIEWS
REFRACTOR STATED ODDS 1:24 ....
*ATOMIC: 1X TO 2.5X BASIC PREVIEWS
ATOMIC STATED ODDS 1:48..............
BBP1 Chipper Jones.............. 2.50 .75
BBP2 Alan Benes................... 1.00 .30
BBP3 Brooks Kieschnick......... 1.00 .30
BBP4 Barry Bonds.................. 6.00 1.80
BBP5 Rey Ordonez................. 1.00 .30
BBP6 Tim Salmon................... 1.50 .45
BBP7 Mike Piazza................... 4.00 1.20
BBP8 Billy Wagner.................. 1.00 .30
BBP9 Andruw Jones............... 2.50 .75
BBP10 Tony Gwynn................ 3.00 .90
BBP11 Paul Wilson.................. 1.00 .30
BBP12 Pokey Reese................ 1.00 .30
BBP13 Frank Thomas.............. 2.50 .75
BBP14 Greg Maddux............... 4.00 1.20
BBP15 Derek Jeter.................. 6.00 1.80
BBP16 Jeff Bagwell................. 1.50 .45
BBP17 Barry Larkin................. 1.50 .45
BBP18 Todd Greene................ 1.00 .30
BBP19 Ruben Rivera............... 1.00 .30
BBP20 Richard Hidalgo........... 1.00 .30
BBP21 Larry Walker................. 1.50 .45
BBP22 Carlos Baerga............. 1.00 .30
BBP23 Derrick Gibson............ 1.00 .30
BBP24 Richie Sexson............. 1.00 .30
BBP25 Mo Vaughn.................. 1.00 .30
BBP26 Hideo Nomo................ 2.50 .75
BBP27 N.Garciaparra............. 5.00 1.50
BBP28 Cal Ripken.................. 8.00 2.40
BBP29 Karim Garcia............... 1.00 .30
BBP30 Ken Griffey Jr.............. 4.00 1.20

1996 Bowman's Best

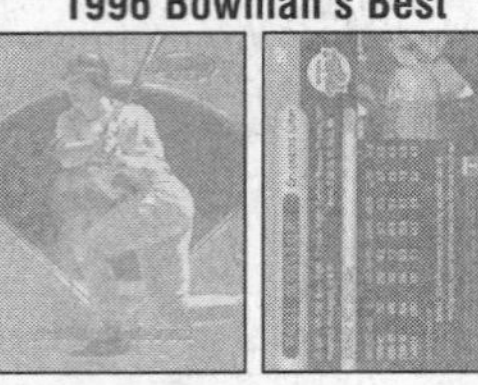
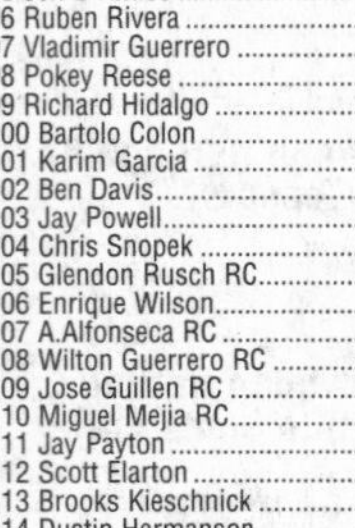

This 180-card set was (produced by Topps) issued in packs of six cards at the cost of $4.99 per pack. The fronts feature a color action player cutout of 90 outstanding veteran players on a chromium gold background design and 90 up and coming prospects and rookies on a silver design. The backs carry a color player portrait, player information and statistics. Card number 33 was never actually issued. Instead, both Roger Clemens and Rafael Palmeiro are erroneously numbered 32. A chrome reprint of the 1952 Bowman Mickey Mantle was inserted at the rate of one in 24 packs. A Refractor version of the Mantle was seeded at 1:96 packs and an Atomic Refractor version was seeded at 1:192. Notable Rookie Cards include Geoff Jenkins and Mike Sweeney.

Nm-Mt Ex-Mt
COMPLETE SET (180)............. 40.00 12.00
1 Hideo Nomo........................ 1.00 .30
2 Edgar Martinez.................... .60 .18
3 Cal Ripken........................ 3.00 .90
4 Wade Boggs........................ .60 .18
5 Cecil Fielder....................... .40 .12
6 Albert Belle......................... .40 .12
7 Chipper Jones.................... 1.00 .30
8 Ryne Sandberg.................. 1.50 .45
9 Tim Salmon......................... .60 .18
10 Barry Bonds.................... 2.50 .75
11 Ken Caminiti...................... .40 .12
12 Ron Gant............................ .40 .12
13 Frank Thomas.................. 1.00 .30
14 Dante Bichette................... .40 .12
15 Jason Kendall.................... .40 .12
16 Mo Vaughn......................... .40 .12
17 Rey Ordonez...................... .40 .12
18 Henry Rodriguez................ .40 .12
19 Ryan Klesko....................... .40 .12
20 Jeff Bagwell....................... .60 .18
21 Randy Johnson................. 1.00 .30
22 Jim Edmonds..................... .40 .12
23 Kenny Lofton...................... .40 .12
24 Andy Pettitte...................... .60 .18
25 Brady Anderson.................. .40 .12
26 Mike Piazza..................... 1.50 .45
27 Greg Vaughn...................... .40 .12
28 Joe Carter.......................... .40 .12
29 Jason Giambi..................... .40 .12
30 Ivan Rodriguez................. 1.00 .30
31 Jeff Conine......................... .40 .12
32 Rafael Palmeiro.................. .60 .18
33 Roger Clemens................. 2.00 .60
34 Chuck Knoblauch............... .40 .12
35 Reggie Sanders.................. .40 .12
36 Andres Galarraga............... .40 .12
37 Paul O'Neill........................ .60 .18
38 Tony Gwynn..................... 1.25 .35
39 Paul Wilson........................ .40 .12
40 Garret Anderson................. .40 .12
41 David Justice...................... .40 .12
42 Eddie Murray.................... 1.00 .30
43 Mike Grace RC................... .50 .15
44 Marty Cordova.................... .40 .12
45 Kevin Appier....................... .40 .12
46 Raul Mondesi...................... .40 .12
47 Jim Thome........................ 1.00 .30
48 Sammy Sosa.................... 1.50 .45
49 Craig Biggio........................ .60 .18
50 Marquis Grissom................ .40 .12
51 Alan Benes......................... .40 .12
52 Manny Ramirez.................. .60 .18
53 Gary Sheffield.................... .60 .18
54 Mike Mussina..................... .60 .18
55 Robin Ventura.................... .40 .12
56 Johnny Damon.................... .60 .18
57 Jose Canseco.................. 1.00 .30
58 Juan Gonzalez.................... .60 .18
59 Tino Martinez...................... .60 .18
60 Brian Hunter....................... .40 .12
61 Fred McGriff....................... .60 .18
62 Jay Buhner......................... .40 .12
63 Carlos Delgado.................. .40 .12
64 Moises Alou........................ .40 .12
65 Roberto Alomar.................. .60 .18
66 Barry Larkin........................ .60 .18
67 Vinny Castilla...................... .40 .12
68 Ray Durham........................ .40 .12
69 Travis Fryman..................... .40 .12
70 Jason Isringhausen............ .40 .12
71 Ken Griffey Jr................... 1.50 .45
72 John Smoltz........................ .60 .18
73 Matt Williams...................... .40 .12
74 Chan Ho Park..................... .40 .12
75 Mark McGwire.................. 3.00 .90
76 Jeffrey Hammonds............. .40 .12
77 Will Clark.......................... 1.00 .30
78 Kirby Puckett................... 1.00 .30
79 Derek Jeter...................... 2.50 .75
80 Derek Bell........................... .40 .12
81 Eric Karros.......................... .40 .12
82 Len Dykstra........................ .40 .12
83 Larry Walker....................... .60 .18
84 Mark Grudzielanek............. .40 .12
85 Greg Maddux.................... 1.50 .45
86 Carlos Baerga..................... .40 .12
87 Paul Molitor........................ .60 .18
88 John Valentin..................... .40 .12
89 Mark Grace........................ .60 .18
90 Ray Lankford...................... .40 .12
91 Andruw Jones.................. 1.00 .30
92 Nomar Garciaparra.......... 2.00 .60
93 Alex Ochoa......................... .40 .12
94 Derrick Gibson.................... .40 .12
95 Jeff D'Amico....................... .40 .12
96 Ruben Rivera...................... .40 .12
97 Vladimir Guerrero............. 2.00 .60
98 Pokey Reese...................... .40 .12
99 Richard Hidalgo.................. .40 .12
100 Bartolo Colon................... .40 .12
101 Karim Garcia.................... .40 .12
102 Ben Davis......................... .40 .12
103 Jay Powell........................ .40 .12
104 Chris Snopek.................... .40 .12
105 Glendon Rusch RC......... 1.00 .30
106 Enrique Wilson................. .40 .12
107 A.Alfonseca RC.............. 1.00 .30
108 Wilton Guerrero RC........ 1.00 .30
109 Jose Guillen RC............. 4.00 1.20
110 Miguel Mejia RC............... .50 .15
111 Jay Payton........................ .40 .12
112 Scott Elarton.................... .40 .12
113 Brooks Kieschnick........... .40 .12
114 Dustin Hermanson........... .40 .12
115 Roger Cedeno.................. .40 .12
116 Matt Wagner.................... .40 .12
117 Lee Daniels...................... .40 .12
118 Ben Grieve....................... .40 .12
119 Ugueth Urbina.................. .40 .12
120 Danny Graves.................. .40 .12
121 Dan Donato RC................ .50 .15
122 Matt Ruebel RC................ .50 .15
123 Mark Sievert RC............... .50 .15
124 Chris Stynes..................... .40 .12
125 Jeff Abbott........................ .40 .12
126 Rocky Coppinger RC........ .50 .15
127 Jermaine Dye.................... .40 .12
128 Todd Greene..................... .40 .12
129 Chris Carpenter................ .40 .12
130 Edgar Renteria................. .40 .12
131 Matt Drews........................ .40 .12
132 Edgard Velazquez RC...... .50 .15
133 Casey Whitten.................. .40 .12
134 Ryan Jones RC................. .50 .15
135 Todd Walker..................... .40 .12
136 Geoff Jenkins RC........... 2.50 .75
137 Matt Morris RC............... 4.00 1.20
138 Richie Sexson.................. .40 .12
139 Todd Dunwoody RC......... .50 .15
140 Gabe Alvarez RC............. .50 .15
141 J.J. Johnson.................... .40 .12
142 Shannon Stewart.............. .40 .12
143 Brad Fullmer.................... .40 .12
144 Julio Santana................... .40 .12
145 Scott Rolen..................... 1.00 .30
146 Amaury Telemaco............ .40 .12
147 Trey Beamon................... .40 .12
148 Billy Wagner.................... .40 .12
149 Todd Hollandsworth......... .40 .12
150 Doug Million..................... .40 .12
151 Javier Valentin RC........... .50 .15
152 Wes Helms RC.............. 1.50 .45
153 Jeff Suppan...................... .40 .12
154 Luis Castillo RC............. 2.50 .75
155 Bob Abreu........................ .40 .12
156 Paul Konerko................... .40 .12
157 Jamey Wright................... .40 .12
158 Eddie Pearson.................. .40 .12
159 Jimmy Haynes.................. .40 .12
160 Derrek Lee........................ .40 .12
161 Damian Moss................... .40 .12
162 Carlos Guillen RC.......... 5.00 1.50
163 Chris Fussell RC.............. .50 .15
164 Mike Sweeney RC.......... 4.00 1.20
165 Donnie Sadler.................. .40 .12
166 Desi Relaford................... .40 .12
167 Steve Gibralter................. .40 .12
168 Neifi Perez....................... .40 .12
169 Antone Williamson........... .40 .12
170 Marty Janzen RC............. .50 .15
171 Todd Helton.................... 2.00 .60
172 Raul Ibanez RC.............. 1.50 .45
173 Bill Selby.......................... .40 .12
174 Shane Monahan RC........ .50 .15
175 Robin Jennings................ .40 .12
176 Bobby Chouinard............. .40 .12
177 Einar Diaz........................ .40 .12
178 Jason Thompson............. .40 .12
179 Rafael Medina RC............ .50 .15
180 Kevin Orie........................ .40 .12
NNO Mickey Mantle............ 10.00 3.00
1952 Bowman Atomic Ref.
NNO Mickey Mantle.............. 5.00 1.50
1952 Bowman Refractor
NNO Mickey Mantle.............. 2.50 .75
1952 Bowman Chrome

1996 Bowman's Best Atomic Refractors

Inserted one in every 48 hobby packs and one in every 80 retail packs, this 180-card set is parallel to the 1996 Bowman's Best set. It is similar in design to the regular set but was printed with sparkling refractor technology.

Nm-Mt Ex-Mt
*GOLD STARS: 6X TO 15X BASIC CARDS
*SILVER STARS: 6X TO 15X BASIC CARDS
*ROOKIES: 3X TO 8X BASIC CARDS..

1996 Bowman's Best Refractors

This 180-card set is parallel to the regular 1996 Bowman Best set and is similar in design. The difference is in the refractive quality of the cards. The cards were inserted at the rate of one in every 12 hobby packs and one in every 20 retail packs.

Nm-Mt Ex-Mt
*GOLD STARS: 3X TO 8X BASIC CARDS
*SILVER STARS: 3X TO 8X BASIC CARDS
*ROOKIES: 1.5X TO 4X BASIC CARDS

1996 Bowman's Best Cuts

Randomly inserted in hobby packs at a rate of one in 24 and retail packs at a rate on one in 40, this chromium card die-cut set features 15 top hobby stars.

Nm-Mt Ex-Mt
COMPLETE SET (15)................ 80.00 24.00
*REFRACTORS: .6X TO 1.5X BASIC CUTS
REF.STATED ODDS 1:48 HOB, 1:80 RET
*ATOMIC: 1X TO 2.5X BASIC CUTS
ATOMIC STATED ODDS 1:96 HOB, 1:160 RET
1 Ken Griffey Jr.................... 6.00 1.80
2 Jason Isringhausen............ 1.50 .45
3 Derek Jeter...................... 10.00 3.00
4 Andruw Jones.................... 4.00 1.20
5 Chipper Jones................... 4.00 1.20
6 Ryan Klesko...................... 1.50 .45
7 Raul Mondesi.................... 1.50 .45
8 Hideo Nomo...................... 4.00 1.20
9 Mike Piazza...................... 6.00 1.80
10 Manny Ramirez............... 2.50 .75
11 Cal Ripken.................... 12.00 3.60
12 Ruben Rivera.................. 1.50 .45
13 Tim Salmon..................... 2.50 .75
14 Frank Thomas................. 4.00 1.20
15 Jim Thome...................... 4.00 1.20

1996 Bowman's Best Mirror Image

Randomly inserted in hobby packs at a rate of one in 48 and retail packs at a rate of one in 80, this 10-card set features four top players on a single card at one of ten different positions. The fronts display a color photo of an AL veteran with a semicircle containing a color portrait of a prospect who plays the same position. The backs carry a color photo of an NL veteran with a semicircle color portrait of a prospect.

Nm-Mt Ex-Mt
COMPLETE SET (10)................ 80.00 24.00
*REFRACTORS: .6X TO 1.5X BASIC CARDS
REFRACTOR ODDS 1:96 HOB, 1:160 RET
*ATOMIC REFRACTORS: 1.25X TO 3X BASIC CARDS
ATOMIC ODDS 1:192 HOB, 1:320 RET
1 Jeff Bagwell........................ 4.00 1.20
Todd Helton
Frank Thomas
Richie Sexson
2 Craig Biggio........................ 4.00 1.20
Luis Castillo
Roberto Alomar
Desi Relaford
3 Chipper Jones..................... 4.00 1.20
Scott Rolen
Wade Boggs
George Arias
4 Barry Larkin...................... 20.00 6.00
Neifi Perez
Cal Ripken
Mark Bellhorn
5 Larry Walker....................... 4.00 1.20
Karim Garcia
Albert Belle
Ruben Rivera
6 Barry Bonds..................... 20.00 6.00
Andruw Jones
Kenny Lofton
Donnie Sadler
7 Tony Gwynn...................... 10.00 3.00
Vladimir Guerrero
Ken Griffey
Ben Grieve
8 Mike Piazza...................... 10.00 3.00
Ben Davis

Ivan Rodriguez
Javier Valentin
Greg Maddux 12.00 3.60
Jamey Wright
Mike Mussina
Bartolo Colon
0 Tom Glavine 4.00 1.20
Billy Wagner
Randy Johnson
Jarrod Washburn

1997 Bowman's Best Preview

andomly inserted in 1997 Bowman Series 1 acks at a rate of one in 12, this 20-card set fea- ures color photos of 10 rookies and 10 veterans hat would be appearing in the 1997 Bowman's est set. The background of each card features a ag of the featured player's homeland.

Nm-Mt Ex-Mt
OMPLETE SET (20) 80.00 24.00
REF: .75X TO 2X BASIC PREVIEWS
EFRACTOR STATED ODDS 1:48
ATOMIC REF: 1.5X TO 4X BASIC PREVIEWS
TOMIC STATED ODDS 1:96
Frank Thomas 4.00 1.20
Ken Griffey Jr. 6.00 1.80
Barry Bonds 10.00 3.00
Derek Jeter 10.00 3.00
Chipper Jones 4.00 1.20
Mark McGwire 12.00 3.60
Cal Ripken 12.00 3.60
Kenny Lofton 1.50 .45
Gary Sheffield 1.50 .45
0 Jeff Bagwell 2.50 .75
1 Wilton Guerrero 1.50 .45
2 Scott Rolen 4.00 1.20
3 Todd Walker 1.50 .45
4 Ruben Rivera 1.50 .45
5 Andruw Jones 1.50 .45
6 Nomar Garciaparra 6.00 1.80
7 Vladimir Guerrero 4.00 1.20
8 Miguel Tejada 5.00 1.50
9 Bartolo Colon 1.50 .45
0 Katsuhiro Maeda 1.50 .45

1997 Bowman's Best

he 1997 Bowman's Best set (produced by opps) was issued in one series totalling 200 ards and was distributed in six-card packs SRP $4.99). The fronts feature borderless color layer photos printed on chromium card stock. he cards of the 100 current veteran stars dis- lay a classic gold design while the cards of the 00 top prospects carry a sleek silver design. ookie Cards include Adrian Beltre, Kris Benson, ose Cruz Jr., Travis Lee, Fernando Tatis, Miguel ejada and Kerry Wood.

Nm-Mt Ex-Mt
OMPLETE SET (200) 40.00 12.00
Ken Griffey Jr. 1.50 .45
Cecil Fielder .40 .12
Albert Belle .40 .12
Todd Hundley .40 .12
Mike Piazza 1.50 .45
Matt Williams .40 .12
Mo Vaughn .40 .12
Ryne Sandberg 1.50 .45
Chipper Jones 1.00 .30
0 Edgar Martinez .60 .18
1 Kenny Lofton .40 .12
2 Ron Gant .40 .12
3 Moises Alou .40 .12
4 Pat Hentgen .40 .12
5 Steve Finley .40 .12
6 Mark Grace .60 .18
7 Jay Buhner .40 .12
8 Jeff Conine .40 .12
9 Jim Edmonds .40 .12
0 Todd Hollandsworth .40 .12
1 Andy Pettitte .60 .18
2 Jim Thome 1.00 .30
3 Eric Young .40 .12
4 Ray Lankford .40 .12
5 Marquis Grissom .40 .12
6 Tony Clark .40 .12
7 Jermaine Allensworth .40 .12
8 Ellis Burks .40 .12
9 Tony Gwynn 1.25 .35
0 Barry Larkin .60 .18
1 John Olerud .40 .12
2 Mariano Rivera .60 .18
3 Paul Molitor .60 .18
4 Ken Caminiti .40 .12
5 Gary Sheffield .40 .12
6 Al Martin .40 .12
7 John Valentin .40 .12
8 Frank Thomas 1.00 .30
9 John Jaha .40 .12
0 Greg Maddux 1.50 .45
1 Alex Fernandez .40 .12
2 Dean Palmer .40 .12
3 Bernie Williams .60 .18
4 Deion Sanders .60 .18
5 Mark McGwire 3.00 .90
6 Brian Jordan .40 .12
7 Bernard Gilkey .40 .12
8 Will Clark 1.00 .30
9 Kevin Appier .40 .12
0 Tom Glavine .60 .18
1 Chuck Knoblauch .40 .12
2 Rondell White .40 .12
3 Greg Vaughn .40 .12
4 Mike Mussina .60 .18
5 Brian McRae .40 .12
6 Chili Davis .40 .12
7 Wade Boggs .60 .18
58 Jeff Bagwell .60 .18
59 Roberto Alomar .60 .18
60 Dennis Eckersley .40 .12
61 Ryan Klesko .40 .12
62 Manny Ramirez .60 .18
63 John Wetteland .40 .12
64 Cal Ripken 3.00 .90
65 Edgar Renteria .40 .12
66 Tino Martinez .60 .18
67 Larry Walker .60 .18
68 Gregg Jefferies .40 .12
69 Lance Johnson .40 .12
70 Carlos Delgado .40 .12
71 Craig Biggio .60 .18
72 Jose Canseco 1.00 .30
73 Barry Bonds 2.50 .75
74 Juan Gonzalez .60 .18
75 Eric Karros .40 .12
76 Reggie Sanders .40 .12
77 Robin Ventura .40 .12
78 Hideo Nomo 1.00 .30
79 David Justice .40 .12
80 Vinny Castilla .40 .12
81 Travis Fryman .40 .12
82 Derek Jeter 2.50 .75
83 Sammy Sosa 1.50 .45
84 Ivan Rodriguez 1.00 .30
85 Rafael Palmeiro .60 .18
86 Roger Clemens 2.00 .60
87 Jason Giambi .40 .12
88 Andres Galarraga .40 .12
89 Jermaine Dye .40 .12
90 Joe Carter .40 .12
91 Brady Anderson .40 .12
92 Derek Bell .40 .12
93 Randy Johnson 1.00 .30
94 Fred McGriff .60 .18
95 John Smoltz .60 .18
96 Harold Baines .40 .12
97 Raul Mondesi .40 .12
98 Tim Salmon .60 .18
99 Carlos Baerga .40 .12
100 Dante Bichette .40 .12
101 Vladimir Guerrero 1.00 .30
102 Richard Hidalgo .40 .12
103 Paul Konerko .40 .12
104 Alex Gonzalez RC 1.00 .30
105 Jason Dickson .40 .12
106 Jose Rosado .40 .12
107 Todd Walker .40 .12
108 Seth Greisinger RC .40 .12
109 Todd Helton 1.00 .30
110 Ben Davis .40 .12
111 Bartolo Colon .40 .12
112 Elieser Marrero .40 .12
113 Jeff D'Amico .40 .12
114 Miguel Tejada RC 6.00 1.80
115 Darin Erstad .40 .12
116 Kris Benson RC 1.50 .45
117 Adrian Beltre RC 8.00 2.40
118 Neifi Perez .40 .12
119 Pokey Reese .40 .12
120 Carl Pavano 1.25 .12
121 Juan Melo .40 .12
122 Kevin McGlinchy RC .40 .12
123 Pat Cline .40 .12
124 Felix Heredia RC .40 .12
125 Aaron Boone .40 .12
126 Glendon Rusch .40 .12
127 Mike Cameron .40 .12
128 Justin Thompson .40 .12
129 Chad Hermansen RC .60 .18
130 Sidney Ponson RC 1.00 .30
131 Willie Martinez RC .40 .12
132 Paul Wilder RC .40 .12
133 Geoff Jenkins .40 .12
134 Roy Halladay RC 1.50 .45
135 Carlos Guillen .40 .12
136 Tony Batista .40 .12
137 Todd Greene .40 .12
138 Luis Castillo .40 .12
139 Jimmy Anderson RC .40 .12
140 Edgard Velazquez .40 .12
141 Chris Snopek .40 .12
142 Ruben Rivera .40 .12
143 Javier Valentin .40 .12
144 Brian Rose .40 .12
145 Fernando Tatis RC .60 .18
146 Dean Crow RC .40 .12
147 Karim Garcia .40 .12
148 Dante Powell .40 .12
149 Hideki Irabu RC .60 .18
150 Matt Morris .40 .12
151 Wes Helms .40 .12
152 Russ Johnson .40 .12
153 Jarrod Washburn .40 .12
154 Kerry Wood RC 12.00 3.60
155 Joe Fontenot RC .40 .12
156 Eugene Kingsale .40 .12
157 Terrence Long .40 .12
158 Calvin Maduro .40 .12
159 Jeff Suppan .40 .12
160 DaRond Stovall .40 .12
161 Mark Redman .40 .12
162 Ken Cloude RC .60 .18
163 Bobby Estalella .40 .12
164 Abraham Nunez RC .40 .12
165 Derrick Gibson .40 .12
166 Mike Drumright RC .40 .12
167 Katsuhiro Maeda .40 .12
168 Jeff Liefer .40 .12
169 Ben Grieve .40 .12
170 Bob Abreu .40 .12
171 Shannon Stewart .40 .12
172 Braden Looper RC .40 .12
173 Brant Brown .40 .12
174 Marlon Anderson .40 .12
175 Brad Fullmer .40 .12
176 Carlos Beltran 3.00 .90
177 Nomar Garciaparra 1.50 .45
178 Derek Lee .40 .12
179 Val.De Los Santos RC .40 .12
180 Dmitri Young .40 .12
181 Jamey Wright .40 .12
182 Hiram Bocachica RC .60 .18
183 Wilton Guerrero .40 .12
184 Chris Carpenter .40 .12
185 Scott Spiezio .40 .12
186 Andruw Jones .40 .12
187 Travis Lee RC .60 .18
188 Jose Cruz Jr. RC 1.00 .30
189 Jose Guillen .40 .12
190 Jeff Abbott .40 .12
191 Ricky Ledee RC .60 .18
192 Mike Sweeney .40 .12
193 Donnie Sadler .40 .12
194 Scott Rolen 1.00 .30
195 Kevin Orie .40 .12
196 Jason Conti RC .40 .12
197 Mark Kotsay RC 1.50 .45
198 Eric Milton RC 1.50 .45
199 Russell Branyan .40 .12
200 Alex Sanchez RC 1.00 .30

1997 Bowman's Best Atomic Refractors

Randomly inserted in packs at a rate of one in 24, cards from this 200 card set parallel the regular Bowman's Best set and were printed with sparkling cross-weave refractor technology.

Nm-Mt Ex-Mt
*STARS: 6X TO 15X BASIC CARDS
*ROOKIES: 4X TO 10X BASIC CARDS

1997 Bowman's Best Refractors

Randomly inserted in packs at a rate of one in 12, this 200 card set is parallel to the regular set and is similar in design. The difference is found in the refractive quality of the cards.

Nm-Mt Ex-Mt
*STARS: 3X TO 8X BASIC CARDS
*ROOKIES: 2X TO 5X BASIC CARDS

1997 Bowman's Best Autographs

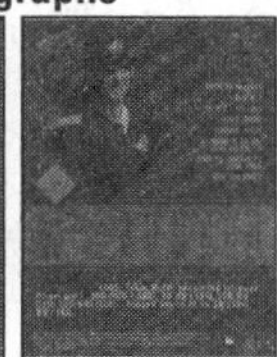

Randomly inserted in packs at a rate of 1:170, this 10-card set features five silver rookie cards and five gold veteran cards with authentic autographs and a "Certified Autograph Issue" stamp.

Nm-Mt Ex-Mt
*REF.STARS: .75X TO 2X BASIC CARDS
REFRACTOR STATED ODDS 1:2036
*ATOMIC STARS: 1.5X TO 4X BASIC CARDS
ATOMIC STATED ODDS 1:6107
SKIP-NUMBERED 10-CARD SET
29 Tony Gwynn 40.00 12.00
33 Paul Molitor 25.00 7.50
82 Derek Jeter 100.00 30.00
91 Brady Anderson 15.00 4.50
98 Tim Salmon 25.00 7.50
107 Todd Walker 15.00 4.50
183 Wilton Guerrero 5.00 1.50
185 Scott Spiezio 5.00 1.50
188 Jose Cruz Jr. 25.00 7.50
194 Scott Rolen 40.00 12.00

1997 Bowman's Best Best Cuts

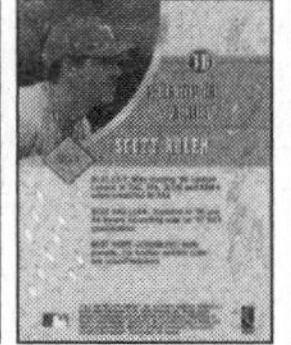

Randomly inserted in packs at a rate of one in 24, this 20-card set features color player photos printed on intricate, Laser Cut Chromium card stock.

Nm-Mt Ex-Mt
COMPLETE SET (20) 150.00 45.00
*REFRACTOR: .6X TO 1.5X BASIC CUTS
REFRACTOR STATED ODDS 1:48
*ATOMIC: 1X TO 2.5X BASIC CUTS 6.00 1.80
ATOMIC STATED ODDS 1:96
BC1 Derek Jeter 15.00 4.50
BC2 Chipper Jones 6.00 1.80
BC3 Frank Thomas 6.00 1.80
BC4 Cal Ripken 20.00 6.00
BC5 Mark McGwire 20.00 6.00
BC6 Ken Griffey Jr. 10.00 3.00
BC7 Jeff Bagwell 4.00 1.20
BC8 Mike Piazza 10.00 3.00
BC9 Ken Caminiti 2.50 .75
BC10 Albert Belle 2.50 .75
BC11 Jose Cruz Jr. 4.00 1.20
BC12 Wilton Guerrero 2.50 .75
BC13 Darin Erstad 2.50 .75
BC14 Andruw Jones 2.50 .75
BC15 Scott Rolen 6.00 1.80
BC16 Jose Guillen 2.50 .75
BC17 Bob Abreu 2.50 .75
BC18 Vladimir Guerrero 6.00 1.80
BC19 Todd Walker 2.50 .75
BC20 Nomar Garciaparra 10.00 3.00

1997 Bowman's Best Mirror Image

Randomly inserted in packs at a rate of one in 48, this 10-card set features color photos of four of the best players in the same position printed on double-sided chromium card stock. Two veterans and two rookies appear on each card. The veteran players are displayed in the larger photos with the rookies appearing in smaller corner photos.

Nm-Mt Ex-Mt
COMPLETE SET (10) 80.00 24.00
*REFRACTORS: .6X TO 1.5X BASIC CARDS
REFRACTOR STATED ODDS 1:96
*ATOMIC REF: 1.25X TO 3X BASIC MI
ATOMIC STATED ODDS 1:192
*INVERTED: 2X VALUE OF NON-INVERTED
INVERTED: RANDOM INSERTS IN PACKS
INVERTED HAVE LARGER ROOKIE PHOTOS
MI1 Nomar Garciaparra 12.00 3.60
Derek Jeter
Hiram Bocachica
Barry Larkin
MI2 Travis Lee 5.00 1.50
Frank Thomas
Derrick Lee
Jeff Bagwell
MI3 Kerry Wood 8.00 2.40
Greg Maddux
Kris Benson
John Smoltz
MI4 Kevin Brown 8.00 2.40
Ivan Rodriguez
Eli Marrero
Mike Piazza
MI5 Jose Cruz Jr. 12.00 3.60
Ken Griffey Jr.
Andruw Jones
Barry Bonds
MI6 Jose Guillen 3.00 .90
Juan Gonzalez
Richard Hidalgo
Gary Sheffield
MI7 Paul Konerko 12.00 3.60
Mark McGwire
Todd Helton
Rafael Palmeiro
MI8 Wilton Guerrero 3.00 .90
Craig Biggio
Donnie Sadler
Chuck Knoblauch
MI9 Russell Branyan 5.00 1.50
Matt Williams
Adrian Beltre
Chipper Jones
MI10 Bob Abreu 5.00 1.50
Kenny Lofton
Vladimir Guerrero
Albert Belle

1998 Bowman's Best

The 1998 Bowman's Best set (produced by Topps) consists of 200 standard size cards and was released in August, 1998. The six-card packs retailed for a suggested price of $5 each. The card fronts feature 100 action photos with a gold background showcasing today's veteran players and 100 photos (combining posed shots with action shots) with a silver background showcasing rookies. The Bowman's Best logo sits in the upper right corner and the featured player's name sits in the lower left corner. Rookie Cards include Ryan Anderson, Troy Glaus, Orlando Hernandez, Carlos Lee, Ruben Mateo and Magglio Ordonez.

Nm-Mt Ex-Mt
COMPLETE SET (200) 40.00 12.00
1 Mark McGwire 2.50 .75
2 Jeromy Burnitz .40 .12
3 Barry Bonds 2.50 .75
4 Dante Bichette .40 .12
5 Chipper Jones 1.00 .30
6 Frank Thomas 1.00 .30
7 Kevin Brown .60 .18
8 Juan Gonzalez .60 .18
9 Jay Buhner .40 .12
10 Chuck Knoblauch .40 .12
11 Cal Ripken 3.00 .90
12 Matt Williams .40 .12
13 Jim Edmonds .40 .12
14 Manny Ramirez .60 .18
15 Tony Clark .40 .12
16 Mo Vaughn .40 .12
17 Bernie Williams .60 .18
18 Scott Rolen 1.00 .30
19 Gary Sheffield .40 .12
20 Albert Belle .40 .12
21 Mike Piazza 1.50 .45
22 John Olerud .40 .12
23 Tony Gwynn 1.25 .35
24 Jay Bell .40 .12
25 Jose Cruz Jr. .40 .12
26 Justin Thompson .40 .12
27 Ken Griffey Jr. 1.50 .45
28 Sandy Alomar Jr. .40 .12
29 Mark Grudzielanek .40 .12
30 Mark Grace .60 .18
31 Ron Gant .40 .12
32 Javy Lopez .40 .12
33 Jeff Bagwell .60 .18
34 Fred McGriff .60 .18
35 Rafael Palmeiro .60 .18
36 Vinny Castilla .40 .12
37 Andy Benes .40 .12
38 Pedro Martinez 1.00 .30
39 Andy Pettitte .60 .18
40 Marty Cordova .40 .12
41 Rusty Greer .40 .12
42 Kevin Orie .40 .12
43 Chan Ho Park .40 .12
44 Ryan Klesko .40 .12
45 Alex Rodriguez 1.50 .45
46 Travis Fryman .40 .12
47 Jeff King .40 .12
48 Roger Clemens 2.00 .60
49 Darin Erstad .40 .12
50 Brady Anderson .40 .12
51 Jason Kendall .40 .12
52 John Valentin .40 .12
53 Ellis Burks .40 .12
54 Brian Hunter .40 .12
55 Paul O'Neill .60 .18
56 Ken Caminiti .40 .12
57 David Justice .40 .12
58 Eric Karros .40 .12
59 Pat Hentgen .40 .12
60 Greg Maddux 1.50 .45
61 Craig Biggio .60 .18
62 Edgar Martinez .60 .18
63 Mike Mussina .60 .18
64 Larry Walker .60 .18
65 Tino Martinez .60 .18
66 Jim Thome 1.00 .30
67 Tom Glavine .60 .18
68 Raul Mondesi .40 .12
69 Marquis Grissom .40 .12
70 Randy Johnson 1.00 .30
71 Steve Finley .40 .12
72 Jose Guillen .40 .12
73 Nomar Garciaparra 1.50 .45
74 Wade Boggs .60 .18
75 Bobby Higginson .40 .12
76 Robin Ventura .40 .12
77 Derek Jeter 2.50 .75
78 Andruw Jones .40 .12
79 Ray Lankford .40 .12
80 Vladimir Guerrero 1.00 .30
81 Kenny Lofton .40 .12
82 Ivan Rodriguez 1.00 .30
83 Neifi Perez .40 .12
84 John Smoltz .60 .18
85 Tim Salmon .60 .18
86 Carlos Delgado .40 .12
87 Sammy Sosa 1.50 .45
88 Jaret Wright .40 .12
89 Roberto Alomar .60 .18
90 Paul Molitor .60 .18
91 Dean Palmer .40 .12
92 Barry Larkin .60 .18
93 Jason Giambi .40 .12
94 Curt Schilling .40 .12
95 Eric Young .40 .12
96 Denny Neagle .40 .12
97 Moises Alou .40 .12
98 Livan Hernandez .40 .12
99 Todd Hundley .40 .12
100 Andres Galarraga .40 .12
101 Travis Lee .40 .12
102 Lance Berkman .60 .18
103 Orlando Cabrera .40 .12
104 Mike Lowell RC 3.00 .90
105 Ben Grieve .40 .12
106 Jae Weong Seo RC 1.00 .30
107 Richie Sexson .40 .12
108 Eli Marrero .40 .12
109 Aramis Ramirez .40 .12
110 Paul Konerko .40 .12
111 Carl Pavano .60 .12
112 Brad Fullmer .40 .12
113 Matt Clement .40 .12
114 Donzell McDonald .40 .12
115 Todd Helton .60 .18
116 Mike Caruso .40 .12
117 Donnie Sadler .40 .12
118 Bruce Chen .40 .12
119 Jarrod Washburn .40 .12
120 Adrian Beltre 1.00 .30
121 Ryan Jackson RC .40 .12
122 Kevin Millar RC 3.00 .90
123 Corey Koskie RC 1.50 .45
124 Dermal Brown .40 .12
125 Kerry Wood 1.00 .30
126 Juan Melo .40 .12
127 Ramon Hernandez .40 .12
128 Roy Halladay .40 .12
129 Ron Wright .40 .12
130 Darnell McDonald RC .60 .18
131 Odalis Perez RC 1.50 .45
132 Alex Cora RC .60 .18
133 Justin Towle .40 .12
134 Juan Encarnacion .40 .12
135 Brian Rose .40 .12
136 Russell Branyan .40 .12
137 Cesar King RC .40 .12
138 Ruben Rivera .40 .12
139 Ricky Ledee .40 .12
140 Vernon Wells .40 .12
141 Luis Rivas RC 1.50 .45
142 Brent Butler .40 .12
143 Karim Garcia .40 .12
144 George Lombard .40 .12
145 Masato Yoshii RC 1.00 .30
146 Braden Looper .40 .12
147 Alex Sanchez .40 .12
148 Kris Benson .40 .12
149 Mark Kotsay .40 .12
150 Richard Hidalgo .40 .12
151 Scott Elarton .40 .12
152 Ryan Minor RC .40 .12
153 Troy Glaus RC 3.00 .90
154 Carlos Lee RC 1.50 .45
155 Michael Coleman .40 .12
156 Jason Grilli RC .40 .12
157 Julio Ramirez RC .40 .12
158 Randy Wolf RC 1.00 .30
159 Ryan Brannan .40 .12
160 Edgard Clemente .40 .12
161 Miguel Tejada .40 .12
162 Chad Hermansen .40 .12
163 Ryan Anderson RC .60 .18
164 Ben Petrick .40 .12

165 Alex Gonzalez .40 .12
166 Ben Davis .40 .12
167 John Patterson .40 .12
168 Cliff Politte .40 .12
169 Randall Simon .40 .12
170 Javier Vazquez .40 .12
171 Kevin Witt .40 .12
172 Geoff Jenkins .40 .12
173 David Ortiz 2.00 .60
174 Derrick Gibson .40 .12
175 Abraham Nunez .40 .12
176 A.J. Hinch .40 .12
177 Ruben Mateo RC .60 .18
178 Magglio Ordonez RC 3.00 .90
179 Todd Dunwoody .40 .12
180 Daryle Ward .40 .12
181 Mike Kinkade RC .40 .12
182 Willie Martinez .40 .12
183 O.Hernandez RC 1.50 .45
184 Eric Milton .40 .12
185 Eric Chavez .40 .12
186 Damian Jackson .40 .12
187 Jim Parque RC .60 .18
188 Dan Reichert RC .60 .18
189 Mike Drumright .40 .12
190 Todd Walker .40 .12
191 Shane Monahan .40 .12
192 Derrek Lee .40 .12
193 Jeremy Giambi RC .60 .18
194 Dan McKinley RC .40 .12
195 Tony Armas Jr. RC .60 .18
196 Matt Anderson RC .60 .18
197 Jim Chamblee RC .40 .12
198 F.Cordero RC 1.00 .30
199 Calvin Pickering .40 .12
200 Reggie Taylor .40 .12

1998 Bowman's Best Atomic Refractors

The 1998 Bowman's Best Atomic Refractor set consists of 200 cards and is a parallel to the 1998 Bowman's Best base set. The cards are randomly inserted in packs at a rate of one in 82. The entire set is sequentially numbered to 100. Each card front featured a kaleidescopic refractive background.

Nm-Mt Ex-Mt
*STARS: 8X TO 20X BASIC CARDS....
*ROOKIES: 5X TO 12X BASIC CARDS
122 Kevin Millar 25.00 7.50

1998 Bowman's Best Refractors

The 1998 Bowman's Best Refractor set consists of 200 cards and is a parallel to the 1998 Bowman's Best base set. The cards are randomly inserted in packs at a rate of one in 20. The entire set is sequentially numbered to 400.

Nm-Mt Ex-Mt
*STARS: 5X TO 12X BASIC CARDS....
*ROOKIES: 2.5X TO 6X BASIC CARDS
122 Kevin Millar 15.00 4.50

1998 Bowman's Best Autographs

Randomly inserted in packs at a rate of one in 180, this 10-card set is an insert to the 1998 Bowman's Best brand. The fronts feature five gold veteran and five silver prospect cards sporting a Topps "Certified Autograph Issue" logo for authentication. The cards are designed in an identical manner to the basic issue 1998 Bowman's Best set except, of course, for the autograph and the certification logo.

Nm-Mt Ex-Mt
*REFRACTORS: .75X TO 2X BASIC AU'S
REFRACTOR STATED ODDS 1:2158 ...
*ATOMICS: 2X TO 4X BASIC AU'S .....
ATOMIC STATED ODDS 1:6437
SKIP-NUMBERED 10-CARD SET
5 Chipper Jones 40.00 12.00
10 Chuck Knoblauch 15.00 4.50
15 Tony Clark 10.00 3.00
20 Albert Belle 15.00 4.50
25 Jose Cruz Jr. 10.00 3.00
105 Ben Grieve 10.00 3.00
110 Paul Konerko 15.00 4.50
115 Todd Helton 25.00 7.50
120 Adrian Beltre 40.00 12.00
125 Kerry Wood 40.00 12.00

1998 Bowman's Best Mirror Image Fusion

Randomly inserted in packs at a rate of one in 12, this 20-card set is an insert to the 1998 Bowman's Best brand. The fronts feature a Major League veteran player with his positional protégé on the flip side. The player's name runs along the bottom of the card.

Nm-Mt Ex-Mt
COMPLETE SET (20) 150.00 45.00
*REFRACTORS: 1.25X TO 3X BASIC MIRROR
REFRACTOR STATED ODDS 1:809
REF.PRINT RUN 100 SERIAL #'d SETS
ATOMIC STATED ODDS 1:3237
ATOMIC PRINT RUN 25 SERIAL #'d SETS
NO ATOMIC PRICING DUE TO SCARCITY
MI1 Frank Thomas 5.00 1.50
David Ortiz
MI2 Chuck Knoblauch 2.50 .75
Enrique Wilson
MI3 Nomar Garciaparra 10.00 3.00
Miguel Tejada
MI4 Alex Rodriguez 10.00 3.00
Mike Caruso
MI5 Cal Ripken 20.00 6.00
Ryan Minor
MI6 Ken Griffey Jr. 10.00 3.00
Ben Grieve
MI7 Juan Gonzalez 4.00 1.20
Juan Encarnacion
MI8 Jose Cruz Jr. 2.50 .75
Ruben Mateo
MI9 Randy Johnson 5.00 1.50
Ryan Anderson
MI10 Ivan Rodriguez 5.00 1.50
A.J. Hinch
MI11 Jeff Bagwell 4.00 1.20
Paul Konerko
MI12 Mark McGwire 15.00 4.50
Travis Lee
MI13 Craig Biggio 4.00 1.20
Chad Hermansen
MI14 Mark Grudzielanek 2.50 .75
Alex Gonzalez
MI15 Chipper Jones 5.00 1.50
Adrian Beltre
MI16 Larry Walker 4.00 1.20
Mark Kotsay
MI17 Tony Gwynn 8.00 2.40
George Lombard
MI18 Barry Bonds 15.00 4.50
Richard Hidalgo
MI19 Greg Maddux 10.00 3.00
Kerry Wood
MI20 Mike Piazza 10.00 3.00
Ben Petrick

1998 Bowman's Best Performers

Randomly inserted in packs at a rate of one in six, this 10-card set is an insert to the 1998 Bowman's Best brand. The card fronts feature full color game-action photos of ten players with the best Minor League stats of 1997. The featured player's name is found below the photo with both Bowman's Best logo and the team logo above the photo.

Nm-Mt Ex-Mt
COMPLETE SET (10) 15.00 4.50
*REFRACTORS: 5X TO 12X BASIC PERF.
REFRACTOR STATED ODDS 1:809
REF.PRINT RUN 200 SERIAL #'d SETS
*ATOMIC: 12.5X TO 30X BASIC PERF.
ATOMIC STATED ODDS 1:3237
ATOMIC PRINT RUN 50 SERIAL #'d SETS
BP1 Ben Grieve 1.50 .45
BP2 Travis Lee 1.50 .45
BP3 Ryan Minor 1.50 .45
BP4 Todd Helton 2.50 .75
BP5 Brad Fullmer 1.50 .45
BP6 Paul Konerko 1.50 .45
BP7 Adrian Beltre 4.00 1.20
BP8 Richie Sexson 1.50 .45
BP9 Aramis Ramirez 1.50 .45
BP10 Russell Branyan 1.50 .45

1999 Bowman's Best

The 1999 Bowman's Best set (produced by Topps) consists of 200 standard size cards. The six-card packs, released in August, 1999, retailed for a suggested price of $5 each. The cards are printed on 27-pt. Serillusion stock and feature 85 veteran stars in a striking gold series, 15 Best Performers bonus subset captured in a bronze series, 50 rookies highlighted in a brilliant blue series and 50 prospects shown in a captivating silver series. The fifty rookies and prospects (cards 151-200) were seeded at a rate of one per pack. Notable Rookie Cards included Pat Burrell, Sean Burroughs, Nick Johnson, Austin Kearns, Corey Patterson and Alfonso Soriano.

Nm-Mt Ex-Mt
COMPLETE SET (200) 50.00 15.00
COMP.SET w/o SP's (150) 25.00 7.50
COMMON CARD (1-150) .40 .12
COMMON (151-200) .50 .15
1 Chipper Jones 1.00 .30
2 Brian Jordan .40 .12
3 David Justice .40 .12
4 Jason Kendall .40 .12
5 Mo Vaughn .40 .12
6 Jim Edmonds .40 .12
7 Wade Boggs .60 .18
8 Jeromy Burnitz .40 .12
9 Todd Hundley .40 .12
10 Rondell White .40 .12
11 Cliff Floyd .40 .12
12 Sean Casey .40 .12
13 Bernie Williams .60 .18
14 Dante Bichette .40 .12
15 Greg Vaughn .40 .12
16 Andres Galarraga .40 .12
17 Ray Durham .40 .12
18 Jim Thome 1.00 .30
19 Gary Sheffield .40 .12
20 Frank Thomas 1.00 .30
21 Orlando Hernandez .40 .12
22 Ivan Rodriguez 1.00 .30
23 Jose Cruz Jr. .40 .12
24 Jason Giambi .40 .12
25 Craig Biggio .60 .18
26 Kerry Wood 1.00 .30
27 Manny Ramirez .60 .18
28 Curt Schilling .40 .12
29 Mike Mussina .60 .18
30 Tim Salmon .60 .18
31 Mike Piazza 1.50 .45
32 Roberto Alomar .60 .18
33 Larry Walker .60 .18
34 Barry Larkin .60 .18
35 Nomar Garciaparra 1.50 .45
36 Paul O'Neill .60 .18
37 Todd Walker .40 .12
38 Eric Karros .40 .12
39 Brad Fullmer .40 .12
40 John Olerud .40 .12
41 Todd Helton .60 .18
42 Raul Mondesi .40 .12
43 Jose Canseco 1.00 .30
44 Matt Williams .40 .12
45 Ray Lankford .40 .12
46 Carlos Delgado .40 .12
47 Darin Erstad .40 .12
48 Vladimir Guerrero 1.00 .30
49 Robin Ventura .40 .12
50 Alex Rodriguez 1.50 .45
51 Vinny Castilla .40 .12
52 Tony Clark .40 .12
53 Pedro Martinez 1.00 .30
54 Rafael Palmeiro .60 .18
55 Scott Rolen .60 .18
56 Tino Martinez .60 .18
57 Tony Gwynn 1.25 .35
58 Barry Bonds 2.50 .75
59 Kenny Lofton .40 .12
60 Javy Lopez .40 .12
61 Mark Grace .60 .18
62 Travis Lee .40 .12
63 Kevin Brown .60 .18
64 Al Leiter .40 .12
65 Albert Belle .40 .12
66 Sammy Sosa 1.50 .45
67 Greg Maddux 1.50 .45
68 Mark Kotsay .40 .12
69 Dmitri Young .40 .12
70 Mark McGwire 2.50 .75
71 Juan Gonzalez .60 .18
72 Andruw Jones .40 .12
73 Derek Jeter 2.50 .75
74 Randy Johnson 1.00 .30
75 Cal Ripken 3.00 .90
76 Shawn Green .40 .12
77 Moises Alou .40 .12
78 Tom Glavine .60 .18
79 Sandy Alomar Jr. .40 .12
80 Ken Griffey Jr. 1.50 .45
81 Ryan Klesko .40 .12
82 Jeff Bagwell .60 .18
83 Ben Grieve .40 .12
84 John Smoltz .60 .18
85 Roger Clemens 2.00 .60
86 Ken Griffey Jr. BP 1.00 .30
87 Roger Clemens BP 1.00 .30
88 Derek Jeter BP 1.25 .35
89 Nomar Garciaparra BP .75 .23
90 Mark McGwire BP 1.25 .35
91 Sammy Sosa BP .75 .23
92 Alex Rodriguez BP .75 .23
93 Greg Maddux BP .75 .23
94 Vladimir Guerrero BP .60 .18
95 Chipper Jones BP .60 .18
96 Kerry Wood BP .60 .18
97 Ben Grieve BP .40 .12
98 Tony Gwynn BP .60 .18
99 Juan Gonzalez BP .40 .12
100 Mike Piazza BP .75 .23
101 Eric Chavez .40 .12
102 Billy Koch .40 .12
103 Dernell Stenson .40 .12
104 Marlon Anderson .40 .12
105 Ron Belliard .40 .12
106 Bruce Chen .40 .12
107 Carlos Beltran .60 .18
108 Chad Hermansen .40 .12
109 Ryan Anderson .40 .12
110 Michael Barrett .40 .12
111 Matt Clement .40 .12
112 Ben Davis .40 .12
113 Calvin Pickering .40 .12
114 Brad Penny .40 .12
115 Paul Konerko .40 .12
116 Alex Gonzalez .40 .12
117 George Lombard .40 .12
118 John Patterson .40 .12
119 Rob Bell .40 .12
120 Ruben Mateo .40 .12
121 Troy Glaus .60 .18
122 Ryan Bradley .40 .12
123 Carlos Lee .40 .12
124 Gabe Kapler .40 .12
125 Ramon Hernandez .40 .12
126 Carlos Febles .40 .12
127 Mitch Meluskey .40 .12
128 Michael Cuddyer .40 .12
129 Pablo Ozuna .40 .12
130 Jayson Werth .40 .12
131 Ricky Ledee .40 .12
132 Jeremy Giambi .40 .12
133 Danny Klassen .40 .12
134 Mark DeRosa .40 .12
135 Randy Wolf .40 .12
136 Roy Halladay .40 .12
137 Derrick Gibson .40 .12
138 Ben Petrick .40 .12
139 Warren Morris .40 .12
140 Lance Berkman .40 .12
141 Russell Branyan .40 .12
142 Adrian Beltre .60 .18
143 Juan Encarnacion .40 .12
144 Fernando Seguignol .40 .12
145 Corey Koskie .40 .12
146 Preston Wilson .40 .12
147 Homer Bush .40 .12
148 Daryle Ward .40 .12
149 Joe McEwing RC .50 .15
150 Peter Bergeron RC .50 .15
151 Pat Burrell RC 2.50 .75
152 Choo Freeman RC .50 .15
153 Matt Belisle RC .50 .15
154 Carlos Pena RC .75 .23
155 A.J. Burnett RC 1.25 .35
156 D.Mientkiewicz RC 1.25 .35
157 Sean Burroughs RC 2.00 .60
158 Mike Zywica RC .50 .15
159 Corey Patterson RC 3.00 .90
160 Austin Kearns RC 4.00 1.20
161 Chip Ambres RC .50 .15
162 Kelly Dransfeldt RC .50 .15
163 Mike Nannini RC .50 .15
164 Mark Mulder RC 3.00 .75
165 Jason Tyner RC .50 .15
166 Bobby Seay RC .50 .15
167 Alex Escobar RC .50 .15
168 Nick Johnson RC 1.25 .35
169 Alfonso Soriano RC 8.00 2.40
170 Clayton Andrews RC .50 .15
171 C.C. Sabathia RC 1.50 .45
172 Matt Holliday RC 1.25 .35
173 Brad Lidge RC 2.50 .75
174 Kit Pellow RC .50 .15
175 J.M. Gold RC .50 .15
176 Roosevelt Brown RC .50 .15
177 Eric Valent RC .50 .15
178 Adam Everett RC .75 .23
179 Jorge Toca RC .50 .15
180 Matt Roney RC .50 .15
181 Andy Brown RC .50 .15
182 Phil Norton RC .50 .15
183 Mickey Lopez RC .50 .15
184 Chris George RC .50 .15
185 Arturo McDowell RC .50 .15
186 Jose Fernandez RC .50 .15
187 Seth Etherton RC .50 .15
188 Josh McKinley RC .50 .15
189 Nate Cornejo RC .50 .15
190 G.Chiaramonte RC .50 .15
191 Mamon Tucker RC .50 .15
192 Ryan Mills RC .50 .15
193 Chad Moeller RC .50 .15
194 Tony Torcato RC .50 .15
195 Jeff Winchester RC .50 .15
196 Rick Elder RC .50 .15
197 Matt Burch RC .50 .15
198 Jeff Urban RC .50 .15
199 Chris Jones RC .50 .15
200 Masao Kida RC .50 .15

1999 Bowman's Best Atomic Refractors

Randomly inserted at a rate of one in 62, this 200-card set is a parallel of the Bowman's Best Base set. Each card in this set is sequentially numbered to 100 and feature a refractive kaleidescope treatment on front.

Nm-Mt Ex-Mt
*STARS: 10X TO 25X BASIC CARDS...
*ROOKIES: 7.5X TO 15X BASIC CARDS

1999 Bowman's Best Refractors

Randomly inserted at a rate of one in 15, this 200-card set is a parallel of the Bowman's Best Base set and features iridescent select metallization technology. Each card in this set is sequentially numbered to 400.

Nm-Mt Ex-Mt
*STARS: 5X TO 12X BASIC CARDS...
*ROOKIES: 4X TO 8X BASIC CARDS..

1999 Bowman's Best Franchise Best Mach I

Randomly inserted in packs at the rate of one in 41, this 10-card set features color photos of some of the Major's top stars printed on die-cut Serillusion stock and sequentially nubered to 3,000.

Nm-Mt Ex-Mt
COMPLETE SET (10) 60.00 18.00
*MACH II: .75X TO 2X MACH I... 4.00 1.20
MACH II STATED ODDS 1:124
MACH II PRINT RUN 1000 SERIAL #'d SETS
*MACH III: 1.25X TO 3X MACH I
MACH III STATED ODDS 1:248
MACH III PRINT RUN 500 SERIAL #'d SETS
FB1 Mark McGwire 10.00 3.00
FB2 Ken Griffey Jr. 6.00 1.80
FB3 Sammy Sosa 6.00 1.80
FB4 Nomar Garciaparra 6.00 1.80
FB5 Alex Rodriguez 6.00 1.80
FB6 Derek Jeter 10.00 3.00
FB7 Mike Piazza 6.00 1.80
FB8 Frank Thomas 4.00 1.20
FB9 Chipper Jones 4.00 1.20
FB10 Juan Gonzalez 2.50 .75

1999 Bowman's Best Franchise Favorites

Randomly inserted in packs at the rate of one in 40, this six-card set features color photos of retired legends and current stars in three versions. Version A pictures the current star; Version B, a retired great; and Version C pairs the current star with the retired legend.

Nm-Mt Ex-Mt
COMPLETE SET (6) 80.00 24.00
FR1A Derek Jeter 20.00 6.00
FR1B Don Mattingly 20.00 6.00
FR1C Derek Jeter 25.00 7.50
Don Mattingly
FR2A Scott Rolen 8.00 2.40
FR2B Mike Schmidt 12.00 3.60
FR2C Scott Rolen 20.00 6.00
Mike Schmidt

1999 Bowman's Best Franchise Favorites Autographs

This six-card set is an autographed parallel version of the regular insert set with the "Topps Certified Autograph Issue" stamp. The insertion rate for these cards are: Versions A and B, 1:1550 packs; and Version C, 1:6174. Version C cards feature autographs from both players.

Nm-Mt Ex-Mt
FR1A Derek Jeter 120.00 36.00
FR1B Don Mattingly 60.00 18.00
FR1C Derek Jeter 300.00 90.00
Don Mattingly
FR2A Scott Rolen 25.00 7.50
FR2B Mike Schmidt 50.00 15.00
FR2C Scott Rolen 120.00 36.00
Mike Schmidt

1999 Bowman's Best Future Foundations Mach I

Randomly inserted into packs at the rate of one in 41, this 10-card set features color photos of some of the top young stars printed on die-cut Serillusion stock and sequentially numbered to 3,000.

Nm-Mt Ex-Mt
COMPLETE SET (10) 30.00 9.00
*MACH II: .75X TO 2X MACH I
MACH II STATED ODDS 1:124
MACH II PRINT RUN 1000 SERIAL #'d SETS
*MACH III: 1.25X TO 3X MACH I
MACH III STATED ODDS 1:248
MACH III PRINT RUN 500 SERIAL #'d SETS
FF1 Ruben Mateo 1.00 .30
FF2 Troy Glaus 1.50 .45
FF3 Eric Chavez 1.50 .45
FF4 Pat Burrell 3.00 .90
FF5 Adrian Beltre 2.50 .75
FF6 Ryan Anderson 1.00 .30
FF7 Alfonso Soriano 5.00 1.50
FF8 Brad Penny 1.00 .30
FF9 Derrick Gibson 1.00 .30
FF10 Bruce Chen 1.00 .30

1999 Bowman's Best Mirror Image

Randomly inserted into packs at the rate of one in 24, this 10-card double-sided set features color photos of a veteran ballplayer on one side and a hot prospect on the other.

Nm-Mt Ex-Mt
COMPLETE SET (10) 60.00 18.00
*REFRACTORS: .75X TO 2X BASIC MIR.IMAGE
REFRACTOR STATED ODDS 1:96

ATOMIC: 1.25X TO 3X BASIC MIR.IMAGE
TOMIC STATED ODDS 1:192
1 Alex Rodriguez 5.00 1.50
Alex Gonzalez
2 Ken Griffey Jr. 5.00 1.50
Ruben Mateo
3 Derek Jeter 8.00 2.40
Alfonso Soriano
4 Sammy Sosa 3.00 .90
Corey Patterson
5 Greg Maddux 5.00 1.50
Bruce Chen
6 Chipper Jones 2.50 .75
Eric Chavez
7 Vladimir Guerrero 2.50 .75
Carlos Beltran
8 Frank Thomas 2.50 .75
Nick Johnson
9 Nomar Garciaparra 5.00 1.50
Pablo Ozuna
10 Mark McGwire 6.00 1.80
Pat Burrell

1999 Bowman's Best Rookie Locker Room Autographs

andomly inserted into packs at the rate of one 248, this five-card set features autographed olor photos of top prospects with the "Topps ertified Autograph Issue" logo stamp.

	Nm-Mt	Ex-Mt
A1 Pat Burrell	15.00	4.50
A2 Michael Barrett	10.00	3.00
A3 Troy Glaus	10.00	3.00
A4 Gabe Kapler	10.00	3.00
A5 Eric Chavez	10.00	3.00

1999 Bowman's Best Rookie Locker Room Game Used Bats

andomly inserted into packs at the rate of one 517, this six-card set features color photos of p players with pieces of game-used bats nbedded into the cards.

	Nm-Mt	Ex-Mt
B1 Pat Burrell	10.00	3.00
B2 Michael Barrett	8.00	2.40
B3 Troy Glaus	8.00	2.40
B4 Gabe Kapler	8.00	2.40
B5 Eric Chavez	8.00	2.40
B6 Richie Sexson	8.00	2.40

1999 Bowman's Best Rookie Locker Room Game Worn Jerseys

andomly inserted into packs at the rate of one 538, this four-card set features color photos some of the hottest young stars with pieces of eir game-used jerseys embedded in the cards.

	Nm-Mt	Ex-Mt
J1 Richie Sexson	10.00	3.00
J2 Michael Barrett	10.00	3.00
J3 Troy Glaus	10.00	3.00
J4 Eric Chavez	10.00	3.00

1999 Bowman's Best Rookie of the Year

andomly inserted into packs at the rate of one 95, this two-card set features color photos of e 1998 American and National League Rookies the Year printed on Serillusion card stock. An utographed version of Ben Grieve's card with e "Topps Certified Autograph Issue" stamp was serted at the rate of 1:1239 packs.

	Nm-Mt	Ex-Mt
ROY1 Ben Grieve	2.50	.75
ROY2 Kerry Wood	2.50	.75
ROY1A Ben Grieve AU	15.00	4.50

2000 Bowman's Best Previews

Randomly inserted into Bowman hobby/retail packs at one in 18, this 10-card insert set features preview cards from the 2000 Bowman's Best product. Card backs carry a "BB" prefix.

	Nm-Mt	Ex-Mt
COMPLETE SET (10)	40.00	12.00
BB1 Derek Jeter	6.00	1.80
BB2 Ken Griffey Jr.	4.00	1.20
BB3 Nomar Garciaparra	4.00	1.20
BB4 Mike Piazza	4.00	1.20
BB5 Alex Rodriguez	4.00	1.20
BB6 Sammy Sosa	4.00	1.20
BB7 Mark McGwire	6.00	1.80
BB8 Pat Burrell	1.00	.30
BB9 Josh Hamilton	1.00	.30
BB10 Adam Piatt	1.00	.30

2000 Bowman's Best

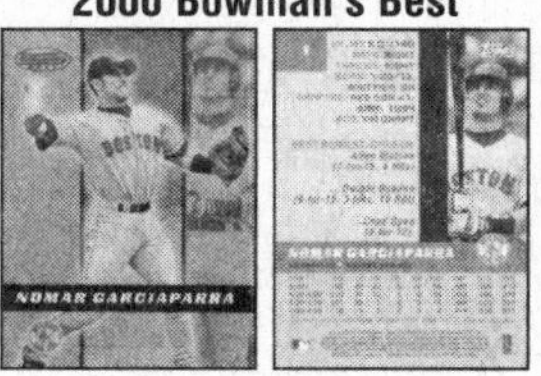

The 2000 Bowman's Best set (produced by Topps) was released in early August, 2000 and features a 200-card base set broken into tiers as follows: Base Veterans/Prospects (1-150) and Rookies (151-200) which were serial numbered to 2999. Each pack contained four cards, and carried a suggested retail of $5.00. Rookie Cards include Rick Asadoorian, Willie Bloomquist, Bobby Bradley, Ben Broussard, Chin-Feng Chen and Barry Zito. The added element of serial-numbered Rookie Cards was extremely popular with collectors and a much-need jolt of life for the Bowman's Best brand (which had been badly overshadowed for two years by the Bowman Chrome Brand).

	Nm-Mt	Ex-Mt
COMP.SET w/o RC's (150)	40.00	12.00
COMMON CARD (1-150)	.40	.12
COMMON (151-200)	5.00	1.50
1 Nomar Garciaparra	1.50	.45
2 Chipper Jones	1.00	.30
3 Tony Clark	.40	.12
4 Bernie Williams	.60	.18
5 Barry Bonds	2.50	.75
6 Jermaine Dye	.40	.12
7 John Olerud	.40	.12
8 Mike Hampton	.40	.12
9 Cal Ripken	3.00	.90
10 Jeff Bagwell	.60	.18
11 Troy Glaus	.40	.12
12 J.D. Drew	.40	.12
13 Jeromy Burnitz	.40	.12
14 Carlos Delgado	.40	.12
15 Shawn Green	.40	.12
16 Kevin Millwood	.40	.12
17 Rondell White	.40	.12
18 Scott Rolen	1.00	.30
19 Jeff Cirillo	.40	.12
20 Barry Larkin	.60	.18
21 Brian Giles	.40	.12
22 Roger Clemens	2.00	.60
23 Manny Ramirez	.60	.18
24 Alex Gonzalez	.40	.12
25 Mark Grace	.60	.18
26 Fernando Tatis	.40	.12
27 Randy Johnson	1.00	.30
28 Roger Cedeno	.40	.12
29 Brian Jordan	.40	.12
30 Kevin Brown	.40	.12
31 Greg Vaughn	.40	.12
32 Roberto Alomar	.60	.18
33 Larry Walker	.60	.18
34 Rafael Palmeiro	.60	.18
35 Curt Schilling	.40	.12
36 Orlando Hernandez	.40	.12
37 Todd Walker	.40	.12
38 Juan Gonzalez	.60	.18
39 Sean Casey	.40	.12
40 Tony Gwynn	1.25	.35
41 Albert Belle	.40	.12
42 Gary Sheffield	.40	.12
43 Michael Barrett	.40	.12
44 Preston Wilson	.40	.12
45 Jim Thome	1.00	.30
46 Shannon Stewart	.40	.12
47 Mo Vaughn	.40	.12
48 Ben Grieve	.40	.12
49 Adrian Beltre	.60	.18
50 Sammy Sosa	1.50	.45
51 Bob Abreu	.40	.12
52 Edgardo Alfonzo	.40	.12
53 Carlos Febles	.40	.12
54 Frank Thomas	1.00	.30
55 Alex Rodriguez	1.50	.45
56 Cliff Floyd	.40	.12
57 Jose Canseco	1.00	.30
58 Erubiel Durazo	.40	.12
59 Tim Hudson	.40	.12
60 Craig Biggio	.60	.18
61 Eric Karros	.40	.12
62 Mike Mussina	.60	.18
63 Robin Ventura	.40	.12
64 Carlos Beltran	.60	.18
65 Pedro Martinez	1.00	.30
66 Gabe Kapler	.40	.12
67 Jason Kendall	.40	.12
68 Derek Jeter	2.50	.75
69 Magglio Ordonez	.40	.12
70 Mike Piazza	1.50	.45
71 Mike Lieberthal	.40	.12
72 Andres Galarraga	.40	.12
73 Raul Mondesi	.40	.12
74 Eric Chavez	.40	.12
75 Greg Maddux	1.50	.45
76 Matt Williams	.40	.12
77 Kris Benson	.40	.12
78 Ivan Rodriguez	1.00	.30
79 Pokey Reese	.40	.12
80 Vladimir Guerrero	1.00	.30
81 Mark McGwire	2.50	.75
82 Vinny Castilla	.40	.12
83 Todd Helton	.60	.18
84 Andruw Jones	.40	.12
85 Ken Griffey Jr.	1.50	.45
86 Mark McGwire BP	1.25	.35
87 Derek Jeter BP	1.25	.35
88 Chipper Jones BP	.60	.18
89 Nomar Garciaparra BP	1.00	.30
90 Sammy Sosa BP	1.00	.30
91 Cal Ripken BP	1.50	.45
92 Juan Gonzalez BP	.40	.12
93 Alex Rodriguez BP	1.00	.30
94 Barry Bonds BP	1.25	.35
95 Sean Casey BP	.40	.12
96 Vladimir Guerrero BP	.60	.18
97 Mike Piazza BP	1.00	.30
98 Shawn Green BP	.40	.12
99 Jeff Bagwell BP	.40	.12
100 Ken Griffey Jr. BP	1.00	.30
101 Rick Ankiel	.40	.12
102 John Patterson	.40	.12
103 David Walling	.40	.12
104 Michael Restovich	.40	.12
105 A.J. Burnett	.40	.12
106 Pablo Ozuna	.40	.12
107 Chad Hermansen	.40	.12
108 Choo Freeman	.40	.12
109 Mark Quinn	.40	.12
110 Corey Patterson	.40	.12
111 Ramon Ortiz	.40	.12
112 Vernon Wells	.40	.12
113 Milton Bradley	.40	.12
114 Gookie Dawkins	.40	.12
115 Sean Burroughs	.40	.12
116 Wily Mo Pena	.40	.12
117 Dee Brown	.40	.12
118 C.C. Sabathia	.40	.12
119 Adam Kennedy	.40	.12
120 Octavio Dotel	.40	.12
121 Kip Wells	.40	.12
122 Ben Petrick	.40	.12
123 Mark Mulder	.40	.12
124 Jason Standridge	.40	.12
125 Adam Piatt	.40	.12
126 Steve Lomasney	.40	.12
127 Jayson Werth	.40	.12
128 Alex Escobar	.40	.12
129 Ryan Anderson	.40	.12
130 Adam Dunn	1.00	.30
131 Ted Lilly	.40	.12
132 Brad Penny	.40	.12
133 Daryle Ward	.40	.12
134 Eric Munson	.40	.12
135 Nick Johnson	.40	.12
136 Jason Jennings	.40	.12
137 Tim Raines Jr.	.40	.12
138 Ruben Mateo	.40	.12
139 Jack Cust	.40	.12
140 Rafael Furcal	.40	.12
141 Eric Gagne	1.50	.45
142 Tony Armas Jr.	.40	.12
143 Mike Paradis	.40	.12
144 Peter Bergeron	.40	.12
145 Alfonso Soriano	1.00	.30
146 Josh Hamilton	.40	.12
147 Michael Cuddyer	.40	.12
148 Jay Gehrke	.40	.12
149 Josh Girdley	.40	.12
150 Pat Burrell	.40	.12
151 Brett Myers RC	8.00	2.40
152 Scott Seabol RC	5.00	1.50
153 Keith Reed RC	5.00	1.50
154 F.Rodriguez RC	25.00	7.50
155 Barry Zito RC	20.00	6.00
156 Pat Manning RC	5.00	1.50
157 Ben Christensen RC	5.00	1.50
158 Corey Myers RC	5.00	1.50
159 Wascar Serrano RC	5.00	1.50
160 Wes Anderson RC	5.00	1.50
161 Andy Tracy RC	5.00	1.50
162 Cesar Saba RC	5.00	1.50
163 Mike Lamb RC	5.00	1.50
164 Bobby Bradley RC	5.00	1.50
165 Vince Faison RC	5.00	1.50
166 Ty Howington RC	5.00	1.50
167 Ken Harvey RC UER Card has pitching stats on the back	8.00	2.40
168 Josh Kalinowski RC	5.00	1.50
169 Ruben Salazar RC	5.00	1.50
170 Aaron Rowand RC	10.00	3.00
171 Ramon Santiago RC	5.00	1.50
172 Scott Sobkowiak RC	5.00	1.50
173 Lyle Overbay RC	10.00	3.00
174 Rico Washington RC	5.00	1.50
175 Rick Asadoorian RC	5.00	1.50
176 Matt Ginter RC	5.00	1.50
177 Jason Stumm RC	5.00	1.50
178 B.J. Garbe RC	5.00	1.50
179 Mike MacDougal RC	5.00	1.50
180 Ryan Christianson RC	5.00	1.50
181 Kurt Ainsworth RC	5.00	1.50
182 Brad Baisley RC	5.00	1.50
183 Ben Broussard RC	8.00	2.40
184 Aaron McNeal RC	5.00	1.50
185 John Sneed RC	5.00	1.50
186 Junior Brignac RC	5.00	1.50
187 Chance Caple RC	5.00	1.50
188 Scott Downs RC	5.00	1.50
189 Matt Cepicky RC	5.00	1.50
190 Chin-Feng Chen RC	25.00	7.50
191 Johan Santana RC	50.00	15.00
192 Brad Baker RC	5.00	1.50
193 Jason Repko RC	5.00	1.50
194 Craig Dingman RC	5.00	1.50
195 Chris Wakeland RC	5.00	1.50
196 Rogelio Arias RC	5.00	1.50
197 Luis Matos RC	5.00	1.50
198 Rob Ramsay	5.00	1.50
199 Willie Bloomquist RC	25.00	7.50
200 Tony Pena Jr. RC	5.00	1.50

2000 Bowman's Best Bets

Randomly inserted into packs at one in 15, this 10-card insert features prospects that are sure bets to excel at the Major League level. Card backs carry a "BBB" prefix.

	Nm-Mt	Ex-Mt
COMPLETE SET (10)	25.00	7.50
BBB1 Pat Burrell	1.50	.45
BBB2 Alfonso Soriano	4.00	1.20
BBB3 Corey Patterson	1.50	.45
BBB4 Eric Munson	1.50	.45
BBB5 Sean Burroughs	1.50	.45
BBB6 Rafael Furcal	1.50	.45
BBB7 Rick Ankiel	1.50	.45
BBB8 Nick Johnson	1.50	.45
BBB9 Ruben Mateo	1.50	.45
BBB10 Josh Hamilton	1.50	.45

2000 Bowman's Best Franchise 2000

Randomly inserted into packs at one in 18, this 25-card set features players that teams build around. Card backs carry an "F" prefix.

	Nm-Mt	Ex-Mt
COMPLETE SET (25)	150.00	45.00
F1 Cal Ripken	20.00	6.00
F2 Nomar Garciaparra	10.00	3.00
F3 Frank Thomas	6.00	1.80
F4 Manny Ramirez	4.00	1.20
F5 Juan Gonzalez	4.00	1.20
F6 Carlos Beltran	4.00	1.20
F7 Derek Jeter	15.00	4.50
F8 Alex Rodriguez	10.00	3.00
F9 Ben Grieve	2.50	.75
F10 Jose Canseco	6.00	1.80
F11 Ivan Rodriguez	6.00	1.80
F12 Mo Vaughn	2.50	.75
F13 Randy Johnson	6.00	1.80
F14 Chipper Jones	6.00	1.80
F15 Sammy Sosa	10.00	3.00
F16 Ken Griffey Jr.	10.00	3.00
F17 Larry Walker	4.00	1.20
F18 Preston Wilson	2.50	.75
F19 Jeff Bagwell	4.00	1.20
F20 Shawn Green	2.50	.75
F21 Vladimir Guerrero	6.00	1.80
F22 Mike Piazza	10.00	3.00
F23 Scott Rolen	6.00	1.80
F24 Tony Gwynn	8.00	2.40
F25 Barry Bonds	15.00	4.50

2000 Bowman's Best Franchise Favorites

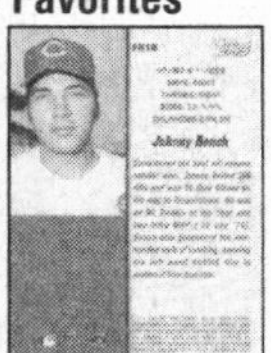

Randomly inserted into packs at one in 17, this six-card insert features players (past and present) that are franchise favorites. Card backs carry a "FR" prefix.

	Nm-Mt	Ex-Mt
COMPLETE SET (6)	30.00	9.00
FR1A Sean Casey	2.50	.75
FR1B Johnny Bench	4.00	1.20
FR1C Sean Casey Johnny Bench	4.00	1.20
FR2A Cal Ripken	10.00	3.00
FR2B Brooks Robinson	2.50	.75
FR2C Cal Ripken Brooks Robinson	10.00	3.00

2000 Bowman's Best Franchise Favorites Autographs

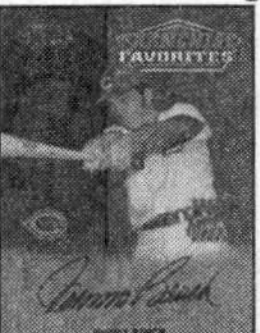
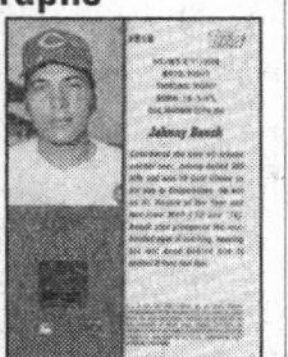

Randomly inserted into packs, this six-card insert is a complete parallel of the Franchise Favorites insert. Each of these cards were autographed by the players, and the set was broken into tiers as folllows: Group A (Sean Casey and Cal Ripken) were inserted at one in 1291, Group B (Johnny Bench and Brooks Robinson) were inserted at one in 1291, and Group C (Casey/Bench, and Ripken/Robinson) were inserted into packs at one in 1,513. The overall odds of getting an autograph cards were one in 574. Card backs carry a "FR" prefix.

	Nm-Mt	Ex-Mt
FR1A Sean Casey A	25.00	7.50
FR1B Johnny Bench B	60.00	18.00
FR1C Sean Casey Johnny Bench	120.00	36.00
FR2A Cal Ripken A	120.00	36.00
FR2B Brooks Robinson B	40.00	12.00
FR2C Cal Ripken Brooks Robinson	300.00	90.00

2000 Bowman's Best Locker Room Collection Autographs

Randomly inserted into packs, this 19-card insert features autographed cards of top Major League prospects. Card backs carry an "LRCA" prefix. Please note that these cards were broken into two groups. Group A cards were inserted at one in 1033 packs, and Group B cards were inserted at one in 61.

	Nm-Mt	Ex-Mt
LRCA1 Carlos Beltran B	40.00	12.00
LRCA2 Rick Ankiel A	15.00	4.50
LRCA3 Vernon Wells A	15.00	4.50
LRCA4 Ruben Mateo A	10.00	3.00
LRCA5 Ben Petrick A	10.00	3.00
LRCA6 Adam Piatt A	10.00	3.00
LRCA7 Eric Munson A	10.00	3.00
LRCA8 Alfonso Soriano A	40.00	12.00
LRCA9 Kerry Wood B	40.00	12.00
LRCA10 Jack Cust A	10.00	3.00
LRCA11 Rafael Furcal A	15.00	4.50
LRCA12 Josh Hamilton A	10.00	3.00
LRCA13 Brad Penny A	15.00	4.50
LRCA14 Dee Brown A	10.00	3.00
LRCA15 Milton Bradley A	15.00	4.50
LRCA16 Ryan Anderson A	10.00	3.00
LRCA17 John Patterson A	10.00	3.00
LRCA18 Nick Johnson A	15.00	4.50
LRCA19 Peter Bergeron A	10.00	3.00

2000 Bowman's Best Locker Room Collection Bats

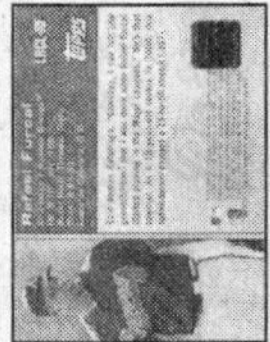

Randomly inserted into packs at one in 376, this 11-card insert features game-used bat cards of some of the hottest prospects in baseball. Card backs carry a "LRCL" prefix.

	Nm-Mt	Ex-Mt
LRCL-AP Adam Piatt	8.00	2.40
LRCL-BP Ben Petrick	8.00	2.40
LRCL-BP Brad Penny	10.00	3.00
LRCL-CB Carlos Beltran	15.00	4.50
LRCL-DB Dee Brown	8.00	2.40
LRCL-EM Eric Munson	8.00	2.40
LRCL-JD J.D. Drew	10.00	3.00
LRCL-PB Pat Burrell	10.00	3.00
LRCL-RA Rick Ankiel	10.00	3.00
LRCL-RF Rafael Furcal	10.00	3.00
LRCL-VW Vernon Wells	10.00	3.00

2000 Bowman's Best Locker Room Collection Jerseys

Randomly inserted into packs at one in 206, this five-card insert features swatches from actual game-used jerseys. Card backs carry a "LRCJ" prefix.

	Nm-Mt	Ex-Mt
LRCJ1 Carlos Beltran	15.00	4.50
LRCJ2 Rick Ankiel	10.00	3.00
LRCJ3 Mark Quinn	8.00	2.40
LRCJ4 Ben Petrick	8.00	2.40
LRCJ5 Adam Piatt	8.00	2.40

2000 Bowman's Best Selections

Randomly inserted into packs at one in 30, this 15-card insert features players that turned out to be outstanding draft selections. Card backs carry a "BBS" prefix.

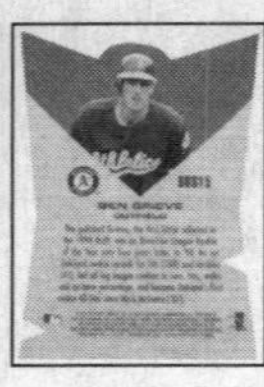

	Nm-Mt	Ex-Mt
COMPLETE SET (15)	120.00	36.00
BBS1 Alex Rodriguez	10.00	3.00
BBS2 Ken Griffey Jr.	10.00	3.00
BBS3 Pat Burrell	2.50	.75
BBS4 Mark McGwire	15.00	4.50
BBS5 Derek Jeter	15.00	4.50
BBS6 Nomar Garciaparra	10.00	3.00
BBS7 Mike Piazza	10.00	3.00
BBS8 Josh Hamilton	2.50	.75
BBS9 Cal Ripken	20.00	6.00
BBS10 Jeff Bagwell	4.00	1.20
BBS11 Chipper Jones	6.00	1.80
BBS12 Jose Canseco	6.00	1.80
BBS13 Carlos Beltran	4.00	1.20
BBS14 Kerry Wood	2.50	.75
BBS15 Ben Grieve	2.50	.75

2000 Bowman's Best Year by Year

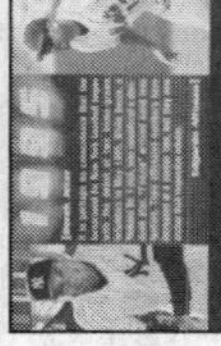

Randomly inserted into packs at one in 23, this 10-card insert features duos that made their Major League debuts in the same year. Card backs carry a "YY" prefix.

	Nm-Mt	Ex-Mt
COMPLETE SET (10)	80.00	24.00
YY1 Sammy Sosa Ken Griffey Jr.	8.00	2.40
YY2 Nomar Garciaparra Vladimir Guerrero	8.00	2.40
YY3 Alex Rodriguez Jeff Cirillo	8.00	2.40
YY4 Mike Piazza Pedro Martinez	8.00	2.40
YY5 Derek Jeter Edgardo Alfonzo	12.00	3.60
YY6 Alfonso Soriano Rick Ankiel	2.00	.60
YY7 Mark McGwire Barry Bonds	12.00	3.60
YY8 Juan Gonzalez Larry Walker	3.00	.90
YY9 Ivan Rodriguez Jeff Bagwell	5.00	1.50
YY10 Shawn Green Manny Ramirez	3.00	.90

2001 Bowman's Best

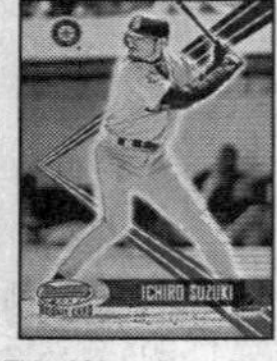
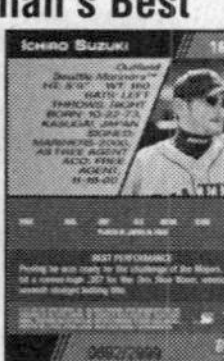

This 200-card set features color action player photos printed in an all new design and leading technology. The set was distributed in five-card packs with a suggested retial price of $5 and includes 35 Rookie and 15 Exclusive Rookie cards sequentially numbered to 2,999.

	Nm-Mt	Ex-Mt
COMP.SET w/o SP's (150)	50.00	15.00
COMMON CARD (1-150)	.40	.12
COMMON (151-200)	5.00	1.50
1 Vladimir Guerrero	1.00	.30
2 Miguel Tejada	.40	.12
3 Geoff Jenkins	.40	.12
4 Jeff Bagwell	.60	.18
5 Todd Helton	.60	.18
6 Ken Griffey Jr.	1.50	.45
7 Nomar Garciaparra	1.50	.45
8 Chipper Jones	1.00	.30
9 Darin Erstad	.40	.12
10 Frank Thomas	1.00	.30
11 Jim Thome	1.00	.30
12 Preston Wilson	.40	.12
13 Kevin Brown	.40	.12
14 Derek Jeter	2.50	.75
15 Scott Rolen	1.00	.30
16 Ryan Klesko	.40	.12
17 Jeff Kent	.40	.12
18 Raul Mondesi	.40	.12
19 Greg Vaughn	.40	.12
20 Bernie Williams	.60	.18
21 Mike Piazza	1.50	.45
22 Richard Hidalgo	.40	.12
23 Dean Palmer	.40	.12
24 Roberto Alomar	.60	.18
25 Sammy Sosa	1.50	.45
26 Randy Johnson	1.00	.30
27 Manny Ramirez	.60	.18
28 Roger Clemens	2.00	.60
29 Terrence Long	.40	.12
30 Jason Kendall	.40	.12
31 Richie Sexson	.40	.12
32 David Wells	.40	.12
33 Andruw Jones	.40	.12
34 Pokey Reese	.40	.12
35 Juan Gonzalez	.60	.18
36 Carlos Beltran	.60	.18
37 Shawn Green	.40	.12
38 Mariano Rivera	.60	.18
39 John Olerud	.40	.12
40 Jim Edmonds	.40	.12
41 Andres Galarraga	.40	.12
42 Carlos Delgado	.40	.12
43 Kris Benson	.40	.12
44 Andy Pettitte	.60	.18
45 Jeff Cirillo	.40	.12
46 Magglio Ordonez	.40	.12
47 Tom Glavine	.60	.18
48 Garret Anderson	.40	.12
49 Cal Ripken	3.00	.90
50 Pedro Martinez	1.00	.30
51 Barry Bonds	2.50	.75
52 Alex Rodriguez	1.50	.45
53 Ben Grieve	.40	.12
54 Edgar Martinez	.60	.18
55 Jason Giambi	.40	.12
56 Jeromy Burnitz	.40	.12
57 Mike Mussina	.60	.18
58 Moises Alou	.40	.12
59 Sean Casey	.40	.12
60 Greg Maddux	1.50	.45
61 Tim Hudson	.40	.12
62 Mark McGwire	2.50	.75
63 Rafael Palmeiro	.60	.18
64 Tony Batista	.40	.12
65 Kazuhiro Sasaki	.40	.12
66 Jorge Posada	.60	.18
67 Johnny Damon	.60	.18
68 Brian Giles	.40	.12
69 Jose Vidro	.40	.12
70 Jermaine Dye	.40	.12
71 Craig Biggio	.60	.18
72 Larry Walker	.60	.18
73 Eric Chavez	.40	.12
74 David Segui	.40	.12
75 Tim Salmon	.60	.18
76 Javy Lopez	.40	.12
77 Paul Konerko	.40	.12
78 Barry Larkin	.60	.18
79 Mike Hampton	.40	.12
80 Bobby Higginson	.40	.12
81 Mark Mulder	.40	.12
82 Pat Burrell	.40	.12
83 Kerry Wood	1.00	.30
84 J.T. Snow	.40	.12
85 Ivan Rodriguez	1.00	.30
86 Edgardo Alfonzo	.40	.12
87 Orlando Hernandez	.40	.12
88 Gary Sheffield	.40	.12
89 Mike Sweeney	.40	.12
90 Carlos Lee	.40	.12
91 Rafael Furcal	.40	.12
92 Troy Glaus	.40	.12
93 Bartolo Colon	.40	.12
94 Cliff Floyd	.40	.12
95 Barry Zito	.60	.18
96 J.D. Drew	.40	.12
97 Eric Karros	.40	.12
98 Jose Valentin	.40	.12
99 Ellis Burks	.40	.12
100 David Justice	.40	.12
101 Larry Barnes	.40	.12
102 Rod Barajas	.40	.12
103 Tony Pena Jr.	.40	.12
104 Jerry Hairston Jr.	.40	.12
105 Keith Ginter	.40	.12
106 Corey Patterson	.40	.12
107 Aaron Rowand	.40	.12
108 Miguel Olivo	.40	.12
109 Goodie Dawkins	.40	.12
110 C.C. Sabathia	.40	.12
111 Ben Petrick	.40	.12
112 Eric Munson	.40	.12
113 Ramon Castro	.40	.12
114 Alex Escobar	.40	.12
115 Josh Hamilton	.40	.12
116 Jason Marquis	.40	.12
117 Ben Davis	.40	.12
118 Alex Cintron	.40	.12
119 Julio Zuleta	.40	.12
120 Ben Broussard	.40	.12
121 Adam Everett	.40	.12
122 Ramon Carvajal RC	.40	.12
123 Felipe Lopez	.40	.12
124 Alfonso Soriano	.60	.18
125 Jayson Werth	.40	.12
126 Donzell McDonald	.40	.12
127 Jason Hart	.40	.12
128 Joe Crede	.40	.12
129 Sean Burroughs	.40	.12
130 Jack Cust	.40	.12
131 Corey Smith	.40	.12
132 Adrian Gonzalez	.40	.12
133 J.R. House	.40	.12
134 Steve Lomasney	.40	.12
135 Tim Raines Jr.	.40	.12
136 Tony Alvarez	.40	.12
137 Doug Mientkiewicz	.40	.12
138 Rocco Baldelli	.60	.18
139 Jason Romano	.40	.12
140 Vernon Wells	.40	.12
141 Mike Bynum	.40	.12
142 Xavier Nady	.40	.12
143 Brad Wilkerson	.40	.12
144 Ben Diggins	.40	.12
145 Aubrey Huff	.40	.12
146 Eric Byrnes	.40	.12
147 Alex Gordon	.40	.12
148 Roy Oswalt	.60	.18
149 Brian Esposito	.40	.12
150 Scott Seabol	.40	.12
151 Erick Almonte RC	5.00	1.50
152 Gary Johnson RC	5.00	1.50
153 Pedro Liriano RC	5.00	1.50
154 Matt White RC	5.00	1.50
155 Luis Montanez RC	5.00	1.50
156 Brad Cresse	5.00	1.50
157 Wilson Betemit RC	5.00	1.50
158 Octavio Martinez RC	5.00	1.50
159 Adam Pettyjohn RC	5.00	1.50
160 Corey Spencer RC	5.00	1.50
161 Mark Burnett RC	5.00	1.50
162 Ichiro Suzuki RC	60.00	18.00
163 Alexis Gomez RC	5.00	1.50
164 Greg Nash RC	5.00	1.50
165 Roberto Miniel RC	5.00	1.50
166 Justin Morneau RC	30.00	9.00
167 Ben Washburn RC	5.00	1.50
168 Bob Keppel RC	8.00	2.40
169 Deivi Mendez RC	5.00	1.50
170 Tsuyoshi Shinjo RC	8.00	2.40
171 Jared Abruzzo RC	5.00	1.50
172 Derrick Van Dusen RC	5.00	1.50
173 Hee Seop Choi RC	8.00	2.40
174 Albert Pujols RC	120.00	36.00
175 Travis Hafner RC	15.00	4.50
176 Ron Davenport RC	5.00	1.50
177 Luis Torres RC	5.00	1.50
178 Jake Peavy RC	20.00	6.00
179 Elvis Corporan RC	5.00	1.50
180 Dave Krynzel	5.00	1.50
181 Tony Blanco RC	8.00	2.40
182 Elpidio Guzman RC	5.00	1.50
183 Matt Butler RC	5.00	1.50
184 Joe Thurston RC	5.00	1.50
185 Andy Beal RC	5.00	1.50
186 Kevin Nulton RC	5.00	1.50
187 Sneideer Santos RC	5.00	1.50
188 Joe Dillon RC	5.00	1.50
189 Jeremy Blevins RC	5.00	1.50
190 Chris Amador RC	5.00	1.50
191 Mark Hendrickson RC	5.00	1.50
192 Willy Aybar RC	8.00	2.40
193 Antoine Cameron RC	5.00	1.50
194 J.J. Johnson RC	5.00	1.50
195 Ryan Ketchner RC	10.00	3.00
196 Bjorn Ivy RC	5.00	1.50
197 Josh Kroeger RC	15.00	4.50
198 Ty Wigginton RC	8.00	2.40
199 Stubby Clapp RC	5.00	1.50
200 Jerrod Riggan RC	5.00	1.50

2001 Bowman's Best Autographs

Randomly inserted in packs at the rate of one in 95, this seven-card set features autographed photos of top players.

	Nm-Mt	Ex-Mt
BBAAG Adrian Gonzalez	10.00	3.00
BBABC Brad Cresse	10.00	3.00
BBAJH Josh Hamilton	10.00	3.00
BBAJR Jon Rauch	10.00	3.00
BBAJRH J.R. House	10.00	3.00
BBASB Sean Burroughs	10.00	3.00
BBATL Terrence Long	10.00	3.00

2001 Bowman's Best Exclusive Autographs

Randomly inserted in packs at the rate of one in 50, this nine-card set features autographed player photos.

	Nm-Mt	Ex-Mt
BBEABI Bjorn Ivy	8.00	2.40
BBEAJB Jeremy Blevins	8.00	2.40
BBEAJJ J.J. Johnson	8.00	2.40
BBEAJR Jerrod Riggan	8.00	2.40
BBEAMH M. Hendrickson	8.00	2.40
BBEASC S. Clapp EXCH	8.00	2.40
BBEASS Sneideer Santos	8.00	2.40
BBEATW Ty Wigginton	10.00	3.00
BBEAWA Willy Aybar	10.00	3.00

2001 Bowman's Best Franchise Favorites Autographs

Randomly inserted in packs, this nine-card set is an autographed parallel version of the regular insert set.

	Nm-Mt	Ex-Mt
FFAAR Alex Rodriguez	100.00	30.00
FFADE Darin Erstad	15.00	4.50
FFADM Don Mattingly	60.00	18.00
FFADW Dave Winfield	25.00	7.50
FFAEJ Darin Erstad Reggie Jackson	80.00	24.00
FFAMW Don Mattingly Dave Winfield	150.00	45.00
FFANR Nolan Ryan	100.00	30.00
FFARJ Reggie Jackson	40.00	12.00
FFARR Nolan Ryan Alex Rodriguez	400.00	120.00

2001 Bowman's Best Franchise Favorites Relics

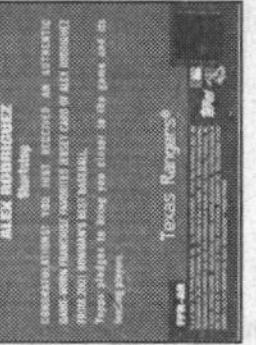

Randomly inserted in packs at the rate of one in 58, this 12-card set features color player photos of franchise favorites along with memorabilia pieces.

	Nm-Mt	Ex-Mt
FFRAR Alex Rodriguez Jsy	25.00	7.50
FFRBB Craig Biggio Jeff Bagwell	40.00	12.00
FFRCB Craig Biggio Uniform	15.00	4.50
FFRDE Darin Erstad Jsy	10.00	3.00
FFRDM Don Mattingly Jsy	40.00	12.00
FFRDW Dave Winfield Jsy	10.00	3.00
FFREJ Darin Erstad Reggie Jackson	40.00	12.00
FFRJB Jeff Bagwell Uniform	15.00	4.50
FFRMW Don Mattingly Dave Winfield	100.00	30.00
FFRNR Nolan Ryan Jsy	50.00	15.00
FFRRJ Reggie Jackson Jsy	15.00	4.50
FFRRR Nolan Ryan Alex Rodriguez	80.00	24.00

2001 Bowman's Best Franchise Futures

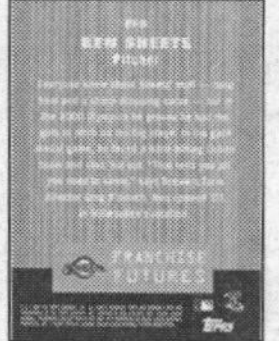

Randomly inserted into packs at the rate of one in 24, this 12-card set displays color photos of top young players.

	Nm-Mt	Ex-Mt
COMPLETE SET (12)	30.00	9.00
FF1 Josh Hamilton	2.00	.60
FF2 Wes Helms	2.00	.60
FF3 Alfonso Soriano	2.00	.60
FF4 Nick Johnson	2.00	.60
FF5 Jose Ortiz	2.00	.60
FF6 Ben Sheets	2.00	.60
FF7 Sean Burroughs	2.00	.60
FF8 Ben Petrick	2.00	.60
FF9 Corey Patterson	2.00	.60
FF10 J.R. House	2.00	.60
FF11 Alex Escobar	2.00	.60
FF12 Travis Hafner	5.00	1.50

2001 Bowman's Best Impact Players

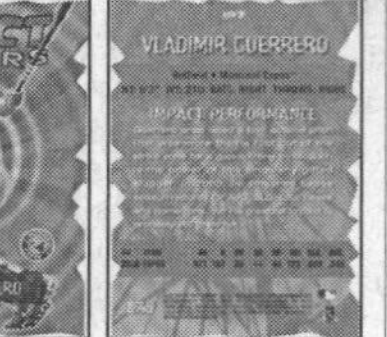

Randomly inserted in packs at the rate of one in seven, this 20-card set features color action photos of top players who have made their mark on the game.

	Nm-Mt	Ex-Mt
COMPLETE SET (20)	30.00	9.00
IP1 Mark McGwire	5.00	1.50
IP2 Sammy Sosa	3.00	.90
IP3 Manny Ramirez	1.25	.35
IP4 Troy Glaus	1.00	.30
IP5 Ken Griffey Jr.	3.00	.90
IP6 Gary Sheffield	1.00	.30
IP7 Vladimir Guerrero	2.00	.60
IP8 Carlos Delgado	1.00	.30
IP9 Jason Giambi	1.00	.30
IP10 Frank Thomas	2.00	.60
IP11 Vernon Wells	1.00	.30
IP12 Carlos Pena	1.00	.30
IP13 Joe Crede	1.00	.30
IP14 Keith Ginter	1.00	.30
IP15 Aubrey Huff	1.00	.30
IP16 Brad Cresse	1.00	.30
IP17 Austin Kearns	1.00	.30
IP18 Nick Johnson	1.00	.30
IP19 Josh Hamilton	1.00	.30
IP20 Corey Patterson	1.00	.30

2001 Bowman's Best Locker Room Collection Jerseys

Randomly inserted in packs at the rate of one in 133, this five-card set features color player photos with swatches of jerseys embedded in the cards and carry the "LRCL" prefix

	Nm-Mt	Ex-Mt
LRCJEC Eric Chavez	10.00	3.00
LRCJJP Jay Payton	8.00	2.40
LRCJMM Mark Mulder	10.00	3.00
LRCJPR Pokey Reese	8.00	2.40
LRCJPW Preston Wilson	10.00	3.00

2001 Bowman's Best Locker Room Collection Lumber

Randomly inserted in packs at the rate of one in 267, this five-card set features color player photos with pieces of actual bats embedded in the cards and carry the "LRCL" prefix.

	Nm-Mt	Ex-Mt
LRCLAG Adrian Gonzalez	10.00	3.00
LRCLCP Corey Patterson	10.00	3.00
LRCLEM Eric Munson	8.00	2.40
LRCLPB Pat Burrell	10.00	3.00
LRCLSB Sean Burroughs	10.00	3.00

2001 Bowman's Best Rookie Fever

Randomly inserted in packs at the rate of one in 10, this 10-card set features color photos of top players during their rookie year. Card backs display the "RF" prefix.

	Nm-Mt	Ex-Mt
COMPLETE SET (10)	15.00	4.50
RF1 Chipper Jones	1.50	.45
RF2 Preston Wilson	1.00	.30
RF3 Todd Helton	1.00	.30
RF4 Jay Payton	1.00	.30
RF5 Ivan Rodriguez	1.50	.45
RF6 Manny Ramirez	1.00	.30
RF7 Derek Jeter	4.00	1.20
RF8 Orlando Hernandez	1.00	.30
RF9 Mark Quinn	1.00	.30
RF10 Terrence Long	1.00	.30

2002 Bowman's Best

This 181 card set was released in August, 2002. The set was issued in five card packs which were issued 10 packs to a box and 10 boxes to a case with an SRP of $15. The first 90 cards of the set featured veteran players while cards 91 through 181 featured prospects or rookies along with either an autograph or a game-used bat piece of the featured player. The higher numbered cards were issued in different seeding ratios and we have notated the group the player belongs to next to their name in our checklist. Card number 181 features Kaz Ishii and was issued as an exchange card which could be redeemed until December 31, 2002.

	Nm-Mt	Ex-Mt
COMP.SET w/o SP's (90)	100.00	30.00
COMMON CARD (1-90)	.75	.23
COMMON AUTO A (91-180)	8.00	2.40
AUTO GROUP A ODDS 1:3		
COMMON AUTO B (91-180)	10.00	3.00
AUTO GROUP B ODDS 1:19		
COMMON BAT (91-180)	5.00	1.50
91-180 BAT STATED ODDS 1:5		
181 ISHII BAT EXCHANGE ODDS 1:131		
1 Josh Beckett	.75	.23
2 Derek Jeter	5.00	1.50
3 Alex Rodriguez	3.00	.90
4 Miguel Tejada	.75	.23
5 Nomar Garciaparra	3.00	.90
6 Aramis Ramirez	.75	.23
7 Jeremy Giambi	.75	.23
8 Bernie Williams	1.25	.35
9 Juan Pierre	.75	.23
10 Chipper Jones	2.00	.60
11 Jimmy Rollins	.75	.23
12 Alfonso Soriano	1.25	.35
13 Mark Prior	3.00	.90
14 Paul Konerko	.75	.23
15 Tim Hudson	.75	.23

6 Doug Mientkiewicz .75 .23
7 Todd Helton 1.25 .35
8 Moises Alou .75 .23
9 Juan Gonzalez 1.25 .35
0 Jorge Posada 1.25 .35
1 Jeff Kent .75 .23
2 Roger Clemens 4.00 1.20
3 Phil Nevin .75 .23
4 Brian Giles .75 .23
5 Carlos Delgado .75 .23
6 Jason Giambi .75 .23
7 Vladimir Guerrero 2.00 .60
8 Cliff Floyd .75 .23
9 Shea Hillenbrand .75 .23
0 Ken Griffey Jr. 3.00 .90
1 Mike Piazza 3.00 .90
2 Carlos Pena .75 .23
3 Larry Walker 1.25 .35
4 Magglio Ordonez .75 .23
5 Mike Mussina 1.25 .35
6 Andruw Jones .75 .23
7 Nick Johnson .75 .23
8 Curt Schilling .75 .23
9 Eric Chavez .75 .23
0 Bartolo Colon .75 .23
1 Eric Hinske .75 .23
2 Sean Burroughs .75 .23
3 Randy Johnson 2.00 .60
4 Adam Dunn 1.25 .35
5 Pedro Martinez 2.00 .60
6 Garret Anderson .75 .23
7 Jim Thome 2.00 .60
8 Gary Sheffield .75 .23
9 Tsuyoshi Shinjo .75 .23
0 Albert Pujols 4.00 1.20
1 Ichiro Suzuki 3.00 .90
2 C.C. Sabathia .75 .23
3 Bobby Abreu .75 .23
4 Ivan Rodriguez 2.00 .60
5 J.D. Drew .75 .23
6 Jacque Jones .75 .23
7 Jason Kendall .75 .23
8 Javier Vazquez .75 .23
9 Jeff Bagwell 1.25 .35
0 Greg Maddux 3.00 .90
1 Jim Edmonds .75 .23
2 Hank Blalock 2.00 .60
3 Jose Vidro .75 .23
4 Kevin Brown .75 .23
5 Mark Teixeira 1.25 .35
6 Sammy Sosa 3.00 .90
7 Lance Berkman .75 .23
8 Mark Mulder .75 .23
9 Marty Cordova .75 .23
70 Frank Thomas 2.00 .60
71 Mike Cameron .75 .23
72 Mike Sweeney .75 .23
73 Barry Bonds 5.00 1.50
74 Troy Glaus .75 .23
75 Barry Zito .75 .23
76 Pat Burrell .75 .23
77 Paul LoDuca .75 .23
78 Rafael Palmeiro 1.25 .35
79 Austin Kearns .75 .23
80 Darin Erstad .75 .23
81 Richie Sexson .75 .23
82 Roberto Alomar 1.25 .35
83 Roy Oswalt .75 .23
84 Ryan Klesko .75 .23
85 Luis Gonzalez .75 .23
86 Scott Rolen 2.00 .60
87 Shannon Stewart .75 .23
88 Shawn Green .75 .23
89 Toby Hall .75 .23
90 Bret Boone .75 .23
91 Casey Kotchman Bat RC 15.00 3.00
92 Jose Valverde AU A RC 10.00 3.00
93 Cole Barthel Bat RC 5.00 1.50
94 Brad Nelson AU A RC 15.00 4.50
95 Mauricio Lara AU A RC 8.00 2.40
96 Ryan Gripp Bat RC 5.00 1.50
97 Brian West AU A RC 8.00 2.40
98 Chris Piersoll AU B RC 10.00 3.00
99 Ryan Church AU B RC 15.00 4.50
100 Javier Colina AU A 8.00 2.40
101 Juan M. Gonzalez AU A RC 8.00 2.40
102 Benito Baez AU A 8.00 2.40
103 Mike Hill Bat RC 5.00 1.50
104 Jason Grove AU B RC 10.00 3.00
105 Koyie Hill AU B 10.00 3.00
106 Mark Outlaw AU A RC 8.00 2.40
107 Jason Bay Bat RC 15.00 4.50
108 Jorge Padilla AU A RC 8.00 2.40
109 Pete Zamora AU A RC 8.00 2.40
110 Joe Mauer AU A RC 60.00 18.00
111 Franklyn German AU A RC 8.00 2.40
112 Chris Flinn AU A RC 8.00 2.40
113 David Wright Bat RC 30.00 9.00
114 An. Martinez AU A RC 8.00 2.40
115 Nic Jackson Bat RC 5.00 1.50
116 Rene Reyes AU A RC 8.00 2.40
117 Colin Young AU A RC 8.00 2.40
118 Joe Orloski AU A RC 8.00 2.40
119 Mike Wilson AU A RC 8.00 2.40
120 Rich Thompson AU A RC 8.00 2.40
121 Jake Mauer AU B RC 10.00 3.00
122 Mario Ramos AU A RC 8.00 2.40
123 Doug Sessions AU B RC 10.00 3.00
124 Doug Devore Bat RC 5.00 1.50
125 Travis Foley AU A RC 8.00 2.40
126 Chris Baker AU A RC 8.00 2.40
127 Michael Floyd AU A RC 8.00 2.40
128 Josh Barfield Bat RC 10.00 3.00
129 Jose Bautista Bat RC 8.00 2.40
130 Gavin Floyd AU A RC 30.00 9.00
131 Jason Botts Bat RC 8.00 2.40
132 Clint Nageotte AU A RC 12.00 3.60
133 Jesus Cota AU B RC 10.00 3.00
134 Ron Calloway Bat RC 5.00 1.50
135 Kevin Cash Bat RC 5.00 1.50
136 Jonny Gomes AU B RC 15.00 4.50
137 Dennis Ulacia AU A RC 8.00 2.40
138 Ryan Snare AU A RC 8.00 2.40
139 Kevin Deaton AU A RC 8.00 2.40
140 Bobby Jenks AU B RC 15.00 4.50
141 Casey Kotchman AU A RC 25.00 7.50
142 Adam Walker AU A RC 8.00 2.40
143 Mike Gonzalez AU A RC 8.00 2.40
144 Ruben Gotay Bat RC 5.00 1.50
145 Jason Grove Bat RC 5.00 1.50
146 Freddy Sanchez AU B RC 10.00 3.00
147 Jason Arnold AU B RC 15.00 4.50
148 Scott Hairston AU A RC 20.00 6.00
149 Jason St. Clair AU B RC 10.00 3.00
150 Chris Tritle Bat RC 5.00 1.50
151 Edwin Yan Bat RC 5.00 1.50
152 Freddy Sanchez Bat RC 5.00 1.50
153 Greg Sain Bat RC 8.00 2.40
154 Yurendell De Caster Bat RC 5.00 1.50
155 Noochie Varner Bat RC 5.00 1.50
156 Nelson Castro AU B RC 10.00 3.00
157 Randall Shelley Bat RC 5.00 1.50
158 Reed Johnson Bat RC 8.00 2.40
159 Ryan Raburn AU A RC 8.00 2.40
160 Jose Morban Bat RC 5.00 1.50
161 Justin Schuda AU A RC 8.00 2.40
162 Henry Pichardo AU A RC 8.00 2.40
163 Josh Bard AU A RC 8.00 2.40
164 Josh Bonifay AU A RC 8.00 2.40
165 Brandon League AU B RC 10.00 3.00
166 Jorge-Julio DePaula AU A RC 10.00 3.00
167 Todd Linden AU B RC 25.00 7.50
168 Francisco Liriano AU A RC 10.00 3.00
169 Chris Snelling AU A RC 8.00 2.40
170 Blake McGinley AU A RC 8.00 2.40
171 Cody McKay AU A RC 8.00 2.40
172 Jason Stanford AU A RC 8.00 2.40
173 Lenny Dinardo AU A RC 8.00 2.40
174 Greg Montalbano AU A RC 8.00 2.40
175 Earl Snyder AU A RC 10.00 3.00
176 Justin Huber AU A RC 10.00 3.00
177 Chris Narveson AU A RC 8.00 2.40
178 Jon Switzer AU A RC 8.00 2.40
179 Ronald Acuna AU A RC 8.00 2.40
180 Chris Duffy Bat RC 5.00 1.50
181 Kazuhisa Ishii Bat RC 10.00 3.00

2002 Bowman's Best Blue

This 181 card set is a parallel of the regular Bowman's Best set. These cards were seeded into packs at different rates which we have notated. These card can be differentiated by their "blue" coloring. Cards numbered from 1 through 90 were issued to a stated print run of 300 serial numbered sets. Card number 181 features Kaz Ishii and was issued as an exchange card which could be redeemed until December 31, 2002.

Nm-Mt Ex-Mt
*BLUE 1-90: 1X TO 2.5X BASIC
1-90 STATED ODDS 1:6
1-90 PRINT RUN 300 SERIAL #'d SETS
*BLUE AUTO: .4X TO 1X BASIC AU A
*BLUE AUTO: .3X TO .8X BASIC AU B
AUTO STATED ODDS 1:6
*BLUE BAT: .4X TO 1X BASIC BAT
BAT STATED ODDS 1:14
ISHII BAT EXCHANGE ODDS 1:335
ISHII BAT EXCHANGE DEADLINE 12/31/02
BLUE BATS FEATURE TEAM LOGOS!
181 Kazuhisa Ishii Bat 10.00 3.00

2002 Bowman's Best Gold

This 181 card set is a parallel of the regular Bowman's Best set. These cards were seeded into packs at different rates which we have notated. These card can be differentiated by their "gold" coloring. Cards numbered from 1 through 90 were limited to a stated print run of 50 serial numbered sets. Card number 181 features Kaz Ishii and was issued as an exchange card which could be redeemed until December 31, 2002.

Nm-Mt Ex-Mt
*GOLD 1-90: 3X TO 8X BASIC
1-90 STATED ODDS 1:31
1-90 PRINT RUN 50 SERIAL #'d SETS
*GOLD AUTO: 1X TO 2.5X BASIC AU A
*GOLD AUTO: .75X TO 2X BASIC AU B
GOLD AUTO STATED ODDS 1:51
*GOLD BAT: 1X TO 2.5X BASIC BAT
GOLD BAT STATED ODDS 1:115
ISHII BAT EXCHANGE ODDS 1:3444
ISHII BAT EXCHANGE DEADLINE 12/31/02
GOLD BATS FEATURE FACSIMILE AUTOS!
181 Kazuhisa Ishii Bat 25.00 7.50

2002 Bowman's Best Red

This 181 card set is a parallel of the regular Bowman's Best set. These cards were seeded into packs at different rates which we have notated. These card can be differentiated by their "red" coloring. Cards numbered from 1 through 90 were limited to a stated print run of 200 serial numbered sets. Card number 181 features Kaz Ishii and was issued as an exchange card which could be redeemed until December 31, 2002.

Nm-Mt Ex-Mt
*RED 1-90: 1.25X TO 3X BASIC
1-90 PRINT RUN 200 SERIAL #'d SETS
*RED AUTO: .6X TO 1.5X BASIC AU A
*RED AUTO: .5X TO 1.2X BASIC AU B
AUTO STATED ODDS 1:17
*RED BATS: .6X TO 1.5X BASIC BATS
BAT STATED ODDS 1:39
ISHII BAT EXCHANGE ODDS 1:1117
ISHII BAT EXCHANGE DEADLINE 12/31/02
RED BATS FEATURE STATISTICS!
181 Kazuhisa Ishii Bat 15.00 4.50

2003 Bowman's Best

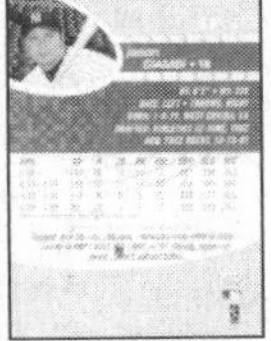

This 130 card set was released in September, 2003. This set was issued in five card packs which contained an autograph card. Each of these packs had an SRP of $15 and these packs were issued 10 to a box and 10 boxes to a case. This set was designed to be checklisted alphabetically as no numbering was used for this set. The first year cards which are autographed have the lettering FY AU RC after their name in the checklist. A few first year players had some cards issued with an bat piece included. Those bat cards were issued one per box-loader pack. In addition, high draft pick Bryan Bullington signed some of the actual boxes and those boxes were issued at a stated rate of one in 106.

MINT NRMT
COMP.SET w/o SP's (50) 40.00 18.00
COMMON CARD 1.00 .45
COMMON AUTO 8.00 3.60
COMMON BAT 4.00 1.80
AB Andrew Brown FY AU RC 10.00 4.50
AK Austin Kearns 1.00 .45
AM Aneudis Mateo FY AU RC 8.00 3.60
AP Albert Pujols 3.00 1.35
AR Alex Rodriguez 2.50 1.10
AS Alfonso Soriano 1.00 .45
AW Aron Weston FY AU RC 8.00 3.60
BB Bryan Bullington FY AU RC 15.00 6.75
BC Bernie Castro FY RC 1.00 .45
BFL Br. Florence FY AU RC 8.00 3.60
BFR Ben Francisco FY AU RC 10.00 4.50
BH Brendan Harris FY AU RC 10.00 4.50
BJH Bo Hart FY RC 1.50 .70
BK Beau Kemp FY AU RC 8.00 3.60
BLB Barry Bonds 4.00 1.80
BM Brian McCann FY AU RC 10.00 4.50
BSG Brian Giles 1.00 .45
BWB Bobby Basham FY AU RC 10.00 4.50
BZ Barry Zito 1.00 .45
CAD Carlos Duran FY AU RC 8.00 3.60
CDC C. De La Cruz FY AU RC 8.00 3.60
CJ Chipper Jones 1.50 .70
CJW C.J. Wilson FY AU 8.00 3.60
CM Charlie Manning FY AU RC 8.00 3.60
CMS Curt Schilling 1.00 .45
CS Cory Stewart FY AU RC 8.00 3.60
CSS Corey Shafer FY AU RC 10.00 4.50
CW Chien-Ming Wang FY RC 2.00 .90
CWA Chien-Ming Wang FY AU 25.00 11.00
DAM D. Moseley FY AU RC 10.00 4.50
DC David Cash FY AU RC 8.00 3.60
DH Dan Haren FY AU RC 10.00 4.50
DJ Derek Jeter 4.00 1.80
DM David Martinez FY AU RC 8.00 3.60
DMM D. McGowan FY AU RC 10.00 4.50
DR Darrell Rasner FY AU RC 8.00 3.60
DW Doug Waechter FY AU RC 10.00 4.50
DY Dustin Yount FY RC 1.50 .70
ERA El. Ramirez FY AU RC 10.00 4.50
ERI Eric Riggs FY AU RC 10.00 4.50
ET Eider Torres FY AU RC 8.00 3.60
FP Felix Pie FY AU RC 25.00 11.00
FS Felix Sanchez FY AU RC 8.00 3.60
FT Ferdin Tejeda FY AU RC 8.00 3.60
GA Greg Aquino FY AU RC 8.00 3.60
GB Gregor Blanco FY AU RC 8.00 3.60
GJA Garret Anderson 1.00 .45
GM Greg Maddux 2.50 1.10
GS G. Schneidmiller FY AU RC 8.00 3.60
HR Hanley Ramirez FY AU RC 25.00 11.00
HRB Hanley Ramirez FY Bat 10.00 4.50
HT Haj Turay FY RC 1.50 .70
IS Ichiro Suzuki 2.50 1.10
JB Jeremy Bonderman FY RC 1.50 .70
JC Jose Contreras FY RC 2.00 .90
JDD J.D. Durbin FY AU RC 10.00 4.50
JFK Jeff Kent 1.00 .45
JG Joey Gomes FY AU RC 8.00 3.60
JGB Joey Gomes FY Bat 4.00 1.80
JGG Jason Giambi 1.00 .45
JK Jason Kubel FY AU RC 25.00 11.00
JKB Jason Kubel FY Bat 10.00 4.50
JLB Jaime Bubela FY AU RC 8.00 3.60
JM Jose Morales FY AU RC 8.00 3.60
JMS Jon-Mark Sprowl FY RC 1.50 .70
JRG Jeremy Griffiths FY AU RC 10.00 4.50
JT Jim Thome 1.50 .70
JV Joe Valentine FY AU RC 8.00 3.60
JW Josh Willingham FY AU RC 10.00 4.50
KBS Kelly Shoppach FY Bat 6.00 2.70
KG Ken Griffey Jr. 2.50 1.10
KJ Kade Johnson FY AU RC 8.00 3.60
KS Kelly Shoppach FY AU RC 12.00 5.50
KY Kevin Youkilis FY AU RC 20.00 9.00
KYE Kevin Youkilis FY Bat 8.00 3.60
LB Lance Berkman 1.00 .45
LF Lew Ford FY AU RC 20.00 9.00
LFJ Lew Ford FY Bat 6.00 2.70
LW Larry Walker 1.00 .45
MB Matt Bruback FY RC 1.00 .45
MD Matt Diaz FY RC 1.50 .70
MDA Matt Diaz FY AU 10.00 4.50
MDH Matt Hensley FY AU RC 8.00 3.60
MM Mark Malaska FY AU RC 8.00 3.60
MH Mi. Hernandez FY AU RC 8.00 3.60
MHI Mi. Hinckley FY AU RC 12.00 5.50
MJP Mike Piazza 2.50 1.10
MK Matt Kata FY AU RC 10.00 4.50
MNH Matt Hagen FY AU RC 10.00 4.50
MO Mike O'Keefe FY RC 1.00 .45
MOR Magglio Ordonez 1.00 .45
MP Mark Prior 1.50 .70
MR Manny Ramirez 1.00 .45
MS Mike Sweeney 1.00 .45
MT Miguel Tejada 1.00 .45
NG Nomar Garciaparra 2.50 1.10
NL Nook Logan FY AU RC 8.00 3.60
OC Ozzie Chavez FY AU RC 8.00 3.60
PB Pat Burrell 1.00 .45
PL Pete LaForest FY AU RC 10.00 4.50
PM Pedro Martinez 1.50 .70
PR Prentice Redman FY AU RC 8.00 3.60
RC Ryan Cameron FY AU RC 8.00 3.60
RD Rajai Davis FY AU RC 10.00 4.50
RH Ryan Howard FY AU RC 40.00 18.00
RHJ Ryan Howard FY Bat 15.00 6.75
RJ Randy Johnson 1.50 .70
RLD Rajai Davis FY Bat 5.00 2.20
RM R. Nivar-Martinez FY RC 1.50 .70
RS Ryan Shealy FY AU RC 10.00 4.50
RSB Ryan Shealy FY Bat 5.00 2.20
RWH Rob. Hammock FY AU RC 10.00 4.50
SG Shawn Green 1.00 .45
SS Sammy Sosa 2.50 1.10
ST Scott Tyler FY AU RC 10.00 4.50
SV Shane Victorino FY RC 1.00 .45
TA Tyler Adamczyk FY AU RC 8.00 3.60
TH Todd Helton 1.00 .45
TI Travis Ishikawa FY AU RC 8.00 3.60
TJ Tyler Johnson FY AU RC 8.00 3.60
TJB T.J. Bohn FY RC 1.00 .45
TKH Torii Hunter 1.00 .45
TO Tim Olson FY AU RC 10.00 4.50
TS T.Story-Harden FY AU RC 8.00 3.60
TSB T.Story-Harden FY Bat 4.00 1.80
TT Terry Tiffee FY RC 1.50 .70
VG Vladimir Guerrero 1.50 .70
WE Willie Eyre FY AU RC 8.00 3.60
WL Wil Ledezma FY AU RC 10.00 4.50
WRC Roger Clemens 3.00 1.35
NNO Bryan Bullington 25.00 11.00
Opened Box AU
NNO Bryan Bullington
Sealed Box AU

2003 Bowman's Best Blue

MINT NRMT
*BLUE: 1.5X TO 4X BASIC
*BLUE FY: 3X TO 8X BASIC FY
BLUE STATED ODDS 1:28
BLUE PRINT RUN 100 SERIAL #'d SETS
*BLUE AUTO: 1X TO 2.5X BASIC AUTO
BLUE AUTO ODDS 1:32
BLUE AUTO PRINT RUN 50 SETS
BLUE AUTO'S NOT SERIAL-NUMBERED
BLUE AU PRINT RUNS PROVIDED BY TOPPS
*BLUE BAT: 1X TO 2.5X BASIC FY BAT
BLUE BAT ODDS 1:22 BOXLOADER PACKS
BLUE BAT PRINT RUN 50 SETS
BLUE BATS NOT SERIAL-NUMBERED
BLUE BAT PRINTS PROVIDED BY TOPPS

2003 Bowman's Best Red

MINT NRMT
*RED: 3X TO 8X BASIC RED
*RED FY: 4X TO 10X BASIC FY
RED STATED ODDS 1:55
RED STATED PRINT RUN 50 SERIAL #'d SETS
RED AUTO ODDS 1:63
RED AUTO PRINT RUN 25 SETS
RED AU PRINT RUNS PROVIDED BY TOPPS
RED AUTOS NOT SERIAL-NUMBERED
NO RED AUTO PRICING DUE TO SCARCITY
RED BAT ODDS 1:44 BOXLOADER PACKS
RED BAT PRINT RUN 25 SETS
RED BAT PRINT RUNS PROVIDED BY TOPPS
RED BATS NOT SERIAL-NUMBERED
NO RED BAT PRICING DUE TO SCARCITY
BWB Bobby Basham FY AU

2003 Bowman's Best Double Play Autographs

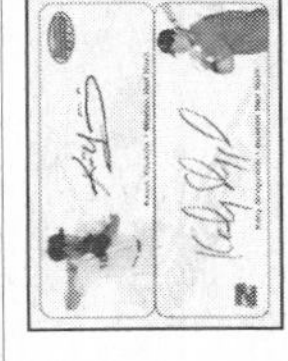

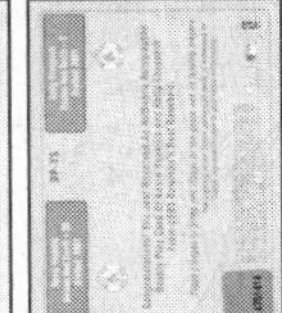

MINT NRMT
STATED ODDS 1:55
EB Elizardo Ramirez 30.00 13.50
Bryan Bullington
GK Joey Gomes 60.00 27.00
Jason Kubel
HV Dan Haren 25.00 11.00
Joe Valentine
LL Nook Logan 25.00 11.00
Wil Ledezma
RS Prentice Redman 15.00 6.75
Gary Schneidmiller
SB Corey Shafer 25.00 11.00
Gregor Blanco
SR Felix Sanchez 15.00 6.75
Darrell Rasner
YS Kevin Youkilis 50.00 22.00
Kelly Shoppach

2003 Bowman's Best Triple Play Autographs

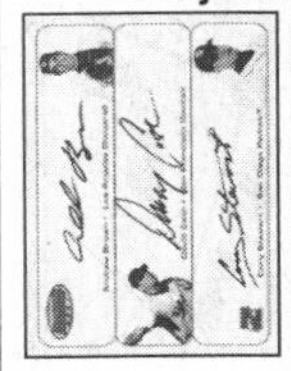

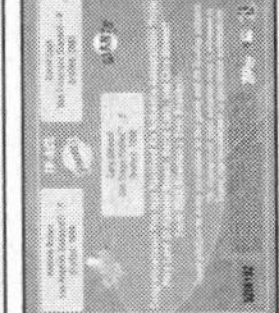

MINT NRMT
STATED ODDS 1:219
BCS Andrew Brown 30.00 13.50
David Cash
Cory Stewart
DRS Rajai Davis 80.00 36.00
Hanley Ramirez
Ryan Shealy

2004 Bowman's Best

This 108-card set was released in September, 2004. The set was issued in five-card packs with an $15 SRP which came 10 packs to a box and 10 boxes to a case. In an interesting twist, the cards are numbered using the initials of the players instead of using a numbering system. Fifty cards in this set feature veteran players and the rest of the set features either rookie cards some of whom signed cardd for this product.

Nm-Mt Ex-Mt
COMP.SET w/o SP'S (50) 25.00 7.50
COMMON CARD 1.00 .30
COMMON RC 1.00 .30
ONE AUTO PER HOBBY PACK
ONE RELIC PER BOX-LOADER PACK
ONE BOX-LOADER PACK PER HOBBY BOX
STAUFFER BOX RANDOM IN HOBBY CASES
OVERALL AU PLATE ODDS 1:391 HOBBY
AU PLATE PRINT RUN 1 SET PER COLOR
BLACK-CYAN-MAGENTA-YELLOW ISSUED
NO AU PLATE PRICING DUE TO SCARCITY
AER Alex Rodriguez 2.50 .75
AG Adam Greenberg FY AU RC 10.00 3.00
AL Anthony Lerew FY RC 1.50 .45
AO Akinori Otsuka FY RC 1.00 .30
AP Albert Pujols 3.00 .90
AS Alfonso Soriano 1.00 .30
BB Bobby Brownlie FY AU RC 15.00 4.50
BEM Brandon Medders FY AU RC 8.00 2.40
BG Brian Giles 1.00 .30
BMS Brad Snyder FY AU RC 12.00 3.60
BP Brayan Pena FY AU RC 8.00 2.40
BS Brad Sullivan FY AU RC 10.00 3.00
CB Carlos Beltran 1.00 .30
CD Carlos Delgado 1.00 .30
CJ Conor Jackson FY AU RC 25.00 7.50
CLH Chin-Lung Hu FY RC 2.00 .60
CMA Craig Ansman FY AU RC 8.00 2.40
CMS Curt Schilling 1.50 .45
CZ Charlie Zink FY AU RC 8.00 2.40
DA David Aardsma FY AU RC 8.00 2.40
DC Dave Crouthers FY AU RC 8.00 2.40
DDN Dustin Nippert FY AU RC 8.00 2.40
DG Danny Gonzalez FY RC 1.00 .30
DK Donald Kelly FY AU RC 8.00 2.40
DL Donald Levinski FY AU RC 8.00 2.40
DM David Murphy FY AU RC 12.00 3.60
DN Dioner Navarro FY AU RC 15.00 4.50
DS Don Sutton FY RC 2.50 .75
EA Erick Aybar FY AU RC 15.00 4.50
EC Eric Chavez 1.00 .30
EH Estee Harris FY AU RC 8.00 2.40
ES Ervin Santana FY AU RC 15.00 4.50
FH Felix Hernandez FY AU RC 30.00 9.00
GA Garret Anderson 1.00 .30
HB Hank Blalock 1.00 .30
HM Hector Made FY RC 1.50 .45
IR Ivan Rodriguez 1.50 .45
IS Ichiro Suzuki 2.50 .75
JA Joaquin Arias FY AU RC 8.00 2.40
JAV Jose Vidro 1.00 .30
JC Juan Cedeno FY AU RC 8.00 2.40
JDS Jason Schmidt 1.00 .30
JE Jesse English FY AU RC 8.00 2.40
JGG Jason Giambi 1.00 .30
JH Jason Hirsh FY AU RC 8.00 2.40
JJC Jon Connolly FY RC 2.00 .60
JK Jon Knott FY AU RC 8.00 2.40
JL Josh Labandeira FY AU RC 8.00 2.40
JLO Javy Lopez 1.00 .30
JP Jorge Posada 1.00 .30
JRG Joey Gathright FY RC 2.00 .60
JS Jeff Salazar FY AU RC 12.00 3.60
JSZ Jason Szuminski FY AU RC 8.00 2.40
JT Jim Thome 1.50 .45
KC Kory Casto FY AU RC 8.00 2.40
KK Kevin Kouzmanoff FY AU RC 10.00 3.00
KM Kazuo Matsui FY Uni RC 15.00 4.50
KRK Kody Kirkland FY Bat RC 8.00 2.40
KS Kyle Sleeth FY RC 2.00 .60
KT Kazuhito Tadano FY Jsy RC 8.00 2.40
LK Logan Kensing FY AU RC 8.00 2.40
LM Lastings Milledge FY AU RC 25.00 7.50
LO Lyle Overbay 1.00 .30
LTH Luke Hughes FY AU RC 8.00 2.40
LWJ Chipper Jones 1.50 .45
MAR Manny Ramirez 1.00 .30
MDC Matt Creighton FY AU RC 8.00 2.40
MG Mike Gosling FY RC 1.00 .30
MJP Mike Piazza 2.50 .75
MO Magglio Ordonez 1.00 .30
MT Miguel Tejada 1.00 .30
MTC Miguel Cabrera 1.00 .30
MV Merkin Valdez FY AU RC 12.00 3.60
MWP Mark Prior 1.50 .45
MY Michael Young 1.00 .30
NAG Nomar Garciaparra 2.50 .75
NG Nick Gorneault FY RC 1.50 .45
NU Nic Ungs FY AU RC 8.00 2.40
OQ Omar Quintanilla FY AU RC 15.00 4.50
PM Paul Maholm FY AU RC 10.00 3.00
PMM Paul McAnulty FY RC 1.50 .45
RB Ryan Budde FY AU RC 8.00 2.40
RC Roger Clemens 3.00 .90
RG Rudy Guillen FY AU RC 12.00 3.60
RJ Randy Johnson 1.50 .45
RN Ricky Nolasco FY AU RC 8.00 2.40
RR Ramon Ramirez FY AU RC 8.00 2.40
RS Richie Sexson 1.00 .30
RT Rob Tejeda FY AU RC 8.00 2.40
SH Shawn Hill FY AU RC 8.00 2.40
SR Scott Rolen 1.50 .45
SS Sammy Sosa 2.50 .75
ST Shingo Takatsu FY Jsy RC 10.00 3.00
TB Travis Blackley FY Jsy RC 8.00 2.40
TD Tyler Davidson FY AU RC 10.00 3.00
TJ Terry Jones FY RC 1.50 .45
TJS Tim Stauffer FY AU RC 10.00 3.00
TLH Todd Helton 1.00 .30
TOH Travis Hanson FY AU RC 8.00 2.40
TRM Tom Mastny FY AU RC 8.00 2.40
TS Todd Self FY RC 1.00 .30
VC Vito Chiaravalloti FY AU RC 10.00 3.00
VG Vladimir Guerrero 1.50 .45
WM Warner Madrigal FY RC 1.50 .45
WS Wardell Starling FY AU RC 8.00 2.40
YM Yadier Molina FY AU RC 20.00 6.00
ZD Zach Duke FY AU RC 20.00 6.00
NNO Tim Stauffer AU Box/100 25.00 7.50

2004 Bowman's Best Green

	Nm-Mt	Ex-Mt
*GREEN: 1.5X TO 4X BASIC		
*GREEN RC'S: 3X TO 8X BASIC RC'S		
GREEN ODDS 1:18		
GREEN PRINT RUN 100 SERIAL #'d SETS		
*GREEN AU'S: .75X TO 2X BASIC AU'S		
GREEN AU ODDS 1:32 HOBBY		
GREEN AU PRINT RUN 50 SETS		
GREEN AUTOS NOT SERIAL-NUMBERED		
AUTO PRINT RUNS PROVIDED BY TOPPS		
*GREEN RELICS: .75X TO 2X BASIC RELICS		
GREEN RELIC ODDS 1:31 HOBBY BOXES		
GREEN RELIC PRINT RUN 50 SETS		
GREEN RELICS NOT SERIAL-NUMBERED		
RELIC PRINT RUNS PROVIDED BY TOPPS		

2004 Bowman's Best Red

	Nm-Mt	Ex-Mt
*RED: 5X TO 12X BASIC		
RED ODDS 1:90 HOBBY		
RED PRINT RUN 20 SERIAL #'d SETS		
NO RED RC PRICING DUE TO SCARCITY		
RED AUTO ODDS 1:156 HOBBY		
RED AU PRINT RUN 10 SETS		
RED AU'S ARE NOT SERIAL-NUMBERED		
PRINT RUN INFO PROVIDED BY TOPPS		
NO RED AU PRICING DUE TO SCARCITY		
RED RELIC ODDS 1:154 HOBBY BOXES		
RED RELIC PRINT RUN 10 SETS		
RED RELICS ARE NOT SERIAL-NUMBERED		
PRINT RUN INFO PROVIDED BY TOPPS		
NO RED RELIC PRICING DUE TO SCARCITY		

2004 Bowman's Best Double Play Autographs

	Nm-Mt	Ex-Mt
STATED ODDS 1:33 HOBBY		
STATED PRINT RUN 236 SETS		
CARDS ARE NOT SERIAL NUMBERED		
PRINT RUN INFO PROVIDED BY TOPPS		
CC Matt Creighton	20.00	6.00
Dave Crouthers		
EN Jesse English	20.00	6.00
Ricky Nolasco		
HJ Travis Hanson	30.00	9.00
Conor Jackson		
MH Lastings Milledge	50.00	15.00
Estee Harris		
MN Brandon Medders	20.00	6.00
Dustin Nippert		
QS Omar Quintanilla	30.00	9.00
Brad Snyder		
SC Tim Stauffer	25.00	7.50
Vito Chiaravalloti		
SK Jeff Salazar	25.00	7.50
Jon Knott		
SV Ervin Santana	30.00	9.00
Merkin Valdez		
UK Nic Ungs	25.00	7.50
Kevin Kouzmanoff		

2004 Bowman's Best Triple Play Autographs

	Nm-Mt	Ex-Mt
STATED ODDS 1:109 HOBBY		
STATED PRINT RUN 236 SETS		
CARDS ARE NOT SERIAL NUMBERED		
PRINT RUN INFO PROVIDED BY TOPPS		
ALS David Aardsma	30.00	9.00
Donald Levinski		
Brad Sullivan		
CBA Juan Cedeno	40.00	12.00
Bobby Brownlie		
Joaquin Arias		
SSV Tim Stauffer	60.00	18.00
Ervin Santana		
Merkin Valdez		

1980 Burger King Pitch/Hit/Run

The cards in this 34-card set measure 2 1/2" by 3 1/2". The "Pitch, Hit, and Run" set was a promotion introduced by Burger King in 1980. The cards carry a Burger King logo on the front and those marked by an asterisk in the checklist contain a different photo from that found in the regularly issued Topps series. For example, Nolan Ryan was shown as a California Angel and Joe Morgan was a Cincinnati Red in the 1980 Topps regular set. Cards 1-11 are pitchers, 12-22 are hitters, and 23-33 are speedsters. Within each subgroup, the players are numbered corresponding to the alphabetical order of their names.

	NM	Ex
COMPLETE SET (34)	25.00	10.00
1 Vida Blue *	.50	.20
2 Steve Carlton	2.00	.80
3 Rollie Fingers	1.00	.40
4 Ron Guidry *	.50	.20
5 Jerry Koosman *	.25	.10
6 Phil Niekro	1.25	.50
7 Jim Palmer *	2.00	.80
8 J.R. Richard	.25	.10
9 Nolan Ryan *	15.00	6.00
Houston Astros		
10 Tom Seaver *	2.50	1.00
11 Bruce Sutter	.25	.10
12 Don Baylor	.50	.20
13 George Brett	6.00	2.40
14 Rod Carew	1.50	.60
15 George Foster	.25	.10
16 Keith Hernandez *	.50	.20
17 Reggie Jackson *	4.00	1.60
18 Fred Lynn *	.50	.20
19 Dave Parker	.25	.10
20 Jim Rice	.25	.10
21 Pete Rose	4.00	1.60
22 Dave Winfield *	3.00	1.20
23 Bobby Bonds *	.50	.20
24 Enos Cabell	.10	.04
25 Cesar Cedeno	.25	.10
26 Julio Cruz	.10	.04
27 Ron LeFlore *	.25	.10
28 Dave Lopes *	.25	.10
29 Omar Moreno *	.25	.10
30 Joe Morgan *	2.50	1.00
Houston Astros		
31 Bill North	.10	.04
32 Frank Taveras	.10	.04
33 Willie Wilson	.25	.10
NNO Checklist Card TP	.05	.02

1996 Circa

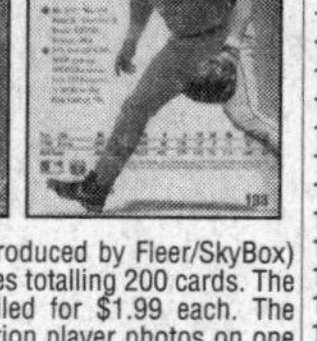

The 1996 Circa set (produced by Fleer/SkyBox) was issued in one series totalling 200 cards. The eight-card packs retailed for $1.99 each. The cards feature color action player photos on one of 28 different background designs and colors indicating the player's major league team. The checklist is grouped alphabetically by team with American League teams preceeding National League teams. The backs carry player information and statistics. Notable Rookie Cards include Darin Erstad and Chris Singleton.

	Nm-Mt	Ex-Mt
COMPLETE SET (200)	25.00	7.50
1 Roberto Alomar	.30	.09
2 Brady Anderson	.20	.06
3 Rocky Coppinger RC	.20	.06
4 Eddie Murray	.50	.15
5 Mike Mussina	.30	.09
6 Randy Myers	.20	.06
7 Rafael Palmeiro	.30	.09
8 Cal Ripken	1.50	.45
9 Jose Canseco	.50	.15
10 Roger Clemens	1.00	.30
11 Mike Greenwell	.20	.06
12 Tim Naehring	.20	.06
13 John Valentin	.20	.06
14 Mo Vaughn	.20	.06
15 Tim Wakefield	.20	.06
16 Jim Abbott	.30	.09
17 Garret Anderson	.20	.06
18 Jim Edmonds	.20	.06
19 Darin Erstad RC	1.50	.45
20 Chuck Finley	.20	.06
21 Troy Percival	.20	.06
22 Tim Salmon	.30	.09
23 J.T. Snow	.20	.06
24 Wilson Alvarez	.20	.06
25 Harold Baines	.20	.06
26 Ray Durham	.20	.06
27 Alex Fernandez	.20	.06
28 Tony Phillips	.20	.06
29 Frank Thomas	.50	.15
30 Robin Ventura	.20	.06
31 Sandy Alomar Jr.	.20	.06
32 Albert Belle	.20	.06
33 Kenny Lofton	.20	.06
34 Dennis Martinez	.20	.06
35 Jose Mesa	.20	.06
36 Charles Nagy	.20	.06
37 Manny Ramirez	.30	.09
38 Jim Thome	.50	.15
39 Travis Fryman	.20	.06
40 Bob Higginson	.20	.06
41 Melvin Nieves	.20	.06
42 Alan Trammell	.20	.06
43 Kevin Appier	.20	.06
44 Johnny Damon	.30	.09
45 Keith Lockhart	.20	.06
46 Jeff Montgomery	.20	.06
47 Joe Randa	.20	.06
48 Bip Roberts	.20	.06
49 Ricky Bones	.20	.06
50 Jeff Cirillo	.20	.06
51 Marc Newfield	.20	.06
52 Dave Nilsson	.20	.06
53 Kevin Seitzer	.20	.06
54 Ron Coomer	.20	.06
55 Marty Cordova	.20	.06
56 Roberto Kelly	.20	.06
57 Chuck Knoblauch	.20	.06
58 Paul Molitor	.30	.09
59 Kirby Puckett	.50	.15
60 Scott Stahoviak	.20	.06
61 Wade Boggs	.30	.09
62 David Cone	.20	.06
63 Cecil Fielder	.20	.06
64 Dwight Gooden	.20	.06
65 Derek Jeter	1.25	.35
66 Tino Martinez	.30	.09
67 Paul O'Neill	.30	.09
68 Andy Pettitte	.30	.09
69 Ruben Rivera	.20	.06
70 Bernie Williams	.30	.09
71 Geronimo Berroa	.20	.06
72 Jason Giambi	.20	.06
73 Mark McGwire	1.25	.35
74 Terry Steinbach	.20	.06
75 Todd Van Poppel	.20	.06
76 Jay Buhner	.20	.06
77 Norm Charlton	.20	.06
78 Ken Griffey Jr.	.75	.23
79 Randy Johnson	.50	.15
80 Edgar Martinez	.30	.09
81 Alex Rodriguez	1.00	.30
82 Paul Sorrento	.20	.06
83 Dan Wilson	.20	.06
84 Will Clark	.50	.15
85 Kevin Elster	.20	.06
86 Juan Gonzalez	.30	.09
87 Rusty Greer	.20	.06
88 Ken Hill	.20	.06
89 Mark McLemore	.20	.06
90 Dean Palmer	.20	.06
91 Roger Pavlik	.20	.06
92 Ivan Rodriguez	.50	.15
93 Joe Carter	.20	.06
94 Carlos Delgado	.20	.06
95 Juan Guzman	.20	.06
96 John Olerud	.20	.06
97 Ed Sprague	.20	.06
98 Jermaine Dye	.20	.06
99 Tom Glavine	.30	.09
100 Marquis Grissom	.20	.06
101 Andruw Jones	.50	.15
102 Chipper Jones	.50	.15
103 David Justice	.20	.06
104 Ryan Klesko	.20	.06
105 Greg Maddux	.75	.23
106 Fred McGriff	.30	.09
107 John Smoltz	.30	.09
108 Brant Brown	.20	.06
109 Mark Grace	.30	.09
110 Brian McRae	.20	.06
111 Ryne Sandberg	.75	.23
112 Sammy Sosa	.75	.23
113 Steve Trachsel	.20	.06
114 Bret Boone	.20	.06
115 Eric Davis	.20	.06
116 Steve Gibralter	.20	.06
117 Barry Larkin	.30	.09
118 Reggie Sanders	.20	.06
119 John Smiley	.20	.06
120 Dante Bichette	.20	.06
121 Ellis Burks	.20	.06
122 Vinny Castilla	.20	.06
123 Andres Galarraga	.20	.06
124 Larry Walker	.30	.09
125 Eric Young	.20	.06
126 Kevin Brown	.20	.06
127 Greg Colbrunn	.20	.06
128 Jeff Conine	.20	.06
129 Charles Johnson	.20	.06
130 Al Leiter	.20	.06
131 Gary Sheffield	.20	.06
132 Devon White	.20	.06
133 Jeff Bagwell	.30	.09
134 Derek Bell	.20	.06
135 Craig Biggio	.30	.09
136 Doug Drabek	.20	.06
137 Brian L.Hunter	.20	.06
138 Darryl Kile	.20	.06
139 Shane Reynolds	.20	.06
140 Brett Butler	.20	.06
141 Eric Karros	.20	.06
142 Ramon Martinez	.20	.06
143 Raul Mondesi	.20	.06
144 Hideo Nomo	.50	.15
145 Chan Ho Park	.20	.06
146 Mike Piazza	.75	.23
147 Moises Alou	.20	.06
148 Yamil Benitez	.20	.06
149 Mark Grudzielanek	.20	.06
150 Pedro Martinez	.50	.15
151 Henry Rodriguez	.20	.06
152 David Segui	.20	.06
153 Rondell White	.20	.06
154 Carlos Baerga	.20	.06
155 John Franco	.20	.06
156 Bernard Gilkey	.20	.06
157 Todd Hundley	.20	.06
158 Jason Isringhausen	.20	.06
159 Lance Johnson	.20	.06
160 Alex Ochoa	.20	.06
161 Rey Ordonez	.20	.06
162 Paul Wilson	.20	.06
163 Ron Blazier	.20	.06
164 Ricky Bottalico	.20	.06
165 Jim Eisenreich	.20	.06
166 Pete Incaviglia	.20	.06
167 Mickey Morandini	.20	.06
168 Ricky Otero	.20	.06
169 Curt Schilling	.20	.06
170 Jay Bell	.20	.06
171 Charlie Hayes	.20	.06
172 Jason Kendall	.20	.06
173 Jeff King	.20	.06
174 Al Martin	.20	.06
175 Alan Benes	.20	.06
176 Royce Clayton	.20	.06
177 Brian Jordan	.20	.06
178 Ray Lankford	.20	.06
179 John Mabry	.20	.06
180 Willie McGee	.20	.06
181 Ozzie Smith	.75	.23
182 Todd Stottlemyre	.20	.06
183 Andy Ashby	.20	.06
184 Ken Caminiti	.20	.06
185 Steve Finley	.20	.06
186 Tony Gwynn	.60	.18
187 Rickey Henderson	.50	.15
188 Wally Joyner	.20	.06
189 Fernando Valenzuela	.20	.06
190 Greg Vaughn	.20	.06
191 Rod Beck	.20	.06
192 Barry Bonds	1.25	.35
193 Shawon Dunston	.20	.06
194 Chris Singleton RC	.30	.09
195 Robby Thompson	.20	.06
196 Matt Williams	.20	.06
197 Barry Bonds CL	.60	.18
198 Ken Griffey Jr. CL	.50	.15
199 Cal Ripken CL	.75	.23
200 Frank Thomas CL	.30	.09

1996 Circa Rave

Randomly inserted in packs at a rate of one in 60, this 200-card set is parallel and similar in design to the regular set except for sparkling foil lettering on front. Each card is individually numbered on back to 150. This set is notable for the fact that it was the one of the earliest parallel sets to feature serial-numbering for each card.

	Nm-Mt	Ex-Mt
*STARS: 25X TO 60X BASIC CARDS		
*ROOKIES: 10X TO 25X BASIC CARDS		

1996 Circa Access

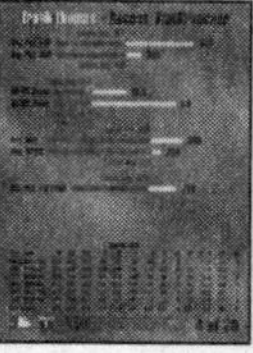

Randomly inserted in packs at a rate of one in 12, this 30-card limited edition set features a fold-out, three-panel card showcasing some of the hottest superstars of the game. The panels display color player photos, player statistics and personal information on team-colored backgrounds. A promotional card featuring Matt Williams was issued to dealers. The card is similar to the basic Access Williams except for the words "Promotional Sample" written across the card front.

	Nm-Mt	Ex-Mt
COMPLETE SET (30)	120.00	36.00
1 Cal Ripken	15.00	4.50
2 Mo Vaughn	2.00	.60
3 Tim Salmon	3.00	.90
4 Frank Thomas	5.00	1.50
5 Albert Belle	2.00	.60
6 Kenny Lofton	2.00	.60
7 Manny Ramirez	3.00	.90
8 Paul Molitor	3.00	.90
9 Kirby Puckett	5.00	1.50
10 Paul O'Neill	3.00	.90
11 Mark McGwire	12.00	3.60
12 Ken Griffey Jr.	8.00	2.40
13 Randy Johnson	5.00	1.50
14 Greg Maddux	8.00	2.40
15 John Smoltz	3.00	.90
16 Sammy Sosa	8.00	2.40
17 Barry Larkin	3.00	.90
18 Gary Sheffield	2.00	.60
19 Jeff Bagwell	3.00	.90
20 Hideo Nomo	5.00	1.50
21 Mike Piazza	8.00	2.40
22 Moises Alou	2.00	.60
23 Henry Rodriguez	2.00	.60
24 Rey Ordonez	2.00	.60
25 Jay Bell	2.00	.60
26 Ozzie Smith	8.00	2.40
27 Tony Gwynn	6.00	1.80
28 Rickey Henderson	5.00	1.50
29 Barry Bonds	12.00	3.60
30 Matt Williams	2.00	.60
P30 Matt Williams	1.00	.30
Promo		

1996 Circa Boss

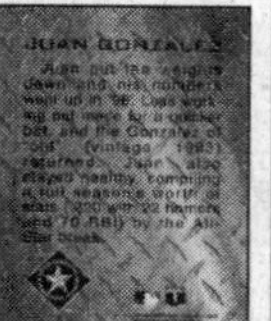

Randomly inserted in packs at a rate of one in six, this 50-card set features a sculpted embossed player image on a team-colored background containing the team logo. The backs carry a information about the player's career. A promotional card featuring Cal Ripken was issued to dealers. The card is similar to the basic Boss Ripken except for the words "Promotional Sample" written across the card front.

	Nm-Mt	Ex-Mt
COMPLETE SET (50)	100.00	30.00
1 Roberto Alomar	1.50	.45
2 Cal Ripken	8.00	2.40
3 Jose Canseco	2.50	.75
4 Mo Vaughn	1.00	.30
5 Tim Salmon	1.50	.45
6 Frank Thomas	2.50	.75
7 Robin Ventura	1.00	.30
8 Albert Belle	1.00	.30
9 Kenny Lofton	1.00	.30
10 Manny Ramirez	1.50	.45
11 Dave Nilsson	1.00	.30
12 Chuck Knoblauch	1.00	.30
13 Paul Molitor	1.50	.45
14 Kirby Puckett	2.50	.75
15 Wade Boggs	1.50	.45
16 Dwight Gooden	1.00	.30
17 Paul O'Neill	1.50	.45
18 Mark McGwire	6.00	1.80
19 Jay Buhner	1.00	.30
20 Ken Griffey Jr.	4.00	1.20
21 Randy Johnson	2.50	.75
22 Will Clark	2.50	.75
23 Juan Gonzalez	1.50	.45
24 Joe Carter	1.00	.30
25 Tom Glavine	1.50	.45
26 Ryan Klesko	1.00	.30
27 Greg Maddux	4.00	1.20
28 John Smoltz	1.50	.45
29 Ryne Sandberg	4.00	1.20
30 Sammy Sosa	4.00	1.20
31 Barry Larkin	1.50	.45
32 Reggie Sanders	1.00	.30
33 Dante Bichette	1.00	.30
34 Andres Galarraga	1.00	.30
35 Charles Johnson	1.00	.30
36 Gary Sheffield	1.00	.30
37 Jeff Bagwell	1.50	.45
38 Hideo Nomo	2.50	.75
39 Mike Piazza	4.00	1.20
40 Moises Alou	1.00	.30
41 Henry Rodriguez	1.00	.30
42 Rey Ordonez	1.00	.30
43 Ricky Otero	1.00	.30
44 Jay Bell	1.00	.30
45 Royce Clayton	1.00	.30
46 Ozzie Smith	4.00	1.20
47 Tony Gwynn	3.00	.90
48 Rickey Henderson	2.50	.75
49 Barry Bonds	6.00	1.80
50 Matt Williams	1.00	.30
P2 Cal Ripken	3.00	.90
Promo		

1997 Circa

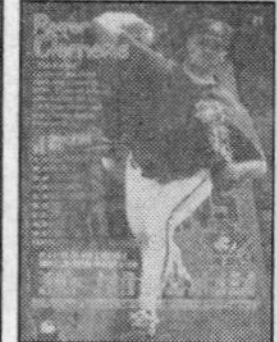

The 1997 Circa set (produced by Fleer/SkyBox) was issued in one series totalling 400 cards and was distributed in eight-card foil packs with a suggested retail price of $1.49. The set contains 393 player cards and seven checklist cards. The fronts feature color player photos with new in-your-face graphics that lift the player off the card. The backs carry in-depth player statistics and "Did you know" information. An Alex Rodriguez promo card (P100) was distributed to dealers. Rookie Cards include Brian Giles.

	Nm-Mt	Ex-Mt
COMPLETE SET (400)	25.00	7.50
1 Kenny Lofton	.20	.06
2 Ray Durham	.20	.06
3 Mariano Rivera	.30	.09
4 Jon Lieber	.20	.06
5 Tim Salmon	.30	.09
6 Mark Grudzielanek	.20	.06
7 Neifi Perez	.20	.06
8 Cal Ripken	1.50	.45
9 John Olerud	.20	.06
10 Edgar Renteria	.20	.06
11 Jose Rosado	.20	.06
12 Mickey Morandini	.20	.06
13 Orlando Miller	.20	.06
14 Ben McDonald	.20	.06
15 Hideo Nomo	.50	.15
16 Fred McGriff	.30	.09
17 Sean Berry	.20	.06
18 Roger Pavlik	.20	.06
19 Aaron Sele	.20	.06
20 Joey Hamilton	.20	.06
21 Roger Clemens	1.00	.30
22 Jose Herrera	.20	.06
23 Ryne Sandberg	.75	.23
24 Ken Griffey Jr.	.75	.23
25 Barry Bonds	1.25	.35
26 Dan Naulty	.20	.06
27 Wade Boggs	.30	.09
28 Ray Lankford	.20	.06
29 Rico Brogna	.20	.06
30 Wally Joyner	.20	.06
31 F.P. Santangelo	.20	.06
32 Vinny Castilla	.20	.06
33 Eddie Murray	.50	.15
34 Kevin Elster	.20	.06
35 Mike Macfarlane	.20	.06
36 Jeff Kent	.20	.06
37 Orlando Merced	.20	.06
38 Jason Isringhausen	.20	.06
39 Chad Ogea	.20	.06
40 Greg Gagne	.20	.06
41 Curt Lyons	.20	.06
42 Mo Vaughn	.20	.06
43 Rusty Greer	.20	.06
44 Shane Reynolds	.20	.06
45 Frank Thomas	.50	.15
46 Chris Hoiles	.20	.06
47 Scott Sanders	.20	.06
48 Mark Lemke	.20	.06
49 Fernando Vina	.20	.06
50 Mark McGwire	1.25	.35
51 Bernie Williams	.30	.09
52 Bobby Higginson	.20	.06
53 Kevin Tapani	.20	.06
54 Rich Becker	.20	.06
55 Felix Heredia RC	.20	.06
56 Delino DeShields	.20	.06
57 Rick Wilkins	.20	.06
58 Edgardo Alfonzo	.20	.06
59 Brett Butler	.20	.06
60 Ed Sprague	.20	.06
61 Joe Randa	.20	.06
62 Ugueth Urbina	.20	.06
63 Todd Greene	.20	.06
64 Devon White	.20	.06
65 Bruce Ruffin	.20	.06
66 Mark Gardner	.20	.06
67 Omar Vizquel	.20	.06
68 Luis Gonzalez	.20	.06
69 Tom Glavine	.30	.09
70 Cal Eldred	.20	.06
71 Wm. VanLandingham	.20	.06
72 Jay Buhner	.20	.06
73 James Baldwin	.20	.06
74 Robin Jennings	.20	.06
75 Terry Steinbach	.20	.06
76 Billy Taylor	.20	.06
77 Armando Benitez	.20	.06
78 Joe Girardi	.20	.06
79 Jay Bell	.20	.06
80 Damon Buford	.20	.06
81 Deion Sanders	.30	.09
82 Bill Haselman	.20	.06
83 John Flaherty	.20	.06
84 Todd Stottlemyre	.20	.06
85 J.T. Snow	.20	.06
86 Felipe Lira	.20	.06
87 Steve Avery	.20	.06
88 Trey Beamon	.20	.06
89 Alex Gonzalez	.20	.06
90 Mark Clark	.20	.06
91 Shane Andrews	.20	.06
92 Randy Myers	.20	.06
93 Gary Gaetti	.20	.06
94 Jeff Blauser	.20	.06

Tony Batista .20 .06
Todd Worrell .20 .06
Jim Edmonds .20 .06
Eric Young .20 .06
Roberto Kelly .20 .06
0 Alex Rodriguez .75 .23
1 Julio Franco .20 .06
2 Jeff Bagwell .30 .09
3 Bobby Witt .20 .06
4 Tino Martinez .30 .09
5 Shannon Stewart .20 .06
6 Brian Banks .20 .06
7 Eddie Taubensee .20 .06
8 Terry Mulholland .20 .06
9 Lyle Mouton .20 .06
0 Jeff Conine .20 .06
1 Johnny Damon .30 .09
2 Quilvio Veras .20 .06
3 Wilton Guerrero .20 .06
4 Dmitri Young .20 .06
5 Garret Anderson .20 .06
6 Bill Pulsipher .20 .06
7 Jacob Brumfield .20 .06
8 Mike Lansing .20 .06
9 Jose Canseco .50 .15
0 Mike Bordick .20 .06
1 Kevin Stocker .20 .06
2 Frankie Rodriguez .20 .06
3 Mike Cameron .20 .06
4 Tony Womack RC .40 .12
5 Bret Boone .20 .06
6 Moises Alou .20 .06
7 Tim Naehring .20 .06
8 Brant Brown .20 .06
9 Todd Zeile .20 .06
0 Dave Nilsson .20 .06
1 Donne Wall .20 .06
2 Jose Mesa .20 .06
3 Mark McLemore .20 .06
4 Mike Stanton .20 .06
5 Dan Wilson .20 .06
6 Jose Offerman .20 .06
7 David Justice .20 .06
8 Kirt Manwaring .20 .06
9 Raul Casanova .20 .06
0 Ron Coomer .20 .06
1 Dave Hollins .20 .06
2 Shawn Estes .20 .06
3 Darren Daulton .20 .06
4 Turk Wendell .20 .06
5 Darrin Fletcher .20 .06
6 Marquis Grissom .20 .06
7 Andy Benes .20 .06
8 Nomar Garciaparra .75 .23
9 Andy Pettitte .30 .09
0 Tony Gwynn .60 .18
1 Robb Nen .20 .06
2 Kevin Seitzer .20 .06
3 Ariel Prieto .20 .06
4 Scott Karl .20 .06
5 Carlos Baerga .20 .06
6 Wilson Alvarez .20 .06
7 Thomas Howard .20 .06
8 Kevin Appier .20 .06
9 Russ Davis .20 .06
0 Justin Thompson .20 .06
1 Pete Schourek .20 .06
2 John Burkett .20 .06
3 Roberto Alomar .30 .09
4 Darren Holmes .20 .06
5 Travis Miller .20 .06
6 Mark Langston .20 .06
7 Juan Guzman .20 .06
8 Pedro Astacio .20 .06
9 Mark Johnson .20 .06
0 Mark Leiter .20 .06
1 Heathcliff Slocumb .20 .06
2 Dante Bichette .20 .06
3 Brian Giles RC 1.00 .30
4 Paul Wilson .20 .06
5 Eric Davis .20 .06
6 Charles Johnson .20 .06
7 Willie Greene .20 .06
8 Geronimo Berroa .20 .06
9 Mariano Duncan .20 .06
30 Robert Person .20 .06
31 David Segui .20 .06
32 Ozzie Guillen .20 .06
33 Osvaldo Fernandez .20 .06
34 Dean Palmer .20 .06
35 Bob Wickman .20 .06
36 Eric Karros .20 .06
37 Travis Fryman .20 .06
38 Andy Ashby .20 .06
39 Scott Stahoviak .20 .06
90 Norm Charlton .20 .06
91 Craig Paquette .20 .06
92 John Smoltz UER .30 .09
Name spelled "Smotlz" on back
93 Orel Hershiser .20 .06
94 Glenallen Hill .20 .06
95 George Arias .20 .06
96 Brian Jordan .20 .06
97 Greg Vaughn .20 .06
98 Rafael Palmeiro .30 .09
99 Darryl Kile .20 .06
00 Derek Jeter 1.25 .35
01 Jose Vizcaino .20 .06
02 Rick Aguilera .20 .06
03 Jason Schmidt .20 .06
04 Trot Nixon .20 .06
05 Tom Pagnozzi .20 .06
06 Mark Wohlers .20 .06
07 Lance Johnson .20 .06
08 Carlos Delgado .20 .06
09 Cliff Floyd .20 .06
10 Kent Mercker .20 .06
11 Matt Mieske .20 .06
12 Ismael Valdes .20 .06
13 Shawon Dunston .20 .06
14 Melvin Nieves .20 .06
15 Tony Phillips .20 .06
16 Scott Spiezio .20 .06
17 Michael Tucker .20 .06
18 Matt Williams .20 .06
19 Ricky Otero .20 .06
20 Kevin Ritz .20 .06
21 Darryl Strawberry .20 .06
22 Troy Percival .20 .06
23 Eugene Kingsale .20 .06
224 Julian Tavarez .20 .06
225 Jermaine Dye .20 .06
226 Jason Kendall .20 .06
227 Sterling Hitchcock .20 .06
228 Jeff Cirillo .20 .06
229 Roberto Hernandez .20 .06
230 Ricky Bottalico .20 .06
231 Bobby Bonilla .20 .06
232 Edgar Martinez .30 .09
233 John Valentin .20 .06
234 Ellis Burks .20 .06
235 Benito Santiago .20 .06
236 Terrell Wade .20 .06
237 Armando Reynoso .20 .06
238 Danny Graves .20 .06
239 Ken Hill .20 .06
240 Dennis Eckersley .20 .06
241 Darin Erstad .20 .06
242 Lee Smith UER .20 .06
Position 2b
243 Cecil Fielder .20 .06
244 Tony Clark .20 .06
245 Scott Erickson .20 .06
246 Bob Abreu .20 .06
247 Ruben Sierra .20 .06
248 Chili Davis .20 .06
249 Darryl Hamilton .20 .06
250 Albert Belle .20 .06
251 Todd Hollandsworth .20 .06
252 Terry Adams .20 .06
253 Rey Ordonez .20 .06
254 Steve Finley .20 .06
255 Jose Valentin .20 .06
256 Royce Clayton .20 .06
257 Sandy Alomar Jr. .20 .06
258 Mike Lieberthal .20 .06
259 Ivan Rodriguez .50 .15
260 Rod Beck .20 .06
261 Ron Karkovice .20 .06
262 Mark Gubicza .20 .06
263 Chris Holt .20 .06
264 Jaime Bluma UER .20 .06
Name spelled "Jamie" on front and back
265 Francisco Cordova .20 .06
266 Javy Lopez .20 .06
267 Reggie Jefferson .20 .06
268 Kevin Brown .20 .06
269 Scott Brosius .20 .06
270 Dwight Gooden .20 .06
271 Marty Cordova .20 .06
272 Jeff Brantley .20 .06
273 Joe Carter .20 .06
274 Todd Jones .20 .06
275 Sammy Sosa .75 .23
276 Randy Johnson .50 .15
277 B.J. Surhoff .20 .06
278 Chan Ho Park .20 .06
279 Jamey Wright .20 .06
280 Manny Ramirez .30 .09
281 John Franco .20 .06
282 Tim Worrell .20 .06
283 Scott Rolen .50 .15
284 Reggie Sanders .20 .06
285 Mike Fetters .20 .06
286 Tim Wakefield .20 .06
287 Trevor Hoffman .20 .06
288 Donovan Osborne .20 .06
289 Phil Nevin .20 .06
290 J.Allensworth .20 .06
291 Rocky Coppinger .20 .06
292 Tim Raines .20 .06
293 Henry Rodriguez .20 .06
294 Paul Sorrento .20 .06
295 Tom Goodwin .20 .06
296 Raul Mondesi .20 .06
297 Allen Watson .20 .06
298 Derek Bell .20 .06
299 Gary Sheffield .20 .06
300 Paul Molitor .30 .09
301 Shawn Green .20 .06
302 Darren Oliver .20 .06
303 Jack McDowell .20 .06
304 Denny Neagle .20 .06
305 Doug Drabek .20 .06
306 Mel Rojas .20 .06
307 Andres Galarraga .20 .06
308 Alex Ochoa .20 .06
309 Gary DiSarcina .20 .06
310 Ron Gant .20 .06
311 Gregg Jefferies .20 .06
312 Ruben Rivera .20 .06
313 Vladimir Guerrero .50 .15
314 Willie Adams .20 .06
315 Bip Roberts .20 .06
316 Mark Grace .30 .09
317 Bernard Gilkey .20 .06
318 Marc Newfield .20 .06
319 Al Leiter .20 .06
320 Otis Nixon .20 .06
321 Tom Candiotti .20 .06
322 Mike Stanley .20 .06
323 Jeff Fassero .20 .06
324 Billy Wagner .20 .06
325 Todd Walker .20 .06
326 Chad Curtis .20 .06
327 Quinton McCracken .20 .06
328 Will Clark .50 .15
329 Andruw Jones .20 .06
330 Robin Ventura .20 .06
331 Curtis Pride .20 .06
332 Barry Larkin .30 .09
333 Jimmy Key .20 .06
334 David Wells .20 .06
335 Mike Holtz .20 .06
336 Paul Wagner .20 .06
337 Greg Maddux .75 .23
338 Curt Schilling .20 .06
339 Steve Trachsel .20 .06
340 John Wetteland .20 .06
341 Rickey Henderson .50 .15
342 Ernie Young .20 .06
343 Harold Baines .20 .06
344 Bobby Jones .20 .06
345 Jeff D'Amico .20 .06
346 John Mabry .20 .06
347 Pedro Martinez .50 .15
348 Mark Lewis .20 .06
349 Dan Miceli .20 .06
350 Chuck Knoblauch .20 .06
351 John Smiley .20 .06
352 Brady Anderson .20 .06
353 Jim Leyritz .20 .06
354 Al Martin .20 .06
355 Pat Hentgen .20 .06
356 Mike Piazza .75 .23
357 Charles Nagy .20 .06
358 Luis Castillo .20 .06
359 Paul O'Neill .30 .09
360 Steve Reed .20 .06
361 Tom Gordon .20 .06
362 Craig Biggio .30 .09
363 Jeff Montgomery .20 .06
364 Jamie Moyer .20 .06
365 Ryan Klesko .20 .06
366 Todd Hundley .20 .06
367 Bobby Estalella .20 .06
368 Jason Giambi .20 .06
369 Brian Hunter .20 .06
370 Ramon Martinez .20 .06
371 Carlos Garcia .20 .06
372 Hal Morris .20 .06
373 Juan Gonzalez .30 .09
374 Brian McRae .20 .06
375 Mike Mussina .30 .09
376 John Ericks .20 .06
377 Larry Walker .30 .09
378 Chris Gomez .20 .06
379 John Jaha .20 .06
380 Rondell White .20 .06
381 Chipper Jones .50 .15
382 David Cone .20 .06
383 Alan Benes .20 .06
384 Troy O'Leary .20 .06
385 Ken Caminiti .20 .06
386 Jeff King .20 .06
387 Mike Hampton .20 .06
388 Jaime Navarro .20 .06
389 Brad Radke .20 .06
390 Joey Cora .20 .06
391 Jim Thome .50 .15
392 Alex Fernandez .20 .06
393 Chuck Finley .20 .06
394 Andruw Jones CL .20 .06
395 Ken Griffey Jr. CL .50 .15
396 Frank Thomas CL .30 .09
397 Alex Rodriguez CL .50 .15
398 Cal Ripken CL .75 .23
399 Mike Piazza CL .50 .15
400 Greg Maddux CL .50 .15
P100 A.Rodriguez Promo 2.00 .60

1997 Circa Rave

Randomly inserted in packs at a rate of one in 30, this hobby exclusive set is a parallel version of the regular set and is similar in design. One hundred fifty of this limited edition set were produced and are sequentially numbered.

Nm-Mt Ex-Mt
*STARS: 25X TO 60X BASIC CARDS..
*ROOKIES: 10X TO 25X BASIC CARDS

1997 Circa Boss

Randomly inserted in packs at a rate of one in six, this 20-card set features color player photos of Baseball's leading men on the field and at bat and are printed on sculpted, embossed cards. The backs carry player information.

Nm-Mt Ex-Mt
COMPLETE SET (20) 40.00 12.00
*SUPER BOSS: 1.5X TO 4X BASIC BOSS
SUPER BOSS STATED ODDS 1:36
1 Jeff Bagwell 1.00 .30
2 Albert Belle .60 .18
3 Barry Bonds 4.00 1.20
4 Ken Caminiti .60 .18
5 Juan Gonzalez 1.00 .30
6 Ken Griffey Jr. 2.50 .75
7 Tony Gwynn 2.00 .60
8 Derek Jeter 4.00 1.20
9 Andruw Jones .60 .18
10 Chipper Jones 1.50 .45
11 Greg Maddux 2.50 .75
12 Mark McGwire 4.00 1.20
13 Mike Piazza 2.50 .75
14 Manny Ramirez 1.00 .30
15 Cal Ripken 5.00 1.50
16 Alex Rodriguez 2.50 .75
17 John Smoltz 1.00 .30
18 Frank Thomas 1.50 .45
19 Mo Vaughn .60 .18
20 Bernie Williams 1.00 .30

1997 Circa Emerald Autographs

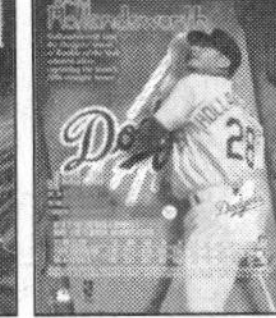

These autographed cards were made available only to those collectors lucky enough to pull one of the scarce Circa Emerald Autograph Redemption cards (randomly seeded into 1:1000 1997 Circa packs). These cards are identical to the regular issue Circa cards except, of course, for the player's autograph on the card front and an embossed Fleer seal for authenticity. The deadline to redeem the cards was May 1st, 1998. In addition, an Emerald Autograph Redemption program entitled "Collect and Win" was featured in 1997 Fleer series two packs. One in every 4 packs contained one of ten different redemption cards. The object was for collectors to piece together all ten cards and then mail them in to receive a complete set of the Circa Emerald Autographs. The catch was that card number seven was extremely shortprinted (official numbers were not released but speculation is that only a handful of number seven cards made their way into packs). The exchange deadline on this "collect and win" promotion was August 1st, 1998.

Nm-Mt Ex-Mt
*EXCH CARDS: .1X TO .25X BASIC AUTO
100 Alex Rodriguez 100.00 30.00
241 Darin Erstad 15.00 4.50
251 T.Hollandsworth AU 10.00 3.00
283 Scott Rolen 30.00 9.00
308 Alex Ochoa 10.00 3.00
325 Todd Walker 15.00 4.50

1997 Circa Fast Track

Randomly inserted in packs at a rate of one in 24, this 10-card set features color player photos of young stars and rookies who will carry baseball into the 21st century. The fronts display the player's image on a flocked background design which shows grass as raised fabric.

Nm-Mt Ex-Mt
COMPLETE SET (10) 40.00 12.00
1 Vladimir Guerrero 4.00 1.20
2 Todd Hollandsworth 1.50 .45
3 Derek Jeter 10.00 3.00
4 Andruw Jones 1.50 .45
5 Chipper Jones 4.00 1.20
6 Andy Pettitte 2.50 .75
7 Mariano Rivera 2.50 .75
8 Alex Rodriguez 6.00 1.80
9 Scott Rolen 4.00 1.20
10 Todd Walker 1.50 .45

1997 Circa Icons

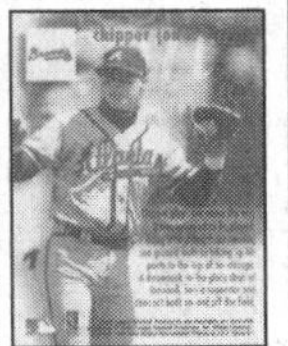

Randomly inserted in packs at a rate of one in 36, this 12-card set features color player images of twelve legendary players printed on 100% holofoil with the word "icon" running across the background. The backs carry player information.

Nm-Mt Ex-Mt
COMPLETE SET (12) 100.00 30.00
1 Juan Gonzalez 3.00 .90
2 Ken Griffey Jr. 8.00 2.40
3 Tony Gwynn 6.00 1.80
4 Derek Jeter 12.00 3.60
5 Chipper Jones 5.00 1.50
6 Greg Maddux 8.00 2.40
7 Mark McGwire 12.00 3.60
8 Mike Piazza 8.00 2.40
9 Cal Ripken 15.00 4.50
10 Alex Rodriguez 8.00 2.40
11 Frank Thomas 5.00 1.50
12 Matt Williams 2.00 .60

1997 Circa Limited Access

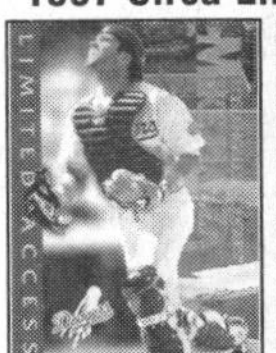

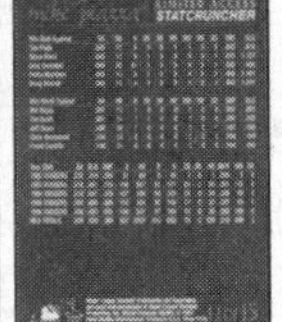

Randomly inserted in retail packs only at a rate of one in 18, this 15-card set features color player photos on die-cut, bi-fold cards which track the players from their youth to the present with in-depth statistical analysis.

Nm-Mt Ex-Mt
COMPLETE SET (15) 150.00 45.00
1 Jeff Bagwell 4.00 1.20
2 Albert Belle 2.50 .75
3 Barry Bonds 15.00 4.50
4 Juan Gonzalez 4.00 1.20
5 Ken Griffey Jr. 10.00 3.00
6 Tony Gwynn 8.00 2.40
7 Derek Jeter 15.00 4.50
8 Chipper Jones 6.00 1.80
9 Greg Maddux 10.00 3.00
10 Mark McGwire 15.00 4.50
11 Mike Piazza 10.00 3.00
12 Cal Ripken 20.00 6.00
13 Alex Rodriguez 10.00 3.00
14 Frank Thomas 6.00 1.80
15 Mo Vaughn 2.50 .75

1997 Circa Rave Reviews

Randomly inserted in packs at a rate of one in 288, this 12-card set features color photos of twelve players who generate incredible numbers off the bat and are printed on 100 percent holofoil. The backs carry player information.

Nm-Mt Ex-Mt
COMPLETE SET (12) 300.00 90.00
1 Albert Belle 6.00 1.80
2 Barry Bonds 40.00 12.00
3 Juan Gonzalez 10.00 3.00
4 Ken Griffey Jr. 25.00 7.50
5 Tony Gwynn 20.00 6.00
6 Greg Maddux 25.00 7.50
7 Mark McGwire 40.00 12.00
8 Eddie Murray 15.00 4.50
9 Mike Piazza 25.00 7.50
10 Cal Ripken 50.00 15.00
11 Alex Rodriguez 25.00 7.50
12 Frank Thomas 15.00 4.50

1998 Circa Thunder

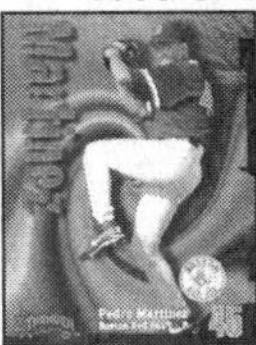

The 1998 Circa Thunder set, produced by Fleer/SkyBox, was issued in one series totalling 300 cards. The eight-card packs retailed for $1.59 each. Collector's should take note that Marquis Grissom's card was erroneously numbered as 8 instead 280. Both Cal Ripken Jr. and Grissom are numbered as 8. In addition, a Cal Ripken promo card was issued prior to the product's public release. The card was distributed in dealer order forms and hobby media releases. It's identical in design to the standard Circa Thunder Ripken except for the text "PROMOTIONAL SAMPLE" written diagonally across the front and back of the card.

Nm-Mt Ex-Mt
COMPLETE SET (300) 25.00 7.50
1 Ben Grieve .20 .06
2 Derek Jeter 1.25 .35
3 Alex Rodriguez .75 .23
4 Paul Molitor .30 .09
5 Nomar Garciaparra .75 .23
6 Fred McGriff .30 .09
7 Kenny Lofton .20 .06
8 Cal Ripken 1.50 .45
9 Matt Williams .20 .06
10 Chipper Jones .50 .15
11 Barry Larkin .30 .09
12 Steve Finley .20 .06
13 Billy Wagner .20 .06
14 Rico Brogna .20 .06
15 Tim Salmon .30 .09
16 Hideo Nomo .50 .15
17 Tony Clark .20 .06
18 Jason Kendall .20 .06
19 Juan Gonzalez .30 .09
20 Jeromy Burnitz .20 .06
21 Roger Clemens 1.00 .30
22 Mark Grace .30 .09
23 Robin Ventura .20 .06
24 Manny Ramirez .30 .09
25 Mark McGwire 1.25 .35
26 Gary Sheffield .20 .06
27 Vladimir Guerrero .50 .15
28 Butch Huskey .20 .06
29 Cecil Fielder .20 .06
30 Rod Myers .20 .06
31 Greg Maddux .75 .23
32 Bill Mueller .20 .06
33 Larry Walker .30 .09
34 Henry Rodriguez .20 .06
35 Mike Mussina .30 .09
36 Ricky Ledee .20 .06
37 Bobby Bonilla .20 .06
38 Curt Schilling .20 .06
39 Luis Gonzalez .20 .06
40 Troy Percival .20 .06
41 Eric Milton .20 .06
42 Mo Vaughn .20 .06
43 Raul Mondesi .20 .06
44 Kenny Rogers .20 .06
45 Frank Thomas .50 .15
46 Jose Canseco .50 .15
47 Tom Glavine .30 .09
48 Rich Butler RC .20 .06
49 Jay Buhner .20 .06
50 Jose Cruz Jr. .20 .06
51 Bernie Williams .30 .09
52 Doug Glanville .20 .06
53 Travis Fryman .20 .06
54 Rey Ordonez .20 .06
55 Jeff Conine .20 .06
56 Trevor Hoffman .20 .06
57 Kirk Rueter .20 .06
UER back Reuter
58 Ron Gant .20 .06
59 Carl Everett .20 .06
60 Joe Carter .20 .06
61 Livan Hernandez .20 .06
62 John Jaha .20 .06
63 Ivan Rodriguez .50 .15
64 Willie Blair .20 .06

65 Todd Helton .30 .09
66 Kevin Young .20 .06
67 Mike Caruso .20 .06
68 Steve Trachsel .20 .06
69 Marty Cordova .20 .06
70 Alex Fernandez .20 .06
71 Eric Karros .20 .06
72 Reggie Sanders .20 .06
73 Russ Davis .20 .06
74 Roberto Hernandez .20 .06
75 Barry Bonds 1.25 .35
76 Alex Gonzalez .20 .06
77 Roberto Alomar .30 .09
78 Troy O'Leary .20 .06
79 Bernard Gilkey .20 .06
80 Ismael Valdes .20 .06
81 Travis Lee .20 .06
82 Brant Brown .20 .06
83 Gary DiSarcina .20 .06
84 Joe Randa .20 .06
85 Jaret Wright .20 .06
86 Quilvio Veras .20 .06
87 Rickey Henderson .50 .15
88 Randall Simon .20 .06
89 Mariano Rivera .30 .09
90 Ugueth Urbina .20 .06
91 Fernando Vina .20 .06
92 Alan Benes .20 .06
93 Dante Bichette .20 .06
94 Karim Garcia .20 .06
95 A.J. Hinch .20 .06
96 Shane Reynolds .20 .06
97 Kevin Stocker .20 .06
98 John Wetteland .20 .06
99 Terry Steinbach .20 .06
100 Ken Griffey Jr. .75 .23
101 Mike Cameron .20 .06
102 Damion Easley .20 .06
103 Randy Myers .20 .06
104 Jason Schmidt .20 .06
105 Jeff King .20 .06
106 Gregg Jefferies .20 .06
107 Sean Casey .20 .06
108 Mark Kotsay .20 .06
109 Brad Fullmer .20 .06
110 Wilson Alvarez .20 .06
111 Sandy Alomar Jr. .20 .06
112 Walt Weiss .20 .06
113 Doug Jones .20 .06
114 Andy Benes .20 .06
115 Paul O'Neill .30 .09
116 Dennis Eckersley .20 .06
117 Todd Greene .20 .06
118 Bobby Jones .20 .06
119 Darrin Fletcher .20 .06
120 Eric Young .20 .06
121 Jeffrey Hammonds .20 .06
122 Mickey Morandini .20 .06
123 Chuck Knoblauch .20 .06
124 Moises Alou .20 .06
125 Miguel Tejada .20 .06
126 Brian Anderson .20 .06
127 Edgar Renteria .20 .06
128 Mike Lansing .20 .06
129 Quinton McCracken .20 .06
130 Ray Lankford .20 .06
131 Andy Ashby .20 .06
132 Kelvim Escobar .20 .06
133 Mike Lowell RC 1.00 .30
134 Randy Johnson .50 .15
135 Andres Galarraga .20 .06
136 Armando Benitez .20 .06
137 Rusty Greer .20 .06
138 Jose Guillen .20 .06
139 Paul Konerko .20 .06
140 Edgardo Alfonzo .20 .06
141 Jim Leyritz .20 .06
142 Mark Clark .20 .06
143 Brian Johnson .20 .06
144 Scott Rolen .50 .15
145 David Cone .20 .06
146 Jeff Shaw .20 .06
147 Shannon Stewart .20 .06
148 Brian Hunter .20 .06
149 Garret Anderson .20 .06
150 Jeff Bagwell .30 .09
151 James Baldwin .20 .06
152 Devon White .20 .06
153 Jim Thome .50 .15
154 Wally Joyner .20 .06
155 Mark Wohlers .20 .06
156 Jeff Cirillo .20 .06
157 Jason Giambi .20 .06
158 Royce Clayton .20 .06
159 Dennis Reyes .20 .06
160 Raul Casanova .20 .06
161 Pedro Astacio .20 .06
162 Todd Dunwoody .20 .06
163 Sammy Sosa .75 .23
164 Todd Hundley .20 .06
165 Wade Boggs .30 .09
166 Robb Nen .20 .06
167 Dan Wilson .20 .06
168 Hideki Irabu .20 .06
169 B.J. Surhoff .20 .06
170 Carlos Delgado .20 .06
171 Fernando Tatis .20 .06
172 Bob Abreu .20 .06
173 David Ortiz .50 .15
174 Tony Womack .20 .06
175 Magglio Ordonez RC 1.25 .35
176 Aaron Boone .20 .06
177 Brian Giles .20 .06
178 Kevin Appier .20 .06
179 Chuck Finley .20 .06
180 Brian Rose .20 .06
181 Ryan Klesko .20 .06
182 Mike Stanley .20 .06
183 Dave Nilsson .20 .06
184 Carlos Perez .20 .06
185 Jeff Blauser .20 .06
186 Richard Hidalgo .20 .06
187 Charles Johnson .20 .06
188 Vinny Castilla .20 .06
189 Joey Hamilton .20 .06
190 Bubba Trammell .20 .06
191 Eli Marrero .20 .06
192 Scott Erickson .20 .06
193 Pat Hentgen .20 .06
194 Jorge Fabregas .20 .06
195 Tino Martinez .30 .09
196 Bobby Higginson .20 .06
197 Dave Hollins .20 .06
198 Rolando Arrojo RC .20 .06
199 Joey Cora .20 .06
200 Mike Piazza .75 .23
201 Reggie Jefferson .20 .06
202 John Smoltz .30 .09
203 Bobby Smith .20 .06
204 Tom Goodwin .20 .06
205 Omar Vizquel .30 .09
206 John Olerud .20 .06
207 Matt Stairs .20 .06
208 Bobby Estalella .20 .06
209 Miguel Cairo .20 .06
210 Shawn Green .20 .06
211 Jon Nunnally .20 .06
212 Al Leiter .20 .06
213 Matt Lawton .20 .06
214 Brady Anderson .20 .06
215 Jeff Kent .20 .06
216 Ray Durham .20 .06
217 Al Martin .20 .06
218 Jeff D'Amico .20 .06
219 Kevin Tapani .20 .06
220 Jim Edmonds .20 .06
221 Jose Vizcaino .20 .06
222 Jay Bell .20 .06
223 Ken Caminiti .20 .06
224 Craig Biggio .30 .09
225 Bartolo Colon .20 .06
226 Neifi Perez .20 .06
227 Delino DeShields .20 .06
228 Javier Lopez .20 .06
229 David Wells .20 .06
230 Brad Rigby .20 .06
231 John Franco .20 .06
232 Michael Coleman .20 .06
233 Edgar Martinez .30 .09
234 Francisco Cordova .20 .06
235 Johnny Damon .30 .09
236 Deivi Cruz .20 .06
237 J.T. Snow .20 .06
238 Enrique Wilson .20 .06
239 Rondell White .20 .06
240 Aaron Sele .20 .06
241 Tony Saunders .20 .06
242 Ricky Bottalico .20 .06
243 Cliff Floyd .20 .06
244 Chili Davis .20 .06
245 Brian McRae .20 .06
246 Brad Radke .20 .06
247 Chan Ho Park .20 .06
248 Lance Johnson .20 .06
249 Rafael Palmeiro .30 .09
250 Tony Gwynn .60 .18
251 Denny Neagle .20 .06
252 Dean Palmer .20 .06
253 Jose Valentin .20 .06
254 Matt Morris .20 .06
255 Ellis Burks .20 .06
256 Jeff Suppan .20 .06
257 Jimmy Key .20 .06
258 Justin Thompson .20 .06
259 Brett Tomko .20 .06
260 Mark Grudzielanek .20 .06
261 Mike Hampton .20 .06
262 Jeff Fassero .20 .06
263 Charles Nagy .20 .06
264 Pedro Martinez .50 .15
265 Todd Zeile .20 .06
266 Will Clark .50 .15
267 Abraham Nunez .20 .06
268 Dave Martinez .20 .06
269 Jason Dickson .20 .06
270 Eric Davis .20 .06
271 Kevin Orie .20 .06
272 Derrek Lee .20 .06
273 Andruw Jones .20 .06
274 Juan Encarnacion .20 .06
275 Carlos Baerga .20 .06
276 Andy Pettitte .30 .09
277 Brent Brede .20 .06
278 Paul Sorrento .20 .06
279 Mike Lieberthal .20 .06
280 Marquis Grissom .20 .06
UER #'d 8 instead of 280
281 Darin Erstad .20 .06
282 Willie Greene .20 .06
283 Derek Bell .20 .06
284 Scott Spiezio .20 .06
285 David Segui .20 .06
286 Albert Belle .20 .06
287 Ramon Martinez .20 .06
288 Jeremi Gonzalez .20 .06
289 Shawn Estes .20 .06
290 Ron Coomer .20 .06
291 John Valentin .20 .06
292 Kevin Brown .30 .09
293 Michael Tucker .20 .06
294 Brian Jordan .20 .06
295 Darryl Kile .20 .06
296 David Justice .20 .06
297 Frank Thomas CL .30 .09
298 Alex Rodriguez CL .50 .15
299 Ken Griffey Jr. CL .50 .15
300 Jose Cruz Jr. CL .20 .06
P8 Cal Ripken Promo 2.00 .60

1998 Circa Thunder Rave

Randomly inserted into packs at an approximate rate of one in every 36 pack box, cards from this 296-card set parallel the basic set. Please note, the four checklist cards included in the regular set were not created in Rave parallel versions. Only 150 Rave sets were printed and each card is serial numbered "of 150" on back. In addition, special silver sparkling foil is used on the player's name and the Thunder logo on the card front.

Nm-Mt Ex-Mt
*STARS: 20X TO 50X BASIC CARDS..
*ROOKIES: 12.5X TO 30X BASIC CARDS

1998 Circa Thunder Boss

Randomly seeded at a rate one in every six packs, cards from this 20-card set feature a collection of the league's top stars.

	Nm-Mt	Ex-Mt
COMPLETE SET (20)	40.00	12.00
1 Jeff Bagwell	1.00	.30
2 Barry Bonds	4.00	1.20
3 Roger Clemens	3.00	.90
4 Jose Cruz Jr.	.60	.18
5 Nomar Garciaparra	2.50	.75
6 Juan Gonzalez	1.00	.30
7 Ken Griffey Jr.	2.50	.75
8 Tony Gwynn	2.00	.60
9 Derek Jeter	4.00	1.20
10 Chipper Jones	1.50	.45
11 Travis Lee	.60	.18
12 Greg Maddux	2.50	.75
13 Pedro Martinez	1.50	.45
14 Mark McGwire	4.00	1.20
15 Mike Piazza	2.50	.75
16 Cal Ripken	5.00	1.50
17 Alex Rodriguez	2.50	.75
18 Scott Rolen	1.50	.45
19 Frank Thomas	1.50	.45
20 Larry Walker	1.00	.30

1998 Circa Thunder Fast Track

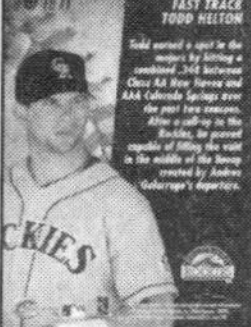

Randomly seeded into packs at a rate of one in 24, cards from this 10-card set feature a selection of talented youngsters on the "fast track" to success. The attractive card fronts feature a color action photo of the player imposed over a glowing gold baseball. In addition, small head shots of all ten players featured in the set are pictured on the right hand side of the card front. The specific player featured on each card has his head shot printed in matching gold holographic imagery.

	Nm-Mt	Ex-Mt
COMPLETE SET (10)	15.00	4.50
1 Jose Cruz Jr.	1.25	.35
2 Juan Encarnacion	1.25	.35
3 Brad Fullmer	1.25	.35
4 Nomar Garciaparra	5.00	1.50
5 Todd Helton	2.00	.60
6 Livan Hernandez	1.25	.35
7 Travis Lee	1.25	.35
8 Neifi Perez	1.25	.35
9 Scott Rolen	3.00	.90
10 Jaret Wright	1.25	.35

1998 Circa Thunder Limited Access

Randomly seeded into retail packs only at a rate of one in 18, cards from this 15-card set feature a selection of the league's top stars doing there thing. These attractive cards actually open up from top to bottom to feature a full length shot of the featured player with an extensive breakdown of 1997 statistics.

	Nm-Mt	Ex-Mt
COMPLETE SET (15)	150.00	45.00
1 Jeff Bagwell	4.00	1.20
2 Roger Clemens	12.00	3.60
3 Jose Cruz Jr.	2.50	.75
4 Nomar Garciaparra	10.00	3.00
5 Juan Gonzalez	4.00	1.20
6 Ken Griffey Jr.	10.00	3.00
7 Tony Gwynn	8.00	2.40
8 Derek Jeter	15.00	4.50
9 Greg Maddux	10.00	3.00
10 Pedro Martinez	6.00	1.80
11 Mark McGwire	15.00	4.50
12 Mike Piazza	10.00	3.00
13 Alex Rodriguez	10.00	3.00
14 Frank Thomas	6.00	1.80
15 Larry Walker	4.00	1.20

1998 Circa Thunder Quick Strike

Randomly seeded into packs at a rate of one in 36, cards from this 12-card set feature a selection of the league's top stars printed on colorful foil-board fronts.

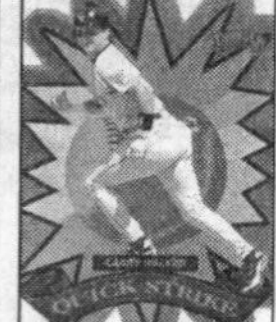

	Nm-Mt	Ex-Mt
COMPLETE SET (12)	80.00	24.00
1 Jeff Bagwell	3.00	.90
2 Roger Clemens	10.00	3.00
3 Jose Cruz Jr.	2.00	.60
4 Nomar Garciaparra	8.00	2.40
5 Ken Griffey Jr.	8.00	2.40
6 Greg Maddux	8.00	2.40
7 Pedro Martinez	5.00	1.50
8 Mark McGwire	12.00	3.60
9 Mike Piazza	8.00	2.40
10 Alex Rodriguez	8.00	2.40
11 Frank Thomas	5.00	1.50
12 Larry Walker	3.00	.90

1998 Circa Thunder Rave Review

Randomly seeded into packs at a rate of one in 288, cards from this tough 15-card set feature a selection of talented major leaguers. The attractive horizontal images feature a color action shot imposed across a bronze foil plaque with the image of a ball field in the background. The card backs feature the reversed plaque imagery with another player photo.

	Nm-Mt	Ex-Mt
COMPLETE SET (15)	250.00	75.00
1 Jeff Bagwell	10.00	3.00
2 Barry Bonds	40.00	12.00
3 Roger Clemens	30.00	9.00
4 Jose Cruz Jr.	6.00	1.80
5 Nomar Garciaparra	25.00	7.50
6 Juan Gonzalez	10.00	3.00
7 Ken Griffey Jr.	25.00	7.50
8 Tony Gwynn	20.00	6.00
9 Derek Jeter	40.00	12.00
10 Greg Maddux	25.00	7.50
11 Mark McGwire	40.00	12.00
12 Mike Piazza	25.00	7.50
13 Alex Rodriguez	25.00	7.50
14 Frank Thomas	15.00	4.50
15 Larry Walker	10.00	3.00

1998 Circa Thunder Thunder Boomers

Randomly seeded into packs at a rate of one in 96, cards from this 12-card set feature a selection of top sluggers. Each card features a color action shot imposed over a see-through cloud-like plastic center, encircled by a imagery of a wooden fence with a massive hole smashed through the middle of it.

	Nm-Mt	Ex-Mt
COMPLETE SET (12)	120.00	36.00
1 Jeff Bagwell	6.00	1.80
2 Barry Bonds	25.00	7.50
3 Jay Buhner	4.00	1.20
4 Andres Galarraga	4.00	1.20
5 Juan Gonzalez	6.00	1.80
6 Ken Griffey Jr.	15.00	4.50
7 Tino Martinez	6.00	1.80
8 Mark McGwire	25.00	7.50
9 Mike Piazza	15.00	4.50
10 Frank Thomas	10.00	3.00
11 Jim Thome	10.00	3.00
12 Larry Walker	6.00	1.80

1987 Classic Game

This 100-card standard-size set was actually distributed as part of a trivia board game. The card backs contain several trivia questions (and answers) which are used to play the game. A dark green border frames the full-color photo. The games were produced by Game Time, Ltd. and were available in toy stores as well as from card dealers. According to the producers of this game, only 75,000 sets were distributed. The set features Bo Jackson, Wally Joyner, and Barry Larkin in their Rookie Card year.

	Nm-Mt	Ex-Mt
COMP.FACT SET (100)	60.00	24.00
1 Pete Rose	2.50	1.00
2 Len Dykstra	.25	.10
3 Darryl Strawberry	.25	.10
4 Keith Hernandez	.25	.10
5 Gary Carter	.75	.30
6 Wally Joyner	.50	.20
7 Andres Thomas	.10	.04
8 Pat Dodson	.10	.04
9 Kirk Gibson	.25	.10
10 Don Mattingly	5.00	2.00
11 Dave Winfield	.75	.30
12 Rickey Henderson	4.00	1.60
13 Dan Pasqua	.10	.04
14 Don Baylor	.25	.10
15 Bo Jackson (Swinging bat in Auburn FB uniform)	10.00	4.00
16 Pete Incaviglia	.25	.10
17 Kevin Bass	.10	.04
18 Barry Larkin	5.00	2.00
19 Dave Magadan	.25	.10
20 Steve Sax	.10	.04
21 Eric Davis	.25	.10
22 Mike Pagliarulo	.10	.04
23 Fred Lynn	.25	.10
24 Reggie Jackson	2.00	.80
25 Larry Parrish	.10	.04
26 Tony Gwynn	5.00	2.00
27 Steve Garvey	.25	.10
28 Glenn Davis	.10	.04
29 Tim Raines	.25	.10
30 Vince Coleman	.10	.04
31 Willie McGee	.25	.10
32 Ozzie Smith	4.00	1.60
33 Dave Parker	.25	.10
34 Tony Pena	.10	.04
35 Ryne Sandberg	4.00	1.60
36 Brett Butler	.25	.10
37 Dale Murphy	.75	.30
38 Bob Horner	.10	.04
39 Pedro Guerrero	.10	.04
40 Brook Jacoby	.10	.04
41 Carlton Fisk	1.00	.40
42 Harold Baines	.50	.20
43 Rob Deer	.10	.04
44 Robin Yount	2.50	1.00
45 Paul Molitor	2.50	1.00
46 Jose Canseco	5.00	2.00
47 George Brett	5.00	2.00
48 Jim Presley	.10	.04
49 Rich Gedman	.10	.04
50 Lance Parrish	.25	.10
51 Eddie Murray	2.50	1.00
52 Cal Ripken	10.00	4.00
53 Kent Hrbek	.10	.04
54 Gary Gaetti	.25	.10
55 Kirby Puckett	5.00	2.00
56 George Bell	.10	.04
57 Tony Fernandez	.10	.04
58 Jesse Barfield	.10	.04
59 Jim Rice	.25	.10
60 Wade Boggs	2.50	1.00
61 Marty Barrett	.10	.04
62 Mike Schmidt	2.50	1.00
63 Von Hayes	.10	.04
64 Jeff Leonard	.10	.04
65 Chris Brown	.10	.04
66 Dave Smith	.10	.04
67 Mike Krukow	.10	.04
68 Ron Guidry	.25	.10
69 Rob Woodward	.10	.04
70 Rob Murphy	.10	.04
71 Andres Galarraga	4.00	1.60
72 Dwight Gooden	.25	.10
73 Bob Ojeda	.10	.04
74 Sid Fernandez	.10	.04
75 Jesse Orosco	.10	.04
76 Roger McDowell	.10	.04
77 John Tudor UER (Misspelled Tutor)	.10	.04
78 Tom Browning	.10	.04
79 Rick Aguilera	.10	.04
80 Lance McCullers	.10	.04
81 Mike Scott	.10	.04
82 Nolan Ryan	10.00	4.00
83 Bruce Hurst	.10	.04
84 Roger Clemens	6.00	2.40
85 Dennis Boyd	.10	.04
86 Dave Righetti	.10	.04
87 Dennis Rasmussen	.10	.04
88 Bret Saberhagen	.25	.10
89 Mark Langston	.10	.04
90 Jack Morris	.25	.10
91 Fernando Valenzuela	.25	.10
92 Orel Hershiser	.25	.10
93 Rick Honeycutt	.10	.04
94 Jeff Reardon	.10	.04
95 John Habyan	.10	.04
96 Goose Gossage	.25	.10
97 Todd Worrell	.10	.04
98 Floyd Youmans	.10	.04
99 Don Aase	.10	.04
100 John Franco	.25	.10

1987 Classic Update Yellow

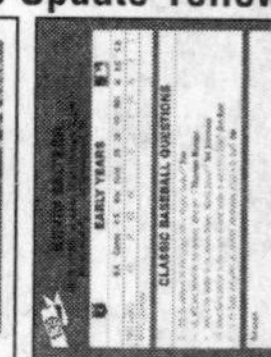

This 50-card standard-size set was actually distributed as part of an update to a trivia board game, but (unlike the original Classic game) was sold without the game. The set is sometimes referred to as the "Travel Edition" of the game. The card backs contain several trivia questions (and answers) which are used to play the game. A yellow border frames the full-color photo. The games were produced by Game Time, Ltd. and were available in toy stores as well as from card dealers. Cards are numbered beginning with 101, as they are an extension of the original set. According to the set's producers, reportedly ɔut 1/3 of the 150,000 sets printed were error s in that they had green backs instead of yel- / backs. This "green back" variation/error set valued at approximately double the prices list- below. Early cards of Barry Bonds and Mark Gwire highlight this set. Most cards issued of ry Bonds tend to be off center. It is believed t the average centering on this card is approx- ately 80/20.

Nm-Mt Ex-Mt
MP.FACT.SET (50) 30.00 12.00
Mike Schmidt 1.00 .40
2 Eric Davis .25 .10
3 Pete Rose 1.25 .50
4 Don Mattingly 1.25 .50
5 Wade Boggs .25 .10
6 Dale Murphy .25 .10
7 Glenn Davis .10 .04
8 Wally Joyner .25 .10
9 Bo Jackson 2.00 .80
0 Cory Snyder .10 .04
1 Jim Lindeman .15 .06
2 Kirby Puckett .40 .16
3 Barry Bonds 15.00 6.00
4 Roger Clemens 1.00 .40
5 Oddibe McDowell .10 .04
6 Bret Saberhagen .15 .06
7 Joe Magrane .15 .06
8 Scott Fletcher .10 .04
9 Mark McLemore .15 .06
0 Joe Niekro .15 .06
Who Me
1 Mark McGwire 10.00 4.00
2 Darryl Strawberry .15 .06
3 Mike Scott .15 .06
4 Andre Dawson .15 .06
5 Jose Canseco .40 .16
6 Kevin McReynolds .10 .04
7 Joe Carter .15 .06
8 Casey Candaele .10 .04
9 Matt Nokes .40 .16
0 Kal Daniels .10 .04
1 Pete Incaviglia .40 .16
2 Benito Santiago .40 .16
3 Barry Larkin 2.00 .80
4 Gary Pettis .10 .04
5 B.J. Surhoff .60 .24
6 Juan Nieves .10 .04
7 Jim Deshaies .10 .04
8 Pete O'Brien .10 .04
9 Kevin Seitzer .15 .06
0 Devon White .60 .24
1 Rob Deer .10 .04
2 Kurt Stillwell .10 .04
3 Edwin Correa .10 .04
4 Dion James .10 .04
5 Danny Tartabull .10 .04
6 Jerry Browne .15 .06
7 Ted Higuera .10 .04
8 Jack Clark .15 .06
9 Ruben Sierra 1.00 .40
0 Mark McGwire and 1.00 .40
Eric Davis

1987 Classic Update Yellow/Green Backs

ese cards parallel the 1987 Classic Yellow set cept the backs are in the style of the regular 87 Classic game set.

Nm-Mt Ex-Mt
MP.FACT.SET (50) 40.00 16.00
REENBACK: .4X TO 1X YELLOW

1988 Classic Blue

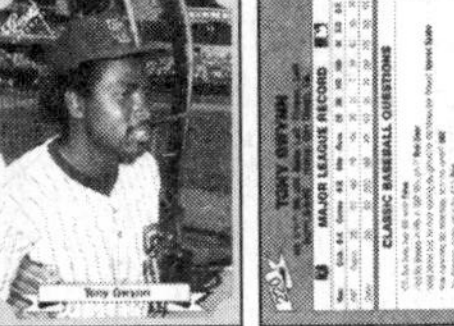

is 50-card blue-bordered standard-size set as actually distributed as part of an update to a via board game, but (unlike the original Classic me) was sold without the game. The card acks contain several trivia questions (and nswers) which are used to play the game. A ue border frames the full color photo. The mes were produced by Game Time, Ltd. and ere available in toy stores as well as from card ealers. Cards are numbered beginning with 201 they are an extension of the original sets.

Nm-Mt Ex-Mt
MP.FACT. SET (50) 10.00 4.00
01 Eric Davis and .15 .06
Dale Murphy
02 B.J. Surhoff .20 .08
03 John Kruk .15 .06
04 Sam Horn .10 .04
05 Jack Clark .15 .06
06 Wally Joyner .15 .06
07 Matt Nokes .10 .04
08 Bo Jackson .25 .10
09 Darryl Strawberry .10 .04
10 Ozzie Smith 1.50 .60
11 Don Mattingly 2.00 .80
12 Mark McGwire 4.00 1.60
13 Eric Davis .15 .06
14 Wade Boggs .75 .30
15 Dale Murphy .25 .10
16 Andre Dawson .25 .10
17 Roger Clemens 2.50 1.00
18 Kevin Seitzer .10 .04
19 Benito Santiago .15 .06
20 Tony Gwynn 2.00 .80
21 Mike Scott .10 .04
22 Steve Bedrosian .10 .04
23 Vince Coleman .10 .04
24 Rick Sutcliffe .10 .04
25 Will Clark 1.00 .40
26 Pete Rose 1.00 .40
27 Mike Greenwell .10 .04
228 Ken Caminiti .25 .10
229 Ellis Burks 1.00 .40
230 Dave Magadan .10 .04
231 Alan Trammell .25 .10
232 Paul Molitor .50 .20
233 Gary Gaetti .15 .06
234 Rickey Henderson 1.00 .40
235 Danny Tartabull UER .10 .04
(Photo actually
Hal McRae)
236 Bobby Bonilla .15 .06
237 Mike Dunne .10 .04
238 Al Leiter .25 .10
239 John Farrell .10 .04
240 Joe Magrane .10 .04
241 Mike Henneman .15 .06
242 George Bell .10 .04
243 Gregg Jefferies .15 .06
244 Jay Buhner .75 .30
245 Todd Benzinger .10 .04
246 Matt Williams .75 .30
247 Mark McGwire and 2.00 .80
Don Mattingly
(Unnumbered; game
instructions on back)
248 George Brett 1.25 .50
249 Jimmy Key .15 .06
250 Mark Langston .10 .04

1988 Classic Red

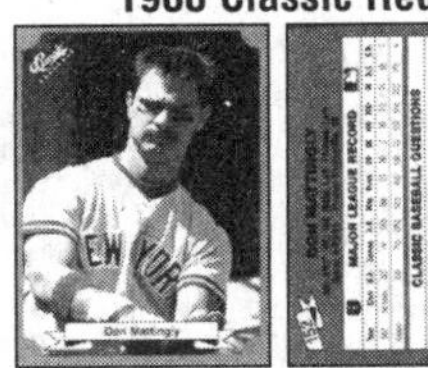

This 50-card red-bordered standard-size set was actually distributed as part of an update to a trivia board game, but (unlike the original Classic game) was sold without the game. The card backs contain several trivia questions (and answers) which are used to play the game. A red border frames the full color photo. The games were produced by Game Time, Ltd. and were available in toy stores as well as from card dealers. Cards are numbered beginning with 151 as they are an extension of the original sets.

Nm-Mt Ex-Mt
COMP. FACT. SET (50) 12.00 4.80
151 Mark McGwire and 2.00 .80
Don Mattingly
152 Don Mattingly 1.50 .60
153 Mark McGwire 2.50 1.00
154 Eric Davis .15 .06
155 Wade Boggs .75 .30
156 Dale Murphy .25 .10
157 Andre Dawson .25 .10
158 Roger Clemens 1.50 .60
159 Kevin Seitzer .15 .06
160 Benito Santiago .15 .06
161 Kal Daniels .10 .04
162 John Kruk .15 .06
163 Bill Ripken .10 .04
164 Kirby Puckett 1.00 .40
165 Jose Canseco .50 .20
166 Matt Nokes .10 .04
167 Mike Schmidt .75 .30
168 Tim Raines .15 .06
169 Ryne Sandberg 1.25 .50
170 Dave Winfield .25 .10
171 Dwight Gooden .15 .06
172 Bret Saberhagen .15 .06
173 Willie McGee .15 .06
174 Jack Morris .15 .06
175 Jeff Leonard .10 .04
176 Cal Ripken 3.00 1.20
177 Pete Incaviglia .10 .04
178 Devon White .10 .04
179 Nolan Ryan 3.00 1.20
180 Ruben Sierra .15 .06
181 Todd Worrell .15 .06
182 Glenn Davis .10 .04
183 Frank Viola .10 .04
184 Cory Snyder .10 .04
185 Tracy Jones .10 .04
186 Terry Steinbach .10 .04
187 Julio Franco .15 .06
188 Larry Sheets .10 .04
189 John Marzano .10 .04
190 Kevin Elster .10 .04
191 Vicente Palacios .10 .04
192 Kent Hrbek .10 .04
193 Eric Bell .10 .04
194 Kelly Downs .10 .04
195 Jose Lind .10 .04
196 Dave Stewart .15 .06
197 Mark McGwire and 2.00 .80
Jose Canseco
198 Phil Niekro .50 .20
Cleveland Indians
199 Phil Niekro .50 .20
Toronto Blue Jays
200 Phil Niekro .50 .20
Atlanta Braves

1989 Classic Light Blue

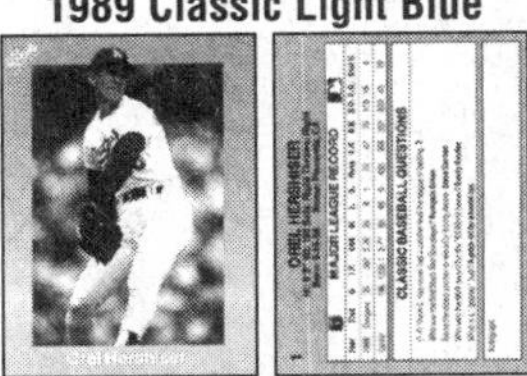

The 1989 Classic set contains 100 standard-size cards. The fronts of these cards have light blue borders. The backs feature 1988 and lifetime stats. The cards were distributed with a baseball boardgame. Reportedly there were 150,000 sets produced.

Nm-Mt Ex-Mt
COMP.FACT.SET (100) 20.00 8.00
1 Orel Hershiser .15 .06
2 Wade Boggs .75 .30
3 Jose Canseco 1.00 .40
4 Mark McGwire 3.00 1.20
5 Don Mattingly 2.00 .80
6 Gregg Jefferies .15 .06
7 Dwight Gooden .15 .06
8 Darryl Strawberry .15 .06
9 Eric Davis .20 .08
10 Joey Meyer .10 .04
11 Joe Carter .20 .08
12 Paul Molitor .75 .30
13 Mark Grace 1.00 .40
14 Kurt Stillwell .10 .04
15 Kirby Puckett 1.00 .40
16 Keith Miller .10 .04
17 Glenn Davis .10 .04
18 Will Clark .50 .20
19 Cory Snyder .10 .04
20 Jose Lind .10 .04
21 Andres Thomas .10 .04
22 Dave Smith .10 .04
23 Mike Scott .10 .04
24 Kevin McReynolds .10 .04
25 B.J. Surhoff .15 .06
26 Mackey Sasser .10 .04
27 Chad Kreuter .10 .04
28 Hal Morris .10 .04
29 Wally Joyner .10 .04
30 Tony Gwynn 2.00 .80
31 Kevin Mitchell .15 .06
32 Dave Winfield .50 .20
33 Billy Bean .20 .08
34 Steve Bedrosian .10 .04
35 Ron Gant .15 .06
36 Len Dykstra .15 .06
37 Andre Dawson .50 .20
38 Brett Butler .15 .06
39 Rob Deer .10 .04
40 Tommy John .15 .06
41 Gary Gaetti .15 .06
42 Tim Raines .15 .06
43 George Bell .10 .04
44 Dwight Evans .15 .06
45 Dennis Martinez .15 .06
46 Andres Galarraga .50 .20
47 George Brett 2.00 .80
48 Mike Schmidt 1.00 .40
49 Dave Stieb .10 .04
50 Rickey Henderson 1.25 .50
51 Craig Biggio 2.00 .80
52 Mark Lemke .10 .04
53 Chris Sabo .10 .04
54 Jeff Treadway .10 .04
55 Kent Hrbek .15 .06
56 Cal Ripken 4.00 1.60
57 Tim Belcher .10 .04
58 Ozzie Smith 1.50 .60
59 Keith Hernandez .15 .06
60 Pedro Guerrero .10 .04
61 Greg Swindell .10 .04
62 Bret Saberhagen .15 .06
63 John Tudor .10 .04
64 Gary Carter .50 .20
65 Kevin Seitzer .10 .04
66 Jesse Barfield .10 .04
67 Luis Medina .10 .04
68 Walt Weiss .10 .04
69 Terry Steinbach .10 .04
70 Barry Larkin .50 .20
71 Pete Rose 1.00 .40
72 Luis Salazar .10 .04
73 Benito Santiago .15 .06
74 Kal Daniels .10 .04
75 Kevin Elster .10 .04
76 Rob Dibble .15 .06
77 Bobby Witt .10 .04
78 Steve Searcy .10 .04
79 Sandy Alomar Jr. .25 .10
80 Chili Davis .15 .06
81 Alvin Davis .10 .04
82 Charlie Leibrandt .10 .04
83 Robin Yount .50 .20
84 Mark Carreon .10 .04
85 Pascual Perez .10 .04
86 Dennis Rasmussen .10 .04
87 Ernie Riles .10 .04
88 Melido Perez .10 .04
89 Doug Jones .10 .04
90 Dennis Eckersley .50 .20
91 Bob Welch .10 .04
92 Bob Milacki .10 .04
93 Jeff Robinson .10 .04
94 Mike Henneman .10 .04
95 Randy Johnson 5.00 2.00
96 Ron Jones .10 .04
97 Jack Armstrong .10 .04
98 Willie McGee .15 .06
99 Ryne Sandberg 1.00 .40
100 David Cone .10 .04
Danny Jackson

1989 Classic Travel Orange

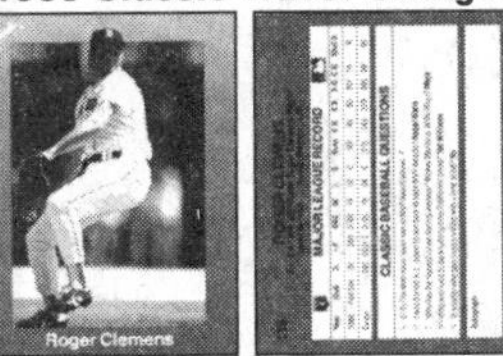

The 1989 Classic Travel Orange set contains 50 standard-size cards. The fronts of the cards have orange borders. The backs feature 1988 and lifetime stats. This subset of cards were distributed as a set in blister packs as "Travel Update I" subsets. Reportedly there were 150,000 sets produced. A first year card of Ken Griffey Jr. highlights this set.

Nm-Mt Ex-Mt
COMP.FACT.SET (50) 15.00 6.00
101 Gary Sheffield 1.50 .60
102 Wade Boggs .15 .06
103 Jose Canseco .25 .10
104 Mark McGwire 1.00 .40
105 Orel Hershiser .10 .04
106 Don Mattingly .60 .24
107 Dwight Gooden .10 .04
108 Darryl Strawberry .10 .04
109 Eric Davis .10 .04
110 H.Meulens UER .05 .02
Listed on card as
Bam Bam Muelens
111 Andy Van Slyke .10 .04
112 Al Leiter .25 .10
113 Matt Nokes .05 .02
114 Mike Krukow .05 .02
115 Tony Fernandez .05 .02
116 Fred McGriff .15 .06
117 Barry Bonds 1.25 .50
118 Gerald Perry .05 .02
119 Roger Clemens .50 .20
120 Kirk Gibson .10 .04
121 Greg Maddux .50 .20
122 Bo Jackson .25 .10
123 Danny Jackson .05 .02
124 Dale Murphy .15 .06
125 David Cone .10 .04
126 Tom Browning .05 .02
127 Roberto Alomar .25 .10
128 Alan Trammell .10 .04
129 Ricky Jordan UER .10 .04
(Misspelled Jordon
on card back)
130 Ramon Martinez .10 .04
131 Ken Griffey Jr. 8.00 3.20
132 Gregg Olson .10 .04
133 Carlos Quintana .05 .02
134 Dave West .05 .02
135 Cameron Drew .05 .02
136 Teddy Higuera .05 .02
137 Sil Campusano .05 .02
138 Mark Gubicza .05 .02
139 Mike Boddicker .05 .02
140 Paul Gibson .05 .02
141 Jose Rijo .10 .04
142 John Costello .05 .02
143 Cecil Espy .05 .02
144 Frank Viola .10 .04
145 Erik Hanson .10 .04
146 Juan Samuel .05 .02
147 Harold Reynolds .10 .04
148 Joe Magrane .05 .02
149 Mike Greenwell .05 .02
150 Darryl Strawberry .10 .04
and Will Clark

1989 Classic Travel Purple

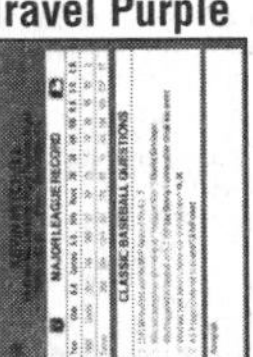

The 1989 Classic "Travel Update II" set contains 50 standard-size cards. The fronts have purple (and gray) borders. The set features "two sport" cards of Bo Jackson and Deion Sanders. In addition, a first year card of Ken Griffey Jr highlights this set. The cards were distributed as a set in blister packs.

Nm-Mt Ex-Mt
COMP.FACT.SET (50) 12.00 4.80
151 Jim Abbott .40 .16
152 Ellis Burks .10 .04
153 Mike Schmidt .50 .20
154 Gregg Jefferies .05 .02
155 Mark Grace .25 .10
156 Jerome Walton .15 .06
157 Bo Jackson .25 .10
158 Jack Clark .10 .04
159 Tom Glavine .25 .10
160 Eddie Murray .25 .10
161 John Dopson .05 .02
162 Ruben Sierra .05 .02
163 Rafael Palmeiro .25 .10
164 Nolan Ryan 1.00 .40
165 Barry Larkin .15 .06
166 Tommy Herr .05 .02
167 Roberto Kelly .05 .02
168 Glenn Davis .05 .02
169 Glenn Braggs .05 .02
170 Juan Bell .05 .02
171 Todd Burns .05 .02
172 Derek Lilliquist .05 .02
173 Orel Hershiser .10 .04
174 John Smoltz .75 .30
175 Ozzie Guillen and .05 .02
Ellis Burks
176 Kirby Puckett .25 .10
177 Robin Ventura .75 .30
178 Allan Anderson .05 .02
179 Steve Sax .05 .02
180 Will Clark .25 .10
181 Mike Devereaux .05 .02
182 Tom Gordon .25 .10
183 Rob Murphy .05 .02
184 Pete O'Brien .05 .02
185 Cris Carpenter .05 .02
186 Tom Brunansky .05 .02
187 Bob Boone .10 .04
188 Lou Whitaker .10 .04
189 Dwight Gooden .10 .04
190 Mark McGwire 1.00 .40
191 John Smiley .05 .02
192 Tommy Gregg .05 .02
193 Ken Griffey Jr. 8.00 3.20
194 Bruce Hurst .05 .02
195 Greg Swindell .05 .02
196 Nelson Liriano .05 .02
197 Randy Myers .10 .04
198 Kevin Mitchell .10 .04
199 Dante Bichette .25 .10
200 Deion Sanders 1.00 .40

1990 Classic Blue

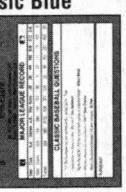

The 1990 Classic Blue (Game) set contains 150 standard-size cards, the largest Classic set to date in terms of player selection. The front borders are blue with magenta splotches. The backs feature 1989 and career total stats. The cards were distributed as a set in blister packs. According to distributors of the set, reportedly there were 200,000 sets produced. Reportedly the Sanders "correction" was made at Sanders own request; less than 10 percent of the sets contain the first version and hence it has the higher value in the checklist below. The complete set price below does not include any of the more difficult variation cards. Early cards of Sammy Sosa and Bernie Williams highlight the set.

Nm-Mt Ex-Mt
COMP. FACT SET (150) 10.00 3.00
1 Nolan Ryan 1.00 .30
2 Bo Jackson .25 .07
3 Gregg Olson .05 .02
4 Tom Gordon .05 .02
5 Robin Ventura .25 .07
6 Will Clark .25 .07
7 Ruben Sierra .05 .02
8 Mark Grace .15 .04
9 Luis DeLosSantos .05 .02
10 Bernie Williams 1.00 .30
11 Eric Davis .10 .03
12 Carney Lansford .10 .03
13 John Smoltz .25 .07
14 Gary Sheffield .25 .07
15 Kent Mercker .10 .03
16 Don Mattingly .60 .18
17 Tony Gwynn .30 .09
18 Ozzie Smith .40 .12
19 Fred McGriff .15 .04
20 Ken Griffey Jr. .75 .23
21A Deion Sanders 3.00 .90
Identified only as
Prime Time on front
21B Deion Sanders .25 .07
Identified as
Deion Prime Time Sanders
on front of card
22 Jose Canseco .25 .07
23 Mitch Williams .05 .02
24 Cal Ripken UER .75 .23
Misspelled Ripkin on back
25 Bob Geren .05 .02
26 Wade Boggs .15 .04
27 Ryne Sandberg .50 .15
28 Kirby Puckett .25 .07
29 Mike Scott .10 .03
30 Dwight Smith .05 .02
31 Craig Worthington .05 .02
32A Ricky Jordan ERR .05 .02
Misspelled Jordon on back
32B Ricky Jordan COR .05 .02
33 Darryl Strawberry .10 .03
34 Jerome Walton .05 .02
35 John Olerud .50 .15
36 Tom Glavine .15 .04
37 Rickey Henderson .25 .07
38 Rolando Roomes .05 .02
39 Mickey Tettleton .10 .03
40 Jim Abbott .15 .04
41 Dave Righetti .10 .03
42 Mike LaValliere .05 .02
43 Rob Dibble .10 .03
44 Pete Harnisch .05 .02
45 Jose Offerman .10 .03
46 Walt Weiss .05 .02
47 Mike Greenwell .05 .02
48 Barry Larkin .15 .04
49 Dave Gallagher .05 .02
50 Junior Felix .05 .02
51 Roger Clemens .50 .15
52 Lonnie Smith .10 .03
53 Jerry Browne .05 .02
54 Greg Briley .05 .02
55 Delino DeShields .10 .03
56 Carmelo Martinez .05 .02
57 Craig Biggio .15 .04
58 Dwight Gooden .10 .03
59 A.L. Fence Busters 1.00 .30
Bo Jackson
Ruben Sierra
Mark McGwire
59B Bo/Rubin/Mark 5.00 1.50
Bo Jackson
Ruben Sierra
Mark McGwire
60 Greg Vaughn .05 .02
61 Roberto Alomar .15 .04
62 Steve Bedrosian .05 .02
63 Devon White .10 .03
64 Kevin Mitchell .05 .02
65 Marquis Grissom .25 .07
66 Brian Holman .05 .02
67 Julio Franco .10 .03
68 Dave West .05 .02
69 Harold Baines .10 .03
70 Eric Anthony .05 .02
71 Glenn Davis .05 .02
72 Mark Langston .05 .02
73 Matt Williams .10 .03
74 Rafael Palmeiro .25 .07
75 Pete Rose Jr. .10 .03
76 Ramon Martinez .05 .02
77 Dwight Evans .10 .03
78 Mackey Sasser .05 .02
79 Mike Schooler .05 .02
80 Dennis Cook .05 .02

81 Orel Hershiser .10 .03
82 Barry Bonds .60 .18
83 Geronimo Berroa .05 .02
84 George Bell .10 .03
85 Andre Dawson .10 .03
86 John Franco .10 .03
87A Clark/Gwynn 3.00 .90
Will Clark
Tony Gwynn
87B N.L. Hit Kings .15 .04
Will Clark
Tony Gwynn
88 Glenallen Hill .05 .02
89 Jeff Ballard .05 .02
90 Todd Zeile .10 .03
91 Frank Viola .10 .03
92 Ozzie Guillen .05 .02
93 Jeffrey Leonard .05 .02
94 Dave Smith .05 .02
95 Dave Parker .10 .03
96 Jose Gonzalez .05 .02
97 Dave Stieb .10 .03
98 Charlie Hayes .05 .02
99 Jesse Barfield .10 .03
100 Joey Belle .10 .03
101 Jeff Reardon .10 .03
102 Bruce Hurst .10 .03
103 Luis Medina .05 .02
104 Mike Moore .05 .02
105 Vince Coleman .05 .02
106 Alan Trammell .10 .03
107 Randy Myers .05 .02
108 Frank Tanana .10 .03
109 Craig Lefferts .05 .02
110 John Wetteland .10 .03
111 Chris Gwynn .05 .02
112 Mark Carreon .05 .02
113 Von Hayes .10 .03
114 Doug Jones .05 .02
115 Andres Galarraga .10 .03
116 Carlton Fisk UER .15 .04
Bellows Falls misspelled
as Bellow Falls on back
117 Paul O'Neill .15 .04
118 Tim Raines .10 .03
119 Tom Brunansky .05 .02
120 Andy Benes .10 .03
121 Mark Portugal .05 .02
122 Willie Randolph .10 .03
123 Jeff Blauser .05 .02
124 Don August .05 .02
125 Chuck Cary .05 .02
126 John Smiley .05 .02
127 Terry Mulholland .05 .02
128 Harold Reynolds .10 .03
129 Hubie Brooks .10 .03
130 Ben McDonald .10 .03
131 Kevin Ritz .05 .02
132 Luis Quinones .05 .02
133A H. Meulens ERR .05 .02
Misspelled Muelens on front
133B H. Meulens COR .05 .02
134 Bill Spiers UER .05 .02
Orangeburg misspelled
as Orangburg on back
135 Andy Hawkins .05 .02
136 Alvin Davis .10 .03
137 Lee Smith .10 .03
138 Joe Carter .10 .03
139 Bret Saberhagen .10 .03
140 Sammy Sosa 5.00 1.50
141 Matt Nokes .05 .02
142 Bert Blyleven .10 .03
143 Bobby Bonilla .10 .03
144 Howard Johnson .10 .03
145 Joe Magrane .05 .02
146 Pedro Guerrero .10 .03
147 Robin Yount .40 .12
148 Dan Gladden .05 .02
149 Steve Sax .10 .03
150A Clark/Mitchell 2.00 .60
Will Clark
Kevin Mitchell
150B Bay Bombers .25 .07
Will Clark
Kevin Mitchell

1990 Classic Update

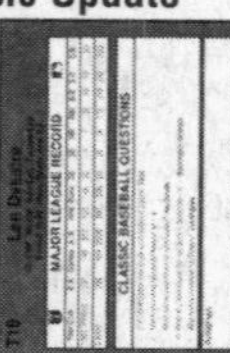

The 1990 Classic Update set was the second set issued by the Classic Game company in 1990. Sometimes referenced as Classic Pink or Red, this set includes a Juan Gonzalez card. This 50-card, standard-size set was issued in late June of 1990. With a few exceptions, the set numbering is in alphabetical order by player's name. Early cards of Juan Gonzalez and Larry Walker highlight this set.

Nm-Mt Ex-Mt
COMP. FACT. SET (50) 6.00 1.80
T1 Gregg Jefferies .05 .02
T2 Steve Adkins .05 .02
T3 Sandy Alomar Jr. .10 .03
T4 Steve Avery .05 .02
T5 Mike Blowers .05 .02
T6 George Brett .75 .23
T7 Tom Browning .05 .02
T8 Ellis Burks .10 .03
T9 Joe Carter .10 .03
T10 Jerald Clark .05 .02
T11 Matt Williams .75 .23
Will Clark
T12 Pat Combs .05 .02
T13 Scott Cooper .05 .02
T14 Mark Davis .05 .02
T15 Storm Davis .05 .02
T16 Larry Walker 1.25 .35
T17 Brian DuBois .05 .02
T18 Len Dykstra .10 .03
T19 John Franco .10 .03
T20 Kirk Gibson .10 .03
T21 Juan Gonzalez 1.50 .45
T22 Tommy Greene .05 .02
T23 Kent Hrbek .10 .03
T24 Mike Huff .05 .02
T25 Bo Jackson .20 .06
T26 Nolan Ryan 2.00 .60
Nolan Knows Bo
T27 Roberto Kelly .05 .02
T28 Mark Langston .05 .02
T29 Ray Lankford .50 .15
T30 Kevin Maas .05 .02
T31 Julio Machado .05 .02
T32 Greg Maddux 1.25 .35
T33 Mark McGwire 1.50 .45
T34 Paul Molitor .20 .06
T35 Hal Morris .05 .02
T36 Dale Murphy .20 .06
T37 Eddie Murray .20 .06
T38 Jaime Navarro .05 .02
T39 Dean Palmer .50 .15
T40 Derek Parks .05 .02
T41 Bobby Rose .05 .02
T42 Wally Joyner .05 .02
T43 Chris Sabo .05 .02
T44 Benito Santiago .10 .03
T45 Mike Stanton .05 .02
T46 Terry Steinbach UER .05 .02
Career BA .725
T47 Dave Stewart .10 .03
T48 Greg Swindell .05 .02
T49 Jose Vizcaino .10 .03
NNO Mark Davis .05 .02
Bret Saberhagen
(Instructions on back)

1990 Classic Yellow

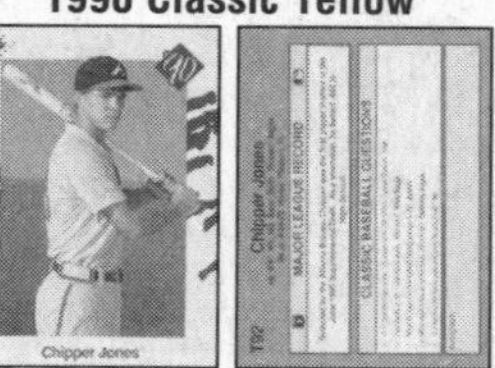

The 1990 Classic III set is also referenced as Classic Yellow. This set also featured number one draft picks of the current year mixed with the other Classic cards. This 100-card standard-size set also contained a special Nolan Ryan commemorative card, Texas Heat. A very early card of Chipper Jones is included in this set. Card T51 was never issued.

Nm-Mt Ex-Mt
COMP.FACT.SET (100) 10.00 3.00
T1 Ken Griffey Jr. .75 .23
T2 John Tudor .05 .02
T3 John Kruk .10 .03
T4 Mark Gardner .05 .02
T5 Scott Radinsky .05 .02
T6 John Burkett .05 .02
T7 Will Clark .25 .07
T8 Gary Carter .60 .18
T9 Ted Higuera .05 .02
T10 Dave Parker .10 .03
T11 Dante Bichette .10 .03
T12 Don Mattingly .60 .18
T13 Greg Harris .05 .02
T14 Dave Hollins .10 .03
T15 Matt Nokes .05 .02
T16 Kevin Tapani .25 .07
T17 Shane Mack .05 .02
T18 Randy Myers .10 .03
T19 Greg Olson .05 .02
T20 Shawn Abner .05 .02
T21 Jim Presley .05 .02
T22 Randy Johnson .50 .12
T23 Edgar Martinez .15 .04
T24 Scott Coolbaugh .05 .02
T25 Jeff Treadway .05 .02
T26 Joe Klink .05 .02
T27 Rickey Henderson .25 .07
T28 Sam Horn .05 .02
T29 Kurt Stillwell .05 .02
T30 Andy Van Slyke .10 .03
T31 Willie Banks .05 .02
T32 Jose Canseco .25 .07
T33 Felix Jose .05 .02
T34 Candy Maldonado .05 .02
T35 Carlos Baerga .10 .03
T36 Keith Hernandez .10 .03
T37 Frank Viola .05 .02
T38 Pete O'Brien .05 .02
T39 Pat Borders .05 .02
T40 Mike Heath .05 .02
T41 Kevin Brown .10 .03
T42 Chris Bosio .05 .02
T43 Shawn Boskie .05 .02
T44 Carlos Quintana .05 .02
T45 Juan Samuel .05 .02
T46 Tim Layana .05 .02
T47 Mike Harkey .05 .02
T48 Gerald Perry .05 .02
T49 Mike Witt .05 .02
T50 Joe Orsulak .05 .02
T51 Not Issued
T52 Willie Blair .05 .02
T53 Gene Larkin .05 .02
T54 Jody Reed .05 .02
T55 Jeff Reardon .10 .03
T56 Kevin McReynolds .05 .02
T57 Mike Marshall .05 .02
Unnumbered
game instructions on back
T58 Eric Yelding .05 .02
T59 Fred Lynn .05 .02
T60 Jim Leyritz .25 .07
T61 John Orton .05 .02
T62 Mike Lieberthal .40 .12
T63 Mike Hartley .05 .02
T64 Kal Daniels .05 .02
T65 Terry Shumpert .05 .02
T66 Sil Campusano .05 .02
T67 Tony Pena .05 .02
T68 Barry Bonds .60 .18
T69 Roger McDowell .05 .02
T70 Kelly Gruber .05 .02
T71 Willie Randolph .10 .03
T72 Rick Parker .05 .02
T73 Bobby Bonilla .10 .03
T74 Jack Armstrong .05 .02
T75 Hubie Brooks .05 .02
T76 Sandy Alomar Jr. .10 .03
T77 Ruben Sierra .05 .02
T78 Erik Hanson .05 .02
T79 Tony Phillips .05 .02
T80 Rondell White .40 .12
T81 Bobby Thigpen .05 .02
T82 Ron Walden .10 .03
T83 Don Peters .10 .03
T84 Nolan Ryan 6TH 1.00 .30
T85 Lance Dickson .10 .03
T86 Ryne Sandberg .40 .12
T87 Eric Christopherson .10 .03
T88 Shane Andrews .10 .03
T89 Marc Newfield .10 .03
T90 Adam Hyzdu .10 .03
T91 Nolan Ryan .50 .15
Reid Ryan
T92 Chipper Jones 3.00 .90
T93 Frank Thomas 1.50 .45
T94 Cecil Fielder .10 .03
T95 Delino DeShields .25 .07
T96 John Olerud .50 .15
T97 David Justice .50 .15
T98 Joe Oliver .05 .02
T99 Alex Fernandez .25 .07
T100 Todd Hundley .25 .07
NNO Micro Players 1.00 .30
Frank Viola
Texas Heat
Don Mattingly
Chipper Jones
(Blue blank back)

1991 Classic Game

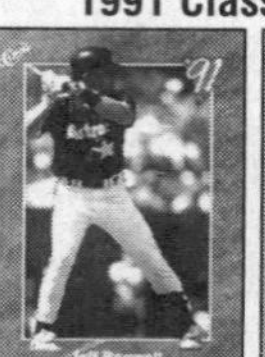

The 1991 Classic Baseball Collector's Edition board game is Classic's first Big Game issue since the 1989 Big Game. 100,000 games were produced, and each one included a board game, action spinner, eight stand-up baseball player pieces, action scoreboard, eight-page picture book with tips from five great baseball players (Carew, Spahn, Schmidt, Brock, and Aaron), 200 player cards, and a certificate of limited edition. The standard-size cards have on the fronts glossy color action photos bordered in purple. The backs are purple and white and have biography, statistics, five trivia questions, and an autograph slot.

Nm-Mt Ex-Mt
COMP. FACT SET (200) 20.00 6.00
1 Frank Viola .05 .02
2 Tim Wallach .05 .02
3 Lou Whitaker .10 .03
4 Brett Butler .10 .03
5 Jim Abbott .10 .03
6 Jack Armstrong .05 .02
7 Craig Biggio .25 .07
8 Brian Barnes .05 .02
9 Dennis(Oil Can) Boyd .05 .02
10 Tom Browning .05 .02
11 Tom Brunansky .05 .02
12 Ellis Burks .10 .03
13 Harold Baines .15 .04
14 Kal Daniels .05 .02
15 Mark Davis .05 .02
16 Storm Davis .05 .02
17 Tom Glavine .50 .15
18 Mike Greenwell .05 .02
19 Kelly Gruber .05 .02
20 Mark Gubicza .05 .02
21 Pedro Guerrero .05 .02
22 Mike Harkey .05 .02
23 Orel Hershiser .10 .03
24 Ted Higuera .05 .02
25 Von Hayes .05 .02
26 Andre Dawson .25 .07
27 Shawon Dunston .05 .02
28 Roberto Kelly .05 .02
29 Joe Magrane .05 .02
30 Dennis Martinez .10 .03
31 Kevin McReynolds .05 .02
32 Matt Nokes .05 .02
33 Dan Plesac .05 .02
34 Dave Parker .10 .03
35 Randy Johnson .75 .23
36 Bret Saberhagen .10 .03
37 Mackey Sasser .05 .02
38 Mike Scott .05 .02
39 Ozzie Smith 1.00 .30
40 Kevin Seitzer .05 .02
41 Ruben Sierra .10 .03
42 Kevin Tapani .05 .02
43 Danny Tartabull .05 .02
44 Robby Thompson .05 .02
45 Andy Van Slyke .10 .03
46 Greg Vaughn .10 .03
47 Harold Reynolds .15 .04
48 Will Clark .25 .07
49 Gary Gaetti .10 .03
50 Joe Grahe .05 .02
51 Carlton Fisk .50 .15
52 Robin Ventura .25 .07
53 Ozzie Guillen .10 .03
54 Tom Candiotti .05 .02
55 Doug Jones .05 .02
56 Eric King .05 .02
57 Kirk Gibson .10 .03
58 Tim Costo .05 .02
59 Robin Yount .50 .15
60 Sammy Sosa 2.00 .60
61 Jesse Barfield .05 .02
62 Marc Newfield .05 .02
63 Jimmy Key .10 .03
64 Felix Jose .05 .02
65 Mark Whiten .05 .02
66 Tommy Greene .05 .02
67 Kent Mercker .05 .02
68 Greg Maddux 1.50 .45
69 Danny Jackson .05 .02
70 Reggie Sanders .10 .03
71 Eric Yelding .05 .02
72 Karl Rhodes .05 .02
73 Fernando Valenzuela .10 .03
74 Chris Nabholz .05 .02
75 Andres Galarraga .25 .07
76 Howard Johnson .05 .02
77 Hubie Brooks .05 .02
78 Terry Mulholland .05 .02
79 Paul Molitor .50 .15
80 Roger McDowell .05 .02
81 Darren Daulton .10 .03
82 Zane Smith .05 .02
83 Ray Lankford .10 .03
84 Bruce Hurst .05 .02
85 Andy Benes .05 .02
86 John Burkett .05 .02
87 Dave Righetti .05 .02
88 Steve Karsay .25 .07
89 D.J. Dozier .05 .02
90 Jeff Bagwell 2.00 .60
91 Joe Carter .10 .03
92 Wes Chamberlain .05 .02
93 Vince Coleman .05 .02
94 Pat Combs .05 .02
95 Jerome Walton .05 .02
96 Jeff Conine .05 .02
97 Alan Trammell .15 .04
98 Don Mattingly 1.00 .30
99 Ramon Martinez .05 .02
100 Dave Magadan .05 .02
101 Greg Swindell UER .05 .02
Misnumbered as T10
102 Dave Stewart .10 .03
103 Gary Sheffield .25 .07
104 George Bell .05 .02
105 Mark Grace .50 .15
106 Steve Sax .05 .02
107 Ryne Sandberg .75 .23
108 Chris Sabo .05 .02
109 Jose Rijo .05 .02
110 Cal Ripken 2.50 .75
111 Kirby Puckett .50 .15
112 Eddie Murray .50 .15
113 Roberto Alomar .25 .07
114 Randy Myers .05 .02
115 Rafael Palmeiro .25 .07
116 John Olerud .15 .04
117 Gregg Jefferies .05 .02
118 Kent Hrbek .10 .03
119 Marquis Grissom .10 .03
120 Ken Griffey Jr. 2.00 .60
121 Dwight Gooden .10 .03
122 Juan Gonzalez .75 .23
123 Ron Gant .10 .03
124 Travis Fryman .25 .07
125 John Franco .10 .03
126 Dennis Eckersley .10 .03
127 Cecil Fielder .10 .03
128 Phil Plantier .05 .02
129 Kevin Mitchell .05 .02
130 Kevin Maas .05 .02
131 Mark McGwire 1.50 .45
132 Ben McDonald .05 .02
133 Len Dykstra .10 .03
134 Delino DeShields .10 .03
135 Jose Canseco .50 .15
136 Eric Davis .10 .03
137 George Brett 1.25 .35
138 Steve Avery .05 .02
139 Eric Anthony .05 .02
140 Bobby Thigpen .05 .02
141 Ken Griffey Sr. .10 .03
142 Barry Larkin .25 .07
143 Jeff Brantley .05 .02
144 Bobby Bonilla .05 .02
145 Jose Offerman .05 .02
146 Mike Mussina 1.50 .45
147 Erik Hanson .05 .02
148 Dale Murphy .40 .12
149 Roger Clemens 1.00 .30
150 Tino Martinez .25 .07
151 Todd Van Poppel .25 .07
152 Mo Vaughn .50 .15
153 Derrick May .05 .02
154 Jack Clark .10 .03
155 Dave Hansen .05 .02
156 Tony Gwynn 1.25 .35
157 Brian McRae .10 .03
158 Matt Williams .15 .04
159 Kirk Dressendorfer .05 .02
160 Scott Erickson .10 .03
161 Tony Fernandez .05 .02
162 Willie McGee .10 .03
163 Fred McGriff .25 .07
164 Leo Gomez .05 .02
165 Bernard Gilkey .05 .02
166 Bobby Witt .05 .02
167 Doug Drabek .05 .02
168 Rob Dibble .05 .02
169 Glenn Davis .05 .02
170 Danny Darwin .05 .02
171 Eric Karros .50 .15
172 Eddie Zosky .05 .02
173 Todd Zeile .05 .02
174 Tim Raines .10 .03
175 Benito Santiago .10 .03
176 Dan Peltier .05 .02
177 Darryl Strawberry .10 .03
178 Hal Morris .05 .02
179 Hensley Meulens .05 .02
180 John Smoltz .25 .07
181 Frank Thomas 1.00 .30
182 Dave Staton .05 .02
183 Scott Chiamparino .05 .02
184 Alex Fernandez .05 .02
185 Mark Lewis .05 .02
186 Bo Jackson .25 .07
187 Mickey Morandini UER .05 .02
Photo is Darren Daulton
188 Cory Snyder .05 .02
189 Rickey Henderson .50 .15
190 Junior Felix .05 .02
191 Milt Cuyler .05 .02
192 Wade Boggs .40 .12
193 Dave Justice .50 .15
Justice Prevails
194 Sandy Alomar Jr. .10 .03
195 Barry Bonds 1.50 .45
196 Nolan Ryan 2.50 .75
197 Rico Brogna .05 .02
198 Steve Decker .05 .02
199 Bob Welch .05 .02
200 Andujar Cedeno .05 .02

1991 Classic I

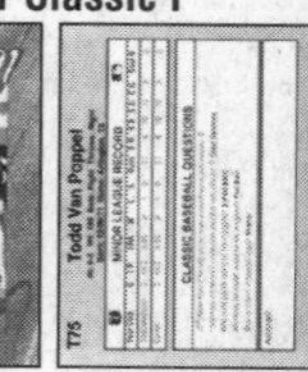

This 100-card standard-size set features man of the most popular players in the game of base ball as well as some of the more excitin prospects. The set includes trivia questions o the backs of the cards. For the most part the se is arranged alphabetically by team and the alphabetically by players within that team.

Nm-Mt Ex-Mt
COMP.FACT SET (100) 8.00 2.40
T1 John Olerud .15 .04
T2 Tino Martinez .25 .07
T3 Ken Griffey Jr. 2.00 .60
T4 Jeromy Burnitz .50 .15
T5 Ron Gant .10 .03
T6 Mike Benjamin .05 .02
T7 Steve Decker .05 .02
T8 Matt Williams .15 .04
T9 Rafael Novoa .05 .02
T10 Kevin Mitchell .05 .02
T11 Dave Justice .25 .07
T12 Leo Gomez .05 .02
T13 Chris Hoiles .05 .02
T14 Ben McDonald .05 .02
T15 David Segui .10 .03
T16 Anthony Telford .05 .02
T17 Mike Mussina 1.50 .45
T18 Roger Clemens 1.25 .35
T19 Wade Boggs .50 .15
T20 Tim Naehring .05 .02
T21 Joe Carter .10 .03
T22 Phil Plantier .05 .02
T23 Rob Dibble .05 .02
T24 Mo Vaughn .40 .12
T25 Lee Stevens .05 .02
T26 Chris Sabo .05 .02
T27 Mark Grace .25 .07
T28 Derrick May .05 .02
T29 Ryne Sandberg .50 .15
T30 Matt Stark .05 .02
T31 Bobby Thigpen .05 .02
T32 Frank Thomas .75 .23
T33 Don Mattingly 1.25 .35
T34 Eric Davis .10 .03
T35 Reggie Jefferson .05 .02
T36 Alex Cole .05 .02
T37 Mark Lewis .05 .02
T38 Tim Costo .05 .02
T39 Sandy Alomar Jr. .10 .03
T40 Travis Fryman .25 .07
T41 Cecil Fielder .10 .03
T42 Milt Cuyler .05 .02
T43 Andujar Cedeno .05 .02
T44 Danny Darwin .05 .02
T45 Randy Hennis .05 .02
T46 George Brett 1.00 .30
T47 Jeff Conine .15 .04
T48 Bo Jackson .25 .07
T49 Brian McRae .10 .03
T50 Brent Mayne .05 .02
T51 Eddie Murray .40 .12
T52 Ramon Martinez .05 .02
T53 Jim Neidlinger .05 .02
T54 Jim Poole .05 .02
T55 Tim McIntosh .05 .02
T56 Randy Veres .05 .02
T57 Kirby Puckett .40 .12
T58 Todd Ritchie .15 .04
T59 Rich Garces .05 .02
T60 Moises Alou .25 .07
T61 Delino DeShields .10 .03
T62 Oscar Azocar .05 .02
T63 Kevin Maas .05 .02
T64 Alan Mills .05 .02
T65 John Franco .10 .03
T66 Chris Jelic .05 .02
T67 Dave Magadan .05 .02
T68 Darryl Strawberry .10 .03
T69 Hensley Meulens .05 .02
T70 Juan Gonzalez .75 .23
T71 Reggie Harris .05 .02
T72 Rickey Henderson .50 .15
T73 Mark McGwire 2.00 .60
T74 Willie McGee .10 .03
T75 Todd Van Poppel .05 .02
T76 Bob Welch .05 .02
T77 Todd Van Poppel .05 .02
Don Peters
David Zancanaro
Kirk Dressendorfer
T78 Len Dykstra .10 .03
T79 Mickey Morandini .05 .02
T80 Wes Chamberlain .05 .02
T81 Barry Bonds 1.25 .35
T82 Doug Drabek .05 .02
T83 Randy Tomlin .05 .02
T84 Scott Chiamparino .05 .02
T85 Rafael Palmeiro .25 .07
T86 Nolan Ryan 2.50 .75
T87 Bobby Witt .05 .02
T88 Fred McGriff .25 .07

89 Dave Stieb	.10	.03
90 Ed Sprague	.10	.03
91 Vince Coleman	.05	.02
92 Rod Brewer	.05	.02
93 Bernard Gilkey	.05	.02
94 Roberto Alomar	.25	.07
95 Chuck Finley	.10	.03
96 Dale Murphy	.25	.07
97 Jose Rijo	.05	.02
98 Hal Morris	.05	.02
99 Friendly Foes	.10	.03
Darryl Strawberry		
Dwight Gooden		
Instructions on back		
NNO Todd Van Poppel	.10	.03
Dave Justice		
Ryne Sandberg		
Kevin Maas		

1991 Classic II

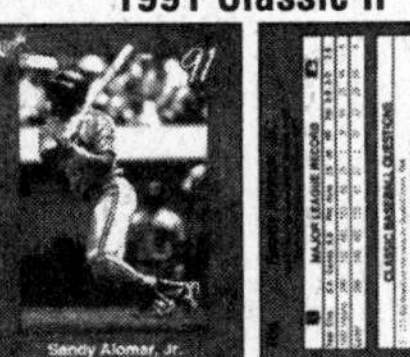

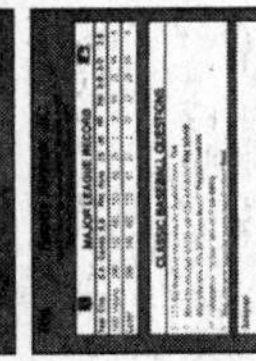

This second issue of the 1991 Classic baseball trivia game contains a small gameboard, accessories, 99 standard-size player cards with trivia questions on the backs, and one "4-in-1" micro player card. The fronts have glossy color action photos with cranberry red borders. The backs have biography, statistics, five trivia questions, and an autograph slot. A first year card of Ivan Rodriguez is featured within this set.

	Nm-Mt	Ex-Mt
COMP. FACT. SET (100)	8.00	2.40
T1 Ken Griffey Jr.	2.50	.75
T2 Wil Cordero	.05	.02
T3 Cal Ripken	3.00	.90
T4 D.J. Dozier	.05	.02
T5 Darrin Fletcher	.05	.02
T6 Glenn Davis	.05	.02
T7 Alex Fernandez	.05	.02
T8 Cory Snyder	.05	.02
T9 Tim Raines	.10	.03
T10 Greg Swindell	.05	.02
T11 Mark Lewis	.05	.02
T12 Rico Brogna	.05	.02
T13 Gary Sheffield	.40	.12
T14 Paul Molitor	.50	.15
T15 Kent Hrbek	.10	.03
T16 Scott Erickson	.10	.03
T17 Steve Sax	.05	.02
T18 Dennis Eckersley	.50	.15
T19 Jose Canseco	.40	.12
T20 Kirk Dressendorfer	.05	.02
T21 Ken Griffey Sr.	.10	.03
T22 Erik Hanson	.05	.02
T23 Dan Peltier	.05	.02
T24 John Olerud	.15	.04
T25 Eddie Zosky	.05	.02
T26 Steve Avery	.05	.02
T27 John Smoltz	.25	.07
T28 Frank Thomas	.60	.18
T29 Jerome Walton	.05	.02
T30 George Bell	.05	.02
T31 Jose Rijo	.05	.02
T32 Randy Myers	.10	.03
T33 Barry Larkin	.25	.07
T34 Eric Anthony	.05	.02
T35 Dave Hansen	.05	.02
T36 Eric Karros	.40	.12
T37 Jose Offerman	.05	.02
T38 Marquis Grissom	.10	.03
T39 Dwight Gooden	.10	.03
T40 Gregg Jefferies	.05	.02
T41 Pat Combs	.05	.02
T42 Todd Zeile	.10	.03
T43 Benito Santiago	.10	.03
T44 Dave Staton	.05	.02
T45 Tony Fernandez	.10	.03
T46 Fred McGriff	.15	.04
T47 Jeff Brantley	.05	.02
T48 Junior Felix	.05	.02
T49 Jack Morris	.10	.03
T50 Chris George	.05	.02
T51 Henry Rodriguez	.10	.03
T52 Paul Marak	.05	.02
T53 Ryan Klesko	.75	.23
T54 Darren Lewis	.05	.02
T55 Lance Dickson	.05	.02
T56 Anthony Young	.05	.02
T57 Willie Banks	.05	.02
T58 Mike Bordick	.15	.04
T59 Roger Salkeld	.05	.02
T60 Steve Karsay	.15	.04
T61 Bernie Williams	.25	.07
T62 Mickey Tettleton	.10	.03
T63 Dave Justice	.25	.07
T64 Steve Decker	.05	.02
T65 Roger Clemens	1.25	.35
T66 Phil Plantier	.05	.02
T67 Ryne Sandberg	.50	.15
T68 Sandy Alomar Jr.	.10	.03
T69 Cecil Fielder	.10	.03
T70 George Brett	1.25	.35
T71 Delino DeShields	.10	.03
T72 Dave Magadan	.05	.02
T73 Darryl Strawberry	.10	.03
T74 Juan Gonzalez	.75	.23
T75 Rickey Henderson	.60	.18
T76 Willie McGee	.10	.03
T77 Todd Van Poppel	.05	.02
T78 Barry Bonds	1.50	.45
T79 Doug Drabek	.05	.02
T80 Nolan Ryan	1.25	.35
300 Game Winner		
T81 Roberto Alomar	.25	.07
T82 Ivan Rodriguez	2.50	.75
T83 Dan Opperman	.05	.02
T84 Jeff Bagwell	2.00	.60
T85 Braulio Castillo	.05	.02
T86 Doug Simons	.05	.02
T87 Wade Taylor	.05	.02
T88 Gary Scott	.05	.02
T89 Dave Stewart	.10	.03
T90 Mike Simms	.05	.02
T91 Luis Gonzalez	1.00	.30
T92 Bobby Bonilla	.10	.03
T93 Tony Gwynn	1.00	.30
T94 Will Clark	.40	.12
T95 Rich Rowland	.05	.02
T96 Alan Trammell	.15	.04
T97 Nolan Ryan	.75	.23
Roger Clemens		
T98 Joe Carter	.10	.03
T99 Jack Clark	.10	.03
T100 Steve Decker	.05	.02
NNO John Olerud	.50	.15
Dwight Gooden		
Jose Canseco		
Darryl Strawberry		

1991 Classic III

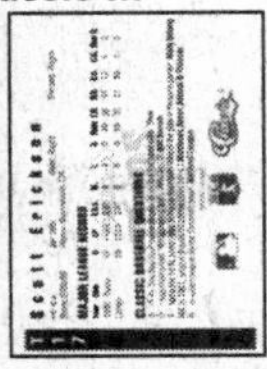

The third issue of the 1991 Classic baseball trivia game contains a small gameboard, accessories, 99 standard-size player cards with trivia questions on the backs, and one "4-in-1" micro player card. The card fronts are glossy color action photos with grayish-green borders. The horizontal backs feature biography, statistics, and five trivia questions. With few exceptions, the cards are arranged in alphabetical order. First year cards of Pedro Martinez and Ivan Rodriguez are featured within this set.

	Nm-Mt	Ex-Mt
COMP.FACT.SET (100)	5.00	1.50
T1 Jim Abbott	.15	.04
T2 Craig Biggio	.15	.04
T3 Wade Boggs	.15	.04
T4 Bobby Bonilla	.10	.03
T5 Ivan Calderon	.05	.02
T6 Jose Canseco	.25	.07
T7 Andy Benes	.05	.02
T8 Wes Chamberlain	.05	.02
T9 Will Clark	.25	.07
T10 Royce Clayton	.05	.02
T11 Gerald Alexander	.05	.02
T12 Chili Davis	.10	.03
T13 Eric Davis	.10	.03
T14 Andre Dawson	.10	.03
T15 Rob Dibble	.10	.03
T16 Chris Donnels	.05	.02
T17 Scott Erickson	.05	.02
T18 Monty Fariss	.05	.02
T19 Ruben Amaro Jr.	.05	.02
T20 Chuck Finley	.10	.03
T21 Carlton Fisk	.15	.04
T22 Carlos Baerga	.05	.02
T23 Ron Gant	.10	.03
T24 Dave Justice	.10	.03
and Ron Gant		
T25 Mike Gardiner	.05	.02
T26 Tom Glavine	.15	.04
T27 Joe Grahe	.05	.02
T28 Derek Bell	.10	.03
T29 Mike Greenwell	.05	.02
T30 Ken Griffey Jr.	.50	.15
T31 Leo Gomez	.05	.02
T32 Tom Goodwin	.05	.02
T33 Tony Gwynn	.30	.09
T34 Mel Hall	.05	.02
T35 Brian Harper	.05	.02
T36 Dave Henderson	.05	.02
T37 Albert Belle	.10	.03
T38 Orel Hershiser	.10	.03
T39 Brian Hunter	.10	.03
T40 Howard Johnson	.05	.02
T41 Felix Jose	.05	.02
T42 Wally Joyner	.10	.03
T43 Jeff Juden	.05	.02
T44 Pat Kelly	.05	.02
T45 Jimmy Key	.10	.03
T46 Chuck Knoblauch	.10	.03
T47 John Kruk	.10	.03
T48 Ray Lankford	.05	.02
T49 Ced Landrum	.05	.02
T50 Scott Livingstone	.05	.02
T51 Kevin Maas	.05	.02
T52 Greg Maddux	.40	.12
T53 Dennis Martinez	.10	.03
T54 Edgar Martinez	.15	.04
T55 Pedro Martinez	3.00	.90
T56 Don Mattingly	.60	.18
T57 Orlando Merced	.05	.02
T58 Keith Mitchell	.05	.02
T59 Kevin Mitchell	.05	.02
T60 Paul Molitor	.15	.04
T61 Jack Morris	.10	.03
T62 Hal Morris	.05	.02
T63 Kevin Morton	.05	.02
T64 Pedro Munoz	.05	.02
T65 Eddie Murray	.25	.07
T66 Jack McDowell	.05	.02
T67 Jeff McNeely	.05	.02
T68 Brian McRae	.10	.03
T69 Kevin McReynolds	.05	.02
T70 Gregg Olson	.05	.02
T71 Rafael Palmeiro	.15	.04
T72 Dean Palmer	.10	.03
T73 Tony Phillips	.05	.02
T74 Kirby Puckett	.25	.07
T75 Carlos Quintana	.05	.02
T76 Pat Rice	.05	.02
T77 Cal Ripken	.75	.23
T78 Ivan Rodriguez	2.00	.60
T79 Nolan Ryan	1.00	.30
T80 Bret Saberhagen	.10	.03
T81 Tim Salmon	1.00	.30
T82 Juan Samuel	.05	.02
T83 Ruben Sierra	.05	.02
T84 Heathcliff Slocumb	.10	.03
T85 Joe Slusarski	.05	.02
T86 John Smiley	.05	.02
T87 Dave Smith	.05	.02
T88 Ed Sprague	.05	.02
T89 Todd Stottlemyre	.05	.02
T90 Mike Timlin	.15	.04
T91 Greg Vaughn	.05	.02
T92 Frank Viola	.10	.03
T93 Chico Walker	.05	.02
T94 Devon White	.10	.03
T95 Matt Williams	.10	.03
T96 Rick Wilkins	.05	.02
T97 Bernie Williams	.25	.07
T98 Nolan Ryan	.50	.15
Goose Gossage		
T99 Gerald Williams	.10	.03
NNO Bobby Bonilla	.25	.07
Will Clark		
Cal Ripken		
Scott Erickson		

1992 Classic Game

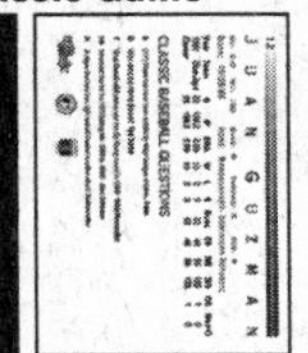

The 1992 Classic Baseball Collector's Edition game contains 200 standard-size cards. The cards were issued in two boxes labeled "Trivia Cards A" and "Trivia Cards B." The game also included an official Major League Action Spinner, eight stand-up baseball hero player pieces, an action scoreboard, a hand-illustrated game board, and a collectible book featuring tips from a new group of baseball legends. According to Classic, production has been limited to 125,000 games. The fronts display glossy color action photos bordered in dark purple. The Classic logo and the year "1992" appear in the top border, while the player's name is given in white lettering in the bottom border. The horizontally oriented backs present biography, statistics (1991 and career), and five baseball trivia questions.

	Nm-Mt	Ex-Mt
COMP. FACT. SET (200)	25.00	7.50
1 Chuck Finley	.20	.06
2 Craig Biggio	.40	.12
3 Luis Gonzalez	.50	.15
4 Pete Harnisch	.10	.03
5 Jeff Juden	.10	.03
6 Harold Baines	.20	.06
7 Kirk Dressendorfer	.10	.03
8 Dennis Eckersley	.40	.12
9 Dave Henderson	.10	.03
10 Dave Stewart	.20	.06
11 Joe Carter	.20	.06
12 Juan Guzman	.10	.03
13 Dave Stieb	.10	.03
14 Todd Stottlemyre	.10	.03
15 Ron Gant	.20	.06
16 Brian Hunter	.10	.03
17 Dave Justice	.40	.12
18 John Smoltz	.20	.06
19 Mike Stanton	.20	.06
20 Chris George	.10	.03
21 Paul Molitor	.50	.15
22 Omar Olivares	.10	.03
23 Lee Smith	.20	.06
24 Ozzie Smith	1.25	.35
25 Todd Zeile	.20	.06
26 George Bell	.20	.06
27 Andre Dawson	.40	.12
28 Shawon Dunston	.10	.03
29 Mark Grace	.40	.12
30 Greg Maddux	2.00	.60
31 Dave Smith	.10	.03
32 Brett Butler	.20	.06
33 Orel Hershiser	.20	.06
34 Eric Karros	.30	.09
35 Ramon Martinez	.10	.03
36 Jose Offerman	.10	.03
37 Juan Samuel	.10	.03
38 Delino DeShields	.20	.06
39 Marquis Grissom	.20	.06
40 Tim Wallach	.10	.03
41 Eric Gunderson	.10	.03
42 Willie McGee	.20	.06
43 Dave Righetti	.10	.03
44 Robby Thompson	.10	.03
45 Matt Williams	.30	.09
46 Sandy Alomar Jr.	.20	.06
47 Reggie Jefferson	.10	.03
48 Mark Lewis	.10	.03
49 Robin Ventura	.40	.12
50 Tino Martinez	.40	.12
51 Roberto Kelly	.10	.03
52 Vince Coleman	.10	.03
53 Dwight Gooden	.20	.06
54 Todd Hundley	.20	.06
55 Kevin Maas	.10	.03
56 Wade Taylor	.10	.03
57 Bryan Harvey	.10	.03
58 Leo Gomez	.10	.03
59 Ben McDonald	.10	.03
60 Ricky Bones	.10	.03
61 Tony Gwynn	1.50	.45
62 Benito Santiago	.20	.06
63 Wes Chamberlain	.10	.03
64 Tommy Greene	.10	.03
65 Dale Murphy	.40	.12
66 Steve Buechele	.10	.03
67 Doug Drabek	.10	.03
68 Joe Grahe	.10	.03
69 Rafael Palmeiro	.40	.12
70 Wade Boggs	.75	.23
71 Ellis Burks	.20	.06
72 Mike Greenwell	.10	.03
73 Mo Vaughn	.30	.09
74 Derek Bell	.10	.03
75 Rob Dibble	.10	.03
76 Barry Larkin	.40	.12
77 Jose Rijo	.10	.03
78 Doug Henry	.10	.03
79 Chris Sabo	.10	.03
80 Pedro Guerrero	.10	.03
81 George Brett	1.50	.45
82 Tom Gordon	.10	.03
83 Mark Gubicza	.10	.03
84 Mark Whiten	.10	.03
85 Brian McRae	.10	.03
86 Danny Jackson	.10	.03
87 Milt Cuyler	.10	.03
88 Travis Fryman	.20	.06
89 Mickey Tettleton	.10	.03
90 Alan Trammell	.40	.12
91 Lou Whitaker	.20	.06
92 Chili Davis	.20	.06
93 Scott Erickson	.20	.06
94 Kent Hrbek	.20	.06
95 Alex Fernandez	.10	.03
96 Carlton Fisk	.75	.23
97 Ramon Garcia	.10	.03
98 Ozzie Guillen	.10	.03
99 Tim Raines	.20	.06
100 Bobby Thigpen	.10	.03
101 Kirby Puckett	.75	.23
102 Bernie Williams	.75	.23
103 Dave Hansen	.10	.03
104 Kevin Tapani	.10	.03
105 Don Mattingly	1.50	.45
106 Frank Thomas	.75	.23
107 Monty Fariss	.10	.03
108 Bo Jackson	.20	.06
109 Jim Abbott	.20	.06
110 Jose Canseco	.40	.12
111 Phil Plantier	.10	.03
112 Brian Williams	.10	.03
113 Mark Langston	.10	.03
114 Wilson Alvarez	.40	.12
115 Roberto Hernandez	.40	.12
116 Darryl Kile	.20	.06
117 Ryan Bowen	.10	.03
118 Rickey Henderson	1.00	.30
119 Mark McGwire	2.50	.75
120 Devon White	.10	.03
121 Roberto Alomar	.40	.12
122 Kelly Gruber	.10	.03
123 Eddie Zosky	.10	.03
124 Tom Glavine	.30	.09
125 Kal Daniels	.10	.03
126 Cal Eldred	.10	.03
127 Deion Sanders	.50	.15
128 Robin Yount	.50	.15
129 Cecil Fielder	.20	.06
130 Ray Lankford	.20	.06
131 Ryne Sandberg	.75	.23
132 Darryl Strawberry	.20	.06
133 Chris Haney	.10	.03
134 Dennis Martinez	.20	.06
135 Bryan Hickerson	.10	.03
136 Will Clark	.75	.23
137 Hal Morris	.10	.03
138 Charles Nagy	.10	.03
139 Jim Thome	1.00	.30
140 Albert Belle	.30	.09
141 Reggie Sanders	.10	.03
142 Scott Cooper	.10	.03
143 David Cone	.40	.12
144 Anthony Young	.10	.03
145 Howard Johnson	.10	.03
146 Arthur Rhodes	.10	.03
147 Scott Aldred	.10	.03
148 Mike Mussina	1.25	.35
149 Fred McGriff	.30	.09
150 Andy Benes	.10	.03
151 Ruben Sierra	.20	.06
152 Len Dykstra	.20	.06
153 Andy Van Slyke	.20	.06
154 Orlando Merced	.10	.03
155 Barry Bonds	1.50	.45
156 John Smiley	.10	.03
157 Julio Franco	.20	.06
158 Juan Gonzalez	.40	.12
159 Ivan Rodriguez	1.50	.45
160 Willie Banks	.10	.03
161 Eric Davis	.30	.09
162 Eddie Murray	.40	.12
163 Dave Fleming	.10	.03
164 Wally Joyner	.10	.03
165 Kevin Mitchell	.20	.06
166 Eddie Taubensee	.10	.03
167 Danny Tartabull	.10	.03
168 Ken Hill	.10	.03
169 Willie Randolph	.20	.06
170 Kevin McReynolds	.10	.03
171 Gregg Jefferies	.10	.03
172 Patrick Lennon	.10	.03
173 Luis Mercedes	.10	.03
174 Glenn Davis	.10	.03
175 Bret Saberhagen	.20	.06
176 Bobby Bonilla	.10	.03
177 Kenny Lofton	.40	.12
178 Jose Lind	.10	.03
179 Royce Clayton	.10	.03
180 Scott Scudder	.10	.03
181 Chuck Knoblauch	.40	.12
182 Terry Pendleton	.10	.03
183 Nolan Ryan	3.00	.90
184 Rob Maurer	.10	.03
185 Brian Bohanon	.10	.03
186 Ken Griffey Jr.	2.50	.75
187 Jeff Bagwell	1.50	.45
188 Steve Avery	.10	.03
189 Roger Clemens	1.50	.45
190 Cal Ripken	3.00	.90
191 Kim Batiste	.10	.03
192 Bip Roberts	.10	.03
193 Greg Swindell	.10	.03
194 Dave Winfield	.40	.12
195 Steve Sax	.10	.03
196 Frank Viola	.10	.03
197 Mo Sanford	.10	.03
198 Kyle Abbott	.10	.03
199 Jack Morris	.20	.06
200 Andy Ashby	.10	.03

1992 Classic I

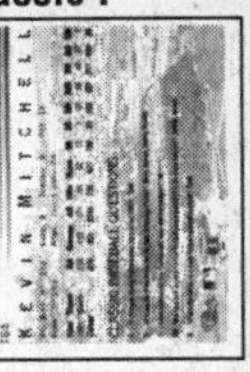

The first issue of the 1992 Classic baseball trivia game contains a small gameboard, accessories, 99 standard-size player cards with trivia questions on the backs, one "4-in-1" micro player card, and four micro player pieces. The cards have on the fronts glossy color action photos bordered in white. A red, gray, and purple stripe with the year "1992" traverses the top of the card. In a horizontal format, the backs feature biography, statistics, and five trivia questions, printed on a ghosted image of the 26 major league city skylines. The cards are numbered on the back and basically arranged in alphabetical order.

	Nm-Mt	Ex-Mt
COMP. FACT. SET (100)	8.00	2.40
T1 Jim Abbott	.10	.03
T2 Kyle Abbott	.05	.02
T3 Scott Aldred	.05	.02
T4 Roberto Alomar	.30	.09
T5 Wilson Alvarez	.05	.02
T6 Andy Ashby	.05	.02
T7 Steve Avery	.05	.02
T8 Jeff Bagwell	1.00	.30
T9 Bret Barberie	.05	.02
T10 Kim Batiste	.05	.02
T11 Derek Bell	.05	.02
T12 Jay Bell	.05	.02
T13 Albert Belle	.10	.03
T14 Andy Benes	.05	.02
T15 Sean Berry	.05	.02
T16 Barry Bonds	1.00	.30
T17 Ryan Bowen	.05	.02
T18 Alejandro Pena	.05	.02
Mark Wohlers		
Kent Mercker		
T19 Scott Brosius	.30	.09
T20 Jay Buhner	.10	.03
T21 David Burba	.05	.02
T22 Jose Canseco	.40	.12
T23 Andujar Cedeno	.05	.02
T24 Will Clark	.50	.15
T25 Royce Clayton	.05	.02
T26 Roger Clemens	1.00	.30
T27 David Cone	.30	.09
T28 Scott Cooper	.05	.02
T29 Chris Cron	.05	.02
T30 Len Dykstra	.10	.03
T31 Cal Eldred	.05	.02
T32 Hector Fajardo	.05	.02
T33 Cecil Fielder	.10	.03
T34 Dave Fleming	.05	.02
T35 Steve Foster	.05	.02
T36 Julio Franco	.10	.03
T37 Carlos Garcia	.05	.02
T38 Tom Glavine	.20	.06
T39 Tom Goodwin	.05	.02
T40 Ken Griffey Jr.	1.50	.45
T41 Chris Haney	.05	.02
T42 Bryan Harvey	.05	.02
T43 Rickey Henderson 939	.75	.23
T44 Carlos Hernandez	.05	.02
T45 Roberto Hernandez	.30	.09
T46 Brook Jacoby	.05	.02
T47 Howard Johnson	.05	.02
T48 Pat Kelly	.05	.02
T49 Darryl Kile	.10	.03
T50 Chuck Knoblauch	.30	.09
T51 Ray Lankford	.30	.09
With Ozzie Smith		
T52 Mark Leiter	.05	.02
T53 Darren Lewis	.05	.02
T54 Scott Livingstone	.05	.02
T55 Shane Mack	.05	.02
T56 Chito Martinez	.05	.02
T57 Dennis Martinez	.10	.03
The Perfect Game		
T58 Don Mattingly	1.00	.30
T59 Paul McClellan	.05	.02
T60 Chuck McElroy	.05	.02
T61 Fred McGriff	.20	.06
T62 Orlando Merced	.05	.02
T63 Luis Mercedes	.05	.02
T64 Kevin Mitchell	.10	.03
T65 Hal Morris	.05	.02
T66 Jack Morris	.10	.03
T67 Mike Mussina	.75	.23
T68 Denny Neagle	.10	.03
T69 Tom Pagnozzi	.05	.02
T70 Terry Pendleton	.05	.02
T71 Phil Plantier	.05	.02
T72 Kirby Puckett	.50	.15
T73 Carlos Quintana	.05	.02
T74 Willie Randolph	.10	.03
T75 Arthur Rhodes	.05	.02
T76 Cal Ripken	2.00	.60
T77 Ivan Rodriguez	1.00	.30
T78 Nolan Ryan	2.00	.60
T79 Ryne Sandberg	.60	.18
T80 Deion Sanders	.50	.15
Deion Drops In		
T81 Reggie Sanders	.10	.03
T82 Mo Sanford	.05	.02
T83 Terry Shumpert	.05	.02
T84 Tim Spehr	.05	.02
T85 Lee Stevens	.05	.02
T86 Darryl Strawberry	.10	.03
T87 Kevin Tapani	.05	.02
T88 Danny Tartabull	.05	.02
T89 Frank Thomas	.60	.18
T90 Jim Thome	.75	.23
T91 Todd Van Poppel	.05	.02
T92 Andy Van Slyke	.05	.02
T93 John Wehner	.05	.02
T94 John Wetteland	.10	.03
T95 Devon White	.05	.02

T96 Brian Williams .05 .02
T97 Mark Wohlers .05 .02
T98 Robin Yount .50 .15
T99 Eddie Zosky .05 .02
NNO0 Barry Bonds 1.00 .30
Roger Clemens
Steve Avery
Nolan Ryan

1992 Classic II

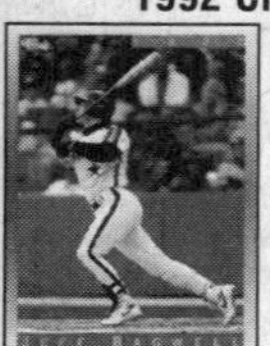

The 1992 Series II baseball trivia board game features 99 standard-size new player trivia standard-size cards, one "4-in-1" micro player card, a game board, and a spinner. The cards display color action player photos on the fronts. The horizontal backs have a biography, statistics (1991 and career), five trivia questions, and a color drawing of the team's uniform. According to Classic, the production run was 175,000 games.

Nm-Mt Ex-Mt
COMP. FACT. SET (100) 10.00 3.00
T1 Jim Abbott .10 .03
T2 Jeff Bagwell 1.00 .30
T3 Jose Canseco .40 .12
T4 Julio Valera .05 .02
T5 Scott Brosius .30 .09
T6 Mark Langston .05 .02
T7 Andy Stankiewicz .05 .02
T8 Gary DiSarcina .05 .02
T9 Pete Harnisch .05 .02
T10 Mark McGwire 1.50 .45
T11 Ricky Bones .05 .02
T12 Steve Avery .05 .02
T13 Deion Sanders .40 .12
T14 Mike Mussina .50 .15
T15 Dave Justice .20 .06
T16 Pat Hentgen .30 .09
T17 Tom Glavine .30 .09
T18 Juan Guzman .05 .02
T19 Ron Gant .10 .03
T20 Kelly Gruber .05 .02
T21 Eric Karros .30 .09
T22 Derrick May .05 .02
T23 Dave Hansen .05 .02
T24 Andre Dawson .20 .06
T25 Eric Davis .10 .03
T26 Ozzie Smith .75 .23
T27 Sammy Sosa 1.25 .35
T28 Lee Smith .10 .03
T29 Ryne Sandberg .50 .15
T30 Robin Yount .40 .12
T31 Matt Williams .20 .06
T32 John Vander Wal .05 .02
T33 Bill Swift .05 .02
T34 Delino DeShields .05 .02
T35 Royce Clayton .05 .02
T36 Moises Alou .10 .03
T37 Will Clark .50 .15
T38 Darryl Strawberry .10 .03
T39 Larry Walker .20 .06
T40 Ramon Martinez .05 .02
T41 Howard Johnson .05 .02
T42 Tino Martinez .30 .09
T43 Dwight Gooden .10 .03
T44 Ken Griffey Jr. 1.50 .45
T45 David Cone .30 .09
T46 Kenny Lofton .30 .09
T47 Bobby Bonilla .10 .03
T48 Carlos Baerga .05 .02
T49 Don Mattingly 1.00 .30
T50 Sandy Alomar Jr. .10 .03
T51 Lenny Dykstra .10 .03
T52 Tony Gwynn 1.00 .30
T53 Felix Jose .05 .02
T54 Rick Sutcliffe .05 .02
T55 Wes Chamberlain .05 .02
T56 Cal Ripken 2.00 .60
T57 Kyle Abbott .05 .02
T58 Leo Gomez .05 .02
T59 Gary Sheffield .30 .09
T60 Anthony Young .05 .02
T61 Roger Clemens 1.00 .30
T62 Rafael Palmeiro .30 .09
T63 Wade Boggs .50 .15
T64 Andy Van Slyke .10 .03
T65 Ruben Sierra .05 .02
T66 Denny Neagle .10 .03
T67 Nolan Ryan 2.00 .60
T68 Doug Drabek .05 .02
T69 Ivan Rodriguez 1.25 .35
T70 Barry Bonds 1.00 .30
T71 Chuck Knoblauch .30 .09
T72 Reggie Sanders .10 .03
T73 Cecil Fielder .10 .03
T74 Barry Larkin .30 .09
T75 Scott Aldred .05 .02
T76 Rob Dibble .05 .02
T77 Brian McRae .05 .02
T78 Tim Belcher .05 .02
T79 George Brett 1.00 .30
T80 Frank Viola .05 .02
T81 Roberto Kelly .05 .02
T82 Jack McDowell .05 .02
T83 Mel Hall .05 .02
T84 Esteban Beltre .05 .02
T85 Robin Ventura .30 .09
T86 George Bell .05 .02
T87 Frank Thomas .60 .18
T88 John Smiley .05 .02
T89 Bobby Thigpen .05 .02
T90 Kirby Puckett .50 .15
T91 Kevin Mitchell .10 .03
T92 Peter Hoy .05 .02
T93 Russ Springer .05 .02
T94 Donovan Osborne .05 .02
T95 Dave Silvestri .05 .02

T96 Chad Curtis .10 .03
T97 Pat Mahomes .05 .02
T98 Danny Tartabull .05 .02
T99 John Doherty .05 .02
NNO0 Ryne Sandberg .50 .15
Mike Mussina
Reggie Sanders
Jose Canseco

1993 Classic Game

The 1993 Classic Game contains 99 trivia standard-size cards, a micro player card, four micro piece stands, a color game board, and a reusable plastic carrying case. As a special bonus, Classic included highlight trivia cards of George Brett and Robin Yount commemorating their 3,000 hits in the 1992 season. The cards feature color action player photos with navy blue borders.

Nm-Mt Ex-Mt
COMP. FACT. SET (100) 12.00 3.60
1 Jim Abbott .10 .03
2 Roberto Alomar .50 .15
3 Moises Alou .10 .03
4 Brady Anderson .10 .03
5 Eric Anthony .05 .02
6 Alex Arias .05 .02
7 Pedro Astacio .05 .02
8 Steve Avery .05 .02
9 Carlos Baerga .05 .02
10 Jeff Bagwell .75 .23
11 George Bell .05 .02
12 Albert Belle .10 .03
13 Craig Biggio .30 .09
14 Barry Bonds 1.25 .35
15 Bobby Bonilla .10 .03
16 Mike Bordick .05 .02
17 George Brett 1.25 .35
3,000th Hit
18 Jose Canseco .50 .15
19 Joe Carter .10 .03
20 Royce Clayton .05 .02
21 Roger Clemens 1.25 .35
22 Greg Colbrunn .05 .02
23 David Cone .30 .09
24 Darren Daulton .10 .03
25 Delino DeShields .05 .02
26 Rob Dibble .05 .02
27 Dennis Eckersley .20 .06
28 Cal Eldred .05 .02
29 Scott Erickson .10 .03
30 Junior Felix .05 .02
31 Tony Fernandez .05 .02
32 Cecil Fielder .10 .03
33 Steve Finley .10 .03
34 Dave Fleming .05 .02
35 Travis Fryman .05 .02
36 Tom Glavine .30 .09
37 Juan Gonzalez .60 .18
38 Ken Griffey Jr. 1.25 .35
39 Marquis Grissom .10 .03
40 Juan Guzman .05 .02
41 Tony Gwynn 1.25 .35
42 Rickey Henderson 1.00 .30
43 Felix Jose .05 .02
44 Wally Joyner .10 .03
45 David Justice .30 .09
46 Eric Karros .20 .06
47 Roberto Kelly .05 .02
48 Ryan Klesko .10 .03
49 Chuck Knoblauch .10 .03
50 John Kruk .10 .03
51 Ray Lankford .10 .03
52 Barry Larkin .30 .09
53 Pat Listach .05 .02
54 Kenny Lofton .30 .09
55 Shane Mack .05 .02
56 Greg Maddux 1.50 .45
57 Dave Magadan .05 .02
58 Edgar Martinez .20 .06
59 Don Mattingly 1.25 .35
60 Ben McDonald .05 .02
61 Jack McDowell .05 .02
62 Fred McGriff .20 .06
63 Mark McGwire 2.00 .60
64 Kevin McReynolds .05 .02
65 Sam Militello .05 .02
66 Paul Molitor .50 .15
67 Jeff Montgomery .10 .03
68 Jack Morris .10 .03
69 Eddie Murray .50 .15
70 Mike Mussina .75 .23
71 Otis Nixon .05 .02
72 Donovan Osborne .05 .02
73 Terry Pendleton .05 .02
74 Mike Piazza 2.50 .75
75 Kirby Puckett .50 .15
76 Cal Ripken Jr. 2.50 .75
77 Bip Roberts .05 .02
78 Ivan Rodriguez .75 .23
79 Nolan Ryan 2.50 .75
80 Ryne Sandberg 1.00 .30
81 Deion Sanders .30 .09
82 Reggie Sanders .10 .03
83 Frank Seminara .05 .02
84 Gary Sheffield .40 .12
85 Ruben Sierra .10 .03
86 John Smiley .05 .02
87 Lee Smith .10 .03
88 Ozzie Smith .75 .23
89 John Smoltz .20 .06
90 Danny Tartabull .05 .02
91 Bob Tewksbury .05 .02
92 Frank Thomas .75 .23
93 Andy Van Slyke .05 .02
94 Mo Vaughn .10 .03
95 Robin Ventura .10 .03

96 Tim Wakefield .10 .03
97 Larry Walker .10 .03
98 Dave Winfield .50 .15
99 Robin Yount 3,000 .50 .15
NNO Mark McGwire 2.00 .60
Sam Militello
Ryan Klesko
Greg Maddux

2004 Classic Clippings

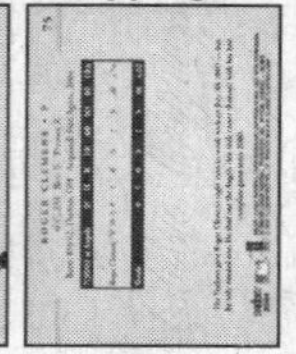

This 110-card set was released in May, 2004. This set was issued in five card packs which came 18 packs to a box and four boxes to a case. Cards number 1 through 75 featured veterans while cards 76 through 100 featured rookies and prospects while cards 101 through 110 featured players making their major league debut at the start of the 2004 season. Cards numbered 76 through 100 were inserted at a rate of one in 18 hobby and one in 108 retail packs and cards numbered 101-110 were random inserts in packs. All cards numbered 76 through 110 were printed to a stated print run of 500 serial numbered sets.

Nm-Mt Ex-Mt
COMP.SET w/o SP's (75) 15.00 4.50
COMMON CARD (1-75) .30 .09
COMMON CARD (76-110) 4.00 1.20
COMMON RC (76-110) 4.00 1.20
PROOFS RANDOM INSERTS IN PACKS
OVERALL PARALLEL ODDS 1:18 H, 1:120 R
PROOFS PRINT RUN 1 SET PER COLOR
BLACK-CYAN-MAGENTA-YELLOW ISSUED
NO PROOFS PRICING DUE TO SCARCITY
1 Juan Pierre .30 .09
2 Derek Jeter 1.50 .45
3 Jose Reyes .30 .09
4 Eric Chavez .30 .09
5 Alex Rodriguez Yanks 1.25 .35
6 Mark Prior .75 .23
7 Carlos Beltran .50 .15
8 Ichiro Suzuki 1.25 .35
9 Shawn Green .30 .09
10 Richie Sexson .30 .09
11 Andruw Jones .30 .09
12 Geoff Jenkins .30 .09
13 Luis Gonzalez .30 .09
14 Garret Anderson .30 .09
15 Adam Dunn .50 .15
16 Nomar Garciaparra 1.25 .35
17 Albert Pujols 1.50 .45
18 Jeff Bagwell .50 .15
19 Rocco Baldelli .30 .09
20 Preston Wilson .30 .09
21 Gary Sheffield .30 .09
22 Magglio Ordonez .30 .09
23 Kerry Wood .75 .23
24 Manny Ramirez .50 .15
25 Randy Johnson .75 .23
26 Ken Griffey Jr. 1.25 .35
27 Rafael Palmeiro .50 .15
28 Vernon Wells .30 .09
29 Mike Piazza 1.25 .35
30 Hank Blalock .30 .09
31 Miguel Cabrera .50 .15
32 Jason Giambi .30 .09
33 Troy Glaus .30 .09
34 Angel Berroa .30 .09
35 Greg Maddux 1.25 .35
36 Lance Berkman .30 .09
37 Austin Kearns .30 .09
38 Hideo Nomo .75 .23
39 Sammy Sosa 1.25 .35
40 Jose Vidro .30 .09
41 Curt Schilling .75 .23
42 Melvin Mora .30 .09
43 Scott Podsednik .30 .09
44 Dontrelle Willis .30 .09
45 Roy Halladay .30 .09
46 Hideki Matsui 1.25 .35
47 Tom Glavine .50 .15
48 Torii Hunter .30 .09
49 Chipper Jones .75 .23
50 Barry Zito .30 .09
51 Vladimir Guerrero .75 .23
52 Jim Thome .75 .23
53 Shannon Stewart .30 .09
54 Miguel Tejada .30 .09
55 Roy Oswalt .30 .09
56 Jason Kendall .30 .09
57 Brian Giles .30 .09
58 Jason Schmidt .30 .09
59 Pedro Martinez .75 .23
60 Bret Boone .30 .09
61 Josh Beckett .30 .09
62 Scott Rolen .75 .23
63 Aubrey Huff .30 .09
64 Pat Burrell .30 .09
65 Mark Teixeira .30 .09
66 Alfonso Soriano .50 .15
67 Carlos Delgado .30 .09
68 Ivan Rodriguez .75 .23
69 Brandon Webb .30 .09
70 Eric Gagne .75 .23
71 Frank Thomas .75 .23
72 Jody Gerut .30 .09
73 Todd Helton .50 .15
74 Andy Pettitte .50 .15
75 Roger Clemens 1.50 .45
76 Rickie Weeks ROO 4.00 1.20
77 Chien-Ming Wang ROO 4.00 1.20
78 Edwin Jackson ROO 4.00 1.20
79 Dallas McPherson ROO 5.00 1.50
80 John Gall ROO RC 5.00 1.50
81 Ryan Wagner ROO 4.00 1.20
82 Clint Barmes ROO 4.00 1.20
83 Khalil Greene ROO 5.00 1.50
84 Chin-Hui Tsao ROO 4.00 1.20
85 Alexis Rios ROO 4.00 1.20
86 Merkin Valdez ROO RC 5.00 1.50
87 Aarom Baldiris ROO RC 5.00 1.50
88 Onil Joseph ROO RC 4.00 1.20
89 Ruddy Yan ROO 4.00 1.20
90 Chad Bentz ROO RC 4.00 1.20
91 Shawn Hill ROO RC 4.00 1.20
92 Delmon Young ROO 5.00 1.50
93 Hector Gimenez ROO RC 4.00 1.20
94 William Bergolla ROO RC 4.00 1.20
95 Ronny Cedeno ROO RC 4.00 1.20
96 Angel Chavez ROO RC 4.00 1.20
97 Justin Leone ROO RC 5.00 1.50
98 Ivan Ochoa ROO RC 4.00 1.20
99 Ian Snell ROO RC 5.00 1.50
100 Rich Harden ROO 4.00 1.20
101 Joe Mauer DEB 5.00 1.50
102 Akinori Otsuka DEB RC 4.00 1.20
103 Bobby Crosby DEB 5.00 1.50
104 Garrett Atkins DEB 4.00 1.20
105 Dan Haren DEB 4.00 1.20
106 Koyie Hill DEB 4.00 1.20
107 Kaz Matsui DEB RC 10.00 3.00
108 Adam LaRoche DEB 4.00 1.20
109 Terrmel Sledge DEB 4.00 1.20
110 Shingo Takatsu DEB RC 6.00 1.80

2004 Classic Clippings First Edition

Nm-Mt Ex-Mt
*1ST ED 1-75: 3X TO 8X BASIC
*1ST ED 76-110: .4X TO 1X BASIC
*1ST ED 76-110: .4X TO 1X BASIC RC
OVERALL PARALLEL ODDS 1:18 H, 1:120 R
STATED PRINT RUN 150 SERIAL #'d SETS
107 Kaz Matsui DEB 10.00 3.00

2004 Classic Clippings All-Star Lineup Swatch

Nm-Mt Ex-Mt
STATED ODDS 1:28 RETAIL
AJ Gary Sheffield 5.00 1.50
Andruw Jones Jsy
Javy Lopez
AP Gary Sheffield 10.00 3.00
Albert Pujols Jsy
Preston Wilson
AR Nomar Garciaparra 10.00 3.00
Alex Rodriguez Jsy
Jason Giambi
AS Carlos Delgado 8.00 2.40
Alfonso Soriano Jsy
Troy Glaus
BZ Roger Clemens 5.00 1.50
Barry Zito Jsy
Roy Halladay
CD Vernon Wells 5.00 1.50
Carlos Delgado Jsy
Roy Halladay
DW Luis Castillo 5.00 1.50
Dontrelle Willis Jsy
Mike Lowell
HB Magglio Ordonez 5.00 1.50
Hank Blalock Jsy
Troy Glaus
HM Ichiro Suzuki 10.00 3.00
Hideki Matsui Base
Garret Anderson
MP Kerry Wood 8.00 2.40
Mark Prior Jsy
Dontrelle Willis
NG Alex Rodriguez 10.00 3.00
Nomar Garciaparra Jsy
Manny Ramirez
RC Alfonso Soriano 10.00 3.00
Roger Clemens Jsy
Jason Giambi
RS Todd Helton 5.00 1.50
Richie Sexson Jsy
Albert Pujols
SR Edgar Renteria 8.00 2.40
Scott Rolen Jsy
Albert Pujols
TH Luis Castillo 8.00 2.40
Todd Helton Jsy
Scott Rolen

2004 Classic Clippings All-Star Lineup Triple Swatch

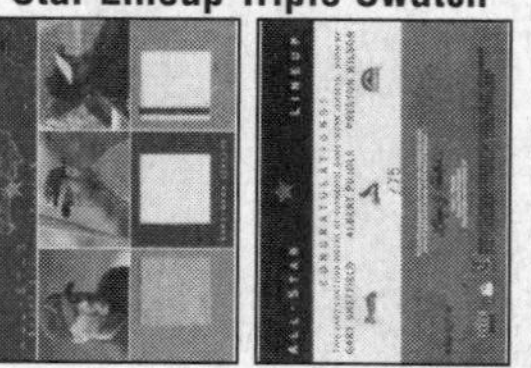

Nm-Mt Ex-Mt
AST PATCH PRINT RUN 25 SERIAL #'d SETS
AST PATCH NO PRICES DUE TO SCARCITY
OVERALL GU ODDS 1:18 H, AU-GU 1:24 R
CARD SMA FEATURES GU BASE SWATCHES
ALL OTHERS ARE JERSEY SWATCHES
CHR Luis Castillo 15.00 4.50
Todd Helton
Scott Rolen
CWL Luis Castillo 10.00 3.00
Dontrelle Willis
Mike Lowell
CZH Roger Clemens 20.00 6.00
Barry Zito
Roy Halladay
DSG Carlos Delgado 15.00 4.50
Alfonso Soriano
Troy Glaus
GRG Nomar Garciaparra 30.00 9.00
Alex Rodriguez
Jason Giambi
HSP Todd Helton 20.00 6.00
Richie Sexson
Albert Pujols
OBG Magglio Ordonez 10.00 3.00
Hank Blalock
Troy Glaus
RGR Alex Rodriguez 25.00 7.50
Nomar Garciaparra
Manny Ramirez
RRP Edgar Renteria 40.00 12.00
Scott Rolen
Albert Pujols
SCG Alfonso Soriano 30.00 9.00
Roger Clemens
Jason Giambi
SJL Gary Sheffield 10.00 3.00
Andruw Jones
Javy Lopez
SMA Ichiro Suzuki Base 40.00 12.00
Hideki Matsui Base
Garret Anderson Base
SPW Gary Sheffield 20.00 6.00
Albert Pujols
Preston Wilson
WDH Vernon Wells 10.00 3.00
Carlos Delgado
Roy Halladay
WPW Kerry Wood 25.00 7.50
Mark Prior
Dontrelle Willis

2004 Classic Clippings Bat Rack Autograph Bronze

Nm-Mt Ex-Mt
OVERALL AU ODDS 1:18 H, AU-GU 1:24 R
STATED PRINT RUN 75 SERIAL #'d SETS
AH Aubrey Huff 15.00 4.50
EM Edgar Martinez 25.00 7.50
GS Gary Sheffield 25.00 7.50
HB Hank Blalock 15.00 4.50
JB Josh Beckett 25.00 7.50
JE Jim Edmonds 25.00 7.50
JR Jose Reyes 15.00 4.50
MC Miguel Cabrera 25.00 7.50
MT Mark Teixeira 25.00 7.50
RA Roberto Alomar 25.00 7.50

2004 Classic Clippings Bat Rack Quad Green

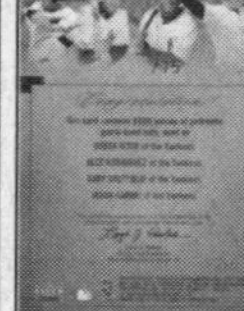

Nm-Mt Ex-Mt
STATED PRINT RUN 75 SERIAL #'d SETS
GOLD PRINT RUN 10 SERIAL #'d SETS
NO GOLD PRICING DUE TO SCARCITY
*RED: .5X TO 1.2X BASIC
RED PRINT RUN 25 SERIAL #'d SETS
OVERALL GU ODDS 1:18 H, AU-GU 1:24 R
BJPR Rocco Baldelli 20.00 6.00
Chipper Jones
Juan Pierre
Manny Ramirez
BLHD Jeff Bagwell 20.00 6.00
Derrek Lee
Aubrey Huff
Carlos Delgado
GTGP Vladimir Guerrero 30.00 9.00
Miguel Tejada
Jason Giambi
Mike Piazza
HRMR Todd Helton 40.00 12.00
Jose Reyes
Kaz Matsui
Scott Rolen
JRMG Derek Jeter 50.00 15.00
Alex Rodriguez
Kaz Matsui
Nomar Garciaparra
JRSG Derek Jeter 50.00 15.00
Alex Rodriguez
Gary Sheffield
Jason Giambi
PPRS Albert Pujols 40.00 12.00
Mark Prior
Alex Rodriguez
Curt Schilling
PRPR Mike Piazza 40.00 12.00
Jose Reyes
Albert Pujols
Scott Rolen
PSCB Juan Pierre 20.00 6.00
Gary Sheffield
Miguel Cabrera
Rocco Baldelli

BG Alfonso Soriano 20.00 6.00
Roberto Alomar
Hank Blalock
Troy Glaus
EJ Sammy Sosa 25.00 7.50
Vladimir Guerrero
Jim Edmonds
Chipper Jones
WS Curt Schilling 25.00 7.50
Nomar Garciaparra
Brandon Webb
Richie Sexson
CB Sammy Sosa.................. 30.00 9.00
Mark Prior
Miguel Cabrera
Josh Beckett
HL Jim Thome 20.00 6.00
Jeff Bagwell
Todd Helton
Derrek Lee
TD Jim Thome 20.00 6.00
Jeff Bagwell
Mark Teixeira
Carlos Delgado

2004 Classic Clippings Bat Rack Triple Green

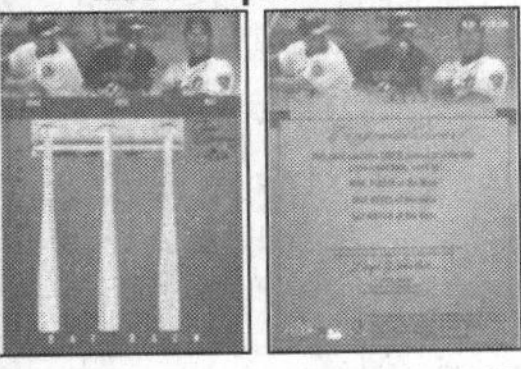

Nm-Mt Ex-Mt
TATED PRINT RUN 175 SERIAL #'d SETS
GOLD: .6X TO 1.5X BASIC...............
OLD PRINT RUN 25 SERIAL #'d SETS
RED: .5X TO 1.2X BASIC..................
ED PRINT RUN 50 SERIAL #'d SETS
VERALL GU ODDS 1:18 H, AU-GU 1:24 R
RS Roberto Alomar................ 15.00 4.50
Jose Reyes
Alfonso Soriano
HD Rocco Baldelli 10.00 3.00
Aubrey Huff
Carlos Delgado
TH Jeff Bagwell..................... 15.00 4.50
Jim Thome
Todd Helton
PB Miguel Cabrera.................. 15.00 4.50
Juan Pierre
Josh Beckett
HG Carlos Delgado 10.00 3.00
Aubrey Huff
Jason Giambi
PJ Vladimir Guerrero............. 15.00 4.50
Juan Pierre
Chipper Jones
PS Vladimir Guerrero 25.00 7.50
Albert Pujols
Sammy Sosa
RB Troy Glaus......................... 15.00 4.50
Scott Rolen
Hank Blalock
RS Nomar Garciaparra............ 20.00 6.00
Manny Ramirez
Curt Schilling
TH Jason Giambi 15.00 4.50
Jim Thome
Todd Helton
MG Derek Jeter 40.00 12.00
Kaz Matsui
Nomar Garciaparra
RS Derek Jeter 40.00 12.00
Alex Rodriguez
Gary Sheffield
PBS Mark Prior......................... 15.00 4.50
Josh Beckett
Curt Schilling
PRE Albert Pujols..................... 40.00 12.00
Scott Rolen
Jim Edmonds
PRM Mike Piazza 25.00 7.50
Jose Reyes
Kaz Matsui
RTC Alex Rodriguez 15.00 4.50
Miguel Tejada
Miguel Cabrera
SBT Alfonso Soriano............... 15.00 4.50
Hank Blalock
Mark Teixeira
SLP Sammy Sosa 30.00 9.00
Derrek Lee
Mark Prior
SRB Gary Sheffield 15.00 4.50
Manny Ramirez
Rocco Baldelli
SWA Richie Sexson 15.00 4.50
Brandon Webb
Roberto Alomar

2004 Classic Clippings Inserts

Nm-Mt Ex-Mt
1-20 PRINT RUN 750 SERIAL #'d SETS
21-25 PRINT RUN 100 SERIAL #'d SETS
STATED ODDS 1:18 HOBBY, 1:150 RETAIL
1 Nolan Ryan 10.00 3.00
2 Mike Schmidt......................... 8.00 2.40
3 Cal Ripken............................ 12.00 3.60
4 Don Mattingly 10.00 3.00
5 Roger Clemens 6.00 1.80
6 Randy Johnson .... 3.00 .90
7 Mark Prior............................. 3.00 .90
8 Jim Thome............................. 3.00 .90
9 Sammy Sosa.......................... 5.00 1.50
10 Pedro Martinez..................... 3.00 .90
11 Chipper Jones....................... 3.00 .90
12 Vladimir Guerrero .... 3.00 .90
13 Albert Pujols 6.00 1.80
14 Ichiro Suzuki........................ 5.00 1.50
15 Derek Jeter........................... 6.00 1.80
16 Alex Rodriguez..................... 5.00 1.50
17 Greg Maddux 5.00 1.50
18 Nomar Garciaparra............... 5.00 1.50
19 Mike Piazza 5.00 1.50
20 Ken Griffey Jr. 5.00 1.50
21 Pie Traynor........................... 8.00 2.40
22 Bill Dickey 8.00 2.40
23 George Sisler 8.00 2.40
24 Ted Williams 20.00 6.00
25 Enos Slaughter...................... 8.00 2.40

2004 Classic Clippings Jersey Rack Autograph Bronze

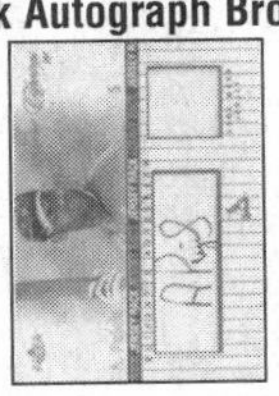

Nm-Mt Ex-Mt
OVERALL AU ODDS 1:18 H, AU-GU 1:24 R
STATED PRINT RUN 149 SERIAL #'d SETS
AB Angel Berroa...................... 10.00 3.00
AP1 Andy Pettitte.................... 40.00 12.00
AP2 Albert Pujols................... 120.00 36.00
BL Barry Larkin....................... 25.00 7.50
BW Brandon Webb 10.00 3.00
CD Carlos Delgado.................. 25.00 7.50
DH Dan Haren......................... 10.00 3.00
DW Dontrelle Willis................. 15.00 4.50
EJ Edwin Jackson 15.00 4.50
GA1 Garret Anderson.............. 25.00 7.50
GA2 Garrett Atkins.................. 10.00 3.00
IR Ivan Rodriguez 40.00 12.00
JG Jody Gerut.......................... 15.00 4.50
KW Kerry Wood 40.00 12.00
MB Marlon Byrd...................... 10.00 3.00
MC Miguel Cabrera.................. 25.00 7.50
MM1 Mark Mulder.................... 15.00 4.50
MM2 Mike Mussina.................. 25.00 7.50
RB Rocco Baldelli 15.00 4.50
RH Roy Halladay 10.00 3.00
RW Ryan Wagner..................... 10.00 3.00
SR Scott Rolen 40.00 12.00
TH Torii Hunter........................ 15.00 4.50

2004 Classic Clippings Jersey Rack Autograph Gold Patch

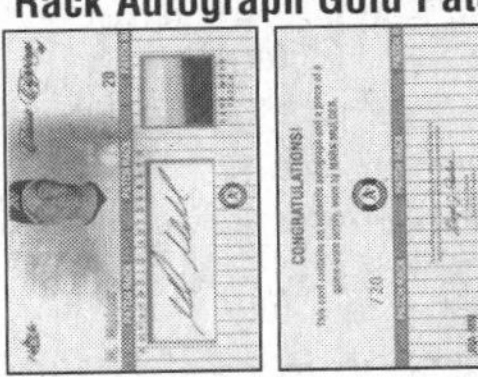

Nm-Mt Ex-Mt
*GOLD PATCH p/r 36-55: 1X TO 2.5X BRZ
*GOLD PATCH p/r 21-35: 1X TO 2.5X BRZ
*GOLD PATCH p/r 16-20: 1.25X TO 3X BRZ
OVERALL AU ODDS 1:18 H, AU-GU 1:24 R
PRINT RUNS B/WN 4-55 COPIES PER
NO PRICING ON QTY OF 11 OR LESS
JB Josh Beckett/21 .... 60.00 18.00

2004 Classic Clippings Jersey Rack Autograph Silver

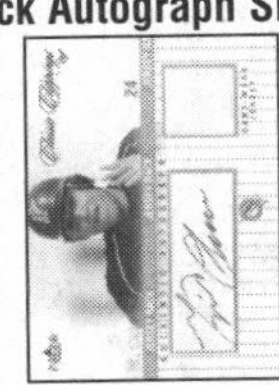

Nm-Mt Ex-Mt
*SILVER: .5X TO 1.2X BRONZE.........
OVERALL AU ODDS 1:18 H, AU-GU 1:24 R
STATED PRINT RUN 50 SERIAL #'d SETS
JB Josh Beckett 30.00 9.00

2004 Classic Clippings Jersey Rack Triple Blue

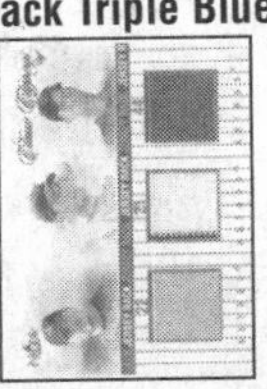

Nm-Mt Ex-Mt
STATED PRINT RUN 225 SERIAL #'d SETS
*BRONZE: .4X TO 1X BASIC..............
BRONZE PRINT RUN 99 SERIAL #'d SETS
GOLD PATCH PRINT RUN 25 SER.#'d SETS
GOLD PATCH NO PRICE DUE TO SCARCITY
*SILVER p/r 64-117: .4X TO 1X BASIC
*SILVER p/r 40-56: .5X TO 1.2X BASIC
*SILVER p/r 20-34: .6X TO 1.5X BASIC
SILVER PRINT RUN B/WN 20-117 COPIES PER
OVERALL GU ODDS 1:18 H, AU-GU 1:24 R
BCP Rocco Baldelli 20.00 6.00
Miguel Cabrera
Albert Pujols
CPB Roger Clemens................. 25.00 7.50
Mark Prior
Josh Beckett
CPO Roger Clemens 20.00 6.00
Andy Pettitte
Roy Oswalt
CWB Miguel Cabrera................ 15.00 4.50
Dontrelle Willis
Josh Beckett
DTS Carlos Delgado................. 15.00 4.50
Miguel Tejada
Alfonso Soriano
GMS Nomar Garciaparra.......... 20.00 6.00
Pedro Martinez
Curt Schilling
JRG Derek Jeter 40.00 12.00
Alex Rodriguez
Jason Giambi
JSW Randy Johnson................ 15.00 4.50
Richie Sexson
Brandon Webb
PRL Mike Piazza 15.00 4.50
Ivan Rodriguez
Javy Lopez
PSR Albert Pujols 25.00 7.50
Sammy Sosa
Manny Ramirez
RJG Alex Rodriguez 50.00 15.00
Derek Jeter
Nomar Garciaparra
SWP Sammy Sosa................... 40.00 12.00
Kerry Wood
Mark Prior
WWB Dontrelle Willis.............. 10.00 3.00
Brandon Webb
Angel Berroa
WWS Dontrelle Willis.............. 15.00 4.50
Kerry Wood
Curt Schilling
ZHM Barry Zito 10.00 3.00
Tim Hudson
Mark Mulder

2004 Classic Clippings Phenom Lineup Autograph Red

Nm-Mt Ex-Mt
STATED PRINT RUN 150 SERIAL #'d SETS
*GOLD: .6X TO 1.5X BASIC...............
GOLD PRINT RUN 50 SERIAL #'d SETS
*SILVER: .5X TO 1.2X BASIC.............
SILVER PRINT RUN 99 SERIAL #'d SETS
OVERALL AU ODDS 1:18 H, AU-GU 1:24 R
AB Nomar Garciaparra 10.00 3.00
Angel Berroa AU
Alex Rodriguez
AL Albert Pujols 10.00 3.00
Adam LaRoche AU
Jim Thome
AR Carlos Delgado.................. 15.00 4.50
Alexis Rios AU
Vernon Wells
BC Nomar Garciaparra 25.00 7.50
Bobby Crosby AU
Alex Rodriguez
CW Hideki Matsui 25.00 7.50
Chien-Ming Wang AU
Jason Giambi
DM Troy Glaus......................... 25.00 7.50
Dallas McPherson AU
Garret Anderson EXCH
DW Mark Prior......................... 15.00 4.50
Dontrelle Willis AU
Kerry Wood
DY Ichiro Suzuki 25.00 7.50
Delmon Young AU
Hideki Matsui
EJ Mark Prior 15.00 4.50
Edwin Jackson AU
Kerry Wood
GS Manny Ramirez 15.00 4.50
Grady Sizemore AU
Garret Anderson
HB Troy Glaus......................... 15.00 4.50
Hank Blalock AU
Alex Rodriguez
JG Albert Pujols 15.00 4.50
John Gall AU
Scott Rolen
JR Kaz Matsui 15.00 4.50
Jose Reyes AU
Rickie Weeks
KG Edgar Renteria................... 40.00 12.00
Khalil Greene AU
Mike Lowell
LN Alex Rodriguez 15.00 4.50
Laynce Nix AU
Garret Anderson
MC Luis Castillo...................... 25.00 7.50
Miguel Cabrera AU
Mike Lowell
MV Edwin Jackson.................. 15.00 4.50
Merkin Valdez AU
Dontrelle Willis
RH1 Roy Halladay 15.00 4.50
Rich Harden AU
Barry Zito EXCH
RH2 Jim Thome 15.00 4.50
Ryan Howard AU
Todd Helton
RW1 Dontrelle Willis............... 10.00 3.00
Ryan Wagner AU
Mark Prior
RW2 Luis Castillo 15.00 4.50
Rickie Weeks AU
Jose Reyes
SP Albert Pujols 15.00 4.50
Scott Podsednik AU
Andruw Jones

2004 Classic Clippings Press Clippings

Nm-Mt Ex-Mt
STATED ODDS 1:6 HOBBY/RETAIL .....
1 Josh Beckett .... 1.00 .30
2 Albert Pujols 5.00 1.50
3 Derek Jeter........................... 5.00 1.50
4 Alex Rodriguez..................... 4.00 1.20
5 Jim Thome............................ 2.50 .75
6 Angel Berroa .... 1.00 .30
7 Dontrelle Willis..................... 1.00 .30
8 Roy Halladay .... 1.00 .30
9 Kerry Wood.......................... 2.50 .75
10 Mark Prior........................... 2.50 .75
11 Roger Clemens 5.00 1.50
12 Hideki Matsui 4.00 1.20
13 Ichiro Suzuki....................... 4.00 1.20
14 Eric Gagne .... 2.50 .75
15 Miguel Cabrera.................... 1.50 .45
16 Nomar Garciaparra.............. 4.00 1.20
17 Hank Blalock .... 1.00 .30
18 Chipper Jones .... 2.50 .75
19 Sammy Sosa........................ 4.00 1.20
20 Alfonso Soriano .... 1.50 .45

2004 Classic Clippings Signature Edition

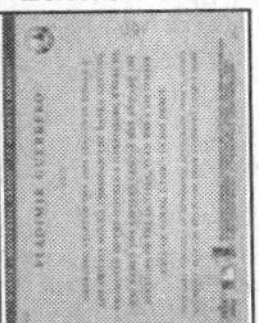

Nm-Mt Ex-Mt
STATED PRINT RUN 50 SERIAL #'d SETS
PURPLE PRINT RUN 1 SERIAL #'d SET
NO PURPLE PRICING DUE TO SCARCITY
OVERALL AU ODDS 1:18 H, AU-GU 1:24 R
AP Albert Pujols..................... 150.00 45.00
CR Cal Ripken 200.00 60.00
DM Don Mattingly.................... 80.00 24.00
EJ Edwin Jackson 20.00 6.00
KG Khalil Greene 50.00 15.00
MP Mark Prior 60.00 18.00
MS Mike Schmidt..................... 80.00 24.00
NR Nolan Ryan 120.00 36.00
RH Rich Harden EXCH 20.00 6.00
RJ Randy Johnson................... 80.00 24.00
RW Rickie Weeks 20.00 6.00
VG Vladimir Guerrero.............. 50.00 15.00

1914 Cracker Jack

The cards in this 144-card set measure approximately 2 1/4" by 3". This "Series of colored pictures of Famous Ball Players and Managers" was issued in packages of Cracker Jack in 1914. The cards have tinted photos set against red backgrounds and many are found with caramel stains. The set also contains Federal League players. The company claims to have printed 15 million cards. The 1914 series can be distinguished from the 1915 issue by the advertising found on the back of the cards. Team names are included for some players to show differences between the 1914 and 1915 issue.

Ex-Mt VG
COMPLETE SET (144)......... 45000.00 22500.00
1 Otto Knabe.......................... 250.00 125.00
2 Frank Baker......................... 400.00 200.00
3 Joe Tinker 400.00 200.00
4 Larry Doyle 175.00 90.00
5 Ward Miller 150.00 75.00
6 Eddie Plank 600.00 300.00
Phila. AL
7 Eddie Collins 450.00 220.00
Phila. AL
8 Rube Oldring........................ 150.00 75.00
9 Artie Hoffman...................... 150.00 75.00
10 John McInnis...................... 150.00 75.00
11 George Stovall 150.00 75.00
12 Connie Mack MG 500.00 250.00
13 Art Wilson 150.00 75.00
14 Sam Crawford.................... 300.00 150.00
15 Reb Russell........................ 150.00 75.00
16 Howie Camnitz 150.00 75.00
17 Roger Bresnahan 350.00 180.00
Catcher
18 Johnny Evers 350.00 180.00
19 Chief Bender 450.00 220.00
Phila. AL
20 Cy Falkenberg 150.00 75.00
21 Heinie Zimmerman............. 150.00 75.00
22 Joe Wood........................... 300.00 150.00
23 Chas.Comiskey OWN 350.00 180.00
24 George Mullen 150.00 75.00
25 Michael Simon 150.00 75.00
26 James Scott 150.00 75.00
27 Bill Carrigan 150.00 75.00
28 Jack Barry 150.00 75.00
29 Vean Gregg 200.00 100.00
Cleveland
30 Ty Cobb........................... 6000.00 3000.00
31 Heinie Wagner.................... 150.00 75.00
32 Mordecai Brown................. 350.00 180.00
33 Amos Strunk....................... 150.00 75.00
34 Ira Thomas......................... 150.00 75.00
35 Harry Hooper 300.00 150.00
36 Ed Walsh............................ 300.00 150.00
37 Grover C. Alexander 800.00 400.00
38 Red Dooin 200.00 100.00
Phila. NL
39 Chick Gandil....................... 350.00 180.00
40 Jimmy Austin...................... 200.00 100.00
St.L. AL
41 Tommy Leach 150.00 75.00
42 Al Bridwell.......................... 150.00 75.00
43 Rube Marquard 350.00 180.00
NY NL
44 Charles Tesreau.................. 150.00 75.00
45 Fred Luderus....................... 150.00 75.00
46 Bob Groom 150.00 75.00
47 Josh Devore........................ 200.00 100.00
Phila. NL
48 Harry Lord 250.00 125.00
49 John Miller.......................... 150.00 75.00
50 John Hummell 150.00 75.00
51 Nap Rucker 175.00 90.00
52 Zach Wheat........................ 350.00 180.00
53 Otto Miller.......................... 150.00 75.00
54 Marty O'Toole.................... 150.00 75.00
55 Dick Hoblitzel 200.00 100.00
Cinc.
56 Clyde Milan........................ 175.00 90.00
57 Walter Johnson.................. 2000.00 1000.00
58 Wally Schang 175.00 90.00
59 Harry Gessler 150.00 75.00
60 Rollie Zeider....................... 250.00 125.00
61 Ray Schalk 300.00 150.00
62 Jay Cashion 300.00 150.00
63 Babe Adams........................ 175.00 90.00
64 Jimmy Archer 150.00 75.00
65 Tris Speaker 700.00 350.00
66 Napoleon Lajoie 800.00 400.00
Cleve.
67 Otis Crandall 150.00 75.00
68 Honus Wagner 2500.00 1250.00
69 John McGraw..................... 450.00 220.00
70 Fred Clarke 300.00 150.00
71 Chief Meyers 175.00 90.00
72 John Boehling 150.00 75.00
73 Max Carey 300.00 150.00
74 Frank Owens 150.00 75.00
75 Miller Huggins 300.00 150.00
76 Claude Hendrix................... 150.00 75.00
77 Hughie Jennings MG 300.00 150.00
78 Fred Merkle........................ 200.00 100.00
79 Ping Bodie 175.00 90.00
80 Ed Ruelbach....................... 175.00 90.00
81 Jim C. Delehanty................ 175.00 90.00
82 Gavvy Cravath 200.00 100.00
83 Russ Ford 150.00 75.00
84 Elmer E. Knetzer 150.00 75.00
85 Buck Herzog 150.00 75.00
86 Burt Shotton 150.00 75.00
87 Forrest Cady........................ 150.00 75.00
88 Christy Mathewson 3000.00 1500.00
Pitching
89 Lawrence Cheney............... 150.00 75.00
90 Frank Smith 150.00 75.00
91 Roger Peckinpaugh............. 175.00 90.00
92 Al Demaree N.Y. NL 200.00 100.00
93 Del Pratt............................. 250.00 125.00
Throwing
94 Eddie Cicotte...................... 325.00 160.00
95 Ray Keating........................ 150.00 75.00
96 Beals Becker 150.00 75.00
97 John(Rube) Benton............. 150.00 75.00
98 Frank LaPorte..................... 150.00 75.00
99 Frank Chance 1500.00 750.00
100 Thomas Seaton 150.00 75.00
101 Frank Schulte................... 150.00 75.00
102 Ray Fisher........................ 150.00 75.00
103 Joe Jackson 8000.00 4000.00
104 Vic Saier........................... 150.00 75.00
105 James Lavender................ 150.00 75.00
106 Joe Birmingham............... 150.00 75.00
107 Tom Downey 150.00 75.00
108 Sherry Magee 200.00 100.00
Phila. NL
109 Fred Blanding................... 150.00 75.00
110 Bob Bescher..................... 150.00 75.00
111 Jim Callahan 300.00 150.00
112 Ed Sweeney 150.00 75.00
113 George Suggs 150.00 75.00
114 Geo.J. Moriarty 175.00 90.00
115 Addison Brennan 150.00 75.00
116 Rollie Zeider..................... 150.00 75.00
117 Ted Easterly..................... 150.00 75.00
118 Ed Konetchy..................... 200.00 100.00
Pittsburgh
119 George Perring.................. 150.00 75.00
120 Mike Doolan..................... 150.00 75.00
121 Hub Perdue 200.00 100.00
Boston NL
122 Owen Bush........................ 150.00 75.00
123 Slim Sallee 150.00 75.00
124 Earl Moore 150.00 75.00

125 Bert Niehoff 200.00 100.00
126 Walter Blair 150.00 75.00
127 Butch Schmidt 150.00 75.00
128 Steve Evans 150.00 75.00
129 Ray Caldwell 150.00 75.00
130 Ivy Wingo 150.00 75.00
131 George Baumgardner 150.00 75.00
132 Les Nunamaker 150.00 75.00
133 Branch Rickey MG 450.00 220.00
134 Armando Marsans 200.00 100.00
Cincinnati
135 Bill Killefer 150.00 75.00
136 Rabbit Maranville 350.00 180.00
137 William Rariden 150.00 75.00
138 Hank Gowdy 150.00 75.00
139 Rebel Oakes 150.00 75.00
140 Danny Murphy 150.00 75.00
141 Cy Barger 150.00 75.00
142 Eugene Packard 150.00 75.00
143 Jake Daubert 175.00 90.00
144 James C. Walsh 200.00 100.00

1915 Cracker Jack

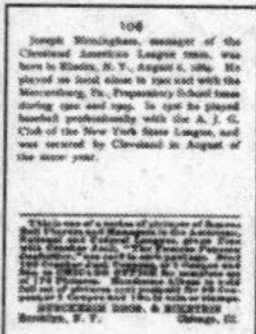

The cards in this 176-card set measure approximately 2 1/4" by 3". When turned over in a lateral motion, a 1915 "series of 176" Cracker Jack card shows the back printing upside-down. Cards were available in boxes of Cracker Jack or from the company for "100 Cracker Jack coupons, or one coupon and 25 cents." An album was available for "50 coupons or one coupon and 10 cents." Because of this send-in offer, the 1915 Cracker Jack cards are noticeably easier to find than the 1914 Cracker Jack cards, although obviously neither set is plentiful. The set essentially duplicates E145-1 (1914 Cracker Jack) except for some additional cards and new poses. Players in the Federal League are indicated by FED in the checklist below.

Ex-Mt VG
COMPLETE SET (176) 35000.00 17500.00
COMMON CARD (1-144) 100.00 50.00
COMM. CARD (145-176) 125.00 60.00
1 Otto Knabe 175.00 90.00
2 Frank Baker 350.00 180.00
3 Joe Tinker 350.00 180.00
4 Larry Doyle 100.00 50.00
5 Ward Miller 100.00 50.00
6 Eddie Plank 500.00 250.00
St.L. FED
7 Eddie Collins 350.00 180.00
Chicago AL
8 Rube Oldring 100.00 50.00
9 Artie Hoffman 100.00 50.00
10 John McInnis 100.00 50.00
11 George Stovall 100.00 50.00
12 Connie Mack MG 400.00 200.00
13 Art Wilson 100.00 50.00
14 Sam Crawford 300.00 150.00
15 Reb Russell 100.00 50.00
16 Howie Camnitz 100.00 50.00
17 Roger Bresnahan 300.00 150.00
18 Johnny Evers 300.00 150.00
19 Chief Bender 350.00 180.00
Baltimore FED
20 Cy Falkenberg 100.00 50.00
21 Heinie Zimmerman 100.00 50.00
22 Joe Wood 250.00 125.00
23 C. Comiskey OWN 300.00 150.00
24 George Mullen 100.00 50.00
25 Michael Simon 100.00 50.00
26 James Scott 100.00 50.00
27 Bill Carrigan 100.00 50.00
28 Jack Barry 100.00 50.00
29 Vean Gregg 125.00 60.00
Boston AL
30 Ty Cobb 4000.00 2000.00
31 Heinie Wagner 100.00 50.00
32 Mordecai Brown 300.00 150.00
33 Amos Strunk 100.00 50.00
34 Ira Thomas 100.00 50.00
35 Harry Hooper 250.00 125.00
36 Ed Walsh 300.00 150.00
37 Grover C. Alexander 600.00 300.00
38 Red Dooin 125.00 60.00
Cincinnati
39 Chick Gandil 300.00 150.00
40 Jimmy Austin 125.00 60.00
Pitts. FED
41 Tommy Leach 100.00 50.00
42 Al Bridwell 100.00 50.00
43 Rube Marquard 350.00 180.00
Brooklyn FED
44 Charles(Jeff) Tesreau 100.00 50.00
45 Fred Luderus 100.00 50.00
46 Bob Groom 100.00 50.00
47 Josh Devore 125.00 60.00
Boston NL
48 Steve O'Neill 125.00 60.00
49 John Miller 100.00 50.00
50 John Hummell 100.00 50.00
51 Nap Rucker 125.00 60.00
52 Zach Wheat 300.00 150.00
53 Otto Miller 100.00 50.00
54 Marty O'Toole 100.00 50.00
55 Dick Hoblitzel 125.00 60.00
Boston AL
56 Clyde Milan 125.00 60.00
57 Walter Johnson 1500.00 750.00
58 Wally Schang 125.00 60.00
59 Harry Gessler 100.00 50.00
60 Oscar Dugey 125.00 60.00
61 Ray Schalk 250.00 125.00
62 Willie Mitchell 125.00 60.00
63 Babe Adams 125.00 60.00
64 Jimmy Archer 100.00 50.00
65 Tris Speaker 600.00 300.00
66 Napoleon Lajoie 600.00 300.00
Phila. AL
67 Otis Crandall 100.00 50.00
68 Honus Wagner 1500.00 750.00
69 John McGraw MG 300.00 150.00
70 Fred Clarke 250.00 125.00
71 Chief Meyers 100.00 50.00
72 John Boehling 100.00 50.00
73 Max Carey 250.00 125.00
74 Frank Owens 100.00 50.00
75 Miller Huggins 300.00 150.00
76 Claude Hendrix 100.00 50.00
77 Hughie Jennings MG 300.00 150.00
78 Fred Merkle 125.00 60.00
79 Ping Bodie 125.00 60.00
80 Ed Ruelbach 125.00 60.00
81 Jim C. Delehanty 125.00 60.00
82 Gavvy Cravath 125.00 60.00
83 Russ Ford 100.00 50.00
84 Elmer E. Knetzer 100.00 50.00
85 Buck Herzog 100.00 50.00
86 Burt Shotton 100.00 50.00
87 Forrest Cady 100.00 50.00
88 Christy Mathewson 1500.00 750.00
Portrait
89 Lawrence Cheney 100.00 50.00
90 Frank Smith 100.00 50.00
91 Roger Peckinpaugh 125.00 60.00
92 Al Demaree 125.00 60.00
Phila. NL
93 Del Pratt 175.00 90.00
Portrait
94 Eddie Cicotte 300.00 150.00
95 Ray Keating 100.00 50.00
96 Beals Becker 100.00 50.00
97 John(Rube) Benton 100.00 50.00
98 Frank LaPorte 100.00 50.00
99 Hal Chase 300.00 150.00
100 Thomas Seaton 100.00 50.00
101 Frank Schulte 100.00 50.00
102 Ray Fisher 100.00 50.00
103 Joe Jackson 8000.00 4000.00
104 Vic Saier 100.00 50.00
105 James Lavender 100.00 50.00
106 Joe Birmingham MG 100.00 50.00
107 Thomas Downey 100.00 50.00
108 Sherry Magee 125.00 60.00
Boston NL
109 Fred Blanding 100.00 50.00
110 Bob Bescher 100.00 50.00
111 Herbie Moran 125.00 60.00
112 Ed Sweeney 100.00 50.00
113 George Suggs 100.00 50.00
114 Geo.J. Moriarty 125.00 60.00
115 Addison Brennan 100.00 50.00
116 Rollie Zeider 100.00 50.00
117 Ted Easterly 100.00 50.00
118 Ed Konetchy 125.00 60.00
Pitts. FED
119 George Perring 100.00 50.00
120 Mike Doolan 100.00 50.00
121 Hub Perdue 125.00 60.00
St. Louis NL
122 Owen Bush 100.00 50.00
123 Slim Sallee 100.00 50.00
124 Earl Moore 100.00 50.00
125 Bert Niehoff 125.00 60.00
Phila. NL
126 Walter Blair 100.00 50.00
127 Butch Schmidt 100.00 50.00
128 Steve Evans 100.00 50.00
129 Ray Caldwell 100.00 50.00
130 Ivy Wingo 100.00 50.00
131 Geo. Baumgardner 100.00 50.00
132 Les Nunamaker 100.00 50.00
133 Branch Rickey MG 300.00 150.00
134 Armando Marsans 125.00 60.00
St.L. FED
135 William Killefer 100.00 50.00
136 Rabbit Maranville 250.00 125.00
137 William Rariden 100.00 50.00
138 Hank Gowdy 100.00 50.00
139 Rebel Oakes 100.00 50.00
140 Danny Murphy 100.00 50.00
141 Cy Barger 100.00 50.00
142 Eugene Packard 100.00 50.00
143 Jake Daubert 100.00 50.00
144 James C. Walsh 100.00 50.00
145 Ted Cather 125.00 60.00
146 George Tyler 125.00 60.00
147 Lee Magee 125.00 60.00
148 Owen Wilson 125.00 60.00
149 Hal Janvrin 125.00 60.00
150 Doc Johnston 125.00 60.00
151 George Whitted 125.00 60.00
152 George McQuillen 125.00 60.00
153 Bill James 125.00 60.00
154 Dick Rudolph 125.00 60.00
155 Joe Connolly 125.00 60.00
156 Jean Dubuc 125.00 60.00
157 George Kaiserling 125.00 60.00
158 Fritz Maisel 125.00 60.00
159 Heinie Groh 125.00 60.00
160 Benny Kauff 125.00 60.00
161 Edd Roush 300.00 150.00
162 George Stallings MG 125.00 60.00
163 Bert Whaling 125.00 60.00
164 Bob Shawkey 125.00 60.00
165 Eddie Murphy 125.00 60.00
166 Joe Bush 125.00 60.00
167 Clark Griffith 300.00 150.00
168 Vin Campbell 125.00 60.00
169 Raymond Collins 125.00 60.00
170 Hans Lobert 125.00 60.00
171 Earl Hamilton 125.00 60.00
172 Erskine Mayer 125.00 60.00
173 Tilly Walker 125.00 60.00
174 Robert Veach 125.00 60.00
175 Joseph Benz 125.00 60.00
176 Hippo Vaughn 175.00 90.00

2002 Diamond Kings

This 160 card set was issued in two separate series. The first 150 cards were issued within the Diamond Kings brand of which was distributed in May, 2002. These cards were issued in four card packs with an SRP of $3.99 which came 24 packs to a box and 20 boxes to a case. Cards numbered 101 through 150 were printed in shorter supply than the other cards. Cards numbered 101 through 121 feature prospect while cards numbered 122 through 150 featured retired veterans. These cards were all issued at a stated rate of one in three packs. Cards 151-160 were issued within packs of 2002 Donruss the Rookies in mid-December, 2002 at the following ratios: hobby 1:10, retail 1:12. This set was noteworthy as Donruss/Playoff created a full set based on the tradition began in 1982 when the first Diamond King cards were created.

Nm-Mt Ex-Mt
COMP.LOW SET (150) 200.00 60.00
COMP.LOW w/o SP's (100) 50.00 15.00
COMP.UPDATE SET (10) 40.00 12.00
COMMON CARD (1-100) .50 .15
COMMON PROSPECT (101-150) 4.00 1.20
COMMON RETIRED (101-150) 4.00 1.20
COMMON CARD (151-160) 4.00 1.20
1 Vladimir Guerrero 1.25 .35
2 Adam Dunn .75 .23
3 Tsuyoshi Shinjo .50 .15
4 Adrian Beltre .75 .23
5 Troy Glaus .50 .15
6 Albert Pujols 2.50 .75
7 Trot Nixon .50 .15
8 Alex Rodriguez 2.00 .60
9 Tom Glavine .75 .23
10 Alfonso Soriano .75 .23
11 Todd Helton .75 .23
12 Joe Torre 1.25 .35
13 Tim Hudson .50 .15
14 Andruw Jones .50 .15
15 Shawn Green .50 .15
16 Aramis Ramirez .50 .15
17 Shannon Stewart .50 .15
18 Barry Bonds 3.00 .90
19 Sean Casey .50 .15
20 Barry Larkin .75 .23
21 Scott Rolen 1.25 .35
22 Barry Zito .50 .15
23 Sammy Sosa 2.00 .60
24 Bartolo Colon .50 .15
25 Ryan Klesko .50 .15
26 Ben Grieve .50 .15
27 Roy Oswalt .50 .15
28 Kazuhiro Sasaki .50 .15
29 Roger Clemens 2.50 .75
30 Bernie Williams .75 .23
31 Roberto Alomar .75 .23
32 Bobby Abreu .50 .15
33 Robert Fick .50 .15
34 Bret Boone .50 .15
35 Rickey Henderson 1.25 .35
36 Brian Giles .50 .15
37 Richie Sexson .50 .15
38 Bud Smith .50 .15
39 Richard Hidalgo .50 .15
40 C. C. Sabathia .50 .15
41 Rich Aurilia .50 .15
42 Carlos Beltran .75 .23
43 Raul Mondesi .50 .15
44 Carlos Delgado .50 .15
45 Randy Johnson 1.25 .35
46 Chan Ho Park .50 .15
47 Rafael Palmeiro .75 .23
48 Chipper Jones 1.25 .35
49 Phil Nevin .50 .15
50 Cliff Floyd .50 .15
51 Pedro Martinez 1.25 .35
52 Craig Biggio .75 .23
53 Paul LoDuca .50 .15
54 Cristian Guzman .50 .15
55 Pat Burrell .50 .15
56 Curt Schilling .50 .15
57 Orlando Cabrera .50 .15
58 Darin Erstad .50 .15
59 Omar Vizquel .75 .23
60 Derek Jeter 3.00 .90
61 Nomar Garciaparra 2.00 .60
62 Edgar Martinez .75 .23
63 Moises Alou .50 .15
64 Eric Chavez .50 .15
65 Mike Sweeney .50 .15
66 Frank Thomas 1.25 .35
67 Mike Piazza 2.00 .60
68 Gary Sheffield .50 .15
69 Mike Mussina .75 .23
70 Greg Maddux 2.00 .60
71 Juan Gonzalez .75 .23
72 Hideo Nomo 1.25 .35
73 Miguel Tejada .50 .15
74 Ichiro Suzuki 2.00 .60
75 Matt Morris .50 .15
76 Ivan Rodriguez 1.25 .35
77 Mark Mulder .50 .15
78 J.D. Drew .50 .15
79 Mark Grace .75 .23
80 Jason Giambi .50 .15
81 Mark Buehrle .50 .15
82 Jose Vidro .50 .15
83 Manny Ramirez .75 .23
84 Jeff Bagwell .75 .23
85 Magglio Ordonez .50 .15
86 Ken Griffey Jr. 2.00 .60
87 Luis Gonzalez .50 .15
88 Jim Edmonds .50 .15
89 Larry Walker .75 .23
90 Jim Thome 1.25 .35
91 Lance Berkman .50 .15
92 Jorge Posada .75 .23
93 Kevin Brown .50 .15
94 Joe Mays .50 .15
95 Kerry Wood 1.25 .35
96 Mark Ellis .50 .15
97 Austin Kearns .50 .15
98 Jorge De La Rosa RC .50 .15
99 Brandon Berger .50 .15
100 Ryan Ludwick .50 .15
101 Marlon Byrd SP 4.00 1.20
102 Brandon Backe SP RC 5.00 1.50
103 Juan Cruz SP 4.00 1.20
104 Anderson Machado SP RC 4.00 1.20
105 So Taguchi SP RC 4.00 1.20
106 Dewon Brazelton SP 4.00 1.20
107 Josh Beckett SP 4.00 1.20
108 John Buck SP 4.00 1.20
109 Jorge Padilla SP RC 4.00 1.20
110 Hee Seop Choi SP 4.00 1.20
111 Angel Berroa SP 4.00 1.20
112 Mark Teixeira SP 4.00 1.20
113 Victor Martinez SP 5.00 1.50
114 Kazuhisa Ishii SP RC 6.00 1.80
115 Dennis Tankersley SP 4.00 1.20
116 Wilson Valdez SP RC 4.00 1.20
117 Antonio Perez SP 4.00 1.20
118 Ed Rogers SP 4.00 1.20
119 Wilson Betemit SP 4.00 1.20
120 Mike Rivera SP 4.00 1.20
121 Mark Prior SP 8.00 2.40
122 Roberto Clemente SP 8.00 2.40
123 Roberto Clemente SP 8.00 2.40
124 Roberto Clemente SP 8.00 2.40
125 Roberto Clemente SP 8.00 2.40
126 Roberto Clemente SP 8.00 2.40
127 Babe Ruth SP 10.00 3.00
128 Ted Williams SP 8.00 2.40
129 Andre Dawson SP 4.00 1.20
130 Eddie Murray SP 5.00 1.50
131 Juan Marichal SP 4.00 1.20
132 Kirby Puckett SP 5.00 1.50
133 Alan Trammell SP 4.00 1.20
134 Bobby Doerr SP 4.00 1.20
135 Carlton Fisk SP 4.00 1.20
136 Eddie Mathews SP 5.00 1.50
137 Mike Schmidt SP 10.00 3.00
138 Catfish Hunter SP 4.00 1.20
139 Nolan Ryan SP 12.00 3.60
140 George Brett SP 12.00 3.60
141 Gary Carter SP 4.00 1.20
142 Paul Molitor SP 4.00 1.20
143 Lou Gehrig SP 6.00 1.80
144 Ryne Sandberg SP 10.00 3.00
145 Tony Gwynn SP 6.00 1.80
146 Ron Santo SP 4.00 1.20
147 Cal Ripken SP 15.00 4.50
148 Al Kaline SP 5.00 1.50
149 Bo Jackson SP 5.00 1.50
150 Don Mattingly SP 12.00 3.60
151 Chris Snelling RC 4.00 1.20
152 Satoru Komiyama RC 4.00 1.20
153 Oliver Perez RC 8.00 2.40
154 Kirk Saarloos RC 4.00 1.20
155 Rene Reyes RC 4.00 1.20
156 Runelvys Hernandez RC 4.00 1.20
157 Rodrigo Rosario RC 4.00 1.20
158 Jason Simontacchi RC 4.00 1.20
159 Miguel Asencio RC 4.00 1.20
160 Aaron Cook RC 4.00 1.20

2002 Diamond Kings Bronze Foil

Inserted at a stated rate of one in six packs, this is a parallel to the Diamond King sets. These cards have white frames with bronze highlights.

Nm-Mt Ex-Mt
*BRONZE 1-100: 1.5X TO 4X BASIC
*BRONZE 101-121: .4X TO 1X BASIC
*BRONZE 122-150: .4X TO 1X BASIC
*BRONZE 151-160: 1X TO 2.5X BASIC

2002 Diamond Kings Gold Foil

Randomly inserted in packs, this is a parallel to the Diamond Kings set. These cards can be differentiated by their having black frames with gold accents. 100 serial-numbered sets were printed.

Nm-Mt Ex-Mt
*GOLD 1-100: 6X TO 15X BASIC
*GOLD 101-121: 1.5X TO 4X BASIC
*GOLD 122-150: 2.5X TO 6X BASIC
*GOLD 151-160: 1.5X TO 4X BASIC
1-150 RANDOM INSERTS IN PACKS
151-160 RANDOM IN DONRUSS ROOK.PACKS

2002 Diamond Kings Silver Foil

Randomly inserted in packs, this is a parallel to the Diamond Kings set. These cards can be differentiated by the grey frames and with silver accents.

Nm-Mt Ex-Mt
*SILVER 1-100: 3X TO 8X BASIC
*SILVER 101-121: .75X TO 2X BASIC
*SILVER 122-150: 1.25X TO 3X BASIC
*SILVER 151-160: 1.25X TO 3X BASIC
151-160 PRINT RUN 250 SERIAL #'d SETS

2002 Diamond Kings Diamond Cut Collection

These 100 cards were inserted at an approx
mate rate of one per hobby box and as rando
inserts in retail packs. These cards feature a m
of autograph and memorabilia cards. The b
cards of Tony Gwynn and Kazuhisa Ishii we
not ready by the time this product packed ou
Thus, exchange cards with a deadline o
November 1st, 2003 were seeded into packs.

Nm-Mt Ex-Mt
DC1 Vladimir Guerrero AU/400 40.00 12.00
DC2 Mark Prior AU/400 80.00 24.00
DC3 Victor Martinez AU/500 40.00 12.00
DC4 Marlon Byrd AU/500 10.00 3.00
DC5 Bud Smith AU/400 10.00 3.00
DC6 Joe Mays AU/500 10.00 3.00
DC7 Troy Glaus AU/500 15.00 4.50
DC8 Ron Santo AU/500 25.00 7.50
DC9 Roy Oswalt AU/500 15.00 4.50
DC10 Angel Berroa AU/500 10.00 3.00
DC11 Mark Buehrle AU/500 15.00 4.50
DC12 John Buck AU/500 10.00 3.00
DC13 Barry Larkin AU/250 50.00 15.00
DC14 Gary Carter AU/250 25.00 7.50
DC15 Mark Teixeira AU/300 25.00 7.50
DC16 Alan Trammell AU/500 15.00 4.50
DC17 Kazuhisa Ishii AU/100 80.00 24.00
DC18 Rafael Palmeiro AU/125 60.00 18.00
DC19 Austin Kearns AU/500 15.00 4.50
DC20 Joe Torre AU/125 60.00 18.00
DC21 J.D. Drew AU/400 25.00 7.50
DC22 So Taguchi AU/400 30.00 9.00
DC23 Juan Marichal AU/500 15.00 4.50
DC24 Bobby Doerr AU/500 25.00 7.50
DC25 Carlos Beltran AU/500 40.00 12.00
DC26 Robert Fick AU/500 10.00 3.00
DC27 Albert Pujols AU/200 120.00 36.00
DC28 Shannon Stewart AU/500 15.00 4.50
DC29 Antonio Perez AU/500 10.00 3.00
DC30 Wilson Betemit AU/500 10.00 3.00
DC31 Alex Rodriguez Jsy/500 15.00 4.50
DC32 Curt Schilling Jsy/500 8.00 2.40
DC33 George Brett Jsy/300 25.00 7.50
DC34 Hideo Nomo Jsy/100 15.00 4.50
DC35 Ivan Rodriguez Jsy/500 10.00 3.00
DC36 Don Mattingly Jsy/200 25.00 7.50
DC37 Joe Mays Jsy/500 8.00 2.40
DC38 Lance Berkman Jsy/400 8.00 2.40
DC39 Tony Gwynn Jsy/500 15.00 4.50
DC40 Darin Erstad Jsy/400 8.00 2.40
DC41 Adrian Beltre Jsy/400 10.00 3.00
DC42 Frank Thomas Jsy/500 10.00 3.00
DC43 Cal Ripken Jsy/300 40.00 12.00
DC44 Jose Vidro Jsy/500 8.00 2.40
DC45 Randy Johnson Jsy/300 10.00 3.00
DC46 Carlos Delgado Jsy/500 8.00 2.40
DC47 Roger Clemens Jsy/400 15.00 4.50
DC48 Luis Gonzalez Jsy/500 8.00 2.40
DC49 Marlon Byrd Jsy/500 8.00 2.40
DC50 Carlton Fisk Jsy/500 10.00 3.00
DC51 Manny Ramirez Jsy/500 10.00 3.00
DC52 Vladimir Guerrero Jsy/500 10.00 3.00
DC53 Barry Larkin Jsy/500 10.00 3.00
DC54 Aramis Ramirez Jsy/500 8.00 2.40
DC55 Todd Helton Jsy/300 10.00 3.00
DC56 Carlos Beltran Jsy/250 10.00 3.00
DC57 Jeff Bagwell Jsy/250 10.00 3.00
DC58 Larry Walker Jsy/500 10.00 3.00
DC59 Al Kaline Jsy/200 10.00 3.00
DC60 Chipper Jones Jsy/500 10.00 3.00
DC61 Bernie Williams Jsy/500 10.00 3.00
DC62 Bud Smith Jsy/500 8.00 2.40
DC63 Edgar Martinez Jsy/500 10.00 3.00
DC64 Pedro Martinez Jsy/500 10.00 3.00
DC65 Andre Dawson Jsy/200 8.00 2.40
DC66 Mike Piazza Jsy/100 25.00 7.50
DC67 Barry Zito Jsy/500 8.00 2.40
DC68 Bo Jackson Jsy/300 10.00 3.00
DC69 Nolan Ryan Jsy/400 40.00 12.00
DC70 Troy Glaus Jsy/500 8.00 2.40
DC71 Jorge Posada Jsy/500 10.00 3.00
DC72 Ted Williams Jsy/100 100.00 30.00
DC73 N.Garciaparra Jsy/500 15.00 4.50
DC74 Catfish Hunter Jsy/100 15.00 4.50
DC75 Gary Carter Jsy/500 8.00 2.40
DC76 Craig Biggio Jsy/500 10.00 3.00
DC77 Andruw Jones Jsy/500 8.00 2.40
DC78 R.Henderson Jsy/300 10.00 3.00
DC79 Greg Maddux Jsy/400 15.00 4.50
DC80 Kerry Wood Jsy/500 10.00 3.00
DC81 Alex Rodriguez Bat/500 15.00 4.50
DC82 Don Mattingly Bat/425 25.00 7.50
DC83 Craig Biggio Bat/500 15.00 4.50
DC84 Kazuhisa Ishii Bat/375 15.00 4.50
DC85 Eddie Murray Bat/500 15.00 4.50
DC86 Carlton Fisk Bat/500 15.00 4.50
DC87 Tsuyoshi Shinjo Bat/500 10.00 3.00
DC88 Bo Jackson Bat/500 15.00 4.50
DC89 Eddie Mathews Bat/100 25.00 7.50
DC90 Chipper Jones Bat/500 15.00 4.50
DC91 Adam Dunn Bat/375 15.00 4.50
DC92 Tony Gwynn Bat/200 15.00 4.50
DC93 Kirby Puckett Bat/500 15.00 4.50
DC94 Andre Dawson Bat/500 10.00 3.00
DC95 Bernie Williams Bat/500 15.00 4.50
DC96 Rob. Clemente Bat/300 80.00 24.00
DC97 Babe Ruth Bat/100 250.00 75.00
DC98 Roberto Alomar Bat/500 15.00 4.50
DC99 Frank Thomas Bat/500 15.00 4.50
DC100 So Taguchi Bat/500 15.00 4.50

2002 Diamond Kings DK Originals

Randomly inserted in packs, these 15 cards are printed to a stated print run of 1000 serial numbered sets. These cards are printed on canvas board with a vintage Diamond King look to them.

Nm-Mt Ex-Mt
COMPLETE SET (15)............... 150.00 45.00
DK1 Alex Rodriguez 12.00 3.60
DK2 Kazuhisa Ishii 10.00 3.00
DK3 Pedro Martinez 8.00 2.40
DK4 Nomar Garciaparra 12.00 3.60
DK5 Albert Pujols.................... 15.00 4.50
DK6 Chipper Jones 8.00 2.40
DK7 So Taguchi 8.00 2.40
DK8 Jeff Bagwell........................ 8.00 2.40
DK9 Vladimir Guerrero................ 8.00 2.40
DK10 Derek Jeter 20.00 6.00
DK11 Sammy Sosa 12.00 3.60
DK12 Ichiro Suzuki 12.00 3.60
DK13 Barry Bonds 20.00 6.00
DK14 Jason Giambi 8.00 2.40
DK15 Mike Piazza 12.00 3.60

2002 Diamond Kings Heritage Collection

Inserted in packs to a stated rate of one in 23 hobby and one in 46 retail packs, these 25 cards featue many of baseball's all-time greats highlighted on canvas board stock.

Nm-Mt Ex-Mt
COMPLETE SET (25)............... 200.00 60.00
HC1 Lou Gehrig 10.00 3.00
HC2 Nolan Ryan........................ 15.00 4.50
HC3 Ryne Sandberg.................. 10.00 3.00
HC4 Ted Williams...................... 12.00 3.60
HC5 Roberto Clemente 15.00 4.50
HC6 Mike Schmidt 12.00 3.60
HC7 Roger Clemens.................. 12.00 3.60
HC8 Kirby Puckett...................... 5.00 1.50
HC9 Andre Dawson..................... 4.00 1.20
HC10 Carlton Fisk 4.00 1.20
HC11 Don Mattingly.................. 15.00 4.50
HC12 Juan Marichal.................... 4.00 1.20
HC13 George Brett 15.00 4.50
HC14 Bo Jackson........................ 5.00 1.50
HC15 Eddie Mathews 5.00 1.50
HC16 Randy Johnson 5.00 1.50
HC17 Alan Trammell 4.00 1.20
HC18 Tony Gwynn 8.00 2.40
HC19 Paul Molitor...................... 4.00 1.20
HC20 Barry Bonds 15.00 4.50
HC21 Eddie Murray.................... 5.00 1.50
HC22 Catfish Hunter 4.00 1.20
HC23 Rickey Henderson 5.00 1.50
HC24 Cal Ripken 20.00 6.00
HC25 Babe Ruth 15.00 4.50

2002 Diamond Kings Recollection Autographs

Randomly inserted in packs, these cards are original Diamond Kings which Donruss/Playoff bought back and had the feature player sign. These cards are all numbered to differing amounts and we have notated that information in our checklist. No pricing is provided on quantities of 25 or less.

Nm-Mt Ex-Mt
47 Alan Trammell 88 DK/110.... 40.00 12.00

2002 Diamond Kings T204

Randomly inserted in packs, these 25 cards are printed to a stated print run of 1000 serial numbered sets. These cards are designed just like the Ramly T204 set which was issued early in the 20th century.

Nm-Mt Ex-Mt
COMPLETE SET (25)............... 250.00 75.00

RC1 Vladimir Guerrero................ 8.00 2.40
RC2 Jeff Bagwell........................ 5.00 1.50
RC3 Barry Bonds 20.00 6.00
RC4 Rickey Henderson 8.00 2.40
RC5 Mike Piazza 12.00 3.60
RC6 Derek Jeter........................ 20.00 6.00
RC7 Kazuhisa Ishii 10.00 3.00
RC8 Ichiro Suzuki 12.00 3.60
RC9 Chipper Jones 8.00 2.40
RC10 Sammy Sosa 12.00 3.60
RC11 Don Mattingly.................. 20.00 6.00
RC12 Shawn Green..................... 5.00 1.50
RC13 Nomar Garciaparra.......... 12.00 3.60
RC14 Luis Gonzalez..................... 5.00 1.50
RC15 Albert Pujols.................... 15.00 4.50
RC16 Cal Ripken 25.00 7.50
RC17 Todd Helton 5.00 1.50
RC18 Hideo Nomo 8.00 2.40
RC19 Alex Rodriguez 12.00 3.60
RC20 So Taguchi 5.00 1.50
RC21 Lance Berkman 5.00 1.50
RC22 Tony Gwynn 10.00 3.00
RC23 Roger Clemens................. 15.00 4.50
RC24 Jason Giambi 5.00 1.50
RC25 Ken Griffey Jr. 12.00 3.60

2002 Diamond Kings Timeline

Issued at a stated rate of one in 60 hobby and one in 120 retail packs, these 10 cards feature two players who have something in common.

Nm-Mt Ex-Mt
COMPLETE SET (10)............... 120.00 36.00
TL1 Lou Gehrig 15.00 4.50
Don Mattingly
TL2 Hideo Nomo....................... 10.00 3.00
Ichiro Suzuki
TL3 Cal Ripken.......................... 20.00 6.00
Alex Rodriguez
TL4 Mike Schmidt..................... 12.00 3.60
Scott Rolen
TL5 Ichiro Suzuki..................... 12.00 3.60
Albert Pujols
TL6 Curt Schilling 10.00 3.00
Randy Johnson
TL7 Chipper Jones.................... 10.00 3.00
Eddie Mathews
TL8 Lou Gehrig 20.00 6.00
Cal Ripken
TL9 Derek Jeter........................ 15.00 4.50
Roger Clemens
TL10 Kazuhisa Ishii 10.00 3.00
SoTaguchi

2003 Diamond Kings

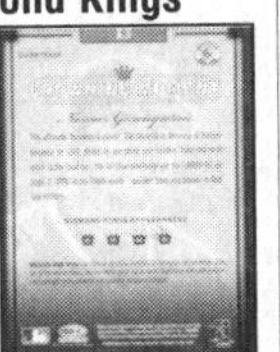

This 200-card set was released in two separate series. The primary Diamond Kings product - containing cards 1-176 from the basic set - was issued in March, 2003. These cards were issued in five card packs with an $4 SRP. These packs came 24 packs to a box and 20 boxes to a case. Cards numbered 151 through 158 feature some of the leading rookie prospects and those cards were issued at a stated rate of one in six. Cards numbered 159 through 175 feature retired greats and those cards were also issued at a stated rate of one in six. Card number 176 feature Cuban refugee Jose Contreras who was signed to a major free agent contract before the 2003 season began. The Contreras card was not on the original checklist. Cards 177-189/191-201 were distributed at a rate of 1:24 packs of DLP Rookies and Traded in December, 2003. Please note, card 190 does not exist.

Nm-Mt Ex-Mt
COMP.LO SET (176)............... 150.00 45.00
COMP.LO SET w/o SP's (150) .. 50.00 15.00
COMMON CARD (1-150) .... .50 .15
COMMON CARD (151-158) .... 2.00 .60
COMMON CARD (159-175) 4.00 1.20
COMMON CARD (177-201) 4.00 1.20
1 Darin Erstad .... .50 .15
2 Garret Anderson........................ .50 .15
3 Troy Glaus................................ .50 .15
4 David Eckstein .... .50 .15
5 Jarrod Washburn .... .50 .15
6 Adam Kennedy........................... .50 .15
7 Jay Gibbons............................... .50 .15
8 Tony Batista .... .50 .15
9 Melvin Mora.............................. .50 .15
10 Rodrigo Lopez .... .50 .15
11 Manny Ramirez .... .75 .23
12 Pedro Martinez....................... 1.25 .35
13 Nomar Garciaparra................ 2.00 .60
14 Rickey Henderson .... 1.25 .35
15 Johnny Damon........................ 1.25 .35
16 Derek Lowe............................. .50 .15
17 Cliff Floyd............................... .50 .15
18 Frank Thomas .... 1.25 .35
19 Magglio Ordonez..................... .50 .15
20 Paul Konerko .... .50 .15
21 Mark Buehrle .... .50 .15
22 C.C. Sabathia .... .50 .15
23 Omar Vizquel .... .75 .23
24 Jim Thome.............................. 1.25 .35
25 Ellis Burks............................... .50 .15
26 Robert Fick.............................. .50 .15
27 Bobby Higginson .... .50 .15
28 Randall Simon .... .50 .15
29 Carlos Pena.............................. .50 .15
30 Carlos Beltran .... .75 .23
31 Paul Byrd .... .50 .15
32 Raul Ibanez .... .50 .15
33 Mike Sweeney .... .50 .15
34 Torii Hunter .... .50 .15
35 Corey Koskie............................ .50 .15
36 A.J. Pierzynski .... .50 .15
37 Cristian Guzman....................... .50 .15
38 Jacque Jones .... .50 .15
39 Derek Jeter............................. 3.00 .90
40 Bernie Williams......................... .75 .23
41 Roger Clemens .... 2.50 .75
42 Mike Mussina........................... .75 .23
43 Jorge Posada .... .75 .23
44 Alfonso Soriano .... .75 .23
45 Jason Giambi .... .50 .15
46 Robin Ventura.......................... .50 .15
47 David Wells .... .50 .15
48 Tim Hudson .... .50 .15
49 Barry Zito .... .50 .15
50 Mark Mulder .... .50 .15
51 Miguel Tejada .... .50 .15
52 Eric Chavez .... .50 .15
53 Jermaine Dye............................ .50 .15
54 Ichiro Suzuki .... 2.00 .60
55 Edgar Martinez......................... .75 .23
56 John Olerud .... .50 .15
57 Dan Wilson .... .50 .15
58 Joel Pineiro.............................. .50 .15
59 Kazuhiro Sasaki .... .50 .15
60 Freddy Garcia .... .50 .15
61 Aubrey Huff.............................. .50 .15
62 Steve Cox................................. .50 .15
63 Randy Winn .... .50 .15
64 Alex Rodriguez .... 2.00 .60
65 Juan Gonzalez.......................... .75 .23
66 Rafael Palmeiro......................... .75 .23
67 Ivan Rodriguez....................... 1.25 .35
68 Kenny Rogers .... .50 .15
69 Carlos Delgado......................... .50 .15
70 Eric Hinske............................... .50 .15
71 Roy Halladay .... .50 .15
72 Vernon Wells............................ .50 .15
73 Shannon Stewart .... .50 .15
74 Curt Schilling .... .50 .15
75 Randy Johnson....................... 1.25 .35
76 Luis Gonzalez........................... .50 .15
77 Mark Grace .... .75 .23
78 Junior Spivey .... .50 .15
79 Greg Maddux .... 2.00 .60
80 Tom Glavine .... .75 .23
81 John Smoltz.............................. .75 .23
82 Chipper Jones .... 1.25 .35
83 Gary Sheffield .... .50 .15
84 Andruw Jones .... .50 .15
85 Kerry Wood .... 1.25 .35
86 Fred McGriff............................. .75 .23
87 Sammy Sosa.......................... 2.00 .60
88 Mark Prior............................. 1.25 .35
89 Ken Griffey Jr. .... 2.00 .60
90 Barry Larkin .... .75 .23
91 Adam Dunn .... .75 .23
92 Sean Casey .... .50 .15
93 Austin Kearns........................... .50 .15
94 Aaron Boone .... .50 .15
95 Larry Walker .... .75 .23
96 Todd Helton .... .75 .23
97 Jason Jennings......................... .50 .15
98 Jay Payton .... .50 .15
99 Josh Beckett .... .50 .15
100 Mike Lowell............................ .50 .15
101 A.J. Burnett............................ .50 .15
102 Jeff Bagwell .... .75 .23
103 Craig Biggio .... .75 .23
104 Lance Berkman .... .50 .15
105 Roy Oswalt............................. .50 .15
106 Wade Miller............................ .50 .15
107 Shawn Green .... .50 .15
108 Adrian Beltre .... .75 .23
109 Hideo Nomo......................... 1.25 .35
110 Kazuhisa Ishii......................... .50 .15
111 Odalis Perez........................... .50 .15
112 Paul Lo Duca .... .50 .15
113 Ben Sheets............................. .50 .15
114 Richie Sexson .... .50 .15
115 Jose Hernandez .... .50 .15
116 Vladimir Guerrero .... 1.25 .35
117 Jose Vidro.............................. .50 .15
118 Tomo Ohka............................. .50 .15
119 Andres Galarraga .... .50 .15
120 Bartolo Colon......................... .50 .15
121 Mike Piazza.......................... 2.00 .60
122 Roberto Alomar .... .75 .23
123 Mo Vaughn .... .50 .15
124 Al Leiter .... .50 .15
125 Edgardo Alfonzo..................... .50 .15
126 Pat Burrell .... .50 .15
127 Bobby Abreu .... .50 .15
128 Mike Lieberthal .... .50 .15
129 Vicente Padilla .... .50 .15
130 Marlon Byrd .... .50 .15
131 Jason Kendall......................... .50 .15
132 Brian Giles .... .50 .15
133 Aramis Ramirez .... .50 .15
134 Kip Wells............................... .50 .15
135 Ryan Klesko .... .50 .15
136 Phil Nevin.............................. .50 .15
137 Brian Lawrence .... .50 .15
138 Sean Burroughs...................... .50 .15
139 Mark Kotsay........................... .50 .15
140 Barry Bonds .... 3.00 .90
141 Jeff Kent................................ .50 .15
142 Benito Santiago...................... .50 .15
143 Kirk Rueter............................. .50 .15
144 Jason Schmidt........................ .50 .15
145 Jim Edmonds........................... .50 .15
146 J.D. Drew .... .50 .15
147 Albert Pujols .... 2.50 .75
148 Tino Martinez .... .75 .23
149 Matt Morris............................ .50 .15
150 Scott Rolen.......................... 1.25 .35
151 Joe Borchard ROO .... 2.00 .60
152 Cliff Lee ROO .... 2.00 .60
153 Brian Tallet ROO.................... 2.00 .60
154 Freddy Sanchez ROO .... 2.00 .60
155 Chone Figgins ROO............... 2.00 .60
156 Kevin Cash ROO .... 2.00 .60
157 Justin Wayne ROO................. 2.00 .60
158 Ben Kozlowski ROO .... 2.00 .60
159 Babe Ruth RET..................... 10.00 3.00
160 Jackie Robinson RET 5.00 1.50
161 Ozzie Smith RET 8.00 2.40
162 Lou Gehrig RET 6.00 1.80
163 Stan Musial RET 6.00 1.80
164 Mike Schmidt RET 10.00 3.00
165 Carlton Fisk RET 5.00 1.50
166 George Brett RET............... 12.00 3.60
167 Dale Murphy RET.................. 8.00 2.40
168 Cal Ripken RET 12.00 3.60
169 Tony Gwynn RET.................... 5.00 1.50
170 Don Mattingly RET.............. 10.00 3.00
171 Jack Morris RET 4.00 1.20
172 Ty Cobb RET 5.00 1.50
173 Nolan Ryan RET................... 10.00 3.00
174 Ryne Sandberg RET................ 8.00 2.40
175 Thurman Munson RET........... 5.00 1.50
176 Jose Contreras ROO RC......... 8.00 2.40
177 Hideki Matsui ROO RC....... 10.00 3.00
178 Jeremy Bonderman ROO RC 5.00 1.50
179 Brandon Webb ROO RC......... 5.00 1.50
180 Adam Loewen ROO RC 5.00 1.50
181 Chien-Ming Wang ROO RC .. 5.00 1.50
182 Hong-Chih Kuo ROO RC 5.00 1.50
183 Clint Barmes ROO RC 5.00 1.50
184 Guillermo Quiroz ROO RC...... 5.00 1.50
185 Edgar Gonzalez ROO RC 4.00 1.20
186 Todd Wellemeyer ROO RC 5.00 1.50
187 Dan Haren ROO RC 5.00 1.50
188 Dustin McGowan ROO RC 5.00 1.50
189 Preston Larrison ROO RC 5.00 1.50
190 Does Not Exist ....
191 Kevin Youkilis ROO RC 6.00 1.80
192 Bubba Nelson ROO RC 5.00 1.50
193 Chris Burke ROO RC 5.00 1.50
194 J.D. Durbin ROO RC 5.00 1.50
195 Ryan Howard ROO RC 10.00 3.00
196 Jason Kubel ROO RC 8.00 2.40
197 Brendan Harris ROO RC 5.00 1.50
198 Brian Bruney ROO RC 5.00 1.50
199 Ramon Nivar ROO RC 5.00 1.50
200 Rickie Weeks ROO RC 10.00 3.00
201 Delmon Young ROO RC 12.00 3.60

2003 Diamond Kings Bronze Foil

Randomly inserted in packs, this is a parallel to the Diamond Kings set. Cards 177-201 were randomly seeded into packs of DLP Rookies and Traded and unlike the first 176 cards are serial numbered to 200 copies per. The bronze cards can be identified by the white frames and the bronze foil used for the cards.

Nm-Mt Ex-Mt
*BRONZE 1-150: 1.5X TO 4X BASIC ..
*BRONZE 151-158: .6X TO 1.5X BASIC
*BRONZE 159-175: .6X TO 1.5X BASIC
*BRONZE 176: .4X TO 1X BASIC.......
*BRZ 177-189/191-201: .5X TO 1.2X BASIC

2003 Diamond Kings Gold Foil

Randomly inserted into packs, this is a parallel to the Diamond Kings insert set. Cards 177-201 were randomly seeded into packs of DLP Rookies and Traded. These cards feature black frames which surround the gold foil usage. Cards 1-176 were issued to a stated print run of 100 serial numbered sets and 177-201 to a stated print run of 50 serial numbered copies per.

Nm-Mt Ex-Mt
*GOLD 1-150: 6X TO 15X BASIC.......
*GOLD 151-158: 2X TO 5X BASIC.......
*GOLD 176: 1X TO 2.5X BASIC.......
*GOLD 177-201: 1.25X TO 3X BASIC.
159 Babe Ruth RET.................. 50.00 15.00
160 Jackie Robinson RET......... 25.00 7.50
161 Ozzie Smith RET 40.00 12.00
162 Lou Gehrig RET 30.00 9.00
163 Stan Musial RET 40.00 12.00
164 Mike Schmidt RET 50.00 15.00
165 Carlton Fisk RET 25.00 7.50
166 George Brett RET 60.00 18.00
167 Dale Murphy RET............... 60.00 18.00
168 Cal Ripken RET 80.00 24.00
169 Tony Gwynn RET................ 30.00 9.00
170 Don Mattingly RET............. 60.00 18.00
171 Jack Morris RET 20.00 6.00
172 Ty Cobb RET 40.00 12.00
173 Nolan Ryan RET................. 60.00 18.00
174 Ryne Sandberg RET........... 60.00 18.00
175 Thurman Munson RET....... 40.00 12.00

2003 Diamond Kings Silver Foil

Randomly inserted into packs, this is a parallel to the Diamond Kings set. Cards 177-201 were randomly seeded into packs of DLP Rookies and Traded. These cards can be identified by the grey frames surrounding the silver foil. Cards 1-176 were serial numbered to 400 and 177-201 were serial numbered to 100.

Nm-Mt Ex-Mt
*SILVER 1-150: 3X TO 8X BASIC ....
*SILVER 151-158: 1X TO 2.5X BASIC
*SILVER 159-175: 1X TO 2.5X BASIC
*SILVER 176: .5X TO 1.2X BASIC.......
*SILVER 177-201: .6X TO 1.5X BASIC

2003 Diamond Kings Diamond Cut Collection

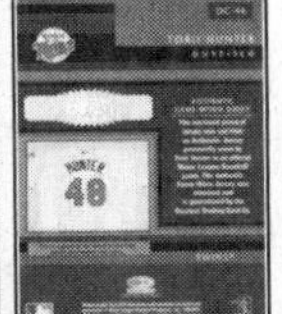

Randomly inserted into packs, this 110 card set features either an autograph or a game-used memorabilia piece. Since these cards are issued to a varying amount of cards, we have notated that information next to the player's name in our checklist.

Nm-Mt Ex-Mt
1 Barry Zito AU/75 .... 60.00 18.00
2 Edgar Martinez AU/125.......... 50.00 15.00
3 Jay Gibbons AU/150 .... 25.00 7.50
4 Joe Borchard AU/150............. 25.00 7.50
5 Marlon Byrd AU/150 .... 25.00 7.50
6 Adam Dunn AU/150............... 40.00 12.00
7 Torii Hunter AU/150 .... 40.00 12.00
8 Vladimir Guerrero AU/25..............
9 Wade Miller AU/150 .... 25.00 7.50
10 Alfonso Soriano AU/100 .... 60.00 18.00
11 Brian Lawrence AU/150 .... 25.00 7.50
12 Cliff Floyd AU/100................ 30.00 9.00
13 Dale Murphy AU/75 .... 80.00 24.00
14 Jack Morris AU/150 .... 30.00 9.00
15 Eric Hinske AU/150.............. 25.00 7.50
16 Jason Jennings AU/150........ 25.00 7.50
17 Mark Buehrle AU/150........... 30.00 9.00
18 Mark Prior AU/150............... 60.00 18.00
19 Mark Mulder AU/150 .... 30.00 9.00
20 Mike Sweeney AU/150 .... 30.00 9.00
21 Nolan Ryan AU/50 .... 250.00 75.00
22 Don Mattingly AU/75 .... 150.00 45.00
23 Andruw Jones AU/75 .... 50.00 15.00
24 Aubrey Huff AU/150............. 30.00 9.00
25 Rickey Henderson AU/25 ....
26 Nolan Ryan Jsy/250 .... 50.00 15.00
27 Ozzie Smith Jsy/400 .... 15.00 4.50
28 Rickey Henderson Jsy/300 .. 10.00 3.00
29 Jack Morris Jsy/500 .... 8.00 2.40
30 George Brett Jsy/350 .... 25.00 7.50
31 Cal Ripken Jsy/300 .... 40.00 12.00
32 Ryne Sandberg Jsy/450....... 20.00 6.00
33 Don Mattingly Jsy/400 .... 25.00 7.50
34 Tony Gwynn Jsy/400............ 15.00 4.50
35 Dale Murphy Jsy/350 .... 10.00 3.00
36 Carlton Fisk Jsy/400 .... 10.00 3.00
37 Stan Musial Jsy/50 ....
38 Lou Gehrig Jsy/50 .... 250.00 75.00
39 Garret Anderson Jsy/450....... 8.00 2.40
40 Pedro Martinez Jsy/400....... 10.00 3.00
41 Nomar Garciaparra Jsy/350 . 15.00 4.50
42 Magglio Ordonez Jsy/450 ...... 8.00 2.40
43 C.C. Sabathia Jsy/500 .... 8.00 2.40
44 Omar Vizquel Jsy/250 .... 15.00 4.50
45 Jim Thome Jsy/500 .... 10.00 3.00
46 Torii Hunter Jsy/500 .... 8.00 2.40
47 Roger Clemens Jsy/500........ 15.00 4.50
48 Alfonso Soriano Jsy/400....... 10.00 3.00
49 Tim Hudson Jsy/500 .... 8.00 2.40
50 Barry Zito Jsy/350 .... 8.00 2.40
51 Mark Mulder Jsy/500.............. 8.00 2.40
52 Miguel Tejada Jsy/400 .... 8.00 2.40
53 John Olerud Jsy/350.............. 8.00 2.40
54 Alex Rodriguez Jsy/500 .... 15.00 4.50
55 Rafael Palmeiro Jsy/500 ...... 10.00 3.00
56 Curt Schilling Jsy/500............ 8.00 2.40
57 Randy Johnson Jsy/400 ...... 10.00 3.00
58 Greg Maddux Jsy/350.......... 15.00 4.50
59 John Smoltz Jsy/400 .... 10.00 3.00
60 Chipper Jones Jsy/450 .... 10.00 3.00
61 Andruw Jones Jsy/500 .... 8.00 2.40
62 Kerry Wood Jsy/500 .... 10.00 3.00
63 Mark Prior Jsy/500 .... 10.00 3.00
64 Adam Dunn Jsy/350 .... 10.00 3.00
65 Larry Walker Jsy/500 .... 10.00 3.00
66 Todd Helton Jsy/500 .... 10.00 3.00
67 Jeff Bagwell Jsy/500 .... 10.00 3.00
68 Roy Oswalt Jsy/500............... 8.00 2.40
69 Hideo Nomo Jsy/150 .... 15.00 4.50
70 Kazuhisa Ishii Jsy/250 .... 10.00 3.00
71 Vladimir Guerrero Jsy/500... 10.00 3.00
72 Mike Piazza Jsy/500............ 15.00 4.50
73 Joe Borchard Jsy/500 .... 8.00 2.40
74 Ryan Klesko Jsy/500.............. 8.00 2.40
75 Shawn Green Jsy/500 .... 8.00 2.40
76 George Brett Bat/350 .... 25.00 7.50
77 Ozzie Smith Bat/450............ 15.00 4.50
78 Cal Ripken Bat/150 .... 50.00 15.00
79 Don Mattingly Bat/400 .... 25.00 7.50
80 Babe Ruth Bat/50.............. 250.00 75.00
81 Dale Murphy Bat/350 .... 10.00 3.00
82 Rickey Henderson Bat/500... 10.00 3.00
83 Ivan Rodriguez Bat/500 ...... 10.00 3.00
84 Marlon Byrd Bat/500.............. 8.00 2.40
85 Eric Chavez Bat/500............... 8.00 2.40
86 Nomar Garciaparra Bat/500 . 15.00 4.50
87 Alex Rodriguez Bat/500 ...... 15.00 4.50
88 Vladimir Guerrero Bat/500... 10.00 3.00
89 Paul Lo Duca Bat/500 .... 8.00 2.40
90 Richie Sexson Bat/500........... 8.00 2.40
91 Mike Piazza Bat/350 .... 15.00 4.50
92 J.D. Drew Bat/500.................. 8.00 2.40
93 Juan Gonzalez Bat/500......... 10.00 3.00
94 Pat Burrell Bat/500................. 8.00 2.40
95 Adam Dunn Bat/250............. 15.00 4.50
96 Mike Schmidt Bat/500 .... 20.00 6.00
97 Ryne Sandberg Bat/500....... 20.00 6.00
98 Edgardo Alfonzo Bat/500 ...... 8.00 2.40
99 Andruw Jones Bat/500 .... 8.00 2.40
100 Carlos Beltran Bat/500....... 10.00 3.00
101 Jeff Bagwell Bat/500 .... 10.00 3.00
102 Lance Berkman Bat/500 .... 8.00 2.40
103 Luis Gonzalez Bat/500 .... 8.00 2.40
104 Carlos Delgado Bat/500 .... 8.00 2.40
105 Jim Edmonds Bat/250 .... 10.00 3.00
106 Alf Soriano Hat-Jsy/75....... 40.00 12.00
107 Greg Maddux Jsy-AU/50.. 200.00 60.00
108 Ty Cobb Pants-Bat/25 ....
109 Adam Dunn Bat-AU/50....... 80.00 24.00
110 R.Henderson Jsy-Bat/50.... 25.00 7.50

2003 Diamond Kings DK Evolution

Issued at a stated rate of one in 18 hobby and one in 36 retail, this 25 card set features both the original photo as well as the artwork.

Nm-Mt Ex-Mt
1 Cal Ripken.............................. 20.00 6.00

2 Ichiro Suzuki 10.00 3.00
3 Randy Johnson 6.00 1.80
4 Pedro Martinez 6.00 1.80
5 Nolan Ryan 15.00 4.50
6 Derek Jeter 15.00 4.50
7 Kerry Wood 6.00 1.80
8 Alex Rodriguez 10.00 3.00
9 Magglio Ordonez 5.00 1.50
10 Greg Maddux 10.00 3.00
11 Todd Helton 5.00 1.50
12 Sammy Sosa 10.00 3.00
13 Lou Gehrig 12.00 3.60
14 Lance Berkman 5.00 1.50
15 Barry Zito 5.00 1.50
16 Barry Bonds 15.00 4.50
17 Tom Glavine 5.00 1.50
18 Shawn Green 5.00 1.50
19 Roger Clemens 12.00 3.60
20 Nomar Garciaparra 10.00 3.00
21 Tony Gwynn 8.00 2.40
22 Vladimir Guerrero 6.00 1.80
23 Albert Pujols 12.00 3.60
24 Chipper Jones 6.00 1.80
25 Alfonso Soriano 5.00 1.50

2003 Diamond Kings Heritage Collection

Issued at a stated rate of one in 23, this 25 card set features a mix of past and present superstars spotlighted with silver holo-foil on canvas board.

Nm-Mt Ex-Mt
1 Ozzie Smith 10.00 3.00
2 Lou Gehrig 12.00 3.60
3 Stan Musial 10.00 3.00
4 Mike Schmidt 12.00 3.60
5 Carlton Fisk 5.00 1.50
6 George Brett 15.00 4.50
7 Dale Murphy 6.00 1.80
8 Cal Ripken 20.00 6.00
9 Tony Gwynn 8.00 2.40
10 Don Mattingly 15.00 4.50
11 Jack Morris 5.00 1.50
12 Ty Cobb 10.00 3.00
13 Nolan Ryan 15.00 4.50
14 Ryne Sandberg 12.00 3.60
15 Thurman Munson 6.00 1.80
16 Ichiro Suzuki 10.00 3.00
17 Derek Jeter 15.00 4.50
18 Greg Maddux 10.00 3.00
19 Sammy Sosa 10.00 3.00
20 Pedro Martinez 6.00 1.80
21 Alex Rodriguez 10.00 3.00
22 Roger Clemens 12.00 3.60
23 Barry Bonds 15.00 4.50
24 Lance Berkman 5.00 1.50
25 Vladimir Guerrero 6.00 1.80

2003 Diamond Kings HOF Heroes Reprints

Issued in the style of the 1983 Donruss Hall of Fame Heroes set, this set was issued at a stated rate of one in 43 hobby and one in 67 retail.

Nm-Mt Ex-Mt
1 Bob Feller 8.00 2.40
2 Al Kaline 8.00 2.40
3 Lou Boudreau 8.00 2.40
4 Duke Snider 8.00 2.40
5 Jackie Robinson 8.00 2.40
6 Early Wynn 8.00 2.40
7 Yogi Berra 8.00 2.40
8 Stan Musial 10.00 3.00
9 Ty Cobb 10.00 3.00
10 Ted Williams 12.00 3.60

2003 Diamond Kings HOF Heroes Reprints Materials

Randomly inserted into packs, these cards parallel the HOF Heroes Reprint set. Each card has a game-used memorabilia piece used by that player during his career. Each of these cards were issued to a stated print run of 50 serial numbered sets.

Nm-Mt Ex-Mt
1 Bob Feller Jsy
2 Al Kaline Bat
3 Lou Boudreau Jsy
4 Duke Snider Bat
5 Jackie Robinson Jsy
6 Early Wynn Jsy
7 Yogi Berra Bat
8 Stan Musial Bat
9 Ty Cobb Bat
10 Ted Williams Jsy

2003 Diamond Kings Recollection

Randomly inserted into packs, these 14 cards feature older repurchased Diamond King subset cards or 1983 Hall of Fame Heroes cards. As each of these cards were issued to a stated print run of 15 or fewer copies, no pricing is available due to market scarcity.

Nm-Mt Ex-Mt
5 Lou Boudreau 83 HOF/3
15 Roberto Clemente 83 HOF/5
16 Roberto Clemente 87 DK/9
17 Ty Cobb 83 DK/10
18 Ty Cobb 83 HOF/5
34 Lou Gehrig 85 DK/10
44 Monte Irvin 83 HOF/5
48 Bob Lemon 83 HOF/5
66 Dan Quisenberry 85 DK/2
69 Jackie Robinson 83 HOF/5
82 Willie Stargell 83 DK/15
83 Willie Stargell 91 DK/6
90 Ted Williams 83 HOF/4
92 Early Wynn 83 HOF/5

2003 Diamond Kings Recollection Autographs

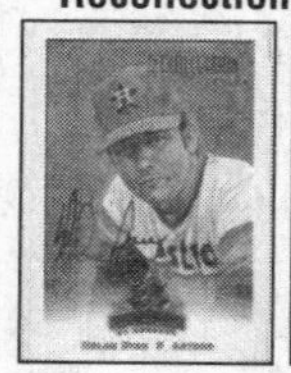

Randomly inserted in packs, these cards feature not only repurchased Donruss Diamond King cards but also an authentic autograph of the featured player. These cards were issued to a varying print run amount and we have notated that information next to the player's name in our checklist. Please note that for cards with a print run of 40 of fewer, no pricing is provided due to market scarcity.

Nm-Mt Ex-Mt
SEE BECKETT.COM FOR PRINT RUNS
NO PRICING ON QTY OF 40 OR LESS
2 Brandon Berger 02 DK/99 15.00 4.50

2003 Diamond Kings Team Timeline

Randomly inserted into packs, these 10 cards feature both an active and retired player from the same team. Each of these cards are printed on canvas board and were issued to a stated print run of 1000 sets.

Nm-Mt Ex-Mt
1 Nolan Ryan 15.00 4.50
Roy Oswalt
2 Dale Murphy 8.00 2.40
Chipper Jones
3 Stan Musial 10.00 3.00
Jim Edmonds
4 George Brett 15.00 4.50
Mike Sweeney
5 Tony Gwynn 8.00 2.40
Ryan Klesko
6 Carlton Fisk 8.00 2.40
Magglio Ordonez
7 Mike Schmidt 20.00 6.00
Pat Burrell
8 Don Mattingly 20.00 6.00
Bernie Williams
9 Ryne Sandberg 15.00 4.50
Kerry Wood
10 Lou Gehrig 12.00 3.60
Alfonso Soriano

2003 Diamond Kings Team Timeline Jerseys

Randomly inserted into packs, this is a parallel to the Team Timeline insert set. Each of these cards feature two game-worn jersey swatches and were issued to a stated print run of 100 serial numbered sets.

Nm-Mt Ex-Mt
1 Nolan Ryan 120.00 36.00

Roy Oswalt
2 Dale Murphy 40.00 12.00
Chipper Jones
3 Stan Musial 50.00 15.00
Jim Edmonds
4 George Brett 80.00 24.00
Mike Sweeney
5 Tony Gwynn 50.00 15.00
Ryan Klesko
6 Carlton Fisk 40.00 12.00
Magglio Ordonez
7 Mike Schmidt 100.00 30.00
Pat Burrell
8 Don Mattingly 100.00 30.00
Bernie Williams
9 Ryne Sandberg 80.00 24.00
Kerry Wood
10 Lou Gehrig 250.00 75.00
Alfonso Soriano/50

2004 Diamond Kings

This 175-card set was released in February, 2004. This set was issued in five-card packs with an $6 SRP which came 12 packs to a box and 16 boxes to a case. This product has a dizzying amount of parallels and insert cards which included DK Materials which had two memorabilia pieces on each card and DK Combos which had not only those two memorabilia pieces but also had an authentic autograph from the player. In addition, many other insert sets were issued including a 134-card recollection autograph insert set as well as many other insert sets. This product; despite the seeming never-ending array of parallel and insert sets which made identifying cards difficult actually became one of the hobby hits of the first part of 2004. Cards numbered 1 through 150 feature current major leaguers while cards 151 through 158 are a flashback featuring some of today's players in an then and now format and cards numbered 159 through 175 is a legends subset. Cards numbered 151 through 175 were randomly inserted into packs.

Nm-Mt Ex-Mt
COMPLETE SET w/Sepia (200) 200.00 60.00
COMPLETE SET (175) 100.00 30.00
COMP.SET w/o SP's (150) 40.00 12.00
COMMON CARD (1-150) .50 .15
COMMON CARD (151-175) 3.00 .90
151-175 RANDOM INSERTS IN PACKS
1 Alex Rodriguez 2.00 .60
2 Andruw Jones .50 .15
3 Nomar Garciaparra 2.00 .60
4 Kerry Wood 1.25 .35
5 Magglio Ordonez .50 .15
6 Victor Martinez .50 .15
7 Jeremy Bonderman .50 .15
8 Josh Beckett .50 .15
9 Jeff Kent .50 .15
10 Carlos Beltran .75 .23
11 Hideo Nomo 1.25 .35
12 Richie Sexson .50 .15
13 Jose Vidro .50 .15
14 Jae Weong Seo .50 .15
15 Alfonso Soriano .75 .23
16 Barry Zito .50 .15
17 Brett Myers .50 .15
18 Brian Giles .50 .15
19 Edgar Martinez .75 .23
20 Jim Edmonds .50 .15
21 Rocco Baldelli .50 .15
22 Mark Teixeira .50 .15
23 Carlos Delgado .50 .15
24 Julius Matos .50 .15
25 Jose Reyes .50 .15
26 Marlon Byrd .50 .15
27 Albert Pujols 2.50 .75
28 Vernon Wells .50 .15
29 Garret Anderson .50 .15
30 Jerome Williams .50 .15
31 Chipper Jones 1.25 .35
32 Rich Harden .50 .15
33 Manny Ramirez .75 .23
34 Derek Jeter 2.50 .75
35 Brandon Webb .50 .15
36 Mark Prior 1.25 .35
37 Roy Halladay .50 .15
38 Frank Thomas 1.25 .35
39 Rafael Palmeiro .75 .23
40 Adam Dunn .75 .23
41 Aubrey Huff .50 .15
42 Todd Helton .75 .23
43 Matt Morris .50 .15
44 Dontrelle Willis .50 .15
45 Lance Berkman .50 .15
46 Mike Sweeney .50 .15
47 Kazuhisa Ishii .50 .15
48 Torii Hunter .50 .15
49 Vladimir Guerrero 1.25 .35
50 Mike Piazza 2.00 .60
51 Alexis Rios .50 .15
52 Shannon Stewart .50 .15
53 Eric Hinske .50 .15
54 Jason Jennings .50 .15
55 Jason Giambi .50 .15
56 Brandon Claussen .50 .15
57 Joe Thurston .50 .15
58 Ramon Nivar .50 .15
59 Jay Gibbons .50 .15
60 Eric Chavez .50 .15
61 Jimmy Gobble .50 .15
62 Walter Young .50 .15
63 Mark Grace .75 .23
64 Austin Kearns .50 .15
65 Bob Abreu .50 .15
66 Hee Seop Choi .50 .15
67 Brandon Phillips .50 .15
68 Rickie Weeks .50 .15
69 Luis Gonzalez .50 .15
70 Mariano Rivera .75 .23
71 Jason Lane .50 .15
72 Xavier Nady .50 .15
73 Runelvys Hernandez .50 .15
74 Aramis Ramirez .50 .15
75 Ichiro Suzuki 2.00 .60
76 Cliff Lee .50 .15
77 Chris Snelling .50 .15
78 Ryan Wagner .50 .15
79 Miguel Tejada .50 .15
80 Juan Gonzalez .75 .23
81 Joe Borchard .50 .15
82 Gary Sheffield .50 .15
83 Wade Miller .50 .15
84 Jeff Bagwell .75 .23
85 Ryan Church .50 .15
86 Adrian Beltre .75 .23
87 Jeff Baker .50 .15
88 Adam Loewen .50 .15
89 Bernie Williams .75 .23
90 Pedro Martinez 1.25 .35
91 Carlos Rivera .50 .15
92 Junior Spivey .50 .15
93 Tim Hudson .50 .15
94 Troy Glaus .50 .15
95 Ken Griffey Jr. 2.00 .60
96 Alexis Gomez .50 .15
97 Antonio Perez .50 .15
98 Dan Haren .50 .15
99 Ivan Rodriguez 1.25 .35
100 Randy Johnson 1.25 .35
101 Lyle Overbay .50 .15
102 Oliver Perez .50 .15
103 Miguel Cabrera .75 .23
104 Scott Rolen 1.25 .35
105 Roger Clemens 2.50 .75
106 Brian Tallet .50 .15
107 Nic Jackson .50 .15
108 Angel Berroa .50 .15
109 Hank Blalock .50 .15
110 Ryan Klesko .50 .15
111 Jose Castillo .50 .15
112 Paul Konerko .50 .15
113 Greg Maddux 2.00 .60
114 Mark Mulder .50 .15
115 Pat Burrell .50 .15
116 Garrett Atkins .50 .15
117 Jeremy Guthrie .50 .15
118 Orlando Cabrera .50 .15
119 Nick Johnson .50 .15
120 Tom Glavine .75 .23
121 Morgan Ensberg .50 .15
122 Sean Casey .50 .15
123 Orlando Hudson .50 .15
124 Hideki Matsui 2.00 .60
125 Craig Biggio .75 .23
126 Adam LaRoche .50 .15
127 Hong-Chih Kuo .50 .15
128 Paul Lo Duca .50 .15
129 Shawn Green .50 .15
130 Luis Castillo .50 .15
131 Joe Crede .50 .15
132 Ken Harvey .50 .15
133 Freddy Sanchez .50 .15
134 Roy Oswalt .50 .15
135 Curt Schilling 1.25 .35
136 Alfredo Amezaga .50 .15
137 Chien-Ming Wang .50 .15
138 Barry Larkin .75 .23
139 Trot Nixon .50 .15
140 Jim Thome 1.25 .35
141 Bret Boone .50 .15
142 Jacque Jones .50 .15
143 Travis Hafner .50 .15
144 Sammy Sosa 2.00 .60
145 Mike Mussina .75 .23
146 Vinny Chulk .50 .15
147 Chad Gaudin .50 .15
148 Delmon Young .75 .23
149 Mike Lowell .50 .15
150 Rickey Henderson 1.25 .35
151 Roger Clemens FB 6.00 1.80
152 Mark Grace FB 4.00 1.20
153 Rickey Henderson FB 4.00 1.20
154 Alex Rodriguez FB 5.00 1.50
155 Rafael Palmeiro FB 4.00 1.20
156 Greg Maddux FB 5.00 1.50
157 Mike Piazza FB 5.00 1.50
158 Mike Mussina FB 4.00 1.20
159 Dale Murphy LGD 4.00 1.20
160 Cal Ripken LGD 10.00 3.00
161 Carl Yastrzemski LGD 5.00 1.50
162 Marty Marion LGD 3.00 .90
163 Don Mattingly LGD 8.00 2.40
164 Robin Yount LGD 5.00 1.50
165 Andre Dawson LGD 3.00 .90
166 Jim Palmer LGD 3.00 .90
167 George Brett LGD 8.00 2.40
168 Whitey Ford LGD 4.00 1.20
169 Roy Campanella LGD 4.00 1.20
170 Roger Maris LGD 4.00 1.20
171 Duke Snider LGD 4.00 1.20
172 Steve Carlton LGD 3.00 .90
173 Stan Musial LGD 5.00 1.50
174 Nolan Ryan LGD 8.00 2.40
175 Deion Sanders LGD 4.00 1.20

2004 Diamond Kings Sepia

Nm-Mt Ex-Mt
*SEPIA: .75X TO 2X BASIC
RANDOM INSERTS IN PACKS

2004 Diamond Kings Bronze

Nm-Mt Ex-Mt
*BRONZE 1-150: 3X TO 8X BASIC
*BRONZE 151-175: 1.25X TO 3X BASIC
RANDOM INSERTS IN PACKS
STATED PRINT RUN 100 SERIAL #'d SETS

2004 Diamond Kings Bronze Sepia

Nm-Mt Ex-Mt
*BRONZE SEPIA: 1.25X TO 3X BASIC
RANDOM INSERTS IN PACKS
STATED PRINT RUN 100 SERIAL #'d SETS

2004 Diamond Kings Platinum

Nm-Mt Ex-Mt
RANDOM INSERTS IN PACKS
STATED PRINT RUN 1 SERIAL #'d SET
NO PRICING DUE TO SCARCITY

2004 Diamond Kings Platinum Sepia

Nm-Mt Ex-Mt
RANDOM INSERTS IN PACKS
STATED PRINT RUN 1 SERIAL #'d SET
NO PRICING DUE TO SCARCITY

2004 Diamond Kings Silver

Nm-Mt Ex-Mt
*SILVER 1-150: 5X TO 12X BASIC
*SILVER 151-175: 2X TO 5X BASIC
RANDOM INSERTS IN PACKS
STATED PRINT RUN 50 SERIAL #'d SETS

2004 Diamond Kings Silver Sepia

Nm-Mt Ex-Mt
*SILVER SEPIA: 2X TO 5X BASIC
RANDOM INSERTS IN PACKS
STATED PRINT RUN 50 SERIAL #'d SETS

2004 Diamond Kings Framed Platinum Grey

Nm-Mt Ex-Mt
RANDOM INSERTS IN PACKS
STATED PRINT RUN 1 SERIAL #'d SET
NO PRICING DUE TO SCARCITY

2004 Diamond Kings Framed Bronze

Nm-Mt Ex-Mt
*FRAMED BRZ 1-150: 1.5X TO 4X BASIC
*FRAMED BRZ 151-175: .75X TO 2X BASIC
STATED ODDS 1:6

2004 Diamond Kings Framed Bronze Sepia

Nm-Mt Ex-Mt
*FRAMED BRZ.SEPIA: .75X TO 2X BASIC
STATED ODDS 1:6

2004 Diamond Kings Framed Gold

Nm-Mt Ex-Mt
*FRAMED GOLD 1-150: 10X TO 25X BASIC
*FRAMED GOLD 150-175: 4X TO 10X BASIC
RANDOM INSERTS IN PACKS
STATED PRINT RUN 25 SERIAL #'d SETS

2004 Diamond Kings Framed Gold Sepia

Nm-Mt Ex-Mt
*FRAMED GOLD SEPIA: 4X TO 10X BASIC
RANDOM INSERTS IN PACKS
STATED PRINT RUN 25 SERIAL #'d SETS

2004 Diamond Kings Framed Platinum Black

Nm-Mt Ex-Mt
RANDOM INSERTS IN PACKS
STATED PRINT RUN 1 SERIAL #'d SET
NO PRICING DUE TO SCARCITY

2004 Diamond Kings Framed Platinum Black Sepia

Nm-Mt Ex-Mt
RANDOM INSERTS IN PACKS
STATED PRINT RUN 1 SERIAL #'d SET
NO PRICING DUE TO SCARCITY

2004 Diamond Kings Framed Platinum Grey Sepia

Nm-Mt Ex-Mt
RANDOM INSERTS IN PACKS
STATED PRINT RUN 1 SERIAL #'d SET
NO PRICING DUE TO SCARCITY

2004 Diamond Kings Framed Platinum White

Nm-Mt Ex-Mt
RANDOM INSERTS IN PACKS
STATED PRINT RUN 1 SERIAL #'d SET
NO PRICING DUE TO SCARCITY

2004 Diamond Kings Framed Platinum White Sepia

Nm-Mt Ex-Mt
RANDOM INSERTS IN PACKS
STATED PRINT RUN 1 SERIAL #'d SET
NO PRICING DUE TO SCARCITY

2004 Diamond Kings Framed Silver

Nm-Mt Ex-Mt
*FRAMED SLV 1-150: 4X TO 10X BASIC
*FRAMED SLV 151-175: 1.5X TO 4X BASIC
RANDOM INSERTS IN PACKS ....
STATED PRINT RUN 100 SERIAL #'d SETS

2004 Diamond Kings Framed Silver Sepia

Nm-Mt Ex-Mt
*FRAMED SLV SEPIA: 1.5X TO 4X BASIC
RANDOM INSERTS IN PACKS ....
STATED PRINT RUN 100 SERIAL #'d SETS

2004 Diamond Kings DK Combos Bronze

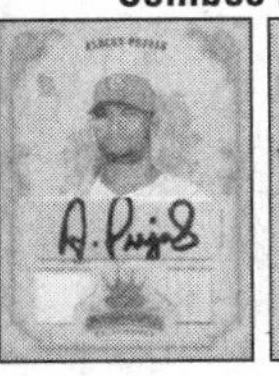

Nm-Mt Ex-Mt
RANDOM INSERTS IN PACKS ....
PRINT RUNS B/WN 1-30 COPIES PER
NO PRICING ON QTY OF 10 OR LESS
26 Marlon Byrd Bat-Jsy/30....... 30.00 9.00
32 Rich Harden Jsy-Jsy/15....... 50.00 15.00
35 Brandon Webb Bat-Jsy/15 ... 40.00 12.00
41 Aubrey Huff Bat-Jsy/15......... 50.00 15.00
53 Eric Hinske Bat-Jsy/30......... 30.00 9.00
57 Joe Thurston Bat-Jsy/25....... 30.00 9.00
59 Jay Gibbons Jsy-Jsy/15........ 40.00 12.00
62 Walter Young Bat-Bat/15....... 40.00 12.00
65 Bob Abreu Bat-Jsy/15.......... 50.00 15.00
71 Jason Lane Bat-Hat/15......... 40.00 12.00
73 Run Hernandez Jsy-Jsy/15 ... 40.00 12.00
74 Aramis Ramirez Bat-Bat/15.. 50.00 15.00
77 Chris Snelling Bat-Bat/15..... 40.00 12.00
81 Joe Borchard Bat-Jsy/15....... 40.00 12.00
92 Junior Spivey Bat-Jsy/15 ..... 40.00 12.00
98 Dan Haren Bat-Jsy/15........... 40.00 12.00
101 Lyle Overbay Bat-Jsy/30 .... 40.00 12.00
103 Miguel Cabrera Bat-Jsy/30. 60.00 18.00
108 Angel Berroa Bat-Pants/30. 30.00 9.00
109 Hank Blalock Bat-Jsy/30 .... 40.00 12.00
111 Jose Castillo Bat-Bat/15..... 40.00 12.00
121 Morgan Ensberg Bat-Jsy/30 40.00 12.00
123 Orlando Hudson Bat-Jsy/30 30.00 9.00
126 Adam LaRoche Bat-Bat/30. 30.00 9.00
127 Hong-Chih Kuo Bat-Bat/15. 80.00 24.00
130 Luis Castillo Bat-Jsy/30 ..... 30.00 9.00
133 Freddy Sanchez Bat-Bat/15 40.00 12.00
136 Alfredo Amezaga Bat-Jsy/15 40.00 12.00
143 Travis Hafner Bat-Jsy/30.... 40.00 12.00
147 Chad Gaudin Jsy-Jsy/25 .... 30.00 9.00

2004 Diamond Kings DK Combos Silver

Nm-Mt Ex-Mt
RANDOM INSERTS IN PACKS ....
PRINT RUNS B/WN 1-15 COPIES PER
NO PRICING ON QTY OF 10 OR LESS
26 Marlon Byrd Bat-Jsy/15....... 40.00 12.00
101 Lyle Overbay Bat-Jsy/15 .... 50.00 15.00
103 Miguel Cabrera Bat-Jsy/15. 80.00 24.00
108 Angel Berroa Bat-Pants/15. 40.00 12.00
109 Hank Blalock Bat-Jsy/15 .... 50.00 15.00
121 Morgan Ensberg Bat-Jsy/15 50.00 15.00
123 Orlando Hudson Bat-Jsy/15 40.00 12.00
126 Adam LaRoche Bat-Bat/15. 40.00 12.00
130 Luis Castillo Bat-Jsy/15..... 40.00 12.00
143 Travis Hafner Bat-Jsy/15.... 50.00 15.00

2004 Diamond Kings DK Combos Framed Bronze

Nm-Mt Ex-Mt
RANDOM INSERTS IN PACKS ....
PRINT RUNS B/WN 1-25 COPIES PER
NO PRICING ON QTY OF 10 OR LESS
26 Marlon Byrd Bat-Jsy/25....... 30.00 9.00
35 Brandon Webb Bat-Jsy/25 ... 30.00 9.00
53 Eric Hinske Bat-Jsy/25......... 30.00 9.00
57 Joe Thurston Bat-Jsy/25....... 30.00 9.00
59 Jay Gibbons Jsy-Jsy/25........ 30.00 9.00
62 Walter Young Bat-Bat/25....... 30.00 9.00
65 Bob Abreu Bat-Jsy/25.......... 40.00 12.00
71 Jason Lane Bat-Hat/25......... 30.00 9.00
74 Aramis Ramirez Bat-Bat/25.. 40.00 12.00
77 Chris Snelling Bat-Bat/25..... 30.00 9.00
81 Joe Borchard Bat-Jsy/25....... 30.00 9.00
92 Junior Spivey Bat-Jsy/25 ..... 30.00 9.00
97 Antonio Perez Bat-Pants/25. 30.00 9.00
98 Dan Haren Bat-Jsy/25........... 30.00 9.00
101 Lyle Overbay Bat-Jsy/25 .... 40.00 12.00
103 Miguel Cabrera Bat-Jsy/25. 60.00 18.00
107 Nic Jackson Bat-Bat/25...... 30.00 9.00
108 Angel Berroa Bat-Pants/25. 30.00 9.00
109 Hank Blalock Bat-Jsy/25 .... 40.00 12.00
110 Ryan Klesko Bat-Jsy/15..... 50.00 15.00
111 Jose Castillo Bat-Bat/25..... 30.00 9.00
112 Paul Konerko Bat-Jsy/15 ... 50.00 15.00
121 Morgan Ensberg Bat-Jsy/25 40.00 12.00
123 Orlando Hudson Bat-Jsy/25 30.00 9.00
126 Adam LaRoche Bat-Bat/25. 30.00 9.00
127 Hong-Chih Kuo Bat-Bat/25. 60.00 18.00
130 Luis Castillo Bat-Jsy/25 ..... 30.00 9.00
133 Freddy Sanchez Bat-Bat/15 40.00 12.00
136 Alfredo Amezaga Bat-Jsy/15 40.00 12.00
143 Travis Hafner Bat-Jsy/15.... 50.00 15.00
147 Chad Gaudin Jsy-Jsy/25 .... 30.00 9.00

2004 Diamond Kings DK Combos Framed Silver

Nm-Mt Ex-Mt
RANDOM INSERTS IN PACKS ....
PRINT RUNS B/WN 1-15 COPIES PER
NO PRICING ON QTY OF 10 OR LESS
110 Ryan Klesko Bat-Jsy/15 ..... 50.00 15.00

2004 Diamond Kings DK Materials Bronze

Nm-Mt Ex-Mt
RANDOM INSERTS IN PACKS ....
PRINT RUNS B/WN 1-150 COPIES PER
NO PRICING ON QTY OF 5 OR LESS..
1 Alex Rodriguez Bat-Jsy/150... 25.00 7.50
2 Andruw Jones Bat-Jsy/150.... 10.00 3.00
3 Nomar Garciaparra Bat-Jsy/150 25.00 7.50
4 Kerry Wood Bat-Jsy/150........ 20.00 6.00
5 Magglio Ordonez Bat-Jsy/150 10.00 3.00
6 Victor Martinez Bat-Bat/100... 10.00 3.00
7 Jeremy Bonderman Jsy-Jsy/30 15.00 4.50
8 Josh Beckett Bat-Jsy/150 ...... 10.00 3.00
9 Jeff Kent Bat-Jsy/150............ 10.00 3.00
10 Carlos Beltran Bat-Jsy/150 .. 15.00 4.50
11 Hideo Nomo Bat-Jsy/150...... 20.00 6.00
12 Richie Sexson Bat-Jsy/150 .. 10.00 3.00
13 Jose Vidro Bat-Jsy/50........... 10.00 3.00
14 Jae Seo Jsy-Jsy/100............ 10.00 3.00
15 Alfonso Soriano Bat-Jsy/150 15.00 4.50
16 Barry Zito Bat-Jsy/100......... 10.00 3.00
17 Brett Myers Jsy-Jsy/30........ 15.00 4.50
18 Brian Giles Bat-Bat/100........ 10.00 3.00
19 Edgar Martinez Bat-Jsy/150. 15.00 4.50
20 Jim Edmonds Bat-Jsy/150... 10.00 3.00
21 Rocco Baldelli Bat-Jsy/100 .. 10.00 3.00
22 Mark Teixeira Bat-Jsy/100.... 10.00 3.00
23 Carlos Delgado Bat-Jsy/150. 10.00 3.00
25 Jose Reyes Bat-Jsy/100....... 10.00 3.00
26 Marlon Byrd Bat-Jsy/100 ...... 10.00 3.00
27 Albert Pujols Bat-Jsy/150 .... 40.00 12.00
28 Vernon Wells Bat-Jsy/150..... 10.00 3.00
29 Garret Anderson Bat-Jsy/15. 25.00 7.50
30 Jerome Williams Jsy-Jsy/100 10.00 3.00
31 Chipper Jones Bat-Jsy/150.. 20.00 6.00
32 Rich Harden Jsy-Jsy/100...... 10.00 3.00
33 Manny Ramirez Bat-Jsy/150 15.00 4.50
34 Derek Jeter Base-Base/100.. 30.00 9.00
35 Brandon Webb Bat-Jsy/100 . 10.00 3.00
36 Mark Prior Bat-Jsy/100......... 20.00 6.00
37 Roy Halladay Jsy-Jsy/100..... 10.00 3.00
38 Frank Thomas Bat-Jsy/150 .. 20.00 6.00
39 Rafael Palmeiro Bat-Jsy/150 15.00 4.50
40 Adam Dunn Bat-Jsy/150....... 15.00 4.50
41 Aubrey Huff Bat-Jsy/30......... 15.00 4.50
42 Todd Helton Bat-Jsy/150...... 15.00 4.50
43 Matt Morris Jsy-Jsy/150....... 10.00 3.00
44 Dontrelle Willis Bat-Jsy/100. 10.00 3.00
45 Lance Berkman Bat-Jsy/150 10.00 3.00
46 Mike Sweeney Bat-Jsy/100 .. 10.00 3.00
47 Kazuhisa Ishii Bat-Jsy/100... 10.00 3.00
48 Torii Hunter Bat-Jsy/100....... 10.00 3.00
49 Vladimir Guerrero Bat-Jsy/100 20.00 6.00
50 Mike Piazza Bat-Jsy/150 ...... 25.00 7.50
51 Alexis Rios Bat-Bat/150 .... 10.00 3.00
52 Shannon Stewart Bat-Bat/100 10.00 3.00
53 Eric Hinske Bat-Jsy/100........ 10.00 3.00
54 Jason Jennings Bat-Jsy/150 10.00 3.00
55 Jason Giambi Bat-Jsy/150 ... 10.00 3.00
56 Brandon Claussen Fld Glv-Shoe/5..
57 Joe Thurston Bat-Jsy/150..... 10.00 3.00
58 Ramon Nivar Bat-Jsy/100 ..... 10.00 3.00
59 Jay Gibbons Jsy-Jsy/100...... 10.00 3.00
60 Eric Chavez Bat-Jsy/150 ...... 10.00 3.00
62 Walter Young Bat-Bat/100..... 10.00 3.00
63 Mark Grace Bat-Jsy/150 .... 15.00 4.50
64 Austin Kearns Bat-Jsy/150.... 10.00 3.00
65 Bob Abreu Bat-Jsy/150......... 10.00 3.00
66 Hee Seop Choi Bat-Jsy/100 . 10.00 3.00
67 Brandon Phillips Bat-Bat/100 10.00 3.00
68 Rickie Weeks Bat-Bat/100..... 10.00 3.00
69 Luis Gonzalez Bat-Jsy/150... 10.00 3.00
70 Mariano Rivera Jsy-Jsy/100 15.00 4.50
71 Jason Lane Bat-Hat/15......... 25.00 7.50
72 Xavier Nady Bat-Hat/5......................
73 Run Hernandez Jsy-Jsy/30 .. 15.00 4.50
74 Aramis Ramirez Bat-Bat/1 ....
75 Ichiro Suzuki Ball-Base/15. 100.00 30.00
77 Chris Snelling Bat-Bat/30...... 15.00 4.50
79 Miguel Tejada Bat-Jsy/150 ... 10.00 3.00
80 Juan Gonzalez Bat-Jsy/150.. 15.00 4.50
81 Joe Borchard Bat-Jsy/15....... 25.00 7.50
82 Gary Sheffield Bat-Jsy/150 .. 10.00 3.00
83 Wade Miller Bat-Jsy/50......... 10.00 3.00
84 Jeff Bagwell Bat-Jsy/150 ...... 15.00 4.50
86 Adrian Beltre Bat-Jsy/100 .... 15.00 4.50
87 Jeff Baker Bat-Bat/100.......... 10.00 3.00
89 Bernie Williams Bat-Jsy/150 15.00 4.50
90 Pedro Martinez Bat-Jsy/100. 20.00 6.00
92 Junior Spivey Bat-Jsy/100 ... 10.00 3.00
93 Tim Hudson Bat-Jsy/150 ...... 10.00 3.00
94 Troy Glaus Bat-Jsy/100......... 10.00 3.00
95 Ken Griffey Jr. Base-Base/100 20.00 6.00
96 Alexis Gomez Bat-Bat/30 ...... 15.00 4.50
97 Antonio Perez Bat-Pants/100 10.00 3.00
98 Dan Haren Bat-Jsy/100......... 10.00 3.00
99 Ivan Rodriguez Bat-Jsy/150. 20.00 6.00
100 Randy Johnson Bat-Jsy/100 20.00 6.00
101 Lyle Overbay Bat-Jsy/100 .. 10.00 3.00
103 Miguel Cabrera Bat-Jsy/100 15.00 4.50
104 Scott Rolen Bat-Jsy/100 .... 20.00 6.00
105 Roger Clemens Bat-Jsy/100 30.00 9.00
107 Nic Jackson Bat-Bat/100..... 10.00 3.00
108 Angel Berroa Bat-Pants/30. 15.00 4.50
109 Hank Blalock Bat-Jsy/100 ... 10.00 3.00
110 Ryan Klesko Bat-Jsy/100 .... 10.00 3.00
111 Jose Castillo Bat-Bat/100 ... 10.00 3.00
112 Paul Konerko Bat-Jsy/100 . 10.00 3.00
113 Greg Maddux Bat-Jsy/100 . 25.00 7.50
114 Mark Mulder Bat-Jsy/100 .. 10.00 3.00
115 Pat Burrell Bat-Jsy/100....... 10.00 3.00
116 Garrett Atkins Jsy-Jsy/100. 10.00 3.00
118 Orlando Cabrera Bat-Jsy/100 10.00 3.00
119 Nick Johnson Bat-Jsy/100 . 10.00 3.00
120 Tom Glavine Bat-Jsy/100 ... 15.00 4.50
121 Morgan Ensberg Bat-Jsy/100 10.00 3.00
122 Sean Casey Bat-Hat/15 ...... 25.00 7.50
123 Orlando Hudson Bat-Jsy/100 10.00 3.00
124 Hideki Matsui Ball-Base/15 120.00 36.00
125 Craig Biggio Bat-Jsy/100 ... 15.00 4.50
126 Adam LaRoche Bat-Bat/100 10.00 3.00
127 Hong-Chih Kuo Bat-Bat/100 10.00 3.00
128 Paul LoDuca Bat-Jsy/100... 10.00 3.00
129 Shawn Green Bat-Jsy/100 . 10.00 3.00
130 Luis Castillo Bat-Jsy/100 ... 10.00 3.00
131 Joe Crede Bat-Btg Glv/5..............
132 Ken Harvey Bat-Bat/100...... 10.00 3.00
133 Freddy Sanchez Bat-Bat/100 10.00 3.00
134 Roy Oswalt Bat-Jsy/100....... 10.00 3.00
135 Curt Schilling Bat-Jsy/100 . 20.00 6.00
136 Alfredo Amezaga Bat-Jsy/15 25.00 7.50
138 Barry Larkin Bat-Jsy/15 ..... 40.00 12.00
139 Trot Nixon Bat-Bat/100 ...... 10.00 3.00
140 Jim Thome Bat-Jsy/100...... 20.00 6.00
141 Bret Boone Bat-Jsy/100 ..... 10.00 3.00
142 Jacque Jones Bat-Jsy/100. 10.00 3.00
143 Travis Hafner Bat-Jsy/100.. 10.00 3.00
144 Sammy Sosa Bat-Jsy/100.. 25.00 7.50
145 Mike Mussina Bat-Jsy/100. 15.00 4.50
147 Chad Gaudin Jsy-Jsy/100 .. 10.00 3.00
149 Mike Lowell Bat-Jsy/100.... 10.00 3.00
150 R.Henderson Bat-Jsy/100 .. 20.00 6.00
151 R.Clemens FB Bat-Jsy/100 30.00 9.00
152 Mark Grace FB Bat-Jsy/15 . 40.00 12.00
153 R.Henderson FB Bat-Jsy/30 30.00 9.00
154 A.Rodriguez FB Bat-Jsy/100 25.00 7.50
155 R.Palmeiro FB Bat-Jsy/100 15.00 4.50
156 G.Maddux FB Bat-Bat/100.. 25.00 7.50
157 Mike Piazza FB Bat-Jsy/100 25.00 7.50
158 M.Mussina FB Bat-Jsy/100 15.00 4.50
159 Dale Murphy LGD Bat-Jsy/30 30.00 9.00
160 Cal Ripken LGD Bat-Jsy/100 50.00 15.00
161 C.Yaz LGD Bat-Jsy/100...... 25.00 7.50
162 M.Marion LGD Jsy-Jsy/30 . 15.00 4.50
163 D.Mattingly LGD Bat-Jsy/100 40.00 12.00
164 R.Yount LGD Bat-Jsy/100 .. 25.00 7.50
165 A.Dawson LGD Bat-Jsy/30. 15.00 4.50
166 Jim Palmer LGD Jsy-Jsy/5 ....
167 George Brett LGD Bat-Jsy/30 60.00 18.00
168 W.Ford LGD Jsy-Pants/30.. 25.00 7.50
169 R.Campy LGD Bat-Pants/15 50.00 15.00
170 R.Maris LGD Bat-Jsy/15 .. 120.00 36.00
171 Duke Snider LGD Bat-Jsy/4 ....
172 S.Carlton LGD Bat-Jsy/100 10.00 3.00
173 Stan Musial LGD Bat-Jsy/30 50.00 15.00
174 Nolan Ryan LGD Bat-Jsy/30 60.00 18.00
175 D.Sanders LGD Bat-Jsy/100 15.00 4.50

2004 Diamond Kings DK Materials Bronze Sepia

Nm-Mt Ex-Mt
RANDOM INSERTS IN PACKS ....
PRINT RUNS B/WN 4-50 COPIES PER
NO PRICING ON QTY OF 5 OR LESS..
151 R.Clemens FB Bat-Jsy/30 .. 50.00 15.00
152 Mark Grace FB Bat-Jsy/15 . 40.00 12.00
153 R.Henderson FB Bat-Jsy/15 50.00 15.00
154 A.Rodriguez FB Bat-Jsy/30 50.00 15.00
155 R.Palmeiro FB Bat-Jsy/50 .. 15.00 4.50
156 G.Maddux FB Bat-Bat/50.... 40.00 12.00
157 Mike Piazza FB Bat-Jsy/50 . 40.00 12.00
158 M.Mussina FB Bat-Jsy/50 .. 15.00 4.50
159 Dale Murphy LGD Bat-Jsy/15 50.00 15.00
160 Cal Ripken LGD Bat-Jsy/50 80.00 24.00
161 C.Yaz LGD Bat-Jsy/50....... 40.00 12.00
162 M.Marion LGD Jsy-Jsy/15 . 25.00 7.50
163 D.Mattingly LGD Bat-Jsy/50 50.00 15.00
164 R.Yount LGD Bat-Jsy/50 .... 40.00 12.00
165 A.Dawson LGD Bat-Jsy/15. 25.00 7.50
166 Jim Palmer LGD Jsy-Jsy/5 ....
167 G.Brett LGD Bat-Jsy/15.... 100.00 30.00
168 W.Ford LGD Jsy-Pants/15.. 40.00 12.00
169 R.Campy LGD Bat-Pants/15 50.00 15.00
170 R.Maris LGD Bat-Jsy/15 .. 120.00 36.00
171 Duke Snider LGD Bat-Jsy/4 ....
172 S.Carlton LGD Bat-Jsy/50 .. 10.00 3.00
173 Stan Musial LGD Bat-Jsy/15 80.00 24.00
174 Nolan Ryan LGD Bat-Jsy/15 100.00 30.00
175 D.Sanders LGD Bat-Jsy/50 15.00 4.50

2004 Diamond Kings DK Materials Gold

Nm-Mt Ex-Mt
RANDOM INSERTS IN PACKS ....
PRINT RUNS B/WN 1-50 COPIES PER
NO PRICING ON QTY OF 5 OR LESS..
1 Alex Rodriguez Bat-Jsy/25..... 50.00 15.00
2 Andruw Jones Bat-Jsy/25...... 15.00 4.50
3 Nomar Garciaparra Bat-Jsy/25 50.00 15.00
4 Kerry Wood Bat-Jsy/25.......... 30.00 9.00
5 Magglio Ordonez Bat-Jsy/25.. 15.00 4.50
6 Victor Martinez Bat-Bat/50...... 10.00 3.00
7 Jeremy Bonderman Jsy-Jsy/5...........
8 Josh Beckett Bat-Jsy/25 .... 15.00 4.50
9 Jeff Kent Bat-Jsy/25.............. 15.00 4.50
10 Carlos Beltran Bat-Jsy/25 .... 25.00 7.50
11 Hideo Nomo Bat-Jsy/25........ 30.00 9.00
12 Richie Sexson Bat-Jsy/25 .... 15.00 4.50
13 Jose Vidro Bat-Jsy/25........... 15.00 4.50
14 Jae Seo Jsy-Jsy/25.............. 15.00 4.50
15 Alfonso Soriano Bat-Jsy/25 . 25.00 7.50
16 Barry Zito Bat-Jsy/25............ 15.00 4.50
17 Brett Myers Jsy-Jsy/5..............
18 Brian Giles Bat-Bat/25.......... 15.00 4.50
19 Edgar Martinez Bat-Jsy/25... 25.00 7.50
20 Jim Edmonds Bat-Jsy/25...... 15.00 4.50
21 Rocco Baldelli Bat-Jsy/25 .... 15.00 4.50
22 Mark Teixeira Bat-Jsy/25...... 15.00 4.50
23 Carlos Delgado Bat-Jsy/25.................
25 Jose Reyes Bat-Jsy/25......... 15.00 4.50
26 Marlon Byrd Bat-Jsy/25 .... 15.00 4.50
27 Albert Pujols Bat-Jsy/25 ...... 60.00 18.00
28 Vernon Wells Bat-Jsy/25....... 15.00 4.50
29 Garret Anderson Bat-Jsy/3..............
30 Jerome Williams Jsy-Jsy/50 10.00 3.00
31 Chipper Jones Bat-Jsy/25..... 30.00 9.00
32 Rich Harden Jsy-Jsy/50........ 10.00 3.00
33 Manny Ramirez Bat-Jsy/25 .. 25.00 7.50
34 Derek Jeter Base-Base/50.... 40.00 12.00
35 Brandon Webb Bat-Jsy/50 ... 10.00 3.00
36 Mark Prior Bat-Jsy/25.......... 30.00 9.00
37 Roy Halladay Jsy-Jsy/25....... 15.00 4.50
38 Frank Thomas Bat-Jsy/25..... 30.00 9.00
39 Rafael Palmeiro Bat-Jsy/50.. 15.00 4.50
40 Adam Dunn Bat-Jsy/25......... 25.00 7.50
41 Aubrey Huff Bat-Jsy/5......................
42 Todd Helton Bat-Jsy/25........ 25.00 7.50
43 Matt Morris Jsy-Jsy/25........ 15.00 4.50
44 Dontrelle Willis Bat-Jsy/25... 15.00 4.50
45 Lance Berkman Bat-Jsy/25 .. 15.00 4.50
46 Mike Sweeney Bat-Jsy/25.... 15.00 4.50
47 Kazuhisa Ishii Bat-Jsy/25...... 15.00 4.50
48 Torii Hunter Bat-Jsy/25 .... 15.00 4.50
49 Vladimir Guerrero Bat-Jsy/25 30.00 9.00
50 Mike Piazza Bat-Jsy/25......... 50.00 15.00
51 Alexis Rios Bat-Bat/25 .... 15.00 4.50
52 Shannon Stewart Bat-Bat/50 10.00 3.00
53 Eric Hinske Bat-Jsy/50......... 10.00 3.00
54 Jason Jennings Bat-Jsy/25 .. 15.00 4.50
55 Jason Giambi Bat-Jsy/25...... 15.00 4.50
56 Brandon Claussen Fld Glv-Shoe/1..
57 Joe Thurston Bat-Jsy/50...... 10.00 3.00
58 Ramon Nivar Bat-Jsy/50....... 10.00 3.00
59 Jay Gibbons Jsy-Jsy/25 .... 15.00 4.50
60 Eric Chavez Bat-Jsy/25 .... 15.00 4.50
62 Walter Young Bat-Bat/50...... 10.00 3.00
63 Mark Grace Bat-Jsy/25 .... 25.00 7.50
64 Austin Kearns Bat-Jsy/25...... 15.00 4.50
65 Bob Abreu Bat-Jsy/25.......... 15.00 4.50
66 Hee Seop Choi Bat-Jsy/25 ... 15.00 4.50
67 Brandon Phillips Bat-Bat/50. 10.00 3.00
68 Rickie Weeks Bat-Bat/50...... 10.00 3.00
69 Luis Gonzalez Bat-Jsy/25..... 15.00 4.50
70 Mariano Rivera Jsy-Jsy/50 .. 15.00 4.50
71 Jason Lane Bat-Hat/3..................
72 Xavier Nady Bat-Hat/2..................
73 Run Hernandez Jsy-Jsy/5 ....
74 Aramis Ramirez Bat-Bat/1 ....
75 Ichiro Suzuki Ball-Base/3 ....
77 Chris Snelling Bat-Bat/5 ....
79 Miguel Tejada Bat-Jsy/50..... 10.00 3.00
80 Juan Gonzalez Bat-Jsy/25.... 25.00 7.50
81 Joe Borchard Bat-Jsy/3..............
82 Gary Sheffield Bat-Jsy/25 ..... 15.00 4.50
83 Wade Miller Bat-Jsy/3..................
84 Jeff Bagwell Bat-Jsy/25 .... 25.00 7.50
86 Adrian Beltre Bat-Jsy/25 ...... 25.00 7.50
87 Jeff Baker Bat-Bat/50............ 10.00 3.00
89 Bernie Williams Bat-Jsy/25.. 25.00 7.50
90 Pedro Martinez Bat-Jsy/25.... 30.00 9.00
92 Junior Spivey Bat-Jsy/25 ..... 15.00 4.50
93 Tim Hudson Bat-Jsy/25 .... 15.00 4.50
94 Troy Glaus Bat-Jsy/25.......... 15.00 4.50
95 Ken Griffey Jr. Base-Base/50 30.00 9.00
96 Alexis Gomez Bat-Bat/5.................
97 Antonio Perez Bat-Pants/50. 10.00 3.00
98 Dan Haren Bat-Jsy/25 .... 15.00 4.50
99 Ivan Rodriguez Bat-Jsy/25... 30.00 9.00
100 Randy Johnson Bat-Jsy/25 30.00 9.00
101 Lyle Overbay Bat-Jsy/50 .... 10.00 3.00
103 Miguel Cabrera Bat-Jsy/25. 25.00 7.50
104 Scott Rolen Bat-Jsy/25 .... 30.00 9.00
105 Roger Clemens Bat-Jsy/25 50.00 15.00
107 Nic Jackson Bat-Bat/30...... 15.00 4.50
108 Angel Berroa Bat-Pants/3...............
109 Hank Blalock Bat-Jsy/25 .... 15.00 4.50
110 Ryan Klesko Bat-Jsy/25 ..... 15.00 4.50
111 Jose Castillo Bat-Bat/50..... 10.00 3.00
112 Paul Konerko Bat-Jsy/25 ... 15.00 4.50
113 Greg Maddux Bat-Jsy/25 ... 50.00 15.00
114 Mark Mulder Bat-Jsy/25 ..... 15.00 4.50
115 Pat Burrell Bat-Jsy/25......... 15.00 4.50
116 Garrett Atkins Jsy-Jsy/50.... 10.00 3.00
118 Orlando Cabrera Bat-Jsy/25 15.00 4.50
119 Nick Johnson Bat-Jsy/25 ... 15.00 4.50
120 Tom Glavine Bat-Jsy/25 ..... 25.00 7.50
121 Morgan Ensberg Bat-Jsy/25 15.00 4.50
122 Sean Casey Bat-Hat/3 ....
123 Orlando Hudson Bat-Jsy/25 15.00 4.50
124 Hideki Matsui Ball-Base/3 ....
125 Craig Biggio Bat-Jsy/25 ..... 25.00 7.50
126 Adam LaRoche Bat-Bat/50. 10.00 3.00
127 Hong-Chih Kuo Bat-Bat/50. 10.00 3.00
128 Paul LoDuca Bat-Jsy/25..... 15.00 4.50
129 Shawn Green Bat-Jsy/25 ... 15.00 4.50
130 Luis Castillo Bat-Jsy/25 ..... 15.00 4.50
131 Joe Crede Bat-Btg Glv/1............
132 Ken Harvey Bat-Bat/50....... 10.00 3.00
133 Freddy Sanchez Bat-Bat/50 10.00 3.00
134 Roy Oswalt Bat-Jsy/50....... 10.00 3.00
135 Curt Schilling Bat-Jsy/25 ... 30.00 9.00
136 Alfredo Amezaga Bat-Jsy/3 ....
138 Barry Larkin Bat-Jsy/3 ....
139 Trot Nixon Bat-Bat/25 .... 15.00 4.50
140 Jim Thome Bat-Jsy/25........ 30.00 9.00
141 Bret Boone Bat-Jsy/5 ....
142 Jacque Jones Bat-Jsy/50 ... 10.00 3.00
143 Travis Hafner Bat-Jsy/50.... 10.00 3.00
144 Sammy Sosa Bat-Jsy/25..... 50.00 15.00
145 Mike Mussina Bat-Jsy/50.... 15.00 4.50
147 Chad Gaudin Jsy-Jsy/25 .... 15.00 4.50
149 Mike Lowell Bat-Jsy/25 .... 15.00 4.50
150 R.Henderson Bat-Jsy/25 .... 30.00 9.00
151 R.Clemens FB Bat-Jsy/25 .. 50.00 15.00
152 Mark Grace FB Bat-Jsy/3 ....
153 R.Henderson FB Bat-Jsy/5 ....
154 A.Rodriguez FB Bat-Jsy/25 50.00 15.00
155 R.Palmeiro FB Bat-Jsy/50 .. 25.00 7.50
156 G.Maddux FB Bat-Bat/50.... 40.00 12.00
157 Mike Piazza FB Bat-Jsy/50 . 40.00 12.00
158 M.Mussina FB Bat-Jsy/50 .. 25.00 7.50
159 Dale Murphy LGD Bat-Jsy/5 ....
160 Cal Ripken LGD Bat-Jsy/50 80.00 24.00
161 C.Yaz LGD Bat-Jsy/50........ 40.00 12.00
162 M.Marion LGD Jsy-Jsy/5 ....
163 D.Mattingly LGD Bat-Jsy/50 50.00 15.00
164 R.Yount LGD Bat-Jsy/50 ..... 40.00 12.00
165 A.Dawson LGD Bat-Jsy/5 ....
166 Jim Palmer LGD Jsy-Jsy/2 ....
167 George Brett LGD Bat-Jsy/5...........
168 W.Ford LGD Jsy-Pants/5...............
169 R.Campy LGD Bat-Pants/3............
170 Roger Maris LGD Bat-Jsy/3 ....
171 Duke Snider LGD Bat-Jsy/1 ....
172 S.Carlton LGD Bat-Jsy/50 .. 10.00 3.00
173 Stan Musial LGD Bat-Jsy/5............
174 Nolan Ryan LGD Bat-Jsy/5 ....
175 D.Sanders LGD Bat-Jsy/50 15.00 4.50

2004 Diamond Kings DK Materials Gold Sepia

Nm-Mt Ex-Mt
RANDOM INSERTS IN PACKS ....
PRINT RUNS B/WN 1-15 COPIES PER
NO PRICING ON QTY OF 5 OR LESS..
151 R.Clemens FB Bat-Jsy/5..............
152 Mark Grace FB Bat-Jsy/3 ....
153 R.Henderson FB Bat-Jsy/3 ....
154 A.Rodriguez FB Bat-Jsy/5 ....
155 R.Palmeiro FB Bat-Jsy/15.. 40.00 12.00
156 G.Maddux FB Bat-Bat/15.... 60.00 18.00
157 Mike Piazza FB Bat-Jsy/15. 60.00 18.00
158 M.Mussina FB Bat-Jsy/15 .. 40.00 12.00
159 Dale Murphy LGD Bat-Jsy/3 ....
160 Cal Ripken LGD Bat-Jsy/15 150.00 45.00
161 C.Yaz LGD Bat-Jsy/15 .... 80.00 24.00
162 M.Marion LGD Jsy-Jsy/3 ....
163 D.Mattingly LGD Bat-Jsy/15 100.00 30.00
164 R.Yount LGD Bat-Jsy/15 .... 80.00 24.00
165 A.Dawson LGD Bat-Jsy/3............
166 Jim Palmer LGD Jsy-Jsy/2 ....
167 George Brett LGD Bat-Jsy/3..........
168 W.Ford LGD Jsy-Pants/3.............
169 R.Campy LGD Bat-Pants/3............
170 Roger Maris LGD Bat-Jsy/3 ....
171 Duke Snider LGD Bat-Jsy/1 ....
172 S.Carlton LGD Bat-Jsy/15 .. 25.00 7.50
173 Stan Musial LGD Bat-Jsy/3..........
174 Nolan Ryan LGD Bat-Jsy/3 ....
175 D.Sanders LGD Bat-Jsy/15 40.00 12.00

2004 Diamond Kings DK Materials Silver

Nm-Mt Ex-Mt
RANDOM INSERTS IN PACKS ....
PRINT RUNS B/WN 1-50 COPIES PER
NO PRICING ON QTY OF 6 OR LESS..
1 Alex Rodriguez Bat-Jsy/50..... 40.00 12.00
2 Andruw Jones Bat-Jsy/50...... 10.00 3.00
3 Nomar Garciaparra Bat-Jsy/50 40.00 12.00
4 Kerry Wood Bat-Jsy/50.......... 25.00 7.50
5 Magglio Ordonez Bat-Jsy/50.. 10.00 3.00
6 Victor Martinez Bat-Bat/50...... 10.00 3.00
7 Jeremy Bonderman Jsy-Jsy/15 25.00 7.50
8 Josh Beckett Bat-Jsy/50 .... 10.00 3.00
9 Jeff Kent Bat-Jsy/50.............. 10.00 3.00
10 Carlos Beltran Bat-Jsy/50 .... 15.00 4.50
11 Hideo Nomo Bat-Jsy/50........ 25.00 7.50
12 Richie Sexson Bat-Jsy/50 .... 10.00 3.00
13 Jose Vidro Bat-Jsy/30........... 15.00 4.50
14 Jae Seo Jsy-Jsy/50.............. 10.00 3.00
15 Alfonso Soriano Bat-Jsy/50 . 15.00 4.50
16 Barry Zito Bat-Jsy/50............ 10.00 3.00
17 Brett Myers Jsy-Jsy/15......... 25.00 7.50
18 Brian Giles Bat-Bat/50.......... 10.00 3.00
19 Edgar Martinez Bat-Jsy/50... 15.00 4.50
20 Jim Edmonds Bat-Jsy/50...... 10.00 3.00
21 Rocco Baldelli Bat-Jsy/50 .... 10.00 3.00
22 Mark Teixeira Bat-Jsy/50...... 10.00 3.00
23 Carlos Delgado Bat-Jsy/50... 10.00 3.00
25 Jose Reyes Bat-Jsy/50......... 10.00 3.00
26 Marlon Byrd Bat-Jsy/50 .... 10.00 3.00
27 Albert Pujols Bat-Jsy/50 ...... 50.00 15.00
28 Vernon Wells Bat-Jsy/50....... 10.00 3.00
29 Garret Anderson Bat-Jsy/6..............
30 Jerome Williams Jsy-Jsy/50 10.00 3.00
31 Chipper Jones Bat-Jsy/50..... 25.00 7.50
32 Rich Harden Jsy-Jsy/50........ 10.00 3.00
33 Manny Ramirez Bat-Jsy/50.. 15.00 4.50
34 Derek Jeter Base-Base/50.... 40.00 12.00
35 Brandon Webb Bat-Jsy/50 ... 10.00 3.00
36 Mark Prior Bat-Jsy/50.......... 25.00 7.50
37 Roy Halladay Jsy-Jsy/50....... 10.00 3.00
38 Frank Thomas Bat-Jsy/50..... 25.00 7.50
39 Rafael Palmeiro Bat-Jsy/50.. 15.00 4.50
40 Adam Dunn Bat-Jsy/50......... 15.00 4.50
41 Aubrey Huff Bat-Jsy/15......... 25.00 7.50
42 Todd Helton Bat-Jsy/50........ 15.00 4.50
43 Matt Morris Jsy-Jsy/50........ 10.00 3.00
44 Dontrelle Willis Bat-Jsy/50... 10.00 3.00
45 Lance Berkman Bat-Jsy/50 .. 10.00 3.00
46 Mike Sweeney Bat-Jsy/50.... 10.00 3.00
47 Kazuhisa Ishii Bat-Jsy/50...... 10.00 3.00
48 Torii Hunter Bat-Jsy/50 .... 10.00 3.00
49 Vladimir Guerrero Bat-Jsy/50 25.00 7.50
50 Mike Piazza Bat-Jsy/50......... 40.00 12.00
51 Alexis Rios Bat-Bat/50 .... 10.00 3.00
52 Shannon Stewart Bat-Bat/50 10.00 3.00
53 Eric Hinske Bat-Jsy/50......... 10.00 3.00
54 Jason Jennings Bat-Jsy/50 .. 10.00 3.00
55 Jason Giambi Bat-Jsy/50...... 10.00 3.00
56 Brandon Claussen Fld Glv-Shoe/1..
57 Joe Thurston Bat-Jsy/50...... 10.00 3.00
58 Ramon Nivar Bat-Jsy/50....... 10.00 3.00
59 Jay Gibbons Jsy-Jsy/50 .... 10.00 3.00
60 Eric Chavez Bat-Jsy/50 .... 10.00 3.00
62 Walter Young Bat-Bat/50...... 10.00 3.00
63 Mark Grace Bat-Jsy/50 .... 15.00 4.50
64 Austin Kearns Bat-Jsy/50...... 10.00 3.00
65 Bob Abreu Bat-Jsy/50.......... 10.00 3.00
66 Hee Seop Choi Bat-Jsy/50 ... 10.00 3.00
67 Brandon Phillips Bat-Bat/50. 10.00 3.00
68 Rickie Weeks Bat-Bat/50...... 10.00 3.00
69 Luis Gonzalez Bat-Jsy/50..... 10.00 3.00
70 Mariano Rivera Jsy-Jsy/50 .. 15.00 4.50
71 Jason Lane Bat-Hat/6..................
72 Xavier Nady Bat-Hat/3..................
73 Run Hernandez Jsy-Jsy/15 .. 25.00 7.50
74 Aramis Ramirez Bat-Bat/1 ....
75 Ichiro Suzuki Ball-Base/6 ....
77 Chris Snelling Bat-Bat/15..... 25.00 7.50
79 Miguel Tejada Bat-Jsy/50..... 10.00 3.00
80 Juan Gonzalez Bat-Jsy/50.... 15.00 4.50
81 Joe Borchard Bat-Jsy/6..............
82 Gary Sheffield Bat-Jsy/50 .... 10.00 3.00
83 Wade Miller Bat-Jsy/6..................
84 Jeff Bagwell Bat-Jsy/50 .... 15.00 4.50
86 Adrian Beltre Bat-Jsy/50 ...... 15.00 4.50
87 Jeff Baker Bat-Bat/50............ 10.00 3.00
89 Bernie Williams Bat-Jsy/50.. 15.00 4.50
90 Pedro Martinez Bat-Jsy/50.... 25.00 7.50
92 Junior Spivey Bat-Jsy/50 ..... 10.00 3.00
93 Tim Hudson Bat-Jsy/50 .... 10.00 3.00
94 Troy Glaus Bat-Jsy/50.......... 10.00 3.00
95 Ken Griffey Jr. Base-Base/50 30.00 9.00
96 Alexis Gomez Bat-Bat/15 ..... 25.00 7.50

97 Antonio Perez Bat-Pants/50. 10.00 3.00
98 Dan Haren Bat-Jsy/50 10.00 3.00
99 Ivan Rodriguez Bat-Jsy/50 25.00 7.50
100 Randy Johnson Bat-Jsy/50 25.00 7.50
101 Lyle Overbay Bat-Jsy/50 10.00 3.00
103 Miguel Cabrera Bat-Jsy/50. 15.00 4.50
104 Scott Rolen Bat-Jsy/50 25.00 7.50
105 Roger Clemens Bat-Jsy/50 40.00 12.00
107 Nic Jackson Bat-Bat/50 10.00 3.00
108 Angel Berroa Bat-Pants/6
109 Hank Blalock Bat-Jsy/50 10.00 3.00
110 Ryan Klesko Bat-Jsy/50 10.00 3.00
111 Jose Castillo Bat-Bat/50 10.00 3.00
112 Paul Konerko Bat-Jsy/50 10.00 3.00
113 Greg Maddux Bat-Jsy/50 40.00 12.00
114 Mark Mulder Bat-Jsy/50 10.00 3.00
115 Pat Burrell Bat-Jsy/50 10.00 3.00
116 Garrett Atkins Jsy-Jsy/50 10.00 3.00
118 Orlando Cabrera Bat-Jsy/50 10.00 3.00
119 Nick Johnson Bat-Jsy/50 10.00 3.00
120 Tom Glavine Bat-Jsy/50 15.00 4.50
121 Morgan Ensberg Bat-Jsy/50 10.00 3.00
122 Sean Casey Bat-Hat/6
123 Orlando Hudson Bat-Jsy/50 10.00 3.00
124 Hideki Matsui Ball-Base/6
125 Craig Biggio Bat-Jsy/50 15.00 4.50
126 Adam LaRoche Bat-Bat/50. 10.00 3.00
127 Hong-Chih Kuo Bat-Bat/50. 10.00 3.00
128 Paul LoDuca Bat-Jsy/50 10.00 3.00
129 Shawn Green Bat-Jsy/50 10.00 3.00
130 Luis Castillo Bat-Jsy/50 10.00 3.00
131 Joe Crede Bat-Btg Glv/1
132 Ken Harvey Bat-Bat/50 10.00 3.00
133 Freddy Sanchez Bat-Bat/50 10.00 3.00
134 Roy Oswalt Bat-Jsy/50 10.00 3.00
135 Curt Schilling Bat-Jsy/50 25.00 7.50
136 Alfredo Amezaga Bat-Jsy/6
138 Barry Larkin Bat-Jsy/6
139 Trot Nixon Bat-Bat/50 10.00 3.00
140 Jim Thome Bat-Jsy/50 25.00 7.50
141 Bret Boone Bat-Jsy/50 10.00 3.00
142 Jacque Jones Bat-Jsy/50 10.00 3.00
143 Travis Hafner Bat-Jsy/50 10.00 3.00
144 Sammy Sosa Bat-Jsy/50 40.00 12.00
145 Mike Mussina Bat-Jsy/50 15.00 4.50
147 Chad Gaudin Jsy-Jsy/50 10.00 3.00
149 Mike Lowell Bat-Jsy/50 10.00 3.00
150 R.Henderson Bat-Jsy/50 25.00 7.50
151 R.Clemens FB Bat-Jsy/50 40.00 12.00
152 Mark Grace FB Bat-Jsy/6
153 R.Henderson FB Bat-Jsy/15 50.00 15.00
154 A.Rodriguez FB Bat-Jsy/30 50.00 15.00
155 R.Palmeiro FB Bat-Jsy/50 15.00 4.50
156 G.Maddux FB Bat-Bat/50 40.00 12.00
157 Mike Piazza FB Bat-Jsy/50 40.00 12.00
158 M.Mussina FB Bat-Jsy/50 15.00 4.50
159 Dale Murphy LGD Bat-Jsy/15
160 Cal Ripken LGD Bat-Jsy/50 80.00 24.00
161 C.Yaz LGD Bat-Jsy/50 40.00 12.00
162 M.Marion LGD Jsy-Jsy/15. 25.00 7.50
163 D.Mattingly LGD Bat-Jsy/50 50.00 15.00
164 R.Yount LGD Bat-Jsy/50 40.00 12.00
165 A.Dawson LGD Bat-Jsy/15. 25.00 7.50
166 Jim Palmer LGD Jsy-Jsy/3
167 G.Brett LGD Bat-Jsy/15 100.00 30.00
168 W.Ford LGD Jsy-Pants/15 40.00 12.00
169 R.Campy LGD Bat-Pants/6
170 Roger Maris LGD Bat-Jsy/6
171 Duke Snider LGD Bat-Jsy/1
172 S.Carlton LGD Bat-Jsy/50 10.00 3.00
173 Stan Musial LGD Bat-Jsy/15 80.00 24.00
174 Nolan Ryan LGD Bat-Jsy/15 100.00 30.00
175 D.Sanders LGD Bat-Jsy/50 15.00 4.50

2004 Diamond Kings DK Materials Silver Sepia

Nm-Mt Ex-Mt
RANDOM INSERTS IN PACKS
PRINT RUNS B/WN 1-30 COPIES PER
NO PRICING ON QTY OF 6 OR LESS
151 R.Clemens FB Bat-Jsy/15 60.00 18.00
152 Mark Grace FB Bat-Jsy/6
153 R.Henderson FB Bat-Jsy/6
154 A.Rodriguez FB Bat-Jsy/15 60.00 18.00
155 R.Palmeiro FB Bat-Jsy/30 25.00 7.50
156 G.Maddux FB Bat-Bat/30 50.00 15.00
157 Mike Piazza FB Bat-Jsy/30 50.00 15.00
158 M.Mussina FB Bat-Jsy/30 25.00 7.50
159 Dale Murphy LGD Bat-Jsy/6
160 Cal Ripken LGD Bat-Jsy/30 100.00 30.00
161 C.Yaz LGD Bat-Jsy/30 50.00 15.00
162 M.Marion LGD Jsy-Jsy/6
163 D.Mattingly LGD Bat-Jsy/30 60.00 18.00
164 R.Yount LGD Bat-Jsy/30 50.00 15.00
165 A.Dawson LGD Bat-Jsy/6
166 Jim Palmer LGD Jsy-Jsy/3
167 George Brett LGD Bat-Jsy/6
168 W.Ford LGD Jsy-Pants/6
169 R.Campy LGD Bat-Pants/6
170 Roger Maris LGD Bat-Jsy/6
171 Duke Snider LGD Bat-Jsy/1
172 S.Carlton LGD Bat-Jsy/30 15.00 4.50
173 Stan Musial LGD Bat-Jsy/6
174 Nolan Ryan LGD Bat-Jsy/6
175 D.Sanders LGD Bat-Jsy/30 25.00 7.50

2004 Diamond Kings DK Materials Framed Bronze

Nm-Mt Ex-Mt
RANDOM INSERTS IN PACKS
PRINT RUNS B/WN 1-100 COPIES PER
NO PRICING ON QTY OF 10 OR LESS
1 Alex Rodriguez Bat-Jsy/100 25.00 7.50
2 Andruw Jones Bat-Jsy/100 10.00 3.00
3 Nomar Garciaparra Bat-Jsy/100 25.00 7.50
4 Kerry Wood Bat-Jsy/100 20.00 6.00
5 Magglio Ordonez Bat-Jsy/100 10.00 3.00
6 Victor Martinez Bat-Bat/100 10.00 3.00
7 Jeremy Bonderman Jsy-Jsy/25 15.00 4.50
8 Josh Beckett Bat-Jsy/100 10.00 3.00
9 Jeff Kent Bat-Jsy/100 10.00 3.00
10 Carlos Beltran Bat-Jsy/100 15.00 4.50
11 Hideo Nomo Bat-Jsy/100 20.00 6.00
12 Richie Sexson Bat-Jsy/100 10.00 3.00
13 Jose Vidro Bat-Jsy/50 10.00 3.00
14 Jae Seo Jsy-Jsy/100 10.00 3.00
15 Alfonso Soriano Bat-Jsy/100 15.00 4.50
16 Barry Zito Bat-Jsy/100 10.00 3.00
17 Brett Myers Jsy-Jsy/25 15.00 4.50
18 Brian Giles Bat-Bat/100 10.00 3.00
19 Edgar Martinez Bat-Jsy/100. 15.00 4.50
20 Jim Edmonds Bat-Jsy/100 10.00 3.00
21 Rocco Baldelli Bat-Jsy/100 10.00 3.00
22 Mark Teixeira Bat-Jsy/100 10.00 3.00
23 Carlos Delgado Bat-Jsy/100. 10.00 3.00
25 Jose Reyes Bat-Jsy/100 10.00 3.00
26 Marlon Byrd Bat-Jsy/100 10.00 3.00
27 Albert Pujols Bat-Jsy/100 40.00 12.00
28 Vernon Wells Bat-Jsy/100 10.00 3.00
29 Garret Anderson Bat-Jsy/25. 15.00 4.50
30 Jerome Williams Jsy-Jsy/100 10.00 3.00
31 Chipper Jones Bat-Jsy/100 20.00 6.00
32 Rich Harden Jsy-Jsy/100 10.00 3.00
33 Manny Ramirez Bat-Jsy/100 15.00 4.50
34 Derek Jeter Base-Base/100 30.00 9.00
35 Brandon Webb Bat-Jsy/100 10.00 3.00
36 Mark Prior Bat-Jsy/100 20.00 6.00
37 Roy Halladay Jsy-Jsy/75 10.00 3.00
38 Frank Thomas Bat-Jsy/100 20.00 6.00
39 Rafael Palmeiro Bat-Jsy/100 15.00 4.50
40 Adam Dunn Bat-Jsy/100 15.00 4.50
41 Aubrey Huff Bat-Jsy/25 15.00 4.50
42 Todd Helton Bat-Jsy/100 15.00 4.50
43 Matt Morris Jsy-Jsy/100 10.00 3.00
44 Dontrelle Willis Bat-Jsy/100. 10.00 3.00
45 Lance Berkman Bat-Jsy/100 10.00 3.00
46 Mike Sweeney Bat-Jsy/100 10.00 3.00
47 Kazuhisa Ishii Bat-Jsy/100 10.00 3.00
48 Torii Hunter Bat-Jsy/100 10.00 3.00
49 Vladimir Guerrero Bat-Jsy/100 20.00 6.00
50 Mike Piazza Bat-Jsy/100 25.00 7.50
51 Alexis Rios Bat-Bat/100 10.00 3.00
52 Shannon Stewart Bat-Bat/100 10.00 3.00
53 Eric Hinske Bat-Jsy/100 10.00 3.00
54 Jason Jennings Bat-Jsy/100 10.00 3.00
55 Jason Giambi Bat-Jsy/100 10.00 3.00
56 Brandon Claussen Fld Glv-Shoe/5
57 Joe Thurston Bat-Jsy/100 10.00 3.00
58 Ramon Nivar Bat-Jsy/100 10.00 3.00
59 Jay Gibbons Jsy-Jsy/100 10.00 3.00
60 Eric Chavez Bat-Jsy/100 10.00 3.00
62 Walter Young Bat-Bat/100 10.00 3.00
63 Mark Grace Bat-Jsy/100 15.00 4.50
64 Austin Kearns Bat-Jsy/50 10.00 3.00
65 Bob Abreu Bat-Jsy/100 10.00 3.00
66 Hee Seop Choi Bat-Jsy/100 10.00 3.00
67 Brandon Phillips Bat-Bat/100 10.00 3.00
68 Rickie Weeks Bat-Bat/100 10.00 3.00
69 Luis Gonzalez Bat-Jsy/100 10.00 3.00
70 Mariano Rivera Jsy-Jsy/100 15.00 4.50
71 Jason Lane Bat-Hat/25 15.00 4.50
72 Xavier Nady Bat-Hat/10
73 Run Hernandez Jsy-Jsy/50 10.00 3.00
74 Aramis Ramirez Bat-Bat/1
75 Ichiro Suzuki Ball-Base/25 80.00 24.00
77 Chris Snelling Bat-Bat/25 15.00 4.50
79 Miguel Tejada Bat-Jsy/100 15.00 4.50
80 Juan Gonzalez Bat-Jsy/100 15.00 4.50
81 Joe Borchard Bat-Jsy/25 15.00 4.50
82 Gary Sheffield Bat-Jsy/100 10.00 3.00
83 Wade Miller Bat-Jsy/25 15.00 4.50
84 Jeff Bagwell Bat-Jsy/100 15.00 4.50
86 Adrian Beltre Bat-Jsy/100 15.00 4.50
87 Jeff Baker Bat-Bat/100 10.00 3.00
89 Bernie Williams Bat-Jsy/100 15.00 4.50
90 Pedro Martinez Bat-Jsy/100. 20.00 6.00
92 Junior Spivey Bat-Jsy/100 10.00 3.00
93 Tim Hudson Bat-Jsy/100 10.00 3.00
94 Troy Glaus Bat-Jsy/100 10.00 3.00
95 Ken Griffey Jr. Base-Base/100 20.00 6.00
96 Alexis Gomez Bat-Bat/30 15.00 4.50
97 Antonio Perez Bat-Pants/100 10.00 3.00
98 Dan Haren Bat-Jsy/100 10.00 3.00
99 Ivan Rodriguez Bat-Jsy/100. 20.00 6.00
100 Randy Johnson Bat-Jsy/100 20.00 6.00
101 Lyle Overbay Bat-Jsy/100 10.00 3.00
103 Miguel Cabrera Bat-Jsy/100 15.00 4.50
104 Scott Rolen Bat-Jsy/100 20.00 6.00
105 Roger Clemens Bat-Jsy/100 30.00 9.00
107 Nic Jackson Bat-Bat/100 10.00 3.00
108 Angel Berroa Bat-Pants/25. 15.00 4.50
109 Hank Blalock Bat-Jsy/100 10.00 3.00
110 Ryan Klesko Bat-Jsy/100 10.00 3.00
111 Jose Castillo Bat-Bat/100 10.00 3.00
112 Paul Konerko Bat-Jsy/50 10.00 3.00
113 Greg Maddux Bat-Jsy/100 25.00 7.50
114 Mark Mulder Bat-Jsy/100 10.00 3.00
115 Pat Burrell Bat-Jsy/100 10.00 3.00
116 Garrett Atkins Jsy-Jsy/100 10.00 3.00
118 Orlando Cabrera Bat-Jsy/100 10.00 3.00
119 Nick Johnson Bat-Jsy/100
120 Tom Glavine Bat-Jsy/100 15.00 4.50
121 Morgan Ensberg Bat-Jsy/100 10.00 3.00
122 Sean Casey Bat-Hat/25 15.00 4.50
123 Orlando Hudson Bat-Jsy/100 10.00 3.00
124 Hideki Matsui Ball-Base/25 80.00 24.00
125 Craig Biggio Bat-Jsy/25 25.00 7.50
126 Adam LaRoche Bat-Bat/100 10.00 3.00
127 Hong-Chih Kuo Bat-Bat/100 10.00 3.00
128 Paul LoDuca Bat-Jsy/100 10.00 3.00
129 Shawn Green Bat-Jsy/100 10.00 3.00
130 Luis Castillo Bat-Jsy/100 10.00 3.00
131 Joe Crede Bat-Btg Glv/5
132 Ken Harvey Bat-Bat/100 10.00 3.00
133 Freddy Sanchez Bat-Bat/100 10.00 3.00
134 Roy Oswalt Bat-Jsy/100 10.00 3.00
135 Curt Schilling Bat-Jsy/100 20.00 6.00
136 Alfredo Amezaga Bat-Jsy/25 15.00 4.50
138 Barry Larkin Bat-Jsy/25 25.00 7.50
139 Trot Nixon Bat-Bat/100 10.00 3.00
140 Jim Thome Bat-Jsy/100 20.00 6.00
141 Bret Boone Bat-Jsy/100 10.00 3.00
142 Jacque Jones Bat-Jsy/100 10.00 3.00
143 Travis Hafner Bat-Jsy/100 10.00 3.00
144 Sammy Sosa Bat-Jsy/100 25.00 7.50
145 Mike Mussina Bat-Jsy/100. 15.00 4.50
147 Chad Gaudin Jsy-Jsy/50 10.00 3.00
149 Mike Lowell Bat-Jsy/100 10.00 3.00
150 R.Henderson Bat-Jsy/100 20.00 6.00
151 R.Clemens FB Bat-Jsy/25 50.00 15.00
152 Mark Grace FB Bat-Jsy/25 25.00 7.50
153 R.Henderson FB Bat-Jsy/25 30.00 9.00
154 A.Rodriguez FB Bat-Jsy/25 50.00 15.00
155 R.Palmeiro FB Bat-Jsy/100 15.00 4.50
156 G.Maddux FB Bat-Bat/100 25.00 7.50
157 Mike Piazza FB Bat-Jsy/100 25.00 7.50
158 M.Mussina FB Bat-Jsy/100 15.00 4.50
159 Dale Murphy LGD Bat-Jsy/25 30.00 9.00
160 Cal Ripken LGD Bat-Jsy/100 50.00 15.00
161 C.Yaz LGD Bat-Jsy/100 25.00 7.50
162 M.Marion LGD Jsy-Jsy/25 15.00 4.50
163 D.Mattingly LGD Bat-Jsy/100 40.00 12.00
164 R.Yount LGD Bat-Jsy/100 25.00 7.50
165 A.Dawson LGD Bat-Jsy/25. 15.00 4.50
166 Jim Palmer LGD Jsy-Jsy/5
167 George Brett LGD Bat-Jsy/25 60.00 18.00
168 W.Ford LGD Jsy-Pants/25 25.00 7.50
169 R.Campy LGD Bat-Jsy/25 30.00 9.00
170 R. Maris LGD Bat-Jsy/25 100.00 30.00
171 Duke Snider LGD Bat-Jsy/4
172 S.Carlton LGD Bat-Jsy/100 10.00 3.00
173 Stan Musial LGD Bat-Jsy/25 50.00 15.00
174 Nolan Ryan LGD Bat-Jsy/25 60.00 18.00
175 D.Sanders LGD Bat-Jsy/100 15.00 4.50

2004 Diamond Kings DK Materials Framed Bronze Sepia

Nm-Mt Ex-Mt
RANDOM INSERTS IN PACKS
PRINT RUNS B/WN 4-50 COPIES PER
NO PRICING ON QTY OF 5 OR LESS
151 R.Clemens FB Bat-Jsy/25 50.00 15.00
152 Mark Grace FB Bat-Jsy/25 25.00 7.50
153 R.Henderson FB Bat-Jsy/25 30.00 9.00
154 A.Rodriguez FB Bat-Jsy/25 50.00 15.00
155 R.Palmeiro FB Bat-Jsy/50 15.00 4.50
156 G.Maddux FB Bat-Bat/50 40.00 12.00
157 Mike Piazza FB Bat-Jsy/50 40.00 12.00
158 M.Mussina FB Bat-Jsy/50 15.00 4.50
159 Dale Murphy LGD Bat-Jsy/15 50.00 15.00
160 Cal Ripken LGD Bat-Jsy/50 80.00 24.00
161 C.Yaz LGD Bat-Jsy/50 40.00 12.00
162 M.Marion LGD Jsy-Jsy/15 25.00 7.50
163 D.Mattingly LGD Bat-Jsy/50 50.00 15.00
164 R.Yount LGD Bat-Jsy/50 40.00 12.00
165 A.Dawson LGD Bat-Jsy/15. 25.00 7.50
166 Jim Palmer LGD Jsy-Jsy/5
167 G.Brett LGD Bat-Jsy/15 100.00 30.00
168 W.Ford LGD Jsy-Pants/15 40.00 12.00
169 R.Campy LGD Bat-Pants/15 50.00 15.00
170 R.Maris LGD Bat-Jsy/15 120.00 36.00
171 Duke Snider LGD Bat-Jsy/5
172 S.Carlton LGD Bat-Jsy/15 25.00 7.50
173 Stan Musial LGD Bat-Jsy/15 80.00 24.00
174 Nolan Ryan LGD Bat-Jsy/15 100.00 30.00
175 D.Sanders LGD Bat-Jsy/50 15.00 4.50

2004 Diamond Kings DK Materials Framed Gold

Nm-Mt Ex-Mt
RANDOM INSERTS IN PACKS
PRINT RUNS B/WN 1-50 COPIES PER
NO PRICING ON QTY OF 10 OR LESS
1 Alex Rodriguez Bat-Jsy/10
2 Andruw Jones Bat-Jsy/10
3 Nomar Garciaparra Bat-Jsy/10
4 Kerry Wood Bat-Jsy/10
5 Magglio Ordonez Bat-Jsy/10
6 Victor Martinez Bat-Bat/50 10.00 3.00
7 Jeremy Bonderman Jsy-Jsy/5
8 Josh Beckett Bat-Jsy/10
9 Jeff Kent Bat-Jsy/10
10 Carlos Beltran Bat-Jsy/10
11 Hideo Nomo Bat-Jsy/10
12 Richie Sexson Bat-Jsy/10
13 Jose Vidro Bat-Jsy/5
14 Jae Seo Jsy-Jsy/10
15 Alfonso Soriano Bat-Jsy/10
16 Barry Zito Bat-Jsy/10
17 Brett Myers Jsy-Jsy/5
18 Brian Giles Bat-Bat/10
19 Edgar Martinez Bat-Jsy/5
20 Jim Edmonds Bat-Jsy/5
21 Rocco Baldelli Bat-Jsy/5
22 Mark Teixeira Bat-Jsy/5
23 Carlos Delgado Bat-Jsy/10
25 Jose Reyes Bat-Jsy/10
26 Marlon Byrd Bat-Jsy/25 15.00 4.50
27 Albert Pujols Bat-Jsy/10
28 Vernon Wells Bat-Jsy/10
29 Garret Anderson Bat-Jsy/10
31 Chipper Jones Bat-Jsy/10
32 Rich Harden Jsy-Jsy/50 10.00 3.00
33 Manny Ramirez Bat-Jsy/10
34 Derek Jeter Base-Base/50 40.00 12.00
35 Brandon Webb Bat-Jsy/50 10.00 3.00
36 Mark Prior Bat-Jsy/10
37 Roy Halladay Jsy-Jsy/10
38 Frank Thomas Bat-Jsy/10
39 Rafael Palmeiro Bat-Jsy/50 15.00 4.50
40 Adam Dunn Bat-Jsy/10
41 Aubrey Huff Bat-Jsy/5
42 Todd Helton Bat-Jsy/10
43 Matt Morris Jsy-Jsy/10
44 Dontrelle Willis Bat-Jsy/10
45 Lance Berkman Bat-Jsy/5
46 Mike Sweeney Bat-Jsy/10
47 Kazuhisa Ishii Bat-Jsy/10
48 Torii Hunter Bat-Jsy/10
49 Vladimir Guerrero Bat-Jsy/10
50 Mike Piazza Bat-Jsy/50 40.00 12.00
51 Alexis Rios Bat-Bat/50 10.00 3.00
52 Shannon Stewart Bat-Bat/50 10.00 3.00
53 Eric Hinske Bat-Jsy/50 10.00 3.00
54 Jason Jennings Bat-Jsy/10
55 Jason Giambi Bat-Jsy/10
56 Brandon Claussen Fld Glv-Shoe/5
57 Joe Thurston Bat-Jsy/50 10.00 3.00
58 Ramon Nivar Bat-Jsy/50 10.00 3.00
59 Jay Gibbons Jsy-Jsy/10
60 Eric Chavez Bat-Jsy/10
62 Walter Young Bat-Bat/50 10.00 3.00
63 Mark Grace Bat-Jsy/5
64 Austin Kearns Bat-Jsy/5
65 Bob Abreu Bat-Jsy/10
66 Hee Seop Choi Bat-Jsy/10
67 Brandon Phillips Bat-Bat/50. 10.00 3.00
68 Rickie Weeks Bat-Bat/50 10.00 3.00
69 Luis Gonzalez Bat-Jsy/10
70 Mariano Rivera Jsy-Jsy/50 15.00 4.50
71 Jason Lane Bat-Hat/5
72 Xavier Nady Bat-Hat/5
73 Run Hernandez Jsy-Jsy/5
74 Aramis Ramirez Bat-Bat/1
75 Ichiro Suzuki Ball-Base/5
77 Chris Snelling Bat-Bat/5
79 Miguel Tejada Bat-Jsy/50 10.00 3.00
80 Juan Gonzalez Bat-Jsy/10
81 Joe Borchard Bat-Jsy/5
82 Gary Sheffield Bat-Jsy/10
83 Wade Miller Bat-Jsy/5
84 Jeff Bagwell Bat-Jsy/10
86 Adrian Beltre Bat-Jsy/5
87 Jeff Baker Bat-Bat/50 10.00 3.00
89 Bernie Williams Bat-Jsy/10
90 Pedro Martinez Bat-Jsy/10
92 Junior Spivey Bat-Jsy/5
93 Tim Hudson Bat-Jsy/5
94 Troy Glaus Bat-Jsy/10
95 Ken Griffey Jr. Base-Base/50 30.00 9.00
96 Alexis Gomez Bat-Bat/5
97 Antonio Perez Bat-Pants/50. 10.00 3.00
98 Dan Haren Bat-Jsy/50 10.00 3.00
99 Ivan Rodriguez Bat-Jsy/10
100 Randy Johnson Bat-Jsy/10
101 Lyle Overbay Bat-Jsy/50 10.00 3.00
103 Miguel Cabrera Bat-Jsy/10
104 Scott Rolen Bat-Jsy/10
105 Roger Clemens Bat-Jsy/10
107 Nic Jackson Bat-Bat/30 15.00 4.50
108 Angel Berroa Bat-Pants/5
109 Hank Blalock Bat-Jsy/5
110 Ryan Klesko Bat-Jsy/10
111 Jose Castillo Bat-Bat/50 10.00 3.00
112 Paul Konerko Bat-Jsy/10
113 Greg Maddux Bat-Jsy/10
114 Mark Mulder Bat-Jsy/10
115 Pat Burrell Bat-Jsy/10
116 Garrett Atkins Jsy-Jsy/50 10.00 3.00
118 Orlando Cabrera Bat-Jsy/5
119 Nick Johnson Bat-Jsy/10
120 Tom Glavine Bat-Jsy/10
121 Morgan Ensberg Bat-Jsy/10
122 Sean Casey Bat-Hat/5
123 Orlando Hudson Bat-Jsy/10
124 Hideki Matsui Ball-Base/5
125 Craig Biggio Bat-Jsy/10
126 Adam LaRoche Bat-Bat/25
127 Hong-Chih Kuo Bat-Bat/50. 10.00 3.00
128 Paul LoDuca Bat-Jsy/10
129 Shawn Green Bat-Jsy/10
130 Luis Castillo Bat-Jsy/10
131 Joe Crede Bat-Btg Glv/5
132 Ken Harvey Bat-Bat/50 10.00 3.00
133 Freddy Sanchez Bat-Bat/50 10.00 3.00
134 Roy Oswalt Bat-Jsy/50 10.00 3.00
135 Curt Schilling Bat-Jsy/10
136 Alfredo Amezaga Bat-Jsy/5
138 Barry Larkin Bat-Jsy/5
139 Trot Nixon Bat-Bat/10
140 Jim Thome Bat-Jsy/10
141 Bret Boone Bat-Jsy/5
142 Jacque Jones Bat-Jsy/50 10.00 3.00
143 Travis Hafner Bat-Jsy/50 10.00 3.00
144 Sammy Sosa Bat-Jsy/10
145 Mike Mussina Bat-Jsy/50 15.00 4.50
147 Chad Gaudin Jsy-Jsy/10
149 Mike Lowell Bat-Jsy/10
150 R.Henderson Bat-Jsy/10
151 R.Clemens FB Bat-Jsy/5
152 Mark Grace FB Bat-Jsy/5
153 R.Henderson FB Bat-Jsy/5
154 A.Rodriguez FB Bat-Jsy/5
155 R.Palmeiro FB Bat-Jsy/50 15.00 4.50
156 G.Maddux FB Bat-Bat/50 40.00 12.00
157 Mike Piazza FB Bat-Jsy/50 40.00 12.00
158 M.Mussina FB Bat-Jsy/50 15.00 4.50
159 Dale Murphy LGD Bat-Jsy/5
160 Cal Ripken LGD Bat-Jsy/50 80.00 24.00
161 C.Yaz LGD Bat-Jsy/50 40.00 12.00
162 M.Marion LGD Jsy-Jsy/5
163 D.Mattingly LGD Bat-Jsy/50 50.00 15.00
164 R.Yount LGD Bat-Jsy/50 40.00 12.00
165 A.Dawson LGD Bat-Jsy/5
166 Jim Palmer LGD Jsy-Jsy/5
167 George Brett LGD Bat-Jsy/5
168 W.Ford LGD Jsy-Pants/5
169 R.Campy LGD Bat-Pants/5
170 Roger Maris LGD Bat-Jsy/5
171 Duke Snider LGD Bat-Jsy/1
172 S.Carlton LGD Bat-Jsy/15 25.00 7.50
173 Stan Musial LGD Bat-Jsy/5
174 Nolan Ryan LGD Bat-Jsy/5
175 D.Sanders LGD Bat-Jsy/50 15.00 4.50

2004 Diamond Kings DK Materials Framed Gold Sepia

Nm-Mt Ex-Mt
RANDOM INSERTS IN PACKS
PRINT RUNS B/WN 1-15 COPIES PER
NO PRICING ON QTY OF 5 OR LESS
151 R.Clemens FB Bat-Jsy/5
152 Mark Grace FB Bat-Jsy/5
153 R.Henderson FB Bat-Jsy/5
154 A.Rodriguez FB Bat-Jsy/5
155 R.Palmeiro FB Bat-Jsy/15 40.00 12.00
156 G.Maddux FB Bat-Bat/15 60.00 18.00
157 Mike Piazza FB Bat-Jsy/15 60.00 18.00
158 M.Mussina FB Bat-Jsy/15 40.00 12.00
159 Dale Murphy LGD Bat-Jsy/5
160 Cal Ripken LGD Bat-Jsy/15 150.00 45.00
161 C.Yaz LGD Bat-Jsy/15 80.00 24.00
162 M.Marion LGD Jsy-Jsy/5
163 D.Mattingly LGD Bat-Jsy/15 100.00 30.00
164 R.Yount LGD Bat-Jsy/15
165 A.Dawson LGD Bat-Jsy/5
166 Jim Palmer LGD Jsy-Jsy/5
167 George Brett LGD Bat-Jsy/5
168 W.Ford LGD Jsy-Pants/5
169 R.Campy LGD Bat-Pants/5
170 Roger Maris LGD Bat-Jsy/5
171 Duke Snider LGD Bat-Jsy/1
172 S.Carlton LGD Bat-Jsy/5
173 Stan Musial LGD Bat-Jsy/5
174 Nolan Ryan LGD Bat-Jsy/5
175 D.Sanders LGD Bat-Jsy/15 40.00 12.00

2004 Diamond Kings DK Materials Framed Silver

Nm-Mt Ex-Mt
RANDOM INSERTS IN PACKS
PRINT RUNS B/WN 1-75 COPIES PER
NO PRICING ON QTY OF 10 OR LESS
1 Alex Rodriguez Bat-Jsy/25 50.00 15.00
2 Andruw Jones Bat-Jsy/25 15.00 4.50
3 Nomar Garciaparra Bat-Jsy/25 50.00 15.00
4 Kerry Wood Bat-Jsy/25 30.00 9.00
5 Magglio Ordonez Bat-Jsy/25 15.00 4.50
6 Victor Martinez Bat-Bat/50 10.00 3.00
7 Jeremy Bonderman Jsy-Jsy/10
8 Josh Beckett Bat-Jsy/25 15.00 4.50
9 Jeff Kent Bat-Jsy/25 15.00 4.50
10 Carlos Beltran Bat-Jsy/25 25.00 7.50
11 Hideo Nomo Bat-Jsy/25 30.00 9.00
12 Richie Sexson Bat-Jsy/25 15.00 4.50
13 Jose Vidro Bat-Jsy/25 15.00 4.50
14 Jae Seo Jsy-Jsy/25 15.00 4.50
15 Alfonso Soriano Bat-Jsy/25 25.00 7.50
16 Barry Zito Bat-Jsy/25 15.00 4.50
17 Brett Myers Jsy-Jsy/10
18 Brian Giles Bat-Bat/25 15.00 4.50
19 Edgar Martinez Bat-Jsy/25 25.00 7.50
20 Jim Edmonds Bat-Jsy/25 15.00 4.50
21 Rocco Baldelli Bat-Jsy/25 15.00 4.50
22 Mark Teixeira Bat-Jsy/25 15.00 4.50
23 Carlos Delgado Bat-Jsy/25 15.00 4.50
25 Jose Reyes Bat-Jsy/25 15.00 4.50
26 Marlon Byrd Bat-Jsy/50 10.00 3.00
27 Albert Pujols Bat-Jsy/25 60.00 18.00
28 Vernon Wells Bat-Jsy/25 15.00 4.50
29 Garret Anderson Bat-Jsy/25. 15.00 4.50
31 Chipper Jones Bat-Jsy/25 30.00 9.00
32 Rich Harden Jsy-Jsy/50 10.00 3.00
33 Manny Ramirez Bat-Jsy/25 25.00 7.50
34 Derek Jeter Base-Base/50 40.00 12.00
35 Brandon Webb Bat-Jsy/50 10.00 3.00
36 Mark Prior Bat-Jsy/25 30.00 9.00
37 Roy Halladay Jsy-Jsy/10
38 Frank Thomas Bat-Jsy/25 30.00 9.00
39 Rafael Palmeiro Bat-Jsy/50 15.00 4.50
40 Adam Dunn Bat-Jsy/25 25.00 7.50
41 Aubrey Huff Bat-Jsy/10
42 Todd Helton Bat-Jsy/25 25.00 7.50
43 Matt Morris Jsy-Jsy/25 15.00 4.50
44 Dontrelle Willis Bat-Jsy/25 15.00 4.50
45 Lance Berkman Bat-Jsy/25 15.00 4.50
46 Mike Sweeney Bat-Jsy/25
47 Kazuhisa Ishii Bat-Jsy/25 15.00 4.50
48 Torii Hunter Bat-Jsy/25 15.00 4.50
49 Vladimir Guerrero Bat-Jsy/25 30.00 9.00
50 Mike Piazza Bat-Jsy/50 40.00 12.00
51 Alexis Rios Bat-Bat/50 10.00 3.00
52 Shannon Stewart Bat-Bat/50 10.00 3.00
53 Eric Hinske Bat-Jsy/50 10.00 3.00
54 Jason Jennings Bat-Jsy/25 15.00 4.50
55 Jason Giambi Bat-Jsy/25 15.00 4.50
56 Brandon Claussen Fld Glv-Shoe/5
57 Joe Thurston Bat-Jsy/50 10.00 3.00
58 Ramon Nivar Bat-Jsy/50 10.00 3.00
59 Jay Gibbons Jsy-Jsy/25 15.00 4.50
60 Eric Chavez Bat-Jsy/25 15.00 4.50
62 Walter Young Bat-Bat/50 10.00 3.00
63 Mark Grace Bat-Jsy/25 25.00 7.50
64 Austin Kearns Bat-Jsy/25 15.00 4.50
65 Bob Abreu Bat-Jsy/25 15.00 4.50
66 Hee Seop Choi Bat-Jsy/25 15.00 4.50
67 Brandon Phillips Bat-Bat/50. 10.00 3.00
68 Rickie Weeks Bat-Bat/50 10.00 3.00
69 Luis Gonzalez Bat-Jsy/25 15.00 4.50
70 Mariano Rivera Jsy-Jsy/75 15.00 4.50
71 Jason Lane Bat-Hat/25 15.00 4.50
72 Xavier Nady Bat-Hat/10
73 Run Hernandez Jsy-Jsy/10
74 Aramis Ramirez Bat-Bat/1
75 Ichiro Suzuki Ball-Base/10
77 Chris Snelling Bat-Bat/10
79 Miguel Tejada Bat-Jsy/50 10.00 3.00
80 Juan Gonzalez Bat-Jsy/25 25.00 7.50
81 Joe Borchard Bat-Jsy/25 15.00 4.50
82 Gary Sheffield Bat-Jsy/25 15.00 4.50
83 Wade Miller Bat-Jsy/25 15.00 4.50
84 Jeff Bagwell Bat-Jsy/25 25.00 7.50
86 Adrian Beltre Bat-Jsy/25 25.00 7.50
87 Jeff Baker Bat-Bat/50 10.00 3.00
89 Bernie Williams Bat-Jsy/25 25.00 7.50
90 Pedro Martinez Bat-Jsy/25 30.00 9.00
92 Junior Spivey Bat-Jsy/25 15.00 4.50
93 Tim Hudson Bat-Jsy/25 15.00 4.50
94 Troy Glaus Bat-Jsy/25 15.00 4.50
95 Ken Griffey Jr. Base-Base/50 30.00 9.00
96 Alexis Gomez Bat-Bat/15
97 Antonio Perez Bat-Pants/50. 10.00 3.00
98 Dan Haren Bat-Jsy/50 10.00 3.00
99 Ivan Rodriguez Bat-Jsy/25 30.00 9.00
100 Randy Johnson Bat-Jsy/25 30.00 9.00
101 Lyle Overbay Bat-Jsy/50 10.00 3.00
103 Miguel Cabrera Bat-Jsy/25. 25.00 7.50
104 Scott Rolen Bat-Jsy/25 30.00 9.00
105 Roger Clemens Bat-Jsy/25 50.00 15.00
107 Nic Jackson Bat-Bat/50 10.00 3.00
108 Angel Berroa Bat-Pants/25. 15.00 4.50
109 Hank Blalock Bat-Jsy/25 15.00 4.50
110 Ryan Klesko Bat-Jsy/25 15.00 4.50
111 Jose Castillo Bat-Bat/50 10.00 3.00
112 Paul Konerko Bat-Jsy/25 15.00 4.50
113 Greg Maddux Bat-Jsy/25 50.00 15.00
114 Mark Mulder Bat-Jsy/25 15.00 4.50
115 Pat Burrell Bat-Jsy/25 15.00 4.50
116 Garrett Atkins Jsy-Jsy/50 10.00 3.00
118 Orlando Cabrera Bat-Jsy/25 15.00 4.50
119 Nick Johnson Bat-Jsy/25 15.00 4.50
120 Tom Glavine Bat-Jsy/25 25.00 7.50
121 Morgan Ensberg Bat-Jsy/25 15.00 4.50
122 Sean Casey Bat-Hat/25 15.00 4.50
123 Orlando Hudson Bat-Jsy/25 15.00 4.50
124 Hideki Matsui Ball-Base/10
125 Craig Biggio Bat-Jsy/25 25.00 7.50
126 Adam LaRoche Bat-Bat/50. 10.00 3.00
127 Hong-Chih Kuo Bat-Bat/50. 10.00 3.00
128 Paul LoDuca Bat-Jsy/25 15.00 4.50
129 Shawn Green Bat-Jsy/25 15.00 4.50
130 Luis Castillo Bat-Jsy/25 15.00 4.50
131 Joe Crede Bat-Btg Glv/5
132 Ken Harvey Bat-Bat/50 10.00 3.00
133 Freddy Sanchez Bat-Bat/50 10.00 3.00
134 Roy Oswalt Bat-Jsy/50 10.00 3.00
135 Curt Schilling Bat-Jsy/25 30.00 9.00
136 Alfredo Amezaga Bat-Jsy/25 15.00 4.50
138 Barry Larkin Bat-Jsy/25 25.00 7.50
139 Trot Nixon Bat-Bat/25 15.00 4.50
140 Jim Thome Bat-Jsy/25 30.00 9.00

41 Bret Boone Bat-Jsy/50 10.00 3.00
42 Jacque Jones Bat-Jsy/50 10.00 3.00
43 Travis Hafner Bat-Jsy/50 10.00 3.00
44 Sammy Sosa Bat-Jsy/25 50.00 15.00
45 Mike Mussina Bat-Jsy/50 15.00 4.50
47 Chad Gaudin Jsy-Jsy/25 15.00 4.50
49 Mike Lowell Bat-Jsy/25 15.00 4.50
50 R.Henderson Bat-Jsy/25 30.00 9.00
51 R.Clemens FB Bat-Jsy/15 60.00 18.00
52 Mark Grace FB Bat-Jsy/15 40.00 12.00
53 R.Henderson FB Bat-Jsy/15 25.00 7.50
54 A.Rodriguez FB Bat-Jsy/15 60.00 18.00
55 R.Palmeiro FB Bat-Jsy/50 15.00 4.50
56 G.Maddux FB Bat-Bat/50 40.00 12.00
57 Mike Piazza FB Bat-Jsy/50 40.00 12.00
58 M.Mussina FB Bat-Jsy/50 15.00 4.50
59 Dale Murphy LGD Bat-Jsy/15 50.00 15.00
60 Cal Ripken LGD Bat-Jsy/50 80.00 24.00
61 C.Yaz LGD Bat-Jsy/50 40.00 12.00
62 M.Marion LGD Jsy-Jsy/15 25.00 7.50
63 D.Mattingly LGD Bat-Jsy/50 50.00 15.00
64 R.Yount LGD Bat-Jsy/50 40.00 12.00
65 A.Dawson LGD Bat-Jsy/15 25.00 7.50
66 Jim Palmer LGD Jsy-Jsy/5
67 G.Brett LGD Bat-Jsy/15 100.00 30.00
68 W.Ford LGD Jsy-Pants/15 40.00 12.00
69 R.Campy LGD Bat-Pants/15 50.00 15.00
70 R.Maris LGD Bat-Jsy/15 120.00 36.00
71 Duke Snider LGD Bat-Jsy/1
72 S.Carlton LGD Bat-Jsy/50 10.00 3.00
73 Stan Musial LGD Bat-Jsy/15 80.00 24.00
74 Nolan Ryan LGD Bat-Jsy/15 100.00 30.00
75 D.Sanders LGD Bat-Jsy/50 15.00 4.50

2004 Diamond Kings DK Materials Framed Silver Sepia

Nm-Mt Ex-Mt
RANDOM INSERTS IN PACKS
PRINT RUNS B/WN 1-30 COPIES PER
NO PRICING ON QTY OF 10 OR LESS
151 R.Clemens FB Bat-Jsy/15 60.00 18.00
152 Mark Grace FB Bat-Jsy/15 40.00 12.00
153 R.Henderson FB Bat-Jsy/15 50.00 15.00
154 A.Rodriguez FB Bat-Jsy/15 60.00 18.00
155 R.Palmeiro FB Bat-Jsy/30 25.00 7.50
156 G.Maddux FB Bat-Bat/30 50.00 15.00
157 Mike Piazza FB Bat-Jsy/30 50.00 15.00
158 M.Mussina FB Bat-Jsy/30 25.00 7.50
159 Dale Murphy LGD Bat-Jsy/1
160 Cal Ripken LGD Bat-Jsy/30 100.00 30.00
161 C.Yaz LGD Bat-Jsy/30 50.00 15.00
162 M.Marion LGD Jsy-Jsy/10
163 D.Mattingly LGD Bat-Jsy/30 60.00 18.00
164 R.Yount LGD Bat-Jsy/30 50.00 15.00
165 A.Dawson LGD Bat-Jsy/10
166 Jim Palmer LGD Jsy-Jsy/5
167 George Brett LGD Bat-Jsy/10
168 W.Ford LGD Jsy-Pants/10
169 R.Campy LGD Bat-Pants/10
170 Roger Maris LGD Bat-Jsy/10
171 Duke Snider LGD Bat-Jsy/1
172 S.Carlton LGD Bat-Jsy/10
173 Stan Musial LGD Bat-Jsy/10
174 Nolan Ryan LGD Bat-Jsy/10
175 D.Sanders LGD Bat-Jsy/30 25.00 7.50

2004 Diamond Kings DK Signatures Bronze

Nm-Mt Ex-Mt
RANDOM INSERTS IN PACKS
PRINT RUNS B/WN 1-200 COPIES PER
NO PRICING ON QTY OF 10 OR LESS
1 Alex Rodriguez/1
2 Andruw Jones/2
4 Kerry Wood/1
5 Magglio Ordonez/2
6 Victor Martinez/200 15.00 4.50
7 Jeremy Bonderman/1
8 Josh Beckett/2
9 Jeff Kent/2
10 Carlos Beltran/8
11 Hideo Nomo/1
12 Richie Sexson/5
13 Jose Vidro/200 10.00 3.00
14 Jae Seo/200 25.00 7.50
17 Brett Myers/200 10.00 3.00
19 Edgar Martinez/25 60.00 18.00
20 Jim Edmonds/1
21 Rocco Baldelli/10
22 Mark Teixeira/5
26 Marlon Byrd/200 10.00 3.00
27 Albert Pujols/1
28 Vernon Wells/10
29 Garret Anderson/5
31 Chipper Jones/1
32 Rich Harden/200 15.00 4.50
35 Brandon Webb/25 15.00 4.50
36 Mark Prior/1
38 Frank Thomas/2
39 Rafael Palmeiro/1
40 Adam Dunn/5
41 Aubrey Huff/100 15.00 4.50
42 Todd Helton/1
44 Dontrelle Willis/15 30.00 9.00
45 Lance Berkman/1
46 Mike Sweeney/8
48 Torii Hunter/100 25.00 7.50
49 Vladimir Guerrero/1
50 Mike Piazza/1
51 Alexis Rios/200 15.00 4.50
52 Shannon Stewart/200 15.00 4.50
53 Eric Hinske/25 15.00 4.50
54 Jason Jennings/15 25.00 7.50
56 Brandon Claussen/200 10.00 3.00
57 Joe Thurston/200 10.00 3.00
58 Ramon Nivar/100 10.00 3.00
59 Jay Gibbons/25 15.00 4.50
60 Eric Chavez/2
61 Jimmy Gobble/100 10.00 3.00
62 Walter Young/200 10.00 3.00
63 Mark Grace/1
64 Austin Kearns/2
65 Bob Abreu/15 30.00 9.00
67 Brandon Phillips/100 10.00 3.00
68 Rickie Weeks/30 25.00 7.50
70 Mariano Rivera/10
71 Jason Lane/200 10.00 3.00
72 Xavier Nady/1
73 Runelvys Hernandez/50 12.00 3.60
74 Aramis Ramirez/100 15.00 4.50
76 Cliff Lee/200 10.00 3.00
77 Chris Snelling/200 10.00 3.00
78 Ryan Wagner/100 10.00 3.00
80 Juan Gonzalez/5
81 Joe Borchard/200 10.00 3.00
82 Gary Sheffield/10
83 Wade Miller/5
84 Jeff Bagwell/1
85 Ryan Church/200 10.00 3.00
86 Adrian Beltre/5
87 Jeff Baker/100 10.00 3.00
88 Adam Loewen/100 10.00 3.00
90 Pedro Martinez/1
91 Carlos Rivera/100 10.00 3.00
92 Junior Spivey/25 15.00 4.50
93 Tim Hudson/2
94 Troy Glaus/5
96 Alexis Gomez/200 10.00 3.00
97 Antonio Perez/46 12.00 3.60
98 Dan Haren/100 10.00 3.00
99 Ivan Rodriguez/5
100 Randy Johnson/1
101 Lyle Overbay/200 15.00 4.50
102 Oliver Perez/200 15.00 4.50
103 Miguel Cabrera/100 25.00 7.50
104 Scott Rolen/2
106 Brian Tallet/200 10.00 3.00
107 Nic Jackson/200 10.00 3.00
108 Angel Berroa/25 15.00 4.50
109 Hank Blalock/25 25.00 7.50
110 Ryan Klesko/8
111 Jose Castillo/200 10.00 3.00
112 Paul Konerko/8
113 Greg Maddux/1
114 Mark Mulder/25 25.00 7.50
116 Garrett Atkins/100 10.00 3.00
117 Jeremy Guthrie/200 10.00 3.00
118 Orlando Cabrera/75 20.00 6.00
120 Tom Glavine/2
121 Morgan Ensberg/200 15.00 4.50
122 Sean Casey/10
123 Orlando Hudson/100 10.00 3.00
125 Craig Biggio/2
126 Adam LaRoche/100 10.00 3.00
127 Hong-Chih Kuo/25 40.00 12.00
128 Paul LoDuca/1
130 Luis Castillo/25 15.00 4.50
131 Joe Crede/100 10.00 3.00
132 Ken Harvey/200 15.00 4.50
133 Freddy Sanchez/50 12.00 3.60
134 Roy Oswalt/8
135 Curt Schilling/1
136 Alfredo Amezaga/90 10.00 3.00
137 Chien-Ming Wang/25 40.00 12.00
139 Trot Nixon/15 30.00 9.00
142 Jacque Jones/25 25.00 7.50
143 Travis Hafner/200 15.00 4.50
144 Sammy Sosa/1
145 Mike Mussina/1
146 Vinny Chulk/200 10.00 3.00
147 Chad Gaudin/100 10.00 3.00
148 Delmon Young/25 40.00 12.00
149 Mike Lowell/25 25.00 7.50
151 Roger Clemens FB/1
152 Mark Grace FB/1
154 Alex Rodriguez FB/1
155 Rafael Palmeiro FB/1
156 Greg Maddux FB/1
157 Mike Piazza FB/1
158 Mike Mussina FB/1
159 Dale Murphy LGD/1
160 Cal Ripken LGD/1
161 Carl Yastrzemski LGD/1
162 Marty Marion LGD/15 30.00 9.00
163 Don Mattingly LGD/1
164 Robin Yount LGD/1
166 Jim Palmer LGD/1
168 Whitey Ford LGD/1
171 Duke Snider LGD/1
172 Steve Carlton LGD/1
173 Stan Musial LGD/1
174 Nolan Ryan LGD/1
175 Deion Sanders LGD/1

2004 Diamond Kings DK Signatures Gold

Nm-Mt Ex-Mt
RANDOM INSERTS IN PACKS
PRINT RUNS B/WN 1-50 COPIES PER
NO PRICING ON QTY OF 12 OR LESS
26 Marlon Byrd/15 25.00 7.50
32 Rich Harden/50 20.00 6.00
51 Alexis Rios/50 20.00 6.00
56 Brandon Claussen/50 12.00 3.60
57 Joe Thurston/50 12.00 3.60
62 Walter Young/50 12.00 3.60
71 Jason Lane/40 12.00 3.60
77 Chris Snelling/50 12.00 3.60
81 Joe Borchard/50 12.00 3.60
85 Ryan Church/50 12.00 3.60
96 Alexis Gomez/50 12.00 3.60
101 Lyle Overbay/50 20.00 6.00
102 Oliver Perez/50 20.00 6.00
106 Brian Tallet/50 12.00 3.60
107 Nic Jackson/50 12.00 3.60
121 Morgan Ensberg/48 20.00 6.00
146 Vinny Chulk/50 12.00 3.60

2004 Diamond Kings DK Signatures Silver

Nm-Mt Ex-Mt
RANDOM INSERTS IN PACKS
PRINT RUNS B/WN 1-100 COPIES PER
NO PRICING ON QTY OF 10 OR LESS
1 Alex Rodriguez/1
2 Andruw Jones/1
4 Kerry Wood/1
5 Magglio Ordonez/1
6 Victor Martinez/49 20.00 6.00
7 Jeremy Bonderman/1
8 Josh Beckett/1
9 Jeff Kent/1
10 Carlos Beltran/5
11 Hideo Nomo/1
12 Richie Sexson/3
13 Jose Vidro/20 20.00 6.00
14 Jae Seo/80 25.00 7.50
17 Brett Myers/90 10.00 3.00
19 Edgar Martinez/15 80.00 24.00
20 Jim Edmonds/1
21 Rocco Baldelli/5
22 Mark Teixeira/3
26 Marlon Byrd/100 10.00 3.00
27 Albert Pujols/1
28 Vernon Wells/5
29 Garret Anderson/3
31 Chipper Jones/1
32 Rich Harden/100 15.00 4.50
35 Brandon Webb/15 25.00 7.50
36 Mark Prior/1
38 Frank Thomas/1
39 Rafael Palmeiro/1
40 Adam Dunn/3
41 Aubrey Huff/40 25.00 7.50
42 Todd Helton/1
44 Dontrelle Willis/5
45 Lance Berkman/1
46 Mike Sweeney/5
48 Torii Hunter/40 40.00 12.00
49 Vladimir Guerrero/1
50 Mike Piazza/1
51 Alexis Rios/100 15.00 4.50
52 Shannon Stewart/30 25.00 7.50
53 Eric Hinske/15 25.00 7.50
54 Jason Jennings/5
56 Brandon Claussen/100 10.00 3.00
57 Joe Thurston/100 10.00 3.00
58 Ramon Nivar/30 15.00 4.50
59 Jay Gibbons/15 25.00 7.50
60 Eric Chavez/1
61 Jimmy Gobble/30 15.00 4.50
62 Walter Young/100 10.00 3.00
63 Mark Grace/1
64 Austin Kearns/1
65 Bob Abreu/6
67 Brandon Phillips/30 15.00 4.50
68 Rickie Weeks/20 25.00 7.50
70 Mariano Rivera/5
71 Jason Lane/100 10.00 3.00
72 Xavier Nady/1
73 Runelvys Hernandez/30 15.00 4.50
74 Aramis Ramirez/30 25.00 7.50
76 Cliff Lee/100 10.00 3.00
77 Chris Snelling/100 10.00 3.00
78 Ryan Wagner/30 15.00 4.50
80 Juan Gonzalez/3
81 Joe Borchard/100 10.00 3.00
82 Gary Sheffield/5
83 Wade Miller/3
84 Jeff Bagwell/1
85 Ryan Church/100 10.00 3.00
86 Adrian Beltre/3
87 Jeff Baker/30 15.00 4.50
88 Adam Loewen/30 15.00 4.50
90 Pedro Martinez/1
91 Carlos Rivera/15
92 Junior Spivey/15 25.00 7.50
93 Tim Hudson/1
94 Troy Glaus/3
96 Alexis Gomez/100 10.00 3.00
97 Antonio Perez/15 25.00 7.50
98 Dan Haren/30 15.00 4.50
99 Ivan Rodriguez/3
100 Randy Johnson/1
101 Lyle Overbay/100 15.00 4.50
102 Oliver Perez/100 15.00 4.50
103 Miguel Cabrera/30 40.00 12.00
104 Scott Rolen/1
105 Roger Clemens/1
106 Brian Tallet/100 10.00 3.00
107 Nic Jackson/100 10.00 3.00
108 Angel Berroa/5
109 Hank Blalock/30 25.00 7.50
110 Ryan Klesko/5
111 Jose Castillo/100 10.00 3.00
112 Paul Konerko/5
113 Greg Maddux/1
114 Mark Mulder/15 30.00 9.00
116 Garrett Atkins/30 15.00 4.50
117 Jeremy Guthrie/30 15.00 4.50
118 Orlando Cabrera/15 30.00 9.00
120 Tom Glavine/1
121 Morgan Ensberg/50 20.00 6.00
122 Sean Casey/5
123 Orlando Hudson/30 15.00 4.50
125 Craig Biggio/1
126 Adam LaRoche/30 15.00 4.50
127 Hong-Chih Kuo/15 50.00 15.00
128 Paul LoDuca/1
130 Luis Castillo/15 25.00 7.50
131 Joe Crede/35 15.00 4.50
132 Ken Harvey/30 25.00 7.50
133 Freddy Sanchez/15 25.00 7.50
134 Roy Oswalt/5
135 Curt Schilling/1
136 Alfredo Amezaga/30 15.00 4.50
137 Chien-Ming Wang/15 50.00 15.00
139 Trot Nixon/6
142 Jacque Jones/10
143 Travis Hafner/30 25.00 7.50
144 Sammy Sosa/1
145 Mike Mussina/1
146 Vinny Chulk/100 10.00 3.00
147 Chad Gaudin/30 15.00 4.50
148 Delmon Young/10
149 Mike Lowell/15 30.00 9.00
151 Roger Clemens FB/1
152 Mark Grace FB/1
154 Alex Rodriguez FB/1
155 Rafael Palmeiro FB/1
156 Greg Maddux FB/1
157 Mike Piazza FB/1
158 Mike Mussina FB/1
159 Dale Murphy LGD/1
160 Cal Ripken LGD/1
161 Carl Yastrzemski LGD/1
162 Marty Marion LGD/10
163 Don Mattingly LGD/1
164 Robin Yount LGD/1
166 Jim Palmer LGD/1
167 George Brett LGD/1
168 Whitey Ford LGD/1
171 Duke Snider LGD/1
172 Steve Carlton LGD/1
173 Stan Musial LGD/1
174 Nolan Ryan LGD/1
175 Deion Sanders LGD/1

2004 Diamond Kings DK Signatures Framed Bronze

Nm-Mt Ex-Mt
RANDOM INSERTS IN PACKS
PRINT RUNS B/WN 1-50 COPIES PER
NO PRICING ON QTY OF 10 OR LESS
1 Alex Rodriguez/1
2 Andruw Jones/5
4 Kerry Wood/1
5 Magglio Ordonez/10
6 Victor Martinez/50 20.00 6.00
7 Jeremy Bonderman/1
8 Josh Beckett/5
9 Jeff Kent/5
10 Carlos Beltran/10
11 Hideo Nomo/1
12 Richie Sexson/10
13 Jose Vidro/25 20.00 6.00
14 Jae Seo/50 30.00 9.00
17 Brett Myers/25 20.00 6.00
19 Edgar Martinez/25 60.00 18.00
20 Jim Edmonds/1
21 Rocco Baldelli/25 25.00 7.50
22 Mark Teixeira/1
26 Marlon Byrd/50 12.00 3.60
27 Albert Pujols/1
28 Vernon Wells/25 25.00 7.50
29 Garret Anderson/10
31 Chipper Jones/1
32 Rich Harden/50 20.00 6.00
35 Brandon Webb/25 20.00 6.00
36 Mark Prior/1
38 Frank Thomas/5
39 Rafael Palmeiro/1
40 Adam Dunn/25 40.00 12.00
41 Aubrey Huff/25 25.00 7.50
42 Todd Helton/1
44 Dontrelle Willis/25 25.00 7.50
45 Lance Berkman/1
46 Mike Sweeney/10
48 Torii Hunter/25 40.00 12.00
49 Vladimir Guerrero/1
50 Mike Piazza/1
51 Alexis Rios/50 20.00 6.00
52 Shannon Stewart/25 25.00 7.50
53 Eric Hinske/25 20.00 6.00
54 Jason Jennings/25 20.00 6.00
56 Brandon Claussen/50 12.00 3.60
57 Joe Thurston/50 12.00 3.60
58 Ramon Nivar/25 20.00 6.00
59 Jay Gibbons/25 20.00 6.00
60 Eric Chavez/10
61 Jimmy Gobble/50 12.00 3.60
62 Walter Young/50 12.00 3.60
63 Mark Grace/1
64 Austin Kearns/5
65 Bob Abreu/25 25.00 7.50
67 Brandon Phillips/50 12.00 3.60
68 Rickie Weeks/25 25.00 7.50
70 Mariano Rivera /10
71 Jason Lane/25 20.00 6.00
72 Xavier Nady/1
73 Runelvys Hernandez/25 20.00 6.00
74 Aramis Ramirez/25 25.00 7.50
76 Cliff Lee/50 12.00 3.60
77 Chris Snelling/50 12.00 3.60
78 Ryan Wagner/25 20.00 6.00
80 Juan Gonzalez/5
81 Joe Borchard/50 12.00 3.60
82 Gary Sheffield/10
83 Wade Miller/5
84 Jeff Bagwell/1
85 Ryan Church/50 12.00 3.60
86 Adrian Beltre/10
87 Jeff Baker/25 20.00 6.00
88 Adam Loewen/25 20.00 6.00
90 Pedro Martinez/1
91 Carlos Rivera/50 12.00 3.60
92 Junior Spivey/5
93 Tim Hudson/10
94 Troy Glaus/25 25.00 7.50
96 Alexis Gomez/50 12.00 3.60
97 Antonio Perez/25 20.00 6.00
98 Dan Haren/25 20.00 6.00
99 Ivan Rodriguez/5
100 Randy Johnson/1
101 Lyle Overbay/50 20.00 6.00
102 Oliver Perez/50 20.00 6.00
103 Miguel Cabrera/50 30.00 9.00
104 Scott Rolen/5
106 Brian Tallet/50 12.00 3.60
107 Nic Jackson/50 12.00 3.60
108 Angel Berroa/25 20.00 6.00
109 Hank Blalock/25 25.00 7.50
110 Ryan Klesko/5
111 Jose Castillo/50 12.00 3.60
112 Paul Konerko/15 30.00 9.00
113 Greg Maddux/1
114 Mark Mulder/25 25.00 7.50
116 Garrett Atkins/50 12.00 3.60
117 Jeremy Guthrie/25 20.00 6.00
118 Orlando Cabrera/25 25.00 7.50
120 Tom Glavine/5
121 Morgan Ensberg/50 20.00 6.00
122 Sean Casey/5
123 Orlando Hudson/50 12.00 3.60
125 Craig Biggio/5
126 Adam LaRoche/50 12.00 3.60
127 Hong-Chih Kuo/25 40.00 12.00
128 Paul LoDuca/1
130 Luis Castillo/25 20.00 6.00
131 Joe Crede/50 12.00 3.60
132 Ken Harvey/25 25.00 7.50
133 Freddy Sanchez/25 20.00 6.00
134 Roy Oswalt/20 25.00 7.50
135 Curt Schilling/1
136 Alfredo Amezaga/25 20.00 6.00
137 Chien-Ming Wang/25 40.00 12.00
139 Trot Nixon/25 25.00 7.50
142 Jacque Jones/25 25.00 7.50
143 Travis Hafner/25 25.00 7.50
144 Sammy Sosa/1
145 Mike Mussina/1
146 Vinny Chulk/50 12.00 3.60
147 Chad Gaudin/25 20.00 6.00
148 Delmon Young/25 40.00 12.00
149 Mike Lowell/25 25.00 7.50
151 Roger Clemens FB/1
152 Mark Grace FB/1
154 Alex Rodriguez FB/1
155 Rafael Palmeiro FB/1
156 Greg Maddux FB/1
157 Mike Piazza FB/1
158 Mike Mussina FB/1
159 Dale Murphy LGD/1
160 Cal Ripken LGD/1
161 Carl Yastrzemski LGD/1
162 Marty Marion LGD/25 25.00 7.50
163 Don Mattingly LGD/1
164 Robin Yount LGD/1
166 Jim Palmer LGD/1
167 George Brett LGD/1
168 Whitey Ford LGD/1
171 Duke Snider LGD/1
172 Steve Carlton LGD/1
173 Stan Musial LGD/1
174 Nolan Ryan LGD/1
175 Deion Sanders LGD/1

2004 Diamond Kings DK Signatures Framed Bronze Sepia

Nm-Mt Ex-Mt
RANDOM INSERTS IN PACKS
PRINT RUNS B/WN 1-25 COPIES PER
NO PRICING ON QTY OF 1 OR LESS
162 Marty Marion LGD/25 25.00 7.50

2004 Diamond Kings DK Signatures Framed Silver

Nm-Mt Ex-Mt
RANDOM INSERTS IN PACKS
PRINT RUNS B/WN 1-25 COPIES PER
NO PRICING ON QTY OF 10 OR LESS
1 Alex Rodriguez/1
2 Andruw Jones/1
4 Kerry Wood/1
5 Magglio Ordonez/10
6 Victor Martinez/15 30.00 9.00
7 Jeremy Bonderman/1
8 Josh Beckett/5
9 Jeff Kent/5
10 Carlos Beltran/10
11 Hideo Nomo/1
12 Richie Sexson/10
13 Jose Vidro/10
14 Jae Seo/15 50.00 15.00
17 Brett Myers/10
19 Edgar Martinez/10
20 Jim Edmonds/1
21 Rocco Baldelli/15 30.00 9.00
22 Mark Teixeira/1
26 Marlon Byrd/15 25.00 7.50
27 Albert Pujols/1
28 Vernon Wells/10
29 Garret Anderson/10
31 Chipper Jones/1
32 Rich Harden/25 25.00 7.50
35 Brandon Webb/15 25.00 7.50
36 Mark Prior/1
38 Frank Thomas/5
39 Rafael Palmeiro/1
40 Adam Dunn/5
41 Aubrey Huff/10
42 Todd Helton/1
44 Dontrelle Willis/10
45 Lance Berkman/1
46 Mike Sweeney/10
47 Kazuhisa Ishii/1
48 Torii Hunter/10
49 Vladimir Guerrero/1
50 Mike Piazza/1
51 Alexis Rios/25 25.00 7.50
52 Shannon Stewart/5
53 Eric Hinske/15
54 Jason Jennings/10
56 Brandon Claussen/25 20.00 6.00
57 Joe Thurston/25 20.00 6.00
58 Ramon Nivar/15 25.00 7.50
59 Jay Gibbons/15 25.00 7.50
60 Eric Chavez/10
61 Jimmy Gobble/15 25.00 7.50
62 Walter Young/25 20.00 6.00
63 Mark Grace/1
64 Austin Kearns/5
65 Bob Abreu/10
67 Brandon Phillips/15 25.00 7.50
68 Rickie Weeks/10
70 Mariano Rivera/5
71 Jason Lane/10
72 Xavier Nady/1
73 Runelvys Hernandez/15 25.00 7.50
74 Aramis Ramirez/10
76 Cliff Lee/15 25.00 7.50
77 Chris Snelling/25 20.00 6.00
78 Ryan Wagner/10
80 Juan Gonzalez/5
81 Joe Borchard/25 20.00 6.00
82 Gary Sheffield/5
83 Wade Miller/3
84 Jeff Bagwell/1
85 Ryan Church/25 20.00 6.00
86 Adrian Beltre/10
87 Jeff Baker/10

88 Adam Loewen/10
90 Pedro Martinez/1
91 Carlos Rivera/15 25.00 7.50
92 Junior Spivey/10
93 Tim Hudson/10
94 Troy Glaus/5
96 Alexis Gomez/25 20.00 6.00
97 Antonio Perez/10
98 Dan Haren/15
99 Ivan Rodriguez/5
100 Randy Johnson/1
101 Lyle Overbay/25 25.00 7.50
102 Oliver Perez/25 25.00 7.50
103 Miguel Cabrera/10
104 Scott Rolen/5
105 Roger Clemens/1
106 Brian Tallet/25 20.00 6.00
107 Nic Jackson/25 20.00 6.00
108 Angel Berroa/5
109 Hank Blalock/10
110 Ryan Klesko/5
111 Jose Castillo/15 25.00 7.50
112 Paul Konerko/10
113 Greg Maddux/1
114 Mark Mulder/10
116 Garrett Atkins/15
117 Jeremy Guthrie/10
118 Orlando Cabrera/10
120 Tom Glavine/5
121 Morgan Ensberg/15 30.00 9.00
122 Sean Casey/5
123 Orlando Hudson/15 25.00 7.50
125 Craig Biggio/5
126 Adam LaRoche/15 25.00 7.50
127 Hong-Chih Kuo/10
128 Paul LoDuca/1
130 Luis Castillo/15 25.00 7.50
131 Joe Crede/10
132 Ken Harvey/15
133 Freddy Sanchez/15 25.00 7.50
134 Roy Oswalt/10
135 Curt Schilling/1
136 Alfredo Amezaga/15 25.00 7.50
137 Chien-Ming Wang/15 50.00 15.00
139 Trot Nixon/10
142 Jacque Jones/10
143 Travis Hafner/10
144 Sammy Sosa/1
145 Mike Mussina/1
146 Vinny Chulk/25 20.00 6.00
147 Chad Gaudin/15 25.00 7.50
148 Delmon Young/10
149 Mike Lowell/15 30.00 9.00
151 Roger Clemens FB/1
152 Mark Grace FB/1
154 Alex Rodriguez FB/1
155 Rafael Palmeiro FB/1
156 Greg Maddux FB/1
157 Mike Piazza FB/1
158 Mike Mussina FB/1
159 Dale Murphy LGD/1
160 Cal Ripken LGD/1
161 Carl Yastrzemski LGD/1
162 Marty Marion LGD/10
163 Don Mattingly LGD/1
164 Robin Yount LGD/1
166 Jim Palmer LGD/1
167 George Brett LGD/1
168 Whitey Ford LGD/1
171 Duke Snider LGD/1
172 Steve Carlton LGD/1
173 Stan Musial LGD/1
174 Nolan Ryan LGD/1
175 Deion Sanders LGD/1

2004 Diamond Kings Diamond Cut Bats

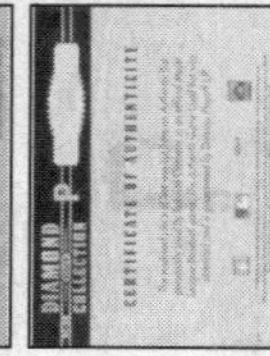

Nm-Mt Ex-Mt
RANDOM INSERTS IN PACKS
PRINT RUNS B/WN 1-100 COPIES PER
NO PRICING ON QTY OF 1 OR LESS
1 Alex Rodriguez/100 25.00 7.50
2 Nomar Garciaparra/100 25.00 7.50
3 Hideo Nomo/100 15.00 4.50
4 Alfonso Soriano/100 15.00 4.50
6 Edgar Martinez/100 15.00 4.50
7 Rocco Baldelli/100 10.00 3.00
8 Mark Teixeira/100 10.00 3.00
9 Albert Pujols/100 30.00 9.00
10 Vernon Wells/100 10.00 3.00
11 Garret Anderson/100 10.00 3.00
14 Brandon Webb/100 10.00 3.00
15 Mark Prior/100 15.00 4.50
16 Rafael Palmeiro/100 15.00 4.50
17 Adam Dunn/100 15.00 4.50
18 Dontrelle Willis/100 10.00 3.00
19 Kazuhisa Ishii/100 10.00 3.00
20 Torii Hunter/100 10.00 3.00
21 Vladimir Guerrero/100 15.00 4.50
22 Mike Piazza/100 25.00 7.50
23 Jason Giambi/100 10.00 3.00
26 Bob Abreu/100 10.00 3.00
27 Hee Seop Choi/100 10.00 3.00
28 Rickie Weeks/100 10.00 3.00
30 Troy Glaus/100 10.00 3.00
31 Ivan Rodriguez/100 15.00 4.50
32 Hank Blalock/100 10.00 3.00
33 Greg Maddux/100 25.00 7.50
34 Nick Johnson/100 10.00 3.00
35 Shawn Green/100 10.00 3.00
36 Sammy Sosa/100 25.00 7.50
37 Dale Murphy/50 25.00 7.50
38 Cal Ripken/50 60.00 18.00
39 Carl Yastrzemski/100 25.00 7.50
41 Don Mattingly/100 30.00 9.00
43 George Brett/50 40.00 12.00

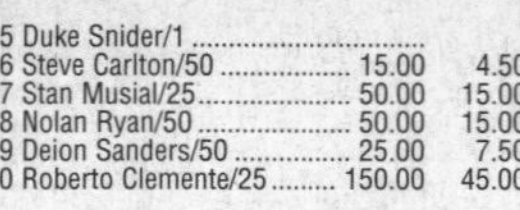

45 Duke Snider/1
46 Steve Carlton/50 15.00 4.50
47 Stan Musial/25 50.00 15.00
48 Nolan Ryan/50 50.00 15.00
49 Deion Sanders/50 25.00 7.50
50 Roberto Clemente/25 150.00 45.00

2004 Diamond Kings Diamond Cut Combos Material

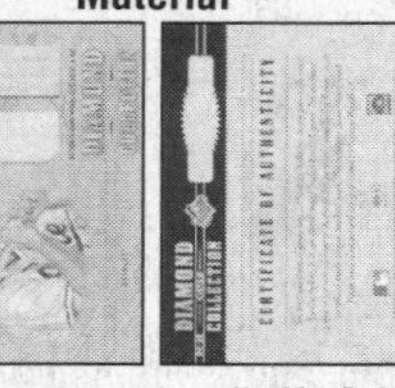

Nm-Mt Ex-Mt
RANDOM INSERTS IN PACKS
PRINT RUNS B/WN 1-50 COPIES PER
NO PRICING ON QTY OF 8 OR LESS
1 Alex Rodriguez Bat-Jsy/50 40.00 12.00
2 Nomar Garciaparra Bat-Jsy/50 40.00 12.00
3 Hideo Nomo Bat-Jsy/25 40.00 12.00
4 Alfonso Soriano Bat-Jsy/50 25.00 7.50
6 Edgar Martinez Bat-Jsy/25 40.00 12.00
7 Rocco Baldelli Bat-Jsy/25 25.00 7.50
8 Mark Teixeira Bat-Jsy/25 40.00 12.00
9 Albert Pujols Bat-Jsy/50 50.00 15.00
10 Vernon Wells Bat-Jsy/25 25.00 7.50
11 Garret Anderson Bat-Jsy/25 25.00 7.50
14 Brandon Webb Bat-Jsy/25 25.00 7.50
15 Mark Prior Bat-Jsy/50 25.00 7.50
16 Rafael Palmeiro Bat-Jsy/25 40.00 12.00
17 Adam Dunn Bat-Jsy/25 40.00 12.00
18 Dontrelle Willis Bat-Jsy/25 25.00 7.50
19 Kazuhisa Ishii Bat-Jsy/25 25.00 7.50
20 Torii Hunter Bat-Jsy/25 25.00 7.50
21 Vladimir Guerrero Bat-Jsy/25 40.00 12.00
22 Mike Piazza Bat-Jsy/50 40.00 12.00
23 Jason Giambi Bat-Jsy/25 25.00 7.50
26 Bob Abreu Bat-Jsy/50 15.00 4.50
27 Hee Seop Choi Bat-Jsy/50 15.00 4.50
30 Troy Glaus Bat-Jsy/25 25.00 7.50
31 Ivan Rodriguez Bat-Jsy/25 40.00 12.00
32 Hank Blalock Bat-Jsy/25 25.00 7.50
33 Greg Maddux Bat-Jsy/50 40.00 12.00
34 Nick Johnson Bat-Jsy/25 25.00 7.50
35 Shawn Green Bat-Jsy/25 25.00 7.50
36 Sammy Sosa Bat-Jsy/50 40.00 12.00
37 Dale Murphy Bat-Jsy/3
38 Cal Ripken Bat-Jsy/8
39 Carl Yastrzemski Bat-Jsy/8
41 Don Mattingly Bat-Jsy/23 80.00 24.00
42 Jim Palmer Jsy-Jsy/22 30.00 9.00
43 George Brett Bat-Jsy/5
44 Whitey Ford Jsy-Pants/16 50.00 15.00
45 Duke Snider Bat-Jsy/1
46 Steve Carlton Bat-Jsy/32 25.00 7.50
47 Stan Musial Bat-Jsy/6
48 Nolan Ryan Bat-Jsy/34 60.00 18.00
49 Deion Sanders Bat-Jsy/24 50.00 15.00
50 Roberto Clemente Bat-Jsy/21

2004 Diamond Kings Diamond Cut Combos Signature

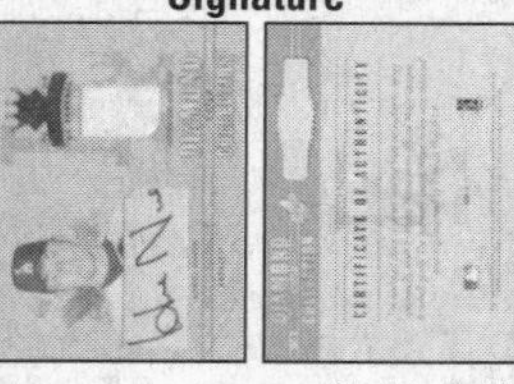

Nm-Mt Ex-Mt
RANDOM INSERTS IN PACKS
PRINT RUNS B/WN 1-32 COPIES PER
NO PRICING ON QTY OF 10 OR LESS
1 Alex Rodriguez Jsy/3
3 Hideo Nomo Jsy/1
5 Brett Myers Jsy/5
6 Edgar Martinez Jsy/5
7 Rocco Baldelli Jsy/10
8 Mark Teixeira Jsy/10
9 Albert Pujols Jsy/5
10 Vernon Wells Jsy/5
11 Garret Anderson Jsy/5
13 Rich Harden Jsy/1
14 Brandon Webb Jsy/10
15 Mark Prior Jsy/5
16 Rafael Palmeiro Jsy/5
17 Adam Dunn Jsy/5
18 Dontrelle Willis Jsy/10
19 Kazuhisa Ishii Jsy/1
20 Torii Hunter Jsy/5
21 Vladimir Guerrero Jsy/5
22 Mike Piazza Jsy/1
26 Bob Abreu Jsy/10
30 Troy Glaus Jsy/10
31 Ivan Rodriguez Jsy/10
32 Hank Blalock Jsy/10
33 Greg Maddux Jsy/1
37 Dale Murphy Jsy/3
38 Cal Ripken Jsy/8
39 Carl Yastrzemski Jsy/8
40 Marty Marion Jsy/25 40.00 12.00
41 Don Mattingly Jsy/23 150.00 45.00
42 Jim Palmer Jsy/22 50.00 15.00
43 George Brett Jsy/1
44 Whitey Ford Jsy/16 80.00 24.00
45 Duke Snider Jsy/4
46 Steve Carlton Jsy/32 60.00 18.00
47 Stan Musial Jsy/6
48 Nolan Ryan Jsy/1
49 Deion Sanders Jsy/1

2004 Diamond Kings Diamond Cut Jerseys

Nm-Mt Ex-Mt
RANDOM INSERTS IN PACKS
PRINT RUNS B/WN 10-100 COPIES PER
NO PRICING ON QTY OF 10 OR LESS
1 Alex Rodriguez/100 25.00 7.50
2 Nomar Garciaparra/100 25.00 7.50
3 Hideo Nomo/100 25.00 7.50
4 Alfonso Soriano/100 15.00 4.50
5 Brett Myers/50 15.00 4.50
6 Edgar Martinez/100 15.00 4.50
7 Rocco Baldelli/100 10.00 3.00
8 Mark Teixeira/100 10.00 3.00
9 Albert Pujols/100 30.00 9.00
10 Vernon Wells/100 10.00 3.00
11 Garret Anderson/50 15.00 4.50
12 Jerome Williams/100 10.00 3.00
13 Rich Harden/100 10.00 3.00
14 Brandon Webb/100 10.00 3.00
15 Mark Prior/100 15.00 4.50
16 Rafael Palmeiro/100 15.00 4.50
17 Adam Dunn/100 15.00 4.50
18 Dontrelle Willis/100 10.00 3.00
19 Kazuhisa Ishii/100 10.00 3.00
20 Torii Hunter/100 10.00 3.00
21 Vladimir Guerrero/50 25.00 7.50
22 Mike Piazza/100 25.00 7.50
23 Jason Giambi/100 10.00 3.00
25 Ramon Nivar/100 10.00 3.00
26 Bob Abreu/100 10.00 3.00
27 Hee Seop Choi/100 10.00 3.00
30 Troy Glaus/100 10.00 3.00
31 Ivan Rodriguez/100 15.00 4.50
32 Hank Blalock/100 10.00 3.00
33 Greg Maddux/100 25.00 7.50
34 Nick Johnson/100 10.00 3.00
35 Shawn Green/100 10.00 3.00
36 Sammy Sosa/100 25.00 7.50
37 Dale Murphy/50 25.00 7.50
38 Cal Ripken/50 60.00 18.00
39 Carl Yastrzemski/100 25.00 7.50
40 Marty Marion/50 15.00 4.50
41 Don Mattingly/100 30.00 9.00
42 Jim Palmer/25 25.00 7.50
43 George Brett/50 40.00 12.00
44 Whitey Ford/25 40.00 12.00
45 Duke Snider/10
46 Steve Carlton/50 15.00 4.50
47 Stan Musial/10
48 Nolan Ryan/50 50.00 15.00
49 Deion Sanders/50 25.00 7.50
50 Roberto Clemente/10

2004 Diamond Kings Diamond Cut Signatures

Nm-Mt Ex-Mt
RANDOM INSERTS IN PACKS
PRINT RUNS B/WN 1-50 COPIES PER
NO PRICING ON QTY OF 10 OR LESS
1 Alex Rodriguez/1
3 Hideo Nomo/1
5 Brett Myers/10
6 Edgar Martinez/5
7 Rocco Baldelli/25 25.00 7.50
8 Mark Teixeira/25 40.00 12.00
9 Albert Pujols/1
10 Vernon Wells/5
11 Garret Anderson/5
13 Rich Harden/50 20.00 6.00
14 Brandon Webb/50 15.00 4.50
15 Mark Prior/5
16 Rafael Palmeiro/5
17 Adam Dunn/5
18 Dontrelle Willis/10
19 Kazuhisa Ishii/1
20 Torii Hunter/25 40.00 12.00
21 Vladimir Guerrero/5
22 Mike Piazza/1
24 Ryan Wagner/50 15.00 4.50
25 Ramon Nivar/50 15.00 4.50
26 Bob Abreu/10
28 Rickie Weeks/50 20.00 6.00
29 Adam Loewen/50 15.00 4.50
30 Troy Glaus/10
31 Ivan Rodriguez/10
32 Hank Blalock/25 25.00 7.50
33 Greg Maddux/1
36 Sammy Sosa/1
37 Dale Murphy/3
38 Cal Ripken/8
39 Carl Yastrzemski/8
40 Marty Marion/25 25.00 7.50
41 Don Mattingly/23 120.00 36.00
42 Jim Palmer/22 30.00 9.00
43 George Brett/1
44 Whitey Ford/16 50.00 15.00
45 Duke Snider/4
46 Steve Carlton/32 40.00 12.00
47 Stan Musial/6
48 Nolan Ryan/34 150.00 45.00
49 Deion Sanders/1

2004 Diamond Kings Gallery of Stars

Nm-Mt Ex-Mt
STATED ODDS 1:37
1 Nolan Ryan 10.00 3.00
2 Cal Ripken 12.00 3.60
3 George Brett 10.00 3.00
4 Don Mattingly 10.00 3.00
5 Deion Sanders 4.00 1.20
6 Mike Piazza 6.00 1.80
7 Hideo Nomo 4.00 1.20
8 Rickey Henderson 4.00 1.20
9 Roger Clemens 8.00 2.40
10 Greg Maddux 6.00 1.80
11 Albert Pujols 8.00 2.40
12 Alex Rodriguez 6.00 1.80
13 Dale Murphy 4.00 1.20
14 Mark Prior 4.00 1.20
15 Dontrelle Willis 3.00 .90

2004 Diamond Kings Gallery of Stars Signatures

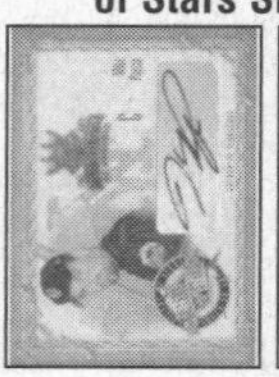

Nm-Mt Ex-Mt
RANDOM INSERTS IN PACKS
PRINT RUNS B/WN 1-10 COPIES PER
NO PRICING DUE TO SCARCITY

2004 Diamond Kings Heritage Collection

Nm-Mt Ex-Mt
RANDOM INSERTS IN PACKS
1 Dale Murphy 4.00 1.20
2 Cal Ripken 12.00 3.60
3 Carl Yastrzemski 6.00 1.80
4 Don Mattingly 10.00 3.00
5 Jim Palmer 3.00 .90
6 Andre Dawson 3.00 .90
7 Roy Campanella 4.00 1.20
8 George Brett 10.00 3.00
9 Duke Snider 4.00 1.20
10 Marty Marion 3.00 .90
11 Deion Sanders 4.00 1.20
12 Whitey Ford 4.00 1.20
13 Stan Musial 6.00 1.80
14 Nolan Ryan 10.00 3.00
15 Steve Carlton 3.00 .90
16 Robin Yount 6.00 1.80
17 Albert Pujols 8.00 2.40
18 Alex Rodriguez 6.00 1.80
19 Mike Piazza 6.00 1.80
20 Roger Clemens 8.00 2.40
21 Hideo Nomo 4.00 1.20
22 Mark Prior 4.00 1.20
23 Roger Maris 4.00 1.20
24 Greg Maddux 6.00 1.80
25 Mark Grace 4.00 1.20

2004 Diamond Kings Heritage Collection Bats

Nm-Mt Ex-Mt
RANDOM INSERTS IN PACKS
PRINT RUNS B/WN 1-50 COPIES PER
NO PRICING ON QTY OF 1 OR LESS
1 Dale Murphy/50 25.00 7.50
2 Cal Ripken/50 60.00 18.00
3 Carl Yastrzemski/50 30.00 9.00
4 Don Mattingly/50 40.00 12.00
6 Andre Dawson/25 25.00 7.50
7 Roy Campanella/25 40.00 12.00
8 George Brett/25 60.00 18.00
9 Duke Snider/1
11 Deion Sanders/50 25.00 7.50
13 Stan Musial/25 50.00 15.00
14 Nolan Ryan/25 60.00 18.00
15 Steve Carlton/25 25.00 7.50
16 Robin Yount/50 30.00 9.00
17 Albert Pujols/50 40.00 12.00
18 Alex Rodriguez/50 30.00 9.00
19 Mike Piazza/50 30.00 9.00
20 Roger Clemens/50 30.00 9.00
21 Hideo Nomo/50 25.00 7.50
22 Mark Prior/50 25.00 7.50
23 Roger Maris/25 80.00 24.00
24 Greg Maddux/50 30.00 9.00
25 Mark Grace/50 25.00 7.50

2004 Diamond Kings Heritage Collection Jerseys

Nm-Mt Ex-Mt
RANDOM INSERTS IN PACKS
PRINT RUNS B/WN 10-50 COPIES PER
NO PRICING ON QTY OF 10 OR LESS
1 Dale Murphy/50 25.00 7.50
2 Cal Ripken/50 60.00 18.00
3 Carl Yastrzemski/50 30.00 9.00
4 Don Mattingly/50 40.00 12.00
5 Jim Palmer/10
6 Andre Dawson/25 25.00 7.50
7 Roy Campanella Pants/25 40.00 12.00
8 George Brett/25 60.00 18.00
9 Duke Snider/10
10 Marty Marion/50 15.00 4.50
11 Deion Sanders/50 25.00 7.50
12 Whitey Ford/25 40.00 12.00
13 Stan Musial/10
14 Nolan Ryan/25 60.00 18.00
15 Steve Carlton/25 25.00 7.50
16 Robin Yount/50 30.00 9.00
17 Albert Pujols/50 40.00 12.00
18 Alex Rodriguez/50 40.00 12.00
19 Mike Piazza/50 30.00 9.00
20 Roger Clemens/50 30.00 9.00
21 Hideo Nomo/50 25.00 7.50
22 Mark Prior/50 25.00 7.50
23 Roger Maris/25 80.00 24.00
24 Greg Maddux/50 30.00 9.00
25 Mark Grace/50 25.00 7.50

2004 Diamond Kings Heritage Collection Signatures

Nm-Mt Ex-Mt
RANDOM INSERTS IN PACKS
PRINT RUNS B/WN 1-16 COPIES PER
NO PRICING ON QTY OF 10 OR LESS
12 Whitey Ford/16 50.00 15.00

2004 Diamond Kings HOF Heroes

Nm-Mt Ex-Mt
RANDOM INSERTS IN PACKS
PRINT RUNS B/WN 100-1000 COPIES PER
1 George Brett #45/1000 10.00 3.00
2 George Brett #45/500 15.00 4.50
3 George Brett #45/250 25.00 7.50
4 Mike Schmidt #46/1000 8.00 2.40
5 Mike Schmidt #46/250 20.00 6.00
6 Nolan Ryan #47/1000 10.00 3.00
7 Nolan Ryan #47/500 15.00 4.50
8 Nolan Ryan #47/250 25.00 7.50
9 Roberto Clemente #48/1000 10.00 3.00
10 Roberto Clemente #48/500 15.00 4.50
11 Roberto Clemente #48/250 25.00 7.50
12 Roberto Clemente #48/100 30.00 9.00
13 Carl Yastrzemski #49/1000 6.00 1.80
14 Robin Yount #50/1000 6.00 1.80
15 Whitey Ford #51/1000 5.00 1.50
16 Duke Snider #52/1000 5.00 1.50
17 Duke Snider #52/250 15.00 4.50
18 Carlton Fisk #53/1000 5.00 1.50
19 Ozzie Smith #54/1000 6.00 1.80
20 Kirby Puckett #55/1000 5.00 1.50
21 Bobby Doerr #56/1000 4.00 1.20
22 Frank Robinson #57/1000 4.00 1.20
23 Ralph Kiner #58/1000 4.00 1.20
24 Al Kaline #59/1000 5.00 1.50
25 Bob Feller #60/1000 4.00 1.20
26 Yogi Berra #61/1000 5.00 1.50
27 Stan Musial #62/1000 6.00 1.80
28 Stan Musial #62/500 10.00 3.00
29 Stan Musial #62/250 15.00 4.50
30 Jim Palmer #63/1000 4.00 1.20
31 Johnny Bench #64/1000 5.00 1.50
32 Steve Carlton #65/1000 4.00 1.20
33 Gary Carter #66/1000 4.00 1.20

4 Roy Campanella #67/1000 ... 5.00 1.50
5 Roy Campanella #67/250 ... 15.00 4.50

2004 Diamond Kings HOF Heroes Bats

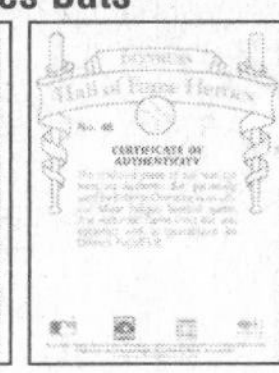

Nm-Mt Ex-Mt
ANDOM INSERTS IN PACKS ...
RINT RUNS B/WN 1-25 COPIES PER
O PRICING ON QTY OF 5 OR LESS ..
George Brett #45/25 ... 50.00 15.00
George Brett #45/25 ... 50.00 15.00
George Brett #45/25 ... 50.00 15.00
Mike Schmidt #46/25 ... 50.00 15.00
Mike Schmidt #46/25 ... 50.00 15.00
Nolan Ryan #47/25 ... 60.00 18.00
Nolan Ryan #47/25 ... 60.00 18.00
Nolan Ryan #47/25 ... 60.00 18.00
Roberto Clemente #48/5 ...
0 Roberto Clemente #48/5 ...
1 Roberto Clemente #48/5 ...
2 Roberto Clemente #48/5 ...
3 Carl Yastrzemski #49/25 ... 50.00 15.00
4 Robin Yount #50/25 ... 50.00 15.00
6 Duke Snider #52/1 ...
7 Duke Snider #52/1 ...
8 Carlton Fisk #53/25 ... 40.00 12.00
9 Ozzie Smith #54/25 ... 50.00 15.00
0 Kirby Puckett #55/25 ... 40.00 12.00
1 Bobby Doerr #56/25 ... 25.00 7.50
2 Frank Robinson #57/25 ... 25.00 7.50
3 Ralph Kiner #58/25 ... 25.00 7.50
4 Al Kaline #59/25 ... 40.00 12.00
6 Yogi Berra #61/5 ...
7 Stan Musial #62/5 ...
8 Stan Musial #62/5 ...
9 Stan Musial #62/5 ...
1 Johnny Bench #64/25 ... 40.00 12.00
2 Steve Carlton #65/25 ... 25.00 7.50
3 Gary Carter #66/25 ... 25.00 7.50
4 Roy Campanella #67/25 ... 40.00 12.00
5 Roy Campanella #67/25 ... 40.00 12.00

2004 Diamond Kings HOF Heroes Combos

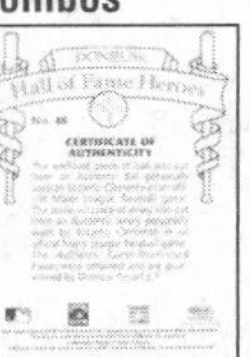

Nm-Mt Ex-Mt
ANDOM INSERTS IN PACKS ...
RINT RUNS B/WN 1-25 COPIES PER
O PRICING ON QTY OF 10 OR LESS
George Brett #45 Bat-Jsy/25 . 60.00 18.00
George Brett #45 Bat-Jsy/25 . 60.00 18.00
George Brett #45 Bat-Jsy/25 . 60.00 18.00
Mike Schmidt #46 Bat-Jsy/25 60.00 18.00
Mike Schmidt #46 Bat-Jsy/25 60.00 18.00
Nolan Ryan #47 Bat-Jsy/25 ... 80.00 24.00
Nolan Ryan #47 Bat-Jsy/25 ... 80.00 24.00
Nolan Ryan #47 Bat-Jsy/25 ... 80.00 24.00
Roberto Clemente #48 Bat-Jsy/5 ...
0 Roberto Clemente #48 Bat-Jsy/5 ...
1 Roberto Clemente #48 Bat-Jsy/5 ...
2 Roberto Clemente #48 Bat-Jsy/5 ...
3 C.Yastrzemski #49 Bat-Jsy/25 60.00 18.00
4 Robin Yount #50 Bat-Jsy/25 60.00 18.00
5 Whitey Ford #51 Jsy-Pants/25 50.00 15.00
6 Duke Snider #52 Bat-Jsy/1 ...
7 Duke Snider #52 Bat-Jsy/1 ...
8 Carlton Fisk #53 Bat-Jsy/25. 50.00 15.00
9 Ozzie Smith #54 Bat-Jsy/25. 60.00 18.00
0 Kirby Puckett #55 Bat-Jsy/25 50.00 15.00
1 Bobby Doerr #56 Bat-Jsy/25 30.00 9.00
2 Frank Robinson #57 Bat-Jsy/10 ...
3 Ralph Kiner #58 Bat-Bat/25 . 30.00 9.00
4 Al Kaline #59 Bat-Jsy/25 ... 50.00 15.00
5 Bob Feller #60 Jsy-Jsy/10 ...
6 Yogi Berra #61 Bat-Jsy/5 ...
7 Stan Musial #62 Bat-Jsy/5 ...
8 Stan Musial #62 Bat-Jsy/5 ...
9 Stan Musial #62 Bat-Jsy/5 ...
0 Jim Palmer #63 Jsy-Jsy/5 ...
1 Johnny Bench #64 Bat-Jsy/1 ...
2 Steve Carlton #65 Bat-Jsy/25 30.00 9.00
3 Gary Carter #66 Bat-Jsy/25 . 30.00 9.00
4 R.Campy #67 Bat-Pants/25.. 50.00 15.00
5 R.Campy #67 Bat-Pants/25.. 50.00 15.00

2004 Diamond Kings HOF Heroes Jerseys

Nm-Mt Ex-Mt
ANDOM INSERTS IN PACKS ...
RINT RUNS B/WN 1-25 COPIES PER
NO PRICING ON QTY OF 10 OR LESS
1 George Brett #45/25 ... 50.00 15.00
2 George Brett #45/25 ... 50.00 15.00
3 George Brett #45/25 ... 50.00 15.00
4 Mike Schmidt #46/25 ... 50.00 15.00
5 Mike Schmidt #46/25 ... 50.00 15.00
6 Nolan Ryan #47/25 ... 60.00 18.00
7 Nolan Ryan #47/25 ... 60.00 18.00
8 Nolan Ryan #47/25 ... 60.00 18.00
9 Roberto Clemente #48/5 ...
10 Roberto Clemente #48/5 ...
11 Roberto Clemente #48/5 ...
12 Roberto Clemente #48/5 ...
13 Carl Yastrzemski #49/25 ... 50.00 15.00
14 Robin Yount #50/25 ... 50.00 15.00
15 Whitey Ford #51/25 ... 40.00 12.00
16 Duke Snider #52/10 ...
17 Duke Snider #52/10 ...
18 Carlton Fisk #53/25 ... 40.00 12.00
19 Ozzie Smith #54/25 ... 50.00 15.00
20 Kirby Puckett #55/25 ... 40.00 12.00
21 Bobby Doerr #56/25 ... 25.00 7.50
22 Frank Robinson #57/10 ...
24 Al Kaline #59/25 ... 40.00 12.00
25 Bob Feller #60/10 ...
26 Yogi Berra #61/5 ...
27 Stan Musial #62/5 ...
28 Stan Musial #62/5 ...
29 Stan Musial #62/5 ...
30 Jim Palmer #63/5 ...
31 Johnny Bench #64/1 ...
32 Steve Carlton #65/25 ... 25.00 7.50
33 Gary Carter #66/25 ... 25.00 7.50
34 Roy Campanella #67/25 ... 40.00 12.00
35 Roy Campanella #67/25 ... 40.00 12.00

2004 Diamond Kings HOF Heroes Signatures

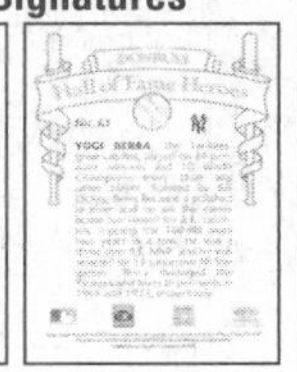

Nm-Mt Ex-Mt
RANDOM INSERTS IN PACKS ...
PRINT RUNS B/WN 4-32 COPIES PER
NO PRICING ON QTY OF 10 OR LESS
1 George Brett #45/5 ...
2 George Brett #45/5 ...
3 George Brett #45/5 ...
6 Nolan Ryan #47/5 ...
7 Nolan Ryan #47/5 ...
8 Nolan Ryan #47/5 ...
13 Carl Yastrzemski #49/8 ...
14 Robin Yount #50/19 ... 100.00 30.00
15 Whitey Ford #51/16 ... 50.00 15.00
16 Duke Snider #52/4 ...
17 Duke Snider #52/4 ...
18 Carlton Fisk #53/5 ...
19 Ozzie Smith #54/5 ...
20 Kirby Puckett #55/5 ...
21 Bobby Doerr #56/10 ...
22 Frank Robinson #57/20 ... 50.00 15.00
23 Ralph Kiner #58/4 ...
24 Al Kaline #59/6 ...
25 Bob Feller #60/19 ... 30.00 9.00
26 Yogi Berra #61/8 ...
27 Stan Musial #62/6 ...
28 Stan Musial #62/6 ...
29 Stan Musial #62/6 ...
30 Jim Palmer #63/22 ... 30.00 9.00
31 Johnny Bench #64/5 ...
32 Steve Carlton #65/32 ... 40.00 12.00
33 Gary Carter #66/5 ...

2004 Diamond Kings Recollection Autographs

Nm-Mt Ex-Mt
RANDOM INSERTS IN PACKS ...
PRINT RUNS B/WN 1-159 COPIES PER
NO PRICING ON QTY OF 14 OR LESS
1 Sandy Alomar Jr. 91 DK/8 ...
2 Rich Aurilia 02 DK/2 ...
3 Jeff Bagwell 93 TP Gall/1 ...
4 Jeff Bagwell 02 DK/2 ...
5 Jeff Bagwell 03 DK/1 ...
6 Clint Barmes 03 DK Black/82. 10.00 3.00
7 Clint Barmes 03 DK Blue/72 .. 12.00 3.60
8 Carlos Beltran 02 DK/23 ... 60.00 18.00
9 Carlos Beltran 03 DK/99 ... 40.00 12.00
10 Adrian Beltre 02 DK/40 ... 30.00 9.00
11 Johnny Bench 83 DK/3 ...
12 Johnny Bench 01 DK Rep/1 ...
13 Yogi Berra 83 HOF/4 ...
14 Craig Biggio 91 DK/10 ...
15 Craig Biggio 03 DK/1 ...
16 Wade Boggs 84 DK/13 ...
17 George Brett 03 DK/1 ...
18 John Buck 02 DK/13 ...
19 Chris Burke 03 DK/150 ... 15.00 4.50
20 Marlon Byrd 02 DK/23 ... 15.00 4.50
21 Marlon Byrd 03 DK/100 ... 10.00 3.00
22 Rod Carew 01 DK Rep/1 ...
23 Steve Carlton 01 DK Rep/6 ...
24 Kevin Cash 03 DK/103 ... 10.00 3.00
25 Jose Cruz 85 DK/59 ... 12.00 3.60
26 J.D. Durbin 03 DK/151 ... 25.00 7.50
27 Jim Edmonds 03 DK/24 ... 40.00 12.00
28 Bob Feller 84 HOF/8 ...
29 Bob Feller 03 DK HOF/18 ... 40.00 12.00
30 Carlton Fisk 02 DK/13 ...
31 Carlton Fisk 02 DK Her/5 ...
32 Julio Franco 87 DK/25 ... 25.00 7.50
33 Freddy Garcia 03 DK/50 ... 20.00 6.00
34 Jay Gibbons 03 DK/100 ... 10.00 3.00
35 Juan Gonzalez 03 DK/10 ...
36 Mark Grace 02 DK/5 ...
37 Mark Grace 03 DK/7 ...
38 Shawn Green 02 DK/2 ...
39 Brendan Harris 03 DK/150 ... 10.00 3.00
40 Rickey Henderson 02 DK/1 ...
41 Rickey Henderson 03 DK/2 ...
42 Ru.Hernandez 02 DK/100 ... 10.00 3.00
43 Eric Hinske 03 DK/20 ... 15.00 4.50
44 Tim Hudson 02 DK/25 ... 40.00 12.00
45 Tim Hudson 03 DK/25 ... 40.00 12.00
46 Aubrey Huff 03 DK/99 ... 15.00 4.50
47 Monte Irvin 84 HOF/7 ...
48 Bo Jackson 02 DK/5 ...
49 Jason Jennings 03 DK/50 ... 12.00 3.60
50 Tommy John 88 DK Black/62 20.00 6.00
51 Tommy John 88 DK Blue/7 ...
52 Howard Johnson 90 DK/52.. 12.00 3.60
53 Andruw Jones 03 DK/14 ...
54 Austin Kearns 02 DK/25 ... 25.00 7.50
55 Austin Kearns 03 DK/25 ... 25.00 7.50
56 Ralph Kiner 83 HOF/5 ...
57 Carney Lansford 85 DK Black/12 ...
58 Carney Lansford 85 DK Blue/4 ...
59 P.Larrison 03 DK Black/74 ... 20.00 6.00
60 Pr.Larrison 03 DK Blue/77 ... 20.00 6.00
61 Greg Maddux 02 DK/1 ...
62 Greg Maddux 03 DK/2 ...
63 Don Mattingly 85 DK/4 ...
64 Don Mattingly 89 DK/5 ...
65 Don Mattingly 02 DK Time/1 ...
66 Don Mattingly 03 DK/5 ...
67 Dustin McGowan 03 DK/159 10.00 3.00
68 Paul Molitor 02 DK Her/5 ...
69 Melvin Mora 03 DK/101 ... 15.00 4.50
70 Joe Morgan 01 DK Rep/2 ...
71 Jack Morris 03 DK/60 ... 20.00 6.00
72 Jack Morris 03 DK Her/19 ... 40.00 12.00
73 Dale Murphy 03 DK Black/3 ...
74 Dale Murphy 03 DK Blue/47 50.00 15.00
75 Dale Murphy 03 DK Her Black/8 ...
76 Dale Murphy 03 DK Her Blue/10 ...
77 Dale Murphy 03 DK Time/18 80.00 24.00
78 Stan Musial 83 HOF/3 ...
79 Stan Musial 03 DK/2 ...
80 Mike Mussina 03 DK/1 ...
81 Phil Niekro 82 DK/10 ...
82 Magglio Ordonez 03 DK/25.. 40.00 12.00
83 Magglio Ordonez 03 DK Ins/10 ...
84 Roy Oswalt 03 DK/10 ...
85 Dave Parker 82 DK/20 ... 25.00 7.50
86 Dave Parker 90 DK/18 ... 40.00 12.00
87 Tony Pena 85 DK/7 ...
88 Jorge Posada 02 DK/25 ... 40.00 12.00
89 Mark Prior 03 DK/25 ... 120.00 36.00
90 Cal Ripken 02 DK/2 ...
91 Cal Ripken 03 DK/3 ...
92 Mike Rivera 02 DK/24 ... 15.00 4.50
93 Robin Roberts 84 HOF Black/6 ...
94 Robin Roberts 84 HOF Blue/1 ...
95 Frank Robinson 83 HOF/8 ...
96 Alex Rodriguez 03 DK/1 ...
97 Ivan Rodriguez 03 DK/22 ... 60.00 18.00
98 Scott Rolen 02 DK/5 ...
99 Scott Rolen 03 DK/2 ...
100 Rodrigo Rosario 02 DK/50. 12.00 3.60
101 Nolan Ryan 02 DK/3 ...
102 Nolan Ryan 03 DK/5 ...
103 Nolan Ryan 03 DK Bronze/1 ...
104 Nolan Ryan 03 DK Evol/1 ...
105 Ron Santo 02 DK/29 ... 40.00 12.00
106 Richie Sexson 02 DK/25 ... 25.00 7.50
107 Richie Sexson 03 DK/25 ... 25.00 7.50
108 Gary Sheffield 03 DK/11 ...
109 Chris Snelling 02 DK/46 ... 12.00 3.60
110 Duke Snider 83 HOF/4 ...
111 J.T. Snow 93 TP Gall Black/1 ...
112 J.T. Snow 93 TP Gall Blue/1 ...
113 Sammy Sosa 99 Retro DK/2 ...
114 Sammy Sosa 01 DK/2 ...
115 Sammy Sosa 03 DK/3 ...
116 Sammy Sosa 03 DK Ins/1 ...
117 Junior Spivey 03 DK Black/12 ...
118 Junior Spivey 03 DK Blue/13 ...
119 Shannon Stewart 02 DK/50 20.00 6.00
120 S.Stewart 03 DK Black/92.. 15.00 4.50
121 Shannon Stewart 03 DK Blue/9 ...
122 Frank Thomas 01 DK Black/1 ...
123 Frank Thomas 01 DK Blue/1 ...
124 Frank Thomas 00 Retro DK Black/2
125 Frank Thomas 00 Retro DK Blue/1
126 G.Thomas 82 DK Black/22. 15.00 4.50
127 G.Thomas 82 DK Blue/20 .. 15.00 4.50
128 Alan Trammell 02 DK/29 ... 25.00 7.50
129 Alan Trammell 02 DK Her/25 25.00 7.50
130 Robin Ventura 03 DK/25 ... 25.00 7.50
131 Jose Vidro 03 DK/25 ... 15.00 4.50
132 Rickie Weeks 03 DK/52 ... 60.00 18.00
133 Kevin Youkilis 03 DK/153 ... 25.00 7.50
134 Barry Zito 03 DK/5 ...

2004 Diamond Kings Team Timeline

Nm-Mt Ex-Mt
STATED ODDS 1:29 ...
1 Deion Sanders ... 4.00 1.20
Andruw Jones
2 Rickie Weeks ... 6.00 1.80
Robin Yount
3 Don Mattingly ... 10.00 3.00
Whitey Ford
4 Chipper Jones ... 4.00 1.20
Dale Murphy
5 Nomar Garciaparra ... 6.00 1.80
Bobby Doerr
6 Mark Prior ... 6.00 1.80
Sammy Sosa
7 Hideo Nomo ... 4.00 1.20
Kazuhisa Ishii
8 Andre Dawson ... 4.00 1.20
Mark Grace
9 Roger Clemens ... 8.00 2.40
Carl Yastrzemski
10 Mike Mussina ... 12.00 3.60
Cal Ripken
11 Stan Musial ... 8.00 2.40
Albert Pujols
12 Jim Palmer ... 4.00 1.20
Mike Mussina
13 Marty Marion ... 6.00 1.80
Stan Musial
14 George Brett ... 10.00 3.00
Mike Sweeney
15 Roger Clemens ... 8.00 2.40
Roger Maris
16 Duke Snider ... 4.00 1.20
Shawn Green
17 Jim Thome ... 8.00 2.40
Mike Schmidt
18 Nolan Ryan ... 10.00 3.00
Alex Rodriguez
19 Roy Campanella ... 6.00 1.80
Mike Piazza

2004 Diamond Kings Team Timeline Bats

Nm-Mt Ex-Mt
RANDOM INSERTS IN PACKS ...
STATED PRINT RUN 25 SERIAL #'d SETS
SNIDER/GREEN PRINT 1 SERIAL #'d CARD
SNIDER/GREEN TOO SCARCE TO PRICE
1 Deion Sanders ... 30.00 9.00
Andruw Jones
2 Rickie Weeks ... 60.00 18.00
Robin Yount
3 Don Mattingly ... 100.00 30.00
Whitey Ford
4 Chipper Jones ... 60.00 18.00
Dale Murphy
5 Nomar Garciaparra ... 50.00 15.00
Bobby Doerr
6 Mark Prior ... 60.00 18.00
Sammy Sosa
7 Hideo Nomo ... 60.00 18.00
Kazuhisa Ishii
8 Andre Dawson ... 30.00 9.00
Mark Grace
9 Roger Clemens ... 60.00 18.00
Carl Yastrzemski
10 Mike Mussina ... 120.00 36.00
Cal Ripken
11 Stan Musial ... 100.00 30.00
Albert Pujols
12 Jim Palmer ... 30.00 9.00
Mike Mussina
13 Marty Marion ...
Stan Musial
14 George Brett ... 50.00 15.00
Mike Sweeney
15 Roger Clemens ... 100.00 30.00
Roger Maris
16 Duke Snider/1 ...
Shawn Green
17 Jim Thome ... 60.00 18.00
Mike Schmidt
18 Nolan Ryan ... 80.00 24.00
Alex Rodriguez
19 Roy Campanella ... 60.00 18.00
Mike Piazza

2004 Diamond Kings Team Timeline Jerseys

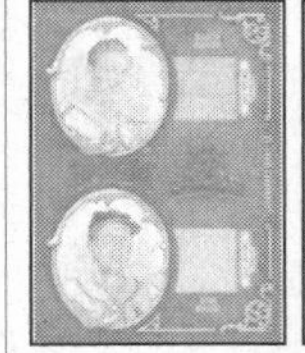

Nm-Mt Ex-Mt
PRINT RUNS B/WN 10-25 COPIES PER
NO PRICING ON QTY OF 10 OR LESS
PRIME PRINT RUN 1 SERIAL #'d SET
NO PRIME PRICING DUE TO SCARCITY
RANDOM INSERTS IN PACKS ...
R.WEEKS IS A BAT SWATCH ...
R.CAMPANELLA IS A PANTS SWATCH
1 Deion Sanders/25 ... 30.00 9.00
Andruw Jones
2 Rickie Weeks/25 ... 60.00 18.00
Robin Yount
3 Don Mattingly/25 ... 100.00 30.00
Whitey Ford
4 Chipper Jones/25 ... 60.00 18.00
Dale Murphy
5 Nomar Garciaparra/25 ... 50.00 15.00
Bobby Doerr
6 Mark Prior/25 ... 60.00 18.00
Sammy Sosa
7 Hideo Nomo/25 ... 60.00 18.00
Kazuhisa Ishii
8 Andre Dawson/25 ... 30.00 9.00
Mark Grace
9 Roger Clemens/25 ... 60.00 18.00
Carl Yastrzemski
10 Mike Mussina/25 ... 120.00 36.00
Cal Ripken
11 Stan Musial/10 ...
Albert Pujols
12 Jim Palmer/10 ...
Mike Mussina
13 Marty Marion/10 ...
Stan Musial
14 George Brett/25 ... 50.00 15.00
Mike Sweeney
15 Roger Clemens/25 ... 100.00 30.00
Roger Maris
16 Duke Snider/10 ...
Shawn Green
17 Jim Thome/25 ... 60.00 18.00
Mike Schmidt
18 Nolan Ryan/25 ... 80.00 24.00
Alex Rodriguez
19 Roy Campanella/25 ... 60.00 18.00
Mike Piazza

2004 Diamond Kings Timeline

Nm-Mt Ex-Mt
STATED ODDS 1:92 ...
1 Roger Clemens ... 8.00 2.40
2 Mark Grace ... 4.00 1.20
3 Mike Mussina ... 4.00 1.20
4 Mike Piazza ... 6.00 1.80
5 Nolan Ryan ... 10.00 3.00
6 Rickey Henderson ... 4.00 1.20

2004 Diamond Kings Timeline Bats

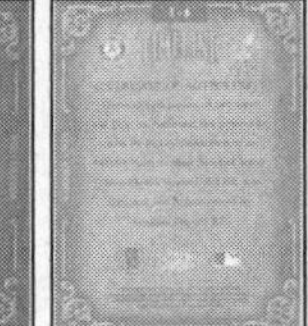

Nm-Mt Ex-Mt
RANDOM INSERTS IN PACKS ...
STATED PRINT RUN 25 SERIAL #'d SETS
1 Roger Clemens Sox-Yanks ... 50.00 15.00
2 Mark Grace Cubs-D'backs ... 40.00 12.00
3 Mike Mussina O's-Yanks ... 40.00 12.00
4 Mike Piazza Dodgers-Mets ... 50.00 15.00
5 Nolan Ryan Astros-Rangers ... 80.00 24.00
6 Rickey Henderson A's-Dodgers 40.00 12.00

2004 Diamond Kings Timeline Jerseys

Nm-Mt Ex-Mt
STATED PRINT RUN 25 SERIAL #'d SETS
PRIME PRINT RUN 1 SERIAL #'d SET
NO PRIME PRICING DUE TO SCARCITY
RANDOM INSERTS IN PACKS ...
1 Roger Clemens Sox-Yanks ... 60.00 18.00
2 Mark Grace Cubs-D'backs ... 50.00 15.00
3 Mike Mussina O's-Yanks ... 50.00 15.00
4 Mike Piazza Dodgers-Mets ... 60.00 18.00
5 Nolan Ryan Astros-Rangers. 100.00 30.00
6 Rickey Henderson A's-Dodgers 50.00 15.00

1934-36 Diamond Stars

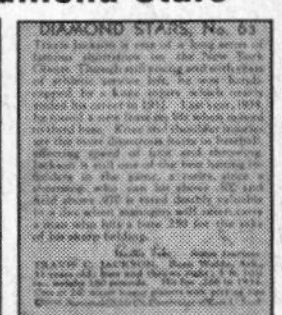

The cards in this 108-card set measure approximately 2 3/8" by 2 7/8". The Diamond Stars set, produced by National Chicle from 1934-36, is also commonly known by its catalog designation, R327. The year of production can be determined by the statistics contained on the back of the card. There are 170 possible front/back combinations counting blue (B) and green (G) backs over all three years. The last twelve cards are repeat players and are quite scarce. The checklist below lists the year(s) and back color(s) for the cards. Cards 32 through 72 were issued only in 1935 with green ink on back. Cards 73 through 84 were issued three ways: 35B, 35G, and 36B. Card numbers 85 through 108 were issued only in 1936 with blue ink on back. The complete set price below refers to the set of all variations listed explicitly below. A blank-backed proof sheet of 12 additional (never-issued) cards was discovered in 1980.

Ex-Mt VG
COMPLETE SET (119) 15000.00 7500.00
COMMON CARD (1-31) 50.00 25.00
COMMON CARD (32-84) 60.00 30.00
COMMON CARD (85-96) 100.00 50.00
COMMON CARD (97-108) 200.00 100.00
WRAP.(1-CENT, BLUE) 250.00 125.00
WRAP.(1-CENT, YELLOW) 200.00 100.00
WRAP.(1-CENT, CLEAR) 200.00 100.00
1 Lefty Grove 750.00 375.00
34G, 35G
2A Al Simmons 150.00 75.00
34G, 35G
Sox on uniform
2B Al Simmons 200.00 100.00
36B
No name on uniform
3 Rabbit Maranville 150.00 75.00
34G, 35G
4 Buddy Myer 60.00 30.00
34G, 35G, 36B
5 Tommy Bridges 60.00 30.00
34G, 35G, 36B
6 Max Bishop 60.00 30.00
34G, 35G
7 Lew Fonseca 60.00 30.00
34G, 35G
8 Joe Vosmik 50.00 25.00
34G, 35G, 36B
9 Mickey Cochrane 175.00 90.00
34G, 35G, 36B
10A Leroy Mahaffey 50.00 25.00
34G, 35G
A's on uniform
10B Leroy Mahaffey 80.00 40.00
36B
No name on uniform
11 Bill Dickey 200.00 100.00
34G, 35G
12A Fred Walker 34G 80.00 40.00
Ruth retires
mentioned on back
12B Fred Walker 35G 80.00 40.00
(Ruth to Boston
mentioned on back
12C Fred Walker 36B 100.00 50.00
13 George Blaeholder 50.00 25.00
34G, 35G
14 Bill Terry 175.00 90.00
34G, 35G
15A Dick Bartell 34G 100.00 50.00
Philadelphia Phillies
on card back
15B Dick Bartell 35G 80.00 40.00
New York Giants
on card back
16 Lloyd Waner 125.00 60.00
34G, 35G, 36B
17 Frankie Frisch 125.00 60.00
34G, 35G
18 Chick Hafey 125.00 60.00
34G, 35G
19 Van Lingle Mungo 80.00 40.00
34G, 35G
20 Frank Hogan 60.00 30.00
34G, 35G
21A Johnny Vergez 34G 80.00 40.00
New York Giants
on card back
21B Johnny Vergez 35G 60.00 30.00
Philadelphia Phillies
on card back
22 Jimmy Wilson 60.00 30.00
34G, 35G, 36B
23 Bill Hallahan 50.00 25.00
34G, 35G
24 Earl Adams 50.00 25.00
34G, 35G
25 Wally Berger 35G 60.00 30.00
26 Pepper Martin 80.00 40.00
35G, 36B
27 Pie Traynor 35G 150.00 75.00
28 Al Lopez 35G 150.00 75.00
29 Red Rolfe 35G 80.00 40.00
30A Heinie Manush 35G 150.00 75.00
W on sleeve
30B Heinie Manush 36B 200.00 100.00
No W on sleeve
31A Kiki Cuyler 35G 125.00 60.00
Chicago Cubs
31B Kiki Cuyler 36B 175.00 90.00
Cincinnati Reds
32 Sam Rice 125.00 60.00
33 Schoolboy Rowe 80.00 40.00
34 Stan Hack 80.00 40.00
35 Earl Averill 125.00 60.00
36A Earnie Lombardi 300.00 150.00
(Sic, Ernie)
36B Ernie Lombardi 200.00 100.00
37 Billy Urbanski 60.00 30.00
38 Ben Chapman 80.00 40.00
39 Carl Hubbell 200.00 100.00
40 Blondy Ryan 60.00 30.00
41 Harvey Hendrick 60.00 30.00
42 Jimmy Dykes 80.00 40.00
43 Ted Lyons 125.00 60.00
44 Rogers Hornsby 400.00 200.00
45 Jo Jo White 60.00 30.00
46 Red Lucas 60.00 30.00
47 Bob Bolton 60.00 30.00
48 Rick Ferrell 125.00 60.00
49 Buck Jordan 60.00 30.00
50 Mel Ott 300.00 150.00
51 Burgess Whitehead 60.00 30.00
52 Tuck Stainback 60.00 30.00
53 Oscar Melillo 60.00 30.00
54A Hank Greenburg 600.00 300.00
(Sic, Greenberg)
54B Hank Greenberg 400.00 200.00
55 Tony Cuccinello 80.00 40.00
56 Gus Suhr 60.00 30.00
57 Cy Blanton 60.00 30.00
58 Glenn Myatt 60.00 30.00
59 Jim Bottomley 125.00 60.00
60 Red Ruffing 150.00 75.00
61 Bill Werber 80.00 40.00
62 Fred Frankhouse 60.00 30.00
63 Travis Jackson 125.00 60.00
64 Jimmie Foxx 400.00 200.00
65 Zeke Bonura 60.00 30.00
66 Ducky Medwick 200.00 100.00
67 Marvin Owen 80.00 40.00
68 Sam Leslie 60.00 30.00
69 Earl Grace 60.00 30.00
70 Hal Trosky 80.00 40.00
71 Ossie Bluege 80.00 40.00
72 Tony Piet 60.00 30.00
73 Fritz Ostermueller 80.00 40.00
35G, 35B, 36B
74 Tony Lazzeri 200.00 100.00
35G, 35B, 36B
75 Jack Burns 80.00 40.00
35G, 35B, 36B
76 Billy Rogell 80.00 40.00
35G, 35B, 36B
77 Charley Gehringer 175.00 90.00
35G, 35B, 36B
78 Joe Kuhel 80.00 40.00
35G, 35B, 36B
79 Willis Hudlin 80.00 40.00
35G, 35B, 36B
80 Lou Chiozza 80.00 40.00
35G, 35B, 36B
81 Bill Delancey 60.00 30.00
35G, 35B, 36B
82A Johnny Babich 80.00 40.00
(Dodgers on uniorm
35G, 35B)
82B Johnny Babich 125.00 60.00
(No name on
uniform; 36B)
83 Paul Waner 150.00 75.00
35G, 35B, 36B
84 Sam Byrd 80.00 40.00
35G, 35B, 36B
85 Moose Solters 100.00 50.00
86 Frank Crosetti 150.00 75.00
87 Steve O'Neill MG 125.00 60.00
88 George Selkirk 125.00 60.00
89 Joe Stripp 125.00 60.00
90 Ray Hayworth 125.00 60.00
91 Bucky Harris MG 200.00 100.00
92 Ethan Allen 100.00 50.00
93 General Crowder 100.00 50.00
94 Wes Ferrell 150.00 75.00
95 Luke Appling 250.00 125.00
96 Lew Riggs 100.00 50.00
97 Al Lopez 400.00 200.00
98 Schoolboy Rowe 200.00 100.00
99 Pie Traynor 500.00 250.00
100 Earl Averill 400.00 200.00
101 Dick Bartell 200.00 100.00
102 Van Lingle Mungo 250.00 125.00
103 Bill Dickey 700.00 350.00
104 Red Rolfe 200.00 100.00
105 Ernie Lombardi 400.00 200.00
106 Red Lucas 200.00 100.00
107 Stan Hack 200.00 100.00
108 Wally Berger 300.00 150.00

1981 Donruss

In 1981 Donruss launched itself into the baseball card market with a 600-card set. Wax packs contained 15 cards as well as a piece of gum. This would be the only year that Donruss was allowed to have any confectionary product in their packs. The standard-size cards are printed on thin stock and more than one pose exists for several popular players. Numerous errors of the first print run were later corrected by the company. These are marked P1 and P2 in our checklist below. According to published reports at the time, approximately 500 sets were made available in uncut sheet form. The key Rookie Cards in this set are Danny Ainge, Tim Raines, and Jeff Reardon.

Nm-Mt Ex-Mt
COMPLETE SET (605) 40.00 16.00
1 Ozzie Smith 3.00 1.20
2 Rollie Fingers .25 .10
3 Rick Wise .10 .04
4 Gene Richards .10 .04
5 Alan Trammell .50 .20
6 Tom Brookens .10 .04
7A Duffy Dyer P1 .25 .10
1980 batting average
has decimal point
7B Duffy Dyer P2 .10 .04
1980 batting average
has no decimal point
8 Mark Fidrych .25 .10
9 Dave Rozema .10 .04
10 Ricky Peters .10 .04
11 Mike Schmidt 2.50 1.00
12 Willie Stargell .50 .20
13 Tim Foli .10 .04
14 Manny Sanguillen .25 .10
15 Grant Jackson .10 .04
16 Eddie Solomon .10 .04
17 Omar Moreno .10 .04
18 Joe Morgan .50 .20
19 Rafael Landestoy .10 .04
20 Bruce Bochy .10 .04
21 Joe Sambito .10 .04
22 Manny Trillo .10 .04
23A Dave Smith RC P1 .50 .20
Line box around stats
is not complete
23B Dave Smith RC P2 .50 .20
Box totally encloses
stats at top
24 Terry Puhl .10 .04
25 Bump Wills .10 .04
26A John Ellis P1 ERR .50 .20
Danny Walton photo on front
26B John Ellis P2 COR .25 .10
27 Jim Kern .10 .04
28 Richie Zisk .10 .04
29 John Mayberry .10 .04
30 Bob Davis .10 .04
31 Jackson Todd .10 .04
32 Alvis Woods .10 .04
33 Steve Carlton .50 .20
34 Lee Mazzilli .25 .10
35 John Stearns .10 .04
36 Roy Lee Jackson .10 .04
37 Mike Scott .25 .10
38 Lamar Johnson .10 .04
39 Kevin Bell .10 .04
40 Ed Farmer .10 .04
41 Ross Baumgarten .10 .04
42 Leo Sutherland .10 .04
43 Dan Meyer .10 .04
44 Ron Reed .10 .04
45 Mario Mendoza .10 .04
46 Rick Honeycutt .10 .04
47 Glenn Abbott .10 .04
48 Leon Roberts .10 .04
49 Rod Carew .50 .20
50 Bert Campaneris .25 .10
51A T.Donahue P1 ERR .25 .10
Name on front
misspelled Donahue
51B Tom Donohue .10 .04
P2 COR
52 Dave Frost .10 .04
53 Ed Halicki .10 .04
54 Dan Ford .10 .04
55 Garry Maddox .10 .04
56A Steve Garvey P1 .25 .10
Surpassed 25 HR
56B Steve Garvey P2 .25 .10
Surpassed 21 HR
57 Bill Russell .25 .10
58 Don Sutton .25 .10
59 Reggie Smith .25 .10
60 Rick Monday .25 .10
61 Ray Knight .25 .10
62 Johnny Bench 1.00 .40
63 Mario Soto .25 .10
64 Doug Bair .10 .04
65 George Foster .25 .10
66 Jeff Burroughs .25 .10
67 Keith Hernandez .25 .10
68 Tom Herr .25 .10
69 Bob Forsch .10 .04
70 John Fulgham .10 .04
71A Bobby Bonds P1 ERR 1.00 .40
986 lifetime HR
71B Bobby Bonds P2 COR .50 .20
326 lifetime HR
72A Rennie Stennett P1 .25 .10
Breaking broke leg
72B Rennie Stennett P2 .10 .04
Word "broke" deleted
73 Joe Strain .10 .04
74 Ed Whitson .10 .04
75 Tom Griffin .10 .04
76 Billy North .10 .04
77 Gene Garber .10 .04
78 Mike Hargrove .10 .04
79 Dave Rosello .10 .04
80 Ron Hassey .10 .04
81 Sid Monge .10 .04
82A J.Charboneau P1 RC 1.00 .40
'78 highlights
For some reason
82B J.Charboneau P2 RC 1.00 .40
Phrase "For some reason" deleted
83 Cecil Cooper .25 .10
84 Sal Bando .25 .10
85 Moose Haas .10 .04
86 Mike Caldwell .10 .04
87A Larry Hisle P1 .25 .10
'77 highlights
line ends with "28 RBI"
87B Larry Hisle P2 .10 .04
Correct line "28 HR"
88 Luis Gomez .10 .04
89 Larry Parrish .25 .10
90 Gary Carter .50 .20
91 Bill Gullickson RC .50 .20
92 Fred Norman .10 .04
93 Tommy Hutton .10 .04
94 Carl Yastrzemski 1.50 .60
95 Glenn Hoffman .10 .04
96 Dennis Eckersley .50 .20
97A Tom Burgmeier P1 .25 .10
ERR Throws: Right
97B Tom Burgmeier P2 .10 .04
COR Throws: Left
98 Win Remmerswaal .10 .04
99 Bob Horner .25 .10
100 George Brett 2.50 1.00
101 Dave Chalk .10 .04
102 Dennis Leonard .10 .04
103 Renie Martin .10 .04
104 Amos Otis .25 .10
105 Graig Nettles .25 .10
106 Eric Soderholm .10 .04
107 Tommy John .25 .10
108 Tom Underwood .10 .04
109 Lou Piniella .25 .10
110 Mickey Klutts .10 .04
111 Bobby Murcer .25 .10
112 Eddie Murray 1.50 .60
113 Rick Dempsey .10 .04
114 Scott McGregor .10 .04
115 Ken Singleton .25 .10
116 Gary Roenicke .10 .04
117 Dave Revering .10 .04
118 Mike Norris .10 .04
119 Rickey Henderson 6.00 2.40
120 Mike Heath .10 .04
121 Dave Cash .10 .04
122 Randy Jones .25 .10
123 Eric Rasmussen .10 .04
124 Jerry Mumphrey .10 .04
125 Richie Hebner .10 .04
126 Mark Wagner .10 .04
127 Jack Morris .50 .20
128 Dan Petry .10 .04
129 Bruce Robbins .10 .04
130 Champ Summers .10 .04
131 Pete Rose P1 3.00 1.20
Last line ends with
see card 251
131B Pete Rose P2 2.00 .80
Last line corrected
see card 371
132 Willie Stargell .50 .20
133 Ed Ott .10 .04
134 Jim Bibby .10 .04
135 Bert Blyleven .25 .10
136 Dave Parker .25 .10
137 Bill Robinson .10 .04
138 Enos Cabell .10 .04
139 Dave Bergman .10 .04
140 J.R. Richard .25 .10
141 Ken Forsch .10 .04
142 Larry Bowa UER .25 .10
Shortshop on front
143 Frank LaCorte UER .10 .04
Photo actually Randy Niemann
144 Denny Walling .10 .04
145 Buddy Bell .25 .10
146 Ferguson Jenkins .25 .10
147 Danny Darwin .25 .10
148 John Grubb .10 .04
149 Alfredo Griffin .10 .04
150 Jerry Garvin .10 .04
151 Paul Mirabella .10 .04
152 Rick Bosetti .10 .04
153 Dick Ruthven .10 .04
154 Frank Taveras .10 .04
155 Craig Swan .10 .04
156 Jeff Reardon RC 1.00 .40
157 Steve Henderson .10 .04
158 Jim Morrison .10 .04
159 Glenn Borgmann .10 .04
160 LaMarr Hoyt RC .50 .20
161 Rich Wortham .10 .04
162 Thad Bosley .10 .04
163 Julio Cruz .10 .04
164A Del Unser P1 .25 .10
No "3B" heading
164B Del Unser P2 .10 .04
Batting record on back
corrected "3B"
165 Jim Anderson .10 .04
166 Jim Beattie .10 .04
167 Shane Rawley .10 .04
168 Joe Simpson .10 .04
169 Rod Carew .50 .20
170 Fred Patek .10 .04
171 Frank Tanana .25 .10
172 Alfredo Martinez .10 .04
173 Chris Knapp .10 .04
174 Joe Rudi .25 .10
175 Greg Luzinski .25 .10
176 Steve Garvey .50 .20
177 Joe Ferguson .10 .04
178 Bob Welch .25 .10
179 Dusty Baker .25 .10
180 Rudy Law .10 .04
181 Dave Concepcion .25 .10
182 Johnny Bench 1.00 .40
183 Mike LaCoss .10 .04
184 Ken Griffey .25 .10
185 Dave Collins .10 .04
186 Brian Asselstine .10 .04
187 Garry Templeton .25 .10
188 Mike Phillips .10 .04
189 Pete Vuckovich .10 .04
190 John Urrea .10 .04
191 Tony Scott .10 .04
192 Darrell Evans .25 .10
193 Milt May .10 .04
194 Bob Knepper .10 .04
195 Randy Moffitt .10 .04
196 Larry Herndon .10 .04
197 Rick Camp .10 .04
198 Andre Thornton .25 .10
199 Tom Veryzer .10 .04
200 Gary Alexander .10 .04
201 Rick Waits .10 .04
202 Rick Manning .10 .04
203 Paul Molitor 1.00 .40
204 Jim Gantner .10 .04
205 Paul Mitchell .10 .04
206 Reggie Cleveland .10 .04
207 Sixto Lezcano .10 .04
208 Bruce Benedict .10 .04
209 Rodney Scott .10 .04
210 John Tamargo .10 .04
211 Bill Lee .25 .10
212 Andre Dawson UER .50 .20
Middle name Fernando
should be Nolan
213 Rowland Office .10 .04
214 Carl Yastrzemski 1.50 .60
215 Jerry Remy .10 .04
216 Mike Torrez .10 .04
217 Skip Lockwood .10 .04
218 Fred Lynn .25 .10
219 Chris Chambliss .25 .10
220 Willie Aikens .10 .04
221 John Wathan .10 .04
222 Dan Quisenberry .10 .04
223 Willie Wilson .25 .10
224 Clint Hurdle .10 .04
225 Bob Watson .10 .04
226 Jim Spencer .10 .04
227 Ron Guidry .25 .10
228 Reggie Jackson 1.00 .40
229 Oscar Gamble .10 .04
230 Jeff Cox .10 .04
231 Luis Tiant .25 .10
232 Rich Dauer .10 .04
233 Dan Graham .10 .04
234 Mike Flanagan .10 .04
235 John Lowenstein .10 .04
236 Benny Ayala .10 .04
237 Wayne Gross .10 .04
238 Rick Langford .10 .04
239 Tony Armas .25 .10
240A Bob Lacey P1 ERR .50 .20
Name misspelled Lacy
240B Bob Lacey P2 COR .10 .04
241 Gene Tenace .25 .10
242 Bob Shirley .10 .04
243 Gary Lucas .10 .04
244 Jerry Turner .10 .04
245 John Wockenfuss .10 .04
246 Stan Papi .10 .04
247 Milt Wilcox .10 .04
248 Dan Schatzeder .10 .04
249 Steve Kemp .10 .04
250 Jim Lentine .10 .04
251 Pete Rose 3.00 1.20
252 Bill Madlock .25 .10
253 Dale Berra .10 .04
254 Kent Tekulve .10 .04
255 Enrique Romo .10 .04
256 Mike Easler .10 .04
257 Chuck Tanner MG .10 .04
258 Art Howe .10 .04
259 Alan Ashby .10 .04
260 Nolan Ryan 5.00 2.00
261A Vern Ruhle P1 ERR .50 .20
Ken Forsch photo on front
261B Vern Ruhle P2 COR .25 .10
262 Bob Boone .25 .10
263 Cesar Cedeno .25 .10
264 Jeff Leonard .25 .10
265 Pat Putnam .10 .04
266 Jon Matlack .10 .04
267 Dave Rajsich .10 .04
268 Billy Sample .10 .04
269 Damaso Garcia .10 .04
270 Tom Buskey .10 .04
271 Joey McLaughlin .10 .04
272 Barry Bonnell .10 .04
273 Tug McGraw .25 .10
274 Mike Jorgensen .10 .04
275 Pat Zachry .10 .04
276 Neil Allen .10 .04
277 Joel Youngblood .10 .04
278 Greg Pryor .10 .04
279 Britt Burns .10 .04
280 Rich Dotson .10 .04
281 Chet Lemon .25 .10
282 Rusty Kuntz .10 .04
283 Ted Cox .10 .04
284 Sparky Lyle .25 .10
285 Larry Cox .10 .04
286 Floyd Bannister .10 .04
287 Byron McLaughlin .10 .04
288 Rodney Craig .10 .04
289 Bobby Grich .25 .10
290 Dickie Thon .10 .04
291 Mark Clear .10 .04
292 Dave Lemanczyk .10 .04
293 Jason Thompson .10 .04
294 Rick Miller .10 .04
295 Lonnie Smith .25 .10
296 Ron Cey .25 .10
297 Steve Yeager .25 .10
298 Bobby Castillo .10 .04
299 Manny Mota .25 .10
300 Jay Johnstone .10 .04
301 Dan Driessen .10 .04
302 Joe Nolan .10 .04
303 Paul Householder .10 .04
304 Harry Spilman .10 .04
305 Cesar Geronimo .10 .04
306A G.Mathews P1 ERR .50 .20
Name misspelled
306B G.Matthews P2 .25 .10
COR
307 Ken Reitz .10 .04
308 Ted Simmons .25 .10
309 John Littlefield .10 .04
310 George Frazier .10 .04
311 Dane Iorg .10 .04
312 Mike Ivie .10 .04
313 Dennis Littlejohn .10 .04
314 Gary Lavelle .10 .04
315 Jack Clark .25 .10
316 Jim Wohlford .10 .04
317 Rick Matula .10 .04
318 Toby Harrah .25 .10
319A D.Kuiper P1 ERR .25 .10
Name misspelled
319B D.Kuiper P2 COR .10 .04
320 Len Barker .25 .10
321 Victor Cruz .10 .04
322 Dell Alston .10 .04
323 Robin Yount 1.50 .60
324 Charlie Moore .10 .04
325 Lary Sorensen .10 .04
326A Gorman Thomas P1 .50 .20
2nd line on back:
"30 HR mark 4th"
326B Gorman Thomas P2 .25 .10
30 HR mark 3rd
327 Bob Rodgers MG .10 .04
328 Phil Niekro .25 .10
329 Chris Speier .10 .04
330A Steve Rodgers P1 .25 .10
ERR Name misspelled
330B S.Rogers P2 COR .25 .10
331 Woodie Fryman .10 .04
332 Warren Cromartie .10 .04
333 Jerry White .10 .04
334 Tony Perez .50 .20
335 Carlton Fisk .50 .20
336 Dick Drago .10 .04
337 Steve Renko .10 .04
338 Jim Rice .25 .10
339 Jerry Royster .10 .04
340 Frank White .25 .10
341 Jamie Quirk .10 .04
342A P.Spittorff P1 ERR .25 .10
Name misspelled
342B Paul Splittorff .10 .04
P2 COR
343 Marty Pattin .10 .04
344 Pete LaCock .10 .04
345 Willie Randolph .25 .10
346 Rick Cerone .10 .04
347 Rich Gossage .25 .10
348 Reggie Jackson 1.00 .40
349 Ruppert Jones .10 .04
350 Dave McKay .10 .04
351 Yogi Berra CO 1.00 .40
352 Doug DeCinces .10 .04

353 Jim Palmer .50 .20
354 Tippy Martinez .10 .04
355 Al Bumbry .10 .04
356 Earl Weaver MG .25 .10
357A Bob Picciolo P1 ERR .25 .10
Name misspelled
357B R.Picciolo P2 COR .10 .04
358 Matt Keough .10 .04
359 Dwayne Murphy .10 .04
360 Brian Kingman .10 .04
361 Bill Fahey .10 .04
362 Steve Mura .10 .04
363 Dennis Kinney .10 .04
364 Dave Winfield .50 .20
365 Lou Whitaker .50 .20
366 Lance Parrish .25 .10
367 Tim Corcoran .10 .04
368 Pat Underwood .10 .04
369 Al Cowens .10 .04
370 Sparky Anderson MG .25 .10
371 Pete Rose 3.00 1.20
372 Phil Garner .25 .10
373 Steve Nicosia .10 .04
374 John Candelaria .25 .10
375 Don Robinson .10 .04
376 Lee Lacy .10 .04
377 John Milner .10 .04
378 Craig Reynolds .10 .04
379A Luis Pujols P1 ERR .25 .10
Name misspelled Pujois
379B Luis Pujols P2 COR .10 .04
380 Joe Niekro .10 .04
381 Joaquin Andujar .25 .10
382 Keith Moreland .10 .04
383 Jose Cruz .25 .10
384 Bill Virdon MG .10 .04
385 Jim Sundberg .25 .10
386 Doc Medich .10 .04
387 Al Oliver .25 .10
388 Jim Norris .10 .04
389 Bob Bailor .10 .04
390 Ernie Whitt .10 .04
391 Otto Velez .10 .04
392 Roy Howell .10 .04
393 Bob Walk RC .50 .20
394 Doug Flynn .10 .04
395 Pete Falcone .10 .04
396 Tom Hausman .10 .04
397 Elliott Maddox .10 .04
398 Mike Squires .10 .04
399 Marvis Foley .10 .04
400 Steve Trout .10 .04
401 Wayne Nordhagen .10 .04
402 Tony LaRussa MG .25 .10
403 Bruce Bochte .10 .04
404 Bake McBride .25 .10
405 Jerry Narron .10 .04
406 Rob Dressler .10 .04
407 Dave Heaverlo .10 .04
408 Tom Paciorek .10 .04
409 Carney Lansford .25 .10
410 Brian Downing .25 .10
411 Don Aase .10 .04
412 Jim Barr .10 .04
413 Don Baylor .25 .10
414 Jim Fregosi MG .10 .04
415 Dallas Green MG .10 .04
416 Dave Lopes .25 .10
417 Jerry Reuss .10 .04
418 Rick Sutcliffe .25 .10
419 Derrel Thomas .10 .04
420 Tom Lasorda MG .50 .20
421 Charlie Leibrandt RC .50 .20
422 Tom Seaver 1.00 .40
423 Ron Oester .10 .04
424 Junior Kennedy .10 .04
425 Tom Seaver 1.00 .40
426 Bobby Cox MG .25 .10
427 Leon Durham RC .50 .20
428 Terry Kennedy .10 .04
429 Silvio Martinez .10 .04
430 George Hendrick .25 .10
431 Red Schoendienst MG .50 .20
432 Johnnie LeMaster .10 .04
433 Vida Blue .25 .10
434 John Montefusco .10 .04
435 Terry Whitfield .10 .04
436 Dave Bristol MG .10 .04
437 Dale Murphy .50 .20
438 Jerry Dybzinski .10 .04
439 Jorge Orta .10 .04
440 Wayne Garland .10 .04
441 Miguel Dilone .10 .04
442 Dave Garcia MG .10 .04
443 Don Money .10 .04
444A B.Martinez P1 ERR .25 .10
Reverse negative
444B Buck Martinez .10 .04
P2 COR
445 Jerry Augustine .10 .04
446 Ben Oglivie .25 .10
447 Jim Slaton .10 .04
448 Doyle Alexander .10 .04
449 Tony Bernazard .10 .04
450 Scott Sanderson .10 .04
451 David Palmer .10 .04
452 Stan Bahnsen .10 .04
453 Dick Williams MG .10 .04
454 Rick Burleson .10 .04
455 Gary Allenson .10 .04
456 Bob Stanley .10 .04
457A J. Tudor P1 ERR RC 1.00 .40
Lifetime W-L 9.7
457B J.Tudor P2 COR RC 1.00 .40
Lifetime W-L 9-7
458 Dwight Evans .50 .20
459 Glenn Hubbard .10 .04
460 U.L. Washington .10 .04
461 Larry Gura .10 .04
462 Rich Gale .10 .04
463 Hal McRae .25 .10
464 Jim Frey MG .10 .04
465 Bucky Dent .25 .10
466 Dennis Werth .10 .04
467 Ron Davis .10 .04
468 Reggie Jackson UER 1.00 .40
32 HR in 1970
should be 23
469 Bobby Brown .10 .04
470 Mike Davis RC .50 .20
471 Gaylord Perry .25 .10
472 Mark Belanger .10 .04
473 Jim Palmer .50 .20
474 Sammy Stewart .10 .04
475 Tim Stoddard .10 .04
476 Steve Stone .10 .04
477 Jeff Newman .10 .04
478 Steve McCatty .10 .04
479 Billy Martin MG .50 .20
480 Mitchell Page .10 .04
481 Steve Carlton CY .25 .10
482 Bill Buckner .25 .10
483A I.DeJesus P1 ERR .25 .10
Lifetime hits 702
483B I.DeJesus P2 COR .10 .04
Lifetime hits 642
484 Cliff Johnson .10 .04
485 Lenny Randle .10 .04
486 Larry Milbourne .10 .04
487 Roy Smalley .10 .04
488 John Castino .10 .04
489 Ron Jackson .10 .04
490A Dave Roberts P1 .25 .10
Career Highlights
Showed pop in
490B Dave Roberts P2 .10 .04
Declared himself
491 George Brett MVP 1.50 .60
492 Mike Cubbage .10 .04
493 Rob Wilfong .10 .04
494 Danny Goodwin .10 .04
495 Jose Morales .10 .04
496 Mickey Rivers .10 .04
497 Mike Edwards .10 .04
498 Mike Sadek .10 .04
499 Lenn Sakata .10 .04
500 Gene Michael MG .10 .04
501 Dave Roberts .10 .04
502 Steve Dillard .10 .04
503 Jim Essian .10 .04
504 Rance Mulliniks .10 .04
505 Darrell Porter .10 .04
506 Joe Torre MG .50 .20
507 Terry Crowley .10 .04
508 Bill Travers .10 .04
509 Nelson Norman .10 .04
510 Bob McClure .10 .04
511 Steve Howe RC .50 .20
512 Dave Rader .10 .04
513 Mick Kelleher .10 .04
514 Kiko Garcia .10 .04
515 Larry Biittner .10 .04
516A Willie Norwood P1 .25 .10
Career Highlights
Spent most of
516B Willie Norwood P2 .10 .04
Traded to Seattle
517 Bo Diaz .10 .04
518 Juan Beniquez .10 .04
519 Scot Thompson .10 .04
520 Jim Tracy RC 1.00 .40
521 Carlos Lezcano .10 .04
522 Joe Amalfitano MG .10 .04
523 Preston Hanna .10 .04
524A Ray Burris P1 .25 .10
Career Highlights
Went on ...
524B Ray Burris P2 .10 .04
Drafted by ...
525 Broderick Perkins .10 .04
526 Mickey Hatcher .10 .04
527 John Goryl MG .10 .04
528 Dick Davis .10 .04
529 Butch Wynegar .10 .04
530 Sal Butera .10 .04
531 Jerry Koosman .25 .10
532A Geoff Zahn P1 .25 .10
(Career Highlights
Was 2nd in
532B Geoff Zahn P2 .10 .04
Signed a 3 year
533 Dennis Martinez .25 .10
534 Gary Thomasson .10 .04
535 Steve Macko .10 .04
536 Jim Kaat .25 .10
537 George Brett 1.50 .60
Rod Carew
538 Tim Raines RC 1.50 .60
539 Keith Smith .10 .04
540 Ken Macha .10 .04
541 Burt Hooton .10 .04
542 Butch Hobson .10 .04
543 Bill Stein .10 .04
544 Dave Stapleton .10 .04
545 Bob Pate .10 .04
546 Doug Corbett .10 .04
547 Darrell Jackson .10 .04
548 Pete Redfern .10 .04
549 Roger Erickson .10 .04
550 Al Hrabosky .25 .10
551 Dick Tidrow .10 .04
552 Dave Ford .10 .04
553 Dave Kingman .25 .10
554A Mike Vail P1 .25 .10
Career Highlights
After two
554B Mike Vail P2 .10 .04
Traded to
555A Jerry Martin P1 .25 .10
Career Highlights
Overcame a
555B Jerry Martin P2 .10 .04
Traded to
556A Jesus Figueroa P1 .25 .10
Career Highlights
Had an
556B Jesus Figueroa P2 .10 .04
Traded to
557 Don Stanhouse .10 .04
558 Barry Foote .10 .04
559 Tim Blackwell .10 .04
560 Bruce Sutter .25 .10
561 Rick Reuschel .25 .10
562 Lynn McGlothen .10 .04
563A Bob Owchinko P1 .25 .10
Career Highlights
Traded to
563B Bob Owchinko P2 .10 .04
Involved in a
564 John Verhoeven .10 .04
565 Ken Landreaux .10 .04
566A Glen Adams P1 ERR .25 .10
Name misspelled
566B G. Adams P2 COR .10 .04
567 Hosken Powell .10 .04
568 Dick Noles .10 .04
569 Danny Ainge RC 1.50 .60
570 Bobby Mattick MG .10 .04
571 Joe Lefebvre .10 .04
572 Bobby Clark .10 .04
573 Dennis Lamp .10 .04
574 Randy Lerch .10 .04
575 Mookie Wilson RC 1.50 .60
576 Ron LeFlore .25 .10
577 Jim Dwyer .10 .04
578 Bill Castro .10 .04
579 Greg Minton .10 .04
580 Mark Littell .10 .04
581 Andy Hassler .10 .04
582 Dave Stieb .25 .10
583 Ken Oberkfell .10 .04
584 Larry Bradford .10 .04
585 Fred Stanley .10 .04
586 Bill Caudill .10 .04
587 Doug Capilla .10 .04
588 George Riley .10 .04
589 Willie Hernandez .10 .04
590 Mike Schmidt MVP 2.50 1.00
591 Steve Stone CY .10 .04
592 Rick Sofield .10 .04
593 Bombo Rivera .10 .04
594 Gary Ward .10 .04
595A Dave Edwards P1 .25 .10
Career Highlights
Sidelined the
595B Dave Edwards P2 .10 .04
Traded to
596 Mike Proly .10 .04
597 Tommy Boggs .10 .04
598 Greg Gross .10 .04
599 Elias Sosa .10 .04
600 Pat Kelly .10 .04
601A Checklist 1-120 P1 .25 .10
ERR Unnumbered
51 Donahue
601B Checklist 1-120 P2 .50 .20
COR Unnumbered
51 Donohue
602 Checklist 121-240 .25 .10
Unnumbered
603A CL 241-360 P1 .25 .10
ERR Unnumbered
306 Mathews
603B CL 241-360 P2 .25 .10
COR Unnumbered
306 Matthews
604A CL 361-480 P1 .25 .10
ERR Unnumbered
379 Pujols
604B CL 361-480 P2 .25 .10
COR Unnumbered
379 Pujols
605A CL 481-600 P1 .25 .10
ERR Unnumbered
566 Glen Adams
605B CL 481-600 P2 .25 .10
COR Unnumbered
566 Glenn Adams

1982 Donruss

The 1982 Donruss set contains 653 numbered standard-size cards and seven unnumbered checklists. The first 26 cards of this set are entitled Diamond Kings (DK) and feature the artwork of Dick Perez of Perez-Steele Galleries. The set was marketed with puzzle pieces in 15-card packs rather than with bubble gum. There are 63 pieces to the puzzle, which, when put together, make a collage of Babe Ruth entitled "Hall of Fame Diamond King." The card stock in this year's Donruss cards is considerably thicker than the 1981 cards. The seven unnumbered checklist cards are arbitrarily assigned numbers 654 through 660 and are listed at the end of the list below. Notable Rookie Cards in this set include Brett Butler, Cal Ripken Jr., Lee Smith and Dave Stewart.

Nm-Mt Ex-Mt
COMPLETE SET (660) 60.00 24.00
COMP.FACT.SET (660) 60.00 24.00
COMP.RUTH PUZZLE 10.00 4.00
1 Pete Rose DK 2.50 1.00
2 Gary Carter DK .20 .08
3 Steve Garvey DK .20 .08
4 Vida Blue DK .20 .08
5 Alan Trammell DK .20 .08
COR
5A Alan Trammel DK ERR .20 .08
(Name misspelled)
6 Len Barker DK .10 .04
7 Dwight Evans DK .20 .08
8 Rod Carew DK .40 .16
9 George Hendrick DK .20 .08
10 Phil Niekro DK .20 .08
11 Richie Zisk DK .10 .04
12 Dave Parker DK .20 .08
13 Nolan Ryan DK 4.00 1.60
14 Ivan DeJesus DK .10 .04
15 George Brett DK 2.00 .80
16 Tom Seaver DK .40 .16
17 Dave Kingman DK .20 .08
18 Dave Winfield DK .20 .08
19 Mike Norris DK .10 .04
20 Carlton Fisk DK .40 .16
21 Ozzie Smith DK 1.50 .60
22 Roy Smalley DK .10 .04
23 Buddy Bell DK .20 .08
24 Ken Singleton DK .20 .08
25 John Mayberry DK .10 .04
26 Gorman Thomas DK .20 .08
27 Earl Weaver MG .20 .08
28 Rollie Fingers .20 .08
29 Sparky Anderson MG .20 .08
30 Dennis Eckersley .40 .16
31 Dave Winfield .20 .08
32 Burt Hooton .10 .04
33 Rick Waits .10 .04
34 George Brett 2.00 .80
35 Steve McCatty .10 .04
36 Steve Rogers .20 .08
37 Bill Stein .10 .04
38 Steve Renko .10 .04
39 Mike Squires .10 .04
40 George Hendrick .20 .08
41 Bob Knepper .10 .04
42 Steve Carlton .40 .16
43 Larry Biittner .10 .04
44 Chris Welsh .10 .04
45 Steve Nicosia .10 .04
46 Jack Clark .20 .08
47 Chris Chambliss .20 .08
48 Ivan DeJesus .10 .04
49 Lee Mazzilli .20 .08
50 Julio Cruz .10 .04
51 Pete Redfern .10 .04
52 Dave Stieb .20 .08
53 Doug Corbett .10 .04
54 Jorge Bell RC 1.00 .40
55 Joe Simpson .10 .04
56 Rusty Staub .20 .08
57 Hector Cruz .10 .04
58 Claudell Washington .10 .04
59 Enrique Romo .10 .04
60 Gary Lavelle .10 .04
61 Tim Flannery .10 .04
62 Joe Nolan .10 .04
63 Larry Bowa .20 .08
64 Sixto Lezcano .10 .04
65 Joe Sambito .10 .04
66 Bruce Kison .10 .04
67 Wayne Nordhagen .10 .04
68 Woodie Fryman .10 .04
69 Billy Sample .10 .04
70 Amos Otis .20 .08
71 Matt Keough .10 .04
72 Toby Harrah .20 .08
73 Dave Righetti RC 1.50 .60
74 Carl Yastrzemski 1.25 .50
75 Bob Welch .20 .08
76 Alan Trammell COR .20 .08
76A Alan Trammel ERR .20 .08
(Name misspelled)
77 Rick Dempsey .10 .04
78 Paul Molitor .40 .16
79 Dennis Martinez .20 .08
80 Jim Slaton .10 .04
81 Champ Summers .10 .04
82 Carney Lansford .20 .08
83 Barry Foote .10 .04
84 Steve Garvey .20 .08
85 Rick Manning .10 .04
86 John Wathan .10 .04
87 Brian Kingman .10 .04
88 Andre Dawson UER .20 .08
(Middle name Fernando
should be Nolan)
89 Jim Kern .10 .04
90 Bobby Grich .20 .08
91 Bob Forsch .10 .04
92 Art Howe .10 .04
93 Marty Bystrom .10 .04
94 Ozzie Smith 1.50 .60
95 Dave Parker .20 .08
96 Doyle Alexander .10 .04
97 Al Hrabosky .10 .04
98 Frank Taveras .10 .04
99 Tim Blackwell .10 .04
100 Floyd Bannister .10 .04
101 Alfredo Griffin .10 .04
102 Dave Engle .10 .04
103 Mario Soto .20 .08
104 Ross Baumgarten .10 .04
105 Ken Singleton .20 .08
106 Ted Simmons .20 .08
107 Jack Morris .20 .08
108 Bob Watson .20 .08
109 Dwight Evans .20 .08
110 Tom Lasorda MG .40 .16
111 Bert Blyleven .20 .08
112 Dan Quisenberry .10 .04
113 Rickey Henderson 2.50 1.00
114 Gary Carter .20 .08
115 Brian Downing .20 .08
116 Al Oliver .20 .08
117 LaMarr Hoyt .10 .04
118 Cesar Cedeno .20 .08
119 Keith Moreland .10 .04
120 Bob Shirley .10 .04
121 Terry Kennedy .10 .04
122 Frank Pastore .10 .04
123 Gene Garber .10 .04
124 Tony Pena .20 .08
125 Allen Ripley .10 .04
126 Randy Martz .10 .04
127 Richie Zisk .10 .04
128 Mike Scott .20 .08
129 Lloyd Moseby .10 .04
130 Rob Wilfong .10 .04
131 Tim Stoddard .10 .04
132 Gorman Thomas .20 .08
133 Dan Petry .10 .04
134 Bob Stanley .10 .04
135 Lou Piniella .20 .08
136 Pedro Guerrero .20 .08
137 Len Barker .10 .04
138 Rich Gale .10 .04
139 Wayne Gross .10 .04
140 Tim Wallach RC 1.00 .40
141 Gene Mauch MG .10 .04
142 Doc Medich .10 .04
143 Tony Bernazard .10 .04
144 Bill Virdon MG .10 .04
145 John Littlefield .10 .04
146 Dave Bergman .10 .04
147 Dick Davis .10 .04
148 Tom Seaver .75 .30
149 Matt Sinatro .10 .04
150 Chuck Tanner MG .10 .04
151 Leon Durham .10 .04
152 Gene Tenace .20 .08
153 Al Bumbry .10 .04
154 Mark Brouhard .10 .04
155 Rick Peters .10 .04
156 Jerry Remy .10 .04
157 Rick Reuschel .20 .08
158 Steve Howe .10 .04
159 Alan Bannister .10 .04
160 U.L. Washington .10 .04
161 Rick Langford .10 .04
162 Bill Gullickson .10 .04
163 Mark Wagner .10 .04
164 Geoff Zahn .10 .04
165 Ron LeFlore .20 .08
166 Dane Iorg .10 .04
167 Joe Niekro .10 .04
168 Pete Rose 2.50 1.00
169 Dave Collins .10 .04
170 Rick Wise .10 .04
171 Jim Bibby .10 .04
172 Larry Herndon .10 .04
173 Bob Horner .20 .08
174 Steve Dillard .10 .04
175 Mookie Wilson .20 .08
176 Dan Meyer .10 .04
177 Fernando Arroyo .10 .04
178 Jackson Todd .10 .04
179 Darrell Jackson .10 .04
180 Alvis Woods .10 .04
181 Jim Anderson .10 .04
182 Dave Kingman .20 .08
183 Steve Henderson .10 .04
184 Brian Asselstine .10 .04
185 Rod Scurry .10 .04
186 Fred Breining .10 .04
187 Danny Boone .10 .04
188 Junior Kennedy .10 .04
189 Sparky Lyle .20 .08
190 Whitey Herzog MG .20 .08
191 Dave Smith .10 .04
192 Ed Ott .10 .04
193 Greg Luzinski .20 .08
194 Bill Lee .20 .08
195 Don Zimmer MG .20 .08
196 Hal McRae .20 .08
197 Mike Norris .10 .04
198 Duane Kuiper .10 .04
199 Rick Cerone .10 .04
200 Jim Rice .20 .08
201 Steve Yeager .20 .08
202 Tom Brookens .10 .04
203 Jose Morales .10 .04
204 Roy Howell .10 .04
205 Tippy Martinez .10 .04
206 Moose Haas .10 .04
207 Al Cowens .10 .04
208 Dave Stapleton .10 .04
209 Bucky Dent .20 .08
210 Ron Cey .20 .08
211 Jorge Orta .10 .04
212 Jamie Quirk .10 .04
213 Jeff Jones .10 .04
214 Tim Raines .40 .16
215 Jon Matlack .10 .04
216 Rod Carew .40 .16
217 Jim Kaat .20 .08
218 Joe Pittman .10 .04
219 Larry Christenson .10 .04
220 Juan Bonilla RC .15 .06
221 Mike Easler .10 .04
222 Vida Blue .20 .08
223 Rick Camp .10 .04
224 Mike Jorgensen .10 .04
225 Jody Davis .10 .04
226 Mike Parrott .10 .04
227 Jim Clancy .10 .04
228 Hosken Powell .10 .04
229 Tom Hume .10 .04
230 Britt Burns .10 .04
231 Jim Palmer .20 .08
232 Bob Rodgers MG .10 .04
233 Milt Wilcox .10 .04
234 Dave Revering .10 .04
235 Mike Torrez .10 .04
236 Robert Castillo .10 .04
237 Von Hayes RC .50 .20
238 Renie Martin .10 .04
239 Dwayne Murphy .10 .04
240 Rodney Scott .10 .04
241 Fred Patek .10 .04
242 Mickey Rivers .10 .04
243 Steve Trout .10 .04
244 Jose Cruz .20 .08
245 Manny Trillo .10 .04
246 Lary Sorensen .10 .04
247 Dave Edwards .10 .04
248 Dan Driessen .10 .04
249 Tommy Boggs .10 .04
250 Dale Berra .10 .04
251 Ed Whitson .10 .04
252 Lee Smith RC 2.00 .80
253 Tom Paciorek .10 .04
254 Pat Zachry .10 .04
255 Luis Leal .10 .04
256 John Castino .10 .04
257 Rich Dauer .10 .04
258 Cecil Cooper .20 .08
259 Dave Rozema .10 .04
260 John Tudor .20 .08
261 Jerry Mumphrey .10 .04
262 Jay Johnstone .10 .04
263 Bo Diaz .10 .04
264 Dennis Leonard .10 .04
265 Jim Spencer .10 .04
266 John Milner .10 .04
267 Don Aase .10 .04
268 Jim Sundberg .20 .08
269 Lamar Johnson .10 .04
270 Frank LaCorte .10 .04
271 Barry Evans .10 .04
272 Enos Cabell .10 .04
273 Del Unser .10 .04
274 George Foster .20 .08
275 Brett Butler RC 1.00 .40
276 Lee Lacy .10 .04
277 Ken Reitz .10 .04
278 Keith Hernandez .20 .08
279 Doug DeCinces .10 .04

280 Charlie Moore .10 .04
281 Lance Parrish .20 .08
282 Ralph Houk MG .10 .04
283 Rich Gossage .20 .08
284 Jerry Reuss .10 .04
285 Mike Stanton .10 .04
286 Frank White .20 .08
287 Bob Owchinko .10 .04
288 Scott Sanderson .10 .04
289 Bump Wills .10 .04
290 Dave Frost .10 .04
291 Chet Lemon .20 .08
292 Tito Landrum .10 .04
293 Vern Ruhle .10 .04
294 Mike Schmidt 2.00 .80
295 Sam Mejias .10 .04
296 Gary Lucas .10 .04
297 John Candelaria .10 .04
298 Jerry Martin .10 .04
299 Dale Murphy .40 .16
300 Mike Lum .10 .04
301 Tom Hausman .10 .04
302 Glenn Abbott .10 .04
303 Roger Erickson .10 .04
304 Otto Velez .10 .04
305 Danny Goodwin .10 .04
306 John Mayberry .10 .04
307 Lenny Randle .10 .04
308 Bob Bailor .10 .04
309 Jerry Morales .10 .04
310 Rufino Linares .10 .04
311 Kent Tekulve .10 .04
312 Joe Morgan .20 .08
313 John Urrea .10 .04
314 Paul Householder .10 .04
315 Garry Maddox .10 .04
316 Mike Ramsey .10 .04
317 Alan Ashby .10 .04
318 Bob Clark .10 .04
319 Tony LaRussa MG .20 .08
320 Charlie Lea .10 .04
321 Danny Darwin .10 .04
322 Cesar Geronimo .10 .04
323 Tom Underwood .10 .04
324 Andre Thornton .10 .04
325 Rudy May .10 .04
326 Frank Tanana .20 .08
327 Dave Lopes .20 .08
328 Richie Hebner .10 .04
329 Mike Flanagan .10 .04
330 Mike Caldwell .10 .04
331 Scott McGregor .10 .04
332 Jerry Augustine .10 .04
333 Stan Papi .10 .04
334 Rick Miller .10 .04
335 Graig Nettles .20 .08
336 Dusty Baker .20 .08
337 Dave Garcia MG .10 .04
338 Larry Gura .10 .04
339 Cliff Johnson .10 .04
340 Warren Cromartie .10 .04
341 Steve Comer .10 .04
342 Rick Burleson .10 .04
343 John Martin RC .15 .06
344 Craig Reynolds .10 .04
345 Mike Proly .10 .04
346 Ruppert Jones .10 .04
347 Omar Moreno .10 .04
348 Greg Minton .10 .04
349 Rick Mahler .10 .04
350 Alex Trevino .10 .04
351 Mike Krukow .10 .04
352A Shane Rawley ERR .40 .16
(Photo actually
Jim Anderson)
352B Shane Rawley COR .10 .04
353 Garth Iorg .10 .04
354 Pete Mackanin .10 .04
355 Paul Moskau .10 .04
356 Richard Dotson .10 .04
357 Steve Stone .10 .04
358 Larry Hisle .10 .04
359 Aurelio Lopez .10 .04
360 Oscar Gamble .10 .04
361 Tom Burgmeier .10 .04
362 Terry Forster .20 .08
363 Joe Charboneau .20 .08
364 Ken Brett .10 .04
365 Tony Armas .20 .08
366 Chris Speier .10 .04
367 Fred Lynn .20 .08
368 Buddy Bell .20 .08
369 Jim Essian .10 .04
370 Terry Puhl .10 .04
371 Greg Gross .10 .04
372 Bruce Sutter .20 .08
373 Joe Lefebvre .10 .04
374 Ray Knight .20 .08
375 Bruce Benedict .10 .04
376 Tim Foli .10 .04
377 Al Holland .10 .04
378 Ken Kravec .10 .04
379 Jeff Burroughs .10 .04
380 Pete Falcone .10 .04
381 Ernie Whitt .10 .04
382 Brad Havens .10 .04
383 Terry Crowley .10 .04
384 Don Money .10 .04
385 Dan Schatzeder .10 .04
386 Gary Allenson .10 .04
387 Yogi Berra CO .75 .30
388 Ken Landreaux .10 .04
389 Mike Hargrove .10 .04
390 Darryl Motley .10 .04
391 Dave McKay .10 .04
392 Stan Bahnsen .10 .04
393 Ken Forsch .10 .04
394 Mario Mendoza .10 .04
395 Jim Morrison .10 .04
396 Mike Ivie .10 .04
397 Broderick Perkins .10 .04
398 Darrell Evans .20 .08
399 Ron Reed .10 .04
400 Johnny Bench .75 .30
401 Steve Bedrosian RC .50 .20
402 Bill Robinson .10 .04
403 Bill Buckner .20 .08
404 Ken Oberkfell .10 .04
405 Cal Ripken RC 40.00 16.00
406 Jim Gantner .10 .04
407 Kirk Gibson .75 .30
408 Tony Perez .40 .16
409 Tommy John UER .20 .08
(Text says 52-56 as
Yankee, should be
52-26)
410 Dave Stewart RC 1.50 .60
411 Dan Spillner .10 .04
412 Willie Aikens .10 .04
413 Mike Heath .10 .04
414 Ray Burris .10 .04
415 Leon Roberts .10 .04
416 Mike Witt .50 .20
417 Bob Molinaro .10 .04
418 Steve Braun .10 .04
419 Nolan Ryan UER 4.00 1.60
(Nisnumbering of
Nolan's no-hitters
on card back)
420 Tug McGraw .20 .08
421 Dave Concepcion .20 .08
422A Juan Eichelberger .40 .16
ERR (Photo actually
Gary Lucas)
422B Juan Eichelberger .10 .04
COR
423 Rick Rhoden .10 .04
424 Frank Robinson MG .40 .16
425 Eddie Miller .10 .04
426 Bill Caudill .10 .04
427 Doug Flynn .10 .04
428 Larry Andersen UER .10 .04
(Misspelled Anderson
on card front)
429 Al Williams .10 .04
430 Jerry Garvin .10 .04
431 Glenn Adams .10 .04
432 Barry Bonnell .10 .04
433 Jerry Narron .10 .04
434 John Stearns .10 .04
435 Mike Tyson .10 .04
436 Glenn Hubbard .10 .04
437 Eddie Solomon .10 .04
438 Jeff Leonard .10 .04
439 Randy Bass RC .50 .20
440 Mike LaCoss .10 .04
441 Gary Matthews .20 .08
442 Mark Littell .10 .04
443 Don Sutton .20 .08
444 John Harris .10 .04
445 Vada Pinson CO .20 .08
446 Elias Sosa .10 .04
447 Charlie Hough .20 .08
448 Willie Wilson .20 .08
449 Fred Stanley .10 .04
450 Tom Veryzer .10 .04
451 Ron Davis .10 .04
452 Mark Clear .10 .04
453 Bill Russell .20 .08
454 Lou Whitaker .20 .08
455 Dan Graham .10 .04
456 Reggie Cleveland .10 .04
457 Sammy Stewart .10 .04
458 Pete Vuckovich .10 .04
459 John Wockenfuss .10 .04
460 Glenn Hoffman .10 .04
461 Willie Randolph .20 .08
462 Fernando Valenzuela .75 .30
463 Ron Hassey .10 .04
464 Paul Splittorff .10 .04
465 Rob Picciolo .10 .04
466 Larry Parrish .10 .04
467 Johnny Grubb .10 .04
468 Dan Ford .10 .04
469 Silvio Martinez .10 .04
470 Kiko Garcia .10 .04
471 Bob Boone .20 .08
472 Luis Salazar .10 .04
473 Randy Niemann .10 .04
474 Tom Griffin .10 .04
475 Phil Niekro .20 .08
476 Hubie Brooks .10 .04
477 Dick Tidrow .10 .04
478 Jim Beattie .10 .04
479 Damaso Garcia .10 .04
480 Mickey Hatcher .10 .04
481 Joe Price .10 .04
482 Ed Farmer .10 .04
483 Eddie Murray .75 .30
484 Ben Oglivie .20 .08
485 Kevin Saucier .10 .04
486 Bobby Murcer .20 .08
487 Bill Campbell .10 .04
488 Reggie Smith .20 .08
489 Wayne Garland .10 .04
490 Jim Wright .10 .04
491 Billy Martin MG .40 .16
492 Jim Fanning MG .10 .04
493 Don Baylor .20 .08
494 Rick Honeycutt .10 .04
495 Carlton Fisk .40 .16
496 Denny Walling .10 .04
497 Bake McBride .20 .08
498 Darrell Porter .10 .04
499 Gene Richards .10 .04
500 Ron Oester .10 .04
501 Ken Dayley .10 .04
502 Jason Thompson .10 .04
503 Milt May .10 .04
504 Doug Bird .10 .04
505 Bruce Bochte .10 .04
506 Neil Allen .10 .04
507 Joey McLaughlin .10 .04
508 Butch Wynegar .10 .04
509 Gary Roenicke .10 .04
510 Robin Yount 1.25 .50
511 Dave Tobik .10 .04
512 Rich Gedman .50 .20
513 Gene Nelson .10 .04
514 Rick Monday .20 .08
515 Miguel Dilone .10 .04
516 Clint Hurdle .10 .04
517 Jeff Newman .10 .04
518 Grant Jackson .10 .04
519 Andy Hassler .10 .04
520 Pat Putnam .10 .04
521 Greg Pryor .10 .04
522 Tony Scott .10 .04
523 Steve Mura .10 .04
524 Johnnie LeMaster .10 .04
525 Dick Ruthven .10 .04
526 John McNamara MG .10 .04
527 Larry McWilliams .10 .04
528 Johnny Ray RC .50 .20
529 Pat Tabler .10 .04
530 Tom Herr .10 .04
531A SD Chicken 1.00 .40
ERR (Without TM)
531B San Diego Chicken 1.00 .40
COR (With TM)
532 Sal Butera .10 .04
533 Mike Griffin .10 .04
534 Kelvin Moore .10 .04
535 Reggie Jackson .40 .16
536 Ed Romero .10 .04
537 Derrel Thomas .10 .04
538 Mike O'Berry .10 .04
539 Jack O'Connor .10 .04
540 Bob Ojeda RC .50 .20
541 Roy Lee Jackson .10 .04
542 Lynn Jones .10 .04
543 Gaylord Perry .20 .08
544A Phil Garner ERR .20 .08
(Reverse negative)
544B Phil Garner COR .20 .08
545 Garry Templeton .20 .08
546 Rafael Ramirez .10 .04
547 Jeff Reardon .20 .08
548 Ron Guidry .20 .08
549 Tim Laudner .10 .04
550 John Henry Johnson .10 .04
551 Chris Bando .10 .04
552 Bobby Brown .10 .04
553 Larry Bradford .10 .04
554 Scott Fletcher RC .50 .20
555 Jerry Royster .10 .04
556 Shooty Babitt UER .10 .04
(Spelled Babbitt
on front)
557 Kent Hrbek RC 1.00 .40
558 Ron Guidry .20 .08
Tommy John
559 Mark Bomback .10 .04
560 Julio Valdez .10 .04
561 Buck Martinez .10 .04
562 Mike A. Marshall RC .50 .20
563 Rennie Stennett .10 .04
564 Steve Crawford .10 .04
565 Bob Babcock .10 .04
566 Johnny Podres CO .20 .08
567 Paul Serna .10 .04
568 Harold Baines .20 .08
569 Dave LaRoche .10 .04
570 Lee May .10 .04
571 Gary Ward .10 .04
572 John Denny .10 .04
573 Roy Smalley .10 .04
574 Bob Brenly RC 1.00 .40
575 Reggie Jackson .20 .08
Dave Winfield
576 Luis Pujols .10 .04
577 Butch Hobson .10 .04
578 Harvey Kuenn MG .10 .04
579 Cal Ripken Sr. CO .20 .08
580 Juan Berenguer .10 .04
581 Benny Ayala .10 .04
582 Vance Law .10 .04
583 Rick Leach .10 .04
584 George Frazier .10 .04
585 Phillies Finest 1.50 .60
Pete Rose
Mike Schmidt
586 Joe Rudi .20 .08
587 Juan Beniquez .10 .04
588 Luis DeLeon .10 .04
589 Craig Swan .10 .04
590 Dave Chalk .10 .04
591 Billy Gardner MG .10 .04
592 Sal Bando .20 .08
593 Bert Campaneris .20 .08
594 Steve Kemp .10 .04
595A Randy Lerch ERR .40 .16
(Braves)
595B Randy Lerch COR .10 .04
(Brewers)
596 Bryan Clark RC .15 .06
597 Dave Ford .10 .04
598 Mike Scioscia .20 .08
599 John Lowenstein .10 .04
600 Rene Lachemann MG .10 .04
601 Mick Kelleher .10 .04
602 Ron Jackson .10 .04
603 Jerry Koosman .20 .08
604 Dave Goltz .10 .04
605 Ellis Valentine .10 .04
606 Lonnie Smith .10 .04
607 Joaquin Andujar .20 .08
608 Garry Hancock .10 .04
609 Jerry Turner .10 .04
610 Bob Bonner .10 .04
611 Jim Dwyer .10 .04
612 Terry Bulling .10 .04
613 Joel Youngblood .10 .04
614 Larry Milbourne .10 .04
615 Gene Roof UER .10 .04
(Name on front
is Phil Roof)
616 Keith Drumwright .10 .04
617 Dave Rosello .10 .04
618 Rickey Keeton .10 .04
619 Dennis Lamp .10 .04
620 Sid Monge .10 .04
621 Jerry White .10 .04
622 Luis Aguayo .10 .04
623 Jamie Easterly .10 .04
624 Steve Sax RC 1.00 .40
625 Dave Roberts .10 .04
626 Rick Bosetti .10 .04
627 Terry Francona RC 1.50 .60
628 Tom Seaver .75 .30
Johnny Bench
629 Paul Mirabella .10 .04
630 Rance Mulliniks .10 .04
631 Kevin Hickey RC .15 .06
632 Reid Nichols .10 .04
633 Dave Geisel .10 .04
634 Ken Griffey .20 .08
635 Bob Lemon MG .40 .16
636 Orlando Sanchez .10 .04
637 Bill Almon .10 .04
638 Danny Ainge .20 .08
639 Willie Stargell .40 .16
640 Bob Sykes .10 .04
641 Ed Lynch .10 .04
642 John Ellis .10 .04
643 Ferguson Jenkins .20 .08
644 Lenn Sakata .10 .04
645 Julio Gonzalez .10 .04
646 Jesse Orosco .10 .04
647 Jerry Dybzinski .10 .04
648 Tommy Davis CO .20 .08
649 Ron Gardenhire RC .50 .20
650 Felipe Alou CO .20 .08
651 Harvey Haddix CO .20 .08
652 Willie Upshaw .50 .20
653 Bill Madlock .20 .08
654A DK Checklist 1-26 .40 .16
ERR (Unnumbered)
(With Trammel)
654B DK Checklist 1-26 .20 .08
COR (Unnumbered)
(With Trammell)
655 Checklist 27-130 .20 .08
(Unnumbered)
656 Checklist 131-234 .20 .08
(Unnumbered)
657 Checklist 235-338 .20 .08
(Unnumbered)
658 Checklist 339-442 .20 .08
(Unnumbered)
659 Checklist 443-544 .20 .08
(Unnumbered)
660 Checklist 545-653 .20 .08
(Unnumbered)

1983 Donruss

The 1983 Donruss baseball set leads off with a 26-card Diamond Kings (DK) series. Of the remaining 634 standard-size cards, two are combination cards, one portrays the San Diego Chicken, one shows the completed Ty Cobb puzzle, and seven are unnumbered checklist cards. The seven unnumbered checklist cards are arbitrarily assigned numbers 654 through 660 and are listed at the end of the list below. All cards measure the standard size. Card fronts feature full color photos around a framed white broder. Several printing variations are available but the complete set price below includes only the more common of each variation pair. Cards were issued in 15-card packs which included a three-piece Ty Cobb puzzle panel (21 different panels were needed to complete the puzzle). Notable Rookie Cards include Wade Boggs, Tony Gwynn and Ryne Sandberg.

Nm-Mt Ex-Mt
COMPLETE SET (660) 60.00 24.00
COMP.FACT.SET (660) 80.00 32.00
COMP.COBB PUZZLE 5.00 2.00
1 Fernando Valenzuela DK .20 .08
2 Rollie Fingers DK .20 .08
3 Reggie Jackson DK .40 .16
4 Jim Palmer DK .20 .08
5 Jack Morris DK .20 .08
6 George Foster DK .20 .08
7 Jim Sundberg DK .20 .08
8 Willie Stargell DK .40 .16
9 Dave Stieb DK .20 .08
10 Joe Niekro DK .10 .04
11 Rickey Henderson DK 1.50 .60
12 Dale Murphy DK .40 .16
13 Toby Harrah DK .20 .08
14 Bill Buckner DK .20 .08
15 Willie Wilson DK .20 .08
16 Steve Carlton DK .40 .16
17 Ron Guidry DK .20 .08
18 Steve Rogers DK .20 .08
19 Kent Hrbek DK .20 .08
20 Keith Hernandez DK .20 .08
21 Floyd Bannister DK .10 .04
22 Johnny Bench DK .75 .30
23 Britt Burns DK .10 .04
24 Joe Morgan DK .20 .08
25 Carl Yastrzemski DK .75 .30
26 Terry Kennedy DK .10 .04
27 Gary Roenicke .10 .04
28 Dwight Bernard .10 .04
29 Pat Underwood .10 .04
30 Gary Allenson .10 .04
31 Ron Guidry .20 .08
32 Burt Hooton .10 .04
33 Chris Bando .10 .04
34 Vida Blue .20 .08
35 Rickey Henderson 1.50 .60
36 Ray Burris .10 .04
37 John Butcher .10 .04
38 Don Aase .10 .04
39 Jerry Koosman .20 .08
40 Bruce Sutter .20 .08
41 Jose Cruz .20 .08
42 Pete Rose 2.50 1.00
43 Cesar Cedeno .20 .08
44 Floyd Chiffer .10 .04
45 Larry McWilliams .10 .04
46 Alan Fowlkes .10 .04
47 Dale Murphy .40 .16
48 Doug Bird .10 .04
49 Hubie Brooks .10 .04
50 Floyd Bannister .10 .04
51 Jack O'Connor .10 .04
52 Steve Senteney .10 .04
53 Gary Gaetti RC 1.00 .40
54 Damaso Garcia .10 .04
55 Gene Nelson .10 .04
56 Mookie Wilson .20 .08
57 Allen Ripley .10 .04
58 Bob Horner .20 .08
59 Tony Pena .10 .04
60 Gary Lavelle .10 .04
61 Tim Lollar .10 .04
62 Frank Pastore .10 .04
63 Garry Maddox .10 .04
64 Bob Forsch .10 .04
65 Harry Spilman .10 .04
66 Geoff Zahn .10 .04
67 Salome Barojas .10 .04
68 David Palmer .10 .04
69 Charlie Hough .20 .08
70 Dan Quisenberry .10 .04
71 Tony Armas .20 .08
72 Rick Sutcliffe .20 .08
73 Steve Balboni .10 .04
74 Jerry Remy .10 .04
75 Mike Scioscia .20 .08
76 John Wockenfuss .10 .04
77 Jim Palmer .20 .08
78 Rollie Fingers .20 .08
79 Joe Nolan .10 .04
80 Pete Vuckovich .10 .04
81 Rick Leach .10 .04
82 Rick Miller .10 .04
83 Graig Nettles .20 .08
84 Ron Cey .20 .08
85 Miguel Dilone .10 .04
86 John Wathan .10 .04
87 Kelvin Moore .10 .04
88A Byrn Smith ERR .20 .08
(Sic, Bryn)
88B Bryn Smith COR .40 .16
89 Dave Hostetler .10 .04
90 Rod Carew .40 .16
91 Lonnie Smith .10 .04
92 Bob Knepper .10 .04
93 Marty Bystrom .10 .04
94 Chris Welsh .10 .04
95 Jason Thompson .10 .04
96 Tom O'Malley .10 .04
97 Phil Niekro .20 .08
98 Neil Allen .10 .04
99 Bill Buckner .20 .08
100 Ed VandeBerg .10 .04
101 Jim Clancy .10 .04
102 Robert Castillo .10 .04
103 Bruce Berenyi .10 .04
104 Carlton Fisk .40 .16
105 Mike Flanagan .10 .04
106 Cecil Cooper .20 .08
107 Jack Morris .20 .08
108 Mike Morgan .10 .04
109 Luis Aponte .10 .04
110 Pedro Guerrero .20 .08
111 Len Barker .10 .04
112 Willie Wilson .20 .08
113 Dave Beard .10 .04
114 Mike Gates .10 .04
115 Reggie Jackson .40 .16
116 George Wright RC .50 .20
117 Vance Law .10 .04
118 Nolan Ryan 4.00 1.60
119 Mike Krukow .10 .04
120 Ozzie Smith 1.25 .50
121 Broderick Perkins .10 .04
122 Tom Seaver .75 .30
123 Chris Chambliss .20 .08
124 Chuck Tanner MG .10 .04
125 Johnnie LeMaster .10 .04
126 Mel Hall RC .50 .20
127 Bruce Bochte .10 .04
128 Charlie Puleo .10 .04
129 Luis Leal .10 .04
130 John Pacella .10 .04
131 Glenn Gulliver .10 .04
132 Don Money .10 .04
133 Dave Rozema .10 .04
134 Bruce Hurst .10 .04
135 Rudy May .10 .04
136 Tom Lasorda MG .40 .16
137 Dan Spillner UER .10 .04
(Photo actually
Ed Whitson)
138 Jerry Martin .10 .04
139 Mike Norris .10 .04
140 Al Oliver .20 .08
141 Daryl Sconiers .10 .04
142 Lamar Johnson .10 .04
143 Harold Baines .20 .08
144 Alan Ashby .10 .04
145 Garry Templeton .20 .08
146 Al Holland .10 .04
147 Bo Diaz .10 .04
148 Dave Concepcion .20 .08
149 Rick Camp .10 .04
150 Jim Morrison .10 .04
151 Randy Martz .10 .04
152 Keith Hernandez .20 .08
153 John Lowenstein .10 .04
154 Mike Caldwell .10 .04
155 Milt Wilcox .10 .04
156 Rich Gedman .10 .04
157 Rich Gossage .20 .08
158 Jerry Reuss .10 .04
159 Ron Hassey .10 .04
160 Larry Gura .10 .04
161 Dwayne Murphy .10 .04
162 Woodie Fryman .10 .04
163 Steve Comer .10 .04
164 Ken Forsch .10 .04
165 Dennis Lamp .10 .04
166 David Green RC .50 .20
167 Terry Puhl .10 .04
168 Mike Schmidt 2.00 .80
(Wearing 37
rather than 20)
169 Eddie Milner .10 .04
170 John Curtis .10 .04
171 Don Robinson .10 .04
172 Rich Gale .10 .04
173 Steve Bedrosian .10 .04
174 Willie Hernandez .10 .04
175 Ron Gardenhire .10 .04
176 Jim Beattie .10 .04
177 Tim Laudner .10 .04
178 Buck Martinez .10 .04
179 Kent Hrbek .20 .08
180 Alfredo Griffin .10 .04
181 Larry Andersen .10 .04
182 Pete Falcone .10 .04

183 Jody Davis .10 .04
184 Glenn Hubbard .10 .04
185 Dale Berra .10 .04
186 Greg Minton .10 .04
187 Gary Lucas .10 .04
188 Dave Van Gorder .10 .04
189 Bob Dernier .10 .04
190 Willie McGee RC 1.00 .40
191 Dickie Thon .10 .04
192 Bob Boone .20 .08
193 Britt Burns .10 .04
194 Jeff Reardon .20 .08
195 Jon Matlack .10 .04
196 Don Slaught RC .50 .20
197 Fred Stanley .10 .04
198 Rick Manning .10 .04
199 Dave Righetti .20 .08
200 Dave Stapleton .10 .04
201 Steve Yeager .20 .08
202 Enos Cabell .10 .04
203 Sammy Stewart .10 .04
204 Moose Haas .10 .04
205 Lenn Sakata .10 .04
206 Charlie Moore .10 .04
207 Alan Trammell .20 .08
208 Jim Rice .20 .08
209 Roy Smalley .10 .04
210 Bill Russell .20 .08
211 Andre Thornton .10 .04
212 Willie Aikens .10 .04
213 Dave McKay .10 .04
214 Tim Blackwell .10 .04
215 Buddy Bell .20 .08
216 Doug DeCinces .10 .04
217 Tom Herr .10 .04
218 Frank LaCorte .10 .04
219 Steve Carlton .40 .16
220 Terry Kennedy .10 .04
221 Mike Easler .10 .04
222 Jack Clark .20 .08
223 Gene Garber .10 .04
224 Scott Holman .10 .04
225 Mike Proly .10 .04
226 Terry Bulling .10 .04
227 Jerry Garvin .10 .04
228 Ron Davis .10 .04
229 Tom Hume .10 .04
230 Marc Hill .10 .04
231 Dennis Martinez .20 .08
232 Jim Gantner .10 .04
233 Larry Pashnick .10 .04
234 Dave Collins .10 .04
235 Tom Burgmeier .10 .04
236 Ken Landreaux .10 .04
237 John Denny .10 .04
238 Hal McRae .20 .08
239 Matt Keough .10 .04
240 Doug Flynn .10 .04
241 Fred Lynn .20 .08
242 Billy Sample .10 .04
243 Tom Paciorek .10 .04
244 Joe Sambito .10 .04
245 Sid Monge .10 .04
246 Ken Oberkfell .10 .04
247 Joe Pittman UER .10 .04
(Photo actually
Juan Eichelberger)
248 Mario Soto .20 .08
249 Claudell Washington .10 .04
250 Rick Rhoden .10 .04
251 Darrell Evans .20 .08
252 Steve Henderson .10 .04
253 Manny Castillo .10 .04
254 Craig Swan .10 .04
255 Joey McLaughlin .10 .04
256 Pete Redfern .10 .04
257 Ken Singleton .20 .08
258 Robin Yount 1.25 .50
259 Elias Sosa .10 .04
260 Bob Ojeda .10 .04
261 Bobby Murcer .20 .08
262 Candy Maldonado RC .50 .20
263 Rick Waits .10 .04
264 Greg Pryor .10 .04
265 Bob Owchinko .10 .04
266 Chris Speier .10 .04
267 Bruce Kison .10 .04
268 Mark Wagner .10 .04
269 Steve Kemp .10 .04
270 Phil Garner .20 .08
271 Gene Richards .10 .04
272 Renie Martin .10 .04
273 Dave Roberts .10 .04
274 Dan Driessen .10 .04
275 Rufino Linares .10 .04
276 Lee Lacy .10 .04
277 Ryne Sandberg RC 10.00 4.00
278 Darrell Porter .10 .04
279 Cal Ripken 6.00 2.40
280 Jamie Easterly .10 .04
281 Bill Fahey .10 .04
282 Glenn Hoffman .10 .04
283 Willie Randolph .20 .08
284 Fernando Valenzuela .20 .08
285 Alan Bannister .10 .04
286 Paul Splittorff .10 .04
287 Joe Rudi .20 .08
288 Bill Gullickson .10 .04
289 Danny Darwin .10 .04
290 Andy Hassler .10 .04
291 Ernesto Escarrega .10 .04
292 Steve Mura .10 .04
293 Tony Scott .10 .04
294 Manny Trillo .10 .04
295 Greg Harris .10 .04
296 Luis DeLeon .10 .04
297 Kent Tekulve .10 .04
298 Atlee Hammaker .10 .04
299 Bruce Benedict .10 .04
300 Fergie Jenkins .20 .08
301 Dave Kingman .20 .08
302 Bill Caudill .10 .04
303 John Castino .10 .04
304 Ernie Whitt .10 .04
305 Randy Johnson .10 .04
306 Garth Iorg .10 .04
307 Gaylord Perry .20 .08
308 Ed Lynch .10 .04
309 Keith Moreland .10 .04
310 Rafael Ramirez .10 .04
311 Bill Madlock .20 .08
312 Milt May .10 .04
313 John Montefusco .10 .04
314 Wayne Krenchicki .10 .04
315 George Vukovich .10 .04
316 Joaquin Andujar .20 .08
317 Craig Reynolds .10 .04
318 Rick Burleson .10 .04
319 Richard Dotson .10 .04
320 Steve Rogers .20 .08
321 Dave Schmidt .10 .04
322 Bud Black RC .50 .20
323 Jeff Burroughs .10 .04
324 Von Hayes .10 .04
325 Butch Wynegar .10 .04
326 Carl Yastrzemski 1.25 .50
327 Ron Roenicke .10 .04
328 Howard Johnson RC 1.00 .40
329 Rick Dempsey UER .10 .04
(Posing as a left-
handed batter)
330A Jim Slaton .10 .04
(Bio printed
black on white)
330B Jim Slaton .20 .08
(Bio printed
black on yellow)
331 Benny Ayala .10 .04
332 Ted Simmons .20 .08
333 Lou Whitaker .20 .08
334 Chuck Rainey .10 .04
335 Lou Piniella .20 .08
336 Steve Sax .20 .08
337 Toby Harrah .20 .08
338 George Brett 2.00 .80
339 Dave Lopes .20 .08
340 Gary Carter .20 .08
341 John Grubb .10 .04
342 Tim Foli .10 .04
343 Jim Kaat .20 .08
344 Mike LaCoss .10 .04
345 Larry Christenson .10 .04
346 Juan Bonilla .10 .04
347 Omar Moreno .10 .04
348 Chili Davis .20 .08
349 Tommy Boggs .10 .04
350 Rusty Staub .20 .08
351 Bump Wills .10 .04
352 Rick Sweet .10 .04
353 Jim Gott RC .50 .20
354 Terry Felton .10 .04
355 Jim Kern .10 .04
356 Bill Almon UER .10 .04
(Expos/Mets in 1983,
not Padres/Mets)
357 Tippy Martinez .10 .04
358 Roy Howell .10 .04
359 Dan Petry .10 .04
360 Jerry Mumphrey .10 .04
361 Mark Clear .10 .04
362 Mike Marshall .10 .04
363 Lary Sorensen .10 .04
364 Amos Otis .20 .08
365 Rick Langford .10 .04
366 Brad Mills .10 .04
367 Brian Downing .20 .08
368 Mike Richardt .10 .04
369 Aurelio Rodriguez .10 .04
370 Dave Smith .10 .04
371 Tug McGraw .20 .08
372 Doug Bair .10 .04
373 Ruppert Jones .10 .04
374 Alex Trevino .10 .04
375 Ken Dayley .10 .04
376 Rod Scurry .10 .04
377 Bob Brenly .10 .04
378 Scot Thompson .10 .04
379 Julio Cruz .10 .04
380 John Stearns .10 .04
381 Dale Murray .10 .04
382 Frank Viola RC 1.50 .60
383 Al Bumbry .10 .04
384 Ben Oglivie .20 .08
385 Dave Tobik .10 .04
386 Bob Stanley .10 .04
387 Andre Robertson .10 .04
388 Jorge Orta .10 .04
389 Ed Whitson .10 .04
390 Don Hood .10 .04
391 Tom Underwood .10 .04
392 Tim Wallach .20 .08
393 Steve Renko .10 .04
394 Mickey Rivers .10 .04
395 Greg Luzinski .20 .08
396 Art Howe .10 .04
397 Alan Wiggins .10 .04
398 Jim Barr .10 .04
399 Ivan DeJesus .10 .04
400 Tom Lawless .10 .04
401 Bob Walk .10 .04
402 Jimmy Smith .10 .04
403 Lee Smith .40 .16
404 George Hendrick .20 .08
405 Eddie Murray .75 .30
406 Marshall Edwards .10 .04
407 Lance Parrish .20 .08
408 Carney Lansford .20 .08
409 Dave Winfield .20 .08
410 Bob Welch .20 .08
411 Larry Milbourne .10 .04
412 Dennis Leonard .10 .04
413 Dan Meyer .10 .04
414 Charlie Lea .10 .04
415 Rick Honeycutt .10 .04
416 Mike Witt .10 .04
417 Steve Trout .10 .04
418 Glenn Brummer .10 .04
419 Denny Walling .10 .04
420 Gary Matthews .20 .08
421 Charlie Leibrandt UER .10 .04
(Liebrandt on
front of card)
422 J.Eichelberger UER .10 .04
Photo actually
Joe Pittman
423 Cecilio Guante UER .10 .04
(Listed as Matt
on card)
424 Bill Laskey .10 .04
425 Jerry Royster .10 .04
426 Dickie Noles .10 .04
427 George Foster .20 .08
428 Mike Moore RC .50 .20
429 Gary Ward .10 .04
430 Barry Bonnell .10 .04
431 Ron Washington .10 .04
432 Rance Mulliniks .10 .04
433 Mike Stanton .10 .04
434 Jesse Orosco .10 .04
435 Larry Bowa .20 .08
436 Biff Pocoroba .10 .04
437 Johnny Ray .10 .04
438 Joe Morgan .20 .08
439 Eric Show RC .50 .20
440 Larry Biittner .10 .04
441 Greg Gross .10 .04
442 Gene Tenace .20 .08
443 Danny Heep .10 .04
444 Bobby Clark .10 .04
445 Kevin Hickey .10 .04
446 Scott Sanderson .10 .04
447 Frank Tanana .20 .08
448 Cesar Geronimo .10 .04
449 Jimmy Sexton .10 .04
450 Mike Hargrove .10 .04
451 Doyle Alexander .10 .04
452 Dwight Evans .20 .08
453 Terry Forster .20 .08
454 Tom Brookens .10 .04
455 Rich Dauer .10 .04
456 Rob Picciolo .10 .04
457 Terry Crowley .10 .04
458 Ned Yost .10 .04
459 Kirk Gibson .20 .08
460 Reid Nichols .10 .04
461 Oscar Gamble .10 .04
462 Dusty Baker .20 .08
463 Jack Perconte .10 .04
464 Frank White .20 .08
465 Mickey Klutts .10 .04
466 Warren Cromartie .10 .04
467 Larry Parrish .10 .04
468 Bobby Grich .20 .08
469 Dane Iorg .10 .04
470 Joe Niekro .10 .04
471 Ed Farmer .10 .04
472 Tim Flannery .10 .04
473 Dave Parker .20 .08
474 Jeff Leonard .10 .04
475 Al Hrabosky .10 .04
476 Ron Hodges .10 .04
477 Leon Durham .10 .04
478 Jim Essian .10 .04
479 Roy Lee Jackson .10 .04
480 Brad Havens .10 .04
481 Joe Price .10 .04
482 Tony Bernazard .10 .04
483 Scott McGregor .10 .04
484 Paul Molitor .40 .16
485 Mike Ivie .10 .04
486 Ken Griffey .20 .08
487 Dennis Eckersley .40 .16
488 Steve Garvey .20 .08
489 Mike Fischlin .10 .04
490 U.L. Washington .10 .04
491 Steve McCatty .10 .04
492 Roy Johnson .10 .04
493 Don Baylor .20 .08
494 Bobby Johnson .10 .04
495 Mike Squires .10 .04
496 Bert Roberge .10 .04
497 Dick Ruthven .10 .04
498 Tito Landrum .10 .04
499 Sixto Lezcano .10 .04
500 Johnny Bench .75 .30
501 Larry Whisenton .10 .04
502 Manny Sarmiento .10 .04
503 Fred Breining .10 .04
504 Bill Campbell .10 .04
505 Todd Cruz .10 .04
506 Bob Bailor .10 .04
507 Dave Stieb .20 .08
508 Al Williams .10 .04
509 Dan Ford .10 .04
510 Gorman Thomas .20 .08
511 Chet Lemon .20 .08
512 Mike Torrez .10 .04
513 Shane Rawley .10 .04
514 Mark Belanger .10 .04
515 Rodney Craig .10 .04
516 Onix Concepcion .10 .04
517 Mike Heath .10 .04
518 Andre Dawson UER .20 .08
(Middle name Fernando,
should be Nolan)
519 Luis Sanchez .10 .04
520 Terry Bogener .10 .04
521 Rudy Law .10 .04
522 Ray Knight .20 .08
523 Joe Lefebvre .10 .04
524 Jim Wohlford .10 .04
525 Julio Franco RC 1.50 .60
526 Ron Oester .10 .04
527 Rick Mahler .10 .04
528 Steve Nicosia .10 .04
529 Junior Kennedy .10 .04
530A Whitey Herzog MG .20 .08
(Bio printed
black on white)
530B Whitey Herzog MG .20 .08
(Bio printed
black on yellow)
531A Don Sutton .20 .08
(Blue border
on photo)
531B Don Sutton .20 .08
(Green border
on photo)
532 Mark Brouhard .10 .04
533A S.Anderson MG .20 .08
Bio printed
black on white
533B S.Anderson MG .20 .08
Bio printed
black on yellow
534 Roger LaFrancois .10 .04
535 George Frazier .10 .04
536 Tom Niedenfuer .10 .04
537 Ed Glynn .10 .04
538 Lee May .10 .04
539 Bob Kearney .10 .04
540 Tim Raines .20 .08
541 Paul Mirabella .10 .04
542 Luis Tiant .20 .08
543 Ron LeFlore .20 .08
544 Dave LaPoint .10 .04
545 Randy Moffitt .10 .04
546 Luis Aguayo .10 .04
547 Brad Lesley .15 .06
548 Luis Salazar .10 .04
549 John Candelaria .10 .04
550 Dave Bergman .10 .04
551 Bob Watson .10 .04
552 Pat Tabler .10 .04
553 Brent Gaff .10 .04
554 Al Cowens .10 .04
555 Tom Brunansky .20 .08
556 Lloyd Moseby .10 .04
557A Pascual Perez ERR 2.00 .80
(Twins in glove)
557B Pascual Perez COR .20 .08
(Braves in glove)
558 Willie Upshaw .10 .04
559 Richie Zisk .10 .04
560 Pat Zachry .10 .04
561 Jay Johnstone .10 .04
562 Carlos Diaz RC .15 .06
563 John Tudor .20 .08
564 Frank Robinson MG .40 .16
565 Dave Edwards .10 .04
566 Paul Householder .10 .04
567 Ron Reed .10 .04
568 Mike Ramsey .10 .04
569 Kiko Garcia .10 .04
570 Tommy John .20 .08
571 Tony LaRussa MG .20 .08
572 Joel Youngblood .10 .04
573 Wayne Tolleson .10 .04
574 Keith Creel .10 .04
575 Billy Martin MG .40 .16
576 Jerry Dybzinski .10 .04
577 Rick Cerone .10 .04
578 Tony Perez .40 .16
579 Greg Brock .10 .04
580 Glenn Wilson .50 .20
581 Tim Stoddard .10 .04
582 Bob McClure .10 .04
583 Jim Dwyer .10 .04
584 Ed Romero .10 .04
585 Larry Herndon .10 .04
586 Wade Boggs RC 8.00 3.20
587 Jay Howell .10 .04
588 Dave Stewart .20 .08
589 Bert Blyleven .20 .08
590 Dick Howser MG .10 .04
591 Wayne Gross .10 .04
592 Terry Francona .20 .08
593 Don Werner .10 .04
594 Bill Stein .10 .04
595 Jesse Barfield .20 .08
596 Bob Molinaro .10 .04
597 Mike Vail .10 .04
598 Tony Gwynn RC 15.00 6.00
599 Gary Rajsich .10 .04
600 Jerry Ujdur .10 .04
601 Cliff Johnson .10 .04
602 Jerry White .10 .04
603 Bryan Clark .10 .04
604 Joe Ferguson .10 .04
605 Guy Sularz .10 .04
606A Ozzie Virgil .20 .08
(Green border
on photo)
606B Ozzie Virgil .20 .08
(Orange border
on photo)
607 Terry Harper .10 .04
608 Harvey Kuenn MG .10 .04
609 Jim Sundberg .20 .08
610 Willie Stargell .40 .16
611 Reggie Smith .20 .08
612 Rob Wilfong .10 .04
613 Joe Niekro .20 .08
Phil Niekro
614 Lee Elia MG .10 .04
615 Mickey Hatcher .10 .04
616 Jerry Hairston .10 .04
617 John Martin .10 .04
618 Wally Backman .10 .04
619 Storm Davis RC .50 .20
620 Alan Knicely .10 .04
621 John Stuper .10 .04
622 Matt Sinatro .10 .04
623 Geno Petralli .50 .20
624 Duane Walker .10 .04
625 Dick Williams MG .10 .04
626 Pat Corrales MG .10 .04
627 Vern Ruhle .10 .04
628 Joe Torre MG .40 .16
629 Anthony Johnson .10 .04
630 Steve Howe .10 .04
631 Gary Woods .10 .04
632 LaMarr Hoyt .10 .04
633 Steve Swisher .10 .04
634 Terry Leach .10 .04
635 Jeff Newman .10 .04
636 Brett Butler .20 .08
637 Gary Gray .10 .04
638 Lee Mazzilli .20 .08
639A Ron Jackson ERR 20.00 8.00
(A's in glove)
639B Ron Jackson COR .10 .04
(Angels in glove,
red border
on photo)
639C Ron Jackson COR .40 .16
(Angels in glove,
green border
on photo)
640 Juan Beniquez .10 .04
641 Dave Rucker .10 .04
642 Luis Pujols .10 .04
643 Rick Monday .20 .08
644 Hosken Powell .10 .04
645 The Chicken .40 .16
646 Dave Engle .10 .04
647 Dick Davis .10 .04
648 Frank Robinson .40 .16
Vida Blue
Joe Morgan
649 Al Chambers .10 .04
650 Jesus Vega .10 .04
651 Jeff Jones .10 .04
652 Marvis Foley .10 .04
653 Ty Cobb Puzzle Card .75 .30
654A Dick Perez/Diamond .40 .16
King Checklist 1-26
(Unnumbered) ERR
(Word "checklist"
omitted from back)
654B Dick Perez/Diamond .40 .16
King Checklist 1-26
(Unnumbered) COR
(Word "checklist"
is on back)
655 Checklist 27-130 .10 .04
(Unnumbered)
656 Checklist 131-234 .10 .04
(Unnumbered)
657 Checklist 235-338 .10 .04
(Unnumbered)
658 Checklist 339-442 .10 .04
(Unnumbered)
659 Checklist 443-544 .10 .04
(Unnumbered)
660 Checklist 545-653 .10 .04
(Unnumbered)

1984 Donruss

The 1984 Donruss set contains a total of 660 standard-size cards; however, only 658 are numbered. The first 26 cards in the set are again Diamond Kings (DK). A new feature, Rated Rookies (RR), was introduced with this set with Bill Madden's 20 selections comprising numbers 27 through 46. Two "Living Legend" cards designated A (featuring Gaylord Perry and Rollie Fingers) and B (featuring Johnny Bench and Carl Yastrzemski) were issued as bonus cards in wax packs, but were not issued in the factory sets sold to hobby dealers. The seven unnumbered checklist cards are arbitrarily assigned numbers 652 through 658 and are listed at the end of the list below. The attractive card front designs changed considerably from the previous two years. And this set has since grown in stature to be recognized as one of the finest produced in the 1980's. The backs contain statistics and are printed in green and black ink. The cards were distributed with a 3-piece puzzle panel of Duke Snider. There are no extra variation cards included in the complete set price below. The variation cards apparently resulted from a different printing for the factory sets as the Darling and Stenhouse no number variations as well as the Perez-Steele errors were corrected in the factory sets which were released later in the year. The Diamond King cards found in packs spelled Perez-Steele as Perez-Steel. Rookie Cards in this set include Joe Carter, Don Mattingly, Darryl Strawberry, and Andy Van Slyke. The Joe Carter card is almost never found well centered.

Nm-Mt Ex-Mt
COMPLETE SET (660) 120.00 47.50
COMP.FACT.SET (658) 150.00 60.00
COMP.SNIDER PUZZLE 5.00 2.00
1 Robin Yount DK COR 2.50 1.00
1A Robin Yount DK ERR 5.00 2.00
2 Dave Concepcion DK .75 .30
COR
2A Dave Concepcion DK .75 .30
ERR (Perez Steel)
3 Dwayne Murphy DK .25 .10
COR
3A Dwayne Murphy DK .25 .10
ERR (Perez Steel)
4 John Castino DK COR .25 .10
4A John Castino DK ERR .25 .10
(Perez Steel)
5 Leon Durham DK COR .75 .30
5A Leon Durham DK ERR .25 .10
(Perez Steel)
6 Rusty Staub DK COR .75 .30
6A Rusty Staub DK ERR .75 .30
(Perez Steel)
7 Jack Clark DK COR .75 .30
7A Jack Clark DK ERR .75 .30
(Perez Steel)
8 Dave Dravecky DK .25 .10
COR
8A Dave Dravecky DK .25 .10
ERR (Perez Steel)
9 Al Oliver DK COR .75 .30
9A Al Oliver DK ERR .75 .30
(Perez Steel)
10 Dave Righetti DK .75 .30
COR
10A Dave Righetti DK .75 .30
ERR (Perez Steel)
11 Hal McRae DK COR .75 .30
11A Hal McRae DK ERR .75 .30
(Perez Steel)
12 Ray Knight DK COR .75 .30
12A Ray Knight DK ERR .75 .30
(Perez Steel)
13 Bruce Sutter DK COR .75 .30
13A Bruce Sutter DK ERR .75 .30
(Perez Steel)
14 Bob Horner DK COR .75 .30
14A Bob Horner DK ERR .75 .30
(Perez Steel)
15 Lance Parrish DK .75 .30
COR
15A Lance Parrish DK .75 .30
ERR (Perez Steel)
16 Matt Young DK COR .75 .30
16A Matt Young DK ERR .75 .30

(Perez Steel)
17 Fred Lynn DK COR .75 .30
17A Fred Lynn DK ERR .75 .30
(Perez Steel)
(A's logo on back
18 Ron Kittle DK COR .25 .10
18A Ron Kittle DK ERR .25 .10
(Perez Steel)
19 Jim Clancy DK COR .25 .10
19A Jim Clancy DK ERR .25 .10
(Perez Steel)
20 Bill Madlock DK COR .75 .30
20A Bill Madlock DK ERR .75 .30
(Perez Steel)
21 Larry Parrish DK .25 .10
COR
21A Larry Parrish DK .25 .10
ERR (Perez Steel)
22 Eddie Murray DK COR 3.00 1.20
22A Eddie Murray DK ERR 3.00 1.20
23 Mike Schmidt DK COR 5.00 2.00
23A M.Schmidt DK ERR 5.00 2.00
24 Pedro Guerrero DK .75 .30
COR
24A Pedro Guerrero DK .75 .30
ERR (Perez Steel)
25 Andre Thornton DK .25 .10
COR
25A Andre Thornton DK .25 .10
ERR (Perez Steel)
26 Wade Boggs DK COR 3.00 1.20
26A Wade Boggs DK ERR 3.00 1.20
27 Joel Skinner RR RC .25 .10
28 Tommy Dunbar RR RC .25 .10
29A M.Stenhouse RC RR .25 .10
ERR No number on back
29B Mike Stenhouse RR 3.00 1.20
COR Numbered on back
30A R.Darling RC RR ERR 1.50 .60
No number on back
30B Ron Darling RR COR 3.00 1.20
(Numbered on back)
31 Dion James RR RC .25 .10
32 Tony Fernandez RR RC 1.50 .60
33 Angel Salazar RR RC .25 .10
34 K. McReynolds RR RC 1.50 .60
35 Dick Schofield RR RC .75 .30
36 Brad Komminsk RR RC .25 .10
37 Tim Teufel RR RC .75 .30
38 Doug Frobel RR RC .25 .10
39 Greg Gagne RR RC .75 .30
40 Mike Fuentes RR RC .25 .10
41 Joe Carter RR RC 5.00 2.00
42 Mike Brown RC RR .25 .10
(Angels OF)
43 Mike Jeffcoat RR RC .25 .10
44 Sid Fernandez RR RC 1.50 .60
45 Brian Dayett RR RC .25 .10
46 Chris Smith RR RC .25 .10
47 Eddie Murray 3.00 1.20
48 Robin Yount 5.00 2.00
49 Lance Parrish 1.50 .60
50 Jim Rice .75 .30
51 Dave Winfield .75 .30
52 Fernando Valenzuela .75 .30
53 George Brett 8.00 3.20
54 Rickey Henderson 5.00 2.00
55 Gary Carter .75 .30
56 Buddy Bell .75 .30
57 Reggie Jackson 1.50 .60
58 Harold Baines .75 .30
59 Ozzie Smith 5.00 2.00
60 Nolan Ryan UER 15.00 6.00
(Text on back refers to 1972 as
the year he struck out 383;
the year was 1973)
61 Pete Rose 10.00 4.00
62 Ron Oester .25 .10
63 Steve Garvey .75 .30
64 Jason Thompson .25 .10
65 Jack Clark .75 .30
66 Dale Murphy 1.50 .60
67 Leon Durham .25 .10
68 Darryl Strawberry RC 5.00 2.00
69 Richie Zisk .25 .10
70 Kent Hrbek .75 .30
71 Dave Stieb .75 .30
72 Ken Schrom .25 .10
73 George Bell .75 .30
74 John Moses .25 .10
75 Ed Lynch .25 .10
76 Chuck Rainey .25 .10
77 Biff Pocoroba .25 .10
78 Cecilio Guante .25 .10
79 Jim Barr .25 .10
80 Kurt Bevacqua .25 .10
81 Tom Foley .25 .10
82 Joe Lefebvre .25 .10
83 Andy Van Slyke RC 1.50 .60
84 Bob Lillis MG .25 .10
85 Ricky Adams .25 .10
86 Jerry Hairston .25 .10
87 Bob James .25 .10
88 Joe Altobelli MG .25 .10
89 Ed Romero .25 .10
90 John Grubb .25 .10
91 John Henry Johnson .25 .10
92 Juan Espino .25 .10
93 Candy Maldonado .25 .10
94 Andre Thornton .25 .10
95 Onix Concepcion .25 .10
96 Donnie Hill UER .25 .10
(Listed as P,
should be 2B)
97 Andre Dawson UER .75 .30
(Wrong middle name,
should be Nolan)
98 Frank Tanana .75 .30
99 Curtis Wilkerson .25 .10
100 Larry Gura .25 .10
101 Dwayne Murphy .25 .10
102 Tom Brennan .25 .10
103 Dave Righetti .75 .30
104 Steve Sax .25 .10
105 Dan Petry .75 .30
106 Cal Ripken 20.00 8.00
107 Paul Molitor UER 1.50 .60
('83 stats should
say .270 BA, 608 AB,
and 164 hits)
108 Fred Lynn .75 .30
109 Neil Allen .25 .10
110 Joe Niekro .25 .10
111 Steve Carlton 1.50 .60
112 Terry Kennedy .25 .10
113 Bill Madlock .75 .30
114 Chili Davis .75 .30
115 Jim Gantner .25 .10
116 Tom Seaver 3.00 1.20
117 Bill Buckner .75 .30
118 Bill Caudill .25 .10
119 Jim Clancy .25 .10
120 John Castino .25 .10
121 Dave Concepcion .75 .30
122 Greg Luzinski .75 .30
123 Mike Boddicker .25 .10
124 Pete Ladd .25 .10
125 Juan Berenguer .25 .10
126 John Montefusco .25 .10
127 Ed Jurak .25 .10
128 Tom Niedenfuer .25 .10
129 Bert Blyleven .75 .30
130 Bud Black .25 .10
131 Gorman Heimueller .25 .10
132 Dan Schatzeder .25 .10
133 Ron Jackson .25 .10
134 Tom Henke RC 1.50 .60
135 Kevin Hickey .25 .10
136 Mike Scott .75 .30
137 Bo Diaz .25 .10
138 Glenn Brummer .25 .10
139 Sid Monge .25 .10
140 Rich Gale .25 .10
141 Brett Butler .75 .30
142 Brian Harper RC .75 .30
143 John Rabb .25 .10
144 Gary Woods .25 .10
145 Pat Putnam .25 .10
146 Jim Acker .25 .10
147 Mickey Hatcher .25 .10
148 Todd Cruz .25 .10
149 Tom Tellmann .25 .10
150 John Wockenfuss .25 .10
151 Wade Boggs UER 8.00 3.20
1983 runs 10; should be 100
152 Don Baylor .75 .30
153 Bob Welch .75 .30
154 Alan Bannister .25 .10
155 Willie Aikens .25 .10
156 Jeff Burroughs .25 .10
157 Bryan Little .25 .10
158 Bob Boone .75 .30
159 Dave Hostetler .25 .10
160 Jerry Dybzinski .25 .10
161 Mike Madden .25 .10
162 Luis DeLeon .25 .10
163 Willie Hernandez .25 .10
164 Frank Pastore .25 .10
165 Rick Camp .25 .10
166 Lee Mazzilli .75 .30
167 Scot Thompson .25 .10
168 Bob Forsch .25 .10
169 Mike Flanagan .25 .10
170 Rick Manning .25 .10
171 Chet Lemon .75 .30
172 Jerry Remy .25 .10
173 Ron Guidry .75 .30
174 Pedro Guerrero .75 .30
175 Willie Wilson .75 .30
176 Carney Lansford .75 .30
177 Al Oliver .75 .30
178 Jim Sundberg .75 .30
179 Bobby Grich .75 .30
180 Rich Dotson .25 .10
181 Joaquin Andujar .75 .30
182 Jose Cruz .75 .30
183 Mike Schmidt 8.00 3.20
184 Gary Redus RC* .75 .30
185 Garry Templeton .75 .30
186 Tony Pena .25 .10
187 Greg Minton .25 .10
188 Phil Niekro .75 .30
189 Ferguson Jenkins .75 .30
190 Mookie Wilson .75 .30
191 Jim Beattie .25 .10
192 Gary Ward .25 .10
193 Jesse Barfield .75 .30
194 Pete Filson .25 .10
195 Roy Lee Jackson .25 .10
196 Rick Sweet .25 .10
197 Jesse Orosco .25 .10
198 Steve Lake .25 .10
199 Ken Dayley .25 .10
200 Manny Sarmiento .25 .10
201 Mark Davis .25 .10
202 Tim Flannery .25 .10
203 Bill Scherrer .25 .10
204 Al Holland .25 .10
205 Dave Von Ohlen .25 .10
206 Mike LaCoss .25 .10
207 Juan Beniquez .25 .10
208 Juan Agosto .25 .10
209 Bobby Ramos .25 .10
210 Al Bumbry .25 .10
211 Mark Brouhard .25 .10
212 Howard Bailey .25 .10
213 Bruce Hurst .25 .10
214 Bob Shirley .25 .10
215 Pat Zachry .25 .10
216 Julio Franco 1.50 .60
217 Mike Armstrong .25 .10
218 Dave Beard .25 .10
219 Steve Rogers .75 .30
220 John Butcher .25 .10
221 Mike Smithson .25 .10
222 Frank White .75 .30
223 Mike Heath .25 .10
224 Chris Bando .25 .10
225 Roy Smalley .25 .10
226 Dusty Baker .75 .30
227 Lou Whitaker .75 .30
228 John Lowenstein .25 .10
229 Ben Oglivie .75 .30
230 Doug DeCinces .25 .10
231 Lonnie Smith .25 .10
232 Ray Knight .75 .30
233 Gary Matthews .75 .30
234 Juan Bonilla .25 .10
235 Rod Scurry .25 .10
236 Atlee Hammaker .25 .10
237 Mike Caldwell .25 .10
238 Keith Hernandez .75 .30
239 Larry Bowa .75 .30
240 Tony Bernazard .25 .10
241 Damaso Garcia .25 .10
242 Tom Brunansky .25 .10
243 Dan Driessen .25 .10
244 Ron Kittle .25 .10
245 Tim Stoddard .25 .10
246 Bob L. Gibson RC .25 .10
(Brewers Pitcher)
247 Marty Castillo .25 .10
248 D.Mattingly RC UER 40.00 16.00
traiing on back
249 Jeff Newman .25 .10
250 Alejandro Pena RC* 1.50 .60
251 Toby Harrah .75 .30
252 Cesar Geronimo .25 .10
253 Tom Underwood .25 .10
254 Doug Flynn .25 .10
255 Andy Hassler .25 .10
256 Odell Jones .25 .10
257 Rudy Law .25 .10
258 Harry Spilman .25 .10
259 Marty Bystrom .25 .10
260 Dave Rucker .25 .10
261 Ruppert Jones .25 .10
262 Jeff R. Jones .25 .10
(Reds OF)
263 Gerald Perry .75 .30
264 Gene Tenace .75 .30
265 Brad Wellman .25 .10
266 Dickie Noles .25 .10
267 Jamie Allen .25 .10
268 Jim Gott .25 .10
269 Ron Davis .25 .10
270 Benny Ayala .25 .10
271 Ned Yost .25 .10
272 Dave Rozema .25 .10
273 Dave Stapleton .25 .10
274 Lou Piniella .75 .30
275 Jose Morales .25 .10
276 Broderick Perkins .25 .10
277 Butch Davis RC .25 .10
278 Tony Phillips RC 1.50 .60
279 Jeff Reardon .75 .30
280 Ken Forsch .25 .10
281 Pete O'Brien RC* .75 .30
282 Tom Paciorek .25 .10
283 Frank LaCorte .25 .10
284 Tim Lollar .25 .10
285 Greg Gross .25 .10
286 Alex Trevino .25 .10
287 Gene Garber .25 .10
288 Dave Parker .75 .30
289 Lee Smith .75 .30
290 Dave LaPoint .25 .10
291 John Shelby .25 .10
292 Charlie Moore .25 .10
293 Alan Trammell .75 .30
294 Tony Armas .75 .30
295 Shane Rawley .25 .10
296 Greg Brock .25 .10
297 Hal McRae .75 .30
298 Mike Davis .25 .10
299 Tim Raines .75 .30
300 Bucky Dent .75 .30
301 Tommy John .75 .30
302 Carlton Fisk 1.50 .60
303 Darrell Porter .25 .10
304 Dickie Thon .25 .10
305 Garry Maddox .25 .10
306 Cesar Cedeno .75 .30
307 Gary Lucas .25 .10
308 Johnny Ray .25 .10
309 Andy McGaffigan .25 .10
310 Claudell Washington .25 .10
311 Ryne Sandberg 12.00 4.80
312 George Foster .75 .30
313 Spike Owen RC .75 .30
314 Gary Gaetti 1.50 .60
315 Willie Upshaw .25 .10
316 Al Williams .25 .10
317 Jorge Orta .25 .10
318 Orlando Mercado .25 .10
319 Junior Ortiz .25 .10
320 Mike Proly .25 .10
321 Randy Johnson UER .25 .10
('72-'82 stats are
from Twins' Randy John-
son, '83 stats are from
Braves' Randy Johnson)
322 Jim Morrison .25 .10
323 Max Venable .25 .10
324 Tony Gwynn 12.00 4.80
325 Duane Walker .25 .10
326 Ozzie Virgil .25 .10
327 Jeff Lahti .25 .10
328 Bill Dawley .25 .10
329 Rob Wilfong .25 .10
330 Marc Hill .25 .10
331 Ray Burris .25 .10
332 Allan Ramirez .25 .10
333 Chuck Porter .25 .10
334 Wayne Krenchicki .25 .10
335 Gary Allenson .25 .10
336 Bobby Meacham .25 .10
337 Joe Beckwith .25 .10
338 Rick Sutcliffe .75 .30
339 Mark Huismann .25 .10
340 Tim Conroy .25 .10
341 Scott Sanderson .25 .10
342 Larry Biittner .25 .10
343 Dave Stewart .75 .30
344 Darryl Motley .25 .10
345 Chris Codiroli .25 .10
346 Rich Behenna .25 .10
347 Andre Robertson .25 .10
348 Mike Marshall .25 .10
349 Larry Herndon .75 .30
350 Rich Dauer .25 .10
351 Cecil Cooper .75 .30
352 Rod Carew 1.50 .60
353 Willie McGee .75 .30
354 Phil Garner .75 .30
355 Joe Morgan .75 .30
356 Luis Salazar .25 .10
357 John Candelaria .25 .10
358 Bill Laskey .25 .10
359 Bob McClure .25 .10
360 Dave Kingman .75 .30
361 Ron Cey .75 .30
362 Matt Young RC .75 .30
363 Lloyd Moseby .25 .10
364 Frank Viola 1.50 .60
365 Eddie Milner .25 .10
366 Floyd Bannister .25 .10
367 Dan Ford .25 .10
368 Moose Haas .25 .10
369 Doug Bair .25 .10
370 Ray Fontenot .25 .10
371 Luis Aponte .25 .10
372 Jack Fimple .25 .10
373 Neal Heaton .25 .10
374 Greg Pryor .25 .10
375 Wayne Gross .25 .10
376 Charlie Lea .25 .10
377 Steve Lubratich .25 .10
378 Jon Matlack .25 .10
379 Julio Cruz .25 .10
380 John Mizerock .25 .10
381 Kevin Gross RC .75 .30
382 Mike Ramsey .25 .10
383 Doug Gwosdz .25 .10
384 Kelly Paris .25 .10
385 Pete Falcone .25 .10
386 Milt May .25 .10
387 Fred Breining .25 .10
388 Craig Lefferts RC .25 .10
389 Steve Henderson .25 .10
390 Randy Moffitt .25 .10
391 Ron Washington .25 .10
392 Gary Roenicke .25 .10
393 Tom Candiotti RC 1.50 .60
394 Larry Pashnick .25 .10
395 Dwight Evans .75 .30
396 Rich Gossage .75 .30
397 Derrel Thomas .25 .10
398 Juan Eichelberger .25 .10
399 Leon Roberts .25 .10
400 Dave Lopes .75 .30
401 Bill Gullickson .25 .10
402 Geoff Zahn .25 .10
403 Billy Sample .25 .10
404 Mike Squires .25 .10
405 Craig Reynolds .25 .10
406 Eric Show .25 .10
407 John Denny .25 .10
408 Dann Bilardello .25 .10
409 Bruce Benedict .25 .10
410 Kent Tekulve .25 .10
411 Mel Hall .75 .30
412 John Stuper .25 .10
413 Rick Dempsey .25 .10
414 Don Sutton .75 .30
415 Jack Morris .75 .30
416 John Tudor .25 .10
417 Willie Randolph .75 .30
418 Jerry Reuss .25 .10
419 Don Slaught .75 .30
420 Steve McCatty .25 .10
421 Tim Wallach .25 .10
422 Larry Parrish .25 .10
423 Brian Downing .75 .30
424 Britt Burns .25 .10
425 David Green .25 .10
426 Jerry Mumphrey .25 .10
427 Ivan DeJesus .25 .10
428 Mario Soto .75 .30
429 Gene Richards .25 .10
430 Dale Berra .25 .10
431 Darrell Evans .75 .30
432 Glenn Hubbard .25 .10
433 Jody Davis .25 .10
434 Danny Heep .25 .10
435 Ed Nunez RC .25 .10
436 Bobby Castillo .25 .10
437 Ernie Whitt .25 .10
438 Scott Ullger .25 .10
439 Doyle Alexander .25 .10
440 Domingo Ramos .25 .10
441 Craig Swan .25 .10
442 Warren Brusstar .25 .10
443 Len Barker .25 .10
444 Mike Easler .25 .10
445 Renie Martin .25 .10
446 D.Rasmussen RC .75 .30
447 Ted Power .25 .10
448 Charles Hudson .25 .10
449 Danny Cox RC .75 .30
450 Kevin Bass .25 .10
451 Daryl Sconiers .25 .10
452 Scott Fletcher .25 .10
453 Bryn Smith .25 .10
454 Jim Dwyer .25 .10
455 Rob Picciolo .25 .10
456 Enos Cabell .25 .10
457 Dennis Boyd .75 .30
458 Butch Wynegar .25 .10
459 Burt Hooton .25 .10
460 Ron Hassey .25 .10
461 Danny Jackson RC .75 .30
462 Bob Kearney .25 .10
463 Terry Francona .75 .30
464 Wayne Tolleson .25 .10
465 Mickey Rivers .25 .10
466 John Wathan .25 .10
467 Bill Almon .25 .10
468 George Vukovich .25 .10
469 Steve Kemp .25 .10
470 Ken Landreaux .25 .10
471 Milt Wilcox .25 .10
472 Tippy Martinez .25 .10
473 Ted Simmons .75 .30
474 Tim Foli .25 .10
475 George Hendrick .75 .30
476 Terry Puhl .25 .10
477 Von Hayes .25 .10
478 Bobby Brown .25 .10
479 Lee Lacy .25 .10
480 Joel Youngblood .25 .10
481 Jim Slaton .25 .10
482 Mike Fitzgerald .25 .10
483 Keith Moreland .25 .10
484 Ron Roenicke .25 .10
485 Luis Leal .25 .10
486 Bryan Oelkers .25 .10
487 Bruce Berenyi .25 .10
488 LaMarr Hoyt .25 .10
489 Joe Nolan .25 .10
490 Marshall Edwards .25 .10
491 Mike Laga .75 .30
492 Rick Cerone .25 .10
493 Rick Miller UER .25 .10
(Listed as Mike
on card front)
494 Rick Honeycutt .25 .10
495 Mike Hargrove .25 .10
496 Joe Simpson .25 .10
497 Keith Atherton .25 .10
498 Chris Welsh .25 .10
499 Bruce Kison .25 .10
500 Bobby Johnson .25 .10
501 Jerry Koosman .75 .30
502 Frank DiPino .25 .10
503 Tony Perez 1.50 .60
504 Ken Oberkfell .25 .10
505 Mark Thurmond .25 .10
506 Joe Price .25 .10
507 Pascual Perez .25 .10
508 Marvell Wynne .75 .30
509 Mike Krukow .25 .10
510 Dick Ruthven .25 .10
511 Al Cowens .25 .10
512 Cliff Johnson .25 .10
513 Randy Bush .25 .10
514 Sammy Stewart .25 .10
515 Bill Schroeder .25 .10
516 Aurelio Lopez .75 .30
517 Mike C. Brown .25 .10
518 Graig Nettles .75 .30
519 Dave Sax .25 .10
520 Jerry Willard .25 .10
521 Paul Splittorff .25 .10
522 Tom Burgmeier .25 .10
523 Chris Speier .25 .10
524 Bobby Clark .25 .10
525 George Wright .25 .10
526 Dennis Lamp .25 .10
527 Tony Scott .25 .10
528 Ed Whitson .25 .10
529 Ron Reed .25 .10
530 Charlie Puleo .25 .10
531 Jerry Royster .25 .10
532 Don Robinson .25 .10
533 Steve Trout .25 .10
534 Bruce Sutter .75 .30
535 Bob Horner .75 .30
536 Pat Tabler .25 .10
537 Chris Chambliss .75 .30
538 Bob Ojeda .25 .10
539 Alan Ashby .25 .10
540 Jay Johnstone .25 .10
541 Bob Dernier .25 .10
542 Brook Jacoby .75 .30
543 U.L. Washington .25 .10
544 Danny Darwin .25 .10
545 Kiko Garcia .25 .10
546 Vance Law UER .25 .10
(Listed as P
on card front)
547 Tug McGraw .75 .30
548 Dave Smith .25 .10
549 Len Matuszek .25 .10
550 Tom Hume .25 .10
551 Dave Dravecky .25 .10
552 Rick Rhoden .25 .10
553 Duane Kuiper .25 .10
554 Rusty Staub .75 .30
555 Bill Campbell .25 .10
556 Mike Torrez .25 .10
557 Dave Henderson .75 .30
558 Len Whitehouse .25 .10
559 Barry Bonnell .25 .10
560 Rick Lysander .25 .10
561 Garth Iorg .25 .10
562 Bryan Clark .25 .10
563 Brian Giles .25 .10
564 Vern Ruhle .25 .10
565 Steve Bedrosian .25 .10
566 Larry McWilliams .25 .10
567 Jeff Leonard UER .25 .10
(Listed as P
on card front)
568 Alan Wiggins .25 .10
569 Jeff Russell RC .75 .30
570 Salome Barojas .25 .10
571 Dane Iorg .25 .10
572 Bob Knepper .25 .10
573 Gary Lavelle .25 .10
574 Gorman Thomas .75 .30
575 Manny Trillo .25 .10
576 Jim Palmer .75 .30
577 Dale Murray .25 .10
578 Tom Brookens .75 .30
579 Rich Gedman .25 .10
580 Bill Doran RC* .75 .30
581 Steve Yeager .75 .30
582 Dan Spillner .25 .10
583 Dan Quisenberry .25 .10
584 Rance Mulliniks .25 .10
585 Storm Davis .25 .10
586 Dave Schmidt .25 .10
587 Bill Russell .75 .30
588 Pat Sheridan .25 .10
589 Rafael Ramirez .25 .10
UER (A's on front)
590 Bud Anderson .25 .10
591 George Frazier .25 .10
592 Lee Tunnell .25 .10
593 Kirk Gibson .75 .30
594 Scott McGregor .25 .10
595 Bob Bailor .25 .10
596 Tom Herr .75 .30
597 Luis Sanchez .25 .10
598 Dave Engle .25 .10
599 Craig McMurtry .25 .10
600 Carlos Diaz .25 .10
601 Tom O'Malley .25 .10
602 Nick Esasky .25 .10
603 Ron Hodges .25 .10
604 Ed VandeBerg .25 .10
605 Alfredo Griffin .25 .10
606 Glenn Hoffman .25 .10
607 Hubie Brooks .25 .10
608 Richard Barnes UER .25 .10
(Photo actually
Neal Heaton)
609 Greg Walker .75 .30
610 Ken Singleton .75 .30

1 Mark Clear .25 .10
2 Buck Martinez .25 .10
3 Ken Griffey .75 .30
4 Reid Nichols .25 .10
5 Doug Sisk .25 .10
6 Bob Brenly .25 .10
7 Joey McLaughlin .25 .10
8 Glenn Wilson .75 .30
9 Bob Stoddard .25 .10
20 Lenn Sakata UER .25 .10
(Listed as Len
on card front)
21 Mike Young RC .25 .10
22 John Stefero .25 .10
23 Carmelo Martinez .25 .10
24 Dave Bergman .25 .10
25 Runnin' Reds UER 3.00 1.20
(Sic, Redbirds)
David Green
Willie McGee
Lonnie Smith
Ozzie Smith
26 Rudy May .25 .10
27 Matt Keough .25 .10
28 Jose DeLeon RC .75 .30
29 Jim Essian .25 .10
0 Darnell Coles RC .75 .30
1 Mike Warren .25 .10
2 Del Crandall MG .25 .10
3 Dennis Martinez .75 .30
4 Mike Moore .25 .10
5 Lary Sorensen .25 .10
6 Ricky Nelson .25 .10
7 Omar Moreno .25 .10
8 Charlie Hough .75 .30
9 Dennis Eckersley 1.50 .60
0 Walt Terrell .25 .10
1 Denny Walling .25 .10
2 Dave Anderson RC .25 .10
3 Jose Oquendo RC .75 .30
4 Bob Stanley .25 .10
5 Dave Geisel .25 .10
6 Scott Garrelts .25 .10
7 Gary Pettis .25 .10
8 Duke Snider 1.50 .60
Puzzle Card
9 Johnnie LeMaster .25 .10
0 Dave Collins .25 .10
1 The Chicken 1.50 .60
2 DK Checklist 1-26 .75 .30
(Unnumbered)
3 Checklist 27-130 .25 .10
(Unnumbered)
4 Checklist 131-234 .25 .10
(Unnumbered)
5 Checklist 235-338 .25 .10
(Unnumbered)
6 Checklist 339-442 .25 .10
(Unnumbered)
7 Checklist 443-546 .25 .10
(Unnumbered)
8 Checklist 547-651 .25 .10
(Unnumbered)
.iving Legends A 2.50 1.00
Gaylord Perry
Rollie Fingers
.iving Legends B 5.00 2.00
Carl Yastrzemski
Johnny Bench

1985 Donruss

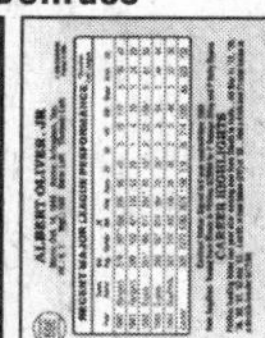

e 1985 Donruss set consists of 660 standard-e cards. Wax packs contained 15 cards and a u Gehrig puzzle panel. The fronts feature full or photos framed by jet black borders (mak- the cards condition sensitive). The first 26 ds of the set feature Diamond Kings (DK), for fourth year in a row; the artwork on the mond Kings was again produced by the ez-Steele Galleries. Cards 27-46 feature ed Rookies (RR). The unnumbered checklist ds are arbitrarily numbered below as num-s 654 through 660. Rookie Cards in this set ude Roger Clemens, Eric Davis, Shawon nston, Dwight Gooden, Orel Hershiser, Jimmy , Terry Pendleton, Kirby Puckett and Bret berhagen.

	Nm-Mt	Ex-Mt
MPLETE SET (660)	60.00	24.00
MP.FACT.SET (660)	80.00	32.00
MP.GEHRIG PUZZLE	4.00	1.60
yne Sandberg DK	1.25	.50
oug DeCinces DK	.15	.06
ichard Dotson DK	.15	.06
ert Blyleven DK	.40	.16
ou Whitaker DK	.40	.16
an Quisenberry DK	.15	.06
on Mattingly DK	2.50	1.00
arney Lansford DK	.40	.16
rank Tanana DK	.40	.16
Willie Upshaw DK	.15	.06
C.Washington DK	.15	.06
Mike Marshall DK	.15	.06
Joaquin Andujar DK	.40	.16
Cal Ripken DK	2.50	1.00
Jim Rice DK	.40	.16
Don Sutton DK	.40	.16
Frank Viola DK	.40	.16
Alvin Davis DK	.40	.16
Mario Soto DK	.40	.16
Jose Cruz DK	.40	.16
Charlie Lea DK	.15	.06
Jesse Orosco DK	.15	.06
Juan Samuel DK	.15	.06
Tony Pena DK	.15	.06
Tony Gwynn DK	1.25	.50
Bob Brenly DK	.15	.06

27 Danny Tartabull RR RC 1.00 .40
28 Mike Bielecki RC .25 .10
29 Steve Lyons RR RC .50 .20
30 Jeff Reed RC .25 .10
31 Tony Brewer RC .25 .10
32 John Morris RC .25 .10
33 Daryl Boston RR RC .25 .10
34 Al Pulido RR .25 .10
35 Steve Kiefer RC .25 .10
36 Larry Sheets RC .25 .10
37 Scott Bradley RC .25 .10
38 Calvin Schiraldi RC .50 .20
39 S.Dunston RR RC 1.00 .40
40 Charlie Mitchell RC .25 .10
41 Billy Hatcher RR RC .50 .20
42 Russ Stephans RC .25 .10
43 Alejandro Sanchez RC .25 .10
44 Steve Jeltz RC .25 .10
45 Jim Traber RC .25 .10
46 Doug Loman RC .25 .10
47 Eddie Murray 1.25 .50
48 Robin Yount 2.00 .80
49 Lance Parrish .40 .16
50 Jim Rice .40 .16
51 Dave Winfield .40 .16
52 Fernando Valenzuela .40 .16
53 George Brett 3.00 1.20
54 Dave Kingman .40 .16
55 Gary Carter .40 .16
56 Buddy Bell .40 .16
57 Reggie Jackson .75 .30
58 Harold Baines .40 .16
59 Ozzie Smith 2.00 .80
60 Nolan Ryan UER 6.00 2.40
(Set strikeout record
in 1973, not 1972)
61 Mike Schmidt 3.00 1.20
62 Dave Parker .40 .16
63 Tony Gwynn 2.50 1.00
64 Tony Pena .15 .06
65 Jack Clark .40 .16
66 Dale Murphy .75 .30
67 Ryne Sandberg 2.50 1.00
68 Keith Hernandez .40 .16
69 Alvin Davis RC* .50 .20
70 Kent Hrbek .40 .16
71 Willie Upshaw .15 .06
72 Dave Engle .15 .06
73 Alfredo Griffin .15 .06
74A Jack Perconte .15 .06
(Career Highlights
takes four lines)
74B Jack Perconte .15 .06
(Career Highlights
takes three lines)
75 Jesse Orosco .15 .06
76 Jody Davis .15 .06
77 Bob Horner .40 .16
78 Larry McWilliams .15 .06
79 Joel Youngblood .15 .06
80 Alan Wiggins .15 .06
81 Ron Oester .15 .06
82 Ozzie Virgil .15 .06
83 Ricky Horton .15 .06
84 Bill Doran .15 .06
85 Rod Carew .75 .30
86 LaMarr Hoyt .15 .06
87 Tim Wallach .15 .06
88 Mike Flanagan .15 .06
89 Jim Sundberg .40 .16
90 Chet Lemon .40 .16
91 Bob Stanley .15 .06
92 Willie Randolph .40 .16
93 Bill Russell .40 .16
94 Julio Franco .40 .16
95 Dan Quisenberry .15 .06
96 Bill Caudill .15 .06
97 Bill Gullickson .15 .06
98 Danny Darwin .15 .06
99 Curtis Wilkerson .15 .06
100 Bud Black .15 .06
101 Tony Phillips .15 .06
102 Tony Bernazard .15 .06
103 Jay Howell .15 .06
104 Burt Hooton .15 .06
105 Milt Wilcox .15 .06
106 Rich Dauer .15 .06
107 Don Sutton .40 .16
108 Mike Witt .15 .06
109 Bruce Sutter .40 .16
110 Enos Cabell .15 .06
111 John Denny .15 .06
112 Dave Dravecky .15 .06
113 Marvell Wynne .15 .06
114 Johnnie LeMaster .15 .06
115 Chuck Porter .15 .06
116 John Gibbons .15 .06
117 Keith Moreland .15 .06
118 Darnell Coles .15 .06
119 Dennis Lamp .15 .06
120 Ron Davis .15 .06
121 Nick Esasky .15 .06
122 Vance Law .15 .06
123 Gary Roenicke .15 .06
124 Bill Schroeder .15 .06
125 Dave Rozema .15 .06
126 Bobby Meacham .15 .06
127 Marty Barrett .15 .06
128 R.J. Reynolds .15 .06
129 Ernie Camacho UER .15 .06
(Photo actually
Rich Thompson)
130 Jorge Orta .15 .06
131 Lary Sorensen .15 .06
132 Terry Francona .40 .16
133 Fred Lynn .40 .16
134 Bob Jones .15 .06
135 Jerry Hairston .15 .06
136 Kevin Bass .15 .06
137 Garry Maddox .15 .06
138 Dave LaPoint .15 .06
139 Kevin McReynolds .40 .16
140 Wayne Krenchicki .15 .06
141 Rafael Ramirez .15 .06
142 Rod Scurry .15 .06
143 Greg Minton .15 .06
144 Tim Stoddard .15 .06
145 Steve Henderson .15 .06
146 George Bell .40 .16
147 Dave Meier .15 .06
148 Sammy Stewart .15 .06
149 Mark Brouhard .15 .06
150 Larry Herndon .15 .06
151 Oil Can Boyd .15 .06
152 Brian Dayett .15 .06
153 Tom Niedenfuer .15 .06
154 Brook Jacoby .15 .06
155 Onix Concepcion .15 .06
156 Tim Conroy .15 .06
157 Joe Hesketh .15 .06
158 Brian Downing .40 .16
159 Tommy Dunbar .15 .06
160 Marc Hill .15 .06
161 Phil Garner .40 .16
162 Jerry Davis .15 .06
163 Bill Campbell .15 .06
164 John Franco RC 1.00 .40
165 Len Barker .15 .06
166 Benny Distefano .15 .06
167 George Frazier .15 .06
168 Tito Landrum .15 .06
169 Cal Ripken 5.00 2.00
170 Cecil Cooper .40 .16
171 Alan Trammell .40 .16
172 Wade Boggs 1.25 .50
173 Don Baylor .40 .16
174 Pedro Guerrero .40 .16
175 Frank White .40 .16
176 Rickey Henderson 1.50 .60
177 Charlie Lea .15 .06
178 Pete O'Brien .15 .06
179 Doug DeCinces .15 .06
180 Ron Kittle .15 .06
181 George Hendrick .40 .16
182 Joe Niekro .15 .06
183 Juan Samuel .15 .06
184 Mario Soto .40 .16
185 Rich Gossage .40 .16
186 Johnny Ray .15 .06
187 Bob Brenly .15 .06
188 Craig McMurtry .15 .06
189 Leon Durham .15 .06
190 Dwight Gooden RC 2.00 .80
191 Barry Bonnell .15 .06
192 Tim Teufel .15 .06
193 Dave Stieb .40 .16
194 Mickey Hatcher .15 .06
195 Jesse Barfield .40 .16
196 Al Cowens .15 .06
197 Hubie Brooks .15 .06
198 Steve Trout .15 .06
199 Glenn Hubbard .15 .06
200 Bill Madlock .40 .16
201 Jeff D. Robinson .15 .06
202 Eric Show .15 .06
203 Dave Concepcion .40 .16
204 Ivan DeJesus .15 .06
205 Neil Allen .15 .06
206 Jerry Mumphrey .15 .06
207 Mike C. Brown .15 .06
208 Carlton Fisk .75 .30
209 Bryn Smith .15 .06
210 Tippy Martinez .15 .06
211 Dion James .15 .06
212 Willie Hernandez .15 .06
213 Mike Easler .15 .06
214 Ron Guidry .40 .16
215 Rick Honeycutt .15 .06
216 Brett Butler .40 .16
217 Larry Gura .15 .06
218 Ray Burris .15 .06
219 Steve Rogers .40 .16
220 Frank Tanana UER .40 .16
(Bats Left listed
twice on card back)
221 Ned Yost .15 .06
222 B.Saberhagen RC UER 1.50 .60
18 career IP on back
223 Mike Davis .15 .06
224 Bert Blyleven .40 .16
225 Steve Kemp .15 .06
226 Jerry Reuss .15 .06
227 Darrell Evans UER .40 .16
(80 homers in 1980)
228 Wayne Gross .15 .06
229 Jim Gantner .40 .16
230 Bob Boone .40 .16
231 Lonnie Smith .15 .06
232 Frank DiPino .15 .06
233 Jerry Koosman .40 .16
234 Graig Nettles .40 .16
235 John Tudor .40 .16
236 John Rabb .15 .06
237 Rick Manning .15 .06
238 Mike Fitzgerald .15 .06
239 Gary Matthews .40 .16
240 Jim Presley .50 .20
241 Dave Collins .15 .06
242 Gary Gaetti .40 .16
243 Dann Bilardello .15 .06
244 Rudy Law .15 .06
245 John Lowenstein .15 .06
246 Tom Tellmann .15 .06
247 Howard Johnson .40 .16
248 Ray Fontenot .15 .06
249 Tony Armas .40 .16
250 Candy Maldonado .15 .06
251 Mike Jeffcoat .15 .06
252 Dane Iorg .15 .06
253 Bruce Bochte .15 .06
254 Pete Rose Expos 4.00 1.60
255 Don Aase .15 .06
256 George Wright .15 .06
257 Britt Burns .15 .06
258 Mike Scott .40 .16
259 Len Matuszek .15 .06
260 Dave Rucker .15 .06
261 Craig Lefferts .15 .06
262 Jay Tibbs .15 .06
263 Bruce Benedict .15 .06
264 Don Robinson .15 .06
265 Gary Lavelle .15 .06
266 Scott Sanderson .15 .06
267 Matt Young .15 .06
268 Ernie Whitt .15 .06
269 Houston Jimenez .15 .06
270 Ken Dixon .15 .06
271 Pete Ladd .15 .06
272 Juan Berenguer .15 .06
273 Roger Clemens RC 40.00 16.00
274 Rick Cerone .15 .06
275 Dave Anderson .15 .06
276 George Vukovich .15 .06
277 Greg Pryor .15 .06
278 Mike Warren .15 .06
279 Bob James .15 .06
280 Bobby Grich .40 .16
281 Mike Mason RC .25 .10
282 Ron Reed .15 .06
283 Alan Ashby .15 .06
284 Mark Thurmond .15 .06
285 Joe Lefebvre .15 .06
286 Ted Power .15 .06
287 Chris Chambliss .40 .16
288 Lee Tunnell .15 .06
289 Rich Bordi .15 .06
290 Glenn Brummer .15 .06
291 Mike Boddicker .15 .06
292 Rollie Fingers .40 .16
293 Lou Whitaker .40 .16
294 Dwight Evans .40 .16
295 Don Mattingly 5.00 2.00
296 Mike Marshall .15 .06
297 Willie Wilson .40 .16
298 Mike Heath .15 .06
299 Tim Raines .40 .16
300 Larry Parrish .15 .06
301 Geoff Zahn .15 .06
302 Rich Dotson .15 .06
303 David Green .15 .06
304 Jose Cruz .40 .16
305 Steve Carlton .40 .16
306 Gary Redus .15 .06
307 Steve Garvey .40 .16
308 Jose DeLeon .15 .06
309 Randy Lerch .15 .06
310 Claudell Washington .15 .06
311 Lee Smith .40 .16
312 Darryl Strawberry 1.25 .50
313 Jim Beattie .15 .06
314 John Butcher .15 .06
315 Damaso Garcia .15 .06
316 Mike Smithson .15 .06
317 Luis Leal .15 .06
318 Ken Phelps .15 .06
319 Wally Backman .15 .06
320 Ron Cey .40 .16
321 Brad Komminsk .15 .06
322 Jason Thompson .15 .06
323 Frank Williams .15 .06
324 Tim Lollar .15 .06
325 Eric Davis RC 1.50 .60
326 Von Hayes .15 .06
327 Andy Van Slyke .40 .16
328 Craig Reynolds .15 .06
329 Dick Schofield .15 .06
330 Scott Fletcher .15 .06
331 Jeff Reardon .40 .16
332 Rick Dempsey .15 .06
333 Ben Oglivie .40 .16
334 Dan Petry .15 .06
335 Jackie Gutierrez .15 .06
336 Dave Righetti .40 .16
337 Alejandro Pena .15 .06
338 Mel Hall .15 .06
339 Pat Sheridan .15 .06
340 Keith Atherton .15 .06
341 David Palmer .15 .06
342 Gary Ward .15 .06
343 Dave Stewart .40 .16
344 Mark Gubicza RC* .50 .20
345 Carney Lansford .40 .16
346 Jerry Willard .15 .06
347 Ken Griffey .40 .16
348 Franklin Stubbs .15 .06
349 Aurelio Lopez .15 .06
350 Al Bumbry .15 .06
351 Charlie Moore .15 .06
352 Luis Sanchez .15 .06
353 Darrell Porter .15 .06
354 Bill Dawley .15 .06
355 Charles Hudson .15 .06
356 Garry Templeton .40 .16
357 Cecilio Guante .15 .06
358 Jeff Leonard .15 .06
359 Paul Molitor .75 .30
360 Ron Gardenhire .15 .06
361 Larry Bowa .40 .16
362 Bob Kearney .15 .06
363 Garth Iorg .15 .06
364 Tom Brunansky .15 .06
365 Brad Gulden .15 .06
366 Greg Walker .15 .06
367 Mike Young .15 .06
368 Rick Waits .15 .06
369 Doug Bair .15 .06
370 Bob Shirley .15 .06
371 Bob Ojeda .15 .06
372 Bob Welch .40 .16
373 Neal Heaton .15 .06
374 Danny Jackson UER .15 .06
(Photo actually
Frank Wills)
375 Donnie Hill .15 .06
376 Mike Stenhouse .15 .06
377 Bruce Kison .15 .06
378 Wayne Tolleson .15 .06
379 Floyd Bannister .15 .06
380 Vern Ruhle .15 .06
381 Tim Corcoran .15 .06
382 Kurt Kepshire .15 .06
383 Bobby Brown .15 .06
384 Dave Van Gorder .15 .06
385 Rick Mahler .15 .06
386 Lee Mazzilli .40 .16
387 Bill Laskey .15 .06
388 Thad Bosley .15 .06
389 Al Chambers .15 .06
390 Tony Fernandez .40 .16
391 Ron Washington .15 .06
392 Bill Swaggerty .15 .06
393 Bob L. Gibson .15 .06
394 Marty Castillo .15 .06
395 Steve Crawford .15 .06
396 Clay Christiansen .15 .06
397 Bob Bailor .15 .06
398 Mike Hargrove .15 .06
399 Charlie Leibrandt .15 .06
400 Tom Burgmeier .15 .06
401 Razor Shines .15 .06
402 Rob Wilfong .15 .06
403 Tom Henke .40 .16
404 Al Jones .15 .06
405 Mike LaCoss .15 .06
406 Luis DeLeon .15 .06
407 Greg Gross .15 .06
408 Tom Hume .15 .06
409 Rick Camp .15 .06
410 Milt May .15 .06
411 Henry Cotto RC .25 .10
412 David Von Ohlen .15 .06
413 Scott McGregor .15 .06
414 Ted Simmons .40 .16
415 Jack Morris .40 .16
416 Bill Buckner .40 .16
417 Butch Wynegar .15 .06
418 Steve Sax .15 .06
419 Steve Balboni .15 .06
420 Dwayne Murphy .15 .06
421 Andre Dawson .40 .16
422 Charlie Hough .40 .16
423 Tommy John .40 .16
424A Tom Seaver ERR .75 .30
(Photo actually
Floyd Bannister)
424B Tom Seaver COR 10.00 4.00
425 Tom Herr .15 .06
426 Terry Puhl .15 .06
427 Al Holland .15 .06
428 Eddie Milner .15 .06
429 Terry Kennedy .15 .06
430 John Candelaria .15 .06
431 Manny Trillo .15 .06
432 Ken Oberkfell .15 .06
433 Rick Sutcliffe .40 .16
434 Ron Darling .40 .16
435 Spike Owen .15 .06
436 Frank Viola .40 .16
437 Lloyd Moseby .15 .06
438 Kirby Puckett RC 10.00 4.00
439 Jim Clancy .15 .06
440 Mike Moore .15 .06
441 Doug Sisk .15 .06
442 Dennis Eckersley .75 .30
443 Gerald Perry .15 .06
444 Dale Berra .15 .06
445 Dusty Baker .40 .16
446 Ed Whitson .15 .06
447 Cesar Cedeno .40 .16
448 Rick Schu .15 .06
449 Joaquin Andujar .40 .16
450 Mark Bailey .15 .06
451 Ron Romanick .15 .06
452 Julio Cruz .15 .06
453 Miguel Dilone .15 .06
454 Storm Davis .15 .06
455 Jaime Cocanower .15 .06
456 Barbaro Garbey .15 .06
457 Rich Gedman .15 .06
458 Phil Niekro .40 .16
459 Mike Scioscia .40 .16
460 Pat Tabler .15 .06
461 Darryl Motley .15 .06
462 Chris Codiroli .15 .06
463 Doug Flynn .15 .06
464 Billy Sample .15 .06
465 Mickey Rivers .15 .06
466 John Wathan .15 .06
467 Bill Krueger .15 .06
468 Andre Thornton .15 .06
469 Rex Hudler .15 .06
470 Sid Bream RC .50 .20
471 Kirk Gibson .40 .16
472 John Shelby .15 .06
473 Moose Haas .15 .06
474 Doug Corbett .15 .06
475 Willie McGee .40 .16
476 Bob Knepper .15 .06
477 Kevin Gross .15 .06
478 Carmelo Martinez .15 .06
479 Kent Tekulve .15 .06
480 Chili Davis .40 .16
481 Bobby Clark .15 .06
482 Mookie Wilson .40 .16
483 Dave Owen .15 .06
484 Ed Nunez .15 .06
485 Rance Mulliniks .15 .06
486 Ken Schrom .15 .06
487 Jeff Russell .15 .06
488 Tom Paciorek .15 .06
489 Dan Ford .15 .06
490 Mike Caldwell .15 .06
491 Scottie Earl .15 .06
492 Jose Rijo RC 1.00 .40
493 Bruce Hurst .15 .06
494 Ken Landreaux .15 .06
495 Mike Fischlin .15 .06
496 Don Slaught .15 .06
497 Steve McCatty .15 .06
498 Gary Lucas .15 .06
499 Gary Pettis .15 .06
500 Marvis Foley .15 .06
501 Mike Squires .15 .06
502 Jim Pankovits .15 .06
503 Luis Aguayo .15 .06
504 Ralph Citarella .15 .06
505 Bruce Bochy .15 .06
506 Bob Owchinko .15 .06
507 Pascual Perez .15 .06
508 Lee Lacy .15 .06
509 Atlee Hammaker .15 .06
510 Bob Dernier .15 .06
511 Ed VandeBerg .15 .06
512 Cliff Johnson .15 .06
513 Len Whitehouse .15 .06
514 Dennis Martinez .40 .16
515 Ed Romero .15 .06
516 Rusty Kuntz .15 .06
517 Rick Miller .15 .06
518 Dennis Rasmussen .15 .06
519 Steve Yeager .40 .16
520 Chris Bando .15 .06
521 U.L. Washington .15 .06
522 Curt Young .15 .06
523 Angel Salazar .15 .06
524 Curt Kaufman .15 .06
525 Odell Jones .15 .06
526 Juan Agosto .15 .06
527 Denny Walling .15 .06
528 Andy Hawkins .15 .06

529 Sixto Lezcano .15 .06
530 Skeeter Barnes RC .25 .10
531 Randy Johnson .15 .06
532 Jim Morrison .15 .06
533 Warren Brusstar .15 .06
534A J.Pendleton ERR RC 1.00 .40
Wrong first name
534B T.Pendleton COR RC 1.00 .40
535 Vic Rodriguez .15 .06
536 Bob McClure .15 .06
537 Dave Bergman .15 .06
538 Mark Clear .15 .06
539 Mike Pagliarulo .15 .06
540 Terry Whitfield .15 .06
541 Joe Beckwith .15 .06
542 Jeff Burroughs .15 .06
543 Dan Schatzeder .15 .06
544 Donnie Scott .15 .06
545 Jim Slaton .15 .06
546 Greg Luzinski .40 .16
547 Mark Salas .15 .06
548 Dave Smith .15 .06
549 John Wockenfuss .15 .06
550 Frank Pastore .15 .06
551 Tim Flannery .15 .06
552 Rick Rhoden .15 .06
553 Mark Davis .15 .06
554 Jeff Dedmon .15 .06
555 Gary Woods .15 .06
556 Danny Heep .15 .06
557 Mark Langston RC 1.00 .40
558 Darrell Brown .15 .06
559 Jimmy Key RC 1.00 .40
560 Rick Lysander .15 .06
561 Doyle Alexander .15 .06
562 Mike Stanton .15 .06
563 Sid Fernandez .40 .16
564 Richie Hebner .15 .06
565 Alex Trevino .15 .06
566 Brian Harper .15 .06
567 Dan Gladden RC .50 .20
568 Luis Salazar .15 .06
569 Tom Foley .15 .06
570 Larry Andersen .15 .06
571 Danny Cox .15 .06
572 Joe Sambito .15 .06
573 Juan Beniquez .15 .06
574 Joel Skinner .15 .06
575 Randy St.Claire .15 .06
576 Floyd Rayford .15 .06
577 Roy Howell .15 .06
578 John Grubb .15 .06
579 Ed Jurak .15 .06
580 John Montefusco .15 .06
581 Orel Hershiser RC 1.50 .60
582 Tom Waddell .15 .06
583 Mark Huismann .15 .06
584 Joe Morgan .40 .16
585 Jim Wohlford .15 .06
586 Dave Schmidt .15 .06
587 Jeff Kunkel .15 .06
588 Hal McRae .40 .16
589 Bill Almon .15 .06
590 Carmelo Castillo .15 .06
591 Omar Moreno .15 .06
592 Ken Howell .15 .06
593 Tom Brookens .15 .06
594 Joe Nolan .15 .06
595 Willie Lozado .15 .06
596 Tom Nieto .15 .06
597 Walt Terrell .15 .06
598 Al Oliver .40 .16
599 Shane Rawley .15 .06
600 Denny Gonzalez .15 .06
601 Mark Grant .15 .06
602 Mike Armstrong .15 .06
603 George Foster .40 .16
604 Dave Lopes .40 .16
605 Salome Barojas .15 .06
606 Roy Lee Jackson .15 .06
607 Pete Filson .15 .06
608 Duane Walker .15 .06
609 Glenn Wilson .15 .06
610 Rafael Santana .15 .06
611 Roy Smith .15 .06
612 Ruppert Jones .15 .06
613 Joe Cowley .15 .06
614 Al Nipper UER .15 .06
(Photo actually
Mike Brown)
615 Gene Nelson .15 .06
616 Joe Carter 1.25 .50
617 Ray Knight .40 .16
618 Chuck Rainey .15 .06
619 Dan Driessen .15 .06
620 Daryl Sconiers .15 .06
621 Bill Stein .15 .06
622 Roy Smalley .15 .06
623 Ed Lynch .15 .06
624 Jeff Stone .15 .06
625 Bruce Berenyi .15 .06
626 Kelvin Chapman .15 .06
627 Joe Price .15 .06
628 Steve Bedrosian .15 .06
629 Vic Mata .15 .06
630 Mike Krukow .15 .06
631 Phil Bradley .50 .20
632 Jim Gott .15 .06
633 Randy Bush .15 .06
634 Tom Browning RC .50 .20
635 Lou Gehrig 1.25 .50
Puzzle Card
636 Reid Nichols .15 .06
637 Dan Pasqua RC .50 .20
638 German Rivera .15 .06
639 Don Schulze .15 .06
640A Mike Jones .15 .06
(Career Highlights,
takes five lines)
640B Mike Jones .15 .06
(Career Highlights,
takes four lines)
641 Pete Rose 4.00 1.60
642 Wade Rowdon .15 .06
643 Jerry Narron .15 .06
644 Darrell Miller .15 .06
645 Tim Hulett RC .25 .10
646 Andy McGaffigan .15 .06
647 Kurt Bevacqua .15 .06
648 John Russell .15 .06
649 Ron Robinson .15 .06
650 Donnie Moore .15 .06
651A Two for the Title 2.00 .80
Dave Winfield
Don Mattingly
(Yellow letters)
651B Two for the Title 5.00 2.00
Dave Winfield
Don Mattingly
(White letters)
652 Tim Laudner .15 .06
653 Steve Farr RC .50 .20
654 DK Checklist 1-26 .15 .06
(Unnumbered)
655 Checklist 27-130 .15 .06
(Unnumbered)
656 Checklist 131-234 .15 .06
(Unnumbered)
657 Checklist 235-338 .15 .06
(Unnumbered)
658 Checklist 339-442 .15 .06
(Unnumbered)
659 Checklist 443-546 .15 .06
(Unnumbered)
660 Checklist 547-653 .15 .06
(Unnumbered)

1985 Donruss Wax Box Cards

The boxes of the 1985 Donruss regular issue baseball cards, in which the wax packs were contained, featured four standard-size cards, with backs. The complete set price of the regular issue set does not include these cards; they are considered a separate set. The cards and are styled the same as the regular Donruss cards. The cards are numbered but with the prefix PC before the number. The value of the panel uncut is slightly greater, perhaps by 25 percent greater, than the value of the individual cards cut up carefully.

	Nm-Mt	Ex-Mt
COMPLETE SET (4)	4.00	1.60
PC1 Dwight Gooden	1.00	.40
PC2 Ryne Sandberg	3.00	1.20
PC3 Ron Kittle	.25	.10
PUZ Lou Gehrig Puzzle Card	.75	.30

1985 Donruss Highlights

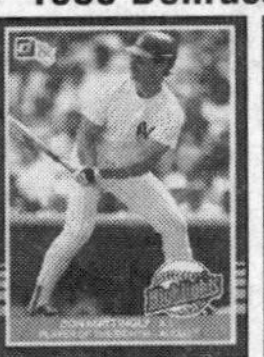
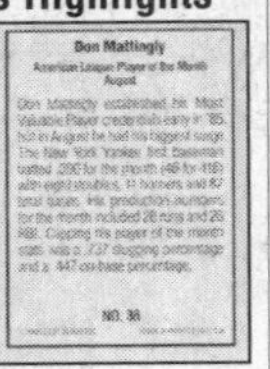

This 56-card standard-size set features the players and pitchers of the month for each league as well as a number of highlight cards commemorating the 1985 season. The Donruss Company dedicated the last two cards to their own selections for Rookies of the Year (ROY). This set proved to be more popular than the Donruss Company had predicted, as their first and only print run was exhausted before card dealers' initial orders were filled.

	Nm-Mt	Ex-Mt
COMP.FACT.SET (56)	15.00	6.00
1 Tom Seaver	.75	.30
2 Rollie Fingers	.50	.20
3 Mike Davis	.10	.04
4 Charlie Leibrandt	.10	.04
5 Dale Murphy	.50	.20
6 Fernando Valenzuela	.20	.08
7 Larry Bowa	.20	.08
8 Dave Concepcion	.20	.08
9 Tony Perez	.50	.20
10 Pete Rose	1.50	.60
11 George Brett	1.50	.60
12 Dave Stieb	.10	.04
13 Dave Parker	.20	.08
14 Andy Hawkins	.10	.04
15 Andy Hawkins	.10	.04
16 Von Hayes	.10	.04
17 Rickey Henderson	.75	.30
18 Jay Howell	.10	.04
19 Pedro Guerrero	.20	.08
20 John Tudor	.10	.04
21 Keith Hernandez Gary Carter	.50	.20
22 Nolan Ryan	5.00	2.00
23 LaMarr Hoyt	.10	.04
24 Oddibe McDowell	.10	.04
25 George Brett	1.50	.60
26 Bret Saberhagen	.50	.20
27 Keith Hernandez	.20	.08
28 Fernando Valenzuela	.20	.08
29 Willie McGee Vince Coleman	.20	.08
30 Tom Seaver	.50	.20
31 Rod Carew	.50	.20
32 Dwight Gooden	.75	.30
33 Dwight Gooden	.75	.30
34 Eddie Murray	.50	.20
35 Don Baylor	.20	.08
36 Don Mattingly	1.50	.60
37 Dave Righetti	.20	.08
38 Willie McGee	.20	.08
39 Shane Rawley	.10	.04
40 Pete Rose	1.50	.60
41 Andre Dawson	.50	.20
42 Rickey Henderson	.75	.30
43 Tom Browning	.20	.08
44 Don Mattingly	1.50	.60
45 Don Mattingly	1.50	.60
46 Charlie Leibrandt	.10	.04
47 Gary Carter	.30	.12
48 Dwight Gooden	.75	.30
49 Wade Boggs	.75	.30
50 Phil Niekro	.50	.20
51 Darrell Evans	.20	.08
52 Willie McGee	.30	.12
53 Dave Winfield	.50	.20
54 Vince Coleman	.20	.08
55 Ozzie Guillen	.50	.20
NNO Checklist Card	.10	.04

1986 Donruss

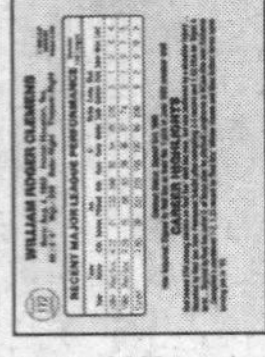

The 1986 Donruss set consists of 660 standard-size cards. Wax packs contained 15 cards plus a Hank Aaron puzzle panel. The card fronts feature blue borders, the standard team logo, player's name, position, and Donruss logo. The first 26 cards of the set are Diamond Kings (DK), for the fifth year in a row; the artwork on the Diamond Kings was again produced by the Perez-Steele Galleries. Cards 27-46 again feature Rated Rookies (RR). The unnumbered checklist cards are arbitrarily numbered below as numbers 654 through 660. Rookie Cards in this set include Jose Canseco, Darren Daulton, Len Dykstra, Cecil Fielder, Andres Galarraga, Fred McGriff and Paul O'Neill.

	Nm-Mt	Ex-Mt
COMPLETE SET (660)	40.00	16.00
COMP.FACT.SET (660)	40.00	16.00
COMP.AARON PUZZLE	2.00	.80
1 Kirk Gibson DK	.25	.10
2 Rich Gossage DK	.25	.10
3 Willie McGee DK	.25	.10
4 George Bell DK	.25	.10
5 Tony Armas DK	.25	.10
6 Chili Davis DK	.25	.10
7 Cecil Cooper DK	.25	.10
8 Mike Boddicker DK	.15	.06
9 Dave Lopes DK	.25	.10
10 Bill Doran DK	.15	.06
11 Bret Saberhagen DK	.25	.10
12 Brett Butler DK	.25	.10
13 Harold Baines DK	.25	.10
14 Mike Davis DK	.15	.06
15 Tony Perez DK	.50	.20
16 Willie Randolph DK	.25	.10
17 Bob Boone DK	.25	.10
18 Orel Hershiser DK	.25	.10
19 Johnny Ray DK	.15	.06
20 Gary Ward DK	.15	.06
21 Rick Mahler DK	.15	.06
22 Phil Bradley DK	.15	.06
23 Jerry Koosman DK	.25	.10
24 Tom Brunansky DK	.15	.06
25 Andre Dawson DK	.15	.06
26 Dwight Gooden DK	.75	.30
27 Kal Daniels RR	.50	.20
28 Fred McGriff RR RC	8.00	3.20
29 Cory Snyder RR	.15	.06
30 Jose Guzman RR RC	.15	.06
31 Ty Gainey RC	.15	.06
32 Johnny Abrego RC	.15	.06
33A A.Galarraga RC RR No accent	1.50	.60
33B A.Galarraga RC RR Accent over e	1.50	.60
34 Dave Shipanoff RC	.15	.06
35 M.McLemore RR RC	1.00	.40
36 Marty Clary RC	.15	.06
37 Paul O'Neill RR RC	4.00	1.60
38 Danny Tartabull RR	.25	.10
39 Jose Canseco RR RC	10.00	4.00
40 Juan Nieves RC	.15	.06
41 Lance McCullers RC	.15	.06
42 Rick Surhoff RC	.15	.06
43 Todd Worrell RR RC	.50	.20
44 Bob Kipper RC	.15	.06
45 John Habyan RR RC	.15	.06
46 Mike Woodard RC	.15	.06
47 Mike Boddicker	.15	.06
48 Robin Yount	1.25	.50
49 Lou Whitaker	.25	.10
50 Oil Can Boyd	.15	.06
51 Rickey Henderson	.75	.30
52 Mike Marshall	.15	.06
53 George Brett	2.00	.80
54 Dave Kingman	.25	.10
55 Hubie Brooks	.15	.06
56 Oddibe McDowell	.15	.06
57 Doug DeCinces	.15	.06
58 Britt Burns	.15	.06
59 Ozzie Smith	1.25	.50
60 Jose Cruz	.25	.10
61 Mike Schmidt	2.00	.80
62 Pete Rose	2.50	1.00
63 Steve Garvey	.25	.10
64 Tony Pena	.15	.06
65 Chili Davis	.25	.10
66 Dale Murphy	.50	.20
67 Ryne Sandberg	1.50	.60
68 Gary Carter	.25	.10
69 Alvin Davis	.15	.06
70 Kent Hrbek	.25	.10
71 George Bell	.25	.10
72 Kirby Puckett	2.00	.80
73 Lloyd Moseby	.15	.06
74 Bob Kearney	.15	.06
75 Dwight Gooden	.75	.30
76 Gary Matthews	.25	.10
77 Rick Mahler	.15	.06
78 Benny Distefano	.15	.06
79 Jeff Leonard	.15	.06
80 Kevin McReynolds	.25	.10
81 Ron Oester	.15	.06
82 John Russell	.15	.06
83 Tommy Herr	.15	.06
84 Jerry Mumphrey	.15	.06
85 Ron Romanick	.15	.06
86 Daryl Boston	.15	.06
87 Andre Dawson	.25	.10
88 Eddie Murray	.75	.30
89 Dion James	.15	.06
90 Chet Lemon	.25	.10
91 Bob Stanley	.15	.06
92 Willie Randolph	.25	.10
93 Mike Scioscia	.25	.10
94 Tom Waddell	.15	.06
95 Danny Jackson	.15	.06
96 Mike Davis	.15	.06
97 Mike Fitzgerald	.15	.06
98 Gary Ward	.15	.06
99 Pete O'Brien	.15	.06
100 Bret Saberhagen	.25	.10
101 Alfredo Griffin	.15	.06
102 Brett Butler	.25	.10
103 Ron Guidry	.25	.10
104 Jerry Reuss	.15	.06
105 Jack Morris	.25	.10
106 Rick Dempsey	.15	.06
107 Ray Burris	.15	.06
108 Brian Downing	.25	.10
109 Willie McGee	.25	.10
110 Bill Doran	.15	.06
111 Kent Tekulve	.15	.06
112 Tony Gwynn	1.25	.50
113 Marvell Wynne	.15	.06
114 David Green	.15	.06
115 Jim Gantner	.15	.06
116 George Foster	.25	.10
117 Steve Trout	.15	.06
118 Mark Langston	.25	.10
119 Tony Fernandez	.15	.06
120 John Butcher	.15	.06
121 Ron Robinson	.15	.06
122 Dan Spillner	.15	.06
123 Mike Young	.15	.06
124 Paul Molitor	.50	.20
125 Kirk Gibson	.25	.10
126 Ken Griffey	.25	.10
127 Tony Armas	.25	.10
128 Mariano Duncan RC*	.50	.20
129 Pat Tabler	.15	.06
130 Frank White	.25	.10
131 Carney Lansford	.25	.10
132 Vance Law	.15	.06
133 Dick Schofield	.15	.06
134 Wayne Tolleson	.15	.06
135 Greg Walker	.15	.06
136 Denny Walling	.15	.06
137 Ozzie Virgil	.15	.06
138 Ricky Horton	.15	.06
139 LaMarr Hoyt	.15	.06
140 Wayne Krenchicki	.15	.06
141 Glenn Hubbard	.15	.06
142 Cecilio Guante	.15	.06
143 Mike Krukow	.15	.06
144 Lee Smith	.25	.10
145 Edwin Nunez	.15	.06
146 Dave Stieb	.25	.10
147 Mike Smithson	.15	.06
148 Ken Dixon	.15	.06
149 Danny Darwin	.15	.06
150 Chris Pittaro	.15	.06
151 Bill Buckner	.25	.10
152 Mike Pagliarulo	.15	.06
153 Bill Russell	.25	.10
154 Brook Jacoby	.15	.06
155 Pat Sheridan	.15	.06
156 Mike Gallego RC	.15	.06
157 Jim Wohlford	.15	.06
158 Gary Pettis	.15	.06
159 Toby Harrah	.25	.10
160 Richard Dotson	.15	.06
161 Bob Knepper	.15	.06
162 Dave Dravecky	.15	.06
163 Greg Gross	.15	.06
164 Eric Davis	.50	.20
165 Gerald Perry	.15	.06
166 Rick Rhoden	.15	.06
167 Keith Moreland	.15	.06
168 Jack Clark	.25	.10
169 Storm Davis	.15	.06
170 Cecil Cooper	.25	.10
171 Alan Trammell	.25	.10
172 Roger Clemens	4.00	1.60
173 Don Mattingly	2.50	1.00
174 Pedro Guerrero	.25	.10
175 Willie Wilson	.25	.10
176 Dwayne Murphy	.15	.06
177 Tim Raines	.25	.10
178 Larry Parrish	.15	.06
179 Mike Witt	.15	.06
180 Harold Baines	.25	.10
181 V.Coleman RC* UER BA 2.67 on back	1.00	.40
182 Jeff Heathcock	.15	.06
183 Steve Carlton	.25	.10
184 Mario Soto	.25	.10
185 Rich Gossage	.25	.10
186 Johnny Ray	.15	.06
187 Dan Gladden	.15	.06
188 Bob Horner	.25	.10
189 Rick Sutcliffe	.25	.10
190 Keith Hernandez	.25	.10
191 Phil Bradley	.15	.06
192 Tom Brunansky	.15	.06
193 Jesse Barfield	.25	.10
194 Frank Viola	.25	.10
195 Willie Upshaw	.15	.06
196 Jim Beattie	.15	.06
197 Darryl Strawberry	.50	.20
198 Ron Cey	.25	.10
199 Steve Bedrosian	.15	.06
200 Steve Kemp	.15	.06
201 Manny Trillo	.15	.06
202 Garry Templeton	.25	.10
203 Dave Parker	.25	.10
204 John Denny	.15	.06
205 Terry Pendleton	.25	.10
206 Terry Puhl	.15	.06
207 Bobby Grich	.25	.10
208 Ozzie Guillen RC*	.50	.20
209 Jeff Reardon	.25	.10
210 Cal Ripken	3.00	1.20
211 Bill Schroeder	.15	.06
212 Dan Petry	.15	.06
213 Jim Rice	.25	.10
214 Dave Righetti	.25	.10
215 Fernando Valenzuela	.25	.10
216 Julio Franco	.25	.10
217 Darryl Motley	.15	.06
218 Dave Collins	.15	.06
219 Tim Wallach	.15	.06
220 George Wright	.15	.06
221 Tommy Dunbar	.15	.06
222 Steve Balboni	.15	.06
223 Jay Howell	.15	.06
224 Joe Carter	.25	.10
225 Ed Whitson	.15	.06
226 Orel Hershiser	.50	.20
227 Willie Hernandez	.15	.06
228 Lee Lacy	.15	.06
229 Rollie Fingers	.25	.10
230 Bob Boone	.25	.10
231 Joaquin Andujar	.25	.10
232 Craig Reynolds	.15	.06
233 Shane Rawley	.15	.06
234 Eric Show	.15	.06
235 Jose DeLeon	.15	.06
236 Jose Uribe	.15	.06
237 Moose Haas	.15	.06
238 Wally Backman	.15	.06
239 Dennis Eckersley	.50	.20
240 Mike Moore	.15	.06
241 Damaso Garcia	.15	.06
242 Tim Teufel	.15	.06
243 Dave Concepcion	.25	.10
244 Floyd Bannister	.15	.06
245 Fred Lynn	.25	.10
246 Charlie Moore	.15	.06
247 Walt Terrell	.15	.06
248 Dave Winfield	.25	.10
249 Dwight Evans	.25	.10
250 Dennis Powell	.15	.06
251 Andre Thornton	.15	.06
252 Onix Concepcion	.15	.06
253 Mike Heath	.15	.06
254A David Palmer ERR (Position 2B)	.15	.06
254B David Palmer COR (Position P)	.50	.20
255 Donnie Moore	.15	.06
256 Curtis Wilkerson	.15	.06
257 Julio Cruz	.15	.06
258 Nolan Ryan	4.00	1.60
259 Jeff Stone	.15	.06
260 John Tudor	.25	.10
261 Mark Thurmond	.15	.06
262 Jay Tibbs	.15	.06
263 Rafael Ramirez	.15	.06
264 Larry McWilliams	.15	.06
265 Mark Davis	.15	.06
266 Bob Dernier	.15	.06
267 Matt Young	.15	.06
268 Jim Clancy	.15	.0
269 Mickey Hatcher	.15	.0
270 Sammy Stewart	.15	.0
271 Bob L. Gibson	.15	.0
272 Nelson Simmons	.15	.0
273 Rich Gedman	.15	.0
274 Butch Wynegar	.15	.0
275 Ken Howell	.15	.0
276 Mel Hall	.15	.0
277 Jim Sundberg	.25	.1
278 Chris Codiroli	.15	.0
279 Herm Winningham	.15	.0
280 Rod Carew	.50	.2
281 Don Slaught	.15	.0
282 Scott Fletcher	.15	.0
283 Bill Dawley	.15	.0
284 Andy Hawkins	.15	.0
285 Glenn Wilson	.15	.0
286 Nick Esasky	.15	.0
287 Claudell Washington	.15	.0
288 Lee Mazzilli	.25	.1
289 Jody Davis	.15	.0
290 Darrell Porter	.15	.0
291 Scott McGregor	.15	.0
292 Ted Simmons	.25	.1
293 Aurelio Lopez	.15	.0
294 Marty Barrett	.15	.0
295 Dale Berra	.15	.0
296 Greg Brock	.15	.0
297 Charlie Leibrandt	.15	.0
298 Bill Krueger	.15	.0
299 Bryn Smith	.15	.0
300 Burt Hooton	.15	.0
301 Stu Cliburn	.15	.0
302 Luis Salazar	.15	.0
303 Ken Dayley	.15	.0
304 Frank DiPino	.15	.0
305 Von Hayes	.15	.0
306 Gary Redus	.15	.0
307 Craig Lefferts	.15	.0
308 Sammy Khalifa	.15	.0
309 Scott Garrelts	.15	.0
310 Rick Cerone	.15	.0
311 Shawon Dunston	.25	.1
312 Howard Johnson	.25	.1
313 Jim Presley	.15	.0
314 Gary Gaetti	.25	.1
315 Luis Leal	.15	.0
316 Mark Salas	.15	.0
317 Bill Caudill	.15	.0
318 Dave Henderson	.15	.0
319 Rafael Santana	.15	.0
320 Leon Durham	.15	.0
321 Bruce Sutter	.25	.1
322 Jason Thompson	.15	.0
323 Bob Brenly	.15	.0
324 Carmelo Martinez	.15	.0
325 Eddie Milner	.15	.0
326 Juan Samuel	.15	.0
327 Tom Nieto	.15	.0
328 Dave Smith	.15	.0
329 Urbano Lugo	.15	.0
330 Joel Skinner	.15	.0
331 Bill Gullickson	.15	.0
332 Floyd Rayford	.15	.0
333 Ben Oglivie	.25	.1
334 Lance Parrish	.25	.1
335 Jackie Gutierrez	.15	.0
336 Dennis Rasmussen	.15	.0
337 Terry Whitfield	.15	.0
338 Neal Heaton	.15	.0
339 Jorge Orta	.15	.0
340 Donnie Hill	.15	.0
341 Joe Hesketh	.15	.0
342 Charlie Hough	.25	.1
343 Dave Rozema	.15	.0
344 Greg Pryor	.15	.0
345 Mickey Tettleton RC	.50	.2
346 George Vukovich	.15	.0

347 Don Baylor .25 .10
348 Carlos Diaz .15 .06
349 Barbaro Garbey .15 .06
350 Larry Sheets .15 .06
351 Ted Higuera RC* .50 .20
352 Juan Beniquez .15 .06
353 Bob Forsch .15 .06
354 Mark Bailey .15 .06
355 Larry Andersen .15 .06
356 Terry Kennedy .15 .06
357 Don Robinson .15 .06
358 Jim Gott .15 .06
359 Earnie Riles .15 .06
360 John Christensen .15 .06
361 Ray Fontenot .15 .06
362 Spike Owen .15 .06
363 Jim Acker .15 .06
364 Ron Davis .15 .06
365 Tom Hume .15 .06
366 Carlton Fisk .50 .20
367 Nate Snell .15 .06
368 Rick Manning .15 .06
369 Darrell Evans .25 .10
370 Ron Hassey .15 .06
371 Wade Boggs .50 .20
372 Rick Honeycutt .15 .06
373 Chris Bando .15 .06
374 Bud Black .15 .06
375 Steve Henderson .15 .06
376 Charlie Lea .15 .06
377 Reggie Jackson .50 .20
378 Dave Schmidt .15 .06
379 Bob James .15 .06
380 Glenn Davis .15 .06
381 Tim Corcoran .15 .06
382 Danny Cox .15 .06
383 Tim Flannery .15 .06
384 Tom Browning .15 .06
385 Rick Camp .15 .06
386 Jim Morrison .15 .06
387 Dave LaPoint .15 .06
388 Dave Lopes .25 .10
389 Al Cowens .15 .06
390 Doyle Alexander .15 .06
391 Tim Laudner .15 .06
392 Don Aase .15 .06
393 Jaime Cocanower .15 .06
394 Randy O'Neal .15 .06
395 Mike Easler .15 .06
396 Scott Bradley .15 .06
397 Tom Niedenfuer .15 .06
398 Jerry Willard .15 .06
399 Lonnie Smith .15 .06
400 Bruce Bochte .15 .06
401 Terry Francona .25 .10
402 Jim Slaton .15 .06
403 Bill Stein .15 .06
404 Tim Hulett .15 .06
405 Alan Ashby .15 .06
406 Tim Stoddard .15 .06
407 Garry Maddox .15 .06
408 Ted Power .15 .06
409 Len Barker .15 .06
410 Denny Gonzalez .15 .06
411 George Frazier .15 .06
412 Andy Van Slyke .25 .10
413 Jim Dwyer .15 .06
414 Paul Householder .15 .06
415 Alejandro Sanchez .15 .06
416 Steve Crawford .15 .06
417 Dan Pasqua .15 .06
418 Enos Cabell .15 .06
419 Mike Jones .15 .06
420 Steve Kiefer .15 .06
421 Tim Burke .15 .06
422 Mike Mason .15 .06
423 Ruppert Jones .15 .06
424 Jerry Hairston .15 .06
425 Tito Landrum .15 .06
426 Jeff Calhoun .15 .06
427 Don Carman .15 .06
428 Tony Perez .50 .20
429 Jerry Davis .15 .06
430 Bob Walk .15 .06
431 Brad Wellman .15 .06
432 Terry Forster .25 .10
433 Billy Hatcher .15 .06
434 Clint Hurdle .15 .06
435 Ivan Calderon RC* .50 .20
436 Pete Filson .15 .06
437 Tom Henke .25 .10
438 Dave Engle .15 .06
439 Tom Filer .15 .06
440 Gorman Thomas .25 .10
441 Rick Aguilera RC .50 .20
442 Scott Sanderson .15 .06
443 Jeff Dedmon .15 .06
444 Joe Orsulak RC* .50 .20
445 Atlee Hammaker .15 .06
446 Jerry Royster .15 .06
447 Buddy Bell .25 .10
448 Dave Rucker .15 .06
449 Ivan DeJesus .15 .06
450 Jim Pankovits .15 .06
451 Jerry Narron .15 .06
452 Bryan Little .15 .06
453 Gary Lucas .15 .06
454 Dennis Martinez .25 .10
455 Ed Romero .15 .06
456 Bob Melvin .15 .06
457 Glenn Hoffman .15 .06
458 Bob Shirley .15 .06
459 Bob Welch .25 .10
460 Carmen Castillo .15 .06
461 Dave Leeper .15 .06
462 Tim Birtsas .15 .06
463 Randy St.Claire .15 .06
464 Chris Welsh .15 .06
465 Greg Harris .15 .06
466 Lynn Jones .15 .06
467 Dusty Baker .25 .10
468 Roy Smith .15 .06
469 Andre Robertson .15 .06
470 Ken Landreaux .15 .06
471 Dave Bergman .15 .06
472 Gary Roenicke .15 .06
473 Pete Vuckovich .15 .06
474 Kirk McCaskill RC .50 .20
475 Jeff Lahti .15 .06
476 Mike Scott .25 .10
477 Darren Daulton RC 1.00 .40
478 Graig Nettles .25 .10
479 Bill Almon .15 .06
480 Greg Minton .15 .06
481 Randy Ready .15 .06
482 Len Dykstra RC 1.50 .60
483 Thad Bosley .15 .06
484 Harold Reynolds RC 1.50 .60
485 Al Oliver .25 .10
486 Roy Smalley .15 .06
487 John Franco .25 .10
488 Juan Agosto .15 .06
489 Al Pardo .15 .06
490 Bill Wegman RC .15 .06
491 Frank Tanana .25 .10
492 Brian Fisher RC .15 .06
493 Mark Clear .15 .06
494 Len Matuszek .15 .06
495 Ramon Romero .15 .06
496 John Wathan .15 .06
497 Rob Picciolo .15 .06
498 U.L. Washington .15 .06
499 John Candelaria .15 .06
500 Duane Walker .15 .06
501 Gene Nelson .15 .06
502 John Mizerock .15 .06
503 Luis Aguayo .15 .06
504 Kurt Kepshire .15 .06
505 Ed Wojna .15 .06
506 Joe Price .15 .06
507 Milt Thompson RC .50 .20
508 Junior Ortiz .15 .06
509 Vida Blue .25 .10
510 Steve Engel .15 .06
511 Karl Best .15 .06
512 Cecil Fielder RC 1.50 .60
513 Frank Eufemia .15 .06
514 Tippy Martinez .15 .06
515 Billy Joe Robidoux .15 .06
516 Bill Scherrer .15 .06
517 Bruce Hurst .15 .06
518 Rich Bordi .15 .06
519 Steve Yeager .25 .10
520 Tony Bernazard .15 .06
521 Hal McRae .25 .10
522 Jose Rijo .25 .10
523 Mitch Webster .15 .06
524 Jack Howell .15 .06
525 Alan Bannister .15 .06
526 Ron Kittle .15 .06
527 Phil Garner .25 .10
528 Kurt Bevacqua .15 .06
529 Kevin Gross .15 .06
530 Bo Diaz .15 .06
531 Ken Oberkfell .15 .06
532 Rick Reuschel .25 .10
533 Ron Meridith .15 .06
534 Steve Braun .15 .06
535 Wayne Gross .15 .06
536 Ray Searage .15 .06
537 Tom Brookens .15 .06
538 Al Nipper .15 .06
539 Billy Sample .15 .06
540 Steve Sax .15 .06
541 Dan Quisenberry .15 .06
542 Tony Phillips .15 .06
543 Floyd Youmans .15 .06
544 Steve Buechele RC .50 .20
545 Craig Gerber .15 .06
546 Joe DeSa .15 .06
547 Brian Harper .15 .06
548 Kevin Bass .15 .06
549 Tom Foley .15 .06
550 Dave Van Gorder .15 .06
551 Bruce Bochy .15 .06
552 R.J. Reynolds .15 .06
553 Chris Brown .15 .06
554 Bruce Benedict .15 .06
555 Warren Brusstar .15 .06
556 Danny Heep .15 .06
557 Darnell Coles .15 .06
558 Greg Gagne .15 .06
559 Ernie Whitt .15 .06
560 Ron Washington .15 .06
561 Jimmy Key .25 .10
562 Billy Swift .15 .06
563 Ron Darling .25 .10
564 Dick Ruthven .15 .06
565 Zane Smith .15 .06
566 Sid Bream .15 .06
567A J.Youngblood ERR .15 .06
Position P
567B J.Youngblood COR .50 .20
Position IF
568 Mario Ramirez .15 .06
569 Tom Runnells .15 .06
570 Rick Schu .15 .06
571 Bill Campbell .15 .06
572 Dickie Thon .15 .06
573 Al Holland .15 .06
574 Reid Nichols .15 .06
575 Bert Roberge .15 .06
576 Mike Flanagan .15 .06
577 Tim Leary .15 .06
578 Mike Laga .15 .06
579 Steve Lyons .15 .06
580 Phil Niekro .25 .10
581 Gilberto Reyes .15 .06
582 Jamie Easterly .15 .06
583 Mark Gubicza .15 .06
584 Stan Javier RC .50 .20
585 Bill Laskey .15 .06
586 Jeff Russell .15 .06
587 Dickie Noles .15 .06
588 Steve Farr .15 .06
589 Steve Ontiveros RC .15 .06
590 Mike Hargrove .15 .06
591 Marty Bystrom .15 .06
592 Franklin Stubbs .15 .06
593 Larry Herndon .15 .06
594 Bill Swaggerty .15 .06
595 Carlos Ponce .15 .06
596 Pat Perry .15 .06
597 Ray Knight .25 .10
598 Steve Lombardozzi .15 .06
599 Brad Havens .15 .06
600 Pat Clements .15 .06
601 Joe Niekro .15 .06
602 Hank Aaron .75 .30
Puzzle Card
603 Dwayne Henry .15 .06
604 Mookie Wilson .25 .10
605 Buddy Biancalana .15 .06
606 Rance Mulliniks .15 .06
607 Alan Wiggins .15 .06
608 Joe Cowley .15 .06
609 Tom Seaver .50 .20
(Green borders on name)
609B Tom Seaver 2.00 .80
(Yellow borders on name)
610 Neil Allen .15 .06
611 Don Sutton .25 .10
612 Fred Toliver .15 .06
613 Jay Baller .15 .06
614 Marc Sullivan .15 .06
615 John Grubb .15 .06
616 Bruce Kison .15 .06
617 Bill Madlock .25 .10
618 Chris Chambliss .25 .10
619 Dave Stewart .25 .10
620 Tim Lollar .15 .06
621 Gary Lavelle .15 .06
622 Charles Hudson .15 .06
623 Joel Davis .15 .06
624 Joe Johnson .15 .06
625 Sid Fernandez .15 .06
626 Dennis Lamp .15 .06
627 Terry Harper .15 .06
628 Jack Lazorko .15 .06
629 Roger McDowell RC* .50 .20
630 Mark Funderburk .15 .06
631 Ed Lynch .15 .06
632 Rudy Law .15 .06
633 Roger Mason RC .15 .06
634 Mike Felder RC .15 .06
635 Ken Schrom .15 .06
636 Bob Ojeda .15 .06
637 Ed VandeBerg .15 .06
638 Bobby Meacham .15 .06
639 Cliff Johnson .15 .06
640 Garth Iorg .15 .06
641 Dan Driessen .15 .06
642 Mike Brown OF .15 .06
643 John Shelby .15 .06
644 Pete Rose RB .75 .30
645 Phil Niekro .25 .10
Joe Niekro
646 Jesse Orosco .15 .06
647 Billy Beane RC 1.00 .40
648 Cesar Cedeno .25 .10
649 Bert Blyleven .25 .10
650 Max Venable .15 .06
651 Vince Coleman .15 .06
Willie McGee
652 Calvin Schiraldi .15 .06
653 Pete Rose KING .75 .30
654 Dia. Kings CL 1-26 .15 .06
Unnumbered
655A CL 1: 27-130 .15 .06
(Unnumbered)
(45 Beane ERR)
655B CL 1: 27-130 .15 .06
(Unnumbered)
(45 Habyan COR)
656 CL 2: 131-234 .15 .06
(Unnumbered)
657 CL 3: 235-338 .15 .06
(Unnumbered)
658 CL 4: 339-442 .15 .06
(Unnumbered)
659 CL 5: 443-546 .15 .06
(Unnumbered)
660 CL 6: 547-653 .15 .06
(Unnumbered)

1986 Donruss Wax Box Cards

The cards in this four-card set measure the standard 2 1/2" by 3 1/2". Cards have essentially the same design as the 1986 Donruss regular issue set. The cards were printed on the bottoms of the regular issue wax pack boxes. The four cards (PC4 to PC6 plus a Hank Aaron puzzle card) are considered a separate set in their own right and are not typically included in a complete set of the regular issue 1986 Donruss cards. The value of the panel uncut is slightly greater, perhaps by 25 percent greater, than the value of the individual cards cut up carefully.

Nm-Mt Ex-Mt
COMPLETE SET (4) 1.00 .40
PC4 Kirk Gibson .40 .16
PC5 Willie Hernandez .10 .04
PC6 Doug DeCinces .10 .04
PUZ Hank Aaron .75 .30
Puzzle Card

1986 Donruss Rookies

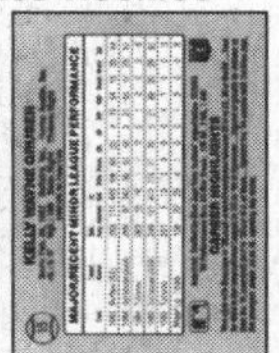

The 1986 Donruss "The Rookies" set features 56 full-color standard-size cards plus a 15-piece puzzle of Hank Aaron. The set was distributed through hobby dealers in a small green, cellophane wrapped factory box. Although the set was wrapped in cellophane, the top card was number one Joyner, resulting in a percentage of the Joyner cards arriving in less than perfect condition. Donruss fixed the problem after it was called to their attention and even went so far as to include a customer service phone number in their second printing. Card fronts are similar in design to the 1986 Donruss regular issue except for the presence of "The Rookies" logo in the lower left corner and a bluish green border instead of a blue border. The key extended Rookie Cards in this set are Barry Bonds, Bobby Bonilla, Will Clark, Bo Jackson, Wally Joyner and John Kruk.

Nm-Mt Ex-Mt
COMP.FACT.SET (56) 50.00 20.00
1 Wally Joyner XRC 1.00 .40
2 Tracy Jones .15 .06
3 Allan Anderson .15 .06
4 Ed Correa .15 .06
5 Reggie Williams .15 .06
6 Charlie Kerfeld .15 .06
7 Andres Galarraga 1.50 .60
8 Bob Tewksbury XRC .50 .20
9 Al Newman .25 .10
10 Andres Thomas .15 .06
11 Barry Bonds XRC 40.00 16.00
12 Juan Nieves .15 .06
13 Mark Eichhorn .15 .06
14 Dan Plesac XRC .50 .20
15 Cory Snyder .15 .06
16 Kelly Gruber .15 .06
17 Kevin Mitchell XRC 1.00 .40
18 Steve Lombardozzi .15 .06
19 Mitch Williams XRC .50 .20
20 John Cerutti .15 .06
21 Todd Worrell .50 .20
22 Jose Canseco 1.50 .60
23 Pete Incaviglia XRC .50 .20
24 Jose Guzman .15 .06
25 Scott Bailes .15 .06
26 Greg Mathews .15 .06
27 Eric King .15 .06
28 Paul Assenmacher .50 .20
29 Jeff Sellers .15 .06
30 Bobby Bonilla XRC 1.00 .40
31 Doug Drabek XRC 1.00 .40
32 Will Clark UER 2.00 .80
(Listed as throwing right, should be left) XRC
33 Bip Roberts XRC .50 .20
34 Jim Deshaies XRC .15 .06
35 Mike LaValliere XRC .50 .20
36 Scott Bankhead .15 .06
37 Dale Sveum .15 .06
38 Bo Jackson XRC 2.00 .80
39 Robby Thompson XRC .50 .20
40 Eric Plunk .15 .06
41 Bill Bathe .15 .06
42 John Kruk XRC 1.50 .60
43 Andy Allanson .15 .06
44 Mark Portugal XRC .50 .20
45 Danny Tartabull .25 .10
46 Bob Kipper .15 .06
47 Gene Walter .15 .06
48 Rey Quinones UER .15 .06
(Misspelled Quinonez)
49 Bobby Witt XRC .50 .20
50 Bill Mooneyham .15 .06
51 John Cangelosi .15 .06
52 Ruben Sierra XRC 1.50 .60
53 Rob Woodward .15 .06
54 Ed Hearn .15 .06
55 Joel McKeon .15 .06
56 Checklist 1-56 .15 .06

1986 Donruss Highlights

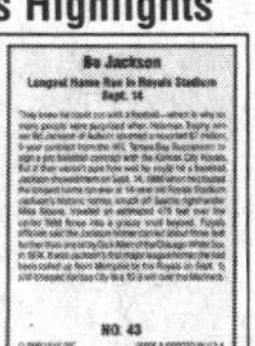

Donruss' second edition of Highlights was released late in 1986. These glossy-coated cards are standard size. Cards commemorate events during the 1986 season, as well as players and pitchers of the month from each league. The set was distributed in its own red, white, blue, and gold box along with a small Hank Aaron puzzle. Card fronts are similar to the regular 1986 Donruss issue except that the Highlights logo is positioned in the lower left-hand corner and the borders are in gold instead of blue. The backs are printed in black and gold on white card stock. A first year card of Jose Canseco highlights this set.

Nm-Mt Ex-Mt
COMP. FACT. SET (56) 5.00 2.00
1 Will Clark 1.00 .40
2 Jose Rijo .10 .04
3 George Brett .60 .24
4 Mike Schmidt .40 .16
5 Roger Clemens .75 .30
6 Roger Clemens .75 .30
7 Kirby Puckett .50 .20
8 Dwight Gooden .40 .16
9 Johnny Ray .10 .04
10 Mickey Mantle 1.00 .40
Reggie Jackson
11 Wade Boggs .25 .10
12 Don Aase .10 .04
13 Wade Boggs .25 .10
14 Jeff Reardon .10 .04
15 Hubie Brooks .10 .04
16 Don Sutton .40 .16
17 Roger Clemens .75 .30
18 Roger Clemens .75 .30
19 Kent Hrbek .15 .06
20 Rick Rhoden .10 .04
21 Kevin Bass .10 .04
22 Bob Horner .10 .04
23 Wally Joyner .25 .10
24 Darryl Strawberry .25 .10
25 Fernando Valenzuela .15 .06
26 Roger Clemens .75 .30
27 Jack Morris .15 .06
28 Scott Fletcher .10 .04
29 Todd Worrell .10 .04
30 Eric Davis .25 .10
31 Bert Blyleven .15 .06
32 Bobby Doerr .25 .10
33 Ernie Lombardi .15 .06
34 Willie McCovey .15 .06
35 Steve Carlton .15 .06
36 Mike Schmidt .40 .16
37 Juan Samuel .10 .04
38 Mike Witt .10 .04
39 Doug DeCinces .10 .04
40 Bill Gullickson .10 .04
41 Dale Murphy .40 .16
42 Joe Carter .40 .16
43 Bo Jackson 1.00 .40
44 Joe Cowley .10 .04
45 Jim Deshaies .10 .04
46 Mike Scott .10 .04
47 Bruce Hurst .10 .04
48 Don Mattingly .60 .24
49 Mike Krukow .10 .04
50 Steve Sax .10 .04
51 John Cangelosi .10 .04
52 Dave Righetti .10 .04
53 Don Mattingly .60 .24
54 Todd Worrell .15 .06
55 Jose Canseco 1.00 .40
56 Checklist Card .10 .04

1987 Donruss

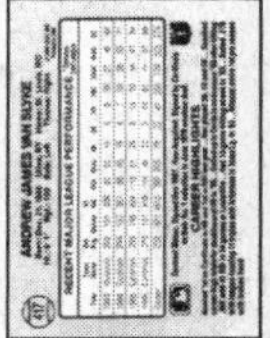

This set consists of 660 standard-size cards. Cards were primarily distributed in 15-card wax packs, rack packs and a factory set. All packs included a Roberto Clemente puzzle panel and the factory sets contained a complete puzzle. The regular-issue cards feature a black and gold border on the front. The backs of the cards in the factory sets are oriented differently than cards taken from wax packs, giving the appearance that one version or the other is upside down when sorting from the card backs. There are no premiums or discounts for either version. The popular Diamond King subset returns for the sixth consecutive year. Some of the Diamond King (1-26) selections are repeats from prior years; Perez-Steele Galleries had indicated in 1987 that a five-year rotation would be maintained in order to avoid depleting the pool of available worthy "kings" on some of the teams. The rich selection of Rookie Cards in this set include Barry Bonds, Bobby Bonilla, Kevin Brown, Will Clark, David Cone, Chuck Finley, Bo Jackson, Wally Joyner, Barry Larkin, Greg Maddux and Rafael Palmeiro.

Nm-Mt Ex-Mt
COMPLETE SET (660) 40.00 16.00
COMP.FACT.SET (660) 50.00 20.00
COMP.CLEMENTE PUZZLE 1.50 .60
1 Wally Joyner DK .40 .16
2 Roger Clemens DK 1.00 .40
3 Dale Murphy DK .25 .10
4 Darryl Strawberry DK .15 .06
5 Ozzie Smith DK .60 .24
6 Jose Canseco DK .40 .16
7 Charlie Hough DK .15 .06
8 Brook Jacoby DK .10 .04
9 Fred Lynn DK .15 .06
10 Rick Rhoden DK .10 .04
11 Chris Brown DK .10 .04
12 Von Hayes DK .10 .04
13 Jack Morris DK .15 .06
14A Kevin McReynolds DK .40 .16
ERR (Yellow strip missing on back)
14B Kevin McReynolds DK .10 .04
COR
15 George Brett DK 1.00 .40
16 Ted Higuera DK .10 .04
17 Hubie Brooks DK .10 .04
18 Mike Scott DK .15 .06
19 Kirby Puckett DK .40 .16
20 Dave Winfield DK .15 .06
21 Lloyd Moseby DK .10 .04
22A Eric Davis DK ERR .40 .16
(Yellow strip missing on back)
22B Eric Davis DK COR .25 .10
23 Jim Presley DK .10 .04
24 Keith Moreland DK .10 .04
25A Greg Walker DK ERR .40 .16
(Yellow strip missing on back)
25B Greg Walker DK COR .10 .04
26 Steve Sax DK .10 .04
27 DK Checklist 1-26 .10 .04
28 B.J. Surhoff RR RC .60 .24
29 Randy Myers RR RC .60 .24
30 Ken Gerhart RC .15 .06
31 Benito Santiago .15 .06
32 Greg Swindell RR RC .40 .16
33 Mike Birkbeck RC .15 .06
34 Terry Steinbach RR RC .60 .24
35 Bo Jackson RR RC 1.50 .60
36 Greg Maddux UER RC 10.00 4.00
middle name misspelled "Allen"
37 Jim Lindeman RC .15 .06
38 Devon White RR RC .60 .24
39 Eric Bell RC .15 .06
40 Willie Fraser RC .15 .06
41 Jerry Browne RR RC .15 .06
42 Chris James RR RC* .15 .06
43 Rafael Palmeiro RR RC 5.00 2.00
44 Pat Dodson RC .15 .06
45 Duane Ward RR RC* .40 .16
46 Mark McGwire RR 8.00 3.20
47 Bruce Fields UER RC .15 .06
(Photo actually Darnell Coles)
48 Eddie Murray .40 .16
49 Ted Higuera .10 .04
50 Kirk Gibson .15 .06
51 Oil Can Boyd .10 .04
52 Don Mattingly 1.25 .50
53 Pedro Guerrero .15 .06

54 George Brett 1.00 .40
55 Jose Rijo .15 .06
56 Tim Raines .15 .06
57 Ed Correa .10 .04
58 Mike Witt .10 .04
59 Greg Walker .10 .04
60 Ozzie Smith .60 .24
61 Glenn Davis .10 .04
62 Glenn Wilson .10 .04
63 Tom Browning .10 .04
64 Tony Gwynn .60 .24
65 R.J. Reynolds .10 .04
66 Will Clark RC 1.50 .60
67 Ozzie Virgil .10 .04
68 Rick Sutcliffe .15 .06
69 Gary Carter .15 .06
70 Mike Moore .10 .04
71 Bert Blyleven .15 .06
72 Tony Fernandez .10 .04
73 Kent Hrbek .15 .06
74 Lloyd Moseby .10 .04
75 Alvin Davis .10 .04
76 Keith Hernandez .15 .06
77 Ryne Sandberg .75 .30
78 Dale Murphy .25 .10
79 Sid Bream .10 .04
80 Chris Brown .10 .04
81 Steve Garvey .15 .06
82 Mario Soto .15 .06
83 Shane Rawley .10 .04
84 Willie McGee .15 .06
85 Jose Cruz .15 .06
86 Brian Downing .15 .06
87 Ozzie Guillen .10 .04
88 Hubie Brooks .10 .04
89 Cal Ripken 1.50 .60
90 Juan Nieves .10 .04
91 Lance Parrish .15 .06
92 Jim Rice .15 .06
93 Ron Guidry .15 .06
94 Fernando Valenzuela .15 .06
95 Andy Allanson .10 .04
96 Willie Wilson .15 .06
97 Jose Canseco .40 .16
98 Jeff Reardon .15 .06
99 Bobby Witt RC .40 .16
100 Checklist 28-133 .10 .04
101 Jose Guzman .10 .04
102 Steve Balboni .10 .04
103 Tony Phillips .10 .04
104 Brook Jacoby .10 .04
105 Dave Winfield .15 .06
106 Orel Hershiser .15 .06
107 Lou Whitaker .15 .06
108 Fred Lynn .15 .06
109 Bill Wegman .10 .04
110 Donnie Moore .10 .04
111 Jack Clark .15 .06
112 Bob Knepper .10 .04
113 Von Hayes .10 .04
114 Bip Roberts RC* .40 .16
115 Tony Pena .10 .04
116 Scott Garrelts .10 .04
117 Paul Molitor .25 .10
118 Darryl Strawberry .15 .06
119 Shawon Dunston .10 .04
120 Jim Presley .10 .04
121 Jesse Barfield .15 .06
122 Gary Gaetti .15 .06
123 Kurt Stillwell .10 .04
124 Joel Davis .10 .04
125 Mike Boddicker .10 .04
126 Robin Yount .60 .24
127 Alan Trammell .15 .06
128 Dave Righetti .15 .06
129 Dwight Evans .15 .06
130 Mike Scioscia .15 .06
131 Julio Franco .15 .06
132 Bret Saberhagen .15 .06
133 Mike Davis .10 .04
134 Joe Hesketh .10 .04
135 Wally Joyner RC .60 .24
136 Don Slaught .10 .04
137 Daryl Boston .10 .04
138 Nolan Ryan 2.00 .80
139 Mike Schmidt 1.00 .40
140 Tommy Herr .10 .04
141 Garry Templeton .15 .06
142 Kal Daniels .10 .04
143 Billy Sample .10 .04
144 Johnny Ray .10 .04
145 Rob Thompson RC* .40 .16
146 Bob Dernier .10 .04
147 Danny Tartabull .10 .04
148 Ernie Whitt .10 .04
149 Kirby Puckett .40 .16
150 Mike Young .10 .04
151 Ernest Riles .10 .04
152 Frank Tanana .15 .06
153 Rich Gedman .10 .04
154 Willie Randolph .15 .06
155 Bill Madlock .15 .06
156 Joe Carter .15 .06
157 Danny Jackson .10 .04
158 Carney Lansford .15 .06
159 Bryn Smith .10 .04
160 Gary Pettis .10 .04
161 Oddibe McDowell .10 .04
162 John Cangelosi .10 .04
163 Mike Scott .15 .06
164 Eric Show .10 .04
165 Juan Samuel .10 .04
166 Nick Esasky .10 .04
167 Zane Smith .10 .04
168 Mike C. Brown OF .10 .04
169 Keith Moreland .10 .04
170 John Tudor .15 .06
171 Ken Dixon .10 .04
172 Jim Gantner .10 .04
173 Jack Morris .15 .06
174 Bruce Hurst .15 .06
175 Dennis Rasmussen .10 .04
176 Mike Marshall .10 .04
177 Dan Quisenberry .10 .04
178 Eric Plunk .10 .04
179 Tim Wallach .10 .04
180 Steve Buechele .10 .04
181 Don Sutton .15 .06
182 Dave Schmidt .10 .04
183 Terry Pendleton .15 .06
184 Jim Deshaies RC * .15 .06
185 Steve Bedrosian .10 .04
186 Pete Rose 1.25 .50
187 Dave Dravecky .10 .04
188 Rick Reuschel .15 .06
189 Dan Gladden .10 .04
190 Rick Mahler .10 .04
191 Thad Bosley .10 .04
192 Ron Darling .15 .06
193 Matt Young .10 .04
194 Tom Brunansky .10 .04
195 Dave Stieb .15 .06
196 Frank Viola .15 .06
197 Tom Henke .10 .04
198 Karl Best .10 .04
199 Dwight Gooden .15 .06
200 Checklist 134-239 .10 .04
201 Steve Trout .10 .04
202 Rafael Ramirez .10 .04
203 Bob Walk .10 .04
204 Roger Mason .10 .04
205 Terry Kennedy .10 .04
206 Ron Oester .10 .04
207 John Russell .10 .04
208 Greg Mathews .10 .04
209 Charlie Kerfeld .10 .04
210 Reggie Jackson .25 .10
211 Floyd Bannister .10 .04
212 Vance Law .10 .04
213 Rich Bordi .10 .04
214 Dan Plesac .10 .04
215 Dave Collins .10 .04
216 Bob Stanley .10 .04
217 Joe Niekro .10 .04
218 Tom Niedenfuer .10 .04
219 Brett Butler .15 .06
220 Charlie Leibrandt .10 .04
221 Steve Ontiveros .10 .04
222 Tim Burke .10 .04
223 Curtis Wilkerson .10 .04
224 Pete Incaviglia RC * .40 .16
225 Lonnie Smith .10 .04
226 Chris Codiroli .10 .04
227 Scott Bailes .10 .04
228 Rickey Henderson .40 .16
229 Ken Howell .10 .04
230 Darnell Coles .10 .04
231 Don Aase .10 .04
232 Tim Leary .10 .04
233 Bob Boone .15 .06
234 Ricky Horton .10 .04
235 Mark Bailey .10 .04
236 Kevin Gross .10 .04
237 Lance McCullers .10 .04
238 Cecilio Guante .10 .04
239 Bob Melvin .10 .04
240 Billy Joe Robidoux .10 .04
241 Roger McDowell .10 .04
242 Leon Durham .10 .04
243 Ed Nunez .10 .04
244 Jimmy Key .15 .06
245 Mike Smithson .10 .04
246 Bo Diaz .10 .04
247 Carlton Fisk .25 .10
248 Larry Sheets .10 .04
249 Juan Castillo RC .15 .06
250 Eric King .10 .04
251 Doug Drabek RC .60 .24
252 Wade Boggs .25 .10
253 Mariano Duncan .10 .04
254 Pat Tabler .10 .04
255 Frank White .15 .06
256 Alfredo Griffin .10 .04
257 Floyd Youmans .10 .04
258 Rob Wilfong .10 .04
259 Pete O'Brien .10 .04
260 Tim Hulett .10 .04
261 Dickie Thon .10 .04
262 Darren Daulton .15 .06
263 Vince Coleman .10 .04
264 Andy Hawkins .10 .04
265 Eric Davis .25 .10
266 Andres Thomas .10 .04
267 Mike Diaz .10 .04
268 Chili Davis .15 .06
269 Jody Davis .10 .04
270 Phil Bradley .10 .04
271 George Bell .15 .06
272 Keith Atherton .10 .04
273 Storm Davis .10 .04
274 Rob Deer .10 .04
275 Walt Terrell .10 .04
276 Roger Clemens 1.00 .40
277 Mike Easler .10 .04
278 Steve Sax .10 .04
279 Andre Thornton .10 .04
280 Jim Sundberg .15 .06
281 Bill Bathe .10 .04
282 Jay Tibbs .10 .04
283 Dick Schofield .10 .04
284 Mike Mason .10 .04
285 Jerry Hairston .10 .04
286 Bill Doran .10 .04
287 Tim Flannery .10 .04
288 Gary Redus .10 .04
289 John Franco .15 .06
290 Paul Assenmacher .40 .16
291 Joe Orsulak .10 .04
292 Lee Smith .15 .06
293 Mike Laga .10 .04
294 Rick Dempsey .10 .04
295 Mike Felder .10 .04
296 Tom Brookens .10 .04
297 Al Nipper .10 .04
298 Mike Pagliarulo .10 .04
299 Franklin Stubbs .10 .04
300 Checklist 240-345 .10 .04
301 Steve Farr .10 .04
302 Bill Mooneyham .10 .04
303 Andres Galarraga .15 .06
304 Scott Fletcher .10 .04
305 Jack Howell .10 .04
306 Russ Morman .10 .04
307 Todd Worrell .10 .04
308 Dave Smith .10 .04
309 Jeff Stone .10 .04
310 Ron Robinson .10 .04
311 Bruce Bochy .10 .04
312 Jim Winn .10 .04
313 Mark Davis .10 .04
314 Jeff Dedmon .10 .04
315 Jamie Moyer RC 1.00 .40
316 Wally Backman .10 .04
317 Ken Phelps .10 .04
318 Steve Lombardozzi .10 .04
319 Rance Mulliniks .10 .04
320 Tim Laudner .10 .04
321 Mark Eichhorn .10 .04
322 Lee Guetterman .10 .04
323 Sid Fernandez .10 .04
324 Jerry Mumphrey .10 .04
325 David Palmer .10 .04
326 Bill Almon .10 .04
327 Candy Maldonado .10 .04
328 John Kruk RC 1.00 .40
329 John Denny .10 .04
330 Milt Thompson .10 .04
331 Mike LaValliere RC * .40 .16
332 Alan Ashby .10 .04
333 Doug Corbett .10 .04
334 Ron Karkovice RC .40 .16
335 Mitch Webster .10 .04
336 Lee Lacy .10 .04
337 Glenn Braggs RC .15 .06
338 Dwight Lowry .10 .04
339 Don Baylor .15 .06
340 Brian Fisher .10 .04
341 Reggie Williams .10 .04
342 Tom Candiotti .10 .04
343 Rudy Law .10 .04
344 Curt Young .10 .04
345 Mike Fitzgerald .10 .04
346 Ruben Sierra RC 1.00 .40
347 Mitch Williams RC * .40 .16
348 Jorge Orta .10 .04
349 Mickey Tettleton .10 .04
350 Ernie Camacho .10 .04
351 Ron Kittle .10 .04
352 Ken Landreaux .10 .04
353 Chet Lemon .15 .06
354 John Shelby .10 .04
355 Mark Clear .10 .04
356 Doug DeCinces .10 .04
357 Ken Dayley .10 .04
358 Phil Garner .15 .06
359 Steve Jeltz .10 .04
360 Ed Whitson .10 .04
361 Barry Bonds RC 15.00 6.00
362 Vida Blue .15 .06
363 Cecil Cooper .15 .06
364 Bob Ojeda .10 .04
365 Dennis Eckersley .25 .10
366 Mike Morgan .10 .04
367 Willie Upshaw .10 .04
368 Allan Anderson .10 .04
369 Bill Gullickson .10 .04
370 Bobby Thigpen RC .40 .16
371 Juan Beniquez .10 .04
372 Charlie Moore .10 .04
373 Dan Petry .10 .04
374 Rod Scurry .10 .04
375 Tom Seaver .25 .10
376 Ed VandeBerg .10 .04
377 Tony Bernazard .10 .04
378 Greg Pryor .10 .04
379 Dwayne Murphy .10 .04
380 Andy McGaffigan .10 .04
381 Kirk McCaskill .10 .04
382 Greg Harris .10 .04
383 Rich Dotson .10 .04
384 Craig Reynolds .10 .04
385 Greg Gross .10 .04
386 Tito Landrum .10 .04
387 Craig Lefferts .10 .04
388 Dave Parker .15 .06
389 Bob Horner .15 .06
390 Pat Clements .10 .04
391 Jeff Leonard .10 .04
392 Chris Speier .10 .04
393 John Moses .10 .04
394 Garth Iorg .10 .04
395 Greg Gagne .10 .04
396 Nate Snell .10 .04
397 Bryan Clutterbuck .10 .04
398 Darrell Evans .15 .06
399 Steve Crawford .10 .04
400 Checklist 346-451 .10 .04
401 Phil Lombardi .10 .04
402 Rick Honeycutt .10 .04
403 Ken Schrom .10 .04
404 Bud Black .10 .04
405 Donnie Hill .10 .04
406 Wayne Krenchicki .10 .04
407 Chuck Finley RC .60 .24
408 Toby Harrah .10 .04
409 Steve Lyons .10 .04
410 Kevin Bass .10 .04
411 Marvell Wynne .10 .04
412 Ron Roenicke .10 .04
413 Tracy Jones .10 .04
414 Gene Garber .10 .04
415 Mike Bielecki .10 .04
416 Frank DiPino .10 .04
417 Andy Van Slyke .15 .06
418 Jim Dwyer .10 .04
419 Ben Oglivie .15 .06
420 Dave Bergman .10 .04
421 Joe Sambito .10 .04
422 Bob Tewksbury RC * .40 .16
423 Len Matuszek .10 .04
424 Mike Kingery RC .15 .06
425 Dave Kingman .15 .06
426 Al Newman .10 .04
427 Gary Ward .10 .04
428 Ruppert Jones .10 .04
429 Harold Baines .15 .06
430 Pat Perry .10 .04
431 Terry Puhl .10 .04
432 Don Carman .10 .04
433 Eddie Milner .10 .04
434 LaMarr Hoyt .10 .04
435 Rick Rhoden .10 .04
436 Jose Uribe .10 .04
437 Ken Oberkfell .10 .04
438 Ron Davis .10 .04
439 Jesse Orosco .10 .04
440 Scott Bradley .10 .04
441 Randy Bush .10 .04
442 John Cerutti .10 .04
443 Roy Smalley .10 .04
444 Kelly Gruber .10 .04
445 Bob Kearney .10 .04
446 Ed Hearn .10 .04
447 Scott Sanderson .10 .04
448 Bruce Benedict .10 .04
449 Junior Ortiz .10 .04
450 Mike Aldrete .10 .04
451 Kevin McReynolds .10 .04
452 Rob Murphy .10 .04
453 Kent Tekulve .10 .04
454 Curt Ford .10 .04
455 Dave Lopes .15 .06
456 Bob Grich .15 .06
457 Jose DeLeon .10 .04
458 Andre Dawson .15 .06
459 Mike Flanagan .10 .04
460 Joey Meyer .15 .06
461 Chuck Cary .10 .04
462 Bill Buckner .15 .06
463 Bob Shirley .10 .04
464 Jeff Hamilton .10 .04
465 Phil Niekro .15 .06
466 Mark Gubicza .10 .04
467 Jerry Willard .10 .04
468 Bob Sebra .10 .04
469 Larry Parrish .10 .04
470 Charlie Hough .15 .06
471 Hal McRae .15 .06
472 Dave Leiper .10 .04
473 Mel Hall .10 .04
474 Dan Pasqua .10 .04
475 Bob Welch .15 .06
476 Johnny Grubb .10 .04
477 Jim Traber .10 .04
478 Chris Bosio RC .40 .16
479 Mark McLemore .15 .06
480 John Morris .10 .04
481 Billy Hatcher .10 .04
482 Dan Schatzeder .10 .04
483 Rich Gossage .15 .06
484 Jim Morrison .10 .04
485 Bob Brenly .10 .04
486 Bill Schroeder .10 .04
487 Mookie Wilson .15 .06
488 Dave Martinez RC .40 .16
489 Harold Reynolds .15 .06
490 Jeff Hearron .10 .04
491 Mickey Hatcher .10 .04
492 Barry Larkin RC 1.50 .60
493 Bob James .10 .04
494 John Habyan .10 .04
495 Jim Adduci .10 .04
496 Mike Heath .10 .04
497 Tim Stoddard .10 .04
498 Tony Armas .15 .06
499 Dennis Powell .10 .04
500 Checklist 452-557 .10 .04
501 Chris Bando .10 .04
502 David Cone RC 1.00 .40
503 Jay Howell .10 .04
504 Tom Foley .10 .04
505 Ray Chadwick .10 .04
506 Mike Loynd RC .15 .06
507 Neil Allen .10 .04
508 Danny Darwin .10 .04
509 Rick Schu .10 .04
510 Jose Oquendo .10 .04
511 Gene Walter .10 .04
512 Terry McGriff .10 .04
513 Ken Griffey .15 .06
514 Benny Distefano .10 .04
515 Terry Mulholland RC .40 .16
516 Ed Lynch .10 .04
517 Bill Swift .10 .04
518 Manny Lee .10 .04
519 Andre David .10 .04
520 Scott McGregor .10 .04
521 Rick Manning .10 .04
522 Willie Hernandez .10 .04
523 Marty Barrett .10 .04
524 Wayne Tolleson .10 .04
525 Jose Gonzalez RC .15 .06
526 Cory Snyder .10 .04
527 Buddy Biancalana .10 .04
528 Moose Haas .10 .04
529 Wilfredo Tejada .10 .04
530 Stu Cliburn .10 .04
531 Dale Mohorcic .10 .04
532 Ron Hassey .10 .04
533 Ty Gainey .10 .04
534 Jerry Royster .10 .04
535 Mike Maddux .10 .04
536 Ted Power .10 .04
537 Ted Simmons .15 .06
538 Rafael Belliard RC .40 .16
539 Chico Walker .10 .04
540 Bob Forsch .10 .04
541 John Stefero .10 .04
542 Dale Sveum .10 .04
543 Mark Thurmond .10 .04
544 Jeff Sellers .10 .04
545 Joel Skinner .10 .04
546 Alex Trevino .10 .04
547 Randy Kutcher .10 .04
548 Joaquin Andujar .15 .06
549 Casey Candaele .10 .04
550 Jeff Russell .10 .04
551 John Candelaria .10 .04
552 Joe Cowley .10 .04
553 Danny Cox .10 .04
554 Denny Walling .10 .04
555 Bruce Ruffin RC .15 .06
556 Buddy Bell .15 .06
557 Jimmy Jones RC .15 .06
558 Bobby Bonilla RC .60 .24
559 Jeff D. Robinson .10 .04
560 Ed Olwine .10 .04
561 Glenallen Hill RC .40 .16
562 Lee Mazzilli .15 .06
563 Mike G. Brown P .10 .04
564 George Frazier .10 .04
565 Mike Sharperson RC .15 .06
566 Mark Portugal RC * .40 .16
567 Rick Leach .10 .04
568 Mark Langston .10 .04
569 Rafael Santana .10 .04
570 Manny Trillo .10 .04
571 Cliff Speck .10 .04
572 Bob Kipper .10 .04
573 Kelly Downs RC .15 .06
574 Randy Asadoor .10 .04
575 Dave Magadan RC .40 .16
576 Marvin Freeman RC .15 .06
577 Jeff Lahti .10 .04
578 Jeff Calhoun .10 .04
579 Gus Polidor .10 .04
580 Gene Nelson .10 .04
581 Tim Teufel .10 .04
582 Odell Jones .10 .04
583 Mark Ryal .10 .04
584 Randy O'Neal .10 .04
585 Mike Greenwell RC .40 .16
586 Ray Knight .15 .06
587 Ralph Bryant .10 .04
588 Carmen Castillo .10 .04
589 Ed Wojna .10 .04
590 Stan Javier .10 .04
591 Jeff Musselman .10 .04
592 Mike Stanley RC .40 .16
593 Darrell Porter .10 .04
594 Drew Hall .10 .04
595 Rob Nelson .10 .04
596 Bryan Oelkers .10 .04
597 Scott Nielsen .10 .04
598 Brian Holton .10 .04
599 Kevin Mitchell RC * .60 .24
600 Checklist 558-660 .10 .04
601 Jackie Gutierrez .10 .04
602 Barry Jones .10 .04
603 Jerry Narron .10 .04
604 Steve Lake .10 .04
605 Jim Pankovits .10 .04
606 Ed Romero .10 .04
607 Dave LaPoint .10 .04
608 Don Robinson .10 .04
609 Mike Krukow .10 .04
610 Dave Valle RC ** .15 .06
611 Len Dykstra .15 .06
612 R.Clemente PUZ .50 .20
613 Mike Trujillo .10 .04
614 Damaso Garcia .10 .04
615 Neal Heaton .10 .04
616 Juan Berenguer .10 .04
617 Steve Carlton .15 .06
618 Gary Lucas .10 .04
619 Geno Petralli .10 .04
620 Rick Aguilera .10 .04
621 Fred McGriff .75 .30
622 Dave Henderson .10 .04
623 Dave Clark RC .15 .06
624 Angel Salazar .10 .04
625 Randy Hunt .10 .04
626 John Gibbons .10 .04
627 Kevin Brown RC 2.00 .80
628 Bill Dawley .10 .04
629 Aurelio Lopez .10 .04
630 Charles Hudson .10 .04
631 Ray Soff .10 .04
632 Ray Hayward .10 .04
633 Spike Owen .10 .04
634 Glenn Hubbard .10 .04
635 Kevin Elster RC .40 .16
636 Mike LaCoss .10 .04
637 Dwayne Henry .10 .04
638 Rey Quinones .10 .04
639 Jim Clancy .10 .04
640 Larry Andersen .10 .04
641 Calvin Schiraldi .10 .04
642 Stan Jefferson .10 .04
643 Marc Sullivan .10 .04
644 Mark Grant .10 .04
645 Cliff Johnson .10 .04
646 Howard Johnson .15 .06
647 Dave Sax .10 .04
648 Dave Stewart .15 .06
649 Danny Heep .10 .04
650 Joe Johnson .10 .04
651 Bob Brower .10 .04
652 Rob Woodward .10 .04
653 John Mizerock .10 .04
654 Tim Pyznarski .10 .04
655 Luis Aquino .10 .04
656 Mickey Brantley .10 .04
657 Doyle Alexander .10 .04
658 Sammy Stewart .10 .04
659 Jim Acker .10 .04
660 Pete Ladd .10 .04

1987 Donruss Wax Box Cards

The cards in this four-card set measure the standard 2 1/2" by 3 1/2". Cards have essentially the same design as the 1987 Donruss regular issue set. The cards were printed on the bottoms of the regular issue wax pack boxes. The four cards (PC10 to PC12 plus a Roberto Clemente puzzle card) are considered a separate set in their own right and are not typically included in a complete set of the regular issue 1987 Donruss cards. The value of the panel uncut is slightly greater, perhaps by 25 percent greater, than the value of the individual cards cut up carefully.

	Nm-Mt	Ex-Mt
COMPLETE SET (4)	2.00	.80
PC10 Dale Murphy	.50	.20
PC11 Jeff Reardon	.25	.10
PC12 Jose Canseco	1.25	.50
PUZ Roberto Clemente (Puzzle Card)	.75	.30

1987 Donruss Rookies

The 1987 Donruss "The Rookies" set features 56 full-color standard-size cards plus a 15-piece puzzle of Roberto Clemente. The set was distributed in factory set form packaged in a small green and black box through hobby dealers. Card fronts are similar in design to the 1987

onruss regular issue except for the presence of 'The Rookies" logo in the lower left corner and a reen border instead of a black border. The key xtended Rookie Cards in this set are Ellis Burks nd Matt Williams. The second Donruss-issued ards of Greg Maddux and Rafael Palmeiro are so in this set. Because it's the first card in the et (of which came in a tightly-sealed cello wrap, ne Mark McGwire card is quite condition sensi-ve.

	Nm-Mt	Ex-Mt
OMP.FACT.SET (56)	25.00	10.00
Mark McGwire	10.00	4.00
Eric Bell	.15	.06
Mark Williamson	.10	.04
Mike Greenwell	.40	.16
Ellis Burks XRC	.60	.24
DeWayne Buice	.10	.04
Mark McLemore	.25	.10
Devon White	.60	.24
Willie Fraser	.15	.06
0 Les Lancaster	.10	.04
1 Ken Williams XRC	.10	.04
2 Matt Nokes XRC	.40	.16
3 Jeff M. Robinson	.10	.04
4 Bo Jackson	1.00	.40
5 Kevin Seitzer XRC	.40	.16
6 Billy Ripken XRC	.40	.16
7 B.J. Surhoff	.60	.24
8 Chuck Crim	.10	.04
9 Mike Birkbeck	.15	.06
0 Chris Bosio	.40	.16
1 Les Straker	.10	.04
2 Mark Davidson	.10	.04
3 Gene Larkin XRC	.40	.16
4 Ken Gerhart	.10	.04
5 Luis Polonia XRC	.40	.16
6 Terry Steinbach	.60	.24
7 Mickey Brantley	.10	.04
8 Mike Stanley	.40	.16
9 Jerry Browne	.15	.06
0 Todd Benzinger XRC	.40	.16
1 Fred McGriff	1.50	.60
2 Mike Henneman XRC	.40	.16
3 Casey Candaele	.10	.04
4 Dave Magadan	.40	.16
5 David Cone	1.00	.40
6 Mike Jackson XRC	.40	.16
7 John Mitchell XRC	.15	.06
8 Mike Dunne	.10	.04
9 John Smiley XRC	.40	.16
0 Joe Magrane XRC	.15	.06
1 Jim Lindeman	.15	.06
2 Shane Mack	.10	.04
3 Stan Jefferson	.10	.04
4 Benito Santiago	.25	.10
5 Matt Williams XRC	2.50	1.00
6 Dave Meads	.10	.04
7 Rafael Palmeiro	5.00	2.00
8 Bill Long	.10	.04
9 Bob Brower	.10	.04
0 James Steels	.10	.04
1 Paul Noce	.10	.04
2 Greg Maddux	8.00	3.20
3 Jeff Musselman	.10	.04
4 Brian Holton	.10	.04
5 Chuck Jackson	.10	.04
6 Checklist 1-56	.10	.04

1987 Donruss Highlights

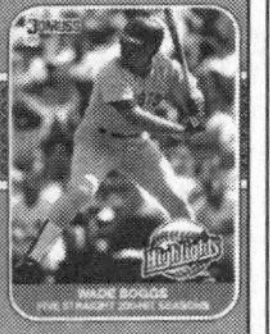

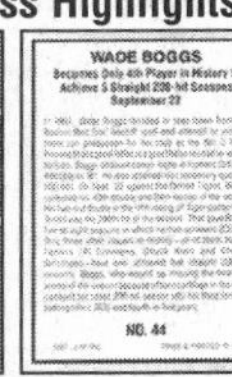

onruss' third (and last) edition of Highlights as released late in 1987. The cards are stan-ard size and are glossy in appearance. Cards ommemorate events during the 1987 season, s well as players and pitchers of the month om each league. The set was distributed in its wn red, black, blue, and gold box along with a nall Roberto Clemente puzzle. Card fronts are milar to the regular 1987 Donruss issue except at the Highlights logo is positioned in the lower ght-hand corner and the borders are in blue stead of black. The backs are printed in black nd gold on white card stock.

	Nm-Mt	Ex-Mt
OMP.FACT.SET (56)	12.00	4.80
Juan Nieves	.10	.04
Mike Schmidt	.40	.16
Eric Davis	.25	.10
Sid Fernandez	.10	.04
Brian Downing	.10	.04
Bret Saberhagen	.15	.06
Tim Raines	.15	.06
Eric Davis	.25	.10
Steve Bedrosian	.10	.04
0 Larry Parrish	.10	.04
1 Jim Clancy	.10	.04
2 Tony Gwynn UER	.40	.16
3 Orel Hershiser	.15	.06
4 Wade Boggs	.25	.10
5 Steve Ontiveros	.10	.04
6 Tim Raines	.15	.06
7 Don Mattingly	.75	.30
8 Ray Dandridge	.15	.06
9 Jim "Catfish" Hunter	.25	.10
0 Billy Williams	.15	.06
1 Bo Diaz	.10	.04
2 Floyd Youmans	.10	.04
3 Don Mattingly	.75	.30
4 Frank Viola	.10	.04
5 Bobby Witt	.15	.06
6 Kevin Seitzer	.40	.16
7 Mark McGwire	3.00	1.20
8 Andre Dawson	.15	.06
9 Paul Molitor	.25	.10
0 Kirby Puckett	.40	.16
1 Andre Dawson	.15	.06
2 Doug Drabek	.40	.16
33 Dwight Evans	.15	.06
34 Mark Langston	.10	.04
35 Wally Joyner	.25	.10
36 Vince Coleman	.10	.04
37 Eddie Murray	.40	.16
38 Cal Ripken	.75	.30
39 Fred McGriff Rob Ducey Ernie Whitt	.15	.06
40 Mark McGwire Jose Canseco	2.00	.80
41 Bob Boone	.15	.06
42 Darryl Strawberry	.15	.06
43 Howard Johnson	.10	.04
44 Wade Boggs	.25	.10
45 Benito Santiago	.15	.06
46 Mark McGwire	3.00	1.20
47 Kevin Seitzer	.40	.16
48 Don Mattingly	.75	.30
49 Darryl Strawberry	.15	.06
50 Pascual Perez	.10	.04
51 Alan Trammell	.15	.06
52 Doyle Alexander	.10	.04
53 Nolan Ryan	1.00	.40
54 Mark McGwire	3.00	1.20
55 Benito Santiago	.15	.06
56 Checklist 1-56	.10	.04

1987 Donruss Opening Day

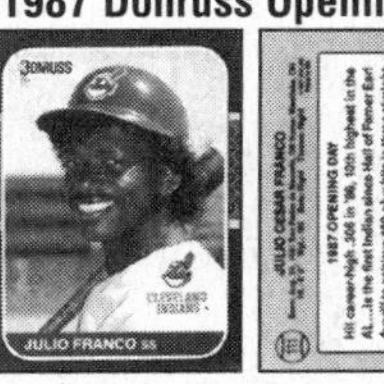

This innovative set of 272 standard-size cards features a card for each of the players in the starting line-ups of all the teams on Opening Day 1987. The set was packaged in a specially designed box. Cards are very similar in design to the 1987 regular Donruss issue except that these "OD" cards have a maroon border instead of a black border. Teams in the same city share a checklist card. A 15-piece puzzle of Roberto Clemente is also included with every complete set. The error on Barry Bonds (picturing Johnny Ray by mistake) was corrected very early in the press run; supposedly less than one percent of the sets have the error. Players in this set in their Rookie Card year include Will Clark, Bo Jackson, Wally Joyner and Barry Larkin.

	Nm-Mt	Ex-Mt
COMP.FACT. SET (272)	50.00	20.00
1 Doug DeCinces	.10	.04
2 Mike Witt	.10	.04
3 George Hendrick	.15	.06
4 Dick Schofield	.10	.04
5 Devon White	.60	.24
6 Butch Wynegar	.10	.04
7 Wally Joyner	.25	.10
8 Mark McLemore	.15	.06
9 Brian Downing	.15	.06
10 Gary Pettis	.10	.04
11 Bill Doran	.10	.04
12 Phil Garner	.15	.06
13 Jose Cruz	.15	.06
14 Kevin Bass	.10	.04
15 Mike Scott	.15	.06
16 Glenn Davis	.10	.04
17 Alan Ashby	.10	.04
18 Billy Hatcher	.10	.04
19 Craig Reynolds	.10	.04
20 Carney Lansford	.15	.06
21 Mike Davis	.10	.04
22 Reggie Jackson	.25	.10
23 Mickey Tettleton	.10	.04
24 Jose Canseco	.40	.16
25 Rob Nelson	.10	.04
26 Tony Phillips	.10	.04
27 Dwayne Murphy	.10	.04
28 Alfredo Griffin	.10	.04
29 Curt Young	.10	.04
30 Willie Upshaw	.10	.04
31 Mike Sharperson	.10	.04
32 Rance Mulliniks	.10	.04
33 Ernie Whitt	.10	.04
34 Jesse Barfield	.15	.06
35 Tony Fernandez	.15	.06
36 Lloyd Moseby	.10	.04
37 Jimmy Key	.15	.06
38 Fred McGriff	.75	.30
39 George Bell	.15	.06
40 Dale Murphy	.25	.10
41 Rick Mahler	.10	.04
42 Ken Griffey	.15	.06
43 Andres Thomas	.10	.04
44 Dion James	.10	.04
45 Ozzie Virgil	.10	.04
46 Ken Oberkfell	.10	.04
47 Gary Roenicke	.10	.04
48 Glenn Hubbard	.10	.04
49 Bill Schroeder	.10	.04
50 Greg Brock	.10	.04
51 Billy Joe Robidoux	.10	.04
52 Glenn Braggs	.15	.06
53 Jim Gantner	.10	.04
54 Paul Molitor	.25	.10
55 Dale Sveum	.10	.04
56 Ted Higuera	.10	.04
57 Rob Deer	.10	.04
58 Robin Yount	.60	.24
59 Jim Lindeman	.15	.06
60 Vince Coleman	.10	.04
61 Tommy Herr	.10	.04
62 Terry Pendleton	.15	.06
63 John Tudor	.15	.06
64 Tony Pena	.10	.04
65 Ozzie Smith	.60	.24
66 Tito Landrum	.10	.04
67 Jack Clark	.15	.06
68 Bob Dernier	.10	.04
69 Rick Sutcliffe	.15	.06
70 Andre Dawson	.15	.06
71 Keith Moreland	.10	.04
72 Jody Davis	.10	.04
73 Brian Dayett	.10	.04
74 Leon Durham	.10	.04
75 Ryne Sandberg	.75	.30
76 Shawon Dunston	.10	.04
77 Mike Marshall	.10	.04
78 Bill Madlock	.15	.06
79 Orel Hershiser	.15	.06
80 Mike Ramsey	.10	.04
81 Ken Landreaux	.10	.04
82 Mike Scioscia	.15	.06
83 Franklin Stubbs	.10	.04
84 Mariano Duncan	.10	.04
85 Steve Sax	.10	.04
86 Mitch Webster	.10	.04
87 Reid Nichols	.10	.04
88 Tim Wallach	.10	.04
89 Floyd Youmans	.10	.04
90 Andres Galarraga	.15	.06
91 Hubie Brooks	.10	.04
92 Jeff Reed	.10	.04
93 Alonzo Powell	.10	.04
94 Vance Law	.10	.04
95 Bob Brenly	.10	.04
96 Will Clark	2.00	.80
97 Chili Davis	.15	.06
98 Mike Krukow	.10	.04
99 Jose Uribe	.10	.04
100 Chris Brown	.10	.04
101 Robby Thompson	.40	.16
102 Candy Maldonado	.10	.04
103 Jeff Leonard	.10	.04
104 Tom Candiotti	.10	.04
105 Chris Bando	.10	.04
106 Cory Snyder	.10	.04
107 Pat Tabler	.10	.04
108 Andre Thornton	.10	.04
109 Joe Carter	.10	.04
110 Tony Bernazard	.10	.04
111 Julio Franco	.15	.06
112 Brook Jacoby	.10	.04
113 Brett Butler	.15	.06
114 Donell Nixon	.10	.04
115 Alvin Davis	.10	.04
116 Mark Langston	.10	.04
117 Harold Reynolds	.15	.06
118 Ken Phelps	.10	.04
119 Mike Kingery	.15	.06
120 Dave Valle	.15	.06
121 Rey Quinones	.10	.04
122 Phil Bradley	.10	.04
123 Jim Presley	.10	.04
124 Keith Hernandez	.15	.06
125 Kevin McReynolds	.10	.04
126 Rafael Santana	.10	.04
127 Bob Ojeda	.10	.04
128 Darryl Strawberry	.15	.06
129 Mookie Wilson	.15	.06
130 Gary Carter	.15	.06
131 Tim Teufel	.10	.04
132 Howard Johnson	.15	.06
133 Cal Ripken	1.50	.60
134 Rick Burleson	.10	.04
135 Fred Lynn	.15	.06
136 Eddie Murray	.40	.16
137 Ray Knight	.15	.06
138 Alan Wiggins	.10	.04
139 John Shelby	.10	.04
140 Mike Boddicker	.10	.04
141 Ken Gerhart	.10	.04
142 Terry Kennedy	.10	.04
143 Steve Garvey	.15	.06
144 Marvell Wynne	.10	.04
145 Kevin Mitchell	.25	.10
146 Tony Gwynn	.60	.24
147 Joey Cora	.40	.16
148 Benito Santiago	.15	.06
149 Eric Show	.10	.04
150 Garry Templeton	.15	.06
151 Carmelo Martinez	.10	.04
152 Von Hayes	.10	.04
153 Lance Parrish	.15	.06
154 Milt Thompson	.10	.04
155 Mike Easler	.10	.04
156 Juan Samuel	.10	.04
157 Steve Jeltz	.10	.04
158 Glenn Wilson	.10	.04
159 Shane Rawley	.10	.04
160 Mike Schmidt	1.00	.40
161 Andy Van Slyke	.15	.06
162 Johnny Ray	.10	.04
163A Barry Bonds ERR (Photo actually Johnny Ray wearing a black shirt)	300.00	120.00
163B Barry Bonds COR	20.00	8.00
164 Junior Ortiz	.10	.04
165 Rafael Belliard	.40	.16
166 Bob Patterson	.10	.04
167 Bobby Bonilla	.60	.24
168 Sid Bream	.10	.04
169 Jim Morrison	.10	.04
170 Jerry Browne	.15	.06
171 Scott Fletcher	.10	.04
172 Ruben Sierra	1.00	.40
173 Larry Parrish	.10	.04
174 Pete O'Brien	.10	.04
175 Pete Incaviglia	.40	.16
176 Don Slaught	.10	.04
177 Oddibe McDowell	.10	.04
178 Charlie Hough	.15	.06
179 Steve Buechele	.10	.04
180 Bob Stanley	.10	.04
181 Wade Boggs	.25	.10
182 Jim Rice	.15	.06
183 Bill Buckner	.15	.06
184 Dwight Evans	.15	.06
185 Spike Owen	.10	.04
186 Don Baylor	.15	.06
187 Marc Sullivan	.10	.04
188 Marty Barrett	.10	.04
189 Dave Henderson	.10	.04
190 Bo Diaz	.10	.04
191 Barry Larkin	2.00	.80
192 Kal Daniels	.10	.04
193 Terry Francona	.15	.06
194 Tom Browning	.10	.04
195 Ron Oester	.10	.04
196 Buddy Bell	.15	.06
197 Eric Davis	.25	.10
198 Dave Parker	.15	.06
199 Steve Balboni	.10	.04
200 Danny Tartabull	.10	.04
201 Ed Hearn	.10	.04
202 Buddy Biancalana	.10	.04
203 Danny Jackson	.10	.04
204 Frank White	.15	.06
205 Bo Jackson	2.00	.80
206 George Brett	1.00	.40
207 Kevin Seitzer	.15	.06
208 Willie Wilson	.15	.06
209 Orlando Mercado	.10	.04
210 Darrell Evans	.15	.06
211 Larry Herndon	.10	.04
212 Jack Morris	.15	.06
213 Chet Lemon	.15	.06
214 Mike Heath	.10	.04
215 Darnell Coles	.10	.04
216 Alan Trammell	.15	.06
217 Terry Harper	.10	.04
218 Lou Whitaker	.15	.06
219 Gary Gaetti	.15	.06
220 Tom Nieto	.10	.04
221 Kirby Puckett	.40	.16
222 Tom Brunansky	.10	.04
223 Greg Gagne	.10	.04
224 Dan Gladden	.10	.04
225 Mark Davidson	.10	.04
226 Bert Blyleven	.15	.06
227 Steve Lombardozzi	.10	.04
228 Kent Hrbek	.15	.06
229 Gary Redus	.10	.04
230 Ivan Calderon	.10	.04
231 Tim Hulett	.10	.04
232 Carlton Fisk	.25	.10
233 Greg Walker	.10	.04
234 Ron Karkovice	.40	.16
235 Ozzie Guillen	.10	.04
236 Harold Baines	.15	.06
237 Donnie Hill	.10	.04
238 Rich Dotson	.10	.04
239 Mike Pagliarulo	.10	.04
240 Joel Skinner	.10	.04
241 Don Mattingly	1.25	.50
242 Gary Ward	.10	.04
243 Dave Winfield	.15	.06
244 Dan Pasqua	.10	.04
245 Wayne Tolleson	.10	.04
246 Willie Randolph	.15	.06
247 Dennis Rasmussen	.10	.04
248 Rickey Henderson	.40	.16
249 Angels Logo	.05	.02
250 Astros Logo	.05	.02
251 A's Logo	.05	.02
252 Blue Jays Logo	.05	.02
253 Braves Logo	.05	.02
254 Brewers Logo	.05	.02
255 Cardinals Logo	.05	.02
256 Dodgers Logo	.05	.02
257 Expos Logo	.05	.02
258 Giants Logo	.05	.02
259 Indians Logo	.05	.02
260 Mariners Logo	.05	.02
261 Orioles Logo	.05	.02
262 Padres Logo	.05	.02
263 Phillies Logo	.05	.02
264 Pirates Logo	.05	.02
265 Rangers Logo	.05	.02
266 Red Sox Logo	.05	.02
267 Reds Logo	.05	.02
268 Royals Logo	.05	.02
269 Tigers Logo	.05	.02
270 Twins Logo	.05	.02
271 Chicago Logos	.05	.02
272 New York Logos	.05	.02

1988 Donruss

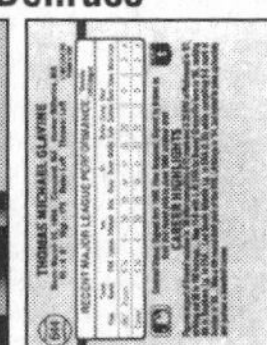

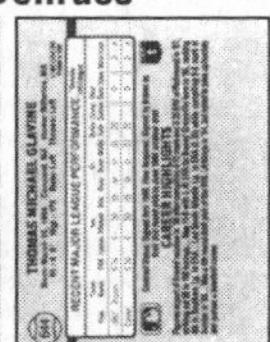

This set consists of 660 standard-size cards. For the seventh straight year, wax packs consisted of 15 cards plus a puzzle panel (featuring Stan Musial this time around). Cards were also distributed in rack packs and retail and hobby factory sets. Card fronts feature a distinctive black and blue border on the front. The card front border design pattern of the factory set card fronts is oriented differently from that of the regular wax pack cards. No premium or discount exists for either version. Subsets include Diamond Kings (1-27) and Rated Rookies (28-47). Cards marked as SP (short printed) from 648-660 are more difficult to find than the other 13 SP's in the lower 600s. These 26 cards listed as SP were apparently pulled from the printing sheet to make room for the 26 Bonus MVP cards. Six of the checklist cards were done two different ways to reflect the inclusion or exclusion of the Bonus MVP cards in the wax packs. In the checklist below, the A variations (for the checklist cards) are from the wax packs and the B variations are from the factory-collated sets. The key Rookie Cards in this set are Roberto Alomar, Jay Bell, Jay Buhner, Ellis Burks, Ken Caminiti, Tom Glavine, Mark Grace and Matt Williams. There was also a Kirby Puckett card issued as the package back of Donruss blister packs; it uses a different photo from both of Kirby's regular and Bonus MVP cards and is unnumbered on the back.

	Nm-Mt	Ex-Mt
COMPLETE SET (660)	10.00	4.00
COMP.FACT.SET (660)	15.00	6.00
COMMON CARD (1-660)	.05	.02
COMMON SP (648-660)	.10	.04
1 Mark McGwire DK	.75	.30
2 Tim Raines DK	.10	.04
3 Benito Santiago DK	.10	.04
4 Alan Trammell DK	.10	.04
5 Danny Tartabull DK	.05	.02
6 Ron Darling DK	.10	.04
7 Paul Molitor DK	.15	.06
8 Devon White DK	.10	.04
9 Andre Dawson DK	.05	.02
10 Julio Franco DK	.10	.04
11 Scott Fletcher DK	.05	.02
12 Tony Fernandez DK	.05	.02
13 Shane Rawley DK	.05	.02
14 Kal Daniels DK	.05	.02
15 Jack Clark DK	.10	.04
16 Dwight Evans DK	.10	.04
17 Tommy John DK	.10	.04
18 Andy Van Slyke DK	.05	.02
19 Gary Gaetti DK	.10	.04
20 Mark Langston DK	.05	.02
21 Will Clark DK	.20	.08
22 Glenn Hubbard DK	.05	.02
23 Billy Hatcher DK	.05	.02
24 Bob Welch DK	.10	.04
25 Ivan Calderon DK	.05	.02
26 Cal Ripken DK	.40	.16
27 DK Checklist 1-26	.05	.02
28 Mackey Sasser RR RC	.25	.10
29 Jeff Treadway RR RC	.25	.10
30 Mike Campbell RR	.05	.02
31 Lance Johnson RR RC	.25	.10
32 Nelson Liriano RR	.05	.02
33 Shawn Abner RR	.05	.02
34 Roberto Alomar RR RC	1.50	.60
35 Shawn Hillegas RR	.05	.02
36 Joey Meyer RR	.05	.02
37 Kevin Elster RR	.05	.02
38 Jose Lind RR RC	.25	.10
39 Kirt Manwaring RR RC	.25	.10
40 Mark Grace RR RC	1.50	.60
41 Jody Reed RR RC	.25	.10
42 John Farrell RR RC	.10	.04
43 Al Leiter RR RC	.50	.20
44 Gary Thurman RR	.05	.02
45 Vicente Palacios RR	.05	.02
46 Eddie Williams RR RC	.10	.04
47 Jack McDowell RR RC	.40	.16
48 Ken Dixon	.05	.02
49 Mike Birkbeck	.05	.02
50 Eric King	.05	.02
51 Roger Clemens	.50	.20
52 Pat Clements	.05	.02
53 Fernando Valenzuela	.10	.04
54 Mark Gubicza	.05	.02
55 Jay Howell	.05	.02
56 Floyd Youmans	.05	.02
57 Ed Correa	.05	.02
58 DeWayne Buice	.05	.02
59 Jose DeLeon	.05	.02
60 Danny Cox	.05	.02
61 Nolan Ryan	1.00	.40
62 Steve Bedrosian	.05	.02
63 Tom Browning	.05	.02
64 Mark Davis	.05	.02
65 R.J. Reynolds	.05	.02
66 Kevin Mitchell	.10	.04
67 Ken Oberkfell	.05	.02
68 Rick Sutcliffe	.10	.04
69 Dwight Gooden	.10	.04
70 Scott Bankhead	.05	.02
71 Bert Blyleven	.10	.04
72 Jimmy Key	.10	.04
73 Les Straker	.05	.02
74 Jim Clancy	.05	.02
75 Mike Moore	.05	.02
76 Ron Darling	.10	.04
77 Ed Lynch	.05	.02
78 Dale Murphy	.15	.06
79 Doug Drabek	.05	.02
80 Scott Garrelts	.05	.02
81 Ed Whitson	.05	.02
82 Rob Murphy	.05	.02
83 Shane Rawley	.05	.02
84 Greg Mathews	.05	.02
85 Jim Deshaies	.05	.02
86 Mike Witt	.05	.02
87 Donnie Hill	.05	.02
88 Jeff Reed	.05	.02
89 Mike Boddicker	.05	.02
90 Ted Higuera	.05	.02
91 Walt Terrell	.05	.02
92 Bob Stanley	.05	.02
93 Dave Righetti	.10	.04
94 Orel Hershiser	.10	.04
95 Chris Bando	.05	.02
96 Bret Saberhagen	.10	.04
97 Curt Young	.05	.02
98 Tim Burke	.05	.02
99 Charlie Hough	.10	.04
100A Checklist 28-137	.05	.02
100B Checklist 28-133	.05	.02
101 Bobby Witt	.05	.02
102 George Brett	.50	.20
103 Mickey Tettleton	.05	.02
104 Scott Bailes	.05	.02
105 Mike Pagliarulo	.05	.02
106 Mike Scioscia	.10	.04
107 Tom Brookens	.05	.02
108 Ray Knight	.10	.04
109 Dan Plesac	.05	.02
110 Wally Joyner	.10	.04
111 Bob Forsch	.05	.02
112 Mike Scott	.10	.04
113 Kevin Gross	.05	.02
114 Benito Santiago	.10	.04
115 Bob Kipper	.05	.02
116 Mike Krukow	.05	.02
117 Chris Bosio	.05	.02
118 Sid Fernandez	.05	.02
119 Jody Davis	.05	.02
120 Mike Morgan	.05	.02
121 Mark Eichhorn	.05	.02
122 Jeff Reardon	.10	.04
123 John Franco	.10	.04
124 Richard Dotson	.05	.02
125 Eric Bell	.05	.02
126 Juan Nieves	.05	.02
127 Jack Morris	.10	.04
128 Rick Rhoden	.05	.02
129 Rich Gedman	.05	.02
130 Ken Howell	.05	.02
131 Brook Jacoby	.05	.02
132 Danny Jackson	.05	.02

133 Gene Nelson .05 .02
134 Neal Heaton .05 .02
135 Willie Fraser .05 .02
136 Jose Guzman .05 .02
137 Ozzie Guillen .05 .02
138 Bob Knepper .05 .02
139 Mike Jackson RC* .25 .10
140 Joe Magrane RC* .25 .10
141 Jimmy Jones .05 .02
142 Ted Power .05 .02
143 Ozzie Virgil .05 .02
144 Felix Fermin .05 .02
145 Kelly Downs .05 .02
146 Shawon Dunston .05 .02
147 Scott Bradley .05 .02
148 Dave Stieb .10 .04
149 Frank Viola .10 .04
150 Terry Kennedy .05 .02
151 Bill Wegman .05 .02
152 Matt Nokes RC* .25 .10
153 Wade Boggs .15 .06
154 Wayne Tolleson .05 .02
155 Mariano Duncan .05 .02
156 Julio Franco .10 .04
157 Charlie Leibrandt .05 .02
158 Terry Steinbach .10 .04
159 Mike Fitzgerald .05 .02
160 Jack Lazorko .05 .02
161 Mitch Williams .05 .02
162 Greg Walker .05 .02
163 Alan Ashby .05 .02
164 Tony Gwynn .30 .12
165 Bruce Ruffin .05 .02
166 Ron Robinson .05 .02
167 Zane Smith .05 .02
168 Junior Ortiz .05 .02
169 Jamie Moyer .10 .04
170 Tony Pena .05 .02
171 Cal Ripken .75 .30
172 B.J. Surhoff .10 .04
173 Lou Whitaker .10 .04
174 Ellis Burks RC .40 .16
175 Ron Guidry .10 .04
176 Steve Sax .05 .02
177 Danny Tartabull .05 .02
178 Carney Lansford .10 .04
179 Casey Candaele .05 .02
180 Scott Fletcher .05 .02
181 Mark McLemore .05 .02
182 Ivan Calderon .05 .02
183 Jack Clark .10 .04
184 Glenn Davis .05 .02
185 Luis Aguayo .05 .02
186 Bo Diaz .05 .02
187 Stan Jefferson .05 .02
188 Sid Bream .05 .02
189 Bob Brenly .05 .02
190 Dion James .05 .02
191 Leon Durham .05 .02
192 Jesse Orosco .05 .02
193 Alvin Davis .05 .02
194 Gary Gaetti .10 .04
195 Fred McGriff .20 .08
196 Steve Lombardozzi .05 .02
197 Rance Mulliniks .05 .02
198 Rey Quinones .05 .02
199 Gary Carter .10 .04
200A Checklist 138-247 .05 .02
200B Checklist 134-239 .05 .02
201 Keith Moreland .05 .02
202 Ken Griffey .10 .04
203 Tommy Gregg .05 .02
204 Will Clark .20 .08
205 John Kruk .10 .04
206 Buddy Bell .10 .04
207 Von Hayes .05 .02
208 Tommy Herr .05 .02
209 Craig Reynolds .05 .02
210 Gary Pettis .05 .02
211 Harold Baines .10 .04
212 Vance Law .05 .02
213 Ken Gerhart .05 .02
214 Jim Gantner .05 .02
215 Chet Lemon .10 .04
216 Dwight Evans .10 .04
217 Don Mattingly .60 .24
218 Franklin Stubbs .05 .02
219 Pat Tabler .05 .02
220 Bo Jackson .20 .08
221 Tony Phillips .05 .02
222 Tim Wallach .05 .02
223 Ruben Sierra .10 .04
224 Steve Buechele .05 .02
225 Frank White .10 .04
226 Alfredo Griffin .05 .02
227 Greg Swindell .05 .02
228 Willie Randolph .10 .04
229 Mike Marshall .05 .02
230 Alan Trammell .10 .04
231 Eddie Murray .20 .08
232 Dale Sveum .05 .02
233 Dick Schofield .05 .02
234 Jose Oquendo .05 .02
235 Bill Doran .05 .02
236 Milt Thompson .05 .02
237 Marvell Wynne .05 .02
238 Bobby Bonilla .10 .04
239 Chris Speier .05 .02
240 Glenn Braggs .05 .02
241 Wally Backman .05 .02
242 Ryne Sandberg .40 .16
243 Phil Bradley .05 .02
244 Kelly Gruber .05 .02
245 Tom Brunansky .05 .02
246 Ron Oester .05 .02
247 Bobby Thigpen .05 .02
248 Fred Lynn .10 .04
249 Paul Molitor .15 .06
250 Darrell Evans .10 .04
251 Gary Ward .05 .02
252 Bruce Hurst .05 .02
253 Bob Welch .10 .04
254 Joe Carter .10 .04
255 Willie Wilson .10 .04
256 Mark McGwire 1.50 .60
257 Mitch Webster .05 .02
258 Brian Downing .10 .04
259 Mike Stanley .05 .02
260 Carlton Fisk .15 .06
261 Billy Hatcher .05 .02
262 Glenn Wilson .05 .02
263 Ozzie Smith .30 .12
264 Randy Ready .05 .02
265 Kurt Stillwell .05 .02
266 David Palmer .05 .02
267 Mike Diaz .05 .02
268 Robby Thompson .05 .02
269 Andre Dawson .10 .04
270 Lee Guetterman .05 .02
271 Willie Upshaw .05 .02
272 Randy Bush .05 .02
273 Larry Sheets .05 .02
274 Rob Deer .05 .02
275 Kirk Gibson .20 .08
276 Marty Barrett .05 .02
277 Rickey Henderson .20 .08
278 Pedro Guerrero .10 .04
279 Brett Butler .10 .04
280 Kevin Seitzer .05 .02
281 Mike Davis .05 .02
282 Andres Galarraga .10 .04
283 Devon White .10 .04
284 Pete O'Brien .05 .02
285 Jerry Hairston .05 .02
286 Kevin Bass .05 .02
287 Carmelo Martinez .05 .02
288 Juan Samuel .05 .02
289 Kal Daniels .05 .02
290 Albert Hall .05 .02
291 Andy Van Slyke .10 .04
292 Lee Smith .10 .04
293 Vince Coleman .05 .02
294 Tom Niedenfuer .05 .02
295 Robin Yount .30 .12
296 Jeff M. Robinson .05 .02
297 Todd Benzinger RC* .25 .10
298 Dave Winfield .10 .04
299 Mickey Hatcher .05 .02
300A Checklist 248-357 .05 .02
300B Checklist 240-345 .05 .02
301 Bud Black .05 .02
302 Jose Canseco .20 .08
303 Tom Foley .05 .02
304 Pete Incaviglia .05 .02
305 Bob Boone .10 .04
306 Bill Long .05 .02
307 Willie McGee .10 .04
308 Ken Caminiti RC .75 .30
309 Darren Daulton .10 .04
310 Tracy Jones .05 .02
311 Greg Booker .05 .02
312 Mike LaValliere .05 .02
313 Chili Davis .10 .04
314 Glenn Hubbard .05 .02
315 Paul Noce .05 .02
316 Keith Hernandez .10 .04
317 Mark Langston .05 .02
318 Keith Atherton .05 .02
319 Tony Fernandez .05 .02
320 Kent Hrbek .10 .04
321 John Cerutti .05 .02
322 Mike Kingery .05 .02
323 Dave Magadan .05 .02
324 Rafael Palmeiro .40 .16
325 Jeff Dedmon .05 .02
326 Barry Bonds 2.00 .80
327 Jeffrey Leonard .05 .02
328 Tim Flannery .05 .02
329 Dave Concepcion .10 .04
330 Mike Schmidt .50 .20
331 Bill Dawley .05 .02
332 Larry Andersen .05 .02
333 Jack Howell .05 .02
334 Ken Williams RC .05 .02
335 Bryn Smith .05 .02
336 Bill Ripken RC* .25 .10
337 Greg Brock .05 .02
338 Mike Heath .05 .02
339 Mike Greenwell .05 .02
340 Claudell Washington .05 .02
341 Jose Gonzalez .05 .02
342 Mel Hall .05 .02
343 Jim Eisenreich .05 .02
344 Tony Bernazard .05 .02
345 Tim Raines .10 .04
346 Bob Brower .05 .02
347 Larry Parrish .05 .02
348 Thad Bosley .05 .02
349 Dennis Eckersley .15 .06
350 Cory Snyder .05 .02
351 Rick Cerone .05 .02
352 John Shelby .05 .02
353 Larry Herndon .05 .02
354 John Habyan .05 .02
355 Chuck Crim .05 .02
356 Gus Polidor .05 .02
357 Ken Dayley .05 .02
358 Danny Darwin .05 .02
359 Lance Parrish .10 .04
360 James Steels .05 .02
361 Al Pedrique .05 .02
362 Mike Aldrete .05 .02
363 Juan Castillo .05 .02
364 Len Dykstra .10 .04
365 Luis Quinones .05 .02
366 Jim Presley .05 .02
367 Lloyd Moseby .05 .02
368 Kirby Puckett .20 .08
369 Eric Davis .10 .04
370 Gary Redus .05 .02
371 Dave Schmidt .05 .02
372 Mark Clear .05 .02
373 Dave Bergman .05 .02
374 Charles Hudson .05 .02
375 Calvin Schiraldi .05 .02
376 Alex Trevino .05 .02
377 Tom Candiotti .05 .02
378 Steve Farr .05 .02
379 Mike Gallego .05 .02
380 Andy McGaffigan .05 .02
381 Kirk McCaskill .05 .02
382 Oddibe McDowell .05 .02
383 Floyd Bannister .05 .02
384 Denny Walling .05 .02
385 Don Carman .05 .02
386 Todd Worrell .05 .02
387 Eric Show .05 .02
388 Dave Parker .10 .04
389 Rick Mahler .05 .02
390 Mike Dunne .05 .02
391 Candy Maldonado .05 .02
392 Bob Dernier .05 .02
393 Dave Valle .05 .02
394 Ernie Whitt .05 .02
395 Juan Berenguer .05 .02
396 Mike Young .05 .02
397 Mike Felder .05 .02
398 Willie Hernandez .05 .02
399 Jim Rice .10 .04
400A Checklist 358-467 .05 .02
400B Checklist 346-451 .05 .02
401 Tommy John .10 .04
402 Brian Holton .05 .02
403 Carmen Castillo .05 .02
404 Jamie Quirk .05 .02
405 Dwayne Murphy .05 .02
406 Jeff Parrett .05 .02
407 Don Sutton .10 .04
408 Jerry Browne .05 .02
409 Jim Winn .05 .02
410 Dave Smith .05 .02
411 Shane Mack .05 .02
412 Greg Gross .05 .02
413 Nick Esasky .05 .02
414 Damaso Garcia .05 .02
415 Brian Fisher .05 .02
416 Brian Dayett .05 .02
417 Curt Ford .05 .02
418 Mark Williamson .05 .02
419 Bill Schroeder .05 .02
420 Mike Henneman RC* .25 .10
421 John Marzano .05 .02
422 Ron Kittle .05 .02
423 Matt Young .05 .02
424 Steve Balboni .05 .02
425 Luis Polonia RC* .25 .10
426 Randy St.Claire .05 .02
427 Greg Harris .05 .02
428 Johnny Ray .05 .02
429 Ray Searage .05 .02
430 Ricky Horton .05 .02
431 Gerald Young .05 .02
432 Rick Schu .05 .02
433 Paul O'Neill .15 .06
434 Rich Gossage .10 .04
435 John Cangelosi .05 .02
436 Mike LaCoss .05 .02
437 Gerald Perry .05 .02
438 Dave Martinez .05 .02
439 Darryl Strawberry .10 .04
440 John Moses .05 .02
441 Greg Gagne .05 .02
442 Jesse Barfield .10 .04
443 George Frazier .05 .02
444 Garth Iorg .05 .02
445 Ed Nunez .05 .02
446 Rick Aguilera .05 .02
447 Jerry Mumphrey .05 .02
448 Rafael Ramirez .05 .02
449 John Smiley RC* .25 .10
450 Atlee Hammaker .05 .02
451 Lance McCullers .05 .02
452 Guy Hoffman .05 .02
453 Chris James .05 .02
454 Terry Pendleton .10 .04
455 Dave Meads .05 .02
456 Bill Buckner .10 .04
457 John Pawlowski .05 .02
458 Bob Sebra .05 .02
459 Jim Dwyer .05 .02
460 Jay Aldrich .05 .02
461 Frank Tanana .10 .04
462 Oil Can Boyd .05 .02
463 Dan Pasqua .05 .02
464 Tim Crews RC .25 .10
465 Andy Allanson .05 .02
466 Bill Pecota RC* .10 .04
467 Steve Ontiveros .05 .02
468 Hubie Brooks .05 .02
469 Paul Kilgus .05 .02
470 Dale Mohorcic .05 .02
471 Dan Quisenberry .05 .02
472 Dave Stewart .10 .04
473 Dave Clark .05 .02
474 Joel Skinner .05 .02
475 Dave Anderson .05 .02
476 Dan Petry .05 .02
477 Carl Nichols .05 .02
478 Ernest Riles .05 .02
479 George Hendrick .10 .04
480 John Morris .05 .02
481 Manny Hernandez .05 .02
482 Jeff Stone .05 .02
483 Chris Brown .05 .02
484 Mike Bielecki .05 .02
485 Dave Dravecky .05 .02
486 Rick Manning .05 .02
487 Bill Almon .05 .02
488 Jim Sundberg .10 .04
489 Ken Phelps .05 .02
490 Tom Henke .05 .02
491 Dan Gladden .05 .02
492 Barry Larkin .15 .06
493 Fred Manrique .05 .02
494 Mike Griffin .05 .02
495 Mark Knudson .05 .02
496 Bill Madlock .10 .04
497 Tim Stoddard .05 .02
498 Sam Horn RC .10 .04
499 Tracy Woodson RC .10 .04
500A Checklist 468-577 .05 .02
500B Checklist 452-557 .05 .02
501 Ken Schrom .05 .02
502 Angel Salazar .05 .02
503 Eric Plunk .05 .02
504 Joe Hesketh .05 .02
505 Greg Minton .05 .02
506 Geno Petralli .05 .02
507 Bob James .05 .02
508 Robbie Wine .05 .02
509 Jeff Calhoun .05 .02
510 Steve Lake .05 .02
511 Mark Grant .05 .02
512 Frank Williams .05 .02
513 Jeff Blauser RC .25 .10
514 Bob Walk .05 .02
515 Craig Lefferts .05 .02
516 Manny Trillo .10 .04
517 Jerry Reed .05 .02
518 Rick Leach .05 .02
519 Mark Davidson .05 .02
520 Jeff Ballard .05 .02
521 Dave Stapleton .05 .02
522 Pat Sheridan .05 .02
523 Al Nipper .05 .02
524 Steve Trout .05 .02
525 Jeff Hamilton .05 .02
526 Tommy Hinzo .05 .02
527 Lonnie Smith .05 .02
528 Greg Cadaret .05 .02
529 Bob McClure UER .05 .02
(Rob on front)
530 Chuck Finley .10 .04
531 Jeff Russell .05 .02
532 Steve Lyons .05 .02
533 Terry Puhl .05 .02
534 Eric Nolte .05 .02
535 Kent Tekulve .05 .02
536 Pat Pacillo .05 .02
537 Charlie Puleo .05 .02
538 Tom Prince .05 .02
539 Greg Maddux 1.00 .40
540 Jim Lindeman .05 .02
541 Pete Stanicek .05 .02
542 Steve Kiefer .05 .02
543A Jim Morrison ERR .15 .06
(No decimal before lifetime average)
543B Jim Morrison COR .05 .02
544 Spike Owen .05 .02
545 Jay Buhner RC .50 .20
546 Mike Devereaux RC .25 .10
547 Jerry Don Gleaton .05 .02
548 Jose Rijo .10 .04
549 Dennis Martinez .10 .04
550 Mike Loynd .05 .02
551 Darrell Miller .05 .02
552 Dave LaPoint .05 .02
553 John Tudor .10 .04
554 Rocky Childress .05 .02
555 Wally Ritchie .05 .02
556 Terry McGriff .05 .02
557 Dave Leiper .05 .02
558 Jeff D. Robinson .05 .02
559 Jose Uribe .05 .02
560 Ted Simmons .10 .04
561 Les Lancaster .05 .02
562 Keith A. Miller RC .25 .10
563 Harold Reynolds .10 .04
564 Gene Larkin RC* .25 .10
565 Cecil Fielder .10 .04
566 Roy Smalley .05 .02
567 Duane Ward .05 .02
568 Bill Wilkinson .05 .02
569 Howard Johnson .10 .04
570 Frank DiPino .05 .02
571 Pete Smith RC .10 .04
572 Darnell Coles .05 .02
573 Don Robinson .05 .02
574 Rob Nelson UER .05 .02
(Career 0 RBI, but 1 RBI in '87)
575 Dennis Rasmussen .05 .02
576 Steve Jeltz UER .05 .02
(Photo actually Juan Samuel; Samuel noted for one batting glove and black bat)
577 Tom Pagnozzi RC .10 .04
578 Ty Gainey .05 .02
579 Gary Lucas .05 .02
580 Ron Hassey .05 .02
581 Herm Winningham .05 .02
582 Rene Gonzales RC .10 .04
583 Brad Komminsk .05 .02
584 Doyle Alexander .05 .02
585 Jeff Sellers .05 .02
586 Bill Gullickson .05 .02
587 Tim Belcher .05 .02
588 Doug Jones RC .25 .10
589 Melido Perez RC .25 .10
590 Rick Honeycutt .05 .02
591 Pascual Perez .05 .02
592 Curt Wilkerson .05 .02
593 Steve Howe .05 .02
594 John Davis .05 .02
595 Storm Davis .05 .02
596 Sammy Stewart .05 .02
597 Neil Allen .05 .02
598 Alejandro Pena .05 .02
599 Mark Thurmond .05 .02
600A Checklist 578-660 .05 .02
BC1-BC26
600B Checklist 558-660 .05 .02
601 Jose Mesa RC .25 .10
602 Don August .05 .02
603 Terry Leach SP .10 .04
604 Tom Newell .05 .02
605 Randall Byers SP .10 .04
606 Jim Gott .05 .02
607 Harry Spilman .05 .02
608 John Candelaria .05 .02
609 Mike Brumley .05 .02
610 Mickey Brantley .05 .02
611 Jose Nunez SP .10 .04
612 Tom Nieto .05 .02
613 Rick Reuschel .10 .04
614 Lee Mazzilli SP .10 .04
615 Scott Lusader .05 .02
616 Bobby Meacham .05 .02
617 Kevin McReynolds SP .10 .04
618 Gene Garber .05 .02
619 Barry Lyons SP .10 .04
620 Randy Myers .10 .04
621 Donnie Moore .05 .02
622 Domingo Ramos .05 .02
623 Ed Romero .05 .02
624 Greg Myers RC .25 .10
625 Ripken Family .40 .16
Cal Ripken Sr.
Cal Ripken Jr.
Billy Ripken
626 Pat Perry .05 .02
627 Andres Thomas SP .10 .04
628 Matt Williams SP RC .75 .30
629 Dave Hengel .05 .02
630 Jeff Musselman SP .10 .04
631 Tim Laudner .05 .02
632 Bob Ojeda SP .10 .04
633 Rafael Santana .05 .02
634 Wes Gardner .05 .02
635 Roberto Kelly SP RC .25 .10
636 Mike Flanagan SP .10 .04
637 Jay Bell RC .40 .16
638 Bob Melvin .05 .02
639 D.Berryhill RC UER .25 .10
Bats: Swithch
640 David Wells SP RC .75 .30
641 Stan Musial PUZ .20 .08
642 Doug Sisk .05 .02
643 Keith Hughes .05 .02
644 Tom Glavine RC 1.50 .60
645 Al Newman .05 .02
646 Scott Sanderson .05 .02
647 Scott Terry .05 .02
648 Tim Teufel SP .10 .04
649 Garry Templeton SP .10 .04
650 Manny Lee SP .10 .04
651 Roger McDowell SP .10 .04
652 Mookie Wilson SP .10 .04
653 David Cone SP .10 .04
654 Ron Gant SP RC .40 .16
655 Joe Price SP .10 .04
656 George Bell SP .10 .04
657 Gregg Jefferies SP RC .25 .10
658 T.Stottlemyre SP RC .25 .10
659 G.Berroa SP RC .25 .10
660 Jerry Royster SP .10 .04
XX Kirby Puckett 1.25 .50
Blister Pack

1988 Donruss Bonus MVP's

Numbered with the prefix "BC" for bonus carc this 26-card set featuring the most valuable play er from each major league team was randoml inserted in the wax and rack packs. The cards ar distinguished by the MVP logo in the upper le corner of the obverse, and cards BC14-BC26 ar considered to be very slightly more difficult t find than cards BC1-BC13.

	Nm-Mt	Ex-Mt
COMPLETE SET (26)	3.00	1.20
BC1 Cal Ripken	.75	.30
BC2 Eric Davis	.10	.04
BC3 Paul Molitor	.15	.06
BC4 Mike Schmidt	.50	.20
BC5 Ivan Calderon	.05	.02
BC6 Tony Gwynn	.30	.12
BC7 Wade Boggs	.15	.06
BC8 Andy Van Slyke	.10	.04
BC9 Joe Carter	.10	.04
BC10 Andre Dawson	.10	.04
BC11 Alan Trammell	.10	.04
BC12 Mike Scott	.10	.04
BC13 Wally Joyner	.10	.04
BC14 Dale Murphy SP	.15	.06
BC15 Kirby Puckett SP	.20	.08
BC16 Pedro Guerrero SP	.10	.04
BC17 Kevin Seitzer SP	.05	.02
BC18 Tim Raines SP	.10	.04
BC19 George Bell SP	.10	.04
BC20 D.Strawberry SP	.10	.04
BC21 Don Mattingly SP	.60	.24
BC22 Ozzie Smith SP	.30	.12
BC23 Mark McGwire SP	1.50	.60
BC24 Will Clark SP	.20	.08
BC25 Alvin Davis SP	.05	.02
BC26 Ruben Sierra SP	.10	.04

1988 Donruss Rookies

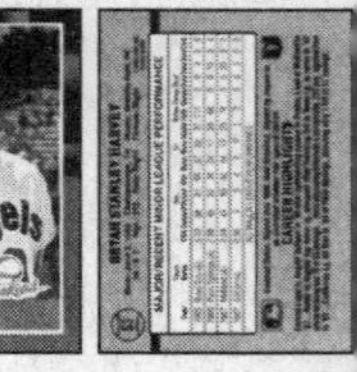

The 1988 Donruss "The Rookies" set features 5 standard-size full-color cards plus a 15-piec puzzle of Stan Musial. This set was distribute exclusively in factory set form in a small, cellc phane-wrapped, green and black through hobb dealers. Card fronts are similar in design to th 1988 Donruss regular issue except for the pres ence of "The Rookies" logo in the lower right co ner and a green and black border instead of blue and black border on the fronts. Extende Rookie Cards in this set include Brady Anderso Edgar Martinez, and Walt Weiss. Notable ear cards were issued of Roberto Alomar, Ma Grace and Jay Buhner.

	Nm-Mt	Ex-Mt
COMP.FACT.SET (56)	10.00	4.00
1 Mark Grace	2.00	.80
2 Mike Campbell	.15	.06
3 Todd Frohwirth	.15	.06
4 Dave Stapleton	.15	.06
5 Shawn Abner	.15	.06
6 Jose Cecena	.15	.06
7 Dave Gallagher	.15	.06
8 Mark Parent	.15	.06
9 Cecil Espy	.15	.06
10 Pete Smith	.15	.06
11 Jay Buhner	1.00	.40
12 Pat Borders XRC	.50	.20
13 Doug Jennings	.15	.06
14 Brady Anderson XRC	.75	.30
15 Pete Stanicek	.15	.06
16 Roberto Kelly	.50	.20
17 Jeff Treadway	.15	.06

8 Walt Weiss XRC* .75 .30
9 Paul Gibson .15 .06
) Tim Crews .15 .06
1 Melido Perez .15 .06
2 Steve Peters .15 .06
3 Craig Worthington .15 .06
4 John Trautwein .15 .06
5 DeWayne Vaughn .15 .06
5 David Wells 1.50 .60
7 Al Leiter 1.00 .40
3 Tim Belcher .15 .06
3 Johnny Paredes .15 .06
) Chris Sabo XRC .40 .16
1 Damon Berryhill .15 .06
2 Randy Milligan XRC* .25 .10
3 Gary Thurman .15 .06
4 Kevin Elster .15 .06
5 Roberto Alomar 1.50 .60
5 E.Martinez UER XRC 2.50 1.00
Photo actually
Edwin Nunez
7 Todd Stottlemyre .15 .06
3 Joey Meyer .15 .06
3 Carl Nichols .15 .06
) Jack McDowell .75 .30
1 Jose Bautista XRC .25 .10
2 Sil Campusano .15 .06
3 John Dopson .15 .06
4 Jody Reed .50 .20
5 Darrin Jackson XRC* .25 .10
5 Mike Capel .15 .06
7 Ron Gant .75 .30
3 John Davis .15 .06
3 Kevin Coffman .15 .06
) Cris Carpenter XRC .25 .10
1 Mackey Sasser .15 .06
2 Luis Alicea XRC .50 .20
3 Bryan Harvey XRC .30 .12
4 Steve Ellsworth .15 .06
5 Mike Macfarlane XRC .50 .20
5 Checklist 1-56 .15 .06

988 Donruss Baseball's Best

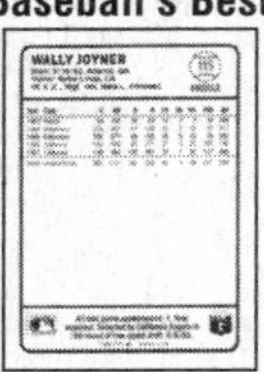

his innovative set of 336 standard-size cards as released by Donruss very late in the 1988 eason to be sold in large national retail chains s a complete packaged set. The set was packged in a specially designed box. Cards are very milar in design to the 1988 regular Donruss sue except that these cards have orange and ack borders instead of blue and black borders. he set is also sometimes referred to as the alloween set because of the orange box and esign of the cards. Six (2 1/2" by 3 1/2") 15-ece puzzles of Stan Musial are also included th every complete set.

Nm-Mt Ex-Mt
OMP.FACT.SET (336) 25.00 10.00
Don Mattingly 1.00 .40
Ron Gant .50 .20
Bob Boone .20 .08
Mark Grace 1.50 .60
Andy Allanson .10 .04
Kal Daniels .10 .04
Floyd Bannister .10 .04
Alan Ashby .10 .04
Marty Barrett .10 .04
0 Tim Belcher .20 .08
1 Harold Baines .20 .08
2 Hubie Brooks .10 .04
3 Doyle Alexander .10 .04
4 Gary Carter .50 .20
5 Glenn Braggs .10 .04
6 Steve Bedrosian .10 .04
7 Barry Bonds 1.00 .40
8 Bert Blyleven .20 .08
9 Tom Brunansky .10 .04
0 John Candelaria .10 .04
1 Shawn Abner .10 .04
2 Jose Canseco .50 .20
3 Brett Butler .20 .08
4 Scott Bradley .10 .04
5 Ivan Calderon .10 .04
6 Rich Gossage .20 .08
7 Brian Downing .10 .04
8 Jim Rice .20 .08
9 Dion James .10 .04
0 Terry Kennedy .10 .04
1 George Bell .10 .04
2 Scott Fletcher .10 .04
3 Bobby Bonilla .20 .08
4 Tim Burke .10 .04
5 Darrell Evans .20 .08
6 Mike Davis .10 .04
7 Shawon Dunston .10 .04
8 Kevin Bass .10 .04
9 George Brett 1.25 .50
0 David Cone .40 .16
1 Ron Darling .10 .04
2 Roberto Alomar 2.00 .80
3 Dennis Eckersley .20 .08
4 Vince Coleman .10 .04
5 Sid Bream .10 .04
6 Gary Gaetti .20 .08
7 Phil Bradley .10 .04
8 Jim Clancy .10 .04
9 Jack Clark .20 .08
0 Mike Krukow .10 .04
1 Henry Cotto .10 .04
2 Rich Dotson .10 .04
3 Jim Gantner .10 .04
4 John Franco .20 .08
5 Pete Incaviglia .10 .04
6 Joe Carter .40 .16
7 Roger Clemens 1.00 .40
8 Gerald Perry .10 .04
9 Jack Howell .10 .04
60 Vance Law .10 .04
61 Jay Bell .50 .20
62 Eric Davis .20 .08
63 Gene Garber .20 .08
64 Glenn Davis .10 .04
65 Wade Boggs .50 .20
66 Kirk Gibson .20 .08
67 Carlton Fisk .50 .20
68 Casey Candaele .10 .04
69 Mike Heath .10 .04
70 Kevin Elster .10 .04
71 Greg Brock .10 .04
72 Don Carman .10 .04
73 Doug Drabek .20 .08
74 Greg Gagne .10 .04
75 Danny Cox .10 .04
76 Rickey Henderson .50 .20
77 Chris Brown .10 .04
78 Terry Steinbach .20 .08
79 Will Clark .50 .20
80 Mickey Brantley .10 .04
81 Ozzie Guillen .20 .08
82 Greg Maddux 1.25 .50
83 Kirk McCaskill .10 .04
84 Dwight Evans .20 .08
85 Ozzie Virgil .10 .04
86 Mike Morgan .10 .04
87 Tony Fernandez .20 .08
88 Jose Guzman .10 .04
89 Mike Dunne .10 .04
90 Andres Galarraga .40 .16
91 Mike Henneman .20 .08
92 Alfredo Griffin .10 .04
93 Rafael Palmeiro .75 .30
94 Jim Deshaies .10 .04
95 Mark Gubicza .10 .04
96 Dwight Gooden .20 .08
97 Howard Johnson .10 .04
98 Mark Davis .10 .04
99 Dave Stewart .20 .08
100 Joe Magrane .10 .04
101 Brian Fisher .10 .04
102 Kent Hrbek .20 .08
103 Kevin Gross .10 .04
104 Tom Henke .10 .04
105 Mike Pagliarulo .10 .04
106 Kelly Downs .10 .04
107 Alvin Davis .10 .04
108 Willie Randolph .20 .08
109 Rob Deer .10 .04
110 Bo Diaz .10 .04
111 Paul Kilgus .10 .04
112 Tom Candiotti .10 .04
113 Dale Murphy .40 .16
114 Rick Mahler .10 .04
115 Wally Joyner .30 .12
116 Ryne Sandberg .50 .20
117 John Farrell .10 .04
118 Nick Esasky .10 .04
119 Bo Jackson .40 .16
120 Bill Doran .10 .04
121 Ellis Burks .75 .30
122 Pedro Guerrero .10 .04
123 Dave LaPoint .10 .04
124 Neal Heaton .10 .04
125 Willie Hernandez .10 .04
126 Roger McDowell .10 .04
127 Ted Higuera .10 .04
128 Von Hayes .10 .04
129 Mike LaValliere .10 .04
130 Dan Gladden .10 .04
131 Willie McGee .20 .08
132 Al Leiter .50 .20
133 Mark Grant .10 .04
134 Bob Welch .10 .04
135 Dave Dravecky .20 .08
136 Mark Langston .10 .04
137 Dan Pasqua .10 .04
138 Rick Sutcliffe .10 .04
139 Dan Petry .10 .04
140 Rich Gedman .10 .04
141 Ken Griffey .20 .08
142 Eddie Murray .50 .20
143 Jimmy Key .20 .08
144 Dale Mohorcic .10 .04
145 Jose Lind .10 .04
146 Dennis Martinez .20 .08
147 Chet Lemon .10 .04
148 Orel Hershiser .20 .08
149 Dave Martinez .10 .04
150 Billy Hatcher .10 .04
151 Charlie Leibrandt .10 .04
152 Keith Hernandez .20 .08
153 Kevin McReynolds .10 .04
154 Tony Gwynn 1.00 .40
155 Stan Javier .10 .04
156 Tony Pena .20 .08
157 Andy Van Slyke .20 .08
158 Gene Larkin .10 .04
159 Chris James .10 .04
160 Fred McGriff .75 .30
161 Rick Rhoden .10 .04
162 Scott Garrelts .10 .04
163 Mike Campbell .10 .04
164 Dave Righetti .10 .04
165 Paul Molitor .50 .20
166 Danny Jackson .10 .04
167 Pete O'Brien .10 .04
168 Julio Franco .20 .08
169 Mark McGwire 2.00 .80
170 Zane Smith .10 .04
171 Johnny Ray .10 .04
172 Les Lancaster .10 .04
173 Mel Hall .10 .04
174 Tracy Jones .10 .04
175 Kevin Seitzer .20 .08
176 Bob Knepper .10 .04
177 Mike Greenwell .10 .04
178 Mike Marshall .10 .04
179 Melido Perez .10 .04
180 Tim Raines .20 .08
181 Jack Morris .20 .08
182 Darryl Strawberry .20 .08
183 Robin Yount .50 .20
184 Lance Parrish .10 .04
185 Darnell Coles .10 .04
186 Kirby Puckett .50 .20
187 Terry Pendleton .20 .08
188 Don Slaught .10 .04
189 Jimmy Jones .10 .04
190 Dave Parker .20 .08
191 Mike Aldrete .10 .04
192 Mike Moore .10 .04
193 Greg Walker .10 .04
194 Calvin Schiraldi .10 .04
195 Dick Schofield .10 .04
196 Jody Reed .20 .08
197 Pete Smith .10 .04
198 Cal Ripken 2.00 .80
199 Lloyd Moseby .10 .04
200 Ruben Sierra .20 .08
201 R.J. Reynolds .10 .04
202 Bryn Smith .10 .04
203 Gary Pettis .10 .04
204 Steve Sax .10 .04
205 Frank DiPino .10 .04
206 Mike Scott UER .10 .04
(1977 Jackson losses
say 1.10, should be 1)
207 Kurt Stillwell .10 .04
208 Mookie Wilson .20 .08
209 Lee Mazzilli .10 .04
210 Lance McCullers .10 .04
211 Rick Honeycutt .10 .04
212 John Tudor .10 .04
213 Jim Gott .10 .04
214 Frank Viola .10 .04
215 Juan Samuel .10 .04
216 Jesse Barfield .10 .04
217 Claudell Washington .10 .04
218 Rick Reuschel .10 .04
219 Jim Presley .10 .04
220 Tommy John .20 .08
221 Dan Plesac .10 .04
222 Barry Larkin .40 .16
223 Mike Stanley .10 .04
224 Cory Snyder .10 .04
225 Andre Dawson .40 .16
226 Ken Oberkfell .10 .04
227 Devon White .20 .08
228 Jamie Moyer .30 .12
229 Brook Jacoby .10 .04
230 Rob Murphy .10 .04
231 Bret Saberhagen .20 .08
232 Nolan Ryan 2.00 .80
233 Bruce Hurst .10 .04
234 Jesse Orosco .20 .08
235 Bobby Thigpen .10 .04
236 Pascual Perez .10 .04
237 Matt Nokes .20 .08
238 Bob Ojeda .10 .04
239 Joey Meyer .10 .04
240 Shane Rawley .10 .04
241 Jeff Robinson .10 .04
242 Jeff Reardon .20 .08
243 Ozzie Smith .40 .16
244 Dave Winfield .50 .20
245 John Kruk .20 .08
246 Carney Lansford .20 .08
247 Candy Maldonado .10 .04
248 Ken Phelps .10 .04
249 Ken Williams .20 .08
250 Al Nipper .10 .04
251 Mark McLemore .10 .04
252 Lee Smith .20 .08
253 Albert Hall .10 .04
254 Billy Ripken .10 .04
255 Kelly Gruber .10 .04
256 Charlie Hough .20 .08
257 John Smiley .20 .08
258 Tim Wallach .20 .08
259 Frank Tanana .20 .08
260 Mike Scioscia .20 .08
261 Damon Berryhill .10 .04
262 Dave Smith .20 .08
263 Willie Wilson .10 .04
264 Len Dykstra .20 .08
265 Randy Myers .30 .12
266 Keith Moreland .10 .04
267 Eric Plunk .10 .04
268 Todd Worrell .20 .08
269 Bob Walk .10 .04
270 Keith Atherton .10 .04
271 Mike Schmidt .50 .20
272 Mike Flanagan .10 .04
273 Rafael Santana .10 .04
274 Robby Thompson .20 .08
275 Rey Quinones .10 .04
276 Cecilio Guante .10 .04
277 B.J. Surhoff .30 .12
278 Chris Sabo .20 .08
279 Mitch Williams .10 .04
280 Greg Swindell .10 .04
281 Alan Trammell .30 .12
282 Storm Davis .10 .04
283 Chuck Finley .30 .12
284 Dave Stieb .20 .08
285 Scott Bailes .10 .04
286 Larry Sheets .10 .04
287 Danny Tartabull .10 .04
288 Checklist Card .10 .04
289 Todd Benzinger .10 .04
290 John Shelby .10 .04
291 Steve Lyons .20 .08
292 Mitch Webster .10 .04
293 Walt Terrell .10 .04
294 Pete Stanicek .10 .04
295 Chris Bosio .10 .04
296 Milt Thompson .10 .04
297 Fred Lynn .20 .08
298 Juan Berenguer .10 .04
299 Ken Dayley .10 .04
300 Joel Skinner .10 .04
301 Benito Santiago .20 .08
302 Ron Hassey .10 .04
303 Jose Uribe .10 .04
304 Harold Reynolds .20 .08
305 Dale Sveum .10 .04
306 Glenn Wilson .10 .04
307 Mike Witt .10 .04
308 Ron Robinson .10 .04
309 Denny Walling .10 .04
310 Joe Orsulak .20 .08
311 David Wells 1.50 .60
312 Steve Buechele .10 .04
313 Jose Oquendo .10 .04
314 Floyd Youmans .10 .04
315 Lou Whitaker .20 .08
316 Fernando Valenzuela .20 .08
317 Mike Boddicker .10 .04
318 Gerald Young .10 .04
319 Frank White .20 .08
320 Bill Wegman .10 .04
321 Tom Niedenfuer .10 .04
322 Ed Whitson .10 .04
323 Curt Young .10 .04
324 Greg Mathews .10 .04
325 Doug Jones .40 .16
326 Tommy Herr .10 .04
327 Kent Tekulve .10 .04
328 Rance Mulliniks .10 .04
329 Checklist Card .10 .04
330 Craig Lefferts .10 .04
331 Franklin Stubbs .10 .04
332 Rick Cerone .10 .04
333 Dave Schmidt .10 .04
334 Larry Parrish .10 .04
335 Tom Browning .10 .04
336 Checklist Card .10 .04

1989 Donruss

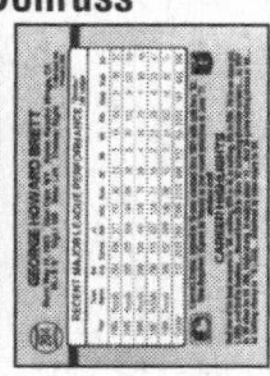

This set consists of 660 standard-size cards. The cards were primarily issued in 15-card wax packs, rack packs and hobby and retail factory sets. Each wax pack also contained a puzzle panel (featuring Warren Spahn this year). The cards feature a distinctive black side border with an alternating coating. Subsets include Diamond Kings (1-27) and Rated Rookies (28-47). There are two variations that occur throughout most of the set. On the card backs "Denotes Led League" can be found with one asterisk to the left or with an asterisk on each side. On the card fronts the horizontal lines on the left and right borders can be glossy or non-glossy. Since both of these variation types are relatively minor and seem equally common, there is no premium value for either type. Rather than short-printing 26 cards in order to make room for printing the Bonus MVP's this year, Donruss apparently chose to double print 106 cards. These double prints are listed below by DP. Rookie Cards in this set include Sandy Alomar Jr., Brady Anderson, Dante Bichette, Craig Biggio, Ken Griffey Jr., Randy Johnson, Curt Schilling, Gary Sheffield and John Smoltz. Similar to the 1988 Donruss set, a special card was issued on blister packs, and features the card number as "Bonus Card".

Nm-Mt Ex-Mt
COMPLETE SET (660) 25.00 10.00
COMP.FACT.SET (672) 25.00 10.00
1 Mike Greenwell DK .05 .02
2 Bobby Bonilla DK DP .10 .04
3 Pete Incaviglia DK .05 .02
4 Chris Sabo DK DP .10 .04
5 Robin Yount DK .40 .16
6 Tony Gwynn DK DP .15 .06
7 Carlton Fisk DK UER .15 .06
(OF on back)
8 Cory Snyder DK .05 .02
9 David Cone DK UER .10 .04
("hurdlers")
10 Kevin Seitzer DK .05 .02
11 Rick Reuschel DK .10 .04
12 Johnny Ray DK .05 .02
13 Dave Schmidt DK .05 .02
14 Andres Galarraga DK .10 .04
15 Kirk Gibson DK .10 .04
16 Fred McGriff DK .15 .06
17 Mark Grace DK .25 .10
18 Jeff M. Robinson DK .05 .02
19 Vince Coleman DK DP .05 .02
20 Dave Henderson DK .05 .02
21 Harold Reynolds DK .05 .02
22 Gerald Perry DK .05 .02
23 Frank Viola DK .10 .04
24 Steve Bedrosian DK .05 .02
25 Glenn Davis DK .05 .02
26 Don Mattingly DK UER .30 .12
(Doesn't mention Don's
previous DK in 1985)
27 DK Checklist 1-26 DP .05 .02
28 S.Alomar Jr. RR RC .40 .16
29 Steve Searcy RR .05 .02
30 Cameron Drew RR .05 .02
31 Gary Sheffield RR RC 1.50 .60
32 Erik Hanson RR RC .25 .10
33 Ken Griffey Jr. RR RC 8.00 3.20
34 Greg W. Harris RR RC .10 .04
35 Gregg Jefferies RR .05 .02
36 Luis Medina RR .05 .02
37 Carlos Quintana RR RC .10 .04
38 Felix Jose RR RC .10 .04
39 Cris Carpenter RR RC* .10 .04
40 Ron Jones RR .10 .04
41 Dave West RR RC .10 .04
42 R.Johnson RC RR UER 4.00 1.20
Card says born in 1964
he was born in 1963
43 Mike Harkey RR RC .10 .04
44 P.Harnisch RR DP RC .25 .10
45 Tom Gordon RR DP RC .40 .16
46 Gregg Olson RC RR DP .25 .10
47 Alex Sanchez RR DP .05 .02
48 Ruben Sierra .05 .02
49 Rafael Palmeiro .25 .10
50 Ron Gant .10 .04
51 Cal Ripken .75 .30
52 Wally Joyner .10 .04
53 Gary Carter .10 .04
54 Andy Van Slyke .10 .04
55 Robin Yount .40 .16
56 Pete Incaviglia .05 .02
57 Greg Brock .05 .02
58 Melido Perez .05 .02
59 Craig Lefferts .05 .02
60 Gary Pettis .05 .02
61 Danny Tartabull .05 .02
62 Guillermo Hernandez .05 .02
63 Ozzie Smith .40 .16
64 Gary Gaetti .10 .04
65 Mark Davis .05 .02
66 Lee Smith .10 .04
67 Dennis Eckersley .15 .06
68 Wade Boggs .15 .06
69 Mike Scott .10 .04
70 Fred McGriff .15 .06
71 Tom Browning .05 .02
72 Claudell Washington .05 .02
73 Mel Hall .05 .02
74 Don Mattingly .60 .24
75 Steve Bedrosian .05 .02
76 Juan Samuel .05 .02
77 Mike Scioscia .10 .04
78 Dave Righetti .10 .04
79 Alfredo Griffin .05 .02
80 Eric Davis UER .10 .04
(165 games in 1988,
should be 135)
81 Juan Berenguer .05 .02
82 Todd Worrell .05 .02
83 Joe Carter .10 .04
84 Steve Sax .05 .02
85 Frank White .10 .04
86 John Kruk .10 .04
87 Rance Mulliniks .05 .02
88 Alan Ashby .05 .02
89 Charlie Leibrandt .05 .02
90 Frank Tanana .10 .04
91 Jose Canseco .25 .10
92 Barry Bonds 1.25 .50
93 Harold Reynolds .10 .04
94 Mark McLemore .05 .02
95 Mark McGwire 1.00 .40
96 Eddie Murray .25 .10
97 Tim Raines .10 .04
98 Robby Thompson .05 .02
99 Kevin McReynolds .05 .02
100 Checklist 28-137 .05 .02
101 Carlton Fisk .15 .06
102 Dave Martinez .05 .02
103 Glenn Braggs .05 .02
104 Dale Murphy .15 .06
105 Ryne Sandberg .40 .16
106 Dennis Martinez .10 .04
107 Pete O'Brien .05 .02
108 Dick Schofield .05 .02
109 Henry Cotto .05 .02
110 Mike Marshall .05 .02
111 Keith Moreland .05 .02
112 Tom Brunansky .05 .02
113 Kelly Gruber UER .05 .02
(Wrong birthdate)
114 Brook Jacoby .05 .02
115 Keith Brown .05 .02
116 Matt Nokes .05 .02
117 Keith Hernandez .10 .04
118 Bob Forsch .05 .02
119 Bert Blyleven UER .10 .04
(... 3000 strikeouts in
1987, should be 1986)
120 Willie Wilson .10 .04
121 Tommy Gregg .05 .02
122 Jim Rice .10 .04
123 Bob Knepper .05 .02
124 Danny Jackson .05 .02
125 Eric Plunk .05 .02
126 Brian Fisher .05 .02
127 Mike Pagliarulo .05 .02
128 Tony Gwynn .30 .12
129 Lance McCullers .05 .02
130 Andres Galarraga .10 .04
131 Jose Uribe .05 .02
132 Kirk Gibson UER .10 .04
(Wrong birthdate)
133 David Palmer .05 .02
134 R.J. Reynolds .05 .02
135 Greg Walker .05 .02
136 Kirk McCaskill UER .05 .02
(Wrong birthdate)
137 Shawon Dunston .05 .02
138 Andy Allanson .05 .02
139 Rob Murphy .05 .02
140 Mike Aldrete .05 .02
141 Terry Kennedy .05 .02
142 Scott Fletcher .05 .02
143 Steve Balboni .05 .02
144 Bret Saberhagen .10 .04
145 Ozzie Virgil .05 .02
146 Dale Sveum .05 .02
147 Darryl Strawberry .10 .04
148 Harold Baines .10 .04
149 George Bell .10 .04
150 Dave Parker .10 .04
151 Bobby Bonilla .10 .04
152 Mookie Wilson .10 .04
153 Ted Power .05 .02
154 Nolan Ryan 1.00 .40
155 Jeff Reardon .10 .04
156 Tim Wallach .05 .02
157 Jamie Moyer .10 .04
158 Rich Gossage .10 .04
159 Dave Winfield .10 .04
160 Von Hayes .05 .02
161 Willie McGee .10 .04
162 Rich Gedman .05 .02
163 Tony Pena .05 .02
164 Mike Morgan .05 .02
165 Charlie Hough .10 .04
166 Mike Stanley .05 .02
167 Andre Dawson .10 .04
168 Joe Boever .05 .02
169 Pete Stanicek .05 .02
170 Bob Boone .10 .04
171 Ron Darling .10 .04
172 Bob Walk .05 .02
173 Rob Deer .05 .02
174 Steve Buechele .05 .02
175 Ted Higuera .05 .02
176 Ozzie Guillen .05 .02
177 Candy Maldonado .05 .02
178 Doyle Alexander .05 .02
179 Mark Gubicza .05 .02
180 Alan Trammell .10 .04
181 Vince Coleman .05 .02
182 Kirby Puckett .25 .10
183 Chris Brown .05 .02

184 Marty Barrett .05 .02
185 Stan Javier .05 .02
186 Mike Greenwell .05 .02
187 Billy Hatcher .05 .02
188 Jimmy Key .10 .04
189 Nick Esasky .05 .02
190 Don Slaught .05 .02
191 Cory Snyder .05 .02
192 John Candelaria .05 .02
193 Mike Schmidt .50 .20
194 Kevin Gross .05 .02
195 John Tudor .10 .04
196 Neil Allen .05 .02
197 Orel Hershiser .10 .04
198 Kal Daniels .05 .02
199 Kent Hrbek .10 .04
200 Checklist 138-247 .05 .02
201 Joe Magrane .05 .02
202 Scott Bailes .05 .02
203 Tim Belcher .05 .02
204 George Brett .60 .24
205 Benito Santiago .10 .04
206 Tony Fernandez .05 .02
207 Gerald Young .05 .02
208 Bo Jackson .25 .10
209 Chet Lemon .10 .04
210 Storm Davis .05 .02
211 Doug Drabek .05 .02
212 Mickey Brantley UER .05 .02
(Photo actually
Nelson Simmons)
213 Devon White .10 .04
214 Dave Stewart .10 .04
215 Dave Schmidt .05 .02
216 Bryn Smith .05 .02
217 Brett Butler .10 .04
218 Bob Ojeda .05 .02
219 Steve Rosenberg .05 .02
220 Hubie Brooks .05 .02
221 B.J. Surhoff .10 .04
222 Rick Mahler .05 .02
223 Rick Sutcliffe .10 .04
224 Neal Heaton .05 .02
225 Mitch Williams .05 .02
226 Chuck Finley .10 .04
227 Mark Langston .05 .02
228 Jesse Orosco .05 .02
229 Ed Whitson .05 .02
230 Terry Pendleton .10 .04
231 Lloyd Moseby .05 .02
232 Greg Swindell .05 .02
233 John Franco .10 .04
234 Jack Morris .10 .04
235 Howard Johnson .10 .04
236 Glenn Davis .05 .02
237 Frank Viola .10 .04
238 Kevin Seitzer .05 .02
239 Gerald Perry .05 .02
240 Dwight Evans .10 .04
241 Jim Deshaies .05 .02
242 Bo Diaz .05 .02
243 Carney Lansford .10 .04
244 Mike LaValliere .05 .02
245 Rickey Henderson .25 .10
246 Roberto Alomar .25 .10
247 Jimmy Jones .05 .02
248 Pascual Perez .05 .02
249 Will Clark .25 .10
250 Fernando Valenzuela .10 .04
251 Shane Rawley .05 .02
252 Sid Bream .05 .02
253 Steve Lyons .05 .02
254 Brian Downing .10 .04
255 Mark Grace .25 .10
256 Tom Candiotti .05 .02
257 Barry Larkin .15 .06
258 Mike Krukow .05 .02
259 Billy Ripken .05 .02
260 Cecilio Guante .05 .02
261 Scott Bradley .05 .02
262 Floyd Bannister .05 .02
263 Pete Smith .05 .02
264 Jim Gantner UER .05 .02
(Wrong birthdate)
265 Roger McDowell .05 .02
266 Bobby Thigpen .05 .02
267 Jim Clancy .05 .02
268 Terry Steinbach .10 .04
269 Mike Dunne .05 .02
270 Dwight Gooden .10 .04
271 Mike Heath .05 .02
272 Dave Smith .05 .02
273 Keith Atherton .05 .02
274 Tim Burke .05 .02
275 Damon Berryhill .05 .02
276 Vance Law .05 .02
277 Rich Dotson .05 .02
278 Lance Parrish .10 .04
279 Denny Walling .05 .02
280 Roger Clemens .50 .20
281 Greg Mathews .05 .02
282 Tom Niedenfuer .05 .02
283 Paul Kilgus .05 .02
284 Jose Guzman .05 .02
285 Calvin Schiraldi .05 .02
286 Charlie Puleo UER .05 .02
(Career ERA 4.24,
should be 4.23)
287 Joe Orsulak .05 .02
288 Jack Howell .05 .02
289 Kevin Elster .05 .02
290 Jose Lind .05 .02
291 Paul Molitor .15 .06
292 Cecil Espy .05 .02
293 Bill Wegman .05 .02
294 Dan Pasqua .05 .02
295 Scott Garrelts UER .05 .02
(Wrong birthdate)
296 Walt Terrell .05 .02
297 Ed Hearn .05 .02
298 Lou Whitaker .10 .04
299 Ken Dayley .05 .02
300 Checklist 248-357 .05 .02
301 Tommy Herr .05 .02
302 Mike Brumley .05 .02
303 Ellis Burks .10 .04
304 Curt Young UER .05 .02
(Wrong birthdate)
305 Jody Reed .05 .02
306 Bill Doran .05 .02
307 David Wells .10 .04
308 Ron Robinson .05 .02
309 Rafael Santana .05 .02
310 Julio Franco .10 .04
311 Jack Clark .10 .04
312 Chris James .05 .02
313 Milt Thompson .05 .02
314 John Shelby .05 .02
315 Al Leiter .25 .10
316 Mike Davis .05 .02
317 Chris Sabo RC * .40 .16
318 Greg Gagne .05 .02
319 Jose Oquendo .05 .02
320 John Farrell .05 .02
321 Franklin Stubbs .05 .02
322 Kurt Stillwell .05 .02
323 Shawn Abner .05 .02
324 Mike Flanagan .05 .02
325 Kevin Bass .05 .02
326 Pat Tabler .05 .02
327 Mike Henneman .05 .02
328 Rick Honeycutt .05 .02
329 John Smiley .05 .02
330 Rey Quinones .05 .02
331 Johnny Ray .05 .02
332 Bob Welch .10 .04
333 Larry Sheets .05 .02
334 Jeff Parrett .05 .02
335 Rick Reuschel UER .10 .04
(For Don Robinson&
should be Jeff)
336 Randy Myers .10 .04
337 Ken Williams .05 .02
338 Andy McGaffigan .05 .02
339 Joey Meyer .05 .02
340 Dion James .05 .02
341 Les Lancaster .05 .02
342 Tom Foley .05 .02
343 Geno Petralli .05 .02
344 Dan Petry .05 .02
345 Alvin Davis .05 .02
346 Mickey Hatcher .05 .02
347 Marvell Wynne .05 .02
348 Danny Cox .05 .02
349 Dave Stieb .10 .04
350 Jay Bell .10 .04
351 Jeff Treadway .05 .02
352 Luis Salazar .05 .02
353 Len Dykstra .10 .04
354 Juan Agosto .05 .02
355 Gene Larkin .05 .02
356 Steve Farr .05 .02
357 Paul Assenmacher .05 .02
358 Todd Benzinger .05 .02
359 Larry Andersen .05 .02
360 Paul O'Neill .15 .06
361 Ron Hassey .05 .02
362 Jim Gott .05 .02
363 Ken Phelps .05 .02
364 Tim Flannery .05 .02
365 Randy Ready .05 .02
366 Nelson Santovenia .05 .02
367 Kelly Downs .05 .02
368 Danny Heep .05 .02
369 Phil Bradley .05 .02
370 Jeff D. Robinson .05 .02
371 Ivan Calderon .05 .02
372 Mike Witt .05 .02
373 Greg Maddux .50 .20
374 Carmen Castillo .05 .02
375 Jose Rijo .10 .04
376 Joe Price .05 .02
377 Rene Gonzales .05 .02
378 Oddibe McDowell .05 .02
379 Jim Presley .05 .02
380 Brad Wellman .05 .02
381 Tom Glavine .25 .10
382 Dan Plesac .05 .02
383 Wally Backman .05 .02
384 Dave Gallagher .05 .02
385 Tom Henke .05 .02
386 Luis Polonia .05 .02
387 Junior Ortiz .05 .02
388 David Cone .10 .04
389 Dave Bergman .05 .02
390 Danny Darwin .05 .02
391 Dan Gladden .05 .02
392 John Dopson .05 .02
393 Frank DiPino .05 .02
394 Al Nipper .05 .02
395 Willie Randolph .10 .04
396 Don Carman .05 .02
397 Scott Terry .05 .02
398 Rick Cerone .05 .02
399 Tom Pagnozzi .05 .02
400 Checklist 358-467 .05 .02
401 Mickey Tettleton .05 .02
402 Curtis Wilkerson .05 .02
403 Jeff Russell .05 .02
404 Pat Perry .05 .02
405 Jose Alvarez RC .10 .04
406 Rick Schu .05 .02
407 Sherman Corbett .05 .02
408 Dave Magadan .05 .02
409 Bob Kipper .05 .02
410 Don August .05 .02
411 Bob Brower .05 .02
412 Chris Bosio .05 .02
413 Jerry Reuss .05 .02
414 Atlee Hammaker .05 .02
415 Jim Walewander .05 .02
416 Mike Macfarlane RC * .25 .10
417 Pat Sheridan .05 .02
418 Pedro Guerrero .10 .04
419 Allan Anderson .05 .02
420 Mark Parent .05 .02
421 Bob Stanley .05 .02
422 Mike Gallego .05 .02
423 Bruce Hurst .05 .02
424 Dave Meads .05 .02
425 Jesse Barfield .10 .04
426 Rob Dibble RC .50 .20
427 Joel Skinner .05 .02
428 Ron Kittle .05 .02
429 Rick Rhoden .05 .02
430 Bob Dernier .05 .02
431 Steve Jeltz .05 .02
432 Rick Dempsey .05 .02
433 Roberto Kelly .05 .02
434 Dave Anderson .05 .02
435 Herm Winningham .05 .02
436 Al Newman .05 .02
437 Jose DeLeon .05 .02
438 Doug Jones .05 .02
439 Brian Holton .05 .02
440 Jeff Montgomery .05 .02
441 Dickie Thon .05 .02
442 Cecil Fielder .10 .04
443 John Fishel .05 .02
444 Jerry Don Gleaton .05 .02
445 Paul Gibson .05 .02
446 Walt Weiss .05 .02
447 Glenn Wilson .05 .02
448 Mike Moore .05 .02
449 Chili Davis .10 .04
450 Dave Henderson .05 .02
451 Jose Bautista RC .10 .04
452 Rex Hudler .05 .02
453 Bob Brenly .05 .02
454 Mackey Sasser .05 .02
455 Daryl Boston .05 .02
456 Mike R. Fitzgerald .05 .02
457 Jeffrey Leonard .05 .02
458 Bruce Sutter .10 .04
459 Mitch Webster .05 .02
460 Joe Hesketh .05 .02
461 Bobby Witt .05 .02
462 Stu Cliburn .05 .02
463 Scott Bankhead .05 .02
464 Ramon Martinez RC .25 .10
465 Dave Leiper .05 .02
466 Luis Alicea RC * .25 .10
467 John Cerutti .05 .02
468 Ron Washington .05 .02
469 Jeff Reed .05 .02
470 Jeff M. Robinson .05 .02
471 Sid Fernandez .05 .02
472 Terry Puhl .05 .02
473 Charlie Lea .05 .02
474 Israel Sanchez .05 .02
475 Bruce Benedict .05 .02
476 Oil Can Boyd .05 .02
477 Craig Reynolds .05 .02
478 Frank Williams .05 .02
479 Greg Cadaret .05 .02
480 Randy Kramer .05 .02
481 Dave Eiland .05 .02
482 Eric Show .05 .02
483 Garry Templeton .10 .04
484 Wallace Johnson .05 .02
485 Kevin Mitchell .10 .04
486 Tim Crews .05 .02
487 Mike Maddux .05 .02
488 Dave LaPoint .05 .02
489 Fred Manrique .05 .02
490 Greg Minton .05 .02
491 Doug Dascenzo UER .05 .02
(Photo actually
Damon Berryhill)
492 Willie Upshaw .05 .02
493 Jack Armstrong RC * .25 .10
494 Kirt Manwaring .05 .02
495 Jeff Ballard .05 .02
496 Jeff Kunkel .05 .02
497 Mike Campbell .05 .02
498 Gary Thurman .05 .02
499 Zane Smith .05 .02
500 Checklist 468-577 DP .05 .02
501 Mike Birkbeck .05 .02
502 Terry Leach .05 .02
503 Shawn Hillegas .05 .02
504 Manny Lee .05 .02
505 Doug Jennings .05 .02
506 Ken Oberkfell .05 .02
507 Tim Teufel .05 .02
508 Tom Brookens .05 .02
509 Rafael Ramirez .05 .02
510 Fred Toliver .05 .02
511 Brian Holman RC * .10 .04
512 Mike Bielecki .05 .02
513 Jeff Pico .05 .02
514 Charles Hudson .05 .02
515 Bruce Ruffin .05 .02
516 L.McWilliams UER .05 .02
New Richland, should
be North Richland
517 Jeff Sellers .05 .02
518 John Costello .05 .02
519 Brady Anderson RC .40 .16
520 Craig McMurtry .05 .02
521 Ray Hayward DP .05 .02
522 Drew Hall DP .05 .02
523 Mark Lemke DP RC .40 .16
524 Oswald Peraza DP .05 .02
525 Bryan Harvey DP RC * .25 .10
526 Rick Aguilera DP .05 .02
527 Tom Prince DP .05 .02
528 Mark Clear DP .05 .02
529 Jerry Browne DP .05 .02
530 Juan Castillo DP .05 .02
531 Jack McDowell DP .10 .04
532 Chris Speier DP .05 .02
533 Darrell Evans DP .10 .04
534 Luis Aquino DP .05 .02
535 Eric King DP .05 .02
536 Ken Hill DP RC .25 .10
537 Randy Bush DP .05 .02
538 Shane Mack DP .05 .02
539 Tom Bolton DP .05 .02
540 Gene Nelson DP .05 .02
541 Wes Gardner DP .05 .02
542 Ken Caminiti DP .10 .04
543 Duane Ward DP .05 .02
544 Norm Charlton DP RC .25 .10
545 Hal Morris DP RC .25 .10
546 Rich Yett DP .05 .02
547 H.Meulens DP RC .10 .04
548 Greg A. Harris DP .05 .02
549 Darren Daulton DP .10 .04
(Posing as right-
handed hitter)
550 Jeff Hamilton DP .05 .02
551 Luis Aguayo DP .05 .02
552 Tim Leary DP .05 .02
(Resembles M.Marshall)
553 Ron Oester DP .05 .02
554 S.Lombardozzi DP .05 .02
555 Tim Jones DP .05 .02
556 Bud Black DP .05 .02
557 Alejandro Pena DP .05 .02
558 Jose DeJesus DP .05 .02
559 D.Rasmussen DP .05 .02
560 Pat Borders DP RC* .25 .10
561 Craig Biggio DP RC .75 .30
562 Luis DeLosSantos DP .05 .02
563 Fred Lynn DP .10 .04
564 Todd Burns DP .05 .02
565 Felix Fermin DP .05 .02
566 Darnell Coles DP .05 .02
567 Willie Fraser DP .05 .02
568 Glenn Hubbard DP .05 .02
569 Craig Worthington DP .05 .02
570 Johnny Paredes DP .05 .02
571 Don Robinson DP .05 .02
572 Barry Lyons DP .05 .02
573 Bill Long DP .05 .02
574 Tracy Jones DP .05 .02
575 Juan Nieves DP .05 .02
576 Andres Thomas DP .05 .02
577 Rolando Roomes DP .05 .02
578 Luis Rivera UER DP .05 .02
(Wrong birthdate)
579 Chad Kreuter DP RC .25 .10
580 Tony Armas DP .10 .04
581 Jay Buhner .10 .04
582 Ricky Horton DP .05 .02
583 Andy Hawkins DP .05 .02
584 Sil Campusano .05 .02
585 Dave Clark .05 .02
586 Van Snider DP .05 .02
587 Todd Frohwirth DP .05 .02
588 W.Spahn DP PUZ .15 .06
589 William Brennan .05 .02
590 German Gonzalez .05 .02
591 Ernie Whitt DP .05 .02
592 Jeff Blauser .05 .02
593 Spike Owen DP .05 .02
594 Matt Williams .25 .10
595 Lloyd McClendon DP .05 .02
596 Steve Ontiveros .05 .02
597 Scott Medvin .05 .02
598 Hipolito Pena DP .05 .02
599 Jerald Clark DP RC .10 .04
600A CL 578-660 DP .05 .02
635 Kurt Schilling
600B CL 578-660 DP .05 .02
635 Curt Schilling;
MVP's not listed
on checklist card
600C CL 578-660 DP .05 .02
635 Curt Schilling;
MVP's listed
following 660
601 Carmelo Martinez DP .05 .02
602 Mike LaCoss .05 .02
603 Mike Devereaux .05 .02
604 Alex Madrid DP .05 .02
605 Gary Redus DP .05 .02
606 Lance Johnson .05 .02
607 Terry Clark DP .05 .02
608 Manny Trillo DP .05 .02
609 Scott Jordan RC .25 .10
610 Jay Howell DP .05 .02
611 Francisco Melendez .05 .02
612 Mike Boddicker .05 .02
613 Kevin Brown DP .25 .10
614 Dave Valle .05 .02
615 Tim Laudner DP .05 .02
616 Andy Nezelek UER .05 .02
(Wrong birthdate)
617 Chuck Crim .05 .02
618 Jack Savage DP .05 .02
619 Adam Peterson .05 .02
620 Todd Stottlemyre .05 .02
621 Lance Blankenship RC .10 .04
622 Miguel Garcia DP .05 .02
623 Keith A. Miller DP .05 .02
624 Ricky Jordan DP RC* .25 .10
625 Ernest Riles DP .05 .02
626 John Moses DP .05 .02
627 Nelson Liriano DP .05 .02
628 Mike Smithson DP .05 .02
629 Scott Sanderson .05 .02
630 Dale Mohorcic .05 .02
631 Marvin Freeman DP .05 .02
632 Mike Young DP .05 .02
633 Dennis Lamp .05 .02
634 Dante Bichette DP RC .40 .16
635 Curt Schilling DP RC 5.00 2.00
636 Scott May DP .05 .02
637 Mike Schooler .05 .02
638 Rick Leach .05 .02
639 Tom Lampkin UER .05 .02
(Throws Left, should
be Throws Right)
640 Brian Meyer .05 .02
641 Brian Harper .05 .02
642 John Smoltz RC 1.00 .40
643 Jose Canseco .15 .06
(40/40 Club)
644 Bill Schroeder .05 .02
645 Edgar Martinez .25 .10
646 Dennis Cook RC .25 .10
647 Barry Jones .05 .02
648 Orel Hershiser .10 .04
(59 and Counting)
649 Rod Nichols .05 .02
650 Jody Davis .05 .02
651 Bob Milacki .05 .02
652 Mike Jackson .05 .02
653 Derek Lilliquist RC .10 .04
654 Paul Mirabella .05 .02
655 Mike Diaz .05 .02
656 Jeff Musselman .05 .02
657 Jerry Reed .05 .02
658 Kevin Blankenship .05 .02
659 Wayne Tolleson .05 .02
660 Eric Hetzel .05 .02
BC Jose Canseco 2.00 .80
Blister Pack

1989 Donruss Bonus MVP's

Rather than short-printing 26 cards in order to make room for printing the Bonus MVP's this year, Donruss apparently chose to double print 106 cards. Numbered with the prefix "BC" for bonus card, the 26-card set featuring the most valuable player from each of the 26 teams was randomly inserted in the wax and rack packs.

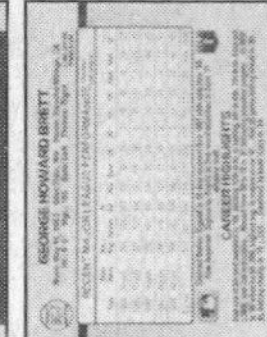

These cards are distinguished by the bold MV logo in the upper background of the obverse and the four doubleprinted cards are denoted b "DP" in the checklist below.

	Nm-Mt	Ex-Mt
COMPLETE SET (26)	1.50	.60
BC1 Kirby Puckett	.25	.10
BC2 Mike Scott	.10	.04
BC3 Joe Carter	.10	.04
BC4 Orel Hershiser	.10	.04
BC5 Jose Canseco	.25	.10
BC6 Darryl Strawberry	.10	.04
BC7 George Brett	.60	.24
BC8 Andre Dawson	.10	.04
BC9 Paul Molitor UER (Brewers logo missing the word Milwaukee)	.15	.06
BC10 Andy Van Slyke	.10	.04
BC11 Dave Winfield	.10	.04
BC12 Kevin Gross	.05	.02
BC13 Mike Greenwell	.05	.02
BC14 Ozzie Smith	.40	.16
BC15 Cal Ripken	.75	.30
BC16 Andres Galarraga	.10	.04
BC17 Alan Trammell	.10	.04
BC18 Kal Daniels	.05	.02
BC19 Fred McGriff	.15	.06
BC20 Tony Gwynn	.30	.12
BC21 Wally Joyner DP	.10	.04
BC22 Will Clark DP	.25	.10
BC23 Ozzie Guillen	.05	.02
BC24 Gerald Perry DP	.05	.02
BC25 Alvin Davis DP	.05	.02
BC26 Ruben Sierra	.05	.02

1989 Donruss Grand Slammers

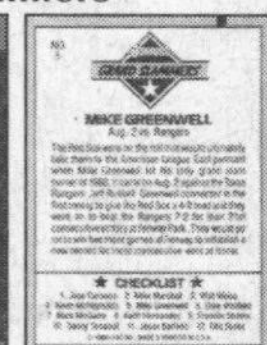

The 1989 Donruss Grand Slammers set contain 12 standard-size cards. Each card in the set ca be found with five different colored border com binations, but no color combination of border appears to be scarcer than any other. The se includes cards for each player who hit one c more grand slams in 1988. The backs detail th players' grand slams. The cards were distribute one per cello pack as well as an insert (com plete) set in each factory set.

	Nm-Mt	Ex-Mt
COMPLETE SET (12)	2.00	.80
1 Jose Canseco	.25	.10
2 Mike Marshall	.05	.02
3 Walt Weiss	.05	.02
4 Kevin McReynolds	.05	.02
5 Mike Greenwell	.05	.02
6 Dave Winfield	.10	.04
7 Mark McGwire	1.00	.40
8 Keith Hernandez	.10	.04
9 Franklin Stubbs	.05	.02
10 Danny Tartabull	.05	.02
11 Jesse Barfield	.10	.04
12 Ellis Burks	.10	.04

1989 Donruss Rookies

The 1989 Donruss Rookies set contains 56 stan dard-size cards. The cards were distribute exclusively in factory set form in small, emeral green, cellophane-wrapped boxes throug hobby dealers. The cards are almost identical design to geular 1989 Donruss except for th green borders. Rookie Cards in this set includ Jim Abbott, Steve Finley, Kenny Rogers an Deion Sanders. Ken Griffey Jr. and Rand Johnson are also featured on a card within th set.

	Nm-Mt	Ex-Mt
COMP.FACT.SET (56)	15.00	6.00
1 Gary Sheffield	1.50	.60
2 Gregg Jefferies	.10	.04
3 Ken Griffey Jr.	5.00	3.20
4 Tom Gordon	.25	.10
5 Billy Spiers RC	.25	.10
6 Deion Sanders RC	1.00	.40
7 Donn Pall	.05	.02
8 Steve Carter	.05	.02
9 Francisco Oliveras	.05	.02
10 Steve Wilson RC	.10	.04
11 Bob Geren RC	.05	.02
12 Tony Castillo RC	.10	.04
13 Kenny Rogers RC	.75	.30

4 Carlos Martinez RC .10 .04
5 Edgar Martinez .25 .10
6 Jim Abbott RC .50 .20
7 Torey Lovullo RC .10 .04
8 Mark Carreon .05 .02
9 Geronimo Berroa .05 .02
20 Luis Medina .05 .02
21 Sandy Alomar Jr. .15 .06
22 Bob Milacki .05 .02
23 Joe Girardi RC .40 .16
24 German Gonzalez .05 .02
25 Craig Worthington .05 .02
26 Jerome Walton RC .25 .10
27 Gary Wayne .05 .02
28 Tim Jones .05 .02
29 Dante Bichette .15 .06
30 Alexis Infante .05 .02
31 Ken Hill .25 .10
32 Dwight Smith RC .25 .10
33 Luis de los Santos .05 .02
34 Eric Yelding .05 .02
35 Gregg Olson .25 .10
36 Phil Stephenson .05 .02
37 Ken Patterson .05 .02
38 Rick Wrona .05 .02
39 Mike Brumley .05 .02
40 Cris Carpenter .05 .02
41 Jeff Brantley RC .25 .10
42 Ron Jones .05 .02
43 Randy Johnson 2.50 .80
44 Kevin Brown .25 .10
45 Ramon Martinez .10 .04
46 Greg W.Harris .05 .02
47 Steve Finley RC .50 .20
48 Randy Kramer .05 .02
49 Erik Hanson .10 .04
50 Matt Merullo .05 .02
51 Mike Devereaux .05 .02
52 Clay Parker .05 .02
53 Omar Vizquel RC .75 .30
54 Derek Lilliquist .05 .02
55 Junior Felix RC .10 .04
56 Checklist 1-56 .05 .02

1989 Donruss Baseball's Best

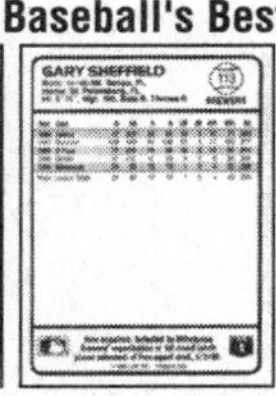

he 1989 Donruss Baseball's Best set contains 36 standard-size glossy cards. The fronts are reen and yellow, and the backs feature career ighlight information. The backs are green, and eature vertically oriented career stats. The cards vere distributed as a set in a blister pack hrough various retail and department store hains. The Sammy Sosa card in this set is the nly major league licensed card issued of him in 989. In addition, early cards of Ken Griffey Jr. nd Randy Johnson are featured in this set.

Nm-Mt Ex-Mt
OMP.FACT.SET (336) 100.00 40.00
Don Mattingly 1.50 .60
Tom Glavine .60 .24
Bert Blyleven .25 .10
Andre Dawson .25 .10
Pete O'Brien .15 .06
Eric Davis .25 .10
George Brett 1.50 .60
Glenn Davis .15 .06
Ellis Burks .25 .10
0 Kirk Gibson .25 .10
1 Carlton Fisk .40 .16
2 Andres Galarraga .25 .10
3 Alan Trammell .25 .10
4 Dwight Gooden .25 .10
5 Paul Molitor .40 .16
6 Roger McDowell .15 .06
7 Doug Drabek .15 .06
8 Kent Hrbek .25 .10
9 Vince Coleman .15 .06
0 Steve Sax .15 .06
1 Roberto Alomar .60 .24
2 Carney Lansford .25 .10
3 Will Clark .60 .24
4 Alvin Davis .15 .06
5 Bobby Thigpen .15 .06
6 Ryne Sandberg 1.00 .40
7 Devon White .25 .10
8 Mike Greenwell .15 .06
9 Dale Murphy .40 .16
0 Jeff Ballard .15 .06
1 Kelly Gruber .15 .06
2 Julio Franco .25 .10
3 Bobby Bonilla .25 .10
4 Tim Wallach .15 .06
5 Lou Whitaker .25 .10
6 Jay Howell .15 .06
7 Greg Maddux 1.25 .50
8 Bill Doran .15 .06
9 Danny Tartabull .15 .06
0 Darryl Strawberry .25 .10
1 Ron Darling .25 .10
2 Tony Gwynn .75 .30
3 Mark McGwire 2.50 1.00
4 Ozzie Smith 1.00 .40
5 Andy Van Slyke .25 .10
6 Juan Berenguer .15 .06
7 Von Hayes .15 .06
8 Tony Fernandez .15 .06
9 Eric Plunk .15 .06
0 Ernest Riles .15 .06
1 Harold Reynolds .25 .10
2 Andy Hawkins .15 .06
3 Robin Yount 1.00 .40
4 Danny Jackson .15 .06
5 Nolan Ryan 2.50 1.00
6 Joe Carter .25 .10
7 Jose Canseco .60 .24
8 Jody Davis .15 .06
9 Lance Parrish .25 .10
60 Mitch Williams .15 .06
61 Brook Jacoby .15 .06
62 Tom Browning .15 .06
63 Kurt Stillwell .15 .06
64 Rafael Ramirez .15 .06
65 Roger Clemens 1.25 .50
66 Mike Scioscia .25 .10
67 Dave Gallagher .15 .06
68 Mark Langston .15 .06
69 Chet Lemon .25 .10
70 Kevin McReynolds .15 .06
71 Rob Deer .15 .06
72 Tommy Herr .15 .06
73 Barry Bonds 3.00 1.20
74 Frank Viola .25 .10
75 Pedro Guerrero .25 .10
76 Dave Righetti UER .15 .06
(ML total of 7 wins incorrect)
77 Bruce Hurst .15 .06
78 Rickey Henderson .60 .24
79 Robby Thompson .15 .06
80 Randy Johnson 8.00 3.20
81 Harold Baines .25 .10
82 Calvin Schiraldi .15 .06
83 Kirk McCaskill .15 .06
84 Lee Smith .25 .10
85 John Smoltz 2.00 .80
86 Mickey Tettleton .15 .06
87 Jimmy Key .25 .10
88 Rafael Palmeiro .60 .24
89 Sid Bream .15 .06
90 Dennis Martinez .25 .10
91 Frank Tanana .25 .10
92 Eddie Murray .60 .24
93 Shawon Dunston .15 .06
94 Mike Scott .25 .10
95 Bret Saberhagen .25 .10
96 David Cone .25 .10
97 Kevin Elster .15 .06
98 Jack Clark .25 .10
99 Dave Stewart .25 .10
100 Jose Oquendo .15 .06
101 Jose Lind .15 .06
102 Gary Gaetti .25 .10
103 Ricky Jordan .50 .20
104 Fred McGriff .40 .16
105 Don Slaught .15 .06
106 Jose Uribe .15 .06
107 Jeffrey Leonard .15 .06
108 Lee Guetterman .15 .06
109 Chris Bosio .15 .06
110 Barry Larkin .40 .16
111 Ruben Sierra .15 .06
112 Greg Swindell .15 .06
113 Gary Sheffield 3.00 1.20
114 Lonnie Smith .15 .06
115 Chili Davis .25 .10
116 Damon Berryhill .15 .06
117 Tom Candiotti .15 .06
118 Kal Daniels .15 .06
119 Mark Gubicza .15 .06
120 Jim Deshaies .15 .06
121 Dwight Evans .25 .10
122 Mike Morgan .15 .06
123 Dan Pasqua .15 .06
124 Bryn Smith .15 .06
125 Doyle Alexander .15 .06
126 Howard Johnson .25 .10
127 Chuck Crim .15 .06
128 Darren Daulton .25 .10
129 Jeff Robinson .15 .06
130 Kirby Puckett .60 .24
131 Joe Magrane .15 .06
132 Jesse Barfield .25 .10
133 Mark Davis UER .15 .06
(Photo actually Dave Leiper)
134 Dennis Eckersley .40 .16
135 Mike Krukow .15 .06
136 Jay Buhner .25 .10
137 Ozzie Guillen .15 .06
138 Rick Sutcliffe .25 .10
139 Wally Joyner .25 .10
140 Wade Boggs .40 .16
141 Jeff Treadway .15 .06
142 Cal Ripken 2.00 .80
143 Dave Stieb .25 .10
144 Pete Incaviglia .15 .06
145 Bob Walk .15 .06
146 Nelson Santovenia .15 .06
147 Mike Heath .15 .06
148 Willie Randolph .25 .10
149 Paul Kilgus .15 .06
150 Billy Hatcher .15 .06
151 Steve Farr .15 .06
152 Gregg Jefferies .25 .10
153 Randy Myers .25 .10
154 Garry Templeton .25 .10
155 Walt Weiss .15 .06
156 Terry Pendleton .25 .10
157 John Smiley .15 .06
158 Greg Gagne .15 .06
159 Len Dykstra .25 .10
160 Nelson Liriano .15 .06
161 Alvaro Espinoza .15 .06
162 Rick Reuschel .25 .10
163 Omar Vizquel UER 1.00 .40
Photo actually Darnell Coles
164 Clay Parker .15 .06
165 Dan Plesac .15 .06
166 John Franco .25 .10
167 Scott Fletcher .15 .06
168 Cory Snyder .15 .06
169 Bo Jackson .60 .24
170 Tommy Gregg .15 .06
171 Jim Abbott 1.00 .40
172 Jerome Walton .50 .20
173 Doug Jones .15 .06
174 Todd Benzinger .15 .06
175 Frank White .25 .10
176 Craig Biggio 2.00 .80
177 John Dopson .15 .06
178 Alfredo Griffin .15 .06
179 Melido Perez .15 .06
180 Tim Burke .15 .06
181 Matt Nokes .15 .06
182 Gary Carter .25 .10
183 Ted Higuera .15 .06
184 Ken Howell .15 .06
185 Rey Quinones .15 .06
186 Wally Backman .15 .06
187 Tom Brunansky .15 .06
188 Steve Balboni .15 .06
189 Marvell Wynne .15 .06
190 Dave Henderson .15 .06
191 Don Robinson .15 .06
192 Ken Griffey Jr. 15.00 8.00
193 Ivan Calderon .15 .06
194 Mike Bielecki .15 .06
195 Johnny Ray .15 .06
196 Rob Murphy .15 .06
197 Andres Thomas .15 .06
198 Phil Bradley .15 .06
199 Junior Felix .25 .10
200 Jeff Russell .15 .06
201 Mike LaValliere .15 .06
202 Kevin Gross .15 .06
203 Keith Moreland .15 .06
204 Mike Marshall .15 .06
205 Dwight Smith .50 .20
206 Jim Clancy .15 .06
207 Kevin Seitzer .15 .06
208 Keith Hernandez .25 .10
209 Bob Ojeda .15 .06
210 Ed Whitson .15 .06
211 Tony Phillips .15 .06
212 Milt Thompson .15 .06
213 Randy Kramer .15 .06
214 Randy Bush .15 .06
215 Randy Ready .15 .06
216 Duane Ward .15 .06
217 Jimmy Jones .15 .06
218 Scott Garrelts .15 .06
219 Scott Bankhead .15 .06
220 Lance McCullers .15 .06
221 B.J. Surhoff .25 .10
222 Chris Sabo .75 .30
223 Steve Buechele .15 .06
224 Joel Skinner .15 .06
225 Orel Hershiser .25 .10
226 Derek Lilliquist .25 .10
227 Claudell Washington .15 .06
228 Lloyd McClendon .15 .06
229 Felix Fermin .15 .06
230 Paul O'Neill .40 .16
231 Charlie Leibrandt .15 .06
232 Dave Smith .15 .06
233 Bob Stanley .15 .06
234 Tim Belcher .15 .06
235 Eric King .15 .06
236 Spike Owen .15 .06
237 Mike Henneman .15 .06
238 Juan Samuel .15 .06
239 Greg Brock .15 .06
240 John Kruk .25 .10
241 Glenn Wilson .15 .06
242 Jeff Reardon .25 .10
243 Todd Worrell .15 .06
244 Dave LaPoint .15 .06
245 Walt Terrell .15 .06
246 Mike Moore .15 .06
247 Kelly Downs .15 .06
248 Dave Valle .15 .06
249 Ron Kittle .15 .06
250 Steve Wilson .25 .10
251 Dick Schofield .15 .06
252 Marty Barrett .15 .06
253 Dion James .15 .06
254 Bob Milacki .15 .06
255 Ernie Whitt .15 .06
256 Kevin Brown .60 .24
257 R.J. Reynolds .15 .06
258 Tim Raines .25 .10
259 Frank Williams .15 .06
260 Jose Gonzalez .15 .06
261 Mitch Webster .15 .06
262 Ken Caminiti .25 .10
263 Bob Boone .25 .10
264 Dave Magadan .15 .06
265 Rick Aguilera .15 .06
266 Chris James .15 .06
267 Bob Welch .25 .10
268 Ken Dayley .15 .06
269 Junior Ortiz .15 .06
270 Allan Anderson .15 .06
271 Steve Jeltz .15 .06
272 George Bell .25 .10
273 Roberto Kelly .15 .06
274 Brett Butler .25 .10
275 Mike Schooler .25 .10
276 Ken Phelps .15 .06
277 Glenn Braggs .15 .06
278 Jose Rijo .25 .10
279 Bobby Witt .15 .06
280 Jerry Browne .15 .06
281 Kevin Mitchell .25 .10
282 Craig Worthington .15 .06
283 Greg Minton .15 .06
284 Nick Esasky .15 .06
285 John Farrell .15 .06
286 Rick Mahler .15 .06
287 Tom Gordon .75 .30
288 Gerald Young .15 .06
289 Jody Reed .15 .06
290 Jeff Hamilton .15 .06
291 Gerald Perry .15 .06
292 Hubie Brooks .15 .06
293 Bo Diaz .15 .06
294 Terry Puhl .15 .06
295 Jim Gantner .15 .06
296 Jeff Parrett .15 .06
297 Mike Boddicker .15 .06
298 Dan Gladden .15 .06
299 Tony Pena .15 .06
300 Checklist Card .15 .06
301 Tom Henke .15 .06
302 Pascual Perez .15 .06
303 Steve Bedrosian .15 .06
304 Ken Hill .50 .20
305 Jerry Reuss .15 .06
306 Jim Eisenreich .15 .06
307 Jack Howell .15 .06
308 Rick Cerone .15 .06
309 Tim Leary .15 .06
310 Joe Orsulak .15 .06
311 Jim Dwyer .15 .06
312 Geno Petralli .15 .06
313 Rick Honeycutt .15 .06
314 Tom Foley .15 .06
315 Kenny Rogers 1.50 .60
316 Mike Flanagan .15 .06
317 Bryan Harvey .15 .06
318 Billy Ripken .15 .06
319 Jeff Montgomery .15 .06
320 Erik Hanson .50 .20
321 Brian Downing .25 .10
322 Gregg Olson .50 .20
323 Terry Steinbach .25 .10
324 Sammy Sosa 25.00 10.00
325 Gene Harris .15 .06
326 Mike Devereaux .15 .06
327 Dennis Cook .50 .20
328 David Wells .25 .10
329 Checklist Card .15 .06
330 Kirt Manwaring .15 .06
331 Jim Presley .15 .06
332 Checklist Card .15 .06
333 Chuck Finley .25 .10
334 Rob Dibble 1.00 .40
335 Cecil Espy .15 .06
336 Dave Parker .25 .10

1990 Donruss

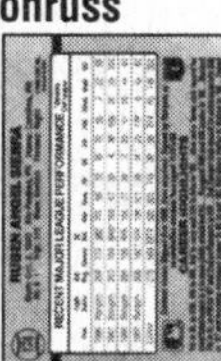

The 1990 Donruss set contains 716 standard-size cards. Cards were issued in wax packs and hobby and retail factory sets. The card fronts feature bright red borders. Subsets include Diamond Kings (1-27) and Rated Rookies (28-47). The set was the largest ever produced by Donruss, unfortunately it also had a large number of errors which were corrected after the cards were released. Most of these feature minor printing flaws and insignificant variations that collectors have found unworthy of price differentials. There are several double-printed cards indicated in our checklist with the set indicated with a "DP" coding. Rookie Cards of note include Juan Gonzalez, David Justice, John Olerud, Dean Palmer, Sammy Sosa, Larry Walker and Bernie Williams.

Nm-Mt Ex-Mt
COMPLETE SET (716) 15.00 4.50
COMP.FACT.SET (728) 15.00 4.50
COMP.YAZ PUZZLE 1.00 .30
1 Bo Jackson DK .15 .04
2 Steve Sax DK .05 .02
3A Ruben Sierra DK ERR .05 .02
(No small line on top border on card back)
3B Ruben Sierra DK COR .05 .02
4 Ken Griffey Jr. DK .40 .12
5 Mickey Tettleton DK .05 .02
6 Dave Stewart DK .05 .02
7 Jim Deshaies DK DP .05 .02
8 John Smoltz DK .25 .07
9 Mike Bielecki DK .05 .02
10A Brian Downing DK .15 .04
ERR (Reverse negative on card front)
10B Brian Downing DK .05 .02
COR
11 Kevin Mitchell DK .05 .02
12 Kelly Gruber DK .05 .02
13 Joe Magrane DK .05 .02
14 John Franco DK .10 .03
15 Ozzie Guillen DK .05 .02
16 Lou Whitaker DK .05 .02
17 John Smiley DK .05 .02
18 Howard Johnson DK .05 .02
19 Willie Randolph DK .10 .03
20 Chris Bosio DK .05 .02
21 Tommy Herr DK DP .05 .02
22 Dan Gladden DK .05 .02
23 Ellis Burks DK .10 .03
24 Pete O'Brien DK .05 .02
25 Bryn Smith DK .05 .02
26 Ed Whitson DK DP .05 .02
27 DK Checklist 1-27 DP .05 .02
(Comments on Perez-Steele on back)
28 Robin Ventura RR .25 .07
29 Todd Zeile RR .10 .03
30 Sandy Alomar Jr. .10 .03
31 Kent Mercker RR RC .25 .07
32 B.McDonald RC UER .25 .07
Middle name Benard not Benjamin
33A J.Gonzalez RC ERR 2.00 .60
Reverse negative
33B J.Gonzalez COR RC 1.50 .45
34 Eric Anthony RR RC .10 .03
35 Mike Fetters RR RC .25 .07
36 Marquis Grissom RC .40 .12
37 Greg Vaughn RR .05 .02
38 Brian DuBois RC .10 .03
39 Steve Avery RR UER .05 .02
(Born in MI, not NJ)
40 Mark Gardner RR RC .10 .03
41 Andy Benes .10 .03
42 D.DeShields RR RC .25 .07
43 Scott Coolbaugh RC .10 .03
44 Pat Combs DP .05 .02
45 Alex Sanchez DP .05 .02
46 Kelly Mann DP RC .10 .03
47 Julio Machado DP RC .10 .03
48 Pete Incaviglia .05 .02
49 Shawon Dunston .05 .02
50 Jeff Treadway .05 .02
51 Jeff Ballard .05 .02
52 Claudell Washington .05 .02
53 Juan Samuel .05 .02
54 John Smiley .05 .02
55 Rob Deer .05 .02
56 Geno Petralli .05 .02
57 Chris Bosio .05 .02
58 Carlton Fisk .15 .04
59 Kirt Manwaring .05 .02
60 Chet Lemon .05 .02
61 Bo Jackson .25 .07
62 Doyle Alexander .05 .02
63 Pedro Guerrero .05 .02
64 Allan Anderson .05 .02
65 Greg W. Harris .05 .02
66 Mike Greenwell .05 .02
67 Walt Weiss .05 .02
68 Wade Boggs .15 .04
69 Jim Clancy .05 .02
70 Junior Felix .05 .02
71 Barry Larkin .15 .04
72 Dave LaPoint .05 .02
73 Joel Skinner .05 .02
74 Jesse Barfield .05 .02
75 Tommy Herr .05 .02
76 Ricky Jordan .05 .02
77 Eddie Murray .25 .07
78 Steve Sax .05 .02
79 Tim Belcher .05 .02
80 Danny Jackson .05 .02
81 Kent Hrbek .10 .03
82 Milt Thompson .05 .02
83 Brook Jacoby .05 .02
84 Mike Marshall .05 .02
85 Kevin Seitzer .05 .02
86 Tony Gwynn .30 .09
87 Dave Stieb .10 .03
88 Dave Smith .05 .02
89 Bret Saberhagen .10 .03
90 Alan Trammell .10 .03
91 Tony Phillips .05 .02
92 Doug Drabek .05 .02
93 Jeffrey Leonard .05 .02
94 Wally Joyner .10 .03
95 Carney Lansford .10 .03
96 Cal Ripken .75 .23
97 Andres Galarraga .10 .03
98 Kevin Mitchell .05 .02
99 Howard Johnson .05 .02
100A Checklist 28-129 .05 .02
100B Checklist 28-125 .05 .02
101 Melido Perez .05 .02
102 Spike Owen .05 .02
103 Paul Molitor .15 .04
104 Geronimo Berroa .05 .02
105 Ryne Sandberg .40 .12
106 Bryn Smith .05 .02
107 Steve Buechele .05 .02
108 Jim Abbott .15 .04
109 Alvin Davis .05 .02
110 Lee Smith .10 .03
111 Roberto Alomar .15 .04
112 Rick Reuschel .05 .02
113A Kelly Gruber ERR .05 .02
(Born 2/22)
113B Kelly Gruber COR .05 .02
(Born 2/26; corrected in factory sets)
114 Joe Carter .10 .03
115 Jose Rijo .05 .02
116 Greg Minton .05 .02
117 Bob Ojeda .05 .02
118 Glenn Davis .05 .02
119 Jeff Reardon .10 .03
120 Kurt Stillwell .05 .02
121 John Smoltz .25 .07
122 Dwight Evans .10 .03
123 Eric Yelding .05 .02
124 John Franco .10 .03
125 Jose Canseco .25 .07
126 Barry Bonds .60 .18
127 Lee Guetterman .05 .02
128 Jack Clark .10 .03
129 Dave Valle .05 .02
130 Hubie Brooks .05 .02
131 Ernest Riles .05 .02
132 Mike Morgan .05 .02
133 Steve Jeltz .05 .02
134 Jeff D. Robinson .05 .02
135 Ozzie Guillen .05 .02
136 Chili Davis .10 .03
137 Mitch Webster .05 .02
138 Jerry Browne .05 .02
139 Bo Diaz .05 .02
140 Robby Thompson .05 .02
141 Craig Worthington .05 .02
142 Julio Franco .10 .03
143 Brian Holman .05 .02
144 George Brett .60 .18
145 Tom Glavine .15 .04
146 Robin Yount .40 .12
147 Gary Carter .10 .03
148 Ron Kittle .05 .02
149 Tony Fernandez .05 .02
150 Dave Stewart .10 .03
151 Gary Gaetti .10 .03
152 Kevin Elster .05 .02
153 Gerald Perry .05 .02
154 Jesse Orosco .05 .02
155 Wally Backman .05 .02
156 Dennis Martinez .10 .03
157 Rick Sutcliffe .10 .03
158 Greg Maddux .40 .12
159 Andy Hawkins .05 .02
160 John Kruk .10 .03
161 Jose Oquendo .05 .02
162 John Dopson .05 .02
163 Joe Magrane .05 .02
164 Bill Ripken .05 .02
165 Fred Manrique .05 .02
166 Nolan Ryan UER 1.00 .30
(Did not lead NL in K's in '89 as he was in AL in '89)
167 Damon Berryhill .05 .02
168 Dale Murphy .25 .07
169 Mickey Tettleton .05 .02
170A Kirk McCaskill ERR .05 .02
(Born 4/19)
170B Kirk McCaskill COR .05 .02
(Born 4/9; corrected in factory sets)
171 Dwight Gooden .10 .03
172 Jose Lind .05 .02
173 B.J. Surhoff .10 .03
174 Ruben Sierra .05 .02
175 Dan Plesac .05 .02

176 Dan Pasqua .05 .02
177 Kelly Downs .05 .02
178 Matt Nokes .05 .02
179 Luis Aquino .05 .02
180 Frank Tanana .05 .02
181 Tony Pena .05 .02
182 Dan Gladden .05 .02
183 Bruce Hurst .05 .02
184 Roger Clemens .50 .15
185 Mark McGwire .60 .18
186 Rob Murphy .05 .02
187 Jim Deshaies .05 .02
188 Fred McGriff .25 .07
189 Rob Dibble .10 .03
190 Don Mattingly .60 .18
191 Felix Fermin .05 .02
192 Roberto Kelly .05 .02
193 Dennis Cook .05 .02
194 Darren Daulton .10 .03
195 Alfredo Griffin .05 .02
196 Eric Plunk .05 .02
197 Orel Hershiser .10 .03
198 Paul O'Neill .15 .04
199 Randy Bush .05 .02
200A Checklist 130-231 .05 .02
200B Checklist 126-223 .05 .02
201 Ozzie Smith .40 .12
202 Pete O'Brien .05 .02
203 Jay Howell .05 .02
204 Mark Gubicza .05 .02
205 Ed Whitson .05 .02
206 George Bell .05 .02
207 Mike Scott .05 .02
208 Charlie Leibrandt .05 .02
209 Mike Heath .05 .02
210 Dennis Eckersley .10 .03
211 Mike LaValliere .05 .02
212 Darnell Coles .05 .02
213 Lance Parrish .05 .02
214 Mike Moore .05 .02
215 Steve Finley .10 .03
216 Tim Raines .10 .03
217A Scott Garrelts ERR .05 .02
(Born 10/20)
217B Scott Garrelts COR .05 .02
(Born 10/30; corrected in factory sets)
218 Kevin McReynolds .05 .02
219 Dave Gallagher .05 .02
220 Tim Wallach .05 .02
221 Chuck Crim .05 .02
222 Lonnie Smith .05 .02
223 Andre Dawson .10 .03
224 Nelson Santovenia .05 .02
225 Rafael Palmeiro .15 .04
226 Devon White .10 .03
227 Harold Reynolds .10 .03
228 Ellis Burks .15 .04
229 Mark Parent .05 .02
230 Will Clark .25 .07
231 Jimmy Key .10 .03
232 John Farrell .05 .02
233 Eric Davis .10 .03
234 Johnny Ray .05 .02
235 Darryl Strawberry .10 .03
236 Bill Doran .05 .02
237 Greg Gagne .05 .02
238 Jim Eisenreich .05 .02
239 Tommy Gregg .05 .02
240 Marty Barrett .05 .02
241 Rafael Ramirez .05 .02
242 Chris Sabo .05 .02
243 Dave Henderson .05 .02
244 Andy Van Slyke .10 .03
245 Alvaro Espinoza .05 .02
246 Garry Templeton .05 .02
247 Gene Harris .05 .02
248 Kevin Gross .05 .02
249 Brett Butler .10 .03
250 Willie Randolph .10 .03
251 Roger McDowell .05 .02
252 Rafael Belliard .05 .02
253 Steve Rosenberg .05 .02
254 Jack Howell .05 .02
255 Marvell Wynne .05 .02
256 Tom Candiotti .05 .02
257 Todd Benzinger .05 .02
258 Don Robinson .05 .02
259 Phil Bradley .05 .02
260 Cecil Espy .05 .02
261 Scott Bankhead .05 .02
262 Frank White .10 .03
263 Andres Thomas .05 .02
264 Glenn Braggs .05 .02
265 David Cone .10 .03
266 Bobby Thigpen .05 .02
267 Nelson Liriano .05 .02
268 Terry Steinbach .05 .02
269 Kirby Puckett UER .25 .07
(Back doesn't consider Joe Torre's .363 in '71)
270 Gregg Jefferies .10 .03
271 Jeff Blauser .05 .02
272 Cory Snyder .05 .02
273 Roy Smith .05 .02
274 Tom Foley .05 .02
275 Mitch Williams .05 .02
276 Paul Kilgus .05 .02
277 Don Slaught .05 .02
278 Von Hayes .05 .02
279 Vince Coleman .05 .02
280 Mike Boddicker .05 .02
281 Ken Dayley .05 .02
282 Mike Devereaux .05 .02
283 Kenny Rogers .10 .03
284 Jeff Russell .05 .02
285 Jerome Walton .05 .02
286 Derek Lilliquist .05 .02
287 Joe Orsulak .05 .02
288 Dick Schofield .05 .02
289 Ron Darling .05 .02
290 Bobby Bonilla .10 .03
291 Jim Gantner .05 .02
292 Bobby Witt .05 .02
293 Greg Brock .05 .02
294 Ivan Calderon .05 .02
295 Steve Bedrosian .05 .02
296 Mike Henneman .05 .02
297 Tom Gordon .10 .03
298 Lou Whitaker .10 .03
299 Terry Pendleton .10 .03
300A Checklist 232-333 .05 .02
300B Checklist 224-321 .05 .02
301 Juan Berenguer .05 .02
302 Mark Davis .05 .02
303 Nick Esasky .05 .02
304 Rickey Henderson .25 .07
305 Rick Cerone .05 .02
306 Craig Biggio .15 .04
307 Duane Ward .05 .02
308 Tom Browning .05 .02
309 Walt Terrell .05 .02
310 Greg Swindell .05 .02
311 Dave Righetti .05 .02
312 Mike Maddux .05 .02
313 Len Dykstra .10 .03
314 Jose Gonzalez .05 .02
315 Steve Balboni .05 .02
316 Mike Scioscia .05 .02
317 Ron Oester .05 .02
318 Gary Wayne .05 .02
319 Todd Worrell .05 .02
320 Doug Jones .05 .02
321 Jeff Hamilton .05 .02
322 Danny Tartabull .05 .02
323 Chris James .05 .02
324 Mike Flanagan .05 .02
325 Gerald Young .05 .02
326 Bob Boone .10 .03
327 Frank Williams .05 .02
328 Dave Parker .10 .03
329 Sid Bream .05 .02
330 Mike Schooler .05 .02
331 Bert Blyleven .10 .03
332 Bob Welch .05 .02
333 Bob Milacki .05 .02
334 Tim Burke .05 .02
335 Jose Uribe .05 .02
336 Randy Myers .10 .03
337 Eric King .05 .02
338 Mark Langston .05 .02
339 Teddy Higuera .05 .02
340 Oddibe McDowell .05 .02
341 Lloyd McClendon .05 .02
342 Pascual Perez .05 .02
343 Kevin Brown UER .10 .03
(Signed is misspelled as signeed on back)
344 Chuck Finley .10 .03
345 Erik Hanson .05 .02
346 Rich Gedman .05 .02
347 Bip Roberts .05 .02
348 Matt Williams .10 .03
349 Tom Henke .05 .02
350 Brad Komminsk .05 .02
351 Jeff Reed .05 .02
352 Brian Downing .05 .02
353 Frank Viola .05 .02
354 Terry Puhl .05 .02
355 Brian Harper .05 .02
356 Steve Farr .05 .02
357 Joe Boever .05 .02
358 Danny Heep .05 .02
359 Larry Andersen .05 .02
360 Rolando Roomes .05 .02
361 Mike Gallego .05 .02
362 Bob Kipper .05 .02
363 Clay Parker .05 .02
364 Mike Pagliarulo .05 .02
365 Ken Griffey Jr. UER .75 .23
(Signed through 1990, should be 1991)
366 Rex Hudler .05 .02
367 Pat Sheridan .05 .02
368 Kirk Gibson .10 .03
369 Jeff Parrett .05 .02
370 Bob Walk .05 .02
371 Ken Patterson .05 .02
372 Bryan Harvey .05 .02
373 Mike Bielecki .05 .02
374 Tom Magrann .05 .02
375 Rick Mahler .05 .02
376 Craig Lefferts .05 .02
377 Gregg Olson .10 .03
378 Jamie Moyer .10 .03
379 Randy Johnson .50 .12
380 Jeff Montgomery .10 .03
381 Marty Clary .05 .02
382 Bill Spiers .05 .02
383 Dave Magadan .05 .02
384 Greg Hibbard RC .10 .03
385 Ernie Whitt .05 .02
386 Rick Honeycutt .05 .02
387 Dave West .05 .02
388 Keith Hernandez .10 .03
389 Jose Alvarez .05 .02
390 Joey Belle .25 .07
391 Rick Aguilera .10 .03
392 Mike Fitzgerald .05 .02
393 Dwight Smith .05 .02
394 Steve Wilson .05 .02
395 Bob Geren .05 .02
396 Randy Ready .05 .02
397 Ken Hill .10 .03
398 Jody Reed .05 .02
399 Tom Brunansky .05 .02
400A Checklist 334-435 .05 .02
400B Checklist 322-419 .05 .02
401 Rene Gonzales .05 .02
402 Harold Baines .10 .03
403 Cecilio Guante .05 .02
404 Joe Girardi .15 .04
405A Sergio Valdez ERR .05 .02
(Card front shows black line crossing S in Sergio)
405B Sergio Valdez COR .05 .02
406 Mark Williamson .05 .02
407 Glenn Hoffman .05 .02
408 Jeff Innis .05 .02
409 Randy Kramer .05 .02
410 Charlie O'Brien .05 .02
411 Charlie Hough .10 .03
412 Gus Polidor .05 .02
413 Ron Karkovice .05 .02
414 Trevor Wilson .05 .02
415 Kevin Ritz .05 .02
416 Gary Thurman .05 .02
417 Jeff M. Robinson .05 .02
418 Scott Terry .05 .02
419 Tim Laudner .05 .02
420 Dennis Rasmussen .05 .02
421 Luis Rivera .05 .02
422 Jim Corsi .05 .02
423 Dennis Lamp .05 .02
424 Ken Caminiti .10 .03
425 David Wells .10 .03
426 Norm Charlton .10 .03
427 Deion Sanders .25 .07
428 Dion James .05 .02
429 Chuck Cary .05 .02
430 Ken Howell .05 .02
431 Steve Lake .05 .02
432 Kal Daniels .05 .02
433 Lance McCullers .05 .02
434 Lenny Harris .05 .02
435 Scott Scudder .05 .02
436 Gene Larkin .05 .02
437 Dan Quisenberry .05 .02
438 Steve Olin RC .25 .07
439 Mickey Hatcher .05 .02
440 Willie Wilson .05 .02
441 Mark Grant .05 .02
442 Mookie Wilson .10 .03
443 Alex Trevino .05 .02
444 Pat Tabler .05 .02
445 Dave Bergman .05 .02
446 Todd Burns .05 .02
447 R.J. Reynolds .05 .02
448 Jay Buhner .10 .03
449 Lee Stevens .10 .03
450 Ron Hassey .05 .02
451 Bob Melvin .05 .02
452 Dave Martinez .05 .02
453 Greg Litton .05 .02
454 Mark Carreon .05 .02
455 Scott Fletcher .05 .02
456 Otis Nixon .05 .02
457 Tony Fossas .05 .02
458 John Russell .05 .02
459 Paul Assenmacher .05 .02
460 Zane Smith .05 .02
461 Jack Daugherty .05 .02
462 Rich Monteleone .05 .02
463 Greg Briley .05 .02
464 Mike Smithson .05 .02
465 Benito Santiago .10 .03
466 Jeff Brantley .05 .02
467 Jose Nunez .05 .02
468 Scott Bailes .05 .02
469 Ken Griffey Sr. .10 .03
470 Bob McClure .05 .02
471 Mackey Sasser .05 .02
472 Glenn Wilson .05 .02
473 Kevin Tapani RC .25 .07
474 Bill Buckner .05 .02
475 Ron Gant .10 .03
476 Kevin Romine .05 .02
477 Juan Agosto .05 .02
478 Herm Winningham .05 .02
479 Storm Davis .05 .02
480 Jeff King .05 .02
481 Kevin Mmahat .05 .02
482 Carmelo Martinez .05 .02
483 Omar Vizquel .25 .07
484 Jim Dwyer .05 .02
485 Bob Knepper .05 .02
486 Dave Anderson .05 .02
487 Ron Jones .05 .02
488 Jay Bell .10 .03
489 Sammy Sosa RC 5.00 1.50
490 Kent Anderson .05 .02
491 Domingo Ramos .05 .02
492 Dave Clark .05 .02
493 Tim Birtsas .05 .02
494 Ken Oberkfell .05 .02
495 Larry Sheets .05 .02
496 Jeff Kunkel .05 .02
497 Jim Presley .05 .02
498 Mike Macfarlane .05 .02
499 Pete Smith .05 .02
500A Checklist 436-537 DP .05 .02
500B Checklist 420-517 .05 .02
501 Gary Sheffield .25 .07
502 Terry Bross .05 .02
503 Jerry Kutzler .05 .02
504 Lloyd Moseby .05 .02
505 Curt Young .05 .02
506 Al Newman .05 .02
507 Keith Miller .05 .02
508 Mike Stanton RC .25 .07
509 Rich Yett .05 .02
510 Tim Drummond .05 .02
511 Joe Hesketh .05 .02
512 Rick Wrona .05 .02
513 Luis Salazar .05 .02
514 Hal Morris .05 .02
515 Terry Mulholland .05 .02
516 John Morris .05 .02
517 Carlos Quintana .05 .02
518 Frank DiPino .05 .02
519 Randy Milligan .05 .02
520 Chad Kreuter .05 .02
521 Mike Jeffcoat .05 .02
522 Mike Harkey .05 .02
523A Andy Nezelek ERR .05 .02
(Wrong birth year)
523B Andy Nezelek COR .15 .04
(Finally corrected in factory sets)
524 Dave Schmidt .05 .02
525 Tony Armas .05 .02
526 Barry Lyons .05 .02
527 Rick Reed RC .25 .07
528 Jerry Reuss .05 .02
529 Dean Palmer RC .25 .07
530 Jeff Peterek .05 .02
531 Carlos Martinez .05 .02
532 Atlee Hammaker .05 .02
533 Mike Brumley .05 .02
534 Terry Leach .05 .02
535 Doug Strange .05 .02
536 Jose DeLeon .05 .02
537 Shane Rawley .05 .02
538 Joey Cora .10 .03
539 Eric Hetzel .05 .02
540 Gene Nelson .05 .02
541 Wes Gardner .05 .02
542 Mark Portugal .05 .02
543 Al Leiter .25 .07
544 Jack Armstrong .05 .02
545 Greg Cadaret .05 .02
546 Rod Nichols .05 .02
547 Luis Polonia .05 .02
548 Charlie Hayes .05 .02
549 Dickie Thon .05 .02
550 Tim Crews .05 .02
551 Dave Winfield .10 .03
552 Mike Davis .05 .02
553 Ron Robinson .05 .02
554 Carmen Castillo .05 .02
555 John Costello .05 .02
556 Bud Black .05 .02
557 Rick Dempsey .05 .02
558 Jim Acker .05 .02
559 Eric Show .05 .02
560 Pat Borders .05 .02
561 Danny Darwin .05 .02
562 Rick Luecken .05 .02
563 Edwin Nunez .05 .02
564 Felix Jose .05 .02
565 John Cangelosi .05 .02
566 Bill Swift .05 .02
567 Bill Schroeder .05 .02
568 Stan Javier .05 .02
569 Jim Traber .05 .02
570 Wallace Johnson .05 .02
571 Donell Nixon .05 .02
572 Sid Fernandez .05 .02
573 Lance Johnson .05 .02
574 Andy McGaffigan .05 .02
575 Mark Knudson .05 .02
576 Tommy Greene RC .10 .03
577 Mark Grace .15 .04
578 Larry Walker RC 1.00 .30
579 Mike Stanley .05 .02
580 Mike Witt DP .05 .02
581 Scott Bradley .05 .02
582 Greg A. Harris .05 .02
583A Kevin Hickey ERR .25 .07
583B Kevin Hickey COR .05 .02
584 Lee Mazzilli .05 .02
585 Jeff Pico .05 .02
586 Joe Oliver .05 .02
587 Willie Fraser DP .05 .02
588 Carl Yastrzemski .25 .07
Puzzle Card DP
589 Kevin Bass DP .05 .02
590 John Moses DP .05 .02
591 Tom Pagnozzi DP .05 .02
592 Tony Castillo DP .05 .02
593 Jerald Clark DP .05 .02
594 Dan Schatzeder .05 .02
595 Luis Quinones DP .05 .02
596 Pete Harnisch DP .05 .02
597 Gary Redus .05 .02
598 Mel Hall .05 .02
599 Rick Schu .05 .02
600A Checklist 538-639 .05 .02
600B Checklist 518-617 .05 .02
601 Mike Kingery DP .05 .02
602 Terry Kennedy DP .05 .02
603 Mike Sharperson DP .05 .02
604 Don Carman DP .05 .02
605 Jim Gott .05 .02
606 Donn Pall DP .05 .02
607 Rance Mulliniks .05 .02
608 Curt Wilkerson DP .05 .02
609 Mike Felder DP .05 .02
610 G.Hernandez DP .05 .02
611 Candy Maldonado DP .05 .02
612 Mark Thurmond DP .05 .02
613 Rick Leach DP .05 .02
614 Jerry Reed DP .05 .02
615 Franklin Stubbs .05 .02
616 Billy Hatcher DP .05 .02
617 Don August DP .05 .02
618 Tim Teufel .05 .02
619 Shawn Hillegas DP .05 .02
620 Manny Lee .05 .02
621 Gary Ward DP .05 .02
622 Mark Guthrie DP .05 .02
623 Jeff Musselman DP .05 .02
624 Mark Lemke DP .05 .02
625 Fernando Valenzuela .10 .03
626 Paul Sorrento DP RC .25 .07
627 Glenallen Hill DP .05 .02
628 Les Lancaster DP .05 .02
629 Vance Law DP .05 .02
630 Randy Velarde DP .05 .02
631 Todd Frohwirth DP .05 .02
632 Willie McGee .10 .03
633 Dennis Boyd DP .05 .02
634 Cris Carpenter DP .05 .02
635 Brian Holton .05 .02
636 Tracy Jones DP .05 .02
637A Terry Steinbach AS .05 .02
(Recent Major League Performance)
637B Terry Steinbach AS .05 .02
(All-Star Game Performance)
638 Brady Anderson .10 .03
639A Jack Morris ERR .10 .03
(Card front shows black line crossing J in Jack)
639B Jack Morris COR .10 .03
640 Jaime Navarro .05 .02
641 Darrin Jackson .05 .02
642 Mike Dyer RC .05 .02
643 Mike Schmidt .50 .15
644 Henry Cotto .05 .02
645 John Cerutti .05 .02
646 Francisco Cabrera .05 .02
647 Scott Sanderson .05 .02
648 Brian Meyer .05 .02
649 Ray Searage .05 .02
650A Bo Jackson AS .25 .07
(Recent Major League Performance)
650B Bo Jackson AS .25 .07
(All-Star Game Performance)
651 Steve Lyons .05 .02
652 Mike LaCoss .05 .02
653 Ted Power .05 .02
654A Howard Johnson AS .05 .02
(Recent Major League Performance)
654B Howard Johnson AS .05 .02
(All-Star Game Performance)
655 Mauro Gozzo .05 .02
656 Mike Blowers RC .10 .03
657 Paul Gibson .05 .02
658 Neal Heaton .05 .02
659 Nolan Ryan 5000K .50 .15
COR (Still an error as Ryan did not lead AL in K's in '75)
659A Nolan Ryan 5000K 1.50 .45
(665 King of Kings back) ERR
660A Harold Baines AS .75 .23
(Black line through star on front; Recent Major League Performance)
660B Harold Baines AS 1.00 .30
(Black line through star on front; All-Star Game Performance)
660C Harold Baines AS .25 .07
(Black line behind star on front; Recent Major League Performance)
660D Harold Baines AS .05 .02
(Black line behind star on front; All-Star Game Performance)
661 Gary Pettis .05 .02
662 Clint Zavaras .05 .02
663A Rick Reuschel AS .05 .02
(Recent Major League Performance)
663B Rick Reuschel AS .05 .02
(All-Star Game Performance)
664 Alejandro Pena .05 .02
665 N.Ryan KING COR .50 .15
665A Nolan Ryan KING 1.50 .45
(659 5000 K back) ERR
665C N.Ryan KING ERR .75 .23
No number on back in factory sets
666 Ricky Horton .05 .02
667 Curt Schilling 1.00 .30
668 Bill Landrum .05 .02
669 Todd Stottlemyre .10 .03
670 Tim Leary .05 .02
671 John Wetteland .25 .07
672 Calvin Schiraldi .05 .02
673A Ruben Sierra AS .05 .02
(Recent Major League Performance)
673B Ruben Sierra AS .05 .02
(All-Star Game Performance)
674A Pedro Guerrero AS .05 .02
(Recent Major League Performance)
674B Pedro Guerrero AS .05 .02
(All-Star Game Performance)
675 Ken Phelps .05 .02
676A Cal Ripken AS .40 .12
(All-Star Game Performance)
676B Cal Ripken AS .75 .23
(Recent Major League Performance)
677 Denny Walling .05 .02
678 Goose Gossage .10 .03
679 Gary Mielke .05 .02
680 Bill Bathe .05 .02
681 Tom Lawless .05 .02
682 Xavier Hernandez RC .05 .02
683A Kirby Puckett AS .15 .04
(Recent Major League Performance)
683B Kirby Puckett AS .15 .04
(All-Star Game Performance)
684 Mariano Duncan .05 .02
685 Ramon Martinez .05 .02
686 Tim Jones .05 .02
687 Tom Filer .05 .02
688 Steve Lombardozzi .05 .02
689 Bernie Williams RC 1.00 .30
690 Chip Hale .05 .02
691 Beau Allred RC .05 .02
692A Ryne Sandberg AS .25 .07
(Recent Major League Performance)
692B Ryne Sandberg AS .25 .07
(All-Star Game Performance)
693 Jeff Huson RC .10 .03
694 Curt Ford .05 .02
695A Eric Davis AS .05 .02
(Recent Major League Performance)
695B Eric Davis AS .05 .02
(All-Star Game Performance)
696 Scott Lusader .05 .02
697A Mark McGwire AS .30 .09
(Recent Major League Performance)
697B Mark McGwire AS .30 .09
(All-Star Game Performance)
698 Steve Cummings RC .05 .02
699 George Canale .05 .02
700A Checklist 640-715 .25 .07
and BC1-BC26
700B Checklist 640-716 .10 .03
and BC1-BC26
700C Checklist 618-716 .05 .02
701A Julio Franco AS .05 .02
(Recent Major League Performance)
701B Julio Franco AS .05 .02
(All-Star Game Performance)

Card	Nm-Mt	Ex-Mt
702 Dave Johnson (P)	.05	.02
703A Dave Stewart AS (Recent Major League Performance)	.05	.02
703B Dave Stewart AS (All-Star Game Performance)	.05	.02
704 Dave Justice RC	.50	.15
705 Tony Gwynn AS (All-Star Game Performance)	.15	.04
705A Tony Gwynn AS (Recent Major League Performance)	.15	.04
706 Greg Myers	.05	.02
707A Will Clark AS (Recent Major League Performance)	.25	.07
707B Will Clark AS (All-Star Game Performance)	.25	.07
708A Benito Santiago AS (Recent Major League Performance)	.05	.02
708B Benito Santiago AS (All-Star Game Performance)	.05	.02
709 Larry McWilliams	.05	.02
710A Ozzie Smith AS (Recent Major League Performance)	.25	.07
710B Ozzie Smith AS Perf	.25	.07
711 John Olerud RC	.50	.15
712A Wade Boggs AS (Recent Major League Performance)	.10	.03
712B Wade Boggs AS (All-Star Game Performance)	.10	.03
713 Gary Eave	.05	.02
714 Bob Tewksbury	.05	.02
715A Kevin Mitchell AS (Recent Major League Performance)	.05	.02
715B Kevin Mitchell AS (All-Star Game Performance)	.05	.02
716 B.Giamatti COMM In Memoriam	.25	.07

1990 Donruss Bonus MVP's

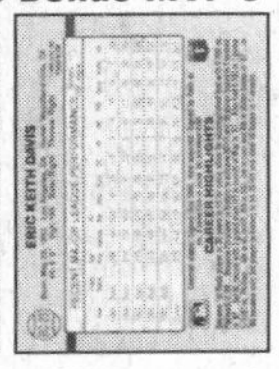

Numbered with the prefix "BC" for bonus card, a 26-card set featuring the most valuable player from each of the 26 teams was randomly inserted in all 1990 Donruss unopened pack formats. The factory sets were distributed without the Bonus Cards; thus there were again new checklist cards printed to reflect the exclusion of the Bonus Cards.

Card	Nm-Mt	Ex-Mt
COMPLETE SET (26)	1.50	.45
BC1 Bo Jackson	.25	.07
BC2 Howard Johnson	.05	.01
BC3 Dave Stewart	.10	.03
BC4 Tony Gwynn	.30	.09
BC5 Orel Hershiser	.10	.03
BC6 Pedro Guerrero	.05	.01
BC7 Tim Raines	.10	.03
BC8 Kirby Puckett	.25	.07
BC9 Alvin Davis	.05	.01
BC10 Ryne Sandberg	.40	.12
BC11 Kevin Mitchell	.05	.01
BC12A John Smoltz ERR (Photo actually Tom Glavine)	.15	.04
BC12B John Smoltz COR	.25	.07
BC13 George Bell	.05	.01
BC14 Julio Franco	.10	.03
BC15 Paul Molitor	.15	.04
BC16 Bobby Bonilla	.10	.03
BC17 Mike Greenwell	.05	.01
BC18 Cal Ripken	.75	.23
BC19 Carlton Fisk	.15	.04
BC20 Chili Davis	.10	.03
BC21 Glenn Davis	.05	.01
BC22 Steve Sax	.05	.01
BC23 Eric Davis DP	.10	.03
BC24 Greg Swindell DP	.05	.01
BC25 Von Hayes DP	.05	.01
BC26 Alan Trammell	.10	.03

1990 Donruss Grand Slammers

This 12-card standard size set was in the 1990 Donruss set as a special card deliniating each 55-card section of the 1990 Factory Set. This set honors those players who connected for grand slam homers during the 1989 season. The cards are in the 1990 Donruss design and the back describes the grand slam homer hit by each player.

Card	Nm-Mt	Ex-Mt
COMPLETE SET (12)	1.50	.45
1 Matt Williams	.10	.03
2 Jeffrey Leonard	.05	.01
3 Chris James	.05	.01
4 Mark McGwire	.60	.18
5 Dwight Evans	.10	.03
6 Will Clark	.25	.07
7 Mike Scioscia	.05	.01
8 Todd Benzinger	.05	.01
9 Fred McGriff	.25	.07
10 Kevin Bass	.05	.01
11 Jack Clark	.10	.03
12 Bo Jackson	.25	.07

1990 Donruss Rookies

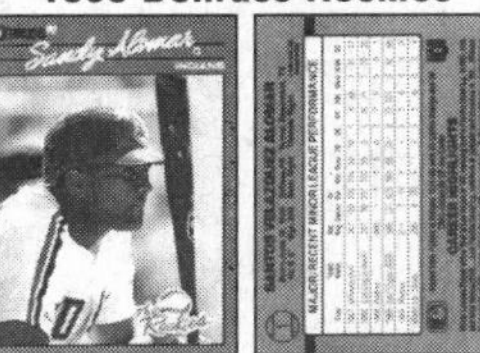

The 1990 Donruss Rookies set marked the fifth consecutive year that Donruss issued a boxed set at season's end honoring the best rookies of the season. This set, which used the 1990 Donruss design but featured a green border, was issued exclusively through the Donruss dealer network to hobby dealers. This 56-card, standard size set came in its own box and the words "The Rookies" are featured prominently on the front of the cards. There are no notable Rookie Cards in this set.

Card	Nm-Mt	Ex-Mt
COMP.FACT.SET (56)	2.00	.60
1 Sandy Alomar Jr. UER (No stitches on baseball on Donruss logo on card front)	.10	.03
2 John Olerud	.50	.15
3 Pat Combs	.05	.02
4 Brian DuBois	.05	.02
5 Felix Jose	.05	.02
6 Delino DeShields	.25	.07
7 Mike Stanton	.05	.02
8 Mike Munoz	.05	.02
9 Craig Grebeck RC	.10	.03
10 Joe Kraemer	.05	.02
11 Jeff Huson	.05	.02
12 Bill Sampen	.05	.02
13 Brian Bohanon RC	.10	.03
14 Dave Justice	.50	.15
15 Robin Ventura	.25	.07
16 Greg Vaughn	.05	.02
17 Wayne Edwards	.05	.02
18 Shawn Boskie RC	.10	.03
19 Carlos Baerga RC	.25	.07
20 Mark Gardner	.05	.02
21 Kevin Appier	.10	.03
22 Mike Harkey	.05	.02
23 Tim Layana	.05	.02
24 Glenallen Hill	.05	.02
25 Jerry Kutzler	.05	.02
26 Mike Blowers	.10	.03
27 Scott Ruskin	.05	.02
28 Dana Kiecker	.05	.02
29 Willie Blair RC	.10	.03
30 Ben McDonald	.05	.02
31 Todd Zeile	.10	.03
32 Scott Coolbaugh	.05	.02
33 Xavier Hernandez	.05	.02
34 Mike Hartley	.05	.02
35 Kevin Tapani	.25	.07
36 Kevin Wickander	.05	.02
37 Carlos Hernandez RC	.25	.07
38 Brian Traxler RC	.10	.03
39 Marty Brown	.05	.02
40 Scott Radinsky RC	.10	.03
41 Julio Machado	.05	.02
42 Steve Avery	.05	.02
43 Mark Lemke	.05	.02
44 Alan Mills RC	.10	.03
45 Marquis Grissom	.25	.07
46 Greg Olson RC	.10	.03
47 Dave Hollins RC	.25	.07
48 Jerald Clark	.05	.02
49 Eric Anthony	.05	.02
50 Tim Drummond	.05	.02
51 John Burkett	.05	.02
52 Brent Knackert RC	.10	.03
53 Jeff Shaw	.05	.02
54 John Orton RC	.10	.03
55 Terry Shumpert	.05	.02
56 Checklist 1-56	.05	.02

1990 Donruss Best AL

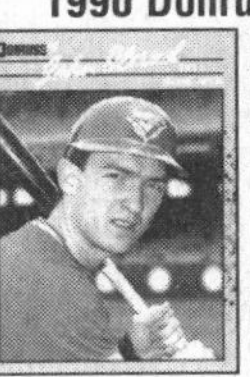
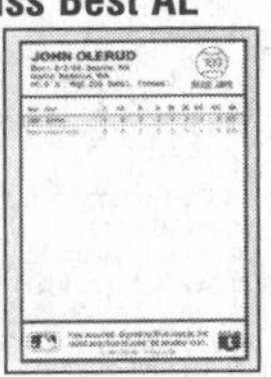

The 1990 Donruss Best of the American League set consists of 144 standard-size cards. This was Donruss' latest version of what had been titled the previous two years as Baseball's Best. In 1990, the sets were split into National and American League and marketed separately. The front design was similar to the regular issue Donruss set except for the front borders being blue while the backs have complete major and minor league statistics as compared to the regular Donruss cards which only cover the past five major-league seasons. An early Sammy Sosa card is featured within this set.

Card	Nm-Mt	Ex-Mt
COMP.FACT.SET (144)	40.00	12.00
1 Ken Griffey Jr.	1.25	.35
2 Bob Milacki	.15	.04
3 Mike Boddicker	.15	.04
4 Bert Blyleven	.20	.06
5 Carlton Fisk	.30	.09
6 Greg Swindell	.15	.04
7 Alan Trammell	.20	.06
8 Mark Davis	.15	.04
9 Chris Bosio	.15	.04
10 Gary Gaetti	.20	.06
11 Matt Nokes	.15	.04
12 Dennis Eckersley	.20	.06
13 Kevin Brown	.20	.06
14 Tom Henke	.15	.04
15 Mickey Tettleton	.15	.04
16 Jody Reed	.15	.04
17 Mark Langston	.15	.04
18 Melido Perez UER (Listed as an Expo rather than White Sox)	.15	.04
19 John Farrell	.15	.04
20 Tony Phillips	.15	.04
21 Bret Saberhagen	.20	.06
22 Robin Yount	.75	.23
23 Kirby Puckett	.50	.15
24 Steve Sax	.15	.04
25 Dave Stewart	.20	.06
26 Alvin Davis	.15	.04
27 Geno Petralli	.15	.04
28 Mookie Wilson	.20	.06
29 Jeff Ballard	.15	.04
30 Ellis Burks	.20	.06
31 Wally Joyner	.20	.06
32 Bobby Thigpen	.15	.04
33 Keith Hernandez	.20	.06
34 Jack Morris	.20	.06
35 George Brett	1.25	.35
36 Dan Plesac	.15	.04
37 Brian Harper	.15	.04
38 Don Mattingly	1.25	.35
39 Dave Henderson	.15	.04
40 Scott Bankhead UER (Asheboro misspelled as Ashboro on card)	.15	.04
41 Rafael Palmeiro	.30	.09
42 Jimmy Key	.20	.06
43 Gregg Olson	.15	.04
44 Tony Pena	.15	.04
45 Jack Howell	.15	.04
46 Eric King	.15	.04
47 Cory Snyder	.15	.04
48 Frank Tanana	.20	.06
49 Nolan Ryan	1.50	.45
50 Bob Boone	.20	.06
51 Dave Parker	.20	.06
52 Allan Anderson	.15	.04
53 Tim Leary	.15	.04
54 Mark McGwire	1.50	.45
55 Dave Valle	.15	.04
56 Fred McGriff	.30	.09
57 Cal Ripken	1.50	.45
58 Roger Clemens	1.00	.30
59 Lance Parrish	.20	.06
60 Robin Ventura	.50	.15
61 Doug Jones	.15	.04
62 Lloyd Moseby	.15	.04
63 Bo Jackson	.50	.15
64 Paul Molitor	.30	.09
65 Kent Hrbek	.20	.06
66 Mel Hall	.15	.04
67 Bob Welch	.20	.06
68 Erik Hanson	.15	.04
69 Harold Baines	.20	.06
70 Junior Felix	.15	.04
71 Craig Worthington	.15	.04
72 Jeff Reardon	.20	.06
73 Johnny Ray	.15	.04
74 Ozzie Guillen	.15	.04
75 Brook Jacoby	.15	.04
76 Chet Lemon	.15	.04
77 Mark Gubicza	.15	.04
78 B.J. Surhoff	.20	.06
79 Rick Aguilera	.20	.06
80 Pascual Perez	.15	.04
81 Jose Canseco	.50	.15
82 Mike Schooler	.15	.04
83 Jeff Huson	.15	.04
84 Kelly Gruber	.15	.04
85 Randy Milligan	.15	.04
86 Wade Boggs	.30	.09
87 Dave Winfield	.20	.06
88 Scott Fletcher	.15	.04
89 Tom Candiotti	.15	.04
90 Mike Heath	.15	.04
91 Kevin Seitzer	.15	.04
92 Ted Higuera	.15	.04
93 Kevin Tapani	.50	.15
94 Roberto Kelly	.15	.04
95 Walt Weiss	.15	.04
96 Checklist Card	.15	.04
97 Sandy Alomar Jr.	.20	.06
98 Pete O'Brien	.15	.04
99 Jeff Russell	.15	.04
100 John Olerud	1.50	.45
101 Pete Harnisch	.15	.04
102 Dwight Evans	.20	.06
103 Chuck Finley	.20	.06
104 Sammy Sosa	15.00	4.50
105 Mike Henneman	.15	.04
106 Kurt Stillwell	.15	.04
107 Greg Vaughn	.15	.04
108 Dan Gladden	.15	.04
109 Jesse Barfield	.15	.04
110 Willie Randolph	.20	.06
111 Randy Johnson	.75	.18
112 Julio Franco	.20	.06
113 Tony Fernandez	.15	.04
114 Ben McDonald	.15	.04
115 Mike Greenwell	.15	.04
116 Luis Polonia	.15	.04
117 Carney Lansford	.20	.06
118 Bud Black	.15	.04
119 Lou Whitaker	.20	.06
120 Jim Eisenreich	.15	.04
121 Gary Sheffield	.50	.15
122 Shane Mack	.15	.04
123 Alvaro Espinoza	.15	.04
124 Rickey Henderson	.50	.15
125 Jeffrey Leonard	.15	.04
126 Gary Pettis	.15	.04
127 Dave Stieb	.20	.06
128 Danny Tartabull	.15	.04
129 Joe Orsulak	.15	.04
130 Tom Brunansky	.15	.04
131 Dick Schofield	.15	.04
132 Candy Maldonado	.15	.04
133 Cecil Fielder	.20	.06
134 Terry Shumpert	.15	.04
135 Greg Gagne	.15	.04
136 Dave Righetti	.20	.06
137 Terry Steinbach	.15	.04
138 Harold Reynolds	.20	.06
139 George Bell	.15	.04
140 Carlos Quintana	.15	.04
141 Ivan Calderon	.15	.04
142 Greg Brock	.15	.04
143 Ruben Sierra	.15	.04
144 Checklist Card	.15	.04

1990 Donruss Best NL

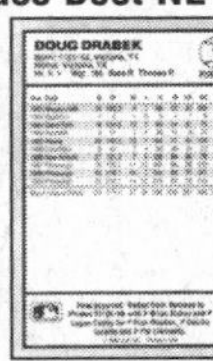

The 1990 Donruss Best of the National League set consists of 144 standard-size cards. This was Donruss' latest version of what had been titled the previous two years as Baseball's Best. In 1990, the sets were split into National and American League and marketed separately. The front design was similar to the regular issue Donruss set except for the front borders being blue while the backs have complete major and minor league statistics as compared to the regular Donruss cards which only cover the past five major-league seasons. An early Larry Walker card is featured within this set.

Card	Nm-Mt	Ex-Mt
COMP.FACT.SET (144)	8.00	2.40
1 Eric Davis	.20	.06
2 Tom Glavine	.30	.09
3 Mike Bielecki	.15	.04
4 Jim Deshaies	.15	.04
5 Mike Scioscia	.15	.04
6 Spike Owen	.15	.04
7 Dwight Gooden	.20	.06
8 Ricky Jordan	.15	.04
9 Doug Drabek	.15	.04
10 Bryn Smith	.15	.04
11 Tony Gwynn	.60	.18
12 John Burkett	.15	.04
13 Nick Esasky	.15	.04
14 Greg Maddux	.75	.23
15 Joe Oliver	.15	.04
16 Mike Scott	.15	.04
17 Tim Belcher	.15	.04
18 Kevin Gross	.15	.04
19 Howard Johnson	.15	.04
20 Darren Daulton	.20	.06
21 John Smiley	.15	.04
22 Ken Dayley	.15	.04
23 Craig Lefferts	.15	.04
24 Will Clark	.50	.15
25 Greg Olson	.15	.04
26 Ryne Sandberg	.60	.18
27 Tom Browning	.15	.04
28 Eric Anthony	.15	.04
29 Juan Samuel	.15	.04
30 Dennis Martinez	.20	.06
31 Kevin Elster	.15	.04
32 Tom Herr	.15	.04
33 Sid Bream	.15	.04
34 Terry Pendleton	.20	.06
35 Roberto Alomar	.30	.09
36 Kevin Bass	.15	.04
37 Jim Presley	.15	.04
38 Les Lancaster	.15	.04
39 Paul O'Neill	.30	.09
40 Dave Smith	.15	.04
41 Kirk Gibson	.20	.06
42 Tim Burke	.15	.04
43 David Cone	.20	.06
44 Ken Howell	.15	.04
45 Barry Bonds	1.25	.35
46 Joe Magrane	.15	.04
47 Andy Benes	.20	.06
48 Gary Carter	.20	.06
49 Pat Combs	.15	.04
50 John Smoltz	.50	.15
51 Mark Grace	.30	.09
52 Barry Larkin	.30	.09
53 Danny Darwin	.15	.04
54 Orel Hershiser	.20	.06
55 Tim Wallach	.15	.04
56 Dave Magadan	.15	.04
57 Roger McDowell	.15	.04
58 Bill Landrum	.15	.04
59 Jose DeLeon	.15	.04
60 Bip Roberts	.15	.04
61 Matt Williams	.20	.06
62 Dale Murphy	.50	.15
63 Dwight Smith	.15	.04
64 Chris Sabo	.15	.04
65 Glenn Davis	.15	.04
66 Jay Howell	.15	.04
67 Andres Galarraga	.20	.06
68 Frank Viola	.20	.06
69 John Kruk	.20	.06
70 Bobby Bonilla	.20	.06
71 Todd Zeile	.20	.06
72 Joe Carter	.20	.06
73 Robby Thompson	.15	.04
74 Jeff Blauser	.15	.04
75 Mitch Williams	.15	.04
76 Rob Dibble	.20	.06
77 Rafael Ramirez	.15	.04
78 Eddie Murray	.50	.15
79 Dave Martinez	.15	.04
80 Darryl Strawberry	.20	.06
81 Dickie Thon	.15	.04
82 Jose Lind	.15	.04
83 Ozzie Smith	.75	.23
84 Bruce Hurst	.15	.04
85 Kevin Mitchell	.15	.04
86 Lonnie Smith	.15	.04
87 Joe Girardi	.15	.04
88 Randy Myers	.20	.06
89 Craig Biggio	.30	.09
90 Fernando Valenzuela	.20	.06
91 Larry Walker	2.00	.60
92 John Franco	.20	.06
93 Dennis Cook	.15	.04
94 Bob Walk	.15	.04
95 Pedro Guerrero	.20	.06
96 Checklist Card	.15	.04
97 Andre Dawson	.20	.06
98 Ed Whitson	.15	.04
99 Steve Bedrosian	.15	.04
100 Oddibe McDowell	.15	.04
101 Todd Benzinger	.15	.04
102 Bill Doran	.15	.04
103 Alfredo Griffin	.15	.04
104 Tim Raines	.20	.06
105 Sid Fernandez	.15	.04
106 Charlie Hayes	.15	.04
107 Mike LaValliere	.15	.04
108 Jose Oquendo	.15	.04
109 Jack Clark	.20	.06
110 Scott Garrelts	.15	.04
111 Ron Gant	.20	.06
112 Shawon Dunston	.15	.04
113 Mariano Duncan	.15	.04
114 Eric Yelding	.15	.04
115 Hubie Brooks	.15	.04
116 Delino DeShields	.20	.06
117 Gregg Jefferies	.15	.04
118 Len Dykstra	.20	.06
119 Andy Van Slyke	.20	.06
120 Lee Smith	.20	.06
121 Benito Santiago	.20	.06
122 Jose Uribe	.15	.04
123 Jeff Treadway	.15	.04
124 Jerome Walton	.15	.04
125 Billy Hatcher	.15	.04
126 Ken Caminiti	.20	.06
127 Kal Daniels	.15	.04
128 Marquis Grissom	.50	.15
129 Kevin McReynolds	.15	.04
130 Wally Backman	.15	.04
131 Willie McGee	.20	.06
132 Terry Kennedy	.15	.04
133 Garry Templeton	.15	.04
134 Lloyd McClendon	.15	.04
135 Daryl Boston	.15	.04
136 Jay Bell	.20	.06
137 Mike Pagliarulo	.15	.04
138 Vince Coleman	.15	.04
139 Brett Butler	.20	.06
140 Von Hayes	.15	.04
141 Ramon Martinez	.15	.04
142 Jack Armstrong	.15	.04
143 Franklin Stubbs	.15	.04
144 Checklist Card	.15	.04

1991 Donruss

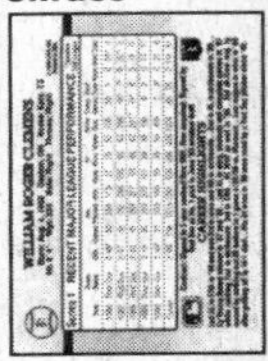

The 1991 Donruss set was issued in two series of 386 and 384 for a total of 770 standard-size cards. This set marked the first time Donruss issued cards in multiple series. The second series was issued approximately three months after the first series was issued. Cards were issued in wax packs and factory sets. As a separate promotion, wax packs were also given away with six and 12-packs of Coke and Diet Coke. First series cards feature blue borders and second series green borders with some stripes and the players name in white against a red background. Subsets include Diamond Kings (1-27), Rated Rookies (28-47/413-432), AL All-Stars (48-56), MVP's (387-412) and NL All-Stars (433-441). There were also special cards to honor the award winners and the heroes of the World Series. On cards 60, 70, 127, 182, 239, 294, 355, 368, and 377, the border stripes are red and yellow. There are no notable Rookie Cards in this set.

Card	Nm-Mt	Ex-Mt
COMPLETE SET (770)	8.00	2.40
COMP.FACT.w/LEAF PREV	10.00	3.00
COMP.FACT.w/STUD. PREV.	10.00	3.00
COMP.STARGELL PUZZLE	1.00	.30
1 Dave Stieb DK	.05	.02
2 Craig Biggio DK	.10	.03
3 Cecil Fielder DK	.05	.02
4 Barry Bonds DK	.30	.09
5 Barry Larkin DK	.10	.03
6 Dave Parker DK	.05	.02
7 Len Dykstra DK	.05	.02
8 Bobby Thigpen DK	.05	.02
9 Roger Clemens DK	.25	.07
10 Ron Gant DK UER (No trademark on team logo on back)	.10	.03
11 Delino DeShields DK	.05	.02
12 R.Alomar DK UER No trademark on team logo on back	.10	.03
13 Sandy Alomar Jr. DK	.05	.02
14 R.Sandberg DK UER Was DK in '85, not '83 as shown	.25	.07
15 Ramon Martinez DK	.05	.02
16 Edgar Martinez DK	.15	.04
17 Dave Magadan DK	.05	.02
18 Matt Williams DK	.05	.02

19 Rafael Palmeiro DK .10 .03
UER (No trademark on team logo on back)
20 Bob Welch DK .05 .02
21 Dave Righetti DK .05 .02
22 Brian Harper DK .05 .02
23 Gregg Olson DK .05 .02
24 Kurt Stillwell DK .05 .02
25 P.Guerrero DK UER .05 .02
No trademark on team logo on back
26 Chuck Finley DK UER .10 .03
(No trademark on team logo on back)
27 DK Checklist 1-27 .05 .02
28 Tino Martinez RR .15 .04
29 Mark Lewis RR .05 .02
30 Bernard Gilkey RR .05 .02
31 Hensley Meulens RR .05 .02
32 Derek Bell RR .10 .03
33 Jose Offerman RR .05 .02
34 Terry Bross RR .05 .02
35 Leo Gomez RR .05 .02
36 Derrick May RR .05 .02
37 Kevin Morton RR .05 .02
38 Moises Alou RR .10 .03
39 Julio Valera RR .05 .02
40 Milt Cuyler RR .05 .02
41 Phil Plantier RR RC .25 .07
42 Scott Chiamparino RR .05 .02
43 Ray Lankford RR .05 .02
44 Mickey Morandini RR .05 .02
45 Dave Hansen RR .05 .02
46 Kevin Belcher RR .05 .02
47 Darrin Fletcher RR .05 .02
48 Steve Sax AS .05 .02
49 Ken Griffey Jr. AS .25 .07
50A J.Canseco AS ERR .10 .03
Team in stat box should be AL, not A's
50B J.Canseco AS COR .25 .07
51 Sandy Alomar Jr. AS .05 .02
52 Cal Ripken AS .40 .12
53 Rickey Henderson AS .15 .04
54 Bob Welch AS .05 .02
55 Wade Boggs AS .10 .03
56 Mark McGwire AS .30 .09
57A Jack McDowell ERR .25 .07
(Career stats do not include 1990)
57B Jack McDowell COR .50 .15
(Career stats do not include 1990)
58 Jose Lind .05 .02
59 Alex Fernandez .05 .02
60 Pat Combs .05 .02
61 Mike Walker .05 .02
62 Juan Samuel .05 .02
63 Mike Blowers UER .05 .02
(Last line has aseball, not baseball)
64 Mark Guthrie .05 .02
65 Mark Salas .05 .02
66 Tim Jones .05 .02
67 Tim Leary .05 .02
68 Andres Galarraga .10 .03
69 Bob Milacki .05 .02
70 Tim Belcher .05 .02
71 Todd Zeile .05 .02
72 Jerome Walton .05 .02
73 Kevin Seitzer .05 .02
74 Jerald Clark .05 .02
75 John Smoltz UER .15 .04
(Born in Detroit, not Warren)
76 Mike Henneman .05 .02
77 Ken Griffey Jr. .50 .15
78 Jim Abbott .15 .04
79 Gregg Jefferies .05 .02
80 Kevin Reimer .05 .02
81 Roger Clemens .50 .15
82 Mike Fitzgerald .05 .02
83 Bruce Hurst UER .05 .02
(Middle name is Lee, not Vee)
84 Eric Davis .10 .03
85 Paul Molitor .15 .04
86 Will Clark .25 .07
87 Mike Bielecki .05 .02
88 Bret Saberhagen .10 .03
89 Nolan Ryan 1.00 .30
90 Bobby Thigpen .05 .02
91 Dickie Thon .05 .02
92 Duane Ward .05 .02
93 Luis Polonia .05 .02
94 Terry Kennedy .05 .02
95 Kent Hrbek .10 .03
96 Danny Jackson .05 .02
97 Sid Fernandez .05 .02
98 Jimmy Key .10 .03
99 Franklin Stubbs .05 .02
100 Checklist 28-103 .05 .02
101 R.J. Reynolds .05 .02
102 Dave Stewart .10 .03
103 Dan Pasqua .05 .02
104 Dan Plesac .05 .02
105 Mark McGwire .60 .18
106 John Farrell .05 .02
107 Don Mattingly .60 .18
108 Carlton Fisk .15 .04
109 Ken Oberkfell .05 .02
110 Darrel Akerfelds .05 .02
111 Gregg Olson .05 .02
112 Mike Scioscia .05 .02
113 Bryn Smith .05 .02
114 Bob Geren .05 .02
115 Tom Candiotti .05 .02
116 Kevin Tapani .05 .02
117 Jeff Treadway .05 .02
118 Alan Trammell .10 .03
119 Pete O'Brien .05 .02
(Blue shading goes through stats)
120 Joel Skinner .05 .02
121 Mike LaValliere .05 .02
122 Dwight Evans .10 .03
123 Jody Reed .05 .02
124 Lee Guetterman .05 .02
125 Tim Burke .05 .02
126 Dave Johnson .05 .02
127 Fernando Valenzuela .10 .03
(Lower large stripe in yellow instead of blue) UER
128 Jose DeLeon .05 .02
129 Andre Dawson .10 .03
130 Gerald Perry .05 .02
131 Greg W. Harris .05 .02
132 Tom Glavine .15 .04
133 Lance McCullers .05 .02
134 Randy Johnson .30 .09
135 Lance Parrish UER .10 .03
(Born in McKeesport, not Clairton)
136 Mackey Sasser .05 .02
137 Geno Petralli .05 .02
138 Dennis Lamp .05 .02
139 Dennis Martinez .10 .03
140 Mike Pagliarulo .05 .02
141 Hal Morris .05 .02
142 Dave Parker .10 .03
143 Brett Butler .10 .03
144 Paul Assenmacher .05 .02
145 Mark Gubicza .05 .02
146 Charlie Hough .10 .03
147 Sammy Sosa .50 .15
148 Randy Ready .05 .02
149 Kelly Gruber .05 .02
150 Devon White .10 .03
151 Gary Carter .10 .03
152 Gene Larkin .05 .02
153 Chris Sabo .05 .02
154 David Cone .10 .03
155 Todd Stottlemyre .05 .02
156 Glenn Wilson .05 .02
157 Bob Walk .05 .02
158 Mike Gallego .05 .02
159 Greg Hibbard .05 .02
160 Chris Bosio .05 .02
161 Mike Moore .05 .02
162 Jerry Browne UER .05 .02
(Born Christiansted, should be St. Croix)
163 Steve Sax UER .05 .02
(No asterisk next to his 1989 At Bats)
164 Melido Perez .05 .02
165 Danny Darwin .05 .02
166 Roger McDowell .05 .02
167 Bill Ripken .05 .02
168 Mike Sharperson .05 .02
169 Lee Smith .10 .03
170 Matt Nokes .05 .02
171 Jesse Orosco .05 .02
172 Rick Aguilera .10 .03
173 Jim Presley .05 .02
174 Lou Whitaker .10 .03
175 Harold Reynolds .10 .03
176 Brook Jacoby .05 .02
177 Wally Backman .05 .02
178 Wade Boggs .15 .04
179 Chuck Cary .05 .02
(Comma after DOB, not on other cards)
180 Tom Foley .05 .02
181 Pete Harnisch .05 .02
182 Mike Morgan .05 .02
183 Bob Tewksbury .05 .02
184 Joe Girardi .05 .02
185 Storm Davis .05 .02
186 Ed Whitson .05 .02
187 Steve Avery UER .05 .02
(Born in New Jersey, should be Michigan)
188 Lloyd Moseby .05 .02
189 Scott Bankhead .05 .02
190 Mark Langston .05 .02
191 Kevin McReynolds .05 .02
192 Julio Franco .10 .03
193 John Dopson .05 .02
194 Dennis Boyd .05 .02
195 Bip Roberts .05 .02
196 Billy Hatcher .05 .02
197 Edgar Diaz .05 .02
198 Greg Litton .05 .02
199 Mark Grace .15 .04
200 Checklist 104-179 .05 .02
201 George Brett .60 .18
202 Jeff Russell .05 .02
203 Ivan Calderon .05 .02
204 Ken Howell .05 .02
205 Tom Henke .05 .02
206 Bryan Harvey .05 .02
207 Steve Bedrosian .05 .02
208 Al Newman .05 .02
209 Randy Myers .05 .02
210 Daryl Boston .05 .02
211 Manny Lee .05 .02
212 Dave Smith .05 .02
213 Don Slaught .05 .02
214 Walt Weiss .05 .02
215 Donn Pall .05 .02
216 Jaime Navarro .05 .02
217 Willie Randolph .10 .03
218 Rudy Seanez .05 .02
219 Jim Leyritz .05 .02
220 Ron Karkovice .05 .02
221 Ken Caminiti .10 .03
222 Von Hayes .05 .02
223 Cal Ripken .75 .23
224 Lenny Harris .05 .02
225 Milt Thompson .05 .02
226 Alvaro Espinoza .05 .02
227 Chris James .05 .02
228 Dan Gladden .05 .02
229 Jeff Blauser .05 .02
230 Mike Heath .05 .02
231 Omar Vizquel .15 .04
232 Doug Jones .05 .02
233 Jeff King .05 .02
234 Luis Rivera .05 .02
235 Ellis Burks .10 .03
236 Greg Cadaret .05 .02
237 Dave Martinez .05 .02
238 Mark Williamson .05 .02
239 Stan Javier .05 .02
240 Ozzie Smith .40 .12
241 Shawn Boskie .05 .02
242 Tom Gordon .05 .02
243 Tony Gwynn .30 .09
244 Tommy Gregg .05 .02
245 Jeff M. Robinson .05 .02
246 Keith Comstock .05 .02
247 Jack Howell .05 .02
248 Keith Miller .05 .02
249 Bobby Witt .05 .02
250 Rob Murphy UER .05 .02
(Shown as on Reds in '89 in stats, should be Red Sox)
251 Spike Owen .05 .02
252 Garry Templeton .05 .02
253 Glenn Braggs .05 .02
254 Ron Robinson .05 .02
255 Kevin Mitchell .05 .02
256 Les Lancaster .05 .02
257 Mel Stottlemyre Jr. .05 .02
258 Kenny Rogers UER .10 .03
(IP listed as 171, should be 172)
259 Lance Johnson .05 .02
260 John Kruk .10 .03
261 Fred McGriff .15 .04
262 Dick Schofield .05 .02
263 Trevor Wilson .05 .02
264 David West .05 .02
265 Scott Scudder .05 .02
266 Dwight Gooden .10 .03
267 Willie Blair .05 .02
268 Mark Portugal .05 .02
269 Doug Drabek .05 .02
270 Dennis Eckersley .10 .03
271 Eric King .05 .02
272 Robin Yount .40 .12
273 Carney Lansford .10 .03
274 Carlos Baerga .05 .02
275 Dave Righetti .10 .03
276 Scott Fletcher .05 .02
277 Eric Yelding .05 .02
278 Charlie Hayes .05 .02
279 Jeff Ballard .05 .02
280 Orel Hershiser .10 .03
281 Jose Oquendo .05 .02
282 Mike Witt .05 .02
283 Mitch Webster .05 .02
284 Greg Gagne .05 .02
285 Greg Olson .05 .02
286 Tony Phillips UER .05 .02
(Born 4/15 should be 4/25)
287 Scott Bradley .05 .02
288 Cory Snyder UER .05 .02
(In text, led is repeated Inglewood is misspelled as Englewood)
289 Jay Bell UER .10 .03
(Born in Pensacola, not Eglin AFB)
290 Kevin Romine .05 .02
291 Jeff D. Robinson .05 .02
292 Steve Frey UER .05 .02
(Bats left, should be right)
293 Craig Worthington .05 .02
294 Tim Crews .05 .02
295 Joe Magrane .05 .02
296 Hector Villanueva .05 .02
297 Terry Shumpert .05 .02
298 Joe Carter .10 .03
299 Kent Mercker UER .05 .02
(IP listed as 53, should be 52)
300 Checklist 180-255 .05 .02
301 Chet Lemon .05 .02
302 Mike Schooler .05 .02
303 Dante Bichette .10 .03
304 Kevin Elster .05 .02
305 Jeff Huson .05 .02
306 Greg A. Harris .05 .02
307 Marquis Grissom UER .10 .03
(Middle name Deon, should be Dean)
308 Calvin Schiraldi .05 .02
309 Mariano Duncan .05 .02
310 Bill Spiers .05 .02
311 Scott Garrelts .05 .02
312 Mitch Williams .05 .02
313 Mike Macfarlane .05 .02
314 Kevin Brown .10 .03
315 Robin Ventura .10 .03
316 Darren Daulton .10 .03
317 Pat Borders .05 .02
318 Mark Eichhorn .05 .02
319 Jeff Brantley .05 .02
320 Shane Mack .05 .02
321 Rob Dibble .10 .03
322 John Franco .10 .03
323 Junior Felix .05 .02
324 Casey Candaele .05 .02
325 Bobby Bonilla .10 .03
326 Dave Henderson .05 .02
327 Wayne Edwards .05 .02
328 Mark Knudson .05 .02
329 Terry Steinbach .05 .02
330 Colby Ward UER .05 .02
(No comma between city and state)
331 Oscar Azocar .05 .02
332 Scott Radinsky .05 .02
333 Eric Anthony .05 .02
334 Steve Lake .05 .02
335 Bob Melvin .05 .02
336 Kal Daniels .05 .02
337 Tom Pagnozzi .05 .02
338 Alan Mills .05 .02
339 Steve Olin .05 .02
340 Juan Berenguer .05 .02
341 Francisco Cabrera .05 .02
342 Dave Bergman .05 .02
343 Henry Cotto .05 .02
344 Sergio Valdez .05 .02
345 Bob Patterson .05 .02
346 John Marzano .05 .02
347 Dana Kiecker .05 .02
348 Dion James .05 .02
349 Hubie Brooks .05 .02
350 Bill Landrum .05 .02
351 Bill Sampen .05 .02
352 Greg Briley .05 .02
353 Paul Gibson .05 .02
354 Dave Eiland .05 .02
355 Steve Finley .10 .03
356 Bob Boone .10 .03
357 Steve Buechele .05 .02
358 Chris Hoiles .05 .02
359 Larry Walker .25 .07
360 Frank DiPino .05 .02
361 Mark Grant .05 .02
362 Dave Magadan .05 .02
363 Robby Thompson .05 .02
364 Lonnie Smith .05 .02
365 Steve Farr .05 .02
366 Dave Valle .05 .02
367 Tim Naehring .05 .02
368 Jim Acker .05 .02
369 Jeff Reardon UER .10 .03
(Born in Pittsfield, not Dalton)
370 Tim Teufel .05 .02
371 Juan Gonzalez .15 .04
372 Luis Salazar .05 .02
373 Rick Honeycutt .05 .02
374 Greg Maddux .40 .12
375 Jose Uribe UER .05 .02
(Middle name Elta, should be Alta)
376 Donnie Hill .05 .02
377 Don Carman .05 .02
378 Craig Grebeck .05 .02
379 Willie Fraser .05 .02
380 Glenallen Hill .05 .02
381 Joe Oliver .05 .02
382 Randy Bush .05 .02
383 Alex Cole .05 .02
384 Norm Charlton .05 .02
385 Gene Nelson .05 .02
386 Checklist 256-331 .05 .02
387 R. Henderson MVP .15 .04
388 Lance Parrish MVP .05 .02
389 Fred McGriff MVP .10 .03
390 Dave Parker MVP .05 .02
391 C. Maldonado MVP .05 .02
392 Ken Griffey Jr. MVP .25 .07
393 Gregg Olson MVP .05 .02
394 Rafael Palmeiro MVP .10 .03
395 Roger Clemens MVP .25 .07
396 George Brett MVP .25 .07
397 Cecil Fielder MVP .05 .02
398 Brian Harper MVP .05 .02
UER Major League Performance, should be Career
399 Bobby Thigpen MVP .05 .02
400 Roberto Kelly MVP .05 .02
UER (Second Base on front and OF on back)
401 Danny Darwin MVP .05 .02
402 Dave Justice MVP .05 .02
403 Lee Smith MVP .05 .02
404 Ryne Sandberg MVP .25 .07
405 Eddie Murray MVP .15 .04
406 Tim Wallach MVP .05 .02
407 Kevin Mitchell MVP .05 .02
408 D. Strawberry MVP .05 .02
409 Joe Carter MVP .05 .02
410 Len Dykstra MVP .05 .02
411 Doug Drabek MVP .05 .02
412 Chris Sabo MVP .05 .02
413 Paul Marak RR .05 .02
414 Tim McIntosh RR .05 .02
415 Brian Barnes RR .10 .03
416 Eric Gunderson RR .05 .02
417 Mike Gardiner RR .05 .02
418 Steve Carter RR .05 .02
419 Gerald Alexander RR .05 .02
420 Rich Garces RR RC .10 .03
421 Chuck Knoblauch RR .10 .03
422 Scott Aldred RR .05 .02
423 W.Chamberlain RR RC .25 .07
424 Lance Dickson RR RC .10 .03
425 Greg Colbrunn RR RC .25 .07
426 Rich DeLucia RR UER .05 .02
(Misspelled Delucia on card)
427 Jeff Conine RR RC .40 .12
428 Steve Decker RR .05 .02
429 Turner Ward RR RC .25 .07
430 Mo Vaughn RR .10 .03
431 Steve Chitren RR .05 .02
432 Mike Benjamin RR .05 .02
433 Ryne Sandberg AS .25 .07
434 Len Dykstra AS .05 .02
435 Andre Dawson AS .05 .02
436A Mike Scioscia AS .05 .02
(White star by name)
436B Mike Scioscia AS .05 .02
(Yellow star by name)
437 Ozzie Smith AS .25 .07
438 Kevin Mitchell AS .05 .02
439 Jack Armstrong AS .05 .02
440 Chris Sabo AS .05 .02
441 Will Clark AS .10 .03
442 Mel Hall .05 .02
443 Mark Gardner .05 .02
444 Mike Devereaux .05 .02
445 Kirk Gibson .10 .03
446 Terry Pendleton .10 .03
447 Mike Harkey .05 .02
448 Jim Eisenreich .05 .02
449 Benito Santiago .10 .03
450 Oddibe McDowell .05 .02
451 Cecil Fielder .10 .03
452 Ken Griffey Sr. .10 .03
453 Bert Blyleven .10 .03
454 Howard Johnson .05 .02
455 Monty Fariss UER .05 .02
(Misspelled Farris on card)
456 Tony Pena .05 .02
457 Tim Raines .10 .03
458 Dennis Rasmussen .05 .02
459 Luis Quinones .05 .02
460 B.J. Surhoff .10 .03
461 Ernest Riles .05 .02
462 Rick Sutcliffe .10 .03
463 Danny Tartabull .05 .02
464 Pete Incaviglia .05 .02
465 Carlos Martinez .05 .02
466 Ricky Jordan .05 .02
467 John Cerutti .05 .02
468 Dave Winfield .10 .03
469 Francisco Oliveras .05 .02
470 Roy Smith .05 .02
471 Barry Larkin .15 .04
472 Ron Darling .05 .02
473 David Wells .10 .03
474 Glenn Davis .05 .02
475 Neal Heaton .05 .02
476 Ron Hassey .05 .02
477 Frank Thomas .25 .07
478 Greg Vaughn .05 .02
479 Todd Burns .05 .02
480 Candy Maldonado .05 .02
481 Dave LaPoint .05 .02
482 Alvin Davis .05 .02
483 Mike Scott .05 .02
484 Dale Murphy .25 .07
485 Ben McDonald .05 .02
486 Jay Howell .05 .02
487 Vince Coleman .05 .02
488 Alfredo Griffin .05 .02
489 Sandy Alomar Jr. .05 .02
490 Kirby Puckett .25 .07
491 Andres Thomas .05 .02
492 Jack Morris .10 .03
493 Matt Young .05 .02
494 Greg Myers .05 .02
495 Barry Bonds .60 .18
496 Scott Cooper UER .05 .02
(No BA for 1990 and career)
497 Dan Schatzeder .05 .02
498 Jesse Barfield .05 .02
499 Jerry Goff .05 .02
500 Checklist 332-408 .05 .02
501 Anthony Telford .05 .02
502 Eddie Murray .25 .07
503 Omar Olivares RC .25 .07
504 Ryne Sandberg .40 .12
505 Jeff Montgomery .05 .02
506 Mark Parent .05 .02
507 Ron Gant .10 .03
508 Frank Tanana .05 .02
509 Jay Buhner .10 .03
510 Max Venable .05 .02
511 Wally Whitehurst .05 .02
512 Gary Pettis .05 .02
513 Tom Brunansky .05 .02
514 Tim Wallach .05 .02
515 Craig Lefferts .05 .02
516 Tim Layana .05 .02
517 Darryl Hamilton .05 .02
518 Rick Reuschel .05 .02
519 Steve Wilson .05 .02
520 Kurt Stillwell .05 .02
521 Rafael Palmeiro .15 .04
522 Ken Patterson .05 .02
523 Len Dykstra .10 .03
524 Tony Fernandez .05 .02
525 Kent Anderson .05 .02
526 Mark Leonard .05 .02
527 Allan Anderson .05 .02
528 Tom Browning .05 .02
529 Frank Viola .10 .03
530 John Olerud .10 .03
531 Juan Agosto .05 .02
532 Zane Smith .05 .02
533 Scott Sanderson .05 .02
534 Barry Jones .05 .02
535 Mike Felder .05 .02
536 Jose Canseco .25 .07
537 Felix Fermin .05 .02
538 Roberto Kelly .05 .02
539 Brian Holman .05 .02
540 Mark Davidson .05 .02
541 Terry Mulholland .05 .02
542 Randy Milligan .05 .02
543 Jose Gonzalez .05 .02
544 Craig Wilson .05 .02
545 Mike Hartley .05 .02
546 Greg Swindell .05 .02
547 Gary Gaetti .10 .03
548 Dave Justice .10 .03
549 Steve Searcy .05 .02
550 Erik Hanson .05 .02
551 Dave Stieb .05 .02
552 Andy Van Slyke .10 .03
553 Mike Greenwell .05 .02
554 Kevin Maas .05 .02
555 Delino DeShields .10 .03
556 Curt Schilling .25 .07
557 Ramon Martinez .05 .02
558 Pedro Guerrero .10 .03
559 Dwight Smith .05 .02
560 Mark Davis .05 .02
561 Shawn Abner .05 .02
562 Charlie Leibrandt .05 .02
563 John Shelby .05 .02
564 Bill Swift .05 .02
565 Mike Fetters .05 .02
566 Alejandro Pena .05 .02
567 Ruben Sierra .10 .03
568 Carlos Quintana .05 .02
569 Kevin Gross .05 .02
570 Derek Lilliquist .05 .02
571 Jack Armstrong .05 .02
572 Greg Brock .05 .02
573 Mike Kingery .05 .02
574 Greg Smith .05 .02
575 Brian McRae RC .25 .07
576 Jack Daugherty .05 .02
577 Ozzie Guillen .05 .02
578 Joe Boever .05 .02
579 Luis Sojo .05 .02
580 Chili Davis .10 .03
581 Don Robinson .05 .02
582 Brian Harper .05 .02
583 Paul O'Neill .15 .04
584 Bob Ojeda .05 .02
585 Mookie Wilson .10 .03
586 Rafael Ramirez .05 .02
587 Gary Redus .05 .02
588 Jamie Quirk .05 .02
589 Shawn Hillegas .05 .02
590 Tom Edens .05 .02
591 Joe Klink .05 .02
592 Charles Nagy .05 .02
593 Eric Plunk .05 .02
594 Tracy Jones .05 .02
595 Craig Biggio .15 .04
596 Jose DeJesus .05 .02

7 Mickey Tettleton .05 .02
8 Chris Gwynn .05 .02
9 Rex Hudler .05 .02
0 Checklist 409-506 .05 .02
1 Jim Gott .05 .02
2 Jeff Manto .05 .02
3 Nelson Liriano .05 .02
4 Mark Lemke .05 .02
5 Clay Parker .05 .02
6 Edgar Martinez .15 .04
7 Mark Whiten .05 .02
8 Ted Power .05 .02
9 Tom Bolton .05 .02
0 Tom Herr .05 .02
1 Andy Hawkins UER .05 .02
Pitched No-Hitter
on 7/1, not 7/2
2 Scott Ruskin .05 .02
3 Ron Kittle .05 .02
4 John Wetteland .10 .03
5 Mike Perez RC .10 .03
6 Dave Clark .05 .02
7 Brent Mayne .05 .02
8 Jack Clark .10 .03
9 Marvin Freeman .05 .02
0 Edwin Nunez .05 .02
1 Russ Swan .05 .02
2 Johnny Ray .05 .02
3 Charlie O'Brien .05 .02
4 Joe Bitker .05 .02
5 Mike Marshall .05 .02
6 Otis Nixon .05 .02
7 Andy Benes .05 .02
8 Ron Oester .05 .02
9 Ted Higuera .05 .02
0 Kevin Bass .05 .02
1 Damon Berryhill .05 .02
2 Bo Jackson .25 .07
3 Brad Arnsberg .05 .02
4 Jerry Willard .05 .02
5 Tommy Greene .05 .02
6 Bob MacDonald .05 .02
7 Kirk McCaskill .05 .02
8 John Burkett .05 .02
9 Paul Abbott RC .10 .03
0 Todd Benzinger .05 .02
1 Todd Hundley .05 .02
2 George Bell .05 .02
3 Javier Ortiz .05 .02
4 Sid Bream .05 .02
5 Bob Welch .05 .02
6 Phil Bradley .05 .02
7 Bill Krueger .05 .02
8 Rickey Henderson .25 .07
9 Kevin Wickander .05 .02
0 Steve Balboni .05 .02
1 Gene Harris .05 .02
2 Jim Deshaies .05 .02
3 Jason Grimsley .05 .02
4 Joe Orsulak .05 .02
5 Jim Poole .05 .02
6 Felix Jose .05 .02
7 Denis Cook .05 .02
8 Tom Brookens .05 .02
9 Junior Ortiz .05 .02
0 Jeff Parrett .05 .02
1 Jerry Don Gleaton .05 .02
2 Brent Knackert .05 .02
3 Rance Mulliniks .05 .02
4 John Smiley .05 .02
5 Larry Andersen .05 .02
6 Willie McGee .10 .03
7 Chris Nabholz .05 .02
8 Brady Anderson .10 .03
9 D.Holmes UER RC .25 .07
19 CG's, should be 0
0 Ken Hill .05 .02
1 Gary Varsho .05 .02
2 Bill Pecota .05 .02
3 Fred Lynn .05 .02
4 Kevin D. Brown .05 .02
5 Dan Petry .05 .02
6 Mike Jackson .05 .02
7 Wally Joyner .10 .03
8 Danny Jackson .05 .02
9 Bill Haselman .05 .02
0 Mike Boddicker .05 .02
1 Mel Rojas .05 .02
2 Roberto Alomar .15 .04
3 Dave Justice ROY .05 .02
4 Chuck Crim .05 .02
5 Matt Williams .10 .03
6 Shawon Dunston .05 .02
7 Jeff Schulz .05 .02
8 John Barfield .05 .02
9 Gerald Young .05 .02
0 Luis Gonzalez RC .50 .15
1 Frank Wills .05 .02
2 Chuck Finley .10 .03
3 S.Alomar Jr. ROY .05 .02
4 Tim Drummond .05 .02
5 Herm Winningham .05 .02
6 Darryl Strawberry .10 .03
7 Al Leiter .10 .03
8 Karl Rhodes .05 .02
9 Stan Belinda .05 .02
0 Checklist 507-604 .05 .02
1 Lance Blankenship .05 .02
2 Willie Stargell PUZ .15 .04
3 Jim Gantner .05 .02
4 Reggie Harris .05 .02
5 Rob Ducey .05 .02
6 Tim Hulett .05 .02
7 Atlee Hammaker .05 .02
8 Xavier Hernandez .05 .02
9 Chuck McElroy .05 .02
10 John Mitchell .05 .02
11 Carlos Hernandez .05 .02
12 Geronimo Pena .05 .02
13 Jim Neidlinger .05 .02
14 John Orton .05 .02
15 Terry Leach .05 .02
16 Mike Stanton .05 .02
17 Walt Terrell .05 .02
18 Luis Aquino .05 .02
19 Bud Black .05 .02
Blue Jays uniform,
but Giants logo
20 Bob Kipper .05 .02
21 Jeff Gray .05 .02

722 Jose Rijo .05 .02
723 Curt Young .05 .02
724 Jose Vizcaino .05 .02
725 Randy Tomlin RC .10 .03
726 Junior Noboa .05 .02
727 Bob Welch CY .05 .02
728 Gary Ward .05 .02
729 Rob Deer .05 .02
(Brewers uniform,
but Tigers logo)
730 David Segui .05 .02
731 Mark Carreon .05 .02
732 Vicente Palacios .05 .02
733 Sam Horn .05 .02
734 Howard Farmer .05 .02
735 Ken Dayley .05 .02
(Cardinals uniform,
but Blue Jays logo)
736 Kelly Mann .05 .02
737 Joe Grahe RC .10 .03
738 Kelly Downs .05 .02
739 Jimmy Kremers .05 .02
740 Kevin Appier .10 .03
741 Jeff Reed .05 .02
742 Jose Rijo WS .05 .02
743 Dave Rohde .05 .02
744 Len Dykstra .15 .04
Dale Murphy
UER (No '91 Donruss
logo on card front)
745 Paul Sorrento .05 .02
746 Thomas Howard .05 .02
747 Matt Stark .05 .02
748 Harold Baines .10 .03
749 Doug Dascenzo .05 .02
750 Doug Drabek CY .05 .02
751 Gary Sheffield .10 .03
752 Terry Lee .05 .02
753 Jim Vatcher .05 .02
754 Lee Stevens .05 .02
755 Randy Veres .05 .02
756 Bill Doran .05 .02
757 Gary Wayne .05 .02
758 Pedro Munoz RC .10 .03
759 Chris Hammond .05 .02
760 Checklist 605-702 .05 .02
761 R.Henderson MVP .15 .04
762 Barry Bonds MVP .30 .09
763 Billy Hatcher WS .05 .02
UER (Line 13, on
should be one)
764 Julio Machado .05 .02
765 Jose Mesa .05 .02
766 Willie Randolph WS .05 .02
767 Scott Erickson .10 .03
768 Travis Fryman .10 .03
769 Rich Rodriguez .05 .02
770 Checklist 703-770 .05 .02
and BC1-BC22

1991 Donruss Bonus Cards

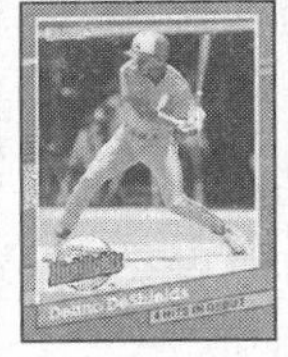
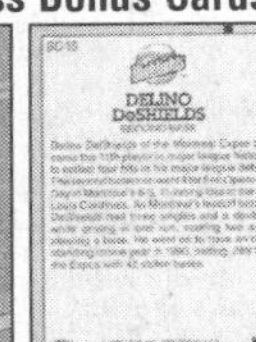

These bonus cards are standard size and were randomly inserted in Donruss packs and highlight outstanding player achievements, the first ten in the first series and the remaining 12 in the second series picking up in time beginning with Valenzuela's no-hitter and continuing until the end of the season.

Nm-Mt Ex-Mt
COMPLETE SET (22) 1.50 .45
BC1 Mark Langston .05 .01
Mike Witt
BC2 Randy Johnson .30 .09
BC3 Nolan Ryan 1.00 .30
No-Hitter
BC4 Dave Stewart .10 .03
BC5 Cecil Fielder .10 .03
BC6 Carlton Fisk .15 .04
BC7 Ryne Sandberg .40 .12
BC8 Gary Carter .10 .03
BC9 Mark McGwire .60 .18
Home Run Milestone
(Back says First
BC10 Bo Jackson .25 .07
BC11 Fernando Valenzuela .05 .02
BC12A Andy Hawkins ERR .05 .01
Pitcher
BC12B Andy Hawkins COR .05 .01
No Hits White Sox
BC13 Melido Perez .05 .01
BC14 T.Mulholland UER .05 .01
Charlie Hayes is
called Chris Hayes
BC15 Nolan Ryan 1.00 .30
300th Win
BC16 Delino DeShields .10 .03
BC17 Cal Ripken .75 .23
BC18 Eddie Murray .25 .07
BC19 George Brett .60 .18
BC20 Bobby Thigpen .05 .01
BC21 Dave Stieb .05 .01
BC22 Willie McGee .10 .03

1991 Donruss Elite

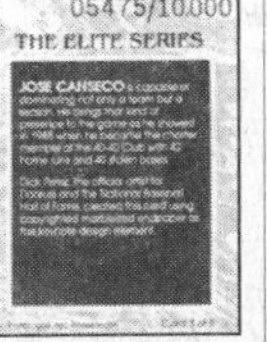

These special cards were randomly inserted in the 1991 Donruss first and second series wax packs. These cards marked the beginning of an eight-year run of Elite inserts. Production was limited to a maximum of 10,000 serial-numbered cards for each card in the Elite series, and lesser production for the Sandberg Signature (5,000) and Ryan Legend (7,500) cards. This was the first time that mainstream insert cards were ever serial numbered allowing for verifiable proof of print runs. The regular Elite cards are photos enclosed in a bronze marble borders which surround an evenly squared photo of the players. The Sandberg Signature card has a green marble border and is signed in a blue sharpie. The Nolan Ryan Legend card is a Dick Perez drawing with silver borders. The cards are all numbered on the back, 1 out of 10,000, etc.

Nm-Mt Ex-Mt
1 Barry Bonds 80.00 24.00
2 George Brett 60.00 18.00
3 Jose Canseco 40.00 12.00
4 Andre Dawson 20.00 6.00
5 Doug Drabek 20.00 6.00
6 Cecil Fielder 20.00 6.00
7 Rickey Henderson 40.00 12.00
8 Matt Williams 20.00 6.00
L1 Nolan Ryan (Legend) 100.00 30.00
S1 Ryne Sandberg 120.00 36.00
(Signature Series)

1991 Donruss Grand Slammers

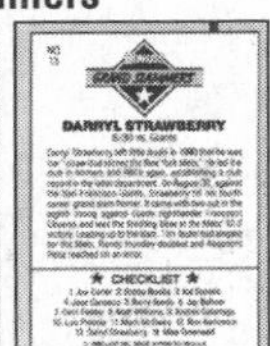

This 14-card standard-size set commemorates players who hit grand slams in 1990. They were distributed in complete set form within factory sets in addition to being seeded at a rate of one per cello pack.

Nm-Mt Ex-Mt
COMPLETE SET (14) 2.00 .60
1 Joe Carter .10 .03
2 Bobby Bonilla .10 .03
3 Kal Daniels .05 .01
4 Jose Canseco .25 .07
5 Barry Bonds .60 .18
6 Jay Buhner .10 .03
7 Cecil Fielder .10 .03
8 Matt Williams .10 .03
9 Andres Galarraga .10 .03
10 Luis Polonia .05 .01
11 Mark McGwire .60 .18
12 Ron Karkovice .05 .01
13 Darryl Strawberry UER .10 .03
(Todd Hundley is
called Randy)
14 Mike Greenwell .05 .01

1991 Donruss Rookies

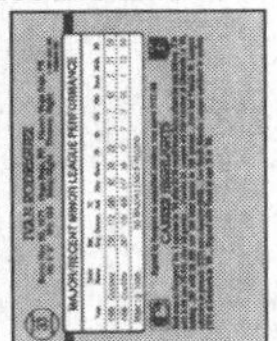

The 56-card 1991 Donruss Rookies set was issued exclusively in factory set form through hobby dealers. The cards measure the standard size and a mini puzzle featuring Hall of Famer Willie Stargell was included with the set. The fronts feature color action player photos, with white and red borders. Rookie Cards include Jeff Bagwell and Ivan Rodriguez.

Nm-Mt Ex-Mt
COMP.FACT.SET (56) 5.00 1.50
1 Pat Kelly RC .10 .03
2 Rich DeLucia .10 .03
3 Wes Chamberlain .10 .03
4 Scott Leius .10 .03
5 Darryl Kile .25 .07
6 Milt Cuyler .10 .03
7 Todd Van Poppel RC .10 .03
8 Ray Lankford .10 .03
9 Brian R. Hunter RC .25 .07
10 Tony Perezchica .10 .03
11 Ced Landrum .10 .03
12 Dave Burba RC .25 .07
13 Ramon Garcia .10 .03
14 Ed Sprague .10 .03
15 Warren Newson .10 .03
16 Paul Faries .10 .03
17 Luis Gonzalez .50 .15
18 Charles Nagy .10 .03
19 Chris Hammond .10 .03
20 Frank Castillo RC .25 .07
21 Pedro Munoz .10 .03
22 Orlando Merced RC .10 .03
23 Jose Melendez .10 .03
24 Kirk Dressendorfer RC .10 .03
25 Heathcliff Slocumb RC .25 .07
26 Doug Simons .10 .03
27 Mike Timlin RC .40 .12
28 Jeff Fassero RC .25 .07
29 Mark Leiter RC .10 .03
30 Jeff Bagwell RC 1.50 .45
31 Brian McRae .25 .07
32 Mark Whiten .10 .03
33 Ivan Rodriguez RC 2.00 .60
34 Wade Taylor .10 .03
35 Darren Lewis .10 .03
36 Mo Vaughn .25 .07
37 Mike Remlinger .10 .03
38 Rick Wilkins RC .10 .03
39 Chuck Knoblauch .25 .07
40 Kevin Morton .10 .03
41 Carlos Rodriguez .10 .03
42 Mark Lewis .10 .03
43 Brent Mayne .10 .03
44 Chris Haney RC .10 .03
45 Denis Boucher RC .10 .03
46 Mike Gardiner .10 .03
47 Jeff Johnson .10 .03
48 Dean Palmer .25 .07
49 Chuck McElroy .10 .03
50 Chris Jones RC .10 .03
51 Scott Kamieniecki RC .10 .03
52 Al Osuna RC .10 .03
53 Rusty Meacham RC .10 .03
54 Chito Martinez .10 .03
55 Reggie Jefferson .10 .03
56 Checklist 1-56 .10 .03

1992 Donruss

The 1992 Donruss set contains 784 standard-size cards issued in two separate series of 396. Cards were issued in first and second series foil wrapped packs in addition to hobby and retail factory sets. One of 21 different puzzle panels featuring Hall of Famer Rod Carew was inserted into each pack. The basic card design features glossy color player photos with white borders. Two-toned blue stripes overlay the top and bottom of the picture. Subsets include Rated Rookies (1-20, 397-421), All-Stars (21-30/422-431) and Highlights (33, 94, 154, 215, 276, 434, 495, 555, 616, 677). The only notable Rookie Card in the set features Scott Brosius.

Nm-Mt Ex-Mt
COMPLETE SET (784) 10.00 3.00
COMP.HOBBY SET (788) 10.00 3.00
COMP.RETAIL SET (788) 10.00 3.00
COMP. SERIES 1 (396) 5.00 1.50
COMP. SERIES 2 (388) 5.00 1.50
COMP.CAREW PUZZLE 1.00 .30
1 Mark Wohlers RR .05 .02
2 Wil Cordero RR .05 .02
3 Kyle Abbott RR .05 .02
4 Dave Nilsson RR .05 .02
5 Kenny Lofton RR .15 .04
6 Luis Mercedes RR .05 .02
7 Roger Salkeld RR .05 .02
8 Eddie Zosky RR .05 .02
9 Todd Van Poppel RR .05 .02
10 Frank Seminara RR RC .10 .03
11 Andy Ashby RR .05 .02
12 Reggie Jefferson RR .05 .02
13 Ryan Klesko RR .10 .03
14 Carlos Garcia RR .05 .02
15 John Ramos RR .05 .02
16 Eric Karros RR .10 .03
17 Patrick Lennon RR .05 .02
18 E.Taubensee RR RC .25 .07
19 Roberto Hernandez RR .05 .02
20 D.J. Dozier RR .05 .02
21 Dave Henderson AS .05 .02
22 Cal Ripken AS .40 .12
23 Wade Boggs AS .10 .03
24 Ken Griffey Jr. AS .25 .07
25 Jack Morris AS .05 .02
26 Danny Tartabull AS .05 .02
27 Cecil Fielder AS .05 .02
28 Roberto Alomar AS .10 .03
29 Sandy Alomar Jr. AS .05 .02
30 Rickey Henderson AS .15 .04
31 Ken Hill .05 .02
32 John Habyan .05 .02
33 Otis Nixon HL .05 .02
34 Tim Wallach .05 .02
35 Cal Ripken .75 .23
36 Gary Carter .10 .03
37 Juan Agosto .05 .02
38 Doug Dascenzo .05 .02
39 Kirk Gibson .10 .03
40 Benito Santiago .10 .03
41 Otis Nixon .05 .02
42 Andy Allanson .05 .02
43 Brian Holman .05 .02
44 Dick Schofield .05 .02
45 Dave Magadan .05 .02
46 Rafael Palmeiro .15 .04
47 Jody Reed .05 .02
48 Ivan Calderon .05 .02
49 Greg W. Harris .05 .02
50 Chris Sabo .05 .02
51 Paul Molitor .15 .04
52 Robby Thompson .05 .02
53 Dave Smith .05 .02
54 Mark Davis .05 .02
55 Kevin Brown .10 .03
56 Donn Pall .05 .02
57 Len Dykstra .10 .03
58 Roberto Alomar .15 .04
59 Jeff D. Robinson .05 .02
60 Willie McGee .10 .03
61 Jay Buhner .10 .03
62 Mike Pagliarulo .05 .02
63 Paul O'Neill .15 .04
64 Hubie Brooks .05 .02
65 Kelly Gruber .05 .02
66 Ken Caminiti .10 .03
67 Gary Redus .05 .02
68 Harold Baines .10 .03
69 Charlie Hough .10 .03
70 B.J. Surhoff .10 .03
71 Walt Weiss .05 .02
72 Shawn Hillegas .05 .02
73 Roberto Kelly .05 .02
74 Jeff Ballard .05 .02
75 Craig Biggio .15 .04
76 Pat Combs .05 .02
77 Jeff M. Robinson .05 .02
78 Tim Belcher .05 .02
79 Cris Carpenter .05 .02
80 Checklist 1-79 .05 .02
81 Steve Avery .05 .02
82 Chris James .05 .02
83 Brian Harper .05 .02
84 Charlie Leibrandt .05 .02
85 Mickey Tettleton .05 .02
86 Pete O'Brien .05 .02
87 Danny Darwin .05 .02
88 Bob Walk .05 .02
89 Jeff Reardon .10 .03
90 Bobby Rose .05 .02
91 Danny Jackson .05 .02
92 John Morris .05 .02
93 Bud Black .05 .02
94 Tommy Greene HL .05 .02
95 Rick Aguilera .10 .03
96 Gary Gaetti .10 .03
97 David Cone .10 .03
98 John Olerud .10 .03
99 Joel Skinner .05 .02
100 Jay Bell .10 .03
101 Bob Milacki .05 .02
102 Norm Charlton .05 .02
103 Chuck Crim .05 .02
104 Terry Steinbach .05 .02
105 Juan Samuel .05 .02
106 Steve Howe .05 .02
107 Rafael Belliard .05 .02
108 Joey Cora .05 .02
109 Tommy Greene .05 .02
110 Gregg Olson .05 .02
111 Frank Tanana .05 .02
112 Lee Smith .10 .03
113 Greg A. Harris .05 .02
114 Dwayne Henry .05 .02
115 Chili Davis .10 .03
116 Kent Mercker .05 .02
117 Brian Barnes .05 .02
118 Rich DeLucia .05 .02
119 Andre Dawson .10 .03
120 Carlos Baerga .05 .02
121 Mike LaValliere .05 .02
122 Jeff Gray .05 .02
123 Bruce Hurst .05 .02
124 Alvin Davis .05 .02
125 John Candelaria .05 .02
126 Matt Nokes .05 .02
127 George Bell .05 .02
128 Bret Saberhagen .10 .03
129 Jeff Russell .05 .02
130 Jim Abbott .15 .04
131 Bill Gullickson .05 .02
132 Todd Zeile .05 .02
133 Dave Winfield .10 .03
134 Wally Whitehurst .05 .02
135 Matt Williams .10 .03
136 Tom Browning .05 .02
137 Marquis Grissom .10 .03
138 Erik Hanson .05 .02
139 Rob Dibble .10 .03
140 Don August .05 .02
141 Tom Henke .05 .02
142 Dan Pasqua .05 .02
143 George Brett .60 .18
144 Jerald Clark .05 .02
145 Robin Ventura .10 .03
146 Dale Murphy .25 .07
147 Dennis Eckersley .10 .03
148 Eric Yelding .05 .02
149 Mario Diaz .05 .02
150 Casey Candaele .05 .02
151 Steve Olin .05 .02
152 Luis Salazar .05 .02
153 Kevin Maas .05 .02
154 Nolan Ryan HL .50 .15
155 Barry Jones .05 .02
156 Chris Hoiles .05 .02
157 Bob Ojeda .05 .02
158 Pedro Guerrero .10 .03
159 Paul Assenmacher .05 .02
160 Checklist 80-157 .05 .02
161 Mike Macfarlane .05 .02
162 Craig Lefferts .05 .02
163 Brian Hunter .05 .02
164 Alan Trammell .10 .03
165 Ken Griffey Jr. .40 .12
166 Lance Parrish .10 .03
167 Brian Downing .05 .02
168 John Barfield .05 .02
169 Jack Clark .10 .03
170 Chris Nabholz .05 .02
171 Tim Teufel .05 .02
172 Chris Hammond .05 .02
173 Robin Yount .40 .12
174 Dave Righetti .10 .03
175 Joe Girardi .05 .02
176 Mike Boddicker .05 .02
177 Dean Palmer .10 .03
178 Greg Hibbard .05 .02
179 Randy Ready .05 .02
180 Devon White .10 .03
181 Mark Eichhorn .05 .02
182 Mike Felder .05 .02
183 Joe Klink .05 .02
184 Steve Bedrosian .05 .02
185 Barry Larkin .15 .04
186 John Franco .10 .03
187 Ed Sprague .05 .02
188 Mark Portugal .05 .02
189 Jose Lind .05 .02
190 Bob Welch .05 .02
191 Alex Fernandez .05 .02
192 Gary Sheffield .10 .03
193 Rickey Henderson .25 .07
194 Rod Nichols .05 .02
195 Scott Kamieniecki .05 .02
196 Mike Flanagan .05 .02
197 Steve Finley .10 .03
198 Darren Daulton .10 .03
199 Leo Gomez .05 .02
200 Mike Morgan .05 .02
201 Bob Tewksbury .05 .02
202 Sid Bream .05 .02
203 Sandy Alomar Jr. .05 .02

204 Greg Gagne .05 .02
205 Juan Berenguer .05 .02
206 Cecil Fielder .10 .03
207 Randy Johnson .25 .07
208 Tony Pena .05 .02
209 Doug Drabek .05 .02
210 Wade Boggs .15 .04
211 Bryan Harvey .05 .02
212 Jose Vizcaino .05 .02
213 Alonzo Powell .05 .02
214 Will Clark .25 .07
215 Rickey Henderson HL .15 .04
216 Jack Morris .10 .03
217 Junior Felix .05 .02
218 Vince Coleman .05 .02
219 Jimmy Key .10 .03
220 Alex Cole .05 .02
221 Bill Landrum .05 .02
222 Randy Milligan .05 .02
223 Jose Rijo .05 .02
224 Greg Vaughn .05 .02
225 Dave Stewart .10 .03
226 Lenny Harris .05 .02
227 Scott Sanderson .05 .02
228 Jeff Blauser .05 .02
229 Ozzie Guillen .05 .02
230 John Kruk .10 .03
231 Bob Melvin .05 .02
232 Milt Cuyler .05 .02
233 Felix Jose .05 .02
234 Ellis Burks .10 .03
235 Pete Harnisch .05 .02
236 Kevin Tapani .05 .02
237 Terry Pendleton .10 .03
238 Mark Gardner .05 .02
239 Harold Reynolds .10 .03
240 Checklist 158-237 .05 .02
241 Mike Harkey .05 .02
242 Felix Fermin .05 .02
243 Barry Bonds .60 .18
244 Roger Clemens .50 .15
245 Dennis Rasmussen .05 .02
246 Jose DeLeon .05 .02
247 Orel Hershiser .10 .03
248 Mel Hall .05 .02
249 Rick Wilkins .05 .02
250 Tom Gordon .05 .02
251 Kevin Reimer .05 .02
252 Luis Polonia .05 .02
253 Mike Henneman .05 .02
254 Tom Pagnozzi .05 .02
255 Chuck Finley .10 .03
256 Mackey Sasser .05 .02
257 John Burkett .05 .02
258 Hal Morris .05 .02
259 Larry Walker .15 .04
260 Bill Swift .05 .02
261 Joe Oliver .05 .02
262 Julio Machado .05 .02
263 Todd Stottlemyre .05 .02
264 Matt Merullo .05 .02
265 Brent Mayne .05 .02
266 Thomas Howard .05 .02
267 Lance Johnson .05 .02
268 Terry Mulholland .05 .02
269 Rick Honeycutt .05 .02
270 Luis Gonzalez .10 .03
271 Jose Guzman .05 .02
272 Jimmy Jones .05 .02
273 Mark Lewis .05 .02
274 Rene Gonzales .05 .02
275 Jeff Johnson .05 .02
276 Dennis Martinez HL .05 .02
277 Delino DeShields .05 .02
278 Sam Horn .05 .02
279 Kevin Gross .05 .02
280 Jose Oquendo .05 .02
281 Mark Grace .15 .04
282 Mark Gubicza .05 .02
283 Fred McGriff .15 .04
284 Ron Gant .10 .03
285 Lou Whitaker .10 .03
286 Edgar Martinez .15 .04
287 Ron Tingley .05 .02
288 Kevin McReynolds .05 .02
289 Ivan Rodriguez .25 .07
290 Mike Gardiner .05 .02
291 Chris Haney .05 .02
292 Darrin Jackson .05 .02
293 Bill Doran .05 .02
294 Ted Higuera .05 .02
295 Jeff Brantley .05 .02
296 Les Lancaster .05 .02
297 Jim Eisenreich .05 .02
298 Ruben Sierra .05 .02
299 Scott Radinsky .05 .02
300 Jose DeJesus .05 .02
301 Mike Timlin .05 .02
302 Luis Sojo .05 .02
303 Kelly Downs .05 .02
304 Scott Bankhead .05 .02
305 Pedro Munoz .05 .02
306 Scott Scudder .05 .02
307 Kevin Elster .05 .02
308 Duane Ward .05 .02
309 Darryl Kile .10 .03
310 Orlando Merced .05 .02
311 Dave Henderson .05 .02
312 Tim Raines .10 .03
313 Mark Lee .05 .02
314 Mike Gallego .05 .02
315 Charles Nagy .05 .02
316 Jesse Barfield .05 .02
317 Todd Frohwirth .05 .02
318 Al Osuna .05 .02
319 Darrin Fletcher .05 .02
320 Checklist 238-316 .05 .02
321 David Segui .05 .02
322 Stan Javier .05 .02
323 Bryn Smith .05 .02
324 Jeff Treadway .05 .02
325 Mark Whiten .05 .02
326 Kent Hrbek .10 .03
327 Dave Justice .10 .03
328 Tony Phillips .05 .02
329 Rob Murphy .05 .02
330 Kevin Morton .05 .02
331 John Smiley .05 .02
332 Luis Rivera .05 .02
333 Wally Joyner .10 .03
334 Heathcliff Slocumb .05 .02
335 Rick Cerone .05 .02
336 Mike Remlinger .05 .02
337 Mike Moore .05 .02
338 Lloyd McClendon .05 .02
339 Al Newman .05 .02
340 Kirk McCaskill .05 .02
341 Howard Johnson .05 .02
342 Greg Myers .05 .02
343 Kal Daniels .05 .02
344 Bernie Williams .15 .04
345 Shane Mack .05 .02
346 Gary Thurman .05 .02
347 Dante Bichette .10 .03
348 Mark McGwire .60 .18
349 Travis Fryman .10 .03
350 Ray Lankford .05 .02
351 Mike Jeffcoat .05 .02
352 Jack McDowell .05 .02
353 Mitch Williams .05 .02
354 Mike Devereaux .05 .02
355 Andres Galarraga .10 .03
356 Henry Cotto .05 .02
357 Scott Bailes .05 .02
358 Jeff Bagwell .25 .07
359 Scott Leius .05 .02
360 Zane Smith .05 .02
361 Bill Pecota .05 .02
362 Tony Fernandez .05 .02
363 Glenn Braggs .05 .02
364 Bill Spiers .05 .02
365 Vicente Palacios .05 .02
366 Tim Burke .05 .02
367 Randy Tomlin .05 .02
368 Kenny Rogers .10 .03
369 Brett Butler .10 .03
370 Pat Kelly .05 .02
371 Bip Roberts .05 .02
372 Gregg Jefferies .05 .02
373 Kevin Bass .05 .02
374 Ron Karkovice .05 .02
375 Paul Gibson .05 .02
376 Bernard Gilkey .05 .02
377 Dave Gallagher .05 .02
378 Bill Wegman .05 .02
379 Pat Borders .05 .02
380 Ed Whitson .05 .02
381 Gilberto Reyes .05 .02
382 Russ Swan .05 .02
383 Andy Van Slyke .10 .03
384 Wes Chamberlain .05 .02
385 Steve Chitren .05 .02
386 Greg Olson .05 .02
387 Brian McRae .05 .02
388 Rich Rodriguez .05 .02
389 Steve Decker .05 .02
390 Chuck Knoblauch .10 .03
391 Bobby Witt .05 .02
392 Eddie Murray .25 .07
393 Juan Gonzalez .15 .04
394 Scott Ruskin .05 .02
395 Jay Howell .05 .02
396 Checklist 317-396 .05 .02
397 Royce Clayton RR .05 .02
398 John Jaha RR RC .25 .07
399 Dan Wilson RR .05 .02
400 Archie Corbin RR .05 .02
401 Barry Manuel RR .05 .02
402 Kim Batiste RR .05 .02
403 Pat Mahomes RR RC .25 .07
404 Dave Fleming RR .05 .02
405 Jeff Juden RR .05 .02
406 Jim Thome RR .25 .07
407 Sam Militello RR .05 .02
408 Jeff Nelson RR RC .25 .07
409 Anthony Young RR .05 .02
410 Tino Martinez RR .15 .04
411 Jeff Mutis RR .05 .02
412 Rey Sanchez RR RC .25 .07
413 Chris Gardner RR .05 .02
414 John Vander Wal RR .05 .02
415 Reggie Sanders RR .05 .02
416 Brian Williams RR RC .10 .03
417 Mo Sanford RR .05 .02
418 D.Weathers RR RC .10 .03
419 Hector Fajardo RR RC .10 .03
420 Steve Foster RR .05 .02
421 Lance Dickson RR .05 .02
422 Andre Dawson AS .05 .02
423 Ozzie Smith AS .25 .07
424 Chris Sabo AS .05 .02
425 Tony Gwynn AS .15 .04
426 Tom Glavine AS .10 .03
427 Bobby Bonilla AS .05 .02
428 Will Clark AS .10 .03
429 Ryne Sandberg AS .25 .07
430 Benito Santiago AS .05 .02
431 Ivan Calderon AS .05 .02
432 Ozzie Smith .40 .12
433 Tim Leary .05 .02
434 Bret Saberhagen HL .05 .02
435 Mel Rojas .05 .02
436 Ben McDonald .05 .02
437 Tim Crews .05 .02
438 Rex Hudler .05 .02
439 Chico Walker .05 .02
440 Kurt Stillwell .05 .02
441 Tony Gwynn .30 .09
442 John Smoltz .15 .04
443 Lloyd Moseby .05 .02
444 Mike Schooler .05 .02
445 Joe Grahe .05 .02
446 Dwight Gooden .10 .03
447 Oil Can Boyd .05 .02
448 John Marzano .05 .02
449 Bret Barberie .05 .02
450 Mike Maddux .05 .02
451 Jeff Reed .05 .02
452 Dale Sveum .05 .02
453 Jose Uribe .05 .02
454 Bob Scanlan .05 .02
455 Kevin Appier .10 .03
456 Jeff Huson .05 .02
457 Ken Patterson .05 .02
458 Ricky Jordan .05 .02
459 Tom Candiotti .05 .02
460 Lee Stevens .05 .02
461 Rod Beck RC .25 .07
462 Dave Valle .05 .02
463 Scott Erickson .05 .02
464 Chris Jones .05 .02
465 Mark Carreon .05 .02
466 Rob Ducey .05 .02
467 Jim Corsi .05 .02
468 Jeff King .05 .02
469 Curt Young .05 .02
470 Bo Jackson .25 .07
471 Chris Bosio .05 .02
472 Jamie Quirk .05 .02
473 Jesse Orosco .05 .02
474 Alvaro Espinoza .05 .02
475 Joe Orsulak .05 .02
476 Checklist 397-477 .05 .02
477 Gerald Young .05 .02
478 Wally Backman .05 .02
479 Juan Bell .05 .02
480 Mike Scioscia .05 .02
481 Omar Olivares .05 .02
482 Francisco Cabrera .05 .02
483 Greg Swindell UER .05 .02
(Shown on Indians,
but listed on Reds)
484 Terry Leach .05 .02
485 Tommy Gregg .05 .02
486 Scott Aldred .05 .02
487 Greg Briley .05 .02
488 Phil Plantier .05 .02
489 Curtis Wilkerson .05 .02
490 Tom Brunansky .05 .02
491 Mike Fetters .05 .02
492 Frank Castillo .05 .02
493 Joe Boever .05 .02
494 Kirt Manwaring .05 .02
495 Wilson Alvarez HL .05 .02
496 Gene Larkin .05 .02
497 Gary DiSarcina .05 .02
498 Frank Viola .10 .03
499 Manuel Lee .05 .02
500 Albert Belle .10 .03
501 Stan Belinda .05 .02
502 Dwight Evans .10 .03
503 Eric Davis .10 .03
504 Darren Holmes .05 .02
505 Mike Bordick .05 .02
506 Dave Hansen .05 .02
507 Lee Guetterman .05 .02
508 Keith Mitchell .05 .02
509 Melido Perez .05 .02
510 Dickie Thon .05 .02
511 Mark Williamson .05 .02
512 Mark Salas .05 .02
513 Milt Thompson .05 .02
514 Mo Vaughn .10 .03
515 Jim Deshaies .05 .02
516 Rich Garces .05 .02
517 Lonnie Smith .05 .02
518 Spike Owen .05 .02
519 Tracy Jones .05 .02
520 Greg Maddux .40 .12
521 Carlos Martinez .05 .02
522 Neal Heaton .05 .02
523 Mike Greenwell .05 .02
524 Andy Benes .05 .02
525 Jeff Schaefer UER .05 .02
(Photo actually
Tino Martinez)
526 Mike Sharperson .05 .02
527 Wade Taylor .05 .02
528 Jerome Walton .05 .02
529 Storm Davis .05 .02
530 Jose Hernandez RC .40 .12
531 Mark Langston .05 .02
532 Rob Deer .05 .02
533 Geronimo Pena .05 .02
534 Juan Guzman .05 .02
535 Pete Schourek .05 .02
536 Todd Benzinger .05 .02
537 Billy Hatcher .05 .02
538 Tom Foley .05 .02
539 Dave Cochrane .05 .02
540 Mariano Duncan .05 .02
541 Edwin Nunez .05 .02
542 Rance Mulliniks .05 .02
543 Carlton Fisk .15 .04
544 Luis Aquino .05 .02
545 Ricky Bones .05 .02
546 Craig Grebeck .05 .02
547 Charlie Hayes .05 .02
548 Jose Canseco .25 .07
549 Andujar Cedeno .05 .02
550 Geno Petralli .05 .02
551 Javier Ortiz .05 .02
552 Rudy Seanez .05 .02
553 Rich Gedman .05 .02
554 Eric Plunk .05 .02
555 Nolan Ryan HL .40 .12
(With Rich Gossage)
556 Checklist 478-555 .05 .02
557 Greg Colbrunn .05 .02
558 Chito Martinez .05 .02
559 Darryl Strawberry .10 .03
560 Luis Alicea .05 .02
561 Dwight Smith .05 .02
562 Terry Shumpert .05 .02
563 Jim Vatcher .05 .02
564 Deion Sanders .15 .04
565 Walt Terrell .05 .02
566 Dave Burba .05 .02
567 Dave Howard .05 .02
568 Todd Hundley .05 .02
569 Jack Daugherty .05 .02
570 Scott Cooper .05 .02
571 Bill Sampen .05 .02
572 Jose Melendez .05 .02
573 Freddie Benavides .05 .02
574 Jim Gantner .05 .02
575 Trevor Wilson .05 .02
576 Ryne Sandberg .40 .12
577 Kevin Seitzer .05 .02
578 Gerald Alexander .05 .02
579 Mike Huff .05 .02
580 Von Hayes .05 .02
581 Derek Bell .10 .03
582 Mike Stanley .05 .02
583 Kevin Mitchell .05 .02
584 Mike Jackson .05 .02
585 Dan Gladden .05 .02
586 Ted Power UER .05 .02
(Wrong year given for
signing with Reds)
587 Jeff Innis .05 .02
588 Bob MacDonald .05 .02
589 Jose Tolentino .05 .02
590 Bob Patterson .05 .02
591 Scott Brosius RC .40 .12
592 Frank Thomas .25 .07
593 Darryl Hamilton .05 .02
594 Kirk Dressendorfer .05 .02
595 Jeff Shaw .05 .02
596 Don Mattingly .60 .18
597 Glenn Davis .05 .02
598 Andy Mota .05 .02
599 Jason Grimsley .05 .02
600 Jim Poole .05 .02
601 Jim Gott .05 .02
602 Stan Royer .05 .02
603 Marvin Freeman .05 .02
604 Denis Boucher .05 .02
605 Denny Neagle .10 .03
606 Mark Lemke .05 .02
607 Jerry Don Gleaton .05 .02
608 Brent Knackert .05 .02
609 Carlos Quintana .05 .02
610 Bobby Bonilla .10 .03
611 Joe Hesketh .05 .02
612 Daryl Boston .05 .02
613 Shawon Dunston .05 .02
614 Danny Cox .05 .02
615 Darren Lewis .05 .02
616 Braves No-Hitter UER .05 .02
Kent Mercker
(Misspelled Merker
on card front)
Alejandro Pena
Mark Wohlers
617 Kirby Puckett .25 .07
618 Franklin Stubbs .05 .02
619 Chris Donnels .05 .02
620 David Wells UER .10 .03
(Career Highlights
in black not red)
621 Mike Aldrete .05 .02
622 Bob Kipper .05 .02
623 Anthony Telford .05 .02
624 Randy Myers .05 .02
625 Willie Randolph .10 .03
626 Joe Slusarski .05 .02
627 John Wetteland .10 .03
628 Greg Cadaret .05 .02
629 Tom Glavine .15 .04
630 Wilson Alvarez .05 .02
631 Wally Ritchie .05 .02
632 Mike Mussina .25 .07
633 Mark Leiter .05 .02
634 Gerald Perry .05 .02
635 Matt Young .05 .02
636 Checklist 556-635 .05 .02
637 Scott Hemond .05 .02
638 David West .05 .02
639 Jim Clancy .05 .02
640 Doug Piatt UER .05 .02
(Not born in 1955 as
on card; incorrect info
on How Acquired)
641 Omar Vizquel .15 .04
642 Rick Sutcliffe .10 .03
643 Glenallen Hill .05 .02
644 Gary Varsho .05 .02
645 Tony Fossas .05 .02
646 Jack Howell .05 .02
647 Jim Campanis .05 .02
648 Chris Gwynn .05 .02
649 Jim Leyritz .05 .02
650 Chuck McElroy .05 .02
651 Sean Berry .05 .02
652 Donald Harris .05 .02
653 Don Slaught .05 .02
654 Rusty Meacham .05 .02
655 Scott Terry .05 .02
656 Ramon Martinez .05 .02
657 Keith Miller .05 .02
658 Ramon Garcia .05 .02
659 Milt Hill .05 .02
660 Steve Frey .05 .02
661 Bob McClure .05 .02
662 Ced Landrum .05 .02
663 Doug Henry RC .10 .03
664 Candy Maldonado .05 .02
665 Carl Willis .05 .02
666 Jeff Montgomery .05 .02
667 Craig Shipley .05 .02
668 Warren Newson .05 .02
669 Mickey Morandini .05 .02
670 Brook Jacoby .05 .02
671 Ryan Bowen .05 .02
672 Bill Krueger .05 .02
673 Rob Mallicoat .05 .02
674 Doug Jones .05 .02
675 Scott Livingstone .05 .02
676 Danny Tartabull .05 .02
677 Joe Carter HL .05 .02
678 Cecil Espy .05 .02
679 Randy Velarde .05 .02
680 Bruce Ruffin .05 .02
681 Ted Wood .05 .02
682 Dan Plesac .05 .02
683 Eric Bullock .05 .02
684 Junior Ortiz .05 .02
685 Dave Hollins .05 .02
686 Dennis Martinez .10 .03
687 Larry Andersen .05 .02
688 Doug Simons .05 .02
689 Tim Spehr .05 .02
690 Calvin Jones .05 .02
691 Mark Guthrie .05 .02
692 Alfredo Griffin .05 .02
693 Joe Carter .10 .03
694 Terry Mathews .05 .02
695 Pascual Perez .05 .02
696 Gene Nelson .05 .02
697 Gerald Williams .05 .02
698 Chris Cron .05 .02
699 Steve Buechele .05 .02
700 Paul McClellan .05 .02
701 Jim Lindeman .05 .02
702 Francisco Oliveras .05 .02
703 Rob Maurer .05 .02
704 Pat Hentgen .05 .02
705 Jaime Navarro .05 .02
706 Mike Magnante RC .10 .03
707 Nolan Ryan 1.00 .3
708 Bobby Thigpen .05 .0
709 John Cerutti .05 .0
710 Steve Wilson .05 .0
711 Hensley Meulens .05 .0
712 Rheal Cormier .05 .0
713 Scott Bradley .05 .0
714 Mitch Webster .05 .0
715 Roger Mason .05 .0
716 Checklist 636-716 .05 .0
717 Jeff Fassero .05 .0
718 Cal Eldred .05 .0
719 Sid Fernandez .05 .0
720 Bob Zupcic RC .10 .0
721 Jose Offerman .05 .0
722 Cliff Brantley .05 .0
723 Ron Darling .05 .0
724 Dave Stieb .05 .0
725 Hector Villanueva .05 .0
726 Mike Hartley .05 .0
727 Arthur Rhodes .05 .0
728 Randy Bush .05 .0
729 Steve Sax .05 .0
730 Dave Otto .05 .0
731 John Wehner .05 .0
732 Dave Martinez .05 .0
733 Ruben Amaro .05 .0
734 Billy Ripken .05 .0
735 Steve Farr .05 .0
736 Shawn Abner .05 .0
737 Gil Heredia RC .25 .0
738 Ron Jones .05 .0
739 Tony Castillo .05 .0
740 Sammy Sosa .40 .1
741 Julio Franco .10 .0
742 Tim Naehring .05 .0
743 Steve Wapnick .05 .0
744 Craig Wilson .05 .0
745 Darrin Chapin .05 .0
746 Chris George .05 .0
747 Mike Simms .05 .0
748 Rosario Rodriguez .05 .0
749 Skeeter Barnes .05 .0
750 Roger McDowell .05 .0
751 Dann Howitt .05 .0
752 Paul Sorrento .05 .0
753 Braulio Castillo .05 .0
754 Yorkis Perez .05 .0
755 Willie Fraser .05 .0
756 Jeremy Hernandez RC .10 .0
757 Curt Schilling .15 .0
758 Steve Lyons .05 .0
759 Dave Anderson .05 .0
760 Willie Banks .05 .0
761 Mark Leonard .05 .0
762 Jack Armstrong .05 .0
(Listed on Indians,
but shown on Reds)
763 Scott Servais .05 .0
764 Ray Stephens .05 .0
765 Junior Noboa .05 .0
766 Jim Olander .05 .0
767 Joe Magrane .05 .0
768 Lance Blankenship .05 .0
769 Mike Humphreys .05 .0
770 Jarvis Brown .05 .0
771 Damon Berryhill .05 .0
772 Alejandro Pena .05 .0
773 Jose Mesa .05 .0
774 Gary Cooper .05 .0
775 Carney Lansford .10 .0
776 Mike Bielecki .05 .0
Shown on Cubs,
but listed on Braves
777 Charlie O'Brien .05 .0
778 Carlos Hernandez .05 .0
779 Howard Farmer .05 .0
780 Mike Stanton .05 .0
781 Reggie Harris .05 .0
782 Xavier Hernandez .05 .0
783 Bryan Hickerson RC .10 .0
784 Checklist 717-784 .05 .0
and BC1-BC8

1992 Donruss Bonus Cards

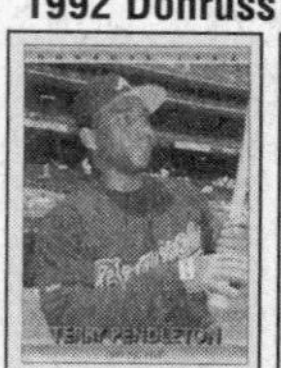
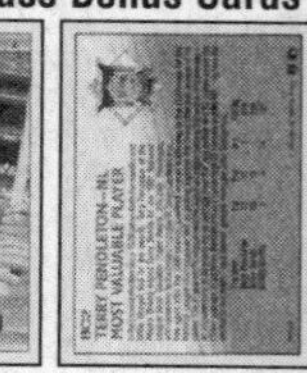

The 1992 Donruss Bonus Cards set contain eight standard-size. The cards are numbered c the back and checklisted below accordingly. Th cards were randomly inserted in foil packs c 1992 Donruss baseball cards.

	Nm-Mt	Ex-Mt
COMPLETE SET (8)	2.00	.60
BC1 Cal Ripken MVP	.75	.23
BC2 Terry Pendleton MVP	.10	.03
BC3 Roger Clemens CY	.50	.15
BC4 Tom Glavine CY	.15	.04
BC5 C.Knoblauch ROY	.10	.03
BC6 Jeff Bagwell ROY	.25	.07
BC7 Colorado Rockies	.05	.01
BC8 Florida Marlins	.05	.01

1992 Donruss Diamond Kings

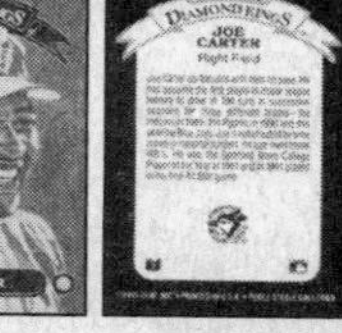

ese standard-size cards were randomly inserted in 1992 Donruss I foil packs (cards 1-13 and checklist only) and in 1992 Donruss II foil cks (cards 14-26). The decision at the time to nsform the popular Diamond King subset into limieted distribution insert set created notable oups of supporters and dissenters. The attrace fronts feature player portraits by noted orts artist Dick Perez. The words "Donruss amond Kings" are superimposed at the card in a gold-trimmed blue and black banner, h the player's name in a similarly designed ck stripe at the card bottom. A very limited ount of 5" by 7" cards were produced. These ues were never formally released but these rds were intended to be premiums in retail oducts.

	Nm-Mt	Ex-Mt
MPLETE SET (27)	20.00	6.00
MPLETE SERIES 1 (14)	16.00	4.80
MPLETE SERIES 2 (13)	4.00	1.20
1 Paul Molitor	1.25	.35
2 Will Clark	2.00	.60
3 Joe Carter	.75	.23
4 Julio Franco	.75	.23
5 Cal Ripken	6.00	1.80
6 Dave Justice	.75	.23
7 George Bell	.40	.12
8 Frank Thomas	2.00	.60
9 Wade Boggs	1.25	.35
10 Scott Sanderson	.40	.12
11 Jeff Bagwell	2.00	.60
12 John Kruk	.75	.23
13 Felix Jose	.40	.12
14 Harold Baines	.75	.23
15 Dwight Gooden	.75	.23
16 Brian McRae	.40	.12
17 Jay Bell	.75	.23
18 Brett Butler	.75	.23
19 Hal Morris	.40	.12
20 Mark Langston	.40	.12
21 Scott Erickson	.40	.12
22 Randy Johnson	2.00	.60
23 Greg Swindell	.40	.12
24 Dennis Martinez	.75	.23
25 Tony Phillips	.40	.12
26 Fred McGriff	1.25	.35
27 Checklist 1-26 DP (Dick Perez)	.40	.12

1992 Donruss Elite

ese cards were random inserts in 1992 onruss first and second series foil packs. Like e previous year, the cards were individually mbered of 10,000. Card fronts feature draatic prismatic borders encasing a full color tion or posed shot of the player. The numberg of the set is essentially a continuation of the ries started the year before. Only 5,000 Ripken gnature Series cards were printed and only 500 Henderson Legends cards were printed. e complete set price does not include cards L2 d S2.

	Nm-Mt	Ex-Mt
Wade Boggs	25.00	7.50
Joe Carter	15.00	4.50
Will Clark	40.00	12.00
Dwight Gooden	15.00	4.50
Ken Griffey Jr.	40.00	12.00
Tony Gwynn	30.00	9.00
Howard Johnson	15.00	4.50
Terry Pendleton	15.00	4.50
Kirby Puckett	25.00	7.50
Frank Thomas	25.00	7.50
Rickey Henderson (Legend Series)	25.00	7.50
2 Cal Ripken (Signature Series)	200.00	60.00

1992 Donruss Update

our cards from this 22-card standard-size set ere included in each retail factory set. Card esign is identical to regular issue 1992 Donruss rds except for the U-prefixed numbering on ack. Card numbers U1-U6 are Rated Rookie rds, while card numbers U7-U9 are Highlights rds. A tough early Kenny Lofton card, his first s a member of the Cleveland Indians, highlights is set.

	Nm-Mt	Ex-Mt
OMPLETE SET (22)	50.00	15.00
1 Pat Listach RR	1.50	.45
2 Andy Stankiewicz RR	1.00	.30
3 Brian Jordan RR	2.50	.75
4 Dan Walters RR	1.00	.30
5 Chad Curtis RR	1.50	.45
6 Kenny Lofton RR	1.50	.45
7 Mark McGwire HL	10.00	3.00
8 Eddie Murray HL	4.00	1.20
9 Jeff Reardon HL	1.50	.45
10 Frank Viola	1.50	.45
11 Gary Sheffield	1.50	.45
12 George Bell	1.00	.30
U13 Rick Sutcliffe	1.50	.45
U14 Wally Joyner	1.50	.45
U15 Kevin Seitzer	1.00	.30
U16 Bill Krueger	1.00	.30
U17 Danny Tartabull	1.00	.30
U18 Dave Winfield	1.50	.45
U19 Gary Carter	1.50	.45
U20 Bobby Bonilla	1.50	.45
U21 Cory Snyder	1.00	.30
U22 Bill Swift	1.00	.30

1992 Donruss Rookies

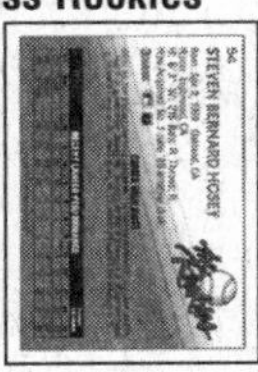

After six years of issuing "The Rookies" as a 56-card boxed set, Donruss expanded it to a 132-card standard-size set and distributed the cards in hobby and retail foil packs. The card design is the same as the 1992 Donruss regular issue except that the two-tone blue color bars have been replaced by green, as in the previous six Donruss Rookies sets. The cards are arranged in alphabetical order and numbered on the back. Rookie Cards in this set include Jeff Kent, Manny Ramirez and Eric Young. In addition an early card of Pedro Martinez is featured.

	Nm-Mt	Ex-Mt
COMPLETE SET (132)	10.00	3.00
1 Kyle Abbott	.05	.02
2 Troy Afenir	.05	.02
3 Rich Amaral RC	.10	.03
4 Ruben Amaro	.05	.02
5 Billy Ashley RC	.10	.03
6 Pedro Astacio RC	.25	.07
7 Jim Austin	.05	.02
8 Robert Ayrault	.05	.02
9 Kevin Baez	.05	.02
10 Esteban Beltre	.05	.02
11 Brian Bohanon	.05	.02
12 Kent Bottenfield RC	.25	.07
13 Jeff Branson	.05	.02
14 Brad Brink	.05	.02
15 John Briscoe	.05	.02
16 Doug Brocail RC	.10	.03
17 Rico Brogna	.05	.02
18 J.T. Bruett	.05	.02
19 Jacob Brumfield	.05	.02
20 Jim Bullinger	.05	.02
21 Kevin Campbell	.05	.02
22 Pedro Castellano RC	.10	.03
23 Mike Christopher	.05	.02
24 Archi Cianfrocco RC	.10	.03
25 Mark Clark RC	.10	.03
26 Craig Colbert	.05	.02
27 Victor Cole	.05	.02
28 Steve Cooke RC	.10	.03
29 Tim Costo	.05	.02
30 Chad Curtis RC	.25	.07
31 Doug Davis	.05	.02
32 Gary DiSarcina	.05	.02
33 John Doherty RC	.10	.03
34 Mike Draper	.05	.02
35 Monty Fariss	.05	.02
36 Bien Figueroa	.05	.02
37 John Flaherty	.05	.02
38 Tim Fortugno	.05	.02
39 Eric Fox RC	.10	.03
40 Jeff Frye RC	.10	.03
41 Ramon Garcia	.05	.02
42 Brent Gates RC	.10	.03
43 Tom Goodwin	.05	.02
44 Buddy Groom RC	.10	.03
45 Jeff Grotewold	.05	.02
46 Juan Guerrero	.05	.02
47 Johnny Guzman RC	.10	.03
48 Shawn Hare RC	.10	.03
49 Ryan Hawblitzel RC	.10	.03
50 Bert Heffernan	.05	.02
51 Butch Henry	.05	.02
52 Cesar Hernandez RC	.10	.03
53 Vince Horsman	.05	.02
54 Steve Hosey	.05	.02
55 Pat Howell	.05	.02
56 Peter Hoy	.05	.02
57 Jonathan Hurst RC	.10	.03
58 Mark Hutton RC	.10	.03
59 Shawn Jeter RC	.10	.03
60 Joel Johnston	.05	.02
61 Jeff Kent RC	1.00	.30
62 Kurt Knudsen RC	.10	.03
63 Kevin Koslofski	.05	.02
64 Danny Leon	.05	.02
65 Jesse Levis	.05	.02
66 Tom Marsh	.05	.02
67 Ed Martel	.05	.02
68 Al Martin RC	.25	.07
69 Pedro Martinez	2.00	.60
70 Derrick May	.05	.02
71 Matt Maysey	.05	.02
72 Russ McGinnis	.05	.02
73 Tim McIntosh	.05	.02
74 Jim McNamara	.05	.02
75 Jeff McNeely	.05	.02
76 Rusty Meacham	.05	.02
77 Tony Menendez	.05	.02
78 Henry Mercedes	.05	.02
79 Paul Miller	.05	.02
80 Joe Millette	.05	.02
81 Blas Minor	.05	.02
82 Dennis Moeller	.05	.02
83 Raul Mondesi	.10	.03
84 Rob Natal	.05	.02
85 Troy Neel RC	.10	.03
86 David Nied RC	.10	.03
87 Jerry Nielson	.05	.02
88 Donovan Osborne	.05	.02
89 John Patterson RC	.10	.03
90 Roger Pavlik RC	.10	.03
91 Dan Peltier	.05	.02
92 Jim Pena	.05	.02
93 William Pennyfeather	.05	.02
94 Mike Perez	.05	.02
95 Hipolito Pichardo RC	.10	.03
96 Greg Pirkl RC	.10	.03
97 Harvey Pulliam	.05	.02
98 Manny Ramirez RC	2.50	.75
99 Pat Rapp RC	.10	.03
100 Jeff Reboulet	.05	.02
101 Darren Reed	.05	.02
102 Shane Reynolds RC	.25	.07
103 Bill Risley	.05	.02
104 Ben Rivera	.05	.02
105 Henry Rodriguez	.05	.02
106 Rico Rossy	.05	.02
107 Johnny Ruffin	.05	.02
108 Steve Scarsone	.05	.02
109 Tim Scott	.05	.02
110 Steve Shifflett	.05	.02
111 Dave Silvestri	.05	.02
112 Matt Stairs RC	.25	.07
113 William Suero	.05	.02
114 Jeff Tackett	.05	.02
115 Eddie Taubensee	.10	.03
116 Rick Trlicek RC	.10	.03
117 Scooter Tucker	.05	.02
118 Shane Turner	.05	.02
119 Julio Valera	.05	.02
120 Paul Wagner RC	.10	.03
121 Tim Wakefield RC	4.00	1.20
122 Mike Walker	.05	.02
123 Bruce Walton	.05	.02
124 Lenny Webster	.05	.02
125 Bob Wickman	.05	.02
126 Mike Williams RC	.25	.07
127 Kerry Woodson	.05	.02
128 Eric Young RC	.25	.07
129 Kevin Young RC	.25	.07
130 Pete Young	.05	.02
131 Checklist 1-66	.05	.02
132 Checklist 67-132	.05	.02

1992 Donruss Rookies Phenoms

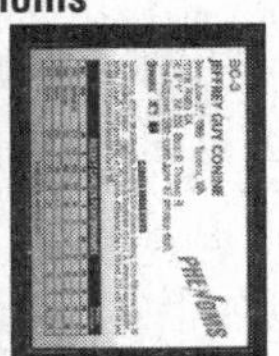

This 20-card standard size set features a selection young prospects. The first twelve cards were randomly inserted into 1992 Donruss The Rookies 12-card foil packs. The last eight were inserted one per 1992 Donruss Rookies 30-card jumbo pack. Each glossy card front features a black border surrounding a full color photo and gold foil type. One of only three MLB-licensed cards of Mike Piazza issued in 1992 is featured within this set.

	Nm-Mt	Ex-Mt
COMP.FOIL SET (12)	30.00	9.00
COMP.JUMBO SET (8)	10.00	3.00
COMM.FOIL (BC1-BC12)	1.00	.30
COMMON (BC13-BC20)	1.00	.30
BC1 Moises Alou	1.50	.45
BC2 Bret Boone	1.50	.45
BC3 Jeff Conine	1.50	.45
BC4 Dave Fleming	1.00	.30
BC5 Tyler Green	1.00	.30
BC6 Eric Karros	1.50	.45
BC7 Pat Listach	1.50	.45
BC8 Kenny Lofton	1.50	.45
BC9 Mike Piazza	20.00	6.00
BC10 Tim Salmon	1.50	.45
BC11 Andy Stankiewicz	1.00	.30
BC12 Dan Walters	1.00	.30
BC13 Ramon Caraballo	1.00	.30
BC14 Brian Jordan	1.50	.45
BC15 Ryan Klesko	1.50	.45
BC16 Sam Militello	1.00	.30
BC17 Frank Seminara	1.00	.30
BC18 Salomon Torres	1.00	.30
BC19 John Valentin	1.50	.45
BC20 Wil Cordero	1.00	.30

1993 Donruss

The 792-card 1993 Donruss set was issued in two series, each with 396 standard-size cards. Cards were distributed in foil packs. The basic card fronts feature glossy color action photos with white borders. At the bottom of the picture, the team logo appears in a team color-coded diamond with the player's name in a color-coded bar extending to the right. A Rated Rookies (RR) subset, sprinkled throughout the set, spotlights 20 young prospects. There are no key Rookie Cards in this set.

	Nm-Mt	Ex-Mt
COMPLETE SET (792)	30.00	9.00
COMP.SERIES 1 (396)	15.00	4.50
COMP.SERIES 2 (396)	15.00	4.50
1 Craig Lefferts	.10	.03
2 Kent Mercker	.10	.03
3 Phil Plantier	.10	.03
4 Alex Arias	.10	.03
5 Julio Valera	.10	.03
6 Dan Wilson	.20	.06
7 Frank Thomas	.50	.15
8 Eric Anthony	.10	.03
9 Derek Lilliquist	.10	.03
10 Rafael Bournigal	.10	.03
11 Manny Alexander RR	.10	.03
12 Bret Barberie	.10	.03
13 Mickey Tettleton	.10	.03
14 Anthony Young	.10	.03
15 Tim Spehr	.10	.03
16 Bob Ayrault	.10	.03
17 Bill Wegman	.10	.03
18 Jay Bell	.20	.06
19 Rick Aguilera	.10	.03
20 Todd Zeile	.10	.03
21 Steve Farr	.10	.03
22 Andy Benes	.10	.03
23 Lance Blankenship	.10	.03
24 Ted Wood	.10	.03
25 Omar Vizquel	.30	.09
26 Steve Avery	.10	.03
27 Brian Bohanon	.10	.03
28 Rick Wilkins	.10	.03
29 Devon White	.20	.06
30 Bobby Ayala RC	.10	.03
31 Leo Gomez	.10	.03
32 Mike Simms	.10	.03
33 Ellis Burks	.20	.06
34 Steve Wilson	.10	.03
35 Jim Abbott	.30	.09
36 Tim Wallach	.10	.03
37 Wilson Alvarez	.10	.03
38 Daryl Boston	.10	.03
39 Sandy Alomar Jr.	.10	.03
40 Mitch Williams	.10	.03
41 Rico Brogna	.10	.03
42 Gary Varsho	.10	.03
43 Kevin Appier	.20	.06
44 Eric Wedge RR RC	.10	.03
45 Dante Bichette	.20	.06
46 Jose Oquendo	.10	.03
47 Mike Trombley	.10	.03
48 Dan Walters	.10	.03
49 Gerald Williams	.10	.03
50 Bud Black	.10	.03
51 Bobby Witt	.10	.03
52 Mark Davis	.10	.03
53 Shawn Barton RC	.10	.03
54 Paul Assenmacher	.10	.03
55 Kevin Reimer	.10	.03
56 Billy Ashley RR	.10	.03
57 Eddie Zosky	.10	.03
58 Chris Sabo	.10	.03
59 Billy Ripken	.10	.03
60 Scooter Tucker	.10	.03
61 Tim Wakefield RR	.50	.15
62 Mitch Webster	.10	.03
63 Jack Clark	.20	.06
64 Mark Gardner	.10	.03
65 Lee Stevens	.10	.03
66 Todd Hundley	.10	.03
67 Bobby Thigpen	.10	.03
68 Dave Hollins	.10	.03
69 Jack Armstrong	.10	.03
70 Alex Cole	.10	.03
71 Mark Carreon	.10	.03
72 Todd Worrell	.10	.03
73 Steve Shifflett	.10	.03
74 Jerald Clark	.10	.03
75 Paul Molitor	.30	.09
76 Larry Carter RC	.10	.03
77 Rich Rowland RR	.10	.03
78 Damon Berryhill	.10	.03
79 Willie Banks	.10	.03
80 Hector Villanueva	.10	.03
81 Mike Gallego	.10	.03
82 Tim Belcher	.10	.03
83 Mike Bordick	.10	.03
84 Craig Biggio	.30	.09
85 Lance Parrish	.20	.06
86 Brett Butler	.20	.06
87 Mike Timlin	.10	.03
88 Brian Barnes	.10	.03
89 Brady Anderson	.20	.06
90 D.J. Dozier	.10	.03
91 Frank Viola	.20	.06
92 Darren Daulton	.20	.06
93 Chad Curtis	.10	.03
94 Zane Smith	.10	.03
95 George Bell	.10	.03
96 Rex Hudler	.10	.03
97 Mark Whiten	.10	.03
98 Tim Teufel	.10	.03
99 Kevin Ritz	.10	.03
100 Jeff Brantley	.10	.03
101 Jeff Conine	.20	.06
102 Vinny Castilla	.20	.06
103 Greg Vaughn	.10	.03
104 Steve Buechele	.10	.03
105 Darren Reed	.10	.03
106 Bip Roberts	.10	.03
107 John Habyan	.10	.03
108 Scott Servais	.10	.03
109 Walt Weiss	.10	.03
110 J.T. Snow RR RC	.30	.09
111 Jay Buhner	.20	.06
112 Darryl Strawberry	.20	.06
113 Roger Pavlik	.10	.03
114 Chris Nabholz	.10	.03
115 Pat Borders	.10	.03
116 Pat Howell	.10	.03
117 Gregg Olson	.10	.03
118 Curt Schilling	.20	.06
119 Roger Clemens	1.00	.30
120 Victor Cole	.10	.03
121 Gary DiSarcina	.10	.03
122 Gary Carter CL Kirt Manwaring	.10	.03
123 Steve Sax	.10	.03
124 Chuck Carr	.10	.03
125 Mark Lewis	.10	.03
126 Tony Gwynn	.60	.18
127 Travis Fryman	.20	.06
128 Dave Burba	.10	.03
129 Wally Joyner	.20	.06
130 John Smoltz	.30	.09
131 Cal Eldred	.10	.03
132 Roberto Alomar CL Devon White	.20	.06
133 Arthur Rhodes	.10	.03
134 Jeff Blauser	.10	.03
135 Scott Cooper	.10	.03
136 Doug Strange	.10	.03
137 Luis Sojo	.10	.03
138 Jeff Branson	.10	.03
139 Alex Fernandez	.10	.03
140 Ken Caminiti	.20	.06
141 Charles Nagy	.10	.03
142 Tom Candiotti	.10	.03
143 Willie Greene RR	.10	.03
144 John Vander Wal	.10	.03
145 Kurt Knudsen	.10	.03
146 John Franco	.20	.06
147 Eddie Pierce RC	.10	.03
148 Kim Batiste	.10	.03
149 Darren Holmes	.10	.03
150 Steve Cooke	.10	.03
151 Terry Jorgensen	.10	.03
152 Mark Clark	.10	.03
153 Randy Velarde	.10	.03
154 Greg W. Harris	.10	.03
155 Kevin Campbell	.10	.03
156 John Burkett	.10	.03
157 Kevin Mitchell	.10	.03
158 Deion Sanders	.30	.09
159 Jose Canseco	.50	.15
160 Jeff Hartsock	.10	.03
161 Tom Quinlan RC	.10	.03
162 Tim Pugh RC	.10	.03
163 Glenn Davis	.10	.03
164 Shane Reynolds	.10	.03
165 Jody Reed	.10	.03
166 Mike Sharperson	.10	.03
167 Scott Lewis	.10	.03
168 Dennis Martinez	.20	.06
169 Scott Radinsky	.10	.03
170 Dave Gallagher	.10	.03
171 Jim Thome	.50	.15
172 Terry Mulholland	.10	.03
173 Milt Cuyler	.10	.03
174 Bob Patterson	.10	.03
175 Jeff Montgomery	.10	.03
176 Tim Salmon RR	.30	.09
177 Franklin Stubbs	.10	.03
178 Donovan Osborne	.10	.03
179 Jeff Reboulet	.10	.03
180 Jeremy Hernandez	.10	.03
181 Charlie Hayes	.10	.03
182 Matt Williams	.20	.06
183 Mike Raczka	.10	.03
184 Francisco Cabrera	.10	.03
185 Rich DeLucia	.10	.03
186 Sammy Sosa	.75	.23
187 Ivan Rodriguez	.50	.15
188 Bret Boone RR	.30	.09
189 Juan Guzman	.10	.03
190 Tom Browning	.10	.03
191 Randy Milligan	.10	.03
192 Steve Finley	.20	.06
193 John Patterson RR	.10	.03
194 Kip Gross	.10	.03
195 Tony Fossas	.10	.03
196 Ivan Calderon	.10	.03
197 Junior Felix	.10	.03
198 Pete Schourek	.10	.03
199 Craig Grebeck	.10	.03
200 Juan Bell	.10	.03
201 Glenallen Hill	.10	.03
202 Danny Jackson	.10	.03
203 John Kiely	.10	.03
204 Bob Tewksbury	.10	.03
205 Kevin Koslofski	.10	.03
206 Craig Shipley	.10	.03
207 John Jaha	.10	.03
208 Royce Clayton	.10	.03
209 Mike Piazza RR	1.50	.45
210 Ron Gant	.20	.06
211 Scott Erickson	.10	.03
212 Doug Dascenzo	.10	.03
213 Andy Stankiewicz	.10	.03
214 Geronimo Berroa	.10	.03
215 Dennis Eckersley	.20	.06
216 Al Osuna	.10	.03
217 Tino Martinez	.30	.09
218 Henry Rodriguez	.10	.03
219 Ed Sprague	.10	.03
220 Ken Hill	.10	.03
221 Chito Martinez	.10	.03
222 Bret Saberhagen	.20	.06
223 Mike Greenwell	.10	.03
224 Mickey Morandini	.10	.03
225 Chuck Finley	.20	.06
226 Denny Neagle	.20	.06
227 Kirk McCaskill	.10	.03
228 Rheal Cormier	.10	.03
229 Paul Sorrento	.10	.03
230 Darrin Jackson	.10	.03
231 Rob Deer	.10	.03
232 Bill Swift	.10	.03
233 Kevin McReynolds	.10	.03
234 Terry Pendleton	.20	.06
235 Dave Nilsson	.10	.03
236 Chuck McElroy	.10	.03
237 Derek Parks	.10	.03
238 Norm Charlton	.10	.03
239 Matt Nokes	.10	.03
240 Juan Guerrero	.10	.03
241 Jeff Parrett	.10	.03
242 Ryan Thompson RR	.10	.03
243 Dave Fleming	.10	.03
244 Dave Hansen	.10	.03
245 Monty Fariss	.10	.03
246 Archi Cianfrocco	.10	.03
247 Pat Hentgen	.10	.03
248 Bill Pecota	.10	.03
249 Ben McDonald	.10	.03
250 Cliff Brantley	.10	.03
251 John Valentin	.10	.03
252 Jeff King	.10	.03
253 Reggie Williams	.10	.03
254 Damon Berryhill CL Alex Arias	.10	.03
255 Ozzie Guillen	.10	.03
256 Mike Perez	.10	.03
257 Thomas Howard	.10	.03
258 Kurt Stillwell	.10	.03
259 Mike Henneman	.10	.03
260 Steve Decker	.10	.03
261 Brent Mayne	.10	.03
262 Otis Nixon	.10	.03
263 Mark Kiefer	.10	.03
264 Don Mattingly CL	.30	.09

Mike Bordick)
265 Richie Lewis RC .10 .03
266 Pat Gomez RC .10 .03
267 Scott Taylor .10 .03
268 Shawon Dunston .10 .03
269 Greg Myers .10 .03
270 Tim Costo .10 .03
271 Greg Hibbard .10 .03
272 Pete Harnisch .10 .03
273 Dave Mlicki .10 .03
274 Orel Hershiser .20 .06
275 Sean Berry RR .10 .03
276 Doug Simons .10 .03
277 John Doherty .10 .03
278 Eddie Murray .50 .15
279 Chris Haney .10 .03
280 Stan Javier .10 .03
281 Jaime Navarro .10 .03
282 Orlando Merced .10 .03
283 Kent Hrbek .20 .06
284 Bernard Gilkey .10 .03
285 Russ Springer .10 .03
286 Mike Maddux .10 .03
287 Eric Fox .10 .03
288 Mark Leonard .10 .03
289 Tim Leary .10 .03
290 Brian Hunter .10 .03
291 Donald Harris .10 .03
292 Bob Scanlan .10 .03
293 Turner Ward .10 .03
294 Hal Morris .10 .03
295 Jimmy Poole .10 .03
296 Doug Jones .10 .03
297 Tony Pena .10 .03
298 Ramon Martinez .10 .03
299 Tim Fortugno .10 .03
300 Marquis Grissom .20 .06
301 Lance Johnson .10 .03
302 Jeff Kent .50 .15
303 Reggie Jefferson .10 .03
304 Wes Chamberlain .10 .03
305 Shawn Hare .10 .03
306 Mike LaValliere .10 .03
307 Gregg Jefferies .10 .03
308 Troy Neel RR .10 .03
309 Pat Listach .10 .03
310 Geronimo Pena .10 .03
311 Pedro Munoz .10 .03
312 Guillermo Velasquez .10 .03
313 Roberto Kelly .10 .03
314 Mike Jackson .10 .03
315 Rickey Henderson .50 .15
316 Mark Lemke .10 .03
317 Erik Hanson .10 .03
318 Derrick May .10 .03
319 Geno Petralli .10 .03
320 Melvin Nieves RR .10 .03
321 Doug Linton .10 .03
322 Rob Dibble .20 .06
323 Chris Hoiles .10 .03
324 Jimmy Jones .10 .03
325 Dave Staton RR .10 .03
326 Pedro Martinez 1.00 .30
327 Paul Quantrill .10 .03
328 Greg Colbrunn .10 .03
329 Hilly Hathaway RC .10 .03
330 Jeff Innis .10 .03
331 Ron Karkovice .10 .03
332 Keith Shepherd RC .10 .03
333 Alan Embree .50 .15
334 Paul Wagner .10 .03
335 Dave Haas .10 .03
336 Ozzie Canseco .10 .03
337 Bill Sampen .10 .03
338 Rich Rodriguez .10 .03
339 Dean Palmer .20 .06
340 Greg Litton .10 .03
341 Jim Tatum RR RC .10 .03
342 Todd Haney RC .10 .03
343 Larry Casian .10 .03
344 Ryne Sandberg .75 .23
345 Sterling Hitchcock RC .20 .06
346 Chris Hammond .10 .03
347 Vince Horsman .10 .03
348 Butch Henry .10 .03
349 Dann Howitt .10 .03
350 Roger McDowell .10 .03
351 Jack Morris .20 .06
352 Bill Krueger .10 .03
353 Cris Colon .10 .03
354 Joe Vitko .10 .03
355 Willie McGee .20 .06
356 Jay Baller .10 .03
357 Pat Mahomes .10 .03
358 Roger Mason .10 .03
359 Jerry Nielsen .10 .03
360 Tom Pagnozzi .10 .03
361 Kevin Baez .10 .03
362 Tim Scott .10 .03
363 Domingo Martinez RC .10 .03
364 Kirt Manwaring .10 .03
365 Rafael Palmeiro .30 .09
366 Ray Lankford .10 .03
367 Tim McIntosh .10 .03
368 Jessie Hollins .10 .03
369 Scott Leius .10 .03
370 Bill Doran .10 .03
371 Sam Militello .10 .03
372 Ryan Bowen .10 .03
373 Dave Henderson .10 .03
374 Dan Smith RR .10 .03
375 Steve Reed RR RC .10 .03
376 Jose Offerman .10 .03
377 Kevin Brown .20 .06
378 Darrin Fletcher .10 .03
379 Duane Ward .10 .03
380 Wayne Kirby RR .10 .03
381 Steve Scarsone .10 .03
382 Mariano Duncan .10 .03
383 Ken Ryan RC .10 .03
384 Lloyd McClendon .10 .03
385 Brian Holman .10 .03
386 Braulio Castillo .10 .03
387 Danny Leon .10 .03
388 Omar Olivares .10 .03
389 Kevin Wickander .10 .03
390 Fred McGriff .30 .09
391 Phil Clark .10 .03
392 Darren Lewis .10 .03
393 Phil Hiatt .10 .03
394 Mike Morgan .10 .03
395 Shane Mack .10 .03
396 Dennis Eckersley CL .20 .06
Art Kusnyer CO
397 David Segui .10 .03
398 Rafael Belliard .10 .03
399 Tim Naehring .10 .03
400 Frank Castillo .10 .03
401 Joe Grahe .10 .03
402 Reggie Sanders .10 .03
403 Roberto Hernandez .10 .03
404 Luis Gonzalez .20 .06
405 Carlos Baerga .10 .03
406 Carlos Hernandez .10 .03
407 Pedro Astacio RR .10 .03
408 Mel Rojas .10 .03
409 Scott Livingstone .10 .03
410 Chico Walker .10 .03
411 Brian McRae .10 .03
412 Ben Rivera .10 .03
413 Ricky Bones .10 .03
414 Andy Van Slyke .20 .06
415 Chuck Knoblauch .20 .06
416 Luis Alicea .10 .03
417 Bob Wickman .10 .03
418 Doug Brocail .10 .03
419 Scott Brosius .20 .06
420 Rod Beck .10 .03
421 Edgar Martinez .30 .09
422 Ryan Klesko .20 .06
423 Nolan Ryan 2.00 .60
424 Rey Sanchez .10 .03
425 Roberto Alomar .30 .09
426 Barry Larkin .30 .09
427 Mike Mussina .30 .09
428 Jeff Bagwell .30 .09
429 Mo Vaughn .20 .06
430 Eric Karros .20 .06
431 John Orton .10 .03
432 Wil Cordero .10 .03
433 Jack McDowell .10 .03
434 Howard Johnson .10 .03
435 Albert Belle .20 .06
436 John Kruk .20 .06
437 Skeeter Barnes .10 .03
438 Don Slaught .10 .03
439 Rusty Meacham .10 .03
440 Tim Laker RR RC .10 .03
441 Robin Yount .75 .23
442 Brian Jordan .20 .06
443 Kevin Tapani .10 .03
444 Gary Sheffield .20 .06
445 Rich Monteleone .10 .03
446 Will Clark .50 .15
447 Jerry Browne .10 .03
448 Jeff Treadway .10 .03
449 Mike Schooler .10 .03
450 Mike Harkey .10 .03
451 Julio Franco .20 .06
452 Kevin Young RR .20 .06
453 Kelly Gruber .10 .03
454 Jose Rijo .10 .03
455 Mike Devereaux .10 .03
456 Andujar Cedeno .10 .03
457 Damion Easley RR .10 .03
458 Kevin Gross .10 .03
459 Matt Young .10 .03
460 Matt Stairs .10 .03
461 Luis Polonia .10 .03
462 Dwight Gooden .20 .06
463 Warren Newson .10 .03
464 Jose DeLeon .10 .03
465 Jose Mesa .10 .03
466 Danny Cox .10 .03
467 Dan Gladden .10 .03
468 Gerald Perry .10 .03
469 Mike Boddicker .10 .03
470 Jeff Gardner .10 .03
471 Doug Henry .10 .03
472 Mike Benjamin .10 .03
473 Dan Peltier RR .10 .03
474 Mike Stanton .10 .03
475 John Smiley .10 .03
476 Dwight Smith .10 .03
477 Jim Leyritz .10 .03
478 Dwayne Henry .10 .03
479 Mark McGwire 1.25 .35
480 Pete Incaviglia .10 .03
481 Dave Cochrane .10 .03
482 Eric Davis .20 .06
483 John Olerud .20 .06
484 Kent Bottenfield .10 .03
485 Mark McLemore .10 .03
486 Dave Magadan .10 .03
487 John Marzano .10 .03
488 Ruben Amaro .10 .03
489 Rob Ducey .10 .03
490 Stan Belinda .10 .03
491 Dan Pasqua .10 .03
492 Joe Magrane .10 .03
493 Brook Jacoby .10 .03
494 Gene Harris .10 .03
495 Mark Leiter .10 .03
496 Bryan Hickerson .10 .03
497 Tom Gordon .10 .03
498 Pete Smith .10 .03
499 Chris Bosio .10 .03
500 Shawn Boskie .10 .03
501 Dave West .10 .03
502 Milt Hill .10 .03
503 Pat Kelly .10 .03
504 Joe Boever .10 .03
505 Terry Steinbach .10 .03
506 Butch Huskey RR .10 .03
507 David Valle .10 .03
508 Mike Scioscia .10 .03
509 Kenny Rogers .20 .06
510 Moises Alou .20 .06
511 David Wells .20 .06
512 Mackey Sasser .10 .03
513 Todd Frohwirth .10 .03
514 Ricky Jordan .10 .03
515 Mike Gardiner .10 .03
516 Gary Redus .10 .03
517 Gary Gaetti .20 .06
518 Checklist .10 .03
519 Carlton Fisk .30 .09
520 Ozzie Smith .75 .23
521 Rod Nichols .10 .03
522 Benito Santiago .20 .06
523 Bill Gullickson .10 .03
524 Robby Thompson .10 .03
525 Mike Macfarlane .10 .03
526 Sid Bream .10 .03
527 Darryl Hamilton .10 .03
528 Checklist .10 .03
529 Jeff Tackett .10 .03
530 Greg Olson .10 .03
531 Bob Zupcic .10 .03
532 Mark Grace .30 .09
533 Steve Frey .10 .03
534 Dave Martinez .10 .03
535 Robin Ventura .20 .06
536 Casey Candaele .10 .03
537 Kenny Lofton .20 .06
538 Jay Howell .10 .03
539 Fern.Ramsey RR RC .10 .03
540 Larry Walker .30 .09
541 Cecil Fielder .20 .06
542 Lee Guetterman .10 .03
543 Keith Miller .10 .03
544 Len Dykstra .20 .06
545 B.J. Surhoff .20 .06
546 Bob Walk .10 .03
547 Brian Harper .10 .03
548 Lee Smith .20 .06
549 Danny Tartabull .10 .03
550 Frank Seminara .10 .03
551 Henry Mercedes .10 .03
552 Dave Righetti .20 .06
553 Ken Griffey Jr. .75 .23
554 Tom Glavine .30 .09
555 Juan Gonzalez .30 .09
556 Jim Bullinger .10 .03
557 Derek Bell .10 .03
558 Cesar Hernandez .10 .03
559 Cal Ripken 1.50 .45
560 Eddie Taubensee .10 .03
561 John Flaherty .10 .03
562 Todd Benzinger .10 .03
563 Hubie Brooks .10 .03
564 Delino DeShields .10 .03
565 Tim Raines .20 .06
566 Sid Fernandez .10 .03
567 Steve Olin .10 .03
568 Tommy Greene .10 .03
569 Buddy Groom .10 .03
570 Randy Tomlin .10 .03
571 Hipolito Pichardo .10 .03
572 Rene Arocha RR RC .20 .06
573 Mike Fetters .10 .03
574 Felix Jose .10 .03
575 Gene Larkin .10 .03
576 Bruce Hurst .10 .03
577 Bernie Williams .30 .09
578 Trevor Wilson .10 .03
579 Bob Welch .10 .03
580 David Justice .20 .06
581 Randy Johnson .50 .15
582 Jose Vizcaino .10 .03
583 Jeff Huson .10 .03
584 Rob Maurer RR .10 .03
585 Todd Stottlemyre .10 .03
586 Joe Oliver .10 .03
587 Bob Milacki .10 .03
588 Rob Murphy .10 .03
589 Greg Pirkl RR .10 .03
590 Lenny Harris .10 .03
591 Luis Rivera .10 .03
592 John Wetteland .20 .06
593 Mark Langston .10 .03
594 Bobby Bonilla .20 .06
595 Esteban Beltre .10 .03
596 Mike Hartley .10 .03
597 Felix Fermin .10 .03
598 Carlos Garcia .10 .03
599 Frank Tanana .10 .03
600 Pedro Guerrero .20 .06
601 Terry Shumpert .10 .03
602 Wally Whitehurst .10 .03
603 Kevin Seitzer .10 .03
604 Chris James .10 .03
605 Greg Gohr RR .10 .03
606 Mark Wohlers .10 .03
607 Kirby Puckett .50 .15
608 Greg Maddux .75 .23
609 Don Mattingly 1.25 .35
610 Greg Cadaret .10 .03
611 Dave Stewart .20 .06
612 Mark Portugal .10 .03
613 Pete O'Brien .10 .03
614 Bob Ojeda .10 .03
615 Joe Carter .20 .06
616 Pete Young .10 .03
617 Sam Horn .10 .03
618 Vince Coleman .10 .03
619 Wade Boggs .30 .09
620 Todd Pratt RC .20 .06
621 Ron Tingley .10 .03
622 Doug Drabek .10 .03
623 Scott Hemond .10 .03
624 Tim Jones .10 .03
625 Dennis Cook .10 .03
626 Jose Melendez .10 .03
627 Mike Munoz .10 .03
628 Jim Pena .10 .03
629 Gary Thurman .10 .03
630 Charlie Leibrandt .10 .03
631 Scott Fletcher .10 .03
632 Andre Dawson .20 .06
633 Greg Gagne .10 .03
634 Greg Swindell .10 .03
635 Kevin Maas .10 .03
636 Xavier Hernandez .10 .03
637 Ruben Sierra .10 .03
638 Dmitri Young RR .20 .06
639 Harold Reynolds .20 .06
640 Tom Goodwin .10 .03
641 Todd Burns .10 .03
642 Jeff Fassero .10 .03
643 Dave Winfield .20 .06
644 Willie Randolph .20 .06
645 Luis Mercedes .10 .03
646 Dale Murphy .50 .15
647 Danny Darwin .10 .03
648 Dennis Moeller .10 .03
649 Chuck Crim .10 .03
650 Checklist .10 .03
651 Shawn Abner .10 .03
652 Tracy Woodson .10 .03
653 Scott Scudder .10 .03
654 Tom Lampkin .10 .03
655 Alan Trammell .20 .06
656 Cory Snyder .10 .03
657 Chris Gwynn .10 .03
658 Lonnie Smith .10 .03
659 Jim Austin .10 .03
660 Rob Picciolo CL .10 .03
661 Tim Hulett .10 .03
662 Marvin Freeman .10 .03
663 Greg A. Harris .10 .03
664 Heathcliff Slocumb .10 .03
665 Mike Butcher .10 .03
666 Steve Foster .10 .03
667 Donn Pall .10 .03
668 Darryl Kile .20 .06
669 Jesse Levis .10 .03
670 Jim Gott .10 .03
671 Mark Hutton RR .10 .03
672 Brian Drahman .10 .03
673 Chad Kreuter .10 .03
674 Tony Fernandez .10 .03
675 Jose Lind .10 .03
676 Kyle Abbott .10 .03
677 Dan Plesac .10 .03
678 Barry Bonds 1.25 .35
679 Chili Davis .20 .06
680 Stan Royer .10 .03
681 Scott Kamieniecki .10 .03
682 Carlos Martinez .10 .03
683 Mike Moore .10 .03
684 Candy Maldonado .10 .03
685 Jeff Nelson .10 .03
686 Lou Whitaker .20 .06
687 Jose Guzman .10 .03
688 Manuel Lee .10 .03
689 Bob MacDonald .10 .03
690 Scott Bankhead .10 .03
691 Alan Mills .10 .03
692 Brian Williams .10 .03
693 Tom Brunansky .10 .03
694 Lenny Webster .10 .03
695 Greg Briley .10 .03
696 Paul O'Neill .30 .09
697 Joey Cora .10 .03
698 Charlie O'Brien .10 .03
699 Junior Ortiz .10 .03
700 Ron Darling .10 .03
701 Tony Phillips .10 .03
702 William Pennyfeather .10 .03
703 Mark Gubicza .10 .03
704 Steve Hosey RR .10 .03
705 Henry Cotto .10 .03
706 David Hulse RC .10 .03
707 Mike Pagliarulo .10 .03
708 Dave Stieb .10 .03
709 Melido Perez .10 .03
710 Jimmy Key .20 .06
711 Jeff Russell .10 .03
712 David Cone .20 .06
713 Russ Swan .10 .03
714 Mark Guthrie .10 .03
715 Checklist .10 .03
716 Al Martin RR .10 .03
717 Randy Knorr .10 .03
718 Mike Stanley .10 .03
719 Rick Sutcliffe .20 .06
720 Terry Leach .10 .03
721 Chipper Jones RR .50 .15
722 Jim Eisenreich .10 .03
723 Tom Henke .10 .03
724 Jeff Frye .10 .03
725 Harold Baines .20 .06
726 Scott Sanderson .10 .03
727 Tom Foley .10 .03
728 Bryan Harvey .10 .03
729 Tom Edens .10 .03
730 Eric Young .10 .03
731 Dave Weathers .10 .03
732 Spike Owen .10 .03
733 Scott Aldred .10 .03
734 Cris Carpenter .10 .03
735 Dion James .10 .03
736 Joe Girardi .10 .03
737 Nigel Wilson RR .10 .03
738 Scott Chiamparino .10 .03
739 Jeff Reardon .20 .06
740 Willie Blair .10 .03
741 Jim Corsi .10 .03
742 Ken Patterson .10 .03
743 Andy Ashby .10 .03
744 Rob Natal .10 .03
745 Kevin Bass .10 .03
746 Freddie Benavides .10 .03
747 Chris Donnels .10 .03
748 Kerry Woodson .10 .03
749 Calvin Jones .10 .03
750 Gary Scott .10 .03
751 Joe Orsulak .10 .03
752 Armando Reynoso .10 .03
753 Monty Fariss .10 .03
754 Billy Hatcher .10 .03
755 Denis Boucher .10 .03
756 Walt Weiss .10 .03
757 Mike Fitzgerald .10 .03
758 Rudy Seanez .10 .03
759 Bret Barberie .10 .03
760 Mo Sanford .10 .03
761 Pedro Castellano .10 .03
762 Chuck Carr .10 .03
763 Steve Howe .10 .03
764 Andres Galarraga .20 .06
765 Jeff Conine .20 .06
766 Ted Power .10 .03
767 Butch Henry .10 .03
768 Steve Decker .10 .03
769 Storm Davis .10 .03
770 Vinny Castilla .20 .06
771 Junior Felix .10 .03
772 Walt Terrell .10 .03
773 Brad Ausmus .10 .03
774 Jamie McAndrew .10 .03
775 Milt Thompson .10 .03
776 Charlie Hayes .10 .03
777 Jack Armstrong .10 .03
778 Dennis Rasmussen .10 .03
779 Darren Holmes .10 .03
780 Alex Arias .10 .03
781 Randy Bush .10 .03
782 Javy Lopez .30 .09
783 Dante Bichette .20 .0
784 John Johnstone RC .10 .0
785 Rene Gonzales .10 .0
786 Alex Cole .10 .0
787 Jeromy Burnitz RR .20 .0
788 Michael Huff .10 .0
789 Anthony Telford .10 .0
790 Jerald Clark .10 .0
791 Joel Johnston .10 .0
792 David Nied RR .10 .0

1993 Donruss Diamond King

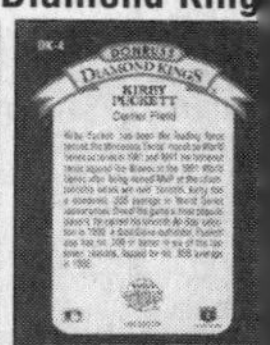

These standard-size cards, commemorati
Donruss' annual selection of the games top pla
ers, were randomly inserted in 1993 Donru
packs. The first 15 cards were available in t
first series of the 1993 Donruss and cards 16-
were inserted with the second series. The car
are gold-foil stamped and feature player portra
by noted sports artist Dick Perez. Card numbe
27-28 honor the first draft picks of the ne
Florida Marlins and Colorado Rockies franchi
es. Collectors 16 years of age and younger co
enter Donruss' Diamond King contest by writi
an essay of 75 words or less explaining w
their favorite Diamond King player was and wh
Winners were awarded one of 30 framed wate
colors at the National Convention, held
Chicago, July 22-25, 1993.

	Nm-Mt	Ex-Mt
COMPLETE SET (31)	30.00	9.0
COMPLETE SERIES 1 (15)	20.00	6.0
COMPLETE SERIES 2 (16)	10.00	3.0
DK1 Ken Griffey Jr.	5.00	1.5
DK2 Ryne Sandberg	5.00	1.5
DK3 Roger Clemens	6.00	1.8
DK4 Kirby Puckett	3.00	.9
DK5 Bill Swift	.60	.1
DK6 Larry Walker	2.00	.6
DK7 Juan Gonzalez	2.00	.6
DK8 Wally Joyner	1.25	.3
DK9 Andy Van Slyke	1.25	.3
DK10 Robin Ventura	1.25	.3
DK11 Bip Roberts	.60	.1
DK12 Roberto Kelly	.60	.1
DK13 Carlos Baerga	.60	.1
DK14 Orel Hershiser	1.25	.3
DK15 Cecil Fielder	1.25	.3
DK16 Robin Yount	5.00	1.5
DK17 Darren Daulton	1.25	.3
DK18 Mark McGwire	8.00	2.4
DK19 Tom Glavine	2.00	.6
DK20 Roberto Alomar	2.00	.6
DK21 Gary Sheffield	1.25	.3
DK22 Bob Tewksbury	.60	.1
DK23 Brady Anderson	1.25	.3
DK24 Craig Biggio	2.00	.6
DK25 Eddie Murray	3.00	.9
DK26 Luis Polonia	.60	.1
DK27 Nigel Wilson	.60	.1
DK28 David Nied	.60	.1
DK29 Pat Listach ROY	.60	.1
DK30 Eric Karros ROY	1.25	.3
DK31 Checklist 1-31	1.00	.3

1993 Donruss Elite

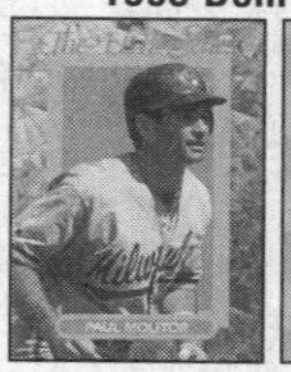

The numbering on the 1993 Elite cards follow
consecutively after that of the 1992 Elite serie
cards, and each of the 10,000 Elite cards is ser
ally numbered. Cards 19-27 were rando
inserts in 1993 Donruss series I foil packs whi
cards 28-36 were inserted in series II packs. Th
backs of the Elite cards also carry the seri
number ("X" of 10,000) as well as the card num
ber. The Signature Series Will Clark card wa
randomly inserted in 1993 Donruss foil pack
he personally autographed 5,000 card
Featuring a Dick Perez portrait, the ten thousan
Legends Series cards honor Robin Yount for hi
3,000th hit achievement.

	Nm-Mt	Ex-Mt
19 Fred McGriff	15.00	4.50
20 Ryne Sandberg	40.00	12.00
21 Eddie Murray	25.00	7.50
22 Paul Molitor	15.00	4.50
23 Barry Larkin	15.00	4.50
24 Don Mattingly	50.00	15.00
25 Dennis Eckersley	15.00	4.50
26 Roberto Alomar	15.00	4.50
27 Edgar Martinez	15.00	4.50
28 Gary Sheffield	15.00	4.50
29 Darren Daulton	15.00	4.50
30 Larry Walker	15.00	4.50
31 Barry Bonds	50.00	15.00
32 Andy Van Slyke	15.00	4.50
33 Mark McGwire	50.00	15.00
34 Cecil Fielder	15.00	4.50
35 Dave Winfield	15.00	4.50
36 Juan Gonzalez	15.00	4.50
L3 Robin Yount (Legend Series)	25.00	7.50
S3 Will Clark AU (Signature Series)	50.00	15.00

1993 Donruss Long Ball Leaders

andomly inserted in 26-card magazine distrib-tor packs (1-9 in series I and 10-18 in series II), hese standard-size cards feature some of MLB's utstanding sluggers.

	Nm-Mt	Ex-Mt
OMPLETE SET (18)	60.00	18.00
OMPLETE SERIES 1 (9)	30.00	9.00
OMPLETE SERIES 2 (9)	30.00	9.00
L1 Rob Deer	1.00	.30
L2 Fred McGriff	3.00	.90
L3 Albert Belle	2.00	.60
L4 Mark McGwire	12.00	3.60
L5 David Justice	2.00	.60
L6 Jose Canseco	5.00	1.50
L7 Kent Hrbek	2.00	.60
L8 Roberto Alomar	3.00	.90
L9 Ken Griffey Jr.	8.00	2.40
L10 Frank Thomas	5.00	1.50
L11 Darryl Strawberry	2.00	.60
L12 Felix Jose	1.00	.30
L13 Cecil Fielder	2.00	.60
L14 Juan Gonzalez	3.00	.90
L15 Ryne Sandberg	8.00	2.40
L16 Gary Sheffield	2.00	.60
L17 Jeff Bagwell	3.00	.90
L18 Larry Walker	3.00	.90

1993 Donruss MVPs

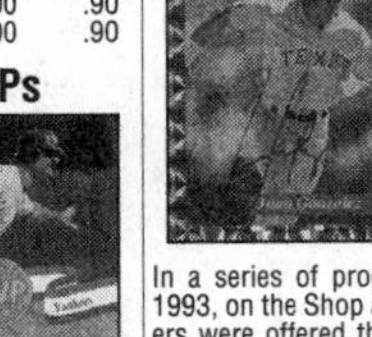

hese twenty-six standard size MVP cards were ssued 13 cards in each series, and they were nserted one per 23-card jumbo packs.

	Nm-Mt	Ex-Mt
OMPLETE SET (26)	30.00	9.00
OMPLETE SERIES 1 (13)	10.00	3.00
OMPLETE SERIES 2 (13)	20.00	6.00
Luis Polonia	.40	.12
Frank Thomas	2.00	.60
George Brett	5.00	1.50
Paul Molitor	1.25	.35
Don Mattingly	5.00	1.50
Roberto Alomar	1.25	.35
Terry Pendleton	.75	.23
Eric Karros	.75	.23
Larry Walker	1.25	.35
0 Eddie Murray	2.00	.60
1 Darren Daulton	.75	.23
2 Ray Lankford	.40	.12
3 Will Clark	2.00	.60
4 Cal Ripken	6.00	1.80
5 Roger Clemens	4.00	1.20
6 Carlos Baerga	.40	.12
7 Cecil Fielder	.75	.23
8 Kirby Puckett	2.00	.60
9 Mark McGwire	5.00	1.50
20 Ken Griffey Jr.	3.00	.90
21 Juan Gonzalez	1.25	.35
22 Ryne Sandberg	3.00	.90
23 Bip Roberts	.40	.12
24 Jeff Bagwell	1.25	.35
25 Barry Bonds	5.00	1.50
26 Gary Sheffield	.75	.23

1993 Donruss Spirit of the Game

These 20 standard-size cards were randomly inserted in 1993 Donruss packs and packed approximately two per box. Cards 1-10 were first-series inserts, and cards 11-20 were second-series inserts. The fronts feature borderless glossy color action player photos.

	Nm-Mt	Ex-Mt
COMPLETE SET (20)	20.00	6.00
COMPLETE SERIES 1 (10)	8.00	2.40
COMPLETE SERIES 2 (10)	12.00	3.60
SG1 Mike Bordick Turning Two	.50	.15
SG2 Dave Justice Play at the Plate	1.00	.30
SG3 Roberto Alomar In There	1.50	.45
SG4 Dennis Eckersley Pumped	1.00	.30
SG5 Juan Gonzalez and Jose Canseco Dynamic Duo	2.50	.75
SG6 George Bell and Frank Thomas ... Gone	2.50	.75
SG7 Wade Boggs and Luis Polonia Safe or Out	1.50	.45
SG8 Will Clark The Thrill	2.50	.75
SG9 Bip Roberts Safe at Home	.50	.15
SG10 Cecil Fielder Rob Deer Mickey Tettleton Thirty 3	.50	.15
SG11 Kenny Lofton Bag Bandit	1.00	.30
SG12 Gary Sheffield Fred McGriff Back to Back	2.50	.75
SG13 Greg Gagne Barry Larkin	.50	.15
SG14 Ryne Sandberg The Ball Stops Here	4.00	1.20
SG15 Carlos Baerga Gary Gaetti Over the Top	.50	.15
SG16 Danny Tartabull At the Wall	.50	.15
SG17 Brady Anderson Head First	1.00	.30
SG18 Frank Thomas Big Hurt	2.50	.75
SG19 Kevin Gross No Hitter	.50	.15
SG20 Robin Yount 3,000 Hits	4.00	1.20

1993 Donruss Elite Dominators

In a series of programs broadcast Dec. 8-13, 1993, on the Shop at Home cable network, viewers were offered the opportunity to purchase a factory-sealed box of either 1993 Donruss I or II, which included one Elite Dominator card produced especially for the promotion. The set retailed for 99.00 plus 6.00 for postage and handling. 5,000 serial-numbered sets were produced and half of the cards for Nolan Ryan, Juan Gonzalez, Paul Molitor, and Don Mattingly were signed by the player. The entire print run of 100,000 cards were reportedly purchased by the Shop at Home network and were to be offered periodically over the network. The production number, out of a total of 5,000 produced, is shown at the bottom.

	Nm-Mt	Ex-Mt
COMP.UNSIG. SET (20)	300.00	90.00
1 Ryne Sandberg	20.00	6.00
2 Fred McGriff	6.00	1.80
3 Greg Maddux	25.00	7.50
4 Ron Gant	5.00	1.50
5 David Justice	8.00	2.40
6 Don Mattingly	20.00	6.00
7 Tim Salmon	12.00	3.60
8 Mike Piazza	40.00	12.00
9 John Olerud	5.00	1.50
10 Nolan Ryan	40.00	12.00
11 Juan Gonzalez	8.00	2.40
12 Ken Griffey Jr.	20.00	6.00
13 Frank Thomas	12.00	3.60
14 Tom Glavine	6.00	1.80
15 George Brett	20.00	6.00
16 Barry Bonds	20.00	6.00
17 Albert Belle	5.00	1.50
18 Paul Molitor	8.00	2.40
19 Cal Ripken	40.00	12.00
20 Roberto Alomar	8.00	2.40
AU6 Don Mattingly AU	50.00	15.00
AU10 Nolan Ryan AU	100.00	30.00
AU11 Juan Gonzalez AU	25.00	7.50
AU18 Paul Molitor AU	30.00	9.00

1994 Donruss

The 1994 Donruss set was issued in two separate series of 330 standard-size cards for a total of 660. Cards were issued in foil wrapped packs. The fronts feature borderless color player action photos on front. There are no notable Rookie Cards in this set.

	Nm-Mt	Ex-Mt
COMPLETE SET (660)	30.00	9.00
COMP.SERIES 1 (330)	15.00	4.50
COMP.SERIES 2 (330)	15.00	4.50
1 Nolan Ryan	4.00	1.20
2 Mike Piazza	1.50	.45
3 Moises Alou	.30	.09
4 Ken Griffey Jr.	1.25	.35
5 Gary Sheffield	.30	.09
6 Roberto Alomar	.50	.15
7 John Kruk	.30	.09
8 Gregg Olson	.15	.04
9 Gregg Jefferies	.15	.04
10 Tony Gwynn	1.00	.30
11 Chad Curtis	.15	.04
12 Craig Biggio	.50	.15
13 John Burkett	.15	.04
14 Carlos Baerga	.15	.04
15 Robin Yount	1.25	.35
16 Dennis Eckersley	.30	.09
17 Dwight Gooden	.30	.09
18 Ryne Sandberg	1.25	.35
19 Rickey Henderson	.75	.23
20 Jack McDowell	.15	.04
21 Jay Bell	.30	.09
22 Kevin Brown	.30	.09
23 Robin Ventura	.30	.09
24 Paul Molitor	.50	.15
25 David Justice	.30	.09
26 Rafael Palmeiro	.50	.15
27 Cecil Fielder	.30	.09
28 Chuck Knoblauch	.30	.09
29 Dave Hollins	.15	.04
30 Jimmy Key	.30	.09
31 Mark Langston	.15	.04
32 Darryl Kile	.30	.09
33 Ruben Sierra	.15	.04
34 Ron Gant	.30	.09
35 Ozzie Smith	1.25	.35
36 Wade Boggs	.50	.15
37 Marquis Grissom	.30	.09
38 Will Clark	.75	.23
39 Kenny Lofton	.30	.09
40 Cal Ripken	2.50	.75
41 Steve Avery	.15	.04
42 Mo Vaughn	.30	.09
43 Brian McRae	.15	.04
44 Mickey Tettleton	.15	.04
45 Barry Larkin	.50	.15
46 Charlie Hayes	.15	.04
47 Kevin Appier	.30	.09
48 Robby Thompson	.15	.04
49 Juan Gonzalez	.50	.15
50 Paul O'Neill	.50	.15
51 Marcos Armas	.15	.04
52 Mike Butcher	.15	.04
53 Ken Caminiti	.30	.09
54 Pat Borders	.15	.04
55 Pedro Munoz	.15	.04
56 Tim Belcher	.15	.04
57 Paul Assenmacher	.15	.04
58 Damon Berryhill	.15	.04
59 Ricky Bones	.15	.04
60 Rene Arocha	.15	.04
61 Shawn Boskie	.15	.04
62 Pedro Astacio	.15	.04
63 Frank Bolick	.15	.04
64 Bud Black	.15	.04
65 Sandy Alomar Jr.	.15	.04
66 Rich Amaral	.15	.04
67 Luis Aquino	.15	.04
68 Kevin Baez	.15	.04
69 Mike Devereaux	.15	.04
70 Andy Ashby	.15	.04
71 Larry Andersen	.15	.04
72 Steve Cooke	.15	.04
73 Mario Diaz	.15	.04
74 Rob Deer	.15	.04
75 Bobby Ayala	.15	.04
76 Freddie Benavides	.15	.04
77 Stan Belinda	.15	.04
78 John Doherty	.15	.04
79 Willie Banks	.15	.04
80 Spike Owen	.15	.04
81 Mike Bordick	.15	.04
82 Chili Davis	.30	.09
83 Luis Gonzalez	.30	.09
84 Ed Sprague	.15	.04
85 Jeff Reboulet	.15	.04
86 Jason Bere	.15	.04
87 Mark Hutton	.15	.04
88 Jeff Blauser	.15	.04
89 Cal Eldred	.15	.04
90 Bernard Gilkey	.15	.04
91 Frank Castillo	.15	.04
92 Jim Gott	.15	.04
93 Greg Colbrunn	.15	.04
94 Jeff Brantley	.15	.04
95 Jeremy Hernandez	.15	.04
96 Norm Charlton	.15	.04
97 Alex Arias	.15	.04
98 John Franco	.30	.09
99 Chris Hoiles	.15	.04
100 Brad Ausmus	.15	.04
101 Wes Chamberlain	.15	.04
102 Mark Dewey	.15	.04
103 Benji Gil	.15	.04
104 John Dopson	.15	.04
105 John Smiley	.15	.04
106 David Nied	.15	.04
107 George Brett	2.00	.60
108 Kirk Gibson	.30	.09
109 Larry Casian	.15	.04
110 Ryne Sandberg CL	.75	.23
111 Brent Gates	.15	.04
112 Damion Easley	.15	.04
113 Pete Harnisch	.15	.04
114 Danny Cox	.15	.04
115 Kevin Tapani	.15	.04
116 Roberto Hernandez	.15	.04
117 Domingo Jean	.15	.04
118 Sid Bream	.15	.04
119 Doug Henry	.15	.04
120 Omar Olivares	.15	.04
121 Mike Harkey	.15	.04
122 Carlos Hernandez	.15	.04
123 Jeff Fassero	.15	.04
124 Dave Burba	.15	.04
125 Wayne Kirby	.15	.04
126 John Cummings	.15	.04
127 Bret Barberie	.15	.04
128 Todd Hundley	.15	.04
129 Tim Hulett	.15	.04
130 Phil Clark	.15	.04
131 Danny Jackson	.15	.04
132 Tom Foley	.15	.04
133 Donald Harris	.15	.04
134 Scott Fletcher	.15	.04
135 Johnny Ruffin	.15	.04
136 Jerald Clark	.15	.04
137 Billy Brewer	.15	.04
138 Dan Gladden	.15	.04
139 Eddie Guardado	.15	.04
140 Cal Ripken CL	.75	.23
141 Scott Hemond	.15	.04
142 Steve Frey	.15	.04
143 Xavier Hernandez	.15	.04
144 Mark Eichhorn	.15	.04
145 Ellis Burks	.30	.09
146 Jim Leyritz	.15	.04
147 Mark Lemke	.15	.04
148 Pat Listach	.15	.04
149 Donovan Osborne	.15	.04
150 Glenallen Hill	.15	.04
151 Orel Hershiser	.30	.09
152 Darrin Fletcher	.15	.04
153 Royce Clayton	.15	.04
154 Derek Lilliquist	.15	.04
155 Mike Felder	.15	.04
156 Jeff Conine	.30	.09
157 Ryan Thompson	.15	.04
158 Ben McDonald	.15	.04
159 Ricky Gutierrez	.15	.04
160 Terry Mulholland	.15	.04
161 Carlos Garcia	.15	.04
162 Tom Henke	.15	.04
163 Mike Greenwell	.15	.04
164 Thomas Howard	.15	.04
165 Joe Girardi	.15	.04
166 Hubie Brooks	.15	.04
167 Greg Gohr	.15	.04
168 Chip Hale	.15	.04
169 Rick Honeycutt	.15	.04
170 Hilly Hathaway	.15	.04
171 Todd Jones	.15	.04
172 Tony Fernandez	.15	.04
173 Bo Jackson	.75	.23
174 Bobby Munoz	.15	.04
175 Greg McMichael	.15	.04
176 Graeme Lloyd	.15	.04
177 Tom Pagnozzi	.15	.04
178 Derrick May	.15	.04
179 Pedro Martinez	.75	.23
180 Ken Hill	.15	.04
181 Bryan Hickerson	.15	.04
182 Jose Mesa	.15	.04
183 Dave Fleming	.15	.04
184 Henry Cotto	.15	.04
185 Jeff Kent	.30	.09
186 Mark McLemore	.15	.04
187 Trevor Hoffman	.30	.09
188 Todd Pratt	.15	.04
189 Blas Minor	.15	.04
190 Charlie Leibrandt	.15	.04
191 Tony Pena	.15	.04
192 Larry Luebbers RC	.15	.04
193 Greg W. Harris	.15	.04
194 David Cone	.30	.09
195 Bill Gullickson	.15	.04
196 Brian Harper	.15	.04
197 Steve Karsay	.15	.04
198 Greg Myers	.15	.04
199 Mark Portugal	.15	.04
200 Pat Hentgen	.15	.04
201 Mike LaValliere	.15	.04
202 Mike Stanley	.15	.04
203 Kent Mercker	.15	.04
204 Dave Nilsson	.15	.04
205 Erik Pappas	.15	.04
206 Mike Morgan	.15	.04
207 Roger McDowell	.15	.04
208 Mike Lansing	.15	.04
209 Kirt Manwaring	.15	.04
210 Randy Milligan	.15	.04
211 Erik Hanson	.15	.04
212 Orestes Destrade	.15	.04
213 Mike Maddux	.15	.04
214 Alan Mills	.15	.04
215 Tim Mauser	.15	.04
216 Ben Rivera	.15	.04
217 Don Slaught	.15	.04
218 Bob Patterson	.15	.04
219 Carlos Quintana	.15	.04
220 Tim Raines CL	.15	.04
221 Hal Morris	.15	.04
222 Darren Holmes	.15	.04
223 Chris Gwynn	.15	.04
224 Chad Kreuter	.15	.04
225 Mike Hartley	.15	.04
226 Scott Lydy	.15	.04
227 Eduardo Perez	.15	.04
228 Greg Swindell	.15	.04
229 Al Leiter	.30	.09
230 Scott Radinsky	.15	.04
231 Bob Wickman	.15	.04
232 Otis Nixon	.15	.04
233 Kevin Reimer	.15	.04
234 Geronimo Pena	.15	.04
235 Kevin Roberson	.15	.04
236 Jody Reed	.15	.04
237 Kirk Rueter	.30	.09
238 Willie McGee	.30	.09
239 Charles Nagy	.15	.04
240 Tim Leary	.15	.04
241 Carl Everett	.30	.09
242 Charlie O'Brien	.15	.04
243 Mike Pagliarulo	.15	.04
244 Kerry Taylor	.15	.04
245 Kevin Stocker	.15	.04
246 Joel Johnston	.15	.04
247 Geno Petralli	.15	.04
248 Jeff Russell	.15	.04
249 Joe Oliver	.15	.04
250 Roberto Mejia	.15	.04
251 Chris Haney	.15	.04
252 Bill Krueger	.15	.04
253 Shane Mack	.15	.04
254 Terry Steinbach	.15	.04
255 Luis Polonia	.15	.04
256 Eddie Taubensee	.15	.04
257 Dave Stewart	.30	.09
258 Tim Raines	.30	.09
259 Bernie Williams	.50	.15
260 John Smoltz	.50	.15
261 Kevin Seitzer	.15	.04
262 Bob Tewksbury	.15	.04
263 Bob Scanlan	.15	.04
264 Henry Rodriguez	.15	.04
265 Tim Scott	.15	.04
266 Scott Sanderson	.15	.04
267 Eric Plunk	.15	.04
268 Edgar Martinez	.50	.15
269 Charlie Hough	.30	.09
270 Joe Orsulak	.15	.04
271 Harold Reynolds	.30	.09
272 Tim Teufel	.15	.04
273 Bobby Thigpen	.15	.04
274 Randy Tomlin	.15	.04
275 Gary Redus	.15	.04
276 Ken Ryan	.15	.04
277 Tim Pugh	.15	.04
278 Jayhawk Owens	.15	.04
279 Phil Hiatt	.15	.04
280 Alan Trammell	.30	.09
281 Dave McCarty	.15	.04
282 Bob Welch	.15	.04
283 J.T. Snow	.30	.09
284 Brian Williams	.15	.04
285 Devon White	.30	.09
286 Steve Sax	.15	.04
287 Tony Tarasco	.15	.04
288 Bill Spiers	.15	.04
289 Allen Watson	.15	.04
290 Rickey Henderson CL	.50	.15
291 Jose Vizcaino	.15	.04
292 Darryl Strawberry	.30	.09
293 John Wetteland	.30	.09
294 Bill Swift	.15	.04
295 Jeff Treadway	.15	.04
296 Tino Martinez	.50	.15
297 Richie Lewis	.15	.04
298 Bret Saberhagen	.30	.09
299 Arthur Rhodes	.15	.04
300 Guillermo Velasquez	.15	.04
301 Milt Thompson	.15	.04
302 Doug Strange	.15	.04
303 Aaron Sele	.15	.04
304 Bip Roberts	.15	.04
305 Bruce Ruffin	.15	.04
306 Jose Lind	.15	.04
307 David Wells	.30	.09
308 Bobby Witt	.15	.04
309 Mark Wohlers	.15	.04
310 B.J. Surhoff	.30	.09
311 Mark Whiten	.15	.04
312 Turk Wendell	.15	.04
313 Raul Mondesi	.30	.09
314 Brian Turang RC	.15	.04
315 Chris Hammond	.15	.04
316 Tim Bogar	.15	.04
317 Brad Pennington	.15	.04
318 Tim Worrell	.15	.04
319 Mitch Williams	.15	.04
320 Rondell White	.30	.09
321 Frank Viola	.30	.09
322 Manny Ramirez	.50	.15
323 Gary Wayne	.15	.04
324 Mike Macfarlane	.15	.04
325 Russ Springer	.15	.04
326 Tim Wallach	.15	.04
327 Salomon Torres	.15	.04
328 Omar Vizquel	.50	.15
329 Andy Tomberlin RC	.15	.04
330 Chris Sabo	.15	.04
331 Mike Mussina	.50	.15
332 Andy Benes	.15	.04
333 Darren Daulton	.30	.09
334 Orlando Merced	.15	.04
335 Mark McGwire	2.00	.60
336 Dave Winfield	.30	.09
337 Sammy Sosa	1.25	.35
338 Eric Karros	.30	.09
339 Greg Vaughn	.15	.04
340 Don Mattingly	2.00	.60
341 Frank Thomas	.75	.23
342 Fred McGriff	.50	.15
343 Kirby Puckett	.75	.23
344 Roberto Kelly	.15	.04
345 Wally Joyner	.30	.09
346 Andres Galarraga	.30	.09
347 Bobby Bonilla	.30	.09
348 Benito Santiago	.30	.09
349 Barry Bonds	2.00	.60
350 Delino DeShields	.15	.04
351 Albert Belle	.30	.09
352 Randy Johnson	.75	.23
353 Tim Salmon	.50	.15
354 John Olerud	.30	.09
355 Dean Palmer	.30	.09
356 Roger Clemens	1.50	.45
357 Jim Abbott	.50	.15
358 Mark Grace	.50	.15
359 Ozzie Guillen	.15	.04
360 Lou Whitaker	.30	.09
361 Jose Rijo	.15	.04
362 Jeff Montgomery	.15	.04
363 Chuck Finley	.30	.09
364 Tom Glavine	.50	.15
365 Jeff Bagwell	.50	.15
366 Joe Carter	.30	.09
367 Ray Lankford	.15	.04
368 Ramon Martinez	.15	.04
369 Jay Buhner	.30	.09
370 Matt Williams	.30	.09
371 Larry Walker	.50	.15
372 Jose Canseco	.75	.23
373 Lenny Dykstra	.30	.09
374 Bryan Harvey	.15	.04
375 Andy Van Slyke	.30	.09
376 Ivan Rodriguez	.75	.23
377 Kevin Mitchell	.15	.04
378 Travis Fryman	.30	.09
379 Duane Ward	.15	.04
380 Greg Maddux	1.25	.35
381 Scott Servais	.15	.04
382 Greg Olson	.15	.04
383 Rey Sanchez	.15	.04
384 Tom Kramer	.15	.04
385 David Valle	.15	.04
386 Eddie Murray	.75	.23
387 Kevin Higgins	.15	.04
388 Dan Wilson	.15	.04
389 Todd Frohwirth	.15	.04
390 Gerald Williams	.15	.04
391 Hipolito Pichardo	.15	.04
392 Pat Meares	.15	.04
393 Luis Lopez	.15	.04
394 Ricky Jordan	.15	.04
395 Bob Walk	.15	.04
396 Sid Fernandez	.15	.04
397 Todd Worrell	.15	.04
398 Darryl Hamilton	.15	.04
399 Randy Myers	.15	.04
400 Rod Brewer	.15	.04
401 Lance Blankenship	.15	.04
402 Steve Finley	.30	.09
403 Phil Leftwich RC	.15	.04

404 Juan Guzman .15 .04
405 Anthony Young .15 .04
406 Jeff Gardner .15 .04
407 Ryan Bowen .15 .04
408 Fernando Valenzuela .30 .09
409 David West .15 .04
410 Kenny Rogers .30 .09
411 Bob Zupcic .15 .04
412 Eric Young .15 .04
413 Bret Boone .30 .09
414 Danny Tartabull .15 .04
415 Bob MacDonald .15 .04
416 Ron Karkovice .15 .04
417 Scott Cooper .15 .04
418 Dante Bichette .30 .09
419 Tripp Cromer .15 .04
420 Billy Ashley .15 .04
421 Roger Smithberg .15 .04
422 Dennis Martinez .30 .09
423 Mike Blowers .15 .04
424 Darren Lewis .15 .04
425 Junior Ortiz .15 .04
426 Butch Huskey .15 .04
427 Jimmy Poole .15 .04
428 Walt Weiss .15 .04
429 Scott Bankhead .15 .04
430 Deion Sanders .50 .15
431 Scott Bullett .15 .04
432 Jeff Huson .15 .04
433 Tyler Green .15 .04
434 Billy Hatcher .15 .04
435 Bob Hamelin .15 .04
436 Reggie Sanders .15 .04
437 Scott Erickson .15 .04
438 Steve Reed .15 .04
439 Randy Velarde .15 .04
440 Tony Gwynn CL .50 .15
441 Terry Leach .15 .04
442 Danny Bautista .15 .04
443 Kent Hrbek .30 .09
444 Rick Wilkins .15 .04
445 Tony Phillips .15 .04
446 Dion James .15 .04
447 Joey Cora .15 .04
448 Andre Dawson .30 .09
449 Pedro Castellano .15 .04
450 Tom Gordon .15 .04
451 Rob Dibble .30 .09
452 Ron Darling .15 .04
453 Chipper Jones .75 .23
454 Joe Grahe .15 .04
455 Domingo Cedeno .15 .04
456 Tom Edens .15 .04
457 Mitch Webster .15 .04
458 Jose Bautista .15 .04
459 Troy O'Leary .15 .04
460 Todd Zeile .15 .04
461 Sean Berry .15 .04
462 Brad Holman RC .15 .04
463 Dave Martinez .15 .04
464 Mark Lewis .15 .04
465 Paul Carey .15 .04
466 Jack Armstrong .15 .04
467 David Telgheder .15 .04
468 Gene Harris .15 .04
469 Danny Darwin .15 .04
470 Kim Batiste .15 .04
471 Tim Wakefield .30 .09
472 Craig Lefferts .15 .04
473 Jacob Brumfield .15 .04
474 Lance Painter .15 .04
475 Milt Cuyler .15 .04
476 Melido Perez .15 .04
477 Derek Parks .15 .04
478 Gary DiSarcina .15 .04
479 Steve Bedrosian .15 .04
480 Eric Anthony .15 .04
481 Julio Franco .30 .09
482 Tommy Greene .15 .04
483 Pat Kelly .15 .04
484 Nate Minchey .15 .04
485 William Pennyfeather .15 .04
486 Harold Baines .30 .09
487 Howard Johnson .15 .04
488 Angel Miranda .15 .04
489 Scott Sanders .15 .04
490 Shawon Dunston .15 .04
491 Mel Rojas .15 .04
492 Jeff Nelson .15 .04
493 Archi Cianfrocco .15 .04
494 Al Martin .15 .04
495 Mike Gallego .15 .04
496 Mike Henneman .15 .04
497 Armando Reynoso .15 .04
498 Mickey Morandini .15 .04
499 Rick Renteria .15 .04
500 Rick Sutcliffe .30 .09
501 Bobby Jones .15 .04
502 Gary Gaetti .30 .09
503 Rick Aguilera .15 .04
504 Todd Stottlemyre .15 .04
505 Mike Mohler .15 .04
506 Mike Stanton .15 .04
507 Jose Guzman .15 .04
508 Kevin Rogers .15 .04
509 Chuck Carr .15 .04
510 Chris Jones .15 .04
511 Brent Mayne .15 .04
512 Greg Harris .15 .04
513 Dave Henderson .15 .04
514 Eric Hillman .15 .04
515 Dan Peltier .15 .04
516 Craig Shipley .15 .04
517 John Valentin .15 .04
518 Wilson Alvarez .15 .04
519 Andujar Cedeno .15 .04
520 Troy Neel .15 .04
521 Tom Candiotti .15 .04
522 Matt Mieske .15 .04
523 Jim Thome .75 .23
524 Lou Frazier .15 .04
525 Mike Jackson .15 .04
526 Pedro Martinez RC .15 .04
527 Roger Pavlik .15 .04
528 Kent Bottenfield .15 .04
529 Felix Jose .15 .04
530 Mark Guthrie .15 .04
531 Steve Farr .15 .04
532 Craig Paquette .15 .04
533 Doug Jones .15 .04
534 Luis Alicea .15 .04
535 Cory Snyder .15 .04
536 Paul Sorrento .15 .04
537 Nigel Wilson .15 .04
538 Jeff King .15 .04
539 Willie Greene .15 .04
540 Kirk McCaskill .15 .04
541 Al Osuna .15 .04
542 Greg Hibbard .15 .04
543 Brett Butler .30 .09
544 Jose Valentin .15 .04
545 Wil Cordero .15 .04
546 Chris Bosio .15 .04
547 Jamie Moyer .30 .09
548 Jim Eisenreich .15 .04
549 Vinny Castilla .30 .09
550 Dave Winfield CL .15 .04
551 John Roper .15 .04
552 Lance Johnson .15 .04
553 Scott Kamieniecki .15 .04
554 Mike Moore .15 .04
555 Steve Buechele .15 .04
556 Terry Pendleton .30 .09
557 Todd Van Poppel .15 .04
558 Rob Butler .15 .04
559 Zane Smith .15 .04
560 David Hulse .15 .04
561 Tim Costo .15 .04
562 John Habyan .15 .04
563 Terry Jorgensen .15 .04
564 Matt Nokes .15 .04
565 Kevin McReynolds .15 .04
566 Phil Plantier .15 .04
567 Chris Turner .15 .04
568 Carlos Delgado .50 .15
569 John Jaha .15 .04
570 Dwight Smith .15 .04
571 John Vander Wal .15 .04
572 Trevor Wilson .15 .04
573 Felix Fermin .15 .04
574 Marc Newfield .15 .04
575 Jeromy Burnitz .30 .09
576 Leo Gomez .15 .04
577 Curt Schilling .30 .09
578 Kevin Young .15 .04
579 Jerry Spradlin RC .15 .04
580 Curt Leskanic .15 .04
581 Carl Willis .15 .04
582 Alex Fernandez .15 .04
583 Mark Holzemer .15 .04
584 Domingo Martinez .15 .04
585 Pete Smith .15 .04
586 Brian Jordan .30 .09
587 Kevin Gross .15 .04
588 J.R. Phillips .15 .04
589 Chris Nabholz .15 .04
590 Bill Wertz .15 .04
591 Derek Bell .15 .04
592 Brady Anderson .30 .09
593 Matt Turner .15 .04
594 Pete Incaviglia .15 .04
595 Greg Gagne .15 .04
596 John Flaherty .15 .04
597 Scott Livingstone .15 .04
598 Rod Bolton .15 .04
599 Mike Perez .15 .04
600 Roger Clemens CL .75 .23
601 Tony Castillo .15 .04
602 Henry Mercedes .15 .04
603 Mike Fetters .15 .04
604 Rod Beck .15 .04
605 Damon Buford .15 .04
606 Matt Whiteside .15 .04
607 Shawn Green .75 .23
608 Midre Cummings .15 .04
609 Jeff McNeely .15 .04
610 Danny Sheaffer .15 .04
611 Paul Wagner .15 .04
612 Torey Lovullo .15 .04
613 Javier Lopez .30 .09
614 Mariano Duncan .15 .04
615 Doug Brocail .15 .04
616 Dave Hansen .15 .04
617 Ryan Klesko .30 .09
618 Eric Davis .30 .09
619 Scott Ruffcorn .15 .04
620 Mike Trombley .15 .04
621 Jaime Navarro .15 .04
622 Rheal Cormier .15 .04
623 Jose Offerman .15 .04
624 David Segui .15 .04
625 Robb Nen .30 .09
626 Dave Gallagher .15 .04
627 Julian Tavarez RC .30 .09
628 Chris Gomez .15 .04
629 Jeffrey Hammonds .15 .04
630 Scott Brosius .30 .09
631 Willie Blair .15 .04
632 Doug Drabek .15 .04
633 Bill Wegman .15 .04
634 Jeff McKnight .15 .04
635 Rich Rodriguez .15 .04
636 Steve Trachsel .15 .04
637 Buddy Groom .15 .04
638 Sterling Hitchcock .15 .04
639 Chuck McElroy .15 .04
640 Rene Gonzales .15 .04
641 Dan Plesac .15 .04
642 Jeff Branson .15 .04
643 Darrell Whitmore .15 .04
644 Paul Quantrill .15 .04
645 Rich Rowland .15 .04
646 Curtis Pride RC .30 .09
647 Erik Plantenberg RC .15 .04
648 Albie Lopez .15 .04
649 Rich Batchelor RC .15 .04
650 Lee Smith .30 .09
651 Cliff Floyd .30 .09
652 Pete Schourek .15 .04
653 Reggie Jefferson .15 .04
654 Bill Haselman .15 .04
655 Steve Hosey .15 .04
656 Mark Clark .15 .04
657 Mark Davis .15 .04
658 Dave Magadan .15 .04
659 Candy Maldonado .15 .04
660 Mark Langston CL .15 .04

1994 Donruss Special Edition

Issued in two series of 50 cards, this 100-card standard-size set of 1994 Donruss Special Edition represents a Gold edition parallel of the best players in the game. The first 50 cards correspond to cards 1-50 in the first series, while the second 50 cards correspond to cards 331-380 in the second series. The cards were issued one per pack or two per jumbo pack.

Nm-Mt Ex-Mt
*STARS: .75X TO 2X BASIC CARDS...

1994 Donruss Anniversary '84

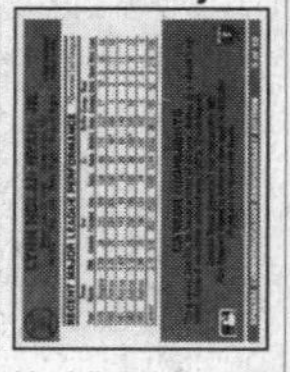

Randomly inserted in hobby foil packs at a rate of one in 12, this ten-card standard-size set reproduces selected cards from the 1984 Donruss baseball set. The cards feature white bordered color player photos on their fronts. The cards are numbered on the back at the bottom right as "X of 10," and also carry the numbers from the original 1984 set at the upper left.

Nm-Mt Ex-Mt
COMPLETE SET (10) 60.00 18.00
1 Joe Carter 2.00 .60
2 Robin Yount 8.00 2.40
3 George Brett 12.00 3.60
4 Rickey Henderson 5.00 1.50
5 Nolan Ryan 25.00 7.50
6 Cal Ripken 15.00 4.50
7 Wade Boggs UER 3.00 .90
1983 runs 10, should be 100
8 Don Mattingly 12.00 3.60
9 Ryne Sandberg 8.00 2.40
10 Tony Gwynn 6.00 1.80

1994 Donruss Award Winner Jumbos

This 10-card set was issued one per jumbo foil and Canadian foil boxes and spotlights players that won various awards in 1993. Cards 1-5 were included in first series boxes and 6-10 with the second series. The cards measure approximately 3 1/2" by 5". Ten-thousand of each card were produced. Card fronts are full-bleed with a color player photo and the Award Winner logo at the top. The backs are individually numbered out of 10,000.

Nm-Mt Ex-Mt
COMPLETE SET (10) 80.00 24.00
COMPLETE SERIES 1 (5) 60.00 18.00
COMPLETE SERIES 2 (5) 20.00 6.00
1 Barry Bonds MVP 20.00 6.00
2 Greg Maddux CY 12.00 3.60
3 Mike Piazza ROY 15.00 4.50
4 Barry Bonds HR King 20.00 6.00
5 Kirby Puckett AS MVP 8.00 2.40
6 Frank Thomas MVP 8.00 2.40
7 Jack McDowell CY 1.50 .45
8 Tim Salmon ROY 5.00 1.50
9 Juan Gonzalez HR King 5.00 1.50
10 Paul Molitor WS MVP 6.00 1.80

1994 Donruss Diamond Kings

This 30-card standard-size set was split in two series. Cards 1-14 and 29 were randomly inserted in first series packs, while cards 15-28 and 30 were inserted in second series packs. With each series, the insertion rate was one in nine. The fronts feature full-bleed player portraits by noted sports artist Dick Perez. The cards are numbered on the back with the prefix DK.

Nm-Mt Ex-Mt
COMPLETE SET (30) 50.00 15.00
*JUMBO DK's: .75X TO 2X BASIC DK'S
ONE JUMBO DK PER RETAIL BOX
DK1 Barry Bonds 6.00 1.80
DK2 Mo Vaughn 1.00 .30
DK3 Steve Avery .50 .15
DK4 Tim Salmon 1.50 .45
DK5 Rick Wilkins .50 .15
DK6 Brian Harper .50 .15
DK7 Andres Galarraga 1.00 .30
DK8 Albert Belle 1.00 .30
DK9 John Kruk 1.00 .30
DK10 Ivan Rodriguez 2.50 .75
DK11 Tony Gwynn 3.00 .90
DK12 Brian McRae .50 .15
DK13 Bobby Bonilla 1.00 .30
DK14 Ken Griffey Jr. 4.00 1.20
DK15 Mike Piazza 5.00 1.50
DK16 Don Mattingly 6.00 1.80
DK17 Barry Larkin 1.50 .45
DK18 Ruben Sierra .50 .15
DK19 Orlando Merced .50 .15
DK20 Greg Vaughn .50 .15
DK21 Gregg Jefferies .50 .15
DK22 Cecil Fielder 1.00 .30
DK23 Moises Alou 1.00 .30
DK24 John Olerud 1.00 .30
DK25 Gary Sheffield 1.00 .30
DK26 Mike Mussina 1.50 .45
DK27 Jeff Bagwell 1.50 .45
DK28 Frank Thomas 2.50 .75
DK29 Dave Winfield 1.00 .30
DK30 Checklist .50 .15

1994 Donruss Dominators

This 20-card, standard-size set was randomly inserted in all packs at a rate of one in 12. The 10 series 1 cards feature the top home run hitters of the '90s, while the 10 series 2 cards depict the decade's batting average leaders.

Nm-Mt Ex-Mt
COMP.SER.1 SET (10) 20.00 6.00
COMP.SER.2 SET (10) 20.00 6.00
*JUMBOS: .75X TO 2X BASIC DOM
ONE JUMBO DOMINATOR PER HOBBY BOX
A1 Cecil Fielder 1.00 .30
A2 Barry Bonds 6.00 1.80
A3 Fred McGriff 1.50 .45
A4 Matt Williams 1.00 .30
A5 Joe Carter 1.00 .30
A6 Juan Gonzalez 1.50 .45
A7 Jose Canseco 2.50 .75
A8 Ron Gant 1.00 .30
A9 Ken Griffey Jr. 4.00 1.20
A10 Mark McGwire 6.00 1.80
B1 Tony Gwynn 3.00 .90
B2 Frank Thomas 2.50 .75
B3 Paul Molitor 1.50 .45
B4 Edgar Martinez 1.50 .45
B5 Kirby Puckett 2.50 .75
B6 Ken Griffey Jr. 4.00 1.20
B7 Barry Bonds 6.00 1.80
B8 Willie McGee 1.00 .30
B9 Lenny Dykstra 1.00 .30
B10 John Kruk 1.00 .30

1994 Donruss Elite

This 12-card set was issued in two series of six. Using a continued numbering system from previous years, cards 37-42 were randomly inserted in first series foil packs with cards 43-48 a second series offering. The cards measure the standard size. Only 10,000 of each card were produced. .

Nm-Mt Ex-Mt
COMPLETE SET (12) 140.00 42.50
COMPLETE SERIES 1 (6) 60.00 18.00
COMPLETE SERIES 2 (6) 80.00 24.00
37 Frank Thomas 10.00 3.00
38 Tony Gwynn 15.00 4.50
39 Tim Salmon 10.00 3.00
40 Albert Belle 10.00 3.00
41 John Kruk 10.00 3.00
42 Juan Gonzalez 10.00 3.00
43 John Olerud 10.00 3.00
44 Barry Bonds 30.00 9.00
45 Ken Griffey Jr. 20.00 6.00
46 Mike Piazza 20.00 6.00
47 Jack McDowell 10.00 3.00
48 Andres Galarraga 10.00 3.00

1994 Donruss Long Ball Leaders

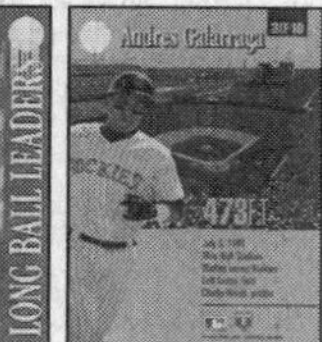

Inserted in second series hobby foil packs at a rate of one in 12, this 10-card standard-size set features some of top home run hitters and the distance of their longest home run of 1993.

Nm-Mt Ex-Mt
COMPLETE SET (10) 30.00 9.00
1 Cecil Fielder 1.50 .45
2 Dean Palmer 1.50 .45
3 Andres Galarraga 1.50 .45
4 Bo Jackson 4.00 1.20
5 Ken Griffey Jr. 6.00 1.80
6 David Justice 1.50 .45
7 Mike Piazza 8.00 2.40
8 Frank Thomas 4.00 1.20
9 Barry Bonds 10.00 3.00
10 Juan Gonzalez 2.50 .75

1994 Donruss MVPs

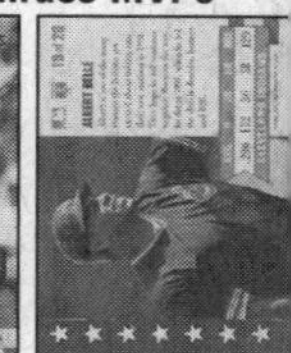

Inserted at a rate of one per first and secon series jumbo pack, this 28-card standard-siz set was split into two series of 14; one player fo each team. The first 14 are of National Leagu players with the latter group being America Leaguers. Full-bleed card fronts feature a action photo of the player with "MVP" in large re (American League) or blue (National) letters the bottom. The player's name and, for Americ League player cards only, team name a beneath the "MVP".

Nm-Mt Ex-Mt
COMPLETE SET (28) 60.00 18.00
COMPLETE SERIES 1 (14) 15.00 4.50
COMPLETE SERIES 2 (14) 50.00 15.00
1 David Justice 1.50 .45
2 Mark Grace 2.50 .75
3 Jose Rijo .75 .23
4 Andres Galarraga 1.50 .45
5 Bryan Harvey .75 .23
6 Jeff Bagwell 2.50 .75
7 Mike Piazza 8.00 2.40
8 Moises Alou 1.50 .45
9 Bobby Bonilla 1.50 .45
10 Len Dykstra 1.50 .45
11 Jeff King .75 .23
12 Gregg Jefferies .75 .23
13 Tony Gwynn 5.00 1.50
14 Barry Bonds 10.00 3.00
15 Cal Ripken Jr. 12.00 3.60
16 Mo Vaughn 1.50 .45
17 Tim Salmon 2.50 .75
18 Frank Thomas 4.00 1.20
19 Albert Belle 1.50 .45
20 Cecil Fielder 1.50 .45
21 Wally Joyner 1.50 .45
22 Greg Vaughn .75 .23
23 Kirby Puckett 4.00 1.20
24 Don Mattingly 10.00 3.00
25 Ruben Sierra .75 .23
26 Ken Griffey Jr. 6.00 1.80
27 Juan Gonzalez 2.50 .75
28 John Olerud 1.50 .45

1994 Donruss Spirit of the Game

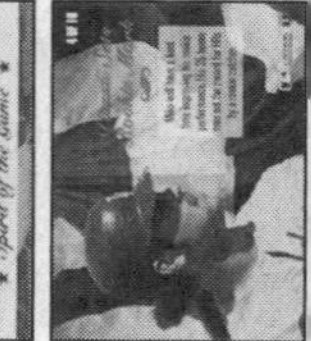

This ten card set features a selction of the game top stars. Cards 1-5 were randomly inserted i first-series magazine jumbo packs and cards 6 10 in second series magazine jumbo packs.

Nm-Mt Ex-Mt
COMPLETE SERIES 1 (5) 25.00 7.50
COMPLETE SERIES 2 (5) 20.00 6.00
*JUMBOS: .75X TO 2X BASIC SOG
ONE JUMBO SPIRIT PER MAG.JUMBO BOX
1 John Olerud 2.00 .60
2 Barry Bonds 12.00 3.60
3 Ken Griffey Jr. 8.00 2.40
4 Mike Piazza 10.00 3.00
5 Juan Gonzalez 3.00 .90
6 Frank Thomas 5.00 1.50
7 Tim Salmon 3.00 .90
8 David Justice 2.00 .60
9 Don Mattingly 12.00 3.60
10 Lenny Dykstra 2.00 .60

1995 Donruss

The 1995 Donruss set consists of 550 standard-size cards. The first series had 330 cards while 220 cards comprised the second series. The fronts feature borderless color action player photos. A second, smaller color player photo in a homeplate shape with team color-coded borders appears in the lower left corner. There are no key Rookie Cards in this set. To preview the product prior to it's public release, Donruss inted up additional quantities of cards 5, 8, 20, 2, 55, 275, 331 and 340 and mailed them to ealers and hobby media.

	Nm-Mt	Ex-Mt
OMPLETE SET (550)	30.00	9.00
OMP.SERIES 1 (330)	20.00	6.00
OMP.SERIES 2 (220)	10.00	3.00
David Justice	.30	.09
Rene Arocha	.15	.04
Sandy Alomar Jr.	.15	.04
Luis Lopez	.15	.04
Mike Piazza	1.25	.35
Bobby Jones	.15	.04
Damion Easley	.15	.04
Barry Bonds	2.00	.60
Mike Mussina	.50	.15
) Kevin Seitzer	.15	.04
John Smiley	.15	.04
2 Wm.VanLandingham	.15	.04
3 Ron Darling	.15	.04
4 Walt Weiss	.15	.04
5 Mike Lansing	.15	.04
6 Allen Watson	.15	.04
7 Aaron Sele	.15	.04
8 Randy Johnson	.75	.23
9 Dean Palmer	.30	.09
0 Jeff Bagwell	.50	.15
1 Curt Schilling	.30	.09
2 Darrell Whitmore	.15	.04
3 Steve Trachsel	.15	.04
4 Dan Wilson	.15	.04
5 Steve Finley	.30	.09
6 Bret Boone	.30	.09
7 Charles Johnson	.30	.09
8 Mike Stanton	.15	.04
9 Ismael Valdes	.15	.04
0 Salomon Torres	.15	.04
1 Eric Anthony	.15	.04
2 Spike Owen	.15	.04
3 Joey Cora	.15	.04
4 Robert Eenhoorn	.15	.04
5 Rick White	.15	.04
6 Omar Vizquel	.50	.15
7 Carlos Delgado	.30	.09
8 Eddie Williams	.15	.04
9 Shawon Dunston	.15	.04
0 Darrin Fletcher	.15	.04
1 Leo Gomez	.15	.04
2 Juan Gonzalez	.50	.15
3 Luis Alicea	.15	.04
4 Ken Ryan	.15	.04
5 Lou Whitaker	.30	.09
6 Mike Blowers	.15	.04
7 Willie Blair	.15	.04
8 Todd Van Poppel	.15	.04
9 Roberto Alomar	.50	.15
0 Ozzie Smith	1.25	.35
1 Sterling Hitchcock	.15	.04
2 Mo Vaughn	.30	.09
3 Rick Aguilera	.15	.04
4 Kent Mercker	.15	.04
5 Don Mattingly	2.00	.60
6 Bob Scanlan	.15	.04
7 Wilson Alvarez	.15	.04
8 Jose Mesa	.15	.04
9 Scott Kamieniecki	.15	.04
0 Todd Jones	.15	.04
1 John Kruk	.30	.09
2 Mike Stanley	.15	.04
3 Tino Martinez	.50	.15
4 Eddie Zambrano	.15	.04
5 Todd Hundley	.15	.04
6 Jamie Moyer	.30	.09
7 Rich Amaral	.15	.04
8 Jose Valentin	.15	.04
9 Alex Gonzalez	.15	.04
0 Kurt Abbott	.15	.04
1 Delino DeShields	.15	.04
2 Brian Anderson	.15	.04
3 John Vander Wal	.15	.04
74 Turner Ward	.15	.04
75 Tim Raines	.30	.09
76 Mark Acre	.15	.04
77 Jose Offerman	.15	.04
78 Jimmy Key	.30	.09
79 Mark Whiten	.15	.04
80 Mark Gubicza	.15	.04
81 Darren Hall	.15	.04
82 Travis Fryman	.30	.09
83 Cal Ripken	2.50	.75
84 Geronimo Berroa	.15	.04
85 Bret Barberie	.15	.04
86 Andy Ashby	.15	.04
87 Steve Avery	.15	.04
88 Rich Becker	.15	.04
89 John Valentin	.15	.04
90 Glenallen Hill	.15	.04
91 Carlos Garcia	.15	.04
92 Dennis Martinez	.30	.09
93 Pat Kelly	.15	.04
94 Orlando Miller	.15	.04
95 Felix Jose	.15	.04
96 Mike Kingery	.15	.04
97 Jeff Kent	.30	.09
98 Pete Incaviglia	.15	.04
99 Chad Curtis	.15	.04
100 Thomas Howard	.15	.04
101 Hector Carrasco	.15	.04
102 Tom Pagnozzi	.15	.04
103 Danny Tartabull	.15	.04
104 Donnie Elliott	.15	.04
105 Danny Jackson	.15	.04
106 Steve Dunn	.15	.04
107 Roger Salkeld	.15	.04
108 Jeff King	.15	.04
109 Cecil Fielder	.30	.09
110 Paul Molitor CL	.30	.09
111 Denny Neagle	.30	.09
112 Troy Neel	.15	.04
113 Rod Beck	.15	.04
114 Alex Rodriguez	2.00	.60
115 Joey Eischen	.15	.04
116 Tom Candiotti	.15	.04
117 Ray McDavid	.15	.04
118 Vince Coleman	.15	.04
119 Pete Harnisch	.15	.04
120 David Nied	.15	.04
121 Pat Rapp	.15	.04
122 Sammy Sosa	1.25	.35
123 Steve Reed	.15	.04
124 Jose Oliva	.15	.04
125 Ricky Bottalico	.15	.04
126 Jose DeLeon	.15	.04
127 Pat Hentgen	.15	.04
128 Will Clark	.75	.23
129 Mark Dewey	.15	.04
130 Greg Vaughn	.15	.04
131 Darren Dreifort	.15	.04
132 Ed Sprague	.15	.04
133 Lee Smith	.30	.09
134 Charles Nagy	.15	.04
135 Phil Plantier	.15	.04
136 Jason Jacome	.15	.04
137 Jose Lima	.15	.04
138 J.R. Phillips	.15	.04
139 J.T. Snow	.30	.09
140 Michael Huff	.15	.04
141 Billy Brewer	.15	.04
142 Jeromy Burnitz	.30	.09
143 Ricky Bones	.15	.04
144 Carlos Rodriguez	.15	.04
145 Luis Gonzalez	.30	.09
146 Mark Lemke	.15	.04
147 Al Martin	.15	.04
148 Mike Bordick	.15	.04
149 Robb Nen	.30	.09
150 Wil Cordero	.15	.04
151 Edgar Martinez	.50	.15
152 Gerald Williams	.15	.04
153 Esteban Beltre	.15	.04
154 Mike Moore	.15	.04
155 Mark Langston	.15	.04
156 Mark Clark	.15	.04
157 Bobby Ayala	.15	.04
158 Rick Wilkins	.15	.04
159 Bobby Munoz	.15	.04
160 Brett Butler CL	.15	.04
161 Scott Erickson	.15	.04
162 Paul Molitor	.50	.15
163 Jon Lieber	.15	.04
164 Jason Grimsley	.15	.04
165 Norberto Martin	.15	.04
166 Javier Lopez	.30	.09
167 Brian McRae	.15	.04
168 Gary Sheffield	.30	.09
169 Marcus Moore	.15	.04
170 John Hudek	.15	.04
171 Kelly Stinnett	.15	.04
172 Chris Gomez	.15	.04
173 Rey Sanchez	.15	.04
174 Juan Guzman	.15	.04
175 Chan Ho Park	.30	.09
176 Terry Shumpert	.15	.04
177 Steve Ontiveros	.15	.04
178 Brad Ausmus	.15	.04
179 Tim Davis	.15	.04
180 Billy Ashley	.15	.04
181 Vinny Castilla	.30	.09
182 Bill Spiers	.15	.04
183 Randy Knorr	.15	.04
184 Brian Hunter	.15	.04
185 Pat Meares	.15	.04
186 Steve Buechele	.15	.04
187 Kirt Manwaring	.15	.04
188 Tim Naehring	.15	.04
189 Matt Mieske	.15	.04
190 Josias Manzanillo	.15	.04
191 Greg McMichael	.15	.04
192 Chuck Carr	.15	.04
193 Midre Cummings	.15	.04
194 Darryl Strawberry	.30	.09
195 Greg Gagne	.15	.04
196 Steve Cooke	.15	.04
197 Woody Williams	.15	.04
198 Ron Karkovice	.15	.04
199 Phil Leftwich	.15	.04
200 Jim Thome	.75	.23
201 Brady Anderson	.30	.09
202 Pedro A.Martinez	.15	.04
203 Steve Karsay	.15	.04
204 Reggie Sanders	.15	.04
205 Bill Risley	.15	.04
206 Jay Bell	.30	.09
207 Kevin Brown	.30	.09
208 Tim Scott	.15	.04
209 Lenny Dykstra	.30	.09
210 Willie Greene	.15	.04
211 Jim Eisenreich	.15	.04
212 Cliff Floyd	.30	.09
213 Otis Nixon	.15	.04
214 Eduardo Perez	.15	.04
215 Manuel Lee	.15	.04
216 Armando Benitez	.30	.09
217 Dave McCarty	.15	.04
218 Scott Livingstone	.15	.04
219 Chad Kreuter	.15	.04
220 Don Mattingly CL	1.00	.30
221 Brian Jordan	.30	.09
222 Matt Whiteside	.15	.04
223 Jim Edmonds	.50	.15
224 Tony Gwynn	1.00	.30
225 Jose Lind	.15	.04
226 Marvin Freeman	.15	.04
227 Ken Hill	.15	.04
228 David Hulse	.15	.04
229 Joe Hesketh	.15	.04
230 Roberto Petagine	.15	.04
231 Jeffrey Hammonds	.15	.04
232 John Jaha	.15	.04
233 John Burkett	.15	.04
234 Hal Morris	.15	.04
235 Tony Castillo	.15	.04
236 Ryan Bowen	.15	.04
237 Wayne Kirby	.15	.04
238 Brent Mayne	.15	.04
239 Jim Bullinger	.15	.04
240 Mike Lieberthal	.30	.09
241 Barry Larkin	.50	.15
242 David Segui	.15	.04
243 Joe Bautista	.15	.04
244 Hector Fajardo	.15	.04
245 Orel Hershiser	.30	.09
246 James Mouton	.15	.04
247 Scott Leius	.15	.04
248 Tom Glavine	.50	.15
249 Danny Bautista	.15	.04
250 Jose Mercedes	.15	.04
251 Marquis Grissom	.30	.09
252 Charlie Hayes	.15	.04
253 Ryan Klesko	.30	.09
254 Vicente Palacios	.15	.04
255 Matias Carrillo	.15	.04
256 Gary DiSarcina	.15	.04
257 Kirk Gibson	.30	.09
258 Garey Ingram	.15	.04
259 Alex Fernandez	.15	.04
260 John Mabry	.15	.04
261 Chris Howard	.15	.04
262 Miguel Jimenez	.15	.04
263 Heathcliff Slocumb	.15	.04
264 Albert Belle	.30	.09
265 Dave Clark	.15	.04
266 Joe Orsulak	.15	.04
267 Joey Hamilton	.15	.04
268 Mark Portugal	.15	.04
269 Kevin Tapani	.15	.04
270 Sid Fernandez	.15	.04
271 Steve Dreyer	.15	.04
272 Denny Hocking	.15	.04
273 Troy O'Leary	.15	.04
274 Milt Cuyler	.15	.04
275 Frank Thomas	.75	.23
276 Jorge Fabregas	.15	.04
277 Mike Gallego	.15	.04
278 Mickey Morandini	.15	.04
279 Roberto Hernandez	.15	.04
280 Henry Rodriguez	.15	.04
281 Garret Anderson	.30	.09
282 Bob Wickman	.15	.04
283 Gar Finnvold	.15	.04
284 Paul O'Neill	.50	.15
285 Royce Clayton	.15	.04
286 Chuck Knoblauch	.30	.09
287 Johnny Ruffin	.15	.04
288 Dave Nilsson	.15	.04
289 David Cone	.30	.09
290 Chuck McElroy	.15	.04
291 Kevin Stocker	.15	.04
292 Jose Rijo	.15	.04
293 Sean Berry	.15	.04
294 Ozzie Guillen	.15	.04
295 Chris Hoiles	.15	.04
296 Kevin Foster	.15	.04
297 Jeff Frye	.15	.04
298 Lance Johnson	.15	.04
299 Mike Kelly	.15	.04
300 Ellis Burks	.30	.09
301 Roberto Kelly	.15	.04
302 Dante Bichette	.30	.09
303 Alvaro Espinoza	.15	.04
304 Alex Cole	.15	.04
305 Rickey Henderson	.75	.23
306 Dave Weathers	.15	.04
307 Shane Reynolds	.15	.04
308 Bobby Bonilla	.30	.09
309 Junior Felix	.15	.04
310 Jeff Fassero	.15	.04
311 Darren Lewis	.15	.04
312 John Doherty	.15	.04
313 Scott Servais	.15	.04
314 Rick Helling	.15	.04
315 Pedro Martinez	.75	.23
316 Wes Chamberlain	.15	.04
317 Bryan Eversgerd	.15	.04
318 Trevor Hoffman	.30	.09
319 John Patterson	.15	.04
320 Matt Walbeck	.15	.04
321 Jeff Montgomery	.15	.04
322 Mel Rojas	.15	.04
323 Eddie Taubensee	.15	.04
324 Ray Lankford	.15	.04
325 Jose Vizcaino	.15	.04
326 Carlos Baerga	.15	.04
327 Jack Voigt	.15	.04
328 Julio Franco	.30	.09
329 Brent Gates	.15	.04
330 Kirby Puckett CL	.50	.15
331 Greg Maddux	1.25	.35
332 Jason Bere	.15	.04
333 Bill Wegman	.15	.04
334 Tuffy Rhodes	.15	.04
335 Kevin Young	.15	.04
336 Andy Benes	.15	.04
337 Pedro Astacio	.15	.04
338 Reggie Jefferson	.15	.04
339 Tim Belcher	.15	.04
340 Ken Griffey Jr.	1.25	.35
341 Mariano Duncan	.15	.04
342 Andres Galarraga	.30	.09
343 Rondell White	.30	.09
344 Cory Bailey	.15	.04
345 Bryan Harvey	.15	.04
346 John Franco	.30	.09
347 Greg Swindell	.15	.04
348 David West	.15	.04
349 Fred McGriff	.50	.15
350 Jose Canseco	.75	.23
351 Orlando Merced	.15	.04
352 Rheal Cormier	.15	.04
353 Carlos Pulido	.15	.04
354 Terry Steinbach	.15	.04
355 Wade Boggs	.50	.15
356 B.J. Surhoff	.30	.09
357 Rafael Palmeiro	.50	.15
358 Anthony Young	.15	.04
359 Tom Brunansky	.15	.04
360 Todd Stottlemyre	.15	.04
361 Chris Turner	.15	.04
362 Joe Boever	.15	.04
363 Jeff Blauser	.15	.04
364 Derek Bell	.15	.04
365 Matt Williams	.30	.09
366 Jeremy Hernandez	.15	.04
367 Joe Girardi	.15	.04
368 Mike Devereaux	.15	.04
369 Jim Abbott	.50	.15
370 Manny Ramirez	.50	.15
371 Kenny Lofton	.30	.09
372 Mark Smith	.15	.04
373 Dave Fleming	.15	.04
374 Dave Stewart	.30	.09
375 Roger Pavlik	.15	.04
376 Hipolito Pichardo	.15	.04
377 Bill Taylor	.15	.04
378 Robin Ventura	.30	.09
379 Bernard Gilkey	.15	.04
380 Kirby Puckett	.75	.23
381 Steve Howe	.15	.04
382 Devon White	.30	.09
383 Roberto Mejia	.15	.04
384 Darrin Jackson	.15	.04
385 Mike Morgan	.15	.04
386 Rusty Meacham	.15	.04
387 Bill Swift	.15	.04
388 Lou Frazier	.15	.04
389 Andy Van Slyke	.30	.09
390 Brett Butler	.30	.09
391 Bobby Witt	.15	.04
392 Jeff Conine	.30	.09
393 Tim Hyers	.15	.04
394 Terry Pendleton	.30	.09
395 Ricky Jordan	.15	.04
396 Eric Plunk	.15	.04
397 Melido Perez	.15	.04
398 Darryl Kile	.30	.09
399 Mark McLemore	.15	.04
400 Greg W.Harris	.15	.04
401 Jim Leyritz	.15	.04
402 Doug Strange	.15	.04
403 Tim Salmon	.50	.15
404 Terry Mulholland	.15	.04
405 Robby Thompson	.15	.04
406 Ruben Sierra	.15	.04
407 Tony Phillips	.15	.04
408 Moises Alou	.30	.09
409 Felix Fermin	.15	.04
410 Pat Listach	.15	.04
411 Kevin Bass	.15	.04
412 Ben McDonald	.15	.04
413 Scott Cooper	.15	.04
414 Jody Reed	.15	.04
415 Deion Sanders	.50	.15
416 Ricky Gutierrez	.15	.04
417 Gregg Jefferies	.15	.04
418 Jack McDowell	.15	.04
419 Al Leiter	.30	.09
420 Tony Longmire	.15	.04
421 Paul Wagner	.15	.04
422 Geronimo Pena	.15	.04
423 Ivan Rodriguez	.75	.23
424 Kevin Gross	.15	.04
425 Kirk McCaskill	.15	.04
426 Greg Myers	.15	.04
427 Roger Clemens	1.50	.45
428 Chris Hammond	.15	.04
429 Randy Myers	.15	.04
430 Roger Mason	.15	.04
431 Bret Saberhagen	.30	.09
432 Jeff Reboulet	.15	.04
433 John Olerud	.30	.09
434 Bill Gullickson	.15	.04
435 Eddie Murray	.75	.23
436 Pedro Munoz	.15	.04
437 Charlie O'Brien	.15	.04
438 Jeff Nelson	.15	.04
439 Mike Macfarlane	.15	.04
440 Don Mattingly CL	1.00	.30
441 Derrick May	.15	.04
442 John Roper	.15	.04
443 Darryl Hamilton	.15	.04
444 Dan Miceli	.15	.04
445 Tony Eusebio	.15	.04
446 Jerry Browne	.15	.04
447 Wally Joyner	.30	.09
448 Brian Harper	.15	.04
449 Scott Fletcher	.15	.04
450 Bip Roberts	.15	.04
451 Pete Smith	.15	.04
452 Chili Davis	.30	.09
453 Dave Hollins	.15	.04
454 Tony Pena	.15	.04
455 Butch Henry	.15	.04
456 Craig Biggio	.50	.15
457 Zane Smith	.15	.04
458 Ryan Thompson	.15	.04
459 Mike Jackson	.15	.04
460 Mark McGwire	2.00	.60
461 John Smoltz	.50	.15
462 Steve Scarsone	.15	.04
463 Greg Colbrunn	.15	.04
464 Shawn Green	.30	.09
465 David Wells	.30	.09
466 Jose Hernandez	.15	.04
467 Chip Hale	.15	.04
468 Tony Tarasco	.15	.04
469 Kevin Mitchell	.15	.04
470 Billy Hatcher	.15	.04
471 Jay Buhner	.30	.09
472 Ken Caminiti	.30	.09
473 Tom Henke	.15	.04
474 Todd Worrell	.15	.04
475 Mark Eichhorn	.15	.04
476 Bruce Ruffin	.15	.04
477 Chuck Finley	.30	.09
478 Marc Newfield	.15	.04
479 Paul Shuey	.15	.04
480 Bob Tewksbury	.15	.04
481 Ramon J.Martinez	.15	.04
482 Melvin Nieves	.15	.04
483 Todd Zeile	.15	.04
484 Benito Santiago	.30	.09
485 Stan Javier	.15	.04
486 Kirk Rueter	.15	.04
487 Andre Dawson	.30	.09
488 Eric Karros	.30	.09
489 Dave Magadan	.15	.04
490 Joe Carter CL	.15	.04
491 Randy Velarde	.15	.04
492 Larry Walker	.50	.15
493 Cris Carpenter	.15	.04
494 Tom Gordon	.15	.04
495 Dave Burba	.15	.04
496 Darren Bragg	.15	.04
497 Darren Daulton	.30	.09
498 Don Slaught	.15	.04
499 Pat Borders	.15	.04
500 Lenny Harris	.15	.04
501 Joe Ausanio	.15	.04
502 Alan Trammell	.30	.09
503 Mike Fetters	.15	.04
504 Scott Ruffcorn	.15	.04
505 Rich Rowland	.15	.04
506 Juan Samuel	.15	.04
507 Bo Jackson	.75	.23
508 Jeff Branson	.15	.04
509 Bernie Williams	.50	.15
510 Paul Sorrento	.15	.04
511 Dennis Eckersley	.30	.09
512 Pat Mahomes	.15	.04
513 Rusty Greer	.30	.09
514 Luis Polonia	.15	.04
515 Willie Banks	.15	.04
516 John Wetteland	.30	.09
517 Mike LaValliere	.15	.04
518 Tommy Greene	.15	.04
519 Mark Grace	.50	.15
520 Bob Hamelin	.15	.04
521 Scott Sanderson	.15	.04
522 Joe Carter	.30	.09
523 Jeff Brantley	.15	.04
524 Andrew Lorraine	.15	.04
525 Rico Brogna	.15	.04
526 Shane Mack	.15	.04
527 Mark Wohlers	.15	.04
528 Scott Sanders	.15	.04
529 Chris Bosio	.15	.04
530 Andujar Cedeno	.15	.04
531 Kenny Rogers	.30	.09
532 Doug Drabek	.15	.04
533 Curt Leskanic	.15	.04
534 Craig Shipley	.15	.04
535 Craig Grebeck	.15	.04
536 Cal Eldred	.15	.04
537 Mickey Tettleton	.15	.04
538 Harold Baines	.30	.09
539 Tim Wallach	.15	.04
540 Damon Buford	.15	.04
541 Lenny Webster	.15	.04
542 Kevin Appier	.30	.09
543 Raul Mondesi	.30	.09
544 Eric Young	.15	.04
545 Russ Davis	.15	.04
546 Mike Benjamin	.15	.04
547 Mike Greenwell	.15	.04
548 Scott Brosius	.30	.09
549 Brian Dorsett	.15	.04
550 Chili Davis CL	.15	.04

1995 Donruss Press Proofs

Parallel to the basic Donruss set, the Press Proofs are distinguished by the player's name, team name and Donruss logo being done in gold foil on front. The words "Press Proof" are also in gold at the top. The first 2,000 cards of the production run were stamped as such (though not serial numbered) and inserted at a rate of one in every 20 first series hobby and retail packs, 1:24 second series hobby and retail packs, 1:18 jumbo packs and 1:24 magazine packs.

	Nm-Mt	Ex-Mt
*STARS: 6X TO 15X BASIC CARDS		

1995 Donruss All-Stars

This 18-card standard-size set was randomly inserted into retail packs. The first series has the nine 1994 American League starters while the second series honored the National League starters. The cards are numbered in the upper right with either an "AL-X" or an "NL-X."

	Nm-Mt	Ex-Mt
COMPLETE SET (18)	150.00	45.00
COMPLETE SERIES 1 (9)	90.00	27.00
COMPLETE SERIES 2 (9)	60.00	18.00
AL1 Jimmy Key	3.00	.90
AL2 Ivan Rodriguez	8.00	2.40
AL3 Frank Thomas	8.00	2.40
AL4 Roberto Alomar	5.00	1.50
AL5 Wade Boggs	5.00	1.50
AL6 Cal Ripken	25.00	7.50
AL7 Joe Carter	3.00	.90
AL8 Ken Griffey Jr.	12.00	3.60
AL9 Kirby Puckett	8.00	2.40
NL1 Greg Maddux	12.00	3.60
NL2 Mike Piazza	12.00	3.60
NL3 Gregg Jefferies	1.50	.45
NL4 Mariano Duncan	1.50	.45
NL5 Matt Williams	3.00	.90
NL6 Ozzie Smith	12.00	3.60
NL7 Barry Bonds	20.00	6.00
NL8 Tony Gwynn	10.00	3.00
NL9 David Justice	3.00	.90

1995 Donruss Bomb Squad

Randomly inserted one in every 24 retail packs and one in every 16 magazine packs, this set features the top six home run hitters in the National and American League. These cards were only included in first series packs. Each of the six cards shows a different slugger on the either side of the card.

	Nm-Mt	Ex-Mt
COMPLETE SET (6)	12.00	3.60
1 Ken Griffey Matt Williams	3.00	.90
2 Frank Thomas Jeff Bagwell	2.00	.60
3 Albert Belle Barry Bonds	5.00	1.50
4 Jose Canseco Fred McGriff	2.00	.60
5 Cecil Fielder	.75	.23

	Nm-Mt	Ex-Mt
Andres Galarraga		
6 Joe Carter	.75	.23
Kevin Mitchell		

1995 Donruss Diamond Kings

The 1995 Donruss Diamond King set consists of 29 standard-size cards that were randomly inserted in packs. The fronts feature water color player portraits by noted sports artist Dick Perez. The player's name and "Diamond Kings" are in gold foil. The backs have a dark blue border with a player photo and text. The cards are numbered on back with a DK prefix.

	Nm-Mt	Ex-Mt
COMPLETE SET (29)	50.00	15.00
COMPLETE SERIES 1 (14)	20.00	6.00
COMPLETE SERIES 2 (15)	30.00	9.00
DK1 Frank Thomas	3.00	.90
DK2 Jeff Bagwell	2.00	.60
DK3 Chili Davis	1.25	.35
DK4 Dante Bichette	1.25	.35
DK5 Ruben Sierra	.60	.18
DK6 Jeff Conine	1.25	.35
DK7 Paul O'Neill	2.00	.60
DK8 Bobby Bonilla	1.25	.35
DK9 Joe Carter	1.25	.35
DK10 Moises Alou	1.25	.35
DK11 Kenny Lofton	1.25	.35
DK12 Matt Williams	1.25	.35
DK13 Kevin Seitzer	.60	.18
DK14 Sammy Sosa	5.00	1.50
DK15 Scott Cooper	.60	.18
DK16 Raul Mondesi	1.25	.35
DK17 Will Clark	3.00	.90
DK18 Lenny Dykstra	1.25	.35
DK19 Kirby Puckett	3.00	.90
DK20 Hal Morris	.60	.18
DK21 Travis Fryman	1.25	.35
DK22 Greg Maddux	5.00	1.50
DK23 Rafael Palmeiro	2.00	.60
DK24 Tony Gwynn	4.00	1.20
DK25 David Cone	1.25	.35
DK26 Al Martin	.60	.18
DK27 Ken Griffey Jr.	5.00	1.50
DK28 Gregg Jefferies	.60	.18
DK29 Checklist	.60	.18

1995 Donruss Dominators

This nine-card standard-size set was randomly inserted in second series hobby packs. Each of these cards features three of the leading players at each position. The horizontal fronts have photos of all three players and identify only their last name. The words "remove protective film" cover a significant portion of the fronts as well. The cards are numbered in the upper right corner as "X" of 9.

	Nm-Mt	Ex-Mt
COMPLETE SET (9)	25.00	7.50
1 David Cone / Mike Mussina / Greg Maddux	3.00	.90
2 Ivan Rodriguez / Mike Piazza / Darren Daulton	3.00	.90
3 Fred McGriff / Frank Thomas / Jeff Bagwell	2.00	.60
4 Roberto Alomar / Carlos Baerga / Craig Biggio	1.25	.35
5 Robin Ventura / Travis Fryman / Matt Williams	.75	.23
6 Cal Ripken / Barry Larkin / Wil Cordero	6.00	1.80
7 Albert Belle / Barry Bonds / Moises Alou	5.00	1.50
8 Ken Griffey / Kenny Lofton / Marquis Grissom	3.00	.90
9 Kirby Puckett / Paul O'Neill / Tony Gwynn	2.50	.75

1995 Donruss Elite

Randomly inserted one in every 210 Series 1 and 2 packs, this set consists of 12 standard-size cards that are numbered (49-60) based on where the previous year's set left off. The fronts contain an action photo surrounded by a marble border. Silver holographic foil borders the card on all four sides. Limited to 10,000, the backs are individually numbered, contain a small photo and write-up.

	Nm-Mt	Ex-Mt
COMPLETE SET (12)	200.00	60.00
COMPLETE SERIES 1 (6)	100.00	30.00
COMPLETE SERIES 2 (6)	100.00	30.00
49 Jeff Bagwell	12.00	3.60
50 Paul O'Neill	12.00	3.60
51 Greg Maddux	25.00	7.50
52 Mike Piazza	25.00	7.50
53 Matt Williams	12.00	3.60
54 Ken Griffey	25.00	7.50
55 Frank Thomas	15.00	4.50
56 Barry Bonds	40.00	12.00
57 Kirby Puckett	15.00	4.50
58 Fred McGriff	12.00	3.60
59 Jose Canseco	15.00	4.50
60 Albert Belle	12.00	3.60

1995 Donruss Long Ball Leaders

Inserted one in every 24 series one hobby packs, this set features eight top home run hitters.

	Nm-Mt	Ex-Mt
COMPLETE SET (8)	20.00	6.00
1 Frank Thomas	2.50	.75
2 Fred McGriff	1.50	.45
3 Ken Griffey	4.00	1.20
4 Matt Williams	1.00	.30
5 Mike Piazza	4.00	1.20
6 Jose Canseco	2.50	.75
7 Barry Bonds	6.00	1.80
8 Jeff Bagwell	1.50	.45

1995 Donruss Mound Marvels

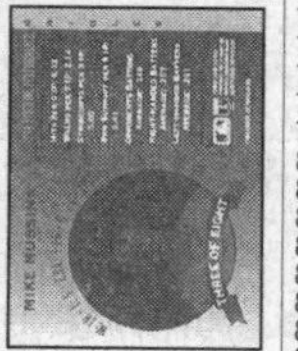

This eight-card standard-size set was randomly inserted into second series magazine jumbo and retail packs at a rate of one every 16 packs. This set features eight of the leading major league starters.

	Nm-Mt	Ex-Mt
COMPLETE SET (8)	20.00	6.00
1 Greg Maddux	6.00	1.80
2 David Cone	1.50	.45
3 Mike Mussina	2.50	.75
4 Bret Saberhagen	1.50	.45
5 Jimmy Key	1.50	.45
6 Doug Drabek	.75	.23
7 Randy Johnson	4.00	1.20
8 Jason Bere	.75	.23

1996 Donruss

The 1996 Donruss set was issued in two series of 330 and 220 cards respectively, for a total of 550. The 12-card packs had a suggested retail price of $1.79. The full-bleed fronts feature full-color action photos with the player's name is in white ink in the upper right. The horizontal backs feature season and career stats, text, vital stats and another photo. Rookie Cards in this set include Mike Cameron.

	Nm-Mt	Ex-Mt
COMPLETE SET (550)	40.00	12.00
COMP.SERIES 1 (330)	25.00	7.50
COMP.SERIES 2 (220)	15.00	4.50
1 Frank Thomas	.75	.23
2 Jason Bates	.30	.09
3 Steve Sparks	.30	.09
4 Scott Servais	.30	.09
5 Angelo Encarnacion RC	.30	.09
6 Scott Sanders	.30	.09
7 Billy Ashley	.30	.09
8 Alex Rodriguez	1.50	.45
9 Sean Bergman	.30	.09
10 Brad Radke	.30	.09
11 Andy Van Slyke	.30	.09
12 Joe Girardi	.30	.09
13 Mark Grudzielanek	.30	.09
14 Rick Aguilera	.30	.09
15 Randy Veres	.30	.09
16 Tim Bogar	.30	.09
17 Dave Veres	.30	.09
18 Kevin Stocker	.30	.09
19 Marquis Grissom	.30	.09
20 Will Clark	.75	.23
21 Jay Bell	.30	.09
22 Allen Battle	.30	.09
23 Frank Rodriguez	.30	.09
24 Terry Steinbach	.30	.09
25 Gerald Williams	.30	.09
26 Sid Roberson	.30	.09
27 Greg Zaun	.30	.09
28 Ozzie Timmons	.30	.09
29 Vaughn Eshelman	.30	.09
30 Ed Sprague	.30	.09
31 Gary DiSarcina	.30	.09
32 Joe Boever	.30	.09
33 Steve Avery	.30	.09
34 Brad Ausmus	.30	.09
35 Kirt Manwaring	.30	.09
36 Gary Sheffield	.30	.09
37 Jason Bere	.30	.09
38 Jeff Manto	.30	.09
39 David Cone	.30	.09
40 Manny Ramirez	.50	.15
41 Sandy Alomar Jr.	.30	.09
42 Curtis Goodwin	.30	.09
43 Tino Martinez	.50	.15
44 Woody Williams	.30	.09
45 Dean Palmer	.30	.09
46 Hipolito Pichardo	.30	.09
47 Jason Giambi	.30	.09
48 Lance Johnson	.30	.09
49 Bernard Gilkey	.30	.09
50 Kirby Puckett	.75	.23
51 Tony Fernandez	.30	.09
52 Alex Gonzalez	.30	.09
53 Bret Saberhagen	.30	.09
54 Lyle Mouton	.30	.09
55 Brian McRae	.30	.09
56 Mark Gubicza	.30	.09
57 Sergio Valdez	.30	.09
58 Darrin Fletcher	.30	.09
59 Steve Parris	.30	.09
60 Johnny Damon	.50	.15
61 Rickey Henderson	.75	.23
62 Darrell Whitmore	.30	.09
63 Roberto Petagine	.30	.09
64 Trenidad Hubbard	.30	.09
65 Heathcliff Slocumb	.30	.09
66 Steve Finley	.30	.09
67 Mariano Rivera	.50	.15
68 Brian L.Hunter	.30	.09
69 Jamie Moyer	.30	.09
70 Ellis Burks	.30	.09
71 Pat Kelly	.30	.09
72 Mickey Tettleton	.30	.09
73 Garret Anderson	.30	.09
74 Andy Pettitte	.50	.15
75 Glenallen Hill	.30	.09
76 Brent Gates	.30	.09
77 Lou Whitaker	.30	.09
78 David Segui	.30	.09
79 Dan Wilson	.30	.09
80 Pat Listach	.30	.09
81 Jeff Bagwell	.50	.15
82 Ben McDonald	.30	.09
83 John Valentin	.30	.09
84 John Jaha	.30	.09
85 Pete Schourek	.30	.09
86 Bryce Florie	.30	.09
87 Brian Jordan	.30	.09
88 Ron Karkovice	.30	.09
89 Al Leiter	.30	.09
90 Tony Longmire	.30	.09
91 Nelson Liriano	.30	.09
92 David Bell	.30	.09
93 Kevin Gross	.30	.09
94 Tom Candiotti	.30	.09
95 Dave Martinez	.30	.09
96 Greg Myers	.30	.09
97 Rheal Cormier	.30	.09
98 Chris Hammond	.30	.09
99 Randy Myers	.30	.09
100 Bill Pulsipher	.30	.09
101 Jason Isringhausen	.30	.09
102 Dave Stevens	.30	.09
103 Roberto Alomar	.50	.15
104 Bob Higginson	.30	.09
105 Eddie Murray	.75	.23
106 Matt Walbeck	.30	.09
107 Mark Wohlers	.30	.09
108 Jeff Nelson	.30	.09
109 Tom Goodwin	.30	.09
110 Cal Ripken CL	1.25	.35
111 Rey Sanchez	.30	.09
112 Hector Carrasco	.30	.09
113 B.J. Surhoff	.30	.09
114 Dan Miceli	.30	.09
115 Dean Hartgraves	.30	.09
116 John Burkett	.30	.09
117 Gary Gaetti	.30	.09
118 Ricky Bones	.30	.09
119 Mike Macfarlane	.30	.09
120 Bip Roberts	.30	.09
121 Dave Mlicki	.30	.09
122 Chili Davis	.30	.09
123 Mark Whiten	.30	.09
124 Herbert Perry	.30	.09
125 Butch Henry	.30	.09
126 Derek Bell	.30	.09
127 Al Martin	.30	.09
128 John Franco	.30	.09
129 W. VanLandingham	.30	.09
130 Mike Bordick	.30	.09
131 Mike Mordecai	.30	.09
132 Robby Thompson	.30	.09
133 Greg Colbrunn	.30	.09
134 Domingo Cedeno	.30	.09
135 Chad Curtis	.30	.09
136 Jose Hernandez	.30	.09
137 Scott Klingenbeck	.30	.09
138 Ryan Klesko	.30	.09
139 John Smiley	.30	.09
140 Charlie Hayes	.30	.09
141 Jay Buhner	.30	.09
142 Doug Drabek	.30	.09
143 Roger Pavlik	.30	.09
144 Todd Worrell	.30	.09
145 Cal Ripken	2.50	.75
146 Steve Reed	.30	.09
147 Chuck Finley	.30	.09
148 Mike Blowers	.30	.09
149 Orel Hershiser	.30	.09
150 Allen Watson	.30	.09
151 Ramon Martinez	.30	.09
152 Melvin Nieves	.30	.09
153 Tripp Cromer	.30	.09
154 Yorkis Perez	.30	.09
155 Stan Javier	.30	.09
156 Mel Rojas	.30	.09
157 Aaron Sele	.30	.09
158 Eric Karros	.30	.09
159 Robb Nen	.30	.09
160 Raul Mondesi	.30	.09
161 John Wetteland	.30	.09
162 Tim Scott	.30	.09
163 Kenny Rogers	.30	.09
164 Melvin Bunch	.30	.09
165 Rod Beck	.30	.09
166 Andy Benes	.30	.09
167 Lenny Dykstra	.30	.09
168 Orlando Merced	.30	.09
169 Tomas Perez	.30	.09
170 Xavier Hernandez	.30	.09
171 Ruben Sierra	.30	.09
172 Alan Trammell	.50	.15
173 Mike Fetters	.30	.09
174 Wilson Alvarez	.30	.09
175 Erik Hanson	.30	.09
176 Travis Fryman	.30	.09
177 Jim Abbott	.50	.15
178 Bret Boone	.30	.09
179 Sterling Hitchcock	.30	.09
180 Pat Mahomes	.30	.09
181 Mark Acre	.30	.09
182 Charles Nagy	.30	.09
183 Rusty Greer	.30	.09
184 Mike Stanley	.30	.09
185 Jim Bullinger	.30	.09
186 Shane Andrews	.30	.09
187 Brian Keyser	.30	.09
188 Tyler Green	.30	.09
189 Mark Grace	.50	.15
190 Bob Hamelin	.30	.09
191 Luis Ortiz	.30	.09
192 Joe Carter	.30	.09
193 Eddie Taubensee	.30	.09
194 Brian Anderson	.30	.09
195 Edgardo Alfonzo	.30	.09
196 Pedro Munoz	.30	.09
197 David Justice	.30	.09
198 Trevor Hoffman	.30	.09
199 Bobby Ayala	.30	.09
200 Tony Eusebio	.30	.09
201 Jeff Russell	.30	.09
202 Mike Hampton	.30	.09
203 Walt Weiss	.30	.09
204 Joey Hamilton	.30	.09
205 Roberto Hernandez	.30	.09
206 Greg Vaughn	.30	.09
207 Felipe Lira	.30	.09
208 Harold Baines	.30	.09
209 Tim Wallach	.30	.09
210 Manny Alexander	.30	.09
211 Tim Laker	.30	.09
212 Chris Haney	.30	.09
213 Brian Maxcy	.30	.09
214 Eric Young	.30	.09
215 Darryl Strawberry	.30	.09
216 Barry Bonds	2.00	.60
217 Tim Naehring	.30	.09
218 Scott Brosius	.30	.09
219 Reggie Sanders	.30	.09
220 Eddie Murray CL	.50	.15
221 Luis Alicea	.30	.09
222 Albert Belle	.30	.09
223 Benji Gil	.30	.09
224 Dante Bichette	.30	.09
225 Bobby Bonilla	.30	.09
226 Todd Stottlemyre	.30	.09
227 Jim Edmonds	.30	.09
228 Todd Jones	.30	.09
229 Shawn Green	.30	.09
230 Javier Lopez	.30	.09
231 Ariel Prieto	.30	.09
232 Tony Phillips	.30	.09
233 James Mouton	.30	.09
234 Jose Oquendo	.30	.09
235 Royce Clayton	.30	.09
236 Chuck Carr	.30	.09
237 Doug Jones	.30	.09
238 Mark McLemore	.30	.09
239 Bill Swift	.30	.09
240 Scott Leius	.30	.09
241 Russ Davis	.30	.09
242 Ray Durham	.30	.09
243 Matt Mieske	.30	.09
244 Brent Mayne	.30	.09
245 Thomas Howard	.30	.09
246 Troy O'Leary	.30	.09
247 Jacob Brumfield	.30	.09
248 Mickey Morandini	.30	.09
249 Todd Hundley	.30	.09
250 Chris Bosio	.30	.09
251 Omar Vizquel	.50	.15
252 Mike Lansing	.30	.09
253 John Mabry	.30	.09
254 Mike Perez	.30	.09
255 Delino DeShields	.30	.09
256 Wil Cordero	.30	.09
257 Mike James	.30	.09
258 Todd Van Poppel	.30	.09
259 Joey Cora	.30	.09
260 Andre Dawson	.30	.09
261 Jerry DiPoto	.30	.09
262 Rick Krivda	.30	.09
263 Glenn Dishman	.30	.09
264 Mike Mimbs	.30	.09
265 John Ericks	.30	.09
266 Jose Canseco	.75	.23
267 Jeff Branson	.30	.09
268 Curt Leskanic	.30	.09
269 Jon Nunnally	.30	.09
270 Scott Stahoviak	.30	.09
271 Jeff Montgomery	.30	.09
272 Hal Morris	.30	.09
273 Esteban Loaiza	.30	.09
274 Rico Brogna	.30	.09
275 Dave Winfield	.30	.09
276 J.R. Phillips	.30	.09
277 Todd Zeile	.30	.09
278 Tom Pagnozzi	.30	.09
279 Mark Lemke	.30	.09
280 Dave Magadan	.30	.09
281 Greg McMichael	.30	.09
282 Mike Morgan	.30	.09
283 Moises Alou	.30	.09
284 Dennis Martinez	.30	.09
285 Jeff Kent	.30	.09
286 Mark Johnson	.30	.09
287 Darren Lewis	.30	.09
288 Brad Clontz	.30	.09
289 Chad Fonville	.30	.09
290 Paul Sorrento	.30	.09
291 Lee Smith	.30	.09
292 Tom Glavine	.50	.15
293 Antonio Osuna	.30	.09
294 Kevin Foster	.30	.09
295 Sandy Martinez	.30	.09
296 Mark Leiter	.30	.09
297 Julian Tavarez	.30	.09
298 Mike Kelly	.30	.09
299 Joe Oliver	.30	.09
300 John Flaherty	.30	.09
301 Don Mattingly	2.00	.60
302 Pat Meares	.30	.09
303 John Doherty	.30	.09
304 Joe Vitiello	.30	.09
305 Vinny Castilla	.30	.09
306 Jeff Brantley	.30	.09
307 Mike Greenwell	.30	.09
308 Midre Cummings	.30	.09
309 Curt Schilling	.50	.15
310 Ken Caminiti	.30	.09
311 Scott Erickson	.30	.09
312 Carl Everett	.30	.09
313 Charles Johnson	.30	.09
314 Alex Diaz	.30	.09
315 Jose Mesa	.30	.09
316 Mark Carreon	.30	.09
317 Carlos Perez	.30	.09
318 Ismael Valdes	.30	.09
319 Frank Castillo	.30	.09
320 Tom Henke	.30	.09
321 Spike Owen	.30	.09
322 Joe Orsulak	.30	.09
323 Paul Menhart	.30	.09
324 Pedro Borbon	.30	.09
325 Paul Molitor CL	.30	.09
326 Jeff Cirillo	.30	.09
327 Edwin Hurtado	.30	.09
328 Orlando Miller	.30	.09
329 Steve Ontiveros	.30	.09
330 Kirby Puckett CL	.50	.15
331 Scott Bullett	.30	.09
332 Andres Galarraga	.30	.09
333 Cal Eldred	.30	.09
334 Sammy Sosa	1.25	.35
335 Don Slaught	.30	.09
336 Jody Reed	.30	.09
337 Roger Cedeno	.30	.09
338 Ken Griffey Jr.	1.25	.35
339 Todd Hollandsworth	.30	.09
340 Mike Trombley	.30	.09
341 Gregg Jefferies	.30	.09
342 Larry Walker	.50	.15
343 Pedro Martinez	.75	.23
344 Dwayne Hosey	.30	.09
345 Terry Pendleton	.30	.09
346 Pete Harnisch	.30	.09
347 Tony Castillo	.30	.09
348 Paul Quantrill	.30	.09
349 Fred McGriff	.50	.15
350 Ivan Rodriguez	.75	.23
351 Butch Huskey	.30	.09
352 Ozzie Smith	1.25	.35
353 Marty Cordova	.30	.09
354 John Wasdin	.30	.09
355 Wade Boggs	.50	.15
356 Dave Nilsson	.30	.09
357 Rafael Palmeiro	.50	.15
358 Luis Gonzalez	.30	.09
359 Reggie Jefferson	.30	.09
360 Carlos Delgado	.30	.09
361 Orlando Palmeiro	.30	.09
362 Chris Gomez	.30	.09
363 John Smoltz	.50	.15
364 Marc Newfield	.30	.09
365 Matt Williams	.30	.09
366 Jesus Tavarez	.30	.09
367 Bruce Ruffin	.30	.09
368 Sean Berry	.30	.09
369 Randy Velarde	.30	.09
370 Tony Pena	.30	.09
371 Jim Thome	.75	.23
372 Jeffrey Hammonds	.30	.09
373 Bob Wolcott	.30	.09
374 Juan Guzman	.30	.09
375 Juan Gonzalez	.50	.15
376 Michael Tucker	.30	.09
377 Doug Johns	.30	.09
378 Mike Cameron RC	1.00	.30
379 Ray Lankford	.30	.09
380 Jose Parra	.30	.09
381 Jimmy Key	.30	.09
382 John Olerud	.30	.09
383 Kevin Ritz	.30	.09
384 Tim Raines	.30	.09
385 Rich Amaral	.30	.09
386 Keith Lockhart	.30	.09
387 Steve Scarsone	.30	.09
388 Cliff Floyd	.30	.09
389 Rich Aude	.30	.09
390 Hideo Nomo	.75	.23
391 Geronimo Berroa	.30	.09
392 Pat Rapp	.30	.09
393 Dustin Hermanson	.30	.09
394 Greg Maddux	1.25	.35
395 Darren Daulton	.30	.09
396 Kenny Lofton	.30	.09
397 Ruben Rivera	.30	.09
398 Billy Wagner	.30	.09
399 Kevin Brown	.30	.09
400 Mike Kingery	.30	.09
401 Bernie Williams	.50	.15
402 Otis Nixon	.30	.09
403 Damion Easley	.30	.09
404 Paul O'Neill	.50	.15
405 Deion Sanders	.50	.15
406 Dennis Eckersley	.30	.09
407 Tony Clark	.30	.09
408 Rondell White	.30	.09
409 Luis Sojo	.30	.09
410 David Hulse	.30	.09

411 Shane Reynolds .30 .09
412 Chris Hoiles .30 .09
413 Lee Tinsley .30 .09
414 Scott Karl .30 .09
415 Ron Gant .30 .09
416 Brian Johnson .30 .09
417 Jose Oliva .30 .09
418 Jack McDowell .30 .09
419 Paul Molitor .50 .15
420 Ricky Bottalico .30 .09
421 Paul Wagner .30 .09
422 Terry Bradshaw .30 .09
423 Bob Tewksbury .30 .09
424 Mike Piazza 1.25 .35
425 Luis Andujar .30 .09
426 Mark Langston .30 .09
427 Stan Belinda .30 .09
428 Kurt Abbott .30 .09
429 Shawon Dunston .30 .09
430 Bobby Jones .30 .09
431 Jose Vizcaino .30 .09
432 Matt Lawton RC .60 .18
433 Pat Hentgen .30 .09
434 Cecil Fielder .30 .09
435 Carlos Baerga .30 .09
436 Rich Becker .30 .09
437 Chipper Jones .75 .23
438 Bill Risley .30 .09
439 Kevin Appier .30 .09
440 Wade Boggs CL .30 .09
441 Jaime Navarro .30 .09
442 Barry Larkin .50 .15
443 Jose Valentin .30 .09
444 Bryan Rekar .30 .09
445 Rick Wilkins .30 .09
446 Quilvio Veras .30 .09
447 Greg Gagne .30 .09
448 Mark Kiefer .30 .09
449 Bobby Witt .30 .09
450 Andy Ashby .30 .09
451 Alex Ochoa .30 .09
452 Jorge Fabregas .30 .09
453 Gene Schall .30 .09
454 Ken Hill .30 .09
455 Tony Tarasco .30 .09
456 Donnie Wall .30 .09
457 Carlos Garcia .30 .09
458 Ryan Thompson .30 .09
459 Marvin Benard RC .40 .12
460 Jose Herrera .30 .09
461 Jeff Blauser .30 .09
462 Chris Hook .30 .09
463 Jeff Conine .30 .09
464 Devon White .30 .09
465 Danny Bautista .30 .09
466 Steve Trachsel .30 .09
467 C.J. Nitkowski .30 .09
468 Mike Devereaux .30 .09
469 David Wells .30 .09
470 Jim Eisenreich .30 .09
471 Edgar Martinez .50 .15
472 Craig Biggio .50 .15
473 Jeff Frye .30 .09
474 Karim Garcia .30 .09
475 Jimmy Haynes .30 .09
476 Darren Holmes .30 .09
477 Tim Salmon .50 .15
478 Randy Johnson .75 .23
479 Eric Plunk .30 .09
480 Scott Cooper .30 .09
481 Chan Ho Park .30 .09
482 Ray McDavid .30 .09
483 Mark Petkovsek .30 .09
484 Greg Swindell .30 .09
485 George Williams .30 .09
486 Yamil Benitez .30 .09
487 Tim Wakefield .30 .09
488 Kevin Tapani .30 .09
489 Derrick May .30 .09
490 Ken Griffey Jr. CL .75 .23
491 Derek Jeter 2.00 .60
492 Jeff Fassero .30 .09
493 Benito Santiago .30 .09
494 Tom Gordon .30 .09
495 Jamie Brewington RC .30 .09
496 Vince Coleman .30 .09
497 Kevin Jordan .30 .09
498 Jeff King .30 .09
499 Mike Simms .30 .09
500 Jose Rijo .30 .09
501 Denny Neagle .30 .09
502 Jose Lima .30 .09
503 Kevin Seitzer .30 .09
504 Alex Fernandez .30 .09
505 Mo Vaughn .30 .09
506 Phil Nevin .30 .09
507 J.T. Snow .30 .09
508 Andujar Cedeno .30 .09
509 Ozzie Guillen .30 .09
510 Mark Clark .30 .09
511 Mark McGwire 2.00 .60
512 Jeff Reboulet .30 .09
513 Armando Benitez .30 .09
514 LaTroy Hawkins .30 .09
515 Brett Butler .30 .09
516 Tavo Alvarez .30 .09
517 Chris Snopek .30 .09
518 Mike Mussina .50 .15
519 Darryl Kile .30 .09
520 Wally Joyner .30 .09
521 Willie McGee .30 .09
522 Kent Mercker .30 .09
523 Mike Jackson .30 .09
524 Troy Percival .30 .09
525 Tony Gwynn 1.00 .30
526 Ron Coomer .30 .09
527 Darryl Hamilton .30 .09
528 Phil Plantier .30 .09
529 Norm Charlton .30 .09
530 Craig Paquette .30 .09
531 Dave Burba .30 .09
532 Mike Henneman .30 .09
533 Terrell Wade .30 .09
534 Eddie Williams .30 .09
535 Robin Ventura .30 .09
536 Chuck Knoblauch .30 .09
537 Les Norman .30 .09
538 Brady Anderson .30 .09
539 Roger Clemens 1.50 .45
540 Mark Portugal .30 .09
541 Mike Matheny .30 .09
542 Jeff Parrett .30 .09
543 Roberto Kelly .30 .09
544 Damon Buford .30 .09
545 Chad Ogea .30 .09
546 Jose Offerman .30 .09
547 Brian Barber .30 .09
548 Danny Tartabull .30 .09
549 Duane Singleton .30 .09
550 Tony Gwynn CL .50 .15

1996 Donruss Press Proofs

Randomly inserted at a rate of one in 12 first series packs and one in 10 second series packs, these cards parallel the regular Donruss issue. Even though they are not sequentially numbered, production on these cards were limited to 2,000 cards. Each card is noted as being a Press Proof in gold foil on the front.

Nm-Mt Ex-Mt
*STARS: 6X TO 15X BASIC CARDS....
*ROOKIES: 4X TO 10X BASIC CARDS

1996 Donruss Diamond Kings

These 31 standard-size cards were randomly inserted into packs and issued in two series of 14 and 17 cards. They were inserted in first series packs at a ratio of approximately one every 60 packs. Second series cards were inserted one every 30 packs. The cards are sequentially numbered in the back lower right as "X" of 10,000. The fronts feature player portraits by noted sports artist Dick Perez. These cards are gold-foil stamped and the portraits are surrounded by gold-foil borders. The backs feature text about the player as well as a player photo. The cards are numbered on the back with a "DK" prefix.

Nm-Mt Ex-Mt
COMPLETE SET (31) 250.00 75.00
COMPLETE SERIES 1 (14) 150.00 45.00
COMPLETE SERIES 2 (17) 100.00 30.00
1 Frank Thomas 12.00 3.60
2 Mo Vaughn 5.00 1.50
3 Manny Ramirez 8.00 2.40
4 Mark McGwire 30.00 9.00
5 Juan Gonzalez 8.00 2.40
6 Roberto Alomar 8.00 2.40
7 Tim Salmon 8.00 2.40
8 Barry Bonds 30.00 9.00
9 Tony Gwynn 15.00 4.50
10 Reggie Sanders 5.00 1.50
11 Larry Walker 8.00 2.40
12 Pedro Martinez 12.00 3.60
13 Jeff King 5.00 1.50
14 Mark Grace 8.00 2.40
15 Greg Maddux 15.00 4.50
16 Don Mattingly 25.00 7.50
17 Gregg Jefferies 4.00 1.20
18 Chad Curtis 4.00 1.20
19 Jason Isringhausen 4.00 1.20
20 B.J. Surhoff 4.00 1.20
21 Jeff Conine 4.00 1.20
22 Kirby Puckett 10.00 3.00
23 Derek Bell 4.00 1.20
24 Wally Joyner 4.00 1.20
25 Brian Jordan 4.00 1.20
26 Edgar Martinez 6.00 1.80
27 Hideo Nomo 10.00 3.00
28 Mike Mussina 6.00 1.80
29 Eddie Murray 10.00 3.00
30 Cal Ripken 30.00 9.00
31 Checklist 4.00 1.20

1996 Donruss Elite

Randomly inserted approximately one in Donruss packs, this 12-card standard-size set is continuously numbered (61-72) from the previous year. First series cards were inserted one every 40 packs. Second series cards were inserted one every 75 packs. The fronts contain an action photo surrounded by a silver border. Limited to 10,000 and sequentially numbered, the backs contain a small photo and write up.

Nm-Mt Ex-Mt
COMPLETE SET (12) 110.00 33.00
COMPLETE SERIES 1 (6) 50.00 15.00
COMPLETE SERIES 2 (6) 60.00 18.00
61 Cal Ripken 30.00 9.00
62 Hideo Nomo 10.00 3.00
63 Reggie Sanders 4.00 1.20
64 Mo Vaughn 4.00 1.20
65 Tim Salmon 6.00 1.80
66 Chipper Jones 10.00 3.00
67 Manny Ramirez 6.00 1.80
68 Greg Maddux 15.00 4.50
69 Frank Thomas 10.00 3.00
70 Ken Griffey Jr. 15.00 4.50
71 Dante Bichette 4.00 1.20
72 Tony Gwynn 12.00 3.60

1996 Donruss Freeze Frame

Randomly inserted in second series packs at a rate of one in 60, this eight-card standard-size set features the top hitters and pitchers in baseball. Just 5,000 of each card were produced and sequentially numbered.

Nm-Mt Ex-Mt
COMPLETE SET (8) 100.00 30.00
1 Frank Thomas 10.00 3.00
2 Ken Griffey Jr. 15.00 4.50
3 Cal Ripken 30.00 9.00
4 Hideo Nomo 10.00 3.00
5 Greg Maddux 15.00 4.50
6 Albert Belle 4.00 1.20
7 Chipper Jones 10.00 3.00
8 Mike Piazza 15.00 4.50

1996 Donruss Hit List

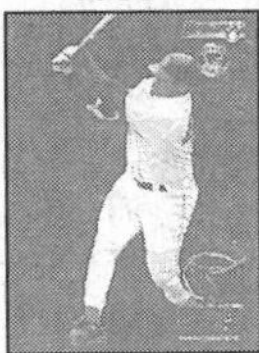

This 16-card standard-size set was randomly inserted in 97 Donruss and salutes the most consistent hitters in the game. The first series cards were inserted one every 105 packs while the second series cards were inserted one every 60 packs. The cards are sequentially numbered out of 10,000.

Nm-Mt Ex-Mt
COMPLETE SET (16) 100.00 30.00
COMPLETE SERIES 1 (8) 60.00 18.00
COMPLETE SERIES 2 (8) 40.00 12.00
1 Tony Gwynn 8.00 2.40
2 Ken Griffey Jr. 10.00 3.00
3 Will Clark 6.00 1.80
4 Mike Piazza 10.00 3.00
5 Carlos Baerga 2.50 .75
6 Mo Vaughn 2.50 .75
7 Mark Grace 4.00 1.20
8 Kirby Puckett 6.00 1.80
9 Frank Thomas 6.00 1.80
10 Barry Bonds 15.00 4.50
11 Jeff Bagwell 4.00 1.20
12 Edgar Martinez 4.00 1.20
13 Tim Salmon 4.00 1.20
14 Wade Boggs 4.00 1.20
15 Don Mattingly 15.00 4.50
16 Eddie Murray 6.00 1.80

1996 Donruss Long Ball Leaders

This eight-card standard-size set was randomly inserted into series one retail packs. They were inserted at a rate of approximately one in every 96 packs. The cards are sequentially numbered out of 5,000. The set highlights eight top sluggers and their farthest home run distance of 1995. The fronts feature a player photo set against a silver-foil background.

Nm-Mt Ex-Mt
COMPLETE SET (8) 120.00 36.00
1 Barry Bonds 30.00 9.00
2 Ryan Klesko 5.00 1.50
3 Mark McGwire 30.00 9.00
4 Raul Mondesi 5.00 1.50
5 Cecil Fielder 5.00 1.50
6 Ken Griffey Jr. 20.00 6.00
7 Larry Walker 8.00 2.40
8 Frank Thomas 12.00 3.60

1996 Donruss Power Alley

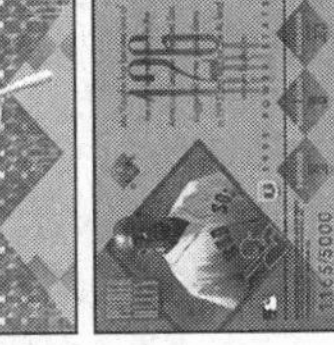

This ten-card standard-size set was randomly inserted into series one hobby packs. They were inserted at a rate of approximately one in every 92 packs. These cards are all sequentially numbered out of 5,000.

Nm-Mt Ex-Mt
COMPLETE SET (10) 80.00 24.00
*DC'S: 1.25X TO 3X BASIC POWER ALLEY
DC SER.1 ODDS 1:920 HOBBY..........
DC PRINT RUN 500 SERIAL #'d SETS
1 Frank Thomas 12.00 3.60
2 Barry Bonds 30.00 9.00
3 Reggie Sanders 5.00 1.50
4 Albert Belle 5.00 1.50
5 Tim Salmon 8.00 2.40
6 Dante Bichette 5.00 1.50
7 Mo Vaughn 5.00 1.50
8 Jim Edmonds 5.00 1.50
9 Manny Ramirez 8.00 2.40
10 Ken Griffey Jr. 20.00 6.00

1996 Donruss Pure Power

Randomly inserted in retail and magazine packs only at a rate of one in eight, this eight-card set features color action player photos of eight of the most powerful players in Major League baseball.

Nm-Mt Ex-Mt
COMPLETE SET (8) 80.00 24.00
1 Raul Mondesi 5.00 1.50
2 Barry Bonds 30.00 9.00
3 Albert Belle 5.00 1.50
4 Frank Thomas 12.00 3.60
5 Mike Piazza 20.00 6.00
6 Dante Bichette 5.00 1.50
7 Manny Ramirez 8.00 2.40
8 Mo Vaughn 5.00 1.50

1996 Donruss Round Trippers

Randomly inserted in second series hobby packs at a rate of one in 55, this 10-card standard-size set honors ten of Baseball's top homerun hitters. Just 5,000 of each card were produced and consecutively numbered.

Nm-Mt Ex-Mt
COMPLETE SET (10) 80.00 24.00
1 Albert Belle 4.00 1.20
2 Barry Bonds 25.00 7.50
3 Jeff Bagwell 6.00 1.80
4 Tim Salmon 6.00 1.80
5 Mo Vaughn 4.00 1.20
6 Ken Griffey Jr. 15.00 4.50
7 Mike Piazza 15.00 4.50
8 Cal Ripken 30.00 9.00
9 Frank Thomas 10.00 3.00
10 Dante Bichette 4.00 1.20

1996 Donruss Showdown

This eight-card standard-size set was randomly inserted in series one packs at a rate of one every 105 packs. These cards feature one top hitter and one top pitcher from each league. The cards are sequentially numbered out of 10,000.

Nm-Mt Ex-Mt
COMPLETE SET (8) 100.00 30.00
1 Frank Thomas 8.00 2.40
Hideo Nomo
2 Barry Bonds 20.00 6.00
Randy Johnson
3 Greg Maddux 12.00 3.60
Ken Griffey Jr.
4 Roger Clemens 10.00 3.00
Tony Gwynn
5 Mike Piazza 12.00 3.60
Mike Mussina
6 Cal Ripken 25.00 7.50
Pedro J.Martinez
7 Tim Wakefield 3.00 .90
Matt Williams
8 Manny Ramirez 5.00 1.50
Carlos Perez

1997 Donruss

The 1997 Donruss set was issued in two separate series of 270 and 180 cards respectively. Both first series and Update cards were distributed in 10-card packs carrying a suggested retail price of $1.99 each. Card fronts feature color action player photos while the backs carry another color player photo with player information and career statistics. The following subsets are included within the set: Checklists (267-270/448-450), Rookies (353-397), Hit List (398-422), King of the Hill (423-437) and Interleague Showdown (438-447). Rookie Cards in this set include Jose Cruz Jr., Brian Giles and Hideki Irabu.

Nm-Mt Ex-Mt
COMPLETE SET (450) 50.00 15.00
COMP. SERIES 1 (270) 25.00 7.50
COMPLETE UPDATE (180) 25.00 7.50
1 Juan Gonzalez .50 .15
2 Jim Edmonds .30 .09
3 Tony Gwynn 1.00 .30
4 Andres Galarraga .30 .09
5 Joe Carter .30 .09
6 Raul Mondesi .30 .09
7 Greg Maddux 1.25 .35
8 Travis Fryman .30 .09
9 Brian Jordan .30 .09
10 Henry Rodriguez .30 .09
11 Manny Ramirez .50 .15
12 Mark McGwire 2.00 .60
13 Marc Newfield .30 .09
14 Craig Biggio .50 .15
15 Sammy Sosa 1.25 .35
16 Brady Anderson .30 .09
17 Wade Boggs .50 .15
18 Charles Johnson .30 .09
19 Matt Williams .30 .09
20 Denny Neagle .30 .09
21 Ken Griffey Jr. 1.25 .35
22 Robin Ventura .30 .09
23 Barry Larkin .50 .15
24 Todd Zeile .30 .09
25 Chuck Knoblauch .30 .09
26 Todd Hundley .30 .09
27 Roger Clemens 1.50 .45
28 Michael Tucker .30 .09
29 Rondell White .30 .09
30 Osvaldo Fernandez .30 .09
31 Ivan Rodriguez .75 .23
32 Alex Fernandez .30 .09
33 Jason Isringhausen .30 .09
34 Chipper Jones .75 .23
35 Paul O'Neill .50 .15
36 Hideo Nomo .75 .23
37 Roberto Alomar .50 .15
38 Derek Bell .30 .09
39 Paul Molitor .50 .15
40 Andy Benes .30 .09
41 Steve Trachsel .30 .09
42 J.T. Snow .30 .09
43 Jason Kendall .30 .09
44 Alex Rodriguez 1.25 .35
45 Joey Hamilton .30 .09
46 Carlos Delgado .30 .09
47 Jason Giambi .30 .09
48 Larry Walker .50 .15
49 Derek Jeter 2.00 .60
50 Kenny Lofton .30 .09
51 Devon White .30 .09
52 Matt Mieske .30 .09
53 Melvin Nieves .30 .09
54 Jose Canseco .75 .23
55 Tino Martinez .50 .15
56 Rafael Palmeiro .50 .15
57 Edgardo Alfonzo .30 .09
58 Jay Buhner .30 .09
59 Shane Reynolds .30 .09
60 Steve Finley .30 .09
61 Bobby Higginson .30 .09
62 Dean Palmer .30 .09
63 Terry Pendleton .30 .09
64 Marquis Grissom .30 .09
65 Mike Stanley .30 .09
66 Moises Alou .30 .09
67 Ray Lankford .30 .09
68 Marty Cordova .30 .09
69 John Olerud .30 .09
70 David Cone .30 .09
71 Benito Santiago .30 .09
72 Ryne Sandberg 1.25 .35
73 Rickey Henderson .75 .23
74 Roger Cedeno .30 .09
75 Wilson Alvarez .30 .09
76 Tim Salmon .50 .15
77 Orlando Merced .30 .09
78 Vinny Castilla .30 .09
79 Ismael Valdes .30 .09
80 Dante Bichette .30 .09
81 Kevin Brown .30 .09
82 Andy Pettitte .50 .15
83 Scott Stahoviak .30 .09
84 Mickey Tettleton .30 .09
85 Jack McDowell .30 .09
86 Tom Glavine .50 .15
87 Gregg Jefferies .30 .09
88 Chili Davis .30 .09
89 Randy Johnson .75 .23
90 John Mabry .30 .09
91 Billy Wagner .30 .09
92 Jeff Cirillo .30 .09
93 Trevor Hoffman .30 .09
94 Juan Guzman .30 .09
95 Geronimo Berroa .30 .09
96 Bernard Gilkey .30 .09
97 Danny Tartabull .30 .09
98 Johnny Damon .50 .15
99 Charlie Hayes .30 .09
100 Reggie Sanders .30 .09
101 Robby Thompson .30 .09
102 Bobby Bonilla .30 .09
103 Reggie Jefferson .30 .09
104 John Smoltz .50 .15
105 Jim Thome .75 .23
106 Ruben Rivera .30 .09
107 Darren Oliver .30 .09
108 Mo Vaughn .30 .09
109 Roger Pavlik .30 .09
110 Terry Steinbach .30 .09
111 Jermaine Dye .30 .09
112 Mark Grudzielanek .30 .09

113 Rick Aguilera .30 .09
114 Jamey Wright .30 .09
115 Eddie Murray .75 .23
116 Brian L. Hunter .30 .09
117 Hal Morris .30 .09
118 Tom Pagnozzi .30 .09
119 Mike Mussina .50 .15
120 Mark Grace .50 .15
121 Cal Ripken 2.50 .75
122 Tom Goodwin .30 .09
123 Paul Sorrento .30 .09
124 Jay Bell .30 .09
125 Todd Hollandsworth .30 .09
126 Edgar Martinez .50 .15
127 George Arias .30 .09
128 Greg Vaughn .30 .09
129 Roberto Hernandez .30 .09
130 Delino DeShields .30 .09
131 Bill Pulsipher .30 .09
132 Joey Cora .30 .09
133 Mariano Rivera .50 .15
134 Mike Piazza 1.25 .35
135 Carlos Baerga .30 .09
136 Jose Mesa .30 .09
137 Will Clark .75 .23
138 Frank Thomas .75 .23
139 John Wetteland .30 .09
140 Shawn Estes .30 .09
141 Garret Anderson .30 .09
142 Andre Dawson .30 .09
143 Eddie Taubensee .30 .09
144 Ryan Klesko .30 .09
145 Rocky Coppinger .30 .09
146 Jeff Bagwell .50 .15
147 Donovan Osborne .30 .09
148 Greg Myers .30 .09
149 Brant Brown .30 .09
150 Kevin Elster .30 .09
151 Bob Wells .30 .09
152 Wally Joyner .30 .09
153 Rico Brogna .30 .09
154 Dwight Gooden .30 .09
155 Jermaine Allensworth .30 .09
156 Ray Durham .30 .09
157 Cecil Fielder .30 .09
158 John Burkett .30 .09
159 Gary Sheffield .30 .09
160 Albert Belle .30 .09
161 Tomas Perez .30 .09
162 David Doster .30 .09
163 John Valentin .30 .09
164 Danny Graves .30 .09
165 Jose Paniagua .30 .09
166 Brian Giles RC 1.50 .45
167 Barry Bonds 2.00 .60
168 Sterling Hitchcock .30 .09
169 Bernie Williams .50 .15
170 Fred McGriff .50 .15
171 George Williams .30 .09
172 Amaury Telemaco .30 .09
173 Ken Caminiti .30 .09
174 Ron Gant .30 .09
175 Dave Justice .30 .09
176 James Baldwin .30 .09
177 Pat Hentgen .30 .09
178 Ben McDonald .30 .09
179 Tim Naehring .30 .09
180 Jim Eisenreich .30 .09
181 Ken Hill .30 .09
182 Paul Wilson .30 .09
183 Marvin Benard .30 .09
184 Alan Benes .30 .09
185 Ellis Burks .30 .09
186 Scott Servais .30 .09
187 David Segui .30 .09
188 Scott Brosius .30 .09
189 Jose Offerman .30 .09
190 Eric Davis .30 .09
191 Brett Butler .30 .09
192 Curtis Pride .30 .09
193 Yamil Benitez .30 .09
194 Chan Ho Park .30 .09
195 Bret Boone .30 .09
196 Omar Vizquel .50 .15
197 Orlando Miller .30 .09
198 Ramon Martinez .30 .09
199 Harold Baines .30 .09
200 Eric Young .30 .09
201 Fernando Vina .30 .09
202 Alex Gonzalez .30 .09
203 Fernando Valenzuela .30 .09
204 Steve Avery .30 .09
205 Ernie Young .30 .09
206 Kevin Appier .30 .09
207 Randy Myers .30 .09
208 Jeff Suppan .30 .09
209 James Mouton .30 .09
210 Russ Davis .30 .09
211 Al Martin .30 .09
212 Troy Percival .30 .09
213 Al Leiter .30 .09
214 Dennis Eckersley .30 .09
215 Mark Johnson .30 .09
216 Eric Karros .30 .09
217 Royce Clayton .30 .09
218 Tony Phillips .30 .09
219 Tim Wakefield .30 .09
220 Alan Trammell .30 .09
221 Eduardo Perez .30 .09
222 Butch Huskey .30 .09
223 Tim Belcher .30 .09
224 Jamie Moyer .30 .09
225 F.P. Santangelo .30 .09
226 Rusty Greer .30 .09
227 Jeff Brantley .30 .09
228 Mark Langston .30 .09
229 Ray Montgomery .30 .09
230 Rich Becker .30 .09
231 Ozzie Smith 1.25 .35
232 Rey Ordonez .30 .09
233 Ricky Otero .30 .09
234 Mike Cameron .30 .09
235 Mike Sweeney .30 .09
236 Mark Lewis .30 .09
237 Luis Gonzalez .30 .09
238 Marcus Jensen .30 .09
239 Ed Sprague .30 .09
240 Jose Valentin .30 .09
241 Jeff Frye .30 .09
242 Charles Nagy .30 .09
243 Carlos Garcia .30 .09
244 Mike Hampton .30 .09
245 B.J. Surhoff .30 .09
246 Wilton Guerrero .30 .09
247 Frank Rodriguez .30 .09
248 Gary Gaetti .30 .09
249 Lance Johnson .30 .09
250 Darren Bragg .30 .09
251 Darryl Hamilton .30 .09
252 John Jaha .30 .09
253 Craig Paquette .30 .09
254 Jaime Navarro .30 .09
255 Shawon Dunston .30 .09
256 Mark Loretta .30 .09
257 Tim Belk .30 .09
258 Jeff Darwin .30 .09
259 Ruben Sierra .30 .09
260 Chuck Finley .30 .09
261 Darryl Strawberry .30 .09
262 Shannon Stewart .30 .09
263 Pedro Martinez .75 .23
264 Neifi Perez .30 .09
265 Jeff Conine .30 .09
266 Orel Hershiser .30 .09
267 Eddie Murray CL .50 .15
268 Paul Molitor CL .30 .09
269 Barry Bonds CL .75 .23
270 Mark McGwire CL 1.00 .30
271 Matt Williams .30 .09
272 Todd Zeile .30 .09
273 Roger Clemens 1.50 .45
274 Michael Tucker .30 .09
275 J.T. Snow .30 .09
276 Kenny Lofton .30 .09
277 Jose Canseco .75 .23
278 Marquis Grissom .30 .09
279 Moises Alou .30 .09
280 Benito Santiago .30 .09
281 Willie McGee .30 .09
282 Chili Davis .30 .09
283 Ron Coomer .30 .09
284 Orlando Merced .30 .09
285 Delino DeShields .30 .09
286 John Wetteland .30 .09
287 Darren Daulton .30 .09
288 Lee Stevens .30 .09
289 Albert Belle .30 .09
290 Sterling Hitchcock .30 .09
291 David Justice .30 .09
292 Eric Davis .30 .09
293 Brian Hunter .30 .09
294 Darryl Hamilton .30 .09
295 Steve Avery .30 .09
296 Joe Vitiello .30 .09
297 Jaime Navarro .30 .09
298 Eddie Murray .75 .23
299 Randy Myers .30 .09
300 Francisco Cordova .30 .09
301 Javier Lopez .30 .09
302 Geronimo Berroa .30 .09
303 Jeffrey Hammonds .30 .09
304 Deion Sanders .50 .15
305 Jeff Fassero .30 .09
306 Curt Schilling .30 .09
307 Robb Nen .30 .09
308 Mark McLemore .30 .09
309 Jimmy Key .30 .09
310 Quilvio Veras .30 .09
311 Bip Roberts .30 .09
312 Esteban Loaiza .30 .09
313 Andy Ashby .30 .09
314 Sandy Alomar Jr. .30 .09
315 Shawn Green .30 .09
316 Luis Castillo .30 .09
317 Benji Gil .30 .09
318 Otis Nixon .30 .09
319 Aaron Sele .30 .09
320 Brad Ausmus .30 .09
321 Troy O'Leary .30 .09
322 Terrell Wade .30 .09
323 Jeff King .30 .09
324 Kevin Seitzer .30 .09
325 Mark Wohlers .30 .09
326 Edgar Renteria .30 .09
327 Dan Wilson .30 .09
328 Brian McRae .30 .09
329 Rod Beck .30 .09
330 Julio Franco .30 .09
331 Dave Nilsson .30 .09
332 Glenallen Hill .30 .09
333 Kevin Elster .30 .09
334 Joe Girardi .30 .09
335 David Wells .30 .09
336 Jeff Blauser .30 .09
337 Darryl Kile .30 .09
338 Jeff Kent .30 .09
339 Jim Leyritz .30 .09
340 Todd Stottlemyre .30 .09
341 Tony Clark .30 .09
342 Chris Hoiles .30 .09
343 Mike Lieberthal .30 .09
344 Matt Lawton .30 .09
345 Alex Ochoa .30 .09
346 Chris Snopek .30 .09
347 Rudy Pemberton .30 .09
348 Eric Owens .30 .09
349 Joe Randa .30 .09
350 John Olerud .30 .09
351 Steve Karsay .30 .09
352 Mark Whiten .30 .09
353 Bob Abreu .30 .09
354 Bartolo Colon .30 .09
355 Vladimir Guerrero .75 .23
356 Darin Erstad .30 .09
357 Scott Rolen .75 .23
358 Andruw Jones .30 .09
359 Scott Spiezio .30 .09
360 Karim Garcia .30 .09
361 Hideki Irabu RC .40 .12
362 Nomar Garciaparra 1.25 .35
363 Dmitri Young .30 .09
364 Bubba Trammell RC .40 .12
365 Kevin Orie .30 .09
366 Jose Rosado .30 .09
367 Jose Guillen .30 .09
368 Brooks Kieschnick .30 .09
369 Pokey Reese .30 .09
370 Glendon Rusch .30 .09
371 Jason Dickson .30 .09
372 Todd Walker .30 .09
373 Justin Thompson .30 .09
374 Todd Greene .30 .09
375 Jeff Suppan .30 .09
376 Trey Beamon .30 .09
377 Damon Mashore .30 .09
378 Wendell Magee .30 .09
379 S. Hasegawa RC .75 .23
380 Bill Mueller RC 3.00 .90
381 Chris Widger .30 .09
382 Tony Graffanino .30 .09
383 Derrek Lee .30 .09
384 Brian Moehler .30 .09
385 Quinton McCracken .30 .09
386 Matt Morris .30 .09
387 Marvin Benard .30 .09
388 Deivi Cruz RC .40 .12
389 Javier Valentin .30 .09
390 Todd Dunwoody .30 .09
391 Derrick Gibson .30 .09
392 Raul Casanova .30 .09
393 George Arias .30 .09
394 Tony Womack RC .50 .15
395 Antone Williamson .30 .09
396 Jose Cruz Jr. RC .50 .15
397 Desi Relaford .30 .09
398 Frank Thomas HIT .50 .15
399 Ken Griffey Jr. HIT .75 .23
400 Cal Ripken HIT 1.25 .35
401 Chipper Jones HIT .50 .15
402 Mike Piazza HIT .75 .23
403 Gary Sheffield HIT .30 .09
404 Alex Rodriguez HIT .75 .23
405 Wade Boggs HIT .30 .09
406 Juan Gonzalez HIT .30 .09
407 Tony Gwynn HIT .50 .15
408 Edgar Martinez HIT .30 .09
409 Jeff Bagwell HIT .30 .09
410 Larry Walker HIT .30 .09
411 Kenny Lofton HIT .30 .09
412 Manny Ramirez HIT .30 .09
413 Mark McGwire HIT 1.00 .30
414 Roberto Alomar HIT .30 .09
415 Derek Jeter HIT 1.00 .30
416 Brady Anderson HIT .30 .09
417 Paul Molitor HIT .30 .09
418 Dante Bichette HIT .30 .09
419 Jim Edmonds HIT .30 .09
420 Mo Vaughn HIT .30 .09
421 Barry Bonds HIT .75 .23
422 Rusty Greer HIT .30 .09
423 Greg Maddux KING .75 .23
424 Andy Pettitte KING .30 .09
425 John Smoltz KING .30 .09
426 Randy Johnson KING .50 .15
427 Hideo Nomo KING .30 .09
428 Roger Clemens KING .75 .23
429 Tom Glavine KING .30 .09
430 Pat Hentgen KING .30 .09
431 Kevin Brown KING .30 .09
432 Mike Mussina KING .30 .09
433 Alex Fernandez KING .30 .09
434 Kevin Appier KING .30 .09
435 David Cone KING .30 .09
436 Jeff Fassero KING .30 .09
437 John Wetteland KING .30 .09
438 Barry Bonds IS .75 .23
Ivan Rodriguez
439 Ken Griffey Jr. IS .75 .23
Andres Galarraga
440 Fred McGriff IS .30 .09
Rafael Palmeiro
441 Barry Larkin IS .50 .15
Jim Thome
442 Sammy Sosa IS .75 .23
Albert Belle
443 Bernie Williams IS .30 .09
Todd Hundley
444 Chuck Knoblauch IS .30 .09
Brian Jordan
445 Mo Vaughn IS .30 .09
Jeff Conine
446 Ken Caminiti IS .30 .09
Jason Giambi
447 Raul Mondesi IS .30 .09
Tim Salmon
448 Cal Ripken CL 1.25 .35
449 Greg Maddux CL .75 .23
450 Ken Griffey Jr. CL .75 .23

1997 Donruss Gold Press Proofs

Randomly inserted in first series at a rate of 1:32 and Update packs at an approximate rate of 1:64, cards from this 450-card set are a die-cut parallel rendition of the more common Silver Press Proof cards. Gold foil stamping further distinguishes them from the Silver Press Proofs. Only 500 gold sets were printed though they are not serial-numbered.

Nm-Mt Ex-Mt
*STARS: 10X TO 25X BASIC CARDS..
*ROOKIES: 3X TO 8X BASIC CARDS..

1997 Donruss Silver Press Proofs

Randomly inserted in first series packs at a rate of one in eight and Update packs at an approximate rate of one in 16, cards from this 450-card Silver foil set parallel the regular 1997 Donruss set. The silver foil stamped words, "Press Proof" down the front right-hand side of the card distinguish them from their regular issue counterparts. Only 2,000 of each card were produced though they are not serial numbered.

Nm-Mt Ex-Mt
*STARS: 4X TO 10X BASIC CARDS....
*ROOKIES: 1.25X TO .3X BASIC CARDS

1997 Donruss Armed and Dangerous

Randomly inserted in hobby packs at a rate of one in 58 packs, this 15-card set features the League's hottest arms in the game. The fronts carry color action player photos with foil printing. The backs display player information and a color player head portrait at the end of a ribbon

representing a medal. Only 5,000 of this set were produced and are sequentially numbered.

Nm-Mt Ex-Mt
COMPLETE SET (15) 120.00 36.00
1 Ken Griffey Jr. 10.00 3.00
2 Raul Mondesi 2.50 .75
3 Chipper Jones 6.00 1.80
4 Ivan Rodriguez 6.00 1.80
5 Randy Johnson 6.00 1.80
6 Alex Rodriguez 10.00 3.00
7 Larry Walker 4.00 1.20
8 Cal Ripken 20.00 6.00
9 Kenny Lofton 2.50 .75
10 Barry Bonds 15.00 4.50
11 Derek Jeter 15.00 4.50
12 Charles Johnson 2.50 .75
13 Greg Maddux 10.00 3.00
14 Roberto Alomar 4.00 1.20
15 Barry Larkin 4.00 1.20

1997 Donruss Diamond Kings

Randomly inserted in all first series packs at a rate of one in 45, this 10-card set commemorates the 15th anniversary of the annual art cards in Donruss baseball sets. Only 10,000 sets were produced each of which is sequentially numbered. Ten cards were printed with the number 1,982 representing the year the insert began and could be redeemed for an original piece of artwork by Diamond Kings artist Dan Gardiner. This was the first year Gardiner painted the Diamond King series.

Nm-Mt Ex-Mt
COMPLETE SET (10) 120.00 36.00
*CANVAS: 1.25X TO 3X BASIC DK'S
CANVAS: RANDOM INS.IN SER.1 PACKS
CANVAS PRINT RUN 500 SERIAL #'d SETS
1 Ken Griffey Jr. 15.00 4.50
2 Cal Ripken 30.00 9.00
3 Mo Vaughn 4.00 1.20
4 Chuck Knoblauch 4.00 1.20
5 Jeff Bagwell 6.00 1.80
6 Henry Rodriguez 4.00 1.20
7 Mike Piazza 15.00 4.50
8 Ivan Rodriguez 10.00 3.00
9 Frank Thomas 10.00 3.00
10 Chipper Jones 10.00 3.00

1997 Donruss Dominators

Randomly inserted in Update packs, cards from this 20-card set feature top stars with either incredible speed, awesome power, or unbelievable pitching ability. Card fronts feature red borders and silver foil stamping.

Nm-Mt Ex-Mt
COMPLETE SET (20) 80.00 24.00
1 Frank Thomas 4.00 1.20
2 Ken Griffey Jr. 6.00 1.80
3 Greg Maddux 6.00 1.80
4 Cal Ripken 12.00 3.60
5 Alex Rodriguez 6.00 1.80
6 Albert Belle 1.50 .45
7 Mark McGwire 10.00 3.00
8 Juan Gonzalez 2.50 .75
9 Chipper Jones 4.00 1.20
10 Hideo Nomo 4.00 1.20
11 Roger Clemens 8.00 2.40
12 John Smoltz 2.50 .75
13 Mike Piazza 6.00 1.80
14 Sammy Sosa 6.00 1.80
15 Matt Williams 1.50 .45
16 Kenny Lofton 1.50 .45
17 Barry Larkin 2.50 .75
18 Rafael Palmeiro 2.50 .75
19 Ken Caminiti 1.50 .45
20 Gary Sheffield 1.50 .45

1997 Donruss Elite Inserts

Randomly inserted in all first series packs, this 12-card set honors perennial all-star players of the League. The fronts feature Micro-etched color action player photos, while the backs carry player information. Only 2,500 of this set were produced and are sequentially numbered.

Nm-Mt Ex-Mt
COMPLETE SET (12) 250.00 75.00
1 Frank Thomas 15.00 4.50
2 Paul Molitor 10.00 3.00
3 Sammy Sosa 25.00 7.50
4 Barry Bonds 40.00 12.00
5 Chipper Jones 15.00 4.50
6 Alex Rodriguez 25.00 7.50
7 Ken Griffey Jr. 25.00 7.50
8 Jeff Bagwell 10.00 3.00
9 Cal Ripken 50.00 15.00
10 Mo Vaughn 6.00 1.80
11 Mike Piazza 25.00 7.50
12 Juan Gonzalez UER 10.00 3.00
name mispelled as Gonzales

1997 Donruss Franchise Features

Randomly inserted in Update hobby packs only at an approximate rate of 1:48, cards from this 15-card set feature color player photos on a unique "movie-poster" style, double-front card design. Each card highlights a superstar veteran on one side displaying a "Now Playing" banner, while the other side features a rookie prospect with a "Coming Attraction" banner. Each card is printed on an all foil card stock and serial numbered to 3,000.

Nm-Mt Ex-Mt
COMPLETE SET (15) 250.00 75.00
1 Ken Griffey Jr. 15.00 4.50
Andruw Jones
2 Frank Thomas 10.00 3.00
Darin Erstad
3 Alex Rodriguez 15.00 4.50
Nomar Garciaparra
4 Chuck Knoblauch 4.00 1.20
Wilton Guerrero
5 Juan Gonzalez 6.00 1.80
Bubba Trammell
6 Chipper Jones 10.00 3.00
Todd Walker
7 Barry Bonds 10.00 3.00
Vladimir Guerrero
8 Mark McGwire 25.00 7.50
Dmitri Young
9 Mike Piazza 15.00 4.50
Mike Sweeney
10 Mo Vaughn 4.00 1.20
Tony Clark
11 Gary Sheffield 4.00 1.20
Jose Guillen
12 Kenny Lofton 4.00 1.20
Shannon Stewart
13 Cal Ripken 30.00 9.00
Scott Rolen
14 Derek Jeter 25.00 7.50
Pokey Reese
15 Tony Gwynn 12.00 3.60
Bob Abreu

1997 Donruss Longball Leaders

Randomly inserted in first series retail packs only, this 15-card set honors the league's most fearsome long-ball hitters. The fronts feature color action player photos and foil stamping. The backs carry player information.

Nm-Mt Ex-Mt
COMPLETE SET (15) 80.00 24.00
1 Frank Thomas 6.00 1.80
2 Albert Belle 2.50 .75
3 Mo Vaughn 2.50 .75
4 Brady Anderson 2.50 .75
5 Greg Vaughn 2.50 .75
6 Ken Griffey Jr. 10.00 3.00
7 Jay Buhner 2.50 .75
8 Juan Gonzalez 4.00 1.20
9 Mike Piazza 10.00 3.00
10 Jeff Bagwell 4.00 1.20
11 Sammy Sosa 10.00 3.00
12 Mark McGwire 15.00 4.50
13 Cecil Fielder 2.50 .75
14 Ryan Klesko 2.50 .75
15 Jose Canseco 6.00 1.80

1997 Donruss Power Alley

This 24-card set features color images of some of the league's top hitters printed on a micro-etched, all-foil card stock with holographic foil stamping. Using a "fractured" printing structure, 12 players utilize a green finish and are numbered to 4,000. Eight players are printed on all blue finish and number to 2,000, with the last four players utilizing a gold finish and are numbered to 1,000.

Nm-Mt Ex-Mt
*GREEN DC's: 2X TO 5X BASIC GREEN
*BLUE DC's: 1.25X TO 3X BASIC BLUE
*GOLD DC's: .75X TO 2X BASIC GOLD
DIE CUTS: RANDOM INS.IN UPDATE PACKS
DIE CUTS PRINT RUN 250 SERIAL #'d SETS

1 Frank Thomas G 15.00 4.50
2 Ken Griffey Jr. G 25.00 7.50
3 Cal Ripken G 50.00 15.00
4 Jeff Bagwell B 6.00 1.80
5 Mike Piazza B 15.00 4.50
6 Andruw Jones GR 2.50 .75
7 Alex Rodriguez G 25.00 7.50
8 Albert Belle GR 2.50 .75
9 Mo Vaughn GR 2.50 .75
10 Chipper Jones B 10.00 3.00
11 Juan Gonzalez B 6.00 1.80
12 Ken Caminiti GR 2.50 .75
13 Manny Ramirez GR 4.00 1.20
14 Mark McGwire GR 15.00 4.50
15 Kenny Lofton B 4.00 1.20
16 Barry Bonds GR 15.00 4.50
17 Gary Sheffield GR 2.50 .75
18 Tony Gwynn GR 8.00 2.40
19 Vladimir Guerrero B 10.00 3.00
20 Ivan Rodriguez B 10.00 3.00
21 Paul Molitor B 6.00 1.80
22 Sammy Sosa GR 10.00 3.00
23 Matt Williams GR 2.50 .75
24 Derek Jeter GR 15.00 4.50

1997 Donruss Rated Rookies

Randomly inserted in all first series packs, this 30-card set honors the top rookie prospects as chosen by Donruss to be the most likely to succeed. The fronts feature color action player photos and silver foil printing. The backs carry a player portrait and player information.

Nm-Mt Ex-Mt
COMPLETE SET (30) 40.00 12.00
1 Jason Thompson 2.00 .60
2 LaTroy Hawkins 2.00 .60
3 Scott Rolen 5.00 1.50
4 Trey Beamon 2.00 .60
5 Kimera Bartee 2.00 .60
6 Nerio Rodriguez 2.00 .60
7 Jeff D'Amico 2.00 .60
8 Quinton McCracken 2.00 .60
9 John Wasdin 2.00 .60
10 Robin Jennings 2.00 .60
11 Steve Gibralter 2.00 .60
12 Tyler Houston 2.00 .60
13 Tony Clark 2.00 .60
14 Ugueth Urbina 2.00 .60
15 Karim Garcia 2.00 .60
16 Raul Casanova 2.00 .60
17 Brooks Kieschnick 2.00 .60
18 Luis Castillo 2.00 .60
19 Edgar Renteria 2.00 .60
20 Andruw Jones 2.00 .60
21 Chad Mottola 2.00 .60
22 Mac Suzuki 2.00 .60
23 Justin Thompson 2.00 .60
24 Darin Erstad 2.00 .60
25 Todd Walker 2.00 .60
26 Todd Greene 2.00 .60
27 Vladimir Guerrero 5.00 1.50
28 Darren Dreifort 2.00 .60
29 John Burke 2.00 .60
30 Damon Mashore 2.00 .60

1997 Donruss Ripken The Only Way I Know

This special autobiographical tribute to Cal Ripken Jr. delivers a one-of-a-kind inside look at the modern day "Iron Man." Cards from this ten card set are printed on all foil card stock with foil stamping, utilizing exclusive photography and excerpts from his book. The first nine cards in the set were randomly seeded into packs of Donruss Update at an approximate rate of 1:24. Card number 10 was available exclusively in his book, "The Only Way I Know." Ripken autographed 2,131 of these number 10 cards and they were randomly inserted into the books. Because of it's separate distribution, card number 10 is not commonly included in complete sets, thus the mainstream set is considered complete with cards 1-9. Only 5,000 of each 1-9 card were produced, each of which are sequentially numbered on back.

Nm-Mt Ex-Mt
COMPLETE SET (9) 100.00 30.00
COMMON CARD (1-9) 12.00 3.60
COMMON CARD (10) 20.00 6.00
10A Cal Ripken AU/2131 200.00 60.00
distributed exclusively with book

1997 Donruss Rocket Launchers

Randomly inserted in first series magazine packs only, this 15-card set honers baseball's top power hitters. The fronts feature color player photos, while the backs carry player information. Only 5,000 sets were produced and all are sequentially numbered.

Nm-Mt Ex-Mt
COMPLETE SET (15) 80.00 24.00
1 Frank Thomas 6.00 1.80
2 Albert Belle 2.50 .75
3 Chipper Jones 6.00 1.80
4 Mike Piazza 10.00 3.00
5 Mo Vaughn 2.50 .75
6 Juan Gonzalez 4.00 1.20
7 Fred McGriff 4.00 1.20
8 Jeff Bagwell 4.00 1.20
9 Matt Williams 2.50 .75
10 Gary Sheffield 2.50 .75
11 Barry Bonds 15.00 4.50
12 Manny Ramirez 4.00 1.20
13 Henry Rodriguez 2.50 .75
14 Jason Giambi 2.50 .75
15 Cal Ripken 20.00 6.00

1997 Donruss Rookie Diamond Kings

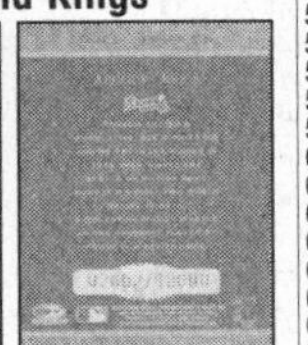

Randomly inserted in Update packs at an approximate rate of 1:24, cards from this 10-card set feature color portraits of some of the season's hottest rookie prospects in gold borders. Only 9,500 of each card were printed and are sequentially numbered. Please note that the numbering of each card runs to 10,000, but the first 500 of each card were Canvas parallels.

Nm-Mt Ex-Mt
COMPLETE SET (10) 60.00 18.00
*CANVAS: 1.25X TO 3X BASIC DK'S
CANVAS PRINT RUN 500 SERIAL #'d SETS
RANDOM INSERTS IN UPDATE PACKS
1 Andruw Jones 4.00 1.20
2 Vladimir Guerrero 10.00 3.00
3 Scott Rolen 10.00 3.00
4 Todd Walker 4.00 1.20
5 Bartolo Colon 4.00 1.20
6 Jose Guillen 4.00 1.20
7 Nomar Garciaparra 15.00 4.50
8 Darin Erstad 4.00 1.20
9 Dmitri Young 4.00 1.20
10 Wilton Guerrero 4.00 1.20

1998 Donruss

The 1998 Donruss set was issued in two series (series one numbers 1-170, series two numbers 171-420) and was distributed in 10-card packs with a suggested retail price of $1.99. The fronts feature color player photos with player information on the backs. The set contains the topical subsets: Fan Club (156-165), Hit List (346-375), The Untouchables (376-385), Spirit of the Game (386-415) and Checklists (416-420). Each Fan Club card carried instructions on how the fan could vote for their favorite players to be included in the 1998 Donruss Update set. Rookie Cards include Kevin Millwood and Magglio Ordonez. Sadly, after an eighteen year run, this was the last Donruss set to be issued due to card manufacturer Pinnacle's bankruptcy in 1998. In 2001, however, Donruss/Playoff procuered a license to produce baseball cards and the Donruss brand was reinstituted after a two year break.

Nm-Mt Ex-Mt
COMPLETE SET (420) 50.00 15.00
COMP.SERIES 1 (170) 20.00 6.00
COMPLETE UPDATE (250) 30.00 9.00
1 Paul Molitor .40 .12
2 Juan Gonzalez .40 .12
3 Darryl Kile .25 .07
4 Randy Johnson .60 .18
5 Tom Glavine .40 .12
6 Pat Hentgen .25 .07
7 David Justice .25 .07
8 Kevin Brown .40 .12
9 Mike Mussina .40 .12
10 Ken Caminiti .25 .07
11 Todd Hundley .25 .07
12 Frank Thomas .60 .18
13 Ray Lankford .25 .07
14 Justin Thompson .25 .07
15 Jason Dickson .25 .07
16 Kenny Lofton .25 .07
17 Ivan Rodriguez .60 .18
18 Pedro Martinez .60 .18
19 Brady Anderson .25 .07
20 Barry Larkin .40 .12
21 Chipper Jones .60 .18
22 Tony Gwynn .75 .23
23 Roger Clemens 1.25 .35
24 Sandy Alomar Jr. .25 .07
25 Tino Martinez .40 .12
26 Jeff Bagwell .40 .12
27 Shawn Estes .25 .07
28 Ken Griffey Jr. 1.00 .30
29 Javier Lopez .25 .07
30 Denny Neagle .25 .07
31 Mike Piazza 1.00 .30
32 Andres Galarraga .25 .07
33 Larry Walker .40 .12
34 Alex Rodriguez 1.00 .30
35 Greg Maddux 1.00 .30
36 Albert Belle .25 .07
37 Barry Bonds 1.50 .45
38 Mo Vaughn .25 .07
39 Kevin Appier .25 .07
40 Wade Boggs .40 .12
41 Garret Anderson .25 .07
42 Jeffrey Hammonds .25 .07
43 Marquis Grissom .25 .07
44 Jim Edmonds .25 .07
45 Brian Jordan .25 .07
46 Raul Mondesi .25 .07
47 John Valentin .25 .07
48 Brad Radke .25 .07
49 Ismael Valdes .25 .07
50 Matt Stairs .25 .07
51 Matt Williams .25 .07
52 Reggie Jefferson .25 .07
53 Alan Benes .25 .07
54 Charles Johnson .25 .07
55 Chuck Knoblauch .25 .07
56 Edgar Martinez .40 .12
57 Nomar Garciaparra 1.00 .30
58 Craig Biggio .40 .12
59 Bernie Williams .40 .12
60 David Cone .25 .07
61 Cal Ripken 2.00 .60
62 Mark McGwire 1.50 .45
63 Roberto Alomar .40 .12
64 Fred McGriff .40 .12
65 Eric Karros .25 .07
66 Robin Ventura .25 .07
67 Darin Erstad .25 .07
68 Michael Tucker .25 .07
69 Jim Thome .60 .18
70 Mark Grace .40 .12
71 Lou Collier .25 .07
72 Karim Garcia .25 .07
73 Alex Fernandez .25 .07
74 J.T. Snow .25 .07
75 Reggie Sanders .25 .07
76 John Smoltz .40 .12
77 Tim Salmon .40 .12
78 Paul O'Neill .40 .12
79 Vinny Castilla .25 .07
80 Rafael Palmeiro .40 .12
81 Jaret Wright .25 .07
82 Jay Buhner .25 .07
83 Brett Butler .25 .07
84 Todd Greene .25 .07
85 Scott Rolen .60 .18
86 Sammy Sosa 1.00 .30
87 Jason Giambi .25 .07
88 Carlos Delgado .25 .07
89 Deion Sanders .40 .12
90 Wilton Guerrero .25 .07
91 Andy Pettitte .40 .12
92 Brian Giles .25 .07
93 Dmitri Young .25 .07
94 Ron Coomer .25 .07
95 Mike Cameron .25 .07
96 Edgardo Alfonzo .25 .07
97 Jimmy Key .25 .07
98 Ryan Klesko .25 .07
99 Andy Benes .25 .07
100 Derek Jeter 1.50 .45
101 Jeff Fassero .25 .07
102 Neifi Perez .25 .07
103 Hideo Nomo .60 .18
104 Andruw Jones .25 .07
105 Todd Helton .40 .12
106 Livan Hernandez .25 .07
107 Brett Tomko .25 .07
108 Shannon Stewart .25 .07
109 Bartolo Colon .25 .07
110 Matt Morris .25 .07
111 Miguel Tejada .25 .07
112 Pokey Reese .25 .07
113 Fernando Tatis .25 .07
114 Todd Dunwoody .25 .07
115 Jose Cruz Jr. .25 .07
116 Chan Ho Park .25 .07
117 Kevin Young .25 .07
118 Rickey Henderson .60 .18
119 Hideki Irabu .25 .07
120 Francisco Cordova .25 .07
121 Al Martin .25 .07
122 Tony Clark .25 .07
123 Curt Schilling .25 .07
124 Rusty Greer .25 .07
125 Jose Canseco .60 .18
126 Edgar Renteria .25 .07
127 Todd Walker .25 .07
128 Wally Joyner .25 .07
129 Bill Mueller .25 .07
130 Jose Guillen .25 .07
131 Manny Ramirez .40 .12
132 Bobby Higginson .25 .07
133 Kevin Orie .25 .07
134 Will Clark .60 .18
135 Dave Nilsson .25 .07
136 Jason Kendall .25 .07
137 Ivan Cruz .25 .07
138 Gary Sheffield .25 .07
139 Bubba Trammell .25 .07
140 Vladimir Guerrero .60 .18
141 Dennis Reyes .25 .07
142 Bobby Bonilla .25 .07
143 Ruben Rivera .25 .07
144 Ben Grieve .25 .07
145 Moises Alou .25 .07
146 Tony Womack .25 .07
147 Eric Young .25 .07
148 Paul Konerko .25 .07
149 Dante Bichette .25 .07
150 Joe Carter .25 .07
151 Rondell White .25 .07
152 Chris Holt .25 .07
153 Shawn Green .25 .07
154 Mark Grudzielanek .25 .07
UER back rudzielanek
155 Jermaine Dye .25 .07
156 Ken Griffey Jr. FC .60 .18
157 Frank Thomas FC .40 .12
158 Chipper Jones FC .40 .12
159 Mike Piazza FC .60 .18
160 Cal Ripken FC 1.00 .30
161 Greg Maddux FC .60 .18
162 Juan Gonzalez FC .25 .07
163 Alex Rodriguez FC .60 .18
164 Mark McGwire FC .75 .23
165 Derek Jeter FC .75 .23
166 Larry Walker CL .25 .07
167 Tony Gwynn CL .40 .12
168 Tino Martinez CL .25 .07
169 Scott Rolen CL .40 .12
170 Nomar Garciaparra CL .60 .18
171 Mike Sweeney .25 .07
172 Dustin Hermanson .25 .07
173 Darren Dreifort .25 .07
174 Ron Gant .25 .07
175 Todd Hollandsworth .25 .07
176 John Jaha .25 .07
177 Kerry Wood .60 .18
178 Chris Stynes .25 .07
179 Kevin Elster .25 .07
180 Derek Bell .25 .07
181 Darryl Strawberry .25 .07
182 Damion Easley .25 .07
183 Jeff Cirillo .25 .07
184 John Thomson .25 .07
185 Dan Wilson .25 .07
186 Jay Bell .25 .07
187 Bernard Gilkey .25 .07
188 Marc Valdes .25 .07
189 Ramon Martinez .25 .07
190 Charles Nagy .25 .07
191 Derek Lowe .25 .07
192 Andy Benes .25 .07
193 Delino DeShields .25 .07
194 Ryan Jackson RC .25 .07
195 Kenny Lofton .25 .07
196 Chuck Knoblauch .25 .07
197 Andres Galarraga .25 .07
198 Jose Canseco .60 .18
199 John Olerud .25 .07
200 Lance Johnson .25 .07
201 Darryl Kile .25 .07
202 Luis Castillo .25 .07
203 Joe Carter .25 .07
204 Dennis Eckersley .25 .07
205 Steve Finley .25 .07
206 Esteban Loaiza .25 .07
207 R.Christenson RC UER .25 .07
birthdate says 1988
208 Deivi Cruz .25 .07
209 Mariano Rivera .40 .12
210 Mike Judd RC .40 .12
211 Billy Wagner .25 .07
212 Scott Spiezio .25 .07
213 Russ Davis .25 .07
214 Jeff Suppan .25 .07
215 Doug Glanville .25 .07
216 Dmitri Young .25 .07
217 Rey Ordonez .25 .07
218 Cecil Fielder .25 .07
219 Masato Yoshii RC .60 .18
220 Raul Casanova .25 .07
221 Rolando Arrojo RC .40 .12
222 Ellis Burks .25 .07
223 Butch Huskey .25 .07
224 Brian Hunter .25 .07
225 Marquis Grissom .25 .07
226 Kevin Brown .40 .12
227 Joe Randa .25 .07
228 Henry Rodriguez .25 .07
229 Omar Vizquel .40 .12
230 Fred McGriff .40 .12
231 Matt Williams .25 .07
232 Moises Alou .25 .07
233 Travis Fryman .25 .07
234 Wade Boggs .40 .12
235 Pedro Martinez .60 .18
236 Rickey Henderson .60 .18
237 Bubba Trammell .25 .07
238 Mike Caruso .25 .07
239 Wilson Alvarez .25 .07
240 Geronimo Berroa .25 .07
241 Eric Milton .25 .07
242 Scott Erickson .25 .07
243 Todd Erdos RC .25 .07
244 Bobby Hughes .25 .07
245 Dave Hollins .25 .07
246 Dean Palmer .25 .07
247 Carlos Baerga .25 .07
248 Jose Silva .25 .07
249 Jose Cabrera RC .25 .07
250 Tom Evans .25 .07
251 Marty Cordova .25 .07
252 Hanley Frias RC .25 .07
253 Javier Valentin .25 .07
254 Mario Valdez .25 .07
255 Joey Cora .25 .07
256 Mike Lansing .25 .07
257 Jeff Kent .25 .07
258 Dave Dellucci RC .60 .18
259 Curtis King RC .25 .07
260 David Segui .25 .07
261 Royce Clayton .25 .07
262 Jeff Blauser .25 .07
263 Manny Aybar RC .25 .07
264 Mike Cather RC .25 .07
265 Todd Zeile .25 .07
266 Richard Hidalgo .25 .07
267 Dante Powell .25 .07
268 Mike DeJean RC .25 .07
269 Ken Cloude .25 .07
270 Danny Klassen .25 .07
271 Sean Casey .25 .07
272 A.J. Hinch .25 .07
273 Rich Butler RC .25 .07
274 Ben Ford RC .25 .07
275 Billy McMillon .25 .07
276 Wilson Delgado .25 .07
277 Orlando Cabrera .25 .07
278 Geoff Jenkins .25 .07
279 Enrique Wilson .25 .07
280 Derrek Lee .25 .07
281 Marc Pisciotta RC .25 .07
282 Abraham Nunez .25 .07
283 Aaron Boone .25 .07
284 Brad Fullmer .25 .07
285 Rob Stanifer RC .25 .07
286 Preston Wilson .25 .07
287 Greg Norton .25 .07
288 Bobby Smith .25 .07
289 Josh Booty .25 .07
290 Russell Branyan .25 .07
291 Jeremi Gonzalez .25 .07
292 Michael Coleman .25 .07
293 Cliff Politte .25 .07
294 Eric Ludwick .25 .07
295 Rafael Medina .25 .07
296 Jason Varitek .60 .18
297 Ron Wright .25 .07
298 Mark Kotsay .25 .07
299 David Ortiz .60 .18
300 Frank Catalanotto RC .60 .18
301 Robinson Checo .25 .07
302 Kevin Millwood RC .75 .23
303 Jacob Cruz .25 .07
304 Javier Vazquez .25 .07
305 Magglio Ordonez RC 1.50 .45
306 Kevin Witt .25 .07
307 Derrick Gibson .25 .07
308 Shane Monahan .25 .07
309 Brian Rose .25 .07
310 Bobby Estalella .25 .07
311 Felix Heredia .25 .07
312 Desi Relaford .25 .07
313 Esteban Yan RC .40 .12
314 Ricky Ledee .25 .07
315 Steve Woodard .25 .07
316 Pat Watkins .25 .07
317 Damian Moss .25 .07
318 Bob Abreu .25 .07
319 Jeff Abbott .25 .07
320 Miguel Cairo .25 .07
321 Rigo Beltran RC .25 .07
322 Tony Saunders .25 .07
323 Randall Simon .25 .07
324 Hiram Bocachica .25 .07
325 Richie Sexson .25 .07
326 Karim Garcia .25 .07
327 Mike Lowell RC 1.25 .35
328 Pat Cline .25 .07
329 Matt Clement .25 .07
330 Scott Elarton .25 .07
331 Manuel Barrios RC .25 .07
332 Bruce Chen .25 .07
333 Juan Encarnacion .25 .07
334 Travis Lee .25 .07
335 Wes Helms .25 .07
336 Chad Fox RC .25 .07
337 Donnie Sadler .25 .07
338 Carlos Mendoza RC .25 .07
339 Damian Jackson .25 .07
340 Julio Ramirez RC .25 .07
341 John Halama RC .40 .12
342 Edwin Diaz .25 .07
343 Felix Martinez .25 .07
344 Eli Marrero .25 .07
345 Carl Pavano .40 .12
346 Vladimir Guerrero HL .40 .12
347 Barry Bonds HL .60 .18
348 Darin Erstad HL .25 .07
349 Albert Belle HL .25 .07
350 Kenny Lofton HL .25 .07
351 Mo Vaughn HL .25 .07
352 Jose Cruz Jr. HL .25 .07
353 Tony Clark HL .25 .07
354 Roberto Alomar HL .25 .07
355 Manny Ramirez HL .25 .07
356 Paul Molitor HL .25 .07
357 Jim Thome HL .40 .12
358 Tino Martinez HL .25 .07
359 Tim Salmon HL .25 .07
360 David Justice HL .25 .07
361 Raul Mondesi HL .25 .07
362 Mark Grace HL .25 .07
363 Craig Biggio HL .25 .07
364 Larry Walker HL .25 .07
365 Mark McGwire HL .75 .23
366 Juan Gonzalez HL .25 .07
367 Derek Jeter HL .75 .23
368 Chipper Jones HL .40 .12
369 Frank Thomas HL .40 .12
370 Alex Rodriguez HL .60 .18
371 Mike Piazza HL .60 .18
372 Tony Gwynn HL .40 .12
373 Jeff Bagwell HL .25 .07
374 N.Garciaparra HL .60 .18
375 Ken Griffey Jr. HL .60 .18
376 Livan Hernandez UN .25 .07
377 Chan Ho Park UN .25 .07
378 Mike Mussina UN .25 .07
379 Andy Pettitte UN .25 .07
380 Greg Maddux UN .60 .18
381 Hideo Nomo UN .40 .12
382 Roger Clemens UN .60 .18
383 Randy Johnson UN .40 .12
384 Pedro Martinez UN .60 .18
385 Jaret Wright UN .25 .07
386 Ken Griffey Jr. SG .60 .18
387 Todd Helton SG .25 .07
388 Paul Konerko SG .25 .07
389 Cal Ripken SG 1.00 .30
390 Larry Walker SG .25 .07
391 Ken Caminiti SG .25 .07
392 Jose Guillen SG .25 .07

393 Jim Edmonds SG .25 .07
394 Barry Larkin SG .25 .07
395 Bernie Williams SG .25 .07
396 Tony Clark SG .25 .07
397 Jose Cruz Jr. SG .25 .07
398 Ivan Rodriguez SG .40 .12
399 Darin Erstad SG .25 .07
400 Scott Rolen SG .40 .12
401 Mark McGwire SG .75 .23
402 Andruw Jones SG .25 .07
403 Juan Gonzalez SG .25 .07
404 Derek Jeter SG .75 .23
405 Chipper Jones SG .40 .12
406 Greg Maddux SG .60 .18
407 Frank Thomas SG .40 .12
408 Alex Rodriguez SG .60 .18
409 Mike Piazza SG .60 .18
410 Tony Gwynn SG .40 .12
411 Jeff Bagwell SG .25 .07
412 N.Garciaparra SG .60 .18
413 Hideo Nomo SG .40 .12
414 Barry Bonds SG .60 .18
415 Ben Grieve SG .25 .07
416 Barry Bonds CL .60 .18
417 Mark McGwire CL .75 .23
418 Roger Clemens CL .60 .18
419 Livan Hernandez CL .25 .07
420 Ken Griffey Jr. CL .60 .18

1998 Donruss Gold Press Proofs

This 420-card set is a limited production, die-cut parallel version of the regular base set. Card fronts are highlighted by a gold foil treatment. Each card is numbered on back as "1 of 500."

Nm-Mt Ex-Mt
*STARS: 10X TO 25X BASIC CARDS
*ROOKIES: 5X TO 12X BASIC CARDS

1998 Donruss Silver Press Proofs

Randomly inserted in packs, this 420-card set is a limited parallel version of the base set printed on silver foil board. Each card is numbered on back as "1 of 1500" produced.

Nm-Mt Ex-Mt
*STARS: 2.5X TO 12X BASIC CARDS
*ROOKIES: 3X TO 6X BASIC CARDS

1998 Donruss Crusade Green

This 100-card set features a selection of the league's top stars. Cards were randomly inserted into three products as follows: 40 players into 1998 Donruss, 30 into 1998 Leaf, and 30 into 1998 Donruss Update. The fronts feature color player photos printed with Limited "refractive" technology. The backs carry player information. Only 250 of each of these Green cards were produced and sequentially numbered. Cards are designated below with a D, L or U suffix to denote their original distribution within Donruss, Leaf or Donruss Update packs. All of the "Call to Arms" (sic CTA) subset cards were mistakenly printed without numbers. Corrected copies were never made.

Nm-Mt Ex-Mt
D SUFFIX ON DONRUSS DISTRIBUTION
L SUFFIX ON LEAF DISTRIBUTION
U SUFFIX ON DON.UPDATE DISTRIBUTION
ALL CTA CARDS ARE UNNUMBERED ERRORS
1 Tim Salmon U 25.00 7.50
2 Garret Anderson U 15.00 4.50
3 Jim Edmonds CTA L 15.00 4.50
4 Darin Erstad CTA L 15.00 4.50
5 Jason Dickson D 15.00 4.50
6 Todd Greene D 15.00 4.50
7 Roberto Alomar CTA 25.00 7.50
8 Cal Ripken D 80.00 24.00
9 Rafael Palmeiro CTA U 25.00 7.50
10 Brady Anderson U 15.00 4.50
11 Mike Mussina L 25.00 7.50
12 Mo Vaughn CTA 15.00 4.50
13 Nomar Garciaparra D 40.00 12.00
14 Frank Thomas CTA U 25.00 7.50
15 Albert Belle CTA L 15.00 4.50
16 Mike Cameron D 15.00 4.50
17 Robin Ventura U 15.00 4.50
18 Manny Ramirez L 25.00 7.50
19 Jim Thome CTA L 25.00 7.50
20 Sandy Alomar Jr. D 15.00 4.50
21 David Justice D 15.00 4.50
22 Matt Williams U 15.00 4.50
23 Tony Clark U 15.00 4.50
24 Bubba Trammell L 15.00 4.50
25 Justin Thompson D 15.00 4.50
26 Bobby Higginson L 15.00 4.50
27 Kevin Appier D 15.00 4.50
28 Paul Molitor L 25.00 7.50
29 C.Knoblauch CTA U 15.00 4.50
30 Todd Walker L 15.00 4.50
31 Bernie Williams U 25.00 7.50
32 Derek Jeter CTA U 60.00 18.00
33 Tino Martinez D 25.00 7.50
34 Andy Pettitte L 25.00 7.50
35 Wade Boggs CTA L 25.00 7.50
36 Hideki Irabu D 15.00 4.50
37 Jose Canseco D 25.00 7.50
38 Jason Giambi U 15.00 4.50
39 Ken Griffey Jr. D 40.00 12.00
40 Alex Rodriguez CTA L 40.00 12.00
41 Randy Johnson L 25.00 7.50
42 Edgar Martinez D 25.00 7.50
43 Jay Buhner CTA U 15.00 4.50
44 Juan Gonzalez CTA U 25.00 7.50
45 Will Clark D 40.00 12.00
46 Ivan Rodriguez L 25.00 7.50
47 Rusty Greer D 15.00 4.50
48 Roger Clemens L 50.00 15.00
49 Carlos Delgado U 15.00 4.50
50 Shawn Green D 15.00 4.50
51 Jose Cruz Jr. D 15.00 4.50
52 Kenny Lofton D 15.00 4.50
53 Chipper Jones D 25.00 7.50
54 Andruw Jones CTA L 15.00 4.50
55 Greg Maddux U 40.00 12.00
56 John Smoltz CTA L 25.00 7.50
57 Tom Glavine U 25.00 7.50
58 Javier Lopez L 15.00 4.50
59 Fred McGriff L 25.00 7.50
60 Mark Grace U 25.00 7.50
61 Sammy Sosa CTA U 40.00 12.00
62 Kevin Orie D 15.00 4.50
63 Barry Larkin CTA U 25.00 7.50
64 Pokey Reese L 15.00 4.50
65 Deion Sanders D 25.00 7.50
66 Andres Galarraga L 15.00 4.50
67 Larry Walker D 25.00 7.50
68 Dante Bichette CTA D 15.00 4.50
69 Neifi Perez U 15.00 4.50
70 Eric Young L 15.00 4.50
71 Todd Helton D 25.00 7.50
72 Gary Sheffield CTA U 15.00 4.50
73 Moises Alou L 15.00 4.50
74 Bobby Bonilla D 15.00 4.50
75 Kevin Brown D 25.00 7.50
76 Ben Grieve L 15.00 4.50
77 Jeff Bagwell CTA U 25.00 7.50
78 Craig Biggio D 25.00 7.50
79 Mike Piazza L 40.00 12.00
80 Raul Mondesi U 15.00 4.50
81 Hideo Nomo CTA U 25.00 7.50
82 Wilton Guerrero D 15.00 4.50
83 Rondell White CTA U 15.00 4.50
84 V.Guerrero CTA U 25.00 7.50
85 Pedro Martinez D 25.00 7.50
86 Edgardo Alfonzo D 15.00 4.50
87 Todd Hundley CTA U 15.00 4.50
88 Scott Rolen D 25.00 7.50
89 Francisco Cordova D 15.00 4.50
90 Jose Guillen D 15.00 4.50
91 Jason Kendall L 15.00 4.50
92 Ray Lankford D 15.00 4.50
93 Mark McGwire CTA D 60.00 18.00
94 Matt Morris D 15.00 4.50
95 Alan Benes L 15.00 4.50
96 Brian Jordan CTA U 15.00 4.50
97 Tony Gwynn L 30.00 9.00
98 Ken Caminiti CTA L 15.00 4.50
99 Barry Bonds CTA U 60.00 18.00
100 Shawn Estes D 15.00 4.50

1998 Donruss Diamond Kings

Randomly inserted in packs, this 20-card set features color player portraits of some of the greatest names in baseball. Only 9,500 sets were produced and are sequentially numbered. The first 500 of each card were printed on actual canvas card stock. In addition, a Frank Thomas sample card was created as a promo for the 1998 Donruss 1 product. The card was sent to all wholesale accounts along with the order forms for the product. The large "SAMPLE" stamp across the back of the card makes it easy to differentiate from Thomas' standard 1998 Diamond King insert card.

Nm-Mt Ex-Mt
COMPLETE SET (20) 100.00 30.00
*CANVAS: 1.25X TO 3X BASIC DIAM.KINGS
CANVAS: RANDOM INSERTS IN PACKS
CANVAS PRINT RUN 500 SERIAL #'d SETS
1 Cal Ripken 20.00 6.00
2 Greg Maddux 10.00 3.00
3 Ivan Rodriguez 6.00 1.80
4 Tony Gwynn 8.00 2.40
5 Paul Molitor 4.00 1.20
6 Kenny Lofton 2.50 .75
7 Andy Pettitte 4.00 1.20
8 Darin Erstad 2.50 .75
9 Randy Johnson 6.00 1.80
10 Derek Jeter 15.00 4.50
11 Hideo Nomo 6.00 1.80
12 David Justice 2.50 .75
13 Bernie Williams 4.00 1.20
14 Roger Clemens 12.00 3.60
15 Barry Larkin 4.00 1.20
16 Andruw Jones 2.50 .75
17 Mike Piazza 10.00 3.00
18 Frank Thomas 6.00 1.80
19 Alex Rodriguez 10.00 3.00
20 Ken Griffey Jr. 10.00 3.00
S20 Frank Thomas Sample 2.00 .60

1998 Donruss Dominators

Randomly inserted in update packs, this 30-card set is an insert to the Donruss base set. The holographic foil-stamped fronts feature color action photos surrounded by an orange background. The featured player's team name sits in the upper right corner and the Donruss logo sits in the upper left corner.

Nm-Mt Ex-Mt
COMPLETE SET (30) 120.00 36.00
1 Roger Clemens 8.00 2.40
2 Tony Clark 1.50 .45
3 Darin Erstad 1.50 .45
4 Jeff Bagwell 2.50 .75
5 Ken Griffey Jr. 6.00 1.80
6 Andruw Jones 1.50 .45
7 Juan Gonzalez 2.50 .75
8 Ivan Rodriguez 4.00 1.20
9 Randy Johnson 4.00 1.20
10 Tino Martinez 2.50 .75
11 Mark McGwire 10.00 3.00
12 Chuck Knoblauch 1.50 .45
13 Jim Thome 4.00 1.20
14 Alex Rodriguez 6.00 1.80
15 Hideo Nomo 4.00 1.20
16 Jose Cruz Jr. 1.50 .45
17 Chipper Jones 4.00 1.20
18 Tony Gwynn 5.00 1.50
19 Barry Bonds 10.00 3.00
20 Mo Vaughn 1.50 .45
21 Cal Ripken 12.00 3.60
22 Greg Maddux 6.00 1.80
23 Manny Ramirez 2.50 .75
24 Andres Galarraga 1.50 .45
25 Vladimir Guerrero 4.00 1.20
26 Albert Belle 1.50 .45
27 Nomar Garciaparra 6.00 1.80
28 Kenny Lofton 1.50 .45
29 Mike Piazza 6.00 1.80
30 Frank Thomas 4.00 1.20

1998 Donruss Elite Inserts

Continuing the popular tradition begun in 1991, Donruss again inserted Elite cards in their packs. These cards which have the work "Elite" written in big cursive letters on the bottom and a small player photo, were serially numbered to 2500 and has the "cream of the crop" of the baseball players. This set was designed to be the last time Donruss would issue Elite cards ending the succsessful eight year run. It's interesting to note that unlike previous Elite inserts, the 1998 cards were not numbered in continuation of the Elite run.

Nm-Mt Ex-Mt
COMPLETE SET (20) 300.00 90.00
1 Jeff Bagwell 8.00 2.40
2 Andruw Jones 5.00 1.50
3 Ken Griffey Jr. 20.00 6.00
4 Derek Jeter 30.00 9.00
5 Juan Gonzalez 8.00 2.40
6 Mark McGwire 30.00 9.00
7 Ivan Rodriguez 12.00 3.60
8 Paul Molitor 8.00 2.40
9 Hideo Nomo 12.00 3.60
10 Mo Vaughn 5.00 1.50
11 Chipper Jones 12.00 3.60
12 Nomar Garciaparra 20.00 6.00
13 Mike Piazza 20.00 6.00
14 Frank Thomas 12.00 3.60
15 Greg Maddux 20.00 6.00
16 Cal Ripken 40.00 12.00
17 Alex Rodriguez 20.00 6.00
18 Jose Cruz Jr. 5.00 1.50
19 Barry Bonds 30.00 9.00
20 Tony Gwynn 15.00 4.50

1998 Donruss FANtasy Team

Randomly inserted in update packs, this 20-card set features the leading votegetters from the online Fan Club. The top vote-getters make up the 1st team FANtasy Team and are sequentially numbered to 1750. The reamining players make up the 2nd team FANtasy Team and are sequentially numbered to 3750. The fronts carry color action photos surrounded by a red, white, and blue star-studded background. Cards number 1-10 feature members from the first team while cards numbered from 11-20 feature members of the second team.

Nm-Mt Ex-Mt
COMPLETE SET (20) 150.00 45.00
*1ST TEAM DC's: 1X TO 2.5X BASIC FANTASY
*2ND TEAM DIE CUTS: 1.5X TO 4X BASIC FANTASY
DIE CUTS PRINT RUN 250 SERIAL #'d SETS
RANDOM INSERTS IN UPDATE PACKS
1 Frank Thomas 10.00 3.00
2 Ken Griffey Jr. 15.00 4.50
3 Cal Ripken 30.00 9.00
4 Jose Cruz Jr. 4.00 1.20
5 Travis Lee 4.00 1.20
6 Greg Maddux 15.00 4.50
7 Alex Rodriguez 15.00 4.50
8 Mark McGwire 25.00 7.50
9 Chipper Jones 10.00 3.00
10 Andruw Jones 4.00 1.20
11 Mike Piazza 10.00 3.00
12 Tony Gwynn 8.00 2.40
13 Larry Walker 4.00 1.20
14 Nomar Garciaparra 10.00 3.00
15 Jaret Wright 2.50 .75
16 Livan Hernandez 2.50 .75
17 Roger Clemens 12.00 3.60
18 Derek Jeter 15.00 4.50
19 Scott Rolen 6.00 1.80
20 Jeff Bagwell 4.00 1.20

1998 Donruss Longball Leaders

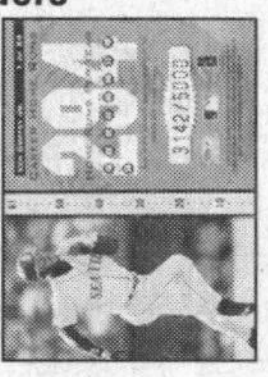

Randomly inserted in first series packs, this 24-card set features color photos of the top sluggers in baseball printed on micro-etched cards. Only 5000 of each card were produced and are sequentially numbered.

Nm-Mt Ex-Mt
COMPLETE SET (24) 120.00 36.00
1 Ken Griffey Jr. 10.00 3.00
2 Mark McGwire 15.00 4.50
3 Tino Martinez 4.00 1.20
4 Barry Bonds 15.00 4.50
5 Frank Thomas 6.00 1.80
6 Albert Belle 2.50 .75
7 Mike Piazza 10.00 3.00
8 Chipper Jones 6.00 1.80
9 Vladimir Guerrero 6.00 1.80
10 Matt Williams 2.50 .75
11 Sammy Sosa 10.00 3.00
12 Tim Salmon 4.00 1.20
13 Raul Mondesi 2.50 .75
14 Jeff Bagwell 4.00 1.20
15 Mo Vaughn 2.50 .75
16 Manny Ramirez 4.00 1.20
17 Jim Thome 6.00 1.80
18 Jim Edmonds 2.50 .75
19 Tony Clark 2.50 .75
20 Nomar Garciaparra 10.00 3.00
21 Juan Gonzalez 4.00 1.20
22 Scott Rolen 6.00 1.80
23 Larry Walker 4.00 1.20
24 Andres Galarraga 2.50 .75

1998 Donruss MLB 99

This 20 card set was inserted into both Donruss Update and Studio packs. These cards feature 20 of the leading Baseball players and were widely available because of the insertion into both of the aforementioned brands.

Nm-Mt Ex-Mt
COMPLETE SET (20) 10.00 3.00
1 Cal Ripken 2.00 .60
2 Nomar Garciaparra 1.00 .30
3 Barry Bonds 1.50 .45
4 Mike Mussina .40 .12
5 Pedro Martinez .60 .18
6 Derek Jeter 1.50 .45
7 Andruw Jones .25 .07
8 Kenny Lofton .25 .07
9 Gary Sheffield .25 .07
10 Raul Mondesi .25 .07
11 Jeff Bagwell .40 .12
12 Tim Salmon .40 .12
13 Tom Glavine .40 .12
14 Ben Grieve .25 .07
15 Matt Williams .25 .07
16 Juan Gonzalez .40 .12
17 Mark McGwire 1.50 .45
18 Bernie Williams .40 .12
19 Andres Galarraga .25 .07
20 Jose Cruz Jr. .25 .07

1998 Donruss Production Line On-Base

Randomly inserted in first series pre-priced packs only, this 20-card set features color player images printed on holographic board with green highlights. Each card is sequentially numbered according to the player's on-base percentage. Print runs for each card is matched with the player's 1997 on-base percentage and is listed individually below after each player's name in our checklist.

Nm-Mt Ex-Mt
1 Frank Thomas/456 20.00 6.00
2 Edgar Martinez/456 12.00 3.60
3 Roberto Alomar/390 12.00 3.60
4 Chuck Knoblauch/390 8.00 2.40
5 Mike Piazza/431 30.00 9.00
6 Barry Larkin/440 12.00 3.60
7 Kenny Lofton/409 8.00 2.40
8 Jeff Bagwell/425 12.00 3.60
9 Barry Bonds/446 50.00 15.00
10 Rusty Greer/405 8.00 2.40
11 Gary Sheffield/424 8.00 2.40
12 Mark McGwire/393 50.00 15.00
13 Chipper Jones/371 20.00 6.00
14 Tony Gwynn/409 25.00 7.50
15 Craig Biggio/415 12.00 3.60
16 Mo Vaughn/420 8.00 2.40
17 Bernie Williams/408 12.00 3.60
18 Ken Griffey Jr./382 30.00 9.00
19 Brady Anderson/393 8.00 2.40
20 Derek Jeter/370 50.00 15.00

1998 Donruss Production Line Power Index

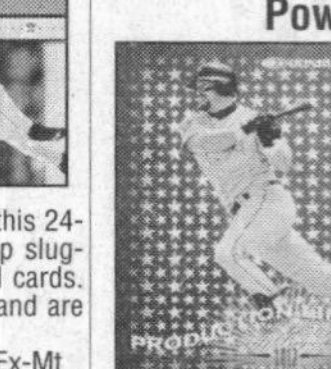

Randomly inserted in first series hobby packs only, this 20-card set features color player images printed on holographic board with blue highlights. Each card is sequentially numbered according to the player's power index. Print runs for each card is matched with the player's 1997 power index percentage and is listed individually below after each player's name in our checklist.

Nm-Mt Ex-Mt
1 Frank Thomas/1067 10.00 3.00
2 Mark McGwire/1039 25.00 7.50
3 Barry Bonds/1031 25.00 7.50
4 Jeff Bagwell/1017 6.00 1.80
5 Ken Griffey Jr./1028 15.00 4.50
6 Alex Rodriguez/846 15.00 4.50
7 Chipper Jones/850 10.00 3.00
8 Mike Piazza/1070 15.00 4.50
9 Mo Vaughn/980 4.00 1.20
10 Brady Anderson/863 4.00 1.20
11 Manny Ramirez/953 6.00 1.80
12 Albert Belle/823 4.00 1.20
13 Jim Thome/1001 10.00 3.00
14 Bernie Williams/952 6.00 1.80
15 Scott Rolen/846 10.00 3.00
16 Vladimir Guerrero/833 10.00 3.00
17 Larry Walker/1172 6.00 1.80
18 David Justice/1013 4.00 1.20
19 Tino Martinez/948 6.00 1.80
20 Tony Gwynn/957 12.00 3.60

1998 Donruss Production Line Slugging

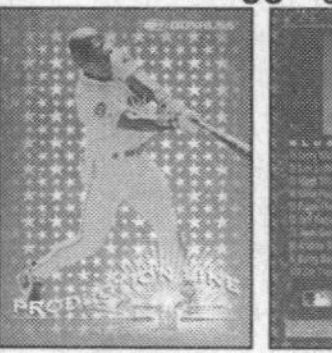

Randomly inserted in first series retail packs only, this 20-card set features color player images printed on holographic board with red highlights. Each card is sequentially numbered according to the player's slugging percentage and is detailed specifically in our checklist.

Nm-Mt Ex-Mt
1 Mark McGwire/646 40.00 12.00
2 Ken Griffey Jr./646 25.00 7.50
3 Andres Galarraga/585 6.00 1.80
4 Barry Bonds/585 40.00 12.00
5 Juan Gonzalez/589 10.00 3.00
6 Mike Piazza/638 25.00 7.50
7 Jeff Bagwell/592 10.00 3.00
8 Manny Ramirez/538 10.00 3.00
9 Jim Thome/579 15.00 4.50
10 Mo Vaughn/560 6.00 1.80
11 Larry Walker/720 10.00 3.00
12 Tino Martinez/577 10.00 3.00
13 Frank Thomas/611 15.00 4.50
14 Tim Salmon/517 10.00 3.00
15 Raul Mondesi/541 6.00 1.80
16 Alex Rodriguez/496 25.00 7.50
17 Nomar Garciaparra/534 25.00 7.50
18 Jose Cruz Jr./499 6.00 1.80
19 Tony Clark/500 6.00 1.80
20 Cal Ripken/402 50.00 15.00

1998 Donruss Rated Rookies

Randomly inserted in packs, this 30-card set features color action photos of some of the top rookie prospects as chosen by Donruss to be the most likely to succeed. The backs carry player information.

Nm-Mt Ex-Mt
COMPLETE SET (30) 40.00 12.00
*MEDALISTS: 2.5X TO 6X BASIC RR
MEDALIST PRINT RUN 250 SETS
RANDOM INSERTS IN PACKS
1 Mark Kotsay 2.00 .60

Card	Nm-Mt	Ex-Mt
Neifi Perez	2.00	.60
Paul Konerko	2.00	.60
Jose Cruz Jr.	2.00	.60
Hideki Irabu	2.00	.60
Mike Cameron	2.00	.60
Jeff Suppan	2.00	.60
Kevin Orie	2.00	.60
Pokey Reese	2.00	.60
0 Todd Dunwoody	2.00	.60
1 Miguel Tejada	2.00	.60
2 Jose Guillen	2.00	.60
3 Bartolo Colon	2.00	.60
4 Derrek Lee	2.00	.60
5 Antone Williamson	2.00	.60
6 Wilton Guerrero	2.00	.60
7 Jaret Wright	2.00	.60
8 Todd Helton	3.00	.90
9 Shannon Stewart	2.00	.60
0 Nomar Garciaparra	8.00	2.40
1 Brett Tomko	2.00	.60
2 Fernando Tatis	2.00	.60
3 Raul Ibanez	2.00	.60
4 Dennis Reyes	2.00	.60
5 Bobby Estalella	2.00	.60
6 Lou Collier	2.00	.60
7 Bubba Trammell	2.00	.60
8 Ben Grieve	2.00	.60
9 Ivan Cruz	2.00	.60
0 Karim Garcia	2.00	.60

1998 Donruss Rookie Diamond Kings

hese cards were randomly inserted in Donruss pdate packs. This 12-card set is an insert to he Donruss base set. The set is sequentially umbered to 10,000. The fronts feature head nd shoulder color prints surrounded by a four-ided border of the top young prospects in oday's MLB.

	Nm-Mt	Ex-Mt
OMPLETE SET (12)	30.00	9.00
CANVAS: 1.25X TO 3X BASIC ROOK.DK'S		
ANVAS PRINT RUN 500 SERIAL #'d SETS		
ANDOM INSERTS IN UPDATE PACKS		
Travis Lee	4.00	1.20
Fernando Tatis	4.00	1.20
Livan Hernandez	4.00	1.20
Todd Helton	6.00	1.80
Derrek Lee	4.00	1.20
Jaret Wright	4.00	1.20
Ben Grieve	4.00	1.20
Paul Konerko	4.00	1.20
Jose Cruz Jr.	4.00	1.20
0 Mark Kotsay	4.00	1.20
1 Todd Greene	4.00	1.20
2 Brad Fullmer	4.00	1.20

1998 Donruss Signature Series Previews

wenty-nine of these 34 cards were randomly nserted into Donruss Update packs. These 29 ards were previewing the then-upcoming 1998 Donruss Signature Series set. Each player igned a slightly different amount of cards so we ave put the amount of cards signed next to the layers name in our checklist. The five addition-l cards (Alou, Casey, Jenkins, Jeter and Wilson) vere never intended for public release. It's elieved that four players (all except Jeter) igned 100 or more cards but failed to return heir cards to the manufacturer (Pinnacle Brands) in time for the Donruss Update packout. Apparently, the cards were stored in Pinnacle's ard vault, but an unknown amount of each card nade their way into the secondary market dur-ng Pinnacle's bankruptcy proceeding when Playoff Inc. bought the holdings. It's believed hat a handful of the Jeter cards were erro-eously sent to Jeter in his 1998 Donruss Signature card agreement (red, green and blue ards for a separate brand). Jeter simply signed all of the cards and sent them back to the man-ufacturer.

	Nm-Mt	Ex-Mt
Sandy Alomar Jr./96	40.00	12.00
2 Moises Alou	50.00	15.00
3 Andy Benes/135	40.00	12.00
Russell Branyan/188	40.00	12.00
Sean Casey	50.00	15.00
Tony Clark/188	40.00	12.00
7 Juan Encarnacion/193	40.00	12.00
3 Brad Fullmer/396	20.00	6.00
3 Juan Gonzalez/108	80.00	24.00
10 Ben Grieve/100	40.00	12.00
11 Todd Helton/101	80.00	24.00
12 Richard Hidalgo/380	20.00	6.00
13 A.J. Hinch/400	20.00	6.00
14 Damian Jackson/15		
15 Geoff Jenkins	120.00	36.00
16 Derek Jeter SP		
17 Chipper Jones/112	120.00	36.00
18 Chuck Knoblauch/98	50.00	15.00
19 Travis Lee/101	40.00	12.00
20 Mike Lowell/450	30.00	9.00
21 Greg Maddux/92	250.00	75.00
22 Kevin Millwood/395	25.00	7.50
23 Magglio Ordonez/420	60.00	18.00
24 David Ortiz/393	50.00	15.00
25 Rafael Palmeiro/107	100.00	30.00
26 Cal Ripken/22		
27 Alex Rodriguez/23		
28 Curt Schilling/100	100.00	30.00
29 Randall Simon/380	20.00	6.00
30 Fernando Tatis/400	20.00	6.00
31 Miguel Tejada/375	30.00	9.00
32 Robin Ventura/95	50.00	15.00
33 Dan Wilson	40.00	12.00
34 Kerry Wood/373	50.00	15.00

2001 Donruss

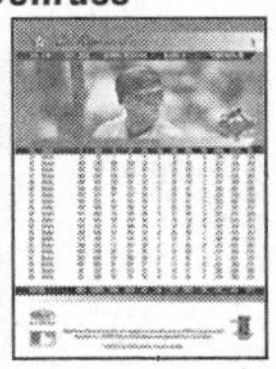

The 2001 Donruss product was released in early May, 2001. The 220-card base set was broken into tiers as follows: Base Veterans (1-150), short-printed Rated Rookies (151-200) serial numbered to 2001, and Fan Club cards (201-220) inserted approximatley one per box. Exchange cards with a redemption deadline of May 1st, 2003 was seeded into packs for card 156 Albert Pujols and 159 Ben Sheets. Each pack contained five cards, and a one card retro pack. Packs carried a suggested retail price of $1.99. Please note that 1999 Retro packs were inserted in Hobby packs, while 2000 Retro packs were inserted into Retail packs. One in every 720 packs contained an exchange card good for a complete set of 2001 Donruss Baseball's Best. One in every 72 packs contained and exchange card good for a complete set of 2001 Donruss the Rookies. The redemption deadline for both exchange cards was January 20th, 2002. The original exchange deadline was November 1st, 2001 but the manufacturer lengthened the redemption period.

	Nm-Mt	Ex-Mt
COMP.SET w/o SP's (150)	25.00	7.50
COMMON CARD (1-150)	.30	.09
COMMON (151-200)	8.00	2.40
COMMON (201-220)	2.50	.75
1 Alex Rodriguez	1.25	.35
2 Barry Bonds	2.00	.60
3 Cal Ripken	2.50	.75
4 Chipper Jones	.75	.23
5 Derek Jeter	2.00	.60
6 Troy Glaus	.30	.09
7 Frank Thomas	.75	.23
8 Greg Maddux	1.25	.35
9 Ivan Rodriguez	.75	.23
10 Jeff Bagwell	.50	.15
11 Jose Canseco	.75	.23
12 Todd Helton	.50	.15
13 Ken Griffey Jr.	1.25	.35
14 Manny Ramirez	.50	.15
15 Mark McGwire	2.00	.60
16 Mike Piazza	1.25	.35
17 Nomar Garciaparra	1.25	.35
18 Pedro Martinez	.75	.23
19 Randy Johnson	.75	.23
20 Rick Ankiel	.30	.09
21 Rickey Henderson	.75	.23
22 Roger Clemens	1.50	.45
23 Sammy Sosa	1.25	.35
24 Tony Gwynn	1.00	.30
25 Vladimir Guerrero	.75	.23
26 Eric Davis	.30	.09
27 Roberto Alomar	.75	.23
28 Mark Mulder	.30	.09
29 Pat Burrell	.30	.09
30 Harold Baines	.30	.09
31 Carlos Delgado	.30	.09
32 J.D. Drew	.30	.09
33 Jim Edmonds	.30	.09
34 Darin Erstad	.30	.09
35 Jason Giambi	.75	.23
36 Tom Glavine	.50	.15
37 Juan Gonzalez	.50	.15
38 Mark Grace	.50	.15
39 Shawn Green	.30	.09
40 Tim Hudson	.30	.09
41 Andruw Jones	.30	.09
42 David Justice	.30	.09
43 Jeff Kent	.30	.09
44 Barry Larkin	.50	.15
45 Pokey Reese	.30	.09
46 Mike Mussina	.50	.15
47 Hideo Nomo	.75	.23
48 Rafael Palmeiro	.50	.15
49 Adam Piatt	.30	.09
50 Scott Rolen	.75	.23
51 Gary Sheffield	.30	.09
52 Bernie Williams	.50	.15
53 Bob Abreu	.30	.09
54 Edgardo Alfonzo	.30	.09
55 Jermaine Clark RC	.50	.15
56 Albert Belle	.30	.09
57 Craig Biggio	.50	.15
58 Andres Galarraga	.30	.09
59 Edgar Martinez	.50	.15
60 Fred McGriff	.50	.15
61 Magglio Ordonez	.30	.09
62 Jim Thome	.75	.23
63 Matt Williams	.30	.09
64 Kerry Wood	.75	.23
65 Moises Alou	.30	.09
66 Brady Anderson	.30	.09
67 Garret Anderson	.30	.09
68 Tony Armas Jr.	.30	.09
69 Tony Batista	.30	.09
70 Jose Cruz Jr.	.30	.09
71 Carlos Beltran	.50	.15
72 Adrian Beltre	.50	.15
73 Kris Benson	.30	.09
74 Lance Berkman	.30	.09
75 Kevin Brown	.30	.09
76 Jay Buhner	.30	.09
77 Jeromy Burnitz	.30	.09
78 Ken Caminiti	.30	.09
79 Sean Casey	.30	.09
80 Luis Castillo	.30	.09
81 Eric Chavez	.30	.09
82 Jeff Cirillo	.30	.09
83 Bartolo Colon	.30	.09
84 David Cone	.30	.09
85 Freddy Garcia	.30	.09
86 Johnny Damon	.50	.15
87 Ray Durham	.30	.09
88 Jermaine Dye	.30	.09
89 Juan Encarnacion	.30	.09
90 Terrence Long	.30	.09
91 Carl Everett	.30	.09
92 Steve Finley	.30	.09
93 Cliff Floyd	.30	.09
94 Brad Fullmer	.30	.09
95 Brian Giles	.30	.09
96 Luis Gonzalez	.30	.09
97 Rusty Greer	.30	.09
98 Jeffrey Hammonds	.30	.09
99 Mike Hampton	.30	.09
100 Orlando Hernandez	.30	.09
101 Richard Hidalgo	.30	.09
102 Geoff Jenkins	.30	.09
103 Jacque Jones	.30	.09
104 Brian Jordan	.30	.09
105 Gabe Kapler	.30	.09
106 Eric Karros	.30	.09
107 Jason Kendall	.30	.09
108 Adam Kennedy	.30	.09
109 Byung-Hyun Kim	.30	.09
110 Ryan Klesko	.30	.09
111 Chuck Knoblauch	.30	.09
112 Paul Konerko	.30	.09
113 Carlos Lee	.30	.09
114 Kenny Lofton	.30	.09
115 Javy Lopez	.30	.09
116 Tino Martinez	.50	.15
117 Ruben Mateo	.30	.09
118 Kevin Millwood	.30	.09
119 Ben Molina	.30	.09
120 Raul Mondesi	.30	.09
121 Trot Nixon	.30	.09
122 John Olerud	.30	.09
123 Paul O'Neill	.50	.15
124 Chan Ho Park	.30	.09
125 Andy Pettitte	.50	.15
126 Jorge Posada	.50	.15
127 Mark Quinn	.30	.09
128 Aramis Ramirez	.30	.09
129 Mariano Rivera	.50	.15
130 Tim Salmon	.50	.15
131 Curt Schilling	.30	.09
132 Richie Sexson	.30	.09
133 John Smoltz	.50	.15
134 J.T. Snow	.30	.09
135 Jay Payton	.30	.09
136 Shannon Stewart	.30	.09
137 B.J. Surhoff	.30	.09
138 Mike Sweeney	.30	.09
139 Fernando Tatis	.30	.09
140 Miguel Tejada	.30	.09
141 Jason Varitek	.50	.15
142 Greg Vaughn	.30	.09
143 Mo Vaughn	.30	.09
144 Robin Ventura UER Listed as playing for Yankees last 2 years Also Bat and Throw information is wrong	.30	.09
145 Jose Vidro	.30	.09
146 Omar Vizquel	.50	.15
147 Larry Walker	.50	.15
148 David Wells	.30	.09
149 Rondell White	.30	.09
150 Preston Wilson	.30	.09
151 Brent Abernathy RR	8.00	2.40
152 Cory Aldridge RR RC	8.00	2.40
153 Gene Altman RR RC	8.00	2.40
154 Josh Beckett RR	8.00	2.40
155 W. Betemit RR RC	8.00	2.40
156 A.Pujols RR/500 RC	120.00	36.00
157 Joe Crede RR	8.00	2.40
158 Jack Cust RR	8.00	2.40
159 Ben Sheets RR/500	40.00	12.00
160 Alex Escobar RR	8.00	2.40
161 A. Hernandez RR RC	8.00	2.40
162 Pedro Feliz RR	8.00	2.40
163 Nate Frese RR RC	8.00	2.40
164 Carlos Garcia RR RC	8.00	2.40
165 Marcus Giles RR	8.00	2.40
166 Alexis Gomez RR RC	8.00	2.40
167 Jason Hart RR	8.00	2.40
168 Eric Hinske RR RC	10.00	3.00
169 Cesar Izturis RR	8.00	2.40
170 Nick Johnson RR	8.00	2.40
171 Mike Young RR	10.00	3.00
172 B. Lawrence RR RC	8.00	2.40
173 Steve Lomasney RR	8.00	2.40
174 Nick Maness RR	8.00	2.40
175 Jose Mieses RR RC	8.00	2.40
176 Greg Miller RR RC	8.00	2.40
177 Eric Munson RR	8.00	2.40
178 Xavier Nady RR	8.00	2.40
179 Blaine Neal RR RC	8.00	2.40
180 Abraham Nunez RR	8.00	2.40
181 Jose Ortiz RR	8.00	2.40
182 Jeremy Owens RR RC	8.00	2.40
183 Pablo Ozuna RR	8.00	2.40
184 Corey Patterson RR	8.00	2.40
185 Carlos Pena RR	8.00	2.40
186 Wily Mo Pena RR	8.00	2.40
187 Timo Perez RR	8.00	2.40
188 A. Pettyjohn RR RC	8.00	2.40
189 Luis Rivas RR	8.00	2.40
190 J. Melian RR RC	8.00	2.40
191 Wilken Ruan RR RC	8.00	2.40
192 D. Sanchez RR RC	8.00	2.40
193 Alfonso Soriano RR	10.00	3.00
194 Rafael Soriano RR RC	10.00	3.00
195 Ichiro Suzuki RR RC	50.00	15.00
196 Billy Sylvester RR RC	8.00	2.40
197 Juan Uribe RR RC	10.00	3.00
198 Eric Valent RR	8.00	2.40
199 C.Valderrama RR RC	8.00	2.40
200 Matt White RR RC	8.00	2.40
201 Alex Rodriguez FC	6.00	1.80
202 Barry Bonds FC	10.00	3.00
203 Cal Ripken FC	12.00	3.60
204 Chipper Jones FC	4.00	1.20
205 Derek Jeter FC	10.00	3.00
206 Troy Glaus FC	2.50	.75
207 Frank Thomas FC	4.00	1.20
208 Greg Maddux FC	6.00	1.80
209 Ivan Rodriguez FC	4.00	1.20
210 Jeff Bagwell FC	2.50	.75
211 Todd Helton FC	2.50	.75
212 Ken Griffey Jr. FC	6.00	1.80
213 Manny Ramirez FC	2.50	.75
214 Mark McGwire FC	10.00	3.00
215 Mike Piazza FC	6.00	1.80
216 Pedro Martinez FC	4.00	1.20
217 Sammy Sosa FC	6.00	1.80
218 Tony Gwynn FC	5.00	1.50
219 Vladimir Guerrero FC	4.00	1.20
220 Nomar Garciaparra FC	6.00	1.80
NNO BB Best Coupon	2.00	.60
NNO The Rookies Coupon	.50	.15

2001 Donruss Stat Line Career

Randomly inserted into 2001 Donruss packs, this 220-card insert parallels the 2001 Donruss base set. Each card is individually serial numbered to a career stat of the given players. Please note that the print runs are listed in our checklist. Exchange cards for Albert Pujols and Ben Sheets with a redemption deadline of May 1st, 2003 were seeded into packs. A special autographed version of Albert Pujols' Stat Line Career card was printed in response to an error in production whereby more Stat Line Career Pujols exchange cards were seeded into packs than the 154 copies intended for release. To honor their commitment to collectors redeeming the exchange card, Donruss had Pujols sign a special non-serial numbered version of the card and sent it out to collectors redeeming the exchange card. Cards with a print run of 25 or fewer are not priced due to market scarcity.

	Nm-Mt	Ex-Mt
*1-150 P/R b/wn 251-400: 2.5X TO 6X		
*1-150 P/R b/wn 201-250: 2.5X TO 6X		
*1-150 P/R b/wn 151-200: 3X TO 8X		
*1-150 P/R b/wn 121-150: 3X TO 8X		
*1-150 P/R b/wn 81-120: 4X TO 10X		
*1-150 P/R b/wn 66-80: 5X TO 12X		
*1-150 P/R b/wn 51-65: 5X TO 12X		
*1-150 P/R b/wn 36-50: 6X TO 15X		
*1-150 P/R b/wn 26-35: 8X TO 20X		
*201-220 P/R b/wn 251-400 .5X TO 1.2X		
*201-220 P/R b/wn 201-250 .5X TO 1.2X		
*201-220 P/R b/wn 151-200 .6X TO 1.5X		
*201-220 P/R b/wn 121-150 .6X TO 1.5X		
*201-220 P/R b/wn 81-120 .75X TO 2X		
*201-220 P/R b/wn 36-50 1.25X TO 3X		
151 B. Abernathy RR/22		
152 Cory Aldridge RR/33	10.00	3.00
153 Gene Altman RR/351	2.00	.60
154 Josh Beckett RR/212	2.50	.75
155 Wilson Betemit RR/15		
156 Albert Pujols RR/154	150.00	45.00
156B Albert Pujols RR AU		
157 Joe Crede RR/357	2.00	.60
158 Jack Cust RR/66	5.00	1.50
159 Ben Sheets RR/159	15.00	4.50
159B Ben Sheets RR AU		
160 Alex Escobar RR/45	8.00	2.40
161 A. Hernandez RR/86	5.00	1.50
162 Pedro Feliz RR/286	2.00	.60
163 Nate Frese RR/119	5.00	1.50
164 Carlos Garcia RR/106	5.00	1.50
165 Marcus Giles RR/320	2.00	.60
166 Alexis Gomez RR/34	10.00	3.00
167 Jason Hart RR/303	2.00	.60
168 Eric Hinske RR/332	2.50	.75
169 Cesar Izturis RR/60	6.00	1.80
170 Nick Johnson RR/308	2.00	.60
171 Mike Young RR/37	12.00	3.60
172 B. Lawrence RR/281	2.00	.60
173 S. Lomasney RR/229	2.50	.75
174 Nick Maness RR/25		
175 Jose Mieses RR/265	2.00	.60
176 Greg Miller RR/328	2.00	.60
177 Eric Munson RR/3		
178 Xavier Nady RR/1		
179 Blaine Neal RR/296	2.00	.60
180 A. Nunez RR/38	8.00	2.40
181 Jose Ortiz RR/7		
182 J. Owens RR/273	2.00	.60
183 Pablo Ozuna RR/333	2.00	.60
184 Corey Patterson RR/11		
185 Carlos Pena RR/52	6.00	1.80
186 Wily Mo Pena RR/114	5.00	1.50
187 Timo Perez RR/49	8.00	2.40
188 A. Pettyjohn RR/20		
189 Luis Rivas RR/310	2.00	.60
190 J. Melian RR/26	10.00	3.00
191 Wilken Ruan RR/215	2.50	.75
192 D. Sanchez RR/19		
193 A. Soriano RR/50	8.00	2.40
194 Rafael Soriano RR/13		
195 Ichiro Suzuki RR/106	120.00	36.00
196 Billy Sylvester RR/11		
197 Juan Uribe RR/157	3.00	.90
198 Eric Valent RR/342	2.00	.60
199 Carlos Valderrama RR/13		
200 Matt White RR/31	10.00	3.00

2001 Donruss Stat Line Season

Randomly inserted into 2001 Donruss packs, this 220-card insert parallels the 2001 Donruss base set. Each card is individually serial numbered to a season stat of the given players. Please note that the print runs are listed in our checklist. Exchange cards for Albert Pujols and Ben Sheets with a redemption deadline of May 1st, 2003 were seeded into packs. Autographed versions of Pujols and Sheets were made available due to an error in production whereby more than the stated amount of Stat Line Season cards for each player were produced. To honor their commitment to collectors - Donruss contracted with the two athletes to sign special non-serial numbered versions of their Stat Line Season card and sent them out to collectors that redeemed the exchange cards. Cards with a print run of 25 or fewer are not priced due to market scarcity.

	Nm-Mt	Ex-Mt
*1-150 P/R b/wn 151-200: 3X TO 8X		
*1-150 P/R b/wn 121-150: 3X TO 8X		
*1-150 P/R b/wn 81-120: 4X TO 10X		
*1-150 P/R b/wn 66-80: 5X TO 12X		
*1-150 P/R b/wn 51-65: 5X TO 12X		
*1-150 P/R b/wn 36-50: 6X TO 15X		
*1-150 P/R b/wn 26-35: 8X TO 20X		
*201-220 P/R b/wn 151-200 .6X TO 1.5X		
*201-220 P/R b/wn 121-150 .6X TO 1.5X		
*201-220 P/R b/wn 81-120 .75X TO 2X		
*201-220 P/R b/wn 66-80 1X TO 2.5X		
*201-220 P/R b/wn 36-50 1.25X TO 3X		
*201-220 P/R b/wn 26-35 1.5X TO 4X		
151 B. Abernathy RR/130	4.00	1.20
152 Cory Aldridge RR/100	5.00	1.50
153 Gene Altman RR/6		
154 Josh Beckett RR/61	6.00	1.80
155 Wilson Betemit RR/89	5.00	1.50
156 Albert Pujols RR/17		
156B Albert Pujols RR AU	400.00	120.00
157 Joe Crede RR/5		
158 Jack Cust RR/131	4.00	1.20
159 Ben Sheets RR/8		
159B Ben Sheets RR AU	60.00	18.00
160 Alex Escobar RR/126	4.00	1.20
161 Adrian Hernandez RR/8		
162 Pedro Feliz RR/2		
163 Nate Frese RR/126	4.00	1.20
164 Carlos Garcia RR/14		
165 Marcus Giles RR/133	4.00	1.20
166 Alexis Gomez RR/117	5.00	1.50
167 Jason Hart RR/31	10.00	3.00
168 Eric Hinske RR/20		
169 Cesar Izturis RR/95	5.00	1.50
170 Nick Johnson RR/145	4.00	1.20
171 Mike Young RR/155	5.00	1.50
172 B. Lawrence RR/165	3.00	.90
173 Steve Lomasney RR/8		
174 Nick Maness RR/127	4.00	1.20
175 Jose Mieses RR/17		
176 Greg Miller RR/10		
177 Eric Munson RR/1		
178 Xavier Nady RR/1		
179 Blaine Neal RR/65	6.00	1.80
180 A. Nunez RR/51	6.00	1.80
181 Jose Ortiz RR/2		
182 Jeremy Owens RR/16		
183 Pablo Ozuna RR/8		
184 Corey Patterson RR/2		
185 Carlos Pena RR/117	5.00	1.50
186 Wily Mo Pena RR/10		
187 Timo Perez RR/14		
188 A. Pettyjohn RR/68	5.00	1.50
189 Luis Rivas RR/18		
190 J. Melian RR/73	5.00	1.50
191 Wilken Ruan RR/165	3.00	.90
192 D.Sanchez RR/121	4.00	1.20
193 Alfonso Soriano RR/2		
194 Rafael Soriano RR/90	5.00	1.50
195 Ichiro Suzuki RR/153	100.00	30.00
196 Billy Sylvester RR/16		
197 Juan Uribe RR/22		
198 Eric Valent RR/22		
199 C.Valderrama RR/137	4.00	1.20
200 Matt White RR/126	4.00	1.20

2001 Donruss 1999 Retro

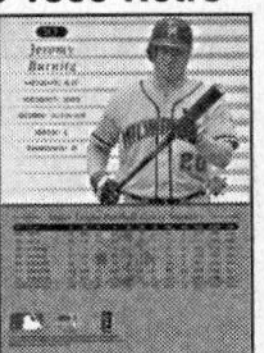

Inserted into hobby packs at one per hobby pack, this 100-card insert features cards that Donruss would have released in 1999 had they been producing baseball cards at the time. The set is broken into tiers as follows: Base Veterans (1-80), and Short-printed Prospects (81-100) serial numbered to 1999. Please note that these cards have a 2001 copyright, thus, are listed under the 2001 products.

	Nm-Mt	Ex-Mt
COMPLETE SET (100)	150.00	45.00
COMP.SET w/o SP's (80)	50.00	15.00
COMMON CARD (1-80)	.60	.18
COMMON CARD (81-100)	5.00	1.50
1 Ken Griffey Jr.	2.50	.75
2 Nomar Garciaparra	2.50	.75
3 Alex Rodriguez	2.50	.75
4 Mark McGwire	4.00	1.20
5 Sammy Sosa	2.50	.75
6 Chipper Jones	1.50	.45
7 Mike Piazza	2.50	.75
8 Barry Larkin	1.00	.30
9 Andruw Jones	.60	.18
10 Albert Belle	.60	.18
11 Jeff Bagwell	1.00	.30
12 Tony Gwynn	2.00	.60
13 Manny Ramirez	1.00	.30
14 Mo Vaughn	.60	.18
15 Barry Bonds	4.00	1.20
16 Frank Thomas	1.50	.45
17 Vladimir Guerrero	1.50	.45
18 Derek Jeter	4.00	1.20
19 Randy Johnson	1.50	.45
20 Greg Maddux	2.50	.75
21 Pedro Martinez	1.50	.45
22 Cal Ripken	5.00	1.50
23 Ivan Rodriguez	1.50	.45
24 Matt Williams	.60	.18
25 Javy Lopez	.60	.18
26 Tim Salmon	1.00	.30

Card	Nm-Mt	Ex-Mt
27 Raul Mondesi	.60	.18
28 Todd Helton	1.00	.30
29 Magglio Ordonez	.60	.18
30 Sean Casey	.60	.18
31 Jeromy Burnitz	.60	.18
32 Jeff Kent	.60	.18
33 Jim Edmonds	.60	.18
34 Jim Thome	1.50	.45
35 Dante Bichette	.60	.18
36 Larry Walker	1.00	.30
37 Will Clark	1.50	.45
38 Omar Vizquel	1.00	.30
39 Mike Mussina	1.00	.30
40 Eric Karros	.60	.18
41 Kenny Lofton	.60	.18
42 David Justice	.60	.18
43 Craig Biggio	1.00	.30
44 J.D. Drew	.60	.18
45 Rickey Henderson	1.50	.45
46 Bernie Williams	1.00	.30
47 Brian Giles	.60	.18
48 Paul O'Neill	1.00	.30
49 Orlando Hernandez	.60	.18
50 Jason Giambi	.60	.18
51 Curt Schilling	.60	.18
52 Scott Rolen	1.50	.45
53 Mark Grace	1.00	.30
54 Moises Alou	.60	.18
55 Jason Kendall	.60	.18
56 Ray Lankford	.60	.18
57 Kerry Wood	1.50	.45
58 Gary Sheffield	.60	.18
59 Ruben Mateo	.60	.18
60 Darin Erstad	.60	.18
61 Troy Glaus	.60	.18
62 Jose Canseco	1.50	.45
63 Wade Boggs	1.00	.30
64 Tom Glavine	1.00	.30
65 Gabe Kapler	.60	.18
66 Juan Gonzalez	1.00	.30
67 Rafael Palmeiro	1.00	.30
68 Richie Sexson	.60	.18
69 Carl Everett	.60	.18
70 David Wells	.60	.18
71 Carlos Delgado	.60	.18
72 Eric Davis	.60	.18
73 Shawn Green	.60	.18
74 Andres Galarraga	.60	.18
75 Edgar Martinez	1.00	.30
76 Roberto Alomar	1.00	.30
77 John Olerud	.60	.18
78 Luis Gonzalez	.60	.18
79 Kevin Brown	.60	.18
80 Roger Clemens	3.00	.90
81 Josh Beckett SP	5.00	1.50
82 Alfonso Soriano SP	8.00	2.40
83 Alex Escobar SP	5.00	1.50
84 Pat Burrell SP	5.00	1.50
85 Eric Chavez SP	5.00	1.50
86 Erubiel Durazo SP	5.00	1.50
87 Abraham Nunez SP	5.00	1.50
88 Carlos Pena SP	5.00	1.50
89 Nick Johnson SP	5.00	1.50
90 Eric Munson SP	5.00	1.50
91 Corey Patterson SP	5.00	1.50
92 Wily Mo Pena SP	5.00	1.50
93 Rafael Furcal SP	5.00	1.50
94 Eric Valent SP	5.00	1.50
95 Mark Mulder SP	5.00	1.50
96 Chad Hutchinson SP	5.00	1.50
97 Freddy Garcia SP	5.00	1.50
98 Tim Hudson SP	5.00	1.50
99 Rick Ankiel SP	5.00	1.50
100 Kip Wells SP	5.00	1.50

2001 Donruss 1999 Retro Stat Line Career

Randomly inserted into 1999 Retro packs, this 100-card insert parallels the 1999 Retro base set. Each card is individually serial numbered to a career stat of the given players. Please note that the print runs are listed in our checklist. Cards with a print run of 25 or fewer are not priced due to market scarcity.

	Nm-Mt	Ex-Mt
*1-80 P/R b/wn 251-400: 1.25X TO 3X		
*1-80 P/R b/wn 201-250: 1.25X TO 3X		
*1-80 P/R b/wn 151-200: 1.5X TO 4X		
*1-80 P/R b/wn 121-150: 1.5X TO 4X		
*1-80 P/R b/wn 81-120: 2X TO 5X		
*1-80 P/R b/wn 66-80: 2.5X TO 6X		
*1-80 P/R b/wn 51-65: 2.5X TO 6X		
*1-80 P/R b/wn 36-50: 3X TO 8X		
*1-80 P/R b/wn 26-35: 4X TO 10X		
81 Josh Beckett/13		
82 Alfonso Soriano/113	4.00	1.20
83 Alex Escobar/181	2.50	.75
84 Pat Burrell/303	2.00	.60
85 Eric Chavez/314	2.00	.60
86 Erubiel Durazo/147	3.00	.90
87 Abraham Nunez/106	4.00	1.20
88 Carlos Pena/46	6.00	1.80
89 Nick Johnson/259	2.00	.60
90 Eric Munson/392	2.00	.60
91 Corey Patterson/117	4.00	1.20
92 Wily Mo Pena/247	2.00	.60
93 Rafael Furcal/137	3.00	.90
94 Eric Valent/53	5.00	1.50
95 Mark Mulder/340	2.00	.60
96 Chad Hutchinson/2		
97 Freddy Garcia/397	2.00	.60
98 Tim Hudson/17		
99 Rick Ankiel/222	2.00	.60
100 Kip Wells/371	2.00	.60

2001 Donruss 1999 Retro Stat Line Season

Randomly inserted into 1999 Retro packs, this 100-card insert parallels the 1999 Retro base set. Each card is individually serial numbered to a season stat of the given players. Please note that the print runs are listed in our checklist. Cards issued to a stated print run of 25 or fewer are not priced due to market scarcity.

	Nm-Mt	Ex-Mt
*1-80 P/R b/wn 251-400: 1.25X TO 3X		
*1-80 P/R b/wn 201-250: 1.25X TO 3X		
*1-80 P/R b/wn 151-200: 1.5X TO 4X		
*1-80 P/R b/wn 121-150: 1.5X TO 4X		
*1-80 P/R b/wn 81-120: 2X TO 5X		
*1-80 P/R b/wn 66-80: 2.5X TO 6X		
*1-80 P/R b/wn 51-65: 2.5X TO 6X		
*1-80 P/R b/wn 36-50: 3X TO 8X		
*1-80 P/R b/wn 26-35: 4X TO 10X		
81 Josh Beckett/178	2.50	.75
82 Alfonso Soriano/7		
83 Alex Escobar/27	8.00	2.40
84 Pat Burrell/7		
85 Eric Chavez/33	8.00	2.40
86 Erubiel Durazo/19		
87 Abraham Nunez/95	4.00	1.20
88 Carlos Pena/319	2.00	.60
89 Nick Johnson/17		
90 Eric Munson/16		
91 Corey Patterson/22		
92 Wily Mo Pena/7		
93 Rafael Furcal/88	4.00	1.20
94 Eric Valent/13		
95 Mark Mulder/113	4.00	1.20
96 Chad Hutchinson/51	5.00	1.50
97 Freddy Garcia/10		
98 Tim Hudson/152	2.50	.75
99 Rick Ankiel/12		
100 Kip Wells/135	2.50	.75

2001 Donruss 1999 Retro Diamond Kings

Randomly inserted into 1999 Retro packs, this 5-card insert set features the "Diamond King" cards that Donruss would have produced had they been producing baseball cards in 1999. Each card is individually serial numbered to 2500.

	Nm-Mt	Ex-Mt
COMPLETE SET (5)	60.00	18.00
*STUDIO: .75X TO 2X BASIC RETRO DK		
STUDIO PRINT RUN 250 SERIAL #'d SETS		
RANDOM INSERTS IN 1999 RETRO PACKS		
1 Scott Rolen	10.00	3.00
2 Sammy Sosa	12.00	3.60
3 Juan Gonzalez	10.00	3.00
4 Ken Griffey Jr.	12.00	3.60
5 Derek Jeter	20.00	6.00

2001 Donruss 2000 Retro

Inserted into retail packs at one per retail pack, this 100-card insert features cards that Donruss would have released in 2000 had they been producing baseball cards at the time. The set is broken into tiers as follows: Base Veterans (1-80), and Short-printed Prospects (81-100) serial numbered to 2000. Please note that these cards have a 2001 copyright, thus, are listed under the 2001 products. Exchange cards originally intended for number 82 C.C. Sabathia and number 95 Ben Sheets were both issued in packs with an expiration date of 05/01/03. It's believed, however, two separate cards were made available for redemption card 95 . . . Ben Sheets and Ichiro Suzuki. It's not known at this time exactly which player was featured on the exchange card number 82.

	Nm-Mt	Ex-Mt
COMPLETE SET (100)	250.00	75.00
COMP.SET w/o SP's (80)	80.00	24.00
COMMON CARD (1-80)	.60	.18
COMMON CARD (81-100)	5.00	1.50
SP * 82/95 WERE AVAIL.ONLY VIA MAIL		
EXCH.CARD 82 NOT KNOWN AT THIS TIME		
1 Vladimir Guerrero	1.50	.45
2 Alex Rodriguez	2.50	.75
3 Ken Griffey Jr.	2.50	.75
4 Nomar Garciaparra	2.50	.75
5 Mike Piazza	2.50	.75
6 Mark McGwire	4.00	1.20
7 Sammy Sosa	2.50	.75
8 Chipper Jones	1.50	.45
9 Jim Edmonds	.60	.18
10 Tony Gwynn	2.00	.60
11 Andruw Jones	.60	.18
12 Albert Belle	.60	.18
13 Jeff Bagwell	1.00	.30
14 Manny Ramirez	1.00	.30
15 Mo Vaughn	.60	.18
16 Barry Bonds	4.00	1.20
17 Frank Thomas	1.50	.45
18 Ivan Rodriguez	1.50	.45
19 Derek Jeter	4.00	1.20
20 Randy Johnson	1.50	.45
21 Greg Maddux	2.50	.75
22 Pedro Martinez	1.50	.45
23 Cal Ripken	5.00	1.50
24 Mark Grace	1.00	.30
25 Javy Lopez	.60	.18
26 Ray Durham	.60	.18
27 Todd Helton	1.00	.30
28 Magglio Ordonez	.60	.18
29 Sean Casey	.60	.18
30 Darin Erstad	.60	.18
31 Barry Larkin	1.00	.30
32 Will Clark	1.50	.45
33 Jim Thome	1.50	.45
34 Dante Bichette	.60	.18
35 Larry Walker	1.00	.30
36 Ken Caminiti	.60	.18
37 Omar Vizquel	1.00	.30
38 Miguel Tejada	.60	.18
39 Eric Karros	.60	.18
40 Gary Sheffield	.60	.18
41 Jeff Cirillo	.60	.18
42 Rondell White	.60	.18
43 Rickey Henderson	1.50	.45
44 Bernie Williams	1.00	.30
45 Brian Giles	.60	.18
46 Paul O'Neill	1.00	.30
47 Orlando Hernandez	.60	.18
48 Ben Grieve	.60	.18
49 Jason Giambi	.60	.18
50 Curt Schilling	.60	.18
51 Scott Rolen	1.50	.45
52 Bobby Abreu	.60	.18
53 Jason Kendall	.60	.18
54 Fernando Tatis	.60	.18
55 Jeff Kent	.60	.18
56 Mike Mussina	1.00	.30
57 Troy Glaus	.60	.18
58 Jose Canseco	1.50	.45
59 Wade Boggs	1.00	.30
60 Fred McGriff	.60	.18
61 Juan Gonzalez	1.00	.30
62 Rafael Palmeiro	1.00	.30
63 Rusty Greer	.60	.18
64 Carl Everett	.60	.18
65 David Wells	.60	.18
66 Carlos Delgado	.60	.18
67 Shawn Green	.60	.18
68 David Justice	.60	.18
69 Edgar Martinez	1.00	.30
70 Andres Galarraga	.60	.18
71 Roberto Alomar	1.00	.30
72 Jermaine Dye	.60	.18
73 John Olerud	.60	.18
74 Luis Gonzalez	.60	.18
75 Craig Biggio	1.00	.30
76 Kevin Millwood	.60	.18
77 Kevin Brown	.60	.18
78 John Smoltz	1.00	.30
79 Roger Clemens	3.00	.90
80 Mike Hampton	.60	.18
81 Tomas De La Rosa SP	5.00	1.50
82 TBD EXCH SP *		
83 Ryan Christenson SP	5.00	1.50
84 Pedro Feliz SP	5.00	1.50
85 Jose Ortiz SP	5.00	1.50
86 Xavier Nady SP	5.00	1.50
87 Julio Zuleta SP	5.00	1.50
88 Jason Hart SP	5.00	1.50
89 Keith Ginter SP	5.00	1.50
90 Brent Abernathy SP	5.00	1.50
91 Timo Perez SP	5.00	1.50
92 Juan Pierre SP	5.00	1.50
93 Tike Redman SP	5.00	1.50
94 Mike Lamb SP	5.00	1.50
95A Ben Sheets SP *	15.00	4.50
95B Ichiro Suzuki SP *	50.00	15.00
96 Kazuhiro Sasaki SP	5.00	1.50
97 Barry Zito SP	8.00	2.40
98 Adam Bernero SP	5.00	1.50
99 Chad Durbin SP	5.00	1.50
100 Matt Ginter SP	5.00	1.50

2001 Donruss 2000 Retro Stat Line Career

Randomly inserted into 2000 Retro packs, this 100-card insert parallels the 2000 Retro base set. Each card is individually serial numbered to a career stat of the given players. Please note that the print runs are listed in our checklist. Cards issued to a stated print run of 25 or fewer are not priced due to market scarcity. Exchange cards were seeded into packs for cards 82 and 95. These cards were originally intended to be redeemed for C.C. Sabathia and Ben Sheets. It's since been discovered that Ichiro Suzuki cards were actually redeemed for card 95.

	Nm-Mt	Ex-Mt
*1-80 P/R b/wn 251-400: 1.25X TO 3X		
*1-80 P/R b/wn 201-250: 1.25X TO 3X		
*1-80 P/R b/wn 151-200: 1.5X TO 4X		
*1-80 P/R b/wn 121-150: 1.5X TO 4X		
*1-80 P/R b/wn 81-120: 2X TO 5X		
*1-80 P/R b/wn 66-80: 2.5X TO 6X		
*1-80 P/R b/wn 51-65: 2.5X TO 6X		
*1-80 P/R b/wn 36-50: 3X TO 8X		
*1-80 P/R b/wn 26-35: 4X TO 10X		
81 Tomas De La Rosa/76	5.00	1.50
82 C.C. Sabathia/6		
83 Ryan Christenson/9		
84 Pedro Feliz/45	5.00	1.50
85 Jose Ortiz/90	4.00	1.20
86 Xavier Nady/175	2.50	.75
87 Julio Zuleta/295	2.00	.60
88 Jason Hart/19		
89 Keith Ginter/188	2.50	.75
90 Brent Abernathy/254	2.00	.60
91 Timo Perez/5		
92 Juan Pierre/104	4.00	1.20
93 Tike Redman/151	2.50	.75
94 Mike Lamb/240	2.00	.60
95 Ichiro Suzuki/159	25.00	7.50
96 Kazuhiro Sasaki/229	2.00	.60
97 Barry Zito/6		
98 Adam Bernero/254	2.00	.60
99 Chad Durbin/3		
100 Matt Ginter/300	2.00	.60

2001 Donruss 2000 Retro Stat Line Season

Randomly inserted into 2000 Retro packs, this 100-card insert parallels the 2000 Retro base set. Each card is individually serial numbered to a season stat of the given players. Please note that the print runs are listed in our checklist. Cards printed to a stated print run of 25 or fewer are not printed due to market scarcity. Exchange cards were seeded into packs for cards 82 and 95. These cards were originally intended to be redeemed for C.C. Sabathia and Ben Sheets. It's since been discovered that Ichiro Suzuki cards were actually redeemed for card 95.

	Nm-Mt	Ex-Mt
*1-80 P/R b/wn 251-400: 1.25X TO 3X		
*1-80 P/R b/wn 201-250: 1.25X TO 3X		
*1-80 P/R b/wn 151-200: 1.5X TO 4X		
*1-80 P/R b/wn 121-150: 1.5X TO 4X		
*1-80 P/R b/wn 81-120: 2X TO 5X		
*1-80 P/R b/wn 66-80: 2.5X TO 6X		
*1-80 P/R b/wn 51-65: 2.5X TO 6X		
*1-80 P/R b/wn 36-50: 3X TO 8X		
*1-80 P/R b/wn 26-35: 4X TO 10X		
81 Tomas De La Rosa/122	2.50	.75
82 C.C. Sabathia/76	25.00	7.50
83 Ryan Christenson/56	5.00	1.50
84 Pedro Feliz/13		
85 Jose Ortiz/107	4.00	1.20
86 Xavier Nady/23		
87 Julio Zuleta/21		
88 Jason Hart/168	2.50	.75
89 Keith Ginter/13		
90 Brent Abernathy/168	2.50	.75
91 Timo Perez/4		
92 Juan Pierre/187	2.50	.75
93 Tike Redman/143	2.50	.75
94 Mike Lamb/177	2.50	.75
95 Ichiro Suzuki/8		
96 Kazuhiro Sasaki/34	8.00	2.40
97 Barry Zito/97	4.00	1.20
98 Adam Bernero/80	5.00	1.50
99 Chad Durbin/3		
100 Matt Ginter/66	5.00	1.50

2001 Donruss 2000 Retro Diamond Kings

Randomly inserted into 2000 Retro packs, this 5-card insert set features the "Diamond King" cards that Donruss would have produced had they been producing baseball cards in 2000. Each card is individually serial numbered to 2500. Card backs carry a "DK" prefix.

	Nm-Mt	Ex-Mt
COMPLETE SET (5)	60.00	18.00
*STUDIO: .75X TO 2X BASIC RETRO DK		
RANDOM IN 2000 RETRO RETAIL PACKS		
STUDIO PRINT RUN 250 SERIAL #'d SETS		
DK1 Frank Thomas	10.00	3.00
DK2 Greg Maddux	12.00	3.60
DK3 Alex Rodriguez	12.00	3.60
DK4 Jeff Bagwell	10.00	3.00
DK5 Manny Ramirez	10.00	3.00

2001 Donruss 2000 Retro Diamond Kings Studio Series Autograph

An exchange card for an Alex Rodriguez autograph with a redemption deadline of May 1st, 2003 was randomly inserted in 2001 Donruss retro 2000 retail packs. The card is a signed version of A-Rod's basic Diamond King Studio Series insert and only 50 serial numbered copies were produced.

	Nm-Mt	Ex-Mt
DK3 Alex Rodriguez	250.00	75.00

2001 Donruss All-Time Diamond Kings

Randomly inserted into 2001 Donruss packs, this 10-card insert features some of the greatest players to have ever grace the front of a "Diamond Kings" card. Card backs carry a "ATDK" prefix. There were 2500 serial numbered sets produced. The Willie Mays and Hank Aaron cards both packed out as exchange cards with a redemption deadline of May 1st, 2003. The Mays card was originally intended to be card number ATDK-9 within this set, but was erroneously numbered ATDK-1 (the same number as the Frank Robinson card) when it was sent out by Donruss. Thus, this set has two card #1's and no card #9.

	Nm-Mt	Ex-Mt
COMPLETE SET (10)	150.00	45.00
*STUDIO: 1X TO 2.5X BASIC ALL-TIME DK		
STUDIO PRINT RUN 200 SERIAL #'d SETS		
STUDIO CARDS ARE SERIAL #'d 51-250		
ATDK1 Willie Mays	25.00	7.50
ATDK1 Frank Robinson	10.00	3.00
ATDK2 Harmon Killebrew	12.00	3.60
ATDK3 Mike Schmidt	20.00	6.00
ATDK4 Reggie Jackson	10.00	3.00
ATDK5 Nolan Ryan	40.00	12.00
ATDK6 George Brett	25.00	7.50
ATDK7 Tom Seaver	10.00	3.00
ATDK8 Hank Aaron	25.00	7.50
ATDK10 Stan Musial	20.00	6.00

2001 Donruss All-Time Diamond Kings Studio Series Autograph

Randomly inserted into 2001 Donruss packs, this 10-card insert is a complete autographed parallel of the 2001 Donruss All-Time Diamond Kings. Card backs carry a "ATDK" prefix. Please note that the serial #ing for these cards is as follows: cards #'d 1/250 through 50/250 are from this Autograph set and cards #'d 51/250 to 250/250 are from the ATDK Studio Series (non-autographed set). Exchange cards with a redemption deadline of May 1st, 2003 were seeded into packs for Hank Aaron, Willie Mays and Nolan Ryan.

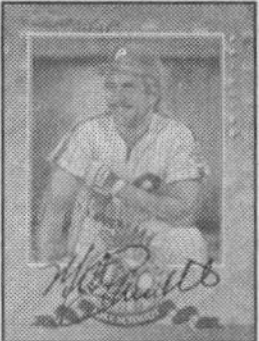
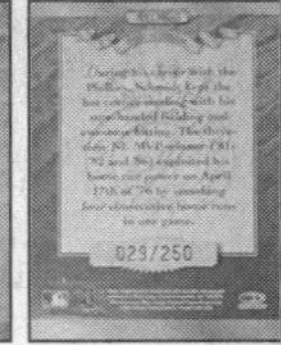

	Nm-Mt	Ex-Mt
AU CARDS ARE #'d 1/250 TO 50/250.		
ATDK1 Willie Mays		
ATDK1 Frank Robinson	80.00	24.00
ATDK2 Harmon Killebrew	120.00	36.00
ATDK3 Mike Schmidt	200.00	60.00
ATDK4 Reggie Jackson	120.00	36.00
ATDK5 Nolan Ryan	250.00	75.00
ATDK6 George Brett	250.00	75.00
ATDK7 Tom Seaver	100.00	30.00
ATDK8 Hank Aaron	250.00	75.00
ATDK10 Stan Musial	150.00	45.00

2001 Donruss Anniversary Originals Autograph

Each of these BGS graded cards were random inserted as box-toppers in boxes of 200 Donruss. Unfortunately, exchange cards with redemption deadline of May 1st, 2003 wer seeded into packs for almost the entire set. (the twelve cards featured in the set - only auto graph cards for Tony Gwynn, David Justice ar Ryne Sandberg actually made their way int packs. Since each card was signed to a differer print run, we have included that information our checklist.

	Nm-Mt	Ex-Mt
82-405 Cal Ripken/23		
83-277 Ryne Sandberg/24		
83-279 Cal Ripken/2		
83-586 Wade Boggs/25		
83-598 Tony Gwynn/24		
84-248 Don Mattingly/25		
87-36 Greg Maddux/25		
87-43 Rafael Palmeiro/250	60.00	18.00
87-361 Barry Bonds/25		
88-34 Roberto Alomar/250	50.00	15.00
88-644 Tom Glavine/250	60.00	18.00
89-42 Randy Johnson/25		
90-704 David Justice/24		

2001 Donruss Bat Kings

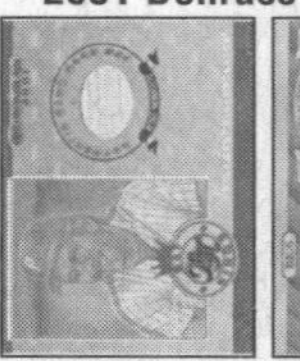

Randomly inserted into packs, this 10-car insert features swatches of actual game-use bat. Card backs carry a "BK" prefix. Each card individually serial numbered to 200. A exchange card with a redemption deadline May 1st, 2003 was seeded into packs for Har Aaron.

	Nm-Mt	Ex-Mt
BK1 Ivan Rodriguez	25.00	7.50
BK2 Tony Gwynn	40.00	12.00
BK3 Barry Bonds	80.00	24.00
BK4 Todd Helton	25.00	7.50
BK5 Troy Glaus	25.00	7.50
BK6 Mike Schmidt	60.00	18.00
BK7 Reggie Jackson	25.00	7.50
BK8 Harmon Killebrew	25.00	7.50
BK9 Frank Robinson	25.00	7.50
BK10 Hank Aaron	100.00	30.00

2001 Donruss Bat Kings Autograph

Randomly inserted into packs, this 10-car insert features swatches of actual game-use bat, as well as, an autograph from the depicte player. Card backs carry a "BK" prefix. Each ca is individually serial numbered to 50. Exchang cards with a redemption deadline of May 1s 2003 were seeded into packs for Barry Bond Troy Glaus, Todd Helton and Ivan Rodrigue Unfortunately, Donruss was not able to get Bar Bonds to sign his Bat King cards - thus a nor autographed version of Bonds' card was se out to collectors. Bonds did, however, agree sign 100 of his vintage Donruss cards (1988 - 2 ɔpies, 1989 -25 copies and 1990 - 50 copies). hese 100 cards were stamped with a ecollection Collection" logo and sent out to ollectors - along with the unsigned Bonds Bat ng card.

	Nm-Mt	Ex-Mt
K1 Ivan Rodriguez	150.00	45.00
K2 Tony Gwynn	150.00	45.00
K3 B.Bonds NO AU Bat	60.00	18.00
K4 Todd Helton	120.00	36.00
K5 Troy Glaus	80.00	24.00
K6 Mike Schmidt	200.00	60.00
K7 Reggie Jackson	150.00	45.00
K8 Harmon Killebrew	150.00	45.00
K9 Frank Robinson	120.00	36.00
K10 Hank Aaron	300.00	90.00

2001 Donruss Diamond Kings

andomly inserted into 2001 Donruss packs, is 20-card insert features players that are lead- s on and off the baseball field. Card backs rry a "DK" prefix. Each card is individually seri- numbered to 2500.

	Nm-Mt	Ex-Mt
OMPLETE SET (20)	250.00	75.00
TUDIO: .75X TO 2X BASIC DK		
TUDIO NO AU PLAYER PRINT 250 #'d SETS		
TUDIO AU PLAYER PRINT 200 #'d SETS		
ANDOM INSERTS IN PACKS		
K1 Alex Rodriguez	12.00	3.60
K2 Cal Ripken	25.00	7.50
K3 Mark McGwire	20.00	6.00
K4 Ken Griffey Jr.	12.00	3.60
K5 Derek Jeter	20.00	6.00
K6 Nomar Garciaparra	12.00	3.60
K7 Mike Piazza	12.00	3.60
K8 Roger Clemens	15.00	4.50
K9 Greg Maddux	12.00	3.60
K10 Chipper Jones	10.00	3.00
K11 Tony Gwynn	10.00	3.00
K12 Barry Bonds	20.00	6.00
K13 Sammy Sosa	12.00	3.60
K14 Vladimir Guerrero	10.00	3.00
K15 Frank Thomas	10.00	3.00
K16 Troy Glaus	10.00	3.00
K17 Todd Helton	10.00	3.00
K18 Ivan Rodriguez	10.00	3.00
K19 Pedro Martinez	10.00	3.00
K20 Carlos Delgado	10.00	3.00

2001 Donruss Diamond Kings Studio Series Autograph

andomly inserted into 2001 Donruss packs, is 11-card insert is a partial parallel of the 2001 amond Kings insert. Each of these auto- aphed cards were serial numbered to 50. change cards with a redemption deadline of ay 1st, 2003 were seeded into packs for Barry onds, Roger Clemens, Troy Glaus, Vladimir uerrero, Todd Helton, Chipper Jones, Alex odriguez and Ivan Rodriguez.

	Nm-Mt	Ex-Mt
K1 Alex Rodriguez	200.00	60.00
K2 Cal Ripken	300.00	90.00
K8 Roger Clemens	200.00	60.00
K9 Greg Maddux	200.00	60.00
K10 Chipper Jones	120.00	36.00
K11 Tony Gwynn	150.00	45.00
K12 Barry Bonds		
K14 Vladimir Guerrero	120.00	36.00
K16 Troy Glaus	80.00	24.00
K17 Todd Helton	100.00	30.00
K18 I. Rodriguez EXCH	120.00	36.00

2001 Donruss Diamond Kings Reprints

andomly inserted into 2001 Donruss packs, is 20-card insert features reprints of past iamond King" cards. Card backs carry a "DKR" efix. Print runs are listed in our checklist. An change card with a redemption deadline of ay 1st, 2003 was seeded into packs for Will ark.

	Nm-Mt	Ex-Mt
OMPLETE SET (20)	200.00	60.00
KR1 Rod Carew/1982	10.00	3.00
KR2 Nolan Ryan/1982	25.00	7.50
KR3 Tom Seaver/1982	10.00	3.00
KR4 Carlton Fisk/1982	10.00	3.00
DKR5 R.Jackson/1983	10.00	3.00
DKR6 S. Carlton/1983	10.00	3.00
DKR7 Johnny Bench/1983	10.00	3.00
DKR8 Joe Morgan/1983	10.00	3.00
DKR9 Mike Schmidt/1984	20.00	6.00
DKR10 Wade Boggs/1984	10.00	3.00
DKR11 Cal Ripken/1985	25.00	7.50
DKR12 Tony Gwynn/1985	12.00	3.60
DKR13 A.Dawson/1986	10.00	3.00
DKR14 Ozzie Smith/1987	15.00	4.50
DKR15 George Brett/1987	25.00	7.50
DKR16 D.Winfield/1987	10.00	3.00
DKR17 Paul Molitor/1988	10.00	3.00
DKR18 Will Clark/1988	15.00	4.50
DKR19 Robin Yount/1989	15.00	4.50
DKR20 K.Griffey Jr./1989	15.00	4.50

2001 Donruss Diamond Kings Reprints Autographs

Randomly inserted into 2001 Donruss packs, this 20-card insert features autographed reprints of past "Diamond King" cards. Card backs carry a "DKR" prefix. Print runs are listed below. Exchange cards with a redemption deadline of May 1st, 2003 were seeded into packs for Wade Boggs, Rod Carew, Steve Carlton, Will Clark, Andre Dawson, Carlton Fisk, Cal Ripken, Nolan Ryan, Ozzie Smith, Dave Winfield and Robin Yount. Ken Griffey Jr. had a card issued serial #'d of 89 copies but he was the only player featured in the set to not sign any of his cards.

	Nm-Mt	Ex-Mt
DKR1 Rod Carew/82	80.00	24.00
DKR2 Nolan Ryan/82	200.00	60.00
DKR3 Tom Seaver/82	80.00	24.00
DKR4 Carlton Fisk/82	80.00	24.00
DKR5 Reggie Jackson/83	100.00	30.00
DKR6 Steve Carlton/83	80.00	24.00
DKR7 Johnny Bench/83	100.00	30.00
DKR8 Joe Morgan/83	60.00	18.00
DKR9 Mike Schmidt/84	175.00	52.50
DKR10 Wade Boggs/84	80.00	24.00
DKR11 Cal Ripken/85	250.00	75.00
DKR12 Tony Gwynn/85	120.00	36.00
DKR13 Andre Dawson/86	60.00	18.00
DKR14 Ozzie Smith/87	100.00	30.00
DKR15 George Brett/87	150.00	45.00
DKR16 Dave Winfield/87	80.00	24.00
DKR17 Paul Molitor/88	80.00	24.00
DKR18 Will Clark/88	120.00	36.00
DKR19 Robin Yount/89	100.00	30.00
DKR20 Ken Griffey Jr. NO AU/89	50.00	15.00

2001 Donruss Elite Series

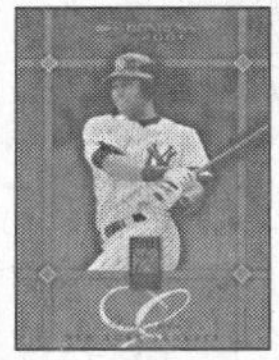
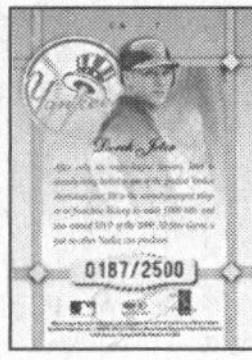

Randomly inserted into 2001 Donruss packs, this 20-card insert features many of the Major Leagues elite players. Card backs carry an "ES" prefix. Each card is individually serial numbered to 2500.

	Nm-Mt	Ex-Mt
COMPLETE SET (20)	150.00	45.00
*DOMINATORS: 6X TO 15X BASIC ELITE		
DOMINATORS PRINT RUN 25 SERIAL #'d SETS		
RANDOM INSERTS IN PACKS		
ES1 Vladimir Guerrero	5.00	1.50
ES2 Cal Ripken	15.00	4.50
ES3 Greg Maddux	8.00	2.40
ES4 Alex Rodriguez	8.00	2.40
ES5 Barry Bonds	12.00	3.60
ES6 Chipper Jones	5.00	1.50
ES7 Derek Jeter	12.00	3.60
ES8 Ivan Rodriguez	5.00	1.50
ES9 Ken Griffey Jr.	8.00	2.40
ES10 Mark McGwire	12.00	3.60
ES11 Mike Piazza	8.00	2.40
ES12 Nomar Garciaparra	8.00	2.40
ES13 Pedro Martinez	5.00	1.50
ES14 Randy Johnson	5.00	1.50
ES15 Roger Clemens	10.00	3.00
ES16 Sammy Sosa	8.00	2.40
ES17 Tony Gwynn	6.00	1.80
ES18 Darin Erstad	4.00	1.20
ES19 Andruw Jones	4.00	1.20
ES20 Bernie Williams	4.00	1.20

2001 Donruss Jersey Kings

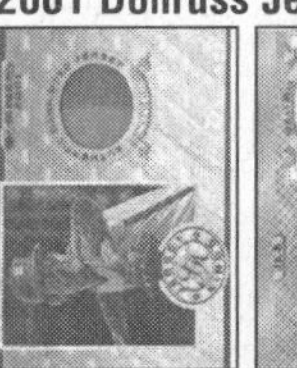
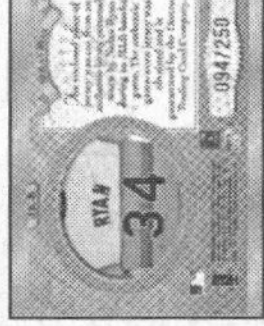

Randomly inserted into packs, this 10-card insert features swatches of actual game-used jerseys. Card backs carry a "JK" prefix. Each card is individually serial numbered to 250. Chipper Jones and Ozzie Smith were available only via mail redemption. Exchange cards with a redemption deadline of May 1st, 2003 for "to be determined" players were seeded originally into packs and many months passed before Chipper Jones and Ozzie Smith were revealed as the players that would be used to fulfill these cards.

	Nm-Mt	Ex-Mt
JK1 Vladimir Guerrero	25.00	7.50
JK2 Cal Ripken	120.00	36.00
JK3 Greg Maddux	50.00	15.00
JK4 Chipper Jones	25.00	7.50
JK5 Roger Clemens	60.00	18.00
JK6 George Brett	60.00	18.00
JK7 Tom Seaver	25.00	7.50
JK8 Nolan Ryan	120.00	36.00
JK9 Stan Musial	60.00	18.00
JK10 Ozzie Smith	40.00	12.00

2001 Donruss Jersey Kings Autograph

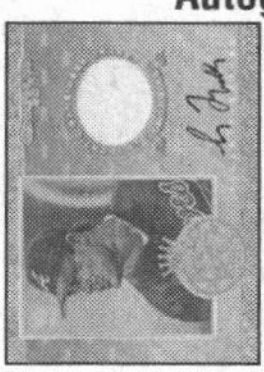

Randomly inserted into packs, this 10-card insert features swatches of actual game-used jerseys, as well as, an autograph from the depicted player. Card backs carry a "JK" prefix. Each card is individually serial numbered to 50. The following players players did not return their cards in time for inclusion in packs: Vladimir Guerrero, Cal Ripken, Chipper Jones, Roger Clemens, Nolan Ryan and Ozzie Smith. Exchange cards with a redemption deadline of May 1st, 2003 were seeded into packs for these players.

	Nm-Mt	Ex-Mt
JK1 Vladimir Guerrero	150.00	45.00
JK2 Cal Ripken	300.00	90.00
JK3 Greg Maddux	200.00	60.00
JK4 Chipper Jones	150.00	45.00
JK5 Roger Clemens	200.00	60.00
JK6 George Brett	200.00	60.00
JK7 Tom Seaver	120.00	36.00
JK8 Nolan Ryan	250.00	75.00
JK9 Stan Musial	200.00	60.00
JK10 Ozzie Smith	150.00	45.00

2001 Donruss Longball Leaders

Randomly inserted into packs, this 20-card insert features some of the Major Leagues top power hitters. Card backs carry a "LL" prefix. Each card is individually serial numbered to 1000.

	Nm-Mt	Ex-Mt
COMPLETE SET (20)	150.00	45.00
LL1 Vladimir Guerrero	8.00	2.40
LL2 Alex Rodriguez	12.00	3.60
LL3 Barry Bonds	20.00	6.00
LL4 Troy Glaus	4.00	1.20
LL5 Frank Thomas	8.00	2.40
LL6 Jeff Bagwell	5.00	1.50
LL7 Todd Helton	5.00	1.50
LL8 Ken Griffey Jr.	12.00	3.60
LL9 Manny Ramirez	5.00	1.50
LL10 Mike Piazza	12.00	3.60
LL11 Sammy Sosa	12.00	3.60
LL12 Carlos Delgado	4.00	1.20
LL13 Jim Edmonds	4.00	1.20
LL14 Jason Giambi	4.00	1.20
LL15 David Justice	4.00	1.20
LL16 Rafael Palmeiro	5.00	1.50
LL17 Gary Sheffield	4.00	1.20
LL18 Jim Thome	8.00	2.40
LL19 Tony Batista	4.00	1.20
LL20 Richard Hidalgo	4.00	1.20

2001 Donruss Production Line

Randomly inserted into packs, this 60-card insert features some of the Major League's most feared hitters. Card backs carry a "PL" prefix. Each card is individually serial numbered to one of three offensive categories: OBP, SLG, and PI. Print runs are listed in our checklist.

	Nm-Mt	Ex-Mt
COMPLETE SET (60)	400.00	120.00
COMMON SLG (21-40)	3.00	.90
COMMON PI (41-60)	2.50	.75
*DIE CUT OBP 1-20: .75X TO 2X BASIC PL		
*DIE CUT SLG 21-40: 1X TO 2.5X BASIC PL		
*DIE CUT PI 41-60: 1.25X TO 3X BASIC PL		
DIE CUT PRINT RUN 100 SERIAL #'d SETS		
PL1 J.Giambi OBP/476	4.00	1.20
PL2 C.Delgado OBP/470	4.00	1.20
PL3 Todd Helton OBP/463	6.00	1.80
PL4 M.Ramirez OBP/457	6.00	1.80
PL5 Barry Bonds OBP/440	25.00	7.50
PL6 G.Sheffield OBP/438	4.00	1.20
PL7 F.Thomas OBP/436	10.00	3.00
PL8 N.Garciaparra OBP/434	15.00	4.50
PL9 Brian Giles OBP/432	4.00	1.20
PL10 E.Alfonzo OBP/425	4.00	1.20
PL11 Jeff Kent OBP/424	4.00	1.20
PL12 J.Bagwell OBP/424	6.00	1.80
PL13 E.Martinez OBP/423	6.00	1.80
PL14 A.Rodriguez OBP/420	15.00	4.50
PL15 L.Castillo OBP/418	4.00	1.20
PL16 Will Clark OBP/418	10.00	3.00
PL17 J.Posada OBP/417	6.00	1.80
PL18 Derek Jeter OBP/416	25.00	7.50
PL19 Bob Abreu OBP/416	4.00	1.20
PL20 M.Alou OBP/416	4.00	1.20
PL21 T.Helton SLG/698	5.00	1.50
PL22 M.Ramirez SLG/697	5.00	1.50
PL23 B.Bonds SLG/688	20.00	6.00
PL24 C.Delgado SLG/664	3.00	.90
PL25 V.Guerrero SLG/664	8.00	2.40
PL26 J.Giambi SLG/647	3.00	.90
PL27 G.Sheffield SLG/643	3.00	.90
PL28 R.Hidalgo SLG/636	3.00	.90
PL29 S. Sosa SLG/634	12.00	3.60
PL30 F. Thomas SLG/625	8.00	2.40
PL31 M. Alou SLG/623	3.00	.90
PL32 J.Bagwell SLG/615	5.00	1.50
PL33 M. Piazza SLG/614	12.00	3.60
PL34 A. Rodriguez SLG/606	12.00	3.60
PL35 Troy Glaus SLG/604	3.00	.90
PL36 N.Garciaparra SLG/599	12.00	3.60
PL37 Jeff Kent SLG/596	3.00	.90
PL38 Brian Giles SLG/594	3.00	.90
PL39 G. Jenkins SLG/588	3.00	.90
PL40 Carl Everett SLG/587	3.00	.90
PL41 Todd Helton PI/1161	4.00	1.20
PL42 M. Ramirez PI/1154	4.00	1.20
PL43 C. Delgado PI/1134	2.50	.75
PL44 Barry Bonds PI/1128	15.00	4.50
PL45 J.Giambi PI/1123	2.50	.75
PL46 G.Sheffield PI/1081	2.50	.75
PL47 V.Guerrero PI/1074	6.00	1.80
PL48 F.Thomas PI/1061	6.00	1.80
PL49 S.Sosa PI/1040	10.00	3.00
PL50 Moises Alou PI/1039	2.50	.75
PL51 Jeff Bagwell PI/1039	4.00	1.20
PL52 N.Garciaparra PI/1033	10.00	3.00
PL53 R.Hidalgo PI/1027	2.50	.75
PL54 A.Rodriguez PI/1026	10.00	3.00
PL55 Brian Giles PI/1026	2.50	.75
PL56 Jeff Kent PI/1020	2.50	.75
PL57 Mike Piazza PI/1012	10.00	3.00
PL58 Troy Glaus PI/1008	2.50	.75
PL59 E.Martinez PI/1002	4.00	1.20
PL60 J.Edmonds PI/994	4.00	1.20

2001 Donruss Recollection Autographs

Two different players signed cards for this program. Barry Bonds and Alex Rodriguez each signed 100 total cards.The Rodriguez cards were randomly inserted in packs as exchange cards and the Bonds cards were issued as concessionary cards for collectors that redeemed a Bat Kings Autograph Bonds. According to representatives at Donruss, Bonds refused to sign the memorabilia bat cards, but did approve signing these Recollection buybacks. The exchange deadline for the Rodriguez cards was May 1st, 2003. The Rodriguez exchange cards that went into packs were numbered RC1-RC4, but the actual autograph cards are not numbered as such. For simplicity's sake we have kept the original RC1-RC4 checklisting.

	Nm-Mt	Ex-Mt
BB1 Barry Bonds 88/25		
BB2 Barry Bonds 89/25		
BB3 Barry Bonds 90/50		
RC1 Alex Rodriguez 97 Don Hit/10		
RC2 Alex Rodriguez 98 Don/20		
RC3 Alex Rodriguez 01 Retro/30	150.00	45.00
RC4 Alex Rodriguez 01 Don/40	150.00	45.00

2001 Donruss Rookie Reprints

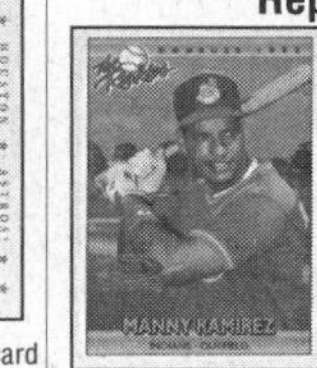

Randomly inserted into packs, this 40-card insert features reprinted Donruss rookie cards from the 80's-90s. Card backs carry a "RR" prefix. Please note that there was an error in production, and there are two number 39's, no number 40. Print runs are listed in our checklist.

	Nm-Mt	Ex-Mt
COMPLETE SET (40)	300.00	90.00
RR1 Cal Ripken/1982	25.00	7.50
RR2 Wade Boggs/1983	5.00	1.50
RR3 Tony Gwynn/1983	12.00	3.60
RR4 Ryne Sandberg/1983	15.00	4.50
RR5 Don Mattingly/1984	25.00	7.50
RR6 Joe Carter/1984	5.00	1.50
RR7 Roger Clemens/1985	20.00	6.00
RR8 Kirby Puckett/1985	8.00	2.40
RR9 Orel Hershiser/1985	5.00	1.50
RR10 A.Galarraga/1986	5.00	1.50
RR11 Jose Canseco/1986	8.00	2.40
RR12 Fred McGriff/1986	5.00	1.50
RR13 Paul O'Neill/1986	5.00	1.50
RR14 Mark McGwire/1987	20.00	6.00
RR15 Barry Bonds/1987	20.00	6.00
RR16 Kevin Brown/1987	5.00	1.50
RR17 David Cone/1987	5.00	1.50
RR18 R.Palmeiro/1987	5.00	1.50
RR19 Barry Larkin/1987	5.00	1.50
RR20 Bo Jackson/1987	8.00	2.40
RR21 Greg Maddux/1987	12.00	3.60
RR22 R. Alomar/1988	5.00	1.50
RR23 Mark Grace/1988	5.00	1.50
RR24 David Wells/1988	5.00	1.50
RR25 Tom Glavine/1988	5.00	1.50
RR26 Matt Williams/1988	5.00	1.50
RR27 Ken Griffey Jr./1989	12.00	3.60
RR28 R. Johnson/1989	8.00	2.40
RR29 Gary Sheffield/1989	5.00	1.50
RR30 Craig Biggio/1989	5.00	1.50
RR31 Curt Schilling/1989	5.00	1.50
RR32 Larry Walker/1990	5.00	1.50
RR33 B. Williams/1990	5.00	1.50
RR34 Sammy Sosa/1990	12.00	3.60
RR35 Juan Gonzalez/1990	5.00	1.50
RR36 David Justice/1990	5.00	1.50
RR37 I.Rodriguez/1991	8.00	2.40
RR38 Jeff Bagwell/1991	5.00	1.50
RR39 Jeff Kent/1992 UER Should have been RR40	5.00	1.50
RR39 M.Ramirez/1991	5.00	1.50

2001 Donruss Rookie Reprints Autograph

Randomly inserted into packs, this 26-card skip-numbered insert features autographed reprinted Donruss rookie cards from the 80's-90s. Card backs carry a "RR" prefix. Print runs are listed in our checklist. Nearly all of these cards packed out in the form of exchange cards - of which carried a May 1st, 2003 redemption deadline. Only autograph cards for Joe Carter, Tony Gwynn, David Justice, Greg Maddux and Ryne Sandberg actually made it into packs. Card RR24 was originally announced as a 1988 Donruss David Wells Reprint (with a print run of 88 copies) but due to contractual problems with the athlete the manufacturer substituted Diamondbacks outfielder Luis Gonzalez (reprinting 91 copies of his 1991 Donruss the Rookies RC).

	Nm-Mt	Ex-Mt
RR1 Cal Ripken/82	150.00	45.00
RR2 W.Boggs/83 EXCH	50.00	15.00
RR3 Tony Gwynn/83	80.00	24.00
RR4 Ryne Sandberg/83	100.00	30.00
RR5 D.Mattingly/84 EXCH	100.00	30.00
RR6 Joe Carter/84	40.00	12.00
RR7 R.Clemens/85 EXCH	120.00	36.00
RR8 K.Puckett/85 EXCH	60.00	18.00
RR9 O.Hershiser/85 EXCH	50.00	15.00
RR10 A.Galarraga/86 EXCH	40.00	12.00
RR15 B.Bonds/87 EXCH	250.00	75.00
RR16 K. Brown/87 EXCH	40.00	12.00
RR17 D.Cone/87 EXCH	40.00	12.00
RR18 R.Palmeiro/87 EXCH	60.00	18.00
RR20 B.Jackson/87 EXCH	80.00	24.00
RR21 Greg Maddux/87	100.00	30.00
RR22 R.Alomar/88 EXCH	50.00	15.00
RR24 D.Wells/88 EXCH	40.00	12.00
RR25 T.Glavine/88 EXCH	60.00	18.00
RR28 R.Johnson/89 EXCH	100.00	30.00
RR29 G.Sheffield/89 EXCH	50.00	15.00
RR31 C.Schilling/89 EXCH	60.00	18.00
RR35 J.Gonzalez/90 EXCH	50.00	15.00
RR36 David Justice/90	40.00	12.00
RR37 I.Rodriguez/91 EXCH	60.00	18.00
RR39 M.Ramirez/92 EXCH	60.00	18.00

2001 Donruss Rookies

This 110-card redemption set was issued via coupons in the 2001 Donruss product. The coupons were issued in packs at a rate of 1:72 and were good for a complete factory sealed set of 2001 Donruss the Rookies. Collector's were to send the coupon along with $24.99 to Playoff by January 20th, 2002. The set also came with one additional Diamond King card (106-110).

	Nm-Mt	Ex-Mt
COMP.FACT.SET (106)	60.00	18.00
COMP.SET w/o SP's (105)	50.00	15.00
R1 Adam Dunn	.75	.23
R2 Ryan Drese RC	.75	.23
R3 Bud Smith RC	.40	.12
R4 Tsuyoshi Shinjo RC	.75	.23
R5 Roy Oswalt	.75	.23

Card	Nm-Mt	Ex-Mt
R6 Wilmy Caceres RC	.40	.12
R7 Willie Harris RC	.40	.12
R8 Andres Torres RC	.40	.12
R9 Brandon Knight RC	.40	.12
R10 Horacio Ramirez RC	.75	.23
R11 Benito Baez RC	.40	.12
R12 Jeremy Affeldt RC	.75	.23
R13 Ryan Jensen RC	.40	.12
R14 Casey Fossum RC	.40	.12
R15 Ramon Vazquez RC	.40	.12
R16 Dustan Mohr RC	.40	.12
R17 Saul Rivera RC	.40	.12
R18 Zach Day RC	.40	.12
R19 Erik Hiljus RC	.40	.12
R20 Cesar Crespo RC	.40	.12
R21 Wilson Guzman RC	.40	.12
R22 Travis Hafner RC	2.50	.75
R23 Grant Balfour RC	.40	.12
R24 Johnny Estrada RC	1.25	.35
R25 Morgan Ensberg RC	1.25	.35
R26 Jack Wilson RC	2.00	.60
R27 Aubrey Huff	.40	.12
R28 Endy Chavez RC	.40	.12
R29 Delvin James RC	.40	.12
R30 Michael Cuddyer	.40	.12
R31 Jason Michaels RC	.40	.12
R32 Martin Vargas RC	.40	.12
R33 Donaldo Mendez RC	.40	.12
R34 Jorge Julio RC	.40	.12
R35 T.Spooneybarger RC	.40	.12
R36 Kurt Ainsworth	.40	.12
R37 Josh Fogg RC	.40	.12
R38 Brian Reith RC	.40	.12
R39 Rick Bauer RC	.40	.12
R40 Tim Redding	.40	.12
R41 Erick Almonte RC	.40	.12
R42 Juan A.Pena RC	.40	.12
R43 Ken Harvey	.40	.12
R44 David Brous RC	.40	.12
R45 Kevin Olsen RC	.40	.12
R46 Henry Mateo RC	.40	.12
R47 Nick Neugebauer	.40	.12
R48 Mike Penney RC	.40	.12
R49 Jay Gibbons RC	1.25	.35
R50 Tim Christman RC	.40	.12
R51 B.Duckworth RC	.40	.12
R52 Brett Jodie RC	.40	.12
R53 Christian Parker RC	.40	.12
R54 Carlos Hernandez	.40	.12
R55 Brandon Larson RC	.40	.12
R56 Nick Punto RC	.40	.12
R57 Elpidio Guzman RC	.40	.12
R58 Joe Beimel RC	.40	.12
R59 Junior Spivey RC	.75	.23
R60 Will Ohman RC	.40	.12
R61 Brandon Lyon RC	.40	.12
R62 Stubby Clapp RC	.40	.12
R63 J.Duchscherer RC	.40	.12
R64 Jimmy Rollins	.40	.12
R65 David Williams RC	.40	.12
R66 Craig Monroe RC	.40	.12
R67 Jose Acevedo RC	.40	.12
R68 Jason Jennings	.40	.12
R69 Josh Phelps	.40	.12
R70 Brian Roberts RC	.40	.12
R71 Claudio Vargas RC	.40	.12
R72 Adam Johnson	.40	.12
R73 Bart Miadich RC	.40	.12
R74 Juan Rivera	.40	.12
R75 Brad Voyles RC	.40	.12
R76 Nate Cornejo	.40	.12
R77 Juan Moreno RC	.40	.12
R78 Brian Rogers RC	.40	.12
R79 R.Rodriguez RC	.40	.12
R80 Geronimo Gil RC	.40	.12
R81 Joe Kennedy RC	.75	.23
R82 Kevin Joseph RC	.40	.12
R83 Josue Perez RC	.40	.12
R84 Victor Zambrano RC	.75	.23
R85 Josh Towers RC	.40	.12
R86 Mike Rivera RC	.40	.12
R87 Mark Prior RC	15.00	4.50
R88 Juan Cruz RC	.40	.12
R89 Dewon Brazelton RC	.75	.23
R90 Angel Berroa RC	1.25	.35
R91 Mark Teixeira RC	6.00	1.80
R92 Cody Ransom RC	.40	.12
R93 Angel Santos RC	.40	.12
R94 Corky Miller RC	.40	.12
R95 Brandon Berger RC	.40	.12
R96 Corey Patterson UPD	.40	.12
R97 A. Pujols UPD UER Homers and RBI Stats wrong	30.00	9.00
R98 Josh Beckett UPD	.40	.12
R99 C.C. Sabathia UPD	.40	.12
R100 A. Soriano UPD	.75	.23
R101 Ben Sheets UPD	.75	.23
R102 Rafael Soriano UPD	.75	.23
R103 Wilson Betemit UPD	.40	.12
R104 Ichiro Suzuki UPD	15.00	4.50
R105 Jose Ortiz UPD	.40	.12

2001 Donruss Rookies Diamond Kings

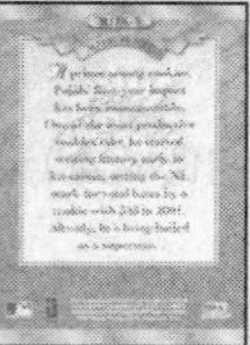

Inserted one per Donruss Rookies set, these five cards feature some of the leading 2001 rookies in a special Diamond King format.

Card	Nm-Mt	Ex-Mt
COMPLETE SET (5)	60.00	18.00
RDK-1 C.C. Sabathia DK	8.00	2.40
RDK-2 T.Shinjo DK	10.00	3.00
RDK-3 Albert Pujols DK	30.00	9.00
RDK-4 Roy Oswalt DK	10.00	3.00
RDK-5 Ichiro Suzuki DK	25.00	7.50

2002 Donruss

This 220 card set was issued in four card packs which had an SRP of $1.99 per pack and were issued 24 to a box and 20 boxes to a case. Cards numbered 151-200 featured leading rookie prospect and were inserted at stated odds of one in four. Card numbered 201-220 were Fan Club subset cards and were inserted at stated odds of one in eight.

Card	Nm-Mt	Ex-Mt
COMPLETE SET (220)	150.00	45.00
COMP.SET w/o SP'S (150)	25.00	7.50
COMMON CARD (1-150)	.30	.09
COMMON CARD (151-200)	3.00	.90
COMMON CARD (201-220)	1.50	.45
1 Alex Rodriguez	1.25	.35
2 Barry Bonds	2.00	.60
3 Derek Jeter	2.00	.60
4 Robert Fick	.30	.09
5 Juan Pierre	.30	.09
6 Torii Hunter	.30	.09
7 Todd Helton	.50	.15
8 Cal Ripken	2.50	.75
9 Manny Ramirez	.50	.15
10 Johnny Damon	.50	.15
11 Mike Piazza	1.25	.35
12 Nomar Garciaparra	1.25	.35
13 Pedro Martinez	.75	.23
14 Brian Giles	.30	.09
15 Albert Pujols	1.50	.45
16 Roger Clemens	1.50	.45
17 Sammy Sosa	1.25	.35
18 Vladimir Guerrero	.75	.23
19 Tony Gwynn	1.00	.30
20 Pat Burrell	.30	.09
21 Carlos Delgado	.30	.09
22 Tino Martinez	.50	.15
23 Jim Edmonds	.30	.09
24 Jason Giambi	.75	.23
25 Tom Glavine	.50	.15
26 Mark Grace	.50	.15
27 Tony Armas Jr.	.30	.09
28 Andruw Jones	.30	.09
29 Ben Sheets	.30	.09
30 Jeff Kent	.30	.09
31 Barry Larkin	.50	.15
32 Joe Mays	.30	.09
33 Mike Mussina	.50	.15
34 Hideo Nomo	.75	.23
35 Rafael Palmeiro	.50	.15
36 Scott Brosius	.30	.09
37 Scott Rolen	.75	.23
38 Gary Sheffield	.30	.09
39 Bernie Williams	.50	.15
40 Bob Abreu	.30	.09
41 Edgardo Alfonzo	.30	.09
42 C.C. Sabathia	.30	.09
43 Jeremy Giambi	.30	.09
44 Craig Biggio	.50	.15
45 Andres Galarraga	.30	.09
46 Edgar Martinez	.50	.15
47 Fred McGriff	.50	.15
48 Magglio Ordonez	.30	.09
49 Jim Thome	.75	.23
50 Matt Williams	.30	.09
51 Kerry Wood	.75	.23
52 Moises Alou	.30	.09
53 Brady Anderson	.30	.09
54 Garret Anderson	.30	.09
55 Juan Gonzalez	.50	.15
56 Bret Boone	.30	.09
57 Jose Cruz Jr.	.30	.09
58 Carlos Beltran	.50	.15
59 Adrian Beltre	.50	.15
60 Joe Kennedy	.30	.09
61 Lance Berkman	.30	.09
62 Kevin Brown	.30	.09
63 Tim Hudson	.30	.09
64 Jeromy Burnitz	.30	.09
65 Jarrod Washburn	.30	.09
66 Sean Casey	.30	.09
67 Eric Chavez	.30	.09
68 Bartolo Colon	.30	.09
69 Freddy Garcia	.30	.09
70 Jermaine Dye	.30	.09
71 Terrence Long	.30	.09
72 Cliff Floyd	.30	.09
73 Luis Gonzalez	.30	.09
74 Ichiro Suzuki	1.25	.35
75 Mike Hampton	.30	.09
76 Richard Hidalgo	.30	.09
77 Geoff Jenkins	.30	.09
78 Gabe Kapler	.30	.09
79 Ken Griffey Jr.	1.25	.35
80 Jason Kendall	.30	.09
81 Josh Towers	.30	.09
82 Ryan Klesko	.30	.09
83 Paul Konerko	.30	.09
84 Carlos Lee	.30	.09
85 Kenny Lofton	.30	.09
86 Josh Beckett	.30	.09
87 Raul Mondesi	.30	.09
88 Trot Nixon	.30	.09
89 John Olerud	.30	.09
90 Paul O'Neill	.50	.15
91 Chan Ho Park	.30	.09
92 Andy Pettitte	.50	.15
93 Jorge Posada	.50	.15
94 Mark Quinn	.30	.09
95 Aramis Ramirez	.30	.09
96 Curt Schilling	.30	.09
97 Richie Sexson	.30	.09
98 John Smoltz	.50	.15
99 Wilson Betemit	.30	.09
100 Shannon Stewart	.30	.09
101 Alfonso Soriano	.50	.15
102 Mike Sweeney	.30	.09
103 Miguel Tejada	.30	.09
104 Greg Vaughn	.30	.09
105 Robin Ventura	.30	.09
106 Jose Vidro	.30	.09
107 Larry Walker	.50	.15
108 Preston Wilson	.30	.09
109 Corey Patterson	.30	.09
110 Mark Mulder	.30	.09
111 Tony Clark	.30	.09
112 Roy Oswalt	.30	.09
113 Jimmy Rollins	.30	.09
114 Kazuhiro Sasaki	.30	.09
115 Barry Zito	.30	.09
116 Javier Vazquez	.30	.09
117 Mike Cameron	.30	.09
118 Phil Nevin	.30	.09
119 Bud Smith	.30	.09
120 Cristian Guzman	.30	.09
121 Al Leiter	.30	.09
122 Brad Radke	.30	.09
123 Bobby Higginson	.30	.09
124 Robert Person	.30	.09
125 Adam Dunn	.50	.15
126 Ben Grieve	.30	.09
127 Rafael Furcal	.30	.09
128 Jay Gibbons	.30	.09
129 Paul LoDuca	.30	.09
130 Wade Miller	.30	.09
131 Tsuyoshi Shinjo	.30	.09
132 Eric Milton	.30	.09
133 Rickey Henderson	.75	.23
134 Roberto Alomar	.50	.15
135 Darin Erstad	.30	.09
136 J.D. Drew	.30	.09
137 Shawn Green	.30	.09
138 Randy Johnson	.75	.23
139 Austin Kearns	.30	.09
140 Jose Canseco	.75	.23
141 Jeff Bagwell	.50	.15
142 Greg Maddux	1.25	.35
143 Mark Buehrle	.30	.09
144 Ivan Rodriguez	.75	.23
145 Frank Thomas	.75	.23
146 Rich Aurilia	.30	.09
147 Troy Glaus	.30	.09
148 Ryan Dempster	.30	.09
149 Chipper Jones	.75	.23
150 Matt Morris	.30	.09
151 Marlon Byrd RR	3.00	.90
152 Ben Howard RR RC	3.00	.90
153 Brandon Backe RR RC	4.00	1.20
154 Jorge De La Rosa RR RC	3.00	.90
155 Corky Miller RR	3.00	.90
156 Dennis Tankersley RR	3.00	.90
157 Kyle Kane RR RC	3.00	.90
158 Justin Duchscherer RR	3.00	.90
159 Brian Mallette RR RC	3.00	.90
160 Chris Baker RR RC	3.00	.90
161 Jason Lane RR	3.00	.90
162 Hee Seop Choi RR	3.00	.90
163 Juan Cruz RR	3.00	.90
164 Rodrigo Rosario RR RC	3.00	.90
165 Matt Guerrier RR	3.00	.90
166 Anderson Machado RR RC	3.00	.90
167 Geronimo Gil RR	3.00	.90
168 Dewon Brazelton RR	3.00	.90
169 Mark Prior RR	10.00	3.00
170 Bill Hall RR	3.00	.90
171 Jorge Padilla RR RC	3.00	.90
172 Jose Cueto RR	3.00	.90
173 Allan Simpson RR RC	3.00	.90
174 Doug Devore RR RC	3.00	.90
175 Josh Pearce RR	3.00	.90
176 Angel Berroa RR	3.00	.90
177 Steve Bechler RR RC	3.00	.90
178 Antonio Perez RR	3.00	.90
179 Mark Teixeira RR	3.00	.90
180 Erick Almonte RR	3.00	.90
181 Orlando Hudson RR	3.00	.90
182 Michael Rivera RR	3.00	.90
183 Raul Chavez RR RC	3.00	.90
184 Juan Pena RR	3.00	.90
185 Travis Hughes RR RC	3.00	.90
186 Ryan Ludwick RR	3.00	.90
187 Ed Rogers RR	3.00	.90
188 Andy Pratt RR RC	3.00	.90
189 Nick Neugebauer RR	3.00	.90
190 Tom Shearn RR RC	3.00	.90
191 Eric Cyr RR	3.00	.90
192 Victor Martinez RR	4.00	1.20
193 Brandon Berger RR	3.00	.90
194 Erik Bedard RR	3.00	.90
195 Fernando Rodney RR	3.00	.90
196 Joe Thurston RR	3.00	.90
197 John Buck RR	3.00	.90
198 Jeff Deardorff RR	3.00	.90
199 Ryan Jamison RR	3.00	.90
200 Alfredo Amezaga RR	3.00	.90
201 Luis Gonzalez FC	1.50	.45
202 Roger Clemens FC	5.00	1.50
203 Barry Zito FC	1.50	.45
204 Bud Smith FC	1.50	.45
205 Magglio Ordonez FC	1.50	.45
206 Kerry Wood FC	2.50	.75
207 Freddy Garcia FC	1.50	.45
208 Adam Dunn FC	1.50	.45
209 Curt Schilling FC	1.50	.45
210 Lance Berkman FC	1.50	.45
211 Rafael Palmeiro FC	1.50	.45
212 Ichiro Suzuki FC	5.00	1.50
213 Bob Abreu FC	1.50	.45
214 Mark Mulder FC	1.50	.45
215 Roy Oswalt FC	1.50	.45
216 Mike Sweeney FC	1.50	.45
217 Paul LoDuca FC	1.50	.45
218 Aramis Ramirez FC	1.50	.45
219 Randy Johnson FC	2.50	.75
220 Albert Pujols FC	5.00	1.50

2002 Donruss Autographs

Inserted randomly in packs, these 19 cards feature signatures of players in the Fan Club subset. Since the cards have different stated print runs, we have listed those print runs in our checklist. Cards with a print run of 25 or fewer are not priced due to market scarcity.

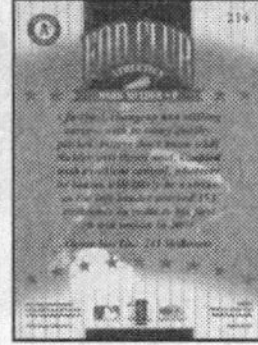

Card	Nm-Mt	Ex-Mt
201 Luis Gonzalez FC/25		
202 Roger Clemens FC/25		
203 Barry Zito FC/200	40.00	12.00
204 Bud Smith FC/200	25.00	7.50
205 Magglio Ordonez FC/200	25.00	7.50
206 Kerry Wood FC/200	40.00	12.00
207 Freddy Garcia FC/200	25.00	7.50
208 Adam Dunn FC/200	40.00	12.00
209 Curt Schilling FC/25		
210 Lance Berkman FC/175	40.00	12.00
211 Rafael Palmeiro FC/25		
213 Bob Abreu FC/200	25.00	7.50
214 Mark Mulder FC/200	25.00	7.50
215 Roy Oswalt FC/200	25.00	7.50
216 Mike Sweeney FC/200	25.00	7.50
217 Paul LoDuca FC/200	25.00	7.50
218 Aramis Ramirez FC/200	25.00	7.50
219 Randy Johnson FC/10		
220 Albert Pujols FC/200	120.00	36.00

2002 Donruss Stat Line Career

Randomly inserted into packs, this is a parallel to the basic Donruss set. These cards feature cards printed on foil-board with silver holo-foil stamping. Each card has a stated print run to a unique career stat. Please note that is a card has a stated print run of 15 or less, no pricing is provided.

Card	Nm-Mt	Ex-Mt
*1-150 P/R b/wn 251-400: 2.5X TO 6X		
*1-150 P/R b/wn 201-250: 2.5X TO 6X		
*1-150 P/R b/wn 151-200: 3X TO 8X.		
*1-150 P/R b/wn 121-150: 3X TO 8X.		
*1-150 P/R b/wn 81-120: 4X TO 10X.		
*1-150 P/R b/wn 66-80: 5X TO 12X...		
*1-150 P/R b/wn 51-65: 5X TO 12X...		
*1-150 P/R b/wn 36-50: 6X TO 15X...		
*201-220 P/R b/wn 251-400 .5X TO 1.2X		
*201-220 P/R b/wn 201-250 .6X TO 1.5X		
*201-220 P/R b/wn 151-200 .75X TO 2X		
*201-220 P/R b/wn 121-150 1X TO 2.5X		
*201-220 P/R b/wn 51-65 1.5X TO 4X		
151 Marlon Byrd RR/232	2.50	.75
152 Ben Howard RR/283	2.00	.60
153 Brandon Backe RR/94	8.00	2.40
154 Jorge De La Rosa RR/54	6.00	1.80
155 Corky Miller RR/184	3.00	.90
156 Dennis Tankersley RR/253	2.00	.60
157 Kyle Kane RR/179	3.00	.90
158 Justin Duchscherer RR/11		
159 Brian Mallette RR/273	2.00	.60
160 Chris Baker RR/270	2.00	.60
161 Jason Lane RR/302	2.00	.60
162 Hee Seop Choi RR/286	2.00	.60
163 Juan Cruz RR/322	2.00	.60
164 Rodrigo Rosario RR/313	2.00	.60
165 Matt Guerrier RR/280	2.00	.60
166 Anderson Machado RR/252	2.00	.60
167 Geronimo Gil RR/293	2.00	.60
168 Dewon Brazelton RR/335	2.00	.60
169 Mark Prior RR/303	8.00	2.40
170 Bill Hall RR/373	2.00	.60
171 Jorge Padilla RR/273	2.00	.60
172 Jose Cueto RR/156	3.00	.90
173 Allan Simpson RR/204	2.50	.75
174 Doug Devore RR/287	2.00	.60
175 Josh Pearce RR/315	2.00	.60
176 Angel Berroa RR/268	2.00	.60
177 Steve Bechler RR/25		
178 Antonio Perez RR/143	4.00	1.20
179 Mark Teixeira RR/165	3.00	.90
180 Erick Almonte RR/4		
181 Orlando Hudson RR/283	2.00	.60
182 Michael Rivera RR/333	2.00	.60
183 Raul Chavez RR/253	2.00	.60
184 Juan Pena RR/293	2.00	.60
185 Travis Hughes RR/174	3.00	.90
186 Ryan Ludwick RR/264	2.00	.60
187 Ed Rogers RR/270	2.00	.60
188 Andy Pratt RR/203	2.50	.75
189 Nick Neugebauer RR/11		
190 Tom Shearn RR/251	2.00	.60
191 Eric Cyr RR/161	3.00	.90
192 Victor Martinez RR/305	3.00	.90
193 Brandon Berger RR/313	2.00	.60
194 Erik Bedard RR/279	2.00	.60
195 Fernando Rodney RR/309	2.00	.60
196 Joe Thurston RR/284	2.00	.60
197 John Buck RR/271	2.00	.60
198 Jeff Deardorff RR/201	2.50	.75
199 Ryan Jamison RR/273	2.00	.60
200 Alfredo Amezaga RR/290	2.00	.60

2002 Donruss Stat Line Season

Randomly inserted into packs, this is a parallel to the basic Donruss set. These cards feature cards printed on foil-board with silver holo-foil stamping. Each card has a stated print run to a unique seasonal stat. Please note that is a card has a stated print run of 15 or less, no pricing is provided.

Card	Nm-Mt	Ex-Mt
*1-150 P/R b/wn 151-200: 3X TO 8X.		
*1-150 P/R b/wn 121-150: 3X TO 8X.		
*1-150 P/R b/wn 81-120: 4X TO 10X.		
*1-150 P/R b/wn 66-80: 5X TO 12X...		
*1-150 P/R b/wn 51-65: 5X TO 12X...		
*1-150 P/R b/wn 36-50: 6X TO 15X...		
*1-150 P/R b/wn 26-35: 8X TO 20X...		
*201-220 P/R b/wn 81-120 1.25X TO 3X		
*201-220 P/R b/wn 66-80 1.5X TO 4X		
*201-220 P/R b/wn 51-65 1.5X TO 4X		
*201-220 P/R b/wn 36-50 2X TO 5X..		
*201-220 P/R b/wn 26-35 2.5X TO 6X		
151 Marlon Byrd RR/89	5.00	1.50
152 Ben Howard RR/29	10.00	3.00
153 Brandon Backe RR/39	12.00	3.60
154 Jorge De La Rosa RR/32	10.00	3.00
155 Corky Miller RR/7		
156 Dennis Tankersley RR/30	10.00	3.00
157 Kyle Kane RR/75	6.00	1.80
158 Justin Duchscherer RR/20		
159 Brian Mallette RR/94	5.00	1.50
160 Chris Baker RR/121	4.00	1.20
161 Jason Lane RR/38	8.00	2.40
162 Hee Seop Choi RR/45	8.00	2.40
163 Juan Cruz RR/39	8.00	2.40
164 Rodrigo Rosario RR/131	4.00	1.20
165 Matt Guerrier RR/118	5.00	1.50
166 Anderson Machado RR/36	8.00	2.40
167 Geronimo Gil RR/17		
168 Dewon Brazelton RR/13		
169 Mark Prior RR/14		
170 Bill Hall RR/65	6.00	1.80
171 Jorge Padilla RR/66	6.00	1.80
172 Jose Cueto RR/62	6.00	1.80
173 Allan Simpson RR/77	6.00	1.80
174 Doug Devore RR/74	6.00	1.80
175 Josh Pearce RR/132	4.00	1.20
176 Angel Berroa RR/63	6.00	1.80
177 Steve Bechler RR/135	4.00	1.20
178 Antonio Perez RR/143	4.00	1.20
179 Mark Teixeira RR/20		
180 Erick Almonte RR/8		
181 Orlando Hudson RR/79	6.00	1.80
182 Michael Rivera RR/4		
183 Raul Chavez RR/5		
184 Juan Pena RR/106	5.00	1.50
185 Travis Hughes RR/86	5.00	1.50
186 Ryan Ludwick RR/103	5.00	1.50
187 Ed Rogers RR/54	6.00	1.80
188 Andy Pratt RR/132	4.00	1.20
189 Nick Neugebauer RR/5		
190 Tom Shearn RR/136	4.00	1.20
191 Eric Cyr RR/131	4.00	1.20
192 Victor Martinez RR/57	10.00	3.00
193 Brandon Berger RR/16		
194 Erik Bedard RR/137	4.00	1.20
195 Fernando Rodney RR/52	6.00	1.80
196 Joe Thurston RR/46	8.00	2.40
197 John Buck RR/73	6.00	1.80
198 Jeff Deardorff RR/100	5.00	1.50
199 Ryan Jamison RR/95	5.00	1.50
200 Alfredo Amezaga RR/37	8.00	2.40

2002 Donruss All-Time Diamond Kings

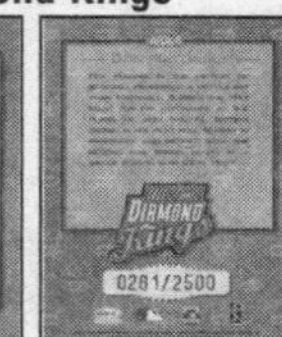

Randomly inserted in packs, these 10 cards feature legendary baseball superstars reproduced on conventional stock with bronze foil. These cards have a stated print run of 2,500 copies.

Card	Nm-Mt	Ex-Mt
*STUDIO: 1X TO 2.5X BASIC ALL-TIME DK		
STUDIO PRINT RUN 250 SERIAL #'d SETS		
1 Ted Williams UER Rogers Hornsby also won the triple crown twice	15.00	4.50
2 Cal Ripken	30.00	9.00
3 Lou Gehrig	15.00	4.50
4 Babe Ruth	25.00	7.50
5 Roberto Clemente	20.00	6.00
6 Don Mattingly	25.00	7.50
7 Kirby Puckett	10.00	3.00
8 Stan Musial	15.00	4.50
9 Yogi Berra	10.00	3.00
10 Ernie Banks	10.00	3.00

2002 Donruss Bat Kings

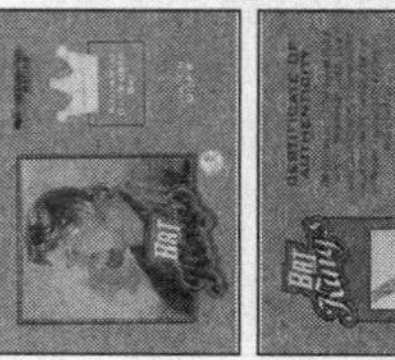

Randomly inserted in packs, these five cards feature a mix of active and retired superstars along with a sliver of each player's game-used bat. The active players have a stated print run of 250 copies while the retired players have a stated print run of 125 copies.

Card	Nm-Mt	Ex-Mt
*STUDIO 1-3: .75X TO 2X BASIC BAT KING		
STUDIO 1-3 PRINT RUN 50 SERIAL #'d SETS		
STUDIO 4-5 PRINT RUN 25 SERIAL #'d SETS		
RANDOM INSERTS IN PACKS		
1 Jason Giambi	15.00	4.50
2 Alex Rodriguez	25.00	7.50
3 Mike Piazza	25.00	7.50
4 Roberto Clemente/125	100.00	30.00
5 Babe Ruth/125	200.00	60.00

2002 Donruss Diamond Kings Inserts

Randomly inserted in packs, these 20 cards feature leading players with silver foil stamping and stated sequential serial numbering to 2500.

Card	Nm-Mt	Ex-Mt
*STUDIO: .75X TO 2X BASIC DK'S		
STUDIO PRINT RUN 250 SERIAL #'d SETS		
RANDOM INSERTS IN PACKS		
1 Nomar Garciaparra	12.00	3.60
2 Shawn Green	10.00	3.00

3 Randy Johnson 10.00 3.00
4 Derek Jeter 20.00 6.00
5 Carlos Delgado 10.00 3.00
6 Roger Clemens 15.00 4.50
7 Jeff Bagwell 10.00 3.00
8 Vladimir Guerrero 10.00 3.00
9 Luis Gonzalez 10.00 3.00
10 Mike Piazza 12.00 3.60
11 Ichiro Suzuki 12.00 3.60
12 Pedro Martinez 10.00 3.00
13 Todd Helton 10.00 3.00
14 Sammy Sosa 12.00 3.60
15 Ivan Rodriguez 10.00 3.00
16 Barry Bonds 20.00 6.00
17 Albert Pujols 15.00 4.50
18 Jim Thome 10.00 3.00
19 Alex Rodriguez 12.00 3.60
20 Jason Giambi 10.00 3.00

2002 Donruss Elite Series

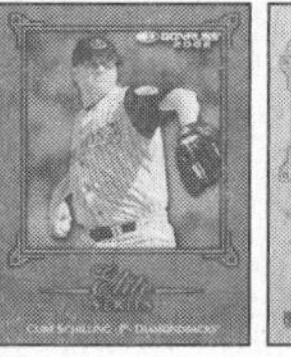

Randomly inserted in packs, these 20 cards feature some of today's most storied performers. These cards are printed on metalized film board and are sequentially numbered to 2,500.

Nm-Mt Ex-Mt
1 Barry Bonds 12.00 3.60
2 Lance Berkman 4.00 1.20
3 Jason Giambi 4.00 1.20
4 Nomar Garciaparra 8.00 2.40
5 Curt Schilling 4.00 1.20
6 Vladimir Guerrero 5.00 1.50
7 Shawn Green 4.00 1.20
8 Jeff Bagwell 4.00 1.20
9 Troy Glaus 4.00 1.20
10 Manny Ramirez 4.00 1.20
11 Eric Chavez 4.00 1.20
12 Carlos Delgado 4.00 1.20
13 Mike Sweeney 4.00 1.20
14 Todd Helton 4.00 1.20
15 Luis Gonzalez 4.00 1.20
16 Enos Slaughter LGD 4.00 1.20
17 Frank Robinson LGD 4.00 1.20
18 Bob Gibson LGD 4.00 1.20
19 Warren Spahn LGD 4.00 1.20
20 Whitey Ford LGD 4.00 1.20

2002 Donruss Elite Series Signatures

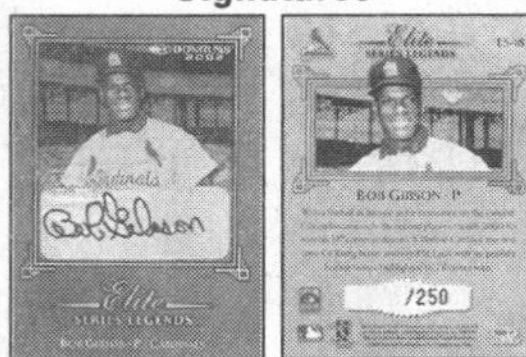

Randomly inserted in packs, these 18 cards feature players who signed cards for the 2002 Donruss Elite product. These cards have different print runs and we have notated that information in our checklist.

Nm-Mt Ex-Mt
2 Lance Berkman/25
3 Jason Giambi/25
4 Nomar Garciaparra/25
5 Curt Schilling/25
6 Vladimir Guerrero/25
7 Shawn Green/25
8 Jeff Bagwell/25
9 Troy Glaus/25
10 Manny Ramirez/25
11 Eric Chavez/25
13 Mike Sweeney/25
14 Todd Helton/25
15 Luis Gonzalez/25
16 Enos Slaughter LGD/250 40.00 12.00
17 Frank Robinson LGD/250 40.00 12.00
18 Bob Gibson LGD/250 40.00 12.00
19 Warren Spahn LGD/250 60.00 18.00
20 Whitey Ford LGD/250 40.00 12.00

2002 Donruss Jersey Kings

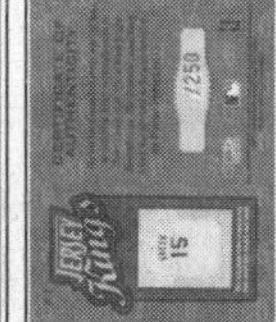

Randomly inserted in packs, these 15 cards feature game-worn jersey swatches of a mix all-time greats and active superstars. The active players have a stated prinrt run of 250 serial numbered sets while the retired players have a stated print run of 125 sets.

Nm-Mt Ex-Mt
*STUDIO 1-12: .75X TO 2X BASIC JSY KINGS
STUDIO 1-12 PRINT RUN 50 SERIAL #'d SETS
STUDIO 13-15 PRINT RUN 25 SERIAL #'d SETS
STUDIO 13-15 TOO SCARCE TO PRICE
RANDOM INSERTS IN PACKS
1 Alex Rodriguez 25.00 7.50
2 Jason Giambi 15.00 4.50
3 Carlos Delgado 15.00 4.50
4 Barry Bonds 40.00 12.00
5 Randy Johnson 25.00 7.50
6 Jim Thome 25.00 7.50
7 Shawn Green 15.00 4.50
8 Pedro Martinez 25.00 7.50
9 Jeff Bagwell 25.00 7.50
10 Vladimir Guerrero 25.00 7.50
11 Ivan Rodriguez 25.00 7.50
12 Nomar Garciaparra 25.00 7.50
13 Don Mattingly/125 40.00 12.00
14 Ted Williams/125 100.00 30.00
15 Lou Gehrig/125 200.00 60.00

2002 Donruss Longball Leaders

Randomly inserted in packs, these 20 cards feature the majors most powerful hitters and they are featured on metalized film board and have a stated print run of 1,000 sequentially numbered sets.

Nm-Mt Ex-Mt
1 Barry Bonds 20.00 6.00
2 Sammy Sosa 12.00 3.60
3 Luis Gonzalez 4.00 1.20
4 Alex Rodriguez 12.00 3.60
5 Shawn Green 4.00 1.20
6 Todd Helton 5.00 1.50
7 Jim Thome 8.00 2.40
8 Rafael Palmeiro 5.00 1.50
9 Richie Sexson 4.00 1.20
10 Troy Glaus 4.00 1.20
11 Manny Ramirez 5.00 1.50
12 Phil Nevin 4.00 1.20
13 Jeff Bagwell 5.00 1.50
14 Carlos Delgado 4.00 1.20
15 Jason Giambi 4.00 1.20
16 Chipper Jones 8.00 2.40
17 Larry Walker 5.00 1.50
18 Albert Pujols 15.00 4.50
19 Brian Giles 4.00 1.20
20 Bret Boone 4.00 1.20

2002 Donruss Production Line

Randomly inserted in packs, these 60 cards feature the msot productive sluggers in three categories: On-Base Percentage, Slugging Percentage and OPS. Cards numbered 1-20 feature On-Base Percentage, while cards numbered 21-40 feature Slugging Percentage and cards numbered 41-60 feature OPS. Since all the cards have different stated print runs, we have listed that information next to the card in our checklist.

Nm-Mt Ex-Mt
COMMON OBP (1-20) 4.00 1.20
COMMON SLG (21-40) 3.00 .90
COMMON OPS (41-60) 2.50 .75
*DIE CUT OBP 1-20: .75X TO 2X BASIC PL
*DIE CUT SLG 21-40: 1X TO 2.5X BASIC PL
*DIE CUT OPS 41-60: 1.25X TO 3X BASIC PL
DIE CUT PRINT RUN 100 SERIAL #'d SETS
DC's ARE 1ST 100 #'d OF EACH PLAYER
RANDOM INSERTS IN PACKS
1 Barry Bonds OBP/415 25.00 7.50
2 Jason Giambi OBP/377 4.00 1.20
3 Larry Walker OBP/349 6.00 1.80
4 Sammy Sosa OBP/337 15.00 4.50
5 Todd Helton OBP/332 6.00 1.80
6 Lance Berkman OBP/330 4.00 1.20
7 Luis Gonzalez OBP/329 4.00 1.20
8 Chipper Jones OBP/327 10.00 3.00
9 Edgar Martinez OBP/323 6.00 1.80
10 Gary Sheffield OBP/317 4.00 1.20
11 Jim Thome OBP/316 10.00 3.00
12 Roberto Alomar OBP/315 6.00 1.80
13 J.D. Drew OBP/314 4.00 1.20
14 Jim Edmonds OBP/310 4.00 1.20
15 Carlos Delgado OBP/308 4.00 1.20
16 Manny Ramirez OBP/305 6.00 1.80
17 Brian Giles OBP/304 4.00 1.20
18 Albert Pujols OBP/303 20.00 6.00
19 John Olerud OBP/301 4.00 1.20
20 Alex Rodriguez OBP/299 15.00 4.50
21 Barry Bonds SLG/763 20.00 6.00
22 Sammy Sosa SLG/637 12.00 3.60
23 Luis Gonzalez SLG/588 3.00 .90
24 Todd Helton SLG/585 5.00 1.50
25 Larry Walker SLG/562 5.00 1.50
26 Jason Giambi SLG/560 3.00 .90
27 Jim Thome SLG/524 8.00 2.40
28 Alex Rodriguez SLG/522 12.00 3.60
29 Lance Berkman SLG/520 3.00 .90
30 J.D. Drew SLG/513 3.00 .90
31 Albert Pujols SLG/510 15.00 4.50
32 Manny Ramirez SLG/509 5.00 1.50
33 Chipper Jones SLG/505 8.00 2.40
34 Shawn Green SLG/498 3.00 .90
35 Brian Giles SLG/490 3.00 .90
36 Juan Gonzalez SLG/490 5.00 1.50
37 Phil Nevin SLG/488 3.00 .90
38 Gary Sheffield SLG/483 3.00 .90
39 Bret Boone SLG/478 3.00 .90
40 Cliff Floyd SLG/478 3.00 .90
41 Barry Bonds OPS/1278 15.00 4.50
42 Sammy Sosa OPS/1074 10.00 3.00
43 Jason Giambi OPS/1037 2.50 .75
44 Todd Helton OPS/1017 4.00 1.20
45 Luis Gonzalez OPS/1017 2.50 .75
46 Larry Walker OPS/1011 4.00 1.20
47 Lance Berkman OPS/950 2.50 .75
48 Jim Thome OPS/940 6.00 1.80
49 Chipper Jones OPS/932 6.00 1.80
50 J.D. Drew OPS/927 2.50 .75
51 Alex Rodriguez OPS/921 10.00 3.00
52 Manny Ramirez OPS/914 4.00 1.20
53 Albert Pujols OPS/913 12.00 3.60
54 Gary Sheffield OPS/900 2.50 .75
55 Brian Giles OPS/894 2.50 .75
56 Phil Nevin OPS/876 2.50 .75
57 Jim Edmonds OPS/874 2.50 .75
58 Shawn Green OPS/870 2.50 .75
59 Cliff Floyd OPS/868 2.50 .75
60 Edgar Martinez OPS/866 4.00 1.20

2002 Donruss Recollection Autographs

Randomly inserted in packs, these 47 cards feature players who signed repurchased copies of their original cards for inclusion in the 2002 Donruss set. Since each player signed a different amount of cards, we have notated that information in our checklist. Please note that due to market scarcity, not all cards can be priced.

Nm-Mt Ex-Mt
8 Gary Carter 87/100 25.00 7.50
9 Gary Carter 89/100 25.00 7.50
11 Joe Carter 87/45
13 Andre Dawson 81/50
14 Andre Dawson 83/50
16 Andre Dawson 87/45
17 Dennis Eckersley 81/45
24 Steve Garvey 87/75 40.00 12.00
46 Tom Seaver 87/60
47 Don Sutton 87/200 25.00 7.50

2002 Donruss Rookie Year Materials Bats

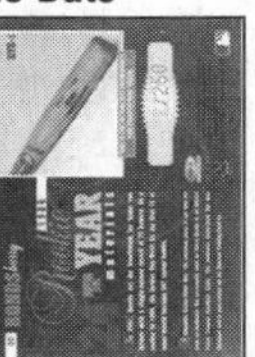

Randomly inserted into packs, these four cards feature a sliver of a game-used bat from the player's rookie season which includes silver holo-foil and are sequentially numbered a stated print run of 250 sequentially numbered sets.

Nm-Mt Ex-Mt
1 Barry Bonds 60.00 18.00
2 Cal Ripken 80.00 24.00
3 Kirby Puckett 40.00 12.00
4 Johnny Bench 40.00 12.00

2002 Donruss Rookie Year Materials Bats ERA

These cards parallel the "Rookie Year Material Bats" insert set. These cards have gold holo-foil and have a stated print run sequentially numbered to the player's debut year. Since those years are all different, we have notated that information in our checklist.

Nm-Mt Ex-Mt
1 Barry Bonds/86 120.00 36.00
2 Cal Ripken/81 150.00 45.00
3 Kirby Puckett/84 80.00 24.00
4 Johnny Bench/68 80.00 24.00

2002 Donruss Rookie Year Materials Jersey

Randomly inserted into packs, these four cards feature a swatch of a game-used jersey from the player's rookie season which includes silver holo-foil and are sequentially numbered a stated print run of either 250 or 50 sequentially numbered sets. The active players have the print run of 250 while the retired players have the print run of 50 sets.

Nm-Mt Ex-Mt
1 Nomar Garciaparra 50.00 15.00
2 Randy Johnson 40.00 12.00

3 Ivan Rodriguez 40.00 12.00
4 Vladimir Guerrero 40.00 12.00
5 Stan Musial/50
6 Yogi Berra/50 100.00 30.00

2002 Donruss Rookie Year Materials Jersey Numbers

These cards parallel the "Rookie Year Material Jerseys" insert set. These cards have gold holo-foil and have a stated print run sequentially numbered to the player's jersey number his rookie season. We have notated that specific stated print information in our checklist.

Nm-Mt Ex-Mt
1 Nomar Garciaparra/5
2 Randy Johnson/51
3 Ivan Rodriguez/7
4 Vladimir Guerrero/27
5 Stan Musial/6
6 Yogi Berra/35

2002 Donruss Rookies

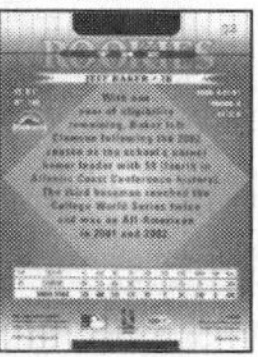

This 110 card set was released in December, 2002. These cards were issued in five card packs which came 24 packs to a box and 16 boxes to a case with an SRP of $3.29 per pack. This set features the top rookies and prospects of the 2002 season.

Nm-Mt Ex-Mt
COMPLETE SET (110) 25.00 7.50
1 Kazuhisa Ishii RC 1.50 .45
2 P.J. Bevis RC .40 .12
3 Jason Simontacchi RC .40 .12
4 John Lackey .25 .07
5 Travis Driskill RC .40 .12
6 Carl Sadler RC .40 .12
7 Tim Kalita RC .40 .12
8 Nelson Castro RC .40 .12
9 Francis Beltran RC .40 .12
10 So Taguchi RC .50 .15
11 Ryan Bukvich RC .40 .12
12 Brian Fitzgerald RC .40 .12
13 Kevin Frederick RC .40 .12
14 Chone Figgins RC .75 .23
15 Marlon Byrd .25 .07
16 Ron Calloway RC .40 .12
17 Jason Lane .25 .07
18 Satoru Komiyama RC .40 .12
19 John Ennis RC .40 .12
20 Juan Brito RC .40 .12
21 Gustavo Chacin RC .50 .15
22 Josh Bard RC .40 .12
23 Brett Myers .25 .07
24 Mike Smith RC .40 .12
25 Eric Hinske .25 .07
26 Jake Peavy .40 .12
27 Todd Donovan RC .40 .12
28 Luis Ugueto RC .40 .12
29 Corey Thurman RC .40 .12
30 Takahito Nomura RC .40 .12
31 Andy Shibilo RC .40 .12
32 Mike Crudale RC .40 .12
33 Earl Snyder RC .50 .15
34 Brian Tallet RC .40 .12
35 Miguel Asencio RC .40 .12
36 Felix Escalona RC .40 .12
37 Drew Henson .40 .12
38 Steve Kent RC .40 .12
39 Rene Reyes RC .40 .12
40 Edwin Almonte RC .40 .12
41 Chris Snelling RC .40 .12
42 Franklyn German RC .40 .12
43 Jeriome Robertson RC .40 .12
44 Colin Young RC .40 .12
45 Jeremy Lambert RC .40 .12
46 Kirk Saarloos RC .40 .12
47 Matt Childers RC .40 .12
48 Justin Wayne .25 .07
49 Jose Valverde RC .50 .15
50 Wily Mo Pena .40 .12
51 Victor Alvarez RC .40 .12
52 Julius Matos RC .40 .12
53 Aaron Cook RC .40 .12
54 Jeff Austin RC .40 .12
55 Adrian Burnside RC .40 .12
56 Brandon Puffer RC .40 .12
57 Jeremy Hill RC .40 .12
58 Jaime Cerda RC .40 .12
59 Aaron Guiel RC .40 .12
60 Ron Chiavacci .25 .07
61 Kevin Cash RC .40 .12
62 Elio Serrano RC .40 .12
63 Julio Mateo RC .40 .12
64 Cam Esslinger RC .40 .12
65 Ken Huckaby RC .40 .12
66 Will Nieves RC .40 .12
67 Luis Martinez RC .40 .12
68 Scotty Layfield RC .40 .12
69 Jeremy Guthrie RC .75 .23
70 Hansel Izquierdo RC .40 .12
71 Shane Nance RC .40 .12
72 Jeff Baker RC 1.50 .45
73 Cliff Bartosh RC .40 .12
74 Mitch Wylie RC .40 .12
75 Oliver Perez RC 3.00 .90
76 Matt Thornton RC .40 .12
77 John Foster RC .40 .12
78 Joe Borchard .25 .07
79 Eric Junge RC .40 .12
80 Jorge Sosa RC .40 .12
81 Runelvys Hernandez RC .40 .12
82 Kevin Mench .25 .07
83 Ben Kozlowski RC .40 .12
84 Trey Hodges RC .40 .12
85 Reed Johnson RC .50 .15
86 Eric Eckenstahler RC .40 .12
87 Franklin Nunez RC .40 .12
88 Victor Martinez .75 .23
89 Kevin Gryboski RC .40 .12
90 Jason Jennings .25 .07
91 Jim Rushford RC .40 .12
92 Jeremy Ward RC .40 .12
93 Adam Walker RC .40 .12
94 Freddy Sanchez RC .40 .12
95 Wilson Valdez RC .40 .12
96 Lee Gardner RC .40 .12
97 Eric Good RC .40 .12
98 Hank Blalock .75 .23
99 Mark Corey RC .40 .12
100 Jason Davis RC .75 .23
101 Mike Gonzalez RC .40 .12
102 David Ross RC .40 .12
103 Tyler Yates RC .50 .15
104 Cliff Lee RC .75 .23
105 Mike Moriarty RC .40 .12
106 Josh Hancock RC .40 .12
107 Jason Beverlin RC .40 .12
108 Clay Condrey RC .40 .12
109 Shawn Sedlacek RC .40 .12
110 Sean Burroughs .40 .12

2002 Donruss Rookies Autographs

Randomly inserted into packs, this is a partial parallel to the Donruss Rookies set. Each players signed between 15 and 100 cards for insertion in this product and cards with a stated print run of 25 or fewer are not priced due to market scarcity.

Nm-Mt Ex-Mt
1 Kazuhisa Ishii/25
2 P.J. Bevis/50 25.00 7.50
7 Tim Kalita/25
9 Francis Beltran/100 10.00 3.00
10 So Taguchi/15
13 Kevin Frederick/100 10.00 3.00
14 Chone Figgins/100 25.00 7.50
15 Marlon Byrd/100 10.00 3.00
17 Jason Lane/100 10.00 3.00
18 Satoru Komiyama/25
19 John Ennis/100 10.00 3.00
22 Josh Bard/100 10.00 3.00
25 Eric Hinske/100 10.00 3.00
28 Luis Ugueto/100 10.00 3.00
29 Corey Thurman/100 10.00 3.00
30 Takahito Nomura/100 25.00 7.50
33 Earl Snyder/100 15.00 4.50
34 Brian Tallet/100 10.00 3.00
36 Felix Escalona/25
37 Drew Henson/50 40.00 12.00
39 Rene Reyes/50 25.00 7.50
40 Edwin Almonte/50 25.00 7.50
41 Chris Snelling/50 15.00 4.50
42 Franklyn German/100 10.00 3.00
45 Jeremy Lambert/100 10.00 3.00
46 Kirk Saarloos/50 15.00 4.50
47 Matt Childers/100 10.00 3.00
50 Wily Mo Pena/100 15.00 4.50
51 Victor Alvarez/100 10.00 3.00
61 Kevin Cash/100 10.00 3.00
62 Elio Serrano/100 10.00 3.00
64 Cam Esslinger/100 10.00 3.00
69 Jeremy Guthrie/100 25.00 7.50
71 Shane Nance/100 10.00 3.00
72 Jeff Baker/100 40.00 12.00
75 Oliver Perez/25
76 Matt Thornton/100 10.00 3.00
78 Joe Borchard/100 10.00 3.00
79 Eric Junge/25
82 Kevin Mench/100 15.00 4.50
83 Ben Kozlowski/100 10.00 3.00
84 Trey Hodges/100 10.00 3.00
85 Reed Johnson/100 15.00 4.50
88 Victor Martinez/100 40.00 12.00
90 Jason Jennings/100 10.00 3.00
95 Wilson Valdez/100 10.00 3.00
97 Eric Good/100 10.00 3.00
98 Hank Blalock/100 40.00 12.00
104 Cliff Lee/100 40.00 12.00
110 Sean Burroughs/50 25.00 7.50

2002 Donruss Rookies Crusade

Randomly inserted into packs, these 50 cards, which were printed on metalized holo-foil board, were printed to a stated print run of 1500 serial numbered sets.

Nm-Mt Ex-Mt
1 Corky Miller 4.00 1.20
2 Jack Cust 4.00 1.20
3 Erik Bedard 4.00 1.20
4 Andres Torres 4.00 1.20
5 Geronimo Gil 4.00 1.20
6 Rafael Soriano 4.00 1.20

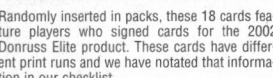

7 Johnny Estrada 4.00 1.20
8 Steve Bechler 4.00 1.20
9 Adam Johnson 4.00 1.20
10 So Taguchi 4.00 1.20
11 Dee Brown 4.00 1.20
12 Kevin Frederick 4.00 1.20
13 Allan Simpson 4.00 1.20
14 Ricardo Rodriguez 4.00 1.20
15 Jason Hart 4.00 1.20
16 Matt Childers 4.00 1.20
17 Jason Jennings 4.00 1.20
18 Anderson Machado 4.00 1.20
19 Fernando Rodney 4.00 1.20
20 Brandon Larson 4.00 1.20
21 Satoru Komiyama 4.00 1.20
22 Francis Beltran 4.00 1.20
23 Joe Thurston 4.00 1.20
24 Josh Pearce 4.00 1.20
25 Carlos Hernandez 4.00 1.20
26 Ben Howard 4.00 1.20
27 Wilson Valdez 4.00 1.20
28 Victor Alvarez 4.00 1.20
29 Cesar Izturis 4.00 1.20
30 Endy Chavez 4.00 1.20
31 Michael Cuddyer 4.00 1.20
32 Bobby Hill 4.00 1.20
33 Willie Harris 4.00 1.20
34 Joe Crede 4.00 1.20
35 Jorge Padilla 4.00 1.20
36 Brandon Backe 5.00 1.50
37 Franklyn German 4.00 1.20
38 Xavier Nady 4.00 1.20
39 Raul Chavez 4.00 1.20
40 Shane Nance 4.00 1.20
41 Brandon Claussen 4.00 1.20
42 Tom Shearn 4.00 1.20
43 Freddy Sanchez 4.00 1.20
44 Chone Figgins 5.00 1.50
45 Cliff Lee 5.00 1.50
46 Brian Mallette 4.00 1.20
47 Mike Rivera 4.00 1.20
48 Elio Serrano 4.00 1.20
49 Rodrigo Rosario 4.00 1.20
50 Earl Snyder 4.00 1.20

2002 Donruss Rookies Crusade Autographs

These 49 cards basically parallel the Rookies Crusade set. These cards were issued to a stated print run of anywhere from 15 to 500 sets. Cards with a print run of 25 or fewer are not priced due to market scarcity.

Nm-Mt Ex-Mt
COMMON CARD p/r 300+ 10.00 3.00
COMMON ROOKIE p/r 300+ 10.00 3.00
COMMON CARD p/r 150-250 10.00 3.00
COMMON CARD p/r 100 15.00 4.50
1 Corky Miller/500 10.00 3.00
2 Jack Cust/500 10.00 3.00
3 Erik Bedard/100 15.00 4.50
4 Andres Torres/500 10.00 3.00
5 Geronimo Gil/500 10.00 3.00
6 Rafael Soriano/500 10.00 3.00
7 Johnny Estrada/400 10.00 3.00
8 Steve Bechler/500 10.00 3.00
9 Adam Johnson/500 10.00 3.00
10 So Taguchi/15
11 Dee Brown/500 10.00 3.00
12 Kevin Frederick/150 10.00 3.00
13 Allan Simpson/150 10.00 3.00
14 Ricardo Rodriguez/500 10.00 3.00
15 Jason Hart/500 10.00 3.00
16 Matt Childers/150 10.00 3.00
17 Jason Jennings/500 10.00 3.00
18 Anderson Machado/500 10.00 3.00
19 Fernando Rodney/500 10.00 3.00
20 Brandon Larson/400 10.00 3.00
21 Satoru Komiyama/25
22 Francis Beltran/500 10.00 3.00
23 Joe Thurston/500 10.00 3.00
24 Josh Pearce/500 10.00 3.00
25 Carlos Hernandez/500 10.00 3.00
26 Ben Howard/500 10.00 3.00
27 Wilson Valdez/500 10.00 3.00
28 Victor Alvarez/500 10.00 3.00
29 Cesar Izturis/500 10.00 3.00
30 Endy Chavez/500 10.00 3.00
31 Michael Cuddyer/375 10.00 3.00
32 Bobby Hill/250 10.00 3.00
33 Willie Harris/300 10.00 3.00
34 Joe Crede/100 15.00 4.50
35 Jorge Padilla/475 10.00 3.00
36 Brandon Backe/350 25.00 7.50
37 Franklyn German/500 10.00 3.00
38 Xavier Nady/500 10.00 3.00
39 Raul Chavez/500 10.00 3.00
40 Shane Nance/500 10.00 3.00
41 Brandon Claussen/150 10.00 3.00
42 Tom Shearn/500 10.00 3.00
44 Chone Figgins/500 15.00 4.50
45 Cliff Lee/500 15.00 4.50
46 Brian Mallette/150 10.00 3.00
47 Mike Rivera/400 10.00 3.00
48 Elio Serrano/500 10.00 3.00
49 Rodrigo Rosario/100 15.00 4.50
50 Earl Snyder/100 25.00 7.50

2002 Donruss Rookies Phenoms

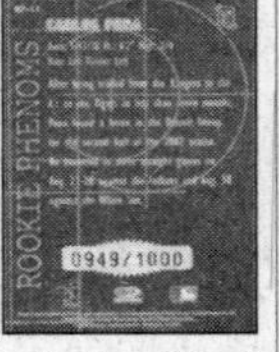

Randomly inserted into packs, these 25 cards, which are set on shimmering double rainbow holo-foil board were sequentially numbered to 1000 serial numbered sets.

Nm-Mt Ex-Mt
1 Kazuhisa Ishii 8.00 2.40
2 Eric Hinske 5.00 1.50
3 Jason Lane 5.00 1.50
4 Victor Martinez 8.00 2.40
5 Mark Prior 10.00 3.00
6 Antonio Perez 5.00 1.50
7 John Buck 5.00 1.50
8 Joe Borchard 5.00 1.50
9 Alexis Gomez 5.00 1.50
10 Sean Burroughs 5.00 1.50
11 Carlos Pena 5.00 1.50
12 Bill Hall 5.00 1.50
13 Alfredo Amezaga 5.00 1.50
14 Ed Rogers 5.00 1.50
15 Mark Teixeira 5.00 1.50
16 Chris Snelling 5.00 1.50
17 Nick Johnson 5.00 1.50
18 Angel Berroa 5.00 1.50
19 Orlando Hudson 5.00 1.50
20 Drew Henson 5.00 1.50
21 Austin Kearns 5.00 1.50
22 Dewon Brazelton 5.00 1.50
23 Dennis Tankersley 5.00 1.50
24 Josh Beckett 5.00 1.50
25 Marlon Byrd 5.00 1.50

2002 Donruss Rookies Phenoms Autographs

These cards parallel the Phenoms insert set. Each of these cards were issued to a stated print run of between 25 and 500 signed copies. As the Ishii was produced to a stated print run of 25 sets, no pricing is provided for that card.

Nm-Mt Ex-Mt
COMMON CARD p/r 300+ 10.00 3.00
COMMON CARD p/r 150-250 10.00 3.00
1 Kazuhisa Ishii/25
2 Eric Hinske/500 10.00 3.00
3 Jason Lane/500 10.00 3.00
4 Victor Martinez/225 30.00 9.00
5 Mark Prior/100 100.00 30.00
6 Antonio Perez/500 10.00 3.00
7 John Buck/100 15.00 4.50
8 Joe Borchard/100 15.00 4.50
9 Alexis Gomez/400 10.00 3.00
10 Sean Burroughs/150 15.00 4.50
11 Carlos Pena/150 10.00 3.00
12 Bill Hall/200 10.00 3.00
13 Alfredo Amezaga/500 10.00 3.00
14 Ed Rogers/500 10.00 3.00
15 Mark Teixeira/100 20.00 6.00
16 Chris Snelling/100 15.00 4.50
17 Nick Johnson/250 15.00 4.50
18 Angel Berroa/500 10.00 3.00
19 Orlando Hudson/400 10.00 3.00
20 Drew Henson/500 20.00 6.00
21 Austin Kearns/75 15.00 4.50
22 Dewon Brazelton/350 10.00 3.00
23 Dennis Tankersley/100 15.00 4.50
24 Josh Beckett/125 20.00 6.00
25 Marlon Byrd/500 10.00 3.00

2002 Donruss Rookies Recollection Autographs

Randomly inserted into packs, these 55 cards feature cards from the 2001 and 2002 Donruss Rookie set which were "bought-back" by Donruss/Playoff for inclusion in this product. These cards were then signed by the player. Due to market scarcity, no pricing is provided for these cards.

Nm-Mt Ex-Mt
1 Jeremy Affeldt 01 DR/25
2 Alfredo Amezaga 02 DN/24
3 Erik Bedard 02 DN/20
4 Angel Berroa 01 DR/50
5 Angel Berroa 02 DN/6
6 Dewon Brazelton 01 DR Black/25
7 Dewon Brazelton 01 DR Blue/23
8 Dewon Brazelton 02 DN/10
9 Juan Cruz 01 DR/25
10 Jorge De La Rosa 02 DN/20
11 Brandon Duckworth 01 DR Black/25
12 Brandon Duckworth 01 DR Blue/25
13 Mark Ellis 02 DK/5
14 Pedro Feliz 01 DN/55
15 Pedro Feliz 01 DN SLC/1
16 Pedro Feliz 01 DN SLS/1
17 Pedro Feliz 01 DN R00 SLC/1
18 Pedro Feliz 01 DN R00 SLS/1
19 Casey Fossum 01 DR/49
20 Jay Gibbons 02 DR Black/20
21 Jay Gibbons 01 DR Blue/28
22 Travis Hafner 01 DR/49
23 Bill Hall 02 DN/20
24 Aubrey Huff 01 DR/19
25 Kazuhisa Ishii 02 DK/5
26 Cesar Izturis 01 DN/45
27 Cesar Izturis 01 DN SLC/1
28 Cesar Izturis 01 DN SLS/1
29 Jason Jennings 01 DR/15
30 Brett Jodie 01 DR Black/27
31 Brett Jodie 01 DR Blue/31
32 Jason Lane 02 DN/1
33 Nick Maness 01 DN/50
34 Victor Martinez 01 ELI/25
35 Donaldo Mendez 01 DR/17
36 Corky Miller 01 DR/49
37 Craig Monroe 01 DR/73
38 Roy Oswalt 01 DR Black/1
39 Roy Oswalt 01 DR Blue/49
40 Adam Pettyjohn 01 DN/55
41 Mark Prior 01 DR Black/1
42 Mark Prior 01 DR Blue/22
43 Brian Reith 01 DR/15
44 Saul Rivera 01 DR/51
45 C.C. Sabathia 01 DR/15
46 Alfonso Soriano 01 DR/15
47 Rafael Soriano 01 DR/99
48 So Taguchi 02 DK/5
49 Mark Teixeira 01 DR/50
50 Mark Teixeira 02 DN/1
51 Mark Teixeira 02 DK/5
52 Claudio Vargas 01 DR/98
53 Martin Vargas 01 DR/97
54 Ramon Vazquez 01 DR/100
55 Brad Voyles 01 DR/25

2003 Donruss

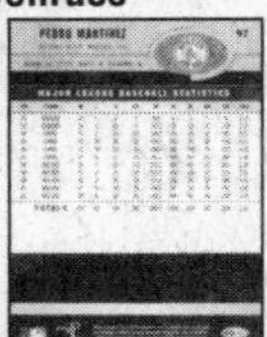

This 400 card set was released in December, 2002. The set was issued in 13 card packs with an SRP of $2.29 which were packed 24 packs to a box and 20 boxes to a case. Subsets in this set include cards numbered Diamond Kings (1-20) and Rated Rookies (21-70). For the first time since Donruss/Playoff returned to card production, this was a baseball set without short printed base cards.

Nm-Mt Ex-Mt
COMPLETE SET (400) 50.00 15.00
COMMON CARD (71-400) .30 .09
COMMON CARD (1-20) .50 .15
COMMON CARD (21-70) .50 .15
1 Vladimir Guerrero DK .75 .23
2 Derek Jeter DK 2.00 .60
3 Adam Dunn DK .50 .15
4 Greg Maddux DK 1.25 .35
5 Lance Berkman DK .50 .15
6 Ichiro Suzuki DK 1.25 .35
7 Mike Piazza DK 1.25 .35
8 Alex Rodriguez DK 1.25 .35
9 Tom Glavine DK .50 .15
10 Randy Johnson DK .75 .23
11 Nomar Garciaparra DK 1.25 .35
12 Jason Giambi DK .50 .15
13 Sammy Sosa DK 1.25 .35
14 Barry Zito DK .50 .15
15 Chipper Jones DK .75 .23
16 Magglio Ordonez DK .50 .15
17 Larry Walker DK .50 .15
18 Alfonso Soriano DK .50 .15
19 Curt Schilling DK .50 .15
20 Barry Bonds DK 2.00 .60
21 Joe Borchard RR .50 .15
22 Chris Snelling RR .50 .15
23 Brian Tallet RR .50 .15
24 Cliff Lee RR .50 .15
25 Freddy Sanchez RR .50 .15
26 Chone Figgins RR .50 .15
27 Kevin Cash RR .50 .15
28 Josh Bard RR .50 .15
29 Jeriome Robertson RR .50 .15
30 Jeremy Hill RR .50 .15
31 Shane Nance RR .50 .15
32 Jake Peavy RR .50 .15
33 Trey Hodges RR .50 .15
34 Eric Eckenstahler RR .50 .15
35 Jim Rushford RR .50 .15
36 Oliver Perez RR .50 .15
37 Kirk Saarloos RR .50 .15
38 Hank Blalock RR .75 .23
39 Francisco Rodriguez RR .50 .15
40 Runelvys Hernandez RR .50 .15
41 Aaron Cook RR .50 .15
42 Josh Hancock RR .50 .15
43 P.J. Bevis RR .50 .15
44 Jon Adkins RR .50 .15
45 Tim Kalita RR .50 .15
46 Nelson Castro RR .50 .15
47 Colin Young RR .50 .15
48 Adrian Burnside RR .50 .15
49 Luis Martinez RR .50 .15
50 Pete Zamora RR .50 .15
51 Todd Donovan RR .50 .15
52 Jeremy Ward RR .50 .15
53 Wilson Valdez RR .50 .15
54 Eric Good RR .50 .15
55 Jeff Baker RR .50 .15
56 Mitch Wylie RR .50 .15
57 Ron Calloway RR .50 .15
58 Jose Valverde RR .50 .15
59 Jason Davis RR .50 .15
60 Scotty Layfield RR .50 .15
61 Matt Thornton RR .50 .15
62 Adam Walker RR .50 .15
63 Gustavo Chacin RR .50 .15
64 Ron Chiavacci RR .50 .15
65 Wiki Nieves RR .50 .15
66 Cliff Bartosh RR .50 .15
67 Mike Gonzalez RR .50 .15
68 Justin Wayne RR .50 .15
69 Eric Junge RR .50 .15
70 Ben Kozlowski RR .50 .15
71 Darin Erstad .30 .09
72 Garret Anderson .30 .09
73 Troy Glaus .30 .09
74 David Eckstein .30 .09
75 Adam Kennedy .30 .09
76 Kevin Appier .30 .09
77 Jarrod Washburn .30 .09
78 Scott Spiezio .30 .09
79 Tim Salmon .50 .15
80 Ramon Ortiz .30 .09
81 Bengie Molina .30 .09
82 Brad Fullmer .30 .09
83 Troy Percival .30 .09
84 David Segui .30 .09
85 Jay Gibbons .30 .09
86 Tony Batista .30 .09
87 Scott Erickson .30 .09
88 Jeff Conine .30 .09
89 Melvin Mora .30 .09
90 Buddy Groom .30 .09
91 Rodrigo Lopez .30 .09
92 Marty Cordova .30 .09
93 Geronimo Gil .30 .09
94 Kenny Lofton .30 .09
95 Shea Hillenbrand .30 .09
96 Manny Ramirez .30 .09
97 Pedro Martinez .75 .23
98 Nomar Garciaparra 1.25 .35
99 Rickey Henderson .75 .23
100 Johnny Damon .75 .23
101 Trot Nixon .30 .09
102 Derek Lowe .30 .09
103 Hee Seop Choi .30 .09
104 Mark Teixeira .30 .09
105 Tim Wakefield .30 .09
106 Jason Varitek .50 .15
107 Frank Thomas .75 .23
108 Joe Crede .30 .09
109 Magglio Ordonez .30 .09
110 Ray Durham .30 .09
111 Mark Buehrle .30 .09
112 Paul Konerko .30 .09
113 Jose Valentin .30 .09
114 Carlos Lee .30 .09
115 Royce Clayton .30 .09
116 C.C. Sabathia .30 .09
117 Ellis Burks .30 .09
118 Omar Vizquel .50 .15
119 Jim Thome .75 .23
120 Matt Lawton .30 .09
121 Travis Fryman .30 .09
122 Earl Snyder .30 .09
123 Ricky Gutierrez .30 .09
124 Einar Diaz .30 .09
125 Danys Baez .30 .09
126 Robert Fick .30 .09
127 Bobby Higginson .30 .09
128 Steve Sparks .30 .09
129 Mike Rivera .30 .09
130 Wendell Magee .30 .09
131 Randall Simon .30 .09
132 Carlos Pena .30 .09
133 Mark Redman .30 .09
134 Juan Acevedo .30 .09
135 Mike Sweeney .30 .09
136 Aaron Guiel .30 .09
137 Carlos Beltran .50 .15
138 Joe Randa .30 .09
139 Paul Byrd .30 .09
140 Shawn Sedlacek .30 .09
141 Raul Ibanez .30 .09
142 Michael Tucker .30 .09
143 Torii Hunter .30 .09
144 Jacque Jones .30 .09
145 David Ortiz .50 .15
146 Corey Koskie .30 .09
147 Brad Radke .30 .09
148 Doug Mientkiewicz .30 .09
149 A.J. Pierzynski .30 .09
150 Dustan Mohr .30 .09
151 Michael Cuddyer .30 .09
152 Eddie Guardado .30 .09
153 Cristian Guzman .30 .09
154 Derek Jeter 2.00 .60
155 Bernie Williams .50 .15
156 Roger Clemens 1.50 .45
157 Mike Mussina .50 .15
158 Jorge Posada .50 .15
159 Alfonso Soriano .50 .15
160 Jason Giambi .30 .09
161 Robin Ventura .30 .09
162 Andy Pettitte .50 .15
163 David Wells .30 .09
164 Nick Johnson .30 .09
165 Jeff Weaver .30 .09
166 Raul Mondesi .30 .09
167 Rondell White .30 .09
168 Tim Hudson .30 .09
169 Barry Zito .30 .09
170 Mark Mulder .30 .09
171 Miguel Tejada .30 .09
172 Eric Chavez .30 .09
173 Billy Koch .30 .09
174 Jermaine Dye .30 .09
175 Scott Hatteberg .30 .09
176 Terrence Long .30 .09
177 David Justice .30 .09
178 Ramon Hernandez .30 .09
179 Ted Lilly .30 .09
180 Ichiro Suzuki 1.25 .35
181 Edgar Martinez .50 .15
182 Mike Cameron .30 .09
183 John Olerud .30 .09
184 Bret Boone .30 .09
185 Dan Wilson .30 .09
186 Freddy Garcia .30 .09
187 Jamie Moyer .30 .09
188 Carlos Guillen .30 .09
189 Ruben Sierra .30 .09
190 Kazuhiro Sasaki .30 .09
191 Mark McLemore .30 .09
192 John Halama .30 .09
193 Joel Pineiro .30 .09
194 Jeff Cirillo .30 .09
195 Rafael Soriano .30 .09
196 Ben Grieve .30 .09
197 Aubrey Huff .30 .09
198 Steve Cox .30 .09
199 Toby Hall .30 .09
200 Randy Winn .30 .09
201 Brent Abernathy .30 .09
202 Chris Gomez .30 .09
203 John Flaherty .30 .09
204 Paul Wilson .30 .09
205 Chan Ho Park .30 .09
206 Alex Rodriguez 1.25 .35
207 Juan Gonzalez .50 .15
208 Rafael Palmeiro .50 .15
209 Ivan Rodriguez .75 .23
210 Rusty Greer .30 .09
211 Kenny Rogers .30 .09
212 Ismael Valdes .30 .09
213 Frank Catalanotto .30 .09
214 Hank Blalock .50 .15
215 Michael Young .50 .15
216 Kevin Mench .30 .09
217 Herbert Perry .30 .09
218 Gabe Kapler .30 .09
219 Carlos Delgado .30 .09
220 Shannon Stewart .30 .09
221 Eric Hinske .30 .09
222 Roy Halladay .30 .09
223 Felipe Lopez .30 .09
224 Vernon Wells .30 .09
225 Josh Phelps .30 .09
226 Jose Cruz .30 .09
227 Curt Schilling .30 .09
228 Randy Johnson .75 .23
229 Luis Gonzalez .30 .09
230 Mark Grace .50 .15
231 Junior Spivey .30 .09
232 Tony Womack .30 .09
233 Matt Williams .30 .09
234 Steve Finley .30 .09
235 Byung-Hyun Kim .30 .09
236 Craig Counsell .30 .09
237 Greg Maddux 1.25 .35
238 Tom Glavine .50 .15
239 John Smoltz .50 .15
240 Chipper Jones .75 .23
241 Gary Sheffield .30 .09
242 Andruw Jones .30 .09
243 Vinny Castilla .30 .09
244 Damian Moss .30 .09
245 Rafael Furcal .30 .09
246 Javy Lopez .30 .09
247 Kevin Millwood .30 .09
248 Kerry Wood .75 .23
249 Fred McGriff .50 .15
250 Sammy Sosa 1.25 .35
251 Alex Gonzalez .30 .09
252 Corey Patterson .30 .09
253 Moises Alou .30 .09
254 Juan Cruz .30 .09
255 Jon Lieber .30 .09
256 Matt Clement .30 .09
257 Mark Prior .75 .23
258 Ken Griffey Jr. 1.25 .35
259 Barry Larkin .50 .15
260 Adam Dunn .50 .15
261 Sean Casey .30 .09
262 Jose Rijo .30 .09
263 Elmer Dessens .30 .09
264 Austin Kearns .30 .09
265 Corky Miller .30 .09
266 Todd Walker .30 .09
267 Chris Reitsma .30 .09
268 Ryan Dempster .30 .09
269 Aaron Boone .30 .09
270 Danny Graves .30 .09
271 Brandon Larson .30 .09
272 Larry Walker .50 .15
273 Todd Helton .50 .15
274 Juan Uribe .30 .09
275 Juan Pierre .30 .09
276 Mike Hampton .30 .09
277 Todd Zeile .30 .09
278 Todd Hollandsworth .30 .09
279 Jason Jennings .30 .09
280 Josh Beckett .30 .09
281 Mike Lowell .30 .09
282 Derrek Lee .30 .09
283 A.J. Burnett .30 .09
284 Luis Castillo .30 .09
285 Tim Raines .30 .09
286 Preston Wilson .30 .09
287 Juan Encarnacion .30 .09
288 Charles Johnson .30 .09
289 Jeff Bagwell .50 .15
290 Craig Biggio .50 .15
291 Lance Berkman .30 .09
292 Daryle Ward .30 .09
293 Roy Oswalt .30 .09
294 Richard Hidalgo .30 .09
295 Octavio Dotel .30 .09
296 Wade Miller .30 .09
297 Julio Lugo .30 .09
298 Billy Wagner .30 .09
299 Shawn Green .30 .09
300 Adrian Beltre .50 .15
301 Paul Lo Duca .30 .09
302 Eric Karros .30 .09
303 Kevin Brown .30 .09
304 Hideo Nomo .75 .23
305 Odalis Perez .30 .09
306 Eric Gagne .75 .23
307 Brian Jordan .30 .09
308 Cesar Izturis .30 .09
309 Mark Grudzielanek .30 .09
310 Kazuhisa Ishii .30 .09
311 Geoff Jenkins .30 .09
312 Richie Sexson .30 .09

313 Jose Hernandez .30 .09
314 Ben Sheets .30 .09
315 Ruben Quevedo .30 .09
316 Jeffrey Hammonds .30 .09
317 Alex Sanchez .30 .09
318 Eric Young .30 .09
319 Takahito Nomura .30 .09
320 Vladimir Guerrero .75 .23
321 Jose Vidro .30 .09
322 Orlando Cabrera .30 .09
323 Michael Barrett .30 .09
324 Javier Vazquez .30 .09
325 Tony Armas Jr. .30 .09
326 Andres Galarraga .30 .09
327 Tomo Ohka .30 .09
328 Bartolo Colon .30 .09
329 Fernando Tatis .30 .09
330 Brad Wilkerson .30 .09
331 Masato Yoshii .30 .09
332 Mike Piazza 1.25 .35
333 Jeromy Burnitz .30 .09
334 Roberto Alomar .50 .15
335 Mo Vaughn .30 .09
336 Al Leiter .30 .09
337 Pedro Astacio .30 .09
338 Edgardo Alfonzo .30 .09
339 Armando Benitez .30 .09
340 Timo Perez .30 .09
341 Jay Payton .30 .09
342 Roger Cedeno .30 .09
343 Rey Ordonez .30 .09
344 Steve Trachsel .30 .09
345 Satoru Komiyama .30 .09
346 Scott Rolen .75 .23
347 Pat Burrell .30 .09
348 Bobby Abreu .30 .09
349 Mike Lieberthal .30 .09
350 Brandon Duckworth .30 .09
351 Jimmy Rollins .30 .09
352 Marlon Anderson .30 .09
353 Travis Lee .30 .09
354 Vicente Padilla .30 .09
355 Randy Wolf .30 .09
356 Jason Kendall .30 .09
357 Brian Giles .30 .09
358 Aramis Ramirez .30 .09
359 Pokey Reese .30 .09
360 Kip Wells .30 .09
361 Josh Fogg .30 .09
362 Mike Williams .30 .09
363 Jack Wilson .30 .09
364 Craig Wilson .30 .09
365 Kevin Young .30 .09
366 Ryan Klesko .30 .09
367 Phil Nevin .30 .09
368 Brian Lawrence .30 .09
369 Mark Kotsay .30 .09
370 Brett Tomko .30 .09
371 Trevor Hoffman .30 .09
372 Deivi Cruz .30 .09
373 Bubba Trammell .30 .09
374 Sean Burroughs .30 .09
375 Barry Bonds 2.00 .60
376 Jeff Kent .30 .09
377 Rich Aurilia .30 .09
378 Tsuyoshi Shinjo .30 .09
379 Benito Santiago .30 .09
380 Kirk Rueter .30 .09
381 Livan Hernandez .30 .09
382 Russ Ortiz .30 .09
383 David Bell .30 .09
384 Jason Schmidt .30 .09
385 Reggie Sanders .30 .09
386 J.T. Snow .30 .09
387 Robb Nen .30 .09
388 Ryan Jensen .30 .09
389 Jim Edmonds .30 .09
390 J.D. Drew .30 .09
391 Albert Pujols 1.50 .45
392 Fernando Vina .30 .09
393 Tino Martinez .50 .15
394 Edgar Renteria .30 .09
395 Matt Morris .30 .09
396 Woody Williams .30 .09
397 Jason Isringhausen .30 .09
398 Placido Polanco .30 .09
399 Eli Marrero .30 .09
400 Jason Simontacchi .30 .09

2003 Donruss Stat Line Career

Randomly inserted into packs, this is a parallel to the 2003 Donruss set. Each card is printed to a number matching some career statistic and the cards are serial numbered to that amount. For those cards with a print run of 25 or fewer, no pricing is provided due to market scarcity.

Nm-Mt Ex-Mt
*STAT LINE 1-20: 2.5X TO 6X BASIC
*21-70 P/R b/wn 251-400: 1.25X TO 3X
*21-70 P/R b/wn 201-250: 1.25X TO 3X
*21-70 P/R b/wn 151-200 1.5X TO 4X
*21-70 P/R b/wn 121-150: 2X TO 5X
*21-70 P/R b/wn 81-120: 2.5X TO 6X
*21-70 P/R b/wn 51-65: 3X TO 8X
*21-70 P/R b/wn 36-50: 4X TO 10X
*21-70 P/R b/wn 26-35: 5X TO 12X
*71-400 P/R b/wn 251-400: 2.5X TO 6X
*71-400 P/R b/wn 201-250: 2.5X TO 6X
*71-400 P/R b/wn 151-200 3X TO 8X
*71-400 P/R b/wn 121-150: 3X TO 8X
*71-400 P/R b/wn 81-120: 4X TO 10X
*71-400 P/R b/wn 66-80: 5X TO 12X
*71-400 P/R b/wn 51-65: 5X TO 12X
*71-400 P/R b/wn 36-50: 6X TO 15X
*71-400 P/R b/wn 26-35: 8X TO 20X
RANDOM INSERTS IN PACKS
SEE BECKETT.COM FOR FOR PRINT RUNS
NO PRICING ON QTY OF 25 OR LESS

2003 Donruss Stat Line Season

Randomly inserted into packs, this is a parallel to the 2003 Donruss set. Each card is printed to a number matching some seasonal statistic and the cards are serial numbered to that amount. For those cards with a print run of 25 or fewer, no pricing is provided due to market scarcity.

Nm-Mt Ex-Mt
*1-20 P/R b/wn 121-150 3X TO 8X
*1-20 P/R b/wn 81-120 4X TO 10X
*1-20 P/R b/wn 66-80 5X TO 12X
*1-20 P/R b/wn 51-65 5X TO 12X
*1-20 P/R b/wn 36-50 6X TO 15X
*1-20 P/R b/wn 26-35 8X TO 20X
*21-70 P/R b/wn 81-120 2.5X TO 6X
*21-70 P/R b/wn 66-80 3X TO 8X
*21-70 P/R b/wn 51-65 3X TO 8X
*21-70 P/R b/wn 36-50 4X TO 10X
*21-70 P/R b/wn 26-35 5X TO 12X
*71-400 P/R b/wn 81-120 4X TO 10X
*71-400 P/R b/wn 66-80 5X TO 12X
*71-400 P/R b/wn 51-65 5X TO 12X
*71-400 P/R b/wn 36-50 6X TO 15X
*71-400 P/R b/wn 26-35 8X TO 20X
RANDOM INSERTS IN PACKS
SEE BECKETT.COM FOR PRINT RUNS
NO PRICING ON QTY OF 25 OR LESS

2003 Donruss All-Stars

Issued at a stated rate of one in 12 retail packs, these 10 cards feature players who are projected to be mainstays on the All-Star team.

Nm-Mt Ex-Mt
1 Ichiro Suzuki 5.00 1.50
2 Alex Rodriguez 5.00 1.50
3 Nomar Garciaparra 5.00 1.50
4 Derek Jeter 8.00 2.40
5 Manny Ramirez 3.00 .90
6 Barry Bonds 8.00 2.40
7 Adam Dunn 3.00 .90
8 Mike Piazza 5.00 1.50
9 Sammy Sosa 5.00 1.50
10 Todd Helton 3.00 .90

2003 Donruss Anniversary 1983

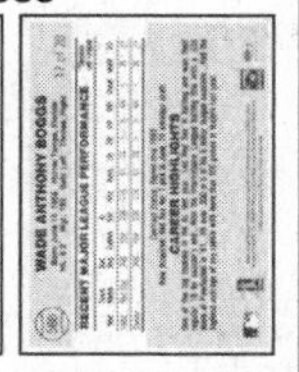

Issued at a stated rate of one in 12, this 20 card set features players who were among the most important players of that era. These cards use the 1983 Donruss design and photos.

Nm-Mt Ex-Mt
1 Dale Murphy 3.00 .90
2 Jim Palmer 3.00 .90
3 Nolan Ryan 8.00 2.40
4 Ozzie Smith 5.00 1.50
5 Tom Seaver 3.00 .90
6 Mike Schmidt 6.00 1.80
7 Steve Carlton 3.00 .90
8 Robin Yount 5.00 1.50
9 Ryne Sandberg 5.00 1.50
10 Cal Ripken 10.00 3.00
11 Fernando Valenzuela 3.00 .90
12 Andre Dawson 3.00 .90
13 George Brett 8.00 2.40
14 Eddie Murray 3.00 .90
15 Dave Winfield 3.00 .90
16 Johnny Bench 3.00 .90
17 Wade Boggs 3.00 .90
18 Tony Gwynn 6.00 1.80
19 San Diego Chicken 3.00 .90
20 Ty Cobb 5.00 1.50

2003 Donruss Bat Kings

Randomly inserted into packs, these 20 cards feature a game bat chip long with a reproduction of a previously used Diamond King card. Cards numbered 1 through 10 have a stated print run of 250 serial numbered sets while cards numbered 11 through 20 have a stated print run of 100 serial numbered sets.

Nm-Mt Ex-Mt
1-10 PRINT RUN 250 SERIAL #'d SETS
11-20 PRINT RUN 100 SERIAL #'d SETS
*STUDIO 1-10: .75X TO 2X BASIC BAT KING
STUDIO 1-10 PRINT RUN 50 SERIAL #'d SETS
STUDIO 11-20 PRINT RUN 25 SERIAL #'d SETS
STUDIO 11-20 NO PRICING DUE TO SCARCITY
RANDOM INSERTS IN PACKS
1 Scott Rolen 99 DK/250 20.00 6.00
2 Frank Thomas 00 DK/250 20.00 6.00
3 Chipper Jones 01 DK/250 20.00 6.00
4 Ivan Rodriguez 01 DK/250 20.00 6.00
5 Stan Musial 01 ATDK/100 50.00 15.00
6 Nomar Garciaparra 02 DK/250 25.00 7.50
7 Vladimir Guerrero 03 DK/250 20.00 6.00
8 Adam Dunn 03 DK/250 20.00 6.00
9 Lance Berkman 03 DK/250 15.00 4.50
10 Magglio Ordonez 03 DK/250 15.00 4.50
11 Ernie Banks 02 ATDK/50
12 Manny Ramirez 95 DK/100 25.00 7.50
13 Mike Piazza 94 DK/100 40.00 12.00
14 Alex Rodriguez 97 DK/100 40.00 12.00
15 Todd Helton 97 RDK/100 25.00 7.50
16 Andre Dawson 85 DK/100 20.00 6.00
17 Cal Ripken 87 DK/100 80.00 24.00
18 Tony Gwynn 88 DK/100 30.00 9.00
19 Don Mattingly 02 ATDK/100 60.00 18.00
20 Ryne Sandberg 90 DK/100 60.00 18.00

2003 Donruss Diamond Kings Inserts

Randomly inserted into packs, these cards parallel the first 20 cards of the regular Donruss set except they are serial numbered to a stated print run of 2500 serial numbered sets. These cards can be easily seperated from the cards inserted into the regular packs as they were printed with a foil stamp.

Nm-Mt Ex-Mt
*STUDIO: .75X TO 2X BASIC DK
STUDIO PRINT RUN 250 SERIAL #'d SETS
RANDOM INSERTS IN PACKS
1 Vladimir Guerrero 10.00 3.00
2 Derek Jeter 20.00 6.00
3 Adam Dunn 10.00 3.00
4 Greg Maddux 12.00 3.60
5 Lance Berkman 10.00 3.00
6 Ichiro Suzuki 12.00 3.60
7 Mike Piazza 12.00 3.60
8 Alex Rodriguez 12.00 3.60
9 Tom Glavine 10.00 3.00
10 Randy Johnson 10.00 3.00
11 Nomar Garciaparra 12.00 3.60
12 Jason Giambi 10.00 3.00
13 Sammy Sosa 12.00 3.60
14 Barry Zito 10.00 3.00
15 Chipper Jones 10.00 3.00
16 Magglio Ordonez 10.00 3.00
17 Larry Walker 10.00 3.00
18 Alfonso Soriano 10.00 3.00
19 Curt Schilling 10.00 3.00
20 Barry Bonds 20.00 6.00

2003 Donruss Elite Series

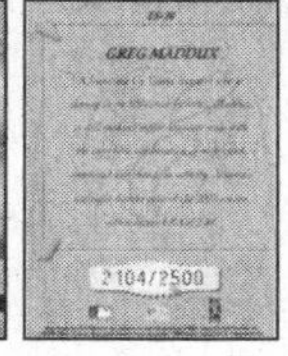

Randomly inserted into packs, this 15 card set, which is issued on metalized film board, features the elite 15 players in baseball. These cards were issued to a stated print run of 2500 serial numbered sets.

Nm-Mt Ex-Mt
DOMINATORS PR.RUN 25 SERIAL #'d SETS
DOMINATORS NO PRICE DUE TO SCARCITY
RANDOM INSERTS IN PACKS
1 Alex Rodriguez 8.00 2.40
2 Barry Bonds 12.00 3.60
3 Ichiro Suzuki 8.00 2.40
4 Vladimir Guerrero 5.00 1.50
5 Randy Johnson 5.00 1.50
6 Pedro Martinez 5.00 1.50
7 Adam Dunn 4.00 1.20
8 Sammy Sosa 8.00 2.40
9 Jim Edmonds 4.00 1.20
10 Greg Maddux 8.00 2.40
11 Kazuhisa Ishii 4.00 1.20
12 Jason Giambi 4.00 1.20
13 Nomar Garciaparra 8.00 2.40
14 Tom Glavine 4.00 1.20
15 Todd Helton 4.00 1.20

2003 Donruss Gamers

Randomly inserted in DLP (Donruss/Leaf/Playoff) rookie packs, these 50 cards have game-worn memorabilia swatches of the featured players.

MINT NRMT
STATED PRINT RUN 500 SERIAL #'d SETS
*JSY NUM: .6X TO 1.5X BASIC
JSY NUM PRINT RUN 100 SERIAL #'d SETS
*POSITION: .6X TO 1.5X BASIC
POSITION PRINT RUN 100 SERIAL #'d SETS
PRIME PRINT RUN 25 SERIAL #'d SETS
NO PRIME PRICING DUE TO SCARCITY
REWARDS PRINT RUN 10 SERIAL #'d SETS
NO REWARDS PRICING DUE TO SCARCITY
RANDOM INSERTS IN DLP R/T PACKS
1 Nomar Garciaparra 15.00 6.75
2 Alex Rodriguez 10.00 4.50
3 Mike Piazza 10.00 4.50
4 Greg Maddux 10.00 4.50
5 Roger Clemens 15.00 6.75
6 Sammy Sosa 15.00 6.75
7 Randy Johnson 8.00 3.60
8 Albert Pujols 15.00 6.75
9 Alfonso Soriano 8.00 3.60
10 Chipper Jones 8.00 3.60
11 Mark Prior 8.00 3.60
12 Hideo Nomo 8.00 3.60
13 Adam Dunn 8.00 3.60
14 Juan Gonzalez 8.00 3.60
15 Vladimir Guerrero 8.00 3.60
16 Pedro Martinez 8.00 3.60
17 Jim Thome 8.00 3.60
18 Brandon Webb 8.00 3.60
19 Mike Mussina 8.00 3.60
20 Mark Teixeira 5.00 2.20
21 Barry Larkin 8.00 3.60
22 Ivan Rodriguez 8.00 3.60
23 Hank Blalock 8.00 3.60
24 Rafael Palmeiro 8.00 3.60
25 Curt Schilling 5.00 2.20
26 Troy Glaus 5.00 2.20
27 Bernie Williams 8.00 3.60
28 Scott Rolen 8.00 3.60
29 Torii Hunter 5.00 2.20
30 Nick Johnson 5.00 2.20
31 Kazuhisa Ishii 5.00 2.20
32 Shawn Green 5.00 2.20
33 Jeff Bagwell 8.00 3.60
34 Lance Berkman 5.00 2.20
35 Roy Oswalt 5.00 2.20
36 Kerry Wood 8.00 3.60
37 Todd Helton 8.00 3.60
38 Manny Ramirez 8.00 3.60
39 Andruw Jones 5.00 2.20
40 Frank Thomas 8.00 3.60
41 Gary Sheffield 5.00 2.20
42 Magglio Ordonez 5.00 2.20
43 Mike Sweeney 5.00 2.20
44 Carlos Beltran 8.00 3.60
45 Richie Sexson 5.00 2.20
46 Jeff Kent 5.00 2.20
47 Carlos Delgado 5.00 2.20
48 Vernon Wells 5.00 2.20
49 Dontrelle Willis 8.00 3.60
50 Jae Weong Seo 5.00 2.20

2003 Donruss Gamers Autographs

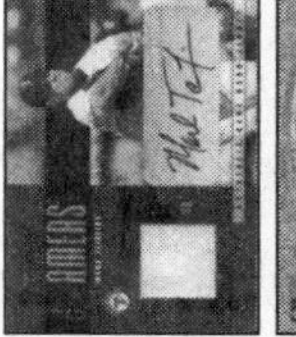
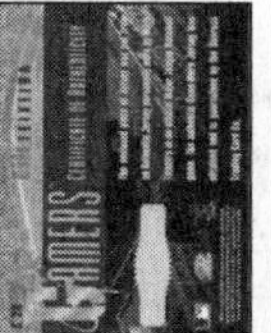

MINT NRMT
RANDOM INSERTS IN DLP R/T PACKS
PRINT RUNS B/WN 5-50 COPIES PER
NO PRICING ON QTY OF 25 OR LESS
2 Alex Rodriguez/5
3 Mike Piazza/5
4 Greg Maddux/5
5 Roger Clemens/5
7 Randy Johnson/5
8 Albert Pujols/5
9 Alfonso Soriano/5
10 Chipper Jones/10
11 Mark Prior/25
12 Hideo Nomo/5
13 Adam Dunn/25
14 Juan Gonzalez/25
15 Vladimir Guerrero/5
16 Pedro Martinez/5
18 Brandon Webb/25
19 Mike Mussina/5
20 Mark Teixeira/50 40.00 18.00
22 Ivan Rodriguez/5
23 Hank Blalock/50 40.00 18.00
24 Rafael Palmeiro/10
25 Curt Schilling/25
26 Troy Glaus/25
27 Bernie Williams/5
28 Scott Rolen/25
29 Torii Hunter/50 30.00 13.50
30 Nick Johnson/25
31 Kazuhisa Ishii/5
32 Shawn Green/5
33 Jeff Bagwell/5
34 Lance Berkman/10
35 Roy Oswalt/50 30.00 13.50
36 Kerry Wood/25
37 Todd Helton/10
39 Andruw Jones/25
40 Frank Thomas/10
41 Gary Sheffield/25
42 Magglio Ordonez/25
43 Mike Sweeney/50 30.00 13.50
44 Carlos Beltran/25
45 Richie Sexson/25
46 Jeff Kent/12
48 Vernon Wells/30 40.00 18.00
49 Dontrelle Willis/50 40.00 18.00
50 Jae Weong Seo/50 40.00 18.00

2003 Donruss Jersey Kings

Randomly inserted into packs, this set features cards which parallel previously issued Diamond King cards along with a game-worn jersey swatch. Cards were printed to a stated print run of either 100 or 250 serial numbered cards and we have put that information next to the player's name in our checklist.

Nm-Mt Ex-Mt
*STUDIO 1-10: .75X TO 2X BASIC JSY KINGS
STUDIO 1-10 PRINT RUN 50 SERIAL #'d SETS

STUDIO 11-20 PRINT RUN 25 SERIAL #'d SETS
STUDIO 11-20 NO PRICE DUE TO SCARCITY
RANDOM INSERTS IN PACKS
1 Juan Gonzalez 99 DK/250 15.00 4.50
2 Greg Maddux 00 DK/250 20.00 6.00
3 Nomar Garciaparra 01 DK/250 25.00 7.50
4 Troy Glaus 01 DK/250 15.00 4.50
5 Reggie Jackson 01 ATDK/100 25.00 7.50
6 Alex Rodriguez 01 DK/250 25.00 7.50
7 Alfonso Soriano 03 DK/250 15.00 4.50
8 Curt Schilling 03 DK/250 15.00 4.50
9 Vladimir Guerrero 03 DK/250 15.00 4.50
10 Adam Dunn 03 DK/250 15.00 4.50
11 Mark Grace 88 DK/100 25.00 7.50
12 Roger Clemens 90 DK/100 40.00 12.00
13 Jeff Bagwell 91 DK/100 25.00 7.50
14 Tom Glavine 92 DK/100 25.00 7.50
15 Mike Piazza 94 DK/100 30.00 9.00
16 Rod Carew 82 DK/100 25.00 7.50
17 Rickey Henderson 82 DK/100 25.00 7.50
18 Mike Schmidt 83 DK/100 40.00 12.00
19 Cal Ripken 85 DK/100 80.00 24.00
20 Dale Murphy 86 DK/100 25.00 7.50

2003 Donruss Jersey Kings Studio Series

This set, which parallels the Jersey King insert set was randomly inserted into packs. Cards numbered 1 through 10 were issued to a stated print run of 50 serial numbered sets and cards numbered 11 through 20 were issued to a stated print run of 25 serial numbered sets. We are not pricing cards numbered 11 through 20 due to market scarcity.

Nm-Mt Ex-Mt
*STUDIO 1-10: .75X TO 2X BASIC JSY KINGS
RANDOM INSERTS IN PACKS
1-10 PRINT RUN 50 SERIAL #'d SETS
11-20 PRINT RUN 25 SERIAL #'d SETS
11-20 NO PRICING DUE TO SCARCITY

2003 Donruss Longball Leaders

Randomly inserted into packs, these 10 cards, honoring some of the leading home run hitters, were printed on metalized film board and were issued to a stated print run of 1000 serial numbered sets.

Nm-Mt Ex-Mt
*SEASON SUM: 1.5X TO 4X BASIC LL
SEASON PRINT RUN BASED ON 02 HR'S
RANDOM INSERTS IN PACKS
1 Alex Rodriguez 12.00 3.60
2 Alfonso Soriano 5.00 1.50
3 Rafael Palmeiro 5.00 1.50
4 Jim Thome 8.00 2.40
5 Jason Giambi 5.00 1.50
6 Sammy Sosa 12.00 3.60
7 Barry Bonds 20.00 6.00
8 Lance Berkman 5.00 1.50
9 Shawn Green 5.00 1.50
10 Vladimir Guerrero 8.00 2.40

2003 Donruss Production Line

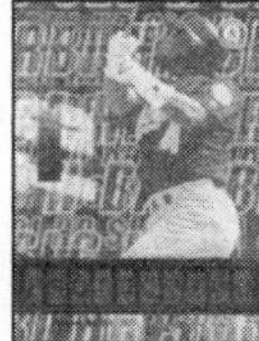

Randomly inserted into packs, these 30 cards feature players who excel in either on base percentage, slugging percentage, batting average or total bases. Each card is printed on metalized film board and was issued to that player's statistical information.

Nm-Mt Ex-Mt
*DIE CUT OPS: 1.25X TO 3X BASIC PL
*DIE CUT OBP/SLG: 1X TO 2.5X BASIC PL
*DIE CUT AVG/TB: .75X TO 2X BASIC PL
DIE CUT PRINT RUN 100 SERIAL #'d SETS
RANDOM INSERTS IN PACKS
1 Alex Rodriguez OPS/1015 10.00 3.00
2 Jim Thome OPS/1122 6.00 1.80
3 Lance Berkman OPS/982 2.50 .75
4 Barry Bonds OPS/1381 15.00 4.50
5 Sammy Sosa OPS/993 10.00 3.00
6 Vladimir Guerrero OPS/1010 6.00 1.80
7 Barry Bonds OBP/582 20.00 6.00
8 Jason Giambi OBP/435 3.00 .90
9 Vladimir Guerrero OBP/417 8.00 2.40
10 Adam Dunn OBP/400 5.00 1.50
11 Chipper Jones OBP/435 8.00 2.40
12 Todd Helton OBP/429 5.00 1.50

13 Rafael Palmeiro SLG/571 5.00 1.50
14 Sammy Sosa SLG/594 12.00 3.60
15 Alex Rodriguez SLG/623 12.00 3.60
16 Larry Walker SLG/602 5.00 1.50
17 Lance Berkman SLG/578 3.00 .90
18 Alfonso Soriano SLG/547 5.00 1.50
19 Ichiro Suzuki AVG/321 15.00 4.50
20 Mike Sweeney AVG/340 4.00 1.20
21 Manny Ramirez AVG/349 6.00 1.80
22 Larry Walker AVG/338 6.00 1.80
23 Barry Bonds AVG/370 25.00 7.50
24 Jim Edmonds AVG/311 4.00 1.20
25 Alfonso Soriano TB/381 6.00 1.80
26 Jason Giambi TB/335 4.00 1.20
27 Miguel Tejada TB/336 4.00 1.20
28 Brian Giles TB/309 4.00 1.20
29 Vladimir Guerrero TB/364 10.00 3.00
30 Pat Burrell TB/319 4.00 1.20

2003 Donruss Timber and Threads

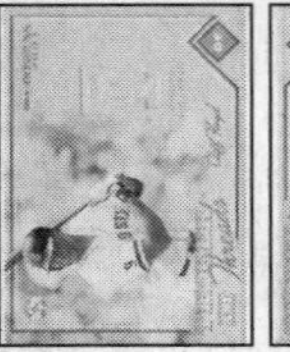

Randomly inserted into packs, these 50 cards feature either a game-used jersey swatch or a game-use bat chip of the featured player. Since these cards have different stated print runs we have put that information next to the player's name in our checklist.

Nm-Mt Ex-Mt
1 Al Kaline Bat/125 25.00 7.50
2 Alex Rodriguez Bat/350 20.00 6.00
3 Carlos Delgado Bat/250 10.00 3.00
4 Cliff Floyd Bat/250 10.00 3.00
5 Eddie Mathews Bat/125 25.00 7.50
6 Edgar Martinez Bat/125 25.00 7.50
7 Ernie Banks Bat/50 40.00 12.00
8 Ivan Rodriguez Bat/125 25.00 7.50
9 J.D. Drew Bat/125 15.00 4.50
10 Jorge Posada Bat/300 15.00 4.50
11 Lou Brock Bat/125 25.00 7.50
12 Mike Piazza Bat/125 25.00 7.50
13 Mike Schmidt Bat/125 60.00 18.00
14 Reggie Jackson Bat/125 25.00 7.50
15 Rickey Henderson Bat/125 25.00 7.50
16 Robin Yount Bat/125 40.00 12.00
17 Rod Carew Bat/125 25.00 7.50
18 Scott Rolen Bat/125 25.00 7.50
19 Shawn Green Bat/200 10.00 3.00
20 Willie Stargell Bat/125 25.00 7.50
21 Alex Rodriguez Jsy/175 30.00 9.00
22 Andruw Jones Jsy/275 10.00 3.00
23 Brooks Robinson Jsy/150 25.00 7.50
24 Chipper Jones Jsy/150 25.00 7.50
25 Greg Maddux Jsy/175 20.00 6.00
26 Hideo Nomo Jsy/300 40.00 12.00
27 Ivan Rodriguez Jsy/225 15.00 4.50
28 Jack Morris Jsy/150 15.00 4.50
29 J.D. Drew Jsy/150 15.00 4.50
30 Jeff Bagwell Jsy/500 15.00 4.50
31 Jim Thome Jsy/200 15.00 4.50
32 John Smoltz Jsy/175 15.00 4.50
33 John Olerud Jsy/450 10.00 3.00
34 Kerry Wood Jsy/200 15.00 4.50
35 Harmon Killebrew Jsy/50
36 Larry Walker Jsy/500 15.00 4.50
37 Magglio Ordonez Jsy/150 15.00 4.50
38 Manny Ramirez Jsy/500 15.00 4.50
39 Mike Piazza Jsy/300 15.00 4.50
40 Mike Sweeney Jsy/200 10.00 3.00
41 Nomar Garciaparra Jsy/200 25.00 7.50
42 Paul Konerko Jsy/500 10.00 3.00
43 Pedro Martinez Jsy/175 15.00 4.50
44 Randy Johnson Jsy/175 15.00 4.50
45 Roger Clemens Jsy/350 25.00 7.50
46 Shawn Green Jsy/250 10.00 3.00
47 Todd Helton Jsy/175 15.00 4.50
48 Tom Glavine Jsy/225 15.00 4.50
49 Tony Gwynn Jsy/150 25.00 7.50
50 Vladimir Guerrero Jsy/450 15.00 4.50

2003 Donruss Rookies

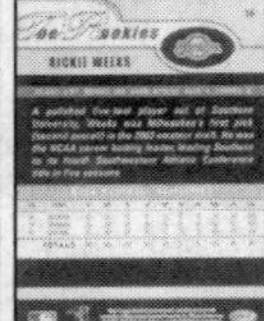

This 65-card set was released in December, 2003. This set was issued as part of the DLP (Donruss/Leaf/Playoff) Rookie Update product in which many of the products issued earlier in the year had Rookie Cards added. Each pack contained eight cards and were sold at an $5 SRP with 24 packs in a box and 12 boxes in a case. In this Rookies set, cards 1-60 feature Rookie Cards while cards numbered 61-65 feature some of the most important players who changed teams during the 2003 season. As mentioned cards from the following DLP products were inserted into these packs: Donruss, Donruss Champions, Donruss Classics, Donruss Diamond Kings, Donruss Elite, Donruss Signature, Donruss Team Heroes, Leaf, Leaf Certified Materials, Leaf Limited, Playoff Absolute Memorabilia, Playoff Prestige and Studio.

MINT NRMT
COMPLETE SET (65) 20.00 9.00
COMMON CARD (1-65) .20 .09
COMMON RC .25 .11
1 Jeremy Bonderman RC .50 .23
2 Adam Loewen RC .60 .25
3 Dan Haren RC .50 .23
4 Jose Contreras RC .60 .25
5 Hideki Matsui RC 2.00 .90
6 Arnie Munoz RC .25 .11
7 Miguel Cabrera .50 .23
8 Andrew Brown RC .40 .18
9 Josh Hall RC .40 .18
10 Josh Stewart RC .25 .11
11 Clint Barmes RC .40 .18
12 Luis Ayala RC .25 .11
13 Brandon Webb RC .60 .25
14 Greg Aquino RC .25 .11
15 Chien-Ming Wang RC .60 .25
16 Rickie Weeks RC 1.50 .70
17 Edgar Gonzalez RC .25 .11
18 Dontrelle Willis .30 .14
19 Bo Hart RC .40 .18
20 Rosman Garcia RC .25 .11
21 Jeremy Griffiths RC .40 .18
22 Craig Brazell RC .40 .18
23 Daniel Cabrera RC .60 .25
24 Fernando Cabrera RC .25 .11
25 Termel Sledge RC .40 .18
26 Ramon Nivar RC .50 .23
27 Rob Hammock RC .40 .18
28 Francisco Rosario RC .25 .11
29 Cory Stewart RC .25 .11
30 Felix Sanchez RC .25 .11
31 Jorge Cordova RC .25 .11
32 Rocco Baldelli .20 .09
33 Beau Kemp RC .25 .11
34 Mike Nakamura RC .25 .11
35 Rett Johnson RC .40 .18
36 Guillermo Quiroz RC .50 .23
37 Hong-Chih Kuo RC .50 .23
38 Ian Ferguson RC .25 .11
39 Franklin Perez RC .25 .11
40 Tim Olson RC .40 .18
41 Jerome Williams .20 .09
42 Rich Fischer RC .25 .11
43 Phil Seibel RC .25 .11
44 Aaron Looper RC .25 .11
45 Jae Weong Seo .20 .09
46 Chad Gaudin RC .25 .11
47 Matt Kata RC .50 .23
48 Ryan Wagner RC .40 .18
49 Michel Hernandez RC .25 .11
50 Diegomar Markwell RC .25 .11
51 Doug Waechter RC .40 .18
52 Mike Nicolas RC .25 .11
53 Prentice Redman RC .25 .11
54 Shane Bazzell RC .25 .11
55 Delmon Young RC 2.00 .90
56 Brian Stokes RC .25 .11
57 Matt Bruback RC .25 .11
58 Nook Logan RC .25 .11
59 Oscar Villarreal RC .25 .11
60 Pete LaForest RC .40 .18
61 Shea Hillenbrand .20 .09
62 Aramis Ramirez .20 .09
63 Aaron Boone .20 .09
64 Roberto Alomar .30 .14
65 Rickey Henderson .50 .23

2003 Donruss Rookies Autographs

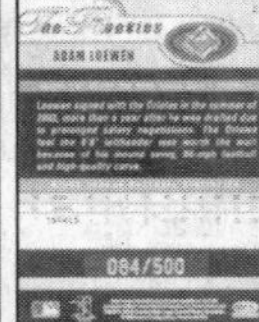

MINT NRMT
RANDOM INSERTS IN DLP R/T PACKS
PRINT RUNS B/WN 10-1000 COPIES PER
NO PRICING ON QTY OF 25 OR LESS
1 Jeremy Bonderman/50 25.00 11.00
2 Adam Loewen/500 15.00 6.75
3 Dan Haren/100 20.00 9.00
4 Jose Contreras/100 25.00 11.00
5 Arnie Munoz/584 10.00 4.50
7 Miguel Cabrera/50 50.00 22.00
8 Andrew Brown/584 15.00 6.75
9 Josh Hall/1000 15.00 6.75
10 Josh Stewart/300 10.00 4.50
11 Clint Barmes/129 15.00 6.75
12 Luis Ayala/1000 10.00 4.50
13 Brandon Webb/100 25.00 11.00
14 Greg Aquino/1000 10.00 4.50
15 Chien-Ming Wang/100 40.00 18.00
16 Rickie Weeks/10
17 Edgar Gonzalez/400 10.00 4.50
18 Dontrelle Willis/25
19 Bo Hart/150 15.00 6.75
20 Rosman Garcia/250 10.00 4.50
21 Jeremy Griffiths/812 15.00 6.75
22 Craig Brazell/205 15.00 6.75
23 Daniel Cabrera/383 15.00 6.75
24 Fernando Cabrera/1000 10.00 4.50
25 Termel Sledge/250 15.00 6.75
26 Ramon Nivar/100 20.00 9.00
27 Rob Hammock/201 15.00 6.75
28 Francisco Rosario/25
29 Cory Stewart/1000 10.00 4.50
30 Felix Sanchez/1000 10.00 4.50
31 Jorge Cordova/1000 10.00 4.50
32 Rocco Baldelli/25
33 Beau Kemp/1000 10.00 4.50
34 Mike Nakamura/1000 10.00 4.50
35 Rett Johnson/1000 15.00 6.75
36 Guillermo Quiroz/90 20.00 9.00
37 Hong-Chih Kuo/50 40.00 18.00
38 Ian Ferguson/1000 10.00 4.50
39 Franklin Perez/1000 10.00 4.50
40 Tim Olson/150 15.00 6.75
41 Jerome Williams/50 25.00 11.00
42 Rich Fischer/734 10.00 4.50
43 Phil Seibel/1000 10.00 4.50
44 Aaron Looper/513 10.00 4.50
45 Jae Weong Seo/50 40.00 18.00
46 Chad Gaudin/19
47 Matt Kata/203 20.00 9.00
48 Ryan Wagner/100 15.00 6.75
49 Michel Hernandez/41
50 Diegomar Markwell/1000 10.00 4.50
51 Doug Waechter/583 15.00 6.75
52 Mike Nicolas/1000 10.00 4.50
53 Prentice Redman/425 10.00 4.50
54 Shane Bazzell/1000 10.00 4.50
55 Delmon Young/75 80.00 36.00
56 Brian Stokes/1000 10.00 4.50
57 Matt Bruback/513 10.00 4.50
58 Nook Logan/150 10.00 4.50
59 Oscar Villarreal/150 10.00 4.50
60 Pete LaForest/250 15.00 6.75

2003 Donruss Rookies Stat Line Career

MINT NRMT
*SLC P/R b/wn 201+: 4X TO 10X
*SLC P/R b/wn 121-200: 5X TO 12X
*SLC P/R b/wn 81-120: 6X TO 15X
*SLC P/R b/wn 66-80: 8X TO 20X
*SLC P/R b/wn 51-65: 8X TO 20X
*SLC RC's P/R b/wn 201+: 4X TO 10X
*SLC RC's P/R b/wn 121-200: 4X TO 10X
*SLC RC's P/R b/wn 81-120: 4X TO 10X
*SLC RC's P/R b/wn 66-80: 5X TO 12X
*SLC RC's P/R b/wn 51-65: 5X TO 12X
*SLC RC's P/R b/wn 36-50: 6X TO 15X
*SLC RC's P/R b/wn 26-35: 8X TO 20X
RANDOM INSERTS IN DLP R/T PACKS
PRINT RUNS B/WN 1-245 COPIES PER
NO PRICING ON QTY OF 25 OR LESS

2003 Donruss Rookies Stat Line Season

MINT NRMT
*SLS P/R b/wn 201+: 4X TO 10X
*SLS P/R b/wn 121-200: 5X TO 12X
*SLS P/R b/wn 66-80: 8X TO 20X
*SLS P/R b/wn 36-50: 10X TO 25X
*SLS P/R b/wn 26-35: 12.5X TO 30X
*SLS RC's P/R b/wn 81-120: 4X TO 10X
*SLS RC's P/R b/wn 66-80: 5X TO 12X
*SLS RC's P/R b/wn 51-65: 5X TO 12X
*SLS RC's P/R b/wn 36-50: 6X TO 15X
*SLS RC's P/R b/wn 26-35: 8X TO 20X
RANDOM INSERTS IN PACKS
PRINT RUNS B/WN 1-130 COPIES PER
NO PRICING ON QTY OF 25 OR LESS

2003 Donruss Rookies Recollection Autographs

MINT NRMT
RANDOM INSERTS IN DLP R/T PACKS
PRINT RUNS B/WN 1-75 COPIES PER
NO PRICING ON QTY OF 5 OR LESS
1 Sandy Alomar Jr. 89 DR/2
2 Sandy Alomar Jr. 90 Black/5
3 Sandy Alomar Jr. 90 Blue/5
4 Jay Buhner 88 DR/5
5 Jose Canseco 86/1
6 Sid Fernandez 84/5
7 Jack McDowell 88/75 25.00 11.00
8 Paul O'Neill 86/5
9 Gary Sheffield 89/5
10 Ruben Sierra 86 DR/1
11 J.T. Snow 93/5
12 Robby Thompson 86 DR/5
13 Matt Williams 87 DR/5

2004 Donruss

This 400-card standard-size set was released in November, 2003. This set was issued in 10 card packs with an $1.99 SRP and those cards came 24 packs to a box and 16 boxes to a case. Please note the following subsets were issued as part of this product: Diamond King (1-25); Rated Rookies (26-70) and Team Checklists (371-400).

MINT NRMT
COMPLETE SET (400) 150.00 70.00
COMP.SET w/o SP's (300) 25.00 11.00
COMMON CARD (71-370) .30 .14
COMMON CARD (1-25/371-400) 2.00 .90
COMMON CARD (26-70) 2.00 .90
1 Derek Jeter DK 4.00 1.80
2 Greg Maddux DK 3.00 1.35
3 Albert Pujols DK 4.00 1.80
4 Ichiro Suzuki DK 3.00 1.35
5 Alex Rodriguez DK 3.00 1.35
6 Roger Clemens DK 4.00 1.80
7 Andruw Jones DK 2.00 .90
8 Barry Bonds DK 5.00 2.20
9 Jeff Bagwell DK 2.00 .90
10 Randy Johnson DK 2.00 .90
11 Scott Rolen DK 2.00 .90
12 Lance Berkman DK 2.00 .90
13 Barry Zito DK 2.00 .90
14 Manny Ramirez DK 2.00 .90
15 Carlos Delgado DK 2.00 .90
16 Alfonso Soriano DK 2.00 .90
17 Todd Helton DK 2.00 .90
18 Mike Mussina DK 2.00 .90
19 Austin Kearns DK 2.00 .90
20 Nomar Garciaparra DK 3.00 1.35
21 Chipper Jones DK 2.00 .90
22 Mark Prior DK 2.00 .90
23 Jim Thome DK 2.00 .90
24 Vladimir Guerrero DK 2.00 .90
25 Pedro Martinez DK 2.00 .90
26 Sergio Mitre RR 2.00 .90
27 Adam Loewen RR 2.00 .90
28 Alfredo Gonzalez RR 2.00 .90
29 Miguel Ojeda RR 2.00 .90
30 Rosman Garcia RR 2.00 .90
31 Arnie Munoz RR 2.00 .90
32 Andrew Brown RR 2.00 .90
33 Josh Hall RR 2.00 .90
34 Josh Stewart RR 2.00 .90
35 Clint Barmes RR 2.00 .90
36 Brandon Webb RR 2.00 .90
37 Chien-Ming Wang RR 3.00 1.35
38 Edgar Gonzalez RR 2.00 .90
39 Alejandro Machado RR 2.00 .90
40 Jeremy Griffiths RR 2.00 .90
41 Craig Brazell RR 2.00 .90
42 Daniel Cabrera RR 3.00 1.35
43 Fernando Cabrera RR 2.00 .90
44 Termel Sledge RR 2.00 .90
45 Rob Hammock RR 2.00 .90
46 Francisco Rosario RR 2.00 .90
47 Francisco Cruceta RR 2.00 .90
48 Rett Johnson RR 2.00 .90
49 Guillermo Quiroz RR 2.00 .90
50 Hong-Chih Kuo RR 3.00 1.35
51 Ian Ferguson RR 2.00 .90
52 Tim Olson RR 2.00 .90
53 Todd Wellemeyer RR 2.00 .90
54 Rich Fischer RR 2.00 .90
55 Phil Seibel RR 2.00 .90
56 Joe Valentine RR 2.00 .90
57 Matt Kata RR 2.00 .90
58 Michael Hessman RR 2.00 .90
59 Michel Hernandez RR 2.00 .90
60 Doug Waechter RR 2.00 .90
61 Prentice Redman RR 2.00 .90
62 Nook Logan RR 2.00 .90
63 Oscar Villarreal RR 2.00 .90
64 Pete LaForest RR 2.00 .90
65 Matt Bruback RR 2.00 .90
66 Dan Haren RR 2.00 .90
67 Greg Aquino RR 2.00 .90
68 Lew Ford RR 3.00 1.35
69 Jeff Duncan RR 2.00 .90
70 Ryan Wagner RR 2.00 .90
71 Bengie Molina .30 .14
72 Brad Fullmer .30 .14
73 Darin Erstad .30 .14
74 David Eckstein .30 .14
75 Garret Anderson .30 .14
76 Jarrod Washburn .30 .14
77 Kevin Appier .30 .14
78 Scott Spiezio .30 .14
79 Tim Salmon .50 .23
80 Troy Glaus .30 .14
81 Troy Percival .30 .14
82 Jason Johnson .30 .14
83 Jay Gibbons .30 .14
84 Melvin Mora .30 .14
85 Sidney Ponson .30 .14
86 Tony Batista .30 .14
87 Bill Mueller .30 .14
88 Byung-Hyun Kim .30 .14
89 David Ortiz .75 .35
90 Derek Lowe .30 .14
91 Johnny Damon .75 .35
92 Casey Fossum .30 .14
93 Manny Ramirez .50 .23
94 Nomar Garciaparra 1.25 .55
95 Pedro Martinez .75 .35
96 Todd Walker .30 .14
97 Trot Nixon .30 .14
98 Bartolo Colon .30 .14
99 Carlos Lee .30 .14
100 D'Angelo Jimenez .30 .14
101 Esteban Loaiza .30 .14
102 Frank Thomas .75 .35
103 Joe Crede .30 .14
104 Jose Valentin .30 .14
105 Magglio Ordonez .30 .14
106 Mark Buehrle .30 .14
107 Paul Konerko .30 .14
108 Brandon Phillips .30 .14
109 C.C Sabathia .30 .14
110 Ellis Burks .30 .14
111 Jeremy Guthrie .30 .14
112 Josh Bard .30 .14
113 Matt Lawton .30 .14
114 Milton Bradley .30 .14
115 Omar Vizquel .50 .23
116 Travis Hafner .30 .14
117 Bobby Higginson .30 .14
118 Carlos Pena .30 .14
119 Dmitri Young .30 .14
120 Eric Munson .30 .14
121 Jeremy Bonderman .30 .14
122 Nate Cornejo .30 .14
123 Omar Infante .30 .14
124 Ramon Santiago .30 .14
125 Angel Berroa .30 .14
126 Carlos Beltran .50 .23
127 Desi Relaford .30 .14
128 Jeremy Affeldt .30 .14
129 Joe Randa .30 .14
130 Ken Harvey .30 .14
131 Mike MacDougal .30 .14
132 Michael Tucker .30 .14
133 Mike Sweeney .30 .14
134 Raul Ibanez .30 .14
135 Runelvys Hernandez .30 .14
136 A.J. Pierzynski .30 .14
137 Brad Radke .30 .14
138 Corey Koskie .30 .14
139 Cristian Guzman .30 .14
140 Doug Mientkiewicz .30 .14
141 Dustan Mohr .30 .14
142 Jacque Jones .30 .14
143 Kenny Rogers .30 .14
144 Bobby Kielty .30 .14
145 Kyle Lohse .30 .14
146 Luis Rivas .30 .14
147 Torii Hunter .30 .14
148 Alfonso Soriano .50 .23
149 Andy Pettitte .50 .23
150 Bernie Williams .50 .23
151 David Wells .30 .14
152 Derek Jeter 1.50 .70
153 Hideki Matsui 1.25 .55
154 Jason Giambi .30 .14
155 Jorge Posada .50 .23
156 Jose Contreras .30 .14
157 Mike Mussina .50 .23
158 Nick Johnson .30 .14
159 Robin Ventura .30 .14
160 Roger Clemens 1.50 .70
161 Barry Zito .30 .14
162 Chris Singleton .30 .14
163 Eric Byrnes .30 .14
164 Eric Chavez .30 .14
165 Erubiel Durazo .30 .14
166 Keith Foulke .30 .14
167 Mark Ellis .30 .14
168 Miguel Tejada .30 .14
169 Mark Mulder .30 .14
170 Ramon Hernandez .30 .14
171 Ted Lilly .30 .14
172 Terrence Long .30 .14
173 Tim Hudson .30 .14
174 Bret Boone .30 .14
175 Carlos Guillen .30 .14
176 Dan Wilson .30 .14
177 Edgar Martinez .50 .23
178 Freddy Garcia .30 .14
179 Gil Meche .30 .14
180 Ichiro Suzuki 1.25 .55
181 Jamie Moyer .30 .14
182 Joel Pineiro .30 .14
183 John Olerud .30 .14
184 Mike Cameron .30 .14
185 Randy Winn .30 .14
186 Ryan Franklin .30 .14
187 Kazuhiro Sasaki .30 .14
188 Aubrey Huff .30 .14
189 Carl Crawford .30 .14
190 Joe Kennedy .30 .14
191 Marlon Anderson .30 .14
192 Rey Ordonez .30 .14
193 Rocco Baldelli .30 .14
194 Toby Hall .30 .14
195 Travis Lee .30 .14
196 Alex Rodriguez 1.25 .55
197 Carl Everett .30 .14
198 Chan Ho Park .30 .14
199 Einar Diaz .30 .14
200 Hank Blalock .30 .14
201 Ismael Valdes .30 .14
202 Juan Gonzalez .50 .23
203 Mark Teixeira .30 .14
204 Mike Young .30 .14
205 Rafael Palmeiro .50 .23
206 Carlos Delgado .30 .14
207 Kelvim Escobar .30 .14
208 Eric Hinske .30 .14
209 Frank Catalanotto .30 .14
210 Josh Phelps .30 .14
211 Orlando Hudson .30 .14
212 Roy Halladay .30 .14
213 Shannon Stewart .30 .14
214 Vernon Wells .30 .14
215 Carlos Baerga .30 .14
216 Curt Schilling .30 .14
217 Junior Spivey .30 .14
218 Luis Gonzalez .30 .14
219 Lyle Overbay .30 .14
220 Mark Grace .50 .23
221 Matt Williams .30 .14
222 Randy Johnson .75 .35
223 Shea Hillenbrand .30 .14
224 Steve Finley .30 .14
225 Andruw Jones .30 .14
226 Chipper Jones .75 .35
227 Gary Sheffield .30 .14
228 Greg Maddux 1.25 .55
229 Javy Lopez .30 .14
230 John Smoltz .50 .23
231 Marcus Giles .30 .14
232 Mike Hampton .30 .14
233 Rafael Furcal .30 .14
234 Robert Fick .30 .14
235 Russ Ortiz .30 .14
236 Alex Gonzalez .30 .14
237 Carlos Zambrano .30 .14
238 Corey Patterson .30 .14
239 Hee Seop Choi .30 .14
240 Kerry Wood .75 .35
241 Mark Bellhorn .30 .14
242 Mark Prior .75 .35
243 Moises Alou .30 .14
244 Sammy Sosa 1.25 .55
245 Aaron Boone .30 .14
246 Adam Dunn .50 .23
247 Austin Kearns .30 .14
248 Barry Larkin .50 .23
249 Felipe Lopez .30 .14
250 Jose Guillen .30 .14
251 Ken Griffey Jr. 1.25 .55
252 Jason LaRue .30 .14
253 Scott Williamson .30 .14
254 Sean Casey .30 .14
255 Shawn Chacon .30 .14
256 Chris Stynes .30 .14
257 Jason Jennings .30 .14
258 Jay Payton .30 .14
259 Jose Hernandez .30 .14
260 Larry Walker .50 .23
261 Preston Wilson .30 .14
262 Ronnie Belliard .30 .14
263 Todd Helton .50 .23
264 A.J. Burnett .30 .14
265 Alex Gonzalez .30 .14
266 Brad Penny .30 .14
267 Derrek Lee .30 .14
268 Ivan Rodriguez .75 .35
269 Josh Beckett .30 .14
270 Juan Encarnacion .30 .14
271 Juan Pierre .30 .14
272 Luis Castillo .30 .14
273 Mike Lowell .30 .14
274 Todd Hollandsworth .30 .14
275 Billy Wagner .30 .14

76 Brad Ausmus	.30	.14
77 Craig Biggio	.50	.23
78 Jeff Bagwell	.50	.23
79 Jeff Kent	.30	.14
80 Lance Berkman	.30	.14
81 Richard Hidalgo	.30	.14
82 Roy Oswalt	.30	.14
83 Wade Miller	.30	.14
84 Adrian Beltre	.50	.23
85 Brian Jordan	.30	.14
86 Cesar Izturis	.30	.14
87 Dave Roberts	.30	.14
88 Eric Gagne	.75	.35
89 Fred McGriff	.50	.23
90 Hideo Nomo	.75	.35
91 Kazuhisa Ishii	.30	.14
92 Kevin Brown	.30	.14
93 Paul Lo Duca	.30	.14
94 Shawn Green	.30	.14
95 Ben Sheets	.30	.14
96 Geoff Jenkins	.30	.14
97 Rey Sanchez	.30	.14
98 Richie Sexson	.30	.14
99 Wes Helms	.30	.14
00 Brad Wilkerson	.30	.14
01 Claudio Vargas	.30	.14
02 Endy Chavez	.30	.14
03 Fernando Tatis	.30	.14
04 Javier Vazquez	.30	.14
05 Jose Vidro	.30	.14
06 Michael Barrett	.30	.14
07 Orlando Cabrera	.30	.14
08 Tony Armas Jr.	.30	.14
09 Vladimir Guerrero	.75	.35
10 Zach Day	.30	.14
11 Al Leiter	.30	.14
12 Cliff Floyd	.30	.14
13 Jae Weong Seo	.30	.14
14 Jeromy Burnitz	.30	.14
15 Mike Piazza	1.25	.55
16 Mo Vaughn	.30	.14
17 Roberto Alomar	.50	.23
18 Roger Cedeno	.30	.14
19 Tom Glavine	.50	.23
20 Jose Reyes	.30	.14
21 Bobby Abreu	.30	.14
22 Brett Myers	.30	.14
23 David Bell	.30	.14
24 Jim Thome	.75	.35
25 Jimmy Rollins	.30	.14
26 Kevin Millwood	.30	.14
27 Marlon Byrd	.30	.14
28 Mike Lieberthal	.30	.14
29 Pat Burrell	.30	.14
30 Randy Wolf	.30	.14
31 Aramis Ramirez	.30	.14
32 Brian Giles	.30	.14
33 Jason Kendall	.30	.14
34 Kenny Lofton	.30	.14
35 Kip Wells	.30	.14
36 Kris Benson	.30	.14
37 Randall Simon	.30	.14
38 Reggie Sanders	.30	.14
39 Albert Pujols	1.50	.70
40 Edgar Renteria	.30	.14
41 Fernando Vina	.30	.14
42 J.D. Drew	.30	.14
43 Jim Edmonds	.30	.14
44 Matt Morris	.30	.14
45 Mike Matheny	.30	.14
46 Scott Rolen	.75	.35
47 Tino Martinez	.50	.23
48 Woody Williams	.30	.14
49 Brian Lawrence	.30	.14
50 Mark Kotsay	.30	.14
51 Mark Loretta	.30	.14
52 Ramon Vazquez	.30	.14
53 Rondell White	.30	.14
54 Ryan Klesko	.30	.14
55 Sean Burroughs	.30	.14
56 Trevor Hoffman	.30	.14
57 Xavier Nady	.30	.14
58 Andres Galarraga	.30	.14
59 Barry Bonds	2.00	.90
60 Benito Santiago	.30	.14
61 Deivi Cruz	.30	.14
62 Edgardo Alfonzo	.30	.14
63 J.T. Snow	.30	.14
64 Jason Schmidt	.30	.14
65 Kirk Rueter	.30	.14
66 Kurt Ainsworth	.30	.14
67 Marquis Grissom	.30	.14
68 Ray Durham	.30	.14
69 Rich Aurilia	.30	.14
70 Tim Worrell	.30	.14
71 Troy Glaus TC	2.00	.90
72 Melvin Mora TC	2.00	.90
73 Nomar Garciaparra TC	3.00	1.35
74 Magglio Ordonez TC	2.00	.90
75 Omar Vizquel TC	2.00	.90
76 Dmitri Young TC	2.00	.90
77 Mike Sweeney TC	2.00	.90
78 Torii Hunter TC	2.00	.90
79 Derek Jeter TC	4.00	1.80
80 Barry Zito TC	2.00	.90
81 Ichiro Suzuki TC	3.00	1.35
82 Rocco Baldelli TC	2.00	.90
83 Alex Rodriguez TC	3.00	1.35
84 Carlos Delgado TC	2.00	.90
85 Randy Johnson TC	2.00	.90
86 Greg Maddux TC	3.00	1.35
87 Sammy Sosa TC	3.00	1.35
88 Ken Griffey Jr. TC	3.00	1.35
89 Todd Helton TC	2.00	.90
90 Ivan Rodriguez TC	2.00	.90
91 Jeff Bagwell TC	2.00	.90
92 Hideo Nomo TC	2.00	.90
93 Richie Sexson TC	2.00	.90
94 Vladimir Guerrero TC	2.00	.90
95 Mike Piazza TC	3.00	1.35
96 Jim Thome TC	2.00	.90
97 Jason Kendall TC	2.00	.90
98 Albert Pujols TC	4.00	1.80
99 Ryan Klesko TC	2.00	.90
00 Barry Bonds TC	5.00	2.20

2004 Donruss Autographs

MINT NRMT

ANDOM INSERTS IN PACKS

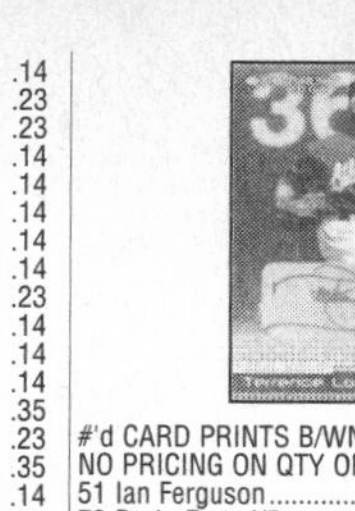

#'d CARD PRINTS B/WN 5-141 COPIES PER
NO PRICING ON QTY OF 12 OR LESS

51 Ian Ferguson	10.00	4.50
73 Darin Erstad/5		
106 Mark Buehrle/141	15.00	6.75
112 Josh Bard	10.00	4.50
123 Omar Infante	10.00	4.50
172 Terrence Long	10.00	4.50
188 Aubrey Huff/143	15.00	6.75
194 Toby Hall	10.00	4.50
217 Junior Spivey/132	10.00	4.50
234 Robert Fick	10.00	4.50
312 Cliff Floyd/12		
349 Brian Lawrence	10.00	4.50

2004 Donruss Press Proofs Black

MINT NRMT

RANDOM INSERTS IN PACKS
STATED PRINT RUN 10 SERIAL #'d SETS
NO PRICING DUE TO SCARCITY

2004 Donruss Press Proofs Blue

MINT NRMT

*PP BLUE 71-370: 4X TO 10X BASIC.
*PP BLUE 1-25/371-400: 1.5X TO 4X BASIC
*PP BLUE 26-70: .75X TO 2X BASIC..
RANDOM INSERTS IN RETAIL PACKS
STATED PRINT RUN 100 SERIAL #'d SETS

2004 Donruss Press Proofs Gold

MINT NRMT

RANDOM INSERTS IN RETAIL PACKS
STATED PRINT RUN 25 SERIAL #'d SETS
NO PRICING DUE TO SCARCITY

2004 Donruss Press Proofs Red

MINT NRMT

*PP RED 71-370: 2.5X TO 6X BASIC..
*PP RED 1-25/371-400: 1X TO 2.5X BASIC
*PP RED 26-70: .5X TO 1.2X BASIC...
STATED ODDS 1:12 RETAIL

2004 Donruss Stat Line Career

MINT NRMT

*71-370 p/r 200-443 2.5X TO 6X
*71-370 p/r 121-200: 3X TO 8X
*71-370 p/r 81-120: 4X TO 10X
*71-370 p/r 66-80: 5X TO 12X
*71-370 p/r 51-65: 5X TO 12X
*71-370 p/r 36-50: 6X TO 15X
*71-370 p/r 26-35: 8X TO 20X
*1-25/371-400 p/r 200-500: 1X TO 2.5X
*1-25/371-400 p/r 121-200: 1.25X TO 3X
*1-25/371-400 p/r 81-120: 1.5X TO 4X
*1-25/371-400 p/r 66-80: 2X TO 5X...
*1-25/371-400 p/r 51-65: 2X TO 5X...
*1-25/371-400 p/r 36-50: 2.5X TO 6X
*1-25/371-400 p/r 26-35: 3X TO 8X...
*26-70 p/r 200-491: .5X TO 1.2X
*26-70 p/r 121-200: .6X TO 1.5X
*26-70 p/r 81-120: .75X TO 2X
*26-70 p/r 66-80: 1X TO 2.5X
*26-70 p/r 51-65: 1X TO 2.5X
*26-70 p/r 36-50: 1.25X TO 3X
*26-70 p/r 26-35: 1.5X TO 4X
RANDOM INSERTS IN PACKS
PRINT RUNS B/WN 6-500 COPIES PER
NO PRICING ON QTY OF 25 OR LESS

2004 Donruss Stat Line Season

MINT NRMT

*71-370 p/r 121-193: 3X TO 8X
*71-370 p/r 81-120: 4X TO 10X
*71-370 p/r 66-80: 5X TO 12X
*71-370 p/r 51-65: 5X TO 12X
*71-370 p/r 36-50: 6X TO 15X
*71-370 p/r 26-35: 8X TO 20X
*1-25/371-400 p/r 201-225:1X TO 2.5X
*1-25/371-400 p/r 121-200: 1.25X TO 3X
*1-25/371-400 p/r 81-120: 1.5X TO 4X
*1-25/371-400 p/r 66-80: 2X TO 5X...
*1-25/371-400 p/r 51-65: 2X TO 5X...
*1-25/371-400 p/r 36-50: 2.5X TO 6X
*1-25/371-400 p/r 26-35: 3X TO 8X...
*26-70 p/r 201-261: .5X TO 1.2X
*26-70 p/r 121-200: .6X TO 1.5X
*26-70 p/r 81-120: .75X TO 2X
*26-70 p/r 66-80: 1X TO 2.5X
*26-70 p/r 51-65: 1X TO 2.5X
*26-70 p/r 36-50: 1.25X TO 3X
*26-70 p/r 26-35: 1.5X TO 4X
RANDOM INSERTS IN PACKS
PRINT RUNS B/WN 1-261 COPIES PER
NO PRICING ON QTY OF 25 OR LESS

2004 Donruss All-Stars American League

MINT NRMT

STATED PRINT RUN 1000 SERIAL #'d SETS
*BLACK: .6X TO 1.5X BASIC
BLACK PRINT RUN 250 SERIAL #'d SETS
RANDOM INSERTS IN PACKS

1 Alex Rodriguez	8.00	3.60
2 Roger Clemens	10.00	4.50
3 Ichiro Suzuki	8.00	3.60
4 Barry Zito	3.00	1.35
5 Garret Anderson	3.00	1.35
6 Derek Jeter	10.00	4.50
7 Manny Ramirez	3.00	1.35
8 Pedro Martinez	5.00	2.20
9 Alfonso Soriano	3.00	1.35
10 Carlos Delgado	3.00	1.35

2004 Donruss All-Stars National League

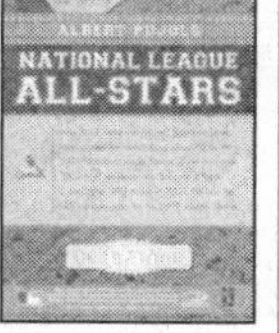

MINT NRMT

STATED PRINT RUN 1000 SERIAL #'d SETS
*BLACK: .6X TO 1.5X BASIC
BLACK PRINT RUN 250 SERIAL #'d SETS
RANDOM INSERTS IN PACKS

1 Barry Bonds	12.00	5.50
2 Andruw Jones	3.00	1.35
3 Scott Rolen	5.00	2.20
4 Austin Kearns	3.00	1.35
5 Mark Prior	5.00	2.20
6 Vladimir Guerrero	5.00	2.20
7 Jeff Bagwell	3.00	1.35
8 Mike Piazza	8.00	3.60
9 Albert Pujols	10.00	4.50
10 Randy Johnson	5.00	2.20

2004 Donruss Bat Kings

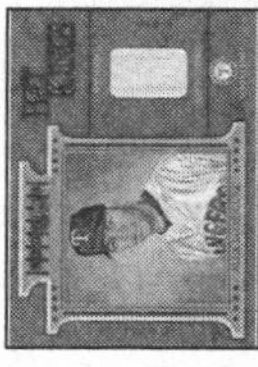

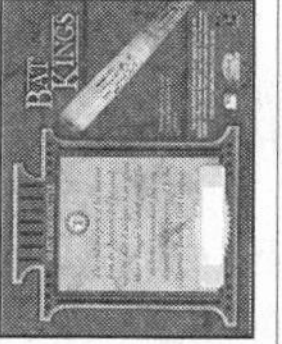

MINT NRMT

1-4 PRINT RUN 250 SERIAL #'d SETS
5-8 PRINT RUN 100 SERIAL #'d SETS
*STUDIO 1-4: .75X TO 2X BASIC
STUDIO 1-4 PRINT RUN 50 SERIAL #'d SETS
STUDIO 5-8 PRINT RUN 25 SERIAL #'d SETS
STUDIO 5-8 NO PRICING DUE TO SCARCITY
RANDOM INSERTS IN PACKS

1 Alex Rodriguez 03	20.00	9.00
2 Albert Pujols 03	25.00	11.00
3 Chipper Jones 03	15.00	6.75
4 Lance Berkman 03	10.00	4.50
5 Cal Ripken 88	80.00	36.00
6 George Brett 87	50.00	22.00
7 Don Mattingly 89	50.00	22.00
8 Roberto Clemente 02	100.00	45.00

2004 Donruss Craftsmen

MINT NRMT

STATED PRINT RUN 2000 SERIAL #'d SETS
*BLACK: 1X TO 2.5X BASIC
BLACK PRINT RUN 275 SERIAL #'d SETS
*MASTER: 1.25X TO 3X BASIC
MASTER PRINT RUN 150 SERIAL #'d SETS
RANDOM INSERTS IN PACKS

1 Alex Rodriguez	5.00	2.20
2 Mark Prior	3.00	1.35
3 Ichiro Suzuki	5.00	2.20
4 Barry Bonds	8.00	3.60
5 Ken Griffey Jr.	5.00	2.20
6 Alfonso Soriano	2.00	.90
7 Mike Piazza	5.00	2.20
8 Chipper Jones	3.00	1.35
9 Derek Jeter	6.00	2.70
10 Randy Johnson	3.00	1.35
11 Sammy Sosa	5.00	2.20
12 Roger Clemens	6.00	2.70
13 Nomar Garciaparra	5.00	2.20
14 Greg Maddux	5.00	2.20
15 Albert Pujols	6.00	2.70

2004 Donruss Diamond Kings Inserts

MINT NRMT

STATED PRINT RUN 2000 SERIAL #'d SETS
*BLACK: .75X TO 2X BASIC
BLACK PRINT RUN 100 SERIAL #'d SETS
*STUDIO: .6X TO 1.5X BASIC
STUDIO PRINT RUN 250 SERIAL #'d SETS

RANDOM INSERTS IN PACKS

1 Derek Jeter	12.00	5.50
2 Greg Maddux	10.00	4.50
3 Albert Pujols	12.00	5.50
4 Ichiro Suzuki	10.00	4.50
5 Alex Rodriguez	10.00	4.50
6 Roger Clemens	12.00	5.50
7 Andruw Jones	8.00	3.60
8 Barry Bonds	15.00	6.75
9 Jeff Bagwell	8.00	3.60
10 Randy Johnson	8.00	3.60
11 Scott Rolen	8.00	3.60
12 Lance Berkman	8.00	3.60
13 Barry Zito	8.00	3.60
14 Manny Ramirez	8.00	3.60
15 Carlos Delgado	8.00	3.60
16 Alfonso Soriano	8.00	3.60
17 Todd Helton	8.00	3.60
18 Mike Mussina	8.00	3.60
19 Austin Kearns	8.00	3.60
20 Nomar Garciaparra	10.00	4.50
21 Chipper Jones	8.00	3.60
22 Mark Prior	8.00	3.60
23 Jim Thome	8.00	3.60
24 Vladimir Guerrero	8.00	3.60
25 Pedro Martinez	8.00	3.60

2004 Donruss Elite Series

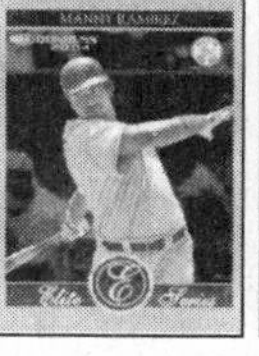

MINT NRMT

RANDOM INSERTS IN PACKS
STATED PRINT RUN 1500 SERIAL #'d SETS
*BLACK: 1X TO 2.5X BASIC
BLACK PRINT RUN 150 SERIAL #'d SETS
DOMINATORS PRINT 25 SERIAL #'d SETS
DOMINATORS NO PRICE DUE TO SCARCITY
RANDOM INSERTS IN PACKS

1 Albert Pujols	10.00	4.50
2 Barry Zito	3.00	1.35
3 Gary Sheffield	3.00	1.35
4 Mike Mussina	3.00	1.35
5 Lance Berkman	3.00	1.35
6 Alfonso Soriano	3.00	1.35
7 Randy Johnson	5.00	2.20
8 Nomar Garciaparra	8.00	3.60
9 Austin Kearns	3.00	1.35
10 Manny Ramirez	3.00	1.35
11 Mark Prior	5.00	2.20
12 Alex Rodriguez	8.00	3.60
13 Derek Jeter	10.00	4.50
14 Barry Bonds	12.00	5.50
15 Roger Clemens	10.00	4.50

2004 Donruss Inside View

MINT NRMT

RANDOM INSERTS IN PACKS
STATED PRINT RUN 1250 SERIAL #'d SETS

1 Derek Jeter	8.00	3.60
2 Greg Maddux	6.00	2.70
3 Albert Pujols	8.00	3.60
4 Ichiro Suzuki	6.00	2.70
5 Alex Rodriguez	6.00	2.70
6 Roger Clemens	8.00	3.60
7 Andruw Jones	2.50	1.10
8 Barry Bonds	10.00	4.50
9 Jeff Bagwell	2.50	1.10
10 Randy Johnson	4.00	1.80
11 Scott Rolen	4.00	1.80
12 Lance Berkman	2.50	1.10
13 Barry Zito	2.50	1.10
14 Manny Ramirez	2.50	1.10
15 Carlos Delgado	2.50	1.10
16 Alfonso Soriano	2.50	1.10
17 Todd Helton	2.50	1.10
18 Mike Mussina	2.50	1.10
19 Austin Kearns	2.50	1.10
20 Nomar Garciaparra	6.00	2.70
21 Chipper Jones	4.00	1.80
22 Mark Prior	4.00	1.80
23 Jim Thome	4.00	1.80
24 Vladimir Guerrero	4.00	1.80
25 Pedro Martinez	4.00	1.80

2004 Donruss Jersey Kings

MINT NRMT

1-6 PRINT RUN 250 SERIAL #'d SETS
7-12 PRINT RUN 100 SERIAL #'d SETS
*STUDIO 1-6: .75X TO 2X BASIC JSY KINGS
STUDIO 1-6 PRINT RUN 50 SERIAL #'d SETS
STUDIO 7-12 PRINT RUN 25 SERIAL #'d SETS
STUDIO 7-12 NO PRICING DUE TO SCARCITY

RANDOM INSERTS IN PACKS

1 Alfonso Soriano 03	15.00	6.75
2 Sammy Sosa 03	20.00	9.00
3 Roger Clemens 03	25.00	11.00
4 Nomar Garciaparra 03	20.00	9.00
5 Mark Prior 03	15.00	6.75
6 Vladimir Guerrero 03	15.00	6.75
7 Don Mattingly 89	50.00	22.00
8 Roberto Clemente 02	100.00	45.00
9 George Brett 87	50.00	22.00
10 Nolan Ryan 01	50.00	22.00
11 Cal Ripken 01	80.00	36.00
12 Mike Schmidt 01	40.00	18.00

2004 Donruss Longball Leaders

MINT NRMT

STATED PRINT RUN 1500 SERIAL #'d SETS
*BLACK: .75X TO 2X BASIC LL
BLACK PRINT RUN 250 SERIAL #'d SETS
*DIE CUT: 1.25X TO 3X BASIC LL
DIE CUT PRINT RUN 50 SERIAL #'d SETS
RANDOM INSERTS IN PACKS

1 Barry Bonds	10.00	4.50
2 Alfonso Soriano	2.50	1.10
3 Adam Dunn	2.50	1.10
4 Alex Rodriguez	6.00	2.70
5 Jim Thome	4.00	1.80
6 Garret Anderson	2.50	1.10
7 Juan Gonzalez	2.50	1.10
8 Jeff Bagwell	2.50	1.10
9 Gary Sheffield	2.50	1.10
10 Sammy Sosa	6.00	2.70

2004 Donruss Mound Marvels

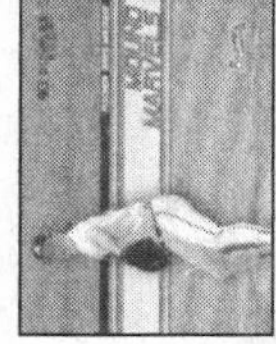

MINT NRMT

STATED PRINT RUN 750 SERIAL #'d SETS
*BLACK: .75X TO 2X BASIC MM
BLACK PRINT RUN 175 SERIAL #'d SETS
RANDOM INSERTS IN PACKS

1 Mark Prior	5.00	2.20
2 Curt Schilling	3.00	1.35
3 Mike Mussina	3.00	1.35
4 Kevin Brown	3.00	1.35
5 Pedro Martinez	5.00	2.20
6 Mark Mulder	3.00	1.35
7 Kerry Wood	5.00	2.20
8 Greg Maddux	8.00	3.60
9 Kevin Millwood	3.00	1.35
10 Barry Zito	3.00	1.35
11 Roger Clemens	10.00	4.50
12 Randy Johnson	5.00	2.20
13 Hideo Nomo	5.00	2.20
14 Tim Hudson	3.00	1.35
15 Tom Glavine	3.00	1.35

2004 Donruss Power Alley Red

MINT NRMT

STATED PRINT RUN 2500 SERIAL #'d SETS
BLACK DC PRINT RUN 1 SERIAL #'d SET
BLACK DC NO PRICING DUE TO SCARCITY
*BLUE: .6X TO 1.5X BASIC RED
BLUE PRINT RUN 1000 SERIAL #'d SETS
*BLUE DC: 1.25X TO 3X BASIC RED..
BLUE DC PRINT RUN 100 SERIAL #'d SETS
GREEN PRINT RUN 25 SERIAL #'d SETS
GREEN NO PRICING DUE TO SCARCITY
GREEN DC 5 SERIAL #'d SETS
GREEN DC NO PRICING DUE TO SCARCITY
*PURPLE: 1X TO 2.5X BASIC RED
PURPLE PRINT RUN 250 SERIAL #'d SETS
PURPLE DC PRINT RUN 25 SERIAL #'d SETS
PURPLE DC NO PRICING DUE TO SCARCITY
*RED DC: 1X TO 2.5X BASIC RED
RED DC PRINT RUN 250 SERIAL #'d SETS

*YELLOW: 1.25X TO 3X BASIC RED ..
YELLOW PRINT RUN 100 SERIAL #'d SETS
YELLOW DC PRINT RUN 10 SERIAL #'d SETS
YELLOW DC NO PRICING DUE TO SCARCITY
RANDOM INSERTS IN PACKS

1 Albert Pujols 6.00 2.70
2 Mike Piazza 5.00 2.20
3 Carlos Delgado 2.00 .90
4 Barry Bonds 8.00 3.60
5 Jim Edmonds 2.00 .90
6 Nomar Garciaparra 5.00 2.20
7 Alfonso Soriano 2.00 .90
8 Alex Rodriguez 5.00 2.20
9 Lance Berkman 2.00 .90
10 Scott Rolen 3.00 1.35
11 Manny Ramirez 2.00 .90
12 Rafael Palmeiro 2.00 .90
13 Sammy Sosa 5.00 2.20
14 Adam Dunn 2.00 .90
15 Andruw Jones 2.00 .90
16 Jim Thome 3.00 1.35
17 Jason Giambi 2.00 .90
18 Jeff Bagwell 2.00 .90
19 Juan Gonzalez 2.00 .90
20 Austin Kearns 2.00 .90

2004 Donruss Production Line Average

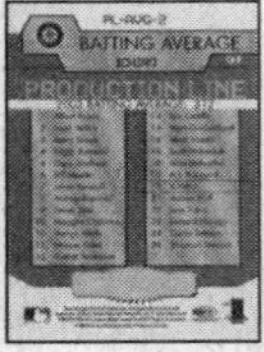

MINT NRMT
PRINT RUNS B/WN 300-359 COPIES PER
*BLACK: .75X TO 2X BASIC AVG........
BLACK PRINT RUN 35 SERIAL #'d SETS
*DIE CUT: .5X TO 1.2X BASIC AVG.....
DIE CUT PRINT RUN 100 SERIAL #'d SETS
RANDOM INSERTS IN PACKS

1 Gary Sheffield/330 5.00 2.20
2 Ichiro Suzuki/312 12.00 5.50
3 Todd Helton/358 5.00 2.20
4 Manny Ramirez/325 5.00 2.20
5 Garret Anderson/315 5.00 2.20
6 Barry Bonds/341 20.00 9.00
7 Albert Pujols/359 15.00 6.75
8 Derek Jeter/324 15.00 6.75
9 Nomar Garciaparra/301 12.00 5.50
10 Hank Blalock/300 5.00 2.20

2004 Donruss Production Line OBP

MINT NRMT
PRINT RUNS B/WN 396-529 COPIES PER
*BLACK: 1X TO 2.5X BASIC OBP........
BLACK PRINT RUN 40 SERIAL #'d SETS
*DIE CUT: .6X TO 1.5X BASIC OBP ....
DIE CUT PRINT RUN 100 SERIAL #'d SETS
RANDOM INSERTS IN PACKS

1 Todd Helton/458 4.00 1.80
2 Albert Pujols/439 12.00 5.50
3 Larry Walker/422 4.00 1.80
4 Barry Bonds/529 15.00 6.75
5 Chipper Jones/402 6.00 2.70
6 Manny Ramirez/427 4.00 1.80
7 Gary Sheffield/419 4.00 1.80
8 Lance Berkman/412 4.00 1.80
9 Alex Rodriguez/396 10.00 4.50
10 Jason Giambi/412 4.00 1.80

2004 Donruss Production Line OPS

MINT NRMT
PRINT RUNS B/WN 910-1278 COPIES PER
*BLACK: .75X TO 2X BASIC OPS........
BLACK PRINT RUN 125 SERIAL #'d SETS
*DIE CUT: .75X TO 2X BASIC OPS .....
DIE CUT PRINT RUN 100 SERIAL #'d SETS
RANDOM INSERTS IN PACKS

1 Albert Pujols/1106 10.00 4.50
2 Barry Bonds/1278 12.00 5.50
3 Gary Sheffield/1023 3.00 1.35
4 Todd Helton/1088 3.00 1.35
5 Scott Rolen/910 5.00 2.20
6 Manny Ramirez/1014 3.00 1.35
7 Alex Rodriguez/995 8.00 3.60
8 Jim Thome/958 5.00 2.20
9 Jason Giambi/939 3.00 1.35
10 Frank Thomas/952 5.00 2.20

2004 Donruss Production Line Slugging

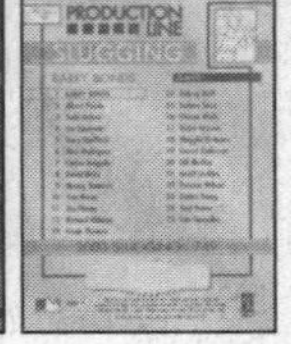

MINT NRMT
PRINT RUNS B/WN 541-749 COPIES PER
*BLACK: .75X TO 2X BASIC SLG........
BLACK PRINT RUN 75 SERIAL #'d SETS
*DIE CUT: .6X TO 1.5X BASIC SLG.....
DIE CUT PRINT RUN 100 SERIAL #'d SETS
RANDOM INSERTS IN PACKS

1 Alex Rodriguez/600 10.00 4.50
2 Frank Thomas/562 6.00 2.70
3 Garret Anderson/541 4.00 1.80
4 Albert Pujols/667 12.00 5.50
5 Sammy Sosa/553 10.00 4.50
6 Gary Sheffield/604 4.00 1.80
7 Manny Ramirez/587 4.00 1.80
8 Jim Edmonds/617 4.00 1.80
9 Barry Bonds/749 15.00 6.75
10 Todd Helton/630 4.00 1.80

2004 Donruss Recollection Autographs

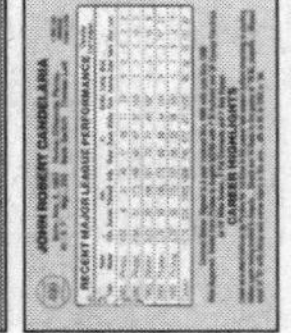

MINT NRMT
RANDOM INSERTS IN PACKS
PRINT RUNS B/WN 1-100 COPIES PER
NO PRICING ON QTY OF 50 OR LESS

27 John Candelaria 88 Black/83 15.00 6.75
39 Jack Clark 87/67 20.00 9.00
40 Jack Clark 88/75 15.00 6.75
69 Sid Fernandez 86/52 20.00 9.00
72 Sid Fernandez 88/58 20.00 9.00
83 George Foster 83/50 20.00 9.00
84 George Foster 84/70 20.00 9.00
85 George Foster 85/50 20.00 9.00
86 George Foster 86/83 15.00 6.75
91 Cliff Lee 03/100 10.00 4.50
92 Terrence Long 01/90 10.00 4.50
93 Melvin Mora 03/50 20.00 9.00
100 Jesse Orosco 86 Blue/65 12.00 5.50
102 Jesse Orosco 87 Blue/90 10.00 4.50
115 Jose Vidro 01/89 10.00 4.50

2004 Donruss Timber and Threads

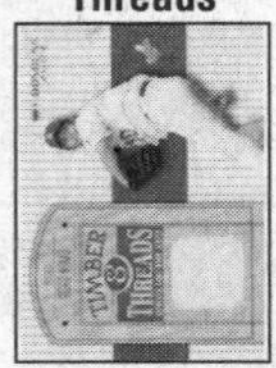

MINT NRMT
STATED ODDS 1:40
*STUDIO: .75X TO 2X BASIC TT
STUDIO RANDOM INSERTS IN PACKS
STUDIO PRINT RUN 50 SERIAL #'d SETS

1 Adam Dunn Jsy 10.00 4.50
2 Alex Rodriguez Blue Jsy 15.00 6.75
3 Alex Rodriguez White Jsy 15.00 6.75
4 Andruw Jones Jsy 8.00 3.60
5 Austin Kearns Jsy 8.00 3.60
6 Carlos Beltran Jsy 10.00 4.50
7 Carlos Lee Jsy 8.00 3.60
8 Frank Thomas Jsy 10.00 4.50
9 Greg Maddux Jsy 10.00 4.50
10 Hideo Nomo Jsy 10.00 4.50
11 Jeff Bagwell Jsy 10.00 4.50
12 Lance Berkman Jsy 8.00 3.60
13 Magglio Ordonez Jsy 8.00 3.60
14 Mike Sweeney Jsy 8.00 3.60
15 Randy Johnson Jsy 10.00 4.50
16 Rocco Baldelli Jsy 8.00 3.60
17 Roger Clemens Jsy 15.00 6.75
18 Sammy Sosa Jsy 15.00 6.75
19 Shawn Green Jsy 8.00 3.60
20 Tom Glavine Jsy 10.00 4.50
21 Adam Dunn Bat 10.00 4.50
22 Andruw Jones Bat 8.00 3.60
23 Bobby Abreu Bat 8.00 3.60
24 Hank Blalock Bat 8.00 3.60
25 Ivan Rodriguez Bat 10.00 4.50
26 Jim Edmonds Bat 8.00 3.60
27 Josh Phelps Bat 8.00 3.60
28 Juan Gonzalez Bat 10.00 4.50
29 Lance Berkman Bat 8.00 3.60
30 Larry Walker Bat 10.00 4.50
31 Magglio Ordonez Bat 8.00 3.60
32 Manny Ramirez Bat 10.00 4.50
33 Mike Piazza Bat 10.00 4.50
34 Nomar Garciaparra Bat 15.00 6.75
35 Paul Lo Duca Bat 8.00 3.60
36 Roberto Alomar Bat 10.00 4.50
37 Rocco Baldelli Bat 8.00 3.60
38 Sammy Sosa Bat 15.00 6.75
39 Vernon Wells Bat 8.00 3.60
40 Vladimir Guerrero Bat 10.00 4.50

2004 Donruss Timber and Threads Autographs

MINT NRMT
RANDOM INSERTS IN PACKS
PRINT RUNS B/WN 5-50 COPIES PER
NO PRICING ON QTY OF 34 OR LESS

2 Alex Rodriguez Blue Jsy/5
5 Austin Kearns Jsy/19
6 Carlos Beltran Jsy/34
7 Carlos Lee Jsy/25
8 Frank Thomas Jsy/5
9 Greg Maddux Jsy/5
10 Hideo Nomo Jsy/5
11 Jeff Bagwell Jsy/5
12 Lance Berkman Jsy/5
13 Magglio Ordonez Jsy/30
14 Mike Sweeney Jsy/25
17 Roger Clemens Jsy/5
19 Shawn Green Jsy/5
20 Tom Glavine Jsy/5
21 Adam Dunn Bat/5
22 Andruw Jones Bat/5
23 Bobby Abreu Bat/50 25.00 11.00
24 Hank Blalock Bat/50 25.00 11.00
25 Ivan Rodriguez Bat/7
26 Jim Edmonds Bat/5
27 Josh Phelps Bat/50 25.00 11.00
28 Juan Gonzalez Bat/5
31 Magglio Ordonez Bat/30
32 Manny Ramirez Bat/5
35 Paul Lo Duca Bat/50 25.00 11.00
36 Roberto Alomar Bat/10
37 Rocco Baldelli Bat/15
40 Vladimir Guerrero Bat/50 60.00 27.00

2005 Donruss

Nm-Mt Ex-Mt
COMPLETE SET (400) 150.00 45.00
COMP.SET w/o SP's (300) 25.00 7.50
COMMON CARD (71-3 .30 .09
COMMON (1-25/371-400) 2.00 .60
COMMON CARD (26-70) 2.00 .60
1-25 STATED ODDS 1:6
26-70 STATED ODDS 1:6
371-400 STATED ODDS 1:6

1 Garret Anderson DK 2.00 .60
2 Vladimir Guerrero DK 2.00 .60
3 Manny Ramirez DK 2.00 .60
4 Kerry Wood DK 2.00 .60
5 Sammy Sosa DK 3.00 .90
6 Magglio Ordonez DK 2.00 .60
7 Adam Dunn DK 2.00 .60
8 Todd Helton DK 2.00 .60
9 Josh Beckett DK 2.00 .60
10 Miguel Cabrera DK 2.00 .60
11 Lance Berkman DK 2.00 .60
12 Carlos Beltran DK 2.00 .60
13 Shawn Green DK 2.00 .60
14 Roger Clemens DK 4.00 1.20
15 Mike Piazza DK 3.00 .90
16 Alex Rodriguez DK 3.00 .90
17 Derek Jeter DK 4.00 1.20
18 Mark Mulder DK 2.00 .60
19 Jim Thome DK 2.00 .60
20 Albert Pujols DK 4.00 1.20
21 Scott Rolen DK 2.00 .60
22 Aubrey Huff DK 2.00 .60
23 Alfonso Soriano DK 2.00 .60
24 Hank Blalock DK 2.00 .60
25 Vernon Wells DK 2.00 .60
26 Kazuo Matsui RR 3.00 .90
27 B.J. Upton RR 3.00 .90
28 Charles Thomas RR 2.00 .60
29 Akinori Otsuka RR 3.00 .90
30 David Aardsma RR 2.00 .60
31 Travis Blackley RR 2.00 .60
32 Brad Halsey RR 2.00 .60
33 David Wright RR 8.00 2.40
34 Kazuhito Tadano RR 3.00 .90
35 Casey Kotchman RR 3.00 .90
36 Khalil Greene RR 5.00 1.50
37 Adrian Gonzalez RR 2.00 .60
38 Zack Greinke RR 3.00 .90
39 Chad Cordero RR 2.00 .60
40 Scott Kazmir RR 5.00 1.50
41 Jeremy Guthrie RR 2.00 .60
42 Noah Lowry RR 2.00 .60
43 Chase Utley RR 3.00 .90
44 Billy Traber RR 2.00 .60
45 Aarom Baldiris RR 2.00 .60
46 Abe Alvarez RR 2.00 .60
47 Angel Chavez RR 2.00 .60
48 Joe Mauer RR 5.00 1.50
49 Joey Gathright RR 3.00 .90
50 John Gall RR 2.00 .60
51 Ronald Belisario RR 2.00 .60
52 Ryan Wing RR 2.00 .60
53 Scott Proctor RR 2.00 .60
54 Yadier Molina RR 3.00 .90
55 Carlos Hines RR 2.00 .60
56 Frankie Francisco RR 2.00 .60
57 Graham Koonce RR 2.00 .60
58 Jake Woods RR 2.00 .60
59 Jason Bartlett RR 2.00 .60
60 Mike Rouse RR 2.00 .60
61 Phil Stockman RR 2.00 .60
62 Renyel Pinto RR 2.00 .60
63 Roberto Novoa RR 2.00 .60
64 Ryan Meaux RR 2.00 .60
65 Dave Crouthers RR 2.00 .60
66 Justin Knoedler RR 2.00 .60
67 Justin Leone RR 2.00 .60
68 Nick Regilio RR 2.00 .60
69 Mike Gosling RR 2.00 .60
70 Onil Joseph RR 2.00 .60
71 Bartolo Colon .30 .09
72 Brad Fullmer .30 .09
73 Chone Figgins .30 .09
74 Darin Erstad .30 .09
75 Francisco Rodriguez .30 .09
76 Garret Anderson .30 .09
77 Jarrod Washburn .30 .09
78 John Lackey .30 .09
79 Jose Guillen .30 .09
80 Robb Quinlan .30 .09
81 Tim Salmon .50 .15
82 Troy Glaus .30 .09
83 Troy Percival .30 .09
84 Vladimir Guerrero .75 .23
85 Brandon Webb .30 .09
86 Casey Fossum .30 .09
87 Luis Gonzalez .30 .09
88 Randy Johnson .75 .23
89 Richie Sexson .30 .09
90 Robby Hammock .30 .09
91 Roberto Alomar .50 .15
92 Adam LaRoche .30 .09
93 Andruw Jones .30 .09
94 Bubba Nelson .30 .09
95 Chipper Jones .75 .23
96 J.D. Drew .30 .09
97 John Smoltz .50 .15
98 Johnny Estrada .30 .09
99 Marcus Giles .30 .09
100 Mike Hampton .30 .09
101 Nick Green .30 .09
102 Rafael Furcal .30 .09
103 Russ Ortiz .30 .09
104 Adam Loewen .30 .09
105 Brian Roberts .30 .09
106 Javy Lopez .30 .09
107 Jay Gibbons .30 .09
108 Larry Bigbie .30 .09
109 Luis Matos .30 .09
110 Melvin Mora .30 .09
111 Miguel Tejada .30 .09
112 Rafael Palmeiro .50 .15
113 Rodrigo Lopez .30 .09
114 Sidney Ponson .30 .09
115 Bill Mueller .30 .09
116 Byung-Hyun Kim .30 .09
117 Curt Schilling .75 .23
118 David Ortiz .75 .23
119 Derek Lowe .30 .09
120 Doug Mientkiewicz .30 .09
121 Jason Varitek .50 .15
122 Johnny Damon .75 .23
123 Keith Foulke .30 .09
124 Kevin Youkilis .30 .09
125 Manny Ramirez .50 .15
126 Orlando Cabrera .30 .09
127 Pedro Martinez .75 .23
128 Trot Nixon .30 .09
129 Aramis Ramirez .30 .09
130 Carlos Zambrano .30 .09
131 Corey Patterson .30 .09
132 Derrek Lee .30 .09
133 Greg Maddux 1.25 .35
134 Kerry Wood .75 .23
135 Mark Prior .75 .23
136 Matt Clement .30 .09
137 Moises Alou .30 .09
138 Nomar Garciaparra 1.25 .35
139 Sammy Sosa 1.25 .35
140 Todd Walker .30 .09
141 Angel Guzman .30 .09
142 Billy Koch .30 .09
143 Carlos Lee .30 .09
144 Frank Thomas .75 .23
145 Magglio Ordonez .30 .09
146 Mark Buehrle .30 .09
147 Paul Konerko .30 .09
148 Wilson Valdez .30 .09
149 Adam Dunn .50 .15
150 Austin Kearns .30 .09
151 Barry Larkin .50 .15
152 Benito Santiago .30 .09
153 Jason LaRue .30 .09
154 Ken Griffey Jr. 1.25 .35
155 Ryan Wagner .30 .09
156 Sean Casey .30 .09
157 Brandon Phillips .30 .09
158 Brian Tallet .30 .09
159 C.C. Sabathia .30 .09
160 Cliff Lee .30 .09
161 Jeremy Guthrie .30 .09
162 Jody Gerut .30 .09
163 Matt Lawton .30 .09
164 Omar Vizquel .50 .15
165 Travis Hafner .30 .09
166 Victor Martinez .30 .09
167 Charles Johnson .30 .09
168 Garrett Atkins .30 .09
169 Jason Jennings .30 .09
170 Jay Payton .30 .09
171 Jeromy Burnitz .30 .09
172 Joe Kennedy .30 .09
173 Larry Walker .50 .15
174 Preston Wilson .30 .09
175 Todd Helton .50 .15
176 Vinny Castilla .30 .09
177 Bobby Higginson .30 .09
178 Brandon Inge .30 .09
179 Carlos Guillen .30 .09
180 Carlos Pena .30 .09
181 Craig Monroe .30 .09
182 Dmitri Young .30 .09
183 Eric Munson .30 .09
184 Fernando Vina .30 .09
185 Ivan Rodriguez .75 .23
186 Jeremy Bonderman .30 .09
187 Rondell White .30 .09
188 A.J. Burnett .30 .09
189 Dontrelle Willis .30 .09
190 Guillermo Mota .30 .09
191 Hee Seop Choi .30 .09
192 Jeff Conine .30 .09
193 Josh Beckett .30 .09
194 Juan Encarnacion .30 .09
195 Juan Pierre .30 .09
196 Luis Castillo .30 .09
197 Miguel Cabrera .50 .15
198 Mike Lowell .30 .09
199 Paul Lo Duca .30 .09
200 Andy Pettitte .50 .15
201 Brad Ausmus .30 .09
202 Carlos Beltran .50 .15
203 Chris Burke .30 .09
204 Craig Biggio .50 .15
205 Jeff Bagwell .50 .15
206 Jeff Kent .30 .09
207 Lance Berkman .30 .09
208 Morgan Ensberg .30 .09
209 Octavio Dotel .30 .09
210 Roger Clemens 1.50 .45
211 Roy Oswalt .30 .09
212 Tim Redding .30 .09
213 Angel Berroa .30 .09
214 Juan Gonzalez .50 .15
215 Ken Harvey .30 .09
216 Mike Sweeney .30 .09
217 Adrian Beltre .50 .15
218 Brad Penny .30 .09
219 Eric Gagne .75 .23
220 Hideo Nomo .75 .23
221 Hong-Chih Kuo .30 .09
222 Jeff Weaver .30 .09
223 Kazuhisa Ishii .30 .09
224 Milton Bradley .30 .09
225 Shawn Green .30 .09
226 Steve Finley .30 .09
227 Danny Kolb .30 .09
228 Geoff Jenkins .30 .09
229 Junior Spivey .30 .09
230 Lyle Overbay .30 .09
231 Rickie Weeks .30 .09
232 Scott Podsednik .30 .09
233 Brad Radke .30 .09
234 Corey Koskie .30 .09
235 Cristian Guzman .30 .09
236 Dustan Mohr .30 .09
237 Eddie Guardado .30 .09
238 J.D. Durbin .30 .09
239 Jacque Jones .30 .09
240 Joe Nathan .30 .09
241 Johan Santana .50 .15
242 Lew Ford .30 .09
243 Michael Cuddyer .30 .09
244 Shannon Stewart .30 .09
245 Torii Hunter .30 .09
246 Brad Wilkerson .30 .09
247 Carl Everett .30 .09
248 Jeff Fassero .30 .09
249 Jose Vidro .30 .09
250 Livan Hernandez .30 .09
251 Michael Barrett .30 .09
252 Tony Batista .30 .09
253 Zach Day .30 .09
254 Al Leiter .30 .09
255 Cliff Floyd .30 .09
256 Jae Weong Seo .30 .09
257 John Olerud .30 .09
258 Jose Reyes .30 .09
259 Mike Cameron .30 .09
260 Mike Piazza 1.25 .35
261 Richard Hidalgo .30 .09
262 Tom Glavine .50 .15
263 Vance Wilson .30 .09
264 Alex Rodriguez 1.25 .35
265 Armando Benitez .30 .09
266 Bernie Williams .50 .15
267 Bubba Crosby .30 .09
268 Chien-Ming Wang .30 .09
269 Derek Jeter 1.50 .45
270 Esteban Loaiza .30 .09
271 Gary Sheffield .30 .09
272 Hideki Matsui 1.25 .35
273 Jason Giambi .30 .09
274 Javier Vazquez .30 .09
275 Jorge Posada .50 .15
276 Jose Contreras .30 .09
277 Kenny Lofton .30 .09
278 Kevin Brown .30 .09
279 Mariano Rivera .50 .15
280 Mike Mussina .50 .15
281 Barry Zito .30 .09
282 Bobby Crosby .50 .15
283 Eric Byrnes .30 .09
284 Eric Chavez .30 .09
285 Erubiel Durazo .30 .09
286 Jermaine Dye .30 .09
287 Mark Kotsay .30 .09
288 Mark Mulder .30 .09
289 Rich Harden .30 .09
290 Tim Hudson .30 .09
291 Billy Wagner .30 .09
292 Bobby Abreu .30 .09
293 Brett Myers .30 .09
294 Eric Milton .30 .09
295 Jim Thome .75 .23
296 Jimmy Rollins .30 .09
297 Kevin Millwood .30 .09
298 Marlon Byrd .30 .09
299 Mike Lieberthal .30 .09
300 Pat Burrell .30 .09
301 Randy Wolf .30 .09
302 Craig Wilson .30 .09
303 Jack Wilson .30 .09
304 Jacob Cruz .30 .09
305 Jason Bay .30 .09
306 Jason Kendall .30 .09
307 Jose Castillo .30 .09
308 Kip Wells .30 .09
309 Brian Giles .30 .09
310 Brian Lawrence .30 .09
311 Chris Oxspring .30 .09
312 David Wells .30 .09
313 Freddy Guzman .30 .09
314 Jake Peavy .30 .09
315 Mark Loretta .30 .09
316 Ryan Klesko .30 .09
317 Sean Burroughs .30 .09
318 Trevor Hoffman .30 .09

319 Xavier Nady .30 .09
320 A.J. Pierzynski .30 .09
321 Edgardo Alfonzo .30 .09
322 J.T. Snow .30 .09
323 Jason Schmidt .30 .09
324 Jerome Williams .30 .09
325 Kirk Rueter .30 .09
326 Bret Boone .30 .09
327 Bucky Jacobsen .30 .09
328 Edgar Martinez .50 .15
329 Freddy Garcia .30 .09
330 Ichiro Suzuki 1.25 .35
331 Jamie Moyer .30 .09
332 Joel Pineiro .30 .09
333 Scott Spiezio .30 .09
334 Shigetoshi Hasegawa .30 .09
335 Albert Pujols 1.50 .45
336 Edgar Renteria .30 .09
337 Jason Isringhausen .30 .09
338 Jim Edmonds .30 .09
339 Matt Morris .30 .09
340 Mike Matheny .30 .09
341 Reggie Sanders .30 .09
342 Scott Rolen .75 .23
343 Woody Williams .30 .09
344 Jeff Suppan .30 .09
345 Aubrey Huff .30 .09
346 Carl Crawford .30 .09
347 Chad Gaudin .30 .09
348 Delmon Young .30 .09
349 Dewon Brazelton .30 .09
350 Jose Cruz Jr. .30 .09
351 Rocco Baldelli .30 .09
352 Tino Martinez .50 .15
353 Toby Hall .30 .09
354 Alfonso Soriano .50 .15
355 Brian Jordan .30 .09
356 Francisco Cordero .30 .09
357 Hank Blalock .30 .09
358 Kenny Rogers .30 .09
359 Kevin Mench .30 .09
360 Laynce Nix .30 .09
361 Mark Teixeira .30 .09
362 Michael Young .30 .09
363 Alex S. Gonzalez .30 .09
364 Alexis Rios .30 .09
365 Carlos Delgado .30 .09
366 Eric Hinske .30 .09
367 Frank Catalanotto .30 .09
368 Josh Phelps .30 .09
369 Roy Halladay .30 .09
370 Vernon Wells .30 .09
371 Vladimir Guerrero TC 2.00 .60
372 Randy Johnson TC 2.00 .60
373 Chipper Jones TC 2.00 .60
374 Miguel Tejada TC 2.00 .60
375 Pedro Martinez TC 2.00 .60
376 Sammy Sosa TC 3.00 .90
377 Frank Thomas TC 2.00 .60
378 Ken Griffey Jr. TC 3.00 .90
379 Victor Martinez TC 2.00 .60
380 Todd Helton TC 2.00 .60
381 Ivan Rodriguez TC 2.00 .60
382 Miguel Cabrera TC 2.00 .60
383 Roger Clemens TC 4.00 1.20
384 Ken Harvey TC 2.00 .60
385 Eric Gagne TC 2.00 .60
386 Lyle Overbay TC 2.00 .60
387 Shannon Stewart TC 2.00 .60
388 Brad Wilkerson TC 2.00 .60
389 Mike Piazza TC 3.00 .90
390 Alex Rodriguez TC 3.00 .90
391 Mark Mulder TC 2.00 .60
392 Jim Thome TC 2.00 .60
393 Jack Wilson TC 2.00 .60
394 Khalil Greene TC 2.00 .60
395 Jason Schmidt TC 2.00 .60
396 Ichiro Suzuki TC 3.00 .90
397 Albert Pujols TC 4.00 1.20
398 Rocco Baldelli TC 2.00 .60
399 Alfonso Soriano TC 2.00 .60
400 Vernon Wells TC 2.00 .60

2005 Donruss 25th Anniversary

Nm-Mt Ex-Mt
*25th ANN 71-370: 10X TO 25X BASIC
*25th ANN 1-25/371-400: 4X TO 10X BASIC
*25th ANN 26-70: 2X TO 5X BASIC
RANDOM INSERTS IN PACKS
STATED PRINT RUN 25 SERIAL #'d SETS

2005 Donruss Press Proofs Black

Nm-Mt Ex-Mt
RANDOM INSERTS IN PACKS
STATED PRINT RUN 10 SERIAL #'d SETS
NO PRICING DUE TO SCARCITY

2005 Donruss Press Proofs Blue

Nm-Mt Ex-Mt
*BLUE 71-370: 4X TO 10X BASIC
*BLUE 1-25/371-400: 1.5X TO 4X BASIC
*BLUE 26-70: .75X TO 2X BASIC
RANDOM INSERTS IN PACKS
STATED PRINT RUN 100 SERIAL #'d SETS

2005 Donruss Press Proofs Gold

Nm-Mt Ex-Mt
*GOLD 71-370: 10X TO 25X BASIC
*GOLD 1-25/371-400: 4X TO 10X BASIC
*GOLD 26-70: 2X TO 5X BASIC
RANDOM INSERTS IN PACKS
STATED PRINT RUN 25 SERIAL #'d SETS

2005 Donruss Press Proofs Red

Nm-Mt Ex-Mt
*RED 71-370: X TO X BASIC
*RED 1-25/371-400: 1X TO 2.5X BASIC
*RED 26-70: .5X TO 1.2X BASIC
RANDOM INSERTS IN PACKS
STATED PRINT RUN 200 SERIAL #'d SETS

2005 Donruss Stat Line Career

Nm-Mt Ex-Mt
*71-370 p/r 200-394 2.5X TO 6X
*71-370 p/r 121-200: 3X TO 8X
*71-370 p/r 81-120: 4X TO 10X
*71-370 p/r 51-80: 5X TO 12X
*71-370 p/r 36-50: 6X TO 15X
*71-370 p/r 26-35: 8X TO 20X
*71-370 p/r 16-25: 10X TO 25X
*1-25/371-400 p/r 200-574:1X TO 2.5X
*1-25/371-400 p/r 121-200: 1.25X TO 3X
*1-25/371-400 p/r 81-120: 1.5X TO 4X
*1-25/371-400 p/r 51-80: 2X TO 5X
*1-25/371-400 p/r 36-50: 2.5X TO 6X
*1-25/371-400 p/r 26-35: 3X TO 8X
*26-70 p/r 200-263: .5X TO 1.2X
*26-70 p/r 121-200: .6X TO 1.5X
*26-70 p/r 81-120: .75X TO 2X
*26-70 p/r 51-80: 1X TO 2.5X
*26-70 p/r 36-50: 1.25X TO 3X
*26-70 p/r 26-35: 1.5X TO 4X
*26-70 p/r 16-25: 2X TO 5X
RANDOM INSERTS IN PACKS
PRINT RUNS B/WN 6-500 COPIES PER
NO PRICING ON QTY OF 15 OR LESS

2005 Donruss Stat Line Season

Nm-Mt Ex-Mt
*71-370 p/r 121-158: 3X TO 8X
*71-370 p/r 81-120: 4X TO 10X
*71-370 p/r 51-80: 5X TO 12X
*71-370 p/r 36-50: 6X TO 15X
*71-370 p/r 26-35: 8X TO 20X
*71-370 p/r 16-25: 10X TO 25X
*1-25/371-400 p/r 81-120: 1.5X TO 4X
*1-25/371-400 p/r 51-80: 2X TO 5X
*1-25/371-400 p/r 36-50: 2.5X TO 6X
*1-25/371-400 p/r 26-35: 3X TO 8X
*1-25/371-400 p/r 16-25: 4X TO 10X
*26-70 p/r 121-200: .6X TO 1.5X
*26-70 p/r 81-120: .75X TO 2X
*26-70 p/r 51-80: 1X TO 2.5X
*26-70 p/r 36-50: 1.25X TO 3X
*26-70 p/r 26-35: 1.5X TO 4X
*26-70 p/r 16-25: 2X TO 5X
RANDOM INSERTS IN PACKS
PRINT RUNS B/WN 1-158 COPIES PER
NO PRICING ON QTY OF 15 OR LESS

2005 Donruss Autographs

Nm-Mt Ex-Mt
RANDOM INSERTS IN PACKS
NO PRICING DUE TO SCARCITY

2005 Donruss '85 Reprints

Nm-Mt Ex-Mt
RANDOM INSERTS IN PACKS
STATED PRINT RUN 1985 SERIAL #'d SETS
1 Eddie Murray 5.00 1.50
2 George Brett 8.00 2.40
3 Nolan Ryan 10.00 3.00
4 Mike Schmidt 8.00 2.40
5 Tony Gwynn 5.00 1.50
7 Cal Ripken 12.00 3.60
8 Dwight Gooden 3.00 .90
9 Roger Clemens 8.00 2.40
10 Don Mattingly 8.00 2.40
11 Kirby Puckett 5.00 1.50
12 Orel Hershiser 3.00 .90

2005 Donruss '85 Reprints Material

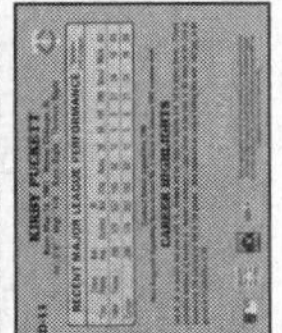

Nm-Mt Ex-Mt
RANDOM INSERTS IN PACKS
STATED PRINT RUN 85 SERIAL #'d SETS
1 Eddie Murray Jsy 25.00 7.50
2 George Brett Jsy 40.00 12.00
3 Nolan Ryan Jkt 40.00 12.00
4 Mike Schmidt Jkt 40.00 12.00
5 Tony Gwynn Jsy 25.00 7.50
7 Cal Ripken Jsy 60.00 18.00
8 Dwight Gooden Jsy
9 Roger Clemens Jsy 40.00 12.00
10 Don Mattingly Jsy 40.00 12.00
11 Kirby Puckett Jsy 25.00 7.50
12 Orel Hershiser Jsy 15.00 4.50

2005 Donruss All-Stars NL

Nm-Mt Ex-Mt
STATED PRINT RUN 1000 SERIAL #'d SETS
*GOLD: .75X TO 2X BASIC
GOLD PRINT RUN 100 SERIAL #'d SETS

RANDOM INSERTS IN PACKS
1 Albert Pujols 10.00 3.00
2 Ben Sheets 3.00 .90
3 Edgar Renteria 3.00 .90
4 Eric Gagne 5.00 1.50
5 Jack Wilson 3.00 .90
6 Jason Schmidt 3.00 .90
7 Jeff Kent 3.00 .90
8 Jim Thome 5.00 1.50
9 Ken Griffey Jr. 8.00 2.40
10 Mike Piazza 8.00 2.40
11 Roger Clemens 10.00 3.00
12 Sammy Sosa 8.00 2.40
13 Scott Rolen 5.00 1.50
14 Sean Casey 3.00 .90
15 Todd Helton 5.00 1.50

2005 Donruss Bat Kings

Nm-Mt Ex-Mt
RANDOM INSERTS IN PACKS
PRINT RUNS B/WN 100-250 COPIES PER
1 Garret Anderson/250 8.00 2.40
2 Vladimir Guerrero/250 10.00 3.00
3 Cal Ripken/100 60.00 18.00
4 Manny Ramirez/250 10.00 3.00
5 Kerry Wood/250 10.00 3.00
6 Sammy Sosa/250 15.00 4.50
7 Magglio Ordonez/250 8.00 2.40
8 Adam Dunn/250 10.00 3.00
9 Todd Helton/250 10.00 3.00
10 Josh Beckett/250 8.00 2.40
11 Miguel Cabrera/250 10.00 3.00
12 Lance Berkman/250 8.00 2.40
13 Carlos Beltran/250 10.00 3.00
14 Shawn Green/250 8.00 2.40
15 Roger Clemens/100 20.00 6.00
16 Mike Piazza/250 15.00 4.50
17 Nolan Ryan/100 50.00 15.00
18 Mark Mulder/250 8.00 2.40
19 Jim Thome/250 10.00 3.00
20 Albert Pujols/250 20.00 6.00
21 Scott Rolen/250 10.00 3.00
22 Aubrey Huff/250 8.00 2.40
23 Alfonso Soriano/250 10.00 3.00

2005 Donruss Bat Kings Signatures

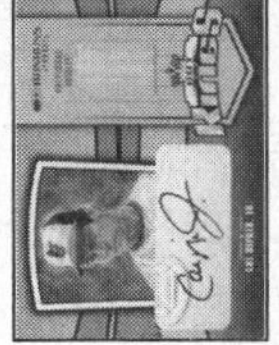

Nm-Mt Ex-Mt
RANDOM INSERTS IN PACKS
PRINT RUNS B/WN 5-10 COPIES PER
NO PRICING DUE TO SCARCITY

2005 Donruss Craftsmen

Nm-Mt Ex-Mt
STATED PRINT RUN 1000 SERIAL #'d SETS
*BLACK: 1.25X TO 3X BASIC
BLACK PRINT RUN 100 SERIAL #'d SETS
*MASTER: 1X TO 2.5X BASIC
MASTER PRINT RUN 250 SERIAL #'d SETS
MASTER BLACK PRINT RUN 10 #'d SETS
NO MASTER BLACK PRICING AVAILABLE
RANDOM INSERTS IN PACKS
1 Albert Pujols 6.00 1.80
2 Alex Rodriguez 5.00 1.50
3 Alfonso Soriano 3.00 .90
4 Andruw Jones 2.00 .60
5 Carlos Beltran 3.00 .90
6 Derek Jeter 6.00 1.80
7 Greg Maddux 5.00 1.50
8 Hank Blalock 2.00 .60
9 Ichiro Suzuki 5.00 1.50
10 Jeff Bagwell 3.00 .90
11 Jim Thome 3.00 .90
12 Josh Beckett 2.00 .60
13 Ken Griffey Jr. 5.00 1.50
14 Manny Ramirez 3.00 .90
15 Mark Mulder 2.00 .60
16 Mark Prior 3.00 .90
17 Mark Teixeira 2.00 .60
18 Miguel Tejada 2.00 .60
19 Mike Mussina 3.00 .90
20 Mike Piazza 5.00 1.50
21 Nomar Garciaparra 5.00 1.50
22 Pedro Martinez 3.00 .90
23 Rafael Palmeiro 3.00 .90
24 Randy Johnson 3.00 .90
25 Roger Clemens 6.00 1.80
26 Sammy Sosa 5.00 1.50
27 Scott Rolen 3.00 .90
28 Tim Hudson 2.00 .60
29 Vernon Wells 2.00 .60
30 Vladimir Guerrero 3.00 .90

2005 Donruss Diamond Kings Inserts

Nm-Mt Ex-Mt
STATED PRINT RUN 2005 SERIAL #'d SETS
*STUDIO: 1X TO 2.5X BASIC
STUDIO PRINT RUN 250 SERIAL #'d SETS
*STUDIO BLACK: 1.25X TO 3X BASIC
STUDIO BLACK PRINT RUN 100 #'d SETS
RANDOM INSERTS IN PACKS
1 Garret Anderson 2.00 .60
2 Vladimir Guerrero 3.00 .90
3 Manny Ramirez 3.00 .90
4 Kerry Wood 3.00 .90
5 Sammy Sosa 5.00 1.50
6 Magglio Ordonez 2.00 .60
7 Adam Dunn 3.00 .90
8 Todd Helton 3.00 .90
9 Josh Beckett 2.00 .60
10 Miguel Cabrera 3.00 .90
11 Lance Berkman 2.00 .60
12 Carlos Beltran 3.00 .90
13 Shawn Green 2.00 .60
14 Roger Clemens 6.00 1.80
15 Mike Piazza 5.00 1.50
16 Alex Rodriguez 5.00 1.50
17 Derek Jeter 6.00 1.80
18 Mark Mulder 2.00 .60
19 Jim Thome 3.00 .90
20 Albert Pujols 6.00 1.80
21 Scott Rolen 3.00 .90
22 Aubrey Huff 2.00 .60
23 Alfonso Soriano 3.00 .90
24 Hank Blalock 2.00 .60
25 Vernon Wells 2.00 .60

2005 Donruss Elite Series

Nm-Mt Ex-Mt
STATED PRINT RUN 1500 SERIAL #'d SETS
*BLACK: .75X TO 2X BASIC
BLACK PRINT RUN 100 SERIAL #'d SETS
*DOMINATOR: .6X TO 1.5X BASIC
DOMINATOR PRINT RUN 250 #'d SETS
*DOM.BLACK: 1.5X TO 4X BASIC
DOM.BLACK PRINT RUN 25 #'d SETS
RANDOM INSERTS IN PACKS
1 Albert Pujols 10.00 3.00
2 Alex Rodriguez 8.00 2.40
3 Alfonso Soriano 5.00 1.50
4 Derek Jeter 10.00 3.00
5 Hank Blalock 3.00 .90
6 Ichiro Suzuki 8.00 2.40
7 Ivan Rodriguez 5.00 1.50
8 Jim Thome 5.00 1.50
9 Ken Griffey Jr. 8.00 2.40
10 Manny Ramirez 5.00 1.50
11 Mark Mulder 3.00 .90
12 Mark Prior 5.00 1.50
13 Michael Young 3.00 .90
14 Miguel Cabrera 5.00 1.50
15 Miguel Tejada 3.00 .90
16 Mike Piazza 8.00 2.40
17 Nomar Garciaparra 8.00 2.40
18 Rafael Palmeiro 5.00 1.50
19 Randy Johnson 5.00 1.50
20 Roger Clemens 10.00 3.00
21 Sammy Sosa 8.00 2.40
22 Scott Rolen 5.00 1.50
23 Tim Hudson 3.00 .90
24 Todd Helton 5.00 1.50
25 Vladimir Guerrero 5.00 1.50

2005 Donruss Fans of the Game

Nm-Mt Ex-Mt
COMPLETE SET (5) 10.00 3.00
RANDOM INSERTS IN PACKS
1 Jesse Ventura 3.00 .90
2 John C. McGinley 2.00 .60
3 Susie Essman 2.00 .60
4 Dean Cain 2.00 .60
5 Meat Loaf 3.00 .90

2005 Donruss Fans of the Game Signatures

Nm-Mt Ex-Mt
RANDOM INSERTS IN PACKS
1 Jesse Ventura 60.00 18.00
2 John C. McGinley 60.00 18.00
3 Susie Essman SP
4 Dean Cain SP
5 Meat Loaf 60.00 18.00

2005 Donruss Inside View

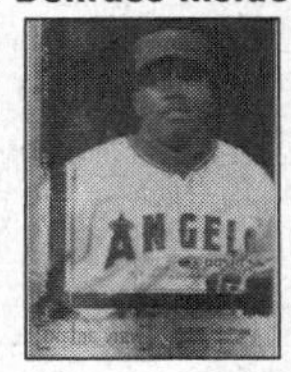

Nm-Mt Ex-Mt
RANDOM INSERTS IN PACKS
NO PRICING DUE TO SCARCITY
NOT INTENDED FOR PUBLIC RELEASE
1 Alex Rodriguez
2 Austin Kearns
3 Barry Larkin
4 C.C. Sabathia
5 Carlos Delgado
6 Chipper Jones
7 Craig Biggio
8 Derek Jeter
9 Derrek Lee
10 Edgar Martinez
11 Garret Anderson
12 Hideo Nomo
13 Ichiro Suzuki
14 Javier Vazquez
15 Javy Lopez
16 Ken Griffey Jr.
17 Magglio Ordonez
18 Rafael Palmeiro
19 Rocco Baldelli
20 Torii Hunter

2005 Donruss Jersey Kings

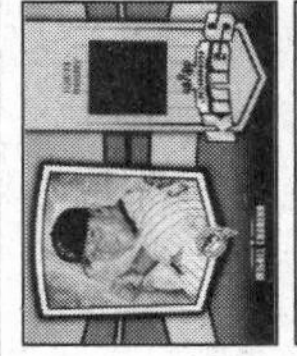

Nm-Mt Ex-Mt
RANDOM INSERTS IN PACKS
PRINT RUNS B/WN 100-250 COPIES PER
1 Garret Anderson/250 8.00 2.40
2 Vladimir Guerrero/250 10.00 3.00
3 Cal Ripken/100 60.00 18.00
4 Manny Ramirez/250 10.00 3.00
5 Kerry Wood/250 10.00 3.00
6 Sammy Sosa/250 15.00 4.50
7 Magglio Ordonez/250 8.00 2.40
8 Adam Dunn/250 10.00 3.00
9 Todd Helton/250 10.00 3.00
10 Josh Beckett/250 8.00 2.40
11 Miguel Cabrera/250 10.00 3.00
12 Lance Berkman/250 8.00 2.40
13 Carlos Beltran/250 10.00 3.00
14 Shawn Green/250 8.00 2.40
15 Roger Clemens/250 15.00 4.50
16 Mike Piazza/250 15.00 4.50
17 Nolan Ryan/100 50.00 15.00
18 Mark Mulder/250 8.00 2.40
19 Jim Thome/250 10.00 3.00
20 Albert Pujols/250 20.00 6.00
21 Scott Rolen/250 10.00 3.00
22 Aubrey Huff/250 8.00 2.40
23 Alfonso Soriano/250 10.00 3.00
24 Hank Blalock/250 8.00 2.40
25 Vernon Wells/250 8.00 2.40

2005 Donruss Jersey Kings Signatures

Nm-Mt Ex-Mt
RANDOM INSERTS IN PACKS

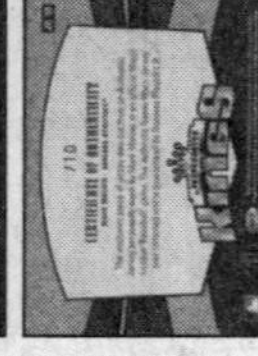

PRINT RUNS B/WN 5-10 COPIES PER
NO PRICING DUE TO SCARCITY

2005 Donruss Longball Leaders

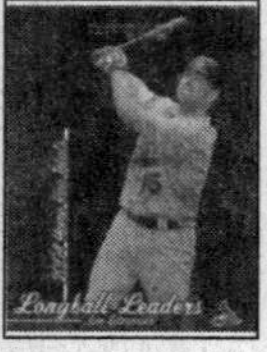

Nm-Mt Ex-Mt
STATED PRINT RUN 1500 SERIAL #'d SETS
*BLACK: .75X TO 2X BASIC
BLACK PRINT RUN 250 SERIAL #'d SETS
*DIE CUT: 1.25X TO 3X BASIC
DIE CUT PRINT RUN 50 SERIAL #'d SETS
BLACK DC PRINT RUN 10 SERIAL #'d SETS
NO BLACK DC PRICING DUE TO SCARCITY
RANDOM INSERTS IN PACKS
1 Adam Dunn 4.00 1.20
2 Adrian Beltre 4.00 1.20
3 Albert Pujols 8.00 2.40
4 Alex Rodriguez 6.00 1.80
5 David Ortiz 4.00 1.20
6 Hank Blalock 2.50 .75
7 J.D. Drew 2.50 .75
8 Jeromy Burnitz 2.50 .75
9 Jim Edmonds 2.50 .75
10 Jim Thome 4.00 1.20
11 Manny Ramirez 4.00 1.20
12 Mark Teixeira 2.50 .75
13 Moises Alou 2.50 .75
14 Paul Konerko 2.50 .75
15 Steve Finley 2.50 .75

2005 Donruss Mound Marvels

Nm-Mt Ex-Mt
STATED PRINT RUN 1000 SERIAL #'d SETS
BLACK PRINT RUN 10 SERIAL #'d SETS
NO BLACK PRICING DUE TO SCARCITY
RANDOM INSERTS IN PACKS
1 Curt Schilling 5.00 1.50
2 Dontrelle Willis 3.00 .90
3 Eric Gagne 5.00 1.50
4 Greg Maddux 8.00 2.40
5 John Smoltz 5.00 1.50
6 Kenny Rogers 3.00 .90
7 Kerry Wood 5.00 1.50
8 Mariano Rivera 5.00 1.50
9 Mark Mulder 3.00 .90
10 Mark Prior 5.00 1.50
11 Mike Mussina 5.00 1.50
12 Pedro Martinez 5.00 1.50
13 Randy Johnson 5.00 1.50
14 Roger Clemens 10.00 3.00
15 Tim Hudson 3.00 .90

2005 Donruss Power Alley Red

Nm-Mt Ex-Mt
STATED PRINT RUN 2500 SERIAL #'d SETS
BLACK PRINT RUN 10 SERIAL #'d SETS
NO BLACK PRICING DUE TO SCARCITY
BLACK DC PRINT RUN 5 SERIAL #'d SETS
NO BLACK DC PRICING DUE TO SCARCITY
*BLUE: .6X TO 1.5X RED
BLUE PRINT RUN 1000 SERIAL #'d SETS
*BLUE DC: 1.25X TO 3X RED
BLUE DC PRINT RUN 100 SERIAL #'d SETS
*GREEN: 2.5X TO 6X RED
GREEN PRINT RUN 25 SERIAL #'d SETS
GREEN DC PRINT RUN 10 SERIAL #'d SETS
NO GREEN DC PRICING DUE TO SCARCITY
*PURPLE: 1X TO 2.5X RED
PURPLE PRINT RUN 250 SERIAL #'d SETS
*PURPLE DC: 1.5X TO 4X RED
PURPLE DC PRINT RUN 50 SERIAL #'d SETS
*RED DC: 1X TO 2.5X RED
RED DC PRINT RUN 250 SERIAL #'d SETS
*YELLOW: 1.25X TO 3X RED
YELLOW PRINT RUN 100 SERIAL #'d SETS
*YELLOW DC: 2.5X TO 6X RED
YELLOW DC PRINT RUN 25 #'d SETS
RANDOM INSERTS IN PACKS
1 Adam Dunn 3.00 .90
2 Adrian Beltre 3.00 .90
3 Albert Pujols 6.00 1.80
4 Alex Rodriguez 5.00 1.50
5 Alfonso Soriano 3.00 .90
6 Gary Sheffield 2.00 .60
7 Hank Blalock 2.00 .60
8 Hideki Matsui 5.00 1.50
9 J.D. Drew 2.00 .60
10 Jeromy Burnitz 2.00 .60
11 Jim Edmonds 2.00 .60
12 Jim Thome 3.00 .90
13 Ken Griffey Jr. 5.00 1.50
14 Manny Ramirez 3.00 .90
15 Mark Teixeira 2.00 .60
16 Miguel Cabrera 3.00 .90
17 Miguel Tejada 2.00 .60
18 Mike Lowell 2.00 .60
19 Mike Piazza 5.00 1.50
20 Moises Alou 2.00 .60
21 Paul Konerko 2.00 .60
22 Sammy Sosa 5.00 1.50
23 Scott Rolen 3.00 .90
24 Todd Helton 3.00 .90
25 Vladimir Guerrero 3.00 .90

2005 Donruss Production Line BA

Nm-Mt Ex-Mt
PRINT RUNS B/WN 324-372 COPIES PER
*BLACK: 1X TO 2.5X BASIC PL
BLACK PRINT RUN 25 SERIAL #'d SETS
*DIE CUT: .5X TO 1.2X BASIC PL
DIE CUT PRINT RUN 100 SERIAL #'d SETS
BLACK DC PRINT RUN 10 SERIAL #'d SETS
NO BLACK DC PRICING DUE TO SCARCITY
RANDOM INSERTS IN PACKS
1 Ichiro Suzuki/372 12.00 3.60
2 Ivan Rodriguez/334 8.00 2.40
3 Juan Pierre/326 5.00 1.50
4 Adrian Beltre/334 8.00 2.40
5 Albert Pujols/331 15.00 4.50
6 Mark Loretta/335 5.00 1.50
7 Melvin Mora/340 5.00 1.50
8 Sean Casey/324 5.00 1.50
9 Todd Helton/347 8.00 2.40
10 Vladimir Guerrero/337 8.00 2.40

2005 Donruss Production Line OBP

Nm-Mt Ex-Mt
PRINT RUNS B/WN 397-469 COPIES PER
*BLACK: 1.25X TO 3X BASIC PL
BLACK PRINT RUN 25 SERIAL #'d SETS
*DIE CUT: .6X TO 1.5X BASIC PL
DIE CUT PRINT RUN 100 SERIAL #'d SETS
BLACK DC PRINT RUN 10 SERIAL #'d SETS
NO BLACK DC PRICING DUE TO SCARCITY
RANDOM INSERTS IN PACKS
1 Albert Pujols/415 12.00 3.60
2 Bobby Abreu/428 4.00 1.20
3 Lance Berkman/450 4.00 1.20
4 J.D. Drew/436 4.00 1.20
5 Jorge Posada/400 6.00 1.80
6 Ichiro Suzuki/414 10.00 3.00
7 Manny Ramirez/397 6.00 1.80
8 Melvin Mora/419 4.00 1.20
9 Todd Helton/469 6.00 1.80
10 Travis Hafner/410 4.00 1.20

2005 Donruss Production Line OPS

Nm-Mt Ex-Mt
PRINT RUNS B/WN 977-1088 COPIES PER
*BLACK: 1X TO 2.5X BASIC PL
BLACK PRINT RUN 50 SERIAL #'d SETS
*DIE CUT: .75X TO 2X BASIC PL
DIE CUT PRINT RUN 100 SERIAL #'d SETS
*BLACK DC: 1.5X TO 4X BASIC PL
BLACK DC PRINT RUN 25 SERIAL #'d SETS
RANDOM INSERTS IN PACKS
1 Albert Pujols/1072 10.00 3.00
2 David Ortiz/983 5.00 1.50
3 Adrian Beltre/1017 5.00 1.50
4 J.D. Drew/1006 3.00 .90
5 Jim Thome/977 5.00 1.50
6 Lance Berkman/1016 3.00 .90
7 Manny Ramirez/1009 5.00 1.50
8 Scott Rolen/1007 5.00 1.50
9 Todd Helton/1088 5.00 1.50
10 Travis Hafner/993 3.00 .90

2005 Donruss Production Line Slugging

Nm-Mt Ex-Mt
PRINT RUNS B/WN 569-657 COPIES PER
*BLACK: .75X TO 2X BASIC PL
BLACK PRINT RUN 50 SERIAL #'d SETS
*DIE CUT: .6X TO 1.5X BASIC PL
DIE CUT PRINT RUN 100 SERIAL #'d SETS
*BLACK DC: 1.2X TO 3X BASIC PL
BLACK DC PRINT RUN 25 SERIAL #'d SETS
RANDOM INSERTS IN PACKS
1 Adrian Beltre/629 6.00 1.80
2 Albert Pujols/657 12.00 3.60
3 Todd Helton/620 6.00 1.80
4 J.D. Drew/569 4.00 1.20
5 Jim Edmonds/643 4.00 1.20
6 Jim Thome/581 6.00 1.80
7 Vladimir Guerrero/598 6.00 1.80
8 Manny Ramirez/613 6.00 1.80
9 Scott Rolen/598 6.00 1.80
10 Travis Hafner/583 4.00 1.20

2005 Donruss Recollection Autographs

Nm-Mt Ex-Mt
RANDOM INSERTS IN PACKS
PRINT RUNS B/WN 1-5 COPIES PER
NO PRICING DUE TO SCARCITY

2005 Donruss Rookies

Nm-Mt Ex-Mt
STATED ODDS 1:23
BLACK PRINT RUN 10 SERIAL #'d SETS
NO BLACK PRICING DUE TO SCARCITY
*BLUE: .5X TO 1.2X BASIC
BLUE PRINT RUN 100 SERIAL #'d SETS
*GOLD: 1.25X TO 3X BASIC
GOLD PRINT RUN 25 SERIAL #'d SETS
*RED: .4X TO 1X BASIC
RED PRINT RUN 200 SERIAL #'d SETS
PARALLELS RANDOM INSERTS IN PACKS
1 Fernando Nieve 3.00 .90
2 Frankie Francisco 3.00 .90
3 Jorge Vasquez 3.00 .90
4 Travis Blackley 3.00 .90
5 Joey Gathright 5.00 1.50
6 Kazuhito Tadano 5.00 1.50
7 Edwin Moreno 3.00 .90
8 Lance Cormier 3.00 .90
9 Justin Knoedler 3.00 .90
10 Orlando Rodriguez 3.00 .90
11 Renyel Pinto 3.00 .90
12 Justin Leone 3.00 .90
13 Dennis Sarfate 3.00 .90
14 Sam Narron 3.00 .90
15 Yadier Molina 5.00 1.50
16 Carlos Vasquez 3.00 .90
17 Ryan Wing 3.00 .90
18 Brad Halsey 3.00 .90
19 Ryan Meaux 3.00 .90
20 Michael Wuertz 3.00 .90
21 Shawn Camp 3.00 .90
22 Ruddy Yan 3.00 .90
23 Don Kelly 3.00 .90
24 Jake Woods 3.00 .90
25 Colby Miller 3.00 .90
26 Abe Alvarez 3.00 .90
27 Mike Rouse 3.00 .90
28 Phil Stockman 3.00 .90
29 Kevin Cave 3.00 .90
30 Chris Shelton 5.00 1.50
31 Tim Bittner 3.00 .90
32 Mariano Gomez 3.00 .90
33 Angel Chavez 3.00 .90
34 Carlos Hines 3.00 .90
35 Aarom Baldiris 3.00 .90
36 Kazuo Matsui 5.00 1.50
37 Nick Regilio 3.00 .90
38 Ivan Ochoa 3.00 .90
39 Graham Koonce 3.00 .90
40 Merkin Valdez 5.00 1.50
41 Greg Dobbs 3.00 .90
42 Chris Oxspring 3.00 .90
43 Dave Crouthers 3.00 .90
44 Freddy Guzman 3.00 .90
45 Akinori Otsuka 5.00 1.50
46 Jesse Crain 3.00 .90
47 Casey Daigle 3.00 .90
48 Roberto Novoa 3.00 .90
49 Eddy Rodriguez 3.00 .90
50 Jason Bartlett 3.00 .90

2005 Donruss Rookies Stat Line Career

Nm-Mt Ex-Mt
*SLC p/r 201-316: .4X TO 1X
*SLC p/r 121-200: .4X TO 1X
*SLC p/r 81-120: .5X TO 1.2X
*SLC p/r 51-80: .6X TO 1.5X
*SLC p/r 36-50: .75X TO 2X
*SLC p/r 26-35: 1X TO 2.5X
*SLC p/r 16-25: 1.25X TO 3X
RANDOM INSERTS IN DLP R/T PACKS
PRINT RUNS B/WN 1-316 COPIES PER
NO PRICING ON QTY OF 15 OR LESS

2005 Donruss Rookies Stat Line Season

Nm-Mt Ex-Mt
*SLS p/r 121-200: .4X TO 1X
*SLS p/r 81-120: .5X TO 1.2X
*SLS p/r 51-80: .6X TO 1.5X
*SLS p/r 36-50: .75X TO 2X
*SLS p/r 26-35: 1X TO 2.5X
*SLS p/r 16-25: 1.25X TO 3X
RANDOM INSERTS IN DLP R/T PACKS
PRINT RUNS B/WN 1-188 COPIES PER
NO PRICING ON QTY OF 15 OR LESS

2005 Donruss Rookies Autographs

Nm-Mt Ex-Mt
COMMON SP 10.00 3.00
RANDOM INSERTS IN PACKS
6/12/14/21/36/40-41/44-47 DO NOT EXIST
SP INFO PROVIDED BY DONRUSS
1 Fernando Nieve 8.00 2.40
2 Frankie Francisco 8.00 2.40
3 Jorge Vasquez 8.00 2.40
4 Travis Blackley 8.00 2.40
5 Joey Gathright 10.00 3.00
7 Edwin Moreno 8.00 2.40
8 Lance Cormier 8.00 2.40
9 Justin Knoedler 8.00 2.40
10 Orlando Rodriguez 8.00 2.40
11 Renyel Pinto 8.00 2.40
13 Dennis Sarfate 8.00 2.40
15 Yadier Molina 10.00 3.00
16 Carlos Vasquez
17 Ryan Wing SP 10.00 3.00
18 Brad Halsey 10.00 3.00
19 Ryan Meaux 8.00 2.40
20 Michael Wuertz 8.00 2.40
22 Ruddy Yan 8.00 2.40
23 Don Kelly 8.00 2.40
24 Jake Woods 8.00 2.40
25 Colby Miller 8.00 2.40
26 Abe Alvarez 10.00 3.00
27 Mike Rouse SP 10.00 3.00
28 Phil Stockman 8.00 2.40
29 Kevin Cave 8.00 2.40
30 Chris Shelton SP 15.00 4.50
31 Tim Bittner 8.00 2.40
32 Mariano Gomez 8.00 2.40
33 Angel Chavez 8.00 2.40
34 Carlos Hines 8.00 2.40
35 Aarom Baldiris 8.00 2.40
37 Nick Regilio 8.00 2.40
38 Ivan Ochoa 8.00 2.40
39 Graham Koonce 8.00 2.40
42 Chris Oxspring 8.00 2.40
43 Dave Crouthers 8.00 2.40
48 Roberto Novoa 8.00 2.40
49 Eddy Rodriguez 8.00 2.40
50 Jason Bartlett 8.00 2.40

2005 Donruss Timber and Threads Bat

Nm-Mt Ex-Mt
RANDOM INSERTS IN PACKS
1 Albert Pujols 15.00 4.50
2 Alfonso Soriano 10.00 3.00
3 Andre Dawson 8.00 2.40
4 Austin Kearns 8.00 2.40
5 Brad Penny 8.00 2.40
6 Carlos Beltran 10.00 3.00
7 Carlos Lee 8.00 2.40
8 Chipper Jones 10.00 3.00
9 Dale Murphy 10.00 3.00
10 Don Mattingly 20.00 6.00
11 Frank Thomas 10.00 3.00
12 Garret Anderson 8.00 2.40
13 Gary Carter 8.00 2.40
14 Hank Blalock 8.00 2.40
15 Jacque Jones 8.00 2.40
17 Jay Gibbons 8.00 2.40
18 Jeff Bagwell 10.00 3.00
20 Jermaine Dye 8.00 2.40
21 Jim Thome 10.00 3.00
22 Jose Vidro 8.00 2.40
23 Lance Berkman 8.00 2.40
24 Laynce Nix 8.00 2.40
25 Magglio Ordonez 8.00 2.40
26 Marcus Giles 8.00 2.40
27 Mark Prior 10.00 3.00
28 Mark Teixeira 8.00 2.40
29 Melvin Mora 8.00 2.40
30 Michael Young 8.00 2.40
31 Miguel Cabrera 10.00 3.00
32 Mike Lowell 8.00 2.40
33 Roy Oswalt 8.00 2.40
34 Sammy Sosa 10.00 3.00
35 Scott Rolen 10.00 3.00
36 Sean Burroughs 8.00 2.40
37 Sean Casey 8.00 2.40
38 Shannon Stewart 8.00 2.40
39 Torii Hunter 8.00 2.40
40 Travis Hafner 8.00 2.40

2005 Donruss Timber and Threads Bat Signature

Nm-Mt Ex-Mt
RANDOM INSERTS IN PACKS
PRINT RUNS B/WN 5-10 COPIES PER
NO PRICING DUE TO SCARCITY

2005 Donruss Timber and Threads Combo

Nm-Mt Ex-Mt
*COMBO: .6X TO 1.5X BAT
RANDOM INSERTS IN PACKS

2005 Donruss Timber and Threads Combo Signature

Nm-Mt Ex-Mt
RANDOM INSERTS IN PACKS
PRINT RUNS B/WN 5-10 COPIES PER
NO PRICING DUE TO SCARCITY

2005 Donruss Timber and Threads Jersey

Nm-Mt Ex-Mt
*JSY: .4X TO 1X BAT
RANDOM INSERTS IN PACKS
19 Jeremy Bonderman 8.00 2.40

2005 Donruss Timber and Threads Jersey Signature

Nm-Mt Ex-Mt
RANDOM INSERTS IN PACKS
PRINT RUNS B/WN 5-10 COPIES PER
NO PRICING DUE TO SCARCITY

2001 Donruss Baseball's Best Bronze

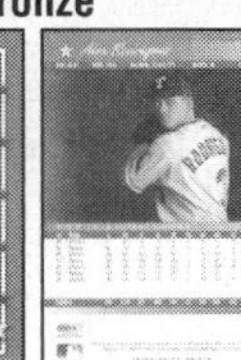

hese 220 cards were available via a coupon andomly seeded into 2001 Donruss baseball acks at stated odds of 1:720. Consumers that ulled the Baseball's Best coupon (or bought it ff the secondary market) then had to mail it into onruss along with a check or money order for 105 prior to the January 20th, 2002 deadline to eceive a factory sealed set 330-card set (of hich contained the 220-card Baseball's Best et plus the 110-card Baseball's Best "The ookies" set. The consumer did not know upon ailing in the coupon whether he or she would e receiving the Bronze, Silver or Gold version of e set of which were disseminated randomly. he 330 cards are glossy-coated parallels of the 20-card basic 2001 Donruss set and the 110-ard 2001 Donruss the Rookies set. Only 999 erial-numbered Bronze sets were created, with ach card carrying serial-numbering on back nd Bronze foil accents on front.

Nm-Mt Ex-Mt
OMP.FACT.SET (330) 200.00 60.00
STARS 1-150: 1.5X TO 4X BASIC CARDS
ROOKIES 151-200: .2X TO .5X BASIC
FAN CLUB 201-220: .4X TO 1X BASIC
56 Albert Pujols RR 50.00 15.00
95 Ichiro Suzuki RR 25.00 7.50

2001 Donruss Baseball's Best Bronze Rookies

ssued as a redemption "update" set to the basic 001 Donruss set, these 105 cards were avail-ble via a coupon which could be mailed into onruss. There were only 999 bronze sets pro-uced.

Nm-Mt Ex-Mt
BRONZE: .6X TO 1.5X BASIC ROOKIES

2001 Donruss Baseball's Best Bronze Rookies Diamond Kings

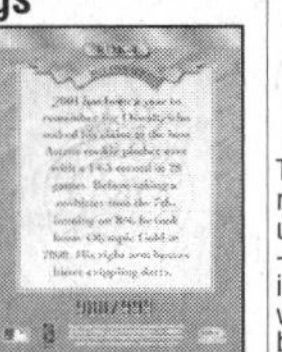

nserted one per Donruss Baseball's Best ronze, these five cards parallel the Donruss ookies Diamond Kings.

Nm-Mt Ex-Mt
BRONZE DK's: .4X TO 1X BASIC DK's

2001 Donruss Baseball's Best Gold

hese 220 cards were available via a coupon andomly seeded into 2001 Donruss baseball acks at stated odds of 1:720. Consumers that ulled the Baseball's Best coupon (or bought it ff the secondary market) then had to mail it into onruss along with a check or money order for 105 prior to the January 20th, 2002 deadline to eceive a factory sealed set 330-card set (of hich contained the 220-card Baseball's Best et plus the 110-card Baseball's Best "The ookies" set. The consumer did not know upon ailing in the coupon whether he or she would e receiving the Bronze, Silver or Gold version of e set of which were disseminated randomly. he 330 cards are glossy-coated parallels of the 20-card basic 2001 Donruss set and the 110-ard 2001 Donruss the Rookies set. Only 99 erial-numbered Gold sets were created, with ach card carrying serial-numbering on back nd Gold foil accents on front.

Nm-Mt Ex-Mt
OMP.FACT.SET (330) 600.00 180.00
STARS 1-150: 4X TO 10X BASIC CARDS
ROOKIES 151-200: .4X TO 1X BASIC
FAN CLUB 201-220: 1X TO 2.5X BASIC

2001 Donruss Baseball's Best Gold Rookies

ssued as a redemption "update" set to the basic 001 Donruss set, these 105 cards were avail-ble via a coupon which could be mailed into Donruss for these 110 cards. There were only 99 old sets produced.

Nm-Mt Ex-Mt
GOLD: 2X TO 5X BASIC ROOKIES ....

2001 Donruss Baseball's Best Gold Rookies Diamond Kings

Inserted one per Donruss Baseball's Best Gold set, these five cards parallel the Donruss Rookies Diamond Kings set.

Nm-Mt Ex-Mt
*GOLD DK'S: 1.25X TO 3X BASIC DK'S

2001 Donruss Baseball's Best Silver

These 220 cards were available via a coupon randomly seeded into 2001 Donruss baseball packs at stated odds of 1:720. Consumers that pulled the Baseball's Best coupon (or bought it off the secondary market) then had to mail it into Donruss along with a check or money order for $105 prior to the January 20th, 2002 deadline to receive a factory sealed set 330-card set (of which contained the 220-card Baseball's Best set plus the 110-card Baseball's Best "The Rookies" set. The consumer did not know upon mailing in the coupon whether he or she would be receiving the Bronze, Silver or Gold version of the set of which were disseminated randomly. The 330 cards are glossy-coated parallels of the 220-card basic 2001 Donruss set and the 110-card 2001 Donruss the Rookies set. Only 499 serial-numbered Silver sets were created, with each card carrying serial-numbering on back and Silver foil accents on front.

Nm-Mt Ex-Mt
COMP.FACT.SET (330) 300.00 90.00
*STARS 1-150: 2.5X TO 6X BASIC CARDS
*ROOKIES 151-200: .3X TO .8X BASIC
*FAN CLUB 201-220: .6X TO 1.5X BASIC

2001 Donruss Baseball's Best Silver Rookies

Issued as a redemption "update" set to the basic 2001 Donruss set, these 105 cards were available via a coupon which could be mailed into Donruss for these 110 cards. There were only 499 silver sets produced.

Nm-Mt Ex-Mt
*SILVER: 1X TO 2.5X BASIC ROOKIES

2001 Donruss Baseball's Best Silver Rookies Diamond Kings

Inserted one per Donruss Baseball's Best Silver set, these five cards parallel the Donruss Rookies Diamond Kings set. These cards were issued to a stated print run of 499 serial numbered sets.

Nm-Mt Ex-Mt
*SILVER DK'S: .6X TO 1.5X BASIC DK'S

2003 Donruss Champions

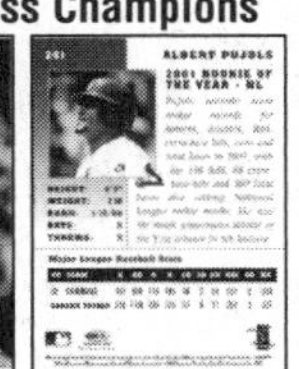

This 309 card set was issued in two separate releases. The primary Donruss Champions product - containing cards 1-301 within the basic set - was released in April, 2003. The set was issued in eight card packs with an $5 SRP. These packs were issued in 24 pack boxes which came 20 boxes to a case. This primary set was originally supposed to be capped at 300 cards but a late addition of Hideki Matsui (card number 301) brought the complete set to 301 cards. In December, 2003, eight additional cards (302-309) were seeded within packs of DLP Rookies and Traded.

Nm-Mt Ex-Mt
COMP.LO SET (301) 50.00 15.00
COMP.UPDATE SET (8) 8.00 2.40
COMMON CARD (302-309) .50 .15
1 Adam Kennedy .30 .09
2 Alfredo Amezaga .30 .09
3 Chone Figgins .30 .09
4 Darin Erstad .50 .15
5 David Eckstein .30 .09
6 Garret Anderson .50 .15
7 Jarrod Washburn .30 .09
8 Nolan Ryan Angels 3.00 .90
9 Tim Salmon .75 .23
10 Troy Glaus .50 .15
11 Troy Percival .50 .15
12 Curt Schilling .50 .15
13 Junior Spivey .30 .09
14 Luis Gonzalez .50 .15
15 Mark Grace .75 .23
16 Randy Johnson 1.25 .35
17 Steve Finley .50 .15
18 Andruw Jones .50 .15
19 Chipper Jones 1.25 .35
20 Dale Murphy 1.25 .35
21 Gary Sheffield .50 .15
22 Greg Maddux 2.00 .60
23 John Smoltz .75 .23
24 Andy Pratt .30 .09
25 Adam LaRoche .30 .09
26 Trey Hodges .30 .09
27 Warren Spahn .75 .23
28 Cal Ripken 4.00 1.20
29 Ed Rogers .30 .09
30 Brian Roberts .30 .09
31 Geronimo Gil .30 .09
32 Jay Gibbons .30 .09
33 Josh Towers .30 .09
34 Casey Fossum .30 .09
35 Cliff Floyd .50 .15
36 Derek Lowe .50 .15
37 Fred Lynn .50 .15
38 Freddy Sanchez .30 .09
39 Manny Ramirez .75 .23
40 Nomar Garciaparra 2.00 .60
41 Pedro Martinez 1.25 .35
42 Rickey Henderson 1.25 .35
43 Shea Hillenbrand .50 .15
44 Trot Nixon .50 .15
45 Bobby Hill .30 .09
46 Corey Patterson .50 .15
47 Fred McGriff .75 .23
48 Hee Seop Choi .30 .09
49 Juan Cruz .30 .09
50 Kerry Wood 1.25 .35
51 Mark Prior 1.25 .35
52 Moises Alou .50 .15
53 Nic Jackson .30 .09
54 Ryne Sandberg 2.50 .75
55 Sammy Sosa 2.00 .60
56 Carlos Lee .50 .15
57 Corwin Malone .30 .09
58 Frank Thomas 1.25 .35
59 Joe Borchard .30 .09
60 Joe Crede .30 .09
61 Magglio Ordonez .50 .15
62 Mark Buehrle .50 .15
63 Paul Konerko .50 .15
64 Tim Hummel .30 .09
65 Jon Adkins .30 .09
66 Adam Dunn .75 .23
67 Austin Kearns .50 .15
68 Barry Larkin .75 .23
69 Jose Acevedo .30 .09
70 Corky Miller .30 .09
71 Eric Davis .50 .15
72 Ken Griffey Jr. 2.00 .60
73 Sean Casey .50 .15
74 Wily Mo Pena .50 .15
75 Bob Feller .50 .15
76 Brian Tallet .30 .09
77 C.C. Sabathia .50 .15
78 Cliff Lee .30 .09
79 Earl Snyder .30 .09
80 Ellis Burks .50 .15
81 Jeremy Guthrie .30 .09
82 Travis Hafner .50 .15
83 Luis Garcia .30 .09
84 Omar Vizquel .75 .23
85 Ricardo Rodriguez .30 .09
86 Ryan Church .30 .09
87 Victor Martinez .75 .23
88 Brandon Phillips .30 .09
89 Jack Cust .30 .09
90 Jason Jennings .30 .09
91 Jeff Baker .30 .09
92 Garrett Atkins .30 .09
93 Juan Uribe .30 .09
94 Larry Walker .75 .23
95 Rene Reyes .30 .09
96 Todd Helton .75 .23
97 Alan Trammell .50 .15
98 Fernando Rodney .30 .09
99 Carlos Pena .30 .09
100 Jack Morris .50 .15
101 Bobby Higginson .50 .15
102 Mike Maroth .30 .09
103 Robert Fick .30 .09
104 Jesus Medrano .30 .09
105 Josh Beckett .50 .15
106 Luis Castillo .30 .09
107 Mike Lowell .50 .15
108 Juan Pierre .50 .15
109 Josh Wilson .30 .09
110 Tim Redding .30 .09
111 Carlos Hernandez .30 .09
112 Craig Biggio .75 .23
113 Henri Stanley .30 .09
114 Jason Lane .30 .09
115 Jeff Bagwell .75 .23
116 John Buck .30 .09
117 Kirk Saarloos .30 .09
118 Lance Berkman .50 .15
119 Nolan Ryan Astros 3.00 .90
120 Richard Hidalgo .30 .09
121 Rodrigo Rosario .30 .09
122 Roy Oswalt .50 .15
123 Tommy Whiteman .30 .09
124 Wade Miller .30 .09
125 Alexis Gomez .30 .09
126 Angel Berroa .30 .09
127 Brandon Berger .30 .09
128 Carlos Beltran .75 .23
129 George Brett 3.00 .90
130 Jimmy Gobble .30 .09
131 Dee Brown .30 .09
132 Mike Sweeney .50 .15
133 Raul Ibanez .30 .09
134 Runelvys Hernandez .30 .09
135 Adrian Beltre .75 .23
136 Brian Jordan .50 .15
137 Cesar Izturis .30 .09
138 Victor Alvarez .30 .09
139 Hideo Nomo 1.25 .35
140 Joe Thurston .30 .09
141 Kazuhisa Ishii .50 .15
142 Kevin Brown .50 .15
143 Odalis Perez .30 .09
144 Paul Lo Duca .50 .15
145 Shawn Green .50 .15
146 Ben Sheets .50 .15
147 Bill Hall .30 .09
148 Nick Neugebauer .30 .09
149 Richie Sexson .50 .15
150 Robin Yount 2.00 .60
151 Shane Nance .30 .09
152 Takahito Nomura .30 .09
153 A.J. Pierzynski .50 .15
154 Joe Mays .30 .09
155 Kirby Puckett 1.25 .35
156 Adam Johnson .30 .09
157 Rob Bowen .30 .09
158 Torii Hunter .50 .15
159 Andres Galarraga .50 .15
160 Endy Chavez .30 .09
161 Javier Vazquez .50 .15
162 Jose Vidro .30 .09
163 Vladimir Guerrero 1.25 .35
164 Dwight Gooden .50 .15
165 Mike Piazza 2.00 .60
166 Roberto Alomar .75 .23
167 Tom Glavine .75 .23
168 Alfonso Soriano .75 .23
169 Bernie Williams .75 .23
170 Brandon Claussen .30 .09
171 Derek Jeter 3.00 .90
172 Don Mattingly 3.00 .90
173 Drew Henson .50 .15
174 Jason Giambi .50 .15
175 Joe Torre MG .75 .23
176 Jorge Posada .75 .23
177 Mike Mussina .75 .23
178 Nick Johnson .30 .09
179 Roger Clemens 2.50 .75
180 Whitey Ford .75 .23
181 Adam Morrissey .30 .09
182 Barry Zito .50 .15
183 David Justice .50 .15
184 Eric Chavez .50 .15
185 Jermaine Dye .50 .15
186 Mark Mulder .50 .15
187 Miguel Tejada .50 .15
188 Reggie Jackson .75 .23
189 Terrence Long .30 .09
190 Tim Hudson .50 .15
191 Anderson Machado .30 .09
192 Bobby Abreu .50 .15
193 Brandon Duckworth .30 .09
194 Jim Thome 1.25 .35
195 Eric Junge .30 .09
196 Jeremy Giambi .30 .09
197 Johnny Estrada .30 .09
198 Jorge Padilla .30 .09
199 Marlon Byrd .30 .09
200 Mike Schmidt 2.50 .75
201 Pat Burrell .50 .15
202 Steve Carlton .50 .15
203 Aramis Ramirez .50 .15
204 Brian Giles .50 .15
205 Carlos Rivera .30 .09
206 Craig Wilson .50 .15
207 Dave Williams .30 .09
208 Jack Wilson .50 .15
209 Jose Castillo .30 .09
210 Kip Wells .30 .09
211 Roberto Clemente 3.00 .90
212 Walter Young .30 .09
213 Ben Howard .30 .09
214 Brian Lawrence .30 .09
215 Cliff Bartosh .30 .09
216 Dennis Tankersley .30 .09
217 Oliver Perez .50 .15
218 Phil Nevin .50 .15
219 Ryan Klesko .50 .15
220 Sean Burroughs .50 .15
221 Tony Gwynn 1.50 .45
222 Xavier Nady .30 .09
223 Mike Rivera .30 .09
224 Barry Bonds 3.00 .90
225 Benito Santiago .50 .15
226 Jason Schmidt .50 .15
227 Jeff Kent .50 .15
228 Kenny Lofton .50 .15
229 Rich Aurilia .30 .09
230 Robb Nen .50 .15
231 Tsuyoshi Shinjo .50 .15
232 Bret Boone .50 .15
233 Chris Snelling .30 .09
234 Edgar Martinez .75 .23
235 Freddy Garcia .50 .15
236 Ichiro Suzuki 2.00 .60
237 John Olerud .50 .15
238 Kazuhiro Sasaki .50 .15
239 Mike Cameron .50 .15
240 Rafael Soriano .30 .09
241 Albert Pujols 2.50 .75
242 J.D. Drew .50 .15
243 Jim Edmonds .50 .15
244 Ozzie Smith 2.00 .60
245 Scott Rolen 1.25 .35
246 So Taguchi .30 .09
247 Stan Musial 2.00 .60
248 Antonio Perez .30 .09
249 Aubrey Huff .50 .15
250 Dewon Brazelton .30 .09
251 Delvin James .30 .09
252 Joe Kennedy .30 .09
253 Toby Hall .30 .09
254 Alex Rodriguez 2.00 .60
255 Ben Kozlowski .30 .09
256 Gerald Laird .30 .09
257 Hank Blalock .75 .23
258 Ivan Rodriguez 1.25 .35
259 Juan Gonzalez .75 .23
260 Kevin Mench .30 .09
261 Mario Ramos .30 .09
262 Mark Teixeira .50 .15
263 Nolan Ryan Rangers 3.00 .90
264 Rafael Palmeiro .75 .23
265 Alexis Rios .75 .23
266 Carlos Delgado .50 .15
267 Eric Hinske .30 .09
268 Josh Phelps .30 .09
269 Kevin Cash .30 .09
270 Orlando Hudson .30 .09
271 Roy Halladay .30 .09
272 Shannon Stewart .50 .15
273 Vernon Wells .50 .15
274 Vinny Chulk .30 .09
275 Jason Anderson .30 .09
276 Craig Brazell RC .60 .18
277 Terrmel Sledge RC .60 .18
278 Ryan Cameron RC .40 .12
279 Clint Barmes RC .60 .18
280 Jhonny Peralta .50 .15
281 Todd Wellemeyer RC .60 .18
282 John Leicester RC .40 .12
283 Brandon Webb RC 1.25 .35
284 Tim Olson RC .60 .18
285 Matt Kata RC 1.00 .30
286 Rob Hammock RC .60 .18
287 Pete LaForest RC .60 .18
288 Nook Logan RC .40 .12
289 Prentice Redman RC .40 .12
290 Joe Valentine RC .40 .12
291 Jose Contreras RC 1.25 .35
292 Josh Stewart RC .40 .12
293 Mike Nicolas RC .40 .12
294 Marshall McDougall .30 .09
295 Travis Chapman .30 .09
296 Jose Morban .30 .09
297 Michael Hessman RC .40 .12
298 Buddy Hernandez RC .40 .12
299 Shane Victorino RC .40 .12
300 Jason Dubois .50 .15
301 Hideki Matsui RC 3.00 .90
302 Ryan Wagner RC .50 .15
303 Adam Loewen RC .60 .18
304 Chien-Ming Wang RC .60 .18
305 Hong-Chih Kuo RC .50 .15
306 Delmon Young RC 2.00 .60
307 Dan Haren RC .50 .15
308 Rickie Weeks RC 1.50 .45
309 Ramon Nivar RC .50 .15

2003 Donruss Champions Autographs

Cards checklisted 1-300 from this set were randomly inserted into Donruss Champions packs. Cards 302-309 were randomly inserted into packs of DLP Rookies and Traded. These cards were issued to different stated print runs and we have notated that information next to the player's name in our checklist. Please note that for cards with stated print runs of 45 or fewer cards we have not priced these cards due to market scarcity.

Nm-Mt Ex-Mt
2 Alfredo Amezaga/325 10.00 3.00
3 Chone Figgins/375 15.00 4.50
4 Darin Erstad/9
8 Nolan Ryan Angels/4
10 Troy Glaus/20
12 Curt Schilling/5
13 Junior Spivey/45 15.00 4.50
14 Luis Gonzalez/5
18 Andruw Jones/20
19 Chipper Jones/10
20 Dale Murphy/20
21 Gary Sheffield/10
24 Andy Pratt/475 10.00 3.00
25 Adam LaRoche/400 10.00 3.00
26 Trey Hodges/305 10.00 3.00
28 Cal Ripken/5
29 Ed Rogers/305 10.00 3.00
30 Brian Roberts/500 10.00 3.00
31 Geronimo Gil/150 10.00 3.00
32 Jay Gibbons/475 10.00 3.00
33 Josh Towers/500 10.00 3.00
34 Casey Fossum/160 10.00 3.00
35 Cliff Floyd/70 25.00 7.50
37 Fred Lynn/80 40.00 12.00
38 Freddy Sanchez/400 10.00 3.00
39 Manny Ramirez/5
40 Nomar Garciaparra/5
41 Pedro Martinez/5
42 Rickey Henderson/5
45 Bobby Hill/5
46 Corey Patterson/100 25.00 7.50
49 Juan Cruz/250 10.00 3.00
50 Kerry Wood/20
51 Mark Prior/50 80.00 24.00
53 Nic Jackson/100 15.00 4.50
56 Carlos Lee/25
57 Corwin Malone/400 10.00 3.00
58 Frank Thomas/5
59 Joe Borchard/215 10.00 3.00
60 Joe Crede/5
61 Magglio Ordonez/25
62 Mark Buehrle/15
64 Tim Hummel/400 10.00 3.00
65 Jon Adkins/400 10.00 3.00
66 Adam Dunn/100 40.00 12.00
67 Austin Kearns/50 25.00 7.50
68 Barry Larkin/9
69 Jose Acevedo/315 10.00 3.00
70 Corky Miller/295 10.00 3.00
71 Eric Davis/45 40.00 12.00
73 Sean Casey/10
74 Wily Mo Pena/450 15.00 4.50
75 Bob Feller/20
76 Brian Tallet/250 10.00 3.00
77 C.C. Sabathia/25
78 Cliff Lee/330 10.00 3.00
79 Earl Snyder/225 10.00 3.00
81 Jeremy Guthrie/400 10.00 3.00
83 Luis Garcia/375 10.00 3.00
86 Ryan Church/395 10.00 3.00
87 Victor Martinez/250 25.00 7.50
88 Brandon Phillips/375 10.00 3.00
89 Jack Cust/498 10.00 3.00
90 Jason Jennings/375 10.00 3.00
91 Jeff Baker/400 10.00 3.00
92 Garrett Atkins/400 10.00 3.00
95 Rene Reyes/350 10.00 3.00
96 Todd Helton/5
97 Alan Trammell/25
98 Fernando Rodney/500 10.00 3.00
100 Jack Morris/50 40.00 12.00
102 Mike Maroth/400 10.00 3.00
103 Robert Fick/15
104 Jesus Medrano/500 10.00 3.00
105 Josh Beckett/14
109 Josh Wilson/400 10.00 3.00
110 Tim Redding/375 10.00 3.00
111 Carlos Hernandez/250 10.00 3.00
112 Craig Biggio/20
113 Henri Stanley/390 10.00 3.00
114 Jason Lane/250 10.00 3.00
117 Kirk Saarloos/149 10.00 3.00
118 Lance Berkman/10
119 Nolan Ryan Astros/4
120 Richard Hidalgo/120 10.00 3.00
121 Rodrigo Rosario/500 10.00 3.00
122 Roy Oswalt/100 25.00 7.50
123 Tommy Whiteman/375 10.00 3.00
124 Wade Miller/125 10.00 3.00

126 Angel Berroa/400 10.00 3.00
127 Brandon Berger/325 10.00 3.00
128 Carlos Beltran/10
129 George Brett/9
130 Jimmy Gobble/400 10.00 3.00
131 Dee Brown/500 10.00 3.00
132 Mike Sweeney/45 25.00 7.50
134 Runelvys Hernandez/400 10.00 3.00
135 Adrian Beltre/20
138 Victor Alvarez/308 10.00 3.00
141 Kazuhisa Ishii/20
142 Kevin Brown/30
144 Paul Lo Duca/45 25.00 7.50
145 Shawn Green/5
146 Ben Sheets/50 25.00 7.50
147 Bill Hall/450 10.00 3.00
148 Nick Neugebauer/375 10.00 3.00
149 Richie Sexson/25
150 Robin Yount/5
151 Shane Nance/150 10.00 3.00
152 Takahito Nomura/50 25.00 7.50
153 A.J. Pierzynski/250 15.00 4.50
154 Joe Mays/5
155 Kirby Puckett/10
156 Adam Johnson/500 10.00 3.00
157 Rob Bowen/375 10.00 3.00
158 Torii Hunter/45 25.00 7.50
159 Andres Galarraga/25
160 Endy Chavez/280 10.00 3.00
161 Javier Vazquez/50 25.00 7.50
162 Jose Vidro/45 15.00 4.50
163 Vladimir Guerrero/20
164 Dwight Gooden/45 40.00 12.00
166 Roberto Alomar/15
167 Tom Glavine/15
168 Alfonso Soriano/10
169 Bernie Williams/10
170 Brandon Claussen/475 10.00 3.00
172 Don Mattingly/20
173 Drew Henson/20
175 Joe Torre/20
177 Mike Mussina/5
178 Nick Johnson/500 10.00 3.00
179 Roger Clemens/5
180 Whitey Ford/10
181 Adam Morrissey/395 10.00 3.00
182 Barry Zito/25
183 David Justice/10
184 Eric Chavez/10
185 Jermaine Dye/125 15.00 4.50
186 Mark Mulder/25
187 Miguel Tejada/15
188 Reggie Jackson/9
189 Terrence Long/250 10.00 3.00
190 Tim Hudson/20
191 Anderson Machado/500 10.00 3.00
192 Bobby Abreu/25
193 Brandon Duckworth/100 15.00 4.50
194 Jim Thome/15
195 Eric Junge/279 10.00 3.00
196 Jeremy Giambi/195 10.00 3.00
198 Jorge Padilla/11
199 Marlon Byrd/10
200 Mike Schmidt/20
202 Steve Carlton/25
203 Aramis Ramirez/20
204 Brian Giles/25
205 Carlos Rivera/400 10.00 3.00
206 Craig Wilson/245 15.00 4.50
207 Dave Williams/265 10.00 3.00
208 Jack Wilson/500 15.00 4.50
209 Jose Castillo/400 10.00 3.00
210 Kip Wells/500 10.00 3.00
212 Walter Young/400 10.00 3.00
213 Ben Howard/500 10.00 3.00
214 Brian Lawrence/500 10.00 3.00
215 Cliff Bartosh/400 10.00 3.00
216 Dennis Tankersley/25
217 Oliver Perez/5
219 Ryan Klesko/20
220 Sean Burroughs/19
221 Tony Gwynn/15
222 Xavier Nady/250 10.00 3.00
223 Mike Rivera/90 15.00 4.50
228 Kenny Lofton/25
233 Chris Snelling/200 10.00 3.00
234 Edgar Martinez/20
235 Freddy Garcia/10
240 Rafael Soriano/500 10.00 3.00
241 Albert Pujols/10
242 J.D. Drew/5
243 Jim Edmonds/10
244 Ozzie Smith/20
245 Scott Rolen/10
246 So Taguchi/10
247 Stan Musial/15
248 Antonio Perez/500 10.00 3.00
249 Aubrey Huff/475 15.00 4.50
250 Dewon Brazelton/50 15.00 4.50
251 Delvin James/400 10.00 3.00
252 Joe Kennedy/250 10.00 3.00
253 Toby Hall/500 10.00 3.00
254 Alex Rodriguez/5
255 Ben Kozlowski/400 10.00 3.00
256 Gerald Laird/450 10.00 3.00
257 Hank Blalock/50 40.00 12.00
258 Ivan Rodriguez/5
259 Juan Gonzalez/20
260 Kevin Mench/475 10.00 3.00
261 Mario Ramos/475 10.00 3.00
262 Mark Teixeira/40 40.00 12.00
263 Nolan Ryan Rangers/4
264 Rafael Palmeiro/5
265 Alexis Rios/400 15.00 4.50
267 Eric Hinske/390 10.00 3.00
268 Josh Phelps/5
269 Kevin Cash/375 10.00 3.00
272 Shannon Stewart/25
274 Vinny Chulk/100 15.00 4.50
275 Jason Anderson/493 25.00 7.50
277 Terrmel Sledge/500 15.00 4.50
278 Ryan Cameron/475 10.00 3.00
279 Clint Barmes/475 15.00 4.50
280 Jhonny Peralta/500 15.00 4.50
281 Todd Wellemeyer/477 15.00 4.50
282 John Leicester/480 10.00 3.00
283 Brandon Webb/500 15.00 4.50
284 Tim Olson/500 15.00 4.50
285 Matt Kata/487 15.00 4.50
286 Rob Hammock/486 15.00 4.50
287 Pete LaForest/500 15.00 4.50
288 Nook Logan/500 10.00 3.00
289 Prentice Redman/488 10.00 3.00
290 Joe Valentine/475 10.00 3.00
291 Jose Contreras/100 25.00 7.50
292 Josh Stewart/485 10.00 3.00
293 Mike Nicolas/500 10.00 3.00
295 Travis Chapman/100 15.00 4.50
296 Jose Morban/475 10.00 3.00
297 Michael Hessman/500 10.00 3.00
298 Buddy Hernandez/500 10.00 3.00
299 Shane Victorino/480 10.00 3.00
300 Jason Dubois/480 15.00 4.50
302 Ryan Wagner/100 15.00 4.50
303 Adam Loewen/100 25.00 7.50
304 Chien-Ming Wang/100 40.00 12.00
305 Hong-Chih Kuo/100 25.00 7.50
306 Delmon Young/25
307 Dan Haren/100 20.00 6.00
308 Rickie Weeks/10
309 Ramon Nivar/100 20.00 6.00

2003 Donruss Champions Autographs Notation

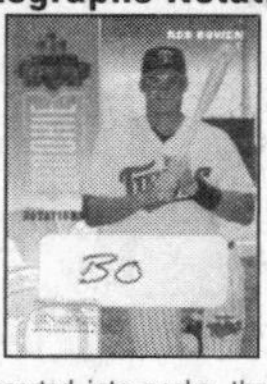

Randomly inserted into packs, these 65 cards feature not only an authentic autograph of the featured player but a notation under their signature. Please note, card 303, Adam Loewen, was distributed within packs of DLP Rookies and Traded. Since the players signed different amounts of cards, we have notated the print run next to the player's name in our checklist. Since none of these cards were issued to stated print run of more than 25 copies, no pricing is provided due to market scarcity.

Nm-Mt Ex-Mt
4 Darin Erstad/1
8 Nolan Ryan/3
13 Junior Spivey/5
32 Jay Gibbons/25
35 Cliff Floyd/1
59 Joe Borchard/10
62 Mark Buehrle/10
68 Barry Larkin/1
70 Corky Miller/5
71 Eric Davis/5
75 Bob Feller/5
79 Earl Snyder/1
83 Luis Garcia/5
86 Ryan Church/5
88 Brandon Phillips/25
89 Jack Cust/2
90 Jason Jennings/25
103 Robert Fick/10
105 Josh Beckett/1
110 Tim Redding/25
113 Henri Stanley/10
117 Kirk Saarloos/1
120 Richard Hidalgo/5
123 Tommy Whiteman/24
129 George Brett/1
132 Mike Sweeney/5
144 Paul Lo Duca/5
148 Nick Neugebauer/25
157 Rob Bowen/25
158 Torii Hunter/5
162 Jose Vidro/5
167 Tom Glavine/5
170 Brandon Claussen/24
173 Drew Henson/5
181 Adam Morrissey/5
188 Reggie Jackson/1
189 Terrence Long/5
190 Tim Hudson/5
196 Jeremy Giambi/5
203 Aramis Ramirez/5
205 Carlos Rivera/25
219 Ryan Klesko/5
220 Sean Burroughs/1
234 Edgar Martinez/5
246 So Taguchi/5
249 Aubrey Huff/25
260 Kevin Mench/25
261 Mario Ramos/25
262 Mark Teixeira/10
267 Eric Hinske/10
269 Kevin Cash/25
275 Jason Anderson/7
278 Ryan Cameron/25
279 Clint Barmes/25
281 Todd Wellemeyer/23
282 Jon Leicester/20
285 Matt Kata/13
286 Rob Hammock/14
289 Prentice Redman/12
290 Joe Valentine/25
292 Josh Stewart/15
296 Jose Morban/25
299 Shane Victorino/20
300 Jason Dubois/20
303 Adam Loewen/10

2003 Donruss Champions Metalized

Randomly inserted into packs, this is a parallel to the Donruss Champions set. Cards 302-309 were randomly seeded within packs of DLP Rookies and Traded. These cards were issued with a special metalized film board and were issued to a stated print run of 100 serial numbered sets.

Nm-Mt Ex-Mt
*METALIZED ACTIVE 1-301: 4X TO 10X
*METALIZED RETIRED 1-301: 8X TO 20X
*METALIZED RC'S 1-301: 1.5X TO 4X
*METALIZED RC'S 302-309: 4X TO 10X

2003 Donruss Champions Call to the Hall

Randomly inserted into packs, these 10 cards feature players who have already been elected to the Hall of Fame. These cards were issued to a stated print run of 2500 serial numbered sets.

Nm-Mt Ex-Mt
HOLO-FOIL PRINT RUN 25 #'d SETS
NO HOLO-FOIL PRICING DUE TO SCARCITY
*METALIZED: 2.5X TO 6X BASIC CALL
METALIZED PRINT RUN 100 #'d SETS
1 Nolan Ryan 10.00 3.00
2 Tom Seaver 5.00 1.50
3 Phil Rizzuto 5.00 1.50
4 Orlando Cepeda 3.00 .90
5 Al Kaline 5.00 1.50
6 Hoyt Wilhelm 3.00 .90
7 Luis Aparicio 3.00 .90
8 Billy Williams 3.00 .90
9 Jim Palmer 3.00 .90
10 Mike Schmidt 8.00 2.40

2003 Donruss Champions Call to the Hall Autographs

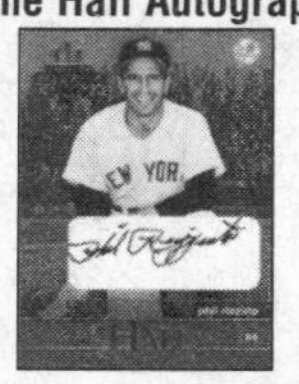

Randomly inserted into packs, these 10 cards parallel the Call to the Hall insert set. These cards feature an authentic autograph of the player featured in the set. Please note, that since Donruss/Playoff use stickers for their autographs, they were able to feature Hoyt Wilhelm who had passed away the previous year.

Nm-Mt Ex-Mt
1 Nolan Ryan/10
2 Tom Seaver/10
3 Phil Rizzuto/25
4 Orlando Cepeda/25
5 Al Kaline/25
6 Hoyt Wilhelm/25
7 Luis Aparicio/25
8 Billy Williams/25
9 Jim Palmer/25
10 Mike Schmidt/10

2003 Donruss Champions Grand Champions

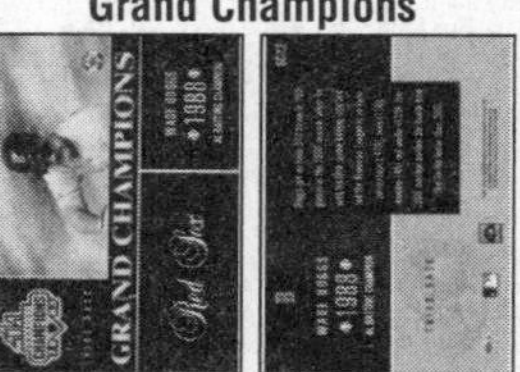

Issued at a stated rate of one in 18 hobby and one in 23 retail, this 25 card sets features a mix of Hall of Famers as well as guaranteed HOFers among active players.

Nm-Mt Ex-Mt
HOLO-FOIL RANDOM INSERTS IN PACKS
HOLO-FOIL PRINT RUN 25 #'d SETS
NO HOLO-FOIL PRICING DUE TO SCARCITY
*METALIZED: 2X TO 5X BASIC GRAND
METALIZED RANDOM INSERTS IN PACKS
METALIZED PRINT RUN 100 SERIAL #'d SETS
1 Stan Musial 8.00 2.40
2 Bob Feller 3.00 .90
3 Reggie Jackson 5.00 1.50
4 George Brett 12.00 3.60
5 Jim Palmer 3.00 .90
6 Harmon Killebrew 5.00 1.50
7 Ernie Banks 5.00 1.50
8 Frank Robinson 5.00 1.50
9 Greg Maddux 8.00 2.40
10 Whitey Ford 5.00 1.50
11 Bob Gibson 5.00 1.50
12 Mike Schmidt 10.00 3.00
13 Nolan Ryan 12.00 3.60
14 Warren Spahn 5.00 1.50
15 Rod Carew 5.00 1.50
16 Hoyt Wilhelm 3.00 .90
17 Duke Snider 5.00 1.50
18 Tom Seaver 5.00 1.50
19 Steve Carlton 3.00 .90
20 Yogi Berra 5.00 1.50
21 Cal Ripken 15.00 4.50
22 Tony Gwynn 6.00 1.80
23 Wade Boggs 5.00 1.50
24 Rickey Henderson 5.00 1.50
25 Roger Clemens 10.00 3.00

2003 Donruss Champions Statistical Champs

Inserted at a stated rate of one in 10 hobby and one in 23 retail, this 30 card set features a mix of active and retired players who have led the

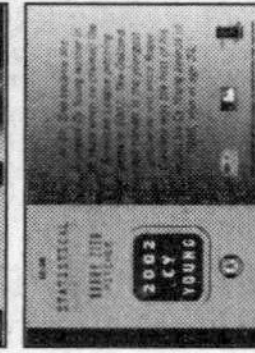

league in various offensive categories.

Nm-Mt Ex-Mt
1 Alex Rodriguez 6.00 1.80
2 Alfonso Soriano 4.00 1.20
3 Curt Schilling 3.00 .90
4 Eddie Mathews 5.00 1.50
5 Fred Lynn 3.00 .90
6 Harmon Killebrew 5.00 1.50
7 Hideo Nomo 4.00 1.20
8 Jim Thome 4.00 1.20
9 Kirby Puckett 4.00 1.20
10 Luis Gonzalez 3.00 .90
11 Manny Ramirez 4.00 1.20
12 Jason Giambi 3.00 .90
13 Mike Schmidt 10.00 3.00
14 Nomar Garciaparra 6.00 1.80
15 Lou Brock 5.00 1.50
16 Randy Johnson 4.00 1.20
17 Reggie Jackson 5.00 1.50
18 Rickey Henderson 4.00 1.20
19 Roberto Clemente 12.00 3.60
20 Barry Zito 3.00 .90
21 Todd Helton 4.00 1.20
22 Tom Seaver 5.00 1.50
23 Tony Gwynn 6.00 1.80
24 Torii Hunter 3.00 .90
25 Troy Glaus 3.00 .90
26 Wade Boggs 5.00 1.50
27 Rod Carew 5.00 1.50
28 Juan Gonzalez 4.00 1.20
29 Sammy Sosa 6.00 1.80
30 Warren Spahn 5.00 1.50

2003 Donruss Champions Statistical Champs Materials

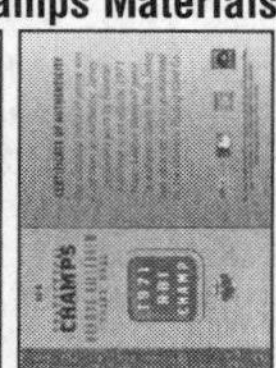

Randomly inserted into packs, this is a parallel to the Statistical Champs insert set. These cards basically feature game-used jersey pieces and were issued to different print runs. We have notated that print run information next to the player's name in our checklist.

Nm-Mt Ex-Mt
1 Alex Rodriguez Jsy/250 25.00 7.50
2 Alfonso Soriano Jsy/25
3 Curt Schilling Jsy/225 10.00 3.00
4 Eddie Mathews Jsy/200 25.00 7.50
5 Fred Lynn Jsy/50 40.00 12.00
6 Harmon Killebrew Jsy/250 25.00 7.50
7 Hideo Nomo Jsy/110 60.00 18.00
8 Jim Thome Jsy/250 15.00 4.50
9 Kirby Puckett Jsy/250 25.00 7.50
10 Luis Gonzalez Jsy/250 10.00 3.00
11 Manny Ramirez Jsy/155 15.00 4.50
12 Jason Giambi Jsy/250 10.00 3.00
13 Mike Schmidt Jsy/250 40.00 12.00
14 Nomar Garciaparra Jsy/99 40.00 12.00
15 Lou Brock Jsy/250 25.00 7.50
16 Randy Johnson Jsy/100 25.00 7.50
17 Reggie Jackson Jsy/200 25.00 7.50
18 Rickey Henderson Jsy/184 15.00 4.50
19 Roberto Clemente Jsy/64
20 Barry Zito Jsy/100 15.00 4.50
21 Todd Helton Jsy/250 15.00 4.50
22 Tom Seaver Jsy/100 40.00 12.00
23 Tony Gwynn Jsy/250 25.00 7.50
24 Torii Hunter Jsy/250 10.00 3.00
25 Troy Glaus Jsy/125 15.00 4.50
26 Wade Boggs Jsy/250 25.00 7.50
27 Rod Carew Hat/150 25.00 7.50
28 Juan Gonzalez Jsy/250 15.00 4.50
29 Sammy Sosa Jsy/250 25.00 7.50
30 Warren Spahn Jsy/150 25.00 7.50

2003 Donruss Champions Team Colors

Issued at a stated rate of one in 10 hobby and one in 23 retail, these 30 cards feature star players from a team set against background colors of the teams colors.

Nm-Mt Ex-Mt
1 Miguel Tejada 3.00 .90
2 Mike Schmidt 10.00 3.00
3 George Brett 12.00 3.60
4 Magglio Ordonez 3.00 .90
5 Ryne Sandberg 10.00 3.00
6 Adam Dunn 4.00 1.20
7 Mark Prior 4.00 1.20
8 Tony Gwynn 6.00 1.80
9 Troy Glaus 3.00 .90
10 Stan Musial 8.00 2.40
11 Kirby Puckett 4.00 1.20
12 Don Mattingly 12.00 3.60
13 Bobby Abreu 3.00 .90
14 Ichiro Suzuki 6.00 1.80
15 Cal Ripken 15.00 4.50
16 Chipper Jones 4.00 1.20
17 Carlos Beltran 4.00 1.20
18 Alfonso Soriano 4.00 1.20
19 Albert Pujols 8.00 2.40
20 Andruw Jones 3.00 .90
21 Bernie Williams 4.00 1.20
22 Todd Helton 4.00 1.20
23 Roberto Clemente 12.00 3.60
24 Jim Thome 4.00 1.20
25 Carlos Delgado 3.00 .90
26 Derek Jeter 10.00 3.00
27 Garret Anderson 3.00 .90
28 Nomar Garciaparra 6.00 1.80
29 Torii Hunter 3.00 .90
30 Vladimir Guerrero 4.00 1.20

2003 Donruss Champions Team Colors Materials

Randomly inserted in packs, this is a parallel t the Team Colors insert set. These cards feature memorabilia piece associated with the player' career. Since each card is serial numbered to different amount, we have notated that informa tion next to the player's name in our checklist.

Nm-Mt Ex-Mt
1 Miguel Tejada Jsy/50 15.00 4.50
2 Mike Schmidt Jsy/200 40.00 12.00
3 George Brett Jsy/200 50.00 15.00
4 Magglio Ordonez Jsy/100 10.00 3.00
5 Ryne Sandberg Jsy/200 40.00 12.00
6 Adam Dunn Jsy/44 25.00 7.50
7 Mark Prior Jsy/200 10.00 3.00
8 Tony Gwynn Jsy/200 20.00 6.00
9 Troy Glaus Jsy/200 8.00 2.40
10 Stan Musial Jsy/200 40.00 12.00
11 Kirby Puckett Jsy/200 15.00 4.50
12 Don Mattingly Jsy/200 60.00 18.00
13 Bobby Abreu Jsy/200 8.00 2.40
14 Ichiro Suzuki Base/200 25.00 7.50
15 Cal Ripken Jsy/200 60.00 18.00
16 Chipper Jones Jsy/200 10.00 3.00
17 Carlos Beltran Jsy/200 10.00 3.00
18 Alfonso Soriano Jsy/25
19 Albert Pujols Base/200 15.00 4.50
20 Andruw Jones Jsy/200 8.00 2.40
21 Bernie Williams Jsy/200 10.00 3.00
22 Todd Helton Jsy/200 10.00 3.00
23 Roberto Clemente Jsy/200. 100.00 30.00
24 Jim Thome Jsy/200 10.00 3.00
25 Carlos Delgado Jsy/200 8.00 2.40
26 Derek Jeter Base/200 25.00 7.50
27 Garret Anderson Jsy/50 15.00 4.50
28 Nomar Garciaparra Jsy/200 25.00 7.50
29 Torii Hunter Jsy/200 8.00 2.40
30 Vladimir Guerrero Jsy/200 10.00 3.00

2003 Donruss Champions Total Game

Inserted at a stated rate of one in nine hobby an one in 12 retail, these 40 cards feature positio players who have well-rounded games.

Nm-Mt Ex-Mt
1 Vladimir Guerrero 4.00 1.20
2 Nomar Garciaparra 6.00 1.80
3 Magglio Ordonez 3.00 .90
4 Garret Anderson 3.00 .90
5 Derek Jeter 10.00 3.00
6 Jim Thome 4.00 1.20
7 Torii Hunter 3.00 .90
8 Todd Helton 4.00 1.20
9 Andruw Jones 3.00 .90
10 Alfonso Soriano 4.00 1.20
11 Luis Gonzalez 3.00 .90
12 Manny Ramirez 4.00 1.20
13 Paul Konerko 3.00 .90
14 Alex Rodriguez 6.00 1.80
15 Carlos Beltran 4.00 1.20
16 Bernie Williams 4.00 1.20
17 Barry Bonds 10.00 3.00
18 Miguel Tejada 3.00 .90
19 Jason Giambi 3.00 .90
20 Ichiro Suzuki 6.00 1.80
21 Ivan Rodriguez 4.00 1.20
22 Rafael Palmeiro 4.00 1.20
23 Carlos Delgado 3.00 .90
24 Vernon Wells 3.00 .90
25 Sammy Sosa 6.00 1.80
26 Chipper Jones 4.00 1.20
27 Adam Dunn 4.00 1.20
28 Larry Walker 4.00 1.20
29 Shawn Green 3.00 .90
30 Richie Sexson 3.00 .90
31 Jose Vidro 3.00 .90
32 Mike Piazza 6.00 1.80
33 Roberto Alomar 4.00 1.20
34 Bobby Abreu 3.00 .90

Pat Burrell 3.00 .90
Brian Giles 3.00 .90
Albert Pujols 8.00 2.40
Lance Berkman 3.00 .90
Ryan Klesko 3.00 .90
Jeff Kent 3.00 .90

2003 Donruss Champions Total Game Materials

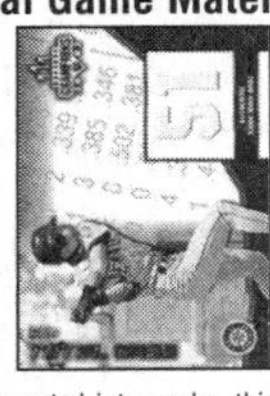

andomly inserted into packs, this is a parallel the Total Game insert set. Each player has a me-used swatch of some item attached to eir career. Since each card is serial numbered a differing amount of cards, we have notated at information next to the player's name in our ecklist.

Nm-Mt Ex-Mt
Vladimir Guerrero Jsy/200 15.00 4.50
Nomar Garciaparra Jsy/200 25.00 7.50
Magglio Ordonez Jsy/100 15.00 4.50
Garret Anderson Jsy/50 20.00 6.00
Derek Jeter Base/200 25.00 7.50
Jim Thome Jsy/200 15.00 4.50
Torii Hunter Jsy/200 10.00 3.00
Todd Helton Jsy/200 15.00 4.50
Andruw Jones Jsy/200 10.00 3.00
Alfonso Soriano Jsy/25
Luis Gonzalez Jsy/200 10.00 3.00
Manny Ramirez Jsy/200 15.00 4.50
Paul Konerko Jsy/200 10.00 3.00
Alex Rodriguez Jsy/200 25.00 7.50
Carlos Beltran Jsy/200 15.00 4.50
Bernie Williams Jsy/200 15.00 4.50
Barry Bonds Base/200 25.00 7.50
Miguel Tejada Jsy/50 20.00 6.00
Jason Giambi Base/200 10.00 3.00
Ichiro Suzuki Base/200 25.00 7.50
Ivan Rodriguez Jsy/100 25.00 7.50
Rafael Palmeiro Jsy/200 15.00 4.50
Carlos Delgado Jsy/200 10.00 3.00
Vernon Wells Jsy/200 10.00 3.00
Sammy Sosa Jsy/200 25.00 7.50
Chipper Jones Jsy/200 15.00 4.50
Adam Dunn Jsy/44 30.00 9.00
Larry Walker Jsy/200 15.00 4.50
Shawn Green Jsy/100 15.00 4.50
Richie Sexson Jsy/200 10.00 3.00
Jose Vidro Jsy/200 10.00 3.00
Mike Piazza Jsy/50 80.00 24.00
Roberto Alomar Jsy/100 25.00 7.50
Bobby Abreu Jsy/200 10.00 3.00
Pat Burrell Jsy/200 10.00 3.00
Brian Giles Jsy/200 10.00 3.00
Albert Pujols Base/200 15.00 4.50
Lance Berkman Jsy/50 20.00 6.00
Ryan Klesko Jsy/200 10.00 3.00
Jeff Kent Jsy/200 10.00 3.00

2003 Donruss Champions World Series Champs

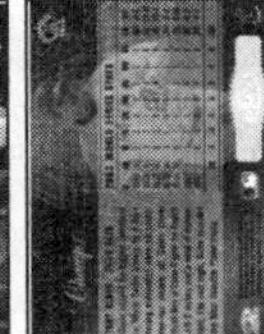

andomly inserted into packs, this 15 card set onors key members of the 2002 Anaheim ngels. These cards were issued to a stated print n of 2,002 serial numbered sets.

Nm-Mt Ex-Mt
OLO-FOIL PRINT RUN 25 #'d SETS
O HOLO-FOIL PRICING DUE TO SCARCITY
METALIZED: 1.25X TO 3X BASIC WS
ETALIZED PRINT RUN 100 #'d SETS
Troy Glaus 3.00 .90
Jarrod Washburn 3.00 .90
Darin Erstad 3.00 .90
Troy Percival 3.00 .90
David Eckstein 3.00 .90
Francisco Rodriguez 3.00 .90
Garret Anderson 3.00 .90
John Lackey 3.00 .90
Tim Salmon 5.00 1.50
Chone Figgins 3.00 .90
1 Adam Kennedy 3.00 .90
2 Scott Spiezio 3.00 .90
3 Ben Molina 3.00 .90
4 Brad Fullmer 3.00 .90
5 Troy Glaus MVP 3.00 .90

2001 Donruss Class of 2001

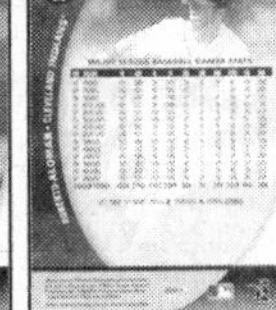

his product was released in mid-December 001, and featured a 300-card base set that was roken into tiers as follows: 100 Base Veterans, 100 Rookies/Prospects serial numbered to 1875, and an additional 100 Rookies/Prospects serial numbered to 625. Each pack contained three cards, and carried a suggested retail price of $3.99. Due to an error in printing, two different players were checklisted as card 252 (John Buck and Adam Johnson) - thus, a total of 301 cards exist for the set, though it's numbering runs from 1-300. Both Buck and Johnson's cards are serial numbered "of 625" on back.

Nm-Mt Ex-Mt
COMP.SET w/o SP's (100) 25.00 7.50
COMMON CARD (1-100) .40 .12
COMMON (101-200) 4.00 1.20
COMMON (201-300) 6.00 1.80
1 Alex Rodriguez 1.50 .45
2 Barry Bonds 2.50 .75
3 Vladimir Guerrero 1.00 .30
4 Jim Edmonds .40 .12
5 Derek Jeter 2.50 .75
6 Jose Canseco 1.00 .30
7 Rafael Furcal .40 .12
8 Cal Ripken 3.00 .90
9 Brad Radke .40 .12
10 Miguel Tejada .40 .12
11 Pat Burrell .40 .12
12 Ken Griffey Jr. 1.50 .45
13 Cliff Floyd .40 .12
14 Luis Gonzalez .40 .12
15 Frank Thomas 1.00 .30
16 Mike Sweeney .40 .12
17 Paul LoDuca .40 .12
18 Lance Berkman .40 .12
19 Tony Gwynn 1.25 .35
20 Chipper Jones 1.00 .30
21 Eric Chavez .40 .12
22 Kerry Wood 1.00 .30
23 Jorge Posada .60 .18
24 J.D. Drew .40 .12
25 Garret Anderson .40 .12
26 Mike Piazza 1.50 .45
27 Kenny Lofton .40 .12
28 Mike Mussina .60 .18
29 Paul Konerko .40 .12
30 Bernie Williams .60 .18
31 Eric Milton .40 .12
32 Shawn Green .40 .12
33 Paul O'Neill .60 .18
34 Juan Gonzalez .60 .18
35 Andres Galarraga .40 .12
36 Gary Sheffield .40 .12
37 Ben Grieve .40 .12
38 Scott Rolen 1.00 .30
39 Mark Grace .60 .18
40 Hideo Nomo 1.00 .30
41 Barry Zito .60 .18
42 Edgar Martinez .60 .18
43 Jarrod Washburn .40 .12
44 Greg Maddux 1.50 .45
45 Mark Buehrle .40 .12
46 Larry Walker .60 .18
47 Trot Nixon .40 .12
48 Nomar Garciaparra 1.50 .45
49 Robert Fick .40 .12
50 Sean Casey .40 .12
51 Joe Mays .40 .12
52 Roger Clemens 2.00 .60
53 Chan Ho Park .40 .12
54 Carlos Delgado .40 .12
55 Phil Nevin .40 .12
56 Jason Giambi .40 .12
57 Raul Mondesi .40 .12
58 Roberto Alomar .60 .18
59 Ryan Klesko .40 .12
60 Andruw Jones .40 .12
61 Gabe Kapler .40 .12
62 Darin Erstad .40 .12
63 Cristian Guzman .40 .12
64 Kazuhiro Sasaki .40 .12
65 Doug Mientkiewicz .40 .12
66 Sammy Sosa 1.50 .45
67 Mike Hampton .40 .12
68 Rickey Henderson 1.00 .30
69 Mark Mulder .40 .12
70 Mark McGwire 2.50 .75
71 Freddy Garcia .40 .12
72 Ivan Rodriguez 1.00 .30
73 Terrence Long .40 .12
74 Jeff Bagwell .60 .18
75 Moises Alou .40 .12
76 Todd Helton .60 .18
77 Preston Wilson .40 .12
78 Pedro Martinez 1.00 .30
79 Bobby Abreu .40 .12
80 Manny Ramirez .60 .18
81 Jose Vidro .40 .12
82 Randy Johnson 1.00 .30
83 Richie Sexson .40 .12
84 Troy Glaus .40 .12
85 Kevin Brown .40 .12
86 Carlos Lee .40 .12
87 Adrian Beltre .60 .18
88 Brian Giles .40 .12
89 Jermaine Dye .40 .12
90 Craig Biggio .60 .18
91 Richard Hidalgo .40 .12
92 Magglio Ordonez .40 .12
93 Aramis Ramirez .40 .12
94 Jeff Kent .40 .12
95 Curt Schilling .40 .12
96 Tim Hudson .40 .12
97 Fred McGriff .60 .18
98 Barry Larkin .60 .18
99 Jim Thome 1.00 .30
100 Tom Glavine .60 .18
101 S.Douglass/1875 RC 4.00 1.20
102 R.MacKowiak/1875 RC 6.00 1.80
103 J.Fikac/1875 RC 4.00 1.20
104 Henry Mateo/1875 RC 4.00 1.20
105 G. Gil/1875 RC 4.00 1.20
106 R. Vazquez/1875 RC 4.00 1.20
107 P. Santana/1875 RC 4.00 1.20
108 Ryan Jensen/1875 RC 4.00 1.20
109 Paul Phillips/1625 RC 4.00 1.20
110 Saul Rivera/1875 RC 4.00 1.20
111 Larry Bigbie/1875 4.00 1.20
112 Josh Phelps/1875 4.00 1.20
113 Justin Kaye/1875 RC 4.00 1.20
114 Kris Keller/1625 RC 4.00 1.20
115 Adam Bernero/1625 4.00 1.20
116 V.Zambrano/1875 RC 6.00 1.80
117 Felipe Lopez/1875 4.00 1.20
118 B.Roberts/1875 RC 4.00 1.20
119 Kurt Ainsworth/1875 4.00 1.20
120 G.Perez/1625 RC 4.00 1.20
121 W.Guzman/1875 RC 4.00 1.20
122 D.Lewis/1875 RC 4.00 1.20
123 Nate Teut/1625 RC 4.00 1.20
124 M. Vargas/1625 RC 4.00 1.20
125 Brandon Inge/1875 4.00 1.20
126 T. Phelps/1875 RC 4.00 1.20
127 Les Walrond/1625 RC 4.00 1.20
128 J. Atchley/1875 RC 4.00 1.20
129 S. Clapp/1875 RC 4.00 1.20
130 Bret Prinz/1875 RC 4.00 1.20
131 Bert Snow/1875 RC 4.00 1.20
132 Joe Crede/1625 4.00 1.20
133 Nick Punto/1875 RC 4.00 1.20
134 C. Hernandez/1875 4.00 1.20
135 Ken Vining/1875 RC 4.00 1.20
136 Luis Pineda/1875 RC 4.00 1.20
137 W. Abreu/1625 RC 4.00 1.20
138 Matt Ginter/1625 4.00 1.20
139 Jason Smith/1875 RC 4.00 1.20
140 Gene Altman/1625 RC 4.00 1.20
141 B. Rogers/1875 RC 4.00 1.20
142 M.Cuddyer/1625 4.00 1.20
143 Mike Penney/1625 RC 4.00 1.20
144 S.Podsednik/1875 RC 15.00 4.50
145 Esix Snead/1625 RC 4.00 1.20
146 S.Watkins/1875 RC 4.00 1.20
147 O.Woodards/1625 RC 4.00 1.20
148 J.Deardorff/1775 RC 4.00 1.20
149 Eric Cyr/1875 RC 4.00 1.20
150 Blaine Neal/1625 RC 4.00 1.20
151 Ben Sheets/1875 6.00 1.80
152 S.Stewart/1875 RC 4.00 1.20
153 M.Koplove/1875 RC 4.00 1.20
154 Kyle Lohse/1875 RC 6.00 1.80
155 F. Rodney/1875 RC 4.00 1.20
156 Aubrey Huff/1625 4.00 1.20
157 Pablo Ozuna/1625 4.00 1.20
158 Bill Ortega/1625 RC 4.00 1.20
159 Toby Hall/1875 4.00 1.20
160 Kevin Olsen/1625 RC 4.00 1.20
161 Will Ohman/1625 RC 4.00 1.20
162 Nate Cornejo/1875 4.00 1.20
163 Jack Cust/1625 4.00 1.20
164 Juan Rivera/1875 4.00 1.20
165 J. Riggan/1875 RC 4.00 1.20
166 D.Mohr/1875 RC 4.00 1.20
167 Doug Nickle/1875 RC 4.00 1.20
168 C.Monroe/1625 RC 4.00 1.20
169 Jason Jennings/1625 4.00 1.20
170 Bart Miadich/1875 RC 4.00 1.20
171 Luis Rivas/1625 4.00 1.20
172 T. Christman/1875 RC 4.00 1.20
173 L. Hudson/1625 RC 4.00 1.20
174 Brett Jodie/1875 RC 4.00 1.20
175 Jorge Julio/1875 RC 4.00 1.20
176 David Espinosa/1625 4.00 1.20
177 Mike Maroth/1625 RC 4.00 1.20
178 Keith Ginter/1625 4.00 1.20
179 J. Moreno/1875 RC 4.00 1.20
180 B. Knight/1875 RC 4.00 1.20
181 Steve Lomasney/1625 4.00 1.20
182 J. Grabow/1625 RC 4.00 1.20
183 Steve Green/1875 RC 4.00 1.20
184 Jason Karnuth/1875 RC 4.00 1.20
185 Bob File/1875 RC 4.00 1.20
186 Brent Abernathy/1625 4.00 1.20
187 M.Ensberg/1875 RC 6.00 1.80
188 Wily Mo Pena/1625 4.00 1.20
189 Ken Harvey/1875 4.00 1.20
190 Josh Pearce/1875 RC 4.00 1.20
191 Cesar Izturis/1625 4.00 1.20
192 Eric Hinske/1625 RC 6.00 1.80
193 Joe Beimel/1875 RC 4.00 1.20
194 Timo Perez/1775 4.00 1.20
195 Troy Mattes/1875 RC 4.00 1.20
196 Eric Valent/1625 4.00 1.20
197 Ed Rogers/1875 RC 4.00 1.20
198 G.Balfour/1875 RC 4.00 1.20
199 Benito Baez/1875 RC 4.00 1.20
200 Vernon Wells/1875 4.00 1.20
201 J.Kennedy PH/525 RC 10.00 3.00
202 W.Betemit PH/525 RC 6.00 1.80
203 C.Parker PH/525 RC 6.00 1.80
204 J.Gibbons PH/525 RC 10.00 3.00
205 C.Garcia PH/425 RC 6.00 1.80
206 J.Wilson PH/525 RC 10.00 3.00
207 J.Estrada PH/425 RC 10.00 3.00
208 W.Ruan PH/425 RC 6.00 1.80
209 B.Duckworth PH/525 RC 6.00 1.80
210 W.Harris PH/625 RC 6.00 1.80
211 M.Byrd PH/525 RC 10.00 3.00
212 C.C. Sabathia PH/600 6.00 1.80
213 D.Tankersley PH/525 RC 6.00 1.80
214 B.Larson PH/425 RC 6.00 1.80
215 A.Gomez PH/425 RC 6.00 1.80
216 Bill Hall PH/525 RC 6.00 1.80
217 A.Perez PH/525 RC 6.00 1.80
218 J.Affeldt PH/425 RC 10.00 3.00
219 J.Spivey PH/625 RC 10.00 3.00
220 C.Fossum PH/425 RC 6.00 1.80
221 B.Lyon PH/625 RC 6.00 1.80
222 A.Santos PH/625 RC 6.00 1.80
223 L.Davis PH/625 RC 6.00 1.80
224 Zach Day PH/425 RC 6.00 1.80
225 D.Williams PH/425 RC 6.00 1.80
226 C.Crespo PH/625 RC 6.00 1.80
227 J.Acevedo PH/425 RC 6.00 1.80
228 T.Hafner PH/625 RC 15.00 4.50
229 O.Hudson PH/525 RC 10.00 3.00
230 J.Mieses PH/425 RC 6.00 1.80
231 R.Rodriguez PH/425 RC 6.00 1.80
232 A.Soriano PH/525 10.00 3.00
233 Jason Hart PH/525 6.00 1.80
234 E.Chavez PH/425 RC 6.00 1.80
235 D.James PH/525 RC 6.00 1.80
236 R.Drese PH/625 RC 10.00 3.00
237 J.Owens PH/425 RC 6.00 1.80
238 B.Voyles PH/425 RC 6.00 1.80
239 Nate Frese PH/425 RC 6.00 1.80
240 Josh Beckett PH/600 6.00 1.80
241 Roy Oswalt PH/525 10.00 3.00
242 J.Uribe PH/475 RC 10.00 3.00
243 C.Aldridge PH/425 RC 6.00 1.80
244 Adam Dunn PH/525 10.00 3.00
245 Bud Smith PH/525 RC 6.00 1.80
246 A.Hernandez PH/525 RC 6.00 1.80
247 M.Guerrier PH/625 RC 6.00 1.80
248 J.Rollins PH/625 6.00 1.80
249 W.Caceres PH/425 RC 6.00 1.80
250 J.Michaels PH/425 RC 6.00 1.80
251 I.Suzuki PH/625 RC 60.00 18.00
252 John Buck PH/525 RC 10.00 3.00
252 Adam Johnson PH/625 6.00 1.80
253 A.Torres PH/525 RC 6.00 1.80
254 A.Amezaga PH/625 RC 6.00 1.80
255 C.Miller PH/525 RC 6.00 1.80
256 R.Soriano PH/425 RC 10.00 3.00
257 D.Mendez PH/425 RC 6.00 1.80
258 V.Martinez PH/625 RC 80.00 24.00
259 C.Patterson PH/525 6.00 1.80
260 H.Ramirez PH/425 RC 10.00 3.00
261 E.Guzman PH/425 RC 6.00 1.80
262 Juan Diaz PH/425 RC 6.00 1.80
263 M.Rivera PH/625 RC 6.00 1.80
264 B.Lawrence PH/425 RC 6.00 1.80
265 J.Perez PH/425 RC 6.00 1.80
266 J.Nunez PH/425 RC 6.00 1.80
267 E.Bedard PH/625 RC 6.00 1.80
268 A.Pujols PH/525 RC 100.00 30.00
269 D.Sanchez PH/425 RC 6.00 1.80
270 C.Ransom PH/625 RC 6.00 1.80
271 G.Miller PH/425 RC 6.00 1.80
272 A.Pettyjohn PH/425 RC 6.00 1.80
273 T.Shinjo PH/625 RC 10.00 3.00
274 C.Vargas PH/425 RC 6.00 1.80
275 J.Duchscherer PH/625 RC 6.00 1.80
276 Tim Spooneybarger PH/625 RC 6.00 1.80
277 R.Bauer PH/625 RC 6.00 1.80
278 Josh Fogg PH/625 RC 6.00 1.80
279 B.Reith PH/425 RC 6.00 1.80
280 S.MacRae PH/625 RC 6.00 1.80
281 R.Ludwick PH/625 RC 6.00 1.80
282 E.Almonte PH/625 RC 6.00 1.80
283 J.Towers PH/525 RC 6.00 1.80
284 J. A.Pena PH/625 RC 6.00 1.80
285 D. Brous PH/425 RC 6.00 1.80
286 Erik Hiljus PH/625 RC 6.00 1.80
287 N.Neugebauer PH/525 6.00 1.80
288 J.Melian PH/625 RC 6.00 1.80
289 B.Sylvester PH/425 RC 6.00 1.80
290 Carlos Valderrama PH/425 RC 6.00 1.80
291 J.Cueto PH/625 RC 6.00 1.80
292 M.White PH/425 RC 6.00 1.80
293 N.Maness PH/425 RC 6.00 1.80
294 J.Lane PH/625 RC 6.00 1.80
295 B.Berger PH/625 RC 6.00 1.80
296 A.Berroa PH/525 RC 10.00 3.00
297 Juan Cruz PH/525 RC 6.00 1.80
298 D.Brazelton PH/525 RC 10.00 3.00
299 M.Prior PH/525 RC 60.00 18.00
300 M.Teixeira PH/525 RC 40.00 12.00

2001 Donruss Class of 2001 First Class

Randomly inserted into packs, this 284-card skip-numbered set parallels the Donruss Class of 2001 base set. Each card was produced with a special holographic foil. Please note that a few of the players were short-printed and are marked accordingly. Cards 1-100 were serial numbered to 100, while cards 101-300 were serial numbered to 50.

Nm-Mt Ex-Mt
*1ST CLASS 1-100: 6X TO 15X BASIC
*1ST CLASS 101-200: .75X TO 2X BASIC
*1ST CLASS 201-300: .5X TO 1.2X BASIC
1 Alex Rodriguez SP/75 25.00 7.50
3 Vladimir Guerrero SP/75 15.00 4.50
10 Miguel Tejada SP/25
14 Luis Gonzalez SP/75 6.00 1.80
15 Frank Thomas SP/75 15.00 4.50
18 Lance Berkman SP/75 6.00 1.80
20 Chipper Jones SP/75 15.00 4.50
22 Kerry Wood SP/75 15.00 4.50
24 J.D. Drew SP/75 6.00 1.80
27 Kenny Lofton SP/75 6.00 1.80
28 Mike Mussina SP/75 10.00 3.00
30 Bernie Williams SP/75 10.00 3.00
32 Shawn Green SP/85 6.00 1.80
34 Juan Gonzalez SP/75 10.00 3.00
35 Andres Galarraga SP/75 6.00 1.80
36 Gary Sheffield SP/75 6.00 1.80
38 Scott Rolen SP/75 15.00 4.50
44 Greg Maddux SP/75 25.00 7.50
48 Nomar Garciaparra SP/85 25.00 7.50
52 Roger Clemens SP/75 30.00 9.00
53 Chan Ho Park SP/85 6.00 1.80
58 Roberto Alomar SP/85 10.00 3.00
59 Ryan Klesko SP/50 6.00 1.80
62 Darin Erstad SP/75 6.00 1.80
72 Ivan Rodriguez SP/75 15.00 4.50
74 Jeff Bagwell SP/85 10.00 3.00
75 Moises Alou SP/75 6.00 1.80
76 Todd Helton SP/75 10.00 3.00
78 Pedro Martinez SP/85 15.00 4.50
80 Manny Ramirez SP/85 10.00 3.00
82 Randy Johnson SP/85 15.00 4.50
85 Kevin Brown SP/75 6.00 1.80
88 Brian Giles SP/75 6.00 1.80
90 Craig Biggio SP/85 10.00 3.00
95 Curt Schilling SP/75 6.00 1.80
98 Barry Larkin SP/85 10.00 3.00
100 Tom Glavine SP/75 10.00 3.00

2001 Donruss Class of 2001 First Class Autographs

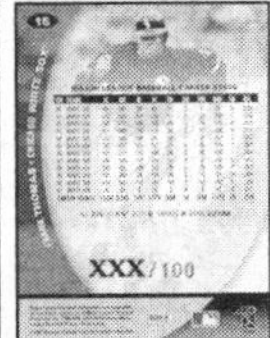

Randomly inserted into packs, this 53-card skip-numbered insert features authentic autographs from some of the hottest players in Major League Baseball. Individual print runs are listed in our checklist.

Nm-Mt Ex-Mt
1 Alex Rodriguez/25
3 Vladimir Guerrero/25
10 Miguel Tejada/75 25.00 7.50
14 Luis Gonzalez/25
15 Frank Thomas/25
17 Paul LoDuca/100 25.00 7.50
18 Lance Berkman/25
20 Chipper Jones/25
21 Eric Chavez/100 25.00 7.50
22 Kerry Wood/25
24 J.D. Drew/25
27 Kenny Lofton/25
28 Mike Mussina/25
30 Bernie Williams/25
32 Shawn Green/15
34 Juan Gonzalez/25
35 Andres Galarraga/25
36 Gary Sheffield/25
38 Scott Rolen/25
41 Barry Zito/100 40.00 12.00
44 Greg Maddux/25
45 Mark Buehrle/100 25.00 7.50
48 Nomar Garciaparra/15
49 Robert Fick/100 25.00 7.50
50 Sean Casey/100 25.00 7.50
51 Joe Mays/100 25.00 7.50
52 Roger Clemens/25
53 Chan Ho Park/15
58 Roberto Alomar/15
59 Ryan Klesko/50
62 Darin Erstad/25
69 Mark Mulder/100 25.00 7.50
72 Ivan Rodriguez/25
73 Terrence Long/100 25.00 7.50
74 Jeff Bagwell/15
75 Moises Alou/25
76 Todd Helton/25
78 Pedro Martinez/15
80 Manny Ramirez/15
81 Jose Vidro/100 25.00 7.50
82 Randy Johnson/15
83 Richie Sexson/100 25.00 7.50
84 Troy Glaus/100 25.00 7.50
85 Kevin Brown/25
88 Brian Giles/25
89 Jermaine Dye/100 25.00 7.50
90 Craig Biggio/15
91 Richard Hidalgo/100 25.00 7.50
93 Aramis Ramirez/100 25.00 7.50
95 Curt Schilling/25
96 Tim Hudson/100 25.00 7.50
98 Barry Larkin/25
100 Tom Glavine/25

2001 Donruss Class of 2001 Rookie Autographs

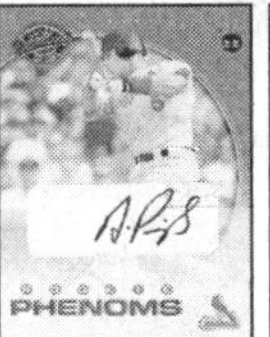
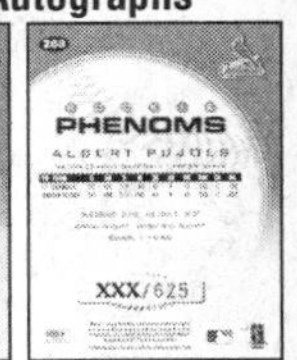

Randomly inserted into packs, this 109-card insert features authentic autographs from some of the hottest young talent in the Minor Leagues. Individual print runs are listed in our checklist.

Nm-Mt Ex-Mt
109 Paul Phillips/250 10.00 3.00
114 Kris Keller/250 10.00 3.00
115 Adam Bernero/250 10.00 3.00
120 George Perez/250 10.00 3.00
123 Nate Teut/250 10.00 3.00
124 Martin Vargas/250 10.00 3.00
127 Les Walrond/250 10.00 3.00
132 Joe Crede/250 10.00 3.00
137 Winston Abreu/250 10.00 3.00
138 Matt Ginter/250 10.00 3.00
140 Gene Altman/250 10.00 3.00
142 Michael Cuddyer/250 10.00 3.00
143 Mike Penney/250 10.00 3.00
145 Esix Snead/250 10.00 3.00
147 O.Woodards/250 10.00 3.00
148 Jeff Deardorff/100 15.00 4.50
150 Blaine Neal/250 10.00 3.00
156 Aubrey Huff/250 15.00 4.50
157 Pablo Ozuna/250 10.00 3.00
158 Bill Ortega/250 10.00 3.00
160 Kevin Olsen/250 10.00 3.00
161 Will Ohman/250 10.00 3.00
163 Jack Cust/250 10.00 3.00
168 Craig Monroe/250 10.00 3.00
169 Jason Jennings/250 10.00 3.00
171 Luis Rivas/250 10.00 3.00
173 Luke Hudson/250 10.00 3.00
176 David Espinosa/250 10.00 3.00
177 Mike Maroth/250 10.00 3.00
178 Keith Ginter/250 10.00 3.00
181 Steve Lomasney/250 10.00 3.00
182 John Grabow/250 10.00 3.00
184 Jason Karnuth/250 10.00 3.00
186 Brent Abernathy/250 10.00 3.00
188 Wily Mo Pena/250 15.00 4.50
191 Cesar Izturis/250 15.00 4.50
192 Eric Hinske/250 15.00 4.50
194 Timo Perez/100 15.00 4.50
196 Eric Valent/250 10.00 3.00
201 Joe Kennedy PH/100 25.00 7.50
202 W.Betemit PH/100 15.00 4.50
203 C.Parker PH/100 15.00 4.50
204 Jay Gibbons PH/100 30.00 9.00
205 Carlos Garcia PH/200 10.00 3.00
206 Jack Wilson PH/100 40.00 12.00
207 J.Estrada PH/200 25.00 7.50
208 Wilkin Ruan PH/200 10.00 3.00
209 B.Duckworth PH/100 15.00 4.50
211 Marlon Byrd PH/100 30.00 9.00
212 C.C. Sabathia PH/25
213 D.Tankersley PH/100 15.00 4.50
214 B.Larson PH/200 10.00 3.00

	Nm-Mt	Ex-Mt
215 Alexis Gomez PH/200	10.00	3.00
216 Bill Hall PH/100	15.00	4.50
217 Antonio Perez PH/100	15.00	4.50
218 J. Affeldt PH/200	15.00	4.50
220 C. Fossum PH/200	10.00	3.00
224 Zach Day PH/200	10.00	3.00
225 D. Williams PH/200	10.00	3.00
227 Jose Acevedo PH/200	10.00	3.00
229 O.Hudson PH/100	25.00	7.50
230 Jose Mieses PH/200	10.00	3.00
231 Ric Rodriguez PH/200	10.00	3.00
232 A. Soriano PH/100	50.00	15.00
233 Jason Hart PH/100	15.00	4.50
234 Endy Chavez PH/200	10.00	3.00
235 Delvin James PH/100	15.00	4.50
237 J. Owens PH/200	10.00	3.00
238 Brad Voyles PH/200	10.00	3.00
239 Nate Frese PH/200	10.00	3.00
240 Josh Beckett PH/25		
241 Roy Oswalt PH/100	30.00	9.00
242 Juan Uribe PH/150	15.00	4.50
243 Cory Aldridge PH/200	10.00	3.00
244 Adam Dunn PH/100	30.00	9.00
245 Bud Smith PH/100	15.00	4.50
246 A.Hernandez PH/100	15.00	4.50
249 W. Caceres PH/200	10.00	3.00
250 J.Michaels PH/200	10.00	3.00
252 John Buck PH/100	25.00	7.50
253 Andres Torres PH/100	15.00	4.50
255 Corky Miller PH/100	15.00	4.50
256 R. Soriano PH/200	15.00	4.50
257 D. Mendez PH/200	10.00	3.00
259 C.Patterson PH/100	20.00	6.00
260 H.Ramirez PH/200	15.00	4.50
261 E.Guzman PH/200	10.00	3.00
262 Juan Diaz PH/200	10.00	3.00
264 B.Lawrence PH/200	10.00	3.00
265 Josue Perez PH/200	10.00	3.00
266 Jose Nunez PH/200	10.00	3.00
268 Albert Pujols PH/100	400.00	120.00
269 D.Sanchez PH/200	10.00	3.00
271 Greg Miller PH/200	10.00	3.00
272 A.Pettyjohn PH/200	10.00	3.00
274 C.Vargas PH/200	10.00	3.00
279 Brian Reith PH/200	10.00	3.00
283 Josh Towers PH/100	15.00	4.50
285 David Brous PH/200	10.00	3.00
287 N.Neugebauer PH/100	15.00	4.50
289 Billy Sylvester PH/200	10.00	3.00
290 C.Valderrama PH/200	10.00	3.00
292 Matt White PH/200	10.00	3.00
293 Nick Maness PH/200	10.00	3.00
296 Angel Berroa PH/100	30.00	9.00
297 Juan Cruz PH/100	15.00	4.50
298 D.Brazelton PH/100	25.00	7.50
299 Mark Prior PH/100	250.00	75.00
300 Mark Teixeira PH/100	150.00	45.00

2001 Donruss Class of 2001 Aces

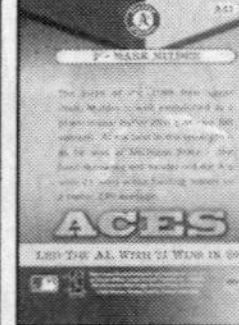

Randomly inserted into packs at one in 30, this 20-card insert features baseball's most prized pitchers. Card backs carry an "A" prefix.

	Nm-Mt	Ex-Mt
COMPLETE SET (20)	100.00	30.00
A1 Roger Clemens	12.00	3.60
A2 Randy Johnson	6.00	1.80
A3 Freddy Garcia	5.00	1.50
A4 Greg Maddux	10.00	3.00
A5 Tim Hudson	5.00	1.50
A6 Curt Schilling	5.00	1.50
A7 Mark Buehrle	5.00	1.50
A8 Matt Morris	5.00	1.50
A9 Joe Mays	5.00	1.50
A10 Javier Vazquez	5.00	1.50
A11 Mark Mulder	5.00	1.50
A12 Wade Miller	5.00	1.50
A13 Barry Zito	5.00	1.50
A14 Pedro Martinez	6.00	1.80
A15 Al Leiter	5.00	1.50
A16 Chan Ho Park	5.00	1.50
A17 John Burkett	5.00	1.50
A18 C.C. Sabathia	5.00	1.50
A19 Jamie Moyer	5.00	1.50
A20 Mike Mussina	5.00	1.50

2001 Donruss Class of 2001 Diamond Aces

This 19-card set is a parallel to the more common Aces insert card. Randomly inserted into packs at an unspecified ratio, each Diamond Aces card features a swatch of game-used memorabilia. All cards utilize jersey swatches except card number A20 Mike Mussina of whom has a Hat swatch instead. Card number A8 was intended to feature Matt Morris, but the card was pulled from the set due to complications in obtaining game-used equipment featuring Morris.

	Nm-Mt	Ex-Mt
A1 Roger Clemens/200	40.00	12.00
A2 Randy Johnson/750	15.00	4.50
A3 Freddy Garcia/350	10.00	3.00
A4 Greg Maddux/750	25.00	7.50
A5 Tim Hudson/550	10.00	3.00
A6 Curt Schilling/525	10.00	3.00
A7 Mark Buehrle/750	10.00	3.00
A8 Does Not Exist		
A9 Joe Mays/750	10.00	3.00
A10 Javier Vazquez/500	10.00	3.00
A11 Mark Mulder/300	10.00	3.00
A12 Wade Miller/525	10.00	3.00
A13 Barry Zito/550	15.00	4.50
A14 Pedro Martinez/550	15.00	4.50
A15 Al Leiter/525	10.00	3.00
A16 Chan Ho Park/400	10.00	3.00
A17 John Burkett/700	10.00	3.00
A18 C.C. Sabathia/550	10.00	3.00
A19 Jamie Moyer/700	10.00	3.00
A20 Mike Mussina Hat/75		

2001 Donruss Class of 2001 BobbleHead

Each box of Donruss Class of 2001 featured one randomly inserted BobbleHead Doll. There were 2000 of each regular doll produced, and 1000 of each ROY doll.

	Nm-Mt	Ex-Mt
1 Ichiro Suzuki	40.00	12.00
2 Cal Ripken	40.00	12.00
3 Derek Jeter	30.00	9.00
4 Mark McGwire	40.00	12.00
5 Albert Pujols	50.00	15.00
6 Ken Griffey Jr.	20.00	6.00
7 Nomar Garciaparra	20.00	6.00
8 Mike Piazza	20.00	6.00
9 Alex Rodriguez	20.00	6.00
10 Manny Ramirez	15.00	4.50
11 Tsuyoshi Shinjo	15.00	4.50
12 Hideo Nomo	15.00	4.50
13 Chipper Jones	15.00	4.50
14 Sammy Sosa	20.00	6.00
15 Roger Clemens	25.00	7.50
16 Tony Gwynn	15.00	4.50
17 Barry Bonds	30.00	9.00
18 Kazuhiro Sasaki	15.00	4.50
19 Pedro Martinez	15.00	4.50
20 Jeff Bagwell	15.00	4.50
21 Ichiro Suzuki ROY	40.00	12.00
22 Albert Pujols ROY	50.00	15.00

2001 Donruss Class of 2001 BobbleHead Cards

The cards were inserted in with the 2001 Donruss BobbleHead dolls, the 22-card set features some of baseball's most prized players. Please note that there were only 2000 of each card product, except for the two ROY cards numbered to 1000 each.

	Nm-Mt	Ex-Mt
COMPLETE SET (22)	200.00	60.00
1 Ichiro Suzuki	25.00	7.50
2 Cal Ripken	20.00	6.00
3 Derek Jeter	15.00	4.50
4 Mark McGwire	20.00	6.00
5 Albert Pujols	30.00	9.00
6 Ken Griffey Jr.	10.00	3.00
7 Nomar Garciaparra	10.00	3.00
8 Mike Piazza	10.00	3.00
9 Alex Rodriguez	10.00	3.00
10 Manny Ramirez	8.00	2.40
11 Tsuyoshi Shinjo	8.00	2.40
12 Hideo Nomo	10.00	3.00
13 Chipper Jones	8.00	2.40
14 Sammy Sosa	10.00	3.00
15 Roger Clemens	12.00	3.60
16 Tony Gwynn	8.00	2.40
17 Barry Bonds	15.00	4.50
18 Kazuhiro Sasaki	8.00	2.40
19 Pedro Martinez	8.00	2.40
20 Jeff Bagwell	8.00	2.40
21 Ichiro Suzuki ROY	30.00	9.00
22 Albert Pujols ROY	40.00	12.00

2001 Donruss Class of 2001 Crusade

Randomly inserted into packs, this 50-card insert features players on a mission. Card backs carry a "C" prefix. Individual print runs are listed in our checklist.

	Nm-Mt	Ex-Mt
C-1 Roger Clemens/275	25.00	7.50
C-2 Luis Gonzalez/275	8.00	2.40
C-3 Troy Glaus/275	8.00	2.40
C-4 Freddy Garcia/300	8.00	2.40
C-5 Sean Casey/285	8.00	2.40
C-6 Bobby Abreu/300	8.00	2.40
C-7 Matt Morris/300	8.00	2.40
C-8 Cal Ripken/275	40.00	12.00
C-9 Miguel Tejada/285	8.00	2.40
C-10 V.Guerrero/275	12.00	3.60
C-11 Mark Buehrle/100	8.00	2.40
C-12 Mike Sweeney/300	8.00	2.40
C-13 Ivan Rodriguez/275	12.00	3.60
C-14 Jeff Bagwell/275	8.00	2.40
C-15 Joe Mays/250	8.00	2.40
C-16 Cliff Floyd/300	8.00	2.40
C-17 Lance Berkman/300	8.00	2.40
C-18 Aramis Ramirez/100	8.00	2.40
C-19 Tony Gwynn/300	15.00	4.50
C-20 S.Stewart/100	8.00	2.40
C-21 Todd Helton/275	8.00	2.40
C-22 Chipper Jones/275	12.00	3.60
C-23 Javier Vazquez/100	8.00	2.40
C-24 Shawn Green/275	8.00	2.40
C-25 Barry Bonds/300	30.00	9.00
C-26 Albert Pujols/250	60.00	18.00
C-27 Wilson Betemit/100	8.00	2.40
C-28 C.C. Sabathia/290	8.00	2.40
C-29 Roy Oswalt/100	8.00	2.40
C-30 Johnny Estrada/100	10.00	3.00
C-31 Nick Johnson/100	8.00	2.40
C-32 Aubrey Huff/100	8.00	2.40
C-33 Corey Patterson/200	8.00	2.40
C-34 Jay Gibbons/100	10.00	3.00
C-35 Marcus Giles/100	8.00	2.40
C-36 Juan Cruz/100	8.00	2.40
C-37 Tsuyoshi Shinjo/300	8.00	2.40
C-38 Ben Sheets/285	8.00	2.40
C-39 Bud Smith/100	8.00	2.40
C-40 Alex Escobar/100	8.00	2.40
C-41 Joe Kennedy/100	8.00	2.40
C-42 Alexis Gomez/100	8.00	2.40
C-43 Jimmy Rollins/300	8.00	2.40
C-44 Josh Towers/100	8.00	2.40
C-45 Joe Crede/100	8.00	2.40
C-46 B.Duckworth/100	8.00	2.40
C-47 Ichiro Suzuki/300	40.00	12.00
C-48 Jose Ortiz/100	8.00	2.40
C-49 Casey Fossum/100	8.00	2.40
C-50 Adam Dunn/200	8.00	2.40

2001 Donruss Class of 2001 Crusade Autographs

Randomly inserted into packs, this 39-card insert features authentic autographs from veterans like Cal Ripken and Chipper Jones. Card backs carry a "C" prefix. Individual print runs are listed in our checklist.

	Nm-Mt	Ex-Mt
C-1 Roger Clemens/25		
C-2 Luis Gonzalez/25		
C-3 Troy Glaus/25		
C-5 Sean Casey/15		
C-8 Cal Ripken/25		
C-9 Miguel Tejada/15		
C-10 Vladimir Guerrero/25		
C-11 Mark Buehrle/200	15.00	4.50
C-13 Ivan Rodriguez/25		
C-14 Jeff Bagwell/25		
C-15 Joe Mays/50		
C-18 Aramis Ramirez/200	15.00	4.50
C-20 S. Stewart/200	15.00	4.50
C-21 Todd Helton/25		
C-22 Chipper Jones/25		
C-23 Javier Vazquez/200	15.00	4.50
C-24 Shawn Green/25		
C-26 Albert Pujols/50	400.00	120.00
C-27 Wilson Betemit/200	15.00	4.50
C-28 C.C. Sabathia/10		
C-29 Roy Oswalt/200	20.00	6.00
C-30 Johnny Estrada/200	25.00	7.50
C-31 Nick Johnson/200	15.00	4.50
C-32 Aubrey Huff/200	15.00	4.50
C-33 Corey Patterson/100	15.00	4.50
C-34 Jay Gibbons/200	25.00	7.50
C-35 Marcus Giles/200	15.00	4.50
C-36 Juan Cruz/200	15.00	4.50
C-38 Ben Sheets/15		
C-39 Bud Smith/200	15.00	4.50
C-40 Alex Escobar/200	15.00	4.50
C-41 Joe Kennedy/200	20.00	6.00
C-42 Alexis Gomez/200	15.00	4.50
C-44 Josh Towers/200	15.00	4.50
C-45 Joe Crede/200	15.00	4.50
C-46 B. Duckworth/200	15.00	4.50
C-48 Jose Ortiz/200	15.00	4.50
C-49 Casey Fossum/200	15.00	4.50
C-50 Adam Dunn/100	40.00	12.00

2001 Donruss Class of 2001 Dominators

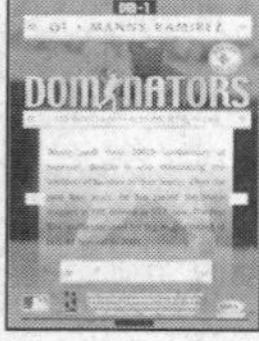

Randomly inserted into packs at one in 20, this 30-card insert features players that dominate their opponents. Card backs carry a "DM" prefix.

	Nm-Mt	Ex-Mt
COMPLETE SET (30)	150.00	45.00
DM-1 Manny Ramirez	5.00	1.50
DM-2 Lance Berkman	5.00	1.50
DM-3 Juan Gonzalez	5.00	1.50
DM-4 Albert Pujols	30.00	9.00
DM-5 Jason Giambi	5.00	1.50
DM-6 Mike Sweeney	5.00	1.50
DM-7 Rafael Palmeiro	5.00	1.50
DM-8 Luis Gonzalez	5.00	1.50
DM-9 Ichiro Suzuki	15.00	4.50
DM-10 Cliff Floyd	5.00	1.50
DM-11 Roberto Alomar	5.00	1.50
DM-12 Paul LoDuca	5.00	1.50
DM-13 Shannon Stewart	5.00	1.50
DM-14 Barry Bonds	15.00	4.50
DM-15 Larry Walker	5.00	1.50
DM-16 Shawn Green	5.00	1.50
DM-17 Moises Alou	5.00	1.50
DM-18 Cal Ripken	20.00	6.00
DM-19 Brian Giles	5.00	1.50
DM-20 Magglio Ordonez	5.00	1.50
DM-21 Jose Vidro	5.00	1.50
DM-22 Edgar Martinez	5.00	1.50
DM-23 Aramis Ramirez	5.00	1.50
DM-24 Tony Gwynn	8.00	2.40
DM-25 Richie Sexson	5.00	1.50
DM-26 Todd Helton	5.00	1.50
DM-27 Garret Anderson	5.00	1.50
DM-28 Chipper Jones	6.00	1.80
DM-29 Troy Glaus	5.00	1.50
DM-30 Jeff Bagwell	5.00	1.50

2001 Donruss Class of 2001 Diamond Dominators

Randomly inserted into packs, this 30-card insert is a complete parallel of the Donruss Class of 2001 Dominators insert each featuring a game-used piece of memorabilia. Card backs carry a "DM" prefix. Individual print runs are listed below.

	Nm-Mt	Ex-Mt
DM-1 Manny Ramirez Bat/725	15.00	4.50
DM-2 Lance Berkman Bat/725	10.00	3.00
DM-3 Juan Gonzalez Bat/500	15.00	4.50
DM-4 Albert Pujols Bat/125	80.00	24.00
DM-5 Jason Giambi Bat/250	10.00	3.00
DM-6 Mike Sweeney Jsy/325	10.00	3.00
DM-7 Rafael Palmeiro Bat/550	15.00	4.50
DM-8 Luis Gonzalez Bat/725	10.00	3.00
DM-9 Ichiro Suzuki Ball/50	100.00	30.00
DM-10 Cliff Floyd Jsy/725	10.00	3.00
DM-11 Roberto Alomar Bat/200	15.00	4.50
DM-12 Paul LoDuca Jsy/600	10.00	3.00
DM-13 Shannon Stewart Bat/725	10.00	3.00
DM-14 Barry Bonds Bat/250	25.00	7.50
DM-15 Larry Walker Bat/725	15.00	4.50
DM-16 Shawn Green Bat/500	10.00	3.00
DM-17 Moises Alou Bat/550	10.00	3.00
DM-18 Cal Ripken Bat/250	40.00	12.00
DM-19 Brian Giles Bat/725	10.00	3.00
DM-20 Magglio Ordonez Bat/725	10.00	3.00
DM-21 Jose Vidro Jsy/725	10.00	3.00
DM-22 Edgar Martinez Jsy/200	15.00	4.50
DM-23 Aramis Ramirez Bat/200	10.00	3.00
DM-24 Tony Gwynn Bat/500	15.00	4.50
DM-25 Richie Sexson Bat/725	10.00	3.00
DM-26 Todd Helton Bat/725	15.00	4.50
DM-27 Garret Anderson Bat/725	10.00	3.00
DM-28 Chipper Jones Bat/725	15.00	4.50
DM-29 Troy Glaus Jsy/200	10.00	3.00
DM-30 Jeff Bagwell Jsy/325	15.00	4.50

2001 Donruss Class of 2001 Rewards

Randomly inserted into packs at one in 212, th 10-card insert features award winning playe Card backs carry a "RW" prefix.

	Nm-Mt	Ex-Mt
RW-1 Jason Giambi MVP	10.00	3.00
RW-2 Ichiro Suzuki MVP	30.00	9.00
RW-3 Roger Clemens CY	30.00	9.00
RW-4 Freddy Garcia CY	10.00	3.0
RW-5 Ichiro Suzuki ROY	30.00	9.0
RW-6 Albert Pujols ROY	40.00	12.0
RW-7 Barry Bonds MVP	30.00	9.0
RW-8 Albert Pujols MVP	40.00	12.0
RW-9 Randy Johnson CY	15.00	4.5
RW-10 Matt Morris CY	10.00	3.0

2001 Donruss Class of 2001 Final Rewards

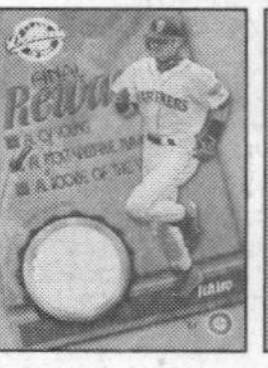

Randomly inserted into packs, this nine-ca insert is a partial parallel of the Donruss Class 2001 Rewards insert. Each card includes a swatch of game-used memorabilia. Individu print runs are listed below.

	Nm-Mt	Ex-Mt
RW-1 Jason Giambi MVP Jsy/250	10.00	3.00
RW-2 Ichiro Suzuki MVP Ball/50	100.00	30.00
RW-3 Roger Clemens CY Jsy/200	20.00	6.00
RW-4 Freddy Garcia CY Jsy/250	10.00	3.00
RW-5 Ichiro Suzuki ROY Ball/50	100.00	30.00
RW-6 Albert Pujols ROY Bat/125	80.00	24.00
RW-7 Barry Bonds MVP Jsy/200	25.00	7.50
RW-8 Albert Pujols MVP Bat/125	80.00	24.00
RW-9 Randy Johnson CY Jsy/250	15.00	4.50

2001 Donruss Class of 2001 Rookie Team

Randomly inserted into packs at one in 83, th 15-card insert features top rookies from t 2001 season. Card backs carry a " RT" prefix.

	Nm-Mt	Ex-Mt
COMPLETE SET (15)	150.00	45.00
RT1 Jay Gibbons	8.00	2.40
RT2 Alfonso Soriano	8.00	2.40
RT3 Jimmy Rollins	5.00	1.50
RT4 Wilson Betemit	5.00	1.50
RT5 Albert Pujols	40.00	12.00
RT6 Johnny Estrada	8.00	2.40
RT7 Ichiro Suzuki	25.00	7.50
RT8 Tsuyoshi Shinjo	8.00	2.40
RT9 Adam Dunn	8.00	2.40
RT10 C.C. Sabathia	5.00	1.50
RT11 Ben Sheets	8.00	2.40
RT12 Roy Oswalt	8.00	2.40
RT13 Bud Smith	5.00	1.50
RT14 Josh Towers	5.00	1.50
RT15 Juan Cruz	5.00	1.50

2001 Donruss Class of 2001 Rookie Team Materials

Randomly inserted into packs, this 15-car insert is a parallel of the Donruss Class of 200 Rookie Team insert. Each card contains a swatc of game-used memorabilia. Individual print rur are listed in our checklist.

	Nm-Mt	Ex-Mt
RT1 Jay Gibbons Btg Glv/100	20.00	6.00
RT2 Alfonso Soriano Btg Glv/100	20.00	6.00
RT3 J.Rollins Jsy/200	10.00	3.00
RT4 Wilson Betemit Hat/100	15.00	4.50
RT5 Albert Pujols Bat/100	80.00	24.00
RT6 Johnny Estrada Shoes/100	20.00	6.00
RT7 Ichiro Suzuki Ball/50	100.00	30.00
RT8 T.Shinjo Shoes/200	15.00	4.50
RT9 Adam Dunn Bat/200	15.00	4.50
RT10 C.C. Sabathia Jsy/200	10.00	3.00
RT11 Ben Sheets Bat/200	15.00	4.50
RT12 Roy Oswalt Btg Glv/50	25.00	7.50
RT13 Bud Smith Jsy/250	10.00	3.00
RT14 J.Towers Pants/200	10.00	3.00
RT15 Juan Cruz Jsy/200	10.00	3.00

2001 Donruss Class of 2001 Yearbook

andomly inserted into packs at one in 24, this 5-card insert features players that had out-standing seasons in 2001. Card backs carry a "B" prefix.

	Nm-Mt	Ex-Mt
OMPLETE SET (25)	150.00	45.00
B-1 Barry Bonds	15.00	4.50
3-2 Mark Mulder	4.00	1.20
B-3 Luis Gonzalez	4.00	1.20
B-4 Lance Berkman	4.00	1.20
B-5 Matt Morris	4.00	1.20
B-6 Roy Oswalt	4.00	1.20
B-7 Todd Helton	4.00	1.20
B-8 Tsuyoshi Shinjo	4.00	1.20
B-9 C.C. Sabathia	4.00	1.20
B-10 Curt Schilling	4.00	1.20
B-11 Rickey Henderson	6.00	1.80
B-12 Jamie Moyer	4.00	1.20
B-13 Shawn Green	4.00	1.20
B-14 Randy Johnson	6.00	1.80
B-15 Jim Thome	6.00	1.80
B-16 Larry Walker	4.00	1.20
B-17 Jimmy Rollins	4.00	1.20
B-18 Kazuhiro Sasaki	4.00	1.20
B-19 Hideo Nomo	6.00	1.80
B-20 Roger Clemens	12.00	3.60
B-21 Bud Smith	4.00	1.20
B-22 Ichiro Suzuki	15.00	4.50
B-23 Albert Pujols	20.00	6.00
B-24 Cal Ripken	20.00	6.00
B-25 Tony Gwynn	8.00	2.40

2001 Donruss Class of 2001 Scrapbook

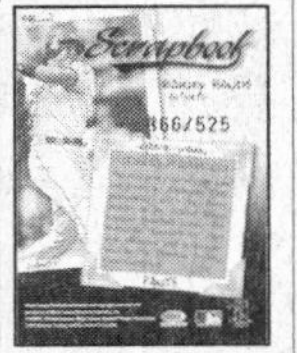

andomly inserted into packs, this 24-card nsert is a partial parallel of the Donruss Class of 001 Yearbook insert. Each card contains a watch of game-used memorabilia. Individual rint runs are listed below.

	Nm-Mt	Ex-Mt
B-1 B.Bonds Pants/525	25.00	7.50
B-2 Mark Mulder/500	10.00	3.00
B-3 Luis Gonzalez/500	10.00	3.00
B-4 Lance Berkman/525	10.00	3.00
B-5 Does Not Exist		
B-6 Roy Oswalt/150	15.00	4.50
B-7 Todd Helton/525	15.00	4.50
B-8 Tsuyoshi Shinjo/75	15.00	4.50
B-9 C.C. Sabathia/500	10.00	3.00
B-10 Curt Schilling/525	10.00	3.00
B-11 R.Henderson Bat/200	15.00	4.50
B-12 Jamie Moyer/500	10.00	3.00
B-13 Shawn Green/525	10.00	3.00
B-14 R.Johnson/500	15.00	4.50
B-15 Jim Thome/400	15.00	4.50
B-16 Larry Walker/500	15.00	4.50
B-17 Jimmy Rollins Base/25		
B-18 K.Sasaki/500	10.00	3.00
B-19 Hideo Nomo/150	25.00	7.50
B-20 Roger Clemens/475	25.00	7.50
B-21 Bud Smith/525	10.00	3.00
B-22 Ichiro Suzuki Ball/75	80.00	24.00
B-23 A.Pujols Bat/150	80.00	24.00
B-24 Cal Ripken/525	40.00	12.00
B-25 T.Gwynn Pants/500	15.00	4.50

2001 Donruss Classics

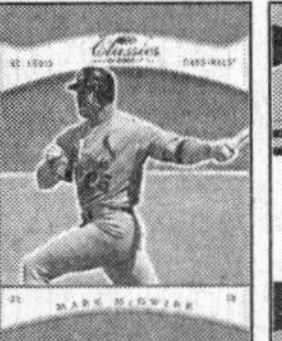
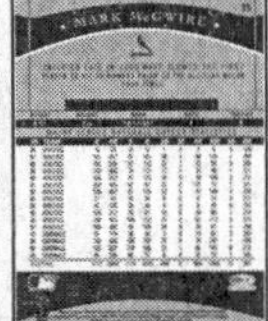

his 200-card set was distributed in six-card acks with a suggested retail price of $11.99. he set features color photos of stars of the ame from the past, present, and future high-ghted with silver tint and foil. Cards 101-150 isplay color photos of rookies and are sequen-ially numbered to 585. Cards 151-200 consist-ng of retired players are sequentially numbered o 1755 and are highlighted with gold tint and oil. Cards 162 (Sandy Koufax LGD) and 185 Robin Roberts LGD) were not intended for pub-c release but a handful of copies made their vay into packs despite the manufacturers efforts o physically pull them from the production rocess. Due to their scarcity, the set is consid-red complete at 198 cards and pricing is navailable on them individually.

	Nm-Mt	Ex-Mt
OMP.SET w/o SP's (100)	25.00	7.50
OMMON CARD (1-100)	.60	.18
COMMON (101-150)	5.00	1.50
COMMON (151-200)	4.00	1.20
1 Alex Rodriguez	2.50	.75
2 Barry Bonds	4.00	1.20
3 Cal Ripken	5.00	1.50
4 Chipper Jones	1.50	.45
5 Derek Jeter	4.00	1.20
6 Troy Glaus	.60	.18
7 Frank Thomas	1.50	.45
8 Greg Maddux	2.50	.75
9 Ivan Rodriguez	1.50	.45
10 Jeff Bagwell	1.00	.30
11 Cliff Floyd	.60	.18
12 Todd Helton	1.00	.30
13 Ken Griffey Jr.	2.50	.75
14 Manny Ramirez	1.00	.30
15 Mark McGwire	4.00	1.20
16 Mike Piazza	2.50	.75
17 Nomar Garciaparra	2.50	.75
18 Pedro Martinez	1.50	.45
19 Randy Johnson	1.50	.45
20 Rick Ankiel	.60	.18
21 Rickey Henderson	1.50	.45
22 Roger Clemens	3.00	.90
23 Sammy Sosa	2.50	.75
24 Tony Gwynn	2.00	.60
25 Vladimir Guerrero	1.50	.45
26 Kazuhiro Sasaki	.60	.18
27 Roberto Alomar	1.00	.30
28 Barry Zito	1.00	.30
29 Pat Burrell	.60	.18
30 Harold Baines	.60	.18
31 Carlos Delgado	.60	.18
32 J.D. Drew	.60	.18
33 Jim Edmonds	.60	.18
34 Darin Erstad	.60	.18
35 Jason Giambi	.60	.18
36 Tom Glavine	1.00	.30
37 Juan Gonzalez	1.00	.30
38 Mark Grace	1.00	.30
39 Shawn Green	.60	.18
40 Tim Hudson	.60	.18
41 Andruw Jones	.60	.18
42 Jeff Kent	.60	.18
43 Barry Larkin	1.00	.30
44 Rafael Furcal	.60	.18
45 Mike Mussina	1.00	.30
46 Hideo Nomo	1.50	.45
47 Rafael Palmeiro	1.00	.30
48 Scott Rolen	1.50	.45
49 Gary Sheffield	.60	.18
50 Bernie Williams	1.00	.30
51 Bob Abreu	.60	.18
52 Edgardo Alfonzo	.60	.18
53 Edgar Martinez	1.00	.30
54 Magglio Ordonez	.60	.18
55 Kerry Wood	1.50	.45
56 Adrian Beltre	.60	.18
57 Lance Berkman	.60	.18
58 Kevin Brown	.60	.18
59 Sean Casey	.60	.18
60 Eric Chavez	.60	.18
61 Bartolo Colon	.60	.18
62 Johnny Damon	1.00	.30
63 Jermaine Dye	.60	.18
64 Juan Encarnacion	.60	.18
65 Carl Everett	.60	.18
66 Brian Giles	.60	.18
67 Mike Hampton	.60	.18
68 Richard Hidalgo	.60	.18
69 Geoff Jenkins	.60	.18
70 Jacque Jones	.60	.18
71 Jason Kendall	.60	.18
72 Ryan Klesko	.60	.18
73 Chan Ho Park	.60	.18
74 Richie Sexson	.60	.18
75 Mike Sweeney	.60	.18
76 Fernando Tatis	.60	.18
77 Miguel Tejada	.60	.18
78 Jose Vidro	.60	.18
79 Larry Walker	1.00	.30
80 Preston Wilson	.60	.18
81 Craig Biggio	1.00	.30
82 Fred McGriff	1.00	.30
83 Jim Thome	1.50	.45
84 Garret Anderson	.60	.18
85 Russell Branyan	.60	.18
86 Tony Batista	.60	.18
87 Terrence Long	.60	.18
88 Brad Fullmer	.60	.18
89 Rusty Greer	.60	.18
90 Orlando Hernandez	.60	.18
91 Gabe Kapler	.60	.18
92 Paul Konerko	.60	.18
93 Carlos Lee	.60	.18
94 Kenny Lofton	.60	.18
95 Raul Mondesi	.60	.18
96 Jorge Posada	1.00	.30
97 Tim Salmon	1.00	.30
98 Greg Vaughn	.60	.18
99 Mo Vaughn	.60	.18
100 Omar Vizquel	1.00	.30
101 Aubrey Huff SP	5.00	1.50
102 Jimmy Rollins SP	5.00	1.50
103 Cory Aldridge SP RC	5.00	1.50
104 Wilmy Caceres SP RC	5.00	1.50
105 Josh Beckett SP	5.00	1.50
106 Wilson Betemit SP RC	5.00	1.50
107 Timo Perez SP	5.00	1.50
108 Albert Pujols SP RC	100.00	30.00
109 Bud Smith SP RC	5.00	1.50
110 Jack Wilson SP RC	10.00	3.00
111 Alex Escobar SP	5.00	1.50
112 J. Estrada SP RC	8.00	2.40
113 Pedro Feliz SP	5.00	1.50
114 Nate Frese SP RC	5.00	1.50
115 Carlos Garcia SP RC	5.00	1.50
116 Brandon Larson SP RC	5.00	1.50
117 Alexis Gomez SP RC	5.00	1.50
118 Jason Hart SP	5.00	1.50
119 Adam Dunn SP	8.00	2.40
120 Marcus Giles SP	5.00	1.50
121 C. Parker SP RC	5.00	1.50
122 J.Melian SP RC	5.00	1.50
123 Endy Chavez SP RC	5.00	1.50
124 A.Hernandez SP RC	5.00	1.50
125 Joe Kennedy SP RC	8.00	2.40
126 Jose Mieses SP RC	5.00	1.50
127 C.C. Sabathia SP	5.00	1.50
128 Eric Munson SP	5.00	1.50
129 Xavier Nady SP	5.00	1.50
130 H. Ramirez SP RC	8.00	2.40
131 Abraham Nunez SP	5.00	1.50
132 Jose Ortiz SP	5.00	1.50
133 Jeremy Owens SP RC	5.00	1.50
134 Claudio Vargas SP RC	5.00	1.50
135 Corey Patterson SP	5.00	1.50
136 Andres Torres SP RC	5.00	1.50
137 Ben Sheets SP	8.00	2.40
138 Joe Crede SP	5.00	1.50
139 A.Pettyjohn SP RC	5.00	1.50
140 E.Guzman SP RC	5.00	1.50
141 Jay Gibbons SP RC	8.00	2.40
142 Wilkin Ruan SP RC	5.00	1.50
143 Tsuyoshi Shinjo SP RC	8.00	2.40
144 Alfonso Soriano SP	8.00	2.40
145 Nick Johnson SP	5.00	1.50
146 Ichiro Suzuki SP RC	60.00	18.00
147 Juan Uribe SP RC	8.00	2.40
148 Jack Cust SP	5.00	1.50
149 C.Valderrama SP RC	5.00	1.50
150 Matt White SP RC	5.00	1.50
151 Hank Aaron LGD	10.00	3.00
152 Ernie Banks LGD	5.00	1.50
153 Johnny Bench LGD	5.00	1.50
154 George Brett LGD	12.00	3.60
155 Lou Brock LGD	5.00	1.50
156 Rod Carew LGD	5.00	1.50
157 Steve Carlton LGD	4.00	1.20
158 Bob Feller LGD	4.00	1.20
159 Bob Gibson LGD	5.00	1.50
160 Reggie Jackson LGD	5.00	1.50
161 Al Kaline LGD	5.00	1.50
162 Sandy Koufax LGD SP		
163 Don Mattingly LGD	12.00	3.60
164 Willie Mays LGD	10.00	3.00
165 Willie McCovey LGD	4.00	1.20
166 Joe Morgan LGD	4.00	1.20
167 Stan Musial LGD	8.00	2.40
168 Jim Palmer LGD	4.00	1.20
169 Brooks Robinson LGD	5.00	1.50
170 Frank Robinson LGD	5.00	1.50
171 Nolan Ryan LGD	12.00	3.60
172 Mike Schmidt LGD	10.00	3.00
173 Tom Seaver LGD	5.00	1.50
174 Warren Spahn LGD	5.00	1.50
175 Robin Yount LGD	8.00	2.40
176 Wade Boggs LGD	5.00	1.50
177 Ty Cobb LGD	8.00	2.40
178 Lou Gehrig LGD	10.00	3.00
179 Luis Aparicio LGD	4.00	1.20
180 Babe Ruth LGD	15.00	4.50
181 Ryne Sandberg LGD	10.00	3.00
182 Yogi Berra LGD	5.00	1.50
183 R.Clemente LGD	12.00	3.60
184 Eddie Murray LGD	5.00	1.50
185 Robin Roberts LGD SP		
186 Duke Snider LGD	5.00	1.50
187 Orlando Cepeda LGD	4.00	1.20
188 Billy Williams LGD	4.00	1.20
189 Juan Marichal LGD	4.00	1.20
190 Harmon Killebrew LGD	5.00	1.50
191 Kirby Puckett LGD	5.00	1.50
192 Carlton Fisk LGD	5.00	1.50
193 Dave Winfield LGD	4.00	1.20
194 Whitey Ford LGD	5.00	1.50
195 Paul Molitor LGD	5.00	1.50
196 Tony Perez LGD	4.00	1.20
197 Ozzie Smith LGD	8.00	2.40
198 Ralph Kiner LGD	5.00	1.50
199 Fergie Jenkins LGD	4.00	1.20
200 Phil Rizzuto LGD	5.00	1.50

2001 Donruss Classics Significant Signatures

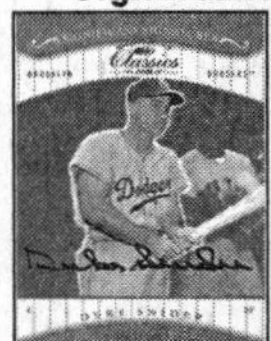
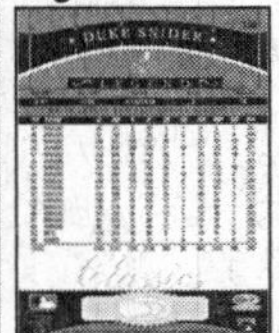

Randomly inserted into packs at the rate of one in 18, this 83-card set is a partial parallel version of the base set. Each card is autographed and displays a rookie/prospect or retired player with platinum tint and holographic foil. Please note, the following cards packed out as redemption cards with an expiration date of September 10th, 2003: Hank Aaron, Luis Aparicio, Ernie Banks, Josh Beckett, Yogi Berra, Rod Carew, Steve Carlton, Orlando Cepeda, Adam Dunn, Johnny Estrada, Bob Feller, Carlton Fisk, Whitey Ford, Bob Gibson, Reggie Jackson, Nick Johnson, Juan Marichal, Willie Mays, Paul Molitor, Joe Morgan, Eddie Murray, Jim Palmer, Corey Patterson, Tony Perez, Kirby Puckett, Phil Rizzuto, Brooks Robinson, Frank Robinson, Nolan Ryan (Astros), C.C. Sabathia, Ryne Sandberg, Ron Santo, Mike Schmidt, Ben Sheets, Ozzie Smith, Billy Williams, Dave Winfield and Robin Yount. Exchange card 162 was originally intended to feature Sandy Koufax but in late 2002 representatives at Donruss switched the redemption to a Nolan Ryan Mets card (Ryan's basic card 171 in the set pictures him as a member of the Texas Rangers). In addition, exchange card 185 was originally intended to feature Robin Roberts but the redemption was switched in late 2002 to Ron Santo.

	Nm-Mt	Ex-Mt
101 Aubrey Huff	10.00	3.00
103 Cory Aldridge	10.00	3.00
105 Josh Beckett SP	25.00	7.50
106 Wilson Betemit	10.00	3.00
107 Timo Perez	8.00	2.40
108 Albert Pujols	300.00	90.00
110 Jack Wilson	20.00	6.00
111 Alex Escobar	8.00	2.40
112 Johnny Estrada	15.00	4.50
113 Pedro Feliz	8.00	2.40
114 Nate Frese	10.00	3.00
115 Carlos Garcia	10.00	3.00
116 Brandon Larson	10.00	3.00
118 Jason Hart	8.00	2.40
119 Adam Dunn SP	25.00	7.50
120 Marcus Giles	10.00	3.00
121 Christian Parker	8.00	2.40
126 Jose Mieses	10.00	3.00
127 C.C.Sabathia SP	15.00	4.50
129 Xavier Nady	8.00	2.40
130 Horacio Ramirez	15.00	4.50
131 Abraham Nunez	8.00	2.40
132 Jose Ortiz	8.00	2.40
133 Jeremy Owens	10.00	3.00
134 Claudio Vargas	10.00	3.00
135 Corey Patterson SP	15.00	4.50
136 Andres Torres	10.00	3.00
137 Ben Sheets SP	25.00	7.50
138 Joe Crede	8.00	2.40
139 Adam Pettyjohn	10.00	3.00
140 Elpidio Guzman	10.00	3.00
141 Jay Gibbons	15.00	4.50
142 Wilkin Ruan	10.00	3.00
144 Alfonso Soriano SP	40.00	12.00
145 Nick Johnson SP	15.00	4.50
147 Juan Uribe	15.00	4.50
149 Carlos Valderrama	10.00	3.00
151 Hank Aaron SP	200.00	60.00
152 Ernie Banks	40.00	12.00
153 Johnny Bench SP	100.00	30.00
154 George Brett SP	175.00	52.50
155 Lou Brock	25.00	7.50
156 Rod Carew	25.00	7.50
157 Steve Carlton	25.00	7.50
158 Bob Feller	20.00	6.00
159 Bob Gibson	25.00	7.50
160 Reggie Jackson SP	100.00	30.00
161 Al Kaline	40.00	12.00
162 Nolan Ryan Astros SP	150.00	45.00
163 Don Mattingly	100.00	30.00
164 Willie Mays SP	200.00	60.00
165 Willie McCovey	25.00	7.50
166 Joe Morgan	20.00	6.00
167 Stan Musial SP	100.00	30.00
168 Jim Palmer	20.00	6.00
169 B. Robinson EXCH	25.00	7.50
170 Frank Robinson	25.00	7.50
171 Nolan Ryan Rangers SP	150.00	45.00
172 Mike Schmidt	80.00	24.00
173 Tom Seaver	25.00	7.50
174 Warren Spahn	40.00	12.00
175 Robin Yount SP	120.00	36.00
176 Wade Boggs SP	80.00	24.00
179 Luis Aparicio	20.00	6.00
181 Ryne Sandberg	80.00	24.00
182 Yogi Berra	40.00	12.00
184 Eddie Murray	60.00	18.00
185 Ron Santo	25.00	7.50
186 Duke Snider	25.00	7.50
187 Orlando Cepeda	20.00	6.00
188 Billy Williams	20.00	6.00
189 Juan Marichal	20.00	6.00
190 Harmon Killebrew	40.00	12.00
191 Kirby Puckett SP	100.00	30.00
192 Carlton Fisk	25.00	7.50
193 Dave Winfield SP	80.00	24.00
194 Whitey Ford	25.00	7.50
195 Paul Molitor SP	80.00	24.00
196 Tony Perez	20.00	6.00
197 Ozzie Smith SP	120.00	36.00
198 Ralph Kiner	25.00	7.50
199 Fergie Jenkins	20.00	6.00
200 Phil Rizzuto	40.00	12.00

2001 Donruss Classics Timeless Tributes

Randomly inserted in packs, this 198-card set is a parallel version of the base set featuring silver or gold holo-foil highlights. The cards are sequentially numbered to 100. Cards 162 and 185 are believed to not exist. It's likely the cards were printed, but due to contractual problems with the featured athletes (Sandy Koufax for card 162 and Robin Roberts for card 185), the manufacturer made the effort to pull and destroy all copies found within the print run during the packout process. A handful of copies of the basic versions of these cards have been confirmed to exist, but given the fact that 1755 of each of those were originally printed versus only 100 of the Timeless Tribute parallels, the likelihood of the parallels sneaking into packs is far slimmer.

	Nm-Mt	Ex-Mt
*TRIBUTE 1-100: 2.5X TO 6X BASIC..		
*TRIBUTE 101-150: .5X TO 1.2X BASIC		
*TRIBUTE 151-200: 1.25X TO 3X BASIC		
108 Albert Pujols	120.00	36.00
146 Ichiro Suzuki	100.00	30.00

2001 Donruss Classics Benchmarks

Randomly inserted in hobby packs at the rate of one in 18 and in retail packs at the rate of one in 72, this 25-card set features color player photos with game-used bench swatches embedded in the cards. Hank Aaron, Willie Stargell and card BM19 were only available as exchange cards. Those cards could be redeemed until September 10, 2003.

	Nm-Mt	Ex-Mt
CARDS 11, 19 AND 24 WERE EXCHANGE		
NO EXCH.PRICING DUE TO SCARCITY		
BM1 Todd Helton	15.00	4.50
BM2 Roberto Clemente	50.00	15.00
BM3 Mark McGwire	40.00	12.00
BM4 Barry Bonds	30.00	9.00
BM5 Bob Gibson	15.00	4.50
BM6 Ken Griffey Jr.	20.00	6.00
BM7 Frank Robinson	15.00	4.50
BM8 Greg Maddux	20.00	6.00
BM9 Reggie Jackson	15.00	4.50
BM10 Sammy Sosa	20.00	6.00
BM11 Willie Stargell EXCH		
BM12 Vladimir Guerrero	15.00	4.50
BM13 Johnny Bench	15.00	4.50
BM14 Tony Gwynn	15.00	4.50
BM15 Mike Schmidt	25.00	7.50
BM16 Ivan Rodriguez	15.00	4.50
BM17 Jeff Bagwell	15.00	4.50
BM18 Cal Ripken	40.00	12.00
BM19 TBD EXCH		
BM20 Kirby Puckett	15.00	4.50
BM21 Frank Thomas	15.00	4.50
BM22 Joe Morgan	10.00	3.00
BM23 Mike Piazza	20.00	6.00
BM24 Hank Aaron EXCH		
BM25 Andruw Jones	10.00	3.00

2001 Donruss Classics Benchmarks Autographs

Randomly inserted in packs, this nine-card set is a partial parallel autographed version of the regular insert set. No autographed cards were seeded into packs. Rather, exchange cards with a redemption deadline of September 10th, 2003 were inserted in their place.

	Nm-Mt	Ex-Mt
BM5 Bob Gibson		
BM7 Frank Robinson		
BM9 Reggie Jackson		
BM12 Vladimir Guerrero		
BM13 Johnny Bench		
BM15 Mike Schmidt		
BM20 Kirby Puckett		
BM22 Joe Morgan		
BM25 Andruw Jones		

2001 Donruss Classics Combos

Randomly inserted in packs, this 45-card set features color action photos of baseball legends. Some cards consist of one player while others display a pairing of two great players. Each card has two or four swatches of game-worn/used memorabilia. One player cards are sequentially numbered to 100 while two player cards are sequentially numbered to 50. The following cards were issued in packs as exchange cards with a redemption deadline of Septemer 10th, 2003: Hank Aaron, Ernie Banks, Wade Boggs, Lou Brock, Steve Carlton, Andre Dawson, Don Mattingly, Jackie Robinson, Ryne Sandberg, Willie Stargell and Billy Williams. In addition, the following dual-player cards packed out as exchange cards (with the same redemption deadline as detailed above): Banks/Williams, Carlton/Schmidt, Clemente/Stargell, Dawson/Sandberg, Mattingly/Boggs, Musial/Brock and Robinson/Snider.

	Nm-Mt	Ex-Mt
1 R.Clemente/100	150.00	45.00
2 Willie Stargell/100	40.00	12.00
3 Babe Ruth/100	600.00	180.00
4 Lou Gehrig/100	400.00	120.00
5 Hank Aaron/100	150.00	45.00
6 Eddie Mathews/100	50.00	15.00
7 Johnny Bench/100	50.00	15.00
8 Joe Morgan/100	25.00	7.50
9 Robin Yount/100	50.00	15.00
10 Paul Molitor/100	40.00	12.00
11 S.Carlton/85 EXCH	25.00	7.50
12 Mike Schmidt/85	60.00	18.00
13 Stan Musial/100	80.00	24.00
14 Lou Brock/100	40.00	12.00
15 Yogi Berra/100	50.00	15.00
16 Phil Rizzuto/100	50.00	15.00
17 Ernie Banks/85	50.00	15.00
18 B. Williams/85 EXCH	25.00	7.50
19 Don Mattingly/100	60.00	18.00
20 Wade Boggs/100	40.00	12.00
21 Jackie Robinson/100	150.00	45.00
22 Duke Snider/100	40.00	12.00
23 Frank Robinson/85	40.00	12.00
24 Brooks Robinson/85	40.00	12.00
25 Orlando Cepeda/100	25.00	7.50
26 Willie McCovey/100	25.00	7.50
27 Ryne Sandberg/100	60.00	18.00
28 Andre Dawson/100	25.00	7.50
29 H.Killebrew/100	50.00	15.00
30 Rod Carew/100	40.00	12.00
31 Roberto Clemente Willie Stargell/50	250.00	75.00
32 Babe Ruth Lou Gehrig	1000.00	300.00
33 Hank Aaron Eddie Mathews	300.00	90.00
34 Johnny Bench Joe Morgan	120.00	36.00

35 Robin Yount 150.00 45.00
Paul Molitor
36 Steve Carlton 200.00 60.00
Mike Schmidt/40
37 Stan Musial 250.00 75.00
Lou Brock/50
38 Yogi Berra 150.00 45.00
Phil Rizzuto/50
39 Ernie Banks 120.00 36.00
Billy Williams/40
40 Don Mattingly 150.00 45.00
Wade Boggs/50
41 Jackie Robinson Jacket-Jsy 200.00 60.00
Duke Snider Bat-Jsy/50
42 Brooks Robinson 100.00 30.00
Frank Robinson
43 Orlando Cepeda 100.00 30.00
Willie McCovey/50
44 Andre Dawson 150.00 45.00
Ryne Sandberg/50
45 Harmon Killebrew 120.00 36.00
Rod Carew

2001 Donruss Classics Combos Autograph

Randomly inserted in packs, this ten-card set is a partial parallel autographed version of the regular insert set. No autographed cards were seeded into packs. Rather, exchange cards with a redmeption deadline of September 10th, 2003 were seeded in their place. Each actual single-player autograph card is serial numbered to 15 copies and dual-player card serial numbered to 10 copies.

Nm-Mt Ex-Mt
CC11 Steve Carlton/15......................
CC12 Mike Schmidt/15......................
CC17 Ernie Banks/15.........................
CC18 Billy Williams/15......................
CC23 Frank Robinson/15....................
CC24 Brooks Robinson/15..................
CC36 Steve Carlton.............................
Mike Schmidt
CC39 Ernie Banks..............................
Billy Williams
CC40 Don Mattingly...........................
Wade Boggs/10
CC42 Brooks Robinson.......................
Frank Robinson

2001 Donruss Classics Legendary Lumberjacks

Randomly inserted in hobby packs at the rate of one in 18 and in retail packs at the rate of one in 72, this 50-card set features color photos of the most skilled sluggers in Baseball. A swatch of a game-used bat was embedded in each card. The following cards packed out as exchange cards with a redemption deadline of September 10th, 2003: Hack Wilson, Hank Aaron, Ernie Banks, Nellie Fox, Jimmie Foxx, Rogers Horsnby, Roger Maris, Willie Stargell and Ted Williams.

Nm-Mt Ex-Mt
STATED ODDS 1:18 HOBBY, 1:72 RETAIL
SP PRINT RUNS PROVIDED BY DONRUSS
SP'S ARE NOT SERIAL-NUMBERED
LL1 Hack Wilson SP/244 * 300.00 90.00
LL2 Chipper Jones.................. 25.00 7.50
LL3 Rogers Hornsby SP/301 * 200.00 60.00
LL4 Nellie Fox SP/300 * ....
LL5 Ivan Rodriguez................. 25.00 7.50
LL6 Jimmie Foxx SP/300 * 300.00 90.00
LL7 Hank Aaron 50.00 15.00
LL8 Yogi Berra SP/400 * ....
LL9 Ernie Banks SP/300 * ....
LL10 George Brett.................... 40.00 12.00
LL11 Ty Cobb SP/100 * 200.00 60.00
LL12 R. Clemente SP............... 150.00 45.00
LL13 Carlton Fisk..................... 15.00 4.50
LL14 Reggie Jackson................ 15.00 4.50
LL15 Al Kaline.......................... 25.00 7.50
LL16 Harmon Killebrew 25.00 7.50
LL17 Ralph Kiner...................... 15.00 4.50
LL18 Roger Maris SP/275 * 250.00 75.00
LL19 Eddie Mathews SP/400 * ....
LL20 Ted Williams SP/300 * 250.00 75.00
LL21 Willie McCovey 15.00 4.50
LL22 Eddie Murray 25.00 7.50
LL23 Joe Morgan SP/268 * ....
LL24 Frank Robinson................ 15.00 4.50
LL25 Tony Perez 10.00 3.00
LL26 Mike Schmidt.................... 40.00 12.00
LL27 Ryne Sandberg 40.00 12.00
LL28 Duke Snider SP/300 * ....
LL29 Willie Stargell SP/500 * ....
LL30 Billy Williams 10.00 3.00
LL31 Dave Winfield................... 10.00 3.00
LL32 Robin Yount..................... 25.00 7.50
LL33 Barry Bonds..................... 50.00 15.00
LL34 Stan Musial SP/300 * ....
LL35 Johnny Bench SP/300 * ....
LL36 Orlando Cepeda 10.00 3.00
LL37 Todd Helton...................... 15.00 4.50
LL38 Frank Thomas.................. 25.00 7.50
LL39 Juan Gonzalez SP/400 * ....
LL40 Cal Ripken SP/200 * ....
LL41 Rafael Palmeiro................ 15.00 4.50
LL42 Troy Glaus SP/100 * ....
LL43 Vladimir Guerrero 25.00 7.50
LL44 Paul Molitor SP/400 * ....
LL45 Tony Gwynn...................... 15.00 4.50
LL46 Rod Carew 15.00 4.50
LL47 Lou Brock 15.00 4.50
LL48 Wade Boggs..................... 15.00 4.50
LL49 Babe Ruth SP/60 * 250.00 75.00
LL50 Lou Gehrig SP/100 * 200.00 60.00

2001 Donruss Classics Stadium Stars

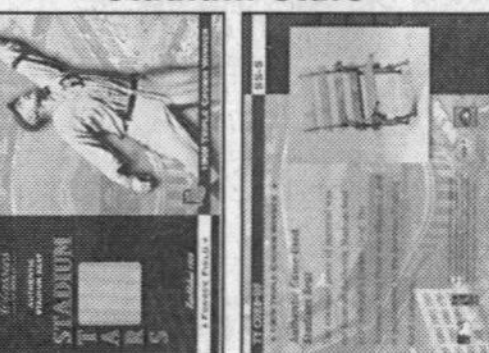

Randomly inserted in hobby packs at the rate of one in 18 and in retail packs at the rate of one in 72, this 25-card set features color action player photos with swatches of stadium seats taken from some of the most heralded ballparks embedded in the cards. An exchange card with a redemption deadline of September 10th, 2003 was seeded into packs for Honus Wagner's card.

Nm-Mt Ex-Mt
SS1 Babe Ruth SP 80.00 24.00
SS2 Cal Ripken 25.00 7.50
SS3 Brooks Robinson.............. 10.00 3.00
SS4 Tony Gwynn SP 15.00 4.50
SS5 Ty Cobb 40.00 12.00
SS6 Vladimir Guerrero SP 15.00 4.50
SS7 Lou Gehrig SP 50.00 15.00
SS8 Nomar Garciaparra 15.00 4.50
SS9 Sammy Sosa SP 15.00 4.50
SS10 Reggie Jackson SP......... 15.00 4.50
SS11 Alex Rodriguez 15.00 4.50
SS12 Derek Jeter 25.00 7.50
SS13 Willie McCovey SP 10.00 3.00
SS14 Mark McGwire................. 25.00 7.50
SS15 Chipper Jones 10.00 3.00
SS16 H. Wagner EXCH 25.00 7.50
SS17 Ken Griffey Jr.................. 15.00 4.50
SS18 Frank Robinson 10.00 3.00
SS19 Barry Bonds SP 25.00 7.50
SS20 Yogi Berra SP................. 15.00 4.50
SS21 Mike Piazza SP 15.00 4.50
SS22 Roger Clemens............... 15.00 4.50
SS23 Duke Snider SP 15.00 4.50
SS24 Frank Thomas.................. 10.00 3.00
SS25 Andruw Jones 8.00 2.40

2001 Donruss Classics Timeless Treasures

Randomly inserted in hobby packs at the rate of one in 420, and in retail packs at the rate of one in 1680, this five-card set features pictures of great players with swatches of memorabilia from five famous events in baseball history.

Nm-Mt Ex-Mt
TT1 M. McGwire Ball SP.......... 200.00 60.00
TT2 Babe Ruth Seat 80.00 24.00
TT3 H. Killebrew Bat SP........... 50.00 15.00
TT4 Derek Jeter Base.............. 50.00 15.00
TT5 Barry Bonds Ball SP 120.00 36.00

2002 Donruss Classics

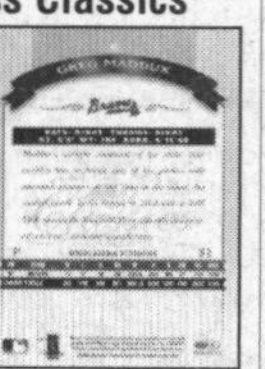

This 200 card standard-size was issued in June, 2002. An additional 25 update cards were seeded into Donruss the Rookies packs distributed in December, 2002. The basic set was released in six card packs which came in two nine-pack mini boxes per full box. The full boxes were issued four boxes to a case and had an SRP of $6 per pack. Cards 1-100 feature veteran active players, while cards 101-150 feature rookies and prospects and cards 151-200 feature retired greats. Cards numbered 101-200 were all printed to a stated print run of 1500 sets and were released two cards per mini-box (or 4 per full box of 18 packs). Update cards 201-225 were also serial-numbered to 1500.

Nm-Mt Ex-Mt
COMP.SET w/o SP's (100)........ 25.00 7.50
COMMON CARD (1-100) .... .60 .18
COMMON (101-150/201-225) 4.00 1.20
COMMON CARD (151-200) 4.00 1.20
1 Alex Rodriguez......................... 2.50 .75
2 Barry Bonds............................. 4.00 1.20
3 C.C. Sabathia .... .60 .18
4 Chipper Jones.......................... 1.50 .45
5 Derek Jeter.............................. 4.00 1.20
6 Troy Glaus................................. .60 .18
7 Frank Thomas .... 1.50 .45
8 Greg Maddux .... 2.50 .75
9 Ivan Rodriguez......................... 1.50 .45
10 Jeff Bagwell .... 1.00 .30
11 Mark Buehrle............................ .60 .18
12 Todd Helton .... 1.00 .30
13 Ken Griffey Jr........................... 2.50 .75
14 Manny Ramirez .... 1.00 .30
15 Brad Penny................................ .60 .18
16 Mike Piazza .... 2.50 .75
17 Nomar Garciaparra................. 2.50 .75
18 Pedro Martinez........................ 1.50 .45
19 Randy Johnson .... 1.50 .45
20 Bud Smith.................................. .60 .18
21 Rickey Henderson .... 1.50 .45
22 Roger Clemens........................ 3.00 .90
23 Sammy Sosa .... 2.50 .75
24 Brandon Duckworth .... .60 .18
25 Vladimir Guerrero .... 1.50 .45
26 Kazuhiro Sasaki .... .60 .18
27 Roberto Alomar .... 1.00 .30
28 Barry Zito.................................... .60 .18
29 Rich Aurilia .... .60 .18
30 Ben Sheets................................. .60 .18
31 Carlos Delgado........................... .60 .18
32 J.D. Drew .... .60 .18
33 Jermaine Dye .... .60 .18
34 Darin Erstad .... .60 .18
35 Jason Giambi .... .60 .18
36 Tom Glavine .... 1.00 .30
37 Juan Gonzalez .... 1.00 .30
38 Luis Gonzalez.............................. .60 .18
39 Shawn Green .... .60 .18
40 Tim Hudson .... .60 .18
41 Andruw Jones .... .60 .18
42 Shannon Stewart .... .60 .18
43 Barry Larkin .... 1.00 .30
44 Wade Miller.................................. .60 .18
45 Mike Mussina .... 1.00 .30
46 Hideo Nomo .... 1.50 .45
47 Rafael Palmeiro.......................... 1.00 .30
48 Scott Rolen .... 1.50 .45
49 Gary Sheffield .... .60 .18
50 Bernie Williams......................... 1.00 .30
51 Bob Abreu .... .60 .18
52 Javier Vazquez .... .60 .18
53 Edgar Martinez.......................... 1.00 .30
54 Magglio Ordonez......................... .60 .18
55 Kerry Wood................................ 1.50 .45
56 Adrian Beltre .... 1.00 .30
57 Lance Berkman .... .60 .18
58 Kevin Brown................................. .60 .18
59 Sean Casey .... .60 .18
60 Eric Chavez .... .60 .18
61 Robert Person............................... .60 .18
62 Jeremy Giambi.............................. .60 .18
63 Freddy Garcia............................... .60 .18
64 Alfonso Soriano .... 1.00 .30
65 Doug Davis .... .60 .18
66 Brian Giles .... .60 .18
67 Moises Alou.................................. .60 .18
68 Richard Hidalgo .... .60 .18
69 Paul LoDuca.................................. .60 .18
70 Aramis Ramirez .... .60 .18
71 Andres Galarraga .... .60 .18
72 Ryan Klesko .... .60 .18
73 Chan Ho Park................................. .60 .18
74 Richie Sexson .... .60 .18
75 Mike Sweeney .... .60 .18
76 Aubrey Huff.................................... .60 .18
77 Miguel Tejada................................. .60 .18
78 Jose Vidro .... .60 .18
79 Larry Walker .... 1.00 .30
80 Roy Oswalt..................................... .60 .18
81 Craig Biggio .... 1.00 .30
82 Juan Pierre..................................... .60 .18
83 Jim Thome.................................... 1.50 .45
84 Josh Towers.................................... .60 .18
85 Alex Escobar .... .60 .18
86 Cliff Floyd.. .60 .18
87 Terrence Long .... .60 .18
88 Curt Schilling .... .60 .18
89 Carlos Beltran .... 1.00 .30
90 Albert Pujols .... 3.00 .90
91 Gabe Kapler .... .60 .18
92 Mark Mulder .... .60 .18
93 Carlos Lee.. .60 .18
94 Robert Fick... .60 .18
95 Raul Mondesi .... .60 .18
96 Ichiro Suzuki................................... 2.50 .75
97 Adam Dunn .... 1.00 .30
98 Corey Patterson .... .60 .18
99 Tsuyoshi Shinjo................................... .60 .18
100 Joe Mays .... .60 .18
101 Juan Cruz ROO 4.00 1.20
102 Marlon Byrd ROO........................... 4.00 1.20
103 Luis Garcia ROO 4.00 1.20
104 Jorge Padilla ROO RC.................... 4.00 1.20
105 Dennis Tankersley ROO................. 4.00 1.20
106 Josh Pearce ROO........................... 4.00 1.20
107 Ramon Vazquez ROO 4.00 1.20
108 Chris Baker ROO RC 4.00 1.20
109 Eric Cyr ROO.................................. 4.00 1.20
110 Reed Johnson ROO RC.................. 5.00 1.50
111 Ryan Jamison ROO 4.00 1.20
112 Antonio Perez ROO 4.00 1.20
113 Satoru Komiyama ROO RC 4.00 1.20
114 Austin Kearns ROO 4.00 1.20
115 Juan Pena ROO 4.00 1.20
116 Orlando Hudson ROO 4.00 1.20
117 Kazuhisa Ishii ROO RC................... 8.00 2.40
118 Erik Bedard ROO 4.00 1.20
119 Luis Ugueto ROO RC 4.00 1.20
120 Ben Howard ROO RC 4.00 1.20
121 Morgan Ensberg ROO 4.00 1.20
122 Doug Devore ROO RC 4.00 1.20
123 Josh Phelps ROO 4.00 1.20
124 Angel Berroa ROO........................... 4.00 1.20
125 Ed Rogers ROO 4.00 1.20
126 Takahito Nomura ROO RC............... 4.00 1.20
127 John Ennis ROO RC 4.00 1.20
128 Bill Hall ROO 4.00 1.20
129 Dewon Brazelton ROO 4.00 1.20
130 Hank Blalock ROO 5.00 1.50
131 So Taguchi ROO RC 5.00 1.50
132 Jorge De La Rosa ROO RC 4.00 1.20
133 Matt Thornton ROO RC..................... 4.00 1.20
134 Brandon Backe ROO RC................... 5.00 1.50
135 Jeff Deardorff ROO 4.00 1.20
136 Steve Smyth ROO 4.00 1.20
137 An. Machado ROO RC....................... 4.00 1.20
138 John Buck ROO 4.00 1.20
139 Mark Prior ROO 8.00 2.40
140 Sean Burroughs ROO 4.00 1.20
141 Alex Herrera ROO 4.00 1.20
142 Francis Beltran ROO RC.................... 4.00 1.20
143 Jason Romano ROO 4.00 1.20
144 Michael Cuddyer ROO 4.00 1.20
145 Steve Bechler ROO RC....................... 4.00 1.20
146 Alfredo Amezaga ROO 4.00 1.20
147 Ryan Ludwick ROO............................. 4.00 1.20
148 Martin Vargas ROO 4.00 1.20
149 Allan Simpson ROO RC 4.00 1.20
150 Mark Teixeira ROO 5.00 1.50
151 Dale Murphy LGD 5.00 1.50
152 Ernie Banks LGD 5.00 1.50
153 Johnny Bench LGD 5.00 1.50
154 George Brett LGD.............................. 10.00 3.00
155 Lou Brock LGD 5.00 1.50
156 Rod Carew LGD 5.00 1.50
157 Steve Carlton LGD 4.00 1.20
158 Joe Torre LGD 5.00 1.50
159 Dennis Eckersley LGD.......................... 4.00 1.20
160 Reggie Jackson LGD............................ 5.00 1.50
161 Al Kaline LGD.. 5.00 1.50
162 Dave Parker LGD 4.00 1.20
163 Don Mattingly LGD 10.00 3.00
164 Tony Gwynn LGD.................................. 5.00 1.50
165 Willie McCovey LGD 4.00 1.20
166 Joe Morgan LGD................................... 4.00 1.20
167 Stan Musial LGD 6.00 1.80
168 Jim Palmer LGD.................................... 4.00 1.20
169 Brooks Robinson LGD 5.00 1.50
170 Bo Jackson LGD 5.00 1.50
171 Nolan Ryan LGD 10.00 3.00
172 Mike Schmidt LGD................................. 8.00 2.40
173 Tom Seaver LGD 5.00 1.50
174 Cal Ripken LGD 12.00 3.60
175 Robin Yount LGD 6.00 1.80
176 Wade Boggs LGD.................................. 5.00 1.50
177 Gary Carter LGD 4.00 1.20
178 Ron Santo LGD 5.00 1.50
179 Luis Aparicio LGD................................. 4.00 1.20
180 Bobby Doerr LGD................................... 5.00 1.50
181 Ryne Sandberg LGD 8.00 2.40
182 Yogi Berra LGD 5.00 1.50
183 Will Clark LGD 5.00 1.50
184 Eddie Murray LGD 5.00 1.50
185 Andre Dawson LGD 4.00 1.20
186 Duke Snider LGD 5.00 1.50
187 Orlando Cepeda LGD 4.00 1.20
188 Billy Williams LGD 4.00 1.20
189 Juan Marichal LGD 4.00 1.20
190 Harmon Killebrew LGD 5.00 1.50
191 Kirby Puckett LGD 5.00 1.50
192 Carlton Fisk LGD..................................... 5.00 1.50
193 Dave Winfield LGD.................................. 4.00 1.20
194 Alan Trammell LGD 4.00 1.20
195 Paul Molitor LGD 5.00 1.50
196 Tony Perez LGD 4.00 1.20
197 Ozzie Smith LGD 6.00 1.80
198 Ralph Kiner LGD...................................... 4.00 1.20
199 Fergie Jenkins LGD 4.00 1.20
200 Phil Rizzuto LGD...................................... 5.00 1.50
201 Oliver Perez ROO RC 10.00 3.00
202 Aaron Cook ROO RC 4.00 1.20
203 Eric Junge ROO RC................................... 4.00 1.20
204 Freddy Sanchez ROO RC 4.00 1.20
205 Cliff Lee ROO RC 5.00 1.50
206 Run. Hernandez ROO RC 4.00 1.20
207 Chone Figgins ROO RC 5.00 1.50
208 Rodrigo Rosario ROO RC 4.00 1.20
209 Kevin Cash ROO RC 4.00 1.20
210 Josh Bard ROO RC.................................... 4.00 1.20
211 Felix Escalona ROO RC 4.00 1.20
212 Jer. Robertson ROO RC 4.00 1.20
213 J. Simontacchi ROO RC............................ 4.00 1.20
214 Shane Nance ROO RC............................... 4.00 1.20
215 Ben Kozlowski ROO RC 4.00 1.20
216 Brian Tallet ROO RC.................................. 4.00 1.20
217 Earl Snyder ROO RC.................................. 5.00 1.50
218 Andy Pratt ROO RC.................................... 4.00 1.20
219 Trey Hodges ROO RC 4.00 1.20
220 Kirk Saarloos ROO RC................................ 4.00 1.20
221 Rene Reyes ROO RC.................................. 4.00 1.20
222 Joe Borchard ROO 4.00 1.20
223 Wilson Valdez ROO RC 4.00 1.20
224 Miguel Asencio ROO RC 4.00 1.20
225 Chris Snelling ROO RC 4.00 1.20

2002 Donruss Classics Significant Signatures

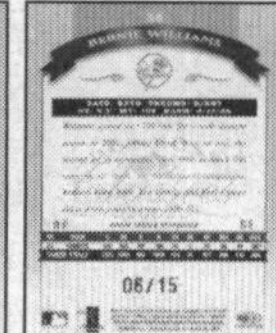

Cards checklisted 1-200 were randomly inserted in basic Donruss Classics packs. Cards 201-225 were randomly inserted in 2002 Donruss the Rookies packs in mid-December, 2002. This is a 202-card, skip-numbered, partial parallel to the Donruss Classics set. Each card has an autographed foil sticker attached to it and since each card has a different stated print run, we have notated that information next to the player's name. Cards with a print run of 25 or less are not priced due to market scarcity. A few signed cards were issued in "personal" form if the number of the signature had something important to their career.

Nm-Mt Ex-Mt
1 Alex Rodriguez/15...........................
3 C.C. Sabathia/20 ....
4 Chipper Jones/15............................
6 Troy Glaus/25..................................
7 Frank Thomas/15.............................
8 Greg Maddux/15..............................
9 Ivan Rodriguez/15...........................
10 Jeff Bagwell/15...............................
11 Mark Buehrle/25.............................
12 Todd Helton/15...............................
14 Manny Ramirez/15..........................
15 Brad Penny/25................................
17 Nomar Garciaparra/15....................
18 Pedro Martinez/15..........................
20 Bud Smith/25..................................
21 Rickey Henderson/15.....................
22 Roger Clemens/15..........................
24 Brandon Duckworth/25...................
25 Vladimir Guerrero/25......................
27 Roberto Alomar/15 ....
28 Barry Zito/25 ....
29 Rich Aurilia/25................................
30 Ben Sheets/25................................
32 J.D. Drew/15...................................
33 Jermaine Dye/25............................
34 Darin Erstad/15..............................
35 Jason Giambi/15.............................
36 Tom Glavine/15...............................
37 Juan Gonzalez/15...........................
38 Luis Gonzalez/15............................
40 Tim Hudson/25................................
41 Andruw Jones/15............................
42 Shannon Stewart/25.......................
43 Barry Larkin/15...............................
44 Wade Miller/25................................
45 Mike Mussina/15.............................
47 Rafael Palmeiro/15.........................
48 Scott Rolen/15................................
49 Gary Sheffield/15............................
50 Bernie Williams/15.........................
51 Bobby Abreu/25..............................
52 Javier Vazquez/25..........................
53 Edgar Martinez/25..........................
55 Kerry Wood/15................................
56 Adrian Beltre/25..............................
57 Lance Berkman/25..........................
58 Kevin Brown/15...............................
59 Sean Casey/20................................
60 Eric Chavez/25................................
61 Robert Person/25............................
62 Jeremy Giambi/25...........................
63 Freddy Garcia/25............................
64 Alfonso Soriano/25.........................
65 Doug Davis/25................................
66 Brian Giles/13.................................
67 Moises Alou/15...............................
68 Richard Hidalgo/25.........................
69 Paul LoDuca/25..............................
70 Aramis Ramirez/25.........................
71 Andres Galarraga/15......................
72 Ryan Klesko/20...............................
74 Richie Sexson/25............................
75 Mike Sweeney/25............................
76 Aubrey Huff/25................................
77 Miguel Tejada/25.............................
78 Jose Vidro/25..................................
80 Roy Oswalt/25.................................
81 Craig Biggio/15...............................
82 Juan Pierre/25.................................
84 Josh Towers/25...............................
85 Alex Escobar/25..............................
86 Cliff Floyd/25...................................
87 Terrence Long/25...........................
88 Curt Schilling/15.............................
89 Carlos Beltran/25............................
90 Albert Pujols/25..............................
91 Gabe Kapler/25...............................
92 Mark Mulder/25...............................
93 Carlos Lee/25..................................
94 Robert Fick/25.................................
97 Adam Dunn/6...................................
98 Corey Patterson/25........................
100 Joe Mays/25.................................
101 Juan Cruz ROO/400 .... 10.00 3.00
102 Marlon Byrd ROO/500 .... 10.00 3.00
103 Luis Garcia ROO/500 .... 10.00 3.00
104 Jorge Padilla ROO/500....... 10.00 3.00
105 Dennis Tankersley ROO/250 15.00 4.50
106 Josh Pearce ROO/500........ 10.00 3.00
107 Ramon Vazquez ROO/500.. 10.00 3.00
108 Chris Baker ROO/500......... 10.00 3.00
109 Eric Cyr ROO/500............... 10.00 3.00
110 Reed Johnson ROO/500 .... 15.00 4.50
111 Ryan Jamison ROO/500..... 10.00 3.00
112 Antonio Perez ROO/500..... 10.00 3.00
113 Satoru Komiyama ROO/50. 25.00 7.50
114 Austin Kearns ROO/500..... 15.00 4.50
115 Juan Pena ROO/500........... 10.00 3.00
116 Orlando Hudson ROO/400 . 10.00 3.00
117 Kazuhisa Ishii ROO/50 ....
118 Erik Bedard ROO/500......... 10.00 3.00
119 Luis Ugueto ROO/250......... 15.00 4.50
120 Ben Howard ROO/500........ 10.00 3.00
121 Morgan Ensberg ROO/500. 15.00 4.50
122 Doug Devore ROO/500 ...... 10.00 3.00
123 Josh Phelps ROO/500........ 10.00 3.00
124 Angel Berroa ROO/500....... 10.00 3.00
125 Ed Rogers ROO/500........... 10.00 3.00
126 Takahito Nomura ROO/25 ....
127 John Ennis ROO/500 .... 10.00 3.00
128 Bill Hall ROO/400............... 10.00 3.00
129 Dewon Brazelton ROO/400 10.00 3.00
130 Hank Blalock ROO/100....... 40.00 12.00
131 So Taguchi ROO/150.......... 40.00 12.00
132 Jorge De La Rosa ROO/500 10.00 3.00
133 Matt Thornton ROO/500 .... 10.00 3.00
134 Brandon Backe ROO/500 ... 25.00 7.50
135 Jeff Deardorff ROO/500 ..... 10.00 3.00
136 Steve Smyth ROO/400....... 10.00 3.00
137 Anderson Machado ROO/500 10.00 3.00
138 John Buck ROO/500 .... 10.00 3.00
139 Mark Prior ROO/250 .... 80.00 24.00
140 Sean Burroughs ROO/50 ... 25.00 7.50
141 Alex Herrera ROO/500 .... 10.00 3.00
142 Francis Beltran ROO/500 ... 10.00 3.00
143 Jason Romano ROO/500 ... 10.00 3.00
144 Michael Cuddyer ROO/400. 10.00 3.00
145 Steve Bechler ROO/500 ..... 10.00 3.00
146 Alfredo Amezaga ROO/500 10.00 3.00
147 Ryan Ludwick ROO/500..... 10.00 3.00
148 Martin Vargas ROO/500..... 10.00 3.00
149 Allan Simpson ROO/500.... 10.00 3.00
150 Mark Teixeira ROO/200...... 25.00 7.50
151 Dale Murphy LGD/25 ....
152 Ernie Banks LGD/25...................
153 Johnny Bench LGD/25 ....
154 George Brett LGD/25..................
155 Lou Brock LGD/100 .... 40.00 12.00
156 Rod Carew LGD/25 ....
157 Steve Carlton LGD/125 ...... 40.00 12.00
158 Joe Torre LGD/25.......................
159 Dennis Eckersley LGD/500. 15.00 4.50
160 Reggie Jackson LGD/25.............
161 Al Kaline LGD/125.............. 50.00 15.00
162 Dave Parker LGD/500 .... 15.00 4.50
163 Don Mattingly LGD/50 ..... 120.00 36.00
164 Tony Gwynn LGD/25..................
165 Willie McCovey LGD/25 ....
166 Joe Morgan LGD/25...................
167 Stan Musial LGD/25...................

68 Jim Palmer LGD/125 25.00 7.50
69 Brooks Robinson LGD/125 40.00 12.00
70 Bo Jackson LGD/25
71 Nolan Ryan LGD/25
72 Mike Schmidt LGD/25
73 Tom Seaver LGD/25
74 Cal Ripken LGD/25
75 Robin Yount LGD/25
76 Wade Boggs LGD/25
77 Gary Carter LGD/150 20.00 6.00
78 Ron Santo LGD/500 25.00 7.50
79 Luis Aparicio LGD/400 15.00 4.50
80 Bobby Doerr LGD/500 15.00 4.50
81 Ryne Sandberg LGD/25
82 Yogi Berra LGD/25
83 Will Clark LGD/50
84 Eddie Murray LGD/25
85 Andre Dawson LGD/200 20.00 6.00
86 Duke Snider LGD/25
87 Orlando Cepeda LGD/125 25.00 7.50
88 Billy Williams LGD/200 20.00 6.00
89 Juan Marichal LGD/500 15.00 4.50
90 Harmon Killebrew LGD/100 50.00 15.00
91 Kirby Puckett LGD/25
92 Carlton Fisk LGD/25
93 Dave Winfield LGD/25
94 Alan Trammell LGD/200 20.00 6.00
95 Paul Molitor LGD/25
96 Tony Perez LGD/150 20.00 6.00
97 Ozzie Smith LGD/25
98 Ralph Kiner LGD/125 25.00 7.50
99 Fergie Jenkins LGD/200 20.00 6.00
100 Phil Rizzuto LGD/125 40.00 12.00
101 Oliver Perez ROO/50 120.00 36.00
103 Eric Junge ROO/50 15.00 4.50
105 Cliff Lee ROO/100 40.00 12.00
107 Chone Figgins ROO/100 25.00 7.50
108 Rodrigo Rosario ROO/250 15.00 4.50
109 Kevin Cash ROO/100 15.00 4.50
110 Josh Bard ROO/100 15.00 4.50
111 Felix Escalona ROO/25
114 Shane Nance ROO/200 15.00 4.50
115 Ben Kozlowski ROO/200 15.00 4.50
116 Brian Tallet ROO/100 15.00 4.50
117 Earl Snyder ROO/100 20.00 6.00
118 Andy Pratt ROO/250 15.00 4.50
119 Trey Hodges ROO/250 15.00 4.50
120 Kirk Saarloos ROO/100 15.00 4.50
121 Rene Reyes ROO/50 15.00 4.50
122 Joe Borchard ROO/100 15.00 4.50
123 Wilson Valdez ROO/100 15.00 4.50
125 Chris Snelling ROO/100 15.00 4.50

2002 Donruss Classics Timeless Tributes

Cards 1-200 were randomly inserted in Donruss Classics packs and cards 201-225 in Donruss the Rookies packs. This is a parallel to the Donruss Classics set. The set is issued to a stated print run of 100 serial-numbered sets.

Nm-Mt Ex-Mt
*TRIBUTE 1-100: 2.5X TO 6X BASIC..
*TRIB.101-150/201-225: .6X TO 1.5X BASIC
*TRIB.151-200: 1.25X TO 3X BASIC..
101 Juan Cruz ROO 6.00 1.80
102 Marlon Byrd ROO 6.00 1.80
103 Luis Garcia ROO 6.00 1.80
104 Jorge Padilla ROO 6.00 1.80
105 Dennis Tankersley ROO 6.00 1.80
106 Josh Pearce ROO 6.00 1.80
107 Ramon Vazquez ROO 6.00 1.80
108 Chris Baker ROO 6.00 1.80
109 Eric Cyr ROO 6.00 1.80
110 Reed Johnson ROO 8.00 2.40
111 Ryan Jamison ROO 6.00 1.80
112 Antonio Perez ROO 6.00 1.80
113 Satoru Komiyama ROO 6.00 1.80
114 Austin Kearns ROO 6.00 1.80
115 Juan Pena ROO 6.00 1.80
116 Orlando Hudson ROO 6.00 1.80
117 Kazuhisa Ishii ROO 12.00 3.60
118 Erik Bedard ROO 6.00 1.80
119 Luis Ugueto ROO 6.00 1.80
120 Ben Howard ROO 6.00 1.80
121 Morgan Ensberg ROO 6.00 1.80
122 Doug Devore ROO 6.00 1.80
123 Josh Phelps ROO 6.00 1.80
124 Angel Berroa ROO 6.00 1.80
125 Ed Rogers ROO 6.00 1.80
126 Takahito Nomura ROO 6.00 1.80
127 John Ennis ROO 6.00 1.80
128 Bill Hall ROO 6.00 1.80
129 Dewon Brazelton ROO 6.00 1.80
130 Hank Blalock ROO 8.00 2.40
131 So Taguchi ROO 8.00 2.40
132 Jorge De La Rosa ROO 6.00 1.80
133 Matt Thornton ROO 6.00 1.80
134 Brandon Backe ROO 8.00 2.40
135 Jeff Deardorff ROO 6.00 1.80
136 Steve Smyth ROO 6.00 1.80
137 Anderson Machado ROO 6.00 1.80
138 John Buck ROO 6.00 1.80
139 Mark Prior ROO 12.00 3.60
140 Sean Burroughs ROO 6.00 1.80
141 Alex Herrera ROO 6.00 1.80
142 Francis Beltran ROO 6.00 1.80
143 Jason Romano ROO 6.00 1.80
144 Michael Cuddyer ROO 6.00 1.80
145 Steve Bechler ROO 6.00 1.80
146 Alfredo Amezaga ROO 6.00 1.80
147 Ryan Ludwick ROO 6.00 1.80
148 Martin Vargas ROO 6.00 1.80
149 Allan Simpson ROO 6.00 1.80
150 Mark Teixeira ROO 8.00 2.40
201 Oliver Perez ROO 25.00 7.50
202 Aaron Cook ROO 6.00 1.80
203 Eric Junge ROO 6.00 1.80
204 Freddy Sanchez ROO 6.00 1.80
205 Cliff Lee ROO 8.00 2.40
206 Runelvys Hernandez ROO 6.00 1.80
207 Chone Figgins ROO 8.00 2.40
208 Rodrigo Rosario ROO 6.00 1.80
209 Kevin Cash ROO 6.00 1.80
210 Josh Bard ROO 6.00 1.80
211 Felix Escalona ROO 6.00 1.80
212 Jeriome Robertson ROO 6.00 1.80
213 Jason Simontacchi ROO 6.00 1.80
214 Shane Nance ROO 6.00 1.80
215 Ben Kozlowski ROO 6.00 1.80
216 Brian Tallet ROO 6.00 1.80
217 Earl Snyder ROO 8.00 2.40
218 Andy Pratt ROO 6.00 1.80
219 Trey Hodges ROO 6.00 1.80
220 Kirk Saarloos ROO 6.00 1.80
221 Rene Reyes ROO 6.00 1.80
222 Joe Borchard ROO 6.00 1.80
223 Wilson Valdez ROO 6.00 1.80
224 Miguel Asencio ROO 6.00 1.80
225 Chris Snelling ROO 6.00 1.80

2002 Donruss Classics Classic Combos

Randomly inserted in packs, each of these 20 cards features two game-used pieces on them. Since each card is printed to a stated print run of 25 or less (which we have notated in our checklist), no pricing is provided for these cards.

Nm-Mt Ex-Mt
1 Eddie Murray Jsy
Cal Ripken Jsy/25
2 George Brett Jsy
Bo Jackson Jsy/25
3 Ted Williams Bat
Jimmie Foxx Bat/25
4 Nolan Ryan Jsy
Steve Carlton Jsy/25
5 Mel Ott Jsy
Babe Ruth Jsy/15
6 Nolan Ryan Jsy
George Brett Jsy/25
7 Babe Ruth Bat
Ty Cobb Bat/15
8 Jackie Robinson Jsy
Duke Snider Jsy/15
9 Nolan Ryan Jsy
George Brett Jsy
Robin Yount Jsy
Orlando Cepeda Jsy/25
10 Rickey Henderson Bat
Ty Cobb Bat/25
11 Ted Williams Jsy
Tony Gwynn Jsy/15
12 Tony Gwynn Bat
Rickey Henderson Bat/25
13 Ty Cobb Bat
Tony Gwynn Bat/25
14 Dave Parker Jsy
Willie Stargell Jsy/25
15 Ted Williams Bat
Ty Cobb Bat/25
16 Jimmie Foxx Bat
Lou Gehrig Bat/15
17 Catfish Hunter Jsy
Reggie Jackson Jsy/25
18 Ted Williams Bat
Ty Cobb Bat
Jimmie Foxx Bat
Lou Gehrig Bat/15
19 Bobby Doerr Jsy
Ted Williams Jsy/15
20 Mike Schmidt Jsy
George Brett Jsy/25

2002 Donruss Classics Classic Singles

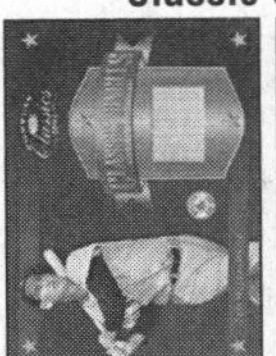

Randomly inserted into packs, these 30 cards feature both a veteran great as well as a game-used memorabilia piece. As these cards have varying print runs, we have notated that information next to the player's name as well as the information as to what memorabilia piece is used.

Nm-Mt Ex-Mt
1 Cal Ripken Jsy/100 50.00 15.00
2 Eddie Murray Jsy/100 15.00 4.50
3 George Brett Jsy/100 25.00 7.50
4 Bo Jackson Jsy/100 15.00 4.50
5 Ted Williams Bat/50 100.00 30.00
6 Jimmie Foxx Sox Bat/50 80.00 24.00
7 Steve Carlton Jsy/50 15.00 4.50
8 Reg Jackson Yanks Jsy/100 15.00 4.50
9 Mel Ott Jsy/50 80.00 24.00
10 Catfish Hunter Jsy/100 15.00 4.50
11 Nolan Ryan Jsy/100 50.00 15.00
12 Rickey Henderson Jsy /100 15.00 4.50
13 Robin Yount Jsy/100 25.00 7.50
14 Orlando Cepeda Jsy/100 10.00 3.00
15 Ty Cobb Bat/50 150.00 45.00
16 Babe Ruth Bat/50 300.00 90.00
17 Dave Parker Jsy/100 10.00 3.00
18 Willie Stargell Jsy/100 15.00 4.50
19 Ernie Banks Bat/100 15.00 4.50
20 Mike Schmidt Jsy/100 25.00 7.50
21 Duke Snider Jsy/50 25.00 7.50
22 Jackie Robinson Jsy/50 100.00 30.00
23 Rickey Henderson Bat/100 15.00 4.50
24 Dale Murphy Bat/100 15.00 4.50
25 Lou Gehrig Bat/50 200.00 60.00
26 Jimmie Foxx A's Bat/50 80.00 24.00
27 Reggie Jackson A's Jsy/100 15.00 4.50
28 Tony Gwynn Bat/100 25.00 7.50
29 Bobby Doerr Jsy/100 10.00 3.00
30 Joe Torre Jsy/100 15.00 4.50

2002 Donruss Classics Legendary Hats

Randomly inserted into packs, this five-card set features not only a retired great but a game-worn swatch of a cap. Each card was printed to a stated print run of 50 serial numbered sets.

Nm-Mt Ex-Mt
1 Don Mattingly 120.00 36.00
2 George Brett 120.00 36.00
3 Wade Boggs 50.00 15.00
4 Reggie Jackson 50.00 15.00
5 Ryne Sandberg 120.00 36.00

2002 Donruss Classics Legendary Leather

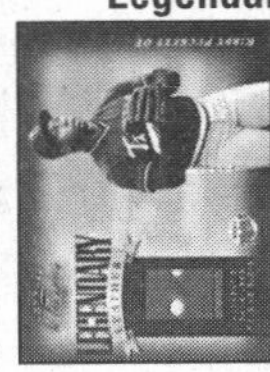
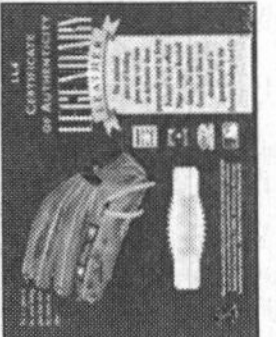

Randomly inserted into packs, this five-card set features not only a retired great but a game-worn swatch of a glove. Each card was printed to a stated print run of 50 serial numbered sets.

Nm-Mt Ex-Mt
1 Don Mattingly Btg Glv 120.00 36.00
2 Wade Boggs Btg Glv 50.00 15.00
3 Tony Gwynn Fld Glv 100.00 30.00
4 Kirby Puckett Fld Glv 80.00 24.00
5 Mike Schmidt Fld Glv 120.00 36.00

2002 Donruss Classics Legendary Lumberjacks

Randomly inserted in packs, this 35 card set features great players of the past along with a game-used bat piece. Since this set was printed to different amounts of cards printed, we have notated the stated print run information next to the player's name.

Nm-Mt Ex-Mt
1 Don Mattingly/500 25.00 7.50
2 George Brett/400 25.00 7.50
3 Stan Musial/100 50.00 15.00
4 Lou Gehrig/50 200.00 60.00
5 Mike Piazza/500 15.00 4.50
6 Mel Ott/50 80.00 24.00
7 Ted Williams/50 100.00 30.00
8 Bo Jackson/500 15.00 4.50
9 Kirby Puckett/500 15.00 4.50
10 Rafael Palmeiro/500 15.00 4.50
11 Andre Dawson/500 10.00 3.00
12 Ozzie Smith/500 15.00 4.50
13 Paul Molitor/500 15.00 4.50
14 Babe Ruth/50 300.00 90.00
15 Carlton Fisk/500 15.00 4.50
16 Rickey Henderson/500 15.00 4.50
17 Gary Carter/500 10.00 3.00
18 Cal Ripken/100 40.00 12.00
19 Eddie Mathews/100 25.00 7.50
20 Luis Aparicio/500 10.00 3.00
21 Al Kaline/100 25.00 7.50
22 Eddie Murray/500 15.00 4.50
23 Yogi Berra/100 25.00 7.50
24 Alex Rodriguez/500 15.00 4.50
25 Tony Gwynn/500 15.00 4.50
26 Roberto Clemente/100 100.00 30.00
27 Mike Schmidt/400 25.00 7.50
28 Reggie Jackson/500 15.00 4.50
29 Ryne Sandberg/500 25.00 7.50
30 Joe Morgan/400 10.00 3.00
31 Joe Torre/500 15.00 4.50
32 Gary Sheffield/500 10.00 3.00
33 Nomar Garciaparra/500 15.00 4.50
34 Jeff Bagwell/500 15.00 4.50
35 Manny Ramirez/500 15.00 4.50

2002 Donruss Classics Legendary Spikes

Randomly inserted into packs, this five-card set features not only a retired great but a game-worn piece of a pair of spikes. Each card was printed to a stated print run of 50 serial numbered sets.

Nm-Mt Ex-Mt
1 Don Mattingly 120.00 36.00
2 Eddie Murray 60.00 18.00
3 Paul Molitor 50.00 15.00
4 Harmon Killebrew 60.00 18.00
5 Mike Schmidt 120.00 36.00

2002 Donruss Classics New Millennium Classics

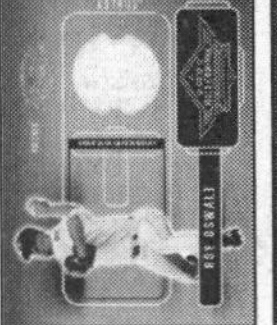

Randomly inserted into packs, these 60 cards feature both an active star as well as a game-used memorabilia piece. As these cards have varying print runs, we have notated that information next to the player's name as well as the information as to what memorabilia piece is used. The Ishii and Taguchi jersey cards were not ready as Donruss went to press and those cards were issued as exchange cards with an deadline of June 1, 2004 to redeem those cards.

Nm-Mt Ex-Mt
*MULTI-COLOR PATCH: 1.25X TO 3X BASIC
1 Curt Schilling Jsy/500 10.00 3.00
2 Vladimir Guerrero Jsy/100 25.00 7.50
3 Jim Thome Jsy/500 15.00 4.50
4 Troy Glaus Jsy/400 10.00 3.00
5 Ivan Rodriguez Jsy/200 20.00 6.00
6 Todd Helton Jsy/400 15.00 4.50
7 Sean Casey Jsy/500 10.00 3.00
8 Scott Rolen Jsy/475 15.00 4.50
9 Ken Griffey Jr. Base/150 15.00 4.50
10 Hideo Nomo Jsy/100 25.00 7.50
11 Tom Glavine Jsy/350 15.00 4.50
12 Pedro Martinez Jsy/100 25.00 7.50
13 Cliff Floyd Jsy/500 10.00 3.00
14 Shawn Green Jsy/125 20.00 6.00
15 Rafael Palmeiro Jsy/250 15.00 4.50
16 Luis Gonzalez Jsy/100 20.00 6.00
17 Lance Berkman Jsy/100 20.00 6.00
18 Frank Thomas Jsy/500 15.00 4.50
19 Randy Johnson Jsy/400 15.00 4.50
20 Moises Alou Jsy/500 10.00 3.00
21 Chipper Jones Jsy/500 15.00 4.50
22 Larry Walker Jsy/300 15.00 4.50
23 Mike Sweeney Jsy/500 10.00 3.00
24 Juan Gonzalez Jsy/300 15.00 4.50
25 Roger Clemens Jsy/100 25.00 7.50
26 Albert Pujols Base/300 15.00 4.50
27 Magglio Ordonez Jsy/500 10.00 3.00
28 Alex Rodriguez Jsy/400 15.00 4.50
29 Jeff Bagwell Jsy/125 25.00 7.50
30 Kazuhiro Sasaki Jsy/500 10.00 3.00
31 Barry Larkin Jsy/300 15.00 4.50
32 Andruw Jones Jsy/350 10.00 3.00
33 Kerry Wood Jsy/200 20.00 6.00
34 Rickey Henderson Jsy/100 25.00 7.50
35 Greg Maddux Jsy/100 25.00 7.50
36 Brian Giles Jsy/400 10.00 3.00
37 Craig Biggio Jsy/100 25.00 7.50
38 Roberto Alomar Jsy/400 15.00 4.50
39 Mike Piazza Jsy/400 15.00 4.50
40 Bernie Williams Jsy/100 25.00 7.50
41 Ichiro Suzuki Ball/100 40.00 12.00
42 Kenny Lofton Jsy/450 10.00 3.00
43 Mark Mulder Jsy/500 10.00 3.00
44 Kazuhisa Ishii Jsy/100 EXCH 25.00 7.50
45 Darin Erstad Jsy/500 10.00 3.00
46 Jose Vidro Jsy/500 10.00 3.00
47 Miguel Tejada Jsy/475 10.00 3.00
48 Roy Oswalt Jsy/500 10.00 3.00
49 So Taguchi Jsy/100 EXCH 25.00 7.50
50 Barry Zito Jsy/500 10.00 3.00
51 Manny Ramirez Jsy/400 15.00 4.50
52 Nomar Garciaparra Jsy/400 15.00 4.50
53 C.C. Sabathia Jsy/500 10.00 3.00
54 Carlos Delgado Jsy/500 10.00 3.00
55 Gary Sheffield Jsy/500 10.00 3.00
56 J.D. Drew Jsy/500 10.00 3.00
57 Barry Bonds Ball/150 40.00 12.00
58 Derek Jeter Ball/150 40.00 12.00
59 Edgar Martinez Jsy/400 15.00 4.50
60 Sammy Sosa Ball/150 25.00 7.50

2002 Donruss Classics Timeless Treasures

Randomly inserted into packs, these 17 cards feature all-time greats along with key pieces of their memorabilia. These cards have different print runs which we have put next to their names. Those cards with a stated print run of 25 or less are not priced due to market scarcity.

Nm-Mt Ex-Mt
1 Ted Williams .406 Avg Jsy/25
2 Ted Williams The Kid Jsy/10
3 Ted Williams Ballgame Jsy/10
4 Ted Williams Splinter Jsy/10
5 Ted Williams Crown Bat/42 100.00 30.00
6 Ted Williams Crown Bat/47 100.00 30.00
7 Ted Williams MVP Bat/46 100.00 30.00
8 Ted Williams MVP Bat/49 100.00 30.00
9 Ted Williams Jsy/9
10 Cal Ripken Iron Man Jsy/98 50.00 15.00
11 Cal Ripken ROY Jsy/82 80.00 24.00
12 Cal Ripken MVP Jsy/83 80.00 24.00
13 Cal Ripken MVP Jsy/91 80.00 24.00
14 Cal Ripken
Lou Gehrig Jsy/25
15 Cal Ripken 2131 Jsy/25
16 Cal Ripken 3000 Hits Jsy/25
17 Cal Ripken Jsy/8

2003 Donruss Classics

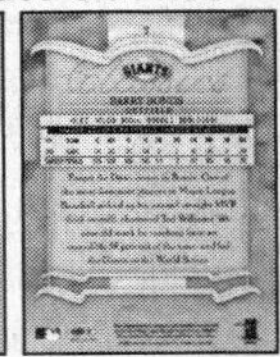

This 211-card set was released in two separate series. The primary Donruss Classics product - containing cards 1-200 from the basic set - was released in April, 2003. This set was issued in seven-card packs with an $6 SRP which were packed 18 to a box and 12 boxes to a case. Cards 201-211 were randomly seeded within packs of DLP Rookies and Traded of which was distributed in December, 2003. The first 100 cards feature active veterans, while cards 101-150 feature retired legends and cards 151-211 feature rookies and leading prospects. Please note that cards 101-200 were issued at a stated rate of one in nine and were issued to a stated print run of 1500 serial numbered sets. Cards 201-211 were serial-numbered to 1000 copies each.

Nm-Mt Ex-Mt
COMP.LO SET w/o SP's (100) 25.00 7.50
COMMON CARD (1-100) .60 .18
COMMON CARD (101-150) 4.00 1.20
COMMON CARD (151-200) 4.00 1.20
COIMMON CARD (201-211) 4.00 1.20
1 Troy Glaus .60 .18
2 Barry Bonds 4.00 1.20
3 Miguel Tejada .60 .18
4 Randy Johnson 1.50 .45
5 Eric Hinske .60 .18
6 Barry Zito .60 .18
7 Jason Jennings .60 .18
8 Derek Jeter 4.00 1.20
9 Vladimir Guerrero 1.50 .45
10 Corey Patterson .60 .18
11 Manny Ramirez 1.00 .30
12 Edgar Martinez 1.00 .30
13 Roy Oswalt .60 .18
14 Andruw Jones .60 .18
15 Alex Rodriguez 2.50 .75
16 Mark Mulder .60 .18
17 Kazuhisa Ishii .60 .18
18 Gary Sheffield .60 .18
19 Jay Gibbons .60 .18
20 Roberto Alomar 1.00 .30
21 A.J. Pierzynski .60 .18
22 Eric Chavez .60 .18
23 Roger Clemens 3.00 .90
24 C.C. Sabathia .60 .18
25 Jose Vidro .60 .18
26 Shannon Stewart .60 .18
27 Mark Teixeira .60 .18
28 Joe Thurston .60 .18
29 Josh Beckett .60 .18
30 Jeff Bagwell 1.00 .30
31 Geronimo Gil .60 .18
32 Curt Schilling .60 .18
33 Frank Thomas 1.50 .45
34 Lance Berkman .60 .18
35 Adam Dunn 1.00 .30
36 Christian Parker .60 .18
37 Jim Thome 1.50 .45
38 Shawn Green .60 .18
39 Drew Henson .60 .18
40 Chipper Jones 1.50 .45
41 Kevin Mench .60 .18
42 Hideo Nomo 1.50 .45
43 Andres Galarraga .60 .18
44 Doug Davis .60 .18
45 Mark Prior 1.50 .45
46 Sean Casey .60 .18
47 Magglio Ordonez .60 .18
48 Tom Glavine 1.00 .30
49 Marlon Byrd .60 .18
50 Albert Pujols 3.00 .90
51 Mark Buehrle .60 .18
52 Aramis Ramirez .60 .18
53 Pat Burrell .60 .18
54 Craig Biggio 1.00 .30
55 Alfonso Soriano 1.00 .30
56 Kerry Wood 1.50 .45
57 Wade Miller .60 .18
58 Hank Blalock 1.00 .30
59 Cliff Floyd .60 .18
60 Jason Giambi .60 .18
61 Carlos Beltran 1.00 .30
62 Brian Roberts .60 .18
63 Paul Lo Duca .60 .18
64 Tim Redding .60 .18
65 Sammy Sosa 2.50 .75
66 Joe Borchard .60 .18
67 Ryan Klesko .60 .18
68 Richie Sexson .60 .18
69 Carlos Lee .60 .18
70 Rickey Henderson 1.50 .45
71 Brian Tallet .60 .18
72 Luis Gonzalez .60 .18
73 Satoru Komiyama .60 .18
74 Tim Hudson .60 .18
75 Ken Griffey Jr. 2.50 .75
76 Adam Johnson .60 .18
77 Bobby Abreu .60 .18
78 Adrian Beltre 1.00 .30

79 Rafael Palmeiro 1.00 .30
80 Ichiro Suzuki 2.50 .75
81 Kenny Lofton .60 .18
82 Brian Giles .60 .18
83 Barry Larkin 1.00 .30
84 Robert Fick .60 .18
85 Ben Sheets .60 .18
86 Scott Rolen 1.50 .45
87 Nomar Garciaparra 2.50 .75
88 Brandon Phillips .60 .18
89 Ben Kozlowski .60 .18
90 Bernie Williams 1.00 .30
91 Pedro Martinez 1.50 .45
92 Todd Helton 1.00 .30
93 Jermaine Dye .60 .18
94 Carlos Delgado .60 .18
95 Mike Piazza 2.50 .75
96 Junior Spivey .60 .18
97 Torii Hunter .60 .18
98 Mike Sweeney .60 .18
99 Ivan Rodriguez 1.50 .45
100 Greg Maddux 2.50 .75
101 Ernie Banks LGD 5.00 1.50
102 Steve Garvey LGD 4.00 1.20
103 George Brett LGD 10.00 3.00
104 Lou Brock LGD 5.00 1.50
105 Hoyt Wilhelm LGD 4.00 1.20
106 Steve Carlton LGD 4.00 1.20
107 Joe Torre LGD 5.00 1.50
108 Dennis Eckersley LGD 4.00 1.20
109 Reggie Jackson LGD 5.00 1.50
110 Al Kaline LGD 5.00 1.50
111 Harold Reynolds LGD 4.00 1.20
112 Don Mattingly LGD 10.00 3.00
113 Tony Gwynn LGD 5.00 1.50
114 Willie McCovey LGD 4.00 1.20
115 Joe Morgan LGD 4.00 1.20
116 Stan Musial LGD 6.00 1.80
117 Jim Palmer LGD 4.00 1.20
118 Brooks Robinson LGD 5.00 1.50
119 Don Sutton LGD 4.00 1.20
120 Nolan Ryan LGD 10.00 3.00
121 Mike Schmidt LGD 8.00 2.40
122 Tom Seaver LGD 5.00 1.50
123 Cal Ripken LGD 12.00 3.60
124 Robin Yount LGD 6.00 1.80
125 Bob Feller LGD 4.00 1.20
126 Joe Carter LGD 4.00 1.20
127 Jack Morris LGD 4.00 1.20
128 Luis Aparicio LGD 4.00 1.20
129 Bobby Doerr LGD 4.00 1.20
130 Dave Parker LGD 4.00 1.20
131 Yogi Berra LGD 5.00 1.50
132 Will Clark LGD 5.00 1.50
133 Fred Lynn LGD 4.00 1.20
134 Andre Dawson LGD 4.00 1.20
135 Duke Snider LGD 5.00 1.50
136 Orlando Cepeda LGD 4.00 1.20
137 Billy Williams LGD 4.00 1.20
138 Dale Murphy LGD 5.00 1.50
139 Harmon Killebrew LGD 5.00 1.50
140 Kirby Puckett LGD 5.00 1.50
141 Carlton Fisk LGD 5.00 1.50
142 Eric Davis LGD 4.00 1.20
143 Alan Trammell LGD 4.00 1.20
144 Paul Molitor LGD 5.00 1.50
145 Jose Canseco LGD 5.00 1.50
146 Ozzie Smith LGD 6.00 1.80
147 Ralph Kiner LGD 4.00 1.20
148 Dwight Gooden LGD 4.00 1.20
149 Phil Rizzuto LGD 5.00 1.50
150 Lenny Dykstra LGD 4.00 1.20
151 Adam LaRoche ROO 4.00 1.20
152 Tim Hummel ROO 4.00 1.20
153 Matt Kata ROO RC 5.00 1.50
154 Jeff Baker ROO 4.00 1.20
155 Josh Stewart ROO RC 4.00 1.20
156 Marshall McDougall ROO 4.00 1.20
157 Jhonny Peralta ROO 4.00 1.20
158 Mike Nicolas ROO RC 4.00 1.20
159 Jeremy Guthrie ROO 4.00 1.20
160 Craig Brazell ROO RC 5.00 1.50
161 Joe Valentine ROO RC 4.00 1.20
162 Buddy Hernandez ROO RC 4.00 1.20
163 Freddy Sanchez ROO 4.00 1.20
164 Shane Victorino ROO RC 4.00 1.20
165 Corwin Malone ROO 4.00 1.20
166 Jason Dubois ROO 4.00 1.20
167 Josh Wilson ROO 4.00 1.20
168 Tim Olson ROO RC 5.00 1.50
169 Cliff Bartosh ROO 4.00 1.20
170 Michael Hessman ROO RC 4.00 1.20
171 Ryan Church ROO 4.00 1.20
172 Garrett Atkins ROO 4.00 1.20
173 Jose Morban ROO 4.00 1.20
174 Ryan Cameron ROO RC 4.00 1.20
175 Todd Wellemeyer ROO RC 5.00 1.50
176 Travis Chapman ROO 4.00 1.20
177 Jason Anderson ROO 4.00 1.20
178 Adam Morrissey ROO 4.00 1.20
179 Jose Contreras ROO RC 5.00 1.50
180 Nic Jackson ROO 4.00 1.20
181 Rob Hammock ROO RC 5.00 1.50
182 Carlos Rivera ROO 4.00 1.20
183 Vinny Chulk ROO 4.00 1.20
184 Pete LaForest ROO RC 5.00 1.50
185 Jon Leicester ROO RC 4.00 1.20
186 Terrmel Sledge ROO RC 5.00 1.50
187 Jose Castillo ROO 4.00 1.20
188 Gerald Laird ROO 4.00 1.20
189 Nook Logan ROO RC 4.00 1.20
190 Clint Barmes ROO RC 5.00 1.50
191 Jesus Medrano ROO 4.00 1.20
192 Henri Stanley ROO 4.00 1.20
193 Hideki Matsui ROO RC 10.00 3.00
194 Walter Young ROO 4.00 1.20
195 Jon Adkins ROO 4.00 1.20
196 Tommy Whiteman ROO 4.00 1.20
197 Rob Bowen ROO 4.00 1.20
198 Brandon Webb ROO RC 5.00 1.50
199 Prentice Redman ROO RC 4.00 1.20
200 Jimmy Gobble ROO 4.00 1.20
201 Jeremy Bonderman ROO RC 5.00 1.50
202 Adam Loewen ROO RC 5.00 1.50
203 Chien-Ming Wang ROO RC 5.00 1.50
204 Hong-Chih Kuo ROO RC 5.00 1.50
205 Ryan Wagner ROO RC 5.00 1.50
206 Dan Haren ROO RC 5.00 1.50
207 Dontrelle Willis ROO 5.00 1.50
208 Rickie Weeks ROO RC 8.00 2.40
209 Ramon Nivar ROO RC 5.00 1.50
210 Chad Gaudin ROO RC 4.00 1.20
211 Delmon Young ROO RC 10.00 3.00

2003 Donruss Classics Significant Signatures

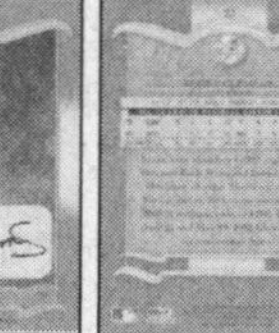

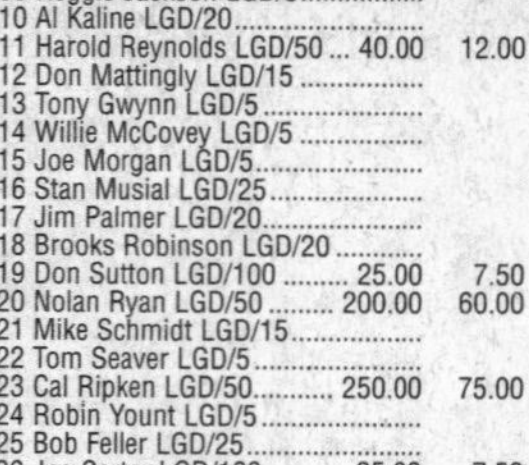

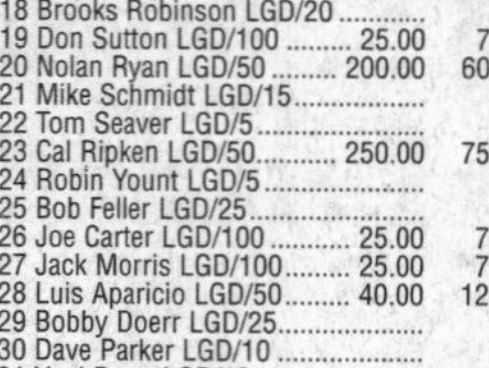

Randomly inserted into packs, this is an almost complete parallel to the basic set. Please note, cards 201-211 were randomly inserted within packs of DLP Rookies and Traded. Each of these cards feature an authentic "sticker" autograph of the featured player on them. Please note that these players signed a different amount of cards ranging between 5-500 copies per and that information is next to the player's name in our checklist. Please note that if the print run is 25 or fewer, no pricing is provided due to market scarcity. Also please note that Hoyt Wilhelm, since he had signed stickers, is able to have signed cards in this set despite having passed on the previous year.

Nm-Mt Ex-Mt
1 Troy Glaus/10
3 Miguel Tejada/5
5 Eric Hinske/250 10.00 3.00
6 Barry Zito/25
7 Jason Jennings/250 10.00 3.00
9 Vladimir Guerrero/5
10 Corey Patterson/100 25.00 7.50
11 Manny Ramirez/5
12 Edgar Martinez/20
13 Roy Oswalt/100 25.00 7.50
14 Andruw Jones/10
15 Alex Rodriguez/5
16 Mark Mulder/100 25.00 7.50
17 Kazuhisa Ishii/5
18 Gary Sheffield/5
19 Jay Gibbons/250 10.00 3.00
20 Roberto Alomar/5
21 A.J. Pierzynski/75 25.00 7.50
22 Eric Chavez/20
23 Roger Clemens/5
24 C.C. Sabathia/5
25 Jose Vidro/75 15.00 4.50
26 Shannon Stewart/25
27 Mark Teixeira/50 40.00 12.00
29 Josh Beckett/5
31 Geronimo Gil/50 15.00 4.50
32 Curt Schilling/5
33 Frank Thomas/5
34 Lance Berkman/5
35 Adam Dunn/100 40.00 12.00
36 Christian Parker/250 10.00 3.00
37 Jim Thome/5
38 Shawn Green/5
39 Drew Henson/100 40.00 12.00
40 Chipper Jones/5
41 Kevin Mench/250 10.00 3.00
43 Andres Galarraga/5
44 Doug Davis/15
45 Mark Prior/50 80.00 24.00
46 Sean Casey/5
47 Magglio Ordonez/5
48 Tom Glavine/10
49 Marlon Byrd/10
50 Albert Pujols/10
51 Mark Buehrle/25
52 Aramis Ramirez/10
53 Pat Burrell/10
54 Craig Biggio/5
55 Alfonso Soriano/5
56 Kerry Wood/15
57 Wade Miller/200 10.00 3.00
58 Hank Blalock/50 40.00 12.00
59 Cliff Floyd/20
61 Carlos Beltran/20
62 Brian Roberts/250 10.00 3.00
63 Paul Lo Duca/100 25.00 7.50
64 Tim Redding/250 10.00 3.00
66 Joe Borchard/100 15.00 4.50
67 Ryan Klesko/20
68 Richie Sexson/20
69 Carlos Lee/25
70 Rickey Henderson/5
71 Brian Tallet/25
72 Luis Gonzalez/5
73 Satoru Komiyama/124 25.00 7.50
74 Tim Hudson/20
76 Adam Johnson/200 10.00 3.00
77 Bobby Abreu/10
78 Adrian Beltre/10
79 Rafael Palmeiro/5
81 Kenny Lofton/5
82 Brian Giles/25
83 Barry Larkin/5
84 Robert Fick/50 15.00 4.50
85 Ben Sheets/20
86 Scott Rolen/5
88 Brandon Phillips/250 10.00 3.00
89 Ben Kozlowski/150 10.00 3.00
90 Bernie Williams/5
91 Pedro Martinez/5
92 Todd Helton/5
93 Jermaine Dye/100 25.00 7.50
96 Junior Spivey/100 15.00 4.50
97 Torii Hunter/50 25.00 7.50
98 Mike Sweeney/25
99 Ivan Rodriguez/5
100 Greg Maddux/5
101 Ernie Banks LGD/5
102 Steve Garvey LGD/100 25.00 7.50
103 George Brett LGD/5
104 Lou Brock LGD/20
105 Hoyt Wilhelm LGD/25
106 Steve Carlton LGD/5
107 Joe Torre LGD/5
108 Dennis Eckersley LGD/50 40.00 12.00
109 Reggie Jackson LGD/5
110 Al Kaline LGD/20
111 Harold Reynolds LGD/50 40.00 12.00
112 Don Mattingly LGD/15
113 Tony Gwynn LGD/5
114 Willie McCovey LGD/5
115 Joe Morgan LGD/5
116 Stan Musial LGD/25
117 Jim Palmer LGD/20
118 Brooks Robinson LGD/20
119 Don Sutton LGD/100 25.00 7.50
120 Nolan Ryan LGD/50 200.00 60.00
121 Mike Schmidt LGD/15
122 Tom Seaver LGD/5
123 Cal Ripken LGD/50 250.00 75.00
124 Robin Yount LGD/5
125 Bob Feller LGD/25
126 Joe Carter LGD/100 25.00 7.50
127 Jack Morris LGD/100 25.00 7.50
128 Luis Aparicio LGD/50 40.00 12.00
129 Bobby Doerr LGD/25
130 Dave Parker LGD/10
131 Yogi Berra LGD/10
132 Will Clark LGD/20
133 Fred Lynn LGD/50 40.00 12.00
134 Andre Dawson LGD/50 40.00 12.00
135 Duke Snider LGD/5
136 Orlando Cepeda LGD/100 25.00 7.50
137 Billy Williams LGD/100 25.00 7.50
138 Dale Murphy LGD/20
139 Harmon Killebrew LGD/15
140 Kirby Puckett LGD/5
141 Carlton Fisk LGD/5
142 Eric Davis LGD/50 40.00 12.00
143 Alan Trammell LGD/50 40.00 12.00
144 Paul Molitor LGD/10
145 Jose Canseco LGD/15
146 Ozzie Smith LGD/5
147 Ralph Kiner LGD/20
148 Dwight Gooden LGD/50 40.00 12.00
149 Phil Rizzuto LGD/20
150 Lenny Dykstra LGD/50 40.00 12.00
151 Adam LaRoche ROO/250 10.00 3.00
152 Tim Hummel ROO/500 10.00 3.00
153 Matt Kata ROO/500 15.00 4.50
154 Jeff Baker ROO/500 10.00 3.00
155 Josh Stewart ROO/177 10.00 3.00
156 Marshall McDougall ROO/500 10.00 3.00
157 Jhonny Peralta ROO/500 10.00 3.00
158 Mike Nicolas ROO/500 10.00 3.00
159 Jeremy Guthrie ROO/500 10.00 3.00
160 Craig Brazell ROO/500 15.00 4.50
161 Joe Valentine ROO/172 10.00 3.00
162 Buddy Hernandez ROO/500 10.00 3.00
163 Freddy Sanchez ROO/500 10.00 3.00
164 Shane Victorino ROO/351 10.00 3.00
165 Corwin Malone ROO/500 10.00 3.00
166 Jason Dubois ROO/500 15.00 4.50
167 Josh Wilson ROO/500 10.00 3.00
168 Tim Olson ROO/500 15.00 4.50
169 Cliff Bartosh ROO/500 10.00 3.00
170 Michael Hessman ROO/427 10.00 3.00
171 Ryan Church ROO/500 10.00 3.00
172 Garrett Atkins ROO/500 10.00 3.00
173 Jose Morban ROO/500 10.00 3.00
174 Ryan Cameron ROO/500 10.00 3.00
175 Todd Wellemeyer ROO/500 15.00 4.50
176 Travis Chapman ROO/477 10.00 3.00
177 Jason Anderson ROO/500 15.00 4.50
178 Adam Morrissey ROO/500 10.00 3.00
179 Jose Contreras ROO/100 25.00 7.50
180 Nic Jackson ROO/500 10.00 3.00
181 Rob Hammock ROO/500 15.00 4.50
182 Carlos Rivera ROO/500 10.00 3.00
183 Vinny Chulk ROO/500 10.00 3.00
184 Pete LaForest ROO/177 15.00 4.50
185 John Leicester ROO/500 10.00 3.00
186 Terrmel Sledge ROO/500 15.00 4.50
187 Jose Castillo ROO/500 10.00 3.00
188 Gerald Laird ROO/500 10.00 3.00
189 Nook Logan ROO/427 10.00 3.00
190 Clint Barmes ROO/100 15.00 4.50
191 Jesus Medrano ROO/500 10.00 3.00
192 Henri Stanley ROO/500 10.00 3.00
194 Walter Young ROO/500 10.00 3.00
195 Jon Adkins ROO/500 10.00 3.00
196 Tommy Whiteman ROO/500 10.00 3.00
197 Rob Bowen ROO/500 10.00 3.00
198 Brandon Webb ROO/500 15.00 4.50
199 Prentice Redman ROO/127 10.00 3.00
200 Jimmy Gobble ROO/500 10.00 3.00
201 Jeremy Bonderman ROO/100 20.00 6.00
202 Adam Loewen ROO/100 25.00 7.50
203 Chien-Ming Wang ROO/50 50.00 15.00
204 Hong-Chih Kuo ROO/25
205 Ryan Wagner ROO/100 15.00 4.50
206 Dan Haren ROO/100 20.00 6.00
207 Dontrelle Willis ROO/25
208 Rickie Weeks ROO/10
209 Ramon Nivar ROO/100 20.00 6.00
210 Chad Gaudin ROO/25
211 Delmon Young ROO/25

2003 Donruss Classics Timeless Tributes

Randomly inserted into packs, this is a complete parallel of the basic Classics set. Please note, cards 201-211 were randomly inserted into packs of DLP Rookies and Traded. Each of these cards were issued to a stated print run of 100 serial numbered sets.

Nm-Mt Ex-Mt
*TRIBUTE 1-100: 2.5X TO 6X BASIC
*TRIB.101-150: 1.25X TO 3X BASIC ..
*TRIBUTE 151-200: .6X TO 1.5X BASIC
*TRIBUTE 201-211: .6X TO 1.5X BASIC

2003 Donruss Classics Classic Combos

Randomly inserted in packs, this 15 card set features two players along with game-used memorabilia of each player. We have noted the print run information next to the player's name in our checklist. Please note that if a card has a stated print run of 25 or fewer we have not priced the card due to market scarcity.

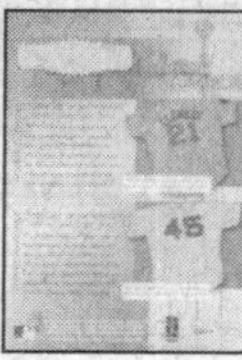

Nm-Mt Ex-Mt
1 Babe Ruth Jsy 600.00 180.00
Lou Gehrig Jsy/50
2 Jackie Robinson Jsy 100.00 30.00
Pee Wee Reese Jsy/50
3 Bobby Doerr Jsy
Fred Lynn Jsy/25
4 Honus Wagner Seat 200.00 60.00
Roberto Clemente Jsy/50
5 Kirby Puckett Jsy
Torri Hunter Jsy/25
6 Ryne Sandberg Jsy
Sammy Sosa Jsy/25
7 Hideo Nomo Jsy
Kazuhisa Ishii Jsy/25
8 Mike Schmidt Jsy
Steve Carlton Jsy/25
9 Paul Molitor Jsy
Robin Yount Jsy/25
10 Duke Snider Jsy
Mike Piazza Jsy/25
11 Al Kaline Jsy
Ty Cobb Bat/25
12 Don Mattingly Jsy
Jason Giambi Jsy/25
13 Ozzie Smith Jsy
Stan Musial Jsy/25
14 Pedro Martinez Jsy
Roger Clemens Jsy/25
15 Thurman Munson Jsy
Yogi Berra Jsy/25

2003 Donruss Classics Classic Singles

Randomly inserted into packs, this 30-card set features a mix of active and retired players along with a memorabilia piece about that player. We have noted the stated print run information next to the player's name in our checklist and if a card was issued to a stated print run of 25 or fewer, there is no pricing due to market scarcity.

Nm-Mt Ex-Mt
1 Babe Ruth Jsy/100 400.00 120.00
2 Lou Gehrig Jsy/80 250.00 75.00
3 Jackie Robinson Jsy/80 100.00 30.00
4 Pee Wee Reese Jsy/25
5 Bobby Doerr Jsy/100 20.00 6.00
6 Fred Lynn Jsy/100 20.00 6.00
7 Honus Wagner Seat/100 50.00 15.00
8 Roberto Clemente Jsy/80 120.00 36.00
9 Kirby Puckett Jsy/100 40.00 12.00
10 Torii Hunter Jsy/100 15.00 4.50
11 Sammy Sosa Jsy/100 25.00 7.50
12 Ryne Sandberg Jsy/100 60.00 18.00
13 Hideo Nomo Jsy/50 120.00 36.00
14 Kazuhisa Ishii Jsy/50 25.00 7.50
15 Mike Schmidt Jsy/100 60.00 18.00
16 Steve Carlton Jsy/100 20.00 6.00
17 Robin Yount Jsy/100 40.00 12.00
18 Paul Molitor Jsy/100 25.00 7.50
19 Mike Piazza Jsy/100 25.00 7.50
20 Duke Snider Jsy/50 40.00 12.00
21 Al Kaline Jsy/50 60.00 18.00
22 Ty Cobb Bat/25
23 Don Mattingly Jsy/100 60.00 18.00
24 Jason Giambi Jsy/100 15.00 4.50
25 Stan Musial Jsy/25
26 Ozzie Smith Jsy/100 40.00 12.00
27 Roger Clemens Jsy/100 30.00 9.00
28 Pedro Martinez Jsy/100 25.00 7.50
29 Thurman Munson Jsy/50 60.00 18.00
30 Yogi Berra Jsy/25

2003 Donruss Classics Dress Code

Randomly inserted into pack, this 75-card set features anywhere from one to four swatches of game-worn/used materials. Each card was issued to different quantities and we have notated that information next to the card in our checklist.

Nm-Mt Ex-Mt
1 Roger Clemens Yanks Jsy/500 15.00 4.50
2 Miguel Tejada Bat-Hat-Jsy/250 20.00 6.00
3 Vladimir Guerrero Jsy/425 10.00 3.00
4 Kazuhisa Ishii Jsy/250 8.00 2.40
5 Chipper Jones Jsy/425 10.00 3.00
6 Troy Glaus Jsy/425 8.00 2.40
7 Rafael Palmeiro Jsy/425 10.00 3.00
8 R.Henderson R.Sox Jsy/250 10.00 3.00
9 Pedro Martinez Jsy/425 10.00 3.00
10 Andruw Jones Jsy/425 8.00 2.40
11 Nomar Garciaparra Jsy/500 15.00 4.50
12 Carlos Delgado Jsy/500 8.00 2.40
13 R.Hend Padres Hat-Jsy/250 20.00 6.00
14 Kerry Wood Hat-Jsy/250 20.00 6.00
15 Lance Berkman Hat-Jsy/50 25.00 7.50
16 Tony Gwynn 80.00 24.00
Hat-Jsy-Pants-Shoe/100
17 Mark Mulder Jsy/425 8.00 2.40
18 Jim Thome Jsy/500 10.00 3.00
19 Mike Piazza Jsy/500 15.00 4.50
20 Mike Mussina Jsy/500 10.00 3.00
21 Luis Gonzalez Jsy/500 8.00 2.40
22 Ryan Klesko Jsy/500 8.00 2.40
23 Richie Sexson Jsy/500 8.00 2.40
24 Curt Schilling Jsy/200 8.00 2.40
25 Alex Rodriguez Rgr Jsy/500 15.00 4.50
26 Bernie Williams Jsy/425 10.00 3.00
27 Cal Ripken Jsy/500 40.00 12.00
28 C.C. Sabathia Jsy/500 8.00 2.40
29 Mike Piazza Bat-Jsy/200 40.00 12.00
30 R.Hend Mets Hat-Jsy/250 20.00 6.00
31 Torii Hunter Jsy/425 8.00 2.40
32 Mark Teixeira Jsy/425 8.00 2.40
33 Dale Murphy Bat-Jsy/300 15.00 4.50
34 Todd Helton Jsy/425 10.00 3.00
35 Eric Chavez Jsy/425 8.00 2.40
36 Vernon Wells Jsy/425 8.00 2.40
37 Jeff Bagwell Hat-Jsy/100 30.00 9.00
38 Nick Johnson Jsy/425 8.00 2.40
39 Tim Hudson Hat-Jsy/250 15.00 4.50
40 Shawn Green Jsy/425 8.00 2.40
41 Mark Buehrle Jsy/500 8.00 2.40
42 Garret Anderson Jsy/100 10.00 3.00
43 Alex Rodriguez M's Jsy/500 15.00 4.50
44 Jason Giambi Jsy/500 8.00 2.40
45 Carlos Beltran Jsy/500 10.00 3.00
46 Adam Dunn Hat-Jsy/100 30.00 9.00
47 Jorge Posada Jsy/425 10.00 3.00
48 Roy Oswalt Hat-Jsy/200 15.00 4.50
49 Rich Aurilia Jsy/500 8.00 2.40
50 Jason Jennings 20.00 6.00
Bat-Hat-Jsy-Shoe/250
51 Mark Prior 50.00 15.00
Fld Glv-Hat-Jsy-Shoe/250
52 Jim Edmonds Jsy/500 8.00 2.40
53 Fred McGriff Jsy/500 10.00 3.00
54 A.Soriano Jsy-Shoe/100 15.00 4.50
55 Jeff Kent Jsy/425 8.00 2.40
56 Hideo Nomo R.Sox Jsy/200 40.00 12.00
57 Manny Ramirez Jsy/425 10.00 3.00
58 Jose Canseco Bat-Jsy/350 15.00 4.50
59 Magglio Ordonez Jsy/500 8.00 2.40
60 Alan Trammell Bat-Jsy/250 15.00 4.50
61 Bobby Abreu Jsy/500 8.00 2.40
62 Rickey Henderson 20.00 6.00
A's Hat-Jsy/200
63 Josh Beckett Jsy/500 8.00 2.40
64 Barry Larkin Jsy/500 10.00 3.00
65 Randy Johnson Jsy/200 10.00 3.00
66 Juan Gonzalez Jsy/500 10.00 3.00
67 Barry Zito Hat-Jsy/125 20.00 6.00
68 Roger Clemens R.Sox Jsy/500 15.00 4.50
69 R.Henderson M's Hat-Jsy/100 30.00 9.00
70 Hideo Nomo Mets Jsy/100 60.00 18.00
71 Paul Konerko Jsy/400 8.00 2.40
72 Pat Burrell Jsy/100 10.00 3.00
73 Frank Thomas Jsy-Pants/500 15.00 4.50
74 Sammy Sosa Jsy/500 15.00 4.50
75 Greg Maddux Btg Glv-Jsy/50 80.00 24.00

2003 Donruss Classics Legendary Hats

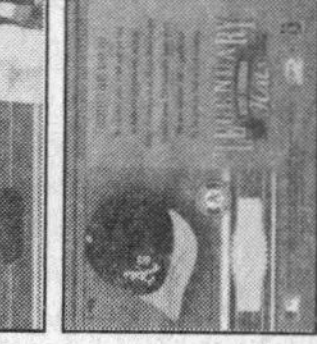

Randomly inserted in packs, this five-card set features a game-worn hat swatch of the featured player. The Roberto Clemente card was issued to a stated print run of 80 serial numbered sets.

Nm-Mt Ex-Mt
1 Roberto Clemente/80 100.00 30.00
2 Kirby Puckett 60.00 18.00
3 Mike Schmidt 120.00 36.00
4 Tony Gwynn 100.00 30.00
5 Rickey Henderson 60.00 18.00

2003 Donruss Classics Legendary Leather

Randomly inserted into packs, this five-card set features a game-used glove piece. Each of these cards were issued to a stated print run of 25 serial numbered sets and there is no pricing due to market scarcity.

Nm-Mt Ex-Mt
1 Nolan Ryan Fld Glv/80 120.00 36.00
2 Jimmie Foxx Fld Glv
3 Steve Carlton Fld Glv
4 Don Mattingly Btg Glv
5 Mike Schmidt Btg Glv

2003 Donruss Classics Legendary Lumberjacks

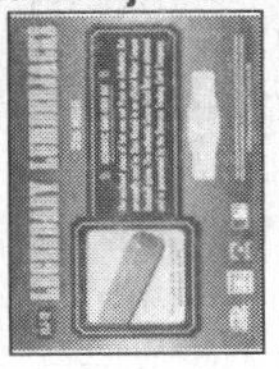

ıdomly inserted into packs, this 35-card set ure retired players along with a game-used swatch. These cards were issued to different ed print runs and we have notated that infor- ition next to their name in our checklist. ase note that for cards with a stated print run 25 or fewer, there is no pricing due to market rcity.

	Nm-Mt	Ex-Mt
abe Ruth/100	200.00	60.00
ou Gehrig/80	150.00	45.00
eorge Brett/250	30.00	9.00
uke Snider/250	25.00	7.50
oberto Clemente/25		
yne Sandberg/400	30.00	9.00
obin Yount/300	20.00	6.00
armon Killebrew/250	25.00	7.50
l Kaline/250	25.00	7.50
Eddie Mathews/225	25.00	7.50
Brooks Robinson/400	20.00	6.00
Stan Musial/11		
Kirby Puckett/375	20.00	6.00
Jose Canseco/400	20.00	6.00
Nellie Fox/325	20.00	6.00
Don Mattingly/400	40.00	12.00
Joe Torre/250	15.00	4.50
Cal Ripken/250	50.00	15.00
Richie Ashburn/250	25.00	7.50
Mike Schmidt/250	30.00	9.00
Dale Murphy/250	25.00	7.50
Thurman Munson/400	20.00	6.00
Tony Gwynn/400	20.00	6.00
Orlando Cepeda/225	15.00	4.50
Ty Cobb/25		
Paul Molitor/325	20.00	6.00
Ralph Kiner/200	15.00	4.50
Frank Robinson/225	25.00	7.50
Yogi Berra/50	60.00	18.00
Reggie Jackson/375	20.00	6.00
Rod Carew/325	20.00	6.00
Carlton Fisk/325	20.00	6.00
Rogers Hornsby/50	80.00	24.00
Mel Ott/125	40.00	12.00
Jimmie Foxx/50	80.00	24.00

2003 Donruss Classics Legendary Spikes

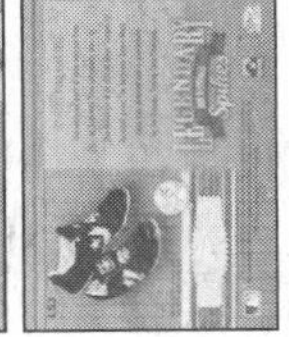

ındomly inserted into packs, this five-card set atureds game-used spike pieces of the fea- ed players. These cards were issued to a stat- print run of 50 serial numbered sets.

	Nm-Mt	Ex-Mt
Kirby Puckett	60.00	18.00
Tony Gwynn	100.00	30.00
Don Mattingly	150.00	45.00
Frank Robinson	50.00	15.00
Gary Carter	40.00	12.00

2003 Donruss Classics Legends of the Fall

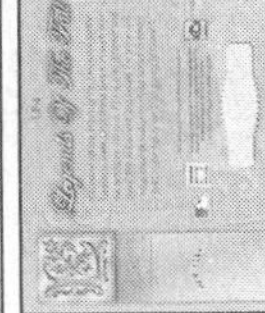

andomly inserted into packs, this 10 card set atured players who were stars of at least one orld Series they played in. Each of these cards ere issued to a stated print run of 2500 serial umbered sets.

	Nm-Mt	Ex-Mt
Reggie Jackson	4.00	1.20
Duke Snider	4.00	1.20
Roberto Clemente	12.00	3.60
Mel Ott	5.00	1.50
Yogi Berra	5.00	1.50
Jackie Robinson	5.00	1.50
Enos Slaughter	4.00	1.20
Willie Stargell	4.00	1.20
Bobby Doerr	4.00	1.20
) Thurman Munson	5.00	1.50

2003 Donruss Classics Legends of the Fall Fabrics

andomly inserted into packs, this is a parallel o the Legends of the Fall insert set. Each of ese cards features a game-worn/used memo- abilia swatch sequentially numbered to varying

quantities. Please note that we have put that stated print run information next to the player's name in our checklist and if the print run is 25 or fewer, no pricing is provided due to market scarcity.

	Nm-Mt	Ex-Mt
1 Reggie Jackson/100	25.00	7.50
2 Duke Snider/25		
3 Roberto Clemente/50	150.00	45.00
4 Mel Ott/25		
5 Yogi Berra/15		
6 Jackie Robinson/50	100.00	30.00
7 Enos Slaughter/25		
8 Willie Stargell/100	25.00	7.50
9 Bobby Doerr/100	20.00	6.00
10 Thurman Munson/25		

2003 Donruss Classics Membership

Randomly inserted into packs, this 15-card set feature members of some of the most prestigious stat groups. Each of these cards were issued to a stated print run of 2500 serial numbered sets.

	Nm-Mt	Ex-Mt
1 Babe Ruth	15.00	4.50
2 Steve Carlton	4.00	1.20
3 Honus Wagner	8.00	2.40
4 Warren Spahn	4.00	1.20
5 Eddie Mathews	5.00	1.50
6 Nolan Ryan	12.00	3.60
7 Rogers Hornsby	4.00	1.20
8 Ernie Banks	5.00	1.50
9 Harmon Killebrew	5.00	1.50
10 Tom Seaver	4.00	1.20
11 Jimmie Foxx	5.00	1.50
12 Ty Cobb	8.00	2.40
13 Frank Robinson	4.00	1.20
14 Mel Ott	5.00	1.50
15 Lou Gehrig	10.00	3.00

2003 Donruss Classics Membership VIP Memorabilia

Randomly inserted in packs, this is a parallel to the Membership insert set. Each of these cards feature a game worn/used memorabilia swatch. Each of these cards were issued to a varying sequential numbering and we have put that information next to the player's name in our checklist. Please note that if a card has a print run of 25 or fewer, no pricing is provided due to market scarcity.

	Nm-Mt	Ex-Mt
1 Babe Ruth Bat/29		
2 Steve Carlton Jsy/81	25.00	7.50
3 Honus Wagner Seat/14		
4 Warren Spahn Jsy/61	50.00	15.00
5 Eddie Mathews Bat/67	60.00	18.00
6 Nolan Ryan Jsy/80	100.00	30.00
7 Rogers Hornsby Bat/31		
8 Ernie Banks Jsy/70	60.00	18.00
9 Harmon Killebrew Jsy/71	60.00	18.00
10 Tom Seaver Jsy/81	40.00	12.00
11 Jimmie Foxx Bat/40	80.00	24.00
12 Ty Cobb Bat/21		
13 Frank Robinson Jsy/71	50.00	15.00
14 Mel Ott Jsy/45	80.00	24.00
15 Lou Gehrig Bat/31		

2003 Donruss Classics Timeless Treasures

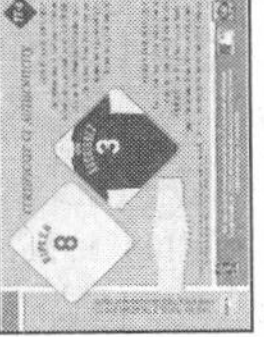

Randomly inserted into packs, these five cards featured some of the game's most legendary players along with two swatches of game-worn/used material sequentially numbered to varying quantities. Please note that for cards with stated print runs of 25 or fewer, no pricing is provided due to market scarcity.

	Nm-Mt	Ex-Mt
1 Stan Musial Jsy	150.00	45.00
Tony Gwynn Jsy/50		
2 Alex Rodriguez Jsy		
Cal Ripken Jsy/25		
3 Roberto Clemente Jsy	150.00	45.00
Vladimir Guerrero Jsy/50		
4 Ernie Banks Jsy		
Sammy Sosa Jsy/25		
5 Don Mattingly Jsy	120.00	36.00
Jason Giambi Jsy/50		

2004 Donruss Classics

This 213-card set was released in April, 2004. The set was issued in six card packs with an $6 SRP which came 18 packs to a box and 14 boxes to a case. The first 150 cards in this set are active veterans while cards 151-175 and 206-211 featured retired greats and cards number 176-205 feature leading prospects. All those cards were printed to a print run of 1999 serial numbered sets. The set closes with three cards featuring leading players who switched teams in the off-season and those cards were issued at a stated rate of one in 18.

	Nm-Mt	Ex-Mt
COMP.SET w/o SP's (153)	25.00	7.50
COMMON CARD (1-150)	.60	.18
COMMON (151-175/206-210)	4.00	1.20
COMMON CARD (176-205)	4.00	1.20
COMMON CARD (211-213)	1.00	.30
1 Albert Pujols	3.00	.90
2 Derek Jeter	3.00	.90
3 Hank Blalock	.60	.18
4 Shannon Stewart	.60	.18
5 Jason Giambi	.60	.18
6 Carlos Lee	.60	.18
7 Trot Nixon	.60	.18
8 Bret Boone	.60	.18
9 Mark Mulder	.60	.18
10 Mariano Rivera	1.00	.30
11 Scott Podsednik	.60	.18
12 Jim Edmonds	.60	.18
13 Mike Lowell	.60	.18
14 Robin Ventura	.60	.18
15 Brian Giles	.60	.18
16 Jose Vidro	.60	.18
17 Manny Ramirez	1.00	.30
18 Alex Rodriguez Rgr	2.50	.75
19 Carlos Beltran	1.00	.30
20 Hideki Matsui	2.50	.75
21 Johan Santana	1.00	.30
22 Richie Sexson	.60	.18
23 Chipper Jones	1.50	.45
24 Steve Finley	.60	.18
25 Mark Prior	1.50	.45
26 Alexis Rios	.60	.18
27 Rafael Palmeiro	1.00	.30
28 Jorge Posada	1.00	.30
29 Barry Zito	.60	.18
30 Jamie Moyer	.60	.18
31 Preston Wilson	.60	.18
32 Miguel Cabrera	1.00	.30
33 Pedro Martinez	1.50	.45
34 Curt Schilling	1.50	.45
35 Hee Seop Choi	.60	.18
36 Dontrelle Willis	.60	.18
37 Rafael Soriano	.60	.18
38 Richard Fischer	.60	.18
39 Brian Tallet	.60	.18
40 Jose Castillo	.60	.18
41 Wade Miller	.60	.18
42 Jose Contreras	.60	.18
43 Runelvys Hernandez	.60	.18
44 Joe Borchard	.60	.18
45 Kazuhisa Ishii	.60	.18
46 Jose Reyes	.60	.18
47 Adam Dunn	1.00	.30
48 Randy Johnson	1.50	.45
49 Brandon Phillips	.60	.18
50 Scott Rolen	1.50	.45
51 Ken Griffey Jr.	2.50	.75
52 Tom Glavine	1.00	.30
53 Cliff Lee	.60	.18
54 Chien-Ming Wang	.60	.18
55 Roy Oswalt	.60	.18
56 Austin Kearns	.60	.18
57 Jhonny Peralta	.60	.18
58 Greg Maddux Braves	2.50	.75
59 Mark Grace	1.00	.30
60 Jae Weong Seo	.60	.18
61 Nic Jackson	.60	.18
62 Roger Clemens	3.00	.90
63 Jimmy Gobble	.60	.18
64 Travis Hafner	.60	.18
65 Paul Konerko	.60	.18
66 Jerome Williams	.60	.18
67 Ryan Klesko	.60	.18
68 Alexis Gomez	.60	.18
69 Omar Vizquel	1.00	.30
70 Zach Day	.60	.18
71 Rickey Henderson	1.50	.45
72 Morgan Ensberg	.60	.18
73 Josh Beckett	.60	.18
74 Garrett Atkins	.60	.18
75 Sean Casey	.60	.18
76 Julio Franco	.60	.18
77 Lyle Overbay	.60	.18
78 Josh Phelps	.60	.18
79 Juan Gonzalez	1.00	.30
80 Rich Harden	.60	.18
81 Bernie Williams	1.00	.30
82 Torii Hunter	.60	.18
83 Angel Berroa	.60	.18
84 Jody Gerut	.60	.18
85 Roberto Alomar	1.00	.30
86 Byung-Hyun Kim	.60	.18
87 Jay Gibbons	.60	.18
88 Chone Figgins	.60	.18
89 Fred McGriff	1.00	.30
90 Rich Aurilia	.60	.18
91 Xavier Nady	.60	.18
92 Marlon Byrd	.60	.18
93 Mike Piazza	2.50	.75
94 Vladimir Guerrero	1.50	.45
95 Shawn Green	.60	.18
96 Jeff Kent	.60	.18
97 Ivan Rodriguez	1.50	.45
98 Jay Payton	.60	.18
99 Barry Larkin	1.00	.30
100 Mike Sweeney	.60	.18
101 Adrian Beltre	1.00	.30
102 Robby Hammock	.60	.18
103 Orlando Hudson	.60	.18
104 Mark Teixeira	.60	.18
105 Hong-Chih Kuo	.60	.18
106 Eric Chavez	.60	.18
107 Nick Johnson	.60	.18
108 Jacque Jones	.60	.18
109 Ken Harvey	.60	.18
110 Aramis Ramirez	.60	.18
111 Victor Martinez	.60	.18
112 Joe Crede	.60	.18
113 Jason Varitek	1.00	.30
114 Troy Glaus	.60	.18
115 Billy Wagner	.60	.18
116 Kerry Wood	1.50	.45
117 Hideo Nomo	1.50	.45
118 Brandon Webb	.60	.18
119 Craig Biggio	1.00	.30
120 Orlando Cabrera	.60	.18
121 Sammy Sosa	2.50	.75
122 Bobby Abreu	.60	.18
123 Andruw Jones	.60	.18
124 Jeff Bagwell	1.00	.30
125 Jim Thome	1.50	.45
126 Javy Lopez	.60	.18
127 Luis Castillo	.60	.18
128 Todd Helton	1.00	.30
129 Roy Halladay	.60	.18
130 Mike Mussina	1.00	.30
131 Eric Byrnes	.60	.18
132 Eric Hinske	.60	.18
133 Nomar Garciaparra	2.50	.75
134 Edgar Martinez	1.00	.30
135 Rocco Baldelli	.60	.18
136 Miguel Tejada	.60	.18
137 Alfonso Soriano Yanks	1.00	.30
138 Carlos Delgado	.60	.18
139 Rafael Furcal	.60	.18
140 Ichiro Suzuki	2.50	.75
141 Aubrey Huff	.60	.18
142 Garret Anderson	.60	.18
143 Vernon Wells	.60	.18
144 Magglio Ordonez	.60	.18
145 Brett Myers	.60	.18
146 Luis Gonzalez	.60	.18
147 Lance Berkman	.60	.18
148 Frank Thomas	1.50	.45
149 Gary Sheffield	.60	.18
150 Tim Hudson	.60	.18
151 Duke Snider LGD	5.00	1.50
152 Carl Yastrzemski LGD	6.00	1.80
153 Whitey Ford LGD	5.00	1.50
154 Cal Ripken LGD	12.00	3.60
155 Dwight Gooden LGD	4.00	1.20
156 Warren Spahn LGD	5.00	1.50
157 Bob Gibson LGD	5.00	1.50
158 Don Mattingly LGD	10.00	3.00
159 Jack Morris LGD	4.00	1.20
160 Jim Bunning LGD	5.00	1.50
161 Fergie Jenkins LGD	4.00	1.20
162 Brooks Robinson LGD	5.00	1.50
163 George Kell LGD	4.00	1.20
164 Darryl Strawberry LGD	4.00	1.20
165 Robin Roberts LGD	4.00	1.20
166 Monte Irvin LGD	4.00	1.20
167 Ernie Banks LGD	5.00	1.50
168 Wade Boggs LGD	5.00	1.50
169 Gaylord Perry LGD	4.00	1.20
170 Keith Hernandez LGD	4.00	1.20
171 Lou Brock LGD	5.00	1.50
172 Frank Robinson LGD	4.00	1.20
173 Nolan Ryan LGD	10.00	3.00
174 Stan Musial LGD	6.00	1.80
175 Eddie Murray LGD	5.00	1.50
176 Byron Gettis ROO	4.00	1.20
177 Merkin Valdez ROO RC	5.00	1.50
178 Rickie Weeks ROO	4.00	1.20
179 Akinori Otsuka ROO RC	4.00	1.20
180 Brian Bruney ROO	4.00	1.20
181 Freddy Guzman ROO RC	5.00	1.50
182 Brendan Harris ROO	4.00	1.20
183 John Gall ROO RC	5.00	1.50
184 Jason Kubel ROO	4.00	1.20
185 Delmon Young ROO	5.00	1.50
186 Ryan Howard ROO UER	4.00	1.20
Stat headers are for a pitcher		
187 Adam Loewen ROO	4.00	1.20
188 J.D. Durbin ROO	4.00	1.20
189 Dan Haren ROO	4.00	1.20
190 Dustin McGowan ROO	4.00	1.20
191 Chad Gaudin ROO	4.00	1.20
192 Preston Larrison ROO	4.00	1.20
193 Ramon Nivar ROO	4.00	1.20
194 Ronald Belisario ROO RC	4.00	1.20
195 Mike Gosling ROO RC	4.00	1.20
196 Kevin Youkilis ROO	4.00	1.20
197 Ryan Wagner ROO	4.00	1.20
198 Bubba Nelson ROO	4.00	1.20
199 Edwin Jackson ROO	4.00	1.20
200 Chris Burke ROO	4.00	1.20
201 Carlos Hines ROO RC	4.00	1.20
202 Greg Dobbs ROO RC	4.00	1.20
203 Jamie Brown ROO RC	4.00	1.20
204 Dave Crouthers ROO RC	4.00	1.20
205 Ian Snell ROO RC	5.00	1.50
206 Gary Carter LGD	4.00	1.20
207 Dale Murphy LGD	5.00	1.50
208 Ryne Sandberg LGD	8.00	2.40
209 Phil Niekro LGD	4.00	1.20
210 Don Sutton LGD	4.00	1.20
211 Alex Rodriguez Yanks SP	5.00	1.50
212 Alfonso Soriano Rgr SP	1.50	.45
213 Greg Maddux Cubs SP	4.00	1.20

2004 Donruss Classics Significant Signatures Green

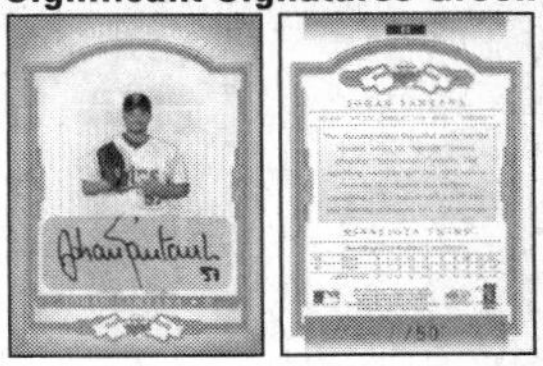

	Nm-Mt	Ex-Mt
RANDOM INSERTS IN PACKS		
PRINT RUNS B/WN 1-100 COPIES PER		
NO PRICING ON QTY OF 15 OR LESS		
3 Hank Blalock/25	25.00	7.50
4 Shannon Stewart/50	20.00	6.00
6 Carlos Lee/10		
7 Trot Nixon/25	25.00	7.50
9 Mark Mulder/10		
10 Mariano Rivera/5		
12 Jim Edmonds/10		
13 Mike Lowell/25	25.00	7.50
14 Robin Ventura/25	25.00	7.50
16 Jose Vidro/10		
17 Manny Ramirez/5		
18 Alex Rodriguez Rgr/1		
19 Carlos Beltran/25	50.00	15.00
21 Johan Santana/50	50.00	15.00
22 Richie Sexson/5		
23 Chipper Jones/1		
24 Steve Finley/25	40.00	12.00
25 Mark Prior/5		
26 Alexis Rios/100	15.00	4.50
27 Rafael Palmeiro/10		
28 Jorge Posada/10		
29 Barry Zito/10		
30 Jamie Moyer/5		
32 Miguel Cabrera/50	30.00	9.00
33 Pedro Martinez/1		
34 Curt Schilling/1		
36 Dontrelle Willis/25	25.00	7.50
37 Rafael Soriano/100	10.00	3.00
38 Richard Fischer/100	10.00	3.00
39 Brian Tallet/100	10.00	3.00
40 Jose Castillo/100	10.00	3.00
41 Wade Miller/25	15.00	4.50
42 Jose Contreras/10		
43 Runelvys Hernandez/20	15.00	4.50
44 Joe Borchard/50	12.00	3.60
47 Adam Dunn/25	40.00	12.00
48 Randy Johnson/1		
49 Brandon Phillips/50	12.00	3.60
50 Scott Rolen/10		
52 Tom Glavine/5		
53 Cliff Lee/50	12.00	3.60
54 Chien-Ming Wang/50	30.00	9.00
55 Roy Oswalt/10		
56 Austin Kearns/10		
57 Jhonny Peralta/100	15.00	4.50
58 Greg Maddux Braves/1		
59 Mark Grace/5		
60 Jae Weong Seo/50	30.00	9.00
61 Nic Jackson/100	10.00	3.00
62 Roger Clemens/1		
63 Jimmy Gobble/45	12.00	3.60
64 Travis Hafner/50	20.00	6.00
65 Paul Konerko/10		
66 Jerome Williams/50	20.00	6.00
67 Ryan Klesko/5		
68 Alexis Gomez/50	12.00	3.60
70 Zach Day/50	12.00	3.60
72 Morgan Ensberg/50	20.00	6.00
73 Josh Beckett/5		
74 Garrett Atkins/99	10.00	3.00
75 Sean Casey/10		
76 Julio Franco/10		
77 Lyle Overbay/100	15.00	4.50
78 Josh Phelps/25	15.00	4.50
79 Juan Gonzalez/25	40.00	12.00
80 Rich Harden/50	20.00	6.00
82 Torii Hunter/10		
83 Angel Berroa/5		
84 Jody Gerut/50	20.00	6.00
85 Roberto Alomar/5		
87 Jay Gibbons/50	12.00	3.60
88 Chone Figgins/50	20.00	6.00
89 Fred McGriff/5		
90 Rich Aurilia/10		
91 Xavier Nady/5		
92 Marlon Byrd/10		
93 Mike Piazza/1		
94 Vladimir Guerrero/5		
95 Shawn Green/1		
97 Ivan Rodriguez/5		
98 Jay Payton/50	12.00	3.60
99 Barry Larkin/25	40.00	12.00
100 Mike Sweeney/1		
101 Adrian Beltre/5		
102 Robby Hammock/50	12.00	3.60
103 Orlando Hudson/50	12.00	3.60
104 Mark Teixeira/10		
105 Hong-Chih Kuo/50	30.00	9.00
106 Eric Chavez/25	25.00	7.50
107 Nick Johnson/10		
108 Jacque Jones/50	20.00	6.00
109 Ken Harvey/100	15.00	4.50
110 Aramis Ramirez/50	20.00	6.00
111 Victor Martinez/50	20.00	6.00
112 Joe Crede/50	12.00	3.60
113 Jason Varitek/25	50.00	15.00
114 Troy Glaus/10		
116 Kerry Wood/5		
117 Hideo Nomo/1		
118 Brandon Webb/25	15.00	4.50
119 Craig Biggio/10		
120 Orlando Cabrera/10		
121 Sammy Sosa/21	200.00	60.00
122 Bobby Abreu/10		
123 Andruw Jones/10		
124 Jeff Bagwell/5		
127 Luis Castillo/25	15.00	4.50
128 Todd Helton/1		
130 Mike Mussina/1		
131 Eric Byrnes/10		

132 Eric Hinske/10
134 Edgar Martinez/25 50.00 15.00
135 Rocco Baldelli/10
136 Miguel Tejada/5
141 Aubrey Huff/5
142 Garret Anderson/5
143 Vernon Wells/10
144 Magglio Ordonez/10
145 Brett Myers/50 12.00 3.60
147 Lance Berkman/5
148 Frank Thomas/5
149 Gary Sheffield/25 40.00 12.00
150 Tim Hudson/10
151 Duke Snider LGD/25 50.00 15.00
152 Carl Yastrzemski LGD/5
153 Whitey Ford LGD/25 50.00 15.00
154 Cal Ripken LGD/5
155 Dwight Gooden LGD/50 25.00 7.50
156 Warren Spahn LGD/10
157 Bob Gibson LGD/5
158 Don Mattingly LGD/25 150.00 45.00
159 Jack Morris LGD/50 15.00 4.50
160 Jim Bunning LGD/25 60.00 18.00
161 Fergie Jenkins LGD/50 25.00 7.50
162 Brooks Robinson LGD/10
163 George Kell LGD/50 25.00 7.50
164 Darryl Strawberry LGD/50 25.00 7.50
165 Robin Roberts LGD/25 50.00 15.00
166 Monte Irvin LGD/25 30.00 9.00
167 Ernie Banks LGD/25 60.00 18.00
168 Wade Boggs LGD/25 60.00 18.00
169 Gaylord Perry LGD/50 15.00 4.50
170 Keith Hernandez LGD/50 25.00 7.50
171 Lou Brock LGD/10
172 Frank Robinson LGD/25 50.00 15.00
173 Nolan Ryan LGD/25 150.00 45.00
174 Stan Musial LGD/25 80.00 24.00
175 Eddie Murray LGD/25 100.00 30.00
176 Byron Gettis ROO/100 10.00 3.00
177 Merkin Valdez ROO/100 20.00 6.00
178 Rickie Weeks ROO/25 25.00 7.50
180 Brian Bruney ROO/100 10.00 3.00
181 Freddy Guzman ROO/100 15.00 4.50
182 Brendan Harris ROO/100 10.00 3.00
183 John Gall ROO/100 25.00 7.50
184 Jason Kubel ROO/100 15.00 4.50
185 Delmon Young ROO/50 50.00 15.00
186 Ryan Howard ROO/100 15.00 4.50
187 Adam Loewen ROO/100 10.00 3.00
188 J.D. Durbin ROO/100 15.00 4.50
189 Dan Haren ROO/100 10.00 3.00
190 Dustin McGowan ROO/100 10.00 3.00
191 Chad Gaudin ROO/100 10.00 3.00
192 Preston Larrison ROO/100 10.00 3.00
193 Ramon Nivar ROO/100 10.00 3.00
195 Mike Gosling ROO/100 10.00 3.00
196 Kevin Youkilis ROO/100 15.00 4.50
197 Ryan Wagner ROO/100 10.00 3.00
198 Bubba Nelson ROO/100 10.00 3.00
199 Edwin Jackson ROO/100 15.00 4.50
200 Chris Burke ROO/100 10.00 3.00
201 Carlos Hines ROO/100 10.00 3.00
202 Greg Dobbs ROO/50 12.00 3.60
203 Jamie Brown ROO/100 10.00 3.00
204 Dave Crouthers ROO/100
205 Ian Snell ROO/100 15.00 4.50
206 Gary Carter LGD/50 25.00 7.50
207 Dale Murphy LGD/50 40.00 12.00
208 Ryne Sandberg LGD/50 80.00 24.00
209 Phil Niekro LGD/50 40.00 12.00
210 Don Sutton LGD/50 25.00 7.50
211 Alex Rodriguez Yanks/1
213 Greg Maddux Cubs/1

2004 Donruss Classics Significant Signatures Red

Nm-Mt Ex-Mt
RANDOM INSERTS IN PACKS
PRINT RUNS B/WN 1-250 COPIES PER
NO PRICING ON QTY OF 15 OR LESS
3 Hank Blalock/50 20.00 6.00
4 Shannon Stewart/100 15.00 4.50
6 Carlos Lee/25 25.00 7.50
7 Trot Nixon/50 20.00 6.00
9 Mark Mulder/25 25.00 7.50
10 Mariano Rivera/5
12 Jim Edmonds/25 40.00 12.00
13 Mike Lowell/50 20.00 6.00
14 Robin Ventura/50 20.00 6.00
16 Jose Vidro/25 15.00 4.50
17 Manny Ramirez/5
18 Alex Rodriguez Rgr/5
19 Carlos Beltran/25 50.00 15.00
21 Johan Santana/100 40.00 12.00
22 Richie Sexson/10
23 Chipper Jones/5
24 Steve Finley/100 25.00 7.50
25 Mark Prior/10
26 Alexis Rios/250 15.00 4.50
27 Rafael Palmeiro/25 100.00 30.00
28 Jorge Posada/25 40.00 12.00
29 Barry Zito/10
30 Jamie Moyer/5
32 Miguel Cabrera/100 25.00 7.50
33 Pedro Martinez/5
34 Curt Schilling/5
36 Dontrelle Willis/100 15.00 4.50
37 Rafael Soriano/250 10.00 3.00
38 Richard Fischer/250 10.00 3.00
39 Brian Tallet/250 10.00 3.00
40 Jose Castillo/250 10.00 3.00
41 Wade Miller/92 10.00 3.00
42 Jose Contreras/25 25.00 7.50
43 Runelvys Hernandez/50 12.00 3.60
44 Joe Borchard/250 10.00 3.00
47 Adam Dunn/25 40.00 12.00
48 Randy Johnson/3
49 Brandon Phillips/70 10.00 3.00
50 Scott Rolen/25 50.00 15.00
52 Tom Glavine/10
53 Cliff Lee/100 10.00 3.00
54 Chien-Ming Wang/250 25.00 7.50
55 Roy Oswalt/25 25.00 7.50
56 Austin Kearns/25 25.00 7.50
57 Jhonny Peralta/250 15.00 4.50
58 Greg Maddux Braves/5
59 Mark Grace/5
60 Jae Weong Seo/100 25.00 7.50
61 Nic Jackson/250 10.00 3.00
62 Roger Clemens/1
63 Jimmy Gobble/200 10.00 3.00
64 Travis Hafner/100 15.00 4.50
65 Paul Konerko/25 25.00 7.50
66 Jerome Williams/250 15.00 4.50
67 Ryan Klesko/5
68 Alexis Gomez/100 10.00 3.00
70 Zach Day/100 10.00 3.00
72 Morgan Ensberg/100 15.00 4.50
73 Josh Beckett/5
74 Garrett Atkins/245 10.00 3.00
75 Sean Casey/10
76 Julio Franco/25 25.00 7.50
77 Lyle Overbay/250 15.00 4.50
78 Josh Phelps/50 12.00 3.60
79 Juan Gonzalez/25 40.00 12.00
80 Rich Harden/150 15.00 4.50
82 Torii Hunter/25 25.00 7.50
83 Angel Berroa/10
84 Jody Gerut/100 15.00 4.50
85 Roberto Alomar/10
87 Jay Gibbons/100 10.00 3.00
88 Chone Figgins/100 15.00 4.50
89 Fred McGriff/5
90 Rich Aurilia/25 15.00 4.50
91 Xavier Nady/10
92 Marlon Byrd/25 15.00 4.50
93 Mike Piazza/10
94 Vladimir Guerrero/10
95 Shawn Green/1
97 Ivan Rodriguez/10
98 Jay Payton/100 10.00 3.00
99 Barry Larkin/25 40.00 12.00
100 Mike Sweeney/1
101 Adrian Beltre/5
102 Robby Hammock/150 10.00 3.00
103 Orlando Hudson/100 10.00 3.00
104 Mark Teixeira/10
105 Hong-Chih Kuo/100 25.00 7.50
106 Eric Chavez/25 25.00 7.50
107 Nick Johnson/25 15.00 4.50
108 Jacque Jones/100 15.00 4.50
109 Ken Harvey/250 15.00 4.50
110 Aramis Ramirez/100 15.00 4.50
111 Victor Martinez/99 15.00 4.50
112 Joe Crede/250 10.00 3.00
113 Jason Varitek/50 50.00 15.00
114 Troy Glaus/25 25.00 7.50
116 Kerry Wood/10
117 Hideo Nomo/1
118 Brandon Webb/50 12.00 3.60
119 Craig Biggio/25 40.00 12.00
120 Orlando Cabrera/50 20.00 6.00
121 Sammy Sosa/25 200.00 60.00
122 Bobby Abreu/25 25.00 7.50
123 Andruw Jones/25 25.00 7.50
124 Jeff Bagwell/25 80.00 24.00
127 Luis Castillo/50 12.00 3.60
128 Todd Helton/5
130 Mike Mussina/5
131 Eric Byrnes/25 25.00 7.50
132 Eric Hinske/25 15.00 4.50
134 Edgar Martinez/50 50.00 15.00
135 Rocco Baldelli/25 25.00 7.50
136 Miguel Tejada/5
141 Aubrey Huff/5
142 Garret Anderson/5
143 Vernon Wells/25 25.00 7.50
144 Magglio Ordonez/25 40.00 12.00
145 Brett Myers/100 10.00 3.00
147 Lance Berkman/5
148 Frank Thomas/5
149 Gary Sheffield/50 30.00 9.00
150 Tim Hudson/25 40.00 12.00
151 Duke Snider LGD/50 40.00 12.00
152 Carl Yastrzemski LGD/10
153 Whitey Ford LGD/50 40.00 12.00
154 Cal Ripken LGD/10
155 Dwight Gooden LGD/100 20.00 6.00
156 Warren Spahn LGD/25 60.00 18.00
157 Bob Gibson LGD/15
158 Don Mattingly LGD/25 150.00 45.00
159 Jack Morris LGD/100 15.00 4.50
160 Jim Bunning LGD/100 40.00 12.00
161 Fergie Jenkins LGD/100 20.00 6.00
162 Brooks Robinson LGD/20 100.00 30.00
163 George Kell LGD/100 20.00 6.00
164 Darryl Strawberry LGD/100 20.00 6.00
165 Robin Roberts LGD/100 25.00 7.50
166 Monte Irvin LGD/100 20.00 6.00
167 Ernie Banks LGD/50 50.00 15.00
168 Wade Boggs LGD/50 50.00 15.00
169 Gaylord Perry LGD/100 15.00 4.50
170 Keith Hernandez LGD/100 20.00 6.00
171 Lou Brock LGD/25 50.00 15.00
172 Frank Robinson LGD/50 40.00 12.00
173 Nolan Ryan LGD/50 120.00 36.00
174 Stan Musial LGD/50 60.00 18.00
175 Eddie Murray LGD/50 80.00 24.00
176 Byron Gettis ROO/250 10.00 3.00
177 Merkin Valdez ROO/250 15.00 4.50
178 Rickie Weeks ROO/50 20.00 6.00
180 Brian Bruney ROO/250 10.00 3.00
181 Freddy Guzman ROO/250 15.00 4.50
182 Brendan Harris ROO/250 10.00 3.00
183 John Gall ROO/250 15.00 4.50
184 Jason Kubel ROO/250 15.00 4.50
185 Delmon Young ROO/100 40.00 12.00
186 Ryan Howard ROO/250 15.00 4.50
187 Adam Loewen ROO/250 10.00 3.00
188 J.D. Durbin ROO/250 15.00 4.50
189 Dan Haren ROO/250 10.00 3.00
190 Dustin McGowan ROO/250 10.00 3.00
191 Chad Gaudin ROO/250 10.00 3.00
192 Preston Larrison ROO/250 10.00 3.00
193 Ramon Nivar ROO/250 10.00 3.00
195 Mike Gosling ROO/250 10.00 3.00
196 Kevin Youkilis ROO/250 15.00 4.50
197 Ryan Wagner ROO/250 10.00 3.00
198 Bubba Nelson ROO/250 10.00 3.00
199 Edwin Jackson ROO/250 15.00 4.50
200 Chris Burke ROO/250 10.00 3.00
201 Carlos Hines ROO/250 10.00 3.00
202 Greg Dobbs ROO/100 10.00 3.00
203 Jamie Brown ROO/250 10.00 3.00
204 Dave Crouthers ROO/250 10.00 3.00
205 Ian Snell ROO/250 15.00 4.50
206 Gary Carter LGD/100 20.00 6.00
207 Dale Murphy LGD/50 40.00 12.00
208 Ryne Sandberg LGD/25 100.00 30.00
209 Phil Niekro LGD/100 25.00 7.50
210 Don Sutton LGD/100 20.00 6.00
211 Alex Rodriguez Yanks/5
213 Greg Maddux Cubs/5

2004 Donruss Classics Timeless Tributes Green

Nm-Mt Ex-Mt
*GREEN 1-150: 3X TO 8X BASIC
*GREEN 151-175/206-210: 1.5X TO 4X BASIC
*GREEN 176-205: .75X TO 2X BASIC
*GREEN 211-213: 2X TO 5X BASIC
RANDOM INSERTS IN PACKS
STATED PRINT RUN 50 SERIAL #'d SETS

2004 Donruss Classics Timeless Tributes Red

Nm-Mt Ex-Mt
*RED 1-150: 2.5X TO 6X BASIC
*RED 151-175/206-210: 1.25X TO 3X BASIC
*RED 176-205: .6X TO 1.5X BASIC
*RED 211-213: 1.5X TO 4X BASIC
RANDOM INSERTS IN PACKS
STATED PRINT RUN 100 SERIAL #'d SETS

2004 Donruss Classics Classic Combos Bat

Nm-Mt Ex-Mt
RANDOM INSERTS IN PACKS
PRINT RUNS B/WN 25-50 COPIES PER
ALL CARDS FEATURE BAT-BAT COMBOS
1 Babe Ruth
Lou Gehrig/25
2 Roy Campanella 40.00 12.00
Pee Wee Reese/50
3 Ted Williams 200.00 60.00
Carl Yastrzemski/25
4 Roberto Clemente 150.00 45.00
Willie Stargell/25
5 Eddie Murray 80.00 24.00
Cal Ripken/50
6 Roger Maris 100.00 30.00
Yogi Berra/25
10 Nolan Ryan 50.00 15.00
Rod Carew/50
11 Don Mattingly 60.00 18.00
Rickey Henderson/50
15 Robin Yount 60.00 18.00
Paul Molitor/50
16 Mark Grace 40.00 12.00
Sammy Sosa/50
17 Ted Williams 150.00 45.00
Bobby Doerr/25
18 Reggie Jackson 40.00 12.00
Rod Carew/50

2004 Donruss Classics Classic Combos Jersey

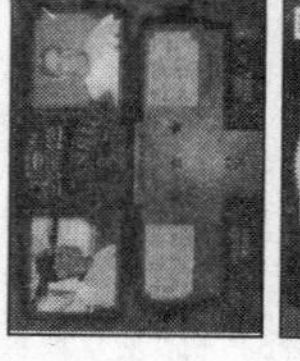

Nm-Mt Ex-Mt
PRINT RUNS B/WN
NO PRICING ON QTY OF 10 OR LESS
PRIME PRINT RUN 1 SERIAL #'d SET
NO PRIME PRICING DUE TO SCARCITY
RANDOM INSERTS IN PACKS
ALL ARE JSY-JSY COMBOS UNLESS NOTED
1 Babe Ruth Pants
Lou Gehrig Pants/15
2 Roy Campanella Pants 50.00 15.00
Pee Wee Reese/25
3 Ted Williams 300.00 90.00
Carl Yastrzemski/15
4 Roberto Clemente 150.00 45.00
Willie Stargell/25
5 Eddie Murray 120.00 36.00
Cal Ripken/25
6 Roger Maris 100.00 30.00
Yogi Berra/25
7 Stan Musial
Bob Gibson/10
8 Whitey Ford 50.00 15.00
Yogi Berra/25
9 Marty Marion 60.00 18.00
Stan Musial/25
10 Nolan Ryan 60.00 18.00
Rod Carew/25
11 Don Mattingly 60.00 18.00
Rickey Henderson/50
12 Jack Morris 25.00 7.50
Alan Trammell/50
13 Whitey Ford 50.00 15.00
Phil Rizzuto/25
14 Marty Marion 40.00 12.00
Red Schoendienst/25
15 Robin Yount 60.00 18.00
Paul Molitor/50
16 Mark Grace 40.00 12.00
Sammy Sosa/50
17 Ted Williams 250.00 75.00
Bobby Doerr/15
18 Reggie Jackson 40.00 12.00
Rod Carew/50

2004 Donruss Classics Classic Combos Quad

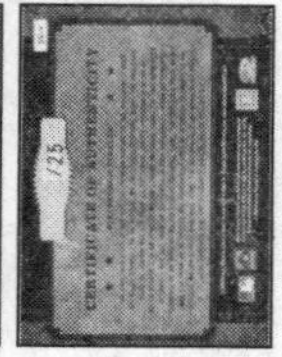

Nm-Mt Ex-Mt
NO PRICING ON QTY OF 5 OR LESS
PRIME PRINT RUN 1 SERIAL #'d SET
NO PRIME PRICING DUE TO SCARCITY
RANDOM INSERTS IN PACKS
1 Babe Ruth Bat-Pants
Lou Gehrig Bat-Pants/5
2 Roy Campanella Bat-Pants 100.00 30.00
Pee Wee Reese Bat-Jsy/25
3 Ted Williams Bat-Jsy 400.00 120.00
Carl Yastrzemski Bat-Jsy/15
4 Roberto Clemente Bat-Jsy 300.00 90.00
Willie Stargell Bat-Jsy/25
5 Eddie Murray Bat-Jsy 200.00 60.00
Cal Ripken Bat-Jsy/25
6 Roger Maris Bat-Jsy 250.00 75.00
Yogi Berra Bat-Jsy/15
10 Nolan Ryan Bat-Jsy 120.00 36.00
Rod Carew Bat-Jsy/25
11 Don Mattingly Bat-Jsy 150.00 45.00
Rickey Henderson Bat-Jsy/25
15 Robin Yount Bat-Jsy 120.00 36.00
Paul Molitor Bat-Jsy/25
16 Mark Grace Bat-Jsy 100.00 30.00
Sammy Sosa Bat-Jsy/25
17 Ted Williams Bat-Jsy 300.00 90.00
Bobby Doerr Bat-Jsy/15
18 Reggie Jackson Bat-Jsy 80.00 24.00
Rod Carew Bat-Jsy/25

2004 Donruss Classics Classic Singles Bat

Nm-Mt Ex-Mt
RANDOM INSERTS IN PACKS
PRINT RUNS B/WN 10-50 COPIES PER
NO PRICING ON QTY OF 10 OR LESS
1 Babe Ruth/15 400.00 120.00
2 Nolan Ryan/10
3 Stan Musial/25 50.00 15.00
4 Ted Williams/25 120.00 36.00
5 Lou Gehrig/50 150.00 45.00
6 Eddie Murray/50 30.00 9.00
7 Roy Campanella/50 30.00 9.00
8 Robin Yount/50 30.00 9.00
9 Roberto Clemente/25 100.00 30.00
10 Don Mattingly/50 50.00 15.00
12 Carl Yastrzemski/50 40.00 12.00
13 Mark Grace/50 25.00 7.50
15 Rickey Henderson/50 30.00 9.00
16 Reggie Jackson/50 25.00 7.50
17 Pee Wee Reese/50 25.00 7.50
20 Roger Maris/25 60.00 18.00
21 Cal Ripken/50 80.00 24.00
23 Willie Stargell/50 25.00 7.50
24 Paul Molitor/50 25.00 7.50
26 Alan Trammell/50 15.00 4.50
27 Sammy Sosa/50 25.00 7.50
28 Bobby Doerr/50 15.00 4.50
29 Rod Carew/50 25.00 7.50
30 Yogi Berra/50 40.00 12.00
32 George Brett/50 50.00 15.00

2004 Donruss Classics Classic Singles Jersey

Nm-Mt Ex-Mt
PRINT RUNS B/WN 10-100 COPIES PER
NO PRICING ON QTY FO 10 OR LESS
PRIME PRINT RUN 1 SERIAL #'d SET
NO PRIME PRICING DUE TO SCARCITY
RANDOM INSERTS IN PACKS
1 Babe Ruth Pants/10

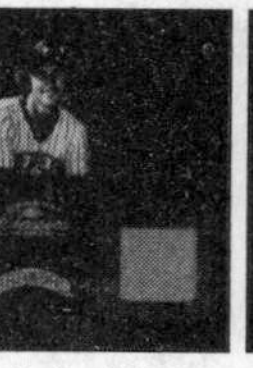

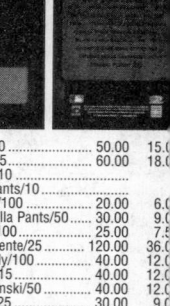

2 Nolan Ryan/50 50.00 15.0
3 Stan Musial/15 60.00 18.0
4 Ted Williams/10
5 Lou Gehrig Pants/10
6 Eddie Murray/100 20.00 6.0
7 Roy Campanella Pants/50 30.00 9.0
8 Robin Yount/100 25.00 7.5
9 Roberto Clemente/25 120.00 36.0
10 Don Mattingly/100 40.00 12.0
11 Bob Gibson/15 40.00 12.0
12 Carl Yastrzemski/50 40.00 12.0
13 Mark Grace/25 30.00 9.0
14 Jack Morris/100 10.00 3.0
15 Rickey Henderson/25 40.00 12.0
16 Reggie Jackson/50 25.00 7.5
17 Pee Wee Reese/25 30.00 9.0
18 Marty Marion/100 10.00 3.0
19 Tommy John/100 10.00 3.0
20 Roger Maris/25 60.00 18.0
21 Cal Ripken/25 120.00 36.0
22 Red Schoendienst/25 20.00 6.0
23 Willie Stargell/100 15.00 4.5
24 Paul Molitor/100 15.00 4.5
25 Whitey Ford/50 25.00 7.5
26 Alan Trammell/100 10.00 3.0
27 Sammy Sosa/100 25.00 7.5
28 Bobby Doerr/50 15.00 4.5
29 Rod Carew/100 15.00 4.5
30 Yogi Berra/15 50.00 15.0
31 Phil Rizzuto/25 30.00 9.0
32 George Brett/25 60.00 18.0

2004 Donruss Classics Classic Singles Jersey-Bat

 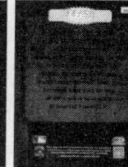

Nm-Mt Ex-M
PRINT RUNS B/WN 5-25 COPIES PER
NO PRICING ON QTY OF 10 OR LESS
PRIME PRINT RUN 1 SERIAL #'d SET
NO PRIME PRICING DUE TO SCARCITY
RANDOM INSERTS IN PACKS
ALL ARE JSY-BAT COMBOS UNLESS NOTED
1 Babe Ruth Pants/5
2 Nolan Ryan/25 60.00 18.0
3 Stan Musial/15 80.00 24.0
4 Ted Williams/10
5 Lou Gehrig Pants/10
6 Eddie Murray/25 50.00 15.0
7 Roy Campanella Pants/25 50.00 15.0
8 Robin Yount/25 60.00 18.0
9 Roberto Clemente/25 200.00 60.0
10 Don Mattingly/25 80.00 24.0
12 Carl Yastrzemski/25 60.00 18.0
13 Mark Grace/25 40.00 12.0
15 Rickey Henderson/25 50.00 15.0
16 Reggie Jackson/25 40.00 12.0
17 Pee Wee Reese/25 40.00 12.0
20 Roger Maris/15 120.00 36.0
21 Cal Ripken/25 150.00 45.0
23 Willie Stargell/25 40.00 12.0
24 Paul Molitor/25 40.00 12.0
26 Alan Trammell/25 25.00 7.5
27 Sammy Sosa/25 50.00 15.0
28 Bobby Doerr/25 25.00 7.5
29 Rod Carew/25 40.00 12.0
30 Yogi Berra/15 60.00 18.0
32 George Brett/25 80.00 24.0

2004 Donruss Classics Dress Code Bat

Nm-Mt Ex-Mt
STATED PRINT RUN 50 SERIAL #'d SETS
S.STEWART PRINT 10 SERIAL #'d CARDS
*DC COMBO MTRL: .5X TO 1.2X BASIC
DC COMBO MTRL PRINT 50 SERIAL #'d SETS
DC COMBO MTRL STEWART 10 #'d CARDS
RANDOM INSERTS IN PACKS
NO S.STEWART PRICING DUE TO SCARCITY
1 Derek Jeter 40.00 12.00
2 Kerry Wood 15.00 4.50
3 Nomar Garciaparra 20.00 6.00
4 Jacque Jones 10.00 3.00
5 Mark Teixeira 10.00 3.00
6 Troy Glaus 10.00 3.00
7 Todd Helton 15.00 4.50
8 Miguel Tejada 10.00 3.00
9 Mike Piazza 20.00 6.00
11 Mike Sweeney 10.00 3.00
12 Albert Pujols 25.00 7.50
13 Rickey Henderson 15.00 4.50

Chipper Jones 15.00 4.50
Don Mattingly 50.00 15.00
Shawn Green 10.00 3.00
Mark Grace 15.00 4.50
Jason Giambi 10.00 3.00
Barry Zito 10.00 3.00
Sammy Sosa 20.00 6.00
Rafael Palmeiro 15.00 4.50
Frank Thomas 15.00 4.50
Manny Ramirez 15.00 4.50
Mike Mussina 15.00 4.50
Magglio Ordonez 10.00 3.00
Rocco Baldelli 10.00 3.00
Andruw Jones 10.00 3.00
Torii Hunter 10.00 3.00
Ivan Rodriguez 15.00 4.50
Jeff Bagwell 15.00 4.50
Mark Mulder 10.00 3.00
Trot Nixon 10.00 3.00
Cal Ripken 80.00 24.00
Dontrelle Willis 10.00 3.00
Hank Blalock 10.00 3.00
Brandon Webb 10.00 3.00
Miguel Cabrera 15.00 4.50
Hideo Nomo 15.00 4.50
Shannon Stewart/10
Tim Hudson 10.00 3.00
Pedro Martinez 15.00 4.50
Hee Seop Choi 10.00 3.00
Randy Johnson 15.00 4.50
Tony Gwynn 25.00 7.50
Mark Prior 15.00 4.50
Eric Chavez 10.00 3.00
Alex Rodriguez 15.00 4.50
Alfonso Soriano 15.00 4.50

2004 Donruss Classics Dress Code Combos Signature

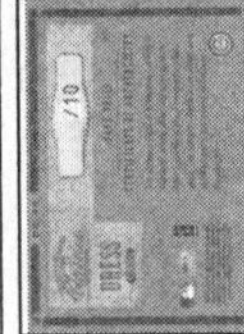

Nm-Mt Ex-Mt
RINT RUNS B/WN 1-25 COPIES PER
PRICING ON QTY OF 10 OR LESS
RIME PRINT RUN 1 SERIAL #'d SET
PRIME PRICING DUE TO SCARCITY
ANDOM INSERTS IN PACKS
Kerry Wood Jsy/5
Jacque Jones Jsy/25 40.00 12.00
Mark Teixeira Jsy/5
Troy Glaus Jsy/5
Todd Helton Jsy/5
Miguel Tejada Jsy/5
Mike Piazza Jsy/5
1 Mike Sweeney Jsy/5
3 Rickey Henderson Jsy/5
4 Chipper Jones Jsy/5
5 Don Mattingly Jsy/5
6 Shawn Green Jsy/1
7 Mark Grace Jsy/5
9 Barry Zito Jsy/5
9 Sammy Sosa Jsy/5
1 Jay Gibbons Jsy/25 25.00 7.50
2 Rafael Palmeiro Jsy/5
3 Frank Thomas Jsy/5
5 Mike Mussina Jsy/5
6 Magglio Ordonez Jsy/5
7 Rocco Baldelli Jsy/10
8 Andruw Jones Jsy/5
9 Torii Hunter Jsy/10
0 Ivan Rodriguez Jsy/5
1 Jeff Bagwell Jsy/5
2 Mark Mulder Jsy/25 40.00 12.00
3 Trot Nixon Jsy/25 40.00 12.00
4 Cal Ripken Jsy/5
5 Dontrelle Willis Jsy/25 40.00 12.00
6 Hank Blalock Jsy/10
7 Brandon Webb Jsy/10
8 Miguel Cabrera Jsy/25 60.00 18.00
9 Hideo Nomo Jsy/5
0 Shannon Stewart Jsy/25 40.00 12.00
1 Tim Hudson Jsy/10
2 Pedro Martinez Jsy/5
4 Randy Johnson Jsy/5
5 Tony Gwynn Jsy/5
6 Mark Prior Jsy/10
7 Eric Chavez Jsy/10
8 Alex Rodriguez Jsy/5
9 Johan Santana Jsy/25 100.00 30.00

2004 Donruss Classics Dress Code Jersey

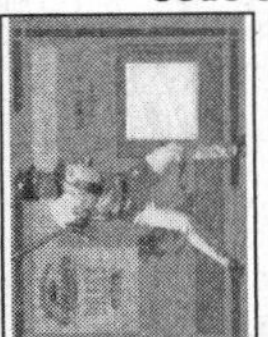
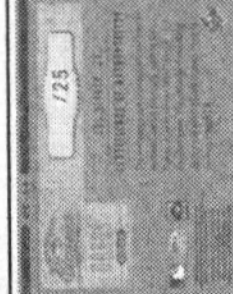

Nm-Mt Ex-Mt
STATED PRINT RUN 100 SERIAL #'d SETS
RIPKEN PRINT RUN 25 SERIAL #'d CARDS
*NUMBER: .4X TO 1X BASIC
*NUMBER RIPKEN: .15X TO .4X BASIC RIPKEN
NUMBER PRINT RUN 100 SERIAL #'d SETS
*PRIME: 1.5X TO 4X BASIC
*PRIME MATTINGLY: .75X TO 2X BASIC MATT
*PRIME RIPKEN: .6X TO 1.2X BASIC RIPKEN
PRIME PRINT RUN 25 SERIAL #'d SETS
PRIME SORIANO PRINT 12 #'d CARDS
NO PRIME SORIANO PRICING AVAILABLE
RANDOM INSERTS IN PACKS

1 Derek Jeter 30.00 9.00
2 Kerry Wood 10.00 3.00
3 Nomar Garciaparra 15.00 4.50
4 Jacque Jones 8.00 2.40
5 Mark Teixeira 8.00 2.40
6 Troy Glaus 8.00 2.40
7 Todd Helton 10.00 3.00
8 Miguel Tejada 8.00 2.40
9 Mike Piazza 15.00 4.50
11 Mike Sweeney 8.00 2.40
12 Albert Pujols 20.00 6.00
13 Rickey Henderson 10.00 3.00
14 Chipper Jones 10.00 3.00
15 Don Mattingly 40.00 12.00
16 Shawn Green 8.00 2.40
17 Mark Grace 10.00 3.00
18 Jason Giambi 8.00 2.40
19 Barry Zito 8.00 2.40
20 Sammy Sosa 15.00 4.50
21 Jay Gibbons 8.00 2.40
22 Rafael Palmeiro 10.00 3.00
23 Frank Thomas 10.00 3.00
24 Manny Ramirez 10.00 3.00
25 Mike Mussina 10.00 3.00
26 Magglio Ordonez 8.00 2.40
27 Rocco Baldelli 8.00 2.40
28 Andruw Jones 8.00 2.40
29 Torii Hunter 8.00 2.40
30 Ivan Rodriguez 10.00 3.00
31 Jeff Bagwell 10.00 3.00
32 Mark Mulder 8.00 2.40
33 Trot Nixon 8.00 2.40
34 Cal Ripken/25 120.00 36.00
35 Dontrelle Willis 8.00 2.40
36 Hank Blalock 8.00 2.40
37 Brandon Webb 8.00 2.40
38 Miguel Cabrera 10.00 3.00
39 Hideo Nomo 10.00 3.00
40 Shannon Stewart 8.00 2.40
41 Tim Hudson 8.00 2.40
42 Pedro Martinez 10.00 3.00
43 Hee Seop Choi 8.00 2.40
44 Randy Johnson 10.00 3.00
45 Tony Gwynn 20.00 6.00
46 Mark Prior 10.00 3.00
47 Eric Chavez 8.00 2.40
48 Alex Rodriguez 10.00 3.00
49 Johan Santana 10.00 3.00
50 Alfonso Soriano 10.00 3.00

2004 Donruss Classics Famous Foursomes

Nm-Mt Ex-Mt
RANDOM INSERTS IN PACKS
STATED PRINT RUN 99 SERIAL #'d SETS
1 Roy Campanella 25.00 7.50
Pee Wee Reese
Jackie Robinson
Duke Snider
2 Stan Musial 25.00 7.50
Bob Gibson
Red Schoendienst
Ken Boyer

2004 Donruss Classics Famous Foursomes Jersey

Nm-Mt Ex-Mt
STATED PRINT RUN 10 SERIAL #'d SETS
PRIME PRINT RUN 1 SERIAL #'d SET
NO PRIME PRICING DUE TO SCARCITY
RANDOM INSERTS IN PACKS
ALL ARE QUAD JSY CARDS UNLESS NOTED
1 Roy Campanella Pants
Pee Wee Reese
Jackie Robinson
Duke Snider
2 Stan Musial
Bob Gibson
Red Schoendienst
Ken Boyer

2004 Donruss Classics Legendary Hats Material

Nm-Mt Ex-Mt
RANDOM INSERTS IN PACKS
PRINT RUNS B/WN 5-25 COPIES PER
NO PRICING ON QTY OF 10 OR LESS
1 Tony Gwynn/10
2 Mike Schmidt/25 80.00 24.00
6 George Brett/25 80.00 24.00
14 Cal Ripken/25 150.00 45.00
16 Kirby Puckett/25 50.00 15.00
20 Reggie Jackson Yanks/25 40.00 12.00
21 Roberto Clemente/5
22 Ernie Banks/25 50.00 15.00
29 Dave Winfield/25 25.00 7.50
40 Wade Boggs/25 40.00 12.00
42 Rickey Henderson A's/25 50.00 15.00
49 Reggie Jackson Angels/25 40.00 12.00
51 Rafael Palmeiro/25 40.00 12.00
52 Sammy Sosa/25 40.00 12.00
55 Steve Carlton/25 25.00 7.50
56 Rod Carew Angels/25 40.00 12.00
60 R.Henderson Angels/25 50.00 15.00

2004 Donruss Classics Legendary Jerseys Material

Nm-Mt Ex-Mt
PRINT RUNS B/WN 5-50 COPIES PER
NO PRICING ON QTY OF 10 OR LESS
PRIME PRINT RUN 1 SERIAL #'d SET
NO PRIME PRICING DUE TO SCARCITY
RANDOM INSERTS IN PACKS
1 Tony Gwynn/50 25.00 7.50
2 Mike Schmidt/25 60.00 18.00
3 Johnny Bench/50 25.00 7.50
4 Roger Maris Yanks/10
5 Ted Williams/10
6 George Brett/25 60.00 18.00
7 Carlton Fisk/50 25.00 7.50
8 Reggie Jackson A's/25 30.00 9.00
9 Joe Morgan/25 20.00 6.00
10 Bo Jackson/25 40.00 12.00
11 Stan Musial/10
12 Andre Dawson/50 15.00 4.50
13 R.Henderson Yanks/25 40.00 12.00
14 Cal Ripken/25 120.00 36.00
15 Dale Murphy/25 30.00 9.00
16 Kirby Puckett/50 30.00 9.00
17 Don Mattingly/50 50.00 15.00
18 Brooks Robinson/50 25.00 7.50
19 Orlando Cepeda/50 15.00 4.50
20 Reggie Jackson Yanks/25 30.00 9.00
21 Roberto Clemente/25 120.00 36.00
22 Ernie Banks/10
23 Frank Robinson/50 15.00 4.50
24 Harmon Killebrew/50 30.00 9.00
25 Willie Stargell/50 25.00 7.50
26 Al Kaline/15 50.00 15.00
27 Carl Yastrzemski/50 40.00 12.00
28 Duke Snider/10
29 Dave Winfield/50 15.00 4.50
30 Eddie Murray/50 30.00 9.00
31 Eddie Mathews/25 40.00 12.00
32 Gary Carter/50 15.00 4.50
33 Rod Carew Twins/25 30.00 9.00
35 Mel Ott/10
36 Paul Molitor/50 25.00 7.50
37 Thurman Munson/15 50.00 15.00
39 Robin Yount/50 30.00 9.00
40 Wade Boggs/50 25.00 7.50
41 Jackie Robinson/5
42 Rickey Henderson A's/25 40.00 12.00
44 Yogi Berra/15 50.00 15.00
46 Luis Aparicio/50 15.00 4.50
47 Phil Rizzuto/25 30.00 9.00
48 Roger Maris A's/25 60.00 18.00
49 Reggie Jackson Angels/50 25.00 7.50
50 Lou Gehrig/5
51 Rafael Palmeiro/50 25.00 7.50
52 Sammy Sosa/50 25.00 7.50
53 Roger Clemens/50 30.00 9.00
54 Nolan Ryan/50 50.00 15.00
55 Steve Carlton/50 15.00 4.50
56 Rod Carew Angels/50 25.00 7.50
57 Whitey Ford/25 30.00 9.00
59 Babe Ruth/5

2004 Donruss Classics Legendary Jerseys Material Number

Nm-Mt Ex-Mt
*NUMBER p/r 50: .4X TO 1X BASIC p/r 50
*NUMBER p/r 25: .5X TO 1.2X BASIC p/r 50
*NUMBER p/r 25: .4X TO 1X BASIC p/r 25
*NUMBER p/r 15: .5X TO 1.2X BASIC p/r 25
*NUMBER p/r 15: .4X TO 1X BASIC p/r 15
RANDOM INSERTS IN PACKS
PRINT RUNS B/WN 3-50 COPIES PER
NO PRICNG ON QTY OF 10 OR LESS
45 Roy Campanella Pants/25 40.00 12.00
58 Fergie Jenkins Pants/25 20.00 6.00

2004 Donruss Classics Legendary Leather Material

Nm-Mt Ex-Mt
RANDOM INSERTS IN PACKS
PRINT RUNS B/WN 5-25 COPIES PER
NO PRICING ON QTY OF 10 OR LESS
1 Tony Gwynn Fld Glv/10
2 Mike Schmidt Fld Glv/10
16 Kirby Puckett Fld Glv/25 50.00 15.00
17 Don Mattingly Btg Glv/10
29 Dave Winfield Fld Glv/10
32 Gary Carter Fld Glv/25 25.00 7.50
34 Jimmie Foxx Fld Glv/10
51 Rafael Palmeiro Fld Glv/25 40.00 12.00
52 Sammy Sosa Btg Glv/25 60.00 18.00
54 Nolan Ryan Fld Glv/5
55 Steve Carlton Fld Glv/25 25.00 7.50
58 Fergie Jenkins Fld Glv/25 25.00 7.50

2004 Donruss Classics Legendary Lumberjacks

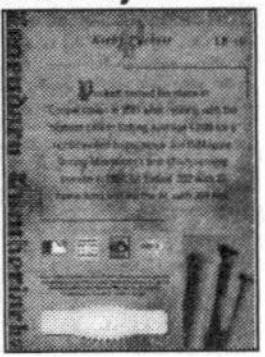

Nm-Mt Ex-Mt
STATED PRINT RUN 1000 SERIAL #'d SETS
*HATS: 1.5X TO 4X LUMBERJACKS
HATS PRINT RUN 50 SERIAL #'d SETS
*JACKETS: 1.5X TO 4X LUMBERJACKS
JACKET PRINT RUN 50 SERIAL #'d SETS
*JERSEYS: .6X TO 1.5X LUMBERJACKS
JERSEY PRINT RUN 500 SERIAL #'d SETS
*LEATHER: 1.2X TO 3X LUMBERJACKS
LEATHER PRINT RUN 100 SERIAL #'d SETS
*PANTS: 1.5X TO 4X LUMBERJACKS
PANTS PRINT RUN 50 SERIAL #'d SETS
*SPIKES: 1.25X TO 3X LUMBERJACKS
SPIKES PRINT RUN 100 SERIAL #'d SETS
RANDOM INSERTS IN PACKS
1 Tony Gwynn 5.00 1.50
2 Mike Schmidt 8.00 2.40
3 Johnny Bench 4.00 1.20
4 Roger Maris Yanks 4.00 1.20
5 Ted Williams 8.00 2.40
6 George Brett 10.00 3.00
7 Carlton Fisk 4.00 1.20
8 Reggie Jackson A's 4.00 1.20
9 Joe Morgan 2.50 .75
10 Bo Jackson 4.00 1.20
11 Stan Musial 6.00 1.80
12 Andre Dawson 2.50 .75
13 Rickey Henderson Yanks 4.00 1.20
14 Cal Ripken 12.00 3.60
15 Dale Murphy 4.00 1.20
16 Kirby Puckett 4.00 1.20
17 Don Mattingly 10.00 3.00
18 Brooks Robinson 4.00 1.20
19 Orlando Cepeda 2.50 .75
20 Reggie Jackson Yanks 4.00 1.20
21 Roberto Clemente 10.00 3.00
22 Ernie Banks 4.00 1.20
23 Frank Robinson 2.50 .75
24 Harmon Killebrew 4.00 1.20
25 Willie Stargell 4.00 1.20
26 Al Kaline 4.00 1.20
27 Carl Yastrzemski 6.00 1.80
28 Duke Snider 4.00 1.20
29 Dave Winfield 2.50 .75
30 Eddie Murray 4.00 1.20
31 Eddie Mathews 4.00 1.20
32 Gary Carter 2.50 .75
33 Rod Carew Twins 4.00 1.20
34 Jimmie Foxx 4.00 1.20
35 Mel Ott 4.00 1.20
36 Paul Molitor 4.00 1.20
37 Thurman Munson 4.00 1.20
38 Rogers Hornsby 4.00 1.20
39 Robin Yount 6.00 1.80
40 Wade Boggs 4.00 1.20
41 Jackie Robinson 4.00 1.20
42 Rickey Henderson A's 4.00 1.20
43 Ty Cobb 5.00 1.50
44 Yogi Berra 4.00 1.20
45 Roy Campanella 4.00 1.20
46 Luis Aparicio 2.50 .75
47 Phil Rizzuto 4.00 1.20
48 Roger Maris A's 4.00 1.20
49 Reggie Jackson Angels 4.00 1.20
50 Lou Gehrig 6.00 1.80
51 Rafael Palmeiro 4.00 1.20
52 Sammy Sosa 6.00 1.80
53 Roger Clemens 8.00 2.40
54 Nolan Ryan 10.00 3.00
55 Steve Carlton 2.50 .75
56 Rod Carew Angels 4.00 1.20
57 Whitey Ford 4.00 1.20
58 Fergie Jenkins 2.50 .75
59 Babe Ruth 10.00 3.00
60 R.Henderson Angels 4.00 1.20

2004 Donruss Classics Legendary Lumberjacks Material

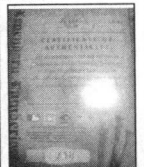

Nm-Mt Ex-Mt
RANDOM INSERTS IN PACKS
PRINT RUNS B/WN 10-100 COPIES PER
NO PRICING ON QTY OF 10 OR LESS
1 Tony Gwynn/100 20.00 6.00
2 Mike Schmidt/100 20.00 6.00
3 Johnny Bench/100 15.00 4.50
4 Roger Maris Yanks/25 60.00 18.00
5 Ted Williams/25 120.00 36.00
6 George Brett/100 40.00 12.00
7 Carlton Fisk/100 15.00 4.50
8 Reggie Jackson A's/100 15.00 4.50
9 Joe Morgan/100 10.00 3.00
10 Bo Jackson/100 20.00 6.00
11 Stan Musial/25 50.00 15.00
12 Andre Dawson/100 10.00 3.00
13 R.Henderson Yanks/100 20.00 6.00
14 Cal Ripken/100 50.00 15.00
15 Dale Murphy/100 15.00 4.50
16 Kirby Puckett/100 20.00 6.00
17 Don Mattingly/100 40.00 12.00
18 Brooks Robinson/100 15.00 4.50
19 Orlando Cepeda/100 10.00 3.00
20 Reggie Jackson Yanks/100 15.00 4.50
21 Roberto Clemente/25 100.00 30.00
22 Ernie Banks/100 20.00 6.00
23 Frank Robinson/100 10.00 3.00
24 Harmon Killebrew/100 20.00 6.00
25 Willie Stargell/100 15.00 4.50
26 Al Kaline/100 20.00 6.00
27 Carl Yastrzemski/100 30.00 9.00
28 Duke Snider/10
29 Dave Winfield/100 10.00 3.00
30 Eddie Murray/100 20.00 6.00
31 Eddie Mathews/50 30.00 9.00
32 Gary Carter/100 10.00 3.00
33 Rod Carew Twins/100 15.00 4.50
34 Jimmie Foxx/10
35 Mel Ott/25 40.00 12.00
36 Paul Molitor/100 15.00 4.50
37 Thurman Munson/50 25.00 7.50
38 Rogers Hornsby/25 80.00 24.00
39 Robin Yount/100 25.00 7.50
40 Wade Boggs/100 15.00 4.50
42 Rickey Henderson A's/50 30.00 9.00
43 Ty Cobb/10
44 Yogi Berra/25 40.00 12.00
45 Roy Campanella/25 40.00 12.00
46 Luis Aparicio/100 10.00 3.00
48 Roger Maris A's/25 60.00 18.00
49 Reggie Jackson Angels/100 15.00 4.50
50 Lou Gehrig/25 200.00 60.00
51 Rafael Palmeiro/100 15.00 4.50
52 Sammy Sosa/100 15.00 4.50
56 Rod Carew Angels/100 15.00 4.50
59 Babe Ruth/10
60 R.Henderson Angels/100 20.00 6.00

2004 Donruss Classics Legendary Pants Material

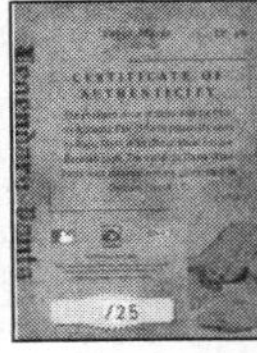

Nm-Mt Ex-Mt
RANDOM INSERTS IN PACKS
PRINT RUNS B/WN 3-50 COPIES PER
NO PRICING ON QTY OF 10 OR LESS
1 Tony Gwynn/25 40.00 12.00
12 Andre Dawson/25 20.00 6.00
24 Harmon Killebrew/50 30.00 9.00
26 Al Kaline/50 30.00 9.00
35 Mel Ott/10
43 Ty Cobb/5
45 Roy Campanella/25 40.00 12.00
46 Luis Aparicio/50 15.00 4.50
47 Phil Rizzuto/50 25.00 7.50
48 Roger Maris A's/25 60.00 18.00
50 Lou Gehrig/4
51 Rafael Palmeiro/25 30.00 9.00
56 Rod Carew Angels/50 25.00 7.50
57 Whitey Ford/25 30.00 9.00
58 Fergie Jenkins/25 20.00 6.00
59 Babe Ruth/3

2004 Donruss Classics Legendary Spikes Material

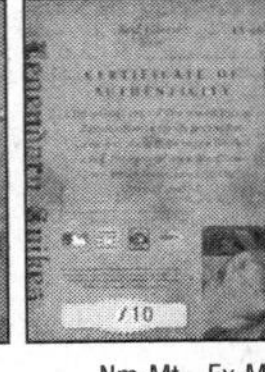

Nm-Mt Ex-Mt
RANDOM INSERTS IN PACKS
NO PRICING ON QTY OF 10 OR LESS
13 R.Henderson Yanks/25 50.00 15.00
17 Don Mattingly/50 80.00 24.00
29 Dave Winfield/50 20.00 6.00
42 Rickey Henderson A's/25 50.00 15.00
51 Rafael Palmeiro/25 40.00 12.00
52 Sammy Sosa/50 40.00 12.00
56 Rod Carew Angels/10
60 R.Henderson Angels/25 50.00 15.00

2004 Donruss Classics Membership

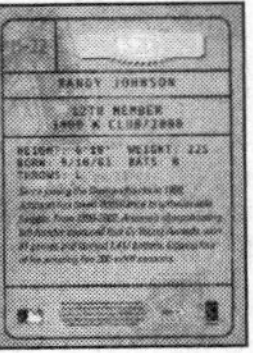

Nm-Mt Ex-Mt
RANDOM INSERTS IN PACKS
STATED PRINT RUN 2499 SERIAL #'d SETS
1 Stan Musial 5.00 1.50
2 Ted Williams 6.00 1.80
3 Early Wynn 2.00 .60
4 Roberto Clemente 8.00 2.40
5 Al Kaline 3.00 .90
6 Bob Gibson 3.00 .90
7 Lou Brock 3.00 .90
8 Carl Yastrzemski 5.00 1.50
9 Gaylord Perry 2.00 .60
10 Fergie Jenkins 2.00 .60

11 Steve Carlton 2.00 .60
12 Reggie Jackson 3.00 .90
13 Rod Carew 3.00 .90
14 Bert Blyleven 2.00 .60
15 Mike Schmidt 6.00 1.80
16 Nolan Ryan 8.00 2.40
17 Robin Yount 5.00 1.50
18 George Brett 8.00 2.40
19 Eddie Murray 3.00 .90
20 Tony Gwynn 4.00 1.20
21 Cal Ripken 10.00 3.00
22 Randy Johnson 3.00 .90
23 Sammy Sosa 5.00 1.50
24 Rafael Palmeiro 3.00 .90
25 Roger Clemens 6.00 1.80

2004 Donruss Classics Membership VIP Bat

Nm-Mt Ex-Mt
RANDOM INSERTS IN PACKS
PRINT RUNS B/WN 10-25 COPIES PER
NO PRICING ON QTY OF 10 OR LESS
1 Stan Musial/25 50.00 15.00
2 Ted Williams/25 120.00 36.00
4 Roberto Clemente/25 100.00 30.00
5 Al Kaline/25 40.00 12.00
7 Lou Brock/25 30.00 9.00
8 Carl Yastrzemski/25 50.00 15.00
11 Steve Carlton/25 20.00 6.00
12 Reggie Jackson/25 30.00 9.00
13 Rod Carew/25 30.00 9.00
15 Mike Schmidt/25 60.00 18.00
16 Nolan Ryan/10
17 Robin Yount/25 40.00 12.00
18 George Brett/10
19 Eddie Murray/25 40.00 12.00
20 Tony Gwynn/25 40.00 12.00
21 Cal Ripken/10
22 Randy Johnson/25 40.00 12.00
23 Sammy Sosa/25 40.00 12.00
24 Rafael Palmeiro/25 30.00 9.00
25 Roger Clemens/25 40.00 12.00

2004 Donruss Classics Membership VIP Combos Material

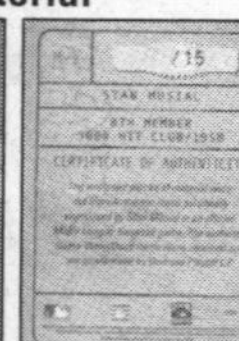

Nm-Mt Ex-Mt
PRINT RUNS B/WN 9-25 COPIES PER
NO PRICING ON QTY OF 10 OR LESS
PRIME PRINT RUN 1 SERIAL #'d SET
NO PRIME PRICING DUE TO SCARCITY
RANDOM INSERTS IN PACKS
1 Stan Musial Bat-Jsy/15 80.00 24.00
2 Ted Williams Bat-Jsy/9
4 Rob Clemente Bat-Jsy/25 200.00 60.00
5 Al Kaline Bat-Pants/25 50.00 15.00
7 Lou Brock Bat-Jsy/10
8 Carl Yastrzemski Bat-Jsy/25 60.00 18.00
10 F.Jenkins Fld Glv-Pants/25 25.00 7.50
11 Steve Carlton Bat-Jsy/25 25.00 7.50
12 Reggie Jackson Bat-Jsy/25 40.00 12.00
13 Rod Carew Bat-Pants/25 40.00 12.00
15 Mike Schmidt Bat-Jsy/25 60.00 18.00
16 Nolan Ryan Bat-Jsy/25 60.00 18.00
17 Robin Yount Bat-Jsy/25 60.00 18.00
18 George Brett Bat-Jsy/25 80.00 24.00
19 Eddie Murray Bat-Jsy/25 50.00 15.00
20 Tony Gwynn Bat-Jsy/25 60.00 18.00
21 Cal Ripken Bat-Jsy/25 150.00 45.00
22 Randy Johnson Bat-Jsy/25 50.00 15.00
23 Sammy Sosa Bat-Jsy/25 50.00 15.00
24 Rafael Palmeiro Bat-Jsy/25 40.00 12.00
25 Roger Clemens Bat-Jsy/25 50.00 15.00

2004 Donruss Classics Membership VIP Combos Signature

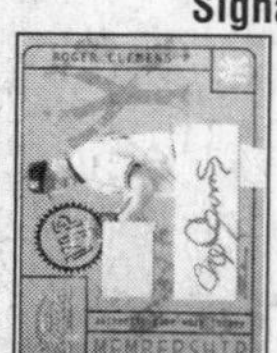

Nm-Mt Ex-Mt
PRINT RUNS B/WN 1-50 COPIES PER
NO PRICING ON QTY OF 5 OR LESS
PRIME PRINT RUN 1 SERIAL #'d SET
NO PRIME PRICING DUE TO SCARCITY
RANDOM INSERTS IN PACKS
1 Stan Musial Jsy/5
5 Al Kaline Pants/25 120.00 36.00
6 Bob Gibson Jsy/5
7 Lou Brock Jsy/5
8 Carl Yastrzemski Jsy/5

9 Gaylord Perry Jsy/50 25.00 7.50
10 Fergie Jenkins Pants/50 40.00 12.00
11 Steve Carlton Jsy/25 80.00 24.00
12 Reggie Jackson Jsy/5
13 Rod Carew Pants/5
14 Bert Blyleven Jsy/50 25.00 7.50
16 Nolan Ryan Jsy/5
17 Robin Yount Jsy/5
18 George Brett Jsy/5
19 Eddie Murray Jsy/5
20 Tony Gwynn Jsy/5
21 Cal Ripken Jsy/5
22 Randy Johnson Jsy/5
23 Sammy Sosa Jsy/5
24 Rafael Palmeiro Jsy/5
25 Roger Clemens Jsy/1

2004 Donruss Classics Membership VIP Jersey

Nm-Mt Ex-Mt
PRINT RUNS B/WN 9-25 COPIES PER
NO PRICING ON QTY OF 10 OR LESS
PRIME PRINT RUN 1 SERIAL #'d SET
NO PRIME PRICING DUE TO SCARCITY
RANDOM INSERTS IN PACKS
1 Stan Musial/15 60.00 18.00
2 Ted Williams/9
3 Early Wynn/10
4 Roberto Clemente/25 120.00 36.00
5 Al Kaline Pants/25 40.00 12.00
6 Bob Gibson/10
7 Lou Brock/10
8 Carl Yastrzemski/25 50.00 15.00
9 Gaylord Perry/25 20.00 6.00
10 Fergie Jenkins Pants/25 20.00 6.00
11 Steve Carlton/25 20.00 6.00
12 Reggie Jackson/25 30.00 9.00
13 Rod Carew/25 30.00 9.00
14 Bert Blyleven/25 20.00 6.00
15 Mike Schmidt/25 60.00 18.00
16 Nolan Ryan/25 60.00 18.00
17 Robin Yount/25 40.00 12.00
18 George Brett/25 60.00 18.00
19 Eddie Murray/25 40.00 12.00
20 Tony Gwynn/25 40.00 12.00
21 Cal Ripken/25 120.00 36.00
22 Randy Johnson/25 40.00 12.00
23 Sammy Sosa/25 40.00 12.00
24 Rafael Palmeiro/25 30.00 9.00
25 Roger Clemens/25 40.00 12.00

2004 Donruss Classics Membership VIP Signatures

Nm-Mt Ex-Mt
RANDOM INSERTS IN PACKS
PRINT RUNS B/WN 1-50 COPIES PER
NO PRICING ON QTY OF 5 OR LESS
1 Stan Musial/5
5 Al Kaline/20 80.00 24.00
6 Bob Gibson/5
7 Lou Brock/5
8 Carl Yastrzemski/5
9 Gaylord Perry/50 15.00 4.50
10 Fergie Jenkins/50 25.00 7.50
11 Steve Carlton/20 50.00 15.00
12 Reggie Jackson/5
13 Rod Carew/5
14 Bert Blyleven/50 15.00 4.50
16 Nolan Ryan/5
17 Robin Yount/5
18 George Brett/5
19 Eddie Murray/5
20 Tony Gwynn/5
21 Cal Ripken/5
22 Randy Johnson/5
23 Sammy Sosa/5
24 Rafael Palmeiro/5
25 Roger Clemens/1

2004 Donruss Classics October Heroes

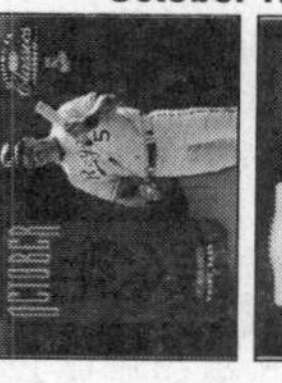

Nm-Mt Ex-Mt
RANDOM INSERTS IN PACKS
STATED PRINT RUN 2499 SERIAL #'d SETS
1 Reggie Jackson 3.00 .90
2 Bob Gibson 3.00 .90
3 Carlton Fisk 3.00 .90
4 Whitey Ford 3.00 .90
5 George Brett 8.00 2.40

6 Roberto Clemente 8.00 2.40
7 Roy Campanella 3.00 .90
8 Babe Ruth 8.00 2.40

2004 Donruss Classics October Heroes Bat

Nm-Mt Ex-Mt
RANDOM INSERTS IN PACKS
PRINT RUNS B/WN 10-25 COPIES PER
NO PRICING OON QTY OF 10 OR LESS
1 Reggie Jackson/25 30.00 9.00
3 Carlton Fisk/25 30.00 9.00
5 George Brett/10
6 Roberto Clemente/25 100.00 30.00
7 Roy Campanella/25 40.00 12.00
8 Babe Ruth/10

2004 Donruss Classics October Heroes Combos Material

Nm-Mt Ex-Mt
PRINT RUNS B/WN 3-25 COPIES PER
NO PRICING ON QTY OF 5 OR LESS
PRIME PRINT RUN 1 SERIAL #'d SET
NO PRIME PRICING DUE TO SCARCITY
RANDOM INSERTS IN PACKS
1 Reggie Jackson Bat-Hat/25 40.00 12.00
3 Carlton Fisk Bat-Jsy/25 40.00 12.00
5 George Brett Bat-Jsy/25 80.00 24.00
6 Roberto Clemente Bat-Jsy/5
7 R.Campanella Bat-Pants/25 50.00 15.00
8 Babe Ruth Bat-Pants/3

2004 Donruss Classics October Heroes Combos Signature

Nm-Mt Ex-Mt
PRINT RUNS B/WN 5-50 COPIES PER
NO PRICING ON QTY OF 5 OR LESS
PRIME PRINT RUN 1 SERIAL #'d SET
NO PRIME PRICING DUE TO SCARCITY
RANDOM INSERTS IN PACKS
1 Reggie Jackson Bat/5
2 Bob Gibson Jsy/5
3 Carlton Fisk Jsy/5
4 Whitey Ford Jsy/50 60.00 18.00
5 George Brett Jsy/5

2004 Donruss Classics October Heroes Fabric

Nm-Mt Ex-Mt
PRINT RUNS B/WN 5-25 COPIES PER
NO PRICING ON QTY OF 5 OR LESS
PRIME PRINT RUN 1 SERIAL #'d SET
NO PRIME PRICING DUE TO SCARCITY
RANDOM INSERTS IN PACKS
2 Bob Gibson Jsy/15 40.00 12.00
3 Carlton Fisk Jsy/25 30.00 9.00
4 Whitey Ford Jsy/25 30.00 9.00
5 George Brett Jsy/25 60.00 18.00
6 Roberto Clemente Jsy/5
7 Roy Campanella Pants/25 40.00 12.00
8 Babe Ruth Pants/5

2004 Donruss Classics October Heroes Signature

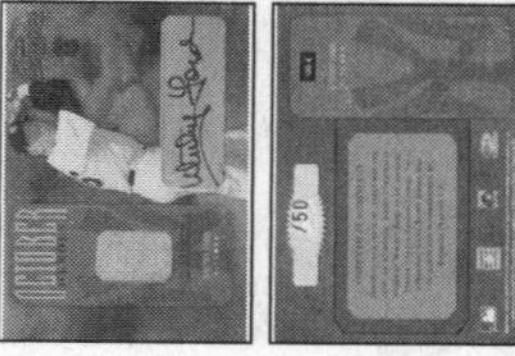

Nm-Mt Ex-Mt
RANDOM INSERTS IN PACKS
PRINT RUNS B/WN 5-50 COPIES PER
NO PRICING ON QTY OF 5 OR LESS
1 Reggie Jackson/5
2 Bob Gibson/5
3 Carlton Fisk/5
4 Whitey Ford/50 40.00 12.00
5 George Brett/5

2004 Donruss Classics Team Colors Bat

Nm-Mt Ex-Mt
RANDOM INSERTS IN PACKS
PRINT RUNS B/WN 10-50 COPIES PER
NO PRICING ON QTY OF 10 OR LESS
2 Steve Garvey/50 15.00 4.50
3 Eric Davis/25 30.00 9.00
4 Al Oliver/50 10.00 3.00
5 Nolan Ryan/10
6 Bobby Doerr/25 20.00 6.00
7 Paul Molitor/50 25.00 7.50
8 Dale Murphy/50 25.00 7.50
11 Jose Canseco/50 30.00 9.00
12 Jim Rice/50 15.00 4.50
13 Will Clark/50 50.00 15.00
14 Alan Trammell/50 15.00 4.50
16 Dwight Evans/50 25.00 7.50
18 Dave Parker Pirates/25 20.00 6.00
21 Andre Dawson Expos/50 15.00 4.50
22 Darryl Strawberry Dgr/50 15.00 4.50
23 George Foster/50 10.00 3.00
26 Bo Jackson/50 30.00 9.00
27 Cal Ripken/50 80.00 24.00
28 Deion Sanders/25 30.00 9.00
29 Don Mattingly/50 50.00 15.00
30 Mark Grace/50 25.00 7.50
31 Fred Lynn/50 10.00 3.00
33 Ernie Banks/25 40.00 12.00
34 Gary Carter/50 15.00 4.50
35 Roger Maris/25 60.00 18.00
36 Ron Santo/50 25.00 7.50
38 Tony Gwynn/50 25.00 7.50

40 Red Schoendienst/25 20.00 6.00
41 Steve Carlton/25 20.00 6.00
42 Wade Boggs/25 30.00 9.00
44 Luis Aparicio/25 20.00 6.00
46 Andre Dawson Cubs/25 20.00 6.00
48 Darryl Strawberry Mets/50 15.00 4.50
49 Dave Parker Reds/50 15.00 4.50

2004 Donruss Classics Team Colors Combos Material

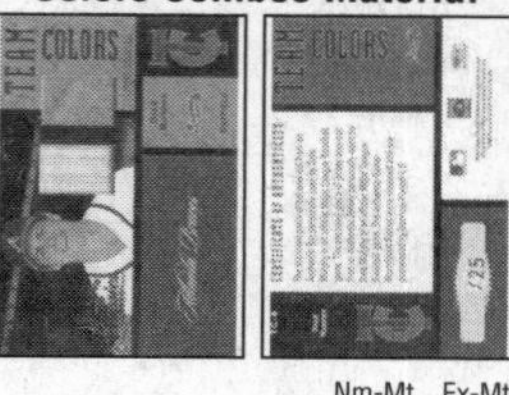

Nm-Mt Ex-Mt
STATED PRINT RUN 25 SERIAL #'d SETS
MARIS PRINT RUN 10 SERIAL #'d CARDS
NO MARIS PRICING DUE TO SCARCITY
PRIME PRINT RUN 1 SERIAL #'d SET
NO PRIME PRICING DUE TO SCARCITY
RANDOM INSERTS IN PACKS
2 Steve Garvey Bat-Jsy 25.00 7.50
3 Eric Davis Bat-Jsy 40.00 12.00
5 Nolan Ryan Bat-Jsy 60.00 18.00
6 Bobby Doerr Bat-Jsy 25.00 7.50
7 Paul Molitor Bat-Jsy 40.00 12.00
8 Dale Murphy Bat-Jsy 40.00 12.00
11 Jose Canseco Bat-Jsy 50.00 15.00
12 Jim Rice Bat-Jsy 25.00 7.50
13 Will Clark Bat-Jsy 80.00 24.00
14 Alan Trammell Bat-Jsy 25.00 7.50
16 Dwight Evans Bat-Jsy 40.00 12.00
18 Dave Parker Pirates Bat-Jsy 25.00 7.50
21 Andre Dawson Expos Bat-Jsy 25.00 7.50
22 Darryl Strawberry Dgr Bat-Jsy 25.00 7.50
23 George Foster Bat-Jsy 20.00 6.00
26 Bo Jackson Bat-Jsy 50.00 15.00
27 Cal Ripken Bat-Jsy 150.00 45.00
28 Deion Sanders Bat-Jsy 40.00 12.00
29 Don Mattingly Bat-Jsy 80.00 24.00
30 Mark Grace Bat-Jsy 40.00 12.00
33 Ernie Banks Bat-Jsy 50.00 15.00
34 Gary Carter Bat-Jacket 25.00 7.50
35 Roger Maris Bat-Jsy/10
38 Tony Gwynn Bat-Jsy 60.00 18.00
40 Red Schoendienst Bat-Jsy 25.00 7.50
41 Steve Carlton Bat-Jsy 25.00 7.50
42 Wade Boggs Bat-Jsy 40.00 12.00
44 Luis Aparicio Bat-Jsy 25.00 7.50
46 Andre Dawson Cubs Bat-Jsy 25.00 7.50
48 D.Strawberry Mets Bat-Jsy 25.00 7.50
49 Dave Parker Reds Bat-Jsy 25.00 7.50

2004 Donruss Classics Team Colors Combos Signature

Nm-Mt Ex-Mt
PRINT RUNS B/WN 2-100 COPIES PER
NO PRICING ON QTY OF 10 OR LESS
PRIME PRINT RUN 1 SERIAL #'d SET
NO PRIME PRICING DUE TO SCARCITY
RANDOM INSERTS IN PACKS
1 L.Dykstra Mets Fld Glv/100 25.00 7.50
2 Steve Garvey Jsy/100 25.00 7.50
3 Eric Davis Jsy/100 40.00 12.00
4 Al Oliver Bat/100 25.00 7.50
5 Nolan Ryan Jsy/5
6 Bobby Doerr Jsy/100 25.00 7.50
7 Paul Molitor Jsy/10
8 Dale Murphy Jsy/10
9 Harold Baines Jsy/100 40.00 12.00
10 Dwight Gooden Jsy/100 25.00 7.50
11 Jose Canseco Jsy/10
12 Jim Rice Jsy/100 25.00 7.50
13 Will Clark Jsy/10
14 Alan Trammell Jsy/100 25.00 7.50
15 Lee Smith Jsy/100 25.00 7.50
16 Dwight Evans Jsy/100 40.00 12.00
17 Tony Oliva Jsy/100 25.00 7.50
18 Dave Parker Pirates Jsy/100 25.00 7.50
19 Jack Morris Jsy/100 25.00 7.50
20 Luis Tiant Jsy/100 25.00 7.50
21 Andre Dawson Expos Jsy/50 40.00 12.00
22 D.Strawberry Dgr Jsy/100 25.00 7.50
23 George Foster Jsy/100 25.00 7.50
24 Marty Marion Jsy/100 25.00 7.50
25 Dennis Eckersley Jsy/100 40.00 12.00
26 Bo Jackson Jsy/10
27 Cal Ripken Jsy/5
28 Deion Sanders Jsy/5
29 Don Mattingly Jacket/10
30 Mark Grace Jsy/10
31 Fred Lynn Jsy/100 25.00 7.50
32 Enos Slaughter Jsy/2
33 Ernie Banks Jsy/25 120.00 36.00
34 Gary Carter Jacket/50 40.00 12.00
36 Ron Santo Bat/25 50.00 15.00
37 Keith Hernandez Jsy/25 50.00 15.00
38 Tony Gwynn Jsy/5
39 Jim Palmer Jsy/50 40.00 12.00
40 Red Schoendienst Jsy/100 25.00 7.50
41 Steve Carlton Jsy/50 60.00 18.00
42 Wade Boggs Jsy/5
43 Tommy John Jsy/100 25.00 7.50
44 Luis Aparicio Jsy/100 25.00 7.50
45 Bob Feller Jsy/100 25.00 7.50
46 Andre Dawson Cubs Jsy/50 40.00 12.00

47 Bert Blyleven Jsy/100 25.00 7.5
48 D.Strawberry Mets Jsy/100 25.00 7.5
49 Dave Parker Reds Jsy/100 25.00 7.5
50 L.Dykstra Phils Btg Glv/30 50.00 15.0

2004 Donruss Classics Team Colors Jersey

Nm-Mt Ex-Mt
PRINT RUNS B/WN 10-100 COPIES PER
NO PRICING ON QTY OF 10 OR LESS
PRIME PRINT RUN 1 SERIAL #'d SET
NO PRIME PRICING DUE TO SCARCITY
RANDOM INSERTS IN PACKS
1 L.Dykstra Mets Fld Glv/25 20.00 6.0
2 Steve Garvey/100 10.00 3.0
3 Eric Davis/25 30.00 9.0
5 Nolan Ryan/50 50.00 15.0
6 Bobby Doerr/25 20.00 6.0
7 Paul Molitor/100 15.00 4.5
8 Dale Murphy/50 25.00 7.5
9 Harold Baines/100 15.00 4.5
10 Dwight Gooden/50 15.00 4.5
11 Jose Canseco/100 20.00 6.0
12 Jim Rice/100 10.00 3.0
13 Will Clark/50 50.00 15.0
14 Alan Trammell/100 10.00 3.0
15 Lee Smith/100 10.00 3.0
16 Dwight Evans/50 25.00 7.5
17 Tony Oliva/100 10.00 3.0
18 Dave Parker Pirates/25 20.00 6.0
19 Jack Morris/100 10.00 3.0
20 Luis Tiant/100 10.00 3.0
21 Andre Dawson Expos/100 10.00 3.0
22 Darryl Strawberry Dgr/100 10.00 3.0
23 George Foster/100 10.00 3.0
24 Marty Marion/50 15.00 4.5
25 Dennis Eckersley/100 10.00 3.0
26 Bo Jackson/50 30.00 9.0
27 Cal Ripken/100 50.00 15.0
28 Deion Sanders/50 25.00 7.5
29 Don Mattingly Jacket/100 40.00 12.0
30 Mark Grace/50 25.00 7.5
31 Fred Lynn/50 15.00 4.5
32 Enos Slaughter/10
33 Ernie Banks/25 40.00 12.00
34 Gary Carter Jacket/10 10.00 3.00
35 Roger Maris/10
37 Keith Hernandez/25 20.00 6.00
38 Tony Gwynn/50 25.00 7.50
39 Jim Palmer/25 20.00 6.00
40 Red Schoendienst/25 20.00 6.00
41 Steve Carlton/25 20.00 6.00
42 Wade Boggs/25 30.00 9.00
43 Tommy John/100 10.00 3.00
44 Luis Aparicio/25 20.00 6.00
45 Bob Feller/10
46 Andre Dawson Cubs/25 20.00 6.00
47 Bert Blyleven/100 10.00 3.00
48 Darryl Strawberry Mets/100 10.00 3.00
49 Dave Parker Reds/100 10.00 3.00

2004 Donruss Classics Team Colors Signatures

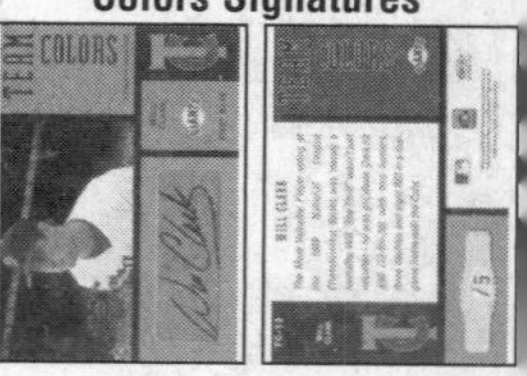

Nm-Mt Ex-Mt
RANDOM INSERTS IN PACKS
PRINT RUNS B/WN 1-50 COPIES PER
NO PRICING ON QTY OF 10 OR LESS
1 Len Dykstra Mets/50 25.00 7.50
2 Steve Garvey/50 25.00 7.50
3 Eric Davis/50 40.00 12.00
4 Al Oliver/50 15.00 4.50
5 Nolan Ryan/5
6 Bobby Doerr/50 25.00 7.50
7 Paul Molitor/5
8 Dale Murphy/5
9 Harold Baines/50 40.00 12.00
10 Dwight Gooden/50 25.00 7.50
11 Jose Canseco/5
12 Jim Rice/50 25.00 7.50
13 Will Clark/5
14 Alan Trammell/50 25.00 7.50
15 Lee Smith/50 25.00 7.50
16 Dwight Evans/50 40.00 12.00
17 Tony Oliva/50 25.00 7.50
18 Dave Parker Pirates/50 25.00 7.50
19 Jack Morris/50 15.00 4.50
20 Luis Tiant/50 15.00 4.50
21 Andre Dawson Expos/25 30.00 9.00
22 Darryl Strawberry Dgr/50 25.00 7.50
23 George Foster/50 15.00 4.50
24 Marty Marion/50 25.00 7.50
25 Dennis Eckersley/50 40.00 12.00
26 Bo Jackson/5
27 Cal Ripken/5
28 Deion Sanders/5
29 Don Mattingly/5
30 Mark Grace/5
31 Fred Lynn/50 15.00 4.50
32 Enos Slaughter/1
33 Ernie Banks/10
34 Gary Carter/25 30.00 9.00
36 Ron Santo/10
37 Keith Hernandez/25 30.00 9.00
38 Tony Gwynn/5
39 Jim Palmer/20 30.00 9.00
40 Red Schoendienst/50 25.00 7.50
41 Steve Carlton/20 50.00 15.00
42 Wade Boggs/5
43 Tommy John/50 15.00 4.50
44 Luis Aparicio/50 25.00 7.50
45 Bob Feller/50 25.00 7.50
46 Andre Dawson Cubs/25 30.00 9.00

' Bert Blyleven/50 15.00 4.50
3 Darryl Strawberry Mets/50 25.00 7.50
Dave Parker Reds/50 25.00 7.50
) Len Dykstra Phils/50 25.00 7.50

2004 Donruss Classics Timeless Triples

Nm-Mt Ex-Mt
ANDOM INSERTS IN PACKS
TATED PRINT RUN 500 SERIAL #'d SETS
Ted Williams 12.00 3.60
Carl Yastrzemski
Carlton Fisk
Lou Gehrig 10.00 3.00
Roger Maris
Thurman Munson
Brooks Robinson 15.00 4.50
Frank Robinson
Cal Ripken
Roger Clemens 8.00 2.40
Andy Pettitte
Roy Oswalt
Greg Maddux 8.00 2.40
Mark Prior
Kerry Wood
Alex Rodriguez 15.00 4.50
Derek Jeter
Gary Sheffield

2004 Donruss Classics Timeless Triples Bat

Nm-Mt Ex-Mt
ANDOM INSERTS IN PACKS
Ted Williams 250.00 75.00
Carl Yastrzemski
Carlton Fisk
Lou Gehrig 300.00 90.00
Roger Maris
Thurman Munson
Brooks Robinson 175.00 52.50
Frank Robinson
Cal Ripken

2004 Donruss Classics Timeless Triples Jersey

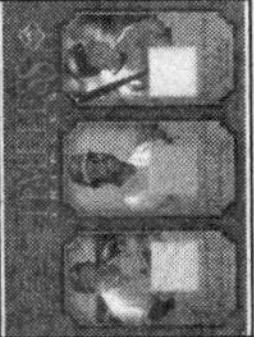

Nm-Mt Ex-Mt
PRINT RUNS B/WN 10-25 COPIES PER
NO PRICING ON QTY OF 10 OR LESS
ALL ARE JSY SWATCHES UNLESS NOTED
GEHRIG IS PANTS SWATCH
PRIME PRINT RUN 1 SERIAL #'d SET
NO PRIME PRICING DUE TO SCARCITY
RANDOM INSERTS IN PACKS
Ted Williams
Carl Yastrzemski
Carlton Fisk/10
2 Lou Gehrig Pants
Roger Maris
Thurman Munson/10
3 Brooks Robinson 200.00 60.00
Frank Robinson
Cal Ripken/25

1998 Donruss Prized Collections Donruss

These cards parallel the 1998 Donruss set. According to published reports, less than 560 sets were produced.

Nm-Mt Ex-Mt
*STARS: 1.25X TO 3X BASIC DONRUSS COLL.

1998 Donruss Prized Collections Elite

These cards parallel the already paralleled Donruss Elite set. According to published reports, less than 220 sets were produced.

Nm-Mt Ex-Mt
*STARS: 1.5X TO 4X BASIC ELITE COLL.

1998 Donruss Prized Collections Leaf

These cards parallel the already parallelled Leaf set. According to published reports, less than 400 sets were produced.

Nm-Mt Ex-Mt
*STARS: 1.25X TO 3X BASIC LEAF COLL.

1998 Donruss Prized Collections Preferred

These cards parallel the already parallelled Donruss Preferred set. According to published reports, less than 55 sets were produced.

Nm-Mt Ex-Mt
*STARS: 1.25X TO 3X BASIC PREF.COLL.

1997 Donruss Elite

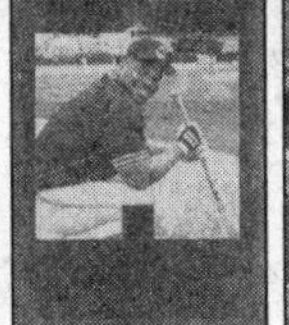

The 1997 Donruss Elite set was issued in one series totalling 150 cards. The product was distributed exclusively to hobby dealers around February, 1997. Each foil-wrapped pack contained eight cards and carried a suggested retail price of $3.49. Player selection was limited to the top stars (plus three player checklist cards) and card design is very similar to the Donruss Elite hockey set that was released one year earlier. Strangely enough, the backs only provide career statistics neglecting statistics from the previous season.

Nm-Mt Ex-Mt
COMPLETE SET (150) 25.00 7.50
1 Juan Gonzalez .60 .18
2 Alex Rodriguez 1.50 .45
3 Frank Thomas 1.00 .30
4 Greg Maddux 1.50 .45
5 Ken Griffey Jr. 1.50 .45
6 Cal Ripken 3.00 .90
7 Mike Piazza 1.50 .45
8 Chipper Jones 1.00 .30
9 Albert Belle .40 .12
10 Andruw Jones .40 .12
11 Vladimir Guerrero 1.00 .30
12 Mo Vaughn .40 .12
UER front Gonzales
13 Ivan Rodriguez 1.00 .30
14 Andy Pettitte .60 .18
15 Tony Gwynn 1.25 .35
16 Barry Bonds 2.50 .75
17 Jeff Bagwell .60 .18
18 Manny Ramirez .60 .18
19 Kenny Lofton .40 .12
20 Roberto Alomar .60 .18
21 Mark McGwire 2.50 .75
22 Ryan Klesko .40 .12
23 Tim Salmon .60 .18
24 Derek Jeter 2.50 .75
25 Eddie Murray 1.00 .30
26 Jermaine Dye .40 .12
27 Ruben Rivera .40 .12
28 Jim Edmonds .40 .12
29 Mike Mussina .60 .18
30 Randy Johnson 1.00 .30
31 Sammy Sosa 1.50 .45
32 Hideo Nomo 1.00 .30
33 Chuck Knoblauch .40 .12
34 Paul Molitor .60 .18
35 Rafael Palmeiro .60 .18
36 Brady Anderson .40 .12
37 Will Clark 1.00 .30
38 Craig Biggio .60 .18
39 Jason Giambi .40 .12
40 Roger Clemens 2.00 .60
41 Jay Buhner .40 .12
42 Edgar Martinez .60 .18
43 Gary Sheffield .40 .12
44 Fred McGriff .60 .18
45 Bobby Bonilla .40 .12
46 Tom Glavine .60 .18
47 Wade Boggs .60 .18
48 Jeff Conine .40 .12
49 John Smoltz .60 .18
50 Jim Thome 1.00 .30
51 Billy Wagner .40 .12
52 Jose Canseco 1.00 .30
53 Javy Lopez .40 .12
54 Cecil Fielder .40 .12
55 Garret Anderson .40 .12
56 Alex Ochoa .40 .12
57 Scott Rolen 1.00 .30
58 Darin Erstad .40 .12
59 Rey Ordonez .40 .12
60 Dante Bichette .40 .12
61 Joe Carter .40 .12
62 Moises Alou .40 .12
63 Jason Isringhausen .40 .12
64 Karim Garcia .40 .12
65 Brian Jordan .40 .12
66 Ruben Sierra .40 .12
67 Todd Hollandsworth .40 .12
68 Paul Wilson .40 .12
69 Ernie Young .40 .12
70 Ryne Sandberg 1.50 .45
71 Raul Mondesi .40 .12
72 George Arias .40 .12
73 Ray Durham .40 .12
74 Dean Palmer .40 .12
75 Shawn Green .40 .12
76 Eric Young .40 .12
77 Jason Kendall .40 .12
78 Greg Vaughn .40 .12
79 Terrell Wade .40 .12
80 Bill Pulsipher .40 .12
81 Bobby Higginson .40 .12
82 Mark Grudzielanek .40 .12
83 Ken Caminiti .40 .12
84 Todd Greene .40 .12
85 Carlos Delgado .40 .12
86 Mark Grace .60 .18
87 Rondell White .40 .12
88 Barry Larkin .60 .18
89 J.T. Snow .40 .12
90 Alex Gonzalez .40 .12
91 Raul Casanova .40 .12
92 Marc Newfield .40 .12
93 Jermaine Allensworth .40 .12
94 John Mabry .40 .12
95 Kirby Puckett 1.00 .30
96 Travis Fryman .40 .12
97 Kevin Brown .40 .12
98 Andres Galarraga .40 .12
99 Marty Cordova .40 .12
100 Henry Rodriguez .40 .12
101 Sterling Hitchcock .40 .12
102 Trey Beamon .40 .12
103 Brett Butler .40 .12
104 Rickey Henderson 1.00 .30
105 Tino Martinez .60 .18
106 Kevin Appier .40 .12
107 Brian Hunter .40 .12
108 Eric Karros .40 .12
109 Andre Dawson .40 .12
110 Darryl Strawberry .40 .12
111 James Baldwin .40 .12
112 Chad Mottola .40 .12
113 Dave Nilsson .40 .12
114 Carlos Baerga .40 .12
115 Chan Ho Park .40 .12
116 John Jaha .40 .12
117 Alan Benes .40 .12
118 Mariano Rivera .60 .18
119 Ellis Burks .40 .12
120 Tony Clark .40 .12
121 Todd Walker .40 .12
122 Dwight Gooden .40 .12
123 Ugueth Urbina .40 .12
124 David Cone .40 .12
125 Ozzie Smith 1.50 .45
126 Kimera Bartee .40 .12
127 Rusty Greer .40 .12
128 Pat Hentgen .40 .12
129 Charles Johnson .40 .12
130 Quinton McCracken .40 .12
131 Troy Percival .40 .12
132 Shane Reynolds .40 .12
133 Charles Nagy .40 .12
134 Tom Goodwin .40 .12
135 Ron Gant .40 .12
136 Dan Wilson .40 .12
137 Matt Williams .40 .12
138 LaTroy Hawkins .40 .12
139 Kevin Seitzer .40 .12
140 Michael Tucker .40 .12
141 Todd Hundley .40 .12
142 Alex Fernandez .40 .12
143 Marquis Grissom .40 .12
144 Steve Finley .40 .12
145 Curtis Pride .40 .12
146 Derek Bell .40 .12
147 Butch Huskey .40 .12
148 Dwight Gooden CL .40 .12
149 Al Leiter CL .40 .12
150 Hideo Nomo CL .40 .12

1997 Donruss Elite Gold Stars

Randomly seeded into one in every nine packs, cards from this set parallel the 150-card base issue. The distinctive gold foil fronts easily differentiate them from their silver-foiled base-issue brethren. The following cards were erroneously printed with a silver (rather than gold) logo on front: 6, 15, 25, 32, 42, 47, 57, 60, 69 and 70. Corrected gold logo versions of these cards do exist but are in far shorter supply though secondary market trading values remain similar to general indifference at this time. The set is considered complete with the erroneous silver logo cards.

Nm-Mt Ex-Mt
*STARS: 4X TO 10X BASIC CARDS

1997 Donruss Elite Leather and Lumber

This ten-card insert set features color action veteran player photos printed on two unique materials. The fronts display a player image on real wood card stock with the end of a baseball bat as background. The backs carry another player photo printed on genuine leather card stock with a baseball and glove as background. Only 500 of each card was produced and are sequentially numbered.

Nm-Mt Ex-Mt
COMPLETE SET (10) 300.00 90.00
1 Ken Griffey Jr. 40.00 12.00
2 Alex Rodriguez 40.00 12.00
3 Frank Thomas 25.00 7.50
4 Chipper Jones 25.00 7.50
5 Ivan Rodriguez 25.00 7.50
6 Cal Ripken 80.00 24.00
7 Barry Bonds 60.00 18.00
8 Chuck Knoblauch 10.00 3.00
9 Manny Ramirez 15.00 4.50
10 Mark McGwire 60.00 18.00

1997 Donruss Elite Passing the Torch

This 12-card insert set features eight players on four double-sided cards. A color portrait of a superstar veteran is displayed on one side with a gold foil background, and a portrait of a rising young star is printed on the flipside. Each of the eight players also has his own card to round out the 12-card set. Only 1500 of this set were produced and are sequentially numbered. However, only 1,350 of each card are available without autographs.

Nm-Mt Ex-Mt
COMPLETE SET (12) 250.00 75.00
1 Cal Ripken 40.00 12.00
2 Alex Rodriguez 20.00 6.00
3 Cal Ripken 50.00 15.00
Alex Rodriguez
4 Kirby Puckett 12.00 3.60
5 Andruw Jones 5.00 1.50
6 Kirby Puckett 10.00 3.00
Andruw Jones
7 Cecil Fielder 5.00 1.50
8 Frank Thomas 12.00 3.60
9 Cecil Fielder 10.00 3.00
Frank Thomas
10 Ozzie Smith 20.00 6.00
11 Derek Jeter 30.00 9.00
12 Ozzie Smith 30.00 9.00
Derek Jeter

1997 Donruss Elite Passing the Torch Autographs

This 12-card set consists of the first 150 sets of the regular "Passing the Torch" set with each card displaying an authentic player autograph. The set features a double front design which captures eight of the league's top superstars, alternating one of four different megastars on the flipside. An individual card for each of the eight players rounds out the set. Each set is sequentially numbered to 150.

Nm-Mt Ex-Mt
1 Cal Ripken 200.00 60.00
2 Alex Rodriguez 200.00 60.00
3 Cal Ripken 600.00 180.00
Alex Rodriguez
4 Kirby Puckett 80.00 24.00
5 Andruw Jones 50.00 15.00
6 Kirby Puckett 100.00 30.00
Andruw Jones
7 Cecil Fielder 30.00 9.00
8 Frank Thomas 80.00 24.00
9 Cecil Fielder 80.00 24.00
Frank Thomas
10 Ozzie Smith 150.00 45.00
11 Derek Jeter 200.00 60.00
12 Ozzie Smith 300.00 90.00
Derek Jeter

1997 Donruss Elite Turn of the Century

This 20-card set showcases the stars of the next millennium and features a color player image on a silver-and-black background. The backs display another player photo with a short paragraph about the player. Only 3,500 of this set were produced and are sequentially numbered.

Nm-Mt Ex-Mt
COMPLETE SET (20) 120.00 36.00
*DIE CUTS: 1.25X TO 3X BASIC TURN CENT.
DC STATED PRINT RUN 500 SERIAL #'d SETS
RANDOM INSERTS IN PACKS
1 Alex Rodriguez 15.00 4.50
2 Andruw Jones 4.00 1.20
3 Chipper Jones 10.00 3.00
4 Todd Walker 4.00 1.20
5 Scott Rolen 10.00 3.00
6 Trey Beamon 4.00 1.20
7 Derek Jeter 25.00 7.50
8 Darin Erstad 4.00 1.20
9 Tony Clark 4.00 1.20
10 Todd Greene 4.00 1.20
11 Jason Giambi 4.00 1.20
12 Justin Thompson 4.00 1.20
13 Ernie Young 4.00 1.20
14 Jason Kendall 4.00 1.20
15 Alex Ochoa 4.00 1.20
16 Brooks Kieschnick 4.00 1.20
17 Bobby Higginson 4.00 1.20
18 Ruben Rivera 4.00 1.20
19 Chan Ho Park 4.00 1.20
20 Chad Mottola 4.00 1.20
P5 Scott Rolen Promo 2.00 .60
P7 Derek Jeter Promo 3.00 .90

1998 Donruss Elite

The 1998 Donruss Elite set was issued in one series totalling 150 cards and distributed in five-card packs with a suggested retail price of $3.99. The fronts feature color player action photos. The backs carry player information. The set contains the topical subset: Generations (118-147). A special embossed Frank Thomas autograph card (parallel to basic issue card number two, except, of course, for Thomas' signature) was available to lucky collectors who pulled a Back to the Future Frank Thomas/David Ortiz card serial numbered between 1 and 100 and redeemed it to Donruss/Leaf.

Nm-Mt Ex-Mt
COMPLETE SET (150) 25.00 7.50
1 Ken Griffey Jr. 1.25 .35
2 Frank Thomas .75 .23
3 Alex Rodriguez 1.25 .35
4 Mike Piazza 1.25 .35
5 Greg Maddux 1.25 .35
6 Cal Ripken 2.50 .75
7 Chipper Jones .75 .23
8 Derek Jeter 2.00 .60
9 Tony Gwynn 1.00 .30
10 Andruw Jones .30 .09
11 Juan Gonzalez .50 .15
12 Jeff Bagwell .50 .15
13 Mark McGwire 2.00 .60
14 Roger Clemens 1.50 .45
15 Albert Belle .30 .09
16 Barry Bonds 2.00 .60
17 Kenny Lofton .30 .09
18 Ivan Rodriguez .75 .23
19 Manny Ramirez .50 .15
20 Jim Thome .75 .23
21 Chuck Knoblauch .30 .09
22 Paul Molitor .50 .15
23 Barry Larkin .50 .15
24 Andy Pettitte .50 .15
25 John Smoltz .50 .15
26 Randy Johnson .75 .23
27 Bernie Williams .50 .15
28 Larry Walker .50 .15
29 Mo Vaughn .30 .09
30 Bobby Higginson .30 .09
31 Edgardo Alfonzo .30 .09
32 Justin Thompson .30 .09
33 Jeff Suppan .30 .09
34 Roberto Alomar .50 .15
35 Hideo Nomo .75 .23
36 Rusty Greer .30 .09
37 Tim Salmon .50 .15
38 Jim Edmonds .30 .09
39 Gary Sheffield .30 .09
40 Ken Caminiti .30 .09
41 Sammy Sosa 1.25 .35
42 Tony Womack .30 .09
43 Matt Williams .30 .09
44 Andres Galarraga .30 .09
45 Garret Anderson .30 .09
46 Rafael Palmeiro .50 .15
47 Mike Mussina .50 .15
48 Craig Biggio .50 .15
49 Wade Boggs .50 .15
50 Tom Glavine .50 .15
51 Jason Giambi .30 .09
52 Will Clark .75 .23
53 David Justice .30 .09
54 Sandy Alomar Jr. .30 .09
55 Edgar Martinez .50 .15
56 Brady Anderson .30 .09
57 Eric Young .30 .09
58 Ray Lankford .30 .09
59 Kevin Brown .50 .15
60 Raul Mondesi .30 .09
61 Bobby Bonilla .30 .09
62 Javier Lopez .30 .09
63 Fred McGriff .50 .15
64 Rondell White .30 .09
65 Todd Hundley .30 .09
66 Mark Grace .50 .15
67 Alan Benes .30 .09
68 Jeff Abbott .30 .09
69 Bob Abreu .30 .09
70 Deion Sanders .50 .15
71 Tino Martinez .50 .15
72 Shannon Stewart .30 .09
73 Homer Bush .30 .09
74 Carlos Delgado .30 .09
75 Raul Ibanez .30 .09
76 Hideki Irabu .30 .09
77 Jose Cruz Jr. .30 .09
78 Tony Clark .30 .09
79 Wilton Guerrero .30 .09
80 Vladimir Guerrero .75 .23
81 Scott Rolen .75 .23
82 Nomar Garciaparra 1.25 .35
83 Darin Erstad .30 .09
84 Chan Ho Park .30 .09
85 Mike Cameron .30 .09
86 Todd Walker .30 .09
87 Todd Dunwoody .30 .09
88 Neifi Perez .30 .09
89 Brett Tomko .30 .09
90 Jose Guillen .30 .09
91 Matt Morris .30 .09
92 Bartolo Colon .30 .09
93 Jaret Wright .30 .09
94 Shawn Estes .30 .09
95 Livan Hernandez .30 .09
96 Bobby Estalella .30 .09
97 Ben Grieve .30 .09
98 Paul Konerko .30 .09
99 David Ortiz .75 .23
100 Todd Helton .50 .15
101 Juan Encarnacion .30 .09
102 Bubba Trammell .30 .09
103 Miguel Tejada .30 .09
104 Jacob Cruz .30 .09
105 Todd Greene .30 .09
106 Kevin Orie .30 .09
107 Mark Kotsay .30 .09
108 Fernando Tatis .30 .09
109 Jay Payton .30 .09
110 Pokey Reese .30 .09
111 Derrek Lee .30 .09
112 Richard Hidalgo .30 .09
113 Ricky Ledee .30 .09
UER front Rickey
114 Lou Collier .30 .09

115 Ruben Rivera .30 .09
116 Shawn Green .30 .09
117 Moises Alou .30 .09
118 Ken Griffey Jr. GEN .75 .23
119 Frank Thomas GEN .50 .15
120 Alex Rodriguez GEN .75 .23
121 Mike Piazza GEN .75 .23
122 Greg Maddux GEN .75 .23
123 Cal Ripken GEN 1.25 .35
124 Chipper Jones GEN .50 .15
125 Derek Jeter GEN 1.00 .30
126 Tony Gwynn GEN .50 .15
127 Andruw Jones GEN .30 .09
128 Juan Gonzalez GEN .30 .09
129 Jeff Bagwell GEN .30 .09
130 Mark McGwire GEN 1.00 .30
131 Roger Clemens GEN .75 .23
132 Albert Belle GEN .30 .09
133 Barry Bonds GEN .75 .23
134 Kenny Lofton GEN .30 .09
135 Ivan Rodriguez GEN .50 .15
136 Manny Ramirez GEN .50 .15
137 Jim Thome GEN .50 .15
138 C.Knoblauch GEN .30 .09
139 Paul Molitor GEN .30 .09
140 Barry Larkin GEN .30 .09
141 Mo Vaughn GEN .30 .09
142 Hideki Irabu GEN .30 .09
143 Jose Cruz Jr. GEN .30 .09
144 Tony Clark GEN .30 .09
145 V.Guerrero GEN .50 .15
146 Scott Rolen GEN .50 .15
147 N.Garciaparra GEN .75 .23
148 Nomar Garciaparra CL .75 .23
149 Larry Walker CL .30 .09
150 Tino Martinez CL .30 .09
AU2 F.Thomas AUTO/100 80.00 24.00

1998 Donruss Elite Aspirations

Randomly inserted in packs, this 150-card set is parallel to the base set. Only 750 of this set were produced and are sequentially numbered.

Nm-Mt Ex-Mt
*STARS: 3X TO 8X BASIC CARDS

1998 Donruss Elite Status

Randomly inserted in packs, this 150-card set is parallel to the base set. Only 100 of this set were produced and are serially numbered.

Nm-Mt Ex-Mt
*STARS: 10X TO 25X BASIC CARDS

1998 Donruss Elite Back to the Future

Randomly inserted in packs, this eight-card set is double-sided and features color images of top veteran and new players on a tile background. Only 1,500 of each card were produced and sequentially numbered.

Nm-Mt Ex-Mt
COMPLETE SET (8) 120.00 36.00
1 Cal Ripken 30.00 9.00
Paul Konerko
2 Jeff Bagwell 6.00 1.80
Todd Helton
3 Eddie Mathews 10.00 3.00
Chipper Jones
4 Juan Gonzalez 6.00 1.80
Ben Grieve
5 Hank Aaron 15.00 4.50
Jose Cruz Jr.
6 Frank Thomas 10.00 3.00
David Ortiz
1-100
7 Nolan Ryan 40.00 12.00
Greg Maddux
8 Alex Rodriguez 15.00 4.50
Nomar Garciaparra

1998 Donruss Elite Back to the Future Autographs

Randomly inserted in packs, this seven-card set is a parallel version of the the regular 1998 Donruss Elite Back to the Future insert set and contains the first 100 cards of the regular set signed by both pictured players. Card number six does not exist. Cal Ripken did not sign card number 1 along with Paul Konerko. Ripken eventually signed 200 separate cards. One hundred special redemptions (rather bland black and white text-based cards) were issued for the Ripken card and randomly seeded into packs. In addition, lucky collectors that pulled one of the first 100 serial numbered Back to the Future Konerko autograph cards could exchange it for a Ripken autograph AND still receive their Konerko autograph back. The first 100 of each card were autographed by both players pictured on the card. There is no autographed card number six. Due to problems in obtaining Frank Thomas' autograph prior to the shipping deadline for the parallel signed Back to the Future cards, the manufacturer was forced to make the first 100 serial numbered cards of card number 6 a redemption for a special Frank Thomas autographed card (a basic 1998 Donruss Elite Thomas card, embossed with a special stamp and signed by Thomas on front). Due to Pinnacle's bankruptcy, the exchange program was abruptly halted in late 1998. Prior to this, the serial numbered 1-100 Thomas/Ortiz cards traded for as much as $300. After this date, the premiums disappeared entirely.

Nm-Mt Ex-Mt
1A Cal Ripken 40.00 12.00
Paul Konerko Redeemed/100
Redeemed card signed only by Konerko
1B C. Ripken AU/200 200.00 60.00
Redeemed card signed only by Ripken
2 Jeff Bagwell 150.00 45.00
Todd Helton
3 Eddie Mathews 250.00 75.00
Chipper Jones
4 Juan Gonzalez 150.00 45.00
Ben Grieve
5 Hank Aaron 200.00 60.00
Jose Cruz Jr.
7 Nolan Ryan 1200.00 350.00
Greg Maddux
8 Alex Rodriguez 600.00 180.00
Nomar Garciaparra

1998 Donruss Elite Craftsmen

Randomly inserted in packs, this 30-card set features color photos of players who are the best at what they do. Only 3,500 of this set were produced and are sequentially numbered.

Nm-Mt Ex-Mt
COMPLETE SET (30) 150.00 45.00
*MASTER: 2.5X TO 6X BASIC CRAFTSMEN
MASTER PRINT RUN 100 SERIAL #'d SETS
RANDOM INSERTS IN PACKS
1 Ken Griffey Jr. 10.00 3.00
2 Frank Thomas 6.00 1.80
3 Alex Rodriguez 10.00 3.00
4 Cal Ripken 20.00 6.00
5 Greg Maddux 10.00 3.00
6 Mike Piazza 10.00 3.00
7 Chipper Jones 6.00 1.80
8 Derek Jeter 15.00 4.50
9 Tony Gwynn 8.00 2.40
10 Nomar Garciaparra 10.00 3.00
11 Scott Rolen 6.00 1.80
12 Jose Cruz Jr. 2.50 .75
13 Tony Clark 2.50 .75
14 Vladimir Guerrero 6.00 1.80
15 Todd Helton 4.00 1.20
16 Ben Grieve 2.50 .75
17 Andruw Jones 2.50 .75
18 Jeff Bagwell 4.00 1.20
19 Mark McGwire 15.00 4.50
20 Juan Gonzalez 4.00 1.20
21 Roger Clemens 12.00 3.60
22 Albert Belle 2.50 .75
23 Barry Bonds 15.00 4.50
24 Kenny Lofton 2.50 .75
25 Ivan Rodriguez 6.00 1.80
26 Paul Molitor 4.00 1.20
27 Barry Larkin UER 4.00 1.20
His team was midentified as the Cardinals
28 Mo Vaughn 2.50 .75
29 Larry Walker 4.00 1.20
30 Tino Martinez 4.00 1.20

1998 Donruss Elite Prime Numbers

Randomly inserted in packs, this 36-card set features three cards each of 12 top players in the league printed with three different numerical backgrounds (of which form a statistical benchmark when placed together). The total number of each card produced depended on the player's particular statistic. Print runs are included below in parentheses at the end of each card description.

Nm-Mt Ex-Mt
1A Ken Griffey Jr. 2 (94) 50.00 15.00
1B Ken Griffey Jr. 9 (204) 25.00 7.50
1C Ken Griffey Jr. 4 (290) 20.00 6.00
2A Frank Thomas 4 (56) 40.00 12.00
2B Frank Thomas 5 (406) 10.00 3.00
2C Frank Thomas 6 (450) 10.00 3.00
3A Mark McGwire 3 (87) 100.00 30.00
3B Mark McGwire 8 (307) 40.00 12.00
3C Mark McGwire 7 (380) 40.00 12.00
4A Cal Ripken 5 (17) 400.00 120.00
4B Cal Ripken 1 (507) 30.00 9.00
4C Cal Ripken 7 (510) 30.00 9.00
5A Mike Piazza 5 (76) 50.00 15.00
5B Mike Piazza 7 (506) 15.00 4.50
5C Mike Piazza 6 (570) 15.00 4.50
6A Chipper Jones 4 (89) 30.00 9.00
6B Chipper Jones 8 (409) 10.00 3.00
6C Chipper Jones 9 (480) 10.00 3.00
7A Tony Gwynn 3 (72) 40.00 12.00
7B Tony Gwynn 7 (302) 15.00 4.50
7C Tony Gwynn 2 (370) 15.00 4.50
8A Barry Bonds 3 (74) 80.00 24.00
8B Barry Bonds 7 (304) 30.00 9.00
8C Barry Bonds 4 (370) 30.00 9.00
9A Jeff Bagwell 4 (25) 60.00 18.00
9B Jeff Bagwell 2 (405) 6.00 1.80
9C Jeff Bagwell 5 (420) 6.00 1.80
10A Juan Gonzalez 5 (89) 25.00 7.50
10B J.Gonzalez 8 (509) 6.00 1.80
10C J.Gonzalez 9 (580) 6.00 1.80
11A Alex Rodriguez 5 (34) 80.00 24.00
11B A.Rodriguez 3 (504) 15.00 4.50
11C A.Rodriguez 4 (530) 15.00 4.50
12A Kenny Lofton 3 (54) 20.00 6.00
12B Kenny Lofton 5 (304) 5.00 1.50
12C Kenny Lofton 4 (350) 5.00 1.50

2001 Donruss Elite

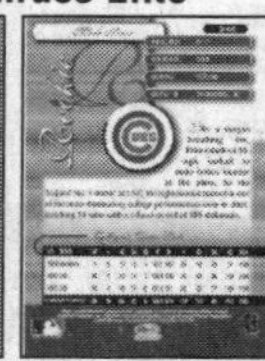

This 200-card hobby only set was distributed in May, 2001 in five-card packs with a suggested retail price of $3.99 and features color photos of some of Baseball's finest players and hot rookies. The low series rookie cards are sequentially numbered to 1000 with the first 100 labeled "Turn of the Century." Cards 201-250 were issued as exchange coupons for unspecified rookies and prospects and randomly seeded into packs at a rate of 1:14. Specific players for each exchange card were announced on Donruss' website in late October, 2001 (and about 15 players were dropped and updated with new players about a month later). The deadline to redeem the coupons was originally 11/01/01 but it was extended to January 20th, 2002. Each coupon carried a cost of $5.99 to redeem. In April of 2002 representatives at Donruss-Playoff released explicit quantities for each of these exchange cards, of which ranged from as few as 377 to as many as 556. All of these cards are actually serial-numbered "XXX/1000" on back but were mailed out in non-sequential order, thus cards serial-numbered as high as 900/1000 etc are in existence but it doesn't mean that 900+ copies were distributed. When the January 20th deadline passed, according to representatives at Donruss-Playoff, the remaining cards were destroyed. Please see our checklist for specific quantities of each card produced.

Nm-Mt Ex-Mt
COMP.SET w/o SP's (150) 25.00 7.50
COMMON CARD (1-150) .30 .09
COMMON (151-200) 8.00 2.40
COMMON CARD (201-250) 10.00 3.00
1 Alex Rodriguez 1.25 .35
2 Barry Bonds 2.00 .60
3 Cal Ripken 2.50 .75
4 Chipper Jones .75 .23
5 Derek Jeter 2.00 .60
6 Troy Glaus .30 .09
7 Frank Thomas .75 .23
8 Greg Maddux 1.25 .35
9 Ivan Rodriguez .75 .23
10 Jeff Bagwell .50 .15
11 Jose Canseco .75 .23
12 Todd Helton .50 .15
13 Ken Griffey Jr. 1.25 .35
14 Manny Ramirez .50 .15
15 Mark McGwire 2.00 .60
16 Mike Piazza 1.25 .35
17 Nomar Garciaparra 1.25 .35
18 Pedro Martinez .75 .23
19 Randy Johnson .75 .23
20 Rick Ankiel .30 .09
21 Rickey Henderson .75 .23
22 Roger Clemens 1.50 .45
23 Sammy Sosa 1.25 .35
24 Tony Gwynn 1.00 .30
25 Vladimir Guerrero .75 .23
26 Eric Davis .30 .09
27 Roberto Alomar .50 .15
28 Mark Mulder .30 .09
29 Pat Burrell .30 .09
30 Harold Baines .30 .09
31 Carlos Delgado .30 .09
32 J.D. Drew .30 .09
33 Jim Edmonds .30 .09
34 Darin Erstad .30 .09
35 Jason Giambi .30 .09
36 Tom Glavine .50 .15
37 Juan Gonzalez .50 .15
38 Mark Grace .50 .15
39 Shawn Green .30 .09
40 Tim Hudson .30 .09
41 Andruw Jones .30 .09
42 David Justice .30 .09
43 Jeff Kent .30 .09
44 Barry Larkin .50 .15
45 Pokey Reese .30 .09
46 Mike Mussina .50 .15
47 Hideo Nomo .75 .23
48 Rafael Palmeiro .50 .15
49 Adam Piatt .30 .09
50 Scott Rolen .75 .23
51 Gary Sheffield .30 .09
52 Bernie Williams .50 .15
53 Bob Abreu .30 .09
54 Edgardo Alfonzo .30 .09
55 Jermaine Clark RC .75 .23
56 Albert Belle .30 .09
57 Craig Biggio .50 .15
58 Andres Galarraga .30 .09
59 Edgar Martinez .50 .15
60 Fred McGriff .50 .15
61 Magglio Ordonez .30 .09
62 Jim Thome .75 .23
63 Matt Williams .30 .09
64 Kerry Wood .75 .23
65 Moises Alou .30 .09
66 Brady Anderson .30 .09
67 Garret Anderson .30 .09
68 Tony Armas Jr. .30 .09
69 Tony Batista .30 .09
70 Jose Cruz Jr. .30 .09
71 Carlos Beltran .50 .15
72 Adrian Beltre .50 .15
73 Kris Benson .30 .09
74 Lance Berkman .30 .09
75 Kevin Brown .30 .09
76 Jay Buhner .30 .09
77 Jeromy Burnitz .30 .09
78 Ken Caminiti .30 .09
79 Sean Casey .30 .09
80 Luis Castillo .30 .09
81 Eric Chavez .30 .09
82 Jeff Cirillo .30 .09
83 Bartolo Colon .30 .09
84 David Cone .30 .09
85 Freddy Garcia .30 .09
86 Johnny Damon .50 .15
87 Ray Durham .30 .09
88 Jermaine Dye .30 .09
89 Juan Encarnacion .30 .09
90 Terrence Long .30 .09
91 Carl Everett .30 .09
92 Steve Finley .30 .09
93 Cliff Floyd .30 .09
94 Brad Fullmer .30 .09
95 Brian Giles .30 .09
96 Luis Gonzalez .30 .09
97 Rusty Greer .30 .09
98 Jeffrey Hammonds .30 .09
99 Mike Hampton .30 .09
100 Orlando Hernandez .30 .09
101 Richard Hidalgo .30 .09
102 Geoff Jenkins .30 .09
103 Jacque Jones .30 .09
104 Brian Jordan .30 .09
105 Gabe Kapler .30 .09
106 Eric Karros .30 .09
107 Jason Kendall .30 .09
108 Adam Kennedy .30 .09
109 Byung-Hyun Kim .30 .09
110 Ryan Klesko .30 .09
111 Chuck Knoblauch .30 .09
112 Paul Konerko .30 .09
113 Carlos Lee .30 .09
114 Kenny Lofton .30 .09
115 Javy Lopez .30 .09
116 Tino Martinez .50 .15
117 Ruben Mateo .30 .09
118 Kevin Millwood .30 .09
119 Ben Molina .30 .09
120 Raul Mondesi .30 .09
121 Trot Nixon .30 .09
122 John Olerud .30 .09
123 Paul O'Neill .50 .15
124 Chan Ho Park .30 .09
125 Andy Pettitte .50 .15
126 Jorge Posada .50 .15
127 Mark Quinn .30 .09
128 Aramis Ramirez .30 .09
129 Mariano Rivera .50 .15
130 Tim Salmon .50 .15
131 Curt Schilling .30 .09
132 Richie Sexson .30 .09
133 John Smoltz .50 .15
134 J.T. Snow .30 .09
135 Jay Payton .30 .09
136 Shannon Stewart .30 .09
137 B.J. Surhoff .30 .09
138 Mike Sweeney .30 .09
139 Fernando Tatis .30 .09
140 Miguel Tejada .30 .09
141 Jason Varitek .50 .15
142 Greg Vaughn .30 .09
143 Mo Vaughn .30 .09
144 Robin Ventura UER .30 .09
Listed as playing for Yankees last 2 years,
Also Bat and Throw information is wrong
145 Jose Vidro .30 .09
146 Omar Vizquel .50 .15
147 Larry Walker .50 .15
148 David Wells .30 .09
149 Rondell White .30 .09
150 Preston Wilson .30 .09
151 Brent Abernathy SP 8.00 2.40
152 Cory Aldridge SP RC 8.00 2.40
153 Gene Altman SP RC 8.00 2.40
154 Josh Beckett SP 8.00 2.40
155 Wilson Betemit SP RC 8.00 2.40
156 Albert Pujols SP RC 300.00 90.00
157 Joe Crede SP 8.00 2.40
158 Jack Cust SP 8.00 2.40
159 Ben Sheets SP 10.00 3.00
160 Alex Escobar SP 8.00 2.40
161 A. Hernandez SP RC 8.00 2.40
162 Pedro Feliz SP 8.00 2.40
163 Nate Frese SP RC 8.00 2.40
164 Carlos Garcia SP RC 8.00 2.40
165 Marcus Giles SP 8.00 2.40
166 Alexis Gomez SP RC 8.00 2.40
167 Jason Hart SP 8.00 2.40
168 Aubrey Huff SP 8.00 2.40
169 Cesar Izturis SP 8.00 2.40
170 Nick Johnson SP 8.00 2.40
171 Jack Wilson SP RC 15.00 4.50
172 B.Lawrence SP RC 8.00 2.40
173 C. Parker SP RC 8.00 2.40
174 Nick Maness SP RC 8.00 2.40
175 Jose Mieses SP RC 8.00 2.40
176 Greg Miller SP RC 8.00 2.40
177 Eric Munson SP 8.00 2.40
178 Xavier Nady SP 8.00 2.40
179 Blaine Neal SP RC 8.00 2.40
180 Abraham Nunez SP 8.00 2.40
181 Jose Ortiz SP 8.00 2.40
182 Jeremy Owens SP RC 8.00 2.40
183 Jay Gibbons SP RC 10.00 3.00
184 Corey Patterson SP 8.00 2.40
185 Carlos Pena SP 8.00 2.40
186 C.C. Sabathia SP 8.00 2.40
187 Timo Perez SP 8.00 2.40
188 A. Pettyjohn SP RC 8.00 2.40
189 D. Mendez SP RC 8.00 2.40
190 J. Melian SP RC 8.00 2.40
191 Wilkin Ruan SP RC 8.00 2.40
192 D. Sanchez SP RC 8.00 2.40
193 Alfonso Soriano SP 10.00 3.00
194 Rafael Soriano SP RC 10.00 3.00
195 Ichiro Suzuki SP RC 120.00 36.00
196 Billy Sylvester SP RC 8.00 2.40
197 Juan Uribe SP RC 10.00 3.00
198 T. Shinjo SP RC 10.00 3.00
199 C. Valderrama SP RC 8.00 2.40
200 Matt White SP RC 8.00 2.40
201 Adam Dunn/468 15.00 4.50
202 Joe Kennedy/465 XRC 15.00 4.50
203 Mike Rivera/427 XRC 10.00 3.00
204 Erick Almonte/401 XRC 10.00 3.00
205 Bran Duckworth EXCH 10.00 3.00
206 Victor Martinez/410 XRC 180.00 55.00
207 Rick Bauer/390 XRC 10.00 3.00
208 Jeff Deardorff/396 XRC 10.00 3.00
209 Antonio Perez/448 XRC 10.00 3.00
210 Bill Hall/404 XRC 10.00 3.00
211 D. Tankersley EXCH 10.00 3.00
212 Jeremy Affeldt/386 XRC 15.00 4.50
213 Junior Spivey/377 XRC 15.00 4.50
214 Casey Fossum/393 XRC 10.00 3.00
215 Brandon Lyon/402 XRC 10.00 3.00
216 Angel Santos/408 XRC 10.00 3.00
217 Cody Ransom/404 XRC 10.00 3.00
218 Jason Lane/424 XRC 10.00 3.00
219 David Williams/408 XRC 10.00 3.00
220 Alex Herrera/405 XRC 10.00 3.00
221 Ryan Drese/378 XRC 15.00 4.50
222 Travis Hafner/419 XRC 60.00 18.00
223 Bud Smith/468 XRC 10.00 3.00
224 Johnny Estrada/415 XRC 25.00 7.50
225 R. Rodriguez EXCH 10.00 3.00
226 Brandon Berger/428 XRC 10.00 3.00
227 Claudio Vargas/395 XRC 10.00 3.00
228 Luis Garcia/438 XRC 10.00 3.00
229 Marlon Byrd/452 XRC 25.00 7.50
230 Hee Seop Choi/479 XRC 25.00 7.50
231 Corky Miller/431 XRC 10.00 3.00
232 J. Duchscherer EXCH 10.00 3.00
233 T. Spooneybarger EXCH 10.00 3.00
234 Roy Oswalt/427 15.00 4.50
235 Willie Harris/418 XRC 10.00 3.00
236 Josh Towers/437 XRC 10.00 3.00
237 Juan A.Pena/400 XRC 10.00 3.00
238 A. Amezaga EXCH 10.00 3.00
239 Geronimo Gil/396 XRC 10.00 3.00
240 Juan Cruz/489 XRC 10.00 3.00
241 Ed Rogers/429 XRC 10.00 3.00
242 Joe Thurston/420 XRC 10.00 3.00
243 O.Hudson EXCH 15.00 4.50
244 John Buck/416 XRC 15.00 4.50
245 Martin Vargas/400 XRC 10.00 3.00
246 David Brous/399 XRC 10.00 3.00
247 D. Brazelton EXCH 15.00 4.50
248 Mark Prior/556 XRC 150.00 45.00
249 Angel Berroa/420 XRC 25.00 7.50
250 Mark Teixeira/543 XRC 80.00 24.00

2001 Donruss Elite Aspirations

Randomly inserted in packs at the rate of one in 62, this 200-card set is a parallel version of the base set printed on holo-foil board with red foil and red tint. Each card was sequentially numbered to the remaining number after subtracting the player's jersey number from 100. Cards with a print run of 25 or fewer are not priced due to market scarcity.

Nm-Mt Ex-Mt
*1-150 PRINT RUN b/wn 81-100: 4X TO 10X
*1-150 PRINT RUN b/wn 66-80: 5X TO 12X
*1-150 PRINT RUN b/wn 51-65: 5X TO 12X
*1-150 PRINT RUN b/wn 36-50: 6X TO 15X
*1-150 PRINT RUN b/wn 26-35: 8X TO 20X
COMMON (151-200) p/r 81-100. 4.00 1.20
MINOR 151-200 p/r 81-100 6.00 1.80
UNLISTED 151-200 p/r 81-100. 15.00 4.50
MINOR 151-200 p/r 66-80 8.00 2.40
SEMISTARS 151-200 p/r 66-80 12.00 3.60
UNLISTED 151-200 p/r 66-80 20.00 6.00
MINOR 151-200 p/r 51-65 10.00 3.00
UNLISTED 151-200 p/r 51-65 25.00 7.50
COMMON (151-200) p/r 36-50 8.00 2.40
MINOR 151-200 p/r 36-50 12.00 3.60
SEMISTARS 151-200 p/r 36-50 20.00 6.00
UNLISTED 151-200 p/r 36-50 30.00 9.00
COMMON (151-200) p/r 26-35. 10.00 3.00
MINOR 151-200 p/r 26-35 15.00 4.50
UNLISTED 151-200 p/r 26-35. 40.00 12.00
UNLISTED 151-200 p/r 21-25 50.00 15.00
MINOR 151-200 p/r 16-20 25.00 7.50
RANDOM INSERTS IN PACKS
SEE BECKETT.COM FOR PRINT RUNS
PRINTS b/wn 1-15 TOO SCARCE TO PRICE
RC'S OF 25 OR LESS TOO SCARCE TO PRICE

2001 Donruss Elite Status

Randomly inserted in packs at the rate of one in 163, this 200-card set is a parallel version of the base set printed on holo-foil board with gold foil and gold tint. Each card is sequentially numbered to the player's jersey number. Cards issued to a stated print run of 25 or fewer are not priced due to market scarcity.

Nm-Mt Ex-Mt
*1-150 PRINT RUN b/wn 81-100: 4X TO 10X
*1-150 PRINT RUN b/wn 66-80: 5X TO 12X
*1-150 PRINT RUN b/wn 51-65: 5X TO 12X
*1-150 PRINT RUN b/wn 36-50: 6X TO 15X
*1-150 PRINT RUN b/wn 26-35: 8X TO 20X
*1-150 PRINT RUN b/wn 21-25: 10X TO 25X
*1-150 PRINT RUN b/wn 16-20: 12.5X TO 30X
MINOR 151-200 p/r 81-100 6.00 1.80
COMMON (151-200) p/r 66-80 5.00 1.50
MINOR 151-200 p/r 66-80 8.00 2.40
UNLISTED 151-200 p/r 66-80 20.00 6.00
COMMON (151-200) p/r 51-65 6.00 1.80
MINOR 151-200 p/r 51-65 10.00 3.00
SEMISTARS 151-200 p/r 51-65 15.00 4.50
UNLISTED 151-200 p/r 51-65 25.00 7.50
MINOR 151-200 p/r 36-50 12.00 3.60
SEMISTARS 151-200 p/r 36-50 20.00 6.00

NOR 151-200 p/r 21-25........ 20.00 6.00
NLISTED 151-200 p/r 21-25... 50.00 15.00
NOR 151-200 p/r 16-20........ 25.00 7.50
EMISTARS 151-200 p/r 16-20 40.00 12.00
NLISTED 151-200 p/r 16-20... 60.00 18.00
ANDOM INSERTS IN PACKS ....
E BECKETT.COM FOR PRINT RUNS
RINTS b/wn 1-15 TOO SCARCE TO PRICE

2001 Donruss Elite Extra Edition Autographs

iese certified autograph cards were made ailable as a compensation by Donruss-Playoff collectors for autograph exchange cards that e manufacturer was unable to fulfill in the 2001 eason. Each card is serial-numbered of 100 on ont. Unlike most Donruss-Playoff autograph ards from 2001, the athletes signed the actual ard rather than signing a sticker (of which was en affixed to the card at a later date). The cards st started to appear on the secondary market April, 2002 but are catalogued as 2001 cards avoid confusion for collectors looking to ref- ence them.

	Nm-Mt	Ex-Mt
34 Roy Oswalt	40.00	12.00
38 Alfredo Amezaga	20.00	6.00
41 Ed Rogers	20.00	6.00

2001 Donruss Elite Turn of the Century Autographs

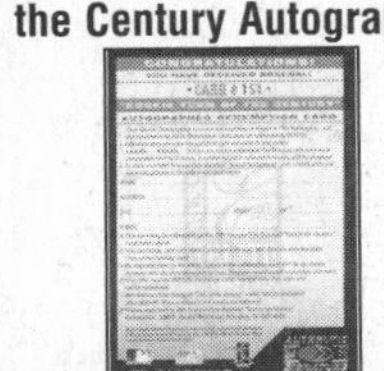

Randomly inserted in packs, these 50 cards fea- ure prospects who signed their cards for the onruss Elite product. Each card had a stated rint run of 100 sets though they are cumula- vely serial-numbered to 1000 (only the first 100 umbered copies of each card Turn of the entury Autographs - the last 900 numbered opies of each card are basic Elite cards). Some layers did not return their cards in time for nclusion in the product and these cards had an edemption deadline of May 1, 2003. Cards umber 195 and 198 at first were not believed to xist, but subsequently were issued without utographs.

	Nm-Mt	Ex-Mt
51 Brent Abernathy	15.00	4.50
52 Cory Aldridge	15.00	4.50
53 Gene Altman	10.00	3.00
54 Josh Beckett	80.00	24.00
55 Wilson Betemit	15.00	4.50
56 Albert Pujols	800.00	240.00
57 Joe Crede	15.00	4.50
58 Jack Cust	15.00	4.50
59 Ben Sheets	40.00	12.00
160 Alex Escobar	15.00	4.50
161 Adrian Hernandez	10.00	3.00
162 Pedro Feliz	15.00	4.50
163 Nate Frese	15.00	4.50
164 Carlos Garcia	15.00	4.50
165 Marcus Giles	25.00	7.50
166 Alexis Gomez	15.00	4.50
167 Jason Hart	15.00	4.50
168 Aubrey Huff	25.00	7.50
169 Cesar Izturis	25.00	7.50
170 Nick Johnson	25.00	7.50
171 Jack Wilson	50.00	15.00
172 Brian Lawrence	15.00	4.50
173 Christian Parker	15.00	4.50
174 Nick Maness	15.00	4.50
175 Jose Mieses	15.00	4.50
176 Greg Miller	15.00	4.50
177 Eric Munson	15.00	4.50
178 Xavier Nady	15.00	4.50
179 Blaine Neal	15.00	4.50
180 Abraham Nunez	15.00	4.50
181 Jose Ortiz	15.00	4.50
182 Jeremy Owens	15.00	4.50
183 Jay Gibbons	40.00	12.00
184 Corey Patterson	25.00	7.50
185 Carlos Pena	15.00	4.50
186 C.C. Sabathia	25.00	7.50
187 Timo Perez	15.00	4.50
188 Adam Pettyjohn	15.00	4.50
189 Donaldo Mendez	10.00	3.00
190 Jackson Melian	15.00	4.50
191 Wilkin Ruan	15.00	4.50
192 Duaner Sanchez	15.00	4.50
193 Alfonso Soriano	80.00	24.00
194 Rafael Soriano	25.00	7.50
195 Ichiro Suzuki NO AU		
196 Billy Sylvester	10.00	3.00
197 Juan Uribe	25.00	7.50
198 Tsuyoshi Shinjo NO AU		
199 Carlos Valderrama	15.00	4.50
200 Matt White	15.00	4.50

2001 Donruss Elite Back 2 Back Jacks

Randomly inserted in packs, this double-sided 45-card set features color photos of one or two players with game-used bat pieces embedded in the cards. Cards with single players are sequentially numbered to 100 while those with doubles were numbered to 50. Exchange cards with a redemption deadline of May 1st, 2003 were seeded into packs for Eddie Mathews, Frank Thomas, Mathews/Glaus combo and F.Robinson/Thomas combo.

	Nm-Mt	Ex-Mt
BB1 Ernie Banks SP/75	25.00	7.50
BB2 Ryne Sandberg SP/75	50.00	15.00
BB3 Babe Ruth	200.00	60.00
BB4 Lou Gehrig	150.00	45.00
BB5 Eddie Mathews	25.00	7.50
BB6 Troy Glaus SP/50	25.00	7.50
BB7 Don Mattingly SP/50	60.00	18.00
BB8 Todd Helton	25.00	7.50
BB9 Wade Boggs	25.00	7.50
BB10 Tony Gwynn	25.00	7.50
BB11 Robin Yount	25.00	7.50
BB12 Paul Molitor SP/50	40.00	12.00
BB13 Mike Schmidt SP/50	50.00	15.00
BB14 Scott Rolen SP/75	25.00	7.50
BB15 Reggie Jackson	25.00	7.50
BB16 Dave Winfield	15.00	4.50
BB17 J. Bench SP/50	40.00	12.00
BB18 Joe Morgan	15.00	4.50
BB19 B. Robinson SP/50	40.00	12.00
BB20 Cal Ripken	50.00	15.00
BB21 Ty Cobb	120.00	36.00
BB22 Al Kaline SP/50	40.00	12.00
BB23 F. Robinson SP/50	40.00	12.00
BB24 Frank Thomas	25.00	7.50
BB25 Roberto Clemente	100.00	30.00
BB26 V. Guerrero SP/50	40.00	12.00
BB27 H.Killebrew SP/50	40.00	12.00
BB28 Kirby Puckett	25.00	7.50
BB29 Yogi Berra SP/75	40.00	12.00
BB30 Phil Rizzuto SP/75	40.00	12.00
BB31 Ernie Banks	100.00	30.00
Ryne Sandberg		
BB32 Babe Ruth	400.00	120.00
Lou Gehrig		
BB33 Eddie Mathews	60.00	18.00
Troy Glaus		
BB34 Don Mattingly	100.00	30.00
Todd Helton		
BB35 Wade Boggs	80.00	24.00
Tony Gwynn		
BB36 Robin Yount	80.00	24.00
Paul Molitor		
BB37 Mike Schmidt	100.00	30.00
Scott Rolen		
BB38 Reggie Jackson	40.00	12.00
Dave Winfield		
BB39 Johnny Bench	60.00	18.00
Joe Morgan		
BB40 Brooks Robinson	120.00	36.00
Cal Ripken		
BB41 Ty Cobb	200.00	60.00
Al Kaline		
BB42 Frank Robinson	60.00	18.00
Frank Thomas		
BB43 Roberto Clemente	120.00	36.00
Vladimir Guerrero		
BB44 Harmon Killebrew	60.00	18.00
Kirby Puckett		
BB45 Yogi Berra		
Phil Rizzuto		

2001 Donruss Elite Back 2 Back Jacks Autograph

Randomly inserted in packs, this 16-card set is a partial parallel autographed version of the regular insert set. Almost every card in the set packed out as an exchange card with a redemption deadline of May 1st, 2003. Only Johnny Bench, Al Kaline and Harmon Killebrew signed cards in time to be seeded directly into packs. Cards with a print run of 25 copies are not priced due to scarcity.

	Nm-Mt	Ex-Mt
BB1 Ernie Banks/25		
BB2 Ryne Sandberg/25		
BB6 Troy Glaus/50	60.00	18.00
BB7 Don Mattingly/50	200.00	60.00
BB12 Paul Molitor/50	80.00	24.00
BB13 Mike Schmidt/50	200.00	60.00
BB14 Scott Rolen/25		
BB17 Johnny Bench/50	120.00	36.00
BB19 Brooks Robinson/50	80.00	24.00
BB22 Al Kaline/50	120.00	36.00
BB23 Frank Robinson/50	80.00	24.00
BB26 Vladimir Guerrero/50	120.00	36.00
BB27 Harmon Killebrew/50	120.00	36.00
BB29 Yogi Berra/25		
BB30 Phil Rizzuto/25		
BB45 Yogi Berra		
Phil Rizzuto		

2001 Donruss Elite Passing the Torch

Randomly inserted in packs, this 24-card set features color action photos of legendary players and up-and-coming phenoms printed on holo-foil board. Cards with single players were sequentially numbered to 1000 while those with two players were numbered to 500.

	Nm-Mt	Ex-Mt
PT1 Stan Musial	12.00	3.60
PT2 Tony Gwynn	10.00	3.00
PT3 Willie Mays	15.00	4.50
PT4 Barry Bonds	20.00	6.00
PT5 Mike Schmidt	15.00	4.50
PT6 Scott Rolen	8.00	2.40
PT7 Cal Ripken	25.00	7.50
PT8 Alex Rodriguez	12.00	3.60
PT9 Hank Aaron	15.00	4.50
PT10 Andruw Jones	5.00	1.50
PT11 Nolan Ryan	20.00	6.00
PT12 Pedro Martinez	8.00	2.40
PT13 Wade Boggs	5.00	1.50
PT14 Nomar Garciaparra	12.00	3.60
PT15 Don Mattingly	20.00	6.00
PT16 Todd Helton	5.00	1.50
PT17 Stan Musial	20.00	6.00
Tony Gwynn		
PT18 Willie Mays	25.00	7.50
Barry Bonds		
PT19 Mike Schmidt	20.00	6.00
Scott Rolen		
PT20 Cal Ripken	40.00	12.00
Alex Rodriguez		
PT21 Hank Aaron	25.00	7.50
Andruw Jones		
PT22 Nolan Ryan	30.00	9.00
Pedro Martinez		
PT23 Wade Boggs	20.00	6.00
Nomar Garciaparra		
PT24 Don Mattingly	30.00	9.00
Todd Helton		

2001 Donruss Elite Passing the Torch Autographs

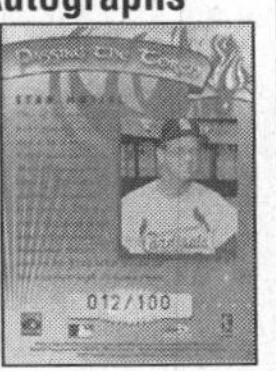

Randomly inserted in packs, this 22-card set is a partial autographed parallel version of the regular insert set printed on double-sided holo-foil board. Cards with single players were sequentially numbered to 100 while those with dual players were numbered to 50. Nearly all of these cards were not available in time for insertion into packs and collectors had until May 1st, 2003 to redeem them. Wade Boggs, Todd Helton, Stan Musial and Nolan Ryan were the only players to return their cards in time for them to be seeded into packs. Cards PT22, PT23 and PT24 were actually 2001 Donruss Elite football exchange cards that were erroneously placed into baseball packs. To honor their commitment to collectors that pulled these cards - the manufacturer created three additional dual autograph baseball cards. These cards are tagged in our checklist with an "FB" status to indicate their origin. The set contains two separate cards numbered PT22 because of this same football snafu - whereby it's theorized that the baseball was originally intended to be complete at 22 cards. The three additional football exchange cards expanded the set to 25 cards and also created two separate PT22 cards.

	Nm-Mt	Ex-Mt
PT1 Stan Musial	120.00	36.00
PT2 Tony Gwynn	80.00	24.00
PT3 Willie Mays	300.00	90.00
PT4 Barry Bonds	300.00	90.00
PT5 Mike Schmidt	120.00	36.00
PT6 Scott Rolen	80.00	24.00
PT7 Cal Ripken	200.00	60.00
PT8 Alex Rodriguez	150.00	45.00
PT9 Hank Aaron	250.00	75.00
PT10 Andruw Jones	50.00	15.00
PT11 Nolan Ryan	150.00	45.00
PT12 P.Martinez EXCH	80.00	24.00
PT13 Wade Boggs	50.00	15.00
PT14 N.Garciaparra EXCH	200.00	60.00
PT15 Don Mattingly	120.00	36.00
PT16 Todd Helton	50.00	15.00
PT17 Stan Musial	200.00	60.00
Tony Gwynn		
PT18 Willie Mays	1200.00	350.00
Barry Bonds		
PT19 Mike Schmidt	200.00	60.00
Scott Rolen		
PT20 Cal Ripken	600.00	180.00
Alex Rodriguez		
PT21 Hank Aaron	300.00	90.00
Andruw Jones		
PT22A Nolan Ryan	500.00	150.00
Roger Clemens FB		
PT22B Nolan Ryan	400.00	120.00
Pedro Martinez BB		
PT23 Wade Boggs	250.00	75.00
Nomar Garciaparra FB		
PT24 Don Mattingly	200.00	60.00
Todd Helton FB		

2001 Donruss Elite Prime Numbers

Randomly inserted in packs at the rate of one in 84, this 30-card set features color action images of 10 stellar performers. Each player has three cards highlighted by a single digit from his high average. The cards are sequentially numbered to the base total of the digit displayed.

	Nm-Mt	Ex-Mt
PN-1A Alex Rodriguez/300	20.00	6.00
PN-1B Alex Rodriguez/50	50.00	15.00
PN-1C Alex Rodriguez/8		
PN-2A Ken Griffey Jr./400	20.00	6.00
PN-2B Ken Griffey Jr./30	60.00	18.00
PN-2C Ken Griffey Jr./8		
PN-3A Mark McGwire/500	30.00	9.00
PN-3B Mark McGwire/50	80.00	24.00
PN-3C Mark McGwire/4		
PN-4A Cal Ripken/400	40.00	12.00
PN-4B Cal Ripken/10		
PN-4C Cal Ripken/7		
PN-5A Derek Jeter/300	30.00	9.00
PN-5B Derek Jeter/20	150.00	45.00
PN-5C Derek Jeter/2		
PN-6A Mike Piazza/300	20.00	6.00
PN-6B Mike Piazza/60	40.00	12.00
PN-6C Mike Piazza/2		
PN-7A N.Garciaparra/300	20.00	6.00
PN-7B N.Garciaparra/70	30.00	9.00
PN-7C Nomar Garciaparra/2		
PN-8A Sammy Sosa/300	20.00	6.00
PN-8B Sammy Sosa/80	30.00	9.00
PN-8C Sammy Sosa/6		
PN-9A V.Guerrero/300	12.00	3.60
PN-9B V.Guerrero/40	30.00	9.00
PN-9C Vladimir Guerrero/5		
PN-10A Tony Gwynn/300	15.00	4.50
PN-10B Tony Gwynn/90	20.00	6.00
PN-10C Tony Gwynn/4		

2001 Donruss Elite Throwback Threads

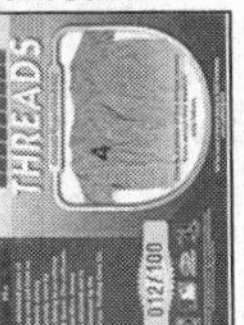

Randomly inserted into packs, this 45-card set features past and present greats with swatches of game-worn jerseys displayed on the cards. Cards with single players are sequentially numbered to 100 while those with doubles are numbered to 50. Exchange cards with a redemption deadline of May 1st, 2003 were seeded into packs for Ernie Banks, Lou Brock, Pedro Martinez, Ozzie Smith and Frank Thomas. In addition, exchange cards packed out for the following dual-player cards: Brock/Ozzie, Banks/Sandberg, F.Robinson/Thomas and Clemens/Pedro. Pricing is not available for cards with a print run of 25 copies due to scarcity.

	Nm-Mt	Ex-Mt
TT1 Stan Musial SP/75	60.00	18.00
TT2 Tony Gwynn SP/75	40.00	12.00
TT3 Willie McCovey	15.00	4.50
TT4 Barry Bonds	50.00	15.00
TT5 Babe Ruth	300.00	90.00
TT6 Lou Gehrig	250.00	75.00
TT7 Mike Schmidt SP/75	50.00	15.00
TT8 Scott Rolen	25.00	7.50
TT9 H.Killebrew SP/75	40.00	12.00
TT10 Kirby Puckett	25.00	7.50
TT11 Al Kaline SP/75	40.00	12.00
TT12 Eddie Mathews	40.00	12.00
TT13 Hank Aaron SP/75	80.00	24.00
TT14 Andruw Jones SP/50	25.00	7.50
TT15 Lou Brock	25.00	7.50
TT16 Ozzie Smith	25.00	7.50
TT17 E.Banks SP/TBD		
TT18 Ryne Sandberg	50.00	15.00
TT19 Roberto Clemente	100.00	30.00
TT20 V. Guerrero SP/50	40.00	12.00
TT21 F.Robinson SP/50	40.00	12.00
TT22 Frank Thomas	25.00	7.50
TT23 B.Robinson SP/50	40.00	12.00
TT24 Cal Ripken	50.00	15.00
TT25 Roger Clemens	25.00	7.50
TT26 Pedro Martinez	25.00	7.50
TT27 Reggie Jackson	25.00	7.50
TT28 Dave Winfield	15.00	4.50
TT29 Don Mattingly SP/50	60.00	18.00
TT30 Todd Helton	25.00	7.50
TT32 Willie McCovey	100.00	30.00
Barry Bonds		
TT33 Babe Ruth	700.00	210.00
Lou Gehrig		
TT34 Mike Schmidt		
Scott Rolen SP/25		
TT35 Harmon Killebrew	80.00	24.00
Kirby Puckett		
TT36 Al Kaline	100.00	30.00
Eddie Mathews		
TT37 Hank Aaron	120.00	36.00
Andruw Jones		
TT38 Lou Brock	80.00	24.00
Ozzie Smith		
TT39 Ernie Banks		
Ryne Sandberg SP/25		
TT40 Roberto Clemente	120.00	36.00
Vladimir Guerrero		
TT41 Frank Robinson	60.00	18.00
Frank Thomas		
TT42 Brooks Robinson	100.00	30.00
Cal Ripken		
TT43 Roger Clemens	80.00	24.00
Pedro Martinez		
TT44 Reggie Jackson	40.00	12.00
Dave Winfield		
TT45 Don Mattingly	80.00	24.00
Todd Helton		

2001 Donruss Elite Throwback Threads Autographs

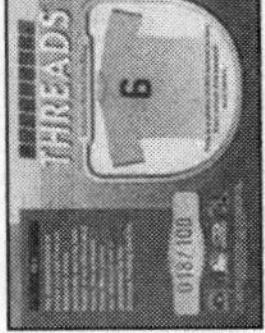

Randomly inserted in packs, this 15-card set is a partial parallel autographed version of the regular insert set. Exchange cards with a May 1st, 2003 redemption deadline were seeded into packs for almost the entire set. Only Al Kaline, Harmon Killebrew and Stan Musial managed to return their cards in time for packout. 2001 Donruss Elite football exchange cards were erroneously seeded into baseball packs for cards TT21 and TT22. Those cards have an "FB" tag added to their listing to denote their origins. The quantity for Ernie Banks signed cards was never revealed by the manufacturer.

	Nm-Mt	Ex-Mt
TT1 Stan Musial/25		
TT2 Tony Gwynn/25		
TT7 Mike Schmidt/25		
TT9 Harmon Killebrew/25		
TT11 Al Kaline/25		
TT13 Hank Aaron/25		
TT14 Andruw Jones/50	100.00	30.00
TT17 Ernie Banks/TBD		
TT20 Vladimir Guerrero/50	150.00	45.00
TT21 Frank Robinson/50 FB		
TT22 Frank Thomas/50 FB		
TT23 Brooks Robinson/50	100.00	30.00
TT29 Don Mattingly/50	200.00	60.00
TT31 Stan Musial		
Tony Gwynn/50		
TT34 Mike Schmidt		
Scott Rolen/25		
TT39 Ernie Banks		
Ryne Sandberg/25		

2001 Donruss Elite Title Waves

Randomly inserted in packs, this 30-card set features the game's most decorated performers highlighted in five different title-winning categories and sequentially numbered to the year they won the title.

	Nm-Mt	Ex-Mt
COMPLETE SET (30)	250.00	75.00
*HOLO: 1.5X TO 4X BASIC WAVES		
HOLO-FOIL PRINT RUN 100 SERIAL #'d SETS		
RANDOM INSERTS IN PACKS		
TW1 Tony Gwynn/1994	8.00	2.40
TW2 Todd Helton/2000	4.00	1.20
TW3 N.Garciaparra/2000	10.00	3.00
TW4 Frank Thomas/1997	6.00	1.80
TW5 Alex Rodriguez/1996	10.00	3.00
TW6 Jeff Bagwell/1994	4.00	1.20
TW7 Mark McGwire/1998	15.00	4.50
TW8 Sammy Sosa/2000	10.00	3.00
TW9 Ken Griffey Jr./1997	10.00	3.00
TW10 Albert Belle/1995	3.00	.90
TW11 Barry Bonds/1993	15.00	4.50
TW12 Jose Canseco/1991	6.00	1.80
TW13 M.Ramirez/1999	4.00	1.20
TW14 Sammy Sosa/1998	10.00	3.00
TW15 A.Galarraga/1996	3.00	.90
TW16 Todd Helton/2000	4.00	1.20
TW17 Ken Griffey Jr./1997	10.00	3.00
TW18 Jeff Bagwell/1994	4.00	1.20
TW19 Mike Piazza/1995	10.00	3.00
TW20 A.Rodriguez/1995	10.00	3.00
TW21 Jason Giambi/2000	3.00	.90
TW22 I.Rodriguez/1999	6.00	1.80
TW23 Greg Maddux/1997	10.00	3.00
TW24 P.Martinez/1994	6.00	1.80
TW25 Derek Jeter/2000	15.00	4.50
TW26 B.Williams/1998	4.00	1.20
TW27 R.Clemens/1999	12.00	3.60
TW28 Chipper Jones/1995	6.00	1.80
TW29 M.McGwire/1990	15.00	4.50
TW30 Cal Ripken/1983	20.00	6.00

2002 Donruss Elite

This 268-card set highlights baseball's premier performers. The standard-size set is made up of 100 veteran players, 50 STAR veteran subset cards and 50 rookie players. The fronts feature full color action shots. The STAR subset cards (101-150) were seeded into packs at a rate of 1:10. The rookie cards (151-200) are sequentially numbered to 1500 but only 1350 of each were actually produced. The first 150 of each rookie card is die-cut and labeled "Turn of the Century" with varying quantities of some autographed. These cards were issued in 5 card packs with a $3.99 SRP which came 20 packs to a box and 20 boxes to a case. Cards 256, 263 and 267-271 were never released.

	Nm-Mt	Ex-Mt
COMP.LO SET w/o SP's (100)	20.00	6.00
COMMON CARD (1-100)	.30	.09
COMMON CARD (101-150)	2.00	.60
COMMON CARD (151-200)	5.00	1.50
COMMON CARD (201-275)	8.00	2.40
1 Vladimir Guerrero	.75	.23
2 Bernie Williams	.50	.15
3 Ichiro Suzuki	1.25	.35
4 Roger Clemens	1.50	.45
5 Greg Maddux	1.25	.35
6 Fred McGriff	.50	.15
7 Jermaine Dye	.30	.09
8 Ken Griffey Jr.	1.25	.35
9 Todd Helton	.50	.15
10 Torii Hunter	.30	.09
11 Pat Burrell	.30	.09
12 Chipper Jones	.75	.23
13 Ivan Rodriguez	.75	.23
14 Roy Oswalt	.30	.09
15 Shannon Stewart	.30	.09
16 Magglio Ordonez	.30	.09
17 Lance Berkman	.30	.09
18 Mark Mulder	.30	.09
19 Al Leiter	.30	.09
20 Sammy Sosa	1.25	.35
21 Scott Rolen	.75	.23
22 Aramis Ramirez	.30	.09
23 Alfonso Soriano	.50	.15
24 Phil Nevin	.30	.09
25 Barry Bonds	2.00	.60
26 Joe Mays	.30	.09
27 Jeff Kent	.30	.09
28 Mark Quinn	.30	.09
29 Adrian Beltre	.50	.15
30 Freddy Garcia	.30	.09
31 Pedro Martinez	.75	.23
32 Darryl Kile	.30	.09
33 Mike Cameron	.30	.09
34 Frank Catalanotto	.30	.09
35 Jose Vidro	.30	.09
36 Jim Thome	.75	.23
37 Javy Lopez	.30	.09
38 Paul Konerko	.30	.09
39 Jeff Bagwell	.50	.15
40 Curt Schilling	.50	.15
41 Miguel Tejada	.30	.09
42 Jim Edmonds	.30	.09
43 Ellis Burks	.30	.09
44 Mark Grace	.50	.15
45 Robb Nen	.30	.09
46 Jeff Conine	.30	.09
47 Derek Jeter	2.00	.60
48 Mike Lowell	.30	.09
49 Javier Vazquez	.30	.09
50 Manny Ramirez	.50	.15
51 Bartolo Colon	.30	.09
52 Carlos Beltran	.50	.15
53 Tim Hudson	.30	.09
54 Rafael Palmeiro	.50	.15
55 Jimmy Rollins	.30	.09
56 Andruw Jones	.30	.09
57 Orlando Cabrera	.30	.09
58 Dean Palmer	.30	.09
59 Bret Boone	.30	.09
60 Carlos Febles	.30	.09
61 Ben Grieve	.30	.09
62 Richie Sexson	.30	.09
63 Alex Rodriguez	1.25	.35
64 Juan Pierre	.30	.09
65 Bobby Higginson	.30	.09
66 Barry Zito	.30	.09
67 Raul Mondesi	.30	.09
68 Albert Pujols	1.50	.45
69 Omar Vizquel	.50	.15
70 Bobby Abreu	.30	.09
71 Corey Koskie	.30	.09
72 Tom Glavine	.50	.15
73 Paul LoDuca	.30	.09
74 Terrence Long	.30	.09
75 Matt Morris	.30	.09
76 Andy Pettitte	.50	.15
77 Rich Aurilia	.30	.09
78 Todd Walker	.30	.09
79 John Olerud UER	.30	.09
Career Header stats are those for a pitcher		
80 Mike Sweeney	.30	.09
81 Ray Durham	.30	.09
82 Fernando Vina	.30	.09
83 Nomar Garciaparra	1.25	.35
84 Mariano Rivera	.50	.15
85 Mike Piazza	1.25	.35
86 Mark Buehrle	.30	.09
87 Adam Dunn	.50	.15
88 Luis Gonzalez	.30	.09
89 Richard Hidalgo	.30	.09
90 Brad Radke	.30	.09
91 Russ Ortiz	.30	.09
92 Brian Giles	.30	.09
93 Billy Wagner	.30	.09
94 Cliff Floyd	.30	.09
95 Eric Milton	.30	.09
96 Bud Smith	.30	.09
97 Wade Miller	.30	.09
98 Jon Lieber	.30	.09
99 Derrek Lee	.30	.09
100 Jose Cruz Jr.	.30	.09
101 Dmitri Young STAR	2.00	.60
102 Mo Vaughn STAR	2.00	.60
103 Tino Martinez STAR	3.00	.90
104 Larry Walker STAR	3.00	.90
105 Chuck Knoblauch STAR	2.00	.60
106 Troy Glaus STAR	2.00	.60
107 Jason Giambi STAR	2.00	.60
108 Travis Fryman STAR	2.00	.60
109 Josh Beckett STAR	2.00	.60
110 Edgar Martinez STAR	3.00	.90
111 Tim Salmon STAR	3.00	.90
112 C.C. Sabathia STAR	2.00	.60
113 Randy Johnson STAR	5.00	1.50
114 Juan Gonzalez STAR	3.00	.90
115 Carlos Delgado STAR	2.00	.60
116 Hideo Nomo STAR	5.00	1.50
117 Kerry Wood STAR	5.00	1.50
118 Brian Jordan STAR	2.00	.60
119 Carlos Pena STAR	2.00	.60
120 Roger Cedeno STAR	2.00	.60
121 Chan Ho Park STAR	2.00	.60
122 Rafael Furcal STAR	2.00	.60
123 Frank Thomas STAR	5.00	1.50
124 Mike Mussina STAR	3.00	.90
125 Rickey Henderson STAR	5.00	1.50
126 Sean Casey STAR	2.00	.60
127 Barry Larkin STAR	3.00	.90
128 Kazuhiro Sasaki STAR	2.00	.60
129 Moises Alou STAR	2.00	.60
130 Jeff Cirillo STAR	2.00	.60
131 Jason Kendall STAR	2.00	.60
132 Gary Sheffield STAR	2.00	.60
133 Ryan Klesko STAR	2.00	.60
134 Kevin Brown STAR	2.00	.60
135 Darin Erstad STAR	2.00	.60
136 Roberto Alomar STAR	3.00	.90
137 Brad Fullmer STAR	2.00	.60
138 Eric Chavez STAR	2.00	.60
139 Ben Sheets STAR	2.00	.60
140 Trot Nixon STAR	2.00	.60
141 Garret Anderson STAR	2.00	.60
142 Shawn Green STAR	2.00	.60
143 Troy Percival STAR	2.00	.60
144 Craig Biggio STAR	3.00	.90
145 Jorge Posada STAR	3.00	.90
146 J.D. Drew STAR	2.00	.60
147 Johnny Damon STAR	3.00	.90
148 Jeromy Burnitz STAR	2.00	.60
149 Robin Ventura STAR	2.00	.60
150 Aaron Sele STAR	2.00	.60
151 Cam Esslinger ROO RC	5.00	1.50
152 Ben Howard ROO RC	5.00	1.50
153 Brandon Backe ROO RC	8.00	2.40
154 Jorge De La Rosa ROO RC	5.00	1.50
155 Austin Kearns ROO	5.00	1.50
156 Carlos Zambrano ROO	5.00	1.50
157 Kyle Kane ROO RC	5.00	1.50
158 So Taguchi ROO RC	8.00	2.40
159 Brian Mallette ROO RC	5.00	1.50
160 Brett Jodie ROO	5.00	1.50
161 Elio Serrano ROO RC	5.00	1.50
162 Joe Thurston ROO	5.00	1.50
163 Kevin Olsen ROO	5.00	1.50
164 Rodrigo Rosario ROO RC	5.00	1.50
165 Matt Guerrier ROO	5.00	1.50
166 And. Machado ROO RC	5.00	1.50
167 Bert Snow ROO	5.00	1.50
168 Franklyn German ROO RC	5.00	1.50
169 Brandon Claussen ROO	5.00	1.50
170 Jason Romano ROO	5.00	1.50
171 Jorge Padilla ROO RC	5.00	1.50
172 Jose Cueto ROO	5.00	1.50
173 Allan Simpson ROO RC	5.00	1.50
174 Doug Devore ROO RC	5.00	1.50
175 Justin Duchscherer ROO	5.00	1.50
176 Josh Pearce ROO	5.00	1.50
177 Steve Bechler ROO RC	5.00	1.50
178 Josh Phelps ROO	5.00	1.50
179 Juan Diaz ROO	5.00	1.50
180 Victor Alvarez ROO RC	5.00	1.50
181 Ramon Vazquez ROO	5.00	1.50
182 Mike Rivera ROO	5.00	1.50
183 Kazuhisa Ishii ROO RC	10.00	3.00
184 Henry Mateo ROO	5.00	1.50
185 Travis Hughes ROO RC	5.00	1.50
186 Zach Day ROO	5.00	1.50
187 Brad Voyles ROO	5.00	1.50
188 Sean Douglass ROO	5.00	1.50
189 Nick Neugebauer ROO	5.00	1.50
190 Tom Shearn ROO RC	5.00	1.50
191 Eric Cyr ROO	5.00	1.50
192 Adam Johnson ROO	5.00	1.50
193 Michael Cuddyer ROO	5.00	1.50
194 Erik Bedard ROO	5.00	1.50
195 Mark Ellis ROO	5.00	1.50
196 Carlos Hernandez ROO	5.00	1.50
197 Deivis Santos ROO	5.00	1.50
198 Morgan Ensberg ROO	5.00	1.50
199 Ryan Jamison ROO	5.00	1.50
200 Cody Ransom ROO	5.00	1.50
201 Chris Snelling ROO RC	8.00	2.40
202 Satoru Komiyama ROO RC	8.00	2.40
203 Jas. Simontacchi ROO RC	8.00	2.40
204 Tim Kalita ROO RC	8.00	2.40
205 Run. Hernandez ROO RC	8.00	2.40
206 Kirk Saarloos ROO RC	8.00	2.40
207 Aaron Cook ROO RC	8.00	2.40
208 Luis Ugueto ROO RC	8.00	2.40
209 Gustavo Chacin ROO RC	3.00	.90
210 Francis Beltran ROO RC	8.00	2.40
211 Takahito Nomura ROO RC	8.00	2.40
212 Oliver Perez ROO RC	15.00	4.50
213 Miguel Asencio ROO RC	8.00	2.40
214 Rene Reyes ROO RC	8.00	2.40
215 Jeff Baker ROO RC	25.00	7.50
216 Jon Adkins ROO RC	8.00	2.40
217 Carlos Rivera ROO RC	8.00	2.40
218 Corey Thurman ROO RC	8.00	2.40
219 Earl Snyder ROO RC	10.00	3.00
220 Felix Escalona ROO RC	8.00	2.40
221 Jeremy Guthrie ROO RC	10.00	3.00
222 Josh Hancock ROO RC	8.00	2.40
223 Ben Kozlowski ROO RC	8.00	2.40
224 Eric Good ROO RC	8.00	2.40
225 Eric Junge ROO RC	8.00	2.40
226 Andy Pratt ROO RC	8.00	2.40
227 Matt Thornton ROO RC	8.00	2.40
228 Jorge Sosa ROO RC	8.00	2.40
229 Mike Smith ROO RC	8.00	2.40
230 Mitch Wylie ROO RC	8.00	2.40
231 John Ennis ROO RC	8.00	2.40
232 Reed Johnson ROO RC	10.00	3.00
233 Joe Borchard ROO	8.00	2.40
234 Ron Calloway ROO RC	8.00	2.40
235 Brian Tallet ROO RC	8.00	2.40
236 Chris Baker ROO RC	8.00	2.40
237 Cliff Lee ROO RC	15.00	4.50
238 Matt Childers ROO RC	8.00	2.40
239 Freddy Sanchez ROO RC	8.00	2.40
240 Chone Figgins ROO RC	10.00	3.00
241 Kevin Cash ROO RC	8.00	2.40
242 Josh Bard ROO RC	8.00	2.40
243 Jer. Robertson ROO RC	8.00	2.40
244 Jeremy Hill ROO RC	8.00	2.40
245 Shane Nance ROO RC	8.00	2.40
246 Wes Obermueller ROO RC	8.00	2.40
247 Trey Hodges ROO RC	8.00	2.40
248 Eric Eckenstahler ROO RC	8.00	2.40
249 Jim Rushford ROO RC	8.00	2.40
250 Jose Castillo ROO RC	15.00	4.50
251 Garrett Atkins ROO RC	10.00	3.00
252 Alexis Rios ROO RC	80.00	24.00
253 Ryan Church ROO RC	10.00	3.00
254 Jimmy Gobble ROO RC	10.00	3.00
255 Corwin Malone ROO RC	8.00	2.40
256 Does Not Exist		
257 Nic Jackson ROO RC	8.00	2.40
258 Tommy Whiteman ROO RC	10.00	3.00
259 Mario Ramos ROO RC	8.00	2.40
260 Rob Bowen ROO RC	8.00	2.40
261 Josh Wilson ROO RC	8.00	2.40
262 Tim Hummel ROO RC	8.00	2.40
263 Does Not Exist		
264 Gerald Laird ROO RC	15.00	4.50
265 Vinny Chulk ROO RC	8.00	2.40
266 Jesus Medrano ROO RC	8.00	2.40
267 Does Not Exist		
268 Does Not Exist		
269 Does Not Exist		
270 Does Not Exist		
271 Does Not Exist		
272 Adam LaRoche ROO RC	30.00	9.00
273 Adam Morrissey ROO RC	8.00	2.40
274 Henri Stanley ROO RC	8.00	2.40
275 Walter Young ROO RC	15.00	4.50

2002 Donruss Elite Aspirations

Randomly inserted into packs, this 200-card set is a parallel to the base set. The cards are standard-size and die-cut on holo-foil board with blue tint and blue foil stamping sequentially numbered to the featured player's jersey number. Due to market scarcity, cards with a print run of less than 25 are not priced.

	Nm-Mt	Ex-Mt
*1-100 PRINT RUN b/wn 26-35 8X TO 20X		
*1-100 PRINT RUN b/wn 36-50 6X TO 15X		
*1-100 PRINT RUN b/wn 51-65 5X TO 12X		
*1-100 PRINT RUN b/wn 66-80 5X TO 12X		
*101-150 PRINT RUN b/wn 26-35 1.25X TO 3X		
*101-150 PRINT RUN b/wn 36-50 1X TO 2.5X		
*101-150 PRINT RUN b/wn 51-65 .75X TO 2X		
UNLISTED 151-200 p/r 81-99	15.00	4.50
COMMON (151-200) p/r 66-80	8.00	2.40
SEMIS 151-200 p/r 66-80	12.00	3.60
UNLISTED 151-200 p/r 66-80	20.00	6.00
COMMON (151-200) p/r 51-65	10.00	3.00
SEMIS 151-200 p/r 51-65	15.00	4.50
UNLISTED 151-200 p/r 51-65	25.00	7.50
COMMON (151-200) p/r 36-50	12.00	3.60
SEMIS 151-200 p/r 36-50	20.00	6.00
UNLISTED 151-200 p/r 36-50	30.00	9.00
COMMON (151-200) p/r 26-35	15.00	4.50
SEMIS 151-200 p/r 26-35	25.00	7.50
UNLISTED 151-200 p/r 26-35	40.00	12.00

RANDOM INSERTS IN PACKS
SEE BECKETT.COM FOR PRINT RUNS
NO PRICING ON QUANTITIES OF 25 OR LESS

2002 Donruss Elite Status

Randomly inserted into packs, this 200-card set is a parallel to the base set. The cards are die-cut on holo-foil board with platinum tint and platinum foil stamping sequentially numbered to the remaining number out of 100 as reduced from the Donruss Elite Aspirations parallel (of which was serial numbered to the featured player's jersey number). We have listed the stated print run next to the player's name in our checklist. Cards with a stated print run of 25 or fewer are not printed due to market scarcity.

	Nm-Mt	Ex-Mt
*1-100 PRINT RUN b/wn 36-50 6X TO 15X		
*1-100 PRINT RUN b/wn 51-65 5X TO 12X		
*1-100 PRINT RUN b/wn 66-80 5X TO 12X		
*1-100 PRINT RUN b/wn 81-98 4X TO 10X		
*101-150 PRINT RUN b/wn 36-50 1X TO 2.5X		
*101-150 PRINT RUN b/wn 51-65 .75X TO 2X		
*101-150 PRINT RUN b/wn 66-80 .75X TO 2X		
*101-150 PRINT RUN b/wn 81-99 .6X TO 1.5X		
COMMON (151-200) p/r 81-99	6.00	1.80
SEMIS 151-200 p/r 81-99	10.00	3.00
UNLISTED 151-200 p/r 81-99	15.00	4.50
COMMON (151-200) p/r 66-80	8.00	2.40
SEMIS 151-200 p/r 66-80	12.00	3.60
UNLISTED 151-200 p/r 66-80	20.00	6.00
COMMON (151-200) p/r 51-65	10.00	3.00
SEMIS 151-200 p/r 51-65	15.00	4.50
UNLISTED 151-200 p/r 51-65	25.00	7.50
COMMON (151-200) p/r 36-50	12.00	3.60
SEMIS 151-200 p/r 36-50	20.00	6.00
UNLISTED 151-200 p/r 36-50	30.00	9.00
COMMON (151-200) p/r 26-35	15.00	4.50
SEMIS 151-200 p/r 26-35	25.00	7.50
UNLISTED 151-200 p/r 26-35	40.00	12.00

RANDOM INSERTS IN PACKS
SEE BECKETT.COM FOR PRINT RUNS
NO PRICING ON QUANTITIES OF 25 OR LESS

2002 Donruss Elite Turn of the Century

Randomly inserted in packs of Elite and Donruss the Rookies, these 71 cards partially parallel the prospect cards in 2002 Donruss Elite. Cards checklisted between 151-200 were distributed in Elite packs and 201-275 in Donruss the Rookies packs. The Turn of the Century parallels are easily identified from basic issue cards by their rounded corners. It's important to note that Turn of the Centruy cards were cumulatively serial-numbered, intermingling the basic Elite cards and the Turn of the Century Autograph cards. For example, card 201 Chris Snelling features serial numbering to 1000. The first 100 numbered copies were devoted to the Turn of the Century sets with Snelling signing cards "1 of 1000" through "50 of 1000". The last 900 numbered cards are his basic Elite Rookie Card. Some players signed all of their Turn of the Century cards and others signed none. We have notated the stated print run next to the player's name in our checklist and cards with a print run of less than 25 are not priced due to market scarcity.

	Nm-Mt	Ex-Mt
154 Jorge De La Rosa/50	8.00	2.40
156 Carlos Zambrano/50	8.00	2.40
157 Kyle Kane/50	8.00	2.40
158 So Taguchi/25		
159 Brian Mallette/50	8.00	2.40
160 Brett Jodie/50	8.00	2.40
165 Matt Guerrier/50	8.00	2.40
168 Franklyn German/50	8.00	2.40
169 Brandon Claussen/50	8.00	2.40
171 Jorge Padilla/50	8.00	2.40
172 Jose Cueto/50	8.00	2.40
176 Josh Pearce/50	8.00	2.40
177 Steve Bechler/50	8.00	2.40
178 Josh Phelps/50	8.00	2.40
180 Victor Alvarez/50	8.00	2.40
182 Michael Rivera/50	10.00	3.00
183 Kazuhisa Ishii/125	25.00	7.50
184 Henry Mateo/50	10.00	3.00
186 Zach Day/50	10.00	3.00
189 Nick Neugebauer/100	8.00	2.40
192 Adam Johnson/125	8.00	2.40
193 Michael Cuddyer/50	10.00	3.00
195 Mark Ellis/25		
196 Carlos Hernandez/150	8.00	2.40
198 Morgan Ensberg/50	10.00	3.00
200 Cody Ransom/150	8.00	2.40
201 Chris Snelling/50	10.00	3.00
202 Satoru Komiyama/75	10.00	3.00
203 Jason Simontacchi/75	10.00	3.00
204 Tim Kalita/100	8.00	2.40
205 Runelvys Hernandez/100	20.00	6.00
206 Kirk Saarloos/50	10.00	3.00
207 Aaron Cook/100	8.00	2.40
208 Luis Ugueto/75	10.00	3.00
209 Gustavo Chacin/75	15.00	4.50
210 Francis Beltran/75	10.00	3.00
211 Takahito Nomura/75	10.00	3.00
212 Oliver Perez/75	40.00	12.00
213 Miguel Asencio/75	10.00	3.00
214 Rene Reyes/75	10.00	3.00
218 Corey Thurman/75	10.00	3.00
219 Earl Snyder/75	15.00	4.50
220 Felix Escalona/75	10.00	3.00
222 Josh Hancock/100	8.00	2.40
225 Eric Junge/75	10.00	3.00
226 Andy Pratt/75	10.00	3.00
227 Matt Thornton/75	10.00	3.00
228 Jorge Sosa/100	8.00	2.40
229 Mike Smith/100	8.00	2.40
230 Mitch Wylie/100	8.00	2.40
231 John Ennis/75	10.00	3.00
232 Reed Johnson/75	15.00	4.50
233 Joe Borchard/75	10.00	3.00
234 Ron Calloway/100	8.00	2.40
235 Brian Tallet/75	10.00	3.00
236 Chris Baker/75	10.00	3.00
237 Cliff Lee/75	25.00	7.50
238 Matt Childers/75	10.00	3.00
239 Freddy Sanchez/100	8.00	2.40
242 Josh Bard/75	10.00	3.00
243 Jeriome Robertson/100	8.00	2.40
244 Jeremy Hill/100	8.00	2.40
245 Shane Nance/75	10.00	3.00
246 Wes Obermueller/100	8.00	2.40
248 Eric Eckenstahler/100	8.00	2.40
249 Jim Rushford/100	8.00	2.40
250 Jose Castillo/100	25.00	7.50
252 Alexis Rios/100	150.00	45.00
257 Nic Jackson/100	8.00	2.40
265 Vinny Chulk/100	8.00	2.40
275 Walter Young/100	25.00	7.50

2002 Donruss Elite Turn of the Century Autographs

Randomly inserted into packs of Elite and Donruss the Rookies, these 95 cards basically parallel the prospect cards in 2002 Donruss Elite. Cards 151-200 were distributed in Elite packs and cards 201-275 in Donruss the Rookies. These cards are all signed by the featured player and we have notated the stated print run information next to the player's name in our checklist. Please note, the cards are serial numbered cumulatively out of 1,500 for cards 151-200 and 1,000 for cards 201-275 - intermingling the basic issue Elite set, the Turn of the Century parallel die cuts and the Turn of the Century Autographs. Actual print runs for the autographs are listed below.

	Nm-Mt	Ex-Mt
151 Cam Esslinger/150	15.00	4.50
152 Ben Howard/150	15.00	4.50
153 Brandon Backe/150	40.00	12.00
154 Jorge De La Rosa/100	15.00	4.50
155 Austin Kearns/150	15.00	4.50
156 Carlos Zambrano/100	25.00	7.50
157 Kyle Kane/100	15.00	4.50
158 So Taguchi/125	25.00	7.50
159 Brian Mallette/100	15.00	4.50
160 Brett Jodie/100	15.00	4.50
161 Elio Serrano/150	15.00	4.50
162 Joe Thurston/150	15.00	4.50
163 Kevin Olsen/150	15.00	4.50
164 Rodrigo Rosario/150	15.00	4.50
165 Matt Guerrier/100	15.00	4.50
166 Anderson Machado/150	15.00	4.50
167 Bert Snow/150	15.00	4.50
168 Franklyn German/100	15.00	4.50
169 Brandon Claussen/100	15.00	4.50
170 Jason Romano/150	15.00	4.50
171 Jorge Padilla/100	15.00	4.50
172 Jose Cueto/100	15.00	4.50
173 Allan Simpson/150	15.00	4.50
174 Doug Devore/150	15.00	4.50
175 Justin Duchscherer/150	15.00	4.50
176 Josh Pearce/100	15.00	4.50
177 Steve Bechler/100	15.00	4.50
178 Josh Phelps/100	15.00	4.50
179 Juan Diaz/150	15.00	4.50
180 Victor Alvarez/100	15.00	4.50
181 Ramon Vazquez/150	15.00	4.50
182 Michael Rivera/100	15.00	4.50
183 Kazuhisa Ishii/25		
184 Henry Mateo/100	15.00	4.50
185 Travis Hughes/150	15.00	4.50
186 Zach Day/100	15.00	4.50
187 Brad Voyles/150	15.00	4.50
188 Sean Douglass/150	15.00	4.50
189 Nick Neugebauer/50	25.00	7.50
190 Tom Shearn/150	15.00	4.50
191 Eric Cyr/150	15.00	4.50
192 Adam Johnson/25		
193 Michael Cuddyer/100	15.00	4.50
194 Erik Bedard/150	15.00	4.50
195 Mark Ellis/125	15.00	4.50
197 Deivis Santos/150	15.00	4.50
198 Morgan Ensberg/100	15.00	4.50
199 Ryan Jamison/150	15.00	4.50
201 Chris Snelling/50	25.00	7.50
202 Satoru Komiyama/25		
204 Tim Kalita/25		
206 Kirk Saarloos/50	25.00	7.50
208 Luis Ugueto/25		
210 Francis Beltran/25		
211 Takahito Nomura/25		
212 Oliver Perez/25		
214 Rene Reyes/25		
215 Jeff Baker/100	80.00	24.00
216 Jon Adkins/100	15.00	4.50
217 Carlos Rivera/100	15.00	4.50
218 Corey Thurman/25		
219 Earl Snyder/25		
220 Felix Escalona/25		
221 Jeremy Guthrie/100	40.00	12.00
223 Ben Kozlowski/100	15.00	4.50
224 Eric Good/100	15.00	4.50
225 Eric Junge/25		
226 Andy Pratt/25		
227 Matt Thornton/25		
231 John Ennis/25		
232 Reed Johnson/25		
233 Joe Borchard/25		
235 Brian Tallet/25		
236 Chris Baker/25		
237 Cliff Lee/25		
238 Matt Childers/25		
240 Chone Figgins/100	40.00	12.00
241 Kevin Cash/100	15.00	4.50
242 Josh Bard/25		
245 Shane Nance/25		
247 Trey Hodges/100	15.00	4.50
251 Garrett Atkins/100	25.00	7.50
253 Ryan Church/100	50.00	15.00
254 Jimmy Gobble/100	40.00	12.00
255 Corwin Malone/100	15.00	4.50
258 Tommy Whiteman/100	25.00	7.50
259 Mario Ramos/100	15.00	4.50
260 Rob Bowen/100	15.00	4.50
261 Josh Wilson/100	15.00	4.50
262 Tim Hummel/100	15.00	4.50
264 Gerald Laird/100	40.00	12.00
266 Jesus Medrano/100	15.00	4.50
272 Adam LaRoche/100	60.00	18.00
273 Adam Morrissey/100	15.00	4.50
274 Henri Stanley/100	15.00	4.50

2002 Donruss Elite All-Star Salutes

Randomly inserted into packs, this 25-card insert set spotlights on the most heralded players. The fronts of the standard-size cards feature full color action shots set on metalized film board with foil and is sequentially numbered to the year the featured player shined in the All-Star Game.

	Nm-Mt	Ex-Mt
COMPLETE SET (25)	150.00	45.00
*CENTURY: 1.25X TO 3X BASIC AS SALUTE		
CENTURY PRINT RUN 100 SERIAL #'d SETS		
1 Ichiro Suzuki/2001	10.00	3.00
2 Tony Gwynn/2001	8.00	2.40
3 Magglio Ordonez/2001	4.00	1.20
4 Cal Ripken/2001	20.00	6.00
5 Roger Clemens/1998	12.00	3.60
6 Kazuhiro Sasaki/2001	4.00	1.20
7 Freddy Garcia/2001	4.00	1.20
8 Luis Gonzalez/2001	4.00	1.20
9 Lance Berkman/2001	4.00	1.20
10 Derek Jeter/2000	15.00	4.50
11 Chipper Jones/2000	6.00	1.80
12 Randy Johnson/2000	6.00	1.80
13 Andruw Jones/2000	4.00	1.20
14 Pedro Martinez/1999	6.00	1.80
15 Jim Thome/1999	6.00	1.80
16 Rafael Palmeiro/1999	4.00	1.20
17 Barry Larkin/1999	4.00	1.20
18 Ivan Rodriguez/1998	6.00	1.80
19 Omar Vizquel/1998	4.00	1.20
20 Edgar Martinez/1997	4.00	1.20
21 Larry Walker/1997	4.00	1.20
22 Javy Lopez/1997	4.00	1.20
23 Mariano Rivera/1997	4.00	1.20
24 Frank Thomas/1995	6.00	1.80
25 Greg Maddux/1994	10.00	3.00

2002 Donruss Elite Back 2 Back Jacks

Randomly inserted into pack, this 30-card insert set showcases both retired and present-day stars. The standard-size fronts are full color action shots that are featured with one or two swatches of game-used bats. Cards featuring one player have a stated print run of 150 sets while cards featuring two players have a stated print run of 75 sets.

	Nm-Mt	Ex-Mt
1 Ivan Rodriguez / Alex Rodriguez	40.00	12.00
2 Kirby Puckett / Dave Winfield	50.00	15.00
3 Ted Williams / Nomar Garciaparra	120.00	36.00
4 Jeff Bagwell / Craig Biggio	50.00	15.00
5 Eddie Murray / Cal Ripken	100.00	30.00
6 Andruw Jones / Chipper Jones	50.00	15.00
7 Roberto Clemente / Willie Stargell	120.00	36.00
8 Lou Gehrig / Don Mattingly	200.00	60.00
9 Larry Walker / Todd Helton	50.00	15.00
10 Manny Ramirez / Trot Nixon	50.00	15.00
11 Ivan Rodriguez	25.00	7.50
12 Alex Rodriguez	25.00	7.50
13 Kirby Puckett	40.00	12.00
14 Dave Winfield	25.00	7.50
15 Ted Williams	100.00	30.00
16 Nomar Garciaparra	25.00	7.50
17 Jeff Bagwell	25.00	7.50
18 Craig Biggio	25.00	7.50
19 Eddie Murray	40.00	12.00
20 Cal Ripken	50.00	15.00
21 Andruw Jones	15.00	4.50
22 Chipper Jones	25.00	7.50
23 Roberto Clemente	100.00	30.00
24 Willie Stargell	25.00	7.50
25 Lou Gehrig	150.00	45.00
26 Don Mattingly	40.00	12.00
27 Larry Walker	25.00	7.50
28 Todd Helton	25.00	7.50
29 Manny Ramirez	25.00	7.50
30 Trot Nixon	15.00	4.50

2002 Donruss Elite Back to the Future

Randomly inserted into packs, this 22-card insert set matches both current and future stars on the fronts and backs respectively. The standard-size card fronts/backs feature full color action shots on metalized film board. 500 serial-numbered copies of each dual-player card were produced and 1000 serial-numbered copies of each single-player card were produced. Card number 6 was originally intended to feature Cardinals rookie So Taguchi paired up with Jim Edmonds and card number 20 was to feature Taguchi by himself, but both cards were pulled from the set before production was finalized, thus this set is complete at 22 cards. Cards featuring one player had a stated print run of 1000 sets and cards featuring two players had a stated print run of 500 sets.

	Nm-Mt	Ex-Mt
1 Scott Rolen / Marlon Byrd	6.00	1.80
2 Joe Crede / Frank Thomas	6.00	1.80
3 Lance Berkman / Jeff Bagwell	6.00	1.80
4 Marcus Giles / Chipper Jones	6.00	1.80
5 Shawn Green / Paul LoDuca	5.00	1.50
7 Kerry Wood / Juan Cruz	6.00	1.80
8 Vladimir Guerrero / Orlando Cabrera	6.00	1.80
9 Scott Rolen	5.00	1.50
10 Marlon Byrd	4.00	1.20
11 Frank Thomas	5.00	1.50
12 Joe Crede	4.00	1.20
13 Jeff Bagwell	4.00	1.20
14 Lance Berkman	4.00	1.20
15 Chipper Jones	5.00	1.50
16 Marcus Giles	4.00	1.20
17 Shawn Green	4.00	1.20
18 Paul LoDuca	4.00	1.20
19 Jim Edmonds	4.00	1.20
21 Kerry Wood	5.00	1.50
22 Juan Cruz	4.00	1.20
23 Vladimir Guerrero	5.00	1.50
24 Orlando Cabrera	4.00	1.20

2002 Donruss Elite Back to the Future Threads

Randomly inserted into packs, this 24-card insert set is a parallel to Donruss Elite Back to the Future. It matches both current and future stars on the fronts and backs respectively. The standard-size card fronts/backs feature full color action shots on metalized film board. The fronts differ by offering one or two swatches of game-worn jerseys. Autograph exchange cards for the Edmonds/Taguchi dual card and So Taguchi's stand alone card were seeded into packs. Please note that only Taguchi was contracted to sign the Edmonds/Taguchi combo card. Both cards had a redemption deadline of October 10th, 2003. Cards featuring one player had a stated print run of 100 sets and cards featuring two players have a stated print run of 50 sets.

	Nm-Mt	Ex-Mt
1 Scott Rolen Jsy / Marlon Byrd Jsy	40.00	12.00
2 Frank Thomas Jsy / Joe Crede Hat	40.00	12.00
3 Jeff Bagwell Jsy / Lance Berkman Jsy	40.00	12.00
4 Chipper Jones Jsy / Marcus Giles Jsy	40.00	12.00
5 Shawn Green Jsy / Paul LoDuca Jsy	25.00	7.50
6 So Taguchi Jsy AU / Jim Edmonds Jsy	50.00	15.00
7 Kerry Wood Jsy / Juan Cruz Jsy	40.00	12.00
8 Vladimir Guerrero Jsy / Orlando Cabrera Jsy	40.00	12.00
9 Scott Rolen	40.00	12.00
10 Marlon Byrd	15.00	4.50
11 Frank Thomas	40.00	12.00
12 Joe Crede Shoes	15.00	4.50
13 Jeff Bagwell	25.00	7.50
14 Lance Berkman	15.00	4.50
15 Chipper Jones	40.00	12.00
16 Marcus Giles	15.00	4.50
17 Shawn Green	15.00	4.50
18 Paul LoDuca	15.00	4.50
19 Jim Edmonds	15.00	4.50
20 So Taguchi AU	40.00	12.00
21 Kerry Wood	40.00	12.00
22 Juan Cruz	15.00	4.50
23 Vladimir Guerrero	40.00	12.00
24 Orlando Cabrera	15.00	4.50

2002 Donruss Elite Career Best

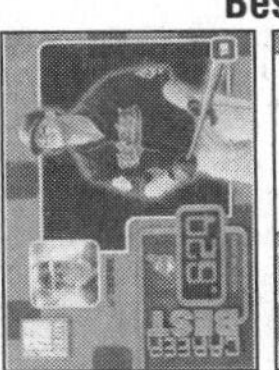

Randomly inserted into packs, this 40-card insert set spotlights on players who established career statistical highs in 2001. Each card is serial numbered to a specific statistical achievement and the cards were randomly seeded into packs. The standard-size card fronts feature color action shots on metalized film board with silver holo-foil stamping. Cards with a stated print run of less than 25 copies are not priced due to market scarcity.

	Nm-Mt	Ex-Mt
1 Albert Pujols OPS/1013	12.00	3.60
2 Alex Rodriguez HR/52	25.00	7.50
3 Alex Rodriguez RBI/135	20.00	6.00
4 Andruw Jones RBI/104	8.00	2.40
5 Barry Bonds HR/73	40.00	12.00
6 Barry Bonds OPS/1379	15.00	4.50
7 Barry Bonds BB/177	30.00	9.00
8 C.C. Sabathia K/171	8.00	2.40
9 Carlos Beltran OPS/876	4.00	1.20
10 Chipper Jones BA/330	8.00	2.40
11 Derek Jeter SB/900	15.00	4.50
12 Eric Chavez RBI/114	8.00	2.40
13 Frank Catalanotto BA/330	5.00	1.50
14 Ichiro Suzuki OPS/838	10.00	3.00
15 Ichiro Suzuki RUN/127	20.00	6.00
16 Ichiro Suzuki 3B/8		
17 J.D. Drew HR/27	30.00	9.00
18 J.D. Drew OPS/1027	4.00	1.20
19 Jason Giambi SLG/660	4.00	1.20
20 Jim Thome HR/49	50.00	15.00
21 Jim Thome SLG/624	6.00	1.80
22 Jorge Posada RBI/95	15.00	4.50
23 Jose Cruz Jr. SLG/856	4.00	1.20
24 Kazuhiro Sasaki SV/45	30.00	9.00
25 Kerry Wood ERA/336	8.00	2.40
26 Lance Berkman OPS/1050	4.00	1.20
27 Magglio Ordonez OB/382	5.00	1.50
28 Mark Mulder ERA/345	5.00	1.50
29 Pat Burrell HR/27	30.00	9.00
30 Pat Burrell SLG/469	5.00	1.50
31 Randy Johnson K/372	8.00	2.40
32 Randy Johnson WIN/21		
33 Richie Sexson SLG/547	4.00	1.20
34 Roberto Alomar OPS/956	4.00	1.20
35 Sammy Sosa RBI/160	20.00	6.00
36 Sammy Sosa OPS/1174	10.00	3.00
37 Shawn Green RBI/125	8.00	2.40
38 Tsuyoshi Shinjo RUN/10		
39 Trot Nixon HIT/150	8.00	2.40
40 Troy Glaus RBI/108	8.00	2.40

2002 Donruss Elite Passing the Torch

Randomly inserted into packs, this 24-card insert set presents baseball legends and rising stars on double-sided holo-foil board. The front/back of these standard-size cards feature color photos of the players. 500 serial-numbered copies of each dual-player card were produced. 1000 serial-numbered copies of single player card were produced.

	Nm-Mt	Ex-Mt
COMPLETE SET (24)	250.00	75.00
1 Fergie Jenkins / Mark Prior	10.00	3.00
2 Nolan Ryan / Roy Oswalt	30.00	9.00
3 Ozzie Smith / J.D. Drew	15.00	4.50
4 George Brett / Carlos Beltran	25.00	7.50
5 Kirby Puckett / Michael Cuddyer	10.00	3.00
6 Johnny Bench / Adam Dunn	10.00	3.00
7 Duke Snider / Paul LoDuca	10.00	3.00
8 Tony Gwynn / Xavier Nady	15.00	4.50
9 Fergie Jenkins	5.00	1.50
10 Mark Prior	10.00	3.00
11 Nolan Ryan	20.00	6.00
12 Roy Oswalt	5.00	1.50
13 Ozzie Smith	12.00	3.60
14 J.D. Drew	5.00	1.50
15 George Brett	20.00	6.00
16 Carlos Beltran	5.00	1.50
17 Kirby Puckett	8.00	2.40
18 Michael Cuddyer	5.00	1.50
19 Johnny Bench	8.00	2.40
20 Adam Dunn	5.00	1.50
21 Duke Snider	5.00	1.50
22 Paul LoDuca	5.00	1.50
23 Tony Gwynn	10.00	3.00
24 Xavier Nady	5.00	1.50

2002 Donruss Elite Passing the Torch Autographs

Randomly inserted into packs, this 24-card autograph set is a parallel to the Donruss Elite Passing the Torch insert set. It presents baseball legends and rising stars on double-sided holo-foil board. The front/back of these standard-size cards also feature color photos of the players, but differ by using color highlight overlays. We have notated the stated print runs next to the player's name in our checklist.

	Nm-Mt	Ex-Mt
1 Fergie Jenkins / Mark Prior/50	120.00	36.00
2 Nolan Ryan / Roy Oswalt/50	200.00	60.00
3 Ozzie Smith / J.D. Drew/50	150.00	45.00
4 George Brett / Carlos Beltran/25		
5 Kirby Puckett / Michael Cuddyer/50	120.00	36.00
6 Johnny Bench / Adam Dunn/50	120.00	36.00
7 Duke Snider / Paul LoDuca/50	120.00	36.00
8 Tony Gwynn / Xavier Nady/50	120.00	36.00
9 Fergie Jenkins/50	50.00	15.00
10 Mark Prior/100	100.00	30.00
11 Nolan Ryan/100	150.00	45.00
12 Roy Oswalt/100	25.00	7.50
13 Ozzie Smith/25		
14 J.D. Drew/100	40.00	12.00
15 George Brett/25		
16 Carlos Beltran/100	60.00	18.00
17 Kirby Puckett/25		
18 Michael Cuddyer/100	25.00	7.50
19 Johnny Bench/100	60.00	18.00
20 Adam Dunn/50	60.00	18.00
21 Duke Snider/100	40.00	12.00
22 Paul LoDuca/100	25.00	7.50
23 Tony Gwynn/100	80.00	24.00
24 Xavier Nady/100	25.00	7.50

2002 Donruss Elite Recollection Autographs

Randomly inserted into packs, these 23 cards featured signed copies of the player's 2001 Donruss Elite card. We have notated the stated print run next to the player's name and cards with a stated print run of 25 or less are not priced due to market scarcity.

	Nm-Mt	Ex-Mt
1 Jeremy Affeldt 01/25		
2 Alfredo Amezaga 01/50	20.00	6.00
3 Angel Berroa 01/25		
4 Dewon Brazelton 01/25		
5 John Buck 01/25		
6 Marlon Byrd 01/25		
7 Juan Cruz 01/25		
8 Brandon Duckworth 01/10		
9 Brandon Duckworth 01/15		
10 Casey Fossum 01/25		
11 Luis Garcia 01/25		
12 Tony Gwynn 01/10		
13 Bill Hall 01/25		
14 Orlando Hudson 01/50	20.00	6.00
15 Ryan Klesko 01/5		
16 Jason Lane 01/24		
17 Corky Miller 01/25		
18 Roy Oswalt 01/25		
19 Antonio Perez 01/50	20.00	6.00
20 Mark Prior 01/25		
21 Mike Rivera 01/50	20.00	6.00
22 Mark Teixeira 01/25		
23 Claudio Vargas 01/50	20.00	6.00
24 Martin Vargas 01/50	20.00	6.00

2002 Donruss Elite Throwback Threads

Randomly inserted into packs, this 64-card insert set offers standard-size cards that display one or two swatches of game-used jerseys from retired legends or current stars. The card front/back features a white border background with color action shots. Card number 28 (intended to be a Rickey Henderson Red Sox card) does not exist in unsigned form. The legendary speedster signed all 100 copies produced and this card can be referenced in the Throwback Threads Autographs parallel set. Cards featuring one player have a stated print run of 100 sets while cards featuring two players have a stated print run of 50 sets.

	Nm-Mt	Ex-Mt
1 Ted Williams / Manny Ramirez	100.00	30.00
2 Carlton Fisk / Mike Piazza	40.00	12.00
3 Bo Jackson / George Brett	80.00	24.00
4 Curt Schilling / Randy Johnson	50.00	15.00
5 Don Mattingly / Lou Gehrig	300.00	90.00
6 Bernie Williams / Dave Winfield	50.00	15.00
7 Rickey Henderson / Ricky Henderson	50.00	15.00
8 Robin Yount / Paul Molitor	60.00	18.00
9 Stan Musial / J.D. Drew	80.00	24.00
10 Andre Dawson / Ryne Sandberg	60.00	18.00
11 Babe Ruth / Reggie Jackson	400.00	120.00
12 Brooks Robinson / Cal Ripken	100.00	30.00
13 Ted Williams / Nomar Garciaparra	100.00	30.00
14 Jackie Robinson / Shawn Green	80.00	24.00
15 Cal Ripken / Tony Gwynn	100.00	30.00
16 Ted Williams	80.00	24.00
17 Manny Ramirez	25.00	7.50
18 Carlton Fisk Red Sox	40.00	12.00
19 Mike Piazza	25.00	7.50
20 Bo Jackson	40.00	12.00
21 George Brett	40.00	12.00
22 Curt Schilling	15.00	4.50
23 Randy Johnson	25.00	7.50
24 Don Mattingly	40.00	12.00
25 Lou Gehrig	250.00	75.00
26 Bernie Williams	25.00	7.50
27 Dave Winfield	25.00	7.50
29 Rickey Henderson Mariners	25.00	7.50
30 Robin Yount	40.00	12.00
31 Paul Molitor	40.00	12.00
32 Stan Musial	60.00	18.00
33 J.D. Drew	15.00	4.50
34 Andre Dawson	25.00	7.50
35 Ryne Sandberg	50.00	15.00
36 Babe Ruth	300.00	90.00
37 Reggie Jackson	40.00	12.00
38 Brooks Robinson	40.00	12.00
39 Cal Ripken Running	80.00	24.00
40 Nomar Garciaparra		
41 Jackie Robinson	80.00	24.00
42 Shawn Green	15.00	4.50
43 Pedro Martinez Grey	25.00	7.50
44 Nolan Ryan Astros	60.00	18.00
45 Kazuhiro Sasaki	15.00	4.50
46 Tony Gwynn	40.00	12.00
47 Carlton Fisk White Sox	40.00	12.00
48 Cal Ripken Batting	80.00	24.00
49 Rod Carew Angels	40.00	12.00
50 Nolan Ryan Rangers	60.00	18.00
51 Alex Rodriguez	25.00	7.50
52 Greg Maddux	25.00	7.50
53 Pedro Martinez White	25.00	7.50
54 Rickey Henderson Padres	25.00	7.50
55 Rod Carew Twins	40.00	12.00
56 Roberto Clemente	100.00	30.00
57 Hideo Nomo	25.00	7.50
58 Rickey Henderson Mets	25.00	7.50
59 Dave Parker	25.00	7.50
60 Eddie Mathews	40.00	12.00
61 Eddie Murray	40.00	12.00
62 Nolan Ryan Angels	60.00	18.00
63 Tom Seaver	40.00	12.00
64 Roger Clemens	40.00	12.00
65 Rickey Henderson A's	25.00	7.50

2002 Donruss Elite Throwback Threads Autographs

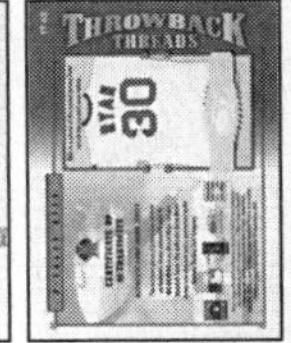

Randomly inserted in packs, these cards partially parallel the Throwback Threads insert set. Other than the Rickey Henderson card, all these cards have stated print runs of 25 or less and we have notated that information in our checklist. Also, due to market scarcity, no pricing is provided for these cards.

	Nm-Mt	Ex-Mt
17 Manny Ramirez/10		
18 Carlton Fisk Red Sox/15		
20 Bo Jackson/10		
21 George Brett/5		
22 Curt Schilling/10		
24 Don Mattingly/20		
26 Bernie Williams/5		
27 Dave Winfield/10		
28 R.Henderson/100	200.00	60.00
30 Robin Yount/10		
31 Paul Molitor/15		
32 Stan Musial/10		
33 J.D. Drew/25		
34 Andre Dawson/15		
35 Ryne Sandberg/20		
37 Reggie Jackson/10		
43 Pedro Martinez/10		
44 Nolan Ryan Astros/10		
46 Tony Gwynn/10		
47 Carlton Fisk White Sox/10		
49 Rod Carew Angels/10		
50 Nolan Ryan Rangers/10		
51 Alex Rodriguez/10		
52 Greg Maddux/10		
55 Rod Carew Twins/10		
59 Dave Parker/25		
61 Eddie Murray/10		
62 Nolan Ryan Angels/10		
63 Tom Seaver/15		

2003 Donruss Elite

This 200 card set was released in June, 2003. The first 180 cards consist of veterans while the final 20 cards are either rookies or leading prospects. This product was issued in five card packs which came 20 packs to a box and 20 boxes to a case with an $5 SRP. The final 20 cards consists of rookies and leading prospects, which were randomly inserted into packs and printed to a stated print run of 1750 serial numbered sets.

	Nm-Mt	Ex-Mt
COMP.SET w/o SP's (180)	20.00	6.00
COMMON CARD (1-180)	.30	.09
COMMON CARD (181-200)	4.00	1.20
1 Darin Erstad	.30	.09
2 David Eckstein	.30	.09
3 Garret Anderson	.30	.09
4 Jarrod Washburn	.30	.09
5 Tim Salmon	.50	.15
6 Troy Glaus	.30	.09
7 Marty Cordova	.30	.09
8 Melvin Mora	.30	.09
9 Rodrigo Lopez	.30	.09
10 Tony Batista	.30	.09
11 Derek Lowe	.30	.09
12 Johnny Damon	.75	.23
13 Manny Ramirez	.50	.15
14 Nomar Garciaparra	1.25	.35
15 Pedro Martinez	.75	.23
16 Shea Hillenbrand	.30	.09
17 Carlos Lee	.30	.09
18 Joe Crede	.30	.09
19 Frank Thomas	.75	.23
20 Magglio Ordonez	.30	.09
21 Mark Buehrle	.30	.09
22 Paul Konerko	.30	.09
23 C.C. Sabathia	.30	.09
24 Ellis Burks	.30	.09
25 Omar Vizquel	.50	.15

26 Brian Tallet .30 .09
27 Bobby Higginson .30 .09
28 Carlos Pena .30 .09
29 Mark Redman .30 .09
30 Steve Sparks .30 .09
31 Carlos Beltran .50 .15
32 Joe Randa .30 .09
33 Mike Sweeney .30 .09
34 Raul Ibanez .30 .09
35 Runelvys Hernandez .30 .09
36 Brad Radke .30 .09
37 Corey Koskie .30 .09
38 Cristian Guzman .30 .09
39 David Ortiz .50 .15
40 Doug Mientkiewicz .30 .09
41 Jacque Jones .30 .09
42 Torii Hunter .30 .09
43 Alfonso Soriano .50 .15
44 Andy Pettitte .50 .15
45 Bernie Williams .50 .15
46 David Wells .30 .09
47 Derek Jeter 2.00 .60
48 Jason Giambi .50 .15
49 Jeff Weaver .30 .09
50 Jorge Posada .50 .15
51 Mike Mussina .50 .15
52 Roger Clemens 1.50 .45
53 Barry Zito .30 .09
54 Eric Chavez .30 .09
55 Jermaine Dye .30 .09
56 Mark Mulder .30 .09
57 Miguel Tejada .30 .09
58 Tim Hudson .30 .09
59 Bret Boone .30 .09
60 Chris Snelling .30 .09
61 Edgar Martinez .50 .15
62 Freddy Garcia .30 .09
63 Ichiro Suzuki 1.25 .35
64 Jamie Moyer .30 .09
65 John Olerud .30 .09
66 Kazuhiro Sasaki .30 .09
67 Aubrey Huff .30 .09
68 Joe Kennedy .30 .09
69 Paul Wilson .30 .09
70 Alex Rodriguez 1.25 .35
71 Chan Ho Park .30 .09
72 Hank Blalock .50 .15
73 Juan Gonzalez .50 .15
74 Kevin Mench .30 .09
75 Rafael Palmeiro .50 .15
76 Carlos Delgado .30 .09
77 Eric Hinske .30 .09
78 Josh Phelps .30 .09
79 Roy Halladay .30 .09
80 Shannon Stewart .30 .09
81 Vernon Wells .30 .09
82 Curt Schilling .30 .09
83 Junior Spivey .30 .09
84 Luis Gonzalez .30 .09
85 Mark Grace .50 .15
86 Randy Johnson .75 .23
87 Steve Finley .30 .09
88 Andruw Jones .30 .09
89 Chipper Jones .75 .23
90 Gary Sheffield .30 .09
91 Greg Maddux 1.25 .35
92 John Smoltz .50 .15
93 Corey Patterson .50 .15
94 Kerry Wood .75 .23
95 Mark Prior .75 .23
96 Moises Alou .30 .09
97 Sammy Sosa 1.25 .35
98 Adam Dunn .50 .15
99 Austin Kearns .30 .09
100 Barry Larkin .50 .15
101 Ken Griffey Jr. 1.25 .35
102 Sean Casey .30 .09
103 Jason Jennings .30 .09
104 Jay Payton .30 .09
105 Larry Walker .50 .15
106 Todd Helton .50 .15
107 A.J. Burnett .30 .09
108 Josh Beckett .30 .09
109 Juan Encarnacion .30 .09
110 Mike Lowell .30 .09
111 Craig Biggio .50 .15
112 Daryle Ward .30 .09
113 Jeff Bagwell .50 .15
114 Lance Berkman .30 .09
115 Roy Oswalt .30 .09
116 Jason Lane .30 .09
117 Adrian Beltre .50 .15
118 Hideo Nomo .75 .23
119 Kazuhisa Ishii .30 .09
120 Kevin Brown .30 .09
121 Odalis Perez .30 .09
122 Paul Lo Duca .30 .09
123 Shawn Green .30 .09
124 Ben Sheets .30 .09
125 Jeffrey Hammonds .30 .09
126 Jose Hernandez .30 .09
127 Richie Sexson .30 .09
128 Bartolo Colon .30 .09
129 Brad Wilkerson .30 .09
130 Javier Vazquez .30 .09
131 Jose Vidro .30 .09
132 Michael Barrett .30 .09
133 Vladimir Guerrero .75 .23
134 Al Leiter .30 .09
135 Mike Piazza 1.25 .35
136 Mo Vaughn .30 .09
137 Pedro Astacio .30 .09
138 Roberto Alomar .50 .15
139 Pat Burrell .30 .09
140 Vicente Padilla .30 .09
141 Jimmy Rollins .30 .09
142 Bobby Abreu .30 .09
143 Marlon Byrd .30 .09
144 Brian Giles .30 .09
145 Jason Kendall .30 .09
146 Aramis Ramirez .30 .09
147 Josh Fogg .30 .09
148 Ryan Klesko .30 .09
149 Phil Nevin .30 .09
150 Sean Burroughs .30 .09
151 Mark Kotsay .30 .09
152 Barry Bonds 2.00 .60
153 Damian Moss .30 .09
154 Jason Schmidt .30 .09
155 Benito Santiago .30 .09
156 Rich Aurilia .30 .09
157 Scott Rolen .75 .23
158 J.D. Drew .30 .09
159 Jim Edmonds .30 .09
160 Matt Morris .30 .09
161 Tino Martinez .50 .15
162 Albert Pujols 1.50 .45
163 Russ Ortiz .30 .09
164 Rey Ordonez .30 .09
165 Paul Byrd .30 .09
166 Kenny Lofton .30 .09
167 Kenny Rogers .30 .09
168 Rickey Henderson .75 .23
169 Fred McGriff .50 .15
170 Charles Johnson .30 .09
171 Mike Hampton .30 .09
172 Jim Thome .75 .23
173 Travis Hafner .30 .09
174 Ivan Rodriguez .75 .23
175 Ray Durham .30 .09
176 Jeremy Giambi .30 .09
177 Jeff Kent .30 .09
178 Cliff Floyd .30 .09
179 Kevin Millwood .30 .09
180 Tom Glavine .50 .15
181 Hideki Matsui ROO RC 10.00 3.00
182 Jose Contreras ROO RC 5.00 1.50
183 Terrmel Sledge ROO RC 5.00 1.50
184 Lew Ford ROO RC 5.00 1.50
185 Jhonny Peralta ROO 4.00 1.20
186 Alexis Rios ROO 5.00 1.50
187 Jeff Baker ROO 4.00 1.20
188 Jeremy Guthrie ROO 4.00 1.20
189 Jose Castillo ROO 4.00 1.20
190 Garrett Atkins ROO 4.00 1.20
191 Jer. Bonderman ROO RC 5.00 1.50
192 Adam LaRoche ROO 4.00 1.20
193 Vinny Chulk ROO 4.00 1.20
194 Walter Young ROO 4.00 1.20
195 Jimmy Gobble ROO 4.00 1.20
196 Prentice Redman ROO RC 4.00 1.20
197 Jason Anderson ROO 4.00 1.20
198 Nic Jackson ROO 4.00 1.20
199 Travis Chapman ROO 4.00 1.20
200 Shane Victorino ROO RC 4.00 1.20

2003 Donruss Elite Aspirations

Nm-Mt Ex-Mt
*1-180 PRINT RUN b/wn 36-50 6X TO 15X
*1-180 PRINT RUN b/wn 51-65: 5X TO 12X
*1-180 PRINT RUN b/wn 66-80 5X TO 12X
*1-180 PRINT RUN b/wn 81-99 4X TO 10X
COMMON (181-200) p/r 81-99 6.00 1.80
SEMIS 181-200 p/r 81-99 10.00 3.00
COMMON (181-200) p/r 51-65 10.00 3.00
SEMIS 181-200 p/r 51-65 15.00 4.50
COMMON (181-200) p/r 36-50 10.00 3.00
COMMON (181-200) p/r 26-35 12.00 3.60
SEMIS 181-200 p/r 26-35 20.00 6.00
RANDOM INSERTS IN PACKS
SEE BECKETT.COM FOR PRINT RUNS
NO PRICING ON QTY OF 25 OR LESS

2003 Donruss Elite Aspirations Gold

Nm-Mt Ex-Mt
RANDOM INSERTS IN PACKS
STATED PRINT RUN 1 SERIAL #'d SET
NO PRICING DUE TO SCARCITY

2003 Donruss Elite Status

Nm-Mt Ex-Mt
*1-180 PRINT RUN b/wn 26-35: 8X TO 20X
*1-180 PRINT RUN b/wn 36-50: 6X TO 15X
*1-180 PRINT RUN b/wn 51-65: 5X TO 12X
*1-180 PRINT RUN b/wn 66-80: 5X TO 12X
*1-180 PRINT RUN b/wn 81-99: 4X TO 10X
COMMON (181-200) p/r 66-80 8.00 2.40
COMMON (181-200) p/r 51-65 10.00 3.00
COMMON (181-200) p/r 36-50 10.00 3.00
RANDOM INSERTS IN PACKS
NO PRICING ON QTY OF 25 OR LESS

2003 Donruss Elite Status Gold

Nm-Mt Ex-Mt
RANDOM INSERTS IN PACKS
STATED PRINT RUN 24 SERIAL #'d SETS
NO PRICING DUE TO SCARCITY

2003 Donruss Elite Turn of the Century Autographs

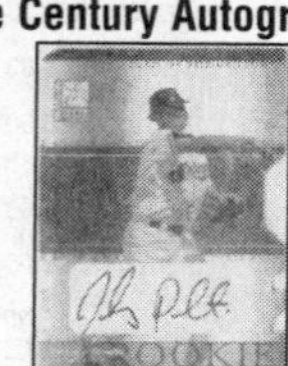

Randomly inserted into packs, this is a partial parallel to the Donruss Elite set and features just the rookie cards with the exception of Hideki Matsui who was under an exclusive contract to Upper Deck. These cards are signed by the player and were issued to a stated print run of 50 serial numbered sets.

Nm-Mt Ex-Mt
182 Jose Contreras ROO 40.00 12.00
183 Terrmel Sledge ROO 25.00 7.50
184 Lew Ford ROO 50.00 15.00
185 Jhonny Peralta ROO 15.00 4.50
186 Alexis Rios ROO 40.00 12.00
187 Jeff Baker ROO 15.00 4.50
188 Jeremy Guthrie ROO 15.00 4.50
189 Jose Castillo ROO 15.00 4.50
190 Garrett Atkins ROO 15.00 4.50
191 Jeremy Bonderman ROO 40.00 12.00
192 Adam LaRoche ROO 15.00 4.50
193 Vinny Chulk ROO 15.00 4.50
194 Walter Young ROO 15.00 4.50
195 Jimmy Gobble ROO 15.00 4.50
196 Prentice Redman ROO 15.00 4.50
197 Jason Anderson ROO 15.00 4.50
198 Nic Jackson ROO 15.00 4.50
199 Travis Chapman ROO 15.00 4.50
200 Shane Victorino ROO 15.00 4.50

2003 Donruss Elite All-Time Career Best

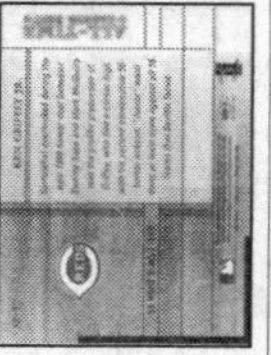

Nm-Mt Ex-Mt
STATED ODDS 1:9
*PARALLEL 1-25 p/r 211-239: 1X TO 2.5X
*PARALLEL 1-25 p/r 105-140: 1.25X TO 3X
*PARALLEL 1-25 p/r 53-60: 2X TO 5X
*PARALLEL 1-25 p/r 39-49: 2.5X TO 6X
*PARALLEL 1-25 p/r 29-31: 3X TO 8X
*PARALLEL 26-50 p/r 393: .6X TO 1.5X
*PARALLEL 26-50 p/r 130-137: 1X TO 2.5X
*PARALLEL 26-50 p/r 55-66: 1.5X TO 4X
*PARALLEL 26-50 p/r 37-49: 2X TO 5X
*PARALLEL 26-50 p/r 35: 2.5X TO 6X
PARALLEL RANDOM INSERTS IN PACKS
PARALLEL PRINTS B/WN 1-393 COPIES PER
NO PARALLEL PRICING ON QTY OF 25 OR LESS
1 Babe Ruth 12.00 3.60
2 Ty Cobb 8.00 2.40
3 Jackie Robinson 4.00 1.20
4 Lou Gehrig 8.00 2.40
5 Thurman Munson 4.00 1.20
6 Nolan Ryan 12.00 3.60
7 Mike Schmidt 8.00 2.40
8 Don Mattingly 10.00 3.00
9 Yogi Berra 4.00 1.20
10 Rod Carew 3.00 .90
11 Reggie Jackson 4.00 1.20
12 Al Kaline 4.00 1.20
13 Harmon Killebrew 4.00 1.20
14 Eddie Mathews 4.00 1.20
15 Stan Musial 6.00 1.80
16 Jim Palmer 3.00 .90
17 Phil Rizzuto 3.00 .90
18 Brooks Robinson 3.00 .90
19 Tom Seaver 3.00 .90
20 Robin Yount 6.00 1.80
21 Carlton Fisk 3.00 .90
22 Dale Murphy 4.00 1.20
23 Cal Ripken 12.00 3.60
24 Tony Gwynn 5.00 1.50
25 Andre Dawson 3.00 .90
26 Derek Jeter 10.00 3.00
27 Ken Griffey Jr. 6.00 1.80
28 Albert Pujols 8.00 2.40
29 Sammy Sosa 6.00 1.80
30 Jason Giambi 3.00 .90
31 Randy Johnson 4.00 1.20
32 Greg Maddux 6.00 1.80
33 Rickey Henderson 4.00 1.20
34 Pedro Martinez 4.00 1.20
35 Jeff Bagwell 3.00 .90
36 Alex Rodriguez 6.00 1.80
37 Vladimir Guerrero 4.00 1.20
38 Chipper Jones 4.00 1.20
39 Shawn Green 3.00 .90
40 Tom Glavine 3.00 .90
41 Curt Schilling 3.00 .90
42 Todd Helton 3.00 .90
43 Roger Clemens 8.00 2.40
44 Lance Berkman 3.00 .90
45 Nomar Garciaparra 6.00 1.80

2003 Donruss Elite All-Time Career Best Materials

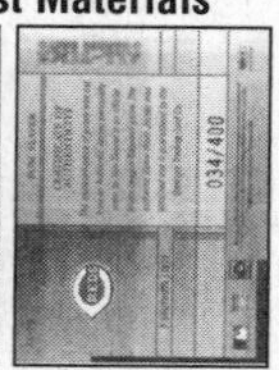

Randomly inserted into packs, this is a parallel to the All-Time Career Best insert set. Each of these cards feature not only the player but also a piece of game-used memorabilia from their career. We have printed what type of material as well as the stated print run next to the player's name in our checklist. Please note that for cards with a stated print run of 25 or fewer, there is no pricing due to market scarcity.

Nm-Mt Ex-Mt
*MULTI-COLOR PATCH: 1.5X TO 4X HI COL
1 Babe Ruth Bat/25
2 Ty Cobb Bat/25
3 Jackie Robinson Jkt/50 80.00 24.00
4 Lou Gehrig Bat/100 150.00 45.00
5 Thurman Munson Bat/200 25.00 7.50
6 Nolan Ryan Jkt/400 50.00 15.00
7 Mike Schmidt Jkt/400 40.00 12.00
8 Don Mattingly Hat/250 50.00 15.00
9 Yogi Berra Bat/100 30.00 9.00
10 Rod Carew Bat/100 15.00 4.50
11 Reggie Jackson Bat/400 15.00 4.50
12 Al Kaline Bat/400 20.00 6.00
13 Harmon Killebrew Pants/400 20.00 6.00
14 Eddie Mathews Bat/200 25.00 7.50
15 Stan Musial Bat/100 50.00 15.00
16 Jim Palmer Jsy/200 20.00 6.00
17 Phil Rizzuto Bat/400 15.00 4.50
18 Brooks Robinson Bat/400 15.00 4.50
19 Tom Seaver Jsy/400 15.00 4.50
20 Robin Yount Bat/400 20.00 6.00
21 Carlton Fisk Bat/400 15.00 4.50
22 Dale Murphy Bat/400 20.00 6.00
23 Cal Ripken Bat/400 40.00 12.00
24 Tony Gwynn Pants/400 15.00 4.50
25 Andre Dawson Bat/400 10.00 3.00
26 Derek Jeter Base/400 20.00 6.00
27 Ken Griffey Jr. Base/400 15.00 4.50
28 Albert Pujols Base/400 15.00 4.50
29 Sammy Sosa Bat/400 15.00 4.50
30 Jason Giambi Bat/400 8.00 2.40
31 Randy Johnson Jsy/400 10.00 3.00
32 Greg Maddux Jsy/400 10.00 3.00
33 Rickey Henderson Bat/400 10.00 3.00
34 Pedro Martinez Jsy/400 10.00 3.00
35 Jeff Bagwell Pants/400 10.00 3.00
36 Alex Rodriguez Bat/400 15.00 4.50
37 Vladimir Guerrero Bat/400 10.00 3.00
38 Chipper Jones Bat/400 10.00 3.00
39 Shawn Green Bat/400 8.00 2.40
40 Tom Glavine Jsy/400 10.00 3.00
41 Curt Schilling Jsy/400 8.00 2.40
42 Todd Helton Bat/400 10.00 3.00
43 Roger Clemens Jsy/400 20.00 6.00
44 Lance Berkman Bat/400 8.00 2.40
45 Nomar Garciaparra Bat/400 15.00 4.50

2003 Donruss Elite All-Time Career Best Materials Parallel

Nm-Mt Ex-Mt
RANDOM INSERTS IN PACKS
PRINT RUNS B/WN 1-393 COPIES PER
NO PRICING ON QTY OF 25 OR LESS
1 Babe Ruth Bat/60 150.00 45.00
2 Ty Cobb Bat/24
3 Jackie Robinson Jkt/19
4 Lou Gehrig Bat/49 150.00 45.00
5 Thurman Munson Bat/105 40.00 12.00
6 Nolan Ryan Jkt/22
7 Mike Schmidt Jkt/48 80.00 24.00
8 Don Mattingly Hat/53 100.00 30.00
9 Yogi Berra Bat/30 80.00 24.00
10 Rod Carew Bat/239 15.00 4.50
11 Reggie Jackson Bat/39 40.00 12.00
12 Al Kaline Bat/29 80.00 24.00
13 Harmon Killebrew Pants/140 30.00 9.00
14 Eddie Mathews Bat/31 80.00 24.00
15 Stan Musial Bat/39 100.00 30.00
16 Jim Palmer Jsy/23
17 Phil Rizzuto Bat/10
18 Brooks Robinson Bat/118 25.00 7.50
19 Tom Seaver Jsy/7
20 Robin Yount Bat/49 60.00 18.00
21 Carlton Fisk Bat/107 25.00 7.50
22 Dale Murphy Bat/44 60.00 18.00
23 Cal Ripken Bat/211 50.00 15.00
24 Tony Gwynn Pants/220 20.00 6.00
25 Andre Dawson Bat/49 25.00 7.50
26 Derek Jeter Base/24
27 Ken Griffey Jr. Base/56 40.00 12.00
28 Albert Pujols Base/37 50.00 15.00
29 Sammy Sosa Bat/66 50.00 15.00
30 Jason Giambi Bat/137 15.00 4.50
31 Randy Johnson Jsy/12
32 Greg Maddux Jsy/20
33 Rickey Henderson Bat/130 20.00 6.00
34 Pedro Martinez Jsy/23
35 Jeff Bagwell Pants/47 25.00 7.50
36 Alex Rodriguez Bat/393 15.00 4.50
37 Vladimir Guerrero Bat/44 40.00 12.00
38 Chipper Jones Bat/45 40.00 12.00
39 Shawn Green Bat/49 25.00 7.50
40 Tom Glavine Jsy/22
41 Curt Schilling Jsy/35 25.00 7.50
42 Todd Helton Bat/59 25.00 7.50
43 Roger Clemens Jsy/1
44 Lance Berkman Bat/55 25.00 7.50
45 Nomar Garciaparra Bat/35 80.00 24.00

2003 Donruss Elite Back to Back Jacks

Randomly inserted into packs, these 50 cards feature game use bat pieces on them. These cards were issued to different print runs depending on what the card number is and we have notated that information in our headers to this set.

Nm-Mt Ex-Mt
1-25 PRINT RUN 250 SERIAL #'d SETS
26-35 PRINT RUN 125 SERIAL #'d SETS
36-40 PRINT RUN 100 SERIAL #'d SETS
41-45 PRINT RUN 75 SERIAL #'d SETS
46-50 PRINT RUN 50 SERIAL #'d SETS
1 Adam Dunn 10.00 3.00
2 Alex Rodriguez 15.00 4.50
3 Alfonso Soriano 10.00 3.00
4 Andruw Jones 8.00 2.40
5 Chipper Jones 10.00 3.00
6 Jason Giambi 8.00 2.40
7 Jeff Bagwell 10.00 3.00
8 Jim Thome 10.00 3.00
9 Juan Gonzalez 10.00 3.00
10 Lance Berkman 8.00 2.40
11 Maggio Ordonez 8.00 2.40
12 Manny Ramirez 10.00 3.00
13 Miguel Tejada 8.00 2.40
14 Mike Piazza 15.00 4.50
15 Nomar Garciaparra 15.00 4.50
16 Rafael Palmeiro 10.00 3.00
17 Rickey Henderson 10.00 3.00
18 Sammy Sosa 15.00 4.50
19 Scott Rolen 10.00 3.00
20 Shawn Green 8.00 2.40
21 Todd Helton 10.00 3.00
22 Vladimir Guerrero 10.00 3.00
23 Ivan Rodriguez 10.00 3.00
24 Eric Chavez 8.00 2.40
25 Larry Walker 10.00 3.00
26 Garret Anderson 20.00 6.00
Troy Glaus
27 Adam Dunn 20.00 6.00
Austin Kearns
28 Alex Rodriguez 30.00 9.00
Rafael Palmeiro
29 Miguel Tejada 20.00 6.00
Eric Chavez
30 Magglio Ordonez 25.00 7.50
Frank Thomas
31 Lance Berkman 20.00 6.00
Jeff Bagwell
32 Nomar Garciaparra 40.00 12.00
Manny Ramirez
33 Vladimir Guerrero 25.00 7.50
Jose Vidro
34 Mike Piazza 25.00 7.50
Roberto Alomar
35 Todd Helton 20.00 6.00
Larry Walker
36 Babe Ruth 150.00 45.00
37 Cal Ripken 80.00 24.00
38 Don Mattingly 60.00 18.00
39 Kirby Puckett 25.00 7.50
40 Roberto Clemente 100.00 30.00
41 Alfonso Soriano 40.00 12.00
Phil Rizzuto
42 Sammy Sosa 60.00 18.00
Andre Dawson
43 Ozzie Smith 60.00 18.00
Scott Rolen
44 Don Mattingly 80.00 24.00
Jason Giambi
45 Rickey Henderson 150.00 45.00
Ty Cobb
46 Joe Morgan 60.00 18.00
Johnny Bench
47 Cal Ripken 150.00 45.00
Brooks Robinson
48 George Brett 150.00 45.00
Bo Jackson
49 Babe Ruth 400.00 120.00
Lou Gehrig
50 Yogi Berra 80.00 24.00
Thurman Munson

2003 Donruss Elite Back to the Future

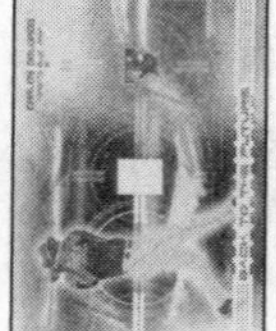
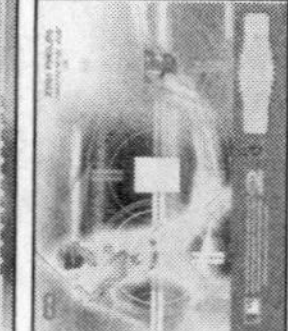

Nm-Mt Ex-Mt
1-10 PRINT RUN 1000 SERIAL #'d SETS
11-15 PRINT RUN 500 SERIAL #'d SETS
RANDOM INSERTS IN PACKS
1 Kerry Wood 5.00 1.50
2 Mark Prior 5.00 1.50
3 Maggio Ordonez 4.00 1.20
4 Joe Borchard 4.00 1.20
5 Lance Berkman 4.00 1.20
6 Jason Lane 4.00 1.20
7 Rafael Palmeiro 4.00 1.20
8 Mark Teixeira 4.00 1.20
9 Carlos Delgado 4.00 1.20
10 Josh Phelps 4.00 1.20
11 Kerry Wood 8.00 2.40
Mark Prior
12 Maggio Ordonez 6.00 1.80
Joe Borchard
13 Lance Berkman 6.00 1.80
Jason Lane
14 Rafael Palmeiro 6.00 1.80
Mark Teixeira
15 Carlos Delgado 6.00 1.80
John Phelps

2003 Donruss Elite Back to the Future Threads

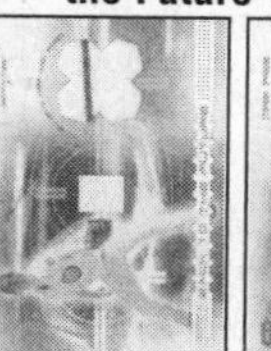
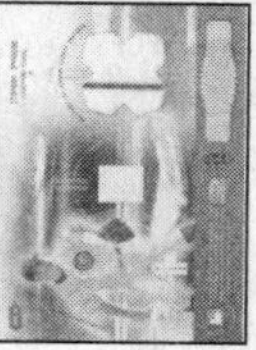

Nm-Mt Ex-Mt
*MULTI-COLOR PATCH: .75X TO 2X HI COL
1-10 PRINT RUN 250 SERIAL #'d SETS
11-15 PRINT RUN 125 SERIAL #'d SETS
RANDOM INSERTS IN PACKS
1 Kerry Wood 15.00 4.50

2 Mark Prior 15.00 4.50
3 Magglio Ordonez 8.00 2.40
4 Joe Borchard 8.00 2.40
5 Lance Berkman 8.00 2.40
6 Jason Lane 8.00 2.40
7 Rafael Palmeiro 10.00 3.00
8 Mark Teixeira 8.00 2.40
9 Carlos Delgado 8.00 2.40
10 Josh Phelps 8.00 2.40
11 Kerry Wood 25.00 7.50
Mark Prior
12 Magglio Ordonez 15.00 4.50
Joe Borchard
13 Lance Berkman 15.00 4.50
Jason Lane
14 Rafael Palmeiro 15.00 4.50
Mark Teixeira
15 Carlos Delgado 15.00 4.50
John Phelps

2003 Donruss Elite Career Bests

Nm-Mt Ex-Mt
RANDOM INSERTS IN PACKS
PRINT RUNS B/WN 4-417 COPIES PER
NO PRICING ON QTY OF 25 OR LESS
1 Randy Johnson WIN/24
2 Curt Schilling WIN/23
3 Garret Anderson 2B/56 10.00 3.00
4 Andruw Jones BB/83 10.00 3.00
5 Kerry Wood CG/4
6 Magglio Ordonez HR/38 12.00 3.60
7 Magglio Ordonez RBI/135 6.00 1.80
8 Adam Dunn HR/26 15.00 4.50
9 Roy Oswalt WIN/19
10 Lance Berkman HR/42 12.00 3.60
11 Lance Berkman RBI/128 6.00 1.80
12 Shawn Green OBP/385 5.00 1.50
13 Alfonso Soriano HR/39 12.00 3.60
14 Alfonso Soriano AVG/300 5.00 1.50
15 Jason Giambi RUN/120 6.00 1.80
16 Derek Jeter SB/32 60.00 18.00
17 Vladimir Guerrero SB/40 20.00 6.00
18 Vladimir Guerrero OBP/417 8.00 2.40
19 Barry Zito WIN/23
20 Miguel Tejada HR/34 15.00 4.50
21 Barry Bonds BB/198 25.00 7.50
22 Barry Bonds AVG/370 20.00 6.00
23 Ichiro Suzuki OBP/388 12.00 3.60
24 Alex Rodriguez HR/57 30.00 9.00
25 Alex Rodriguez RBI/142 20.00 6.00

2003 Donruss Elite Career Bests Materials

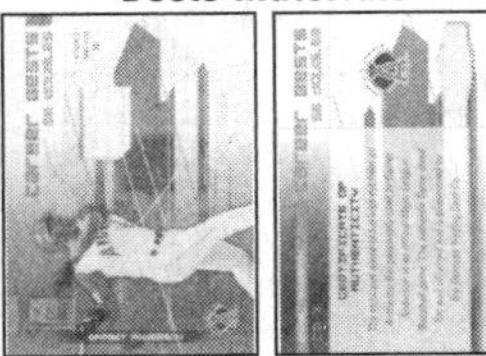

Nm-Mt Ex-Mt
RANDOM INSERTS IN PACKS
STATED PRINT RUN 500 SERIAL #'d SETS
1 Randy Johnson WIN Jsy 10.00 3.00
2 Curt Schilling WIN Jsy 8.00 2.40
3 Garret Anderson 2B Bat 8.00 2.40
4 Andruw Jones BB Bat 8.00 2.40
5 Kerry Wood CG Shoe 15.00 4.50
6 Magglio Ordonez HR Bat 8.00 2.40
7 Magglio Ordonez RBI Bat 8.00 2.40
8 Adam Dunn HR Bat 10.00 3.00
9 Roy Oswalt WIN Jsy 8.00 2.40
10 Lance Berkman HR Bat 8.00 2.40
11 Lance Berkman RBI Bat 8.00 2.40
12 Shawn Green OBP Bat 8.00 2.40
13 Alfonso Soriano HR Bat 10.00 3.00
14 Alfonso Soriano AVG Bat 10.00 3.00
15 Jason Giambi RUN Bat 8.00 2.40
16 Derek Jeter SB Base 20.00 6.00
17 Vladimir Guerrero SB Bat 10.00 3.00
18 Vladimir Guerrero OBP Bat 10.00 3.00
19 Barry Zito WIN Jsy 8.00 2.40
20 Miguel Tejada HR Bat 8.00 2.40
21 Barry Bonds BB Base 20.00 6.00
22 Barry Bonds AVG Base 20.00 6.00
23 Ichiro Suzuki OBP Base 20.00 6.00
24 Alex Rodriguez HR Jsy 15.00 4.50
25 Alex Rodriguez RBI Jsy 15.00 4.50

2003 Donruss Elite Career Bests Materials Autographs

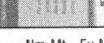

Nm-Mt Ex-Mt
RANDOM INSERTS IN PACKS
PRINT RUNS B/WN 5-250 COPIES PER
NO PRICING ON QTY OF 25 OR LESS
2 Curt Schilling WIN Jsy/5
3 Garret Anderson 2B Bat/75 50.00 15.00
4 Andruw Jones BB Bat/10
5 Kerry Wood CG Shoe/15
6 Magglio Ordonez HR Bat/10
7 Magglio Ordonez RBI Bat/10
8 Adam Dunn HR Bat/100 60.00 18.00
9 Roy Oswalt WIN Jsy/250 40.00 12.00
10 Lance Berkman HR Bat/25
11 Lance Berkman RBI Bat/25
13 Alfonso Soriano HR Bat/5
14 Alfonso Soriano AVG Bat/5
17 Vlad Guerrero SB Bat/50 100.00 30.00
18 Vlad Guerrero OBP Bat/50 100.00 30.00
19 Barry Zito WIN Jsy/75 60.00 18.00
20 Miguel Tejada HR Bat/25
24 Alex Rodriguez HR Jsy/5
25 Alex Rodriguez RBI Jsy/5

2003 Donruss Elite Highlights

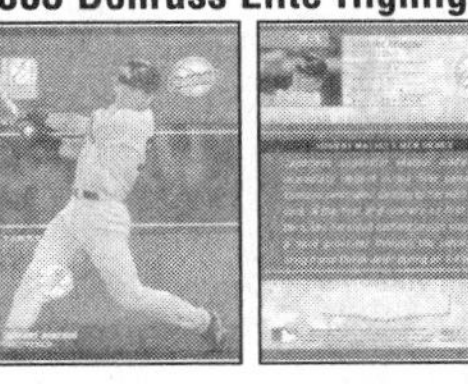

Nm-Mt Ex-Mt
RANDOM INSERTS IN PACKS
STATED PRINT RUN 500 SERIAL #'d SETS
1 Sammy Sosa 500 HR 12.00 3.60
2 Rafael Palmeiro 500 HR 8.00 2.40
3 Hideki Matsui Debut 10.00 3.00
4 Jose Contreras Debut 8.00 2.40
5 Kevin Millwood No-Hit 5.00 1.50

2003 Donruss Elite Highlights Autographs

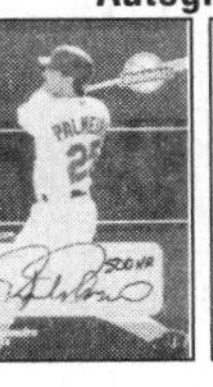
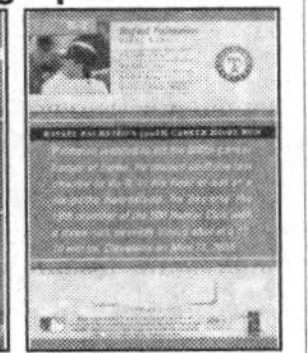

Nm-Mt Ex-Mt
RANDOM INSERTS IN PACKS
STATED PRINT RUN 50 SERIAL #'d SETS
2 Rafael Palmeiro 500 HR 100.00 30.00
4 Jose Contreras Debut 40.00 12.00

2003 Donruss Elite Passing the Torch

Nm-Mt Ex-Mt
1-10 PRINT RUN 1000 SERIAL #'d SETS
11-15 PRINT RUN 500 SERIAL #'d SETS
RANDOM INSERTS IN PACKS
1 Stan Musial 10.00 3.00
2 Jim Edmonds 4.00 1.20
3 Dale Murphy 6.00 1.80
4 Andruw Jones 4.00 1.20
5 Roger Clemens 12.00 3.60
6 Mark Prior 6.00 1.80
7 Tom Seaver 6.00 1.80
8 Tom Glavine 6.00 1.80
9 Mike Schmidt 12.00 3.60
10 Pat Burrell 4.00 1.20
11 Stan Musial 15.00 4.50
Jim Edmonds
12 Dale Murphy 10.00 3.00
Andruw Jones
13 Roger Clemens 15.00 4.50
Mark Prior
14 Tom Seaver 10.00 3.00
Tom Glavine
15 Mike Schmidt 20.00 6.00
Pat Burrell

2003 Donruss Elite Passing the Torch Autographs

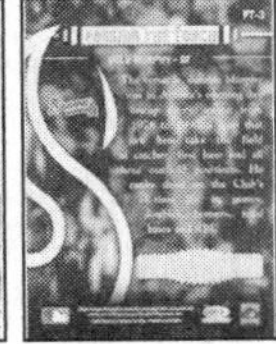

Randomly inserted into packs, these cards feature the continuation of the popular Passing the Torch Autograph insert set. The first 10 cards feature individual autographs while the final five cards feature dual autographs of the players.

Nm-Mt Ex-Mt
1-10 PRINT RUN 50 SERIAL #'d SETS
11-15 PRINT RUN 25 SERIAL #'d SETS
NO 11-15 PRICING DUE TO SCARCITY
RANDOM INSERTS IN PACKS
1 Stan Musial 120.00 36.00
2 Jim Edmonds 80.00 24.00
3 Dale Murphy 80.00 24.00
4 Andruw Jones 50.00 15.00
5 Roger Clemens 200.00 60.00
6 Mark Prior 100.00 30.00
7 Tom Seaver 80.00 24.00
8 Tom Glavine 80.00 24.00
9 Mike Schmidt 150.00 45.00
10 Pat Burrell 50.00 15.00
11 Stan Musial
Jim Edmonds
12 Dale Murphy
Andruw Jones
13 Roger Clemens
Mark Prior
14 Tom Seaver
Tom Glavine
15 Mike Schmidt
Pat Burrell

2003 Donruss Elite Recollection Autographs

Randomly inserted into packs, these 65 cards feature cards prepared for previous Donruss Elite products and they feature both autographs and a recollection collection stamp on all the cards. Please note that we have notated the stated print run next to the player's name and specific card in our checklist. For cards with print runs of 25 or fewer, no pricing is available due to market scarcity.

Nm-Mt Ex-Mt
1 Jeremy Affeldt 01/75 25.00 7.50
2 Erick Almonte 01/75 10.00 3.00
3 Jeff Bagwell 02/1
4 Adrian Beltre 02/36 30.00 9.00
5 Adrian Beltre 02 Asp/5
6 Adrian Beltre 02 Sta/3
7 Brandon Berger 01/83 10.00 3.00
8 Angel Berroa 01/28 50.00 15.00
9 John Buck 01/25
10 Mark Buehrle 02/23
11 Marlon Byrd 01/24
12 Jose Castillo 02/23
13 Jeff Deardorff 01/53 10.00 3.00
14 Ryan Drese 01/100 40.00 12.00
15 J.D. Drew 01/15
16 J.D. Drew 02/10
17 J.D. Drew 02 CB/5
18 Jim Edmonds 01/15
19 Jim Edmonds 02/5
20 Jim Edmonds 02 BTF/5
21 Luis Garcia 01/28 25.00 7.50
22 Geronimo Gil 01/75 10.00 3.00
23 Mark Grace 02/2
24 Shawn Green 01/2
25 Shawn Green 02/2
26 Shawn Green 02 BTF/2
27 Shawn Green 02 CB/2
28 Travis Hafner 01 Black/52 40.00 12.00
29 Travis Hafner 01 Blue/23
30 Bill Hall 01/27 25.00 7.50
31 Orlando Hudson 01 Black/12
32 Orlando Hudson 01 Blue /13
33 Tim Hudson 01/25
34 Tim Hudson 02/25
35 Gerald Laird 02/46 50.00 15.00
36 Jason Lane 01/27 25.00 7.50
37 Adam LaRoche 02/25
38 Cliff Lee 01/25
39 Kenny Lofton 01/25
40 Greg Maddux 01/5
41 Greg Maddux 01 TW/5
42 Greg Maddux 02/10
43 Greg Maddux 02 AS/5
44 Victor Martinez 01/52 150.00 45.00
45 Corky Miller 01/25
46 Roy Oswalt 01 Black/61 25.00 7.50
47 Roy Oswalt 01 Blue/9
48 Roy Oswalt 02/24
49 Mark Prior 01/10
50 Mike Rivera 01/3
51 Ricardo Rodriguez 01/75 10.00 3.00
52 Freddy Sanchez 02/25
53 Gary Sheffield 01/25
54 Gary Sheffield 02/14
55 Bud Smith 01/50 20.00 6.00
56 Bud Smith 02/28 20.00 6.00
57 Chris Snelling 02/25
58 Junior Spivey 01/45 30.00 9.00
59 Tim Spooneybarger 01/100 10.00 3.00
60 Shannon Stewart 01/24
61 Shannon Stewart 02/35 25.00 7.50
62 Dennis Tankersley 01/15
63 Mark Teixeira 01/19
64 Claudio Vargas 01/51 10.00 3.00
65 Martin Vargas 01/10

2003 Donruss Elite Throwback Threads

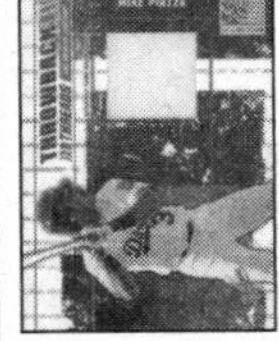
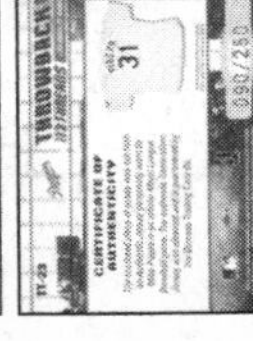

Randomly inserted into packs, these 100 cards feature not only the player's featured but also a game-worn uniform piece from during their career. Please note that the final 10 cards in the checklist feature either two different pieces from a player's career or two pieces from players who have something in common.

Nm-Mt Ex-Mt
1-45 PRINT RUN 250 SERIAL #'d SETS
46-75 PRINT RUN 125 SERIAL #'d SETS
76-90 PRINT RUN 100 SERIAL #'d SETS
91-95 PRINT RUN 75 SERIAL #'d SETS
96-100 PRINT RUN RUN 50 SERIAL #'d SETS
*MULTI-COLOR PATCH: .75X TO 2X HI COL
1 Randy Johnson D'backs 10.00 3.00
2 Randy Johnson M's 10.00 3.00
3 Roger Clemens Yanks 25.00 7.50
4 Roger Clemens Red Sox 25.00 7.50
5 Manny Ramirez 10.00 3.00
6 Greg Maddux 15.00 4.50
7 Jason Giambi Yanks 8.00 2.40
8 Jason Giambi A's 8.00 2.40
9 Alex Rodriguez Rgr 15.00 4.50
10 Alex Rodriguez M's 15.00 4.50
11 Miguel Tejada 8.00 2.40
12 Alfonso Soriano 10.00 3.00
13 Nomar Garciaparra 15.00 4.50
14 Pedro Martinez Red Sox 10.00 3.00
15 Pedro Martinez Expos 10.00 3.00
16 Andruw Jones 8.00 2.40
17 Chipper Jones 10.00 3.00
18 Barry Zito 8.00 2.40
19 Mark Mulder 8.00 2.40
20 Lance Berkman 8.00 2.40
21 Magglio Ordonez 8.00 2.40
22 Mike Piazza Mets 15.00 4.50
23 Mike Piazza Dodgers 15.00 4.50
24 Rickey Henderson Padres 10.00 3.00
25 Rickey Henderson Mets 10.00 3.00
26 Rickey Henderson M's 10.00 3.00
27 Sammy Sosa 15.00 4.50
28 Shawn Green 8.00 2.40
29 Troy Glaus 8.00 2.40
30 Vladimir Guerrero 10.00 3.00
31 Adam Dunn 10.00 3.00
32 Jeff Bagwell 10.00 3.00
33 Curt Schilling 8.00 2.40
34 Hideo Nomo Dodgers 40.00 12.00
35 Hideo Nomo Red Sox 40.00 12.00
36 Hideo Nomo Mets 40.00 12.00
37 Kerry Wood 10.00 3.00
38 Mark Prior 10.00 3.00
39 Roberto Alomar 10.00 3.00
40 Todd Helton 10.00 3.00
41 Jim Thome 10.00 3.00
42 Rafael Palmeiro 10.00 3.00
43 Juan Gonzalez 10.00 3.00
44 Vernon Wells 8.00 2.40
45 Torii Hunter 8.00 2.40
46 Randy Johnson D'backs 25.00 7.50
Randy Johnson M's
47 Roger Clemens Yankees 50.00 15.00
Roger Clemens Red Sox
48 Jason Giambi Yankees 20.00 6.00
Jason Giambi A's
49 Alex Rodriguez Rangers 40.00 12.00
Alex Rodriguez M's
50 Pedro Martinez Red Sox 25.00 7.50
Pedro Martinez Expos
51 Mike Piazza Mets 40.00 12.00
Mike Piazza Dodgers
52 Rickey Henderson A's 25.00 7.50
Rickey Henderson M's
53 Rickey Henderson Padres 25.00 7.50
Rickey Henderson Mets
54 Rickey Henderson Angels 25.00 7.50
Rickey Henderson Padres
55 Hideo Nomo Dodgers 50.00 15.00
Hideo Nomo Red Sox
56 Randy Johnson D'backs 25.00 7.50
Randy Johnson Expos
57 Randy Johnson 25.00 7.50
Curt Schilling
58 Alfonso Soriano 25.00 7.50
Jason Giambi
59 Barry Zito 20.00 6.00
Mark Mulder
60 Andruw Jones 25.00 7.50
Chipper Jones
61 Greg Maddux 60.00 18.00
Tom Glavine
62 Lance Berkman 25.00 7.50
Jeff Bagwell
63 Roger Clemens 30.00 9.00
Mark Prior
64 Alex Rodriguez 30.00 9.00
Rafael Palmeiro
65 Jim Thome 25.00 7.50
Roberto Alomar
66 Mike Piazza 25.00 7.50
Roberto Alomar
67 Sammy Sosa 40.00 12.00
Mark Grace
68 Todd Helton 25.00 7.50
Larry Walker
69 Adam Dunn 25.00 7.50
Austin Kearns
70 Alex Rodriguez 25.00 7.50
Ivan Rodriguez
71 Bobby Abreu 20.00 6.00
Marlon Byrd
72 Miguel Tejada 20.00 6.00
Eric Chavez
73 Greg Maddux 40.00 12.00
John Smoltz
74 Kerry Wood 10.00 3.00
Mark Prior
75 Barry Zito 20.00 6.00
Tim Hudson
76 Babe Ruth 400.00 120.00
77 Ty Cobb 120.00 36.00
78 Jackie Robinson 100.00 30.00
79 Lou Gehrig 150.00 45.00
80 Thurman Munson 50.00 15.00
81 Nolan Ryan Astros 50.00 15.00
82 Don Mattingly 50.00 15.00
83 Mike Schmidt 40.00 12.00
84 Reggie Jackson 25.00 7.50
85 George Brett 50.00 15.00
86 Cal Ripken 60.00 18.00
87 Tony Gwynn 25.00 7.50
88 Yogi Berra 25.00 7.50
89 Stan Musial 50.00 15.00
90 Jim Palmer 20.00 6.00
91 Thurman Munson 60.00 18.00
Jorge Posada
92 Dale Murphy 60.00 18.00
Chipper Jones
93 Don Mattingly 100.00 30.00
Jason Giambi
94 Andre Dawson 60.00 18.00
Sammy Sosa
95 Nolan Ryan 80.00 24.00
Mark Prior
96 Babe Ruth 500.00 150.00
Lou Gehrig
97 Tom Seaver 60.00 18.00
Joe Morgan
98 Harmon Killebrew 60.00 18.00
Rod Carew
99 Nolan Ryan Rangers 120.00 36.00
Nolan Ryan Angels
100 Reggie Jackson Yankees 60.00 18.00
Reggie Jackson A's

2003 Donruss Elite Throwback Threads Autographs

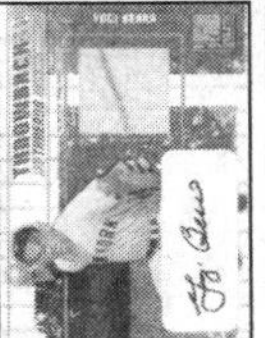
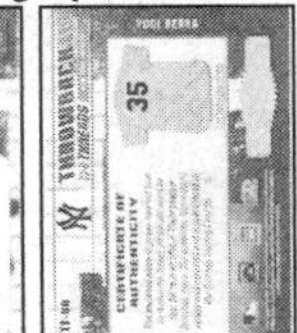

Randomly inserted into packs, this is a quasi-parallel to the Throwback Threads insert set. These cards were signed by the player featured and issued to stated print runs of between five and 75 copies per. Please note that if a player signed 25 or fewer copies, there is no pricing due to market scarcity.

Nm-Mt Ex-Mt
3 Roger Clemens Yanks/15
4 Roger Clemens Red Sox/5
6 Greg Maddux/5
9 Alex Rodriguez Rgr/5
10 Alex Rodriguez M's/5
12 Alfonso Soriano/5
14 Pedro Martinez Red Sox/5
15 Pedro Martinez Expos/5
16 Andruw Jones/25
17 Chipper Jones/20
18 Barry Zito/25
19 Mark Mulder/10
20 Lance Berkman/25
21 Magglio Ordonez/15
24 Rickey Henderson Padres/10
25 Rickey Henderson Mets/5
26 Rickey Henderson M's/5
27 Sammy Sosa/15
29 Troy Glaus/15
30 Vladimir Guerrero/50 100.00 30.00
31 Adam Dunn/50 100.00 30.00
37 Kerry Wood/50 100.00 30.00
38 Mark Prior/75 100.00 30.00
39 Roberto Alomar/50 100.00 30.00
40 Todd Helton/15
41 Jim Thome/25
45 Torii Hunter/25
81 Nolan Ryan Angels/25
82 Don Mattingly/25
83 Mike Schmidt/25
84 Reggie Jackson/25
85 George Brett/15
86 Cal Ripken/15
87 Tony Gwynn/25
88 Yogi Berra/25
89 Stan Musial/25
90 Jim Palmer/25

2003 Donruss Elite Throwback Threads Prime

Nm-Mt Ex-Mt
1-45 PRINT RUN 25 SERIAL #'d SETS
46-75 PRINT RUN 15 SERIAL #'d SETS
76-95 PRINT RUN 10 SERIAL #'d SETS
96-100 PRINT RUN 5 SERIAL #'d SETS

2003 Donruss Elite Extra Edition

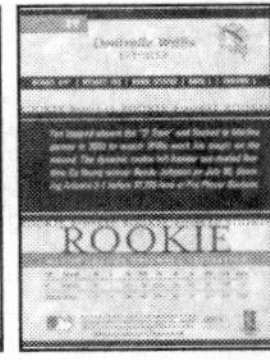

These cards were also inserted as part of the overall DLP Rookie/Traded Packs. Each of these cards feature Rookie Cards and are all issued to a stated print run of 900 serial numbered sets. Please note that cards numbered 42, 51, 54 and 56 do not exist for this set.

MINT NRMT
1 Adam Loewen RC 5.00 2.20
2 Brandon Webb RC 5.00 2.20
3 Chien-Ming Wang RC 5.00 2.20
4 Hong-Chih Kuo RC 5.00 2.20
5 Clint Barmes RC 5.00 2.20
6 Guillermo Quiroz RC 5.00 2.20
7 Edgar Gonzalez RC 4.00 1.80
8 Todd Wellemeyer RC 5.00 2.20
9 Alfredo Gonzalez RC 4.00 1.80
10 Craig Brazell RC 5.00 2.20

11 Tim Olson RC 5.00 2.20
12 Rich Fischer RC 4.00 1.80
13 Daniel Cabrera RC 8.00 3.60
14 Francisco Rosario RC 4.00 1.80
15 Francisco Cruceta RC 4.00 1.80
16 Alejandro Machado RC 4.00 1.80
17 Andrew Brown RC 5.00 2.20
18 Rob Hammock RC 5.00 2.20
19 Arnie Munoz RC 4.00 1.80
20 Felix Sanchez RC 4.00 1.80
21 Nook Logan RC 4.00 1.80
22 Cory Stewart RC 4.00 1.80
23 Michel Hernandez RC 4.00 1.80
24 Rett Johnson RC 5.00 2.20
25 Josh Hall RC 5.00 2.20
26 Doug Waechter RC 5.00 2.20
27 Matt Kata RC 5.00 2.20
28 Dan Haren RC 5.00 2.20
29 Dontrelle Willis 5.00 2.20
30 Ramon Nivar RC 5.00 2.20
31 Chad Gaudin RC 4.00 1.80
32 Rickie Weeks RC 12.00 5.50
33 Ryan Wagner RC 5.00 2.20
34 Kevin Correia RC 4.00 1.80
35 Bo Hart RC 5.00 2.20
36 Oscar Villarreal RC 4.00 1.80
37 Josh Willingham RC 5.00 2.20
38 Jeff Duncan RC 5.00 2.20
39 David DeJesus RC 5.00 2.20
40 Dustin McGowan RC 5.00 2.20
41 Preston Larrison RC 5.00 2.20
42 Does Not Exist
43 Kevin Youkilis RC 8.00 3.60
44 Bubba Nelson RC 5.00 2.20
45 Chris Burke RC 5.00 2.20
46 J.D. Durbin RC 5.00 2.20
47 Ryan Howard RC 12.00 5.50
48 Jason Kubel RC 10.00 4.50
49 Brendan Harris RC 5.00 2.20
50 Brian Bruney RC 5.00 2.20
51 Does Not Exist
52 Byron Gettis RC 4.00 1.80
53 Edwin Jackson RC 12.00 5.50
54 Does Not Exist
55 Daniel Garcia RC 4.00 1.80
56 Does Not Exist
57 Chad Cordero RC 4.00 1.80
58 Delmon Young RC 15.00 6.75

2003 Donruss Elite Extra Edition Aspirations

MINT NRMT
*ASP P/R b/wn 51-65: 1X TO 2.5X
*ASP RC's P/R b/wn 81-120: .6X TO 1.5X
*ASP RC's P/R b/wn 66-80: .75X TO 2X
*ASP RC's P/R b/wn 51-65: .75X TO 2X
*ASP RC's P/R b/wn 36-50: 1X TO 2.5X
*ASP RC's P/R b/wn 26-35: 1.25X TO 3X
RANDOM INSERTS IN DLP R/T PACKS
PRINT RUNS B/WN 24-98 COPIES PER
NO PRICING ON QTY OF 25 OR LESS
CARDS 42/51/54/56 DO NOT EXIST

2003 Donruss Elite Extra Edition Aspirations Gold

MINT NRMT
RANDOM INSERTS IN DLP R/T PACKS
STATED PRINT RUN 1 SERIAL #'d SET
NO PRICING DUE TO SCARCITY
CARDS 42/51/54/56 DO NOT EXIST

2003 Donruss Elite Extra Edition Status

MINT NRMT
*STATUS P/R b/wn 26-35: 1.5X TO 4X
*STATUS RC's P/R b/wn 66-80: .75X TO 2X
*STATUS RC's P/R b/wn 51-65: .75X TO 2X
*STATUS RC's P/R b/wn 36-50: 1X TO 2.5X
*STATUS RC's P/R b/wn 26-35: 1.25X TO 3X
RANDOM INSERTS IN DLP R/T PACKS
PRINT RUNS B/WN 2-76 COPIES PER
NO PRICING ON QTY OF 25 OR LESS
CARDS 42/51/54/56 DO NOT EXIST

2003 Donruss Elite Extra Edition Status Gold

MINT NRMT
RANDOM INSERTS IN DLP R/T PACKS
STATED PRINT RUN 24 SERIAL #'d SETS
NO PRICING DUE TO SCARCITY
CARDS 42/51/54/56 DO NOT EXIST

2003 Donruss Elite Extra Edition Turn of the Century

MINT NRMT
*TOC P/R b/wn 66-80: .75X TO 2X
*TOC RC's P/R b/wn 66-80: .75X TO 2X
RANDOM INSERTS IN DLP R/T PACKS
PRINT RUNS B/WN 75-100 COPIES PER

2003 Donruss Elite Extra Edition Turn of the Century Autographs

MINT NRMT
RANDOM INSERTS IN DLP R/T PACKS
STATED PRINT RUN 100 SERIAL #'d SETS
CARDS 29/32/34 PRINT RUN 25 #'d SETS
NO PRICING ON QTY OF 25 OR LESS
1 Adam Loewen 25.00 11.00
2 Brandon Webb 25.00 11.00
3 Chien-Ming Wang 50.00 22.00
4 Hong-Chih Kuo 40.00 18.00
5 Clint Barmes 15.00 6.75
6 Guillermo Quiroz 20.00 9.00
7 Edgar Gonzalez 10.00 4.50
8 Todd Wellemeyer 15.00 6.75
9 Alfredo Gonzalez 10.00 4.50
10 Craig Brazell 15.00 6.75
11 Tim Olson 15.00 6.75
12 Rich Fischer 10.00 4.50
13 Daniel Cabrera 30.00 13.50
14 Francisco Rosario 10.00 4.50
15 Francisco Cruceta 10.00 4.50
16 Alejandro Machado 10.00 4.50
17 Andrew Brown 15.00 6.75
18 Rob Hammock 15.00 6.75
19 Arnie Munoz 10.00 4.50
20 Felix Sanchez 10.00 4.50
21 Nook Logan 10.00 4.50
22 Cory Stewart 10.00 4.50
23 Michel Hernandez 10.00 4.50
24 Rett Johnson 15.00 6.75
25 Josh Hall 15.00 6.75
26 Doug Waechter 15.00 6.75
27 Matt Kata 20.00 9.00
28 Dan Haren 20.00 9.00
29 Dontrelle Willis/25
30 Ramon Nivar 20.00 9.00
31 Chad Gaudin 10.00 4.50
32 Rickie Weeks/25
33 Ryan Wagner 15.00 6.75
34 Kevin Correia/25
35 Bo Hart 15.00 6.75
36 Oscar Villarreal 10.00 4.50
37 Josh Willingham 15.00 6.75
38 Jeff Duncan 15.00 6.75
40 Dustin McGowan 20.00 9.00
41 Preston Larrison 10.00 4.50
43 Kevin Youkilis 40.00 18.00
44 Bubba Nelson 15.00 6.75
45 Chris Burke 20.00 9.00
46 J.D. Durbin 20.00 9.00
47 Ryan Howard 60.00 27.00
48 Jason Kubel 60.00 27.00
49 Brendan Harris 15.00 6.75
50 Brian Bruney 15.00 6.75
52 Byron Gettis 10.00 4.50
53 Edwin Jackson 50.00 22.00
55 Daniel Garcia 10.00 4.50
58 Delmon Young 150.00 70.00

2004 Donruss Elite

This 205 card set was released in May, 2004. The set was issued in five card packs with an $5 SRP which came 20 packs to a box and 12 boxes to a case. The first 150 cards of this set featured veterans while cards numbered 151 through 180 featured rookie cards printed to varying print runs. We have notated those specfic print runs next to the players name in our checklist. Cards numbered 181 through 200 feature retired greats which were randomly inserted into packs and those cards were issued to a stated print run of 1000 serial numbered sets. Please note, that although there is two separate numberings (including 201-205) for the Fans of the Game insert set, we have moved those cards into an insert set listing. Card number 169 was not issued.

Nm-Mt Ex-Mt
COMP.SET w/o SP's (150) 25.00 7.50
COMMON CARD 1-150 .30 .09
COMMON AUTO (151-180) 8.00 2.40
COMMON CARD (181-200) 3.00 .90
CARD NUMBER 169 DOES NOT EXIST
1 Troy Glaus .30 .09
2 Darin Erstad .30 .09
3 Garret Anderson .30 .09
4 Tim Salmon .50 .15
5 Bartolo Colon .30 .09
6 Jose Guillen .30 .09
7 Miguel Tejada .30 .09
8 Adam Loewen .30 .09
9 Jay Gibbons .30 .09
10 Melvin Mora .30 .09
11 Javy Lopez .30 .09
12 Pedro Martinez .75 .23
13 Curt Schilling .75 .23
14 David Ortiz .75 .23
15 Keith Foulke .30 .09
16 Nomar Garciaparra 1.25 .35
17 Magglio Ordonez .30 .09
18 Frank Thomas .75 .23
19 Carlos Lee .30 .09
20 Paul Konerko .30 .09
21 Mark Buehrle .30 .09
22 Jody Gerut .30 .09
23 Victor Martinez .30 .09
24 C.C. Sabathia .30 .09
25 Ellis Burks .30 .09
26 Bobby Higginson .30 .09
27 Jeremy Bonderman .30 .09
28 Fernando Vina .30 .09
29 Carlos Pena .30 .09
30 Dmitri Young .30 .09
31 Carlos Beltran .50 .15
32 Benito Santiago .30 .09
33 Mike Sweeney .30 .09
34 Angel Berroa .30 .09
35 Runelvys Hernandez .30 .09
36 Johan Santana .50 .15
37 Doug Mientkiewicz .30 .09
38 Shannon Stewart .30 .09
39 Torii Hunter .30 .09
40 Derek Jeter 1.50 .45
41 Jason Giambi .30 .09
42 Bernie Williams .50 .15
43 Alfonso Soriano .50 .15
44 Gary Sheffield .30 .09
45 Mike Mussina .50 .15
46 Jorge Posada .50 .15
47 Hideki Matsui 1.25 .35
48 Kevin Brown .30 .09
49 Javier Vazquez .30 .09
50 Mariano Rivera .50 .15
51 Eric Chavez .30 .09
52 Tim Hudson .30 .09
53 Mark Mulder .30 .09
54 Barry Zito .30 .09
55 Ichiro Suzuki 1.25 .35
56 Edgar Martinez .50 .15
57 Bret Boone .30 .09
58 John Olerud .30 .09
59 Scott Spiezio .30 .09
60 Aubrey Huff .30 .09
61 Rocco Baldelli .30 .09
62 Jose Cruz Jr. .30 .09
63 Delmon Young .50 .15
64 Mark Teixeira .30 .09
65 Hank Blalock .30 .09
66 Michael Young .30 .09
67 Alex Rodriguez 1.25 .35
68 Carlos Delgado .30 .09
69 Eric Hinske .30 .09
70 Roy Halladay .30 .09
71 Vernon Wells .30 .09
72 Randy Johnson .75 .23
73 Richie Sexson .30 .09
74 Brandon Webb .30 .09
75 Luis Gonzalez .30 .09
76 Steve Finley .30 .09
77 Chipper Jones .75 .23
78 Andruw Jones .30 .09
79 Marcus Giles .30 .09
80 Rafael Furcal .30 .09
81 J.D. Drew .30 .09
82 Sammy Sosa 1.25 .35
83 Kerry Wood .75 .23
84 Mark Prior .75 .23
85 Derrek Lee .30 .09
86 Moises Alou .30 .09
87 Corey Patterson .30 .09
88 Ken Griffey Jr. 1.25 .35
89 Austin Kearns .30 .09
90 Adam Dunn .50 .15
91 Barry Larkin .50 .15
92 Todd Helton .50 .15
93 Larry Walker .50 .15
94 Preston Wilson .30 .09
95 Charles Johnson .30 .09
96 Luis Castillo .30 .09
97 Josh Beckett .30 .09
98 Mike Lowell .30 .09
99 Miguel Cabrera .50 .15
100 Juan Pierre .30 .09
101 Dontrelle Willis .30 .09
102 Andy Pettitte .50 .15
103 Wade Miller .30 .09
104 Jeff Bagwell .50 .15
105 Craig Biggio .50 .15
106 Lance Berkman .30 .09
107 Jeff Kent .30 .09
108 Roy Oswalt .30 .09
109 Hideo Nomo .75 .23
110 Adrian Beltre .50 .15
111 Paul Lo Duca .30 .09
112 Shawn Green .30 .09
113 Fred McGriff .50 .15
114 Eric Gagne .75 .23
115 Geoff Jenkins .30 .09
116 Rickie Weeks .30 .09
117 Scott Podsednik .30 .09
118 Nick Johnson .30 .09
119 Orlando Cabrera .30 .09
120 Jose Vidro .30 .09
121 Kazuo Matsui RC 2.50 .75
122 Tom Glavine .50 .15
123 Al Leiter .30 .09
124 Mike Piazza 1.25 .35
125 Jose Reyes .30 .09
126 Mike Cameron .30 .09
127 Pat Burrell .30 .09
128 Jim Thome .75 .23
129 Mike Lieberthal .30 .09
130 Bobby Abreu .30 .09
131 Kip Wells .30 .09
132 Jack Wilson .30 .09
133 Pokey Reese .30 .09
134 Brian Giles .30 .09
135 Sean Burroughs .30 .09
136 Ryan Klesko .30 .09
137 Trevor Hoffman .30 .09
138 Jason Schmidt .30 .09
139 J.T. Snow .30 .09
140 A.J. Pierzynski .30 .09
141 Ray Durham .30 .09
142 Jim Edmonds .30 .09
143 Albert Pujols 1.50 .45
144 Edgar Renteria .30 .09
145 Scott Rolen .75 .23
146 Matt Morris .30 .09
147 Ivan Rodriguez .75 .23
148 Vladimir Guerrero .75 .23
149 Greg Maddux 1.25 .35
150 Kevin Millwood .30 .09
151 Hector Gimenez AU/750 RC 8.00 2.40
152 Willy Taveras AU/750 RC 10.00 3.00
153 Ruddy Yan AU/750 8.00 2.40
154 Graham Koonce AU/750 8.00 2.40
155 Jose Capellan AU/750 RC 30.00 9.00
156 Onil Joseph AU/750 RC 8.00 2.40
157 John Gall AU/1000 RC 10.00 3.00
158 Carlos Hines AU/750 RC 8.00 2.40
159 Jerry Gil AU/750 RC 8.00 2.40
160 Mike Gosling AU/750 RC 8.00 2.40
161 Jason Frasor AU/750 RC 8.00 2.40
162 Justin Knoedler AU/750 RC 8.00 2.40
163 Merkin Valdez AU/750 RC 15.00 4.50
164 Angel Chavez AU/1000 RC 8.00 2.40
165 Ivan Ochoa AU/750 RC 8.00 2.40
166 Greg Dobbs AU/750 RC 8.00 2.40
167 Ronald Belisario AU/750 RC 8.00 2.40
168 Aarom Baldiris AU/750 RC 10.00 3.00
169 Does Not Exist
170 Dave Crouthers AU/750 RC 8.00 2.40
171 Freddy Guzman AU/750 RC 10.00 3.00
172 Akinori Otsuka AU/250 RC 40.00 12.00
173 Ian Snell AU/750 RC 10.00 3.00
174 Nick Regilio AU/1000 RC 8.00 2.40
175 Jamie Brown AU/750 RC 8.00 2.40
176 Jerome Gamble AU/750 RC 8.00 2.40
177 Roberto Novoa AU/1000 RC 10.00 3.00
178 Sean Henn AU/1000 RC 8.00 2.40
179 Ramon Ramirez AU/1000 RC 8.00 2.40
180 Jason Bartlett AU/1000 RC 10.00 3.00
181 Bob Gibson RET 4.00 1.20
182 Cal Ripken RET 10.00 3.00
183 Carl Yastrzemski RET 5.00 1.50
184 Dale Murphy RET 4.00 1.20
185 Don Mattingly RET 8.00 2.40
186 Eddie Murray RET 4.00 1.20
187 George Brett RET 8.00 2.40
188 Jackie Robinson RET 4.00 1.20
189 Jim Palmer RET 3.00 .90
190 Lou Gehrig RET 5.00 1.50
191 Mike Schmidt RET 6.00 1.80
192 Ozzie Smith RET 5.00 1.50
193 Nolan Ryan RET 8.00 2.40
194 Reggie Jackson RET 4.00 1.20
195 Roberto Clemente RET 8.00 2.40
196 Robin Yount RET 5.00 1.50
197 Stan Musial RET 5.00 1.50
198 Ted Williams RET 6.00 1.80
199 Tony Gwynn RET 4.00 1.20
200 Ty Cobb RET 4.00 1.20

2004 Donruss Elite Aspirations

Nm-Mt Ex-Mt
*1-150 PRINT RUN b/wn 81-99: 4X TO 10X
*1-150 PRINT RUN b/wn 66-80: 5X TO 12X
*1-150 PRINT RUN b/wn 51-65: 5X TO 12X
*1-150 PRINT RUN b/wn 36-50: 6X TO 15X
*1-150 PRINT RUN b/wn 26-35: 8X TO 20X
*1-150 PRINT RUN b/wn 16-25: 10X TO 25X
*151-180 P/R 81-99: .3X TO .8X AU 750+
*151-180 P/R 66-80: .4X TO 1X AU 750+
*151-180 P/R 51-65: .4X TO 1X AU 750+
*151-180 P/R 36-50: .5X TO 1.2X AU 750+
*151-180 P/R 26-35: .6X TO 1.5X AU 750+
*151-180 P/R 81-99: .2X TO .5X AU 250
*181-200 P/R b/wn 81-99: 1.25X TO 3X
*181-200 P/R b/wn 66-80: 1.5X TO 4X
*181-200 P/R b/wn 51-65: 1.5X TO 4X
RANDOM INSERTS IN PACKS
PRINT RUNS B/WN 19-99 COPIES PER
1-150/181-200 NO PRICING ON 15 OR LESS
151-180 NO PRICING ON 25 OR LESS
121 Kazuo Matsui/75 25.00 7.50
169 Kazuo Matsui ROO/75 25.00 7.50

2004 Donruss Elite Status

Nm-Mt Ex-Mt
*1-150 PRINT RUN b/wn 66-80: 5X TO 12X
*1-150 PRINT RUN b/wn 51-65: 5X TO 12X
*1-150 PRINT RUN b/wn 36-50: 6X TO 15X
*1-150 PRINT RUN b/wn 26-35: 8X TO 20X
*1-150 PRINT RUN b/wn 16-25: 10X TO 25X
*151-180 P/R 81: .3X TO .8X AU 750+
*151-180 P/R 66-80: .4X TO 1X AU 750+
*151-180 P/R 51-65: .4X TO 1X AU 750+
*151-180 P/R 36-50: .5X TO 1.2X AU 750+
*181-200 P/R b/wn 36-50: 2X TO 5X
*181-200 P/R b/wn 26-35: 2.5X TO 6X
*181-200 P/R b/wn 16-25: 3X TO 8X
RANDOM INSERTS IN PACKS
PRINT RUNS B/WN 1-81 COPIES PER
1-120/122-50/181-200 NO PRICE 15 OR LESS
121/151-180 NO PRICING ON 25 OR LESS

2004 Donruss Elite Status Gold

Nm-Mt Ex-Mt
*GOLD 1-120/122-150: 10X TO 25X BASIC
*GOLD 181-200: 3X TO 8X BASIC
RANDOM INSERTS IN PACKS
STATED PRINT RUN 24 SERIAL #'d SETS
121/151-180 NO PRICING DUE TO SCARCITY

2004 Donruss Elite Turn of the Century

Nm-Mt Ex-Mt
*TOC 1-120/122-150: 1.5X TO 4X BASIC
*TOC 121: 1.25X TO 3X BASIC
1-150 PRINT RUN 750 SERIAL #'d SETS
*TOC 181-200: .75X TO 2X BASIC
181-200 PRINT RUN 250 SERIAL #'d SETS
RANDOM INSERTS IN PACKS
CARDS 151-180 DO NOT EXIST

2004 Donruss Elite Back 2 Back Jacks

Nm-Mt Ex-Mt
RANDOM INSERTS IN PACKS
SINGLE PRINT RUNS B/WN 25-125 PER
DUAL PRINT RUNS B/WN 25-50 PER
1 Albert Pujols/125 20.00 6.00
2 Alex Rodriguez Rgr/125 12.00 3.60
3 Alfonso Soriano/125 10.00 3.00
4 Andruw Jones/125 8.00 2.40
5 Chipper Jones/125 10.00 3.00
6 Derek Jeter/125 20.00 6.00
7 Frank Thomas/125 10.00 3.00
8 Miguel Cabrera/125 10.00 3.00
9 Jason Giambi/125 8.00 2.40
10 Jim Thome/125 10.00 3.00
11 Mike Piazza/125 12.00 3.60
12 Nomar Garciaparra/25 40.00 12.00
13 Sammy Sosa/125 12.00 3.60
14 Shawn Green/125 8.00 2.40
15 Vladimir Guerrero/125 10.00 3.00
16 Andruw Jones 25.00 7.50
Chipper Jones /50
17 Alfonso Soriano 40.00 12.00
Derek Jeter /50
18 Jeff Bagwell 25.00 7.50
Lance Berkman /50
19 Alex Rodriguez 25.00 7.50
Rafael Palmeiro /50
20 Adam Dunn 25.00 7.50
Austin Kearns/25
21 Al Kaline/100 20.00 6.00
22 Babe Ruth/50 200.00 60.00
23 Cal Ripken/100 50.00 15.00
24 Dale Murphy/100 15.00 4.50
25 Don Mattingly/100 20.00 6.00
26 George Brett/100 20.00 6.00
27 Lou Gehrig/100 100.00 30.00
28 Mike Schmidt/100 20.00 6.00
29 Roberto Clemente/100 60.00 18.00
30 Roy Campanella/100 25.00 7.50
31 Babe Ruth 250.00 75.00
Roger Maris /25
32 Harmon Killebrew 50.00 15.00
Kirby Puckett /50
33 Paul Molitor 50.00 15.00
Robin Yount /50
34 Reggie Jackson 25.00 7.50
Reggie Jackson /50
35 Lou Gehrig 200.00 60.00
Ty Cobb /50
36 Don Mattingly 40.00 12.00
Jason Giambi /50
37 Ted Williams 100.00 30.00
Nomar Garciaparra /50
38 Andre Dawson 30.00 9.00
Sammy Sosa /50
39 Dale Murphy 25.00 7.50
Chipper Jones /50
40 Stan Musial 40.00 12.00
Jim Edmonds /50

2004 Donruss Elite Back 2 Back Jacks Combos

Nm-Mt Ex-Mt
*COMBO 1-15: .75X TO 2X B2B p/r 125
*COMBO 1-15: .4X TO 1X B2B p/r 25
*COMBO 16-20: .6X TO 1.5X B2B p/r 50
*COMBO 16-20: .5X TO 1.2X B2B p/r 25
*COMBO 21-30 p/r 50:.6X TO 1.5X BTBp/r100
*COMBO 21-30 p/r 25: 1X TO 2.5X BTB p/r 100
*COMBO 21-30 p/r 25: .6X TO 1.5X BTB p/r 50
*COMBO 31-40 p/r 25: .6X TO 1.5X B2B p/r 50
RANDOM INSERTS IN PACKS
SINGLE PRINT RUNS B/WN 25-50 PER
DUAL PRINT RUNS B/WN 10-25 PER
NO PRICING ON QTY OF 10 OR LESS
12 N.Garciaparra Bat-Jsy/50 40.00 12.00
22 Babe Ruth Bat-Jsy/25 500.00 150.00
27 Lou Gehrig Bat-Jsy/25 250.00 75.00
35 Lou Gehrig Bat-Jsy 400.00 120.00
Ty Cobb Bat-Jsy/25
37 Ted Williams Bat-Jsy 150.00 45.00
Nomar Garciaparra Bat-Jsy/25

2004 Donruss Elite Back to the Future

Nm-Mt Ex-Mt
1-6 PRINT RUN 500 SERIAL #'d SETS
6-9 PRINT RUN 250 SERIAL #'d SETS
*BLACK 1-6: 1X TO 2.5X BASIC
*BLACK 7-9: 1.25X TO 3X BASIC
BLACK 1-6 PRINT RUN 50 SERIAL #'d SETS
BLACK 7-9 PRINT RUN 25 SERIAL #'d SETS
*GOLD 1-6: .6X TO 1.5X BASIC
*GOLD 7-9: .75X TO 2X BASIC
GOLD 1-6 PRINT RUN 100 SERIAL #'d SETS
GOLD 7-9 PRINT RUN 50 SERIAL #'d SETS
*RED 1-6: .5X TO 1.2X BASIC
*RED 7-9: .5X TO 1.2X BASIC
RED 1-6 PRINT RUN 250 SERIAL #'d SETS
RED 7-9 PRINT RUN 125 SERIAL #'d SETS
RANDOM INSERTS IN PACKS
1 Tim Hudson 3.00 .90
2 Rich Harden 3.00 .90
3 Alex Rodriguez Rgr 6.00 1.80
4 Hank Blalock 3.00 .90
5 Sammy Sosa 6.00 1.80
6 Hee Seop Choi 3.00 .90
7 Tim Hudson 4.00 1.20
Rich Harden
8 Alex Rodriguez 8.00 2.40
Hank Blalock
9 Sammy Sosa 8.00 2.40
Hee Seop Choi

2004 Donruss Elite Back to the Future Jerseys

Nm-Mt Ex-Mt
1-6 PRINT RUN 200 SERIAL #'d SETS

7-9 PRINT RUN 100 SERIAL #'d SETS
*PRIME: 1.25X TO 3X BASIC
PRIME 1-6 PRINT RUN 50 SERIAL #'d SETS
PRIME 7-9 PRINT RUN 25 SERIAL #'d SETS
RANDOM INSERTS IN PACKS
1 Tim Hudson 6.00 1.80
2 Rich Harden 6.00 1.80
3 Alex Rodriguez Rgr 10.00 3.00
4 Hank Blalock 6.00 1.80
5 Sammy Sosa 10.00 3.00
6 Hee Seop Choi 6.00 1.80
7 Tim Hudson 10.00 3.00
Rich Harden
8 Alex Rodriguez 15.00 4.50
Hank Blalock
9 Sammy Sosa 15.00 4.50
Hee Seop Choi

2004 Donruss Elite Career Best

Nm-Mt Ex-Mt
STATED PRINT RUN 1000 SERIAL #'d SETS
*BLACK: 1.25X TO 3X BASIC
BLACK PRINT RUN 100 SERIAL #'d SETS
*GOLD p/r 220-390: 1X TO 2.5X BASIC
*GOLD p/r 130-193: 1X TO 2.5X BASIC
*GOLD p/r 113-116: 1.25X TO 3X BASIC
*GOLD p/r 40-57: 2X TO 5X BASIC
*GOLD p/r 23-33: 3X TO 8X BASIC
*GOLD p/r 18-20: 4X TO 10X BASIC
GOLD PRINT RUNS B/WN 14-393 PER
NO GOLD PRICING ON QTY OF 14 OR LESS
RANDOM INSERTS IN PACKS
1 Albert Pujols 4.00 1.20
2 Alex Rodriguez Rgr 3.00 .90
3 Alfonso Soriano 2.00 .60
4 Andruw Jones 1.50 .45
5 Barry Zito 1.50 .45
6 Cal Ripken 8.00 2.40
7 Chipper Jones 2.00 .60
8 Curt Schilling 1.50 .45
9 Derek Jeter 4.00 1.20
10 Don Mattingly 6.00 1.80
11 Dontrelle Willis 2.00 .60
12 Doc Gooden 2.00 .60
13 Eddie Murray 2.50 .75
14 Frank Thomas 2.00 .60
15 Gary Sheffield 1.50 .45
16 George Brett 6.00 1.80
17 Greg Maddux 3.00 .90
18 Hideo Nomo 3.00 .90
19 Ichiro Suzuki 3.00 .90
20 Ivan Rodriguez 2.00 .60
21 Jason Giambi 1.50 .45
22 Jeff Bagwell 2.00 .60
23 Jim Thome 2.00 .60
24 Kerry Wood 2.00 .60
25 Lance Berkman 1.50 .45
26 Magglio Ordonez 1.50 .45
27 Mark Prior 2.00 .60
28 Mike Piazza 3.00 .90
29 Mike Schmidt 5.00 1.50
30 Nomar Garciaparra 3.00 .90
31 Pedro Martinez 2.00 .60
32 Randy Johnson 2.00 .60
33 Roger Clemens 3.00 .90
34 Sammy Sosa 3.00 .90
35 Tony Gwynn 3.00 .90

2004 Donruss Elite Career Best Bats

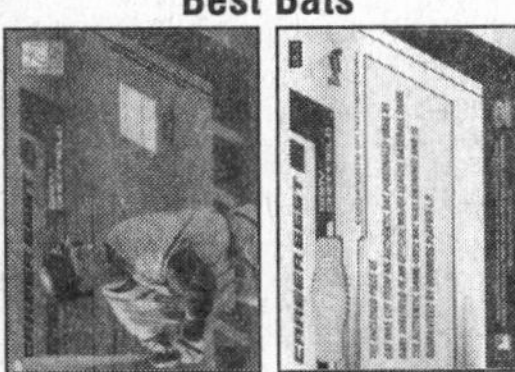

Nm-Mt Ex-Mt
PRINT RUNS B/WN 100-200 COPIES PER
*COMBO p/r 50: 1X TO 2.5X BASIC p/r 200
*COMBO p/r 50: .75X TO 2X BASIC p/r 100
*COMBO p/r 25: 1.25X TO 3X BASIC p/r 200
COMBO PRINT RUNS B/WN 25-50 PER
RANDOM INSERTS IN PACKS
1 Albert Pujols/200 15.00 4.50
2 Alex Rodriguez Rgr/200 10.00 3.00
3 Alfonso Soriano/200 8.00 2.40
4 Andruw Jones/200 6.00 1.80
5 Barry Zito/200 6.00 1.80
6 Cal Ripken/200 40.00 12.00
7 Chipper Jones/200 8.00 2.40
8 Curt Schilling/200 6.00 1.80
9 Derek Jeter/200 15.00 4.50
10 Don Mattingly/200 20.00 6.00
11 Dontrelle Willis/100 8.00 2.40
12 Doc Gooden/200 8.00 2.40
13 Eddie Murray/200 10.00 3.00
14 Frank Thomas/200 8.00 2.40
15 Gary Sheffield/200 6.00 1.80
16 George Brett/200 20.00 6.00
17 Greg Maddux/100 12.00 3.60
18 Hideo Nomo/100 10.00 3.00
20 Ivan Rodriguez/200 8.00 2.40
21 Jason Giambi/200 6.00 1.80
22 Jeff Bagwell/200 8.00 2.40
23 Jim Thome/200 8.00 2.40
24 Kerry Wood/100 10.00 3.00
25 Lance Berkman/200 6.00 1.80
26 Magglio Ordonez/200 6.00 1.80
27 Mark Prior/100 10.00 3.00
28 Mike Piazza/200 10.00 3.00
29 Mike Schmidt/200 15.00 4.50
30 Nomar Garciaparra/200 10.00 3.00
31 Pedro Martinez/200 8.00 2.40
32 Randy Johnson/200 8.00 2.40
33 Roger Clemens/200 15.00 4.50
34 Sammy Sosa/200 10.00 3.00
35 Tony Gwynn/200 15.00 4.50

2004 Donruss Elite Career Best Jerseys

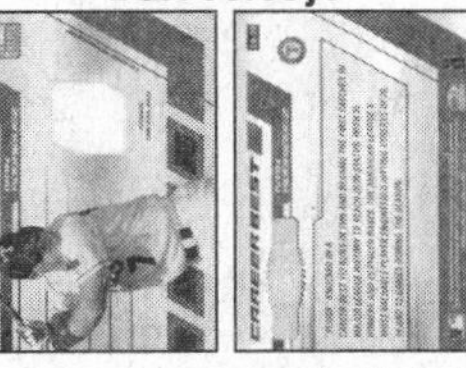

Nm-Mt Ex-Mt
PRINT RUNS B/WN 50-200 COPIES PER
*PRIME p/r 50: 1.25X TO 3X BASIC p/r 200
*PRIME p/r 25: 1.5X TO 4X BASIC p/r 200
*PRIME p/r 25: 1X TO 2.5X BASIC p/r 100
*PRIME p/r 25: 1X TO 2.5X BASIC p/r 50
PRIME PRINT RUNS B/WN 25-50 COPIES PER
RANDOM INSERTS IN PACKS
1 Albert Pujols/200 15.00 4.50
2 Alex Rodriguez/200 10.00 3.00
3 Alfonso Soriano/200 8.00 2.40
4 Andruw Jones/200 6.00 1.80
5 Barry Zito/200 6.00 1.80
6 Cal Ripken/50 60.00 18.00
7 Chipper Jones/200 8.00 2.40
8 Curt Schilling/200 6.00 1.80
9 Derek Jeter/200 15.00 4.50
10 Don Mattingly/50 30.00 9.00
11 Dontrelle Willis/200 6.00 1.80
12 Doc Gooden/200 8.00 2.40
13 Eddie Murray/200 10.00 3.00
14 Frank Thomas/200 8.00 2.40
15 Gary Sheffield/200 6.00 1.80
16 George Brett/50 30.00 9.00
17 Greg Maddux/200 10.00 3.00
18 Hideo Nomo/200 10.00 3.00
20 Ivan Rodriguez/200 8.00 2.40
21 Jason Giambi/200 6.00 1.80
22 Jeff Bagwell/200 8.00 2.40
23 Jim Thome/200 8.00 2.40
24 Kerry Wood/200 8.00 2.40
25 Lance Berkman/200 6.00 1.80
26 Magglio Ordonez/200 6.00 1.80
27 Mark Prior/200 8.00 2.40
28 Mike Piazza/200 10.00 3.00
29 Mike Schmidt/100 25.00 7.50
30 Nomar Garciaparra/200 10.00 3.00
31 Pedro Martinez/200 8.00 2.40
32 Randy Johnson/200 8.00 2.40
33 Roger Clemens/200 15.00 4.50
34 Sammy Sosa/200 10.00 3.00
35 Tony Gwynn/50 25.00 7.50

2004 Donruss Elite Fans of the Game

Nm-Mt Ex-Mt
RANDOM INSERTS IN PACKS
201 James Gandolfini 3.00 .90
202 Freddy Adu 3.00 .90
203 Summer Sanders 2.00 .60
204 Janet Evans 2.00 .60
205 Brandi Chastain 3.00 .90

2004 Donruss Elite Fans of the Game Autographs

This five card insert set, which was randomly inserted into packs, was the lead-off insert of inserting autograph cards of living celebrities from other fields into major sport mainstream packs. Among the players in these packs were teenage soccer sensation Freddy Adu and star of Television show "The Sopranos" James Gandolfini.

Nm-Mt Ex-Mt
RANDOM INSERTS IN PACKS
201 James Gandolfini 120.00 36.00
202 Freddy Adu 80.00 24.00
203 Summer Sanders 40.00 12.00
204 Janet Evans 40.00 12.00
205 Brandi Chastain 80.00 24.00

2004 Donruss Elite Passing the Torch

Nm-Mt Ex-Mt
1-30 PRINT RUN 1000 SERIAL #'d SETS

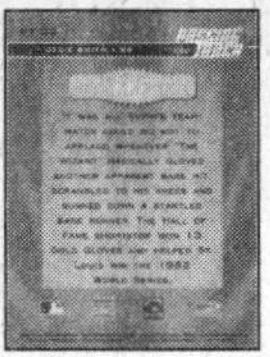

31-45 PRINT RUN 500 SERIAL #'d SETS
*BLACK 1-30: .75X TO 2X BASIC
*BLACK 31-45: 1X TO 2.5X BASIC
BLACK 1-30 PRINT RUN 100 #'d SETS
BLACK 31-45 PRINT RUN 50 #'d SETS
*BLUE 1-30: .6X TO 1.5X BASIC
*BLUE 31-45: .6X TO 1.5X BASIC
BLUE 1-30 PRINT RUN 250 #'d SETS
BLUE 31-45 PRINT RUN 125 #'d SETS
*GOLD 1-30: 1.25X TO 3X BASIC
*GOLD 31-45: 1.5X TO 4X BASIC
GOLD 1-30 PRINT RUN 50 #'d SETS
GOLD 31-45 PRINT RUN 25 #'d SETS
*GREEN 1-30: .5X TO 1.2X BASIC
*GREEN 31-45: .5X TO 1.2X BASIC
GREEN 1-30 PRINT RUN 500 #'d SETS
GREEN 31-45 PRINT RUN 250 #'d SETS
RANDOM INSERTS IN PACKS
1 Whitey Ford 4.00 1.20
2 Andy Pettitte 3.00 .90
3 Willie McCovey 3.00 .90
4 Will Clark 4.00 1.20
5 Stan Musial 6.00 1.80
6 Albert Pujols 6.00 1.80
7 Andre Dawson 3.00 .90
8 Vladimir Guerrero 3.00 .90
9 Dale Murphy 4.00 1.20
10 Chipper Jones 3.00 .90
11 Joe Morgan 3.00 .90
12 Barry Larkin 4.00 1.20
13 Catfish Hunter 4.00 1.20
14 Tim Hudson 2.50 .75
15 Jim Rice 3.00 .90
16 Manny Ramirez 3.00 .90
17 Greg Maddux 5.00 1.50
18 Mark Prior 3.00 .90
19 Don Mattingly 10.00 3.00
20 Jason Giambi 2.50 .75
21 Roy Campanella 4.00 1.20
22 Mike Piazza 5.00 1.50
23 Ozzie Smith 6.00 1.80
24 Scott Rolen 3.00 .90
25 Roger Clemens 6.00 1.80
26 Mike Mussina 3.00 .90
27 Babe Ruth 8.00 2.40
28 Roger Maris 4.00 1.20
29 Nolan Ryan 10.00 3.00
30 Roy Oswalt 2.50 .75
31 Whitey Ford 5.00 1.50
Andy Pettitte
32 Willie McCovey 5.00 1.50
Will Clark
33 Stan Musial 8.00 2.40
Albert Pujols
34 Andre Dawson 5.00 1.50
Vladimir Guerrero
35 Dale Murphy 5.00 1.50
Chipper Jones
36 Joe Morgan 5.00 1.50
Barry Larkin
37 Catfish Hunter 5.00 1.50
Tim Hudson
38 Jim Rice 5.00 1.50
Manny Ramirez
39 Greg Maddux 6.00 1.80
Mark Prior
40 Don Mattingly 12.00 3.60
Jason Giambi
41 Roy Campanella 6.00 1.80
Mike Piazza
42 Ozzie Smith 8.00 2.40
Scott Rolen
43 Roger Clemens 8.00 2.40
Mike Mussina
44 Babe Ruth 10.00 3.00
Roger Maris
45 Nolan Ryan 12.00 3.60
Roy Oswalt

2004 Donruss Elite Passing the Torch Autographs

Nm-Mt Ex-Mt
RANDOM INSERTS IN PACKS
SINGLE PRINT RUNS B/WN 5-50 PER
DUAL PRINT RUNS B/WN 1-5 COPIES PER
NO PRICING ON QTY OF 10 OR LESS
1 Whitey Ford/10
3 Willie McCovey/10
4 Will Clark/15 150.00 45.00
6 Stan Musial/10
7 Andre Dawson/50 20.00 6.00
8 Vladimir Guerrero/5
9 Dale Murphy/50 40.00 12.00
10 Chipper Jones/5
11 Joe Morgan/15 40.00 12.00
12 Barry Larkin/10
14 Tim Hudson/15 60.00 18.00
15 Jim Rice/50 20.00 6.00
16 Manny Ramirez/5
17 Greg Maddux/5
18 Mark Prior/15 150.00 45.00
19 Don Mattingly/10
22 Mike Piazza/5
23 Ozzie Smith/5
24 Scott Rolen/15 80.00 24.00
25 Roger Clemens/5
26 Mike Mussina/5
29 Nolan Ryan/10
30 Roy Oswalt/50 20.00 6.00
32 Willie McCovey
Will Clark/5
33 Stan Musial
Albert Pujols/5
34 Andre Dawson
Vladimir Guerrero/5
35 Dale Murphy
Chipper Jones/5
36 Joe Morgan
Barry Larkin/5
38 Jim Rice
Manny Ramirez/5
39 Greg Maddux
Mark Prior/5
42 Ozzie Smith
Scott Rolen/5
43 Roger Clemens
Mike Mussina/5
44 Babe Ruth
Roger Maris/1
45 Nolan Ryan
Roy Oswalt/5

2004 Donruss Elite Passing the Torch Bats

Nm-Mt Ex-Mt
1-30 PRINT RUNS B/WN 25-200 COPIES PER
31-45 PRINT RUNS B/WN 25-50 COPIES PER
RANDOM INSERTS IN PACKS
2 Andy Pettitte/200 8.00 2.40
3 Willie McCovey/100 10.00 3.00
4 Will Clark/100 15.00 4.50
5 Stan Musial/100 30.00 9.00
6 Albert Pujols/200 15.00 4.50
7 Andre Dawson/100 10.00 3.00
8 Vladimir Guerrero/200 8.00 2.40
9 Dale Murphy/100 15.00 4.50
10 Chipper Jones/200 8.00 2.40
11 Joe Morgan/200 8.00 2.40
12 Barry Larkin/200 8.00 2.40
14 Tim Hudson/200 6.00 1.80
15 Jim Rice/200 8.00 2.40
16 Manny Ramirez/200 8.00 2.40
17 Greg Maddux/200 10.00 3.00
18 Mark Prior/200 8.00 2.40
19 Don Mattingly/100 20.00 6.00
20 Jason Giambi/200 6.00 1.80
21 Roy Campanella/50 30.00 9.00
22 Mike Piazza/200 10.00 3.00
23 Ozzie Smith/200 15.00 4.50
24 Scott Rolen/200 8.00 2.40
25 Roger Clemens/200 15.00 4.50
26 Mike Mussina/200 8.00 2.40
27 Babe Ruth/25 200.00 60.00
28 Roger Maris/50 50.00 15.00
29 Nolan Ryan/100 25.00 7.50
30 Roy Oswalt/200 6.00 1.80
32 Willie McCovey 25.00 7.50
Will Clark /50
33 Stan Musial 50.00 15.00
Albert Pujols /50
34 Andre Dawson 25.00 7.50
Vladimir Guerrero /50
35 Dale Murphy 25.00 7.50
Chipper Jones /50
36 Joe Morgan 25.00 7.50
Barry Larkin /50
38 Jim Rice 25.00 7.50
Manny Ramirez /50
39 Greg Maddux 40.00 12.00
Mark Prior /50
40 Don Mattingly 40.00 12.00
Jason Giambi /50
41 Roy Campanella 40.00 12.00
Mike Piazza /25
42 Ozzie Smith 30.00 9.00
Scott Rolen /50
43 Roger Clemens 30.00 9.00
Mike Mussina /50
44 Babe Ruth 250.00 75.00
Roger Maris /25
45 Nolan Ryan 40.00 12.00
Roy Oswalt /50

2004 Donruss Elite Passing the Torch Jerseys

Nm-Mt Ex-Mt
1-30 PRINT RUNS B/WN 25-200 COPIES PER
31-45 PRINT RUNS B/WN 25-50 COPIES PER
RANDOM INSERTS IN PACKS
1 Whitey Ford/100 15.00 4.50
2 Andy Pettitte/200 8.00 2.40
3 Willie McCovey/100 10.00 3.00
4 Will Clark/100 15.00 4.50
5 Stan Musial/100 30.00 9.00
6 Albert Pujols/200 15.00 4.50
7 Andre Dawson/200 8.00 2.40
8 Vladimir Guerrero/200 8.00 2.40
9 Dale Murphy/100 15.00 4.50
10 Chipper Jones/200 8.00 2.40
11 Joe Morgan/100 10.00 3.00
12 Barry Larkin/200 8.00 2.40
13 Catfish Hunter/100 15.00 4.50
14 Tim Hudson/200 6.00 1.80
15 Jim Rice/200 8.00 2.40
16 Manny Ramirez/200 8.00 2.40
18 Mark Prior/200 8.00 2.40
19 Don Mattingly/100 25.00 7.50
20 Jason Giambi/200 6.00 1.80
21 Roy Campanella/50 30.00 9.00
22 Mike Piazza/200 10.00 3.00
23 Ozzie Smith/100 20.00 6.00
24 Scott Rolen/200 8.00 2.40
25 Roger Clemens/200 15.00 4.50
26 Mike Mussina/200 8.00 2.40
27 Babe Ruth/25 400.00 120.00
28 Roger Maris/50 60.00 18.00
29 Nolan Ryan/100 30.00 9.00
30 Roy Oswalt/200 6.00 1.80
31 Whitey Ford 25.00 7.50
Andy Pettitte/50
32 Willie McCovey 25.00 7.50
Will Clark/50
33 Stan Musial 50.00 15.00
Albert Pujols/50
34 Andre Dawson 25.00 7.50
Vladimir Guerrero/50
35 Dale Murphy 25.00 7.50
Chipper Jones/50
36 Joe Morgan 25.00 7.50
Barry Larkin/50
37 Catfish Hunter 25.00 7.50
Tim Hudson/50
38 Jim Rice 25.00 7.50
Manny Ramirez/50
40 Don Mattingly 40.00 12.00
Jason Giambi/50
41 Roy Campanella 50.00 15.00
Mike Piazza/25
42 Ozzie Smith 30.00 9.00
Scott Rolen/50
43 Roger Clemens 30.00 9.00
Mike Mussina/50
44 Babe Ruth
Roger Maris/25
45 Nolan Ryan 50.00 15.00
Roy Oswalt/50

2004 Donruss Elite Recollection Autographs

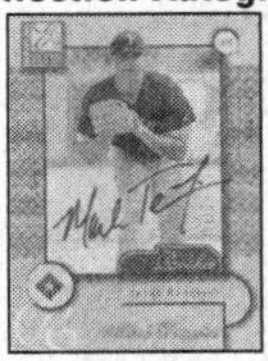

Nm-Mt Ex-Mt
RANDOM INSERTS IN PACKS
PRINT RUNS B/WN 1-95 COPIES PER
NO PRICING ON QTY OF 14 OR LESS
1 Jeremy Affeldt 01/25 25.00 7.50
2 Erick Almonte 01/26 15.00 4.50
3 Rich Aurilia 02/2
4 Jeff Baker 02/25 40.00 12.00
5 Brandon Berger 01/25 15.00 4.50
6 Marlon Byrd 01/24 25.00 7.50
7 Juan Cruz 01/5
8 Ryan Drese 02/45 25.00 7.50
9 Brandon Duckworth 01/16 20.00 6.00
10 Casey Fossum 01/23 20.00 6.00
11 Geronimo Gil 01/25 15.00 4.50
12 Mark Grace 02/2
13 Jeremy Guthrie 02/25 20.00 6.00
14 Nic Jackson 02/95 10.00 3.00
15 Barry Larkin 01 PCRD/4
16 Greg Maddux 01 Ser/1
17 Antonio Perez 01/3
18 Mark Prior 01/14
19 Ivan Rodriguez 01 Ser/3
20 Ivan Rodriguez 01 SerDom/3
21 Ricardo Rodriguez 01/25 15.00 4.50
22 Ruben Sierra 97 GS/1
23 Bud Smith 01/25 15.00 4.50
24 Sammy Sosa 01/1
25 Junior Spivey 01/20 20.00 6.00
26 Tim Spooneybarger 01/25 15.00 4.50
27 Mark Teixeira 01/6
28 Martin Vargas 01/37 10.00 3.00

2004 Donruss Elite Team

Nm-Mt Ex-Mt
STATED PRINT RUN 1500 SERIAL #'d SETS
*BLACK: 1X TO 2.5X BASIC
BLACK PRINT RUN 150 SERIAL #'d SETS
*GOLD: .75X TO 2X BASIC
GOLD PRINT RUN 250 SERIAL #'d SETS
RANDOM INSERTS IN PACKS
1 Cal Ripken 10.00 3.00
Eddie Murray
Jim Palmer
2 Derek Jeter 5.00 1.50
Roger Clemens
Bernie Williams
Andy Pettitte

3 Johnny Bench 5.00 1.50
Tony Perez
George Foster
Dave Concepcion
4 Josh Beckett 2.50 .75
Dontrelle Willis
Ivan Rodriguez
5 Randy Johnson 2.50 .75
Curt Schilling
Luis Gonzalez
Mark Grace
6 Derek Jeter 5.00 1.50
Wade Boggs
Darryl Strawberry
7 Chipper Jones 5.00 1.50
Tom Glavine
Greg Maddux
Ryan Klesko
8 Doc Gooden 2.50 .75
Gary Carter
Darryl Strawberry
9 Jackie Robinson 3.00 .90
Roy Campanella
Duke Snider
10 Phil Rizzuto 3.00 .90
Yogi Berra
Whitey Ford
11 Stan Musial 5.00 1.50
Red Schoendienst
Marty Marion
Enos Slaughter

2004 Donruss Elite Team Bats

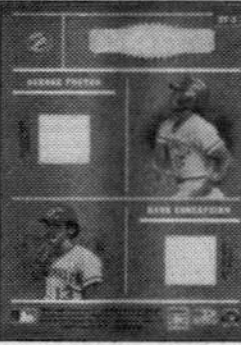

Nm-Mt Ex-Mt
RANDOM INSERTS IN PACKS
STATED PRINT RUN 100 SERIAL #'d SETS
2 Derek Jeter 40.00 12.00
Roger Clemens
Bernie Williams
Andy Pettitte
3 Johnny Bench 50.00 15.00
Tony Perez
George Foster
Dave Concepcion
4 Josh Beckett 15.00 4.50
Dontrelle Willis
Ivan Rodriguez
5 Randy Johnson 25.00 7.50
Curt Schilling
Luis Gonzalez
Mark Grace
6 Derek Jeter 30.00 9.00
Wade Boggs
Darryl Strawberry
7 Chipper Jones 30.00 9.00
Tom Glavine
Greg Maddux
Ryan Klesko
8 Doc Gooden 15.00 4.50
Gary Carter
Darryl Strawberry

2004 Donruss Elite Team Jerseys

Nm-Mt Ex-Mt
RANDOM INSERTS IN PACKS
STATED PRINT RUN 100 SERIAL #'d SETS
JACKIE/CAMPY/SNIDER PRINT 50 #'d CARDS
ROY CAMPANELLA SWATCH IS PANTS
1 Cal Ripken 60.00 18.00
Eddie Murray
Jim Palmer
2 Derek Jeter 40.00 12.00
Roger Clemens
Bernie Williams
Andy Pettitte
4 Josh Beckett 15.00 4.50
Dontrelle Willis
Ivan Rodriguez
5 Randy Johnson 25.00 7.50
Curt Schilling
Luis Gonzalez
Mark Grace
6 Derek Jeter 30.00 9.00
Wade Boggs
Darryl Strawberry
7 Chipper Jones 30.00 9.00
Tom Glavine
Greg Maddux
Ryan Klesko
9 Jackie Robinson 80.00 24.00
Roy Campanella Pants
Duke Snider/50
10 Phil Rizzuto 40.00 12.00
Yogi Berra
Whitey Ford
11 Stan Musial 60.00 18.00
Red Schoendienst
Marty Marion
Enos Slaughter

2004 Donruss Elite Throwback Threads

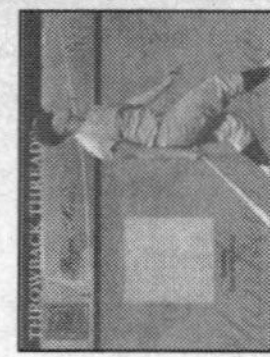

Nm-Mt Ex-Mt
1-20 PRINT RUN 150 SERIAL #'d SETS
21-30 PRINT RUN 75 SERIAL #'d SETS
RUTH 31 PRINT RUN 50 #'d CARDS..
32-50 PRINT RUN 100 SERIAL #'d SETS
RUTH/GEHRIG 51 PRINT 25 #'d CARDS
52-60 PRINT RUN 50 SERIAL #'d SETS
*PRIME 1-20: 1.5X TO 4X BASIC 1-20
*PRIME 21-30: 1X TO 2.5X BASIC 21-30
*PRIME 31-50: 1.25X TO 3X BASIC 31-50
PRIME SINGLE PRINTS B/WN 10-25 PER
PRIME DUAL PRINTS B/WN 5-15 PER
NO PRIME PRICING ON QTY OF 10 OR LESS
RANDOM INSERTS IN PACKS
CARD NUMBER 3 DOES NOT EXIST...
1 Albert Pujols/150 15.00 4.50
2 Alex Rodriguez Rgr/150 10.00 3.00
4 Chipper Jones/150 8.00 2.40
5 Derek Jeter/150 15.00 4.50
6 Greg Maddux/150 10.00 3.00
7 Hideo Nomo/150 10.00 3.00
8 Miguel Cabrera/150 8.00 2.40
9 Ivan Rodriguez/150 8.00 2.40
10 Jason Giambi/150 6.00 1.80
11 Jeff Bagwell/150 8.00 2.40
12 Lance Berkman/150 6.00 1.80
13 Mark Prior/150 8.00 2.40
14 Mike Piazza/150 10.00 3.00
15 Nomar Garciaparra/150 10.00 3.00
16 Pedro Martinez/150 8.00 2.40
17 Randy Johnson/150 8.00 2.40
18 Sammy Sosa/150 10.00 3.00
19 Shawn Green/150 6.00 1.80
20 Vladimir Guerrero/150 8.00 2.40
21 Adam Dunn 20.00 6.00
Austin Kearns /75
22 Barry Zito 15.00 4.50
Mark Mulder /75
23 Curt Schilling 15.00 4.50
Curt Schilling /75
24 Derek Jeter 30.00 9.00
Jason Giambi /75
25 Dontrelle Willis 15.00 4.50
Josh Beckett /75
26 Frank Thomas 20.00 6.00
Magglio Ordonez /75
27 Jim Thome 20.00 6.00
Jim Thome /75
28 Kerry Wood 25.00 7.50
Mark Prior /75
29 Hank Blalock 15.00 4.50
Mark Teixeira /75
30 Albert Pujols 40.00 12.00
Scott Rolen /75
31 Babe Ruth/50 300.00 90.00
32 Cal Ripken/100 50.00 15.00
33 Carl Yastrzemski/100 25.00 7.50
34 Deion Sanders/100 15.00 4.50
35 Don Mattingly/100 25.00 7.50
36 George Brett/100 25.00 7.50
37 Jim Palmer/100 10.00 3.00
38 Kirby Puckett/100 15.00 4.50
39 Lou Gehrig/100 200.00 60.00
40 Mark Grace/100 15.00 4.50
41 Mike Schmidt/100 25.00 7.50
42 Nolan Ryan/100 30.00 9.00
43 Ozzie Smith/100 20.00 6.00
44 Reggie Jackson/100 15.00 4.50
45 Rickey Henderson/100 15.00 4.50
46 Roberto Clemente/100 80.00 24.00
47 Roger Clemens/100 20.00 6.00
48 Roger Maris/100 50.00 15.00
49 Roy Campanella Pants/100 25.00 7.50
50 Tony Gwynn/100 20.00 6.00
51 Babe Ruth 500.00 150.00
Lou Gehrig /25
52 Cal Ripken 60.00 18.00
Eddie Murray /50
53 Ted Williams 100.00 30.00
Carl Yastrzemski /50
54 Andre Dawson 20.00 6.00
Gary Carter /50
55 Reggie Jackson 25.00 7.50
Rod Carew /50
56 Derek Jeter 50.00 15.00
Phil Rizzuto /50
57 Nolan Ryan 50.00 15.00
Roy Oswalt /50
58 Roger Clemens 30.00 9.00
Mike Mussina /50
59 Albert Pujols 50.00 15.00
Stan Musial /50
60 Nomar Garciaparra 100.00 30.00
Ted Williams /50

2004 Donruss Elite Throwback Threads Autographs

Nm-Mt Ex-Mt
STATED PRINT RUN 25 SERIAL #'d SETS
PRIME PRINT RUNS B/WN 5-10 COPIES PER
NO PRIME PRICING DUE TO SCARCITY
RANDOM INSERTS IN PACKS
9 Ivan Rodriguez/25 80.00 24.00
13 Mark Prior/25 150.00 45.00
18 Sammy Sosa/25 200.00 60.00
35 Don Mattingly/25 150.00 45.00
37 Jim Palmer/25 50.00 15.00

2002 Donruss Originals

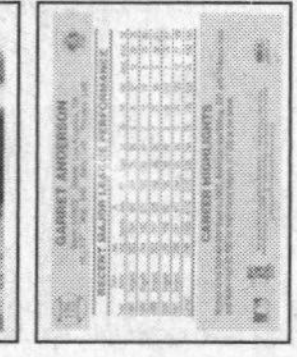

This 425 card set was issued in two separate series. The Donruss Originals product, containing cards 1-400, was released in September, 2002. This product was issued in five card packs which were seeded 24 packs to a box and 20 boxes to a case with each pack having a suggested retail price of $3. Fifty cards in this set were printed to a quantity of approximately 20 percent fewer than the other 350 cards in this set. All 50 cards are tagged as SP's in our checklist. This set was issued in the styles of the 1982, 1984, 1986 and 1988 Donruss sets but featured active 2002 players. The "style year" of the card is listed next to the player's name in our checklist. In addition, puzzle pieces featuring the late Ted Williams were randomly inserted into packs. Cards 401-425 were randomly seeded into hobby and retail packs of 2002 Donruss the Rookies (of which was released in mid-December 2002) at the following ratios: hobby 1:3, retail 1:4. These update cards feature a selection of prospects.

Nm-Mt Ex-Mt
COMP.LOW SET (400) 200.00 60.00
COMP.UPDATE SET (25) 25.00 7.50
COMMON CARD (1-400) .40 .12
COMMON SP 1.00 .30
COMMON CARD (401-425) .75 .23
COMP.WILLIAMS PUZZLE (63) 40.00 12.00
1 So Taguchi 82 RR RC .60 .18
2 Allan Simpson 82 RR RC .40 .12
3 Brian Mallette 82 RR RC .40 .12
4 Ben Howard 82 RR RC .40 .12
5 Kazuhisa Ishii 82 RR RC 2.50 .75
6 Francis Beltran 82 RR RC .40 .12
7 Jorge Padilla 82 RR RC .40 .12
8 Brandon Puffer 82 RR RC .40 .12
9 Oliver Perez 82 RR RC 4.00 1.20
10 Kirk Saarloos 82 RR RC .40 .12
11 Travis Driskill 82 RR RC .40 .12
12 Jeremy Lambert 82 RR RC .40 .12
13 John Foster 82 RR RC .40 .12
14 Steve Kent 82 RR RC .40 .12
15 Shawn Sedlacek 82 RR RC .40 .12
16 Alex Rodriguez 82 1.50 .45
17 Lance Berkman 82 .40 .12
18 Kevin Brown 82 .40 .12
19 Garret Anderson 82 .40 .12
20 Bobby Abreu 82 .40 .12
21 Richard Hidalgo 82 .40 .12
22 Matt Morris 82 .40 .12
23 Manny Ramirez 82 SP 1.50 .45
24 Derek Jeter 82 2.50 .75
25 Kerry Wood 82 1.00 .30
26 Mark Grace 82 .60 .18
27 Edgar Martinez 82 .60 .18
28 Nomar Garciaparra 82 1.50 .45
29 Roberto Alomar 82 SP 1.50 .45
30 Jason Giambi 82 .40 .12
31 Juan Gonzalez 82 SP 1.50 .45
32 Albert Pujols 82 2.00 .60
33 Juan Cruz 82 .40 .12
34 Troy Glaus 82 .40 .12
35 Greg Maddux 82 1.50 .45
36 Adam Dunn 82 SP 1.50 .45
37 J.D. Drew 82 .40 .12
38 Tsuyoshi Shinjo 82 .40 .12
39 Vladimir Guerrero 82 1.00 .30
40 Barry Bonds 82 2.50 .75
41 Carlos Delgado 82 .40 .12
42 Ken Griffey Jr. 82 1.50 .45
43 Carlos Pena 82 .40 .12
44 Jeff Kent 82 .40 .12
45 Roger Clemens 82 SP 4.00 1.20
46 Frank Thomas 82 1.00 .30
47 Larry Walker 82 .60 .18
48 Pedro Martinez 82 1.00 .30
49 Moises Alou 82 .40 .12
50 Andruw Jones 82 SP 1.00 .30
51 Luis Gonzalez 82 .40 .12
52 Adrian Beltre 82 .60 .18
53 Bobby Hill 82 .40 .12
54 Roy Oswalt 82 .40 .12
55 Tim Hudson 82 .40 .12
56 Trot Nixon 82 .40 .12
57 Jeff Bagwell 82 .60 .18
58 Bernie Williams 82 .60 .18
59 Magglio Ordonez 82 SP 1.00 .30
60 Bartolo Colon 82 .40 .12
61 Shawn Green 82 .40 .12
62 Mark Buehrle 82 .40 .12
63 Sean Casey 82 .40 .12
64 Rickey Henderson 82 1.00 .30
65 Aramis Ramirez 82 SP 1.00 .30
66 Ichiro Suzuki 82 1.50 .45
67 Cliff Floyd 82 .40 .12
68 Darin Erstad 82 .40 .12
69 Paul LoDuca 82 .40 .12
70 Ivan Rodriguez 82 1.00 .30
71 Mo Vaughn 82 .40 .12
72 Todd Helton 82 SP 1.50 .45
73 Raul Mondesi 82 .40 .12
74 Sammy Sosa 82 1.50 .45
75 Cristian Guzman 82 .40 .12
76 Jimmy Rollins 82 .40 .12
77 Hideo Nomo 82 1.00 .30
78 C.C. Sabathia 82 .40 .12
79 Wade Miller 82 .40 .12
80 Drew Henson 82 SP 1.00 .30
81 Chipper Jones 82 1.00 .30
82 Miguel Tejada 82 .40 .12
83 Freddy Garcia 82 .40 .12
84 Richie Sexson 82 .40 .12
85 Robin Ventura 82 .40 .12
86 Jose Vidro 82 .40 .12
87 Rich Aurilla 82 .40 .12
88 Scott Rolen 82 1.00 .30
89 Carlos Beltran 82 .60 .18
90 Austin Kearns 82 SP 1.00 .30
91 Kazuhiro Sasaki 82 .40 .12
92 Carlos Hernandez 82 .40 .12
93 Randy Johnson 82 1.00 .30
94 Jim Thome 82 1.00 .30
95 Curt Schilling 82 .40 .12
96 Alfonso Soriano 82 SP 1.50 .45
97 Barry Larkin 82 .60 .18
98 Rafael Palmeiro 82 .60 .18
99 Tom Glavine 82 .60 .18
100 Barry Zito 82 .40 .12
101 Craig Biggio 82 .60 .18
102 Mike Piazza 82 1.50 .45
103 Ben Sheets 82 .40 .12
104 Mark Mulder 82 .40 .12
105 Mike Mussina 82 .60 .18
106 Jim Edmonds 82 .40 .12
107 Paul Konerko 82 .40 .12
108 Pat Burrell 82 .40 .12
109 Chan Ho Park 82 .40 .12
110 Mike Sweeney 82 .40 .12
111 Phil Nevin 82 .40 .12
112 Brian Giles 82 .40 .12
113 Eric Chavez 82 SP 1.00 .30
114 Corey Patterson 82 .40 .12
115 Gary Sheffield 82 .40 .12
116 Kazuhisa Ishii 84 RR RC 2.50 .75
117 Kyle Kane 84 RR RC .40 .12
118 Eric Junge 84 RR RC .40 .12
119 Luis Ugueto 84 RR RC .40 .12
120 Cam Esslinger 84 RR RC .40 .12
121 Earl Snyder 84 RR RC .60 .18
122 Oliver Perez 84 RR RC 4.00 1.20
123 Victor Alvarez 84 RR RC .40 .12
124 Tom Shearn 84 RR RC .40 .12
125 Corey Thurman 84 RR RC .40 .12
126 Satoru Komiyama 84 RR RC .40 .12
127 Hansel Izquierdo 84 RR RC .40 .12
128 Elio Serrano 84 RR RC .40 .12
129 Mike Crudale 84 RR RC .40 .12
130 Chris Snelling 84 RR RC .40 .12
131 Nomar Garciaparra 84 1.50 .45
132 Roger Clemens 84 2.00 .60
133 Hank Blalock 84 1.00 .30
134 Eric Chavez 84 .40 .12
135 Corey Patterson 84 .40 .12
136 Richie Sexson 84 .40 .12
137 Freddy Garcia 84 .40 .12
138 Miguel Tejada 84 .40 .12
139 Alex Rodriguez 84 SP 3.00 .90
140 Adrian Beltre 84 .60 .18
141 Bobby Abreu 84 .40 .12
142 Bret Boone 84 .40 .12
143 Tim Hudson 84 .40 .12
144 Roy Oswalt 84 .40 .12
145 Derek Jeter 84 2.50 .75
146 Rich Aurilla 84 .40 .12
147 Mark Grace 84 .60 .18
148 Kerry Wood 84 SP 2.00 .60
149 Geronimo Gil 84 .40 .12
150 Mark Buehrle 84 .40 .12
151 Jim Edmonds 84 .40 .12
152 Ichiro Suzuki 84 1.50 .45
153 Juan Gonzalez 84 .60 .18
154 Darin Erstad 84 .40 .12
155 Barry Bonds 84 SP 5.00 1.50
156 Greg Maddux 84 1.50 .45
157 Adam Dunn 84 .60 .18
158 Todd Helton 84 .60 .18
159 Roberto Alomar 84 .60 .18
160 Sammy Sosa 84 1.50 .45
161 Sean Burroughs 84 .40 .12
162 Albert Pujols 84 2.00 .60
163 Carlos Delgado 84 .40 .12
164 Frank Thomas 84 1.00 .30
165 Ken Griffey Jr. 84 1.50 .45
166 Jason Giambi 84 1.00 .30
167 Chipper Jones 84 1.00 .30
168 Ivan Rodriguez 84 1.00 .30
169 Pedro Martinez 84 SP 2.00 .60
170 Gary Sheffield 84 .40 .12
171 Andruw Jones 84 .40 .12
172 Luis Gonzalez 84 SP 1.00 .30
173 Raul Mondesi 84 .40 .12
174 Jose Vidro 84 .40 .12
175 Garret Anderson 84 SP 1.00 .30
176 Scott Rolen 84 1.00 .30
177 Kazuhiro Sasaki 84 .40 .12
178 Jeff Bagwell 84 .60 .18
179 Manny Ramirez 84 .60 .18
180 Jim Thome 84 1.00 .30
181 Ben Sheets 84 .40 .12
182 Randy Johnson 84 1.00 .30
183 Lance Berkman 84 .40 .12
184 Shawn Green 84 .40 .12
185 Rickey Henderson 84 SP 2.00 .60
186 Edgar Martinez 84 .60 .18
187 Barry Larkin 84 .60 .18
188 Bernie Williams 84 .60 .18
189 Luis Aparicio 84 .60 .18
190 Troy Glaus 84 SP 1.00 .30
191 Mike Mussina 84 .60 .18
192 Pee Wee Reese 84 .60 .18
193 Craig Biggio 84 .60 .18
194 Vladimir Guerrero 84 1.00 .30
195 J.D. Drew 84 .40 .12
196 Jeff Kent 84 .40 .12
197 Dewon Brazelton 84 .40 .12
198 Tsuyoshi Shinjo 84 SP 1.00 .30
199 Sean Casey 84 .40 .12
200 Hideo Nomo 84 1.00 .30
201 C.C. Sabathia 84 .40 .12
202 Larry Walker 84 .60 .18
203 Mark Teixeira 84 .60 .18
204 Mike Sweeney 84 SP 1.00 .30
205 Moises Alou 84 .40 .12
206 Mark Prior 84 1.50 .45
207 Javier Vazquez 84 .40 .12
208 Phil Nevin 84 SP 1.00 .30
209 Harmon Killebrew 84 1.00 .30
210 Brian Giles 84 .40 .12
211 Carlos Beltran 84 .60 .18
212 Don Drysdale 84 1.00 .30
213 Matt Morris 84 .40 .12
214 Trot Nixon 84 .40 .12
215 Magglio Ordonez 84 .40 .12
216 Curt Schilling 84 SP 1.00 .30
217 Mark Mulder 84 .40 .12
218 Alfonso Soriano 84 .60 .18
219 Rafael Palmeiro 84 SP 1.50 .45
220 Tom Glavine 84 .60 .18
221 Barry Zito 84 .40 .12
222 Mike Piazza 84 1.50 .45
223 Bartolo Colon 84 .40 .12
224 Cliff Floyd 84 .40 .12
225 Paul LoDuca 84 SP 1.00 .30
226 Cristian Guzman 84 .40 .12
227 Mo Vaughn 84 .40 .12
228 Aramis Ramirez 84 .40 .12
229 Pat Burrell 84 .40 .12
230 Chan Ho Park 84 .40 .12
231 Satoru Komiyama 86 RR RC .40 .12
232 Brandon Backe 86 RR RC 1.00 .30
233 Anderson Machado 86 RR RC .40 .12
234 Doug Devore 86 RR RC .40 .12
235 Steve Bechler 86 RR RC .40 .12
236 John Ennis 86 RR RC .40 .12
237 Rodrigo Rosario 86 RR RC .40 .12
238 Jorge Sosa 86 RR RC .40 .12
239 Ken Huckaby 86 RR RC .40 .12
240 Mike Moriarty 86 RR RC .40 .12
241 Kirk Saarloos 86 RR RC .40 .12
242 Kevin Frederick 86 RR RC .40 .12
243 Aaron Guiel 86 RR RC .40 .12
244 Jose Rodriguez 86 RR RC .40 .12
245 So Taguchi 86 RR RC .60 .18
246 Albert Pujols 86 2.00 .60
247 Derek Jeter 86 2.50 .75
248 Brian Giles 86 .40 .12
249 Mike Cameron 86 .40 .12
250 Josh Beckett 86 .40 .12
251 Ken Griffey Jr. 86 SP 3.00 .90
252 Aramis Ramirez 86 .40 .12
253 Miguel Tejada 86 .40 .12
254 Carlos Delgado 86 .40 .12
255 Pedro Martinez 86 1.00 .30
256 Raul Mondesi 86 .40 .12
257 Roger Clemens 86 2.00 .60
258 Gary Sheffield 86 .40 .12
259 Jose Vidro 86 SP 1.00 .30
260 Alex Rodriguez 86 1.50 .45
261 Larry Walker 86 .60 .18
262 Mark Mulder 86 .40 .12
263 Scott Rolen 86 1.00 .30
264 Tim Hudson 86 .40 .12
265 Manny Ramirez 86 .60 .18
266 Rich Aurilla 86 .40 .12
267 Roy Oswalt 86 .40 .12
268 Mark Grace 86 .60 .18
269 Lance Berkman 86 SP 1.00 .30
270 Nomar Garciaparra 86 SP 3.00 .90
271 Barry Bonds 86 2.50 .75
272 Ryan Klesko 86 .40 .12
273 Ichiro Suzuki 86 1.50 .45
274 Shawn Green 86 .40 .12
275 Darin Erstad 86 .40 .12
276 Bernie Williams 86 .60 .18
277 Greg Maddux 86 SP 3.00 .90
278 Eric Hinske 86 .40 .12
279 Randy Johnson 86 1.00 .30
280 Todd Helton 86 .60 .18
281 Sammy Sosa 86 SP 3.00 .90
282 Nick Johnson 86 .40 .12
283 Jose Cruz Jr. 86 .40 .12
284 Frank Thomas 86 1.00 .30
285 Tsuyoshi Shinjo 86 .40 .12
286 Troy Glaus 86 .40 .12
287 Jason Giambi 86 .40 .12
288 Chipper Jones 86 SP 2.00 .60
289 Roberto Alomar 86 .60 .18
290 Bobby Hill 86 .40 .12
291 Garret Anderson 86 .40 .12
292 Andruw Jones 86 .40 .12
293 Luis Gonzalez 86 .40 .12
294 Mike Mussina 86 .60 .18
295 Ivan Rodriguez 86 SP 2.00 .60
296 Barry Larkin 86 .60 .18
297 Kazuhiro Sasaki 86 .40 .12
298 Alfonso Soriano 86 .60 .18
299 Jeff Bagwell 86 SP 1.50 .45
300 Bobby Abreu 86 .40 .12
301 Ben Sheets 86 .40 .12
302 Curt Schilling 86 .40 .12
303 Jim Thome 86 1.00 .30
304 Kerry Wood 86 1.00 .30
305 Mark Buehrle 86 SP 1.00 .30
306 Rickey Henderson 86 1.00 .30
307 Rafael Palmeiro 86 .60 .18
308 Jim Edmonds 86 .40 .12
309 Mike Piazza 86 1.50 .45
310 Edgar Martinez 86 .60 .18
311 Tom Glavine 86 .60 .18
312 Adrian Beltre 86 .60 .18
313 Adam Dunn 86 .60 .18
314 Craig Biggio 86 .60 .18
315 Vladimir Guerrero 86 SP 2.00 .60
316 Bret Boone 86 .40 .12
317 Hideo Nomo 86 SP 2.00 .60
318 Jeff Kent 86 .40 .12
319 Juan Gonzalez 86 .60 .18
320 Sean Casey 86 .40 .12
321 C.C. Sabathia 86 .40 .12
322 J.D. Drew 86 .40 .12
323 Torii Hunter 86 SP 1.00 .30
324 Chan Ho Park 86 .40 .12
325 Mike Sweeney 86 .40 .12
326 Javier Vazquez 86 .40 .12
327 Jorge Posada 86 .60 .18
328 Barry Zito 86 .40 .12
329 Willie McCovey 86 .40 .12
330 Kevin Brown 86 .40 .12
331 Mo Vaughn 86 .40 .12
332 Carlos Beltran 86 .60 .18
333 Bobby Doerr 86 .40 .12
334 Matt Morris 86 .40 .12
335 Trot Nixon 86 SP 1.00 .30
336 Magglio Ordonez 86 .40 .12
337 Paul LoDuca 86 .40 .12
338 Phil Nevin 86 .40 .12

339 Eric Chavez 86 .40 .12
340 Corey Patterson 86 .40 .12
341 Richie Sexson 86 .40 .12
342 Pat Burrell 86 SP 1.00 .30
343 Freddy Garcia 86 .40 .12
344 Bartolo Colon 86 .40 .12
345 Cliff Floyd 86 .40 .12
346 Deivis Santos 88 RR .40 .12
347 Felix Escalona 88 RR RC .40 .12
348 Miguel Asencio 88 RR RC .40 .12
349 Takahito Nomura 88 RR RC .40 .12
350 Jorge Padilla 88 RR RC .40 .12
351 Torii Hunter 88 .40 .12
352 Ichiro Suzuki 88 1.50 .45
353 Jay Gibbons 88 .40 .12
354 Alfonso Soriano 88 .60 .18
355 Mark Buehrle 88 .40 .12
356 Shawn Green 88 SP 1.00 .30
357 Barry Larkin 88 .60 .18
358 Josh Fogg 88 .40 .12
359 Shannon Stewart 88 .40 .12
360 Andruw Jones 88 .40 .12
361 Juan Gonzalez 88 .60 .18
362 Ken Griffey Jr. 88 1.50 .45
363 Tim Hudson 88 .40 .12
364 Roy Oswalt 88 SP 1.00 .30
365 Carlos Delgado 88 .40 .12
366 Albert Pujols 88 SP 4.00 1.20
367 Willie Stargell 88 .60 .18
368 Roger Clemens 88 2.00 .60
369 Luis Gonzalez 88 .40 .12
370 Barry Zito 88 .40 .12
371 Alex Rodriguez 88 1.50 .45
372 Troy Glaus 88 .40 .12
373 Vladimir Guerrero 88 1.00 .30
374 Jeff Bagwell 88 .60 .18
375 Randy Johnson 88 1.00 .30
376 Manny Ramirez 88 .60 .18
377 Derek Jeter 88 SP 5.00 1.50
378 C.C. Sabathia 88 .40 .12
379 Rickey Henderson 88 1.00 .30
380 J.D. Drew 88 SP 1.00 .30
381 Nomar Garciaparra 88 1.50 .45
382 Darin Erstad 88 .40 .12
383 Ben Sheets 88 .40 .12
384 Frank Thomas 88 1.00 .30
385 Barry Bonds 88 2.50 .75
386 Pedro Martinez 88 1.00 .30
387 Mark Mulder 88 .40 .12
388 Greg Maddux 88 1.50 .45
389 Todd Helton 88 .60 .18
390 Lance Berkman 88 .40 .12
391 Sammy Sosa 88 1.50 .45
392 Mike Piazza 88 SP 3.00 .90
393 Chipper Jones 88 1.00 .30
394 Adam Dunn 88 .60 .18
395 Jason Giambi 88 .40 .12
396 Eric Chavez 88 .40 .12
397 Bobby Abreu 88 .40 .12
398 Aramis Ramirez 88 .40 .12
399 Paul LoDuca 88 .40 .12
400 Miguel Tejada 88 .40 .12
401 Runelvys Hernandez 82 RC .75 .23
402 Wilson Valdez 82 RC .75 .23
403 Brian Tallet 82 RC .75 .23
404 Chone Figgins 82 RC 2.00 .60
405 Jeriome Robertson 82 RC .75 .23
406 Shane Nance 84 RC .75 .23
407 Aaron Cook 84 RC .75 .23
408 Trey Hodges 84 RC .75 .23
409 Matt Childers 84 RC .75 .23
410 Mitch Wylie 84 RC .75 .23
411 Rene Reyes 84 RC .75 .23
412 Mike Smith 84 RC .75 .23
413 Jason Simontacchi 84 RC .40 .12
414 Luis Martinez 84 RC .75 .23
415 Kevin Cash 84 RC .75 .23
416 Todd Donovan 86 RC .75 .23
417 Scotty Layfield 86 RC .75 .23
418 Joe Borchard 86 .75 .23
419 Adrian Burnside 86 RC .75 .23
420 Ben Kozlowski 86 RC .75 .23
421 Clay Condrey 88 RC .75 .23
422 Cliff Lee 88 RC 2.00 .60
423 Josh Bard 88 RC .75 .23
424 Freddy Sanchez 88 RC .75 .23
425 Ron Calloway 88 RC .75 .23

2002 Donruss Originals Aqueous

Randomly inserted in packs, these cards which are known as the Aqueous cards are actually "glossy" in nature and parallel the entire 2002 Donruss Originals set.

Nm-Mt Ex-Mt
*AQUEOUS: 3X TO 8X BASIC
*AQUEOUS: 1.5X TO 4X BASIC SP's
*AQUEOUS: 1.25X TO 3X BASIC RC's

2002 Donruss Originals All-Stars

Inserted at stated odds of one in 30 hobby and one in 120 retail, this 25 card set features a mix of the leading active players as well as some of the greats of the 1980's.

Nm-Mt Ex-Mt
1 George Brett 12.00 3.60
2 Rickey Henderson 5.00 1.50
3 Mike Schmidt 12.00 3.60
4 Vladimir Guerrero 5.00 1.50
5 Tony Gwynn 8.00 2.40
6 Curt Schilling 5.00 1.50
7 Don Mattingly 15.00 4.50
8 Roberto Alomar 5.00 1.50
9 Cal Ripken 20.00 6.00
10 Carlton Fisk 5.00 1.50
11 Roger Clemens 10.00 3.00
12 Jeff Bagwell 5.00 1.50
13 Kirby Puckett 5.00 1.50
14 Nolan Ryan 15.00 4.50
15 Ryne Sandberg 12.00 3.60
16 Ivan Rodriguez 5.00 1.50
17 Sammy Sosa 8.00 2.40
18 Greg Maddux 8.00 2.40
19 Alex Rodriguez 8.00 2.40
20 Todd Helton 5.00 1.50
21 Randy Johnson 5.00 1.50
22 Troy Glaus 5.00 1.50
23 Ichiro Suzuki 8.00 2.40
24 Barry Bonds 12.00 3.60
25 Derek Jeter 12.00 3.60

2002 Donruss Originals Box Bottoms

Issued at the bottom of each Donruss Originals box was this four card blank-backed set featuring a design from each of the 1980's even years that Donruss produced cards during.

Nm-Mt Ex-Mt
COMPLETE SET (4) 2.00 .60
NNO Kazuhisa Ishii 82 .50 .15
NNO Nomar Garciaparra 84 .50 .15
NNO Roger Clemens 86 .50 .15
NNO Mike Piazza 88 .50 .15

2002 Donruss Originals Champions

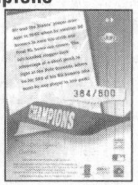

Randomly inserted in packs this 25 card set was issued to a stated print run of 800 serial numbered sets and featured a mix of the best players of today along with some all time greats.

Nm-Mt Ex-Mt
1 Nolan Ryan 20.00 6.00
2 George Brett 15.00 4.50
3 Edgar Martinez 8.00 2.40
4 Mike Schmidt 15.00 4.50
5 Randy Johnson 8.00 2.40
6 Tony Gwynn 10.00 3.00
7 John Smoltz 8.00 2.40
8 Roger Clemens 15.00 4.50
9 Mel Ott 8.00 2.40
10 Todd Helton 8.00 2.40
11 Bernie Williams 8.00 2.40
12 Troy Glaus 8.00 2.40
13 Steve Carlton 8.00 2.40
14 Ryne Sandberg 15.00 4.50
15 Ted Williams UER 12.00 3.60
Williams played in the AL, card says NL
16 Alex Rodriguez M's 12.00 3.60
17 Lou Boudreau 8.00 2.40
18 Luis Gonzalez 8.00 2.40
19 Rickey Henderson 8.00 2.40
20 Jose Canseco 8.00 2.40
21 Stan Musial 10.00 3.00
22 Randy Johnson 8.00 2.40
23 Don Mattingly 20.00 6.00
24 Nomar Garciaparra 12.00 3.60
25 Wade Boggs 8.00 2.40

2002 Donruss Originals Champions Materials

Randomly inserted in packs, this parallel to the Champions insert set features game-used jersey swatches of the featured player. Since the cards have different print runs, we have notated that information next to the player's name in our checklist.

Nm-Mt Ex-Mt
1 Nolan Ryan/78 50.00 15.00
2 George Brett/80 50.00 15.00
3 Edgar Martinez/92 25.00 7.50
4 Mike Schmidt/80 40.00 12.00
5 Randy Johnson/94 25.00 7.50
6 Tony Gwynn/84 25.00 7.50
7 John Smoltz/96 25.00 7.50
8 Roger Clemens/88 25.00 7.50
9 Mel Ott/42
10 Todd Helton/100 25.00 7.50
11 Bernie Williams/98 25.00 7.50
12 Troy Glaus/100 15.00 4.50
13 Steve Carlton/80 15.00 4.50
14 Ryne Sandberg/90 40.00 12.00
15 Ted Williams/42
16 Alex Rodriguez M's/96 25.00 7.50
17 Lou Boudreau/44 25.00 7.50
18 Luis Gonzalez/99 15.00 4.50
19 Rickey Henderson/82 25.00 7.50
20 Jose Canseco/88 25.00 7.50
21 Stan Musial/50
22 Randy Johnson/88 25.00 7.50
23 Don Mattingly/84 50.00 15.00
24 Nomar Garciaparra/100 25.00 7.50
25 Wade Boggs/88 25.00 7.50

2002 Donruss Originals Embossed Notation

Randomly inserted in packs, these 97 cards represent cards which were "bought back" by Donruss/Playoff. Each card have not only an "embossing" on the front but also an "inscription" which indicated that it was purchased for this product. In addition, these cards were not serial numbered so we are using the stated print runs in our checklist provided by the company. Please note that each card has a stated print run of one copy so no pricing is provided.

Nm-Mt Ex-Mt
1 Yogi Berra 1982 HOF
2 Wade Boggs 1986 AS
3 George Brett 1982 AS
4 George Brett 1982 HOF
5 George Brett 1984 AS
6 George Brett 1984 HOF
7 George Brett 1986 AS
8 George Brett 1986 HOF
9 George Brett 1986 HL HOF
10 George Brett 1988 AS
11 George Brett 1988 HOF
12 Rod Carew 1982 AS
13 Rod Carew 1982 HOF
14 Rod Carew 1984 HOF
15 Rod Carew 1986 HOF
16 Steve Carlton 1982 AS
17 Steve Carlton 1982 CY
18 Steve Carlton 1982 HOF
19 Steve Carlton 1984 HOF
20 Gary Carter 1982 AS
21 Gary Carter 1984 AS
22 Gary Carter 1984 AS MVP
23 Gary Carter 1986 AS
24 Roger Clemens 1986 AS
25 Andre Dawson 1982 AS
26 Carlton Fisk 1982 AS
27 Carlton Fisk 1982 HOF
28 Carlton Fisk 1984 HOF
29 Carlton Fisk 1986 HOF
30 Tony Gwynn 1986 AS
31 Rickey Henderson 1982 AS
32 Rickey Henderson 1984 AS
33 Rickey Henderson 1986 AS
34 Rickey Henderson 1988 AS
35 Reggie Jackson 1984 AS
36 Reggie Jackson 1984 HOF
37 Reggie Jackson 1986 HOF
38 Fergie Jenkins 1982 HOF
39 Ferguson Jenkins 1984 HOF
40 Fred Lynn 1982 AS
41 Greg Maddux 1988 AS
42 Don Mattingly 1986 AS
43 Don Mattingly 1988 AS
44 Paul Molitor 1982 HOF
45 Paul Molitor 1984 HOF
46 Paul Molitor 1986 HOF
47 Dale Murphy 1982 AS
48 Dale Murphy 1982 MVP
49 Dale Murphy 1984 AS
50 Dale Murphy 1986 AS
51 Eddie Murray 1982 AS
52 Eddie Murray 1982 HOF
53 Eddie Murray 1984 AS
54 Eddie Murray 1984 HOF
55 Eddie Murray 1986 AS
56 Eddie Murray 1986 HOF
57 Phil Niekro 1982 AS
58 Phil Niekro 1982 HOF
59 Phil Niekro 1984 HOF
60 Phil Niekro 1986 HOF
61 Jim Palmer 1982 HOF
62 Jim Palmer 1984 HOF
63 Dave Parker 1986 AS
64 Kirby Puckett 1986 AS
65 Kirby Puckett 1986 HOF
66 Kirby Puckett 1986 HL HOF
67 Kirby Puckett 1988 AS
68 Cal Ripken 1984 AS
69 Cal Ripken 1986 AS
70 Cal Ripken 1986 AS
71 Cal Ripken 1988 AS
72 Nolan Ryan 1986 HOF
73 Ryne Sandberg 1986 AS
74 Mike Schmidt 1984 HOF
75 Mike Schmidt 1986 AS
76 Mike Schmidt 1986 HOF
77 Mike Schmidt 1986 HL HOF #4
78 Mike Schmidt 1986 HL HOF #36
79 Mike Schmidt 1988 HOF
80 Tom Seaver 1984 HOF
81 Tom Seaver 1986 HOF
82 Ozzie Smith 1984 AS
83 Ozzie Smith 1984 HOF
84 Ozzie Smith 1986 AS
85 Ozzie Smith 1986 HOF
86 Willie Stargell 1982 HOF
87 Dave Winfield 1982 AS
88 Dave Winfield 1982 HOF
89 Dave Winfield 1984 AS
90 Dave Winfield 1984 HOF
91 Dave Winfield 1986 AS
92 Dave Winfield 1986 HOF
93 Robin Yount 1982 AS
94 Robin Yount 1982 HOF
95 Robin Yount 1982 MVP
96 Robin Yount 1984 HOF
97 Robin Yount 1986 HOF

2002 Donruss Originals Gamers

Randomly inserted into packs, these 50 cards feature a mix of players along with a game-used jersey swatch of the featured player. Since players have varying print runs, we have notated that information next to their name in our checklist.

Nm-Mt Ex-Mt
1 Alfonso Soriano/400 15.00 4.50
2 Shawn Green/500 10.00 3.00
3 Curt Schilling/250 15.00 4.50
4 Hideo Nomo Red Sox/100 80.00 24.00
5 Toby Hall/500 10.00 3.00
6 Andruw Jones/500 10.00 3.00
7 Cliff Floyd/500 10.00 3.00
8 Mark Ellis/500 10.00 3.00
9 Gabe Kapler/500 10.00 3.00
10 Andres Galarraga/500 10.00 3.00
11 Freddy Garcia/500 10.00 3.00
12 Tsuyoshi Shinjo/200 15.00 4.50
13 Robin Ventura/500 10.00 3.00
14 Paul LoDuca/500 10.00 3.00
15 Manny Ramirez/500 15.00 4.50
16 Garret Anderson/250 15.00 4.50
17 Joe Kennedy/500 10.00 3.00
18 Roger Clemens/500 20.00 6.00
19 Gary Sheffield/500 10.00 3.00
20 Vernon Wells/500 10.00 3.00
21 Matt Guerrier/500
22 Hideo Nomo Dodgers/100 80.00 24.00
23 Tim Hudson/500 10.00 3.00
24 Larry Bigbie/500 10.00 3.00
25 Larry Walker/500 15.00 4.50
26 Ryan Ludwick/500
27 John Olerud/500 10.00 3.00
28 Chipper Jones/500 15.00 4.50
29 Tony Gwynn/500 15.00 4.50
30 Juan Gonzalez/500 15.00 4.50
31 Jacque Jones/500 10.00 3.00
32 Frank Thomas/500 15.00 4.50
33 Luis Gonzalez/500 10.00 3.00
34 Geoff Jenkins/500 10.00 3.00
35 J.D. Drew/500 10.00 3.00
36 Edgardo Alfonzo/500 10.00 3.00
37 Todd Helton/500 15.00 4.50
38 Brad Penny/500 10.00 3.00
39 Robert Fick/500 10.00 3.00
40 Will Clark/500 15.00 4.50
41 Tony Armas Jr./500 10.00 3.00
42 Nick Johnson/400 10.00 3.00
43 Ben Grieve/500 10.00 3.00
44 Vladimir Guerrero/500 15.00 4.50
45 Jason Jennings/500 10.00 3.00
46 Carlos Lee/500 10.00 3.00
47 Carlos Delgado/500 10.00 3.00
48 Chan Ho Park/500 10.00 3.00
49 Juan Diaz/500 10.00 3.00
50 Alex Rodriguez M's/400 20.00 6.00

2002 Donruss Originals Hit List

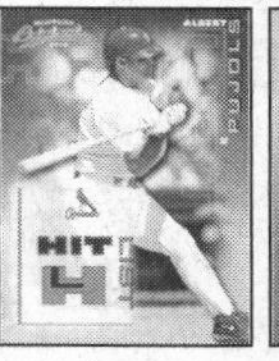
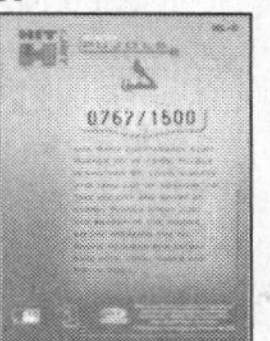

Randomly inserted into packs, this 20 card set features some of the leading hitters in Baseball and these cards are printed to a stated print run of 1500 serial numbered sets.

Nm-Mt Ex-Mt
1 Ichiro Suzuki 6.00 1.80
2 Shawn Green 4.00 1.20
3 Alex Rodriguez 6.00 1.80
4 Nomar Garciaparra 6.00 1.80
5 Derek Jeter 10.00 3.00
6 Barry Bonds 10.00 3.00
7 Mike Piazza 6.00 1.80
8 Albert Pujols 8.00 2.40
9 Chipper Jones 4.00 1.20
10 Sammy Sosa 6.00 1.80
11 Rickey Henderson 4.00 1.20
12 Frank Thomas 4.00 1.20
13 Jeff Bagwell 4.00 1.20
14 Vladimir Guerrero 4.00 1.20
15 Todd Helton 4.00 1.20
16 Adam Dunn 4.00 1.20
17 Rafael Palmeiro 4.00 1.20
18 Manny Ramirez 4.00 1.20
19 Lance Berkman 4.00 1.20
20 Jason Giambi A's 4.00 1.20

2002 Donruss Originals Hit List Total Bases

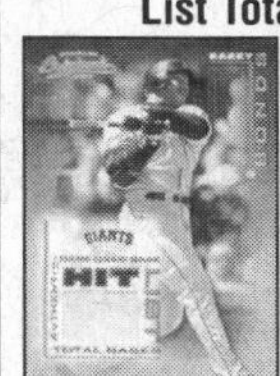
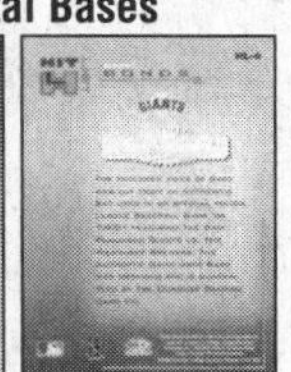

Randomly inserted into packs, this is a parallel of the Hit List insert set. Each card features a game-used piece and we have notated what type of memorabilia next to the player's name in our checklist.

Nm-Mt Ex-Mt
1 Ichiro Suzuki Base/316 25.00 7.50
2 Shawn Green Bat/370 15.00 4.50
3 Alex Rodriguez Rgr Bat/393 20.00 6.00
4 Nomar Garciaparra Bat/365 15.00 4.50
5 Derek Jeter Base/346 25.00 7.50
6 Barry Bonds Base/411 25.00 7.50
7 Mike Piazza Dodgers Bat/355 15.00 4.50
8 Albert Pujols Base/360 15.00 4.50
9 Chipper Jones Bat/359 15.00 4.50
10 Sammy Sosa Base/425 15.00 4.50
11 Rickey Henderson Bat/285 15.00 4.50
12 Frank Thomas Bat/364 15.00 4.50
13 Jeff Bagwell Bat/363 15.00 4.50
14 Vladimir Guerrero Bat/379 15.00 4.50
15 Todd Helton Bat/405 15.00 4.50
16 Adam Dunn Bat/141 15.00 4.50
17 Rafael Palmeiro Bat/356 15.00 4.50
18 Manny Ramirez Bat/346 15.00 4.50
19 Lance Berkman Bat/358 15.00 4.50
20 Jason Giambi A's Base/343 10.00 3.00

2002 Donruss Originals Making History

Randomly inserted into packs, this 10 card set features players on the verge of either setting records or achieving important milestones in baseball history. Each of these cards were issued to a stated print run of 800 serial numbered sets.

Nm-Mt Ex-Mt
1 Rafael Palmeiro 8.00 2.40
2 Roger Clemens 15.00 4.50
3 Greg Maddux 12.00 3.60
4 Randy Johnson 8.00 2.40
5 Barry Bonds 20.00 6.00
6 Mike Piazza 12.00 3.60
7 Roberto Alomar 8.00 2.40
8 Rickey Henderson 8.00 2.40
9 Sammy Sosa 12.00 3.60
10 Tom Glavine 8.00 2.40

2002 Donruss Originals Making History Materials

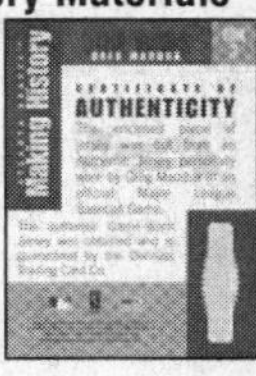

Randomly inserted into packs, these 10 cards parallel the Making History insert set. Each card features a game-used memorabilia piece and were issued to a stated print run of 100 serial numbered sets.

Nm-Mt Ex-Mt
1 Rafael Palmeiro Jsy 25.00 7.50
2 Roger Clemens Jsy 40.00 12.00
3 Greg Maddux Jsy 25.00 7.50
4 Randy Johnson Jsy 25.00 7.50
5 Barry Bonds Base 40.00 12.00
6 Mike Piazza Jsy 25.00 7.50
7 Roberto Alomar Jsy 25.00 7.50
8 Rickey Henderson Jsy 25.00 7.50
9 Sammy Sosa Base 25.00 7.50
10 Tom Glavine Jsy 25.00 7.50

2002 Donruss Originals Mound Marvels

Inserted into packs at stated odds of one in 40 hobby and one in 72 retail, these 15 cards feature some of the leading pitchers in the game. Roger Clemens has two cards in this set.

Nm-Mt Ex-Mt
1 Roger Clemens 8/20/01 8.00 2.40
2 Matt Morris 4.00 1.20
3 Pedro Martinez 4.00 1.20
4 Randy Johnson 4.00 1.20
5 Wade Miller 4.00 1.20
6 Tim Hudson 4.00 1.20
7 Mike Mussina 4.00 1.20
8 C.C. Sabathia 4.00 1.20
9 Kazuhiro Sasaki 4.00 1.20
10 Curt Schilling 4.00 1.20
11 Hideo Nomo 4.00 1.20
12 Roger Clemens 10/30/01 8.00 2.40
13 Mark Buehrle 4.00 1.20
14 Barry Zito 4.00 1.20
15 Roy Oswalt 4.00 1.20

2002 Donruss Originals Mound Marvels High Heat

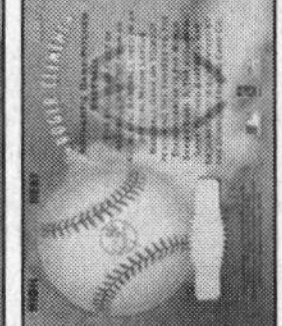

Randomly inserted into packs, this is a parallel of the Mound Marvels insert set. These cards all feature pieces of game-used balls on them are are issued to a stated print run of 100 serial numbered sets.

Nm-Mt Ex-Mt
1 Roger Clemens 8/20/01 50.00 15.00
2 Matt Morris 20.00 6.00
3 Pedro Martinez 25.00 7.50
4 Randy Johnson 25.00 7.50
5 Wade Miller 20.00 6.00
6 Tim Hudson 20.00 6.00
7 Mike Mussina 25.00 7.50
8 C.C. Sabathia 20.00 6.00
9 Kazuhiro Sasaki 20.00 6.00
10 Curt Schilling 20.00 6.00
11 Hideo Nomo 80.00 24.00
12 Roger Clemens 10/30/01 50.00 15.00
13 Mark Buehrle 20.00 6.00
14 Barry Zito 20.00 6.00
15 Roy Oswalt 20.00 6.00

2002 Donruss Originals Nifty Fifty Bats

Randomly inserted into packs, these fifty cards feature game-used bat pieces and are issued to a stated print run of 50 serial numbered sets.

Nm-Mt Ex-Mt
1 Alex Rodriguez Rangers 40.00 12.00
2 Kerry Wood 25.00 7.50
3 Ivan Rodriguez 25.00 7.50
4 Geronimo Gil 12.00 3.60
5 Vladimir Guerrero 25.00 7.50
6 Corky Miller 12.00 3.60
7 Todd Helton 25.00 7.50
8 Rickey Henderson Padres 25.00 7.50
9 Andruw Jones 20.00 6.00
10 Barry Bonds Ball 60.00 18.00
11 Tom Glavine 25.00 7.50
12 Mark Teixeira 25.00 7.50
13 Mike Piazza Mets 40.00 12.00
14 Austin Kearns 20.00 6.00
15 Rickey Henderson M's 25.00 7.50
16 Derek Jeter Ball 50.00 15.00
17 Barry Larkin 25.00 7.50
18 Jeff Bagwell 25.00 7.50
19 Bernie Williams 25.00 7.50
20 Frank Thomas 25.00 7.50
21 Lance Berkman 20.00 6.00
22 Marlon Byrd 12.00 3.60
23 Randy Johnson 25.00 7.50
24 Ichiro Suzuki Ball 60.00 18.00
25 Darin Erstad 20.00 6.00
26 Jason Lane 12.00 3.60
27 Roberto Alomar 25.00 7.50
28 Ken Griffey Jr. Ball 40.00 12.00
29 Tsuyoshi Shinjo 20.00 6.00
30 Pedro Martinez 25.00 7.50
31 Rickey Henderson Mets 25.00 7.50
32 Albert Pujols Ball 50.00 15.00
33 Nomar Garciaparra 40.00 12.00
34 Troy Glaus 20.00 6.00
35 Chipper Jones 25.00 7.50
36 Adam Dunn 25.00 7.50
37 Jason Giambi Ball 20.00 6.00
38 Greg Maddux 40.00 12.00
39 Mike Piazza Dodgers 40.00 12.00
40 So Taguchi 25.00 7.50
41 Manny Ramirez 25.00 7.50
42 Scott Rolen 25.00 7.50
43 Sammy Sosa Ball 40.00 12.00
44 Shawn Green 20.00 6.00
45 Rickey Henderson Red Sox 25.00 7.50
46 Alex Rodriguez M's 40.00 12.00
47 Hideo Nomo Red Sox 40.00 12.00
48 Kazuhisa Ishii 25.00 7.50
49 Luis Gonzalez 20.00 6.00
50 Jim Thome 25.00 7.50

2002 Donruss Originals Nifty Fifty Combos

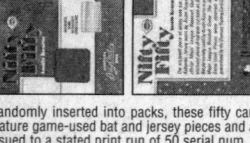

Randomly inserted into packs, these fifty cards feature game-used bat and jersey pieces and are issued to a stated print run of 50 serial num bered sets. A few cards feature other types of memorabilia and we have notated that information next to the player's name in our checklist.

Nm-Mt Ex-Mt
1 Alex Rodriguez Rangers 50.00 15.00
2 Kerry Wood 40.00 12.00
3 Ivan Rodriguez 40.00 12.00
4 Geronimo Gil 20.00 6.00
5 Vladimir Guerrero 40.00 12.00
6 Corky Miller 20.00 6.00
7 Todd Helton 40.00 12.00
8 Rickey Henderson Padres 40.00 12.00
9 Andruw Jones 30.00 9.00
10 Barry Bonds Base/Ball 80.00 24.00
11 Tom Glavine 40.00 12.00
12 Mark Teixeira 40.00 12.00
13 Mike Piazza Mets 50.00 15.00
14 Austin Kearns 30.00 9.00
15 Rickey Henderson M's 40.00 12.00
16 Derek Jeter Base/Ball 60.00 18.00
17 Barry Larkin 40.00 12.00
18 Jeff Bagwell 40.00 12.00
19 Bernie Williams 40.00 12.00
20 Frank Thomas 40.00 12.00
21 Lance Berkman 30.00 9.00
22 Marlon Byrd 20.00 6.00
23 Randy Johnson 40.00 12.00
24 Ichiro Suzuki Base/Ball 80.00 24.00
25 Darin Erstad 30.00 9.00
26 Jason Lane 20.00 6.00
27 Roberto Alomar 40.00 12.00
28 Ken Griffey Jr. Base/Ball 50.00 15.00
29 Tsuyoshi Shinjo 30.00 9.00
30 Pedro Martinez 40.00 12.00
31 Rickey Henderson Mets 40.00 12.00
32 Albert Pujols Base/Ball 60.00 18.00
33 Nomar Garciaparra 50.00 15.00
34 Troy Glaus 30.00 9.00
35 Chipper Jones 40.00 12.00
36 Adam Dunn 40.00 12.00
37 Jason Giambi Base/Ball 30.00 9.00
38 Greg Maddux 50.00 15.00
39 Mike Piazza Dodgers 50.00 15.00
40 So Taguchi 40.00 12.00
41 Manny Ramirez 40.00 12.00
42 Scott Rolen 40.00 12.00
43 Sammy Sosa Base/Ball 50.00 15.00
44 Shawn Green 30.00 9.00
45 Rickey Henderson Red Sox 40.00 12.00
46 Alex Rodriguez M's 50.00 15.00
47 Hideo Nomo Red Sox 50.00 15.00
48 Kazuhisa Ishii 40.00 12.00
49 Luis Gonzalez 30.00 9.00
50 Jim Thome 40.00 12.00

2002 Donruss Originals Nifty Fifty Jerseys

Randomly inserted into packs, these fifty cards feature game-used jersey pieces and are issued to a stated print run of 50 serial numbered sets.

Nm-Mt Ex-Mt
1 Alex Rodriguez Rangers
2 Kerry Wood 25.00 7.50
3 Ivan Rodriguez 25.00 7.50
4 Geronimo Gil 12.00 3.60
5 Vladimir Guerrero 25.00 7.50
6 Corky Miller 12.00 3.60
7 Todd Helton 25.00 7.50
8 Rickey Henderson Padres 25.00 7.50
9 Andruw Jones 20.00 6.00
10 Barry Bonds Base
11 Tom Glavine 25.00 7.50
12 Mark Teixeira 25.00 7.50
13 Mike Piazza Mets 40.00 12.00
14 Austin Kearns 20.00 6.00
15 Rickey Henderson M's 25.00 7.50
16 Derek Jeter Base 50.00 15.00
17 Barry Larkin 25.00 7.50
18 Jeff Bagwell 25.00 7.50
19 Bernie Williams 25.00 7.50
20 Frank Thomas 25.00 7.50
21 Lance Berkman 20.00 6.00
22 Marlon Byrd 12.00 3.60
23 Randy Johnson 25.00 7.50
24 Ichiro Suzuki Base 60.00 18.00
25 Darin Erstad 20.00 6.00
26 Jason Lane 12.00 3.60
27 Roberto Alomar 25.00 7.50
28 Ken Griffey Jr. Base 40.00 12.00
29 Tsuyoshi Shinjo 20.00 6.00
30 Pedro Martinez 25.00 7.50
31 Rickey Henderson Mets 25.00 7.50
32 Albert Pujols Base 50.00 15.00
33 Nomar Garciaparra 40.00 12.00
34 Troy Glaus 20.00 6.00
35 Chipper Jones 25.00 7.50
36 Adam Dunn 25.00 7.50
37 Jason Giambi Base 20.00 6.00
38 Greg Maddux 40.00 12.00
39 Mike Piazza Dodgers 40.00 12.00
40 So Taguchi 25.00 7.50
41 Manny Ramirez 25.00 7.50
42 Scott Rolen 25.00 7.50
43 Sammy Sosa Base 40.00 12.00
44 Shawn Green 20.00 6.00
45 Rickey Henderson Red Sox 25.00 7.50
46 Alex Rodriguez M's 40.00 12.00
47 Hideo Nomo Red Sox 40.00 12.00
48 Kazuhisa Ishii 25.00 7.50
49 Luis Gonzalez 20.00 6.00
50 Jim Thome 25.00 7.50

2002 Donruss Originals On The Record

Randomly inserted into packs, this 15 card sets feature players and some of their most famous accomplishments. These cards were issued to a stated print run of 800 serial numbered sets.

Nm-Mt Ex-Mt
1 Ty Cobb HR 9 10.00 3.00
2 Jimmie Foxx 8.00 2.40
3 Lou Gehrig 15.00 4.50
4 Dale Murphy 20.00 6.00
5 Steve Carlton 8.00 2.40
6 Randy Johnson 8.00 2.40
7 Greg Maddux 12.00 3.60
8 Roger Clemens 15.00 4.50
9 Yogi Berra 8.00 2.40
10 Don Mattingly 20.00 6.00
11 Rickey Henderson 8.00 2.40
12 Stan Musial 10.00 3.00
13 Jackie Robinson 8.00 2.40
14 Roberto Clemente 40.00 12.00
15 Mike Schmidt 15.00 4.50

2002 Donruss Originals On The Record Materials

Randomly inserted into packs, these cards parallel the On the Record insert set and each of these cards feature a game-used memorabilia piece. Each card has a stated print run to a year in which they either accomplished an important feat or won a major award and we have notated that information in our checklist.

Nm-Mt Ex-Mt
1 Ty Cobb Bat/9
2 Jimmie Foxx Bat/33
3 Lou Gehrig Jsy/34
4 Dale Murphy Jsy/83 15.00 4.50
5 Steve Carlton Jsy/72 15.00 4.50
6 Randy Johnson Jsy/100 15.00 4.50
7 Greg Maddux Jsy/93 20.00 6.00
8 Roger Clemens Jsy/87 25.00 7.50
9 Yogi Berra Jsy/51 15.00 4.50
10 Don Mattingly Jsy/85 40.00 12.00
11 Rickey Henderson Jsy/90 15.00 4.50
12 Stan Musial Jsy/43
13 Jackie Robinson Jsy/49
14 Roberto Clemente Jsy/66 100.00 30.00
15 Mike Schmidt Jsy/80 40.00 12.00

2002 Donruss Originals Power Alley

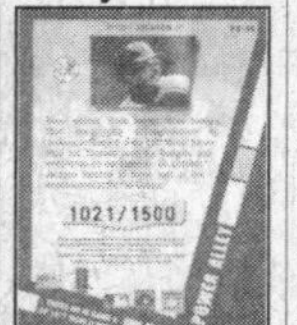

Randomly inserted into packs, these 15 cards feature some of the leading power hitters of 2002 along with some of the best power hitters of Donruss' early years. Each card was issued to a stated print run of 1500 serial numbered sets.

Nm-Mt Ex-Mt
*DIE CUTS: 1.25X TO 3X BASIC ALLEY
DIE CUT PRINT RUN 100 SERIAL #'d SETS
1 Barry Bonds 10.00 3.00
2 Sammy Sosa 6.00 1.80
3 Lance Berkman 4.00 1.20
4 Luis Gonzalez 4.00 1.20
5 Alex Rodriguez 6.00 1.80
6 Troy Glaus 4.00 1.20
7 Vladimir Guerrero 4.00 1.20
8 Jason Giambi 4.00 1.20
9 Mike Piazza 6.00 1.80
10 Todd Helton 4.00 1.20
11 Mike Schmidt 8.00 2.40
12 Don Mattingly 10.00 3.00
13 Andre Dawson 4.00 1.20
14 Reggie Jackson 4.00 1.20
15 Dale Murphy 10.00 3.00

2002 Donruss Originals Recollection Autographs Notation

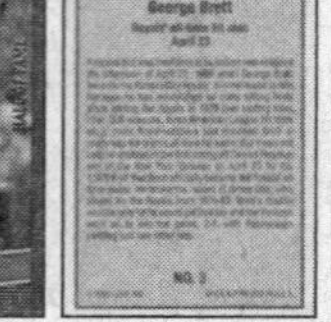

Randomly inserted into packs, these 88 cards feature original Donruss cards "bought back" for insertion into 2002 Donruss Originals packs. Each card has a "recollection" logo as well as an inscription. Since each of these cards have a stated print run of one copy, there is no pricing provided due to scarcity.

Nm-Mt Ex-Mt
1 Johnny Bench 82 HOF
2 Wade Boggs 86 AS
3 George Brett 82 AS
4 George Brett 82 HOF
5 George Brett 84 AS
6 George Brett 84 HOF
7 George Brett 86 AS
8 George Brett 86 HOF
9 George Brett 88 AS
10 George Brett 88 HOF
11 Jose Canseco 86 AS
12 Jose Canseco 88 AS
13 Jose Canseco 88 MVP
14 Rod Carew 82 AS
15 Rod Carew 84 HOF
16 Steve Carlton 82 CY
17 Steve Carlton 84 HOF
18 Steve Carlton 86 HOF
19 Carlton Fisk 82 AS
20 Carlton Fisk 82 HOF
21 Carlton Fisk 84 HOF
22 Carlton Fisk 86 HOF
23 Steve Garvey 84 AS
24 Tony Gwynn 84 AS
25 Tony Gwynn 86 AS
26 Rickey Henderson 88 AS
27 Reggie Jackson 82 HOF
28 Reggie Jackson 82 MVP
29 Reggie Jackson 84 AS
30 Reggie Jackson 84 HOF
31 Reggie Jackson 86 HOF
32 Fergie Jenkins 82 HOF
33 Fergie Jenkins 84 HOF
34 Fred Lynn 82 AS
35 Greg Maddux 88 AS
36 Greg Maddux 88 AS
37 Don Mattingly 84 AS
38 Don Mattingly 86 AS
39 Don Mattingly 88 AS
40 Don Mattingly 88 AS
41 Paul Molitor 82 HOF
42 Paul Molitor 84 HOF
43 Paul Molitor 86 HOF
44 Paul Molitor 88 AS
45 Joe Morgan 82 HOF
46 Joe Morgan 84 HOF
47 Jack Morris 84 AS
48 Jim Palmer 82 HOF
49 Jim Palmer 84 HOF
50 Dave Parker 86 AS
51 Tony Perez 82 HOF
52 Tony Perez 84 HOF
53 Tony Perez 86 HOF
54 Kirby Puckett 86 AS
55 Kirby Puckett 86 HOF
56 Kirby Puckett 88 MVP AS
57 Nolan Ryan 82 HOF
58 Nolan Ryan 84 HOF
59 Nolan Ryan 86 HOF
60 Nolan Ryan 88 HOF
61 Ryne Sandberg 84 AS
62 Ryne Sandberg 84 HOF
63 Ryne Sandberg 84 MVP
64 Ryne Sandberg 86 AS
65 Ryne Sandberg 86 HOF
66 Mike Schmidt 82 AS
67 Mike Schmidt 82 HOF
68 Mike Schmidt 84 AS
69 Mike Schmidt 84 HOF
70 Mike Schmidt 86 AS
71 Mike Schmidt 86 HOF
72 Mike Schmidt 86 MVP
73 Mike Schmidt 86 HL #4 MVP
74 Mike Schmidt 86 HL #36 MVP
75 Mike Schmidt 88 HOF
76 Tom Seaver 82 HOF
77 Tom Seaver 86 HOF
78 Don Sutton 82 HOF
79 Don Sutton 84 HOF
80 Don Sutton 86 HOF
81 Alan Trammell 84 AS
82 Alan Trammell 88 AS
83 Dave Winfield 82 AS
84 Dave Winfield 82 HOF
85 Dave Winfield 84 AS
86 Dave Winfield 84 HOF
87 Dave Winfield 86 AS
88 Dave Winfield 86 HOF

2002 Donruss Originals Signature Marks

Randomly inserted into packs, these 50 cards feature signed cards. Since these cards have some varying stated print run information, we have notated that information next to their name in our checklist.

Nm-Mt Ex-Mt
1 Kazuhisa Ishii/50
2 Eric Hinske/200 10.00 3.00
3 Cesar Izturis/200 10.00 3.00
4 Roy Oswalt/100 15.00 4.50
5 Jack Cust/200 10.00 3.00
6 Nick Johnson/200 15.00 4.50
7 Jason Hart/200 10.00 3.00
8 Mark Prior/100 80.00 24.00
9 Luis Garcia/200 10.00 3.00
10 Jay Gibbons/200 10.00 3.00
11 Corky Miller/200 10.00 3.00
12 Antonio Perez/100 10.00 3.00
13 Andres Torres/200 10.00 3.00
14 Brandon Claussen/200 10.00 3.00
15 Ed Rogers/200 10.00 3.00
16 Jorge Padilla/200 10.00 3.00
17 Francis Beltran/200 10.00 3.00
18 Kip Wells/200 10.00 3.00
19 Ryan Ludwick/200 10.00 3.00
20 Juan Cruz/100
21 Juan Diaz/200 10.00 3.00
22 Marcus Giles/200 15.00 4.50
23 Joe Kennedy/200 10.00 3.00
24 Wade Miller/100 10.00 3.00
25 Corey Patterson/100 15.00 4.50
26 Angel Berroa/200 10.00 3.00
27 Ricardo Rodriguez/200 10.00 3.00
28 Toby Hall/200 10.00 3.00
29 Carlos Pena/50 15.00 4.50
30 Jason Jennings/200 10.00 3.00
31 Rafael Soriano/200 10.00 3.00
32 Marlon Byrd/100 10.00 3.00
33 Rodrigo Rosario/200 10.00 3.00
34 Rick Ankiel/200
35 Brent Abernathy/200 10.00 3.00
36 Bill Hall/200 10.00 3.00
37 Fernando Rodney/200
38 Josh Pearce/200 10.00 3.00
39 Brian Lawrence/200 10.00 3.00
40 Tim Redding/200 10.00 3.00
41 Matt Guerrier/200
42 Jeremy Giambi/200 10.00 3.00
43 Victor Martinez/200 40.00 12.00
44 Hank Blalock/50 50.00 15.00
45 Larry Bigbie/200
46 Geronimo Gil/200 10.00 3.00
47 So Taguchi/50 40.00 12.00
48 Austin Kearns/200 15.00 4.50
49 Alfonso Soriano/50 50.00 15.00
50 Jose Ortiz/100

2002 Donruss Originals What If 1978

Issued as part of the What If series which were inserted at an overall rate of one in 12 hobby and one in 24 retail. These cards feature players active in 1978 along with what their cards could have looked like if Donruss had been producing cards at that time.

Nm-Mt Ex-Mt
1 Paul Molitor RR 8.00 2.40
2 Alan Trammell RR 5.00 1.50
3 Ozzie Smith RR 15.00 4.50
4 George Brett 15.00 4.50
5 Johnny Bench 10.00 3.00
6 Rod Carew 8.00 2.40
7 Carlton Fisk 8.00 2.40
8 Reggie Jackson 8.00 2.40
9 Dale Murphy 15.00 4.50
10 Joe Morgan 5.00 1.50
11 Eddie Murray 20.00 6.00
12 Jim Palmer 5.00 1.50
13 Tom Seaver 8.00 2.40
14 Willie Stargell 8.00 2.40
15 Dave Winfield 5.00 1.50
16 Dave Parker 5.00 1.50
17 Mike Schmidt 15.00 4.50
18 Eddie Mathews 10.00 3.00
19 Lou Brock 8.00 2.40
20 Willie McCovey 5.00 1.50
21 Andre Dawson 5.00 1.50
22 Dennis Eckersley 5.00 1.50
23 Robin Yount 10.00 3.00
24 Nolan Ryan 15.00 4.50
25 Steve Carlton 5.00 1.50
26 Paul Molitor 8.00 2.40
27 Ozzie Smith 10.00 3.00

2002 Donruss Originals What If 1980

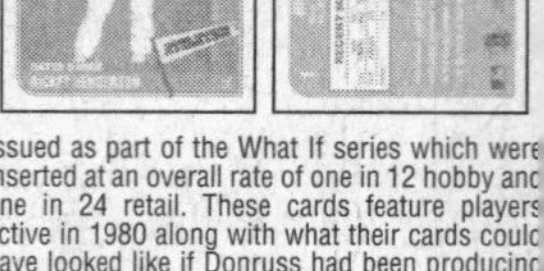

Issued as part of the What If series which were inserted at an overall rate of one in 12 hobby and one in 24 retail. These cards feature players active in 1980 along with what their cards could have looked like if Donruss had been producing cards at that time.

Nm-Mt Ex-Mt
1 Rickey Henderson RR 10.00 3.00
2 Johnny Bench 10.00 3.00
3 George Brett 15.00 4.50
4 Steve Carlton 5.00 1.50
5 Rod Carew 8.00 2.40
6 Gary Carter 5.00 1.50
7 Carlton Fisk 8.00 2.40
8 Reggie Jackson 8.00 2.40
9 Dave Parker 5.00 1.50
10 Dale Murphy 15.00 4.50
11 Paul Molitor 8.00 2.40
12 Mike Schmidt 15.00 4.50
13 Alan Trammell 5.00 1.50
14 Dave Winfield 5.00 1.50
15 Robin Yount 10.00 3.00
16 Joe Morgan 5.00 1.50
17 Jim Palmer 5.00 1.50
18 Nolan Ryan 15.00 4.50
19 Tom Seaver 8.00 2.40
20 Ozzie Smith 10.00 3.00
21 Willie McCovey 5.00 1.50
22 Andre Dawson 5.00 1.50
23 Eddie Murray 10.00 3.00
24 Al Kaline 10.00 3.00
25 Duke Snider 8.00 2.40

2002 Donruss Originals What If Rookies

Issued as part of the What If series which were inserted at an overall rate of one in 12 hobby and one in 24 retail. These cards feature players active in the 1980's along with what their cards would have looked like if Donruss had made a card of the featured player that year.

Nm-Mt Ex-Mt
1 Wade Boggs 82 RR 8.00 2.40

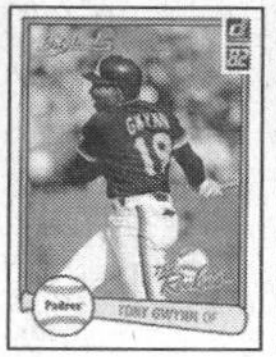

Card	Nm-Mt	Ex-Mt
2 Ryne Sandberg 82 RR	15.00	4.50
3 Cal Ripken 82 RR	25.00	7.50
4 Tony Gwynn 82	10.00	3.00
5 Don Mattingly 82	25.00	7.50
6 Wade Boggs 82	8.00	2.40
7 Roger Clemens 84 RR	15.00	4.50
8 Kirby Puckett 84 RR	10.00	3.00
9 Eric Davis 84 RR	5.00	1.50
10 Dwight Gooden 84 RR	5.00	1.50
11 Eric Davis 84	5.00	1.50
12 Roger Clemens 84	15.00	4.50
13 Kirby Puckett 84	10.00	3.00
14 Dwight Gooden 84	5.00	1.50
15 Barry Bonds 86 RR	15.00	4.50
16 Will Clark 86	10.00	3.00
17 Barry Larkin 86	8.00	2.40
18 Greg Maddux 86	15.00	4.50
19 Rafael Palmeiro 86	8.00	2.40
20 Craig Biggio 88	8.00	2.40
21 Gary Sheffield 88	5.00	1.50
22 Randy Johnson 88	10.00	3.00
23 Curt Schilling 88	5.00	1.50

1997 Donruss Signature

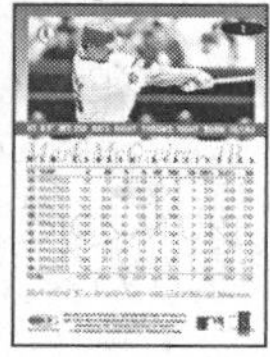

Distributed in five-card packs with one authentic autographed card per pack, this 100-card set was issued in two series. However, these regular cards were issued with both series and one could make sets from either series. These packs carried a suggested retail price of $14.99. The fronts feature color player photos with player information on the backs. The only Rookie Cards of note in this set are Jose Cruz Jr. and Mark Kotsay.

Card	Nm-Mt	Ex-Mt
COMPLETE SET (100)	50.00	15.00
1 Mark McGwire	3.00	.90
2 Kenny Lofton	.50	.15
3 Tony Gwynn	1.50	.45
4 Tony Clark	.50	.15
5 Tim Salmon	.75	.23
6 Ken Griffey Jr.	2.00	.60
7 Mike Piazza	2.00	.60
8 Greg Maddux	2.00	.60
9 Roberto Alomar	.75	.23
10 Andres Galarraga	.50	.15
11 Roger Clemens	2.50	.75
12 Bernie Williams	.75	.23
13 Rondell White	.50	.15
14 Kevin Appier	.50	.15
15 Ray Lankford	.50	.15
16 Frank Thomas	1.25	.35
17 Will Clark	1.25	.35
18 Chipper Jones	1.25	.35
19 Jeff Bagwell	.75	.23
20 Manny Ramirez	.75	.23
21 Ryne Sandberg	2.00	.60
22 Paul Molitor	.75	.23
23 Gary Sheffield	.50	.15
24 Jim Edmonds	.50	.15
25 Barry Larkin	.75	.23
26 Rafael Palmeiro	.75	.23
27 Alan Benes	.50	.15
28 Dave Justice	.50	.15
29 Randy Johnson	1.25	.35
30 Barry Bonds	3.00	.90
31 Mo Vaughn	.50	.15
32 Michael Tucker	.50	.15
33 Larry Walker	.75	.23
34 Tino Martinez	.75	.23
35 Jose Guillen	.50	.15
36 Carlos Delgado	.50	.15
37 Jason Dickson	.50	.15
38 Tom Glavine	.75	.23
39 Raul Mondesi	.50	.15
40 Jose Cruz Jr. RC	.75	.23
41 Johnny Damon	.75	.23
42 Mark Grace	.75	.23
43 Juan Gonzalez	.75	.23
44 Vladimir Guerrero	1.25	.35
45 Kevin Brown	.50	.15
46 Justin Thompson	.50	.15
47 Eric Young	.50	.15
48 Ron Coomer	.50	.15
49 Mark Kotsay RC	1.25	.35
50 Scott Rolen	1.25	.35
51 Derek Jeter	3.00	.90
52 Jim Thome	1.25	.35
53 Fred McGriff	.75	.23
54 Albert Belle	.50	.15
55 Garret Anderson	.50	.15
56 Wilton Guerrero	.50	.15
57 Jose Canseco	1.25	.35
58 Cal Ripken	4.00	1.20
59 Sammy Sosa	2.00	.60
60 Dmitri Young	.50	.15
61 Alex Rodriguez	2.00	.60
62 Javier Lopez	.50	.15
63 Sandy Alomar Jr.	.50	.15
64 Joe Carter	.50	.15
65 Dante Bichette	.50	.15
66 Al Martin	.50	.15
67 Darin Erstad	.50	.15
68 Pokey Reese	.50	.15
69 Brady Anderson	.50	.15
70 Andruw Jones	.50	.15
71 Ivan Rodriguez	1.25	.35
72 Nomar Garciaparra	2.00	.60
73 Moises Alou	.50	.15
74 Andy Pettitte	.75	.23
75 Jay Buhner	.50	.15
76 Craig Biggio	.75	.23
77 Wade Boggs	.75	.23
78 Shawn Estes	.50	.15
79 Neifi Perez	.50	.15
80 Rusty Greer	.50	.15
81 Pedro Martinez	1.25	.35
82 Mike Mussina	.75	.23
83 Jason Giambi	.50	.15
84 Hideo Nomo	1.25	.35
85 Todd Hundley	.50	.15
86 Deion Sanders	.75	.23
87 Mike Cameron	.50	.15
88 Bobby Bonilla	.50	.15
89 Todd Greene	.50	.15
90 Kevin Orie	.50	.15
91 Ken Caminiti	.50	.15
92 Chuck Knoblauch	.50	.15
93 Matt Morris	.50	.15
94 Matt Williams	.50	.15
95 Pat Hentgen	.50	.15
96 John Smoltz	.75	.23
97 Edgar Martinez	.75	.23
98 Jason Kendall	.50	.15
99 Ken Griffey Jr. CL	1.25	.35
100 Frank Thomas CL	.75	.23

1997 Donruss Signature Platinum Press Proofs

Randomly inserted in packs, this set is a holo foil parallel version of the base set. Only 150 of this set were produced. Each card is numbered "1 of 150" on the back. Some cards were mistakenly printed with the "1 of 150 backs" but did not have the platinum press proof front. These cards are valued at approximately the same price as the values below.

	Nm-Mt	Ex-Mt
*STARS: 10X TO 25X BASIC CARDS		
*ROOKIES: 4X TO 10X BASIC CARDS		

1997 Donruss Signature Autographs

Inserted one per pack, this 117-card set features color player autographed photos. The first 100 cards each player signed were blue, sequentially numbered to 1000, and designated as "Century Marks." The next 100 cards signed were green, sequentially numbered 101-1100, and designated as "Millenium Marks." Player autographs surpassing 1100 were red and were not numbered. Some autographed signature cards were not available at first and were designated by blank-backed redemption cards which could be redeemed by mail for the player's autograph card. The cards are checklisted below in alphabetical order. Asterisk cards were found in both Series A and B. Print runs for how many cards each player signed is noted next to the players name. Exchange cards for Raul Mondesi and Edgar Renteria were seeded into packs. Notable cards of players in their Rookie Card seasons include Brian Giles and Miguel Tejada. The Miguel Tejada and David Ortiz cards were signed in either black or blue ink. At this time, there is no price differential for either version of these cards.

Card	Nm-Mt	Ex-Mt
1 Jeff Abbott/3900	4.00	1.20
2 Bob Abreu/3900	10.00	3.00
3 Edgardo Alfonzo/3900	4.00	1.20
4 Roberto Alomar/150 *	50.00	15.00
5 Sandy Alomar Jr./1400	6.00	1.80
6 Moises Alou/900	15.00	4.50
7 Garret Anderson/3900	15.00	4.50
8 Andy Ashby/3900	4.00	1.20
9 Trey Beamon/3900	4.00	1.20
10 Alan Benes/3900	4.00	1.20
11 Geronimo Berroa/3900	4.00	1.20
12 Wade Boggs/150 *	120.00	36.00
13 Kevin Brown C/3900	4.00	1.20
14 Brett Butler/1400	15.00	4.50
15 Mike Cameron/3900	10.00	3.00
16 Giovanni Carrara/2900	4.00	1.20
17 Luis Castillo/3900	10.00	3.00
18 Tony Clark/3900	4.00	1.20
19 Will Clark/1400	25.00	7.50
20 Lou Collier/3900	4.00	1.20
21 Bartolo Colon/3900	10.00	3.00
22 Ron Coomer/3900	4.00	1.20
23 Marty Cordova/3900	4.00	1.20
24 Jacob Cruz/3900 *	4.00	1.20
25 Jose Cruz Jr./900 *	10.00	3.00
26 Russ Davis/3900	4.00	1.20
27 Jason Dickson/3900	4.00	1.20
28 Todd Dunwoody/3900	4.00	1.20
29 Jermaine Dye/3900	10.00	3.00
30 Jim Edmonds/3900	15.00	4.50
31 Darin Erstad/900 *	15.00	4.50
32 Bobby Estalella/3900	4.00	1.20
33 Shawn Estes/3900	4.00	1.20
34 Jeff Fassero/3900	4.00	1.20
35 Andres Galarraga/900	15.00	4.50
36 Karim Garcia/3900	4.00	1.20
37 Derrick Gibson/3900	4.00	1.20
38 Brian Giles/3900	15.00	4.50
39 Tom Glavine/150	80.00	24.00
40 Rick Gorecki/900	6.00	1.80
41 Shawn Green/1900	15.00	4.50
42 Todd Greene/3900	4.00	1.20
43 Rusty Greer/3900	10.00	3.00
44 Ben Grieve/3900	4.00	1.20
45 M.Grudzielanek/3900	4.00	1.20
46 V.Guerrero/1900 *	25.00	7.50
47 Wilton Guerrero/2150	4.00	1.20
48 Jose Guillen/2900	10.00	3.00
49 J.Hammonds/2150	4.00	1.20
50 Todd Helton/1400	25.00	7.50
51 T.Hollandsworth/2900	4.00	1.20
52 Trenidad Hubbard/900	6.00	1.80
53 Todd Hundley/1400	6.00	1.80
54 Bobby Jones/3900	4.00	1.20
55 Brian Jordan/1400	15.00	4.50
56 David Justice/900	15.00	4.50
57 Eric Karros/650	15.00	4.50
58 Jason Kendall/3900	10.00	3.00
59 Jimmy Key/3900	15.00	4.50
60 B.Kieschnick/3900	4.00	1.20
61 Ryan Klesko/225	30.00	9.00
62 Paul Konerko/3900	10.00	3.00
63 Mark Kotsay/2400	10.00	3.00
64 Ray Lankford/3900	4.00	1.20
65 Barry Larkin/150 *	50.00	15.00
66 Derrek Lee/3900	10.00	3.00
67 Esteban Loaiza/3900	4.00	1.20
68 Javier Lopez/1400	15.00	4.50
69 Edgar Martinez/150 *	80.00	24.00
70 Pedro Martinez/900	60.00	18.00
71 Rafael Medina/3900	4.00	1.20
72 Raul Mondesi/650	15.00	4.50
73 Matt Morris/3900	15.00	4.50
74 Paul O'Neill/900	25.00	7.50
75 Kevin Orie/3900	4.00	1.20
76 David Ortiz/3900	40.00	12.00
77 Rafael Palmeiro/900	40.00	12.00
78 Jay Payton/3900	4.00	1.20
79 Neifi Perez/3900	4.00	1.20
80 Manny Ramirez/900	40.00	12.00
81 Joe Randa/3900	4.00	1.20
82 Pokey Reese/3900	10.00	3.00
83 Edgar Renteria SP	25.00	7.50
84 Dennis Reyes/3900	4.00	1.20
85 Henry Rodriguez/3900	4.00	1.20
86 Scott Rolen/1900 *	25.00	7.50
87 Kirk Rueter/2900	10.00	3.00
88 Ryne Sandberg/400	60.00	18.00
89 Dwight Smith/2900	4.00	1.20
90 J.T. Snow/900	15.00	4.50
91 Scott Spiezio/3900	4.00	1.20
92 Shannon Stewart/2900	10.00	3.00
93 Jeff Suppan/1900	4.00	1.20
94 Mike Sweeney/3900	10.00	3.00
95 Miguel Tejada/3900	20.00	6.00
96 Justin Thompson/2400	4.00	1.20
97 Brett Tomko/3900	4.00	1.20
98 Bubba Trammell/3900	8.00	2.40
99 Michael Tucker/3900	4.00	1.20
100 Javier Valentin/3900	4.00	1.20
101 Mo Vaughn/150 *	30.00	9.00
102 Robin Ventura/1400	15.00	4.50
103 Terrell Wade/3900	4.00	1.20
104 Billy Wagner/3900	15.00	4.50
105 Larry Walker/900	40.00	12.00
106 Todd Walker/2400	10.00	3.00
107 Rondell White/3900	10.00	3.00
108 Kevin Wickander/900	4.00	1.20
109 Chris Widger/3900	4.00	1.20
110 Matt Williams/150 *	30.00	9.00
111 A.Williamson/3900	4.00	1.20
112 Dan Wilson/3900	4.00	1.20
113 Tony Womack/3900	8.00	2.40
114 Jaret Wright/3900	15.00	3.00
115 Dmitri Young/3900	10.00	3.00
116 Eric Young/3900	4.00	1.20
117 Kevin Young/3900	4.00	1.20
NNO F.Thomas Sample Fascimile Autograph	2.00	.60

1997 Donruss Signature Autographs Century

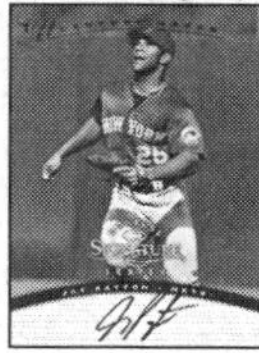

Randomly inserted in packs, this set, identified with blue card fronts, features the first 100 cards signed by each player. The cards are sequentially numbered. Raul Mondesi, Eddie Murray, Edgar Renteria and Jim Thome were seeded in packs as exchange cards. The cards are checklisted below in alphabetical order. A number of Nomar Garciaparra Century marks were lost or destroyed during packaging and only 62 of these cards were inserted into packs.

Card	Nm-Mt	Ex-Mt
1 Jeff Abbott	25.00	7.50
2 Bob Abreu	40.00	12.00
3 Edgardo Alfonzo	25.00	7.50
4 Roberto Alomar *	80.00	24.00
5 Sandy Alomar Jr.	25.00	7.50
6 Moises Alou	40.00	12.00
7 Garret Anderson	80.00	24.00
8 Andy Ashby	25.00	7.50
9 Jeff Bagwell	150.00	45.00
10 Trey Beamon	25.00	7.50
11 Albert Belle	40.00	12.00
12 Alan Benes	25.00	7.50
13 Geronimo Berroa	25.00	7.50
14 Wade Boggs *	100.00	30.00
15 Barry Bonds	400.00	120.00
16 Bobby Bonilla *	40.00	12.00
17 Kevin Brown	80.00	24.00
18 Kevin Brown C	25.00	7.50
19 Jay Buhner	40.00	12.00
20 Brett Butler	40.00	12.00
21 Mike Cameron	40.00	12.00
22 Giovanni Carrara	25.00	7.50
23 Luis Castillo	40.00	12.00
24 Tony Clark	25.00	7.50
25 Will Clark	100.00	30.00
26 Roger Clemens *	250.00	75.00
27 Lou Collier	25.00	7.50
28 Bartolo Colon	40.00	12.00
29 Ron Coomer	25.00	7.50
30 Marty Cordova	25.00	7.50
31 Jacob Cruz *	25.00	7.50
32 Jose Cruz Jr. *	40.00	12.00
33 Russ Davis	25.00	7.50
34 Jason Dickson	25.00	7.50
35 Todd Dunwoody	25.00	7.50
36 Jermaine Dye	40.00	12.00
37 Jim Edmonds	80.00	24.00
38 Darin Erstad *	40.00	12.00
39 Bobby Estalella	25.00	7.50
40 Shawn Estes	25.00	7.50
41 Jeff Fassero	25.00	7.50
42 Andres Galarraga	40.00	12.00
43 Karim Garcia	25.00	7.50
44 N. Garciaparra SP62 *	400.00	120.00
45 Derrick Gibson	25.00	7.50
46 Brian Giles	60.00	18.00
47 Tom Glavine	100.00	30.00
48 Juan Gonzalez	80.00	24.00
49 Rick Gorecki	25.00	7.50
50 Shawn Green	80.00	24.00
51 Todd Greene	25.00	7.50
52 Rusty Greer	40.00	12.00
53 Ben Grieve	25.00	7.50
54 Mark Grudzielanek	25.00	7.50
55 Vladimir Guerrero *	100.00	30.00
56 Wilton Guerrero	25.00	7.50
57 Jose Guillen	40.00	12.00
58 Tony Gwynn *	120.00	36.00
59 Jeffrey Hammonds	25.00	7.50
60 Todd Helton	100.00	30.00
61 Todd Hollandsworth	25.00	7.50
62 Trenidad Hubbard	25.00	7.50
63 Todd Hundley	25.00	7.50
64 Derek Jeter *	300.00	90.00
65 Andruw Jones *	80.00	24.00
66 Bobby Jones	25.00	7.50
67 Chipper Jones *	120.00	36.00
68 Brian Jordan	40.00	12.00
69 David Justice	40.00	12.00
70 Eric Karros	40.00	12.00
71 Jason Kendall	40.00	12.00
72 Jimmy Key	80.00	24.00
73 Brooks Kieschnick	25.00	7.50
74 Ryan Klesko	40.00	12.00
75 Chuck Knoblauch *	40.00	12.00
76 Paul Konerko	40.00	12.00
77 Mark Kotsay	40.00	12.00
78 Ray Lankford	25.00	7.50
79 Barry Larkin *	80.00	24.00
80 Derrek Lee	40.00	12.00
81 Esteban Loaiza	25.00	7.50
82 Javier Lopez	40.00	12.00
83 Greg Maddux *	250.00	75.00
84 Edgar Martinez *	100.00	30.00
85 Pedro Martinez	150.00	45.00
86 Tino Martinez *	100.00	30.00
87 Rafael Medina	25.00	7.50
88 Raul Mondesi	40.00	12.00
89 Matt Morris	80.00	24.00
90 Eddie Murray EXCH*	120.00	36.00
91 Mike Mussina	80.00	24.00
92 Paul O'Neill	80.00	24.00
93 Kevin Orie	25.00	7.50
94 David Ortiz	150.00	45.00
95 Rafael Palmeiro	100.00	30.00
96 Jay Payton	25.00	7.50
97 Neifi Perez	25.00	7.50
98 Andy Pettitte *	100.00	30.00
99 Manny Ramirez	100.00	30.00
100 Joe Randa	25.00	7.50
101 Pokey Reese	40.00	12.00
102 Edgar Renteria	80.00	12.00
103 Dennis Reyes	25.00	7.50
104 Cal Ripken	300.00	90.00
105 Alex Rodriguez	250.00	75.00
106 Henry Rodriguez	25.00	7.50
107 Ivan Rodriguez	100.00	30.00
108 Scott Rolen *	100.00	30.00
109 Kirk Rueter	40.00	12.00
110 Ryne Sandberg	120.00	36.00
111 Gary Sheffield *	80.00	24.00
112 Dwight Smith	25.00	7.50
113 J.T. Snow	40.00	12.00
114 Scott Spiezio	25.00	7.50
115 Shannon Stewart	40.00	12.00
116 Jeff Suppan	25.00	7.50
117 Mike Sweeney	40.00	12.00
118 Miguel Tejada	80.00	24.00
119 Frank Thomas	100.00	30.00
120 Jim Thome	100.00	30.00
121 Justin Thompson	25.00	7.50
122 Brett Tomko	25.00	7.50
123 Bubba Trammell	25.00	7.50
124 Michael Tucker	25.00	7.50
125 Javier Valentin	25.00	7.50
126 Mo Vaughn *	40.00	12.00
127 Robin Ventura	40.00	12.00
128 Terrell Wade	25.00	7.50
129 Billy Wagner	80.00	24.00
130 Larry Walker	100.00	30.00
131 Todd Walker	40.00	12.00
132 Rondell White	40.00	12.00
133 Kevin Wickander	25.00	7.50
134 Chris Widger	25.00	7.50
135 Bernie Williams	120.00	36.00
136 Matt Williams *	40.00	12.00
137 Antone Williamson	25.00	7.50
138 Dan Wilson	25.00	7.50
139 Tony Womack	25.00	7.50
140 Jaret Wright	50.00	12.00
141 Dmitri Young	40.00	12.00
142 Eric Young	25.00	7.50
143 Kevin Young	25.00	7.50

1997 Donruss Signature Autographs Millennium

Randomly inserted in packs, this set, identified with green card fronts, features the second group of 100 cards signed by each player. The cards are sequentially numbered 101-1,100 (except for some shortprinted cards in quantities of 400, 650 or 900) and are checklisted in alphabetical order. It has been noted that there are

some cards in circulation that lack serial numbering. Edgar Renteria was seeded into packs as an exchange card and has been verified by representatives at Donruss as being a short-print. Eddie Murray, Raul Mondesi and Jim Thome were also exchange cards.

Card	Nm-Mt	Ex-Mt
1 Jeff Abbott	8.00	2.40
2 Bob Abreu	15.00	4.50
3 Edgardo Alfonzo	8.00	2.40
4 Roberto Alomar *	25.00	7.50
5 Sandy Alomar Jr.	8.00	2.40
6 Moises Alou	15.00	4.50
7 Garret Anderson	25.00	7.50
8 Andy Ashby	8.00	2.40
9 Jeff Bagwell/400	100.00	30.00
10 Trey Beamon	8.00	2.40
11 Albert Belle/400	25.00	7.50
12 Alan Benes	8.00	2.40
13 Geronimo Berroa	8.00	2.40
14 Wade Boggs *	40.00	12.00
15 Barry Bonds/400	250.00	75.00
16 Bobby Bonilla/900 *	15.00	4.50
17 Kevin Brown/900	25.00	7.50
18 Kevin Brown C	8.00	2.40
19 Jay Buhner/900	15.00	4.50
20 Brett Butler	15.00	4.50
21 Mike Cameron	15.00	4.50
22 Giovanni Carrara	8.00	2.40
23 Luis Castillo	15.00	4.50
24 Tony Clark	8.00	2.40
25 Will Clark	40.00	12.00
26 Roger Clemens/400 *	150.00	45.00
27 Lou Collier	8.00	2.40
28 Bartolo Colon	15.00	4.50
29 Ron Coomer	8.00	2.40
30 Marty Cordova	8.00	2.40
31 Jacob Cruz	8.00	2.40
32 Jose Cruz Jr. *	15.00	4.50
33 Russ Davis	8.00	2.40
34 Jason Dickson	8.00	2.40
35 Todd Dunwoody	8.00	2.40
36 Jermaine Dye	15.00	4.50
37 Jim Edmonds	25.00	7.50
38 Darin Erstad *	15.00	4.50
39 Bobby Estalella	8.00	2.40
40 Shawn Estes	8.00	2.40
41 Jeff Fassero	8.00	2.40
42 Andres Galarraga	15.00	4.50
43 Karim Garcia	8.00	2.40
44 N.Garciaparra/650 *	120.00	36.00
45 Derrick Gibson	8.00	2.40
46 Brian Giles	25.00	7.50
47 Tom Glavine	40.00	12.00
48 Juan Gonzalez/900	25.00	7.50
49 Rick Gorecki	8.00	2.40
50 Shawn Green	25.00	7.50
51 Todd Greene	8.00	2.40
52 Rusty Greer	15.00	4.50
53 Ben Grieve	8.00	2.40
54 Mark Grudzielanek	8.00	2.40
55 Vladimir Guerrero *	40.00	12.00
56 Wilton Guerrero	8.00	2.40
57 Jose Guillen	15.00	4.50
58 Tony Gwynn/900 *	40.00	12.00
59 Jeffrey Hammonds	8.00	2.40
60 Todd Helton	40.00	12.00
61 Todd Hundley	8.00	2.40
62 Todd Hollandsworth	8.00	2.40
63 Trenidad Hubbard	8.00	2.40
64 Derek Jeter/400 *	175.00	52.50
65 Andruw Jones/900 *	25.00	7.50
66 Bobby Jones	8.00	2.40
67 Chipper Jones/900 *	40.00	12.00
68 Brian Jordan	15.00	4.50
69 David Justice	15.00	4.50
70 Eric Karros	15.00	4.50
71 Jason Kendall	15.00	4.50
72 Jimmy Key	25.00	7.50
73 Brooks Kieschnick	8.00	2.40
74 Ryan Klesko	15.00	4.50
75 C.Knoblauch/900 *	15.00	4.50
76 Paul Konerko	15.00	4.50
77 Mark Kotsay	15.00	4.50
78 Ray Lankford	8.00	2.40
79 Barry Larkin *	25.00	7.50
80 Derrek Lee	15.00	4.50
81 Esteban Loaiza	8.00	2.40
82 Javier Lopez	15.00	4.50
83 Greg Maddux/400 *	100.00	30.00
84 Edgar Martinez *	40.00	12.00
85 Pedro Martinez	60.00	18.00
86 Tino Martinez/900 *	40.00	12.00
87 Rafael Medina	8.00	2.40
88 Raul Mondesi	15.00	4.50
89 Matt Morris	25.00	7.50
90 Eddie Murray/900 *	50.00	15.00
91 Mike Mussina/900	25.00	7.50
92 Paul O'Neill	25.00	7.50
93 Kevin Orie	8.00	2.40
94 David Ortiz	50.00	15.00
95 Rafael Palmeiro	40.00	12.00
96 Jay Payton	8.00	2.40
97 Neifi Perez	8.00	2.40
98 Andy Pettitte/900 *	40.00	12.00
99 Manny Ramirez	40.00	12.00
100 Joe Randa	8.00	2.40
101 Pokey Reese	15.00	4.50
102 Edgar Renteria SP	40.00	12.00
103 Dennis Reyes	8.00	2.40
104 Cal Ripken/400	150.00	45.00
105 Alex Rodriguez/400	150.00	45.00
106 Henry Rodriguez	8.00	2.40
107 Ivan Rodriguez/900	40.00	12.00
108 Scott Rolen *	40.00	12.00
109 Kirk Rueter	15.00	4.50
110 Ryne Sandberg	50.00	15.00

111 Gary Sheffield/400 * 40.00 12.00
112 Dwight Smith 8.00 2.40
113 J.T. Snow 15.00 4.50
114 Scott Spiezio 8.00 2.40
115 Shannon Stewart 15.00 4.50
116 Jeff Suppan 8.00 2.40
117 Mike Sweeney 15.00 4.50
118 Miguel Tejada 30.00 9.00
119 Frank Thomas/400 80.00 24.00
120 Jim Thome/900 40.00 12.00
121 Justin Thompson 8.00 2.40
122 Brett Tomko 8.00 2.40
123 Bubba Trammell 10.00 3.00
124 Michael Tucker 8.00 2.40
125 Javier Valentin 8.00 2.40
126 Mo Vaughn * 15.00 4.50
127 Robin Ventura 15.00 4.50
128 Terrell Wade 8.00 2.40
129 Billy Wagner 25.00 7.50
130 Larry Walker 40.00 12.00
131 Todd Walker 15.00 4.50
132 Rondell White 15.00 4.50
133 Kevin Wickander 8.00 2.40
134 Chris Widger 8.00 2.40
135 Bernie Williams/400 100.00 30.00
136 Matt Williams * 15.00 4.50
137 Antone Williamson 8.00 2.40
138 Dan Wilson 8.00 2.40
139 Tony Womack 10.00 3.00
140 Jaret Wright 20.00 4.50
141 Dmitri Young 15.00 4.50
142 Eric Young 8.00 2.40
143 Kevin Young 8.00 2.40

1997 Donruss Signature Notable Nicknames

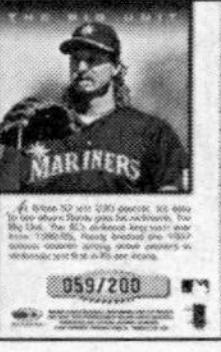

Randomly inserted in packs, this 10-card set features photos of players with notable nicknames. Only 200 of this serial numbered set were produced. The cards are unnumbered and checklisted in alphabetical order. Roger Clemens signed a good deal of his cards without using his "Rocket" nickname. In addition, some Frank Thomas cards have been seen signed without "The Big Hurt" nickname. There is no difference in value between the two versions.

Nm-Mt Ex-Mt
1 Ernie Banks 150.00 45.00
Mr. Cub
2 Tony Clark 60.00 18.00
The Tiger
3 Roger Clemens 450.00 135.00
The Rocket
4 Reggie Jackson 150.00 45.00
Mr. October
5 Randy Johnson 350.00 105.00
The Big Unit
6 Stan Musial 200.00 60.00
The Man
7 Ivan Rodriguez 150.00 45.00
Pudge
8 Frank Thomas 150.00 45.00
The Big Hurt
9 Mo Vaughn 80.00 24.00
The Hit Dog
10 Billy Wagner 120.00 36.00
The Kid

1997 Donruss Signature Significant Signatures

Randomly inserted in packs, this 22-card set features photos with autographs of legendary Hall of Fame players. Only 2000 of each card was produced and serially numbered. The cards are checklisted below in alphabetical order. Reggie Jackson signed his cards in 2 different color inks. The cards he signed in silver are in shorter supply and are valued higher.

Nm-Mt Ex-Mt
1 Ernie Banks 40.00 12.00
2 Johnny Bench 40.00 12.00
3 Yogi Berra 40.00 12.00
4 George Brett 60.00 18.00
5 Lou Brock 40.00 12.00
6 Rod Carew 40.00 12.00
7 Steve Carlton 40.00 12.00
8 Larry Doby 60.00 18.00
9 Carlton Fisk 40.00 12.00
10 Bob Gibson 40.00 12.00
11 Reggie Jackson 40.00 12.00
11A R.Jackson Silver Ink 120.00 36.00
12 Al Kaline 40.00 12.00
13 Harmon Killebrew 40.00 12.00
14 Don Mattingly 50.00 15.00
15 Stan Musial 50.00 15.00
16 Jim Palmer 25.00 7.50
17 Brooks Robinson 40.00 12.00
18 Frank Robinson 25.00 7.50
19 Mike Schmidt 50.00 15.00
20 Tom Seaver 40.00 12.00
21 Duke Snider 40.00 12.00
22 Carl Yastrzemski 50.00 15.00

1998 Donruss Signature

The 140-card 1998 Donruss Signature set was distributed in five-card packs with one authentic autographed card per pack and a suggested retail price of $14.99. The fronts feature color action player photos in white borders. The backs carry player information and career statistics. Due to Pinnacle's bankruptcy, these cards were later released by Playoff. This set was released in very late December, 1998. Notable Rookie Cards in this set include J.D. Drew, Troy Glaus, Orlando Hernandez, Gabe Kapler, Kevin Millwood and Magglio Ordonez.

Nm-Mt Ex-Mt
COMPLETE SET (140) 50.00 15.00
1 David Justice .40 .12
2 Derek Jeter 2.50 .75
3 Nomar Garciaparra 1.50 .45
4 Ryan Klesko .40 .12
5 Jeff Bagwell .60 .18
6 Dante Bichette .40 .12
7 Ivan Rodriguez 1.00 .30
8 Albert Belle .40 .12
9 Cal Ripken 3.00 .90
10 Craig Biggio .60 .18
11 Barry Larkin .60 .18
12 Jose Guillen .40 .12
13 Will Clark 1.00 .30
14 J.T. Snow .40 .12
15 Chuck Knoblauch .40 .12
16 Todd Walker .40 .12
17 Scott Rolen 1.00 .30
18 Rickey Henderson 1.00 .30
19 Juan Gonzalez .60 .18
20 Justin Thompson .40 .12
21 Roger Clemens 2.00 .60
22 Ray Lankford .40 .12
23 Jose Cruz Jr. .40 .12
24 Ken Griffey Jr. 1.50 .45
25 Andruw Jones .40 .12
26 Darin Erstad .40 .12
27 Jim Thome 1.00 .30
28 Wade Boggs .60 .18
29 Ken Caminiti .40 .12
30 Todd Hundley .40 .12
31 Mike Piazza 1.50 .45
32 Sammy Sosa 1.50 .45
33 Larry Walker .60 .18
34 Matt Williams .40 .12
35 Frank Thomas 1.00 .30
36 Gary Sheffield .40 .12
37 Alex Rodriguez 1.50 .45
38 Hideo Nomo 1.00 .30
39 Kenny Lofton .40 .12
40 John Smoltz .60 .18
41 Mo Vaughn .40 .12
42 Edgar Martinez .60 .18
43 Paul Molitor .60 .18
44 Rafael Palmeiro .60 .18
45 Barry Bonds 2.50 .75
46 Vladimir Guerrero 1.00 .30
47 Carlos Delgado .40 .12
48 Bobby Higginson .40 .12
49 Greg Maddux 1.50 .45
50 Jim Edmonds .40 .12
51 Randy Johnson 1.00 .30
52 Mark McGwire 2.50 .75
53 Rondell White .40 .12
54 Raul Mondesi .40 .12
55 Manny Ramirez .60 .18
56 Pedro Martinez 1.00 .30
57 Tim Salmon .60 .18
58 Moises Alou .40 .12
59 Fred McGriff .60 .18
60 Garret Anderson .40 .12
61 Sandy Alomar Jr. .40 .12
62 Chan Ho Park .40 .12
63 Mark Kotsay .40 .12
64 Mike Mussina .60 .18
65 Tom Glavine .60 .18
66 Tony Clark .40 .12
67 Mark Grace .60 .18
68 Tony Gwynn 1.25 .35
69 Tino Martinez .60 .18
70 Kevin Brown .60 .18
71 Todd Greene .40 .12
72 Andy Pettitte .60 .18
73 Livan Hernandez .40 .12
74 Curt Schilling .40 .12
75 Andres Galarraga .40 .12
76 Rusty Greer .40 .12
77 Jay Buhner .40 .12
78 Bobby Bonilla .40 .12
79 Chipper Jones 1.00 .30
80 Eric Young .40 .12
81 Jason Giambi .40 .12
82 Javy Lopez .40 .12
83 Roberto Alomar .60 .18
84 Bernie Williams .60 .18
85 A.J. Hinch .40 .12
86 Kerry Wood 1.00 .30
87 Juan Encarnacion .40 .12
88 Brad Fullmer .40 .12
89 Ben Grieve .40 .12
90 Magglio Ordonez RC 8.00 2.40
91 Todd Helton .60 .18
92 Richard Hidalgo .40 .12
93 Paul Konerko .40 .12
94 Aramis Ramirez .40 .12
95 Ricky Ledee .40 .12
96 Derrek Lee .40 .12
97 Travis Lee .40 .12
98 Matt Anderson RC .60 .18
99 Jaret Wright .40 .12
100 David Ortiz 1.00 .30
101 Carl Pavano .60 .12
102 O.Hernandez RC 1.50 .45
103 Fernando Tatis .40 .12
104 Miguel Tejada .40 .12
105 Rolando Arrojo RC .60 .18
106 Kevin Millwood RC 1.50 .45
107 Ken Griffey Jr. CL 1.00 .30
108 Frank Thomas CL .60 .18
109 Cal Ripken CL 1.50 .45
110 Greg Maddux CL 1.00 .30
111 John Olerud .40 .12
112 David Cone .40 .12
113 Vinny Castilla .40 .12
114 Jason Kendall .40 .12
115 Brian Jordan .40 .12
116 Hideki Irabu .40 .12
117 Bartolo Colon .40 .12
118 Greg Vaughn .40 .12
119 David Segui .40 .12
120 Bruce Chen .40 .12
121 Julio Ramirez RC .40 .12
122 Troy Glaus RC 8.00 2.40
123 Jeremy Giambi RC .60 .18
124 Ryan Minor RC .40 .12
125 Richie Sexson .40 .12
126 Dermal Brown .40 .12
127 Adrian Beltre 1.00 .30
128 Carlos Chavez .40 .12
129 J.D. Drew RC 8.00 2.40
130 Gabe Kapler RC 1.00 .30
131 Masato Yoshii RC 1.00 .30
132 Mike Lowell RC 4.00 1.20
133 Jim Parque RC .60 .18
134 Roy Halladay .40 .12
135 Carlos Lee RC 1.50 .45
136 Jin Ho Cho RC .40 .12
137 Michael Barrett .40 .12
138 F.Seguignol RC .40 .12
139 Odalis Perez RC UER 1.50 .45
Back pictures John Rocker
140 Mark McGwire CL 1.25 .35

1998 Donruss Signature Proofs

Randomly inserted in packs, this 140-card set is a holo-foil treated parallel version of the base set. Only 150 sets were produced and numbered "1 of 150."

Nm-Mt Ex-Mt
*STARS: 6X TO 15X BASIC CARDS....
*ROOKIES: 1.5X TO 4X BASIC CARDS

1998 Donruss Signature Autographs

Inserted one per pack, this 98-card set features color action player images on a red foil background with the player's autograph in the lower portion of the card. The numbers following the player's name in our checklist indicate how many cards that player signed. The first 100 cards signed by each player are blue, sequentially-numbered and designated as "Century Marks." The next 1,000 signed are green, sequentially numbered and designated as "Millennium Marks." The cards are unnumbered and checklisted below in alphabetical order. An unnumbered Travis Lee sample card was distributed many months prior to the product's release. It's important to note that sample card features a facsimile autograph of Lee's.

Nm-Mt Ex-Mt
1 Roberto Alomar/150 40.00 12.00
2 Sandy Alomar Jr./700 10.00 3.00
3 Moises Alou/900 20.00 6.00
4 Gabe Alvarez/2900 4.00 1.20
5 Wilson Alvarez/1600 4.00 1.20
6 Jay Bell/1500 10.00 3.00
7 Adrian Beltre/1900 40.00 12.00
8 Andy Benes/2600 4.00 1.20
9 Aaron Boone/3400 10.00 3.00
10 Russell Branyan/1650 4.00 1.20
11 Orlando Cabrera/3100 10.00 3.00
12 Mike Cameron/1150 10.00 3.00
13 Joe Carter/400 20.00 6.00
14 Sean Casey/2275 10.00 3.00
15 Bruce Chen/150 15.00 4.50
16 Tony Clark/2275 4.00 1.20
17 Will Clark/1400 25.00 7.50
18 Matt Clement/1400 10.00 1.20
19 Pat Cline/1400 4.00 1.20
20 Ken Cloude/3400 4.00 1.20
21 Michael Coleman/2800 4.00 1.20
22 David Cone/25
23 Jeff Conine/1400 10.00 3.00
24 Jacob Cruz/3200 4.00 1.20
25 Russ Davis/3500 4.00 1.20
26 Jason Dickson/1400 4.00 1.20
27 Todd Dunwoody/3500 4.00 1.20
28 Juan Encarnacion/3400 4.00 1.20
29 Darin Erstad/700 20.00 6.00
30 Bobby Estalella/3400 4.00 1.20
31 Jeff Fassero/3400 4.00 1.20
32 John Franco/1800 10.00 3.00
33 Brad Fullmer/3100 4.00 1.20
34 Jason Giambi/3100 25.00 7.50
35 Derrick Gibson/1200 4.00 1.20
36 Todd Greene/1400 4.00 1.20
37 Ben Grieve/1400 4.00 1.20
38 M.Grudzielanek/3200 4.00 1.20
39 V.Guerrero/2100 40.00 12.00
40 Wilton Guerrero/1900 4.00 1.20
41 Jose Guillen/2400 10.00 3.00
42 Todd Helton/1300 25.00 7.50
43 Richard Hidalgo/3400 4.00 1.20
44 A.J. Hinch/2900 4.00 1.20
45 Butch Huskey/1900 4.00 1.20
46 Raul Ibanez/3300 4.00 1.20
47 Damian Jackson/900 10.00 3.00
48 Geoff Jenkins/3100 10.00 3.00
49 Eric Karros/650 20.00 6.00
50 Ryan Klesko/400 20.00 6.00
51 Mark Kotsay/3600 10.00 3.00
52 Ricky Ledee/2200 4.00 1.20
53 Derrek Lee/3400 10.00 3.00
54 Travis Lee/150 15.00 4.50
55 Javier Lopez/650 20.00 6.00
56 Mike Lowell/3500 15.00 4.50
57 Greg Maddux/12
58 Eli Marrero/3400 4.00 1.20
59 Al Martin/1300 4.00 1.20
60 Rafael Medina/1400 4.00 1.20
61 Scott Morgan/900 10.00 3.00
62 Abraham Nunez/3500 4.00 1.20
63 Paul O'Neill/1000 25.00 7.50
64 Luis Ordaz/2700 4.00 1.20
65 Magglio Ordonez/3200 25.00 7.50
66 Kevin Orie/1350 4.00 1.20
67 David Ortiz/3400 25.00 7.50
68 Rafael Palmeiro/1000 40.00 12.00
69 Carl Pavano/2600 25.00 3.00
70 Neifi Perez/3300 4.00 1.20
71 Dante Powell/3050 4.00 1.20
72 Aramis Ramirez/2800 10.00 3.00
73 Mariano Rivera/900 50.00 15.00
74 Felix Rodriguez/1400 4.00 1.20
75 Henry Rodriguez/3400 4.00 1.20
76 Scott Rolen/1900 40.00 12.00
77 Brian Rose/1400 4.00 1.20
78 Curt Schilling/900 40.00 12.00
79 Richie Sexson/3500 10.00 3.00
80 Randall Simon/3500 4.00 1.20
81 J.T. Snow/400 20.00 6.00
82 Jeff Suppan/1400 4.00 1.20
83 Fernando Tatis/3900 4.00 1.20
84 Miguel Tejada/3800 10.00 3.00
85 Brett Tomko/3400 4.00 1.20
86 Bubba Trammell/3900 4.00 1.20
87 Ismael Valdes/1900 4.00 1.20
88 Robin Ventura/1400 10.00 3.00
89 Billy Wagner/3900 25.00 7.50
90 Todd Walker/1900 10.00 3.00
91 Daryle Ward/400 10.00 3.00
92 Rondell White/3400 10.00 3.00
93 A.Williamson/3350 4.00 1.20
94 Dan Wilson/2400 4.00 1.20
95 Enrique Wilson/3400 4.00 1.20
96 Preston Wilson/2100 10.00 3.00
97 Tony Womack/3500 4.00 1.20
98 Kerry Wood/3400 40.00 12.00
NNO Travis Lee Sample 1.00 .30
Facsimile Autograph

1998 Donruss Signature Autographs Century

Randomly inserted in packs, this 122-card set is a sequentially numbered, blue parallel version of the Signature Autographs insert set and features the first 100 cards signed by each pictured player. The cards are unnumbered and checklisted in alphabetical order.

Nm-Mt Ex-Mt
1 Roberto Alomar 80.00 24.00
2 Sandy Alomar Jr. 25.00 7.50
3 Moises Alou 40.00 12.00
4 Gabe Alvarez 25.00 7.50
5 Wilson Alvarez 25.00 7.50
6 Brady Anderson 40.00 12.00
7 Jay Bell 40.00 12.00
8 Albert Belle 40.00 12.00
9 Adrian Beltre 100.00 30.00
10 Andy Benes 25.00 7.50
11 Wade Boggs 100.00 30.00
12 Barry Bonds 400.00 120.00
13 Aaron Boone 40.00 12.00
14 Russell Branyan 25.00 7.50
15 Jay Buhner 40.00 12.00
16 Ellis Burks 40.00 12.00
17 Orlando Cabrera 40.00 12.00
18 Mike Cameron 40.00 12.00
19 Ken Caminiti 80.00 24.00
20 Joe Carter 40.00 12.00
21 Sean Casey 40.00 12.00
22 Bruce Chen 25.00 7.50
23 Tony Clark 25.00 7.50
24 Will Clark 100.00 30.00
25 Roger Clemens 200.00 60.00
26 Matt Clement 40.00 7.50
27 Pat Cline 25.00 7.50
28 Ken Cloude 25.00 7.50
29 Michael Coleman 25.00 7.50
30 David Cone 40.00 12.00
31 Jeff Conine 40.00 12.00
32 Jacob Cruz 25.00 7.50
33 Jose Cruz Jr. 25.00 7.50
34 Russ Davis 25.00 7.50
35 Jason Dickson 25.00 7.50
36 Todd Dunwoody 25.00 7.50
37 Scott Elarton 25.00 7.50
38 Darin Erstad 40.00 12.00
39 Bobby Estalella 25.00 7.50
40 Jeff Fassero 25.00 7.50
41 John Franco 40.00 12.00
42 Brad Fullmer 25.00 7.50
43 Andres Galarraga 40.00 12.00
44 Nomar Garciaparra 200.00 60.00
45 Jason Giambi 80.00 24.00
46 Derrick Gibson 25.00 7.50
47 Tom Glavine 100.00 30.00
48 Juan Gonzalez 80.00 24.00
49 Todd Greene 25.00 7.50
50 Ben Grieve 25.00 7.50
51 Mark Grudzielanek 25.00 7.50
52 Vladimir Guerrero 100.00 30.00
53 Wilton Guerrero 25.00 7.50
54 Jose Guillen 40.00 12.00
55 Tony Gwynn 120.00 36.00
56 Todd Helton 80.00 24.00
57 Richard Hidalgo 25.00 7.50
58 A.J. Hinch 25.00 7.50
59 Butch Huskey 25.00 7.50
60 Raul Ibanez 25.00 7.50
61 Damian Jackson 25.00 7.50
62 Geoff Jenkins 40.00 12.00
63 Derek Jeter 250.00 75.00
64 Randy Johnson 150.00 45.00
65 Chipper Jones 120.00 36.00
66 Eric Karros/50 40.00 12.00
67 Ryan Klesko 40.00 12.00
68 Chuck Knoblauch 40.00 12.00
69 Mark Kotsay 40.00 12.00
70 Ricky Ledee 25.00 7.50
71 Derrek Lee 40.00 12.00
72 Travis Lee 25.00 7.50
73 Javier Lopez 40.00 12.00
74 Mike Lowell 50.00 15.00
75 Greg Maddux 200.00 60.00
76 Eli Marrero 25.00 7.50
77 Al Martin 25.00 7.50
78 Rafael Medina 25.00 7.50
79 Paul Molitor 80.00 24.00
80 Scott Morgan 25.00 7.50
81 Mike Mussina 80.00 24.00
82 Abraham Nunez 25.00 7.50
83 Paul O'Neill 80.00 24.00
84 Luis Ordaz 25.00 7.50
85 Magglio Ordonez 80.00 24.00
86 Kevin Orie 25.00 7.50
87 David Ortiz 80.00 24.00
88 Rafael Palmeiro 100.00 30.00
89 Carl Pavano 80.00 12.00
90 Neifi Perez 25.00 7.50
91 Andy Pettitte 100.00 30.00
92 Aramis Ramirez 40.00 12.00
93 Cal Ripken 250.00 75.00
94 Mariano Rivera 120.00 36.00
95 Alex Rodriguez 200.00 60.00
96 Felix Rodriguez 25.00 7.50
97 Henry Rodriguez 25.00 7.50
98 Ivan Rodriguez 100.00 30.00
99 Scott Rolen 100.00 30.00
100 Brian Rose 25.00 7.50
101 Curt Schilling 100.00 30.00
102 Richie Sexson 40.00 12.00
103 Randall Simon 25.00 7.50
104 J.T. Snow 40.00 12.00
105 Darryl Strawberry 150.00 45.00
106 Jeff Suppan 25.00 7.50
107 Fernando Tatis 25.00 7.50
108 Brett Tomko 25.00 7.50
109 Bubba Trammell 25.00 7.50
110 Ismael Valdes 25.00 7.50
111 Robin Ventura 40.00 12.00
112 Billy Wagner 80.00 24.00
113 Todd Walker 40.00 12.00
114 Daryle Ward 25.00 7.50
115 Rondell White 40.00 12.00
116 Matt Williams/80 40.00 12.00
117 Antone Williamson 25.00 7.50
118 Dan Wilson 25.00 7.50
119 Enrique Wilson 25.00 7.50
120 Preston Wilson 40.00 12.00
121 Tony Womack 25.00 7.50
122 Kerry Wood 100.00 30.00

1998 Donruss Signature Autographs Millennium

Randomly inserted in packs, this 125-card set is a sequentially numbered, green foil parallel version of the Signature Autographs insert set and features the next 1,000 cards signed by each pictured player after the initial 100. In numerous cases, players signed less than 1,000 cards. Print runs for these short-prints are specified after the player's name in the checklist. The cards are unnumbered and checklisted below in alphabetical order.

Nm-Mt Ex-Mt
1 Roberto Alomar 25.00 7.50
2 Sandy Alomar Jr. 8.00 2.40
3 Moises Alou 15.00 4.50
4 Gabe Alvarez 8.00 2.40
5 Wilson Alvarez 8.00 2.40
6 Brady Anderson/800 15.00 4.50
7 Jay Bell 15.00 4.50
8 Albert Belle/400 40.00 12.00
9 Adrian Beltre 40.00 12.00
10 Andy Benes 8.00 2.40
11 Wade Boggs/900 40.00 12.00
12 Barry Bonds/400 250.00 75.00
13 Aaron Boone 15.00 4.50
14 Russell Branyan 8.00 2.40
15 Jay Buhner/400 40.00 12.00
16 Ellis Burks/900 15.00 4.50
17 Orlando Cabrera 15.00 4.50
18 Mike Cameron 15.00 4.50
19 Ken Caminiti/900 15.00 4.50
20 Joe Carter 15.00 4.50
21 Sean Casey 15.00 4.50
22 Bruce Chen 8.00 2.40
23 Tony Clark 8.00 2.40
24 Will Clark 40.00 12.00
25 Roger Clemens/400 150.00 45.00
26 Matt Clement/900 15.00 2.40
27 Pat Cline 8.00 2.40
28 Ken Cloude 8.00 2.40
29 Michael Coleman 8.00 2.40
30 David Cone 15.00 4.50

31 Jeff Conine 15.00 4.50
32 Jacob Cruz 8.00 2.40
33 Jose Cruz Jr./850 8.00 2.40
34 Russ Davis/950 8.00 2.40
35 Jason Dickson/950 8.00 2.40
36 Todd Dunwoody 8.00 2.40
37 Scott Elarton/900 8.00 2.40
38 Juan Encarnacion 8.00 2.40
39 Darin Erstad 15.00 4.50
40 Bobby Estalella 8.00 2.40
41 Jeff Fassero 8.00 2.40
42 John Franco/950 15.00 4.50
43 Brad Fullmer 8.00 2.40
44 Andres Galarraga/900 15.00 4.50
45 Nomar Garciaparra/400 120.00 36.00
46 Jason Giambi 25.00 7.50
47 Derrick Gibson 8.00 2.40
48 Tom Glavine/700 40.00 12.00
49 Juan Gonzalez 25.00 7.50
50 Todd Greene 8.00 2.40
51 Ben Grieve 8.00 2.40
52 Mark Grudzielanek 8.00 2.40
53 Vladimir Guerrero 40.00 12.00
54 Wilton Guerrero 8.00 2.40
55 Jose Guillen 15.00 4.50
56 Tony Gwynn/900 40.00 12.00
57 Todd Helton 25.00 7.50
58 Richard Hidalgo 8.00 2.40
59 A.J. Hinch 8.00 2.40
60 Butch Huskey 8.00 2.40
61 Raul Ibanez 8.00 2.40
62 Damian Jackson 8.00 2.40
63 Geoff Jenkins 15.00 4.50
64 Derek Jeter/400 175.00 52.50
65 Randy Johnson/800 80.00 24.00
66 Chipper Jones/900 40.00 12.00
67 Eric Karros 15.00 4.50
68 Ryan Klesko 15.00 4.50
69 Chuck Knoblauch/900 15.00 4.50
70 Mark Kotsay 15.00 4.50
71 Ricky Ledee 8.00 2.40
72 Derrek Lee 15.00 4.50
73 Travis Lee 8.00 2.40
74 Javier Lopez/800 15.00 4.50
75 Mike Lowell 25.00 7.50
76 Greg Maddux/400 100.00 30.00
77 Eli Marrero 8.00 2.40
78 Al Martin/950 8.00 2.40
79 Rafael Medina/850 8.00 2.40
80 Paul Molitor/900 25.00 7.50
81 Scott Morgan 8.00 2.40
82 Mike Mussina/900 25.00 7.50
83 Abraham Nunez 8.00 2.40
84 Paul O'Neill/900 25.00 7.50
85 Luis Ordaz 8.00 2.40
86 Magglio Ordonez 40.00 12.00
87 Kevin Orie 8.00 2.40
88 David Ortiz 25.00 7.50
89 Rafael Palmeiro/900 40.00 12.00
90 Carl Pavano 25.00 4.50
91 Neifi Perez 8.00 2.40
92 Andy Pettitte/900 40.00 12.00
93 Dante Powell/950 8.00 2.40
94 Aramis Ramirez 15.00 4.50
95 Cal Ripken/375 150.00 45.00
96 Mariano Rivera 50.00 15.00
97 Alex Rodriguez/350 150.00 45.00
98 Felix Rodriguez 8.00 2.40
99 Henry Rodriguez 8.00 2.40
100 Ivan Rodriguez 40.00 12.00
101 Scott Rolen 40.00 12.00
102 Brian Rose 8.00 2.40
103 Curt Schilling 40.00 12.00
104 Richie Sexson 15.00 4.50
105 Randall Simon 8.00 2.40
106 J.T. Snow 15.00 4.50
107 Darryl Strawberry/900 40.00 12.00
108 Jeff Suppan 8.00 2.40
109 Fernando Tatis 8.00 2.40
110 Miguel Tejada 15.00 4.50
111 Brett Tomko 8.00 2.40
112 Bubba Trammell 8.00 2.40
113 Ismael Valdes 8.00 2.40
114 Robin Ventura 15.00 4.50
115 Billy Wagner/900 25.00 7.50
116 Todd Walker 15.00 4.50
117 Daryle Ward 8.00 2.40
118 Rondell White 15.00 4.50
119 Matt Williams/820 15.00 4.50
120 Antone Williamson 8.00 2.40
121 Dan Wilson 8.00 2.40
122 Enrique Wilson 8.00 2.40
123 Preston Wilson/400 40.00 12.00
124 Tony Womack 8.00 2.40
125 Kerry Wood 40.00 12.00

1998 Donruss Signature Significant Signatures

Randomly inserted in packs, this 18-card set features color photos with autographs of some of baseball's all-time great players. Only 2,000 of this sequentially-numbered set were produced. Sandy Koufax was on the original checklist but his cards were not returned in time for the pack out. Thus, officials at Donruss made the Billy Williams card an exchange card. Each collector that pulled a Billy Williams card could send it in to Donruss for a Koufax card. In addition, the signed Williams card was sent back too. Special exchange cards were created for Nolan Ryan and Ozzie Smith. The cards were randomly seeded into packs and then redeemed to Donruss for the real autograph cards. The exchange deadline for cards R1-R3 was December 31st, 1999. All three "R-Series" exchange cards (Ryan, Koufax and Smith) feature refractive, shiny fronts whereas the other cards seeded in packs are printed on basic foilboard. The Koufax card has been seen featuring two separate styles of foil serial-numbering on back: the standard thin-lettered foil numbering seen on all other cards from this set and a unique thicker, shorter foil numbering seen only on the Koufax. It's not known at this time as to why the Los Angeles Koufax variation has two separate styles of font used for serial-numbering. A mysterious non-refractive Sandy Koufax card, picturing him wearing a Brooklyn Dodgers cap and lacking any "R-Series" checklist numbering on back surfaced some time after the product's initial release. Like the Koufax LA card, the Brooklyn variation is also serial-numbered to 2000 on back though it's not known if 2000 copies actually exist. It's also not known at this time how this Brooklyn card made it's way into the secondary market. Representatives at Donruss-Playoff were unable to provide us with information on this matter given that the company was technically owned by Pinnacle in 1998 and then purchased out of bankruptcy in 2001 by the new Donruss-Playoff Corporation. The Catfish Hunter card was signed in either blue or blank ink.

Nm-Mt Ex-Mt
1 Ernie Banks 40.00 12.00
2 Yogi Berra 40.00 12.00
3 George Brett 60.00 18.00
4 Catfish Hunter 60.00 18.00
5 Al Kaline 40.00 12.00
6 Harmon Killebrew 40.00 12.00
7 Ralph Kiner 25.00 7.50
9 Eddie Mathews 60.00 18.00
10 Don Mattingly 60.00 18.00
11 Willie McCovey 25.00 7.50
12 Stan Musial 50.00 15.00
13 Phil Rizzuto SP/1000 50.00 15.00
14 N.Ryan EXCH 15.00 4.50
15 O.Smith EXCH 5.00 1.50
16 Duke Snider 25.00 7.50
17 Don Sutton 25.00 7.50
18 Billy Williams 25.00 7.50
18A B.Williams Redeemed 5.00 1.50
R1 Nolan Ryan 100.00 30.00
R2 Ozzie Smith 40.00 12.00
R3 Sandy Koufax LA 200.00 60.00
NNO Sandy Koufax Brooklyn 200.00 60.00

2001 Donruss Signature

This 311 card set was issued 25 cards to a "gift" box. The 25 card boxes had a SRP of $49.99 per box and the boxes were issued eight to a mini case. Cards numbered from 111 through 165 were inserted at an approximate rate of one per box and were serial numbered to 330. Cards numbered 166 to 311 were issued at an approximate rate of two per box and were serial numbered to 800.

Nm-Mt Ex-Mt
COMP.SET w/o SP'S (110) 50.00 15.00
COMMON CARD (1-110) 1.00 .30
COMMON (111-165) 10.00 3.00
COMMON AU RC (111-165) 10.00 3.00
COMMON NO AU (111-165) 8.00 2.40
COMMON (166-311) 5.00 1.50
COMMON RC (166-311) 5.00 1.50
1 Alex Rodriguez 4.00 1.20
2 Barry Bonds 6.00 1.80
3 Cal Ripken 8.00 2.40
4 Chipper Jones 2.50 .75
5 Derek Jeter 6.00 1.80
6 Troy Glaus 1.00 .30
7 Frank Thomas 2.50 .75
8 Greg Maddux 4.00 1.20
9 Ivan Rodriguez 2.50 .75
10 Jeff Bagwell 1.50 .45
11 John Olerud 1.00 .30
12 Todd Helton 1.50 .45
13 Ken Griffey Jr. 4.00 1.20
14 Manny Ramirez 1.50 .45
15 Mark McGwire 6.00 1.80
16 Mike Piazza 4.00 1.20
17 Nomar Garciaparra 4.00 1.20
18 Moises Alou 1.00 .30
19 Aramis Ramirez 1.00 .30
20 Curt Schilling 1.00 .30
21 Pat Burrell 1.00 .30
22 Doug Mientkiewicz 1.00 .30
23 Carlos Delgado 1.00 .30
24 J.D. Drew 1.00 .30
25 Cliff Floyd 1.00 .30
26 Freddy Garcia 1.00 .30
27 Roberto Alomar 1.50 .45
28 Barry Zito 1.50 .45
29 Juan Encarnacion 1.00 .30
30 Paul Konerko 1.00 .30
31 Mark Mulder 1.00 .30
32 Andy Pettitte 1.50 .45
33 Jim Edmonds 1.00 .30
34 Darin Erstad 1.00 .30
35 Jason Giambi 1.00 .30
36 Tom Glavine 1.50 .45
37 Juan Gonzalez 1.50 .45
38 Fred McGriff 1.50 .45
39 Shawn Green 1.00 .30
40 Tim Hudson 1.00 .30
41 Andruw Jones 1.00 .30
42 Jeff Kent 1.00 .30
43 Barry Larkin 1.50 .45
44 Brad Radke 1.00 .30
45 Mike Mussina 1.50 .45
46 Hideo Nomo 2.50 .75
47 Rafael Palmeiro 1.50 .45
48 Scott Rolen 2.50 .75
49 Gary Sheffield 1.00 .30
50 Bernie Williams 1.50 .45
51 Bob Abreu 1.00 .30
52 Edgardo Alfonzo 1.00 .30
53 Edgar Martinez 1.50 .45
54 Magglio Ordonez 1.00 .30
55 Kerry Wood 2.50 .75
56 Adrian Beltre 1.50 .45
57 Lance Berkman 1.00 .30
58 Kevin Brown 2.50 .75
59 Sean Casey 1.00 .30
60 Eric Chavez 1.00 .30
61 Bartolo Colon 1.00 .30
62 Sammy Sosa 4.00 1.20
63 Jermaine Dye 1.00 .30
64 Tony Gwynn 3.00 .90
65 Carl Everett 1.00 .30
66 Brian Giles 1.00 .30
67 Mike Hampton 1.00 .30
68 Richard Hidalgo 1.00 .30
69 Geoff Jenkins 1.00 .30
70 Tony Clark 1.00 .30
71 Roger Clemens 5.00 1.50
72 Ryan Klesko 1.00 .30
73 Chan Ho Park 1.00 .30
74 Richie Sexson 1.00 .30
75 Mike Sweeney 1.00 .30
76 Kazuhiro Sasaki 1.00 .30
77 Miguel Tejada 1.00 .30
78 Jose Vidro 1.00 .30
79 Larry Walker 1.50 .45
80 Preston Wilson 1.00 .30
81 Craig Biggio 1.50 .45
82 Andres Galarraga 1.00 .30
83 Jim Thome 2.50 .75
84 Vladimir Guerrero 2.50 .75
85 Rafael Furcal 1.00 .30
86 Cristian Guzman 1.00 .30
87 Terrence Long 1.00 .30
88 Bret Boone 1.00 .30
89 Wade Miller 1.00 .30
90 Eric Milton 1.00 .30
91 Gabe Kapler 1.00 .30
92 Johnny Damon 1.50 .45
93 Carlos Lee 1.00 .30
94 Kenny Lofton 1.00 .30
95 Raul Mondesi 1.00 .30
96 Jorge Posada 1.50 .45
97 Mark Grace 1.50 .45
98 Robert Fick 1.00 .30
99 Joe Mays 1.00 .30
100 Aaron Sele 1.00 .30
101 Ben Grieve 1.00 .30
102 Luis Gonzalez 1.00 .30
103 Ray Durham 1.00 .30
104 Mark Quinn 1.00 .30
105 Jose Canseco 2.50 .75
106 David Justice 1.00 .30
107 Pedro Martinez 2.50 .75
108 Randy Johnson 2.50 .75
109 Phil Nevin 1.00 .30
110 Rickey Henderson 2.50 .75
111 Alex Escobar AU 10.00 3.00
112 J.Estrada AU RC 25.00 7.50
113 Pedro Feliz AU 10.00 3.00
114 Nate Frese AU RC 10.00 3.00
115 R. Rodriguez AU RC 10.00 3.00
116 B.Larson AU RC 10.00 3.00
117 Alexis Gomez AU RC 10.00 3.00
118 Jason Hart AU 10.00 3.00
119 C.C. Sabathia AU 15.00 4.50
120 Endy Chavez AU RC 10.00 3.00
121 C.Parker AU RC 10.00 3.00
122 Jackson Melian RC 8.00 2.40
123 Joe Kennedy AU RC 15.00 4.50
124 A.Hernandez AU RC 10.00 3.00
125 Cesar Izturis AU 15.00 4.50
126 Jose Mieses AU RC 10.00 3.00
127 Roy Oswalt AU 25.00 7.50
128 Eric Munson AU 10.00 3.00
129 Xavier Nady AU 10.00 3.00
130 H.Ramirez AU RC 15.00 4.50
131 Abraham Nunez AU 10.00 3.00
132 Jose Ortiz AU 10.00 3.00
133 Jeremy Owens AU RC 10.00 3.00
134 Claudio Vargas AU RC 10.00 3.00
135 Corey Patterson AU 15.00 4.50
136 Carlos Pena 8.00 2.40
137 Bud Smith AU RC 10.00 3.00
138 Adam Dunn AU 25.00 7.50
139 A.Pettyjohn AU RC 10.00 3.00
140 E.Guzman AU RC 10.00 3.00
141 Jay Gibbons AU RC 25.00 7.50
142 Wilkin Ruan AU RC 10.00 3.00
143 Tsuyoshi Shinjo RC 10.00 3.00
144 Alfonso Soriano AU 40.00 12.00
145 Marcus Giles AU 15.00 4.50
146 Ichiro Suzuki RC 80.00 24.00
147 Juan Uribe AU RC 15.00 4.50
148 David Williams AU RC 10.00 3.00
149 C. Valderrama AU RC 10.00 3.00
150 Matt White AU RC 10.00 3.00
151 Albert Pujols AU RC 425.00 130.00
152 D.Mendez AU RC 10.00 3.00
153 Cory Aldridge AU RC 10.00 3.00
154 B. Duckworth AU RC 10.00 3.00
155 Josh Beckett AU 25.00 7.50
156 W.Betemit AU RC 10.00 3.00
157 Ben Sheets AU 25.00 7.50
158 Andres Torres AU RC 10.00 3.00
159 Aubrey Huff AU 15.00 4.50
160 Jack Wilson AU RC 40.00 12.00
161 Rafael Soriano AU RC 15.00 4.50
162 Nick Johnson AU 15.00 4.50
163 Carlos Garcia AU RC 10.00 3.00
164 Josh Towers AU RC 10.00 3.00
165 J.Michaels AU RC 10.00 3.00
166 Ryan Drese RC 8.00 2.40
167 Dewon Brazelton RC 8.00 2.40
168 Kevin Olsen RC 5.00 1.50
169 Benito Baez RC 5.00 1.50
170 Mark Prior RC 50.00 15.00
171 Wilmy Caceres RC 5.00 1.50
172 Mark Teixeira RC 30.00 9.00
173 Willie Harris RC 5.00 1.50
174 Mike Koplove RC 5.00 1.50
175 Brandon Knight RC 5.00 1.50
176 John Grabow RC 5.00 1.50
177 Jeremy Affeldt RC 8.00 2.40
178 Brandon Inge 5.00 1.50
179 Casey Fossum RC 5.00 1.50
180 Scott Stewart RC 5.00 1.50
181 Luke Hudson RC 5.00 1.50
182 Ken Vining RC 5.00 1.50
183 Toby Hall 5.00 1.50
184 Eric Knott RC 5.00 1.50
185 Kris Foster RC 5.00 1.50
186 David Brous RC 5.00 1.50
187 Roy Smith RC 5.00 1.50
188 Grant Balfour RC 5.00 1.50
189 Jeremy Fikac RC 5.00 1.50
190 Morgan Ensberg RC 8.00 2.40
191 Ryan Freel RC 5.00 1.50
192 Ryan Jensen RC 5.00 1.50
193 Lance Davis RC 5.00 1.50
194 Delvin James RC 5.00 1.50
195 Timo Perez 5.00 1.50
196 Michael Cuddyer 5.00 1.50
197 Bob File RC 5.00 1.50
198 Martin Vargas RC 5.00 1.50
199 Kris Keller RC 5.00 1.50
200 T.Spooneybarger RC 5.00 1.50
201 Adam Everett 5.00 1.50
202 Josh Fogg RC 5.00 1.50
203 Kip Wells 5.00 1.50
204 Rick Bauer RC 5.00 1.50
205 Brent Abernathy 5.00 1.50
206 Erick Almonte RC 5.00 1.50
207 Pedro Santana RC 5.00 1.50
208 Ken Harvey 5.00 1.50
209 Jerrod Riggan RC 5.00 1.50
210 Nick Punto RC 5.00 1.50
211 Steve Green RC 5.00 1.50
212 Nick Neugebauer 5.00 1.50
213 Chris George 5.00 1.50
214 Mike Penney RC 5.00 1.50
215 Bret Prinz RC 5.00 1.50
216 Tim Christman RC 5.00 1.50
217 Sean Douglass RC 5.00 1.50
218 Brett Jodie RC 5.00 1.50
219 Juan Diaz RC 5.00 1.50
220 Carlos Hernandez 5.00 1.50
221 Alex Cintron 5.00 1.50
222 Juan Cruz RC 5.00 1.50
223 Larry Bigbie 5.00 1.50
224 Junior Spivey RC 8.00 2.40
225 Luis Rivas 5.00 1.50
226 Brandon Lyon RC 5.00 1.50
227 Tony Cogan RC 5.00 1.50
228 J.Duchscherer RC 5.00 1.50
229 Tike Redman 5.00 1.50
230 Jimmy Rollins 5.00 1.50
231 Scott Podsednik RC 20.00 6.00
232 Jose Acevedo RC 5.00 1.50
233 Luis Pineda RC 5.00 1.50
234 Josh Phelps 5.00 1.50
235 Paul Phillips RC 5.00 1.50
236 Brian Roberts RC 5.00 1.50
237 O.Woodards RC 5.00 1.50
238 Bart Miadich RC 5.00 1.50
239 Les Walrond RC 5.00 1.50
240 Brad Voyles RC 5.00 1.50
241 Joe Crede 5.00 1.50
242 Juan Moreno RC 5.00 1.50
243 Matt Ginter 5.00 1.50
244 Brian Rogers RC 5.00 1.50
245 Pablo Ozuna 5.00 1.50
246 Geronimo Gil RC 5.00 1.50
247 Mike Maroth RC 5.00 1.50
248 Josue Perez RC 5.00 1.50
249 Dee Brown 5.00 1.50
250 Victor Zambrano RC 8.00 2.40
251 Nick Maness RC 5.00 1.50
252 Kyle Lohse RC 8.00 2.40
253 Greg Miller RC 5.00 1.50
254 Henry Mateo RC 5.00 1.50
255 Duaner Sanchez RC 5.00 1.50
256 Rob MacKowiak RC 8.00 2.40
257 Steve Lomasney 5.00 1.50
258 Angel Santos RC 5.00 1.50
259 Winston Abreu RC 5.00 1.50
260 Brandon Berger RC 5.00 1.50
261 Tomas De La Rosa 5.00 1.50
262 Ramon Vazquez RC 5.00 1.50
263 Mickey Callaway RC 5.00 1.50
264 Corky Miller RC 5.00 1.50
265 Keith Ginter 5.00 1.50
266 Cody Ransom RC 5.00 1.50
267 Doug Nickle RC 5.00 1.50
268 Derrick Lewis RC 5.00 1.50
269 Eric Hinske RC 8.00 2.40
270 Travis Phelps RC 5.00 1.50
271 Eric Valent 5.00 1.50
272 Michael Rivera RC 5.00 1.50
273 Esix Snead RC 5.00 1.50
274 Troy Mattes RC 5.00 1.50
275 Jermaine Clark RC 5.00 1.50
276 Nate Cornejo 5.00 1.50
277 George Perez RC 5.00 1.50
278 Juan Rivera 5.00 1.50
279 Justin Atchley RC 5.00 1.50
280 Adam Johnson 5.00 1.50
281 Gene Altman RC 5.00 1.50
282 Jason Jennings 5.00 1.50
283 Scott MacRae RC 5.00 1.50
284 Craig Monroe RC 5.00 1.50
285 Bert Snow RC 5.00 1.50
286 Stubby Clapp RC 5.00 1.50
287 Jack Cust 5.00 1.50
288 Will Ohman RC 5.00 1.50
289 Wily Mo Pena 5.00 1.50
290 Joe Beimel RC 5.00 1.50
291 Jason Karnuth RC 5.00 1.50
292 Bill Ortega RC 5.00 1.50
293 Nate Teut RC 5.00 1.50
294 Erik Hiljus RC 5.00 1.50
295 Jason Smith RC 5.00 1.50
296 Juan A.Pena RC 5.00 1.50
297 David Espinosa 5.00 1.50
298 Tim Redding 5.00 1.50
299 Brian Lawrence RC 5.00 1.50
300 Brian Reith RC 5.00 1.50
301 Chad Durbin 5.00 1.50
302 Kurt Ainsworth 5.00 1.50
303 Blaine Neal RC 5.00 1.50
304 Jorge Julio RC 5.00 1.50
305 Adam Bernero 5.00 1.50
306 Travis Hafner RC 12.00 3.60
307 Dustan Mohr RC 5.00 1.50
308 Cesar Crespo RC 5.00 1.50
309 Billy Sylvester RC 5.00 1.50
310 Zach Day RC 5.00 1.50
311 Angel Berroa RC 8.00 2.40

2001 Donruss Signature Proofs

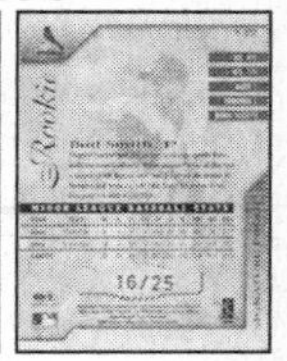

Randomly inserted in gift boxes, these 311 cards parallel the Donruss Signature set. Cards numbered 1-110 were issued to a print run of 175 sets while cards numbered 111-311 were issued to a print run of 25 sets. Please note that all cards numbered between 111 and 165 were autographed in addition to a few other scattered cards throughout the set. Due to market scarcity, no pricing is provided for cards numbered 111-311.

Nm-Mt Ex-Mt
*PROOFS 1-110: 1.5X TO 4X BASIC ..
111 Alex Escobar AU
112 Johnny Estrada AU
113 Pedro Feliz AU
114 Nate Frese AU
115 Ricardo Rodriguez AU
116 Brandon Larson AU
117 Alexis Gomez AU
118 Jason Hart AU
119 C.C. Sabathia AU
120 Endy Chavez AU
121 Christian Parker AU
122 Jackson Melian
123 Joe Kennedy AU
124 Adrian Hernandez AU
125 Cesar Izturis AU
126 Jose Mieses AU
127 Roy Oswalt AU
128 Eric Munson AU
129 Xavier Nady AU
130 Horacio Ramirez AU
131 Abraham Nunez AU
132 Jose Ortiz AU
133 Jeremy Owens AU
134 Claudio Vargas AU
135 Corey Patterson AU
136 Carlos Pena AU
137 Bud Smith AU
138 Adam Dunn AU
139 Adam Pettyjohn AU
140 Elpidio Guzman AU
141 Jay Gibbons AU
142 Wilkin Ruan AU
143 Tsuyoshi Shinjo
144 Alfonso Soriano AU
145 Marcus Giles AU
146 Ichiro Suzuki
147 Juan Uribe AU
148 David Williams AU
149 Carlos Valderrama AU
150 Matt White AU
151 Albert Pujols AU
152 Donaldo Mendez AU
153 Cory Aldridge AU
154 Brandon Duckworth AU
155 Josh Beckett AU
156 Wilson Betemit AU
157 Ben Sheets AU
158 Andres Torres AU
159 Aubrey Huff AU
160 Jack Wilson AU
161 Rafael Soriano AU
162 Nick Johnson AU
163 Carlos Garcia AU
164 Josh Towers AU
165 Jason Michaels AU
167 Dewon Brazelton AU
172 Mark Teixeira AU
179 Casey Fossum AU
194 Delvin James AU
196 Michael Cuddyer AU
222 Juan Cruz AU
241 Joe Crede AU
249 Dee Brown AU
265 Keith Ginter AU
269 Eric Hinske AU
271 Eric Valent AU
280 Adam Johnson AU
282 Jason Jennings AU
287 Jack Cust AU
289 Wily Mo Pena AU
297 David Espinosa AU
311 Angel Berroa AU

2001 Donruss Signature Award Winning Signatures

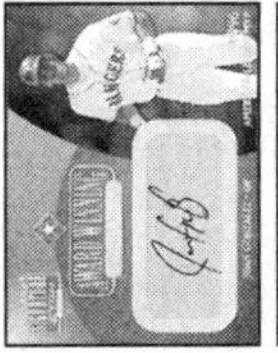
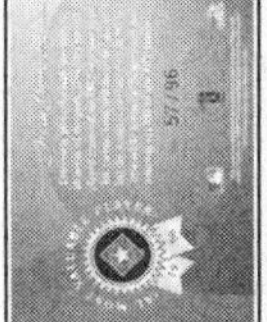

Randomly inserted in gift boxes, these cards feature signature from various players who won awards and the cards have stated print runs to that year they won an award. Please see our checklist for specific print run information.

Nm-Mt Ex-Mt
1 Jeff Bagwell/94 100.00 30.00

Card	Nm-Mt	Ex-Mt
2 Carlos Beltran/99	50.00	15.00
3 Johnny Bench/68	100.00	30.00
4 Yogi Berra/55	60.00	18.00
5 Craig Biggio/97	50.00	15.00
6 Barry Bonds/93	250.00	75.00
7 Rod Carew/77	80.00	24.00
8 Orlando Cepeda/67	30.00	9.00
9 Andre Dawson/77	30.00	9.00
10 D.Eckersley CY/92	30.00	9.00
11 D.Eckersley MVP/92	30.00	9.00
12 Whitey Ford/61	60.00	18.00
13 Jason Giambi/100	25.00	7.50
14 Bob Gibson/68	50.00	15.00
15 Juan Gonzalez/96	40.00	12.00
16 Orel Hershiser/88	40.00	12.00
17 Al Kaline/67	100.00	30.00
18 Fred Lynn/75 MVP	30.00	9.00
19 Fred Lynn/75 ROY	30.00	9.00
20 Jim Palmer/76	30.00	9.00
21 Cal Ripken/83	150.00	45.00
22 Phil Rizzuto/50	50.00	15.00
23 Brooks Robinson/64	50.00	15.00
24 Scott Rolen/97	50.00	15.00
25 Ryne Sandberg/84	120.00	36.00
26 Warren Spahn/57	60.00	18.00
27 Frank Thomas/94	50.00	15.00
28 Billy Williams/61	30.00	9.00
29 Kerry Wood/98	50.00	15.00
30 Robin Yount/89	80.00	24.00

2001 Donruss Signature Award Winning Signatures Masters Series

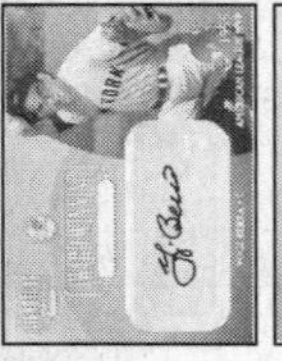
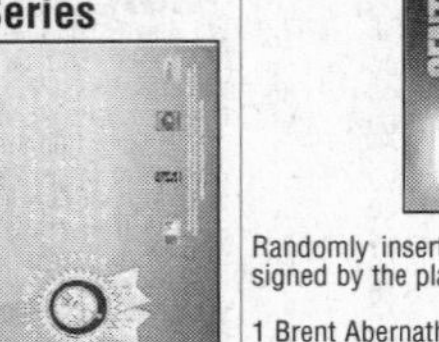

Randomly inserted in gift boxes, these cards feature various award winners who signed cards relating to various awards they won during their career.

Card	Nm-Mt	Ex-Mt
1 Jeff Bagwell		
2 Carlos Beltran	50.00	15.00
3 Johnny Bench		
4 Yogi Berra		
5 Craig Biggio	50.00	15.00
6 Barry Bonds		
7 Rod Carew		
8 Orlando Cepeda	25.00	7.50
9 Andre Dawson	25.00	7.50
10 Dennis Eckersley CY	25.00	7.50
11 Dennis Eckersley MVP	25.00	7.50
12 Whitey Ford	80.00	24.00
13 Jason Giambi		
14 Bob Gibson	40.00	12.00
15 Juan Gonzalez		
16 Orel Hershiser	100.00	30.00
17 Al Kaline	80.00	24.00
18 Fred Lynn MVP	25.00	7.50
19 Fred Lynn ROY	25.00	7.50
20 Jim Palmer	25.00	7.50
21 Cal Ripken		
22 Phil Rizzuto	40.00	12.00
23 Brooks Robinson	40.00	12.00
24 Scott Rolen	50.00	15.00
25 Ryne Sandberg		
26 Warren Spahn	50.00	15.00
27 Frank Thomas		
28 Billy Williams	25.00	7.50
29 Kerry Wood	50.00	15.00
30 Robin Yount		

2001 Donruss Signature Century Marks

Randomly inserted in gift boxes, these 48 cards feature signed cards of the featured players to various amounts. Please see our checklist to get the specific information on how many cards each player signed for this part of the promotion.

Card	Nm-Mt	Ex-Mt
1 Brent Abernathy/184	10.00	3.00
2 Roberto Alomar/102	40.00	12.00
3 Rick Ankiel/119	10.00	3.00
4 Lance Berkman/121	25.00	7.50
5 Mark Buehrle/224	15.00	4.50
6 Wilmy Caceres/194	10.00	3.00
7 Eric Chavez/170	15.00	4.50
8 Joe Crede/154	10.00	3.00
9 Jack Cust/178	10.00	3.00
10 B. Duckworth/183	10.00	3.00
11 David Espinosa/199	10.00	3.00
12 Johnny Estrada/198	15.00	4.50
13 Pedro Feliz/180	10.00	3.00
14 Robert Fick/232	10.00	3.00
15 Cliff Floyd/146	15.00	4.50
16 Casey Fossum/100	10.00	3.00
17 Jay Gibbons/175	15.00	4.50
18 Keith Ginter/163	10.00	3.00
19 Troy Glaus/144	15.00	4.50
20 Luis Gonzalez/101	15.00	4.50
21 Vladimir Guerrero/187	40.00	12.00
22 Richard Hidalgo/173	10.00	3.00
23 Tim Hudson/145	25.00	7.50
24 Adam Johnson/130	10.00	3.00
25 Gabe Kapler/150	10.00	3.00
26 Joe Kennedy/219	15.00	4.50
27 Ryan Klesko/176	15.00	4.50
28 Carlos Lee/179	15.00	4.50
29 Terrence Long/180	10.00	3.00
30 Edgar Martinez/110	40.00	12.00
31 Joe Mays/209	10.00	3.00
32 Greg Miller/194	10.00	3.00
33 Wade Miller/180	10.00	3.00
34 Mark Mulder/203	15.00	4.50
35 Xavier Nady/180	10.00	3.00
36 Magglio Ordonez/104	15.00	4.50
37 Jose Ortiz/187	10.00	3.00
38 Roy Oswalt/192	25.00	7.50
39 Wily Mo Pena/203	15.00	4.50
40 Brad Penny/198	10.00	3.00
41 Aramis Ramirez/241	15.00	4.50
42 Luis Rivas/163	10.00	3.00
43 Alex Rodriguez/110	150.00	45.00
44 Scott Rolen/106	40.00	12.00
45 Mike Sweeney/99	15.00	4.50
46 Eric Valent/163	10.00	3.00
47 Kip Wells/223	10.00	3.00
48 Kerry Wood/109	40.00	12.00

2001 Donruss Signature Century Marks Masters Series

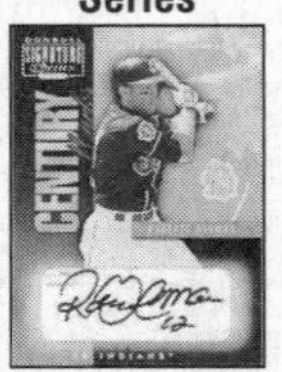

Randomly inserted in packs, these cards were signed by the players.

Card	Nm-Mt	Ex-Mt
1 Brent Abernathy	10.00	3.00
2 Roberto Alomar	50.00	15.00
3 Rick Ankiel	10.00	3.00
4 Lance Berkman	25.00	7.50
5 Mark Buehrle	15.00	4.50
6 Wilmy Caceres	10.00	3.00
7 Eric Chavez	15.00	4.50
8 Joe Crede	10.00	3.00
9 Jack Cust	10.00	3.00
10 Brandon Duckworth	10.00	3.00
11 David Espinosa	10.00	3.00
12 Johnny Estrada	15.00	4.50
13 Pedro Feliz	10.00	3.00
14 Robert Fick	10.00	3.00
15 Cliff Floyd	15.00	4.50
16 Casey Fossum	10.00	3.00
17 Jay Gibbons	15.00	4.50
18 Keith Ginter	10.00	3.00
19 Troy Glaus	40.00	12.00
20 Luis Gonzalez		
21 Vladimir Guerrero		
22 Richard Hidalgo	10.00	3.00
23 Tim Hudson	25.00	7.50
24 Adam Johnson	10.00	3.00
25 Gabe Kapler	10.00	3.00
26 Joe Kennedy	15.00	4.50
27 Ryan Klesko	15.00	4.50
28 Carlos Lee	15.00	4.50
29 Terrence Long	10.00	3.00
30 Edgar Martinez	40.00	12.00
31 Joe Mays	10.00	3.00
32 Greg Miller	10.00	3.00
33 Wade Miller	10.00	3.00
34 Mark Mulder	15.00	4.50
35 Xavier Nady	10.00	3.00
36 Magglio Ordonez	15.00	4.50
37 Jose Ortiz	10.00	3.00
38 Roy Oswalt	25.00	7.50
39 Wily Mo Pena	15.00	4.50
40 Brad Penny	10.00	3.00
41 Aramis Ramirez	15.00	4.50
42 Luis Rivas	10.00	3.00
43 Alex Rodriguez		
44 Scott Rolen		
45 Mike Sweeney	15.00	4.50
46 Eric Valent	10.00	3.00
47 Kip Wells	10.00	3.00
48 Kerry Wood		

2001 Donruss Signature Milestone Marks

Randomly inserted in gift boxes, these 36 cards feature players autographs on a card related to specific highlights from each player's career. Since each player signed a different number of cards, please see our checklist for more detailed information on how many of each card was signed.

Card	Nm-Mt	Ex-Mt
1 Ernie Banks/285	50.00	15.00
2 Yogi Berra/120	60.00	18.00
3 Wade Boggs/98	120.00	36.00
4 Barry Bonds/55	250.00	75.00
5 G. Brett 3000 Hits/27		
6 George Brett 1500 RBI/23		
7 Lou Brock/83	30.00	9.00
8 Rod Carew/110	50.00	15.00
9 Steve Carlton/75	50.00	15.00
10 Gary Carter/213	20.00	6.00
11 Bobby Doerr/192	20.00	6.00
12 Bob Feller/202	20.00	6.00
13 Whitey Ford/186	30.00	9.00
14 Steve Garvey/175	20.00	6.00
15 Tony Gwynn/99	60.00	18.00
16 Fergie Jenkins/149	20.00	6.00
17 Al Kaline/149	60.00	18.00
18 Harmon Killebrew/127	50.00	15.00
19 Ralph Kiner/105	20.00	6.00
20 Willie McCovey/20		
21 Paul Molitor/96	60.00	18.00
22 E. Murray 3000 Hits/46	150.00	45.00
23 Eddie Murray 1500 RBI/17		
24 Stan Musial/109	80.00	24.00
25 Phil Niekro/300	20.00	6.00
26 Tony Perez/146	20.00	6.00
27 Cal Ripken/25		
28 Frank Robinson/136	30.00	9.00
29 M. Schmidt 500 HR/40		
30 Mike Schmidt 1500 RBI/23		
31 Enos Slaughter/117	30.00	9.00
32 Warren Spahn/300	50.00	15.00
33 Alan Trammell/154	20.00	6.00
34 Hoyt Wilhelm/227	20.00	6.00
35 D.Winfield Padres/31		
36 Dave Winfield Yankees/15		

2001 Donruss Signature Milestone Marks Masters Series

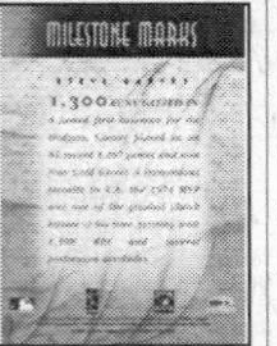

Randomly inserted in packs, these cards were signed by the players. Card number one does not exist for this set.

Card	Nm-Mt	Ex-Mt
1 Does Not Exist		
2 Yogi Berra		
3 Wade Boggs		
4 Barry Bonds		
5 George Brett 3000 Hits		
6 George Brett 1500 RBI		
7 Lou Brock	30.00	9.00
8 Rod Carew		
9 Steve Carlton	60.00	18.00
10 Gary Carter	20.00	6.00
11 Bobby Doerr	20.00	6.00
12 Bob Feller	20.00	6.00
13 Whitey Ford	80.00	24.00
14 Steve Garvey	20.00	6.00
15 Tony Gwynn		
16 Fergie Jenkins	20.00	6.00
17 Al Kaline	100.00	30.00
18 Harmon Killebrew	80.00	24.00
19 Ralph Kiner	20.00	6.00
20 Willie McCovey		
21 Paul Molitor	120.00	36.00
22 Eddie Murray 3000 Hits		
23 Eddie Murray 1500 RBI		
24 Stan Musial		
25 Phil Niekro	20.00	6.00
26 Tony Perez	20.00	6.00
27 Cal Ripken		
28 Frank Robinson	30.00	9.00
29 Mike Schmidt 500 HR		
30 Mike Schmidt 1500 RBI		
31 Enos Slaughter	30.00	9.00
32 Warren Spahn		
33 Alan Trammell	20.00	6.00
34 Hoyt Wilhelm	20.00	6.00
35 Dave Winfield Padres		
36 Dave Winfield Yankees		

2001 Donruss Signature Notable Nicknames

Randomly inserted in gift boxes, these 18 cards feature players along with their nickname. Each player signed 100 of these cards for inclusion in this product.

Card	Nm-Mt	Ex-Mt
1 Ernie Banks Mr. Cub	100.00	30.00
2 Orlando Cepeda Baby Bull	60.00	18.00
3 Will Clark The Thrill	200.00	60.00
4 Roger Clemens The Rocket	350.00	105.00
5 Andre Dawson The Hawk	60.00	18.00
6 Bob Feller Rapid Robert	60.00	18.00
7 Carlton Fisk Pudge	100.00	30.00
8 Andres Galarraga Big Cat	60.00	18.00
9 Luis Gonzalez 4	60.00	18.00
10 Reggie Jackson Mr. October	100.00	30.00
11 Harmon Killebrew Killer	100.00	30.00
12 Stan Musial The Man	150.00	45.00
13 Brooks Robinson Hoover	100.00	30.00
14 Nolan Ryan The Express	300.00	90.00
15 Ryne Sandberg Ryno	200.00	60.00
16 Enos Slaughter Country	100.00	30.00
17 Duke Snider 4	100.00	30.00
18 Frank Thomas MVP	150.00	45.00

2001 Donruss Signature Notable Nicknames Masters Series

Randomly inserted into gift boxes, these 18 cards featured signed cards of star players along with their nicknames.

Card	Nm-Mt	Ex-Mt
1 Ernie Banks Mr. Cub	150.00	45.00
2 Orlando Cepeda Baby Bull	80.00	24.00
3 Will Clark The Thrill	200.00	60.00
4 Roger Clemens The Rocket		
5 Andre Dawson The Hawk	80.00	24.00
6 Bob Feller Rapid Robert	80.00	24.00
7 Carlton Fisk Pudge	120.00	36.00
8 Andres Galarraga Big Cat	80.00	24.00
9 Luis Gonzalez 4	80.00	24.00
10 Reggie Jackson Mr. October		
11 Harmon Killebrew Killer	150.00	45.00
12 Stan Musial The Man		
13 Brooks Robinson Hoover	120.00	36.00
14 Nolan Ryan The Express	500.00	150.00
15 Ryne Sandberg Rhino	300.00	90.00
16 Enos Slaughter Country	120.00	36.00
17 Duke Snider 4		
18 Frank Thomas MVP		

2001 Donruss Signature Stats

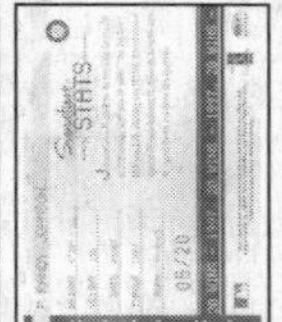

Randomly inserted into gift boxes, these 52 cards feature players who signed cards relating to a key stat in their career. Since each card is signed to a different amount, please see our checklist for specific information about each card.

Card	Nm-Mt	Ex-Mt
1 Roberto Alomar/120	40.00	12.00
2 Moises Alou/124	15.00	4.50
3 Luis Aparicio/313	15.00	4.50
4 Lance Berkman/297	25.00	7.50
5 Wade Boggs/51	150.00	45.00
6 Lou Brock/118	25.00	7.50
7 Gary Carter/32		
8 Joe Carter/121	15.00	4.50
9 Sean Casey/103	15.00	4.50
10 Darin Erstad/100	15.00	4.50
11 Bob Feller/26		
12 Cliff Floyd/45	15.00	4.50
13 Whitey Ford/72	60.00	18.00
14 Andres Galarraga/150	15.00	4.50
15 Bob Gibson/112	25.00	7.50
16 Brian Giles/123	15.00	4.50
17 Troy Glaus/102	15.00	4.50
18 Luis Gonzalez/114	15.00	4.50
19 Vladimir Guerrero/131	40.00	12.00
20 Tony Gwynn/17		
21 Richard Hidalgo/314	10.00	3.00
22 Bo Jackson/32		
23 Fergie Jenkins/25		
24 Randy Johnson/20		
25 Al Kaline/128	60.00	18.00
26 Gabe Kapler/302	10.00	3.00
27 Ralph Kiner/54	40.00	12.00
28 Ryan Klesko/23		
29 Carlos Lee/261	15.00	4.50
30 Kenny Lofton/210	25.00	7.50
31 Edgar Martinez/145	40.00	12.00
32 Joe Mays/115	10.00	3.00
33 Paul Molitor/41	80.00	24.00
34 Mark Mulder/88	25.00	7.50
35 Phil Niekro/23		
36 Magglio Ordonez/126	15.00	4.50
37 Rafael Palmeiro/47	60.00	18.00
38 Jim Palmer/23		
39 Chan Ho Park/18		
40 Kirby Puckett/31		
41 Manny Ramirez/45	80.00	24.00
42 Alex Rodriguez/132	150.00	45.00
43 Ivan Rodriguez/113	40.00	12.00
44 Curt Schilling/15		
45 Tom Seaver/25		
46 Shannon Stewart/319	15.00	4.50
47 Mike Sweeney/144	15.00	4.50
48 Miguel Tejada/115	15.00	4.50
49 Joe Torre/230	40.00	12.00
50 Javier Vazquez/405	15.00	4.50
51 Jose Vidro/330	10.00	3.00
52 Hoyt Wilhelm/243	15.00	4.50

2001 Donruss Signature Stats Masters Series

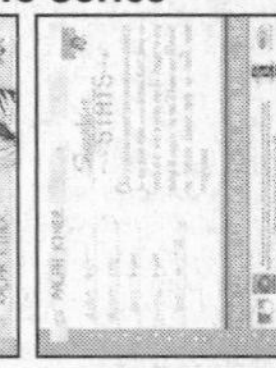

Randomly inserted into gift boxes, these 52 cards featured signed cards of star players along with information about a key stat.

Card	Nm-Mt	Ex-Mt
1 Roberto Alomar	60.00	18.00
2 Moises Alou	15.00	4.50
3 Luis Aparicio	15.00	4.50
4 Lance Berkman	25.00	7.50
5 Wade Boggs		
6 Lou Brock	80.00	24.00
7 Gary Carter	15.00	4.50
8 Joe Carter	15.00	4.50
9 Sean Casey	15.00	4.50
10 Darin Erstad	60.00	18.00
11 Bob Feller	15.00	4.50
12 Cliff Floyd	15.00	4.50
13 Whitey Ford	80.00	24.00
14 Andres Galarraga	60.00	18.00
15 Bob Gibson	50.00	15.00
16 Brian Giles	15.00	4.50
17 Troy Glaus	30.00	9.00
18 Luis Gonzalez		
19 Vladimir Guerrero		
20 Tony Gwynn		
21 Richard Hidalgo	10.00	3.00
22 Bo Jackson	120.00	36.00
23 Fergie Jenkins	15.00	4.50
24 Randy Johnson		
25 Al Kaline	80.00	24.00
26 Gabe Kapler	10.00	3.00
27 Ralph Kiner	25.00	7.50
28 Ryan Klesko	15.00	4.50
29 Carlos Lee	15.00	4.50
30 Kenny Lofton	25.00	7.50
31 Edgar Martinez	50.00	15.00
32 Joe Mays	10.00	3.00
33 Paul Molitor		
34 Mark Mulder	15.00	4.50
35 Phil Niekro	15.00	4.50
36 Magglio Ordonez	15.00	4.50
37 Rafael Palmeiro		
38 Jim Palmer	40.00	12.00
39 Chan Ho Park	200.00	60.00
40 Kirby Puckett		
41 Manny Ramirez		
42 Alex Rodriguez		
43 Ivan Rodriguez		
44 Curt Schilling	60.00	18.00
45 Tom Seaver		
46 Shannon Stewart	15.00	4.50
47 Mike Sweeney	15.00	4.50
48 Miguel Tejada	15.00	4.50
49 Joe Torre	100.00	30.00
50 Javier Vazquez	15.00	4.50
51 Jose Vidro	10.00	3.00
52 Hoyt Wilhelm		

2001 Donruss Signature Team Trademarks

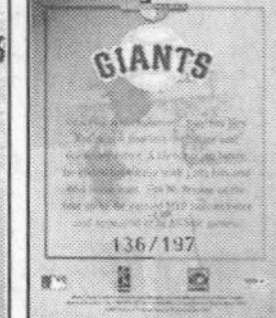

Randomly inserted into gift boxes, these 58 cards feature signed cards of a player as well as information about the team they played for. Since each player signed a different amount of cards for this promotion, we have included detailed information in our checklist.

Card	Nm-Mt	Ex-Mt
1 Rick Ankiel/179	20.00	6.00
2 Ernie Banks/180	60.00	18.00
3 Johnny Bench/20		
4 Yogi Berra/124	60.00	18.00
5 Wade Boggs/89	120.00	36.00
6 Barry Bonds/77	250.00	75.00
7 Lou Brock/29		
8 Steve Carlton/174	30.00	9.00
9 Sean Casey/123	20.00	6.00
10 Orlando Cepeda/100	20.00	6.00
11 Roger Clemens RS/30		
12 Roger Clemens Yankees/21		
13 Andre Dawson/176	20.00	6.00
14 Bobby Doerr/193	30.00	9.00
15 Whitey Ford/94	50.00	15.00
16 Does Not Exist		
17 Steve Garvey/182	20.00	6.00
18 Bob Gibson/98	40.00	12.00
19 Juan Gonzalez/70	100.00	30.00
20 Shawn Green/109	20.00	6.00
21 Orel Hershiser/210	50.00	15.00

22 Reggie Jackson/73 .... 80.00 24.00
23 Fergie Jenkins/213 .... 20.00 6.00
24 Chipper Jones/74 .... 80.00 24.00
25 Pedro Martinez/27 ....
26 Don Mattingly/72 .... 150.00 45.00
27 Willie Mays/197 .... 150.00 45.00
28 Willie McCovey/26 .... 80.00 24.00
29 Joe Morgan/33 ....
30 Eddie Murray/45 .... 120.00 36.00
31 Stan Musial/65 .... 100.00 30.00
32 Mike Mussina Balt./85 .... 80.00 24.00
33 M.Mussina Yanks/95 .... 80.00 24.00
34 Phil Niekro/187 .... 20.00 6.00
35 Rafael Palmeiro/99 .... 50.00 15.00
36 Jim Palmer/142 .... 20.00 6.00
37 Tony Perez/73 .... 20.00 6.00
38 Manny Ramirez/57 .... 60.00 18.00
39 Cal Ripken/47 .... 300.00 90.00
40 Phil Rizzuto/98 .... 50.00 15.00
41 Brooks Robinson/146 .... 30.00 9.00
42 F.Robinson Orioles/118 .... 30.00 9.00
43 F.Robinson Reds/116 .... 30.00 9.00
44 Alex Rodriguez/100 .... 150.00 45.00
45 Ivan Rodriguez/62 .... 80.00 24.00
46 Scott Rolen/39 ....
47 Nolan Ryan/153 .... 150.00 45.00
48 Ryne Sandberg/52 .... 150.00 45.00
49 Curt Schilling/63 .... 40.00 12.00
50 Mike Schmidt/107 .... 100.00 30.00
51 Tom Seaver/25 ....
52 Gary Sheffield/194 .... 30.00 9.00
53 Enos Slaughter/215 .... 30.00 9.00
54 Duke Snider/47 .... 80.00 24.00
55 Warren Spahn/140 .... 40.00 12.00
56 Joe Torre/90 .... 60.00 18.00
57 Billy Williams/194 .... 20.00 6.00
58 Kerry Wood/52 .... 60.00 18.00

2001 Donruss Signature Team Trademarks Masters Series

Randomly inserted into gift boxes, these 56 cards featured signed cards of star players along with information about the team they played for. Card number 27 does not exist in this set.

Nm-Mt Ex-Mt

Rick Ankiel ....
Does Not Exist ....
Johnny Bench ....
Yogi Berra ....
Wade Boggs ....
Barry Bonds ....
Lou Brock ....
Steve Carlton 60.00 18.00
Sean Casey ....
10 Orlando Cepeda 15.00 4.50
11 Roger Clemens Red Sox ....
12 Roger Clemens Yankees ....
13 Andre Dawson 15.00 4.50
14 Bobby Doerr 15.00 4.50
15 Whitey Ford ....
16 Nomar Garciaparra 200.00 60.00
17 Steve Garvey 15.00 4.50
18 Bob Gibson 60.00 18.00
19 Juan Gonzalez ....
20 Shawn Green ....
21 Orel Hershiser 80.00 24.00
22 Reggie Jackson ....
23 Fergie Jenkins 15.00 4.50
24 Chipper Jones ....
25 Pedro Martinez ....
26 Don Mattingly 150.00 45.00
27 Does Not Exist ....
28 Willie McCovey ....
29 Joe Morgan ....
30 Eddie Murray ....
31 Stan Musial ....
32 Mike Mussina Orioles ....
33 Mike Mussina Yankees ....
34 Phil Niekro 15.00 4.50
35 Rafael Palmeiro ....
36 Jim Palmer 25.00 7.50
37 Tony Perez 15.00 4.50
38 Manny Ramirez ....
39 Cal Ripken ....
40 Phil Rizzuto 50.00 15.00
41 Brooks Robinson 50.00 15.00
42 Frank Robinson Orioles 80.00 24.00
43 Frank Robinson Reds ....
44 Alex Rodriguez ....
45 Ivan Rodriguez ....
46 Scott Rolen ....
47 Nolan Ryan 200.00 60.00
48 Ryne Sandberg ....
49 Curt Schilling 40.00 12.00
50 Mike Schmidt ....
51 Tom Seaver 60.00 18.00
52 Gary Sheffield 20.00 6.00
53 Enos Slaughter 20.00 6.00
54 Duke Snider ....
55 Warren Spahn 50.00 15.00
56 Joe Torre ....
57 Billy Williams 15.00 4.50
58 Kerry Wood ....

2003 Donruss Signature

This 150 card set was released in August, 2003. This set was issued in four card packs issued in a special "box". These pack/boxes had a $50 SRP. Cards numbered 1-100 feature veterans in team alphabetical order while cards numbered 101 through 150 feature rookies. Unlike most Donruss/Playoff products, these rookie cards were not shortprinted.

MINT NRMT

COMMON CARD (1-100) .... 1.00 .45

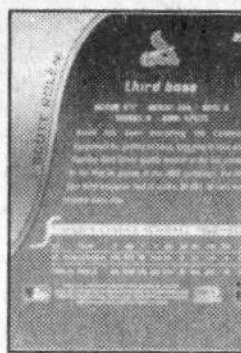

COMMON CARD (101-150) .... 1.00 .45
1 Garret Anderson .... 1.00 .45
2 Tim Salmon .... 1.50 .70
3 Troy Glaus .... 1.00 .45
4 Curt Schilling .... 1.00 .45
5 Luis Gonzalez .... 1.00 .45
6 Mark Grace .... 1.50 .70
7 Matt Williams .... 1.00 .45
8 Randy Johnson 2.50 1.10
9 Andruw Jones .... 1.00 .45
10 Chipper Jones 2.50 1.10
11 Gary Sheffield .... 1.00 .45
12 Greg Maddux 4.00 1.80
13 Johnny Damon 2.50 1.10
14 Manny Ramirez .... 1.50 .70
15 Nomar Garciaparra 4.00 1.80
16 Pedro Martinez 2.50 1.10
17 Corey Patterson .... 1.00 .45
18 Kerry Wood 2.50 1.10
19 Mark Prior 2.50 1.10
20 Sammy Sosa 4.00 1.80
21 Bartolo Colon .... 1.00 .45
22 Frank Thomas 2.50 1.10
23 Maggilo Ordonez .... 1.00 .45
24 Paul Konerko .... 1.00 .45
25 Adam Dunn .... 1.50 .70
26 Austin Kearns .... 1.00 .45
27 Barry Larkin .... 1.50 .70
28 Ken Griffey Jr. 4.00 1.80
29 C.C. Sabathia .... 1.00 .45
30 Omar Vizquel .... 1.50 .70
31 Larry Walker .... 1.50 .70
32 Todd Helton .... 1.50 .70
33 Ivan Rodriguez 2.50 1.10
34 Josh Beckett .... 1.00 .45
35 Craig Biggio .... 1.50 .70
36 Jeff Bagwell .... 1.50 .70
37 Jeff Kent .... 1.00 .45
38 Lance Berkman .... 1.00 .45
39 Richard Hidalgo .... 1.00 .45
40 Roy Oswalt .... 1.00 .45
41 Carlos Beltran .... 1.50 .70
42 Mike Sweeney .... 1.00 .45
43 Runelvys Hernandez .... 1.00 .45
44 Hideo Nomo 2.50 1.10
45 Kazuhisa Ishii .... 1.00 .45
46 Paul Lo Duca .... 1.00 .45
47 Shawn Green .... 1.00 .45
48 Ben Sheets .... 1.00 .45
49 Richie Sexson .... 1.00 .45
50 A.J. Pierzynski .... 1.00 .45
51 Torii Hunter .... 1.00 .45
52 Javier Vazquez .... 1.00 .45
53 Jose Vidro .... 1.00 .45
54 Vladimir Guerrero 2.50 1.10
55 Cliff Floyd .... 1.00 .45
56 David Cone .... 1.00 .45
57 Mike Piazza 4.00 1.80
58 Roberto Alomar .... 1.50 .70
59 Tom Glavine .... 1.50 .70
60 Alfonso Soriano .... 1.50 .70
61 Derek Jeter 6.00 2.70
62 Drew Henson .... 1.00 .45
63 Jason Giambi .... 1.50 .70
64 Mike Mussina .... 1.50 .70
65 Nick Johnson .... 1.00 .45
66 Roger Clemens 5.00 2.20
67 Barry Zito .... 1.00 .45
68 Eric Chavez .... 1.00 .45
69 Mark Mulder .... 1.00 .45
70 Miguel Tejada .... 1.00 .45
71 Tim Hudson .... 1.00 .45
72 Bobby Abreu .... 1.00 .45
73 Jim Thome 2.50 1.10
74 Kevin Millwood .... 1.00 .45
75 Pat Burrell .... 1.00 .45
76 Brian Giles .... 1.00 .45
77 Jason Kendall .... 1.00 .45
78 Kenny Lofton .... 1.00 .45
79 Phil Nevin .... 1.00 .45
80 Ryan Klesko .... 1.00 .45
81 Andres Galarraga .... 1.00 .45
82 Barry Bonds 6.00 2.70
83 Rich Aurilia .... 1.00 .45
84 Edgar Martinez .... 1.50 .70
85 Freddy Garcia .... 1.00 .45
86 Ichiro Suzuki 4.00 1.80
87 Albert Pujols 5.00 2.20
88 Jim Edmonds .... 1.00 .45
89 Scott Rolen 2.50 1.10
90 So Taguchi .... 1.00 .45
91 Rocco Baldelli .... 1.00 .45
92 Alex Rodriguez 4.00 1.80
93 Hank Blalock .... 1.50 .70
94 Juan Gonzalez .... 1.50 .70
95 Mark Teixeira .... 1.00 .45
96 Rafael Palmeiro .... 1.50 .70
97 Carlos Delgado .... 1.00 .45
98 Eric Hinske .... 1.00 .45
99 Roy Halladay .... 1.00 .45
100 Vernon Wells .... 1.00 .45
101 Hideki Matsui ROO RC 10.00 4.50
102 Jose Contreras ROO RC 3.00 1.35
103 Jer. Bonderman ROO RC 2.50 1.10
104 Bernie Castro ROO RC .... 1.00 .45
105 Alfredo Gonzalez ROO RC .... 1.00 .45
106 Arnie Munoz ROO RC .... 1.00 .45
107 Andrew Brown ROO RC .... 1.50 .70
108 Josh Hall ROO RC .... 1.50 .70
109 Josh Stewart ROO RC .... 1.00 .45
110 Clint Barmes ROO RC .... 1.50 .70
111 Brandon Webb ROO RC 3.00 1.35
112 Chien-Ming Wang ROO RC 3.00 1.35
113 Edgar Gonzalez ROO RC .... 1.00 .45
114 Al. Machado ROO RC .... 1.00 .45
115 Jeremy Griffiths ROO RC .... 1.50 .70
116 Craig Brazell ROO RC .... 1.50 .70
117 Shane Bazzell ROO RC .... 1.00 .45
118 Fernando Cabrera ROO RC .... 1.00 .45
119 Terrmel Sledge ROO RC .... 1.50 .70
120 Rob Hammock ROO RC .... 1.50 .70
121 Francisco Rosario ROO RC .... 1.00 .45
122 Francisco Cruceta ROO RC .... 1.00 .45
123 Rett Johnson ROO RC .... 1.50 .70
124 Guillermo Quiroz ROO RC 2.50 1.10
125 Hong-Chih Kuo ROO RC 2.50 1.10
126 Ian Ferguson ROO RC .... 1.00 .45
127 Tim Olson ROO RC .... 1.50 .70
128 Todd Wellemeyer ROO RC .... 1.50 .70
129 Rich Fischer ROO RC .... 1.00 .45
130 Phil Seibel ROO RC .... 1.00 .45
131 Joe Valentine ROO RC .... 1.00 .45
132 Matt Kata ROO RC 2.50 1.10
133 Michael Hessman ROO RC .... 1.00 .45
134 Michel Hernandez ROO RC .... 1.00 .45
135 Doug Waechter ROO RC .... 1.50 .70
136 Prentice Redman ROO RC .... 1.00 .45
137 Nook Logan ROO RC .... 1.00 .45
138 Oscar Villarreal ROO RC .... 1.00 .45
139 Pete LaForest ROO RC .... 1.50 .70
140 Matt Bruback ROO RC .... 1.00 .45
141 Dontrelle Willis ROO .... 1.50 .70
142 Greg Aquino ROO RC .... 1.00 .45
143 Lew Ford ROO RC 4.00 1.80
144 Jeff Duncan ROO RC .... 1.50 .70
145 Dan Haren ROO RC 2.50 1.10
146 Miguel Ojeda ROO RC .... 1.00 .45
147 Rosman Garcia ROO RC .... 1.00 .45
148 Felix Sanchez ROO RC .... 1.00 .45
149 Jon Leicester ROO RC .... 1.00 .45
150 Roger Deago ROO RC .... 1.00 .45

2003 Donruss Signature Century Proofs

MINT NRMT

*CENTURY 1-100: 2X TO 5X BASIC ...
*CENTURY 101-150: 1X TO 2.5X BASIC
RANDOM INSERTS IN PACKS ....
STATED PRINT RUN 100 SERIAL #'d SETS

2003 Donruss Signature Decade Proofs

MINT NRMT

RANDOM INSERTS IN PACKS ....
STATED PRINT RUN 10 SERIAL #'d SETS
NO PRICING DUE TO SCARCITY ....

2003 Donruss Signature Autographs

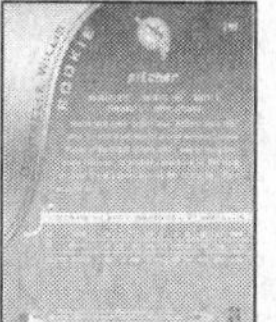

Randomly inserted into packs; these 50 cards parallel the basic set and feature autographs of the featured players. The first 47 of these cards (checklisted from 1-102) are not serial numbered but we are giving print run information in our checklist provided by Donruss/Playoff. Cards 151-153 were distributed as random inserts within packs of DLP Rookies and Traded and each is serial numbered to 200. No pricing is provided for cards with print runs of 28 or fewer due to scarcity.

MINT NRMT

1 Garret Anderson 15.00 6.75
6 Mark Grace SP/141 .... 50.00 22.00
7 Matt Williams 15.00 6.75
8 Randy Johnson SP/50 .... 80.00 36.00
10 Chipper Jones SP/50 .... 60.00 27.00
12 Greg Maddux SP/25 ....
14 Manny Ramirez SP/50 .... 50.00 22.00
16 Pedro Martinez SP/5 ....
27 Barry Larkin SP/159 .... 40.00 18.00
32 Todd Helton SP/5 ....
33 Ivan Rodriguez SP/50 .... 50.00 22.00
36 Jeff Bagwell SP/25 ....
38 Lance Berkman SP/75 .... 40.00 18.00
39 Richard Hidalgo 10.00 4.50
40 Roy Oswalt SP/150 .... 15.00 6.75
42 Mike Sweeney 15.00 6.75
44 Hideo Nomo SP/25 ....
45 Kazuhisa Ishii SP/25 ....
50 A.J. Pierzynski 15.00 6.75
51 Torii Hunter 15.00 6.75
53 Jose Vidro 10.00 4.50
54 Vladimir Guerrero 25.00 11.00
55 Cliff Floyd 15.00 6.75
56 David Cone SP/35 .... 25.00 11.00
57 Mike Piazza SP/5 ....
58 Roberto Alomar SP/50 .... 40.00 18.00
62 Drew Henson SP/28 ....
64 Mike Mussina SP/5 ....
65 Nick Johnson 10.00 4.50
67 Barry Zito SP/150 .... 15.00 6.75
68 Eric Chavez 15.00 6.75
69 Mark Mulder SP/50 .... 25.00 11.00
72 Bobby Abreu 15.00 6.75
78 Kenny Lofton SP/229 .... 25.00 11.00
80 Ryan Klesko SP/150 .... 15.00 6.75
81 Andres Galarraga 15.00 6.75
83 Rich Aurilia SP/122 .... 15.00 6.75
84 Edgar Martinez 25.00 11.00
88 Jim Edmonds SP/25 ....
89 Scott Rolen SP/200 .... 25.00 11.00
90 So Taguchi SP/220 .... 15.00 6.75
92 Alex Rodriguez SP/25 ....
95 Mark Teixeira SP/150 .... 25.00 11.00
96 Rafael Palmeiro SP/25 ....
100 Vernon Wells 15.00 6.75
102 Jose Contreras ROO 25.00 11.00
141 D.Willis ROO SP/150 .... 25.00 11.00
151 Delmon Young ROO 60.00 27.00
152 Rickie Weeks ROO 30.00 13.50
153 Edwin Jackson ROO 30.00 13.50

2003 Donruss Signature Autographs Century

MINT NRMT

1-RANDOM INSERTS IN PACKS ....
151-154 RANDOM IN DLP R/T PACKS
1-102 PRINT RUN 100 SERIAL #'d SETS
151-154 PRINT RUN 21 SERIAL #'d SETS
NO PRICING ON QTY OF 25 OR LESS
CARD 154 IS NOT SIGNED ....
1 Garret Anderson 25.00 11.00
7 Matt Williams 25.00 11.00
27 Barry Larkin 50.00 22.00
39 Richard Hidalgo 15.00 6.75
42 Mike Sweeney 25.00 11.00
50 A.J. Pierzynski 25.00 11.00
51 Torii Hunter 25.00 11.00
53 Jose Vidro 15.00 6.75
54 Vladimir Guerrero 40.00 18.00
55 Cliff Floyd 25.00 11.00
62 Drew Henson 40.00 18.00
65 Nick Johnson 15.00 6.75
69 Mark Mulder 25.00 11.00
72 Bobby Abreu 25.00 11.00
78 Kenny Lofton 40.00 18.00
81 Andres Galarraga 25.00 11.00
84 Edgar Martinez 40.00 18.00
89 Scott Rolen 40.00 18.00
90 So Taguchi 25.00 11.00
100 Vernon Wells 25.00 11.00
102 Jose Contreras ROO 40.00 18.00
151 Delmon Young ROO ....
152 Rickie Weeks ROO ....
153 Edwin Jackson ROO ....

2003 Donruss Signature Autographs Decade

MINT NRMT

1-102 RANDOM INSERTS IN PACKS ..
151-154 RANDOM IN DLP R/T PACKS
STATED PRINT RUN 10 SERIAL #'d SETS
NO PRICING DUE TO SCARCITY ....
CARD 154 IS NOT SIGNED ....

2003 Donruss Signature Autographs Notations

Randomly inserted into packs, these cards feature not only authentic autographs from the featured player but also a special "notation" next to their name in the checklist. Since each card has a different print run we have put that information next to the card in our checklist. Please note that for cards with print runs of 30 or fewer, no pricing is provided.

MINT NRMT

1A Garret Anderson #16/75 .... 25.00 11.00
1B Garret Anderson 7-27-94/45 30.00 13.50
1C Garret Anderson WSC 02/75 25.00 11.00
6 Mark Grace Amazing/5 ....
7A Matt Williams #9/250 .... 15.00 6.75
7B Matt Williams 01 WS/50 .... 30.00 13.50
10A Chipper Jones 96-01 AS/25 ....
10B Chipper Jones MVP 99/25 ....
32 Todd Helton 02 AS/15 ....
33 Ivan Rodriguez #7/5 ....
36 Jeff Bagwell Baggy/5 ....
38A Lance Berkman #17/15 ....
38B Lance Berkman #22/5 ....
38C Lance Berkman #27/1 ....
38D Lance Berkman 02/1 ....
38E Lance Berkman Rice Owls/5 ....
38F Lance Berkman Rice Univ./5 ....
38G Lance Berkman William/1 ....
40 Roy Oswalt #44/25 ....
45 Kazuhisa Ishii #17/35 .... 50.00 22.00
50 A.J. Pierzynski 02 AS/200 .... 15.00 6.75
51A Torii Hunter 02 AS/25 ....
51B Torii Hunter #48/20 ....
53A Jose Vidro #3/40 .... 20.00 9.00
53B Jose Vidro AS 00/15 ....
53C Jose Vidro 2X AS/6 ....
55 Cliff Floyd #30/5 ....
57A Mike Piazza #31/5 ....
57B Mike Piazza ROY 93/1 ....
62A Drew Henson UM #7/2 ....
62B Drew Henson QB #7/24 ....
62C Drew Henson DH #7/73 .... 40.00 18.00
68A Eric Chavez #3/50 .... 30.00 13.50
68B Eric Chavez Chavy/25 ....
69 Mark Mulder MSU/30 ....
78 Kenny Lofton #7/150 .... 25.00 11.00
80 Ryan Klesko #30/75 .... 25.00 11.00
83 Rich Aurilia #35/61 .... 20.00 9.00
84A Edgar Martinez #11/250 .... 25.00 11.00
84B E.Martinez BT 92-95/60 .... 50.00 22.00
92A Alex Rodriguez #3/5 ....
92B Alex Rodriguez WCS 93/5 ....
92C Alex Rodriguez Westminster/1 ....
96 Rafael Palmeiro 500 HR/25 ....
100 Vernon Wells #10/75 .... 25.00 11.00

2003 Donruss Signature Autographs Notations Century

MINT NRMT

RANDOM INSERTS IN PACKS ....
STATED PRINT RUN 100 SERIAL #'d SETS
1A Garret Anderson #16 .... 25.00 11.00
1B Garret Anderson 7-27-94 .... 25.00 11.00
7A Matt Williams #9 .... 25.00 11.00
7B Matt Williams 01 WS 25.00 11.00
50 A.J. Pierzynski 02 AS 25.00 11.00
68A Eric Chavez #3 .... 25.00 11.00
78 Kenny Lofton #7 .... 40.00 18.00
84A Edgar Martinez #11 .... 40.00 18.00

2003 Donruss Signature Autographs Notations Decade

MINT NRMT

RANDOM INSERTS IN PACKS ....
STATED PRINT RUN 10 SERIAL #'d SETS
NO PRICING DUE TO SCARCITY ....

2003 Donruss Signature Cuts

Randomly inserted into packs, these 15 cards feature "cut" signatures from the featured player. Each of these cards have different print runs and we have notated that print run information in our checklist. Please note for cards with 25 or fewer copies, no pricing is provided.

MINT NRMT

4 Curt Schilling/7 ....
8 Randy Johnson/40 .... 80.00 36.00
10 Chipper Jones/9 ....
33 Ivan Rodriguez/122 .... 40.00 18.00
54 Vladimir Guerrero/34 .... 50.00 22.00
58 Roberto Alomar/100 .... 40.00 18.00
59 Tom Glavine/9 ....
64 Mike Mussina/82 .... 50.00 22.00
66 Roger Clemens/9 ....
73 Jim Thome/127 .... 40.00 18.00
80 Ryan Klesko/35 .... 30.00 13.50
81 Andres Galarraga/51 .... 30.00 13.50
89 Scott Rolen/36 .... 50.00 22.00
94 Juan Gonzalez/9 ....
96 Rafael Palmeiro/13 ....

2003 Donruss Signature Cuts Decade

MINT NRMT

RANDOM INSERTS IN PACKS ....
STATED PRINT RUN 10 SERIAL #'d SETS
NO PRICING DUE TO SCARCITY ....

2003 Donruss Signature Authentic Cuts

Randomly inserted into packs, these three cards feature cut signatures of the most legendary players in baseball history. We have notated the print run next to the player's name in our checklist and due to market scarcity, no pricing is provided for these cards.

MINT NRMT

1 Ty Cobb/3 ....
2 Babe Ruth/1 ....
3 Lou Gehrig/1 ....

2003 Donruss Signature INKredible Three

Randomly inserted into packs, these five cards feature three signatures on each card from players with a common team allegiance. Each of these cards were issued to a stated print run of 50 serial numbered sets.

MINT NRMT

1 Barry Zito 400.00 180.00
Mark Mulder
Tim Hudson
2 Greg Maddux 400.00 180.00
Chipper Jones
Andruw Jones
3 Kerry Wood 500.00 220.00
Mark Prior
Ernie Banks
4 Kirby Puckett 250.00 110.00
Harmon Killebrew
Torii Hunter
5 Vladimir Guerrero 150.00 70.00
Jose Vidro
Javier Vazquez

2003 Donruss Signature INKredible Four

Randomly inserted into packs, these 10 cards feature four signatures from players with a common team allegiance. Each of these cards were issued to a stated print run of 25 serial numbered sets and no pricing is provided due to market scarcity.

MINT NRMT
1 Jeff Bagwell
Craig Biggio
Lance Berkman
Roy Oswalt
2 Mike Schmidt
Steve Carlton
Pat Burrell
Jim Thome
3 Carlos Lee
Magglio Ordonez
Frank Thomas
Mark Buehrle
4 Brooks Robinson
Frank Robinson
Cal Ripken
Jim Palmer
5 Pedro Martinez
Manny Ramirez
Rickey Henderson
Bobby Doerr
6 Mike Sweeney
Carlos Beltran
Bo Jackson
George Brett
7 Randy Johnson
Curt Schilling
Mark Grace
Junior Spivey
8 Dwight Gooden
Lenny Dykstra
Tom Glavine
Roberto Alomar
9 Alex Rodriguez
Rafael Palmeiro
Nolan Ryan
Ferguson Jenkins
10 Roberto Alomar
Joe Carter
Ryan Klesko
Tony Gwynn

2003 Donruss Signature INKredible Six

Randomly inserted into packs, these five cards feature six signatures on each card with a common thread tying together all the players. Each of these cards were issued to a stated print run of 10 serial numbered sets and no pricing is provided due to market scarcity.

MINT NRMT
1 Adam Dunn
Tom Seaver
Johnny Bench
Austin Kearns
Joe Morgan
Barry Larkin
2 Albert Pujols
Stan Musial
Jim Edmonds
Scott Rolen
Lou Brock
Ozzie Smith
3 Andre Dawson
Ernie Banks
Mark Prior
Ryne Sandberg
Kerry Wood
Mark Grace
4 Yogi Berra
Whitey Ford
Rickey Henderson
Don Mattingly
Phil Rizzuto
Reggie Jackson
5 Alex Rodriguez
Roger Clemens
Hideo Nomo
George Brett
Don Mattingly
Nolan Ryan

2003 Donruss Signature Legends of Summer

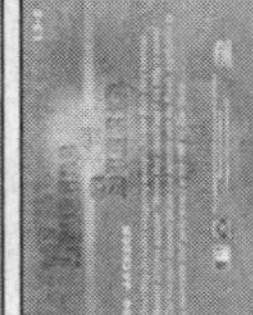

Randomly inserted into packs, these 40 cards feature some of the best retired players. Each of these cards were issued to a stated print run of 250 serial numbered sets.

MINT NRMT
*CENTURY: .6X TO 1.5X BASIC
CENTURY PRINT RUN 100 SERIAL #'d SETS
DECADE PRINT RUN 10 SERIAL #'d SETS
NO DECADE PRICING DUE TO SCARCITY
RANDOM INSERTS IN PACKS
1 Al Kaline 8.00 3.60
2 Alan Trammell 5.00 2.20
3 Andre Dawson 5.00 2.20
4 Babe Ruth 15.00 6.75
5 Billy Williams 5.00 2.20
6 Bo Jackson 8.00 3.60
7 Bob Feller 5.00 2.20
8 Bobby Doerr 5.00 2.20
9 Brooks Robinson 5.00 2.20
10 Dale Murphy 8.00 3.60
11 Dennis Eckersley 5.00 2.20
12 Don Mattingly 15.00 6.75
13 Duke Snider 5.00 2.20
14 Eric Davis 5.00 2.20
15 Frank Robinson 5.00 2.20
16 Fred Lynn 5.00 2.20
17 Gary Carter 5.00 2.20
18 Harmon Killebrew 8.00 3.60
19 Jack Morris 5.00 2.20
20 Jim Palmer 5.00 2.20
21 Jim Abbott 5.00 2.20
22 Joe Morgan 5.00 2.20
23 Joe Torre 5.00 2.20
24 Johnny Bench 8.00 3.60
25 Jose Canseco 8.00 3.60
26 Kirby Puckett 8.00 3.60
27 Lenny Dykstra 5.00 2.20
28 Lou Brock 5.00 2.20
29 Ralph Kiner 5.00 2.20
30 Mike Schmidt 12.00 5.50
31 Nolan Ryan Rgr 15.00 6.75
32 Nolan Ryan Angels 15.00 6.75
33 Orel Hershiser 5.00 2.20
34 Phil Rizzuto 5.00 2.20
35 Orlando Cepeda 5.00 2.20
36 Ryne Sandberg 12.00 5.50
37 Stan Musial 10.00 4.50
38 Steve Garvey 5.00 2.20
39 Tony Perez 5.00 2.20
40 Ty Cobb 10.00 4.50

2003 Donruss Signature Legends of Summer Autographs

Randomly inserted into packs, this is a partial parallel of the Legends of Summer set. A few cards were issued in smaller quantities and we have notated that information (as provided by Donruss/Playoff) in our checklist.

MINT NRMT
1 Al Kaline 25.00 11.00
2 Alan Trammell 15.00 6.75
3 Andre Dawson 15.00 6.75
5 Billy Williams 15.00 6.75
6 Bo Jackson SP/100 60.00 27.00
7 Bob Feller 15.00 6.75
8 Bobby Doerr 15.00 6.75
9 Brooks Robinson 25.00 11.00
10 Dale Murphy SP/75 40.00 18.00
11 Dennis Eckersley 15.00 6.75
12 Don Mattingly SP/50 100.00 45.00
13 Duke Snider SP/225 25.00 11.00
14 Eric Davis 15.00 6.75
15 Frank Robinson 15.00 6.75
16 Fred Lynn 15.00 6.75
17 Gary Carter 15.00 6.75
18 Harmon Killebrew SP/171 25.00 11.00
19 Jack Morris 15.00 6.75
20 Jim Palmer 15.00 6.75
21 Jim Abbott 15.00 6.75
22 Joe Morgan SP/125 25.00 11.00
23 Joe Torre 15.00 6.75
24 Johnny Bench SP/75 40.00 18.00
25 Jose Canseco SP/75 40.00 18.00
26 Kirby Puckett SP/75 50.00 22.00
27 Lenny Dykstra 15.00 6.75
28 Lou Brock 25.00 11.00
29 Ralph Kiner 15.00 6.75
30 Mike Schmidt SP/75 80.00 36.00
31 Nolan Ryan Rgr SP/75 150.00 70.00
33 Orel Hershiser 25.00 11.00
34 Phil Rizzuto 25.00 11.00
35 Orlando Cepeda 15.00 6.75
36 Ryne Sandberg SP/75 80.00 36.00
37 Stan Musial SP/200 60.00 27.00
38 Steve Garvey 15.00 6.75
39 Tony Perez 15.00 6.75

2003 Donruss Signature Legends of Summer Autographs Century

MINT NRMT
RANDOM INSERTS IN PACKS
STATED PRINT RUN 100 SERIAL #'d SETS
1 Al Kaline 40.00 18.00
2 Alan Trammell 25.00 11.00
3 Andre Dawson 25.00 11.00
5 Billy Williams 25.00 11.00
6 Bo Jackson 60.00 27.00
7 Bob Feller 25.00 11.00
8 Bobby Doerr 25.00 11.00
9 Brooks Robinson 40.00 18.00
11 Dennis Eckersley 25.00 11.00
12 Don Mattingly 80.00 36.00
14 Eric Davis 25.00 11.00
15 Frank Robinson 25.00 11.00
16 Fred Lynn 25.00 11.00
17 Gary Carter 25.00 11.00
19 Jack Morris 25.00 11.00
20 Jim Palmer 25.00 11.00
21 Jim Abbott 25.00 11.00
23 Joe Torre 25.00 11.00
27 Lenny Dykstra 25.00 11.00
28 Lou Brock 40.00 18.00
29 Ralph Kiner 25.00 11.00
33 Orel Hershiser 80.00 36.00
34 Phil Rizzuto 40.00 18.00
35 Orlando Cepeda 25.00 11.00
36 Ryne Sandberg 80.00 36.00
37 Stan Musial 60.00 27.00
38 Steve Garvey 25.00 11.00
39 Tony Perez 25.00 11.00

2003 Donruss Signature Legends of Summer Autographs Decade

MINT NRMT
RANDOM INSERTS IN PACKS
STATED PRINT RUN 10 SERIAL #'d SETS
NO PRICING DUE TO SCARCITY

2003 Donruss Signature Legends of Summer Autographs Notations

This parallel to the Legends of Summer insert set features not only authentic autographs from some of the featured players but also special notations added by the player. Since there are varying print runs on these cards we have provided that information next to the player's name in our checklist. Please note that cards with a print run of 25 or fewer are not priced due to market scarcity.

MINT NRMT
1A Al Kaline #6/200 25.00 11.00
1B Al Kaline HOF '80/200 25.00 11.00
1C Al Kaline Mr. Tiger/200 25.00 11.00
2 A.Trammell 84 WS MVP/250 15.00 6.75
3A Andre Dawson #8/165 15.00 6.75
3B Andre Dawson 87 MVP/250 15.00 6.75
5B Billy Williams 61 ROY/250 15.00 6.75
5C Billy Williams 87 HOF/150 15.00 6.75
7A Bob Feller #19/250 15.00 6.75
7B Bob Feller HOF 62/250 15.00 6.75
7C Bob Feller Triple Crown/200
8A Bobby Doerr #1/250 15.00 6.75
8B Bobby Doerr HOF 86/250 15.00 6.75
8C Bobby Doerr MVP 44/250 15.00 6.75
9A B.Robinson 64 MVP/150 25.00 11.00
9B B.Robinson 70 WS MVP/50 50.00 22.00
10A Dale Murphy MVP 82/50 50.00 22.00
10B Dale Murphy MVP 83/50 50.00 22.00
11A D.Eckersley 92 CY/250 15.00 6.75
11B D.Eckersley 92 CY-MVP/250 15.00 6.75
11C D.Eckersley 92 MVP/250 15.00 6.75
13 Duke Snider HOF 80/25
14A Eric Davis #44/250 15.00 6.75
14B Eric Davis 87 AS/150 15.00 6.75
14C Eric Davis 90 WS/200 15.00 6.75
16A Fred Lynn 75 MVP-ROY/240 15.00 6.75
16B Fred Lynn 75-83 AS/250 15.00 6.75
17 Gary Carter The Kid/5
18A H.Killebrew #3/75 40.00 18.00
18B H.Killebrew 69 MVP/50 50.00 22.00
18C H.Killebrew 573 HR/50 50.00 22.00
18D H.Killebrew HOF 84/125 40.00 18.00
19A J.Morris 91 WS MVP/250 15.00 6.75
19B Jack Morris 92 WS/250 15.00 6.75
20A Jim Palmer 73 CY/190 15.00 6.75
20B Jim Palmer 75 CY/140 15.00 6.75
20C Jim Palmer 76 CY/50 30.00 13.50
21A Jim Abbott 4-8-89/200 15.00 6.75
21B Jim Abbott 9-4-93/100 25.00 11.00
21C Jim Abbott 6-15-99/75 25.00 11.00
21D Jim Abbott U of Mich/50 30.00 13.50
21E Jim Abbott Yanks/25
24A Johnny Bench #5/20
24B Johnny Bench HOF/1
24C Johnny Bench HOF 89/5
24D Johnny Bench MVP 70/1
24E Johnny Bench MVP 72/1
27 Lenny Dykstra 86 WS/226 15.00 6.75
28A Lou Brock SB 938/25
28B Lou Brock HOF 85/50 50.00 22.00
29A Ralph Kiner #4/150 15.00 6.75
29B Ralph Kiner 48-53 AS/25
29C Ralph Kiner HOF/200 15.00 6.75
29D Ralph Kiner HOF 75/100 25.00 11.00
31 Nolan Ryan Rgr 5714 SO/25
35A O.Cepeda Baby Bull/75 50.00 22.00
35B O.Cepeda MVP 67/40 30.00 13.50
35C O.Cepeda 58 ROY/40 30.00 13.50
35D O.Cepeda 67 WS/40 30.00 13.50
35E O.Cepeda 68 WS/40 30.00 13.50
36A Ryne Sandberg #23/5
36B Ryne Sandberg Cubs/20
36C Ryne Sandberg 84 MVP/25
38A Steve Garvey #6/150 15.00 6.75
38B Steve Garvey 74 MVP/25
38C Steve Garvey 78 AS MVP/50 30.00 13.50
38D Steve Garvey 81 WS/75 25.00 11.00
39A Tony Perez #24/250 15.00 6.75
39B Tony Perez HOF 02/175 15.00 6.75
39C Tony Perez WS 75/125 25.00 11.00
39D Tony Perez WS 76/75 25.00 11.00

2003 Donruss Signature Legends of Summer Autographs Notations Century

MINT NRMT
RANDOM INSERTS IN PACKS
STATED PRINT RUN 100 SERIAL #'d SETS
1A Al Kaline #6 40.00 18.00
1B Al Kaline HOF 80 40.00 18.00
1C Al Kaline Mr. Tiger 40.00 18.00
2 Alan Trammell 84 WS MVP 25.00 11.00
3A Andre Dawson #8 25.00 11.00
3B Andre Dawson 87 MVP 25.00 11.00
5A Billy Williams #26 25.00 11.00
5B Billy Williams 61 ROY 25.00 11.00
5C Billy Williams 87 HOF 25.00 11.00
7A Bob Feller #19 25.00 11.00
7B Bob Feller HOF 62 25.00 11.00
7C Bob Feller Triple Crown 25.00 11.00
8A Bobby Doerr #1 25.00 11.00
8B Bobby Doerr HOF 86 25.00 11.00
8C Bobby Doerr MVP 44 25.00 11.00
11A Dennis Eckersley 92 CY 25.00 11.00
11B D.Eckersley 92 CY-MVP 25.00 11.00
11C Dennis Eckersley 92 MVP 25.00 11.00
14A Eric Davis #44 25.00 11.00
14B Eric Davis 87 AS 25.00 11.00
14C Eric Davis 90 WS 25.00 11.00
16A Fred Lynn 75 MVP-ROY 25.00 11.00
16B Fred Lynn 75-83 AS 25.00 11.00
19A Jack Morris 91 WS MVP 25.00 11.00
19B Jack Morris 92 WS 25.00 11.00
20A Jim Palmer 73 CY 25.00 11.00
20B Jim Palmer 75 CY 25.00 11.00
20C Jim Palmer 76 CY 25.00 11.00
21A Jim Abbott 4-8-89 25.00 11.00
21B Jim Abbott 9-4-93 25.00 11.00
21C Jim Abbott 6-15-99 25.00 11.00
21D Jim Abbott U of Mich 25.00 11.00
21E Jim Abbott Yanks 25.00 11.00
27 Lenny Dykstra 86 WS 25.00 11.00
29A Ralph Kiner #4 25.00 11.00
29B Ralph Kiner 48-53 AS 25.00 11.00
29C Ralph Kiner HOF 25.00 11.00
29D Ralph Kiner HOF 75 25.00 11.00
38A Steve Garvey #6 25.00 11.00
38B Steve Garvey 74 MVP 25.00 11.00
38C Steve Garvey 78 AS MVP 25.00 11.00
38D Steve Garvey 81 WS 25.00 11.00
39A Tony Perez #24 25.00 11.00
39B Tony Perez HOF 02 25.00 11.00
39C Tony Perez WS 75 25.00 11.00
39D Tony Perez WS 76 25.00 11.00

2003 Donruss Signature Legends of Summer Autographs Notations Decade

MINT NRMT
RANDOM INSERTS IN PACKS
STATED PRINT RUN 10 SERIAL #'d SETS
NO PRICING DUE TO SCARCITY

2003 Donruss Signature Notable Nicknames

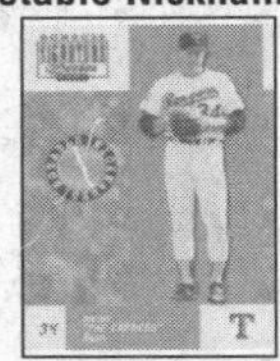

Randomly inserted into packs, these 20 cards players who are commonly known by a nickname. Each of these cards were issued to a stated print run of 750 serial numbered sets.

MINT NRMT
*CENTURY: .6X TO 1.5X BASIC
CENTURY PRINT RUN 100 SERIAL #'d SETS
DECADE PRINT RUN 10 SERIAL #'d SETS
NO DECADE PRICING DUE TO SCARCITY
RANDOM INSERTS IN PACKS
1 Andre Dawson 5.00 2.20
2 Torii Hunter 5.00 2.20
3 Brooks Robinson 5.00 2.20
4 Carlton Fisk 5.00 2.20
5 Mike Mussina 5.00 2.20
6 Don Mattingly 15.00 6.75
7 Duke Snider 5.00 2.20
8 Eric Davis 5.00 2.20
9 Frank Thomas 6.00 2.70
10 Randy Johnson 6.00 2.70
11 Lenny Dykstra 5.00 2.20
12 Ivan Rodriguez 6.00 2.70
13 Nolan Ryan 15.00 6.75
14 Phil Rizzuto 5.00 2.20
15 Reggie Jackson 5.00 2.20
16 Roger Clemens 12.00 5.50
17 Ryne Sandberg 12.00 5.50
18 Stan Musial 10.00 4.50
19 Luis Gonzalez 5.00 2.20
20 Will Clark 6.00 2.70

2003 Donruss Signature Notable Nicknames Autographs

Randomly inserted in packs, these cards parallel the regular Notable Nickname set but also include an authentic autograph from the featured player as well as his nickname. Most of these cards were issued to a stated print run of 100 copies but a few were issued in smaller quantities and that information is notated in our checklist. For those cards with a print run of 25 or fewer, no pricing is provided due to market scarcity.

MINT NRMT
1 Andre Dawson 50.00 22.00
2 Torii Hunter 50.00 22.00
3 Brooks Robinson 80.00 36.00
4 Carlton Fisk 80.00 36.00
5 Mike Mussina 100.00 45.00
6 Don Mattingly 150.00 70.00
7 Duke Snider 80.00 36.00
8 Eric Davis/40 80.00 36.00
9 Frank Thomas 100.00 45.00
10 Randy Johnson 120.00 55.00
11 Lenny Dykstra 30.00 13.50
12 Ivan Rodriguez/75 80.00 36.00
13 Nolan Ryan/15
14 Phil Rizzuto 80.00 36.00
15 Reggie Jackson 80.00 36.00
16 Roger Clemens 200.00 90.00
17 Ryne Sandberg 100.00 45.00
18 Stan Musial 120.00 55.00
19 Luis Gonzalez 50.00 22.00
20 Will Clark 80.00 36.00

2003 Donruss Signature Notable Nicknames Autographs Decade

MINT NRMT
RANDOM INSERTS IN PACKS
STATED PRINT RUN 10 SERIAL #'d SETS
NO PRICING DUE TO SCARCITY

2003 Donruss Signature Player Collection Autographs

Randomly inserted in packs, these cards featur authentic autographs on "player collection cards. Since each of these cards were issued t a different print run, we have notated that infor mation next to the player's name in our check list.

MINT NRMT
1 Roberto Alomar/75 40.00 18.00
2 Adrian Beltre/104 40.00 18.00
3 Lance Berkman/50 50.00 22.00
4 Craig Biggio Btg/26
5 Craig Biggio Fldg/26
6 Joe Borchard/53 20.00 9.00
7 Roger Clemens Pitch/9
8 Roger Clemens Stretch/4
9 J.D. Drew/52 50.00 22.00
10 Jim Edmonds/52 50.00 22.00
11 Tony Gwynn/11
12 Todd Helton/50 50.00 22.00
13 Jason Jennings/49 20.00 9.00
14 Andruw Jones Away/25
15 Andruw Jones Home/25
16 Chipper Jones/51 60.00 27.00
17 Paul Konerko/26
18 Paul Lo Duca/227 15.00 6.75
19 Magglio Ordonez/102 25.00 11.00
20 Roy Oswalt/10
21 Rafael Palmeiro/25
22 Mark Prior/27 100.00 45.00
23 Cal Ripken/22
24 Alex Rodriguez M's/24
25 Alex Rodriguez Rgr/25
26 Ivan Rodriguez/52 50.00 22.00
27 Richie Sexson/50 30.00 13.50
28 Alfonso Soriano/11
29A Matt Williams/19
29B Matt Williams/483 15.00 6.75

2003 Donruss Signature Tean Trademarks

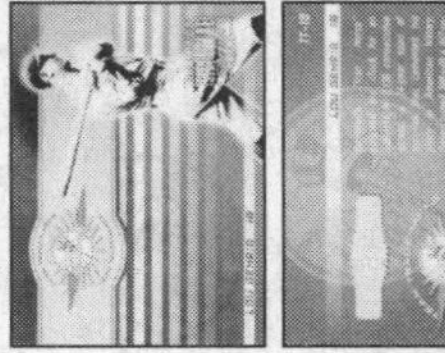

Randomly inserted into packs, these cards fea ture the term "team trademark" on the card. Eac of these cards were issued to a stated print ru of 500 serial numbered sets.

MINT NRMT
*CENTURY: .75X TO 2X BASIC
CENTURY PRINT RUN 100 SERIAL #'d SETS
DECADE PRINT RUN 10 SERIAL #'d SETS
NO DECADE PRICING DUE TO SCARCITY
RANDOM INSERTS IN PACKS
1 Adam Dunn 4.00 1.80
2 Andre Dawson 4.00 1.80
3 Babe Ruth 12.00 5.50
4 Barry Bonds 12.00 5.50
5 Brooks Robinson 4.00 1.80
6 Cal Ripken 15.00 6.75
7 Derek Jeter 12.00 5.50
8 Don Mattingly 12.00 5.50
9 Frank Robinson 4.00 1.80
10 Fred Lynn 4.00 1.80
11 Gary Carter 4.00 1.80
12 George Brett 12.00 5.50
13 Greg Maddux 8.00 3.60
14 Ichiro Suzuki 8.00 3.60
15 Jim Palmer 4.00 1.80
16 Jose Contreras 5.00 2.20
17 Kerry Wood 5.00 2.20

18 Lou Gehrig	8.00	3.60
19 Magglio Ordonez	4.00	1.80
20 Mark Grace	4.00	1.80
21 Mike Schmidt	10.00	4.50
22 Nolan Ryan Rgr	12.00	5.50
23 Nolan Ryan Astros	12.00	5.50
24 Reggie Jackson	4.00	1.80
25 Rickey Henderson	5.00	2.20
26 Roberto Clemente	10.00	4.50
27 Roger Clemens Sox	10.00	4.50
28 Roger Clemens Yanks	10.00	4.50
29 Ryne Sandberg	10.00	4.50
30 Sammy Sosa	8.00	3.60
31 Stan Musial	8.00	3.60
32 Steve Carlton	4.00	1.80
33 Tim Hudson	4.00	1.80
34 Tom Glavine	4.00	1.80
35 Tom Seaver	4.00	1.80
36 Tony Gwynn	6.00	2.70
37 Torii Hunter	4.00	1.80
38 Ty Cobb	8.00	3.60
39 Vladimir Guerrero	5.00	2.20
40 Will Clark	5.00	2.20

2003 Donruss Signature Team Trademarks Autographs

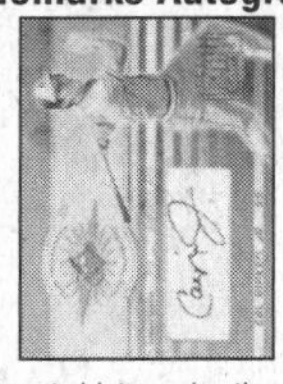

Randomly inserted into packs, these cards partially parallel the Team Trademark insert set. Each of these cards feature an authentic autograph from the featured player. Since there are some different print runs we have notated that information in our checklist next to the player's name. For those cards with print runs of 25 or fewer, no pricing is provided due to market scarcity.

	MINT	NRMT
1 Adam Dunn/50	50.00	22.00
2 Andre Dawson/250	15.00	6.75
5 Brooks Robinson/250	25.00	11.00
6 Cal Ripken/50	200.00	90.00
8 Don Mattingly/75	100.00	45.00
10 Fred Lynn/250	15.00	6.75
11 Gary Carter/250	15.00	6.75
12 George Brett/50	120.00	55.00
13 Greg Maddux/50	120.00	55.00
16 Jose Contreras/250	25.00	11.00
17 Kerry Wood/50	50.00	22.00
19 Magglio Ordonez/75	25.00	11.00
20 Mark Grace/25		
23 Nolan Ryan Astros/50	150.00	70.00
24 Reggie Jackson/75	40.00	18.00
25 Rickey Henderson/50	100.00	45.00
27 Roger Clemens Sox/50	150.00	70.00
28 Roger Clemens Yanks/50	150.00	70.00
29 Ryne Sandberg/100	80.00	36.00
31 Stan Musial/200	60.00	27.00
32 Steve Carlton/150	25.00	11.00
33 Tim Hudson/100	50.00	22.00
34 Tom Glavine/50	50.00	22.00
35 Tom Seaver/50	50.00	22.00
36 Tony Gwynn/50	80.00	36.00
37 Torii Hunter/250	15.00	6.75
39 Vladimir Guerrero/250	25.00	11.00
40 Will Clark/125	40.00	18.00

2003 Donruss Signature Team Trademarks Autographs Century

	MINT	NRMT
RANDOM INSERTS IN PACKS		
STATED PRINT RUN 100 SERIAL #'d SETS		
1 Andre Dawson	25.00	11.00
5 Brooks Robinson	40.00	18.00
9 Frank Robinson	25.00	11.00
10 Fred Lynn	25.00	11.00
11 Gary Carter	25.00	11.00
15 Jim Palmer	25.00	11.00
16 Jose Contreras	40.00	18.00
20 Mark Grace	60.00	27.00
29 Ryne Sandberg	80.00	36.00
31 Stan Musial	60.00	27.00
32 Steve Carlton	40.00	18.00
34 Tom Glavine	40.00	18.00
37 Torii Hunter	25.00	11.00
39 Vladimir Guerrero	40.00	18.00

2003 Donruss Signature Team Trademarks Autographs Decade

	MINT	NRMT
RANDOM INSERTS IN PACKS		
STATED PRINT RUN 10 SERIAL #'d SETS		
NO PRICING DUE TO SCARCITY		

2003 Donruss Signature Team Trademarks Autographs Notations

Randomly inserted into packs, these cards feature not only authentic autographs from the featured player as well as a special notation added to that autographs. Each of these cards have varying print runs and we have added that information in our checklist next to the player's name. For those cards with a stated print run of 25 or fewer copies, no pricing is provided due to market scarcity.

	MINT	NRMT
2A Andre Dawson #10/250	15.00	6.75
2B Andre Dawson ROY 77/150	15.00	6.75

5A B.Robinson 64 MVP/75	50.00	22.00
5B B.Robinson 70 WS MVP/125	40.00	18.00
10A Fred Lynn 75-83 AS/50	30.00	13.50
11 Gary Carter The Kid/25		
12 George Brett #5/25		
15A Jim Palmer 73 CY/32	30.00	13.50
15B Jim Palmer 75 CY/128	25.00	11.00
15C Jim Palmer 76 CY/150	15.00	6.75
17 Kerry Wood ROY 98/25		
24A Reggie Jackson #44/5		
24B Reggie Jackson 99/20		
29A Ryne Sandberg #23/40	120.00	55.00
29B Ryne Sandberg Cubs/5		
29C Ryne Sandberg 84 MVP/55	100.00	45.00
32A Steve Carlton 72 CY/50	50.00	22.00
32B Steve Carlton 77 CY/50	50.00	22.00
32C Steve Carlton 80 CY/50	50.00	22.00
32D Steve Carlton 82 CY/50	50.00	22.00
33A Tim Hudson Black Angus/5		
33B Tim Hudson Huddy/50	60.00	27.00
37A Torii Hunter #48/20		
40A Will Clark 89 MVP/52	80.00	36.00
40B Will Clark 89 WS/52	80.00	36.00

2003 Donruss Signature Team Trademarks Autographs Notations Century

	MINT	NRMT
RANDOM INSERTS IN PACKS		
STATED PRINT RUN 100 SERIAL #'d SETS		
2A Andre Dawson #10	25.00	11.00
2B Andre Dawson ROY 77	25.00	11.00
10A Fred Lynn 75-83 AS	25.00	11.00
10B Fred Lynn 75 MVP-ROY	25.00	11.00
15A Jim Palmer 73 CY	25.00	11.00
15B Jim Palmer 75 CY	25.00	11.00
15C Jim Palmer 76 CY	25.00	11.00

2003 Donruss Signature Team Trademarks Autographs Notations Decade

	MINT	NRMT
RANDOM INSERTS IN PACKS		
STATED PRINT RUN 10 SERIAL #'d SETS		
NO PRICING DUE TO SCARCITY		

2003 Donruss Team Heroes

This 548 card set was distributed in two separate series. The primary Team Heroes product - containing cards 1-540 from the basic set - was released very late in December, 2002. These cards were issued in 13 card packs with an SRP of $3 per pack. This product was issued in 24 pack boxes which came 20 boxes to a case. Several great players, were issued as members of two or more different teams. Update cards 541-548 were distributed as commonly available cards within packs of 2003 DLP Rookies and Traded of which was released in December, 2003. Due to a problem in production, these update cards feature a glossy sheen, differentiating them from the remaining 540 cards within the basic set. Furthermore, they may be confused with the Team Heroes Glossy parallel cards of which were issued as random inserts in basic Team Heroes packs.

	Nm-Mt	Ex-Mt
COMP.LO SET (540)	80.00	24.00
COMP.UPDATE SET (8)	8.00	2.40
COMMON CARD (541-548)	.30	.09
1 Adam Kennedy	.30	.09
2 Steve Green	.30	.09
3 Rod Carew Angels	.75	.23
4 Alfredo Amezaga	.30	.09
5 Reggie Jackson Angels	.75	.23
6 Jarrod Washburn	.30	.09
7 Nolan Ryan Angels	3.00	.90
8 Tim Salmon	.50	.15
9 Garret Anderson	.30	.09
10 Darin Erstad	.30	.09
11 Elpidio Guzman	.30	.09
12 David Eckstein	.30	.09
13 Troy Percival	.30	.09
14 Troy Glaus	.30	.09
15 Doug Devore	.30	.09
16 Tony Womack	.30	.09
17 Matt Williams	.30	.09
18 Junior Spivey	.30	.09
19 Mark Grace	.50	.15
20 Curt Schilling	.30	.09
21 Erubiel Durazo	.30	.09
22 Craig Counsell	.30	.09
23 Byung-Hyun Kim	.30	.09
24 Randy Johnson D'backs	.75	.23
25 Luis Gonzalez	.30	.09
26 John Smoltz	.50	.15
27 Tim Spooneybarger	.30	.09
28 Dale Murphy	1.25	.35
29 Warren Spahn	.75	.23
30 Jason Marquis	.30	.09
31 Kevin Millwood	.30	.09
32 Javy Lopez	.30	.09
33 Vinny Castilla	.30	.09
34 Julio Franco	.30	.09
35 Trey Hodges	.30	.09
36 Chipper Jones	.75	.23
37 Gary Sheffield	.30	.09
38 Billy Sylvester	.30	.09
39 Tom Glavine	.50	.15
40 Rafael Furcal	.30	.09
41 Cory Aldridge	.30	.09
42 Greg Maddux Braves	1.25	.35
43 John Ennis	.30	.09
44 Wes Helms	.30	.09
45 Horacio Ramirez	.30	.09
46 Derrick Lewis	.30	.09
47 Marcus Giles	.30	.09
48 Eddie Mathews	1.25	.35
49 Wilson Betemit	.30	.09
50 Andruw Jones	.30	.09
51 Josh Towers	.30	.09
52 Ed Rogers	.30	.09
53 Kris Foster	.30	.09
54 Brooks Robinson	.75	.23
55 Cal Ripken	4.00	1.20
56 Brian Roberts	.30	.09
57 Luis Rivera	.30	.09
58 Rodrigo Lopez	.30	.09
59 Geronimo Gil	.30	.09
60 Erik Bedard	.30	.09
61 Jim Palmer	.50	.15
62 Jay Gibbons	.30	.09
63 Travis Driskill	.30	.09
64 Larry Bigbie	.30	.09
65 Eddie Murray	1.25	.35
66 Hoyt Wilhelm	.50	.15
67 Bobby Doerr	.50	.15
68 Pedro Martinez	.75	.23
69 Roger Clemens Red Sox	1.50	.45
70 Nomar Garciaparra	1.25	.35
71 Trot Nixon	.30	.09
72 Dennis Eckersley Red Sox	.50	.15
73 John Burkett	.30	.09
74 Tim Wakefield	.30	.09
75 Wade Boggs Red Sox	.75	.23
76 Cliff Floyd	.30	.09
77 Casey Fossum	.30	.09
78 Johnny Damon	.75	.23
79 Fred Lynn	.50	.15
80 Rickey Henderson Red Sox	.75	.23
81 Juan Diaz	.30	.09
82 Manny Ramirez	.50	.15
83 Carlton Fisk Red Sox	.75	.23
84 Jorge De La Rosa	.30	.09
85 Shea Hillenbrand	.30	.09
86 Derek Lowe	.30	.09
87 Jason Varitek	.50	.15
88 Carlos Baerga	.30	.09
89 Freddy Sanchez	.30	.09
90 Ugueth Urbina	.30	.09
91 Rey Sanchez	.30	.09
92 Josh Hancock	.30	.09
93 Tony Clark	.30	.09
94 Dustin Hermanson	.30	.09
95 Ryne Sandberg	2.50	.75
96 Fred McGriff	.50	.15
97 Alex Gonzalez	.30	.09
98 Mark Bellhorn	.30	.09
99 Fergie Jenkins	.50	.15
100 Jon Lieber	.30	.09
101 Francis Beltran	.30	.09
102 Greg Maddux Cubs	1.25	.35
103 Nate Frese	.30	.09
104 Andre Dawson Cubs	.75	.23
105 Carlos Zambrano	.30	.09
106 Steve Smyth	.30	.09
107 Ernie Banks	1.25	.35
108 Will Ohman	.30	.09
109 Kerry Wood	.75	.23
110 Bobby Hill	.30	.09
111 Moises Alou	.30	.09
112 Hee Seop Choi	.30	.09
113 Corey Patterson	.30	.09
114 Sammy Sosa	1.25	.35
115 Mark Prior	.75	.23
116 Juan Cruz	.30	.09
117 Ron Santo	.75	.23
118 Billy Williams	.50	.15
119 Antonio Alfonseca	.30	.09
120 Matt Clement	.30	.09
121 Carlton Fisk White Sox	.75	.23
122 Joe Crede	.30	.09
123 Magglio Ordonez	.30	.09
124 Frank Thomas	.75	.23
125 Joe Borchard	.30	.09
126 Royce Clayton	.30	.09
127 Luis Aparicio	.50	.15
128 Willie Harris	.30	.09
129 Kyle Kane	.30	.09
130 Paul Konerko	.30	.09
131 Matt Ginter	.30	.09
132 Carlos Lee	.30	.09
133 Mark Buehrle	.30	.09
134 Adam Dunn	.50	.15
135 Eric Davis	.50	.15
136 Johnny Bench	1.25	.35
137 Joe Morgan	.50	.15
138 Austin Kearns	.30	.09
139 Barry Larkin	.50	.15
140 Ken Griffey Jr. Reds	1.25	.35
141 Luis Pineda	.30	.09
142 Corky Miller	.30	.09
143 Brandon Larson	.30	.09
144 Wily Mo Pena	.30	.09
145 Lance Davis	.30	.09
146 Tom Seaver Reds	.75	.23
147 Luke Hudson	.30	.09
148 Sean Casey	.30	.09
149 Tony Perez	.50	.15
150 Todd Walker	.30	.09
151 Aaron Boone	.30	.09
152 Jose Rijo	.30	.09
153 Ryan Dempster	.30	.09
154 Danny Graves	.30	.09
155 Matt Lawton	.30	.09
156 Cliff Lee	.30	.09
157 Ryan Drese	.30	.09
158 Danys Baez	.30	.09
159 Einar Diaz	.30	.09
160 Milton Bradley	.30	.09
161 Earl Snyder	.30	.09
162 Ellis Burks	.30	.09
163 Lou Boudreau	.50	.15
164 Bob Feller	.50	.15
165 Ricardo Rodriguez	.30	.09
166 Victor Martinez	.50	.15
167 Alex Herrera	.30	.09
168 Omar Vizquel	.50	.15
169 David Elder	.30	.09
170 C.C. Sabathia	.30	.09
171 Alex Escobar	.30	.09
172 Brian Tallet	.30	.09
173 Jim Thome	.75	.23
174 Rene Reyes	.30	.09
175 Juan Uribe	.30	.09
176 Jason Romano	.30	.09
177 Juan Pierre	.30	.09
178 Jason Jennings	.30	.09
179 Jose Ortiz	.30	.09
180 Larry Walker	.50	.15
181 Cam Esslinger	.30	.09
182 Todd Helton	.50	.15
183 Aaron Cook	.30	.09
184 Jack Cust	.30	.09
185 Jack Morris Tigers	.50	.15
186 Mike Rivera	.30	.09
187 Bobby Higginson	.30	.09
188 Fernando Rodney	.30	.09
189 Al Kaline	1.25	.35
190 Carlos Pena	.30	.09
191 Alan Trammell	.50	.15
192 Mike Maroth	.30	.09
193 Adam Pettyjohn	.30	.09
194 David Espinosa	.30	.09
195 Adam Bernero	.30	.09
196 Franklyn German	.30	.09
197 Robert Fick	.30	.09
198 Andres Torres	.30	.09
199 Luis Castillo	.30	.09
200 Preston Wilson	.30	.09
201 Pablo Ozuna	.30	.09
202 Brad Penny	.30	.09
203 Josh Beckett	.30	.09
204 Charles Johnson	.30	.09
205 Wilson Valdez	.30	.09
206 A.J. Burnett	.30	.09
207 Abraham Nunez	.30	.09
208 Mike Lowell	.30	.09
209 Jose Cueto	.30	.09
210 Jeriome Robertson	.30	.09
211 Jeff Bagwell	.50	.15
212 Kirk Saarloos	.30	.09
213 Craig Biggio	.50	.15
214 Rodrigo Rosario	.30	.09
215 Roy Oswalt	.30	.09
216 John Buck	.30	.09
217 Tim Redding	.30	.09
218 Morgan Ensberg	.30	.09
219 Richard Hidalgo	.30	.09
220 Wade Miller	.30	.09
221 Lance Berkman	.30	.09
222 Raul Chavez	.30	.09
223 Carlos Hernandez	.30	.09
224 Greg Miller	.30	.09
225 Tom Shearn	.30	.09
226 Jason Lane	.30	.09
227 Nolan Ryan Astros	3.00	.90
228 Billy Wagner	.30	.09
229 Octavio Dotel	.30	.09
230 Shane Reynolds	.30	.09
231 Julio Lugo	.30	.09
232 Daryle Ward	.30	.09
233 Mike Sweeney	.30	.09
234 Angel Berroa	.30	.09
235 George Brett	3.00	.90
236 Brad Voyles	.30	.09
237 Brandon Berger	.30	.09
238 Chad Durbin	.30	.09
239 Alexis Gomez	.30	.09
240 Jeremy Affeldt	.30	.09
241 Bo Jackson	1.25	.35
242 Dee Brown	.30	.09
243 Tony Cogan	.30	.09
244 Carlos Beltran	.50	.15
245 Joe Randa	.30	.09
246 Pee Wee Reese	.75	.23
247 Andy Ashby	.30	.09
248 Cesar Izturis	.30	.09
249 Duke Snider	.75	.23
250 Mark Grudzielanek	.30	.09
251 Chin-Feng Chen	.30	.09
252 Brian Jordan	.30	.09
253 Steve Garvey	.50	.15
254 Odalis Perez	.30	.09
255 Hideo Nomo	.75	.23
256 Kevin Brown	.30	.09
257 Eric Karros	.30	.09
258 Joe Thurston	.30	.09
259 Carlos Garcia	.30	.09
260 Shawn Green	.30	.09
261 Paul Lo Duca	.30	.09
262 Kazuhisa Ishii	.30	.09
263 Victor Alvarez	.30	.09
264 Eric Gagne	.75	.23
265 Don Sutton	.50	.15
266 Orel Hershiser	.50	.15
267 Dave Roberts	.30	.09
268 Adrian Beltre	.50	.15
269 Don Drysdale	1.25	.35
270 Jackie Robinson	1.25	.35
271 Tyler Houston	.30	.09
272 Omar Daal	.30	.09
273 Marquis Grissom	.30	.09
274 Paul Quantrill	.30	.09
275 Paul Molitor	.75	.23
276 Jose Hernandez	.30	.09
277 Takahito Nomura	.30	.09
278 Nick Neugebauer	.30	.09
279 Jose Mieses	.30	.09
280 Richie Sexson	.30	.09
281 Matt Childers	.30	.09
282 Bill Hall	.30	.09
283 Ben Sheets	.30	.09
284 Brian Mallette	.30	.09
285 Geoff Jenkins	.30	.09
286 Robin Yount	2.00	.60
287 Jeff Deardorff	.30	.09
288 Luis Rivas	.30	.09
289 Harmon Killebrew	1.25	.35
290 Michael Cuddyer	.30	.09
291 Torii Hunter	.30	.09
292 Kevin Frederick	.30	.09
293 Adam Johnson	.30	.09
294 Jack Morris Twins	.50	.15
295 Rod Carew Twins	.75	.23
296 Kirby Puckett	1.25	.35
297 Joe Mays	.30	.09
298 Jacque Jones	.30	.09
299 Cristian Guzman	.30	.09
300 Kyle Lohse	.30	.09
301 Eric Milton	.30	.09
302 Brad Radke	.30	.09
303 Doug Mientkiewicz	.30	.09
304 Corey Koskie	.30	.09
305 Jose Vidro	.30	.09
306 Claudio Vargas	.30	.09
307 Gary Carter Expos	.50	.15
308 Andre Dawson Expos	.75	.23
309 Henry Mateo	.30	.09
310 Andres Galarraga	.30	.09
311 Zach Day	.30	.09
312 Bartolo Colon	.30	.09
313 Endy Chavez	.30	.09
314 Javier Vazquez	.30	.09
315 Michael Barrett	.30	.09
316 Vladimir Guerrero	.75	.23
317 Orlando Cabrera	.30	.09
318 Al Leiter	.30	.09
319 Timo Perez	.30	.09
320 Rey Ordonez	.30	.09
321 Gary Carter	.50	.15
322 Armando Benitez	.30	.09
323 Dwight Gooden	.50	.15
324 Pedro Astacio	.30	.09
325 Roberto Alomar	.50	.15
326 Edgardo Alfonzo	.30	.09
327 Nolan Ryan Mets	3.00	.90
328 Mo Vaughn	.30	.09
329 Ryan Jamison	.30	.09
330 Satoru Komiyama	.30	.09
331 Mike Piazza	1.25	.35
332 Tom Seaver Mets	.75	.23
333 Jorge Posada	.50	.15
334 Derek Jeter	2.00	.60
335 Babe Ruth	3.00	.90
336 Lou Gehrig	2.00	.60
337 Andy Pettitte	.50	.15
338 Mariano Rivera	.50	.15
339 Robin Ventura	.30	.09
340 Yogi Berra	1.25	.35
341 Phil Rizzuto	.75	.23
342 Bernie Williams	.50	.15
343 Alfonso Soriano	.50	.15
344 Drew Henson	.30	.09
345 Erick Almonte	.30	.09
346 Rondell White	.30	.09
347 Christian Parker	.30	.09
348 Joe Torre MG Yankees	.75	.23
349 Nick Johnson	.30	.09
350 Raul Mondesi	.30	.09
351 Brandon Claussen	.30	.09
352 Reggie Jackson Yankees	.75	.23
353 Roger Clemens Yankees	1.50	.45
354 Don Mattingly	3.00	.90
355 Jason Giambi	.30	.09
356 Adrian Hernandez	.30	.09
357 Jeff Weaver	.30	.09
358 Mike Mussina	.50	.15
359 Brett Jodie	.30	.09
360 David Wells	.30	.09
361 Enos Slaughter Yankees	.50	.15
362 Whitey Ford	.75	.23
363 Eric Chavez	.30	.09
364 Miguel Tejada	.30	.09
365 Barry Zito	.30	.09
366 Bert Snow	.30	.09
367 Rickey Henderson A's	.75	.23
368 Juan Pena	.30	.09
369 Terrence Long	.30	.09
370 Dennis Eckersley A's	.50	.15
371 Mark Ellis	.30	.09
372 Tim Hudson	.30	.09
373 Jose Canseco	1.25	.35
374 Reggie Jackson A's	.75	.23
375 Mark Mulder	.30	.09
376 David Justice	.30	.09
377 Jermaine Dye	.30	.09
378 Brett Myers	.30	.09
379 Lenny Dykstra	.50	.15
380 Vicente Padilla	.30	.09
381 Bobby Abreu	.30	.09
382 Pat Burrell	.30	.09
383 Jorge Padilla	.30	.09
384 Jeremy Giambi	.30	.09
385 Mike Lieberthal	.30	.09
386 Anderson Machado	.30	.09
387 Marlon Byrd	.30	.09
388 Bud Smith	.30	.09
389 Eric Valent	.30	.09
390 Elio Serrano	.30	.09
391 Jimmy Rollins	.30	.09
392 Brandon Duckworth	.30	.09
393 Robin Roberts	.50	.15
394 Marlon Anderson	.30	.09
395 Robert Person	.30	.09
396 Johnny Estrada	.30	.09
397 Mike Schmidt	3.00	.90
398 Eric Junge	.30	.09
399 Jason Michaels	.30	.09
400 Steve Carlton	.50	.15
401 Placido Polanco	.30	.09
402 John Grabow	.30	.09
403 Tomas De La Rosa	.30	.09
404 Tike Redman	.30	.09
405 Willie Stargell	.75	.23
406 Dave Williams	.30	.09
407 John Candelaria	.30	.09
408 Jack Wilson	.30	.09
409 Matt Guerrier	.30	.09
410 Jason Kendall	.30	.09
411 Josh Fogg	.30	.09
412 Aramis Ramirez	.30	.09
413 Dave Parker	.50	.15
414 Roberto Clemente	2.50	.75
415 Kip Wells	.30	.09
416 Brian Giles	.30	.09
417 Honus Wagner	1.25	.35
418 Ramon Vazquez	.30	.09
419 Oliver Perez	.30	.09
420 Ryan Klesko	.30	.09

421 Brian Lawrence .30 .09
422 Ben Howard .30 .09
423 Ozzie Smith Padres 2.00 .60
424 Dennis Tankersley .30 .09
425 Tony Gwynn 1.00 .30
426 Sean Burroughs .30 .09
427 Xavier Nady .30 .09
428 Phil Nevin .30 .09
429 Trevor Hoffman .30 .09
430 Jake Peavy .30 .09
431 Cody Ransom .30 .09
432 Kenny Lofton .30 .09
433 Mel Ott .75 .23
434 Tsuyoshi Shinjo .30 .09
435 Deivis Santos .30 .09
436 Rich Aurilia .30 .09
437 Will Clark Giants 1.25 .35
438 Pedro Feliz .30 .09
439 J.T. Snow .30 .09
440 Robb Nen .30 .09
441 Carlos Valderrama .30 .09
442 Willie McCovey .50 .15
443 Jeff Kent .30 .09
444 Orlando Cepeda .50 .15
445 Barry Bonds 2.00 .60
446 Alex Rodriguez M's 1.25 .35
447 Allan Simpson .30 .09
448 Antonio Perez .30 .09
449 Edgar Martinez .50 .15
450 Freddy Garcia .30 .09
451 Chris Snelling .30 .09
452 Matt Thornton .30 .09
453 Kazuhiro Sasaki .30 .09
454 Harold Reynolds .50 .15
455 Randy Johnson M's .75 .23
456 Bret Boone .30 .09
457 Rafael Soriano .30 .09
458 Luis Ugueto .30 .09
459 Ken Griffey Jr. M's 1.25 .35
460 Ichiro Suzuki 1.25 .35
461 Jamie Moyer .30 .09
462 Joel Pineiro .30 .09
463 Jeff Cirillo .30 .09
464 John Olerud .30 .09
465 Mike Cameron .30 .09
466 Ruben Sierra .30 .09
467 Mark McLemore .30 .09
468 Carlos Guillen .30 .09
469 Dan Wilson .30 .09
470 Shigetoshi Hasegawa .30 .09
471 Ben Davis .30 .09
472 Ozzie Smith Cards 2.00 .60
473 Matt Morris .30 .09
474 Edgar Renteria .30 .09
475 Les Walrond .30 .09
476 Albert Pujols 1.50 .45
477 Stan Musial 2.00 .60
478 J.D. Drew .30 .09
479 Josh Pearce .30 .09
480 Enos Slaughter Cards .50 .15
481 Jason Simontacchi .30 .09
482 Jeremy Lambert .30 .09
483 Tino Martinez .50 .15
484 Rogers Hornsby 1.25 .35
485 Rick Ankiel .30 .09
486 Jim Edmonds .30 .09
487 Scott Rolen .75 .23
488 Kevin Joseph .30 .09
489 Fernando Vina .30 .09
490 Jason Isringhausen .30 .09
491 Lou Brock .75 .23
492 Joe Torre Cards .75 .23
493 Bob Gibson .75 .23
494 Chuck Finley .30 .09
495 So Taguchi .30 .09
496 Ben Grieve .30 .09
497 Toby Hall .30 .09
498 Brent Abernathy .30 .09
499 Brandon Backe .30 .09
500 Felix Escalona .30 .09
501 Matt White .30 .09
502 Randy Winn .30 .09
503 Carl Crawford .30 .09
504 Dewon Brazelton .30 .09
505 Joe Kennedy .30 .09
506 Wade Boggs D-Rays .75 .23
507 Aubrey Huff .30 .09
508 Alex Rodriguez Rangers 1.25 .35
509 Ivan Rodriguez .75 .23
510 Will Clark Rangers 1.25 .35
511 Hank Blalock .50 .15
512 Travis Hughes .30 .09
513 Travis Hafner .30 .09
514 Ryan Ludwick .30 .09
515 Doug Davis .30 .09
516 Juan Gonzalez .50 .15
517 Jason Hart .30 .09
518 Mark Teixeira .30 .09
519 Nolan Ryan Rangers 3.00 .90
520 Rafael Palmeiro .50 .15
521 Kevin Mench .30 .09
522 Chan Ho Park .30 .09
523 Kenny Rogers .30 .09
524 Rusty Greer .30 .09
525 Michael Young .50 .15
526 Carlos Delgado .30 .09
527 Vernon Wells .30 .09
528 Orlando Hudson .30 .09
529 Shannon Stewart .30 .09
530 Joe Carter .50 .15
531 Chris Baker .30 .09
532 Eric Hinske .30 .09
533 Corey Thurman .30 .09
534 Josh Phelps .30 .09
535 Reed Johnson .30 .09
536 Brian Bowles .30 .09
537 Roy Halladay .30 .09
538 Jose Cruz Jr. .30 .09
539 Kelvim Escobar .30 .09
540 Chris Carpenter .30 .09
541 Rickie Weeks RC 1.50 .45
542 Hideki Matsui RC 2.00 .60
543 Ramon Nivar RC .60 .18
544 Adam Loewen RC .60 .18
545 Brandon Webb RC .60 .18
546 Dan Haren RC .50 .15
547 Delmon Young RC 2.00 .60
548 Ryan Wagner RC .40 .12

2003 Donruss Team Heroes Autographs

Randomly inserted into packs, this is a partial parallel to the Team Heroes set. Cards 541-548 were randomly seeded into packs of DLP Rookies and Traded. Each player signed a different amount of cards for this set and that information is noted next to the player's name in our checklist. It's important to note, though the manufacturer did publicly release print runs for all cards within this set, only those cards prtoduced in quantities of 100 or fewer copies actually carry foil serial-numbering on front. For those cards with a stated print run of 25 or fewer, no pricing is provided due to market scarcity. This set includes the first ever certified autographs for ESPN announcer Harold Reynolds and pitcher John Candelaria.

Nm-Mt Ex-Mt
2 Steve Green/25
3 Rod Carew Angels/10
4 Alfredo Amezaga/250 10.00 3.00
5 Reggie Jackson Angels/5
7 Nolan Ryan Angels/10
10 Darin Erstad/5
11 Elpidio Guzman/100 15.00 4.50
14 Troy Glaus/15
15 Doug Devore/122 15.00 4.50
20 Curt Schilling/5
25 Luis Gonzalez/5
28 Dale Murphy/15
35 Trey Hodges/250 10.00 3.00
36 Chipper Jones/10
37 Gary Sheffield/10
38 Billy Sylvester/250 10.00 3.00
39 Tom Glavine/15
41 Cory Aldridge/250 10.00 3.00
42 Greg Maddux Braves/5
43 John Ennis/25
45 Horacio Ramirez/200 10.00 3.00
46 Derrick Lewis/250 10.00 3.00
47 Marcus Giles/200 15.00 4.50
49 Wilson Betemit/75 15.00 4.50
50 Andruw Jones/15
51 Josh Towers/110 15.00 4.50
52 Ed Rogers/250 10.00 3.00
53 Kris Foster/250 10.00 3.00
54 Brooks Robinson/20
55 Cal Ripken/5
56 Brian Roberts/250 10.00 3.00
57 Luis Rivera/25
59 Geronimo Gil/60 15.00 4.50
60 Erik Bedard/250 10.00 3.00
61 Jim Palmer/5
62 Jay Gibbons/181 10.00 3.00
64 Larry Bigbie/100 25.00 7.50
65 Eddie Murray/10
66 Hoyt Wilhelm/25
67 Bobby Doerr/25
68 Pedro Martinez/5
69 Roger Clemens Red Sox/10
70 Nomar Garciaparra/10
72 Dennis Eckersley Red Sox/25
75 Wade Boggs Red Sox/10
76 Cliff Floyd/25
77 Casey Fossum/250 10.00 3.00
79 Fred Lynn/50 25.00 7.50
80 Rickey Henderson Red Sox/10
81 Juan Diaz/250 10.00 3.00
82 Manny Ramirez/5
83 Carlton Fisk Red Sox/5
84 Jorge De La Rosa/250 10.00 3.00
95 Ryne Sandberg/15
99 Fergie Jenkins/50 25.00 7.50
101 Francis Beltran/250 10.00 3.00
102 Greg Maddux Cubs/5
103 Nate Frese/250 10.00 3.00
104 Andre Dawson Cubs/25
105 Carlos Zambrano/150 25.00 7.50
106 Steve Smyth/25
107 Ernie Banks/15
108 Will Ohman/50 15.00 4.50
110 Bobby Hill/150 10.00 3.00
113 Corey Patterson/25
115 Mark Prior/50 80.00 24.00
116 Juan Cruz/50 15.00 4.50
117 Ron Santo/25
118 Billy Williams/10
121 Carlton Fisk White Sox/5
122 Joe Crede/250 10.00 3.00
123 Magglio Ordonez/25
124 Frank Thomas/5
125 Joe Borchard/250 10.00 3.00
127 Luis Aparicio/50 25.00 7.50
128 Willie Harris/129 15.00 4.50
129 Kyle Kane/100 15.00 4.50
131 Matt Ginter/250 10.00 3.00
132 Carlos Lee/50 25.00 7.50
133 Mark Buehrle/50 25.00 7.50
134 Adam Dunn/25
135 Eric Davis/75 25.00 7.50
136 Johnny Bench/10
137 Joe Morgan/15
138 Austin Kearns/71 25.00 7.50
139 Barry Larkin/15
141 Luis Pineda/25
142 Corky Miller/250 10.00 3.00
143 Brandon Larson/143 10.00 3.00
144 Wily Mo Pena/250 15.00 4.50
146 Tom Seaver Reds/15
147 Luke Hudson/50 15.00 4.50
148 Sean Casey/25
149 Tony Perez/50 25.00 7.50
156 Cliff Lee/250 10.00 3.00
161 Earl Snyder/250 10.00 3.00
165 Ricardo Rodriguez/250 10.00 3.00
166 Victor Martinez/200 25.00 7.50
167 Alex Herrera/250 10.00 3.00
170 C.C. Sabathia/20
171 Alex Escobar/125 15.00 4.50
172 Brian Tallet/250 10.00 3.00
173 Jim Thome/15
174 Rene Reyes/250 10.00 3.00
175 Juan Uribe/33
176 Jason Romano/50 15.00 4.50
177 Juan Pierre/66 25.00 7.50
178 Jason Jennings/250 10.00 3.00
179 Jose Ortiz/250 10.00 3.00
181 Cam Esslinger/250 10.00 3.00
182 Todd Helton/10
184 Jack Cust/250 10.00 3.00
185 Jack Morris Tigers/50 25.00 7.50
186 Mike Rivera/250 10.00 3.00
188 Fernando Rodney/250 10.00 3.00
189 Al Kaline/15
190 Carlos Pena/96 15.00 4.50
191 Alan Trammell/25
192 Mike Maroth/250 10.00 3.00
193 Adam Pettyjohn/250 10.00 3.00
194 David Espinosa/250 10.00 3.00
195 Adam Bernero/250 10.00 3.00
196 Franklyn German/250 10.00 3.00
197 Robert Fick/50 15.00 4.50
198 Andres Torres/250 10.00 3.00
201 Pablo Ozuna/250 10.00 3.00
203 Josh Beckett/20
205 Wilson Valdez/250 10.00 3.00
207 Abraham Nunez/250 10.00 3.00
209 Jose Cueto/25
211 Jeff Bagwell/10
212 Kirk Saarloos/250 10.00 3.00
213 Craig Biggio/10
214 Rodrigo Rosario/250 10.00 3.00
215 Roy Oswalt/50 25.00 7.50
216 John Buck/25
217 Tim Redding/250 10.00 3.00
218 Morgan Ensberg/250 10.00 3.00
219 Richard Hidalgo/100 15.00 4.50
220 Wade Miller/200 10.00 3.00
221 Lance Berkman/25
222 Raul Chavez/125 25.00 7.50
223 Carlos Hernandez/250 10.00 3.00
224 Greg Miller/90 15.00 4.50
225 Tom Shearn/25
226 Jason Lane/250 10.00 3.00
227 Nolan Ryan Astros/10
233 Mike Sweeney/25
234 Angel Berroa/200 10.00 3.00
235 George Brett/10
236 Brad Voyles/200 10.00 3.00
237 Brandon Berger/250 10.00 3.00
238 Chad Durbin/250 10.00 3.00
239 Alexis Gomez/165 10.00 3.00
240 Jeremy Affeldt/250 10.00 3.00
241 Bo Jackson/5
242 Dee Brown/50 15.00 4.50
243 Tony Cogan/250 10.00 3.00
244 Carlos Beltran/25
248 Cesar Izturis/200 10.00 3.00
249 Duke Snider/5
253 Steve Garvey/75 40.00 12.00
256 Kevin Brown/15
258 Joe Thurston/108 15.00 4.50
259 Carlos Garcia/100 15.00 4.50
260 Shawn Green/10
261 Paul Lo Duca/50 25.00 7.50
262 Kazuhisa Ishii/15
263 Victor Alvarez/250 10.00 3.00
265 Don Sutton/50 25.00 7.50
266 Orel Hershiser/15
268 Adrian Beltre/25
275 Paul Molitor/10
277 Takahito Nomura/100 25.00 7.50
278 Nick Neugebauer/25
279 Jose Mieses/50 15.00 4.50
280 Richie Sexson/5
281 Matt Childers/50 15.00 4.50
283 Ben Sheets/100 25.00 7.50
284 Brian Mallette/250 10.00 3.00
286 Robin Yount/15
287 Jeff Deardorff/100 15.00 4.50
288 Luis Rivas/200 15.00 4.50
289 Harmon Killebrew/15
290 Michael Cuddyer/250 10.00 3.00
291 Torii Hunter/100 25.00 7.50
292 Kevin Frederick/25
293 Adam Johnson/25
294 Jack Morris Twins/50 25.00 7.50
295 Rod Carew Twins/10
296 Kirby Puckett/10
297 Joe Mays/5
305 Jose Vidro/50 15.00 4.50
306 Claudio Vargas/150 10.00 3.00
307 Gary Carter Expos/20
308 Andre Dawson Expos/25
309 Henry Mateo/250 10.00 3.00
310 Andres Galarraga 15
311 Zach Day/250 10.00 3.00
313 Endy Chavez/250 10.00 3.00
314 Javier Vazquez/50 25.00 7.50
316 Vladimir Guerrero/15
319 Timo Perez/29
321 Gary Carter/20
323 Dwight Gooden/75
325 Roberto Alomar/15
327 Nolan Ryan Mets/10
329 Ryan Jamison/25
330 Satoru Komiyama/25
332 Tom Seaver Mets/15
340 Yogi Berra/15
341 Phil Rizzuto/15
342 Bernie Williams/10
343 Alfonso Soriano/25
344 Drew Henson/50 40.00 12.00
345 Erick Almonte/250 10.00 3.00
347 Christian Parker/200 10.00 3.00
348 Joe Torre Yankees/5
351 Brandon Claussen/250 10.00 3.00
352 Reggie Jackson Yankees/5
353 Roger Clemens Yankees/10
354 Don Mattingly/15
356 Adrian Hernandez/200 10.00 3.00
358 Mike Mussina/5
359 Brett Jodie/250 10.00 3.00
363 Eric Chavez/25
364 Miguel Tejada/20
365 Barry Zito/25
366 Bert Snow/250 10.00 3.00
367 Rickey Henderson A's/10
368 Juan Pena/250 10.00 3.00
369 Terrence Long/25
370 Dennis Eckersley A's/25
371 Mark Ellis/150 10.00 3.00
372 Tim Hudson/15
373 Jose Canseco/15
374 Reggie Jackson A's/5
375 Mark Mulder/25
376 David Justice/5
377 Jermaine Dye/15
379 Lenny Dykstra/75 25.00 7.50
381 Bobby Abreu/20
383 Jorge Padilla/250 10.00 3.00
384 Jeremy Giambi/100 15.00 4.50
386 Anderson Machado/250 10.00 3.00
387 Marlon Byrd/200 10.00 3.00
388 Bud Smith/125 15.00 4.50
389 Eric Valent/100 15.00 4.50
390 Elio Serrano/250 10.00 3.00
392 Brandon Duckworth/100 15.00 4.50
395 Robert Person/100 15.00 4.50
396 Johnny Estrada/209 15.00 4.50
397 Mike Schmidt/10
398 Eric Junge/250 10.00 3.00
399 Jason Michaels/221 10.00 3.00
400 Steve Carlton/20
402 John Grabow/250 10.00 3.00
403 Tomas De La Rosa/25
404 Tike Redman/25
406 Dave Williams/250 10.00 3.00
407 John Candelaria/100 25.00 7.50
408 Jack Wilson/250 15.00 4.50
409 Matt Guerrier/200 10.00 3.00
412 Aramis Ramirez/50 25.00 7.50
413 Dave Parker/50 25.00 7.50
415 Kip Wells/250 10.00 3.00
416 Brian Giles/25
418 Ramon Vazquez/200 10.00 3.00
419 Oliver Perez/150 15.00 4.50
420 Ryan Klesko/15
421 Brian Lawrence/250 10.00 3.00
422 Ben Howard/250 10.00 3.00
423 Ozzie Smith Padres/15
425 Tony Gwynn/15
426 Sean Burroughs/25
427 Xavier Nady/50 15.00 4.50
431 Cody Ransom/100 15.00 4.50
432 Kenny Lofton/15
435 Deivis Santos/100 15.00 4.50
436 Rich Aurilia/5
437 Will Clark Giants/10
438 Pedro Feliz/50 15.00 4.50
441 Carlos Valderrama/250 10.00 3.00
442 Willie McCovey/15
444 Orlando Cepeda/25
446 Alex Rodriguez M's/5
447 Allan Simpson/250 10.00 3.00
448 Antonio Perez/250 10.00 3.00
449 Edgar Martinez/15
450 Freddy Garcia/5
451 Chris Snelling/100 15.00 4.50
452 Matt Thornton/200 10.00 3.00
454 Harold Reynolds/100 25.00 7.50
457 Rafael Soriano/250 10.00 3.00
458 Luis Ugueto/50 15.00 4.50
472 Ozzie Smith Cards/15
475 Les Walrond/50 15.00 4.50
476 Albert Pujols/15
477 Stan Musial/15
478 J.D. Drew/10
479 Josh Pearce/200 10.00 3.00
482 Jeremy Lambert/25
485 Rick Ankiel/15
487 Scott Rolen/15
491 Lou Brock/15
492 Joe Torre Cards/10
497 Toby Hall/200 10.00 3.00
498 Brent Abernathy/250 10.00 3.00
499 Brandon Backe/250 15.00 4.50
500 Felix Escalona/50 15.00 4.50
501 Matt White/25
504 Dewon Brazelton/100 15.00 4.50
505 Joe Kennedy/200 10.00 3.00
506 Wade Boggs D-Rays/10
507 Aubrey Huff/100 25.00 7.50
508 Alex Rodriguez Rangers/5
509 Ivan Rodriguez/5
510 Will Clark Rangers/15
511 Hank Blalock/25
512 Travis Hughes/200 10.00 3.00
513 Travis Hafner/10
514 Ryan Ludwick/250 10.00 3.00
515 Doug Davis/250 10.00 3.00
516 Juan Gonzalez/5
517 Jason Hart/123 15.00 4.50
518 Mark Teixeira/50 40.00 12.00
519 Nolan Ryan Rangers/10
520 Rafael Palmeiro/10
521 Kevin Mench/250 10.00 3.00
528 Orlando Hudson/120 15.00 4.50
529 Shannon Stewart/25
530 Joe Carter/20
531 Chris Baker/200 10.00 3.00
532 Eric Hinske/250 10.00 3.00
533 Corey Thurman/250 10.00 3.00
534 Josh Phelps/150 10.00 3.00
535 Reed Johnson/250 10.00 3.00
536 Brian Bowles/250 10.00 3.00
541 Rickie Weeks/10
543 Ramon Nivar/100 20.00 6.00
544 Adam Loewen/100 25.00 7.50
545 Brandon Webb/100 25.00 7.50
546 Dan Haren/100 20.00 6.00
547 Delmon Young/25
548 Ryan Wagner/100 15.00 4.50

2003 Donruss Team Heroes Glossy

Issued one per pack, this is a parallel to the Donruss Team Heroes set. These cards can be differentiated from the regular cards as the fronts have a glossy sheen.

Nm-Mt Ex-Mt
*ACTIVE PLAYERS: 1.25X TO 3X BASIC
*RETIRED PLAYERS: 2X TO 5X BASIC

2003 Donruss Team Heroes Stat Line

Randomly inserted in packs, this is a parallel to the Donruss Team Heroes set. Cards 541-548 were randomly inserted into packs of DLP Rookies and Traded. Each card is sequentially numbered to a different quantity depending on the stat involved in producing the card. If the card was issued to a stated print run of 25 of fewer for a player active at time of issue or 36 or fewer for a player retired at time of issue, we are not providing pricing due to market scarcity.

Nm-Mt Ex-Mt
*ACTIVE P/R b/wn 201-250: 2.5X TO 6X
*ACTIVE P/R b/wn 151-200: 3X TO 8X
*ACTIVE P/R b/wn 121-150: 3X TO 8X
*ACTIVE P/R b/wn 81-120: 4X TO 10X
*ACTIVE P/R b/wn 66-80: 5X TO 12X.
*ACTIVE P/R b/wn 51-65: 5X TO 12X.
*ACTIVE P/R b/wn 36-50: 6X TO 15X.
*ACTIVE P/R b/wn 26-35: 8X TO 20X.
*RETIRED P/R b/wn 201-250: 2.5X TO 6X
*RETIRED P/R b/wn 151-200: 3X TO 8X
*RETIRED P/R b/wn 121-150: 3X TO 8X
*RETIRED P/R b/wn 81-120: 4X TO 10X
*RETIRED P/R b/wn 66-80: 5X TO 12X
*RETIRED P/R b/wn 51-65: 5X TO 12X
*RETIRED P/R b/wn 36-50: 6X TO 15X
*RC's P/R b/wn 36-50: 6X TO 15X
*RC's P/R b/wn 26-35: 8X TO 20X
541-548 RANDOM IN DLP R/T PACKS
1 Adam Kennedy/148 2.50 .75
2 Steve Green/4
3 Rod Carew Angels/38 12.00 3.60
4 Alfredo Amezaga/7
5 Reggie Jackson Angels/39 12.00 3.60
6 Jarrod Washburn/139 2.50 .75
7 Nolan Ryan Angels/61 40.00 12.00
8 Tim Salmon/138 4.00 1.20
9 Garret Anderson/123 2.50 .75
10 Darin Erstad/177 2.50 .75
11 Elpidio Guzman/112 3.00 .90
12 David Eckstein/178 2.50 .75
13 Troy Percival/68 4.00 1.20
14 Troy Glaus/111 3.00 .90
15 Doug Devore/114 3.00 .90
16 Tony Womack/160 2.50 .75
17 Matt Williams/56 4.00 1.20
18 Junior Spivey/162 2.50 .75
19 Mark Grace/75 6.00 1.80
20 Curt Schilling/23
21 Erubiel Durazo/58 4.00 1.20
22 Craig Counsell/123 2.50 .75
23 Byung-Hyun Kim/92 3.00 .90
24 Randy Johnson D'backs/24
25 Luis Gonzalez/151 2.50 .75
26 John Smoltz/85 5.00 1.50
27 Tim Spooneybarger/51 4.00 1.20
28 Dale Murphy/39 20.00 6.00
29 Warren Spahn/63 10.00 3.00
30 Jason Marquis/84 3.00 .90
31 Kevin Millwood/178 2.50 .75
32 Javy Lopez/81 3.00 .90
33 Vinny Castilla/126 2.50 .75
34 Julio Franco/96 3.00 .90
35 Trey Hodges/6
36 Chipper Jones/100 8.00 2.40
37 Gary Sheffield/84 3.00 .90
38 Billy Sylvester/53 4.00 1.20
39 Tom Glavine/127 4.00 1.20
40 Rafael Furcal/175 2.50 .75
41 Cory Aldridge/17
42 Greg Maddux Braves/118 12.00 3.60
43 John Ennis/1
44 Wes Helms/51 4.00 1.20
45 Horacio Ramirez/69 4.00 1.20
46 Derrick Lewis/61 4.00 1.20
47 Marcus Giles/49 5.00 1.50
48 Eddie Mathews/47 20.00 6.00
49 Wilson Betemit/89 3.00 .90
50 Andruw Jones/148 2.50 .75
51 Josh Towers/13
52 Ed Rogers/5
53 Kris Foster/14
54 Brooks Robinson/16
55 Cal Ripken/44 60.00 18.00
56 Brian Roberts/29 6.00 1.80
57 Luis Rivera/1
58 Rodrigo Lopez/136 2.50 .75
59 Geronimo Gil/98 3.00 .90
60 Erik Bedard/1
61 Jim Palmer/20
62 Jay Gibbons/121 2.50 .75
63 Travis Driskill/78 4.00 1.20
64 Larry Bigbie/3
65 Eddie Murray/124 10.00 3.00
66 Hoyt Wilhelm/143 4.00 1.20
67 Bobby Doerr/27
68 Pedro Martinez/20
69 Roger Clemens Red Sox/20
70 Nomar Garciaparra/24
71 Trot Nixon/136 2.50 .75
72 Dennis Eckersley Red Sox/20
73 John Burkett/124 2.50 .75
74 Tim Wakefield/134 2.50 .75
75 Wade Boggs Red Sox/24
76 Cliff Floyd/150 2.50 .75
77 Casey Fossum/101 3.00 .90
78 Johnny Damon/178 6.00 1.80
79 Fred Lynn/16
80 Rickey Henderson Red Sox/8
81 Juan Diaz/2
82 Manny Ramirez/107 5.00 1.50
83 Carlton Fisk Red Sox/22
84 Jorge De La Rosa/110 3.00 .90
85 Shea Hillenbrand/186 2.50 .75
86 Derek Lowe/21
87 Jason Varitek/124 4.00 1.20
88 Carlos Baerga/52 4.00 1.20
89 Freddy Sanchez/3
90 Ugueth Urbina/71 4.00 1.20
91 Rey Sanchez/102 3.00 .90
92 Josh Hancock/6
93 Tony Clark/57 4.00 1.20
94 Dustin Hermanson/13
95 Ryne Sandberg/123 20.00 6.00
96 Fred McGriff/143 4.00 1.20
97 Alex Gonzalez/127 2.50 .75

98 Mark Bellhorn/115 3.00 .90
99 Fergie Jenkins/20
100 Jon Lieber/87 3.00 .90
101 Francis Beltran/11
102 Greg Maddux Cubs/20
103 Nate Frese/24
104 Andre Dawson Cubs/49 12.00 3.60
105 Carlos Zambrano/93 3.00 .90
106 Steve Smyth/16
107 Ernie Banks/143 10.00 3.00
108 Will Ohman/12
109 Kerry Wood/12
110 Bobby Hill/20
111 Moises Alou/133 2.50 .75
112 Hee Seop Choi/9
113 Corey Patterson/150 2.50 .75
114 Sammy Sosa/49 20.00 6.00
115 Mark Prior/6
116 Juan Cruz/81 3.00 .90
117 Ron Santo/5
118 Billy Williams/137 4.00 1.20
119 Antonio Alfonseca/61 4.00 1.20
120 Matt Clement/215 2.00 .60
121 Carlton Fisk White Sox/107 8.00 2.40
122 Joe Crede/57 4.00 1.20
123 Magglio Ordonez/38 5.00 1.50
124 Frank Thomas/132 6.00 1.80
125 Joe Borchard/5
126 Royce Clayton/86 3.00 .90
127 Luis Aparicio/92 5.00 1.50
128 Willie Harris/14
129 Kyle Kane/9
130 Paul Konerko/173 2.50 .75
131 Matt Ginter/37 5.00 1.50
132 Carlos Lee/130 2.50 .75
133 Mark Buehrle/19
134 Adam Dunn/26 10.00 3.00
135 Eric Davis/27 10.00 3.00
136 Johnny Bench/40 20.00 6.00
137 Joe Morgan/17
138 Austin Kearns/13
139 Barry Larkin/124 4.00 1.20
140 Ken Griffey Jr. Reds/52 15.00 4.50
141 Luis Pineda/31 6.00 1.80
142 Corky Miller/29 6.00 1.80
143 Brandon Larson/14
144 Wily Mo Pena/4
145 Lance Davis/78 4.00 1.20
146 Tom Seaver Reds/61 10.00 3.00
147 Luke Hudson/7
148 Sean Casey/111 3.00 .90
149 Tony Perez/79 6.00 1.80
150 Todd Walker/183 2.50 .75
151 Aaron Boone/146 2.50 .75
152 Jose Rijo/38 5.00 1.50
153 Ryan Dempster/151 2.50 .75
154 Danny Graves/58 4.00 1.20
155 Matt Lawton/98 3.00 .90
156 Cliff Lee/6
157 Ryan Drese/102 3.00 .90
158 Danys Baez/130 2.50 .75
159 Einar Diaz/66 4.00 1.20
160 Milton Bradley/81 3.00 .90
161 Earl Snyder/11
162 Ellis Burks/156 2.50 .75
163 Lou Boudreau/46 8.00 2.40
164 Bob Feller/27
165 Ricardo Rodriguez/24
166 Victor Martinez/9
167 Alex Herrera/5
168 Omar Vizquel/160 4.00 1.20
169 David Elder/23
170 C.C. Sabathia/149 2.50 .75
171 Alex Escobar/10
172 Brian Tallet/5
173 Jim Thome/52 10.00 3.00
174 Rene Reyes/133 2.50 .75
175 Juan Uribe/136 2.50 .75
176 Jason Romano/23
177 Juan Pierre/170 2.50 .75
178 Jason Jennings/16
179 Jose Ortiz/48 5.00 1.50
180 Larry Walker/26 10.00 3.00
181 Cam Esslinger/29 6.00 1.80
182 Todd Helton/30 10.00 3.00
183 Aaron Cook/14
184 Jack Cust/11
185 Jack Morris Tigers/17
186 Mike Rivera/30 6.00 1.80
187 Bobby Higginson/125 2.50 .75
188 Fernando Rodney/10
189 Al Kaline/137 10.00 3.00
190 Carlos Pena/96 3.00 .90
191 Alan Trammell/55 6.00 1.80
192 Mike Maroth/58 4.00 1.20
193 Adam Pettyjohn/40 5.00 1.50
194 David Espinosa/90 3.00 .90
195 Adam Bernero/69 4.00 1.20
196 Franklyn German/6
197 Robert Fick/150 2.50 .75
198 Andres Torres/14
199 Luis Castillo/185 2.50 .75
200 Preston Wilson/124 2.50 .75
201 Pablo Ozuna/13
202 Brad Penny/93 3.00 .90
203 Josh Beckett/6
204 Charles Johnson/53 4.00 1.20
205 Wilson Valdez/98 3.00 .90
206 A.J. Burnett/203 2.00 .60
207 Abraham Nunez/2
208 Mike Lowell/165 2.50 .75
209 Jose Cueto/47 5.00 1.50
210 Jeriome Robertson/6
211 Jeff Bagwell/31 10.00 3.00
212 Kirk Saarloos/54 4.00 1.20
213 Craig Biggio/15
214 Rodrigo Rosario/94 3.00 .90
215 Roy Oswalt/19
216 John Buck/118 3.00 .90
217 Tim Redding/63 4.00 1.20
218 Morgan Ensberg/32 6.00 1.80
219 Richard Hidalgo/91 3.00 .90
220 Wade Miller/144 2.50 .75
221 Lance Berkman/42 5.00 1.50
222 Raul Chavez/1
223 Carlos Hernandez/93 3.00 .90
224 Greg Miller/51 4.00 1.20
225 Tom Shearn/80 4.00 1.20
226 Jason Lane/20
227 Nolan Ryan Astros/38 50.00 15.00
228 Billy Wagner/88 3.00 .90
229 Octavio Dotel/118 3.00 .90
230 Shane Reynolds/47 5.00 1.50
231 Julio Lugo/84 3.00 .90
232 Daryle Ward/125 2.50 .75
233 Mike Sweeney/160 2.50 .75
234 Angel Berroa/17
235 George Brett/45 50.00 15.00
236 Brad Voyles/26 6.00 1.80
237 Brandon Berger/27 6.00 1.80
238 Chad Durbin/5
239 Alexis Gomez/2
240 Jeremy Affeldt/67 4.00 1.20
241 Bo Jackson/32
242 Dee Brown/12
243 Tony Cogan/62 4.00 1.20
244 Carlos Beltran/174 4.00 1.20
245 Joe Randa/155 2.50 .75
246 Pee Wee Reese/33
247 Andy Ashby/107 3.00 .90
248 Cesar Izturis/102 3.00 .90
249 Duke Snider/136 6.00 1.80
250 Mark Grudzielanek/145 2.50 .75
251 Chin-Feng Chen/1
252 Brian Jordan/134 2.50 .75
253 Steve Garvey/115 5.00 1.50
254 Odalis Perez/155 2.50 .75
255 Hideo Nomo/16
256 Kevin Brown/58 4.00 1.20
257 Eric Karros/142 2.50 .75
258 Joe Thurston/6
259 Carlos Garcia/9
260 Shawn Green/42 5.00 1.50
261 Paul Lo Duca/163 2.50 .75
262 Kazuhisa Ishii/14
263 Victor Alvarez/7
264 Eric Gagne/114 8.00 2.40
265 Don Sutton/21
266 Orel Hershiser/59 6.00 1.80
267 Dave Roberts/117 3.00 .90
268 Adrian Beltre/151 4.00 1.20
269 Don Drysdale/58 15.00 4.50
270 Jackie Robinson/39 20.00 6.00
271 Tyler Houston/90 3.00 .90
272 Omar Daal/105 3.00 .90
273 Marquis Grissom/95 3.00 .90
274 Paul Quantrill/53 4.00 1.20
275 Paul Molitor/114 8.00 2.40
276 Jose Hernandez/151 2.50 .75
277 Takahito Nomura/9
278 Nick Neugebauer/47 5.00 1.50
279 Jose Mieses/55 4.00 1.20
280 Richie Sexson/102 3.00 .90
281 Matt Childers/6
282 Bill Hall/7
283 Ben Sheets/170 2.50 .75
284 Brian Mallette/5
285 Geoff Jenkins/59 4.00 1.20
286 Robin Yount/29
287 Jeff Deardorff/108 3.00 .90
288 Luis Rivas/81 3.00 .90
289 Harmon Killebrew/44 20.00 6.00
290 Michael Cuddyer/29 6.00 1.80
291 Torii Hunter/29 6.00 1.80
292 Kevin Frederick/5
293 Adam Johnson/112 3.00 .90
294 Jack Morris Twins/18
295 Rod Carew Twins/128 6.00 1.80
296 Kirby Puckett/31
297 Joe Mays/38 5.00 1.50
298 Jacque Jones/173 2.50 .75
299 Cristian Guzman/170 2.50 .75
300 Kyle Lohse/124 2.50 .75
301 Eric Milton/121 2.50 .75
302 Brad Radke/62 4.00 1.20
303 Doug Mientkiewicz/122 2.50 .75
304 Corey Koskie/131 2.50 .75
305 Jose Vidro/19
306 Claudio Vargas/95 3.00 .90
307 Gary Carter Expos/105 5.00 1.50
308 Andre Dawson Expos/107 8.00 2.40
309 Henry Mateo/4
310 Andres Galarraga/76 4.00 1.20
311 Zach Day/25
312 Bartolo Colon/149 2.50 .75
313 Endy Chavez/37 5.00 1.50
314 Javier Vazquez/179 2.50 .75
315 Michael Barrett/99 3.00 .90
316 Vladimir Guerrero/39 12.00 3.60
317 Orlando Cabrera/148 2.50 .75
318 Al Leiter/172 2.50 .75
319 Timo Perez/131 2.50 .75
320 Rey Ordonez/117 3.00 .90
321 Gary Carter/105 5.00 1.50
322 Armando Benitez/79 4.00 1.20
323 Dwight Gooden/24
324 Pedro Astacio/152 2.50 .75
325 Roberto Alomar/11
326 Edgardo Alfonzo/151 2.50 .75
327 Nolan Ryan Mets/92 30.00 9.00
328 Mo Vaughn/126 2.50 .75
329 Ryan Jamison/90 3.00 .90
330 Satoru Komiyama/33 6.00 1.80
331 Mike Piazza/33 25.00 7.50
332 Tom Seaver Mets/25
333 Jorge Posada/20
334 Derek Jeter/18
335 Babe Ruth/60 40.00 12.00
336 Lou Gehrig/23
337 Andy Pettitte/97 5.00 1.50
338 Mariano Rivera/45 8.00 2.40
339 Robin Ventura/115 3.00 .90
340 Yogi Berra/30
341 Phil Rizzuto/36 12.00 3.60
342 Bernie Williams/19
343 Alfonso Soriano/39 8.00 2.40
344 Drew Henson/1
345 Erick Almonte/97 3.00 .90
346 Rondell White/109 3.00 .90
347 Christian Parker/1
348 Joe Torre Yankees/103 8.00 2.40
349 Nick Johnson/15
350 Raul Mondesi/65 4.00 1.20
351 Brandon Claussen/73 4.00 1.20
352 Reggie Jackson Yankees/5
353 Roger Clemens Yankees/13
354 Don Mattingly/53 40.00 12.00
355 Jason Giambi/41 5.00 1.50
356 Adrian Hernandez/9
357 Jeff Weaver/132 2.50 .75
358 Mike Mussina/18
359 Brett Jodie/14
360 David Wells/137 2.50 .75
361 Enos Slaughter Yankees/148 4.00 1.20
362 Whitey Ford/25
363 Eric Chavez/161 2.50 .75
364 Miguel Tejada/34 6.00 1.80
365 Barry Zito/23
366 Bert Snow/54 4.00 1.20
367 Rickey Henderson A's/108 8.00 2.40
368 Juan Pena/34 6.00 1.80
369 Terrence Long/141 2.50 .75
370 Dennis Eckersley A's/33
371 Mark Ellis/94 3.00 .90
372 Tim Hudson/15
373 Jose Canseco/100 12.00 3.60
374 Reggie Jackson A's/117 8.00 2.40
375 Mark Mulder/19
376 David Justice/106 3.00 .90
377 Jermaine Dye/123 2.50 .75
378 Brett Myers/34 6.00 1.80
379 Lenny Dykstra/19
380 Vicente Padilla/128 2.50 .75
381 Bobby Abreu/20
382 Pat Burrell/37 5.00 1.50
383 Jorge Padilla/124 2.50 .75
384 Jeremy Giambi/81 3.00 .90
385 Mike Lieberthal/133 2.50 .75
386 Anderson Machado/113 3.00 .90
387 Marlon Byrd/8
388 Bud Smith/22
389 Eric Valent/2
390 Elio Serrano/45 5.00 1.50
391 Jimmy Rollins/156 2.50 .75
392 Brandon Duckworth 167 2.50 .75
393 Robin Roberts/28 10.00 3.00
394 Marlon Anderson 139 2.50 .75
395 Robert Person/61 4.00 1.20
396 Johnny Estrada/2
397 Mike Schmidt/30
398 Eric Junge/11
399 Jason Michaels/28 6.00 1.80
400 Steve Carlton/20
401 Placido Polanco/158 2.50 .75
402 John Grabow/97 3.00 .90
403 Tomas De La Rosa/78 4.00 1.20
404 Tike Redman/84 3.00 .90
405 Willie Stargell/48 12.00 3.60
406 Dave Williams/33 6.00 1.80
407 John Candelaria/177 2.50 .75
408 Jack Wilson/133 2.50 .75
409 Matt Guerrier/130 2.50 .75
410 Jason Kendall/154 2.50 .75
411 Josh Fogg/113 3.00 .90
412 Aramis Ramirez/122 2.50 .75
413 Dave Parker/125 4.00 1.20
414 Roberto Clemente/29
415 Kip Wells/134 2.50 .75
416 Brian Giles/148 2.50 .75
417 Honus Wagner/61 15.00 4.50
418 Ramon Vazquez/116 3.00 .90
419 Oliver Perez/94 3.00 .90
420 Ryan Klesko/162 2.50 .75
421 Brian Lawrence/149 2.50 .75
422 Ben Howard/10
423 Ozzie Smith Padres/40 30.00 9.00
424 Dennis Tankersley/39 5.00 1.50
425 Tony Gwynn/49 15.00 4.50
426 Sean Burroughs/52 4.00 1.20
427 Xavier Nady/136 2.50 .75
428 Phil Nevin/116 3.00 .90
429 Trevor Hoffman/69 4.00 1.20
430 Jake Peavy/90 3.00 .90
431 Cody Ransom/2
432 Kenny Lofton/139 2.50 .75
433 Mel Ott/151 6.00 1.80
434 Tsuyoshi Shinjo/86 3.00 .90
435 Deivis Santos/152 2.50 .75
436 Rich Aurilia/138 2.50 .75
437 Will Clark Giants/116 12.00 3.60
438 Pedro Feliz/37 5.00 1.50
439 J.T. Snow/104 3.00 .90
440 Robb Nen/81 3.00 .90
441 Carlos Valderrama/127 2.50 .75
442 Willie McCovey/126 4.00 1.20
443 Jeff Kent/37 5.00 1.50
444 Orlando Cepeda/96 5.00 1.50
445 Barry Bonds/46 30.00 9.00
446 Alex Rodriguez M's/46 20.00 6.00
447 Allan Simpson/99 3.00 .90
448 Antonio Perez/62 4.00 1.20
449 Edgar Martinez/91 5.00 1.50
450 Freddy Garcia/181 2.50 .75
451 Chris Snelling/4
452 Matt Thornton/44 5.00 1.50
453 Kazuhiro Sasaki/73 4.00 1.20
454 Harold Reynolds/60 6.00 1.80
455 Randy Johnson M's/53 10.00 3.00
456 Bret Boone/169 2.50 .75
457 Rafael Soriano/32 6.00 1.80
458 Luis Ugueto/19
459 Ken Griffey Jr. M's/56 15.00 4.50
460 Ichiro Suzuki/51 15.00 4.50
461 Jamie Moyer/147 2.50 .75
462 Joel Pineiro/136 2.50 .75
463 Jeff Cirillo/121 2.50 .75
464 John Olerud/166 2.50 .75
465 Mike Cameron/130 2.50 .75
466 Ruben Sierra/113 3.00 .90
467 Mark McLemore/91 3.00 .90
468 Carlos Guillen/124 2.50 .75
469 Dan Wilson /106 3.00 .90
470 Shigetoshi Hasegawa/39 5.00 1.50
471 Ben Davis/59 4.00 1.20
472 Ozzie Smith Cards/57 25.00 7.50
473 Matt Morris/171 2.50 .75
474 Edgar Renteria/166 2.50 .75
475 Les Walrond/142 2.50 .75
476 Albert Pujols/34 30.00 9.00
477 Stan Musial/31
478 J.D. Drew/107 3.00 .90
479 Josh Pearce/1
480 Enos Slaughter Cards/130 4.00 1.20
481 Jason Simontacchi/72 4.00 1.20
482 Jeremy Lambert/21
483 Tino Martinez/134 4.00 1.20
484 Rogers Hornsby/42 20.00 6.00
485 Rick Ankiel/27 6.00 1.80
486 Jim Edmonds/148 2.50 .75
487 Scott Rolen/14
488 Kevin Joseph/2
489 Fernando Vina/168 2.50 .75
490 Jason Isringhausen/68 4.00 1.20
491 Lou Brock/52 10.00 3.00
492 Joe Torre Cards/100 8.00 2.40
493 Bob Gibson/22
494 Chuck Finley/174 2.50 .75
495 So Taguchi/6
496 Ben Grieve/121 2.50 .75
497 Toby Hall/85 3.00 .90
498 Brent Abernathy/112 3.00 .90
499 Brandon Backe/6
500 Felix Escalona/34 6.00 1.80
501 Matt White/58 4.00 1.20
502 Randy Winn/181 2.50 .75
503 Carl Crawford/67 4.00 1.20
504 Dewon Brazelton/5
505 Joe Kennedy/109 3.00 .90
506 Wade Boggs D-Rays/60 10.00 3.00
507 Aubrey Huff/142 2.50 .75
508 Alex Rodriguez Rangers/57 15.00 4.50
509 Ivan Rodriguez/19
510 Will Clark Rangers/102 12.00 3.60
511 Hank Blalock/31 10.00 3.00
512 Travis Hughes/137 2.50 .75
513 Travis Hafner/15
514 Ryan Ludwick/19
515 Doug Davis/28 6.00 1.80
516 Juan Gonzalez/78 6.00 1.80
517 Jason Hart/4
518 Mark Teixeira/69 4.00 1.20
519 Nolan Ryan Rangers/51 40.00 12.00
520 Rafael Palmeiro/43 8.00 2.40
521 Kevin Mench/95 3.00 .90
522 Chan Ho Park/9
523 Kenny Rogers/107 3.00 .90
524 Rusty Greer/59 4.00 1.20
525 Michael Young/150 4.00 1.20
526 Carlos Delgado/33 6.00 1.80
527 Vernon Wells/167 2.50 .75
528 Orlando Hudson/53 4.00 1.20
529 Shannon Stewart/175 2.50 .75
530 Joe Carter/121 4.00 1.20
531 Chris Baker/42 5.00 1.50
532 Eric Hinske/24
533 Corey Thurman/56 4.00 1.20
534 Josh Phelps/82 3.00 .90
535 Reed Johnson/46 5.00 1.50
536 Brian Bowles/19
537 Roy Halladay/168 2.50 .75
538 Jose Cruz Jr./114 3.00 .90
539 Kelvim Escobar/85 3.00 .90
540 Chris Carpenter/45 5.00 1.50
541 Rickie Weeks/27
542 Hideki Matsui/50 40.00 12.00
543 Ramon Nivar/39 8.00 2.40
544 Adam Loewen/25
545 Brandon Webb/10
546 Dan Haren/10
547 Delmon Young/7
548 Ryan Wagner/15

2003 Donruss Team Heroes Timeline Threads

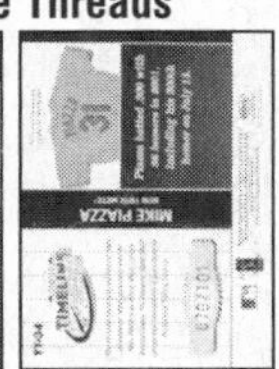

Randomly inserted into packs, these 50 cards feature game-used jersey swatches from a mix of active and retired players. These cards are serial numbered to some year which matches an important year in the player's career.

Nm-Mt Ex-Mt
1 Bobby Doerr/39 30.00 9.00
2 Phil Rizzuto/47 50.00 15.00
3 Yogi Berra/47 60.00 18.00
4 Pee Wee Reese/58 30.00 9.00
5 Stan Musial/42
6 Al Kaline/64 50.00 15.00
7 Orlando Cepeda/65 25.00 7.50
8 Eddie Mathews/66 50.00 15.00
9 Lou Brock/66 30.00 9.00
10 Juan Marichal/67 25.00 7.50
11 Ernie Banks/68 50.00 15.00
12 Willie Stargell/68 30.00 9.00
13 Jim Palmer/69 25.00 7.50
14 Luis Aparicio/69 25.00 7.50
15 Tom Seaver/69 30.00 9.00
16 Harmon Killebrew/71 50.00 15.00
17 Joe Morgan/74 25.00 7.50
18 Brooks Robinson/76 30.00 9.00
19 Mike Schmidt/81 80.00 24.00
20 Willie McCovey/77 25.00 7.50
21 Robin Yount/78 50.00 15.00
22 Reggie Jackson/79 30.00 9.00
23 Rod Carew/85 50.00 15.00
24 Nolan Ryan/91 100.00 30.00
25 Tony Gwynn/98 30.00 9.00
26 Alex Rodriguez/100 40.00 12.00
27 Carlos Delgado/101 20.00 6.00
28 Lance Berkman/102 20.00 6.00
29 Randy Johnson/100 30.00 9.00
30 Josh Beckett/101 20.00 6.00
31 Eric Davis/89 25.00 7.50
32 Todd Helton/100 25.00 7.50
33 Jose Canseco/89 50.00 15.00
34 Mike Piazza/101 40.00 12.00
35 Fred Lynn/75 25.00 7.50
36 Mike Sweeney/101 20.00 6.00
37 Miguel Tejada/101 20.00 6.00
38 Curt Schilling/101 20.00 6.00
39 Dale Murphy/87 50.00 15.00
40 Jim Thome/101 30.00 9.00
41 Adam Dunn/102 25.00 7.50
42 Nomar Garciaparra/100 40.00 12.00
43 Vladimir Guerrero/100 30.00 9.00
44 Alfonso Soriano/102 25.00 7.50
45 Wade Boggs/90 30.00 9.00
46 Randy Johnson/89 30.00 9.00
47 Hal Newhouser/55 25.00 7.50
48 Chipper Jones/93 30.00 9.00
49 Andruw Jones/96 20.00 6.00
50 Frank Thomas/94 30.00 9.00

2004 Donruss Team Heroes

Issued only as a retail product, this 465 card set was released in May, 2004. The set was issued in eight card packs with an $2 SRP which came 24 packs to a box and 20 boxes to a case. Cards numbered 1 through 440 feature a mix of active and retired players while cards numbered 441 through 465 feature players who were traded in the off-season. According to Donruss, those final 25 cards are approximately twice as hard to pull as the other cards in this set.

Nm-Mt Ex-Mt
COMPLETE SET (465) 100.00 30.00
COMMON RETIRED (1-440) .50 .15
COMMON SP (441-465) 1.00 .30
441-465 APPX. 2X TOUGHER THAN 1-440
441-465 DIST.INFO PROVIDED BY DONRUSS
1 Troy Glaus .30 .09
2 Garret Anderson .30 .09
3 John Lackey .30 .09
4 Jarrod Washburn .30 .09
5 Bengie Molina .30 .09
6 Adam Kennedy .30 .09
7 Francisco Rodriguez .30 .09
8 Darin Erstad .30 .09
9 Ramon Ortiz .30 .09
10 Chone Figgins .30 .09
11 Rich Fischer .30 .09
12 David Eckstein .30 .09
13 Troy Percival .30 .09
14 Tim Salmon .50 .15
15 Nolan Ryan Angels 3.00 .90
16 Luis Gonzalez .30 .09
17 Matt Kata .30 .09
18 Randy Johnson .75 .23
19 Oscar Villarreal .30 .09
20 Tim Olson .30 .09
21 Rob Hammock .30 .09
22 Alex Cintron .30 .09
23 Brian Bruney .30 .09
24 Brandon Webb .30 .09
25 Greg Aquino .30 .09
26 Shea Hillenbrand .30 .09
27 Steve Finley .30 .09
28 Rod Barajas .30 .09
29 Mike Hampton .30 .09
30 Adam LaRoche .30 .09
31 Russ Ortiz .30 .09
32 Chipper Jones .75 .23
33 John Smoltz .50 .15
34 Andruw Jones .30 .09
35 Bubba Nelson .30 .09
36 Johnny Estrada .30 .09
37 Marcus Giles .30 .09
38 Rafael Furcal .30 .09
39 Horacio Ramirez .30 .09
40 Dale Murphy 1.25 .35
41 Gaylord Perry Braves .50 .15
42 Mark DeRosa .30 .09
43 Adam Loewen .30 .09
44 Jerry Hairston Jr. .30 .09
45 Jose Morban .30 .09
46 Daniel Cabrera .30 .09
47 Jay Gibbons .30 .09
48 Larry Bigbie .30 .09
49 Luis Matos .30 .09
50 Rodrigo Lopez .30 .09
51 Melvin Mora .30 .09
52 Cal Ripken 4.00 1.20
53 Geronimo Gil .30 .09
54 Tony Batista .30 .09
55 Jason Johnson .30 .09
56 Jason Varitek .50 .15
57 Bill Mueller .30 .09
58 Todd Walker .30 .09
59 Trot Nixon .30 .09
60 Tim Wakefield .30 .09
61 Kevin Youkilis .30 .09
62 David Ortiz .75 .23
63 Johnny Damon .75 .23
64 Derek Lowe .30 .09
65 Pedro Martinez .75 .23
66 Carl Yastrzemski 2.00 .60
67 Bobby Doerr .50 .15
68 Matt Clement .30 .09
69 Sammy Sosa 1.25 .35
70 Randall Simon .30 .09
71 Nate Frese .30 .09
72 Carlos Zambrano .30 .09
73 Moises Alou .30 .09
74 Mark Prior .75 .23
75 Jason DuBois .30 .09
76 Nic Jackson .30 .09
77 Corey Patterson .30 .09
78 John Webb .30 .09
79 Kerry Wood .75 .23
80 Aramis Ramirez .30 .09
81 Brendan Harris .30 .09
82 Kenny Lofton .30 .09
83 Alex Gonzalez .30 .09
84 Gary Matthews Sr. .50 .15
85 Mark Grace .50 .15
86 Mark Grudzielanek .30 .09
87 Joe Borowski .30 .09
88 Joe Crede .30 .09
89 Mark Buehrle .30 .09
90 Paul Konerko .30 .09
91 Magglio Ordonez .30 .09
92 Corwin Malone .30 .09
93 Frank Thomas .75 .23
94 Jose Valentin .30 .09
95 Miguel Olivo .30 .09

96 Esteban Loaiza .30 .09
97 Carlos Lee .30 .09
98 Harold Baines .50 .15
99 Jason LaRue .30 .09
100 Sean Casey .30 .09
101 Adam Dunn .50 .15
102 Josh Hall .30 .09
103 Danny Graves .30 .09
104 Barry Larkin .50 .15
105 Ken Griffey Jr. 1.25 .35
106 Brandon Claussen .30 .09
107 Austin Kearns .30 .09
108 D'Angelo Jimenez .30 .09
109 Ryan Wagner .30 .09
110 Tim Hummel .30 .09
111 Johnny Bench 1.25 .35
112 Eric Davis .50 .15
113 Jose Rijo .50 .15
114 Travis Hafner .30 .09
115 Jody Gerut .30 .09
116 Fernando Cabrera .30 .09
117 Jhonny Peralta .30 .09
118 Ryan Church .30 .09
119 Francisco Cruceta .30 .09
120 Omar Vizquel .50 .15
121 Jason Davis .30 .09
122 Jeremy Guthrie .30 .09
123 C.C. Sabathia .30 .09
124 Milton Bradley .30 .09
125 Cliff Lee .30 .09
126 Victor Martinez .30 .09
127 Bob Feller .50 .15
128 Casey Blake .30 .09
129 Josh Bard .30 .09
130 Billy Traber .30 .09
131 Coco Crisp .30 .09
132 Larry Walker .50 .15
133 Jason Jennings .30 .09
134 Garrett Atkins .30 .09
135 Rene Reyes .30 .09
136 Chin-Hui Tsao .30 .09
137 Preston Wilson .30 .09
138 Jeff Baker .30 .09
139 Charles Johnson .30 .09
140 Shawn Chacon .30 .09
141 Todd Helton .50 .15
142 Jay Payton .30 .09
143 Omar Infante .30 .09
144 Bobby Higginson .30 .09
145 Dmitri Young .30 .09
146 Jorge Cordova .30 .09
147 Jeremy Bonderman .30 .09
148 Brandon Inge .30 .09
149 Franklyn German .30 .09
150 Nook Logan .30 .09
151 Alex Sanchez .30 .09
152 Craig Monroe .30 .09
153 Preston Larrison .30 .09
154 Carlos Pena .30 .09
155 Alan Trammell .50 .15
156 Jack Morris .50 .15
157 Eric Munson .30 .09
158 Mike Maroth .30 .09
159 Josh Beckett .30 .09
160 Josh Willingham .30 .09
161 Mike Lowell .30 .09
162 Luis Castillo .30 .09
163 Wilson Valdez .30 .09
164 Miguel Cabrera .50 .15
165 Alex Gonzalez .30 .09
166 Carl Pavano .30 .09
167 Dontrelle Willis .50 .15
168 Juan Pierre .30 .09
169 Juan Encarnacion .30 .09
170 Brad Penny .30 .09
171 Ivan Rodriguez Marlins .75 .23
172 Josh Wilson .30 .09
173 Jeff Conine .30 .09
174 Mark Redman .30 .09
175 A.J. Burnett .30 .09
176 Jeff Bagwell .50 .15
177 Octavio Dotel .30 .09
178 Craig Biggio .50 .15
179 John Buck .30 .09
180 Rodrigo Rosario .30 .09
181 Tommy Whiteman .30 .09
182 Kirk Saarloos .30 .09
183 Jason Lane .30 .09
184 Wade Miller .30 .09
185 Lance Berkman .30 .09
186 Roy Oswalt .30 .09
187 Tim Redding .30 .09
188 Jeff Kent .30 .09
189 Chris Burke .30 .09
190 Morgan Ensberg .30 .09
191 Nolan Ryan Astros 3.00 .90
192 Geoff Blum .30 .09
193 Jeremy Affeldt .30 .09
194 Mike Sweeney .30 .09
195 Angel Berroa .30 .09
196 Jimmy Gobble .30 .09
197 Ken Harvey .30 .09
198 Carlos Beltran .50 .15
199 Alexis Gomez .30 .09
200 Byron Gettis .30 .09
201 Mike MacDougal .30 .09
202 David DeJesus .30 .09
203 Runelvys Hernandez .30 .09
204 George Brett 3.00 .90
205 Amos Otis .50 .15
206 Joe Randa .30 .09
207 Aaron Guiel .30 .09
208 Eric Gagne .75 .23
209 Shawn Green .30 .09
210 Kevin Brown .30 .09
211 Cesar Izturis .30 .09
212 Kazuhisa Ishii .30 .09
213 Joe Thurston .30 .09
214 Odalis Perez .30 .09
215 Rickey Henderson .75 .23
216 Hideo Nomo .75 .23
217 Hong-Chi Kuo .30 .09
218 Edwin Jackson .30 .09
219 Paul Lo Duca .30 .09
220 Adrian Beltre .50 .15
221 Duke Snider .75 .23
222 Steve Garvey .50 .15
223 Rickie Weeks .30 .09
224 Bill Hall .30 .09
225 Doug Davis .30 .09
226 Geoff Jenkins .30 .09
227 Matt Childers .30 .09
228 Dan Kolb .30 .09
229 Scott Podsednik .30 .09
230 Pedro Liriano .30 .09
231 Ben Sheets .30 .09
232 Robin Yount 2.00 .60
233 Gorman Thomas .50 .15
234 Ben Oglivie .50 .15
235 Matt LeCroy .30 .09
236 Cristian Guzman .30 .09
237 Lew Ford .30 .09
238 J.C. Romero .30 .09
239 Rob Bowen .30 .09
240 Corey Koskie .30 .09
241 Jacque Jones .30 .09
242 Brad Radke .30 .09
243 Shannon Stewart .30 .09
244 J.D. Durbin .30 .09
245 Doug Mientkiewicz .30 .09
246 Jason Kubel .30 .09
247 Torii Hunter .30 .09
248 Johan Santana .50 .15
249 Kirby Puckett 1.25 .35
250 Luis Rivas .30 .09
251 Orlando Cabrera .30 .09
252 Tony Armas Jr. .30 .09
253 Brad Wilkerson .30 .09
254 Endy Chavez .30 .09
255 Jose Vidro .30 .09
256 Zach Day .30 .09
257 Livan Hernandez .30 .09
258 Terrmel Sledge .30 .09
259 Michael Barrett .30 .09
260 Gary Carter .50 .15
261 Andre Dawson .50 .15
262 Craig Brazell .30 .09
263 Mike Piazza 1.25 .35
264 Jeff Duncan .30 .09
265 Jason Anderson .30 .09
266 Tom Glavine .50 .15
267 Danny Garcia .30 .09
268 Ty Wigginton .30 .09
269 Al Leiter .30 .09
270 Jeremy Griffiths .30 .09
271 Jose Reyes .50 .15
272 Prentice Redman .30 .09
273 Cliff Floyd .30 .09
274 Jae Seo .30 .09
275 Nolan Ryan Mets 3.00 .90
276 Keith Hernandez .50 .15
277 Jason Phillips .30 .09
278 Kazuo Matsui RC 2.50 .75
279 Jose Contreras .30 .09
280 Aaron Boone .30 .09
281 Mike Mussina .50 .15
282 Jason Giambi .30 .09
283 Hideki Matsui 1.25 .35
284 Derek Jeter 1.50 .45
285 Mariano Rivera .50 .15
286 Chien-Ming Wang .30 .09
287 Bernie Williams .50 .15
288 Alfonso Soriano Yanks .50 .15
289 Jorge Posada .50 .15
290 Michel Hernandez .30 .09
291 Erik Almonte .30 .09
292 Don Mattingly 3.00 .90
293 Roger Clemens Yanks 1.50 .45
294 Gaylord Perry Rgr .50 .15
295 Tommy John .50 .15
296 Tim Hudson .30 .09
297 Rich Harden .30 .09
298 Eric Chavez .30 .09
299 Adam Morrissey .30 .09
300 Mark Mulder .30 .09
301 Eric Byrnes .30 .09
302 Jermaine Dye .30 .09
303 Barry Zito .30 .09
304 Erubiel Durazo .30 .09
305 Mark Ellis .30 .09
306 Bobby Crosby .50 .15
307 Shane Bazzell .30 .09
308 Mario Ramos .30 .09
309 Jose Canseco 1.25 .35
310 Placido Polanco .30 .09
311 Jimmy Rollins .30 .09
312 Jim Thome .75 .23
313 Brett Myers .30 .09
314 Jason Michaels .30 .09
315 Vicente Padilla .30 .09
316 Bobby Abreu .30 .09
317 Ryan Howard .30 .09
318 Chase Utley .30 .09
319 Pat Burrell .30 .09
320 Randy Wolf .30 .09
321 Franklin Perez .30 .09
322 Marlon Byrd .30 .09
323 Kevin Millwood .30 .09
324 Mike Lieberthal .30 .09
325 Anderson Machado .30 .09
326 Travis Chapman .30 .09
327 Steve Carlton .50 .15
328 Greg Luzinski .50 .15
329 David Bell .30 .09
330 Craig Wilson .30 .09
331 Kris Benson .30 .09
332 Jose Castillo .30 .09
333 Josh Fogg .30 .09
334 Jason Kendall .30 .09
335 Walter Young .30 .09
336 Oliver Perez .30 .09
337 Jason Bay .30 .09
338 Duaner Sanchez .30 .09
339 Jack Wilson .30 .09
340 Carlos Rivera .30 .09
341 Kip Wells .30 .09
342 Freddy Sanchez .30 .09
343 Roberto Clemente 3.00 .90
344 Al Oliver .50 .15
345 Phil Nevin .30 .09
346 Trevor Hoffman .30 .09
347 Ryan Klesko .30 .09
348 Khalil Greene .75 .23
349 Freddy Guzman RC .50 .15
350 Brian Giles .30 .09
351 Brian Lawrence .30 .09
352 Sean Burroughs .30 .09
353 Ben Howard .30 .09
354 Xavier Nady .30 .09
355 Mark Loretta .30 .09
356 Ramon Vazquez .30 .09
357 Tony Gwynn 1.50 .45
358 Adam Eaton .30 .09
359 Merkin Valdez RC 1.00 .30
360 Kevin Correia .30 .09
361 Edgardo Alfonzo .30 .09
362 Mike Cameron .30 .09
363 Ray Durham .30 .09
364 Jesse Foppert .30 .09
365 Robb Nen .30 .09
366 Marquis Grissom .30 .09
367 Jerome Williams .30 .09
368 Jason Schmidt .30 .09
369 Will Clark 1.25 .35
370 Bret Boone .30 .09
371 Freddy Garcia .30 .09
372 Dan Wilson .30 .09
373 Rhett Johnson .30 .09
374 Kazuhiro Sasaki .30 .09
375 Ichiro Suzuki 1.25 .35
376 Edgar Martinez .50 .15
377 Jamie Moyer .30 .09
378 Joel Pineiro .30 .09
379 Carlos Guillen .30 .09
380 Randy Winn .30 .09
381 J.J. Putz .30 .09
382 John Olerud .30 .09
383 Matt Thornton .30 .09
384 Rafael Soriano .30 .09
385 Gil Meche .30 .09
386 Albert Pujols 1.50 .45
387 Woody Williams .30 .09
388 Dan Haren .30 .09
389 Matt Morris .30 .09
390 Jim Edmonds .30 .09
391 Edgar Renteria .30 .09
392 Scott Rolen .75 .23
393 J.D. Drew .30 .09
394 Bo Hart .30 .09
395 Stan Musial 2.00 .60
396 Red Schoendienst .50 .15
397 Terry Pendleton .50 .15
398 Mike Matheny .30 .09
399 Dewon Brazelton .30 .09
400 Chad Gaudin .30 .09
401 Aubrey Huff .30 .09
402 Victor Zambrano .30 .09
403 Antonio Perez .30 .09
404 Carl Crawford .30 .09
405 Joe Kennedy .30 .09
406 Pete LaForest .30 .09
407 Delmon Young .50 .15
408 Rocco Baldelli .30 .09
409 Doug Waechter .30 .09
410 Brian Stokes .30 .09
411 Edwin Almonte .30 .09
412 Toby Hall .30 .09
413 Lance Carter .30 .09
414 Greg Maddux Braves 1.25 .35
415 Hank Blalock .50 .15
416 Colby Lewis .30 .09
417 Mark Teixeira .50 .15
418 Gerald Laird .30 .09
419 Ricardo Rodriguez .30 .09
420 Ben Kozlowski .30 .09
421 Kevin Mench .30 .09
422 Michael Young .30 .09
423 Ramon Nivar .30 .09
424 Laynce Nix .30 .09
425 Nolan Ryan Rgr 3.00 .90
426 Einar Diaz .30 .09
427 Carlos Delgado .30 .09
428 Eric Hinske .30 .09
429 Dustin McGowan .30 .09
430 Frank Catalanotto .30 .09
431 Kevin Cash .30 .09
432 Roy Halladay .30 .09
433 Orlando Hudson .30 .09
434 Francisco Rosario .30 .09
435 Guillermo Quiroz .30 .09
436 Vernon Wells .30 .09
437 Josh Phelps .30 .09
438 Alexis Rios .30 .09
439 Reed Johnson .30 .09
440 Chris Woodward .30 .09
441 Bartolo Colon SP 1.00 .30
442 Richie Sexson SP 1.00 .30
443 Greg Maddux Cubs SP 3.00 .90
444 Javy Lopez SP 1.00 .30
445 Gary Sheffield SP 1.00 .30
446 Curt Schilling SP 2.00 .60
447 Nomar Garciaparra SP 3.00 .90
448 Manny Ramirez SP 1.25 .35
449 Derrek Lee SP 1.00 .30
450 Roberto Alomar SP 1.25 .35
451 Ivan Rodriguez Tigers SP 2.00 .60
452 Junior Spivey SP 1.00 .30
453 Alfonso Soriano Rgr SP 1.25 .35
454 Vladimir Guerrero SP 2.00 .60
455 Nick Johnson SP 1.00 .30
456 Javier Vazquez SP 1.00 .30
457 Andy Pettitte SP 1.25 .35
458 Miguel Tejada SP 1.00 .30
459 Rich Aurilia SP 1.00 .30
460 A.J. Pierzynski SP 1.00 .30
461 Raul Ibanez SP 1.00 .30
462 Roger Clemens Astros SP 4.00 1.20
463 Juan Gonzalez SP 1.25 .35
464 Rafael Palmeiro SP 1.25 .35
465 Alex Rodriguez Yanks SP 3.00 .90

2004 Donruss Team Heroes Autographs

Nm-Mt Ex-Mt

STATED ODDS 1:24
#'d CARD PRINTS B/WN 1-86 COPIES PER
NO PRICING ON QTY OF 48 OR LESS
1 Troy Glaus/5
2 Garret Anderson/1
10 Chone Figgins 15.00 4.50
11 Rich Fischer 8.00 2.40
15 Nolan Ryan Angels/5
17 Matt Kata 8.00 2.40
19 Oscar Villarreal 8.00 2.40
20 Tim Olson 8.00 2.40
21 Rob Hammock/57 10.00 3.00
23 Brian Bruney 8.00 2.40
24 Brandon Webb/1
25 Greg Aquino 8.00 2.40
27 Steve Finley/1
30 Adam LaRoche/5
32 Chipper Jones/1
34 Andruw Jones/5
35 Bubba Nelson 8.00 2.40
36 Johnny Estrada/3
37 Marcus Giles/3
38 Rafael Furcal/1
40 Dale Murphy/10
41 Gaylord Perry Braves/10
43 Adam Loewen/1
45 Jose Morban 8.00 2.40
46 Daniel Cabrera 10.00 3.00
47 Jay Gibbons/10
49 Luis Matos/1
52 Cal Ripken/1
56 Jason Varitek/5
59 Trot Nixon/10
61 Kevin Youkilis/50 15.00 4.50
65 Pedro Martinez/1
66 Carl Yastrzemski/1
67 Bobby Doerr/10
69 Sammy Sosa/5
71 Nate Frese 8.00 2.40
74 Mark Prior/5
75 Jason DuBois 8.00 2.40
76 Nic Jackson 8.00 2.40
78 John Webb 8.00 2.40
80 Aramis Ramirez/10
81 Brendan Harris 8.00 2.40
84 Gary Matthews Sr. 15.00 4.50
85 Mark Grace/1
88 Joe Crede/5
89 Mark Buehrle/5
90 Paul Konerko/1
91 Magglio Ordonez/5
92 Corwin Malone 8.00 2.40
93 Frank Thomas/1
97 Carlos Lee/5
98 Harold Baines/10
100 Sean Casey/5
101 Adam Dunn/5
102 Josh Hall/25
104 Barry Larkin/1
106 Brandon Claussen 8.00 2.40
107 Austin Kearns/5
109 Ryan Wagner/10
110 Tim Hummel 8.00 2.40
111 Johnny Bench/1
112 Eric Davis/10
114 Travis Hafner/10
115 Jody Gerut/10
116 Fernando Cabrera 8.00 2.40
117 Jhonny Peralta 10.00 3.00
118 Ryan Church 8.00 2.40
119 Francisco Cruceta/75 10.00 3.00
122 Jeremy Guthrie/5
127 Bob Feller/10
135 Rene Reyes/14
138 Jeff Baker/5
141 Todd Helton/1
142 Jay Payton/5
146 Jorge Cordova 8.00 2.40
147 Jeremy Bonderman/2
149 Franklyn German 8.00 2.40
150 Nook Logan 8.00 2.40
153 Preston Larrison 8.00 2.40
155 Alan Trammell/5
156 Jack Morris/10
159 Josh Beckett/1
160 Josh Willingham 8.00 2.40
162 Luis Castillo/10
163 Wilson Valdez 8.00 2.40
164 Miguel Cabrera/5
167 Dontrelle Willis/5
172 Josh Wilson 8.00 2.40
176 Jeff Bagwell/1
178 Craig Biggio/1
179 John Buck/18
180 Rodrigo Rosario 8.00 2.40
181 Tommy Whiteman 8.00 2.40
182 Kirk Saarloos/5
183 Jason Lane/10
186 Roy Oswalt/5
187 Tim Redding/22
189 Chris Burke 8.00 2.40
191 Nolan Ryan Astros/5
195 Angel Berroa/5
196 Jimmy Gobble/2
197 Ken Harvey 10.00 3.00
198 Carlos Beltran/5
199 Alexis Gomez/10
200 Byron Gettis 8.00 2.40
203 Runelvys Hernandez/1
204 George Brett/1
205 Amos Otis 15.00 4.50
209 Shawn Green/1
211 Cesar Izturis 8.00 2.40
212 Kazuhisa Ishii/1
213 Joe Thurston/5
216 Hideo Nomo/1
217 Hong-Chi Kuo/10
218 Edwin Jackson/10
221 Duke Snider/10
222 Steve Garvey/10
223 Rickie Weeks/5
225 Doug Davis 8.00 2.40
227 Matt Childers 8.00 2.40
230 Pedro Liriano 8.00 2.40
232 Robin Yount/1
233 Gorman Thomas 15.00 4.50
234 Ben Oglivie/86 20.00 6.00
237 Lew Ford 10.00 3.00
238 J.C. Romero 8.00 2.40
239 Rob Bowen 8.00 2.40
241 Jacque Jones/5
243 Shannon Stewart/10
246 Jason Kubel/50 15.00 4.50
247 Torii Hunter/5
248 Johan Santana/5
249 Kirby Puckett/1
251 Orlando Cabrera/5
254 Endy Chavez/3
255 Jose Vidro/5
256 Zach Day/10
258 Terrmel Sledge 8.00 2.40
260 Gary Carter/10
261 Andre Dawson/1
262 Craig Brazell 8.00 2.40
263 Mike Piazza/1
264 Jeff Duncan 8.00 2.40
265 Jason Anderson 8.00 2.40
266 Tom Glavine/1
267 Danny Garcia 8.00 2.40
270 Jeremy Griffiths 8.00 2.40
272 Prentice Redman 8.00 2.40
273 Cliff Floyd/5
274 Jae Seo/5
275 Nolan Ryan Mets/5
276 Keith Hernandez/10
279 Jose Contreras/5
281 Mike Mussina/1
285 Mariano Rivera/5
286 Chien-Ming Wang/5
287 Bernie Williams/1
289 Jorge Posada/5
290 Michel Hernandez/9
291 Erik Almonte/66 10.00 3.00
292 Don Mattingly/5
294 Gaylord Perry Rgr/10
295 Tommy John/10
296 Tim Hudson/5
297 Rich Harden/10
298 Eric Chavez/10
299 Adam Morrissey/16
300 Mark Mulder/5
301 Eric Byrnes/10
302 Jermaine Dye/5
303 Barry Zito/1
307 Shane Bazzell 8.00 2.40
308 Mario Ramos 8.00 2.40
309 Jose Canseco/5
314 Jason Michaels/42
316 Bobby Abreu/10
321 Franklin Perez 8.00 2.40
322 Marlon Byrd/5
325 Anderson Machado/50 10.00 3.00
326 Travis Chapman 8.00 2.40
327 Steve Carlton/5
328 Greg Luzinski 15.00 4.50
330 Craig Wilson/1
331 Kris Benson 8.00 2.40
332 Jose Castillo/5
335 Walter Young/67 10.00 3.00
336 Oliver Perez/20
338 Duaner Sanchez 8.00 2.40
340 Carlos Rivera/3
342 Freddy Sanchez/2
344 Al Oliver/5
345 Phil Nevin/1
347 Ryan Klesko/1
349 Freddy Guzman/6
350 Brian Giles/1
352 Sean Burroughs/1
353 Ben Howard 8.00 2.40
357 Tony Gwynn/1
359 Merkin Valdez/50 25.00 7.50
360 Kevin Correia 8.00 2.40
367 Jerome Williams/10
369 Will Clark/5
371 Freddy Garcia/1
373 Rhett Johnson/76 10.00 3.00
376 Edgar Martinez/10
377 Jamie Moyer/5
381 J.J. Putz 8.00 2.40
383 Matt Thornton/50 10.00 3.00
384 Rafael Soriano 8.00 2.40
388 Dan Haren/10
390 Jim Edmonds/1
392 Scott Rolen/1
393 J.D. Drew/1
394 Bo Hart/4
395 Stan Musial/1
396 Red Schoendienst/10
397 Terry Pendleton/10
399 Dewon Brazelton/10
401 Aubrey Huff/10
403 Antonio Perez/1
405 Joe Kennedy/10
406 Pete LaForest 8.00 2.40
407 Delmon Young/10
408 Rocco Baldelli/5
410 Brian Stokes 8.00 2.40
411 Edwin Almonte 8.00 2.40
415 Hank Blalock/5
417 Mark Teixeira/5
418 Gerald Laird/6
419 Ricardo Rodriguez 8.00 2.40
420 Ben Kozlowski 8.00 2.40
421 Kevin Mench/8
423 Ramon Nivar/5
425 Nolan Ryan Rgr/5
431 Kevin Cash 8.00 2.40
433 Orlando Hudson/10
434 Francisco Rosario/48
435 Guillermo Quiroz/10
436 Vernon Wells/5
437 Josh Phelps/5
438 Alexis Rios/10
442 Richie Sexson/5
443 Greg Maddux Cubs/1
444 Javy Lopez/1
445 Gary Sheffield/5
446 Curt Schilling/1
448 Manny Ramirez/1
450 Roberto Alomar/5
452 Junior Spivey/10
454 Vladimir Guerrero/1
455 Nick Johnson/5
456 Javier Vazquez/10
459 Rich Aurilia/5
463 Juan Gonzalez/1
464 Rafael Palmeiro/1
465 Alex Rodriguez Yanks/1

2004 Donruss Team Heroes Showdown Bronze

Nm-Mt Ex-Mt

BRONZE 1-440: 2.5X TO 6X BASIC ..
BRONZE 1-440: 2X TO 5X BASIC RC
BRONZE 441-465: 1X TO 2.5X BASIC SP
ANDOM INSERTS IN PACKS ....
TATED PRINT RUN 150 SERIAL #'d SETS

2004 Donruss Team Heroes Showdown Gold

Nm-Mt Ex-Mt

ANDOM INSERTS IN PACKS ....
TATED PRINT RUN 10 SERIAL #'d SETS
O PRICING DUE TO SCARCITY ....

2004 Donruss Team Heroes Showdown Silver

Nm-Mt Ex-Mt

SILVER 1-440: 5X TO 12X BASIC .....
SILVER 1-440: 4X TO 10X BASIC RC
SILVER 441-465: 2X TO 5X BASIC SP
ANDOM INSERTS IN PACKS ....
TATED PRINT RUN 50 SERIAL #'d SETS

2004 Donruss Timelines

his 50-card set was released in January, 2004. hese cards were issued in five-card packs with a $50 SRP which came four packs to a box and ght boxes to a case.

	Nm-Mt	Ex-Mt
OMPLETE SET (50)	50.00	15.00
Adam Dunn	2.00	.60
Albert Pujols	6.00	1.80
Alex Rodriguez	5.00	1.50
Alfonso Soriano	2.00	.60
Andruw Jones	2.00	.60
Austin Kearns	2.00	.60
Miguel Cabrera	2.00	.60
Barry Zito	2.00	.60
Carlos Beltran	2.00	.60
0 Carlos Delgado	2.00	.60
1 Chipper Jones	3.00	.90
2 Curt Schilling	2.00	.60
3 Derek Jeter	6.00	1.80
4 Frank Thomas	3.00	.90
5 Garret Anderson	2.00	.60
6 Gary Sheffield	2.00	.60
7 Greg Maddux	5.00	1.50
8 Hank Blalock	2.00	.60
9 Hideki Matsui	5.00	1.50
0 Hideo Nomo	3.00	.90
1 Ichiro Suzuki	5.00	1.50
2 Ivan Rodriguez	3.00	.90
3 Jason Giambi	2.00	.60
4 Jeff Bagwell	2.00	.60
5 Jim Thome	3.00	.90
6 Juan Gonzalez	2.00	.60
7 Ken Griffey Jr.	5.00	1.50
8 Kevin Brown	2.00	.60
9 Kerry Wood	3.00	.90
0 Lance Berkman	2.00	.60
1 Magglio Ordonez	2.00	.60
2 Manny Ramirez	2.00	.60
3 Mark Prior	3.00	.90
4 Mike Mussina	2.00	.60
5 Mike Piazza	5.00	1.50
6 Nomar Garciaparra	5.00	1.50
7 Pedro Martinez	3.00	.90
8 Rafael Palmeiro	2.00	.60
9 Randy Johnson	3.00	.90
0 Richie Sexson	2.00	.60
1 Roger Clemens	6.00	1.80
2 Roy Halladay	2.00	.60
3 Sammy Sosa	5.00	1.50
4 Scott Rolen	3.00	.90
5 Shawn Green	2.00	.60
6 Tim Hudson	2.00	.60
7 Todd Helton	2.00	.60
8 Torii Hunter	2.00	.60
9 Vernon Wells	2.00	.60
0 Vladimir Guerrero	3.00	.90

2004 Donruss Timelines Gold

Nm-Mt Ex-Mt

GOLD: 2.5X TO 6X BASIC ....
ANDOM INSERTS IN PACKS ....
TATED PRINT RUN 25 SERIAL #'d SETS

2004 Donruss Timelines Platinum

Nm-Mt Ex-Mt

ANDOM INSERTS IN PACKS ....
TATED PRINT RUN 1 SERIAL #'d SET
O PRICING DUE TO SCARCITY ....

2004 Donruss Timelines Silver

Nm-Mt Ex-Mt

SILVER: 1X TO 2.5X BASIC..............
ANDOM INSERTS IN PACKS ....
TATED PRINT RUN 100 SERIAL #'d SETS

2004 Donruss Timelines Autograph Gold

Nm-Mt Ex-Mt

TATED PRINT RUN 25 SERIAL #'d SETS
LATINUM PRINT RUN 1 SERIAL #'d SET
O PLATINUM PRICING DUE TO SCARCITY

RANDOM INSERTS IN PACKS ....

1 Adam Dunn	40.00	12.00
7 Miguel Cabrera	40.00	12.00
9 Carlos Beltran	50.00	15.00
15 Garret Anderson	25.00	7.50
18 Hank Blalock	25.00	7.50
22 Ivan Rodriguez	50.00	15.00
26 Juan Gonzalez	40.00	12.00
31 Magglio Ordonez	40.00	12.00
33 Mark Prior	120.00	36.00
44 Scott Rolen	50.00	15.00
48 Torii Hunter	25.00	7.50
49 Vernon Wells	25.00	7.50
50 Vladimir Guerrero	50.00	15.00

2004 Donruss Timelines Material

Nm-Mt Ex-Mt

STATED ODDS 1:2.................................
*COMBO: 1X TO 2.5X BASIC...............
*COMBO: .5X TO 1.2X BASIC SP ....
COMBO PRINT RUN 125 SERIAL #'d SETS
COMBOS FEATURE BAT-JSY SWATCHES
*PRIME: 1X TO 2.5X BASIC................
PRIME PRINT RUN 125 SERIAL #'d SETS
PRIME M.CABRERA PRINT 10 #'d CARDS
NO PRIME M.CABRERA PRICING AVAIL.

1 Adam Dunn Jsy	10.00	3.00
2 Albert Pujols Jsy	15.00	4.50
3 Alex Rodriguez Jsy	15.00	4.50
4 Alfonso Soriano Jsy	10.00	3.00
5 Andruw Jones Jsy	8.00	2.40
7 Miguel Cabrera Jsy SP	20.00	6.00
10 Carlos Delgado Jsy	8.00	2.40
11 Chipper Jones Jsy	10.00	3.00
14 Frank Thomas Jsy	10.00	3.00
17 Greg Maddux Jsy	10.00	3.00
20 Hideo Nomo Jsy	15.00	4.50
22 Ivan Rodriguez Bat	10.00	3.00
23 Jason Giambi Bat	8.00	2.40
24 Jeff Bagwell Bat	10.00	3.00
25 Jim Thome Jsy	10.00	3.00
26 Juan Gonzalez Bat	10.00	3.00
30 Lance Berkman Jsy	8.00	2.40
33 Mark Prior Jsy	10.00	3.00
35 Mike Piazza Jsy	10.00	3.00
36 Nomar Garciaparra Jsy	15.00	4.50
37 Pedro Martinez Jsy	10.00	3.00
39 Randy Johnson Jsy	10.00	3.00
41 Roger Clemens Jsy	15.00	4.50
43 Sammy Sosa Jsy	15.00	4.50
45 Shawn Green Jsy	8.00	2.40
47 Todd Helton Jsy	10.00	3.00
49 Vernon Wells Jsy	8.00	2.40

2004 Donruss Timelines Material Autograph

Nm-Mt Ex-Mt

PRINT RUNS B/WN 1-50 COPIES PER
NO PRICING ON QTY OF 5 OR LESS..
PRIME PRINT RUN 1 SERIAL #'d SET
NO PRIME PRICING DUE TO SCARCITY
RANDOM INSERTS IN PACKS ....

1 Adam Dunn Jsy/5		
2 Albert Pujols Jsy/5		
3 Alex Rodriguez Jsy/5		
4 Alfonso Soriano Jsy/1		
5 Andruw Jones Jsy/5		
7 Miguel Cabrera Bat/25	60.00	18.00
11 Chipper Jones Jsy/5		
14 Frank Thomas Jsy/5		
17 Greg Maddux Jsy/5		
20 Hideo Nomo Jsy/5		
22 Ivan Rodriguez Bat/25	120.00	36.00
24 Jeff Bagwell Bat/5		
26 Juan Gonzalez Bat/5		
30 Lance Berkman Jsy/5		
33 Mark Prior Jsy/50	100.00	30.00
35 Mike Piazza Jsy/5		
39 Randy Johnson Jsy/5		
41 Roger Clemens Jsy/5		
45 Shawn Green Jsy/5		
49 Vernon Wells Jsy/50	40.00	12.00

2004 Donruss Timelines Boys of Summer

Nm-Mt Ex-Mt

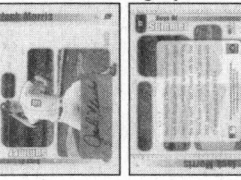

STATED PRINT RUN 250 SERIAL #'d SETS
*GOLD: 2X TO 5X BASIC ....
GOLD PRINT RUN 25 SERIAL #'d SETS
PLATINUM 1 SERIAL #'d SET............
NO PLATINUM PRICING DUE TO SCARCITY
*SILVER: .6X TO 1.5X BASIC.............
SILVER PRINT RUN 100 SERIAL #'d SETS
RANDOM INSERTS IN PACKS ....

1 Alan Trammell	5.00	1.50
2 Marty Marion	5.00	1.50
3 Andre Dawson	5.00	1.50
4 Bo Jackson	8.00	2.40
5 Cal Ripken	20.00	6.00
6 Steve Garvey	5.00	1.50
7 Dale Murphy	8.00	2.40
8 Darren Daulton	5.00	1.50
9 Darryl Strawberry	5.00	1.50
10 Dave Parker	5.00	1.50
11 Doc Gooden	5.00	1.50
12 Don Mattingly	15.00	4.50
13 Eric Davis	5.00	1.50
14 Dwight Evans	5.00	1.50
15 Fred Lynn	5.00	1.50
16 Graig Nettles	5.00	1.50
17 Jay Buhner	5.00	1.50
18 Jim Rice	5.00	1.50
19 Jose Canseco	8.00	2.40
20 Keith Hernandez	5.00	1.50
21 Rickey Henderson	8.00	2.40
22 Jack Morris	5.00	1.50
23 Tony Gwynn	10.00	3.00
24 Vida Blue	5.00	1.50
25 Will Clark	15.00	4.50

2004 Donruss Timelines Boys of Summer Autograph

Nm-Mt Ex-Mt

PLATINUM PRINT RUN 1 SERIAL #'d SET
NO PLATINUM PRICING DUE TO SCARCITY
RANDOM INSERTS IN PACKS ....

2 Marty Marion	15.00	4.50
3 Andre Dawson	15.00	4.50
6 Steve Garvey	15.00	4.50
8 Darren Daulton	15.00	4.50
9 Darryl Strawberry	15.00	4.50
10 Dave Parker	15.00	4.50
11 Doc Gooden	15.00	4.50
13 Eric Davis	15.00	4.50
15 Fred Lynn	15.00	4.50
16 Graig Nettles	15.00	4.50
17 Jay Buhner	15.00	4.50
20 Keith Hernandez	15.00	4.50
22 Jack Morris	15.00	4.50
24 Vida Blue	15.00	4.50

2004 Donruss Timelines Boys of Summer Autograph Gold

Nm-Mt Ex-Mt

*GOLD: 1X TO 2.5X BASIC BOYS AUTO
RANDOM INSERTS IN PACKS ....
STATED PRINT RUN 25 SERIAL #'d SETS

1 Alan Trammell	30.00	9.00
12 Don Mattingly	120.00	36.00
14 Dwight Evans	50.00	15.00
18 Jim Rice	30.00	9.00
25 Will Clark	120.00	36.00

2004 Donruss Timelines Boys of Summer Autograph Silver

Nm-Mt Ex-Mt

*SILVER: .6X TO 1.5X BASIC BOYS AUTO
RANDOM INSERTS IN PACKS ....
STATED PRINT RUN 100 SERIAL #'d SETS

2004 Donruss Timelines Boys of Summer Material

Nm-Mt Ex-Mt

*COMBO: 1X TO 2.5X BASIC..............
COMBO PRINT RUN 100 SERIAL #'d SETS
MOST COMBOS ARE BAT-JSY SWATCHES
*PRIME: 1X TO 2.5X BASIC................
PRIME PRINT RUN 100 SERIAL #'d SETS
RANDOM INSERTS IN PACKS ....

3 Andre Dawson Jsy	8.00	2.40
4 Bo Jackson Jsy	15.00	4.50
5 Cal Ripken Jsy	40.00	12.00
7 Dale Murphy Bat	15.00	4.50
9 Darryl Strawberry Jsy	8.00	2.40
11 Doc Gooden Jsy	8.00	2.40
12 Don Mattingly Jacket	20.00	6.00
19 Jose Canseco Bat	15.00	4.50
21 Rickey Henderson Jsy	15.00	4.50
22 Jack Morris Jsy	8.00	2.40
23 Tony Gwynn Jsy	15.00	4.50
25 Will Clark Jsy	15.00	4.50

2004 Donruss Timelines Boys of Summer Material Autograph

Nm-Mt Ex-Mt

PRINT RUNS B/WN 5-150 COPIES PER
NO PRICING ON QTY OF 10 OR LESS
PRIME PRINT RUN 1 SERIAL #'d SET
NO PRIME PRICING DUE TO SCARCITY
RANDOM INSERTS IN PACKS ....

3 Andre Dawson Jsy/50	30.00	9.00
4 Bo Jackson Jsy/5		
5 Cal Ripken Jsy/5		
7 Dale Murphy Bat/10		
9 Darryl Strawberry Jsy/150	20.00	6.00
11 Doc Gooden Jsy/100	25.00	7.50
12 Don Mattingly Jacket/25	150.00	45.00
19 Jose Canseco Bat/5		
21 Rickey Henderson Jsy/5		
22 Jack Morris Jsy/150	20.00	6.00
23 Tony Gwynn Jsy/10		
25 Will Clark Jsy/15		

2004 Donruss Timelines Call to the Hall

Nm-Mt Ex-Mt

STATED PRINT RUN 250 SERIAL #'d SETS
*GOLD: 2X TO 5X BASIC ....
GOLD PRINT RUN 25 SERIAL #'d SETS
PLATINUM PRINT RUN 1 SERIAL #'d SET
NO PLATINUM PRICING DUE TO SCARCITY
*SILVER: .6X TO 1.5X BASIC.............
SILVER PRINT RUN 100 SERIAL #'d SETS
RANDOM INSERTS IN PACKS ....

1 Babe Ruth	15.00	4.50
2 Billy Williams	5.00	1.50
3 Bob Feller	5.00	1.50
4 Bobby Doerr	5.00	1.50
5 Carlton Fisk	5.00	1.50
6 Gary Carter	5.00	1.50
7 George Brett	15.00	4.50
8 Carl Yastrzemski	10.00	3.00
9 Harmon Killebrew	8.00	2.40
10 Jim Palmer	5.00	1.50
11 Joe Morgan	5.00	1.50
12 Johnny Bench	8.00	2.40
13 Kirby Puckett	8.00	2.40
14 Gaylord Perry	5.00	1.50
15 Mike Schmidt	12.00	3.60
16 Nolan Ryan	15.00	4.50
17 Ozzie Smith	10.00	3.00
18 Phil Rizzuto	5.00	1.50
19 Reggie Jackson	5.00	1.50
20 Roberto Clemente	15.00	4.50
21 Robin Yount	10.00	3.00
22 Rod Carew	5.00	1.50
23 Rollie Fingers	5.00	1.50
24 Steve Carlton	5.00	1.50
25 Tom Seaver	5.00	1.50

2004 Donruss Timelines Call to the Hall Autograph

Nm-Mt Ex-Mt

PLATINUM PRINT RUN 1 SERIAL #'d SET
NO PLATINUM PRICING DUE TO SCARCITY
RANDOM INSERTS IN PACKS ....

3 Bob Feller	20.00	6.00
4 Bobby Doerr	15.00	4.50
14 Gaylord Perry	15.00	4.50
23 Rollie Fingers	15.00	4.50

2004 Donruss Timelines Call to the Hall Autograph Gold

Nm-Mt Ex-Mt

*GOLD: 1X TO 2.5X BASIC CALL AUTO
RANDOM INSERTS IN PACKS ....
STATED PRINT RUN 25 SERIAL #'d SETS

2 Billy Williams	40.00	12.00
6 Gary Carter	40.00	12.00
10 Jim Palmer	40.00	12.00
18 Phil Rizzuto	60.00	18.00
24 Steve Carlton	50.00	15.00

2004 Donruss Timelines Call to the Hall Autograph Silver

Nm-Mt Ex-Mt

*SILVER: .6X TO 1.5X BASIC CALL AUTO
RANDOM INSERTS IN PACKS ....
STATED PRINT RUN 100 SERIAL #'d SETS

3 Bob Feller	40.00	12.00

2004 Donruss Timelines Call to the Hall Material

Nm-Mt Ex-Mt

CLEMENTE PRINT RUN 100 #'d CARDS
B.RUTH PRINT RUN 50 #'d CARDS....
ALL OTHER CARDS ARE NOT SERIAL #'d
*COMBO: 1X TO 2.5X BASIC...............
COMBO PRINT RUN 125 SERIAL #'d SETS
MOST COMBOS ARE BAT-JSY SWATCHES
RANDOM INSERTS IN PACKS ....

1 Babe Ruth Jsy/50	600.00	180.00
4 Bobby Doerr Bat	8.00	2.40
6 Gary Carter Jacket	8.00	2.40
7 George Brett Bat	20.00	6.00
8 Carl Yastrzemski Bat	20.00	6.00
13 Kirby Puckett Bat	15.00	4.50
15 Mike Schmidt Bat	20.00	6.00
16 Nolan Ryan Jsy	20.00	6.00
17 Ozzie Smith Bat	15.00	4.50
19 Reggie Jackson Bat	10.00	3.00
20 Roberto Clemente Bat/100	60.00	18.00

2004 Donruss Timelines Call to the Hall Material Autograph

Nm-Mt Ex-Mt

RANDOM INSERTS IN PACKS ....
PRINT RUNS B/WN 5-100 COPIES PER
NO PRICING ON QTY OF 5 OR LESS..

4 Bobby Doerr Bat/100	30.00	9.00
6 Gary Carter Jacket/25	50.00	15.00
7 George Brett Bat/5		
8 Carl Yastrzemksi Bat/5		
13 Kirby Puckett Bat/5		
16 Nolan Ryan Jsy/5		
17 Ozzie Smith Bat/5		
19 Reggie Jackson Bat/25	80.00	24.00

2004 Donruss Timelines Recollection Autographs

Issued at a stated rate of one in two, this set features an astounding 1576 cards procured by Donruss/Playoff from hobby sources as "buy-back" cards feature many of the best players of the 80's, 90's and the present time who signed copies of these cards in a quantity from anywhere from 1 to 225 of the featured cards. Each of these cards have a recollection autograph embossing on the front and stated serial numbering on the back. Please note that for cards issued to a stated print run of 15 or fewer that no pricing is provided.

	Nm-Mt	Ex-Mt
1 Sandy Alomar Jr. 89/25	15.00	4.50
2 Sandy Alomar Jr. 90 Black/5		
3 Sandy Alomar Jr. 90 Blue/13		
4 Sandy Alomar Jr. 90 DR/5		
5 Sandy Alomar Jr. 91 Black/15		
5A Sandy Alomar Jr. 91 Blue/5		
6 San Alomar Jr. 91 AS Black/32	15.00	4.50
7 Sandy Alomar Jr. 91 AS Blue/13		
8 Sandy Alomar Jr. 91 DK Black/15		
9 Sandy Alomar Jr. 91 DK Blue/10		
10 Sandy Alomar Jr. 91 ROY Black/8		
11 Sandy Alomar Jr. 91 ROY Blue/15		
12 Sandy Alomar Jr. 92 Black/20	15.00	4.50
13 Sandy Alomar Jr. 92 Blue/14		
14 Sandy Alomar Jr. 92 AS Black/13		
15 Sandy Alomar Jr. 92 AS Blue/11		
16 Sandy Alomar Jr. 93 Black/14		
17 Sandy Alomar Jr. 93 Blue/7		
18 Sandy Alomar Jr. 94/15		
19 Sandy Alomar Jr. 95/5		
20 Sandy Alomar Jr. 96/14		
21 Sandy Alomar Jr. 97/16	25.00	7.50
22 Sandy Alomar Jr. 97 PP/1		
23 Sandy Alomar Jr. 98 Black/18	25.00	7.50
24 Sandy Alomar Jr. 98 Blue/2		
25 Sandy Alomar Jr. 98 PP/3		
26 Rich Aurilia 02/10		
27 Rich Aurilia 03/10		
28 Wally Backman 83/38	12.00	3.60
29 Wally Backman 85/97	10.00	3.00
30 Wally Backman 86/67	12.00	3.60
31 Wally Backman 87/38	12.00	3.60
32 Wally Backman 88/190	10.00	3.00
33 Wally Backman 89/30	15.00	4.50
34 Wally Backman 89 BB/1		
35 Wally Backman 89 TR/2		
36 Wally Backman 90/74	12.00	3.60
37 Wally Backman 91/79	12.00	3.60
38 Wally Backman 92/59	12.00	3.60
39 Jeff Bagwell 92/1		
40 Jeff Bagwell 93 MVP/1		
41 Jeff Bagwell 00 Retro DK/2		
42 Jeff Bagwell 02/1		
43 Jeff Bagwell 03/1		
44 H.Baines 82 Black/15		
45 H.Baines 82 Blue/15		
46 H.Baines 83 Black/8		
47 H.Baines 83 Blue/20	40.00	12.00
48 H.Baines 84 Black/20	40.00	12.00
49 H.Baines 84 Blue/10		
50 H.Baines 85 Black/1		
51 H.Baines 85 Blue/10		
52 H.Baines 86 Black/5		
53 H.Baines 86 Blue/2		
54 H.Baines 86 DK Black/32	40.00	12.00
55 H.Baines 86 DK Blue/14		
56 H.Baines 87 Blue/59	30.00	9.00
57 H.Baines 87 Black/7		
58 H.Baines 88 Black/1		
59 H.Baines 88 Blue/26	40.00	12.00
60 H.Baines 88 AS/2		
61 H.Baines 88 BB/1		
62 H.Baines 89 Black/33	40.00	12.00
63 H.Baines 89 Blue/39	30.00	9.00
64 H.Baines 90 Black/1		
65 H.Baines 90 Blue/28	40.00	12.00
66 H.Baines 90 AS/19	60.00	18.00
67 H.Baines 91/6		
68 H.Baines 92 Black/7		
69 H.Baines 92 Blue/17	60.00	18.00
70 H.Baines 93/9		
71 H.Baines 94/9		
72 H.Baines 95/3		
73 H.Baines 96/3		
74 H.Baines 97/11		
75 H.Baines 97 GPP/1		
76 H.Baines 01/5		
77 Dusty Baker 81/36	20.00	6.00
78 Dusty Baker 82/20	25.00	7.50
79 Dusty Baker 83/36	20.00	6.00
80 Dusty Baker 84/37	20.00	6.00
81 Dusty Baker 85/30	25.00	7.50
82 Dusty Baker 86/35	25.00	7.50
83 Jesse Barfield 83/42	12.00	3.60
84 Jesse Barfield 84/63	12.00	3.60
85 Jesse Barfield 85/88	10.00	3.00
86 Jesse Barfield 86/41	12.00	3.60
87 Jesse Barfield 87/61	12.00	3.60
88 Jesse Barfield 88/42	12.00	3.60
89 Jesse Barfield 88 BB/1		
90 Jesse Barfield 89/41	12.00	3.60
91 Jesse Barfield 90/42	12.00	3.60
92 Jesse Barfield 91 Black/2		
93 Jesse Barfield 91 Blue/27	15.00	4.50
94 Jesse Barfield 92 Black/1		
95 Jesse Barfield 92 Blue/28	15.00	4.50
96 Don Baylor 81 Black/30	15.00	4.50
97 Don Baylor 81 Blue/47	12.00	3.60
98 Don Baylor 82 Black/27	15.00	4.50
99 Don Baylor 82 Blue/56	12.00	3.60
100 Don Baylor 83 Black/23	15.00	4.50
101 Don Baylor 83 Blue/23	15.00	4.50
102 Don Baylor 84 Black/15		
103 Don Baylor 84 Blue/12		
104 Don Baylor 85 Black/20	15.00	4.50
105 Don Baylor 85 Blue/4		
106 Don Baylor 86 Black/42	12.00	3.60
107 Don Baylor 86 Blue/28	15.00	4.50
108 Don Baylor 87 Black/28	15.00	4.50
109 Don Baylor 87 Blue/37	12.00	3.60
110 Josh Beckett 99 Retro/3		
111 Josh Beckett 02/1		
112 Josh Beckett 03/1		
113 Carlos Beltran 01/56	50.00	15.00
114 Carlos Beltran 02/34	50.00	15.00
115 Adrian Beltre 01/5		
116 Adrian Beltre 02/5		
117 Adrian Beltre 03/3		
118 Johnny Bench 81 #62/5		
119 Johnny Bench 81 #182/1		
120 Johnny Bench 82/15		
121 Johnny Bench 82 w/Seaver/4		
122 Johnny Bench 83/6		
123 Kris Benson 01/104	10.00	3.00
124 Kris Benson 01 SLC/6		
125 Yogi Berra 82/5		
126 Craig Biggio 89/5		
127 Craig Biggio 90/1		
128 Craig Biggio 91/1		
129 Vida Blue 81/5		
130 Vida Blue 82/26	15.00	4.50
131 Vida Blue 82 DK/16	25.00	7.50
132 Vida Blue 83/26	15.00	4.50
133 Vida Blue 83 MVP/20	15.00	4.50
134 Vida Blue 86/51	12.00	3.60
135 Vida Blue 87/28	15.00	4.50
136 Bert Blyleven 81 Black/14		
137 Bert Blyleven 81 Blue/3		
138 Bert Blyleven 82 Black/5		
139 Bert Blyleven 82 Blue/12		
140 Bert Blyleven 83 Black/4		
141 Bert Blyleven 83 Blue/1		
142 Bert Blyleven 84 Black/6		
143 Bert Blyleven 84 Blue/23	15.00	4.50
144 Bert Blyleven 85 Black/52	12.00	3.60
145 Bert Blyleven 85 Blue/4		
146 Bert Blyleven 85 DK Black/5		
147 Bert Blyleven 85 DK Blue/40	12.00	3.60
148 Bert Blyleven 86 Black/5		
149 Bert Blyleven 86 Blue/1		
150 Bert Blyleven 87 Black/32	15.00	4.50
151 Bert Blyleven 87 Blue/2		
152 Bert Blyleven 88 Black/15		
153 Bert Blyleven 88 Blue/101	10.00	3.00
154 Bert Blyleven 88 BB Black/3		
155 Bert Blyleven 88 BB Blue/1		
156 Bert Blyleven 89 Black/39	12.00	3.60
157 Bert Blyleven 89 Blue/2		
158 Bert Blyleven 89 BB/1		
159 Bert Blyleven 90 Black/57	12.00	3.60
160 Bert Blyleven 90 Blue/2		
161 Bert Blyleven 91 Black/52	12.00	3.60
162 Bert Blyleven 91 Blue/10		
163 Wade Boggs 83/7		
164 Wade Boggs 84/1		
165 Wade Boggs 85/3		
166 Wade Boggs 85 HL/1		
167 Wade Boggs 86/2		
168 Wade Boggs 87/1		
169 Wade Boggs 87 HL #14/1		
170 Wade Boggs 87 HL #44/1		
171 Wade Boggs 88/1		
172 Wade Boggs 88 AS #31/1		
173 Wade Boggs 88 AS #7/1		
174 Wade Boggs 88 BB/1		
175 Wade Boggs 88 MVP/1		
176 Wade Boggs 89/1		
177 Wade Boggs 90/1		
178 Wade Boggs 90 AS/1		
179 Wade Boggs 90 BB/1		
180 Wade Boggs 91/1		
181 Wade Boggs 91 AS/1		
182 Wade Boggs 92/1		
183 Wade Boggs 92 AS/1		
184 Wade Boggs 93/1		
185 Wade Boggs 94/2		
186 Wade Boggs 94 SE/2		
187 Wade Boggs 95/3		
188 Wade Boggs 96/4		
189 Wade Boggs 97/10		
190 Wade Boggs 97 HIT/9		
191 Wade Boggs 98/13		
192 Wade Boggs 99 Retro/1		
193 Wade Boggs 00 Retro/1		
194 Wade Boggs 01 RR/1		
195 George Brett 82/1		
196 George Brett 84/1		
197 George Brett 86 HL/1		
198 George Brett 87 DK/1		
199 George Brett 88 BB/1		
200 Bill Buckner 81/25	25.00	7.50
201 Bill Buckner 82/25	25.00	7.50
202 Bill Buckner 83/25	25.00	7.50
203 Bill Buckner 83 DK/33	25.00	7.50
204 Bill Buckner 84/25	25.00	7.50
205 Bill Buckner 85 Black/21	25.00	7.50
206 Bill Buckner 85 Blue/4		
207 Bill Buckner 86/25	25.00	7.50
208 Bill Buckner 87/25	25.00	7.50
209 Bill Buckner 88 Black/24	25.00	7.50
210 Bill Buckner 88 Blue/1		
211 Bill Buckner 90 Black/2		
212 Bill Buckner 90 Blue/23	25.00	7.50
213 Jay Buhner 88/15		
214 Jay Buhner 88 DR/5		
215 Jay Buhner 89/11		
216 Jay Buhner 90/14		
217 Jay Buhner 91/14		
218 Jay Buhner 91 GS/1		
219 Jay Buhner 92/19	40.00	12.00
220 Jay Buhner 93/20	25.00	7.50
221 Jay Buhner 94/16	40.00	12.00
222 Jay Buhner 95/3		
223 Jay Buhner 96/4		
224 Jay Buhner 97/19	40.00	12.00
225 Jay Buhner 98/18	40.00	12.00
226 Jay Buhner 98 SPP/4		
227 Jay Buhner 01/5		
228 Marlon Byrd 02/28	15.00	4.50
229 Jose Canseco 86/4		
230 Jose Canseco 87/5		
231 Jose Canseco 87 DK/16	80.00	24.00
232 Jose Canseco 88/18	80.00	24.00
233 Jose Canseco 88 BB/1		
234 Jose Canseco 89/4		
235 Jose Canseco 89 40-40/17	80.00	24.00
236 Jose Canseco 89 GS/3		
237 Jose Canseco 89 MVP/4		
238 Jose Canseco 90/12		
239 Jose Canseco 91/3		
240 Jose Canseco 91 AS/7		
241 Jose Canseco 92/13		
242 Jose Canseco 93/18	80.00	24.00
243 Jose Canseco 94/1		
244 Jose Canseco 94 LL/1		
245 Jose Canseco 95/8		
246 Jose Canseco 96/1		
247 Jose Canseco 97 #54/6		
248 Jose Canseco 97 #277/2		
249 Jose Canseco 98/2		
250 Jose Canseco 98 SPP/1		
251 Rod Carew 81 #49/5		
252 Rod Carew 81 #169/3		
253 Rod Carew 81 w/Brett/1		
254 Rod Carew 82/3		
255 Rod Carew 82 DK/2		
256 Rod Carew 83/4		
257 Rod Carew 84/5		
258 Rod Carew 85/2		
259 Rod Carew 86/2		
260 Steve Carlton 81/29	40.00	12.00
261 Steve Carlton 81 CY/30	40.00	12.00
262 Steve Carlton 82/30	40.00	12.00
263 Steve Carlton 83/57	30.00	9.00
264 Steve Carlton 83 DK/25	40.00	12.00
265 Steve Carlton 84/3		
266 Steve Carlton 85/48	30.00	9.00
267 Steve Carlton 86/15		
268 Steve Carlton 87/7		
269 Steve Carlton 03 A83/1		
270 Gary Carter 81/27	25.00	7.50
271 Gary Carter 82/36	20.00	6.00
272 Gary Carter 82 DK/16	40.00	12.00
273 Gary Carter 83/42	20.00	6.00
274 Gary Carter 84/13		
275 Gary Carter 85/19	40.00	12.00
276 Gary Carter 86/61	20.00	6.00
277 Gary Carter 87/75	20.00	6.00
278 Gary Carter 88/47	20.00	6.00
279 Gary Carter 88 BB/1		
280 Gary Carter 89 Black/16	40.00	12.00
281 Gary Carter 89 Blue/15		
282 Gary Carter 89 BB/1		
283 Gary Carter 90 Black/1		
284 Gary Carter 90 Blue/12		
285 Gary Carter 91/26	25.00	7.50
286 Gary Carter 91 HL Black/1		
287 Gary Carter 91 HL Blue/21		
288 Gary Carter 92 Black/12		
289 Gary Carter 92 Blue/4		
290 Gary Carter 93 CL/19	40.00	12.00
291 Jack Clark 84 DK/17	40.00	12.00
292 Jack Clark 88 DK/67	20.00	6.00
293 Will Clark 87/10		
294 Will Clark 88/3		
295 Will Clark 88 BB/1		
296 Will Clark 88 DK/2		
297 Will Clark 89/5		
298 Will Clark 89 AS/2		
299 Will Clark 89 GS/1		
300 Will Clark 89 MVP/4		
301 Will Clark 90/4		
302 Will Clark 91/3		
303 Will Clark 92/6		
304 Will Clark 94/1		
305 Will Clark 95/1		
306 Will Clark 96/1		
307 Will Clark 99 Retro/2		
308 Will Clark 00 Retro/4		
309 Roger Clemens 86/1		
310 Roger Clemens 86 HL #5/1		
311 Roger Clemens 86 HL #6/1		
312 Roger Clemens 86 HL #17/1		
313 Roger Clemens 86 HL #18/1		
314 Roger Clemens 86 HL #26/1		
315 Roger Clemens 87/1		
316 Roger Clemens 88/1		
317 Roger Clemens 88 BB/1		
318 Roger Clemens 89/1		
319 Roger Clemens 90/1		
320 Roger Clemens 91/1		
321 Roger Clemens 91 MVP/1		
322 Roger Clemens 92/1		
323 Roger Clemens 95/1		
324 Roger Clemens 98 SPP/1		
325 Roger Clemens 99 Retro/2		
326 Roger Clemens 00 Retro/1		
327 Roger Clemens 01/1		
328 Roger Clemens 02/1		
329 Jose Cruz Sr. 81/39	12.00	3.60
330 Jose Cruz Sr. 82/50	12.00	3.60
331 Jose Cruz Sr. 83/50	12.00	3.60
332 Jose Cruz Sr. 84/50	12.00	3.60
333 Jose Cruz Sr. 85/49	12.00	3.60
334 Jose Cruz Sr. 86/50	12.00	3.60
335 Jose Cruz Sr. 87/57	12.00	3.60
336 Darren Daulton 86/24	25.00	7.50
337 Darren Daulton 87 Black/32	25.00	7.50
338 Darren Daulton 87 Blue/68	20.00	6.00
339 Darren Daulton 88 Black/21	25.00	7.50
340 Darren Daulton 88 Blue/18	40.00	12.00
341 Darren Daulton 89 Black/30	25.00	7.50
342 Darren Daulton 89 Blue/104	15.00	4.50
343 Darren Daulton 90/2		
344 Darren Daulton 91/7		
345 Darren Daulton 92 Black/7		
346 Darren Daulton 92 Blue/1		
347 Darren Daulton 93 Black/10		
348 Darren Daulton 93 Blue/23	25.00	7.50
349 Darren Daulton 93 DK/1		
350 Darren Daulton 94/10		
351 Darren Daulton 96/12		
352 Darren Daulton 97/3		
353 Darren Daulton 97 SPP/1		
354 Alvin Davis 85 DK/1		
355 Eric Davis 85/4		
356 Eric Davis 86/5		
357 Eric Davis 87/62	20.00	6.00
358 Eric Davis 87 DK COR Black/2		
359 E.Davis 87 DK COR Blue/39	20.00	6.00
360 Eric Davis 87 DK ERR/6		
361 Eric Davis 87 HL/1		
362 Eric Davis 88/80	20.00	6.00
363 Eric Davis 88 AS/1		
364 Eric Davis 88 BB/1		
365 Eric Davis 88 MVP/36	20.00	6.00
366 Eric Davis 89/71	20.00	6.00
367 Eric Davis 90/42	20.00	6.00
368 Eric Davis 90 AS/41	20.00	6.00
369 Eric Davis 91/66	20.00	6.00
370 Eric Davis 91 BC/102	15.00	4.50
371 Eric Davis 92/49	20.00	6.00
372 Eric Davis 93/20	25.00	7.50
373 Eric Davis 94/44	20.00	6.00
374 Eric Davis 97 #190/40	20.00	6.00
375 Eric Davis 97 #292/30	25.00	7.50
376 Eric Davis 99 Retro/95	15.00	4.50
377 Eric Davis 01/122	15.00	4.50
378 Eric Davis 01 SLS/6		
379 Andre Dawson 81/25	25.00	7.50
380 Andre Dawson 82 Black/20		
381 Andre Dawson 82 Blue/4		
382 Andre Dawson 83 Black/20	25.00	7.50
383 Andre Dawson 83 Blue/4		
384 Andre Dawson 84 Black/33	25.00	7.50
385 Andre Dawson 84 Blue/1		
386 Andre Dawson 85 Black/17	40.00	12.00
387 Andre Dawson 85 Blue/14		
388 Andre Dawson 86 Black/29	25.00	7.50
389 Andre Dawson 86 Blue/10		
390 A.Dawson 86 DK Black/34	25.00	7.50
391 A.Dawson 86 DK Blue/19	40.00	12.00
392 Andre Dawson 87 Black/19	40.00	12.00
393 Andre Dawson 87 Blue/18	40.00	12.00
394 Andre Dawson 87 HL #28/10		
395 Andre Dawson 87 HL #31/10		
396 Andre Dawson 88 Black/20	25.00	7.50
397 Andre Dawson 88 Blue/1		
398 Andre Dawson 88 AS/5		
399 Andre Dawson 88 BB/1		
400 A.Dawson 88 DK Black/35	25.00	7.50
401 A.Dawson 88 DK Blue/30	25.00	7.50
402 Andre Dawson 88 MVP/19	40.00	12.00
403 Andre Dawson 89 Black/20	25.00	7.50
404 Andre Dawson 89 Blue/10		
405 Andre Dawson 89 BB/1		
406 A.Dawson 89 MVP Black/20	25.00	7.50
407 Andre Dawson 89 MVP Blue/1		
408 Andre Dawson 90 Black/18	40.00	12.00
409 Andre Dawson 90 Blue/2		
410 Andre Dawson 91/20	25.00	7.50
411 A.Dawson 91 AS Black/20	25.00	7.50
412 Andre Dawson 91 AS Blue/1		
413 Andre Dawson 92 Blue/30	25.00	7.50
414 Andre Dawson 92 AS Black/12		
415 Andre Dawson 92 AS Blue/9		
416 Andre Dawson 93/19	40.00	12.00
417 Andre Dawson 94/10		
418 Andre Dawson 95/20		
419 Andre Dawson 96/15		
420 Andre Dawson 97/18	40.00	12.00
421 Lenny Dykstra 86/17	40.00	12.00
422 Lenny Dykstra 87/80	20.00	6.00
423 Lenny Dykstra 88/88	15.00	4.50
424 Lenny Dykstra 88 BB/1		
425 Lenny Dykstra 89/71	20.00	6.00
426 Lenny Dykstra 89 BB/1		
427 Lenny Dykstra 90/51	20.00	6.00
428 Lenny Dykstra 91/43	20.00	6.00
429 Lenny Dykstra 91 AS/37	20.00	6.00
430 Lenny Dykstra 91 DK/23		
431 Lenny Dykstra 91 MVP/21	25.00	7.50
432 Lenny Dykstra 91 w/Murphy/5		
433 Lenny Dykstra 92/64	20.00	6.00
434 Lenny Dykstra 93/32	25.00	7.50
435 Lenny Dykstra 94/21	25.00	7.50
436 Lenny Dykstra 95/25	25.00	7.50
437 Jim Edmonds 95/2		
438 Jim Edmonds 97/7		
439 Jim Edmonds 97 HIT/3		
440 Jim Edmonds 98/1		
441 Jim Edmonds 98 GPP SG/1		
442 Jim Edmonds 98 SPP/1		
443 Jim Edmonds 98 SPP SG/1		
444 Jim Edmonds 99 Retro/25	40.00	12.00
445 Jim Edmonds 00 Retro/25	40.00	12.00
446 Jim Edmonds 01/25	40.00	12.00
447 Jim Edmonds 02/6		
448 Dwight Evans 81/36	20.00	6.00
449 Dwight Evans 82/16	40.00	12.00
450 Dwight Evans 82 DK/4		
451 Dwight Evans 83/42	20.00	6.00
452 Dwight Evans 84/16	40.00	12.00
453 Dwight Evans 85/29	25.00	7.50
454 Dwight Evans 86/28	25.00	7.50
455 Dwight Evans 87/25	25.00	7.50
456 Dwight Evans 87 HL/10		
457 Dwight Evans 88/25	25.00	7.50
458 Dwight Evans 88 BB/1		
459 Dwight Evans 88 DK/30	25.00	7.50
460 Dwight Evans 89/16	40.00	12.00
461 Dwight Evans 91/4		
462 Dwight Evans 92/7		
463 Sid Fernandez 84/8		
464 Sid Fernandez 85/1		
465 Sid Fernandez 87/30	25.00	7.50
466 Sid Fernandez 88/56	20.00	6.00
467 Sid Fernandez 89/26	25.00	7.50
468 Sid Fernandez 90/1		
469 Sid Fernandez 91/14		
470 Sid Fernandez 92/8		
471 Sid Fernandez 93/4		
472 Sid Fernandez 94/8		
473 Sid Fernandez 95/4		
474 Rollie Fingers 81/56	20.00	6.00
475 Rollie Fingers 82/42	20.00	6.00
476 Rollie Fingers 82/63	20.00	6.00
477 Rollie Fingers 83 DK/24	25.00	7.50
478 Rollie Fingers 85/34	25.00	7.50
479 Rollie Fingers 86/43	20.00	6.00
480 Carlton Fisk 82 DK/11		
481 Carlton Fisk 83/3		
482 Carlton Fisk 85/1		
483 Carlton Fisk 87/4		
484 George Foster 83 DK/10		
485 John Franco 85/37	12.00	3.60
486 John Franco 86/41	12.00	3.60
487 John Franco 87/112	10.00	3.00
488 John Franco 88/225	10.00	3.00
489 John Franco 88 BB/1		
490 John Franco 89/83	10.00	3.00
491 John Franco 90/50	12.00	3.60
492 John Franco 90 DK/57	12.00	3.60
493 John Franco 91/72	12.00	3.60
494 John Franco 92/66	12.00	3.60
495 John Franco 93/64	12.00	3.60
496 John Franco 94/21	15.00	4.50
497 John Franco 95/19	25.00	7.50
498 John Franco 96/25	15.00	4.50
499 Julio Franco 83/14		
500 Julio Franco 84/15		
501 Julio Franco 85/30	25.00	7.50
502 Julio Franco 86/46	20.00	6.00
503 Julio Franco 87/59	20.00	6.00
504 Julio Franco 88/122	15.00	4.50
505 Julio Franco 88 BB/1		
506 Julio Franco 88 DK/75	15.00	4.50
507 Julio Franco 89/48	20.00	6.00
508 Julio Franco 90/46	20.00	6.00
509 Julio Franco 90 AS/26	25.00	7.50
510 Julio Franco 90 MVP/1		
511 Julio Franco 91/62	20.00	6.00
512 Julio Franco 92/38	20.00	6.00
513 Julio Franco 93/33	25.00	7.50
514 Julio Franco 94/18		
515 Julio Franco 95/21	25.00	7.50
516 Julio Franco 97/14		
517 Freddy Garcia 01/50	20.00	6.00
518 Freddy Garcia 01 SLC/1		
519 Freddy Garcia 01 SLS/1		
520 Freddy Garcia 02/27	25.00	7.50
521 Freddy Garcia 03/25	25.00	7.50
522 Jay Gibbons 01 DR/50	12.00	3.60
523 Jay Gibbons 02/3		
524 Jay Gibbons 03/24	15.00	4.50
525 Juan Gonzalez 90/10		
526 Juan Gonzalez 90 RevNeg/5		
527 D.Gooden 85/31	40.00	12.00
528 D.Gooden 86/9		
529 D.Gooden 86 DK/28	25.00	7.50
530 D.Gooden 87 Black/9		
531 D.Gooden 87 Blue/99	15.00	4.50
532 D.Gooden 88 Black/27	25.00	7.50
533 D.Gooden 88 Blue/121	15.00	4.50
534 D.Gooden 88 BB/2		
535 D.Gooden 89 Black/48	20.00	6.00
536 D.Gooden 89 Blue/49	20.00	6.00
537 D.Gooden 89 AS/1		
538 D.Gooden 90 Black/2		
539 D.Gooden 90 Blue/87	15.00	4.50
540 D.Gooden 91 Black/12		
541 D.Gooden 91 Blue/71	20.00	6.00
542 D.Gooden 92 Black/23	25.00	7.50
543 D.Gooden 92 Blue/6		
544 D.Gooden 93 Black/12		
545 D.Gooden 93 Blue/12		
546 D.Gooden 94 Black/3		
547 D.Gooden 94 Blue/20	25.00	7.50
548 D.Gooden 97 Black/16	40.00	12.00
549 D.Gooden 97 Blue/4		
550 Mark Grace 88/5		
551 Mark Grace 90/1		
552 Mark Grace 91/1		
553 Mark Grace 92/1		
554 Mark Grace 99 Retro/1		
555 Mark Grace 01/1		
556 Mark Grace 02/1		
557 Mark Grace 03/1		
558 Bobby Grich 81/88	10.00	3.00
559 Bobby Grich 82/88	10.00	3.00
560 Bobby Grich 83/70	12.00	3.60
561 Bobby Grich 84/73	12.00	3.60
562 Bobby Grich 85/84	10.00	3.00
563 Bobby Grich 86/67	12.00	3.60
564 Bobby Grich 87/90	10.00	3.00
565 Tony Gwynn 83/8		
566 Todd Helton 99 Retro/6		
567 Todd Helton 00 Retro/1		
568 Todd Helton 01/2		
569 Todd Helton 01 DK/2		
570 Todd Helton 01 FC/2		
571 Todd Helton 01 LL/2		
572 Todd Helton 01 LLDC/1		
573 Todd Helton 01 PL #3/1		
574 Todd Helton 01 PL #21/1		
575 Todd Helton 02/7		
576 Rickey Henderson 82/1		
577 Rickey Henderson 83/3		
578 Rickey Henderson 85/2		
579 Rickey Henderson 85 HL #17/1		
580 Rickey Henderson 85 HL #42/1		
581 Rickey Henderson 88/1		
582 Rickey Henderson 88 AS/2		
583 Rickey Henderson 88 BB/1		
584 Rickey Henderson 89/3		
585 Rickey Henderson 90/1		
586 Rickey Henderson 91/1		
587 Rickey Henderson 91 AS/2		
588 Rickey Henderson 91 AW/1		
589 Rickey Henderson 91 MVP/2		
590 Rickey Henderson 92/1		
591 Rickey Henderson 92 AS/2		
592 Rickey Henderson 92 HL/2		
593 Rickey Henderson 93/2		
594 Rickey Henderson 94/1		
595 Rickey Henderson 94 SE/1		
596 Rickey Henderson 95/2		
597 Rickey Henderson 96/1		
598 Rickey Henderson 98/1		
599 Rickey Henderson 00 Retro/1		
600 Rickey Henderson 01/1		
601 Keith Hernandez 81/19	40.00	12.00
602 Keith Hernandez 82/36	20.00	6.00
603 Keith Hernandez 83/39	20.00	6.00
604 Keith Hernandez 83 DK/25	25.00	7.50
605 Keith Hernandez 84/36	20.00	6.00
606 Keith Hernandez 85/80	20.00	6.00
607 Keith Hernandez 86/66	20.00	6.00
608 Keith Hernandez 87/123	15.00	4.50
609 Keith Hernandez 88 Black/91	15.00	4.50
610 Keith Hernandez 88 Blue/74	20.00	6.00
611 Keith Hernandez 88 BB/1		
612 Keith Hernandez 89/76	20.00	6.00
613 Keith Hernandez 89 BB/1		
614 Keith Hernandez 89 GS Green/2		
615 Keith Hernandez 89 GS Purple/4		
616 Keith Hernandez 89 GS Black/1		
617 Keith Hernandez 90/87	15.00	4.50
618 Eric Hinske 03/20	15.00	4.50
619 Eric Hinske 04/1		
620 Charlie Hough 82/60	12.00	3.60
621 Charlie Hough 83/56	12.00	3.60
622 Charlie Hough 84/79	12.00	3.60
623 Charlie Hough 85/69	12.00	3.60
624 Charlie Hough 86/58	12.00	3.60
625 Charlie Hough 87/150	10.00	3.00
626 Charlie Hough 87 DK/81	10.00	3.00
627 Charlie Hough 88/184	10.00	3.00
628 Charlie Hough 88 BB/1		
629 Charlie Hough 89/51	12.00	3.60
630 Charlie Hough 90/45	12.00	3.60
631 Charlie Hough 91/88	10.00	3.00
632 Charlie Hough 92/55	12.00	3.60
633 Charlie Hough 94/19	25.00	7.50
634 Art Howe 81/43	12.00	3.60
635 Art Howe 82 Black/37	12.00	3.60
636 Art Howe 82 Blue/57	12.00	3.60

637 Art Howe 83 Black/20 15.00 4.50
638 Art Howe 83 Blue/54 12.00 3.60
639 Tim Hudson 01/2
640 Tim Hudson 02/13
641 Tim Hudson 03/39 30.00 9.00
642 Aubrey Huff 04/3
643 Bo Jackson 86 DR/3
644 Bo Jackson 86 HL/3
645 Bo Jackson 90 DK/1
646 Bo Jackson 92/1
647 Fergie Jenkins 81/21 25.00 7.50
648 Fergie Jenkins 82/57 20.00 6.00
649 Fergie Jenkins 83/29 25.00 7.50
650 Fergie Jenkins 84/45 20.00 6.00
651 Tommy John 81 Black/15
652 Tommy John 81 Blue/6
653 Tommy John 82 Black/15
654 Tommy John 82 Blue/23 15.00 4.50
655 Tommy John 82 w/Guidry/11
656 Tommy John 83 Black/4
657 Tommy John 83 Blue/35 15.00 4.50
658 Tommy John 84 Black/15
659 Tommy John 84 Blue/31 15.00 4.50
660 Tommy John 85 Black/19 25.00 7.50
661 Tommy John 85 Blue/25 15.00 4.50
662 Tommy John 88 Black/66 12.00 3.60
663 Tommy John 88 Blue/25 15.00 4.50
664 Tommy John 88 DK Blue/50 12.00 3.60
665 Howard Johnson 83/28 15.00 4.50
666 Howard Johnson 85/29 15.00 4.50
667 Howard Johnson 86/24 15.00 4.50
668 Howard Johnson 87 Black/1
669 Howard Johnson 87 Blue/24 15.00 4.50
670 Howard Johnson 87 HL/9
671 Howard Johnson 88/25 15.00 4.50
672 Howard Johnson 89/25 15.00 4.50
673 Howard Johnson 90/25 15.00 4.50
674 Howard Johnson 90 AS/28 15.00 4.50
675 Howard Johnson 90 MVP/24 15.00 4.50
676 Howard Johnson 91/25 15.00 4.50
677 Howard Johnson 92 Black/26 15.00 4.50
678 Howard Johnson 92 Blue/4
679 Howard Johnson 93/17 25.00 7.50
680 Howard Johnson 94/24 15.00 4.50
681 Nick Johnson 99 Retro/53 12.00 3.60
682 Nick Johnson 99 Retro SLC/2
683 Nick Johnson 99 Retro SLS/2
684 Nick Johnson 01/55 12.00 3.60
685 Nick Johnson 01 SLC/2
686 Nick Johnson 01 SLS/2
687 Randy Johnson 89/1
688 Randy Johnson 90/1
689 Randy Johnson 91/1
690 Randy Johnson 92/1
691 Randy Johnson 95/1
692 Randy Johnson 96/1
693 Randy Johnson 99 Retro/1
694 Randy Johnson 01/1
695 Randy Johnson 02/1
696 Randy Johnson 03/1
697 Andruw Jones 99 Retro/10
698 Chipper Jones 96/2
699 Chipper Jones 99 Retro/2
700 Chipper Jones 00 Retro/2
701 Chipper Jones 01/2
702 Chipper Jones 01 DK/2
703 Chipper Jones 02/1
704 Dave Justice 90/24 40.00 12.00
705 Dave Justice 91/3
706 Dave Justice 91 MVP/9
707 Dave Justice 91 ROY/9
708 Dave Justice 92/8
709 Dave Justice 93/8
710 Dave Justice 94/16 60.00 18.00
711 Dave Justice 95/10
712 Dave Justice 96/3
713 Dave Justice 97 #175/2
714 Dave Justice 97 #291/4
715 Dave Justice 97 GPP #291/1
716 Dave Justice 97 SPP #175/2
717 Dave Justice 97 TSPE/2
718 Dave Justice 98/2
719 Dave Justice 98 GPP/1
720 Dave Justice 98 SPP/2
721 Dave Justice 99 Retro/10
722 Dave Justice 00 Retro/10
723 Dave Justice 01/25 40.00 12.00
724 Austin Kearns 02/14
725 Austin Kearns 03 Black/48 20.00 6.00
726 Austin Kearns 03 Blue/2
727 Jimmy Key 85/8
728 Jimmy Key 86/54 30.00 9.00
729 Jimmy Key 87/92 25.00 7.50
730 Jimmy Key 87 OD/3
731 Jimmy Key 88/74 30.00 9.00
732 Jimmy Key 89/64 30.00 9.00
733 Jimmy Key 90/42 30.00 9.00
734 Jimmy Key 91/20 40.00 12.00
735 Jimmy Key 92/38 30.00 9.00
736 Jimmy Key 93/23 40.00 12.00
737 Jimmy Key 94/19 60.00 18.00
738 Jimmy Key 94 SE/1
739 Jimmy Key 95/17 60.00 18.00
740 Jimmy Key 96/31 40.00 12.00
741 Jimmy Key 97/16 60.00 18.00
742 Jimmy Key 98/2
743 Carney Lansford 81 Black/87 10.00 3.00
744 Carney Lansford 81 Blue/9
745 Carney Lansford 82 Black/36 12.00 3.60
746 Carney Lansford 82 Blue/23 15.00 4.50
747 Carney Lansford 83 Black/10
748 Carney Lansford 83 Blue/29 15.00 4.50
749 Carney Lansford 84 Black/9
750 Carney Lansford 84 Blue/12
751 Carney Lansford 85/21 15.00 4.50
752 Carney Lansford 86/54 12.00 3.60
753 Carney Lansford 87/76 12.00 3.60
754 Carney Lansford 88 BB/1
755 Carney Lansford 88 Black/2
756 Carney Lansford 88 Blue/66 12.00 3.60
757 Carney Lansford 89/17 25.00 7.50
758 Carney Lansford 90/3
759 Carney Lansford 91/19 25.00 7.50
760 Carney Lansford 92/6
761 Carlos Lee 01/110 15.00 4.50
762 Carlos Lee 01 SLS/2
763 Carlos Lee 02/6
764 Kenny Lofton 92/1
765 Greg Luzinski 81 Black/15
766 Greg Luzinski 81 Blue/72 20.00 6.00
767 Greg Luzinski 82/67 20.00 6.00
768 Greg Luzinski 83/52 20.00 6.00
769 Greg Luzinski 84/43 20.00 6.00
770 Greg Luzinski 85/44 20.00 6.00
771 Fred Lynn 81 Black/43 20.00 6.00
772 Fred Lynn 81 Blue/23 25.00 7.50
773 Fred Lynn 82 Black/17 40.00 12.00
774 Fred Lynn 82 Blue/37 20.00 6.00
775 Fred Lynn 83 Black/1
776 Fred Lynn 83 Blue/42 20.00 6.00
777 Fred Lynn 84 Blue/25 25.00 7.50
778 Fred Lynn 84 Black/9
779 Fred Lynn 84 DK/21 25.00 7.50
780 Fred Lynn 85 Black/5
781 Fred Lynn 85 Blue/28 25.00 7.50
782 Fred Lynn 86 Black/43 20.00 6.00
783 Fred Lynn 86 Blue/8
784 Fred Lynn 87 Black/38 20.00 6.00
785 Fred Lynn 87 Blue/25 25.00 7.50
786 Fred Lynn 87 DK/82 15.00 4.50
787 Fred Lynn 88 Black/30 25.00 7.50
788 Fred Lynn 88 Blue/14
789 Fred Lynn 88 BB/1
790 Fred Lynn 89 Black/5
791 Fred Lynn 89 Blue/50 20.00 6.00
792 Fred Lynn 91/18 40.00 12.00
793 Greg Maddux 87/4
794 Greg Maddux 87 DR/5
795 Greg Maddux 88/1
796 Greg Maddux 89/1
797 Greg Maddux 90/1
798 Greg Maddux 91/1
799 Greg Maddux 92/1
800 Greg Maddux 93/1
801 Greg Maddux 94/1
802 Greg Maddux 95/1
803 Greg Maddux 96/1
804 Greg Maddux 98/1
805 Greg Maddux 98 DOM/1
806 Greg Maddux 99 Retro/1
807 Greg Maddux 00 Retro DK/1
808 Greg Maddux 01/1
809 Greg Maddux 01 DK/1
810 Greg Maddux 02/1
811 Greg Maddux 03 DK/1
812 Edgar Martinez 89/39 50.00 15.00
813 Edgar Martinez 91 DK/7
814 Edgar Martinez 92/9
815 Edgar Martinez 93/10
816 Edgar Martinez 94/3
817 Edgar Martinez 96/13
818 Edgar Martinez 97/3
819 Edgar Martinez 98/3
820 E.Martinez 99 Retro/42 50.00 15.00
821 E.Martinez 00 Retro/43 50.00 15.00
822 Edgar Martinez 01/58 50.00 15.00
823 Edgar Martinez 02/25 50.00 15.00
824 Pedro Martinez 92 DR/2
825 Pedro Martinez 93/1
826 Pedro Martinez 95/1
827 Pedro Martinez 96/1
828 Pedro Martinez 98/1
829 Pedro Martinez 01/1
830 Pedro Martinez 01 DK/1
831 Pedro Martinez 01 FC/1
832 Gary Matthews Sr. 81 COR/14
833 Gary Matthews Sr. 81 ERR/7
834 Gary Matthews Sr. 82/76 12.00 3.60
835 Gary Matthews Sr. 83/52 12.00 3.60
836 G.Matthews Sr. 84 Black/49 12.00 3.60
837 Gary Matthews Sr. 84 Blue/11
838 Gary Matthews Sr. 85/45 12.00 3.60
839 Gary Matthews Sr. 86/54 12.00 3.60
840 Don Mattingly 85/1
841 Don Mattingly 86/3
842 Don Mattingly 87/2
843 Don Mattingly 87 HL #17/5
844 Don Mattingly 87 HL #23/5
845 Don Mattingly 88/2
846 Don Mattingly 88 BB/1
847 Don Mattingly 88 MVP/2
848 Don Mattingly 89/2
849 Don Mattingly 90/2
850 Don Mattingly 91/2
851 Don Mattingly 92/2
852 Don Mattingly 93/3
853 Don Mattingly 94/5
854 Don Mattingly 95/3
855 Don Mattingly 95 CL/1
856 Jack McDowell 88/213 15.00 4.50
857 Jack McDowell 89/114 15.00 4.50
858 Jack McDowell 91/19 40.00 12.00
859 Jack McDowell 92/26 25.00 7.50
860 Jack McDowell 93/11
861 Jack McDowell 94/8
862 Jack McDowell 94 SE/3
863 Jack McDowell 95/5
864 Jack McDowell 96/17 40.00 12.00
865 Jack McDowell 97/6
866 Jack McDowell 97 SPP/1
867 Fred McGriff 86/20
868 Fred McGriff 88/1
869 Fred McGriff 89 DK/3
870 Fred McGriff 90/1
871 Fred McGriff 91/1
872 Fred McGriff 91 MVP/2
873 Fred McGriff 92/1
874 Fred McGriff 93/1
875 Fred McGriff 93 SOG/1
876 Fred McGriff 94/1
877 Fred McGriff 94 DOM/1
878 Fred McGriff 97/1
879 Fred McGriff 97 SPP/1
880 Fred McGriff 98 #64/1
881 Fred McGriff 98 GPP #64/1
882 Fred McGriff 98 SPP #230/1
883 Fred McGriff 00 Retro/1
884 Fred McGriff 01/1
885 Paul Molitor 81/6
886 Paul Molitor 82/5
887 Paul Molitor 83/9
888 Paul Molitor 84/2
889 Paul Molitor 85/4
890 Paul Molitor 86/6
891 Paul Molitor 87/1
892 Paul Molitor 87 HL/2
893 Paul Molitor 88/4
894 Paul Molitor 88 BB/1
895 Paul Molitor 88 DK/7
896 Paul Molitor 88 MVP/2
897 Paul Molitor 89/4
898 Paul Molitor 89 MVP/2
899 Paul Molitor 90/1
900 Paul Molitor 90 MVP/3
901 Paul Molitor 91/1
902 Paul Molitor 92/2
903 Paul Molitor 92 DK/1
904 Paul Molitor 93/2
905 Paul Molitor 94/2
906 Paul Molitor 94 SE/2
907 Paul Molitor 95/2
908 Paul Molitor 95 CL/1
909 Paul Molitor 96 CL/1
910 Paul Molitor 97/4
911 Paul Molitor 97 CL/1
912 Paul Molitor 97 HIT/2
913 Paul Molitor 98/6
914 Paul Molitor 98 HIT/1
915 Joe Morgan 81/7
916 Joe Morgan 82/6
917 Joe Morgan 82 DK/15
918 Joe Morgan 83/1
919 Joe Morgan 83 w/F.Rob/4
920 Joe Morgan 84/2
921 Joe Morgan 85/10
922 Jack Morris 81/31 25.00 7.50
923 Jack Morris 82/56 20.00 6.00
924 Jack Morris 83/48 20.00 6.00
925 Jack Morris 83 DK/14
926 Jack Morris 84/36 20.00 6.00
927 Jack Morris 85/42 20.00 6.00
928 Jack Morris 86/45 20.00 6.00
929 Jack Morris 87/123 15.00 4.50
930 Jack Morris 87 DK/106 15.00 4.50
931 Jack Morris 88/139 15.00 4.50
932 Jack Morris 88 AS/6
933 Jack Morris 88 BB/1
934 Jack Morris 89/107 15.00 4.50
935 Jack Morris 90/71 20.00 6.00
936 Jack Morris 91/34 25.00 7.50
937 Jack Morris 92/59 20.00 6.00
938 Jack Morris 92 AS/40 20.00 6.00
939 Jack Morris 93/78 20.00 6.00
940 Jamie Moyer 87/50 20.00 6.00
941 Jamie Moyer 88/24 25.00 7.50
942 Jamie Moyer 88 BB/1
943 Jamie Moyer 89/44 20.00 6.00
944 Jamie Moyer 90/35 25.00 7.50
945 Jamie Moyer 94/19 40.00 12.00
946 Jamie Moyer 95/29 25.00 7.50
947 Jamie Moyer 96/16 40.00 12.00
948 Jamie Moyer 97/11
949 Jamie Moyer 03/21 25.00 7.50
950 Dale Murphy 81 Black/21 50.00 15.00
951 Dale Murphy 81 Blue/14
952 Dale Murphy 82/9
953 Dale Murphy 83 Black/2
954 Dale Murphy 83 Blue/24 50.00 15.00
955 Dale Murphy 83 DK Black/1
956 Dale Murphy 83 DK Blue/11
957 Dale Murphy 84 Black/3
958 Dale Murphy 84 Blue/11
959 Dale Murphy 85 Black/8
960 Dale Murphy 85 Blue/13
961 Dale Murphy 86 Black/1
962 Dale Murphy 86 Blue/10
963 Dale Murphy 87 Black/2
964 Dale Murphy 87 Blue/37 50.00 15.00
965 Dale Murphy 87 DK Black/5
966 Dale Murphy 87 DK Blue/64 50.00 15.00
967 Dale Murphy 88 Black/3
968 Dale Murphy 88 Blue/40 50.00 15.00
969 Dale Murphy 88 AS Black/1
970 Dale Murphy 88 AS Blue/1
971 Dale Murphy 88 BB/1
972 Dale Murphy 88 MVP Black/2
973 Dale Murphy 88 MVP Blue/18
974 Dale Murphy 89 Black/5
975 Dale Murphy 89 Blue/40 50.00 15.00
976 Dale Murphy 90 Black/4
977 Dale Murphy 90 Blue/15
978 Dale Murphy 91 Black/2
979 Dale Murphy 91 Blue/4
980 Dale Murphy 92 Black/17 80.00 24.00
981 Dale Murphy 92 Blue/4
982 Dale Murphy 93 Black/12
983 Dale Murphy 93 Blue/3
984 Eddie Murray 81 Black/1
985 Eddie Murray 81 Blue/1
986 Eddie Murray 82/2
987 Eddie Murray 83/2
988 Eddie Murray 85/2
989 Eddie Murray 86 Black/1
990 Eddie Murray 86 Blue/1
991 Eddie Murray 87/2
992 Eddie Murray 87 HL/1
993 Eddie Murray 88/2
994 Eddie Murray 89/2
995 Eddie Murray 90/2
996 Eddie Murray 91 Black/1
997 Eddie Murray 91 Blue/1
998 Eddie Murray 91 BC Black/1
999 Eddie Murray 91 BC Blue/1
1000 Eddie Murray 91 MVP/2
1001 Eddie Murray 92/2
1002 Eddie Murray 93 Black/1
1003 Eddie Murray 93 Blue/1
1004 Eddie Murray 94/1
1005 Eddie Murray 95/2
1006 Stan Musial 01 ATDK/1
1007 Mike Mussina 95/3
1008 Mike Mussina 99 Retro/5
1009 Mike Mussina 00 Retro/5
1010 Mike Mussina 01/5
1011 Mike Mussina 02/5
1012 Graig Nettles 81 Black/6
1013 Graig Nettles 81 Blue/6
1014 Graig Nettles 82 Black/15
1015 Graig Nettles 82 Blue/27 25.00 7.50
1016 Graig Nettles 83 Black/15
1017 Graig Nettles 83 Blue/48 20.00 6.00
1018 Graig Nettles 84 Black/37 20.00 6.00
1019 Graig Nettles 84 Blue/13
1020 Graig Nettles 85 Black/23 25.00 7.50
1021 Graig Nettles 85 Blue/10
1022 Graig Nettles 86 Black/41 20.00 6.00
1023 Graig Nettles 86 Blue/11
1024 Phil Niekro 81/13
1025 Phil Niekro 82/15
1026 Phil Niekro 83/15
1027 Phil Niekro 83 w/Joe/2
1028 Phil Niekro 84/10
1029 Phil Niekro 85/9
1030 Phil Niekro 86/10
1031 Phil Niekro 86 w/Joe/10
1032 Phil Niekro 87/8
1033 Trot Nixon 01/110 15.00 4.50
1034 Trot Nixon 02/27 25.00 7.50
1035 Trot Nixon 03/25 25.00 7.50
1036 Al Oliver 81/65 12.00 3.60
1037 Al Oliver 82/60 12.00 3.60
1038 Al Oliver 83/49 12.00 3.60
1039 Al Oliver 84 Black/61 12.00 3.60
1040 Al Oliver 84 Blue/1
1041 Al Oliver 84 DK/29 15.00 4.50
1042 Al Oliver 85/55 12.00 3.60
1043 Al Oliver 86/58 12.00 3.60
1044 Paul O'Neill 86/21 40.00 12.00
1045 Paul O'Neill 88/1
1046 Paul O'Neill 89/15
1047 Paul O'Neill 91/10
1048 Paul O'Neill 92/3
1049 Paul O'Neill 93/2
1050 Paul O'Neill 96 GPP/3
1051 Paul O'Neill 99 Retro/10
1052 Paul O'Neill 00 Retro/12
1053 Paul O'Neill 01/29 40.00 12.00
1054 Paul O'Neill 02/29 40.00 12.00
1055 M.Ordonez 99 Retro/25 50.00 15.00
1056 M.Ordonez 00 Retro/25 50.00 15.00
1057 Magglio Ordonez 01/25 50.00 15.00
1058 Magglio Ordonez 02/25 50.00 15.00
1059 Jesse Orosco 85 DK Black/4
1060 Jesse Orosco 85 DK Blue/25 15.00 4.50
1061 Roy Oswalt 01 DR/30 25.00 7.50
1062 Roy Oswalt 02/11
1063 Roy Oswalt 02 FC/1
1064 Roy Oswalt 03/31 25.00 7.50
1065 Amos Otis 81/43 20.00 6.00
1066 Amos Otis 82/52 20.00 6.00
1067 Amos Otis 83/41 20.00 6.00
1068 Rafael Palmeiro 87/35 100.00 30.00
1069 Rafael Palmeiro 89/2
1070 Rafael Palmeiro 90/1
1071 Rafael Palmeiro 91/1
1072 Rafael Palmeiro 91 MVP/2
1073 Rafael Palmeiro 92/5
1074 Rafael Palmeiro 96/1
1075 Rafael Palmeiro 01/1
1076 Jim Palmer 81 #353 Black/11
1077 Jim Palmer 81 #353 Blue/11
1078 J.Palmer 81 #473 Black/16 40.00 12.00
1079 J.Palmer 81 #473 Blue/19 40.00 12.00
1080 Jim Palmer 82/49 20.00 6.00
1081 Jim Palmer 83/6
1082 Jim Palmer 83 DK/20
1083 Jim Palmer 84/17 40.00 12.00
1084 Dave Parker 81/18
1085 Dave Parker 82/31 25.00 7.50
1086 Dave Parker 83/39 20.00 6.00
1087 Dave Parker 84 Black/21 25.00 7.50
1088 Dave Parker 84 Blue/15 40.00 12.00
1089 Dave Parker 85 Black/1
1090 Dave Parker 85 Blue/19 40.00 12.00
1091 Dave Parker 86 Black/5
1092 Dave Parker 86 Blue/23 25.00 7.50
1093 Dave Parker 87 Black/66 20.00 6.00
1094 Dave Parker 87 Blue/11
1095 Dave Parker 88/85 15.00 4.50
1096 Dave Parker 89/21 25.00 7.50
1097 Dave Parker 90 Black/8
1098 Dave Parker 90 Blue/18 40.00 12.00
1099 Dave Parker 91/15
1100 Dave Parker 91 MVP/20 25.00 7.50
1101 Tony Pena 82/61 12.00 3.60
1102 Tony Pena 83/51 12.00 3.60
1103 Tony Pena 84/45 12.00 3.60
1104 Tony Pena 85/22 15.00 4.50
1105 Tony Pena 86/29 15.00 4.50
1106 Tony Pena 87/69 12.00 3.60
1107 Tony Pena 88/46 12.00 3.60
1108 Tony Pena 88 BB/1
1109 Tony Pena 89/36 12.00 3.60
1110 Tony Pena 90/16 25.00 7.50
1111 Tony Pena 91/17 25.00 7.50
1112 Tony Pena 92/30 15.00 4.50
1113 Tony Pena 93/43 12.00 3.60
1114 Tony Pena 94/8
1115 Tony Pena 95/3
1116 Tony Pena 96/11
1117 Tony Pena 96 GPP/1
1118 Terry Pendleton 85 COR/6
1119 Terry Pendleton 85 ERR/16 25.00 7.50
1120 Terry Pendleton 86/48 12.00 3.60
1121 Terry Pendleton 87/53 12.00 3.60
1122 Terry Pendleton 88/58 12.00 3.60
1123 Terry Pendleton 88 BB/1
1124 Terry Pendleton 89/54 12.00 3.60
1125 Terry Pendleton 90/60 12.00 3.60
1126 Terry Pendleton 91 Black/3
1127 Terry Pendleton 91 Blue/36 12.00 3.60
1128 Terry Pendleton 92/18 25.00 7.50
1129 Terry Pendleton 92 BC/4
1130 Terry Pendleton 93/43 12.00 3.60
1131 Terry Pendleton 94/27
1132 Terry Pendleton 95/13
1133 Terry Pendleton 96/17 25.00 7.50
1134 Terry Pendleton 97/21 15.00 4.50
1135 Gaylord Perry 81/91 15.00 4.50
1136 Gaylord Perry 82/79 20.00 6.00
1137 Gaylord Perry 83/55 20.00 6.00
1138 Jorge Posada 01/109 60.00 18.00
1139 Jorge Posada 01 PL/5
1140 Jorge Posada 01 PLDC/1
1141 Jorge Posada 02/4
1142 Kirby Puckett 85/8
1143 Kirby Puckett 87/21 80.00 24.00
1144 Harold Reynolds 86/32 25.00 7.50
1145 Harold Reynolds 87/65 20.00 6.00
1146 Harold Reynolds 88/65 20.00 6.00
1147 Harold Reynolds 89/22 25.00 7.50
1148 Harold Reynolds 89 BB/1
1149 Harold Reynolds 89 DK/12
1150 Harold Reynolds 90/4
1151 Harold Reynolds 91/13
1152 Harold Reynolds 92/26 25.00 7.50
1153 Harold Reynolds 93/16 40.00 12.00
1154 Harold Reynolds 94/6
1155 Jim Rice 81/13
1156 Jim Rice 82 Black/23 25.00 7.50
1157 Jim Rice 82 Blue/7
1158 Jim Rice 83/25 25.00 7.50
1159 Jim Rice 84/20 25.00 7.50
1160 Jim Rice 85/17 40.00 12.00
1161 Jim Rice 85 DK Black/23 25.00 7.50
1162 Jim Rice 85 DK Blue/2
1163 Jim Rice 86/28 25.00 7.50
1164 Jim Rice 87 Black/6
1165 Jim Rice 87 Blue/18 40.00 12.00
1166 Jim Rice 88/25 25.00 7.50
1167 Jim Rice 88 BB/1
1168 Jim Rice 89/12
1169 Cal Ripken 84/1
1170 Cal Ripken 85 DK/2
1171 Cal Ripken 86/1
1172 Cal Ripken 87/1
1173 Cal Ripken 87 HL/1
1174 Cal Ripken 88/1
1175 Cal Ripken 88 BC/1
1176 Cal Ripken 88 DK/2
1177 Cal Ripken 89/1
1178 Cal Ripken 90/1
1179 Cal Ripken 90 AS/1
1180 Cal Ripken 91/1
1181 Cal Ripken 91 AS/1
1182 Cal Ripken 92/1
1183 Cal Ripken 92 AS/1
1184 Cal Ripken 93 MVP/1
1185 Cal Ripken 99 Retro/1
1186 Cal Ripken 00 Retro/1
1187 Cal Ripken 01/1
1188 Cal Ripken 01 DK/1
1189 Cal Ripken 02/1
1190 M.Rivera 96/1
1191 M.Rivera 97/9
1192 M.Rivera 01 Black/27 100.00 30.00
1193 M.Rivera 01 Blue/23 100.00 30.00
1194 Frank Robinson 82/47 30.00 9.00
1195 Frank Robinson 83/36 30.00 9.00
1196 Frank Robinson 83 w/Morgan/10
1197 Frank Robinson 01 ATDK/1
1198 Alex Rodriguez 95/6
1199 Alex Rodriguez 97/1
1200 Alex Rodriguez 98/2
1201 Alex Rodriguez 98 FC/6
1202 Alex Rodriguez 98 HL/1
1203 Alex Rodriguez 99 Retro/1
1204 Alex Rodriguez 00 Retro/1
1205 Alex Rodriguez 00 Retro DK/1
1206 Alex Rodriguez 01/1
1207 Alex Rodriguez 01 DKSS/1
1208 Alex Rodriguez 02/1
1209 Ivan Rodriguez 91 DR/3
1210 Ivan Rodriguez 92/14
1211 Ivan Rodriguez 93/28 80.00 24.00
1212 Ivan Rodriguez 94/5
1213 Ivan Rodriguez 94 SE/3
1214 Ivan Rodriguez 95/2
1215 Ivan Rodriguez 96/16 120.00 36.00
1216 Ivan Rodriguez 97/5
1217 Ivan Rodriguez 98/2
1218 Ivan Rodriguez 98 SPP SG/1
1219 Ivan Rodriguez 99 Retro/10
1220 Ivan Rodriguez 99 Retro SLC/3
1221 Ivan Rodriguez 00 Retro/5
1222 Ivan Rodriguez 00 Retro SLC/3
1223 Ivan Rodriguez 01/5
1224 Ivan Rodriguez 01 DK/2
1225 Ivan Rodriguez 01 DKS/3
1226 Ivan Rodriguez 01 FC/5
1227 Ivan Rodriguez 01 RR/3
1228 Ivan Rodriguez 01 SLC/3
1229 Ivan Rodriguez 02/4
1230 Scott Rolen 98 SPP/1
1231 Scott Rolen 99 Retro/3
1232 Scott Rolen 99 Retro DK/3
1233 Scott Rolen 00 Retro/3
1234 Scott Rolen 01/2
1235 Scott Rolen 02/1
1236 Scott Rolen 03/1
1237 Nolan Ryan 83/2
1238 Nolan Ryan 85/3
1239 Nolan Ryan 86/2
1240 Nolan Ryan 87/5
1241 Nolan Ryan 87 HL/7
1242 Nolan Ryan 88/2
1243 Nolan Ryan 89/4
1244 Nolan Ryan 90/25 200.00 60.00
1245 Nolan Ryan 92/1
1246 Nolan Ryan 92 HL/1
1247 Nolan Ryan 92 HL w/Gossage/1
1248 Nolan Ryan 01 ATDK/1
1249 Ryne Sandberg 89/15
1249A Ryne Sandberg 89 Black/1
1250 Deion Sanders 89 DR/3
1251 Deion Sanders 90/4
1252 Deion Sanders 92/11
1253 Curt Schilling 89/67 50.00 15.00
1254 Richie Sexson 99 Retro/30 25.00 7.50
1255 Richie Sexson 01/30 25.00 7.50
1256 Richie Sexson 02/29 25.00 7.50
1257 Gary Sheffield 89/19 100.00 30.00
1258 Gary Sheffield 89 DR/10
1259 Gary Sheffield 90/1
1260 Gary Sheffield 91/2
1261 Gary Sheffield 92/1
1262 Gary Sheffield 94/2
1263 Gary Sheffield 96/1
1264 Gary Sheffield 99 Retro/2
1265 Gary Sheffield 00 Retro/1
1266 Gary Sheffield 02/1
1267 Ruben Sierra 86 DR/4
1268 Ruben Sierra 87 Black/121 15.00 4.50
1269 Ruben Sierra 87 Blue/101 15.00 4.50
1270 Ruben Sierra 88 Black/18 25.00 7.50
1271 Ruben Sierra 88 Blue/2
1272 Ruben Sierra 88 BB/1
1273 Ruben Sierra 88 MVP Black/12
1274 Ruben Sierra 88 MVP Blue/1
1275 Ruben Sierra 89/9
1276 R.Sierra 89 MVP Black/26 15.00 4.50
1277 Ruben Sierra 89 MVP Blue/3
1278 Ruben Sierra 91 Black/1
1279 Ruben Sierra 91 Blue/7
1280 Ruben Sierra 92/15
1281 Ruben Sierra 93 Black/1
1282 Ruben Sierra 93 Blue/6
1283 Ruben Sierra 94/4
1284 Ruben Sierra 95 DK/1
1285 Ruben Sierra 97 Black/9

1286 Ruben Sierra 97 Blue/2
1287 Lee Smith 83/9
1288 Duke Snider 84/26 40.00 12.00
1289 J.T. Snow 93 Black/34 15.00 4.50
1290 J.T. Snow 93 Blue/3
1291 J.T. Snow 94/1
1292 J.T. Snow 95 Black/1
1293 J.T. Snow 95 Blue/13
1294 J.T. Snow 96 Black/6
1295 J.T. Snow 96 Blue/19 25.00 7.50
1296 J.T. Snow 97 #42 Black/2
1297 J.T. Snow 97 #42 Blue/21 15.00 4.50
1298 J.T. Snow 97 #275 Black/2
1299 J.T. Snow 97 #275 Blue/13
1300 J.T. Snow 98 Black/19 25.00 7.50
1301 J.T. Snow 98 Blue/2
1302 J.T. Snow 98 SPP Black/1
1303 J.T. Snow 98 SPP Blue/1
1304 J.T. Snow 01 Black/81 10.00 3.00
1305 J.T. Snow 01 Blue/19 25.00 7.50
1306 J.T. Snow 03 Black/7
1307 J.T. Snow 03 Blue/2
1308 Sammy Sosa 90/15
1309 Sammy Sosa 91/4
1310 Sammy Sosa 92/2
1311 Sammy Sosa 93/1
1312 Sammy Sosa 95/4
1313 Sammy Sosa 96/2
1314 Sammy Sosa 99 Retro/3
1315 Sammy Sosa 00 Retro/2
1316 Sammy Sosa 01/3
1317 Sammy Sosa 01 PL/1
1318 Sammy Sosa 01 RR/1
1319 Sammy Sosa 02/2
1320 Warren Spahn 89/1
1321 Junior Spivey 03/20 15.00 4.50
1322 Terry Steinbach 87/22 15.00 4.50
1323 Terry Steinbach 87 DR/1
1324 Terry Steinbach 88/41
1325 Terry Steinbach 88 BB/1
1326 Terry Steinbach 89/34 15.00 4.50
1327 Terry Steinbach 90/30 15.00 4.50
1328 Terry Steinbach 90 AS/10
1329 Terry Steinbach 91/11
1330 Terry Steinbach 92 Black/6
1331 Terry Steinbach 92 Blue/10
1332 Terry Steinbach 93 Black/3
1333 Terry Steinbach 93 Blue/11
1334 Terry Steinbach 94 Black/1
1335 Terry Steinbach 94 Blue/5
1336 Terry Steinbach 95/3
1337 Terry Steinbach 96/4
1338 Terry Steinbach 96 GPP/5
1339 Terry Steinbach 97 Black/8
1340 Terry Steinbach 97 Blue/13
1341 Shannon Stewart 01/108 15.00 4.50
1342 Shannon Stewart 02/36 20.00 6.00
1343 Shannon Stewart 03/36 20.00 6.00
1344 Dave Stieb 81/3
1345 Dave Stieb 82/15
1346 Dave Stieb 83/24
1347 Dave Stieb 83 DK/9
1348 Dave Stieb 84/30 25.00 7.50
1349 Dave Stieb 85/19 40.00 12.00
1350 Dave Stieb 86/23 25.00 7.50
1351 Dave Stieb 87/99 15.00 4.50
1352 Dave Stieb 88/51 20.00 6.00
1353 Dave Stieb 88 BB/1
1354 Dave Stieb 89/36 20.00 6.00
1355 Dave Stieb 89 BB/1
1356 Dave Stieb 90/29 25.00 7.50
1357 Dave Stieb 91/10
1358 Dave Stieb 91 DK/17 40.00 12.00
1359 Dave Stieb 91 HL/3
1360 Dave Stieb 92/13
1361 Dave Stieb 93/12
1362 Darryl Strawberry 84/13
1363 Darryl Strawberry 85/30 25.00 7.50
1364 Darryl Strawberry 86/11
1365 Darryl Strawberry 86 HL/9
1366 Darryl Strawberry 87/83 15.00 4.50
1367 Darryl Strawberry 87 DK/81 15.00 4.50
1368 Darryl Strawberry 87 HL #42/10
1369 Darryl Strawberry 87 HL #49/11
1370 Darryl Strawberry 88/71 20.00 6.00
1371 Darryl Strawberry 88 AS/9
1372 Darryl Strawberry 88 BB/1
1373 D.Strawberry 88 MVP/38 20.00 6.00
1374 Darryl Strawberry 89/67 20.00 6.00
1375 Darryl Strawberry 89 BB/2
1376 D.Strawberry 89 MVP/63 20.00 6.00
1377 Darryl Strawberry 90/84 15.00 4.50
1378 Darryl Strawberry 91/33 25.00 7.50
1379 Darryl Strawberry 91 GS Blue/1
1380 Darryl Strawberry 91 GS Green/4
1381 D.Strawberry 91 MVP/33 25.00 7.50
1382 Darryl Strawberry 92/23 25.00 7.50
1383 Darryl Strawberry 92 McD/2
1384 Darryl Strawberry 93/41 20.00 6.00
1385 Darryl Strawberry 94/9
1386 Darryl Strawberry 95/22 25.00 7.50
1387 Darryl Strawberry 96/8
1388 Darryl Strawberry 97/36 20.00 6.00
1389 Darryl Strawberry 97 PP/1
1390 Darryl Strawberry 98/8
1391 Darryl Strawberry 98 GPP/1
1392 Darryl Strawberry 98 SPP/1
1393 B.J. Surhoff 87/108 15.00 4.50
1394 B.J. Surhoff 87 DR/15
1395 B.J. Surhoff 88/69 20.00 6.00
1396 B.J. Surhoff 88 BB/1
1397 B.J. Surhoff 89/44 20.00 6.00
1398 B.J. Surhoff 90/3
1399 B.J. Surhoff 91/13
1400 B.J. Surhoff 92/21 25.00 7.50
1401 B.J. Surhoff 93/10
1402 B.J. Surhoff 95/1
1403 B.J. Surhoff 97/2
1404 B.J. Surhoff 01/92 15.00 4.50
1405 B.J. Surhoff 01 SLS/9
1406 Frank Thomas 91/1
1407 Frank Thomas 92/1
1408 Frank Thomas 93/2
1409 Frank Thomas 93 SOG/1
1410 Frank Thomas 94/2
1411 Frank Thomas 94 SE/1
1412 Frank Thomas 95/1
1413 Frank Thomas 97/2
1414 Frank Thomas 98/1
1415 Frank Thomas 98 FC/2
1416 Frank Thomas 99 Retro/1
1417 Frank Thomas 00 Retro/1
1418 Frank Thomas 01/1
1419 Frank Thomas 01 LL/1
1420 Frank Thomas 02/1
1421 Gorman Thomas 81 Black/26
1422 Gorman Thomas 81 Blue/12
1423 G.Thomas 82 Black/35 12.00 3.60
1424 Gorman Thomas 82 Blue/30 15.00 4.50
1425 G.Thomas 83 Black/28 15.00 4.50
1426 Gorman Thomas 83 Blue/34 15.00 4.50
1427 G.Thomas 84 Black/33 15.00 4.50
1428 Gorman Thomas 84 Blue/37 12.00 3.60
1429 G.Thomas 86 Black/27 15.00 4.50
1430 Gorman Thomas 86 Blue/31 15.00 4.50
1431 Robby Thompson 86 DR/10
1432 Robby Thompson 87/36 12.00 3.60
1433 Robby Thompson 88 BB/1
1434 R.Thompson 88 Black/77 12.00 3.60
1435 R.Thompson 88 Blue/62 12.00 3.60
1436 Robby Thompson 89/57 12.00 3.60
1437 Robby Thompson 90/65 12.00 3.60
1438 Robby Thompson 91/46 12.00 3.60
1439 Robby Thompson 92/25 15.00 4.50
1440 Robby Thompson 93/17 25.00 7.50
1441 Robby Thompson 94/20 15.00 4.50
1442 Robby Thompson 95/14
1443 Robby Thompson 96/21 15.00 4.50
1444 Robby Thompson 97/27 15.00 4.50
1445 Luis Tiant 81/3
1446 Luis Tiant 83/27 15.00 4.50
1447 Alan Trammell 81/5
1448 Alan Trammell 82 COR/8
1449 Alan Trammell 82 ERR/11
1450 A.Trammell 82 DK COR/21 25.00 7.50
1451 Alan Trammell 82 DK ERR/2
1452 Alan Trammell 83 Black/21 25.00 7.50
1453 Alan Trammell 83 Blue/1
1454 Alan Trammell 84/6
1455 Alan Trammell 85/2
1456 Alan Trammell 86/15
1457 Alan Trammell 87 Black/38 20.00 6.00
1458 Alan Trammell 87 Blue/10
1459 Alan Trammell 87 HL/10
1460 Alan Trammell 88/89 15.00 4.50
1461 Alan Trammell 88 BB/1
1462 Alan Trammell 88 DK/77 20.00 6.00
1463 Alan Trammell 88 MVP/18 40.00 12.00
1464 Alan Trammell 89 Black/9
1465 Alan Trammell 89 Blue/13
1466 A.Tram 89 MVP Black/20 25.00 7.50
1467 Alan Trammell 89 MVP Blue/11
1468 Alan Trammell 90/1
1469 Alan Trammell 90 MVP/2
1470 Alan Trammell 91/12
1471 Alan Trammell 92/13
1472 Alan Trammell 93/16 40.00 12.00
1473 Alan Trammell 94 Black/1
1474 Alan Trammell 94 Blue/3
1475 Alan Trammell 95/1
1476 Alan Trammell 97/7
1477 Jason Varitek 01/110 40.00 12.00
1478 Robin Ventura 90/5
1479 Robin Ventura 90 DR/2
1480 Robin Ventura 91/17 40.00 12.00
1481 Robin Ventura 92/18 40.00 12.00
1482 Robin Ventura 93/9
1483 Robin Ventura 96 PP/1
1484 Robin Ventura 97/1
1485 Robin Ventura 98 SPP/3
1486 Robin Ventura 01/34 25.00 7.50
1487 Robin Ventura 02/34 25.00 7.50
1488 Frank White 81/5
1489 Frank White 82/24 15.00 4.50
1490 Frank White 83/25 15.00 4.50
1491 Frank White 84/28
1492 Frank White 85/11
1493 Frank White 86/15
1494 Frank White 87/15
1495 Frank White 88/47 12.00 3.60
1496 Frank White 88 BB/1
1497 Frank White 89/23 15.00 4.50
1498 Frank White 90/3
1499 Bernie Williams 90/5
1500 Matt Williams 87 DR/9
1501 Matt Williams 88/78 25.00 7.50
1502 Matt Williams 88/38 30.00 9.00
1503 Matt Williams 90/5
1504 Matt Williams 91/4
1505 Matt Williams 91 DK/10
1506 Matt Williams 91 GS/2
1507 Matt Williams 92/19 60.00 18.00
1508 Matt Williams 93/24 40.00 12.00
1509 Matt Williams 94/2
1510 Matt Williams 95/21 40.00 12.00
1511 Matt Williams 96/3
1512 Matt Williams 97 #19/10
1513 Matt Williams 97 #271/6
1514 Matt Williams 97 PP #19/2
1515 Matt Williams 98/2
1516 M.Williams 99 Retro/50 30.00 9.00
1517 Matt Williams 01/35 40.00 12.00
1518 Matt Williams 02/28 40.00 12.00
1519 Mookie Wilson 81/50
1520 Mookie Wilson 82/39 20.00 6.00
1521 Mookie Wilson 83/24 25.00 7.50
1522 Mookie Wilson 84/26 25.00 7.50
1523 Mookie Wilson 85/50 20.00 6.00
1524 Mookie Wilson 86/40 20.00 6.00
1525 Mookie Wilson 87/35 25.00 7.50
1526 Mookie Wilson 88/4
1527 Mookie Wilson 88 BB/1
1528 Mookie Wilson 89/28 25.00 7.50
1529 Mookie Wilson 90/20 25.00 7.50
1530 Mookie Wilson 91/25 25.00 7.50
1531 Dave Winfield 81/5
1532 Dave Winfield 82/4
1533 Dave Winfield 82 DK/4
1534 Dave Winfield 82 w/Reggie/3
1535 Dave Winfield 83/3
1536 Dave Winfield 84/2
1537 Dave Winfield 85/3
1538 Dave Winfield 86/2
1539 Dave Winfield 87/2
1540 Dave Winfield 87 DK/2
1541 Dave Winfield 88/2
1542 Dave Winfield 88 AS/2
1543 Dave Winfield 88 BB/1
1544 Dave Winfield 89/2
1545 Dave Winfield 89 AS/2
1546 Dave Winfield 89 BC/2
1547 Dave Winfield 89 GS/2
1548 Dave Winfield 90/2
1549 Dave Winfield 91/2
1550 Dave Winfield 92/4
1551 Dave Winfield 93/2
1552 Carl Yastrzemski 81 #94/2
1553 Carl Yastrzemski 81 #214/3
1554 Carl Yastrzemski 82/3
1555 Carl Yastrzemski 83/3
1556 Carl Yastrzemski 83 DK/3
1557 Carl Yastrzemski 90/4
1558 Robin Yount 82/3
1559 Robin Yount 83/3
1560 Robin Yount 84/2
1561 Robin Yount 84 DK/2
1562 Robin Yount 85/3
1563 Robin Yount 86/2
1564 Robin Yount 87/1
1565 Robin Yount 88/2
1566 Robin Yount 88 BB/1
1567 Robin Yount 89/1
1568 Robin Yount 89 DK/3
1569 Robin Yount 90/3
1570 Robin Yount 91/2
1571 Robin Yount 92/3
1572 Robin Yount 93/1
1573 Robin Yount 94/1
1574 Barry Zito 02/4
1575 Barry Zito 03/25 40.00 12.00
1576 Barry Zito 03 DK/5

2004 Donruss World Series

Nm-Mt Ex-Mt
COMP.SET w/o SP's (175) 40.00 12.00
COMP.SOX CHAMPS (25) 20.00 6.00
COMMON ACTIVE (1-175) .40 .12
COMMON RETIRED (1-175) .50 .15
176-200: OVERALL AU-GU ODDS 5 PER BOX
176-200 PRINT RUNS B/WN 487-1000 PER
COMMON (201-224/WS1) 1.00 .30
201-224/WS1 ISSUED IN SOX CHAMPS SET
1 Bartolo Colon .40 .12
2 Darin Erstad .40 .12
3 Garret Anderson .40 .12
4 Tim Salmon .60 .18
5 Troy Glaus .40 .12
6 Vladimir Guerrero 1.00 .30
7 Brandon Webb .40 .12
8 Luis Gonzalez .40 .12
9 Randy Johnson 1.00 .30
10 Roberto Alomar .60 .18
11 Shea Hillenbrand .40 .12
12 Steve Finley .40 .12
13 Andruw Jones .40 .12
14 Chipper Jones 1.00 .30
15 J.D. Drew .40 .12
16 Marcus Giles .40 .12
17 Rafael Furcal .40 .12
18 Javy Lopez .40 .12
19 Jay Gibbons .40 .12
20 Luis Matos .40 .12
21 Melvin Mora .40 .12
22 Miguel Tejada .40 .12
23 Rafael Palmeiro .60 .18
24 Curt Schilling 1.00 .30
25 Dwight Evans .50 .15
26 Fred Lynn .50 .15
27 Jason Varitek .60 .18
28 Jim Rice .50 .15
29 Johnny Damon 1.00 .30
30 Luis Tiant .50 .15
31 Manny Ramirez .60 .18
32 Nomar Garciaparra 1.50 .45
33 Pedro Martinez 1.00 .30
34 Trot Nixon .40 .12
35 Aramis Ramirez .40 .12
36 Corey Patterson .40 .12
37 Derrek Lee .40 .12
38 Greg Maddux 1.50 .45
39 Kerry Wood 1.00 .30
40 Mark Prior 1.00 .30
41 Moises Alou .40 .12
42 Sammy Sosa 1.50 .45
43 Carlos Lee .40 .12
44 Frank Thomas 1.00 .30
45 Luis Aparicio .50 .15
46 Magglio Ordonez .40 .12
47 Mark Buehrle .40 .12
48 Paul Konerko .40 .12
49 Adam Dunn .60 .18
50 Austin Kearns .40 .12
51 Barry Larkin .60 .18
52 Dave Concepcion .50 .15
53 George Foster .50 .15
54 Joe Morgan .50 .15
55 Sean Casey .40 .12
56 Tony Perez .50 .15
57 C.C. Sabathia .40 .12
58 Jody Gerut .40 .12
59 Omar Vizquel .60 .18
60 Victor Martinez .40 .12
61 Charles Johnson .40 .12
62 Jeromy Burnitz .40 .12
63 Larry Walker .60 .18
64 Preston Wilson .40 .12
65 Todd Helton .60 .18
66 Alan Trammell .50 .15
67 Dmitri Young .40 .12
68 Ivan Rodriguez 1.00 .30
69 Jeremy Bonderman .40 .12
70 A.J. Burnett .40 .12
71 Brad Penny .40 .12
72 Dontrelle Willis .40 .12
73 Josh Beckett .40 .12
74 Juan Pierre .40 .12
75 Luis Castillo .40 .12
76 Miguel Cabrera .60 .18
77 Mike Lowell .40 .12
78 Andy Pettitte .60 .18
79 Craig Biggio .60 .18
80 Jeff Bagwell .60 .18
81 Jeff Kent .40 .12
82 Lance Berkman .40 .12
83 Roger Clemens 2.00 .60
84 Roy Oswalt .40 .12
85 Wade Miller .40 .12
86 Angel Berroa .40 .12
87 Carlos Beltran .60 .18
88 Juan Gonzalez .60 .18
89 Ken Harvey .40 .12
90 Mike Sweeney .40 .12
91 Adrian Beltre .60 .18
92 Hideo Nomo 1.00 .30
93 Kazuhisa Ishii .40 .12
94 Milton Bradley .40 .12
95 Orel Hershiser .50 .15
96 Paul Lo Duca .40 .12
97 Shawn Green .40 .12
98 Ben Sheets .40 .12
99 Geoff Jenkins .40 .12
100 Junior Spivey .40 .12
101 Rickie Weeks .40 .12
102 Scott Podsednik .40 .12
103 Jack Morris .50 .15
104 Jacque Jones .40 .12
105 Johan Santana .60 .18
106 Shannon Stewart .40 .12
107 Torii Hunter .40 .12
108 Jose Vidro .40 .12
109 Orlando Cabrera Sox .60 .18
110 Al Leiter .40 .12
111 Darryl Strawberry .50 .15
112 Dwight Gooden .50 .15
113 Jose Reyes .40 .12
114 Kazuo Matsui RC 2.50 .75
115 Keith Hernandez .50 .15
116 Lenny Dykstra .50 .15
117 Mike Piazza 1.50 .45
118 Tom Glavine .60 .18
119 Alex Rodriguez 1.50 .45
120 Bernie Williams .60 .18
121 Derek Jeter 2.00 .60
122 Gary Sheffield .40 .12
123 Jason Giambi .40 .12
124 Javier Vazquez .40 .12
125 Jorge Posada .60 .18
126 Kenny Lofton .40 .12
127 Kevin Brown .40 .12
128 Mariano Rivera .60 .18
129 Mike Mussina .60 .18
130 Barry Zito .40 .12
131 Eric Chavez .40 .12
132 Jermaine Dye .40 .12
133 Mark Mulder .40 .12
134 Rich Harden .40 .12
135 Tim Hudson .40 .12
136 Brett Myers .40 .12
137 Jim Thome 1.00 .30
138 Kevin Millwood .40 .12
139 Marlon Byrd .40 .12
140 Mike Lieberthal .40 .12
141 Pat Burrell .40 .12
142 Steve Carlton .50 .15
143 Dave Parker .50 .15
144 Jason Kendall .40 .12
145 Brian Giles .40 .12
146 Jay Payton .40 .12
147 Ryan Klesko .40 .12
148 J.T. Snow .40 .12
149 Jason Schmidt .40 .12
150 Bret Boone .40 .12
151 Edgar Martinez .60 .18
152 Jamie Moyer .40 .12
153 Rich Aurilia .40 .12
154 Shigetoshi Hasegawa .40 .12
155 Albert Pujols 2.00 .60
156 Dan Haren .40 .12
157 Edgar Renteria .40 .12
158 Fernando Vina .40 .12
159 Jim Edmonds .40 .12
160 Matt Morris .40 .12
161 Scott Rolen 1.00 .30
162 Aubrey Huff .40 .12
163 Carl Crawford .40 .12
164 Dewon Brazelton .40 .12
165 Fred McGriff .60 .18
166 Rocco Baldelli .60 .18
167 Alfonso Soriano .60 .18
168 Hank Blalock .40 .12
169 Kenny Rogers .40 .12
170 Mark Teixeira .40 .12
171 Michael Young .40 .12
172 Carlos Delgado .40 .12
173 Eric Hinske .40 .12
174 Roy Halladay .40 .12
175 Vernon Wells .40 .12
176 Ivan Ochoa AU/487 RC 8.00 2.40
177 Jason Bartlett AU/1000 RC 10.00 3.00
178 J.Labandeira AU/703 RC 8.00 2.40
179 Phil Stockman AU/1000 RC 8.00 2.40
180 Ronny Cedeno AU/715 RC 8.00 2.40
181 Shawn Camp AU/1000 RC 8.00 2.40
182 Ruddy Yan AU/1000 8.00 2.40
183 Roberto Novoa AU/568 RC 10.00 3.00
184 Just Knoedler AU/1000 RC 8.00 2.40
185 Jesse Harper AU/1000 RC 8.00 2.40
186 Jas Szuminski AU/1000 RC 8.00 2.40
187 Jamie Brown AU/800 RC 8.00 2.40
188 Ed Rodriguez AU/1000 RC 10.00 3.00
189 Dennis Sarfate AU/1000 RC 8.00 2.40
190 Ryan Meaux AU/1000 RC 8.00 2.40
191 Ch.Thomas AU/1000 RC 15.00 4.50
192 F.Francisco AU/1000 RC 8.00 2.40
193 Orl Rodriguez AU/500 RC 8.00 2.40
194 Joey Gathright AU/1000 RC 12.00 3.60
195 Renyel Pinto AU/1000 RC 10.00 3.00
196 Justin Leone AU/1000 RC 10.00 3.00
197 Tim Bausher AU/834 RC 8.00 2.40
198 Trav Blackley AU/1000 RC 10.00 3.00
199 Yadier Molina AU/500 RC 20.00 6.00
200 Brad Halsey AU/500 RC 10.00 3.00
201 Curt Schilling WSC 3.00 .90
202 Pedro Martinez WSC 3.00 .90
203 Derek Lowe WSC 1.00 .30
204 Tim Wakefield WSC 1.00 .30
205 Bronson Arroyo WSC 1.00 .30
206 Mike Timlin WSC 1.00 .30
207 Curtis Leskanic WSC 1.00 .30
208 Mike Myers WSC 1.00 .30
209 Alan Embree WSC 1.00 .30
210 Keith Foulke WSC 2.00 .60
211 Jason Varitek WSC 2.00 .60
212 Doug Mirabelli WSC 1.00 .30
213 Doug Mientkiewicz WSC 1.00 .30
214 Mark Bellhorn WSC 2.00 .60
215 Pokey Reese WSC 1.00 .30
216 Orlando Cabrera WSC 2.00 .60
217 Bill Mueller WSC 2.00 .60
218 Kevin Youkilis WSC 1.00 .30
219 Manny Ramirez WSC 2.00 .60
220 Johnny Damon WSC 3.00 .90
221 Dave Roberts WSC 1.00 .30
222 Trot Nixon WSC 1.00 .30
223 Gabe Kapler WSC 1.00 .30
224 David Ortiz WSC 3.00 .90
WS1 Pedro Martinez 3.00 .90
Curt Schilling
David Ortiz

2004 Donruss World Series HoloFoil 100

Nm-Mt Ex-Mt
*HOLO 1-175: 3X TO 8X BASIC
*HOLO 1-175: 2.5X TO 6X BASIC RC's
*HOLO 176-200: .2X TO .5X BAS.p/r 703-1000
*HOLO 176-200: .2X TO .5X BAS.p/r 487-568
RANDOM INSERTS IN PACKS
STATED PRINT RUN 100 SERIAL #'d SETS

2004 Donruss World Series HoloFoil 50

Nm-Mt Ex-Mt
*HOLO 1-175: 5X TO 12X BASIC
*HOLO 1-175: 4X TO 10X BASIC RC's
*HOLO 176-200: .3X TO .8X BAS.p/r 703-1000
*HOLO 176-200: .3X TO .8X BAS.p/r 487-568
RANDOM INSERTS IN PACKS
STATED PRINT RUN 50 SERIAL #'d SETS

2004 Donruss World Series HoloFoil 25

Nm-Mt Ex-Mt
*HOLO 1-175: 8X TO 20X BASIC
RANDOM INSERTS IN PACKS
STATED PRINT RUN 25 SERIAL #'d SETS
NO RC YR PRICING DUE TO SCARCITY

2004 Donruss World Series HoloFoil 10

Nm-Mt Ex-Mt
RANDOM INSERTS IN PACKS
STATED PRINT RUN 10 SERIAL #'d SETS
NO PRICING DUE TO SCARCITY

2004 Donruss World Series Material Bat

Nm-Mt Ex-Mt
*BAT: .5X TO 1.2X AL/NL p/r 250
*BAT: .4X TO 1X AL/NL p/r 100
OVERALL AU-GU ODDS FIVE PER BOX
STATED PRINT RUN 100 SERIAL #'d SETS
10 Roberto Alomar 8.00 2.40
15 J.D. Drew 5.00 1.50
18 Javy Lopez 5.00 1.50
27 Jason Varitek 8.00 2.40
29 Johnny Damon 10.00 3.00
32 Nomar Garciaparra 12.00 3.60
34 Trot Nixon 5.00 1.50
37 Derrek Lee 5.00 1.50
41 Moises Alou 5.00 1.50
45 Luis Aparicio 8.00 2.40
46 Magglio Ordonez 5.00 1.50
51 Barry Larkin 8.00 2.40
53 George Foster 8.00 2.40
54 Joe Morgan 8.00 2.40
55 Sean Casey 5.00 1.50
56 Tony Perez 8.00 2.40
61 Charles Johnson 5.00 1.50
66 Alan Trammell 8.00 2.40
68 Ivan Rodriguez 10.00 3.00
74 Juan Pierre 5.00 1.50
75 Luis Castillo 5.00 1.50
78 Andy Pettitte 8.00 2.40
83 Roger Clemens 12.00 3.60
84 Roy Oswalt 5.00 1.50
87 Carlos Beltran 8.00 2.40
88 Juan Gonzalez 8.00 2.40
89 Ken Harvey 5.00 1.50
107 Torii Hunter 5.00 1.50
108 Jose Vidro 5.00 1.50
109 Orlando Cabrera Sox 8.00 2.40
112 Dwight Gooden 8.00 2.40
113 Jose Reyes 5.00 1.50
114 Kazuo Matsui 15.00 4.50
115 Keith Hernandez 8.00 2.40
116 Lenny Dykstra 8.00 2.40
122 Gary Sheffield 5.00 1.50
125 Jorge Posada 8.00 2.40
126 Kenny Lofton 5.00 1.50
127 Kevin Brown 5.00 1.50
132 Jermaine Dye 5.00 1.50
145 Brian Giles 5.00 1.50
151 Edgar Martinez 8.00 2.40
153 Rich Aurilia 5.00 1.50
157 Edgar Renteria 5.00 1.50
167 Alfonso Soriano 8.00 2.40
170 Mark Teixeira 5.00 1.50

71 Michael Young 5.00 1.50
72 Carlos Delgado 5.00 1.50

2004 Donruss World Series Material Fabric AL/NL

Nm-Mt Ex-Mt
OVERALL AU-GU ODDS FIVE PER BOX
STATED PRINT RUN 250 SERIAL #'d SETS
2 Darin Erstad Jsy 5.00 1.50
3 Garret Anderson Jsy 5.00 1.50
4 Tim Salmon Jsy 8.00 2.40
5 Troy Glaus Jsy 5.00 1.50
6 Vladimir Guerrero Jsy 8.00 2.40
7 Brandon Webb Pants 5.00 1.50
8 Luis Gonzalez Jsy 5.00 1.50
9 Randy Johnson Pants/100 10.00 3.00
12 Steve Finley Jsy 5.00 1.50
13 Andruw Jones Jsy 5.00 1.50
14 Chipper Jones Jsy 8.00 2.40
16 Marcus Giles Jsy 5.00 1.50
17 Rafael Furcal Jsy 5.00 1.50
19 Jay Gibbons Jsy 5.00 1.50
20 Luis Matos Jsy 5.00 1.50
21 Melvin Mora Jsy 5.00 1.50
22 Miguel Tejada Jsy 5.00 1.50
23 Rafael Palmeiro Jsy/100 8.00 2.40
25 Dwight Evans Jsy 8.00 2.40
26 Fred Lynn Jsy 8.00 2.40
28 Jim Rice Jsy 8.00 2.40
31 Manny Ramirez Jsy 8.00 2.40
33 Pedro Martinez Jsy 8.00 2.40
35 Aramis Ramirez Jsy 5.00 1.50
38 Greg Maddux Jsy/100 12.00 3.60
39 Kerry Wood Pants 8.00 2.40
40 Mark Prior Jsy 8.00 2.40
42 Sammy Sosa Jsy 10.00 3.00
43 Carlos Lee Jsy 5.00 1.50
44 Frank Thomas Jsy 8.00 2.40
47 Mark Buehrle Jsy 5.00 1.50
48 Paul Konerko Jsy 5.00 1.50
49 Adam Dunn Jsy 8.00 2.40
50 Austin Kearns Jsy 5.00 1.50
52 Dave Concepcion Jsy 8.00 2.40
57 C.C. Sabathia Jsy 5.00 1.50
58 Jody Gerut Jsy 5.00 1.50
59 Omar Vizquel Jsy 8.00 2.40
60 Victor Martinez Jsy 5.00 1.50
63 Larry Walker Jsy 8.00 2.40
64 Preston Wilson Jsy 5.00 1.50
65 Todd Helton Jsy 8.00 2.40
70 A.J. Burnett Jsy 5.00 1.50
71 Brad Penny Jsy 5.00 1.50
72 Dontrelle Willis Jsy 5.00 1.50
73 Josh Beckett Jsy 5.00 1.50
76 Miguel Cabrera Jsy 8.00 2.40
77 Mike Lowell Jsy 5.00 1.50
79 Craig Biggio Jsy 8.00 2.40
80 Jeff Bagwell Pants 8.00 2.40
81 Jeff Kent Jsy 5.00 1.50
82 Lance Berkman Jsy 5.00 1.50
86 Angel Berroa Pants 5.00 1.50
90 Mike Sweeney Jsy 5.00 1.50
91 Adrian Beltre Jsy 8.00 2.40
92 Hideo Nomo Jsy 8.00 2.40
93 Kazuhisa Ishii Jsy 5.00 1.50
95 Orel Hershiser Jsy/100 8.00 2.40
96 Paul Lo Duca Jsy 5.00 1.50
97 Shawn Green Jsy 5.00 1.50
98 Ben Sheets Pants 5.00 1.50
99 Geoff Jenkins Jsy 5.00 1.50
104 Jacque Jones Jsy 5.00 1.50
105 Johan Santana Jsy 8.00 2.40
106 Shannon Stewart Jsy 5.00 1.50
110 Al Leiter Jsy 5.00 1.50
111 Darryl Strawberry Jsy 8.00 2.40
117 Mike Piazza Jsy 10.00 3.00
118 Tom Glavine Jsy 8.00 2.40
120 Bernie Williams Jsy 8.00 2.40
123 Jason Giambi Jsy 5.00 1.50
128 Mariano Rivera Jsy 8.00 2.40
129 Mike Mussina Jsy 8.00 2.40
130 Barry Zito Jsy 5.00 1.50
131 Eric Chavez Jsy 5.00 1.50
133 Mark Mulder Jsy 5.00 1.50
135 Tim Hudson Jsy 5.00 1.50
136 Brett Myers Jsy 5.00 1.50
137 Jim Thome Jsy 8.00 2.40
138 Kevin Millwood Jsy 5.00 1.50
139 Marlon Byrd Jsy 5.00 1.50
141 Pat Burrell Jsy 5.00 1.50
142 Steve Carlton Jsy/100 8.00 2.40
143 Dave Parker Jsy/100 8.00 2.40
147 Ryan Klesko Jsy 5.00 1.50
152 Jamie Moyer Jsy 5.00 1.50
155 Albert Pujols Jsy/100 20.00 6.00
156 Dan Haren Jsy 5.00 1.50
159 Jim Edmonds Jsy 5.00 1.50
161 Scott Rolen Jsy 8.00 2.40
162 Aubrey Huff Jsy 5.00 1.50
163 Carl Crawford Jsy 5.00 1.50
164 Dewon Brazelton Jsy 5.00 1.50
165 Fred McGriff Jsy 8.00 2.40
166 Rocco Baldelli Jsy 5.00 1.50
168 Hank Blalock Jsy 5.00 1.50
174 Roy Halladay Jsy 5.00 1.50
175 Vernon Wells Jsy 5.00 1.50

2004 Donruss World Series Material Fabric Number

Nm-Mt Ex-Mt
*NBR p/r 75: .5X TO 1.2X AL/NL p/r 250
*NBR p/r 36-65: .75X TO 2X AL/NL p/r 250
*NBR p/r 36-65: .6X TO 1.5X AL/NL p/r 100
*NBR p/r 20-35: 1.25X TO 3X AL/NL p/r 250
*NBR p/r 20-35: 1X TO 2.5X AL/NL p/r 100

*NBR p/r 15-19: 1.5X TO 4X AL/NL p/r 250
*NBR p/r 15-19: 1.25X TO 3X AL/NL p/r 100
OVERALL AU-GU ODDS FIVE PER BOX
PRINT RUNS B/WN 1-75 #'d COPIES PER
NO PRICING ON QTY OF 14 OR LESS
30 Luis Tiant Jsy/23 15.00 4.50
46 Magglio Ordonez Jsy/30 12.00 3.60
53 George Foster Jsy/15 20.00 6.00
98 Ben Sheets Pants/15 15.00 4.50
107 Torii Hunter Jsy/48 8.00 2.40
125 Jorge Posada Jsy/20 20.00 6.00

2004 Donruss World Series Signature

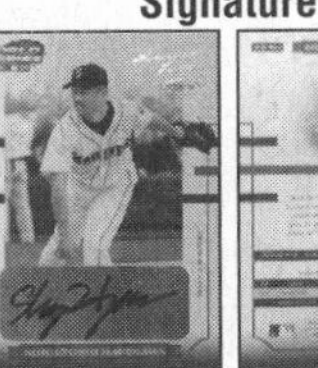

Nm-Mt Ex-Mt
1-175 AU-GU ODDS FIVE PER BOX
1-175 PRINT RUNS B/WN 5-25 COPIES PER
1-175 NO PRICING ON QTY OF 10 OR LESS
201-222 ODDS 1:75 SOX CHAMPS SETS
201-222 ARE NOT SERIAL-NUMBERED
201-222 SP INFO PROVIDED BY DONRUSS
3 Garret Anderson/25 25.00 7.50
7 Brandon Webb/25 15.00 4.50
10 Roberto Alomar/5
11 Shea Hillenbrand/25 25.00 7.50
12 Steve Finley/25 25.00 7.50
13 Andruw Jones/5
16 Marcus Giles/25 25.00 7.50
17 Rafael Furcal/25 25.00 7.50
19 Jay Gibbons/25 15.00 4.50
20 Luis Matos/25 15.00 4.50
21 Melvin Mora/25 25.00 7.50
23 Rafael Palmeiro/5
25 Dwight Evans/25 40.00 12.00
26 Fred Lynn/25 25.00 7.50
28 Jim Rice/25 25.00 7.50
30 Luis Tiant/25 25.00 7.50
31 Manny Ramirez/5
33 Pedro Martinez/5
34 Trot Nixon/25 25.00 7.50
35 Aramis Ramirez/25 25.00 7.50
37 Derrek Lee/25 25.00 7.50
39 Kerry Wood/5
40 Mark Prior/25 60.00 18.00
42 Sammy Sosa/5
43 Carlos Lee/25 15.00 4.50
44 Frank Thomas/5
45 Luis Aparicio/25 25.00 7.50
46 Magglio Ordonez/25 25.00 7.50
47 Mark Buehrle/25 25.00 7.50
49 Adam Dunn/25 40.00 12.00
50 Austin Kearns/25 25.00 7.50
52 Dave Concepcion/25 25.00 7.50
53 George Foster/25 25.00 7.50
54 Joe Morgan/5
55 Sean Casey/10
56 Tony Perez/25 40.00 12.00
57 C.C. Sabathia/25 25.00 7.50
58 Jody Gerut/25 15.00 4.50
60 Victor Martinez/25 25.00 7.50
64 Preston Wilson/25 25.00 7.50
66 Alan Trammell/25 25.00 7.50
69 Jeremy Bonderman/25 15.00 4.50
71 Brad Penny/25 15.00 4.50
76 Miguel Cabrera/25 40.00 12.00
77 Mike Lowell/10
78 Andy Pettitte/5
79 Craig Biggio/5
80 Jeff Bagwell/5
83 Roger Clemens/5
84 Roy Oswalt/25 25.00 7.50
85 Wade Miller/25 15.00 4.50
86 Angel Berroa/25 15.00 4.50
87 Carlos Beltran/25 50.00 15.00
89 Ken Harvey/25 15.00 4.50
92 Hideo Nomo/5
94 Milton Bradley/25 25.00 7.50
95 Orel Hershiser/5
96 Paul Lo Duca/25 25.00 7.50
97 Shawn Green/5
101 Rickie Weeks/25 25.00 7.50
102 Scott Podsednik/25 25.00 7.50
103 Jack Morris/25 25.00 7.50
104 Jacque Jones/25 25.00 7.50
105 Johan Santana/25 50.00 15.00
106 Shannon Stewart/25 25.00 7.50
107 Torii Hunter/25 25.00 7.50
108 Jose Vidro/25 15.00 4.50
109 Orlando Cabrera Sox/25 50.00 15.00
111 Darryl Strawberry/25 25.00 7.50
112 Dwight Gooden/25 25.00 7.50
113 Jose Reyes/9
115 Keith Hernandez/25 25.00 7.50
116 Lenny Dykstra/25 25.00 7.50
117 Mike Piazza/5
120 Bernie Williams/5
125 Jorge Posada/5
132 Jermaine Dye/25 25.00 7.50
133 Mark Mulder/25 25.00 7.50
134 Rich Harden/25 25.00 7.50
135 Tim Hudson/5
139 Marlon Byrd/25 15.00 4.50
142 Steve Carlton/25 40.00 12.00
143 Dave Parker/25 25.00 7.50
146 Jay Payton/25 15.00 4.50
148 J.T. Snow/25 25.00 7.50
151 Edgar Martinez/10
152 Jamie Moyer/10
154 Shigetoshi Hasegawa/25 50.00 15.00
155 Albert Pujols/5
156 Dan Haren/25 15.00 4.50
159 Jim Edmonds/5
161 Scott Rolen/10
162 Aubrey Huff/25 25.00 7.50
163 Carl Crawford/25 25.00 7.50
164 Dewon Brazelton/25 15.00 4.50
167 Alfonso Soriano/10
168 Hank Blalock/25 25.00 7.50
170 Mark Teixeira/25 40.00 12.00
171 Michael Young/25 25.00 7.50
175 Vernon Wells/10
201 Curt Schilling WSC SP
202 Pedro Martinez WSC SP
210 Keith Foulke WSC
211 Jason Varitek WSC SP
216 Orlando Cabrera WSC
218 Kevin Youkilis WSC
219 Manny Ramirez WSC SP
222 Trot Nixon WSC

2004 Donruss World Series Blue

Nm-Mt Ex-Mt
COMPLETE SET (100) 80.00 24.00
COMMON ACTIVE (1-100) .75 .23
COMMON RETIRED (1-100) 1.00 .30
ONE PER PACK
1 Josh Beckett .75 .23
2 Miguel Cabrera 1.25 .35
3 Derrek Lee .75 .23
4 Mike Lowell .75 .23
5 Brad Penny .75 .23
6 Ivan Rodriguez 2.00 .60
7 Dontrelle Willis .75 .23
8 Luis Castillo .75 .23
9 Garret Anderson .75 .23
10 Troy Glaus 1.25 .35
11 John Lackey .75 .23
12 Chone Figgins .75 .23
13 Tim Salmon 1.25 .35
14 Darin Erstad .75 .23
15 Troy Percival .75 .23
16 Steve Finley .75 .23
17 Mark Grace 1.50 .45
18 Randy Johnson 2.00 .60
19 Curt Schilling D'backs .75 .23
20 Luis Gonzalez .75 .23
21 Andy Pettitte 1.25 .35
22 Bernie Williams 1.25 .35
23 Jorge Posada 1.25 .35
24 Mariano Rivera 1.25 .35
25 Roger Clemens 4.00 1.20
26 Jose Canseco Yanks 2.50 .75
27 David Justice 1.00 .30
28 Paul O'Neill Yanks 1.50 .45
29 Darryl Strawberry Yanks 1.00 .30
30 David Wells .75 .23
31 Wade Boggs 1.50 .45
32 Charles Johnson .75 .23
33 Cliff Floyd .75 .23
34 Moises Alou .75 .23
35 Edgar Renteria .75 .23
36 Chipper Jones 2.00 .60
37 Tom Glavine 1.25 .35
38 John Smoltz 1.25 .35
39 Greg Maddux 3.00 .90
40 Ryan Klesko .75 .23
41 Javy Lopez .75 .23
42 Fred McGriff 1.25 .35
43 Roberto Alomar 1.25 .35
44 Joe Carter 1.00 .30
45 Rickey Henderson Jays 2.50 .75
46 Paul Molitor 1.50 .45
47 Jack Morris Jays 1.00 .30
48 Jack Morris Twins 1.00 .30
49 Kirby Puckett 2.50 .75
50 Eric Davis 1.00 .30
51 Barry Larkin 1.25 .35
52 Paul O'Neill Reds 1.50 .45
53 Dennis Eckersley 1.50 .45
54 Jose Canseco A's 2.50 .75
55 Rickey Henderson A's 2.50 .75
56 Dave Parker A's 1.00 .30
57 Orel Hershiser 1.50 .45
58 Kirk Gibson Dodgers 1.50 .45
59 Bert Blyleven Twins 1.00 .30
60 Dwight Gooden 1.00 .30
61 Gary Carter 1.00 .30
62 Lenny Dykstra 1.00 .30
63 Keith Hernandez Mets 1.00 .30
64 Darryl Strawberry Mets 1.00 .30
65 George Brett 5.00 1.50
66 Kirk Gibson Tigers 1.50 .45
67 Alan Trammell 1.00 .30
68 Jim Palmer 1.00 .30
69 Eddie Murray 2.50 .75
70 Cal Ripken 8.00 2.40
71 Keith Hernandez Cards 1.00 .30
72 Ozzie Smith 4.00 1.20
73 Steve Garvey 1.00 .30
74 Steve Carlton 1.00 .30
75 Mike Schmidt 5.00 1.50
76 John Candelaria 1.00 .30
77 Bert Blyleven Pirates 1.00 .30
78 Dave Parker Pirates 1.00 .30
79 Willie Stargell 79 1.50 .45
80 Reggie Jackson Yanks 1.50 .45
81 Johnny Bench 2.50 .75
82 Dave Concepcion 1.00 .30
83 George Foster 1.00 .30
84 Joe Morgan 1.00 .30
85 Tony Perez 1.00 .30
86 Rollie Fingers 1.00 .30
87 Catfish Hunter 1.50 .45
88 Reggie Jackson A's 1.50 .45
89 Al Oliver 1.00 .30
90 Roberto Clemente 5.00 1.50
91 Willie Stargell 71 1.50 .45
92 Brooks Robinson 1.50 .45
93 Frank Robinson 1.00 .30
94 Nolan Ryan 6.00 1.80
95 Tom Seaver 1.50 .45
96 Al Kaline 2.50 .75
97 Bob Gibson 1.50 .45
98 Lou Brock 1.50 .45
99 Orlando Cepeda 1.00 .30
100 Duke Snider 1.50 .45

2004 Donruss World Series Blue Material Bat

Nm-Mt Ex-Mt
*BAT: .6X TO 1.5X BLUE WS p/r 67-103
OVERALL AU-GU ODDS FIVE PER BOX
STATED PRINT RUN 50 SERIAL #'d SETS
8 Luis Castillo 8.00 2.40
17 Mark Grace 15.00 4.50
23 Jorge Posada 12.00 3.60
27 David Justice 10.00 3.00
28 Paul O'Neill Yanks 15.00 4.50
34 Moises Alou 8.00 2.40
35 Edgar Renteria 8.00 2.40
42 Fred McGriff 12.00 3.60
43 Roberto Alomar 12.00 3.60
44 Joe Carter 10.00 3.00
45 Rickey Henderson Jays 20.00 6.00
46 Paul Molitor 15.00 4.50
49 Kirby Puckett 20.00 6.00
50 Eric Davis 10.00 3.00
52 Paul O'Neill Reds 15.00 4.50
56 Dave Parker A's 10.00 3.00
58 Kirk Gibson Dodgers 15.00 4.50
62 Lenny Dykstra 10.00 3.00
63 Keith Hernandez Mets 10.00 3.00
66 Kirk Gibson Tigers 15.00 4.50
67 Alan Trammell 10.00 3.00
72 Ozzie Smith 25.00 7.50
73 Steve Garvey 10.00 3.00
84 Joe Morgan 10.00 3.00
85 Tony Perez 10.00 3.00
89 Al Oliver 10.00 3.00
90 Roberto Clemente 60.00 18.00
92 Brooks Robinson 15.00 4.50
93 Frank Robinson 10.00 3.00
96 Al Kaline 20.00 6.00
99 Orlando Cepeda 10.00 3.00

2004 Donruss World Series Blue Material Fabric AL/NL

Nm-Mt Ex-Mt
*AL/NL p/r 100: .4X TO 1X WS p/r 67-103
*AL/NL p/r 50: .6X TO 1.5X WS p/r 67-103
*AL/NL p/r 50: .4X TO 1X WS p/r 55
OVERALL AU-GU ODDS FIVE PER BOX
PRINT RUNS B/WN 5-100 COPIES PER
NO PRICING ON QTY OF 10 OR LESS

2004 Donruss World Series Blue Material Fabric WS

Nm-Mt Ex-Mt
OVERALL AU-GU ODDS FIVE PER BOX
PRINT RUNS B/WN 55-103 COPIES PER
1 Josh Beckett Jsy/103 5.00 1.50
2 Miguel Cabrera Jsy/103 8.00 2.40
3 Derrek Lee Jsy/103 5.00 1.50
4 Mike Lowell Jsy/103 5.00 1.50
5 Brad Penny Jsy/103 5.00 1.50
6 Ivan Rodriguez Jsy/103 10.00 3.00
7 Dontrelle Willis Jsy/103 5.00 1.50
9 Garret Anderson Jsy/102 5.00 1.50
10 Troy Glaus Jsy/102 5.00 1.50
13 Tim Salmon Jsy/102 8.00 2.40
14 Darin Erstad Jsy/102 5.00 1.50
15 Troy Percival Jsy/102 5.00 1.50
16 Steve Finley Jsy/101 5.00 1.50
18 Randy Johnson Pants/101 10.00 3.00
19 C.Schill D'backs Jsy/101 5.00 1.50
20 Luis Gonzalez Jsy/101 5.00 1.50
21 Andy Pettitte Jsy/100 8.00 2.40
22 Bernie Williams Jsy/100 8.00 2.40
24 Mariano Rivera Jsy/100 8.00 2.40
25 Roger Clemens Jsy/100 12.00 3.60
29 D.Strawberry Yanks Jsy/99 8.00 2.40
30 David Wells Jsy/99 5.00 1.50
31 Wade Boggs Jsy/96 12.00 3.60
32 Charles Johnson Jsy/97 5.00 1.50
33 Cliff Floyd Jsy/97 5.00 1.50
36 Chipper Jones Jsy/95 10.00 3.00
37 Tom Glavine Jsy/95 8.00 2.40
39 Greg Maddux Jsy/95 12.00 3.60
40 Ryan Klesko Jsy/95 5.00 1.50
41 Javy Lopez Jsy/95 5.00 1.50
51 Barry Larkin Jsy/90 8.00 2.40
54 Jose Canseco A's Jsy/89 15.00 4.50
55 R.Henderson A's Jsy/89 15.00 4.50
57 Orel Hershiser Jsy/88 12.00 3.60
59 Bert Blyleven Twins Jsy/87 8.00 2.40
60 Dwight Gooden Jsy/86 8.00 2.40
61 Gary Carter Jkt/86 8.00 2.40
64 D.Strawberry Mets Jsy/86 8.00 2.40
65 George Brett Jsy/85 20.00 6.00
68 Jim Palmer Pants/83 8.00 2.40
69 Eddie Murray Jsy/83 15.00 4.50
70 Cal Ripken Jsy/83 50.00 15.00
71 K.Hernandez Cards Jsy/82 8.00 2.40
74 Steve Carlton Jsy/80 8.00 2.40
75 Mike Schmidt Jkt/80 20.00 6.00
78 Dave Parker Pirates Jsy/79 8.00 2.40
79 Willie Stargell 79 Jsy/79 12.00 3.60
80 R.Jackson Yanks Jsy/78 12.00 3.60
81 Johnny Bench Jsy/75 15.00 4.50
82 Dave Concepcion Jsy/75 8.00 2.40
83 George Foster Jsy/75 8.00 2.40
86 Rollie Fingers Jsy/74 8.00 2.40
87 Catfish Hunter Jsy/74 12.00 3.60
88 Reggie Jackson A's Jkt/73 12.00 3.60
91 Willie Stargell 71 Jsy/71 12.00 3.60
98 Lou Brock Jkt/67 12.00 3.60
100 Duke Snider Pants/55 15.00 4.50

2004 Donruss World Series Blue Signature

Nm-Mt Ex-Mt
OVERALL AU-GU ODDS FIVE PER BOX
PRINT RUNS B/WN 5-50 COPIES PER
NO PRICING ON QTY OF 10 OR LESS
1 Josh Beckett/5
2 Miguel Cabrera/25 40.00 12.00
3 Derrek Lee/25 25.00 7.50
4 Mike Lowell/10
5 Brad Penny/25 15.00 4.50
7 Dontrelle Willis/5
9 Garret Anderson/25 25.00 7.50
11 John Lackey/50 12.00 3.60
12 Chone Figgins/25 15.00 4.50
16 Steve Finley/25 25.00 7.50
17 Mark Grace/5
18 Randy Johnson/5
21 Andy Pettitte/5
22 Bernie Williams/5
23 Jorge Posada/5
25 Roger Clemens/5
26 Jose Canseco Yanks/5
27 David Justice/5
28 Paul O'Neill Yanks/5
29 Darryl Strawberry Yanks/25 25.00 7.50
42 Fred McGriff/25 50.00 15.00
43 Roberto Alomar/5
44 Joe Carter/10
45 Rickey Henderson Jays/5
46 Paul Molitor/5
47 Jack Morris Jays/25 25.00 7.50
48 Jack Morris Twins/25 25.00 7.50
50 Eric Davis/25 25.00 7.50
52 Paul O'Neill Reds/5
53 Dennis Eckersley/25 40.00 12.00
54 Jose Canseco A's/5
55 Rickey Henderson A's/5
56 Dave Parker A's/25 25.00 7.50
57 Orel Hershiser/5
58 Kirk Gibson Dodgers/10
59 Bert Blyleven Twins/25 25.00 7.50
60 Dwight Gooden/25 25.00 7.50
61 Gary Carter/10
62 Lenny Dykstra/25 25.00 7.50
63 Keith Hernandez Mets/25 25.00 7.50
64 Darryl Strawberry Mets/25 25.00 7.50
65 George Brett/5
66 Kirk Gibson Tigers/10
67 Alan Trammell/25 25.00 7.50
68 Jim Palmer/25 25.00 7.50
69 Eddie Murray/5
70 Cal Ripken/5
71 Keith Hernandez Cards/25 25.00 7.50
72 Ozzie Smith/5
73 Steve Garvey/10
74 Steve Carlton/10
75 Mike Schmidt/5
76 John Candelaria/25 25.00 7.50
77 Bert Blyleven Pirates/25 25.00 7.50
78 Dave Parker Pirates/25 25.00 7.50
81 Johnny Bench/5
82 Dave Concepcion/25 25.00 7.50
83 George Foster/25 25.00 7.50
84 Joe Morgan/5
85 Tony Perez/25 40.00 12.00
86 Rollie Fingers/25 25.00 7.50
89 Al Oliver/25 25.00 7.50
92 Brooks Robinson/10
93 Frank Robinson/10
94 Nolan Ryan/10
95 Tom Seaver/5
96 Al Kaline/10
97 Bob Gibson/10
98 Lou Brock/10
100 Duke Snider/10

2004 Donruss World Series Face Off

Nm-Mt Ex-Mt
STATED PRINT RUN 500 SERIAL #'d SETS
*HOLO: 2X TO 5X BASIC
HOLOFOIL PRINT RUN 25 SERIAL #'d SETS
RANDOM INSERTS IN PACKS

1 Roger Clemens 8.00 2.40
Mike Piazza
2 Mike Mussina 4.00 1.20
Ivan Rodriguez
3 Mark Grace 5.00 1.50
Jorge Posada
4 Greg Maddux 6.00 1.80
Jim Thome
5 Rickey Henderson 5.00 1.50
Curt Schilling
6 Kirby Puckett 5.00 1.50
Tom Glavine
7 Dennis Eckersley 5.00 1.50
Will Clark
8 Bernie Williams 5.00 1.50
Randy Johnson
9 Cal Ripken 15.00 4.50
Steve Carlton
10 Tom Seaver 5.00 1.50
Reggie Jackson
11 Mike Schmidt 10.00 3.00
George Brett
12 Wade Boggs 5.00 1.50
Keith Hernandez
13 Dwight Gooden 4.00 1.20
Dwight Evans
14 Johnny Bench 5.00 1.50
Catfish Hunter
15 Jim Palmer 4.00 1.20
Dave Parker
16 Bob Gibson 5.00 1.50
Al Kaline
17 Carl Yastrzemski 8.00 2.40
Lou Brock
18 Duke Snider 5.00 1.50
Whitey Ford
19 Carlton Fisk 5.00 1.50
Tony Perez
20 Roberto Clemente 10.00 3.00
Frank Robinson

2004 Donruss World Series Face Off Material

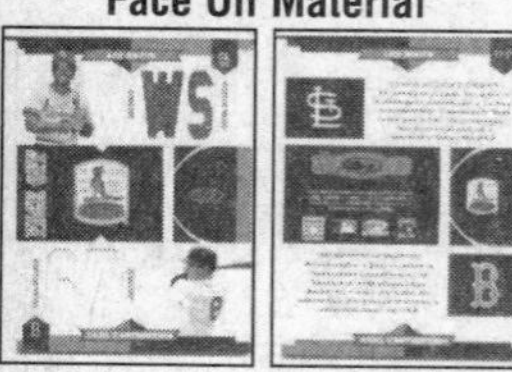

Nm-Mt Ex-Mt
OVERALL AU-GU ODDS FIVE PER BOX
PRINT RUNS B/WN 10-100 COPIES PER
NO PRICING ON QTY OF 10 OR LESS

1 Roger Clemens Jsy 25.00 7.50
Mike Piazza Jsy/100
2 Mike Mussina Jsy 20.00 6.00
Ivan Rodriguez Jsy/100
3 Mark Grace Jsy
Jorge Posada Jsy/10
4 Greg Maddux Jsy 40.00 12.00
Jim Thome Jsy/25
5 Rickey Henderson Jsy 20.00 6.00
Curt Schilling Jsy/100
6 Kirby Puckett Jsy 25.00 7.50
Tom Glavine Jsy/100
8 Bernie Williams Jsy 20.00 6.00
Randy Johnson Pants/100
9 Cal Ripken Jsy 80.00 24.00
Steve Carlton Jsy/50
11 Mike Schmidt Jkt 50.00 15.00
George Brett Jsy/50
13 Dwight Gooden Jsy 30.00 9.00
Dwight Evans Jsy/50
15 Jim Palmer Jsy 15.00 4.50
Dave Parker Jsy/50
17 Carl Yastrzemski Jsy 50.00 15.00
Lou Brock Jkt/50
18 Duke Snider Pants 25.00 7.50
Whitey Ford Jsy/50
19 Carlton Fisk Jsy 25.00 7.50
Tony Perez Fld Glv/50
20 Roberto Clemente Jsy
Frank Robinson Jsy/10

2004 Donruss World Series Fans of the Game

Nm-Mt Ex-Mt
STATED ODDS 1:24

1 Val Kilmer 3.00 .90
2 Stan Lee 3.00 .90
3 Apolo Anton Ohno 2.00 .60
4 Gene Shalit 2.00 .60
5 Leeann Tweeden 3.00 .90

2004 Donruss World Series Fans of the Game Signatures

Nm-Mt Ex-Mt
RANDOM INSERTS IN PACKS

1 Val Kilmer 60.00 18.00
2 Stan Lee 60.00 18.00
3 Apolo Anton Ohno 40.00 12.00
4 Gene Shalit 25.00 7.50
5 Leeann Tweeden 50.00 15.00

2004 Donruss World Series Legends of the Fall

Nm-Mt Ex-Mt
STATED PRINT RUN 500 SERIAL #'d SETS
*HOLO: 2X TO 5X BASIC
HOLOFOIL PRINT RUN 25 SERIAL #'d SETS
RANDOM INSERTS IN PACKS

1 Bob Gibson 5.00 1.50
2 Brooks Robinson 5.00 1.50
3 Cal Ripken 15.00 4.50
4 Carl Yastrzemski 8.00 2.40
5 Carlton Fisk 5.00 1.50
6 Derek Jeter 8.00 2.40
7 Duke Snider 5.00 1.50
8 Eddie Murray 5.00 1.50
9 Frank Robinson 4.00 1.20
10 Gary Carter 4.00 1.20
11 George Brett 10.00 3.00
12 Jim Palmer 4.00 1.20
13 Johnny Bench 5.00 1.50
14 Mariano Rivera 5.00 1.50
15 Mike Schmidt 10.00 3.00
16 Phil Rizzuto 5.00 1.50
17 Red Schoendienst 4.00 1.20
18 Reggie Jackson 5.00 1.50
19 Rickey Henderson 5.00 1.50
20 Whitey Ford 5.00 1.50

2004 Donruss World Series Legends of the Fall Material

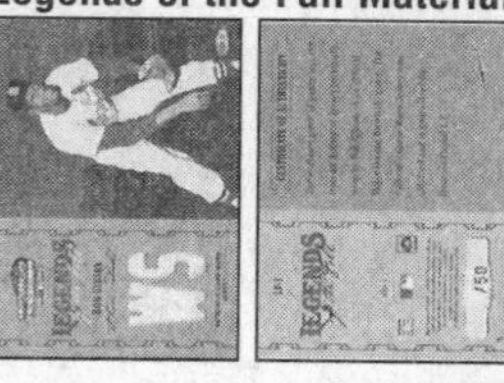

Nm-Mt Ex-Mt
OVERALL AU-GU ODDS FIVE PER BOX
PRINT RUNS B/WN 25-100 COPIES PER

1 Bob Gibson Jsy/50 15.00 4.50
2 Brooks Robinson Bat/100 12.00 3.60
3 Cal Ripken Jkt/100 40.00 12.00
4 Carl Yastrzemski Bat/50 25.00 7.50
5 Carlton Fisk Bat/50 15.00 4.50
7 Duke Snider Pants/50 15.00 4.50
8 Eddie Murray Jsy/50 20.00 6.00
9 Frank Robinson Bat/100 8.00 2.40
10 Gary Carter Jkt/100 8.00 2.40
11 George Brett Bat/50 30.00 9.00
12 Jim Palmer Pants/25 15.00 4.50
13 Johnny Bench Bat/100 15.00 4.50
14 Mariano Rivera Jsy/100 12.00 3.60
15 Mike Schmidt Jkt/50 30.00 9.00
16 Phil Rizzuto Pants/50 15.00 4.50
17 Red Schoendienst Bat/100 8.00 2.40
18 Reggie Jackson Bat/100 12.00 3.60
19 Rickey Henderson Bat/100 15.00 4.50

2004 Donruss World Series Legends of the Fall Signature

Nm-Mt Ex-Mt
*SIG p/r 50: .4X TO 1X SIG MTL p/r 100
*SIG p/r 25: .4X TO 1X SIG MTL p/r 50
*SIG p/r 25: .3X TO .8X SIG MTL p/r 25
OVERALL AU-GU ODDS FIVE PER BOX
PRINT RUNS B/WN 5-50 COPIES PER
NO PRICING ON QTY OF 10 OR LESS

2004 Donruss World Series Legends of the Fall Signature Material

Nm-Mt Ex-Mt
OVERALL AU-GU ODDS FIVE PER BOX
PRINT RUNS B/WN 5-100 COPIES PER
NO PRICING ON QTY OF 10 OR LESS

1 Bob Gibson Jsy/25 50.00 15.00
2 Brooks Robinson Bat/50 40.00 12.00
3 Cal Ripken Jkt/5
4 Carl Yastrzemski Bat/5
5 Carlton Fisk Bat/10
7 Duke Snider Pants/50 40.00 12.00
8 Eddie Murray Jsy/5
9 Frank Robinson Bat/50 40.00 12.00
10 Gary Carter Jkt/50 25.00 7.50
11 George Brett Bat/5
12 Jim Palmer Pants/25 30.00 9.00
13 Johnny Bench Bat/25 80.00 24.00
15 Mike Schmidt Jkt/10
16 Phil Rizzuto Pants/50 40.00 12.00
17 Red Schoendienst Bat/100 20.00 6.00
18 Reggie Jackson Bat/10
19 Rickey Henderson Bat/10

2004 Donruss World Series MVP

Nm-Mt Ex-Mt
STATED PRINT RUN 1000 SERIAL #'d SETS
*HOLO: 1.5X TO 4X BASIC
HOLOFOIL PRINT RUN 50 SERIAL #'d SETS
RANDOM INSERTS IN PACKS

1 Whitey Ford 4.00 1.20
2 Bob Gibson 4.00 1.20
3 Frank Robinson 3.00 .90
4 Brooks Robinson 4.00 1.20
5 Roberto Clemente 8.00 2.40
6 Reggie Jackson 4.00 1.20
7 Rollie Fingers 3.00 .90
8 Johnny Bench 4.00 1.20
9 Reggie Jackson 4.00 1.20
10 Mike Schmidt 8.00 2.40
11 Alan Trammell 3.00 .90
12 Orel Hershiser 3.00 .90
13 Jack Morris 3.00 .90
14 Paul Molitor 4.00 1.20
15 Tom Glavine 4.00 1.20

2004 Donruss World Series MVP Material

Nm-Mt Ex-Mt
OVERALL AU-GU ODDS FIVE PER BOX
PRINT RUNS B/WN 10-100 COPIES PER
NO PRICING ON QTY OF 10 OR LESS

1 Whitey Ford Jsy/50 15.00 4.50
2 Bob Gibson Jsy/50 15.00 4.50
3 Frank Robinson Jsy/25 15.00 4.50
5 Roberto Clemente Jsy/10
6 Reggie Jackson Jkt/100 12.00 3.60
7 Rollie Fingers Jsy/100 8.00 2.40
8 Johnny Bench Jsy/10
9 Reggie Jackson Jsy/25 25.00 7.50
10 Mike Schmidt Jsy/50 30.00 9.00
12 Orel Hershiser Jsy/100 8.00 2.40
15 Tom Glavine Jsy/100 12.00 3.60

2004 Donruss World Series MVP Signature

Nm-Mt Ex-Mt
OVERALL AU-GU ODDS FIVE PER BOX
PRINT RUNS B/WN 5-25 COPIES PER
NO PRICING ON QTY OF 10 OR LESS

11 Alan Trammell/25 25.00 7.50
13 Jack Morris/25 25.00 7.50

2004 Donruss World Series MVP Signature Material

Nm-Mt Ex-Mt
OVERALL AU-GU ODDS FIVE PER BOX
PRINT RUNS B/WN 5-100 COPIES PER
NO PRICING ON QTY OF 10 OR LESS

1 Whitey Ford Jsy/10
2 Bob Gibson Jsy/50 40.00 12.00
3 Frank Robinson Shoe/50 40.00 12.00
7 Rollie Fingers Jsy/100 20.00 6.00
8 Johnny Bench Jsy/5
10 Mike Schmidt Jkt/5
12 Orel Hershiser Jsy/25 30.00 9.00

2004 Donruss World Series October Heroes

Nm-Mt Ex-Mt
STATED PRINT RUN 500 SERIAL #'d SETS
*HOLO: 2X TO 5X BASIC
HOLOFOIL PRINT RUN 25 SERIAL #'d SETS
RANDOM INSERTS IN PACKS

1 Alan Trammell 4.00 1.20
2 Andy Pettitte 4.00 1.20
3 Catfish Hunter 5.00 1.50
4 Chipper Jones 4.00 1.20
5 Dave Concepcion 4.00 1.20
6 David Wells 3.00 .90
7 Jack Morris 4.00 1.20
8 Joe Morgan 4.00 1.20
9 Josh Beckett 3.00 .90
10 Kirby Puckett 5.00 1.50
11 Kirk Gibson 5.00 1.50
12 Marty Marion 4.00 1.20
13 Miguel Cabrera 4.00 1.20
14 Paul Molitor 5.00 1.50
15 Paul O'Neill 5.00 1.50
16 Randy Johnson 4.00 1.20
17 Roger Clemens 8.00 2.40
18 Steve Carlton 4.00 1.20
19 Steve Garvey 4.00 1.20
20 Wade Boggs 5.00 1.50

2004 Donruss World Series October Heroes Material

Nm-Mt Ex-Mt
OVERALL AU-GU ODDS FIVE PER BOX
PRINT RUNS B/WN 25-100 COPIES PER

1 Alan Trammell Jsy/25 15.00 4.50
2 Andy Pettitte Jsy/100 8.00 2.40
3 Catfish Hunter Jsy/25 25.00 7.50
4 Chipper Jones Jsy/100 10.00 3.00
5 Dave Concepcion Jsy/100 8.00 2.40
6 David Wells Jsy/25 12.00 3.60
9 Josh Beckett Jsy/100 5.00 1.50
10 Kirby Puckett Jsy/25 30.00 9.00
12 Marty Marion Jsy/25 15.00 4.50
13 Miguel Cabrera Jsy/100 8.00 2.40
16 Randy Johnson Pants/50 15.00 4.50
17 Roger Clemens Jsy/100 12.00 3.60
18 Steve Carlton Jsy/100 8.00 2.40
19 Steve Garvey Jsy/100 8.00 2.40
20 Wade Boggs Jsy/100 12.00 3.60

2004 Donruss World Series October Heroes Signature

Nm-Mt Ex-Mt
*SIG p/r 25: .5X TO 1.2X SIG MTL p/r 100
*SIG p/r 25: .4X TO 1X SIG MTL p/r 50
OVERALL AU-GU ODDS FIVE PER BOX
PRINT RUNS B/WN 1-25 COPIES PER
NO PRICING ON QTY OF 10 OR LESS

7 Jack Morris/25 25.00 7.50

2004 Donruss World Series October Legends

Nm-Mt Ex-Mt
STATED PRINT RUN 500 SERIAL #'d SETS
*HOLO: 2X TO 5X BASIC
HOLOFOIL PRINT RUN 25 SERIAL #'d SETS

RANDOM INSERTS IN PACKS

1 Bob Gibson 5.00 1.50
2 Cal Ripken 15.00 4.50
3 Carl Yastrzemski 8.00 2.40
4 Carlton Fisk 5.00 1.50
5 Duke Snider 5.00 1.50
6 Eddie Murray 5.00 1.50
7 Frank Robinson 4.00 1.20
8 George Brett 10.00 3.00
9 Joe Morgan 4.00 1.20
10 Johnny Bench 5.00 1.50
11 Lou Brock 5.00 1.50
12 Mike Schmidt 10.00 3.00
13 Paul Molitor 5.00 1.50
14 Phil Rizzuto 5.00 1.50
15 Reggie Jackson 5.00 1.50
16 Robin Yount 8.00 2.40
17 Stan Musial 8.00 2.40
18 Steve Carlton 4.00 1.20
19 Whitey Ford 5.00 1.50
20 Willie McCovey 5.00 1.50

2004 Donruss World Series October Legends Material

Nm-Mt Ex-Mt
OVERALL AU-GU ODDS FIVE PER BOX
PRINT RUNS B/WN 10-100 COPIES PER
NO PRICING ON QTY OF 10 OR LESS

1 Bob Gibson Jsy/50 15.00 4.50
2 Cal Ripken Jsy/50 60.00 18.00
3 Carl Yastrzemski Jsy/50 25.00 7.50
4 Carlton Fisk Jsy/100 12.00 3.60
5 Duke Snider Jsy/25 25.00 7.50
6 Eddie Murray Jsy/100 15.00 4.50
7 Frank Robinson Jsy/50 10.00 3.00
8 George Brett Jsy/50 30.00 9.00
10 Johnny Bench Jsy/50 20.00 6.00
11 Lou Brock Jkt/100 12.00 3.60
12 Mike Schmidt Jkt/100 20.00 6.00
13 Paul Molitor Jsy/10
14 Phil Rizzuto Pants/25 25.00 7.50
15 Reggie Jackson Jkt/100 12.00 3.60
16 Robin Yount Jsy/100 15.00 4.50
17 Stan Musial Jsy/10
18 Steve Carlton Jsy/100 8.00 2.40
19 Whitey Ford Pants/25 25.00 7.50
20 Willie McCovey Jsy/25 25.00 7.50

2004 Donruss World Series October Legends Signature

Nm-Mt Ex-Mt
*SIG p/r 25: .5X TO 1.2X SIG MTL p/r 100
*SIG p/r 25: .4X TO 1X SIG MTL p/r 50
OVERALL AU-GU ODDS FIVE PER BOX
PRINT RUNS B/WN 5-25 COPIES PER
NO PRICING ON QTY OF 10 OR LESS

2004 Donruss World Series October Legends Signature Material

Nm-Mt Ex-Mt
OVERALL AU-GU ODDS FIVE PER BOX
PRINT RUNS B/WN 5-100 COPIES PER
NO PRICING ON QTY OF 10 OR LESS

1 Bob Gibson Jsy/50 40.00 12.00
2 Cal Ripken Jsy/5
3 Carl Yastrzemski Jsy/5
4 Carlton Fisk Jsy/15 60.00 18.00
5 Duke Snider Jsy/50 40.00 12.00
6 Eddie Murray Jsy/5
7 Frank Robinson Jsy/50 40.00 12.00
8 George Brett Jsy/5
10 Johnny Bench Jsy/10
11 Lou Brock Jkt/100 30.00 9.00
12 Mike Schmidt Jkt/10
13 Paul Molitor Jsy/25 50.00 15.00
14 Phil Rizzuto Pants/50 40.00 12.00
16 Robin Yount Jsy/25 80.00 24.00
17 Stan Musial Jsy/25 100.00 30.00
18 Steve Carlton Jsy/100 30.00 9.00
19 Whitey Ford Pants/25 50.00 15.00
20 Willie McCovey Jsy/25 50.00 15.00

2004 Donruss World Series Playoff All-Stars

Nm-Mt Ex-Mt
STATED PRINT RUN 500 SERIAL #'d SETS

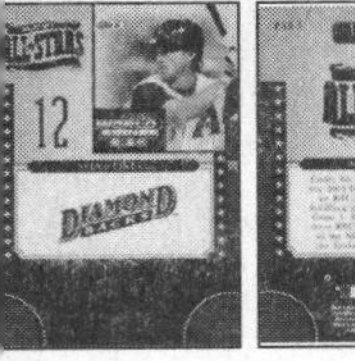

OLO: 2X TO 5X BASIC
LOFOIL PRINT RUN 25 SERIAL #'d SETS
NDOM INSERTS IN PACKS
Mark Prior 4.00 1.20
Sammy Sosa 6.00 1.80
Steve Finley 3.00 .90
David Ortiz 4.00 1.20
Mike Piazza 6.00 1.80
Edgar Martinez 4.00 1.20
Roy Oswalt 3.00 .90
Johan Santana 4.00 1.20
Jacque Jones 3.00 .90
Will Clark 5.00 1.50
Albert Pujols 8.00 2.40
Andre Dawson 4.00 1.20
Nolan Ryan 12.00 3.60
Fred Lynn 4.00 1.20
Jim Rice 4.00 1.20
Dwight Evans 4.00 1.20
Harmon Killebrew 5.00 1.50
Maury Wills 4.00 1.20
Mark Mulder 3.00 .90
Frank Thomas 4.00 1.20

2004 Donruss World Series Playoff All-Stars Material 1

Nm-Mt Ex-Mt
VERALL AU-GU ODDS FIVE PER BOX
RINT RUNS B/WN 50-100 COPIES PER
Mark Prior Jsy/100 10.00 3.00
Sammy Sosa Jsy/100 12.00 3.60
Steve Finley Jsy/100 5.00 1.50
David Ortiz Jsy/100 15.00 4.50
Mike Piazza Jsy/100 12.00 3.60
Edgar Martinez Jsy/50 12.00 3.60
Roy Oswalt Jsy/100 5.00 1.50
Johan Santana Jsy/100 10.00 3.00
Jacque Jones Jsy/100 5.00 1.50
Will Clark Bat/100 15.00 4.50
Albert Pujols Jsy/100 20.00 6.00
Andre Dawson Jsy/100 8.00 2.40
Nolan Ryan Jsy/100 25.00 7.50
Fred Lynn Jsy/50 10.00 3.00
Jim Rice Jsy/50 10.00 3.00
Dwight Evans Jsy/50 10.00 3.00
Harmon Killebrew Jsy/50 20.00 6.00
Mark Mulder Jsy/50 8.00 2.40
Frank Thomas Jsy/100 10.00 3.00

2004 Donruss World Series Playoff All-Stars Material 2

Nm-Mt Ex-Mt
MTL2 p/r 100: .6X TO 1.5X MTL1 p/r 100
MTL2 p/r 100: .4X TO 1X MTL1 p/r 50
MTL2 p/r 50: 1X TO 2.5X MTL1 p/r 100
MTL2 p/r 50: .6X TO 1.5X MTL1 p/r 50
VERALL AU-GU ODDS FIVE PER BOX
RINT RUNS B/WN 50-100 COPIES PER

2004 Donruss World Series Playoff All-Stars Material 3

Nm-Mt Ex-Mt
MTL3 p/r 100: .75X TO 2X MTL1 p/r 100
MTL3 p/r 100: .6X TO 1.5X MTL1 p/r 50
MTL3 p/r 50: 1.25X TO 3X MTL1 p/r 100
MTL3 p/r 50: .75X TO 2X MTL1 p/r 50
MTL3 p/r 25: 1.25X TO 3X MTL1 p/r 50
VERALL AU-GU ODDS FIVE PER BOX
RINT RUNS B/WN 25-100 COPIES PER

2004 Donruss World Series Playoff All-Stars Signature

Nm-Mt Ex-Mt
SIG p/r 25: .5X TO 1.2X SIG MTL p/r 100
SIG p/r 25: .4X TO 1X SIG MTL p/r 50

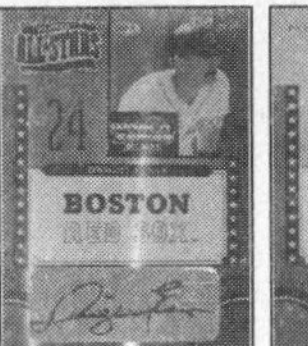

*SIG p/r 25: .3X TO .8X SIG MTL p/r 25
OVERALL AU-GU ODDS FIVE PER BOX
PRINT RUNS B/WN 5-25 COPIES PER
NO PRICING ON QTY OF 10 OR LESS
1 Mark Prior/25 60.00 18.00
13 Nolan Ryan/25 120.00 36.00
18 Maury Wills/25 25.00 7.50

2004 Donruss World Series Playoff All-Stars Signature Material 1

Nm-Mt Ex-Mt
OVERALL AU-GU ODDS FIVE PER BOX
PRINT RUNS B/WN 5-100 COPIES PER
NO PRICING ON QTY OF 10 OR LESS
1 Mark Prior Jsy/10
2 Sammy Sosa Jsy/5
3 Steve Finley Jsy/100 20.00 6.00
4 David Ortiz Jsy/100 50.00 15.00
5 Mike Piazza Jsy/5
6 Edgar Martinez Jsy/50 40.00 12.00
7 Roy Oswalt Jsy/100 20.00 6.00
8 Johan Santana Jsy/100 40.00 12.00
9 Jacque Jones Jsy/100 20.00 6.00
10 Will Clark Bat/25 80.00 24.00
11 Albert Pujols Jsy/5
12 Andre Dawson Jsy/100 20.00 6.00
13 Nolan Ryan Jsy/5
14 Fred Lynn Jsy/25 30.00 9.00
15 Jim Rice Jsy/25 30.00 9.00
16 Dwight Evans Jsy/50 40.00 12.00
17 Harmon Killebrew Jsy/10
19 Mark Mulder Jsy/25 30.00 9.00
20 Frank Thomas Jsy/25 60.00 18.00

2004 Donruss World Series Playoff All-Stars Signature Material 2

Nm-Mt Ex-Mt
*SM2 p/r 100: .5X TO 1.2X SM1 p/r 100
*SM2 p/r 50: .6X TO 1.5X SM1 p/r 100
*SM2 p/r 50: .5X TO 1.2X SM1 p/r 50
*SM2 p/r 50: .4X TO 1X SM1 p/r 25 ..
*SM2 p/r 25: .6X TO 1.5X SM1 p/r 50
*SM2 p/r 25: .5X TO 1.2X SM1 p/r 25
OVERALL AU-GU ODDS FIVE PER BOX
PRINT RUNS B/WN 5-100 COPIES PER
NO PRICING ON QTY OF 10 OR LESS
17 H.Killebrew Bat-Jsy/25 80.00 24.00

2004 Donruss World Series Playoff All-Stars Signature Material 3

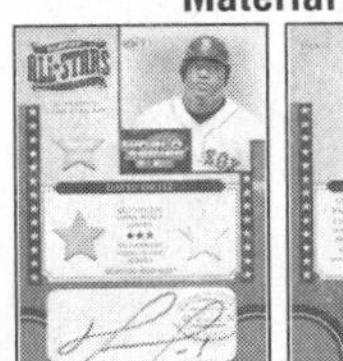

Nm-Mt Ex-Mt
*SM3 p/r 100: .6X TO 1.5X SM1 p/r 100
*SM3 p/r 100: .5X TO 1.2X SM1 p/r 50
*SM3 p/r 100: .4X TO 1X SM1 p/r 25
*SM3 p/r 50: .6X TO 1.5X SM1 p/r 50
*SM3 p/r 50: .5X TO 1.2X SM1 p/r 25
OVERALL AU-GU ODDS FIVE PER BOX
PRINT RUNS B/WN 5-100 COPIES PER
NO PRICING ON QTY OF 10 OR LESS

2004 Donruss World Series Records

Nm-Mt Ex-Mt
STATED PRINT RUN 1000 SERIAL #'d SETS
*HOLO: 1.5X TO 4X BASIC
HOLOFOIL PRINT RUN 50 SERIAL #'d SETS
RANDOM INSERTS IN PACKS
1 Lou Brock 4.00 1.20
2 Yogi Berra 4.00 1.20
3 Reggie Jackson 4.00 1.20

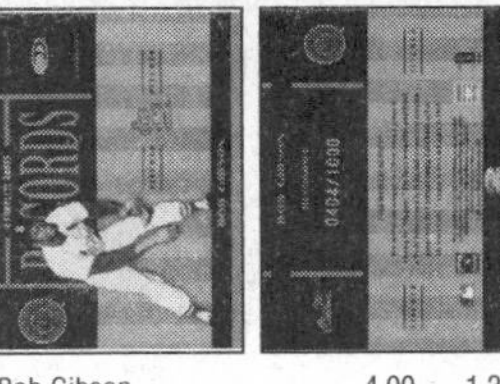

4 Bob Gibson 4.00 1.20
5 Whitey Ford 4.00 1.20

2004 Donruss World Series Records Material

Nm-Mt Ex-Mt
OVERALL AU-GU ODDS FIVE PER BOX
PRINT RUNS B/WN 10-100 COPIES PER
NO PRICING ON QTY OF 10 OR LESS
1 Lou Brock Bat/100 12.00 3.60
2 Yogi Berra Bat/50 20.00 6.00
3 Reggie Jackson Bat/100 12.00 3.60
4 Bob Gibson Hat/10
5 Whitey Ford Pants/25 25.00 7.50

2004 Donruss World Series Records Signature

Nm-Mt Ex-Mt
*SIG p/r 25: .5X TO 1.2X SIG MTL p/r 100
OVERALL AU-GU ODDS FIVE PER BOX
PRINT RUNS B/WN 10-25 COPIES PER
NO PRICING ON QTY OF 10 OR LESS

2004 Donruss World Series Records Signature Material

Nm-Mt Ex-Mt
COMPLETE SET (5)
OVERALL AU-GU ODDS FIVE PER BOX
PRINT RUNS B/WN 10-100 COPIES PER
NO PRICING ON QTY OF 10 OR LESS
1 Lou Brock Bat/100 30.00 9.00
2 Yogi Berra Bat/10
3 Reggie Jackson Bat/20 50.00 15.00
4 Bob Gibson Hat/10
5 Whitey Ford Pants/10

2004 Donruss World Series Signature Trio

Nm-Mt Ex-Mt
OVERALL AU-GU ODDS FIVE PER BOX
PRINT RUNS B/WN 5-25 COPIES PER
NO PRICING ON QTY OF 10 OR LESS
1 Josh Beckett
Miguel Cabrera
Dontrelle Willis/10
2 Derrek Lee 50.00 15.00
Brad Penny
Mike Lowell/25
3 John Lackey 80.00 24.00
Chone Figgins
Garret Anderson/25
4 Mark Grace
Randy Johnson
Steve Finley/5
5 Jorge Posada
Bernie Williams
Roger Clemens/5
7 Chipper Jones
Fred McGriff
David Justice/10
8 Roberto Alomar 150.00 45.00
Paul Molitor
Jack Morris/25
9 Eric Davis 120.00 36.00
Barry Larkin
Paul O'Neill/25
10 Dennis Eckersley 150.00 45.00
Jose Canseco
Dave Parker/25
11 Keith Hernandez 80.00 24.00
Dwight Gooden
Gary Carter/25
12 Darryl Strawberry 80.00 24.00
Lenny Dykstra
George Foster/25
13 Alan Trammell 120.00 36.00
Kirk Gibson
Jack Morris/25
14 Jim Palmer
Eddie Murray
Cal Ripken/5
15 Bert Blyleven 80.00 24.00
John Candelaria
Dave Parker/25
16 Johnny Bench
Joe Morgan
Tony Perez/5
17 Dave Concepcion
George Foster
Johnny Bench/5
18 Jim Palmer
Frank Robinson
Brooks Robinson/10
19 Bob Gibson
Lou Brock
Orlando Cepeda/6
20 Stan Musial
Red Schoendienst
Marty Marion/10

2004 Donruss World Series Souvenirs Playoff

Nm-Mt Ex-Mt
OVERALL AU-GU ODDS FIVE PER BOX
STATED PRINT RUN 100 SERIAL #'d SETS
1 Chipper Jones Ball 15.00 4.50
2 Randy Johnson Ball 15.00 4.50
3 Albert Pujols Ball 25.00 7.50
4 Jason Schmidt Ball 10.00 3.00
5 Gary Sheffield Ball 10.00 3.00
6 Miguel Tejada Ball 10.00 3.00
7 J.D. Drew Ball 10.00 3.00
8 John Smoltz Ball 15.00 4.50
9 Eric Milton Ball 10.00 3.00
10 Mark Grace Ball 15.00 4.50
11 Tim Hudson Ball 10.00 3.00
12 Jeff Bagwell Ball 15.00 4.50
13 Jim Edmonds Ball 10.00 3.00
14 Sammy Sosa Ball 15.00 4.50
15 Albert Pujols Ball 25.00 7.50

2004 Donruss World Series Souvenirs WS

Nm-Mt Ex-Mt
OVERALL AU-GU ODDS FIVE PER BOX
STATED PRINT RUN 100 SERIAL #'d SETS
1 Jason Schmidt Ball 10.00 3.00
2 Troy Glaus Base 10.00 3.00
3 Reggie Sanders Base 10.00 3.00
4 Tim Salmon Base 15.00 4.50
5 Garret Anderson Base 10.00 3.00
6 Francisco Rodriguez Base 10.00 3.00
7 Rich Aurilia Ball 10.00 3.00
8 Jeff Kent Ball 10.00 3.00
9 Darin Erstad Base 10.00 3.00
10 Troy Glaus Base 10.00 3.00
11 Jeff Kent Ball 10.00 3.00
12 Scott Spiezio Base 10.00 3.00
13 Troy Percival Base 10.00 3.00
14 Garret Anderson Base 10.00 3.00
15 Darin Erstad Base 10.00 3.00

2004 Donruss World Series Triple Threads

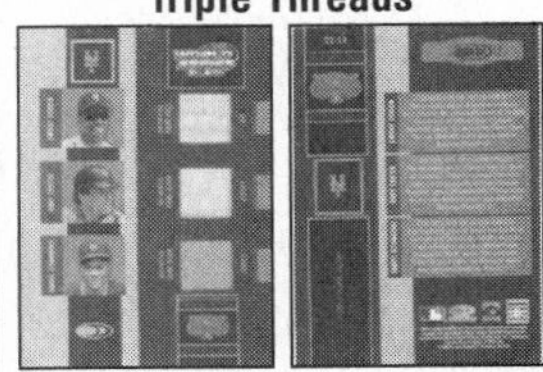

Nm-Mt Ex-Mt
OVERALL AU-GU ODDS FIVE PER BOX
PRINT RUNS B/WN 50-100 PER
B ='S BAT, J ='S JSY, P ='S PANTS
1 Josh Beckett Jsy 20.00 6.00
Miguel Cabrera Jsy
Mike Lowell Bat/100
2 Luis Castillo Bat 25.00 7.50
Ivan Rodriguez Jsy
Dontrelle Willis Jsy/100
3 Garret Anderson Bat 25.00 7.50
Troy Glaus Jsy
Tim Salmon Jsy/100
4 Curt Schilling Jsy 30.00 9.00
Mark Grace Bat
Randy Johnson Pants/50
5 Jorge Posada Bat 30.00 9.00
Bernie Williams Jsy
Roger Clemens Jsy/50
6 Andy Pettitte Jsy 25.00 7.50
Wade Boggs Jsy
Mariano Rivera Jsy/50
7 Charles Johnson Bat 12.00 3.60
Cliff Floyd Jsy
Moises Alou Bat/100
8 Chipper Jones Jsy 40.00 12.00
Tom Glavine Jsy
Greg Maddux Jsy/100
9 Joe Carter Jsy 30.00 9.00
Rickey Henderson Bat
David Wells Jsy/100
10 Eric Davis Bat 25.00 7.50
Barry Larkin Bat
Paul O'Neill Bat/100
11 Dwight Gooden Bat 25.00 7.50
Gary Carter Jsy
Darryl Strawberry Jsy/100
12 Frank White Bat 40.00 12.00
Willie Wilson Bat
George Brett Jsy/100
13 Jim Palmer Jsy 150.00 45.00
Eddie Murray Jsy
Cal Ripken Jkt/50
14 Willie Stargell Jsy 25.00 7.50
Dave Parker Jsy
Bill Madlock Bat/100
15 Johnny Bench Bat 40.00 12.00
Joe Morgan Bat
Tony Perez Bat/100
16 Dave Concepcion Jsy 50.00 15.00
George Foster Jsy
Johnny Bench Bat/50
17 Al Oliver Bat 100.00 30.00
Roberto Clemente Bat
Willie Stargell Jsy/50
18 Jim Palmer Jsy 30.00 9.00
Frank Robinson Jsy
Brooks Robinson Bat/50
19 Bob Gibson Jsy 30.00 9.00
Lou Brock Bat
Orlando Cepeda Bat/50
20 Stan Musial Bat 50.00 15.00
Red Schoendienst Bat
Marty Marion Jsy/50

1941 Double Play

The cards in this 75-card set measure approximately 2 1/2" by 3 1/8" was a blank-backed issue distributed by Gum Products. It consists of 75 numbered cards (two consecutive numbers per card), each depicting two players in sepia tone photographs. Cards 81-100 contain action poses, and the last 50 numbers of the set are slightly harder to find. Cards that have been cut in half to form "singles" have a greatly reduced value. These cards have a value from five to ten percent of the uncut strips and are very difficult to sell. The player on the left has an odd number and the other player has an even number. We are using only the odd numbers to identify these panels. Each penny pack contained two cards and they were issued 100 packs to a box.

Ex-Mt VG
COMPLETE SET (150) 5000.00 2500.00
COMMON PAIRS (1-100) 25.00 12.50
COMMON (101-150) 30.00 15.00
WRAPPER (1-CENT) 500.00 250.00
1 Larry French 60.00 30.00
Vance Page
3 Billy Herman 50.00 25.00
Stan Hack
5 Lonny Frey 40.00 20.00
Johnny VanderMeer
7 Paul Derringer 40.00 20.00
Bucky Walters
9 Frank McCormick 25.00 12.50
Billy Werber
11 Johnny Ripple 50.00 25.00
Ernie Lombardi
13 Alex Kampouris 25.00 12.50
Whitlow Wyatt
15 Mickey Owen 50.00 25.00
Paul Waner
17 Cookie Lavagetto 30.00 15.00
Pete Reiser
19 James Wasdell 30.00 15.00
Dolph Camilli
21 Dixie Walker 50.00 25.00
Joe Medwick
23 Pee Wee Reese 200.00 100.00
Kirby Higbe
25 Harry Danning 25.00 12.50
Cliff Melton
27 Harry Gumbert 25.00 12.50
Burgess Whitehead
29 Joe Orengo 25.00 12.50
Joe Moore
31 Mel Ott 100.00 50.00
Norman Young
33 Lee Handley 50.00 25.00
Arky Vaughan
35 Bob Klinger 25.00 12.50
Stanley Brown
37 Terry Moore 30.00 15.00

Card	Nm-Mt	Ex-Mt
Gus Mancuso		
39 Johnny Mize	150.00	75.00
Enos Slaughter		
41 Johnny Cooney	25.00	12.50
Sibby Sisti		
43 Max West	25.00	12.50
Carvel Rowell		
45 Danny Litwhiler	25.00	12.50
Merrill May		
47 Frank Hayes	25.00	12.50
Al Brancato		
49 Bob Johnson	30.00	15.00
Bill Nagel		
51 Bobo Newsom	100.00	50.00
Hank Greenberg		
53 Barney McCosky	75.00	38.00
Charlie Gehringer		
55 Mike Higgins	30.00	15.00
Dick Bartell		
57 Ted Williams	500.00	250.00
Jim Tabor		
59 Joe Cronin	200.00	100.00
Jimmy Foxx		
61 Lefty Gomez	250.00	125.00
Phil Rizzuto		
63 Joe DiMaggio	750.00	375.00
Charlie Keller		
65 Red Rolfe	100.00	50.00
Bill Dickey		
67 Joe Gordon	100.00	50.00
Red Ruffing		
69 Mike Tresh	60.00	30.00
Luke Appling		
71 Moose Solters	25.00	12.50
Johnny Rigney		
73 Buddy Myer	30.00	15.00
Ben Chapman		
75 Cecil Travis	30.00	15.00
George Case		
77 Joe Krakauskas	125.00	60.00
Bob Feller		
79 Ken Keltner	30.00	15.00
Hal Trosky		
81 Ted Williams	600.00	300.00
Joe Cronin		
83 Joe Gordon	40.00	20.00
Charlie Keller		
85 Hank Greenberg	200.00	100.00
Red Ruffing		
87 Hal Trosky	30.00	15.00
George Case		
89 Mel Ott	100.00	50.00
Burgess Whitehead		
91 Harry Danning	25.00	12.50
Harry Gumbert		
93 Norman Young	25.00	12.50
Cliff Melton		
95 Jimmy Ripple	30.00	15.00
Bucky Walters		
97 Stan Hack	30.00	15.00
Bob Klinger		
99 Johnny Mize	75.00	38.00
Dan Litwhiler		
101 Dom Dallesandro	30.00	15.00
Augie Galan		
103 Bill Lee	40.00	20.00
Phil Cavarretta		
105 Lefty Grove	150.00	75.00
Bobby Doerr		
107 Frank Pytlak	60.00	30.00
Dom DiMaggio		
109 Jerry Priddy	40.00	20.00
Johnny Murphy		
111 Tommy Henrich	50.00	25.00
Marius Russo		
113 Frank Crosetti	50.00	25.00
Johnny Sturm		
115 Ival Goodman	30.00	15.00
Myron McCormick		
117 Eddie Joost	30.00	15.00
Ernie Koy		
119 Lloyd Waner	60.00	30.00
Hank Majeski		
121 Buddy Hassett	30.00	15.00
Eugene Moore		
123 Nick Etten	30.00	15.00
Johnny Rizzo		
125 Sam Chapman	30.00	15.00
Wally Moses		
127 Johnny Babich	30.00	15.00
Dick Siebert		
129 Nelson Potter	30.00	15.00
Benny McCoy		
131 Clarence Campbell	75.00	38.00
Lou Boudreau		
133 Rollie Hemsley	40.00	20.00
Mel Harder		
135 Gerald Walker	30.00	15.00
Joe Heving		
137 Johnny Rucker	30.00	15.00
Ace Adams		
139 Morris Arnovich	100.00	50.00
Carl Hubbell		
141 Lew Riggs	75.00	38.00
Leo Durocher		
143 Fred Fitzsimmons	30.00	15.00
Joe Vosmik		
145 Frank Crespi	30.00	15.00
Jim Brown		
147 Don Heffner	30.00	15.00
Harlond Clift		
149 Debs Garms	40.00	20.00
Elbie Fletcher		

1995 Emotion

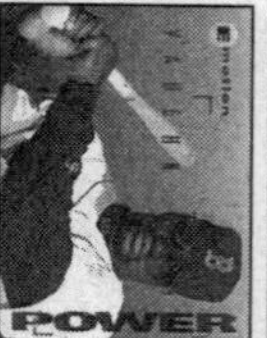

This 200-card standard-size set was produced by Fleer/SkyBox. The first-year brand has double-thick card stock with borderless fronts. Card fronts and backs are either horizontal or vertical. On the front of each player card is a theme such as Class (Cal Ripken) and Confident (Barry Bonds). The backs have two player photos, '94 stats and career numbers. The checklist is arranged alphabetically by team with AL preceding NL. Notable Rookie Cards include Hideo Nomo.

	Nm-Mt	Ex-Mt
COMPLETE SET (200)	40.00	12.00
1 Brady Anderson	.40	.12
2 Kevin Brown	.40	.12
3 Curtis Goodwin	.20	.06
4 Jeffrey Hammonds	.20	.06
5 Ben McDonald	.20	.06
6 Mike Mussina	.60	.18
7 Rafael Palmeiro	.60	.18
8 Cal Ripken Jr.	3.00	.90
9 Jose Canseco	1.00	.30
10 Roger Clemens	2.00	.60
11 Vaughn Eshelman	.20	.06
12 Mike Greenwell	.20	.06
13 Erik Hanson	.20	.06
14 Tim Naehring	.20	.06
15 Aaron Sele	.20	.06
16 John Valentin	.20	.06
17 Mo Vaughn	.40	.12
18 Chili Davis	.40	.12
19 Gary DiSarcina	.20	.06
20 Chuck Finley	.40	.12
21 Tim Salmon	.60	.18
22 Lee Smith	.40	.12
23 J.T. Snow	.40	.12
24 Jim Abbott	.60	.18
25 Jason Bere	.20	.06
26 Ray Durham	.40	.12
27 Ozzie Guillen	.20	.06
28 Tim Raines	.40	.12
29 Frank Thomas	1.00	.30
30 Robin Ventura	.40	.12
31 Carlos Baerga	.20	.06
32 Albert Belle	.40	.12
33 Orel Hershiser	.40	.12
34 Kenny Lofton	.40	.12
35 Dennis Martinez	.40	.12
36 Eddie Murray	1.00	.30
37 Manny Ramirez	.60	.18
38 Julian Tavarez	.20	.06
39 Jim Thome	1.00	.30
40 Dave Winfield	.40	.12
41 Chad Curtis	.20	.06
42 Cecil Fielder	.40	.12
43 Travis Fryman	.40	.12
44 Kirk Gibson	.40	.12
45 Bobby Higginson RC	1.00	.30
46 Alan Trammell	.40	.12
47 Lou Whitaker	.40	.12
48 Kevin Appier	.40	.12
49 Gary Gaetti	.40	.12
50 Jeff Montgomery	.20	.06
51 Jon Nunnally	.20	.06
52 Ricky Bones	.20	.06
53 Cal Eldred	.20	.06
54 Joe Oliver	.20	.06
55 Kevin Seitzer	.20	.06
56 Marty Cordova	.20	.06
57 Chuck Knoblauch	.40	.12
58 Kirby Puckett	1.00	.30
59 Wade Boggs	.60	.18
60 Derek Jeter	2.50	.75
61 Jimmy Key	.40	.12
62 Don Mattingly	2.50	.75
63 Jack McDowell	.20	.06
64 Paul O'Neill	.60	.18
65 Andy Pettitte	.60	.18
66 Ruben Rivera	.20	.06
67 Mike Stanley	.20	.06
68 John Wetteland	.40	.12
69 Geronimo Berroa	.20	.06
70 Dennis Eckersley	.40	.12
71 Rickey Henderson	1.00	.30
72 Mark McGwire	2.50	.75
73 Steve Ontiveros	.20	.06
74 Ruben Sierra	.20	.06
75 Terry Steinbach	.20	.06
76 Jay Buhner	.40	.12
77 Ken Griffey Jr.	1.50	.45
78 Randy Johnson	1.00	.30
79 Edgar Martinez	.60	.18
80 Tino Martinez	.60	.18
81 Marc Newfield	.20	.06
82 Alex Rodriguez	2.50	.75
83 Will Clark	1.00	.30
84 Benji Gil	.20	.06
85 Juan Gonzalez	.60	.18
86 Rusty Greer	.40	.12
87 Dean Palmer	.40	.12
88 Ivan Rodriguez	1.00	.30
89 Kenny Rogers	.40	.12
90 Roberto Alomar	.60	.18
91 Joe Carter	.40	.12
92 David Cone	.40	.12
93 Alex Gonzalez	.20	.06
94 Shawn Green	.40	.12
95 Pat Hentgen	.20	.06
96 Paul Molitor	.60	.18
97 John Olerud	.40	.12
98 Devon White	.40	.12
99 Steve Avery	.20	.06
100 Tom Glavine	.60	.18
101 Marquis Grissom	.40	.12
102 Chipper Jones	1.00	.30
103 David Justice	.40	.12
104 Ryan Klesko	.40	.12
105 Javier Lopez	.40	.12
106 Greg Maddux	1.50	.45
107 Fred McGriff	.60	.18
108 John Smoltz	.60	.18
109 Shawon Dunston	.20	.06
110 Mark Grace	.60	.18
111 Brian McRae	.20	.06
112 Randy Myers	.20	.06
113 Sammy Sosa	1.50	.45
114 Steve Trachsel	.20	.06
115 Bret Boone	.40	.12
116 Ron Gant	.40	.12
117 Barry Larkin	.60	.18
118 Deion Sanders	.60	.18
119 Reggie Sanders	.20	.06
120 Pete Schourek	.20	.06
121 John Smiley	.20	.06
122 Jason Bates	.20	.06
123 Dante Bichette	.40	.12
124 Vinny Castilla	.40	.12
125 Andres Galarraga	.40	.12
126 Larry Walker	.60	.18
127 Greg Colbrunn	.20	.06
128 Jeff Conine	.40	.12
129 Andre Dawson	.40	.12
130 Chris Hammond	.20	.06
131 Charles Johnson	.40	.12
132 Gary Sheffield	.40	.12
133 Quilvio Veras	.20	.06
134 Jeff Bagwell	.60	.18
135 Derek Bell	.20	.06
136 Craig Biggio	.60	.18
137 Jim Dougherty RC	.25	.07
138 John Hudek	.20	.06
139 Orlando Miller	.20	.06
140 Phil Plantier	.20	.06
141 Eric Karros	.40	.12
142 Ramon Martinez	.20	.06
143 Raul Mondesi	.40	.12
144 Hideo Nomo RC	2.00	.60
145 Mike Piazza	1.50	.45
146 Ismael Valdes	.20	.06
147 Todd Worrell	.20	.06
148 Moises Alou	.40	.12
149 Yamil Benitez RC	.25	.07
150 Wil Cordero	.20	.06
151 Jeff Fassero	.20	.06
152 Cliff Floyd	.40	.12
153 Pedro Martinez	1.00	.30
154 Carlos Perez RC	.50	.15
155 Tony Tarasco	.20	.06
156 Rondell White	.40	.12
157 Edgardo Alfonzo	.40	.12
158 Bobby Bonilla	.40	.12
159 Rico Brogna	.20	.06
160 Bobby Jones	.20	.06
161 Bill Pulsipher	.20	.06
162 Bret Saberhagen	.40	.12
163 Ricky Bottalico	.20	.06
164 Darren Daulton	.40	.12
165 Lenny Dykstra	.40	.12
166 Charlie Hayes	.20	.06
167 Dave Hollins	.20	.06
168 Gregg Jefferies	.20	.06
169 Michael Mimbs RC	.25	.07
170 Curt Schilling	.40	.12
171 Heathcliff Slocumb	.20	.06
172 Jay Bell	.40	.12
173 Micah Franklin RC	.25	.07
174 Mark Johnson RC	.50	.15
175 Jeff King	.20	.06
176 Al Martin	.20	.06
177 Dan Miceli	.20	.06
178 Denny Neagle	.40	.12
179 Bernard Gilkey	.20	.06
180 Ken Hill	.20	.06
181 Brian Jordan	.40	.12
182 Ray Lankford	.20	.06
183 Ozzie Smith	1.50	.45
184 Andy Benes	.20	.06
185 Ken Caminiti	.40	.12
186 Steve Finley	.40	.12
187 Tony Gwynn	1.25	.35
188 Joey Hamilton	.20	.06
189 Melvin Nieves	.20	.06
190 Scott Sanders	.20	.06
191 Rod Beck	.20	.06
192 Barry Bonds	2.50	.75
193 Royce Clayton	.20	.06
194 Glenallen Hill	.20	.06
195 Darren Lewis	.20	.06
196 Mark Portugal	.20	.06
197 Matt Williams	.40	.12
198 Checklist 1-82	.20	.06
199 Checklist 83-162	.20	.06
200 CL 163-200/Inserts	.20	.06
P8 Cal Ripken Promo	2.00	.60

1995 Emotion Masters

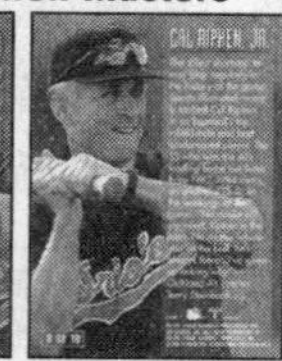

The theme of this 10-card standard-size set is the showcasing of players that come through in the clutch. Randomly inserted at a rate of one in eight packs, a player photo is superimposed over a larger photo that is ghosted in a color emblematic of that team. The player's name and the Emotion logo are at the bottom. The backs have a photo to the left and text to the right. Both sides of the card are shaded in the color scheme of the player's team.

	Nm-Mt	Ex-Mt
COMPLETE SET (10)	40.00	12.00
1 Barry Bonds	8.00	2.40
2 Juan Gonzalez	2.00	.60
3 Ken Griffey Jr.	5.00	1.50
4 Tony Gwynn	4.00	1.20
5 Kenny Lofton	1.25	.35
6 Greg Maddux	5.00	1.50
7 Raul Mondesi	1.25	.35
8 Cal Ripken	10.00	3.00
9 Frank Thomas	3.00	.90
10 Matt Williams	1.25	.35

1995 Emotion N-Tense

Randomly inserted at a rate of one in 37 packs, this 12-card standard-size set features fronts that have a player photo surrounded by a swirling color scheme and a large holographic "N" in the background. The backs feature a like color scheme with text and player photo.

	Nm-Mt	Ex-Mt
COMPLETE SET (12)	100.00	30.00
1 Jeff Bagwell	5.00	1.50
2 Albert Belle	3.00	.90
3 Barry Bonds	20.00	6.00
4 Cecil Fielder	3.00	.90
5 Ron Gant	3.00	.90
6 Ken Griffey Jr.	12.00	3.60
7 Mark McGwire	20.00	6.00
8 Mike Piazza	12.00	3.60
9 Manny Ramirez	5.00	1.50
10 Frank Thomas	8.00	2.40
11 Mo Vaughn	3.00	.90
12 Matt Williams	3.00	.90

1995 Emotion Ripken

This 15-card Cal Ripken standard-size set features great moments from the career of the Baltimore Orioles' great. Inserted at a rate of one in 12 packs, cards 1-10 feature moments actually selected by the record-breaking shortstop. Referred to as "Timeless", an action photo of Ripken is superimposed over a silver background that includes a watch and another photo at the top. The backs elaborate on the event or events which Cal selected. This text is superimposed over a large photo. A five-card mail-in set (described on wrapper) was also made available. The expiration was 3/1/96.

	Nm-Mt	Ex-Mt
COMPLETE SET (10)	40.00	12.00
COMMON CARD (1-10)	5.00	1.50
COMMON MAIL (11-15)	5.00	1.50

1995 Emotion Rookies

This 10-card standard-size set was inserted at a rate of one in five packs. Card fronts feature an action photo superimposed over background that is in a color consistent with that of the team's. The backs have a player photo and a write-up.

	Nm-Mt	Ex-Mt
COMPLETE SET (10)	25.00	7.50
1 Edgardo Alfonzo	1.00	.30
2 Jason Bates	1.00	.30
3 Marty Cordova	1.00	.30
4 Ray Durham	1.00	.30
5 Alex Gonzalez	1.00	.30
6 Shawn Green	1.00	.30
7 Charles Johnson	1.00	.30
8 Chipper Jones	2.00	.60
9 Hideo Nomo	4.00	1.20
10 Alex Rodriguez	8.00	2.40

1996 Emotion-XL

The 1996 Emotion-XL set (produced by Fleer/SkyBox) was issued in one series totalling 300 standard-size cards. The seven-card packs retailed for $4.99 each. The fronts feature a color action player photo with either a blue, green or maroon frame and the player's name and team printed in a foil-stamped medallion. A descriptive term describing the player completes the front. The backs carry player information and statistics. The cards are grouped alphabetically by team with AL preceding NL. A Manny Ramirez promo card was distributed to dealers and hobby media to preview the set.

	Nm-Mt	Ex-Mt
COMPLETE SET (300)	60.00	18.00
1 Roberto Alomar	1.25	.35
2 Brady Anderson	.75	.23
3 Bobby Bonilla	.75	.23
4 Jeffrey Hammonds	.75	.23
5 Chris Hoiles	.75	.23
6 Mike Mussina	1.25	.35
7 Randy Myers	.75	.23
8 Rafael Palmeiro	1.25	.35
9 Cal Ripken	6.00	1.80
10 B.J. Surhoff	.75	.2
11 Jose Canseco	2.00	.6
12 Roger Clemens	4.00	1.2
13 Wil Cordero	.75	.2
14 Mike Greenwell	.75	.2
15 Dwayne Hosey	.75	.2
16 Tim Naehring	.75	.2
17 Troy O'Leary	.75	.2
18 Mike Stanley	.75	.2
19 John Valentin	.75	.2
20 Mo Vaughn	.75	.2
21 Jim Abbott	1.25	.3
22 Garret Anderson	.75	.2
23 George Arias	.75	.2
24 Chili Davis	.75	.2
25 Jim Edmonds	.75	.2
26 Chuck Finley	.75	.2
27 Todd Greene	.75	.2
28 Mark Langston	.75	.2
29 Troy Percival	.75	.2
30 Tim Salmon	1.25	.3
31 Lee Smith	.75	.2
32 J.T. Snow	.75	.2
33 Harold Baines	.75	.2
34 Jason Bere	.75	.2
35 Ray Durham	.75	.2
36 Alex Fernandez	.75	.2
37 Ozzie Guillen	.75	.2
38 Darren Lewis	.75	.2
39 Lyle Mouton	.75	.2
40 Tony Phillips	.75	.2
41 Danny Tartabull	.75	.2
42 Frank Thomas	2.00	.6
43 Robin Ventura	.75	.2
44 Sandy Alomar Jr.	.75	.2
45 Carlos Baerga	.75	.2
46 Albert Belle	.75	.2
47 Julio Franco	.75	.2
48 Orel Hershiser	.75	.2
49 Kenny Lofton	.75	.2
50 Dennis Martinez	.75	.2
51 Jack McDowell	.75	.2
52 Jose Mesa	.75	.2
53 Eddie Murray	2.00	.6
54 Charles Nagy	.75	.2
55 Manny Ramirez	1.25	.35
56 Jim Thome	2.00	.6
57 Omar Vizquel	1.25	.35
58 Chad Curtis	.75	.23
59 Cecil Fielder	.75	.23
60 Travis Fryman	.75	.23
61 Chris Gomez	.75	.23
62 Felipe Lira	.75	.23
63 Alan Trammell	.75	.23
64 Kevin Appier	.75	.23
65 Johnny Damon	1.25	.35
66 Tom Goodwin	.75	.23
67 Mark Gubicza	.75	.23
68 Jeff Montgomery	.75	.23
69 Jon Nunnally	.75	.23
70 Bip Roberts	.75	.23
71 Ricky Bones	.75	.23
72 Chuck Carr	.75	.23
73 John Jaha	.75	.23
74 Ben McDonald	.75	.23
75 Matt Mieske	.75	.23
76 Dave Nilsson	.75	.23
77 Kevin Seitzer	.75	.23
78 Greg Vaughn	.75	.23
79 Rick Aguilera	.75	.23
80 Marty Cordova	.75	.23
81 Roberto Kelly	.75	.23
82 Chuck Knoblauch	.75	.23
83 Pat Meares	.75	.23
84 Paul Molitor	1.25	.35
85 Kirby Puckett	2.00	.60
86 Brad Radke	.75	.23
87 Wade Boggs	1.25	.35
88 David Cone	.75	.23
89 Dwight Gooden	.75	.23
90 Derek Jeter	5.00	1.50
91 Tino Martinez	1.25	.35
92 Paul O'Neill	1.25	.35
93 Andy Pettitte	1.25	.35
94 Tim Raines	.75	.23
95 Ruben Rivera	.75	.23
96 Kenny Rogers	.75	.23
97 Ruben Sierra	.75	.23
98 John Wetteland	.75	.23
99 Bernie Williams	1.25	.35
100 Allen Battle	.75	.23
101 Geronimo Berroa	.75	.23
102 Brent Gates	.75	.23
103 Doug Johns	.75	.23
104 Mark McGwire	5.00	1.50
105 Pedro Munoz	.75	.23
106 Ariel Prieto	.75	.23
107 Terry Steinbach	.75	.23
108 Todd Van Poppel	.75	.23
109 Chris Bosio	.75	.23
110 Jay Buhner	.75	.23
111 Joey Cora	.75	.23
112 Russ Davis	.75	.23
113 Ken Griffey Jr.	3.00	.90
114 Sterling Hitchcock	.75	.23
115 Randy Johnson	2.00	.60
116 Edgar Martinez	1.25	.35
117 Alex Rodriguez	4.00	1.20
118 Paul Sorrento	.75	.23
119 Dan Wilson	.75	.23
120 Will Clark	2.00	.60
121 Juan Gonzalez	1.25	.35
122 Rusty Greer	.75	.23
123 Kevin Gross	.75	.23
124 Ken Hill	.75	.23
125 Dean Palmer	.75	.23
126 Roger Pavlik	.75	.23
127 Ivan Rodriguez	2.00	.60
128 Mickey Tettleton	.75	.23
129 Joe Carter	.75	.23
130 Carlos Delgado	.75	.23
131 Alex Gonzalez	.75	.23
132 Shawn Green	.75	.23
133 Erik Hanson	.75	.23
134 Pat Hentgen	.75	.23
135 Otis Nixon	.75	.23
136 John Olerud	.75	.23
137 Ed Sprague	.75	.23
138 Steve Avery	.75	.23
139 Jermaine Dye	.75	.23

0 Tom Glavine 1.25 .35
1 Marquis Grissom .75 .23
2 Chipper Jones 2.00 .60
3 David Justice .75 .23
4 Ryan Klesko .75 .23
5 Javier Lopez .75 .23
46 Greg Maddux 3.00 .90
7 Fred McGriff 1.25 .35
8 Jason Schmidt 1.25 .35
9 John Smoltz 1.25 .35
0 Mark Wohlers .75 .23
1 Jim Bullinger .75 .23
2 Frank Castillo .75 .23
3 Kevin Foster .75 .23
4 Luis Gonzalez .75 .23
5 Mark Grace 1.25 .35
6 Brian McRae .75 .23
7 Jaime Navarro .75 .23
8 Rey Sanchez .75 .23
9 Ryne Sandberg 3.00 .90
0 Sammy Sosa 3.00 .90
1 Bret Boone .75 .23
2 Jeff Brantley .75 .23
3 Vince Coleman .75 .23
4 Steve Gibralter .75 .23
5 Barry Larkin 1.25 .35
6 Hal Morris .75 .23
7 Mark Portugal .75 .23
8 Reggie Sanders .75 .23
9 Pete Schourek .75 .23
70 John Smiley .75 .23
71 Jason Bates .75 .23
72 Dante Bichette .75 .23
73 Ellis Burks .75 .23
74 Vinny Castilla .75 .23
75 Andres Galarraga .75 .23
76 Kevin Ritz .75 .23
77 Bill Swift .75 .23
78 Larry Walker 1.25 .35
79 Walt Weiss .75 .23
80 Eric Young .75 .23
81 Kurt Abbott .75 .23
82 Kevin Brown .75 .23
83 John Burkett .75 .23
84 Greg Colbrunn .75 .23
85 Jeff Conine .75 .23
86 Chris Hammond .75 .23
87 Charles Johnson .75 .23
88 Terry Pendleton .75 .23
89 Pat Rapp .75 .23
90 Gary Sheffield .75 .23
91 Quilvio Veras .75 .23
92 Devon White .75 .23
93 Jeff Bagwell 1.25 .35
94 Derek Bell .75 .23
95 Sean Berry .75 .23
96 Craig Biggio 1.25 .35
97 Doug Drabek .75 .23
98 Tony Eusebio .75 .23
99 Mike Hampton .75 .23
00 Brian L.Hunter .75 .23
01 Derrick May .75 .23
02 Orlando Miller .75 .23
03 Shane Reynolds .75 .23
04 Mike Blowers .75 .23
05 Tom Candiotti .75 .23
06 Delino DeShields .75 .23
07 Greg Gagne .75 .23
08 Karim Garcia .75 .23
09 Todd Hollandsworth .75 .23
10 Eric Karros .75 .23
11 Ramon Martinez .75 .23
12 Raul Mondesi .75 .23
13 Hideo Nomo 2.00 .60
14 Chan Ho Park .75 .23
15 Mike Piazza 3.00 .90
16 Ismael Valdes .75 .23
17 Todd Worrell .75 .23
18 Moises Alou .75 .23
19 Yamil Benitez .75 .23
20 Jeff Fassero .75 .23
21 Darrin Fletcher .75 .23
22 Cliff Floyd .75 .23
23 Pedro Martinez 2.00 .60
24 Carlos Perez .75 .23
25 Mel Rojas .75 .23
26 David Segui .75 .23
27 Rondell White .75 .23
28 Rico Brogna .75 .23
29 Carl Everett .75 .23
30 John Franco .75 .23
231 Bernard Gilkey .75 .23
232 Todd Hundley .75 .23
233 Jason Isringhausen .75 .23
234 Lance Johnson .75 .23
235 Bobby Jones .75 .23
236 Jeff Kent .75 .23
237 Rey Ordonez .75 .23
238 Bill Pulsipher .75 .23
239 Jose Vizcaino .75 .23
240 Paul Wilson .75 .23
241 Ricky Bottalico .75 .23
242 Darren Daulton .75 .23
243 Lenny Dykstra .75 .23
244 Jim Eisenreich .75 .23
245 Sid Fernandez .75 .23
246 Gregg Jefferies .75 .23
247 Mickey Morandini .75 .23
248 Benito Santiago .75 .23
249 Curt Schilling .75 .23
250 Mark Whiten .75 .23
251 Todd Zeile .75 .23
252 Jay Bell .75 .23
253 Carlos Garcia .75 .23
254 Charlie Hayes .75 .23
255 Jason Kendall .75 .23
256 Jeff King .75 .23
257 Al Martin .75 .23
258 Orlando Merced .75 .23
259 Dan Miceli .75 .23
260 Denny Neagle .75 .23
261 Alan Benes .75 .23
262 Andy Benes .75 .23
263 Royce Clayton .75 .23
264 Dennis Eckersley .75 .23
265 Gary Gaetti .75 .23
266 Ron Gant .75 .23
267 Brian Jordan .75 .23
268 Ray Lankford .75 .23
269 John Mabry .75 .23
270 Tom Pagnozzi .75 .23
271 Ozzie Smith 3.00 .90
272 Todd Stottlemyre .75 .23
273 Andy Ashby .75 .23
274 Brad Ausmus .75 .23
275 Ken Caminiti .75 .23
276 Steve Finley .75 .23
277 Tony Gwynn 2.50 .75
278 Joey Hamilton .75 .23
279 Rickey Henderson 2.00 .60
280 Trevor Hoffman .75 .23
281 Wally Joyner .75 .23
282 Jody Reed .75 .23
283 Bob Tewksbury .75 .23
284 Fernando Valenzuela .75 .23
285 Rod Beck .75 .23
286 Barry Bonds 5.00 1.50
287 Mark Carreon .75 .23
288 Shawon Dunston .75 .23
289 O.Fernandez RC .75 .23
290 Glenallen Hill .75 .23
291 Stan Javier .75 .23
292 Mark Leiter .75 .23
293 Kirt Manwaring .75 .23
294 Robby Thompson .75 .23
295 W.VanLandingham .75 .23
296 Allen Watson .75 .23
297 Matt Williams .75 .23
298 Checklist .75 .23
299 Checklist .75 .23
300 Checklist .75 .23
P55 Manny Ramirez 1.00 .30
Promo

1996 Emotion-XL D-Fense

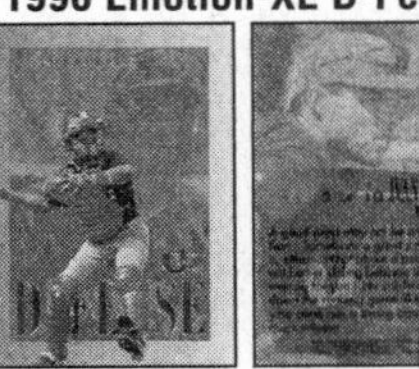

Randomly inserted in packs at a rate of one in four, this 10-card set showcases outstanding defensive players. The fronts feature a color action player cut-out on a sepia portait background with silver foil print and border. The backs carry information about the player on another sepia portrait background.

	Nm-Mt	Ex-Mt
COMPLETE SET (10)	25.00	7.50
1 Roberto Alomar	1.50	.45
2 Barry Bonds	6.00	1.80
3 Mark Grace	1.50	.45
4 Ken Griffey Jr.	4.00	1.20
5 Kenny Lofton	1.00	.30
6 Greg Maddux	4.00	1.20
7 Raul Mondesi	1.00	.30
8 Cal Ripken	8.00	2.40
9 Ivan Rodriguez	2.50	.75
10 Matt Williams	1.00	.30

1996 Emotion-XL Legion of Boom

Randomly inserted in packs at a rate of one in 36, this 12-card set features the game's big hitters on cards with translucent card backs. The fronts carry a color action player cut-out with silver foil print.

	Nm-Mt	Ex-Mt
COMPLETE SET (12)	150.00	45.00
1 Albert Belle	5.00	1.50
2 Barry Bonds	30.00	9.00
3 Juan Gonzalez	8.00	2.40
4 Ken Griffey Jr.	20.00	6.00
5 Mark McGwire	30.00	9.00
6 Mike Piazza	20.00	6.00
7 Manny Ramirez	8.00	2.40
8 Tim Salmon	8.00	2.40
9 Sammy Sosa	20.00	6.00
10 Frank Thomas	12.00	3.60
11 Mo Vaughn	5.00	1.50
12 Matt Williams	5.00	1.50

1996 Emotion-XL N-Tense

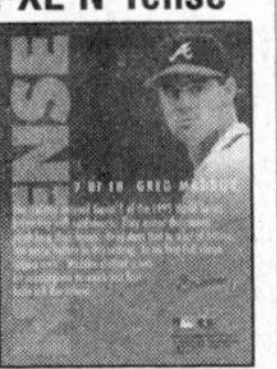

Randomly inserted in packs at a rate of one in 12, this 10-card set highlights top-clutch performers on special, front N-shaped die-cut cards. The backs carry information about the player on a player portrait background.

	Nm-Mt	Ex-Mt
COMPLETE SET (10)	60.00	18.00
1 Albert Belle	2.00	.60
2 Barry Bonds	12.00	3.60
3 Jose Canseco	5.00	1.50
4 Ken Griffey Jr.	8.00	2.40
5 Tony Gwynn	6.00	1.80
6 Randy Johnson	5.00	1.50
7 Greg Maddux	8.00	2.40
8 Cal Ripken	15.00	4.50
9 Frank Thomas	5.00	1.50
10 Matt Williams	2.00	.60

1996 Emotion-XL Rare Breed

Randomly inserted in packs at a rate of one in 100, this 10-card set showcases young stars on lenticular cards. The fronts feature color action player cut-outs on a baseball graphics background. The backs carry player information over a color player portrait.

	Nm-Mt	Ex-Mt
COMPLETE SET (10)	120.00	36.00
1 Garret Anderson	10.00	3.00
2 Marty Cordova	8.00	2.40
3 Brian L.Hunter	8.00	2.40
4 Jason Isringhausen	10.00	3.00
5 Charles Johnson	10.00	3.00
6 Chipper Jones	25.00	7.50
7 Raul Mondesi	10.00	3.00
8 Hideo Nomo	25.00	7.50
9 Manny Ramirez	15.00	4.50
10 Rondell White	10.00	3.00

2001 eTopps

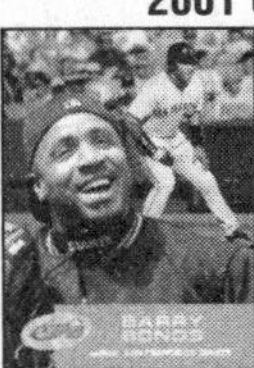

One of the more unique products of the year 2001 made its long-awaited debut (after months of technical setbacks) in mid-September. eTopps was distributed and marketed in a manner unlike any other brand of cards before them. The only place they were initially offered for sale was at the eTopps website (www.eTopps.com). Starting in late September on a weekly basis - and for about three months, Topps released IPO's (aka Initial Player Offerings) on a handful of cards to the point where all 150 eTopps baseball cards were available. A pre-determined number of shares were given for each player based upon Topps estimation of popularity (a.k.a. they offered 10,000 Ichiro's and only 4,000 Rafael Furcal's). Price per card during IPO status typically ranged from $3.50 per card to $9.50 per card - again based on popularity. The one week IPO period was the only time these cards were ever offered for sale by Topps and most importantly Topps only printed the exact amount of cards that were ordered during that window of time. Thus, even though Topps had offered 4,000 shares of Jeff Bagwell, only 485 copies were ordered - thus that's all they produced. Consumers had the option to have their cards held by Topps whereby they could automatically trade them to other collectors (much like one would buy and sell stocks) on the eTopps "floor" - a special section of eBay created for this product, or have the card mailed to them ($6.95 for the first card and 85 cents for each additional).

	Nm-Mt	Ex-Mt
1 Nomar Garciaparra/1315		
2 Chipper Jones/674		
3 Jeff Bagwell/485		
4 Randy Johnson/1499		
7 Adam Dunn/4197		
8 J.D. Drew/767		
9 Larry Walker/420		
10 Edgardo Alfonzo/338		
11 Lance Berkman/595		
12 Tony Gwynn/828		
13 Andruw Jones/908		
15 Troy Glaus/862		
17 Sammy Sosa/2487		
21 Darin Erstad/664		
22 Barry Bonds/1567		
27 Derek Jeter/1041		
29 Curt Schilling/2125		
30 Roberto Alomar/448		
31 Luis Gonzalez/1104		
32 Jimmy Rollins/1307		
34 Joe Crede/1050		
39 Sean Casey/537		
46 Alex Rodriguez/2212		
47 Tom Glavine/437		
50 Jose Ortiz/738		
51 Cal Ripken/2201		
52 Bob Abreu/677		
55 Alex Escobar/931		
56 Ivan Rodriguez/698		
59 Jeff Kent/452		
62 Rick Ankiel/752		
65 Craig Biggio/410		
66 Carlos Delgado/398		
68 Greg Maddux/1031		
69 Kerry Wood/1056		
71 Todd Helton/978		
72 Mariano Rivera/824		
73 Jason Kendall/672		
75 Scott Rolen/498		
76 Kazuhiro Sasaki/5000		
77 Roy Oswalt/915		
78 C.C. Sabathia/1974		
83 Brian Giles/400		
87 Rafael Furcal/646		
88 Mike Mussina/793		
89 Gary Sheffield/359		
92 Mark McGwire/2908		
94 Tsuyoshi Shinjo/3000		
99 Jose Vidro/443		
100 Ichiro Suzuki/10000	20.00	6.00
105 Manny Ramirez/1074		
109 Juan Gonzalez/558		
112 Ken Griffey Jr./2398		
114 Tim Hudson/663		
115 Nick Johnson/1217		
118 Jason Giambi/897		
122 Rafael Palmeiro/464		
124 V. Guerrero/854		
125 Vernon Wells/349		
127 Roger Clemens/1462		
128 Frank Thomas/834		
129 Carlos Beltran/489		
130 Pat Burrell/1253		
131 Pedro Martinez/1038		
132 Mike Piazza/1379		
135 Luis Montanez/5000		
140 Sean Burroughs/5000		
141 Barry Zito/843		
142 Bobby Bradley/5000		
143 Albert Pujols/5000	50.00	15.00
144 Ben Sheets/1713		
145 Alfonso Soriano/1699		
146 Josh Hamilton/5000		
147 Eric Munson/5000		
150 Mark Mulder/4335		

2002 eTopps

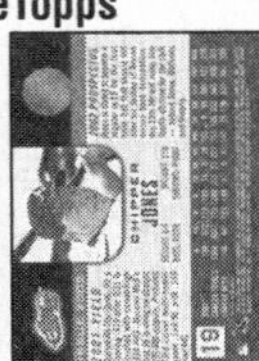

For the second consecutive year, Topps issued a set only available through their on-line services. ETopps was distributed and marketed in a manner unlike any other brand of cards before them. The only place they were initially offered for sale was at the eTopps website (www.eTopps.com). Starting with the beginning of the 2002 season and continuing through the 2002 All-Star break these cards were made available on a weekly basis. A pre-determined number of shares (ranging from as few as 2,000 to as many as 6,000) were given for each player based upon Topps estimation of popularity. For 2002, your "portfolio" could increase if the players in the set met certain statistical goals for the season. Price per card during IPO status typically ranged from approximately $4 per card to $9 per card - again based on popularity. The one week IPO period was the only time these cards were ever offered for sale by Topps and most importantly Topps only printed the exact amount of cards that were ordered during that window of time. These print runs are displayed in our checklist. Consumers had the option to have their cards held by Topps, whereby they could automatically sell them or buy more to and from other collectors (much like one would buy and sell stocks) on the eTopps "floor" - a special section of eBay created for this product, or have the card mailed to them ($6.95 for the first card and 85 cents for each additional).

	Nm-Mt	Ex-Mt
1 Ichiro Suzuki/9477		
2 Jason Giambi/5142		
3 Roberto Alomar/2711		
4 Bret Boone/2000		
5 Frank Catalanotto/2000		
6 Alex Rodriguez/6393		
7 Jim Thome/2927		
8 Toby Hall/2000		
9 Troy Glaus/4323		
10 Derek Jeter/8000		
11 Alfonso Soriano/5000		
12 Eric Chavez/4334		
13 Preston Wilson/2000		
14 Bernie Williams/4436		
15 Larry Walker/2546		
16 Todd Helton/3430		
17 Moises Alou/2856		
18 Lance Berkman/5000		
19 Chipper Jones/4734		
20 Andruw Jones/4849		
21 Barry Bonds/6658		
22 Sammy Sosa/8000		
23 Luis Gonzalez/2671		
24 Shawn Green/4438		
25 Jeff Bagwell/3359		
26 Albert Pujols/5531		
27 Rafael Palmeiro/2700		
28 Jimmy Rollins/5000		
29 Vladimir Guerrero/6000		
30 Jeff Kent/3000		
31 Ken Griffey Jr./4569		
32 Magglio Ordonez/4000		
33 Mike Piazza/4202		
34 Pedro Martinez/6000		
35 Mark Mulder/4000		
36 Roger Clemens/4567		
37 Freddy Garcia/4986		
38 Tim Hudson/2000		
39 Mike Mussina/3708		
40 Joe Mays/3000		
41 Barry Zito/3590		
42 Jermaine Dye/2693		
43 Mariano Rivera/3709		
44 Randy Johnson/6211		
45 Curt Schilling/5190		
46 Greg Maddux/4008		
47 Javier Vazquez/3000		
48 Kerry Wood/3346		
49 Wilson Betemit/2377		
50 Adam Dunn/6000		
51 Josh Beckett/5000		
52 Paul LoDuca/3998		
53 Ben Sheets/3842		
54 Eric Valent/5000		
55 Brian Giles/2000		
56 Mo Vaughn/2772		
57 C.C. Sabathia/2525		
58 Nick Johnson/5000		
59 Miguel Tejada/4000		
60 Carlos Delgado/3604		
61 Tsuyoshi Shinjo/3000		
62 Juan Gonzalez/2361		
63 Mike Sweeney/3173		
64 Ivan Rodriguez/3000		
65 Bud Smith/3000		
66 Brandon Duckworth/2000		
67 Xavier Nady/4000		
68 D'Angelo Jimenez/1725		
69 Roy Oswalt/3523		
70 J.D. Drew/3195		
71 Cliff Floyd/3725		
72 Kevin Brown/3000		
73 Gary Sheffield/3593		
74 Aramis Ramirez/3000		
75 Nomar Garciaparra/5090		
76 Phil Nevin/2348		
77 Juan Cruz/4000		
78 Hideo Nomo/2857		
79 Chris George/3000		
80 Matt Morris/3000		
81 Corey Patterson/4000		
82 Joel Pineiro/4776		
83 Mark Buehrle/3000		
84 Shannon Stewart/1992		
85 Kazuhiro Sasaki/4000		
86 Carlos Pena/4000		
87 Brad Penny/3000		
88 Rich Aurilia/2795		
89 Wade Miller/4000		
90 Tim Raines Jr./5000		
91 Kazuhisa Ishii/6000		
92 Hank Blalock/5000		
93 So Taguchi/5000		
94 Mark Prior/5000		
95 Rickey Henderson/4013		
96 Austin Kearns/6000		
97 Tom Glavine/3000		
98 Manny Ramirez/4905		
99 Shea Hillenbrand/4000		
100 Junior Spivey/5000		
101 Derek Lowe/4911		
102 Torii Hunter/4000		
103 Juan Rivera/4000		
104 Eric Hinske/5000		
105 Bobby Hill/3000		
106 Rafael Soriano/4000		
107 Jim Edmonds/3851		

2003 eTopps

For the third consecutive season, Topps issued cards through their eTopps network. The distribution of these cards began in March, 2003. These cards were printed to match the amount of orders received and were available at an original cost of between $4 and $9.50. Please note, card 117 was never issued - thus, though the set is numbered 1-123 only 122 cards were produced.

	Nm-Mt	Ex-Mt
1 Troy Glaus		
2 Manny Ramirez		
3 Magglio Ordonez		
4 Jim Thome		
5 Torii Hunter		
6 Jason Giambi		
7 Tim Hudson		
8 Ichiro Suzuki		
9 Aubrey Huff		
10 Alex Rodriguez		
11 Francisco Rodriguez		
12 Joe Borchard		
13 Mark Teixeira		
14 Marlon Byrd		
15 Carlos Delgado		
16 Tom Glavine		
17 Curt Schilling		
18 Mark Prior		
19 Ken Griffey Jr.		
20 Todd Helton		
21 Jeff Bagwell		
22 Shawn Green		
23 Vladimir Guerrero		
24 Roberto Alomar		
25 Brian Giles		
26 Barry Bonds		
27 Albert Pujols		
28 Nomar Garciaparra		
29 Alfonso Soriano		
30 Barry Zito		
31 Edgar Martinez		
32 Ivan Rodriguez		
33 Greg Maddux		
34 Sammy Sosa		
35 Austin Kearns		
36 Craig Biggio		
37 Mike Piazza		
38 Andruw Jones		
39 Jeff Kent		
40 Roy Oswalt		
41 Miguel Tejada		
42 Derek Jeter		
43 Pedro Martinez		
44 Jarrod Washburn		
45 Randy Johnson		
46 Bernie Williams		
47 Chipper Jones		
48 Gary Sheffield		
49 Larry Walker		

50 Lance Berkman		
51 Garret Anderson		
52 Jason Schmidt		
53 Rodrigo Lopez		
54 Oliver Perez		
55 Derek Lowe		
56 Vicente Padilla		
57 Paul Konerko		
58 Bartolo Colon		
59 Omar Vizquel		
60 Adam Dunn		
61 Carlos Pena		
62 Richie Sexson		
63 Paul Byrd		
64 Eric Gagne		
65 Brad Radke		
66 A.J. Burnett		
67 Brandon Phillips		
68 Mike Hampton		
69 Tim Salmon		
70 Roger Clemens		
71 Jake Peavy		
72 Pat Burrell		
73 Ben Sheets		
74 Fred McGriff		
75 John Smoltz		
76 Josh Phelps		
77 John Olerud		
78 Eric Chavez		
79 Jeff Weaver		
80 Scott Rolen		
81 Carl Crawford		
82 Rafael Palmeiro		
83 Roy Halladay		
84 Josh Beckett		
85 Jorge Posada		
86 Mark Mulder		
87 Eric Milton		
88 Angel Berroa		
89 Jason Lane		
90 Kerry Wood		
91 Brad Wilkerson		
92 Orlando Hudson		
93 Mike Mussina		
94 Hee Seop Choi		
95 Chris Snelling		
96 Tomo Ohka		
97 Andy Pettitte		
98 Drew Henson		
99 Chin-Feng Chen		
100 Jason Jennings		
101 Hideki Matsui		
102 Jose Contreras		
103 Rocco Baldelli		
104 Jeremy Bonderman		
105 Jesse Foppert		
106 Randy Wolf		
107 Kevin Millwood		
108 Eric Byrnes		
109 Edgar Renteria		
110 Jose Reyes		
111 Dontrelle Willis		
112 Mike Lowell		
113 Jerome Williams		
114 Esteban Loaiza		
115 Gil Meche		
116 Ty Wigginton		
117 Does Not Exist		
118 Brett Myers		
119 Miguel Cabrera		
120 Brandon Webb		
121 Aaron Heilman		
122 Rich Harden		
123 Morgan Ensberg		

1997 E-X2000

This 100-card set (produced by Fleer/SkyBox) was distributed in two-card foil packs with a suggested retail price of $3.99. An oversized Alex Rodriguez card shipped in its own holder was mailed to dealers who ordered E-X 2000 cases. They are numbered out of 3,000 and priced below. Also priced below is the redemption card for a baseball signed by Rodriguez. 100 of these cards were produced and the redemption deadline was May 1, 1998.

	Nm-Mt	Ex-Mt
COMPLETE SET (100)	80.00	24.00
1 Jim Edmonds	.75	.23
2 Darin Erstad	.75	.23
3 Eddie Murray	2.00	.60
4 Roberto Alomar	1.25	.35
5 Brady Anderson	.75	.23
6 Mike Mussina	1.25	.35
7 Rafael Palmeiro	1.25	.35
8 Cal Ripken	6.00	1.80
9 Steve Avery	.75	.23
10 Nomar Garciaparra	3.00	.90
11 Mo Vaughn	.75	.23
12 Albert Belle	.75	.23
13 Mike Cameron	.75	.23
14 Ray Durham	.75	.23
15 Frank Thomas	2.00	.60
16 Robin Ventura	.75	.23
17 Manny Ramirez	1.25	.35
18 Jim Thome	2.00	.60
19 Matt Williams	.75	.23
20 Tony Clark	.75	.23
21 Travis Fryman	.75	.23
22 Bob Higginson	.75	.23
23 Kevin Appier	.75	.23
24 Johnny Damon	1.25	.35
25 Jermaine Dye	.75	.23
26 Jeff Cirillo	.75	.23
27 Ben McDonald	.75	.23
28 Chuck Knoblauch	.75	.23
29 Paul Molitor	1.25	.35
30 Todd Walker	.75	.23
31 Wade Boggs	1.25	.35
32 Cecil Fielder	.75	.23
33 Derek Jeter	5.00	1.50
34 Andy Pettitte	1.25	.35
35 Ruben Rivera	.75	.23
36 Bernie Williams	1.25	.35
37 Jose Canseco	2.00	.60
38 Mark McGwire	5.00	1.50
39 Jay Buhner	.75	.23
40 Ken Griffey Jr.	3.00	.90
41 Randy Johnson	2.00	.60
42 Edgar Martinez	1.25	.35
43 Alex Rodriguez	3.00	.90
44 Dan Wilson	.75	.23
45 Will Clark	2.00	.60
46 Juan Gonzalez	1.25	.35
47 Ivan Rodriguez	2.00	.60
48 Joe Carter	.75	.23
49 Roger Clemens	4.00	1.20
50 Juan Guzman	.75	.23
51 Pat Hentgen	.75	.23
52 Tom Glavine	1.25	.35
53 Andruw Jones	.75	.23
54 Chipper Jones	2.00	.60
55 Ryan Klesko	.75	.23
56 Kenny Lofton	.75	.23
57 Greg Maddux	3.00	.90
58 Fred McGriff	1.25	.35
59 John Smoltz	1.25	.35
60 Mark Wohlers	.75	.23
61 Mark Grace	1.25	.35
62 Ryne Sandberg	3.00	.90
63 Sammy Sosa	3.00	.90
64 Barry Larkin	1.25	.35
65 Deion Sanders	1.25	.35
66 Reggie Sanders	.75	.23
67 Dante Bichette	.75	.23
68 Ellis Burks	.75	.23
69 Andres Galarraga	.75	.23
70 Moises Alou	.75	.23
71 Kevin Brown	.75	.23
72 Cliff Floyd	.75	.23
73 Edgar Renteria	.75	.23
74 Gary Sheffield	.75	.23
75 Bob Abreu	.75	.23
76 Jeff Bagwell	1.25	.35
77 Craig Biggio	1.25	.35
78 Todd Hollandsworth	.75	.23
79 Eric Karros	.75	.23
80 Raul Mondesi	.75	.23
81 Hideo Nomo	2.00	.60
82 Mike Piazza	3.00	.90
83 Vladimir Guerrero	2.00	.60
84 Henry Rodriguez	.75	.23
85 Todd Hundley	.75	.23
86 Alex Ochoa	.75	.23
87 Rey Ordonez	.75	.23
88 Gregg Jefferies	.75	.23
89 Scott Rolen	2.00	.60
90 Jermaine Allensworth	.75	.23
91 Jason Kendall	.75	.23
92 Ken Caminiti	.75	.23
93 Tony Gwynn	2.50	.75
94 Rickey Henderson	2.00	.60
95 Barry Bonds	5.00	1.50
96 J.T. Snow	.75	.23
97 Dennis Eckersley	.75	.23
98 Ron Gant	.75	.23
99 Brian Jordan	.75	.23
100 Ray Lankford	.75	.23
101 Checklist	.75	.23
102 Checklist	.75	.23
P43 Alex Rodriguez	1.50	.45
Three card promo strip		
S43 Alex Rodriguez	10.00	3.00
Mailed to Dealers who ordered Cases		
Card is numbered out of 3,000		
NNO Alex Rodriguez	100.00	30.00
Ball Exch 100 produced		

1997 E-X2000 Credentials

Randomly inserted in packs at the approximate rate of one in 60, this 100-card set is parallel to the base set with an etched holofoil border. The stated print run was less than 299 sets.

	Nm-Mt	Ex-Mt
*STARS: 3X TO 8X BASIC CARDS		

1997 E-X2000 Essential Credentials

Randomly inserted in packs at the rate of one in 200, this 100-card set is parallel to the base set with an etched refractive holographic foil border. Less than 99 sets were produced and are sequentially numbered.

	Nm-Mt	Ex-Mt
*STARS: 8X TO 20X BASIC CARDS		

1997 E-X2000 A Cut Above

Randomly inserted in packs at the rate of one in 288, this 10-card set features color images of "power hitters" on a holographic foil, die-cut sawblade background.

	Nm-Mt	Ex-Mt
COMPLETE SET (10)	250.00	75.00
1 Frank Thomas	20.00	6.00
2 Ken Griffey Jr.	30.00	9.00
3 Alex Rodriguez	30.00	9.00
4 Albert Belle	8.00	2.40
5 Juan Gonzalez	12.00	3.60
6 Mark McGwire	50.00	15.00
7 Mo Vaughn	8.00	2.40
8 Manny Ramirez	12.00	3.60
9 Barry Bonds	50.00	15.00
10 Fred McGriff	12.00	3.60

1997 E-X2000 Emerald Autographs

This six-card set features autographed color player photos of some of the hottest young stars in baseball. In addition to an authentic black-ink autograph, each card is embossed with a SkyBox logo about the size of a quarter. These cards were obtained by exchanging a redemption card by mail before the May 1, 1998, deadline.

	Nm-Mt	Ex-Mt
*EXCH.CARDS: .1X TO .25X BASIC AUTO		
2 Darin Erstad	15.00	4.50
30 Todd Walker	15.00	4.50
43 Alex Rodriguez	100.00	30.00
78 Todd Hollandsworth	15.00	4.50
86 Alex Ochoa	15.00	4.50
89 Scott Rolen	40.00	12.00

1997 E-X2000 Hall or Nothing

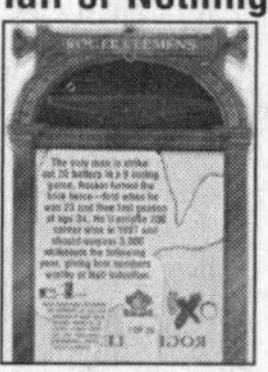

Randomly inserted in packs at the rate of one in 20, this 20-card set features color images of future Cooperstown Hall of Fame candidates printed on 30-pt. acrylic card stock with etched cooper foil borders and gold foil stamping.

	Nm-Mt	Ex-Mt
COMPLETE SET (20)	120.00	36.00
1 Frank Thomas	5.00	1.50
2 Ken Griffey Jr.	8.00	2.40
3 Eddie Murray	5.00	1.50
4 Cal Ripken	15.00	4.50
5 Ryne Sandberg	8.00	2.40
6 Wade Boggs	3.00	.90
7 Roger Clemens	10.00	3.00
8 Tony Gwynn	6.00	1.80
9 Alex Rodriguez	8.00	2.40
10 Mark McGwire	12.00	3.60
11 Barry Bonds	12.00	3.60
12 Greg Maddux	8.00	2.40
13 Juan Gonzalez	3.00	.90
14 Albert Belle	2.00	.60
15 Mike Piazza	8.00	2.40
16 Jeff Bagwell	3.00	.90
17 Dennis Eckersley	2.00	.60
18 Mo Vaughn	2.00	.60
19 Roberto Alomar	3.00	.90
20 Kenny Lofton	2.00	.60

1997 E-X2000 Star Date 2000

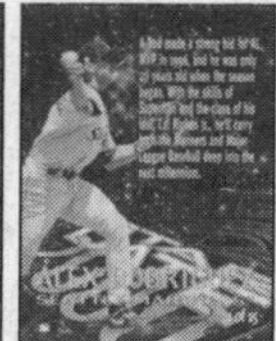

Randomly inserted in packs at the rate of one in nine, this 15-card set features color images of young star players printed on holographic foil with swirls of spot glitter coating.

	Nm-Mt	Ex-Mt
COMPLETE SET (15)	30.00	9.00
1 Alex Rodriguez	5.00	1.50
2 Andruw Jones	1.25	.35
3 Andy Pettitte	2.00	.60
4 Brooks Kieschnick	1.25	.35
5 Chipper Jones	3.00	.90
6 Darin Erstad	1.25	.35
7 Derek Jeter	8.00	2.40
8 Jason Kendall	1.25	.35
9 Jermaine Dye	1.25	.35
10 Neifi Perez	1.25	.35
11 Scott Rolen	3.00	.90
12 Todd Hollandsworth	1.25	.35
13 Todd Walker	1.25	.35
14 Tony Clark	1.25	.35
15 Vladimir Guerrero	3.00	.90

1998 E-X2001

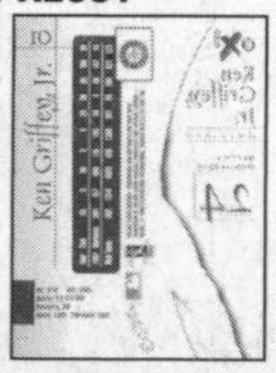

The 1998 E-X2001 set (made by Fleer/SkyBox) was issued in one series totalling 100 cards and distributed exclusively to hobby outlets. Cards were issued in two-card packs carrying a $3.99 suggested retail price. The cards are stunningly attractive, featuring full color action shots printed on clear acetate stock with sparkling foil backgrounds. An unnumbered Kerry Wood exchange card was randomly seeded into 1 in every 50 packs (the same pull rate as any other basic issue card). Unlike the acetate stock basic cards, this Wood exchange card was printed on paper stock and could be redeemed until March 31st, 1999 for a real E-X2001 acetate stock Wood card (number 101). In addition, an Alex Rodriguez sample card was issued a few months prior to the product's release. This sample card was distributed to dealers and hobby media to preview the upcoming release. The card is identical to a standard Alex Rodriguex E-X2001 except for the text "PROMOTIONAL SAMPLE" printed diagonally across the card back. There are no key Rookie Cards in this set.

	Nm-Mt	Ex-Mt
COMPLETE SET (100)	80.00	24.00
1 Alex Rodriguez	3.00	.90
2 Barry Bonds	5.00	1.50
3 Greg Maddux	3.00	.90
4 Roger Clemens	4.00	1.20
5 Juan Gonzalez	1.25	.35
6 Chipper Jones	2.00	.60
7 Derek Jeter	5.00	1.50
8 Frank Thomas	2.00	.60
9 Cal Ripken	6.00	1.80
10 Ken Griffey Jr.	3.00	.90
11 Mark McGwire	5.00	1.50
12 Hideo Nomo	2.00	.60
13 Tony Gwynn	2.50	.75
14 Ivan Rodriguez	2.00	.60
15 Mike Piazza	3.00	.90
16 Roberto Alomar	1.25	.35
17 Jeff Bagwell	1.25	.35
18 Andruw Jones	.75	.23
19 Albert Belle	.75	.23
20 Mo Vaughn	.75	.23
21 Kenny Lofton	.75	.23
22 Gary Sheffield	.75	.23
23 Tony Clark	.50	.15
24 Mike Mussina	1.25	.35
25 Barry Larkin	1.25	.35
26 Moises Alou	.75	.23
27 Brady Anderson	.75	.23
28 Andy Pettitte	1.25	.35
29 Sammy Sosa	3.00	.90
30 Raul Mondesi	.75	.23
31 Andres Galarraga	.75	.23
32 Chuck Knoblauch	.75	.23
33 Jim Thome	2.00	.60
34 Craig Biggio	1.25	.35
35 Jay Buhner	.75	.23
36 Rafael Palmeiro	1.25	.35
37 Curt Schilling	.75	.23
38 Tino Martinez	1.25	.35
39 Pedro Martinez	2.00	.60
40 Jose Canseco	2.00	.60
41 Jeff Cirillo	.50	.15
42 Dean Palmer	.75	.23
43 Tim Salmon	1.25	.35
44 Jason Giambi	.75	.23
45 Bobby Higginson	.75	.23
46 Jim Edmonds	.75	.23
47 David Justice	.75	.23
48 John Olerud	.75	.23
49 Ray Lankford	.50	.15
50 Al Martin	.50	.15
51 Mike Lieberthal	.75	.23
52 Henry Rodriguez	.50	.15
53 Edgar Renteria	.75	.23
54 Eric Karros	.75	.23
55 Marquis Grissom	.75	.23
56 Wilson Alvarez	.50	.15
57 Darryl Kile	.75	.23
58 Jeff King	.50	.15
59 Shawn Estes	.50	.15
60 Tony Womack	.50	.15
61 Willie Greene	.50	.15
62 Ken Caminiti	.75	.23
63 Vinny Castilla	.75	.23
64 Mark Grace	1.25	.35
65 Ryan Klesko	.75	.23
66 Robin Ventura	.75	.23
67 Todd Hundley	.50	.15
68 Travis Fryman	.75	.23
69 Edgar Martinez	1.25	.35
70 Matt Williams	.75	.23
71 Paul Molitor	1.25	.35
72 Kevin Brown	1.25	.35
73 Randy Johnson	2.00	.60
74 Bernie Williams	1.25	.35
75 Manny Ramirez	1.25	.35
76 Fred McGriff	1.25	.35
77 Tom Glavine	1.25	.35
78 Carlos Delgado	.75	.23
79 Larry Walker	1.25	.35
80 Hideki Irabu	.50	.15
81 Ryan McGuire	.50	.15
82 Justin Thompson	.50	.15
83 Kevin Orie	.50	.15
84 Jon Nunnally	.50	.15
85 Mark Kotsay	.50	.15
86 Todd Walker	.50	.15
87 Jason Dickson	.50	.15
88 Fernando Tatis	.50	.15
89 Karim Garcia	.50	.15
90 Ricky Ledee	.50	.15
91 Paul Konerko	.75	.23
92 Jaret Wright	.50	.15
93 Darin Erstad	.75	.23
94 Livan Hernandez	.50	.15
95 Nomar Garciaparra	3.00	.90
96 Jose Cruz Jr.	.50	.15
97 Scott Rolen	2.00	.60
98 Ben Grieve	.50	.15
99 Vladimir Guerrero	2.00	.60
100 Travis Lee	.50	.15
101 K.Wood Redemption	5.00	1.50
NNO Kerry Wood EXCH	2.50	.75
NNO A.Rodriguez Sample	1.50	.45

1998 E-X2001 Essential Credentials Future

These cards were randomly inserted in E-X200 packs. For this parallel version, the amount cards produced is inverse to the card numbe Each card is individually serial numbered on th lower edge of the card back. For conveniece, th amount of each player produced is listed next their listing. Cards between 76 and 100 are n priced due to scarcity.

	Nm-Mt	Ex-Mt
1 Alex Rodriguez (100)	60.00	18.00
2 Barry Bonds (99)	100.00	30.00
3 Greg Maddux (98)	60.00	18.00
4 Roger Clemens (97)	80.00	24.00
5 Juan Gonzalez (96)	25.00	7.50
6 Chipper Jones (95)	40.00	12.00
7 Derek Jeter (94)	100.00	30.00
8 Frank Thomas (93)	40.00	12.00
9 Cal Ripken (92)	120.00	36.00
10 Ken Griffey Jr. (91)	60.00	18.00
11 Mark McGwire (90)	100.00	30.00
12 Hideo Nomo (89)	40.00	12.00
13 Tony Gwynn (88)	50.00	15.00
14 Ivan Rodriguez (87)	40.00	12.00
15 Mike Piazza (86)	60.00	18.00
16 Roberto Alomar (85)	25.00	7.50
17 Jeff Bagwell (84)	25.00	7.50
18 Andruw Jones (83)	25.00	7.50
19 Albert Belle (82)	25.00	7.50
20 Mo Vaughn (81)	25.00	7.50
21 Kenny Lofton (80)	25.00	7.50
22 Gary Sheffield (79)	25.00	7.50
23 Tony Clark (78)	15.00	4.50
24 Mike Mussina (77)	25.00	7.50
25 Barry Larkin (76)	25.00	7.50
26 Moises Alou (75)	25.00	7.50
27 Brady Anderson (74)	25.00	7.50
28 Andy Pettitte (73)	25.00	7.50
29 Sammy Sosa (72)	60.00	18.00
30 Raul Mondesi (71)	25.00	7.50
31 Andres Galarraga (70)	25.00	7.50
32 Chuck Knoblauch (69)	20.00	6.00
33 Jim Thome (68)	50.00	15.00
34 Craig Biggio (67)	30.00	9.00
35 Jay Buhner (66)	20.00	6.00
36 Rafael Palmeiro (65)	30.00	9.00
37 Curt Schilling (64)	20.00	6.00
38 Tino Martinez (63)	30.00	9.00
39 Pedro Martinez (62)	50.00	15.00
40 Jose Canseco (61)	50.00	15.00
41 Jeff Cirillo (60)	12.00	3.60
42 Dean Palmer (59)	20.00	6.00
43 Tim Salmon (58)	30.00	9.00
44 Jason Giambi (57)	20.00	6.00
45 Bobby Higginson (56)	20.00	6.00
46 Jim Edmonds (55)	20.00	6.00
47 David Justice (54)	20.00	6.00
48 John Olerud (53)	20.00	6.00
49 Ray Lankford (52)	12.00	3.60
50 Al Martin (51)	12.00	3.60
51 Mike Lieberthal (50)	25.00	7.50
52 Henry Rodriguez (49)	15.00	4.50
53 Edgar Renteria (48)	25.00	7.50
54 Eric Karros (47)	25.00	7.50
55 Marquis Grissom (46)	25.00	7.50
56 Wilson Alvarez (45)	15.00	4.50
57 Darryl Kile (44)	25.00	7.50
58 Jeff King (43)	15.00	4.50
59 Shawn Estes (42)	15.00	4.50
60 Tony Womack (41)	15.00	4.50
61 Willie Greene (40)	15.00	4.50
62 Ken Caminiti (39)	25.00	7.50
63 Vinny Castilla (38)	25.00	7.50
64 Mark Grace (37)	40.00	12.00
65 Ryan Klesko (36)	25.00	7.50
66 Robin Ventura (35)	40.00	12.00
67 Todd Hundley (34)	30.00	9.00
68 Travis Fryman (33)	40.00	12.00
69 Edgar Martinez (32)	50.00	15.00
70 Matt Williams (31)	40.00	12.00
71 Paul Molitor (30)	50.00	15.00
72 Kevin Brown (29)	50.00	15.00
73 Randy Johnson (28)	80.00	24.00
74 Bernie Williams (27)	50.00	15.00
75 Manny Ramirez (26)	50.00	15.00
76 Fred McGriff (25)		
77 Tom Glavine (24)		
78 Carlos Delgado (23)		
79 Larry Walker (22)		
80 Hideki Irabu (21)		
81 Ryan McGuire (20)		
82 Justin Thompson (19)		
83 Kevin Orie (18)		
84 Jon Nunnally (17)		
85 Mark Kotsay (16)		
86 Todd Walker (15)		
87 Jason Dickson (14)		
88 Fernando Tatis (13)		
89 Karim Garcia (12)		
90 Ricky Ledee (11)		
91 Paul Konerko (10)		
92 Jaret Wright (9)		
93 Darin Erstad (8)		
94 Livan Hernandez (7)		
95 Nomar Garciaparra (6)		
96 Jose Cruz Jr. (5)		
97 Scott Rolen (4)		
98 Ben Grieve (3)		
99 Vladimir Guerrero (2)		
100 Travis Lee (1)		

1998 E-X2001 Essential Credentials Now

These cards were randomly inserted in E-X2001 packs. For this parallel version, the amount of cards produced is equal to their card number. Each card in individually serial numbered on the lower edge of the card back. Again like in the Essential Credentials Future, we have put the amount of cards produced next to the players name. Cards numbered between 1 and 25 are not priced due to scarcity.

	Nm-Mt	Ex-Mt
1 Alex Rodriguez (1)		
2 Barry Bonds (2)		
3 Greg Maddux (3)		

Roger Clemens (4)
Juan Gonzalez (5)
Chipper Jones (6)
Derek Jeter (7)
Frank Thomas (8)
Cal Ripken (9)
0 Ken Griffey Jr. (10)
1 Mark McGwire (11)
2 Hideo Nomo (12)
3 Tony Gwynn (13)
4 Ivan Rodriguez (14)
5 Mike Piazza (15)
6 Roberto Alomar (16)
7 Jeff Bagwell (17)
8 Andruw Jones (18)
9 Albert Belle (19)
0 Mo Vaughn (20)
1 Kenny Lofton (21)
2 Gary Sheffield (22)
3 Tony Clark (23)
4 Mike Mussina (24)
5 Barry Larkin (25)
6 Moises Alou (26) 40.00 12.00
7 Brady Anderson (27) 40.00 12.00
8 Andy Pettitte (28) 50.00 15.00
9 Sammy Sosa (29) 120.00 36.00
0 Raul Mondesi (30) 40.00 12.00
1 Andres Galarraga (31) 40.00 12.00
2 Chuck Knoblauch (32) 40.00 12.00
3 Jim Thome (33) 60.00 18.00
4 Craig Biggio (34) 50.00 15.00
5 Jay Buhner (35) 40.00 12.00
6 Rafael Palmeiro (36) 40.00 12.00
7 Curt Schilling (37) 25.00 7.50
8 Tino Martinez (38) 40.00 12.00
9 Pedro Martinez (39) 50.00 15.00
0 Jose Canseco (40) 50.00 15.00
1 Jeff Cirillo (41) 15.00 4.50
2 Dean Palmer (42) 25.00 7.50
3 Tim Salmon (43) 40.00 12.00
44 Jason Giambi (44) 25.00 7.50
45 Bobby Higginson (45) 25.00 7.50
46 Jim Edmonds (46) 25.00 7.50
47 David Justice (47) 25.00 7.50
48 John Olerud (48) 25.00 7.50
49 Ray Lankford (49) 15.00 4.50
50 Al Martin (50) 15.00 4.50
51 Mike Lieberthal (51) 20.00 6.00
52 Henry Rodriguez (52) 12.00 3.60
53 Edgar Renteria (53) 20.00 6.00
54 Eric Karros (54) 20.00 6.00
55 Marquis Grissom (55) 20.00 6.00
56 Wilson Alvarez (56) 12.00 3.60
57 Darryl Kile (57) 20.00 6.00
58 Jeff King (58) 12.00 3.60
59 Shawn Estes (59) 12.00 3.60
60 Tony Womack (60) 12.00 3.60
61 Willie Greene (61) 12.00 3.60
62 Ken Caminiti (62) 20.00 6.00
63 Vinny Castilla (63) 20.00 6.00
64 Mark Grace (64) 25.00 7.50
65 Ryan Klesko (65) 20.00 6.00
66 Robin Ventura (66) 20.00 6.00
67 Todd Hundley (67) 12.00 3.60
68 Travis Fryman (68) 20.00 6.00
69 Edgar Martinez (69) 25.00 7.50
70 Matt Williams (70) 20.00 6.00
71 Paul Molitor (71) 25.00 7.50
72 Kevin Brown (72) 25.00 7.50
73 Randy Johnson (73) 40.00 12.00
74 Bernie Williams (74) 25.00 7.50
75 Manny Ramirez (75) 40.00 12.00
76 Fred McGriff (76) 25.00 7.50
77 Tom Glavine (77) 25.00 7.50
78 Carlos Delgado (78) 15.00 4.50
79 Larry Walker (79) 25.00 7.50
80 Hideki Irabu (80) 10.00 3.00
81 Ryan McGuire (81) 10.00 3.00
82 Justin Thompson (82) 10.00 3.00
83 Kevin Orie (83) 10.00 3.00
84 Jon Nunnally (84) 10.00 3.00
85 Mark Kotsay (85) 10.00 3.00
86 Todd Walker (86) 10.00 3.00
87 Jason Dickson (87) 10.00 3.00
88 Fernando Tatis (88) 10.00 3.00
89 Karim Garcia (89) 10.00 3.00
90 Ricky Ledee (90) 10.00 3.00
91 Paul Konerko (91) 15.00 4.50
92 Jaret Wright (92) 10.00 3.00
93 Darin Erstad (93) 15.00 4.50
94 Livan Hernandez (94) 10.00 3.00
95 N.Garciaparra (95) 60.00 18.00
96 Jose Cruz Jr. (96) 10.00 3.00
97 Scott Rolen (97) 40.00 12.00
98 Ben Grieve (98) 10.00 3.00
99 Vladimir Guerrero (99) 40.00 12.00
100 Travis Lee (100) 10.00 3.00

1998 E-X2001 Cheap Seat Treats

Randomly inserted in packs at a rate of one in 24, this 20-card set is an insert to the SkyBox E-X2001 brand. Each die-cut card is shaped like a folding chair with silver foil stamping and features a color player photo of some of today's greatest sluggers.

	Nm-Mt	Ex-Mt
COMPLETE SET (20)	100.00	30.00
1 Frank Thomas	8.00	2.40
2 Ken Griffey Jr.	12.00	3.60
3 Mark McGwire	20.00	6.00
4 Tino Martinez	5.00	1.50
5 Larry Walker	5.00	1.50
6 Juan Gonzalez	5.00	1.50
7 Mike Piazza	12.00	3.60
8 Jeff Bagwell	5.00	1.50

9 Tony Clark 2.00 .60
10 Albert Belle 3.00 .90
11 Andres Galarraga 3.00 .90
12 Jim Thome 8.00 2.40
13 Mo Vaughn 3.00 .90
14 Barry Bonds 20.00 6.00
15 Vladimir Guerrero 8.00 2.40
16 Scott Rolen 8.00 2.40
17 Travis Lee 2.00 .60
18 David Justice 3.00 .90
19 Jose Cruz Jr. 2.00 .60
20 Andruw Jones 3.00 .90

1998 E-X2001 Destination Cooperstown

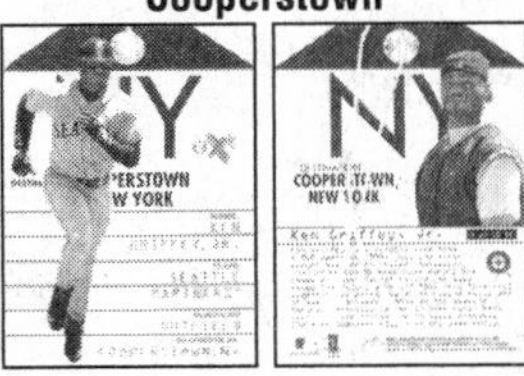

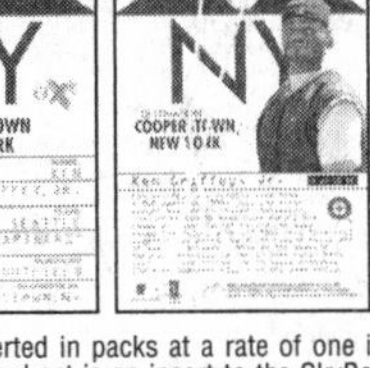

Randomly inserted in packs at a rate of one in 720, this 15-card set is an insert to the SkyBox E-X2001 brand. Each card is designed to resemble a luggage destination tag including a piece of string tied to a hole at the top of each card and honors future Hall-of Famers with color player photos. The cards also provide the featured player's name, team, and position.

	Nm-Mt	Ex-Mt
1 Alex Rodriguez	40.00	12.00
2 Frank Thomas	25.00	7.50
3 Cal Ripken	80.00	24.00
4 Roger Clemens	50.00	15.00
5 Greg Maddux	40.00	12.00
6 Chipper Jones	25.00	7.50
7 Ken Griffey Jr.	40.00	12.00
8 Mark McGwire	60.00	18.00
9 Tony Gwynn	30.00	9.00
10 Mike Piazza	40.00	12.00
11 Jeff Bagwell	15.00	4.50
12 Jose Cruz Jr.	10.00	3.00
13 Derek Jeter	60.00	18.00
14 Hideo Nomo	40.00	12.00
15 Ivan Rodriguez	25.00	7.50

1998 E-X2001 Signature 2001

Randomly inserted in packs at a rate of one in 60, this 17-card set is an insert to the SkyBox E-X2001 brand. The exclusive insert features color action photos and autographs signed by some of MLB's brightest young stars.

	Nm-Mt	Ex-Mt
1 Ricky Ledee	10.00	3.00
2 Derrick Gibson	10.00	3.00
3 Mark Kotsay	15.00	4.50
4 Kevin Millwood	15.00	4.50
5 Brad Fullmer	10.00	3.00
6 Todd Walker	15.00	4.50
7 Ben Grieve	10.00	3.00
8 Tony Clark	10.00	3.00
9 Jaret Wright	10.00	3.00
10 Randall Simon	10.00	3.00
11 Paul Konerko	15.00	4.50
12 Todd Helton	40.00	12.00
13 David Ortiz	40.00	12.00
14 Alex Gonzalez	10.00	3.00
15 Bobby Estalella	10.00	3.00
16 Alex Rodriguez SP	120.00	36.00
17 Mike Lowell	25.00	7.50

1998 E-X2001 Star Date 2001

Randomly inserted in packs at a rate of one in 12, this 15-card set is an insert to the SkyBox E-X2001 brand. The fronts feature a background of space-age graphics and gold-foil stamping on plastic stock. The color action photos showcase some of the hottest up-and-coming stars in the MLB.

	Nm-Mt	Ex-Mt
COMPLETE SET (15)	15.00	4.50
1 Travis Lee	1.00	.30
2 Jose Cruz Jr.	1.00	.30
3 Paul Konerko	1.00	.30
4 Bobby Estalella	1.00	.30
5 Magglio Ordonez	4.00	1.20
6 Juan Encarnacion	1.00	.30
7 Richard Hidalgo	1.00	.30
8 Abraham Nunez	1.00	.30
9 Sean Casey	1.00	.30
10 Todd Helton	1.50	.45
11 Brad Fullmer	1.00	.30
12 Ben Grieve	1.00	.30
13 Livan Hernandez	1.00	.30
14 Jaret Wright	1.00	.30
15 Todd Dunwoody	1.00	.30

1999 E-X Century

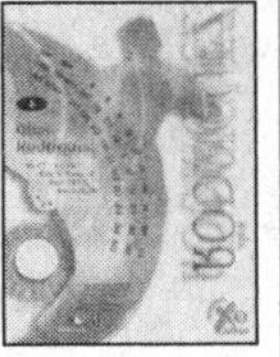

This 120-card set features color action player photos silhouetted on extra thick transparent plastic card stock. Each pack contained three cards and carried a suggested retail price of $5.99. The set contains a 30-card Rookie short-printed subset (91-120) with an insertion rate of 1:2 packs. A promotional sample card featuring Ben Grieve was distributed to dealer accounts and hobby media shortly before the product's national release. This card can be easily identified by the "PROMOTIONAL SAMPLE" text running across the back. Notable Rookie Cards include Pat Burrell.

	Nm-Mt	Ex-Mt
COMPLETE SET (120)	80.00	24.00
COMP.SET w/o SP's (90)	40.00	12.00
COMMON CARD (1-90)	.50	.15
COMMON SP (91-120)	1.00	.30
1 Scott Rolen	2.00	.60
2 Nomar Garciaparra	3.00	.90
3 Mike Piazza	3.00	.90
4 Tony Gwynn	2.50	.75
5 Sammy Sosa	3.00	.90
6 Alex Rodriguez	3.00	.90
7 Vladimir Guerrero	2.00	.60
8 Chipper Jones	2.00	.60
9 Derek Jeter	5.00	1.50
10 Kerry Wood	2.00	.60
11 Juan Gonzalez	1.25	.35
12 Frank Thomas	2.00	.60
13 Mo Vaughn	.75	.23
14 Greg Maddux	3.00	.90
15 Jeff Bagwell	1.25	.35
16 Mark McGwire	5.00	1.50
17 Ken Griffey Jr.	3.00	.90
18 Roger Clemens	4.00	1.20
19 Cal Ripken	6.00	1.80
20 Travis Lee	.50	.15
21 Todd Helton	1.25	.35
22 Darin Erstad	.75	.23
23 Pedro Martinez	2.00	.60
24 Barry Bonds	5.00	.45
25 Andruw Jones	.75	.23
26 Larry Walker	1.25	.35
27 Albert Belle	.75	.23
28 Ivan Rodriguez	2.00	.60
29 Magglio Ordonez	.75	.23
30 Andres Galarraga	.75	.23
31 Mike Mussina	1.25	.35
32 Randy Johnson	2.00	.60
33 Tom Glavine	1.25	.35
34 Barry Larkin	1.25	.35
35 Jim Thome	2.00	.60
36 Gary Sheffield	.75	.23
37 Bernie Williams	1.25	.35
38 Carlos Delgado	.75	.23
39 Rafael Palmeiro	1.25	.35
40 Edgar Renteria	.75	.23
41 Brad Fullmer	.50	.15
42 David Wells	.75	.23
43 Dante Bichette	.75	.23
44 Jaret Wright	.50	.15
45 Ricky Ledee	.50	.15
46 Ray Lankford	.50	.15
47 Mark Grace	1.25	.35
48 Jeff Cirillo	.50	.15
49 Rondell White	.75	.23
50 Jeromy Burnitz	.75	.23
51 Sean Casey	.75	.23
52 Rolando Arrojo	.50	.15
53 Jason Giambi	.75	.23
54 John Olerud	.75	.23
55 Will Clark	2.00	.60
56 Raul Mondesi	.75	.23
57 Scott Brosius	.75	.23
58 Bartolo Colon	.75	.23
59 Steve Finley	.75	.23
60 Javy Lopez	.75	.23
61 Tim Salmon	1.25	.35
62 Roberto Alomar	1.25	.35
63 Vinny Castilla	.75	.23
64 Craig Biggio	1.25	.35
65 Jose Guillen	.75	.23
66 Greg Vaughn	.50	.15
67 Jose Canseco	2.00	.60
68 Shawn Green	.75	.23
69 Curt Schilling	.75	.23
70 Orlando Hernandez	.50	.15
71 Jose Cruz Jr.	.50	.15
72 Alex Gonzalez	.50	.15
73 Tino Martinez	1.25	.35
74 Todd Hundley	.50	.15
75 Brian Giles	.75	.23
76 Cliff Floyd	.75	.23
77 Paul O'Neill	1.25	.35
78 Ken Caminiti	.75	.23
79 Ron Gant	.75	.23
80 Juan Encarnacion	.50	.15
81 Ben Grieve	.50	.15
82 Brian Jordan	.75	.23
83 Rickey Henderson	2.00	.60
84 Tony Clark	.50	.15
85 Shannon Stewart	.75	.23
86 Robin Ventura	.75	.23
87 Todd Walker	.50	.15
88 Kevin Brown	1.25	.35
89 Moises Alou	.75	.23
90 Manny Ramirez	1.25	.35
91 Gabe Alvarez SP	1.00	.30
92 Jeremy Giambi SP	1.00	.30
93 Adrian Beltre SP	1.00	.30
94 George Lombard SP	1.00	.30
95 Ryan Minor SP	1.00	.30
96 Kevin Witt SP	1.00	.30
97 Scott Hunter SP RC	1.00	.30
98 Carlos Guillen SP	1.00	.30
99 Derrick Gibson SP	1.00	.30
100 Trot Nixon SP	1.00	.30
101 Troy Glaus SP	1.00	.25
102 Armando Rios SP	1.00	.30
103 Preston Wilson SP	1.00	.30
104 Pat Burrell SP RC	2.50	.75
105 J.D. Drew SP	1.00	.30
106 Bruce Chen SP	1.00	.30
107 Matt Clement SP	1.00	.30
108 Carlos Beltran SP	1.00	.30
109 Carlos Febles SP	1.00	.30
110 Rob Fick SP	1.00	.30
111 Russell Branyan SP	1.00	.30
112 R.Brown SP RC	1.00	.30
113 Corey Koskie SP	1.00	.30
114 M.Encarnacion SP RC	1.00	.30
115 Peter Tucci SP	1.00	.30
116 Eric Chavez SP	1.00	.30
117 Gabe Kapler SP	1.00	.30
118 Marlon Anderson SP	1.00	.30
119 A.J. Burnett SP RC	1.50	.45
120 Ryan Bradley SP	1.00	.30
P81 Ben Grieve Sample	1.00	.30

1999 E-X Century Essential Credentials Future

Randomly inserted into packs, this 120-card set is a sequentially numbered gold foil parallel version of the E-X Century base set. The print run for each card follows the player's name in the checklist below.

	Nm-Mt	Ex-Mt
1 Scott Rolen (120)	20.00	6.00
2 N.Garciaparra (119)	50.00	15.00
3 Mike Piazza (118)	50.00	15.00
4 Tony Gwynn (117)	40.00	12.00
5 Sammy Sosa (116)	50.00	15.00
6 Alex Rodriguez (115)	50.00	15.00
7 Vladimir Guerrero (114)	20.00	6.00
8 Chipper Jones (113)	20.00	6.00
9 Derek Jeter (112)	80.00	24.00
10 Kerry Wood (111)	20.00	6.00
11 Juan Gonzalez (110)	20.00	6.00
12 Frank Thomas (109)	20.00	6.00
13 Mo Vaughn (108)	15.00	4.50
14 Greg Maddux (107)	50.00	15.00
15 Jeff Bagwell (106)	20.00	6.00
16 Mark McGwire (105)	80.00	24.00
17 Ken Griffey Jr. (104)	50.00	15.00
18 Roger Clemens (103)	60.00	18.00
19 Cal Ripken (102)	100.00	30.00
20 Travis Lee (101)	12.00	3.60
21 Todd Helton (100)	20.00	6.00
22 Darin Erstad (99)	12.00	3.60
23 Pedro Martinez (98)	30.00	9.00
24 Barry Bonds (97)	100.00	30.00
25 Andruw Jones (96)	12.00	3.60
26 Larry Walker (95)	20.00	6.00
27 Albert Belle (94)	12.00	3.60
28 Ivan Rodriguez (93)	30.00	9.00
29 Magglio Ordonez (92)	12.00	3.60
30 Andres Galarraga (91)	12.00	3.60
31 Mike Mussina (90)	20.00	6.00
32 Randy Johnson (89)	30.00	9.00
33 Tom Glavine (88)	20.00	6.00
34 Barry Larkin (87)	20.00	6.00
35 Jim Thome (86)	30.00	9.00
36 Gary Sheffield (85)	12.00	3.60
37 Bernie Williams (84)	20.00	6.00
38 Carlos Delgado (83)	12.00	3.60
39 Rafael Palmeiro (82)	20.00	6.00
40 Edgar Renteria (81)	12.00	3.60
41 Brad Fullmer (80)	10.00	3.00
42 David Wells (79)	12.00	3.60
43 Dante Bichette (78)	12.00	3.60
44 Jaret Wright (77)	10.00	3.00
45 Ricky Ledee (76)	10.00	3.00
46 Ray Lankford (75)	10.00	3.00
47 Mark Grace (74)	20.00	6.00
48 Jeff Cirillo (73)	10.00	3.00
49 Rondell White (72)	12.00	3.60
50 Jeromy Burnitz (71)	12.00	3.60
51 Sean Casey (70)	15.00	4.50
52 Rolando Arrojo (69)	12.00	3.60
53 Jason Giambi (68)	15.00	4.50
54 John Olerud (67)	15.00	4.50
55 Will Clark (66)	40.00	12.00
56 Raul Mondesi (65)	15.00	4.50
57 Scott Brosius (64)	15.00	3.70
58 Bartolo Colon (63)	15.00	4.50
59 Steve Finley (62)	15.00	4.50
60 Javy Lopez (61)	15.00	4.50
61 Tim Salmon (60)	25.00	7.50
62 Roberto Alomar (59)	25.00	7.50
63 Vinny Castilla (58)	15.00	4.50
64 Craig Biggio (57)	25.00	7.50
65 Jose Guillen (56)	15.00	4.50
66 Greg Vaughn (55)	12.00	3.60
67 Jose Canseco (54)	40.00	12.00
68 Shawn Green (53)	15.00	4.50
69 Curt Schilling (52)	15.00	4.50
70 O.Hernandez (51)	12.00	3.60
71 Jose Cruz Jr. (50)	12.00	3.60
72 Alex Gonzalez (49)	12.00	3.60
73 Tino Martinez (48)	30.00	9.00
74 Todd Hundley (47)	12.00	3.60
75 Brian Giles (46)	20.00	6.00
76 Cliff Floyd (45)	20.00	6.00
77 Paul O'Neill (44)	30.00	9.00
78 Ken Caminiti (43)	20.00	6.00
79 Ron Gant (42)	20.00	6.00
80 Juan Encarnacion (41)	12.00	3.60
81 Ben Grieve (40)	12.00	3.60
82 Brian Jordan (39)	20.00	6.00
83 Rickey Henderson (38)	50.00	15.00
84 Tony Clark (37)	12.00	3.60
85 Shannon Stewart (36)	20.00	6.00
86 Robin Ventura (35)	25.00	7.50
87 Todd Walker (34)	15.00	4.50
88 Kevin Brown (33)	40.00	12.00
89 Moises Alou (32)	25.00	7.50
90 Manny Ramirez (31)	40.00	12.00
91 Gabe Alvarez (30)	15.00	4.50
92 Jeremy Giambi (29)	15.00	4.50
93 Adrian Beltre (28)	40.00	12.00
94 George Lombard (27)	15.00	4.50
95 Ryan Minor (26)	15.00	4.50
96 Kevin Witt (25)		
97 Scott Hunter (24)		
98 Carlos Guillen (23)		
99 Derrick Gibson (22)		
100 Trot Nixon (21)		
101 Troy Glaus (20)		
102 Armando Rios (19)		
103 Preston Wilson (18)		
104 Pat Burrell (17)		
105 J.D. Drew (16)		
106 Bruce Chen (15)		
107 Matt Clement (14)		
108 Carlos Beltran (13)		
109 Carlos Febles (12)		
110 Rob Fick (11)		
111 Russell Branyan (10)		
112 Roosevelt Brown (9)		
113 Corey Koskie (8)		
114 Mario Encarnacion (7)		
115 Peter Tucci (6)		
116 Eric Chavez (5)		
117 Gabe Kapler (4)		
118 Marlon Anderson (3)		
119 A.J. Burnett (2)		
120 Ryan Bradley (1)		

1999 E-X Century Essential Credentials Now

Randomly inserted into packs, this 120-card set is a silver foil parallel version of the E-X Century base set. Each card is sequentially numbered to the pictured player's card number and follows the player's name in the checklist below.

	Nm-Mt	Ex-Mt
1 Scott Rolen (1)		
2 Nomar Garciaparra (2)		
3 Mike Piazza (3)		
4 Tony Gwynn (4)		
5 Sammy Sosa (5)		
6 Alex Rodriguez (6)		
7 Vladimir Guerrero (7)		
8 Chipper Jones (8)		
9 Derek Jeter (9)		
10 Kerry Wood (10)		
11 Juan Gonzalez (11)		
12 Frank Thomas (12)		
13 Mo Vaughn (13)		
14 Greg Maddux (14)		
15 Jeff Bagwell (15)		
16 Mark McGwire (16)		
17 Ken Griffey Jr. (17)		
18 Roger Clemens (18)		
19 Cal Ripken (19)		
20 Travis Lee (20)		
21 Todd Helton (21)		
22 Darin Erstad (22)		
23 Pedro Martinez (23)		
24 Barry Bonds (24)		
25 Andruw Jones (25)		
26 Larry Walker (26)	50.00	15.00
27 Albert Belle (27)	40.00	12.00
28 Ivan Rodriguez (28)	60.00	18.00
29 Magglio Ordonez (29)	40.00	12.00
30 Andres Galarraga (30)	40.00	12.00
31 Mike Mussina (31)	50.00	15.00
32 Randy Johnson (32)	60.00	18.00
33 Tom Glavine (33)	50.00	15.00
34 Barry Larkin (34)	50.00	15.00
35 Jim Thome (35)	60.00	18.00
36 Gary Sheffield (36)	20.00	6.00
37 Bernie Williams (37)	30.00	9.00
38 Carlos Delgado (38)	20.00	16.00
39 Rafael Palmeiro (39)	30.00	9.00
40 Edgar Renteria (40)	20.00	6.00
41 Brad Fullmer (41)	12.00	3.60
42 David Wells (42)	20.00	6.00
43 Dante Bichette (43)	20.00	6.00
44 Jaret Wright (44)	12.00	3.60
45 Ricky Ledee (45)	12.00	3.60
46 Ray Lankford (46)	12.00	3.60
47 Mark Grace (47)	30.00	9.00
48 Jeff Cirillo (48)	12.00	3.60
49 Rondell White (49)	20.00	6.00
50 Jeromy Burnitz (50)	20.00	6.00
51 Sean Casey (51)	15.00	4.50
52 Rolando Arrojo (52)	12.00	3.60
53 Jason Giambi (53)	15.00	4.50
54 John Olerud (54)	15.00	4.50
55 Will Clark (55)	40.00	12.00
56 Raul Mondesi (56)	15.00	4.50
57 Scott Brosius (57)	15.00	4.50
58 Bartolo Colon (58)	15.00	4.50
59 Steve Finley (59)	15.00	4.50
60 Javy Lopez (60)	15.00	4.50
61 Tim Salmon (61)	25.00	7.50
62 Roberto Alomar (62)	25.00	7.50
63 Vinny Castilla (63)	15.00	4.50
64 Craig Biggio (64)	25.00	7.50
65 Jose Guillen (65)	15.00	4.50
66 Greg Vaughn (66)	12.00	3.60
67 Jose Canseco (67)	40.00	12.00
68 Shawn Green (68)	15.00	4.50
69 Curt Schilling (69)	15.00	4.50
70 O.Hernandez (70)	12.00	3.60
71 Jose Cruz Jr. (71)	10.00	3.00
72 Alex Gonzalez (72)	10.00	3.00
73 Tino Martinez (73)	20.00	6.00
74 Todd Hundley (74)	10.00	3.00
75 Brian Giles (75)	12.00	3.60
76 Cliff Floyd (76)	12.00	3.60
77 Paul O'Neill (77)	20.00	6.00
78 Ken Caminiti (78)	12.00	3.60
79 Ron Gant (79)	12.00	3.60
80 Juan Encarnacion (80)	10.00	3.00
81 Ben Grieve (81)	10.00	3.00
82 Brian Jordan (82)	12.00	3.60
83 Rickey Henderson (83)	30.00	9.00
84 Tony Clark (84)	10.00	3.00
85 Shannon Stewart (85)	12.00	3.60
86 Robin Ventura (86)	12.00	3.60
87 Todd Walker (87)	10.00	3.00
88 Kevin Brown (88)	20.00	6.00
89 Moises Alou (89)	12.00	3.60
90 Manny Ramirez (90)	20.00	6.00
91 Gabe Alvarez (91)	10.00	3.00
92 Jeremy Giambi (92)	10.00	3.00
93 Adrian Beltre (93)	20.00	6.00

94 George Lombard (94) 10.00 3.00
95 Ryan Minor (95) 10.00 3.00
96 Kevin Witt (96) 10.00 3.00
97 Scott Hunter (97) 10.00 3.00
98 Carlos Guillen (98) 12.00 3.60
99 Derrick Gibson (99) 10.00 3.00
100 Trot Nixon (100) 12.00 3.60
101 Troy Glaus (101) 10.00 3.00
102 Armando Rios (102) 6.00 1.80
103 Preston Wilson (103) 10.00 3.00
104 Pat Burrell (104) 40.00 12.00
105 J.D. Drew (105) 10.00 3.00
106 Bruce Chen (106) 6.00 1.80
107 Matt Clement (107) 6.00 1.80
108 Carlos Beltran (108) 15.00 4.50
109 Carlos Febles (109) 6.00 6.00
110 Rob Fick (110) 6.00 1.80
111 Russell Branyan (111) 6.00 1.80
112 R.Brown (112) 6.00 1.80
113 Corey Koskie (113) 10.00 3.00
114 M.Encarnacion (114) 6.00 1.80
115 Peter Tucci (115) 6.00 1.80
116 Eric Chavez (116) 10.00 3.00
117 Gabe Kapler (117) 6.00 1.80
118 M.Anderson (118) 6.00 1.80
119 A.J. Burnett (119) 25.00 7.50
120 Ryan Bradley (120) 6.00 1.80

1999 E-X Century Authen-Kicks

Randomly inserted into packs, this nine-card set features color cut-outs of top young players with swatches of their game-worn shoes embedded in the cards beside black-and-white head shots of the players in the background. The print run for each card follows the player's name in our checklist.

Nm-Mt Ex-Mt
B1/R1 AU PRINT RUN 8 #'d OF EACH
NO B1/R1 PRICING DUE TO SCARCITY
1 J.D. Drew/160 .... 25.00 7.50
2 Travis Lee/175 .... 15.00 4.50
3 Kevin Millwood/165 .... 25.00 7.50
4 Bruce Chen/205 .... 15.00 4.50
5 Troy Glaus/205 .... 25.00 7.50
6 Todd Helton/205 .... 40.00 12.00
7 Ricky Ledee/180 .... 15.00 4.50
8 Scott Rolen/205 .... 50.00 15.00
9 Jeremy Giambi/205 .... 15.00 4.50
B1 J.D. Drew Black AU/8 ....
R1 J.D. Drew Red AU/8 ....

1999 E-X Century E-X Quisite

Randomly inserted into packs at the rate of one in 18, this 15-card set features color cut-outs of top young players printed on cards with an unique interior die-cut design.

Nm-Mt Ex-Mt
COMPLETE SET (15) 40.00 12.00
1 Troy Glaus .... 1.50 .45
2 J.D. Drew .... 1.50 .45
3 Pat Burrell .... 3.00 .90
4 Russell Branyan .... 1.50 .45
5 Kerry Wood 6.00 1.80
6 Eric Chavez .... 1.50 .45
7 Ben Grieve .... 1.50 .45
8 Gabe Kapler .... 1.50 .45
9 Adrian Beltre .... 1.50 .45
10 Todd Helton 4.00 1.20
11 Roosevelt Brown .... 1.50 .45
12 Marlon Anderson .... 1.50 .45
13 Jeremy Giambi .... 1.50 .45
14 Magglio Ordonez .... 2.50 .75
15 Travis Lee .... 1.50 .23

1999 E-X Century Favorites for Fenway '99

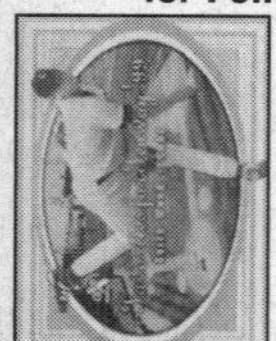

Randomly inserted into packs at the rate of one in 36, this 20-card set features color cut-outs of All-Star Game starters silhouetted in front of The Green Monster, Fenway Park.

Nm-Mt Ex-Mt
COMPLETE SET (20) 300.00 90.00
1 Mo Vaughn 4.00 1.20
2 Nomar Garciaparra 15.00 4.50
3 Frank Thomas 10.00 3.00
4 Ken Griffey Jr. 15.00 4.50
5 Roger Clemens 20.00 6.00
6 Alex Rodriguez 15.00 4.50
7 Derek Jeter 25.00 7.50
8 Juan Gonzalez 6.00 1.80
9 Cal Ripken 30.00 9.00
10 Ivan Rodriguez 10.00 3.00
11 J.D. Drew 5.00 1.50
12 Barry Bonds 25.00 7.50
13 Tony Gwynn 12.00 3.60
14 Vladimir Guerrero 10.00 3.00
15 Chipper Jones 10.00 3.00
16 Kerry Wood 10.00 3.00
17 Mike Piazza 15.00 4.50
18 Sammy Sosa 15.00 4.50
19 Scott Rolen 10.00 3.00
20 Mark McGwire 25.00 7.50

1999 E-X Century Milestones of the Century

Randomly inserted into packs, this 10-card set features color action photos of players with top statistical performances from the 1998 season printed on a multi-layered card design. Each card is sequentially numbered to the pictured player's 1998 statistical performance and follows the player's name in our checklist.

Nm-Mt Ex-Mt
1 Kerry Wood/20 ....
2 Mark McGwire/70 .... 120.00 36.00
3 Sammy Sosa/66 .... 60.00 18.00
4 Ken Griffey Jr./350 .... 30.00 9.00
5 Roger Clemens/98 .... 60.00 18.00
6 Cal Ripken/17 ....
7 Alex Rodriguez/40 .... 80.00 24.00
8 Barry Bonds/400 .... 40.00 12.00
9 N.Y. Yankees/114 .... 80.00 24.00
10 Travis Lee/98 .... 5.00 1.50

2000 E-X

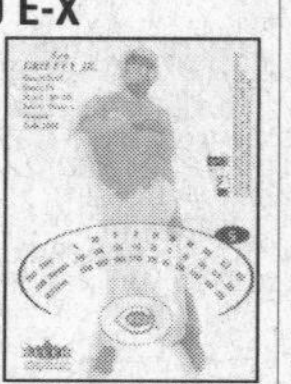

The 2000 E-X product was released in June, 2000 as a 90-card set. The set featured 60-player cards and 30-short printed prospect cards. Each of the prospect cards were individually serial numbered to 3499. Each pack contained three cards and carried a suggested retail price of $3.99.

Nm-Mt Ex-Mt
COMPLETE SET (90) 100.00 30.00
COMP.SET w/o SP's (60) 20.00 6.00
COMMON CARD (1-60) .... .40 .12
COMMON PROS (61-90) 4.00 1.20
1 Alex Rodriguez .... 1.50 .45
2 Jeff Bagwell .... .60 .18
3 Mike Piazza .... 1.50 .45
4 Tony Gwynn .... 1.25 .35
5 Ken Griffey Jr. .... 1.50 .45
6 Juan Gonzalez .... .60 .18
7 Vladimir Guerrero .... 1.00 .30
8 Cal Ripken .... 3.00 .90
9 Mo Vaughn .... .40 .12
10 Chipper Jones .... 1.00 .30
11 Derek Jeter .... 2.50 .75
12 Nomar Garciaparra .... 1.50 .45
13 Mark McGwire .... 2.50 .75
14 Sammy Sosa .... 1.50 .45
15 Pedro Martinez .... 1.00 .30
16 Greg Maddux .... 1.50 .45
17 Frank Thomas .... 1.00 .30
18 Shawn Green .... .40 .12
19 Carlos Beltran .... .60 .18
20 Roger Clemens .... 2.00 .60
21 Randy Johnson .... 1.00 .30
22 Bernie Williams .... .60 .18
23 Carlos Delgado .... .40 .12
24 Manny Ramirez .... .60 .18
25 Freddy Garcia .... .40 .12
26 Barry Bonds .... 2.50 .75
27 Tim Hudson .... .40 .12
28 Larry Walker .... .60 .18
29 Raul Mondesi .... .40 .12
30 Ivan Rodriguez .... 1.00 .30
31 Magglio Ordonez .... .40 .12
32 Scott Rolen .... 1.00 .30
33 Mike Mussina .... .60 .18
34 J.D. Drew .... .40 .12
35 Tom Glavine .... .60 .18
36 Barry Larkin .... .60 .18
37 Jim Thome .... 1.00 .30
38 Erubiel Durazo .... .40 .12
39 Curt Schilling .... .40 .12
40 Orlando Hernandez .... .40 .12
41 Rafael Palmeiro .... .60 .18
42 Gabe Kapler .... .40 .12
43 Mark Grace .... .60 .18
44 Jeff Cirillo .... .40 .12
45 Jeromy Burnitz .... .40 .12
46 Sean Casey .... .40 .12
47 Kevin Millwood .... .40 .12
48 Vinny Castilla .... .40 .12
49 Jose Canseco .... 1.00 .30
50 Roberto Alomar .... .60 .18
51 Craig Biggio .... .60 .18
52 Preston Wilson .... .40 .12
53 Jeff Weaver .... .40 .12
54 Robin Ventura .... .40 .12
55 Ben Grieve .... .40 .12
56 Troy Glaus .... .40 .12
57 Jacque Jones .... .40 .12
58 Brian Giles .... .40 .12
59 Kevin Brown .... .40 .12
60 Todd Helton .... .60 .18
61 Ben Petrick PROS 4.00 1.20
62 C.Hermansen PROS 4.00 1.20
63 Kevin Barker PROS 4.00 1.20
64 Matt LeCroy PROS 4.00 1.20
65 Brad Penny PROS 4.00 1.20
66 D.T. Cromer PROS 4.00 1.20
67 Steve Lomasney PROS 4.00 1.20
68 Cole Liniak PROS 4.00 1.20
69 B.J. Ryan PROS 4.00 1.20
70 Wilton Veras PROS 4.00 1.20
71 A.McNeal PROS RC 4.00 1.20
72 Nick Johnson PROS 4.00 1.20
73 Adam Piatt PROS 4.00 1.20
74 Adam Kennedy PROS 4.00 1.20
75 Cesar King PROS 4.00 1.20
76 Peter Bergeron PROS 4.00 1.20
77 Rob Bell PROS 4.00 1.20
78 Wily Pena PROS 4.00 1.20
79 Ruben Mateo PROS 4.00 1.20
80 Kip Wells PROS 4.00 1.20
81 Alex Escobar PROS 4.00 1.20
82 Danys Baez PROS RC 4.00 1.20
83 Travis Dawkins PROS 4.00 1.20
84 Mark Quinn PROS 4.00 1.20
85 Jimmy Anderson PROS 4.00 1.20
86 Rick Ankiel PROS 4.00 1.20
87 Alfonso Soriano PROS 5.00 1.50
88 Pat Burrell PROS 4.00 1.20
89 Eric Munson PROS 4.00 1.20
90 Josh Beckett PROS 5.00 1.50

2000 E-X Essential Credentials Future

Randomly inserted into packs, this 90-card insert is a complete parallel of the E-X base set. Print runs for each of these cards are provided after the player's name in our checklist.

Nm-Mt Ex-Mt
1 Alex Rodriguez (60) 80.00 24.00
2 Jeff Bagwell (59) 30.00 9.00
3 Mike Piazza (58) 80.00 24.00
4 Tony Gwynn (57) 60.00 18.00
5 Ken Griffey Jr. (56) 80.00 24.00
6 Juan Gonzalez (55) 30.00 9.00
7 Vladimir Guerrero (54) 40.00 12.00
8 Cal Ripken (53) 150.00 45.00
9 Mo Vaughn (52) 30.00 9.00
10 Chipper Jones (51) 40.00 12.00
11 Derek Jeter (50) 120.00 36.00
12 N.Garciaparra (49) 80.00 24.00
13 Mark McGwire (48) 120.00 36.00
14 Sammy Sosa (47) 80.00 24.00
15 Pedro Martinez (46) 40.00 12.00
16 Greg Maddux (45) 80.00 24.00
17 Frank Thomas (44) 40.00 12.00
18 Shawn Green (43) 20.00 6.00
19 Carlos Beltran (42) 40.00 12.00
20 Roger Clemens (41) 100.00 30.00
21 Randy Johnson (40) 40.00 12.00
22 Bernie Williams (39) 40.00 12.00
23 Carlos Delgado (38) 20.00 6.00
24 Manny Ramirez (37) 40.00 12.00
25 Freddy Garcia (36) 20.00 6.00
26 Barry Bonds (35) 150.00 45.00
27 Tim Hudson (34) 40.00 12.00
28 Larry Walker (33) 50.00 15.00
29 Raul Mondesi (32) 40.00 12.00
30 Ivan Rodriguez (31) 60.00 18.00
31 Magglio Ordonez (30) 40.00 12.00
32 Scott Rolen (29) 60.00 18.00
33 Mike Mussina (28) 50.00 15.00
34 J.D. Drew (27) 40.00 12.00
35 Tom Glavine (26) 50.00 15.00
36 Barry Larkin (25) ....
37 Jim Thome (24) ....
38 Erubiel Durazo (23) ....
39 Curt Schilling (22) ....
40 O.Hernandez (21) ....
41 Rafael Palmeiro (20) ....
42 Gabe Kapler (19) ....
43 Mark Grace (18) ....
44 Jeff Cirillo (17) ....
45 Jeromy Burnitz (16) ....
46 Sean Casey (15) ....
47 Kevin Millwood (14) ....
48 Vinny Castilla (13) ....
49 Jose Canseco (12) ....
50 Roberto Alomar (11) ....
51 Craig Biggio (10) ....
52 Preston Wilson (9) ....
53 Jeff Weaver (8) ....
54 Robin Ventura (7) ....
55 Ben Grieve (6) ....
56 Troy Glaus (5) ....
57 Jacque Jones (4) ....
58 Brian Giles (3) ....
59 Kevin Brown (2) ....
60 Todd Helton (1) ....
61 Ben Petrick (30) 25.00 7.50
62 Chad Hermansen (29) 25.00 7.50
63 Kevin Barker (28) 25.00 7.50
64 Matt LeCroy (27) 25.00 7.50
65 Brad Penny (26) 25.00 7.50
66 D.T. Cromer (25) ....
67 Steve Lomasney (24) ....
68 Cole Liniak (23) ....
69 B.J. Ryan (22) ....
70 Wilton Veras (21) ....
71 Aaron McNeal (20) ....
72 Nick Johnson (19) ....
73 Adam Piatt (18) ....
74 Adam Kennedy (17) ....
75 Cesar King (16) ....
76 Peter Bergeron (15) ....
77 Rob Bell (14) ....
78 Wily Pena (13) ....
79 Ruben Mateo (12) ....
80 Kip Wells (11) ....
81 Alex Escobar (10) ....
82 Danys Baez (9) ....
83 Travis Dawkins (8) ....
84 Mark Quinn (7) ....
85 Jimmy Anderson (6) ....
86 Rick Ankiel (5) ....
87 Alfonso Soriano (4) ....
88 Pat Burrell (3) ....
89 Eric Munson (2) ....
90 Josh Beckett (1) ....

2000 E-X Essential Credentials Now

Randomly inserted into packs, this 90-card insert is a complete parallel of the E-X base set. Print runs for each of these cards are provided after the player's name in our checklist.

Nm-Mt Ex-Mt
1 Alex Rodriguez (1) ....
2 Jeff Bagwell (2) ....
3 Mike Piazza (3) ....
4 Tony Gwynn (4) ....
5 Ken Griffey Jr. (5) ....
6 Juan Gonzalez (6) ....
7 Vladimir Guerrero (7) ....
8 Cal Ripken (8) ....
9 Mo Vaughn (9) ....
10 Chipper Jones (10) ....
11 Derek Jeter (11) ....
12 Nomar Garciaparra (12) ....
13 Mark McGwire (13) ....
14 Sammy Sosa (14) ....
15 Pedro Martinez (15) ....
16 Greg Maddux (16) ....
17 Frank Thomas (17) ....
18 Shawn Green (18) ....
19 Carlos Beltran (19) ....
20 Roger Clemens (20) ....
21 Randy Johnson (21) ....
22 Bernie Williams (22) ....
23 Carlos Delgado (23) ....
24 Manny Ramirez (24) ....
25 Freddy Garcia (25) ....
26 Barry Bonds (26) 150.00 45.00
27 Tim Hudson (27) ....
28 Larry Walker (28) 50.00 15.00
29 Raul Mondesi (29) 40.00 12.00
30 Ivan Rodriguez (30) 60.00 18.00
31 Magglio Ordonez (31) 40.00 12.00
32 Scott Rolen (32) 60.00 18.00
33 Mike Mussina (33) 50.00 15.00
34 J.D. Drew (34) 40.00 12.00
35 Tom Glavine (35) 50.00 15.00
36 Barry Larkin (36) 30.00 9.00
37 Jim Thome (37) 50.00 15.00
38 Erubiel Durazo (38) 20.00 6.00
39 Curt Schilling (39) 25.00 7.50
40 O.Hernandez (40) 20.00 6.00
41 Rafael Palmeiro (41) 30.00 9.00
42 Gabe Kapler (42) 20.00 6.00
43 Mark Grace (43) 30.00 9.00
44 Jeff Cirillo (44) 20.00 6.00
45 Jeromy Burnitz (45) 25.00 7.50
46 Sean Casey (46) 25.00 7.50
47 Kevin Millwood (47) 25.00 7.50
48 Vinny Castilla (48) 25.00 7.50
49 Jose Canseco (49) 50.00 15.00
50 Roberto Alomar (50) 30.00 9.00
51 Craig Biggio (51) 25.00 7.50
52 Preston Wilson (52) 20.00 6.00
53 Jeff Weaver (53) 15.00 4.50
54 Robin Ventura (54) 20.00 6.00
55 Ben Grieve (55) 15.00 4.50
56 Troy Glaus (56) 20.00 6.00
57 Jacque Jones (57) 20.00 6.00
58 Brian Giles (58) 20.00 6.00
59 Kevin Brown (59) 25.00 7.50
60 Todd Helton (60) 25.00 7.50
61 Ben Petrick (1) ....
62 Chad Hermansen (2) ....
63 Kevin Barker (3) ....
64 Matt LeCroy (4) ....
65 Brad Penny (5) ....
66 D.T. Cromer (6) ....
67 Steve Lomasney (7) ....
68 Cole Liniak (8) ....
69 B.J. Ryan (9) ....
70 Wilton Veras (10) ....
71 Aaron McNeal (11) ....
72 Nick Johnson (12) ....
73 Adam Piatt (13) ....
74 Adam Kennedy (14) ....
75 Cesar King (15) ....
76 Peter Bergeron (16) ....
77 Rob Bell (17) ....
78 Wily Pena (18) ....
79 Ruben Mateo (19) ....
80 Kip Wells (20) ....
81 Alex Escobar (21) ....
82 Danys Baez (22) ....
83 Travis Dawkins (23) ....
84 Mark Quinn (24) ....
85 Jimmy Anderson (25) ....
86 Rick Ankiel (26) 60.00 18.00
87 Alfonso Soriano (27) 60.00 18.00
88 Pat Burrell (28) 60.00 18.00
89 Eric Munson (29) 50.00 15.00
90 Josh Beckett (30) 60.00 18.00

2000 E-X E-Xceptional Red

Randomly inserted into packs, this 15-card insert features some of the hottest major league ballplayers. Each card is individually numbered to 1999. Card backs carry a "XC" prefix.

Nm-Mt Ex-Mt
COMPLETE SET (15) 150.00 45.00
*BLUE: 1.25X TO 3X RED
BLUE PRINT RUN 250 SERIAL #'d SETS
*GREEN: .6X TO 1.5X RED
GREEN PRINT RUN 999 SERIAL #'d SETS
RANDOM INSERTS IN PACKS ....
XC1 Ken Griffey Jr. 10.00 3.00
XC2 Derek Jeter 15.00 4.50
XC3 Nomar Garciaparra 10.00 3.00
XC4 Mark McGwire 15.00 4.50
XC5 Sammy Sosa 10.00 3.00
XC6 Mike Piazza 10.00 3.00
XC7 Alex Rodriguez 10.00 3.00
XC8 Cal Ripken 20.00 6.00
XC9 Chipper Jones 6.00 1.80
XC10 Pedro Martinez 6.00 1.80
XC11 Jeff Bagwell 4.00 1.20
XC12 Greg Maddux 10.00 3.00
XC13 Roger Clemens 12.00 3.60
XC14 Tony Gwynn 8.00 2.40
XC15 Frank Thomas 6.00 1.80

2000 E-X E-Xciting

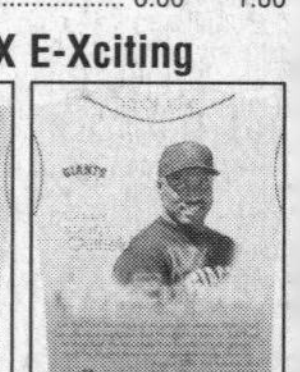

Randomly inserted into packs at one in 24, this 10-card insert set features some of the most exciting players in modern major league baseball. Card backs carry a "XT" prefix.

Nm-Mt Ex-Mt
COMPLETE SET (10) 60.00 18.00
XT1 Mark McGwire 10.00 3.00
XT2 Ken Griffey Jr. 6.00 1.80
XT3 Randy Johnson 4.00 1.20
XT4 Sammy Sosa 6.00 1.80
XT5 Manny Ramirez .... 2.50 .75
XT6 Jose Canseco 4.00 1.20
XT7 Derek Jeter 10.00 3.00
XT8 Scott Rolen 4.00 1.20
XT9 Juan Gonzalez .... 2.50 .75
XT10 Barry Bonds 10.00 3.00

2000 E-X E-Xplosive

Randomly inserted into packs, this 20-card set features some of the most explosive players in major league baseball. Each card is individually serial numbered to 2499. Card backs carry a "XP" prefix.

Nm-Mt Ex-Mt
COMPLETE SET (20) 200.00 60.00
XP1 Tony Gwynn 8.00 2.40
XP2 Alex Rodriguez 10.00 3.00
XP3 Pedro Martinez 4.00 1.20
XP4 Sammy Sosa 10.00 3.00
XP5 Cal Ripken 20.00 6.00
XP6 Adam Piatt 4.00 1.20
XP7 Pat Burrell 4.00 1.20
XP8 J.D. Drew 4.00 1.20
XP9 Mike Piazza 10.00 3.00
XP10 Shawn Green 4.00 1.20
XP11 Troy Glaus 4.00 1.20
XP12 Randy Johnson 4.00 1.20
XP13 Juan Gonzalez 4.00 1.20
XP14 Chipper Jones 4.00 1.20
XP15 Ivan Rodriguez 4.00 1.20
XP16 Nomar Garciaparra 10.00 3.00
XP17 Ken Griffey Jr. 10.00 3.00
XP18 Nick Johnson 4.00 1.20
XP19 Mark McGwire 15.00 4.50
XP20 Frank Thomas 4.00 1.20

2000 E-X Generation E-X

Randomly inserted into packs at one in eight, this15-card insert set features some of the hottest young talent in major league baseball. Card backs carry a "GX" prefix.

Nm-Mt Ex-Mt
COMPLETE SET (15) 50.00 15.00
GX1 Rick Ankiel .... 3.00 .90
GX2 Josh Beckett .... 3.00 .90
GX3 Carlos Beltran .... 1.50 .45
GX4 Pat Burrell .... 3.00 .90
GX5 Freddy Garcia .... 3.00 .90
GX6 Alex Rodriguez 6.00 1.80
GX7 Derek Jeter 10.00 3.00
GX8 Tim Hudson .... 3.00 .90
GX9 Shawn Green .... 3.00 .90
GX10 Eric Munson .... 3.00 .90
GX11 Adam Piatt 4.00 1.20
GX12 Adam Kennedy .... 1.50 .45
GX13 Nick Johnson 4.00 1.20
GX14 Alfonso Soriano .... 3.00 .90
GX15 Nomar Garciaparra 6.00 1.80

2000 E-X Genuine Coverage

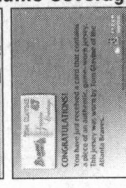

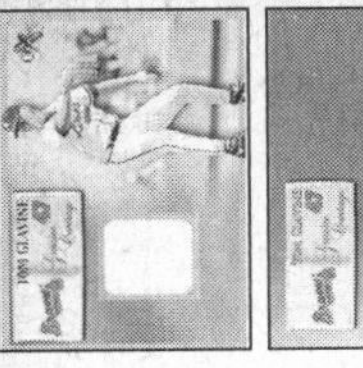

andomly inserted into packs at one in 144, this 0-card insert set features swatches from actual ame-used jerseys. Cards are numbered based n each player's actual uniform number.

	Nm-Mt	Ex-Mt
Derek Jeter	30.00	9.00
Alex Rodriguez	15.00	4.50
Cal Ripken	30.00	9.00
0 Chipper Jones	15.00	4.50
1 Edgar Martinez	15.00	4.50
5 Barry Bonds	25.00	7.50
3 Raul Mondesi	10.00	3.00
7 Tom Glavine	15.00	4.50
2 Tim Hudson	10.00	3.00

2001 E-X

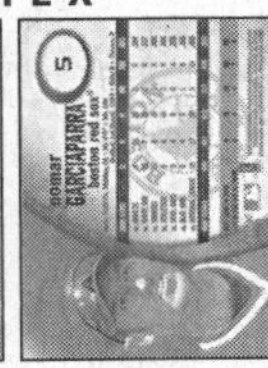

he 2001 E-X product was released in mid-May, 001, and featured a 130-card base set that was roken into tiers as follows: Base Veterans (1-00), and Rookies/Prospects (101-130) (individually serial numbered). Each pack contained 5 ards, and carried a suggested retail price of 4.99. An additional ten cards (131-140) featuring a selection of top prospects was distributed n late December, 2001 within Fleer Platinum RC packs. Each of these cards is serial-numbered to 99 copies.

	Nm-Mt	Ex-Mt
COMP.SET w/o SP's (100)	25.00	7.50
COMMON CARD (1-100)	.50	.15
COMMON (101-130)	8.00	2.40
COMMON (131-140)	10.00	3.00
1 Jason Kendall	.50	.15
2 Derek Jeter	3.00	.90
3 Greg Vaughn	.50	.15
4 Eric Chavez	.50	.15
5 Nomar Garciaparra	2.00	.60
6 Roberto Alomar	.75	.23
7 Barry Larkin	.75	.23
8 Matt Lawton	.50	.15
9 Larry Walker	.75	.23
10 Chipper Jones	1.25	.35
11 Scott Rolen	1.25	.35
12 Carlos Lee	.50	.15
13 Adrian Beltre	.75	.23
14 Ben Grieve	.50	.15
15 Mike Sweeney	.50	.15
16 John Olerud	.50	.15
17 Gabe Kapler	.50	.15
18 Brian Giles	.50	.15
19 Luis Gonzalez	.50	.15
20 Sammy Sosa	2.00	.60
21 Roger Clemens	2.50	.75
22 Vladimir Guerrero	1.25	.35
23 Ken Griffey Jr.	2.00	.60
24 Mark McGwire	3.00	.90
25 Orlando Hernandez	.50	.15
26 Shannon Stewart	.50	.15
27 Fred McGriff	.75	.23
28 Lance Berkman	.50	.15
29 Carlos Delgado	.50	.15
30 Mike Piazza	2.00	.60
31 Juan Encarnacion	.50	.15
32 David Justice	.50	.15
33 Greg Maddux	2.00	.60
34 Frank Thomas	1.25	.35
35 Jason Giambi	.50	.15
36 Ruben Mateo	.50	.15
37 Todd Helton	.75	.23
38 Jim Edmonds	.50	.15
39 Steve Finley	.50	.15
40 Tom Glavine	.75	.23
41 Mo Vaughn	.50	.15
42 Phil Nevin	.50	.15
43 Richie Sexson	.50	.15
44 Craig Biggio	.75	.23
45 Kerry Wood	1.25	.35
46 Pat Burrell	.50	.15
47 Edgar Martinez	.75	.23
48 Jim Thome	1.25	.35
49 Jeff Bagwell	.75	.23
50 Bernie Williams	.75	.23
51 Andruw Jones	.50	.15
52 Gary Sheffield	.50	.15
53 Johnny Damon	.75	.23
54 Rondell White	.50	.15
55 J.D. Drew	.50	.15
56 Tony Batista	.50	.15
57 Paul Konerko	.50	.15
58 Rafael Palmeiro	.75	.23
59 Cal Ripken	4.00	1.20
60 Darin Erstad	.50	.15
61 Ivan Rodriguez	1.25	.35
62 Barry Bonds	3.00	.90
63 Edgardo Alfonzo	.50	.15
64 Ellis Burks	.50	.15
65 Mike Lieberthal	.50	.15
66 Robin Ventura	.50	.15
67 Richard Hidalgo	.50	.15
68 Magglio Ordonez	.50	.15
69 Kazuhiro Sasaki	.50	.15
70 Miguel Tejada	.50	.15
71 David Wells	.50	.15
72 Troy Glaus	.50	.15
73 Jose Vidro	.50	.15
74 Shawn Green	.50	.15
75 Barry Zito	.75	.23
76 Jermaine Dye	.50	.15
77 Geoff Jenkins	.50	.15
78 Jeff Kent	.50	.15
79 Al Leiter	.50	.15
80 Deivi Cruz	.50	.15
81 Eric Karros	.50	.15
82 Albert Belle	.50	.15
83 Pedro Martinez	1.25	.35
84 Raul Mondesi	.50	.15
85 Preston Wilson	.50	.15
86 Rafael Furcal	.50	.15
87 Rick Ankiel	.50	.15
88 Randy Johnson	1.25	.35
89 Kevin Brown	.50	.15
90 Sean Casey	.50	.15
91 Mike Mussina	.75	.23
92 Alex Rodriguez	2.00	.60
93 Andres Galarraga	.50	.15
94 Juan Gonzalez	.75	.23
95 Manny Ramirez	.75	.23
96 Mark Grace	.75	.23
97 Carl Everett	.50	.15
98 Tony Gwynn	1.50	.45
99 Mike Hampton	.50	.15
100 Ken Caminiti	.50	.15
101 Jason Hart/1749	8.00	2.40
102 Corey Patterson/1199	8.00	2.40
103 Timo Perez/1999	8.00	2.40
104 Marcus Giles/1999	8.00	2.40
105 I. Suzuki/1999 RC	60.00	18.00
106 Aubrey Huff/1499	8.00	2.40
107 Joe Crede/1999	8.00	2.40
108 Larry Barnes/1499	8.00	2.40
109 Esix Snead/1999 RC	8.00	2.40
110 Kenny Kelly/2249	8.00	2.40
111 Justin Miller/2249	8.00	2.40
112 Jack Cust/1999	8.00	2.40
113 Xavier Nady/999	8.00	2.40
114 Eric Munson/1499	8.00	2.40
115 E. Guzman/1749 RC	8.00	2.40
116 Juan Pierre/2189	8.00	2.40
117 W. Abreu/1749 RC	8.00	2.40
118 Keith Ginter/1999	8.00	2.40
119 Jace Brewer/2699	8.00	2.40
120 P. Crawford/2249	8.00	2.40
121 Jason Tyner/2249	8.00	2.40
122 Tike Redman/1999	8.00	2.40
123 John Riedling/2499	8.00	2.40
124 Jose Ortiz/1499	8.00	2.40
125 O. Mairena/2499	8.00	2.40
126 Eric Byrnes/2249	8.00	2.40
127 Brian Cole/999	8.00	2.40
128 Adam Piatt/2249	8.00	2.40
129 Nate Rolison/2499	8.00	2.40
130 Keith McDonald/2249	8.00	2.40
131 Albert Pujols/499 RC	100.00	30.00
132 Bud Smith/499 RC	10.00	3.00
133 T.Shinjo/499 RC	15.00	4.50
134 W.Betemit/499 RC	10.00	3.00
135 A.Hernandez/499 RC	10.00	3.00
136 J.Melian/499 RC	10.00	3.00
137 Jay Gibbons/499 RC	15.00	4.50
138 J.Estrada/499 RC	15.00	4.50
139 M.Ensberg/499 RC	15.00	4.50
140 Drew Henson/499 RC	15.00	4.50
NNO Derek Jeter Base Inks AU/500	150.00	45.00
MM2 Derek Jeter Monumental Moments	12.00	3.60
NNO Derek Jeter Monumental Moments AU/96	120.00	36.00

2001 E-X Prospect Autographs

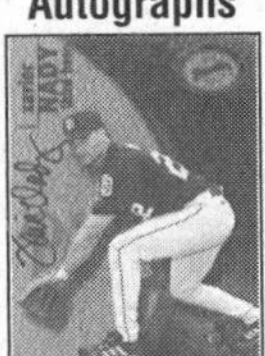

Randomly inserted into packs, this 29-card insert is actually an autographed parallel of cards 101-130 in the 2001 E-X base set (with exception of card 105). Please note that the print runs are listed below for each card.

	Nm-Mt	Ex-Mt
101 Jason Hart/250	15.00	4.50
102 Corey Patterson/800	20.00	6.00
103 Timo Perez/1000	15.00	4.50
104 Marcus Giles/500	20.00	6.00
106 Aubrey Huff/500	20.00	6.00
107 Joe Crede/500	15.00	4.50
108 Larry Barnes/500	15.00	4.50
109 Esix Snead/500	20.00	6.00
110 Kenny Kelly/250	15.00	4.50
111 Justin Miller/250	15.00	4.50
112 Jack Cust/1000	15.00	4.50
113 Xavier Nady/1000	15.00	4.50
114 Eric Munson/1500	15.00	4.50
115 Elpidio Guzman/250	20.00	6.00
116 Juan Pierre/810	20.00	6.00
117 Winston Abreu/250	15.00	4.50
118 Keith Ginter/500	15.00	4.50
119 Jace Brewer/300	15.00	4.50
120 Paxton Crawford/250	15.00	4.50
121 Jason Tyner/250	15.00	4.50
122 Tike Redman/250	15.00	4.50
123 John Riedling/500	15.00	4.50
124 Jose Ortiz/500	15.00	4.50
125 Oswaldo Mairena/500	15.00	4.50
126 Eric Byrnes/250	20.00	6.00
127 Brian Cole/200	20.00	6.00
128 Adam Piatt/250	15.00	4.50
129 Nate Rolison/500	15.00	4.50
130 Keith McDonald/250	15.00	4.50

2001 E-X Essential Credentials

Randomly inserted into packs, this 130-card insert is a complete parallel of the 2001 E-X base set. Please note that cards 1-100 are individually serial numbered to 299, while cards 101-130 are serial numbered to 29.

	Nm-Mt	Ex-Mt
COMMON CARD (1-100)	5.00	1.50
*STARS 1-100: 5X TO 12X BASIC CARDS		
COMMON (101-130)	20.00	6.00

2001 E-X Behind the Numbers Game Jersey

Randomly inserted into packs at one in 33, this 44-card insert features game used jersey swatches for some of the greatest players of all-time. Card backs carry a "BH" prefix.

	Nm-Mt	Ex-Mt
BH1 Johnny Bench	15.00	4.50
BH2 Wade Boggs	15.00	4.50
BH3 George Brett	25.00	7.50
BH4 Lou Brock	15.00	4.50
BH5 Rollie Fingers	10.00	3.00
BH6 Carlton Fisk	15.00	4.50
BH7 Reggie Jackson	15.00	4.50
BH8 Al Kaline	15.00	4.50
BH9 Willie Mays		
BH10 Willie McCovey	10.00	3.00
BH11 Paul Molitor	15.00	4.50
BH12 Eddie Murray	15.00	4.50
BH13 Jim Palmer	10.00	3.00
BH14 Ozzie Smith	15.00	4.50
BH15 Nolan Ryan	50.00	15.00
BH16 Mike Schmidt	25.00	7.50
BH17 Tom Seaver	15.00	4.50
BH18 Dave Winfield	10.00	3.00
BH19 Ted Williams	100.00	30.00
BH20 Robin Yount	15.00	4.50
BH21 Brady Anderson	10.00	3.00
BH22 Rick Ankiel	10.00	3.00
BH23 Albert Belle	10.00	3.00
BH24 Adrian Beltre	15.00	4.50
BH25 Barry Bonds	40.00	12.00
BH26 Eric Chavez	10.00	3.00
BH27 J.D. Drew	10.00	3.00
BH28 Darin Erstad	10.00	3.00
BH29 Troy Glaus	10.00	3.00
BH30 Mark Grace	15.00	4.50
BH31 Ben Grieve	10.00	3.00
BH32 Tony Gwynn	20.00	6.00
BH33 Todd Helton	15.00	4.50
BH34 Derek Jeter	40.00	12.00
BH35 Jeff Kent	10.00	3.00
BH36 Jason Kendall	10.00	3.00
BH37 Greg Maddux	20.00	6.00
BH38 John Olerud	10.00	3.00
BH39 Cal Ripken	40.00	12.00
BH40 Chipper Jones	15.00	4.50
BH41 John Smoltz	15.00	4.50
BH42 Frank Thomas	15.00	4.50
BH43 Robin Ventura	10.00	3.00
BH44 Bernie Williams	15.00	4.50

2001 E-X Behind the Numbers Game Jersey Autograph

Randomly inserted into packs, this 42-card insert is a partial parallel of the 2001 E-X Behind the Numbers insert. Each card in this set is autographed, and the stated print run for each card is listed below for your convenience.

	Nm-Mt	Ex-Mt
1 Brady Anderson/9		
2 Rick Ankiel/66	40.00	12.00
3 Albert Belle/88	50.00	15.00
4 Adrian Beltre/29	60.00	18.00
5 Johnny Bench/5		
6 Wade Boggs/26	200.00	60.00
7 Barry Bonds/25		
8 George Brett/5		
9 Lou Brock/20		
10 Eric Chavez/3		
11 J.D. Drew/7		
12 Darin Erstad/17		
13 Rollie Fingers/34	100.00	30.00
14 Carlton Fisk/27	200.00	60.00
15 Troy Glaus/25		
16 Mark Grace/17		
17 Ben Grieve/14		
18 Tony Gwynn/19		
19 Todd Helton/17		
20 Reggie Jackson/44	150.00	45.00
21 Derek Jeter/2		
22 Chipper Jones/10		
23 Al Kaline/6		
24 Jason Kendall/18		
25 Jeff Kent/21		
26 Greg Maddux/31	300.00	90.00
27 Willie McCovey/44	100.00	30.00
28 Paul Molitor/4		
29 Eddie Murray/33	200.00	60.00
30 John Olerud/5		
31 Jim Palmer/22		
32 Cal Ripken/8		
33 Nolan Ryan/34	500.00	150.00
34 Mike Schmidt/20		
35 Tom Seaver/41	150.00	45.00
36 Ozzie Smith/1		
37 John Smoltz/29	120.00	36.00
38 Frank Thomas/35	150.00	45.00
39 Robin Ventura/4		
40 Bernie Williams/51	150.00	45.00
41 Dave Winfield/31	150.00	45.00
42 Robin Yount/19		

2001 E-X Extra Innings

Randomly inserted into retail packs at one in 20, this 10-card insert features players that keep on going long after 9-innings. Card backs carry an "XI" prefix.

	Nm-Mt	Ex-Mt
COMPLETE SET (10)	100.00	30.00
XI1 Mark McGwire	12.00	3.60
XI2 Sammy Sosa	8.00	2.40
XI3 Chipper Jones	5.00	1.50
XI4 Mike Piazza	8.00	2.40
XI5 Cal Ripken	15.00	4.50
XI6 Ken Griffey Jr.	8.00	2.40
XI7 Alex Rodriguez	8.00	2.40
XI8 Vladimir Guerrero	5.00	1.50
XI9 Nomar Garciaparra	8.00	2.40
XI10 Derek Jeter	12.00	3.60

2001 E-X Wall of Fame

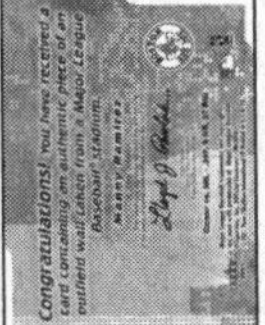

Randomly inserted into packs at one in 24, this 30-card insert features swatches of the outfield walls used in Major League ballparks. Please note that the cards are not numbered, and are listed below in alphabetical order for convenience.

	Nm-Mt	Ex-Mt
1 Jeff Bagwell	10.00	3.00
2 Barry Bonds	25.00	7.50
3 Pat Burrell	8.00	2.40
4 Roger Clemens	15.00	4.50
5 Nomar Garciaparra	15.00	4.50
6 Jason Giambi	8.00	2.40
7 Troy Glaus	8.00	2.40
8 Juan Gonzalez	10.00	3.00
9 Ken Griffey Jr.	15.00	4.50
10 Vladimir Guerrero	10.00	3.00
11 Tony Gwynn	15.00	4.50
12 Todd Helton	10.00	3.00
13 Geoff Jenkins	8.00	2.40
14 Derek Jeter	25.00	7.50
15 Andruw Jones	8.00	2.40
16 Chipper Jones	10.00	3.00
17 Jason Kendall	8.00	2.40
18 Greg Maddux	10.00	3.00
19 Pedro Martinez	10.00	3.00
20 Mark McGwire	40.00	12.00
21 Paul Molitor	10.00	3.00
22 Mike Piazza	10.00	3.00
23 Manny Ramirez	10.00	3.00
24 Cal Ripken	40.00	12.00
25 Alex Rodriguez	15.00	4.50
26 Ivan Rodriguez	10.00	3.00
27 Scott Rolen	10.00	3.00
28 Sammy Sosa	15.00	4.50
29 Frank Thomas	10.00	3.00
30 Robin Yount	10.00	3.00

2002 E-X

This 139 card set was issued in May, 2002. It was released in four card packs which came 24 packs to a box and four boxes to a case. The price for hobby packs (which had many more inserts) was $5 per pack and the retail packs were $3 per pack. The first 100 cards featured veterans while the last 40 cards featured rookies and prospects. Cards numbered 101 through 125 were printed to specific serial numbers while cards numbered 126-140 were issued at a stated rate of one in 24 hobby or retail packs. Though the set is checklisted 1-140, card 133 does not exist. It was originally intended to feature Yankees prospect Drew Henson, but Fleer's exclusive contract with the ballplayer expired two weeks prior to the release of E-X.

	Nm-Mt	Ex-Mt
COMP.SET w/o SP's (100)	25.00	7.50
COMMON CARD (1-100)	.50	.15
COMMON CARD (101-120)	5.00	1.50
COMMON CARD (121-125)	5.00	1.50
COMMON CARD (126-140)	5.00	1.50
1 Alex Rodriguez	2.00	.60
2 Albert Pujols	2.50	.75
3 Ken Griffey Jr.	2.00	.60
4 Vladimir Guerrero	1.25	.35
5 Sammy Sosa	2.00	.60
6 Ichiro Suzuki	2.00	.60
7 Jorge Posada	.75	.23
8 Matt Williams	.50	.15
9 Adrian Beltre	.75	.23
10 Pat Burrell	.50	.15
11 Roger Cedeno	.50	.15
12 Tony Clark	.50	.15
13 Steve Finley	.50	.15
14 Rafael Furcal	.50	.15
15 Rickey Henderson	1.25	.35
16 Richard Hidalgo	.50	.15
17 Jason Kendall	.50	.15
18 Tino Martinez	.75	.23
19 Scott Rolen	1.25	.35
20 Shannon Stewart	.50	.15
21 Jose Vidro	.50	.15
22 Preston Wilson	.50	.15
23 Raul Mondesi	.50	.15
24 Lance Berkman	.50	.15
25 Rick Ankiel	.50	.15
26 Kevin Brown	.50	.15
27 Jeromy Burnitz	.50	.15
28 Jeff Cirillo	.50	.15
29 Carl Everett	.50	.15
30 Eric Chavez	.50	.15
31 Freddy Garcia	.50	.15
32 Mark Grace	.75	.23
33 David Justice	.50	.15
34 Fred McGriff	.75	.23
35 Mike Mussina	.75	.23
36 John Olerud	.50	.15
37 Magglio Ordonez	.50	.15
38 Curt Schilling	.50	.15
39 Aaron Sele	.50	.15
40 Robin Ventura	.50	.15
41 Adam Dunn	.75	.23
42 Jeff Bagwell	.75	.23
43 Barry Bonds	3.00	.90
44 Roger Clemens	2.50	.75
45 Cliff Floyd	.50	.15
46 Jason Giambi	.50	.15
47 Juan Gonzalez	.75	.23
48 Luis Gonzalez	.50	.15
49 Cristian Guzman	.50	.15
50 Todd Helton	.75	.23
51 Derek Jeter	3.00	.90
52 Rafael Palmeiro	.75	.23
53 Mike Sweeney	.50	.15
54 Ben Grieve	.50	.15
55 Phil Nevin	.50	.15
56 Mike Piazza	2.00	.60
57 Moises Alou	.50	.15
58 Ivan Rodriguez	1.25	.35
59 Manny Ramirez	.75	.23
60 Brian Giles	.50	.15
61 Jim Thome	1.25	.35
62 Larry Walker	.75	.23
63 Bobby Abreu	.50	.15
64 Troy Glaus	.50	.15
65 Garret Anderson	.50	.15
66 Roberto Alomar	.75	.23
67 Bret Boone	.50	.15
68 Marty Cordova	.50	.15
69 Craig Biggio	.75	.23
70 Omar Vizquel	.75	.23
71 Jermaine Dye	.50	.15
72 Darin Erstad	.50	.15
73 Carlos Delgado	.50	.15
74 Nomar Garciaparra	2.00	.60
75 Greg Maddux	2.00	.60
76 Tom Glavine	.75	.23
77 Frank Thomas	1.25	.35
78 Shawn Green	.50	.15
79 Bobby Higginson	.50	.15
80 Jeff Kent	.50	.15
81 Chuck Knoblauch	.50	.15
82 Paul Konerko	.50	.15
83 Carlos Lee	.50	.15
84 Jon Lieber	.50	.15
85 Paul LoDuca	.50	.15
86 Mike Lowell	.50	.15
87 Edgar Martinez	.75	.23
88 Doug Mientkiewicz	.50	.15
89 Pedro Martinez	1.25	.35
90 Randy Johnson	1.25	.35
91 Aramis Ramirez	.50	.15
92 J.D. Drew	.50	.15
93 Chris Richard	.50	.15
94 Jimmy Rollins	.50	.15
95 Ryan Klesko	.50	.15
96 Gary Sheffield	.50	.15
97 Chipper Jones	1.25	.35
98 Greg Vaughn	.50	.15
99 Mo Vaughn	.50	.15
100 Bernie Williams	.75	.23
101 John Foster NT/2999 RC	5.00	1.50
102 J. DeLaRosa NT/2999 RC	5.00	1.50
103 Ed. Almonte NT/2999 RC	5.00	1.50
104 Chris Booker NT/2999 RC	5.00	1.50
105 Victor Alvarez NT/2999 RC	5.00	1.50
106 Cliff Bartosh NT/2999 RC	5.00	1.50
107 Felix Escalona NT/2999 RC	5.00	1.50
108 C. Thurman NT/2999 RC	5.00	1.50
109 Kazuhisa Ishii NT/2999 RC	10.00	3.00
110 Mig. Asencio NT/2999 RC	5.00	1.50
111 P.J. Bevis NT/2499 RC	5.00	1.50
112 Gus. Chacin NT/2499 RC	8.00	2.40
113 Steve Kent NT/2499 RC	5.00	1.50
114 Tak. Nomura NT/2499 RC	5.00	1.50
115 Adam Walker NT/2499 RC	5.00	1.50
116 So Taguchi NT/2499 RC	8.00	2.40
117 Reed Johnson NT/2499 RC	8.00	2.40
118 Rod Rosario NT/2499 RC	5.00	1.50
119 Luis Martinez NT/2499 RC	5.00	1.50
120 Sat Komiyama NT/2499 RC	5.00	1.50
121 Sean Burroughs NT/1999	5.00	1.50
122 Hank Blalock NT/1999	8.00	2.40
123 Marlon Byrd NT/1999	5.00	1.50
124 Nick Johnson NT/1999	5.00	1.50

Card	Nm-Mt	Ex-Mt
125 Mark Teixeira NT/1999	8.00	2.40
126 David Espinosa NT	5.00	1.50
127 Adrian Burnside NT RC	5.00	1.50
128 Mark Corey NT RC	5.00	1.50
129 Matt Thornton NT RC	5.00	1.50
130 Dane Sardinha NT	5.00	1.50
131 Juan Rivera NT	5.00	1.50
132 Austin Kearns NT	5.00	1.50
133 Does Not Exist		
134 Ben Broussard NT	5.00	1.50
135 Orlando Hudson NT	5.00	1.50
136 Carlos Pena NT	5.00	1.50
137 Kenny Kelly NT	5.00	1.50
138 Bill Hall NT	5.00	1.50
139 Ron Chiavacci NT	5.00	1.50
140 Mark Prior NT	12.00	3.60

2002 E-X Essential Credentials Future

Randomly inserted in packs, these 125 cards have two distinct patterns of serial numbering. Cards numbered 1 through 60 are inversely numbered and have a game used piece on them while cards numbered 61 through 125 are also inversley numbered.

Card	Nm-Mt	Ex-Mt
1 Alex Rodriguez Jsy/60	60.00	18.00
2 Albert Pujols Base/59	60.00	18.00
3 Ken Griffey Jr. Base/58	60.00	18.00
4 Vladimir Guerrero Base/57	40.00	12.00
5 Sammy Sosa Base/56	60.00	18.00
6 Ichiro Suzuki Base/55		
7 Jorge Posada Bat/54	30.00	9.00
8 Matt Williams Bat/53	25.00	7.50
9 Adrian Beltre Bat/52	30.00	9.00
10 Pat Burrell Bat/51	25.00	7.50
11 Roger Cedeno Bat/50	25.00	7.50
12 Tony Clark Bat/49	25.00	7.50
13 Steve Finley Bat/48	30.00	9.00
14 Rafael Furcal Bat/47	30.00	9.00
15 Rickey Henderson Bat/46	50.00	15.00
16 Richard Hidalgo Bat/45	25.00	7.50
17 Jason Kendall Bat/44	30.00	9.00
18 Tino Martinez Bat/43	40.00	12.00
19 Scott Rolen Bat/42	50.00	15.00
20 Shannon Stewart Bat/41	30.00	9.00
21 Jose Vidro Bat/40	25.00	7.50
22 Preston Wilson Bat/39	30.00	9.00
23 Raul Mondesi Bat/38	30.00	9.00
24 Lance Berkman Bat/37	30.00	9.00
25 Rick Ankiel Jsy/36	25.00	7.50
26 Kevin Brown Jsy/35	40.00	12.00
27 Jeromy Burnitz Bat/34	40.00	12.00
28 Jeff Cirillo Jsy/33	30.00	9.00
29 Carl Everett Jsy/32	40.00	12.00
30 Eric Chavez Bat/31	40.00	12.00
31 Freddy Garcia Jsy/30	40.00	12.00
32 Mark Grace Jsy/29	50.00	15.00
33 David Justice Jsy/28	40.00	12.00
34 Fred McGriff Jsy/27	50.00	15.00
35 Mike Mussina Jsy/26		
36 John Olerud Jsy/25		
37 Magglio Ordonez Jsy/24		
38 Curt Schilling Jsy/23		
39 Aaron Sele Jsy/22		
40 Robin Ventura Jsy/21		
41 Adam Dunn Bat/20		
42 Jeff Bagwell Jsy/19		
43 Barry Bonds Pants/18		
44 Roger Clemens Bat/17		
45 Cliff Floyd Bat/16		
46 Jason Giambi Base/15		
47 Juan Gonzalez Jsy/14		
48 Luis Gonzalez Base/13		
49 Cristian Guzman Bat/12		
50 Todd Helton Base/11		
51 Derek Jeter Bat/10		
52 Rafael Palmeiro Bat/9		
53 Mike Sweeney Bat/8		
54 Ben Grieve Jsy/7		
55 Phil Nevin Bat/6		
56 Mike Piazza Base/5		
57 Moises Alou Bat/4		
58 Ivan Rodriguez Jsy/3		
59 Manny Ramirez Base/2		
60 Brian Giles Bat/1		
61 Jim Thome/125	20.00	6.00
62 Larry Walker/124	12.00	3.60
63 Bobby Abreu/123	8.00	2.40
64 Troy Glaus/122	8.00	2.40
65 Garret Anderson/121	8.00	2.40
66 Roberto Alomar/120	12.00	3.60
67 Bret Boone/119	8.00	2.40
68 Marty Cordova/118	8.00	2.40
69 Craig Biggio/117	12.00	3.60
70 Omar Vizquel/116	12.00	3.60
71 Jermaine Dye/115	8.00	2.40
72 Darin Erstad/114	8.00	2.40
73 Carlos Delgado/113	8.00	2.40
74 Nomar Garciaparra/112	30.00	9.00
75 Greg Maddux/111	30.00	9.00
76 Tom Glavine/110	12.00	3.60
77 Frank Thomas/109	20.00	6.00
78 Shawn Green/108	8.00	2.40
79 Bobby Higginson/107	8.00	2.40
80 Jeff Kent/106	8.00	2.40
81 Chuck Knoblauch/105	8.00	2.40
82 Paul Konerko/104	8.00	2.40
83 Carlos Lee/103	8.00	2.40
84 Jon Lieber/102	8.00	2.40
85 Paul LoDuca/101	8.00	2.40
86 Mike Lowell/100	8.00	2.40
87 Edgar Martinez/99	12.00	3.60
88 Doug Mientkiewicz/98	8.00	2.40
89 Pedro Martinez/97	20.00	6.00
90 Randy Johnson/96	20.00	6.00
91 Aramis Ramirez/95	8.00	2.40
92 J.D. Drew/94	8.00	2.40
93 Chris Richard/93	8.00	2.40
94 Jimmy Rollins/92	8.00	2.40
95 Ryan Klesko/91	8.00	2.40
96 Gary Sheffield/90	8.00	2.40
97 Chipper Jones/89	20.00	6.00
98 Greg Vaughn/88	8.00	2.40
99 Mo Vaughn/87	8.00	2.40
100 Bernie Williams/86	12.00	3.60
101 John Foster NT/85	8.00	2.40
102 Jorge De La Rosa NT/84	8.00	2.40
103 Edwin Almonte NT/83	8.00	2.40
104 Chris Booker NT/82	8.00	2.40
105 Victor Alvarez NT/81	8.00	2.40
106 Cliff Bartosh NT/80	10.00	3.00
107 Felix Escalona NT/79	10.00	3.00
108 Corey Thurman NT/78	10.00	3.00
109 Kazuhisa Ishii NT/77	25.00	7.50
110 Miguel Asencio NT/76	10.00	3.00
111 P.J. Bevis NT/75	10.00	3.00
112 Gustavo Chacin NT/74	15.00	4.50
113 Steve Kent NT/73	10.00	3.00
114 Takahito Nomura NT/72	10.00	3.00
115 Adam Walker NT/71	10.00	3.00
116 So Taguchi NT/70	15.00	4.50
117 Reed Johnson NT/69	15.00	4.50
118 Rodrigo Rosario NT/68	10.00	3.00
119 Luis Martinez NT/67	10.00	3.00
120 Satoru Komiyama NT/66	10.00	3.00
121 Sean Burroughs NT/65	12.00	3.60
122 Hank Blalock NT/64	30.00	9.00
123 Marlon Byrd NT/63	12.00	3.60
124 Nick Johnson NT/62	12.00	3.60
125 Mark Teixeira NT/61	20.00	6.00

2002 E-X Essential Credentials Now

Randomly inserted in packs, these 125 cards are printed to a stated print run matching their card number. In addition, the first 60 cards of the set have a game-used piece mounted to the card.

Card	Nm-Mt	Ex-Mt
1 Alex Rodriguez Jsy/1		
2 Albert Pujols Base/2		
3 Ken Griffey Jr. Base/3		
4 Vladimir Guerrero Base/4		
5 Sammy Sosa Base/5		
6 Ichiro Suzuki Base/6		
7 Jorge Posada Bat/7		
8 Matt Williams Bat/8		
9 Adrian Beltre Bat/9		
10 Pat Burrell Bat/10		
11 Roger Cedeno Bat/11		
12 Tony Clark Bat/12		
13 Steve Finley Bat/13		
14 Rafael Furcal Bat/14		
15 Rickey Henderson Bat/15		
16 Richard Hidalgo Bat/16		
17 Jason Kendall Bat/17		
18 Tino Martinez Bat/18		
19 Scott Rolen Bat/19		
20 Shannon Stewart Bat/20		
21 Jose Vidro Bat/21		
22 Preston Wilson Bat/22		
23 Raul Mondesi Bat/23		
24 Lance Berkman Bat/24		
25 Rick Ankiel Jsy/25		
26 Kevin Brown Jsy/26	40.00	12.00
27 Jeromy Burnitz Bat/27	40.00	12.00
28 Jeff Cirillo Jsy/28	30.00	9.00
29 Carl Everett Jsy/29	40.00	12.00
30 Eric Chavez Bat/30	40.00	12.00
31 Freddy Garcia Jsy/31	40.00	12.00
32 Mark Grace Jsy/32	50.00	15.00
33 David Justice Jsy/33	40.00	12.00
34 Fred McGriff Jsy/34	50.00	15.00
35 Mike Mussina Jsy/35		
36 John Olerud Jsy/36	30.00	9.00
37 Magglio Ordonez Jsy/37	30.00	9.00
38 Curt Schilling Jsy/38	30.00	9.00
39 Aaron Sele Jsy/39	25.00	7.50
40 Robin Ventura Jsy/40	30.00	9.00
41 Adam Dunn Bat/41	40.00	12.00
42 Jeff Bagwell Jsy/42	40.00	12.00
43 Barry Bonds Pants/43	120.00	36.00
44 Roger Clemens Bat/44	100.00	30.00
45 Cliff Floyd Bat/45	30.00	9.00
46 Jason Giambi Base/46	30.00	9.00
47 Juan Gonzalez Jsy/47	40.00	12.00
48 Luis Gonzalez Base/48	30.00	9.00
49 Cristian Guzman Bat/49	25.00	7.50
50 Todd Helton Base/50	40.00	12.00
51 Derek Jeter Bat/51	120.00	36.00
52 Rafael Palmeiro Bat/52	30.00	9.00
53 Mike Sweeney Bat/53	25.00	7.50
54 Ben Grieve Jsy/54	20.00	6.00
55 Phil Nevin Bat/55	25.00	7.50
56 Mike Piazza Base/56	60.00	18.00
57 Moises Alou Bat/57	25.00	7.50
58 Ivan Rodriguez Jsy/58	40.00	12.00
59 Manny Ramirez Base/59	30.00	9.00
60 Brian Giles Bat/60	25.00	7.50
61 Jim Thome/61	30.00	9.00
62 Larry Walker/62	20.00	6.00
63 Bobby Abreu/63	12.00	3.60
64 Troy Glaus/64	12.00	3.60
65 Garret Anderson/65	12.00	3.60
66 Roberto Alomar/66	15.00	4.50
67 Bret Boone/67	10.00	3.00
68 Marty Cordova/68	10.00	3.00
69 Craig Biggio/69	15.00	4.50
70 Omar Vizquel/70	15.00	4.50
71 Jermaine Dye/71	10.00	3.00
72 Darin Erstad/72	10.00	3.00
73 Carlos Delgado/73	10.00	3.00
74 Nomar Garciaparra/74	40.00	12.00
75 Greg Maddux/75	40.00	12.00
76 Tom Glavine/76	15.00	4.50
77 Frank Thomas/77	25.00	7.50
78 Shawn Green/78	10.00	3.00
79 Bobby Higginson/79	10.00	3.00
80 Jeff Kent/80	10.00	3.00
81 Chuck Knoblauch/81	8.00	2.40
82 Paul Konerko/82	8.00	2.40
83 Carlos Lee/83	8.00	2.40
84 Jon Lieber/84	8.00	2.40
85 Paul LoDuca/85	8.00	2.40
86 Mike Lowell/86	8.00	2.40
87 Edgar Martinez/87	12.00	3.60
88 Doug Mientkiewicz/88	8.00	2.40
89 Pedro Martinez/89	20.00	6.00
90 Randy Johnson/90	20.00	6.00
91 Aramis Ramirez/91	8.00	2.40
92 J.D. Drew/92	8.00	2.40
93 Chris Richard/93	8.00	2.40
94 Jimmy Rollins/94	8.00	2.40
95 Ryan Klesko/95	8.00	2.40
96 Gary Sheffield/96	8.00	2.40
97 Chipper Jones/97	20.00	6.00
98 Greg Vaughn/98	8.00	2.40
99 Mo Vaughn/99	8.00	2.40
100 Bernie Williams/100	12.00	3.60
101 John Foster NT/101	8.00	2.40
102 Jorge De La Rosa NT/102	8.00	2.40
103 Edwin Almonte NT/103	8.00	2.40
104 Chris Booker NT/104	8.00	2.40
105 Victor Alvarez NT/105	8.00	2.40
106 Cliff Bartosh NT/106	8.00	2.40
107 Felix Escalona NT/107	8.00	2.40
108 Corey Thurman NT/108	8.00	2.40
109 Kazuhisa Ishii NT/109	25.00	7.50
110 Miguel Asencio NT/110	8.00	2.40
111 P.J. Bevis NT/111	8.00	2.40
112 Gustavo Chacin NT/112	12.00	3.60
113 Steve Kent NT/113	8.00	2.40
114 Takahito Nomura NT/114	8.00	2.40
115 Adam Walker NT/115	8.00	2.40
116 So Taguchi NT/116	12.00	3.60
117 Reed Johnson NT/117	12.00	3.60
118 Rodrigo Rosario NT/118	8.00	2.40
119 Luis Martinez NT/119	8.00	2.40
120 Satoru Komiyama NT/120	8.00	2.40
121 Sean Burroughs NT/121	8.00	2.40
122 Hank Blalock NT/122	20.00	6.00
123 Marlon Byrd NT/123	8.00	2.40
124 Nick Johnson NT/124	8.00	2.40
125 Mark Teixeira NT/125	12.00	3.60

2002 E-X Behind the Numbers

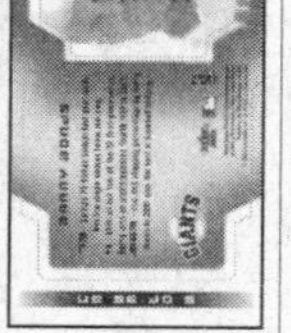

Inserted at stated odds of one in eight hobby and one in 12 retail, these 35 cards pays tribute to special numbers for hitters and pitchers.

Card	Nm-Mt	Ex-Mt
COMPLETE SET (35)	120.00	36.00
1 Ichiro Suzuki	6.00	1.80
2 Jason Giambi	2.50	.75
3 Mike Piazza	6.00	1.80
4 Brian Giles	2.50	.75
5 Barry Bonds	10.00	3.00
6 Pedro Martinez	4.00	1.20
7 Nomar Garciaparra	6.00	1.80
8 Randy Johnson	4.00	1.20
9 Craig Biggio	2.50	.75
10 Manny Ramirez	2.50	.75
11 Mike Mussina	2.50	.75
12 Kerry Wood	4.00	1.20
13 Jim Edmonds	2.50	.75
14 Ivan Rodriguez	4.00	1.20
15 Jeff Bagwell	2.50	.75
16 Roger Clemens	8.00	2.40
17 Chipper Jones	4.00	1.20
18 Shawn Green	2.50	.75
19 Albert Pujols	8.00	2.40
20 Andruw Jones	2.50	.75
21 Luis Gonzalez	2.50	.75
22 Todd Helton	2.50	.75
23 Jorge Posada	2.50	.75
24 Scott Rolen	4.00	1.20
25 Ben Sheets	2.50	.75
26 Alfonso Soriano	2.50	.75
27 Greg Maddux	6.00	1.80
28 Gary Sheffield	2.50	.75
29 Barry Zito	2.50	.75
30 Alex Rodriguez	6.00	1.80
31 Larry Walker	2.50	.75
32 Derek Jeter	10.00	3.00
33 Ken Griffey Jr.	6.00	1.80
34 Vladimir Guerrero	4.00	1.20
35 Sammy Sosa	6.00	1.80

2002 E-X Behind the Numbers Game Jersey

This partial parallel, issued at a stated rate of one in 24 hobby packs and one in 130 retail packs, features not only the Behind the Numbers insert card but a swatch of game used memorabilia.

Card	Nm-Mt	Ex-Mt
1 Jeff Bagwell	15.00	4.50
2 Craig Biggio Jsy/Pants	15.00	4.50
3 Barry Bonds SP/50		
4 Roger Clemens	25.00	7.50
5 Jim Edmonds	10.00	3.00
6 Brian Giles	10.00	3.00
7 Luis Gonzalez	10.00	3.00
8 Shawn Green	10.00	3.00
9 Todd Helton	15.00	4.50
10 Derek Jeter SP	40.00	12.00
11 Randy Johnson SP	15.00	4.50
12 Andruw Jones	10.00	3.00
13 Chipper Jones	15.00	4.50
14 Greg Maddux	15.00	4.50
15 Pedro Martinez	15.00	4.50
16 Mike Mussina	15.00	4.50
17 Mike Piazza Pants	15.00	4.50
18 Jorge Posada	15.00	4.50
19 Manny Ramirez	15.00	4.50
20 Alex Rodriguez	20.00	6.00
21 Ivan Rodriguez	15.00	4.50
22 Scott Rolen	15.00	4.50
23 Alfonso Soriano SP	15.00	4.50
24 Barry Zito	10.00	3.00

2002 E-X Behind the Numbers Game Jersey Dual

Randomly inserted in packs, these seven cards feature two swatches of jerseys from players who wear the same uniform number. These cards have a stated print run of 25 serial number sets and there is no pricing due to scarcity.

Card	Nm-Mt	Ex-Mt
1 Craig Biggio / Ivan Rodriguez		
2 Barry Bonds / Andruw Jones		
3 Jim Edmonds / Shawn Green		
4 Brian Giles / Manny Ramirez		
5 Greg Maddux / Mike Piazza		
6 Scott Rolen / Todd Helton		
7 Alfonso Soriano / Larry Walker		

2002 E-X Barry Bonds 4X MVP

Randomly inserted in packs, these four cards have a stated print run to the years in which Barry Bonds won the MVP award.

Card	Nm-Mt	Ex-Mt
COMMON CARD (1-4)	10.00	3.00

2002 E-X Game Essentials

Randomly inserted in packs, these 35 cards feature players along with a piece of their game-used gear.

*PATCH PREMIUM: 1.5X TO 3X LISTED PRICE

Card	Nm-Mt	Ex-Mt
1 Carlos Beltran Jsy	15.00	4.50
2 Barry Bonds Btg Glv SP		
3 Barry Bonds Wristband SP		
4 Kevin Brown Pants	10.00	3.00
5 Jeromy Burnitz Jsy	10.00	3.00
6 Carlos Delgado Bat	10.00	3.00
7 Jason Hart Bat SP		
8 Rickey Henderson Bat	15.00	4.50
9 Rickey Henderson Jsy	15.00	4.50
10 Drew Henson Bat	10.00	3.00
11 Drew Henson Cleat	10.00	3.00
12 Drew Henson Fld Glv	15.00	4.50
13 Derek Jeter Cleat	50.00	15.00
14 Jason Kendall Jsy	10.00	3.00
15 Jeff Kent Jsy SP		
16 Barry Larkin Fld Glv	25.00	7.50
17 Javy Lopez Jsy	10.00	3.00
18 Raul Mondesi Btg Glv	15.00	4.50
19 Raul Mondesi Jsy	10.00	3.00
20 Rafael Palmeiro Bat	15.00	4.50
21 Rafael Palmeiro Pants	15.00	4.50
22 Adam Piatt Jsy	10.00	3.00
23 Brad Radke Jsy	10.00	3.00
24 Cal Ripken Jsy	40.00	12.00
25 Mariano Rivera Jsy	15.00	4.50
26 Alex Rodriguez Btg Glv	25.00	7.50
27 Alex Rodriguez Cleat SP		
28 Ivan Rodriguez Cleat SP		
29 Kazuhiro Sasaki Jsy	10.00	3.00
30 J.T. Snow Jsy SP		
31 Mo Vaughn Jsy	10.00	3.00
32 Robin Ventura Btg Glv	15.00	4.50
33 Robin Ventura Jsy	10.00	3.00
34 Jose Vidro Jsy	10.00	3.00
35 Matt Williams Jsy	10.00	3.00

2002 E-X HardWear

Inserted in packs at stated odds of one in 7 hobby and one in 216 retail, these 10 cards fe ture players who play the game with prope aggressiveness.

Card	Nm-Mt	Ex-Mt
COMPLETE SET (10)	100.00	30.00
1 Ivan Rodriguez	8.00	2.40
2 Mike Piazza	12.00	3.60
3 Derek Jeter	20.00	6.00
4 Barry Bonds	20.00	6.00
5 Todd Helton	8.00	2.40
6 Roberto Alomar	8.00	2.40
7 Albert Pujols	15.00	4.50
8 Ichiro Suzuki	12.00	3.60
9 Ken Griffey Jr.	12.00	3.60
10 Jason Giambi	8.00	2.40

2002 E-X Hit and Run

Inserted at stated odds of one in 12 hobby an one in 72 retail, these 30 cards feature player who do the best job of hitting a baseball.

Card	Nm-Mt	Ex-Mt
COMPLETE SET (30)	100.00	30.00
1 Adam Dunn	2.50	.75
2 Derek Jeter	10.00	3.00
3 Frank Thomas	4.00	1.20
4 Albert Pujols	8.00	2.40
5 J.D. Drew	2.50	.75
6 Richard Hidalgo	2.50	.75
7 John Olerud	2.50	.75
8 Roberto Alomar	2.50	.75
9 Pat Burrell	2.50	.75
10 Darin Erstad	2.50	.75
11 Mark Grace	2.50	.75
12 Chipper Jones	4.00	1.20
13 Jose Vidro	2.50	.75
14 Cliff Floyd	2.50	.75
15 Mo Vaughn	2.50	.75
16 Nomar Garciaparra	6.00	1.80
17 Ivan Rodriguez	4.00	1.20
18 Luis Gonzalez	2.50	.75
19 Jason Giambi	2.50	.75
20 Bernie Williams	2.50	.75
21 Mike Piazza	6.00	1.80
22 Barry Bonds	10.00	3.00
23 Jose Ortiz	2.50	.75
24 Magglio Ordonez	2.50	.75
25 Troy Glaus	2.50	.75
26 Alex Rodriguez	6.00	1.80
27 Ichiro Suzuki	6.00	1.80
28 Sammy Sosa	6.00	1.80
29 Ken Griffey Jr.	6.00	1.80
30 Vladimir Guerrero	4.00	1.20

2002 E-X Hit and Run Game Base

Inserted in packs at stated odds of one in 120 hobby and one in 360 retail, this 10-card partial parallel set to the Hit and Run set includes a game base piece.

Card	Nm-Mt	Ex-Mt
1 J.D. Drew	8.00	2.40
2 Adam Dunn	10.00	3.00
3 Jason Giambi	8.00	2.40
4 Troy Glaus	8.00	2.40
5 Ken Griffey Jr.	15.00	4.50
6 Vladimir Guerrero	10.00	3.00
7 Albert Pujols	15.00	4.50
8 Sammy Sosa	15.00	4.50
9 Ichiro Suzuki	15.00	4.50
10 Bernie Williams	10.00	3.00

2002 E-X Hit and Run Game Bat

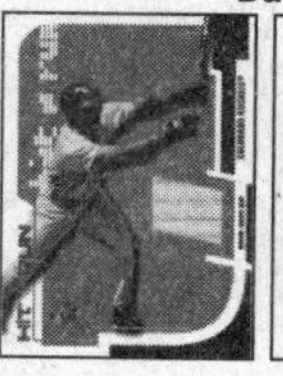

Inserted in packs at a stated rate of one in 24 hobby and one in 130 retail packs, this 19-card partial parallel set features not only players from the Hit and Run insert set but a game bat sliver attached to the card.

Card	Nm-Mt	Ex-Mt
1 Roberto Alomar	12.00	3.60
2 J.D. Drew	8.00	2.40
3 Darin Erstad	8.00	2.40
4 Cliff Floyd	8.00	2.40
5 Nomar Garciaparra	25.00	7.50

6 Luis Gonzalez 8.00 2.40
7 Richard Hidalgo 8.00 2.40
8 Derek Jeter 30.00 9.00
9 Chipper Jones 12.00 3.60
10 John Olerud 8.00 2.40
11 Magglio Ordonez 8.00 2.40
12 Jose Ortiz 8.00 2.40
13 Mike Piazza 15.00 4.50
14 Alex Rodriguez 20.00 6.00
15 Ivan Rodriguez 12.00 3.60
16 Frank Thomas 12.00 3.60
17 Mo Vaughn 8.00 2.40
18 Jose Vidro 8.00 2.40
19 Bernie Williams 12.00 3.60

2002 E-X Hit and Run Game Bat and Base

Inserted in packs at a stated rate of one in 240 hobby and one in 720 retail packs, these eight cards are a partial parallel to the Hit and Run insert set. These cards feature both a piece of a game bat and a base used by the featured players.

Nm-Mt Ex-Mt
1 Roberto Alomar 15.00 4.50
2 Barry Bonds SP
3 Nomar Garciaparra 40.00 12.00
4 Derek Jeter 50.00 15.00
5 Chipper Jones 25.00 7.50
6 Mike Piazza 30.00 9.00
7 Alex Rodriguez 40.00 12.00
8 Mo Vaughn 15.00 4.50

2002 E-X Derek Jeter 4X Champ

Randomly inserted in packs, these four cards honor the four years that Fleer representative Derek Jeter was on a World Series Champion. These cards have a stated print run of the season in which Jeter finished as a champion.

Nm-Mt Ex-Mt
COMMON CARD (1-4) 10.00 3.00

2003 E-X

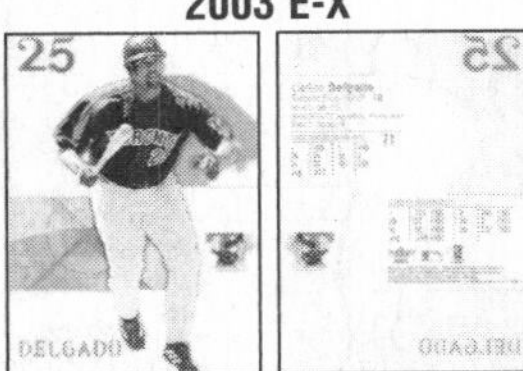

This 102 card set was issued in October, 2003. This set was issued in three card packs which had an $6 SRP and were issued 20 packs to a box and 12 boxes to a case. The first 72 cards featured common veterans while cards 73 through 82 feature shorter printed veterans and cards numbered 83 through 86 feature 2003 rookies and cards numbered 87 through 102 feature Rookie Cards of the player.

MINT NRMT
COMP.SET w/o SP's (72) 40.00 18.00
COMMON CARD (1-72) .50 .23
COMMON CARD (73-82) 4.00 1.80
COMMON CARD (83-86) 4.00 1.80
COMMON CARD (87-102) 4.00 1.80
1 Troy Glaus .50 .23
2 Darin Erstad .50 .23
3 Garret Anderson .50 .23
4 Curt Schilling .50 .23
5 Randy Johnson 1.25 .55
6 Luis Gonzalez .50 .23
7 Greg Maddux 2.00 .90
8 Chipper Jones 1.25 .55
9 Andruw Jones .50 .23
10 Melvin Mora .50 .23
11 Jay Gibbons .50 .23
12 Nomar Garciaparra 2.00 .90
13 Pedro Martinez 1.25 .55
14 Manny Ramirez .75 .35
15 Sammy Sosa 2.00 .90
16 Kerry Wood 1.25 .55
17 Magglio Ordonez .50 .23
18 Frank Thomas 1.25 .55
19 Roberto Alomar .75 .35
20 Barry Larkin .75 .35
21 Adam Dunn .75 .35
22 Austin Kearns .50 .23
23 Omar Vizquel .75 .35
24 Larry Walker .75 .35
25 Todd Helton .75 .35
26 Preston Wilson .50 .23
27 Dmitri Young .50 .23
28 Ivan Rodriguez 1.25 .55
29 Mike Lowell .50 .23
30 Jeff Kent .50 .23
31 Jeff Bagwell .75 .35
32 Roy Oswalt .50 .23
33 Craig Biggio .75 .35
34 Mike Sweeney .50 .23
35 Carlos Beltran .75 .35
36 Shawn Green .50 .23
37 Kazuhisa Ishii .50 .23
38 Richie Sexson .50 .23
39 Torii Hunter .50 .23
40 Jacque Jones .50 .23
41 Jose Vidro .50 .23
42 Vladimir Guerrero 1.25 .55
43 Mike Piazza 2.00 .90
44 Tom Glavine .75 .35
45 Roger Clemens 2.50 1.10
46 Jason Giambi .50 .23
47 Bernie Williams .75 .35
48 Alfonso Soriano .75 .35
49 Mike Mussina .75 .35
50 Barry Zito .50 .23
51 Miguel Tejada .50 .23
52 Eric Chavez .50 .23
53 Eric Byrnes .50 .23
54 Jim Thome 1.25 .55
55 Kevin Millwood .50 .23
56 Brian Giles .50 .23
57 Xavier Nady .50 .23
58 Barry Bonds 3.00 1.35
59 Bret Boone .50 .23
60 Edgar Martinez .75 .35
61 Kazuhiro Sasaki .50 .23
62 Edgar Renteria .50 .23
63 J.D. Drew .50 .23
64 Scott Rolen 1.25 .55
65 Jim Edmonds .50 .23
66 Aubrey Huff .50 .23
67 Alex Rodriguez 2.00 .90
68 Juan Gonzalez .75 .35
69 Hank Blalock .75 .35
70 Mark Teixeira .50 .23
71 Carlos Delgado .50 .23
72 Vernon Wells .50 .23
73 Shea Hillenbrand SP 4.00 1.80
74 Gary Sheffield SP 4.00 1.80
75 Mark Prior SP 5.00 2.20
76 Ken Griffey Jr. SP 12.00 5.50
77 Lance Berkman SP 4.00 1.80
78 Hideo Nomo SP 15.00 6.75
79 Derek Jeter SP 20.00 9.00
80 Ichiro Suzuki SP 12.00 5.50
81 Albert Pujols SP 15.00 6.75
82 Rafael Palmeiro SP 5.00 2.20
83 Jose Reyes ROO SP 4.00 1.80
84 Rocco Baldelli ROO SP 4.00 1.80
85 Hee Seop Choi ROO SP 4.00 1.80
86 Dontrelle Willis ROO SP 5.00 2.20
87 Robb Hammock ROO SP RC 5.00 2.20
88 Brandon Webb ROO SP RC 5.00 2.20
89 Matt Kata ROO SP RC 5.00 2.20
90 T.Wellemeyer ROO SP RC 5.00 2.20
91 Fran Cruceta ROO SP RC 4.00 1.80
92 Clint Barmes ROO SP RC 5.00 2.20
93 Jer Bonderman ROO SP RC 5.00 2.20
94 David Matranga ROO SP RC 4.00 1.80
95 Ryan Wagner ROO SP RC 5.00 2.20
96 Jeremy Griffiths ROO SP RC 5.00 2.20
97 Hideki Matsui ROO SP RC 15.00 6.75
98 Jose Contreras ROO SP RC 8.00 3.60
99 C.Wang ROO SP RC 5.00 2.20
100 Bo Hart ROO SP RC 5.00 2.20
101 Danny Haren ROO SP RC 5.00 2.20
102 Rickie Weeks ROO SP RC 10.00 4.50

2003 E-X Essential Credentials Future

MINT NRMT
*EC FUTURE 1-22: 4X TO 10X BASIC.
*EC FUTURE 23-52: 5X TO 12X BASIC
*EC FUTURE 53-67: 6X TO 15X BASIC
*EC FUTURE 68-72: 8X TO 20X BASIC
*EC FUTURE 73-77: 1.5X TO 4X BASIC
RANDOM INSERTS IN PACKS
PRINT RUNS B/WN 1-102 COPIES PER
78-102 NOT PRICED DUE TO SCARCITY

2003 E-X Essential Credentials Now

MINT NRMT
*EC NOW 26-30: 10X TO 25X BASIC.
*EC NOW 31-35: 8X TO 20X BASIC
*EC NOW 36-50: 6X TO 15X BASIC
*EC NOW 51-72: 5X TO 12X BASIC
*EC NOW 73-80: .75X TO 2X BASIC
*EC NOW 81-82: .6X TO 1.5X BASIC
*EC NOW 83-102: .75X TO 2X BASIC
*EC NOW 83-102: .75X TO 2X BASIC RC'S
RANDOM INSERTS IN PACKS
PRINT RUNS B/WN 1-102 COPIES PER
1-25 NO PRICING DUE TO SCARCITY

2003 E-X Behind the Numbers

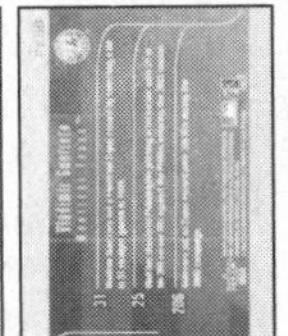

MINT NRMT
STATED ODDS 1:80
1 Derek Jeter 20.00 9.00
2 Alex Rodriguez 12.00 5.50
3 Randy Johnson 8.00 3.60
4 Chipper Jones 8.00 3.60
5 Jim Thome 8.00 3.60
6 Alfonso Soriano 8.00 3.60
7 Adam Dunn 8.00 3.60
8 Nomar Garciaparra 12.00 5.50
9 Roger Clemens 15.00 6.75
10 Gary Sheffield 5.00 2.20
11 Vladimir Guerrero 8.00 3.60
12 Greg Maddux 12.00 5.50
13 Sammy Sosa 12.00 5.50
14 Mike Piazza 12.00 5.50
15 Troy Glaus 5.00 2.20

2003 E-X Behind the Numbers Game Jersey 500

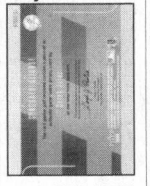

MINT NRMT
PRINT RUN 500 SERIAL #'d SETS
*BTN 199: .5X TO 1.2X BTN 500
BTN 199 PRINT RUN 199 #'d SETS
*BTN 99 MULTI-PATCH: 1.25X TO 3X BTN 500
*BTN 99 ONE COLOR: .75X TO 2X BTN 500
BTN 99 PRINT RUN 99 #'d SETS
BTN 99 ARE MOSTLY PATCH CARDS.
RANDOM INSERTS IN PACKS
AD Adam Dunn 8.00 3.60
AR Alex Rodriguez 12.00 5.50
AS Alfonso Soriano 8.00 3.60
BM Brett Myers 5.00 2.20
BZ Barry Zito 5.00 2.20
CJ Chipper Jones 8.00 3.60
DJ Derek Jeter 20.00 9.00
DW Dontrelle Willis 8.00 3.60
GM Greg Maddux 10.00 4.50
GS Gary Sheffield 5.00 2.20
HB Hank Blalock 8.00 3.60
JT Jim Thome 8.00 3.60
LB Lance Berkman 5.00 2.20
MB Marlon Byrd 5.00 2.20
MP Mike Piazza 10.00 4.50
NG Nomar Garciaparra 12.00 5.50
RA Roberto Alomar 8.00 3.60
RB Rocco Baldelli 5.00 2.20
RC Roger Clemens 12.00 5.50
RJ Randy Johnson 8.00 3.60
RP Rafael Palmeiro 8.00 3.60
SS Sammy Sosa 12.00 5.50
TG Troy Glaus 5.00 2.20
TGL Tom Glavine 8.00 3.60
VG Vladimir Guerrero 8.00 3.60

2003 E-X Behind the Numbers Game Jersey Autographs

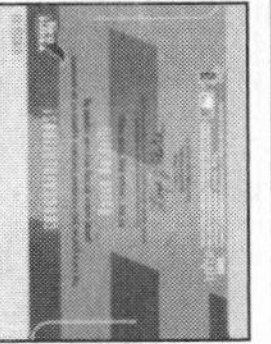

Please note there is no expiration date to redeem the Marlon Byrd autographs.

MINT NRMT
RANDOM INSERTS IN PACKS
PRINT RUNS B/WN 5-35 COPIES PER
DW Dontrelle Willis/35 50.00 22.00
HB Hank Blalock/9
MB Marlon Byrd/29 EXCH 25.00 11.00
RB Rocco Baldelli/5

2003 E-X Behind the Numbers Game Jersey Number

MINT NRMT
RANDOM INSERTS IN PACKS
PRINT RUNS B/WN 2-75 COPIES PER
NO PRICING ON QTY OF 25 OR LESS
AD Adam Dunn/44 20.00 9.00
AR Alex Rodriguez/3
AS Alfonso Soriano/12
BM Brett Myers/39 15.00 6.75
BZ Barry Zito/75 10.00 4.50
CJ Chipper Jones/10
DJ Derek Jeter/2
DW Dontrelle Willis/35 25.00 11.00
GM Greg Maddux/31 40.00 18.00
GS Gary Sheffield/11
HB Hank Blalock/9
JT Jim Thome/25
LB Lance Berkman/17
MB Marlon Byrd/29 20.00 9.00
MP Mike Piazza/31 40.00 18.00
NG Nomar Garciaparra/5
RA Roberto Alomar/12
RB Rocco Baldelli/5
RC Roger Clemens/22
RJ Randy Johnson/51 15.00 6.75
RP Rafael Palmeiro/25
SS Sammy Sosa/21
TG Troy Glaus/25
TGL Tom Glavine/47 20.00 9.00
VG Vladimir Guerrero/27 25.00 11.00

2003 E-X Diamond Essentials

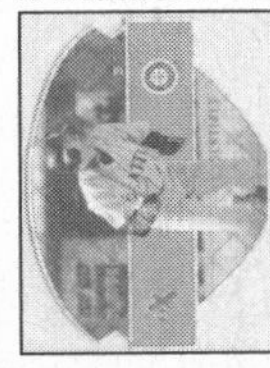

MINT NRMT
STATED ODDS 1:480
NO MORE THAN 30 SETS PRODUCED
PRINT RUN INFO PROVIDED BY FLEER
NO PRICING DUE TO SCARCITY
1 Randy Johnson
2 Ichiro Suzuki
3 Albert Pujols
4 Barry Bonds
5 Hideki Matsui
6 Derek Jeter
7 Chipper Jones
8 Sammy Sosa
9 Jeff Bagwell
10 Mike Piazza
11 Pedro Martinez
12 Mark Prior
13 Jason Giambi
14 Jose Reyes
15 Alfonso Soriano

2003 E-X Diamond Essentials Autographs

Please note there is no scheduled expiration date to redeem these Albert Pujols autographs.

MINT NRMT
RANDOM INSERTS IN PACKS
PRINT RUNS B/WN 100-299 COPIES PER
AP Albert Pujols/100 EXCH 150.00 70.00
DW Dontrelle Willis/265 25.00 11.00
RB Rocco Baldelli/299 15.00 6.75
RW Ryan Wagner/199 15.00 6.75

2003 E-X Diamond Essentials Game Jersey 345

MINT NRMT
STATED PRINT RUN 345 SERIAL #'d SETS
*DE 245: .5X TO 1.2X DE 345
DE 245 PRINT RUN 245 #'d SETS
*DE 145: .6X TO 1.5X DE 345
DE 145 PRINT RUN 145 #'d SETS
*DE 55 MULTI-PATCH: 1.25X TO 3X DE 345
*DE 55 ONE COLOR: 1X TO 2.5X DE 345
DE 55 PRINT RUN 55 #'d SETS
DE 55 ARE MOSTLY PATCH CARDS
DE 5 PRINT RUN 5 #'d SETS
NO DE 5 PRICING DUE TO SCARCITY
CJ Chipper Jones 8.00 3.60
DJ Derek Jeter 20.00 9.00
JB Jeff Bagwell 8.00 3.60
JG Jason Giambi 5.00 2.20
JR Jose Reyes 5.00 2.20
MP Mike Piazza 12.00 5.50
MP Mark Prior 8.00 3.60
PM Pedro Martinez 8.00 3.60
RJ Randy Johnson 8.00 3.60
SS Sammy Sosa 12.00 5.50

2003 E-X Emerald Essentials

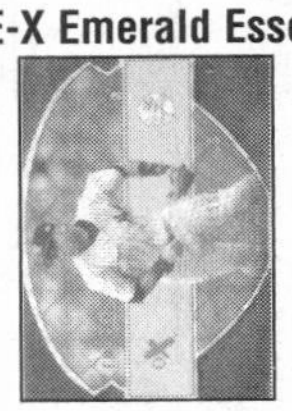

MINT NRMT
STATED ODDS 1:240
NO PRICING DUE TO SCARCITY
1 Austin Kearns
2 Alfonso Soriano
3 Miguel Tejada
4 Troy Glaus
5 Adam Dunn
6 Hideo Nomo
7 Kerry Wood
8 Nomar Garciaparra
9 Roger Clemens
10 Derek Jeter

2003 E-X Emerald Essentials Autographs

Please note that there is no expiration date to redeem the Marlon Byrd autographs.

MINT NRMT
RANDOM INSERTS IN PACKS
PRINT RUNS B/WN 29-299 COPIES PER
BW Brandon Webb/299 20.00 9.00
HB Hank Blalock/299 25.00 11.00
MB Marlon Byrd/29 EXCH

2003 E-X Emerald Essentials Game Jersey 375

MINT NRMT
STATED PRINT RUN 375 SERIAL #'d SETS
*EE 250: .5X TO 1.2X EE 375
EE 250 PRINT RUN 250 #'d SETS
*EE 175: .6X TO 1.5X EE 375
EE 175 PRINT RUN 175 #'d SETS
*EE 60 SWATCH: 1X TO 2.5X EE 375
*EE 60 MULTI-PATCH: 1.25X TO 3X EE 375
EE 60 PRINT RUN 60 #'d SETS
ABOUT HALF OF EE 60'S ARE PATCH CARDS
EE 15 PRINT RUN 15 #'d SETS
NO EE 15 PRICING DUE TO SCARCITY
AD Adam Dunn 8.00 3.60
AK Austin Kearns 5.00 2.20
AR Alex Rodriguez 12.00 5.50
AS Alfonso Soriano 8.00 3.60
HN Hideo Nomo 15.00 6.75
KW Kerry Wood 8.00 3.60
MT Miguel Tejada 5.00 2.20
NG Nomar Garciaparra 12.00 5.50
RC Roger Clemens 12.00 5.50
TG Troy Glaus 5.00 2.20

2003 E-X X-tra Innings

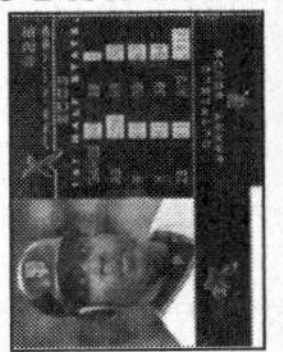

MINT NRMT
STATED ODDS 1:32
1 Ichiro Suzuki 8.00 3.60
2 Albert Pujols 10.00 4.50
3 Barry Bonds 12.00 5.50
4 Jason Giambi 4.00 1.80
5 Pedro Martinez 5.00 2.20
6 Mark Prior 5.00 2.20
7 Derek Jeter 12.00 5.50
8 Curt Schilling 4.00 1.80
9 Jeff Bagwell 5.00 2.20
10 Alex Rodriguez 8.00 3.60

2004 E-X

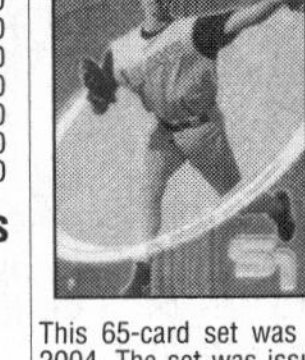
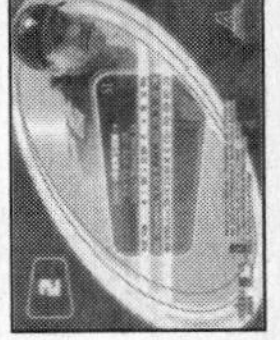

This 65-card set was released in late August, 2004. The set was issued in seven -card packs with an $200 SRP which came 12 "packs" to a case. The first 40-cards of this set featured veterans while the final 25 cards feature Rookie Cards and leading prospects which were inserted at a stated rate of one per pack. Those cards (41-65) were issued to a stated print run of 350 serial numbered sets with the first 150 of those cards being die-cut.

Nm-Mt Ex-Mt
COMMON CARD (1-40) 2.00 .60
COMMON CARD (41-65) 5.00 1.50
SEE PARALLEL SET FOR DIE CUT PRICES
1 Vladimir Guerrero 3.00 .90
2 Randy Johnson 3.00 .90
3 Chipper Jones 3.00 .90
4 Miguel Tejada 2.00 .60
5 Pedro Martinez 3.00 .90
6 Nomar Garciaparra 5.00 1.50
7 Sammy Sosa 5.00 1.50
8 Greg Maddux 5.00 1.50
9 Frank Thomas 3.00 .90
10 Ken Griffey Jr. 5.00 1.50
11 Omar Vizquel 3.00 .90
12 Todd Helton 3.00 .90
13 Ivan Rodriguez 3.00 .90
14 Miguel Cabrera 3.00 .90
15 Dontrelle Willis 2.00 .60
16 Jeff Bagwell 3.00 .90
17 Roger Clemens 6.00 1.80
18 Carlos Beltran 3.00 .90
19 Hideo Nomo 3.00 .90
20 Scott Podsednik 2.00 .60
21 Torii Hunter 2.00 .60
22 Jose Vidro 2.00 .60
23 Mike Piazza 5.00 1.50
24 Hideki Matsui 5.00 1.50
25 Alex Rodriguez 5.00 1.50
26 Derek Jeter 6.00 1.80
27 Tim Hudson 2.00 .60

28 Jim Thome 3.00 .90
29 Craig Wilson 2.00 .60
30 Brian Giles 2.00 .60
31 Jason Schmidt 2.00 .60
32 Ichiro Suzuki 5.00 1.50
33 Scott Rolen 3.00 .90
34 Albert Pujols 6.00 1.80
35 Rocco Baldelli 2.00 .60
36 Alfonso Soriano 3.00 .90
37 Carlos Delgado 2.00 .60
38 Curt Schilling 3.00 .90
39 Mark Prior 3.00 .90
40 Josh Beckett 2.00 .60
41 Merkin Valdez ROO RC 8.00 2.40
42 Akinori Otsuka ROO RC 5.00 1.50
43 Ian Snell ROO RC 8.00 2.40
44 Kaz Matsui ROO RC 15.00 4.50
45 Jason Bartlett ROO RC 8.00 2.40
46 Dennis Sarfate ROO RC 5.00 1.50
47 Sean Henn ROO RC 5.00 1.50
48 David Aardsma ROO RC 5.00 1.50
49 Casey Kotchman ROO 5.00 1.50
50 John Gall ROO RC 8.00 2.40
51 William Bergolla ROO RC 5.00 1.50
52 Angel Chavez ROO RC 5.00 1.50
53 Hector Gimenez ROO RC 5.00 1.50
54 Aaron Baldiris ROO RC 8.00 2.40
55 Justin Leone ROO RC 8.00 2.40
56 Onil Joseph ROO RC 5.00 1.50
57 Freddy Guzman ROO RC 5.00 1.50
58 Andres Blanco ROO RC 5.00 1.50
59 Greg Dobbs ROO RC 5.00 1.50
60 Joe Mauer ROO 8.00 2.40
61 Luis Gonzalez ROO RC 5.00 1.50
62 Chris Saenz ROO RC 5.00 1.50
63 Zack Greinke ROO 5.00 1.50
64 Jose Capellan ROO RC 10.00 3.00
65 Brad Halsey ROO RC 8.00 2.40

2004 E-X Die Cuts

Nm-Mt Ex-Mt
*DIE CUTS 41-65: .5X TO 1.2X BASIC
41-65 OVERALL ODDS ONE PER PACK
STATED PRINT RUN 150 SERIAL #'d SETS
DIE CUTS ARE 1ST 150 SERIAL #'d COPIES

2004 E-X Essential Credentials Future

Nm-Mt Ex-Mt
*FUTURE p/r 51-65: 1.5X TO 4X BASIC
*FUTURE p/r 36-50: 2X TO 5X BASIC
*FUTURE p/r 26-35: 2.5X TO 6X BASIC
OVERALL PARALLEL ODDS 1:3
PRINT RUNS B/WN 1-65 COPIES PER
NO PRICING ON QTY OF 25 OR LESS

2004 E-X Essential Credentials Now

Nm-Mt Ex-Mt
*NOW p/r 51-65: .75X TO 2X BASIC
*NOW p/r 41-50: 1X TO 2.5X BASIC
*NOW p/r
*NOW p/r 26-35: 2.5X TO 6X BASIC
*NOW p/r 16-25: 3X TO 8X BASIC
OVERALL PARALLEL ODDS 1:3
PRINT RUNS B/WN 1-65 COPIES PER
NO PRICING ON QTY OF 14 OR LESS

2004 E-X Check Mates

The cards with the TBD's were not found in our analyst searching for cards in the product.

Nm-Mt Ex-Mt
OVERALL AUTO ODDS ONE PER PACK
PRINT RUNS B/WN 1-25 COPIES PER
NO PRICING ON QTY OF 1 COPY PER
EXCHANGE DEADLINE INDEFINITE
APSM Albert Pujols 400.00 120.00
Stan Musial/25
BRLG Babe Ruth
Lou Gehrig/1
CYDS Carl Yastrzemski
Duke Snider/25
EBRS Ernie Banks 200.00 60.00
Ryne Sandberg/25
EMRP Eddie Murray 150.00 45.00
Rafael Palmeiro/25
HWTC Honus Wagner
Ty Cobb/1
MRPM Manny Ramirez
Pedro Martinez/25
RJDM Reggie Jackson 250.00 75.00
Don Mattingly/25
RJGM Randy Johnson 250.00 75.00
Greg Maddux/25 EXCH
RYKP Robin Yount 200.00 60.00
Kirby Puckett/25 EXCH
WBTG Wade Boggs 175.00 52.50
Tony Gwynn/25
YBJB Yogi Berra
Johnny Bench/25

2004 E-X Classic ConnExions Game Used Double

Nm-Mt Ex-Mt
STATED PRINT RUN 22 SERIAL #'d SETS
DOUBLE EMERALD PRINT RUN 1 #'d SET
NO DOUBLE EMERALD PRICING AVAILABLE
OVERALL GU ODDS ONE PER PACK
BRJF Babe Ruth Bat 250.00 75.00
Jimmie Foxx Bat
CRBR Cal Ripken Jsy 150.00 45.00
Brooks Robinson Bat

CRNR Cal Ripken Jsy 150.00 45.00
Nolan Ryan Jsy
CRRY Cal Ripken Jsy 120.00 36.00
Robin Yount Jsy
DMRJ Don Mattingly Jsy 80.00 24.00
Reggie Jackson Jsy
DMTM Don Mattingly Jsy 100.00 30.00
Thurman Munson Jsy
DWCY Dave Winfield Jsy 50.00 15.00
Carl Yastrzemski Jsy
EMCR Eddie Murray Jsy 150.00 45.00
Cal Ripken Jsy
EMRJ Eddie Murray Jsy 60.00 18.00
Reggie Jackson Jsy
HKAK Harmon Killebrew Pants 60.00 18.00
Al Kaline Pants
HWHG Hack Wilson Bat 100.00 30.00
Hank Greenberg Bat
JBCF Johnny Bench Jsy 60.00 18.00
Carlton Fisk Pants
JCRH Jose Canseco Jsy 60.00 18.00
Rickey Henderson Jsy
KPDM Kirby Puckett Jsy 80.00 24.00
Don Mattingly Jsy
LBRC Lou Brock Jsy 40.00 12.00
Rod Carew Jsy
MSEM Mike Schmidt Jsy 150.00 45.00
Eddie Mathews Pants
NRTS Nolan Ryan Jsy 120.00 36.00
Tom Seaver Jsy
PMRY Paul Molitor Jsy 80.00 24.00
Robin Yount Jsy
RCRJ Rod Carew Jsy 40.00 12.00
Reggie Jackson Jsy
RHLB Rickey Henderson Jsy 60.00 18.00
Lou Brock Jsy
RMBR Roger Maris Bat 300.00 90.00
Babe Ruth Bat
TGRH Tony Gwynn Jsy 80.00 24.00
Rickey Henderson Jsy
TWCY Ted Williams Bat 200.00 60.00
Carl Yastrzemski Bat
WBCY Wade Boggs Bat 60.00 18.00
Carl Yastrzemski Jsy
WBDM Wade Boggs Jsy 60.00 18.00
Don Mattingly Jsy
WBTG Wade Boggs Bat 60.00 18.00
Tony Gwynn Jsy
WMWS Willie McCovey Bat 40.00 12.00
Willie Stargell Bat
WSWF Warren Spahn Jsy 40.00 12.00
Whitey Ford Pants
YBRC Yogi Berra Bat 60.00 18.00
Roy Campanella Bat

2004 E-X Classic ConnExions Game Used Triple

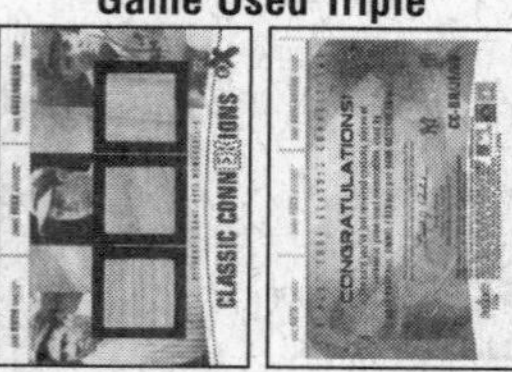

Nm-Mt Ex-Mt
STATED PRINT RUN 13 SERIAL #'d SETS
TRIPLE EMERALD PRINT RUN 1 #'d SET
NO TRIPLE EMERALD PRICING AVAILABLE
OVERALL GU ODDS ONE PER PACK
B = BAT, J = JSY, P = PANTS
BCB Yogi Berra Bat
Roy Campanella Bat
Johnny Bench Jsy
BCH Lou Brock Jsy
Rod Carew Jsy
Rickey Henderson Jsy
BGM Wade Boggs Bat
Tony Gwynn Jsy
Don Mattingly Jsy
KKY Harmon Killebrew Pants
Al Kaline Pants
Carl Yastrzemski Jsy
MMJ Don Mattingly Jsy
Thurman Munson Jsy
Reggie Jackson Jsy
RFG Babe Ruth Bat
Jimmie Foxx Bat
Hank Greenberg Bat
RMR Brooks Robinson Bat
Eddie Murray Jsy
Cal Ripken Jsy
SMR Mike Schmidt Jsy
Eddie Mathews Pants
Cal Ripken Jsy
WRF Ted Williams Bat
Babe Ruth Bat
Jimmie Foxx Bat
WYB Ted Williams Bat
Carl Yastrzemski Jsy
Wade Boggs Bat

2004 E-X Clearly Authentics Black Patch

Nm-Mt Ex-Mt
*3-COLOR PATCHES: ADD 20% PREMIUM
*4-COLOR PATCHES: ADD 50% PREMIUM
*5-COLOR PATCHES: ADD 100% PREMIUM
*JSY TAG PATCHES: ADD 100% PREMIUM
OVERALL GU ODDS ONE PER PACK

STATED PRINT RUN 75 SERIAL #'d SETS
AD Adam Dunn 20.00 6.00
AJ Andruw Jones 15.00 4.50
AP Albert Pujols 50.00 15.00
AR Alex Rodriguez 40.00 12.00
AS Alfonso Soriano 20.00 6.00
BG Brian Giles 15.00 4.50
BZ Barry Zito 15.00 4.50
CJ Chipper Jones 25.00 7.50
CR Cal Ripken 80.00 24.00
CS Curt Schilling 25.00 7.50
DM Don Mattingly 50.00 15.00
DW Dontrelle Willis 15.00 4.50
EG Eric Gagne 25.00 7.50
EM Eddie Murray 40.00 12.00
FT Frank Thomas 25.00 7.50
GM Greg Maddux 30.00 9.00
HB Hank Blalock 15.00 4.50
HM Hideki Matsui 60.00 18.00
HN Hideo Nomo 40.00 12.00
IR Ivan Rodriguez 25.00 7.50
JB Jeff Bagwell 20.00 6.00
JB2 Josh Beckett 15.00 4.50
JG2 Jason Giambi 15.00 4.50
JT Jim Thome 25.00 7.50
KM Kaz Matsui 50.00 15.00
KW Kerry Wood 25.00 7.50
LB Lance Berkman 15.00 4.50
MC Miguel Cabrera 20.00 6.00
MO Magglio Ordonez 15.00 4.50
MP Mark Prior 25.00 7.50
MP2 Mike Piazza 40.00 12.00
MR Manny Ramirez 20.00 6.00
MT Mark Teixeira 15.00 4.50
MT2 Miguel Tejada 15.00 4.50
OS Ozzie Smith 40.00 12.00
PB Pat Burrell 15.00 4.50
PM Paul Molitor 25.00 7.50
PR Pedro Martinez 25.00 7.50
RB Rocco Baldelli 15.00 4.50
RC Roger Clemens 40.00 12.00
RC2 Rod Carew 25.00 7.50
RH Rickey Henderson 30.00 9.00
RJ Randy Johnson 25.00 7.50
RP Rafael Palmeiro 20.00 6.00
RW Rickie Weeks 15.00 4.50
SG Shawn Green 15.00 4.50
SR Scott Rolen 25.00 7.50
SS Sammy Sosa 30.00 9.00
TG Troy Glaus 15.00 4.50
TG2 Tony Gwynn 40.00 12.00
TH Todd Helton 20.00 6.00
TH2 Torii Hunter 15.00 4.50
TH3 Tim Hudson 15.00 4.50
VG Vladimir Guerrero 25.00 7.50

2004 E-X Clearly Authentics Bronze Jersey-Patch

Nm-Mt Ex-Mt
*BRONZE JSY-PATCH: .6X TO 1.5X BASIC
*3-COLOR PATCHES: ADD 20% PREMIUM
*4-COLOR PATCHES: ADD 50% PREMIUM
*5-COLOR PATCHES: ADD 100% PREMIUM
*JSY TAG PATCHES: ADD 100% PREMIUM
OVERALL GU ODDS ONE PER PACK
STATED PRINT RUN 35 SERIAL #'d SETS
CY Carl Yastrzemski 60.00 18.00
RJ2 Reggie Jackson 40.00 12.00

2004 E-X Clearly Authentics Burgundy Triple Patch

Nm-Mt Ex-Mt
OVERALL GU ODDS ONE PER PACK
STATED PRINT RUN 13 SERIAL #'d SETS
NO PRICING DUE TO SCARCITY

2004 E-X Clearly Authentics Pewter Bat-Patch

Nm-Mt Ex-Mt
*PEWTER BAT-PATCH: .6X TO 1.5X BASIC
*3-COLOR PATCHES: ADD 20% PREMIUM
*4-COLOR PATCHES: ADD 50% PREMIUM
*5-COLOR PATCHES: ADD 100% PREMIUM
*JSY TAG PATCHES: ADD 100% PREMIUM
OVERALL GU ODDS ONE PER PACK
STATED PRINT RUN 44 SERIAL #'d SETS
CY Carl Yastrzemski 60.00 18.00
RJ2 Reggie Jackson 40.00 12.00

2004 E-X Clearly Authentics Royal Blue Bat-Jersey-Patch

Nm-Mt Ex-Mt
OVERALL GU ODDS ONE PER PACK
STATED PRINT RUN 8 SERIAL #'d SETS
NO PRICING DUE TO SCARCITY

2004 E-X Clearly Authentics Tan Double Patch

Nm-Mt Ex-Mt
*TAN DOUBLE PATCH: .75X TO 2X BASIC
*3-COLOR PATCHES: ADD 20% PREMIUM
*4-COLOR PATCHES: ADD 50% PREMIUM
*5-COLOR PATCHES: ADD 100% PREMIUM
*JSY TAG PATCHES: ADD 100% PREMIUM
OVERALL GU ODDS ONE PER PACK
STATED PRINT RUN 22 SERIAL #'d SETS
CY Carl Yastrzemski 80.00 24.00
RJ2 Reggie Jackson 50.00 15.00

2004 E-X Clearly Authentics Double MLB Logo

Nm-Mt Ex-Mt
OVERALL GU ODDS ONE PER PACK
STATED PRINT RUN 1 SERIAL #'d SET
NO PRICING DUE TO SCARCITY
AJCJ Andruw Jones
Chipper Jones
APSR Albert Pujols
Scott Rolen
ASAR Alfonso Soriano
Alex Rodriguez
BZTH Barry Zito
Tim Hudson
CSPM Curt Schilling
Pedro Martinez
FTMO Frank Thomas
Magglio Ordonez
GMMP Greg Maddux
Mark Prior
GMRC Greg Maddux
Roger Clemens
HBMT Hank Blalock
Mark Teixeira
HMJG Hideki Matsui
Jason Giambi
HNEG Hideo Nomo
Eric Gagne
HNHM Hideo Nomo
Hideki Matsui
IRMP Ivan Rodriguez
Mike Piazza
JTPB Jim Thome
Pat Burrell
KWMP Kerry Wood
Mark Prior
LBJB Lance Berkman
Jeff Bagwell
MGRP Mark Grace
Rafael Palmeiro
MRVG Manny Ramirez
Vladimir Guerrero
RJRC Randy Johnson
Roger Clemens
TGVG Troy Glaus
Vladimir Guerrero

2004 E-X Clearly Authentics Signature Black Jersey

Nm-Mt Ex-Mt
*3-COLOR PATCHES: ADD 20% PREMIUM
*4-COLOR PATCHES: ADD 50% PREMIUM
*5-COLOR PATCHES: ADD 100% PREMIUM
*JSY TAG PATCHES: ADD 100% PREMIUM
OVERALL AUTO ODDS ONE PER PACK
PRINT RUNS B/WN 17-50 COPIES PER
EXCHANGE DEADLINE INDEFINITE
AP Albert Pujols/50 200.00 60.00
BW Bernie Williams/42 50.00 15.00
BZ Barry Zito/18 40.00 12.00
CJ Chipper Jones/50 60.00 18.00
DW Dontrelle Willis/50 25.00 7.50
FT Frank Thomas/50 60.00 18.00
GM Greg Maddux/37 EXCH 80.00 24.00
GS Gary Sheffield/50 40.00 12.00
HB Hank Blalock/50 25.00 7.50
IR Ivan Rodriguez/50 50.00 15.00
JB Josh Beckett/50 40.00 12.00
JD J.D. Drew/50 40.00 12.00
KW Kerry Wood/34 60.00 18.00
MC Miguel Cabrera/50 40.00 12.00
MP1 Mike Piazza/37 120.00 36.00
MR1 Manny Ramirez/50 60.00 18.00
MR2 Mariano Rivera/50 80.00 24.00
PM Pedro Martinez/23 120.00 36.00
RC Roger Clemens/50 150.00 45.00
RJ Randy Johnson/17 120.00 36.00
RO Roy Oswalt/49 25.00 7.50
RP Rafael Palmeiro/43 60.00 18.00
TG Troy Glaus/50 40.00 12.00
TH Todd Helton/50 40.00 12.00
VG Vladimir Guerrero/50 60.00 18.00

2004 E-X Clearly Authentics Signature Emerald MLB Logo

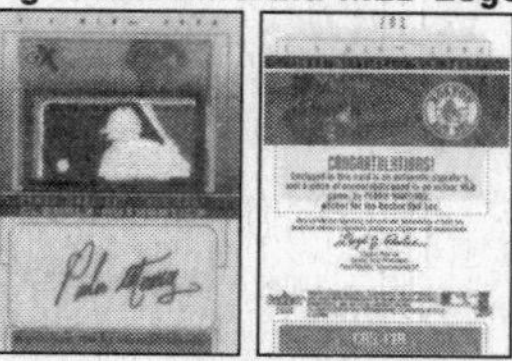

Nm-Mt Ex-Mt
OVERALL AUTO ODDS ONE PER PACK
STATED PRINT RUN 1 SERIAL #'d SET
NO PRICING DUE TO SCARCITY
EXCHANGE DEADLINE INDEFINITE

2004 E-X Clearly Authentics Signature Pewter Jersey

Nm-Mt Ex-Mt
*PTR p/r 36-41: .4X TO 1X BLK p/r 50
*PTR p/r 20-27: .5X TO 1.2X BLK p/r 50
*3-COLOR PATCHES: ADD 20% PREMIUM
*4-COLOR PATCHES: ADD 50% PREMIUM
*5-COLOR PATCHES: ADD 100% PREMIUM
*JSY TAG PATCHES: ADD 100% PREMIUM
OVERALL AUTO ODDS ONE PER PACK
PRINT RUNS B/WN 7-41 COPIES PER
NO PRICING ON QTY OF 10 OR LESS

2004 E-X Clearly Authentics Signature Tan Patch

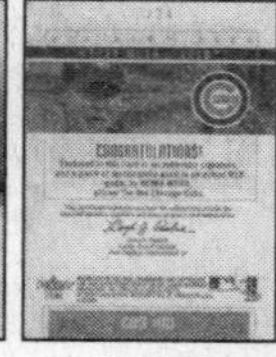

Nm-Mt Ex-Mt
*TAN p/r 75: .4X TO .1X BLK p/r 18
*TAN p/r 42-51: .6X TO 1.5X BLK p/r 42-50
*TAN p/r 42-51: .4X TO 1X BLK p/r 23
*TAN p/r 42-51: .4X TO 1X BLK p/r 17
*TAN p/r 21-35: .6X TO 1.5X BLK p/r 37-50
*TAN p/r 21-35: .5X TO 1.2X BLK p/r 34
*TAN p/r 17: .75X TO 2X BLK p/r 50
*3-COLOR PATCHES: ADD 20% PREMIUM
*4-COLOR PATCHES: ADD 50% PREMIUM
*5-COLOR PATCHES: ADD 100% PREMIUM
*JSY TAG PATCHES: ADD 100% PREMIUM
OVERALL AUTO ODDS ONE PER PACK
PRINT RUNS B/WN 5-75 COPIES PER
NO PRICING ON QTY OF 11 OR LESS
EXCHANGE DEADLINE INDEFINITE
RC Roger Clemens/22 200.00 60.00

2004 E-X ConnExions Dual Autograph

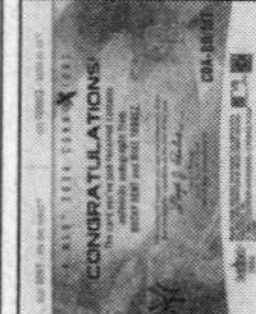

Nm-Mt Ex-Mt
OVERALL AUTO ODDS ONE PER PACK
PRINT RUNS B/WN 25-50 COPIES PER
EXCHANGE DEADLINE INDEFINITE
ABCB Adrian Beltre 100.00 30.00
Carlos Beltran/25
BBMW Bill Buckner 60.00 18.00
Mookie Wilson/50
BDMT Bucky Dent 50.00 15.00
Mike Torrez/50
BGMG Brian Giles 60.00 18.00
Marcus Giles/25
BJDS Bo Jackson
Deion Sanders/25
BZTH Barry Zito 80.00 24.00
Tim Hudson/25
CKJM Casey Kotchman 60.00 18.00
Joe Mauer/50
CLMO Carlos Lee 60.00 18.00
Magglio Ordonez/25
CWJW Craig Wilson 60.00 18.00
Jack Wilson/25
DWMC Dontrelle Willis 80.00 24.00
Miguel Cabrera/25
EGBW Eric Gagne 80.00 24.00
Billy Wagner/25 EXCH
JDTN Johnny Damon 100.00 30.00
Trot Nixon/25
JNPN Joe Niekro 50.00 15.00
Phil Niekro/50
KGDE Kirk Gibson 80.00 24.00
Dennis Eckersley/25
MTHB Mark Teixeira 80.00 24.00
Hank Blalock/25
MYKG Michael Young 80.00 24.00
Khalil Greene/50
RWDY Rickie Weeks 80.00 24.00
Delmon Young/25
SPLO Scott Podsednik 60.00 18.00
Lyle Overbay/25
SSTH Shannon Stewart 60.00 18.00
Torii Hunter/25

2004 E-X Double Barrel

Nm-Mt Ex-Mt
OVERALL GU ODDS ONE PER PACK
STATED PRINT RUN 1 SERIAL #'d SET
NO PRICING DUE TO SCARCITY
AJCJ Andruw Jones
Chipper Jones

AKAD Austin Kearns
Adam Dunn
BWGS Bernie Williams
Gary Sheffield
DMRJ Don Mattingly
Reggie Jackson
IRAR Ivan Rodriguez
Alex Rodriguez
KMHM Kaz Matsui
Hideki Matsui
KPTH Kirby Puckett
Torii Hunter
LBJB Lance Berkman
Jeff Bagwell
MPGC Mike Piazza
Gary Carter
MRSS Manny Ramirez
Sammy Sosa
MTHB Mark Teixeira
Hank Blalock
RCOC Roberto Clemente
Orlando Cepeda
RJCS Randy Johnson
Curt Schilling
RPJT Rafael Palmeiro
Jim Thome
TGVG Troy Glaus
Vladimir Guerrero
TWCY Ted Williams
Carl Yastrzemski
WBTG Wade Boggs
Tony Gwynn
WSWM Willie Stargell
Willie McCovey

2004 E-X Signings of the Times Best Year

	Nm-Mt	Ex-Mt
OVERALL AUTO ODDS ONE PER PACK		
PRINT RUNS B/WN 48-94 COPIES PER		
EXCHANGE DEADLINE INDEFINITE		
BJ Bo Jackson Jsy/89	60.00	18.00
CY Carl Yastrzemski Bat/67	80.00	24.00
DM Don Mattingly Jsy/85	80.00	24.00
DS Duke Snider Bat/55	50.00	15.00
DS2 Deion Sanders Jsy/92	60.00	18.00
EB Ernie Banks Bat/58	80.00	24.00
EM Eddie Murray Jsy/83	60.00	18.00
GB George Brett Jsy/80	100.00	30.00
JB Johnny Bench Jsy/72	60.00	18.00
JC Jose Canseco Jsy/88	50.00	15.00
KP Kirby Puckett Bat/88	60.00	18.00
MS Mike Schmidt Jsy/80	100.00	30.00
NR Nolan Ryan Jsy/73	150.00	45.00
OS Ozzie Smith Jsy/87	60.00	18.00
RH Rickey Henderson Jsy/90	80.00	24.00
RJ Reggie Jackson Jsy/73	60.00	18.00
RS Ryne Sandberg Bat/90	80.00	24.00
RY Robin Yount Jsy/82 EXCH	60.00	18.00
SM Stan Musial Bat/48	80.00	24.00
TG Tony Gwynn Jsy/94	60.00	18.00
TS Tom Seaver Jsy/69	50.00	15.00
WB Wade Boggs Bat/87	40.00	12.00
WC Will Clark Jsy/91	50.00	15.00
YB Yogi Berra Bat/54	80.00	24.00

2004 E-X Signings of the Times Debut Year

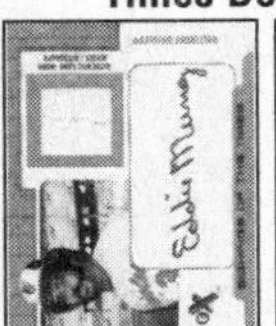

Nm-Mt Ex-Mt
*DEBUT p/r 66-89: .4X TO 1X BEST p/r 69-94
*DEBUT p/r 41-61: .4X TO 1X BEST p/r 48-58
OVERALL AUTO ODDS ONE PER PACK
PRINT RUNS B/WN 41-89 COPIES PER
EXCHANGE DEADLINE INDEFINITE ....

2004 E-X Signings of the Times HOF Year

	Nm-Mt	Ex-Mt
*HOF p/r 69-99: .4X TO 1X BEST p/r 67-82		
*HOF p/r 69-99: .6X TO .8X BEST p/r 48-58		
OVERALL AUTO ODDS ONE PER PACK		
PRINT RUNS B/WN 1-99 COPIES PER		
NO PRICING ON QTY OF 3 OR LESS..		
EXCHANGE DEADLINE INDEFINITE		
CY Carl Yastrzemski Bat/89	80.00	24.00
DS Duke Snider Bat/80	40.00	12.00
EB Ernie Banks Bat/77	60.00	18.00
EM Eddie Murray Jsy/3		

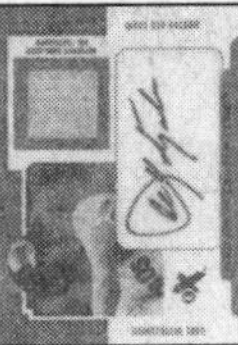

GB George Brett Jsy/99	100.00	30.00
JB Johnny Bench Jsy/89	60.00	18.00
KP Kirby Puckett Bat/1		
MS Mike Schmidt Jsy/95	100.00	30.00
NR Nolan Ryan Jsy/99	150.00	45.00
OS Ozzie Smith Jsy/2		
RJ Reggie Jackson Jsy/93	60.00	18.00
RY Robin Yount Jsy/99 EXCH	60.00	18.00
SM Stan Musial Bat/69	60.00	18.00
TS Tom Seaver Jsy/92	50.00	15.00
YB Yogi Berra Bat/72	60.00	18.00

2004 E-X Signings of the Times Pewter

Nm-Mt Ex-Mt
*PTR p/r 36-60: .5X TO 1.2X BEST p/r 83-92
*PTR p/r 36-60: .4X TO 1X BEST p/r 48
*PTR p/r 21-33: .6X TO 1.5X BEST p/r 85-94
*PTR p/r 21-33: .5X TO 1.2X BEST p/r 54-58
OVERALL AUTO ODDS ONE PER PACK
PRINT RUNS B/WN 21-60 COPIES PER

1993 Finest

This 199-card standard-size single series set is widely recognized as one of the most important issues of the 1990's. The Finest brand was Topps first attempt at the super-premium card market. Production was announced at 4,000 cases and cards were distributed exclusively through hobby dealers in the fall of 1993. This was the first time in the history of the hobby that a major manufacturer publicly released production figures. Cards were issued in seven-card foil fin-wrapped packs that carried a suggested retail price of $3.99. The product was a smashing success upon release with pack prices immediately soaring well above suggested retail prices. The popularity of the product has continued to grow throughout the years as it's place in hobby lore is now well solidified. The cards have silver-blue metallic finishes on their fronts and feature color player action photos. The set's title appears at the top, and the player's name is shown at the bottom. J.T. Snow is the only Rookie Card of note in this set.

	Nm-Mt	Ex-Mt
COMPLETE SET (199)	100.00	30.00
1 David Justice	2.50	.75
2 Lou Whitaker	2.50	.75
3 Bryan Harvey	1.50	.45
4 Carlos Garcia	1.50	.45
5 Sid Fernandez	1.50	.45
6 Brett Butler	2.50	.75
7 Scott Cooper	1.50	.45
8 B.J. Surhoff	2.50	.75
9 Steve Finley	2.50	.75
10 Curt Schilling	2.50	.75
11 Jeff Bagwell	4.00	1.20
12 Alex Cole	1.50	.45
13 John Olerud	2.50	.75
14 John Smiley	1.50	.45
15 Bip Roberts	1.50	.45
16 Albert Belle	2.50	.75
17 Duane Ward	1.50	.45
18 Alan Trammell	2.50	.75
19 Andy Benes	1.50	.45
20 Reggie Sanders	1.50	.45
21 Todd Zeile	1.50	.45
22 Rick Aguilera	1.50	.45
23 Dave Hollins	1.50	.45
24 Jose Rijo	1.50	.45
25 Matt Williams	2.50	.75
26 Sandy Alomar Jr.	1.50	.45
27 Alex Fernandez	1.50	.45
28 Ozzie Smith	10.00	3.00
29 Ramon Martinez	1.50	.45
30 Bernie Williams	4.00	1.20
31 Gary Sheffield	2.50	.75
32 Eric Karros	2.50	.75
33 Frank Viola	2.50	.75
34 Kevin Young	2.50	.75
35 Ken Hill	1.50	.45
36 Tony Fernandez	1.50	.45
37 Tim Wakefield	4.00	1.20
38 John Kruk	2.50	.75
39 Chris Sabo	1.50	.45
40 Marquis Grissom	2.50	.75
41 Glenn Davis	1.50	.45
42 Jeff Montgomery	1.50	.45
43 Kenny Lofton	2.50	.75
44 John Burkett	1.50	.45
45 Darryl Hamilton	1.50	.45
46 Jim Abbott	4.00	1.20
47 Ivan Rodriguez	6.00	1.80
48 Eric Young	1.50	.45
49 Mitch Williams	1.50	.45
50 Harold Reynolds	2.50	.75
51 Brian Harper	1.50	.45
52 Rafael Palmeiro	4.00	1.20
53 Bret Saberhagen	2.50	.75
54 Jeff Conine	2.50	.75
55 Ivan Calderon	1.50	.45
56 Juan Guzman	1.50	.45
57 Carlos Baerga	1.50	.45
58 Charles Nagy	1.50	.45
59 Wally Joyner	2.50	.75
60 Charlie Hayes	1.50	.45
61 Shane Mack	1.50	.45
62 Pete Harnisch	1.50	.45
63 George Brett	15.00	4.50
64 Lance Johnson	1.50	.45
65 Ben McDonald	1.50	.45
66 Bobby Bonilla	2.50	.75
67 Terry Steinbach	1.50	.45
68 Ron Gant	2.50	.75
69 Doug Jones	1.50	.45
70 Paul Molitor	4.00	1.20
71 Brady Anderson	2.50	.75
72 Chuck Finley	2.50	.75
73 Mark Grace	4.00	1.20
74 Mike Devereaux	1.50	.45
75 Tony Phillips	1.50	.45
76 Chuck Knoblauch	2.50	.75
77 Tony Gwynn	8.00	2.40
78 Kevin Appier	2.50	.75
79 Sammy Sosa	10.00	3.00
80 Mickey Tettleton	1.50	.45
81 Felix Jose	1.50	.45
82 Mark Langston	1.50	.45
83 Gregg Jefferies	1.50	.45
84 Andre Dawson AS	2.50	.75
85 Greg Maddux AS	10.00	3.00
86 Rickey Henderson AS	6.00	1.80
87 Tom Glavine AS	4.00	1.20
88 Roberto Alomar AS	4.00	1.20
89 Darryl Strawberry AS	2.50	.75
90 Wade Boggs AS	4.00	1.20
91 Bo Jackson AS	6.00	1.80
92 Mark McGwire AS	15.00	4.50
93 Robin Ventura AS	2.50	.75
94 Joe Carter AS	2.50	.75
95 Lee Smith AS	2.50	.75
96 Cal Ripken AS	20.00	6.00
97 Larry Walker AS	4.00	1.20
98 Don Mattingly AS	15.00	4.50
99 Jose Canseco AS	6.00	1.80
100 Dennis Eckersley AS	2.50	.75
101 Terry Pendleton AS	2.50	.75
102 Frank Thomas AS	6.00	1.80
103 Barry Bonds AS	15.00	4.50
104 Roger Clemens AS	12.00	3.60
105 Ryne Sandberg AS	10.00	3.00
106 Fred McGriff AS	4.00	1.20
107 Nolan Ryan AS	25.00	7.50
108 Will Clark AS	6.00	1.80
109 Pat Listach AS	1.50	.45
110 Ken Griffey Jr. AS	10.00	3.00
111 Cecil Fielder AS	2.50	.75
112 Kirby Puckett AS	6.00	1.80
113 Dwight Gooden AS	2.50	.75
114 Barry Larkin AS	4.00	1.20
115 David Cone AS	2.50	.75
116 Juan Gonzalez AS	4.00	1.20
117 Kent Hrbek	2.50	.75
118 Tim Wallach	1.50	.45
119 Craig Biggio	4.00	1.20
120 Roberto Kelly	1.50	.45
121 Gregg Olson	1.50	.45
122 Eddie Murray UER 122 career strikeouts should be 1224	6.00	1.80
123 Wil Cordero	1.50	.45
124 Jay Buhner	2.50	.75
125 Carlton Fisk	4.00	1.20
126 Eric Davis	2.50	.75
127 Doug Drabek	1.50	.45
128 Ozzie Guillen	1.50	.45
129 John Wetteland	2.50	.75
130 Andres Galarraga	2.50	.75
131 Ken Caminiti	2.50	.75
132 Tom Candiotti	1.50	.45
133 Pat Borders	1.50	.45
134 Kevin Brown	2.50	.75
135 Travis Fryman	2.50	.75
136 Kevin Mitchell	1.50	.45
137 Greg Swindell	1.50	.45
138 Benito Santiago	2.50	.75
139 Reggie Jefferson	1.50	.45
140 Chris Bosio	1.50	.45
141 Deion Sanders	4.00	1.20
142 Scott Erickson	1.50	.45
143 Howard Johnson	1.50	.45
144 Orestes Destrade	1.50	.45
145 Jose Guzman	1.50	.45
146 Chad Curtis	1.50	.45
147 Cal Eldred	1.50	.45
148 Willie Greene	1.50	.45
149 Tommy Greene	1.50	.45
150 Erik Hanson	1.50	.45
151 Bob Welch	1.50	.45
152 John Jaha	1.50	.45
153 Harold Baines	2.50	.75
154 Randy Johnson	6.00	1.80
155 Al Martin	1.50	.45
156 J.T. Snow RC	4.00	1.20
157 Mike Mussina	4.00	1.20
158 Ruben Sierra	1.50	.45
159 Dean Palmer	2.50	.75
160 Steve Avery	1.50	.45
161 Julio Franco	2.50	.75
162 Dave Winfield	2.50	.75
163 Tim Salmon	4.00	1.20
164 Tom Henke	1.50	.45
165 Mo Vaughn	2.50	.75
166 John Smoltz	4.00	1.20
167 Danny Tartabull	1.50	.45
168 Delino DeShields	1.50	.45
169 Charlie Hough	2.50	.75
170 Paul O'Neill	4.00	1.20
171 Darren Daulton	2.50	.75
172 Jack McDowell	1.50	.45
173 Junior Felix	1.50	.45
174 Jimmy Key	2.50	.75
175 George Bell	1.50	.45
176 Mike Stanton	1.50	.45
177 Len Dykstra	2.50	.75
178 Norm Charlton	1.50	.45
179 Eric Anthony	1.50	.45
180 Rob Dibble	2.50	.75
181 Otis Nixon	1.50	.45
182 Randy Myers	1.50	.45
183 Tim Raines	2.50	.75
184 Orel Hershiser	2.50	.75
185 Andy Van Slyke	2.50	.75
186 Mike Lansing RC	2.50	.75
187 Ray Lankford	1.50	.45
188 Mike Morgan	1.50	.45
189 Moises Alou	2.50	.75
190 Edgar Martinez	4.00	1.20
191 John Franco	2.50	.75
192 Robin Yount	10.00	3.00
193 Bob Tewksbury	1.50	.45
194 Jay Bell	2.50	.75
195 Luis Gonzalez	2.50	.75
196 Dave Fleming	1.50	.45
197 Mike Greenwell	1.50	.45
198 David Nied	1.50	.45
199 Mike Piazza	15.00	4.50

1993 Finest Refractors

Randomly inserted in packs at a rate of one in 18, these 199 standard-size cards are identical to the regular-issue 1993 Topps Finest except that their fronts have been laminated with a plastic diffraction grating that gives the card a colorful 3-D appearance. Because of the known production numbers, these cards are believed to have a print run of 241 of each card. It is believed that there might be short printed cards in this set. Topps, however, has never publicly released any verification of shortprinted singles, but some of the singles are accepted as being tough to find due to poor regional distribution and hoarding. Due to their high value, these cards are extremely condition sensitive, with much attention paid to centering and minor scratches on the card fronts.

	Nm-Mt	Ex-Mt
28 Ozzie Smith	120.00	36.00
41 Glenn Davis*	120.00	36.00
47 Ivan Rodriguez *	200.00	60.00
63 George Brett	200.00	60.00
77 Tony Gwynn	120.00	36.00
79 Sammy Sosa *	200.00	60.00
81 Felix Jose*	100.00	30.00
85 Greg Maddux AS	200.00	60.00
88 Roberto Alomar AS	100.00	30.00
91 Bo Jackson AS	120.00	36.00
92 Mark McGwire AS	400.00	120.00
96 Cal Ripken AS	800.00	240.00
98 Don Mattingly AS	250.00	75.00
99 Jose Canseco AS !	120.00	36.00
102 Frank Thomas AS	250.00	75.00
103 Barry Bonds AS	500.00	150.00
104 Roger Clemens AS	200.00	60.00
105 Ryne Sandberg AS	150.00	45.00
107 Nolan Ryan AS !	700.00	210.00
108 Will Clark AS	120.00	36.00
110 Ken Griffey Jr. AS !	400.00	120.00
112 Kirby Puckett AS	120.00	36.00
114 Barry Larkin AS	100.00	30.00
116 Juan Gonzalez AS *	250.00	75.00
122 Eddie Murray UER 122 career strikeouts should be 1224	120.00	36.00
154 Randy Johnson	150.00	45.00
157 Mike Mussina	100.00	30.00
192 Robin Yount	120.00	36.00
199 Mike Piazza	250.00	75.00

1993 Finest Jumbos

These oversized (approximately 4" by 6") cards were inserted one per sealed box of 1993 Topps Finest packs and feature reproductions of 33 players from that set's All-Star subset (84-116). Some hobby dealers believe because of the known production numbers that slightly less than 1,500 of each of these cards were produced.

	Nm-Mt	Ex-Mt
COMPLETE SET (33)	500.00	150.00
*STARS: 1X TO 2.5X BASIC CARDS...		

1994 Finest Pre-Production

This 40-card preview standard-size set is identical in design to the basic Finest set. Cards were randomly inserted at a rate of one in 36 in second series Topps packs and three cards were issued with each Topps factory set. The card numbers on back correspond to those of the regular issue. The only way to distinguish between the preview and basic cards is "Pre-Production" in small red letters on back.

	Nm-Mt	Ex-Mt
COMPLETE SET (40)	150.00	45.00
22P Deion Sanders	12.00	3.60
23P Jose Offerman	5.00	1.50
26P Alex Fernandez	5.00	1.50
31P Steve Finley	8.00	2.40
35P Andres Galarraga	8.00	2.40
43P Reggie Sanders	5.00	1.50
47P Dave Hollins	5.00	1.50
52P David Cone	8.00	2.40
59P Dante Bichette	8.00	2.40
61P Orlando Merced	5.00	1.50
62P Brian McRae	5.00	1.50
66P Mike Mussina	12.00	3.60
76P Mike Stanley	5.00	1.50
78P Mark McGwire	50.00	15.00
79P Pat Listach	5.00	1.50
82P Dwight Gooden	8.00	2.40
84P Phil Plantier	5.00	1.50
90P Jeff Russell	5.00	1.50
92P Gregg Jefferies	5.00	1.50
93P Jose Guzman	5.00	1.50
100P John Smoltz	12.00	3.60
102P Jim Thome	20.00	6.00
121P Moises Alou	8.00	2.40
125P Devon White	8.00	2.40
126P Ivan Rodriguez	20.00	6.00
130P Dave Magadan	5.00	1.50
136P Ozzie Smith	30.00	9.00
141P Chris Hoiles	5.00	1.50
149P Jim Abbott	12.00	3.60
151P Bill Swift	5.00	1.50
154P Edgar Martinez	12.00	3.60
157P J.T. Snow	8.00	2.40
159P Alan Trammell	8.00	2.40
163P Roberto Kelly	5.00	1.50
166P Scott Erickson	5.00	1.50
168P Scott Cooper	5.00	1.50
169P Rod Beck	5.00	1.50
177P Dean Palmer	8.00	2.40
182P Todd Van Poppel	5.00	1.50
185P Paul Sorrento	5.00	1.50

1994 Finest

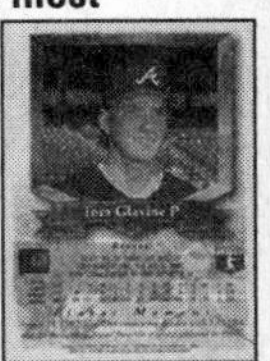

The 1994 Topps Finest baseball set consists of two series of 220 cards each, for a total of 440 standard-size cards. Each series includes 40 special design Finest cards: 20 top 1993 rookies (1-20), 20 top 1994 rookies (421-440) and 40 top veterans (201-240). It's believed that these subset cards are in slightly shorter supply than the basic issue cards, but the manufacturer has never confirmed this. These glossy and metallic cards have a color photo on front with green and gold borders. A color photo on back is accompanied by statistics and a "Finest Moment" note. Some series 2 packs contained either one or two series 1 cards. The only notable Rookie Card is Chan Ho Park.

	Nm-Mt	Ex-Mt
COMPLETE SET (440)	120.00	36.00
COMP. SERIES 1 (220)	60.00	18.00
COMP. SERIES 2 (220)	60.00	18.00
1 Mike Piazza FIN	6.00	1.80
2 Kevin Stocker FIN	.75	.23
3 Greg McMichael FIN	.75	.23
4 Jeff Conine FIN	1.25	.35
5 Rene Arocha FIN	.75	.23
6 Aaron Sele FIN	.75	.23
7 Brent Gates FIN	.75	.23
8 Chuck Carr FIN	.75	.23
9 Kirk Rueter FIN	1.25	.35
10 Mike Lansing FIN	.75	.23
11 Al Martin FIN	.75	.23
12 Jason Bere FIN	.75	.23
13 Troy Neel FIN	.75	.23
14 Armando Reynoso FIN	.75	.23
15 Jeromy Burnitz FIN	1.25	.35
16 Rich Amaral FIN	.75	.23
17 David McCarty FIN	.75	.23
18 Tim Salmon FIN	2.00	.60
19 Steve Cooke FIN	.75	.23
20 Wil Cordero FIN	.75	.23
21 Kevin Tapani	.75	.23
22 Deion Sanders	2.00	.60
23 Jose Offerman	.75	.23
24 Mark Langston	.75	.23
25 Ken Hill	.75	.23
26 Alex Fernandez	.75	.23
27 Jeff Blauser	.75	.23
28 Royce Clayton	.75	.23
29 Brad Ausmus	.75	.23
30 Ryan Bowen	.75	.23
31 Steve Finley	1.25	.35
32 Charlie Hayes	.75	.23
33 Jeff Kent	1.25	.35
34 Mike Henneman	.75	.23
35 Andres Galarraga	1.25	.35
36 Wayne Kirby	.75	.23
37 Joe Oliver	.75	.23
38 Terry Steinbach	.75	.23
39 Ryan Thompson	.75	.23
40 Luis Alicea	.75	.23
41 Randy Velarde	.75	.23
42 Bob Tewksbury	.75	.23
43 Reggie Sanders	.75	.23
44 Brian Williams	.75	.23
45 Joe Orsulak	.75	.23
46 Jose Lind	.75	.23
47 Dave Hollins	.75	.23
48 Graeme Lloyd	.75	.23
49 Jim Gott	.75	.23
50 Andre Dawson	1.25	.35
51 Steve Buechele	.75	.23
52 David Cone	1.25	.35
53 Ricky Gutierrez	.75	.23
54 Lance Johnson	.75	.23
55 Tino Martinez	2.00	.60
56 Phil Hiatt	.75	.23
57 Carlos Garcia	.75	.23
58 Danny Darwin	.75	.23
59 Dante Bichette	1.25	.35
60 Scott Kamieniecki	.75	.23
61 Orlando Merced	.75	.23
62 Brian McRae	.75	.23
63 Pat Kelly	.75	.23
64 Tom Henke	.75	.23
65 Jeff King	.75	.23
66 Mike Mussina	2.00	.60
67 Tim Pugh	.75	.23
68 Robby Thompson	.75	.23
69 Paul O'Neill	2.00	.60
70 Hal Morris	.75	.23
71 Ron Karkovice	.75	.23
72 Joe Girardi	.75	.23
73 Eduardo Perez	.75	.23
74 Raul Mondesi	1.25	.35
75 Mike Gallego	.75	.23
76 Mike Stanley	.75	.23
77 Kevin Roberson	.75	.23
78 Mark McGwire	8.00	2.40
79 Pat Listach	.75	.23

80 Eric Davis 1.25 .35
81 Mike Bordick .75 .23
82 Dwight Gooden 1.25 .35
83 Mike Moore .75 .23
84 Phil Plantier .75 .23
85 Darren Lewis .75 .23
86 Rick Wilkins .75 .23
87 Darryl Strawberry 1.25 .35
88 Rob Dibble 1.25 .35
89 Greg Vaughn .75 .23
90 Jeff Russell .75 .23
91 Mark Lewis .75 .23
92 Gregg Jefferies .75 .23
93 Jose Guzman .75 .23
94 Kenny Rogers 1.25 .35
95 Mark Lemke .75 .23
96 Mike Morgan .75 .23
97 Andujar Cedeno .75 .23
98 Orel Hershiser 1.25 .35
99 Greg Swindell .75 .23
100 John Smoltz 2.00 .60
101 Pedro A.Martinez RC .75 .23
102 Jim Thome 3.00 .90
103 David Segui .75 .23
104 Charles Nagy .75 .23
105 Shane Mack .75 .23
106 John Jaha .75 .23
107 Tom Candiotti .75 .23
108 David Wells 1.25 .35
109 Bobby Jones .75 .23
110 Bob Hamelin .75 .23
111 Bernard Gilkey .75 .23
112 Chili Davis 1.25 .35
113 Todd Stottlemyre .75 .23
114 Derek Bell .75 .23
115 Mark McLemore .75 .23
116 Mark Whiten .75 .23
117 Mike Devereaux .75 .23
118 Terry Pendleton 1.25 .35
119 Pat Meares .75 .23
120 Pete Harnisch .75 .23
121 Moises Alou 1.25 .35
122 Jay Buhner 1.25 .35
123 Wes Chamberlain .75 .23
124 Mike Perez .75 .23
125 Devon White 1.25 .35
126 Ivan Rodriguez 3.00 .90
127 Don Slaught .75 .23
128 John Valentin .75 .23
129 Jaime Navarro .75 .23
130 Dave Magadan .75 .23
131 Brady Anderson 1.25 .35
132 Juan Guzman .75 .23
133 John Wetteland 1.25 .35
134 Dave Stewart 1.25 .35
135 Scott Servais .75 .23
136 Ozzie Smith 5.00 1.50
137 Darrin Fletcher .75 .23
138 Jose Mesa .75 .23
139 Wilson Alvarez .75 .23
140 Pete Incaviglia .75 .23
141 Chris Hoiles .75 .23
142 Darryl Hamilton .75 .23
143 Chuck Finley 1.25 .35
144 Archi Cianfrocco .75 .23
145 Bill Wegman .75 .23
146 Joey Cora .75 .23
147 Darrell Whitmore .75 .23
148 David Hulse .75 .23
149 Jim Abbott 2.00 .60
150 Curt Schilling 1.25 .35
151 Bill Swift .75 .23
152 Tommy Greene .75 .23
153 Roberto Mejia .75 .23
154 Edgar Martinez 2.00 .60
155 Roger Pavlik .75 .23
156 Randy Tomlin .75 .23
157 J.T. Snow 1.25 .35
158 Bob Welch .75 .23
159 Alan Trammell 1.25 .35
160 Ed Sprague .75 .23
161 Ben McDonald .75 .23
162 Derrick May .75 .23
163 Roberto Kelly .75 .23
164 Bryan Harvey .75 .23
165 Ron Gant 1.25 .35
166 Scott Erickson .75 .23
167 Anthony Young .75 .23
168 Scott Cooper .75 .23
169 Rod Beck .75 .23
170 John Franco 1.25 .35
171 Gary DiSarcina .75 .23
172 Dave Fleming .75 .23
173 Wade Boggs 2.00 .60
174 Kevin Appier 1.25 .35
175 Jose Bautista .75 .23
176 Wally Joyner 1.25 .35
177 Dean Palmer 1.25 .35
178 Tony Phillips .75 .23
179 John Smiley .75 .23
180 Charlie Hough 1.25 .35
181 Scott Fletcher .75 .23
182 Todd Van Poppel .75 .23
183 Mike Blowers .75 .23
184 Willie McGee 1.25 .35
185 Paul Sorrento .75 .23
186 Eric Young .75 .23
187 Bret Barberie .75 .23
188 Manuel Lee .75 .23
189 Jeff Branson .75 .23
190 Jim Deshaies .75 .23
191 Ken Caminiti 1.25 .35
192 Tim Raines 1.25 .35
193 Joe Grahe .75 .23
194 Hipolito Pichardo .75 .23
195 Denny Neagle 1.25 .35
196 Jeff Gardner .75 .23
197 Mike Benjamin .75 .23
198 Milt Thompson .75 .23
199 Bruce Ruffin .75 .23
200 Chris Hammond UER .75 .23
(Back of card has Mariners; should be Marlins)
201 Tony Gwynn FIN 4.00 1.20
202 Robin Ventura FIN 1.25 .35
203 Frank Thomas FIN 3.00 .90
204 Kirby Puckett FIN 3.00 .90
205 Roberto Alomar FIN 2.00 .60
206 Dennis Eckersley FIN 1.25 .35
207 Joe Carter FIN 1.25 .35
208 Albert Belle FIN 1.25 .35
209 Greg Maddux FIN 5.00 1.50
210 Ryne Sandberg FIN 5.00 1.50
211 Juan Gonzalez FIN 2.00 .60
212 Jeff Bagwell FIN 2.00 .60
213 Randy Johnson FIN 3.00 .90
214 Matt Williams FIN 1.25 .35
215 Dave Winfield FIN 1.25 .35
216 Larry Walker FIN 2.00 .60
217 Roger Clemens FIN 6.00 1.80
218 Kenny Lofton FIN 1.25 .35
219 Cecil Fielder FIN 1.25 .35
220 Darren Daulton FIN 1.25 .35
221 John Olerud FIN 1.25 .35
222 Jose Canseco FIN 3.00 .90
223 Rickey Henderson FIN 3.00 .90
224 Fred McGriff FIN 2.00 .60
225 Gary Sheffield FIN 1.25 .35
226 Jack McDowell FIN .75 .23
227 Rafael Palmeiro FIN 2.00 .60
228 Travis Fryman FIN 1.25 .35
229 Marquis Grissom FIN 1.25 .35
230 Barry Bonds FIN 8.00 2.40
231 Carlos Baerga FIN .75 .23
232 Ken Griffey Jr. FIN 5.00 1.50
233 David Justice FIN 1.25 .35
234 Bobby Bonilla FIN 1.25 .35
235 Cal Ripken FIN 10.00 3.00
236 Sammy Sosa FIN 5.00 1.50
237 Len Dykstra FIN 1.25 .35
238 Will Clark FIN 3.00 .90
239 Paul Molitor FIN 2.00 .60
240 Barry Larkin FIN 2.00 .60
241 Bo Jackson 3.00 .90
242 Mitch Williams .75 .23
243 Ron Darling .75 .23
244 Darryl Kile 1.25 .35
245 Geronimo Berroa .75 .23
246 Gregg Olson .75 .23
247 Brian Harper .75 .23
248 Rheal Cormier .75 .23
249 Rey Sanchez .75 .23
250 Jeff Fassero .75 .23
251 Sandy Alomar Jr. .75 .23
252 Chris Bosio .75 .23
253 Andy Stankiewicz .75 .23
254 Harold Baines 1.25 .35
255 Andy Ashby .75 .23
256 Tyler Green .75 .23
257 Kevin Brown 1.25 .35
258 Mo Vaughn 1.25 .35
259 Mike Harkey .75 .23
260 Dave Henderson .75 .23
261 Kent Hrbek 1.25 .35
262 Darrin Jackson .75 .23
263 Bob Wickman .75 .23
264 Spike Owen .75 .23
265 Todd Jones .75 .23
266 Pat Borders .75 .23
267 Tom Glavine 2.00 .60
268 Dave Nilsson .75 .23
269 Rich Batchelor .75 .23
270 Delino DeShields .75 .23
271 Felix Fermin .75 .23
272 Orestes Destrade .75 .23
273 Mickey Morandini .75 .23
274 Otis Nixon .75 .23
275 Ellis Burks 1.25 .35
276 Greg Gagne .75 .23
277 John Doherty .75 .23
278 Julio Franco 1.25 .35
279 Bernie Williams 2.00 .60
280 Rick Aguilera .75 .23
281 Mickey Tettleton .75 .23
282 David Nied .75 .23
283 Johnny Ruffin .75 .23
284 Dan Wilson .75 .23
285 Omar Vizquel 2.00 .60
286 Willie Banks .75 .23
287 Erik Pappas .75 .23
288 Cal Eldred .75 .23
289 Bobby Witt .75 .23
290 Luis Gonzalez 1.25 .35
291 Greg Pirkl .75 .23
292 Alex Cole .75 .23
293 Ricky Bones .75 .23
294 Denis Boucher .75 .23
295 John Burkett .75 .23
296 Steve Trachsel .75 .23
297 Ricky Jordan .75 .23
298 Mark Dewey .75 .23
299 Jimmy Key 1.25 .35
300 Mike Macfarlane .75 .23
301 Tim Belcher .75 .23
302 Carlos Reyes .75 .23
303 Greg A. Harris .75 .23
304 Brian Anderson RC 1.25 .35
305 Terry Mulholland .75 .23
306 Felix Jose .75 .23
307 Darren Holmes .75 .23
308 Jose Rijo .75 .23
309 Paul Wagner .75 .23
310 Bob Scanlan .75 .23
311 Mike Jackson .75 .23
312 Jose Vizcaino .75 .23
313 Rob Butler .75 .23
314 Kevin Seitzer .75 .23
315 Geronimo Pena .75 .23
316 Hector Carrasco .75 .23
317 Eddie Murray 3.00 .90
318 Roger Salkeld .75 .23
319 Todd Hundley .75 .23
320 Danny Jackson .75 .23
321 Kevin Young .75 .23
322 Mike Greenwell .75 .23
323 Kevin Mitchell .75 .23
324 Chuck Knoblauch 1.25 .35
325 Danny Tartabull .75 .23
326 Vince Coleman .75 .23
327 Marvin Freeman .75 .23
328 Andy Benes .75 .23
329 Mike Kelly .75 .23
330 Karl Rhodes .75 .23
331 Allen Watson .75 .23
332 Damion Easley .75 .23
333 Reggie Jefferson .75 .23
334 Kevin McReynolds .75 .23
335 Arthur Rhodes .75 .23
336 Brian R. Hunter .75 .23
337 Tom Browning .75 .23
338 Pedro Munoz .75 .23
339 Billy Ripken .75 .23
340 Gene Harris .75 .23
341 Fernando Vina .75 .23
342 Sean Berry .75 .23
343 Pedro Astacio .75 .23
344 B.J. Surhoff 1.25 .35
345 Doug Drabek .75 .23
346 Jody Reed .75 .23
347 Ray Lankford .75 .23
348 Steve Farr .75 .23
349 Eric Anthony .75 .23
350 Pete Smith .75 .23
351 Lee Smith 1.25 .35
352 Mariano Duncan .75 .23
353 Doug Strange .75 .23
354 Tim Bogar .75 .23
355 Dave Weathers .75 .23
356 Eric Karros 1.25 .35
357 Randy Myers .75 .23
358 Chad Curtis .75 .23
359 Steve Avery .75 .23
360 Brian Jordan 1.25 .35
361 Tim Wallach .75 .23
362 Pedro Martinez 3.00 .90
363 Bip Roberts .75 .23
364 Lou Whitaker 1.25 .35
365 Luis Polonia .75 .23
366 Benito Santiago 1.25 .35
367 Brett Butler 1.25 .35
368 Shawon Dunston .75 .23
369 Kelly Stinnett RC 1.25 .35
370 Chris Turner .75 .23
371 Ruben Sierra .75 .23
372 Greg A. Harris .75 .23
373 Xavier Hernandez .75 .23
374 Howard Johnson .75 .23
375 Duane Ward .75 .23
376 Roberto Hernandez .75 .23
377 Scott Leius .75 .23
378 Dave Valle .75 .23
379 Sid Fernandez .75 .23
380 Doug Jones .75 .23
381 Zane Smith .75 .23
382 Craig Biggio 2.00 .60
383 Rick White RC .75 .23
384 Tom Pagnozzi .75 .23
385 Chris James .75 .23
386 Bret Boone 1.25 .35
387 Jeff Montgomery 1.25 .35
388 Chad Kreuter .75 .23
389 Greg Hibbard .75 .23
390 Mark Grace 2.00 .60
391 Phil Leftwich RC .75 .23
392 Don Mattingly 8.00 2.40
393 Ozzie Guillen .75 .23
394 Gary Gaetti 1.25 .35
395 Erik Hanson .75 .23
396 Scott Brosius 1.25 .35
397 Tom Gordon .75 .23
398 Bill Gullickson .75 .23
399 Matt Mieske .75 .23
400 Pat Hentgen .75 .23
401 Walt Weiss .75 .23
402 Greg Blosser .75 .23
403 Stan Javier .75 .23
404 Doug Henry .75 .23
405 Ramon Martinez .75 .23
406 Frank Viola 1.25 .35
407 Mike Hampton 1.25 .35
408 Andy Van Slyke 1.25 .35
409 Bobby Ayala .75 .23
410 Todd Zeile .75 .23
411 Jay Bell 1.25 .35
412 Dennis Martinez 1.25 .35
413 Mark Portugal .75 .23
414 Bobby Munoz .75 .23
415 Kirt Manwaring .75 .23
416 John Kruk 1.25 .35
417 Trevor Hoffman 1.25 .35
418 Chris Sabo .75 .23
419 Bret Saberhagen 1.25 .35
420 Chris Nabholz .75 .23
421 James Mouton FIN .75 .23
422 Tony Tarasco FIN .75 .23
423 Carlos Delgado FIN 2.00 .60
424 Rondell White FIN 1.25 .35
425 Javier Lopez FIN 1.25 .35
426 Chan Ho Park FIN RC 2.00 .60
427 Cliff Floyd FIN 1.25 .35
428 Dave Staton FIN .75 .23
429 J.R. Phillips FIN .75 .23
430 Manny Ramirez FIN 2.00 .60
431 Kurt Abbott FIN RC 1.25 .35
432 Melvin Nieves FIN .75 .23
433 Alex Gonzalez FIN .75 .23
434 Rick Helling FIN .75 .23
435 Danny Bautista FIN .75 .23
436 Matt Walbeck FIN .75 .23
437 Ryan Klesko FIN 1.25 .35
438 Steve Karsay FIN .75 .23
439 Salomon Torres FIN .75 .23
440 Scott Ruffcorn FIN .75 .23

1994 Finest Refractors

The 1994 Topps Finest Refractors baseball set consists of two series of 220 cards each, for a total of 440 cards. These special cards were inserted at a rate of one in every nine packs. They are identical to the basic Finest card except for a more intense luster and 3-D appearance.

Nm-Mt Ex-Mt
*STARS: 2.5X TO 6X BASIC CARDS...
*ROOKIES: 1.5X TO 4X BASIC CARDS

1994 Finest Jumbos

Inserted one per Finest box, this 80-card oversized set (3 1/2" by 5") was issued in two series of 40. Each of the 80 cards is identical in design to the special "Finest" cards from the basic Finest set except for the size. The "Finest" subset was designated to showcase top rookies, prospects and veterans. The card numbering is the same as the corresponding basic issue cards. Hence, the first series comprises of cards 1-20 and 201-220. The second series is cards 221-240 and 421-440.

Nm-Mt Ex-Mt
*JUMBOS: 1.25X TO 3X BASIC CARDS

1995 Finest

Consisting of 330 standard-size cards, this set (produced by Topps) was issued in series of 220 and 110. A protective film, designed to keep the card from scratching and to maintain original gloss, covers the front. With the Finest logo at the top, a silver baseball diamond design surrounded by green (field) form the background to an action photo. Horizontally designed backs have a photo to the right with statistical information to the left. A Finest Moment, or career highlight, is also included. Rookie Cards in this set include Bobby Higginson and Hideo Nomo.

Nm-Mt Ex-Mt
COMPLETE SET (330) 60.00 18.00
COMP. SERIES 1 (220) 50.00 15.00
COMP. SERIES 2 (110) 15.00 4.50
1 Raul Mondesi 1.00 .30
2 Kurt Abbott .50 .15
3 Chris Gomez .50 .15
4 Manny Ramirez 1.50 .45
5 Rondell White 1.00 .30
6 William VanLandingham .50 .15
7 Jon Lieber .50 .15
8 Ryan Klesko 1.00 .30
9 John Hudek .50 .15
10 Joey Hamilton .50 .15
11 Bob Hamelin .50 .15
12 Brian Anderson .50 .15
13 Mike Lieberthal 1.00 .30
14 Rico Brogna .50 .15
15 Rusty Greer 1.00 .30
16 Carlos Delgado 1.00 .30
17 Jim Edmonds 1.50 .45
18 Steve Trachsel .50 .15
19 Matt Walbeck .50 .15
20 Armando Benitez 1.00 .30
21 Steve Karsay .50 .15
22 Jose Oliva .50 .15
23 Cliff Floyd 1.00 .30
24 Kevin Foster .50 .15
25 Javier Lopez 1.00 .30
26 Jose Valentin .50 .15
27 James Mouton .50 .15
28 Hector Carrasco .50 .15
29 Orlando Miller .50 .15
30 Garret Anderson 1.00 .30
31 Marvin Freeman .50 .15
32 Brett Butler 1.00 .30
33 Roberto Kelly .50 .15
34 Rod Beck .50 .15
35 Jose Rijo .50 .15
36 Edgar Martinez 1.50 .45
37 Jim Thome 2.50 .75
38 Rick Wilkins .50 .15
39 Wally Joyner 1.00 .30
40 Wil Cordero .50 .15
41 Tommy Greene .50 .15
42 Travis Fryman 1.00 .30
43 Don Slaught .50 .15
44 Brady Anderson 1.00 .30
45 Matt Williams 1.00 .30
46 Rene Arocha .50 .15
47 Rickey Henderson 2.50 .75
48 Mike Mussina 1.50 .45
49 Greg McMichael .50 .15
50 Jody Reed .50 .15
51 Tino Martinez 1.50 .45
52 Dave Clark .50 .15
53 John Valentin .50 .15
54 Bret Boone 1.00 .30
55 Walt Weiss .50 .15
56 Kenny Lofton 1.00 .30
57 Scott Leius .50 .15
58 Eric Karros 1.00 .30
59 John Olerud 1.00 .30
60 Chris Hoiles .50 .15
61 Sandy Alomar Jr. .50 .15
62 Tim Wallach .50 .15
63 Cal Eldred .50 .15
64 Tom Glavine 1.50 .45
65 Mark Grace 1.50 .45
66 Rey Sanchez .50 .15
67 Bobby Ayala .50 .15
68 Dante Bichette 1.00 .30
69 Andres Galarraga 1.00 .30
70 Chuck Carr .50 .15
71 Bobby Witt .50 .15
72 Steve Avery .50 .15
73 Bobby Jones .50 .15
74 Delino DeShields .50 .15
75 Kevin Tapani .50 .15
76 Randy Johnson 2.50 .75
77 David Nied .50 .15
78 Pat Hentgen .50 .15
79 Tim Salmon 1.50 .45
80 Todd Zeile .50 .15
81 John Wetteland 1.00 .30
82 Albert Belle 1.00 .30
83 Ben McDonald .50 .15
84 Bobby Munoz .50 .15
85 Bip Roberts .50 .15
86 Mo Vaughn 1.00 .30
87 Chuck Finley 1.00 .30
88 Chuck Knoblauch 1.00 .30
89 Frank Thomas 2.50 .75
90 Danny Tartabull .50 .15
91 Dean Palmer 1.00 .30
92 Len Dykstra 1.00 .30
93 J.R. Phillips .50 .15
94 Tom Candiotti .50 .15
95 Marquis Grissom .50 .15
96 Barry Larkin 1.50 .45
97 Bryan Harvey .50 .15
98 David Justice 1.00 .30
99 David Cone 1.00 .30
100 Wade Boggs 1.50 .45
101 Jason Bere .50 .15
102 Hal Morris .50 .15
103 Fred McGriff 1.50 .45
104 Bobby Bonilla 1.00 .30
105 Jay Buhner 1.00 .30
106 Allen Watson .50 .15
107 Mickey Tettleton .50 .15
108 Kevin Appier 1.00 .30
109 Ivan Rodriguez 2.50 .75
110 Carlos Garcia .50 .15
111 Andy Benes .50 .15
112 Eddie Murray 2.50 .75
113 Mike Piazza 4.00 1.20
114 Greg Vaughn .50 .15
115 Paul Molitor 1.50 .45
116 Terry Steinbach .50 .15
117 Jeff Bagwell 1.50 .45
118 Ken Griffey Jr. 4.00 1.20
119 Gary Sheffield 1.00 .30
120 Cal Ripken 8.00 2.40
121 Jeff Kent 1.00 .30
122 Jay Bell 1.00 .30
123 Will Clark 2.50 .75
124 Cecil Fielder 1.00 .30
125 Alex Fernandez .50 .15
126 Don Mattingly 6.00 1.80
127 Reggie Sanders .50 .15
128 Moises Alou 1.00 .30
129 Craig Biggio 1.50 .45
130 Eddie Williams .50 .15
131 John Franco 1.00 .30
132 John Kruk 1.00 .30
133 Jeff King .50 .15
134 Royce Clayton .50 .15
135 Doug Drabek .50 .15
136 Ray Lankford .50 .15
137 Roberto Alomar 1.50 .45
138 Todd Hundley .50 .15
139 Alex Cole .50 .15
140 Shawon Dunston .50 .15
141 John Roper .50 .15
142 Mark Langston .50 .15
143 Tom Pagnozzi .50 .15
144 Wilson Alvarez .50 .15
145 Scott Cooper .50 .15
146 Kevin Mitchell .50 .15
147 Mark Whiten .50 .15
148 Jeff Conine 1.00 .30
149 Chili Davis 1.00 .30
150 Luis Gonzalez 1.00 .30
151 Juan Guzman .50 .15
152 Mike Greenwell .50 .15
153 Mike Henneman .50 .15
154 Rick Aguilera .50 .15
155 Dennis Eckersley 1.00 .30
156 Darrin Fletcher .50 .15
157 Darren Lewis .50 .15
158 Juan Gonzalez 1.50 .45
159 Dave Hollins .50 .15
160 Jimmy Key 1.00 .30
161 Roberto Hernandez .50 .15
162 Randy Myers .50 .15
163 Joe Carter 1.00 .30
164 Darren Daulton 1.00 .30
165 Mike Macfarlane .50 .15
166 Bret Saberhagen 1.00 .30
167 Kirby Puckett 2.50 .75
168 Lance Johnson .50 .15
169 Mark McGwire 6.00 1.80
170 Jose Canseco 2.50 .75
171 Mike Stanley .50 .15
172 Lee Smith 1.00 .30
173 Robin Ventura 1.00 .30
174 Greg Gagne .50 .15
175 Brian McRae .50 .15
176 Mike Bordick .50 .15
177 Rafael Palmeiro 1.50 .45
178 Kenny Rogers 1.00 .30
179 Chad Curtis .50 .15
180 Devon White 1.00 .30
181 Paul O'Neill 1.50 .45
182 Ken Caminiti 1.00 .30
183 Dave Nilsson .50 .15
184 Tim Naehring .50 .15
185 Roger Clemens 5.00 1.50
186 Otis Nixon .50 .15
187 Tim Raines 1.00 .30
188 Denny Martinez 1.00 .30
189 Pedro Martinez 2.50 .75
190 Jim Abbott 1.50 .45
191 Ryan Thompson .50 .15
192 Barry Bonds 6.00 1.80
193 Joe Girardi .50 .15
194 Steve Finley 1.00 .30
195 John Jaha .50 .15
196 Tony Gwynn 3.00 .90
197 Sammy Sosa 4.00 1.20
198 John Burkett .50 .15
199 Carlos Baerga .50 .15
200 Ramon Martinez .50 .15
201 Aaron Sele .50 .15
202 Eduardo Perez .50 .15
203 Alan Trammell 1.00 .30
204 Orlando Merced .50 .15
205 Deion Sanders 1.50 .45
206 Robb Nen 1.00 .30
207 Jack McDowell .50 .15
208 Ruben Sierra .50 .15
209 Bernie Williams 1.50 .45
210 Kevin Seitzer .50 .15
211 Charles Nagy .50 .15
212 Tony Phillips .50 .15
213 Greg Maddux 4.00 1.20
214 Jeff Montgomery .50 .15
215 Larry Walker 1.50 .45
216 Andy Van Slyke 1.00 .30
217 Ozzie Smith 4.00 1.20
218 Geronimo Pena .50 .15
219 Gregg Jefferies .50 .15
220 Lou Whitaker 1.00 .30
221 Chipper Jones 2.50 .75
222 Benji Gil .50 .15
223 Tony Phillips .50 .15
224 Trevor Wilson .50 .15
225 Tony Tarasco .50 .15
226 Roberto Petagine .50 .15
227 Mike Macfarlane .50 .15
228 Hideo Nomo RCUER 8.00 2.40
(In 3rd line agianst)

229 Mark McLemore .50 .15
230 Ron Gant 1.00 .30
231 Andujar Cedeno .50 .15
232 Mike Mimbs RC .50 .15
233 Jim Abbott 1.50 .45
234 Ricky Bones .50 .15
235 Marty Cordova .50 .15
236 Mark Johnson RC 1.25 .35
237 Marquis Grissom 1.00 .30
238 Tom Henke .50 .15
239 Terry Pendleton 1.00 .30
240 John Wetteland 1.00 .30
241 Lee Smith 1.00 .30
242 Jaime Navarro .50 .15
243 Luis Alicea .50 .15
244 Scott Cooper .50 .15
245 Gary Gaetti 1.00 .30
246 Edgardo Alfonzo UER 1.00 .30
(Incomplete career BA)
247 Brad Clontz .50 .15
248 Dave Mlicki .50 .15
249 Dave Winfield 1.00 .30
250 Mark Grudzielanek RC 1.25 .35
251 Alex Gonzalez .50 .15
252 Kevin Brown 1.00 .30
253 Esteban Loaiza .50 .15
254 Vaughn Eshelman .50 .15
255 Bill Swift .50 .15
256 Brian McRae .50 .15
257 Bobby Higginson RC 2.00 .60
258 Jack McDowell .50 .15
259 Scott Stahoviak .50 .15
260 Jon Nunnally .50 .15
261 Charlie Hayes .50 .15
262 Jacob Brumfield .50 .15
263 Chad Curtis .50 .15
264 Heathcliff Slocumb .50 .15
265 Mark Whiten .50 .15
266 Mickey Tettleton .50 .15
267 Jose Mesa .50 .15
268 Doug Jones .50 .15
269 Trevor Hoffman 1.00 .30
270 Paul Sorrento .50 .15
271 Shane Andrews .50 .15
272 Brett Butler 1.00 .30
273 Curtis Goodwin .50 .15
274 Larry Walker 1.50 .45
275 Phil Plantier .50 .15
276 Ken Hill .50 .15
277 Vinny Castilla UER 1.00 .30
Rockies spelled Rockie
278 Billy Ashley .50 .15
279 Derek Jeter 6.00 1.80
280 Bob Tewksbury .50 .15
281 Jose Offerman .50 .15
282 Glenallen Hill .50 .15
283 Tony Fernandez .50 .15
284 Mike Devereaux .50 .15
285 John Burkett .50 .15
286 Geronimo Berroa .50 .15
287 Quilvio Veras .50 .15
288 Jason Bates .50 .15
289 Lee Tinsley .50 .15
290 Derek Bell .50 .15
291 Jeff Fassero .50 .15
292 Ray Durham 1.00 .30
293 Chad Ogea .50 .15
294 Bill Pulsipher .50 .15
295 Phil Nevin 1.00 .30
296 Carlos Perez RC 1.25 .35
297 Roberto Kelly .50 .15
298 Tim Wakefield 1.00 .30
299 Jeff Manto .50 .15
300 Brian Hunter .50 .15
301 C.J. Nitkowski .50 .15
302 Dustin Hermanson .50 .15
303 John Mabry .50 .15
304 Orel Hershiser 1.00 .30
305 Ron Villone .50 .15
306 Sean Bergman .50 .15
307 Tom Goodwin .50 .15
308 Al Reyes .50 .15
309 Todd Stottlemyre .50 .15
310 Rich Becker .50 .15
311 Joey Cora .50 .15
312 Ed Sprague .50 .15
313 John Smoltz UER 1.50 .45
(3rd line; from spelled as form)
314 Frank Castillo .50 .15
315 Chris Hammond .50 .15
316 Ismael Valdes .50 .15
317 Pete Harnisch .50 .15
318 Bernard Gilkey .50 .15
319 John Kruk 1.00 .30
320 Marc Newfield .50 .15
321 Brian Johnson .50 .15
322 Mark Portugal .50 .15
323 David Hulse .50 .15
324 Luis Ortiz UER .50 .15
(Below spelled beloe)
325 Mike Benjamin .50 .15
326 Brian Jordan 1.00 .30
327 Shawn Green 1.00 .30
328 Joe Oliver .50 .15
329 Felipe Lira .50 .15
330 Andre Dawson 1.00 .30

1995 Finest Refractors

This set is a parallel to the basic Finest set, including the use of protective coating, the difference can be found in the refractive sheen. The cards were inserted at a rate of one in 12 packs.

Nm-Mt Ex-Mt
*STARS: 4X TO 10X BASIC CARDS....
*ROOKIES: 3X TO 8X BASIC CARDS..

1995 Finest Flame Throwers

Randomly inserted in first series packs at a rate of 1:48, this nine-card set showcases strikeout leaders who bring on the heat. With a protective coating, a player photo is superimposed over a fiery orange background.

Nm-Mt Ex-Mt
COMPLETE SET (9) 40.00 12.00
FT1 Jason Bere 3.00 .90
FT2 Roger Clemens 30.00 9.00
FT3 Juan Guzman 3.00 .90
FT4 John Hudek 3.00 .90

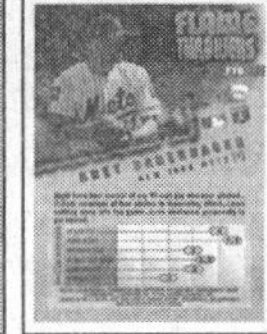

FT5 Randy Johnson 15.00 4.50
FT6 Pedro Martinez 15.00 4.50
FT7 Jose Rijo 3.00 .90
FT8 Bret Saberhagen 6.00 1.80
FT9 John Wetteland 6.00 1.80

1995 Finest Power Kings

Randomly inserted in series one packs at a rate of one in 24, Power Kings is an 18-card set highlighting top sluggers. With a protective coating, the fronts feature chromium technology that allows the player photo to be further enhanced as if to jump out from a blue lightning bolt background.

Nm-Mt Ex-Mt
COMPLETE SET (18) 150.00 45.00
PK1 Bob Hamelin 2.50 .75
PK2 Raul Mondesi 5.00 1.50
PK3 Ryan Klesko 5.00 1.50
PK4 Carlos Delgado 5.00 1.50
PK5 Manny Ramirez 8.00 2.40
PK6 Mike Piazza 20.00 6.00
PK7 Jeff Bagwell 8.00 2.40
PK8 Mo Vaughn 5.00 1.50
PK9 Frank Thomas 12.00 3.60
PK10 Ken Griffey Jr. 20.00 6.00
PK11 Albert Belle 5.00 1.50
PK12 Sammy Sosa 20.00 6.00
PK13 Dante Bichette 5.00 1.50
PK14 Gary Sheffield 5.00 1.50
PK15 Matt Williams 5.00 1.50
PK16 Fred McGriff 8.00 2.40
PK17 Barry Bonds 30.00 9.00
PK18 Cecil Fielder 5.00 1.50

1996 Finest

The 1996 Finest set (produced by Topps) was issued in two series of 191 cards and 168 cards respectively, for a total of 359 cards. The six-card foil packs originally retailed for $5.00 each. A protective film, designed to keep the card from scratching and to maintain original gloss, covers the front. This product provides collectors with the opportunity to complete a number of sets within sets, each with a different degree of insertion. Each card is numbered twice to indicate the set count and the theme count. Series 1 set covers four distinct themes: Finest Phenoms, Finest Intimidators, Finest Gamers and Finest Sterling. Within the first three themes, some players will be common (bronze trim), some uncommon (silver) and some rare (gold). Finest Sterling consists of star players included within one of the other three themes, but featured with a new design and different photography. The breakdown for the player selection of common, uncommon and rare cards is completely random. There are 110 common, 55 uncommon (1:4 packs) and 25 rare cards (1:24 packs). Series 2 covers four distict themes also with common, uncommon and rare cards seeded at the same ratio. The four themes are: Finest Franchises which features 36 team leaders and bonafide superstars, Finest Additions which features 47 players who have switched teams in '96, Finest Prodigies which features 45 best up-and-coming players, and Finest Sterling with 39 top stars. In addition to the cards' special borders, each card will also have either "common," "uncommon", or "rare" written within the numbering box on the card backs to let collectors know which type of card they hold.

Nm-Mt Ex-Mt
COMP.BRONZE SER.1 (110) 25.00 7.50
COMP.BRONZE SER.2 (110) 25.00 7.50
COMMON BRONZE .50 .15
COMMON GOLD 5.00 1.50
COMMON SILVER 2.50 .75
B5 Roberto Hernandez B .50 .15
B8 Terry Pendleton B .50 .15
B12 Ken Caminiti B .50 .15
B15 Dan Miceli B .50 .15
B16 Chipper Jones B 1.25 .35
B17 John Wetteland B .50 .15
B19 Tim Naehring B .50 .15
B21 Eddie Murray B 1.25 .35
B23 Kevin Appier B .50 .15
B24 Ken Griffey Jr. B 2.00 .60
B26 Brian McRae B .50 .15
B27 Pedro Martinez B 1.25 .35
B28 Brian Jordan B .50 .15
B29 Mike Fetters B .50 .15
B30 Carlos Delgado B .50 .15
B31 Shane Reynolds B .50 .15
B32 Terry Steinbach B .50 .15
B34 Mark Leiter B .50 .15
B36 David Segui B .50 .15
B40 Fred McGriff B .75 .23
B44 Glenallen Hill B .50 .15
B45 Brady Anderson B .50 .15
B47 Jim Thome B 1.25 .35
B48 Frank Thomas B 1.25 .35
B49 Chuck Knoblauch B .50 .15
B50 Len Dykstra B .50 .15
B53 Tom Pagnozzi B .50 .15
B55 Ricky Bones B .50 .15
B56 David Justice B .50 .15
B57 Steve Avery B .50 .15
B58 Robby Thompson B .50 .15
B61 Tony Gwynn B 1.50 .45
B63 Denny Neagle B .50 .15
B67 Robin Ventura B .50 .15
B70 Kevin Seitzer B .50 .15
B71 Ramon Martinez B .50 .15
B75 Brian L.Hunter B .50 .15
B76 Alan Benes B .50 .15
B80 Ozzie Guillen B .50 .15
B82 Benji Gil B .50 .15
B85 Todd Hundley B .50 .15
B87 Pat Hentgen B .50 .15
B89 Chuck Finley B .50 .15
B92 Derek Jeter B 3.00 .90
B93 Paul O'Neill B .75 .23
B94 Darrin Fletcher B .50 .15
B96 Delino DeShields B .50 .15
B97 Tim Salmon B .75 .23
B98 John Olerud B .50 .15
B101 Tim Wakefield B .50 .15
B103 Dave Stevens B .50 .15
B104 Orlando Merced B .50 .15
B106 Jay Bell B .50 .15
B107 John Burkett B .50 .15
B108 Chris Hoiles B .50 .15
B110 Dave Nilsson B .50 .15
B111 Rod Beck B .50 .15
B113 Mike Piazza B 2.00 .60
B114 Mark Langston B .50 .15
B116 Rico Brogna B .50 .15
B118 Tom Goodwin B .50 .15
B119 Bryan Rekar B .50 .15
B120 David Cone B .50 .15
B122 Andy Pettitte B .75 .23
B123 Chili Davis B .50 .15
B124 John Smoltz B .75 .23
B125 H.Slocumb B .50 .15
B126 Dante Bichette B .50 .15
B128 Alex Gonzalez B .50 .15
B129 Jeff Montgomery B .50 .15
B131 Denny Martinez B .50 .15
B132 Mel Rojas B .50 .15
B133 Derek Bell B .50 .15
B134 Trevor Hoffman B .50 .15
B136 Darren Daulton B .50 .15
B137 Pete Schourek B .50 .15
B138 Phil Nevin B .50 .15
B139 Andres Galarraga B .50 .15
B140 Chad Fonville B .50 .15
B144 J.T. Snow B .50 .15
B146 Barry Bonds B 3.00 .90
B147 Orel Hershiser B .50 .15
B148 Quilvio Veras B .50 .15
B149 Will Clark B 1.25 .35
B150 Jose Rijo B .50 .15
B152 Travis Fryman B .50 .15
B154 Alex Fernandez B .50 .15
B155 Wade Boggs B .75 .23
B156 Troy Percival B .50 .15
B157 Moises Alou B .50 .15
B158 Javy Lopez B .50 .15
B159 Jason Giambi B .50 .15
B162 Mark McGwire B 3.00 .90
B163 Eric Karros B .50 .15
B166 Mickey Tettleton B .50 .15
B167 Barry Larkin B .75 .23
B169 Ruben Sierra B .50 .15
B170 Bill Swift B .50 .15
B172 Chad Curtis B .50 .15
B173 Dean Palmer B .50 .15
B175 Bobby Bonilla B .50 .15
B176 Greg Colbrunn B .50 .15
B177 Jose Mesa B .50 .15
B178 Mike Greenwell B .50 .15
B181 Doug Drabek B .50 .15
B183 Wilson Alvarez B .50 .15
B184 Marty Cordova B .50 .15
B185 Hal Morris B .50 .15
B187 Carlos Garcia B .50 .15
B190 Marquis Grissom B .50 .15
B193 Will Clark B 1.25 .35
B194 Paul Molitor B .75 .23
B195 Kenny Rogers B .50 .15
B196 Reggie Sanders B .50 .15
B199 Raul Mondesi B .50 .15
B200 Lance Johnson B .50 .15
B201 Alvin Morman B .50 .15
B202 Jack McDowell B .50 .15
B203 Randy Myers B .50 .15
B205 Harold Baines B .50 .15
B206 Marty Cordova B .50 .15
B207 Rich Hunter B RC .50 .15
B208 Al Leiter B .50 .15
B209 Greg Gagne B .50 .15
B210 Ben McDonald B .50 .15
B212 Terry Adams B .50 .15
B213 Paul Sorrento B .50 .15
B214 Albert Belle B .50 .15
B215 Mike Blowers B .50 .15
B216 Jim Edmonds B .50 .15
B217 Felipe Crespo B .50 .15
B219 Shawon Dunston B .50 .15
B220 Jimmy Haynes B .50 .15
B221 Jose Canseco B 1.25 .35
B222 Eric Davis B .50 .15
B224 Tim Raines B .50 .15
B225 Tony Phillips B .50 .15
B226 Charlie Hayes B .50 .15
B227 Eric Owens B .50 .15
B228 Roberto Alomar B .75 .23
B233 Kenny Lofton B .50 .15
B236 Mark McGwire B 3.00 .90
B237 Jay Buhner B .50 .15
B238 Craig Biggio B .75 .23
B240 Barry Bonds B 3.00 .90
B244 Ron Gant B .50 .15
B245 Paul Wilson B .50 .15
B246 T.Hollandsworth B .50 .15
B247 Todd Zeile B .50 .15
B248 David Justice B .50 .15
B250 Moises Alou B .50 .15
B251 Bob Wolcott B .50 .15
B252 David Wells B .50 .15
B253 Juan Gonzalez B .75 .23
B254 Andres Galarraga B .50 .15
B255 Dave Hollins B .50 .15
B257 Sammy Sosa B 2.00 .60
B258 Ivan Rodriguez B 1.25 .35
B259 Bip Roberts B .50 .15
B260 Tino Martinez B .75 .23
B262 Mike Stanley B .50 .15
B264 Butch Huskey B .50 .15
B265 Jeff Conine B .50 .15
B267 Mark Grace B .75 .23
B268 Jason Schmidt B .75 .23
B269 Otis Nixon B .50 .15
B271 Kirby Puckett B 1.25 .35
B273 Andy Benes B .50 .15
B275 Mike Piazza B 2.00 .60
B276 Rey Ordonez B .50 .15
B278 Gary Gaetti B .50 .15
B280 Robin Ventura B .50 .15
B281 Cal Ripken B 4.00 1.20
B282 Carlos Baerga B .50 .15
B283 Roger Cedeno B .50 .15
B285 Terrell Wade B .50 .15
B286 Kevin Brown B .50 .15
B287 Rafael Palmeiro B .75 .23
B288 Mo Vaughn B .50 .15
B292 Bob Tewksbury B .50 .15
B297 T.J. Mathews B .50 .15
B298 Manny Ramirez B .75 .23
B299 Jeff Bagwell B .75 .23
B301 Wade Boggs B .75 .23
B303 Steve Gibralter B .50 .15
B304 B.J. Surhoff B .50 .15
B306 Royce Clayton B .50 .15
B307 Sal Fasano B .50 .15
B309 Gary Sheffield B .50 .15
B310 Ken Hill B .50 .15
B311 Joe Girardi B .50 .15
B312 Matt Lawton B RC 1.00 .30
B314 Julio Franco B .50 .15
B315 Joe Carter B .50 .15
B316 Brooks Kieschnick B .50 .15
B318 H.Slocumb B .50 .15
B319 Barry Larkin B .75 .23
B320 Tony Gwynn B 1.50 .45
B322 Frank Thomas B 1.25 .35
B323 Edgar Martinez B .75 .23
B325 Henry Rodriguez B .50 .15
B326 Marvin Benard B RC .50 .15
B329 Ugueth Urbina B .50 .15
B331 Roger Salkeld B .50 .15
B332 Edgar Renteria B .50 .15
B333 Ryan Klesko B .50 .15
B334 Ray Lankford B .50 .15
B336 Justin Thompson B .50 .15
B339 Mark Clark B .50 .15
B340 Ruben Rivera B .50 .15
B342 Matt Williams B .50 .15
B343 F.Cordova B RC .50 .15
B344 Cecil Fielder B .50 .15
B348 Mark Grudzielanek B .50 .15
B349 Ron Coomer B .50 .15
B351 Rich Aurilia B RC 1.00 .30
B352 Jose Herrera B .50 .15
B356 Tony Clark B .50 .15
B358 Dan Naulty B .50 .15
B359 Checklist B .50 .15
G4 Marty Cordova G 5.00 1.50
G6 Tony Gwynn G 15.00 4.50
G9 Albert Belle G 5.00 1.50
G18 Kirby Puckett G 12.00 3.60
G20 Karim Garcia G 5.00 1.50
G25 Cal Ripken G 40.00 12.00
G33 Hideo Nomo G 12.00 3.60
G39 Ryne Sandberg G 20.00 6.00
G42 Jeff Bagwell G 4.00 1.20
G51 Jason Isringhausen G 5.00 1.50
G64 Mo Vaughn G 5.00 1.50
G66 Dante Bichette G 5.00 1.50
G74 Mark McGwire G 30.00 9.00
G81 Kenny Lofton G 5.00 1.50
G83 Jim Edmonds G 5.00 1.50
G90 Mike Mussina G 8.00 2.40
G100 Jeff Conine G 5.00 1.50
G102 Johnny Damon G 8.00 2.40
G105 Barry Bonds G 30.00 9.00
G117 Jose Canseco G 12.00 3.60
G135 Ken Griffey Jr. G 20.00 6.00
G141 Chipper Jones G 12.00 3.60
G145 Greg Maddux G 20.00 6.00
G164 Jay Buhner G 5.00 1.50
G186 Frank Thomas G 12.00 3.60
G191 Checklist G 5.00 1.50
G192 Chipper Jones G 12.00 3.60
G197 Roberto Alomar G 8.00 2.40
G198 Dennis Eckersley G 5.00 1.50
G202 George Arias G 5.00 1.50
G232 Hideo Nomo G 12.00 3.60
G243 Chris Snopek G 5.00 1.50
G249 Tim Salmon G 8.00 2.40
G266 Matt Williams G 5.00 1.50
G270 Randy Johnson G 12.00 3.60
G279 Paul Molitor G 8.00 2.40
G290 Cecil Fielder G 5.00 1.50
G294 L.Hernandez G RC 8.00 2.40
G300 Marty Janzen G RC 5.00 1.50
G308 Ron Gant G 5.00 1.50
G321 Ryan Klesko G 5.00 1.50
G324 Jermaine Dye G 5.00 1.50
G330 Jason Giambi G 5.00 1.50
G335 Edgar Martinez G 8.00 2.40
G338 Rey Ordonez G 5.00 1.50
G347 Sammy Sosa G 20.00 6.00
G354 Juan Gonzalez G 8.00 2.40
G355 Craig Biggio G 8.00 2.40
S1 Greg Maddux S UER 10.00 3.00
95 stats listed as Mariners
S2 Bernie Williams S 4.00 1.20
S3 Ivan Rodriguez S 6.00 1.80
S7 Barry Larkin S 4.00 1.20
S10 Ray Lankford S 2.50 .75
S11 Mike Piazza S 10.00 3.00
S13 Larry Walker S 4.00 1.20
S14 Matt Williams S 2.50 .75
S22 Tim Salmon S 4.00 1.20
S35 Edgar Martinez S 4.00 1.20
S37 Gregg Jefferies S 2.50 .75
S38 Bill Pulsipher S 2.50 .75
S41 Shawn Green S 2.50 .75
S43 Jim Abbott S 4.00 1.20
S46 Roger Clemens S 12.00 3.60
S52 Rondell White S 2.50 .75
S54 Dennis Eckersley S 2.50 .75
S59 Hideo Nomo S 6.00 1.80
S60 Gary Sheffield S 2.50 .75
S62 Will Clark S 6.00 1.80
S65 Bret Boone S 2.50 .75
S68 Rafael Palmeiro S 4.00 1.20
S69 Carlos Baerga S 2.50 .75
S72 Tom Glavine S 4.00 1.20
S73 Garret Anderson S 2.50 .75
S77 Randy Johnson S 6.00 1.80
S78 Jeff King S 2.50 .75
S79 Kirby Puckett S 6.00 1.80
S84 Cecil Fielder S 2.50 .75
S86 Reggie Sanders S 2.50 .75
S88 Ryan Klesko S 2.50 .75
S91 John Valentin S 2.50 .75
S95 Manny Ramirez S 4.00 1.20
S99 Vinny Castilla S 2.50 .75
S109 Carlos Perez S 2.50 .75
S112 Craig Biggio S 4.00 1.20
S115 Juan Gonzalez S 4.00 1.20
S121 Ray Durham S 2.50 .75
S127 C.J. Nitkowski S 2.50 .75
S130 Raul Mondesi S 2.50 .75
S142 Lee Smith S 2.50 .75
S143 Joe Carter S 2.50 .75
S151 Mo Vaughn S 2.50 .75
S153 Frank Rodriguez S 2.50 .75
S160 Steve Finley S 2.50 .75
S161 Jeff Bagwell S 4.00 1.20
S165 Cal Ripken S 20.00 6.00
S168 Lyle Mouton S 2.50 .75
S171 Sammy Sosa S 10.00 3.00
S174 John Franco S 2.50 .75
S179 Greg Vaughn S 2.50 .75
S180 Mark Wohlers S 2.50 .75
S182 Paul O'Neill S 4.00 1.20
S188 Albert Belle S 2.50 .75
S189 Mark Grace S 4.00 1.20
S211 Ernie Young S 2.50 .75
S218 Fred McGriff S 4.00 1.20
S223 Kimera Bartee S 2.50 .75
S229 Rickey Henderson S 6.00 1.80
S230 Sterling Hitchcock S 2.50 .75
S231 Bernard Gilkey S 2.50 .75
S234 Ryne Sandberg S 10.00 3.00
S235 Greg Maddux S 10.00 3.00
S239 Todd Stottlemyre S 2.50 .75
S241 Jason Kendall S 2.50 .75
S242 Paul O'Neill S 4.00 1.20
S256 Devon White S 2.50 .75
S261 Chuck Knoblauch S 2.50 .75
S263 Wally Joyner S 2.50 .75
S272 Andy Fox S 2.50 .75
S274 Sean Berry S 2.50 .75
S277 Benito Santiago S 2.50 .75
S284 Chad Mottola S 2.50 .75
S289 Dante Bichette S 2.50 .75
S291 Dwight Gooden S 2.50 .75
S293 Kevin Mitchell S 2.50 .75
S295 Russ Davis S 2.50 .75
S296 Chan Ho Park S 2.50 .75
S302 Larry Walker S 4.00 1.20
S305 Ken Griffey Jr. S 10.00 3.00
S313 Billy Wagner S 2.50 .75
S317 Mike Grace S RC 2.50 .75
S327 Kenny Lofton S 2.50 .75
S328 Derek Bell S 2.50 .75
S337 Gary Sheffield S 2.50 .75
S341 Mark Grace S 4.00 1.20
S345 Andres Galarraga S 2.50 .75
S346 Brady Anderson S 2.50 .75
S350 Derek Jeter S 12.00 3.60
S353 Jay Buhner S 2.50 .75
S357 Tino Martinez S 4.00 1.20

1996 Finest Refractors

This 359-card set is parallel to the basic 1996 Finest set. The first 191 cards are parallel to the regular Series 1 with the second 168 cards parallel to regular Series 2. The word "refractor" is printed above the numbers on the card backs. The rate of insertion is one in 12 for a Bronze refractor (common), one in 48 for a Silver refractor (uncommon), and one in 288 for a Gold refractor (rare).

Nm-Mt Ex-Mt
*BRONZE STARS: 4X to 10X BASIC CARDS
*GOLD STARS: .75X TO 2X BASIC CARDS
*SILVER STARS: 1.25X TO 3X BASIC CARDS

1997 Finest

The 1997 Finest set (produced by Topps) was issued in two series of 175 cards each and was distributed in six-card packs with a suggested retail price of $5.00. The fronts feature a borderless action player photo while the backs carry player information with another player photo. Series one is divided into five distinct themes: Finest Hurlers (top pitchers), Finest Blue Chips (up-and-coming future stars), Finest Power (long-ball hitters), Finest Warriors (superstar players), and Finest Masters (hottest players). Series two is also divided into five distinct themes: Finest Power (power hitters and pitchers), Finest Masters (top players), Finest Blue Chips (top new players), Finest Competitors (hottest players), and Finest Acquisitions (latest trades and new signings). All five themes of each series have common cards (1-100 and 176-275) designated with bronze trim, uncommon (101-150 and 276-325) with silver trim and an insertion rate of one in four for both series, and rare (151-175 and 326-350) with gold trim and an insertion rate of one in 24 for both series. The cards are numbered on the backs within the whole set and within the theme set. Notable Rookie Cards include Brian Giles.

	Nm-Mt	Ex-Mt
COMP.BRONZE SER.1 (100)	30.00	9.00
COMP.BRONZE SER.2 (100)	30.00	9.00
COM.BRON.(1-100/176-275)	.50	.15
COMP.SILVER SER.1 (50)	120.00	36.00
COMP.SILVER SER.2 (50)	150.00	45.00
COM.SILV.(101-150/276-325)	2.00	.60
COMP.GOLD SER.1 (25)	300.00	90.00
COMP.GOLD SER.2 (25)	250.00	75.00
COM.GOLD (151-175/326-350)	5.00	1.50

BICHETTE/JETER BOTH NUMBERED 155
BICHETTE UER SHOULD BE NUMBER 5

1 Barry Bonds B 3.00 .90
2 Ryne Sandberg B 2.00 .60
3 Brian Jordan B .50 .15
4 Rocky Coppinger B .50 .15
5 Dante Bichette B UER .50 .15
Card is erroneously numbered 155
6 Al Martin B .50 .15
7 Charles Nagy B .50 .15
8 Otis Nixon B .50 .15
9 Mark Johnson B .50 .15
10 Jeff Bagwell B .75 .23
11 Ken Hill B .50 .15
12 Willie Adams B .50 .15
13 Raul Mondesi B .50 .15
14 Reggie Sanders B .50 .15
15 Derek Jeter B 3.00 .90
16 Jermaine Dye B .50 .15
17 Edgar Renteria B .50 .15
18 Travis Fryman B .50 .15
19 Roberto Hernandez B .50 .15
20 Sammy Sosa B 2.00 .60
21 Garret Anderson B .50 .15
22 Rey Ordonez B .50 .15
23 Glenallen Hill B .50 .15
24 Dave Nilsson B .50 .15
25 Kevin Brown B .50 .15
26 Brian McRae B .50 .15
27 Joey Hamilton B .50 .15
28 Jamey Wright B .50 .15
29 Frank Thomas B 1.25 .35
30 Mark McGwire B 3.00 .90
31 Ramon Martinez B .50 .15
32 Jaime Bluma B .50 .15
33 Frank Rodriguez B .50 .15
34 Andy Benes B .50 .15
35 Jay Buhner B .50 .15
36 Justin Thompson B .50 .15
37 Darin Erstad B .50 .15
38 Gregg Jefferies B .50 .15
39 Jeff D'Amico B .50 .15
40 Pedro Martinez B 1.25 .35
41 Nomar Garciaparra B 2.00 .60
42 Jose Valentin B .50 .15
43 Pat Hentgen B .50 .15
44 Will Clark B 1.25 .35
45 Bernie Williams B .75 .23
46 Luis Castillo B .50 .15
47 B.J. Surhoff B .50 .15
48 Greg Gagne B .50 .15
49 Pete Schourek B .50 .15
50 Mike Piazza B 2.00 .60
51 Dwight Gooden B .50 .15
52 Javy Lopez B .50 .15
53 Chuck Finley B .50 .15
54 James Baldwin B .50 .15
55 Jack McDowell B .50 .15
56 Royce Clayton B .50 .15
57 Carlos Delgado B .50 .15
58 Neifi Perez B .50 .15
59 Eddie Taubensee B .50 .15
60 Rafael Palmeiro B .75 .23
61 Marty Cordova B .50 .15
62 Wade Boggs B .75 .23
63 Rickey Henderson B 1.25 .35
64 Mike Hampton B .50 .15
65 Troy Percival B .50 .15
66 Barry Larkin B .75 .23
67 J.Allensworth B .50 .15
68 Mark Clark B .50 .15
69 Mike Lansing B .50 .15
70 Mark Grudzielanek B .50 .15
71 Todd Stottlemyre B .50 .15
72 Juan Guzman B .50 .15
73 John Burkett B .50 .15
74 Wilson Alvarez B .50 .15
75 Ellis Burks B .50 .15
76 Bobby Higginson B .50 .15
77 Ricky Bottalico B .50 .15
78 Omar Vizquel B .75 .23
79 Paul Sorrento B .50 .15
80 Denny Neagle B .50 .15
81 Roger Pavlik B .50 .15
82 Mike Lieberthal B .50 .15
83 Devon White B .50 .15
84 John Olerud B .50 .15
85 Kevin Appier B .50 .15
86 Joe Girardi B .50 .15
87 Paul O'Neill B .75 .23
88 Mike Sweeney B .50 .15
89 John Smiley B .50 .15
90 Ivan Rodriguez B 1.25 .35
91 Randy Myers B .50 .15
92 Bip Roberts B .50 .15
93 Jose Mesa B .50 .15
94 Paul Wilson B .50 .15
95 Mike Mussina B .75 .23
96 Ben McDonald B .50 .15
97 John Mabry B .50 .15
98 Tom Goodwin B .50 .15
99 Edgar Martinez B .75 .23
100 Andruw Jones B .50 .15
101 Jose Canseco S 5.00 1.50
102 Billy Wagner S 2.00 .60
103 Dante Bichette S 2.00 .60
104 Curt Schilling S 2.00 .60
105 Dean Palmer S 2.00 .60
106 Larry Walker S 3.00 .90
107 Bernie Williams S 3.00 .90
108 Chipper Jones S 5.00 1.50
109 Gary Sheffield S 2.00 .60
110 Randy Johnson S 5.00 1.50
111 Roberto Alomar S 3.00 .90
112 Todd Walker S 2.00 .60
113 Sandy Alomar Jr. S 2.00 .60
114 John Jaha S 2.00 .60
115 Ken Caminiti S UER 2.00 .60
Card is numbered 135
116 Ryan Klesko S 2.00 .60
117 Mariano Rivera S 3.00 .90
118 Jason Giambi S 2.00 .60
119 Lance Johnson S 2.00 .60
120 Robin Ventura S 2.00 .60
121 Todd Hollandsworth S 2.00 .60
122 Johnny Damon S 2.00 .60
123 W. VanLandingham S 2.00 .60
124 Jason Kendall S 2.00 .60
125 Vinny Castilla S 2.00 .60
126 Harold Baines S 2.00 .60
127 Joe Carter S 2.00 .60
128 Craig Biggio S 3.00 .90
129 Tony Clark S 2.00 .60
130 Ron Gant S 2.00 .60
131 David Segui S 2.00 .60
132 Steve Trachsel S 2.00 .60
133 Scott Rolen S 5.00 1.50
134 Mike Stanley S 2.00 .60
135 Cal Ripken S 15.00 4.50
136 John Smoltz S 3.00 .90
137 Bobby Jones S 2.00 .60
138 Manny Ramirez S 3.00 .90
139 Ken Griffey Jr. S 8.00 2.40
140 Chuck Knoblauch S 2.00 .60
141 Mark Grace S 3.00 .90
142 Chris Snopek S 2.00 .60
143 Hideo Nomo S 5.00 1.50
144 Tim Salmon S 3.00 .90
145 David Cone S 2.00 .60
146 Eric Young S 2.00 .60
147 Jeff Brantley S 2.00 .60
148 Jim Thome S 5.00 1.50
149 Trevor Hoffman S 2.00 .60
150 Juan Gonzalez S 3.00 .90
151 Mike Piazza G 20.00 6.00
152 Ivan Rodriguez G 12.00 3.60
153 Mo Vaughn G 5.00 1.50
154 Brady Anderson G 5.00 1.50
155 Mark McGwire G 30.00 9.00
156 Rafael Palmeiro G 8.00 2.40
157 Barry Larkin G 8.00 2.40
158 Greg Maddux G 20.00 6.00
159 Jeff Bagwell G 8.00 2.40
160 Frank Thomas G 12.00 3.60
161 Ken Caminiti G 5.00 1.50
162 Andruw Jones G 5.00 1.50
163 Dennis Eckersley G 5.00 1.50
164 Jeff Conine G 5.00 1.50
165 Jim Edmonds G 5.00 1.50
166 Derek Jeter G 30.00 9.00
167 Vladimir Guerrero G 12.00 3.60
168 Sammy Sosa G 20.00 6.00
169 Tony Gwynn G 15.00 4.50
170 Andres Galarraga G 5.00 1.50
171 Todd Hundley G 5.00 1.50
172 Jay Buhner G UER 5.00 1.50
Card is numbered 164
173 Paul Molitor G 8.00 2.40
174 Kenny Lofton G 5.00 1.50
175 Barry Bonds G 30.00 9.00
176 Gary Sheffield B .50 .15
177 Dmitri Young B .50 .15
178 Jay Bell B .50 .15
179 David Wells B .50 .15
180 Walt Weiss B .50 .15
181 Paul Molitor B .75 .23
182 Jose Guillen B .50 .15
183 Al Leiter B .50 .15
184 Mike Fetters B .50 .15
185 Mark Langston B .50 .15
186 Fred McGriff B .75 .23
187 Darrin Fletcher B .50 .15
188 Brant Brown B .50 .15
189 Geronimo Berroa B .50 .15
190 Jim Thome B 1.25 .35
191 Jose Vizcaino B .50 .15
192 Andy Ashby B .50 .15
193 Rusty Greer B .50 .15
194 Brian Hunter B .50 .15
195 Chris Hoiles B .50 .15
196 Orlando Merced B .50 .15
197 Brett Butler B .50 .15
198 Derek Bell B .50 .15
199 Bobby Bonilla B .50 .15
200 Alex Ochoa B .50 .15
201 Wally Joyner B .50 .15
202 Mo Vaughn B .50 .15
203 Doug Drabek B .50 .15
204 Tino Martinez B .75 .23
205 Roberto Alomar B .75 .23
206 Brian Giles B RC 3.00 .90
207 Todd Worrell B .50 .15
208 Alan Benes B .50 .15
209 Jim Leyritz B .50 .15
210 Darryl Hamilton B .50 .15
211 Jimmy Key B .50 .15
212 Juan Gonzalez B .75 .23
213 Vinny Castilla B .50 .15
214 Chuck Knoblauch B .50 .15
215 Tony Phillips B .50 .15
216 Jeff Cirillo B .50 .15
217 Carlos Garcia B .50 .15
218 Brooks Kieschnick B .50 .15
219 Marquis Grissom B .50 .15
220 Dan Wilson B .50 .15
221 Greg Vaughn B .50 .15
222 John Wetteland B .50 .15
223 Andres Galarraga B .50 .15
224 Ozzie Guillen B .50 .15
225 Kevin Elster B .50 .15
226 Bernard Gilkey B .50 .15
227 Mike Macfarlane B .50 .15
228 Heathcliff Slocumb B .50 .15
229 Wendell Magee Jr. B .50 .15
230 Carlos Baerga B .50 .15
231 Kevin Seitzer B .50 .15
232 Henry Rodriguez B .50 .15
233 Roger Clemens B 2.50 .75
234 Mark Wohlers B .50 .15
235 Eddie Murray B 1.25 .35
236 Todd Zeile B .50 .15
237 J.T. Snow B .50 .15
238 Ken Griffey Jr. B 2.00 .60
239 Sterling Hitchcock B .50 .15
240 Albert Belle B .50 .15
241 Terry Steinbach B .50 .15
242 Robb Nen B .50 .15
243 Mark McLemore B .50 .15
244 Jeff King B .50 .15
245 Tony Clark B .50 .15
246 Tim Salmon B .75 .23
247 Benito Santiago B .50 .15
248 Robin Ventura B .50 .15
249 Bubba Trammell B RC .50 .15
250 Chili Davis B .50 .15
251 John Valentin B .50 .15
252 Cal Ripken B 4.00 1.20
253 Matt Williams B .50 .15
254 Jeff Kent B .50 .15
255 Eric Karros B .50 .15
256 Ray Lankford B .50 .15
257 Ed Sprague B .50 .15
258 Shane Reynolds B .50 .15
259 Jaime Navarro B .50 .15
260 Eric Davis B .50 .15
261 Orel Hershiser B .50 .15
262 Mark Grace B .75 .23
263 Rod Beck B .50 .15
264 Ismael Valdes B .50 .15
265 Manny Ramirez B .75 .23
266 Ken Caminiti B .50 .15
267 Tim Naehring B .50 .15
268 Jose Rosado B .50 .15
269 Greg Colbrunn B .50 .15
270 Dean Palmer B .50 .15
271 David Justice B .50 .15
272 Scott Spiezio B .50 .15
273 Chipper Jones B 1.25 .35
274 Mel Rojas B .50 .15
275 Bartolo Colon B .50 .15
276 Darin Erstad S 2.00 .60
277 Sammy Sosa S 6.00 1.80
278 Rafael Palmeiro S 3.00 .90
279 Frank Thomas S 5.00 1.50
280 Ruben Rivera S 2.00 .60
281 Hal Morris S 2.00 .60
282 Jay Buhner S 2.00 .60
283 Kenny Lofton S 2.00 .60
284 Jose Canseco S 5.00 1.50
285 Alex Fernandez S 2.00 .60
286 Todd Helton S 5.00 1.50
287 Andy Pettitte S 3.00 .90
288 John Franco S 2.00 .60
289 Ivan Rodriguez S 5.00 1.50
290 Ellis Burks S 2.00 .60
291 Julio Franco S 2.00 .60
292 Mike Piazza S 8.00 2.40
293 Brian Jordan S 2.00 .60
294 Greg Maddux S 8.00 2.40
295 Bob Abreu S 2.00 .60
296 Rondell White S 2.00 .60
297 Moises Alou S 2.00 .60
298 Tony Gwynn S 6.00 1.80
299 Deion Sanders S 3.00 .90
300 Jeff Montgomery S 2.00 .60
301 Ray Durham S 2.00 .60
302 John Wasdin S 2.00 .60
303 Ryne Sandberg S 8.00 2.40
304 Delino DeShields S 2.00 .60
305 Mark McGwire S 12.00 3.60
306 Andruw Jones S 2.00 .60
307 Kevin Orie S 2.00 .60
308 Matt Williams S 2.00 .60
309 Karim Garcia S 2.00 .60
310 Derek Jeter S 12.00 3.60
311 Mo Vaughn S 2.00 .60
312 Brady Anderson S 2.00 .60
313 Barry Bonds S 12.00 3.60
314 Steve Finley S 2.00 .60
315 Vladimir Guerrero S 5.00 1.50
316 Matt Morris S 2.00 .60
317 Tom Glavine S 3.00 .90
318 Jeff Bagwell S 3.00 .90
319 Albert Belle S 2.00 .60
320 Hideki Irabu S RC 2.00 .60
321 Andres Galarraga S 2.00 .60
322 Cecil Fielder S 2.00 .60
323 Barry Larkin S 3.00 .90
324 Todd Hundley S 2.00 .60
325 Fred McGriff S 3.00 .90
326 Gary Sheffield G 5.00 1.50
327 Craig Biggio G 8.00 2.40
328 Raul Mondesi G 5.00 1.50
329 Edgar Martinez G 8.00 2.40
330 Chipper Jones G 12.00 3.60
331 Bernie Williams G 8.00 2.40
332 Juan Gonzalez G 8.00 2.40
333 Ron Gant G 5.00 1.50
334 Cal Ripken G 40.00 12.00
335 Larry Walker G 8.00 2.40
336 Matt Williams G 5.00 1.50
337 Jose Cruz Jr. G RC 8.00 2.40
338 Joe Carter G 5.00 1.50
339 Wilton Guerrero G 5.00 1.50
340 Cecil Fielder G 5.00 1.50
341 Todd Walker G 5.00 1.50
342 Ken Griffey Jr. G 20.00 6.00
343 Ryan Klesko G 5.00 1.50
344 Roger Clemens G 25.00 7.50
345 Hideo Nomo G 12.00 3.60
346 Dante Bichette G 5.00 1.50
347 Albert Belle G 5.00 1.50
348 Randy Johnson G 12.00 3.60
349 Manny Ramirez G 8.00 2.40
350 John Smoltz G 8.00 2.40

1997 Finest Embossed

This 150-card set is parallel to regular set numbers 101-175 of Finest Series 1 and 276-350 of Finest Series 2. There is an embossed version of cards 101-150 and 276-325 with an insertion rate of one in 16 for each series. There is an embossed die-cut version of cards 151-175 and 326-350 with an insertion rate of one in 96 packs for each series.

Nm-Mt Ex-Mt
*SILV.STARS: .60X TO 1.5X BASIC CARD
*SILVER ROOKIES: .5X TO 1.25X BASIC
*GOLD STARS: .75X TO 2X BASIC CARD
*GOLD ROOKIES: .5X TO 1.2X BASIC CARD

1997 Finest Embossed Refractors

This 150-card set is a parallel version of the regular Finest Embossed set and is similar in design. The difference is found in the refractive quality of the cards.

Nm-Mt Ex-Mt
*SILVER STARS: 2.5X TO 6X BASIC CARDS
*SILVER ROOKIES: 2X TO 5X BASIC CARDS
*SER.1 GOLD STARS: 2X TO 5X BASIC
*SER.2 GOLD STARS: 2X TO 5X BASIC
*SER.2 GOLD RC'S: 1.25X TO 3X BASIC

1997 Finest Refractors

This 350-card set is parallel and similar in design to the regular Finest set. The distinction is in the refractive quality of the card. Cards 1-100 and 176-275 have an insertion rate of one in 12 in each series packs. Cards 101-150 and 276-325 have an insertion rate of one in 48 in each series packs. Cards 151-175 and 326-350 have an insertion rate of one in 288.

Nm-Mt Ex-Mt
*BRONZE STARS: 4X TO 10X BASIC CARD
*BRONZE RC'S: 1.25X TO 3X BASIC CARD
*SILVER STARS: 1.25X TO 3X BASIC CARD
*SILVER ROOKIES: 1X TO 2.5X BASIC CARD
*GOLD STARS: 1.25X TO 3X BASIC CARD
*GOLD ROOKIES: .75X TO 2X BASIC CARD

1998 Finest

This 275-card set (produced by Topps) was distributed in first and second series six-card packs with a suggested retail price of $5. Series one contains cards 1-150 and series two contains cards 151-275. Each card features action color player photos printed on 26 pt. card stock with each postion identified by a different card design. The backs carry player information and career statistics.

	Nm-Mt	Ex-Mt
COMPLETE SET (275)	50.00	15.00
COMP.SERIES 1 (150)	25.00	7.50
COMP.SERIES 2 (125)	25.00	7.50

1 Larry Walker .60 .18
2 Andruw Jones .40 .12
3 Ramon Martinez .25 .07
4 Geronimo Berroa .25 .07
5 David Justice .40 .12
6 Rusty Greer .40 .12
7 Chad Ogea .25 .07
8 Tom Goodwin .25 .07
9 Tino Martinez .60 .18
10 Jose Guillen .40 .12
11 Jeffrey Hammonds .25 .07
12 Brian McRae .25 .07
13 Jeremi Gonzalez .25 .07
14 Craig Counsell .25 .07
15 Mike Piazza 1.50 .45
16 Greg Maddux 1.50 .45
17 Todd Greene .25 .07
18 Rondell White .40 .12
19 Kirk Rueter .25 .07
20 Tony Clark .25 .07
21 Brad Radke .40 .12
22 Jaret Wright .25 .07
23 Carlos Delgado .40 .12
24 Dustin Hermanson .25 .07
25 Gary Sheffield .40 .12
26 Jose Canseco 1.00 .30
27 Kevin Young .40 .12
28 David Wells .40 .12
29 Mariano Rivera .60 .18
30 Reggie Sanders .25 .07
31 Mike Cameron .40 .12
32 Bobby Witt .25 .07
33 Kevin Orie .25 .07
34 Royce Clayton .25 .07
35 Edgar Martinez .60 .18
36 Neifi Perez .25 .07
37 Kevin Appier .40 .12
38 Darryl Hamilton .25 .07
39 Michael Tucker .25 .07
40 Roger Clemens 2.00 .60
41 Carl Everett .40 .12
42 Mike Sweeney .40 .12
43 Pat Meares .25 .07
44 Brian Giles .40 .12
45 Matt Morris .40 .12
46 Jason Dickson .25 .07
47 Rich Loiselle RC .40 .12
48 Joe Girardi .25 .07
49 Steve Trachsel .25 .07
50 Ben Grieve .25 .07
51 Brian Johnson .25 .07
52 Hideki Irabu .40 .12
53 J.T. Snow .40 .12
54 Mike Hampton .40 .12
55 Dave Nilsson .25 .07
56 Alex Fernandez .25 .07
57 Brett Tomko .25 .07
58 Wally Joyner .40 .12
59 Kelvim Escobar .25 .07
60 Roberto Alomar .60 .18
61 Todd Jones .25 .07
62 Paul O'Neill .60 .18
63 Jamie Moyer .40 .12
64 Mark Wohlers .25 .07
65 Jose Cruz Jr. .25 .07
66 Troy Percival .40 .12
67 Rick Reed .25 .07
68 Will Clark 1.00 .30
69 Jamey Wright .25 .07
70 Mike Mussina .60 .18
71 David Cone .40 .12
72 Ryan Klesko .40 .12
73 Scott Hatteberg .25 .07
74 James Baldwin .25 .07
75 Tony Womack .25 .07
76 Carlos Perez .25 .07
77 Charles Nagy .25 .07
78 Jeromy Burnitz .40 .12
79 Shane Reynolds .25 .07
80 Cliff Floyd .40 .12
81 Jason Kendall .40 .12
82 Chad Curtis .25 .07
83 Matt Karchner .25 .07
84 Ricky Bottalico .25 .07
85 Sammy Sosa 1.50 .45
86 Javy Lopez .40 .12
87 Jeff Kent .40 .12
88 Shawn Green .40 .12
89 Joey Cora .25 .07
90 Tony Gwynn 1.25 .35
91 Bob Tewksbury .25 .07
92 Derek Jeter 2.50 .75
93 Eric Davis .40 .12
94 Jeff Fassero .25 .07
95 Denny Neagle .25 .07
96 Ismael Valdes .25 .07
97 Tim Salmon .60 .18
98 Mark Grudzielanek .25 .07
99 Curt Schilling .40 .12
100 Ken Griffey Jr. 1.50 .45
101 Edgardo Alfonzo .25 .07
102 Vinny Castilla .40 .12
103 Jose Rosado .25 .07
104 Scott Erickson .25 .07
105 Alan Benes .25 .07
106 Shannon Stewart .40 .12
107 Delino DeShields .25 .07
108 Mark Loretta .40 .12
109 Todd Hundley .25 .07
110 Chuck Knoblauch .40 .12
111 Todd Helton .60 .18
112 F.P. Santangelo .25 .07
113 Jeff Cirillo .25 .07
114 Omar Vizquel .60 .18
115 John Valentin .25 .07
116 Damion Easley .25 .07
117 Matt Lawton .25 .07
118 Jim Thome 1.00 .30
119 Sandy Alomar Jr. .25 .07
120 Albert Belle .40 .12
121 Chris Stynes .25 .07
122 Butch Huskey .25 .07
123 Shawn Estes .25 .07
124 Terry Adams .25 .07
125 Ivan Rodriguez 1.00 .30
126 Ron Gant .40 .12
127 John Mabry .25 .07
128 Jeff Shaw .25 .07
129 Jeff Montgomery .25 .07
130 Justin Thompson .25 .07
131 Livan Hernandez .25 .07
132 Ugueth Urbina .25 .07
133 Scott Servais .25 .07
134 Troy O'Leary .25 .07
135 Cal Ripken 3.00 .90
136 Quilvio Veras .25 .07
137 Pedro Astacio .25 .07
138 Willie Greene .25 .07
139 Lance Johnson .25 .07
140 Nomar Garciaparra 1.50 .45
141 Jose Offerman .25 .07
142 Scott Rolen 1.00 .30
143 Derek Bell .25 .07
144 Johnny Damon .60 .18
145 Mark McGwire 2.50 .75
146 Chan Ho Park .40 .12
147 Edgar Renteria .40 .12
148 Eric Young .25 .07
149 Craig Biggio .60 .18
150 Checklist (1-150) .25 .07
151 Frank Thomas 1.00 .30
152 John Wetteland .40 .12
153 Mike Lansing .25 .07
154 Pedro Martinez 1.00 .30
155 Rico Brogna .25 .07
156 Kevin Brown .60 .18
157 Alex Rodriguez 1.50 .45
158 Wade Boggs .60 .18
159 Richard Hidalgo .25 .07
160 Mark Grace .60 .18
161 Jose Mesa .25 .07
162 John Olerud .40 .12
163 Tim Belcher .25 .07
164 Chuck Finley .40 .12
165 Brian Hunter .25 .07
166 Joe Carter .40 .12
167 Stan Javier .25 .07
168 Jay Bell .40 .12
169 Ray Lankford .40 .12
170 John Smoltz .60 .18
171 Ed Sprague .25 .07
172 Jason Giambi .40 .12
173 Todd Walker .25 .07
174 Paul Konerko .40 .12
175 Rey Ordonez .25 .07
176 Dante Bichette .40 .12
177 Bernie Williams .60 .18
178 Jon Nunnally .25 .07
179 Rafael Palmeiro .60 .18
180 Jay Buhner .40 .12
181 Devon White .40 .12
182 Jeff D'Amico .25 .07
183 Walt Weiss .40 .12
184 Scott Spiezio .25 .07
185 Moises Alou .40 .12
186 Carlos Baerga .25 .07
187 Todd Zeile .40 .12
188 Gregg Jefferies .40 .12
189 Mo Vaughn .40 .12
190 Terry Steinbach .25 .07
191 Ray Durham .40 .12
192 Robin Ventura .40 .12
193 Jeff Reed .25 .07
194 Ken Caminiti .40 .12
195 Eric Karros .40 .12

96 Wilson Alvarez .25 .07
97 Gary Gaetti .25 .07
98 Andres Galarraga .40 .12
99 Alex Gonzalez .25 .07
'00 Garret Anderson .40 .12
'01 Andy Benes .25 .07
'02 Harold Baines .40 .12
'03 Ron Coomer .25 .07
'04 Dean Palmer .40 .12
'05 Reggie Jefferson .25 .07
'06 John Burkett .25 .07
'07 Jermaine Allensworth .25 .07
'08 Bernard Gilkey .25 .07
'09 Jeff Bagwell .60 .18
'10 Kenny Lofton .40 .12
'11 Bobby Jones .25 .07
'12 Bartolo Colon .40 .12
'13 Jim Edmonds .40 .12
'14 Pat Hentgen .25 .07
'15 Matt Williams .40 .12
'16 Bob Abreu .40 .12
'17 Jorge Posada .60 .18
'18 Marty Cordova .25 .07
'19 Ken Hill .25 .07
'20 Steve Finley .40 .12
'21 Jeff King .25 .07
'22 Quinton McCracken .25 .07
'23 Matt Stairs .25 .07
'24 Darin Erstad .40 .12
'25 Fred McGriff .60 .18
'26 Marquis Grissom .40 .12
'27 Doug Glanville .25 .07
'28 Tom Glavine .60 .18
'29 John Franco .40 .12
'30 Darren Bragg .25 .07
'31 Barry Larkin .60 .18
'32 Trevor Hoffman .40 .12
'33 Brady Anderson .40 .12
'34 Al Martin .25 .07
'35 B.J. Surhoff .40 .12
'36 Ellis Burks .40 .12
'37 Randy Johnson 1.00 .30
'38 Mark Clark .25 .07
'39 Tony Saunders .25 .07
'40 Hideo Nomo 1.00 .30
'41 Brad Fullmer .25 .07
'42 Chipper Jones 1.00 .30
'43 Jose Valentin .25 .07
'44 Manny Ramirez .60 .18
'45 Derrek Lee .40 .12
'46 Jimmy Key .40 .12
'47 Tim Naehring .25 .07
'48 Bobby Higginson .40 .12
'49 Charles Johnson .40 .12
'50 Chili Davis .40 .12
'51 Tom Gordon .25 .07
'52 Mike Lieberthal .40 .12
'53 Billy Wagner .40 .12
'54 Juan Guzman .25 .07
'55 Todd Stottlemyre .25 .07
'56 Brian Jordan .40 .12
'57 Barry Bonds 2.50 .75
'58 Dan Wilson .25 .07
'59 Paul Molitor .60 .18
'60 Juan Gonzalez .60 .18
'61 Francisco Cordova .25 .07
'62 Cecil Fielder .40 .12
'63 Travis Lee .25 .07
'64 Kevin Tapani .25 .07
'65 Raul Mondesi .40 .12
'66 Travis Fryman .40 .12
'67 Armando Benitez .25 .07
'68 Pokey Reese .25 .07
'69 Rick Aguilera .25 .07
'70 Andy Pettitte .60 .18
'71 Jose Vizcaino .25 .07
'72 Kerry Wood 1.00 .30
'73 Vladimir Guerrero 1.00 .30
'74 John Smiley .25 .07
'75 Checklist (151-275) .25 .07

1998 Finest No-Protectors

andomly inserted in retail packs at the rate of ne in two and one in every HTA pack, this 275-ard set is parallel to the base set only without e Finest Protector covering and features doue-sided Finest technology.

Nm-Mt Ex-Mt
OMPLETE SET (275) 350.00 105.00
OMP. SERIES 1 (150) 200.00 60.00
OMP. SERIES 2 (125) 150.00 45.00
STARS: 2X TO 4X BASIC CARDS

1998 Finest No-Protectors Refractors

andomly inserted in retail packs at the rate of ne in 24 and in HTA packs at the rate of one in), this 275-card set is parallel to the regular nest No-Protector set. The difference is seen in e refractive quality of the card.

Nm-Mt Ex-Mt
STARS: 5X TO 12X BASIC CARDS

1998 Finest Oversize

hese sixteen 3" by 5" cards were inserted one very three hobby boxes. Though not actually on e cards, first series cards have been assigned A prefix and second series a B prefix to clari- our listing. The cards are parallel to the regu- r Finest cards except numbering "of 8". They ere issued as chiptoppers in the boxes.

Nm-Mt Ex-Mt
OMPLETE SERIES 1 (8) 120.00 36.00
OMPLETE SERIES 2 (8) 80.00 24.00
REFRACTORS: .75X TO 2X BASIC OVERSIZE
EF.ODDS 1:6 HOBBY/HTA BOXES
1 Mark McGwire 15.00 4.50
2 Cal Ripken 20.00 6.00
3 Nomar Garciaparra 10.00 3.00
4 Mike Piazza 10.00 3.00
5 Greg Maddux 10.00 3.00
6 Jose Cruz Jr. 1.50 .45
7 Roger Clemens 12.00 3.60
8 Ken Griffey Jr. 10.00 3.00
B1 Frank Thomas 6.00 1.80
B2 Bernie Williams 4.00 1.20
B3 Randy Johnson 6.00 1.80
B4 Chipper Jones 6.00 1.80
B5 Manny Ramirez 4.00 1.20
B6 Barry Bonds 15.00 4.50
B7 Juan Gonzalez 4.00 1.20
B8 Jeff Bagwell 4.00 1.20

1998 Finest Refractors

Randomly inserted in retail packs at the rate of one in 12 and in HTA packs at the rate of one in five, this 275-card set is parallel to the base set. The difference is found in the refractive quality of the card.

Nm-Mt Ex-Mt
*STARS: 5X TO 12X BASIC CARDS

1998 Finest Centurions

Randomly inserted in Series one hobby packs at a rate of 1:153 and Home Team Advantage packs at a rate of 1:71, cards from this 20-card set feature action color photos of top players who will lead the game into the next century. Each card is sequentially numbered on back to 500. Unfortunately, an unknown quantity of unnumbered Centurions made their way into the secondary market in 1999. It's believed that these cards were quality control extras. To further compound this situation, some unscrupulous parties attempted to serial-number the cards. The fake cards have flat gold foil numbering. The real cards have bright foil numbering.

Nm-Mt Ex-Mt
COMPLETE SET (20) 100.00 30.00
*REF: 2X TO 5X BASIC CENTURIONS
SER.1 REF.ODDS 1:1020 HOBBY, 1:471 HTA
REFRACTOR PR.RUN 75 SERIAL #'d SETS
C1 Andruw Jones 2.00 .60
C2 Vladimir Guerrero 5.00 1.50
C3 Nomar Garciaparra 8.00 2.40
C4 Scott Rolen 5.00 1.50
C5 Ken Griffey Jr. 8.00 2.40
C6 Jose Cruz Jr. 1.25 .35
C7 Barry Bonds 12.00 3.60
C8 Mark McGwire 12.00 3.60
C9 Juan Gonzalez 3.00 .90
C10 Jeff Bagwell 3.00 .90
C11 Frank Thomas 5.00 1.50
C12 Paul Konerko 2.00 .60
C13 Alex Rodriguez 8.00 2.40
C14 Mike Piazza 8.00 2.40
C15 Travis Lee 1.25 .35
C16 Chipper Jones 5.00 1.50
C17 Larry Walker 3.00 .90
C18 Mo Vaughn 2.00 .60
C19 Livan Hernandez 1.25 .35
C20 Jaret Wright 1.25 .35

1998 Finest Centurions Refractors

Randomly inserted in Series one packs at a rate of 1 in 1020 hobby packs and one in 471 HTA packs, this 20-card set is parallel to the regular Centurions set. The difference is seen in the refractive quality of the cards. Each card is sequentially numbered to 75 on back and carries an "R" directly underneath the card number.

Nm-Mt Ex-Mt
*REFRACTORS: 1.5X TO 4X CENTURIONS

1998 Finest The Man

Randomly inserted in packs at a rate of one in 119, this 20-card set is an insert to the 1998 Finest base set. The entire set is sequentially numbered to 500.

Nm-Mt Ex-Mt
COMPLETE SET (20) 400.00 120.00
*REF: 1X TO 2.5X BASIC THE MAN
REF.SER.2 ODDS 1:793
REFRACTOR PR.RUN 75 SERIAL #'d SETS
TM1 Ken Griffey Jr. 25.00 7.50
TM2 Barry Bonds 40.00 12.00
TM3 Frank Thomas 15.00 4.50
TM4 Chipper Jones 15.00 4.50
TM5 Cal Ripken 50.00 15.00
TM6 Nomar Garciaparra 25.00 7.50
TM7 Mark McGwire 40.00 12.00
TM8 Mike Piazza 25.00 7.50
TM9 Derek Jeter 40.00 12.00
TM10 Alex Rodriguez 25.00 7.50
TM11 Jose Cruz Jr. 4.00 1.20
TM12 Larry Walker 10.00 3.00
TM13 Jeff Bagwell 10.00 3.00
TM14 Tony Gwynn 20.00 6.00
TM15 Travis Lee 4.00 1.20
TM16 Juan Gonzalez 10.00 3.00
TM17 Scott Rolen 15.00 4.50
TM18 Randy Johnson 15.00 4.50
TM19 Roger Clemens 30.00 9.00
TM20 Greg Maddux 25.00 7.50

1998 Finest Mystery Finest 1

Randomly inserted in first series hobby packs at the rate of one in 36 and Home Team Advantage packs at the rate of one in 15, cards from this 50-card set feature color action photos of 20 top players on double-sided cards. Each player is matched with three different players on the opposite side or another photo of himself. Each side is covered with the Finest opaque protector.

Nm-Mt Ex-Mt
*REFRACTOR: 1X TO 2.5X BASIC MYSTERY
REF.SER.1 ODDS 1:144 HOBBY, 1:64 HTA
M1 Frank Thomas 15.00 4.50
Ken Griffey Jr.
M2 Frank Thomas 15.00 4.50
Mike Piazza
M3 Frank Thomas 25.00 7.50
Mark McGwire
M4 Frank Thomas 10.00 3.00
Frank Thomas
M5 Ken Griffey Jr. 15.00 4.50
Mike Piazza
M6 Ken Griffey Jr. 25.00 7.50
Mark McGwire
M7 Ken Griffey Jr. 15.00 4.50
Ken Griffey Jr.
M8 Mike Piazza 25.00 7.50
Mark McGwire
M9 Mike Piazza 20.00 6.00
Mike Piazza
M10 Mark McGwire 30.00 9.00
Mark McGwire
M11 Nomar Garciaparra 15.00 4.50
Jose Cruz Jr.
M12 Nomar Garciaparra 20.00 6.00
Derek Jeter
M13 Nomar Garciaparra 15.00 4.50
Andruw Jones
M14 Nomar Garciaparra 20.00 6.00
Nomar Garciaparra
M15 Jose Cruz Jr. 25.00 7.50
Derek Jeter
M16 Jose Cruz Jr. 4.00 1.20
Andruw Jones
M17 Jose Cruz Jr. 4.00 1.20
Jose Cruz Jr.
M18 Derek Jeter 25.00 7.50
Andruw Jones
M19 Derek Jeter 30.00 9.00
Derek Jeter
M20 Andruw Jones 4.00 1.20
Andruw Jones
M21 Cal Ripken 25.00 7.50
Tony Gwynn
M22 Cal Ripken 30.00 9.00
Barry Bonds
M23 Cal Ripken 30.00 9.00
Greg Maddux
M24 Cal Ripken 40.00 12.00
Cal Ripken
M25 Tony Gwynn 30.00 9.00
Barry Bonds
M26 Tony Gwynn 15.00 4.50
Greg Maddux
M27 Tony Gwynn 15.00 4.50
Tony Gwynn
M28 Barry Bonds 30.00 9.00
Greg Maddux
M29 Barry Bonds 30.00 9.00
Barry Bonds
M30 Greg Maddux 20.00 6.00
Greg Maddux
M31 Juan Gonzalez 6.00 1.80
Larry Walker
M32 Juan Gonzalez 6.00 1.80
Andres Galarraga
M33 Juan Gonzalez 10.00 3.00
Chipper Jones
M34 Juan Gonzalez 6.00 1.80
Juan Gonzalez
M35 Larry Walker 6.00 1.80
Andres Galarraga
M36 Larry Walker 10.00 3.00
Chipper Jones
M37 Larry Walker 6.00 1.80
Larry Walker
M38 Andres Galarraga 10.00 3.00
Chipper Jones
M39 Andres Galarraga 4.00 1.20
Andres Galarraga
M40 Chipper Jones 10.00 3.00
Chipper Jones
M41 Gary Sheffield 15.00 4.50
Sammy Sosa
M42 Gary Sheffield 6.00 1.80
Jeff Bagwell
M43 Gary Sheffield 6.00 1.80
Tino Martinez
M44 Gary Sheffield 4.00 1.20
Gary Sheffield
M45 Sammy Sosa 20.00 6.00
Jeff Bagwell
M46 Sammy Sosa 15.00 4.50
Tino Martinez
M47 Sammy Sosa 20.00 6.00
Sammy Sosa
M48 Jeff Bagwell 6.00 1.80
Tino Martinez
M49 Jeff Bagwell 6.00 1.80
Jeff Bagwell
M50 Tino Martinez 6.00 1.80
Tino Martinez

1998 Finest Mystery Finest 2

Randomly inserted in second series hobby packs at the rate of one in 36 and Home Team Advantage packs at the rate of one in 15, cards from this 50-card set feature color action photos of 20 top players on double-sided cards. Each player is matched with three different players on the opposite side or another photo of himself. Each side is covered with the Finest opaque protector.

Nm-Mt Ex-Mt
COMPLETE SET (40) 300.00 90.00
*REFRACTOR: 1X TO 2.5X BASIC MYSTERY
REF.SER.2 ODDS 1:144
M1 Nomar Garciaparra 15.00 4.50
Frank Thomas
M2 Nomar Garciaparra 15.00 4.50
Albert Belle
M3 Nomar Garciaparra 15.00 4.50
Scott Rolen
M4 Frank Thomas 10.00 3.00
Albert Belle
M5 Frank Thomas 10.00 3.00
Scott Rolen
M6 Albert Belle 10.00 3.00
Scott Rolen
M7 Ken Griffey Jr. 15.00 4.50
Jose Cruz Jr.
M8 Ken Griffey Jr. 15.00 4.50
Alex Rodriguez
M9 Ken Griffey Jr. 20.00 6.00
Roger Clemens
M10 Jose Cruz Jr. 15.00 4.50
Alex Rodriguez
M11 Jose Cruz Jr. 20.00 6.00
Roger Clemens
M12 Alex Rodriguez 15.00 4.50
Roger Clemens
M13 Mike Piazza 30.00 9.00
Barry Bonds
M14 Mike Piazza 25.00 7.50
Derek Jeter
M15 Mike Piazza 15.00 4.50
Bernie Williams
M16 Barry Bonds 30.00 9.00
Derek Jeter
M17 Barry Bonds 15.00 4.50
Bernie Williams
M18 Deter Jeter 25.00 7.50
Bernie Williams
M19 Mark McGwire 25.00 7.50
Jeff Bagwell
M20 Mark McGwire 25.00 7.50
Mo Vaughn
M21 Mark McGwire 25.00 7.50
Jim Thome
M22 Jeff Bagwell 6.00 1.80
Mo Vaughn
M23 Jeff Bagwell 10.00 3.00
Jim Thome
M24 Mo Vaughn 10.00 3.00
Jim Thome
M25 Juan Gonzalez 6.00 1.80
Travis Lee
M26 Juan Gonzalez 6.00 1.80
Ben Grieve
M27 Juan Gonzalez 6.00 1.80
Fred McGriff
M28 Travis Lee 4.00 1.20
Ben Grieve
M29 Travis Lee 6.00 1.80
Fred McGriff
M30 Ben Grieve 6.00 1.80
Fred McGriff
M31 Albert Belle 4.00 1.20
Albert Belle
M32 Scott Rolen 10.00 3.00
Scott Rolen
M33 Alex Rodriguez 20.00 6.00
Alex Rodriguez
M34 Roger Clemens 20.00 6.00
Roger Clemens
M35 Bernie Williams 6.00 1.80
Bernie Williams
M36 Mo Vaughn 4.00 1.20
Mo Vaughn
M37 Jim Thome 10.00 3.00
Jim Thome
M38 Travis Lee 4.00 1.20
Travis Lee
M39 Fred McGriff 6.00 1.80
Fred McGriff
M40 Ben Grieve 4.00 1.20
Ben Grieve

1998 Finest Mystery Finest Oversize

One of these three different cards was randomly seeded as chiptoppers (lying on top of the packs, but within the sealed box) at a rate of 1:6 series two Home Team Collector boxes. Besides the obvious difference in size, these cards are also numbered differently than the standard-sized cards, but beyond that they're essentially straight parallels of their standard sized siblings.

Nm-Mt Ex-Mt
COMPLETE SET (3) 40.00 12.00
SER.2 STATED ODDS 1:6 HTA BOXES
*REFRACTOR: .75X TO 2X OVERSIZE
SER.2 REF.STATED ODDS 1:12 HTA BOXES
1 Ken Griffey Jr. 10.00 3.00
Alex Rodriguez
2 Derek Jeter 15.00 4.50
Bernie Williams
3 Mark McGwire 15.00 4.50
Jeff Bagwell

1998 Finest Power Zone

Randomly inserted in series one hobby packs at the rate of one in 72 and in series one Home Team Advantage packs at the rate of one in 32, this 20-card set features color action photos of top players printed with new "Flop Inks" technology which actually changes the color of the card when it is held at different angles.

Nm-Mt Ex-Mt
COMPLETE SET (20) 200.00 60.00
P1 Ken Griffey Jr. 20.00 6.00
P2 Jeff Bagwell 8.00 2.40
P3 Jose Cruz Jr. 3.00 .90
P4 Barry Bonds 30.00 9.00
P5 Mark McGwire 30.00 9.00
P6 Jim Thome 12.00 3.60
P7 Mo Vaughn 5.00 1.50
P8 Gary Sheffield 5.00 1.50
P9 Andres Galarraga 5.00 1.50
P10 Nomar Garciaparra 20.00 6.00
P11 Rafael Palmeiro 8.00 2.40
P12 Sammy Sosa 20.00 6.00
P13 Jay Buhner 5.00 1.50
P14 Tony Clark 3.00 .90
P15 Mike Piazza 20.00 6.00
P16 Larry Walker 8.00 2.40
P17 Albert Belle 5.00 1.50
P18 Tino Martinez 8.00 2.40
P19 Juan Gonzalez 8.00 2.40
P20 Frank Thomas 12.00 3.60

1998 Finest Stadium Stars

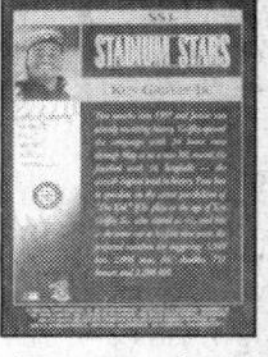

Randomly inserted in packs at a rate of one in 72, this 24-card set features a selection of the majors top hitters set against an attractive foil-glowing stadium background.

Nm-Mt Ex-Mt
COMPLETE SET (24) 300.00 90.00
SS1 Ken Griffey Jr. 20.00 6.00
SS2 Alex Rodriguez 20.00 6.00
SS3 Mo Vaughn 5.00 1.50
SS4 Nomar Garciaparra 20.00 6.00
SS5 Frank Thomas 12.00 3.60
SS6 Albert Belle 5.00 1.50
SS7 Derek Jeter 30.00 9.00
SS8 Chipper Jones 12.00 3.60
SS9 Cal Ripken 40.00 12.00
SS10 Jim Thome 12.00 3.60
SS11 Mike Piazza 20.00 6.00
SS12 Juan Gonzalez 8.00 2.40
SS13 Jeff Bagwell 8.00 2.40
SS14 Sammy Sosa 20.00 6.00
SS15 Jose Cruz Jr. 3.00 .90
SS16 Gary Sheffield 5.00 1.50
SS17 Larry Walker 8.00 2.40
SS18 Tony Gwynn 15.00 4.50
SS19 Mark McGwire 30.00 9.00
SS20 Barry Bonds 30.00 9.00
SS21 Tino Martinez 8.00 2.40
SS22 Manny Ramirez 8.00 2.40
SS23 Ken Caminiti 5.00 1.50
SS24 Andres Galarraga 5.00 1.50

1999 Finest

This 300-card set (produced by Topps) was distributed in first and second series six-card packs with a suggested retail price of $5. The fronts feature color action player photos printed on 27 pt. card stock using Chromium technology. The backs carry player information. The set includes the following subsets: Gems (101-120), Sensations (121-130) Rookies (131-150/277-299), Sterling (251-265) and Gamers (266-276). Card number 300 is a special Hank Aaron/Mark McGwire tribute. Cards numbered from 101 through 150 and 251 through 300 were short printed and seeded at a rate of one per hobby, one per retail and two per Home Team Advantage pack. Notable Rookie Cards include Pat Burrell, Sean Burroughs, Nick Johnson, Austin Kearns, Corey Patterson and Alfonso Soriano.

Nm-Mt Ex-Mt
COMPLETE SET (300) 100.00 30.00
COMP.SERIES 1 (150) 50.00 15.00
COMP.SERIES 2 (150) 50.00 15.00
COMP.SER.1 w/o SP's (100) 20.00 6.00

COMP.SER.2 w/o SP's (100)..... 20.00 6.00
COMMON (1-100/151-250) .50 .12
COMMON (101-150/251-300) .50 .15
1 Darin Erstad .40 .12
2 Javy Lopez .40 .12
3 Vinny Castilla .40 .12
4 Jim Thome 1.00 .30
5 Tino Martinez .60 .18
6 Mark Grace .60 .18
7 Shawn Green .40 .12
8 Dustin Hermanson .40 .12
9 Kevin Young .40 .12
10 Tony Clark .40 .12
11 Scott Brosius .40 .12
12 Craig Biggio .60 .18
13 Brian McRae .40 .12
14 Chan Ho Park .40 .12
15 Manny Ramirez .60 .18
16 Chipper Jones 1.00 .30
17 Rico Brogna .40 .12
18 Quinton McCracken .40 .12
19 J.T. Snow .40 .12
20 Tony Gwynn 1.25 .35
21 Juan Guzman .40 .12
22 John Valentin .40 .12
23 Rick Helling .40 .12
24 Sandy Alomar Jr. .40 .12
25 Frank Thomas 1.00 .30
26 Jorge Posada .60 .18
27 Dmitri Young .40 .12
28 Rick Reed .40 .12
29 Kevin Tapani .40 .12
30 Troy Glaus .60 .18
31 Kenny Rogers .40 .12
32 Jeromy Burnitz .40 .12
33 Mark Grudzielanek .40 .12
34 Mike Mussina .60 .18
35 Scott Rolen 1.00 .30
36 Neifi Perez .40 .12
37 Brad Radke .40 .12
38 Darryl Strawberry .40 .12
39 Robb Nen .40 .12
40 Moises Alou .40 .12
41 Eric Young .40 .12
42 Livan Hernandez .40 .12
43 John Wetteland .40 .12
44 Matt Lawton .40 .12
45 Ben Grieve .40 .12
46 Fernando Tatis .40 .12
47 Travis Fryman .40 .12
48 David Segui .40 .12
49 Bob Abreu .40 .12
50 Nomar Garciaparra 1.50 .45
51 Paul O'Neill .60 .18
52 Jeff King .40 .12
53 Francisco Cordova .40 .12
54 John Olerud .40 .12
55 Vladimir Guerrero 1.00 .30
56 Fernando Vina .40 .12
57 Shane Reynolds .40 .12
58 Chuck Finley .40 .12
59 Rondell White .40 .12
60 Greg Vaughn .40 .12
61 Ryan Minor .40 .12
62 Tom Gordon .40 .12
63 Damion Easley .40 .12
64 Ray Durham .40 .12
65 Orlando Hernandez .40 .12
66 Bartolo Colon .40 .12
67 Jaret Wright .40 .12
68 Royce Clayton .40 .12
69 Tim Salmon .60 .18
70 Mark McGwire 2.50 .75
71 Alex Gonzalez .40 .12
72 Tom Glavine .60 .18
73 David Justice .40 .12
74 Omar Vizquel .60 .18
75 Juan Gonzalez .60 .18
76 Bobby Higginson .40 .12
77 Todd Walker .40 .12
78 Dante Bichette .40 .12
79 Kevin Millwood .40 .12
80 Roger Clemens 2.00 .60
81 Kerry Wood 1.00 .30
82 Cal Ripken 3.00 .90
83 Jay Bell .40 .12
84 Barry Bonds 2.50 .75
85 Alex Rodriguez 1.50 .45
86 Doug Glanville .40 .12
87 Jason Kendall .40 .12
88 Sean Casey .40 .12
89 Aaron Sele .40 .12
90 Derek Jeter 2.50 .75
91 Andy Ashby .40 .12
92 Rusty Greer .40 .12
93 Rod Beck .40 .12
94 Matt Williams .40 .12
95 Mike Piazza 1.50 .45
96 Wally Joyner .40 .12
97 Barry Larkin .60 .18
98 Eric Milton .40 .12
99 Gary Sheffield .40 .12
100 Greg Maddux 1.50 .45
101 Ken Griffey Jr. GEM 2.50 .75
102 Frank Thomas GEM 1.25 .35
103 N.Garciaparra GEM 2.50 .75
104 Mark McGwire GEM 4.00 1.20
105 Alex Rodriguez GEM 2.50 .75
106 Tony Gwynn GEM 2.00 .60
107 Juan Gonzalez GEM .75 .23
108 Jeff Bagwell GEM .75 .23
109 Sammy Sosa GEM 2.50 .75
110 V.Guerrero GEM 1.25 .35
111 Roger Clemens GEM 3.00 .90
112 Barry Bonds GEM 4.00 1.20
113 Darin Erstad GEM .50 .15
114 Mike Piazza GEM 2.50 .75
115 Derek Jeter GEM 4.00 1.20
116 Chipper Jones GEM 1.25 .35
117 Larry Walker GEM .75 .23
118 Scott Rolen GEM 1.25 .35
119 Cal Ripken GEM 5.00 1.50
120 Greg Maddux GEM 2.50 .75
121 Troy Glaus SENS .50 .15
122 Ben Grieve SENS .50 .15
123 Ryan Minor SENS .50 .15
124 Kerry Wood SENS 1.25 .35
125 Travis Lee SENS .50 .15
126 Adrian Beltre SENS .75 .23
127 Brad Fullmer SENS .50 .15
128 Aramis Ramirez SENS .50 .15
129 Eric Chavez SENS .50 .15
130 Todd Helton SENS .75 .23
131 Pat Burrell RC 2.50 .75
132 Ryan Mills RC .50 .15
133 Austin Kearns RC 4.00 1.20
134 Josh McKinley RC .50 .15
135 Adam Everett RC .75 .23
136 Marlon Anderson .50 .15
137 Bruce Chen .50 .15
138 Matt Clement .50 .15
139 Alex Gonzalez .50 .15
140 Roy Halladay .50 .15
141 Calvin Pickering .50 .15
142 Randy Wolf .50 .15
143 Ryan Anderson .50 .15
144 Ruben Mateo .50 .15
145 Alex Escobar RC .50 .15
146 Jeremy Giambi .50 .15
147 Lance Berkman .50 .15
148 Michael Barrett .50 .15
149 Preston Wilson .50 .15
150 Gabe Kapler .50 .15
151 Roger Clemens 2.00 .60
152 Jay Buhner .40 .12
153 Brad Fullmer .40 .12
154 Ray Lankford .40 .12
155 Jim Edmonds .40 .12
156 Jason Giambi .40 .12
157 Bret Boone .40 .12
158 Jeff Cirillo .40 .12
159 Rickey Henderson 1.00 .30
160 Edgar Martinez .60 .18
161 Ron Gant .40 .12
162 Mark Kotsay .40 .12
163 Trevor Hoffman .40 .12
164 Jason Schmidt .40 .12
165 Brett Tomko .40 .12
166 David Ortiz .60 .18
167 Dean Palmer .40 .12
168 Hideki Irabu .40 .12
169 Mike Cameron .40 .12
170 Pedro Martinez 1.00 .30
171 Tom Goodwin .40 .12
172 Brian Hunter .40 .12
173 Al Leiter .40 .12
174 Charles Johnson .40 .12
175 Curt Schilling .40 .12
176 Robin Ventura .40 .12
177 Travis Lee .40 .12
178 Jeff Shaw .40 .12
179 Ugueth Urbina .40 .12
180 Roberto Alomar .60 .18
181 Cliff Floyd .40 .12
182 Adrian Beltre .60 .18
183 Tony Womack .40 .12
184 Brian Jordan .40 .12
185 Randy Johnson 1.00 .30
186 Mickey Morandini .40 .12
187 Todd Hundley .40 .12
188 Jose Valentin .40 .12
189 Eric Davis .40 .12
190 Ken Caminiti .40 .12
191 David Wells .40 .12
192 Ryan Klesko .40 .12
193 Garret Anderson .40 .12
194 Eric Karros .40 .12
195 Ivan Rodriguez 1.00 .30
196 Aramis Ramirez .40 .12
197 Mike Lieberthal .40 .12
198 Will Clark 1.00 .30
199 Rey Ordonez .40 .12
200 Ken Griffey Jr. 1.50 .45
201 Jose Guillen .40 .12
202 Scott Erickson .40 .12
203 Paul Konerko .40 .12
204 Johnny Damon .60 .18
205 Larry Walker .60 .18
206 Denny Neagle .40 .12
207 Jose Offerman .40 .12
208 Andy Pettitte .60 .18
209 Bobby Jones .40 .12
210 Kevin Brown .60 .18
211 John Smoltz .60 .18
212 Henry Rodriguez .40 .12
213 Tim Belcher .40 .12
214 Carlos Delgado .40 .12
215 Andruw Jones .40 .12
216 Andy Benes .40 .12
217 Fred McGriff .60 .18
218 Edgar Renteria .40 .12
219 Miguel Tejada .40 .12
220 Bernie Williams .60 .18
221 Justin Thompson .40 .12
222 Marty Cordova .40 .12
223 Delino DeShields .40 .12
224 Ellis Burks .40 .12
225 Kenny Lofton .40 .12
226 Steve Finley .40 .12
227 Eric Chavez .40 .12
228 Jose Cruz Jr. .40 .12
229 Marquis Grissom .40 .12
230 Jeff Bagwell .60 .18
231 Jose Canseco 1.00 .30
232 Edgardo Alfonzo .40 .12
233 Richie Sexson .40 .12
234 Jeff Kent .40 .12
235 Rafael Palmeiro .60 .18
236 David Cone .40 .12
237 Gregg Jefferies .40 .12
238 Mike Lansing .40 .12
239 Mariano Rivera .60 .18
240 Albert Belle .40 .12
241 Chuck Knoblauch .40 .12
242 Derek Bell .40 .12
243 Pat Hentgen .40 .12
244 Andres Galarraga .40 .12
245 Mo Vaughn .40 .12
246 Wade Boggs .60 .18
247 Devon White .40 .12
248 Todd Helton .60 .18
249 Raul Mondesi .40 .12
250 Sammy Sosa 1.50 .45
251 Nomar Garciaparra ST 2.50 .75
252 Mark McGwire ST 4.00 1.20
253 Alex Rodriguez ST 2.50 .75
254 Juan Gonzalez ST .75 .23
255 Vladimir Guerrero ST 1.25 .35
256 Ken Griffey Jr. ST 2.50 .75
257 Mike Piazza ST 2.50 .75
258 Derek Jeter ST 4.00 1.20
259 Albert Belle ST .50 .15
260 Greg Vaughn ST .50 .15
261 Sammy Sosa ST 2.50 .75
262 Greg Maddux ST 2.50 .75
263 Frank Thomas ST 1.25 .35
264 Mark Grace ST .75 .23
265 Ivan Rodriguez ST 1.25 .35
266 Roger Clemens GM 3.00 .90
267 Mo Vaughn GM .50 .15
268 Jim Thome GM 1.25 .35
269 Darin Erstad GM .50 .15
270 Chipper Jones GM 1.25 .35
271 Larry Walker GM .75 .23
272 Cal Ripken GM 5.00 1.50
273 Scott Rolen GM 1.25 .35
274 Randy Johnson GM 1.25 .35
275 Tony Gwynn GM 2.00 .60
276 Barry Bonds GM 4.00 1.20
277 Sean Burroughs RC 2.00 .60
278 J.M. Gold RC .50 .15
279 Carlos Lee .50 .15
280 George Lombard .50 .15
281 Carlos Beltran .75 .23
282 Fernando Seguignol .50 .15
283 Eric Chavez .50 .15
284 Carlos Pena RC .75 .23
285 Corey Patterson RC 3.00 .90
286 Alfonso Soriano RC 8.00 2.40
287 Nick Johnson RC 1.25 .35
288 Jorge Toca RC .50 .15
289 A.J. Burnett RC 1.25 .35
290 Andy Brown RC .50 .15
291 D.Mientkiewicz RC 1.25 .35
292 Bobby Seay RC .50 .15
293 Chip Ambres RC .50 .15
294 C.C. Sabathia RC 1.50 .45
295 Choo Freeman RC .50 .15
296 Eric Valent RC .50 .15
297 Matt Belisle RC .50 .15
298 Jason Tyner RC .50 .15
299 Masao Kida RC .50 .15
300 Hank Aaron 3.00 .90
Mark McGwire

1999 Finest Gold Refractors

This 300-card set is a die-cut gold foil parallel version of the base set. Only 100 serially numbered sets were produced. Cards were randomly inserted in hobby and retail packs. Series one packs were at the rate of one in 82 and HTA packs at a rate of one in 38. Series 2 packs were at the rate of one in 57 and HTA packs at a rate of one in 26.

Nm-Mt Ex-Mt
*STARS 1-100/151-250: 10X TO 25X BASIC
*STARS 101-150/251-300: 6X TO 15X BAS.
*ROOKIES: 4X TO 10X BASIC

1999 Finest Refractors

Randomly inserted in series one and two packs at the rate of one in 12 hobby/retail and one in five HTA, this 300-card set is a parallel version of the base set and is similar in design. The difference is found in the refractive quality of the card.

Nm-Mt Ex-Mt
*STARS 1-100/151-250: 3X TO 8X BASIC
*STARS 101-150/251-300: 2X TO 5X BASIC
*ROOKIES: 1.5X TO 4X BASIC

1999 Finest Aaron Award Contenders

Randomly inserted into Series two packs at different rates depending on the player, this nine-card set features color action photos of players vying for the Hank Aaron Award.

Nm-Mt Ex-Mt
COMPLETE SET (9) 60.00 18.00
HA1 SER.2 ODDS 1:216, 1:108 HTA
HA2 SER.2 ODDS 1:108, 1:54 HTA
HA3 SER.2 ODDS 1:72, 1:36 HTA
HA4 SER.2 ODDS 1:54, 1:27 HTA
HA5 SER.2 ODDS 1:43, 1:21 HTA
HA6 SER.2 ODDS 1:36, 1:18 HTA
HA7 SER.2 ODDS 1:31, 1:15 HTA
HA8 SER.2 ODDS 1:27, 1:13 HTA
HA9 SER.2 ODDS 1:24, 1:12 HTA
*REFRACTORS: 1.5X TO 4X BASIC AARON AW
REF HA1 SER.2 ODDS 1:1728, 1:864 HTA
REF HA2 SER.2 ODDS 1:864, 1:432 HTA
REF HA3 SER.2 ODDS 1:576, 1:288 HTA
REF HA4 SER.2 ODDS 1:432, 1:216 HTA
REF HA5 SER.2 ODDS 1:344, 1:172 HTA
REF HA6 SER.2 ODDS 1:288, 1:144 HTA
REF HA7 SER.2 ODDS 1:248, 1:124 HTA
REF HA8 SER.2 ODDS 1:216, 1:108 HTA
REF HA9 SER.2 ODDS 1:192, 1:96 HTA
HA1 Juan Gonzalez 8.00 2.40
HA2 Vladimir Guerrero 10.00 3.00
HA3 Nomar Garciaparra 12.00 3.60
HA4 Albert Belle 3.00 .90
HA5 Frank Thomas 5.00 1.50
HA6 Sammy Sosa 6.00 1.80
HA7 Alex Rodriguez 5.00 1.50
HA8 Ken Griffey Jr. 4.00 1.20
HA9 Mark McGwire 5.00 1.50

1999 Finest Complements

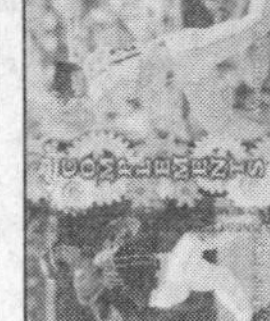

Randomly inserted into Series two packs at the rate of one in 56, this seven-card set features color action photos of 14 stars who complement each other's skills and share a common bond paired together on cards printed with advanced "Split Screen" technology which combines Refractor and Non-Refractor technology on the same card. Each card has three variations as follows: 1) Non-Refractor/Refractor, 2) Refractor/Non-Refractor, and 3) Refractor/Refractor.

Nm-Mt Ex-Mt
COMPLETE SET (7) 50.00 15.00
RIGHT/LEFT REF.VARIATIONS EQUAL VALUE
*DUAL REF: 1.25X TO 3X BASIC COMP.
DUAL REF.SER.2 ODDS 1:168, 1:81 HTA
C1 Mike Piazza 6.00 1.80
Ivan Rodriguez
C2 Tony Gwynn 5.00 1.50
Wade Boggs
C3 Kerry Wood 8.00 2.40
Roger Clemens
C4 Juan Gonzalez 6.00 1.80
Sammy Sosa
C5 Derek Jeter 10.00 3.00
Nomar Garciaparra
C6 Mark McGwire 10.00 3.00
Frank Thomas
C7 Vladimir Guerrero 4.00 1.20
Andruw Jones

1999 Finest Double Feature

Randomly inserted into Series two packs at the rate of one in 56, this seven-card set features color photos of fourteen paired teammates printed on cards using Split Screen technology combining Refractor and Non-Refractor technology on the same card. There are three different versions of each card as follows: 1) Non-Refractor/Refractor, 2) Refractor/Non-Refractor, and 3) Refractor/Refractor.

Nm-Mt Ex-Mt
COMPLETE SET (7) 40.00 12.00
RIGHT/LEFT REF.VARIATIONS EQUAL VALUE
*DUAL REF: 1.25X TO 3X BASIC DOUB.FEAT.
*DUAL REF BURRELL: 1.25X TO 3X HI COLUM
DUAL REF.SER.2 ODDS 1:168, 1:81 HTA
DF1 Ken Griffey Jr. 6.00 1.80
Alex Rodriguez
DF2 Chipper Jones 4.00 1.20
Andruw Jones
DF3 Darin Erstad 1.50 .45
Mo Vaughn
DF4 Craig Biggio 2.50 .75
Jeff Bagwell
DF5 Ben Grieve 1.50 .45
Eric Chavez
DF6 Albert Belle 12.00 3.60
Cal Ripken
DF7 Scott Rolen 2.50 .75
Pat Burrell

1999 Finest Franchise Records

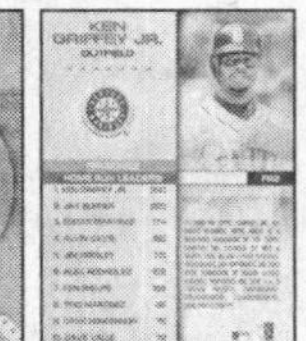

Randomly inserted into Series two packs at the rate of one in 129, this ten-card set features color action photos of all-time and single-season franchise statistic holders. A refractive parallel version of this set was also produced and inserted in Series two packs at the rate of one in 378.

Nm-Mt Ex-Mt
COMPLETE SET (10) 150.00 45.00
*REFRACTORS: .75X TO 2X BASIC FRAN.REC.
REF.SER.2 ODDS 1:378, 1:189 HTA
FR1 Frank Thomas 10.00 3.00
FR2 Ken Griffey Jr. 15.00 4.50
FR3 Mark McGwire 25.00 7.50
FR4 Juan Gonzalez 6.00 1.80
FR5 Nomar Garciaparra 15.00 4.50
FR6 Mike Piazza 15.00 4.50
FR7 Cal Ripken 30.00 9.00
FR8 Sammy Sosa 15.00 4.50
FR9 Barry Bonds 25.00 7.50
FR10 Tony Gwynn 12.00 3.60

1999 Finest Future's Finest

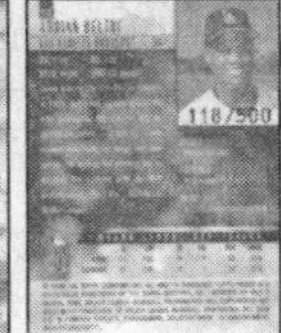

Randomly inserted into Series two packs at the rate of one in 171, this 10-card set features color photos of top young stars printed on card stock using Refractive Finest technology. The cards are sequentially numbered to 500.

Nm-Mt Ex-Mt
COMPLETE SET (10) 100.00 30.00
FF1 Pat Burrell 12.00 3.60
FF2 Troy Glaus 10.00 3.00
FF3 Eric Chavez 10.00 3.00
FF4 Ryan Anderson 10.00 3.00
FF5 Ruben Mateo 10.00 3.00
FF6 Gabe Kapler 10.00 3.00
FF7 Alex Gonzalez 10.00 3.00
FF8 Michael Barrett 10.00 3.00
FF9 Adrian Beltre 10.00 3.00
FF10 Fernando Seguignol 10.00 3.00

1999 Finest Leading Indicators

Randomly inserted in Series one packs at th rate of one in 24, this 10-card set features colc action photos highlighting the 1998 home ru totals of superstar players and printed on carc using a heat-sensitvie, thermal-ink technolog When a collector touched the baseball field bacl ground in left, center, or right field, the heat fro his finger revealed the pictured player's '9 home run totals in that direction.

Nm-Mt Ex-Mt
COMPLETE SET (10) 50.00 15.00
L1 Mark McGwire 10.00 3.00
L2 Sammy Sosa 6.00 1.80
L3 Ken Griffey Jr. 6.00 1.80
L4 Greg Vaughn 1.50 .45
L5 Albert Belle 1.50 .45
L6 Juan Gonzalez 2.50 .75
L7 Andres Galarraga 1.50 .45
L8 Alex Rodriguez 6.00 1.80
L9 Barry Bonds 10.00 3.00
L10 Jeff Bagwell 2.50 .75

1999 Finest Milestones

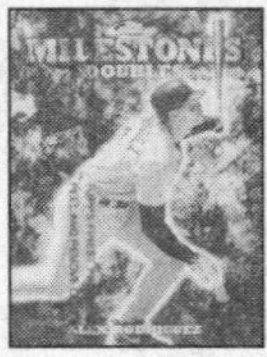

Randomly inserted into packs at the rate of or in 29, this 40-card set features color photos players who have the highest statistics in fo categories: Hits, Home Runs, RBI's ar Doubles. The cards are printed with Refract technology and sequentially numbered based c the category as follows: Hits to 3,000, Hom Runs to 500, RBIs to 1,400, and Doubles to 50

Nm-Mt Ex-Mt
M1 Tony Gwynn HIT 5.00 1.50
M2 Cal Ripken HIT 12.00 3.60
M3 Wade Boggs HIT 2.50 .75
M4 Ken Griffey Jr. HIT 6.00 1.80
M5 Frank Thomas HIT 4.00 1.20
M6 Barry Bonds HIT 10.00 3.00
M7 Travis Lee HIT 1.50 .45
M8 Alex Rodriguez HIT 6.00 1.80
M9 Derek Jeter HIT 10.00 3.00
M10 V.Guerrero HIT 4.00 1.20
M11 Mark McGwire HR 30.00 9.00
M12 Ken Griffey Jr. HR 20.00 6.00
M13 Vladimir Guerrero HR 12.00 3.60
M14 Alex Rodriguez HR 20.00 6.00
M15 Barry Bonds HR 30.00 9.00
M16 Sammy Sosa HR 20.00 6.00
M17 Albert Belle HR 5.00 1.50
M18 Frank Thomas HR 12.00 3.60
M19 Jose Canseco HR 12.00 3.60
M20 Mike Piazza HR 20.00 6.00
M21 Jeff Bagwell RBI 4.00 1.20
M22 Barry Bonds RBI 15.00 4.50
M23 Ken Griffey Jr. RBI 10.00 3.00
M24 Albert Belle RBI 2.50 .75
M25 Juan Gonzalez RBI 4.00 1.20
M26 Vinny Castilla RBI 2.50 .75
M27 Mark McGwire RBI 15.00 4.50
M28 Alex Rodriguez RBI 10.00 3.00
M29 N.Garciaparra RBI 10.00 3.00
M30 Frank Thomas RBI 6.00 1.80
M31 Barry Bonds 2B 30.00 9.00
M32 Albert Belle 2B 5.00 1.50
M33 Ben Grieve 2B 5.00 1.50
M34 Craig Biggio 2B 8.00 2.40
M35 Vladimir Guerrero 2B 12.00 3.60
M36 N.Garciaparra 2B 20.00 6.00
M37 Alex Rodriguez 2B 20.00 6.00
M38 Derek Jeter 2B 30.00 9.00
M39 Ken Griffey Jr. 2B 20.00 6.00
M40 Brad Fullmer 2B 5.00 1.50

1999 Finest Peel and Revea Sparkle

Randomly inserted in Series one packs at th rate of one in 30, this 20-card set features col action player images on a sparkle background.

This set was considered Common and the protective coating had to be peeled from the card front and back to reveal the level.

Nm-Mt Ex-Mt
COMPLETE SET (20) 120.00 36.00
*HYPERPLAID: .6X TO 1.5X SPARKLE
HYPERPLAID SER.1 ODDS 1:60 H/R,1:30 HTA
*STADIUM STARS: 1.25X TO 3X SPARKLE
STAD.STAR SER.1 ODDS 1:120 H/R, 1:60 HTA
1 Kerry Wood 5.00 1.50
2 Mark McGwire 12.00 3.60
3 Sammy Sosa 8.00 2.40
4 Ken Griffey Jr. 8.00 2.40
5 Nomar Garciaparra 8.00 2.40
6 Greg Maddux 8.00 2.40
7 Derek Jeter 12.00 3.60
8 Andres Galarraga 2.00 .60
9 Alex Rodriguez 8.00 2.40
10 Frank Thomas 5.00 1.50
11 Roger Clemens 10.00 3.00
12 Juan Gonzalez 3.00 .90
13 Ben Grieve 2.00 .60
14 Jeff Bagwell 3.00 .90
15 Todd Helton 3.00 .90
16 Chipper Jones 5.00 1.50
17 Barry Bonds 12.00 3.60
18 Travis Lee 2.00 .60
19 Vladimir Guerrero 5.00 1.50
20 Pat Burrell 3.00 .90

1999 Finest Prominent Figures

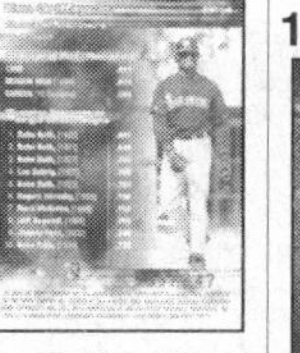

Randomly inserted in Series one packs with various insertion rates, this 50-card set features color action photos of ten superstars in each of five statistical categories and printed with refractor technology. The categories are: Home Runs (with an insertion rate of 1:1,749) and sequentially numbered to 70, Slugging Percentage (1:145) numbered to 847, Batting Average (1:289) numbered to 424, Runs Batted In (1:644) numbered to 190, and Total Bases (1:268) numbered to 457.

Nm-Mt Ex-Mt
PF1 Mark McGwire HR 100.00 30.00
PF2 Sammy Sosa HR 60.00 18.00
PF3 Ken Griffey Jr. HR 60.00 18.00
PF4 Mike Piazza HR 60.00 18.00
PF5 Juan Gonzalez HR 25.00 7.50
PF6 Greg Vaughn HR 15.00 4.50
PF7 Alex Rodriguez HR 60.00 18.00
PF8 Manny Ramirez HR 25.00 7.50
PF9 Jeff Bagwell HR 25.00 7.50
PF10 Andres Galarraga HR 15.00 4.50
PF11 Mark McGwire SLG 20.00 6.00
PF12 Sammy Sosa SLG 12.00 3.60
PF13 Juan Gonzalez SLG 5.00 1.50
PF14 Ken Griffey Jr. SLG 12.00 3.60
PF15 Barry Bonds SLG 20.00 6.00
PF16 Greg Vaughn SLG 3.00 .90
PF17 Larry Walker SLG 5.00 1.50
PF18 A.Galarraga SLG 3.00 .90
PF19 Jeff Bagwell SLG 5.00 1.50
PF20 Albert Belle SLG 3.00 .90
PF21 Tony Gwynn BAT 12.00 3.60
PF22 Mike Piazza BAT 15.00 4.50
PF23 Larry Walker BAT 6.00 1.80
PF24 Alex Rodriguez BAT 15.00 4.50
PF25 John Olerud BAT 4.00 1.20
PF26 Frank Thomas BAT 10.00 3.00
PF27 Bernie Williams BAT 6.00 1.80
PF28 Chipper Jones BAT 10.00 3.00
PF29 Jim Thome BAT 10.00 3.00
PF30 Barry Bonds BAT 25.00 7.50
PF31 Juan Gonzalez RBI 10.00 3.00
PF32 Sammy Sosa RBI 25.00 7.50
PF33 Mark McGwire RBI 40.00 12.00
PF34 Albert Belle RBI 6.00 1.80
PF35 Ken Griffey Jr. RBI 25.00 7.50
PF36 Jeff Bagwell RBI 10.00 3.00
PF37 Chipper Jones RBI 15.00 4.50
PF38 Vinny Castilla RBI 6.00 1.80
PF39 Alex Rodriguez RBI 25.00 7.50
PF40 A.Galarraga RBI 6.00 1.80
PF41 Sammy Sosa TB 15.00 4.50
PF42 Mark McGwire TB 25.00 7.50
PF43 Albert Belle TB 4.00 1.20
PF44 Ken Griffey Jr. TB 15.00 4.50
PF45 Jeff Bagwell TB 6.00 1.80
PF46 Juan Gonzalez TB 6.00 1.80
PF47 Barry Bonds TB 25.00 7.50
PF48 V.Guerrero TB 10.00 3.00
PF49 Larry Walker TB 6.00 1.80
PF50 Alex Rodriguez TB 15.00 4.50

1999 Finest Split Screen

Randomly inserted in Series one packs at the rate of one in 28, this 14-card set features action color photos of two players paired together on the same card and printed using a special refractor and non-refractor technology. Each card was printed with right/left refractor variations.

Nm-Mt Ex-Mt
COMPLETE SET (14) 100.00 30.00
RIGHT/LEFT REF.VARIATIONS EQUAL VALUE
*DUAL REF: 1.25X TO 3X BASIC SCREEN
DUAL REF.SER.1 ODDS 1:82 H/R, 1:42 HTA
SS1 Mark McGwire 10.00 3.00
Sammy Sosa
SS2 Ken Griffey Jr. 6.00 1.80
Alex Rodriguez
SS3 Nomar Garciaparra 10.00 3.00
Derek Jeter
SS4 Barry Bonds 10.00 3.00
Albert Belle
SS5 Cal Ripken 12.00 3.60
Tony Gwynn
SS6 Manny Ramirez 2.50 .75
Juan Gonzalez
SS7 Frank Thomas 4.00 1.20
Andres Galarraga
SS8 Scott Rolen 4.00 1.20
Chipper Jones
SS9 Ivan Rodriguez 6.00 1.80
Mike Piazza
SS10 Kerry Wood 8.00 2.40
Roger Clemens
SS11 Greg Maddux 6.00 1.80
Tom Glavine
SS12 Troy Glaus 1.50 .45
Eric Chavez
SS13 Ben Grieve 2.50 .75
Todd Helton
SS14 Travis Lee 2.50 .75
Pat Burrell

1999 Finest Team Finest Blue

Randomly inserted in Series one and Series two packs at the rate of one in 82 first series and one in 57 second series. Also distributed in HTA packs at a rate of one in 38 first series and one in 26 second series. This 20-card set features color action player images printed using prismatic Chromium technology with blue highlights and is sequentially numbered to 1500. Cards 1-10 were distributed in first series packs and 11-20 in second series packs.

Nm-Mt Ex-Mt
COMP.BLUE SET (20) 150.00 45.00
*BLUE REF: .75X TO 2X BASIC BLUE.
BLUE REF.SER.1 ODDS 1:816 HOB, 1:377 HTA
BLUE REF.SER.2 ODDS 1:571 HOB, 1:263 HTA
BLUE REF.PRINT RUN 150 SERIAL #'d SETS
*RED: .5X TO 1.2X BASIC BLUE
RED SER.2 ODDS 1:18 HTA
RED SER.1 ODDS 1:25 HTA
RED PRINT RUN 500 SERIAL #'d SETS
*RED REF: 2.5X TO 6X BASIC BLUE
RED REF.SER.1 ODDS 1:254 HTA
RED REF.SER.2 ODDS 1:184 HTA
RED REF.PRINT RUN 50 SERIAL #'d SETS
*GOLD: .6X TO 1.5X BASIC BLUE
GOLD SER.1 ODDS 1:51 HTA
GOLD SER.2 ODDS 1:37 HTA
GOLD PRINT RUN 250 SERIAL #'d SETS
*GOLD REF: 4X TO 10X BASIC BLUE.
GOLD REF.SER.1 ODDS 1:510 HTA
GOLD REF.SER.2 ODDS 1:369 HTA
GOLD REF.PRINT RUN 25 SERIAL #'d SETS
TF1 Greg Maddux 6.00 1.80
TF2 Mark McGwire 10.00 3.00
TF3 Sammy Sosa 6.00 1.80
TF4 Juan Gonzalez 2.50 .75
TF5 Alex Rodriguez 6.00 1.80
TF6 Travis Lee 2.00 .60
TF7 Roger Clemens 8.00 2.40
TF8 Darin Erstad 2.00 .60
TF9 Todd Helton 2.50 .75
TF10 Mike Piazza 6.00 1.80
TF11 Kerry Wood 4.00 1.20
TF12 Ken Griffey Jr. 6.00 1.80
TF13 Frank Thomas 4.00 1.20
TF14 Jeff Bagwell 2.50 .75
TF15 Nomar Garciaparra 6.00 1.80
TF16 Derek Jeter 10.00 3.00
TF17 Chipper Jones 4.00 1.20
TF18 Barry Bonds 10.00 3.00
TF19 Tony Gwynn 5.00 1.50
TF20 Ben Grieve 2.00 .60

2000 Finest

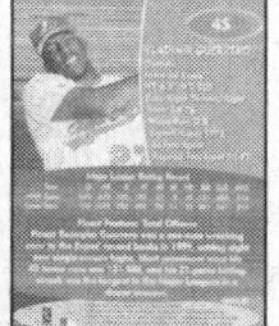

Produced by Topps, the 2000 Finest Series one product was released in April, 2000 as a 147-card set. The Finest Series two product was released in July, 2000 as a 140-card set. Each hobby and retail pack contained six cards and carried a suggested retail price of $4.99. Each HTA pack contained 13 cards and carried a suggested retail price of $10.00. The set includes 179-player cards, 20 first series Rookie Cards (cards 101-120) each serial numbered to 2000 and 20 second series Rookie Cards (cards 247-266) each serial numbered to 3000, 15 Features subset cards (cards 121-135), 10 Counterparts subset cards (numbers 267-276), and 20 Gems subset cards (numbers 136-145 and 277-286). The set also includes two versions of card number 146 Ken Griffey Jr. wearing his Reds uniform (a portrait and action shot). Rookie Cards were seeded at a rate of 1:23 hobby/retail packs and 1:6 HTA packs. Features and Counterparts subset cards were inserted one every eight hobby and retail packs and one every three HTA packs. Gems subset cards were inserted one every 24 hobby and retail packs and one every nine HTA packs. Notable Rookie Cards include Rick Asadoorian and Bobby Bradley. Finally, 20 "Graded Gems" exchange cards were randomly seeded into packs (10 per series). The lucky handful of collectors that found these cards could send them into Topps for a complete Gems subset, each of which was professionally graded "Gem Mint 10" by PSA.

Nm-Mt Ex-Mt
COMP.SERIES 1 w/o SP's (100) 25.00 7.50
COMP.SERIES 2 w/o SP's (100) 25.00 7.50
COMMON (1-100/147-246) .40 .12
COMMON (101-120) 4.00 1.20
COMMON (121-135) 1.50 .45
COMMON (136-145/277-286) 2.00 .60
COMMON (247-266) 4.00 1.20
COMMON (267-276) 1.00 .30
1 Nomar Garciaparra 1.50 .45
2 Chipper Jones 1.00 .30
3 Erubiel Durazo .40 .12
4 Robin Ventura .60 .18
5 Garret Anderson .40 .12
6 Dean Palmer .40 .12
7 Mariano Rivera .60 .18
8 Rusty Greer .40 .12
9 Jim Thome 1.00 .30
10 Jeff Bagwell .60 .18
11 Jason Giambi 1.00 .30
12 Jeromy Burnitz .40 .12
13 Mark Grace .60 .18
14 Russ Ortiz .40 .12
15 Kevin Brown .60 .18
16 Kevin Millwood .40 .12
17 Scott Williamson .40 .12
18 Orlando Hernandez .40 .12
19 Todd Walker .40 .12
20 Carlos Beltran .60 .18
21 Ruben Rivera .40 .12
22 Curt Schilling .60 .18
23 Brian Giles .40 .12
24 Eric Karros .40 .12
25 Preston Wilson .40 .12
26 Al Leiter .40 .12
27 Juan Encarnacion .40 .12
28 Tim Salmon .60 .18
29 B.J. Surhoff .40 .12
30 Bernie Williams .60 .18
31 Lee Stevens .40 .12
32 Pokey Reese .40 .12
33 Mike Sweeney .40 .12
34 Corey Koskie .40 .12
35 Roberto Alomar .60 .18
36 Tim Hudson .60 .18
37 Tom Glavine .60 .18
38 Jeff Kent .40 .12
39 Mike Lieberthal .40 .12
40 Barry Larkin .60 .18
41 Paul O'Neill .60 .18
42 Rico Brogna .40 .12
43 Brian Daubach .40 .12
44 Rich Aurilia .40 .12
45 Vladimir Guerrero 1.00 .30
46 Luis Castillo .40 .12
47 Bartolo Colon .40 .12
48 Kevin Appier .40 .12
49 Mo Vaughn .40 .12
50 Alex Rodriguez 1.50 .45
51 Randy Johnson 1.00 .30
52 Kris Benson .40 .12
53 Tony Clark .40 .12
54 Chad Allen .40 .12
55 Larry Walker .60 .18
56 Freddy Garcia .40 .12
57 Paul Konerko .40 .12
58 Edgardo Alfonzo .40 .12
59 Brady Anderson .40 .12
60 Derek Jeter 2.50 .75
61 John Smoltz .60 .18
62 Doug Glanville .40 .12
63 Shannon Stewart .40 .12
64 Greg Maddux 1.50 .45
65 Mark McGwire 2.50 .75
66 Gary Sheffield .40 .12
67 Kevin Young .40 .12
68 Tony Gwynn 1.25 .35
69 Rey Ordonez .40 .12
70 Cal Ripken 3.00 .90
71 Todd Helton .60 .18
72 Brian Jordan .40 .12
73 Jose Canseco 1.00 .30
74 Luis Gonzalez .40 .12
75 Barry Bonds 2.50 .75
76 Jermaine Dye .40 .12
77 Jose Offerman .40 .12
78 Magglio Ordonez .40 .12
79 Fred McGriff .60 .18
80 Ivan Rodriguez 1.00 .30
81 Josh Hamilton .40 .12
82 Vernon Wells .40 .12
83 Mark Mulder .40 .12
84 John Patterson .40 .12
85 Nick Johnson .40 .12
86 Pablo Ozuna .40 .12
87 A.J. Burnett .40 .12
88 Jack Cust .40 .12
89 Adam Piatt .40 .12
90 Rob Ryan .40 .12
91 Sean Burroughs .40 .12
92 D'Angelo Jimenez .40 .12
93 Chad Hermansen .40 .12
94 Robert Fick .40 .12
95 Ruben Mateo .40 .12
96 Alex Escobar .40 .12
97 Wily Pena .40 .12
98 Corey Patterson .40 .12
99 Eric Munson .40 .12
100 Pat Burrell .40 .12
101 Michael Tejera RC 4.00 1.20
102 Bobby Bradley RC 4.00 1.20
103 Larry Bigbie RC 6.00 1.80
104 B.J. Garbe RC 4.00 1.20
105 Josh Kalinowski RC 4.00 1.20
106 Brett Myers RC 6.00 1.80
107 Chris Mears RC 4.00 1.20
108 Aaron Rowand RC 8.00 2.40
109 Corey Myers RC 4.00 1.20
110 John Sneed RC 4.00 1.20
111 Ryan Christianson RC 4.00 1.20
112 Kyle Snyder 4.00 1.20
113 Mike Paradis 4.00 1.20
114 Chance Caple RC 4.00 1.20
115 Ben Christensen RC 4.00 1.20
116 Brad Baker RC 4.00 1.20
117 Rob Purvis RC 4.00 1.20
118 Rick Asadoorian RC 4.00 1.20
119 Ruben Salazar RC 4.00 1.20
120 Julio Zuleta RC 4.00 1.20
121 Alex Rodriguez 2.50 .75
Ken Griffey Jr.
122 Nomar Garciaparra 3.00 .90
Derek Jeter
123 Mark Mcgwire 4.00 1.20
Sammy Sosa
124 Randy Johnson 2.50 .75
Pedro Martinez
125 Ivan Rodriguez 2.50 .75
Mike Piazza
126 Manny Ramirez 1.50 .45
Roberto Alomar
127 Chipper Jones 2.50 .75
Andruw Jones
128 Cal Ripken 5.00 1.50
Tony Gwynn
129 Jeff Bagwell 1.50 .45
Craig Biggio
130 Barry Bonds 4.00 1.20
Vladimir Guerrero
131 Nick Johnson 2.50 .75
Alfonso Soriano
132 Josh Hamilton 4.00 1.20
Pat Burrell
133 Corey Patterson 1.50 .45
Ruben Mateo
134 Larry Walker 1.50 .45
Todd Helton
135 Rey Ordonez 1.50 .45
Edgardo Alfonzo
136 Derek Jeter GEM 8.00 2.40
137 Alex Rodriguez GEM 5.00 1.50
138 Chipper Jones GEM 5.00 1.50
139 Mike Piazza GEM 5.00 1.50
140 Mark McGwire GEM 8.00 2.40
141 Ivan Rodriguez GEM 5.00 1.50
142 Cal Ripken GEM 10.00 3.00
143 V.Guerrero GEM 5.00 1.50
144 Randy Johnson GEM 5.00 1.50
145 Jeff Bagwell GEM 3.00 .90
146 K.Griffey Jr. ACTION 1.50 .45
146A Ken Griffey Jr. PORT 1.50 .45
147 Andruw Jones .40 .12
148 Kerry Wood 1.00 .30
149 Jim Edmonds .40 .12
150 Pedro Martinez 1.00 .30
151 Warren Morris .40 .12
152 Trevor Hoffman .40 .12
153 Ryan Klesko .40 .12
154 Andy Pettitte .60 .18
155 Frank Thomas 1.00 .30
156 Damion Easley .40 .12
157 Cliff Floyd .40 .12
158 Ben Davis .40 .12
159 John Valentin .40 .12
160 Rafael Palmeiro .60 .18
161 Andy Ashby .40 .12
162 J.D. Drew .40 .12
163 Jay Bell .40 .12
164 Adam Kennedy .40 .12
165 Manny Ramirez .60 .18
166 John Halama .40 .12
167 Octavio Dotel .40 .12
168 Darin Erstad .40 .12
169 Jose Lima .40 .12
170 Andres Galarraga .40 .12
171 Scott Rolen 1.00 .30
172 Delino DeShields .40 .12
173 J.T. Snow .40 .12
174 Tony Womack .40 .12
175 John Olerud .40 .12
176 Jason Kendall .40 .12
177 Carlos Lee .40 .12
178 Eric Milton .40 .12
179 Jeff Cirillo .40 .12
180 Gabe Kapler .40 .12
181 Greg Vaughn .40 .12
182 Denny Neagle .40 .12
183 Tino Martinez .60 .18
184 Doug Mientkiewicz .40 .12
185 Juan Gonzalez .60 .18
186 Ellis Burks .40 .12
187 Mike Hampton .40 .12
188 Royce Clayton .40 .12
189 Mike Mussina .60 .18
190 Carlos Delgado .40 .12
191 Ben Grieve .40 .12
192 Fernando Tatis .40 .12
193 Matt Williams .40 .12
194 Rondell White .40 .12
195 Shawn Green .40 .12
196 Hideki Irabu .40 .12
197 Troy Glaus .40 .12
198 Roger Cedeno .40 .12
199 Ray Lankford .40 .12
200 Sammy Sosa 1.50 .45
201 Kenny Lofton .40 .12
202 Edgar Martinez .60 .18
203 Mark Kotsay .40 .12
204 David Wells .40 .12
205 Craig Biggio .60 .18
206 Ray Durham .40 .12
207 Troy O'Leary .40 .12
208 Rickey Henderson 1.00 .30
209 Bob Abreu .40 .12
210 Neifi Perez .40 .12
211 Carlos Febles .40 .12
212 Chuck Knoblauch .40 .12
213 Moises Alou .40 .12
214 Omar Vizquel .60 .18
215 Vinny Castilla .40 .12
216 Javy Lopez .40 .12
217 Johnny Damon .60 .18
218 Roger Clemens 2.00 .60
219 Miguel Tejada .40 .12
220 Carl Everett .40 .12
221 Matt Lawton .40 .12
222 Albert Belle .40 .12
223 Adrian Beltre .60 .18
224 Dante Bichette .40 .12
225 Raul Mondesi .40 .12
226 Mike Piazza 1.50 .45
227 Brad Penny .40 .12
228 Kip Wells .40 .12
229 Adam Everett .40 .12
230 Eddie Yarnall .40 .12
231 Matt LeCroy .40 .12
232 Jason Tyner .40 .12
233 Rick Ankiel .40 .12
234 Lance Berkman .40 .12
235 Rafael Furcal .40 .12
236 Dee Brown .40 .12
237 Gookie Dawkins .40 .12
238 Eric Valent .40 .12
239 Peter Bergeron .40 .12
240 Alfonso Soriano 1.00 .30
241 Adam Dunn 1.00 .30
242 Jorge Toca .40 .12
243 Ryan Anderson .40 .12
244 Jason Dellaero .40 .12
245 Jason Grilli .40 .12
246 Milton Bradley .40 .12
247 Scott Downs RC 4.00 1.20
248 Keith Reed RC 4.00 1.20
249 Edgar Cruz RC 4.00 1.20
250 Wes Anderson RC 4.00 1.20
251 Lyle Overbay RC 8.00 2.40
252 Mike Lamb RC 4.00 1.20
253 Vince Faison RC 4.00 1.20
254 Chad Alexander 4.00 1.20
255 Chris Wakeland RC 4.00 1.20
256 Aaron McNeal RC 4.00 1.20
257 Tomo Ohka RC 4.00 1.20
258 Ty Howington RC 4.00 1.20
259 Javier Colina RC 4.00 1.20
260 Jason Jennings 4.00 1.20
261 Ramon Santiago RC 4.00 1.20
262 Johan Santana RC 50.00 15.00
263 Quincy Foster RC 4.00 1.20
264 Junior Brignac RC 4.00 1.20
265 Rico Washington RC 4.00 1.20
266 Scott Sobkowiak RC 4.00 1.20
267 Pedro Martinez 2.50 .75
Rick Ankiel
268 Manny Ramirez 2.50 .75
Vladimir Guerrero
269 A.J.Burnett 1.00 .30
Mark Mulder
270 Mike Piazza 2.50 .75
Eric Munson
271 Josh Hamilton 1.00 .30
Corey Patterson
272 Ken Griffey Jr. 2.00 .60
Sammy Sosa
273 Derek Jeter 4.00 1.20
Alfonso Soriano
274 Mark McGwire 4.00 1.20
Pat Burrell
275 Chipper Jones 4.00 1.20
Cal Ripken
276 Nomar Garciaparra 2.50 .75
Alex Rodriguez
277 Pedro Martinez GEM 5.00 1.50
278 Tony Gwynn GEM 4.00 1.20
279 Barry Bonds GEM 8.00 2.40
280 Juan Gonzalez GEM 3.00 .90
281 Larry Walker GEM 3.00 .90
282 N.Garciaparra GEM 5.00 1.50
283 Ken Griffey Jr. GEM 5.00 1.50
284 Manny Ramirez GEM 3.00 .90
285 Shawn Green GEM 2.00 .60
286 Sammy Sosa GEM 5.00 1.50
NNO Graded Gems Ser.1 EXCH/10
NNO Graded Gems Ser.2 EXCH/10

2000 Finest Gold Refractors

Randomly inserted in packs, this 287-card set parallels the base set. The set includes 179-player cards, 40 Rookie Cards (numbers 101-120 and 247-266) each serial numbered to 100, 15 Features subset cards (numbers 121-135), 10 Counterparts subset cards (numbers 267-276), and 20 Gems subset cards (numbers 136-145 and 277-286). The set also includes two versions of card number 146 Ken Griffey Jr. wearing his Reds uniform (a portrait and action shot). Rookie/Veteran Cards were seeded at a rate of 1:240 hobby/retail packs and TBD HTA packs. Features and Counterparts subset cards were inserted one every 960 hobby and retail packs and one every 400 HTA packs. Gems subset cards were inserted one every 2880 hobby and retail packs and one every 1200 HTA packs. All cards are featured on gold die-cut technology.

Nm-Mt Ex-Mt
*STARS 1-100/146-246: 20X TO 50X BASIC
*ROOKIES 101-120: 2.5X TO 6X BASIC
*ROOKIES 247-266: 2.5X TO 6X BASIC
*FEATURES 121-135: 4X TO 10X BASIC
*GEMS 136-145/277-286: 4X TO 10X BASIC
*COUNTER 267-276: 4X TO 10X BASIC

2000 Finest Refractors

Randomly inserted in packs, this 146-card set parallels the base set. The set includes 179-player cards, 40 Rookie Cards (numbers 101-120 and 247-266) each serial numbered to 500, 15 Features subset cards (numbers 121-135), 10 Counterparts subset cards (numbers 267-276), and 20 Gems subset cards (numbers 136-145 and 277-286). The set also includes two versions of card number 146 Ken Griffey Jr. wearing his Reds uniform (a portrait and action shot). Rookie/Veteran Cards were seeded at a rate of 1:24 hobby/retail packs and 1:6 HTA packs. Features and Counterparts subset cards were inserted one every 96 hobby and retail packs and one every 40 HTA packs. Gems subset cards were inserted one every 288 hobby and retail packs and one every 120 HTA packs.

Nm-Mt Ex-Mt
*STARS 1-100/146-246: 6X TO 15X BASIC
*ROOKIES 101-120: 1X TO 2.5X BASIC
*FEATURES 121-135: 1.5X TO 4X BASIC
*GEMS 136-145/277-286: 1.5X TO 4X BASIC
*ROOKIES 247-266: 1X TO 2.5X BASIC RC'S
*COUNTER 267-276: 1.5X TO 4X BASIC

2000 Finest Gems Oversize

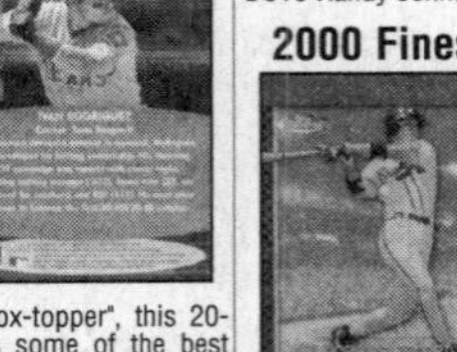

Randomly inserted as a "box-topper", this 20-card oversized set features some of the best players in major league baseball. Please note that cards 1-10 were inserted into series one boxes, and cards 11-20 were inserted into series two boxes.

Nm-Mt Ex-Mt
COMPLETE SERIES 1 (10) 60.00 18.00
COMPLETE SERIES 2 (10) 50.00 15.00
*REF: .4X TO 1X BASIC GEMS OVERSIZE
REFRACTORS ONE PER HTA CHIP-TOPPER
1 Derek Jeter 10.00 3.00
2 Alex Rodriguez 6.00 1.80
3 Chipper Jones 4.00 1.20
4 Mike Piazza 6.00 1.80
5 Mark McGwire 10.00 3.00
6 Ivan Rodriguez 4.00 1.20
7 Cal Ripken 12.00 3.60
8 Vladimir Guerrero 4.00 1.20
9 Randy Johnson 4.00 1.20
10 Jeff Bagwell 2.50 .75
11 Nomar Garciaparra 6.00 1.80
12 Ken Griffey Jr. 6.00 1.80
13 Manny Ramirez 2.50 .75
14 Shawn Green 1.50 .45
15 Sammy Sosa 6.00 1.80
16 Pedro Martinez 4.00 1.20
17 Tony Gwynn 5.00 1.50
18 Barry Bonds 10.00 3.00
19 Juan Gonzalez 2.50 .75
20 Larry Walker 2.50 .75

2000 Finest Ballpark Bounties

Randomly inserted into first and second series packs at one in 24 hobby/retail and 1:12 HTA, this insert set features 30 MLB players who are "wanted" for their pure talent. Card backs carry a "BB" prefix. Please note that cards 1-15 were inserted into series one packs, while cards 16-30 were inserted into series two packs.

Nm-Mt Ex-Mt
COMPLETE SERIES 1 (15) 80.00 24.00
COMPLETE SERIES 2 (15) 100.00 30.00
BB1 Chipper Jones 5.00 1.50
BB2 Mike Piazza 8.00 2.40
BB3 Vladimir Guerrero 5.00 1.50
BB4 Sammy Sosa 8.00 2.40
BB5 Nomar Garciaparra 8.00 2.40
BB6 Manny Ramirez 3.00 .90
BB7 Jeff Bagwell 3.00 .90
BB8 Scott Rolen 5.00 1.50
BB9 Carlos Beltran 3.00 .90
BB10 Pedro Martinez 5.00 1.50
BB11 Greg Maddux 8.00 2.40
BB12 Josh Hamilton 2.00 .60
BB13 Adam Piatt 2.00 .60
BB14 Pat Burrell 2.00 .60
BB15 Alfonso Soriano 5.00 1.50
BB16 Alex Rodriguez 8.00 2.40
BB17 Derek Jeter 12.00 3.60
BB18 Cal Ripken 15.00 4.50
BB19 Larry Walker 3.00 .90
BB20 Barry Bonds 12.00 3.60
BB21 Ken Griffey Jr. 8.00 2.40
BB22 Mark McGwire 12.00 3.60
BB23 Ivan Rodriguez 5.00 1.50
BB24 Andruw Jones 2.00 .60
BB25 Todd Helton 3.00 .90
BB26 Randy Johnson 5.00 1.50
BB27 Ruben Mateo 2.00 .60
BB28 Corey Patterson 2.00 .60
BB29 Sean Burroughs 2.00 .60
BB30 Eric Munson 2.00 .60

2000 Finest Dream Cast

Randomly inserted into series two packs at one in 36 hobby/retail packs and one in 13 HTA packs, this 10-card insert features players that have skills people dream about having. Card backs carry a "DC" prefix.

Nm-Mt Ex-Mt
COMPLETE SET (10) 100.00 30.00

DC1 Mark McGwire 15.00 4.50
DC2 Roberto Alomar 4.00 1.20
DC3 Chipper Jones 6.00 1.80
DC4 Derek Jeter 15.00 4.50
DC5 Barry Bonds 15.00 4.50
DC6 Ken Griffey Jr. 10.00 3.00
DC7 Sammy Sosa 10.00 3.00
DC8 Mike Piazza 10.00 3.00
DC9 Pedro Martinez 6.00 1.80
DC10 Randy Johnson 6.00 1.80

2000 Finest For the Record

Randomly inserted in first series packs at a rate of 1:71 hobby or retail and 1:33 HTA, this insert set features 30 serial-numbered cards. Each player has three versions that are sequentially numbered to the distance of the left, center, and right field walls of their home ballpark. Card backs carry a "FR" prefix.

Nm-Mt Ex-Mt
FR1A Derek Jeter/318 30.00 9.00
FR1B Derek Jeter/408 30.00 9.00
FR1C Derek Jeter/314 30.00 9.00
FR2A Mark McGwire/330 30.00 9.00
FR2B Mark McGwire/402 30.00 9.00
FR2C Mark McGwire/330 30.00 9.00
FR3A Ken Griffey Jr./331 15.00 4.50
FR3B Ken Griffey Jr./405 15.00 4.50
FR3C Ken Griffey Jr./327 15.00 4.50
FR4A Alex Rodriguez/331 20.00 6.00
FR4B Alex Rodriguez/405 20.00 6.00
FR4C Alex Rodriguez/327 20.00 6.00
FR5A N.Garciaparra/310 15.00 4.50
FR5B N.Garciaparra/390 15.00 4.50
FR5C N.Garciaparra/302 15.00 4.50
FR6A Cal Ripken/333 40.00 12.00
FR6B Cal Ripken/410 40.00 12.00
FR6C Cal Ripken/318 40.00 12.00
FR7A Sammy Sosa/355 15.00 4.50
FR7B Sammy Sosa/400 15.00 4.50
FR7C Sammy Sosa/353 15.00 4.50
FR8A Manny Ramirez/325 10.00 3.00
FR8B Manny Ramirez/410 10.00 3.00
FR8C Manny Ramirez/325 10.00 3.00
FR9A Mike Piazza/338 15.00 4.50
FR9B Mike Piazza/410 15.00 4.50
FR9C Mike Piazza/338 15.00 4.50
FR10A Chipper Jones/335 10.00 3.00
FR10B Chipper Jones/401 10.00 3.00
FR10C Chipper Jones/330 10.00 3.00

2000 Finest Going the Distance

Randomly inserted in first series hobby and retail packs at one in 24 and HTA packs at a rate of one in 12, this 12-card insert set features some of the best hitters in major league baseball. Card backs carry a "GTD" prefix.

Nm-Mt Ex-Mt
COMPLETE SET (12) 80.00 24.00
GTD1 Tony Gwynn 5.00 1.50
GTD2 Alex Rodriguez 6.00 1.80
GTD3 Derek Jeter 10.00 3.00
GTD4 Chipper Jones 4.00 1.20
GTD5 Nomar Garciaparra 6.00 1.80
GTD6 Sammy Sosa 6.00 1.80
GTD7 Ken Griffey Jr. 6.00 1.80
GTD8 Vladimir Guerrero 4.00 1.20
GTD9 Mark McGwire 10.00 3.00
GTD10 Mike Piazza 6.00 1.80
GTD11 Manny Ramirez 2.50 .75
GTD12 Cal Ripken 12.00 3.60

2000 Finest Moments

Randomly inserted into series two hobby and retail packs at one in nine, and HTA packs at one in four, this four-card insert features great moments from the 1999 baseball season. Card backs carry a "FM" prefix.

Nm-Mt Ex-Mt
COMPLETE SET (4) 6.00 1.80
*REFRACTORS: .75X TO 2X BASIC MOMENTS
SER.2 REF.ODDS 1:20 H/R 1:9 HTA
FM1 Chipper Jones 1.50 .45
FM2 Ivan Rodriguez 1.50 .45
FM3 Tony Gwynn 2.00 .60
FM4 Wade Boggs 1.50 .45

2000 Finest Moments Refractors Autograph

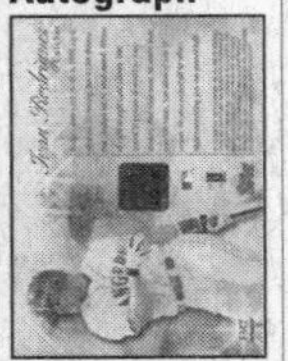

Randomly inserted into series two hobby/retail packs at one in 425, and in HTA packs at one in 196, this four-card set is a complete parallel of the Finest Moments insert. This set is autographed by the player depicted on the card. Card backs carry a "FM" prefix.

Nm-Mt Ex-Mt
FM1 Chipper Jones 40.00 12.00
FM2 Ivan Rodriguez 40.00 12.00
FM3 Tony Gwynn 50.00 15.00
FM4 Wade Boggs 40.00 12.00

2001 Finest

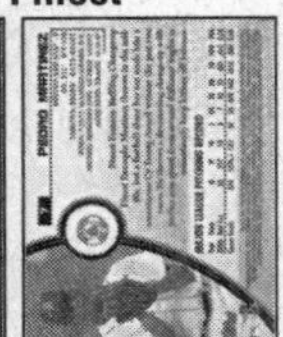

This 140-card set was distributed in six-card hobby packs with a suggested retail price of $6. Printed on 27 pt. card stock, the set features color action photos of 100 veteran players, 30 draft picks and prospects printed with the "Rookie Card" logo and sequentially numbered to 999, and 10 standout veterans sequentially numbered to 1999.

Nm-Mt Ex-Mt
COMP.SET w/o SP's 25.00 7.50
COMMON CARD (1-110) .40 .12
COMMON SP 10.00 3.00
COMMON (111-140) 10.00 3.00
1 Mike Piazza SP 20.00 6.00
2 Andruw Jones .40 .12
3 Jason Giambi .40 .12
4 Fred McGriff .60 .18
5 Vladimir Guerrero SP 1.00 .30
6 Adrian Gonzalez .40 .12
7 Pedro Martinez 1.00 .30
8 Mike Lieberthal .40 .12
9 Warren Morris .40 .12
10 Juan Gonzalez .60 .18
11 Jose Canseco 1.00 .30
12 Jose Valentin .40 .12
13 Jeff Cirillo .40 .12
14 Pokey Reese .40 .12
15 Scott Rolen 1.00 .30
16 Greg Maddux 1.50 .45
17 Carlos Delgado .40 .12
18 Rick Ankiel .40 .12
19 Steve Finley .40 .12
20 Shawn Green .40 .12
21 Orlando Cabrera .40 .12
22 Roberto Alomar .60 .18
23 John Olerud .40 .12
24 Albert Belle .40 .12
25 Edgardo Alfonzo .40 .12
26 Rafael Palmeiro .60 .18
27 Mike Sweeney .40 .12
28 Bernie Williams .60 .18
29 Larry Walker .60 .18
30 Barry Bonds SP 25.00 7.50
31 Orlando Hernandez .40 .12
32 Randy Johnson 1.00 .30
33 Shannon Stewart .40 .12
34 Mark Grace .60 .18
35 Alex Rodriguez SP 25.00 7.50
36 Tino Martinez .60 .18
37 Carlos Febles .40 .12
38 Al Leiter .40 .12
39 Omar Vizquel .60 .18
40 Chuck Knoblauch .40 .12
41 Tim Salmon .60 .18
42 Brian Jordan .40 .12
43 Edgar Renteria .40 .12
44 Preston Wilson .40 .12
45 Mariano Rivera .60 .18
46 Gabe Kapler .40 .12
47 Jason Kendall .40 .12
48 Rickey Henderson 1.00 .30
49 Luis Gonzalez .40 .12
50 Tom Glavine .60 .18
51 Jeromy Burnitz .40 .12
52 Garret Anderson .40 .12
53 Craig Biggio .60 .18
54 Vinny Castilla .40 .12
55 Jeff Kent .40 .12
56 Gary Sheffield .40 .12
57 Jorge Posada .60 .18
58 Sean Casey .40 .12
59 Johnny Damon .60 .18
60 Dean Palmer .40 .12
61 Todd Helton .60 .18
62 Barry Larkin .60 .18
63 Robin Ventura .40 .12
64 Kenny Lofton .40 .12
65 Sammy Sosa SP 15.00 4.50
66 Rafael Furcal .40 .12
67 Jay Bell .40 .12
68 J.T. Snow .40 .12
69 Jose Vidro .40 .12
70 Ivan Rodriguez 1.00 .30
71 Jermaine Dye .40 .12
72 Chipper Jones SP 10.00 3.00
73 Fernando Vina .40 .12
74 Ben Grieve .40 .12
75 Mark McGwire SP 25.00 7.50
76 Matt Williams .40 .12
77 Mark Grudzielanek .40 .12
78 Mike Hampton .40 .12
79 Brian Giles .40 .12
80 Tony Gwynn 1.25 .35
81 Carlos Beltran .60 .18
82 Ray Durham .40 .12
83 Brad Radke .40 .12
84 David Justice .40 .12
85 Frank Thomas 1.00 .30
86 Todd Zeile .40 .12
87 Pat Burrell .40 .12
88 Jim Thome 1.00 .30
89 Greg Vaughn .40 .12
90 Ken Griffey Jr. SP 15.00 4.50
91 Mike Mussina .60 .18
92 Magglio Ordonez .40 .12
93 Bob Abreu .40 .12
94 Alex Gonzalez .40 .12
95 Kevin Brown .40 .12
96 Jay Buhner .40 .12
97 Roger Clemens 2.00 .60
98 Nomar Garciaparra SP 15.00 4.50
99 Derrek Lee .40 .12
100 Derek Jeter SP 25.00 7.50
101 Adrian Beltre .60 .18
102 Geoff Jenkins .40 .12
103 Javy Lopez .40 .12
104 Raul Mondesi .40 .12
105 Troy Glaus .40 .12
106 Jeff Bagwell .60 .18
107 Eric Karros .40 .12
108 Mo Vaughn .40 .12
109 Cal Ripken 3.00 .90
110 Manny Ramirez .60 .18
111 Scott Heard PROS 10.00 3.00
112 L. Montanez PROS RC 10.00 3.00
113 Ben Diggins PROS 10.00 3.00
114 Shaun Boyd PROS RC 10.00 3.00
115 Sean Burnett PROS 10.00 3.00
116 Carmen Cali PROS RC 10.00 3.00
117 D.Thompson PROS 10.00 3.00
118 D.Parrish PROS RC 10.00 3.00
119 D.Rich PROS RC 10.00 3.00
120 Chad Petty PROS RC 10.00 3.00
121 S.Smyth PROS RC 10.00 3.00
122 John Lackey PROS 10.00 3.00
123 M.Galante PROS RC 10.00 3.00
124 D.Borrell PROS RC 10.00 3.00
125 Bob Keppel PROS RC 15.00 4.50
126 J.Wayne PROS RC 10.00 3.00
127 J.R. House PROS 10.00 3.00
128 Brian Sellier PROS RC 10.00 3.00
129 Dan Moylan PROS RC 10.00 3.00
130 Scott Pratt PROS RC 10.00 3.00
131 Victor Hall PROS RC 10.00 3.00
132 Joel Pineiro PROS 20.00 6.00
133 J.Axelson PROS RC 10.00 3.00
134 Jose Reyes PROS RC 50.00 15.00
135 G. Runser PROS RC 10.00 3.00
136 B. Hebson PROS RC 10.00 3.00
137 S.Serrano PROS RC 10.00 3.00
138 K. Joseph PROS RC 10.00 3.00
139 J. Richardson PROS RC 10.00 3.00
140 M. Fischer PROS RC 10.00 3.00

2001 Finest Refractors

This 140-card set is a parallel version of the base set and is distinguished by the refractive quality of the cards. The 100 veteran cards are sequentially numbered to 499, the 30 draft picks and prospects to 241, and the 10 standout veterans to 399.

Nm-Mt Ex-Mt
*1-110 REF: 4X TO 10X BASIC 1-110
*SP REF: .5X TO 1.2X BASIC SP
*111-140 REF: .75X TO 2X BASIC 111-140

2001 Finest All-Stars

Randomly inserted in packs at the rate of one in five, this 10-card set features color photos of the preeminent players at their respective postions. A refractive parallel version of this insert set was also produced and inserted in packs at the rate of one in 20.

Nm-Mt Ex-Mt
COMPLETE SET (10) 60.00 18.00
*REF: 1X TO 2.5X BASIC ALL-STARS.
REFRACTOR ODDS 1:40 HOBBY, 1:20 HTA
FAS1 Mark McGwire 10.00 3.00
FAS2 Derek Jeter 10.00 3.00
FAS3 Alex Rodriguez 6.00 1.80
FAS4 Chipper Jones 4.00 1.20
FAS5 Nomar Garciaparra 6.00 1.80
FAS6 Sammy Sosa 6.00 1.80
FAS7 Mike Piazza 6.00 1.80
FAS8 Barry Bonds 10.00 3.00
FAS9 Vladimir Guerrero 4.00 1.20
FAS10 Ken Griffey Jr. 6.00 1.80

2001 Finest Autographs

Randomly inserted in packs at the rate of one in 22, this 29-card set features autographed color photos of players who made the moments. All of

these cards are refractors and carry the Topps "Certified Autograph" stamp and the Topps "Genuine Issue" sticker.

Nm-Mt Ex-Mt
FA-AG Adrian Gonzalez 10.00 3.00
FA-AH Adam Hyzdu 10.00 3.00
FA-AK Adam Kennedy 10.00 3.00
FA-AP Albert Pujols 250.00 75.00
FA-BD Ben Diggins 10.00 3.00
FA-BM Ben Molina 10.00 3.00
FA-BS Ben Sheets 15.00 4.50
FA-BZ Barry Zito 15.00 4.50
FA-BKC Brian Cole 10.00 3.00
FA-CD Chad Durham 10.00 3.00
FA-CP Carlos Pena 10.00 3.00
FA-DK Dave Krynzel 10.00 3.00
FA-DCP Corey Patterson 10.00 3.00
FA-JC Joe Crede 10.00 3.00
FA-JH Jason Hart 10.00 3.00
FA-JM Justin Morneau 60.00 18.00
FA-JO Jose Ortiz 10.00 3.00
FA-JP Jay Payton 10.00 3.00
FA-JHH Josh Hamilton 10.00 3.00
FA-JRH J.R. House 10.00 3.00
FA-KG Keith Ginter 10.00 3.00
FA-KM Kevin Mench 10.00 3.00
FA-MB Milton Bradley 10.00 3.00
FA-MQ Mark Quinn 10.00 3.00
FA-MR Mark Redman 10.00 3.00
FA-RF Rafael Furcal 10.00 3.00
FA-SB Sean Burnett 10.00 3.00
FA-TF Troy Farnsworth 10.00 3.00
FA-TL Terrence Long 10.00 3.00

2001 Finest Moments

Randomly inserted in packs at the rate of one in 12, this 25-card set features color photos of players involved in great moments from the 2000 season plus both active and retired 3000 Hit Club members. A refractive parallel version of this set was also produced with an insertion rate of 1:40.

Nm-Mt Ex-Mt
COMPLETE SET (25) 120.00 36.00
*REF: .75X TO 2X BASIC MOMENTS
REFRACTOR ODDS 1:40 HOBBY, 1:20 HTA
FM1 Pat Burrell 2.50 .75
FM2 Adam Kennedy 2.50 .75
FM3 Mike Lamb 2.50 .75
FM4 Rafael Furcal 2.50 .75
FM5 Terrence Long 2.50 .75
FM6 Jay Payton 2.50 .75
FM7 Mark Quinn 2.50 .75
FM8 Ben Molina 2.50 .75
FM9 Kazuhiro Sasaki 2.50 .75
FM10 Mark Redman 2.50 .75
FM11 Barry Bonds 15.00 4.50
FM12 Alex Rodriguez 10.00 3.00
FM13 Roger Clemens 12.00 3.60
FM14 Jim Edmonds 2.50 .75
FM15 Jason Giambi 2.50 .75
FM16 Todd Helton 4.00 1.20
FM17 Troy Glaus 2.50 .75
FM18 Carlos Delgado 2.50 .75
FM19 Darin Erstad 2.50 .75
FM20 Cal Ripken 20.00 6.00
FM21 Paul Molitor 4.00 1.20
FM22 Robin Yount 10.00 3.00
FM23 George Brett 15.00 4.50
FM24 Dave Winfield 2.50 .75
FM25 Eddie Murray 6.00 1.80

2001 Finest Moments Refractors Autograph

Randomly inserted in packs at the rate of one in 250, this 10-card set features autographed player photos with the Topps "Certified Autograph" stamp and the Topps "Genuine Issue" sticker printed on these refractive cards. Exchange cards with a redemption deadline of April 30, 2003 were seeded into packs for Cal Ripken, Eddie Murray and Robin Yount.

Nm-Mt Ex-Mt
FMA-BB Barry Bonds 250.00 75.00
FMA-CR Cal Ripken 150.00 45.00
FMA-DW Dave Winfield 40.00 12.00
FMA-EM Eddie Murray 60.00 18.00
FMA-GB George Brett 100.00 30.00
FMA-JG Jason Giambi 40.00 12.00
FMA-PM Paul Molitor 40.00 12.00

FMA-RY Robin Yount 60.00 18.00
FMA-TG Troy Glaus 40.00 12.00
FMA-TH Todd Helton 40.00 12.00

2001 Finest Origins

Randomly inserted in packs at the rate of one in seven, this 15-card set features some of today's best ballplayers who didn't make the 1993 Finest cut. These cards are printed in the 1993 classic Finest card design. A refractive parallel version of this set was also produced with an insertion rate of 1:40.

Nm-Mt Ex-Mt
COMPLETE SET (15) 40.00 12.00
*REF: 1X TO 2.5X BASIC ORIGINS
REFRACTOR ODDS 1:40 HOBBY, 1:20 HTA
FO1 Derek Jeter 12.00 3.60
FO2 Jason Kendall 2.00 .60
FO3 Jose Vidro 2.00 .60
FO4 Preston Wilson 2.00 .60
FO5 Jim Edmonds 2.00 .60
FO6 Vladimir Guerrero 5.00 1.50
FO7 Andruw Jones 2.00 .60
FO8 Scott Rolen 5.00 1.50
FO9 Edgardo Alfonzo 2.00 .60
FO10 Mike Sweeney 2.00 .60
FO11 Alex Rodriguez 8.00 2.40
FO12 Jermaine Dye 2.00 .60
FO13 Charles Johnson 2.00 .60
FO14 Darren Dreifort 2.00 .60
FO15 Neifi Perez 2.00 .60

2002 Finest

This 110 card set was issued in five card pack with an SRP of $6 per pack which were packed six per mini box with three mini boxes per full box and twelve boxes per case. Cards number 101 through 110 are Rookie Cards which were all autographed by the featured player. One of these autograph cards were inserted into each six pack mini box.

Nm-Mt Ex-Mt
COMP.SET w/o SP's (100) 25.00 7.50
COMMON CARD (1-100) .50 .15
COMMON CARD (101-110) 10.00 3.00
1 Mike Mussina .75 .23
2 Steve Sparks .50 .15
3 Randy Johnson 1.25 .35
4 Orlando Cabrera .50 .15
5 Jeff Kent .50 .15
6 Carlos Delgado .50 .15
7 Ivan Rodriguez 1.25 .35
8 Jose Cruz .50 .15
9 Jason Giambi .50 .15
10 Brad Penny .50 .15
11 Moises Alou .50 .15
12 Mike Piazza 2.00 .60
13 Ben Grieve .50 .15
14 Derek Jeter 3.00 .90
15 Roy Oswalt .50 .15
16 Pat Burrell .50 .15
17 Preston Wilson .50 .15
18 Kevin Brown .50 .15
19 Barry Bonds 3.00 .90
20 Phil Nevin .50 .15
21 Aramis Ramirez .50 .15
22 Carlos Beltran .75 .23
23 Chipper Jones 1.25 .35
24 Curt Schilling .50 .15
25 Jorge Posada .75 .23
26 Alfonso Soriano .75 .23
27 Cliff Floyd .50 .15
28 Rafael Palmeiro .75 .23
29 Terrence Long .50 .15
30 Ken Griffey Jr. 2.00 .60
31 Jason Kendall .50 .15
32 Jose Vidro .50 .15
33 Jermaine Dye .50 .15
34 Bobby Higginson .50 .15
35 Albert Pujols 2.50 .75
36 Miguel Tejada .50 .15
37 Jim Edmonds .50 .15
38 Barry Zito .50 .15
39 Jimmy Rollins .50 .15
40 Rafael Furcal .50 .15
41 Omar Vizquel .75 .23
42 Kazuhiro Sasaki .50 .15
43 Brian Giles .50 .15
44 Darin Erstad .50 .15
45 Mariano Rivera .75 .23
46 Troy Percival .50 .15
47 Mike Sweeney .50 .15
48 Vladimir Guerrero 1.25 .35
49 Troy Glaus .50 .15
50 So Taguchi RC 3.00 .90
51 Edgardo Alfonzo .50 .15
52 Roger Clemens 2.50 .75
53 Eric Chavez .50 .15
54 Alex Rodriguez 2.00 .60
55 Cristian Guzman .50 .15
56 Jeff Bagwell .75 .23
57 Bernie Williams .75 .23
58 Kerry Wood 1.25 .35
59 Ryan Klesko .50 .15
60 Ichiro Suzuki 2.00 .60
61 Larry Walker .75 .23
62 Nomar Garciaparra 2.00 .60
63 Craig Biggio .75 .23
64 J.D. Drew .50 .15
65 Juan Pierre .50 .15
66 Roberto Alomar .75 .23
67 Luis Gonzalez .50 .15
68 Bud Smith .50 .15
69 Magglio Ordonez .50 .15
70 Scott Rolen 1.25 .35
71 Tsuyoshi Shinjo .50 .15
72 Paul Konerko .50 .15
73 Garret Anderson .50 .15
74 Tim Hudson .50 .15
75 Adam Dunn .75 .23
76 Gary Sheffield .50 .15
77 Johnny Damon Sox 1.25 .35
78 Todd Helton .75 .23
79 Geoff Jenkins .50 .15
80 Shawn Green .50 .15
81 C.C. Sabathia .50 .15
82 Kazuhisa Ishii RC UER 4.00 1.20
2001 ERA is incorrect
83 Rich Aurilia .50 .15
84 Mike Hampton .50 .15
85 Ben Sheets .50 .15
86 Andruw Jones .50 .15
87 Richie Sexson .50 .15
88 Jim Thome 1.25 .35
89 Sammy Sosa 2.00 .60
90 Greg Maddux 2.00 .60
91 Pedro Martinez 1.25 .35
92 Jeromy Burnitz .50 .15
93 Raul Mondesi .50 .15
94 Bret Boone .50 .15
95 Jerry Hairston .50 .15
96 Mike Rivera .50 .15
97 Juan Cruz .50 .15
98 Morgan Ensberg .50 .15
99 Nathan Haynes .50 .15
100 Xavier Nady .50 .15
101 Nic Jackson FY AU RC 10.00 3.00
102 Mauricio Lara FY AU RC 10.00 3.00
103 Freddy Sanchez FY AU RC 10.00 3.00
104 Clint Nageotte FY AU RC 15.00 4.50
105 Beltran Perez FY AU RC 10.00 3.00
106 Garrett Gentry FY AU RC 10.00 3.00
107 Chad Qualls FY AU RC 10.00 3.00
108 Jason Bay FY AU RC 50.00 15.00
109 Michael Hill FY AU RC 10.00 3.00
110 Brian Tallet FY AU RC 10.00 3.00

2002 Finest Refractors

Inserted in packs at stated odds of one in two mini boxes, these cards parallel the 2002 Finest set. These cards have the patented topps "refractor" sheen and have a stated print run of 499 serial numbered sets.

Nm-Mt Ex-Mt
*REFRACTORS 1-100: 2.5X TO 6X BASIC
*REF.RC'S 1-100: 1.5X TO 4X BASIC
101 Nic Jackson FY 5.00 1.50
102 Mauricio Lara FY 5.00 1.50
103 Freddy Sanchez FY 5.00 1.50
104 Clint Nageotte FY 10.00 3.00
105 Beltran Perez FY 5.00 1.50
106 Garett Gentry FY 5.00 1.50
107 Chad Qualls FY 5.00 1.50
108 Jason Bay FY 25.00 7.50
109 Michael Hill FY 5.00 1.50
110 Brian Tallet FY 5.00 1.50

2002 Finest Xfractors

Inserted at a rate of one in three mini boxes, these cards parallel the Finest set. These cards have a uniquely patterned finest design and are printed to a stated print run of 299 serial numbered sets.

Nm-Mt Ex-Mt
*XF 1-100: 3X TO 8X BASIC
*XF RC'S 1-100: 2X TO 5X BASIC
*XF 101-110: .5X TO 1.2X REFRACTOR

2002 Finest Xfractors Protectors

Inserted at a rate of one in seven mini boxes, these cards parallel the Finest set. These cards have a uniquely patterned finest design and were created with a "finest protector" and are printed to a stated print run of 99 serial numbered sets.

Nm-Mt Ex-Mt
*XF PROT. 1-100: 6X TO 15X BASIC
*XF PROT.RC'S 1-100: 4X TO 10X BASIC
*XF PROT 101-110: .75X TO 2X REFRACTOR

2002 Finest Bat Relics

Inserted at a stated rate of one in 12 mini boxes these 15 cards feature a bat slice from the featured player.

Nm-Mt Ex-Mt
FBR-AJ Andruw Jones 10.00 3.00
FBR-AP Albert Pujols 20.00 6.00
FBR-AR Alex Rodriguez 15.00 4.50
FBR-AS Alfonso Soriano 15.00 4.50
FBR-BB Barry Bonds 25.00 7.50
FBR-BO Bret Boone 10.00 3.00
FBR-BW Bernie Williams 15.00 4.50
FBR-CJ Chipper Jones 15.00 4.50
FBR-IR Ivan Rodriguez 15.00 4.50
FBR-LG Luis Gonzalez 10.00 3.00
FBR-MP Mike Piazza 15.00 4.50
FBR-NG Nomar Garciaparra 15.00 4.50
FBR-TG Tony Gwynn 15.00 4.50
FBR-TH Todd Helton 15.00 4.50
FBR-TS Tsuyoshi Shinjo 10.00 3.00

2002 Finest Jersey Relics

Inserted at a stated rate of one in four mini boxes, these 24 cards feature the player photo along with a game-used jersey swatch.

Nm-Mt Ex-Mt
FJR-AJ Andruw Jones 10.00 3.00
FJR-AR Alex Rodriguez 15.00 4.50
FJR-BB Barry Bonds 25.00 7.50
FJR-BO Bret Boone 10.00 3.00
FJR-CD Carlos Delgado 10.00 3.00
FJR-CJ Chipper Jones 15.00 4.50
FJR-CS Curt Schilling 10.00 3.00
FJR-FT Frank Thomas 15.00 4.50
FJR-GM Greg Maddux 15.00 4.50
FJR-HN Hideo Nomo 15.00 4.50
FJR-IR Ivan Rodriguez 15.00 4.50
FJR-JB Jeff Bagwell 15.00 4.50
FJR-LG Luis Gonzalez 10.00 3.00
FJR-LW Larry Walker 15.00 4.50
FJR-MG Mark Grace 15.00 4.50
FJR-MP Mike Piazza 15.00 4.50
FJR-PM Pedro Martinez 15.00 4.50
FJR-RA Roberto Alomar 15.00 4.50
FJR-RH Rickey Henderson 15.00 4.50
FJR-RP Rafael Palmeiro 15.00 4.50
FJR-SG Shawn Green 10.00 3.00
FJR-TG Tony Gwynn 15.00 4.50
FJR-TH Todd Helton 15.00 4.50
FJR-TS Tsuyoshi Shinjo 10.00 3.00

2002 Finest Moments Autographs

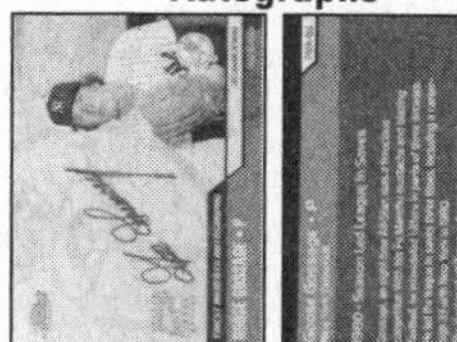

Inserted at a stated rate of one in three mini boxes, these cards feature leading retired players who signed cards honoring their greatest career moment.

Nm-Mt Ex-Mt
FMA-BG Bob Gibson 25.00 7.50
FMA-BR Bobby Richardson 25.00 7.50
FMA-BT Bobby Thomson 15.00 4.50
FMA-DL Don Larsen 25.00 7.50
FMA-DM Don Mattingly 80.00 24.00
FMA-FJ Fergie Jenkins 15.00 4.50
FMA-GG Goose Gossage 15.00 4.50
FMA-GP Gaylord Perry 15.00 4.50
FMA-JB Jim Bunning 40.00 12.00
FMA-JS Johnny Sain 15.00 4.50
FMA-LA Luis Aparicio 15.00 4.50
FMA-MS Mike Schmidt 80.00 24.00
FMA-RS Red Schoendienst 15.00 4.50
FMA-YB Yogi Berra 40.00 12.00
FMA-BRO Brooks Robinson 25.00 7.50

2003 Finest

This 110 card set was released in May, 2003. This product was issued in six pack mini-boxes with an SRP of $36. The first 100 cards are veterans while the final 10 cards featured autographed cards of leading rookies and prospects. Those cards (101-110) were issued at a stated rate of one in four mini boxes.

Nm-Mt Ex-Mt
COMP.SET w/o SP's (100) 25.00 7.50
COMMON CARD (1-100) .50 .15
COMMON CARD (101-110) 15.00 4.50
1 Sammy Sosa 2.00 .60
2 Paul Konerko .50 .15
3 Todd Helton .75 .23
4 Mike Lowell .50 .15
5 Lance Berkman .50 .15
6 Kazuhisa Ishii .50 .15
7 A.J. Pierzynski .50 .15
8 Jose Vidro .50 .15
9 Roberto Alomar .75 .23
10 Derek Jeter 3.00 .90
11 Barry Zito .50 .15
12 Jimmy Rollins .50 .15
13 Brian Giles .50 .15
14 Ryan Klesko .50 .15
15 Rich Aurilia .50 .15
16 Jim Edmonds .50 .15
17 Aubrey Huff .50 .15
18 Ivan Rodriguez 1.25 .35
19 Eric Hinske .50 .15
20 Barry Bonds 3.00 .90
21 Darin Erstad .50 .15
22 Curt Schilling .50 .15
23 Andruw Jones .50 .15
24 Jay Gibbons .50 .15
25 Nomar Garciaparra 2.00 .60
26 Kerry Wood 1.25 .35
27 Magglio Ordonez .50 .15
28 Austin Kearns .50 .15
29 Jason Jennings .50 .15
30 Jason Giambi .50 .15
31 Tim Hudson .50 .15
32 Edgar Martinez .75 .23
33 Carl Crawford .50 .15
34 Hee Seop Choi .50 .15
35 Vladimir Guerrero 1.25 .35
36 Jeff Kent .50 .15
37 John Smoltz .75 .23
38 Frank Thomas 1.25 .35
39 Cliff Floyd .50 .15
40 Mike Piazza 2.00 .60
41 Mark Prior 1.25 .35
42 Tim Salmon .75 .23
43 Shawn Green .50 .15
44 Bernie Williams .75 .23
45 Jim Thome 1.25 .35
46 John Olerud .50 .15
47 Orlando Hudson .50 .15
48 Mark Teixeira .50 .15
49 Gary Sheffield .50 .15
50 Ichiro Suzuki 2.00 .60
51 Tom Glavine .75 .23
52 Torii Hunter .50 .15
53 Craig Biggio .75 .23
54 Carlos Beltran .75 .23
55 Bartolo Colon .50 .15
56 Jorge Posada .75 .23
57 Pat Burrell .50 .15
58 Edgar Renteria .50 .15
59 Rafael Palmeiro .75 .23
60 Alfonso Soriano .75 .23
61 Brandon Phillips .50 .15
62 Luis Gonzalez .50 .15
63 Manny Ramirez .75 .23
64 Garret Anderson .50 .15
65 Ken Griffey Jr. 2.00 .60
66 A.J. Burnett .50 .15
67 Mike Sweeney .50 .15
68 Doug Mientkiewicz .50 .15
69 Eric Chavez .50 .15
70 Adam Dunn .75 .23
71 Shea Hillenbrand .50 .15
72 Troy Glaus .50 .15
73 Rodrigo Lopez .50 .15
74 Moises Alou .50 .15
75 Chipper Jones 1.25 .35
76 Bobby Abreu .50 .15
77 Mark Mulder .50 .15
78 Kevin Brown .50 .15
79 Josh Beckett .50 .15
80 Larry Walker .75 .23
81 Randy Johnson 1.25 .35
82 Greg Maddux 2.00 .60
83 Johnny Damon 1.25 .35
84 Omar Vizquel .75 .23
85 Jeff Bagwell .75 .23
86 Carlos Pena .50 .15
87 Roy Oswalt .50 .15
88 Richie Sexson .50 .15
89 Roger Clemens 2.50 .75
90 Miguel Tejada .50 .15
91 Vicente Padilla .50 .15
92 Phil Nevin .50 .15
93 Edgardo Alfonzo .50 .15
94 Bret Boone .50 .15
95 Albert Pujols 2.50 .75
96 Carlos Delgado .50 .15
97 Jose Contreras RC 1.50 .45
98 Scott Rolen 1.25 .35
99 Pedro Martinez 1.25 .35
100 Alex Rodriguez 2.00 .60
101 Adam LaRoche AU 15.00 4.50
102 Andy Marte AU RC 40.00 12.00
103 Daryl Clark AU RC 15.00 4.50
104 J.D. Durbin AU RC 15.00 4.50
105 Craig Brazell AU RC 15.00 4.50
106 Brian Burgamy AU RC 10.00 3.00
107 Tyler Johnson AU RC 10.00 3.00
108 Joey Gomes AU RC 10.00 3.00
109 Bryan Bullington AU RC 25.00 7.50
110 Byron Gettis AU RC 10.00 3.00

2003 Finest Refractors

This is a complete parallel of the basic Finest set. Cards numbered 1-100 were issued at a stated rate of one per mini-box and cards numbered 101-110 were issued at a stated rate of one every 34 mini-boxes.

Nm-Mt Ex-Mt
*REFRACTORS 1-100: 2X TO 5X BASIC
*REFRACTOR RC'S 1-100: 1.25X TO 3X BASIC
*REFRACTORS 101-110: .75X TO 2X BASIC

2003 Finest X-Fractors

Inserted at a stated rate of one in seven mini-boxes, this is a parallel to the Finest set. These cards were issued to a stated print run of 99 serial numbered sets.

Nm-Mt Ex-Mt
*X-FRACTORS 1-100: 6X TO 15X BASIC
*X-FRACTOR RC'S 1-100: 4X TO 10X BASIC
*X-FRACTORS 101-110: 1X TO 2.5X BASIC

2003 Finest Uncirculated Gold X-Fractors

Issued as a box topper for the big box which contained all the mini-boxes, this is a parallel to the basic set. These cards are sealed in plastic holders and were issued to a stated print run of 199 serial numbered sets.

Nm-Mt Ex-Mt
*GOLD X-F 1-100: 5X TO 12X BASIC
*GOLD X-F RC'S 1-100: 3X TO 8X BASIC
*GOLD X-F 101-110: .75X TO 2X BASIC

2003 Finest Bat Relics

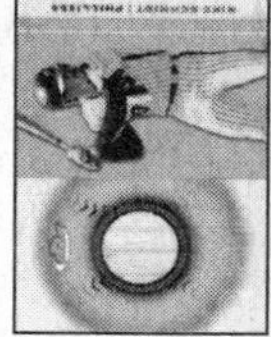

These cards were inserted at different rates depending on what group the bat relic belonged to. We have notated what group the player belonged to next to their name in our checklist.

Nm-Mt Ex-Mt
GROUP A STATED ODDS 1:104 MINI-BOXES
GROUP B STATED ODDS 1:32 MINI-BOXES
GROUP C STATED ODDS 1:29 MINI-BOXES
GROUP D STATED ODDS 1:42 MINI-BOXES
GROUP E STATED ODDS 1:40 MINI-BOXES
GROUP F STATED ODDS 1:23 MINI-BOXES
GROUP G STATED ODDS 1:18 MINI-BOXES
GROUP H STATED ODDS 1:24 MINI-BOXES
GROUP I STATED ODDS 1:12 MINI-BOXES
GROUP J STATED ODDS 1:22 MINI-BOXES
GROUP K STATED ODDS 1:21 MINI-BOXES
AD Adam Dunn H 10.00 3.00
AK Austin Kearns F 8.00 2.40
AP Albert Pujols I 15.00 4.50
AR Alex Rodriguez E 15.00 4.50
AS Alfonso Soriano H 10.00 3.00
BB Barry Bonds F 20.00 6.00
CJ Chipper Jones G 15.00 4.50
CR Cal Ripken B 40.00 12.00
DM Dale Murphy I 15.00 4.50
GM Greg Maddux F 15.00 4.50
IR Ivan Rodriguez G 15.00 4.50
JB Jeff Bagwell D 10.00 3.00
JT Jim Thome D 15.00 4.50
KP Kirby Puckett K 15.00 4.50
LB Lance Berkman C 8.00 2.40
MP Mike Piazza E 15.00 4.50
MR Manny Ramirez I 10.00 3.00
MS Mike Schmidt C 25.00 7.50
MT Miguel Tejada I 8.00 2.40
NG Nomar Garciaparra A 25.00 7.50
PM Paul Molitor C 15.00 4.50
RC Rod Carew K 10.00 3.00
RCL Roger Clemens J 15.00 4.50
RH Rickey Henderson B 15.00 4.50
RP Rafael Palmeiro J 10.00 3.00
TH Todd Helton B 10.00 3.00
WB Wade Boggs G 10.00 3.00

2003 Finest Moments Refractors Autographs

Inserted at different odds depening on whether the card was issued as part of group A or group B, this 12 card set features authentic signatures of baseball legends. Johnny Sain did not return his card in time for inclusion in this product and the exchange cards could be redeemed until April 30, 2005.

Nm-Mt Ex-Mt
GROUP A STATED ODDS 1:113 MINI-BOXES
GROUP B STATED ODDS 1:5 MINI-BOXES
EXCHANGE DEADLINE 04/30/05
DL Don Larsen B 25.00 7.50
EB Ernie Banks A 60.00 18.00
GC Gary Carter B 15.00 4.50
GF George Foster B 15.00 4.50
GG Goose Gossage B 15.00 4.50
GP Gaylord Perry B 15.00 4.50
JP Jim Palmer B 15.00 4.50
JS Johnny Sain B EXCH 15.00 4.50
KH Keith Hernandez B 15.00 4.50
LB Lou Brock B 25.00 7.50
OC Orlando Cepeda B 15.00 4.50
PB Paul Blair B 15.00 4.50
WMA Willie Mays A 150.00 45.00

2003 Finest Uniform Relics

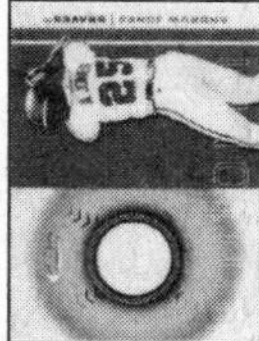

These 22 cards were inserted in different odds depending on what group the player belonged to. We have notated what group the player belonged to next to their name in our checklist.

Nm-Mt Ex-Mt
GROUP A STATED ODDS 1:28 MINI-BOXES
GROUP B STATED ODDS 1:11 MINI-BOXES
GROUP C STATED ODDS 1:11 MINI-BOXES
GROUP D STATED ODDS 1:10 MINI-BOXES
GROUP E STATED ODDS 1:19 MINI-BOXES
GROUP F STATED ODDS 1:12 MINI-BOXES
GROUP G STATED ODDS 1:34 MINI-BOXES
GROUP H STATED ODDS 1:17 MINI-BOXES
AD Adam Dunn B 10.00 3.00
AJ Andruw Jones H 8.00 2.40
AP Albert Pujols D 15.00 4.50

AR Alex Rodriguez F 15.00 4.50
AS Alfonso Soriano A 10.00 3.00
BB Barry Bonds D 20.00 6.00
CJ Chipper Jones B 15.00 4.50
CS Curt Schilling B 8.00 2.40
EC Eric Chavez B 8.00 2.40
GM Greg Maddux C 15.00 4.50
LG Luis Gonzalez D 8.00 2.40
LW Larry Walker C 10.00 3.00
MM Mark Mulder C 8.00 2.40
MP Mike Piazza C 15.00 4.50
MR Manny Ramirez E 10.00 3.00
MSW Mike Sweeney F 8.00 2.40
RJ Randy Johnson H 15.00 4.50
RO Roy Oswalt G 8.00 2.40
RP Rafael Palmeiro E 10.00 3.00
SS Sammy Sosa D 20.00 6.00
TH Todd Helton F 10.00 3.00
WM Willie Mays A 50.00 15.00

2004 Finest

This 122 card set was released in May, 2004. The set was issued in 30-card packs with a $40 SRP. Those packs were issued three to a box and 12 boxes to a case. The first 100 cards in this set feature veterans while cards 101-110 feature veteran players with a game-used jersey swatch on the card and cards 111-122 feature autograph rookie cards. Please note that Jeff Allison, David Murphy and Lastings Milledge did not sign their cards in time for pack out and those cards could be redeemed until April 30, 2006.

Nm-Mt Ex-Mt
COMP.SET w/o SP's (100) 25.00 7.50
COMMON CARD (1-100) .50 .15
COMMON CARD (101-110) 8.00 2.40
101-110 STATED ODDS 1:7 MINI-BOXES
COMMON CARD (111-122) 10.00 3.00
111-122 STATED ODDS 1:3 MINI-BOXES
EXCHANGE DEADLINE 04/30/06
1 Juan Pierre .50 .15
2 Derek Jeter 2.50 .75
3 Garret Anderson .50 .15
4 Javy Lopez .50 .15
5 Corey Patterson .50 .15
6 Todd Helton .75 .23
7 Roy Oswalt .50 .15
8 Shawn Green .50 .15
9 Vladimir Guerrero 1.25 .35
10 Jorge Posada .75 .23
11 Jason Kendall .50 .15
12 Scott Rolen 1.25 .35
13 Randy Johnson 1.25 .35
14 Bill Mueller .50 .15
15 Magglio Ordonez .50 .15
16 Larry Walker .75 .23
17 Lance Berkman .50 .15
18 Richie Sexson .50 .15
19 Orlando Cabrera .50 .15
20 Alfonso Soriano .75 .23
21 Kevin Millwood .50 .15
22 Edgar Martinez .75 .23
23 Aubrey Huff .50 .15
24 Carlos Delgado .50 .15
25 Vernon Wells .50 .15
26 Mark Teixeira .50 .15
27 Troy Glaus .50 .15
28 Jeff Kent .50 .15
29 Hideo Nomo 1.25 .35
30 Torii Hunter .50 .15
31 Hank Blalock .50 .15
32 Brandon Webb .50 .15
33 Tony Batista .50 .15
34 Bret Boone .50 .15
35 Ryan Klesko .50 .15
36 Barry Zito .50 .15
37 Edgar Renteria .50 .15
38 Geoff Jenkins .50 .15
39 Jeff Bagwell .75 .23
40 Dontrelle Willis .50 .15
41 Adam Dunn .75 .23
42 Mark Buehrle .50 .15
43 Esteban Loaiza .50 .15
44 Angel Berroa .50 .15
45 Ivan Rodriguez 1.25 .35
46 Jose Vidro .50 .15
47 Mark Mulder .50 .15
48 Roger Clemens 2.50 .75
49 Jim Edmonds .50 .15
50 Eric Gagne 1.25 .35
51 Marcus Giles .50 .15
52 Curt Schilling 1.25 .35
53 Ken Griffey Jr. 2.00 .60
54 Jason Schmidt .50 .15
55 Miguel Tejada .50 .15
56 Dmitri Young .50 .15
57 Mike Lowell .50 .15
58 Mike Sweeney .50 .15
59 Scott Podsednik .50 .15
60 Miguel Cabrera .75 .23
61 Johan Santana .75 .23
62 Bernie Williams .75 .23
63 Eric Chavez .50 .15
64 Bobby Abreu .50 .15
65 Brian Giles .50 .15
66 Michael Young .50 .15
67 Paul Lo Duca .50 .15
68 Austin Kearns .50 .15
69 Jody Gerut .50 .15
70 Kerry Wood 1.25 .35
71 Luis Matos .50 .15
72 Greg Maddux 2.00 .60
73 Alex Rodriguez Yanks 2.00 .60
74 Mike Lieberthal .50 .15
75 Jim Thome 1.25 .35
76 Javier Vazquez .50 .15
77 Bartolo Colon .50 .15
78 Manny Ramirez .75 .23
79 Jacque Jones .50 .15
80 Johnny Damon 1.25 .35
81 Carlos Beltran .75 .23
82 C.C. Sabathia .50 .15
83 Preston Wilson .50 .15
84 Luis Castillo .50 .15
85 Kevin Brown .50 .15
86 Shannon Stewart .50 .15
87 Cliff Floyd .50 .15
88 Mike Mussina .75 .23
89 Rafael Furcal .50 .15
90 Roy Halladay .50 .15
91 Frank Thomas 1.25 .35
92 Melvin Mora .50 .15
93 Andruw Jones .50 .15
94 Luis Gonzalez .50 .15
95 David Ortiz 1.25 .35
96 Gary Sheffield .50 .15
97 Tim Hudson .50 .15
98 Phil Nevin .50 .15
99 Ichiro Suzuki 2.00 .60
100 Albert Pujols 2.50 .75
101 Nomar Garciaparra SR Jsy 15.00 4.50
102 Sammy Sosa SR Jsy 15.00 4.50
103 Josh Beckett SR Jsy 8.00 2.40
104 Jason Giambi SR Jsy 8.00 2.40
105 Rocco Baldelli SR Jsy 8.00 2.40
106 Jose Reyes SR Jsy 8.00 2.40
107 Chipper Jones SR Jsy 10.00 3.00
108 Pedro Martinez SR Jsy 10.00 3.00
109 Mike Piazza SR Jsy 15.00 4.50
110 Mark Prior SR Jsy 10.00 3.00
111 Craig Ansman AU RC 10.00 3.00
112 Jeff Allison AU RC EXCH 15.00 4.50
113 David Murphy AU RC EXCH 15.00 4.50
114 Jason Hirsh AU RC 10.00 3.00
115 Matt Moses AU RC 15.00 4.50
116 Estee Harris AU RC 10.00 3.00
117 Logan Kensing AU RC 10.00 3.00
118 L.Milledge AU RC EXCH 30.00 9.00
119 Merkin Valdez AU RC 15.00 4.50
120 Travis Blackley AU RC 15.00 4.50
121 Vito Chiaravalloti AU RC 15.00 4.50
122 Dioner Navarro AU RC 20.00 6.00

2004 Finest Gold Refractors

Nm-Mt Ex-Mt
*GOLD REF 1-100: 6X TO 15X BASIC
1-100 STATED ODDS 1:11
*GOLD REF 101-110: 1.25X TO 3X BASIC
101-110 STATED ODDS 1:102
*GOLD REF 111-122: 2X TO 4X BASIC
111-122 STATED ODDS 1:85
STATED PRINT RUN 50 SERIAL #'d SETS
EXCHANGE DEADLINE 04/30/06

2004 Finest Refractors

Nm-Mt Ex-Mt
*REFRACTORS 1-100: 2X TO 5X BASIC
1-100 APPX.ODDS 3 IN EVERY 4 MINI-BOXES
*REFRACTORS 101-110: .5X TO 1.2X BASIC
101-110 STATED ODDS 1:26 MINI-BOXES
*REFRACTORS 111-122: .6X TO 1.5X BASIC
111-122 STATED ODDS 1:22 MINI-BOXES
EXCHANGE DEADLINE 04/30/06
118 Lastings Milledge AU EXCH 50.00 15.00

2004 Finest Uncirculated Gold X-Fractors

Nm-Mt Ex-Mt
*GOLD X-F 1-100: 4X TO 10X BASIC
*GOLD X-F 101-110: .75X TO 2X BASIC
*GOLD X-F 111-122: 1X TO 2.5X BASIC
ONE PER BASIC SEALED BOX
STATED PRINT RUN 139 SERIAL #'d SETS
EXCHANGE DEADLINE 04/30/06
118 Lastings Milledge AU EXCH 80.00 24.00

2004 Finest Moments Autographs

Nm-Mt Ex-Mt
GROUP A ODDS 1:86 MINI-BOXES
GROUP B ODDS 1:102 MINI-BOXES
GROUP C ODDS 1:5 MINI-BOXES
DS Duke Snider A 40.00 12.00
EK Ed Kranepool C 15.00 4.50
GS George Foster C 10.00 3.00
JA Jim Abbott A 25.00 7.50
JP Johnny Podres C 10.00 3.00
LD Lenny Dykstra C 10.00 3.00
OC Orlando Cepeda C 15.00 4.50
RY Robin Yount A 50.00 15.00
VB Vida Blue C 10.00 3.00
WM Willie Mays B 150.00 45.00

2004 Finest Relics

Nm-Mt Ex-Mt
GROUP A ODDS 1:3 MINI-BOXES
GROUP B ODDS 1:4 MINI-BOXES
AB Angel Berroa Bat B 8.00 2.40
AD Adam Dunn Jsy A 10.00 3.00
AG Adrian Gonzalez Bat A 8.00 2.40
AJ Andruw Jones Bat A 8.00 2.40
AP Andy Pettitte Uni B 10.00 3.00
AP1 Albert Pujols Uni A 20.00 6.00
AP2 Albert Pujols Bat A 20.00 6.00

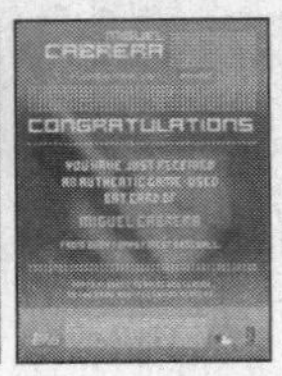

AR1 A.Rodriguez Rgr Jsy A 15.00 4.50
AR2 A.Rodriguez Yanks Jsy A 25.00 7.50
AS Alfonso Soriano Bat A 10.00 3.00
BM1 B.Myers Arm Down Jsy A 8.00 2.40
BM2 B.Myers Arm Up Jsy A 8.00 2.40
BW Bernie Williams Bat B 10.00 3.00
BZ Barry Zito Jsy A 8.00 2.40
CCS C.C. Sabathia Jsy A 8.00 2.40
CG Cristian Guzman Jsy A 8.00 2.40
CS Curt Schilling Jsy A 8.00 2.40
DE Darin Erstad Bat A 8.00 2.40
DL Derek Lowe Uni A 8.00 2.40
DW Dontrelle Willis Uni B 8.00 2.40
DY Delmon Young Bat B 10.00 3.00
EC Eric Chavez Uni B 8.00 2.40
FT Frank Thomas Jsy A 10.00 3.00
GM Greg Maddux Jsy A 15.00 4.50
GS Gary Sheffield Bat A 8.00 2.40
HB1 Hank Blalock Jsy A 8.00 2.40
HB2 Hank Blalock Jsy B 8.00 2.40
IR1 I.Rodriguez Running Jsy A 10.00 3.00
IR2 I.Rodriguez w/Glove Jsy A 10.00 3.00
IR3 Ivan Rodriguez Bat B 10.00 3.00
JB Jeff Bagwell Jsy A 10.00 3.00
JL Javy Lopez Jsy A 8.00 2.40
JP Juan Pierre Bat A 8.00 2.40
JPB1 Josh Beckett Jsy A 8.00 2.40
JR1 Jose Reyes White Jsy A 8.00 2.40
JR2 Jose Reyes Bat A 8.00 2.40
JR3 Jose Reyes Black Jsy B 8.00 2.40
JS John Smoltz Uni A 10.00 3.00
JT Jim Thome Jsy A 10.00 3.00
KI Kazuhisa Ishii Jsy A 8.00 2.40
KM Kevin Millwood Jsy A 8.00 2.40
KS Kazuhiro Sasaki Jsy A 8.00 2.40
KW1 Kerry Wood Jsy A 10.00 3.00
KW2 Kerry Wood Bat A 10.00 3.00
LB1 Lance Berkman Bat A 8.00 2.40
LB2 Lance Berkman Jsy A 8.00 2.40
LG Luis Gonzalez Jsy B 8.00 2.40
LW Larry Walker Jsy A 10.00 3.00
MB Marlon Byrd Jsy A 8.00 2.40
MC Miguel Cabrera Bat B 10.00 3.00
ML1 Mike Lowell Grey Jsy A 8.00 2.40
ML2 Mike Lowell Black Jsy B 8.00 2.40
MM Mark Mulder Uni B 8.00 2.40
MO1 Maggio Ordonez Jsy A 8.00 2.40
MO2 Maggio Ordonez Bat A 8.00 2.40
MP Mark Prior Bat A 10.00 3.00
MR Mariano Rivera Uni A 10.00 3.00
MT1 Miguel Tejada Bat A 8.00 2.40
MT2 Miguel Tejada Uni A 8.00 2.40
NG Nomar Garciaparra Bat A 15.00 4.50
PB Pat Burrell Jsy A 8.00 2.40
PW Preston Wilson Bat A 8.00 2.40
RB1 R.Baldelli Bat Down Jsy B 8.00 2.40
RB3 R.Baldelli Bat on Ball Jsy B 8.00 2.40
RH Rich Harden Uni B 8.00 2.40
RJ Randy Johnson Jsy A 10.00 3.00
RP1 Rafael Palmeiro Bat A 10.00 3.00
RP2 Rafael Palmeiro Uni A 10.00 3.00
RP3 Rafael Palmeiro Jsy B 10.00 3.00
SB Sean Burroughs Bat A 8.00 2.40
SG Shawn Green Jsy A 8.00 2.40
SR Scott Rolen Bat A 10.00 3.00
SS Sammy Sosa Bat A 15.00 4.50
TG Troy Glaus Bat A 8.00 2.40
TH Tim Hudson Uni B 8.00 2.40
TH1 Todd Helton Bat A 10.00 3.00
TH2 Todd Helton Jsy A 10.00 3.00
TKH1 Torii Hunter Bat A 8.00 2.40
TKH2 Torii Hunter Jsy B 8.00 2.40
VG Vladimir Guerrero Jsy B 10.00 3.00
VW Vernon Wells Jsy A 8.00 2.40

1993 Flair

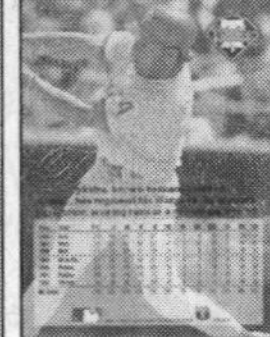

This 300-card standard-size set represents Fleer's entrance into the super-premium category of trading cards. Cards were distributed exclusively in specially encased "hardpacks". The cards are made from heavy 24 point board card stock, with an additional three points of high-gloss laminate on each side, and feature full-bleed color fronts that sport two photos of each player, one superposed upon the other. The cards are numbered alphabetically within teams with National League preceding American league. There are no key Rookie Cards in this set.

Nm-Mt Ex-Mt
COMPLETE SET (300) 50.00 15.00
1 Steve Avery .25 .07
2 Jeff Blauser .25 .07
3 Ron Gant .50 .15
4 Tom Glavine .75 .23
5 David Justice .50 .15
6 Mark Lemke .25 .07
7 Greg Maddux 2.00 .60
8 Fred McGriff .75 .23
9 Terry Pendleton .50 .15
10 Deion Sanders .75 .23
11 John Smoltz .75 .23
12 Mike Stanton .25 .07
13 Steve Buechele .25 .07
14 Mark Grace .75 .23
15 Greg Hibbard .25 .07
16 Derrick May .25 .07
17 Chuck McElroy .25 .07
18 Mike Morgan .25 .07
19 Randy Myers .25 .07
20 Ryne Sandberg 2.00 .60
21 Dwight Smith .25 .07
22 Sammy Sosa 2.00 .60
23 Jose Vizcaino .25 .07
24 Tim Belcher .25 .07
25 Rob Dibble .50 .15
26 Roberto Kelly .25 .07
27 Barry Larkin .75 .23
28 Kevin Mitchell .25 .07
29 Hal Morris .25 .07
30 Joe Oliver .25 .07
31 Jose Rijo .25 .07
32 Bip Roberts .25 .07
33 Chris Sabo .25 .07
34 Reggie Sanders .25 .07
35 Dante Bichette .50 .15
36 Willie Blair .25 .07
37 Jerald Clark .25 .07
38 Alex Cole .25 .07
39 Andres Galarraga .50 .15
40 Joe Girardi .25 .07
41 Charlie Hayes .25 .07
42 Chris Jones .25 .07
43 David Nied .25 .07
44 Eric Young .25 .07
45 Alex Arias .25 .07
46 Jack Armstrong .25 .07
47 Bret Barberie .25 .07
48 Chuck Carr .25 .07
49 Jeff Conine .50 .15
50 Orestes Destrade .25 .07
51 Chris Hammond .25 .07
52 Bryan Harvey .25 .07
53 Benito Santiago .50 .15
54 Gary Sheffield .50 .15
55 Walt Weiss .25 .07
56 Eric Anthony .25 .07
57 Jeff Bagwell .75 .23
58 Craig Biggio .75 .23
59 Ken Caminiti .50 .15
60 Andujar Cedeno .25 .07
61 Doug Drabek .25 .07
62 Steve Finley .50 .15
63 Luis Gonzalez .50 .15
64 Pete Harnisch .25 .07
65 Doug Jones .25 .07
66 Darryl Kile .50 .15
67 Greg Swindell .25 .07
68 Brett Butler .50 .15
69 Jim Gott .25 .07
70 Orel Hershiser .50 .15
71 Eric Karros .50 .15
72 Pedro Martinez 2.50 .75
73 Ramon Martinez .25 .07
74 Roger McDowell .25 .07
75 Mike Piazza 3.00 .90
76 Jody Reed .25 .07
77 Tim Wallach .25 .07
78 Moises Alou .50 .15
79 Greg Colbrunn .25 .07
80 Wil Cordero .25 .07
81 Delino DeShields .25 .07
82 Jeff Fassero .25 .07
83 Marquis Grissom .50 .15
84 Ken Hill .25 .07
85 Mike Lansing RC .50 .15
86 Dennis Martinez .50 .15
87 Larry Walker .75 .23
88 John Wetteland .50 .15
89 Bobby Bonilla .50 .15
90 Vince Coleman .25 .07
91 Dwight Gooden .25 .07
92 Todd Hundley .25 .07
93 Howard Johnson .25 .07
94 Eddie Murray 1.25 .35
95 Joe Orsulak .25 .07
96 Bret Saberhagen .50 .15
97 Darren Daulton .50 .15
98 Mariano Duncan .25 .07
99 Len Dykstra .50 .15
100 Jim Eisenreich .25 .07
101 Tommy Greene .25 .07
102 Dave Hollins .25 .07
103 Pete Incaviglia .25 .07
104 Danny Jackson .25 .07
105 John Kruk .50 .15
106 Terry Mulholland .25 .07
107 Curt Schilling .50 .15
108 Mitch Williams .25 .07
109 Stan Belinda .25 .07
110 Jay Bell .50 .15
111 Steve Cooke .25 .07
112 Carlos Garcia .25 .07
113 Jeff King .25 .07
114 Al Martin .25 .07
115 Orlando Merced .25 .07
116 Don Slaught .25 .07
117 Andy Van Slyke .50 .15
118 Tim Wakefield 1.25 .35
119 Rene Arocha RC .50 .15
120 Bernard Gilkey .25 .07
121 Gregg Jefferies .25 .07
122 Ray Lankford .25 .07
123 Donovan Osborne .25 .07
124 Tom Pagnozzi .25 .07
125 Erik Pappas .25 .07
126 Geronimo Pena .25 .07
127 Lee Smith .50 .15
128 Ozzie Smith 2.00 .60
129 Bob Tewksbury .25 .07
130 Mark Whiten .25 .07
131 Derek Bell .25 .07
132 Andy Benes .25 .07
133 Tony Gwynn 1.50 .45
134 Gene Harris .25 .07
135 Trevor Hoffman .50 .15
136 Phil Plantier .25 .07
137 Rod Beck .25 .07
138 Barry Bonds 3.00 .90
139 John Burkett .25 .07
140 Will Clark 1.25 .35
141 Royce Clayton .25 .07
142 Mike Jackson .25 .07
143 Darren Lewis .25 .07
144 Kirt Manwaring .25 .07
145 Willie McGee .50 .15
146 Bill Swift .25 .07
147 Robby Thompson .25 .07
148 Matt Williams .50 .15
149 Brady Anderson .50 .15
150 Mike Devereaux .25 .07
151 Chris Hoiles .25 .07
152 Ben McDonald .25 .07
153 Mark McLemore .25 .07
154 Mike Mussina .75 .23
155 Gregg Olson .25 .07
156 Harold Reynolds .50 .15
157 Cal Ripken UER 4.00 1.20
(Back refers to his games streak going into 1992; should be 1993) Also streak is spelled steak
158 Rick Sutcliffe .50 .15
159 Fernando Valenzuela .50 .15
160 Roger Clemens 2.50 .75
161 Scott Cooper .25 .07
162 Andre Dawson .50 .15
163 Scott Fletcher .25 .07
164 Mike Greenwell .25 .07
165 Greg A. Harris .25 .07
166 Billy Hatcher .25 .07
167 Jeff Russell .25 .07
168 Mo Vaughn .50 .15
169 Frank Viola .50 .15
170 Chad Curtis .25 .07
171 Chili Davis .50 .15
172 Gary DiSarcina .25 .07
173 Damion Easley .25 .07
174 Chuck Finley .50 .15
175 Mark Langston .25 .07
176 Luis Polonia .25 .07
177 Tim Salmon .75 .23
178 Scott Sanderson .25 .07
179 J.T.Snow RC .75 .23
180 Wilson Alvarez .25 .07
181 Ellis Burks .50 .15
182 Joey Cora .25 .07
183 Alex Fernandez .25 .07
184 Ozzie Guillen .25 .07
185 Roberto Hernandez .25 .07
186 Bo Jackson 1.25 .35
187 Lance Johnson .25 .07
188 Jack McDowell .25 .07
189 Frank Thomas 1.25 .35
190 Robin Ventura .50 .15
191 Carlos Baerga .25 .07
192 Albert Belle .50 .15
193 Wayne Kirby .25 .07
194 Derek Lilliquist .25 .07
195 Kenny Lofton .50 .15
196 Carlos Martinez .25 .07
197 Jose Mesa .25 .07
198 Eric Plunk .25 .07
199 Paul Sorrento .25 .07
200 John Doherty .25 .07
201 Cecil Fielder .50 .15
202 Travis Fryman .50 .15
203 Kirk Gibson .50 .15
204 Mike Henneman .25 .07
205 Chad Kreuter .25 .07
206 Scott Livingstone .25 .07
207 Tony Phillips .25 .07
208 Mickey Tettleton .25 .07
209 Alan Trammell .50 .15
210 David Wells .50 .15
211 Lou Whitaker .50 .15
212 Kevin Appier .50 .15
213 George Brett 3.00 .90
214 David Cone .50 .15
215 Tom Gordon .25 .07
216 Phil Hiatt .25 .07
217 Felix Jose .25 .07
218 Wally Joyner .50 .15
219 Jose Lind .25 .07
220 Mike Macfarlane .25 .07
221 Brian McRae .25 .07
222 Jeff Montgomery .25 .07
223 Cal Eldred .25 .07
224 Darryl Hamilton .25 .07
225 John Jaha .25 .07
226 Pat Listach .25 .07
227 Graeme Lloyd RC .50 .15
228 Kevin Reimer .25 .07
229 Bill Spiers .25 .07
230 B.J. Surhoff .50 .15
231 Greg Vaughn .25 .07
232 Robin Yount 2.00 .60
233 Rick Aguilera .25 .07
234 Jim Deshaies .25 .07
235 Brian Harper .25 .07
236 Kent Hrbek .50 .15
237 Chuck Knoblauch .50 .15
238 Shane Mack .25 .07
239 David McCarty .25 .07
240 Pedro Munoz .25 .07
241 Mike Pagliarulo .25 .07
242 Kirby Puckett 1.25 .35
243 Dave Winfield .50 .15
244 Jim Abbott .75 .23
245 Wade Boggs .75 .23
246 Pat Kelly .25 .07
247 Jimmy Key .50 .15
248 Jim Leyritz .25 .07
249 Don Mattingly 3.00 .90
250 Matt Nokes .25 .07
251 Paul O'Neill .75 .23
252 Mike Stanley .25 .07
253 Danny Tartabull .25 .07
254 Bob Wickman .25 .07
255 Bernie Williams .75 .23
256 Mike Bordick .25 .07
257 Dennis Eckersley .50 .15
258 Brent Gates .25 .07
259 Rich Gossage .50 .15
260 Rickey Henderson 1.25 .35
261 Mark McGwire 3.00 .90
262 Ruben Sierra .25 .07
263 Terry Steinbach .25 .07
264 Bob Welch .25 .07
265 Bobby Witt .25 .07
266 Rich Amaral .25 .07
267 Chris Bosio .25 .07
268 Jay Buhner .50 .15
269 Norm Charlton .25 .07
270 Ken Griffey Jr. 2.00 .60
271 Erik Hanson .25 .07
272 Randy Johnson 1.25 .35
273 Edgar Martinez .75 .23
274 Tino Martinez .75 .23

275 Dave Valle .25 .07
276 Omar Vizquel .75 .23
277 Kevin Brown .50 .15
278 Jose Canseco 1.25 .35
279 Julio Franco .50 .15
280 Juan Gonzalez .75 .23
281 Tom Henke .25 .07
282 David Hulse RC .25 .07
283 Rafael Palmeiro .75 .23
284 Dean Palmer .50 .15
285 Ivan Rodriguez 1.25 .35
286 Nolan Ryan 5.00 1.50
287 Roberto Alomar .75 .23
288 Pat Borders .25 .07
289 Joe Carter .50 .15
290 Juan Guzman .25 .07
291 Pat Hentgen .25 .07
292 Paul Molitor .75 .23
293 John Olerud .50 .15
294 Ed Sprague .25 .07
295 Dave Stewart .50 .15
296 Duane Ward .25 .07
297 Devon White .50 .15
298 Checklist 1-100 .25 .07
299 Checklist 101-200 .25 .07
300 Checklist 201-300 .25 .07

1993 Flair Wave of the Future

his 20-card standard-size limited edition insert et features a selction of top prospects. Cards vere randomly seeded into1993 Flair packs. ach card is made of the same thick card stock s the regular-issue set and features full-bleed olor player action photos on the fronts, with the lair logo, player's name, and the "Wave of the uture" name and logo in gold foil, all superim- osed upon an ocean breaker. A Rookie Year Jim dmonds card is a highlight of this set.

Nm-Mt Ex-Mt
OMPLETE SET (20) 40.00 12.00
Jason Bere 1.00 .30
Jeromy Burnitz 2.00 .60
Russ Davis 2.00 .60
Jim Edmonds 8.00 2.40
Cliff Floyd 2.00 .60
Jeffrey Hammonds 1.00 .30
Trevor Hoffman 2.00 .60
Domingo Jean 1.00 .30
David McCarty 1.00 .30
0 Bobby Munoz 1.00 .30
1 Brad Pennington 1.00 .30
2 Mike Piazza 10.00 3.00
3 Manny Ramirez 4.00 1.20
4 John Roper 1.00 .30
5 Tim Salmon 2.50 .75
6 Aaron Sele 1.00 .30
7 Allen Watson 1.00 .30
8 Rondell White 2.00 .60
9 Darrell Whitmore UER 1.00 .30
(Nigel Wilson back)
0 Nigel Wilson UER 1.00 .30
(Darrell Whitmore back)

1994 Flair

or the second consecutive year Fleer issued eir premium-level Flair brand. The set consists 450 full bleed cards in two series of 250 and 00. The card stock is thicker than the tradition- standard card. Card fronts feature two photos ith the player's name and team name at the ottom in gold foil. The cards are grouped alpha- etically by team within each league with AL pre- eding NL. Notable Rookie Cards include Chan o Park and Alex Rodriguez. An Aaron Sele romo card was distributed to dealers and obby media to preview the product.

Nm-Mt Ex-Mt
OMPLETE SET (450) 80.00 24.00
OMP. SERIES 1 (250) 20.00 6.00
OMP. SERIES 2 (200) 60.00 18.00
Harold Baines .50 .15
Jeffrey Hammonds .25 .07
Chris Hoiles .25 .07
Ben McDonald .25 .07
Mark McLemore .25 .07
Jamie Moyer .50 .15
Jim Poole .25 .07
Cal Ripken Jr. 4.00 1.20
Chris Sabo .25 .07
) Scott Bankhead .25 .07
Scott Cooper .25 .07
2 Danny Darwin .25 .07
3 Andre Dawson .50 .15
4 Billy Hatcher .25 .07
5 Aaron Sele .25 .07
6 John Valentin .25 .07
7 Dave Valle .25 .07
8 Mo Vaughn .50 .15
9 Brian Anderson RC .50 .15
0 Gary DiSarcina .25 .07
1 Jim Edmonds 1.25 .35
2 Chuck Finley .50 .15
3 Bo Jackson 1.25 .35
4 Mark Leiter .25 .07
25 Greg Myers .25 .07
26 Eduardo Perez .25 .07
27 Tim Salmon .75 .23
28 Wilson Alvarez .25 .07
29 Jason Bere .25 .07
30 Alex Fernandez .25 .07
31 Ozzie Guillen .25 .07
32 Joe Hall RC .25 .07
33 Darrin Jackson .25 .07
34 Kirk McCaskill .25 .07
35 Tim Raines .50 .15
36 Frank Thomas 1.25 .35
37 Carlos Baerga .25 .07
38 Albert Belle .50 .15
39 Mark Clark .25 .07
40 Wayne Kirby .25 .07
41 Dennis Martinez .50 .15
42 Charles Nagy .25 .07
43 Manny Ramirez .75 .23
44 Paul Sorrento .25 .07
45 Jim Thome 1.25 .35
46 Eric Davis .50 .15
47 John Doherty .25 .07
48 Junior Felix .25 .07
49 Cecil Fielder .50 .15
50 Kirk Gibson .50 .15
51 Mike Moore .25 .07
52 Tony Phillips .25 .07
53 Alan Trammell .50 .15
54 Kevin Appier .50 .15
55 Stan Belinda .25 .07
56 Vince Coleman .25 .07
57 Greg Gagne .25 .07
58 Bob Hamelin .25 .07
59 Dave Henderson .25 .07
60 Wally Joyner .50 .15
61 Mike Macfarlane .25 .07
62 Jeff Montgomery .25 .07
63 Ricky Bones .25 .07
64 Jeff Bronkey .25 .07
65 Alex Diaz RC .25 .07
66 Cal Eldred .25 .07
67 Darryl Hamilton .25 .07
68 John Jaha .25 .07
69 Mark Kiefer .25 .07
70 Kevin Seitzer .25 .07
71 Turner Ward .25 .07
72 Rich Becker .25 .07
73 Scott Erickson .25 .07
74 Keith Garagozzo RC .25 .07
75 Kent Hrbek .50 .15
76 Scott Leius .25 .07
77 Kirby Puckett 1.25 .35
78 Matt Walbeck .25 .07
79 Dave Winfield .50 .15
80 Mike Gallego .25 .07
81 Xavier Hernandez .25 .07
82 Jimmy Key .50 .15
83 Jim Leyritz .25 .07
84 Don Mattingly 3.00 .90
85 Matt Nokes .25 .07
86 Paul O'Neill .75 .23
87 Melido Perez .25 .07
88 Danny Tartabull .25 .07
89 Mike Bordick .25 .07
90 Ron Darling .25 .07
91 Dennis Eckersley .50 .15
92 Stan Javier .25 .07
93 Steve Karsay .25 .07
94 Mark McGwire 3.00 .90
95 Troy Neel .25 .07
96 Terry Steinbach .25 .07
97 Bill Taylor RC .50 .15
98 Eric Anthony .25 .07
99 Chris Bosio .25 .07
100 Tim Davis .25 .07
101 Felix Fermin .25 .07
102 Dave Fleming .25 .07
103 Ken Griffey Jr. 2.00 .60
104 Greg Hibbard .25 .07
105 Reggie Jefferson .25 .07
106 Tino Martinez .75 .23
107 Jack Armstrong .25 .07
108 Will Clark 1.25 .35
109 Juan Gonzalez .75 .23
110 Rick Helling .25 .07
111 Tom Henke .25 .07
112 David Hulse .25 .07
113 Manuel Lee .25 .07
114 Doug Strange .25 .07
115 Roberto Alomar .75 .23
116 Joe Carter .50 .15
117 Carlos Delgado .75 .23
118 Pat Hentgen .25 .07
119 Paul Molitor .75 .23
120 John Olerud .50 .15
121 Dave Stewart .50 .15
122 Todd Stottlemyre .25 .07
123 Mike Timlin .25 .07
124 Jeff Blauser .25 .07
125 Tom Glavine .75 .23
126 David Justice .50 .15
127 Mike Kelly .25 .07
128 Ryan Klesko .50 .15
129 Javier Lopez .50 .15
130 Greg Maddux 2.00 .60
131 Fred McGriff .75 .23
132 Kent Mercker .25 .07
133 Mark Wohlers .25 .07
134 Willie Banks .25 .07
135 Steve Buechele .25 .07
136 Shawon Dunston .25 .07
137 Jose Guzman .25 .07
138 Glenallen Hill .25 .07
139 Randy Myers .25 .07
140 Karl Rhodes .25 .07
141 Ryne Sandberg 2.00 .60
142 Steve Trachsel .25 .07
143 Bret Boone .50 .15
144 Tom Browning .25 .07
145 Hector Carrasco .25 .07
146 Barry Larkin .75 .23
147 Hal Morris .25 .07
148 Jose Rijo .25 .07
149 Reggie Sanders .25 .07
150 John Smiley .25 .07
151 Dante Bichette .50 .15
152 Ellis Burks .50 .15
153 Joe Girardi .25 .07
154 Mike Harkey .25 .07
155 Roberto Mejia .25 .07
156 Marcus Moore .25 .07
157 Armando Reynoso .25 .07
158 Bruce Ruffin .25 .07
159 Eric Young .25 .07
160 Kurt Abbott RC .50 .15
161 Jeff Conine .50 .15
162 Orestes Destrade .25 .07
163 Chris Hammond .25 .07
164 Bryan Harvey .25 .07
165 Dave Magadan .25 .07
166 Gary Sheffield .50 .15
167 David Weathers .25 .07
168 Andujar Cedeno .25 .07
169 Tom Edens .25 .07
170 Luis Gonzalez .50 .15
171 Pete Harnisch .25 .07
172 Todd Jones .25 .07
173 Darryl Kile .50 .15
174 James Mouton .25 .07
175 Scott Servais .25 .07
176 Mitch Williams .25 .07
177 Pedro Astacio .25 .07
178 Orel Hershiser .50 .15
179 Raul Mondesi .50 .15
180 Jose Offerman .25 .07
181 Chan Ho Park RC .75 .23
182 Mike Piazza 2.50 .75
183 Cory Snyder .25 .07
184 Tim Wallach .25 .07
185 Todd Worrell .25 .07
186 Sean Berry .25 .07
187 Wil Cordero .25 .07
188 Darrin Fletcher .25 .07
189 Cliff Floyd .50 .15
190 Marquis Grissom .50 .15
191 Rod Henderson .25 .07
192 Ken Hill .25 .07
193 Pedro Martinez 1.25 .35
194 Kirk Rueter .50 .15
195 Jeromy Burnitz .50 .15
196 John Franco .50 .15
197 Dwight Gooden .50 .15
198 Todd Hundley .25 .07
199 Bobby Jones .25 .07
200 Jeff Kent .50 .15
201 Mike Maddux .25 .07
202 Ryan Thompson .25 .07
203 Jose Vizcaino .25 .07
204 Darren Daulton .50 .15
205 Lenny Dykstra .50 .15
206 Jim Eisenreich .25 .07
207 Dave Hollins .25 .07
208 Danny Jackson .25 .07
209 Doug Jones .25 .07
210 Jeff Juden .25 .07
211 Ben Rivera .25 .07
212 Kevin Stocker .25 .07
213 Milt Thompson .25 .07
214 Jay Bell .50 .15
215 Steve Cooke .25 .07
216 Mark Dewey .25 .07
217 Al Martin .25 .07
218 Orlando Merced .25 .07
219 Don Slaught .25 .07
220 Zane Smith .25 .07
221 Rick White RC .25 .07
222 Kevin Young .25 .07
223 Rene Arocha .25 .07
224 Rheal Cormier .25 .07
225 Brian Jordan .50 .15
226 Ray Lankford .50 .15
227 Mike Perez .25 .07
228 Ozzie Smith 2.00 .60
229 Mark Whiten .25 .07
230 Todd Zeile .25 .07
231 Derek Bell .25 .07
232 Archi Cianfrocco .25 .07
233 Ricky Gutierrez .25 .07
234 Trevor Hoffman .50 .15
235 Phil Plantier .25 .07
236 Dave Staton .25 .07
237 Wally Whitehurst .25 .07
238 Todd Benzinger .25 .07
239 Barry Bonds 3.00 .90
240 John Burkett .25 .07
241 Royce Clayton .25 .07
242 Bryan Hickerson .25 .07
243 Mike Jackson .25 .07
244 Darren Lewis .25 .07
245 Kirt Manwaring .25 .07
246 Mark Portugal .25 .07
247 Salomon Torres .25 .07
248 Checklist .25 .07
249 Checklist .25 .07
250 Checklist .25 .07
251 Brady Anderson .50 .15
252 Mike Devereaux .25 .07
253 Sid Fernandez .25 .07
254 Leo Gomez .25 .07
255 Mike Mussina .75 .23
256 Mike Oquist .25 .07
257 Rafael Palmeiro .75 .23
258 Lee Smith .50 .15
259 Damon Berryhill .25 .07
260 Wes Chamberlain .25 .07
261 Roger Clemens 2.50 .75
262 Gar Finnvold RC .25 .07
263 Mike Greenwell .25 .07
264 Tim Naehring .25 .07
265 Otis Nixon .25 .07
266 Ken Ryan .25 .07
267 Chad Curtis .25 .07
268 Chili Davis .50 .15
269 Damion Easley .25 .07
270 Jorge Fabregas .25 .07
271 Mark Langston .25 .07
272 Phil Leftwich RC .25 .07
273 Harold Reynolds .50 .15
274 J.T. Snow .50 .15
275 Joey Cora .50 .15
276 Julio Franco .50 .15
277 Roberto Hernandez .25 .07
278 Lance Johnson .25 .07
279 Ron Karkovice .25 .07
280 Jack McDowell .25 .07
281 Robin Ventura .50 .15
282 Sandy Alomar Jr. .25 .07
283 Kenny Lofton .50 .15
284 Jose Mesa .25 .07
285 Jack Morris .50 .15
286 Eddie Murray 1.25 .35
287 Chad Ogea .25 .07
288 Eric Plunk .25 .07
289 Paul Shuey .25 .07
290 Omar Vizquel .75 .23
291 Danny Bautista .25 .07
292 Travis Fryman .50 .15
293 Greg Gohr .25 .07
294 Chris Gomez .25 .07
295 Mickey Tettleton .25 .07
296 Lou Whitaker .50 .15
297 David Cone .50 .15
298 Gary Gaetti .50 .15
299 Tom Gordon .25 .07
300 Felix Jose .25 .07
301 Jose Lind .25 .07
302 Brian McRae .25 .07
303 Mike Fetters .25 .07
304 Brian Harper .25 .07
305 Pat Listach .25 .07
306 Matt Mieske .25 .07
307 Dave Nilsson .25 .07
308 Jody Reed .25 .07
309 Greg Vaughn .25 .07
310 Bill Wegman .25 .07
311 Rick Aguilera .25 .07
312 Alex Cole .25 .07
313 Denny Hocking .25 .07
314 Chuck Knoblauch .50 .15
315 Shane Mack .25 .07
316 Pat Meares .25 .07
317 Kevin Tapani .25 .07
318 Jim Abbott .75 .23
319 Wade Boggs .75 .23
320 Sterling Hitchcock .25 .07
321 Pat Kelly .25 .07
322 Terry Mulholland .25 .07
323 Luis Polonia .25 .07
324 Mike Stanley .25 .07
325 Bob Wickman .25 .07
326 Bernie Williams .75 .23
327 Mark Acre RC .25 .07
328 Geronimo Berroa .25 .07
329 Scott Brosius .50 .15
330 Brent Gates .25 .07
331 Rickey Henderson 1.25 .35
332 Carlos Reyes RC .25 .07
333 Ruben Sierra .25 .07
334 Bobby Witt .25 .07
335 Bobby Ayala .25 .07
336 Jay Buhner .50 .15
337 Randy Johnson 1.25 .35
338 Edgar Martinez .75 .23
339 Bill Risley .25 .07
340 Alex Rodriguez RC 40.00 12.00
341 Roger Salkeld .25 .07
342 Dan Wilson .25 .07
343 Kevin Brown .50 .15
344 Jose Canseco 1.25 .35
345 Dean Palmer .50 .15
346 Ivan Rodriguez 1.25 .35
347 Kenny Rogers .50 .15
348 Pat Borders .25 .07
349 Juan Guzman .25 .07
350 Ed Sprague .25 .07
351 Devon White .50 .15
352 Steve Avery .25 .07
353 Roberto Kelly .25 .07
354 Mark Lemke .25 .07
355 Greg McMichael .25 .07
356 Terry Pendleton .50 .15
357 John Smoltz .75 .23
358 Mike Stanton .25 .07
359 Tony Tarasco .25 .07
360 Mark Grace .75 .23
361 Derrick May .25 .07
362 Rey Sanchez .25 .07
363 Sammy Sosa 2.00 .60
364 Rick Wilkins .25 .07
365 Jeff Brantley .25 .07
366 Tony Fernandez .25 .07
367 Chuck McElroy .25 .07
368 Kevin Mitchell .25 .07
369 John Roper .25 .07
370 Johnny Ruffin .25 .07
371 Deion Sanders .75 .23
372 Marvin Freeman .25 .07
373 Andres Galarraga .50 .15
374 Charlie Hayes .25 .07
375 Nelson Liriano .25 .07
376 David Nied .25 .07
377 Walt Weiss .25 .07
378 Bret Barberie .25 .07
379 Jerry Browne .25 .07
380 Chuck Carr .25 .07
381 Greg Colbrunn .25 .07
382 Charlie Hough .50 .15
383 Kurt Miller .25 .07
384 Benito Santiago .50 .15
385 Jeff Bagwell .75 .23
386 Craig Biggio .75 .23
387 Ken Caminiti .50 .15
388 Doug Drabek .25 .07
389 Steve Finley .50 .15
390 John Hudek RC .25 .07
391 Orlando Miller .25 .07
392 Shane Reynolds .25 .07
393 Brett Butler .50 .15
394 Tom Candiotti .25 .07
395 Delino DeShields .25 .07
396 Kevin Gross .25 .07
397 Eric Karros .50 .15
398 Ramon Martinez .25 .07
399 Henry Rodriguez .25 .07
400 Moises Alou .50 .15
401 Jeff Fassero .25 .07
402 Mike Lansing .25 .07
403 Mel Rojas .25 .07
404 Larry Walker .75 .23
405 John Wetteland .50 .15
406 Gabe White .25 .07
407 Bobby Bonilla .50 .15
408 Josias Manzanillo .25 .07
409 Bret Saberhagen .50 .15
410 David Segui .25 .07
411 Mariano Duncan .25 .07
412 Tommy Greene .25 .07
413 Billy Hatcher .25 .07
414 Ricky Jordan .25 .07
415 John Kruk .50 .15
416 Bobby Munoz .25 .07
417 Curt Schilling .50 .15
418 Fernando Valenzuela .50 .15
419 David West .25 .07
420 Carlos Garcia .25 .07
421 Brian Hunter .25 .07
422 Jeff King .25 .07
423 Jon Lieber .25 .07
424 Ravelo Manzanillo .25 .07
425 Denny Neagle .50 .15
426 Andy Van Slyke .50 .15
427 Bryan Eversgerd RC .25 .07
428 Bernard Gilkey .25 .07
429 Gregg Jefferies .25 .07
430 Tom Pagnozzi .25 .07
431 Bob Tewksbury .25 .07
432 Allen Watson .25 .07
433 Andy Ashby .25 .07
434 Andy Benes .25 .07
435 Donnie Elliott .25 .07
436 Tony Gwynn 1.50 .45
437 Joey Hamilton .25 .07
438 Tim Hyers RC .25 .07
439 Luis Lopez .25 .07
440 Bip Roberts .25 .07
441 Scott Sanders .25 .07
442 Rod Beck .25 .07
443 Dave Burba .25 .07
444 Darryl Strawberry .50 .15
445 Bill Swift .25 .07
446 Robby Thompson .25 .07
447 B.VanLandingham RC .25 .07
448 Matt Williams .50 .15
449 Checklist .25 .07
450 Checklist .25 .07
P15 Aaron Sele Promo 1.00 .30

1994 Flair Hot Gloves

Randomly inserted in second series packs at a rate of one in 24, this set highlights 10 of the game's top players that also have outstanding defensive ability. The cards feature a special die-cut "glove" design with the player appearing within the glove. The back has a short write-up and a photo.

Nm-Mt Ex-Mt
COMPLETE SET (10) 120.00 36.00
1 Barry Bonds 25.00 7.50
2 Will Clark 10.00 3.00
3 Ken Griffey Jr. 15.00 4.50
4 Kenny Lofton 4.00 1.20
5 Greg Maddux 15.00 4.50
6 Don Mattingly 25.00 7.50
7 Kirby Puckett 10.00 3.00
8 Cal Ripken Jr. 30.00 9.00
9 Tim Salmon 6.00 1.80
10 Matt Williams 4.00 1.20

1994 Flair Hot Numbers

This 10-card set was randomly inserted in first series packs at a rate of one in 24. Metallic fronts feature a player photo with various numbers or statistics serving as background. The backs have a small photo centered in the middle surrounded by text highlighting achievements.

Nm-Mt Ex-Mt
COMPLETE SET (10) 80.00 24.00
1 Roberto Alomar 5.00 1.50
2 Carlos Baerga 1.50 .45
3 Will Clark 8.00 2.40
4 Fred McGriff 5.00 1.50
5 Paul Molitor 5.00 1.50
6 John Olerud 3.00 .90
7 Mike Piazza 15.00 4.50
8 Cal Ripken Jr. 25.00 7.50
9 Ryne Sandberg 12.00 3.60
10 Frank Thomas 8.00 2.40

1994 Flair Infield Power

Randomly inserted in second series packs at a rate of one in five, this 10-card standard-size set spotlights major league infielders who are power hitters. Card fronts feature a horizontal format with two photos of the player. The backs contain a short write-up with emphasis on power num bers and a small photo.

Nm-Mt Ex-Mt
COMPLETE SET (10) 15.00 4.50
1 Jeff Bagwell 1.25 .35

2 Will Clark	2.00	.60
3 Darren Daulton	.75	.23
4 Don Mattingly	5.00	1.50
5 Fred McGriff	1.25	.35
6 Rafael Palmeiro	1.25	.35
7 Mike Piazza	4.00	1.20
8 Cal Ripken Jr.	6.00	1.80
9 Frank Thomas	2.00	.60
10 Matt Williams	.75	.23

1994 Flair Outfield Power

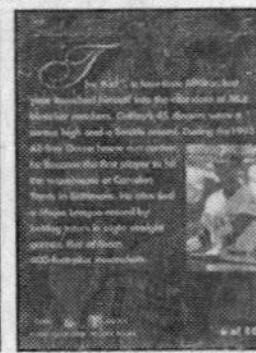

This 10-card standard-size set was randomly inserted in both first and second series packs at a rate of one in five. Two photos on the front feature the player fielding and hitting. The back contains a small photo and text.

	Nm-Mt	Ex-Mt
COMPLETE SET (10)	20.00	6.00
1 Albert Belle	1.00	.30
2 Barry Bonds	6.00	1.80
3 Joe Carter	1.00	.30
4 Lenny Dykstra	1.00	.30
5 Juan Gonzalez	1.50	.45
6 Ken Griffey Jr.	4.00	1.20
7 David Justice	1.00	.30
8 Kirby Puckett	2.50	.75
9 Tim Salmon	1.50	.45
10 Dave Winfield	1.00	.30

1994 Flair Wave of the Future

This 20-card standard-size set takes a look at potential big league stars. The cards were randomly inserted in packs at a rate of one in five -- the first 10 in series one, the second 10 in series two. The fronts and backs have the player superimposed over a wavy colored background. The front has the Wave of the Future logo and a paragraph or two about the player along with a photo on the back. This set is highlighted by an early Alex Rodriguez card.

	Nm-Mt	Ex-Mt
COMPLETE SER.1 (10)	15.00	4.50
COMPLETE SER.2 (10)	40.00	12.00
A1 Kurt Abbott	2.00	.60
A2 Carlos Delgado	2.50	.75
A3 Steve Karsay	1.00	.30
A4 Ryan Klesko	2.00	.60
A5 Javier Lopez	2.00	.60
A6 Raul Mondesi	2.00	.60
A7 James Mouton	1.00	.30
A8 Chan Ho Park	2.50	.75
A9 Dave Staton	1.00	.30
A10 Rick White	1.00	.30
B1 Mark Acre	1.00	.30
B2 Chris Gomez	1.00	.30
B3 Joey Hamilton	1.00	.30
B4 John Hudek	1.00	.30
B5 Jon Lieber	1.00	.30
B6 Matt Mieske	1.00	.30
B7 Orlando Miller	1.00	.30
B8 Alex Rodriguez	30.00	9.00
B9 Tony Tarasco	1.00	.30
B10 W.VanLandingham	1.00	.30

1995 Flair

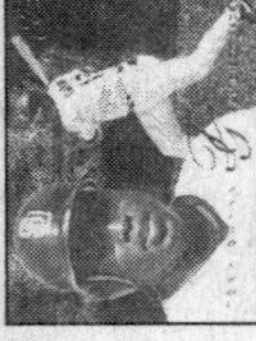

This set (produced by Fleer) was issued in two series of 216 cards for a total of 432 standard-size cards. Horizontally designed fronts have a 100 percent etched foil surface containing two player photos. The backs feature a full-bleed photo with yearly statistics superimposed. The checklist is arranged alphabetically by league with AL preceding NL. Rookie Cards include Bobby Higginson and Hideo Nomo.

	Nm-Mt	Ex-Mt
COMPLETE SET (432)	50.00	15.00
COMP. SERIES 1 (216)	30.00	9.00
COMP. SERIES 2 (216)	20.00	6.00
1 Brady Anderson	.50	.15
2 Harold Baines	.50	.15
3 Leo Gomez	.25	.07
4 Alan Mills	.25	.07
5 Jamie Moyer	.50	.15
6 Mike Mussina	.75	.23
7 Mike Oquist	.25	.07
8 Arthur Rhodes	.25	.07
9 Cal Ripken Jr.	4.00	1.20
10 Roger Clemens	2.50	.75
11 Scott Cooper	.25	.07
12 Mike Greenwell	.25	.07
13 Aaron Sele	.25	.07
14 John Valentin	.25	.07
15 Mo Vaughn	.50	.15
16 Chad Curtis	.25	.07
17 Gary DiSarcina	.25	.07
18 Chuck Finley	.50	.15
19 Andrew Lorraine	.25	.07
20 Spike Owen	.25	.07
21 Tim Salmon	.75	.23
22 J.T. Snow	.50	.15
23 Wilson Alvarez	.25	.07
24 Jason Bere	.25	.07
25 Ozzie Guillen	.25	.07
26 Mike LaValliere	.25	.07
27 Frank Thomas	1.25	.35
28 Robin Ventura	.50	.15
29 Carlos Baerga	.25	.07
30 Albert Belle	.50	.15
31 Jason Grimsley	.25	.07
32 Dennis Martinez	.50	.15
33 Eddie Murray	1.25	.35
34 Charles Nagy	.25	.07
35 Manny Ramirez	.75	.23
36 Paul Sorrento	.25	.07
37 John Doherty	.25	.07
38 Cecil Fielder	.50	.15
39 Travis Fryman	.50	.15
40 Chris Gomez	.25	.07
41 Tony Phillips	.25	.07
42 Lou Whitaker	.50	.15
43 David Cone	.50	.15
44 Gary Gaetti	.50	.15
45 Mark Gubicza	.25	.07
46 Bob Hamelin	.25	.07
47 Wally Joyner	.50	.15
48 Rusty Meacham	.25	.07
49 Jeff Montgomery	.25	.07
50 Ricky Bones	.25	.07
51 Cal Eldred	.25	.07
52 Pat Listach	.25	.07
53 Matt Mieske	.25	.07
54 Dave Nilsson	.25	.07
55 Greg Vaughn	.25	.07
56 Bill Wegman	.25	.07
57 Chuck Knoblauch	.50	.15
58 Scott Leius	.25	.07
59 Pat Mahomes	.25	.07
60 Pat Meares	.25	.07
61 Pedro Munoz	.25	.07
62 Kirby Puckett	1.25	.35
63 Wade Boggs	.75	.23
64 Jimmy Key	.50	.15
65 Jim Leyritz	.25	.07
66 Don Mattingly	3.00	.90
67 Paul O'Neill	.75	.23
68 Melido Perez	.25	.07
69 Danny Tartabull	.25	.07
70 John Briscoe	.25	.07
71 Scott Brosius	.50	.15
72 Ron Darling	.25	.07
73 Brent Gates	.25	.07
74 Rickey Henderson	1.25	.35
75 Stan Javier	.25	.07
76 Mark McGwire	3.00	.90
77 Todd Van Poppel	.25	.07
78 Bobby Ayala	.25	.07
79 Mike Blowers	.25	.07
80 Jay Buhner	.50	.15
81 Ken Griffey Jr.	2.00	.60
82 Randy Johnson	1.25	.35
83 Tino Martinez	.75	.23
84 Jeff Nelson	.25	.07
85 Alex Rodriguez	3.00	.90
86 Will Clark	1.25	.35
87 Jeff Frye	.25	.07
88 Juan Gonzalez	.75	.23
89 Rusty Greer	.50	.15
90 Darren Oliver	.25	.07
91 Dean Palmer	.50	.15
92 Ivan Rodriguez	1.25	.35
93 Matt Whiteside	.25	.07
94 Roberto Alomar	.75	.23
95 Joe Carter	.50	.15
96 Tony Castillo	.25	.07
97 Juan Guzman	.25	.07
98 Pat Hentgen	.25	.07
99 Mike Huff	.25	.07
100 John Olerud	.50	.15
101 Woody Williams	.25	.07
102 Roberto Kelly	.25	.07
103 Ryan Klesko	.50	.15
104 Javier Lopez	.50	.15
105 Greg Maddux	2.00	.60
106 Fred McGriff	.75	.23
107 Jose Oliva	.25	.07
108 John Smoltz	.75	.23
109 Tony Tarasco	.25	.07
110 Mark Wohlers	.25	.07
111 Jim Bullinger	.25	.07
112 Shawon Dunston	.25	.07
113 Derrick May	.25	.07
114 Randy Myers	.25	.07
115 Karl Rhodes	.25	.07
116 Rey Sanchez	.25	.07
117 Steve Trachsel	.25	.07
118 Eddie Zambrano	.25	.07
119 Bret Boone	.50	.15
120 Brian Dorsett	.25	.07
121 Hal Morris	.25	.07
122 Jose Rijo	.25	.07
123 John Roper	.25	.07
124 Reggie Sanders	.25	.07
125 Pete Schourek	.25	.07
126 John Smiley	.25	.07
127 Ellis Burks	.50	.15
128 Vinny Castilla	.50	.15
129 Marvin Freeman	.25	.07
130 Andres Galarraga	.50	.15
131 Mike Munoz	.25	.07
132 David Nied	.25	.07
133 Bruce Ruffin	.25	.07
134 Walt Weiss	.25	.07
135 Eric Young	.25	.07
136 Greg Colbrunn	.25	.07
137 Jeff Conine	.50	.15
138 Jeremy Hernandez	.25	.07
139 Charles Johnson	.50	.15
140 Robb Nen	.50	.15
141 Gary Sheffield	.50	.15
142 Dave Weathers	.25	.07
143 Jeff Bagwell	.75	.23
144 Craig Biggio	.75	.23
145 Tony Eusebio	.25	.07
146 Luis Gonzalez	.50	.15
147 John Hudek	.25	.07
148 Darryl Kile	.50	.15
149 Dave Veres	.25	.07
150 Billy Ashley	.25	.07
151 Pedro Astacio	.25	.07
152 Rafael Bournigal	.25	.07
153 Delino DeShields	.25	.07
154 Raul Mondesi	.50	.15
155 Mike Piazza	2.00	.60
156 Rudy Seanez	.25	.07
157 Ismael Valdes	.25	.07
158 Tim Wallach	.25	.07
159 Todd Worrell	.25	.07
160 Moises Alou	.50	.15
161 Cliff Floyd	.50	.15
162 Gil Heredia	.25	.07
163 Mike Lansing	.25	.07
164 Pedro Martinez	1.25	.35
165 Kirk Rueter	.25	.07
166 Tim Scott	.25	.07
167 Jeff Shaw	.25	.07
168 Rondell White	.50	.15
169 Bobby Bonilla	.50	.15
170 Rico Brogna	.25	.07
171 Todd Hundley	.25	.07
172 Jeff Kent	.50	.15
173 Jim Lindeman	.25	.07
174 Joe Orsulak	.25	.07
175 Bret Saberhagen	.50	.15
176 Toby Borland	.25	.07
177 Darren Daulton	.50	.15
178 Lenny Dykstra	.50	.15
179 Jim Eisenreich	.25	.07
180 Tommy Greene	.25	.07
181 Tony Longmire	.25	.07
182 Bobby Munoz	.25	.07
183 Kevin Stocker	.25	.07
184 Jay Bell	.50	.15
185 Steve Cooke	.25	.07
186 Ravelo Manzanillo	.25	.07
187 Al Martin	.25	.07
188 Denny Neagle	.50	.15
189 Don Slaught	.25	.07
190 Paul Wagner	.25	.07
191 Rene Arocha	.25	.07
192 Bernard Gilkey	.25	.07
193 Jose Oquendo	.25	.07
194 Tom Pagnozzi	.25	.07
195 Ozzie Smith	2.00	.60
196 Allen Watson	.25	.07
197 Mark Whiten	.25	.07
198 Andy Ashby	.25	.07
199 Donnie Elliott	.25	.07
200 Bryce Florie	.25	.07
201 Tony Gwynn	1.50	.45
202 Trevor Hoffman	.50	.15
203 Brian Johnson	.25	.07
204 Tim Mauser	.25	.07
205 Bip Roberts	.25	.07
206 Rod Beck	.25	.07
207 Barry Bonds	3.00	.90
208 Royce Clayton	.25	.07
209 Darren Lewis	.25	.07
210 Mark Portugal	.25	.07
211 Kevin Rogers	.25	.07
212 W.VanLandingham	.25	.07
213 Matt Williams	.50	.15
214 Checklist	.25	.07
215 Checklist	.25	.07
216 Checklist	.25	.07
217 Bret Barberie	.25	.07
218 Armando Benitez	.50	.15
219 Kevin Brown	.50	.15
220 Sid Fernandez	.25	.07
221 Chris Hoiles	.25	.07
222 Doug Jones	.25	.07
223 Ben McDonald	.25	.07
224 Rafael Palmeiro	.75	.23
225 Andy Van Slyke	.50	.15
226 Jose Canseco	1.25	.35
227 Vaughn Eshelman	.25	.07
228 Mike Macfarlane	.25	.07
229 Tim Naehring	.25	.07
230 Frank Rodriguez	.25	.07
231 Lee Tinsley	.25	.07
232 Mark Whiten	.25	.07
233 Garret Anderson	.50	.15
234 Chili Davis	.50	.15
235 Jim Edmonds	.75	.23
236 Mark Langston	.25	.07
237 Troy Percival	.50	.15
238 Tony Phillips	.25	.07
239 Lee Smith	.50	.15
240 Jim Abbott	.75	.23
241 James Baldwin	.25	.07
242 Mike Devereaux	.25	.07
243 Ray Durham	.50	.15
244 Alex Fernandez	.25	.07
245 Roberto Hernandez	.25	.07
246 Lance Johnson	.25	.07
247 Ron Karkovice	.25	.07
248 Tim Raines	.50	.15
249 Sandy Alomar Jr.	.25	.07
250 Orel Hershiser	.50	.15
251 Julian Tavarez	.25	.07
252 Jim Thome	1.25	.35
253 Omar Vizquel	.75	.23
254 Dave Winfield	.50	.15
255 Chad Curtis	.25	.07
256 Kirk Gibson	.50	.15
257 Mike Henneman	.25	.07
258 Bob Higginson RC	1.00	.30
259 Felipe Lira	.25	.07
260 Rudy Pemberton	.25	.07
261 Alan Trammell	.50	.15
262 Kevin Appier	.50	.15
263 Pat Borders	.25	.07
264 Tom Gordon	.25	.07
265 Jose Lind	.25	.07
266 Jon Nunnally	.25	.07
267 Dilson Torres RC	.25	.07
268 Michael Tucker	.25	.07
269 Jeff Cirillo	.25	.07
270 Darryl Hamilton	.25	.07
271 David Hulse	.25	.07
272 Mark Kiefer	.25	.07
273 Graeme Lloyd	.25	.07
274 Joe Oliver	.25	.07
275 Al Reyes RC	.25	.07
276 Kevin Seitzer	.25	.07
277 Rick Aguilera	.25	.07
278 Marty Cordova	.25	.07
279 Scott Erickson	.25	.07
280 LaTroy Hawkins	.25	.07
281 Brad Radke RC	1.00	.30
282 Kevin Tapani	.25	.07
283 Tony Fernandez	.25	.07
284 Sterling Hitchcock	.25	.07
285 Pat Kelly	.25	.07
286 Jack McDowell	.25	.07
287 Andy Pettitte	.75	.23
288 Mike Stanley	.25	.07
289 John Wetteland	.50	.15
290 Bernie Williams	.75	.23
291 Mark Acre	.25	.07
292 Geronimo Berroa	.25	.07
293 Dennis Eckersley	.50	.15
294 Steve Ontiveros	.25	.07
295 Ruben Sierra	.25	.07
296 Terry Steinbach	.25	.07
297 Dave Stewart	.50	.15
298 Todd Stottlemyre	.25	.07
299 Darren Bragg	.25	.07
300 Joey Cora	.25	.07
301 Edgar Martinez	.75	.23
302 Bill Risley	.25	.07
303 Ron Villone	.25	.07
304 Dan Wilson	.25	.07
305 Benji Gil	.25	.07
306 Wilson Heredia	.25	.07
307 Mark McLemore	.25	.07
308 Otis Nixon	.25	.07
309 Kenny Rogers	.50	.15
310 Jeff Russell	.25	.07
311 Mickey Tettleton	.25	.07
312 Bob Tewksbury	.25	.07
313 David Cone	.50	.15
314 Carlos Delgado	.50	.15
315 Alex Gonzalez	.25	.07
316 Shawn Green	.50	.15
317 Paul Molitor	.75	.23
318 Ed Sprague	.25	.07
319 Devon White	.50	.15
320 Steve Avery	.25	.07
321 Jeff Blauser	.25	.07
322 Brad Clontz	.25	.07
323 Tom Glavine	.75	.23
324 Marquis Grissom	.50	.15
325 Chipper Jones	1.25	.35
326 David Justice	.50	.15
327 Mark Lemke	.25	.07
328 Kent Mercker	.25	.07
329 Jason Schmidt	1.25	.35
330 Steve Buechele	.25	.07
331 Kevin Foster	.25	.07
332 Mark Grace	.75	.23
333 Brian McRae	.25	.07
334 Sammy Sosa	2.00	.60
335 Ozzie Timmons	.25	.07
336 Rick Wilkins	.25	.07
337 Hector Carrasco	.25	.07
338 Ron Gant	.50	.15
339 Barry Larkin	.75	.23
340 Deion Sanders	.75	.23
341 Benito Santiago	.50	.15
342 Roger Bailey	.25	.07
343 Jason Bates	.25	.07
344 Dante Bichette	.50	.15
345 Joe Girardi	.25	.07
346 Bill Swift	.25	.07
347 Mark Thompson	.25	.07
348 Larry Walker	.75	.23
349 Kurt Abbott	.25	.07
350 John Burkett	.25	.07
351 Chuck Carr	.25	.07
352 Andre Dawson	.50	.15
353 Chris Hammond	.25	.07
354 Charles Johnson	.50	.15
355 Terry Pendleton	.50	.15
356 Quilvio Veras	.25	.07
357 Derek Bell	.25	.07
358 Jim Dougherty RC	.25	.07
359 Doug Drabek	.25	.07
360 Todd Jones	.25	.07
361 Orlando Miller	.25	.07
362 James Mouton	.25	.07
363 Phil Plantier	.25	.07
364 Shane Reynolds	.25	.07
365 Todd Hollandsworth	.25	.07
366 Eric Karros	.50	.15
367 Ramon Martinez	.25	.07
368 Hideo Nomo RC	3.00	.90
369 Jose Offerman	.25	.07
370 Antonio Osuna	.25	.07
371 Todd Williams	.25	.07
372 Shane Andrews	.25	.07
373 Wil Cordero	.25	.07
374 Jeff Fassero	.25	.07
375 Darrin Fletcher	.25	.07
376 Mark Grudzielanek RC	.50	.15
377 Carlos Perez RC	.50	.15
378 Mel Rojas	.25	.07
379 Tony Tarasco	.25	.07
380 Edgardo Alfonzo	.50	.15
381 Brett Butler	.50	.15
382 Carl Everett	.50	.15
383 John Franco	.50	.15
384 Pete Harnisch	.25	.07
385 Bobby Jones	.25	.07
386 Dave Mlicki	.25	.07
387 Jose Vizcaino	.25	.07
388 Ricky Bottalico	.25	.07
389 Tyler Green	.25	.07
390 Charlie Hayes	.25	.07
391 Dave Hollins	.25	.07
392 Gregg Jefferies	.25	.07
393 Michael Mimbs RC	.25	.07
394 Mickey Morandini	.25	.07
395 Curt Schilling	.50	.15
396 Heathcliff Slocumb	.25	.07
397 J.Christiansen RC	.25	.07
398 Midre Cummings	.25	.07
399 Carlos Garcia	.25	.07
400 Mark Johnson RC	.25	.07
401 Jeff King	.25	.07
402 Jon Lieber	.25	.07
403 Esteban Loaiza	.25	.07
404 Orlando Merced	.25	.07
405 Gary Wilson RC	.25	.07
406 Scott Cooper	.25	.07
407 Tom Henke	.25	.07
408 Ken Hill	.25	.07
409 Danny Jackson	.25	.07
410 Brian Jordan	.50	.15
411 Ray Lankford	.25	.07
412 John Mabry	.25	.07
413 Todd Zeile	.25	.07
414 Andy Benes	.25	.07
415 Andres Berumen	.25	.07
416 Ken Caminiti	.50	.15
417 Andujar Cedeno	.25	.07
418 Steve Finley	.50	.15
419 Joey Hamilton	.25	.07
420 Dustin Hermanson	.25	.07
421 Melvin Nieves	.25	.07
422 Roberto Petagine	.25	.07
423 Eddie Williams	.25	.07
424 Glenallen Hill	.25	.07
425 Kirt Manwaring	.25	.07
426 Terry Mulholland	.25	.07
427 J.R. Phillips	.25	.07
428 Joe Rosselli	.25	.07
429 Robby Thompson	.25	.07
430 Checklist	.25	.07
431 Checklist	.25	.07
432 Checklist	.25	.07

1995 Flair Hot Gloves

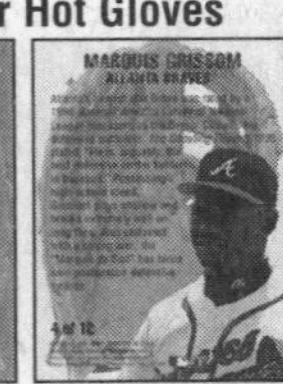

This 12-card standard-size set features players that are known for their defensive prowess Randomly inserted in series two packs at a rat of one in 25, a player photo is superimpose over an embossed design of a bronze glove.

	Nm-Mt	Ex-Mt
COMPLETE SET (12)	80.00	24.00
1 Roberto Alomar	6.00	1.80
2 Barry Bonds	25.00	7.50
3 Ken Griffey Jr.	15.00	4.50
4 Marquis Grissom	4.00	1.20
5 Barry Larkin	6.00	1.80
6 Darren Lewis	2.00	.60
7 Kenny Lofton	4.00	1.20
8 Don Mattingly	25.00	7.50
9 Cal Ripken	30.00	9.00
10 Ivan Rodriguez	10.00	3.00
11 Devon White	4.00	1.20
12 Matt Williams	4.00	1.20

1995 Flair Hot Numbers

Randomly inserted in series one packs at a rat of one in nine, this 10-card standard-size se showcases top players. A player photo on fron is superimposed over a gold background tha contains player stats from 1994.

	Nm-Mt	Ex-Mt
COMPLETE SET (10)	50.00	15.00
1 Jeff Bagwell	2.50	.75
2 Albert Belle	1.50	.45
3 Barry Bonds	10.00	3.00
4 Ken Griffey Jr.	6.00	1.80
5 Kenny Lofton	4.00	1.20
6 Greg Maddux	6.00	1.80
7 Mike Piazza	6.00	1.80
8 Cal Ripken	12.00	3.60
9 Frank Thomas	4.00	1.20
10 Matt Williams	1.50	.45

1995 Flair Infield Power

Randomly inserted in second series packs at rate of one in six, this 10-card standard-size s features sluggers that man the infield. A play photo on front is surrounded by multiple colo schemes with a horizontal back offering a playe photo and highlights.

	Nm-Mt	Ex-Mt
COMPLETE SET (10)	12.00	3.60
1 Jeff Bagwell	1.25	.35
2 Darren Daulton	.75	.23
3 Cecil Fielder	.75	.23
4 Andres Galarraga	.75	.23
5 Fred McGriff	1.25	.35
6 Rafael Palmeiro	1.25	.35
7 Mike Piazza	3.00	.90
8 Frank Thomas	2.00	.60
9 Mo Vaughn	.75	.23
10 Matt Williams	.75	.23

1995 Flair Outfield Power

Randomly inserted in first series packs at a ra of one in six, this 10-card standard-size set fe tures sluggers that patrol the outfield. A play photo on front is surrounded by multiple col schemes with a horizontal back offering a play photo and highlights.

	Nm-Mt	Ex-Mt
COMPLETE SET (10)	12.00	3.60
1 Albert Belle	.75	.23
2 Dante Bichette	.75	.23
3 Barry Bonds	5.00	1.50
4 Jose Canseco	2.00	.60
5 Joe Carter	.75	.23
6 Juan Gonzalez	1.25	.35
7 Ken Griffey Jr.	3.00	.90
8 Kirby Puckett	2.00	.60
9 Gary Sheffield	.75	.23
10 Ruben Sierra	.40	.12

1995 Flair Ripken

Titled "Enduring", this 10-card standard-size set is a tribute to Cal Ripken's career through the '94 season. Cards were randomly inserted in second series packs at a rate of one in 12. Full-bleed fronts have the set title in silver foil toward the bottom. The backs have a photo and a write-up on a specific achievement as selected by Cal. A five-card mail-in wrapper offer completes the set. The expiration date on this offer was March 1, 1996.

	Nm-Mt	Ex-Mt
COMPLETE SET (10)	80.00	24.00
COMMON CARD (1-10)	10.00	3.00
COMMON MAIL (11-15)	5.00	1.50

1995 Flair Today's Spotlight

This 12-card die-cut set was randomly inserted in first series packs at a rate of one in 25 packs. The upper portion of the player photo on front has the spotlight effect as the remainder of the photo is darkened.

	Nm-Mt	Ex-Mt
COMPLETE SET (12)	100.00	30.00
1 Jeff Bagwell	8.00	2.40
2 Jason Bere	2.50	.75
3 Cliff Floyd	5.00	1.50
4 Chuck Knoblauch	5.00	1.50
5 Kenny Lofton	12.00	3.60
6 Javier Lopez	5.00	1.50
7 Raul Mondesi	5.00	1.50
8 Mike Mussina	8.00	2.40
9 Mike Piazza	20.00	6.00
10 Manny Ramirez	8.00	2.40
11 Tim Salmon	8.00	2.40
12 Frank Thomas	12.00	3.60

1995 Flair Wave of the Future

Spotlighting 10 of the game's hottest young stars, cards were randomly inserted in second series packs at a rate of one in nine. An action photo is superimposed over primarily a solid background save for the player's name, team and same name which appear several times.

	Nm-Mt	Ex-Mt
COMPLETE SET (10)	25.00	7.50
1 Jason Bates	1.00	.30
2 Armando Benitez	1.50	.45
3 Marty Cordova	1.00	.30
4 Ray Durham	1.50	.45
5 Vaughn Eshelman	1.00	.30
6 Carl Everett	1.50	.45
7 Shawn Green	1.50	.45
8 Dustin Hermanson	1.00	.30
9 Chipper Jones	4.00	1.20
10 Hideo Nomo	5.00	1.50

1996 Flair

Released in July, 1996, this 400-card set (produced by Fleer) was issued in one series and sold in seven-card packs at a suggested retail price of $4.99. Gold and Silver etched foil front variations exist for all cards. These color variations were printed in similar quantities and are valued equally. The fronts and backs each carry a color action player cut-out on a player portrait background with player statistics on the backs. The cards are grouped alphabetically within teams and checklisted below alphabetically according to teams for each league. Notable Rookie Cards include Tony Batista.

	Nm-Mt	Ex-Mt
COMPLETE SET (400)	100.00	30.00
1 Roberto Alomar	1.50	.45
2 Brady Anderson	1.00	.30
3 Bobby Bonilla	1.00	.30
4 Scott Erickson	1.00	.30
5 Jeffrey Hammonds	1.00	.30
6 Jimmy Haynes	1.00	.30
7 Chris Hoiles	1.00	.30
8 Kent Mercker	1.00	.30
9 Mike Mussina	1.50	.45
10 Randy Myers	1.00	.30
11 Rafael Palmeiro	1.50	.45
12 Cal Ripken	8.00	2.40
13 B.J. Surhoff	1.00	.30
14 David Wells	1.00	.30
15 Jose Canseco	2.50	.75
16 Roger Clemens	5.00	1.50
17 Wil Cordero	1.00	.30
18 Tom Gordon	1.00	.30
19 Mike Greenwell	1.00	.30
20 Dwayne Hosey	1.00	.30
21 Jose Malave	1.00	.30
22 Tim Naehring	1.00	.30
23 Troy O'Leary	1.00	.30
24 Aaron Sele	1.00	.30
25 Heathcliff Slocumb	1.00	.30
26 Mike Stanley	1.00	.30
27 Jeff Suppan	1.00	.30
28 John Valentin	1.00	.30
29 Mo Vaughn	1.00	.30
30 Tim Wakefield	1.00	.30
31 Jim Abbott	1.50	.45
32 Garret Anderson	1.00	.30
33 George Arias	1.00	.30
34 Chili Davis	1.00	.30
35 Gary DiSarcina	1.00	.30
36 Jim Edmonds	1.00	.30
37 Chuck Finley	1.00	.30
38 Todd Greene	1.00	.30
39 Mark Langston	1.00	.30
40 Troy Percival	1.00	.30
41 Tim Salmon	1.50	.45
42 Lee Smith	1.00	.30
43 J.T. Snow	1.00	.30
44 Randy Velarde	1.00	.30
45 Tim Wallach	1.00	.30
46 Wilson Alvarez	1.00	.30
47 Harold Baines	1.00	.30
48 Jason Bere	1.00	.30
49 Ray Durham	1.00	.30
50 Alex Fernandez	1.00	.30
51 Ozzie Guillen	1.00	.30
52 Roberto Hernandez	1.00	.30
53 Ron Karkovice	1.00	.30
54 Darren Lewis	1.00	.30
55 Lyle Mouton	1.00	.30
56 Tony Phillips	1.00	.30
57 Chris Snopek	1.00	.30
58 Kevin Tapani	1.00	.30
59 Danny Tartabull	1.00	.30
60 Frank Thomas	2.50	.75
61 Robin Ventura	1.00	.30
62 Sandy Alomar Jr.	1.00	.30
63 Carlos Baerga	1.00	.30
64 Albert Belle	1.00	.30
65 Julio Franco	1.00	.30
66 Orel Hershiser	1.00	.30
67 Kenny Lofton	1.00	.30
68 Dennis Martinez	1.00	.30
69 Jack McDowell	1.00	.30
70 Jose Mesa	1.00	.30
71 Eddie Murray	2.50	.75
72 Charles Nagy	1.00	.30
73 Tony Pena	1.00	.30
74 Manny Ramirez	1.50	.45
75 Julian Tavarez	1.00	.30
76 Jim Thome	2.50	.75
77 Omar Vizquel	1.50	.45
78 Chad Curtis	1.00	.30
79 Cecil Fielder	1.00	.30
80 Travis Fryman	1.00	.30
81 Chris Gomez	1.00	.30
82 Bob Higginson	1.00	.30
83 Mark Lewis	1.00	.30
84 Felipe Lira	1.00	.30
85 Alan Trammell	1.00	.30
86 Kevin Appier	1.00	.30
87 Johnny Damon	1.50	.45
88 Tom Goodwin	1.00	.30
89 Mark Gubicza	1.00	.30
90 Bob Hamelin	1.00	.30
91 Keith Lockhart	1.00	.30
92 Jeff Montgomery	1.00	.30
93 Jon Nunnally	1.00	.30
94 Bip Roberts	1.00	.30
95 Michael Tucker	1.00	.30
96 Joe Vitiello	1.00	.30
97 Ricky Bones	1.00	.30
98 Chuck Carr	1.00	.30
99 Jeff Cirillo	1.00	.30
100 Mike Fetters	1.00	.30
101 John Jaha	1.00	.30
102 Mike Matheny	1.00	.30
103 Ben McDonald	1.00	.30
104 Matt Mieske	1.00	.30
105 Dave Nilsson	1.00	.30
106 Kevin Seitzer	1.00	.30
107 Steve Sparks	1.00	.30
108 Jose Valentin	1.00	.30
109 Greg Vaughn	1.00	.30
110 Rick Aguilera	1.00	.30
111 Rich Becker	1.00	.30
112 Marty Cordova	1.00	.30
113 LaTroy Hawkins	1.00	.30
114 Dave Hollins	1.00	.30
115 Roberto Kelly	1.00	.30
116 Chuck Knoblauch	1.50	.45
117 Matt Lawton RC	1.50	.45
118 Pat Meares	1.00	.30
119 Paul Molitor	1.50	.45
120 Kirby Puckett	2.50	.75
121 Brad Radke	1.00	.30
122 Frank Rodriguez	1.00	.30
123 Scott Stahoviak	1.00	.30
124 Matt Walbeck	1.00	.30
125 Wade Boggs	1.50	.45
126 David Cone	1.00	.30
127 Joe Girardi	1.00	.30
128 Dwight Gooden	1.00	.30
129 Derek Jeter	6.00	1.80
130 Jimmy Key	1.00	.30
131 Jim Leyritz	1.00	.30
132 Tino Martinez	1.50	.45
133 Paul O'Neill	1.50	.45
134 Andy Pettitte	1.50	.45
135 Tim Raines	1.00	.30
136 Ruben Rivera	1.00	.30
137 Kenny Rogers	1.00	.30
138 Ruben Sierra	1.00	.30
139 John Wetteland	1.00	.30
140 Bernie Williams	1.50	.45
141 Tony Batista RC	1.50	.45
142 Allen Battle	1.00	.30
143 Geronimo Berroa	1.00	.30
144 Mike Bordick	1.00	.30
145 Scott Brosius	1.00	.30
146 Steve Cox	1.00	.30
147 Brent Gates	1.00	.30
148 Jason Giambi	1.00	.30
149 Doug Johns	1.00	.30
150 Mark McGwire	6.00	1.80
151 Pedro Munoz	1.00	.30
152 Ariel Prieto	1.00	.30
153 Terry Steinbach	1.00	.30
154 Todd Van Poppel	1.00	.30
155 Bobby Ayala	1.00	.30
156 Chris Bosio	1.00	.30
157 Jay Buhner	1.00	.30
158 Joey Cora	1.00	.30
159 Russ Davis	1.00	.30
160 Ken Griffey Jr.	4.00	1.20
161 Sterling Hitchcock	1.00	.30
162 Randy Johnson	2.50	.75
163 Edgar Martinez	1.50	.45
164 Alex Rodriguez	5.00	1.50
165 Paul Sorrento	1.00	.30
166 Dan Wilson	1.00	.30
167 Will Clark	2.50	.75
168 Benji Gil	1.00	.30
169 Juan Gonzalez	1.50	.45
170 Rusty Greer	1.00	.30
171 Kevin Gross	1.00	.30
172 Darryl Hamilton	1.00	.30
173 Mike Henneman	1.00	.30
174 Ken Hill	1.00	.30
175 Mark McLemore	1.00	.30
176 Dean Palmer	1.00	.30
177 Roger Pavlik	1.00	.30
178 Ivan Rodriguez	2.50	.75
179 Mickey Tettleton	1.00	.30
180 Bobby Witt	1.00	.30
181 Joe Carter	1.00	.30
182 Felipe Crespo	1.00	.30
183 Alex Gonzalez	1.00	.30
184 Shawn Green	1.00	.30
185 Juan Guzman	1.00	.30
186 Erik Hanson	1.00	.30
187 Pat Hentgen	1.00	.30
188 Sandy Martinez	1.00	.30
189 Otis Nixon	1.00	.30
190 John Olerud	1.00	.30
191 Paul Quantrill	1.00	.30
192 Bill Risley	1.00	.30
193 Ed Sprague	1.00	.30
194 Steve Avery	1.00	.30
195 Jeff Blauser	1.00	.30
196 Brad Clontz	1.00	.30
197 Jermaine Dye	1.00	.30
198 Tom Glavine	1.50	.45
199 Marquis Grissom	1.00	.30
200 Chipper Jones	2.50	.75
201 David Justice	1.00	.30
202 Ryan Klesko	1.00	.30
203 Mark Lemke	1.00	.30
204 Javier Lopez	1.00	.30
205 Greg Maddux	4.00	1.20
206 Fred McGriff	1.50	.45
207 Greg McMichael	1.00	.30
208 Wonderful Monds RC	1.00	.30
209 Jason Schmidt	1.50	.45
210 John Smoltz	1.50	.45
211 Mark Wohlers	1.00	.30
212 Jim Bullinger	1.00	.30
213 Frank Castillo	1.00	.30
214 Kevin Foster	1.00	.30
215 Luis Gonzalez	1.00	.30
216 Mark Grace	1.50	.45
217 Robin Jennings	1.00	.30
218 Doug Jones	1.00	.30
219 Dave Magadan	1.00	.30
220 Brian McRae	1.00	.30
221 Jaime Navarro	1.00	.30
222 Rey Sanchez	1.00	.30
223 Ryne Sandberg	4.00	1.20
224 Scott Servais	1.00	.30
225 Sammy Sosa	4.00	1.20
226 Ozzie Timmons	1.00	.30
227 Bret Boone	1.00	.30
228 Jeff Branson	1.00	.30
229 Jeff Brantley	1.00	.30
230 Dave Burba	1.00	.30
231 Vince Coleman	1.00	.30
232 Steve Gibralter	1.00	.30
233 Mike Kelly	1.00	.30
234 Barry Larkin	1.50	.45
235 Hal Morris	1.00	.30
236 Mark Portugal	1.00	.30
237 Jose Rijo	1.00	.30
238 Reggie Sanders	1.00	.30
239 Pete Schourek	1.00	.30
240 John Smiley	1.00	.30
241 Eddie Taubensee	1.00	.30
242 Jason Bates	1.00	.30
243 Dante Bichette	1.00	.30
244 Ellis Burks	1.00	.30
245 Vinny Castilla	1.00	.30
246 Andres Galarraga	1.00	.30
247 Darren Holmes	1.00	.30
248 Curt Leskanic	1.00	.30
249 Steve Reed	1.00	.30
250 Kevin Rtiz	1.00	.30
251 Bret Saberhagen	1.00	.30
252 Bill Swift	1.00	.30
253 Larry Walker	1.50	.45
254 Walt Weiss	1.00	.30
255 Eric Young	1.00	.30
256 Kurt Abbott	1.00	.30
257 Kevin Brown	1.00	.30
258 John Burkett	1.00	.30
259 Greg Colbrunn	1.00	.30
260 Jeff Conine	1.00	.30
261 Andre Dawson	1.00	.30
262 Chris Hammond	1.00	.30
263 Charles Johnson	1.00	.30
264 Al Leiter	1.00	.30
265 Robb Nen	1.00	.30
266 Terry Pendleton	1.00	.30
267 Pat Rapp	1.00	.30
268 Gary Sheffield	1.00	.30
269 Quilvio Veras	1.00	.30
270 Devon White	1.00	.30
271 Bob Abreu	1.00	.30
272 Jeff Bagwell	1.50	.45
273 Derek Bell	1.00	.30
274 Sean Berry	1.00	.30
275 Craig Biggio	1.50	.45
276 Doug Drabek	1.00	.30
277 Tony Eusebio	1.00	.30
278 Richard Hidalgo	1.00	.30
279 Brian L.Hunter	1.00	.30
280 Todd Jones	1.00	.30
281 Derrick May	1.00	.30
282 Orlando Miller	1.00	.30
283 James Mouton	1.00	.30
284 Shane Reynolds	1.00	.30
285 Greg Swindell	1.00	.30
286 Mike Blowers	1.00	.30
287 Brett Butler	1.00	.30
288 Tom Candiotti	1.00	.30
289 Roger Cedeno	1.00	.30
290 Delino DeShields	1.00	.30
291 Greg Gagne	1.00	.30
292 Karim Garcia	1.00	.30
293 Todd Hollandsworth	1.00	.30
294 Eric Karros	1.00	.30
295 Ramon Martinez	1.00	.30
296 Raul Mondesi	1.00	.30
297 Hideo Nomo	2.50	.75
298 Mike Piazza	4.00	1.20
299 Ismael Valdes	1.00	.30
300 Todd Worrell	1.00	.30
301 Moises Alou	1.00	.30
302 Shane Andrews	1.00	.30
303 Yamil Benitez	1.00	.30
304 Jeff Fassero	1.00	.30
305 Darrin Fletcher	1.00	.30
306 Cliff Floyd	1.00	.30
307 Mark Grudzielanek	1.00	.30
308 Mike Lansing	1.00	.30
309 Pedro Martinez	2.50	.75
310 Ryan McGuire	1.00	.30
311 Carlos Perez	1.00	.30
312 Mel Rojas	1.00	.30
313 David Segui	1.00	.30
314 Rondell White	1.00	.30
315 Edgardo Alfonzo	1.00	.30
316 Rico Brogna	1.00	.30
317 Carl Everett	1.00	.30
318 John Franco	1.00	.30
319 Bernard Gilkey	1.00	.30
320 Todd Hundley	1.00	.30
321 Jason Isringhausen	1.00	.30
322 Lance Johnson	1.00	.30
323 Bobby Jones	1.00	.30
324 Jeff Kent	1.00	.30
325 Rey Ordonez	1.00	.30
326 Bill Pulsipher	1.00	.30
327 Jose Vizcaino	1.00	.30
328 Paul Wilson	1.00	.30
329 Ricky Bottalico	1.00	.30
330 Darren Daulton	1.00	.30
331 David Doster	1.00	.30
332 Lenny Dykstra	1.00	.30
333 Jim Eisenreich	1.00	.30
334 Sid Fernandez	1.00	.30
335 Gregg Jefferies	1.00	.30
336 Mickey Morandini	1.00	.30
337 Benito Santiago	1.00	.30
338 Curt Schilling	1.00	.30
339 Kevin Stocker	1.00	.30
340 David West	1.00	.30
341 Mark Whiten	1.00	.30
342 Todd Zeile	1.00	.30
343 Jay Bell	1.00	.30
344 John Ericks	1.00	.30
345 Carlos Garcia	1.00	.30
346 Charlie Hayes	1.00	.30
347 Jason Kendall	1.00	.30
348 Jeff King	1.00	.30
349 Mike Kingery	1.00	.30
350 Al Martin	1.00	.30
351 Orlando Merced	1.00	.30
352 Dan Miceli	1.00	.30
353 Denny Neagle	1.00	.30
354 Alan Benes	1.00	.30
355 Andy Benes	1.00	.30
356 Royce Clayton	1.00	.30
357 Dennis Eckersley	1.00	.30
358 Gary Gaetti	1.00	.30
359 Ron Gant	1.00	.30
360 Brian Jordan	1.00	.30
361 Ray Lankford	1.00	.30
362 John Mabry	1.00	.30
363 T.J. Mathews	1.00	.30
364 Mike Morgan	1.00	.30
365 Donovan Osborne	1.00	.30
366 Tom Pagnozzi	1.00	.30
367 Ozzie Smith	4.00	1.20
368 Todd Stottlemyre	1.00	.30
369 Andy Ashby	1.00	.30
370 Brad Ausmus	1.00	.30
371 Ken Caminiti	1.00	.30
372 Andujar Cedeno	1.00	.30
373 Steve Finley	1.00	.30
374 Tony Gwynn	3.00	.90
375 Joey Hamilton	1.00	.30
376 Rickey Henderson	2.50	.75
377 Trevor Hoffman	1.00	.30
378 Wally Joyner	1.00	.30
379 Marc Newfield	1.00	.30
380 Jody Reed	1.00	.30
381 Bob Tewksbury	1.00	.30
382 Fernando Valenzuela	1.00	.30
383 Rod Beck	1.00	.30
384 Barry Bonds	6.00	1.80
385 Mark Carreon	1.00	.30
386 Shawon Dunston	1.00	.30
387 O.Fernandez RC	1.00	.30
388 Glenallen Hill	1.00	.30
389 Stan Javier	1.00	.30
390 Mark Leiter	1.00	.30
391 Kirt Manwaring	1.00	.30
392 Robby Thompson	1.00	.30
393 W.VanLandingham	1.00	.30
394 Allen Watson	1.00	.30
395 Matt Williams	1.00	.30
396 Checklist 1-92	1.00	.30
397 Checklist 93-180	1.00	.30
398 Checklist 181-272	1.00	.30
399 Checklist 273-365	1.00	.30
400 CL 366-400/Inserts	1.00	.30
P12 Cal Ripken Jr PROMO		

1996 Flair Diamond Cuts

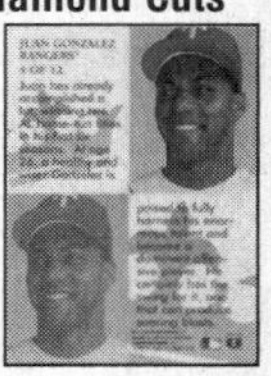

Randomly inserted in packs at a rate of one in 20, this 12-card set showcases the game's greatest stars with rainbow holofoil and glitter coating on the card.

	Nm-Mt	Ex-Mt
COMPLETE SET (12)	100.00	30.00
1 Jeff Bagwell	4.00	1.20
2 Albert Belle	2.50	.75
3 Barry Bonds	15.00	4.50
4 Juan Gonzalez	4.00	1.20
5 Ken Griffey Jr.	10.00	3.00
6 Greg Maddux	10.00	3.00
7 Eddie Murray	6.00	1.80
8 Mike Piazza	10.00	3.00
9 Cal Ripken	20.00	6.00
10 Frank Thomas	6.00	1.80
11 Mo Vaughn	2.50	.75
12 Matt Williams	2.50	.75

1996 Flair Hot Gloves

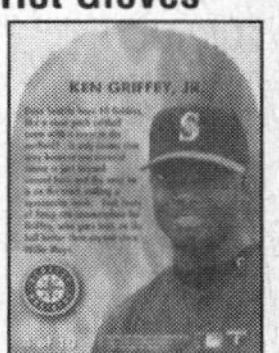

Randomly inserted in hobby packs only at a rate of one in 90, this 10-card set is printed on special, thermo-embossed die-cut cards and spotlights the best defensive players.

	Nm-Mt	Ex-Mt
COMPLETE SET (10)	120.00	36.00
1 Roberto Alomar	10.00	3.00
2 Barry Bonds	40.00	12.00
3 Will Clark	15.00	4.50
4 Ken Griffey Jr.	25.00	7.50
5 Kenny Lofton	6.00	1.80
6 Greg Maddux	25.00	7.50
7 Mike Piazza	25.00	7.50
8 Cal Ripken	50.00	15.00
9 Ivan Rodriguez	15.00	4.50
10 Matt Williams	6.00	1.80

1996 Flair Powerline

Randomly inserted in packs at a rate of one in six, this 10-card set features baseball's leading power hitters. The fronts display a color action close-up player photo with a green overlay indicating his power. The backs carry a player portrait and a statement about the player's hitting power.

	Nm-Mt	Ex-Mt
COMPLETE SET (10)	30.00	9.00
1 Albert Belle	1.00	.30
2 Barry Bonds	6.00	1.80
3 Juan Gonzalez	1.50	.45
4 Ken Griffey Jr.	4.00	1.20
5 Mark McGwire	6.00	1.80
6 Mike Piazza	4.00	1.20
7 Manny Ramirez	1.50	.45
8 Sammy Sosa	4.00	1.20
9 Frank Thomas	2.50	.75
10 Matt Williams	1.00	.30

1996 Flair Wave of the Future

Randomly inserted in packs at a rate of one in 72, this 20-card set highlights the top 1996 rookies and prospects on lenticular cards.

	Nm-Mt	Ex-Mt
COMPLETE SET (20)	200.00	60.00
1 Bob Abreu	10.00	3.00
2 George Arias	10.00	3.00
3 Tony Batista	15.00	4.50
4 Alan Benes	10.00	3.00

Card	Nm-Mt	Ex-Mt
5 Yamil Benitez	10.00	3.00
6 Steve Cox	10.00	3.00
7 David Doster	10.00	3.00
8 Jermaine Dye	10.00	3.00
9 Osvaldo Fernandez	10.00	3.00
10 Karim Garcia	10.00	3.00
11 Steve Gibralter	10.00	3.00
12 Todd Greene	10.00	3.00
13 Richard Hidalgo	10.00	3.00
14 Robin Jennings	10.00	3.00
15 Jason Kendall	10.00	3.00
16 Jose Malave	10.00	3.00
17 Wonderful Monds	10.00	3.00
18 Rey Ordonez	10.00	3.00
19 Ruben Rivera	10.00	3.00
20 Paul Wilson	10.00	3.00

2002 Flair

This 138 card set was issued in April, 2002. These cards were issued in five card packs which came 20 boxes to a case with a cost of $7 per pack. Each unopened box also contained a "Sweet Swatch" box topper. The last 38 cards in the set are future fame cards featuring leading prospects in the game. These cards have a stated print run of 1750 serial numbered sets.

	Nm-Mt	Ex-Mt
COMP.SET w/o SP's (100)	25.00	7.50
COMMON CARD (1-100)	.50	.15
COMMON CARD (101-138)	5.00	1.50
1 Scott Rolen	1.25	.35
2 Derek Jeter	3.00	.90
3 Sean Casey	.50	.15
4 Hideo Nomo	1.25	.35
5 Craig Biggio	.75	.23
6 Randy Johnson	1.25	.35
7 J.D. Drew	.50	.15
8 Greg Maddux	2.00	.60
9 Paul LoDuca	.50	.15
10 John Olerud	.50	.15
11 Barry Larkin	.75	.23
12 Mark Grace	.75	.23
13 Jimmy Rollins	.50	.15
14 Todd Helton	.75	.23
15 Jim Edmonds	.50	.15
16 Roy Oswalt	.50	.15
17 Phil Nevin	.50	.15
18 Tim Salmon	.75	.23
19 Magglio Ordonez	.50	.15
20 Roger Clemens	2.50	.75
21 Raul Mondesi	.50	.15
22 Edgar Martinez	.75	.23
23 Pedro Martinez	1.25	.35
24 Edgardo Alfonzo	.50	.15
25 Bernie Williams	.75	.23
26 Gary Sheffield	.50	.15
27 D'Angelo Jimenez	.50	.15
28 Toby Hall	.50	.15
29 Joe Mays	.50	.15
30 Alfonso Soriano	.75	.23
31 Mike Piazza	2.00	.60
32 Lance Berkman	.50	.15
33 Jim Thome	1.25	.35
34 Ben Sheets	.50	.15
35 Brandon Inge	.50	.15
36 Luis Gonzalez	.50	.15
37 Jeff Kent	.50	.15
38 Ben Grieve	.50	.15
39 Carlos Delgado	.50	.15
40 Pat Burrell	.50	.15
41 Mark Buehrle	.50	.15
42 Cristian Guzman	.50	.15
43 Shawn Green	.50	.15
44 Nomar Garciaparra	2.00	.60
45 Carlos Beltran	.75	.23
46 Troy Glaus	.75	.23
47 Paul Konerko	.50	.15
48 Moises Alou	.50	.15
49 Kerry Wood	1.25	.35
50 Jose Vidro	.50	.15
51 Juan Encarnacion	.50	.15
52 Bobby Abreu	.50	.15
53 C.C. Sabathia	.50	.15
54 Alex Rodriguez	2.00	.60
55 Albert Pujols	2.50	.75
56 Bret Boone	.50	.15
57 Orlando Hernandez	.50	.15
58 Jason Kendall	.50	.15
59 Tim Hudson	.50	.15
60 Darin Erstad	.50	.15
61 Mike Mussina	.75	.23
62 Ken Griffey Jr.	2.00	.60
63 Adrian Beltre	.75	.23
64 Jeff Bagwell	.75	.23
65 Vladimir Guerrero	1.25	.35
66 Mike Sweeney	.50	.15
67 Sammy Sosa	2.00	.60
68 Andruw Jones	.50	.15
69 Richie Sexson	.50	.15
70 Matt Morris	.50	.15
71 Ivan Rodriguez	1.25	.35
72 Shannon Stewart	.50	.15
73 Barry Bonds	3.00	.90
74 Matt Williams	.50	.15
75 Jason Giambi	.50	.15
76 Brian Giles	.50	.15
77 Cliff Floyd	.50	.15
78 Tino Martinez	.75	.23
79 Juan Gonzalez	.75	.23
80 Frank Thomas	1.25	.35
81 Ichiro Suzuki	2.00	.60
82 Barry Zito	.50	.15
83 Chipper Jones	1.25	.35
84 Adam Dunn	.75	.23
85 Kazuhiro Sasaki	.50	.15
86 Mark Quinn	.50	.15
87 Rafael Palmeiro	.75	.23
88 Jeromy Burnitz	.50	.15
89 Curt Schilling	.50	.15
90 Chris Richard	.50	.15
91 Jon Lieber	.50	.15
92 Doug Mientkiewicz	.50	.15
93 Roberto Alomar	.75	.23
94 Rich Aurilia	.50	.15
95 Eric Chavez	.50	.15
96 Larry Walker	.75	.23
97 Manny Ramirez	.75	.23
98 Tony Clark	.50	.15
99 Tsuyoshi Shinjo	.50	.15
100 Josh Beckett	.50	.15
101 Dewon Brazelton FF	5.00	1.50
102 Jeremy Lambert FF RC	5.00	1.50
103 Andres Torres FF	5.00	1.50
104 Matt Childers FF RC	5.00	1.50
105 Wilson Betemit FF	5.00	1.50
106 Willie Harris FF	5.00	1.50
107 Drew Henson FF	5.00	1.50
108 Rafael Soriano FF	5.00	1.50
109 Carlos Valderrama FF	5.00	1.50
110 Victor Martinez FF	8.00	2.40
111 Juan Rivera FF	5.00	1.50
112 Felipe Lopez FF	5.00	1.50
113 Brandon Duckworth FF	5.00	1.50
114 Jeremy Owens FF	5.00	1.50
115 Aaron Cook FF RC	5.00	1.50
116 Derrick Lewis FF	5.00	1.50
117 Mark Teixeira FF	8.00	2.40
118 Ken Harvey FF	5.00	1.50
119 Tim Spooneybarger FF	5.00	1.50
120 Bill Hall FF	5.00	1.50
121 Adam Pettyjohn FF	5.00	1.50
122 Ramon Castro FF	5.00	1.50
123 Marlon Byrd FF	5.00	1.50
124 Matt White FF	5.00	1.50
125 Eric Cyr FF	5.00	1.50
126 Morgan Ensberg FF	5.00	1.50
127 Horacio Ramirez FF	5.00	1.50
128 Ron Calloway FF RC	5.00	1.50
129 Nick Punto FF	5.00	1.50
130 Joe Kennedy FF	5.00	1.50
131 So Taguchi FF RC	8.00	2.40
132 Austin Kearns FF	5.00	1.50
133 Mark Prior FF	12.00	3.60
134 Kazuhisa Ishii FF RC	10.00	3.00
135 Steve Torrealba FF	5.00	1.50
136 Adam Walker FF RC	5.00	1.50
137 Travis Hafner FF	5.00	1.50
138 Zach Day FF	5.00	1.50

2002 Flair Collection

Randomly inserted into packs, this is a parallel set to the basic Flair set. These cards are serial numbered to 175 for the lower number cards and to 50 for the future fame set.

Nm-Mt Ex-Mt
*COLLECTION 1-100: 3X TO 8X BASIC
*COLLECTION 101-138: 1X TO 2.5X BASIC

2002 Flair Jersey Heights

This 25-card set features game-used jersey swatches from a selection of major league stars. The cards were seeded into packs at a rate of 1:18 hobby and 1:100 retail. Though the cards are not serial-numbered in any way, representatives at Fleer confirmed that the following players were produced in slightly lower quantities: Barry Bonds, Roger Clemens, J.D. Drew, Greg Maddux and Alex Rodriguez. In addition, based upon analysis of secondary market trading volume by our staff, the following cards are perceived to be in greater supply: Jeff Bagwell, Jim Edmonds, Randy Johnson, Chipper Jones, Ivan Rodriguez, Curt Schilling and Larry Walker.

	Nm-Mt	Ex-Mt
1 Edgardo Alfonzo	8.00	2.40
2 Jeff Bagwell *	8.00	2.40
3 Craig Biggio	8.00	2.40
4 Barry Bonds SP	25.00	7.50
5 Sean Casey	8.00	2.40
6 Roger Clemens SP	25.00	7.50
7 Carlos Delgado	8.00	2.40
8 J.D. Drew SP	8.00	2.40
9 Jim Edmonds *	8.00	2.40
10 Nomar Garciaparra	20.00	6.00
11 Shawn Green	8.00	2.40
12 Todd Helton	8.00	2.40
13 Derek Jeter *	25.00	7.50
14 Randy Johnson *	10.00	3.00
15 Chipper Jones *	10.00	3.00
16 Barry Larkin	8.00	2.40
17 Greg Maddux SP	15.00	4.50
18 Pedro Martinez	10.00	3.00
19 Rafael Palmeiro	8.00	2.40
20 Mike Piazza	15.00	4.50
21 Manny Ramirez	8.00	2.40
22 Alex Rodriguez SP	15.00	4.50
23 Ivan Rodriguez *	10.00	3.00
24 Curt Schilling *	8.00	2.40
25 Larry Walker *	8.00	2.40

2002 Flair Jersey Heights Dual Swatch

Randomly inserted in packs, these 12 cards features not only two players (usually teammates) with something in common but also a jersey swatch from each player featured. These cards have a stated print run of 100 serial numbered sets.

	Nm-Mt	Ex-Mt
1 Randy Johnson	40.00	12.00
Curt Schilling		
2 Pedro Martinez	80.00	24.00
Nomar Garciaparra		
3 Edgardo Alfonzo	40.00	12.00
Mike Piazza		
4 Derek Jeter	100.00	30.00
Roger Clemens		
5 Greg Maddux	40.00	12.00
Chipper Jones		
6 Jim Edmonds	25.00	7.50
J.D. Drew		
7 Jeff Bagwell	40.00	12.00
Craig Biggio		
8 Rafael Palmeiro	40.00	12.00
Ivan Rodriguez		
9 Carlos Delgado	25.00	7.50
Shawn Green		
10 Todd Helton	40.00	12.00
Larry Walker		
11 Sean Casey	40.00	12.00
Barry Larkin		
12 Alex Rodriguez	40.00	12.00
Manny Ramirez		

2002 Flair Jersey Heights Hot Numbers Patch

Randomly inserted into packs, these 24 cards feature a jersey patch from the featured player. These cards have a stated print run of 100 serial numbered sets.

	Nm-Mt	Ex-Mt
1 Edgardo Alfonzo	25.00	7.50
2 Jeff Bagwell	40.00	12.00
3 Craig Biggio	40.00	12.00
4 Sean Casey	25.00	7.50
5 Roger Clemens		
6 Carlos Delgado	25.00	7.50
7 J.D. Drew	25.00	7.50
8 Jim Edmonds	25.00	7.50
9 Nomar Garciaparra	80.00	24.00
10 Shawn Green	25.00	7.50
11 Todd Helton	40.00	12.00
12 Derek Jeter	100.00	30.00
13 Randy Johnson	40.00	12.00
14 Chipper Jones	40.00	12.00
15 Barry Larkin	40.00	12.00
16 Greg Maddux	60.00	18.00
17 Pedro Martinez	40.00	12.00
18 Rafael Palmeiro	40.00	12.00
19 Mike Piazza	60.00	18.00
20 Manny Ramirez	40.00	12.00
21 Alex Rodriguez	60.00	18.00
22 Ivan Rodriguez	40.00	12.00
23 Curt Schilling	25.00	7.50
24 Larry Walker	40.00	12.00

2002 Flair Power Tools Bats

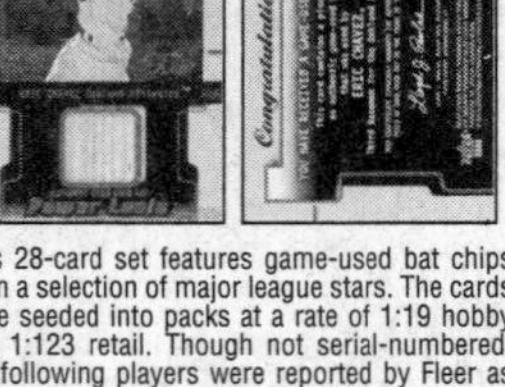

This 28-card set features game-used bat chips from a selection of major league stars. The cards were seeded into packs at a rate of 1:19 hobby and 1:123 retail. Though not serial-numbered, the following players were reported by Fleer as being short prints: Jeff Bagwell, Pat Burrell, J.D. Drew, Rafael Palmeiro, Scott Rolen, Reggie Sanders and Jim Thome. All of these cards are immeasurably tougher to pull from packs than others from this set. Please refer to our checklist for specific print run quantities on these short prints. In addition, based on market research by our staff, the following players appear to be in greater supply than other cards from this set: Bret Boone, Ivan Rodriguez and Tsuyoshi Shinjo.

	Nm-Mt	Ex-Mt
1 Roberto Alomar	8.00	2.40
2 Jeff Bagwell SP/150	15.00	4.50
3 Craig Biggio	8.00	2.40
4 Barry Bonds	20.00	6.00
5 Bret Boone *	8.00	2.40
6 Pat Burrell SP/225	15.00	4.50
7 Eric Chavez	8.00	2.40
8 J.D. Drew SP/150	15.00	4.50
9 Jim Edmonds	8.00	2.40
10 Juan Gonzalez	8.00	2.40
11 Luis Gonzalez	8.00	2.40
12 Shawn Green	8.00	2.40
13 Derek Jeter	20.00	6.00
14 Doug Mientkiewicz	8.00	2.40
15 Magglio Ordonez	8.00	2.40
16 Rafael Palmeiro SP/100	15.00	4.50
17 Mike Piazza	15.00	4.50
18 Alex Rodriguez	15.00	4.50
19 Ivan Rodriguez *	10.00	3.00
20 Scott Rolen SP/42		
21 Reggie Sanders SP/120	15.00	4.50
22 Gary Sheffield	8.00	2.40
23 Tsuyoshi Shinjo *	8.00	2.40
24 Miguel Tejada	8.00	2.40
25 Frank Thomas	10.00	3.00
26 Jim Thome SP/225	15.00	4.50
27 Larry Walker	8.00	2.40
28 Bernie Williams	8.00	2.40

2002 Flair Power Tools Bats Gold

Randomly inserted into packs, these 28 cards parallel the Power Tools insert set. These cards have gold borders and have a stated print run of 100 serial numbered sets.

	Nm-Mt	Ex-Mt
1 Roberto Alomar	15.00	4.50
2 Jeff Bagwell	15.00	4.50
3 Craig Biggio	15.00	4.50
4 Barry Bonds	50.00	15.00
5 Bret Boone	12.00	3.60
6 Pat Burrell	12.00	3.60
7 Eric Chavez	12.00	3.60
8 J.D. Drew	12.00	3.60
9 Jim Edmonds	12.00	3.60
10 Juan Gonzalez	15.00	4.50
11 Luis Gonzalez	12.00	3.60
12 Shawn Green	12.00	3.60
13 Derek Jeter	50.00	15.00
14 Doug Mientkiewicz	12.00	3.60
15 Magglio Ordonez	12.00	3.60
16 Rafael Palmeiro	15.00	4.50
17 Mike Piazza	25.00	7.50
18 Alex Rodriguez	25.00	7.50
19 Ivan Rodriguez	15.00	4.50
20 Scott Rolen	15.00	4.50
21 Reggie Sanders	12.00	3.60
22 Gary Sheffield	12.00	3.60
23 Tsuyoshi Shinjo	12.00	3.60
24 Miguel Tejada	12.00	3.60
25 Frank Thomas	15.00	4.50
26 Jim Thome	15.00	4.50
27 Larry Walker	15.00	4.50
28 Bernie Williams	15.00	4.50

2002 Flair Power Tools Dual Bats

Randomly inserted into packs, these 15 cards feature not only two players but bat chips from each of the featured players. A few cards were issued in lesser quantity and we have notated those cards along with the stated print run in our checklist. Please note that these cards are not serial numbered.

Nm-Mt Ex-Mt
*GOLD: 1X TO 2.5X BASIC DUAL BAT
GOLD RANDOM INSERTS IN PACKS..
GOLD PRINT RUN 50 SERIAL #'d SETS
GOLD CARDS 7 AND 13 DO NOT EXIST

	Nm-Mt	Ex-Mt
1 Eric Chavez	15.00	4.50
Miguel Tejada		
2 Barry Bonds	30.00	9.00
Tsuyoshi Shinjo		
3 Jim Edmonds	15.00	4.50
J.D. Drew		
4 Jeff Bagwell	25.00	7.50
Craig Biggio		
5 Bernie Williams	40.00	12.00
Derek Jeter		
6 Roberto Alomar	25.00	7.50
Mike Piazza		
7 Sean Casey		
Jim Thome SP/40		
8 Pat Burrell	20.00	6.00
Scott Rolen		
9 Gary Sheffield	15.00	4.50
Shawn Green		
10 Ivan Rodriguez	25.00	7.50
Alex Rodriguez		
11 Juan Gonzalez	15.00	4.50
Rafael Palmeiro		
12 Magglio Ordonez	20.00	6.00
Frank Thomas		
13 Larry Walker	15.00	4.50
Todd Helton SP/225		
14 Luis Gonzalez	15.00	4.50
Reggie Sanders		
15 Doug Mientkiewicz	15.00	4.50
Bret Boone		

2002 Flair Sweet Swatch

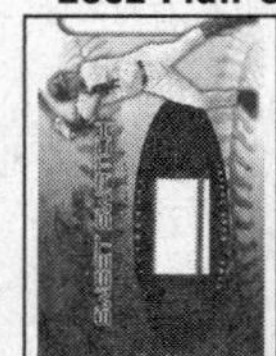

Issued one per hobby box as a "box-topper", these cards feature a larger jersey swatch from the featured players. Each player was issued to a different print run and we have notated the stated print run in our checklist.

	Nm-Mt	Ex-Mt
1 Jeff Bagwell/490	15.00	4.50
2 Josh Beckett/500	15.00	4.50
3 Darin Erstad/525	15.00	4.50
4 Freddy Garcia/620	15.00	4.50
5 Brian Giles Pants/445	15.00	4.50
6 Juan Gonzalez/505	15.00	4.50
7 Mark Grace/795	15.00	4.50
8 Derek Jeter/525	40.00	12.00
9 Jason Kendall/990	15.00	4.50
10 Paul LoDuca/440	15.00	4.50
11 Greg Maddux/475	15.00	4.50
12 Magglio Ordonez/495	15.00	4.50
13 Rafael Palmeiro/535	15.00	4.50
14 Mike Piazza/1000	15.00	4.50
15 Alex Rodriguez/550	25.00	7.50
16 Ivan Rodriguez/475	15.00	4.50
17 Tim Salmon/465	15.00	4.50
18 Kazuhiro Sasaki/770	15.00	4.50
19 Alfonso Soriano/775	15.00	4.50
20 Larry Walker/430	15.00	4.50
21 Ted Williams/250	150.00	45.00

2002 Flair Sweet Swatch Bat Autograph

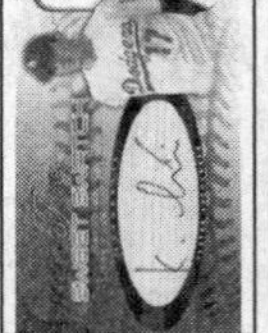

Randomly inserted as hobby box toppers, these cards feature not only a bat chip from the featured player but also an autograph. Each card was printed to a different amount and we have notated that stated print run information next to the player's name in our checklist. Some of the Drew Henson cards and all of the Derek Jeter cards were issued as exchange cards and those cards could be redeemed until April 30th, 2003.

Nm-Mt Ex-Mt
GOLD PARALLELS RANDOM BOX-TOPPERS
GOLD PRINT RUN 15 SERIAL #'d SETS
GOLD NOT PRICED DUE TO SCARCITY

	Nm-Mt	Ex-Mt
1 Barry Bonds/35	350.00	105.00
2 Dewon Brazelton/185	20.00	6.00
3 Marlon Byrd/185	20.00	6.00
4 Ron Cey/285	25.00	7.50
5 David Espinosa/485	20.00	6.00
6 Drew Henson/785	40.00	12.00
7 Kazuhisa Ishii/335	40.00	12.00
8 Derek Jeter/375	120.00	36.00
9 Al Kaline/285	60.00	18.00
10 Don Mattingly/85	200.00	60.00
11 Paul Molitor/85	60.00	18.00
12 Dale Murphy/285	80.00	24.00
13 Tony Perez/115	25.00	7.50
14 Mark Prior/285	100.00	30.00
15 Albert Pujols/50		
16 Brooks Robinson/185	40.00	12.00
17 Dane Sardinha/485	20.00	6.00
18 Ben Sheets/85	50.00	15.00
19 Ozzie Smith/185	100.00	30.00
20 So Taguchi/335	40.00	12.00
21 Mark Teixeira/185	40.00	12.00
22 Maury Wills/285	25.00	7.50

2002 Flair Sweet Swatch Patch

This 20-card over-sized set is a premium parallel version of the basic Sweet Swatch inserts. The cards were randomly seeded exclusively into hobby boxes as box-toppers. Unlike the basic cards, each of these parallels features a piece of jersey patch (often with very colorful pieces of the player's name or a team logo taken from their game used jersey). Each card was serial-numbered by hand. In general, between 50-80 copies of each card were produced, but please reference our checklist for specific quantities. Ted Williams (15 copies) and Derek Jeter (20 copies) are the scarcest cards in this set. Also, Pirates outfielder Brian Giles was the only player to have a basic Sweet Swatch card that was NOT featured in this Patch parallel because Fleer used a pair of his game-used pants for the basic card (thus no patch swatches were available).

Nm-Mt Ex-Mt
*PREMIUM PATCHES: 2X LISTED PRICES
1 OF 1 PARALLEL RANDOM BOX-TOPPER
NO 1 OF 1 PRICING DUE TO SCARCITY

	Nm-Mt	Ex-Mt
1 Jeff Bagwell/45	100.00	30.00
2 Josh Beckett/60	80.00	24.00
3 Darin Erstad/50	80.00	24.00
4 Freddy Garcia/50	80.00	24.00
5 Juan Gonzalez/55	100.00	30.00
6 Mark Grace/75	100.00	30.00
7 Derek Jeter/20		
8 Jason Kendall/120	60.00	18.00
9 Paul LoDuca/50	80.00	24.00
10 Greg Maddux/50	150.00	45.00
11 Magglio Ordonez/55	80.00	24.00
12 Rafael Palmeiro/60	100.00	30.00
13 Mike Piazza/95	150.00	45.00
14 Alex Rodriguez/50	150.00	45.00
15 Ivan Rodriguez/50	120.00	36.00
16 Tim Salmon/40	100.00	30.00
17 Kazuhiro Sasaki/80	80.00	24.00
18 Alfonso Soriano/35	100.00	30.00
19 Larry Walker/60	100.00	30.00
20 Ted Williams/15		

2003 Flair

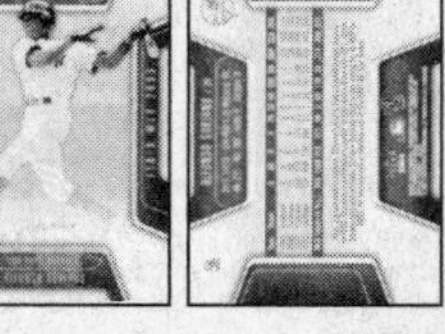

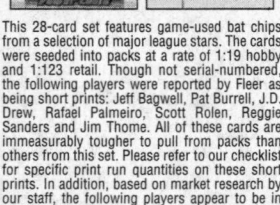

his 135 card set was issued in two separate eleases. The primary Flair product was released June, 2003. These cards were issued in five ard packs with an $6 SRP which came 20 packs a box and 12 boxes to a case. Cards numered 1-90 feature veterans while cards numered 91-125 feature rookies. The cards 91 rough 125 were issued to a stated print run of 00 serial numbered sets. Cards 126-135 were andomly seeded into packs of Fleer Rookies and reats of which was distributed in December, 003. Each of these update cards featured a top rospect and was serial numbered to 500 opies.

Nm-Mt Ex-Mt
OMP.LO SET w/o SP's (90) 25.00 7.50
OMMON CARD (1-90) .... .50 .15
OMMON CARD (91-135) 5.00 1.50
Hideo Nomo 1.25 .35
Derek Jeter 3.00 .90
Junior Spivey .50 .15
Rich Aurilia .50 .15
Luis Gonzalez .50 .15
Sean Burroughs .50 .15
Pedro Martinez 1.25 .35
Randy Winn .50 .15
Carlos Delgado .50 .15
) Pat Burrell .50 .15
1 Barry Larkin .75 .23
2 Roberto Alomar .75 .23
3 Tony Batista .50 .15
4 Barry Bonds 3.00 .90
5 Craig Biggio .75 .23
6 Ivan Rodriguez 1.25 .35
7 Javier Vazquez .50 .15
8 Joe Borchard .50 .15
9 Josh Phelps .50 .15
0 Omar Vizquel .75 .23
1 Tom Glavine .75 .23
2 Darin Erstad .50 .15
3 Hee Seop Choi .50 .15
4 Roger Clemens 2.50 .75
5 Michael Cuddyer .50 .15
6 Mike Sweeney .50 .15
7 Phil Nevin .50 .15
8 Torii Hunter .50 .15
9 Vladimir Guerrero 1.25 .35
0 Ellis Burks .50 .15
1 Jimmy Rollins .50 .15
2 Ken Griffey Jr. 2.00 .60
3 Magglio Ordonez .50 .15
4 Mark Prior 1.25 .35
5 Mike Lieberthal .50 .15
6 Jorge Posada .75 .23
7 Rodrigo Lopez .50 .15
8 Todd Helton .75 .23
9 Adam Kennedy .50 .15
0 Curt Schilling .50 .15
1 Jim Thome 1.25 .35
2 Josh Beckett .50 .15
3 Carlos Pena .50 .15
4 Jason Kendall .50 .15
5 Sammy Sosa 2.00 .60
6 Scott Rolen 1.25 .35
7 Alex Rodriguez 2.00 .60
8 Aubrey Huff .50 .15
9 Bobby Abreu .50 .15
0 Jeff Kent .50 .15
1 Joe Randa .50 .15
2 Lance Berkman .50 .15
3 Orlando Cabrera .50 .15
4 Richie Sexson .50 .15
5 Albert Pujols 2.00 .60
6 Alfonso Soriano .75 .23
7 Greg Maddux 2.00 .60
8 Jason Giambi .50 .15
9 Jeff Bagwell .75 .23
0 Kerry Wood 1.25 .35
1 Manny Ramirez .75 .23
2 Eric Chavez .50 .15
3 Preston Wilson .50 .15
4 Shawn Green .50 .15
5 Shea Hillenbrand .50 .15
6 Austin Kearns .50 .15
7 Cliff Floyd .50 .15
8 Edgardo Alfonzo .50 .15
9 J.D. Drew .50 .15
0 Larry Walker .75 .23
1 Mike Piazza 2.00 .60
2 Andruw Jones .50 .15
3 Ben Grieve .50 .15
4 Eric Hinske .50 .15
5 Geoff Jenkins .50 .15
6 Kazuhiro Sasaki .50 .15
7 Matt Morris .50 .15
8 Miguel Tejada .50 .15
9 Aramis Ramirez .50 .15
0 Troy Glaus .50 .15
1 Ichiro Suzuki 2.00 .60
2 Mark Teixeira .50 .15
3 Nomar Garciaparra 2.00 .60
4 Chipper Jones 1.25 .35
5 Frank Thomas 1.25 .35
6 Paul Lo Duca .50 .15
7 Bernie Williams .75 .23
8 Adam Dunn .75 .23
9 Randy Johnson 1.25 .35
0 Barry Zito .50 .15
1 Lew Ford FF RC 10.00 3.00
2 Joe Valentine FF RC 5.00 1.50
3 Jhonny Peralta FF 5.00 1.50
4 Hideki Matsui FF RC 20.00 6.00
5 Francisco Rosario FF RC 5.00 1.50
6 Adam LaRoche FF 5.00 1.50
7 Josh Hall FF RC 8.00 2.40
8 Chien-Ming Wang FF RC 10.00 3.00
9 Josh Willingham FF RC 8.00 2.40
00 Guillermo Quiroz FF RC 8.00 2.40
01 Terrmel Sledge FF RC 8.00 2.40
02 Prentice Redman FF RC 5.00 1.50
03 Matt Bruback FF RC 5.00 1.50
04 Alejandro Machado FF RC 5.00 1.50
05 Shane Victorino FF RC 5.00 1.50
06 Chris Waters FF RC 5.00 1.50
07 Jose Contreras FF RC 10.00 3.00
08 Pete LaForest FF RC 8.00 2.40
09 Nook Logan FF RC 5.00 1.50
10 Hector Luna FF RC 5.00 1.50
11 Daniel Cabrera FF RC 10.00 3.00
12 Matt Kata FF RC 8.00 2.40
113 Rontrez Johnson FF RC 5.00 1.50
114 Josh Stewart FF RC 5.00 1.50
115 Michael Hessman FF RC 5.00 1.50
116 Felix Sanchez FF RC 5.00 1.50
117 Michel Hernandez FF RC 5.00 1.50
118 Arnaldo Munoz FF RC 5.00 1.50
119 Ian Ferguson FF RC 5.00 1.50
120 Clint Barmes FF RC 8.00 2.40
121 Brian Stokes FF RC 5.00 1.50
122 Craig Brazell FF RC 8.00 2.40
123 John Webb FF 5.00 1.50
124 Tim Olson FF RC 8.00 2.40
125 Jeremy Bonderman FF RC 8.00 2.40
126 Jeff Duncan RC 8.00 2.40
127 Rickie Weeks RC 12.00 3.60
128 Brandon Webb RC 10.00 3.00
129 Robby Hammock RC 8.00 2.40
130 Jon Leicester RC 5.00 1.50
131 Ryan Wagner RC 8.00 2.40
132 Bo Hart RC 8.00 2.40
133 Edwin Jackson RC 12.00 3.60
134 Sergio Mitre RC 8.00 2.40
135 Delmon Young RC 15.00 4.50

2003 Flair Collection Row 1

Nm-Mt Ex-Mt
*ROW 1 1-90: 2.5X TO 6X BASIC
*ROW 1 91-125: .4X TO 1X BASIC
RANDOM INSERTS IN PACKS
STATED PRINT RUN 150 SERIAL #'d SETS

2003 Flair Collection Row 2

Nm-Mt Ex-Mt
RANDOM INSERTS IN PACKS
STATED PRINT RUN 25 SERIAL #'d SETS
NO PRICING DUE TO SCARCITY

2003 Flair Diamond Cuts Jersey

Issued at a stated rate of one in 10, these 15 cards feature jersey swatches from some of baseball's leading players.

Nm-Mt Ex-Mt
STATED ODDS 1:10
*GOLD: 1X TO 2.5X BASIC
GOLD RANDOM INSERTS IN PACKS
GOLD PRINT RUN 100 SERIAL #'d SETS
AR Alex Rodriguez 10.00 3.00
AS Alfonso Soriano 8.00 2.40
BZ Barry Zito 5.00 1.50
CJ Chipper Jones 8.00 2.40
DJ Derek Jeter 15.00 4.50
GM Greg Maddux 10.00 3.00
JD J.D. Drew 5.00 1.50
MP Mike Piazza 10.00 3.00
PB Pat Burrell 5.00 1.50
RA Roberto Alomar 8.00 2.40
RC Roger Clemens 10.00 3.00
RO Roy Oswalt 5.00 1.50
SR Scott Rolen 8.00 2.40
TG Troy Glaus 5.00 1.50
VG Vladimir Guerrero 8.00 2.40

2003 Flair Hot Numbers Patch

Randomly inserted into packs, these 15 cards feature game-used "patch pieces" from leading baseball players. Each of these cards were issued to a stated print run of 100 serial numbered sets.

Nm-Mt Ex-Mt
AR Alex Rodriguez 40.00 12.00
AS Alfonso Soriano 30.00 9.00
BZ Barry Zito 25.00 7.50
CJ Chipper Jones 30.00 9.00
DJ Derek Jeter 60.00 18.00
GM Greg Maddux 40.00 12.00
JD J.D. Drew 25.00 7.50
MP Mike Piazza 40.00 12.00
PB Pat Burrell 25.00 7.50
RA Roberto Alomar 30.00 9.00
RC Roger Clemens
RO Roy Oswalt 25.00 7.50
SR Scott Rolen 30.00 9.00
TG Troy Glaus 25.00 7.50
VG Vladimir Guerrero 30.00 9.00

2003 Flair Hot Numbers Dual Patch

Randomly inserted into packs, these cards feature two "patch" swatches from leading baseball players. Each of these cards were issued to a stated print run of 25 serial numbered sets and no pricing is available due to market scarcity.

Nm-Mt Ex-Mt
ARVG Alex Rodriguez
Vladimir Guerrero
ASDJ Alfonso Soriano
Derek Jeter
ASRA Alfonso Soriano
Roberto Alomar
CJPB Chipper Jones
Pat Burrell
DJAR Derek Jeter
Alex Rodriguez
JDSR J.D. Drew
Scott Rolen
PBJD Pat Burrell
J.D. Drew
RAMP Roberto Alomar
Mike Piazza
SRCJ Scott Rolen
Chipper Jones
VGMP Vladimir Guerrero
Mike Piazza

2003 Flair Power Tools Bats

Randomly inserted into packs, these 18 cards feature game-used bat chips from leading players. Each of these cards were issued to a stated print run of 500 serial numbered sets.

Nm-Mt Ex-Mt
*GOLD: .6X TO 1.5X BASIC
GOLD PRINT RUN 100 SERIAL #'d SETS
RANDOM INSERTS IN PACKS
AD Adam Dunn 10.00 3.00
AJ Andruw Jones 8.00 2.40
AK Austin Kearns 8.00 2.40
AR Alex Rodriguez 15.00 4.50
AS Alfonso Soriano 10.00 3.00
BW Bernie Williams 10.00 3.00
DJ Derek Jeter 20.00 6.00
HSC Hee-Seop Choi 8.00 2.40
JB Jeff Bagwell 10.00 3.00
JGI Jason Giambi 8.00 2.40
JGO Juan Gonzalez 10.00 3.00
JT Jim Thome 10.00 3.00
LB Lance Berkman 8.00 2.40
MP Mike Piazza 15.00 4.50
MT Miguel Tejada 8.00 2.40
NG Nomar Garciaparra 15.00 4.50
SR Scott Rolen 10.00 3.00
SS Sammy Sosa 15.00 4.50

2003 Flair Power Tools Dual Bats

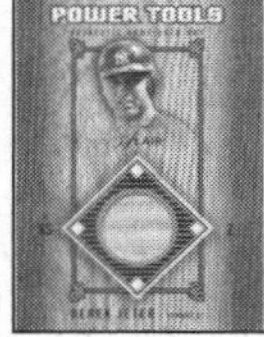

Randomly inserted into packs, these cards feature two "game-used" bat chips of the featured players. Each of these cards were issued to a stated print run of 200 serial numbered sets.

Nm-Mt Ex-Mt
ADAK Adam Dunn 20.00 6.00
Austin Kearns
ARNG Alex Rodriguez 30.00 9.00
Nomar Garciaparra
DJAS Derek Jeter 40.00 12.00
Alfonso Soriano
JGBW Jason Giambi 20.00 6.00
Bernie Williams
JGMP Jason Giambi 25.00 7.50
Mike Piazza
JTSS Jim Thome 20.00 6.00
Sammy Sosa
LBJB Lance Berkman 20.00 6.00
Jeff Bagwell
MTAR Miguel Tejada 20.00 6.00
Alex Rodriguez
NBDJ Nomar Garciaparra 40.00 12.00
Derek Jeter

2003 Flair Sweet Swatch Autos Jumbo

Randomly inserted in jumbo packs, these seven cards feature authentic autographs from leading players. There are three different varieties of Derek Jeter autographs. Please note that we have put the stated serial numbered print run next to the player's name in our checklist.

Nm-Mt Ex-Mt
GOLD PRINT RUN 25 SERIAL #'d SETS
NO GOLD PRICING DUE TO SCARCITY
MASTERPIECE PRINT 1 SERIAL #'d SET
NO M'PIECE PRICING DUE TO SCARCITY
RANDOM INSERTS IN JUMBO PACKS
AD Adam Dunn/218 50.00 15.00
DJ Derek Jeter/312 100.00 30.00
DJA Derek Jeter/30
DJW Derek Jeter/50
JB Jeff Bagwell/218 50.00 15.00
RJ Randy Johnson/218 80.00 24.00
TG Troy Glaus/116 40.00 12.00

2003 Flair Sweet Swatch Jersey

Randomly inserted into packs, these 18 cards feature game-used jersey swatches from some of baseball's star players.

Nm-Mt Ex-Mt
*JUMBO 50: 1X TO 2.5X BASIC
JUMBO 50 PRINT RUN 50 SERIAL #'d SETS
*JUMBO 150: .6X TO 1.5X BASIC
JUMBO 150 PRINT RUN 150 SERIAL #'d SETS
JUMBO MASTERPIECE 1 SERIAL #'d SET
NO JUMBO M'PIECE PRICING AVAILABLE
JUMBOS RANDOM IN JUMBO PACKS
SSAD Adam Dunn 10.00 3.00
SSAR Alex Rodriguez 15.00 4.50
SSAS Alfonso Soriano 10.00 3.00
SSBW Bernie Williams 10.00 3.00
SSCJ Chipper Jones 10.00 3.00
SSDJ Derek Jeter 20.00 6.00
SSHN Hideo Nomo 15.00 4.50
SSJG Jason Giambi 8.00 2.40
SSKS Kazuhiro Sasaki 8.00 2.40
SSLB Lance Berkman 8.00 2.40
SSMP Mark Prior 10.00 3.00
SSMT Miguel Tejada 8.00 2.40
SSNG Nomar Garciaparra 15.00 4.50
SSPM Pedro Martinez 10.00 3.00
SSRC Roger Clemens 15.00 4.50
SSRJ Randy Johnson 10.00 3.00
SSSS Sammy Sosa 15.00 4.50
SSVG Vladimir Guerrero 10.00 3.00

2003 Flair Sweet Swatch Jersey Jumbo

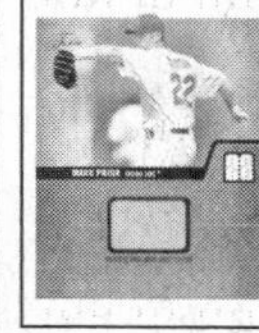

Inserted at a stated rate of one per jumbo pack, these 18 cards feature jersey swatches from some of baseball's leading players.

Nm-Mt Ex-Mt
ADSSJ Adam Dunn/1090 10.00 3.00
ARSSJ Alex Rodriguez/55 40.00 12.00
ASSSJ Alfonso Soriano/57 25.00 7.50
BWSSJ Bernie Williams/1420 10.00 3.00
CJSSJ Chipper Jones/80 25.00 7.50
DJSSJ Derek Jeter/47 50.00 15.00
HNSSJ Hideo Nomo/970 10.00 3.00
JGSSJ Jason Giambi/350 10.00 3.00
KSSSJ Kazuhiro Sasaki/505 10.00 3.00
LBSSJ Lance Berkman/1465 8.00 2.40
MPSSJ Mark Prior/1195 10.00 3.00
MTSSJ Miguel Tejada/518 10.00 3.00
NGSSJ Nomar Garciaparra/727 20.00 6.00
PMSSJ Pedro Martinez/1480 10.00 3.00
RCSSJ Roger Clemens/97 30.00 9.00
RJSSJ Randy Johnson/274 15.00 4.50
SSSSJ Sammy Sosa/279 20.00 6.00
VGSSJ Vladimir Guerrero/46 40.00 12.00

2003 Flair Sweet Swatch Jersey Dual Jumbo

Randomly inserted into jumbo packs, these eight cards feature two jersey swatches from some of baseball's leading players. Each of these cards were issued to a stated print run of 25 serial numbered sets and no pricing is available due to market scarcity.

Nm-Mt Ex-Mt
ADLB Adam Dunn
Lance Berkman
DJBW Derek Jeter
Bernie Williams
JGAS Jason Giambi
Alfonso Soriano
KSHN Kazuhiro Sasaki
Hideo Nomo
MTAR Miguel Tejada
Alex Rodriguez
NMPM Nomar Garciaparra
Pedro Martinez
RJMP Randy Johnson
Mark Prior
VGCJ Vladimir Guerrero
Chipper Jones

2003 Flair Sweet Swatch Patch

Randomly inserted into packs, these 18 cards feature patches from some of baseball's superstars. Each of these cards were issued to a stated print run of 50 serial numbered sets.

Nm-Mt Ex-Mt
SSPAD Adam Dunn
SSPAR Alex Rodriguez 50.00 15.00
SSPAS Alfonso Soriano 40.00 12.00
SSPBW Bernie Williams 40.00 12.00
SSPCJ Chipper Jones 40.00 12.00
SSPDJ Derek Jeter 80.00 24.00
SSPHN Hideo Nomo 40.00 12.00
SSPJG Jason Giambi 30.00 9.00
SSPKS Kazuhiro Sasaki 30.00 9.00
SSPLB Lance Berkman 30.00 9.00
SSPMP Mark Prior 40.00 12.00
SSPMT Miguel Tejada 30.00 9.00
SSPNG Nomar Garciaparra 50.00 15.00
SSPPM Pedro Martinez 40.00 12.00
SSPRC Roger Clemens 60.00 18.00
SSPRJ Randy Johnson 40.00 12.00
SSPSS Sammy Sosa 50.00 15.00
SSPVG Vladimir Guerrero 40.00 12.00

2003 Flair Sweet Swatch Patch Jumbo

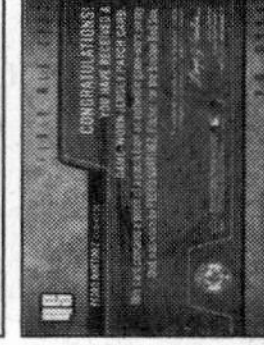

Randomly inserted in jumbo packs, these 18 cards feature patch pieces of leading players. Each of these cards were produced to differing print runs and we have notated the print run next to the player's name in our checklist. If any card was issued to a stated print run of 25 or fewer cards, there is no pricing due to market scarcity.

Nm-Mt Ex-Mt
ADSSPE Adam Dunn/130 40.00 12.00
ARSSPE Alex Rodriguez/298 50.00 15.00
ASSSPE Alfonso Soriano/28
BWSSPE Bernie Williams/123 40.00 12.00
CJSSPE Chipper Jones/284 30.00 9.00
DJSSPE Derek Jeter/35
HNSSPE Hideo Nomo/114 60.00 18.00
JGSSPE Jason Giambi/26
KSSSPE Kazuhiro Sasaki/90 30.00 9.00
LBSSPE Lance Berkman/287 25.00 7.50
MPSSPE Mark Prior/290 30.00 9.00
MTSSPE Miguel Tejada/183 25.00 7.50
NGSSPE Nomar Garciaparra/124 50.00 15.00
PMSSPE Pedro Martinez/185 30.00 9.00
RCSSPE Roger Clemens/1
RJSSPE Randy Johnson/46 50.00 15.00
SSSSPE Sammy Sosa/190 50.00 15.00
VGSSPE Vladimir Guerrero/290 30.00 9.00

2003 Flair Wave of the Future Memorabilia

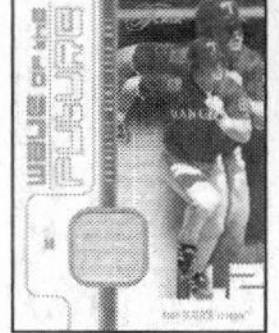
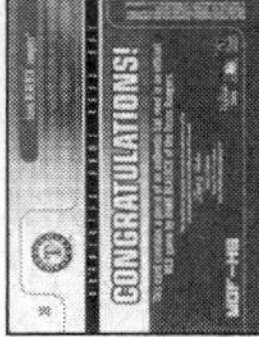

Randomly inserted into packs, these six cards feature not only some of the up and coming young prospects but also an game-used memorabilia piece. Each of these cards were issued to a stated print run of 500 serial numbered sets.

Nm-Mt Ex-Mt
*GOLD: .6X TO 1.5X BASIC
GOLD PRINT RUN 100 SERIAL #'d SETS
RANDOM INSERTS IN PACKS
AH Aubrey Huff Bat 8.00 2.40
AK Austin Kearns Jsy 8.00 2.40
CC Carl Crawford Bat 8.00 2.40
HB Hank Blalock Bat 10.00 3.00
JP Josh Phelps Jsy 8.00 2.40
SB Sean Burroughs Jsy 8.00 2.40

2004 Flair

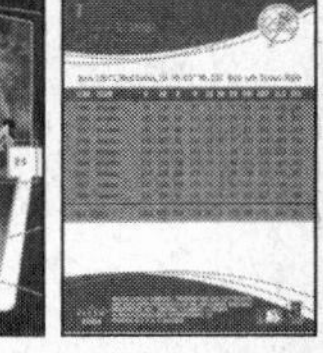

This 82 card set was released in April, 2004. It was issued in 12-card hobby packs with an $120 SRP packs (little boxes) which were packed 12 to a case. This set was also issued in four-card retail packs with an $3 SRP. The retail packs were issued 24 packs to a box and 20 boxes to a case. The first 60 cards in this set feature veterans while the final 22 cards feature leading rookies and prospects entering the 2004 season. The final 22 cards were issued at a stated rate of one per hobby pack and one in 200 retail packs and were issued to a stated print run of 799 serial numbered sets.

Nm-Mt Ex-Mt
COMMON CARD (61-82) 4.00 1.20
1 Brandon Webb 1.50 .45
2 Todd Helton 2.00 .60

3 Jeff Bagwell 2.00 .60
4 Shawn Green 1.50 .45
5 Vladimir Guerrero 3.00 .90
6 Tom Glavine 2.00 .60
7 Jason Giambi 1.50 .45
8 Barry Zito 1.50 .45
9 Jason Kendall 1.50 .45
10 Carlos Delgado 1.50 .45
11 Curt Schilling 3.00 .90
12 Ken Griffey Jr. 5.00 1.50
13 Mike Piazza 5.00 1.50
14 Alfonso Soriano 2.00 .60
15 Albert Pujols 6.00 1.80
16 Chipper Jones 3.00 .90
17 Alex Rodriguez 5.00 1.50
18 Miguel Tejada 1.50 .45
19 Pedro Martinez 3.00 .90
20 Mark Prior 3.00 .90
21 Magglio Ordonez 1.50 .45
22 Scott Podsednik 1.50 .45
23 Shannon Stewart 1.50 .45
24 Rocco Baldelli 1.50 .45
25 Darin Erstad 1.50 .45
26 Omar Vizquel 2.00 .60
27 Angel Berroa 1.50 .45
28 Jose Vidro 1.50 .45
29 Rich Harden 1.50 .45
30 Andruw Jones 1.50 .45
31 Troy Glaus 1.50 .45
32 Sammy Sosa 5.00 1.50
33 Dontrelle Willis 1.50 .45
34 Ivan Rodriguez 3.00 .90
35 Nomar Garciaparra 5.00 1.50
36 Josh Beckett 1.50 .45
37 Jose Reyes 1.50 .45
38 Scott Rolen 3.00 .90
39 Greg Maddux 5.00 1.50
40 Andy Pettitte 2.00 .60
41 Jason Schmidt 1.50 .45
42 Edgar Martinez 2.00 .60
43 Manny Ramirez 2.00 .60
44 Torii Hunter 1.50 .45
45 Mark Teixeira 1.50 .45
46 Hideo Nomo 3.00 .90
47 Brian Giles 1.50 .45
48 Adam Dunn 2.00 .60
49 Fernando Vina 1.50 .45
50 Hideki Matsui 5.00 1.50
51 Jim Thome 3.00 .90
52 Hank Blalock 1.50 .45
53 Miguel Cabrera 2.00 .60
54 Randy Johnson 3.00 .90
55 Javy Lopez 1.50 .45
56 Frank Thomas 3.00 .90
57 Roger Clemens 6.00 1.80
58 Marlon Byrd 1.50 .45
59 Derek Jeter 6.00 1.80
60 Ichiro Suzuki 5.00 1.50
61 Kaz Matsui C04 RC 8.00 2.40
62 Chad Bentz C04 RC 4.00 1.20
63 Greg Dobbs C04 RC 4.00 1.20
64 John Gall C04 RC 5.00 1.50
65 Cory Sullivan C04 RC 4.00 1.20
66 Hector Gimenez C04 RC 4.00 1.20
67 Graham Koonce C04 4.00 1.20
68 Jason Bartlett C04 RC 5.00 1.50
69 Angel Chavez C04 RC 4.00 1.20
70 Ronny Cedeno C04 RC 4.00 1.20
71 Don Kelly C04 RC 4.00 1.20
72 Ivan Ochoa C04 RC 4.00 1.20
73 Ruddy Yan C04 4.00 1.20
74 Mike Gosling C04 RC 4.00 1.20
75 Alfredo Simon C04 RC 4.00 1.20
76 Jerome Gamble C04 RC 4.00 1.20
77 Chris Aguila C04 RC 4.00 1.20
78 Mike Rouse C04 RC 4.00 1.20
79 Justin Leone C04 RC 5.00 1.50
80 Merkin Valdez C04 RC 5.00 1.50
81 Aaron Baldiris C04 RC 5.00 1.50
82 Chris Shelton C04 RC 5.00 1.50

2004 Flair Collection Row 1

Nm-Mt Ex-Mt
*ROW 1 1-60: 1.25X TO 3X BASIC
*ROW 1 61-82: .6X TO 1.5X BASIC
OVERALL PARALLEL ODDS 1:6 HOBBY
ROW 1 STATED ODDS 1:55 RETAIL
STATED PRINT RUN 100 SERIAL #'d SETS
61 Kaz Matsui C04 15.00 4.50

2004 Flair Collection Row 2

Nm-Mt Ex-Mt
OVERALL PARALLEL ODDS 1:6 HOBBY
STATED PRINT RUN 1 SERIAL #'d SET
NO PRICING DUE TO SCARCITY

2004 Flair Autograph

Nm-Mt Ex-Mt
PRINT RUNS B/WN 60-280 COPIES PER
*CROWN: .4X TO 1X p/r 122-280
*CROWN: .4X TO 1X p/r 60-96
CROWN PRINT RUN 100 SERIAL #'d SETS
MASTERPIECE PRINT RUN 1 SER.#'d SET
NO M'PIECE PRICING DUE TO SCARCITY
*PARCHMENT: .75X TO 2X p/r 122-280
*PARCHMENT: .6X TO 1.5X p/r 60-96
PARCHMENT PRINT RUN 25 SER.#'d SETS
NO RC YR PARCHMENT PRICING AVAIL.
PLATINUM PRINT RUN 10 SERIAL #'d SETS
NO PLATINUM PRICING DUE TO SCARCITY
OVERALL AU ODDS 1:1 HOBBY
OVERALL AU-GU ODDS 1:24 RETAIL
AB1 Aarom Baldiris/180 15.00 4.50
AB2 Angel Berroa/178 10.00 3.00
AJ Andruw Jones/163 15.00 4.50
ALR Adam LaRoche/280 10.00 3.00
AR Alexis Rios/185 15.00 4.50
BC Bobby Crosby/87 40.00 12.00
BN Bubba Nelson/185 10.00 3.00
BW Brandon Webb/122 10.00 3.00
CMW Chien-Ming Wang/178 40.00 12.00
CP Corey Patterson/172 15.00 4.50
CS Chris Shelton/170 15.00 4.50
DH Dan Haren/195 10.00 3.00
DW Dontrelle Willis/73 25.00 7.50
DY Delmon Young/177 25.00 7.50
EJ Edwin Jackson/193 15.00 4.50
GA Garrett Atkins/195 10.00 3.00
GK Graham Koonce/175 10.00 3.00
GS Grady Sizemore/197 15.00 4.50
JB1 Jason Bartlett/95 15.00 4.50
JB2 Josh Beckett/65 40.00 12.00
JE Jim Edmonds/73 40.00 12.00
JG John Gall/94 15.00 4.50
JL Josh Labandeira/166 10.00 3.00
JP Juan Pierre/94 15.00 4.50
JUL Justin Leone/180 15.00 4.50
JV Javier Vazquez/187 15.00 4.50
KG Khalil Greene/195 40.00 12.00
KW0 Kerry Wood/73 50.00 15.00
MC Miguel Cabrera/172 25.00 7.50
MM Mike Mussina/69 40.00 12.00
MN Michael Nakamura/180 10.00 3.00
MP Mark Prior/60 80.00 24.00
MR Mike Rouse/195 10.00 3.00
MV Merkin Valdez/179 15.00 4.50
RB Rocco Baldelli/180 15.00 4.50
RH Ryan Howard/185 15.00 4.50
RM Ryan Meaux/180 10.00 3.00
RW1 Ryan Wagner/175 10.00 3.00
RW2 Rickie Weeks/169 15.00 4.50
SP Scott Podsednik/96 25.00 7.50

2004 Flair Autograph Die Cut

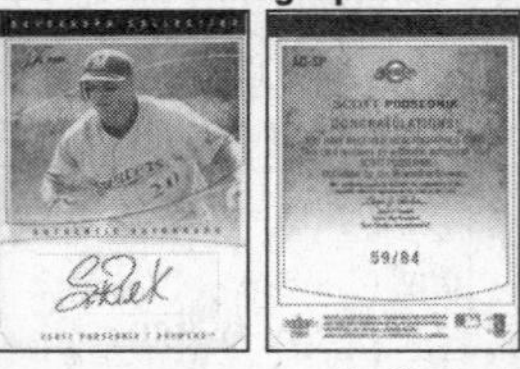

Nm-Mt Ex-Mt
OVERALL AU ODDS 1:1 HOBBY
PRINT RUNS B/WN 10-113 COPIES PER
NO PRICING ON QTY OF 19 OR LESS
AB1 Aarom Baldiris/17
AB2 Angel Berroa/17
ALR Adam LaRoche/10
BC Bobby Crosby/102 40.00 12.00
BN Bubba Nelson/10
BW Brandon Webb/10
CMW Chien-Ming Wang/17
CP Corey Patterson/16
CS Chris Shelton/17
DH Dan Haren/10
DW Dontrelle Willis/10
EJ Edwin Jackson/16
GA Garrett Atkins/10
JB1 Jason Bartlett/113 15.00 4.50
JG John Gall/94 15.00 4.50
JL Josh Labandeira/19
JP Juan Pierre/80 25.00 7.50
KG Khalil Greene/10
MC Miguel Cabrera/14
MN Michael Nakamura/10
RH Ryan Howard/10
RM Ryan Meaux/10
RW1 Ryan Wagner/16
RW2 Rickie Weeks/16
SP Scott Podsednik/84 25.00 7.50

2004 Flair Cuts and Glory 100

Nm-Mt Ex-Mt
STATED PRINT RUN 100 SERIAL #'d SETS
*CUTS/GLORY 50: .5X TO 1X BASIC
CUTS/GLORY 50 PRINT RUN 50 #'d SETS
CUTS/GLORY 15 PRINT RUN 15 #'d SETS
C/G 15 NO PRICING DUE TO SCARCITY
CUTS/GLORY 3 PRINT RUN 3 #'d SETS
C/G 3 NO PRICING DUE TO SCARCITY
CUTS/GLORY 1 PRINT RUN 1 #'d SETS
C/G 1 NO PRICING DUE TO SCARCITY
OVERALL AU ODDS 1:1 HOBBY
OVERALL AU-GU ODDS 1:24 RETAIL
EXCHANGE DEADLINE INDEFINITE
AD Adam Dunn 40.00 12.00
AK Austin Kearns 25.00 7.50
AP Albert Pujols 150.00 45.00
CD Carlos Delgado 40.00 12.00
CJ Chipper Jones 60.00 18.00
EG Eric Gagne 50.00 15.00
EM Edgar Martinez 40.00 12.00
FT Frank Thomas 60.00 18.00
GA Garret Anderson 25.00 7.50
GM Greg Maddux EXCH 100.00 30.00
HB Hank Blalock 25.00 7.50
JR Jose Reyes 25.00 7.50
LG Luis Gonzalez 25.00 7.50
MB Marlon Byrd 15.00 4.50
MO Magglio Ordonez 25.00 7.50
MT Mark Teixeira 40.00 12.00
RH Ricky Henderson 80.00 24.00
RJ Randy Johnson 60.00 18.00
SR Scott Rolen 50.00 15.00
TH Torii Hunter 25.00 7.50
VG Vladimir Guerrero 50.00 15.00

2004 Flair Diamond Cuts Game Used Blue

Nm-Mt Ex-Mt
STATED PRINT RUN 250 SERIAL #'d SETS
*BLUE DC: 1X TO 2.5X BLUE
BLUE DC PRINT RUN 25 SERIAL #'d SETS
*COPPER: .6X TO 1.5X BLUE
COPPER PRINT RUN 75 SERIAL #'d SETS
COPPER DC PRINT RUN 8 SERIAL #'d SETS
NO COPPER DC PRICING DUE TO SCARCITY
*GOLD p/r 38-55: 1.25X TO 3X BLUE
*GOLD p/r 21-35: 1.5X TO 4X BLUE
GOLD PRINT RUNS B/WN 2-55 COPIES PER
NO GOLD PRICING ON QTY OF 10 OR LESS
GOLD DC PRINT RUN 3 SERIAL #'d SETS
NO GOLD DC PRICING DUE TO SCARCITY
*PEWTER: .5X TO 1.2X BLUE
PEWTER PRINT RUN 125 SERIAL #'d SETS
PEWTER DC PRINT RUN 13 SER.#'d SETS
NO PEWTER DC PRICING DUE TO SCARCITY
*PLATINUM p/r 36-43: 1.25X TO 3X BLUE
*PLATINUM p/r 21-29: 1.5X TO 4X BLUE
*PLATINUM p/r 16-18: 2X TO 5X BLUE
PLAT.PRINT RUNS B/WN 5-43 COPIES PER
NO PLAT.PRICING ON QTY OF 14 OR LESS
PLATINUM DC PRINT RUN 1 SERIAL #'d SET
NO PLAT.DC PRICING DUE TO SCARCITY
PURPLE PRINT RUN 1 SERIAL #'d SET
NO PURPLE PRICING DUE TO SCARCITY
*RED: .4X TO 1X BLUE
RED PRINT RUN 175 SERIAL #'d SETS
RED DC: 1.25X TO 3X BLUE
RED DC PRINT RUN 18 SERIAL #'d SETS
*SILVER: 1.25X TO 3X BLUE
SILVER PRINT RUN 50 SERIAL #'d SETS
SILVER DC PRINT RUN 5 SERIAL #'d SETS
NO SILVER DC PRICING DUE TO SCARCITY
OVERALL GU ODDS 3 PER HOBBY PACK
ALL ARE JERSEY CARDS UNLESS NOTED
AJ Andruw Jones 5.00 1.50
ALP Albert Pujols 15.00 4.50
ANP Andy Pettitte 8.00 2.40
CJ Chipper Jones 8.00 2.40
CS Curt Schilling 8.00 2.40
DJ Derek Jeter 15.00 4.50
DW Dontrelle Willis 5.00 1.50
HB Hank Blalock 5.00 1.50
HM Hideki Matsui Base 15.00 4.50
IS Ichiro Suzuki Base 15.00 4.50
JB Josh Beckett 5.00 1.50
JR Jose Reyes 5.00 1.50
MAP Mark Prior 8.00 2.40
MIP Mike Piazza 12.00 3.60
MT Mark Teixeira 5.00 1.50
NG Nomar Garciaparra 12.00 3.60
PM Pedro Martinez 8.00 2.40
RC Roger Clemens 15.00 4.50
SR Scott Rolen 8.00 2.40
SS Sammy Sosa 12.00 3.60

2004 Flair Diamond Cuts Game Used Dual Gold

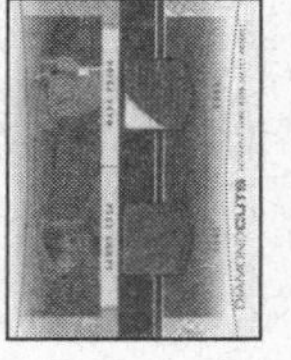

Nm-Mt Ex-Mt
OVERALL GU ODDS 3 PER HOBBY PACK
STATED PRINT RUN 10 SERIAL #'d SETS
NO PRICING DUE TO SCARCITY
CJAJ Chipper Jones
Andruw Jones
CSPM Curt Schilling
Pedro Martinez
HBMT Hank Blalock
Mark Teixeira
ISHM Ichiro Suzuki
Hideki Matsui
JBDW Josh Beckett
Dontrelle Willis
JRMP Jose Reyes
Mike Piazza
NGDJ Nomar Garciaparra
Derek Jeter
RCAP Roger Clemens
Andy Pettitte
SRAP Scott Rolen
Albert Pujols
SSMP Sammy Sosa
Mark Prior

2004 Flair Hot Numbers

Nm-Mt Ex-Mt
STATED ODDS 1:16 RETAIL
STATED PRINT RUN 500 SERIAL #'d SETS
*GOLD p/r 51-75: .75X TO 2X BASIC
*GOLD p/r 38-48: 1X TO 2.5X BASIC
*GOLD p/r 21-35: 1.25X TO 3X BASIC
*GOLD p/r 17: 1.5X TO 4X BASIC
GOLD ODDS 1:275 RETAIL
GOLD PRINT RUNS B/WN 2-75 COPIES PER
NO GOLD PRICING ON QTY OF 13 OR LESS
1 Chipper Jones 5.00 1.50
2 Derek Jeter 10.00 3.00
3 Alex Rodriguez 8.00 2.40
4 Torii Hunter 4.00 1.20
5 Nomar Garciaparra 8.00 2.40
6 Troy Glaus 4.00 1.20
7 Tom Glavine 5.00 1.50
8 Albert Pujols 10.00 3.00
9 Kerry Wood 5.00 1.50
10 Hideo Nomo 5.00 1.50
11 Rocco Baldelli 4.00 1.20
12 Mark Prior 5.00 1.50
13 Hank Blalock 4.00 1.20
14 Mark Teixeira 4.00 1.20
15 Curt Schilling 5.00 1.50
16 Randy Johnson 5.00 1.50
17 Barry Larkin 5.00 1.50
18 Vladimir Guerrero 5.00 1.50
19 Brandon Webb 4.00 1.20
20 Todd Helton 5.00 1.50
21 Jeff Bagwell 5.00 1.50
22 Barry Zito 4.00 1.20
23 Sammy Sosa 8.00 2.40
24 Pedro Martinez 5.00 1.50
25 Jim Thome 5.00 1.50
26 Frank Thomas 5.00 1.50
27 Greg Maddux 8.00 2.40
28 Jason Giambi 4.00 1.20
29 Manny Ramirez 5.00 1.50
30 Josh Beckett 4.00 1.20
31 Mike Piazza 8.00 2.40
32 Hideki Matsui 8.00 2.40
33 Ichiro Suzuki 8.00 2.40
34 Ken Griffey Jr. 8.00 2.40
35 Mike Mussina 5.00 1.50

2004 Flair Hot Numbers Game Used Blue

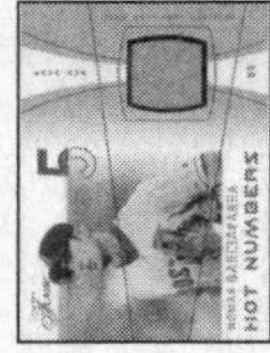

Nm-Mt Ex-Mt
STATED PRINT RUN 250 SERIAL #'d SETS
*BLUE DC: 1X TO 2.5X BLUE
BLUE DC PRINT RUN 25 SERIAL #'d SETS
COPPER: .6X TO 1.5X BLUE
COPPER PRINT RUN 75 SERIAL #'d SETS
COPPER DC PRINT RUN 8 SERIAL #'d SETS
NO COPPER DC PRICING DUE TO SCARCITY
*GOLD p/r 38-55: 1.25X TO 3X BLUE
*GOLD p/r 21-35: 1.5X TO 4X BLUE
*GOLD p/r 17: 2X TO 5X BLUE
GOLD PRINT RUNS B/WN 2-55 COPIES PER
NO GOLD PRICING ON QTY OF 13 OR LESS
GOLD DC PRINT RUN 3 SERIAL #'d SETS
NO GOLD DC PRICING DUE TO SCARCITY
*PEWTER: .5X TO 1.2X BLUE
PEWTER PRINT RUN 125 SERIAL #'d SETS
PEWTER DC PRINT RUN 13 SER.#'d SETS
NO PEWTER DC PRICING DUE TO SCARCITY
*PLATINUM p/r 37-47: 1.25X TO 3X BLUE
*PLATINUM p/r 25-33: 1.5X TO 4X BLUE
*PLATINUM p/r 16-18: 2X TO 5X BLUE
PLAT.PRINT RUNS B/WN 2-47 COPIES PER
NO PLAT.PRICING ON QTY OF 14 OR LESS
PLATINUM DC PRINT RUN 1 SERIAL #'d SET
NO PLAT.DC PRICING DUE TO SCARCITY
PURPLE PRINT RUN 1 SERIAL #'d SET
NO PURPLE PRICING DUE TO SCARCITY
*RED: .4X TO 1X BLUE
RED PRINT RUN 175 SERIAL #'d SETS
*RED DC: 1.25X TO 3X BLUE
RED DC PRINT RUN 18 SERIAL #'d SETS
*SILVER: 1.25X TO 3X BLUE
SILVER PRINT RUN 50 SERIAL #'d SETS
SILVER DC PRINT RUN 5 SERIAL #'d SETS
NO SILVER DC PRICING DUE TO SCARCITY
OVERALL GU ODDS 3 PER HOBBY PACK
AP Albert Pujols 15.00 4.50
AR Alex Rodriguez 15.00 4.50
BL Barry Larkin 8.00 2.40
BW Brandon Webb 5.00 1.50
CJ Chipper Jones 8.00 2.40
CS Curt Schilling 8.00 2.40
DJ Derek Jeter 15.00 4.50
FT Frank Thomas 8.00 2.40
GM Greg Maddux 12.00 3.60
HB Hank Blalock 5.00 1.50
HN Hideo Nomo 8.00 2.40
JEB Jeff Bagwell 8.00 2.40
JG Jason Giambi 5.00 1.50
JOB Josh Beckett 5.00 1.50
JT Jim Thome 8.00 2.40
KW Kerry Wood 8.00 2.40
MAP Mark Prior 8.00 2.40
MIP Mike Piazza 12.00 3.60
MM Mike Mussina 8.00 2.40
MR Manny Ramirez 8.00 2.40
MT Mark Teixeira 5.00 1.50
NG Nomar Garciaparra 12.00 3.60
PM Pedro Martinez 8.00 2.40
RB Rocco Baldelli 5.00 1.50
RJ Randy Johnson 8.00 2.40
SS Sammy Sosa 12.00 3.60
TH Todd Helton 8.00 2.40
TOG Tom Glavine 8.00 2.40
TRG Troy Glaus 5.00 1.50
VG Vladimir Guerrero 8.00 2.40

2004 Flair Lettermen

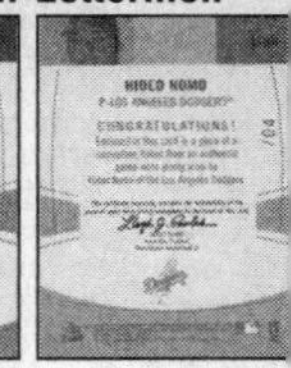

Nm-Mt Ex-Mt
OVERALL GU ODDS 3 PER HOBBY PACK
PRINT RUNS B/WN 4-11 COPIES PER
NO PRICING DUE TO SCARCITY
AP Albert Pujols/6
AR Alex Rodriguez/9
DW Dontrelle Willis/5
HB Hank Blalock/7
HN Hideo Nomo/4
JB Josh Beckett/7
JT Jim Thome/5
MP Mark Prior/5
MT Mark Teixeira/8
NG Nomar Garciaparra/11
PM Pedro Martinez/8
RB Rocco Baldelli/8
SS Sammy Sosa/4
TH Torii Hunter/6
VG Vladimir Guerrero/8

2004 Flair Power Tools Game Used Blue

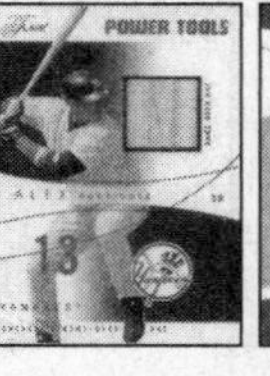
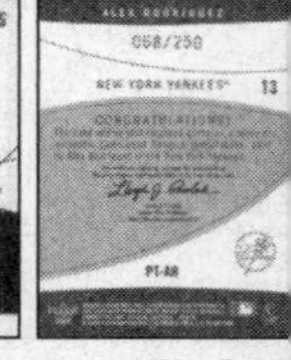

Nm-Mt Ex-Mt
STATED PRINT RUN 250 SERIAL #'d SETS
*BLUE DC: 1X TO 2.5X BLUE
BLUE DC PRINT RUN 25 SERIAL #'d SETS
*COPPER: .75X TO 2X BLUE
COPPER PRINT RUN 75 SERIAL #'d SETS
COPPER DC PRINT RUN 8 SERIAL #'d SETS
NO COPPER DC PRICING DUE TO SCARCITY
*GOLD p/r 44: 1.5X TO 4X BLUE
*GOLD p/r 20-31: 2X TO 5X BLUE
GOLD PRINT RUNS B/WN 2-44 COPIES PER
NO GOLD PRICING ON QTY OF 13 OR LESS
GOLD DC PRINT RUN 3 SERIAL #'d SETS
NO GOLD DC PRICING DUE TO SCARCITY
*PEWTER: .75X TO 2X BLUE
PEWTER PRINT RUN 125 SERIAL #'d SETS
PEWTER DC 13 SERIAL #'d SETS
NO PEWTER DC PRICING DUE TO SCARCITY
*PLATINUM p/r 37-47: 1.5X TO 4X BLUE
*PLATINUM p/r 25-30: 2X TO 5X BLUE
PLAT.PRINT RUN B/WN 10-47 COPIES PER
NO PLAT.PRICING ON QTY OF 11 OR LESS
PLATINUM DC PRINT RUN 1 SERIAL #'d SET
NO PLAT.DC PRICING DUE TO SCARCITY
PURPLE PRINT RUN 1 SERIAL #'d SET
NO PURPLE PRICING DUE TO SCARCITY
*RED: .4X TO 1X BLUE
RED PRINT RUN 175 SERIAL #'d SETS
*RED DC: 1.25X TO 3X BLUE
RED DC PRINT RUN 18 SERIAL #'d SETS
*SILVER: 1X TO 2.5X BLUE
SILVER PRINT RUN 50 SERIAL #'d SETS
SILVER DC PRINT RUN 5 SERIAL #'d SETS
NO SILVER DC PRICING DUE TO SCARCITY
OVERALL GU ODDS 3 PER HOBBY PACK
AD Adam Dunn 8.00 2.40
AP Albert Pujols 15.00 4.50
AR Alex Rodriguez 15.00 4.50
AS Alfonso Soriano 8.00 2.40
CJ Chipper Jones 8.00 2.40
DJ Derek Jeter 15.00 4.50
JG Jason Giambi 5.00 1.50
JP Jorge Posada 8.00 2.40
JT Jim Thome 8.00 2.40
MP Mike Piazza 12.00 3.60
MR Manny Ramirez 8.00 2.40
NG Nomar Garciaparra 12.00 3.60
RB Rocco Baldelli 5.00 1.50
SS Sammy Sosa 12.00 3.60
VG Vladimir Guerrero 8.00 2.40

2004 Flair Significant Cuts

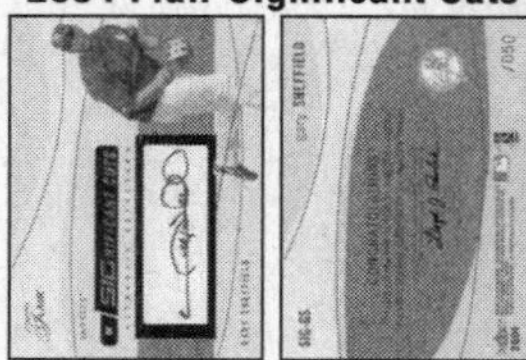

Nm-Mt Ex-Mt
OVERALL AU ODDS 1:1 HOBBY
PRINT RUNS B/WN 1-200 COPIES PER
NO PRICING ON QTY OF 10 OR LESS
AP1 Andy Pettitte/50 60.00 18.00
AP2 Albert Pujols/20
BL Barry Larkin/75 40.00 12.00
BR Babe Ruth/1
BT Bill Terry/3
CG Charlie Gehringer/2
CJ Chipper Jones/22
CR Cal Ripken/25 250.00 75.00
DE Dennis Eckersley/75 40.00 12.00
DM Don Mattingly/25 120.00 36.00

S Enos Slaughter/3
F Frankie Frisch/1
S Gary Sheffield/50 40.00 12.00
R Ivan Rodriguez/50 50.00 15.00
B1 Josh Beckett/10
B2 Johnny Bench/25 60.00 18.00
R Jose Reyes/25 30.00 9.00
S John Smoltz/75 60.00 18.00
MR Mariano Rivera/50 80.00 24.00
MS Mike Schmidt/25 150.00 45.00
MT Miguel Tejada/25 30.00 9.00
R Nolan Ryan/25 175.00 52.50
M Paul Molitor/75 40.00 12.00
A Roberto Alomar/50 40.00 12.00
H Roy Halladay/50 15.00 4.50
P Rafael Palmeiro/25 60.00 18.00
C Ty Cobb/3
C Vince Carter/200 50.00 15.00

2003 Flair Greats

his 133 card set was released in December, 002. These cards were issued in five card packs ith an SRP of $6. These cards were issued in 0 pack boxes which came 12 boxes to a case. ards numbered 96 through 133 were inserted our per special home team boxes which also ad 20 packs in a box but only had 4 boxes to a ase. A promo card of Al Kaline was also issued efore the product was issued and we have laced that card at the end of our set listings.

Nm-Mt Ex-Mt
OMP.SET w/o SP's (95) 40.00 12.00
OMMON CARD (1-95) 1.00 .30
OMMON CARD (96-133) 5.00 1.50
Ozzie Smith 4.00 1.20
Red Schoendienst 1.00 .30
Harmon Killebrew 2.50 .75
Ralph Kiner 1.00 .30
Johnny Bench 2.50 .75
Al Kaline 2.50 .75
Bobby Doerr 1.00 .30
Cal Ripken 8.00 2.40
Enos Slaughter 1.00 .30
0 Phil Rizzuto 1.50 .45
1 Luis Aparicio 1.00 .30
2 Pee Wee Reese 1.50 .45
3 Richie Ashburn 1.50 .45
4 Ernie Banks 2.50 .75
5 Earl Weaver 1.00 .30
6 Whitey Ford 1.50 .45
7 Brooks Robinson 1.50 .45
8 Lou Boudreau 1.00 .30
9 Robin Yount 4.00 1.20
0 Mike Schmidt 5.00 1.50
1 Bob Lemon 1.00 .30
2 Stan Musial 4.00 1.20
3 Joe Morgan 1.00 .30
4 Early Wynn 1.00 .30
5 Willie Stargell 1.50 .45
6 Yogi Berra 2.50 .75
7 Juan Marichal 1.00 .30
8 Rick Ferrell 1.00 .30
9 Rod Carew 1.50 .45
0 Jim Bunning 1.00 .30
1 Ferguson Jenkins 1.00 .30
2 Steve Carlton 1.00 .30
3 Larry Doby 1.00 .30
4 Nolan Ryan 6.00 1.80
5 Phil Niekro UER 1.00 .30
Career win total in blurb is wrong
6 Billy Williams 1.00 .30
7 Hal Newhouser 1.00 .30
8 Bob Feller 1.00 .30
9 Lou Brock 1.50 .45
0 Monte Irvin 1.00 .30
1 Eddie Mathews 2.50 .75
2 Rollie Fingers 1.00 .30
3 Gaylord Perry 1.00 .30
4 Reggie Jackson 1.50 .45
5 Bob Gibson 1.50 .45
6 Robin Roberts 1.50 .45
7 Tom Seaver 1.50 .45
8 Willie McCovey 1.00 .30
9 Hoyt Wilhelm 1.00 .30
0 George Kell 1.00 .30
1 Warren Spahn 1.50 .45
2 Catfish Hunter 1.50 .45
3 Dom DiMaggio 1.00 .30
4 Joe Medwick 1.00 .30
5 Johnny Pesky 1.00 .30
6 Steve Garvey 1.00 .30
7 Harry Heilmann 1.00 .30
8 Dave Winfield 1.00 .30
9 Andre Dawson 1.00 .30
0 Jimmie Foxx 2.50 .75
1 Buddy Bell 1.00 .30
2 Gabby Hartnett 1.00 .30
3 Babe Ruth 8.00 2.40
4 Dizzy Dean 1.50 .45
5 Hank Greenberg 2.50 .75
6 Don Drysdale 2.50 .75
7 Gary Carter 1.00 .30
8 Wade Boggs 1.50 .45
9 Tony Perez 1.00 .30
0 Mickey Cochrane 1.50 .45
1 Bill Dickey 1.50 .45
2 George Brett 6.00 1.80
3 Honus Wagner 2.50 .75
4 George Sisler 1.00 .30
5 Walter Johnson 2.50 .75
6 Ron Santo 1.50 .45
7 Roy Campanella 2.50 .75
8 Roger Maris 2.50 .75
9 Kirby Puckett 2.50 .75
0 Alan Trammell 1.00 .30
1 Don Mattingly 6.00 1.80
2 Ty Cobb 3.00 .90
83 Lou Gehrig 5.00 1.50
84 Jackie Robinson 2.50 .75
85 Billy Martin 1.50 .45
86 Paul Molitor 1.50 .45
87 Duke Snider 1.50 .45
88 Thurman Munson 2.50 .75
89 Luke Appling 1.00 .30
90 Ernie Lombardi 1.00 .30
91 Rube Waddell 1.00 .30
92 Travis Jackson 1.00 .30
93 Joe Sewell 1.00 .30
94 King Kelly 1.50 .45
95 Heinie Manush 1.00 .30
96 Bobby Doerr HT 5.00 1.50
97 Johnny Pesky HT 5.00 1.50
98 Wade Boggs HT 8.00 2.40
99 Tony Conigliaro HT 8.00 2.40
100 Carlton Fisk HT 8.00 2.40
101 Rico Petrocelli HT 5.00 1.50
102 Jim Rice HT 5.00 1.50
103 Al Lopez HT 5.00 1.50
104 Pee Wee Reese HT 8.00 2.40
105 Tommy Lasorda HT 5.00 1.50
106 Gil Hodges HT 8.00 2.40
107 Jackie Robinson HT 8.00 2.40
108 Duke Snider HT 8.00 2.40
109 Don Drysdale HT 8.00 2.40
110 Steve Garvey HT 5.00 1.50
111 Hoyt Wilhelm HT 5.00 1.50
112 Juan Marichal HT 5.00 1.50
113 Monte Irvin HT 5.00 1.50
114 Willie McCovey HT 5.00 1.50
115 Travis Jackson HT 5.00 1.50
116 Bobby Bonds HT 5.00 1.50
117 Orlando Cepeda HT 5.00 1.50
118 Whitey Ford HT 8.00 2.40
119 Phil Rizzuto HT 8.00 2.40
120 Reggie Jackson HT 8.00 2.40
121 Yogi Berra HT 8.00 2.40
122 Roger Maris HT 8.00 2.40
123 Don Mattingly HT 25.00 7.50
124 Babe Ruth HT 15.00 4.50
125 Dave Winfield HT 5.00 1.50
126 Bob Gibson HT 8.00 2.40
127 Enos Slaughter HT 5.00 1.50
128 Joe Medwick HT 5.00 1.50
129 Lou Brock HT 8.00 2.40
130 Ozzie Smith HT 10.00 3.00
131 Stan Musial HT 10.00 3.00
132 Steve Carlton HT 5.00 1.50
133 Dizzy Dean HT 8.00 2.40
P6 Al Kaline 2.00 .60
Promotional Sample

2003 Flair Greats Ballpark Heroes

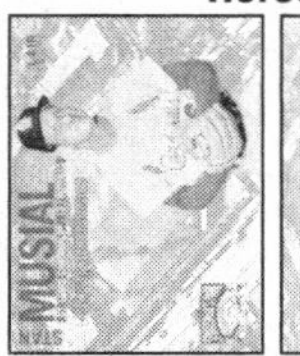

Issued at a stated rate of one in 10, these nine cards feature some of baseball's greatest players.

Nm-Mt Ex-Mt
1 Nolan Ryan 6.00 1.80
2 Babe Ruth 8.00 2.40
3 Honus Wagner 2.50 .75
4 Ty Cobb 4.00 1.20
5 Ernie Banks 2.50 .75
6 Mike Schmidt 5.00 1.50
7 Duke Snider 2.50 .75
8 Cal Ripken 8.00 2.40
9 Stan Musial 4.00 1.20

2003 Flair Greats Bat Rack Classics Quads

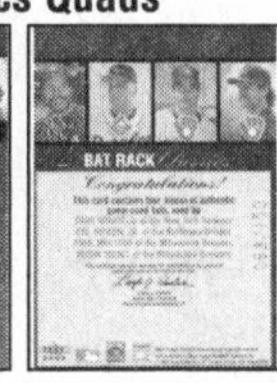

Randomly inserted into packs, these five cards feature game-used bat chips from four players all on the same card. These cards were issued to a stated print run of 150 serial numbered sets.

Nm-Mt Ex-Mt
1 Don Mattingly 120.00 36.00
Joe Morgan
Cal Ripken
Brooks Robinson
2 Eddie Murray 60.00 18.00
Eddie Mathews
Reggie Jackson
Willie McCovey
3 Tony Perez 80.00 24.00
Don Mattingly
Hank Greenberg
Willie Stargell
4 Ryne Sandberg 60.00 18.00
Ron Santo
Billy Williams
Andre Dawson
5 Dave Winfield 80.00 24.00
Cal Ripken
Paul Molitor
Robin Yount

2003 Flair Greats Bat Rack Classics Trios

Randomly inserted into packs, these five cards feature game-used bat chips from three players

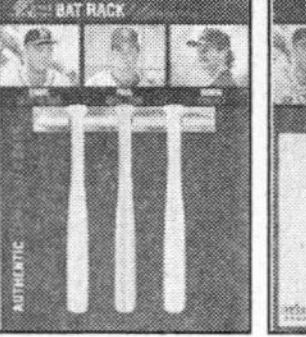
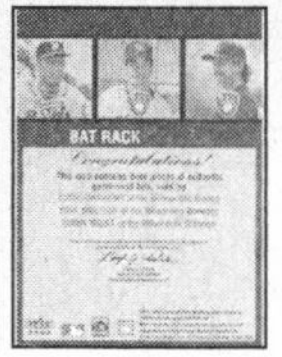

all on the same card. These cards were issued to a stated print run of 300 serial numbered sets.

Nm-Mt Ex-Mt
1 Tommy Agee 25.00 7.50
Jerry Grote
Bud Harrelson
2 Johnny Bench 40.00 12.00
Joe Morgan
Tony Perez
3 Hank Greenberg 50.00 15.00
Harry Heilman
George Kell
4 Reggie Jackson 50.00 15.00
Don Mattingly
Dave Winfield
5 Eddie Mathews 50.00 15.00
Paul Molitor
Robin Yount
6 Eddie Murray 80.00 24.00
Cal Ripken
Brooks Robinson
7 Dave Parker 25.00 7.50
Willie Stargell
8 Ryne Sandberg 50.00 15.00
Ron Santo
Billy Williams

2003 Flair Greats Classic Numbers

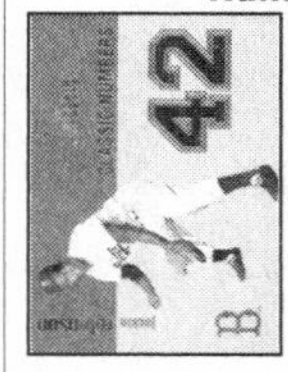

Inserted into packs at a stated rate of one in 20, these 13 cards feature some of the most famous uniform numbers ever.

Nm-Mt Ex-Mt
1 Jackie Robinson 6.00 1.80
2 Willie McCovey 4.00 1.20
3 Brooks Robinson 4.00 1.20
4 Reggie Jackson 4.00 1.20
5 Ozzie Smith 10.00 3.00
6 Johnny Bench 6.00 1.80
7 Yogi Berra 6.00 1.80
8 Cal Ripken 20.00 6.00
9 George Brett 15.00 4.50
10 Thurman Munson 6.00 1.80
11 Joe Morgan 4.00 1.20
12 Nolan Ryan 15.00 4.50
13 Steve Carlton 4.00 1.20

2003 Flair Greats Classic Numbers Game Used

Inserted at stated odds of one in 24 hobby packs and one in 27 home team packs, these 11 cards feature game-worn material from 11 of the players from the Classic Numbers set. A few players were issued in shorter supply and we have notated that information along with their announced print run information next to the player's name in our checklist.

Nm-Mt Ex-Mt
PATCH RANDOM INSERTS IN PACKS.
PATCH PRINT RUN 25 SERIAL #'d SETS
NO PATCH PRICING DUE TO SCARCITY
1 Johnny Bench Jsy 20.00 6.00
2 Yogi Berra Pants SP/75 25.00 7.50
3 George Brett Jsy 25.00 7.50
4 Steve Carlton Jsy 20.00 6.00
5 Willie McCovey Jsy SP/125 15.00 4.50
6 Joe Morgan Pants SP/200 15.00 4.50
7 Thurman Munson Pants 30.00 9.00
8 Cal Ripken Jsy 30.00 9.00
9 Nolan Ryan Jsy 50.00 15.00
10 Ryne Sandberg Jsy 25.00 7.50
11 Ozzie Smith Jsy 20.00 6.00

2003 Flair Greats Classic Numbers Game Used Dual

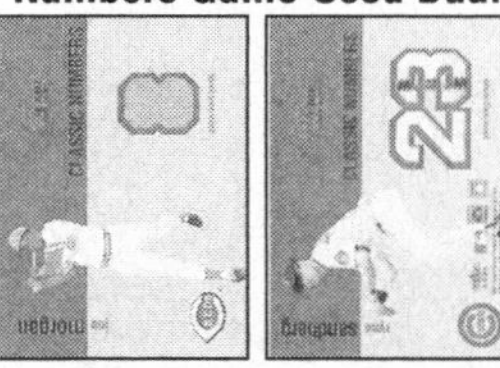

Randomly inserted into packs, these eight cards feature two players along with game-worn swatches of each of these players. Each of these cards was issued to a stated print run of 250 serial numbered sets.

Nm-Mt Ex-Mt
1 Johnny Bench Jsy 40.00 12.00
Thurman Munson Pants
2 Yogi Berra Pants 40.00 12.00
Thurman Munson Pants
3 Yogi Berra Pants 60.00 18.00
Cal Ripken Jsy
4 George Brett Jsy 80.00 24.00
Nolan Ryan Jsy
5 Willie McCovey Jsy 25.00 7.50
Johnny Bench Jsy
6 Joe Morgan Pants 40.00 12.00
Ryne Sandberg Jsy
7 Cal Ripken Pants 60.00 18.00
Ozzie Smith Jsy
8 Nolan Ryan Jsy 60.00 18.00
Steve Carlton Jsy

2003 Flair Greats Cut of History Autographs

Randomly inserted into packs, these cards feature authentic autographs of the featured player. These cards were issued to different print runs and we have notated that information in our checklist.

Nm-Mt Ex-Mt
1 Johnny Bench/161 60.00 18.00
2 Steve Carlton/506 25.00 7.50
3 Dom DiMaggio/402 50.00 15.00
4 Tony Kubek/161 50.00 15.00
5 Cal Ripken/155 175.00 52.50
6 Alan Trammell/211 25.00 7.50

2003 Flair Greats Cut of History Game Used

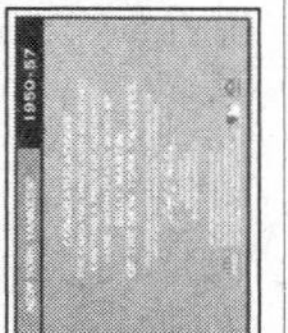

Issued at a stated rate of one in ten packs, these 27 cards feature game-used pieces of 27 of baseball's all time greats. A few players were issued in smaller quantity and we have notated that information along with their stated print run next to their name in our checklist.

Nm-Mt Ex-Mt
1 Luis Aparicio Jsy 8.00 2.40
2 Frank Baker Bat SP/50 50.00 15.00
3 Buddy Bell Bat 8.00 2.40
4 Wade Boggs Jsy SP/250 20.00 6.00
5 Steve Carlton Pants 8.00 2.40
6 Gary Carter Jsy 8.00 2.40
7 Dennis Eckersley Jsy 8.00 2.40
8 Hank Greenberg Bat SP/100 50.00 15.00
9 Catfish Hunter Jsy SP/200 20.00 6.00
10 Reggie Jackson Bat 10.00 3.00
11 Ferguson Jenkins Pants 8.00 2.40
12 Roger Maris Jsy SP/250 60.00 18.00
13 Billy Martin Pants 10.00 3.00
14 Willie McCovey Pants 8.00 2.40
15 Joe Medwick Bat 20.00 6.00
16 Eddie Murray Jsy 10.00 3.00
17 Graig Nettles Bat 8.00 2.40
18 Phil Niekro Pants 8.00 2.40
19 Paul O'Neill Jsy 10.00 3.00
20 Jim Palmer Pants 8.00 2.40
21 Kirby Puckett Bat 10.00 3.00
22 Cal Ripken Pants 25.00 7.50
23 Tom Seaver Pants 10.00 3.00
24A Alan Trammell Bat 8.00 2.40
24B Alan Trammell Jsy 8.00 2.40
25 Hoyt Wilhelm Jsy 8.00 2.40
26 Early Wynn Jsy 8.00 2.40

2003 Flair Greats Cut of History Game Used Gold

This set parallels the Cut of History Game Used set. Each of these cards were issued to a stated print run of 100 serial numbered sets.

Nm-Mt Ex-Mt
*GOLD: .75X TO 2X BASIC
*GOLD: .5X TO 1.2X BASIC SP'S

2003 Flair Greats of the Grain

Randomly inserted into packs, these nine cards feature all-time greats laser etched on to a wood swatch. These cards were issued to a stated print run of 50 serial numbered sets. Please note that these cards do not contain game-used wood on them.

Nm-Mt Ex-Mt
1 George Brett 150.00 45.00
2 Ty Cobb 100.00 30.00
3 Lou Gehrig 80.00 24.00
4 Eddie Mathews 80.00 24.00
5 Don Mattingly 150.00 45.00
6 Stan Musial 100.00 30.00
7 Cal Ripken 120.00 36.00
8 Babe Ruth 120.00 36.00
9 Mike Schmidt 100.00 30.00

2003 Flair Greats Hall of Fame Postmark

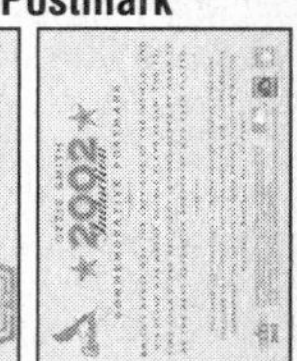

Randomly inserted into packs, these cards honor the day that Ozzie Smith was inducted into the Hall of Fame. Some of these cards were autographed and we have noted the print run for both of these cards in our checklist.

Nm-Mt Ex-Mt
1 Ozzie Smith/2002 25.00 7.50
2 Ozzie Smith AU/202 100.00 30.00

2003 Flair Greats Home Team Cuts Game Used

These cards were issued at an overall rate of one in 20 for both single or dual game used cards in the home team boxes. A few cards were issued in smaller quantities than the others and we have notated that information in our checklist.

Nm-Mt Ex-Mt
1 Wade Boggs Jsy SP/250 20.00 6.00
2 Bobby Bonds Bat 10.00 3.00
3 Carlton Fisk Jsy 15.00 4.50
4 Steve Garvey Jsy 10.00 3.00
5 Reggie Jackson Bat 15.00 4.50
6 Tom Lasorda Jsy SP/150 15.00 4.50
7 Juan Marichal Pants 10.00 3.00
8 Roger Maris Jsy SP/150 80.00 24.00
9 Billy Martin Pants 15.00 4.50
10 Willie McCovey Pants SP/200 15.00 4.50
11 Joe Medwick Bat SP/250 25.00 7.50
12 P.Reese Pants SP/75 20.00 6.00
13 Jim Rice Bat 10.00 3.00
14 R.Schoendienst Pants SP/200 15.00 4.50
15 Ozzie Smith Bat 20.00 6.00
16 Duke Snider Pants 15.00 4.50
17 Dave Winfield Bat 10.00 3.00

2003 Flair Greats Home Team Cuts Game Used Dual

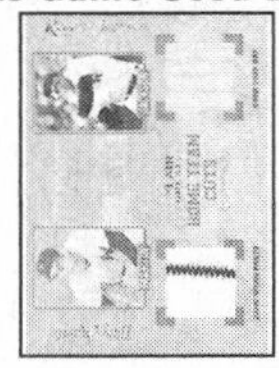

These cards were issued at an overall rate of one in 20 for both single or dual game used cards in the home team boxes. A few cards were issued in smaller quantities than the others and we have notated that information in our checklist.

Nm-Mt Ex-Mt
1 Bobby Bonds Bat 40.00 12.00
Willie McCovey Pants/100
2 Carlton Fisk Jsy 30.00 9.00
Jim Rice Bat/100
3 Billy Martin Pants 30.00 9.00
Reggie Jackson Bat/175
4 Pee Wee Reese Pants 30.00 9.00
Duke Snider Pants/100
5 Red Schoendienst Pants 25.00 7.50
Joe Medwick Bat/125

2003 Flair Greats Sweet Swatch Classic Bat

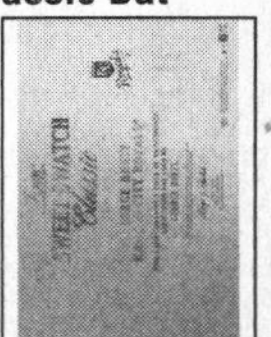

Randomly inserted into jumbo packs, these 12 cards feature game-used bat pieces of the featured players. Each player was issued to a different print run and we have notated that information in our checklist.

	Nm-Mt	Ex-Mt
1 Johnny Bench/175	25.00	7.50
2 George Brett/320	40.00	12.00
3 Jose Canseco/175	25.00	7.50
4 Orlando Cepeda/165	20.00	6.00
5 Andre Dawson/310	15.00	4.50
6 Reggie Jackson/155	25.00	7.50
7 Eddie Mathews/185	25.00	7.50
8 Don Mattingly/340	50.00	15.00
9 Willie McCovey/155	20.00	6.00
10 Kirby Puckett/165	25.00	7.50
11 Pee Wee Reese/165	25.00	7.50
12 Cal Ripken/305	50.00	15.00

2003 Flair Greats Sweet Swatch Classic Bat Image

These four cards partially parallel the sweet swatch classic bat insert set. Each of these cards were issued to a stated print run of less than 50 copies.

	Nm-Mt	Ex-Mt
1 Johnny Bench/36	80.00	24.00
2 Tony Kubek/35	60.00	18.00
3 Cal Ripken/42	150.00	45.00
4 Alan Trammell/44	60.00	18.00

2003 Flair Greats Sweet Swatch Classic Bat Image Autographs

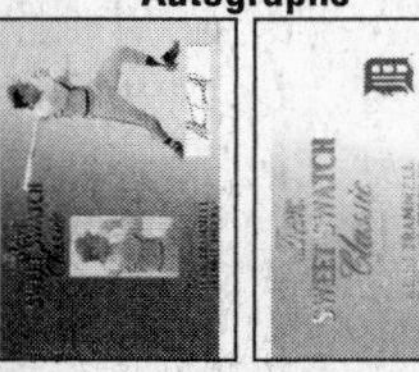

These four cards partially parallel the sweet swatch classic bat insert image set along with the player's autograph. Each of these cards were issued to a stated print run of 40 serial numbered sets.

	Nm-Mt	Ex-Mt
1 Johnny Bench	120.00	36.00
2 Tony Kubek	100.00	30.00
3 Cal Ripken	250.00	75.00
4 Alan Trammell	80.00	24.00

2003 Flair Greats Sweet Swatch Classic Jersey

Randomly inserted into jumbo packs, these 72 cards feature game-used jersey swatches of the featured players. Each player was issued to a different print run and we have notated that information in our checklist.

	Nm-Mt	Ex-Mt
1 Johnny Bench Jsy/410	20.00	6.00
2 George Brett Jsy/384	40.00	12.00
3 Jose Canseco Jsy/1329	15.00	4.50
4 Jerry Coleman Jsy/528	20.00	6.00
5 Andre Dawson Jsy/335	20.00	6.00
6 Carlton Fisk Jsy/1200	15.00	4.50
7 Gil Hodges Jsy/545	20.00	6.00
8 Juan Marichal Jsy/385	20.00	6.00
9 Don Mattingly Jsy/880	40.00	12.00
10 Paul Molitor Jsy/592	20.00	6.00
11 Jim Palmer Jsy/335	20.00	6.00
12 Kirby Puckett Jsy/445	20.00	6.00
13 Cal Ripken Jsy/557	40.00	12.00
14 Nolan Ryan Jsy/590	50.00	15.00
15 Ryne Sandberg Jsy/374	30.00	9.00
17 Robin Yount Jsy/340	25.00	7.50
19 Tom Seaver Jsy/385	20.00	6.00

2003 Flair Greats Sweet Swatch Classic Patch

This 16 card set partially parallels the sweet swatch classic jersey set. Each of these cards feature a game-used patch piece and we have notated the stated print run in our checklist.

	Nm-Mt	Ex-Mt
PATCH MASTERPIECE PRINT RUN 1 #'d SET		
NO PATCH MP PRICING DUE TO SCARCITY		
1 Johnny Bench/59	80.00	24.00
2 George Brett/53	150.00	45.00
3 Jose Canseco/177	60.00	18.00
4 Jerry Coleman/37	50.00	15.00
5 Andre Dawson/58	50.00	15.00
6 Carlton Fisk/51	80.00	24.00
7 Juan Marichal/48	50.00	15.00
8 Don Mattingly/106	150.00	45.00
9 Paul Molitor/96	60.00	18.00
10 Jim Palmer/63	60.00	18.00
11 Kirby Puckett/72	80.00	24.00
12 Cal Ripken/69	150.00	45.00
13 Nolan Ryan/60	150.00	45.00
14 Ryne Sandberg/40	150.00	45.00
15 Tom Seaver/66	60.00	18.00
16 Robin Yount/66	100.00	30.00

1997 Flair Showcase Row 2

The 1997 Flair Showcase set (produced by Fleer) was issued in one series totalling 540 cards and was distributed in five-card packs with a suggested retail price of $4.99. Three groups of 60 cards were inserted at different rates: Cards numbered from one through 60 were inserted 1.5 cards per pack, cards numbered from 61 through 120 were inserted one every 1.5 packs and cards numbered from 61 through 120 were inserted at a rate of one per pack. This hobby exclusive set is divided into three 180-card sets (Row 2/Style, Row 1/Grace, and Row 0/Showcase) and features holographic foil fronts with an action photo of the player silhouetted over a larger black-and-white head-shot image in the background. The thick card stock is laminated with a shiny glossy coating for a super-premium "feel." Also inserted one in every pack was a Million Dollar Moments card. Rookie Cards include Brian Giles. Finally, 25 serial-numbered Alex Rodriguez Emerald Exchange cards (good for a signed Rodriguez glove) were randomly seeded into packs. The card fronts were very similar in design to the regular Row 2 Rodriguez, except for green foil accents. The card back, however, consisted entirely of text explaining prize guidelines. The deadline to exchange the card was 8/1/98.

	Nm-Mt	Ex-Mt
COMPLETE SET (180)	80.00	24.00
COMMON CARD (1-60)	.50	.15
ROW 2 1-60 ODDS 1.5:1		
COMMON (61-120)	.75	.23
ROW 2 61-120 ODDS 1:1.5		
COMMON (121-180)	.60	.18
ROW 2 121-180 STATED ODDS 1:1		
A.ROD GLOVE EXCH RANDOM IN PACKS		
A.ROD GLOVE EXCH.DEADLINE: 8/1/98		
1 Andruw Jones	.50	.15
2 Derek Jeter	3.00	.90
3 Alex Rodriguez	2.00	.60
4 Paul Molitor	.75	.23
5 Jeff Bagwell	.75	.23
6 Scott Rolen	1.25	.35
7 Kenny Lofton	.50	.15
8 Cal Ripken	4.00	1.20
9 Brady Anderson	.50	.15
10 Chipper Jones	1.25	.35
11 Todd Greene	.50	.15
12 Todd Walker	.50	.15
13 Billy Wagner	.50	.15
14 Craig Biggio	.75	.23
15 Kevin Orie	.50	.15
16 Hideo Nomo	1.25	.35
17 Kevin Appier	.50	.15
18 B.Trammell RC	.50	.15
19 Juan Gonzalez	.75	.23
20 Randy Johnson	1.25	.35
21 Roger Clemens	2.50	.75
22 Johnny Damon	.75	.23
23 Ryne Sandberg	2.00	.60
24 Ken Griffey Jr.	2.00	.60
25 Barry Bonds	3.00	.90
26 Nomar Garciaparra	2.00	.60
27 Vladimir Guerrero	1.25	.35
28 Ron Gant	.50	.15
29 Joe Carter	.50	.15
30 Tim Salmon	.75	.23
31 Mike Piazza	2.00	.60
32 Barry Larkin	.75	.23
33 Manny Ramirez	.75	.23
34 Sammy Sosa	2.00	.60
35 Frank Thomas	1.25	.35
36 Melvin Nieves	.50	.15
37 Tony Gwynn	1.50	.45
38 Gary Sheffield	.50	.15
39 Darin Erstad	.50	.15
40 Ken Caminiti	.50	.15
41 Jermaine Dye	.50	.15
42 Mo Vaughn	.50	.15
43 Raul Mondesi	.50	.15
44 Greg Maddux	2.00	.60
45 Chuck Knoblauch	.50	.15
46 Andy Pettitte	.75	.23
47 Deion Sanders	.75	.23
48 Albert Belle	.50	.15
49 Jamey Wright	.50	.15
50 Rey Ordonez	.50	.15
51 Bernie Williams	.75	.23
52 Mark McGwire	3.00	.90
53 Mike Mussina	.75	.23
54 Bob Abreu	.50	.15
55 Reggie Sanders	.50	.15
56 Brian Jordan	.50	.15
57 Ivan Rodriguez	1.25	.35
58 Roberto Alomar	.75	.23
59 Tim Naehring	.50	.15
60 Edgar Renteria	.50	.15
61 Dean Palmer	.75	.23
62 Benito Santiago	.75	.23
63 David Cone	.75	.23
64 Carlos Delgado	.75	.23
65 Brian Giles RC	2.00	.60
66 Alex Ochoa	.75	.23
67 Rondell White	.75	.23
68 Robin Ventura	.75	.23
69 Eric Karros	.75	.23
70 Jose Valentin	.75	.23
71 Rafael Palmeiro	1.25	.35
72 Chris Snopek	.75	.23
73 David Justice	.75	.23
74 Tom Glavine	1.25	.35
75 Rudy Pemberton	.75	.23
76 Larry Walker	1.25	.35
77 Jim Thome	2.00	.60
78 Charles Johnson	.75	.23
79 Dante Powell	.75	.23
80 Derrek Lee	.75	.23
81 Jason Kendall	.75	.23
82 Todd Hollandsworth	.75	.23
83 Bernard Gilkey	.75	.23
84 Mel Rojas	.75	.23
85 Dmitri Young	.75	.23
86 Bret Boone	.75	.23
87 Pat Hentgen	.75	.23
88 Bobby Bonilla	.75	.23
89 John Wetteland	.75	.23
90 Todd Hundley	.75	.23
91 Wilton Guerrero	.75	.23
92 Geronimo Berroa	.75	.23
93 Al Martin	.75	.23
94 Danny Tartabull	.75	.23
95 Brian McRae	.75	.23
96 Steve Finley	.75	.23
97 Todd Stottlemyre	.75	.23
98 John Smoltz	1.25	.35
99 Matt Williams	.75	.23
100 Eddie Murray	2.00	.60
101 Henry Rodriguez	.75	.23
102 Marty Cordova	.75	.23
103 Juan Guzman	.75	.23
104 Chili Davis	.75	.23
105 Eric Young	.75	.23
106 Jeff Abbott	.75	.23
107 Shannon Stewart	.75	.23
108 Rocky Coppinger	.75	.23
109 Jose Canseco	2.00	.60
110 Dante Bichette	.75	.23
111 Dwight Gooden	.75	.23
112 Scott Brosius	.75	.23
113 Steve Avery	.75	.23
114 Andres Galarraga	.75	.23
115 Sandy Alomar Jr.	.75	.23
116 Ray Lankford	.75	.23
117 Jorge Posada	1.25	.35
118 Ryan Klesko	.75	.23
119 Jay Buhner	.75	.23
120 Jose Guillen	.75	.23
121 Paul O'Neill	1.00	.30
122 Jimmy Key	.60	.18
123 Hal Morris	.60	.18
124 Travis Fryman	.60	.18
125 Jim Edmonds	.60	.18
126 Jeff Cirillo	.60	.18
127 Fred McGriff	1.00	.30
128 Alan Benes	.60	.18
129 Derek Bell	.60	.18
130 Tony Graffanino	.60	.18
131 Shawn Green	.60	.18
132 Denny Neagle	.60	.18
133 Alex Fernandez	.60	.18
134 Mickey Morandini	.60	.18
135 Royce Clayton	.60	.18
136 Jose Mesa	.60	.18
137 Edgar Martinez	1.00	.30
138 Curt Schilling	.60	.18
139 Lance Johnson	.60	.18
140 Andy Benes	.60	.18
141 Charles Nagy	.60	.18
142 Mariano Rivera	1.00	.30
143 Mark Wohlers	.60	.18
144 Ken Hill	.60	.18
145 Jay Bell	.60	.18
146 Bob Higginson	.60	.18
147 Mark Grudzielanek	.60	.18
148 Ray Durham	.60	.18
149 John Olerud	.60	.18
150 Joey Hamilton	.60	.18
151 Trevor Hoffman	.60	.18
152 Dan Wilson	.60	.18
153 J.T. Snow	.60	.18
154 Marquis Grissom	.60	.18
155 Yamil Benitez	.60	.18
156 Rusty Greer	.60	.18
157 Darryl Kile	.60	.18
158 Ismael Valdes	.60	.18
159 Jeff Conine	.60	.18
160 Darren Daulton	.60	.18
161 Chan Ho Park	.60	.18
162 Troy Percival	.60	.18
163 Wade Boggs	1.00	.30
164 Dave Nilsson	.60	.18
165 Vinny Castilla	.60	.18
166 Kevin Brown	.60	.18
167 Dennis Eckersley	.60	.18
168 Wendell Magee Jr.	.60	.18
169 John Jaha	.60	.18
170 Garret Anderson	.60	.18
171 Jason Giambi	.60	.18
172 Mark Grace	1.00	.30
173 Tony Clark	.60	.18
174 Moises Alou	.60	.18
175 Brett Butler	.60	.18
176 Cecil Fielder	.60	.18
177 Chris Widger	.60	.18
178 Doug Drabek	.60	.18
179 Ellis Burks	.60	.18
180 S. Hasegawa RC	1.50	.45
NNO Alex Rodriguez Glove EXCH/25	2.00	.60

1997 Flair Showcase Row 1

Randomly inserted in packs at various rates: Cards number 1 through 60 at a rate of one in 2.5 packs, cards numbered 61 through 120 at one every two packs and cards numbered from 121 through 180 at a rate of one every three packs. This 180-card Grace set is parallel to the base Flair Showcase Row 2 (Style) set and features holographic foil fronts with an action photo of the player silhouetted over a larger color head-shot image in the background.

	Nm-Mt	Ex-Mt
*STARS 1-60: .75X TO 2X ROW 2		
*STARS 61-120: .4X TO 1X ROW 2		
*ROOKIES 61-120: .5X TO 1.25X ROW 2		
*ROOKIES 61-120: .5X TO 1.25X ROW 2		

1997 Flair Showcase Row 0

Randomly inserted in various rates depending on the card number: Cards numbered one through 60 were inserted one every 24 packs, cards numbered 61 through 120 at a rate of one per 12 and cards numbered 121 through 180 at a rate of one every five packs. This 180-card Showcase set is parallel to the base Flair Showcase Row 2 (Style) set and features holographic foil fronts with a head-shot image of the player silhouetted over a larger player action-shot in the background.

	Nm-Mt	Ex-Mt
*STARS 1-60: 4X TO 10X ROW 2		
*STARS 61-120: 1.25X TO 3X ROW 2		
*ROOKIES 61-120: 1.5X TO 4X ROW 2		
*STARS 121-180: 1X TO 2.5X ROW 2		

1997 Flair Showcase Legacy Collection Row 2

Randomly inserted in packs at a rate of one in 30 (cumulatively between all three rows of Legacy), this 180-card set is parallel to the regular set. Only 100 sequentially numbered sets were produced, each featuring an "alternate" player photo printed on a matte finish/foil stamped card.

	Nm-Mt	Ex-Mt
*LC ROW 2 1-60: 20X TO 50X BASIC		
*LC ROW 2 61-120: 12.5X TO 30X BASIC		
*LC ROW 2 RC'S 61-120: 10X TO 25X BASIC		
*LC ROW 2 121-180: 15X TO 40X BASIC		

1997 Flair Showcase Legacy Collection Row 1

Randomly inserted in packs at a rate of one in 30 (cumulatively between all three rows of Legacy), this 180-card set is parallel to the regular set. Only 100 sequentially numbered sets were produced, each featuring an "alternate" player photo printed on a matte finish/foil stamped card.

	Nm-Mt	Ex-Mt
*LC ROW 1 1-60: 20X TO 50X BASIC		
*LC ROW 1 61-120: 12.5X TO 30X BASIC		
*LC ROW 1 RC'S 61-120: 10X TO 25X BASIC		
*LC ROW 1 121-180: 15X TO 40X BASIC		

1997 Flair Showcase Legacy Collection Row 0

Randomly inserted in packs at a rate of one in 30 (cumulatively between all three rows of Legacy), this 180-card set is parallel to the regular set. Only 100 sequentially numbered sets were produced, each featuring an "alternate" player photo printed on a matte finish/foil stamped card.

	Nm-Mt	Ex-Mt
*LC ROW 0 1-60: 20X TO 50X BASIC		
*LC ROW 0 61-120: 12.5X TO 30X BASIC		
*LC ROW 0 RC'S 61-120: 10X TO 25X BASIC		
*LC ROW 0 121-180: 15X TO 40X BASIC		

1997 Flair Showcase Diamond Cuts

Randomly inserted in packs at a rate of one in 20, this 20-card set features color images of baseball's brightest stars silhouetted on a holo-foil-stamped die-cut diamond-design background.

	Nm-Mt	Ex-Mt
COMPLETE SET (20)	150.00	45.00
1 Jeff Bagwell	4.00	1.20
2 Albert Belle	2.50	.75
3 Ken Caminiti	2.50	.75
4 Juan Gonzalez	4.00	1.20
5 Ken Griffey Jr.	10.00	3.00
6 Tony Gwynn	8.00	2.40
7 Todd Hundley	4.00	1.20
8 Andruw Jones	2.50	.75
9 Chipper Jones	6.00	1.80
10 Greg Maddux	10.00	3.00
11 Mark McGwire	15.00	4.50
12 Mike Piazza	10.00	3.00
13 Derek Jeter	15.00	4.50
14 Manny Ramirez	4.00	1.20
15 Cal Ripken	20.00	6.00
16 Alex Rodriguez	10.00	3.00
17 Frank Thomas	6.00	1.80
18 Mo Vaughn	2.50	.75
19 Bernie Williams	4.00	1.20
20 Matt Williams	4.00	1.20

1997 Flair Showcase Hot Gloves

Randomly inserted in packs at a rate of one in 90, this 15-card set features color images of baseball's top glovemen silhouetted against a die-cut flame and glove background with temperature-sensitive inks.

	Nm-Mt	Ex-Mt
1 Roberto Alomar	12.00	3.60
2 Barry Bonds	50.00	15.00
3 Juan Gonzalez	12.00	3.60
4 Ken Griffey Jr.	30.00	9.00
5 Marquis Grissom	10.00	3.00
6 Derek Jeter	50.00	15.00
7 Chipper Jones	20.00	6.00
8 Barry Larkin	12.00	3.60
9 Kenny Lofton	8.00	2.40
10 Greg Maddux	30.00	9.00
11 Mike Piazza	30.00	9.00
12 Cal Ripken	60.00	18.00
13 Alex Rodriguez	30.00	9.00
14 Ivan Rodriguez	20.00	6.00
15 Frank Thomas	20.00	6.00

1997 Flair Showcase Wave of the Future

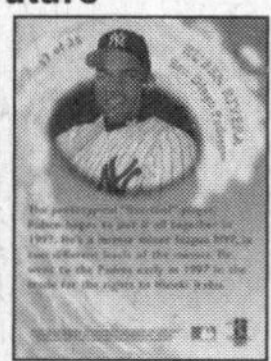

Randomly inserted in packs at a rate of one in four, this 27-card set features color images of top rookies silhouetted against a background of an embossed wave design with simulated sand.

	Nm-Mt	Ex-Mt
COMPLETE SET (27)	40.00	12.00
STATED ODDS 1:4		
1 Todd Greene	1.00	.30
2 Andruw Jones	1.50	.45
3 Randall Simon	1.50	.45
4 Wady Almonte	1.00	.30
5 Pat Cline	1.00	.30
6 Jeff Abbott	1.00	.30
7 Justin Towle	1.00	.30
8 Richie Sexson	1.50	.45
9 Bubba Trammell	1.50	.45
10 Bob Abreu	1.50	.45
11 David Arias-Ortiz	10.00	3.00
12 Todd Walker	1.00	.30
13 Orlando Cabrera	3.00	1.20
14 Vladimir Guerrero	3.00	.90
15 Ricky Ledee	1.50	.45
16 Jorge Posada	2.00	.60
17 Ruben Rivera	1.00	.30
18 Scott Spiezio	1.00	.30
19 Scott Rolen	3.00	.90
20 Emil Brown	1.00	.30
21 Jose Guillen	1.50	.45
22 T.J. Staton	1.00	.30
23 Eli Marrero	1.00	.30
24 Fernando Tatis	1.50	.45
25 Ryan Jones	1.00	.30
WF1 Hideki Irabu	1.50	.45
WF2 Jose Cruz Jr.	2.00	.60

1998 Flair Showcase Row 3

This set (produced by Fleer) was issued in fiv card packs which retailed for $4.99 per pack an were released in July, 1998. Each player was fea tured in four rows with Row 3 being the easies to obtain from opening packs. This 120 card se features two photos of the player on the fron The Row 3 cards were inserted in different ratio depending on which numbers they are. Th complete odds are listed below for each group c 30 cards. Cards numbered 1-30 were seede one every 9/10th of a pack; cards numbered 31 60 were seeded one every 1.1 packs; card numbered 61-90 were seeded one every 1. packs and cards 91-120 were seeded one ever two packs. Rookie Cards include Maggli Ordonez.

	Nm-Mt	Ex-Mt
COMPLETE SET (120)	60.00	18.00
COMMON CARD (1-30)	.50	.15
COMMON CARD (31-60)	.50	.15
COMMON CARD (61-90)	.60	.18
COMMON CARD (91-120)	.75	.23
1 Ken Griffey Jr.	2.00	.60
2 Travis Lee	.50	.15
3 Frank Thomas	1.25	.35
4 Ben Grieve	.50	.15
5 Nomar Garciaparra	2.00	.60
6 Jose Cruz Jr.	.50	.15
7 Alex Rodriguez	2.00	.60
8 Cal Ripken	4.00	1.20
9 Mark McGwire	3.00	.90
10 Chipper Jones	1.25	.35
11 Paul Konerko	.50	.15
12 Todd Helton	.75	.23
13 Greg Maddux	2.00	.60
14 Derek Jeter	3.00	.90
15 Jaret Wright	.50	.15
16 Livan Hernandez	.50	.15
17 Mike Piazza	2.00	.60
18 Juan Encarnacion	.50	.15
19 Tony Gwynn	1.50	.45
20 Scott Rolen	1.25	.35
21 Roger Clemens	2.50	.75
22 Tony Clark	.50	.15
23 Albert Belle	.50	.15
24 Mo Vaughn	.50	.15
25 Andruw Jones	.50	.15
26 Jason Dickson	.50	.15
27 Fernando Tatis	.50	.15
28 Ivan Rodriguez	1.25	.35
29 Ricky Ledee	.50	.15
30 Darin Erstad	.50	.15
31 Brian Rose	.50	.15
32 Magglio Ordonez RC	5.00	1.50
33 Larry Walker	.75	.23
34 Bobby Higginson	.50	.15
35 Chili Davis	.50	.15
36 Barry Bonds	3.00	.90
37 Vladimir Guerrero	1.25	.35
38 Jeff Bagwell	.75	.23
39 Kenny Lofton	.50	.15
40 Ryan Klesko	.50	.15
41 Mike Cameron	.50	.15
42 Charles Johnson	.50	.15
43 Andy Pettitte	.75	.23
44 Juan Gonzalez	.75	.23
45 Tim Salmon	.75	.23
46 Hideki Irabu	.50	.15
47 Paul Molitor	.75	.23
48 Edgar Renteria	.50	.15
49 Manny Ramirez	.75	.23
50 Jim Edmonds	.50	.15
51 Bernie Williams	.75	.23
52 Roberto Alomar	.75	.23
53 David Justice	.50	.15
54 Rey Ordonez	.50	.15
55 Ken Caminiti	.50	.15
56 Jose Guillen	.50	.15
57 Randy Johnson	1.25	.35
58 Brady Anderson	.50	.15
59 Hideo Nomo	1.25	.35
60 Tino Martinez	.75	.23
61 John Smoltz	1.00	.30
62 Joe Carter	.60	.18
63 Matt Williams	.60	.18
64 Robin Ventura	.60	.18
65 Barry Larkin	1.00	.30
66 Dante Bichette	.60	.18

67 Travis Fryman .60 .18
68 Gary Sheffield .60 .18
69 Eric Karros .60 .18
70 Matt Stairs .60 .18
71 Al Martin .60 .18
72 Jay Buhner .60 .18
73 Ray Lankford .60 .18
74 Carlos Delgado .60 .18
75 Edgardo Alfonzo .60 .18
76 Rondell White .60 .18
77 Chuck Knoblauch .60 .18
78 Raul Mondesi .60 .18
79 Johnny Damon 1.00 .30
80 Matt Morris .60 .18
81 Tom Glavine 1.00 .30
82 Kevin Brown 1.00 .30
83 Garret Anderson .60 .18
84 Mike Mussina 1.00 .30
85 Pedro Martinez 1.50 .45
86 Craig Biggio 1.00 .30
87 Darryl Kile .60 .18
88 Rafael Palmeiro 1.00 .30
89 Jim Thome 1.50 .45
90 Andres Galarraga .60 .18
91 Sammy Sosa 3.00 .90
92 Willie Greene .75 .23
93 Vinny Castilla .75 .23
94 Justin Thompson .75 .23
95 Jeff King .75 .23
96 Jeff Cirillo .75 .23
97 Mark Grudzielanek .75 .23
98 Brad Radke .75 .23
99 John Olerud .75 .23
100 Curt Schilling .75 .23
101 Steve Finley .75 .23
102 J.T. Snow .75 .23
103 Edgar Martinez 1.25 .35
104 Wilson Alvarez .75 .23
105 Rusty Greer .75 .23
106 Pat Hentgen .75 .23
107 David Cone .75 .23
108 Fred McGriff 1.25 .35
109 Jason Giambi .75 .23
110 Tony Womack .75 .23
111 Bernard Gilkey .75 .23
112 Alan Benes .75 .23
113 Mark Grace 1.25 .35
114 Reggie Sanders .75 .23
115 Moises Alou .75 .23
116 John Jaha .75 .23
117 Henry Rodriguez .75 .23
118 Dean Palmer .75 .23
119 Mike Lieberthal .75 .23
120 Shawn Estes .75 .23

1998 Flair Showcase Row 2

These Row 2 cards are parallel to regular base set. Similar to the other rows there is different pull ratios for each group of 30 cards as follows. Cards numbered 1 through 30 are seeded one every two packs; cards numbered from 31 through 60 are seeded one every 2.5 packs; cards numbered from 61 through 90 are seeded one every four packs and cards numbered from 91-120 are seeded one every 3.5 packs.

Nm-Mt Ex-Mt
COMPLETE SET (120) 100.00 30.00
*STARS 1-30: .6X TO 1.5X ROW 3
*STARS 31-60: .5X TO 1.25X ROW 3.
*STARS 61-90: .6X TO 1.5X ROW 3
*STARS 91-120: .5X TO 1.25X ROW 3

1998 Flair Showcase Row 1

These Row 1 cards are parallel to regular base set. Similar to the other rows there is different pull ratios for each group of 30 cards as follows. Cards numbered from 1 through 30 are inserted one every 16 packs; cards numbered from 31 through 60 are inserted one every 24 packs; cards numbered from 61 through 90 are inserted one every six packs and cards numbered from 91 through 120 are inserted one every 10 packs.

Nm-Mt Ex-Mt
*STARS 1-30: 2X TO 5X ROW 3
*STARS 31-60: 2.5X TO 6X ROW 3
*ROOKIES 31-60: 2.5X TO 6X ROW 3
*STARS 61-90: .75X TO 2X ROW 3
*STARS 91-120: 1X TO 2.5X ROW 3..

1998 Flair Showcase Row 0

These Row 0 cards are parallel to regular base set. These cards are serial numbered and get more plentiful as they are numbered higher in the set. Serial numbering is as follows: Cards numbered from 1 through 30 are serial numbered to 250, cards numbered from 31 through 60 are serial numbered to 500, cards numbered from 61 through 90 are serial numbered to 1000 and cards numbered 91 through 120 are serial numbered to 2000.

Nm-Mt Ex-Mt
*STARS 1-30: 6X TO 15X ROW 3
*STARS 31-60: 5X TO 12X ROW 3
*ROOKIES 31-60: 5X TO 12X ROW 3.
*STARS 61-90: 3X TO 8X ROW 3
*STARS 91-120: 1.5X TO 4X ROW 3..

1998 Flair Showcase Legacy Collection Row 3

Yet another parallel version of the Flair Showcase set, these cards are serial numbered to 100 each.

Nm-Mt Ex-Mt
*STARS 1-30: 12.5X TO 30X BASIC ROW 3
*STARS 31-60: 12.5X TO 30X BASIC ROW 3
*ROOKIES 31-60: 8X TO 20X BASIC ROW 3
*STARS 61-90: 8X TO 20X ROW 3
*STARS 91-120: 8X TO 20X BASIC ROW 3

1998 Flair Showcase Legacy Collection Row 2

Yet another parallel version of the Flair Showcase set, these cards are serial numbered to 100 each.

Nm-Mt Ex-Mt
*STARS 1-30: 12.5X TO 30X BASIC ROW 3
*STARS 31-60: 12.5X TO 30X BASIC ROW 3
*ROOKIES 31-60: 8X TO 20X BASIC ROW 2
*STARS 61-90: 8X TO 20X ROW 3
*STARS 91-120: 8X TO 20X BASIC ROW 3

1998 Flair Showcase Legacy Collection Row 1

Yet another parallel version of the Flair Showcase set, these cards are serial numbered to 100 each.

Nm-Mt Ex-Mt
*STARS 1-30: 12.5X TO 30X BASIC ROW 3
*STARS 31-60: 12.5X TO 30X BASIC ROW 3
*ROOKIES 31-60: 8X TO 20X BASIC ROW 1
*STARS 61-90: 8X TO 20X ROW 3
*STARS 91-120: 8X TO 20X BASIC ROW 3

1998 Flair Showcase Legacy Collection Row 0

Yet another parallel version of the Flair Showcase set, these cards are serial numbered to 100 each.

Nm-Mt Ex-Mt
*STARS 1-30: 12.5X TO 30X BASIC ROW 3
*STARS 31-60: 12.5X TO 30X BASIC ROW 3
*ROOKIES 31-60: 8X TO 20X BASIC ROW 3
*STARS 61-90: 8X TO 20X ROW 3
*STARS 91-120: 8X TO 20X BASIC ROW 3

1998 Flair Showcase Perfect 10

Sequentially numbered to 10, this 10-card insert features color player photography using silk-screen technology. While no pricing is available due to scarcity, we provide a checklist for identification purposes.

Nm-Mt Ex-Mt
1 Ken Griffey Jr.
2 Cal Ripken
3 Frank Thomas
4 Mike Piazza
5 Greg Maddux
6 Nomar Garciaparra
7 Mark McGwire
8 Scott Rolen
9 Alex Rodriguez
10 Roger Clemens

1998 Flair Showcase Wave of the Future

Randomly inserted in packs at a rate of one in 20, this 12-card insert feature color action photography on cards filled with vegetable oil and sparkles in an attempt to mimic ocean waters.

Nm-Mt Ex-Mt
COMPLETE SET (12) 25.00 7.50
1 Travis Lee 2.00 .60
2 Todd Helton 3.00 .90
3 Ben Grieve 2.00 .60
4 Juan Encarnacion 2.00 .60
5 Brad Fullmer 2.00 .60
6 Ruben Rivera 2.00 .60
7 Paul Konerko 2.00 .60
8 Derrek Lee 2.00 .60
9 Mike Lowell 5.00 1.50
10 Magglio Ordonez 5.00 1.50
11 Rich Butler 2.00 .60
12 Eli Marrero 2.00 .60

1999 Flair Showcase Row 3

This 144-card set was distributed in five-card packs with a suggested retail price of $4.99 and features two color player photos on the front with full rainbow holofoil, silver foil and embossing. This base set is considered the "Power" level. The set was broken into three separate tiers of 28 card subsets as follows: Cards numbered from 1 through 48 were seeded one every .9 packs; cards numbered 49 through 96 were seeded one every 1.1 packs and cards numbered 97 through 144 were seeded one every 1.2 packs. Rookie Cards include Pat Burrell.

Nm-Mt Ex-Mt
COMPLETE SET (144) 60.00 18.00
COMMON CARD (1-48) .50 .15
COMMON CARD (49-96) .50 .15
COMMON CARD (97-144) .60 .18
1 Mark McGwire 3.00 .90
2 Sammy Sosa 2.00 .60
3 Ken Griffey Jr. 2.00 .60
4 Chipper Jones 1.25 .35
5 Ben Grieve .50 .15
6 J.D. Drew .50 .15
7 Jeff Bagwell .75 .23
8 Cal Ripken 4.00 1.20
9 Tony Gwynn 1.50 .45
10 Nomar Garciaparra 2.00 .60
11 Travis Lee .50 .15
12 Troy Glaus UER .50 .15
Spelled Tony on back
13 Mike Piazza 2.00 .60
14 Alex Rodriguez 2.00 .60
15 Kevin Brown .75 .23
16 Darin Erstad .50 .15
17 Scott Rolen 1.25 .35
18 Micah Bowie RC .50 .15
19 Juan Gonzalez .75 .23
20 Kerry Wood 1.25 .35
21 Roger Clemens 2.50 .75
22 Derek Jeter 3.00 .90
23 Pat Burrell RC 2.50 .75
24 Tim Salmon .75 .23
25 Barry Bonds 3.00 .90
26 Roosevelt Brown RC .50 .15
27 Vladimir Guerrero 1.25 .35
28 Randy Johnson 1.25 .35
29 Mo Vaughn .50 .15
30 Fernando Seguignol .50 .15
31 Greg Maddux 2.00 .60
32 Tony Clark .50 .15
33 Eric Chavez .50 .15
34 Kris Benson .50 .15
35 Frank Thomas 1.25 .35
36 Mario Encarnacion RC .50 .15
37 Gabe Kapler .50 .15
38 Jeremy Giambi .50 .15
39 Peter Tucci .50 .15
40 Manny Ramirez .75 .23
41 Albert Belle .50 .15
42 Warren Morris .50 .15
43 Michael Barrett .50 .15
44 Andruw Jones .50 .15
45 Carlos Delgado .50 .15
46 Jaret Wright .50 .15
47 Juan Encarnacion .50 .15
48 Scott Hunter RC .50 .15
49 Tino Martinez .75 .23
50 Craig Biggio .75 .23
51 Jim Thome 1.25 .35
52 Vinny Castilla .50 .15
53 Tom Glavine .75 .23
54 Bob Higginson .50 .15
55 Moises Alou .50 .15
56 Robin Ventura .50 .15
57 Bernie Williams .75 .23
58 Pedro Martinez 1.25 .35
59 Greg Vaughn .50 .15
60 Ray Lankford .50 .15
61 Jose Canseco 1.25 .35
62 Ivan Rodriguez 1.25 .35
63 Shawn Green .50 .15
64 Rafael Palmeiro .75 .23
65 Ellis Burks .50 .15
66 Jason Kendall .50 .15
67 David Wells .50 .15
68 Rondell White .50 .15
69 Gary Sheffield .50 .15
70 Ken Caminiti .50 .15
71 Cliff Floyd .50 .15
72 Larry Walker .75 .23
73 Bartolo Colon .50 .15
74 Barry Larkin .75 .23
75 Calvin Pickering .50 .15
76 Jim Edmonds .50 .15
77 Henry Rodriguez .50 .15
78 Roberto Alomar .75 .23
79 Andres Galarraga .50 .15
80 Richie Sexson .50 .15
81 Todd Helton .75 .23
82 Damion Easley .50 .15
83 Livan Hernandez .50 .15
84 Carlos Beltran .75 .23
85 Todd Hundley .50 .15
86 Todd Walker .50 .15
87 Scott Brosius .50 .15
88 Bob Abreu .50 .15
89 Corey Koskie .50 .15
90 Ruben Rivera .50 .15
91 Edgar Renteria .50 .15
92 Quinton McCracken .50 .15
93 Bernard Gilkey .50 .15
94 Shannon Stewart .50 .15
95 Dustin Hermanson .50 .15
96 Mike Caruso .50 .15
97 Alex Gonzalez .60 .18
98 Raul Mondesi .60 .18
99 David Cone .60 .18
100 Curt Schilling .60 .18
101 Brian Giles .60 .18
102 Edgar Martinez 1.00 .30
103 Rolando Arrojo .60 .18
104 Derek Bell .60 .18
105 Denny Neagle .60 .18
106 Marquis Grissom .60 .18
107 Bret Boone .60 .18
108 Mike Mussina 1.00 .30
109 John Smoltz 1.00 .30
110 Brett Tomko .60 .18
111 David Justice .60 .18
112 Andy Pettitte 1.00 .30
113 Eric Karros .60 .18
114 Dante Bichette .60 .18
115 Jeromy Burnitz .60 .18
116 Paul Konerko .60 .18
117 Steve Finley .60 .18
118 Ricky Ledee .60 .18
119 Edgardo Alfonzo .60 .18
120 Dean Palmer .60 .18
121 Rusty Greer .60 .18
122 Luis Gonzalez .60 .18
123 Randy Winn .60 .18
124 Jeff Kent .60 .18
125 Doug Glanville .60 .18
126 Justin Thompson .60 .18
127 Bret Saberhagen .60 .18
128 Wade Boggs 1.00 .30
129 Al Leiter .60 .18
130 Paul O'Neill 1.00 .30
131 Chan Ho Park .60 .18
132 Johnny Damon 1.00 .30
133 Darryl Kile .60 .18
134 Reggie Sanders .60 .18
135 Kevin Millwood .60 .18
136 Charles Johnson .60 .18
137 Ray Durham .60 .18
138 Rico Brogna .60 .18
139 Matt Williams .60 .18
140 Sandy Alomar Jr. .60 .18
141 Jeff Cirillo .60 .18
142 Devon White .60 .18
143 Andy Benes .60 .18
144 Mike Stanley .60 .18

1999 Flair Showcase Row 2

This 144-card set is parallel to the Row 1 or base set and features two action player photos with embossed jersey-like background printed on full rainbow holofoil cards. This set is called the "Passion" level. Seeding rates are as follows, cards numbered one through 48 are seeded one every three packs; cards numbered 49 through 96 are seeded one every 1.33 packs and cards numbered 97-144 are seeded one every two packs.

Nm-Mt Ex-Mt
COMPLETE SET (144)
*STARS 1-48: 1X TO 2.5X ROW 3
*ROOKIES 1-48: 1.25X TO 3X ROW 3
*STARS 49-96: .5X TO 1.25X ROW 3
*STARS 97-144: .5X TO 1.25X ROW 3

1999 Flair Showcase Row 1

This 144-card set is parallel to the base set and features three photos of the same player on a plastic laminate individual numbered card. Cards 1-48 are serially numbered to 1500; Cards 49-96 to 3000; Cards 97-144 to 6000. This set is the "Showcase" level.

Nm-Mt Ex-Mt
*STARS 1-48: 4X TO 10X ROW 3
*ROOKIES 1-48: 4X TO 10X ROW 3...
*STARS 49-96: 2.5X TO 6X ROW 3
*STARS 97-144: 1.25X TO 3X ROW 3

1999 Flair Showcase Legacy Collection Row 3

Randomly inserted into packs, this 144-card set is the Power parallel version of the Legacy Collection set.

Nm-Mt Ex-Mt
*STARS 1-48: 12.5X TO 30X BASIC ROW 3
*ROOKIES 1-48: 8X TO 20X BASIC ROW 3
*STARS 49-96: 12.5X TO 30X BASIC ROW 3
*STARS 97-144: 10X TO 25X BASIC ROW 3

1999 Flair Showcase Legacy Collection Row 2

Randomly inserted into packs, this 144-card set is the Passion parallel version of the Legacy Collection set.

Nm-Mt Ex-Mt
*STARS 1-48: 12.5X TO 30X BASIC ROW 3
*ROOKIES 1-48: 8X TO 20X BASIC ROW 3
*STARS 49-96: 12.5X TO 30X BASIC ROW 3
*STARS 97-144: 10X TO 25X BASIC ROW 3

1999 Flair Showcase Legacy Collection Row 1

Randomly inserted into packs, this 144-card set is the Showcase parallel version of the Legacy Collection set.

Nm-Mt Ex-Mt
*STARS 1-48: 12.X TO 30X BASIC ROW 3
*ROOKIES 1-48: 8X TO 20X BASIC ROW 3
*STARS 49-96: 12.5X TO 30X BASIC ROW 3
*STARS 97-144: 10X TO 25X BASIC ROW 3

1999 Flair Showcase Measure of Greatness

Randomly inserted into packs, this 15-card set features color photos of superstars who are closing in on milestones of all-time great players. Only 500 serial-numbered cards were produced.

Nm-Mt Ex-Mt
COMPLETE SET (15) 400.00 120.00
1 Roger Clemens 30.00 9.00
2 Nomar Garciaparra 25.00 7.50
3 Juan Gonzalez 10.00 3.00
4 Ken Griffey Jr. 25.00 7.50
5 Vladimir Guerrero 15.00 4.50
6 Tony Gwynn 20.00 6.00
7 Derek Jeter 40.00 12.00
8 Chipper Jones 15.00 4.50
9 Mark McGwire 40.00 12.00
10 Mike Piazza 25.00 7.50
11 Manny Ramirez 10.00 3.00
12 Cal Ripken 50.00 15.00
13 Alex Rodriguez 25.00 7.50
14 Sammy Sosa 25.00 7.50
15 Frank Thomas 15.00 4.50

1999 Flair Showcase Wave of the Future

Randomly inserted into packs, this 15-card set features color photos of young stars. Each card is serially numbered to 1000.

Nm-Mt Ex-Mt
COMPLETE SET (15) 100.00 30.00
1 Kerry Wood 10.00 3.00
2 Ben Grieve 5.00 1.50
3 J.D. Drew 5.00 1.50
4 Juan Encarnacion 5.00 1.50
5 Travis Lee 5.00 1.50
6 Todd Helton 8.00 2.40
7 Troy Glaus 5.00 1.50
8 Ricky Ledee 5.00 1.50
9 Eric Chavez 5.00 1.50
10 Ben Davis 5.00 1.50
11 George Lombard 5.00 1.50
12 Jeremy Giambi 5.00 1.50
13 Roosevelt Brown 5.00 1.50
14 Pat Burrell 12.00 3.60
15 Preston Wilson 5.00 1.50

1959 Fleer Ted Williams

The cards in this 80-card set measure 2 1/2" by 3 1/2". The 1959 Fleer set, with a catalog designation of R418-1, portrays the life of Ted Williams. The wording of the wrapper, "Baseball's Greatest Series," has led to speculation that Fleer contemplated similar sets honoring other baseball immortals, but chose to develop instead the format of the 1960 and 1961 issues. These packs contained either six or eight cards. The packs cost a nickel and were packed 24 to a box which were packed 24 to a case. Card number 68, which was withdrawn early in production, is considered scarce and has even been counterfeited; the fake has a rosy coloration and a cross-hatch pattern visible over the picture area. The card numbering is arranged essentially in chronological order.

NM Ex
COMPLETE SET (80) 1800.00 900.00
WRAPPER (6-CARD) 125.00 60.00
WRAPPER (8-CARD) 150.00 75.00
1 Ted Williams 100.00 50.00
The Early Years
Choosing up sides
on the sandlots
2 Ted Williams 100.00 50.00
Babe Ruth
Meeting boyhood idol
Babe Ruth
3 Ted Williams 15.00 7.50
Practice Makes Perfect
At place practicing on the sandlots
4 Ted Williams 15.00 7.50
Learns Fine Points
Sliding at Herbert Hoover High
5 Ted Williams 15.00 7.50
Ted's Fame Spreads
At plate at Herbert Hoover High
6 Ted Williams 25.00 12.50
Ted Turns Pro
Portrait
San Diego Padres
PCL League
uniform)
7 Ted Williams 15.00 7.50
From Mound to Plate
At plate
San Diego Padres, PCL
8 Ted Williams 15.00 7.50
1937 First Full Season
Making a leaping catch
9 Ted Williams 20.00 10.00
Eddie Collins
First Step to Majors
10 Ted Williams 15.00 7.50
Gunning as Pastime
Wearing hunting gear, taking aim
11 Ted Williams 40.00 20.00
Jimmie Foxx
First Spring Training
12 Ted Williams 20.00 10.00
Burning Up Minors
Pitching for Minneapolis
American Association
13 Ted Williams 15.00 7.50
1939 Shows Will Stay
Follow-through
14 Ted Williams 15.00 7.50
Outstanding Rookie '39
Follow-through
15 Ted Williams 20.00 10.00
Licks Sophomore Jinx
Sliding into third base
for a triple
16 Ted Williams 15.00 7.50
1941 Greatest Year
Follow-through at plate
17 Ted Williams 40.00 20.00
How Ted Hit .400
Youthful Williams
as he looked in '41
18 Ted Williams 20.00 10.00
1941 All Star Hero
Crossing plate
after home run
19 Ted Williams 15.00 7.50
Wins Triple Crown
Crossing plate at Fenway Park
20 Ted Williams 15.00 7.50
On to Naval Training
In training plane
at Amherst College
21 Ted Williams 15.00 7.50
Honors for Williams
Receiving 1942 Sporting News POY
22 Ted Williams 15.00 7.50
1944 Ted Solos
In cockpit at
Pensacola, FL Navy Air Station
23 Ted Williams 15.00 7.50
Williams Wins Wings
Wearing Naval
Aviation Cadet uniform
24 Ted Williams 15.00 7.50
1945 Sharpshooter
Taking Naval eye test
25 Ted Williams 15.00 7.50
1945 Ted Discharged
In cockpit, giving
the thumbs up
26 Ted Williams 15.00 7.50
Off to Flying Start
In batters box
spring training, 1946
27 Ted Williams 15.00 7.50
7/9/46 One Man Show
Riding blooper pitch out of park
28 Ted Williams 15.00 7.50
The Williams Shift
Diagram of Cleveland Indians
position shift to defense Williams
29 Ted Williams 20.00 10.00
Ted Hits for Cycle
Close-up of follow through
30 Ted Williams 15.00 7.50
Beating Williams Shift
Crossing plate after home run
31 Ted Williams 20.00 10.00
Sox Lose Series
Sliding across plate
Sept. 14, 1946
32 Ted Williams 15.00 7.50
Joseph Cashman
Most Valuable Player

Receiving MVP Award
33 Ted Williams 15.00 7.50
Another Triple Crown
Famous Williams' Grip
34 Ted Williams 15.00 7.50
Runs Scored Record
Sliding into 2nd base
in 1947 AS Game
35 Ted Williams 15.00 7.50
Sox Miss Pennant
Checking weight on
new 36 oz. hickory bat
36 Ted Williams 15.00 7.50
Banner Year for Ted
Bunting down the
3rd base line
37 Ted Williams 15.00 7.50
1949 Sox Miss Again
Two moods: grim and determined
smiling and happy
38 Ted Williams 15.00 7.50
1949 Power Rampage
Full shot of his
batting follow through
39 Ted Williams 25.00 12.50
Joe Cronin
Eddie Collins
1950 Great Start
Signing $125,000 contract
40 Ted Williams 15.00 7.50
Ted Crashes into Wall
Making catch in
1950 All Star game
and crashing into wall
41 Ted Williams 15.00 7.50
1950 Ted Recovers
Recuperating from elbow operation
in hospital
42 Ted Williams 15.00 7.50
Tom Yawkey
Slowed by Injury
43 Ted Williams 15.00 7.50
Double Play Lead
Leaping high to
make great catch
44 Ted Williams 15.00 7.50
Back to Marines
Hanging up number 9
prior to leaving for Marines
45 Ted Williams 15.00 7.50
Farewell to Baseball
Honored at Fenway Park
prior to return to service
46 Ted Williams 15.00 7.50
Ready for Combat
Drawing jet pilot equipment
in Willow Grove
47 Ted Williams 15.00 7.50
Ted Crash Lands Jet
In flying gear
and jet he crash landed in
48 Ted Williams 20.00 10.00
Ford Frick
1953 Ted Returns
Throwing out 1st ball
at All-Star Game in Cincinnati
49 Ted Williams 15.00 7.50
Smash Return
Giving his arm
whirlpool treatment
50 Ted Williams 25.00 12.50
1954 Spring Injury
Full batting pose at plate
51 Ted Williams 15.00 7.50
Ted is Patched Up
In first workout after
fractured collar bone
52 Ted Williams 20.00 10.00
1954 Ted's Comeback
Hitting a home run
against Detroit
53 Ted Williams 15.00 7.50
Comeback is Success
Beating catcher's
tag at home plate
54 Ted Williams 15.00 7.50
Ted Hooks Big One
With prize catch
1235 lb. black marlin
55 Ted Williams 20.00 10.00
Joe Cronin
Retirement "No Go"
Returning from retirement
56 Ted Williams 15.00 7.50
2,000th Hit
8/11/55
57 Ted Williams 20.00 10.00
400th Homer
In locker room
58 Ted Williams 15.00 7.50
Williams Hits .388
Four-picture sequence
of his batting swing
59 Ted Williams 15.00 7.50
Hot September for Ted
Full shot of follow through
at plate
60 Ted Williams 15.00 7.50
More Records for Ted
Swinging and missing
61 Ted Williams 20.00 10.00
1957 Outfielder
Warming up prior
to ball game
62 Ted Williams 15.00 7.50
1958 Sixth Batting Title
Slamming pitch into stands
63 Ted Williams 80.00 40.00
Ted's All-Star Record
Portrait and facsimile autograph
64 Ted Williams 15.00 7.50
Barbara Williams
Daughter and Daddy
In uniform holding his daughter
65 Ted Williams 20.00 10.00
1958 August 30
Determination on face
connecting with ball
66 Ted Williams 15.00 7.50
1958 Powerhouse
Stance and follow through
in batters box
67 Ted Williams 40.00 20.00
Sam Snead
Two Famous Fishermen
testing fishing equipment
68 Ted Williams 700.00 350.00
Bucky Harris
Ted Signs for 1959 SP
signing contract
69 Ted Williams 15.00 7.50
A Future Ted Williams
With eager, young newcomer
70 Ted Williams 40.00 20.00
Jim Thorpe
at Sportsmen's Show
71 Ted Williams 15.00 7.50
Hitting Fund. 1
Proper gripping of
a baseball bat
72 Ted Williams 15.00 7.50
Hitting Fund. 2
Checking his swing
73 Ted Williams 15.00 7.50
Hitting Fund. 3
Stance and follow-through
74 Ted Williams 15.00 7.50
Here's How
Demonstrating in locker room
an aspect of hitting
75 Ted Williams 50.00 25.00
Eddie Collins
Babe Ruth
Williams' Value to Sox
76 Ted Williams 15.00 7.50
On Base Record
Awaiting intentional walk
to first base
77 Ted Williams 15.00 7.50
Ted Relaxes
Displaying bonefish
which he caught
78 Ted Williams 15.00 7.50
Rep. Joe Martin
Justice Earl Warren
Honors for Williams
Clark Griffith Memorial Award
79 Ted Williams 25.00 12.50
Where Ted Stands
Wielding giant eight foot bat
when honored as modern-day Paul
Bunyan
80 Ted Williams 40.00 20.00
Ted's Goals for 1959
Admiring his portrait

1960 Fleer

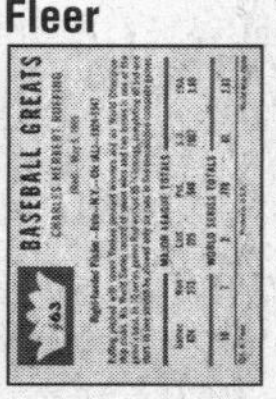

The cards in this 79-card set measure 2 1/2" by 3 1/2". The cards from the 1960 Fleer series of Baseball Greats are sometimes mistaken for 1930s cards by collectors not familiar with this set. The cards each contain a tinted photo of a baseball immortal, and were issued in one series. There are no known scarcities, although a number 80 card (Pepper Martin reverse with Eddie Collins, Joe Tinker or Lefty Grove obverse) exists (this is not considered part of the set). The catalog designation for 1960 Fleer is R418-2. The cards were printed on a 96-card sheet with 17 double prints. These are noted in the checklist below by DP. On the sheet the second Eddie Collins card is typically found in the number 80 position. According to correspondence sent from Fleers at the time -- no card 80 was issued because of contract problems. Some cards have been discovered with wrong backs. The cards were issued in nickel packs which were packed 24 to a box.

	NM	Ex
COMPLETE SET (79)	600.00	240.00
WRAPPER	100.00	40.00

1 Napoleon Lajoie DP 30.00 12.00
2 Christy Mathewson 15.00 6.00
3 Babe Ruth 100.00 40.00
4 Carl Hubbell 8.00 3.20
5 Grover C. Alexander 8.00 3.20
6 Walter Johnson DP 10.00 4.00
7 Chief Bender 4.00 1.60
8 Roger Bresnahan 4.00 1.60
9 Mordecai Brown 4.00 1.60
10 Tris Speaker 8.00 3.20
11 Arky Vaughan DP 4.00 1.60
12 Zach Wheat 4.00 1.60
13 George Sisler 4.00 1.60
14 Connie Mack 8.00 3.20
15 Clark Griffith 4.00 1.60
16 Lou Boudreau DP 8.00 3.20
17 Ernie Lombardi 4.00 1.60
18 Heinie Manush 4.00 1.60
19 Marty Marion 6.00 2.40
20 Eddie Collins DP 4.00 1.60
21 Rabbit Maranville DP 4.00 1.60
22 Joe Medwick 4.00 1.60
23 Ed Barrow 4.00 1.60
24 Mickey Cochrane 6.00 2.40
25 Jimmy Collins 4.00 1.60
26 Bob Feller DP 15.00 6.00
27 Luke Appling 6.00 2.40
28 Lou Gehrig 80.00 32.00
29 Gabby Hartnett 4.00 1.60
30 Chuck Klein 4.00 1.60
31 Tony Lazzeri DP 6.00 2.40
32 Al Simmons 4.00 1.60
33 Wilbert Robinson 4.00 1.60
34 Sam Rice 4.00 1.60
35 Herb Pennock 4.00 1.60
36 Mel Ott DP 8.00 3.20
37 Lefty O'Doul 4.00 1.60
38 Johnny Mize 8.00 3.20
39 Edmund(Bing) Miller 4.00 1.60
40 Joe Tinker 4.00 1.60
41 Frank Baker DP 4.00 1.60
42 Ty Cobb 60.00 24.00
43 Paul Derringer 4.00 1.60
44 Cap Anson 4.00 1.60
45 Jim Bottomley 4.00 1.60
46 Eddie Plank DP 4.00 1.60
47 Denton(Cy) Young 10.00 4.00
48 Hack Wilson 6.00 2.40
49 Ed Walsh UER 4.00 1.60
(Photo actually
Ed Walsh Jr.)
50 Frank Chance 4.00 1.60
51 Dazzy Vance DP 4.00 1.60
52 Bill Terry 6.00 2.40
53 Jimmie Foxx 10.00 4.00
54 Lefty Gomez 8.00 3.20
55 Branch Rickey 4.00 1.60
56 Ray Schalk DP 4.00 1.60
57 Johnny Evers 4.00 1.60
58 Charley Gehringer 6.00 2.40
59 Burleigh Grimes 4.00 1.60
60 Lefty Grove 8.00 3.20
61 Rube Waddell DP 4.00 1.60
62 John(Honus) Wagner 15.00 6.00
63 Red Ruffing 4.00 1.60
64 Kenesaw M. Landis 4.00 1.60
65 Harry Heilmann 4.00 1.60
66 John McGraw DP 4.00 1.60
67 Hughie Jennings 4.00 1.60
68 Hal Newhouser 6.00 2.40
69 Waite Hoyt 4.00 1.60
70 Bobo Newsom 4.00 1.60
71 Earl Averill DP 4.00 1.60
72 Ted Williams 80.00 32.00
73 Warren Giles 6.00 2.40
74 Ford Frick 6.00 2.40
75 Kiki Cuyler 4.00 1.60
76 Paul Waner DP 6.00 2.40
77 Pie Traynor 4.00 1.60
78 Lloyd Waner 4.00 1.60
79 Ralph Kiner 10.00 4.00
80A Pepper Martin SP 2500.00 1000.00
Eddie Collins
pictured on obverse
80B Pepper Martin SP 2000.00 800.00
Lefty Grove
pictured on obverse
80C Pepper Martin SP 2000.00 800.00
Joe Tinker on Front

1961 Fleer

The cards in this 154-card set measure 2 1/2" by 3 1/2". In 1961, Fleer continued its Baseball Greats format by issuing this series of cards. The set was released in two distinct series, 1-88 and 89-154 (of which the latter is more difficult to obtain). The players within each series are conveniently numbered in alphabetical order. The catalog number for this set is F418-3. In each first series pack Fleer inserted a Major League team decal and a pennant sticker honoring past World Series winners. The cards were issued in nickel packs which were issued 24 to a box.

	NM	Ex
COMPLETE SET (154)	1200.00	475.00
COMMON CARD (1-88)	3.00	1.20
COMMON CARD (89-154)	8.00	3.20
WRAPPER (5-CENT)	100.00	40.00

1 Frank Baker CL 50.00 15.00
Ty Cobb
Zack Wheat
2 Grover C. Alexander 6.00 2.40
3 Nick Altrock 3.00 1.20
4 Cap Anson 4.00 1.60
5 Earl Averill 4.00 1.60
6 Frank Baker 4.00 1.60
7 Dave Bancroft 4.00 1.60
8 Chief Bender 4.00 1.60
9 Jim Bottomley 4.00 1.60
10 Roger Bresnahan 4.00 1.60
11 Mordecai Brown 4.00 1.60
12 Max Carey 4.00 1.60
13 Jack Chesbro 4.00 1.60
14 Ty Cobb 50.00 20.00
15 Mickey Cochrane 4.00 1.60
16 Eddie Collins 6.00 2.40
17 Earle Combs 4.00 1.60
18 Charles Comiskey 4.00 1.60
19 Kiki Cuyler 4.00 1.60
20 Paul Derringer 3.00 1.20
21 Howard Ehmke 3.00 1.20
22 Billy Evans 4.00 1.60
23 Johnny Evers 4.00 1.60
24 Urban Faber 4.00 1.60
25 Bob Feller 12.00 4.80
26 Wes Ferrell 3.00 1.20
27 Lew Fonseca 3.00 1.20
28 Jimmie Foxx 6.00 2.40
29 Ford Frick 3.00 1.20
30 Frankie Frisch 4.00 1.60
31 Lou Gehrig 80.00 32.00
32 Charley Gehringer 4.00 1.60
33 Warren Giles 3.00 1.20
34 Lefty Gomez 4.00 1.60
35 Goose Goslin 4.00 1.60
36 Clark Griffith 4.00 1.60
37 Burleigh Grimes 4.00 1.60
38 Lefty Grove 6.00 2.40
39 Chick Hafey 4.00 1.60
40 Jesse Haines 4.00 1.60
41 Gabby Hartnett 4.00 1.60
42 Harry Heilmann 4.00 1.60
43 Rogers Hornsby 6.00 2.40
44 Waite Hoyt 4.00 1.60
45 Carl Hubbell 6.00 2.40
46 Miller Huggins 4.00 1.60
47 Hughie Jennings 4.00 1.60
48 Ban Johnson 4.00 1.60
49 Walter Johnson 12.00 4.80
50 Ralph Kiner 6.00 2.40
51 Chuck Klein 4.00 1.60
52 Johnny Kling 3.00 1.20
53 Kenesaw M. Landis 4.00 1.60
54 Tony Lazzeri 4.00 1.60
55 Ernie Lombardi 4.00 1.60
56 Dolf Luque 3.00 1.20
57 Heinie Manush 4.00 1.60
58 Marty Marion 3.00 1.20
59 Christy Mathewson 12.00 4.80
60 John McGraw 4.00 1.60
61 Joe Medwick 4.00 1.60
62 Edmund(Bing) Miller 3.00 1.20
63 Johnny Mize 4.00 1.60
64 John Mostil 3.00 1.20
65 Art Nehf 3.00 1.20
66 Hal Newhouser 4.00 1.60
67 Bobo Newsom 3.00 1.20
68 Mel Ott 6.00 2.40
69 Allie Reynolds 3.00 1.20
70 Sam Rice 4.00 1.60
71 Eppa Rixey 4.00 1.60
72 Edd Roush 4.00 1.60
73 Schoolboy Rowe 3.00 1.20
74 Red Ruffing 4.00 1.60
75 Babe Ruth 125.00 50.00
76 Joe Sewell 4.00 1.60
77 Al Simmons 4.00 1.60
78 George Sisler 4.00 1.60
79 Tris Speaker 4.00 1.60
80 Fred Toney 3.00 1.20
81 Dazzy Vance 4.00 1.60
82 Hippo Vaughn 3.00 1.20
83 Ed Walsh 4.00 1.60
84 Lloyd Waner 4.00 1.60
85 Paul Waner 4.00 1.60
86 Zack Wheat 4.00 1.60
87 Hack Wilson 4.00 1.60
88 Jimmy Wilson 3.00 1.20
89 George Sisler CL 60.00 18.00
Pie Traynor
90 Babe Adams 8.00 3.20
91 Dale Alexander 8.00 3.20
92 Jim Bagby 8.00 3.20
93 Ossie Bluege 8.00 3.20
94 Lou Boudreau 10.00 4.00
95 Tommy Bridges 8.00 3.20
96 Donie Bush 8.00 3.20
97 Dolph Camilli 8.00 3.20
98 Frank Chance 10.00 4.00
99 Jimmy Collins 10.00 4.00
100 Stan Coveleskie 10.00 4.00
101 Hugh Critz 8.00 3.20
102 Alvin Crowder 8.00 3.20
103 Joe Dugan 8.00 3.20
104 Bibb Falk 8.00 3.20
105 Rick Ferrell 10.00 4.00
106 Art Fletcher 8.00 3.20
107 Dennis Galehouse 8.00 3.20
108 Chick Galloway 8.00 3.20
109 Mule Haas 8.00 3.20
110 Stan Hack 8.00 3.20
111 Bump Hadley 8.00 3.20
112 Billy Hamilton 10.00 4.00
113 Joe Hauser 8.00 3.20
114 Babe Herman 8.00 3.20
115 Travis Jackson 10.00 4.00
116 Eddie Joost 8.00 3.20
117 Addie Joss 10.00 4.00
118 Joe Judge 8.00 3.20
119 Joe Kuhel 8.00 3.20
120 Napoleon Lajoie 12.00 4.80
121 Dutch Leonard 8.00 3.20
122 Ted Lyons 10.00 4.00
123 Connie Mack 12.00 4.80
124 Rabbit Maranville 10.00 4.00
125 Fred Marberry 8.00 3.20
126 Joe McGinnity 10.00 4.00
127 Oscar Melillo 8.00 3.20
128 Ray Mueller 8.00 3.20
129 Kid Nichols 10.00 4.00
130 Lefty O'Doul 10.00 4.00
131 Bob O'Farrell 8.00 3.20
132 Roger Peckinpaugh 8.00 3.20
133 Herb Pennock 10.00 4.00
134 George Pipgras 8.00 3.20
135 Eddie Plank 10.00 4.00
136 Ray Schalk 10.00 4.00
137 Hal Schumacher 8.00 3.20
138 Luke Sewell 8.00 3.20
139 Bob Shawkey 8.00 3.20
140 Riggs Stephenson 8.00 3.20
141 Billy Sullivan 8.00 3.20
142 Bill Terry 12.00 4.80
143 Joe Tinker 10.00 4.00
144 Pie Traynor 10.00 4.00
145 Hal Trosky 8.00 3.20
146 George Uhle 8.00 3.20
147 Johnny VanderMeer 10.00 4.00
148 Arky Vaughan 10.00 4.00
149 Rube Waddell 10.00 4.00
150 Honus Wagner 50.00 20.00
151 Dixie Walker 8.00 3.20
152 Ted Williams 125.00 50.00
153 Cy Young 40.00 16.00
154 Ross Youngs 40.00 16.00

1963 Fleer

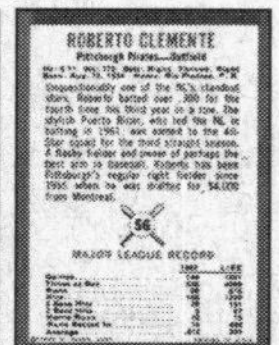

The Fleer set of current baseball players was marketed in 1963 in a gum card-style waxed wrapper package which contained a cherry cookie instead of gum. The five cent packs were packaged 24 to a box. The cards were printed in sheets of 66 with the scarce card of Joe Adcock (number 46) replaced by the unnumbered checklist card for the final press run. The complete set price includes the checklist card. The catalog designation for this set is R418-4. The key Rookie Card in this set is Maury Wills. The set is basically arranged numerically in alphabetical order by teams which are also in alphabetical order.

	NM	Ex
COMPLETE SET (67)	1500.00	800.00
WRAPPER (5-CENT)	100.00	40.00

1 Steve Barber 25.00 7.50
2 Ron Hansen 15.00 6.00
3 Milt Pappas 20.00 8.00
4 Brooks Robinson 100.00 40.00
5 Willie Mays 175.00 70.00
6 Lou Clinton 15.00 6.00
7 Bill Monbouquette 15.00 6.00
8 Carl Yastrzemski 100.00 40.00
9 Ray Herbert 15.00 6.00
10 Jim Landis 15.00 6.00
11 Dick Donovan 15.00 6.00
12 Tito Francona 15.00 6.00
13 Jerry Kindall 15.00 6.00
14 Frank Lary 20.00 8.00
15 Dick Howser 20.00 8.00
16 Jerry Lumpe 15.00 6.00
17 Norm Siebern 15.00 6.00
18 Don Lee 15.00 6.00
19 Albie Pearson 20.00 8.00
20 Bob Rodgers 20.00 8.00
21 Leon Wagner 15.00 6.00
22 Jim Kaat 25.00 10.00
23 Vic Power 20.00 8.00
24 Rich Rollins 20.00 8.00
25 Bobby Richardson 25.00 10.00
26 Ralph Terry 20.00 8.00
27 Tom Cheney 15.00 6.00
28 Chuck Cottier 15.00 6.00
29 Jimmy Piersall 20.00 8.00
30 Dave Stenhouse 15.00 6.00
31 Glen Hobbie 15.00 6.00
32 Ron Santo 25.00 10.00
33 Gene Freese 15.00 6.00
34 Vada Pinson 25.00 10.00
35 Bob Purkey 15.00 6.00
36 Joe Amalfitano 15.00 6.00
37 Bob Aspromonte 15.00 6.00
38 Dick Farrell 15.00 6.00
39 Al Spangler 15.00 6.00
40 Tommy Davis 20.00 8.00
41 Don Drysdale 80.00 32.00
42 Sandy Koufax 200.00 80.00
43 Maury Wills RC 100.00 40.00
44 Frank Bolling 15.00 6.00
45 Warren Spahn 80.00 32.00
46 Joe Adcock SP 150.00 60.00
47 Roger Craig 20.00 8.00
48 Al Jackson 20.00 8.00
49 Rod Kanehl 20.00 8.00
50 Ruben Amaro 15.00 6.00
51 Johnny Callison 20.00 8.00
52 Clay Dalrymple 15.00 6.00
53 Don Demeter 15.00 6.00
54 Art Mahaffey 15.00 6.00
55 Smoky Burgess 20.00 8.00
56 Roberto Clemente 175.00 70.00
57 Roy Face 20.00 8.00
58 Vern Law 20.00 8.00
59 Bill Mazeroski 30.00 12.00
60 Ken Boyer 25.00 10.00
61 Bob Gibson 80.00 32.00
62 Gene Oliver 15.00 6.00
63 Bill White 20.00 8.00
64 Orlando Cepeda 30.00 12.00
65 Jim Davenport 15.00 6.00
66 Billy O'Dell 25.00 7.50
NNO Checklist card 500.00 160.00

1981 Fleer

This issue of cards marks Fleer's first modern era entry into the current player baseball card market since 1963. Unopened packs contained 17 cards as well as a piece of gum. Unopened boxes contained 38 packs. As a matter of fact, the boxes actually told the retailer there was extra profit as they were charged as if there were 36 packs in the box. Cards are grouped in team order and teams are ordered based upon their standings from the 1980 season with the World Series champion Philadelphia Phillies starting off the set. Cards 638-660 feature specials and checklists. The cards of pitchers in this set erroneously show a heading (on the card backs) of "Batting Record" over their career pitching statistics. There were three distinct printings: the two following the primary run were designed to correct numerous errors. The variations caused by these multiple printings are noted in the checklist below (P1, P2, or P3). The Craig Nettles variation was corrected before the end of the first printing and thus is not included in the complete set consideration due to scarcity. The key Rookie Cards in this set are Danny Ainge, Harold Baines, Kirk Gibson, Jeff Reardon, and Fernando Valenzuela, whose first name was erroneously spelled Fernand on the card front.

	Nm-Mt	Ex-Mt
COMPLETE SET (660)	40.00	16.00

1 Pete Rose UER 3.00 1.20
270 hits in 63
should be 170
2 Larry Bowa .... .25 .10
3 Manny Trillo .... .10 .04
4 Bob Boone .... .25 .10
5 Mike Schmidt 2.50 1.00
See also 640A
6 Steve Carlton P1 .... .50 .20
Golden Arm
Back 1066 Cardinals
Number on back 6
6B Steve Carlton P2 .... 1.50 .60
Pitcher of Year
Back 1066 Cardinals
6C Steve Carlton P3 .... 2.00 .80

1966 Cardinals
7 Tug McGraw .25 .10
See 657A
8 Larry Christenson .10 .04
9 Bake McBride .25 .10
10 Greg Luzinski .25 .10
11 Ron Reed .10 .04
12 Dickie Noles .10 .04
13 Keith Moreland .10 .04
14 Bob Walk RC .50 .20
15 Lonnie Smith .25 .10
16 Dick Ruthven .10 .04
17 Sparky Lyle .25 .10
18 Greg Gross .10 .04
19 Garry Maddox .10 .04
20 Nino Espinosa .10 .04
21 George Vukovich .10 .04
22 John Vukovich .10 .04
23 Ramon Aviles .10 .04
24A Kevin Saucier P1 .10 .04
Name on back Ken
24B Kevin Saucier P2 .10 .04
Name on back Ken
24C Kevin Saucier P3 .50 .20
Name on back Kevin
25 Randy Lerch .10 .04
26 Del Unser .10 .04
27 Tim McCarver .25 .10
28 George Brett 2.50 1.00
See also 655A
29 Willie Wilson .25 .10
See also 653A
30 Paul Splittorff .10 .04
31 Dan Quisenberry .10 .04
32A Amos Otis P1 .25 .10
(Batting Pose
Outfield
32 on back
32B Amos Otis P2 .25 .10
Series Starter
483 on back
33 Steve Busby .10 .04
34 U.L. Washington .10 .04
35 Dave Chalk .10 .04
36 Darrell Porter .10 .04
37 Marty Pattin .10 .04
38 Larry Gura .10 .04
39 Renie Martin .10 .04
40 Rich Gale .10 .04
41A Hal McRae P1 .50 .20
(Royals on front
in black letters
41B Hal McRae P2 .25 .10
(Royals on front
in blue letters
42 Dennis Leonard .10 .04
43 Willie Aikens .10 .04
44 Frank White .25 .10
45 Clint Hurdle .10 .04
46 John Wathan .10 .04
47 Pete LaCock .10 .04
48 Rance Mulliniks .10 .04
49 Jeff Twitty .10 .04
50 Jamie Quirk .10 .04
51 Art Howe .10 .04
52 Ken Forsch .10 .04
53 Vern Ruhle .10 .04
54 Joe Niekro .10 .04
55 Frank LaCorte .10 .04
56 J.R. Richard .25 .10
57 Nolan Ryan 5.00 2.00
58 Enos Cabell .10 .04
59 Cesar Cedeno .25 .10
60 Jose Cruz .25 .10
61 Bill Virdon MG .10 .04
62 Terry Puhl .10 .04
63 Joaquin Andujar .25 .10
64 Alan Ashby .10 .04
65 Joe Sambito .10 .04
66 Denny Walling .10 .04
67 Jeff Leonard .25 .10
68 Luis Pujols .10 .04
69 Bruce Bochy .10 .04
70 Rafael Landestoy .10 .04
71 Dave Smith RC .50 .20
72 Danny Heep .10 .04
73 Julio Gonzalez .10 .04
74 Craig Reynolds .10 .04
75 Gary Woods .10 .04
76 Dave Bergman .10 .04
77 Randy Niemann .10 .04
78 Joe Morgan .50 .20
79 Reggie Jackson 1.00 .40
See also 650A
80 Bucky Dent .25 .10
81 Tommy John .25 .10
82 Luis Tiant .25 .10
83 Rick Cerone .10 .04
84 Dick Howser MG .10 .04
85 Lou Piniella .25 .10
86 Ron Davis .10 .04
87A Graig Nettles ERR 5.00 2.00
Name on back spelled Craig
87B Graig Nettles COR .25 .10
Graig
88 Ron Guidry .25 .10
89 Rich Gossage .25 .10
90 Rudy May .10 .04
91 Gaylord Perry .25 .10
92 Eric Soderholm .10 .04
93 Bob Watson .10 .04
94 Bobby Murcer .25 .10
95 Bobby Brown .10 .04
96 Jim Spencer .10 .04
97 Tom Underwood .10 .04
98 Oscar Gamble .10 .04
99 Johnny Oates .25 .10
100 Fred Stanley .10 .04
101 Ruppert Jones .10 .04
102 Dennis Werth .10 .04
103 Joe Lefebvre .10 .04
104 Brian Doyle .10 .04
105 Aurelio Rodriguez .10 .04
106 Doug Bird .10 .04
107 Mike Griffin RC .15 .06
108 Tim Lollar .10 .04
109 Willie Randolph .25 .10
110 Steve Garvey .50 .20
111 Reggie Smith .25 .10
112 Don Sutton .25 .10
113 Burt Hooton .10 .04
114A Dave Lopes P1 .50 .20
Small hand on back
114B Dave Lopes P2 .25 .10
No hand
115 Dusty Baker .25 .10
116 Tom Lasorda MG .50 .20
117 Bill Russell .25 .10
118 Jerry Reuss UER .10 .04
Home omitted
119 Terry Forster .25 .10
120A Bob Welch P1 .25 .10
(Name on back is Bob
120B Bob Welch P2 .25 .10
Name on back is Robert
121 Don Stanhouse .10 .04
122 Rick Monday .25 .10
123 Derrel Thomas .10 .04
124 Joe Ferguson .10 .04
125 Rick Sutcliffe .25 .10
126A Ron Cey P1 .25 .10
Small hand on back
126B Ron Cey P2 .25 .10
No hand
127 Dave Goltz .10 .04
128 Jay Johnstone .10 .04
129 Steve Yeager .25 .10
130 Gary Weiss .10 .04
131 Mike Scioscia RC 1.50 .60
132 Vic Davalillo .10 .04
133 Doug Rau .10 .04
134 Pepe Frias .10 .04
135 Mickey Hatcher .10 .04
136 Steve Howe RC .50 .20
137 Robert Castillo .10 .04
138 Gary Thomasson .10 .04
139 Rudy Law .10 .04
140 F.Valenzuela RC UER 2.00 .80
Misspelled Fernand on card
141 Manny Mota .25 .10
142 Gary Carter .50 .20
143 Steve Rogers .25 .10
144 Warren Cromartie .10 .04
145 Andre Dawson .50 .20
146 Larry Parrish .10 .04
147 Rowland Office .10 .04
148 Ellis Valentine .10 .04
149 Dick Williams MG .10 .04
150 Bill Gullickson RC .50 .20
151 Elias Sosa .10 .04
152 John Tamargo .10 .04
153 Chris Speier .10 .04
154 Ron LeFlore .25 .10
155 Rodney Scott .10 .04
156 Stan Bahnsen .10 .04
157 Bill Lee .25 .10
158 Fred Norman .10 .04
159 Woodie Fryman .10 .04
160 David Palmer .10 .04
161 Jerry White .10 .04
162 Roberto Ramos .10 .04
163 John D'Acquisto .10 .04
164 Tommy Hutton .10 .04
165 Charlie Lea .10 .04
166 Scott Sanderson .10 .04
167 Ken Macha .10 .04
168 Tony Bernazard .10 .04
169 Jim Palmer .50 .20
170 Steve Stone .10 .04
171 Mike Flanagan .10 .04
172 Al Bumbry .10 .04
173 Doug DeCinces .10 .04
174 Scott McGregor .10 .04
175 Mark Belanger .10 .04
176 Tim Stoddard .10 .04
177A Rick Dempsey P1 .25 .10
Small hand on front
177B Rick Dempsey P2 .10 .04
No hand
178 Earl Weaver MG .25 .10
179 Tippy Martinez .10 .04
180 Dennis Martinez .25 .10
181 Sammy Stewart .10 .04
182 Rich Dauer .10 .04
183 Lee May .10 .04
184 Eddie Murray 1.50 .60
185 Benny Ayala .10 .04
186 John Lowenstein .10 .04
187 Gary Roenicke .10 .04
188 Ken Singleton .25 .10
189 Dan Graham .10 .04
190 Terry Crowley .10 .04
191 Kiko Garcia .10 .04
192 Dave Ford .10 .04
193 Mark Corey .10 .04
194 Lenn Sakata .10 .04
195 Doug DeCinces .10 .04
196 Johnny Bench 1.00 .40
197 Dave Concepcion .25 .10
198 Ray Knight .25 .10
199 Ken Griffey .25 .10
200 Tom Seaver 1.00 .40
201 Dave Collins .10 .04
202A George Foster P1 .50 .20
Slugger
Number on back 216
202B George Foster P2 .50 .20
Slugger
Number on back 202
203 Junior Kennedy .10 .04
204 Frank Pastore .10 .04
205 Dan Driessen .10 .04
206 Hector Cruz .10 .04
207 Paul Moskau .10 .04
208 Charlie Leibrandt RC .50 .20
209 Harry Spilman .10 .04
210 Joe Price .10 .04
211 Tom Hume .10 .04
212 Joe Nolan .10 .04
213 Doug Bair .10 .04
214 Mario Soto .10 .04
215A Bill Bonham P1 .50 .20
(Small hand on back)
215B Bill Bonham P2 .10 .04
(No hand)
216 George Foster .25 .10
(See 202)
217 Paul Householder .10 .04
218 Ron Oester .10 .04
219 Sam Mejias .10 .04
220 Sheldon Burnside .10 .04
221 Carl Yastrzemski 1.50 .60
222 Jim Rice .25 .10
223 Fred Lynn .25 .10
224 Carlton Fisk .50 .20
225 Rick Burleson .10 .04
226 Dennis Eckersley .50 .20
227 Butch Hobson .10 .04
228 Tom Burgmeier .10 .04
229 Garry Hancock .10 .04
230 Don Zimmer MG .25 .10
231 Steve Renko .10 .04
232 Dwight Evans .50 .20
233 Mike Torrez .10 .04
234 Bob Stanley .10 .04
235 Jim Dwyer .10 .04
236 Dave Stapleton .10 .04
237 Glenn Hoffman .10 .04
238 Jerry Remy .10 .04
239 Dick Drago .10 .04
240 Bill Campbell .10 .04
241 Tony Perez .50 .20
242 Phil Niekro .50 .20
243 Dale Murphy .50 .20
244 Bob Horner .25 .10
245 Jeff Burroughs .25 .10
246 Rick Camp .10 .04
247 Bobby Cox MG .25 .10
248 Bruce Benedict .10 .04
249 Gene Garber .10 .04
250 Jerry Royster .10 .04
251A Gary Matthews P1 .50 .20
Small hand on back
251B Gary Matthews P2 .25 .10
No hand
252 Chris Chambliss .25 .10
253 Luis Gomez .10 .04
254 Bill Nahorodny .10 .04
255 Doyle Alexander .10 .04
256 Brian Asselstine .10 .04
257 Biff Pocoroba .10 .04
258 Mike Lum .10 .04
259 Charlie Spikes .10 .04
260 Glenn Hubbard .10 .04
261 Tommy Boggs .10 .04
262 Al Hrabosky UER .25 .10
Card lists him as 5' 1"
263 Rick Matula .10 .04
264 Preston Hanna .10 .04
265 Larry Bradford .10 .04
266 Rafael Ramirez .10 .04
267 Larry McWilliams .10 .04
268 Rod Carew .50 .20
269 Bobby Grich .25 .10
270 Carney Lansford .25 .10
271 Don Baylor .25 .10
272 Joe Rudi .25 .10
273 Dan Ford .10 .04
274 Jim Fregosi MG .10 .04
275 Dave Frost .10 .04
276 Frank Tanana .25 .10
277 Dickie Thon .10 .04
278 Jason Thompson .10 .04
279 Rick Miller .10 .04
280 Bert Campaneris .25 .10
281 Tom Donohue .10 .04
282 Brian Downing .25 .10
283 Fred Patek .10 .04
284 Bruce Kison .10 .04
285 Dave LaRoche .10 .04
286 Don Aase .10 .04
287 Jim Barr .10 .04
288 Alfredo Martinez .10 .04
289 Larry Harlow .10 .04
290 Andy Hassler .10 .04
291 Dave Kingman .25 .10
292 Bill Buckner .25 .10
293 Rick Reuschel .25 .10
294 Bruce Sutter .25 .10
295 Jerry Martin .10 .04
296 Scot Thompson .10 .04
297 Ivan DeJesus .10 .04
298 Steve Dillard .10 .04
299 Dick Tidrow .10 .04
300 Randy Martz .10 .04
301 Lenny Randle .10 .04
302 Lynn McGlothen .10 .04
303 Cliff Johnson .10 .04
304 Tim Blackwell .10 .04
305 Dennis Lamp .10 .04
306 Bill Caudill .10 .04
307 Carlos Lezcano .10 .04
308 Jim Tracy RC 1.00 .40
309 Doug Capilla UER .10 .04
Cubs on front but
Braves on back
310 Willie Hernandez .10 .04
311 Mike Vail .10 .04
312 Mike Krukow .10 .04
313 Barry Foote .10 .04
314 Larry Biittner .10 .04
315 Mike Tyson .10 .04
316 Lee Mazzilli .25 .10
317 John Stearns .10 .04
318 Alex Trevino .10 .04
319 Craig Swan .10 .04
320 Frank Taveras .10 .04
321 Steve Henderson .10 .04
322 Neil Allen .10 .04
323 Mark Bomback .10 .04
324 Mike Jorgensen .10 .04
325 Joe Torre MG .50 .20
326 Elliott Maddox .10 .04
327 Pete Falcone .10 .04
328 Ray Burris .10 .04
329 Claudell Washington .10 .04
330 Doug Flynn .10 .04
331 Joel Youngblood .10 .04
332 Bill Almon .10 .04
333 Tom Hausman .10 .04
334 Pat Zachry .10 .04
335 Jeff Reardon RC 1.00 .40
336 Wally Backman RC .50 .20
337 Dan Norman .10 .04
338 Jerry Morales .10 .04
339 Ed Farmer .10 .04
340 Bob Molinaro .10 .04
341 Todd Cruz .10 .04
342A Britt Burns P1 .50 .20
Small hand on front
342B Britt Burns P2 .25 .10
No hand
343 Kevin Bell .10 .04
344 Tony LaRussa MG .25 .10
345 Steve Trout .10 .04
346 Harold Baines RC 3.00 1.20
347 Richard Wortham .10 .04
348 Wayne Nordhagen .10 .04
349 Mike Squires .10 .04
350 Lamar Johnson .10 .04
351 Rickey Henderson 3.00 1.20
Most Stolen Bases AL
352 Francisco Barrios .10 .04
353 Thad Bosley .10 .04
354 Chet Lemon .25 .10
355 Bruce Kimm .10 .04
356 Richard Dotson .10 .04
357 Jim Morrison .10 .04
358 Mike Proly .10 .04
359 Greg Pryor .10 .04
360 Dave Parker .25 .10
361 Omar Moreno .10 .04
362A Kent Tekulve P1 .10 .04
Back 1071 Waterbury
and 1078 Pirates
362B Kent Tekulve P2 .10 .04
1971 Waterbury and
1978 Pirates
363 Willie Stargell .50 .20
364 Phil Garner .25 .10
365 Ed Ott .10 .04
366 Don Robinson .10 .04
367 Chuck Tanner MG .10 .04
368 Jim Rooker .10 .04
369 Dale Berra .10 .04
370 Jim Bibby .10 .04
371 Steve Nicosia .10 .04
372 Mike Easler .10 .04
373 Bill Robinson .10 .04
374 Lee Lacy .10 .04
375 John Candelaria .25 .10
376 Manny Sanguillen .25 .10
377 Rick Rhoden .10 .04
378 Grant Jackson .10 .04
379 Tim Foli .10 .04
380 Rod Scurry .10 .04
381 Bill Madlock .25 .10
382A Kurt Bevacqua .25 .10
P1 ERR
P on cap backwards
382B Kurt Bevacqua P2 .10 .04
COR
383 Bert Blyleven .25 .10
384 Eddie Solomon .10 .04
385 Enrique Romo .10 .04
386 John Milner .10 .04
387 Mike Hargrove .10 .04
388 Jorge Orta .10 .04
389 Toby Harrah .25 .10
390 Tom Veryzer .10 .04
391 Miguel Dilone .10 .04
392 Dan Spillner .10 .04
393 Jack Brohamer .10 .04
394 Wayne Garland .10 .04
395 Sid Monge .10 .04
396 Rick Waits .10 .04
397 Joe Charboneau RC 1.00 .40
398 Gary Alexander .10 .04
399 Jerry Dybzinski .10 .04
400 Mike Stanton .10 .04
401 Mike Paxton .10 .04
402 Gary Gray .10 .04
403 Rick Manning .10 .04
404 Bo Diaz .10 .04
405 Ron Hassey .10 .04
406 Ross Grimsley .10 .04
407 Victor Cruz .10 .04
408 Len Barker .25 .10
409 Bob Bailor .10 .04
410 Otto Velez .10 .04
411 Ernie Whitt .10 .04
412 Jim Clancy .10 .04
413 Barry Bonnell .10 .04
414 Dave Stieb .25 .10
415 Damaso Garcia .10 .04
416 John Mayberry .10 .04
417 Roy Howell .10 .04
418 Danny Ainge RC 1.50 .60
419A Jesse Jefferson P1 .10 .04
Back says Pirates
419B Jesse Jefferson P2 .10 .04
Back says Pirates
419C Jesse Jefferson P3 .50 .20
Back says Blue Jays
420 Joey McLaughlin .10 .04
421 Lloyd Moseby RC .50 .20
422 Alvis Woods .10 .04
423 Garth Iorg .10 .04
424 Doug Ault .10 .04
425 Ken Schrom .10 .04
426 Mike Willis .10 .04
427 Steve Braun .10 .04
428 Bob Davis .10 .04
429 Jerry Garvin .10 .04
430 Alfredo Griffin .10 .04
431 Bob Mattick MG .10 .04
432 Vida Blue .25 .10
433 Jack Clark .25 .10
434 Willie McCovey .50 .20
435 Mike Ivie .10 .04
436A Darrel Evans P1 ERR .50 .20
(Name on front Darrel
436B Darrell Evans P2 COR .50 .20
Name on front Darrell
437 Terry Whitfield .10 .04
438 Rennie Stennett .10 .04
439 John Montefusco .10 .04
440 Jim Wohlford .10 .04
441 Bill North .10 .04
442 Milt May .10 .04
443 Max Venable .10 .04
444 Ed Whitson .10 .04
445 Al Holland .10 .04
446 Randy Moffitt .10 .04
447 Bob Knepper .10 .04
448 Gary Lavelle .10 .04
449 Greg Minton .10 .04
450 Johnnie LeMaster .10 .04
451 Larry Herndon .10 .04
452 Rich Murray .10 .04
453 Joe Pettini .10 .04
454 Allen Ripley .10 .04
455 Dennis Littlejohn .10 .04
456 Tom Griffin .10 .04
457 Alan Hargesheimer .10 .04
458 Joe Strain .10 .04
459 Steve Kemp .10 .04
460 Sparky Anderson MG .25 .10
461 Alan Trammell .50 .20
462 Mark Fidrych .25 .10
463 Lou Whitaker .50 .20
464 Dave Rozema .10 .04
465 Milt Wilcox .10 .04
466 Champ Summers .10 .04
467 Lance Parrish .25 .10
468 Dan Petry .10 .04
469 Pat Underwood .10 .04
470 Rick Peters .10 .04
471 Al Cowens .10 .04
472 John Wockenfuss .10 .04
473 Tom Brookens .10 .04
474 Richie Hebner .10 .04
475 Jack Morris .50 .20
476 Jim Lentine .10 .04
477 Bruce Robbins .10 .04
478 Mark Wagner .10 .04
479 Tim Corcoran .10 .04
480A Stan Papi P1 .25 .10
Front as Pitcher
480B Stan Papi P2 .10 .04
Front as Shortstop
481 Kirk Gibson RC 2.00 .80
482 Dan Schatzeder .10 .04
483A Amos Otis P1 .25 .10
See card 32
483B Amos Otis P2 .25 .10
See card 32
484 Dave Winfield .50 .20
485 Rollie Fingers .25 .10
486 Gene Richards .10 .04
487 Randy Jones .10 .04
488 Ozzie Smith 3.00 1.20
489 Gene Tenace .25 .10
490 Bill Fahey .10 .04
491 John Curtis .10 .04
492 Dave Cash .10 .04
493A Tim Flannery P1 .25 .10
Batting right
493B Tim Flannery P2 .10 .04
Batting left
494 Jerry Mumphrey .10 .04
495 Bob Shirley .10 .04
496 Steve Mura .10 .04
497 Eric Rasmussen .10 .04
498 Broderick Perkins .10 .04
499 Barry Evans .10 .04
500 Chuck Baker .10 .04
501 Luis Salazar RC .50 .20
502 Gary Lucas .10 .04
503 Mike Armstrong .10 .04
504 Jerry Turner .10 .04
505 Dennis Kinney .10 .04
506 Willie Montanez UER .10 .04
Spelled Willy on card front
507 Gorman Thomas .25 .10
508 Ben Oglivie .25 .10
509 Larry Hisle .10 .04
510 Sal Bando .25 .10
511 Robin Yount 1.50 .60
512 Mike Caldwell .10 .04
513 Sixto Lezcano .10 .04
514A Bill Travers P1 ERR .25 .10
Jerry Augustine
with Augustine back
514B Bill Travers P2 COR .10 .04
515 Paul Molitor 1.00 .40
516 Moose Haas .10 .04
517 Bill Castro .10 .04
518 Jim Slaton .10 .04
519 Lary Sorensen .10 .04
520 Bob McClure .10 .04
521 Charlie Moore .10 .04
522 Jim Gantner .10 .04
523 Reggie Cleveland .10 .04
524 Don Money .10 .04
525 Bill Travers .10 .04
526 Buck Martinez .10 .04
527 Dick Davis .10 .04
528 Ted Simmons .25 .10
529 Garry Templeton .25 .10
530 Ken Reitz .10 .04
531 Tony Scott .10 .04
532 Ken Oberkfell .10 .04
533 Bob Sykes .10 .04
534 Keith Smith .10 .04
535 John Littlefield .10 .04
536 Jim Kaat .25 .10
537 Bob Forsch .10 .04
538 Mike Phillips .10 .04
539 Terry Landrum .10 .04
540 Leon Durham RC .50 .20
541 Terry Kennedy .10 .04
542 George Hendrick .25 .10
543 Dane Iorg .10 .04
544 Mark Littell .10 .04
545 Keith Hernandez .25 .10
546 Silvio Martinez .10 .04
547A Don Hood P1 ERR .25 .10
Pete Vuckovich
with Vuckovich back
547B Don Hood P2 COR .10 .04
548 Bobby Bonds .25 .10
549 Mike Ramsey RC .15 .06
550 Tom Herr .10 .04
551 Roy Smalley .10 .04
552 Jerry Koosman .25 .10
553 Ken Landreaux .10 .04
554 John Castino .10 .04
555 Doug Corbett .10 .04
556 Bombo Rivera .10 .04
557 Ron Jackson .10 .04
558 Butch Wynegar .10 .04
559 Hosken Powell .10 .04
560 Pete Redfern .10 .04
561 Roger Erickson .10 .04
562 Glenn Adams .10 .04
563 Rick Sofield .10 .04
564 Geoff Zahn .10 .04
565 Pete Mackanin .10 .04
566 Mike Cubbage .10 .04

567 Darrell Jackson .10 .04
568 Dave Edwards .10 .04
569 Rob Wilfong .10 .04
570 Sal Butera .10 .04
571 Jose Morales .10 .04
572 Rick Langford .10 .04
573 Mike Norris .10 .04
574 Rickey Henderson 6.00 2.40
575 Tony Armas .25 .10
576 Dave Revering .10 .04
577 Jeff Newman .10 .04
578 Bob Lacey .10 .04
579 Brian Kingman .10 .04
580 Mitchell Page .10 .04
581 Billy Martin MG .50 .20
582 Rob Picciolo .10 .04
583 Mike Heath .10 .04
584 Mickey Klutts .10 .04
585 Orlando Gonzalez .10 .04
586 Mike Davis RC .50 .20
587 Wayne Gross .10 .04
588 Matt Keough .10 .04
589 Steve McCatty .10 .04
590 Dwayne Murphy .10 .04
591 Mario Guerrero .10 .04
592 Dave McKay .10 .04
593 Jim Essian .10 .04
594 Dave Heaverlo .10 .04
595 Maury Wills MG .25 .10
596 Juan Beniquez .10 .04
597 Rodney Craig .10 .04
598 Jim Anderson .10 .04
599 Floyd Bannister .10 .04
600 Bruce Bochte .10 .04
601 Julio Cruz .10 .04
602 Ted Cox .10 .04
603 Dan Meyer .10 .04
604 Larry Cox .10 .04
605 Bill Stein .10 .04
606 Steve Garvey .50 .20
Most Hits NL
607 Dave Roberts .10 .04
608 Leon Roberts .10 .04
609 Reggie Walton .10 .04
610 Dave Edler .10 .04
611 Larry Milbourne .10 .04
612 Kim Allen .10 .04
613 Mario Mendoza .10 .04
614 Tom Paciorek .10 .04
615 Glenn Abbott .10 .04
616 Joe Simpson .10 .04
617 Mickey Rivers .10 .04
618 Jim Kern .10 .04
619 Jim Sundberg .25 .10
620 Richie Zisk .10 .04
621 Jon Matlack .10 .04
622 Ferguson Jenkins .25 .10
623 Pat Corrales MG .10 .04
624 Ed Figueroa .10 .04
625 Buddy Bell .25 .10
626 Al Oliver .25 .10
627 Doc Medich .10 .04
628 Bump Wills .10 .04
629 Rusty Staub .25 .10
630 Pat Putnam .10 .04
631 John Grubb .10 .04
632 Danny Darwin .10 .04
633 Ken Clay .10 .04
634 Jim Norris .10 .04
635 John Butcher .10 .04
636 Dave Roberts .10 .04
637 Billy Sample .10 .04
638 Carl Yastrzemski 1.50 .60
639 Cecil Cooper .25 .10
640 Mike Schmidt P1 2.50 1.00
Portrait
Third Base
number on back 5
640B Mike Schmidt P2 2.50 1.00
1980 Home Run King
640 on back
641A CL: Phils/Royals P1 .25 .10
41 is Hal McRae
641B CL: Phils/Royals P2 .25 .10
41 is Hal McRae
Double Threat
642 CL: Astros/Yankees .10 .04
643 CL: Expos/Dodgers .10 .04
644A CL: Reds/Orioles P1 .25 .10
202 is George Foster
Joe Nolan pitcher
should be catcher
644B CL: Reds/Orioles P2 .25 .10
202 is Foster Slugger
Joe Nolan pitcher
should be catcher
645 Pete Rose 1.50 .60
Larry Bowa
Mike Schmidt
Triple Threat P1
No number on back
645B Pete Rose 2.50 1.00
Larry Bowa
Mike Schmidt
Triple Threat P2
Back numbered 645
646 CL: Braves/Red Sox .10 .04
647 CL: Cubs/Angels .10 .04
648 CL: Mets/White Sox .10 .04
649 CL: Indians/Pirates .10 .04
650 Reggie Jackson 1.00 .40
Mr. Baseball P1
Number on back 79
650B Reggie Jackson .50 .20
Mr. Baseball P2
Number on back 650
651 CL: Giants/Blue Jays .10 .04
652A CL:Tigers/Padres P1 .25 .10
483 is listed
652B CL:Tigers/Padres P2 .25 .10
483 is deleted
653A Willie Wilson P1 .25 .10
Most Hits Most Runs
Number on back 29
653B Willie Wilson P2 .25 .10
Most Hits Most Runs
Number on back 653
654A Checklist Brewers .25 .10
Cards P1
514 Jerry Augustine
547 Pete Vuckovich
654B Checklist Brewers .25 .10
Cards P2
514 Billy Travers
547 Don Hood
655 George Brett P1 2.50 1.00
.390 Average
Number on back 28
655B George Brett P2 2.50 1.00
.390 Average
Number on back 655
656 CL:Twins/Oakland A's .25 .10
657A Tug McGraw P1 .25 .10
Game Saver
Number on back 7
657B Tug McGraw P2 .25 .10
Game Saver
Number on back 657
658 CL: Rangers/Mariners .10 .04
659A Checklist P1 .10 .04
of Special Cards
Last lines on front
Wilson Most Hits
659B Checklist P2 .10 .04
of Special Cards
Last lines on front
Otis Series Starter
660 Steve Carlton P1 .50 .20
Golden Arm
(Number on back 660
Back 1066 Cardinals
660B Steve Carlton P2 2.00 .80
Golden Arm
1966 Cardinals

1982 Fleer

The 1982 Fleer set contains 660-card standard-size cards, of which are grouped in team order based upon standings from the previous season. Cards numbered 628 through 646 are special cards highlighting some of the stars and leaders of the 1981 season. The last 14 cards in the set (647-660) are checklist cards. The backs feature player statistics and a full-color team logo in the upper right-hand corner of each card. The complete set price below does not include any of the more valuable variation cards listed. Fleer was not allowed to insert bubble gum or other confectionary products into these packs; therefore logo stickers were included in these 15-card packs. Notable Rookie Cards in this set include Cal Ripken Jr., Lee Smith, and Dave Stewart.

Nm-Mt Ex-Mt
COMPLETE SET (660) 50.00 20.00
1 Dusty Baker .20 .08
2 Robert Castillo .10 .04
3 Ron Cey .20 .08
4 Terry Forster .20 .08
5 Steve Garvey .20 .08
6 Dave Goltz .10 .04
7 Pedro Guerrero .20 .08
8 Burt Hooton .10 .04
9 Steve Howe .10 .04
10 Jay Johnstone .10 .04
11 Ken Landreaux .10 .04
12 Dave Lopes .20 .08
13 Mike A. Marshall RC .50 .20
14 Bobby Mitchell .10 .04
15 Rick Monday .20 .08
16 Tom Niedenfuer RC .50 .20
17 Ted Power RC .15 .06
18 Jerry Reuss UER .10 .04
("Home:" omitted)
19 Ron Roenicke .10 .04
20 Bill Russell .20 .08
21 Steve Sax RC 1.00 .40
22 Mike Scioscia .20 .08
23 Reggie Smith .20 .08
24 Dave Stewart RC 1.50 .60
25 Rick Sutcliffe .20 .08
26 Derrel Thomas .10 .04
27 Fernando Valenzuela .75 .30
28 Bob Welch .20 .08
29 Steve Yeager .20 .08
30 Bobby Brown .10 .04
31 Rick Cerone .10 .04
32 Ron Davis .10 .04
33 Bucky Dent .20 .08
34 Barry Foote .10 .04
35 George Frazier .10 .04
36 Oscar Gamble .10 .04
37 Rich Gossage .20 .08
38 Ron Guidry .20 .08
39 Reggie Jackson .40 .16
40 Tommy John .20 .08
41 Rudy May .10 .04
42 Larry Milbourne .10 .04
43 Jerry Mumphrey .10 .04
44 Bobby Murcer .20 .08
45 Gene Nelson .10 .04
46 Graig Nettles .20 .08
47 Johnny Oates .20 .08
48 Lou Piniella .20 .08
49 Willie Randolph .20 .08
50 Rick Reuschel .20 .08
51 Dave Revering .10 .04
52 Dave Righetti RC 1.50 .60
53 Aurelio Rodriguez .10 .04
54 Bob Watson .10 .04
55 Dennis Werth .10 .04
56 Dave Winfield .20 .08
57 Johnny Bench .75 .30
58 Bruce Berenyi .10 .04
59 Larry Biittner .10 .04
60 Scott Brown .10 .04
61 Dave Collins .10 .04
62 Geoff Combe .10 .04
63 Dave Concepcion .20 .08
64 Dan Driessen .10 .04
65 Joe Edelen .10 .04
66 George Foster .20 .08
67 Ken Griffey .20 .08
68 Paul Householder .10 .04
69 Tom Hume .10 .04
70 Junior Kennedy .10 .04
71 Ray Knight .20 .08
72 Mike LaCoss .10 .04
73 Rafael Landestoy .10 .04
74 Charlie Leibrandt .10 .04
75 Sam Mejias .10 .04
76 Paul Moskau .10 .04
77 Joe Nolan .10 .04
78 Mike O'Berry .10 .04
79 Ron Oester .10 .04
80 Frank Pastore .10 .04
81 Joe Price .10 .04
82 Tom Seaver .75 .30
83 Mario Soto .20 .08
84 Mike Vail .10 .04
85 Tony Armas .20 .08
86 Shooty Babitt .10 .04
87 Dave Beard .10 .04
88 Rick Bosetti .10 .04
89 Keith Drumwright .10 .04
90 Wayne Gross .10 .04
91 Mike Heath .10 .04
92 Rickey Henderson 2.50 1.00
93 Cliff Johnson .10 .04
94 Jeff Jones .10 .04
95 Matt Keough .10 .04
96 Brian Kingman .10 .04
97 Mickey Klutts .10 .04
98 Rick Langford .10 .04
99 Steve McCatty .10 .04
100 Dave McKay .10 .04
101 Dwayne Murphy .10 .04
102 Jeff Newman .10 .04
103 Mike Norris .10 .04
104 Bob Owchinko .10 .04
105 Mitchell Page .10 .04
106 Rob Picciolo .10 .04
107 Jim Spencer .10 .04
108 Fred Stanley .10 .04
109 Tom Underwood .10 .04
110 Joaquin Andujar .20 .08
111 Steve Braun .10 .04
112 Bob Forsch .10 .04
113 George Hendrick .20 .08
114 Keith Hernandez .20 .08
115 Tom Herr .20 .08
116 Dane Iorg .10 .04
117 Jim Kaat .20 .08
118 Tito Landrum .10 .04
119 Sixto Lezcano .10 .04
120 Mark Littell .10 .04
121 John Martin RC .15 .06
122 Silvio Martinez .10 .04
123 Ken Oberkfell .10 .04
124 Darrell Porter .10 .04
125 Mike Ramsey .10 .04
126 Orlando Sanchez .10 .04
127 Bob Shirley .10 .04
128 Lary Sorensen .10 .04
129 Bruce Sutter .20 .08
130 Bob Sykes .10 .04
131 Garry Templeton .20 .08
132 Gene Tenace .20 .08
133 Jerry Augustine .10 .04
134 Sal Bando .20 .08
135 Mark Brouhard .10 .04
136 Mike Caldwell .10 .04
137 Reggie Cleveland .10 .04
138 Cecil Cooper .20 .08
139 Jamie Easterly .10 .04
140 Marshall Edwards .10 .04
141 Rollie Fingers .20 .08
142 Jim Gantner .10 .04
143 Moose Haas .10 .04
144 Larry Hisle .10 .04
145 Roy Howell .10 .04
146 Rickey Keeton .10 .04
147 Randy Lerch .10 .04
148 Paul Molitor .40 .16
149 Don Money .10 .04
150 Charlie Moore .10 .04
151 Ben Oglivie .20 .08
152 Ted Simmons .20 .08
153 Jim Slaton .10 .04
154 Gorman Thomas .20 .08
155 Robin Yount 1.25 .50
156 Pete Vuckovich .10 .04
(Should precede Yount
in the team order)
157 Benny Ayala .10 .04
158 Mark Belanger .10 .04
159 Al Bumbry .10 .04
160 Terry Crowley .10 .04
161 Rich Dauer .10 .04
162 Doug DeCinces .10 .04
163 Rick Dempsey .10 .04
164 Jim Dwyer .10 .04
165 Mike Flanagan .10 .04
166 Dave Ford .10 .04
167 Dan Graham .10 .04
168 Wayne Krenchicki .10 .04
169 John Lowenstein .10 .04
170 Dennis Martinez .20 .08
171 Tippy Martinez .10 .04
172 Scott McGregor .10 .04
173 Jose Morales .10 .04
174 Eddie Murray .75 .30
175 Jim Palmer .20 .08
176 Cal Ripken RC 40.00 16.00
Fleer Ripken cards from 1982 through 1993 erroneously have 22 games played in 1981;not 23.
177 Gary Roenicke .10 .04
178 Lenn Sakata .10 .04
179 Ken Singleton .20 .08
180 Sammy Stewart .10 .04
181 Tim Stoddard .10 .04
182 Steve Stone .10 .04
183 Stan Bahnsen .10 .04
184 Ray Burris .10 .04
185 Gary Carter .20 .08
186 Warren Cromartie .10 .04
187 Andre Dawson .20 .08
188 Terry Francona RC 1.50 .60
189 Woodie Fryman .10 .04
190 Bill Gullickson .10 .04
191 Grant Jackson .10 .04
192 Wallace Johnson .10 .04
193 Charlie Lea .10 .04
194 Bill Lee .20 .08
195 Jerry Manuel .10 .04
196 Brad Mills .10 .04
197 John Milner .10 .04
198 Rowland Office .10 .04
199 David Palmer .10 .04
200 Larry Parrish .10 .04
201 Mike Phillips .10 .04
202 Tim Raines .40 .16
203 Bobby Ramos .10 .04
204 Jeff Reardon .20 .08
205 Steve Rogers .20 .08
206 Scott Sanderson .10 .04
207 Rodney Scott UER .40 .16
(Photo actually
Tim Raines)
208 Elias Sosa .10 .04
209 Chris Speier .10 .04
210 Tim Wallach RC 1.00 .40
211 Jerry White .10 .04
212 Alan Ashby .10 .04
213 Cesar Cedeno .20 .08
214 Jose Cruz .20 .08
215 Kiko Garcia .10 .04
216 Phil Garner .20 .08
217 Danny Heep .10 .04
218 Art Howe .10 .04
219 Bob Knepper .10 .04
220 Frank LaCorte .10 .04
221 Joe Niekro .10 .04
222 Joe Pittman .10 .04
223 Terry Puhl .10 .04
224 Luis Pujols .10 .04
225 Craig Reynolds .10 .04
226 J.R. Richard .20 .08
227 Dave Roberts .10 .04
228 Vern Ruhle .10 .04
229 Nolan Ryan 4.00 1.60
230 Joe Sambito .10 .04
231 Tony Scott .10 .04
232 Dave Smith .10 .04
233 Harry Spilman .10 .04
234 Don Sutton .20 .08
235 Dickie Thon .10 .04
236 Denny Walling .10 .04
237 Gary Woods .10 .04
238 Luis Aguayo .10 .04
239 Ramon Aviles .10 .04
240 Bob Boone .20 .08
241 Larry Bowa .20 .08
242 Warren Brusstar .10 .04
243 Steve Carlton .40 .16
244 Larry Christenson .10 .04
245 Dick Davis .10 .04
246 Greg Gross .10 .04
247 Sparky Lyle .20 .08
248 Garry Maddox .10 .04
249 Gary Matthews .20 .08
250 Bake McBride .20 .08
251 Tug McGraw .20 .08
252 Keith Moreland .10 .04
253 Dickie Noles .10 .04
254 Mike Proly .10 .04
255 Ron Reed .10 .04
256 Pete Rose 2.50 1.00
257 Dick Ruthven .10 .04
258 Mike Schmidt 2.00 .80
259 Lonnie Smith .10 .04
260 Manny Trillo .10 .04
261 Del Unser .10 .04
262 George Vukovich .10 .04
263 Tom Brookens .10 .04
264 George Cappuzzello .10 .04
265 Marty Castillo .10 .04
266 Al Cowens .10 .04
267 Kirk Gibson .75 .30
268 Richie Hebner .10 .04
269 Ron Jackson .10 .04
270 Lynn Jones .10 .04
271 Steve Kemp .10 .04
272 Rick Leach .10 .04
273 Aurelio Lopez .10 .04
274 Jack Morris .20 .08
275 Kevin Saucier .10 .04
276 Lance Parrish .20 .08
277 Rick Peters .10 .04
278 Dan Petry .10 .04
279 Dave Rozema .10 .04
280 Stan Papi .10 .04
281 Dan Schatzeder .10 .04
282 Champ Summers .10 .04
283 Alan Trammell .20 .08
284 Lou Whitaker .20 .08
285 Milt Wilcox .10 .04
286 John Wockenfuss .10 .04
287 Gary Allenson .10 .04
288 Tom Burgmeier .10 .04
289 Bill Campbell .10 .04
290 Mark Clear .10 .04
291 Steve Crawford .10 .04
292 Dennis Eckersley .40 .16
293 Dwight Evans .20 .08
294 Rich Gedman .50 .20
295 Garry Hancock .10 .04
296 Glenn Hoffman .10 .04
297 Bruce Hurst .10 .04
298 Carney Lansford .20 .08
299 Rick Miller .10 .04
300 Reid Nichols .10 .04
301 Bob Ojeda RC .50 .20
302 Tony Perez .40 .16
303 Chuck Rainey .10 .04
304 Jerry Remy .10 .04
305 Jim Rice .20 .08
306 Joe Rudi .20 .08
307 Bob Stanley .10 .04
308 Dave Stapleton .10 .04
309 Frank Tanana .20 .08
310 Mike Torrez .10 .04
311 John Tudor .20 .08
312 Carl Yastrzemski 1.25 .50
313 Buddy Bell .20 .08
314 Steve Comer .10 .04
315 Danny Darwin .10 .04
316 John Ellis .10 .04
317 John Grubb .10 .04
318 Rick Honeycutt .10 .04
319 Charlie Hough .20 .08
320 Ferguson Jenkins .20 .08
321 John Henry Johnson .10 .04
322 Jim Kern .10 .04
323 Jon Matlack .10 .04
324 Doc Medich .10 .04
325 Mario Mendoza .10 .04
326 Al Oliver .20 .08
327 Pat Putnam .10 .04
328 Mickey Rivers .10 .04
329 Leon Roberts .10 .04
330 Billy Sample .10 .04
331 Bill Stein .10 .04
332 Jim Sundberg .20 .08
333 Mark Wagner .10 .04
334 Bump Wills .10 .04
335 Bill Almon .10 .04
336 Harold Baines .20 .08
337 Ross Baumgarten .10 .04
338 Tony Bernazard .10 .04
339 Britt Burns .10 .04
340 Richard Dotson .10 .04
341 Jim Essian .10 .04
342 Ed Farmer .10 .04
343 Carlton Fisk .40 .16
344 Kevin Hickey RC .15 .06
345 LaMarr Hoyt .10 .04
346 Lamar Johnson .10 .04
347 Jerry Koosman .20 .08
348 Rusty Kuntz .10 .04
349 Dennis Lamp .10 .04
350 Ron LeFlore .20 .08
351 Chet Lemon .20 .08
352 Greg Luzinski .20 .08
353 Bob Molinaro .10 .04
354 Jim Morrison .10 .04
355 Wayne Nordhagen .10 .04
356 Greg Pryor .10 .04
357 Mike Squires .10 .04
358 Steve Trout .10 .04
359 Alan Bannister .10 .04
360 Len Barker .10 .04
361 Bert Blyleven .20 .08
362 Joe Charboneau .20 .08
363 John Denny .10 .04
364 Bo Diaz .10 .04
365 Miguel Dilone .10 .04
366 Jerry Dybzinski .10 .04
367 Wayne Garland .10 .04
368 Mike Hargrove .10 .04
369 Toby Harrah .20 .08
370 Ron Hassey .10 .04
371 Von Hayes RC .50 .20
372 Pat Kelly .10 .04
373 Duane Kuiper .10 .04
374 Rick Manning .10 .04
375 Sid Monge .10 .04
376 Jorge Orta .10 .04
377 Dave Rosello .10 .04
378 Dan Spillner .10 .04
379 Mike Stanton .10 .04
380 Andre Thornton .10 .04
381 Tom Veryzer .10 .04
382 Rick Waits .10 .04
383 Doyle Alexander .10 .04
384 Vida Blue .20 .08
385 Fred Breining .10 .04
386 Enos Cabell .10 .04
387 Jack Clark .20 .08
388 Darrell Evans .20 .08
389 Tom Griffin .10 .04
390 Larry Herndon .10 .04
391 Al Holland .10 .04
392 Gary Lavelle .10 .04
393 Johnnie LeMaster .10 .04
394 Jerry Martin .10 .04
395 Milt May .10 .04
396 Greg Minton .10 .04
397 Joe Morgan .20 .08
398 Joe Pettini .10 .04
399 Allen Ripley .10 .04
400 Billy Smith .10 .04
401 Rennie Stennett .10 .04
402 Ed Whitson .10 .04
403 Jim Wohlford .10 .04
404 Willie Aikens .10 .04
405 George Brett 2.00 .80
406 Ken Brett .10 .04
407 Dave Chalk .10 .04
408 Rich Gale .10 .04
409 Cesar Geronimo .10 .04
410 Larry Gura .10 .04
411 Clint Hurdle .10 .04
412 Mike Jones .10 .04
413 Dennis Leonard .10 .04
414 Renie Martin .10 .04
415 Lee May .10 .04
416 Hal McRae .20 .08
417 Darryl Motley .10 .04
418 Rance Mulliniks .10 .04
419 Amos Otis .20 .08
420 Ken Phelps .10 .04
421 Jamie Quirk .10 .04
422 Dan Quisenberry .10 .04
423 Paul Splittorff .10 .04
424 U.L. Washington .10 .04
425 John Wathan .10 .04
426 Frank White .20 .08
427 Willie Wilson .20 .08
428 Brian Asselstine .10 .04
429 Bruce Benedict .10 .04
430 Tommy Boggs .10 .04
431 Larry Bradford .10 .04
432 Rick Camp .10 .04
433 Chris Chambliss .20 .08
434 Gene Garber .10 .04
435 Preston Hanna .10 .04
436 Bob Horner .20 .08
437 Glenn Hubbard .10 .04
438A All Hrabosky ERR 8.00 3.20
(Height 5'1"
All on reverse)
438B Al Hrabosky ERR .40 .16
(Height 5'1")
438C Al Hrabosky .20 .08
(Height 5'10")
439 Rufino Linares .10 .04

0 Rick Mahler .10 .04
1 Ed Miller .10 .04
2 John Montefusco .10 .04
3 Dale Murphy .40 .16
4 Phil Niekro .20 .08
5 Gaylord Perry .20 .08
6 Biff Pocoroba .10 .04
7 Rafael Ramirez .10 .04
8 Jerry Royster .10 .04
9 Claudell Washington .10 .04
0 Don Aase .10 .04
1 Don Baylor .20 .08
2 Juan Beniquez .10 .04
3 Rick Burleson .10 .04
4 Bert Campaneris .20 .08
5 Rod Carew .40 .16
6 Bob Clark .10 .04
7 Brian Downing .20 .08
8 Dan Ford .10 .04
9 Ken Forsch .10 .04
0A Dave Frost (5 mm .10 .04
space before ERA)
0B Dave Frost .10 .04
(1 mm space)
1 Bobby Grich .20 .08
2 Larry Harlow .10 .04
3 John Harris .10 .04
4 Andy Hassler .10 .04
5 Butch Hobson .10 .04
6 Jesse Jefferson .10 .04
7 Bruce Kison .10 .04
8 Fred Lynn .20 .08
9 Angel Moreno .10 .04
0 Ed Ott .10 .04
1 Fred Patek .10 .04
2 Steve Renko .10 .04
3 Mike Witt .50 .20
4 Geoff Zahn .10 .04
5 Gary Alexander .10 .04
6 Dale Berra .10 .04
7 Kurt Bevacqua .10 .04
8 Jim Bibby .10 .04
9 John Candelaria .10 .04
0 Victor Cruz .10 .04
1 Mike Easler .10 .04
2 Tim Foli .10 .04
3 Lee Lacy .10 .04
4 Vance Law .10 .04
5 Bill Madlock .20 .08
6 Willie Montanez .10 .04
7 Omar Moreno .10 .04
8 Steve Nicosia .10 .04
9 Dave Parker .20 .08
0 Tony Pena .20 .08
1 Pascual Perez .10 .04
2 Johnny Ray RC .50 .20
3 Rick Rhoden .10 .04
4 Bill Robinson .10 .04
5 Don Robinson .10 .04
6 Enrique Romo .10 .04
7 Rod Scurry .10 .04
8 Eddie Solomon .10 .04
9 Willie Stargell .40 .16
0 Kent Tekulve .10 .04
1 Jason Thompson .10 .04
2 Glenn Abbott .10 .04
3 Jim Anderson .10 .04
4 Floyd Bannister .10 .04
5 Bruce Bochte .10 .04
6 Jeff Burroughs .10 .04
7 Bryan Clark RC .15 .06
8 Ken Clay .10 .04
9 Julio Cruz .10 .04
0 Dick Drago .10 .04
1 Gary Gray .10 .04
2 Dan Meyer .10 .04
3 Jerry Narron .10 .04
4 Tom Paciorek .10 .04
5 Casey Parsons .10 .04
6 Lenny Randle .10 .04
7 Shane Rawley .10 .04
8 Joe Simpson .10 .04
9 Richie Zisk .10 .04
20 Neil Allen .10 .04
21 Bob Bailor .10 .04
22 Hubie Brooks .10 .04
23 Mike Cubbage .10 .04
24 Pete Falcone .10 .04
25 Doug Flynn .10 .04
26 Tom Hausman .10 .04
27 Ron Hodges .10 .04
28 Randy Jones .10 .04
29 Mike Jorgensen .10 .04
30 Dave Kingman .20 .08
31 Ed Lynch .10 .04
32 Mike G. Marshall .10 .04
33 Lee Mazzilli .20 .08
34 Dyar Miller .10 .04
35 Mike Scott .20 .08
36 Rusty Staub .20 .08
37 John Stearns .10 .04
38 Craig Swan .10 .04
39 Frank Taveras .10 .04
40 Alex Trevino .10 .04
41 Ellis Valentine .10 .04
42 Mookie Wilson .20 .08
43 Joel Youngblood .10 .04
44 Pat Zachry .10 .04
45 Glenn Adams .10 .04
46 Fernando Arroyo .10 .04
47 John Verhoeven .10 .04
48 Sal Butera .10 .04
49 John Castino .10 .04
50 Don Cooper .10 .04
51 Doug Corbett .10 .04
52 Dave Engle .10 .04
53 Roger Erickson .10 .04
54 Danny Goodwin .10 .04
55A Darrell Jackson .40 .16
(Black cap)
55B Darrell Jackson .20 .08
(Red cap with T)
55C Darrell Jackson 3.00 1.20
(Red cap, no emblem)
56 Pete Mackanin .10 .04
57 Jack O'Connor .10 .04
58 Hosken Powell .10 .04
59 Pete Redfern .10 .04
60 Roy Smalley .10 .04
61 Chuck Baker UER .10 .04
(Shortshop on front)
562 Gary Ward .10 .04
563 Rob Wilfong .10 .04
564 Al Williams .10 .04
565 Butch Wynegar .10 .04
566 Randy Bass RC .50 .20
567 Juan Bonilla RC .15 .06
568 Danny Boone .10 .04
569 John Curtis .10 .04
570 Juan Eichelberger .10 .04
571 Barry Evans .10 .04
572 Tim Flannery .10 .04
573 Ruppert Jones .10 .04
574 Terry Kennedy .10 .04
575 Joe Lefebvre .10 .04
576A John Littlefield ERR 150.00 60.00
(Left handed;
reverse negative)
576B John Littlefield COR .20 .08
(Right handed)
577 Gary Lucas .10 .04
578 Steve Mura .10 .04
579 Broderick Perkins .10 .04
580 Gene Richards .10 .04
581 Luis Salazar .10 .04
582 Ozzie Smith 1.50 .60
583 John Urrea .10 .04
584 Chris Welsh .10 .04
585 Rick Wise .10 .04
586 Doug Bird .10 .04
587 Tim Blackwell .10 .04
588 Bobby Bonds .20 .08
589 Bill Buckner .20 .08
590 Bill Caudill .10 .04
591 Hector Cruz .10 .04
592 Jody Davis .10 .04
593 Ivan DeJesus .10 .04
594 Steve Dillard .10 .04
595 Leon Durham .10 .04
596 Rawly Eastwick .20 .08
597 Steve Henderson .10 .04
598 Mike Krukow .10 .04
599 Mike Lum .10 .04
600 Randy Martz .10 .04
601 Jerry Morales .10 .04
602 Ken Reitz .10 .04
603 Lee Smith RC ERR 2.00 .80
(Cubs logo reversed)
603B Lee Smith RC COR 6.00 2.40
604 Dick Tidrow .10 .04
605 Jim Tracy .20 .08
606 Mike Tyson .10 .04
607 Ty Waller .10 .04
608 Danny Ainge .20 .08
609 Jorge Bell RC 1.00 .40
610 Mark Bomback .10 .04
611 Barry Bonnell .10 .04
612 Jim Clancy .10 .04
613 Damaso Garcia .10 .04
614 Jerry Garvin .10 .04
615 Alfredo Griffin .10 .04
616 Garth Iorg .10 .04
617 Luis Leal .10 .04
618 Ken Macha .10 .04
619 John Mayberry .10 .04
620 Joey McLaughlin .10 .04
621 Lloyd Moseby .10 .04
622 Dave Stieb .20 .08
623 Jackson Todd .10 .04
624 Willie Upshaw .50 .20
625 Otto Velez .10 .04
626 Ernie Whitt .10 .04
627 Alvis Woods .10 .04
628 All Star Game .20 .08
Cleveland, Ohio
629 Frank White .20 .08
Bucky Dent
630 Dan Driessen .20 .08
Dave Concepcion
George Foster
631 Bruce Sutter .10 .04
Top NL Relief Pitcher
632 Steve Carlton .20 .08
Carlton Fisk
633 Carl Yastrzemski .75 .30
3000th Game
634 Johnny Bench .75 .30
Tom Seaver
635 Fernando Valenzuela .10 .04
Gary Carter
636A Fernando Valenzuela: .40 .16
NL SO King "he" NL
636B Fernando Valenzuela: .40 .16
NL SO King "the" NL
637 Mike Schmidt .75 .30
Home Run King
638 Gary Carter .10 .04
Dave Parker
639 Perfect Game UER .20 .08
Len Barker
Bo Diaz
(Catcher actually
Ron Hassey)
640 Pete Rose .75 .30
Pete Rose Jr.
641 Lonnie Smith .75 .30
Mike Schmidt
Steve Carlton
642 Fred Lynn .20 .08
Dwight Evans
643 Rickey Henderson 1.25 .50
Most Hits and Runs
644 Rollie Fingers .20 .08
Most Saves AL
645 Tom Seaver .20 .08
Most 1981 Wins
646 Yankee Powerhouse .20 .08
Reggie Jackson
Dave Winfield
(Comma on back
after outfielder)
646B Yankee Powerhouse .20 .08
Reggie Jackson
Dave Winfield
(No comma)
647 CL: Yankees/Dodgers .10 .04
648 CL: A's/Reds .10 .04
649 CL: Cards/Brewers .10 .04
650 CL: Expos/Orioles .10 .04
651 CL: Astros/Phillies .10 .04
652 CL: Tigers/Red Sox .10 .04
653 CL: Rangers/White Sox .10 .04
654 CL: Giants/Indians .10 .04
655 CL: Royals/Braves .10 .04
656 CL: Angels/Pirates .10 .04
657 CL: Mariners/Mets .10 .04
658 CL: Padres/Twins .10 .04
659 CL: Blue Jays/Cubs .10 .04
660 Specials Checklist .10 .04

1983 Fleer

In 1983, for the third straight year, Fleer produced a baseball series of 660 standard-size cards. Of these, 1-628 are player cards, 629-646 are special cards, and 647-660 are checklist cards. The player cards are again ordered alphabetically within team and teams seeded in descending order based upon the previous season's standings. The front of each card has a colorful team logo at bottom left and the player's name and position at lower right. The reverses are done in shades of brown on white. Wax packs consisted of 15 cards plus logo stickers in a 38-pack box. Notable Rookie Cards include Wade Boggs, Tony Gwynn and Ryne Sandberg.

Nm-Mt Ex-Mt
COMPLETE SET (660) 60.00 24.00
1 Joaquin Andujar .20 .08
2 Doug Bair .10 .04
3 Steve Braun .10 .04
4 Glenn Brummer .10 .04
5 Bob Forsch .10 .04
6 David Green RC .50 .20
7 George Hendrick .20 .08
8 Keith Hernandez .20 .08
9 Tom Herr .10 .04
10 Dane Iorg .10 .04
11 Jim Kaat .20 .08
12 Jeff Lahti .10 .04
13 Tito Landrum .10 .04
14 Dave LaPoint .10 .04
15 Willie McGee RC 1.00 .40
16 Steve Mura .10 .04
17 Ken Oberkfell .10 .04
18 Darrell Porter .10 .04
19 Mike Ramsey .10 .04
20 Gene Roof .10 .04
21 Lonnie Smith .10 .04
22 Ozzie Smith 1.25 .50
23 John Stuper .10 .04
24 Bruce Sutter .20 .08
25 Gene Tenace .20 .08
26 Jerry Augustine .10 .04
27 Dwight Bernard .10 .04
28 Mark Brouhard .10 .04
29 Mike Caldwell .10 .04
30 Cecil Cooper .20 .08
31 Jamie Easterly .10 .04
32 Marshall Edwards .10 .04
33 Rollie Fingers .20 .08
34 Jim Gantner .10 .04
35 Moose Haas .10 .04
36 Roy Howell .10 .04
37 Pete Ladd .10 .04
38 Bob McClure .10 .04
39 Doc Medich .10 .04
40 Paul Molitor .40 .16
41 Don Money .10 .04
42 Charlie Moore .10 .04
43 Ben Oglivie .20 .08
44 Ed Romero .10 .04
45 Ted Simmons .20 .08
46 Jim Slaton .10 .04
47 Don Sutton .20 .08
48 Gorman Thomas .20 .08
49 Pete Vuckovich .10 .04
50 Ned Yost .10 .04
51 Robin Yount 1.25 .50
52 Benny Ayala .10 .04
53 Bob Bonner .10 .04
54 Al Bumbry .10 .04
55 Terry Crowley .10 .04
56 Storm Davis RC .50 .20
57 Rich Dauer .10 .04
58 Rick Dempsey UER .10 .04
(Posing batting lefty)
59 Jim Dwyer .10 .04
60 Mike Flanagan .10 .04
61 Dan Ford .10 .04
62 Glenn Gulliver .10 .04
63 John Lowenstein .10 .04
64 Dennis Martinez .20 .08
65 Tippy Martinez .10 .04
66 Scott McGregor .10 .04
67 Eddie Murray .75 .30
68 Joe Nolan .10 .04
69 Jim Palmer .20 .08
70 Cal Ripken 6.00 2.40
71 Gary Roenicke .10 .04
72 Lenn Sakata .10 .04
73 Ken Singleton .20 .08
74 Sammy Stewart .10 .04
75 Tim Stoddard .10 .04
76 Don Aase .10 .04
77 Don Baylor .20 .08
78 Juan Beniquez .10 .04
79 Bob Boone .20 .08
80 Rick Burleson .10 .04
81 Rod Carew .40 .16
82 Bobby Clark .10 .04
83 Doug Corbett .10 .04
84 John Curtis .10 .04
85 Doug DeCinces .10 .04
86 Brian Downing .20 .08
87 Joe Ferguson .10 .04
88 Tim Foli .10 .04
89 Ken Forsch .10 .04
90 Dave Goltz .10 .04
91 Bobby Grich .20 .08
92 Andy Hassler .10 .04
93 Reggie Jackson .40 .16
94 Ron Jackson .10 .04
95 Tommy John .20 .08
96 Bruce Kison .10 .04
97 Fred Lynn .20 .08
98 Ed Ott .10 .04
99 Steve Renko .10 .04
100 Luis Sanchez .10 .04
101 Rob Wilfong .10 .04
102 Mike Witt .10 .04
103 Geoff Zahn .10 .04
104 Willie Aikens .10 .04
105 Mike Armstrong .10 .04
106 Vida Blue .20 .08
107 Bud Black RC .50 .20
108 George Brett 2.00 .80
109 Bill Castro .10 .04
110 Onix Concepcion .10 .04
111 Dave Frost .10 .04
112 Cesar Geronimo .10 .04
113 Larry Gura .10 .04
114 Steve Hammond .10 .04
115 Don Hood .10 .04
116 Dennis Leonard .10 .04
117 Jerry Martin .10 .04
118 Lee May .10 .04
119 Hal McRae .20 .08
120 Amos Otis .20 .08
121 Greg Pryor .10 .04
122 Dan Quisenberry .10 .04
123 Don Slaught RC .50 .20
124 Paul Splittorff .10 .04
125 U.L. Washington .10 .04
126 John Wathan .10 .04
127 Frank White .20 .08
128 Willie Wilson .20 .08
129 Steve Bedrosian UER .10 .04
(Height 6'33")
130 Bruce Benedict .10 .04
131 Tommy Boggs .10 .04
132 Brett Butler .20 .08
133 Rick Camp .10 .04
134 Chris Chambliss .20 .08
135 Ken Dayley .10 .04
136 Gene Garber .10 .04
137 Terry Harper .10 .04
138 Bob Horner .20 .08
139 Glenn Hubbard .10 .04
140 Rufino Linares .10 .04
141 Rick Mahler .10 .04
142 Dale Murphy .40 .16
143 Phil Niekro .20 .08
144 Pascual Perez .10 .04
145 Biff Pocoroba .10 .04
146 Rafael Ramirez .10 .04
147 Jerry Royster .10 .04
148 Ken Smith .10 .04
149 Bob Walk .10 .04
150 Claudell Washington .10 .04
151 Bob Watson .10 .04
152 Larry Whisenton .10 .04
153 Porfirio Altamirano .10 .04
154 Marty Bystrom .10 .04
155 Steve Carlton .40 .16
156 Larry Christenson .10 .04
157 Ivan DeJesus .10 .04
158 John Denny .10 .04
159 Bob Dernier .10 .04
160 Bo Diaz .10 .04
161 Ed Farmer .10 .04
162 Greg Gross .10 .04
163 Mike Krukow .10 .04
164 Garry Maddox .10 .04
165 Gary Matthews .20 .08
166 Tug McGraw .20 .08
167 Bob Molinaro .10 .04
168 Sid Monge .10 .04
169 Ron Reed .10 .04
170 Bill Robinson .10 .04
171 Pete Rose 2.50 1.00
172 Dick Ruthven .10 .04
173 Mike Schmidt 2.00 .80
174 Manny Trillo .10 .04
175 Ozzie Virgil .10 .04
176 George Vukovich .10 .04
177 Gary Allenson .10 .04
178 Luis Aponte .10 .04
179 Wade Boggs RC 8.00 3.20
180 Tom Burgmeier .10 .04
181 Mark Clear .10 .04
182 Dennis Eckersley .40 .16
183 Dwight Evans .20 .08
184 Rich Gedman .10 .04
185 Glenn Hoffman .10 .04
186 Bruce Hurst .10 .04
187 Carney Lansford .20 .08
188 Rick Miller .10 .04
189 Reid Nichols .10 .04
190 Bob Ojeda .10 .04
191 Tony Perez .40 .16
192 Chuck Rainey .10 .04
193 Jerry Remy .10 .04
194 Jim Rice .20 .08
195 Bob Stanley .10 .04
196 Dave Stapleton .10 .04
197 Mike Torrez .10 .04
198 John Tudor .20 .08
199 Julio Valdez .10 .04
200 Carl Yastrzemski 1.25 .50
201 Dusty Baker .20 .08
202 Joe Beckwith .10 .04
203 Greg Brock .10 .04
204 Ron Cey .20 .08
205 Terry Forster .20 .08
206 Steve Garvey .20 .08
207 Pedro Guerrero .20 .08
208 Burt Hooton .10 .04
209 Steve Howe .10 .04
210 Ken Landreaux .10 .04
211 Mike Marshall .10 .04
212 Candy Maldonado RC .50 .20
213 Rick Monday .20 .08
214 Tom Niedenfuer .10 .04
215 Jorge Orta .10 .04
216 Jerry Reuss UER .10 .04
("Home:" omitted)
217 Ron Roenicke .10 .04
218 Vicente Romo .10 .04
219 Bill Russell .20 .08
220 Steve Sax .20 .08
221 Mike Scioscia .20 .08
222 Dave Stewart .20 .08
223 Derrel Thomas .10 .04
224 Fernando Valenzuela .20 .08
225 Bob Welch .20 .08
226 Ricky Wright .10 .04
227 Steve Yeager .20 .08
228 Bill Almon .10 .04
229 Harold Baines .20 .08
230 Salome Barojas .10 .04
231 Tony Bernazard .10 .04
232 Britt Burns .10 .04
233 Richard Dotson .10 .04
234 Ernesto Escarrega .10 .04
235 Carlton Fisk .40 .16
236 Jerry Hairston .10 .04
237 Kevin Hickey .10 .04
238 LaMarr Hoyt .10 .04
239 Steve Kemp .10 .04
240 Jim Kern .10 .04
241 Ron Kittle RC 1.00 .40
242 Jerry Koosman .20 .08
243 Dennis Lamp .10 .04
244 Rudy Law .10 .04
245 Vance Law .10 .04
246 Ron LeFlore .20 .08
247 Greg Luzinski .20 .08
248 Tom Paciorek .10 .04
249 Aurelio Rodriguez .10 .04
250 Mike Squires .10 .04
251 Steve Trout .10 .04
252 Jim Barr .10 .04
253 Dave Bergman .10 .04
254 Fred Breining .10 .04
255 Bob Brenly .10 .04
256 Jack Clark .20 .08
257 Chili Davis .20 .08
258 Darrell Evans .20 .08
259 Alan Fowlkes .10 .04
260 Rich Gale .10 .04
261 Atlee Hammaker .10 .04
262 Al Holland .10 .04
263 Duane Kuiper .10 .04
264 Bill Laskey .10 .04
265 Gary Lavelle .10 .04
266 Johnnie LeMaster .10 .04
267 Renie Martin .10 .04
268 Milt May .10 .04
269 Greg Minton .10 .04
270 Joe Morgan .20 .08
271 Tom O'Malley .10 .04
272 Reggie Smith .20 .08
273 Guy Sularz .10 .04
274 Champ Summers .10 .04
275 Max Venable .10 .04
276 Jim Wohlford .10 .04
277 Ray Burris .10 .04
278 Gary Carter .20 .08
279 Warren Cromartie .10 .04
280 Andre Dawson .20 .08
281 Terry Francona .20 .08
282 Doug Flynn .10 .04
283 Woodie Fryman .10 .04
284 Bill Gullickson .10 .04
285 Wallace Johnson .10 .04
286 Charlie Lea .10 .04
287 Randy Lerch .10 .04
288 Brad Mills .10 .04
289 Dan Norman .10 .04
290 Al Oliver .20 .08
291 David Palmer .10 .04
292 Tim Raines .20 .08
293 Jeff Reardon .20 .08
294 Steve Rogers .20 .08
295 Scott Sanderson .10 .04
296 Dan Schatzeder .10 .04
297 Bryn Smith .10 .04
298 Chris Speier .10 .04
299 Tim Wallach .20 .08
300 Jerry White .10 .04
301 Joel Youngblood .10 .04
302 Ross Baumgarten .10 .04
303 Dale Berra .10 .04
304 John Candelaria .10 .04
305 Dick Davis .10 .04
306 Mike Easler .10 .04
307 Richie Hebner .10 .04
308 Lee Lacy .10 .04
309 Bill Madlock .20 .08
310 Larry McWilliams .10 .04
311 John Milner .10 .04
312 Omar Moreno .10 .04
313 Jim Morrison .10 .04
314 Steve Nicosia .10 .04
315 Dave Parker .20 .08
316 Tony Pena .10 .04
317 Johnny Ray .10 .04
318 Rick Rhoden .10 .04
319 Don Robinson .10 .04
320 Enrique Romo .10 .04
321 Manny Sarmiento .10 .04
322 Rod Scurry .10 .04
323 Jimmy Smith .10 .04
324 Willie Stargell .40 .16
325 Jason Thompson .10 .04
326 Kent Tekulve .10 .04
327A Tom Brookens .10 .04
(Short .375" brown box
shaded in on card back)
327B Tom Brookens .10 .04
(Longer 1.25" brown box
shaded in on card back)
328 Enos Cabell .10 .04
329 Kirk Gibson .20 .08
330 Larry Herndon .10 .04
331 Mike Ivie .10 .04
332 Howard Johnson RC 1.00 .40
333 Lynn Jones .10 .04
334 Rick Leach .10 .04
335 Chet Lemon .20 .08
336 Jack Morris .20 .08
337 Lance Parrish .20 .08
338 Larry Pashnick .10 .04
339 Dan Petry .10 .04
340 Dave Rozema .10 .04
341 Dave Rucker .10 .04
342 Elias Sosa .10 .04

343 Dave Tobik .10 .04
344 Alan Trammell .20 .08
345 Jerry Turner .10 .04
346 Jerry Ujdur .10 .04
347 Pat Underwood .10 .04
348 Lou Whitaker .20 .08
349 Milt Wilcox .10 .04
350 Glenn Wilson .50 .20
351 John Wockenfuss .10 .04
352 Kurt Bevacqua .10 .04
353 Juan Bonilla .10 .04
354 Floyd Chiffer .10 .04
355 Luis DeLeon .10 .04
356 Dave Dravecky RC 1.00 .40
357 Dave Edwards .10 .04
358 Juan Eichelberger .10 .04
359 Tim Flannery .10 .04
360 Tony Gwynn RC 15.00 6.00
361 Ruppert Jones .10 .04
362 Terry Kennedy .10 .04
363 Joe Lefebvre .10 .04
364 Sixto Lezcano .10 .04
365 Tim Lollar .10 .04
366 Gary Lucas .10 .04
367 John Montefusco .10 .04
368 Broderick Perkins .10 .04
369 Joe Pittman .10 .04
370 Gene Richards .10 .04
371 Luis Salazar .10 .04
372 Eric Show RC .50 .20
373 Garry Templeton .20 .08
374 Chris Welsh .10 .04
375 Alan Wiggins .10 .04
376 Rick Cerone .10 .04
377 Dave Collins .10 .04
378 Roger Erickson .10 .04
379 George Frazier .10 .04
380 Oscar Gamble .10 .04
381 Rich Gossage .20 .08
382 Ken Griffey .20 .08
383 Ron Guidry .20 .08
384 Dave LaRoche .10 .04
385 Rudy May .10 .04
386 John Mayberry .10 .04
387 Lee Mazzilli .20 .08
388 Mike Morgan .10 .04
389 Jerry Mumphrey .10 .04
390 Bobby Murcer .20 .08
391 Graig Nettles .20 .08
392 Lou Piniella .20 .08
393 Willie Randolph .20 .08
394 Shane Rawley .10 .04
395 Dave Righetti .20 .08
396 Andre Robertson .10 .04
397 Roy Smalley .10 .04
398 Dave Winfield .20 .08
399 Butch Wynegar .10 .04
400 Chris Bando .10 .04
401 Alan Bannister .10 .04
402 Len Barker .10 .04
403 Tom Brennan .10 .04
404 Carmelo Castillo .10 .04
405 Miguel Dilone .10 .04
406 Jerry Dybzinski .10 .04
407 Mike Fischlin .10 .04
408 Ed Glynn UER .10 .04
(Photo actually
Bud Anderson)
409 Mike Hargrove .10 .04
410 Toby Harrah .20 .08
411 Ron Hassey .10 .04
412 Von Hayes .10 .04
413 Rick Manning .10 .04
414 Bake McBride .20 .08
415 Larry Milbourne .10 .04
416 Bill Nahorodny .10 .04
417 Jack Perconte .10 .04
418 Lary Sorensen .10 .04
419 Dan Spillner .10 .04
420 Rick Sutcliffe .20 .08
421 Andre Thornton .10 .04
422 Rick Waits .10 .04
423 Eddie Whitson .10 .04
424 Jesse Barfield .20 .08
425 Barry Bonnell .10 .04
426 Jim Clancy .10 .04
427 Damaso Garcia .10 .04
428 Jerry Garvin .10 .04
429 Alfredo Griffin .10 .04
430 Garth Iorg .10 .04
431 Roy Lee Jackson .10 .04
432 Luis Leal .10 .04
433 Buck Martinez .10 .04
434 Joey McLaughlin .10 .04
435 Lloyd Moseby .10 .04
436 Rance Mulliniks .10 .04
437 Dale Murray .10 .04
438 Wayne Nordhagen .10 .04
439 Geno Petralli .50 .20
440 Hosken Powell .10 .04
441 Dave Stieb .20 .08
442 Willie Upshaw .10 .04
443 Ernie Whitt .10 .04
444 Alvis Woods .10 .04
445 Alan Ashby .10 .04
446 Jose Cruz .20 .08
447 Kiko Garcia .10 .04
448 Phil Garner .20 .08
449 Danny Heep .10 .04
450 Art Howe .10 .04
451 Bob Knepper .10 .04
452 Alan Knicely .10 .04
453 Ray Knight .20 .08
454 Frank LaCorte .10 .04
455 Mike LaCoss .10 .04
456 Randy Moffitt .10 .04
457 Joe Niekro .10 .04
458 Terry Puhl .10 .04
459 Luis Pujols .10 .04
460 Craig Reynolds .10 .04
461 Bert Roberge .10 .04
462 Vern Ruhle .10 .04
463 Nolan Ryan 4.00 1.60
464 Joe Sambito .10 .04
465 Tony Scott .10 .04
466 Dave Smith .10 .04
467 Harry Spilman .10 .04
468 Dickie Thon .10 .04
469 Denny Walling .10 .04
470 Larry Andersen .10 .04
471 Floyd Bannister .10 .04
472 Jim Beattie .10 .04
473 Bruce Bochte .10 .04
474 Manny Castillo .10 .04
475 Bill Caudill .10 .04
476 Bryan Clark .10 .04
477 Al Cowens .10 .04
478 Julio Cruz .10 .04
479 Todd Cruz .10 .04
480 Gary Gray .10 .04
481 Dave Henderson .10 .04
482 Mike Moore RC .50 .20
483 Gaylord Perry .20 .08
484 Dave Revering .10 .04
485 Joe Simpson .10 .04
486 Mike Stanton .10 .04
487 Rick Sweet .10 .04
488 Ed VandeBerg .10 .04
489 Richie Zisk .10 .04
490 Doug Bird .10 .04
491 Larry Bowa .20 .08
492 Bill Buckner .20 .08
493 Bill Campbell .10 .04
494 Jody Davis .10 .04
495 Leon Durham .10 .04
496 Steve Henderson .10 .04
497 Willie Hernandez .10 .04
498 Ferguson Jenkins .20 .08
499 Jay Johnstone .10 .04
500 Junior Kennedy .10 .04
501 Randy Martz .10 .04
502 Jerry Morales .10 .04
503 Keith Moreland .10 .04
504 Dickie Noles .10 .04
505 Mike Proly .10 .04
506 Allen Ripley .10 .04
507 R.Sandberg RC UER 10.00 4.00
Should say High School
in Spokane, Washington
508 Lee Smith .40 .16
509 Pat Tabler .10 .04
510 Dick Tidrow .10 .04
511 Bump Wills .10 .04
512 Gary Woods .10 .04
513 Tony Armas .20 .08
514 Dave Beard .10 .04
515 Jeff Burroughs .10 .04
516 John D'Acquisto .10 .04
517 Wayne Gross .10 .04
518 Mike Heath .10 .04
519 R.Henderson UER 1.50 .60
Brock record listed
as 120 steals
520 Cliff Johnson .10 .04
521 Matt Keough .10 .04
522 Brian Kingman .10 .04
523 Rick Langford .10 .04
524 Dave Lopes .20 .08
525 Steve McCatty .10 .04
526 Dave McKay .10 .04
527 Dan Meyer .10 .04
528 Dwayne Murphy .10 .04
529 Jeff Newman .10 .04
530 Mike Norris .10 .04
531 Bob Owchinko .10 .04
532 Joe Rudi .20 .08
533 Jimmy Sexton .10 .04
534 Fred Stanley .10 .04
535 Tom Underwood .10 .04
536 Neil Allen .10 .04
537 Wally Backman .10 .04
538 Bob Bailor .10 .04
539 Hubie Brooks .10 .04
540 Carlos Diaz RC .25 .10
541 Pete Falcone .10 .04
542 George Foster .20 .08
543 Ron Gardenhire .10 .04
544 Brian Giles .10 .04
545 Ron Hodges .10 .04
546 Randy Jones .10 .04
547 Mike Jorgensen .10 .04
548 Dave Kingman .20 .08
549 Ed Lynch .10 .04
550 Jesse Orosco .10 .04
551 Rick Ownbey .10 .04
552 Charlie Puleo .10 .04
553 Gary Rajsich .10 .04
554 Mike Scott .20 .08
555 Rusty Staub .20 .08
556 John Stearns .10 .04
557 Craig Swan .10 .04
558 Ellis Valentine .10 .04
559 Tom Veryzer .10 .04
560 Mookie Wilson .20 .08
561 Pat Zachry .10 .04
562 Buddy Bell .20 .08
563 John Butcher .10 .04
564 Steve Comer .10 .04
565 Danny Darwin .10 .04
566 Bucky Dent .20 .08
567 John Grubb .10 .04
568 Rick Honeycutt .10 .04
569 Dave Hostetler .10 .04
570 Charlie Hough .20 .08
571 Lamar Johnson .10 .04
572 Jon Matlack .10 .04
573 Paul Mirabella .10 .04
574 Larry Parrish .10 .04
575 Mike Richardt .10 .04
576 Mickey Rivers .10 .04
577 Billy Sample .10 .04
578 Dave Schmidt .10 .04
579 Bill Stein .10 .04
580 Jim Sundberg .20 .08
581 Frank Tanana .20 .08
582 Mark Wagner .10 .04
583 George Wright RC .50 .20
584 Johnny Bench .75 .30
585 Bruce Berenyi .10 .04
586 Larry Biittner .10 .04
587 Cesar Cedeno .20 .08
588 Dave Concepcion .20 .08
589 Dan Driessen .10 .04
590 Greg Harris .10 .04
591 Ben Hayes .10 .04
592 Paul Householder .10 .04
593 Tom Hume .10 .04
594 Wayne Krenchicki .10 .04
595 Rafael Landestoy .10 .04
596 Charlie Leibrandt .10 .04
597 Eddie Milner .10 .04
598 Ron Oester .10 .04
599 Frank Pastore .10 .04
600 Joe Price .10 .04
601 Tom Seaver .75 .30
602 Bob Shirley .10 .04
603 Mario Soto .20 .08
604 Alex Trevino .10 .04
605 Mike Vail .10 .04
606 Duane Walker .10 .04
607 Tom Brunansky .20 .08
608 Bobby Castillo .10 .04
609 John Castino .10 .04
610 Ron Davis .10 .04
611 Lenny Faedo .10 .04
612 Terry Felton .10 .04
613 Gary Gaetti RC 1.00 .40
614 Mickey Hatcher .10 .04
615 Brad Havens .10 .04
616 Kent Hrbek .20 .08
617 Randy Johnson .10 .04
618 Tim Laudner .10 .04
619 Jeff Little .10 .04
620 Bobby Mitchell .10 .04
621 Jack O'Connor .10 .04
622 John Pacella .10 .04
623 Pete Redfern .10 .04
624 Jesus Vega .10 .04
625 Frank Viola RC 1.50 .60
626 Ron Washington .10 .04
627 Gary Ward .10 .04
628 Al Williams .10 .04
629 Carl Yastrzemski .75 .30
Dennis Eckersley
Mark Clear
630 Gaylord Perry .10 .04
Terry Bulling 5/6/82
631 Dave Concepcion .20 .08
Manny Trillo
632 Robin Yount .75 .30
Buddy Bell
633 Dave Winfield .10 .04
Kent Hrbek
634 Willie Stargell .75 .30
Pete Rose
635 Toby Harrah .20 .08
Andre Thornton
636 Ozzie Smith .75 .30
Lonnie Smith
637 Bo Diaz .10 .04
Gary Carter
638 Carlton Fisk .20 .08
Gary Carter
639 Rickey Henderson IA .75 .30
640 Ben Oglivie .40 .16
Reggie Jackson
641 Joel Youngblood .10 .04
August 4, 1982
642 Ron Hassey .20 .08
Len Barker
643 Black and Blue .20 .08
Vida Blue
644 Black and Blue .10 .04
Bud Black
645 Reggie Jackson Power .20 .08
646 Rickey Henderson Speed .75 .30
647 CL: Cards/Brewers .10 .04
648 CL: Orioles/Angels .10 .04
649 CL: Royals/Braves .10 .04
650 CL: Phillies/Red Sox .10 .04
651 CL: Dodgers/White Sox .10 .04
652 CL: Giants/Expos .10 .04
653 CL: Pirates/Tigers .10 .04
654 CL: Padres/Yankees .10 .04
655 CL: Indians/Blue Jays .10 .04
656 CL: Astros/Mariners .10 .04
657 CL: Cubs/A's .10 .04
658 CL: Mets/Rangers .10 .04
659 CL: Reds/Twins .10 .04
660 CL: Specials/Teams .10 .04

1984 Fleer

The 1984 Fleer card 660-card standard-size set featured fronts with full-color team logos along with the player's name and position and the Fleer identification. Wax packs again consisted of 15 cards plus logo stickers. The set features many imaginative photos, several multi-player cards, and many more action shots than the 1983 card set. The backs are quite similar to the 1983 backs except that blue rather than brown ink is used. The player cards are alphabetized within team and the teams are ordered by their 1983 season finish and won-lost record. Specials (626-646) and checklist cards (647-660) make up the end of the set. The key Rookie Cards in this set are Don Mattingly, Darryl Strawberry and Andy Van Slyke.

Nm-Mt Ex-Mt
COMPLETE SET (660) 50.00 20.00
1 Mike Boddicker .15 .06
2 Al Bumbry .15 .06
3 Todd Cruz .15 .06
4 Rich Dauer .15 .06
5 Storm Davis .15 .06
6 Rick Dempsey .15 .06
7 Jim Dwyer .15 .06
8 Mike Flanagan .15 .06
9 Dan Ford .15 .06
10 John Lowenstein .15 .06
11 Dennis Martinez .40 .16
12 Tippy Martinez .15 .06
13 Scott McGregor .15 .06
14 Eddie Murray 1.50 .60
15 Joe Nolan .15 .06
16 Jim Palmer .40 .16
17 Cal Ripken 10.00 4.00
18 Gary Roenicke .15 .06
19 Lenn Sakata .15 .06
20 John Shelby .15 .06
21 Ken Singleton .40 .16
22 Sammy Stewart .15 .06
23 Tim Stoddard .15 .06
24 Marty Bystrom .15 .06
25 Steve Carlton .75 .30
26 Ivan DeJesus .15 .06
27 John Denny .15 .06
28 Bob Dernier .15 .06
29 Bo Diaz .15 .06
30 Kiko Garcia .15 .06
31 Greg Gross .15 .06
32 Kevin Gross RC .50 .20
33 Von Hayes .15 .06
34 Willie Hernandez .15 .06
35 Al Holland .15 .06
36 Charles Hudson .15 .06
37 Joe Lefebvre .15 .06
38 Sixto Lezcano .15 .06
39 Garry Maddox .15 .06
40 Gary Matthews .40 .16
41 Len Matuszek .15 .06
42 Tug McGraw .40 .16
43 Joe Morgan .40 .16
44 Tony Perez .75 .30
45 Ron Reed .15 .06
46 Pete Rose 5.00 2.00
47 Juan Samuel RC 1.00 .40
48 Mike Schmidt 4.00 1.60
49 Ozzie Virgil .15 .06
50 Juan Agosto .15 .06
51 Harold Baines .40 .16
52 Floyd Bannister .15 .06
53 Salome Barojas .15 .06
54 Britt Burns .15 .06
55 Julio Cruz .15 .06
56 Richard Dotson .15 .06
57 Jerry Dybzinski .15 .06
58 Carlton Fisk .75 .30
59 Scott Fletcher .15 .06
60 Jerry Hairston .15 .06
61 Kevin Hickey .15 .06
62 Marc Hill .15 .06
63 LaMarr Hoyt .15 .06
64 Ron Kittle .15 .06
65 Jerry Koosman .40 .16
66 Dennis Lamp .15 .06
67 Rudy Law .15 .06
68 Vance Law .15 .06
69 Greg Luzinski .40 .16
70 Tom Paciorek .15 .06
71 Mike Squires .15 .06
72 Dick Tidrow .15 .06
73 Greg Walker .50 .20
74 Glenn Abbott .15 .06
75 Howard Bailey .15 .06
76 Doug Bair .15 .06
77 Juan Berenguer .15 .06
78 Tom Brookens .40 .16
79 Enos Cabell .15 .06
80 Kirk Gibson .40 .16
81 John Grubb .15 .06
82 Larry Herndon .40 .16
83 Wayne Krenchicki .15 .06
84 Rick Leach .15 .06
85 Chet Lemon .40 .16
86 Aurelio Lopez .40 .16
87 Jack Morris .40 .16
88 Lance Parrish .75 .30
89 Dan Petry .40 .16
90 Dave Rozema .15 .06
91 Alan Trammell .40 .16
92 Lou Whitaker .40 .16
93 Milt Wilcox .15 .06
94 Glenn Wilson .40 .16
95 John Wockenfuss .15 .06
96 Dusty Baker .40 .16
97 Joe Beckwith .15 .06
98 Greg Brock .15 .06
99 Jack Fimple .15 .06
100 Pedro Guerrero .40 .16
101 Rick Honeycutt .15 .06
102 Burt Hooton .15 .06
103 Steve Howe .15 .06
104 Ken Landreaux .15 .06
105 Mike Marshall .15 .06
106 Rick Monday .40 .16
107 Jose Morales .15 .06
108 Tom Niedenfuer .15 .06
109 Alejandro Pena RC* 1.00 .40
110 Jerry Reuss UER .15 .06
("Home:" omitted)
111 Bill Russell .40 .16
112 Steve Sax .15 .06
113 Mike Scioscia .40 .16
114 Derrel Thomas .15 .06
115 Fernando Valenzuela .40 .16
116 Bob Welch .40 .16
117 Steve Yeager .40 .16
118 Pat Zachry .15 .06
119 Don Baylor .40 .16
120 Bert Campaneris .40 .16
121 Rick Cerone .15 .06
122 Ray Fontenot .15 .06
123 George Frazier .15 .06
124 Oscar Gamble .15 .06
125 Rich Gossage .40 .16
126 Ken Griffey .40 .16
127 Ron Guidry .40 .16
128 Jay Howell .15 .06
129 Steve Kemp .15 .06
130 Matt Keough .15 .06
131 Don Mattingly RC 20.00 8.00
132 John Montefusco .15 .06
133 Omar Moreno .15 .06
134 Dale Murray .15 .06
135 Graig Nettles .40 .16
136 Lou Piniella .40 .16
137 Willie Randolph .40 .16
138 Shane Rawley .15 .06
139 Dave Righetti .40 .16
140 Andre Robertson .15 .06
141 Bob Shirley .15 .06
142 Roy Smalley .15 .06
143 Dave Winfield .40 .16
144 Butch Wynegar .15 .06
145 Jim Acker .15 .06
146 Doyle Alexander .15 .06
147 Jesse Barfield .40 .1
148 Jorge Bell .40 .1
149 Barry Bonnell .15 .0
150 Jim Clancy .15 .0
151 Dave Collins .15 .0
152 Tony Fernandez RC 1.00 .4
153 Damaso Garcia .15 .0
154 Dave Geisel .15 .0
155 Jim Gott .15 .0
156 Alfredo Griffin .15 .0
157 Garth Iorg .15 .0
158 Roy Lee Jackson .15 .0
159 Cliff Johnson .15 .0
160 Luis Leal .15 .0
161 Buck Martinez .15 .0
162 Joey McLaughlin .15 .0
163 Randy Moffitt .15 .0
164 Lloyd Moseby .15 .0
165 Rance Mulliniks .15 .0
166 Jorge Orta .15 .0
167 Dave Stieb .40 .1
168 Willie Upshaw .15 .0
169 Ernie Whitt .15 .0
170 Len Barker .15 .0
171 Steve Bedrosian .15 .0
172 Bruce Benedict .15 .0
173 Brett Butler .40 .1
174 Rick Camp .15 .0
175 Chris Chambliss .40 .1
176 Ken Dayley .15 .0
177 Pete Falcone .15 .0
178 Terry Forster .40 .1
179 Gene Garber .15 .0
180 Terry Harper .15 .0
181 Bob Horner .40 .1
182 Glenn Hubbard .15 .06
183 Randy Johnson .15 .06
184 Craig McMurtry .15 .06
185 Donnie Moore .15 .06
186 Dale Murphy .75 .30
187 Phil Niekro .40 .16
188 Pascual Perez .15 .06
189 Biff Pocoroba .15 .06
190 Rafael Ramirez .15 .06
191 Jerry Royster .15 .06
192 Claudell Washington .15 .06
193 Bob Watson .15 .06
194 Jerry Augustine .15 .06
195 Mark Brouhard .15 .06
196 Mike Caldwell .15 .06
197 Tom Candiotti RC 1.00 .40
198 Cecil Cooper .40 .16
199 Rollie Fingers .40 .16
200 Jim Gantner .15 .06
201 Bob L. Gibson RC .25 .10
202 Moose Haas .15 .06
203 Roy Howell .15 .06
204 Pete Ladd .15 .06
205 Rick Manning .15 .06
206 Bob McClure .15 .06
207 Paul Molitor UER .75 .30
('83 stats should say
.270 BA and 608 AB)
208 Don Money .15 .06
209 Charlie Moore .15 .06
210 Ben Oglivie .40 .16
211 Chuck Porter .15 .06
212 Ed Romero .15 .06
213 Ted Simmons .40 .16
214 Jim Slaton .15 .06
215 Don Sutton .40 .16
216 Tom Tellmann .15 .06
217 Pete Vuckovich .15 .06
218 Ned Yost .15 .06
219 Robin Yount 2.50 1.00
220 Alan Ashby .15 .06
221 Kevin Bass .15 .06
222 Jose Cruz .40 .16
223 Bill Dawley .15 .06
224 Frank DiPino .15 .06
225 Bill Doran RC* .50 .20
226 Phil Garner .40 .16
227 Art Howe .15 .06
228 Bob Knepper .15 .06
229 Ray Knight .40 .16
230 Frank LaCorte .15 .06
231 Mike LaCoss .15 .06
232 Mike Madden .15 .06
233 Jerry Mumphrey .15 .06
234 Joe Niekro .15 .06
235 Terry Puhl .15 .06
236 Luis Pujols .15 .06
237 Craig Reynolds .15 .06
238 Vern Ruhle .15 .06
239 Nolan Ryan 8.00 3.20
240 Mike Scott .40 .16
241 Tony Scott .15 .06
242 Dave Smith .15 .06
243 Dickie Thon .15 .06
244 Denny Walling .15 .06
245 Dale Berra .15 .06
246 Jim Bibby .15 .06
247 John Candelaria .15 .06
248 John DeLeon RC .50 .20
249 Mike Easler .15 .06
250 Cecilio Guante .15 .06
251 Richie Hebner .15 .06
252 Lee Lacy .15 .06
253 Bill Madlock .40 .16
254 Milt May .15 .06
255 Lee Mazzilli .40 .16
256 Larry McWilliams .15 .06
257 Jim Morrison .15 .06
258 Dave Parker .40 .16
259 Tony Pena .15 .06
260 Johnny Ray .15 .06
261 Rick Rhoden .15 .06
262 Don Robinson .15 .06
263 Manny Sarmiento .15 .06
264 Rod Scurry .15 .06
265 Kent Tekulve .15 .06
266 Gene Tenace .40 .16
267 Jason Thompson .15 .06
268 Lee Tunnell .15 .06
269 Marvell Wynne .50 .20
270 Ray Burris .15 .06
271 Gary Carter .40 .16
272 Warren Cromartie .15 .06
273 Andre Dawson .40 .16
274 Doug Flynn .15 .06

5 Terry Francona .40 .16
6 Bill Gullickson .15 .06
7 Bob James .15 .06
8 Charlie Lea .15 .06
9 Bryan Little .15 .06
0 Al Oliver .40 .16
1 Tim Raines .40 .16
2 Bobby Ramos .15 .06
3 Jeff Reardon .40 .16
4 Steve Rogers .40 .16
5 Scott Sanderson .15 .06
6 Dan Schatzeder .15 .06
7 Bryn Smith .15 .06
8 Chris Speier .15 .06
9 Manny Trillo .15 .06
0 Mike Vail .15 .06
1 Tim Wallach .15 .06
2 Chris Welsh .15 .06
3 Jim Wohlford .15 .06
4 Kurt Bevacqua .15 .06
5 Juan Bonilla .15 .06
6 Bobby Brown .15 .06
7 Luis DeLeon .15 .06
8 Dave Dravecky .15 .06
9 Tim Flannery .15 .06
0 Steve Garvey .40 .16
1 Tony Gwynn 6.00 2.40
2 Andy Hawkins .15 .06
3 Ruppert Jones .15 .06
4 Terry Kennedy .15 .06
5 Tim Lollar .15 .06
6 Gary Lucas .15 .06
7 Kevin McReynolds RC 1.00 .40
8 Sid Monge .15 .06
9 Mario Ramirez .15 .06
0 Gene Richards .15 .06
1 Luis Salazar .15 .06
2 Eric Show .15 .06
3 Elias Sosa .15 .06
4 Garry Templeton .40 .16
5 Mark Thurmond .15 .06
6 Ed Whitson .15 .06
7 Alan Wiggins .15 .06
8 Neil Allen .15 .06
9 Joaquin Andujar .40 .16
0 Steve Braun .15 .06
1 Glenn Brummer .15 .06
2 Bob Forsch .15 .06
3 David Green .15 .06
4 George Hendrick .40 .16
5 Tom Herr .15 .06
6 Dane Iorg .15 .06
7 Jeff Lahti .15 .06
8 Dave LaPoint .15 .06
9 Willie McGee .40 .16
0 Ken Oberkfell .15 .06
1 Darrell Porter .15 .06
2 Jamie Quirk .15 .06
3 Mike Ramsey .15 .06
4 Floyd Rayford .15 .06
5 Lonnie Smith .15 .06
6 Ozzie Smith 2.50 1.00
7 John Stuper .15 .06
8 Bruce Sutter .40 .16
9 A.Van Slyke RC UER 1.00 .40
Batting and throwing
both wrong on card back
0 Dave Von Ohlen .15 .06
1 Willie Aikens .15 .06
2 Mike Armstrong .15 .06
3 Bud Black .15 .06
4 George Brett 4.00 1.60
5 Onix Concepcion .15 .06
6 Keith Creel .15 .06
7 Larry Gura .15 .06
8 Don Hood .15 .06
9 Dennis Leonard .15 .06
0 Hal McRae .40 .16
1 Amos Otis .40 .16
2 Gaylord Perry .40 .16
3 Greg Pryor .15 .06
4 Dan Quisenberry .15 .06
5 Steve Renko .15 .06
6 Leon Roberts .15 .06
7 Pat Sheridan .15 .06
8 Joe Simpson .15 .06
9 Don Slaught .40 .16
0 Paul Splittorff .15 .06
1 U.L. Washington .15 .06
2 John Wathan .15 .06
3 Frank White .40 .16
4 Willie Wilson .40 .16
5 Jim Barr .15 .06
6 Dave Bergman .15 .06
7 Fred Breining .15 .06
8 Bob Brenly .15 .06
9 Jack Clark .40 .16
70 Chili Davis .40 .16
71 Mark Davis .15 .06
72 Darrell Evans .40 .16
73 Atlee Hammaker .15 .06
74 Mike Krukow .15 .06
75 Duane Kuiper .15 .06
76 Bill Laskey .15 .06
77 Gary Lavelle .15 .06
78 Johnnie LeMaster .15 .06
79 Jeff Leonard .15 .06
80 Randy Lerch .15 .06
81 Renie Martin .15 .06
82 Andy McGaffigan .15 .06
83 Greg Minton .15 .06
84 Tom O'Malley .15 .06
85 Max Venable .15 .06
86 Brad Wellman .15 .06
87 Joel Youngblood .15 .06
88 Gary Allenson .15 .06
89 Luis Aponte .15 .06
90 Tony Armas .40 .16
91 Doug Bird .15 .06
92 Wade Boggs 4.00 1.60
93 Dennis Boyd .40 .16
94 Mike Brown UER .25 .10
(shown with record
of 31-104)
95 Mark Clear .15 .06
96 Dennis Eckersley .75 .30
97 Dwight Evans .40 .16
98 Rich Gedman .15 .06
99 Glenn Hoffman .15 .06
00 Bruce Hurst .15 .06
401 John Henry Johnson .15 .06
402 Ed Jurak .15 .06
403 Rick Miller .15 .06
404 Jeff Newman .15 .06
405 Reid Nichols .15 .06
406 Bob Ojeda .15 .06
407 Jerry Remy .15 .06
408 Jim Rice .40 .16
409 Bob Stanley .40 .16
410 Dave Stapleton .15 .06
411 John Tudor .40 .16
412 Carl Yastrzemski 1.50 .60
413 Buddy Bell .40 .16
414 Larry Biittner .15 .06
415 John Butcher .15 .06
416 Danny Darwin .15 .06
417 Bucky Dent .40 .16
418 Dave Hostetler .15 .06
419 Charlie Hough .40 .16
420 Bobby Johnson .15 .06
421 Odell Jones .15 .06
422 Jon Matlack .15 .06
423 Pete O'Brien RC* .50 .20
424 Larry Parrish .15 .06
425 Mickey Rivers .15 .06
426 Billy Sample .15 .06
427 Dave Schmidt .15 .06
428 Mike Smithson .15 .06
429 Bill Stein .15 .06
430 Dave Stewart .40 .16
431 Jim Sundberg .40 .16
432 Frank Tanana .40 .16
433 Dave Tobik .15 .06
434 Wayne Tolleson .15 .06
435 George Wright .15 .06
436 Bill Almon .15 .06
437 Keith Atherton .15 .06
438 Dave Beard .15 .06
439 Tom Burgmeier .15 .06
440 Jeff Burroughs .15 .06
441 Chris Codiroli .15 .06
442 Tim Conroy .15 .06
443 Mike Davis .15 .06
444 Wayne Gross .15 .06
445 Garry Hancock .15 .06
446 Mike Heath .15 .06
447 Rickey Henderson 2.50 1.00
448 Donnie Hill .15 .06
449 Bob Kearney .15 .06
450 Bill Krueger RC .25 .10
451 Rick Langford .15 .06
452 Carney Lansford .40 .16
453 Dave Lopes .40 .16
454 Steve McCatty .15 .06
455 Dan Meyer .15 .06
456 Dwayne Murphy .15 .06
457 Mike Norris .15 .06
458 Ricky Peters .15 .06
459 Tony Phillips RC 1.00 .40
460 Tom Underwood .15 .06
461 Mike Warren .15 .06
462 Johnny Bench 1.50 .60
463 Bruce Berenyi .15 .06
464 Dann Bilardello .15 .06
465 Cesar Cedeno .40 .16
466 Dave Concepcion .40 .16
467 Dan Driessen .15 .06
468 Nick Esasky .15 .06
469 Rich Gale .15 .06
470 Ben Hayes .15 .06
471 Paul Householder .15 .06
472 Tom Hume .15 .06
473 Alan Knicely .15 .06
474 Eddie Milner .15 .06
475 Ron Oester .15 .06
476 Kelly Paris .15 .06
477 Frank Pastore .15 .06
478 Ted Power .15 .06
479 Joe Price .15 .06
480 Charlie Puleo .15 .06
481 Gary Redus RC* .50 .20
482 Bill Scherrer .15 .06
483 Mario Soto .40 .16
484 Alex Trevino .15 .06
485 Duane Walker .15 .06
486 Larry Bowa .40 .16
487 Warren Brusstar .15 .06
488 Bill Buckner .40 .16
489 Bill Campbell .15 .06
490 Ron Cey .40 .16
491 Jody Davis .15 .06
492 Leon Durham .15 .06
493 Mel Hall .40 .16
494 Ferguson Jenkins .40 .16
495 Jay Johnstone .15 .06
496 Craig Lefferts RC .25 .10
497 Carmelo Martinez .15 .06
498 Jerry Morales .15 .06
499 Keith Moreland .15 .06
500 Dickie Noles .15 .06
501 Mike Proly .15 .06
502 Chuck Rainey .15 .06
503 Dick Ruthven .15 .06
504 Ryne Sandberg 6.00 2.40
505 Lee Smith .40 .16
506 Steve Trout .15 .06
507 Gary Woods .15 .06
508 Juan Beniquez .15 .06
509 Bob Boone .40 .16
510 Rick Burleson .15 .06
511 Rod Carew .75 .30
512 Bobby Clark .15 .06
513 John Curtis .15 .06
514 Doug DeCinces .15 .06
515 Brian Downing .40 .16
516 Tim Foli .15 .06
517 Ken Forsch .15 .06
518 Bobby Grich .40 .16
519 Andy Hassler .15 .06
520 Reggie Jackson .75 .30
521 Ron Jackson .15 .06
522 Tommy John .40 .16
523 Bruce Kison .15 .06
524 Steve Lubratich .15 .06
525 Fred Lynn .40 .16
526 Gary Pettis .15 .06
527 Luis Sanchez .15 .06
528 Daryl Sconiers .15 .06
529 Ellis Valentine .15 .06
530 Rob Wilfong .15 .06
531 Mike Witt .15 .06
532 Geoff Zahn .15 .06
533 Bud Anderson .15 .06
534 Chris Bando .15 .06
535 Alan Bannister .15 .06
536 Bert Blyleven .40 .16
537 Tom Brennan .15 .06
538 Jamie Easterly .15 .06
539 Juan Eichelberger .15 .06
540 Jim Essian .15 .06
541 Mike Fischlin .15 .06
542 Julio Franco .75 .30
543 Mike Hargrove .15 .06
544 Toby Harrah .40 .16
545 Ron Hassey .15 .06
546 Neal Heaton .15 .06
547 Bake McBride .40 .16
548 Broderick Perkins .15 .06
549 Lary Sorensen .15 .06
550 Dan Spillner .15 .06
551 Rick Sutcliffe .40 .16
552 Pat Tabler .15 .06
553 Gorman Thomas .40 .16
554 Andre Thornton .15 .06
555 George Vukovich .15 .06
556 Darrell Brown .15 .06
557 Tom Brunansky .15 .06
558 Randy Bush .15 .06
559 Bobby Castillo .15 .06
560 John Castino .15 .06
561 Ron Davis .15 .06
562 Dave Engle .15 .06
563 Lenny Faedo .15 .06
564 Pete Filson .15 .06
565 Gary Gaetti .75 .30
566 Mickey Hatcher .15 .06
567 Kent Hrbek .40 .16
568 Rusty Kuntz .15 .06
569 Tim Laudner .15 .06
570 Rick Lysander .15 .06
571 Bobby Mitchell .15 .06
572 Ken Schrom .15 .06
573 Ray Smith .15 .06
574 Tim Teufel RC .50 .20
575 Frank Viola .75 .30
576 Gary Ward .15 .06
577 Ron Washington .15 .06
578 Len Whitehouse .15 .06
579 Al Williams .15 .06
580 Bob Bailor .15 .06
581 Mark Bradley .15 .06
582 Hubie Brooks .15 .06
583 Carlos Diaz .15 .06
584 George Foster .40 .16
585 Brian Giles .15 .06
586 Danny Heep .15 .06
587 Keith Hernandez .40 .16
588 Ron Hodges .15 .06
589 Scott Holman .15 .06
590 Dave Kingman .40 .16
591 Ed Lynch .15 .06
592 Jose Oquendo RC .50 .20
593 Jesse Orosco .15 .06
594 Junior Ortiz .15 .06
595 Tom Seaver 1.50 .60
596 Doug Sisk .15 .06
597 Rusty Staub .40 .16
598 John Stearns .15 .06
599 Darryl Strawberry RC 3.00 1.20
600 Craig Swan .15 .06
601 Walt Terrell .15 .06
602 Mike Torrez .15 .06
603 Mookie Wilson .40 .16
604 Jamie Allen .15 .06
605 Jim Beattie .15 .06
606 Tony Bernazard .15 .06
607 Manny Castillo .15 .06
608 Bill Caudill .15 .06
609 Bryan Clark .15 .06
610 Al Cowens .15 .06
611 Dave Henderson .40 .16
612 Steve Henderson .15 .06
613 Orlando Mercado .15 .06
614 Mike Moore .15 .06
615 Ricky Nelson UER .15 .06
(Jamie Nelson's
stats on back)
616 Spike Owen RC .50 .20
617 Pat Putnam .15 .06
618 Ron Roenicke .15 .06
619 Mike Stanton .15 .06
620 Bob Stoddard .15 .06
621 Rick Sweet .15 .06
622 Roy Thomas .15 .06
623 Ed VandeBerg .15 .06
624 Matt Young RC .50 .20
625 Richie Zisk .15 .06
626 Fred Lynn IA .40 .16
627 Manny Trillo IA .15 .06
628 Steve Garvey IA .15 .06
629 Rod Carew IA .40 .16
630 Wade Boggs IA 1.50 .60
631 Tim Raines IA .15 .06
632 Al Oliver IA .40 .16
633 Steve Sax IA .15 .06
634 Dickie Thon IA .15 .06
635 Dan Quisenberry .15 .06
Tippy Martinez
636 Joe Morgan 1.50 .60
Pete Rose
Tony Perez
637 Lance Parrish .75 .30
Bob Boone
638 George Brett 2.00 .80
Gaylord Perry
639 Dave Righetti .75 .30
Mike Warren
Bob Forsch
640 Johnny Bench 1.50 .60
Carl Yastrzemski
641 Gaylord Perry IA .15 .06
642 Steve Carlton IA .40 .16
643 Joe Altobelli MG .15 .06
Paul Owens MG
644 Rick Dempsey WS .15 .06
645 Mike Boddicker WS .15 .06
646 Scott McGregor WS .15 .06
647 CL: Orioles/Royals .15 .06
Joe Altobelli MG
648 CL: Phillies/Giants .15 .06
Paul Owens MG
649 CL: White Sox/Red Sox .75 .30
Tony LaRussa MG
650 CL: Tigers/Rangers .75 .30
Sparky Anderson MG
651 CL: Dodgers/A's .75 .30
Tommy Lasorda MG
652 CL: Yankees/Reds .75 .30
Billy Martin MG
653 CL: Blue Jays/Cubs .40 .16
Bobby Cox MG
654 CL: Braves/Angels .75 .30
Joe Torre MG
655 CL: Brewers/Indians .15 .06
Rene Lachemann MG
656 CL: Astros/Twins .15 .06
Bob Lillis MG
657 CL: Pirates/Mets .15 .06
Chuck Tanner MG
658 CL: Expos/Mariners .15 .06
Bill Virdon MG
659 CL: Padres/Specials .40 .16
Dick Williams MG
660 CL: Cardinals/Teams .75 .30
Whitey Herzog MG

1984 Fleer Update

This set was Fleer's first update set and portrayed players with their proper team for the current year and rookies who were not in their regular issue. Like the Topps Traded sets of the time, the Fleer Update sets were distributed in factory set form through hobby dealers only. The set was quite popular with collectors, and, apparently, the print run was relatively short, as the set was quickly in short supply and exhibited a rapid and dramatic price increase in the mid to late 1980's. The cards are numbered on the back with a U prefix and placed in alphabetical order by player name. The key (extended) Rookie Cards in this set are Roger Clemens, John Franco, Dwight Gooden, Jimmy Key, Mark Langston, Kirby Puckett, and Bret Saberhagen. Collectors are urged to be careful if purchasing single cards of Clemens, Darling, Gooden, Puckett, Rose, or Saberhagen as these specific cards have been illegally reprinted. These fakes are blurry when compared to the real cards and have noticeably different printing dot patterns under 8X or greater magnification..

Nm-Mt Ex-Mt
COMP.FACT.SET (132) 350.00 140.00
1 Willie Aikens 1.00 .40
2 Luis Aponte 1.00 .40
3 Mark Bailey 1.00 .40
4 Bob Bailor 1.00 .40
5 Dusty Baker 1.50 .60
6 Steve Balboni 1.00 .40
7 Alan Bannister 1.00 .40
8 Marty Barrett XRC 2.00 .80
9 Dave Beard 1.00 .40
10 Joe Beckwith 1.00 .40
11 Dave Bergman 1.00 .40
12 Tony Bernazard 1.00 .40
13 Bruce Bochte 1.00 .40
14 Barry Bonnell 1.00 .40
15 Phil Bradley 2.00 .80
16 Fred Breining 1.00 .40
17 Mike C. Brown 1.00 .40
18 Bill Buckner 1.50 .60
19 Ray Burris 1.00 .40
20 John Butcher 1.00 .40
21 Brett Butler 1.50 .60
22 Enos Cabell 1.00 .40
23 Bill Campbell 1.00 .40
24 Bill Caudill 1.00 .40
25 Bobby Clark 1.00 .40
26 Bryan Clark 1.00 .40
27 Roger Clemens XRC 225.00 90.00
28 Jaime Cocanower 1.00 .40
29 Ron Darling XRC* 5.00 2.00
30 Alvin Davis XRC 2.00 .80
31 Bob Dernier 1.00 .40
32 Carlos Diaz 1.00 .40
33 Mike Easler 1.00 .40
34 Dennis Eckersley 2.50 1.00
35 Jim Essian 1.00 .40
36 Darrell Evans 1.50 .60
37 Mike Fitzgerald 1.00 .40
38 Tim Foli 1.00 .40
39 John Franco XRC 5.00 2.00
40 George Frazier 1.00 .40
41 Rich Gale 1.00 .40
42 Barbaro Garbey 1.00 .40
43 Dwight Gooden XRC 15.00 6.00
44 Rich Gossage 1.50 .60
45 Wayne Gross 1.00 .40
46 Mark Gubicza XRC 2.00 .80
47 Jackie Gutierrez 1.00 .40
48 Toby Harrah 1.50 .60
49 Ron Hassey 1.00 .40
50 Richie Hebner 1.00 .40
51 Willie Hernandez 1.00 .40
52 Ed Hodge 1.00 .40
53 Ricky Horton 1.00 .40
54 Art Howe 1.00 .40
55 Dane Iorg 1.00 .40
56 Brook Jacoby 2.00 .80
57 Dion James XRC* 1.00 .40
58 Mike Jeffcoat XRC 1.00 .40
59 Ruppert Jones 1.00 .40
60 Bob Kearney 1.00 .40
61 Jimmy Key XRC 5.00 2.00
62 Dave Kingman 1.50 .60
63 Brad Komminsk XRC 1.00 .40
64 Jerry Koosman 1.50 .60
65 Wayne Krenchicki 1.00 .40
66 Rusty Kuntz 1.00 .40
67 Frank LaCorte 1.00 .40
68 Dennis Lamp 1.00 .40
69 Tito Landrum 1.00 .40
70 Mark Langston XRC 5.00 2.00
71 Rick Leach 1.00 .40
72 Craig Lefferts 1.00 .40
73 Gary Lucas 1.00 .40
74 Jerry Martin 1.00 .40
75 Carmelo Martinez 1.00 .40
76 Mike Mason XRC 1.00 .40
77 Gary Matthews 1.50 .60
78 Andy McGaffigan 1.00 .40
79 Joey McLaughlin 1.00 .40
80 Joe Morgan 1.50 .60
81 Darryl Motley 1.00 .40
82 Graig Nettles 1.50 .60
83 Phil Niekro 1.50 .60
84 Ken Oberkfell 1.00 .40
85 Al Oliver 1.50 .60
86 Jorge Orta 1.00 .40
87 Amos Otis 1.50 .60
88 Bob Owchinko 1.00 .40
89 Dave Parker 1.50 .60
90 Jack Perconte 1.00 .40
91 Tony Perez 2.50 1.00
92 Gerald Perry 2.00 .80
93 Kirby Puckett XRC 60.00 24.00
94 Shane Rawley 1.00 .40
95 Floyd Rayford 1.00 .40
96 Ron Reed 1.00 .40
97 R.J. Reynolds 1.00 .40
98 Gene Richards 1.00 .40
99 Jose Rijo XRC 5.00 2.00
100 Jeff D. Robinson 1.00 .40
101 Ron Romanick 1.00 .40
102 Pete Rose 12.00 4.80
103 Bret Saberhagen XRC 8.00 3.20
104 Scott Sanderson 1.00 .40
105 Dick Schofield XRC* 2.00 .80
106 Tom Seaver 4.00 1.60
107 Jim Slaton 1.00 .40
108 Mike Smithson 1.00 .40
109 Lary Sorensen 1.00 .40
110 Tim Stoddard 1.00 .40
111 Jeff Stone 1.00 .40
112 Champ Summers 1.00 .40
113 Jim Sundberg 1.50 .60
114 Rick Sutcliffe 1.50 .60
115 Craig Swan 1.00 .40
116 Derrel Thomas 1.00 .40
117 Gorman Thomas 1.50 .60
118 Alex Trevino 1.00 .40
119 Manny Trillo 1.00 .40
120 John Tudor 1.50 .60
121 Tom Underwood 1.00 .40
122 Mike Vail 1.00 .40
123 Tom Waddell 1.00 .40
124 Gary Ward 1.00 .40
125 Terry Whitfield 1.00 .40
126 Curtis Wilkerson 1.00 .40
127 Frank Williams 1.00 .40
128 Glenn Wilson 1.50 .60
129 John Wockenfuss 1.00 .40
130 Ned Yost 1.00 .40
131 Mike Young RC 1.00 .40
132 Checklist 1-132 1.00 .40

1985 Fleer

The 1985 Fleer set consists of 660 standard-size cards. Wax packs contained 15 cards plus logo stickers. Card fronts feature a full color photo, team logo along with the player's name and position. The borders enclosing the photo are color-coded to correspond to the player's team. The cards are ordered alphabetically within team. The teams are ordered based on their respective performance during the prior year. Subsets include Specials (626-643) and Major League Prospects (644-653). The black and white photo on the reverse is included for the third straight year. Rookie Cards include Roger Clemens, Eric Davis, Shawon Dunston, John Franco, Dwight Gooden, Orel Hershiser, Jimmy Key, Mark Langston, Terry Pendleton, Kirby Puckett and Bret Saberhagen

Nm-Mt Ex-Mt
COMPLETE SET (660) 80.00 32.00
1 Doug Bair .15 .06
2 Juan Berenguer .15 .06
3 Dave Bergman .15 .06
4 Tom Brookens .15 .06
5 Marty Castillo .15 .06
6 Darrell Evans .40 .16
7 Barbaro Garbey .15 .06
8 Kirk Gibson .40 .16
9 John Grubb .15 .06
10 Willie Hernandez .15 .06
11 Larry Herndon .15 .06
12 Howard Johnson .40 .16
13 Ruppert Jones .15 .06
14 Rusty Kuntz .15 .06
15 Chet Lemon .40 .16
16 Aurelio Lopez .15 .06
17 Sid Monge .15 .06
18 Jack Morris .40 .16
19 Lance Parrish .40 .16
20 Dan Petry .15 .06
21 Dave Rozema .15 .06
22 Bill Scherrer .15 .06
23 Alan Trammell .40 .16
24 Lou Whitaker .40 .16
25 Milt Wilcox .15 .06
26 Kurt Bevacqua .15 .06
27 Greg Booker .15 .06
28 Bobby Brown .15 .06
29 Luis DeLeon .15 .06
30 Dave Dravecky .15 .06
31 Tim Flannery .15 .06
32 Steve Garvey .40 .16
33 Rich Gossage .40 .16
34 Tony Gwynn 2.50 1.00
35 Greg Harris .15 .06
36 Andy Hawkins .15 .06
37 Terry Kennedy .15 .06
38 Craig Lefferts .15 .06
39 Tim Lollar .15 .06
40 Carmelo Martinez .15 .06
41 Kevin McReynolds .40 .16

42 Graig Nettles .40 .16
43 Luis Salazar .15 .06
44 Eric Show .15 .06
45 Garry Templeton .40 .16
46 Mark Thurmond .15 .06
47 Ed Whitson .15 .06
48 Alan Wiggins .15 .06
49 Rich Bordi .15 .06
50 Larry Bowa .40 .16
51 Warren Brusstar .15 .06
52 Ron Cey .40 .16
53 Henry Cotto RC .25 .10
54 Jody Davis .15 .06
55 Bob Dernier .15 .06
56 Leon Durham .15 .06
57 Dennis Eckersley .75 .30
58 George Frazier .15 .06
59 Richie Hebner .15 .06
60 Dave Lopes .40 .16
61 Gary Matthews .40 .16
62 Keith Moreland .15 .06
63 Rick Reuschel .40 .16
64 Dick Ruthven .15 .06
65 Ryne Sandberg 2.50 1.00
66 Scott Sanderson .15 .06
67 Lee Smith .40 .16
68 Tim Stoddard .15 .06
69 Rick Sutcliffe .40 .16
70 Steve Trout .15 .06
71 Gary Woods .15 .06
72 Wally Backman .15 .06
73 Bruce Berenyi .15 .06
74 Hubie Brooks UER .15 .06
(Kelvin Chapman's
stats on card back)
75 Kelvin Chapman .15 .06
76 Ron Darling .40 .16
77 Sid Fernandez .40 .16
78 Mike Fitzgerald .15 .06
79 George Foster .40 .16
80 Brent Gaff .15 .06
81 Ron Gardenhire .15 .06
82 Dwight Gooden RC 2.00 .80
83 Tom Gorman .15 .06
84 Danny Heep .15 .06
85 Keith Hernandez .40 .16
86 Ray Knight .40 .16
87 Ed Lynch .15 .06
88 Jose Oquendo .15 .06
89 Jesse Orosco .15 .06
90 Rafael Santana .15 .06
91 Doug Sisk .15 .06
92 Rusty Staub .40 .16
93 Darryl Strawberry 1.25 .50
94 Walt Terrell .15 .06
95 Mookie Wilson .40 .16
96 Jim Acker .15 .06
97 Willie Aikens .15 .06
98 Doyle Alexander .15 .06
99 Jesse Barfield .40 .16
100 George Bell .40 .16
101 Jim Clancy .15 .06
102 Dave Collins .15 .06
103 Tony Fernandez .40 .16
104 Damaso Garcia .15 .06
105 Jim Gott .15 .06
106 Alfredo Griffin .15 .06
107 Garth Iorg .15 .06
108 Roy Lee Jackson .15 .06
109 Cliff Johnson .15 .06
110 Jimmy Key RC 1.00 .40
111 Dennis Lamp .15 .06
112 Rick Leach .15 .06
113 Luis Leal .15 .06
114 Buck Martinez .15 .06
115 Lloyd Moseby .15 .06
116 Rance Mulliniks .15 .06
117 Dave Stieb .40 .16
118 Willie Upshaw .15 .06
119 Ernie Whitt .15 .06
120 Mike Armstrong .15 .06
121 Don Baylor .40 .16
122 Marty Bystrom .15 .06
123 Rick Cerone .15 .06
124 Joe Cowley .15 .06
125 Brian Dayett .15 .06
126 Tim Foli .15 .06
127 Ray Fontenot .15 .06
128 Ken Griffey .40 .16
129 Ron Guidry .40 .16
130 Toby Harrah .40 .16
131 Jay Howell .15 .06
132 Steve Kemp .15 .06
133 Don Mattingly 5.00 2.00
134 Bobby Meacham .15 .06
135 John Montefusco .15 .06
136 Omar Moreno .15 .06
137 Dale Murray .15 .06
138 Phil Niekro .40 .16
139 Mike Pagliarulo .15 .06
140 Willie Randolph .40 .16
141 Dennis Rasmussen .15 .06
142 Dave Righetti .40 .16
143 Jose Rijo RC 1.00 .40
144 Andre Robertson .15 .06
145 Bob Shirley .15 .06
146 Dave Winfield .40 .16
147 Butch Wynegar .15 .06
148 Gary Allenson .15 .06
149 Tony Armas .40 .16
150 Marty Barrett .15 .06
151 Wade Boggs 1.25 .50
152 Dennis Boyd .15 .06
153 Bill Buckner .40 .16
154 Mark Clear .15 .06
155 Roger Clemens RC 40.00 16.00
156 Steve Crawford .15 .06
157 Mike Easler .15 .06
158 Dwight Evans .40 .16
159 Rich Gedman .15 .06
160 Jackie Gutierrez .40 .16
(Wade Boggs
shown on deck)
161 Bruce Hurst .15 .06
162 John Henry Johnson .15 .06
163 Rick Miller .15 .06
164 Reid Nichols .15 .06
165 Al Nipper .15 .06
166 Bob Ojeda .15 .06
167 Jerry Remy .15 .06
168 Jim Rice .40 .16
169 Bob Stanley .15 .06
170 Mike Boddicker .15 .06
171 Al Bumbry .15 .06
172 Todd Cruz .15 .06
173 Rich Dauer .15 .06
174 Storm Davis .15 .06
175 Rick Dempsey .15 .06
176 Jim Dwyer .15 .06
177 Mike Flanagan .15 .06
178 Dan Ford .15 .06
179 Wayne Gross .15 .06
180 John Lowenstein .15 .06
181 Dennis Martinez .40 .16
182 Tippy Martinez .15 .06
183 Scott McGregor .15 .06
184 Eddie Murray 1.25 .50
185 Joe Nolan .15 .06
186 Floyd Rayford .15 .06
187 Cal Ripken 5.00 2.00
188 Gary Roenicke .15 .06
189 Lenn Sakata .15 .06
190 John Shelby .15 .06
191 Ken Singleton .40 .16
192 Sammy Stewart .15 .06
193 Bill Swaggerty .15 .06
194 Tom Underwood .15 .06
195 Mike Young .15 .06
196 Steve Balboni .15 .06
197 Joe Beckwith .15 .06
198 Bud Black .15 .06
199 George Brett 3.00 1.20
200 Onix Concepcion .15 .06
201 Mark Gubicza RC* .50 .20
202 Larry Gura .15 .06
203 Mark Huismann .15 .06
204 Dane Iorg .15 .06
205 Danny Jackson .15 .06
206 Charlie Leibrandt .15 .06
207 Hal McRae .40 .16
208 Darryl Motley .15 .06
209 Jorge Orta .15 .06
210 Greg Pryor .15 .06
211 Dan Quisenberry .15 .06
212 Bret Saberhagen RC 1.50 .60
213 Pat Sheridan .15 .06
214 Don Slaught .15 .06
215 U.L. Washington .15 .06
216 John Wathan .15 .06
217 Frank White .40 .16
218 Willie Wilson .40 .16
219 Neil Allen .15 .06
220 Joaquin Andujar .40 .16
221 Steve Braun .15 .06
222 Danny Cox .15 .06
223 Bob Forsch .15 .06
224 David Green .15 .06
225 George Hendrick .40 .16
226 Tom Herr .15 .06
227 Ricky Horton .15 .06
228 Art Howe .15 .06
229 Mike Jorgensen .15 .06
230 Kurt Kepshire .15 .06
231 Jeff Lahti .15 .06
232 Tito Landrum .15 .06
233 Dave LaPoint .15 .06
234 Willie McGee .40 .16
235 Tom Nieto .15 .06
236 Terry Pendleton RC 1.00 .40
237 Darrell Porter .15 .06
238 Dave Rucker .15 .06
239 Lonnie Smith .15 .06
240 Ozzie Smith 2.00 .80
241 Bruce Sutter .40 .16
242 Andy Van Slyke UER .40 .16
(Bats Right,
Throws Left)
243 Dave Von Ohlen .15 .06
244 Larry Andersen .15 .06
245 Bill Campbell .15 .06
246 Steve Carlton .40 .16
247 Tim Corcoran .15 .06
248 Ivan DeJesus .15 .06
249 John Denny .15 .06
250 Bo Diaz .15 .06
251 Greg Gross .15 .06
252 Kevin Gross .15 .06
253 Von Hayes .15 .06
254 Al Holland .15 .06
255 Charles Hudson .15 .06
256 Jerry Koosman .40 .16
257 Joe Lefebvre .15 .06
258 Sixto Lezcano .15 .06
259 Garry Maddox .15 .06
260 Len Matuszek .15 .06
261 Tug McGraw .40 .16
262 Al Oliver .40 .16
263 Shane Rawley .15 .06
264 Juan Samuel .15 .06
265 Mike Schmidt 3.00 1.20
266 Jeff Stone .15 .06
267 Ozzie Virgil .15 .06
268 Glenn Wilson .15 .06
269 John Wockenfuss .15 .06
270 Darrell Brown .15 .06
271 Tom Brunansky .15 .06
272 Randy Bush .15 .06
273 John Butcher .15 .06
274 Bobby Castillo .15 .06
275 Ron Davis .15 .06
276 Dave Engle .15 .06
277 Pete Filson .15 .06
278 Gary Gaetti .40 .16
279 Mickey Hatcher .15 .06
280 Ed Hodge .15 .06
281 Kent Hrbek .40 .16
282 Houston Jimenez .15 .06
283 Tim Laudner .15 .06
284 Rick Lysander .15 .06
285 Dave Meier .15 .06
286 Kirby Puckett RC 10.00 4.00
287 Pat Putnam .15 .06
288 Ken Schrom .15 .06
289 Mike Smithson .15 .06
290 Tim Teufel .15 .06
291 Frank Viola .40 .16
292 Ron Washington .15 .06
293 Don Aase .15 .06
294 Juan Beniquez .15 .06
295 Bob Boone .40 .16
296 Mike C. Brown .15 .06
297 Rod Carew .75 .30
298 Doug Corbett .15 .06
299 Doug DeCinces .15 .06
300 Brian Downing .40 .16
301 Ken Forsch .15 .06
302 Bobby Grich .40 .16
303 Reggie Jackson .75 .30
304 Tommy John .40 .16
305 Curt Kaufman .15 .06
306 Bruce Kison .15 .06
307 Fred Lynn .40 .16
308 Gary Pettis .15 .06
309 Ron Romanick .15 .06
310 Luis Sanchez .15 .06
311 Dick Schofield .15 .06
312 Daryl Sconiers .15 .06
313 Jim Slaton .15 .06
314 Derrel Thomas .15 .06
315 Rob Wilfong .15 .06
316 Mike Witt .15 .06
317 Geoff Zahn .15 .06
318 Len Barker .15 .06
319 Steve Bedrosian .15 .06
320 Bruce Benedict .15 .06
321 Rick Camp .15 .06
322 Chris Chambliss .40 .16
323 Jeff Dedmon .15 .06
324 Terry Forster .40 .16
325 Gene Garber .15 .06
326 Albert Hall .15 .06
327 Terry Harper .15 .06
328 Bob Horner .40 .16
329 Glenn Hubbard .15 .06
330 Randy Johnson .15 .06
331 Brad Komminsk .15 .06
332 Rick Mahler .15 .06
333 Craig McMurtry .15 .06
334 Donnie Moore .15 .06
335 Dale Murphy .75 .30
336 Ken Oberkfell .15 .06
337 Pascual Perez .15 .06
338 Gerald Perry .15 .06
339 Rafael Ramirez .15 .06
340 Jerry Royster .15 .06
341 Alex Trevino .15 .06
342 Claudell Washington .15 .06
343 Alan Ashby .15 .06
344 Mark Bailey .15 .06
345 Kevin Bass .15 .06
346 Enos Cabell .15 .06
347 Jose Cruz .40 .16
348 Bill Dawley .15 .06
349 Frank DiPino .15 .06
350 Bill Doran .15 .06
351 Phil Garner .40 .16
352 Bob Knepper .15 .06
353 Mike LaCoss .15 .06
354 Jerry Mumphrey .15 .06
355 Joe Niekro .15 .06
356 Terry Puhl .15 .06
357 Craig Reynolds .15 .06
358 Vern Ruhle .15 .06
359 Nolan Ryan 6.00 2.40
360 Joe Sambito .15 .06
361 Mike Scott .40 .16
362 Dave Smith .15 .06
363 Julio Solano .15 .06
364 Dickie Thon .15 .06
365 Denny Walling .15 .06
366 Dave Anderson .15 .06
367 Bob Bailor .15 .06
368 Greg Brock .15 .06
369 Carlos Diaz .15 .06
370 Pedro Guerrero .40 .16
371 Orel Hershiser RC 1.50 .60
372 Rick Honeycutt .15 .06
373 Burt Hooton .15 .06
374 Ken Howell .15 .06
375 Ken Landreaux .15 .06
376 Candy Maldonado .15 .06
377 Mike Marshall .15 .06
378 Tom Niedenfuer .15 .06
379 Alejandro Pena .15 .06
380 Jerry Reuss UER .15 .06
("Home:" omitted)
381 R.J. Reynolds .15 .06
382 German Rivera .15 .06
383 Bill Russell .40 .16
384 Steve Sax .40 .16
385 Mike Scioscia .40 .16
386 Franklin Stubbs .15 .06
387 Fernando Valenzuela .40 .16
388 Bob Welch .40 .16
389 Terry Whitfield .15 .06
390 Steve Yeager .40 .16
391 Pat Zachry .15 .06
392 Fred Breining .15 .06
393 Gary Carter .40 .16
394 Andre Dawson .40 .16
395 Miguel Dilone .15 .06
396 Dan Driessen .15 .06
397 Doug Flynn .15 .06
398 Terry Francona .40 .16
399 Bill Gullickson .15 .06
400 Bob James .15 .06
401 Charlie Lea .15 .06
402 Bryan Little .15 .06
403 Gary Lucas .15 .06
404 David Palmer .15 .06
405 Tim Raines .40 .16
406 Mike Ramsey .15 .06
407 Jeff Reardon .40 .16
408 Steve Rogers .40 .16
409 Dan Schatzeder .15 .06
410 Bryn Smith .15 .06
411 Mike Stenhouse .15 .06
412 Tim Wallach .15 .06
413 Jim Wohlford .15 .06
414 Bill Almon .15 .06
415 Keith Atherton .15 .06
416 Bruce Bochte .15 .06
417 Tom Burgmeier .15 .06
418 Ray Burris .15 .06
419 Bill Caudill .15 .06
420 Chris Codiroli .15 .06
421 Tim Conroy .15 .06
422 Mike Davis .15 .06
423 Jim Essian .15 .06
424 Mike Heath .15 .06
425 Rickey Henderson 1.50 .60
426 Donnie Hill .15 .06
427 Dave Kingman .40 .16
428 Bill Krueger .40 .16
429 Carney Lansford .40 .16
430 Steve McCatty .15 .06
431 Joe Morgan .40 .16
432 Dwayne Murphy .15 .06
433 Tony Phillips .15 .06
434 Lary Sorensen .15 .06
435 Mike Warren .15 .06
436 Curt Young .15 .06
437 Luis Aponte .15 .06
438 Chris Bando .15 .06
439 Tony Bernazard .15 .06
440 Bert Blyleven .40 .16
441 Brett Butler .40 .16
442 Ernie Camacho .15 .06
443 Joe Carter 1.25 .50
444 Carmelo Castillo .15 .06
445 Jamie Easterly .15 .06
446 Steve Farr RC .50 .20
447 Mike Fischlin .15 .06
448 Julio Franco .40 .16
449 Mel Hall .15 .06
450 Mike Hargrove .15 .06
451 Neal Heaton .15 .06
452 Brook Jacoby .15 .06
453 Mike Jeffcoat .15 .06
454 Don Schulze .15 .06
455 Roy Smith .15 .06
456 Pat Tabler .15 .06
457 Andre Thornton .15 .06
458 George Vukovich .15 .06
459 Tom Waddell .15 .06
460 Jerry Willard .15 .06
461 Dale Berra .15 .06
462 John Candelaria .15 .06
463 Jose DeLeon .15 .06
464 Doug Frobel .15 .06
465 Cecilio Guante .15 .06
466 Brian Harper .15 .06
467 Lee Lacy .15 .06
468 Bill Madlock .40 .16
469 Lee Mazzilli .40 .16
470 Larry McWilliams .15 .06
471 Jim Morrison .15 .06
472 Tony Pena .15 .06
473 Johnny Ray .15 .06
474 Rick Rhoden .15 .06
475 Don Robinson .15 .06
476 Rod Scurry .15 .06
477 Kent Tekulve .15 .06
478 Jason Thompson .15 .06
479 John Tudor .40 .16
480 Lee Tunnell .15 .06
481 Marvell Wynne .15 .06
482 Salome Barojas .15 .06
483 Dave Beard .15 .06
484 Jim Beattie .15 .06
485 Barry Bonnell .15 .06
486 Phil Bradley .50 .20
487 Al Cowens .15 .06
488 Alvin Davis RC* .50 .20
489 Dave Henderson .15 .06
490 Steve Henderson .15 .06
491 Bob Kearney .15 .06
492 Mark Langston RC 1.00 .40
493 Larry Milbourne .15 .06
494 Paul Mirabella .15 .06
495 Mike Moore .15 .06
496 Edwin Nunez .15 .06
497 Spike Owen .15 .06
498 Jack Perconte .15 .06
499 Ken Phelps .15 .06
500 Jim Presley .50 .20
501 Mike Stanton .15 .06
502 Bob Stoddard .15 .06
503 Gorman Thomas .40 .16
504 Ed VandeBerg .15 .06
505 Matt Young .15 .06
506 Juan Agosto .15 .06
507 Harold Baines .40 .16
508 Floyd Bannister .15 .06
509 Britt Burns .15 .06
510 Julio Cruz .15 .06
511 Richard Dotson .15 .06
512 Jerry Dybzinski .15 .06
513 Carlton Fisk .75 .30
514 Scott Fletcher .15 .06
515 Jerry Hairston .15 .06
516 Marc Hill .15 .06
517 LaMarr Hoyt .15 .06
518 Ron Kittle .15 .06
519 Rudy Law .15 .06
520 Vance Law .15 .06
521 Greg Luzinski .40 .16
522 Gene Nelson .15 .06
523 Tom Paciorek .15 .06
524 Ron Reed .15 .06
525 Bert Roberge .15 .06
526 Tom Seaver .75 .30
527 Roy Smalley .15 .06
528 Dan Spillner .15 .06
529 Mike Squires .15 .06
530 Greg Walker .15 .06
531 Cesar Cedeno .40 .16
532 Dave Concepcion .40 .16
533 Eric Davis RC 1.50 .60
534 Nick Esasky .15 .06
535 Tom Foley .15 .06
536 John Franco UER RC 1.00 .40
(Koufax misspelled
as Kofax on back)
537 Brad Gulden .15 .06
538 Tom Hume .15 .06
539 Wayne Krenchicki .15 .06
540 Andy McGaffigan .15 .06
541 Eddie Milner .15 .06
542 Ron Oester .15 .06
543 Bob Owchinko .15 .06
544 Dave Parker .40 .16
545 Frank Pastore .15 .06
546 Tony Perez .75 .30
547 Ted Power .15 .06
548 Joe Price .15 .06
549 Gary Redus .15 .06
550 Pete Rose 4.00 1.60
551 Jeff Russell .15 .06
552 Mario Soto .40 .16
553 Jay Tibbs .15 .0
554 Duane Walker .15 .0
555 Alan Bannister .15 .0
556 Buddy Bell .40 .1
557 Danny Darwin .15 .0
558 Charlie Hough .40 .1
559 Bobby Jones .15 .0
560 Odell Jones .15 .0
561 Jeff Kunkel .15 .0
562 Mike Mason RC .25 .1
563 Pete O'Brien .15 .0
564 Larry Parrish .15 .0
565 Mickey Rivers .15 .0
566 Billy Sample .15 .0
567 Dave Schmidt .15 .0
568 Donnie Scott .15 .0
569 Dave Stewart .40 .1
570 Frank Tanana .40 .1
571 Wayne Tolleson .15 .0
572 Gary Ward .15 .0
573 Curtis Wilkerson .15 .0
574 George Wright .15 .0
575 Ned Yost .15 .0
576 Mark Brouhard .15 .0
577 Mike Caldwell .15 .0
578 Bobby Clark .15 .0
579 Jaime Cocanower .15 .0
580 Cecil Cooper .40 .1
581 Rollie Fingers .40 .16
582 Jim Gantner .15 .06
583 Moose Haas .15 .06
584 Dion James .15 .06
585 Pete Ladd .15 .06
586 Rick Manning .15 .06
587 Bob McClure .15 .06
588 Paul Molitor .75 .30
589 Charlie Moore .15 .06
590 Ben Oglivie .40 .16
591 Chuck Porter .15 .06
592 Randy Ready RC* .25 .10
593 Ed Romero .15 .06
594 Bill Schroeder .15 .06
595 Ray Searage .15 .06
596 Ted Simmons .40 .16
597 Jim Sundberg .40 .16
598 Don Sutton .40 .16
599 Tom Tellmann .15 .06
600 Rick Waits .15 .06
601 Robin Yount 2.00 .80
602 Dusty Baker .40 .16
603 Bob Brenly .15 .06
604 Jack Clark .40 .16
605 Chili Davis .40 .16
606 Mark Davis .15 .06
607 Dan Gladden RC .50 .20
608 Atlee Hammaker .15 .06
609 Mike Krukow .15 .06
610 Duane Kuiper .15 .06
611 Bob Lacey .15 .06
612 Bill Laskey .15 .06
613 Gary Lavelle .15 .06
614 Johnnie LeMaster .15 .06
615 Jeff Leonard .15 .06
616 Randy Lerch .15 .06
617 Greg Minton .15 .06
618 Steve Nicosia .15 .06
619 Gene Richards .15 .06
620 Jeff D. Robinson .15 .06
621 Scot Thompson .15 .06
622 Manny Trillo .15 .06
623 Brad Wellman .15 .06
624 Frank Williams .15 .06
625 Joel Youngblood .15 .06
626 Cal Ripken IA 3.00 1.20
627 Mike Schmidt IA 1.25 .50
628 Sparky Anderson IA .40 .16
629 Dave Winfield .40 .16
Rickey Henderson
630 Mike Schmidt 2.00 .80
Ryne Sandberg
631 Darryl Strawberry 1.25 .50
Gary Carter
Steve Garvey
Ozzie Smith
632 Gary Carter .15 .06
Charlie Lea
633 Steve Garvey .40 .16
Rich Gossage
634 Dwight Gooden 1.25 .50
Juan Samuel
635 Willie Upshaw IA .15 .06
636 Lloyd Moseby IA .15 .06
637 HOLLAND: Al Holland .15 .06
638 TUNNELL .15 .06
Lee Tunnell
639 Reggie Jackson IA .40 .16
640 4000th Hit IA 1.25 .50
641 Cal Ripken Jr. 3.00 1.20
Cal Ripken Sr.
642 Cubs Division Champs .40 .16
643 Two Perfect Games .40 .16
and One No-Hitter:
Mike Witt
David Palmer
Jack Morris
644 Willie Lozado and .15 .06
Vic Mata
645 Kelly Gruber RC and .50 .20
Randy O'Neal
646 Jose Roman .15 .06
Joel Skinner
647 Steve Kiefer RC and 1.00 .40
Danny Tartabull
648 Rob Dee RC and .50 .20
Alejandro Sanchez
649 Billy Hatcher RC and 1.00 .40
Shawon Dunston
650 Ron Robinson and .15 .06
Mike Bielecki
651 Zane Smith RC and .50 .20
Paul Zuvella
652 Joe Hesketh RC and .50 .20
Glenn Davis
653 John Russell and .15 .06
Steve Jeltz
654 CL: Tigers/Padres .15 .06
and Cubs/Mets
655 CL: Blue Jays/Yankees .15 .06
and Red Sox/Orioles
656 CL: Royals/Cardinals .15 .06

and Phillies/Twins
57 CL: Angels/Braves .15 .06
and Astros/Dodgers
58 CL: Expos/A's .15 .06
and Indians/Pirates
59 CL: Mariners/White Sox .15 .06
and Reds/Rangers
60 CL: Brewers/Giants .15 .06
and Special Cards

1985 Fleer Update

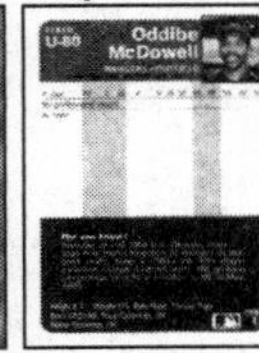

his 132-card standard-size update set was ssued in factory set form exclusively through obby dealers. Design is identical to the regular-ssue 1985 Fleer cards except for the U prefixed ard numbers on back. Cards are ordered alpha-etically by the player's name. This set features ne extended Rookie Cards of Vince Coleman, Darren Daulton, Ozzie Guillen and Mickey ettleton.

Nm-Mt Ex-Mt
COMP.FACT.SET (132) 6.00 2.40
Don Aase .15 .06
Bill Almon .15 .06
Dusty Baker .40 .16
Dale Berra .15 .06
Karl Best .15 .06
Tim Birtsas .15 .06
Vida Blue .40 .16
Rich Bordi .15 .06
Daryl Boston XRC* .25 .10
0 Hubie Brooks .15 .06
1 Chris Brown .25 .10
2 Tom Browning XRC* .50 .20
3 Al Bumbry .15 .06
4 Tim Burke .15 .06
5 Ray Burris .15 .06
6 Jeff Burroughs .15 .06
7 Ivan Calderon XRC .50 .20
8 Jeff Calhoun .15 .06
9 Bill Campbell .15 .06
20 Don Carman .15 .06
21 Gary Carter .40 .16
22 Bobby Castillo .15 .06
23 Bill Caudill .15 .06
24 Rick Cerone .15 .06
25 Jack Clark .40 .16
26 Pat Clements .15 .06
27 Stu Cliburn .15 .06
28 Vince Coleman XRC 1.00 .40
29 Dave Collins .15 .06
30 Fritz Connally .15 .06
31 Henry Cotto .25 .10
32 Danny Darwin .15 .06
33 Darren Daulton XRC 1.00 .40
34 Jerry Davis .15 .06
35 Brian Dayett .15 .06
36 Ken Dixon .15 .06
37 Tommy Dunbar .15 .06
38 Mariano Duncan XRC .50 .20
39 Bob Fallon .15 .06
40 Brian Fisher XRC .25 .10
41 Mike Fitzgerald .15 .06
42 Ray Fontenot .15 .06
43 Greg Gagne XRC* .50 .20
44 Oscar Gamble .15 .06
45 Jim Gott .15 .06
46 David Green .15 .06
47 Alfredo Griffin .15 .06
48 Ozzie Guillen XRC .50 .20
49 Toby Harrah .40 .16
50 Ron Hassey .15 .06
51 Rickey Henderson 2.50 1.00
52 Steve Henderson .15 .06
53 George Hendrick .40 .16
54 Teddy Higuera XRC .50 .20
55 Al Holland .15 .06
56 Burt Hooton .15 .06
57 Jay Howell .15 .06
58 LaMarr Hoyt .15 .06
59 Tim Hulett XRC* .25 .10
60 Bob James .15 .06
61 Cliff Johnson .15 .06
62 Howard Johnson .40 .16
63 Ruppert Jones .15 .06
64 Steve Kemp .15 .06
65 Bruce Kison .15 .06
66 Mike LaCoss .15 .06
67 Lee Lacy .15 .06
68 Dave LaPoint .15 .06
69 Gary Lavelle .15 .06
70 Vance Law .15 .06
71 Manny Lee XRC .25 .10
72 Sixto Lezcano .15 .06
73 Tim Lollar .15 .06
74 Urbano Lugo .15 .06
75 Fred Lynn .40 .16
76 Steve Lyons XRC .50 .20
77 Mickey Mahler .15 .06
78 Ron Mathis .15 .06
79 Len Matuszek .15 .06
80 O.McDowell XRC UER .50 .20
Part of bio
actually Roger's
81 R.McDowell XRC UER .50 .20
Part of bio
actually Oddibe's
82 Donnie Moore .15 .06
83 Ron Musselman .15 .06
84 Al Oliver .40 .16
85 Joe Orsulak XRC .50 .20
86 Dan Pasqua XRC* .50 .20
87 Chris Pittaro .15 .06
88 Rick Reuschel .40 .16
89 Earnie Riles .15 .06
90 Jerry Royster .15 .06
91 Dave Rozema .15 .06
92 Dave Rucker .15 .06
93 Vern Ruhle .15 .06
94 Mark Salas .15 .06
95 Luis Salazar .15 .06
96 Joe Sambito .15 .06
97 Billy Sample .15 .06
98 Alejandro Sanchez XRC .25 .10
99 Calvin Schiraldi XRC .50 .20
100 Rick Schu .15 .06
101 Larry Sheets XRC .25 .10
102 Ron Shephard .15 .06
103 Nelson Simmons .15 .06
104 Don Slaught .15 .06
105 Roy Smalley .15 .06
106 Lonnie Smith .15 .06
107 Nate Snell .15 .06
108 Lary Sorensen .15 .06
109 Chris Speier .15 .06
110 Mike Stenhouse .15 .06
111 Tim Stoddard .15 .06
112 John Stuper .15 .06
113 Jim Sundberg .40 .16
114 Bruce Sutter .40 .16
115 Don Sutton .40 .16
116 Bruce Tanner .15 .06
117 Kent Tekulve .15 .06
118 Walt Terrell .15 .06
119 Mickey Tettleton XRC .50 .20
120 Rich Thompson .15 .06
121 Louis Thornton .15 .06
122 Alex Trevino .15 .06
123 John Tudor .40 .16
124 Jose Uribe .15 .06
125 Dave Valle XRC .50 .20
126 Dave Von Ohlen .15 .06
127 Curt Wardle .15 .06
128 U.L. Washington .15 .06
129 Ed Whitson .15 .06
130 Herm Winningham .15 .06
131 Rich Yett .15 .06
132 Checklist U1-U132 .15 .06

1986 Fleer

The 1986 Fleer set consists of 660-card standard-size cards. Wax packs included 15 cards plus logo stickers. Card fronts feature dark blue borders (resulting in extremely condition sensitive cards commonly found with chipped edges), a team logo along with the player's name and position. The player cards are alphabetized within team and the teams are ordered by their 1985 season finish and won-lost record. Subsets include Specials (626-643) and Major League Prospects (644-653). The Dennis and Tippy Martinez cards were apparently switched in the set numbering, as their adjacent numbers (279 and 280) were reversed on the Orioles checklist card. The set includes the Rookie Cards of Rick Aguilera, Jose Canseco, Darren Daulton, Len Dykstra, Cecil Fielder, Andres Galarraga and Paul O'Neill.

Nm-Mt Ex-Mt
COMPLETE SET (660) 40.00 16.00
COMP.FACT.SET (660) 40.00 16.00
1 Steve Balboni .15 .06
2 Joe Beckwith .15 .06
3 Buddy Biancalana .15 .06
4 Bud Black .15 .06
5 George Brett 2.00 .80
6 Onix Concepcion .15 .06
7 Steve Farr .15 .06
8 Mark Gubicza .15 .06
9 Dane Iorg .15 .06
10 Danny Jackson .15 .06
11 Lynn Jones .15 .06
12 Mike Jones .15 .06
13 Charlie Leibrandt .15 .06
14 Hal McRae .25 .10
15 Omar Moreno .15 .06
16 Darryl Motley .15 .06
17 Jorge Orta .15 .06
18 Dan Quisenberry .15 .06
19 Bret Saberhagen .25 .10
20 Pat Sheridan .15 .06
21 Lonnie Smith .15 .06
22 Jim Sundberg .25 .10
23 John Wathan .15 .06
24 Frank White .25 .10
25 Willie Wilson .25 .10
26 Joaquin Andujar .25 .10
27 Steve Braun .15 .06
28 Bill Campbell .15 .06
29 Cesar Cedeno .25 .10
30 Jack Clark .25 .10
31 Vince Coleman RC* 1.00 .40
32 Danny Cox .15 .06
33 Ken Dayley .15 .06
34 Ivan DeJesus .15 .06
35 Bob Forsch .15 .06
36 Brian Harper .15 .06
37 Tom Herr .15 .06
38 Ricky Horton .15 .06
39 Kurt Kepshire .15 .06
40 Jeff Lahti .15 .06
41 Tito Landrum .15 .06
42 Willie McGee .25 .10
43 Tom Nieto .15 .06
44 Terry Pendleton .25 .10
45 Darrell Porter .15 .06
46 Ozzie Smith 1.25 .50
47 John Tudor .25 .10
48 Andy Van Slyke .25 .10
49 Todd Worrell RC .50 .20
50 Jim Acker .15 .06
51 Doyle Alexander .15 .06
52 Jesse Barfield .25 .10
53 George Bell .25 .10
54 Jeff Burroughs .15 .06
55 Bill Caudill .15 .06
56 Jim Clancy .15 .06
57 Tony Fernandez .15 .06
58 Tom Filer .15 .06
59 Damaso Garcia .15 .06
60 Tom Henke .25 .10
61 Garth Iorg .15 .06
62 Cliff Johnson .15 .06
63 Jimmy Key .25 .10
64 Dennis Lamp .15 .06
65 Gary Lavelle .15 .06
66 Buck Martinez .15 .06
67 Lloyd Moseby .15 .06
68 Rance Mulliniks .15 .06
69 Al Oliver .25 .10
70 Dave Stieb .25 .10
71 Louis Thornton .15 .06
72 Willie Upshaw .15 .06
73 Ernie Whitt .15 .06
74 Rick Aguilera RC .50 .20
75 Wally Backman .15 .06
76 Gary Carter .25 .10
77 Ron Darling .25 .10
78 Len Dykstra RC 1.50 .60
79 Sid Fernandez .15 .06
80 George Foster .25 .10
81 Dwight Gooden .75 .30
82 Tom Gorman .15 .06
83 Danny Heep .15 .06
84 Keith Hernandez .25 .10
85 Howard Johnson .25 .10
86 Ray Knight .25 .10
87 Terry Leach .15 .06
88 Ed Lynch .15 .06
89 Roger McDowell RC* .50 .20
90 Jesse Orosco .15 .06
91 Tom Paciorek .15 .06
92 Ronn Reynolds .15 .06
93 Rafael Santana .15 .06
94 Doug Sisk .15 .06
95 Rusty Staub .25 .10
96 Darryl Strawberry .50 .20
97 Mookie Wilson .25 .10
98 Neil Allen .15 .06
99 Don Baylor .25 .10
100 Dale Berra .15 .06
101 Rich Bordi .15 .06
102 Marty Bystrom .15 .06
103 Joe Cowley .15 .06
104 Brian Fisher RC .15 .06
105 Ken Griffey .25 .10
106 Ron Guidry .25 .10
107 Ron Hassey .15 .06
108 R.Henderson UER .75 .30
SB Record of 120, sic
109 Don Mattingly 2.50 1.00
110 Bobby Meacham .15 .06
111 John Montefusco .15 .06
112 Phil Niekro .25 .10
113 Mike Pagliarulo .15 .06
114 Dan Pasqua .15 .06
115 Willie Randolph .25 .10
116 Dave Righetti .25 .10
117 Andre Robertson .15 .06
118 Billy Sample .15 .06
119 Bob Shirley .15 .06
120 Ed Whitson .15 .06
121 Dave Winfield .25 .10
122 Butch Wynegar .15 .06
123 Dave Anderson .15 .06
124 Bob Bailor .15 .06
125 Greg Brock .15 .06
126 Enos Cabell .15 .06
127 Bobby Castillo .15 .06
128 Carlos Diaz .15 .06
129 Mariano Duncan RC* .50 .20
130 Pedro Guerrero .25 .10
131 Orel Hershiser .50 .20
132 Rick Honeycutt .15 .06
133 Ken Howell .15 .06
134 Ken Landreaux .15 .06
135 Bill Madlock .25 .10
136 Candy Maldonado .15 .06
137 Mike Marshall .15 .06
138 Len Matuszek .15 .06
139 Tom Niedenfuer .15 .06
140 Alejandro Pena .15 .06
141 Jerry Reuss .15 .06
142 Bill Russell .25 .10
143 Steve Sax .15 .06
144 Mike Scioscia .25 .10
145 Fernando Valenzuela .25 .10
146 Bob Welch .25 .10
147 Terry Whitfield .15 .06
148 Juan Beniquez .15 .06
149 Bob Boone .25 .10
150 John Candelaria .15 .06
151 Rod Carew .50 .20
152 Stu Cliburn .15 .06
153 Doug DeCinces .15 .06
154 Brian Downing .25 .10
155 Ken Forsch .15 .06
156 Craig Gerber .15 .06
157 Bobby Grich .25 .10
158 George Hendrick .25 .10
159 Al Holland .15 .06
160 Reggie Jackson .50 .20
161 Ruppert Jones .15 .06
162 Urbano Lugo .15 .06
163 Kirk McCaskill RC .50 .20
164 Donnie Moore .15 .06
165 Gary Pettis .15 .06
166 Ron Romanick .15 .06
167 Dick Schofield .15 .06
168 Daryl Sconiers .15 .06
169 Jim Slaton .15 .06
170 Don Sutton .25 .10
171 Mike Witt .15 .06
172 Buddy Bell .25 .10
173 Tom Browning .25 .10
174 Dave Concepcion .25 .10
175 Eric Davis .50 .20
176 Bo Diaz .15 .06
177 Nick Esasky .15 .06
178 John Franco .25 .10
179 Tom Hume .15 .06
180 Wayne Krenchicki .15 .06
181 Andy McGaffigan .15 .06
182 Eddie Milner .15 .06
183 Ron Oester .15 .06
184 Dave Parker .25 .10
185 Frank Pastore .15 .06
186 Tony Perez .50 .20
187 Ted Power .15 .06
188 Joe Price .15 .06
189 Gary Redus .15 .06
190 Ron Robinson .15 .06
191 Pete Rose 2.50 1.00
192 Mario Soto .25 .10
193 John Stuper .15 .06
194 Jay Tibbs .15 .06
195 Dave Van Gorder .15 .06
196 Max Venable .15 .06
197 Juan Agosto .15 .06
198 Harold Baines .25 .10
199 Floyd Bannister .15 .06
200 Britt Burns .15 .06
201 Julio Cruz .15 .06
202 Joel Davis .15 .06
203 Richard Dotson .15 .06
204 Carlton Fisk .50 .20
205 Scott Fletcher .15 .06
206 Ozzie Guillen RC* .50 .20
207 Jerry Hairston .15 .06
208 Tim Hulett .15 .06
209 Bob James .15 .06
210 Ron Kittle .15 .06
211 Rudy Law .15 .06
212 Bryan Little .15 .06
213 Gene Nelson .15 .06
214 Reid Nichols .15 .06
215 Luis Salazar .15 .06
216 Tom Seaver .50 .20
217 Dan Spillner .15 .06
218 Bruce Tanner .15 .06
219 Greg Walker .15 .06
220 Dave Wehrmeister .15 .06
221 Juan Berenguer .15 .06
222 Dave Bergman .15 .06
223 Tom Brookens .15 .06
224 Darrell Evans .25 .10
225 Barbaro Garbey .15 .06
226 Kirk Gibson .25 .10
227 John Grubb .15 .06
228 Willie Hernandez .15 .06
229 Larry Herndon .15 .06
230 Chet Lemon .25 .10
231 Aurelio Lopez .15 .06
232 Jack Morris .25 .10
233 Randy O'Neal .15 .06
234 Lance Parrish .25 .10
235 Dan Petry .15 .06
236 Alejandro Sanchez .15 .06
237 Bill Scherrer .15 .06
238 Nelson Simmons .15 .06
239 Frank Tanana .25 .10
240 Walt Terrell .15 .06
241 Alan Trammell .25 .10
242 Lou Whitaker .25 .10
243 Milt Wilcox .15 .06
244 Hubie Brooks .15 .06
245 Tim Burke .15 .06
246 Andre Dawson .25 .10
247 Mike Fitzgerald .15 .06
248 Terry Francona .25 .10
249 Bill Gullickson .15 .06
250 Joe Hesketh .15 .06
251 Bill Laskey .15 .06
252 Vance Law .15 .06
253 Charlie Lea .15 .06
254 Gary Lucas .15 .06
255 David Palmer .15 .06
256 Tim Raines .25 .10
257 Jeff Reardon .25 .10
258 Bert Roberge .15 .06
259 Dan Schatzeder .15 .06
260 Bryn Smith .15 .06
261 Randy St.Claire .15 .06
262 Scot Thompson .15 .06
263 Tim Wallach .15 .06
264 U.L. Washington .15 .06
265 Mitch Webster .15 .06
266 Herm Winningham .15 .06
267 Floyd Youmans .15 .06
268 Don Aase .15 .06
269 Mike Boddicker .15 .06
270 Rich Dauer .15 .06
271 Storm Davis .15 .06
272 Rick Dempsey .15 .06
273 Ken Dixon .15 .06
274 Jim Dwyer .15 .06
275 Mike Flanagan .15 .06
276 Wayne Gross .15 .06
277 Lee Lacy .15 .06
278 Fred Lynn .25 .10
279 Tippy Martinez .15 .06
280 Dennis Martinez .25 .10
281 Scott McGregor .15 .06
282 Eddie Murray .75 .30
283 Floyd Rayford .15 .06
284 Cal Ripken 3.00 1.20
285 Gary Roenicke .15 .06
286 Larry Sheets .15 .06
287 John Shelby .15 .06
288 Nate Snell .15 .06
289 Sammy Stewart .15 .06
290 Alan Wiggins .15 .06
291 Mike Young .15 .06
292 Alan Ashby .15 .06
293 Mark Bailey .15 .06
294 Kevin Bass .15 .06
295 Jeff Calhoun .15 .06
296 Jose Cruz .25 .10
297 Glenn Davis .15 .06
298 Bill Dawley .15 .06
299 Frank DiPino .15 .06
300 Bill Doran .15 .06
301 Phil Garner .25 .10
302 Jeff Heathcock .15 .06
303 Charlie Kerfeld .15 .06
304 Bob Knepper .15 .06
305 Ron Mathis .15 .06
306 Jerry Mumphrey .15 .06
307 Jim Pankovits .15 .06
308 Terry Puhl .15 .06
309 Craig Reynolds .15 .06
310 Nolan Ryan 4.00 1.60
311 Mike Scott .25 .10
312 Dave Smith .15 .06
313 Dickie Thon .15 .06
314 Denny Walling .15 .06
315 Kurt Bevacqua .15 .06
316 Al Bumbry .15 .06
317 Jerry Davis .15 .06
318 Luis DeLeon .15 .06
319 Dave Dravecky .15 .06
320 Tim Flannery .15 .06
321 Steve Garvey .25 .10
322 Rich Gossage .25 .10
323 Tony Gwynn 1.25 .50
324 Andy Hawkins .15 .06
325 LaMarr Hoyt .15 .06
326 Roy Lee Jackson .15 .06
327 Terry Kennedy .15 .06
328 Craig Lefferts .15 .06
329 Carmelo Martinez .15 .06
330 Lance McCullers .15 .06
331 Kevin McReynolds .15 .06
332 Graig Nettles .25 .10
333 Jerry Royster .15 .06
334 Eric Show .15 .06
335 Tim Stoddard .15 .06
336 Garry Templeton .25 .10
337 Mark Thurmond .15 .06
338 Ed Wojna .15 .06
339 Tony Armas .25 .10
340 Marty Barrett .15 .06
341 Wade Boggs .50 .20
342 Dennis Boyd .15 .06
343 Bill Buckner .25 .10
344 Mark Clear .15 .06
345 Roger Clemens 4.00 1.60
346 Steve Crawford .15 .06
347 Mike Easler .15 .06
348 Dwight Evans .25 .10
349 Rich Gedman .15 .06
350 Jackie Gutierrez .15 .06
351 Glenn Hoffman .15 .06
352 Bruce Hurst .15 .06
353 Bruce Kison .15 .06
354 Tim Lollar .15 .06
355 Steve Lyons .15 .06
356 Al Nipper .15 .06
357 Bob Ojeda .15 .06
358 Jim Rice .25 .10
359 Bob Stanley .15 .06
360 Mike Trujillo .15 .06
361 Thad Bosley .15 .06
362 Warren Brusstar .15 .06
363 Ron Cey .25 .10
364 Jody Davis .15 .06
365 Bob Dernier .15 .06
366 Shawon Dunston .25 .10
367 Leon Durham .15 .06
368 Dennis Eckersley .50 .20
369 Ray Fontenot .15 .06
370 George Frazier .15 .06
371 Billy Hatcher .15 .06
372 Dave Lopes .25 .10
373 Gary Matthews .25 .10
374 Ron Meridith .15 .06
375 Keith Moreland .15 .06
376 Reggie Patterson .15 .06
377 Dick Ruthven .15 .06
378 Ryne Sandberg 1.50 .60
379 Scott Sanderson .15 .06
380 Lee Smith .25 .10
381 Lary Sorensen .15 .06
382 Chris Speier .15 .06
383 Rick Sutcliffe .25 .10
384 Steve Trout .15 .06
385 Gary Woods .15 .06
386 Bert Blyleven .25 .10
387 Tom Brunansky .15 .06
388 Randy Bush .15 .06
389 John Butcher .15 .06
390 Ron Davis .15 .06
391 Dave Engle .15 .06
392 Frank Eufemia .15 .06
393 Pete Filson .15 .06
394 Gary Gaetti .25 .10
395 Greg Gagne .15 .06
396 Mickey Hatcher .15 .06
397 Kent Hrbek .25 .10
398 Tim Laudner .15 .06
399 Rick Lysander .15 .06
400 Dave Meier .15 .06
401 Kirby Puckett UER 2.00 .80
Card has him in NL,
should be AL
402 Mark Salas .15 .06
403 Ken Schrom .15 .06
404 Roy Smalley .15 .06
405 Mike Smithson .15 .06
406 Mike Stenhouse .15 .06
407 Tim Teufel .15 .06
408 Frank Viola .25 .10
409 Ron Washington .15 .06
410 Keith Atherton .15 .06
411 Dusty Baker .25 .10
412 Tim Birtsas .15 .06
413 Bruce Bochte .15 .06
414 Chris Codiroli .15 .06
415 Dave Collins .15 .06
416 Mike Davis .15 .06
417 Alfredo Griffin .15 .06
418 Mike Heath .15 .06
419 Steve Henderson .15 .06
420 Donnie Hill .15 .06
421 Jay Howell .15 .06
422 Tommy John .25 .10
423 Dave Kingman .25 .10
424 Bill Krueger .15 .06
425 Rick Langford .15 .06
426 Carney Lansford .25 .10
427 Steve McCatty .15 .06
428 Dwayne Murphy .15 .06
429 Steve Ontiveros RC .15 .06
430 Tony Phillips .15 .06
431 Jose Rijo .25 .10
432 Mickey Tettleton RC .50 .20
433 Luis Aguayo .15 .06
434 Larry Andersen .15 .06
435 Steve Carlton .25 .10
436 Don Carman .15 .06
437 Tim Corcoran .15 .06
438 Darren Daulton RC 1.00 .40
439 John Denny .15 .06
440 Tom Foley .15 .06
441 Greg Gross .15 .06
442 Kevin Gross .15 .06
443 Von Hayes .15 .06
444 Charles Hudson .15 .06
445 Garry Maddox .15 .06
446 Shane Rawley .15 .06
447 Dave Rucker .15 .06
448 John Russell .15 .06
449 Juan Samuel .15 .06
450 Mike Schmidt 2.00 .80
451 Rick Schu .15 .06
452 Dave Shipanoff .15 .06

453 Dave Stewart .25 .10
454 Jeff Stone .15 .06
455 Kent Tekulve .15 .06
456 Ozzie Virgil .15 .06
457 Glenn Wilson .15 .06
458 Jim Beattie .15 .06
459 Karl Best .15 .06
460 Barry Bonnell .15 .06
461 Phil Bradley .15 .06
462 Ivan Calderon RC* .50 .20
463 Al Cowens .15 .06
464 Alvin Davis .15 .06
465 Dave Henderson .15 .06
466 Bob Kearney .15 .06
467 Mark Langston .25 .10
468 Bob Long .15 .06
469 Mike Moore .15 .06
470 Edwin Nunez .15 .06
471 Spike Owen .15 .06
472 Jack Perconte .15 .06
473 Jim Presley .15 .06
474 Donnie Scott .15 .06
475 Bill Swift .15 .06
476 Danny Tartabull .25 .10
477 Gorman Thomas .25 .10
478 Roy Thomas .15 .06
479 Ed VandeBerg .15 .06
480 Frank Wills .15 .06
481 Matt Young .15 .06
482 Ray Burris .15 .06
483 Jaime Cocanower .15 .06
484 Cecil Cooper .25 .10
485 Danny Darwin .15 .06
486 Rollie Fingers .25 .10
487 Jim Gantner .15 .06
488 Bob L. Gibson .15 .06
489 Moose Haas .15 .06
490 Teddy Higuera RC* .50 .20
491 Paul Householder .15 .06
492 Pete Ladd .15 .06
493 Rick Manning .15 .06
494 Bob McClure .15 .06
495 Paul Molitor .50 .20
496 Charlie Moore .15 .06
497 Ben Oglivie .25 .10
498 Randy Ready .15 .06
499 Earnie Riles .15 .06
500 Ed Romero .15 .06
501 Bill Schroeder .15 .06
502 Ray Searage .15 .06
503 Ted Simmons .25 .10
504 Pete Vuckovich .15 .06
505 Rick Waits .15 .06
506 Robin Yount 1.25 .50
507 Len Barker .15 .06
508 Steve Bedrosian .15 .06
509 Bruce Benedict .15 .06
510 Rick Camp .15 .06
511 Rick Cerone .15 .06
512 Chris Chambliss .25 .10
513 Jeff Dedmon .15 .06
514 Terry Forster .25 .10
515 Gene Garber .15 .06
516 Terry Harper .15 .06
517 Bob Horner .25 .10
518 Glenn Hubbard .15 .06
519 Joe Johnson .15 .06
520 Brad Komminsk .15 .06
521 Rick Mahler .15 .06
522 Dale Murphy .50 .20
523 Ken Oberkfell .15 .06
524 Pascual Perez .15 .06
525 Gerald Perry .15 .06
526 Rafael Ramirez .15 .06
527 Steve Shields .15 .06
528 Zane Smith .15 .06
529 Bruce Sutter .25 .10
530 Milt Thompson RC .50 .20
531 Claudell Washington .15 .06
532 Paul Zuvella .15 .06
533 Vida Blue .25 .10
534 Bob Brenly .15 .06
535 Chris Brown .15 .06
536 Chili Davis .25 .10
537 Mark Davis .15 .06
538 Rob Deer .15 .06
539 Dan Driessen .15 .06
540 Scott Garrelts .15 .06
541 Dan Gladden .15 .06
542 Jim Gott .15 .06
543 David Green .15 .06
544 Atlee Hammaker .15 .06
545 Mike Jeffcoat .15 .06
546 Mike Krukow .15 .06
547 Dave LaPoint .15 .06
548 Jeff Leonard .15 .06
549 Greg Minton .15 .06
550 Alex Trevino .15 .06
551 Manny Trillo .15 .06
552 Jose Uribe .15 .06
553 Brad Wellman .15 .06
554 Frank Williams .15 .06
555 Joel Youngblood .15 .06
556 Alan Bannister .15 .06
557 Glenn Brummer .15 .06
558 Steve Buechele RC .50 .20
559 Jose Guzman RC .15 .06
560 Toby Harrah .25 .10
561 Greg Harris .15 .06
562 Dwayne Henry .15 .06
563 Burt Hooton .15 .06
564 Charlie Hough .25 .10
565 Mike Mason .15 .06
566 Oddibe McDowell .15 .06
567 Dickie Noles .15 .06
568 Pete O'Brien .15 .06
569 Larry Parrish .15 .06
570 Dave Rozema .15 .06
571 Dave Schmidt .15 .06
572 Don Slaught .15 .06
573 Wayne Tolleson .15 .06
574 Duane Walker .15 .06
575 Gary Ward .15 .06
576 Chris Welsh .15 .06
577 Curtis Wilkerson .15 .06
578 George Wright .15 .06
579 Chris Bando .15 .06
580 Tony Bernazard .15 .06
581 Brett Butler .25 .10
582 Ernie Camacho .15 .06
583 Joe Carter .25 .10
584 Carmen Castillo .15 .06
585 Jamie Easterly .15 .06
586 Julio Franco .25 .10
587 Mel Hall .15 .06
588 Mike Hargrove .15 .06
589 Neal Heaton .15 .06
590 Brook Jacoby .15 .06
591 Otis Nixon RC .50 .20
592 Jerry Reed .15 .06
593 Vern Ruhle .15 .06
594 Pat Tabler .15 .06
595 Rich Thompson .15 .06
596 Andre Thornton .15 .06
597 Dave Von Ohlen .15 .06
598 George Vukovich .15 .06
599 Tom Waddell .15 .06
600 Curt Wardle .15 .06
601 Jerry Willard .15 .06
602 Bill Almon .15 .06
603 Mike Bielecki .15 .06
604 Sid Bream .15 .06
605 Mike C. Brown .15 .06
606 Pat Clements .15 .06
607 Jose DeLeon .15 .06
608 Denny Gonzalez .15 .06
609 Cecilio Guante .15 .06
610 Steve Kemp .15 .06
611 Sammy Khalifa .15 .06
612 Lee Mazzilli .25 .10
613 Larry McWilliams .15 .06
614 Jim Morrison .15 .06
615 Joe Orsulak RC* .50 .20
616 Tony Pena .15 .06
617 Johnny Ray .15 .06
618 Rick Reuschel .25 .10
619 R.J. Reynolds .15 .06
620 Rick Rhoden .15 .06
621 Don Robinson .15 .06
622 Jason Thompson .15 .06
623 Lee Tunnell .15 .06
624 Jim Winn .15 .06
625 Marvell Wynne .15 .06
626 Dwight Gooden IA .50 .20
627 Don Mattingly IA 1.25 .50
628 Pete Rose 4192 .50 .20
629 Rod Carew 3000 Hits .25 .10
630 Tom Seaver .25 .10
Phil Niekro
631 Don Baylor Ouch .25 .10
632 Darryl Strawberry .25 .10
Tim Raines
633 Cal Ripken 1.50 .60
Alan Trammell
634 Wade Boggs 1.00 .40
George Brett
635 Bob Horner .50 .20
Dale Murphy
636 Willie McGee .25 .10
Vince Coleman
637 Vince Coleman IA .25 .10
638 Pete Rose .75 .30
Dwight Gooden
639 Wade Boggs 1.25 .50
Don Mattingly
640 Dale Murphy .50 .20
Steve Garvey
Dave Parker
641 Fernando Valenzuela .50 .20
Dwight Gooden
642 Jimmy Key .25 .10
Dave Stieb
643 Carlton Fisk .25 .10
Rich Gedman
644 Gene Walter RC and 2.00 .80
Benito Santiago
645 Mike Woodard and .15 .06
Colin Ward
646 Kal Daniels RC and 4.00 1.60
Paul O'Neill
647 Andres Galarraga RC 1.50 .60
Fred Toliver
648 Bob Kipper and .15 .06
Curt Ford
649 Jose Canseco RC and 8.00 3.20
Eric Plunk
650 Mark McLemore RC 1.00 .40
Gus Polidor
651 Rob Woodward and .15 .06
Mickey Brantley
652 Billy Joe Robidoux .15 .06
Mark Funderburk
653 Cecil Fielder RC and 1.50 .60
Cory Snyder
654 CL: Royals/Cardinals .15 .06
Blue Jays/Mets
655 CL: Yankees/Dodgers .15 .06
Angels/Reds UER
(168 Darly Sconiers)
656 CL: White Sox/Tigers .15 .06
Expos/Orioles
(279 Dennis&
280 Tippy)
657 CL: Astros/Padres .15 .06
Red Sox/Cubs
658 CL: Twins/A's .15 .06
Phillies/Mariners
659 CL: Brewers/Braves .15 .06
Giants/Rangers
660 CL: Indians/Pirates .15 .06
Special Cards

1986 Fleer All-Stars

Randomly inserted in wax and cello packs, this 12-card standard-size set features top stars. The cards feature red backgrounds (American Leaguers) and blue backgrounds (National Leaguers). The 12 selections cover each position, left and right-handed starting pitchers, a reliever, and a designated hitter.

Nm-Mt Ex-Mt
COMPLETE SET (12) 25.00 10.00
1 Don Mattingly 8.00 3.20
2 Tom Herr .50 .20
3 George Brett 6.00 2.40
4 Gary Carter .75 .30
5 Cal Ripken 10.00 4.00
6 Dave Parker .75 .30
7 Rickey Henderson UER 2.50 1.00
(Misspelled Ricky
on card back)
8 Pedro Guerrero .75 .30
9 Dan Quisenberry .50 .20
10 Dwight Gooden 2.50 1.00
11 Gorman Thomas .75 .30
12 John Tudor .75 .30

1986 Fleer Future Hall of Famers

These six standard-size cards were issued one per Fleer three-packs. This set features players that Fleer predicts will be "Future Hall of Famers." The card backs describe career highlights, records, and honors won by the player.

Nm-Mt Ex-Mt
COMPLETE SET (6) 15.00 6.00
1 Pete Rose 6.00 2.40
2 Steve Carlton .60 .24
3 Tom Seaver 1.25 .50
4 Rod Carew 1.25 .50
5 Nolan Ryan 10.00 4.00
6 Reggie Jackson 1.25 .50

1986 Fleer Wax Box Cards

The cards in this eight-card set measure the standard size and were found on the bottom of the Fleer regular issue wax pack and cello pack boxes as four-card panel. Cards have essentially the same design as the 1986 Fleer regular issue set. These eight cards (C1 to C8) are considered a separate set in their own right and are not typically included in a complete set of the regular issue 1986 Fleer cards. The value of the panel uncut is slightly greater, perhaps by 25 percent greater, than the value of the individual cards cut up carefully.

Nm-Mt Ex-Mt
COMPLETE SET (8) 6.00 2.40
C1 Royals Logo .25 .10
C2 George Brett 3.00 1.20
C3 Ozzie Guillen .75 .30
C4 Dale Murphy .75 .30
C5 Cardinals Logo .25 .10
C6 Tom Browning .25 .10
C7 Gary Carter 1.00 .40
C8 Carlton Fisk 1.00 .40

1986 Fleer Update

This 132-card standard-size set was distributed in factory set form through hobby dealers. In addition to the complete set of 132 cards, the box also contains 25 Team Logo Stickers.The card fronts look very similar to the 1986 Fleer regular issue. These cards are just as condition sensitive with most cards having chippled edges straight out of the box. The cards are numbered (with a U prefix) alphabetically according to player's last name. The extended Rookie Cards in this set include Barry Bonds, Bobby Bonilla, Will Clark, Wally Joyner and John Kruk.

Nm-Mt Ex-Mt
COMP.FACT.SET (132) 60.00 24.00
1 Mike Aldrete .15 .06
2 Andy Allanson .15 .06
3 Neil Allen .15 .06
4 Joaquin Andujar .25 .10
5 Paul Assenmacher .50 .20
6 Scott Bailes .15 .06
7 Jay Baller .15 .06
8 Scott Bankhead .15 .06
9 Bill Bathe .15 .06
10 Don Baylor .25 .10
11 Billy Beane XRC 1.00 .40
12 Steve Bedrosian .15 .06
13 Juan Beniquez .15 .06
14 Barry Bonds XRC 50.00 20.00
15 Bobby Bonilla UER 1.00 .40
(Wrong birthday) XRC
16 Rich Bordi .15 .06
17 Bill Campbell .15 .06
18 Tom Candiotti .15 .06
19 John Cangelosi .15 .06
20 Jose Canseco UER 1.50 .60
(Headings on back
for a pitcher)
21 Chuck Cary .15 .06
22 Juan Castillo XRC .15 .06
23 Rick Cerone .15 .06
24 John Cerutti .15 .06
25 Will Clark XRC 2.00 .80
26 Mark Clear .15 .06
27 Darnell Coles .15 .06
28 Dave Collins .15 .06
29 Tim Conroy .15 .06
30 Ed Correa .15 .06
31 Joe Cowley .15 .06
32 Bill Dawley .15 .06
33 Rob Deer .15 .06
34 John Denny .15 .06
35 Jim Deshaies XRC .15 .06
36 Doug Drabek XRC 1.00 .40
37 Mike Easler .15 .06
38 Mark Eichhorn .15 .06
39 Dave Engle .15 .06
40 Mike Fischlin .15 .06
41 Scott Fletcher .15 .06
42 Terry Forster .25 .10
43 Terry Francona .25 .10
44 Andres Galarraga 1.50 .60
45 Lee Guetterman .15 .06
46 Bill Gullickson .15 .06
47 Jackie Gutierrez .15 .06
48 Moose Haas .15 .06
49 Billy Hatcher .15 .06
50 Mike Heath .15 .06
51 Guy Hoffman .15 .06
52 Tom Hume .15 .06
53 Pete Incaviglia XRC .50 .20
54 Dane Iorg .15 .06
55 Chris James XRC .15 .06
56 Stan Javier XRC* .50 .20
57 Tommy John .25 .10
58 Tracy Jones .15 .06
59 Wally Joyner XRC 1.00 .40
60 Wayne Krenchicki .15 .06
61 John Kruk XRC 1.50 .60
62 Mike LaCoss .15 .06
63 Pete Ladd .15 .06
64 Dave LaPoint .15 .06
65 Mike LaValliere XRC .50 .20
66 Rudy Law .15 .06
67 Dennis Leonard .15 .06
68 Steve Lombardozzi .15 .06
69 Aurelio Lopez .15 .06
70 Mickey Mahler .15 .06
71 Candy Maldonado .15 .06
72 Roger Mason XRC* .15 .06
73 Greg Mathews .15 .06
74 Andy McGaffigan .15 .06
75 Joel McKeon .15 .06
76 Kevin Mitchell XRC 1.00 .40
77 Bill Mooneyham .15 .06
78 Omar Moreno .15 .06
79 Jerry Mumphrey .15 .06
80 Al Newman .25 .10
81 Phil Niekro .25 .10
82 Randy Niemann .15 .06
83 Juan Nieves .15 .06
84 Bob Ojeda .15 .06
85 Rick Ownbey .15 .06
86 Tom Paciorek .15 .06
87 David Palmer .15 .06
88 Jeff Parrett XRC .15 .06
89 Pat Perry .15 .06
90 Dan Plesac .15 .06
91 Darrell Porter .15 .06
92 Luis Quinones .15 .06
93 Rey Quinones UER .15 .06
(Misspelled Quinonez)
94 Gary Redus .15 .06
95 Jeff Reed .15 .06
96 Bip Roberts XRC .50 .20
97 Billy Joe Robidoux .15 .06
98 Gary Roenicke .15 .06
99 Ron Roenicke .15 .06
100 Angel Salazar .15 .06
101 Joe Sambito .15 .06
102 Billy Sample .15 .06
103 Dave Schmidt .15 .06
104 Ken Schrom .15 .06
105 Ruben Sierra XRC 1.50 .60
106 Ted Simmons .25 .10
107 Sammy Stewart .15 .06
108 Kurt Stillwell .15 .06
109 Dale Sveum .15 .06
110 Tim Teufel .15 .06
111 Bob Tewksbury XRC .50 .20
112 Andres Thomas .15 .06
113 Jason Thompson .15 .06
114 Milt Thompson .50 .20
115 R. Thompson XRC .50 .20
116 Jay Tibbs .15 .06
117 Fred Toliver .15 .06
118 Wayne Tolleson .15 .06
119 Alex Trevino .15 .06
120 Manny Trillo .15 .06
121 Ed VandeBerg .15 .06
122 Ozzie Virgil .15 .06
123 Tony Walker .15 .06
124 Gene Walter .15 .06
125 Duane Ward XRC .50 .20
126 Jerry Willard .15 .06
127 Mitch Williams XRC .50 .20
128 Reggie Williams .15 .06
129 Bobby Witt XRC .50 .20
130 Marvell Wynne .15 .06
131 Steve Yeager .25 .10
132 Checklist 1-132 .15 .06

1987 Fleer

This set consists of 660 standard-size cards. Cards were primarily issued in 17-card wax packs, rack packs and hobby and retail factory sets. The wax packs were packed 36 to a box and 20 boxes to a case. The rack packs were packed 24 to a box and 3 boxes to a case. Card fronts feature a distinctive light blue and white blended border encasing a color photo. Cards are again organized numerically by teams with team ordering based on the previous seasons record. The last 36 cards in the set consist of Specials (625-643), Rookie Pairs (644-653), and checklists (654-660). The key Rookie Cards in this set are Barry Bonds, Bobby Bonilla, Will Clark, Chuck Finley, Bo Jackson, Wally Joyner, John Kruk, Barry Larkin and Devon White.

Nm-Mt Ex-Mt
COMPLETE SET (660) 80.00 32.00
COMP.FACT.SET (672) 80.00 32.00
1 Rick Aguilera .15 .06
2 Richard Anderson .15 .06
3 Wally Backman .15 .06
4 Gary Carter .25 .10
5 Ron Darling .25 .10
6 Len Dykstra .25 .10
7 Kevin Elster RC .50 .20
8 Sid Fernandez .15 .06
9 Dwight Gooden .25 .10
10 Ed Hearn .15 .06
11 Danny Heep .15 .06
12 Keith Hernandez .25 .10
13 Howard Johnson .25 .10
14 Ray Knight .25 .10
15 Lee Mazzilli .25 .10
16 Roger McDowell .15 .06
17 Kevin Mitchell RC * 1.25 .50
18 Randy Niemann .15 .06
19 Bob Ojeda .15 .06
20 Jesse Orosco .15 .06
21 Rafael Santana .15 .06
22 Doug Sisk .15 .06
23 Darryl Strawberry .25 .10
24 Tim Teufel .15 .06
25 Mookie Wilson .25 .10
26 Tony Armas .25 .10
27 Marty Barrett .25 .10
28 Don Baylor .25 .10
29 Wade Boggs .40 .16
30 Oil Can Boyd .15 .06
31 Bill Buckner .25 .10
32 Roger Clemens 1.50 .60
33 Steve Crawford .15 .06
34 Dwight Evans .25 .10
35 Rich Gedman .15 .06
36 Dave Henderson .15 .06
37 Bruce Hurst .15 .06
38 Tim Lollar .15 .06
39 Al Nipper .15 .06
40 Spike Owen .15 .06
41 Jim Rice .25 .10
42 Ed Romero .15 .06
43 Joe Sambito .15 .06
44 Calvin Schiraldi .15 .06
45 Tom Seaver UER .40 .16
Lifetime saves total 0, should be 1
46 Jeff Sellers .15 .06
47 Bob Stanley .15 .06
48 Sammy Stewart .15 .06
49 Larry Andersen .15 .06
50 Alan Ashby .15 .06
51 Kevin Bass .15 .06
52 Jeff Calhoun .15 .06
53 Jose Cruz .25 .10
54 Danny Darwin .15 .06
55 Glenn Davis .15 .06
56 Jim Deshaies RC * .25 .10
57 Bill Doran .15 .06
58 Phil Garner .25 .10
59 Billy Hatcher .15 .06
60 Charlie Kerfeld .15 .06
61 Bob Knepper .15 .06
62 Dave Lopes .25 .10
63 Aurelio Lopez .15 .06
64 Jim Pankovits .15 .06
65 Terry Puhl .15 .06
66 Craig Reynolds .15 .06
67 Nolan Ryan 3.00 1.20
68 Mike Scott .25 .10
69 Dave Smith .15 .06
70 Dickie Thon .15 .06
71 Tony Walker .15 .06
72 Denny Walling .15 .06
73 Bob Boone .25 .10
74 Rick Burleson .15 .06
75 John Candelaria .15 .06
76 Doug Corbett .15 .06
77 Doug DeCinces .15 .06
78 Brian Downing .25 .10
79 Chuck Finley RC 1.25 .50
80 Terry Forster .25 .10
81 Bob Grich .25 .10
82 George Hendrick .25 .10
83 Jack Howell .15 .06
84 Reggie Jackson .40 .16
85 Ruppert Jones .15 .06
86 Wally Joyner RC 1.25 .50
87 Gary Lucas .15 .06
88 Kirk McCaskill .15 .06
89 Donnie Moore .15 .06
90 Gary Pettis .15 .06
91 Vern Ruhle .15 .06
92 Dick Schofield .15 .06
93 Don Sutton .25 .10
94 Rob Wilfong .15 .06
95 Mike Witt .15 .06
96 Doug Drabek RC 1.25 .50
97 Mike Easler .15 .06
98 Mike Fischlin .15 .06
99 Brian Fisher .15 .06
100 Ron Guidry .25 .10
101 Rickey Henderson .60 .24
102 Tommy John .25 .10
103 Ron Kittle .15 .06
104 Don Mattingly 2.00 .80
105 Bobby Meacham .15 .06
106 Joe Niekro .15 .06
107 Mike Pagliarulo .15 .06
108 Dan Pasqua .15 .06
109 Willie Randolph .25 .10
110 Dennis Rasmussen .15 .06
111 Dave Righetti .25 .10
112 Gary Roenicke .15 .06
113 Rod Scurry .15 .06
114 Bob Shirley .15 .06
115 Joel Skinner .15 .06
116 Tim Stoddard .15 .06
117 Bob Tewksbury RC * .50 .20
118 Wayne Tolleson .15 .06
119 Claudell Washington .15 .06
120 Dave Winfield .25 .10
121 Steve Buechele .15 .06
122 Ed Correa .15 .06
123 Scott Fletcher .15 .06
124 Jose Guzman .15 .06
125 Toby Harrah .25 .10
126 Greg Harris .15 .06
127 Charlie Hough .25 .10
128 Pete Incaviglia RC * .50 .20
129 Mike Mason .15 .06
130 Oddibe McDowell .15 .06
131 Dale Mohorcic .15 .06
132 Pete O'Brien .15 .06
133 Tom Paciorek .15 .06
134 Larry Parrish .15 .06
135 Geno Petralli .15 .06
136 Darrell Porter .15 .06
137 Jeff Russell .15 .06
138 Ruben Sierra RC 2.00 .80
139 Don Slaught .15 .06
140 Gary Ward .15 .06
141 Curtis Wilkerson .15 .06
142 Mitch Williams RC * .50 .20
143 Bobby Witt RC UER .50 .20
(Tulsa misspelled as
Tusla; ERA should
be 6.43, not .643)
144 Dave Bergman .15 .06
145 Tom Brookens .15 .06
146 Bill Campbell .15 .06
147 Chuck Cary .15 .06
148 Darnell Coles .15 .06
149 Dave Collins .15 .06
150 Darrell Evans .25 .10
151 Kirk Gibson .25 .10
152 John Grubb .15 .06
153 Willie Hernandez .15 .06
154 Larry Herndon .15 .06
155 Eric King .15 .06
156 Chet Lemon .25 .10
157 Dwight Lowry .15 .06
158 Jack Morris .25 .10
159 Randy O'Neal .15 .06
160 Lance Parrish .25 .10
161 Dan Petry .15 .06
162 Pat Sheridan .15 .06

63 Jim Slaton .15 .06
64 Frank Tanana .25 .10
65 Walt Terrell .15 .06
66 Mark Thurmond .15 .06
67 Alan Trammell .25 .10
68 Lou Whitaker .25 .10
69 Luis Aguayo .15 .06
70 Steve Bedrosian .15 .06
71 Don Carman .15 .06
72 Darren Daulton .25 .10
73 Greg Gross .15 .06
74 Kevin Gross .15 .06
75 Von Hayes .15 .06
76 Charles Hudson .15 .06
77 Tom Hume .15 .06
78 Steve Jeltz .15 .06
79 Mike Maddux .15 .06
80 Shane Rawley .15 .06
81 Gary Redus .15 .06
82 Ron Roenicke .15 .06
83 Bruce Ruffin RC .25 .10
84 John Russell .15 .06
85 Juan Samuel .15 .06
86 Dan Schatzeder .15 .06
87 Mike Schmidt 1.50 .60
88 Rick Schu .15 .06
89 Jeff Stone .15 .06
90 Kent Tekulve .15 .06
91 Milt Thompson .15 .06
92 Glenn Wilson .15 .06
93 Buddy Bell .25 .10
94 Tom Browning .15 .06
95 Sal Butera .15 .06
96 Dave Concepcion .25 .10
97 Kal Daniels .15 .06
98 Eric Davis .40 .16
99 John Denny .15 .06
00 Bo Diaz .15 .06
01 Nick Esasky .15 .06
02 John Franco .25 .10
03 Bill Gullickson .15 .06
04 Barry Larkin RC 3.00 1.20
05 Eddie Milner .15 .06
06 Rob Murphy .15 .06
07 Ron Oester .15 .06
08 Dave Parker .25 .10
09 Tony Perez .40 .16
10 Ted Power .15 .06
11 Joe Price .15 .06
12 Ron Robinson .15 .06
13 Pete Rose 2.00 .80
14 Mario Soto .25 .10
15 Kurt Stillwell .15 .06
16 Max Venable .15 .06
17 Chris Welsh .15 .06
18 Carl Willis RC .25 .10
19 Jesse Barfield .25 .10
20 George Bell .25 .10
21 Bill Caudill .15 .06
22 John Cerutti .15 .06
23 Jim Clancy .15 .06
24 Mark Eichhorn .15 .06
25 Tony Fernandez .15 .06
26 Damaso Garcia .15 .06
27 Kelly Gruber ERR .15 .06
(Wrong birth year)
228 Tom Henke .15 .06
229 Garth Iorg .15 .06
230 Joe Johnson .15 .06
231 Cliff Johnson .15 .06
232 Jimmy Key .25 .10
233 Dennis Lamp .15 .06
234 Rick Leach .15 .06
235 Buck Martinez .15 .06
236 Lloyd Moseby .15 .06
237 Rance Mulliniks .15 .06
238 Dave Stieb .25 .10
239 Willie Upshaw .15 .06
240 Ernie Whitt .15 .06
241 Andy Allanson .15 .06
242 Scott Bailes .15 .06
243 Chris Bando .15 .06
244 Tony Bernazard .15 .06
245 John Butcher .15 .06
246 Brett Butler .25 .10
247 Ernie Camacho .15 .06
248 Tom Candiotti .15 .06
249 Joe Carter .25 .10
250 Carmen Castillo .15 .06
251 Julio Franco .25 .10
252 Mel Hall .15 .06
253 Brook Jacoby .15 .06
254 Phil Niekro .25 .10
255 Otis Nixon .15 .06
256 Dickie Noles .15 .06
257 Bryan Oelkers .15 .06
258 Ken Schrom .15 .06
259 Don Schulze .15 .06
260 Cory Snyder .15 .06
261 Pat Tabler .15 .06
262 Andre Thornton .15 .06
263 Rich Yett .15 .06
264 Mike Aldrete .15 .06
265 Juan Berenguer .15 .06
266 Vida Blue .25 .10
267 Bob Brenly .15 .06
268 Chris Brown .15 .06
269 Will Clark RC 3.00 1.20
270 Chili Davis .25 .10
271 Mark Davis .15 .06
272 Kelly Downs RC .25 .10
273 Scott Garrelts .15 .06
274 Dan Gladden .15 .06
275 Mike Krukow .15 .06
276 Randy Kutcher .15 .06
277 Mike LaCoss .15 .06
278 Jeff Leonard .15 .06
279 Candy Maldonado .15 .06
280 Roger Mason .15 .06
281 Bob Melvin .15 .06
282 Greg Minton .15 .06
283 Jeff D. Robinson .15 .06
284 Harry Spilman .15 .06
285 R.Thompson RC* .50 .20
286 Jose Uribe .15 .06
287 Frank Williams .15 .06
288 Joel Youngblood .15 .06
289 Jack Clark .25 .10
290 Vince Coleman .15 .06
291 Tim Conroy .15 .06
292 Danny Cox .15 .06
293 Ken Dayley .15 .06
294 Curt Ford .15 .06
295 Bob Forsch .15 .06
296 Tom Herr .15 .06
297 Ricky Horton .15 .06
298 Clint Hurdle .15 .06
299 Jeff Lahti .15 .06
300 Steve Lake .15 .06
301 Tito Landrum .15 .06
302 Mike LaValliere RC * .50 .20
303 Greg Mathews .15 .06
304 Willie McGee .25 .10
305 Jose Oquendo .15 .06
306 Terry Pendleton .25 .10
307 Pat Perry .15 .06
308 Ozzie Smith 1.00 .40
309 Ray Soff .15 .06
310 John Tudor .25 .10
311 Andy Van Slyke UER .25 .10
(Bats R, Throws L)
312 Todd Worrell .15 .06
313 Dann Bilardello .15 .06
314 Hubie Brooks .15 .06
315 Tim Burke .15 .06
316 Andre Dawson .25 .10
317 Mike Fitzgerald .15 .06
318 Tom Foley .15 .06
319 Andres Galarraga .25 .10
320 Joe Hesketh .15 .06
321 Wallace Johnson .15 .06
322 Wayne Krenchicki .15 .06
323 Vance Law .15 .06
324 Dennis Martinez .25 .10
325 Bob McClure .15 .06
326 Andy McGaffigan .15 .06
327 Al Newman .15 .06
328 Tim Raines .25 .10
329 Jeff Reardon .25 .10
330 Luis Rivera RC .25 .10
331 Bob Sebra .15 .06
332 Bryn Smith .15 .06
333 Jay Tibbs .15 .06
334 Tim Wallach .15 .06
335 Mitch Webster .15 .06
336 Jim Wohlford .15 .06
337 Floyd Youmans .15 .06
338 Chris Bosio RC .50 .20
339 Glenn Braggs RC .25 .10
340 Rick Cerone .15 .06
341 Mark Clear .15 .06
342 Bryan Clutterbuck .15 .06
343 Cecil Cooper .25 .10
344 Rob Deer .15 .06
345 Jim Gantner .15 .06
346 Ted Higuera .15 .06
347 John Henry Johnson .15 .06
348 Tim Leary .15 .06
349 Rick Manning .15 .06
350 Paul Molitor .40 .16
351 Charlie Moore .15 .06
352 Juan Nieves .15 .06
353 Ben Oglivie .25 .10
354 Dan Plesac .15 .06
355 Ernest Riles .15 .06
356 Billy Joe Robidoux .15 .06
357 Bill Schroeder .15 .06
358 Dale Sveum .15 .06
359 Gorman Thomas .25 .10
360 Bill Wegman .15 .06
361 Robin Yount 1.00 .40
362 Steve Balboni .15 .06
363 Scott Bankhead .15 .06
364 Buddy Biancalana .15 .06
365 Bud Black .15 .06
366 George Brett 1.50 .60
367 Steve Farr .15 .06
368 Mark Gubicza .15 .06
369 Bo Jackson RC 3.00 1.20
370 Danny Jackson .15 .06
371 Mike Kingery RC .25 .10
372 Rudy Law .15 .06
373 Charlie Leibrandt .15 .06
374 Dennis Leonard .15 .06
375 Hal McRae .25 .10
376 Jorge Orta .15 .06
377 Jamie Quirk .15 .06
378 Dan Quisenberry .15 .06
379 Bret Saberhagen .25 .10
380 Angel Salazar .15 .06
381 Lonnie Smith .15 .06
382 Jim Sundberg .25 .10
383 Frank White .25 .10
384 Willie Wilson .25 .10
385 Joaquin Andujar .25 .10
386 Doug Bair .15 .06
387 Dusty Baker .25 .10
388 Bruce Bochte .15 .06
389 Jose Canseco .60 .24
390 Chris Codiroli .15 .06
391 Mike Davis .15 .06
392 Alfredo Griffin .15 .06
393 Moose Haas .15 .06
394 Donnie Hill .15 .06
395 Jay Howell .15 .06
396 Dave Kingman .25 .10
397 Carney Lansford .25 .10
398 Dave Leiper .15 .06
399 Bill Mooneyham .15 .06
400 Dwayne Murphy .15 .06
401 Steve Ontiveros .15 .06
402 Tony Phillips .15 .06
403 Eric Plunk .15 .06
404 Jose Rijo .25 .10
405 Terry Steinbach RC 1.25 .50
406 Dave Stewart .25 .10
407 Mickey Tettleton .15 .06
408 Dave Von Ohlen .15 .06
409 Jerry Willard .15 .06
410 Curt Young .15 .06
411 Bruce Bochy .15 .06
412 Dave Dravecky .15 .06
413 Tim Flannery .15 .06
414 Steve Garvey .25 .10
415 Rich Gossage .25 .10
416 Tony Gwynn 1.00 .40
417 Andy Hawkins .15 .06
418 LaMarr Hoyt .15 .06
419 Terry Kennedy .15 .06
420 John Kruk RC 2.00 .80
421 Dave LaPoint .15 .06
422 Craig Lefferts .15 .06
423 Carmelo Martinez .15 .06
424 Lance McCullers .15 .06
425 Kevin McReynolds .15 .06
426 Graig Nettles .25 .10
427 Bip Roberts RC .50 .20
428 Jerry Royster .15 .06
429 Benito Santiago .25 .10
430 Eric Show .15 .06
431 Bob Stoddard .15 .06
432 Garry Templeton .25 .10
433 Gene Walter .15 .06
434 Ed Whitson .15 .06
435 Marvell Wynne .15 .06
436 Dave Anderson .15 .06
437 Greg Brock .15 .06
438 Enos Cabell .15 .06
439 Mariano Duncan .15 .06
440 Pedro Guerrero .25 .10
441 Orel Hershiser .25 .10
442 Rick Honeycutt .15 .06
443 Ken Howell .15 .06
444 Ken Landreaux .15 .06
445 Bill Madlock .25 .10
446 Mike Marshall .15 .06
447 Len Matuszek .15 .06
448 Tom Niedenfuer .15 .06
449 Alejandro Pena .15 .06
450 Dennis Powell .15 .06
451 Jerry Reuss .15 .06
452 Bill Russell .25 .10
453 Steve Sax .15 .06
454 Mike Scioscia .25 .10
455 Franklin Stubbs .15 .06
456 Alex Trevino .15 .06
457 Fernando Valenzuela .25 .10
458 Ed VandeBerg .15 .06
459 Bob Welch .25 .10
460 Reggie Williams .15 .06
461 Don Aase .15 .06
462 Juan Beniquez .15 .06
463 Mike Boddicker .15 .06
464 Juan Bonilla .15 .06
465 Rich Bordi .15 .06
466 Storm Davis .15 .06
467 Rick Dempsey .15 .06
468 Ken Dixon .15 .06
469 Jim Dwyer .15 .06
470 Mike Flanagan .15 .06
471 Jackie Gutierrez .15 .06
472 Brad Havens .15 .06
473 Lee Lacy .15 .06
474 Fred Lynn .25 .10
475 Scott McGregor .15 .06
476 Eddie Murray .60 .24
477 Tom O'Malley .15 .06
478 Cal Ripken Jr. 2.50 1.00
479 Larry Sheets .15 .06
480 John Shelby .15 .06
481 Nate Snell .15 .06
482 Jim Traber .15 .06
483 Mike Young .15 .06
484 Neil Allen .15 .06
485 Harold Baines .25 .10
486 Floyd Bannister .15 .06
487 Daryl Boston .15 .06
488 Ivan Calderon .15 .06
489 John Cangelosi .15 .06
490 Steve Carlton .25 .10
491 Joe Cowley .15 .06
492 Julio Cruz .15 .06
493 Bill Dawley .15 .06
494 Jose DeLeon .15 .06
495 Richard Dotson .15 .06
496 Carlton Fisk .40 .16
497 Ozzie Guillen .15 .06
498 Jerry Hairston .15 .06
499 Ron Hassey .15 .06
500 Tim Hulett .15 .06
501 Bob James .15 .06
502 Steve Lyons .15 .06
503 Joel McKeon .15 .06
504 Gene Nelson .15 .06
505 Dave Schmidt .15 .06
506 Ray Searage .15 .06
507 Bobby Thigpen RC .50 .20
508 Greg Walker .15 .06
509 Jim Acker .15 .06
510 Doyle Alexander .15 .06
511 Paul Assenmacher .50 .20
512 Bruce Benedict .15 .06
513 Chris Chambliss .25 .10
514 Jeff Dedmon .15 .06
515 Gene Garber .15 .06
516 Ken Griffey .25 .10
517 Terry Harper .15 .06
518 Bob Horner .25 .10
519 Glenn Hubbard .15 .06
520 Rick Mahler .15 .06
521 Omar Moreno .15 .06
522 Dale Murphy .40 .16
523 Ken Oberkfell .15 .06
524 Ed Olwine .15 .06
525 David Palmer .15 .06
526 Rafael Ramirez .15 .06
527 Billy Sample .15 .06
528 Ted Simmons .25 .10
529 Zane Smith .15 .06
530 Bruce Sutter .25 .10
531 Andres Thomas .15 .06
532 Ozzie Virgil .15 .06
533 Allan Anderson .15 .06
534 Keith Atherton .15 .06
535 Billy Beane .25 .10
536 Bert Blyleven .25 .10
537 Tom Brunansky .15 .06
538 Randy Bush .15 .06
539 George Frazier .15 .06
540 Gary Gaetti .25 .10
541 Greg Gagne .15 .06
542 Mickey Hatcher .15 .06
543 Neal Heaton .15 .06
544 Kent Hrbek .25 .10
545 Roy Lee Jackson .15 .06
546 Tim Laudner .15 .06
547 Steve Lombardozzi .15 .06
548 Mark Portugal RC * .50 .20
549 Kirby Puckett .60 .24
550 Jeff Reed .15 .06
551 Mark Salas .15 .06
552 Roy Smalley .15 .06
553 Mike Smithson .15 .06
554 Frank Viola .25 .10
555 Thad Bosley .15 .06
556 Ron Cey .25 .10
557 Jody Davis .15 .06
558 Ron Davis .15 .06
559 Bob Dernier .15 .06
560 Frank DiPino .15 .06
561 Shawon Dunston UER .15 .06
(Wrong birth year
listed on card back)
562 Leon Durham .15 .06
563 Dennis Eckersley .40 .16
564 Terry Francona .25 .10
565 Dave Gumpert .15 .06
566 Guy Hoffman .15 .06
567 Ed Lynch .15 .06
568 Gary Matthews .25 .10
569 Keith Moreland .15 .06
570 Jamie Moyer RC 2.00 .80
571 Jerry Mumphrey .15 .06
572 Ryne Sandberg 1.25 .50
573 Scott Sanderson .15 .06
574 Lee Smith .25 .10
575 Chris Speier .15 .06
576 Rick Sutcliffe .25 .10
577 Manny Trillo .15 .06
578 Steve Trout .15 .06
579 Karl Best .15 .06
580 Scott Bradley .15 .06
581 Phil Bradley .15 .06
582 Mickey Brantley .15 .06
583 Mike G. Brown P .15 .06
584 Alvin Davis .15 .06
585 Lee Guetterman .15 .06
586 Mark Huismann .15 .06
587 Bob Kearney .15 .06
588 Pete Ladd .15 .06
589 Mark Langston .15 .06
590 Mike Moore .15 .06
591 Mike Morgan .15 .06
592 John Moses .15 .06
593 Ken Phelps .15 .06
594 Jim Presley .15 .06
595 Rey Quinones UER .15 .06
(Quinonez on front)
596 Harold Reynolds .25 .10
597 Billy Swift .15 .06
598 Danny Tartabull .15 .06
599 Steve Yeager .25 .10
600 Matt Young .15 .06
601 Bill Almon .15 .06
602 Rafael Belliard RC .50 .20
603 Mike Bielecki .15 .06
604 Barry Bonds RC 60.00 24.00
605 Bobby Bonilla RC 1.25 .50
606 Sid Bream .15 .06
607 Mike C. Brown .15 .06
608 Pat Clements .15 .06
609 Mike Diaz .15 .06
610 Cecilio Guante .15 .06
611 Barry Jones .15 .06
612 Bob Kipper .15 .06
613 Larry McWilliams .15 .06
614 Jim Morrison .15 .06
615 Joe Orsulak .15 .06
616 Junior Ortiz .15 .06
617 Tony Pena .15 .06
618 Johnny Ray .15 .06
619 Rick Reuschel .25 .10
620 R.J. Reynolds .15 .06
621 Rick Rhoden .15 .06
622 Don Robinson .15 .06
623 Bob Walk .15 .06
624 Jim Winn .15 .06
625 Pete Incaviglia .60 .24
Jose Canseco
626 Don Sutton .25 .10
Phil Niekro
627 Dave Righetti .15 .06
Don Aase
628 Wally Joyner .40 .16
Jose Canseco
629 Gary Carter .25 .10
Sid Fernandez
Dwight Gooden
Keith Hernandez
Darryl Strawberry
630 Mike Scott .15 .06
Mike Krukow
631 Fernando Valenzuela .15 .06
John Franco
632 Bob Horner 4 Homers .15 .06
633 Jose Canseco .60 .24
Jim Rice
Kirby Puckett
634 Gary Carter .60 .24
Roger Clemens
635 Steve Carlton 4000K's .25 .10
636 Glenn Davis .60 .24
Eddie Murray
637 Wade Boggs .25 .10
Keith Hernandez
638 Don Mattingly 1.00 .40
Darryl Strawberry
639 Dave Parker .60 .24
Ryne Sandberg
640 Dwight Gooden .60 .24
Roger Clemens
641 Mike Witt .15 .06
Charlie Hough
642 Juan Samuel .25 .10
Tim Raines
643 Harold Baines .25 .10
Jesse Barfield
644 Dave Clark RC and .50 .20
Greg Swindell
645 Ron Karkovice RC .50 .20
Russ Morman
646 Devon White RC and 1.25 .50
Willie Fraser
647 Mike Stanley RC and .50 .20
Jerry Browne
648 Dave Magadan RC .50 .20
Phil Lombardi
649 Jose Gonzalez RC .25 .10
Ralph Bryant
650 Jimmy Jones RC and .25 .10
Randy Asadoor
651 Tracy Jones RC and .25 .10
Marvin Freeman
652 John Stefero and .50 .20
Kevin Seitzer RC
653 Rob Nelson and .25 .10
Steve Fireovid
654 CL: Mets/Red Sox .15 .06
Astros/Angels
655 CL: Yankees/Rangers .15 .06
Tigers/Phillies
656 CL: Reds/Blue Jays .15 .06
Indians/Giants
ERR (230/231 wrong)
657 CL: Cardinals/Expos .15 .06
Brewers/Royals
658 CL: A's/Padres .15 .06
Dodgers/Orioles
659 CL: White Sox/Braves .15 .06
Twins/Cubs
660 CL: Mariners/Pirates .15 .06
Special Cards
ER (580/581 wrong)

1987 Fleer Glossy

This set parallels the regular 1987 Fleer issue and signified a short-lived three year run of Glossy parallel cards likely produced in response to Topps' run of Tiffany parallel sets. The cards were issued in a special tin which also included a glossy version of the World Series set. These 672 standard-size are differentiated only by the gloss on the front. This set was produced in fairly large quantities, although still significantly less than regular issue cards. According to widely held beliefs in the hobby, somewhere between 75 and 100 thousand of these sets were produced.

	Nm-Mt	Ex-Mt
COMP.FACT.SET (672)	130.00	52.50

*STARS: .5X TO 1.2X BASIC CARDS..
*ROOKIES: .5X TO 1.2X BASIC CARDS
FACTORY SET PRICE IS FOR SEALED SETS
OPENED SETS SELL FOR 50-60% OF SEALED

1987 Fleer All-Stars

This 12-card standard-size set was distributed as an insert in packs of the Fleer regular issue. The cards are designed with a color player photo superimposed on a gray or black background with yellow stars. The player's name, team, and position are printed in orange on black or gray at the bottom of the obverse. The card backs are done predominantly in gray, red, and black and are numbered on the back in the upper right hand corner.

	Nm-Mt	Ex-Mt
COMPLETE SET (12)	20.00	8.00
1 Don Mattingly	6.00	2.40
2 Gary Carter	.75	.30
3 Tony Fernandez	.50	.20
4 Steve Sax	.50	.20
5 Kirby Puckett	2.00	.80
6 Mike Schmidt	5.00	2.00
7 Mike Easler	.50	.20
8 Todd Worrell	.50	.20
9 George Bell	.75	.30
10 Fernando Valenzuela	.75	.30
11 Roger Clemens	5.00	2.00
12 Tim Raines	.75	.30

1987 Fleer Headliners

This six-card standard-size set was distributed one per rack pack as well as with three-pack wax pack rack packs. The obverse features the player photo against a beige background with irregular red stripes. The checklist below also lists each player's team affiliation. The set is sequenced in alphabetical order.

	Nm-Mt	Ex-Mt
COMPLETE SET (6)	6.00	2.40
1 Wade Boggs	.60	.24
2 Jose Canseco	1.00	.40
3 Dwight Gooden	.40	.16
4 Rickey Henderson	1.00	.40
5 Keith Hernandez	.40	.16
6 Jim Rice	.40	.16

1987 Fleer Wax Box Cards

The cards in this 16-card set measure the standard, 2 1/2" by 3 1/2". Cards have essentially the same design as the 1987 Fleer regular issue set. The cards were printed on the bottoms of the regular issue wax pack boxes. These 16 cards (C1 to C16) are considered a separate set in their own right and are not typically included in a complete set of the regular issue 1987 Fleer cards. The value of the panel uncut is slightly greater, perhaps by 25 percent greater, than the value of the individual cards cut up carefully.

	Nm-Mt	Ex-Mt
COMPLETE SET (16)	10.00	4.00
C1 Mets Logo	.10	.04
C2 Jesse Barfield	.10	.04
C3 George Brett	3.00	1.20
C4 Dwight Gooden	.50	.20
C5 Boston Logo	.10	.04
C6 Keith Hernandez	.25	.10
C7 Wally Joyner	.75	.30
C8 Dale Murphy	.75	.30
C9 Astros Logo	.10	.04
C10 Dave Parker	.25	.10
C11 Kirby Puckett	1.00	.40
C12 Dave Righetti	.10	.04
C13 Angels Logo	.10	.04
C14 Ryne Sandberg	2.00	.80
C15 Mike Schmidt	1.50	.60
C16 Robin Yount	.75	.30

1987 Fleer World Series

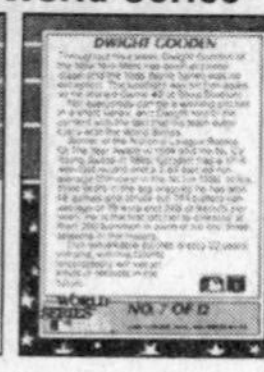

This 12-card standard-size set of features highlights of the previous year's World Series between the Mets and the Red Sox. The sets were packaged as a complete set insert with the collated sets (of the 1987 Fleer regular issue) which were sold by Fleer directly to hobby card dealers; they were not available in the general retail candy store outlets.

Nm-Mt Ex-Mt
COMPLETE SET (12) 2.00 .80
1 Bruce Hurst .15 .06
2 Keith Hernandez and .25 .10
Wade Boggs
3 Roger Clemens HOR 1.50 .60
4 Gary Carter .25 .10
5 Ron Darling .25 .10
6 Marty Barrett .15 .06
7 Dwight Gooden .25 .10
8 Strategy at Work .25 .10
(Mets Conference)
9 Dwight Evans .25 .10
Congratulated by Rich Gedman
10 Dave Henderson .15 .06
11 Ray Knight .25 .10
Darryl Strawberry
12 Ray Knight .25 .10

1987 Fleer Update

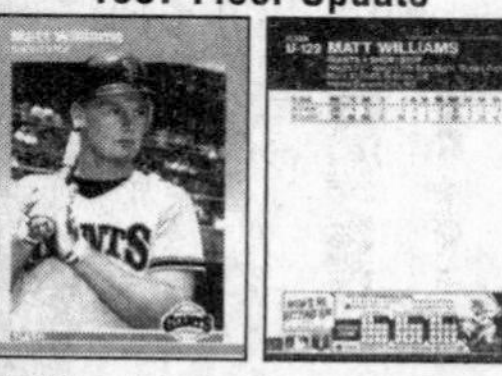

This 132-card standard-size set was distributed exclusively in factory set form through hobby dealers. In addition to the complete set of 132 cards, the box also contained 25 Team Logo stickers. The cards look very similar to the 1987 Fleer regular issue except for the U-prefixed numbering on back. Cards are ordered alphabetically according to player's last name. The key extended Rookie Cards in this set are Ellis Burks, Greg Maddux, Fred McGriff and Matt Williams. In addition an early card of legendary slugger Mark McGwire highlights this set.

Nm-Mt Ex-Mt
COMP.FACT.SET (132) 15.00 6.00
1 Scott Bankhead .10 .04
2 Eric Bell .15 .06
3 Juan Beniquez .10 .04
4 Juan Berenguer .10 .04
5 Mike Birkbeck .15 .06
6 Randy Bockus .10 .04
7 Rod Booker .10 .04
8 Thad Bosley .10 .04
9 Greg Brock .10 .04
10 Bob Brower .10 .04
11 Chris Brown .10 .04
12 Jerry Browne .15 .06
13 Ralph Bryant .10 .04
14 DeWayne Buice .10 .04
15 Ellis Burks XRC .75 .30
16 Casey Candaele .10 .04
17 Steve Carlton .15 .06
18 Juan Castillo .15 .06
19 Chuck Crim .10 .04
20 Mark Davidson .10 .04
21 Mark Davis .10 .04
22 Storm Davis .10 .04
23 Bill Dawley .10 .04
24 Andre Dawson .15 .06
25 Brian Dayett .10 .04
26 Rick Dempsey .10 .04
27 Ken Dowell .10 .04
28 Dave Dravecky .10 .04
29 Mike Dunne .10 .04
30 Dennis Eckersley .25 .10
31 Cecil Fielder .15 .06
32 Brian Fisher .10 .04
33 Willie Fraser .15 .06
34 Ken Gerhart .10 .04
35 Jim Gott .10 .04
36 Dan Gladden .10 .04
37 Mike Greenwell XRC* .30 .12
38 Cecilio Guante .10 .04
39 Albert Hall .10 .04
40 Atlee Hammaker .10 .04
41 Mickey Hatcher .10 .04
42 Mike Heath .10 .04
43 Neal Heaton .10 .04
44 Mike Henneman XRC .30 .12
45 Guy Hoffman .10 .04
46 Charles Hudson .10 .04
47 Chuck Jackson .10 .04
48 Mike Jackson XRC .30 .12
49 Reggie Jackson .25 .10
50 Chris James .10 .04
51 Dion James .10 .04
52 Stan Javier .10 .04
53 Stan Jefferson .10 .04
54 Jimmy Jones .15 .06
55 Tracy Jones .10 .04
56 Terry Kennedy .10 .04
57 Mike Kingery .15 .06
58 Ray Knight .15 .06
59 Gene Larkin XRC .30 .12
60 Mike LaValliere .30 .12
61 Jack Lazorko .10 .04
62 Terry Leach .10 .04
63 Rick Leach .10 .04
64 Craig Lefferts .10 .04
65 Jim Lindeman .15 .06
66 Bill Long .10 .04
67 Mike Loynd XRC .15 .06
68 Greg Maddux XRC 8.00 3.20
69 Bill Madlock .15 .06
70 Dave Magadan .30 .12
71 Joe Magrane XRC .15 .06
72 Fred Manrique .10 .04
73 Mike Mason .10 .04
74 Lloyd McClendon XRC .30 .12
75 Fred McGriff 1.00 .40
76 Mark McGwire 5.00 2.00
77 Mark McLemore .15 .06
78 Kevin McReynolds .10 .04
79 Dave Meads .10 .04
80 Greg Minton .10 .04
81 John Mitchell XRC .15 .06
82 Kevin Mitchell .25 .10
83 John Morris .10 .04
84 Jeff Musselman .10 .04
85 Randy Myers XRC .75 .30
86 Gene Nelson .10 .04
87 Joe Niekro .10 .04
88 Tom Nieto .10 .04
89 Reid Nichols .10 .04
90 Matt Nokes XRC .30 .12
91 Dickie Noles .10 .04
92 Edwin Nunez .10 .04
93 Jose Nunez .10 .04
94 Paul O'Neill .40 .16
95 Jim Paciorek .10 .04
96 Lance Parrish .15 .06
97 Bill Pecota XRC .15 .06
98 Tony Pena .10 .04
99 Luis Polonia XRC .30 .12
100 Randy Ready .10 .04
101 Jeff Reardon .15 .06
102 Gary Redus .10 .04
103 Rick Rhoden .10 .04
104 Wally Ritchie .10 .04
105 Jeff M. Robinson UER .10 .04
(Wrong Jeff's
stats on back)
106 Mark Salas .10 .04
107 Dave Schmidt .10 .04
108 Kevin Seitzer UER .30 .12
(Wrong birth year)
109 John Shelby .10 .04
110 John Smiley XRC .30 .12
111 Lary Sorensen .10 .04
112 Chris Speier .10 .04
113 Randy St.Claire .10 .04
114 Jim Sundberg .15 .06
115 B.J. Surhoff XRC .75 .30
116 Greg Swindell .30 .12
117 Danny Tartabull .10 .04
118 Dorn Taylor .10 .04
119 Lee Tunnell .10 .04
120 Ed VandeBerg .10 .04
121 Andy Van Slyke .15 .06
122 Gary Ward .10 .04
123 Devon White .75 .30
124 Alan Wiggins .10 .04
125 Bill Wilkinson .10 .04
126 Jim Winn .10 .04
127 Frank Williams .10 .04
128 Ken Williams XRC .10 .04
129 Matt Williams XRC 1.50 .60
130 Herm Winningham .10 .04
131 Matt Young .10 .04
132 Checklist 1-132 .10 .04

1987 Fleer Update Glossy

This set parallels the regular Fleer Update issue. The cards were issued in a special tin. These 132 standard-size are differentiated only by the gloss on the front. This set was produced in fairly large quantities, although still significantly less than regular issue cards. Similar to the regular Glossy set -- it is believed that between 75 and 100 thousand of these sets were produced.

Nm-Mt Ex-Mt
COMP.FACT.SET (132) 15.00 6.00
*STARS: .4X TO 1X BASIC CARDS
*ROOKIES: .4X TO 1X BASIC CARDS

1987 Fleer Hottest Stars

This 44-card boxed standard-size set was produced by Fleer for distribution by Revco stores all over the country. The cards feature full color fronts and red, white, and black backs. The card fronts are easily distinguished by their solid red outside borders and and white and blue inner borders framing the player's picture. The box for the cards proclaims "1987 Limited Edition Baseball's Hottest Stars" and is styled in the same manner and color scheme as the cards themselves. The checklist for the set is given on the back of the set box. The card numbering is in alphabetical order by player's name. An early card of Barry Bonds highlights this set.

Nm-Mt Ex-Mt
COMP.FACT.SET (44) 60.00 24.00
1 Joaquin Andujar .10 .04
2 Harold Baines .15 .06
3 Kevin Bass .10 .04
4 Don Baylor .15 .06
5 Barry Bonds 50.00 20.00
6 George Brett 1.00 .40
7 Tom Brunansky .10 .04
8 Brett Butler .15 .06
9 Jose Canseco .40 .16
10 Roger Clemens 1.50 .60
11 Ron Darling .10 .04
12 Eric Davis .15 .06
13 Andre Dawson .15 .06
14 Doug DeCinces .10 .04
15 Leon Durham .10 .04
16 Mark Eichhorn .10 .04
17 Scott Garrelts .10 .04
18 Dwight Gooden .15 .06
19 Dave Henderson .10 .04
20 Rickey Henderson .40 .16
21 Keith Hernandez .15 .06
22 Ted Higuera .10 .04
23 Bob Horner .15 .06
24 Pete Incaviglia .15 .06
25 Wally Joyner .25 .10
26 Mark Langston .10 .04
27 Don Mattingly UER 1.25 .50
(Pirates logo
on back)
28 Dale Murphy .40 .16
29 Kirk McCaskill .10 .04
30 Willie McGee .15 .06
31 Dave Righetti .15 .06
32 Pete Rose 1.25 .50
33 Bruce Ruffin .10 .04
34 Steve Sax .10 .04
35 Mike Schmidt 1.00 .40
36 Larry Sheets .10 .04
37 Eric Show .10 .04
38 Dave Smith .10 .04
39 Cory Snyder .10 .04
40 Frank Tanana .15 .06
41 Alan Trammell .15 .06
42 Reggie Williams .10 .04
43 Mookie Wilson .15 .06
44 Todd Worrell .15 .06

1988 Fleer

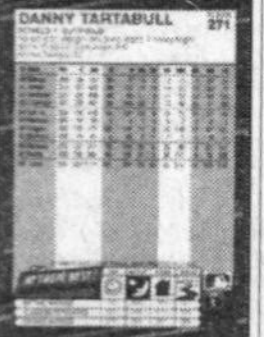

This set consists of 660 standard-size cards. Cards were primarily issued in 15-card wax packs and hobby and retail factory sets. Each wax pack contained one of 26 different "Stadium Card" stickers. Card fronts feature a distinctive white background with red and blue diagonal stripes across the card. As in years past cards are organized numerically by teams and team order is based upon the previous season's record. Subsets include Specials (622-640), Rookie Pairs (641-653), and checklists (654-660). Rookie Cards in this set include Jay Bell, Ellis Burks, Ken Caminiti, Ron Gant, Tom Glavine, Mark Grace, Edgar Martinez, Jack McDowell and Matt Williams.

Nm-Mt Ex-Mt
COMPLETE SET (660) 15.00 6.00
COMP.RETAIL SET (660) 15.00 6.00
COMP.HOBBY SET (672) 15.00 6.00
1 Keith Atherton .10 .04
2 Don Baylor .15 .06
3 Juan Berenguer .10 .04
4 Bert Blyleven .15 .06
5 Tom Brunansky .10 .04
6 Randy Bush .10 .04
7 Steve Carlton .15 .06
8 Mark Davidson .10 .04
9 George Frazier .10 .04
10 Gary Gaetti .15 .06
11 Greg Gagne .10 .04
12 Dan Gladden .10 .04
13 Kent Hrbek .15 .06
14 Gene Larkin RC* .40 .16
15 Tim Laudner .10 .04
16 Steve Lombardozzi .10 .04
17 Al Newman .10 .04
18 Joe Niekro .10 .04
19 Kirby Puckett .30 .12
20 Jeff Reardon .15 .06
21A Dan Schatzeder ERR .15 .06
(Misspelled Schatzader
on both sides of the card)
21B Dan Schatzeder COR .10 .04
22 Roy Smalley .10 .04
23 Mike Smithson .10 .04
24 Les Straker .10 .04
25 Frank Viola .15 .06
26 Jack Clark .15 .06
27 Vince Coleman .10 .04
28 Danny Cox .10 .04
29 Bill Dawley .10 .04
30 Ken Dayley .10 .04
31 Doug DeCinces .10 .04
32 Curt Ford .10 .04
33 Bob Forsch .10 .04
34 David Green .10 .04
35 Tom Herr .10 .04
36 Ricky Horton .10 .04
37 Lance Johnson RC .40 .16
38 Steve Lake .10 .04
39 Jim Lindeman .10 .04
40 Joe Magrane RC* .40 .16
41 Greg Mathews .10 .04
42 Willie McGee .15 .06
43 John Morris .10 .04
44 Jose Oquendo .10 .04
45 Tony Pena .10 .04
46 Terry Pendleton .15 .06
47 Ozzie Smith .50 .20
48 John Tudor .15 .06
49 Lee Tunnell .10 .04
50 Todd Worrell .15 .06
51 Doyle Alexander .10 .04
52 Dave Bergman .10 .04
53 Tom Brookens .10 .04
54 Darrell Evans .15 .06
55 Kirk Gibson .30 .12
56 Mike Heath .10 .04
57 Mike Henneman RC* .40 .16
58 Willie Hernandez .10 .04
59 Larry Herndon .10 .04
60 Eric King .10 .04
61 Chet Lemon .15 .06
62 Scott Lusader .10 .04
63 Bill Madlock .15 .06
64 Jack Morris .15 .06
65 Jim Morrison .10 .04
66 Matt Nokes RC* .40 .16
67 Dan Petry .10 .04
68A Jeff M. Robinson .20 .08
ERR, Stats for Jeff D. Robinson
on card back
Born 12-13-60
68B Jeff M. Robinson .10 .04
COR, Born 12-14-61
69 Pat Sheridan .10 .04
70 Nate Snell .10 .04
71 Frank Tanana .15 .06
72 Walt Terrell .10 .04
73 Mark Thurmond .10 .04
74 Alan Trammell .15 .06
75 Lou Whitaker .15 .06
76 Mike Aldrete .10 .04
77 Bob Brenly .10 .04
78 Will Clark .30 .12
79 Chili Davis .15 .06
80 Kelly Downs .10 .04
81 Dave Dravecky .10 .04
82 Scott Garrelts .10 .04
83 Atlee Hammaker .10 .04
84 Dave Henderson .10 .04
85 Mike Krukow .10 .04
86 Mike LaCoss .10 .04
87 Craig Lefferts .10 .04
88 Jeff Leonard .10 .04
89 Candy Maldonado .10 .04
90 Eddie Milner .10 .04
91 Bob Melvin .10 .04
92 Kevin Mitchell .15 .06
93 Jon Perlman .10 .04
94 Rick Reuschel .15 .06
95 Don Robinson .10 .04
96 Chris Speier .10 .04
97 Harry Spilman .10 .04
98 Robby Thompson .15 .06
99 Jose Uribe .10 .04
100 Mark Wasinger .10 .04
101 Matt Williams RC 1.50 .60
102 Jesse Barfield .15 .06
103 George Bell .15 .06
104 Juan Beniquez .10 .04
105 John Cerutti .10 .04
106 Jim Clancy .10 .04
107 Rob Ducey .10 .04
108 Mark Eichhorn .10 .04
109 Tony Fernandez .10 .04
110 Cecil Fielder .15 .06
111 Kelly Gruber .10 .04
112 Tom Henke .10 .04
113A Garth Iorg ERR .20 .08
(Misspelled Iorq
on card front)
113B Garth Iorg COR .10 .04
114 Jimmy Key .15 .06
115 Rick Leach .10 .04
116 Manny Lee .10 .04
117 Nelson Liriano .10 .04
118 Fred McGriff .30 .12
119 Lloyd Moseby .10 .04
120 Rance Mulliniks .10 .04
121 Jeff Musselman .10 .04
122 Jose Nunez .10 .04
123 Dave Stieb .15 .06
124 Willie Upshaw .10 .04
125 Duane Ward .10 .04
126 Ernie Whitt .10 .04
127 Rick Aguilera .15 .06
128 Wally Backman .10 .04
129 Mark Carreon RC .15 .06
130 Gary Carter .15 .06
131 David Cone .15 .06
132 Ron Darling .15 .06
133 Len Dykstra .15 .06
134 Sid Fernandez .10 .04
135 Dwight Gooden .15 .06
136 Keith Hernandez .15 .06
137 Gregg Jefferies RC .40 .16
138 Howard Johnson .15 .06
139 Terry Leach .10 .04
140 Barry Lyons .10 .04
141 Dave Magadan .10 .04
142 Roger McDowell .10 .04
143 Kevin McReynolds .10 .04
144 Keith A. Miller RC .40 .16
145 John Mitchell RC .15 .06
146 Randy Myers .15 .06
147 Bob Ojeda .10 .04
148 Jesse Orosco .10 .04
149 Rafael Santana .10 .04
150 Doug Sisk .10 .04
151 Darryl Strawberry .15 .06
152 Tim Teufel .10 .04
153 Gene Walter .10 .04
154 Mookie Wilson .15 .06
155 Jay Aldrich .10 .04
156 Chris Bosio .10 .04
157 Glenn Braggs .10 .04
158 Greg Brock .10 .04
159 Juan Castillo .10 .04
160 Mark Clear .10 .04
161 Cecil Cooper .15 .06
162 Chuck Crim .10 .04
163 Rob Deer .10 .04
164 Mike Felder .10 .04
165 Jim Gantner .10 .04
166 Ted Higuera .10 .04
167 Steve Kiefer .10 .04
168 Rick Manning .10 .04
169 Paul Molitor .20 .08
170 Juan Nieves .10 .04
171 Dan Plesac .10 .04
172 Earnest Riles .10 .04
173 Bill Schroeder .10 .04
174 Steve Stanicek .10 .04
175 B.J. Surhoff .15 .06
176 Dale Sveum .10 .04
177 Bill Wegman .10 .04
178 Robin Yount .50 .20
179 Hubie Brooks .10 .04
180 Tim Burke .10 .04
181 Casey Candaele .10 .04
182 Mike Fitzgerald .10 .04
183 Tom Foley .10 .04
184 Andres Galarraga .15 .06
185 Neal Heaton .10 .04
186 Wallace Johnson .10 .04
187 Vance Law .10 .04
188 Dennis Martinez .15 .06
189 Bob McClure .10 .04
190 Andy McGaffigan .10 .04
191 Reid Nichols .10 .04
192 Pascual Perez .10 .04
193 Tim Raines .15 .06
194 Jeff Reed .10 .04
195 Bob Sebra .10 .04
196 Bryn Smith .10 .04
197 Randy St.Claire .10 .04
198 Tim Wallach .10 .04
199 Mitch Webster .10 .04
200 Herm Winningham .10 .04
201 Floyd Youmans .10 .04
202 Brad Arnsberg .10 .04
203 Rick Cerone .10 .04
204 Pat Clements .10 .04
205 Henry Cotto .10 .04
206 Mike Easler .10 .04
207 Ron Guidry .15 .06
208 Bill Gullickson .10 .04
209 Rickey Henderson .30 .12
210 Charles Hudson .10 .04
211 Tommy John .15 .06
212 Roberto Kelly RC .40 .16
213 Ron Kittle .10 .04
214 Don Mattingly 1.00 .40
215 Bobby Meacham .10 .04
216 Mike Pagliarulo .10 .04
217 Dan Pasqua .10 .04
218 Willie Randolph .15 .06
219 Rick Rhoden .10 .04
220 Dave Righetti .15 .06
221 Jerry Royster .10 .04
222 Tim Stoddard .10 .04
223 Wayne Tolleson .10 .04
224 Gary Ward .10 .04
225 Claudell Washington .10 .04
226 Dave Winfield .15 .06
227 Buddy Bell .15 .06
228 Tom Browning .10 .04
229 Dave Concepcion .15 .06
230 Kal Daniels .10 .04
231 Eric Davis .15 .06
232 Bo Diaz .10 .04
233 Nick Esasky .10 .04
(Has a dollar sign
before '87 SB totals)
234 John Franco .15 .06
235 Guy Hoffman .10 .04
236 Tom Hume .10 .04
237 Tracy Jones .10 .04
238 Bill Landrum .10 .04
239 Barry Larkin .20 .08
240 Terry McGriff .10 .04
241 Rob Murphy .10 .04
242 Ron Oester .10 .04
243 Dave Parker .15 .06
244 Pat Perry .10 .04
245 Ted Power .10 .04
246 Dennis Rasmussen .10 .04
247 Ron Robinson .10 .04
248 Kurt Stillwell .10 .04
249 Jeff Treadway RC .40 .16
250 Frank Williams .10 .04
251 Steve Balboni .10 .04
252 Bud Black .10 .04
253 Thad Bosley .10 .04
254 George Brett .75 .30
255 John Davis .10 .04
256 Steve Farr .10 .04
257 Gene Garber .10 .04
258 Jerry Don Gleaton .10 .04
259 Mark Gubicza .10 .04
260 Bo Jackson .30 .12
261 Danny Jackson .10 .04
262 Ross Jones .10 .04
263 Charlie Leibrandt .10 .04
264 Bill Pecota RC* .15 .06
265 Melido Perez RC .40 .16
266 Jamie Quirk .10 .04
267 Dan Quisenberry .10 .04
268 Bret Saberhagen .15 .06
269 Angel Salazar .10 .04
270 Kevin Seitzer UER .15 .06
(Wrong birth year)
271 Danny Tartabull .10 .04
272 Gary Thurman .10 .04
273 Frank White .15 .06
274 Willie Wilson .15 .06
275 Tony Bernazard .10 .04
276 Jose Canseco .30 .12
277 Mike Davis .10 .04
278 Storm Davis .10 .04
279 Dennis Eckersley .20 .08
280 Alfredo Griffin .10 .04
281 Rick Honeycutt .10 .04
282 Jay Howell .10 .04
283 Reggie Jackson .20 .08
284 Dennis Lamp .10 .04
285 Carney Lansford .15 .06
286 Mark McGwire 2.50 1.00
287 Dwayne Murphy .10 .04
288 Gene Nelson .10 .04
289 Steve Ontiveros .10 .04
290 Tony Phillips .10 .04
291 Eric Plunk .10 .04
292 Luis Polonia RC* .40 .16
293 Rick Rodriguez .10 .04
294 Terry Steinbach .15 .06
295 Dave Stewart .15 .06
296 Curt Young .10 .04
297 Luis Aguayo .10 .04
298 Steve Bedrosian .10 .04
299 Jeff Calhoun .10 .04
300 Don Carman .10 .04
301 Todd Frohwirth .10 .04
302 Greg Gross .10 .04
303 Kevin Gross .10 .04
304 Von Hayes .10 .04
305 Keith Hughes .10 .04

306 Mike Jackson RC* .40 .16
307 Chris James .10 .04
308 Steve Jeltz .10 .04
309 Mike Maddux .10 .04
310 Lance Parrish .15 .06
311 Shane Rawley .10 .04
312 Wally Ritchie .10 .04
313 Bruce Ruffin .10 .04
314 Juan Samuel .10 .04
315 Mike Schmidt .75 .30
316 Rick Schu .10 .04
317 Jeff Stone .10 .04
318 Kent Tekulve .10 .04
319 Milt Thompson .10 .04
320 Glenn Wilson .10 .04
321 Rafael Belliard .10 .04
322 Barry Bonds 3.00 1.20
323 Bobby Bonilla UER .15 .06
(Wrong birth year)
324 Sid Bream .10 .04
325 John Cangelosi .10 .04
326 Mike Diaz .10 .04
327 Doug Drabek .10 .04
328 Mike Dunne .10 .04
329 Brian Fisher .10 .04
330 Brett Gideon .10 .04
331 Terry Harper .10 .04
332 Bob Kipper .10 .04
333 Mike LaValliere .10 .04
334 Jose Lind RC .40 .16
335 Junior Ortiz .10 .04
336 Vicente Palacios .10 .04
337 Bob Patterson .10 .04
338 Al Pedrique .10 .04
339 R.J. Reynolds .10 .04
340 John Smiley RC* .40 .16
341 Andy Van Slyke UER .15 .06
(Wrong batting and
throwing listed)
342 Bob Walk .10 .04
343 Marty Barrett .10 .04
344 Todd Benzinger RC* .40 .16
345 Wade Boggs .20 .08
346 Tom Bolton .10 .04
347 Oil Can Boyd .10 .04
348 Ellis Burks RC .50 .20
349 Roger Clemens .75 .30
350 Steve Crawford .10 .04
351 Dwight Evans .15 .06
352 Wes Gardner .10 .04
353 Rich Gedman .10 .04
354 Mike Greenwell .10 .04
355 Sam Horn RC .15 .06
356 Bruce Hurst .10 .04
357 John Marzano .10 .04
358 Al Nipper .10 .04
359 Spike Owen .10 .04
360 Jody Reed RC .40 .16
361 Jim Rice .15 .06
362 Ed Romero .10 .04
363 Kevin Romine .10 .04
364 Joe Sambito .10 .04
365 Calvin Schiraldi .10 .04
366 Jeff Sellers .10 .04
367 Bob Stanley .10 .04
368 Scott Bankhead .10 .04
369 Phil Bradley .10 .04
370 Scott Bradley .10 .04
371 Mickey Brantley .10 .04
372 Mike Campbell .10 .04
373 Alvin Davis .10 .04
374 Lee Guetterman .10 .04
375 Dave Hengel .10 .04
376 Mike Kingery .10 .04
377 Mark Langston .10 .04
378 Edgar Martinez RC 4.00 1.60
379 Mike Moore .10 .04
380 Mike Morgan .10 .04
381 John Moses .10 .04
382 Donell Nixon .10 .04
383 Edwin Nunez .10 .04
384 Ken Phelps .10 .04
385 Jim Presley .10 .04
386 Rey Quinones .10 .04
387 Jerry Reed .10 .04
388 Harold Reynolds .15 .06
389 Dave Valle .10 .04
390 Bill Wilkinson .10 .04
391 Harold Baines .15 .06
392 Floyd Bannister .10 .04
393 Daryl Boston .10 .04
394 Ivan Calderon .10 .04
395 Jose DeLeon .10 .04
396 Richard Dotson .10 .04
397 Carlton Fisk .20 .08
398 Ozzie Guillen .10 .04
399 Ron Hassey .10 .04
400 Donnie Hill .10 .04
401 Bob James .10 .04
402 Dave LaPoint .10 .04
403 Bill Lindsey .10 .04
404 Bill Long .10 .04
405 Steve Lyons .10 .04
406 Fred Manrique .10 .04
407 Jack McDowell RC .50 .20
408 Gary Redus .10 .04
409 Ray Searage .10 .04
410 Bobby Thigpen .10 .04
411 Greg Walker .10 .04
412 Ken Williams RC .10 .04
413 Jim Winn .10 .04
414 Jody Davis .10 .04
415 Andre Dawson .15 .06
416 Brian Dayett .10 .04
417 Bob Dernier .10 .04
418 Frank DiPino .10 .04
419 Shawon Dunston .10 .04
420 Leon Durham .10 .04
421 Les Lancaster .10 .04
422 Ed Lynch .10 .04
423 Greg Maddux 1.50 .60
424 Dave Martinez .10 .04
425A Keith Moreland ERR 1.50 .60
(Photo actually
Jody Davis)
425B Keith Moreland COR .15 .06
(Bat on shoulder)
426 Jamie Moyer .15 .06
427 Jerry Mumphrey .10 .04
428 Paul Noce .10 .04
429 Rafael Palmeiro .60 .24
430 Wade Rowdon .10 .04
431 Ryne Sandberg .60 .24
432 Scott Sanderson .10 .04
433 Lee Smith .15 .06
434 Jim Sundberg .15 .06
435 Rick Sutcliffe .15 .06
436 Manny Trillo .10 .04
437 Juan Agosto .10 .04
438 Larry Andersen .10 .04
439 Alan Ashby .10 .04
440 Kevin Bass .10 .04
441 Ken Caminiti RC 1.00 .40
442 Rocky Childress .10 .04
443 Jose Cruz .15 .06
444 Danny Darwin .10 .04
445 Glenn Davis .10 .04
446 Jim Deshaies .10 .04
447 Bill Doran .10 .04
448 Ty Gainey .10 .04
449 Billy Hatcher .10 .04
450 Jeff Heathcock .10 .04
451 Bob Knepper .10 .04
452 Rob Mallicoat .10 .04
453 Dave Meads .10 .04
454 Craig Reynolds .10 .04
455 Nolan Ryan 1.50 .60
456 Mike Scott .15 .06
457 Dave Smith .10 .04
458 Denny Walling .10 .04
459 Robbie Wine .10 .04
460 Gerald Young .10 .04
461 Bob Brower .10 .04
462A Jerry Browne ERR 1.50 .60
(Photo actually
Bob Brower,
white player)
462B Jerry Browne COR .15 .06
(Black player)
463 Steve Buechele .10 .04
464 Edwin Correa .10 .04
465 Cecil Espy .10 .04
466 Scott Fletcher .10 .04
467 Jose Guzman .10 .04
468 Greg Harris .10 .04
469 Charlie Hough .15 .06
470 Pete Incaviglia .10 .04
471 Paul Kilgus .10 .04
472 Mike Loynd .10 .04
473 Oddibe McDowell .10 .04
474 Dale Mohorcic .10 .04
475 Pete O'Brien .10 .04
476 Larry Parrish .10 .04
477 Geno Petralli .10 .04
478 Jeff Russell .10 .04
479 Ruben Sierra .15 .06
480 Mike Stanley .10 .04
481 Curtis Wilkerson .10 .04
482 Mitch Williams .10 .04
483 Bobby Witt .10 .04
484 Tony Armas .15 .06
485 Bob Boone .15 .06
486 Bill Buckner .15 .06
487 DeWayne Buice .10 .04
488 Brian Downing .15 .06
489 Chuck Finley .15 .06
490 Willie Fraser UER .10 .04
(Wrong bio stats,
for George Hendrick)
491 Jack Howell .10 .04
492 Ruppert Jones .10 .04
493 Wally Joyner .15 .06
494 Jack Lazorko .10 .04
495 Gary Lucas .10 .04
496 Kirk McCaskill .10 .04
497 Mark McLemore .10 .04
498 Darrell Miller .10 .04
499 Greg Minton .10 .04
500 Donnie Moore .10 .04
501 Gus Polidor .10 .04
502 Johnny Ray .10 .04
503 Mark Ryal .10 .04
504 Dick Schofield .10 .04
505 Don Sutton .15 .06
506 Devon White .15 .06
507 Mike Witt .10 .04
508 Dave Anderson .10 .04
509 Tim Belcher .10 .04
510 Ralph Bryant .10 .04
511 Tim Crews RC .40 .16
512 Mike Devereaux RC .40 .16
513 Mariano Duncan .10 .04
514 Pedro Guerrero .15 .06
515 Jeff Hamilton .10 .04
516 Mickey Hatcher .10 .04
517 Brad Havens .10 .04
518 Orel Hershiser .15 .06
519 Shawn Hillegas .10 .04
520 Ken Howell .10 .04
521 Tim Leary .10 .04
522 Mike Marshall .10 .04
523 Steve Sax .10 .04
524 Mike Scioscia .15 .06
525 Mike Sharperson .10 .04
526 John Shelby .10 .04
527 Franklin Stubbs .10 .04
528 Fernando Valenzuela .15 .06
529 Bob Welch .15 .06
530 Matt Young .10 .04
531 Jim Acker .10 .04
532 Paul Assenmacher .10 .04
533 Jeff Blauser RC .40 .16
534 Joe Boever .10 .04
535 Martin Clary .10 .04
536 Kevin Coffman .10 .04
537 Jeff Dedmon .10 .04
538 Ron Gant RC .50 .20
539 Tom Glavine RC 3.00 1.20
540 Ken Griffey .15 .06
541 Albert Hall .10 .04
542 Glenn Hubbard .10 .04
543 Dion James .10 .04
544 Dale Murphy .20 .08
545 Ken Oberkfell .10 .04
546 David Palmer .10 .04
547 Gerald Perry .10 .04
548 Charlie Puleo .10 .04
549 Ted Simmons .15 .06
550 Zane Smith .10 .04
551 Andres Thomas .10 .04
552 Ozzie Virgil .10 .04
553 Don Aase .10 .04
554 Jeff Ballard .10 .04
555 Eric Bell .10 .04
556 Mike Boddicker .10 .04
557 Ken Dixon .10 .04
558 Jim Dwyer .10 .04
559 Ken Gerhart .10 .04
560 Rene Gonzales RC .15 .06
561 Mike Griffin .10 .04
562 John Habyan UER .10 .04
(Misspelled Hayban on
both sides of card)
563 Terry Kennedy .10 .04
564 Ray Knight .15 .06
565 Lee Lacy .10 .04
566 Fred Lynn .15 .06
567 Eddie Murray .30 .12
568 Tom Niedenfuer .10 .04
569 Bill Ripken RC* .40 .16
570 Cal Ripken 1.25 .50
571 Dave Schmidt .10 .04
572 Larry Sheets .10 .04
573 Pete Stanicek .10 .04
574 Mark Williamson .10 .04
575 Mike Young .10 .04
576 Shawn Abner .10 .04
577 Greg Booker .10 .04
578 Chris Brown .10 .04
579 Keith Comstock .10 .04
580 Joey Cora RC .40 .16
581 Mark Davis .10 .04
582 Tim Flannery .20 .08
(With surfboard)
583 Goose Gossage .15 .06
584 Mark Grant .10 .04
585 Tony Gwynn .50 .20
586 Andy Hawkins .10 .04
587 Stan Jefferson .10 .04
588 Jimmy Jones .10 .04
589 John Kruk .15 .06
590 Shane Mack .10 .04
591 Carmelo Martinez .10 .04
592 Lance McCullers UER .10 .04
(6'11" tall)
593 Eric Nolte .10 .04
594 Randy Ready .10 .04
595 Luis Salazar .10 .04
596 Benito Santiago .15 .06
597 Eric Show .10 .04
598 Garry Templeton .15 .06
599 Ed Whitson .10 .04
600 Scott Bailes .10 .04
601 Chris Bando .10 .04
602 Jay Bell RC .50 .20
603 Brett Butler .15 .06
604 Tom Candiotti .10 .04
605 Joe Carter .15 .06
606 Carmen Castillo .10 .04
607 Brian Dorsett .10 .04
608 John Farrell RC .15 .06
609 Julio Franco .15 .06
610 Mel Hall .10 .04
611 Tommy Hinzo .10 .04
612 Brook Jacoby .10 .04
613 Doug Jones RC .40 .16
614 Ken Schrom .10 .04
615 Cory Snyder .10 .04
616 Sammy Stewart .10 .04
617 Greg Swindell .10 .04
618 Pat Tabler .10 .04
619 Ed VandeBerg .10 .04
620 Eddie Williams RC .15 .06
621 Rich Yett .10 .04
622 Wally Joyner .15 .06
Cory Snyder
623 George Bell .10 .04
Pedro Guerrero
624 Mark McGwire 1.00 .40
Jose Canseco
625 Dave Righetti .10 .04
Dan Plesac
626 Bret Saberhagen .15 .06
Mike Witt
Jack Morris
627 John Franco .10 .04
Steve Bedrosian
628 Ozzie Smith .30 .12
Ryne Sandberg
629 Mark McGwire HL 1.25 .50
630 Mike Greenwell .30 .12
Ellis Burks
Todd Benzinger
631 Tony Gwynn .20 .08
Tim Raines
632 Mike Scott .15 .06
Orel Hershiser
633 Pat Tabler 1.25 .50
Mark McGwire
634 Tony Gwynn .20 .08
Vince Coleman
635 Tony Fernandez .50 .20
Cal Ripken
Alan Trammell
636 Mike Schmidt .30 .12
Gary Carter
637 Darryl Strawberry .15 .06
Eric Davis
638 Matt Nokes .20 .08
Kirby Puckett
639 Keith Hernandez .15 .06
Dale Murphy
640 Billy Ripken .75 .30
Cal Ripken
641 Mark Grace RC and 3.00 1.20
Darrin Jackson
642 Damon Berryhill RC .40 .16
Jeff Montgomery RC
643 Felix Fermin .15 .06
Jesse Reid RC
644 Greg Myers .40 .16
Greg Tabor RC
645 Joey Meyer .15 .06
Jim Eppard RC
646 Adam Peterson .40 .16
Randy Velarde RC
647 Pete Smith .40 .16
Chris Gwynn RC
648 Tom Newell and .15 .06
Greg Jelks RC
649 Mario Diaz .15 .06
Clay Parker RC
650 Jack Savage and .15 .06
Todd Simmons RC
651 John Burkett .40 .16
Kirt Manwaring RC
652 Dave Otto .50 .20
Walt Weiss RC
653 Jeff King .40 .16
Randell Byers RC
654 CL: Twins/Cards .10 .04
Tigers/Giants UER
(90 Bob Melvin,
91 Eddie Milner)
655 CL: Blue Jays/Mets .10 .04
Brewers/Expos UER
(Mets listed before
Blue Jays on card)
656 CL: Yankees/Reds .10 .04
Royals/A's
657 CL: Phillies/Pirates .10 .04
Red Sox/Mariners
658 CL: White Sox/Cubs .10 .04
Astros/Rangers
659 CL: Angels/Dodgers .10 .04
Braves/Orioles
660 CL: Padres/Indians .10 .04
Rookies/Specials

1988 Fleer Glossy

This 660 card set is a parallel to the regular Fleer issue. The cards are the same as the regular issue except for the glossy sheen on the front. The cards (along with the 12-card World Series insert set) were issued in a factory tin distributed exclusively through hobby dealers. Since many dealers had problems selling their 1987 sets, production was reduced for the 1988 issues. It is believed that between 40 and 60 thousand of these sets were produced,

Nm-Mt Ex-Mt
COMP.FACT.SET (672) 25.00 10.00
*STARS: .6X TO 1.5X BASIC CARDS
*ROOKIES: 1.25X TO 3X BASIC CARDS

1988 Fleer All-Stars

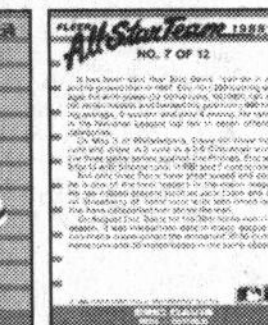

These 12 standard-size cards were inserted randomly in wax and cello packs of the 1988 Fleer set. The cards show the player silhouetted against a light green background with dark green stripes. The player's name, team, and position are printed in yellow at the bottom of the obverse. The card backs are done predominantly in green, white, and black. The players are the "best" at each position, three pitchers, eight position players, and a designated hitter.

Nm-Mt Ex-Mt
COMPLETE SET (12) 6.00 2.40
1 Matt Nokes 1.50 .60
2 Tom Henke .40 .16
3 Ted Higuera .40 .16
4 Roger Clemens 3.00 1.20
5 George Bell .60 .24
6 Andre Dawson .60 .24
7 Eric Davis .60 .24
8 Wade Boggs .75 .30
9 Alan Trammell .60 .24
10 Juan Samuel .40 .16
11 Jack Clark .60 .24
12 Paul Molitor .75 .30

1988 Fleer Headliners

This six-card standard-size set was distributed one per rack pack. The obverse features the player photo superimposed on a gray newsprint background. The cards are printed in red, black, and white on the back describing why that particular player made headlines the previous season. The set is sequenced in alphabetical order.

Nm-Mt Ex-Mt
COMPLETE SET (6) 6.00 2.40
1 Don Mattingly 1.25 .50
2 Mark McGwire 4.00 1.60
3 Jack Morris .20 .08
4 Darryl Strawberry .20 .08
5 Dwight Gooden .20 .08
6 Tim Raines .20 .08

1988 Fleer Wax Box Cards

The cards in this 16-card set measure the standard size. Cards have essentially the same design as the 1988 Fleer regular issue set. The cards were printed on the bottoms of the regular issue wax pack boxes. These 16 cards (C1 to C16) are considered a separate set in their own right and are not typically included in a complete set of the regular issue 1988 Fleer cards. The value of the panel uncut is slightly greater, perhaps by 25 percent greater, than the value of the individual cards cut up carefully.

Nm-Mt Ex-Mt
COMPLETE SET (16) 8.00 3.20
C1 Cardinals Logo .10 .04
C2 Dwight Evans .25 .10
C3 Andres Galarraga 1.00 .40
C4 Wally Joyner .25 .10
C5 Twins Logo .10 .04
C6 Dale Murphy 1.00 .40
C7 Kirby Puckett 1.25 .50
C8 Shane Rawley .10 .04
C9 Giants Logo .10 .04
C10 Ryne Sandberg 2.50 1.00
C11 Mike Schmidt 1.25 .50
C12 Kevin Seitzer .10 .04
C13 Tigers Logo .10 .04
C14 Dave Stewart .25 .10
C15 Tim Wallach .10 .04
C16 Todd Worrell .25 .10

1988 Fleer World Series

This 12-card standard-size set features highlights of the previous year's World Series between the Minnesota Twins and the St. Louis Cardinals. The sets were packaged as a complete set insert with the collated sets (of the 1988 Fleer regular issue) which were sold by Fleer directly to hobby card dealers; they were not available in the general retail candy store outlets. The set numbering is essentially in chronological order of the events from the immediate past World Series.

Nm-Mt Ex-Mt
COMPLETE SET (12) 2.00 .80
1 Dan Gladden .10 .04
2 Randy Bush .10 .04
3 John Tudor .15 .06
4 Ozzie Smith .50 .20
5 Todd Worrell .10 .04
Tony Pena
6 Vince Coleman .10 .04
7 Tom Herr .10 .04
Dan Driessen
8 Kirby Puckett .30 .12
9 Kent Hrbek .15 .06
10 Tom Herr .10 .04
11 Don Baylor .15 .06
12 Frank Viola .15 .06

1988 Fleer Update

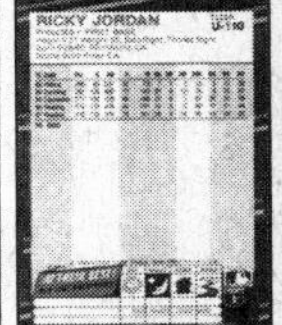

This 132-card standard-size set was distributed exclusively in factory set form in a red, white and blue, cellophane-wrapped box through hobby dealers. In addition to the complete set of 132 cards, the box also contained 25 Team Logo stickers. The cards look very similar to the 1988 Fleer regular issue except for the U-prefixed numbering on back. Cards are ordered alphabetically by player's last name. This was the first Fleer Update set to adopt the Fleer "alphabetical within team" numbering system. The key extended Rookie Cards in this set are Roberto Alomar, Craig Biggio Al Leiter, John Smoltz and David Wells.

Nm-Mt Ex-Mt
COMP.FACT.SET (132) 8.00 3.20
1 Jose Bautista XRC .25 .10
2 Joe Orsulak .10 .04
3 Doug Sisk .10 .04
4 Craig Worthington .10 .04
5 Mike Boddicker .10 .04
6 Rick Cerone .10 .04
7 Larry Parrish .10 .04
8 Lee Smith .20 .08
9 Mike Smithson .10 .04
10 John Trautwein .10 .04
11 Sherman Corbett .10 .04
12 Chili Davis .20 .08
13 Jim Eppard .10 .04
14 Bryan Harvey XRC .50 .20
15 John Davis .10 .04
16 Dave Gallagher .10 .04
17 Ricky Horton .10 .04
18 Dan Pasqua .10 .04
19 Melido Perez .10 .04
20 Jose Segura .10 .04
21 Andy Allanson .10 .04
22 Jon Perlman .10 .04
23 Domingo Ramos .10 .04
24 Rick Rodriguez .10 .04
25 Willie Upshaw .10 .04
26 Paul Gibson .10 .04
27 Don Heinkel .10 .04
28 Ray Knight .20 .08
29 Gary Pettis .10 .04
30 Luis Salazar .10 .04
31 Mike Macfarlane XRC .50 .20
32 Jeff Montgomery .50 .20
33 Ted Power .10 .04
34 Israel Sanchez .10 .04
35 Kurt Stillwell .10 .04
36 Pat Tabler .10 .04
37 Don August .10 .04
38 Darryl Hamilton XRC .50 .20
39 Jeff Leonard .10 .04
40 Joey Meyer .10 .04

41 Allan Anderson .10 .04
42 Brian Harper .10 .04
43 Tom Herr .10 .04
44 Charlie Lea .10 .04
45 John Moses .10 .04
(Listed as Hohn on checklist card)
46 John Candelaria .10 .04
47 Jack Clark .20 .08
48 Richard Dotson .10 .04
49 Al Leiter XRC* 1.00 .40
50 Rafael Santana .10 .04
51 Don Slaught .10 .04
52 Todd Burns .10 .04
53 Dave Henderson .10 .04
54 Doug Jennings .10 .04
55 Dave Parker .20 .08
56 Walt Weiss .75 .30
57 Bob Welch .20 .08
58 Henry Cotto .10 .04
59 Mario Diaz UER .10 .04
(Listed as Marion on card front)
60 Mike Jackson .20 .08
61 Bill Swift .10 .04
62 Jose Cecena .10 .04
63 Ray Hayward .10 .04
64 Jim Steels UER .10 .04
(Listed as Jim Steele on card back)
65 Pat Borders XRC .50 .20
66 Sil Campusano .10 .04
67 Mike Flanagan .10 .04
68 Todd Stottlemyre XRC .50 .20
69 David Wells XRC 1.25 .50
70 Jose Alvarez XRC .25 .10
71 Paul Runge .10 .04
72 Cesar Jimenez .10 .04
(Card was intended for German Jiminez& it's his photo)
73 Pete Smith .10 .04
74 John Smoltz XRC 3.00 1.20
75 Damon Berryhill .25 .10
76 Goose Gossage .20 .08
77 Mark Grace 1.50 .60
78 Darrin Jackson .25 .10
79 Vance Law .10 .04
80 Jeff Pico .10 .04
81 Gary Varsho .10 .04
82 Tim Birtsas .10 .04
83 Rob Dibble XRC 1.00 .40
84 Danny Jackson .10 .04
85 Paul O'Neill .30 .12
86 Jose Rijo .20 .08
87 Chris Sabo XRC .75 .30
88 John Fishel .10 .04
89 Craig Biggio XRC 2.00 .80
90 Terry Puhl .10 .04
91 Rafael Ramirez .10 .04
92 Louie Meadows .10 .04
93 Kirk Gibson .50 .20
94 Alfredo Griffin .10 .04
95 Jay Howell .10 .04
96 Jesse Orosco .10 .04
97 Alejandro Pena .10 .04
98 Tracy Woodson XRC* .25 .10
99 John Dopson .10 .04
100 Brian Holman XRC .25 .10
101 Rex Hudler .10 .04
102 Jeff Parrett .10 .04
103 Nelson Santovenia .10 .04
104 Kevin Elster .10 .04
105 Jeff Innis .10 .04
106 Mackey Sasser XRC* .50 .20
107 Phil Bradley .10 .04
108 Danny Clay .10 .04
109 Greg A.Harris .10 .04
110 Ricky Jordan XRC .50 .20
111 David Palmer .10 .04
112 Jim Gott .10 .04
113 Tommy Gregg UER .10 .04
(Photo actually Randy Milligan)
114 Barry Jones .10 .04
115 Randy Milligan XRC* .25 .10
116 Luis Alicea XRC .50 .20
117 Tom Brunansky .10 .04
118 John Costello .10 .04
119 Jose DeLeon .10 .04
120 Bob Horner .20 .08
121 Scott Terry .10 .04
122 Roberto Alomar XRC 3.00 1.20
123 Dave Leiper .10 .04
124 Keith Moreland .10 .04
125 Mark Parent .10 .04
126 Dennis Rasmussen .10 .04
127 Randy Bockus .10 .04
128 Brett Butler .20 .08
129 Donell Nixon .10 .04
130 Earnest Riles .10 .04
131 Roger Samuels .10 .04
132 Checklist U1-U132 .10 .04

1988 Fleer Update Glossy

This 132 card set is a parallel to the regular Fleer Update issue. Except for a glossy sheen on the front, the cards are identical to the regular Fleer issue. The cards were issued through hobby dealers in a special tin box. The cards are not as plentiful as the regular Fleer update set. Similar to the regular Glossy set, it is believed that between 40 and 60 thousand of these sets were produced.

Nm-Mt Ex-Mt
COMP.FACT.SET (132) 25.00 10.00
*STARS: 1X TO 2.5X BASIC CARDS
*ROOKIES: 1.25X TO 3X BASIC CARDS

1989 Fleer

This set consists of 660 standard-size cards. Cards were primarily issued in 15-card wax packs, rack packs and hobby and retail factory sets. Card fronts feature a distinctive gray border background with white and yellow trim. Cards are again organized alphabetically within teams and teams ordered by previous season record. The last 33 cards in the set consist of Specials (628-639), Rookie Pairs (640-653), and checklists (654-660). Approximately half of the California Angels players have white rather than yellow halos. Certain Oakland A's player cards have red instead of green lines for front photo borders. Checklist cards are available either with or without positions listed for each player. Rookie Cards in this set include Craig Biggio, Ken Griffey Jr., Randy Johnson, Gary Sheffield, and John Smoltz. An interesting variation was discovered in late 1999 by Beckett Grading Services on the Randy Johnson RC (card number 381). It seems the most common version features a crudely-blacked out image of an outfield billboard. A scarcer version clearly reveals the words "Marlboro" on the billboard. A value for this variation is not provided due to scarcity. One of the hobby's most notorious errors and variations hails from this product. Card number 616, Billy Ripken, was originally published with a four-letter word imprinted on the bat. Needless to say, this caused quite a stir in 1989 and the card was quickly reprinted. Because of this, several different variations were printed with the final solution (and the most common version of this card) being a black box covering the bat knob. The first variation is still actively sought after in the hobby and the other versions are still sought after by collectors seeking a "master" set.

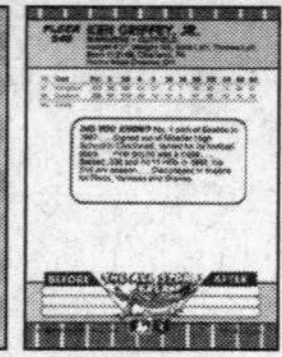

Nm-Mt Ex-Mt
COMPLETE SET (660) 15.00 6.00
COMP.FACT.SET (672) 15.00 6.00
1 Don Baylor .10 .04
2 Lance Blankenship RC .10 .04
3 Todd Burns UER .05 .02
(Wrong birthdate; before/after All-Star stats missing)
4 Greg Cadaret UER .05 .02
(All-Star Break stats show 3 losses, should be 2
5 Jose Canseco .25 .10
6 Storm Davis .05 .02
7 Dennis Eckersley .15 .06
8 Mike Gallego .05 .02
9 Ron Hassey .05 .02
10 Dave Henderson .05 .02
11 Rick Honeycutt .05 .02
12 Glenn Hubbard .05 .02
13 Stan Javier .05 .02
14 Doug Jennings .05 .02
15 Felix Jose RC .10 .04
16 Carney Lansford .10 .04
17 Mark McGwire 1.00 .40
18 Gene Nelson .05 .02
19 Dave Parker .10 .04
20 Eric Plunk .05 .02
21 Luis Polonia .05 .02
22 Terry Steinbach .10 .04
23 Dave Stewart .10 .04
24 Walt Weiss .05 .02
25 Bob Welch .10 .04
26 Curt Young .05 .02
27 Rick Aguilera .05 .02
28 Wally Backman .05 .02
29 Mark Carreon UER .05 .02
(After All-Star Break batting 7.14)
30 Gary Carter .10 .04
31 David Cone .10 .04
32 Ron Darling .10 .04
33 Len Dykstra .10 .04
34 Kevin Elster .05 .02
35 Sid Fernandez .05 .02
36 Dwight Gooden .10 .04
37 Keith Hernandez .10 .04
38 Gregg Jefferies .05 .02
39 Howard Johnson .10 .04
40 Terry Leach .05 .02
41 Dave Magadan UER .05 .02
(Bio says 15 doubles, should be 13)
42 Bob McClure .05 .02
43 Roger McDowell UER .05 .02
(Led Mets with 58, should be 62)
44 Kevin McReynolds .05 .02
45 Keith A. Miller .05 .02
46 Randy Myers .10 .04
47 Bob Ojeda .05 .02
48 Mackey Sasser .05 .02
49 Darryl Strawberry .10 .04
50 Tim Teufel .05 .02
51 Dave West RC .10 .04
52 Mookie Wilson .10 .04
53 Dave Anderson .05 .02
54 Tim Belcher .05 .02
55 Mike Davis .05 .02
56 Mike Devereaux .05 .02
57 Kirk Gibson .10 .04
58 Alfredo Griffin .05 .02
59 Chris Gwynn .05 .02
60 Jeff Hamilton .05 .02
61A Danny Heep ERR .25 .10
Lake Hills
61B Danny Heep COR .05 .02
San Antonio
62 Orel Hershiser .10 .04
63 Brian Holton .05 .02
64 Jay Howell .05 .02
65 Tim Leary .05 .02
66 Mike Marshall .05 .02
67 Ramon Martinez RC .25 .10
68 Jesse Orosco .05 .02
69 Alejandro Pena .05 .02
70 Steve Sax .05 .02
71 Mike Scioscia .10 .04
72 Mike Sharperson .05 .02
73 John Shelby .05 .02
74 Franklin Stubbs .05 .02
75 John Tudor .10 .04
76 Fernando Valenzuela .10 .04
77 Tracy Woodson .05 .02
78 Marty Barrett .05 .02
79 Todd Benzinger .05 .02
80 Mike Boddicker UER .05 .02
(Rochester in '76, should be '78)
81 Wade Boggs .15 .06
82 Oil Can Boyd .05 .02
83 Ellis Burks .10 .04
84 Rick Cerone .05 .02
85 Roger Clemens .50 .20
86 Steve Curry .05 .02
87 Dwight Evans .10 .04
88 Wes Gardner .05 .02
89 Rich Gedman .05 .02
90 Mike Greenwell .05 .02
91 Bruce Hurst .05 .02
92 Dennis Lamp .05 .02
93 Spike Owen .05 .02
94 Larry Parrish UER .05 .02
(Before All-Star Break batting 1.90)
95 Carlos Quintana RC .10 .04
96 Jody Reed .05 .02
97 Jim Rice .10 .04
98A Kevin Romine ERR .25 .10
(Photo actually Randy Kutcher batting)
98B Kevin Romine COR .05 .02
(Arms folded)
99 Lee Smith .10 .04
100 Mike Smithson .05 .02
101 Bob Stanley .05 .02
102 Allan Anderson .05 .02
103 Keith Atherton .05 .02
104 Juan Berenguer .05 .02
105 Bert Blyleven .10 .04
106 Eric Bullock UER .05 .02
Bats/Throws Right, should be Left
107 Randy Bush .05 .02
108 John Christensen .05 .02
109 Mark Davidson .05 .02
110 Gary Gaetti .10 .04
111 Greg Gagne .05 .02
112 Dan Gladden .05 .02
113 German Gonzalez .05 .02
114 Brian Harper .05 .02
115 Tom Herr .05 .02
116 Kent Hrbek .10 .04
117 Gene Larkin .05 .02
118 Tim Laudner .05 .02
119 Charlie Lea .05 .02
120 Steve Lombardozzi .05 .02
121A John Moses ERR .25 .10
Tempe
121B John Moses COR .05 .02
Phoenix
122 Al Newman .05 .02
123 Mark Portugal .05 .02
124 Kirby Puckett .25 .10
125 Jeff Reardon .10 .04
126 Fred Toliver .05 .02
127 Frank Viola .10 .04
128 Doyle Alexander .05 .02
129 Dave Bergman .05 .02
130A Tom Brookens ERR .75 .30
(Mike Heath back)
130B Tom Brookens COR .05 .02
131 Paul Gibson .05 .02
132A Mike Heath ERR .75 .30
(Tom Brookens back)
132B Mike Heath COR .05 .02
133 Don Heinkel .05 .02
134 Mike Henneman .05 .02
135 Guillermo Hernandez .05 .02
136 Eric King .05 .02
137 Chet Lemon .10 .04
138 Fred Lynn UER .10 .04
'74 and '75 stats missing
139 Jack Morris .10 .04
140 Matt Nokes .05 .02
141 Gary Pettis .05 .02
142 Ted Power .05 .02
143 Jeff M. Robinson .05 .02
144 Luis Salazar .05 .02
145 Steve Searcy .05 .02
146 Pat Sheridan .05 .02
147 Frank Tanana .10 .04
148 Alan Trammell .10 .04
149 Walt Terrell .05 .02
150 Jim Walewander .05 .02
151 Lou Whitaker .10 .04
152 Tim Birtsas .05 .02
153 Tom Browning .05 .02
154 Keith Brown .05 .02
155 Norm Charlton RC .25 .10
156 Dave Concepcion .10 .04
157 Kal Daniels .05 .02
158 Eric Davis .10 .04
159 Bo Diaz .05 .02
160 Rob Dibble RC .50 .20
161 Nick Esasky .05 .02
162 John Franco .10 .04
163 Danny Jackson .05 .02
164 Barry Larkin .15 .06
165 Rob Murphy .05 .02
166 Paul O'Neill .15 .06
167 Jeff Reed .05 .02
168 Jose Rijo .10 .04
169 Ron Robinson .05 .02
170 Chris Sabo RC .40 .16
171 Candy Sierra .05 .02
172 Van Snider .05 .02
173A Jeff Treadway 5.00 2.00
(Target registration mark above head on front in light blue)
173B Jeff Treadway .05 .02
(No target on front)
174 Frank Williams UER .05 .02
(After All-Star Break stats are jumbled)
175 Herm Winningham .05 .02
176 Jim Adduci .05 .02
177 Don August .05 .02
178 Mike Birkbeck .05 .02
179 Chris Bosio .05 .02
180 Glenn Braggs .05 .02
181 Greg Brock .05 .02
182 Mark Clear .05 .02
183 Chuck Crim .05 .02
184 Rob Deer .05 .02
185 Tom Filer .05 .02
186 Jim Gantner .05 .02
187 Darryl Hamilton RC .25 .10
188 Ted Higuera .05 .02
189 Odell Jones .05 .02
190 Jeffrey Leonard .05 .02
191 Joey Meyer .05 .02
192 Paul Mirabella .05 .02
193 Paul Molitor .15 .06
194 Charlie O'Brien .05 .02
195 Dan Plesac .05 .02
196 Gary Sheffield RC 1.50 .60
197 B.J. Surhoff .10 .04
198 Dale Sveum .05 .02
199 Bill Wegman .05 .02
200 Robin Yount .40 .16
201 Rafael Belliard .05 .02
202 Barry Bonds 1.25 .50
203 Bobby Bonilla .10 .04
204 Sid Bream .10 .04
205 Benny Distefano .05 .02
206 Doug Drabek .05 .02
207 Mike Dunne .05 .02
208 Felix Fermin .05 .02
209 Brian Fisher .05 .02
210 Jim Gott .05 .02
211 Bob Kipper .05 .02
212 Dave LaPoint .05 .02
213 Mike LaValliere .05 .02
214 Jose Lind .05 .02
215 Junior Ortiz .05 .02
216 Vicente Palacios .05 .02
217 Tom Prince .05 .02
218 Gary Redus .05 .02
219 R.J. Reynolds .05 .02
220 Jeff D. Robinson .05 .02
221 John Smiley .05 .02
222 Andy Van Slyke .10 .04
223 Bob Walk .05 .02
224 Glenn Wilson .05 .02
225 Jesse Barfield .10 .04
226 George Bell .10 .04
227 Pat Borders RC .25 .10
228 John Cerutti .05 .02
229 Jim Clancy .05 .02
230 Mark Eichhorn .05 .02
231 Tony Fernandez .05 .02
232 Cecil Fielder .10 .04
233 Mike Flanagan .05 .02
234 Kelly Gruber .05 .02
235 Tom Henke .05 .02
236 Jimmy Key .10 .04
237 Rick Leach .05 .02
238 Manny Lee UER .05 .02
(Bio says regular shortstop, sic, Tony Fernandez)
239 Nelson Liriano .05 .02
240 Fred McGriff .15 .06
241 Lloyd Moseby .05 .02
242 Rance Mulliniks .05 .02
243 Jeff Musselman .05 .02
244 Dave Stieb .10 .04
245 Todd Stottlemyre .05 .02
246 Duane Ward .05 .02
247 David Wells .10 .04
248 Ernie Whitt UER .05 .02
(HR total 21, should be 121)
249 Luis Aguayo .05 .02
250A Neil Allen ERR .75 .30
Sarasota, FL
250B Neil Allen COR .05 .02
Syosset, NY
251 John Candelaria .05 .02
252 Jack Clark .10 .04
253 Richard Dotson .05 .02
254 Rickey Henderson .25 .10
255 Tommy John .10 .04
256 Roberto Kelly .05 .02
257 Al Leiter .25 .10
258 Don Mattingly .60 .24
259 Dale Mohorcic .05 .02
260 Hal Morris RC .25 .10
261 Scott Nielsen .05 .02
262 Mike Pagliarulo UER .05 .02
(Wrong birthdate)
263 Hipolito Pena .05 .02
264 Ken Phelps .05 .02
265 Willie Randolph .10 .04
266 Rick Rhoden .05 .02
267 Dave Righetti .10 .04
268 Rafael Santana .05 .02
269 Steve Shields .05 .02
270 Joel Skinner .05 .02
271 Don Slaught .05 .02
272 Claudell Washington .05 .02
273 Gary Ward .05 .02
274 Dave Winfield .10 .04
275 Luis Aquino .05 .02
276 Floyd Bannister .05 .02
277 George Brett .60 .24
278 Bill Buckner .10 .04
279 Nick Capra .05 .02
280 Jose DeJesus .05 .02
281 Steve Farr .05 .02
282 Jerry Don Gleaton .05 .02
283 Mark Gubicza .05 .02
284 Tom Gordon RC UER .40 .16
(16.2 innings in '88, should be 15.2)
285 Bo Jackson .25 .10
286 Charlie Leibrandt .05 .02
287 Mike Macfarlane RC .25 .10
288 Jeff Montgomery .05 .02
289 Bill Pecota UER .05 .02
(Photo actually Brad Wellman)
290 Jamie Quirk .05 .02
291 Bret Saberhagen .10 .04
292 Kevin Seitzer .05 .02
293 Kurt Stillwell .05 .02
294 Pat Tabler .05 .02
295 Danny Tartabull .05 .02
296 Gary Thurman .05 .02
297 Frank White .10 .04
298 Willie Wilson .10 .04
299 Roberto Alomar .25 .10
300 S.Alomar Jr. RC UER .40 .16
Wrong birthdate, says 6/16/66, should say 6/18/66
301 Chris Brown .05 .02
302 Mike Brumley UER .05 .02
(133 hits in '88, should be 134)
303 Mark Davis .05 .02
304 Mark Grant .05 .02
305 Tony Gwynn .30 .12
306 Greg W. Harris RC .10 .04
307 Andy Hawkins .05 .02
308 Jimmy Jones .05 .02
309 John Kruk .10 .04
310 Dave Leiper .05 .02
311 Carmelo Martinez .05 .02
312 Lance McCullers .05 .02
313 Keith Moreland .05 .02
314 Dennis Rasmussen .05 .02
315 Randy Ready UER .05 .02
(1214 games in '88, should be 114)
316 Benito Santiago .10 .04
317 Eric Show .05 .02
318 Todd Simmons .05 .02
319 Garry Templeton .10 .04
320 Dickie Thon .05 .02
321 Ed Whitson .05 .02
322 Marvell Wynne .05 .02
323 Mike Aldrete .05 .02
324 Brett Butler .10 .04
325 Will Clark UER .25 .10
(Three consecutive 100 RBI seasons)
326 Kelly Downs UER .05 .02
('88 stats missing)
327 Dave Dravecky .05 .02
328 Scott Garrelts .05 .02
329 Atlee Hammaker .05 .02
330 Charlie Hayes RC .25 .10
331 Mike Krukow .05 .02
332 Craig Lefferts .05 .02
333 Candy Maldonado .05 .02
334 Kirt Manwaring UER .05 .02
(Bats Rights)
335 Bob Melvin .05 .02
336 Kevin Mitchell .10 .04
337 Donell Nixon .05 .02
338 Tony Perezchica .05 .02
339 Joe Price .05 .02
340 Rick Reuschel .10 .04
341 Earnest Riles .05 .02
342 Don Robinson .05 .02
343 Chris Speier .05 .02
344 Robby Thompson UER .05 .02
(West Plam Beach)
345 Jose Uribe .05 .02
346 Matt Williams .25 .10
347 Trevor Wilson RC .10 .04
348 Juan Agosto .05 .02
349 Larry Andersen .05 .02
350A Alan Ashby ERR 2.00 .80
(Throws Rig)
350B Alan Ashby COR .05 .02
351 Kevin Bass .05 .02
352 Buddy Bell .10 .04
353 Craig Biggio RC .75 .30
354 Danny Darwin .05 .02
355 Glenn Davis .05 .02
356 Jim Deshaies .05 .02
357 Bill Doran .05 .02
358 John Fishel .05 .02
359 Billy Hatcher .05 .02
360 Bob Knepper .05 .02
361 L.Meadows UER .05 .02
Bio says 10 EBH's and 6 SB's in '88, should be 3 and 4
362 Dave Meads .05 .02
363 Jim Pankovits .05 .02
364 Terry Puhl .05 .02
365 Rafael Ramirez .05 .02
366 Craig Reynolds .05 .02
367 Mike Scott .10 .04
(Card number listed as 368 on Astros CL)
368 Nolan Ryan 1.00 .40
(Card number listed as 367 on Astros CL)
369 Dave Smith .05 .02
370 Gerald Young .05 .02
371 Hubie Brooks .05 .02
372 Tim Burke .05 .02
373 John Dopson .05 .02
374 Mike R. Fitzgerald .05 .02
375 Tom Foley .05 .02
376 Andres Galarraga UER .10 .04
(Home: Caracus)
377 Neal Heaton .05 .02
378 Joe Hesketh .05 .02
379 Brian Holman RC .10 .04
380 Rex Hudler .05 .02
381 R.Johnson RC UER 4.00 1.20
Innings for '85 and '86 shown as 27 and 120, should be 27.1 and 119.2
381B R. Johnson Marlboro VAR
382 Wallace Johnson .05 .02
383 Tracy Jones .05 .02
384 Dave Martinez .05 .02
385 Dennis Martinez .10 .04
386 Andy McGaffigan .05 .02
387 Otis Nixon .05 .02
388 Johnny Paredes .05 .02
389 Jeff Parrett .05 .02
390 Pascual Perez .05 .02
391 Tim Raines .10 .04

392 Luis Rivera .05 .02
393 Nelson Santovenia .05 .02
394 Bryn Smith .05 .02
395 Tim Wallach .05 .02
396 Andy Allanson UER .05 .02
1214 hits in '88,
should be 114
397 Rod Allen .05 .02
398 Scott Bailes .05 .02
399 Tom Candiotti .05 .02
400 Joe Carter .10 .04
401 Carmen Castillo UER .05 .02
(After All-Star Break
batting 2.50)
402 Dave Clark UER .05 .02
(Card front shows
position as Rookie;
after All-Star Break
batting 3.14)
403 John Farrell UER .05 .02
(Typo in runs
allowed in '88)
404 Julio Franco .10 .04
405 Don Gordon .05 .02
406 Mel Hall .05 .02
407 Brad Havens .05 .02
408 Brook Jacoby .05 .02
409 Doug Jones .05 .02
410 Jeff Kaiser .05 .02
411 Luis Medina .05 .02
412 Cory Snyder .05 .02
413 Greg Swindell .05 .02
414 Ron Tingley UER .05 .02
(Hit HR in first ML
at-bat, should be
first AL at-bat)
415 Willie Upshaw .05 .02
416 Ron Washington .05 .02
417 Rich Yett .05 .02
418 Damon Berryhill .05 .02
419 Mike Bielecki .05 .02
420 Doug Dascenzo .05 .02
421 Jody Davis UER .05 .02
(Braves stats for
'88 missing)
422 Andre Dawson .10 .04
423 Frank DiPino .05 .02
424 Shawon Dunston .05 .02
425 Rich Gossage .10 .04
426 Mark Grace UER .25 .10
(Minor League stats
for '88 missing)
427 Mike Harkey RC .10 .04
428 Darrin Jackson .10 .04
429 Les Lancaster .05 .02
430 Vance Law .05 .02
431 Greg Maddux .50 .20
432 Jamie Moyer .10 .04
433 Al Nipper .05 .02
434 Rafael Palmeiro UER .25 .10
170 hits in '88,
should be 178
435 Pat Perry .05 .02
436 Jeff Pico .05 .02
437 Ryne Sandberg .40 .16
438 Calvin Schiraldi .05 .02
439 Rick Sutcliffe .10 .04
440A Manny Trillo ERR 2.00 .80
(Throws Rig)
440B Manny Trillo COR .05 .02
441 Gary Varsho UER .05 .02
(Wrong birthdate;
.303 should be .302;
11/28 should be 9/19)
442 Mitch Webster .05 .02
443 Luis Alicea RC .25 .10
444 Tom Brunansky .05 .02
445 Vince Coleman UER .05 .02
Third straight with 83
should be fourth straight with 81
446 John Costello UER .05 .02
(Home California,
should be New York)
447 Danny Cox .05 .02
448 Ken Dayley .05 .02
449 Jose DeLeon .05 .02
450 Curt Ford .05 .02
451 Pedro Guerrero .10 .04
452 Bob Horner .10 .04
453 Tim Jones .05 .02
454 Steve Lake .05 .02
455 Joe Magrane UER .05 .02
(Des Moines& IO)
456 Greg Mathews .05 .02
457 Willie McGee .10 .04
458 Larry McWilliams .05 .02
459 Jose Oquendo .05 .02
460 Tony Pena .05 .02
461 Terry Pendleton .10 .04
462 Steve Peters UER .05 .02
(Lives in Harrah,
not Harah)
463 Ozzie Smith .40 .16
464 Scott Terry .05 .02
465 Denny Walling .05 .02
466 Todd Worrell .05 .02
467 Tony Armas UER .10 .04
(Before All-Star Break
batting 2.39)
468 Dante Bichette RC .40 .16
469 Bob Boone .10 .04
470 Terry Clark .05 .02
471 Stu Cliburn .05 .02
472 Mike Cook UER .05 .02
(TM near Angels logo
missing from front)
473 Sherman Corbett .05 .02
474 Chili Davis .10 .04
475 Brian Downing .10 .04
476 Jim Eppard .05 .02
477 Chuck Finley .10 .04
478 Willie Fraser .05 .02
479 Bryan Harvey UER RC .25 .10
ML record shows 0-0,
should be 7-5
480 Jack Howell .05 .02
481 Wally Joyner UER .10 .04
(Yorba Linda, GA)
482 Jack Lazorko .05 .02
483 Kirk McCaskill .05 .02
484 Mark McLemore .05 .02
485 Greg Minton .05 .02
486 Dan Petry .05 .02
487 Johnny Ray .05 .02
488 Dick Schofield .05 .02
489 Devon White .10 .04
490 Mike Witt .05 .02
491 Harold Baines .10 .04
492 Daryl Boston .05 .02
493 Ivan Calderon UER .05 .02
('80 stats shifted)
494 Mike Diaz .05 .02
495 Carlton Fisk .15 .06
496 Dave Gallagher .05 .02
497 Ozzie Guillen .05 .02
498 Shawn Hillegas .05 .02
499 Lance Johnson .05 .02
500 Barry Jones .05 .02
501 Bill Long .05 .02
502 Steve Lyons .05 .02
503 Fred Manrique .05 .02
504 Jack McDowell .10 .04
505 Donn Pall .05 .02
506 Kelly Paris .05 .02
507 Dan Pasqua .05 .02
508 Ken Patterson .05 .02
509 Melido Perez .05 .02
510 Jerry Reuss .05 .02
511 Mark Salas .05 .02
512 Bobby Thigpen UER .05 .02
('86 ERA 4.69,
should be 4.68)
513 Mike Woodard .05 .02
514 Bob Brower .05 .02
515 Steve Buechele .05 .02
516 Jose Cecena .05 .02
517 Cecil Espy .05 .02
518 Scott Fletcher .05 .02
519 Cecilio Guante .05 .02
('87 Yankee stats
are off-centered)
520 Jose Guzman .05 .02
521 Ray Hayward .05 .02
522 Charlie Hough .10 .04
523 Pete Incaviglia .05 .02
524 Mike Jeffcoat .05 .02
525 Paul Kilgus .05 .02
526 Chad Kreuter RC .25 .10
527 Jeff Kunkel .05 .02
528 Oddibe McDowell .05 .02
529 Pete O'Brien .05 .02
530 Geno Petralli .05 .02
531 Jeff Russell .05 .02
532 Ruben Sierra .05 .02
533 Mike Stanley .05 .02
534A Ed VandeBerg ERR 2.00 .80
(Throws Lef)
534B Ed VandeBerg COR .05 .02
535 Curtis Wilkerson ERR .05 .02
(Pitcher headings
at bottom)
536 Mitch Williams .05 .02
537 Bobby Witt UER .05 .02
('85 ERA .643,
should be 6.43)
538 Steve Balboni .05 .02
539 Scott Bankhead .05 .02
540 Scott Bradley .05 .02
541 Mickey Brantley .05 .02
542 Jay Buhner .10 .04
543 Mike Campbell .05 .02
544 Darnell Coles .05 .02
545 Henry Cotto .05 .02
546 Alvin Davis .05 .02
547 Mario Diaz .05 .02
548 Ken Griffey Jr. RC 8.00 3.20
549 Erik Hanson RC .25 .10
550 Mike Jackson UER .05 .02
(Lifetime ERA 3.345,
should be 3.45)
551 Mark Langston .05 .02
552 Edgar Martinez .25 .10
553 Bill McGuire .05 .02
554 Mike Moore .05 .02
555 Jim Presley .05 .02
556 Rey Quinones .05 .02
557 Jerry Reed .05 .02
558 Harold Reynolds .10 .04
559 Mike Schooler .05 .02
560 Bill Swift .05 .02
561 Dave Valle .05 .02
562 Steve Bedrosian .05 .02
563 Phil Bradley .05 .02
564 Don Carman .05 .02
565 Bob Dernier .05 .02
566 Marvin Freeman .05 .02
567 Todd Frohwirth .05 .02
568 Greg Gross .05 .02
569 Kevin Gross .05 .02
570 Greg A. Harris .05 .02
571 Von Hayes .05 .02
572 Chris James .05 .02
573 Steve Jeltz .05 .02
574 Ron Jones UER .10 .04
(Led IL in '88 with
85, should be 75)
575 Ricky Jordan RC .25 .10
576 Mike Maddux .05 .02
577 David Palmer .05 .02
578 Lance Parrish .10 .04
579 Shane Rawley .05 .02
580 Bruce Ruffin .05 .02
581 Juan Samuel .05 .02
582 Mike Schmidt .50 .20
583 Kent Tekulve .05 .02
584 Milt Thompson UER .05 .02
(19 hits in '88,
should be 109)
585 Jose Alvarez RC .10 .04
586 Paul Assenmacher .05 .02
587 Bruce Benedict .05 .02
588 Jeff Blauser .05 .02
589 Terry Blocker .05 .02
590 Ron Gant .10 .04
591 Tom Glavine .25 .10
592 Tommy Gregg .05 .02
593 Albert Hall .05 .02
594 Dion James .05 .02
595 Rick Mahler .05 .02
596 Dale Murphy .15 .06
597 Gerald Perry .05 .02
598 Charlie Puleo .05 .02
599 Ted Simmons .10 .04
600 Pete Smith .05 .02
601 Zane Smith .05 .02
602 John Smoltz RC 1.00 .40
603 Bruce Sutter .10 .04
604 Andres Thomas .05 .02
605 Ozzie Virgil .05 .02
606 Brady Anderson RC .40 .16
607 Jeff Ballard .05 .02
608 Jose Bautista RC .10 .04
609 Ken Gerhart .05 .02
610 Terry Kennedy .05 .02
611 Eddie Murray .25 .10
612 Carl Nichols UER .05 .02
(Before All-Star Break
batting 1.88)
613 Tom Niedenfuer .05 .02
614 Joe Orsulak .05 .02
615 Oswald Peraza UER .05 .02
(Shown as Oswaldo)
616A Bill Ripken ERR 20.00 8.00
(Rick Face written
on knob of bat)
616B Bill Ripken 80.00 32.00
(Bat knob
whited out)
616C Bill Ripken 5.00 2.00
(Words on bat knob
scribbled out in White)
616D Bill Ripken 20.00 8.00
Words on Bat
scribbled out in Black
616E Bill Ripken DP .10 .04
(Black box covering
bat knob)
617 Cal Ripken .75 .30
618 Dave Schmidt .05 .02
619 Rick Schu .05 .02
620 Larry Sheets .05 .02
621 Doug Sisk .05 .02
622 Pete Stanicek .05 .02
623 Mickey Tettleton .05 .02
624 Jay Tibbs .05 .02
625 Jim Traber .05 .02
626 Mark Williamson .05 .02
627 Craig Worthington .05 .02
628 Jose Canseco 40/40 .15 .06
629 Tom Browning Perfect .05 .02
630 Roberto Alomar .25 .10
Sandy Alomar Jr. UER
(Names on card listed
in wrong order)
631 Will Clark .25 .10
Rafael Palmeiro UER
(Gallaraga, sic;
Clark 3 consecutive
100 RBI seasons;
third with 102 RBI's)
632 Darryl Strawberry .10 .04
Will Clark UER (Homeruns
should be two words)
633 Wade Boggs .10 .04
Carney Lansford UER
(Boggs hit .366 in
'86, should be '88)
634 Jose Canseco .50 .20
Terry Steinbach
Mark McGwire
635 Mark Davis .05 .02
Dwight Gooden
636 Danny Jackson .05 .02
David Cone UER
Hersheiser, sic
637 Chris Sabo .10 .04
Bobby Bonilla UER
Bobby Bonds, sic
638 Andres Galarraga UER .05 .02
(Misspelled Gallaraga
on card back)
Gerald Perry
639 Kirby Puckett .15 .06
Eric Davis
640 Steve Wilson and .05 .02
Cameron Drew
641 Kevin Brown and .25 .10
Kevin Reimer
642 Brad Pounders RC .10 .04
Jerald Clark
643 Mike Capel and .05 .02
Drew Hall
644 Joe Girardi RC and .40 .16
Rolando Roomes
645 Lenny Harris RC and .25 .10
Marty Brown
646 Luis DeLosSantos .05 .02
and Jim Campbell
647 Randy Kramer and .05 .02
Miguel Garcia
648 Torey Lovullo RC and .10 .04
Robert Palacios
649 Jim Corsi and .05 .02
Bob Milacki
650 Grady Hall and .05 .02
Mike Rochford
651 Terry Taylor RC .10 .04
Vance Lovelace
652 Ken Hill RC and .25 .10
Dennis Cook
653 Scott Service and .05 .02
Shane Turner
654 CL: Oakland/Mets .05 .02
Dodgers/Red Sox
(10 Henderson;
68 Jess Orosco)
655A CL: Twins/Tigers ERR .05 .02
Reds/Brewers
(179 Boslo and
Twins/Tigers positions
listed)
655B CL: Twins/Tigers COR .05 .02
Reds/Brewers
(179 Boslo but
Twins/Tigers positions
not listed)
656 CL: Pirates/Blue Jays .05 .02
Yankees/Royals
(225 Jess Barfield)
657 CL: Padres/Giants .05 .02
Astros/Expos
(367/368 wrong)
658 CL: Indians/Cubs .05 .02
Cardinals/Angels
(449 Deleon)
659 CL: White Sox/Rangers .05 .02
Mariners/Phillies
660 CL: Braves/Orioles .05 .02
Specials/Checklists
(632 hyphenated diff-
erently and 650 Hali;
595 Rich Mahler;
619 Rich Schu)

1989 Fleer Glossy

This 660 card set turned out to be the final parallel glossy issue for Fleer. These cards are identical to the regular Fleer cards except for the glossy sheen on the front. As many dealers did not order this product, this set is considerably scarcer than the regular 1989 Fleer set and the preceding years of Glossy parallels. Unlike the previous two seasons, the update set was not issued in Glossy form. It is estimated that Fleer made approximately 30,000 of these sets. The Ken Griffey Jr. card from this set is regarded as one of the most important early parallels in hobby history and is more often than not found with poor centering.

Nm-Mt Ex-Mt
COMP.FACT.SET (672) 120.00 47.50
*STARS: 2X TO 5X BASIC CARDS
*ROOKIES: 3X TO 8X BASIC CARDS

1989 Fleer All-Stars

This twelve-card standard-size subset was randomly inserted in Fleer wax and cello packs. The players selected are the 1989 Fleer Major League All-Star team. One player has been selected for each position along with a DH and three pitchers. The cards feature a distinctive green background on the card fronts. The set is sequenced in alphabetical order.

Nm-Mt Ex-Mt
COMPLETE SET (12) 5.00 2.00
1 Bobby Bonilla .75 .30
2 Jose Canseco 2.00 .80
3 Will Clark 2.00 .80
4 Dennis Eckersley 1.25 .50
5 Julio Franco .75 .30
6 Mike Greenwell .40 .16
7 Orel Hershiser .75 .30
8 Paul Molitor 1.25 .50
9 Mike Scioscia .75 .30
10 Darryl Strawberry .75 .30
11 Alan Trammell .75 .30
12 Frank Viola .75 .30

1989 Fleer For The Record

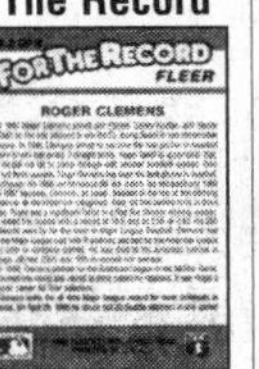

This six-card standard-size insert set was distributed one per rack pack. The set is subtitled "For The Record" and commemorates record-breaking events for those players from the previous season. The card backs are printed in red, black, and gray on white card stock. The set is sequenced in alphabetical order.

Nm-Mt Ex-Mt
COMPLETE SET (6) 8.00 3.20
1 Wade Boggs 1.00 .40
2 Roger Clemens 3.00 1.20
3 Andres Galarraga .60 .24
4 Kirk Gibson .60 .24
5 Greg Maddux 3.00 1.20
6 Don Mattingly UER 4.00 1.60
(Won batting title
'83& should say '84)

1989 Fleer Wax Box Cards

The cards in this 28-card set measure the standard 2 1/2" by 3 1/2". Cards have essentially the same design as the 1989 Fleer regular issue set. The cards were printed on the bottoms of the regular issue wax pack boxes. These 28 cards (C1 to C28) are considered a separate set in their own right and are not typically included in a complete set of the regular issue 1989 Fleer cards. The value of the panel uncut is slightly greater, perhaps by 25 percent greater, than the value of the individual cards cut up carefully. The wax box cards are further distinguished by the gray card stock used.

Nm-Mt Ex-Mt
COMPLETE SET (28) 10.00 4.00
C1 Mets Logo .15 .06
C2 Wade Boggs .75 .30
C3 George Brett 1.50 .60
C4 Jose Canseco UER 1.50 .60
('88 strikeouts 121
and career strike-
outs 49, should
be 128 and 491)
C5 A's Logo .15 .06
C6 Will Clark 1.00 .40
C7 David Cone .60 .24
C8 Andres Galarraga UER .60 .24
(Career average .289
should be .269)
C9 Dodgers Logo .15 .06
C10 Kirk Gibson .25 .10
C11 Mike Greenwell .15 .06
C12 Tony Gwynn 2.50 1.00
C13 Tigers Logo .15 .06
C14 Orel Hershiser .25 .10
C15 Danny Jackson .15 .06
C16 Wally Joyner .25 .10
C17 Red Sox Logo .15 .06
C18 Yankees Logo .15 .06
C19 Fred McGriff UER 1.00 .40
(Career BA of .289
should be .269)
C20 Kirby Puckett 2.00 .80
C21 Chris Sabo .15 .06
C22 Kevin Seitzer .15 .06
C23 Pirates Logo .15 .06
C24 Astros Logo .15 .06
C25 Darryl Strawberry .25 .10
C26 Alan Trammell .40 .16
C27 Andy Van Slyke .15 .06
C28 Frank Viola .15 .06

1989 Fleer World Series

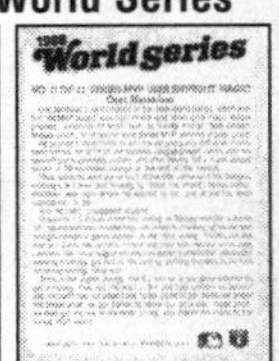

This 12-card standard-size set features highlights of the previous year's World Series between the Dodgers and the Athletics. The sets were packaged as a complete set insert with the collated sets (of the 1989 Fleer regular issue) which were sold by Fleer directly to hobby card dealers; they were not available in the general retail candy store outlets. The Kirk Gibson card from this set highlights one of the most famous home runs in World Series history.

Nm-Mt Ex-Mt
COMPLETE SET (12) 2.00 .80
1 Mickey Hatcher .05 .02
2 Tim Belcher .05 .02
3 Jose Canseco .25 .10
4 Mike Scioscia .10 .04
5 Kirk Gibson .10 .04
6 Orel Hershiser .10 .04
7 Mike Marshall .05 .02
8 Mark McGwire 1.00 .40
9 Steve Sax UER .05 .02
actually 42 steals in '88
10 Walt Weiss .05 .02
11 Orel Hershiser .10 .04
12 Dodger Blue .10 .04
World Champs

1989 Fleer Update

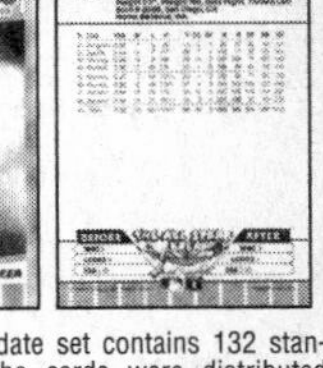

The 1989 Fleer Update set contains 132 standard-size cards. The cards were distributed exclusively in factory set form in grey and white, cellophane wrapped boxes through hobby dealers. The cards are identical in design to regular issue 1989 Fleer cards except for the U-prefixed numbering on back. The set numbering is in team order with players within teams ordered alphabetically. The set includes special cards for Nolan Ryan's 5,000th strikeout and Mike Schmidt's retirement. Rookie Cards include Kevin Appier, Joey (Albert) Belle, Deion Sanders, Greg Vaughn, Robin Ventura and Todd Zeile.

Nm-Mt Ex-Mt
COMP.FACT.SET (132) 5.00 2.00
1 Phil Bradley .05 .02
2 Mike Devereaux .05 .02
3 Steve Finley RC .50 .20
4 Kevin Hickey .05 .02
5 Brian Holton .05 .02
6 Bob Milacki .05 .02
7 Randy Milligan .05 .02
8 John Dopson .05 .02
9 Nick Esasky .05 .02
10 Rob Murphy .05 .02
11 Jim Abbott RC* .50 .20
12 Bert Blyleven .10 .04
13 Jeff Manto RC .10 .04
14 Bob McClure .05 .02
15 Lance Parrish .10 .04
16 Lee Stevens RC .25 .10
17 Claudell Washington .05 .02
18 Mark Davis RC .25 .10
19 Eric King .05 .02
20 Ron Kittle .05 .02
21 Matt Merullo .05 .02
22 Steve Rosenberg .05 .02
23 Robin Ventura RC .75 .30
24 Keith Atherton .05 .02
25 Joey Belle RC 1.00 .40
26 Jerry Browne .05 .02
27 Felix Fermin .05 .02
28 Brad Komminsk .05 .02

29 Pete O'Brien .05 .02
30 Mike Brumley .05 .02
31 Tracy Jones .05 .02
32 Mike Schwabe .05 .02
33 Gary Ward .05 .02
34 Frank Williams .05 .02
35 Kevin Appier RC .50 .20
36 Bob Boone .10 .04
37 Luis DeLosSantos .05 .02
38 Jim Eisenreich .05 .02
39 Jaime Navarro RC .10 .04
40 Bill Spiers RC .25 .10
41 Greg Vaughn RC .40 .16
42 Randy Veres .05 .02
43 Wally Backman .05 .02
44 Shane Rawley .05 .02
45 Steve Balboni .05 .02
46 Jesse Barfield .10 .04
47 Alvaro Espinoza .05 .02
48 Bob Geren RC .05 .02
49 Mel Hall .05 .02
50 Andy Hawkins .05 .02
51 Hensley Meulens RC .10 .04
52 Steve Sax .05 .02
53 Deion Sanders RC 1.00 .40
54 Rickey Henderson .25 .10
55 Mike Moore .05 .02
56 Tony Phillips .05 .02
57 Greg Briley .10 .04
58 Gene Harris RC .10 .04
59 Randy Johnson 2.50 .80
60 Jeffrey Leonard .05 .02
61 Dennis Powell .05 .02
62 Omar Vizquel RC .75 .30
63 Kevin Brown .25 .10
64 Julio Franco .10 .04
65 Jamie Moyer .10 .04
66 Rafael Palmeiro .25 .10
67 Nolan Ryan 1.50 .60
68 Francisco Cabrera RC .10 .04
69 Junior Felix RC .10 .04
70 Al Leiter .25 .10
71 Alex Sanchez .05 .02
72 Geronimo Berroa .05 .02
73 Derek Lilliquist RC .10 .04
74 Lonnie Smith .10 .04
75 Jeff Treadway .05 .02
76 Paul Kilgus .05 .02
77 Lloyd McClendon .05 .02
78 Scott Sanderson .05 .02
79 Dwight Smith RC .25 .10
80 Jerome Walton RC .25 .10
81 Mitch Williams .05 .02
82 Steve Wilson .10 .04
83 Todd Benzinger .05 .02
84 Ken Griffey Sr. .10 .04
85 Rick Mahler .05 .02
86 Rolando Roomes .05 .02
87 Scott Scudder RC .10 .04
88 Jim Clancy .05 .02
89 Rick Rhoden .05 .02
90 Dan Schatzeder .05 .02
91 Mike Morgan .05 .02
92 Eddie Murray .25 .10
93 Willie Randolph .10 .04
94 Ray Searage .05 .02
95 Mike Aldrete .05 .02
96 Kevin Gross .05 .02
97 Mark Langston .05 .02
98 Spike Owen .05 .02
99 Zane Smith .05 .02
100 Don Aase .05 .02
101 Barry Lyons .05 .02
102 Juan Samuel .05 .02
103 Wally Whitehurst RC .10 .04
104 Dennis Cook .05 .02
105 Len Dykstra .10 .04
106 Charlie Hayes .25 .10
107 Tommy Herr .05 .02
108 Ken Howell .05 .02
109 John Kruk .10 .04
110 Roger McDowell .05 .02
111 Terry Mulholland .05 .02
112 Jeff Parrett .05 .02
113 Neal Heaton .05 .02
114 Jeff King .05 .02
115 Randy Kramer .05 .02
116 Bill Landrum .05 .02
117 Cris Carpenter RC * .10 .04
118 Frank DiPino .05 .02
119 Ken Hill .25 .10
120 Dan Quisenberry .05 .02
121 Milt Thompson .05 .02
122 Todd Zeile RC .40 .16
123 Jack Clark .10 .04
124 Bruce Hurst .05 .02
125 Mark Parent .05 .02
126 Bip Roberts .05 .02
127 Jeff Brantley RC UER .25 .10
(Photo actually Joe Kmak)
128 Terry Kennedy .05 .02
129 Mike LaCoss .05 .02
130 Greg Litton .05 .02
131 Mike Schmidt .75 .30
132 Checklist 1-132 .05 .02

1990 Fleer

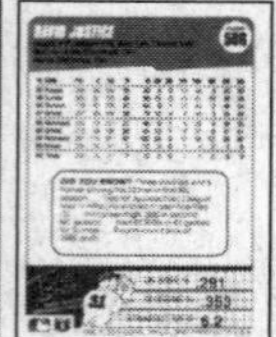

The 1990 Fleer set contains 660 standard-size cards. Cards were primarily issued in wax packs, rack packs and hobby and retail factory sets. Card fronts feature white outer borders with ribbon-like, colored inner borders. The set is again ordered numerically by teams based upon the previous season's record. Subsets include Decade Greats (621-630), Superstar Combinations (631-639), Rookie Prospects (640-653) and checklists (654-660). Rookie Cards of note include Moises Alou, Juan Gonzalez, David Justice, Sammy Sosa and Larry Walker.

	Nm-Mt	Ex-Mt
COMPLETE SET (660)	15.00	4.50
COMP.RETAIL SET (660)	15.00	4.50
COMP.HOBBY SET (672)	15.00	4.50

1 Lance Blankenship .05 .02
2 Todd Burns .05 .02
3 Jose Canseco .25 .07
4 Jim Corsi .05 .02
5 Storm Davis .05 .02
6 Dennis Eckersley .10 .03
7 Mike Gallego .05 .02
8 Ron Hassey .05 .02
9 Dave Henderson .05 .02
10 Rickey Henderson .25 .07
11 Rick Honeycutt .05 .02
12 Stan Javier .05 .02
13 Felix Jose .05 .02
14 Carney Lansford .10 .03
15 Mark McGwire UER .60 .18
(1989 runs listed as 4, should be 74)
16 Mike Moore .05 .02
17 Gene Nelson .05 .02
18 Dave Parker .10 .03
19 Tony Phillips .05 .02
20 Terry Steinbach .05 .02
21 Dave Stewart .10 .03
22 Walt Weiss .05 .02
23 Bob Welch .05 .02
24 Curt Young .05 .02
25 Paul Assenmacher .05 .02
26 Damon Berryhill .05 .02
27 Mike Bielecki .05 .02
28 Kevin Blankenship .05 .02
29 Andre Dawson .10 .03
30 Shawon Dunston .05 .02
31 Joe Girardi .15 .04
32 Mark Grace .15 .04
33 Mike Harkey .05 .02
34 Paul Kilgus .05 .02
35 Les Lancaster .05 .02
36 Vance Law .05 .02
37 Greg Maddux .40 .12
38 Lloyd McClendon .05 .02
39 Jeff Pico .05 .02
40 Ryne Sandberg .40 .12
41 Scott Sanderson .05 .02
42 Dwight Smith .05 .02
43 Rick Sutcliffe .10 .03
44 Jerome Walton .05 .02
45 Mitch Webster .05 .02
46 Curt Wilkerson .05 .02
47 Dean Wilkins .05 .02
48 Mitch Williams .05 .02
49 Steve Wilson .05 .02
50 Steve Bedrosian .05 .02
51 Mike Benjamin RC .10 .03
52 Jeff Brantley .05 .02
53 Brett Butler .10 .03
54 Will Clark UER .10 .03
(Did You Know says first in runs, should say tied for first)
55 Kelly Downs .05 .02
56 Scott Garrelts .05 .02
57 Atlee Hammaker .05 .02
58 Terry Kennedy .05 .02
59 Mike LaCoss .05 .02
60 Craig Lefferts .05 .02
61 Greg Litton .05 .02
62 Candy Maldonado .05 .02
63 Kirt Manwaring UER .05 .02
(No '88 Phoenix stats as noted in box)
64 Randy McCament .05 .02
65 Kevin Mitchell .05 .02
66 Donell Nixon .05 .02
67 Ken Oberkfell .05 .02
68 Rick Reuschel .05 .02
69 Ernest Riles .05 .02
70 Don Robinson .05 .02
71 Pat Sheridan .05 .02
72 Chris Speier .05 .02
73 Robby Thompson .05 .02
74 Jose Uribe .05 .02
75 Matt Williams .10 .03
76 George Bell .05 .02
77 Pat Borders .05 .02
78 John Cerutti .05 .02
79 Junior Felix .05 .02
80 Tony Fernandez .05 .02
81 Mike Flanagan .05 .02
82 Mauro Gozzo .05 .02
83 Kelly Gruber .05 .02
84 Tom Henke .05 .02
85 Jimmy Key .10 .03
86 Manny Lee .05 .02
87 Nelson Liriano UER .05 .02
(Should say "led the IL" instead of "led the TL")
88 Lee Mazzilli .05 .02
89 Fred McGriff .25 .07
90 Lloyd Moseby .05 .02
91 Rance Mulliniks .05 .02
92 Alex Sanchez .05 .02
93 Dave Stieb .10 .03
94 Todd Stottlemyre .10 .03
95 Duane Ward UER .05 .02
(Double line of '87 Syracuse stats)
96 David Wells .10 .03
97 Ernie Whitt .05 .02
98 Frank Wills .05 .02
99 Mookie Wilson .10 .03
100 Kevin Appier .10 .03
101 Luis Aquino .05 .02
102 Bob Boone .10 .03
103 George Brett .60 .18
104 Jose DeJesus .05 .02
105 Luis De Los Santos .05 .02
106 Jim Eisenreich .05 .02
107 Steve Farr .05 .02
108 Tom Gordon .10 .03
109 Mark Gubicza .05 .02
110 Bo Jackson .25 .07
111 Terry Leach .05 .02
112 Charlie Leibrandt .05 .02
113 Rick Luecken .05 .02
114 Mike Macfarlane .05 .02
115 Jeff Montgomery .10 .03
116 Bret Saberhagen .10 .03
117 Kevin Seitzer .05 .02
118 Kurt Stillwell .05 .02
119 Pat Tabler .05 .02
120 Danny Tartabull .05 .02
121 Gary Thurman .05 .02
122 Frank White .10 .03
123 Willie Wilson .05 .02
124 Matt Winters .05 .02
125 Jim Abbott .15 .04
126 Tony Armas .05 .02
127 Dante Bichette .25 .07
128 Bert Blyleven .10 .03
129 Chili Davis .10 .03
130 Brian Downing .05 .02
131 Mike Fetters RC .25 .07
132 Chuck Finley .10 .03
133 Willie Fraser .05 .02
134 Bryan Harvey .05 .02
135 Jack Howell .05 .02
136 Wally Joyner .10 .03
137 Jeff Manto .05 .02
138 Kirk McCaskill .05 .02
139 Bob McClure .05 .02
140 Greg Minton .05 .02
141 Lance Parrish .05 .02
142 Dan Petry .05 .02
143 Johnny Ray .05 .02
144 Dick Schofield .05 .02
145 Lee Stevens .10 .03
146 Claudell Washington .05 .02
147 Devon White .10 .03
148 Mike Witt .05 .02
149 Roberto Alomar .15 .04
150 Sandy Alomar Jr. .10 .03
151 Andy Benes .10 .03
152 Jack Clark .10 .03
153 Pat Clements .05 .02
154 Joey Cora .10 .03
155 Mark Davis .05 .02
156 Mark Grant .05 .02
157 Tony Gwynn .30 .09
158 Greg W. Harris .05 .02
159 Bruce Hurst .05 .02
160 Darrin Jackson .05 .02
161 Chris James .05 .02
162 Carmelo Martinez .05 .02
163 Mike Pagliarulo .05 .02
164 Mark Parent .05 .02
165 Dennis Rasmussen .05 .02
166 Bip Roberts .05 .02
167 Benito Santiago .10 .03
168 Calvin Schiraldi .05 .02
169 Eric Show .05 .02
170 Garry Templeton .05 .02
171 Ed Whitson .05 .02
172 Brady Anderson .10 .03
173 Jeff Ballard .05 .02
174 Phil Bradley .05 .02
175 Mike Devereaux .05 .02
176 Steve Finley .10 .03
177 Pete Harnisch .05 .02
178 Kevin Hickey .05 .02
179 Brian Holton .05 .02
180 Ben McDonald RC .25 .07
181 Bob Melvin .05 .02
182 Bob Milacki .05 .02
183 Randy Milligan UER .05 .02
(Double line of '87 stats)
184 Gregg Olson .10 .03
185 Joe Orsulak .05 .02
186 Bill Ripken .05 .02
187 Cal Ripken .75 .23
188 Dave Schmidt .05 .02
189 Larry Sheets .05 .02
190 Mickey Tettleton .05 .02
191 Mark Thurmond .05 .02
192 Jay Tibbs .05 .02
193 Jim Traber .05 .02
194 Mark Williamson .05 .02
195 Craig Worthington .05 .02
196 Don Aase .05 .02
197 Blaine Beatty .05 .02
198 Mark Carreon .05 .02
199 Gary Carter .10 .03
200 David Cone .10 .03
201 Ron Darling .05 .02
202 Kevin Elster .05 .02
203 Sid Fernandez .05 .02
204 Dwight Gooden .10 .03
205 Keith Hernandez .10 .03
206 Jeff Innis .05 .02
207 Gregg Jefferies .10 .03
208 Howard Johnson .05 .02
209 Barry Lyons UER .05 .02
(Double line of '87 stats)
210 Dave Magadan .05 .02
211 Kevin McReynolds .05 .02
212 Jeff Musselman .05 .02
213 Randy Myers .10 .03
214 Bob Ojeda .05 .02
215 Juan Samuel .05 .02
216 Mackey Sasser .05 .02
217 Darryl Strawberry .10 .03
218 Tim Teufel .05 .02
219 Frank Viola .05 .02
220 Juan Agosto .05 .02
221 Larry Andersen .05 .02
222 Eric Anthony RC .10 .03
223 Kevin Bass .05 .02
224 Craig Biggio .15 .04
225 Ken Caminiti .10 .03
226 Jim Clancy .05 .02
227 Danny Darwin .05 .02
228 Glenn Davis .05 .02
229 Jim Deshaies .05 .02
230 Bill Doran .05 .02
231 Bob Forsch .05 .02
232 Brian Meyer .05 .02
233 Terry Puhl .05 .02
234 Rafael Ramirez .05 .02
235 Rick Rhoden .05 .02
236 Dan Schatzeder .05 .02
237 Mike Scott .05 .02
238 Dave Smith .05 .02
239 Alex Trevino .05 .02
240 Glenn Wilson .05 .02
241 Gerald Young .05 .02
242 Tom Brunansky .05 .02
243 Cris Carpenter .05 .02
244 Alex Cole RC .10 .03
245 Vince Coleman .05 .02
246 John Costello .05 .02
247 Ken Dayley .05 .02
248 Jose DeLeon .05 .02
249 Frank DiPino .05 .02
250 Pedro Guerrero .05 .02
251 Ken Hill .10 .03
252 Joe Magrane .05 .02
253 Willie McGee UER .10 .03
(No decimal point before 353)
254 John Morris .05 .02
255 Jose Oquendo .05 .02
256 Tony Pena .05 .02
257 Terry Pendleton .10 .03
258 Ted Power .05 .02
259 Dan Quisenberry .05 .02
260 Ozzie Smith .40 .12
261 Scott Terry .05 .02
262 Milt Thompson .05 .02
263 Denny Walling .05 .02
264 Todd Worrell .05 .02
265 Todd Zeile .10 .03
266 Marty Barrett .05 .02
267 Mike Boddicker .05 .02
268 Wade Boggs .15 .04
269 Ellis Burks .15 .04
270 Rick Cerone .05 .02
271 Roger Clemens .50 .15
272 John Dopson .05 .02
273 Nick Esasky .05 .02
274 Dwight Evans .10 .03
275 Wes Gardner .05 .02
276 Rich Gedman .05 .02
277 Mike Greenwell .05 .02
278 Danny Heep .05 .02
279 Eric Hetzel .05 .02
280 Dennis Lamp .05 .02
281 Rob Murphy UER .05 .02
('89 stats say Reds, should say Red Sox)
282 Joe Price .05 .02
283 Carlos Quintana .05 .02
284 Jody Reed .05 .02
285 Luis Rivera .05 .02
286 Kevin Romine .05 .02
287 Lee Smith .10 .03
288 Mike Smithson .05 .02
289 Bob Stanley .05 .02
290 Harold Baines .10 .03
291 Kevin Brown .10 .03
292 Steve Buechele .05 .02
293 Scott Coolbaugh .05 .02
294 Jack Daugherty .05 .02
295 Cecil Espy .05 .02
296 Julio Franco .10 .03
297 Juan Gonzalez RC 1.50 .45
298 Cecilio Guante .05 .02
299 Drew Hall .05 .02
300 Charlie Hough .10 .03
301 Pete Incaviglia .05 .02
302 Mike Jeffcoat .05 .02
303 Chad Kreuter .05 .02
304 Jeff Kunkel .05 .02
305 Rick Leach .05 .02
306 Fred Manrique .05 .02
307 Jamie Moyer .10 .03
308 Rafael Palmeiro .15 .04
309 Geno Petralli .05 .02
310 Kevin Reimer .05 .02
311 Kenny Rogers .10 .03
312 Jeff Russell .05 .02
313 Nolan Ryan 1.00 .30
314 Ruben Sierra .05 .02
315 Bobby Witt .05 .02
316 Chris Bosio .05 .02
317 Glenn Braggs UER .05 .02
(Stats say 111 K's, but bio says 117 K's)
318 Greg Brock .05 .02
319 Chuck Crim .05 .02
320 Rob Deer .05 .02
321 Mike Felder .05 .02
322 Tom Filer .05 .02
323 Tony Fossas .05 .02
324 Jim Gantner .05 .02
325 Darryl Hamilton .05 .02
326 Teddy Higuera .05 .02
327 Mark Knudson .05 .02
328 Bill Krueger UER .05 .02
('86 stats missing)
329 Tim McIntosh RC .10 .03
330 Paul Molitor .15 .04
331 Jaime Navarro .05 .02
332 Charlie O'Brien .05 .02
333 Jeff Peterek .05 .02
334 Dan Plesac .05 .02
335 Jerry Reuss .05 .02
336 Gary Sheffield UER .25 .07
(Bio says played for 3 teams in '87, but stats say in '88)
337 Bill Spiers .05 .02
338 B.J. Surhoff .10 .03
339 Greg Vaughn .05 .02
340 Robin Yount .40 .12
341 Hubie Brooks .05 .02
342 Tim Burke .05 .02
343 Mike Fitzgerald .05 .02
344 Tom Foley .05 .02
345 Andres Galarraga .10 .03
346 Damaso Garcia .05 .02
347 Marquis Grissom RC .40 .12
348 Kevin Gross .05 .02
349 Joe Hesketh .05 .02
350 Jeff Huson RC .05 .02
351 Wallace Johnson .05 .02
352 Mark Langston .05 .02
353A Dave Martinez 2.00 .60
(Yellow on front)
353B Dave Martinez .05 .02
(Red on front)
354 Dennis Martinez UER .10 .03
('87 ERA is 616, should be 6.16)
355 Andy McGaffigan .05 .02
356 Otis Nixon .05 .02
357 Spike Owen .05 .02
358 Pascual Perez .05 .02
359 Tim Raines .10 .03
360 Nelson Santovenia .05 .02
361 Bryn Smith .05 .02
362 Zane Smith .05 .02
363 Larry Walker RC 1.00 .30
364 Tim Wallach .05 .02
365 Rick Aguilera .10 .03
366 Allan Anderson .05 .02
367 Wally Backman .05 .02
368 Doug Baker .05 .02
369 Juan Berenguer .05 .02
370 Randy Bush .05 .02
371 Carmelo Castillo .05 .02
372 Mike Dyer RC .05 .02
373 Gary Gaetti .10 .03
374 Greg Gagne .05 .02
375 Dan Gladden .05 .02
376 G.Gonzalez UER .05 .02
Bio says 31 saves in '88, but stats say 30
377 Brian Harper .05 .02
378 Kent Hrbek .10 .03
379 Gene Larkin .05 .02
380 Tim Laudner UER .05 .02
(No decimal point before '85 BA of 238)
381 John Moses .05 .02
382 Al Newman .05 .02
383 Kirby Puckett .25 .07
384 Shane Rawley .05 .02
385 Jeff Reardon .10 .03
386 Roy Smith .05 .02
387 Gary Wayne .05 .02
388 Dave West .05 .02
389 Tim Belcher .05 .02
390 Tim Crews UER .05 .02
(Stats say 163 IP for '83, but bio says 136)
391 Mike Davis .05 .02
392 Rick Dempsey .05 .02
393 Kirk Gibson .10 .03
394 Jose Gonzalez .05 .02
395 Alfredo Griffin .05 .02
396 Jeff Hamilton .05 .02
397 Lenny Harris .05 .02
398 Mickey Hatcher .05 .02
399 Orel Hershiser .10 .03
400 Jay Howell .05 .02
401 Mike Marshall .05 .02
402 Ramon Martinez .05 .02
403 Mike Morgan .05 .02
404 Eddie Murray .25 .07
405 Alejandro Pena .05 .02
406 Willie Randolph .10 .03
407 Mike Scioscia .05 .02
408 Ray Searage .05 .02
409 Fernando Valenzuela .10 .03
410 Jose Vizcaino RC .25 .07
411 John Wetteland .25 .07
412 Jack Armstrong .05 .02
413 Todd Benzinger UER .05 .02
(Bio says .323 at Pawtucket, but stats say .321)
414 Tim Birtsas .05 .02
415 Tom Browning .05 .02
416 Norm Charlton .05 .02
417 Eric Davis .10 .03
418 Rob Dibble .10 .03
419 John Franco .10 .03
420 Ken Griffey Sr. .10 .03
421 Chris Hammond RC .10 .03
(No 1989 used for "Did Not Play" stat, actually did play for Nashville in 1989)
422 Danny Jackson .05 .02
423 Barry Larkin .15 .04
424 Tim Leary .05 .02
425 Rick Mahler .05 .02
426 Joe Oliver .05 .02
427 Paul O'Neill .15 .04
428 Luis Quinones UER .05 .02
('86-'88 stats are omitted from card but included in totals)
429 Jeff Reed .05 .02
430 Jose Rijo .05 .02
431 Ron Robinson .05 .02
432 Rolando Roomes .05 .02
433 Chris Sabo .05 .02
434 Scott Scudder .05 .02
435 Herm Winningham .05 .02
436 Steve Balboni .05 .02
437 Jesse Barfield .05 .02
438 Mike Blowers RC .10 .03
439 Tom Brookens .05 .02
440 Greg Cadaret .05 .02
441 Alvaro Espinoza UER .05 .02
(Career games say 218, should be 219)
442 Bob Geren .05 .02
443 Lee Guetterman .05 .02
444 Mel Hall .05 .02
445 Andy Hawkins .05 .02
446 Roberto Kelly .05 .02
447 Don Mattingly .60 .18
448 Lance McCullers .05 .02
449 Hensley Meulens .05 .02
450 Dale Mohorcic .05 .02
451 Clay Parker .05 .02
452 Eric Plunk .05 .02
453 Dave Righetti .05 .02
454 Deion Sanders .25 .07
455 Steve Sax .05 .02
456 Don Slaught .05 .02
457 Walt Terrell .05 .02
458 Dave Winfield .10 .03

459 Jay Bell .10 .03
460 Rafael Belliard .05 .02
461 Barry Bonds .60 .18
462 Bobby Bonilla .10 .03
463 Sid Bream .05 .02
464 Benny Distefano .05 .02
465 Doug Drabek .05 .02
466 Jim Gott .05 .02
467 Billy Hatcher UER .05 .02
(.1 hits for Cubs
in 1984)
468 Neal Heaton .05 .02
469 Jeff King .05 .02
470 Bob Kipper .05 .02
471 Randy Kramer .05 .02
472 Bill Landrum .05 .02
473 Mike LaValliere .05 .02
474 Jose Lind .05 .02
475 Junior Ortiz .05 .02
476 Gary Redus .05 .02
477 Rick Reed RC .25 .07
478 R.J. Reynolds .05 .02
479 Jeff D. Robinson .05 .02
480 John Smiley .05 .02
481 Andy Van Slyke .10 .03
482 Bob Walk .05 .02
483 Andy Allanson .05 .02
484 Scott Bailes .05 .02
485 Joey Belle UER .25 .07
(Has Jay Bell
"Did You Know")
Later changed his name to Albert
486 Bud Black .05 .02
487 Jerry Browne .05 .02
488 Tom Candiotti .05 .02
489 Joe Carter .10 .03
490 Dave Clark .05 .02
(No '84 stats)
491 John Farrell .05 .02
492 Felix Fermin .05 .02
493 Brook Jacoby .05 .02
494 Dion James .05 .02
495 Doug Jones .05 .02
496 Brad Komminsk .05 .02
497 Rod Nichols .05 .02
498 Pete O'Brien .05 .02
499 Steve Olin RC .10 .03
500 Jesse Orosco .05 .02
501 Joel Skinner .05 .02
502 Cory Snyder .05 .02
503 Greg Swindell .05 .02
504 Rich Yett .05 .02
505 Scott Bankhead .05 .02
506 Scott Bradley .05 .02
507 Greg Briley UER .05 .02
(28 SB's in bio,
but 27 in stats)
508 Jay Buhner .10 .03
509 Darnell Coles .05 .02
510 Keith Comstock .05 .02
511 Henry Cotto .05 .02
512 Alvin Davis .05 .02
513 Ken Griffey Jr. .75 .23
514 Erik Hanson .05 .02
515 Gene Harris .05 .02
516 Brian Holman .05 .02
517 Mike Jackson .05 .02
518 Randy Johnson .50 .12
519 Jeffrey Leonard .05 .02
520 Edgar Martinez .15 .04
521 Dennis Powell .05 .02
522 Jim Presley .05 .02
523 Jerry Reed .05 .02
524 Harold Reynolds .10 .03
525 Mike Schooler .05 .02
526 Bill Swift .05 .02
527 Dave Valle .05 .02
528 Omar Vizquel .25 .07
529 Ivan Calderon .05 .02
530 Carlton Fisk UER .15 .04
(Bellow Falls, should
be Bellows Falls)
531 Scott Fletcher .05 .02
532 Dave Gallagher .05 .02
533 Ozzie Guillen .05 .02
534 Greg Hibbard RC .10 .03
535 Shawn Hillegas .05 .02
536 Lance Johnson .05 .02
537 Eric King .05 .02
538 Ron Kittle .05 .02
539 Steve Lyons .05 .02
540 Carlos Martinez .05 .02
541 Tom McCarthy .05 .02
542 Matt Merullo .05 .02
(Had 5 ML runs scored
entering '90, not 6)
543 Donn Pall UER .05 .02
(Stats say pro career
began in '85,
bio says '88)
544 Dan Pasqua .05 .02
545 Ken Patterson .05 .02
546 Melido Perez .05 .02
547 Steve Rosenberg .05 .02
548 Sammy Sosa RC 5.00 1.50
549 Bobby Thigpen .05 .02
550 Robin Ventura .25 .07
551 Greg Walker .05 .02
552 Don Carman .05 .02
553 Pat Combs .05 .02
(6 walks for Phillies
in '89 in stats,
brief bio says 4)
554 Dennis Cook .05 .02
555 Darren Daulton .10 .03
556 Len Dykstra .10 .03
557 Curt Ford .05 .02
558 Charlie Hayes .05 .02
559 Von Hayes .05 .02
560 Tommy Herr .05 .02
561 Ken Howell .05 .02
562 Steve Jeltz .05 .02
563 Ron Jones .05 .02
564 Ricky Jordan UER .05 .02
(Duplicate line of
statistics on back)
565 John Kruk .10 .03
566 Steve Lake .05 .02
567 Roger McDowell .05 .02
568 Terry Mulholland UER .05 .02
(Did You Know refers
to Dave Magadan)
569 Dwayne Murphy .05 .02
570 Jeff Parrett .05 .02
571 Randy Ready .05 .02
572 Bruce Ruffin .05 .02
573 Dickie Thon .05 .02
574 Jose Alvarez UER .05 .02
('78 and '79 stats
are reversed)
575 Geronimo Berroa .05 .02
576 Jeff Blauser .05 .02
577 Joe Boever .05 .02
578 Marty Clary UER .05 .02
(No comma between
city and state)
579 Jody Davis .05 .02
580 Mark Eichhorn .05 .02
581 Darrell Evans .10 .03
582 Ron Gant .10 .03
583 Tom Glavine .15 .04
584 Tommy Greene RC .10 .03
585 Tommy Gregg .05 .02
586 Dave Justice RC UER .50 .15
(Actually had 16 2B
in Sumter in '86)
587 Mark Lemke .05 .02
588 Derek Lilliquist .05 .02
589 Oddibe McDowell .05 .02
590 Kent Mercker RC ERA .05 .02
(Bio says 2.75 ERA,
stats say 2.68 ERA)
591 Dale Murphy .25 .07
592 Gerald Perry .05 .02
593 Lonnie Smith .05 .02
594 Pete Smith .05 .02
595 John Smoltz .25 .07
596 Mike Stanton RC UER .25 .07
(No comma between
city and state)
597 Andres Thomas .05 .02
598 Jeff Treadway .05 .02
599 Doyle Alexander .05 .02
600 Dave Bergman .05 .02
601 Brian DuBois .05 .02
602 Paul Gibson .05 .02
603 Mike Heath .05 .02
604 Mike Henneman .05 .02
605 Guillermo Hernandez .05 .02
606 Shawn Holman .05 .02
607 Tracy Jones .05 .02
608 Chet Lemon .05 .02
609 Fred Lynn .05 .02
610 Jack Morris .10 .03
611 Matt Nokes .05 .02
612 Gary Pettis .05 .02
613 Kevin Ritz .05 .02
614 Jeff M. Robinson .05 .02
('88 stats are
not in line)
615 Steve Searcy .05 .02
616 Frank Tanana .05 .02
617 Alan Trammell .10 .03
618 Gary Ward .05 .02
619 Lou Whitaker .10 .03
620 Frank Williams .05 .02
621A George Brett '80 2.00 .60
ERR (Had 10 .390
hitting seasons)
621B George Brett '80 .30 .09
COR
622 Fern.Valenzuela '81 .05 .02
623 Dale Murphy '82 .15 .04
624A Cal Ripken '83 ERR 5.00 1.50
(Misspelled Ripkin
on card back)
624B Cal Ripken '83 COR .40 .12
625 Ryne Sandberg '84 .25 .07
626 Don Mattingly '85 .20 .06
627 Roger Clemens '86 .25 .07
628 George Bell '87 .05 .02
629 J.Canseco '88 UER .10 .03
Reggie won MVP in
'83, should say '73
630A Will Clark '89 ERR 1.00 .30
(32 total bases
on card back)
630B Will Clark '89 COR .25 .07
(321 total bases;
technically still
an error, listing
only 24 runs)
631 Mark Davis .05 .02
Mitch Williams
632 Wade Boggs .10 .03
Mike Greenwell
633 Mark Gubicza .05 .02
Jeff Russell
634 Tony Fernandez .25 .07
Cal Ripken
635 Kirby Puckett .15 .04
Bo Jackson
636 Nolan Ryan .40 .12
Mike Scott
637 Will Clark .10 .03
Kevin Mitchell
638 Don Mattingly .30 .09
Mark McGwire
639 Howard Johnson .25 .07
Ryne Sandberg
640 Rudy Seanez RC .10 .03
Colin Charland
641 George Canale RC .25 .07
Kevin Maas UER
(Canale listed as INF
on front, 1B on back)
642 Kelly Mann .25 .07
and Dave Hansen RC
643 Greg Smith .10 .03
and Stu Tate
644 Tom Drees .10 .03
and Dann Howitt
645 Mike Roesler RC .10 .03
and Derrick May
646 Scott Hemond .10 .03
and Mark Gardner RC
647 John Orton .10 .03
and Scott Leius RC
648 Rich Monteleone .10 .03
and Dana Williams
649 Mike Huff .10 .03
and Steve Frey
650 Chuck McElroy .75 .23
and Moises Alou RC
651 Bobby Rose .25 .07
and Mike Hartley
652 Matt Kinzer .10 .03
and Wayne Edwards
653 Delino DeShields RC .25 .07
and Jason Grimsley
654 CL: A's/Cubs .05 .02
Giants/Blue Jays
655 CL: Royals/Angels .05 .02
Padres/Orioles
656 CL: Mets/Astros .05 .02
Cards/Red Sox
657 CL: Rangers/Brewers .05 .02
Expos/Twins
658 CL: Dodgers/Reds .05 .02
Yankees/Pirates
659 CL: Indians/Mariners .05 .02
White Sox/Phillies
660A CL: Braves/Tigers .05 .02
Specials/Checklists
(Checklist-660 in small-
er print on card front)
660B CL: Braves/Tigers .05 .02
Specials/Checklists
(Checklist-660 in nor-
mal print on card front)

1990 Fleer Canadian

The 1990 Fleer Canadian set contains 660 standard-size cards. The cards were distributed in wax packs exclusively in Canada. The Canadian set differs from the U.S. version only in that it shows copyright "FLEER LTD./LTEE PTD. IN CANADA" on the card backs. Although these Canadian cards were undoubtedly produced in much lesser quantities compared to the U.S. issue, the fact that the versions are so similar has kept the demand down over the years.

Nm-Mt Ex-Mt
COMPLETE SET (660) 60.00 18.00
*STARS: 2X to 5X BASIC CARDS
*ROOKIES: 2X to 4X BASIC CARDS

1990 Fleer All-Stars

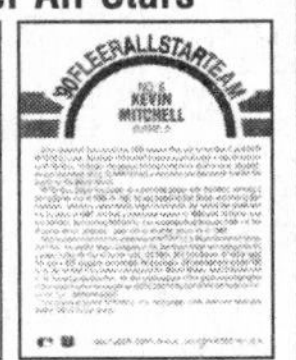

The 1990 Fleer All-Star insert set includes 12 standard-size cards. The set was randomly inserted in 33-card cellos and wax packs. The set is sequenced in alphabetical order. The fronts are white with a light gray screen and bright red stripes. The player selection for the set is Fleer's opinion of the best Major Leaguer at each position.

Nm-Mt Ex-Mt
COMPLETE SET (12) 3.00 .90
1 Harold Baines .25 .07
2 Will Clark .25 .07
3 Mark Davis .15 .04
4 Howard Johnson UER .15 .04
(In middle of 5th
line, the is
misspelled th)
5 Joe Magrane .15 .04
6 Kevin Mitchell .15 .04
7 Kirby Puckett .60 .18
8 Cal Ripken 2.00 .60
9 Ryne Sandberg 1.00 .30
10 Mike Scott UER .15 .04
Astros spelled Asatros on back
11 Ruben Sierra .15 .04
12 Mickey Tettleton .15 .04

1990 Fleer League Standouts

This six-card standard-size insert set was distributed one per 45-card rack pack. The set is subtitled "Standouts" and commemorates outstanding events for those players from the previous season.

Nm-Mt Ex-Mt
COMPLETE SET (6) 6.00 1.80
1 Barry Larkin 1.25 .35
2 Don Mattingly 5.00 1.50
3 Darryl Strawberry .75 .23
4 Jose Canseco 2.00 .60
5 Wade Boggs 1.25 .35
6 Mark Grace UER 1.25 .35
(Chris Sabo misspelled
as Cris)

1990 Fleer Soaring Stars

The 1990 Fleer Soaring Stars set was issued exclusively in jumbo cello packs. This 12-card, standard-size set features some of the most popular young players entering the 1990 season. The set gives the visual impression of rockets exploding in the air to honor these young players.

Nm-Mt Ex-Mt
COMPLETE SET (12) 15.00 4.50
1 Todd Zeile 1.00 .30
2 Mike Stanton .50 .15
3 Larry Walker 2.00 .60
4 Robin Ventura 2.00 .60
5 Scott Coolbaugh .50 .15
6 Ken Griffey Jr. 5.00 1.50
7 Tom Gordon 1.00 .30
8 Jerome Walton .50 .15
9 Junior Felix .50 .15
10 Jim Abbott 1.50 .45
11 Ricky Jordan .50 .15
12 Dwight Smith .50 .15

1990 Fleer Wax Box Cards

The 1990 Fleer wax box cards comprise seven different box bottoms with four cards each, for a total of 28 standard-size cards. The outer front borders are white; the inner, ribbon-like borders are different depending on the team. The vertically oriented backs are gray. The cards are numbered with a "C" prefix.

Nm-Mt Ex-Mt
COMPLETE SET (28) 12.00 3.60
C1 Giants Logo .10 .03
C2 Tim Belcher .10 .03
C3 Roger Clemens 2.50 .75
C4 Eric Davis .25 .07
C5 Glenn Davis .10 .03
C6 Cubs Logo .10 .03
C7 John Franco .25 .07
C8 Mike Greenwell .10 .03
C9 A's Logo .10 .03
C10 Ken Griffey Jr. 3.00 .90
C11 Pedro Guerrero .10 .03
C12 Tony Gwynn 2.50 .75
C13 Blue Jays Logo .10 .03
C14 Orel Hershiser .25 .07
C15 Bo Jackson .25 .07
C16 Howard Johnson .10 .03
C17 Mets Logo .10 .03
C18 Cardinals Logo .10 .03
C19 Don Mattingly 2.50 .75
C20 Mark McGwire 4.00 1.20
C21 Kevin Mitchell .10 .03
C22 Kirby Puckett 1.00 .30
C23 Royals Logo .10 .03
C24 Orioles Logo .10 .03
C25 Ruben Sierra .25 .07
C26 Dave Stewart .25 .07
C27 Jerome Walton .10 .03
C28 Robin Yount .75 .23

1990 Fleer World Series

This 12-card standard-size set was issued as an insert in with the Fleer factory sets, celebrating the 1989 World Series. This set marked the fourth year that Fleer issued a special World Series set in their factory (or vend) set. The design of these cards are different from the regular Fleer issue as the photo is framed by a white border with red and blue World Series cards and the player description in black.

Nm-Mt Ex-Mt
COMPLETE SET (12) 1.00 .30
1 Mike Moore .05 .01
2 Kevin Mitchell .05 .01
3 Terry Steinbach .05 .01
4 Will Clark .10 .03
5 Jose Canseco .25 .07
6 Walt Weiss .05 .01
7 Terry Steinbach .05 .01
8 Dave Stewart .10 .03
9 Dave Parker .10 .03
10 Dave Parker .10 .03
Jose Canseco
Will Clark
11 Rickey Henderson .25 .07
12 Oakland A's Celebrate .10 .03
Baseball's Best in 89

1990 Fleer Update

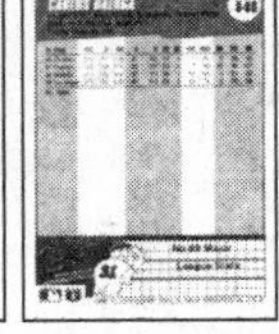

The 1990 Fleer Update set contains 132 standard-size cards. This set marked the seventh consecutive year Fleer issued an end of season Update set. The set was issued exclusively as a boxed set through hobby dealers. The set is checklisted alphabetically by team for each league and then alphabetically within each team. The fronts are styled the same as the 1990 Fleer regular issue set. The backs are numbered with the prefix "U" for Update. Rookie Cards in this set include Travis Fryman, Todd Hundley, John Olerud and Frank Thomas.

Nm-Mt Ex-Mt
COMP.FACT.SET (132) 4.00 1.20
1 Steve Avery .05 .02
2 Francisco Cabrera .05 .02
3 Nick Esasky .05 .02
4 Jim Kremers .05 .02
5 Greg Olson RC .10 .03
6 Jim Presley .05 .02
7 Shawn Boskie RC .10 .03
8 Joe Kraemer .05 .02
9 Luis Salazar .05 .02
10 Hector Villanueva .05 .02
11 Glenn Braggs .05 .02
12 Mariano Duncan .05 .02
13 Billy Hatcher .05 .02
14 Tim Layana .05 .02
15 Hal Morris .05 .02
16 Javier Ortiz .05 .02
17 Dave Rohde .05 .02
18 Eric Yelding .05 .02
19 Hubie Brooks .05 .02
20 Kal Daniels .05 .02
21 Dave Hansen .05 .02
22 Mike Hartley .05 .02
23 Stan Javier .05 .02
24 Jose Offerman RC .25 .07
25 Juan Samuel .05 .02
26 Dennis Boyd .05 .02
27 Delino DeShields .25 .07
28 Steve Frey .05 .02
29 Mark Gardner .05 .02
30 Chris Nabholz RC .10 .03
31 Bill Sampen .05 .02
32 Dave Schmidt .05 .02
33 Daryl Boston .05 .02
34 Chuck Carr RC .10 .03
35 John Franco .10 .03
36 Todd Hundley RC .25 .07
37 Julio Machado .05 .02
38 Alejandro Pena .05 .02
39 Darren Reed .05 .02
40 Kelvin Torve .05 .02
41 Darrel Akerfelds .05 .02
42 Jose DeJesus .05 .02
43 Dave Hollins RC UER .25 .07
(Misspelled Dane
on card back)
44 Carmelo Martinez .05 .02
45 Brad Moore .05 .02
46 Dale Murphy .25 .07
47 Wally Backman .05 .02
48 Stan Belinda RC .10 .03
49 Bob Patterson .05 .02
50 Ted Power .05 .02
51 Don Slaught .05 .02
52 Geronimo Pena RC .10 .03
53 Lee Smith .10 .03
54 John Tudor .05 .02
55 Joe Carter .10 .03
56 Thomas Howard .05 .02
57 Craig Lefferts .05 .02
58 Rafael Valdez .05 .02
59 Dave Anderson .05 .02
60 Kevin Bass .05 .02
61 John Burkett .05 .02
62 Gary Carter .10 .03
63 Rick Parker .05 .02
64 Trevor Wilson .05 .02
65 Chris Hoiles RC .25 .07
66 Tim Hulett .05 .02
67 Dave Johnson .05 .02
68 Curt Schilling 1.00 .30
69 David Segui RC .25 .07
70 Tom Brunansky .05 .02
71 Greg A. Harris .05 .02
72 Dana Kiecker .05 .02
73 Tim Naehring RC .10 .03
74 Tony Pena .05 .02
75 Jeff Reardon .10 .03
76 Jerry Reed .05 .02
77 Mark Eichhorn .05 .02
78 Mark Langston .05 .02
79 John Orton .05 .02
80 Luis Polonia .05 .02
81 Dave Winfield .10 .03
82 Cliff Young .05 .02
83 Wayne Edwards .05 .02
84 Alex Fernandez RC .25 .07
85 Craig Grebeck RC .10 .03
86 Scott Radinsky RC .10 .03
87 Frank Thomas RC 1.50 .45
88 Beau Allred RC .05 .02
89 Sandy Alomar Jr. .05 .02
90 Carlos Baerga RC .25 .07
91 Kevin Bearse .05 .02
92 Chris James .05 .02
93 Candy Maldonado .05 .02
94 Jeff Manto .05 .02
95 Cecil Fielder .10 .03
96 Travis Fryman RC .40 .12
97 Lloyd Moseby .05 .02
98 Edwin Nunez .05 .02
99 Tony Phillips .05 .02
100 Larry Sheets .05 .02
101 Mark Davis .05 .02
102 Storm Davis .05 .02
103 Gerald Perry .05 .02
104 Terry Shumpert .05 .02
105 Edgar Diaz .05 .02
106 Dave Parker .10 .03
107 Tim Drummond .05 .02
108 Junior Ortiz .05 .02
109 Park Pittman .05 .02
110 Kevin Tapani RC .25 .07
111 Oscar Azocar .05 .02
112 Jim Leyritz RC .25 .07
113 Kevin Maas .10 .03
114 Alan Mills RC .10 .03
115 Matt Nokes .05 .02
116 Pascual Perez .05 .02
117 Ozzie Canseco .05 .02
118 Scott Sanderson .05 .02
119 Tino Martinez .25 .07
120 Jeff Schaefer RC .05 .02

121 Matt Young .05 .02
122 Brian Bohanon RC .10 .03
123 Jeff Huson .05 .02
124 Ramon Manon .05 .02
125 Gary Mielke UER .05 .02
(Shown as Blue Jay on front)
126 Willie Blair RC .10 .03
127 Glenallen Hill .05 .02
128 John Olerud RC UER .50 .15
(Listed as throwing right, should be left)
129 Luis Sojo .05 .02
130 Mark Whiten RC .25 .07
131 Nolan Ryan 1.00 .30
132 Checklist U1-U132 .05 .02

1991 Fleer

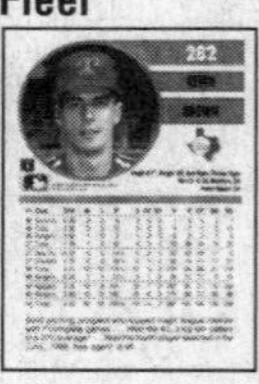

The 1991 Fleer set consists of 720 standard-size cards. Cards were primarily issued in wax packs, cello packs and factory sets. This set does not have what had been a Fleer tradition in prior years, the two-player Rookie Cards and there are less two-player special cards than in prior years. The design features bright yellow borders with the information in black indicating name, position, and team. The set is again ordered numerically by teams, followed by combination cards, rookie prospect pairs, and checklists. There are no notable Rookie Cards in this set. A number of the cards in the set can be found with photos cropped (very slightly) differently as Fleer used two separate printers in their attempt to maximize production.

	Nm-Mt	Ex-Mt
COMPLETE SET (720)	8.00	2.40
COMP.RETAIL SET (732)	10.00	3.00
COMP.HOBBY SET (732)	10.00	3.00

1 Troy Afenir .05 .02
2 Harold Baines .10 .03
3 Lance Blankenship .05 .02
4 Todd Burns .05 .02
5 Jose Canseco .25 .07
6 Dennis Eckersley .10 .03
7 Mike Gallego .05 .02
8 Ron Hassey .05 .02
9 Dave Henderson .05 .02
10 Rickey Henderson .25 .07
11 Rick Honeycutt .05 .02
12 Doug Jennings .05 .02
13 Joe Klink .05 .02
14 Carney Lansford .10 .03
15 Darren Lewis .05 .02
16 Willie McGee UER .10 .03
(Height 6'11")
17 Mark McGwire UER .60 .18
(183 extra base hits in 1987)
18 Mike Moore .05 .02
19 Gene Nelson .05 .02
20 Dave Otto .05 .02
21 Jamie Quirk .05 .02
22 Willie Randolph .10 .03
23 Scott Sanderson .05 .02
24 Terry Steinbach .05 .02
25 Dave Stewart .10 .03
26 Walt Weiss .05 .02
27 Bob Welch .05 .02
28 Curt Young .05 .02
29 Wally Backman .05 .02
30 Stan Belinda UER .05 .02
(Born in Huntington, should be State College)
31 Jay Bell .10 .03
32 Rafael Belliard .05 .02
33 Barry Bonds .60 .18
34 Bobby Bonilla .10 .03
35 Sid Bream .05 .02
36 Doug Drabek .05 .02
37 Carlos Garcia RC .10 .03
38 Neal Heaton .05 .02
39 Jeff King .05 .02
40 Bob Kipper .05 .02
41 Bill Landrum .05 .02
42 Mike LaValliere .05 .02
43 Jose Lind .05 .02
44 Carmelo Martinez .05 .02
45 Bob Patterson .05 .02
46 Ted Power .05 .02
47 Gary Redus .05 .02
48 R.J. Reynolds .05 .02
49 Don Slaught .05 .02
50 John Smiley .05 .02
51 Zane Smith .05 .02
52 Randy Tomlin RC .10 .03
53 Andy Van Slyke .10 .03
54 Bob Walk .05 .02
55 Jack Armstrong .05 .02
56 Todd Benzinger .05 .02
57 Glenn Braggs .05 .02
58 Keith Brown .05 .02
59 Tom Browning .05 .02
60 Norm Charlton .05 .02
61 Eric Davis .10 .03
62 Rob Dibble .10 .03
63 Bill Doran .05 .02
64 Mariano Duncan .05 .02
65 Chris Hammond .05 .02
66 Billy Hatcher .05 .02
67 Danny Jackson .05 .02
68 Barry Larkin .15 .04
69 Tim Layana .05 .02
(Black line over made in first text line)
70 Terry Lee .05 .02
71 Rick Mahler .05 .02
72 Hal Morris .05 .02
73 Randy Myers .05 .02
74 Ron Oester .05 .02
75 Joe Oliver .05 .02
76 Paul O'Neill .15 .04
77 Luis Quinones .05 .02
78 Jeff Reed .05 .02
79 Jose Rijo .05 .02
80 Chris Sabo .05 .02
81 Scott Scudder .05 .02
82 Herm Winningham .05 .02
83 Larry Andersen .05 .02
84 Marty Barrett .05 .02
85 Mike Boddicker .05 .02
86 Wade Boggs .15 .04
87 Tom Bolton .05 .02
88 Tom Brunansky .05 .02
89 Ellis Burks .10 .03
90 Roger Clemens .50 .15
91 Scott Cooper .05 .02
92 John Dopson .05 .02
93 Dwight Evans .10 .03
94 Wes Gardner .05 .02
95 Jeff Gray .05 .02
96 Mike Greenwell .05 .02
97 Greg A. Harris .05 .02
98 Daryl Irvine .05 .02
99 Dana Kiecker .05 .02
100 Randy Kutcher .05 .02
101 Dennis Lamp .05 .02
102 Mike Marshall .05 .02
103 John Marzano .05 .02
104 Rob Murphy .05 .02
105 Tim Naehring .05 .02
106 Tony Pena .05 .02
107 Phil Plantier RC .25 .07
108 Carlos Quintana .05 .02
109 Jeff Reardon .10 .03
110 Jerry Reed .05 .02
111 Jody Reed .05 .02
112 Luis Rivera UER .05 .02
(Born 1/3/84)
113 Kevin Romine .05 .02
114 Phil Bradley .05 .02
115 Ivan Calderon .05 .02
116 Wayne Edwards .05 .02
117 Alex Fernandez .05 .02
118 Carlton Fisk .15 .04
119 Scott Fletcher .05 .02
120 Craig Grebeck .05 .02
121 Ozzie Guillen .05 .02
122 Greg Hibbard .05 .02
123 Lance Johnson UER .05 .02
(Born Cincinnati, should be Lincoln Heights)
124 Barry Jones .05 .02
125 Ron Karkovice .05 .02
126 Eric King .05 .02
127 Steve Lyons .05 .02
128 Carlos Martinez .05 .02
129 Jack McDowell UER .05 .02
(Stanford misspelled as Standford on back)
130 Donn Pall .05 .02
(No dots over any i's in text)
131 Dan Pasqua .05 .02
132 Ken Patterson .05 .02
133 Melido Perez .05 .02
134 Adam Peterson .05 .02
135 Scott Radinsky .05 .02
136 Sammy Sosa .50 .15
137 Bobby Thigpen .05 .02
138 Frank Thomas .25 .07
139 Robin Ventura .10 .03
140 Daryl Boston .05 .02
141 Chuck Carr .05 .02
142 Mark Carreon .05 .02
143 David Cone .10 .03
144 Ron Darling .05 .02
145 Kevin Elster .05 .02
146 Sid Fernandez .05 .02
147 John Franco .10 .03
148 Dwight Gooden .10 .03
149 Tom Herr .05 .02
150 Todd Hundley .05 .02
151 Gregg Jefferies .05 .02
152 Howard Johnson .05 .02
153 Dave Magadan .05 .02
154 Kevin McReynolds .05 .02
155 Keith Miller UER .05 .02
(Text says Rochester in '87, stats say Tide-water, mixed up with other Keith Miller)
156 Bob Ojeda .05 .02
157 Tom O'Malley .05 .02
158 Alejandro Pena .05 .02
159 Darren Reed .05 .02
160 Mackey Sasser .05 .02
161 Darryl Strawberry .10 .03
162 Tim Teufel .05 .02
163 Kelvin Torve .05 .02
164 Julio Valera .05 .02
165 Frank Viola .10 .03
166 Wally Whitehurst .05 .02
167 Jim Acker .05 .02
168 Derek Bell .10 .03
169 George Bell .05 .02
170 Willie Blair .05 .02
171 Pat Borders .05 .02
172 John Cerutti .05 .02
173 Junior Felix .05 .02
174 Tony Fernandez .05 .02
175 Kelly Gruber UER .05 .02
(Born in Houston, should be Bellaire)
176 Tom Henke .05 .02
177 Glenallen Hill .05 .02
178 Jimmy Key .10 .03
179 Manny Lee .05 .02
180 Fred McGriff .15 .04
181 Rance Mulliniks .05 .02
182 Greg Myers .05 .02
183 John Olerud UER .10 .03
(Listed as throwing right, should be left)
184 Luis Sojo .05 .02
185 Dave Stieb .05 .02
186 Todd Stottlemyre .05 .02
187 Duane Ward .05 .02
188 David Wells .10 .03
189 Mark Whiten .05 .02
190 Ken Williams .05 .02
191 Frank Wills .05 .02
192 Mookie Wilson .10 .03
193 Don Aase .05 .02
194 Tim Belcher UER .05 .02
(Born Sparta, Ohio, should say Mt. Gilead)
195 Hubie Brooks .05 .02
196 Dennis Cook .05 .02
197 Tim Crews .05 .02
198 Kal Daniels .05 .02
199 Kirk Gibson .10 .03
200 Jim Gott .05 .02
201 Alfredo Griffin .05 .02
202 Chris Gwynn .05 .02
203 Dave Hansen .05 .02
204 Lenny Harris .05 .02
205 Mike Hartley .05 .02
206 Mickey Hatcher .05 .02
207 Carlos Hernandez .05 .02
208 Orel Hershiser .10 .03
209 Jay Howell UER .05 .02
(No 1982 Yankee stats)
210 Mike Huff .05 .02
211 Stan Javier .05 .02
212 Ramon Martinez .05 .02
213 Mike Morgan .05 .02
214 Eddie Murray .25 .07
215 Jim Neidlinger .05 .02
216 Jose Offerman .05 .02
217 Jim Poole .05 .02
218 Juan Samuel .05 .02
219 Mike Scioscia .05 .02
220 Ray Searage .05 .02
221 Mike Sharperson .05 .02
222 Fernando Valenzuela .10 .03
223 Jose Vizcaino .05 .02
224 Mike Aldrete .05 .02
225 Scott Anderson .05 .02
226 Dennis Boyd .05 .02
227 Tim Burke .05 .02
228 Delino DeShields .10 .03
229 Mike Fitzgerald .05 .02
230 Tom Foley .05 .02
231 Steve Frey .05 .02
232 Andres Galarraga .10 .03
233 Mark Gardner .05 .02
234 Marquis Grissom .10 .03
235 Kevin Gross .05 .02
(No date given for first Expos win)
236 Drew Hall .05 .02
237 Dave Martinez .05 .02
238 Dennis Martinez .10 .03
239 Dale Mohorcic .05 .02
240 Chris Nabholz .05 .02
241 Otis Nixon .05 .02
242 Junior Noboa .05 .02
243 Spike Owen .05 .02
244 Tim Raines .10 .03
245 Mel Rojas UER .05 .02
(Stats show 3.60 ERA& bio says 3.19 ERA)
246 Scott Ruskin .05 .02
247 Bill Sampen .05 .02
248 Nelson Santovenia .05 .02
249 Dave Schmidt .05 .02
250 Larry Walker .25 .07
251 Tim Wallach .05 .02
252 Dave Anderson .05 .02
253 Kevin Bass .05 .02
254 Steve Bedrosian .05 .02
255 Jeff Brantley .05 .02
256 John Burkett .05 .02
257 Brett Butler .10 .03
258 Gary Carter .10 .03
259 Will Clark .25 .07
260 Steve Decker RC .10 .03
261 Kelly Downs .05 .02
262 Scott Garrelts .05 .02
263 Terry Kennedy .05 .02
264 Mike LaCoss .05 .02
265 Mark Leonard .05 .02
266 Greg Litton .05 .02
267 Kevin Mitchell .05 .02
268 Randy O'Neal .05 .02
269 Rick Parker .05 .02
270 Rick Reuschel .05 .02
271 Ernest Riles .05 .02
272 Don Robinson .05 .02
273 Robby Thompson .05 .02
274 Mark Thurmond .05 .02
275 Jose Uribe .05 .02
276 Matt Williams .10 .03
277 Trevor Wilson .05 .02
278 Gerald Alexander .05 .02
279 Brad Arnsberg .05 .02
280 Kevin Belcher .05 .02
281 Joe Bitker .05 .02
282 Kevin Brown .10 .03
283 Steve Buechele .05 .02
284 Jack Daugherty .05 .02
285 Julio Franco .10 .03
286 Juan Gonzalez .15 .04
287 Bill Haselman .05 .02
288 Charlie Hough .10 .03
289 Jeff Huson .05 .02
290 Pete Incaviglia .05 .02
291 Mike Jeffcoat .05 .02
292 Jeff Kunkel .05 .02
293 Gary Mielke .05 .02
294 Jamie Moyer .10 .03
295 Rafael Palmeiro .15 .04
296 Geno Petralli .05 .02
297 Gary Pettis .05 .02
298 Kevin Reimer .05 .02
299 Kenny Rogers .10 .03
300 Jeff Russell .05 .02
301 John Russell .05 .02
302 Nolan Ryan 1.00 .30
303 Ruben Sierra .05 .02
304 Bobby Witt .05 .02
305 Jim Abbott UER .15 .04
(Text on back states he won Sullivan Award (outstanding amateur athlete) in 1989;should be '88)
306 Kent Anderson .05 .02
307 Dante Bichette .10 .03
308 Bert Blyleven .10 .03
309 Chili Davis .10 .03
310 Brian Downing .05 .02
311 Mark Eichhorn .05 .02
312 Mike Fetters .05 .02
313 Chuck Finley .10 .03
314 Willie Fraser .05 .02
315 Bryan Harvey .05 .02
316 Donnie Hill .05 .02
317 Wally Joyner .10 .03
318 Mark Langston .05 .02
319 Kirk McCaskill .05 .02
320 John Orton .05 .02
321 Lance Parrish .10 .03
322 Luis Polonia UER .05 .02
(1984 Madfison, should be Madison)
323 Johnny Ray .05 .02
324 Bobby Rose .05 .02
325 Dick Schofield .05 .02
326 Rick Schu .05 .02
327 Lee Stevens .05 .02
328 Devon White .10 .03
329 Dave Winfield .10 .03
330 Cliff Young .05 .02
331 Dave Bergman .05 .02
332 Phil Clark RC .10 .03
333 Darnell Coles .05 .02
334 Milt Cuyler .05 .02
335 Cecil Fielder .10 .03
336 Travis Fryman .10 .03
337 Paul Gibson .05 .02
338 Jerry Don Gleaton .05 .02
339 Mike Heath .05 .02
340 Mike Henneman .05 .02
341 Chet Lemon .05 .02
342 Lance McCullers .05 .02
343 Jack Morris .10 .03
344 Lloyd Moseby .05 .02
345 Edwin Nunez .05 .02
346 Clay Parker .05 .02
347 Dan Petry .05 .02
348 Tony Phillips .05 .02
349 Jeff M. Robinson .05 .02
350 Mark Salas .05 .02
351 Mike Schwabe .05 .02
352 Larry Sheets .05 .02
353 John Shelby .05 .02
354 Frank Tanana .05 .02
355 Alan Trammell .10 .03
356 Gary Ward .05 .02
357 Lou Whitaker .10 .03
358 Beau Allred .05 .02
359 Sandy Alomar Jr. .05 .02
360 Carlos Baerga .05 .02
361 Kevin Bearse .05 .02
362 Tom Brookens .05 .02
363 Jerry Browne UER .05 .02
(No dot over i in first text line)
364 Tom Candiotti .05 .02
365 Alex Cole .05 .02
366 John Farrell UER .05 .02
(Born in Neptune, should be Monmouth)
367 Felix Fermin .05 .02
368 Keith Hernandez .10 .03
369 Brook Jacoby .05 .02
370 Chris James .05 .02
371 Dion James .05 .02
372 Doug Jones .05 .02
373 Candy Maldonado .05 .02
374 Steve Olin .05 .02
375 Jesse Orosco .05 .02
376 Rudy Seanez .05 .02
377 Joel Skinner .05 .02
378 Cory Snyder .05 .02
379 Greg Swindell .05 .02
380 Sergio Valdez .05 .02
381 Mike Walker .05 .02
382 Colby Ward .05 .02
383 Turner Ward RC .25 .07
384 Mitch Webster .05 .02
385 Kevin Wickander .05 .02
386 Darrel Akerfelds .05 .02
387 Joe Boever .05 .02
388 Rod Booker .05 .02
389 Sil Campusano .05 .02
390 Don Carman .05 .02
391 Wes Chamberlain RC .25 .07
392 Pat Combs .05 .02
393 Darren Daulton .10 .03
394 Jose DeJesus .05 .02
395A Len Dykstra .10 .03
Name spelled Lenny on back
395B Len Dykstra .10 .03
Name spelled Len on back
396 Jason Grimsley .05 .02
397 Charlie Hayes .05 .02
398 Von Hayes .05 .02
399 David Hollins UER .05 .02
(Atl-bats& should say at-bats)
400 Ken Howell .05 .02
401 Ricky Jordan .05 .02
402 John Kruk .10 .03
403 Steve Lake .05 .02
404 Chuck Malone .05 .02
405 Roger McDowell UER .05 .02
(Says Phillies is saves, should say in)
406 Chuck McElroy .05 .02
407 Mickey Morandini .05 .02
408 Terry Mulholland .05 .02
409 Dale Murphy .25 .07
410A Randy Ready ERR .05 .02
(No Brewers stats listed for 1983)
410B Randy Ready COR .05 .02
411 Bruce Ruffin .05 .02
412 Dickie Thon .05 .02
413 Paul Assenmacher .05 .02
414 Damon Berryhill .05 .02
415 Mike Bielecki .05 .02
416 Shawn Boskie .05 .02
417 Dave Clark .05 .02
418 Doug Dascenzo .05 .02
419A Andre Dawson ERR .10 .03
(No stats for 1976)
419B Andre Dawson COR .10 .03
420 Shawon Dunston .05 .02
421 Joe Girardi .05 .02
422 Mark Grace .15 .04
423 Mike Harkey .05 .02
424 Les Lancaster .05 .02
425 Bill Long .05 .02
426 Greg Maddux .40 .12
427 Derrick May .05 .02
428 Jeff Pico .05 .02
429 Domingo Ramos .05 .02
430 Luis Salazar .05 .02
431 Ryne Sandberg .40 .12
432 Dwight Smith .05 .02
433 Greg Smith .05 .02
434 Rick Sutcliffe .10 .03
435 Gary Varsho .05 .02
436 Hector Villanueva .05 .02
437 Jerome Walton .05 .02
438 Curtis Wilkerson .05 .02
439 Mitch Williams .05 .02
440 Steve Wilson .05 .02
441 Marvell Wynne .05 .02
442 Scott Bankhead .05 .02
443 Scott Bradley .05 .02
444 Greg Briley .05 .02
445 Mike Brumley UER .05 .02
(Text 40 SB's in 1988, stats say 41)
446 Jay Buhner .10 .03
447 Dave Burba RC .25 .07
448 Henry Cotto .05 .02
449 Alvin Davis .05 .02
450 Ken Griffey Jr. .50 .15
(Bat around .300)
450A Ken Griffey Jr. 1.00 .30
(Bat .300)
451 Erik Hanson .05 .02
452 Gene Harris UER .05 .02
(63 career runs, should be 73)
453 Brian Holman .05 .02
454 Mike Jackson .05 .02
455 Randy Johnson .30 .09
456 Jeffrey Leonard .05 .02
457 Edgar Martinez .15 .04
458 Tino Martinez .15 .04
459 Pete O'Brien UER .05 .02
(1987 BA .266, should be .286)
460 Harold Reynolds .10 .03
461 Mike Schooler .05 .02
462 Bill Swift .05 .02
463 David Valle .05 .02
464 Omar Vizquel .15 .04
465 Matt Young .05 .02
466 Brady Anderson .10 .03
467 Jeff Ballard UER .05 .02
(Missing top of right parenthesis after Saberhagen in last text line)
468 Juan Bell .05 .02
469A Mike Devereaux .10 .03
(First line of text ends with six)
469B Mike Devereaux .10 .03
(First line of text ends with runs)
470 Steve Finley .10 .03
471 Dave Gallagher .05 .02
472 Leo Gomez .05 .02
473 Rene Gonzales .05 .02
474 Pete Harnisch .05 .02
475 Kevin Hickey .05 .02
476 Chris Hoiles .05 .02
477 Sam Horn .05 .02
478 Tim Hulett .05 .02
(Photo shows National Leaguer sliding into second base)
479 Dave Johnson .05 .02
480 Ron Kittle UER .05 .02
(Edmonton misspelled as Edmundton)
481 Ben McDonald .05 .02
482 Bob Melvin .05 .02
483 Bob Milacki .05 .02
484 Randy Milligan .05 .02
485 John Mitchell .05 .02
486 Gregg Olson .05 .02
487 Joe Orsulak .05 .02
488 Joe Price .05 .02
489 Bill Ripken .05 .02
490 Cal Ripken .75 .23
491 Curt Schilling .25 .07
492 David Segui .05 .02
493 Anthony Telford .05 .02
494 Mickey Tettleton .05 .02
495 Mark Williamson .05 .02
496 Craig Worthington .05 .02
497 Juan Agosto .05 .02
498 Eric Anthony .05 .02
499 Craig Biggio .15 .04
500 Ken Caminiti UER .10 .03
(Born 4/4, should be 4/21)
501 Casey Candaele .05 .02
502 Andujar Cedeno .05 .02
503 Danny Darwin .05 .02
504 Mark Davidson .05 .02
505 Glenn Davis .05 .02
506 Jim Deshaies .05 .02
507 Luis Gonzalez RC .50 .15
508 Bill Gullickson .05 .02
509 Xavier Hernandez .05 .02
510 Brian Meyer .05 .02
511 Ken Oberkfell .05 .02
512 Mark Portugal .05 .02
513 Rafael Ramirez .05 .02
514 Karl Rhodes .05 .02
515 Mike Scott .05 .02
516 Mike Simms .05 .02
517 Dave Smith .05 .02
518 Franklin Stubbs .05 .02
519 Glenn Wilson .05 .02

20 Eric Yelding UER .05 .02
(Text has 63 steals, stats have 64, which is correct)
21 Gerald Young .05 .02
22 Shawn Abner .05 .02
23 Roberto Alomar .15 .04
24 Andy Benes .05 .02
25 Joe Carter .10 .03
26 Jack Clark .10 .03
27 Joey Cora .05 .02
28 Paul Faries .05 .02
29 Tony Gwynn .30 .09
30 Atlee Hammaker .05 .02
31 Greg W. Harris .05 .02
32 Thomas Howard .05 .02
33 Bruce Hurst .05 .02
34 Craig Lefferts .05 .02
35 Derek Lilliquist .05 .02
36 Fred Lynn .05 .02
37 Mike Pagliarulo .05 .02
38 Mark Parent .05 .02
39 Dennis Rasmussen .05 .02
40 Bip Roberts .05 .02
41 Richard Rodriguez .05 .02
42 Benito Santiago .10 .03
43 Calvin Schiraldi .05 .02
44 Eric Show .05 .02
45 Phil Stephenson .05 .02
46 Garry Templeton UER .05 .02
(Born 3/24/57, should be 3/24/56)
47 Ed Whitson .05 .02
48 Eddie Williams .05 .02
49 Kevin Appier .10 .03
50 Luis Aquino .05 .02
51 Bob Boone .10 .03
52 George Brett .60 .18
53 Jeff Conine RC .40 .12
54 Steve Crawford .05 .02
55 Mark Davis .05 .02
56 Storm Davis .05 .02
57 Jim Eisenreich .05 .02
58 Steve Farr .05 .02
59 Tom Gordon .05 .02
60 Mark Gubicza .05 .02
61 Bo Jackson .25 .07
62 Mike Macfarlane .05 .02
63 Brian McRae RC .25 .07
64 Jeff Montgomery .05 .02
65 Bill Pecota .05 .02
66 Gerald Perry .05 .02
67 Bret Saberhagen .10 .03
68 Jeff Schulz .05 .02
69 Kevin Seitzer .05 .02
70 Terry Shumpert .05 .02
71 Kurt Stillwell .05 .02
72 Danny Tartabull .05 .02
73 Gary Thurman .05 .02
74 Frank White .10 .03
75 Willie Wilson .05 .02
76 Chris Bosio .05 .02
77 Greg Brock .05 .02
78 George Canale .05 .02
79 Chuck Crim .05 .02
80 Rob Deer .05 .02
81 Edgar Diaz .05 .02
82 Tom Edens .05 .02
83 Mike Felder .05 .02
84 Jim Gantner .05 .02
85 Darryl Hamilton .05 .02
86 Ted Higuera .05 .02
87 Mark Knudson .05 .02
88 Bill Krueger .05 .02
89 Tim McIntosh .05 .02
90 Paul Mirabella .05 .02
91 Paul Molitor .15 .04
92 Jaime Navarro .05 .02
93 Dave Parker .10 .03
94 Dan Plesac .05 .02
95 Ron Robinson .05 .02
96 Gary Sheffield .10 .03
97 Bill Spiers .05 .02
98 B.J. Surhoff .10 .03
99 Greg Vaughn .05 .02
00 Randy Veres .05 .02
01 Robin Yount .40 .12
02 Rick Aguilera .10 .03
03 Allan Anderson .05 .02
04 Juan Berenguer .05 .02
05 Randy Bush .05 .02
06 Carmelo Castillo .05 .02
07 Tim Drummond .05 .02
08 Scott Erickson .05 .02
09 Gary Gaetti .10 .03
10 Greg Gagne .05 .02
11 Dan Gladden .05 .02
12 Mark Guthrie .05 .02
13 Brian Harper .05 .02
14 Kent Hrbek .10 .03
15 Gene Larkin .05 .02
16 Terry Leach .05 .02
17 Nelson Liriano .05 .02
18 Shane Mack .05 .02
19 John Moses .05 .02
20 Pedro Munoz RC .10 .03
21 Al Newman .05 .02
22 Junior Ortiz .05 .02
23 Kirby Puckett .25 .07
24 Roy Smith .05 .02
25 Kevin Tapani .05 .02
26 Gary Wayne .05 .02
27 David West .05 .02
28 Cris Carpenter .05 .02
29 Vince Coleman .05 .02
30 Ken Dayley .05 .02
31A Jose DeLeon ERR .05 .02
(missing '79 Bradenton stats)
31B Jose DeLeon COR .05 .02
(with '79 Bradenton stats)
32 Frank DiPino .05 .02
33 Bernard Gilkey .05 .02
34A P.Guerrero ERR .10 .03
career SB shown as "$91"
34B Pedro Guerrero COR .10 .03
35 Ken Hill .05 .02
36 Felix Jose .05 .02
37 Ray Lankford .05 .02
38 Joe Magrane .05 .02
639 Tom Niedenfuer .05 .02
640 Jose Oquendo .05 .02
641 Tom Pagnozzi .05 .02
642 Terry Pendleton .10 .03
643 Mike Perez RC .10 .03
644 Bryn Smith .05 .02
645 Lee Smith .10 .03
646 Ozzie Smith .40 .12
647 Scott Terry .05 .02
648 Bob Tewksbury .05 .02
649 Milt Thompson .05 .02
650 John Tudor .05 .02
651 Denny Walling .05 .02
652 Craig Wilson .05 .02
653 Todd Worrell .05 .02
654 Todd Zeile .05 .02
655 Oscar Azocar .05 .02
656 Steve Balboni UER .05 .02
(Born 1/5/57, should be 1/16)
657 Jesse Barfield .05 .02
658 Greg Cadaret .05 .02
659 Chuck Cary .05 .02
660 Rick Cerone .05 .02
661 Dave Eiland .05 .02
662 Alvaro Espinoza .05 .02
663 Bob Geren .05 .02
664 Lee Guetterman .05 .02
665 Mel Hall .05 .02
666 Andy Hawkins .05 .02
667 Jimmy Jones .05 .02
668 Roberto Kelly .05 .02
669 Dave LaPoint UER .05 .02
(No '81 Brewers stats, totals also are wrong)
670 Tim Leary .05 .02
671 Jim Leyritz .05 .02
672 Kevin Maas .05 .02
673 Don Mattingly .60 .18
674 Matt Nokes .05 .02
675 Pascual Perez .05 .02
676 Eric Plunk .05 .02
677 Dave Righetti .10 .03
678 Jeff D. Robinson .05 .02
679 Steve Sax .05 .02
680 Mike Witt .05 .02
681 Steve Avery UER .05 .02
(Born in New Jersey, should say Michigan)
682 Mike Bell .05 .02
683 Jeff Blauser .05 .02
684 F.Cabrera UER .05 .02
Born 10/16, should say 10/10
685 Tony Castillo .05 .02
686 Marty Clary UER .05 .02
(Shown pitching righty, but bio has left)
687 Nick Esasky .05 .02
688 Ron Gant .10 .03
689 Tom Glavine .15 .04
690 Mark Grant .05 .02
691 Tommy Gregg .05 .02
692 Dwayne Henry .05 .02
693 Dave Justice .10 .03
694 Jimmy Kremers .05 .02
695 Charlie Leibrandt .05 .02
696 Mark Lemke .05 .02
697 Oddibe McDowell .05 .02
698 Greg Olson .05 .02
699 Jeff Parrett .05 .02
700 Jim Presley .05 .02
701 Victor Rosario .05 .02
702 Lonnie Smith .05 .02
703 Pete Smith .05 .02
704 John Smoltz .15 .04
705 Mike Stanton .05 .02
706 Andres Thomas .05 .02
707 Jeff Treadway .05 .02
708 Jim Vatcher .05 .02
709 Ryne Sandberg .25 .07
Cecil Fielder
710 Barry Bonds .75 .23
Ken Griffey Jr.
711 Bobby Bonilla .10 .03
Barry Larkin
712 Bobby Thigpen .05 .02
John Franco
713 Andre Dawson .25 .07
Ryne Sandberg UER
(Ryno misspelled Rhino)
714 CL:A's/Pirates .05 .02
Reds/Red Sox
715 CL:White Sox/Mets .05 .02
Blue Jays/Dodgers
716 CL:Expos/Giants .05 .02
Rangers/Angels
717 CL:Tigers/Indians .05 .02
Phillies/Cubs
718 CL:Mariners/Orioles .05 .02
Astros/Padres
719 CL:Royals/Brewers .05 .02
Twins/Cardinals
720 CL:Yankees/Braves .05 .02
Superstars/Specials

1991 Fleer All-Stars

For the sixth consecutive year Fleer issued an All-Star insert set. This year the cards were only available as random inserts in Fleer cello packs. This ten-card standard-size set is reminiscent of the 1971 Topps Greatest Moments set with two pictures on the (black-bordered) front as well as a photo on the back.

Nm-Mt Ex-Mt
COMPLETE SET (10) 15.00 4.50
1 Ryne Sandberg 3.00 .90
2 Barry Larkin 1.25 .35
3 Matt Williams .75 .23
4 Cecil Fielder .75 .23
5 Barry Bonds 5.00 1.50
6 Rickey Henderson 2.00 .60
7 Ken Griffey Jr. 4.00 1.20
8 Jose Canseco 2.00 .60
9 Benito Santiago .75 .23
10 Roger Clemens 4.00 1.20

1991 Fleer Pro-Visions

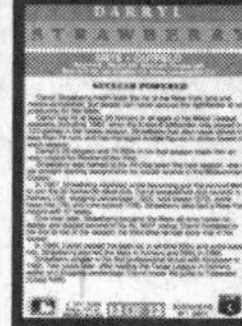

This 12-card standard-size insert set features paintings by artist Terry Smith framed by distinctive black borders on each card front. The cards were randomly inserted in wax and rack packs. An additional four-card set was issued only in 1991 Fleer factory sets. Those cards are numbered F1-F4. Unlike the 12 cards inserted in packs, these factory set cards feature white borders on front.

Nm-Mt Ex-Mt
COMPLETE REG.SET (12) 4.00 1.20
COMP.FACT.SET (4) 2.00 .60
1 Kirby Puckett UER .75 .23
(.326 average, should be .328)
2 Will Clark UER .75 .23
(On tenth line, pennant misspelled pennent)
3 Ruben Sierra UER .15 .04
(No apostrophe in hasn't)
4 Mark McGwire UER 2.00 .60
(Fisk won ROY in '72, not '82)
5 Bo Jackson .75 .23
(Bio says 6', others have him at 6'1")
6 Jose Canseco UER .75 .23
(Bio 6'3", 230& text has 6'4", 240)
7 Dwight Gooden UER .30 .09
(2.80 ERA in Lynchburg, should be 2.50)
8 Mike Greenwell UER .15 .04
(.328 BA and 87 RBI, should be .325 and 95)
9 Roger Clemens 1.50 .45
10 Eric Davis .30 .09
11 Don Mattingly 2.00 .60
12 Darryl Strawberry .30 .09
F1 Barry Bonds 2.00 .60
F2 Rickey Henderson .75 .23
F3 Ryne Sandberg 1.25 .35
F4 Dave Stewart .30 .09

1991 Fleer Wax Box Cards

These cards were issued on the bottom of 1991 Fleer wax boxes. This set celebrated the spate of no-hitters in 1990 and were printed on three different boxes. These standard size cards, come four to a box, three about the no-hitters and one team logo card on each box. The cards are blank backed and are numbered on the front in a subtle way. They are ordered below as they are numbered, which is by chronological order of their no-hitters. Only the player cards are listed below since there was a different team logo card on each box.

Nm-Mt Ex-Mt
COMPLETE SET (9) 4.00 1.20
1 Mark Langston .10 .03
and Mike Witt
2 Randy Johnson 1.00 .30
3 Nolan Ryan 3.00 .90
4 Dave Stewart .20 .06
5 Fernando Valenzuela .20 .06
6 Andy Hawkins .10 .03
7 Melido Perez .10 .03
8 Terry Mulholland .10 .03
9 Dave Stieb .20 .06

1991 Fleer World Series

This eight-card set captures highlights from the 1990 World Series between the Cincinnati Reds and the Oakland Athletics. The set was only available as an insert with the 1991 Fleer factory sets. The standard-size cards have on the fronts color action photos, bordered in blue on a white card face. The words "World Series '90" appears in red and blue lettering above the pictures. The backs have a similar design, only with a summary of an aspect of the Series on a yellow background.

Nm-Mt Ex-Mt
COMPLETE SET (8) .75 .23
1 Eric Davis .10 .03
2 Billy Hatcher .05 .01
3 Jose Canseco .25 .07
4 Rickey Henderson .25 .07
5 Chris Sabo .05 .01
6 Dave Stewart .10 .03
7 Jose Rijo .05 .01
8 Reds Celebrate .05 .01

1991 Fleer Update

The 1991 Fleer Update set contains 132 standard-size cards. The cards were distributed exclusively in factory set form through hobby dealers. Card design is identical to regular issue 1991 Fleer cards with the notable bright yellow borders except for the U-prefixed numbering on back. The cards are ordered alphabetically by team. The key Rookie Cards in this set are Jeff Bagwell and Ivan Rodriguez.

Nm-Mt Ex-Mt
COMP.FACT.SET (132) 5.00 1.50
1 Glenn Davis .05 .02
2 Dwight Evans .10 .03
3 Jose Mesa .05 .02
4 Jack Clark .10 .03
5 Danny Darwin .05 .02
6 Steve Lyons .05 .02
7 Mo Vaughn .10 .03
8 Floyd Bannister .05 .02
9 Gary Gaetti .10 .03
10 Dave Parker .10 .03
11 Joey Cora .05 .02
12 Charlie Hough .10 .03
13 Matt Merullo .05 .02
14 Warren Newson .05 .02
15 Tim Raines .10 .03
16 Albert Belle .10 .03
17 Glenallen Hill .05 .02
18 Shawn Hillegas .05 .02
19 Mark Lewis .05 .02
20 Charles Nagy .05 .02
21 Mark Whiten .05 .02
22 John Cerutti .05 .02
23 Rob Deer .05 .02
24 Mickey Tettleton .05 .02
25 Warren Cromartie .05 .02
26 Kirk Gibson .10 .03
27 David Howard .05 .02
28 Brent Mayne .05 .02
29 Dante Bichette .10 .03
30 Mark Lee RC .05 .02
31 Julio Machado .05 .02
32 Edwin Nunez .05 .02
33 Willie Randolph .10 .03
34 Franklin Stubbs .05 .02
35 Bill Wegman .05 .02
36 Chili Davis .10 .03
37 Chuck Knoblauch .10 .03
38 Scott Leius .05 .02
39 Jack Morris .10 .03
40 Mike Pagliarulo .05 .02
41 Lenny Webster .05 .02
42 John Habyan .05 .02
43 Steve Howe .05 .02
44 Jeff Johnson .05 .02
45 Scott Kamieniecki RC .05 .02
46 Pat Kelly RC .05 .02
47 Hensley Meulens .05 .02
48 Wade Taylor .05 .02
49 Bernie Williams .25 .07
50 Kirk Dressendorfer RC .05 .02
51 Ernest Riles .05 .02
52 Rich DeLucia .05 .02
53 Tracy Jones .05 .02
54 Bill Krueger .05 .02
55 Alonzo Powell .05 .02
56 Jeff Schaefer .05 .02
57 Russ Swan .05 .02
58 John Barfield .05 .02
59 Rich Gossage .10 .03
60 Jose Guzman .05 .02
61 Dean Palmer .10 .03
62 Ivan Rodriguez RC 2.00 .60
63 Roberto Alomar .15 .04
64 Tom Candiotti .05 .02
65 Joe Carter .10 .03
66 Ed Sprague .05 .02
67 Pat Tabler .05 .02
68 Mike Timlin RC .15 .04
69 Devon White .10 .03
70 Rafael Belliard .05 .02
71 Juan Berenguer .05 .02
72 Sid Bream .05 .02
73 Marvin Freeman .05 .02
74 Kent Mercker .05 .02
75 Otis Nixon .05 .02
76 Terry Pendleton .10 .03
77 George Bell .05 .02
78 Danny Jackson .05 .02
79 Chuck McElroy .05 .02
80 Gary Scott .05 .02
81 Heathcliff Slocumb RC .10 .03
82 Dave Smith .05 .02
83 Rick Wilkins RC .05 .02
84 Freddie Benavides .05 .02
85 Ted Power .05 .02
86 Mo Sanford .05 .02
87 Jeff Bagwell RC 1.50 .45
88 Steve Finley .10 .03
89 Pete Harnisch .05 .02
90 Darryl Kile .10 .03
91 Brett Butler .10 .03
92 John Candelaria .05 .02
93 Gary Carter .10 .03
94 Kevin Gross .05 .02
95 Bob Ojeda .05 .02
96 Darryl Strawberry .10 .03
97 Ivan Calderon .05 .02
98 Ron Hassey .05 .02
99 Gilberto Reyes .05 .02
100 Hubie Brooks .05 .02
101 Rick Cerone .05 .02
102 Vince Coleman .05 .02
103 Jeff Innis .05 .02
104 Pete Schourek RC .05 .02
105 Andy Ashby RC .25 .07
106 Wally Backman .05 .02
107 Darrin Fletcher .05 .02
108 Tommy Greene .05 .02
109 John Morris .05 .02
110 Mitch Williams .05 .02
111 Lloyd McClendon .05 .02
112 Orlando Merced RC .05 .02
113 Vicente Palacios .05 .02
114 Gary Varsho .05 .02
115 John Wehner .05 .02
116 Rex Hudler .05 .02
117 Tim Jones .05 .02
118 Geronimo Pena .05 .02
119 Gerald Perry .05 .02
120 Larry Andersen .05 .02
121 Jerald Clark .05 .02
122 Scott Coolbaugh .05 .02
123 Tony Fernandez .05 .02
124 Darrin Jackson .05 .02
125 Fred McGriff .15 .04
126 Jose Mota RC .05 .02
127 Tim Teufel .05 .02
128 Bud Black .05 .02
129 Mike Felder .05 .02
130 Willie McGee .10 .03
131 Dave Righetti .10 .03
132 Checklist U1-U132 .05 .02

1992 Fleer

The 1992 Fleer set contains 720 standard-size cards issued in one comprehensive series. The cards were distributed in plastic wrapped packs, 35-card cello packs, 42-card rack packs and factory sets. The card fronts shade from metallic pale green to white as one moves down the face. The team logo and player's name appear to the right of the picture, running the length of the card. The cards are ordered alphabetically within and according to teams for each league with AL preceding NL. Topical subsets feature Major League Prospects (652-680), Record Setters (681-687), League Leaders (688-697), Super Star Specials (698-707) and Pro Visions (708-713). Rookie Cards include Scott Brosius and Vinny Castilla.

Nm-Mt Ex-Mt
COMPLETE SET (720) 10.00 3.00
COMP.HOBBY SET (732) 20.00 6.00
COMP.RETAIL SET (732) 20.00 6.00
1 Brady Anderson .10 .03
2 Jose Bautista .10 .03
3 Juan Bell .10 .03
4 Glenn Davis .10 .03
5 Mike Devereaux .10 .03
6 Dwight Evans .10 .03
7 Mike Flanagan .10 .03
8 Leo Gomez .10 .03
9 Chris Hoiles .10 .03
10 Sam Horn .10 .03
11 Tim Hulett .10 .03
12 Dave Johnson .10 .03
13 Chito Martinez .10 .03
14 Ben McDonald .10 .03
15 Bob Melvin .10 .03
16 Luis Mercedes .10 .03
17 Jose Mesa .10 .03
18 Bob Milacki .10 .03
19 Randy Milligan .10 .03
20 Mike Mussina UER .25 .07
(Card back refers to him as Jeff)
21 Gregg Olson .10 .03
22 Joe Orsulak .10 .03
23 Jim Poole .10 .03
24 Arthur Rhodes .10 .03
25 Billy Ripken .10 .03
26 Cal Ripken .75 .23
27 David Segui .10 .03
28 Roy Smith .10 .03
29 Anthony Telford .10 .03
30 Mark Williamson .10 .03
31 Craig Worthington .10 .03
32 Wade Boggs .15 .04
33 Tom Bolton .10 .03
34 Tom Brunansky .10 .03
35 Ellis Burks .10 .03
36 Jack Clark .10 .03
37 Roger Clemens .50 .15
38 Danny Darwin .10 .03
39 Mike Greenwell .10 .03
40 Joe Hesketh .10 .03
41 Daryl Irvine .10 .03
42 Dennis Lamp .10 .03
43 Tony Pena .10 .03
44 Phil Plantier .10 .03
45 Carlos Quintana .10 .03
46 Jeff Reardon .10 .03
47 Jody Reed .10 .03
48 Luis Rivera .10 .03
49 Mo Vaughn .15 .04
50 Jim Abbott .15 .04
51 Kyle Abbott .10 .03
52 Ruben Amaro .10 .03
53 Scott Bailes .10 .03
54 Chris Beasley .10 .03
55 Mark Eichhorn .10 .03
56 Mike Fetters .10 .03
57 Chuck Finley .10 .03
58 Gary Gaetti .10 .03
59 Dave Gallagher .10 .03
60 Donnie Hill .10 .03

61 Bryan Harvey UER .10 .03
(Lee Smith led the Majors with 47 saves)
62 Wally Joyner .10 .03
63 Mark Langston .10 .03
64 Kirk McCaskill .10 .03
65 John Orton .10 .03
66 Lance Parrish .10 .03
67 Luis Polonia .10 .03
68 Bobby Rose .10 .03
69 Dick Schofield .10 .03
70 Luis Sojo .10 .03
71 Lee Stevens .10 .03
72 Dave Winfield .10 .03
73 Cliff Young .10 .03
74 Wilson Alvarez .10 .03
75 Esteban Beltre .10 .03
76 Joey Cora .10 .03
77 Brian Drahman .10 .03
78 Alex Fernandez .10 .03
79 Carlton Fisk .15 .04
80 Scott Fletcher .10 .03
81 Craig Grebeck .10 .03
82 Ozzie Guillen .10 .03
83 Greg Hibbard .10 .03
84 Charlie Hough .10 .03
85 Mike Huff .10 .03
86 Bo Jackson .25 .07
87 Lance Johnson .10 .03
88 Ron Karkovice .10 .03
89 Jack McDowell .10 .03
90 Matt Merullo .10 .03
91 Warren Newson .10 .03
92 Donn Pall UER .10 .03
(Called Dunn on card back)
93 Dan Pasqua .10 .03
94 Ken Patterson .10 .03
95 Melido Perez .10 .03
96 Scott Radinsky .10 .03
97 Tim Raines .10 .03
98 Sammy Sosa .40 .12
99 Bobby Thigpen .10 .03
100 Frank Thomas .25 .07
101 Robin Ventura .10 .03
102 Mike Aldrete .10 .03
103 Sandy Alomar Jr. .10 .03
104 Carlos Baerga .10 .03
105 Albert Belle .10 .03
106 Willie Blair .10 .03
107 Jerry Browne .10 .03
108 Alex Cole .10 .03
109 Felix Fermin .10 .03
110 Glenallen Hill .10 .03
111 Shawn Hillegas .10 .03
112 Chris James .10 .03
113 Reggie Jefferson .10 .03
114 Doug Jones .10 .03
115 Eric King .10 .03
116 Mark Lewis .10 .03
117 Carlos Martinez .10 .03
118 Charles Nagy UER .10 .03
(Throws right, but card says left)
119 Rod Nichols .10 .03
120 Steve Olin .10 .03
121 Jesse Orosco .10 .03
122 Rudy Seanez .10 .03
123 Joel Skinner .10 .03
124 Greg Swindell .10 .03
125 Jim Thome .25 .07
126 Mark Whiten .10 .03
127 Scott Aldred .10 .03
128 Andy Allanson .10 .03
129 John Cerutti .10 .03
130 Milt Cuyler .10 .03
131 Mike Dalton .10 .03
132 Rob Deer .10 .03
133 Cecil Fielder .10 .03
134 Travis Fryman .10 .03
135 Dan Gakeler .10 .03
136 Paul Gibson .10 .03
137 Bill Gullickson .10 .03
138 Mike Henneman .10 .03
139 Pete Incaviglia .10 .03
140 Mark Leiter .10 .03
141 Scott Livingstone .10 .03
142 Lloyd Moseby .10 .03
143 Tony Phillips .10 .03
144 Mark Salas .10 .03
145 Frank Tanana .10 .03
146 Walt Terrell .10 .03
147 Mickey Tettleton .10 .03
148 Alan Trammell .10 .03
149 Lou Whitaker .10 .03
150 Kevin Appier .10 .03
151 Luis Aquino .10 .03
152 Todd Benzinger .10 .03
153 Mike Boddicker .10 .03
154 George Brett .60 .18
155 Storm Davis .10 .03
156 Jim Eisenreich .10 .03
157 Kirk Gibson .10 .03
158 Tom Gordon .10 .03
159 Mark Gubicza .10 .03
160 David Howard .10 .03
161 Mike Macfarlane .10 .03
162 Brent Mayne .10 .03
163 Brian McRae .10 .03
164 Jeff Montgomery .10 .03
165 Bill Pecota .10 .03
166 Harvey Pulliam .10 .03
167 Bret Saberhagen .10 .03
168 Kevin Seitzer .10 .03
169 Terry Shumpert .10 .03
170 Kurt Stillwell .10 .03
171 Danny Tartabull .10 .03
172 Gary Thurman .10 .03
173 Dante Bichette .10 .03
174 Kevin D. Brown .10 .03
175 Chuck Crim .10 .03
176 Jim Gantner .10 .03
177 Darryl Hamilton .10 .03
178 Ted Higuera .10 .03
179 Darren Holmes .10 .03
180 Mark Lee .10 .03
181 Julio Machado .10 .03
182 Paul Molitor .15 .04
183 Jaime Navarro .10 .03
184 Edwin Nunez .10 .03
185 Dan Plesac .10 .03
186 Willie Randolph .10 .03
187 Ron Robinson .10 .03
188 Gary Sheffield .10 .03
189 Bill Spiers .10 .03
190 B.J. Surhoff .10 .03
191 Dale Sveum .10 .03
192 Greg Vaughn .10 .03
193 Bill Wegman .10 .03
194 Robin Yount .40 .12
195 Rick Aguilera .10 .03
196 Allan Anderson .10 .03
197 Steve Bedrosian .10 .03
198 Randy Bush .10 .03
199 Larry Casian .10 .03
200 Chili Davis .10 .03
201 Scott Erickson .10 .03
202 Greg Gagne .10 .03
203 Dan Gladden .10 .03
204 Brian Harper .10 .03
205 Kent Hrbek .10 .03
206 C.Knoblauch UER .10 .03
Career hit total of 59 is wrong
207 Gene Larkin .10 .03
208 Terry Leach .10 .03
209 Scott Leius .10 .03
210 Shane Mack .10 .03
211 Jack Morris .10 .03
212 Pedro Munoz .10 .03
213 Denny Neagle .10 .03
214 Al Newman .10 .03
215 Junior Ortiz .10 .03
216 Mike Pagliarulo .10 .03
217 Kirby Puckett .25 .07
218 Paul Sorrento .10 .03
219 Kevin Tapani .10 .03
220 Lenny Webster .10 .03
221 Jesse Barfield .10 .03
222 Greg Cadaret .10 .03
223 Dave Eiland .10 .03
224 Alvaro Espinoza .10 .03
225 Steve Farr .10 .03
226 Bob Geren .10 .03
227 Lee Guetterman .10 .03
228 John Habyan .10 .03
229 Mel Hall .10 .03
230 Steve Howe .10 .03
231 Mike Humphreys .10 .03
232 Scott Kamieniecki .10 .03
233 Pat Kelly .10 .03
234 Roberto Kelly .10 .03
235 Tim Leary .10 .03
236 Kevin Maas .10 .03
237 Don Mattingly .60 .18
238 Hensley Meulens .10 .03
239 Matt Nokes .10 .03
240 Pascual Perez .10 .03
241 Eric Plunk .10 .03
242 John Ramos .10 .03
243 Scott Sanderson .10 .03
244 Steve Sax .10 .03
245 Wade Taylor .10 .03
246 Randy Velarde .10 .03
247 Bernie Williams .15 .04
248 Troy Afenir .10 .03
249 Harold Baines .10 .03
250 Lance Blankenship .10 .03
251 Mike Bordick .10 .03
252 Jose Canseco .25 .07
253 Steve Chitren .10 .03
254 Ron Darling .10 .03
255 Dennis Eckersley .10 .03
256 Mike Gallego .10 .03
257 Dave Henderson .10 .03
258 R.Henderson UER .25 .07
Wearing 24 on front and 22 on back
259 Rick Honeycutt .10 .03
260 Brook Jacoby .10 .03
261 Carney Lansford .10 .03
262 Mark McGwire .60 .18
263 Mike Moore .10 .03
264 Gene Nelson .10 .03
265 Jamie Quirk .10 .03
266 Joe Slusarski .10 .03
267 Terry Steinbach .10 .03
268 Dave Stewart .10 .03
269 Todd Van Poppel .10 .03
270 Walt Weiss .10 .03
271 Bob Welch .10 .03
272 Curt Young .10 .03
273 Scott Bradley .10 .03
274 Greg Briley .10 .03
275 Jay Buhner .10 .03
276 Henry Cotto .10 .03
277 Alvin Davis .10 .03
278 Rich DeLucia .10 .03
279 Ken Griffey Jr. .40 .12
280 Erik Hanson .10 .03
281 Brian Holman .10 .03
282 Mike Jackson .10 .03
283 Randy Johnson .25 .07
284 Tracy Jones .10 .03
285 Bill Krueger .10 .03
286 Edgar Martinez .15 .04
287 Tino Martinez .15 .04
288 Rob Murphy .10 .03
289 Pete O'Brien .10 .03
290 Alonzo Powell .10 .03
291 Harold Reynolds .10 .03
292 Mike Schooler .10 .03
293 Russ Swan .10 .03
294 Bill Swift .10 .03
295 Dave Valle .10 .03
296 Omar Vizquel .15 .04
297 Gerald Alexander .10 .03
298 Brad Arnsberg .10 .03
299 Kevin Brown .10 .03
300 Jack Daugherty .10 .03
301 Mario Diaz .10 .03
302 Brian Downing .10 .03
303 Julio Franco .10 .03
304 Juan Gonzalez .15 .04
305 Rich Gossage .10 .03
306 Jose Guzman .10 .03
307 Jose Hernandez RC .40 .12
308 Jeff Huson .10 .03
309 Mike Jeffcoat .10 .03
310 Terry Mathews .10 .03
311 Rafael Palmeiro .15 .04
312 Dean Palmer .10 .03
313 Geno Petralli .10 .03
314 Gary Pettis .10 .03
315 Kevin Reimer .10 .03
316 Ivan Rodriguez .25 .07
317 Kenny Rogers .10 .03
318 Wayne Rosenthal .10 .03
319 Jeff Russell .10 .03
320 Nolan Ryan 1.00 .30
321 Ruben Sierra .10 .03
322 Jim Acker .10 .03
323 Roberto Alomar .15 .04
324 Derek Bell .10 .03
325 Pat Borders .10 .03
326 Tom Candiotti .10 .03
327 Joe Carter .10 .03
328 Rob Ducey .10 .03
329 Kelly Gruber .10 .03
330 Juan Guzman .10 .03
331 Tom Henke .10 .03
332 Jimmy Key .10 .03
333 Manny Lee .10 .03
334 Al Leiter .10 .03
335 Bob MacDonald .10 .03
336 Candy Maldonado .10 .03
337 Rance Mulliniks .10 .03
338 Greg Myers .10 .03
339 John Olerud UER .10 .03
(1991 BA has .256, but text says .258)
340 Ed Sprague .10 .03
341 Dave Stieb .10 .03
342 Todd Stottlemyre .10 .03
343 Mike Timlin .10 .03
344 Duane Ward .10 .03
345 David Wells .10 .03
346 Devon White .10 .03
347 Mookie Wilson .10 .03
348 Eddie Zosky .10 .03
349 Steve Avery .10 .03
350 Mike Bell .10 .03
351 Rafael Belliard .10 .03
352 Juan Berenguer .10 .03
353 Jeff Blauser .10 .03
354 Sid Bream .10 .03
355 Francisco Cabrera .10 .03
356 Marvin Freeman .10 .03
357 Ron Gant .10 .03
358 Tom Glavine .15 .04
359 Brian Hunter .10 .03
360 Dave Justice .10 .03
361 Charlie Leibrandt .10 .03
362 Mark Lemke .10 .03
363 Kent Mercker .10 .03
364 Keith Mitchell .10 .03
365 Greg Olson .10 .03
366 Terry Pendleton .10 .03
367 Armando Reynoso RC .25 .07
368 Deion Sanders .15 .04
369 Lonnie Smith .10 .03
370 Pete Smith .10 .03
371 John Smoltz .15 .04
372 Mike Stanton .10 .03
373 Jeff Treadway .10 .03
374 Mark Wohlers .10 .03
375 Paul Assenmacher .10 .03
376 George Bell .10 .03
377 Shawn Boskie .10 .03
378 Frank Castillo .10 .03
379 Andre Dawson .10 .03
380 Shawon Dunston .10 .03
381 Mark Grace .15 .04
382 Mike Harkey .10 .03
383 Danny Jackson .10 .03
384 Les Lancaster .10 .03
385 Ced Landrum .10 .03
386 Greg Maddux .40 .12
387 Derrick May .10 .03
388 Chuck McElroy .10 .03
389 Ryne Sandberg .40 .12
390 Heathcliff Slocumb .10 .03
391 Dave Smith .10 .03
392 Dwight Smith .10 .03
393 Rick Sutcliffe .10 .03
394 Hector Villanueva .10 .03
395 Chico Walker .10 .03
396 Jerome Walton .10 .03
397 Rick Wilkins .10 .03
398 Jack Armstrong .10 .03
399 Freddie Benavides .10 .03
400 Glenn Braggs .10 .03
401 Tom Browning .10 .03
402 Norm Charlton .10 .03
403 Eric Davis .10 .03
404 Rob Dibble .10 .03
405 Bill Doran .10 .03
406 Mariano Duncan .10 .03
407 Kip Gross .10 .03
408 Chris Hammond .10 .03
409 Billy Hatcher .10 .03
410 Chris Jones .10 .03
411 Barry Larkin .15 .04
412 Hal Morris .10 .03
413 Randy Myers .10 .03
414 Joe Oliver .10 .03
415 Paul O'Neill .15 .04
416 Ted Power .10 .03
417 Luis Quinones .10 .03
418 Jeff Reed .10 .03
419 Jose Rijo .10 .03
420 Chris Sabo .10 .03
421 Reggie Sanders .10 .03
422 Scott Scudder .10 .03
423 Glenn Sutko .10 .03
424 Eric Anthony .10 .03
425 Jeff Bagwell .25 .07
426 Craig Biggio .15 .04
427 Ken Caminiti .10 .03
428 Casey Candaele .10 .03
429 Mike Capel .10 .03
430 Andujar Cedeno .10 .03
431 Jim Corsi .10 .03
432 Mark Davidson .10 .03
433 Steve Finley .10 .03
434 Luis Gonzalez .10 .03
435 Pete Harnisch .10 .03
436 Dwayne Henry .10 .03
437 Xavier Hernandez .10 .03
438 Jimmy Jones .10 .03
439 Darryl Kile .10 .03
440 Rob Mallicoat .10 .03
441 Andy Mota .10 .03
442 Al Osuna .10 .03
443 Mark Portugal .10 .03
444 Scott Servais .10 .03
445 Mike Simms .10 .03
446 Gerald Young .10 .03
447 Tim Belcher .10 .03
448 Brett Butler .10 .03
449 John Candelaria .10 .03
450 Gary Carter .10 .03
451 Dennis Cook .10 .03
452 Tim Crews .10 .03
453 Kal Daniels .10 .03
454 Jim Gott .10 .03
455 Alfredo Griffin .10 .03
456 Kevin Gross .10 .03
457 Chris Gwynn .10 .03
458 Lenny Harris .10 .03
459 Orel Hershiser .10 .03
460 Jay Howell .10 .03
461 Stan Javier .10 .03
462 Eric Karros .10 .03
463 Ramon Martinez UER .10 .03
(Card says bats right, should be left)
464 Roger McDowell UER .10 .03
(Wins add up to 54, totals have 51)
465 Mike Morgan .10 .03
466 Eddie Murray .25 .07
467 Jose Offerman .10 .03
468 Bob Ojeda .10 .03
469 Juan Samuel .10 .03
470 Mike Scioscia .10 .03
471 Darryl Strawberry .10 .03
472 Bret Barberie .10 .03
473 Brian Barnes .10 .03
474 Eric Bullock .10 .03
475 Ivan Calderon .10 .03
476 Delino DeShields .10 .03
477 Jeff Fassero .10 .03
478 Mike Fitzgerald .10 .03
479 Steve Frey .10 .03
480 Andres Galarraga .10 .03
481 Mark Gardner .10 .03
482 Marquis Grissom .10 .03
483 Chris Haney .10 .03
484 Barry Jones .10 .03
485 Dave Martinez .10 .03
486 Dennis Martinez .10 .03
487 Chris Nabholz .10 .03
488 Spike Owen .10 .03
489 Gilberto Reyes .10 .03
490 Mel Rojas .10 .03
491 Scott Ruskin .10 .03
492 Bill Sampen .10 .03
493 Larry Walker .15 .04
494 Tim Wallach .10 .03
495 Daryl Boston .10 .03
496 Hubie Brooks .10 .03
497 Tim Burke .10 .03
498 Mark Carreon .10 .03
499 Tony Castillo .10 .03
500 Vince Coleman .10 .03
501 David Cone .10 .03
502 Kevin Elster .10 .03
503 Sid Fernandez .10 .03
504 John Franco .10 .03
505 Dwight Gooden .10 .03
506 Todd Hundley .10 .03
507 Jeff Innis .10 .03
508 Gregg Jefferies .10 .03
509 Howard Johnson .10 .03
510 Dave Magadan .10 .03
511 Terry McDaniel .10 .03
512 Kevin McReynolds .10 .03
513 Keith Miller .10 .03
514 Charlie O'Brien .10 .03
515 Mackey Sasser .10 .03
516 Pete Schourek .10 .03
517 Julio Valera .10 .03
518 Frank Viola .10 .03
519 Wally Whitehurst .10 .03
520 Anthony Young .10 .03
521 Andy Ashby .10 .03
522 Kim Batiste .10 .03
523 Joe Boever .10 .03
524 Wes Chamberlain .10 .03
525 Pat Combs .10 .03
526 Danny Cox .10 .03
527 Darren Daulton .10 .03
528 Jose DeJesus .10 .03
529 Len Dykstra .10 .03
530 Darrin Fletcher .10 .03
531 Tommy Greene .10 .03
532 Jason Grimsley .10 .03
533 Charlie Hayes .10 .03
534 Von Hayes .10 .03
535 Dave Hollins .10 .03
536 Ricky Jordan .10 .03
537 John Kruk .10 .03
538 Jim Lindeman .10 .03
539 Mickey Morandini .10 .03
540 Terry Mulholland .10 .03
541 Dale Murphy .25 .07
542 Randy Ready .10 .03
543 Wally Ritchie UER .10 .03
(Letters in data are cut off on card)
544 Bruce Ruffin .10 .03
545 Steve Searcy .10 .03
546 Dickie Thon .10 .03
547 Mitch Williams .10 .03
548 Stan Belinda .10 .03
549 Jay Bell .10 .03
550 Barry Bonds .60 .18
551 Bobby Bonilla .10 .03
552 Steve Buechele .10 .03
553 Doug Drabek .10 .03
554 Neal Heaton .10 .03
555 Jeff King .10 .03
556 Bob Kipper .10 .03
557 Bill Landrum .10 .03
558 Mike LaValliere .10 .03
559 Jose Lind .10 .03
560 Lloyd McClendon .10 .03
561 Orlando Merced .10 .03
562 Bob Patterson .10 .03
563 Joe Redfield .10 .03
564 Gary Redus .10 .03
565 Rosario Rodriguez .10 .03
566 Don Slaught .10 .03
567 John Smiley .10 .03
568 Zane Smith .10 .03
569 Randy Tomlin .10 .03
570 Andy Van Slyke .10 .03
571 Gary Varsho .10 .03
572 Bob Walk .10 .03
573 John Wehner UER .10 .03
(Actually played for Carolina in 1991, not Cards)
574 Juan Agosto .10 .03
575 Cris Carpenter .10 .03
576 Jose DeLeon .10 .03
577 Rich Gedman .10 .03
578 Bernard Gilkey .10 .03
579 Pedro Guerrero .10 .03
580 Ken Hill .10 .03
581 Rex Hudler .10 .03
582 Felix Jose .10 .03
583 Ray Lankford .10 .03
584 Omar Olivares .10 .03
585 Jose Oquendo .10 .03
586 Tom Pagnozzi .10 .03
587 Geronimo Pena .10 .03
588 Mike Perez .10 .03
589 Gerald Perry .10 .03
590 Bryn Smith .10 .03
591 Lee Smith .10 .03
592 Ozzie Smith .40 .12
593 Scott Terry .10 .03
594 Bob Tewksbury .10 .03
595 Milt Thompson .10 .03
596 Todd Zeile .10 .03
597 Larry Andersen .10 .03
598 Oscar Azocar .10 .03
599 Andy Benes .10 .03
600 Ricky Bones .10 .03
601 Jerald Clark .10 .03
602 Pat Clements .10 .03
603 Paul Faries .10 .03
604 Tony Fernandez .10 .03
605 Tony Gwynn .30 .09
606 Greg W. Harris .10 .03
607 Thomas Howard .10 .03
608 Bruce Hurst .10 .03
609 Darrin Jackson .10 .03
610 Tom Lampkin .10 .03
611 Craig Lefferts .10 .03
612 Jim Lewis RC .10 .03
613 Mike Maddux .10 .03
614 Fred McGriff .15 .04
615 Jose Melendez .10 .03
616 Jose Mota .10 .03
617 Dennis Rasmussen .10 .03
618 Bip Roberts .10 .03
619 Rich Rodriguez .10 .03
620 Benito Santiago .10 .03
621 Craig Shipley .10 .03
622 Tim Teufel .10 .03
623 Kevin Ward .10 .03
624 Ed Whitson .10 .03
625 Dave Anderson .10 .03
626 Kevin Bass .10 .03
627 Rod Beck RC .40 .12
628 Bud Black .10 .03
629 Jeff Brantley .10 .03
630 John Burkett .10 .03
631 Will Clark .25 .07
632 Royce Clayton .10 .03
633 Steve Decker .10 .03
634 Kelly Downs .10 .03
635 Mike Felder .10 .03
636 Scott Garrelts .10 .03
637 Eric Gunderson .10 .03
638 Bryan Hickerson RC .10 .03
639 Darren Lewis .10 .03
640 Greg Litton .10 .03
641 Kirt Manwaring .10 .03
642 Paul McClellan .10 .03
643 Willie McGee .10 .03
644 Kevin Mitchell .10 .03
645 Francisco Oliveras .10 .03
646 Mike Remlinger .10 .03
647 Dave Righetti .10 .03
648 Robby Thompson .10 .03
649 Jose Uribe .10 .03
650 Matt Williams .10 .03
651 Trevor Wilson .10 .03
652 T.Goodwin MLP UER .10 .03
Timed in 3.5, should be be timed
653 Terry Bross MLP .10 .03
654 M.Christopher MLP .10 .03
655 Kenny Lofton MLP .15 .04
656 Chris Cron MLP .10 .03
657 Willie Banks MLP .10 .03
658 Pat Rice MLP .10 .03
659A R.Maurer MLP ERR .75 .23
Name misspelled as Mauer on card front
659B R.Maurer MLP COR .10 .03
660 Don Harris MLP .10 .03
661 Henry Rodriguez MLP .10 .03
662 Cliff Brantley MLP .10 .03
663 M.Linskey MLP UER .10 .03
220 pounds in data, 200 in text
664 Gary DiSarcina MLP .10 .03
665 Gil Heredia RC .25 .07
666 V.Castilla MLP RC .75 .23
667 Paul Abbott MLP .10 .03
668 M.Fariss MLP UER .10 .03
Called Paul on back
669 Jarvis Brown MLP .10 .03
670 Wayne Kirby MLP RC .10 .03
671 S.Brosius MLP RC .40 .12
672 Bob Hamelin MLP .10 .03
673 Joel Johnston MLP .10 .03
674 Tim Spehr MLP .10 .03
675A J.Gardner MLP ERR .75 .23
P on front,

should be SS
675B Jeff Gardner MLP COR .10 .03
676 Rico Rossy MLP .10 .03
677 R.Hernandez MLP RC .10 .03
678 Ted Wood MLP .10 .03
679 Cal Eldred MLP .10 .03
680 Sean Berry MLP .10 .03
681 Rickey Henderson RS .15 .04
682 Nolan Ryan RS .50 .15
683 Dennis Martinez RS .10 .03
684 Wilson Alvarez RS .10 .03
685 Joe Carter RS .10 .03
686 Dave Winfield RS .10 .03
687 David Cone RS .10 .03
688 Jose Canseco LL UER .10 .03
(Text on back has 42 stolen bases in '88; should be 40)
689 Howard Johnson LL .10 .03
690 Julio Franco LL .10 .03
691 Terry Pendleton LL .10 .03
692 Cecil Fielder LL .10 .03
693 Scott Erickson LL .10 .03
694 Tom Glavine LL .10 .03
695 Dennis Martinez LL .10 .03
696 Bryan Harvey LL .10 .03
697 Lee Smith LL .10 .03
698 Roberto Alomar .10 .03
Sandy Alomar Jr.
699 Bobby Bonilla .10 .03
Will Clark
700 Mark Wohlers .10 .03
Kent Mercker
Alejandro Pena
701 Stacy Jones .15 .04
Bo Jackson
Gregg Olson
Frank Thomas
702 Paul Molitor .15 .04
Brett Butler
703 Cal Ripken .40 .12
Joe Carter
704 Barry Larkin .15 .04
Kirby Puckett
705 Mo Vaughn .10 .03
Cecil Fielder
706 Ramon Martinez .10 .03
Ozzie Guillen
707 Harold Baines .10 .03
Wade Boggs
708 Robin Yount PV .25 .07
709 K.Griffey Jr. PV UER .25 .07
Missing quotations on back; BA has .322, but was actually .327
710 Nolan Ryan PV .50 .15
711 Cal Ripken PV .40 .12
712 Frank Thomas PV .15 .04
713 Dave Justice PV .10 .03
714 Checklist 1-101 .10 .03
715 Checklist 102-194 .10 .03
716 Checklist 195-296 .10 .03
717 Checklist 297-397 .10 .03
718 Checklist 398-494 .10 .03
719 Checklist 495-596 .10 .03
720A CL 597-720 ERR .10 .03
659 Rob Mauer
720B CL 597-720 COR .10 .03
659 Rob Maurer

1992 Fleer All-Stars

Cards from this 24-card standard-size set were randomly inserted in plastic wrap packs. Selected members of the American and National League 1991 All-Star squads comprise this set.

Nm-Mt Ex-Mt
COMPLETE SET (24) 30.00 9.00
1 Felix Jose .75 .23
2 Tony Gwynn 2.50 .75
3 Barry Bonds 5.00 1.50
4 Bobby Bonilla .75 .23
5 Mike LaValliere .75 .23
6 Tom Glavine 1.25 .35
7 Ramon Martinez .75 .23
8 Lee Smith .75 .23
9 Mickey Tettleton .75 .23
10 Scott Erickson .75 .23
11 Frank Thomas 2.00 .60
12 Danny Tartabull .75 .23
13 Will Clark 2.00 .60
14 Ryne Sandberg 3.00 .90
15 Terry Pendleton .75 .23
16 Barry Larkin 1.25 .35
17 Rafael Palmeiro 1.25 .35
18 Julio Franco .75 .23
19 Robin Ventura .75 .23
20 Cal Ripken UER 6.00 1.80
(Candidte; total bases misspelled as based)
21 Joe Carter .75 .23
22 Kirby Puckett 2.00 .60
23 Ken Griffey Jr. 3.00 .90
24 Jose Canseco 2.00 .60

1992 Fleer Clemens

Roger Clemens served as a spokesperson for Fleer during 1992 and was the exclusive subject of this 15-card standard-size set. The first 12-card Clemens "Career Highlights" subseries was randomly inserted in 1992 Fleer packs. Two-thousand signed cards were randomly inserted in wax packs and could also be won by entering a drawing. However, these cards are uncertifiable as they do not have any distinguishable marks. Moreover, a three-card Clemens subset (13-15) was available through a special mail-in offer. The glossy color photos on the fronts are

bordered in black and accented with gold stripes and lettering on the top of the card.

Nm-Mt Ex-Mt
COMPLETE SET (12) 12.00 3.60
COMMON CARD (1-12) 1.00 .30
COMMON MAIL (13-15) 1.00 .30
AU Roger Clemens AU 60.00 18.00
Uncertified Signature
NNO Roger Clemens 6.00 1.80
Paul Mullan Promo

1992 Fleer Lumber Company

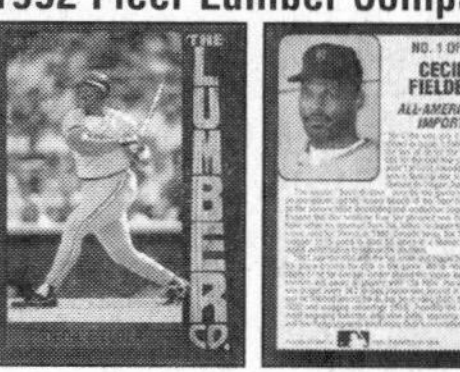

The 1992 Fleer Lumber Company standard-size set features nine outstanding hitters in Major League Baseball. This set was only available as a bonus in Fleer hobby factory sets.

Nm-Mt Ex-Mt
COMPLETE SET (9) 10.00 3.00
L1 Cecil Fielder .75 .23
L2 Mickey Tettleton .75 .23
L3 Darryl Strawberry .75 .23
L4 Ryne Sandberg 3.00 .90
L5 Jose Canseco 2.00 .60
L6 Matt Williams UER .75 .23
In 17th line, cycle is spelled cyle
L7 Cal Ripken 6.00 1.80
L8 Barry Bonds 5.00 1.50
L9 Ron Gant .75 .23

1992 Fleer Rookie Sensations

Cards from the 20-card Fleer Rookie Sensations set were randomly inserted in 1992 Fleer 35-card cello packs. The cards were extremely popular upon release resulting in packs selling for levels far above suggested retail levels. The glossy color photos on the fronts have a white border on a royal blue card face. The words "Rookie Sensations" appear above the picture in gold foil lettering, while the player's name appears on a gold foil plaque beneath the picture. Through a mail-in offer for ten Fleer baseball card wrappers and 1.00 for postage and handling, Fleer offered an uncut 8 1/2" by 11" numbered promo sheet picturing ten of the 20-card set on each side in a reduced-size front-only format. The offer indicated an expiration date of July 31, 1992, or whenever the production quantity of 250,000 sheets was exhausted.

Nm-Mt Ex-Mt
COMPLETE SET (20) 50.00 15.00
1 Frank Thomas 5.00 1.50
2 Todd Van Poppel 1.50 .45
3 Orlando Merced 1.50 .45
4 Jeff Bagwell 5.00 1.50
5 Jeff Fassero 1.50 .45
6 Darren Lewis 1.50 .45
7 Milt Cuyler 1.50 .45
8 Mike Timlin 1.50 .45
9 Brian McRae 1.50 .45
10 Chuck Knoblauch 2.00 .60
11 Rich DeLucia 1.50 .45
12 Ivan Rodriguez 5.00 1.50
13 Juan Guzman 1.50 .45
14 Steve Chitren 1.50 .45
15 Mark Wohlers 1.50 .45
16 Wes Chamberlain 1.50 .45
17 Ray Lankford 1.50 .45
18 Chito Martinez 1.50 .45
19 Phil Plantier 1.50 .45
20 Scott Leius UER 1.50 .45
(Misspelled Lieus on card front)

1992 Fleer Smoke 'n Heat

This 12-card standard-size set features outstanding major league pitchers, especially the premier fastball pitchers in both leagues. These cards were only available in Fleer's 1992 Christmas factory set.

Nm-Mt Ex-Mt
COMPLETE SET (12) 10.00 3.00
S1 Lee Smith .75 .23
S2 Jack McDowell .75 .23
S3 David Cone .75 .23
S4 Roger Clemens 4.00 1.20
S5 Nolan Ryan 8.00 2.40
S6 Scott Erickson .75 .23
S7 Tom Glavine 1.25 .35
S8 Dwight Gooden .75 .23
S9 Andy Benes .75 .23
S10 Steve Avery .75 .23
S11 Randy Johnson 2.00 .60
S12 Jim Abbott 1.25 .35

1992 Fleer Team Leaders

Cards from the 20-card Fleer Team Leaders set were randomly inserted in 1992 Fleer 42-card rack packs.

Nm-Mt Ex-Mt
COMPLETE SET (20) 40.00 12.00
1 Don Mattingly 10.00 3.00
2 Howard Johnson 1.50 .45
3 Chris Sabo UER 1.50 .45
(Where he it, should be Where he hit)
4 Carlton Fisk 2.50 .75
5 Kirby Puckett 4.00 1.20
6 Cecil Fielder 1.50 .45
7 Tony Gwynn 5.00 1.50
8 Will Clark 4.00 1.20
9 Bobby Bonilla 1.50 .45
10 Len Dykstra 1.50 .45
11 Tom Glavine 2.50 .75
12 Rafael Palmeiro 2.50 .75
13 Wade Boggs 2.50 .75
14 Joe Carter 1.50 .45
15 Ken Griffey Jr. 6.00 1.80
16 Darryl Strawberry 1.50 .45
17 Cal Ripken 12.00 3.60
18 Danny Tartabull 1.50 .45
19 Jose Canseco 4.00 1.20
20 Andre Dawson 1.50 .45

1992 Fleer Update

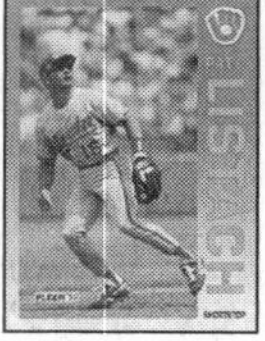

The 1992 Fleer Update set contains 132 standard-size cards. Cards were distributed exclusively in factory sets through hobby dealers. Factory sets included a four-card, black-bordered '92 Headliners' insert set for a total of 136 cards. Due to lackluster retail response for previous Fleer Update sets, wholesale orders for this product were low, resulting in a short print run. As word got out that the cards were in short supply, the secondary market prices soared not soon after release. The basic card design is identical to the regular issue 1992 Fleer cards except for the U-prefixed numbering on back. The cards are checklisted alphabetically within and according to teams for each league with AL preceding NL. Rookie Cards in this set include Jeff Kent and Mike Piazza. The Piazza card is widely recognized as one of the more desirable singles issued in the 1990's.

Nm-Mt Ex-Mt
COMP.FACT.SET (136) 100.00 30.00
COMPLETE SET (132) 80.00 24.00
1 Todd Frohwirth .50 .15
2 Alan Mills .50 .15
3 Rick Sutcliffe 1.00 .30
4 John Valentin RC 1.50 .45
5 Frank Viola 1.00 .30
6 Bob Zupcic RC .50 .15
7 Mike Butcher .50 .15
8 Chad Curtis RC 1.50 .45
9 Damion Easley RC 1.50 .45
10 Tim Salmon 2.50 .75
11 Julio Valera .50 .15
12 George Bell .50 .15
13 Roberto Hernandez .50 .15
14 Shawn Jeter RC .50 .15
15 Thomas Howard .50 .15
16 Jesse Levis .50 .15
17 Kenny Lofton 1.50 .45
18 Paul Sorrento .50 .15
19 Rico Brogna .50 .15
20 John Doherty RC .50 .15
21 Dan Gladden .50 .15
22 Buddy Groom RC .50 .15
23 Shawn Hare RC .50 .15
24 John Kiely .50 .15
25 Kurt Knudsen .50 .15
26 Gregg Jefferies .50 .15
27 Wally Joyner 1.00 .30
28 Kevin Koslofski .50 .15
29 Kevin McReynolds .50 .15
30 Rusty Meacham .50 .15
31 Keith Miller .50 .15
32 Hipolito Pichardo RC .50 .15
33 Jim Austin .50 .15
34 Scott Fletcher .50 .15
35 John Jaha RC 1.50 .45
36 Pat Listach RC 1.50 .45
37 Dave Nilsson .50 .15
38 Kevin Seitzer .50 .15
39 Tom Edens .50 .15
40 Pat Mahomes RC 1.50 .45
41 John Smiley .50 .15
42 Charlie Hayes .50 .15
43 Sam Militello .50 .15
44 Andy Stankiewicz .50 .15
45 Danny Tartabull .50 .15
46 Bob Wickman .50 .15
47 Jerry Browne .50 .15
48 Kevin Campbell .50 .15
49 Vince Horsman .50 .15
50 Troy Neel RC .50 .15
51 Ruben Sierra .50 .15
52 Bruce Walton .50 .15
53 Willie Wilson .50 .15
54 Bret Boone 2.50 .75
55 Dave Fleming .50 .15
56 Kevin Mitchell .50 .15
57 Jeff Nelson RC 2.50 .75
58 Shane Turner .50 .15
59 Jose Canseco 2.50 .75
60 Jeff Frye RC .50 .15
61 Danny Leon .50 .15
62 Roger Pavlik RC .50 .15
63 David Cone 1.00 .30
64 Pat Hentgen .50 .15
65 Randy Knorr .50 .15
66 Jack Morris 1.00 .30
67 Dave Winfield 1.00 .30
68 David Nied RC .50 .15
69 Otis Nixon .50 .15
70 Alejandro Pena .50 .15
71 Jeff Reardon 1.00 .30
72 Alex Arias RC .50 .15
73 Jim Bullinger .50 .15
74 Mike Morgan .50 .15
75 Rey Sanchez RC 1.50 .45
76 Bob Scanlan .50 .15
77 Sammy Sosa 4.00 1.20
78 Scott Bankhead .50 .15
79 Tim Belcher .50 .15
80 Steve Foster .50 .15
81 Willie Greene .50 .15
82 Bip Roberts .50 .15
83 Scott Ruskin .50 .15
84 Greg Swindell .50 .15
85 Juan Guerrero .50 .15
86 Butch Henry .50 .15
87 Doug Jones .50 .15
88 Brian Williams RC .50 .15
89 Tom Candiotti .50 .15
90 Eric Davis 1.00 .30
91 Carlos Hernandez .50 .15
92 Mike Piazza RC 60.00 18.00
93 Mike Sharperson .50 .15
94 Eric Young RC 1.50 .45
95 Moises Alou 1.00 .30
96 Greg Colbrunn .50 .15
97 Wil Cordero .50 .15
98 Ken Hill .50 .15
99 John Vander Wal RC 1.50 .45
100 John Wetteland 1.00 .30
101 Bobby Bonilla 1.00 .30
102 Eric Hillman RC .50 .15
103 Pat Howell .50 .15
104 Jeff Kent RC 10.00 3.00
105 Dick Schofield .50 .15
106 Ryan Thompson RC .50 .15
107 Chico Walker .50 .15
108 Juan Bell .50 .15
109 Mariano Duncan .50 .15
110 Jeff Grotewold .50 .15
111 Ben Rivera .50 .15
112 Curt Schilling 1.50 .45
113 Victor Cole .50 .15
114 Al Martin RC 1.50 .45
115 Roger Mason .50 .15
116 Blas Minor .50 .15
117 Tim Wakefield RC 5.00 1.50
118 Mark Clark RC .50 .15
119 Rheal Cormier .50 .15
120 Donovan Osborne .50 .15
121 Todd Worrell .50 .15
122 Jeremy Hernandez RC .50 .15
123 Randy Myers .50 .15
124 Frank Seminara RC .50 .15
125 Gary Sheffield 1.00 .30
126 Dan Walters .50 .15
127 Steve Hosey .50 .15
128 Mike Jackson .50 .15
129 Jim Pena .50 .15
130 Cory Snyder .50 .15
131 Bill Swift .50 .15
132 Checklist U1-U132 .50 .15

1992 Fleer Update Headliners

Each 1992 Fleer Update factory set included a four-card set of Headliner inserts. The cards are numbered separately and have a completely different design to the base cards. Each Headliner features UV coating and black borders. The set features a selection of stars that made headlines in the 1991 season. Cards are numbered on back X of 4.

Nm-Mt Ex-Mt
COMPLETE SET (4) 8.00 2.40
1 Ken Griffey Jr. 3.00 .90
2 Robin Yount 3.00 .90
3 Jeff Reardon .75 .23
4 Cecil Fielder .75 .23

1993 Fleer

The 720-card 1993 Fleer baseball set contains two series of 360 standard-size cards. Cards were distributed in plastic wrapped packs, cello packs, jumbo packs and rack packs. For the first time in years, Fleer did not issue a factory set. In fact, Fleer discontinued issuing factory sets from 1993 through 1998. The cards are checklisted below alphabetically within and according to teams for each league with NL preceding AL. Topical subsets include League Leaders (344-348/704-708), Round Trippers (349-353/709-713), and Super Star Specials (354-357/714-717). Each series concludes with checklists (358-360/718-720). There are no key Rookie Cards in this set.

Nm-Mt Ex-Mt
COMPLETE SET (720) 40.00 12.00
COMP.SERIES 1 (360) 20.00 6.00
COMP.SERIES 2 (360) 20.00 6.00
1 Steve Avery .10 .03
2 Sid Bream .10 .03
3 Ron Gant .20 .06
4 Tom Glavine .30 .09
5 Brian Hunter .10 .03
6 Ryan Klesko .20 .06
7 Charlie Leibrandt .10 .03
8 Kent Mercker .10 .03
9 David Nied .10 .03
10 Otis Nixon .10 .03
11 Greg Olson .10 .03
12 Terry Pendleton .20 .06
13 Deion Sanders .30 .09
14 John Smoltz .30 .09
15 Mike Stanton .10 .03
16 Mark Wohlers .10 .03
17 Paul Assenmacher .10 .03
18 Steve Buechele .10 .03
19 Shawon Dunston .10 .03
20 Mark Grace .30 .09
21 Derrick May .10 .03
22 Chuck McElroy .10 .03
23 Mike Morgan .10 .03
24 Rey Sanchez .10 .03
25 Ryne Sandberg .75 .23
26 Bob Scanlan .10 .03
27 Sammy Sosa .75 .23
28 Rick Wilkins .10 .03
29 Bobby Ayala RC .10 .03
30 Tim Belcher .10 .03
31 Jeff Branson .10 .03
32 Norm Charlton .10 .03
33 Steve Foster .10 .03
34 Willie Greene .10 .03
35 Chris Hammond .10 .03
36 Milt Hill .10 .03
37 Hal Morris .10 .03
38 Joe Oliver .10 .03
39 Paul O'Neill .30 .09
40 Tim Pugh RC .10 .03
41 Jose Rijo .10 .03
42 Bip Roberts .10 .03
43 Chris Sabo .10 .03
44 Reggie Sanders .10 .03
45 Eric Anthony .10 .03
46 Jeff Bagwell .30 .09
47 Craig Biggio .30 .09
48 Joe Boever .10 .03
49 Casey Candaele .10 .03
50 Steve Finley .20 .06
51 Luis Gonzalez .20 .06
52 Pete Harnisch .10 .03
53 Xavier Hernandez .10 .03
54 Doug Jones .10 .03
55 Eddie Taubensee .10 .03
56 Brian Williams .10 .03
57 Pedro Astacio .10 .03
58 Todd Benzinger .10 .03
59 Brett Butler .20 .06
60 Tom Candiotti .10 .03
61 Lenny Harris .10 .03
62 Carlos Hernandez .10 .03
63 Orel Hershiser .20 .06
64 Eric Karros .20 .06
65 Ramon Martinez .10 .03
66 Jose Offerman .10 .03
67 Mike Scioscia .10 .03
68 Mike Sharperson .10 .03
69 Eric Young .10 .03
70 Moises Alou .20 .06
71 Ivan Calderon .10 .03
72 Archi Cianfrocco .10 .03
73 Wil Cordero .10 .03
74 Delino DeShields .10 .03
75 Mark Gardner .10 .03
76 Ken Hill .10 .03
77 Tim Laker RC .10 .03
78 Chris Nabholz .10 .03
79 Mel Rojas .10 .03
80 John Vander Wal UER .10 .03
(Misspelled Vander Wall in letters on back)
81 Larry Walker .30 .09
82 Tim Wallach .10 .03
83 John Wetteland .20 .06
84 Bobby Bonilla .20 .06
85 Daryl Boston .10 .03
86 Sid Fernandez .10 .03
87 Eric Hillman .10 .03
88 Todd Hundley .10 .03
89 Howard Johnson .10 .03
90 Jeff Kent .50 .15
91 Eddie Murray .50 .15
92 Bill Pecota .10 .03
93 Bret Saberhagen .20 .06
94 Dick Schofield .10 .03

95 Pete Schourek .10 .03
96 Anthony Young .10 .03
97 Ruben Amaro .10 .03
98 Juan Bell .10 .03
99 Wes Chamberlain .10 .03
100 Darren Daulton .20 .06
101 Mariano Duncan .10 .03
102 Mike Hartley .10 .03
103 Ricky Jordan .10 .03
104 John Kruk .20 .06
105 Mickey Morandini .10 .03
106 Terry Mulholland .10 .03
107 Ben Rivera .10 .03
108 Curt Schilling .20 .06
109 Keith Shepherd RC .10 .03
110 Stan Belinda .10 .03
111 Jay Bell .20 .06
112 Barry Bonds 1.25 .35
113 Jeff King .10 .03
114 Mike LaValliere .10 .03
115 Jose Lind .10 .03
116 Roger Mason .10 .03
117 Orlando Merced .10 .03
118 Bob Patterson .10 .03
119 Don Slaught .10 .03
120 Zane Smith .10 .03
121 Randy Tomlin .10 .03
122 Andy Van Slyke .20 .06
123 Tim Wakefield .50 .15
124 Rheal Cormier .10 .03
125 Bernard Gilkey .10 .03
126 Felix Jose .10 .03
127 Ray Lankford .10 .03
128 Bob McClure .10 .03
129 Donovan Osborne .10 .03
130 Tom Pagnozzi .10 .03
131 Geronimo Pena .10 .03
132 Mike Perez .10 .03
133 Lee Smith .20 .06
134 Bob Tewksbury .10 .03
135 Todd Worrell .10 .03
136 Todd Zeile .10 .03
137 Jerald Clark .10 .03
138 Tony Gwynn .60 .18
139 Greg W. Harris .10 .03
140 Jeremy Hernandez .10 .03
141 Darrin Jackson .10 .03
142 Mike Maddux .10 .03
143 Fred McGriff .30 .09
144 Jose Melendez .10 .03
145 Rich Rodriguez .10 .03
146 Frank Seminara .10 .03
147 Gary Sheffield .20 .06
148 Kurt Stillwell .10 .03
149 Dan Walters .10 .03
150 Rod Beck .10 .03
151 Bud Black .10 .03
152 Jeff Brantley .10 .03
153 John Burkett .10 .03
154 Will Clark .50 .15
155 Royce Clayton .10 .03
156 Mike Jackson .10 .03
157 Darren Lewis .10 .03
158 Kirt Manwaring .10 .03
159 Willie McGee .20 .06
160 Cory Snyder .10 .03
161 Bill Swift .10 .03
162 Trevor Wilson .10 .03
163 Brady Anderson .20 .06
164 Glenn Davis .10 .03
165 Mike Devereaux .10 .03
166 Todd Frohwirth .10 .03
167 Leo Gomez .10 .03
168 Chris Hoiles .10 .03
169 Ben McDonald .10 .03
170 Randy Milligan .10 .03
171 Alan Mills .10 .03
172 Mike Mussina .30 .09
173 Gregg Olson .10 .03
174 Arthur Rhodes .10 .03
175 David Segui .10 .03
176 Ellis Burks .20 .06
177 Roger Clemens 1.00 .30
178 Scott Cooper .10 .03
179 Danny Darwin .10 .03
180 Tony Fossas .10 .03
181 Paul Quantrill .10 .03
182 Jody Reed .10 .03
183 John Valentin .10 .03
184 Mo Vaughn .20 .06
185 Frank Viola .20 .06
186 Bob Zupcic .10 .03
187 Jim Abbott .30 .09
188 Gary DiSarcina .10 .03
189 Damion Easley .10 .03
190 Junior Felix .10 .03
191 Chuck Finley .20 .06
192 Joe Grahe .10 .03
193 Bryan Harvey .10 .03
194 Mark Langston .10 .03
195 John Orton .10 .03
196 Luis Polonia .10 .03
197 Tim Salmon .30 .09
198 Luis Sojo .10 .03
199 Wilson Alvarez .10 .03
200 George Bell .10 .03
201 Alex Fernandez .10 .03
202 Craig Grebeck .10 .03
203 Ozzie Guillen .10 .03
204 Lance Johnson .10 .03
205 Ron Karkovice .10 .03
206 Kirk McCaskill .10 .03
207 Jack McDowell .10 .03
208 Scott Radinsky .10 .03
209 Tim Raines .20 .06
210 Frank Thomas .50 .15
211 Robin Ventura .20 .06
212 Sandy Alomar Jr. .10 .03
213 Carlos Baerga .10 .03
214 Dennis Cook .10 .03
215 Thomas Howard .10 .03
216 Mark Lewis .10 .03
217 Derek Lilliquist .10 .03
218 Kenny Lofton .20 .06
219 Charles Nagy .10 .03
220 Steve Olin .10 .03
221 Paul Sorrento .10 .03
222 Jim Thome .50 .15
223 Mark Whiten .10 .03
224 Milt Cuyler .10 .03
225 Rob Deer .10 .03
226 John Doherty .10 .03
227 Cecil Fielder .20 .06
228 Travis Fryman .20 .06
229 Mike Henneman .10 .03
230 John Kiely UER .10 .03
(Card has batting stats of Pat Kelly)
231 Kurt Knudsen .10 .03
232 Scott Livingstone .10 .03
233 Tony Phillips .10 .03
234 Mickey Tettleton .10 .03
235 Kevin Appier .20 .06
236 George Brett 1.25 .35
237 Tom Gordon .10 .03
238 Gregg Jefferies .10 .03
239 Wally Joyner .20 .06
240 Kevin Koslofski .10 .03
241 Mike Macfarlane .10 .03
242 Brian McRae .10 .03
243 Rusty Meacham .10 .03
244 Keith Miller .10 .03
245 Jeff Montgomery .10 .03
246 Hipolito Pichardo .10 .03
247 Ricky Bones .10 .03
248 Cal Eldred .10 .03
249 Mike Fetters .10 .03
250 Darryl Hamilton .10 .03
251 Doug Henry .10 .03
252 John Jaha .10 .03
253 Pat Listach .10 .03
254 Paul Molitor .30 .09
255 Jaime Navarro .10 .03
256 Kevin Seitzer .10 .03
257 B.J. Surhoff .20 .06
258 Greg Vaughn .10 .03
259 Bill Wegman .10 .03
260 Robin Yount .75 .23
261 Rick Aguilera .10 .03
262 Chili Davis .20 .06
263 Scott Erickson .10 .03
264 Greg Gagne .10 .03
265 Mark Guthrie .10 .03
266 Brian Harper .10 .03
267 Kent Hrbek .20 .06
268 Terry Jorgensen .10 .03
269 Gene Larkin .10 .03
270 Scott Leius .10 .03
271 Pat Mahomes .10 .03
272 Pedro Munoz .10 .03
273 Kirby Puckett .50 .15
274 Kevin Tapani .10 .03
275 Carl Willis .10 .03
276 Steve Farr .10 .03
277 John Habyan .10 .03
278 Mel Hall .10 .03
279 Charlie Hayes .10 .03
280 Pat Kelly .10 .03
281 Don Mattingly 1.25 .35
282 Sam Militello .10 .03
283 Matt Nokes .10 .03
284 Melido Perez .10 .03
285 Andy Stankiewicz .10 .03
286 Danny Tartabull .10 .03
287 Randy Velarde .10 .03
288 Bob Wickman .10 .03
289 Bernie Williams .30 .09
290 Lance Blankenship .10 .03
291 Mike Bordick .10 .03
292 Jerry Browne .10 .03
293 Dennis Eckersley .20 .06
294 Rickey Henderson .50 .15
295 Vince Horsman .10 .03
296 Mark McGwire 1.25 .35
297 Jeff Parrett .10 .03
298 Ruben Sierra .10 .03
299 Terry Steinbach .10 .03
300 Walt Weiss .10 .03
301 Bob Welch .10 .03
302 Willie Wilson .10 .03
303 Bobby Witt .10 .03
304 Bret Boone .30 .09
305 Jay Buhner .20 .06
306 Dave Fleming .10 .03
307 Ken Griffey Jr. .75 .23
308 Erik Hanson .10 .03
309 Edgar Martinez .30 .09
310 Tino Martinez .30 .09
311 Jeff Nelson .10 .03
312 Dennis Powell .10 .03
313 Mike Schooler .10 .03
314 Russ Swan .10 .03
315 Dave Valle .10 .03
316 Omar Vizquel .30 .09
317 Kevin Brown .30 .09
318 Todd Burns .10 .03
319 Jose Canseco .50 .15
320 Julio Franco .20 .06
321 Jeff Frye .10 .03
322 Juan Gonzalez .30 .09
323 Jose Guzman .10 .03
324 Jeff Huson .10 .03
325 Dean Palmer .20 .06
326 Kevin Reimer .10 .03
327 Ivan Rodriguez .50 .15
328 Kenny Rogers .20 .06
329 Dan Smith .10 .03
330 Roberto Alomar .30 .09
331 Derek Bell .10 .03
332 Pat Borders .10 .03
333 Joe Carter .20 .06
334 Kelly Gruber .10 .03
335 Tom Henke .10 .03
336 Jimmy Key .20 .06
337 Manuel Lee .10 .03
338 Candy Maldonado .10 .03
339 John Olerud .20 .06
340 Todd Stottlemyre .10 .03
341 Duane Ward .10 .03
342 Devon White .20 .06
343 Dave Winfield .20 .06
344 Edgar Martinez LL .20 .06
345 Cecil Fielder LL .10 .03
346 Kenny Lofton LL .10 .03
347 Jack Morris LL .10 .03
348 Roger Clemens LL .50 .15
349 Fred McGriff RT .20 .06
350 Barry Bonds RT .60 .18
351 Gary Sheffield RT .10 .03
352 Darren Daulton RT .10 .03
353 Dave Hollins RT .10 .03
354 Pedro Martinez .50 .15
Ramon Martinez
355 Ivan Rodriguez .50 .15
Kirby Puckett
356 Ryne Sandberg .50 .15
Gary Sheffield
357 Roberto Alomar .20 .06
Chuck Knoblauch
Carlos Baerga
358 Checklist 1-120 .10 .03
359 Checklist 121-240 .10 .03
360 Checklist 241-360 .10 .03
361 Rafael Belliard .10 .03
362 Damon Berryhill .10 .03
363 Mike Bielecki .10 .03
364 Jeff Blauser .10 .03
365 Francisco Cabrera .10 .03
366 Marvin Freeman .10 .03
367 David Justice .20 .06
368 Mark Lemke .10 .03
369 Alejandro Pena .10 .03
370 Jeff Reardon .20 .06
371 Lonnie Smith .10 .03
372 Pete Smith .10 .03
373 Shawn Boskie .10 .03
374 Jim Bullinger .10 .03
375 Frank Castillo .10 .03
376 Doug Dascenzo .10 .03
377 Andre Dawson .20 .06
378 Mike Harkey .10 .03
379 Greg Hibbard .10 .03
380 Greg Maddux .75 .23
381 Ken Patterson .10 .03
382 Jeff D. Robinson .10 .03
383 Luis Salazar .10 .03
384 Dwight Smith .10 .03
385 Jose Vizcaino .10 .03
386 Scott Bankhead .10 .03
387 Tom Browning .10 .03
388 Darnell Coles .10 .03
389 Rob Dibble .20 .06
390 Bill Doran .10 .03
391 Dwayne Henry .10 .03
392 Cesar Hernandez .10 .03
393 Roberto Kelly .10 .03
394 Barry Larkin .30 .09
395 Dave Martinez .10 .03
396 Kevin Mitchell .10 .03
397 Jeff Reed .10 .03
398 Scott Ruskin .10 .03
399 Greg Swindell .10 .03
400 Dan Wilson .20 .06
401 Andy Ashby .10 .03
402 Freddie Benavides .10 .03
403 Dante Bichette .20 .06
404 Willie Blair .10 .03
405 Denis Boucher .10 .03
406 Vinny Castilla .20 .06
407 Braulio Castillo .10 .03
408 Alex Cole .10 .03
409 Andres Galarraga .20 .06
410 Joe Girardi .10 .03
411 Butch Henry .10 .03
412 Darren Holmes .10 .03
413 Calvin Jones .10 .03
414 Steve Reed RC .10 .03
415 Kevin Ritz .10 .03
416 Jim Tatum RC .10 .03
417 Jack Armstrong .10 .03
418 Bret Barberie .10 .03
419 Ryan Bowen .10 .03
420 Cris Carpenter .10 .03
421 Chuck Carr .10 .03
422 Scott Chiamparino .10 .03
423 Jeff Conine .20 .06
424 Jim Corsi .10 .03
425 Steve Decker .10 .03
426 Chris Donnels .10 .03
427 Monty Fariss .10 .03
428 Bob Natal .10 .03
429 Pat Rapp .10 .03
430 Dave Weathers .10 .03
431 Nigel Wilson .10 .03
432 Ken Caminiti .20 .06
433 Andujar Cedeno .10 .03
434 Tom Edens .10 .03
435 Juan Guerrero .10 .03
436 Pete Incaviglia .10 .03
437 Jimmy Jones .10 .03
438 Darryl Kile .20 .06
439 Rob Murphy .10 .03
440 Al Osuna .10 .03
441 Mark Portugal .10 .03
442 Scott Servais .10 .03
443 John Candelaria .10 .03
444 Tim Crews .10 .03
445 Eric Davis .20 .06
446 Tom Goodwin .10 .03
447 Jim Gott .10 .03
448 Kevin Gross .10 .03
449 Dave Hansen .10 .03
450 Jay Howell .10 .03
451 Roger McDowell .10 .03
452 Bob Ojeda .10 .03
453 Henry Rodriguez .10 .03
454 Darryl Strawberry .20 .06
455 Mitch Webster .10 .03
456 Steve Wilson .10 .03
457 Brian Barnes .10 .03
458 Sean Berry .10 .03
459 Jeff Fassero .10 .03
460 Darrin Fletcher .10 .03
461 Marquis Grissom .20 .06
462 Dennis Martinez .20 .06
463 Spike Owen .10 .03
464 Matt Stairs .10 .03
465 Sergio Valdez .10 .03
466 Kevin Bass .10 .03
467 Vince Coleman .10 .03
468 Mark Dewey .10 .03
469 Kevin Elster .10 .03
470 Tony Fernandez .10 .03
471 John Franco .20 .06
472 Dave Gallagher .10 .03
473 Paul Gibson .10 .03
474 Dwight Gooden .20 .06
475 Lee Guetterman .10 .03
476 Jeff Innis .10 .03
477 Dave Magadan .10 .03
478 Charlie O'Brien .10 .03
479 Willie Randolph .20 .06
480 Mackey Sasser .10 .03
481 Ryan Thompson .10 .03
482 Chico Walker .10 .03
483 Kyle Abbott .10 .03
484 Bob Ayrault .10 .03
485 Kim Batiste .10 .03
486 Cliff Brantley .10 .03
487 Jose DeLeon .10 .03
488 Len Dykstra .20 .06
489 Tommy Greene .10 .03
490 Jeff Grotewold .10 .03
491 Dave Hollins .10 .03
492 Danny Jackson .10 .03
493 Stan Javier .10 .03
494 Tom Marsh .10 .03
495 Greg Mathews .10 .03
496 Dale Murphy .50 .15
497 Todd Pratt RC .20 .06
498 Mitch Williams .10 .03
499 Danny Cox .10 .03
500 Doug Drabek .10 .03
501 Carlos Garcia .10 .03
502 Lloyd McClendon .10 .03
503 Denny Neagle .20 .06
504 Gary Redus .10 .03
505 Bob Walk .10 .03
506 John Wehner .10 .03
507 Luis Alicea .10 .03
508 Mark Clark .10 .03
509 Pedro Guerrero .20 .06
510 Rex Hudler .10 .03
511 Brian Jordan .20 .06
512 Omar Olivares .10 .03
513 Jose Oquendo .10 .03
514 Gerald Perry .10 .03
515 Bryn Smith .10 .03
516 Craig Wilson .10 .03
517 Tracy Woodson .10 .03
518 Larry Andersen .10 .03
519 Andy Benes .10 .03
520 Jim Deshaies .10 .03
521 Bruce Hurst .10 .03
522 Randy Myers .10 .03
523 Benito Santiago .20 .06
524 Tim Scott .10 .03
525 Tim Teufel .10 .03
526 Mike Benjamin .10 .03
527 Dave Burba .10 .03
528 Craig Colbert .10 .03
529 Mike Felder .10 .03
530 Bryan Hickerson .10 .03
531 Chris James .10 .03
532 Mark Leonard .10 .03
533 Greg Litton .10 .03
534 Francisco Oliveras .10 .03
535 John Patterson .10 .03
536 Jim Pena .10 .03
537 Dave Righetti .20 .06
538 Robby Thompson .10 .03
539 Jose Uribe .10 .03
540 Matt Williams .20 .06
541 Storm Davis .10 .03
542 Sam Horn .10 .03
543 Tim Hulett .10 .03
544 Craig Lefferts .10 .03
545 Chito Martinez .10 .03
546 Mark McLemore .10 .03
547 Luis Mercedes .10 .03
548 Bob Milacki .10 .03
549 Joe Orsulak .10 .03
550 Billy Ripken .10 .03
551 Cal Ripken Jr. 1.50 .45
552 Rick Sutcliffe .20 .06
553 Jeff Tackett .10 .03
554 Wade Boggs .30 .09
555 Tom Brunansky .10 .03
556 Jack Clark .20 .06
557 John Dopson .10 .03
558 Mike Gardiner .10 .03
559 Mike Greenwell .10 .03
560 Greg A. Harris .10 .03
561 Billy Hatcher .10 .03
562 Joe Hesketh .10 .03
563 Tony Pena .10 .03
564 Phil Plantier .10 .03
565 Luis Rivera .10 .03
566 Herm Winningham .10 .03
567 Matt Young .10 .03
568 Bert Blyleven .20 .06
569 Mike Butcher .10 .03
570 Chuck Crim .10 .03
571 Chad Curtis .10 .03
572 Tim Fortugno .10 .03
573 Steve Frey .10 .03
574 Gary Gaetti .20 .06
575 Scott Lewis .10 .03
576 Lee Stevens .10 .03
577 Ron Tingley .10 .03
578 Julio Valera .10 .03
579 Shawn Abner .10 .03
580 Joey Cora .10 .03
581 Chris Cron .10 .03
582 Carlton Fisk .30 .09
583 Roberto Hernandez .10 .03
584 Charlie Hough .20 .06
585 Terry Leach .10 .03
586 Donn Pall .10 .03
587 Dan Pasqua .10 .03
588 Steve Sax .10 .03
589 Bobby Thigpen .10 .03
590 Albert Belle .20 .06
591 Felix Fermin .10 .03
592 Glenallen Hill .10 .03
593 Brook Jacoby .10 .03
594 Reggie Jefferson .10 .03
595 Carlos Martinez .10 .03
596 Jose Mesa .10 .03
597 Rod Nichols .10 .03
598 Junior Ortiz .10 .03
599 Eric Plunk .10 .03
600 Ted Power .10 .03
601 Scott Scudder .10 .03
602 Kevin Wickander .10 .03
603 Skeeter Barnes .10 .03
604 Mark Carreon .10 .03
605 Dan Gladden .10 .03
606 Bill Gullickson .10 .03
607 Chad Kreuter .10 .03
608 Mark Leiter .10 .03
609 Mike Munoz .10 .03
610 Rich Rowland .10 .03
611 Frank Tanana .10 .03
612 Walt Terrell .10 .03
613 Alan Trammell .20 .06
614 Lou Whitaker .20 .06
615 Luis Aquino .10 .03
616 Mike Boddicker .10 .03
617 Jim Eisenreich .10 .03
618 Mark Gubicza .10 .03
619 David Howard .10 .03
620 Mike Magnante .10 .03
621 Brent Mayne .10 .03
622 Kevin McReynolds .10 .03
623 Ed Pierce RC .10 .03
624 Bill Sampen .10 .03
625 Steve Shifflett .10 .03
626 Gary Thurman .10 .03
627 Curt Wilkerson .10 .03
628 Chris Bosio .10 .03
629 Scott Fletcher .10 .03
630 Jim Gantner .10 .03
631 Dave Nilsson .10 .03
632 Jesse Orosco .10 .03
633 Dan Plesac .10 .03
634 Ron Robinson .10 .03
635 Bill Spiers .10 .03
636 Franklin Stubbs .10 .03
637 Willie Banks .10 .03
638 Randy Bush .10 .03
639 Chuck Knoblauch .20 .06
640 Shane Mack .10 .03
641 Mike Pagliarulo .10 .03
642 Jeff Reboulet .10 .03
643 John Smiley .10 .03
644 Mike Trombley .10 .03
645 Gary Wayne .10 .03
646 Lenny Webster .10 .03
647 Tim Burke .10 .03
648 Mike Gallego .10 .03
649 Dion James .10 .03
650 Jeff Johnson .10 .03
651 Scott Kamieniecki .10 .03
652 Kevin Maas .10 .03
653 Rich Monteleone .10 .03
654 Jerry Nielsen .10 .03
655 Scott Sanderson .10 .03
656 Mike Stanley .10 .03
657 Gerald Williams .10 .03
658 Curt Young .10 .03
659 Harold Baines .20 .06
660 Kevin Campbell .10 .03
661 Ron Darling .10 .03
662 Kelly Downs .10 .03
663 Eric Fox .10 .03
664 Dave Henderson .10 .03
665 Rick Honeycutt .10 .03
666 Mike Moore .10 .03
667 Jamie Quirk .10 .03
668 Jeff Russell .10 .03
669 Dave Stewart .20 .06
670 Greg Briley .10 .03
671 Dave Cochrane .10 .03
672 Henry Cotto .10 .03
673 Rich DeLucia .10 .03
674 Brian Fisher .10 .03
675 Mark Grant .10 .03
676 Randy Johnson .50 .15
677 Tim Leary .10 .03
678 Pete O'Brien .10 .03
679 Lance Parrish .20 .06
680 Harold Reynolds .20 .06
681 Shane Turner .10 .03
682 Jack Daugherty .10 .03
683 David Hulse RC .10 .03
684 Terry Mathews .10 .03
685 Al Newman .10 .03
686 Edwin Nunez .10 .03
687 Rafael Palmeiro .30 .09
688 Roger Pavlik .10 .03
689 Geno Petralli .10 .03
690 Nolan Ryan 2.00 .60
691 David Cone .20 .06
692 Alfredo Griffin .10 .03
693 Juan Guzman .10 .03
694 Pat Hentgen .10 .03
695 Randy Knorr .10 .03
696 Bob MacDonald .10 .03
697 Jack Morris .20 .06
698 Ed Sprague .10 .03
699 Dave Stieb .10 .03
700 Pat Tabler .10 .03
701 Mike Timlin .10 .03
702 David Wells .20 .06
703 Eddie Zosky .10 .03
704 Gary Sheffield LL .10 .03
705 Darren Daulton LL .10 .03
706 Marquis Grissom LL .10 .03
707 Greg Maddux LL .50 .15
708 Bill Swift LL .10 .03
709 Juan Gonzalez RT .20 .06
710 Mark McGwire RT .60 .18
711 Cecil Fielder RT .10 .03
712 Albert Belle RT .20 .06
713 Joe Carter RT .10 .03
714 Cecil Fielder SS .30 .09
Frank Thomas
715 Larry Walker SS .30 .09
Darren Daulton
716 Edgar Martinez SS .20 .06
Robin Ventura
717 Roger Clemens SS .50 .15
Dennis Eckersley
718 Checklist 361-480 .10 .03
719 Checklist 481-600 .10 .03
720 Checklist 601-720 .10 .03

1993 Fleer All-Stars

This 24-card standard-size set featuring members of the American and National league All-Star squads, was randomly inserted in wax packs. 12 American League players were seeded in series 1 packs and 12 National League players in series 2.

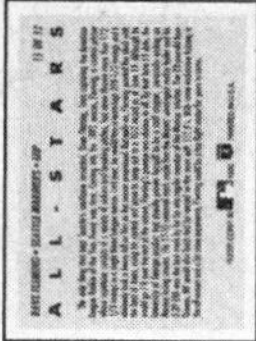

	Nm-Mt	Ex-Mt
COMPLETE SET (24)	40.00	12.00
COMPLETE SER.1 (12)	25.00	7.50
COMPLETE SER.2 (12)	15.00	4.50
AL1 Frank Thomas	3.00	.90
AL2 Roberto Alomar	2.00	.60
AL3 Edgar Martinez	2.00	.60
AL4 Pat Listach	.60	.18
AL5 Cecil Fielder	1.25	.35
AL6 Juan Gonzalez	2.00	.60
AL7 Ken Griffey Jr.	5.00	1.50
AL8 Joe Carter	1.25	.35
AL9 Kirby Puckett	3.00	.90
AL10 Brian Harper	.60	.18
AL11 Dave Fleming	.60	.18
AL12 Jack McDowell	.60	.18
NL1 Fred McGriff	2.00	.60
NL2 Delino DeShields	.60	.18
NL3 Gary Sheffield	1.25	.35
NL4 Barry Larkin	2.00	.60
NL5 Felix Jose	.60	.18
NL6 Larry Walker	2.00	.60
NL7 Barry Bonds	8.00	2.40
NL8 Andy Van Slyke	1.25	.35
NL9 Darren Daulton	1.25	.35
NL10 Greg Maddux	5.00	1.50
NL11 Tom Glavine	2.00	.60
NL12 Lee Smith	1.25	.35

1993 Fleer Glavine

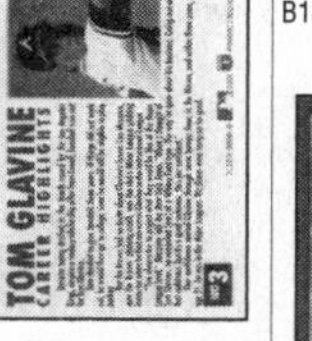

As part of the Signature Series, this 12-card standard-size set spotlights Tom Glavine. An additional three cards (13-15) were available via a mail-in offer and are generally considered to be a separate set. The mail-in offer expired on September 30, 1993. Reportedly, a filmmaking problem during production resulted in eight variations in this 12-card insert set. Different backs appear on eight of the 12 cards. Cards 1-4 and 7-10 in wax packs feature card-back text variations from those included in the rack and jumbo magazine packs. The text differences occur in the first few words of text on the card back. No corrections were made in Series I. The correct Glavine cards appeared in Series I wax, rack, and jumbo magazine packs. In addition, Tom Glavine signed cards for this set. Unlike some of the previous autograph cards from Fleer, these cards were certified as authentic by the manufacturer.

	Nm-Mt	Ex-Mt
COMPLETE SET (12)	4.00	1.20
COMMON CARD (1-12)	.50	.15
COMMON MAIL (13-15)	2.00	.60
AU Tom Glavine AU (Certified signature)	50.00	15.00

1993 Fleer Golden Moments

Cards from this six-card standard-size set, featuring memorable moments from the previous season, were randomly inserted in 1993 Fleer wax packs, three each in series 1 and 2.

	Nm-Mt	Ex-Mt
COMPLETE SET (6)	12.00	3.60
COMPLETE SER.1 (3)	4.00	1.20
COMPLETE SER.2 (3)	8.00	2.40
A1 George Brett	6.00	1.80
A2 Mickey Morandini	.50	.15
A3 Dave Winfield	1.00	.30
B1 Dennis Eckersley	1.00	.30
B2 Bip Roberts	.50	.15
B3 Frank Thomas and Juan Gonzalez	2.50	.75

1993 Fleer Major League Prospects

Cards from this 36-card standard-size set, featuring a selection of prospects, were randomly inserted in wax packs, 18 in each series. Early Cards of Pedro Martinez and Mike Piazza are featured within this set.

	Nm-Mt	Ex-Mt
COMPLETE SET (36)	30.00	9.00
COMPLETE SERIES 1 (18)	20.00	6.00
COMPLETE SERIES 2 (18)	10.00	3.00
A1 Melvin Nieves	.50	.15
A2 Sterling Hitchcock	.75	.23
A3 Tim Costo	.50	.15
A4 Manny Alexander	.50	.15
A5 Alan Embree	2.00	.60
A6 Kevin Young	.75	.23
A7 J.T. Snow	1.25	.35
A8 Russ Springer	.50	.15
A9 Billy Ashley	.50	.15
A10 Kevin Rogers	.50	.15
A11 Steve Hosey	.50	.15
A12 Eric Wedge	.50	.15
A13 Mike Piazza	8.00	2.40
A14 Jesse Levis	.50	.15
A15 Rico Brogna	.50	.15
A16 Alex Arias	.50	.15
A17 Rod Brewer	.50	.15
A18 Troy Neel	.50	.15
B1 Scooter Tucker	.50	.15
B2 Kerry Woodson	.50	.15
B3 Greg Colbrunn	.50	.15
B4 Pedro Martinez	6.00	1.80
B5 Dave Silvestri	.50	.15
B6 Kent Bottenfield	.50	.15
B7 Rafael Bournigal	.50	.15
B8 J.T. Bruett	.50	.15
B9 Dave Mlicki	.50	.15
B10 Paul Wagner	.50	.15
B11 Mike Williams	.50	.15
B12 Henry Mercedes	.50	.15
B13 Scott Taylor	.50	.15
B14 Dennis Moeller	.50	.15
B15 Javy Lopez	1.25	.35
B16 Steve Cooke	.50	.15
B17 Pete Young	.50	.15
B18 Ken Ryan	.50	.15

1993 Fleer Pro-Visions

Cards from this six-card standard-size set, featuring a selection of superstars in fantasy paintings, were randomly inserted in poly packs, three each in series one and series two.

	Nm-Mt	Ex-Mt
COMPLETE SET (6)	5.00	1.50
COMPLETE SERIES 1 (3)	3.00	.90
COMPLETE SERIES 2 (3)	2.00	.60
A1 Roberto Alomar	2.00	.60
A2 Dennis Eckersley	1.25	.35
A3 Gary Sheffield	1.25	.35
B1 Andy Van Slyke	1.25	.35
B2 Tom Glavine	2.00	.60
B3 Cecil Fielder	1.25	.35

1993 Fleer Rookie Sensations

Cards from this 20-card standard-size set, featuring a selection of 1993's top rookies, were randomly inserted in cello packs, 10 in each series.

	Nm-Mt	Ex-Mt
COMPLETE SET (20)	20.00	6.00
COMPLETE SERIES 1 (10)	10.00	3.00
COMPLETE SERIES 2 (10)	10.00	3.00
RSA1 Kenny Lofton	2.00	.60
RSA2 Cal Eldred	1.00	.30
RSA3 Pat Listach	1.00	.30
RSA4 Roberto Hernandez	1.00	.30
RSA5 Dave Fleming	1.00	.30
RSA6 Eric Karros	2.00	.60
RSA7 Reggie Sanders	1.00	.30
RSA8 Derrick May	1.00	.30
RSA9 Mike Perez	1.00	.30
RSA10 Donovan Osborne	1.00	.30
RSB1 Moises Alou	2.00	.60
RSB2 Pedro Astacio	1.00	.30
RSB3 Jim Austin	1.00	.30
RSB4 Chad Curtis	1.00	.30
RSB5 Gary DiSarcina	1.00	.30
RSB6 Scott Livingstone	1.00	.30
RSB7 Sam Militello	1.00	.30
RSB8 Arthur Rhodes	1.00	.30
RSB9 Tim Wakefield	5.00	1.50
RSB10 Bob Zupcic	1.00	.30

1993 Fleer Team Leaders

One Team Leader or Tom Glavine insert was seeded into each Fleer rack pack. Series 1 racks included 10 American League players, while series 2 racks included 10 National League players.

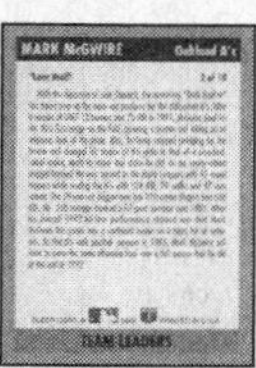

	Nm-Mt	Ex-Mt
COMPLETE SERIES 1 (10)	50.00	15.00
COMPLETE SERIES 2 (10)	20.00	6.00
AL1 Kirby Puckett	5.00	1.50
AL2 Mark McGwire	12.00	3.60
AL3 Pat Listach	1.00	.30
AL4 Roger Clemens	10.00	3.00
AL5 Frank Thomas	5.00	1.50
AL6 Carlos Baerga	1.00	.30
AL7 Brady Anderson	2.00	.60
AL8 Juan Gonzalez	3.00	.90
AL9 Roberto Alomar	3.00	.90
AL10 Ken Griffey Jr.	8.00	2.40
NL1 Will Clark	5.00	1.50
NL2 Terry Pendleton	2.00	.60
NL3 Ray Lankford	1.00	.30
NL4 Eric Karros	2.00	.60
NL5 Gary Sheffield	2.00	.60
NL6 Ryne Sandberg	8.00	2.40
NL7 Marquis Grissom	2.00	.60
NL8 John Kruk	2.00	.60
NL9 Jeff Bagwell	3.00	.90
NL10 Andy Van Slyke	2.00	.60

1993 Fleer Final Edition

This 300-card standard-size set was issued exclusively in factory set form (along with ten Diamond Tribute inserts) to update and feature rookies not in the regular 1993 Fleer set. The cards are identical in design to regular issue 1993 Fleer cards except for the F-prefixed numbering. Cards are ordered alphabetically within teams with NL preceding AL. The set closes with checklist cards (298-300). The only key Rookie Card in this set features Jim Edmonds.

	Nm-Mt	Ex-Mt
COMP.FACT.SET (310)	10.00	3.00
COMPLETE SET (300)	8.00	2.40
1 Steve Bedrosian	.10	.03
2 Jay Howell	.10	.03
3 Greg Maddux	.75	.23
4 Greg McMichael RC	.15	.04
5 Tony Tarasco RC	.15	.04
6 Jose Bautista	.10	.03
7 Jose Guzman	.10	.03
8 Greg Hibbard	.10	.03
9 Candy Maldonado	.10	.03
10 Randy Myers	.10	.03
11 Matt Walbeck RC	.40	.12
12 Turk Wendell	.10	.03
13 Willie Wilson	.10	.03
14 Greg Cadaret	.10	.03
15 Roberto Kelly	.10	.03
16 Randy Milligan	.10	.03
17 Kevin Mitchell	.10	.03
18 Jeff Reardon	.20	.06
19 John Roper	.10	.03
20 John Smiley	.10	.03
21 Andy Ashby	.10	.03
22 Dante Bichette	.20	.06
23 Willie Blair	.10	.03
24 Pedro Castellano	.10	.03
25 Vinny Castilla	.20	.06
26 Jerald Clark	.10	.03
27 Alex Cole	.10	.03
28 Scott Fredrickson RC	.15	.04
29 Jay Gainer RC	.15	.04
30 Andres Galarraga	.20	.06
31 Joe Girardi	.10	.03
32 Ryan Hawblitzel	.10	.03
33 Charlie Hayes	.10	.03
34 Darren Holmes	.10	.03
35 Chris Jones	.10	.03
36 David Nied	.10	.03
37 J.Owens RC	.15	.04
38 Lance Painter RC	.40	.12
39 Jeff Parrett	.10	.03
40 Steve Reed	.10	.03
41 Armando Reynoso	.10	.03
42 Bruce Ruffin	.10	.03
43 Danny Sheaffer RC	.15	.04
44 Keith Shepherd	.10	.03
45 Jim Tatum	.10	.03
46 Gary Wayne	.10	.03
47 Eric Young	.10	.03
48 Luis Aquino	.10	.03
49 Alex Arias	.10	.03
50 Jack Armstrong	.10	.03
51 Bret Barberie	.10	.03
52 Geronimo Berroa	.10	.03
53 Ryan Bowen	.10	.03
54 Greg Briley	.10	.03
55 Cris Carpenter	.10	.03
56 Chuck Carr	.10	.03
57 Jeff Conine	.20	.06
58 Jim Corsi	.10	.03
59 Orestes Destrade	.10	.03
60 Junior Felix	.10	.03
61 Chris Hammond	.10	.03
62 Bryan Harvey	.10	.03
63 Charlie Hough	.20	.06
64 Joe Klink	.10	.03
65 Richie Lewis RC UER (Refers to place of birth and residence as Illinois instead of Indiana)	.15	.04
66 Mitch Lyden RC	.15	.04
67 Bob Natal	.10	.03
68 Scott Pose RC	.15	.04
69 Rich Renteria	.10	.03
70 Benito Santiago	.20	.06
71 Gary Sheffield	.20	.06
72 Matt Turner RC	.15	.04
73 Walt Weiss	.10	.03
74 Darrell Whitmore RC	.15	.04
75 Nigel Wilson	.10	.03
76 Kevin Bass	.10	.03
77 Doug Drabek	.10	.03
78 Tom Edens	.10	.03
79 Chris James	.10	.03
80 Greg Swindell	.10	.03
81 Omar Daal RC	.40	.12
82 Raul Mondesi	.20	.06
83 Jody Reed	.10	.03
84 Cory Snyder	.10	.03
85 Rick Trlicek	.10	.03
86 Tim Wallach	.10	.03
87 Todd Worrell	.10	.03
88 Tavo Alvarez	.10	.03
89 Frank Bolick	.10	.03
90 Kent Bottenfield	.10	.03
91 Greg Colbrunn	.10	.03
92 Cliff Floyd	.20	.06
93 Lou Frazier RC	.15	.04
94 Mike Gardiner	.10	.03
95 Mike Lansing RC	.40	.12
96 Bill Risley	.10	.03
97 Jeff Shaw	.10	.03
98 Kevin Baez	.10	.03
99 Tim Bogar RC	.15	.04
100 Jeromy Burnitz	.20	.06
101 Mike Draper	.10	.03
102 Darrin Jackson	.10	.03
103 Mike Maddux	.10	.03
104 Joe Orsulak	.10	.03
105 Doug Saunders RC	.15	.04
106 Frank Tanana	.10	.03
107 Dave Telgheder RC	.15	.04
108 Larry Andersen	.10	.03
109 Jim Eisenreich	.10	.03
110 Pete Incaviglia	.10	.03
111 Danny Jackson	.10	.03
112 David West	.10	.03
113 Al Martin	.10	.03
114 Blas Minor	.10	.03
115 Dennis Moeller	.10	.03
116 William Pennyfeather	.10	.03
117 Rich Robertson RC	.15	.04
118 Ben Shelton	.10	.03
119 Lonnie Smith	.10	.03
120 Freddie Toliver	.10	.03
121 Paul Wagner	.10	.03
122 Kevin Young	.20	.06
123 Rene Arocha RC	.40	.12
124 Gregg Jefferies	.10	.03
125 Paul Kilgus	.10	.03
126 Les Lancaster	.10	.03
127 Joe Magrane	.10	.03
128 Rob Murphy	.10	.03
129 Erik Pappas	.10	.03
130 Stan Royer	.10	.03
131 Ozzie Smith	.75	.23
132 Tom Urbani RC	.15	.04
133 Mark Whiten	.10	.03
134 Derek Bell	.10	.03
135 Doug Brocail	.10	.03
136 Phil Clark	.10	.03
137 Mark Ettles RC	.15	.04
138 Jeff Gardner	.10	.03
139 Pat Gomez RC	.15	.04
140 Ricky Gutierrez	.10	.03
141 Gene Harris	.10	.03
142 Kevin Higgins	.10	.03
143 Trevor Hoffman	.20	.06
144 Phil Plantier	.10	.03
145 Kerry Taylor RC	.15	.04
146 Guillermo Velasquez	.10	.03
147 Wally Whitehurst	.10	.03
148 Tim Worrell RC	.40	.12
149 Todd Benzinger	.10	.03
150 Barry Bonds	1.25	.35
151 Greg Brummett RC	.15	.04
152 Mark Carreon	.10	.03
153 Dave Martinez	.10	.03
154 Jeff Reed	.10	.03
155 Kevin Rogers	.10	.03
156 Harold Baines	.20	.06
157 Damon Buford	.10	.03
158 Paul Carey RC	.15	.04
159 Jeffrey Hammonds	.10	.03
160 Jamie Moyer	.20	.06
161 Sherman Obando RC	.15	.04
162 John O'Donoghue RC	.15	.04
163 Brad Pennington	.10	.03
164 Jim Poole	.10	.03
165 Harold Reynolds	.20	.06
166 Fernando Valenzuela	.20	.06
167 Jack Voigt RC	.15	.04
168 Mark Williamson	.10	.03
169 Scott Bankhead	.10	.03
170 Greg Blosser	.10	.03
171 Jim Byrd RC	.15	.04
172 Ivan Calderon	.10	.03
173 Andre Dawson	.20	.06
174 Scott Fletcher	.10	.03
175 Jose Melendez	.10	.03
176 Carlos Quintana	.10	.03
177 Jeff Russell	.10	.03
178 Aaron Sele	.10	.03
179 Rod Correia RC	.15	.04
180 Chili Davis	.20	.06
181 Jim Edmonds RC	5.00	1.50
182 Rene Gonzales	.10	.03
183 Hilly Hathaway RC	.15	.04
184 Torey Lovullo	.10	.03
185 Greg Myers	.10	.03
186 Gene Nelson	.10	.03
187 Troy Percival	.30	.09
188 Scott Sanderson	.10	.03
189 Darryl Scott RC	.15	.04
190 J.T. Snow RC	.60	.18
191 Russ Springer	.10	.03
192 Jason Bere	.10	.03
193 Rodney Bolton	.10	.03
194 Ellis Burks	.20	.06
195 Bo Jackson	.50	.15
196 Mike LaValliere	.10	.03
197 Scott Ruffcorn	.10	.03
198 Jeff Schwarz	.10	.03
199 Jerry DiPoto	.10	.03
200 Alvaro Espinoza	.10	.03
201 Wayne Kirby	.10	.03
202 Tom Kramer RC	.15	.04
203 Jesse Levis	.10	.03
204 Manny Ramirez	.50	.15
205 Jeff Treadway	.10	.03
206 Bill Wertz RC	.15	.04
207 Cliff Young	.10	.03
208 Matt Young	.10	.03
209 Kirk Gibson	.20	.06
210 Greg Gohr	.10	.03
211 Bill Krueger	.10	.03
212 Bob MacDonald	.10	.03
213 Mike Moore	.10	.03
214 David Wells	.20	.06
215 Billy Brewer	.10	.03
216 David Cone	.20	.06
217 Greg Gagne	.10	.03
218 Mark Gardner	.10	.03
219 Chris Haney	.10	.03
220 Phil Hiatt	.10	.03
221 Jose Lind	.10	.03
222 Juan Bell	.10	.03
223 Tom Brunansky	.10	.03
224 Mike Ignasiak	.10	.03
225 Joe Kmak	.10	.03
226 Tom Lampkin	.10	.03
227 Graeme Lloyd RC	.40	.12
228 Carlos Maldonado	.10	.03
229 Matt Mieske	.10	.03
230 Angel Miranda	.10	.03
231 Troy O'Leary RC	.40	.12
232 Kevin Reimer	.10	.03
233 Larry Casian	.10	.03
234 Jim Deshaies	.10	.03
235 Eddie Guardado RC	.60	.18
236 Chip Hale	.10	.03
237 Mike Maksudian RC	.15	.04
238 David McCarty	.10	.03
239 Pat Meares RC	.40	.12
240 George Tsamis RC	.15	.04
241 Dave Winfield	.20	.06
242 Jim Abbott	.30	.09
243 Wade Boggs	.30	.09
244 Andy Cook RC	.15	.04
245 Russ Davis RC	.15	.04
246 Mike Humphreys	.10	.03
247 Jimmy Key	.20	.06
248 Jim Leyritz	.10	.03
249 Bobby Munoz	.10	.03
250 Paul O'Neill	.30	.09
251 Spike Owen	.10	.03
252 Dave Silvestri	.10	.03
253 Marcos Armas RC	.15	.04
254 Brent Gates	.10	.03
255 Rich Gossage	.20	.06
256 Scott Lydy RC	.15	.04
257 Henry Mercedes	.10	.03
258 Mike Mohler RC	.40	.12
259 Troy Neel	.10	.03
260 Edwin Nunez	.10	.03
261 Craig Paquette	.10	.03
262 Kevin Seitzer	.10	.03
263 Rich Amaral	.10	.03
264 Mike Blowers	.10	.03
265 Chris Bosio	.10	.03
266 Norm Charlton	.10	.03
267 Jim Converse RC	.15	.04
268 John Cummings RC	.15	.04
269 Mike Felder	.10	.03
270 Mike Hampton	.20	.06
271 Bill Haselman	.10	.03
272 Dwayne Henry	.10	.03
273 Greg Litton	.10	.03
274 Mackey Sasser	.10	.03
275 Lee Tinsley	.10	.03
276 David Wainhouse	.10	.03
277 Jeff Bronkey	.10	.03
278 Benji Gil	.10	.03
279 Tom Henke	.10	.03
280 Charlie Leibrandt	.10	.03
281 Robb Nen	.20	.06
282 Bill Ripken	.10	.03
283 Jon Shave RC	.15	.04
284 Doug Strange	.10	.03
285 Matt Whiteside RC	.15	.04
286 Scott Brow RC	.15	.04
287 Willie Canate RC	.15	.04
288 Tony Castillo	.10	.03
289 Domingo Cedeno RC	.15	.04
290 Darnell Coles	.10	.03
291 Danny Cox	.10	.03
292 Mark Eichhorn	.10	.03
293 Tony Fernandez	.10	.03
294 Al Leiter	.20	.06
295 Paul Molitor	.30	.09
296 Dave Stewart	.20	.06
297 Woody Williams RC	.60	.18
298 Checklist F1-F100	.10	.03
299 Checklist F101-F200	.10	.03
300 Checklist F201-F300	.10	.03

1993 Fleer Final Edition Diamond Tribute

Each Fleer Final Edition factory set contained a complete 10-card set of Diamond Tribute inserts. These cards are numbered separately and feature a totally different design from the base cards. Each card is numbered "X" of 10 on back.

	Nm-Mt	Ex-Mt
COMPLETE SET (10)	4.00	1.20
1 Wade Boggs	.50	.15

2 George Brett 2.00 .60
3 Andre Dawson .30 .09
4 Carlton Fisk .50 .15
5 Paul Molitor .50 .15
6 Nolan Ryan 3.00 .90
7 Lee Smith .30 .09
8 Ozzie Smith 1.25 .35
9 Dave Winfield .30 .09
10 Robin Yount 1.25 .35

1994 Fleer

The 1994 Fleer baseball set consists of 720 standard-size cards. Cards were distributed in hobby, retail, and jumbo packs. The cards are numbered on the back, grouped alphabetically within teams, and checklisted below alphabetically according to teams for each league with AL preceding NL. The set closes with a Superstar Specials (706-713) subset. There are no key Rookie Cards in this set.

Nm-Mt Ex-Mt
COMPLETE SET (720) 40.00 12.00
1 Brady Anderson .30 .09
2 Harold Baines .30 .09
3 Mike Devereaux .15 .04
4 Todd Frohwirth .15 .04
5 Jeffrey Hammonds .15 .04
6 Chris Hoiles .15 .04
7 Tim Hulett .15 .04
8 Ben McDonald .15 .04
9 Mark McLemore .15 .04
10 Alan Mills .15 .04
11 Jamie Moyer .30 .09
12 Mike Mussina .50 .15
13 Gregg Olson .15 .04
14 Mike Pagliarulo .15 .04
15 Brad Pennington .15 .04
16 Jim Poole .15 .04
17 Harold Reynolds .30 .09
18 Arthur Rhodes .15 .04
19 Cal Ripken Jr. 2.50 .75
20 David Segui .15 .04
21 Rick Sutcliffe .30 .09
22 Fernando Valenzuela .30 .09
23 Jack Voigt .15 .04
24 Mark Williamson .15 .04
25 Scott Bankhead .15 .04
26 Roger Clemens 1.50 .45
27 Scott Cooper .15 .04
28 Danny Darwin .15 .04
29 Andre Dawson .30 .09
30 Rob Deer .15 .04
31 John Dopson .15 .04
32 Scott Fletcher .15 .04
33 Mike Greenwell .15 .04
34 Greg A. Harris .15 .04
35 Billy Hatcher .15 .04
36 Bob Melvin .15 .04
37 Tony Pena .15 .04
38 Paul Quantrill .15 .04
39 Carlos Quintana .15 .04
40 Ernest Riles .15 .04
41 Jeff Russell .15 .04
42 Ken Ryan .15 .04
43 Aaron Sele .15 .04
44 John Valentin .15 .04
45 Mo Vaughn .30 .09
46 Frank Viola .30 .09
47 Bob Zupcic .15 .04
48 Mike Butcher .15 .04
49 Rod Correia .15 .04
50 Chad Curtis .15 .04
51 Chili Davis .30 .09
52 Gary DiSarcina .15 .04
53 Damion Easley .15 .04
54 Jim Edmonds .75 .23
55 Chuck Finley .30 .09
56 Steve Frey .15 .04
57 Rene Gonzales .15 .04
58 Joe Grahe .15 .04
59 Hilly Hathaway .15 .04
60 Stan Javier .15 .04
61 Mark Langston .15 .04
62 Phil Leftwich RC .15 .04
63 Torey Lovullo .15 .04
64 Joe Magrane .15 .04
65 Greg Myers .15 .04
66 Ken Patterson .15 .04
67 Eduardo Perez .15 .04
68 Luis Polonia .15 .04
69 Tim Salmon .50 .15
70 J.T. Snow .30 .09
71 Ron Tingley .15 .04
72 Julio Valera .15 .04
73 Wilson Alvarez .15 .04
74 Tim Belcher .15 .04
75 George Bell .15 .04
76 Jason Bere .15 .04
77 Rod Bolton .15 .04
78 Ellis Burks .30 .09
79 Joey Cora .15 .04
80 Alex Fernandez .15 .04
81 Craig Grebeck .15 .04
82 Ozzie Guillen .15 .04
83 Roberto Hernandez .15 .04
84 Bo Jackson .75 .23
85 Lance Johnson .15 .04
86 Ron Karkovice .15 .04
87 Mike LaValliere .15 .04
88 Kirk McCaskill .15 .04
89 Jack McDowell .15 .04
90 Warren Newson .15 .04
91 Dan Pasqua .15 .04
92 Scott Radinsky .15 .04
93 Tim Raines .30 .09
94 Steve Sax .15 .04
95 Jeff Schwarz .15 .04
96 Frank Thomas .75 .23
97 Robin Ventura .30 .09
98 Sandy Alomar Jr. .15 .04
99 Carlos Baerga .15 .04
100 Albert Belle .30 .09
101 Mark Clark .15 .04
102 Jerry DiPoto .15 .04
103 Alvaro Espinoza .15 .04
104 Felix Fermin .15 .04
105 Jeremy Hernandez .15 .04
106 Reggie Jefferson .15 .04
107 Wayne Kirby .15 .04
108 Tom Kramer .15 .04
109 Mark Lewis .15 .04
110 Derek Lilliquist .15 .04
111 Kenny Lofton .30 .09
112 Candy Maldonado .15 .04
113 Jose Mesa .15 .04
114 Jeff Mutis .15 .04
115 Charles Nagy .15 .04
116 Bob Ojeda .15 .04
117 Junior Ortiz .15 .04
118 Eric Plunk .15 .04
119 Manny Ramirez .50 .15
120 Paul Sorrento .15 .04
121 Jim Thome .75 .23
122 Jeff Treadway .15 .04
123 Bill Wertz .15 .04
124 Skeeter Barnes .15 .04
125 Milt Cuyler .15 .04
126 Eric Davis .30 .09
127 John Doherty .15 .04
128 Cecil Fielder .30 .09
129 Travis Fryman .30 .09
130 Kirk Gibson .30 .09
131 Dan Gladden .15 .04
132 Greg Gohr .15 .04
133 Chris Gomez .15 .04
134 Bill Gullickson .15 .04
135 Mike Henneman .15 .04
136 Kurt Knudsen .15 .04
137 Chad Kreuter .15 .04
138 Bill Krueger .15 .04
139 Scott Livingstone .15 .04
140 Bob MacDonald .15 .04
141 Mike Moore .15 .04
142 Tony Phillips .15 .04
143 Mickey Tettleton .15 .04
144 Alan Trammell .30 .09
145 David Wells .30 .09
146 Lou Whitaker .30 .09
147 Kevin Appier .30 .09
148 Stan Belinda .15 .04
149 George Brett 2.00 .60
150 Billy Brewer .15 .04
151 Hubie Brooks .15 .04
152 David Cone .30 .09
153 Gary Gaetti .30 .09
154 Greg Gagne .15 .04
155 Tom Gordon .15 .04
156 Mark Gubicza .15 .04
157 Chris Gwynn .15 .04
158 John Habyan .15 .04
159 Chris Haney .15 .04
160 Phil Hiatt .15 .04
161 Felix Jose .15 .04
162 Wally Joyner .30 .09
163 Jose Lind .15 .04
164 Mike Macfarlane .15 .04
165 Mike Magnante .15 .04
166 Brent Mayne .15 .04
167 Brian McRae .15 .04
168 Kevin McReynolds .15 .04
169 Keith Miller .15 .04
170 Jeff Montgomery .15 .04
171 Hipolito Pichardo .15 .04
172 Rico Rossy .15 .04
173 Juan Bell .15 .04
174 Ricky Bones .15 .04
175 Cal Eldred .15 .04
176 Mike Fetters .15 .04
177 Darryl Hamilton .15 .04
178 Doug Henry .15 .04
179 Mike Ignasiak .15 .04
180 John Jaha .15 .04
181 Pat Listach .15 .04
182 Graeme Lloyd .15 .04
183 Matt Mieske .15 .04
184 Angel Miranda .15 .04
185 Jaime Navarro .15 .04
186 Dave Nilsson .15 .04
187 Troy O'Leary .15 .04
188 Jesse Orosco .15 .04
189 Kevin Reimer .15 .04
190 Kevin Seitzer .15 .04
191 Bill Spiers .15 .04
192 B.J. Surhoff .30 .09
193 Dickie Thon .15 .04
194 Jose Valentin .15 .04
195 Greg Vaughn .15 .04
196 Bill Wegman .15 .04
197 Robin Yount 1.25 .35
198 Rick Aguilera .15 .04
199 Willie Banks .15 .04
200 Bernardo Brito .15 .04
201 Larry Casian .15 .04
202 Scott Erickson .15 .04
203 Eddie Guardado .15 .04
204 Mark Guthrie .15 .04
205 Chip Hale .15 .04
206 Brian Harper .15 .04
207 Mike Hartley .15 .04
208 Kent Hrbek .30 .09
209 Terry Jorgensen .15 .04
210 Chuck Knoblauch .30 .09
211 Gene Larkin .15 .04
212 Shane Mack .15 .04
213 David McCarty .15 .04
214 Pat Meares .15 .04
215 Pedro Munoz .15 .04
216 Derek Parks .15 .04
217 Kirby Puckett .75 .23
218 Jeff Reboulet .15 .04
219 Kevin Tapani .15 .04
220 Mike Trombley .15 .04
221 George Tsamis .15 .04
222 Carl Willis .15 .04
223 Dave Winfield .30 .09
224 Jim Abbott .50 .15
225 Paul Assenmacher .15 .04
226 Wade Boggs .50 .15
227 Russ Davis .15 .04
228 Steve Farr .15 .04
229 Mike Gallego .15 .04
230 Paul Gibson .15 .04
231 Steve Howe .15 .04
232 Dion James .15 .04
233 Domingo Jean .15 .04
234 Scott Kamieniecki .15 .04
235 Pat Kelly .15 .04
236 Jimmy Key .30 .09
237 Jim Leyritz .15 .04
238 Kevin Maas .15 .04
239 Don Mattingly 2.00 .60
240 Rich Monteleone .15 .04
241 Bobby Munoz .15 .04
242 Matt Nokes .15 .04
243 Paul O'Neill .50 .15
244 Spike Owen .15 .04
245 Melido Perez .15 .04
246 Lee Smith .30 .09
247 Mike Stanley .15 .04
248 Danny Tartabull .15 .04
249 Randy Velarde .15 .04
250 Bob Wickman .15 .04
251 Bernie Williams .50 .15
252 Mike Aldrete .15 .04
253 Marcos Armas .15 .04
254 Lance Blankenship .15 .04
255 Mike Bordick .15 .04
256 Scott Brosius .30 .09
257 Jerry Browne .15 .04
258 Ron Darling .15 .04
259 Kelly Downs .15 .04
260 Dennis Eckersley .30 .09
261 Brent Gates .15 .04
262 Rich Gossage .30 .09
263 Scott Hemond .15 .04
264 Dave Henderson .15 .04
265 Rick Honeycutt .15 .04
266 Vince Horsman .15 .04
267 Scott Lydy .15 .04
268 Mark McGwire 2.00 .60
269 Mike Mohler .15 .04
270 Troy Neel .15 .04
271 Edwin Nunez .15 .04
272 Craig Paquette .15 .04
273 Ruben Sierra .30 .09
274 Terry Steinbach .15 .04
275 Todd Van Poppel .15 .04
276 Bob Welch .15 .04
277 Bobby Witt .15 .04
278 Rich Amaral .15 .04
279 Mike Blowers .15 .04
280 Bret Boone UER .30 .09
(Name spelled Brett on front)
281 Chris Bosio .15 .04
282 Jay Buhner .30 .09
283 Norm Charlton .15 .04
284 Mike Felder .15 .04
285 Dave Fleming .15 .04
286 Ken Griffey Jr. 1.25 .35
287 Erik Hanson .15 .04
288 Bill Haselman .15 .04
289 Brad Holman RC .15 .04
290 Randy Johnson .75 .23
291 Tim Leary .15 .04
292 Greg Litton .15 .04
293 Dave Magadan .15 .04
294 Edgar Martinez .50 .15
295 Tino Martinez .50 .15
296 Jeff Nelson .15 .04
297 Erik Plantenberg RC .15 .04
298 Mackey Sasser .15 .04
299 Brian Turang RC .15 .04
300 Dave Valle .15 .04
301 Omar Vizquel .50 .15
302 Brian Bohanon .15 .04
303 Kevin Brown .30 .09
304 Jose Canseco UER .75 .23
(Back mentions 1991 as his 40/40 MVP season; should be '88)
305 Mario Diaz .15 .04
306 Julio Franco .30 .09
307 Juan Gonzalez .50 .15
308 Tom Henke .15 .04
309 David Hulse .15 .04
310 Manuel Lee .15 .04
311 Craig Lefferts .15 .04
312 Charlie Leibrandt .15 .04
313 Rafael Palmeiro .50 .15
314 Dean Palmer .30 .09
315 Roger Pavlik .15 .04
316 Dan Peltier .15 .04
317 Gene Petralli .15 .04
318 Gary Redus .15 .04
319 Ivan Rodriguez .75 .23
320 Kenny Rogers .30 .09
321 Nolan Ryan 3.00 .90
322 Doug Strange .15 .04
323 Matt Whiteside .15 .04
324 Roberto Alomar .50 .15
325 Pat Borders .15 .04
326 Joe Carter .30 .09
327 Tony Castillo .15 .04
328 Darnell Coles .15 .04
329 Danny Cox .15 .04
330 Mark Eichhorn .15 .04
331 Tony Fernandez .15 .04
332 Alfredo Griffin .15 .04
333 Juan Guzman .15 .04
334 Rickey Henderson .75 .23
335 Pat Hentgen .15 .04
336 Randy Knorr .15 .04
337 Al Leiter .30 .09
338 Paul Molitor .50 .15
339 Jack Morris .30 .09
340 John Olerud .30 .09
341 Dick Schofield .15 .04
342 Ed Sprague .15 .04
343 Dave Stewart .30 .09
344 Todd Stottlemyre .15 .04
345 Mike Timlin .15 .04
346 Duane Ward .15 .04
347 Turner Ward .15 .04
348 Devon White .30 .09
349 Woody Williams .30 .09
350 Steve Avery .15 .04
351 Steve Bedrosian .15 .04
352 Rafael Belliard .15 .04
353 Damon Berryhill .15 .04
354 Jeff Blauser .15 .04
355 Sid Bream .15 .04
356 Francisco Cabrera .15 .04
357 Marvin Freeman .15 .04
358 Ron Gant .30 .09
359 Tom Glavine .50 .15
360 Jay Howell .15 .04
361 David Justice .30 .09
362 Ryan Klesko .30 .09
363 Mark Lemke .15 .04
364 Javier Lopez .30 .09
365 Greg Maddux 1.25 .35
366 Fred McGriff .50 .15
367 Greg McMichael .15 .04
368 Kent Mercker .15 .04
369 Otis Nixon .15 .04
370 Greg Olson .15 .04
371 Bill Pecota .15 .04
372 Terry Pendleton .30 .09
373 Deion Sanders .50 .15
374 Pete Smith .15 .04
375 John Smoltz .50 .15
376 Mike Stanton .15 .04
377 Tony Tarasco .15 .04
378 Mark Wohlers .15 .04
379 Jose Bautista .15 .04
380 Shawn Boskie .15 .04
381 Steve Buechele .15 .04
382 Frank Castillo .15 .04
383 Mark Grace .50 .15
384 Jose Guzman .15 .04
385 Mike Harkey .15 .04
386 Greg Hibbard .15 .04
387 Glenallen Hill .15 .04
388 Steve Lake .15 .04
389 Derrick May .15 .04
390 Chuck McElroy .15 .04
391 Mike Morgan .15 .04
392 Randy Myers .15 .04
393 Dan Plesac .15 .04
394 Kevin Roberson .15 .04
395 Rey Sanchez .15 .04
396 Ryne Sandberg 1.25 .35
397 Bob Scanlan .15 .04
398 Dwight Smith .15 .04
399 Sammy Sosa 1.25 .35
400 Jose Vizcaino .15 .04
401 Rick Wilkins .15 .04
402 Willie Wilson .15 .04
403 Eric Yelding .15 .04
404 Bobby Ayala .15 .04
405 Jeff Branson .15 .04
406 Tom Browning .15 .04
407 Jacob Brumfield .15 .04
408 Tim Costo .15 .04
409 Rob Dibble .30 .09
410 Willie Greene .15 .04
411 Thomas Howard .15 .04
412 Roberto Kelly .15 .04
413 Bill Landrum .15 .04
414 Barry Larkin .50 .15
415 Larry Luebbers RC .15 .04
416 Kevin Mitchell .15 .04
417 Hal Morris .15 .04
418 Joe Oliver .15 .04
419 Tim Pugh .15 .04
420 Jeff Reardon .30 .09
421 Jose Rijo .15 .04
422 Bip Roberts .15 .04
423 John Roper .15 .04
424 Johnny Ruffin .15 .04
425 Chris Sabo .15 .04
426 Juan Samuel .15 .04
427 Reggie Sanders .15 .04
428 Scott Service .15 .04
429 John Smiley .15 .04
430 Jerry Spradlin RC .15 .04
431 Kevin Wickander .15 .04
432 Freddie Benavides .15 .04
433 Dante Bichette .30 .09
434 Willie Blair .15 .04
435 Daryl Boston .15 .04
436 Kent Bottenfield .15 .04
437 Vinny Castilla .30 .09
438 Jerald Clark .15 .04
439 Alex Cole .15 .04
440 Andres Galarraga .30 .09
441 Joe Girardi .15 .04
442 Greg W. Harris .15 .04
443 Charlie Hayes .15 .04
444 Darren Holmes .15 .04
445 Chris Jones .15 .04
446 Roberto Mejia .15 .04
447 David Nied .15 .04
448 Jayhawk Owens .15 .04
449 Jeff Parrett .15 .04
450 Steve Reed .15 .04
451 Armando Reynoso .15 .04
452 Bruce Ruffin .15 .04
453 Mo Sanford .15 .04
454 Danny Sheaffer .15 .04
455 Jim Tatum .15 .04
456 Gary Wayne .15 .04
457 Eric Young .15 .04
458 Luis Aquino .15 .04
459 Alex Arias .15 .04
460 Jack Armstrong .15 .04
461 Bret Barberie .15 .04
462 Ryan Bowen .15 .04
463 Chuck Carr .15 .04
464 Jeff Conine .30 .09
465 Henry Cotto .15 .04
466 Orestes Destrade .15 .04
467 Chris Hammond .15 .04
468 Bryan Harvey .15 .04
469 Charlie Hough .30 .09
470 Joe Klink .15 .04
471 Richie Lewis .15 .04
472 Bob Natal .15 .04
473 Pat Rapp .15 .04
474 Rich Renteria .15 .04
475 Rich Rodriguez .15 .04
476 Benito Santiago .30 .09
477 Gary Sheffield .30 .09
478 Matt Turner .15 .04
479 David Weathers .15 .04
480 Walt Weiss .15 .04
481 Darrell Whitmore .15 .04
482 Eric Anthony .15 .04
483 Jeff Bagwell .50 .15
484 Kevin Bass .15 .04
485 Craig Biggio .50 .15
486 Ken Caminiti .30 .09
487 Andujar Cedeno .15 .04
488 Chris Donnels .15 .04
489 Doug Drabek .15 .04
490 Steve Finley .30 .09
491 Luis Gonzalez .30 .09
492 Pete Harnisch .15 .04
493 Xavier Hernandez .15 .04
494 Doug Jones .15 .04
495 Todd Jones .15 .04
496 Darryl Kile .30 .09
497 Al Osuna .15 .04
498 Mark Portugal .15 .04
499 Scott Servais .15 .04
500 Greg Swindell .15 .04
501 Eddie Taubensee .15 .04
502 Jose Uribe .15 .04
503 Brian Williams .15 .04
504 Billy Ashley .15 .04
505 Pedro Astacio .15 .04
506 Brett Butler .30 .09
507 Tom Candiotti .15 .04
508 Omar Daal .15 .04
509 Jim Gott .15 .04
510 Kevin Gross .15 .04
511 Dave Hansen .15 .04
512 Carlos Hernandez .15 .04
513 Orel Hershiser .30 .09
514 Eric Karros .30 .09
515 Pedro Martinez .75 .23
516 Ramon Martinez .15 .04
517 Roger McDowell .15 .04
518 Raul Mondesi .30 .09
519 Jose Offerman .15 .04
520 Mike Piazza 1.50 .45
521 Jody Reed .15 .04
522 Henry Rodriguez .15 .04
523 Mike Sharperson .15 .04
524 Cory Snyder .15 .04
525 Darryl Strawberry .30 .09
526 Rick Trlicek .15 .04
527 Tim Wallach .15 .04
528 Mitch Webster .15 .04
529 Steve Wilson .15 .04
530 Todd Worrell .15 .04
531 Moises Alou .30 .09
532 Brian Barnes .15 .04
533 Sean Berry .15 .04
534 Greg Colbrunn .15 .04
535 Delino DeShields .15 .04
536 Jeff Fassero .15 .04
537 Darrin Fletcher .15 .04
538 Cliff Floyd .30 .09
539 Lou Frazier .15 .04
540 Marquis Grissom .30 .09
541 Butch Henry .15 .04
542 Ken Hill .15 .04
543 Mike Lansing .15 .04
544 Brian Looney RC .15 .04
545 Dennis Martinez .30 .09
546 Chris Nabholz .15 .04
547 Randy Ready .15 .04
548 Mel Rojas .15 .04
549 Kirk Rueter .30 .09
550 Tim Scott .15 .04
551 Jeff Shaw .15 .04
552 Tim Spehr .15 .04
553 John Vander Wal .15 .04
554 Larry Walker .50 .15
555 John Wetteland .30 .09
556 Rondell White .30 .09
557 Tim Bogar .15 .04
558 Bobby Bonilla .30 .09
559 Jeromy Burnitz .30 .09
560 Sid Fernandez .15 .04
561 John Franco .30 .09
562 Dave Gallagher .15 .04
563 Dwight Gooden .30 .09
564 Eric Hillman .15 .04
565 Todd Hundley .15 .04
566 Jeff Innis .15 .04
567 Darrin Jackson .15 .04
568 Howard Johnson .15 .04
569 Bobby Jones .15 .04
570 Jeff Kent .30 .09
571 Mike Maddux .15 .04
572 Jeff McKnight .15 .04
573 Eddie Murray .75 .23
574 Charlie O'Brien .15 .04
575 Joe Orsulak .15 .04
576 Bret Saberhagen .30 .09
577 Pete Schourek .15 .04
578 Dave Telgheder .15 .04
579 Ryan Thompson .15 .04
580 Anthony Young .15 .04
581 Ruben Amaro .15 .04
582 Larry Andersen .15 .04
583 Kim Batiste .15 .04
584 Wes Chamberlain .15 .04
585 Darren Daulton .30 .09
586 Mariano Duncan .15 .04
587 Lenny Dykstra .30 .09
588 Jim Eisenreich .15 .04
589 Tommy Greene .15 .04
590 Dave Hollins .15 .04
591 Pete Incaviglia .15 .04
592 Danny Jackson .15 .04
593 Ricky Jordan .15 .04
594 John Kruk .30 .09
595 Roger Mason .15 .04
596 Mickey Morandini .15 .04
597 Terry Mulholland .15 .04
598 Todd Pratt .15 .04
599 Ben Rivera .15 .04
600 Curt Schilling .30 .09
601 Kevin Stocker .15 .04
602 Milt Thompson .15 .04
603 David West .15 .04
604 Mitch Williams .15 .04
605 Jay Bell .30 .09
606 Dave Clark .15 .04
607 Steve Cooke .15 .04

608 Tom Foley .15 .04
609 Carlos Garcia .15 .04
610 Joel Johnston .15 .04
611 Jeff King .15 .04
612 Al Martin .15 .04
613 Lloyd McClendon .15 .04
614 Orlando Merced .15 .04
615 Blas Minor .15 .04
616 Denny Neagle .30 .09
617 Mark Petkovsek RC .15 .04
618 Tom Prince .15 .04
619 Don Slaught .15 .04
620 Zane Smith .15 .04
621 Randy Tomlin .15 .04
622 Andy Van Slyke .30 .09
623 Paul Wagner .15 .04
624 Tim Wakefield .30 .09
625 Bob Walk .15 .04
626 Kevin Young .15 .04
627 Luis Alicea .15 .04
628 Rene Arocha .15 .04
629 Rod Brewer .15 .04
630 Rheal Cormier .15 .04
631 Bernard Gilkey .15 .04
632 Lee Guetterman .15 .04
633 Gregg Jefferies .15 .04
634 Brian Jordan .30 .09
635 Les Lancaster .15 .04
636 Ray Lankford .15 .04
637 Rob Murphy .15 .04
638 Omar Olivares .15 .04
639 Jose Oquendo .15 .04
640 Donovan Osborne .15 .04
641 Tom Pagnozzi .15 .04
642 Erik Pappas .15 .04
643 Geronimo Pena .15 .04
644 Mike Perez .15 .04
645 Gerald Perry .15 .04
646 Ozzie Smith 1.25 .35
647 Bob Tewksbury .15 .04
648 Allen Watson .15 .04
649 Mark Whiten .15 .04
650 Tracy Woodson .15 .04
651 Todd Zeile .15 .04
652 Andy Ashby .15 .04
653 Brad Ausmus .15 .04
654 Billy Bean .15 .04
655 Derek Bell .15 .04
656 Andy Benes .15 .04
657 Doug Brocail .15 .04
658 Jarvis Brown .15 .04
659 Archi Cianfrocco .15 .04
660 Phil Clark .15 .04
661 Mark Davis .15 .04
662 Jeff Gardner .15 .04
663 Pat Gomez .15 .04
664 Ricky Gutierrez .15 .04
665 Tony Gwynn 1.00 .30
666 Gene Harris .15 .04
667 Kevin Higgins .15 .04
668 Trevor Hoffman .30 .09
669 Pedro Martinez RC .15 .04
670 Tim Mauser .15 .04
671 Melvin Nieves .15 .04
672 Phil Plantier .15 .04
673 Frank Seminara .15 .04
674 Craig Shipley .15 .04
675 Kerry Taylor .15 .04
676 Tim Teufel .15 .04
677 Guillermo Velasquez .15 .04
678 Wally Whitehurst .15 .04
679 Tim Worrell .15 .04
680 Rod Beck .15 .04
681 Mike Benjamin .15 .04
682 Todd Benzinger .15 .04
683 Bud Black .15 .04
684 Barry Bonds 2.00 .60
685 Jeff Brantley .15 .04
686 Dave Burba .15 .04
687 John Burkett .15 .04
688 Mark Carreon .15 .04
689 Will Clark .75 .23
690 Royce Clayton .15 .04
691 Bryan Hickerson .15 .04
692 Mike Jackson .15 .04
693 Darren Lewis .15 .04
694 Kirt Manwaring .15 .04
695 Dave Martinez .15 .04
696 Willie McGee .30 .09
697 John Patterson .15 .04
698 Jeff Reed .15 .04
699 Kevin Rogers .15 .04
700 Scott Sanderson .15 .04
701 Steve Scarsone .15 .04
702 Billy Swift .15 .04
703 Robby Thompson .15 .04
704 Matt Williams .30 .09
705 Trevor Wilson .15 .04
706 Fred McGriff .30 .09
Ron Gant
David Justice
707 John Olerud .30 .09
Paul Molitor
708 Mike Mussina .30 .09
Jack McDowell
709 Lou Whitaker .30 .09
Alan Trammell
710 Rafael Palmeiro .30 .09
Juan Gonzalez
711 Brett Butler .50 .15
Tony Gwynn
712 Kirby Puckett .50 .15
Chuck Knoblauch
713 Mike Piazza .75 .23
Eric Karros
714 Checklist 1 .15 .04
715 Checklist 2 .15 .04
716 Checklist 3 .15 .04
717 Checklist 4 .15 .04
718 Checklist 5 .15 .04
719 Checklist 6 .15 .04
720 Checklist 7 .15 .04
P659 Tim Salmon Promo 1.00 .30

1994 Fleer All-Rookies

Collectors could redeem an All-Rookie Team exchange card by mail for this nine-card set of top 1994 rookies at each position as chosen by Fleer. The expiration date to remeem this set was

September 30, 1994. None of these players were in the basic 1994 Fleer set. The exchange card was randomly inserted into all 1994 Fleer packs.

	Nm-Mt	Ex-Mt
COMPLETE SET (9)	8.00	2.40
M1 Kurt Abbott	1.00	.30
M2 Rich Becker	.50	.15
M3 Carlos Delgado	1.50	.45
M4 Jorge Fabregas	.50	.15
M5 Bob Hamelin	.50	.15
M6 John Hudek	.50	.15
M7 Tim Hyers	.50	.15
M8 Luis Lopez	.50	.15
M9 James Mouton	.50	.15
NNO Exp. All-Rookie Exch.	.50	.15

1994 Fleer All-Stars

Fleer issued this 50-card standard-size set in 1994, to commemorate the All-Stars of the 1993 season. The cards were exclusively available in the Fleer wax packs at a rate of one in two. The set features 25 American League (1-25) and 25 National League (26-50) All-Stars. Each league's all-stars are sequenced in alphabetical order.

	Nm-Mt	Ex-Mt
COMPLETE SET (50)	25.00	7.50
1 Roberto Alomar	.60	.18
2 Carlos Baerga	.20	.06
3 Albert Belle	.40	.12
4 Wade Boggs	.60	.18
5 Joe Carter	.40	.12
6 Scott Cooper	.20	.06
7 Cecil Fielder	.40	.12
8 Travis Fryman	.40	.12
9 Juan Gonzalez	.60	.18
10 Ken Griffey Jr.	1.50	.45
11 Pat Hentgen	.20	.06
12 Randy Johnson	1.00	.30
13 Jimmy Key	.40	.12
14 Mark Langston	.20	.06
15 Jack McDowell	.20	.06
16 Paul Molitor	.60	.18
17 Jeff Montgomery	.20	.06
18 Mike Mussina	.60	.18
19 John Olerud	.40	.12
20 Kirby Puckett	1.00	.30
21 Cal Ripken	3.00	.90
22 Ivan Rodriguez	1.00	.30
23 Frank Thomas	1.00	.30
24 Greg Vaughn	.20	.06
25 Duane Ward	.20	.06
26 Steve Avery	.20	.06
27 Rod Beck	.20	.06
28 Jay Bell	.40	.12
29 Andy Benes	.20	.06
30 Jeff Blauser	.20	.06
31 Barry Bonds	2.50	.75
32 Bobby Bonilla	.40	.12
33 John Burkett	.20	.06
34 Darren Daulton	.40	.12
35 Andres Galarraga	.40	.12
36 Tom Glavine	.60	.18
37 Mark Grace	.60	.18
38 Marquis Grissom	.40	.12
39 Tony Gwynn	1.25	.35
40 Bryan Harvey	.20	.06
41 Dave Hollins	.20	.06
42 David Justice	.40	.12
43 Darryl Kile	.40	.12
44 John Kruk	.40	.12
45 Barry Larkin	.60	.18
46 Terry Mulholland	.20	.06
47 Mike Piazza	2.00	.60
48 Ryne Sandberg	1.50	.45
49 Gary Sheffield	.40	.12
50 John Smoltz	.60	.18

1994 Fleer Award Winners

Randomly inserted in foil packs at a rate of one in 37, this six-card standard-size set spotlights six outstanding players who received awards.

	Nm-Mt	Ex-Mt
COMPLETE SET (6)	8.00	2.40
1 Frank Thomas	1.25	.35
2 Barry Bonds	3.00	.90
3 Jack McDowell	.25	.07
4 Greg Maddux	2.00	.60
5 Tim Salmon	.75	.23
6 Mike Piazza	2.50	.75

1994 Fleer Golden Moments

These standard-size cards were issued one per blue retail jumbo pack. The fronts feature borderless color player action photos. A shrink-wrapped package containing a jumbo set was issued one per Fleer hobby case. Jumbos were later issued for retail purposes with a production number of 10,000. The standard-size cards are not individually numbered.

	Nm-Mt	Ex-Mt
COMPLETE SET (10)	30.00	9.00
*JUMBOS: .4X TO 1X BASIC GM		
ONE JUMBO SET PER HOBBY CASE ..		
JUMBOS ALSO REPACKAGED FOR RETAIL		
1 Mark Whiten	.60	.18
2 Carlos Baerga	.60	.18
3 Dave Winfield	1.25	.35
4 Ken Griffey Jr.	5.00	1.50
5 Bo Jackson	3.00	.90
6 George Brett	8.00	2.40
7 Nolan Ryan	12.00	3.60
8 Fred McGriff	2.00	.60
9 Frank Thomas	3.00	.90
10 Chris Bosio	.60	.18
Jim Abbott		
Darryl Kile		

1994 Fleer League Leaders

Randomly inserted in all pack types at a rate of one in 17, this 28-card set features six statistical leaders each for the American (1-6) and the National (7-12) Leagues.

	Nm-Mt	Ex-Mt
COMPLETE SET (12)	5.00	1.50
1 John Olerud	.40	.12
2 Albert Belle	.40	.12
3 Rafael Palmeiro	.50	.15
4 Kenny Lofton	.40	.12
5 Jack McDowell	.25	.07
6 Kevin Appier	.40	.12
7 Andres Galarraga	.40	.12
8 Barry Bonds	1.50	.45
9 Lenny Dykstra	.40	.12
10 Chuck Carr	.25	.07
11 Tom Glavine UER	.50	.15
No number on back of card		
12 Greg Maddux	2.50	.75

1994 Fleer Lumber Company

Randomly inserted in jumbo packs at a rate of one in five, this ten-card standard-size set features the best hitters in the game. The cards are numbered alphabetically.

	Nm-Mt	Ex-Mt
COMPLETE SET (10)	10.00	3.00
1 Albert Belle	.50	.15
2 Barry Bonds	3.00	.90
3 Ron Gant	.50	.15
4 Juan Gonzalez	.75	.23
5 Ken Griffey Jr.	2.00	.60
6 David Justice	.50	.15
7 Fred McGriff	.75	.23
8 Rafael Palmeiro	.75	.23
9 Frank Thomas	1.25	.35
10 Matt Williams	.50	.15

1994 Fleer Major League Prospects

Randomly inserted in all pack types at a rate of one in six, this 35-card standard-size set showcases some of the outstanding young players in Major League Baseball. The cards are numbered on the back "X of 35" and are sequenced in alphabetical order.

	Nm-Mt	Ex-Mt
COMPLETE SET (35)	15.00	4.50
1 Kurt Abbott	.75	.23
2 Brian Anderson	.75	.23
3 Rich Aude	.25	.07
4 Cory Bailey	.25	.07
5 Danny Bautista	.25	.07
6 Marty Cordova	.25	.07
7 Tripp Cromer	.25	.07
8 Midre Cummings	.25	.07
9 Carlos Delgado	1.25	.35
10 Steve Dreyer	.25	.07
11 Steve Dunn	.25	.07
12 Jeff Granger	.25	.07
13 Tyrone Hill	.25	.07
14 Denny Hocking	.25	.07
15 John Hope	.25	.07
16 Butch Huskey	.25	.07
17 Miguel Jimenez	.25	.07
18 Chipper Jones	2.00	.60
19 Steve Karsay	.25	.07
20 Mike Kelly	.25	.07
21 Mike Lieberthal	.75	.23
22 Albie Lopez	.25	.07
23 Jeff McNeely	.25	.07
24 Danny Miceli	.25	.07
25 Nate Minchey	.25	.07
26 Marc Newfield	.25	.07
27 Darren Oliver	.75	.23
28 Luis Ortiz	.25	.07
29 Curtis Pride	.75	.23
30 Roger Salkeld	.25	.07
31 Scott Sanders	.25	.07
32 Dave Staton	.25	.07
33 Salomon Torres	.25	.07
34 Steve Trachsel	.25	.07
35 Chris Turner	.25	.07

1994 Fleer Pro-Visions

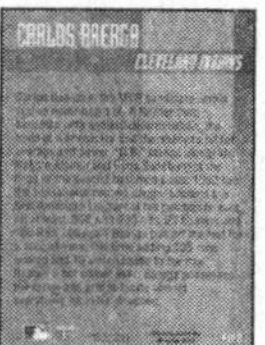

Randomly inserted in all pack types at a rate of one in 12, this nine-card standard-size set features on its fronts colorful artistic player caricatures with surrealistic backgrounds drawn by illustrator Wayne Still. When all nine cards are placed in order in a collector sheet, the backgrounds fit together to form a composite. The cards are numbered on the back "X of 9."

	Nm-Mt	Ex-Mt
COMPLETE SET (9)	4.00	1.20
1 Darren Daulton	.40	.12
2 John Olerud	.40	.12
3 Matt Williams	.40	.12
4 Carlos Baerga	.20	.06
5 Ozzie Smith	1.50	.45
6 Juan Gonzalez	.60	.18
7 Jack McDowell	.20	.06
8 Mike Piazza	2.00	.60
9 Tony Gwynn	1.25	.35

1994 Fleer Rookie Sensations

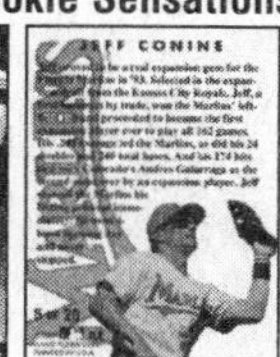

Randomly inserted in jumbo packs at a rate of one in four, this 20-card standard-size set features outstanding rookies. The fronts are "double exposed," with a player action cutout superimposed over a second photo. The cards are numbered on the back "X of 20" and are sequenced in alphabetical order.

	Nm-Mt	Ex-Mt
COMPLETE SET (20)	20.00	6.00
1 Rene Arocha	1.00	.30
2 Jason Bere	1.00	.30
3 Jeromy Burnitz	2.00	.60
4 Chuck Carr	1.00	.30
5 Jeff Conine	2.00	.60
6 Steve Cooke	1.00	.30
7 Cliff Floyd	2.00	.60
8 Jeffrey Hammonds	1.00	.30
9 Wayne Kirby	1.00	.30
10 Mike Lansing	1.00	.30
11 Al Martin	1.00	.30
12 Greg McMichael	1.00	.30
13 Troy Neel	1.00	.30
14 Mike Piazza	10.00	3.00
15 Armando Reynoso	1.00	.30
16 Kirk Rueter	2.00	.60
17 Tim Salmon	3.00	.90
18 Aaron Sele	1.00	.30
19 J.T. Snow	2.00	.60
20 Kevin Stocker	1.00	.30

1994 Fleer Salmon

Spotlighting American League Rookie of the Year Tim Salmon, this 15-card standard size set was issued in two forms. Cards 1-12 were randomly inserted in packs (one in eight) and 13-15 were available through a mail-in offer. Ten wrappers and 1.50 were necessary to acquire the mail-ins. The mail-in expiration date was September 30, 1994. Salmon autographed more than 2,000 of his cards.

	Nm-Mt	Ex-Mt
COMPLETE SET (12)	15.00	4.50
COMMON CARD (1-12)	1.00	.30
COMMON MAIL (13-15)	1.00	.30
AU Tim Salmon AU	25.00	7.50
(Certified autograph)		

1994 Fleer Smoke 'n Heat

Randomly inserted in wax packs at a rate of one in 36, this 12-card standard-size set showcases the best pitchers in the game. The cards are numbered on the back "X of 12." and are sequenced in alphabetical order.

	Nm-Mt	Ex-Mt
COMPLETE SET (12)	60.00	18.00
1 Roger Clemens	10.00	3.00
2 David Cone	2.00	.60
3 Juan Guzman	1.00	.30
4 Pete Harnisch	1.00	.30
5 Randy Johnson	5.00	1.50
6 Mark Langston	1.00	.30
7 Greg Maddux	8.00	2.40
8 Mike Mussina	3.00	.90
9 Jose Rijo	1.00	.30
10 Nolan Ryan	20.00	6.00
11 Curt Schilling	2.00	.60
12 John Smoltz	3.00	.90

1994 Fleer Team Leaders

Randomly inserted in all pack types, this 28-card standard-size set features Fleer's selected top player from each of the 28 major league teams. The card numbering is arranged alphabetically by city according to the American (1-14) and the National (15-28) Leagues.

	Nm-Mt	Ex-Mt
COMPLETE SET (28)	25.00	7.50
1 Cal Ripken	4.00	1.20
2 Mo Vaughn	.50	.15
3 Tim Salmon	.75	.23
4 Frank Thomas	1.25	.35
5 Carlos Baerga	.25	.07
6 Cecil Fielder	.50	.15
7 Brian McRae	.25	.07
8 Greg Vaughn	.25	.07
9 Kirby Puckett	1.25	.35
10 Don Mattingly	3.00	.90
11 Mark McGwire	3.00	.90
12 Ken Griffey Jr.	2.00	.60
13 Juan Gonzalez	.75	.23
14 Paul Molitor	.75	.23
15 David Justice	.50	.15
16 Ryne Sandberg	2.00	.60
17 Barry Larkin	.75	.23
18 Andres Galarraga	.50	.15
19 Gary Sheffield	.50	.15
20 Jeff Bagwell	.75	.23
21 Mike Piazza	2.50	.75
22 Marquis Grissom	.50	.15
23 Bobby Bonilla	.50	.15
24 Lenny Dykstra	.50	.15
25 Jay Bell	.50	.15
26 Gregg Jefferies	.25	.07
27 Tony Gwynn	1.50	.45
28 Will Clark	1.25	.35

1994 Fleer Update

This 200-card standard-size set highlights traded players in their new uniforms and promising young rookies. The Update set was exclusively distributed in factory set form through hobby dealers. A ten card Diamond Tribute set was included in each factory set for a total of 210 cards. The cards are numbered on the back, grouped alphabetically by team by league with AL preceding NL. Key Rookie Cards include Chan Ho Park and Alex Rodriguez.

	Nm-Mt	Ex-Mt
COMP.FACT.SET (210)	50.00	15.00
1 Mark Eichhorn	.25	.07

2 Sid Fernandez .25 .07
3 Leo Gomez .25 .07
4 Mike Oquist .25 .07
5 Rafael Palmeiro .75 .23
6 Chris Sabo .25 .07
7 Dwight Smith .25 .07
8 Lee Smith .50 .15
9 Damon Berryhill .25 .07
10 Wes Chamberlain .25 .07
11 Gar Finnvold .25 .07
12 Chris Howard .25 .07
13 Tim Naehring .25 .07
14 Otis Nixon .25 .07
15 Brian Anderson RC .50 .15
16 Jorge Fabregas .25 .07
17 Rex Hudler .25 .07
18 Bo Jackson 1.25 .35
19 Mark Leiter .25 .07
20 Spike Owen .25 .07
21 Harold Reynolds .50 .15
22 Chris Turner .25 .07
23 Dennis Cook .25 .07
24 Jose DeLeon .25 .07
25 Julio Franco .50 .15
26 Joe Hall .25 .07
27 Darrin Jackson .25 .07
28 Dane Johnson .25 .07
29 Norberto Martin .25 .07
30 Scott Sanderson .25 .07
31 Jason Grimsley .25 .07
32 Dennis Martinez .50 .15
33 Jack Morris .50 .15
34 Eddie Murray 1.25 .35
35 Chad Ogea .25 .07
36 Tony Pena .25 .07
37 Paul Shuey .25 .07
38 Omar Vizquel .75 .23
39 Danny Bautista .25 .07
40 Tim Belcher .25 .07
41 Joe Boever .25 .07
42 Storm Davis .25 .07
43 Junior Felix .25 .07
44 Mike Gardiner .25 .07
45 Buddy Groom .25 .07
46 Juan Samuel .25 .07
47 Vince Coleman .25 .07
48 Bob Hamelin .25 .07
49 Dave Henderson .25 .07
50 Rusty Meacham .25 .07
51 Terry Shumpert .25 .07
52 Jeff Bronkey .25 .07
53 Alex Diaz .25 .07
54 Brian Harper .25 .07
55 Jose Mercedes .25 .07
56 Jody Reed .25 .07
57 Bob Scanlan .25 .07
58 Turner Ward .25 .07
59 Rich Becker .25 .07
60 Alex Cole .25 .07
61 Denny Hocking .25 .07
62 Scott Leius .25 .07
63 Pat Mahomes .25 .07
64 Carlos Pulido .25 .07
65 Dave Stevens .25 .07
66 Matt Walbeck .25 .07
67 Xavier Hernandez .25 .07
68 Sterling Hitchcock .25 .07
69 Terry Mulholland .25 .07
70 Luis Polonia .25 .07
71 Gerald Williams .25 .07
72 Mark Acre RC .25 .07
73 Geronimo Berroa .25 .07
74 Rickey Henderson 1.25 .35
75 Stan Javier .25 .07
76 Steve Karsay .25 .07
77 Carlos Reyes .25 .07
78 Bill Taylor RC .50 .15
79 Eric Anthony .25 .07
80 Bobby Ayala .25 .07
81 Tim Davis .25 .07
82 Felix Fermin .25 .07
83 Reggie Jefferson .25 .07
84 Keith Mitchell .25 .07
85 Bill Risley .25 .07
86 Alex Rodriguez RC 40.00 12.00
87 Roger Salkeld .25 .07
88 Dan Wilson .25 .07
89 Cris Carpenter .25 .07
90 Will Clark 1.25 .35
91 Jeff Frye .25 .07
92 Rick Helling .25 .07
93 Chris James .25 .07
94 Oddibe McDowell .25 .07
95 Billy Ripken .25 .07
96 Carlos Delgado .75 .23
97 Alex Gonzalez .25 .07
98 Shawn Green 1.25 .35
99 Darren Hall .25 .07
100 Mike Huff .25 .07
101 Mike Kelly .25 .07
102 Roberto Kelly .25 .07
103 Charlie O'Brien .25 .07
104 Jose Oliva .25 .07
105 Gregg Olson .25 .07
106 Willie Banks .25 .07
107 Jim Bullinger .25 .07
108 Chuck Crim .25 .07
109 Shawon Dunston .25 .07
110 Karl Rhodes .25 .07
111 Steve Trachsel .25 .07
112 Anthony Young .25 .07
113 Eddie Zambrano .25 .07
114 Bret Boone .50 .15
115 Jeff Brantley .25 .07
116 Hector Carrasco .25 .07
117 Tony Fernandez .25 .07
118 Tim Fortugno .25 .07
119 Erik Hanson .25 .07
120 Chuck McElroy .25 .07
121 Deion Sanders .75 .23
122 Ellis Burks .50 .15
123 Marvin Freeman .25 .07
124 Mike Harkey .25 .07
125 Howard Johnson .25 .07
126 Mike Kingery .25 .07
127 Nelson Liriano .25 .07
128 Marcus Moore .25 .07
129 Mike Munoz .25 .07
130 Kevin Ritz .25 .07
131 Walt Weiss .25 .07
132 Kurt Abbott RC .50 .15
133 Jerry Browne .25 .07
134 Greg Colbrunn .25 .07
135 Jeremy Hernandez .25 .07
136 Dave Magadan .25 .07
137 Kurt Miller .25 .07
138 Robb Nen .50 .15
139 Jesus Tavarez RC .25 .07
140 Sid Bream .25 .07
141 Tom Edens .25 .07
142 Tony Eusebio .25 .07
143 John Hudek RC .25 .07
144 Brian L. Hunter .25 .07
145 Orlando Miller .25 .07
146 James Mouton .25 .07
147 Shane Reynolds .25 .07
148 Rafael Bournigal .25 .07
149 Delino DeShields .25 .07
150 Garey Ingram RC .25 .07
151 Chan Ho Park RC .75 .23
152 Wil Cordero .25 .07
153 Pedro Martinez 1.25 .35
154 Randy Milligan .25 .07
155 Lenny Webster .25 .07
156 Rico Brogna .25 .07
157 Josias Manzanillo .25 .07
158 Kevin McReynolds .25 .07
159 Mike Remlinger .25 .07
160 David Segui .25 .07
161 Pete Smith .25 .07
162 Kelly Stinnett RC .50 .15
163 Jose Vizcaino .25 .07
164 Billy Hatcher .25 .07
165 Doug Jones .25 .07
166 Mike Lieberthal .50 .15
167 Tony Longmire .25 .07
168 Bobby Munoz .25 .07
169 Paul Quantrill .25 .07
170 Heathcliff Slocumb .25 .07
171 Fernando Valenzuela .50 .15
172 Mark Dewey .25 .07
173 Brian R. Hunter .25 .07
174 Jon Lieber .25 .07
175 Ravelo Manzanillo .25 .07
176 Dan Miceli .25 .07
177 Rick White .25 .07
178 Bryan Eversgerd .25 .07
179 John Habyan .25 .07
180 Terry McGriff .25 .07
181 Vicente Palacios .25 .07
182 Rich Rodriguez .25 .07
183 Rick Sutcliffe .50 .15
184 Donnie Elliott .25 .07
185 Joey Hamilton .25 .07
186 Tim Hyers RC .25 .07
187 Luis Lopez .25 .07
188 Ray McDavid .25 .07
189 Bip Roberts .25 .07
190 Scott Sanders .25 .07
191 Eddie Williams .25 .07
192 Steve Frey .25 .07
193 Pat Gomez .25 .07
194 Rich Monteleone .25 .07
195 Mark Portugal .25 .07
196 Darryl Strawberry .50 .15
197 Salomon Torres .25 .07
198 W.VanLandingham RC .25 .07
199 Checklist .25 .07
200 Checklist .25 .07

1994 Fleer Update Diamond Tribute

Each 1994 Fleer Update factory set contained a complete 10-card set of Diamond Tribute inserts. This was the third and final year that Fleer included an insert set in their factory boxed update sets. The 1994 Diamond Tribute inserts feature a player action shot cut out against a backdrop of clouds and baseballs. The selection once again focuses on the game's top veterans. Cards are numbered "X" of 10 on the back.

Nm-Mt Ex-Mt
COMPLETE SET (10) 2.00 .60
1 Barry Bonds 1.00 .30
2 Joe Carter .15 .04
3 Will Clark .40 .12
4 Roger Clemens .75 .23
5 Tony Gwynn .50 .15
6 Don Mattingly 1.00 .30
7 Fred McGriff .25 .07
8 Eddie Murray .40 .12
9 Kirby Puckett .40 .12
10 Cal Ripken 1.25 .35

1995 Fleer

The 1995 Fleer set consists of 600 standard-size cards issued as one series. Each pack contained at least one insert card with some 'Hot Packs' containing nothing but insert cards. Full-bleed fronts have two player photos and, atypical of baseball cards fronts, biographical information such as height, weight, etc. The backgrounds are multi-colored. The backs are horizontal and contain year-by-year statistics along with a photo. There was a different design for each of baseball's six divisions. The checklist is arranged alphabetically by teams within each league with AL preceding NL. To preview the product prior to it's public release, Fleer printed up additional quantities of cards 26, 78, 155, 235, 285, 351, 509 and 514 and mailed them to dealers and hobby media.

Nm-Mt Ex-Mt
COMPLETE SET (600) 50.00 15.00
1 Brady Anderson .30 .09
2 Harold Baines .30 .09
3 Damon Buford .15 .04
4 Mike Devereaux .15 .04
5 Mark Eichhorn .15 .04
6 Sid Fernandez .15 .04
7 Leo Gomez .15 .04
8 Jeffrey Hammonds .15 .04
9 Chris Hoiles .15 .04
10 Rick Krivda .15 .04
11 Ben McDonald .15 .04
12 Mark McLemore .15 .04
13 Alan Mills .15 .04
14 Jamie Moyer .30 .09
15 Mike Mussina .50 .15
16 Mike Oquist .15 .04
17 Rafael Palmeiro .50 .15
18 Arthur Rhodes .15 .04
19 Cal Ripken Jr. 2.50 .75
20 Chris Sabo .15 .04
21 Lee Smith .30 .09
22 Jack Voigt .15 .04
23 Damon Berryhill .15 .04
24 Tom Brunansky .15 .04
25 Wes Chamberlain .15 .04
26 Roger Clemens 1.50 .45
27 Scott Cooper .15 .04
28 Andre Dawson .30 .09
29 Gar Finnvold .15 .04
30 Tony Fossas .15 .04
31 Mike Greenwell .15 .04
32 Joe Hesketh .15 .04
33 Chris Howard .15 .04
34 Chris Nabholz .15 .04
35 Tim Naehring .15 .04
36 Otis Nixon .15 .04
37 Carlos Rodriguez .15 .04
38 Rich Rowland .15 .04
39 Ken Ryan .15 .04
40 Aaron Sele .15 .04
41 John Valentin .15 .04
42 Mo Vaughn .30 .09
43 Frank Viola .30 .09
44 Danny Bautista .15 .04
45 Joe Boever .15 .04
46 Milt Cuyler .15 .04
47 Storm Davis .15 .04
48 John Doherty .15 .04
49 Junior Felix .15 .04
50 Cecil Fielder .30 .09
51 Travis Fryman .30 .09
52 Mike Gardiner .15 .04
53 Kirk Gibson .30 .09
54 Chris Gomez .15 .04
55 Buddy Groom .15 .04
56 Mike Henneman .15 .04
57 Chad Kreuter .15 .04
58 Mike Moore .15 .04
59 Tony Phillips .15 .04
60 Juan Samuel .15 .04
61 Mickey Tettleton .15 .04
62 Alan Trammell .30 .09
63 David Wells .30 .09
64 Lou Whitaker .30 .09
65 Jim Abbott .50 .15
66 Joe Ausanio .15 .04
67 Wade Boggs .50 .15
68 Mike Gallego .15 .04
69 Xavier Hernandez .15 .04
70 Sterling Hitchcock .15 .04
71 Steve Howe .15 .04
72 Scott Kamieniecki .15 .04
73 Pat Kelly .15 .04
74 Jimmy Key .30 .09
75 Jim Leyritz .15 .04
76 Don Mattingly UER 2.00 .60
Photo is a reversed negative
77 Terry Mulholland .15 .04
78 Paul O'Neill .50 .15
79 Melido Perez .15 .04
80 Luis Polonia .15 .04
81 Mike Stanley .15 .04
82 Danny Tartabull .15 .04
83 Randy Velarde .15 .04
84 Bob Wickman .15 .04
85 Bernie Williams .50 .15
86 Gerald Williams .15 .04
87 Roberto Alomar .50 .15
88 Pat Borders .15 .04
89 Joe Carter .30 .09
90 Tony Castillo .15 .04
91 Brad Cornett RC .15 .04
92 Carlos Delgado .30 .09
93 Alex Gonzalez .15 .04
94 Shawn Green .30 .09
95 Juan Guzman .15 .04
96 Darren Hall .15 .04
97 Pat Hentgen .15 .04
98 Mike Huff .15 .04
99 Randy Knorr .15 .04
100 Al Leiter .30 .09
101 Paul Molitor .50 .15
102 John Olerud .30 .09
103 Dick Schofield .15 .04
104 Ed Sprague .15 .04
105 Dave Stewart .30 .09
106 Todd Stottlemyre .15 .04
107 Devon White .30 .09
108 Woody Williams .15 .04
109 Wilson Alvarez .15 .04
110 Paul Assenmacher .15 .04
111 Jason Bere .15 .04
112 Dennis Cook .15 .04
113 Joey Cora .15 .04
114 Jose DeLeon .15 .04
115 Alex Fernandez .15 .04
116 Julio Franco .30 .09
117 Craig Grebeck .15 .04
118 Ozzie Guillen .15 .04
119 Roberto Hernandez .15 .04
120 Darrin Jackson .15 .04
121 Lance Johnson .15 .04
122 Ron Karkovice .15 .04
123 Mike LaValliere .15 .04
124 Norberto Martin .15 .04
125 Kirk McCaskill .15 .04
126 Jack McDowell .15 .04
127 Tim Raines .30 .09
128 Frank Thomas .75 .23
129 Robin Ventura .30 .09
130 Sandy Alomar Jr. .15 .04
131 Carlos Baerga .15 .04
132 Albert Belle .30 .09
133 Mark Clark .15 .04
134 Alvaro Espinoza .15 .04
135 Jason Grimsley .15 .04
136 Wayne Kirby .15 .04
137 Kenny Lofton .30 .09
138 Albie Lopez .15 .04
139 Dennis Martinez .30 .09
140 Jose Mesa .15 .04
141 Eddie Murray .75 .23
142 Charles Nagy .15 .04
143 Tony Pena .15 .04
144 Eric Plunk .15 .04
145 Manny Ramirez .50 .15
146 Jeff Russell .15 .04
147 Paul Shuey .15 .04
148 Paul Sorrento .15 .04
149 Jim Thome .75 .23
150 Omar Vizquel .50 .15
151 Dave Winfield .30 .09
152 Kevin Appier .30 .09
153 Billy Brewer .15 .04
154 Vince Coleman .15 .04
155 David Cone .30 .09
156 Gary Gaetti .30 .09
157 Greg Gagne .15 .04
158 Tom Gordon .15 .04
159 Mark Gubicza .15 .04
160 Bob Hamelin .15 .04
161 Dave Henderson .15 .04
162 Felix Jose .15 .04
163 Wally Joyner .30 .09
164 Jose Lind .15 .04
165 Mike Macfarlane .15 .04
166 Mike Magnante .15 .04
167 Brent Mayne .15 .04
168 Brian McRae .15 .04
169 Rusty Meacham .15 .04
170 Jeff Montgomery .15 .04
171 Hipolito Pichardo .15 .04
172 Terry Shumpert .15 .04
173 Michael Tucker .15 .04
174 Ricky Bones .15 .04
175 Jeff Cirillo .15 .04
176 Alex Diaz .15 .04
177 Cal Eldred .15 .04
178 Mike Fetters .15 .04
179 Darryl Hamilton .15 .04
180 Brian Harper .15 .04
181 John Jaha .15 .04
182 Pat Listach .15 .04
183 Graeme Lloyd .15 .04
184 Jose Mercedes .15 .04
185 Matt Mieske .15 .04
186 Dave Nilsson .15 .04
187 Jody Reed .15 .04
188 Bob Scanlan .15 .04
189 Kevin Seitzer .15 .04
190 Bill Spiers .15 .04
191 B.J. Surhoff .30 .09
192 Jose Valentin .15 .04
193 Greg Vaughn .15 .04
194 Turner Ward .15 .04
195 Bill Wegman .15 .04
196 Rick Aguilera .15 .04
197 Rich Becker .15 .04
198 Alex Cole .15 .04
199 Marty Cordova .15 .04
200 Steve Dunn .15 .04
201 Scott Erickson .15 .04
202 Mark Guthrie .15 .04
203 Chip Hale .15 .04
204 LaTroy Hawkins .15 .04
205 Denny Hocking .15 .04
206 Chuck Knoblauch .30 .09
207 Scott Leius .15 .04
208 Shane Mack .15 .04
209 Pat Mahomes .15 .04
210 Pat Meares .15 .04
211 Pedro Munoz .15 .04
212 Kirby Puckett .75 .23
213 Jeff Reboulet .15 .04
214 Dave Stevens .15 .04
215 Kevin Tapani .15 .04
216 Matt Walbeck .15 .04
217 Carl Willis .15 .04
218 Brian Anderson .15 .04
219 Chad Curtis .15 .04
220 Chili Davis .30 .09
221 Gary DiSarcina .15 .04
222 Damion Easley .15 .04
223 Jim Edmonds .50 .15
224 Chuck Finley .30 .09
225 Joe Grahe .15 .04
226 Rex Hudler .15 .04
227 Bo Jackson .75 .23
228 Mark Langston .15 .04
229 Phil Leftwich .15 .04
230 Mark Leiter .15 .04
231 Spike Owen .15 .04
232 Bob Patterson .15 .04
233 Troy Percival .30 .09
234 Eduardo Perez .15 .04
235 Tim Salmon .50 .15
236 J.T. Snow .30 .09
237 Chris Turner .15 .04
238 Mark Acre .15 .04
239 Geronimo Berroa .15 .04
240 Mike Bordick .15 .04
241 John Briscoe .15 .04
242 Scott Brosius .30 .09
243 Ron Darling .15 .04
244 Dennis Eckersley .30 .09
245 Brent Gates .15 .04
246 Rickey Henderson .75 .23
247 Stan Javier .15 .04
248 Steve Karsay .15 .04
249 Mark McGwire 2.00 .60
250 Troy Neel .15 .04
251 Steve Ontiveros .15 .04
252 Carlos Reyes .15 .04
253 Ruben Sierra .15 .04
254 Terry Steinbach .15 .04
255 Bill Taylor .15 .04
256 Todd Van Poppel .15 .04
257 Bobby Witt .15 .04
258 Rich Amaral .15 .04
259 Eric Anthony .15 .04
260 Bobby Ayala .15 .04
261 Mike Blowers .15 .04
262 Chris Bosio .15 .04
263 Jay Buhner .30 .09
264 John Cummings .15 .04
265 Tim Davis .15 .04
266 Felix Fermin .15 .04
267 Dave Fleming .15 .04
268 Goose Gossage .30 .09
269 Ken Griffey Jr. 1.25 .35
270 Reggie Jefferson .15 .04
271 Randy Johnson .75 .23
272 Edgar Martinez .50 .15
273 Tino Martinez .50 .15
274 Greg Pirkl .15 .04
275 Bill Risley .15 .04
276 Roger Salkeld .15 .04
277 Luis Sojo .15 .04
278 Mac Suzuki .15 .04
279 Dan Wilson .15 .04
280 Kevin Brown .30 .09
281 Jose Canseco .75 .23
282 Cris Carpenter .15 .04
283 Will Clark .75 .23
284 Jeff Frye .15 .04
285 Juan Gonzalez .50 .15
286 Rick Helling .15 .04
287 Tom Henke .15 .04
288 David Hulse .15 .04
289 Chris James .15 .04
290 Manuel Lee .15 .04
291 Oddibe McDowell .15 .04
292 Dean Palmer .30 .09
293 Roger Pavlik .15 .04
294 Bill Ripken .15 .04
295 Ivan Rodriguez .75 .23
296 Kenny Rogers .30 .09
297 Doug Strange .15 .04
298 Matt Whiteside .15 .04
299 Steve Avery .15 .04
300 Steve Bedrosian .15 .04
301 Rafael Belliard .15 .04
302 Jeff Blauser .15 .04
303 Dave Gallagher .15 .04
304 Tom Glavine .50 .15
305 David Justice .30 .09
306 Mike Kelly .15 .04
307 Roberto Kelly .15 .04
308 Ryan Klesko .30 .09
309 Mark Lemke .15 .04
310 Javier Lopez .30 .09
311 Greg Maddux 1.25 .35
312 Fred McGriff .50 .15
313 Greg McMichael .15 .04
314 Kent Mercker .15 .04
315 Charlie O'Brien .15 .04
316 Jose Oliva .15 .04
317 Terry Pendleton .30 .09
318 John Smoltz .50 .15
319 Mike Stanton .15 .04
320 Tony Tarasco .15 .04
321 Terrell Wade .15 .04
322 Mark Wohlers .15 .04
323 Kurt Abbott .15 .04
324 Luis Aquino .15 .04
325 Bret Barberie .15 .04
326 Ryan Bowen .15 .04
327 Jerry Browne .15 .04
328 Chuck Carr .15 .04
329 Matias Carrillo .15 .04
330 Greg Colbrunn .15 .04
331 Jeff Conine .30 .09
332 Mark Gardner .15 .04
333 Chris Hammond .15 .04
334 Bryan Harvey .15 .04
335 Richie Lewis .15 .04
336 Dave Magadan .15 .04
337 Terry Mathews .15 .04
338 Robb Nen .30 .09
339 Yorkis Perez .15 .04
340 Pat Rapp .15 .04
341 Benito Santiago .30 .09
342 Gary Sheffield .30 .09
343 Dave Weathers .15 .04
344 Moises Alou .30 .09
345 Sean Berry .15 .04
346 Wil Cordero .15 .04
347 Joey Eischen .15 .04
348 Jeff Fassero .15 .04
349 Darrin Fletcher .15 .04
350 Cliff Floyd .30 .09
351 Marquis Grissom .30 .09
352 Butch Henry .15 .04
353 Gil Heredia .15 .04
354 Ken Hill .15 .04
355 Mike Lansing .15 .04
356 Pedro Martinez .75 .23
357 Mel Rojas .15 .04
358 Kirk Rueter .15 .04
359 Tim Scott .15 .04
360 Jeff Shaw .15 .04
361 Larry Walker .50 .15
362 Lenny Webster .15 .04
363 John Wetteland .30 .09
364 Rondell White .30 .09
365 Bobby Bonilla .30 .09
366 Rico Brogna .30 .09
367 Jeromy Burnitz .30 .09
368 John Franco .30 .09
369 Dwight Gooden .30 .09
370 Todd Hundley .15 .04
371 Jason Jacome .15 .04
372 Bobby Jones .15 .04
373 Jeff Kent .30 .09
374 Jim Lindeman .15 .04

375 Josias Manzanillo	.15	.04
376 Roger Mason	.15	.04
377 Kevin McReynolds	.15	.04
378 Joe Orsulak	.15	.04
379 Bill Pulsipher	.15	.04
380 Bret Saberhagen	.30	.09
381 David Segui	.15	.04
382 Pete Smith	.15	.04
383 Kelly Stinnett	.15	.04
384 Ryan Thompson	.15	.04
385 Jose Vizcaino	.15	.04
386 Toby Borland	.15	.04
387 Ricky Bottalico	.15	.04
388 Darren Daulton	.30	.09
389 Mariano Duncan	.15	.04
390 Lenny Dykstra	.30	.09
391 Jim Eisenreich	.15	.04
392 Tommy Greene	.15	.04
393 Dave Hollins	.15	.04
394 Pete Incaviglia	.15	.04
395 Danny Jackson	.15	.04
396 Doug Jones	.15	.04
397 Ricky Jordan	.15	.04
398 John Kruk	.30	.09
399 Mike Lieberthal	.30	.09
400 Tony Longmire	.15	.04
401 Mickey Morandini	.15	.04
402 Bobby Munoz	.15	.04
403 Curt Schilling	.30	.09
404 Heathcliff Slocumb	.15	.04
405 Kevin Stocker	.15	.04
406 Fernando Valenzuela	.30	.09
407 David West	.15	.04
408 Willie Banks	.15	.04
409 Jose Bautista	.15	.04
410 Steve Buechele	.15	.04
411 Jim Bullinger	.15	.04
412 Chuck Crim	.15	.04
413 Shawon Dunston	.15	.04
414 Kevin Foster	.15	.04
415 Mark Grace	.50	.15
416 Jose Hernandez	.15	.04
417 Glenallen Hill	.15	.04
418 Brooks Kieschnick	.15	.04
419 Derrick May	.15	.04
420 Randy Myers	.15	.04
421 Dan Plesac	.15	.04
422 Karl Rhodes	.15	.04
423 Rey Sanchez	.15	.04
424 Sammy Sosa	1.25	.35
425 Steve Trachsel	.15	.04
426 Rick Wilkins	.15	.04
427 Anthony Young	.15	.04
428 Eddie Zambrano	.15	.04
429 Bret Boone	.30	.09
430 Jeff Branson	.15	.04
431 Jeff Brantley	.15	.04
432 Hector Carrasco	.15	.04
433 Brian Dorsett	.15	.04
434 Tony Fernandez	.15	.04
435 Tim Fortugno	.15	.04
436 Erik Hanson	.15	.04
437 Thomas Howard	.15	.04
438 Kevin Jarvis	.15	.04
439 Barry Larkin	.50	.15
440 Chuck McElroy	.15	.04
441 Kevin Mitchell	.15	.04
442 Hal Morris	.15	.04
443 Jose Rijo	.15	.04
444 John Roper	.15	.04
445 Johnny Ruffin	.15	.04
446 Deion Sanders	.50	.15
447 Reggie Sanders	.15	.04
448 Pete Schourek	.15	.04
449 John Smiley	.15	.04
450 Eddie Taubensee	.15	.04
451 Jeff Bagwell	.50	.15
452 Kevin Bass	.15	.04
453 Craig Biggio	.50	.15
454 Ken Caminiti	.30	.09
455 Andujar Cedeno	.15	.04
456 Doug Drabek	.15	.04
457 Tony Eusebio	.15	.04
458 Mike Felder	.15	.04
459 Steve Finley	.30	.09
460 Luis Gonzalez	.30	.09
461 Mike Hampton	.30	.09
462 Pete Harnisch	.15	.04
463 John Hudek	.15	.04
464 Todd Jones	.15	.04
465 Darryl Kile	.30	.09
466 James Mouton	.15	.04
467 Shane Reynolds	.15	.04
468 Scott Servais	.15	.04
469 Greg Swindell	.15	.04
470 Dave Veres RC	.40	.12
471 Brian Williams	.15	.04
472 Jay Bell	.30	.09
473 Jacob Brumfield	.15	.04
474 Dave Clark	.15	.04
475 Steve Cooke	.15	.04
476 Midre Cummings	.15	.04
477 Mark Dewey	.15	.04
478 Tom Foley	.15	.04
479 Carlos Garcia	.15	.04
480 Jeff King	.15	.04
481 Jon Lieber	.15	.04
482 Ravelo Manzanillo	.15	.04
483 Al Martin	.15	.04
484 Orlando Merced	.15	.04
485 Danny Miceli	.15	.04
486 Denny Neagle	.30	.09
487 Lance Parrish	.30	.09
488 Don Slaught	.15	.04
489 Zane Smith	.15	.04
490 Andy Van Slyke	.30	.09
491 Paul Wagner	.15	.04
492 Rick White	.15	.04
493 Luis Alicea	.15	.04
494 Rene Arocha	.15	.04
495 Rheal Cormier	.15	.04
496 Bryan Eversgerd	.15	.04
497 Bernard Gilkey	.15	.04
498 John Habyan	.15	.04
499 Gregg Jefferies	.15	.04
500 Brian Jordan	.30	.09
501 Ray Lankford	.15	.04
502 John Mabry	.15	.04
503 Terry McGriff	.15	.04
504 Tom Pagnozzi	.15	.04
505 Vicente Palacios	.15	.04
506 Geronimo Pena	.15	.04
507 Gerald Perry	.15	.04
508 Rich Rodriguez	.15	.04
509 Ozzie Smith	1.25	.35
510 Bob Tewksbury	.15	.04
511 Allen Watson	.15	.04
512 Mark Whiten	.15	.04
513 Todd Zeile	.15	.04
514 Dante Bichette	.30	.09
515 Willie Blair	.15	.04
516 Ellis Burks	.30	.09
517 Marvin Freeman	.15	.04
518 Andres Galarraga	.30	.09
519 Joe Girardi	.15	.04
520 Greg W. Harris	.15	.04
521 Charlie Hayes	.15	.04
522 Mike Kingery	.15	.04
523 Nelson Liriano	.15	.04
524 Mike Munoz	.15	.04
525 David Nied	.15	.04
526 Steve Reed	.15	.04
527 Kevin Ritz	.15	.04
528 Bruce Ruffin	.15	.04
529 John Vander Wal	.15	.04
530 Walt Weiss	.15	.04
531 Eric Young	.15	.04
532 Billy Ashley	.15	.04
533 Pedro Astacio	.15	.04
534 Rafael Bournigal	.15	.04
535 Brett Butler	.30	.09
536 Tom Candiotti	.15	.04
537 Omar Daal	.15	.04
538 Delino DeShields	.15	.04
539 Darren Dreifort	.15	.04
540 Kevin Gross	.15	.04
541 Orel Hershiser	.30	.09
542 Garey Ingram	.15	.04
543 Eric Karros	.30	.09
544 Ramon Martinez	.15	.04
545 Raul Mondesi	.30	.09
546 Chan Ho Park	.30	.09
547 Mike Piazza	1.25	.35
548 Henry Rodriguez	.15	.04
549 Rudy Seanez	.15	.04
550 Ismael Valdes	.15	.04
551 Tim Wallach	.15	.04
552 Todd Worrell	.15	.04
553 Andy Ashby	.15	.04
554 Brad Ausmus	.15	.04
555 Derek Bell	.15	.04
556 Andy Benes	.15	.04
557 Phil Clark	.15	.04
558 Donnie Elliott	.15	.04
559 Ricky Gutierrez	.15	.04
560 Tony Gwynn	1.00	.30
561 Joey Hamilton	.15	.04
562 Trevor Hoffman	.30	.09
563 Luis Lopez	.15	.04
564 Pedro A. Martinez	.15	.04
565 Tim Mauser	.15	.04
566 Phil Plantier	.15	.04
567 Bip Roberts	.15	.04
568 Scott Sanders	.15	.04
569 Craig Shipley	.15	.04
570 Jeff Tabaka	.15	.04
571 Eddie Williams	.15	.04
572 Rod Beck	.15	.04
573 Mike Benjamin	.15	.04
574 Barry Bonds	2.00	.60
575 Dave Burba	.15	.04
576 John Burkett	.15	.04
577 Mark Carreon	.15	.04
578 Royce Clayton	.15	.04
579 Steve Frey	.15	.04
580 Bryan Hickerson	.15	.04
581 Mike Jackson	.15	.04
582 Darren Lewis	.15	.04
583 Kirt Manwaring	.15	.04
584 Rich Monteleone	.15	.04
585 John Patterson	.15	.04
586 J.R. Phillips	.15	.04
587 Mark Portugal	.15	.04
588 Joe Rosselli	.15	.04
589 Darryl Strawberry	.30	.09
590 Bill Swift	.15	.04
591 Robby Thompson	.15	.04
592 W.VanLandingham	.15	.04
593 Matt Williams	.30	.09
594 Checklist	.15	.04
595 Checklist	.15	.04
596 Checklist	.15	.04
597 Checklist	.15	.04
598 Checklist	.15	.04
599 Checklist	.15	.04
600 Checklist	.15	.04

1995 Fleer All-Fleer

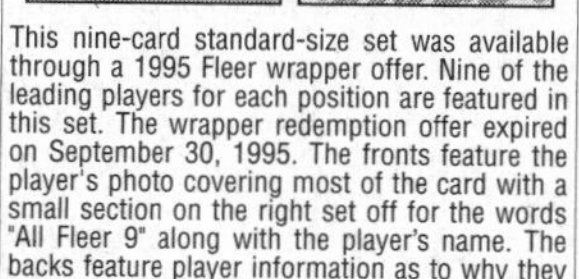

This nine-card standard-size set was available through a 1995 Fleer wrapper offer. Nine of the leading players for each position are featured in this set. The wrapper redemption offer expired on September 30, 1995. The fronts feature the player's photo covering most of the card with a small section on the right set off for the words "All Fleer 9" along with the player's name. The backs feature player information as to why they are among the best in the game.

	Nm-Mt	Ex-Mt
COMPLETE SET (9)	10.00	3.00
1 Mike Piazza	1.25	.35
2 Frank Thomas	.75	.23
3 Roberto Alomar	.50	.15
4 Cal Ripken	2.50	.75
5 Matt Williams	.30	.09
6 Barry Bonds	2.00	.60
7 Ken Griffey Jr.	1.25	.35
8 Tony Gwynn	1.00	.30
9 Greg Maddux	1.25	.35

1995 Fleer All-Rookies

This nine-card standard-size set was available through a Rookie Exchange redemption card randomly inserted in packs. The redemption deadline was 9/30/95. This set features players who made their major league debut in 1995. The fronts have an action photo with a grainy background. The player's name and team are in gold foil at the bottom. Horizontal backs have a player photo the left and minor league highlights to the right.

	Nm-Mt	Ex-Mt
COMPLETE SET (9)	3.00	.90
M1 Edgardo Alfonzo	.50	.15
M2 Jason Bates	.25	.07
M3 Brian Boehringer	.25	.07
M4 Darren Bragg	.25	.07
M5 Brad Clontz	.25	.07
M6 Jim Dougherty	.25	.07
M7 Todd Hollandsworth	.25	.07
M8 Rudy Pemberton	.25	.07
M9 Frank Rodriguez	.25	.07
NNO Exp. All-Rookie Exch.	.25	.07

1995 Fleer All-Stars

Randomly inserted in all pack types at a rate of one in three, this 25-card standard-size set showcases those that participated in the 1994 mid-season classic held in Pittsburgh. Horizontally designed, the fronts contain photos of American League stars with the back protraying the National League player from the same position. On each side, the 1994 All-Star Game logo appears in gold foil as does either the A.L. or N.L. logo in silver foil.

	Nm-Mt	Ex-Mt
COMPLETE SET (25)	10.00	3.00
1 Ivan Rodriguez Mike Piazza	1.50	.45
2 Frank Thomas Gregg Jefferies	1.00	.30
3 Robert Alomar Mariano Duncan	.60	.18
4 Wade Boggs Matt Williams	.60	.18
5 Cal Ripken Jr. Ozzie Smith	3.00	.90
6 Joe Carter Barry Bonds	2.50	.75
7 Ken Griffey Jr. Tony Gwynn	1.50	.45
8 Kirby Puckett David Justice	1.00	.30
9 Jimmy Key Greg Maddux	1.50	.45
10 Chuck Knoblauch Wil Cordero	.40	.12
11 Scott Cooper Ken Caminiti	.40	.12
12 Will Clark Carlos Garcia	1.00	.30
13 Paul Molitor Jeff Bagwell	.60	.18
14 Travis Fryman Craig Biggio	.60	.18
15 Mickey Tettleton Fred McGriff	.60	.18
16 Kenny Lofton Moises Alou	.40	.12
17 Albert Belle Marquis Grissom	.40	.12
18 Paul O'Neill Dante Bichette	.60	.18
19 David Cone Ken Hill	.40	.12
20 Mike Mussina Doug Drabek	.60	.18
21 Randy Johnson John Hudek	1.00	.30
22 Pat Hentgen Danny Jackson	.20	.06
23 Wilson Alvarez Rod Beck	.20	.06
24 Lee Smith Randy Myers	.40	.12
25 Jason Bere Doug Jones	.20	.06

1995 Fleer Award Winners

Randomly inserted in all pack types at a rate of one in 24, this six card standard-size set highlights the major award winners of 1994. Card fronts feature action photos that are full-bleed on the right border and have gold border on the left. Within the gold border are the player's name and Fleer Award Winner. The backs contain a photo with text that references 1994 accomplishments.

	Nm-Mt	Ex-Mt
COMPLETE SET (6)	5.00	1.50
1 Frank Thomas	1.25	.35
2 Jeff Bagwell	.75	.23
3 David Cone	.50	.15
4 Greg Maddux	2.00	.60
5 Bob Hamelin	.25	.07
6 Raul Mondesi	.50	.15

1995 Fleer League Leaders

Randomly inserted in all pack types at a rate of one in 12, this 10-card standard-size set features 1994 American and National League leaders in various categories. The horizontal cards have player photos on front and back. The back also has a brief write-up concerning the accomplishment.

	Nm-Mt	Ex-Mt
COMPLETE SET (10)	8.00	2.40
1 Paul O'Neill	.75	.23
2 Ken Griffey Jr.	2.00	.60
3 Kirby Puckett	1.25	.35
4 Jimmy Key	.50	.15
5 Randy Johnson	1.25	.35
6 Tony Gwynn	1.50	.45
7 Matt Williams	.50	.15
8 Jeff Bagwell	.75	.23
9 Greg Maddux Ken Hill	2.00	.60
10 Andy Benes	.25	.07

1995 Fleer Lumber Company

Randomly inserted in retail packs at a rate of one in 24, this standard-size set highlights 10 of the game's top sluggers. Full-bleed card fronts feature an action photo with the Lumber Company logo, which includes the player's name, toward the bottom of the photo. Card backs have a player photo and woodgrain background with a write-up that highlights individual achievements.

	Nm-Mt	Ex-Mt
COMPLETE SET (10)	30.00	9.00
1 Jeff Bagwell	2.50	.75
2 Albert Belle	1.50	.45
3 Barry Bonds	10.00	3.00
4 Jose Canseco	4.00	1.20
5 Joe Carter	1.50	.45
6 Ken Griffey Jr.	6.00	1.80
7 Fred McGriff	2.50	.75
8 Kevin Mitchell	.75	.23
9 Frank Thomas	4.00	1.20
10 Matt Williams	1.50	.45

1995 Fleer Major League Prospects

Randomly inserted in all pack types at a rate of one in six, this 10-card standard-size set spotlights major league hopefuls. Card fronts feature a player photo with the words "Major League Prospects" serving as part of the background. The player's name and team appear in silver foil at the bottom. The backs have a photo and a write-up on his minor league career.

	Nm-Mt	Ex-Mt
COMPLETE SET (10)	10.00	3.00
1 Garret Anderson	.50	.15
2 James Baldwin	.25	.07
3 Alan Benes	.25	.07
4 Armando Benitez	.50	.15
5 Ray Durham	.50	.15
6 Brian L. Hunter	.25	.07
7 Derek Jeter	4.00	1.20
8 Charles Johnson	.50	.15
9 Orlando Miller	.25	.07
10 Alex Rodriguez	4.00	1.20

1995 Fleer Pro-Visions

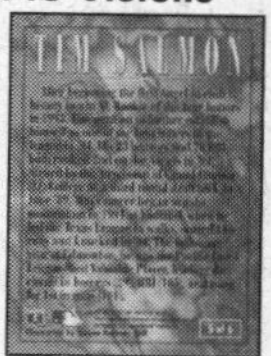

Randomly inserted in all pack types at a rate of one in nine, this six card standard-size set features top players illustrated by Wayne Anthony Still. The colorful artwork on front features the player in a surrealistic setting. The backs offer write-up on the player's previous season.

	Nm-Mt	Ex-Mt
COMPLETE SET (6)	3.00	.90
1 Mike Mussina	.50	.15
2 Raul Mondesi	.30	.09
3 Jeff Bagwell	.50	.15
4 Greg Maddux	1.25	.35
5 Tim Salmon	.50	.15
6 Manny Ramirez	.50	.15

1995 Fleer Rookie Sensations

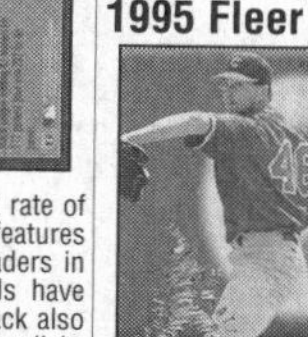

Randomly inserted in 18-card packs, this 20-card standard-size set features top rookies from the 1994 season. The fronts have full-bleed color photos with the team and player's name in gold foil along the right edge. The backs also have full-bleed color photos along with player information.

	Nm-Mt	Ex-Mt
COMPLETE SET (20)	40.00	12.00
1 Kurt Abbott	2.00	.60
2 Rico Brogna	2.00	.60
3 Hector Carrasco	2.00	.60
4 Kevin Foster	2.00	.60
5 Chris Gomez	2.00	.60
6 Darren Hall	2.00	.60
7 Bob Hamelin	2.00	.60
8 Joey Hamilton	2.00	.60
9 John Hudek	2.00	.60
10 Ryan Klesko	4.00	1.20
11 Javier Lopez	4.00	1.20
12 Matt Mieske	2.00	.60
13 Raul Mondesi	4.00	1.20
14 Manny Ramirez	5.00	1.50
15 Shane Reynolds	2.00	.60
16 Bill Risley	2.00	.60
17 Johnny Ruffin	2.00	.60
18 Steve Trachsel	2.00	.60
19 W.VanLandingham	2.00	.60
20 Rondell White	4.00	1.20

1995 Fleer Team Leaders

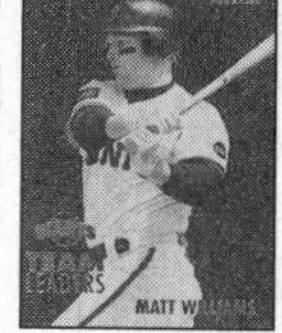

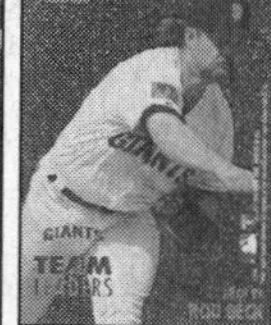

Randomly inserted in 12-card hobby packs at a rate of one in 24, this 28-card standard-size set features top players from each team. Each team is represented with card the has the team's leading hitter on one side with the leading pitcher on the other side. The team logo, "Team Leaders" and the player's name are gold foil stamped on front and back.

	Nm-Mt	Ex-Mt
COMPLETE SET (28)	100.00	30.00
1 Cal Ripken Jr. Mike Mussina	25.00	7.50
2 Mo Vaughn Roger Clemens	15.00	4.50
3 Tim Salmon Chuck Finley	5.00	1.50
4 Frank Thomas Jack McDowell	8.00	2.40
5 Albert Belle Dennis Martinez	3.00	.90
6 Cecil Fielder Mike Moore	3.00	.90
7 Bob Hamelin David Cone	3.00	.90
8 Greg Vaughn Ricky Bones	1.50	.45
9 Kirby Puckett Rick Aguilera	8.00	2.40
10 Don Mattingly Jimmy Key	20.00	6.00
11 Ruben Sierra Dennis Eckersley	3.00	.90
12 Ken Griffey Jr. Randy Johnson	12.00	3.60
13 Jose Canseco Kenny Rogers	8.00	2.40
14 Joe Carter Pat Hentgen	3.00	.90
15 David Justice Greg Maddux	12.00	3.60
16 Sammy Sosa Steve Trachsel	12.00	3.60

17 Kevin Mitchell 1.50 .45
Jose Rijo
18 Dante Bichette 3.00 .90
Bruce Ruffin
19 Jeff Conine 3.00 .90
Robb Nen
20 Jeff Bagwell 5.00 1.50
Doug Drabek
21 Mike Piazza 12.00 3.60
Ramon Martinez
22 Moises Alou 3.00 .90
Ken Hill
23 Bobby Bonilla 3.00 .90
Bret Saberhagen
24 Darren Daulton 3.00 .90
Danny Jackson
25 Jay Bell 3.00 .90
Zane Smith
26 Gregg Jefferies 1.50 .45
Bob Tewksbury
27 Tony Gwynn 10.00 3.00
Andy Benes
28 Matt Williams 3.00 .90
Rod Beck

1995 Fleer Update

This 200-card standard-size set features many players who were either rookies in 1995 or played for new teams. These cards were issued in either 12-card packs with a suggested retail price of $1.49 or 18-card packs that had a suggested retail price of $2.29. Each Fleer Update pack included one card from several insert sets produced with this product. Hot packs featuring only these insert cards were included one every 72 packs. The full-bleed fronts have two player photos and, atypical of baseball card fronts, biographical information such as height, weight, etc. The backgrounds are multi-colored. The backs are horizontal, have yearly statistics, a photo, and are numbered with the prefix "U". The checklist is arranged alphabetically by team within each league's divisions. Key Rookie Cards in this set include Bobby Higginson and Hideo Nomo.

Nm-Mt Ex-Mt
COMPLETE SET (200) 15.00 4.50
1 Manny Alexander .10 .03
2 Bret Barberie .10 .03
3 Armando Benitez .20 .06
4 Kevin Brown .20 .06
5 Doug Jones .10 .03
6 Sherman Obando .10 .03
7 Andy Van Slyke .20 .06
8 Stan Belinda .10 .03
9 Jose Canseco .50 .15
10 Vaughn Eshelman .10 .03
11 Mike Macfarlane .10 .03
12 Troy O'Leary .10 .03
13 Steve Rodriguez .10 .03
14 Lee Tinsley .10 .03
15 Tim Vanegmond .10 .03
16 Mark Whiten .10 .03
17 Sean Bergman .10 .03
18 Chad Curtis .10 .03
19 John Flaherty .10 .03
20 Bob Higginson RC .75 .23
21 Felipe Lira .10 .03
22 Shannon Penn .10 .03
23 Todd Steverson .10 .03
24 Sean Whiteside .10 .03
25 Tony Fernandez .10 .03
26 Jack McDowell .10 .03
27 Andy Pettitte .30 .09
28 John Wetteland .20 .06
29 David Cone .20 .06
30 Mike Timlin .10 .03
31 Duane Ward .10 .03
32 Jim Abbott .30 .09
33 James Baldwin .10 .03
34 Mike Devereaux .10 .03
35 Ray Durham .20 .06
36 Tim Fortugno .10 .03
37 Scott Ruffcorn .10 .03
38 Chris Sabo .10 .03
39 Paul Assenmacher .10 .03
40 Bud Black .10 .03
41 Orel Hershiser .20 .06
42 Julian Tavarez .10 .03
43 Dave Winfield .20 .06
44 Pat Borders .10 .03
45 Melvin Bunch RC .10 .03
46 Tom Goodwin .10 .03
47 Jon Nunnally .10 .03
48 Joe Randa .10 .03
49 Dilson Torres RC .10 .03
50 Joe Vitiello .10 .03
51 David Hulse .10 .03
52 Scott Karl .10 .03
53 Mark Kiefer .10 .03
54 Derrick May .10 .03
55 Joe Oliver .10 .03
56 Al Reyes RC .10 .03
57 Steve Sparks RC .40 .12
58 Jerald Clark .10 .03
59 Eddie Guardado .10 .03
60 Kevin Maas .10 .03
61 David McCarty .10 .03
62 Brad Radke RC .75 .23
63 Scott Stahoviak .10 .03
64 Garret Anderson .20 .06
65 Shawn Boskie .10 .03
66 Mike James .10 .03
67 Tony Phillips .10 .03
68 Lee Smith .20 .06
69 Mitch Williams .10 .03
70 Jim Corsi .10 .03
71 Mark Harkey .10 .03
72 Dave Stewart .20 .06
73 Todd Stottlemyre .10 .03
74 Joey Cora .10 .03
75 Chad Kreuter .10 .03
76 Jeff Nelson .10 .03
77 Alex Rodriguez 1.25 .35
78 Ron Villone .10 .03
79 Bob Wells RC .40 .12
80 Jose Alberro RC .10 .03
81 Terry Burrows .10 .03
82 Kevin Gross .10 .03
83 Wilson Heredia .10 .03
84 Mark McLemore .10 .03
85 Otis Nixon .10 .03
86 Jeff Russell .10 .03
87 Mickey Tettleton .10 .03
88 Bob Tewksbury .10 .03
89 Pedro Borbon .10 .03
90 Marquis Grissom .20 .06
91 Chipper Jones .50 .15
92 Mike Mordecai .10 .03
93 Jason Schmidt .50 .15
94 John Burkett .10 .03
95 Andre Dawson .20 .06
96 Matt Dunbar RC .10 .03
97 Charles Johnson .20 .06
98 Terry Pendleton .20 .06
99 Rich Scheid .10 .03
100 Quilvio Veras .10 .03
101 Bobby Witt .10 .03
102 Eddie Zosky .10 .03
103 Shane Andrews .10 .03
104 Reid Cornelius .10 .03
105 Chad Fonville RC .10 .03
106 Mark Grudzielanek RC .40 .12
107 Roberto Kelly .10 .03
108 Carlos Perez RC .40 .12
109 Tony Tarasco .10 .03
110 Brett Butler .20 .06
111 Carl Everett .20 .06
112 Pete Harnisch .10 .03
113 Doug Henry .10 .03
114 Kevin Lomon RC .10 .03
115 Blas Minor .10 .03
116 Dave Mlicki .10 .03
117 Ricky Otero RC .10 .03
118 Norm Charlton .10 .03
119 Tyler Green .10 .03
120 Gene Harris .10 .03
121 Charlie Hayes .10 .03
122 Gregg Jefferies .10 .03
123 Michael Mimbs RC .10 .03
124 Paul Quantrill .10 .03
125 Frank Castillo .10 .03
126 Brian McRae .10 .03
127 Jaime Navarro .10 .03
128 Mike Perez .10 .03
129 Tanyon Sturtze .10 .03
130 Ozzie Timmons .10 .03
131 John Courtright .10 .03
132 Ron Gant .20 .06
133 Xavier Hernandez .10 .03
134 Brian Hunter .10 .03
135 Benito Santiago .20 .06
136 Pete Smith .10 .03
137 Scott Sullivan .10 .03
138 Derek Bell .10 .03
139 Doug Brocail .10 .03
140 Ricky Gutierrez .10 .03
141 Pedro A.Martinez .10 .03
142 Orlando Miller .10 .03
143 Phil Plantier .10 .03
144 Craig Shipley .10 .03
145 Rich Aude .10 .03
146 J.Christiansen RC .10 .03
147 Freddy Adrian Garcia RC .10 .03
148 Jim Gott .10 .03
149 Mark Johnson RC .40 .12
150 Esteban Loaiza .10 .03
151 Dan Plesac .10 .03
152 Gary Wilson RC .10 .03
153 Allen Battle .10 .03
154 Terry Bradshaw .10 .03
155 Scott Cooper .10 .03
156 Tripp Cromer .10 .03
157 John Frascatore RC .10 .03
158 John Habyan .10 .03
159 Tom Henke .10 .03
160 Ken Hill .10 .03
161 Danny Jackson .10 .03
162 Donovan Osborne .10 .03
163 Tom Urbani .10 .03
164 Roger Bailey .10 .03
165 Jorge Brito RC .10 .03
166 Vinny Castilla .20 .06
167 Darren Holmes .10 .03
168 Roberto Mejia .10 .03
169 Bill Swift .10 .03
170 Mark Thompson .10 .03
171 Larry Walker .30 .09
172 Greg Hansell .10 .03
173 Dave Hansen .10 .03
174 Carlos Hernandez .10 .03
175 Hideo Nomo RC 1.50 .45
176 Joe Offerman .10 .03
177 Antonio Osuna .10 .03
178 Reggie Williams .10 .03
179 Todd Williams .10 .03
180 Andres Berumen .10 .03
181 Ken Caminiti .20 .06
182 Andujar Cedeno .10 .03
183 Steve Finley .20 .06
184 Bryce Florie .10 .03
185 Dustin Hermanson .10 .03
186 Ray Holbert .10 .03
187 Melvin Nieves .10 .03
188 Roberto Petagine .10 .03
189 Jody Reed .10 .03
190 Fernando Valenzuela .20 .06
191 Brian Williams .10 .03
192 Mark Dewey .10 .03
193 Glenallen Hill .10 .03
194 Chris Hook RC .10 .03
195 Terry Mulholland .10 .03
196 Steve Scarsone .10 .03
197 Trevor Wilson .10 .03
198 Checklist .10 .03
199 Checklist .10 .03
200 Checklist .10 .03

1995 Fleer Update Diamond Tribute

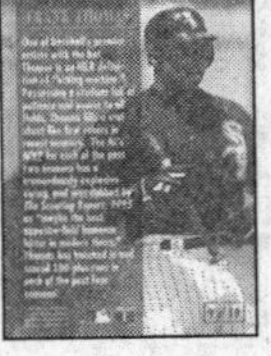

This 10-card standard-size set featuring some of baseball's leading stars were inserted at a stated rate of one in five packs. The cards are numbered in the lower right with an "X" of 10.

Nm-Mt Ex-Mt
COMPLETE SET (10) 8.00 2.40
1 Jeff Bagwell .50 .15
2 Albert Belle .30 .09
3 Barry Bonds 2.00 .60
4 David Cone .30 .09
5 Dennis Eckersley .30 .09
6 Ken Griffey Jr. 1.25 .35
7 Rickey Henderson .75 .23
8 Greg Maddux 1.25 .35
9 Frank Thomas .75 .23
10 Matt Williams .30 .09

1995 Fleer Update Headliners

Inserted one every three packs, this 20-card standard-size set features various major league stars. The cards are numbered in the lower left as "X" of 20.

Nm-Mt Ex-Mt
COMPLETE SET (20) 12.00 3.60
1 Jeff Bagwell .50 .15
2 Albert Belle .30 .09
3 Barry Bonds 2.00 .60
4 Jose Canseco .75 .23
5 Joe Carter .30 .09
6 Will Clark .75 .23
7 Roger Clemens 1.50 .45
8 Lenny Dykstra .30 .09
9 Cecil Fielder .30 .09
10 Juan Gonzalez .50 .15
11 Ken Griffey Jr. 1.25 .35
12 Kenny Lofton .30 .09
13 Greg Maddux 1.25 .35
14 Fred McGriff .50 .15
15 Mike Piazza 1.25 .35
16 Kirby Puckett .75 .23
17 Tim Salmon .50 .15
18 Frank Thomas .75 .23
19 Mo Vaughn .30 .09
20 Matt Williams .30 .09

1995 Fleer Update Rookie Update

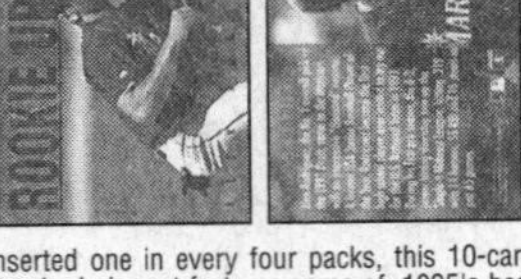

Inserted one in every four packs, this 10-card standard-size set features some of 1995's best rookies. The cards are numbered as "X of 10". Chipper Jones and Hideo Nomo are among the players included in this set.

Nm-Mt Ex-Mt
COMPLETE SET (10) 10.00 3.00
1 Shane Andrews .25 .07
2 Ray Durham .50 .15
3 Shawn Green .50 .15
4 Charles Johnson .50 .15
5 Chipper Jones 1.50 .45
6 Esteban Loaiza .25 .07
7 Hideo Nomo 2.00 .60
8 Jon Nunnally .25 .07
9 Alex Rodriguez 4.00 1.20
10 Julian Tavarez .25 .07

1995 Fleer Update Smooth Leather

Inserted one every five jumbo packs, this 10-card standard-size set features many leading defensive wizards. The card fronts feature a player photo. Underneath the player photo, is his name along with the words "smooth leather" on the bottom. The right corner features a glove. All of this information as well as the "Fleer 95" logo is in gold print. All of this is on a card with a special leather-like coating. The back features a photo as well as fielding information. The cards are numbered in the lower left as "X of 10" and are sequenced in alphabetical order.

Nm-Mt Ex-Mt
COMPLETE SET (10) 25.00 7.50
1 Roberto Alomar 1.50 .45
2 Barry Bonds 6.00 1.80
3 Ken Griffey Jr. 4.00 1.20
4 Marquis Grissom 1.00 .30
5 Darren Lewis .50 .15
6 Kenny Lofton 1.00 .30
7 Don Mattingly 6.00 1.80
8 Cal Ripken 8.00 2.40
9 Ivan Rodriguez 2.50 .75
10 Matt Williams 1.00 .30

1995 Fleer Update Soaring Stars

This nine-card standard-size set was inserted one every 36 packs. The fronts feature the player's photo set against a prismatic background of baseballs. The player's name, the "Soaring Stars" logo as well as a star are all printed in gold foil at the bottom. The back has a player photo, his name as well as some career information. The cards are numbered in the upper right "X of 9" and are sequenced in alphabetical order.

Nm-Mt Ex-Mt
COMPLETE SET (9) 25.00 7.50
1 Moises Alou UER 2.50 .75
(says .399 BA in 1994)
2 Jason Bere 1.25 .35
3 Jeff Conine 2.50 .75
4 Cliff Floyd 2.50 .75
5 Pat Hentgen 1.25 .35
6 Kenny Lofton 2.50 .75
7 Raul Mondesi 2.50 .75
8 Mike Piazza 10.00 3.00
9 Tim Salmon 4.00 1.20

1996 Fleer

The 1996 Fleer baseball set consists of 600 standard-size cards issued in one series. Cards were issued in 11-card packs with a suggested retail price of $1.49. Borderless fronts are matte-finished and have full-color action shots with the player's name, team and position stamped in gold foil. Backs contain a biography and career stats on the top and a full-color head shot with a 1995 synopsis on the bottom. The matte finish on the cards was designed so collectors could have an easier surface for cards to be autographed. Fleer included in each pack a "Thanks a Million" scratch-off game card redeemable for instant-win prizes and a chance to bat for a million-dollar prize in a Major League park. Rookie Cards in this set include Matt Lawton and Mike Sweeney. A Cal Ripken promo was distributed to dealers and hobby media to preview the set.

Nm-Mt Ex-Mt
COMPLETE SET (600) 80.00 24.00
1 Manny Alexander .30 .09
2 Brady Anderson .30 .09
3 Harold Baines .30 .09
4 Armando Benitez .30 .09
5 Bobby Bonilla .30 .09
6 Kevin Brown .30 .09
7 Scott Erickson .30 .09
8 Curtis Goodwin .30 .09
9 Jeffrey Hammonds .30 .09
10 Jimmy Haynes .30 .09
11 Chris Hoiles .30 .09
12 Doug Jones .30 .09
13 Rick Krivda .30 .09
14 Jeff Manto .30 .09
15 Ben McDonald .30 .09
16 Jamie Moyer .30 .09
17 Mike Mussina .50 .15
18 Jesse Orosco .30 .09
19 Rafael Palmeiro .50 .15
20 Cal Ripken 2.50 .75
21 Rick Aguilera .30 .09
22 Luis Alicea .30 .09
23 Stan Belinda .30 .09
24 Jose Canseco .75 .23
25 Roger Clemens 1.50 .45
26 Vaughn Eshelman .30 .09
27 Mike Greenwell .30 .09
28 Erik Hanson .30 .09
29 Dwayne Hosey .30 .09
30 Mike Macfarlane UER .30 .09
31 Tim Naehring .30 .09
32 Troy O'Leary .30 .09
33 Aaron Sele .30 .09
34 Zane Smith .30 .09
35 Jeff Suppan .30 .09
36 Lee Tinsley .30 .09
37 John Valentin .30 .09
38 Mo Vaughn .30 .09
39 Tim Wakefield .30 .09
40 Jim Abbott .50 .15
41 Brian Anderson .30 .09
42 Garret Anderson .30 .09
43 Chili Davis .30 .09
44 Gary DiSarcina .30 .09
45 Damion Easley .30 .09
46 Jim Edmonds .30 .09
47 Chuck Finley .30 .09
48 Todd Greene .30 .09
49 Mike Harkey .30 .09
50 Mike James .30 .09
51 Mark Langston .30 .09
52 Greg Myers .30 .09
53 Orlando Palmeiro .30 .09
54 Bob Patterson .30 .09
55 Troy Percival .30 .09
56 Tony Phillips .30 .09
57 Tim Salmon .50 .15
58 Lee Smith .30 .09
59 J.T. Snow .30 .09
60 Randy Velarde .30 .09
61 Wilson Alvarez .30 .09
62 Luis Andujar .30 .09
63 Jason Bere .30 .09
64 Ray Durham .30 .09
65 Alex Fernandez .30 .09
66 Ozzie Guillen .30 .09
67 Roberto Hernandez .30 .09
68 Lance Johnson .30 .09
69 Matt Karchner .30 .09
70 Ron Karkovice .30 .09
71 Norberto Martin .30 .09
72 Dave Martinez .30 .09
73 Kirk McCaskill .30 .09
74 Lyle Mouton .30 .09
75 Tim Raines .30 .09
76 Mike Sirotka RC .50 .15
77 Frank Thomas .75 .23
78 Larry Thomas .30 .09
79 Robin Ventura .30 .09
80 Sandy Alomar Jr. .30 .09
81 Paul Assenmacher .30 .09
82 Carlos Baerga .30 .09
83 Albert Belle .30 .09
84 Mark Clark .30 .09
85 Alan Embree .30 .09
86 Alvaro Espinoza .30 .09
87 Orel Hershiser .30 .09
88 Ken Hill .30 .09
89 Kenny Lofton .30 .09
90 Dennis Martinez .30 .09
91 Jose Mesa .30 .09
92 Eddie Murray .75 .23
93 Charles Nagy .30 .09
94 Chad Ogea .30 .09
95 Tony Pena .30 .09
96 Herb Perry .30 .09
97 Eric Plunk .30 .09
98 Jim Poole .30 .09
99 Manny Ramirez .50 .15
100 Paul Sorrento .30 .09
101 Julian Tavarez .30 .09
102 Jim Thome .75 .23
103 Omar Vizquel .50 .15
104 Dave Winfield .30 .09
105 Danny Bautista .30 .09
106 Joe Boever .30 .09
107 Chad Curtis .30 .09
108 John Doherty .30 .09
109 Cecil Fielder .30 .09
110 John Flaherty .30 .09
111 Travis Fryman .30 .09
112 Chris Gomez .30 .09
113 Bob Higginson .30 .09
114 Mark Lewis .30 .09
115 Jose Lima .30 .09
116 Felipe Lira .30 .09
117 Brian Maxcy .30 .09
118 C.J. Nitkowski .30 .09
119 Phil Plantier .30 .09
120 Clint Sodowsky .30 .09
121 Alan Trammell .30 .09
122 Lou Whitaker .30 .09
123 Kevin Appier .30 .09
124 Johnny Damon .50 .15
125 Gary Gaetti .30 .09
126 Tom Goodwin .30 .09
127 Tom Gordon .30 .09
128 Mark Gubicza .30 .09
129 Bob Hamelin .30 .09
130 David Howard .30 .09
131 Jason Jacome .30 .09
132 Wally Joyner .30 .09
133 Keith Lockhart .30 .09
134 Brent Mayne .30 .09
135 Jeff Montgomery .30 .09
136 Jon Nunnally .30 .09
137 Juan Samuel .30 .09
138 Mike Sweeney RC 1.50 .45
139 Michael Tucker .30 .09
140 Joe Vitiello .30 .09
141 Ricky Bones .30 .09
142 Chuck Carr .30 .09
143 Jeff Cirillo .30 .09
144 Mike Fetters .30 .09
145 Darryl Hamilton .30 .09
146 David Hulse .30 .09
147 John Jaha .30 .09
148 Scott Karl .30 .09
149 Mark Kiefer .30 .09
150 Pat Listach .30 .09
151 Mark Loretta .30 .09
152 Mike Matheny .30 .09
153 Matt Mieske .30 .09
154 Dave Nilsson .30 .09
155 Joe Oliver .30 .09
156 Al Reyes .30 .09
157 Kevin Seitzer .30 .09
158 Steve Sparks .30 .09
159 B.J. Surhoff .30 .09
160 Jose Valentin .30 .09
161 Greg Vaughn .30 .09
162 Fernando Vina .30 .09

163 Rich Becker .30 .09
164 Ron Coomer .30 .09
165 Marty Cordova .30 .09
166 Chuck Knoblauch .30 .09
167 Matt Lawton RC .75 .23
168 Pat Meares .30 .09
169 Paul Molitor .50 .15
170 Pedro Munoz .30 .09
171 Jose Parra .30 .09
172 Kirby Puckett .75 .23
173 Brad Radke .30 .09
174 Jeff Reboulet .30 .09
175 Rich Robertson .30 .09
176 Frank Rodriguez .30 .09
177 Scott Stahoviak .30 .09
178 Dave Stevens .30 .09
179 Matt Walbeck .30 .09
180 Wade Boggs .50 .15
181 David Cone .30 .09
182 Tony Fernandez .30 .09
183 Joe Girardi .30 .09
184 Derek Jeter 2.00 .60
185 Scott Kamieniecki .30 .09
186 Pat Kelly .30 .09
187 Jim Leyritz .30 .09
188 Tino Martinez .50 .15
189 Don Mattingly 2.00 .60
190 Jack McDowell .30 .09
191 Jeff Nelson .30 .09
192 Paul O'Neill .50 .15
193 Melido Perez .30 .09
194 Andy Pettitte .50 .15
195 Mariano Rivera .50 .15
196 Ruben Sierra .30 .09
197 Mike Stanley .30 .09
198 Darryl Strawberry .30 .09
199 John Wetteland .30 .09
200 Bob Wickman .30 .09
201 Bernie Williams .50 .15
202 Mark Acre .30 .09
203 Geronimo Berroa .30 .09
204 Mike Bordick .30 .09
205 Scott Brosius .30 .09
206 Dennis Eckersley .30 .09
207 Brent Gates .30 .09
208 Jason Giambi .30 .09
209 Rickey Henderson .75 .23
210 Jose Herrera .30 .09
211 Stan Javier .30 .09
212 Doug Johns .30 .09
213 Mark McGwire 2.00 .60
214 Steve Ontiveros .30 .09
215 Craig Paquette .30 .09
216 Ariel Prieto .30 .09
217 Carlos Reyes .30 .09
218 Terry Steinbach .30 .09
219 Todd Stottlemyre .30 .09
220 Danny Tartabull .30 .09
221 Todd Van Poppel .30 .09
222 John Wasdin .30 .09
223 George Williams .30 .09
224 Steve Wojciechowski .30 .09
225 Rich Amaral .30 .09
226 Bobby Ayala .30 .09
227 Tim Belcher .30 .09
228 Andy Benes .30 .09
229 Chris Bosio .30 .09
230 Darren Bragg .30 .09
231 Jay Buhner .30 .09
232 Norm Charlton .30 .09
233 Vince Coleman .30 .09
234 Joey Cora .30 .09
235 Russ Davis .30 .09
236 Alex Diaz .30 .09
237 Felix Fermin .30 .09
238 Ken Griffey Jr. 1.25 .35
239 Sterling Hitchcock .30 .09
240 Randy Johnson .75 .23
241 Edgar Martinez .50 .15
242 Bill Risley .30 .09
243 Alex Rodriguez 1.50 .12
244 Luis Sojo .30 .09
245 Dan Wilson .30 .09
246 Bob Wolcott .30 .09
247 Will Clark .75 .23
248 Jeff Frye .30 .09
249 Benji Gil .30 .09
250 Juan Gonzalez .50 .15
251 Rusty Greer .30 .09
252 Kevin Gross .30 .09
253 Roger McDowell .30 .09
254 Mark McLemore .30 .09
255 Otis Nixon .30 .09
256 Luis Ortiz .30 .09
257 Mike Pagliarulo .30 .09
258 Dean Palmer .30 .09
259 Roger Pavlik .30 .09
260 Ivan Rodriguez .75 .23
261 Kenny Rogers .30 .09
262 Jeff Russell .30 .09
263 Mickey Tettleton .30 .09
264 Bob Tewksbury .30 .09
265 Dave Valle .30 .09
266 Matt Whiteside .30 .09
267 Roberto Alomar .50 .15
268 Joe Carter .30 .09
269 Tony Castillo .30 .09
270 Domingo Cedeno .30 .09
271 Tim Crabtree UER .30 .09
272 Carlos Delgado .30 .09
273 Alex Gonzalez .30 .09
274 Shawn Green .30 .09
275 Juan Guzman .30 .09
276 Pat Hentgen .30 .09
277 Al Leiter .30 .09
278 Sandy Martinez .30 .09
279 Paul Menhart .30 .09
280 John Olerud .30 .09
281 Paul Quantrill .30 .09
282 Ken Robinson .30 .09
283 Ed Sprague .30 .09
284 Mike Timlin .30 .09
285 Steve Avery .30 .09
286 Rafael Belliard .30 .09
287 Jeff Blauser .30 .09
288 Pedro Borbon .30 .09
289 Brad Clontz .30 .09
290 Mike Devereaux .30 .09
291 Tom Glavine .50 .15
292 Marquis Grissom .30 .09
293 Chipper Jones .75 .23
294 David Justice .30 .09
295 Mike Kelly .30 .09
296 Ryan Klesko .30 .09
297 Mark Lemke .30 .09
298 Javier Lopez .30 .09
299 Greg Maddux 1.25 .35
300 Fred McGriff .50 .15
301 Greg McMichael .30 .09
302 Kent Mercker .30 .09
303 Mike Mordecai .30 .09
304 Charlie O'Brien .30 .09
305 Eduardo Perez .30 .09
306 Luis Polonia .30 .09
307 Jason Schmidt .50 .15
308 John Smoltz .50 .15
309 Terrell Wade .30 .09
310 Mark Wohlers .30 .09
311 Scott Bullett .30 .09
312 Jim Bullinger .30 .09
313 Larry Casian .30 .09
314 Frank Castillo .30 .09
315 Shawon Dunston .30 .09
316 Kevin Foster .30 .09
317 Matt Franco .30 .09
318 Luis Gonzalez .30 .09
319 Mark Grace .50 .15
320 Jose Hernandez .30 .09
321 Mike Hubbard .30 .09
322 Brian McRae .30 .09
323 Randy Myers .30 .09
324 Jaime Navarro .30 .09
325 Mark Parent .30 .09
326 Mike Perez .30 .09
327 Rey Sanchez .30 .09
328 Ryne Sandberg 1.25 .35
329 Scott Servais .30 .09
330 Sammy Sosa 1.25 .35
331 Ozzie Timmons .30 .09
332 Steve Trachsel .30 .09
333 Todd Zeile .30 .09
334 Bret Boone .30 .09
335 Jeff Branson .30 .09
336 Jeff Brantley .30 .09
337 Dave Burba .30 .09
338 Hector Carrasco .30 .09
339 Mariano Duncan .30 .09
340 Ron Gant .30 .09
341 Lenny Harris .30 .09
342 Xavier Hernandez .30 .09
343 Thomas Howard .30 .09
344 Mike Jackson .30 .09
345 Barry Larkin .50 .15
346 Darren Lewis .30 .09
347 Hal Morris .30 .09
348 Eric Owens .30 .09
349 Mark Portugal .30 .09
350 Jose Rijo .30 .09
351 Reggie Sanders .30 .09
352 Benito Santiago .30 .09
353 Pete Schourek .30 .09
354 John Smiley .30 .09
355 Eddie Taubensee .30 .09
356 Jerome Walton .30 .09
357 David Wells .30 .09
358 Roger Bailey .30 .09
359 Jason Bates .30 .09
360 Dante Bichette .30 .09
361 Ellis Burks .30 .09
362 Vinny Castilla .30 .09
363 Andres Galarraga .30 .09
364 Darren Holmes .30 .09
365 Mike Kingery .30 .09
366 Curt Leskanic .30 .09
367 Quinton McCracken .30 .09
368 Mike Munoz .30 .09
369 David Nied .30 .09
370 Steve Reed .30 .09
371 Bryan Rekar .30 .09
372 Kevin Ritz .30 .09
373 Bruce Ruffin .30 .09
374 Bret Saberhagen .30 .09
375 Bill Swift .30 .09
376 John Vander Wal .30 .09
377 Larry Walker .50 .15
378 Walt Weiss .30 .09
379 Eric Young .30 .09
380 Kurt Abbott .30 .09
381 Alex Arias .30 .09
382 Jerry Browne .30 .09
383 John Burkett .30 .09
384 Greg Colbrunn .30 .09
385 Jeff Conine .30 .09
386 Andre Dawson .30 .09
387 Chris Hammond .30 .09
388 Charles Johnson .30 .09
389 Terry Mathews .30 .09
390 Robb Nen .30 .09
391 Joe Orsulak .30 .09
392 Terry Pendleton .30 .09
393 Pat Rapp .30 .09
394 Gary Sheffield .30 .09
395 Jesus Tavarez .30 .09
396 Marc Valdes .30 .09
397 Quilvio Veras .30 .09
398 Randy Veres .30 .09
399 Devon White .30 .09
400 Jeff Bagwell .50 .15
401 Derek Bell .30 .09
402 Craig Biggio .50 .15
403 John Cangelosi .30 .09
404 Jim Dougherty .30 .09
405 Doug Drabek .30 .09
406 Tony Eusebio .30 .09
407 Ricky Gutierrez .30 .09
408 Mike Hampton .30 .09
409 Dean Hartgraves .30 .09
410 John Hudek .30 .09
411 Brian L. Hunter .30 .09
412 Todd Jones .30 .09
413 Darryl Kile .30 .09
414 Dave Magadan .30 .09
415 Derrick May .30 .09
416 Orlando Miller .30 .09
417 James Mouton .30 .09
418 Shane Reynolds .30 .09
419 Greg Swindell .30 .09
420 Jeff Tabaka .30 .09
421 Dave Veres .30 .09
422 Billy Wagner .30 .09
423 Donne Wall .30 .09
424 Rick Wilkins .30 .09
425 Billy Ashley .30 .09
426 Mike Blowers .30 .09
427 Brett Butler .30 .09
428 Tom Candiotti .30 .09
429 Juan Castro .30 .09
430 John Cummings .30 .09
431 Delino DeShields .30 .09
432 Joey Eischen .30 .09
433 Chad Fonville .30 .09
434 Greg Gagne .30 .09
435 Dave Hansen .30 .09
436 Carlos Hernandez .30 .09
437 Todd Hollandsworth .30 .09
438 Eric Karros .30 .09
439 Roberto Kelly .30 .09
440 Ramon Martinez .30 .09
441 Raul Mondesi .30 .09
442 Hideo Nomo .75 .23
443 Antonio Osuna .30 .09
444 Chan Ho Park .30 .09
445 Mike Piazza 1.25 .35
446 Felix Rodriguez .30 .09
447 Kevin Tapani .30 .09
448 Ismael Valdes .30 .09
449 Todd Worrell .30 .09
450 Moises Alou .30 .09
451 Shane Andrews .30 .09
452 Yamil Benitez .30 .09
453 Sean Berry .30 .09
454 Wil Cordero .30 .09
455 Jeff Fassero .30 .09
456 Darrin Fletcher .30 .09
457 Cliff Floyd .30 .09
458 Mark Grudzielanek .30 .09
459 Gil Heredia .30 .09
460 Tim Laker .30 .09
461 Mike Lansing .30 .09
462 Pedro J.Martinez .75 .23
463 Carlos Perez .30 .09
464 Curtis Pride .30 .09
465 Mel Rojas .30 .09
466 Kirk Rueter .30 .09
467 F.P. Santangelo .30 .09
468 Tim Scott .30 .09
469 David Segui .30 .09
470 Tony Tarasco .30 .09
471 Rondell White .30 .09
472 Edgardo Alfonzo .30 .09
473 Tim Bogar .30 .09
474 Rico Brogna .30 .09
475 Damon Buford .30 .09
476 Paul Byrd .30 .09
477 Carl Everett .30 .09
478 John Franco .30 .09
479 Todd Hundley .30 .09
480 Butch Huskey .30 .09
481 Jason Isringhausen .30 .09
482 Bobby Jones .30 .09
483 Chris Jones .30 .09
484 Jeff Kent .30 .09
485 Dave Mlicki .30 .09
486 Robert Person .30 .09
487 Bill Pulsipher .30 .09
488 Kelly Stinnett .30 .09
489 Ryan Thompson .30 .09
490 Jose Vizcaino .30 .09
491 Howard Battle .30 .09
492 Toby Borland .30 .09
493 Ricky Bottalico .30 .09
494 Darren Daulton .30 .09
495 Lenny Dykstra .30 .09
496 Jim Eisenreich .30 .09
497 Sid Fernandez .30 .09
498 Tyler Green .30 .09
499 Charlie Hayes .30 .09
500 Gregg Jefferies .30 .09
501 Kevin Jordan .30 .09
502 Tony Longmire .30 .09
503 Tom Marsh .30 .09
504 Michael Mimbs .30 .09
505 Mickey Morandini .30 .09
506 Gene Schall .30 .09
507 Curt Schilling .30 .09
508 Heathcliff Slocumb .30 .09
509 Kevin Stocker .30 .09
510 Andy Van Slyke .30 .09
511 Lenny Webster .30 .09
512 Mark Whiten .30 .09
513 Mike Williams .30 .09
514 Jay Bell .30 .09
515 Jacob Brumfield .30 .09
516 Jason Christiansen .30 .09
517 Dave Clark .30 .09
518 Midre Cummings .30 .09
519 Angelo Encarnacion .30 .09
520 John Ericks .30 .09
521 Carlos Garcia .30 .09
522 Mark Johnson .30 .09
523 Jeff King .30 .09
524 Nelson Liriano .30 .09
525 Esteban Loaiza .30 .09
526 Al Martin .30 .09
527 Orlando Merced .30 .09
528 Dan Miceli .30 .09
529 Ramon Morel .30 .09
530 Denny Neagle .30 .09
531 Steve Parris .30 .09
532 Dan Plesac .30 .09
533 Don Slaught .30 .09
534 Paul Wagner .30 .09
535 John Wehner .30 .09
536 Kevin Young .30 .09
537 Allen Battle .30 .09
538 David Bell .30 .09
539 Alan Benes .30 .09
540 Scott Cooper .30 .09
541 Tripp Cromer .30 .09
542 Tony Fossas .30 .09
543 Bernard Gilkey .30 .09
544 Tom Henke .30 .09
545 Brian Jordan .30 .09
546 Ray Lankford .30 .09
547 John Mabry .30 .09
548 T.J. Mathews .30 .09
549 Mike Morgan .30 .09
550 Jose Oliva .30 .09
551 Jose Oquendo .30 .09
552 Donovan Osborne .30 .09
553 Tom Pagnozzi .30 .09
554 Mark Petkovsek .30 .09
555 Danny Sheaffer .30 .09
556 Ozzie Smith 1.25 .35
557 Mark Sweeney .30 .09
558 Allen Watson .30 .09
559 Andy Ashby .30 .09
560 Brad Ausmus .30 .09
561 Willie Blair .30 .09
562 Ken Caminiti .30 .09
563 Andujar Cedeno .30 .09
564 Glenn Dishman .30 .09
565 Steve Finley .30 .09
566 Bryce Florie .30 .09
567 Tony Gwynn 1.00 .30
568 Joey Hamilton .30 .09
569 Dustin Hermanson .30 .09
570 Trevor Hoffman .30 .09
571 Brian Johnson .30 .09
572 Marc Kroon .30 .09
573 Scott Livingstone .30 .09
574 Marc Newfield .30 .09
575 Melvin Nieves .30 .09
576 Jody Reed .30 .09
577 Bip Roberts .30 .09
578 Scott Sanders .30 .09
579 Fernando Valenzuela .30 .09
580 Eddie Williams .30 .09
581 Rod Beck .30 .09
582 Marvin Benard RC .30 .09
583 Barry Bonds 2.00 .60
584 Jamie Brewington RC .30 .09
585 Mark Carreon .30 .09
586 Royce Clayton .30 .09
587 Shawn Estes .30 .09
588 Glenallen Hill .30 .09
589 Mark Leiter .30 .09
590 Kirt Manwaring .30 .09
591 David McCarty .30 .09
592 Terry Mulholland .30 .09
593 John Patterson .30 .09
594 J.R. Phillips .30 .09
595 Deion Sanders .50 .15
596 Steve Scarsone .30 .09
597 Robby Thompson .30 .09
598 Sergio Valdez .30 .09
599 W.Van Landingham .30 .09
600 Matt Williams .30 .09
P20 Cal Ripken 3.00 .90
Promo

1996 Fleer Tiffany

The Tiffany Collection is a 600-card parallel set that has a special UV coating that replaces the matte finish of the regular cards and silver holographic foil that takes the place of gold foil for lettering. These cards were inserted in regular packs at one card per pack.

Nm-Mt Ex-Mt
*STARS: 2X TO 5X BASIC CARDS
*ROOKIES: 4X TO 10X BASIC CARDS

1996 Fleer Checklists

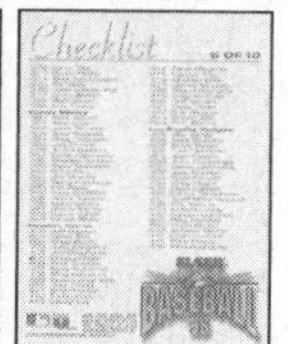

Checklist cards were seeded one per six regular packs and have glossy, borderless fronts with full-color shots of the Major League's best. "Checklist" and the player's name are stamped in gold foil. Backs list the entire rundown of '96 Fleer cards printed in black type on a white background.

	Nm-Mt	Ex-Mt
COMPLETE SET (10)	4.00	1.20
1 Barry Bonds	1.00	.30
2 Ken Griffey Jr.	.60	.18
3 Chipper Jones	.40	.12
4 Greg Maddux	.60	.18
5 Mike Piazza	.60	.18
6 Manny Ramirez	.25	.07
7 Cal Ripken	1.25	.35
8 Frank Thomas	.40	.12
9 Mo Vaughn	.15	.04
10 Matt Williams	.15	.04

1996 Fleer Golden Memories

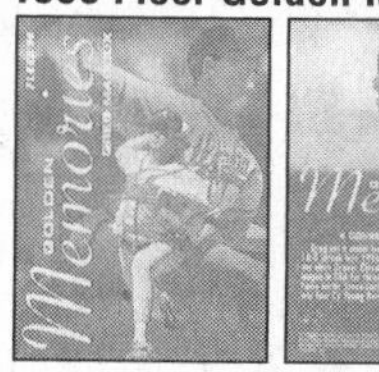

Randomly inserted at a rate of one in 10 regular packs, this 10-card standard-size set features important highlights of the 1995 season. Fronts have two action shots, one serving as a background, the other a full-color cutout. "Golden Memories" and player's name are printed vertically in white type. Backs contain a biography, player close-up and career statistics.

	Nm-Mt	Ex-Mt
COMPLETE SET (10)	8.00	2.40
1 Albert Belle	.40	.12
2 Barry Bonds Sammy Sosa	1.50	.45
3 Greg Maddux	1.50	.45
4 Edgar Martinez	.60	.18
5 Ramon Martinez	.40	.12
6 Mark McGwire	2.50	.75
7 Eddie Murray	1.00	.30
8 Cal Ripken	3.00	.90
9 Frank Thomas	1.00	.30
10 Alan Trammell Lou Whitaker	.40	.12

1996 Fleer Lumber Company

This retail-exclusive 12-card set was inserted one in every nine packs and features RBI and HR power hitters. The fronts display a color action player cut-out on a wood background with embossed printing. The backs carry a player photo and information about the player.

	Nm-Mt	Ex-Mt
COMPLETE SET (12)	25.00	7.50
1 Albert Belle	1.00	.30
2 Dante Bichette	1.00	.30
3 Barry Bonds	6.00	1.80
4 Ken Griffey Jr.	4.00	1.20
5 Mark McGwire	6.00	1.80
6 Mike Piazza	4.00	1.20
7 Manny Ramirez	1.50	.45
8 Tim Salmon	1.50	.45
9 Sammy Sosa	4.00	1.20
10 Frank Thomas	2.50	.75
11 Mo Vaughn	1.00	.30
12 Matt Williams	1.00	.30

1996 Fleer Postseason Glory

Randomly inserted in regular packs at a rate of one in five, this five-card standard-size set highlights great moments of the 1996 Divisional, League Championship and World Series games. Horizontal, white-bordered fronts feature a player in three full-color action cutouts with black strips on top and bottom. "Post-Season Glory" appears on top and the player's name is printed in silver hologram foil. White-bordered backs are split between a full-color player close-up and a description of his post-season play printed in white type on a black background.

	Nm-Mt	Ex-Mt
COMPLETE SET (5)	2.00	.60
1 Tom Glavine	.25	.07
2 Ken Griffey Jr.	.60	.18
3 Orel Hershiser	.15	.04
4 Randy Johnson	.40	.12
5 Jim Thome	.40	.12

1996 Fleer Prospects

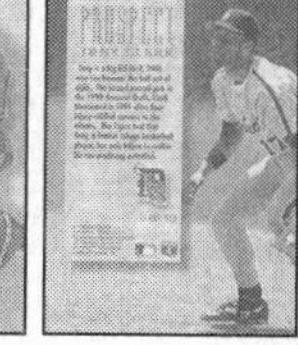

Randomly inserted at a rate of one in six regular packs, this ten-card standard-size set focuses on players moving up through the farm system. Borderless fronts have full-color head shots on one-color backgrounds. "Prospect" and the player's name are stamped in silver hologram foil. Backs feature a full-color action shot with a synopsis of talent printed in a green box.

	Nm-Mt	Ex-Mt
COMPLETE SET (10)	4.00	1.20
1 Yamil Benitez	.50	.15
2 Roger Cedeno	.50	.15
3 Tony Clark	.50	.15
4 Micah Franklin	.50	.15
5 Karim Garcia	.50	.15
6 Todd Greene	.50	.15
7 Alex Ochoa	.50	.15
8 Ruben Rivera	.50	.15
9 Chris Snopek	.50	.15
10 Shannon Stewart	1.00	.30

1996 Fleer Road Warriors

Randomly inserted in regular packs at a rate of one in 13, this 10-card standard-size set focuses on players who thrive on the road. Fronts feature a full-color player cutout set against a winding rural highway background. "Road Warriors" is printed in reverse type with a hazy white border and the player's name is printed in white type underneath. Backs include the player's road stats, biography and a close-up shot.

	Nm-Mt	Ex-Mt
COMPLETE SET (10)	12.00	3.60
1 Derek Bell	.50	.15
2 Tony Gwynn	1.50	.45
3 Greg Maddux	2.00	.60
4 Mark McGwire	3.00	.90
5 Mike Piazza	2.00	.60
6 Manny Ramirez	.75	.23
7 Tim Salmon	.75	.23
8 Frank Thomas	1.25	.35
9 Mo Vaughn	.50	.15
10 Matt Williams	.50	.15

1996 Fleer Rookie Sensations

Randomly inserted at a rate of one in 11 regular packs, this 15-card standard-size set highlights 1995's best rookies. Borderless, horizontal fronts have a full-color action shot and a silver hologram strip containing the player's name and team logo. Horizontal backs have full-color head shots with a player profile all printed on a white background.

	Nm-Mt	Ex-Mt
COMPLETE SET (15)	15.00	4.50
1 Garret Anderson	1.25	.35
2 Marty Cordova	1.25	.35
3 Johnny Damon	2.00	.60
4 Ray Durham	1.25	.35
5 Carl Everett	1.25	.35
6 Shawn Green	1.25	.35
7 Brian L.Hunter	1.25	.35
8 Jason Isringhausen	1.25	.35
9 Charles Johnson	1.25	.35
10 Chipper Jones	3.00	.90
11 John Mabry	1.25	.35
12 Hideo Nomo	3.00	.90
13 Troy Percival	1.25	.35
14 Andy Pettitte	2.00	.60
15 Quilvio Veras	1.25	.35

1996 Fleer Smoke 'n Heat

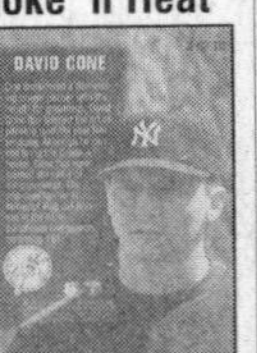

Randomly inserted at a rate of one in nine regular packs, this 10-card standard-size set celebrates the pitchers with rifle arms and a high strikeout count. Fronts feature a full-color player cutout set against a red flame background. "Smoke 'n Heat" and the player's name are printed in gold type. Backs feature the pitcher's 1995 numbers, a biography and career stats along with a full-color close-up.

	Nm-Mt	Ex-Mt
COMPLETE SET (10)	6.00	1.80
1 Kevin Appier	.50	.15
2 Roger Clemens	2.50	.75
3 David Cone	.50	.15
4 Chuck Finley	.50	.15
5 Randy Johnson	1.25	.35
6 Greg Maddux	2.00	.60
7 Pedro Martinez	1.25	.35
8 Hideo Nomo	1.25	.35
9 John Smoltz	.75	.23
10 Todd Stottlemyre	.50	.15

1996 Fleer Team Leaders

This hobby-exclusive 28-card set was randomly inserted one in every nine packs and features statistical and inspirational leaders. The fronts display color action player cut-out on a foil background of the team name and logo. The backs carry a player portrait and player information.

	Nm-Mt	Ex-Mt
COMPLETE SET (28)	60.00	18.00
1 Cal Ripken	10.00	3.00
2 Mo Vaughn	1.25	.35
3 Jim Edmonds	1.25	.35
4 Frank Thomas	3.00	.90
5 Kenny Lofton	1.25	.35
6 Travis Fryman	1.25	.35
7 Gary Gaetti	1.25	.35
8 B.J. Surhoff	1.25	.35
9 Kirby Puckett	3.00	.90
10 Don Mattingly	8.00	2.40
11 Mark McGwire	8.00	2.40
12 Ken Griffey Jr.	5.00	1.50
13 Juan Gonzalez	2.00	.60
14 Joe Carter	1.25	.35
15 Greg Maddux	5.00	1.50
16 Sammy Sosa	5.00	1.50
17 Barry Larkin	2.00	.60
18 Dante Bichette	1.25	.35
19 Jeff Conine	1.25	.35
20 Jeff Bagwell	2.00	.60
21 Mike Piazza	5.00	1.50
22 Rondell White	1.25	.35
23 Rico Brogna	1.25	.35
24 Darren Daulton	1.25	.35
25 Jeff King	1.25	.35
26 Ray Lankford	1.25	.35
27 Tony Gwynn	4.00	1.20
28 Barry Bonds	8.00	2.40

1996 Fleer Tomorrow's Legends

Randomly inserted in regular packs at a rate of one in 13, this 10-card set focuses on young talent with bright futures. Multicolored fronts have four panels of art that serve as a background and a full-color player cutout. "Tomorrow's Legends" and player's name are printed in white type at the bottom. Backs include the player's '95 stats, biography and a full-color close-up shot.

	Nm-Mt	Ex-Mt
COMPLETE SET (10)	10.00	3.00
1 Garret Anderson	.75	.23
2 Jim Edmonds	.75	.23
3 Brian L.Hunter	.75	.23
4 Jason Isringhausen	.75	.23
5 Charles Johnson	.75	.23
6 Chipper Jones	2.00	.60
7 Ryan Klesko	.75	.23
8 Hideo Nomo	2.00	.60
9 Manny Ramirez	1.25	.35
10 Rondell White	.75	.23

1996 Fleer Zone

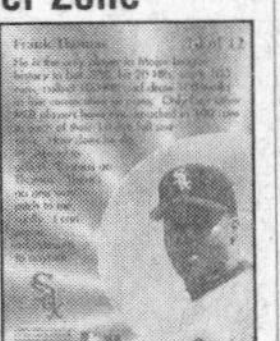

This 12-card set was randomly inserted one in every 90 packs and features "unstoppable" hitters and "unhittable" pitchers. The fronts display a color action player cut-out printed on holographic foil. The backs carry a player portrait with information as to why they were selected for this set.

	Nm-Mt	Ex-Mt
COMPLETE SET (12)	100.00	30.00
1 Albert Belle	3.00	.90
2 Barry Bonds	20.00	6.00
3 Ken Griffey Jr.	12.00	3.60
4 Tony Gwynn	10.00	3.00
5 Randy Johnson	8.00	2.40
6 Kenny Lofton	3.00	.90
7 Greg Maddux	12.00	3.60
8 Edgar Martinez	5.00	1.50
9 Mike Piazza	12.00	3.60
10 Frank Thomas	8.00	2.40
11 Mo Vaughn	3.00	.90
12 Matt Williams	3.00	.90

1996 Fleer Update

The 1996 Fleer Update set was issued in one series totalling 250 cards. The 11-card packs retailed for $1.49 each. The fronts feature color action player photos. The backs carry complete player stats and a "Did you know?" fact. The cards are grouped alphabetically within teams and checklisted below alphabetically according to teams for each league with AL preceding NL. The set contains the subset: Encore (U211-U245). Notable Rookie Cards include Tony Batista, Mike Cameron, Matt Mantei and Chris Singleton.

	Nm-Mt	Ex-Mt
COMPLETE SET (250)	30.00	9.00
U1 Roberto Alomar	.50	.15
U2 Mike Devereaux	.30	.09
U3 Scott McClain RC	.30	.09
U4 Roger McDowell	.30	.09
U5 Kent Mercker	.30	.09
U6 Jimmy Myers RC	.30	.09
U7 Randy Myers	.30	.09
U8 B.J. Surhoff	.30	.09
U9 Tony Tarasco	.30	.09
U10 David Wells	.30	.09
U11 Wil Cordero	.30	.09
U12 Tom Gordon	.30	.09
U13 Reggie Jefferson	.30	.09
U14 Jose Malave	.30	.09
U15 Kevin Mitchell	.30	.09
U16 Jamie Moyer	.30	.09
U17 Heathcliff Slocumb	.30	.09
U18 Mike Stanley	.30	.09
U19 George Arias	.30	.09
U20 Jorge Fabregas	.30	.09
U21 Don Slaught	.30	.09
U22 Randy Velarde	.30	.09
U23 Harold Baines	.30	.09
U24 Mike Cameron RC	1.00	.30
U25 Darren Lewis	.30	.09
U26 Tony Phillips	.30	.09
U27 Bill Simas	.30	.09
U28 Chris Snopek	.30	.09
U29 Kevin Tapani	.30	.09
U30 Danny Tartabull	.30	.09
U31 Julio Franco	.30	.09
U32 Jack McDowell	.30	.09
U33 Kimera Bartee	.30	.09
U34 Mark Lewis	.30	.09
U35 Melvin Nieves	.30	.09
U36 Mark Parent	.30	.09
U37 Eddie Williams	.30	.09
U38 Tim Belcher	.30	.09
U39 Sal Fasano	.30	.09
U40 Chris Haney	.30	.09
U41 Mike Macfarlane	.30	.09
U42 Jose Offerman	.30	.09
U43 Joe Randa	.30	.09
U44 Bip Roberts	.30	.09
U45 Chuck Carr	.30	.09
U46 Bobby Hughes	.30	.09
U47 Graeme Lloyd	.30	.09
U48 Ben McDonald	.30	.09
U49 Kevin Wickander	.30	.09
U50 Rick Aguilera	.30	.09
U51 Mike Durant	.30	.09
U52 Chip Hale	.30	.09
U53 LaTroy Hawkins	.30	.09
U54 Dave Hollins	.30	.09
U55 Roberto Kelly	.30	.09
U56 Paul Molitor	.50	.15
U57 Dan Naulty	.30	.09
U58 Mariano Duncan	.30	.09
U59 Andy Fox	.30	.09
U60 Joe Girardi	.30	.09
U61 Dwight Gooden	.30	.09
U62 Jimmy Key	.30	.09
U63 Matt Luke	.30	.09
U64 Tino Martinez	.50	.15
U65 Jeff Nelson	.30	.09
U66 Tim Raines	.30	.09
U67 Ruben Rivera	.30	.09
U68 Kenny Rogers	.30	.09
U69 Gerald Williams	.30	.09
U70 Tony Batista RC	.60	.18
U71 Allen Battle	.30	.09
U72 Jim Corsi	.30	.09
U73 Steve Cox	.30	.09
U74 Pedro Munoz	.30	.09
U75 Phil Plantier	.30	.09
U76 Scott Spiezio	.30	.09
U77 Ernie Young	.30	.09
U78 Russ Davis	.30	.09
U79 Sterling Hitchcock	.30	.09
U80 Edwin Hurtado	.30	.09
U81 Raul Ibanez RC	.60	.18
U82 Mike Jackson	.30	.09
U83 Ricky Jordan	.30	.09
U84 Paul Sorrento	.30	.09
U85 Doug Strange	.30	.09
U86 M.Brandenburg RC	.30	.09
U87 Damon Buford	.30	.09
U88 Kevin Elster	.30	.09
U89 Darryl Hamilton	.30	.09
U90 Ken Hill	.30	.09
U91 Ed Vosberg	.30	.09
U92 Craig Worthington	.30	.09
U93 Tilson Brito RC	.30	.09
U94 Giovanni Carrara RC	.30	.09
U95 Felipe Crespo	.30	.09
U96 Erik Hanson	.30	.09
U97 Marty Janzen RC	.30	.09
U98 Otis Nixon	.30	.09
U99 Charlie O'Brien	.30	.09
U100 Robert Perez	.30	.09
U101 Paul Quantrill	.30	.09
U102 Bill Risley	.30	.09
U103 Juan Samuel	.30	.09
U104 Jermaine Dye	.30	.09
U105 W.Monds RC	.30	.09
U106 Dwight Smith	.30	.09
U107 Jerome Walton	.30	.09
U108 Terry Adams	.30	.09
U109 Leo Gomez	.30	.09
U110 Robin Jennings	.30	.09
U111 Doug Jones	.30	.09
U112 Brooks Kieschnick	.30	.09
U113 Dave Magadan	.30	.09
U114 Jason Maxwell RC	.30	.09
U115 Rodney Myers RC	.30	.09
U116 Eric Anthony	.30	.09
U117 Vince Coleman	.30	.09
U118 Eric Davis	.30	.09
U119 Steve Gibralter	.30	.09
U120 Curtis Goodwin	.30	.09
U121 Willie Greene	.30	.09
U122 Mike Kelly	.30	.09
U123 Marcus Moore	.30	.09
U124 Chad Mottola	.30	.09
U125 Chris Sabo	.30	.09
U126 Roger Salkeld	.30	.09
U127 Pedro Castellano	.30	.09
U128 Trenidad Hubbard	.30	.09
U129 Jayhawk Owens	.30	.09
U130 Jeff Reed	.30	.09
U131 Kevin Brown	.30	.09
U132 Al Leiter	.30	.09
U133 Matt Mantei RC	.40	.12
U134 Dave Weathers	.30	.09
U135 Devon White	.30	.09
U136 Bob Abreu	.30	.09
U137 Sean Berry	.30	.09
U138 Doug Brocail	.30	.09
U139 Richard Hidalgo	.30	.09
U140 Alvin Morman	.30	.09
U141 Mike Blowers	.30	.09
U142 Roger Cedeno	.30	.09
U143 Greg Gagne	.30	.09
U144 Karim Garcia	.30	.09
U145 Wilton Guerrero RC	.40	.12
U146 Israel Alcantara RC	.30	.09
U147 Omar Daal	.30	.09
U148 Ryan McGuire	.30	.09
U149 Sherman Obando	.30	.09
U150 Jose Paniagua	.30	.09
U151 Henry Rodriguez	.30	.09
U152 Andy Stankiewicz	.30	.09
U153 Dave Veres	.30	.09
U154 Juan Acevedo	.30	.09
U155 Mark Clark	.30	.09
U156 Bernard Gilkey	.30	.09
U157 Pete Harnisch	.30	.09
U158 Lance Johnson	.30	.09
U159 Brent Mayne	.30	.09
U160 Rey Ordonez	.30	.09
U161 Kevin Roberson	.30	.09
U162 Paul Wilson	.30	.09
U163 David Doster RC	.30	.09
U164 Mike Grace RC	.30	.09
U165 Rich Hunter RC	.30	.09
U166 Pete Incaviglia	.30	.09
U167 Mike Lieberthal	.30	.09
U168 Terry Mulholland	.30	.09
U169 Ken Ryan	.30	.09
U170 Benito Santiago	.30	.09
U171 Kevin Sefcik RC	.30	.09
U172 Lee Tinsley	.30	.09
U173 Todd Zeile	.30	.09
U174 F.Cordova RC	.40	.12
U175 Danny Darwin	.30	.09
U176 Charlie Hayes	.30	.09
U177 Jason Kendall	.30	.09
U178 Mike Kingery	.30	.09
U179 Jon Lieber	.30	.09
U180 Zane Smith	.30	.09
U181 Luis Alicea	.30	.09
U182 Cory Bailey	.30	.09
U183 Andy Benes	.30	.09
U184 Pat Borders	.30	.09
U185 Mike Busby RC	.30	.09
U186 Royce Clayton	.30	.09
U187 Dennis Eckersley	.30	.09
U188 Gary Gaetti	.30	.09
U189 Ron Gant	.30	.09
U190 Aaron Holbert	.30	.09
U191 Willie McGee	.30	.09
U192 Miguel Mejia RC	.30	.09
U193 Jeff Parrett	.30	.09
U194 Todd Stottlemyre	.30	.09
U195 Sean Bergman	.30	.09
U196 Archi Cianfrocco	.30	.09
U197 Rickey Henderson	.75	.23
U198 Wally Joyner	.30	.09
U199 Craig Shipley	.30	.09
U200 Bob Tewksbury	.30	.09
U201 Tim Worrell	.30	.09
U202 Rich Aurilia RC	.60	.18
U203 Doug Creek	.30	.09
U204 Shawon Dunston	.30	.09
U205 O.Fernandez RC	.30	.09
U206 Mark Gardner	.30	.09
U207 Stan Javier	.30	.09
U208 Marcus Jensen	.30	.09
U209 Chris Singleton RC	.40	.12
U210 Allen Watson	.30	.09
U211 Jeff Bagwell ENC	.50	.15
U212 Derek Bell ENC	.30	.09
U213 Albert Belle ENC	.30	.09
U214 Wade Boggs ENC	.50	.15
U215 Barry Bonds ENC	2.00	.60
U216 Jose Canseco ENC	.75	.23
U217 Marty Cordova ENC	.30	.09
U218 Jim Edmonds ENC	.30	.09
U219 Cecil Fielder ENC	.30	.09
U220 A.Galarraga ENC	.30	.09
U221 Juan Gonzalez ENC	.50	.15
U222 Mark Grace ENC	.50	.15
U223 Ken Griffey Jr. ENC	1.25	.35
U224 Tony Gwynn ENC	1.00	.30
U225 J. Isringhausen ENC	.30	.09
U226 Derek Jeter ENC	2.00	.60
U227 Randy Johnson ENC	.75	.23
U228 Chipper Jones ENC	.75	.23
U229 Ryan Klesko ENC	.30	.09
U230 Barry Larkin ENC	.50	.15
U231 Kenny Lofton ENC	.30	.09
U232 Greg Maddux ENC	1.25	.35
U233 Raul Mondesi ENC	.30	.09
U234 Hideo Nomo ENC	.75	.23
U235 Mike Piazza ENC	1.25	.35
U236 Manny Ramirez ENC	.50	.15
U237 Cal Ripken ENC	1.50	.45
U238 Tim Salmon ENC	.50	.15
U239 Ryne Sandberg ENC	1.25	.35
U240 Reggie Sanders ENC	.30	.09
U241 Gary Sheffield ENC	.30	.09
U242 Sammy Sosa ENC	1.25	.35
U243 Frank Thomas ENC	.75	.23
U244 Mo Vaughn ENC	.30	.09
U245 Matt Williams ENC	.30	.09
U246 Barry Bonds CL	1.00	.30
U247 Ken Griffey Jr. CL	.75	.23
U248 Rey Ordonez CL	.30	.09
U249 Ryne Sandberg CL	.75	.23
U250 Frank Thomas CL	.50	.15

1996 Fleer Update Tiffany

Inserted one per pack, these 250 cards parallel the basic Fleer Update cards. Unlike the basic cards, Tiffany inserts feature a layer of UV coating and a special logo on each card front.

	Nm-Mt	Ex-Mt
COMPLETE SET (250)	120.00	36.00

*STARS: 1.25X TO 3X BASIC CARDS.
*ROOKIES: 2X TO 5X BASIC CARDS..

1996 Fleer Update Diamond Tribute

Randomly inserted in packs at a rate of one in 100, this 10-card set spotlights future Hall of Famers with holographic foils in a diamond design.

	Nm-Mt	Ex-Mt
COMPLETE SET (10)	150.00	45.00
1 Wade Boggs	6.00	1.80
2 Barry Bonds	25.00	7.50
3 Ken Griffey Jr.	15.00	4.50
4 Tony Gwynn	12.00	3.60
5 Rickey Henderson	10.00	3.00
6 Greg Maddux	15.00	4.50
7 Eddie Murray	10.00	3.00
8 Cal Ripken	30.00	9.00
9 Ozzie Smith	15.00	4.50
10 Frank Thomas	10.00	3.00

1996 Fleer Update Headliners

Randomly inserted exclusively in retail packs at a rate of one in 20, cards from this 20-card set feature raised textured printing. The fronts carry color action player photos with the word "headliner" running continuously across the background.

	Nm-Mt	Ex-Mt
COMPLETE SET (20)	40.00	12.00
1 Roberto Alomar	1.25	.35
2 Jeff Bagwell	1.25	.35
3 Albert Belle	.75	.23
4 Barry Bonds	5.00	1.50
5 Cecil Fielder	.75	.23
6 Juan Gonzalez	1.25	.35
7 Ken Griffey Jr.	3.00	.90
8 Tony Gwynn	2.50	.75
9 Randy Johnson	2.00	.60
10 Chipper Jones	2.00	.60
11 Ryan Klesko	.75	.23
12 Kenny Lofton	.75	.23
13 Greg Maddux	3.00	.90
14 Hideo Nomo	2.00	.60
15 Mike Piazza	3.00	.90
16 Manny Ramirez	1.25	.35
17 Cal Ripken	6.00	1.80
18 Tim Salmon	1.25	.35
19 Frank Thomas	2.00	.60
20 Matt Williams	.75	.23

1996 Fleer Update New Horizons

Randomly inserted in hobby packs only at a rate of one in five, this 20-card set features 1996 rookies and prospects. The fronts carry player action color photos printed on foil cards. The backs display a player portrait and information about the player.

	Nm-Mt	Ex-Mt
COMPLETE SET (20)	15.00	4.50
1 Bob Abreu	.50	.15
2 George Arias	.50	.15
3 Tony Batista	1.00	.30
4 Steve Cox	.50	.15
5 Jermaine Dye	.50	.15
6 Andy Fox	.50	.15
7 Mike Grace	.50	.15
8 Todd Greene	.50	.15
9 Wilton Guerrero	.50	.15
10 Richard Hidalgo	.50	.15
11 Raul Ibanez	1.50	.45
12 Robin Jennings	.50	.15
13 Marcus Jensen	.50	.15
14 Jason Kendall	.50	.15
15 Jason Maxwell	.50	.15
16 Ryan McGuire	.50	.15
17 Miguel Mejia	.50	.15
18 Wonderful Monds	.50	.15
19 Rey Ordonez	.50	.15
20 Paul Wilson	.50	.15

1996 Fleer Update Smooth Leather

Randomly inserted in packs at a rate of one in five, this 10-card set features defensive stars. The fronts display color player photos and gold foil printing. The backs carry a player portrait

and information about why the player was selected for this set.

	Nm-Mt	Ex-Mt
COMPLETE SET (10)	10.00	3.00
1 Roberto Alomar	.60	.18
2 Barry Bonds	2.50	.75
3 Will Clark	1.00	.30
4 Ken Griffey Jr.	1.50	.45
5 Kenny Lofton	.40	.12
6 Greg Maddux	1.50	.45
7 Raul Mondesi	.40	.12
8 Rey Ordonez	.40	.12
9 Cal Ripken	3.00	.90
10 Matt Williams	.40	.12

1996 Fleer Update Soaring Stars

Randomly inserted in packs at a rate of one in 11, this 10-card set features 10 of the hottest young players. The fronts carry color player cut-outs on a background of soaring baseballs in etched foil. The backs display another player photo on the same background with player information.

	Nm-Mt	Ex-Mt
COMPLETE SET (10)	25.00	7.50
1 Jeff Bagwell	1.25	.35
2 Barry Bonds	5.00	1.50
3 Juan Gonzalez	1.25	.35
4 Ken Griffey Jr.	3.00	.90
5 Chipper Jones	2.00	.60
6 Greg Maddux	3.00	.90
7 Mike Piazza	3.00	.90
8 Manny Ramirez	1.25	.35
9 Frank Thomas	2.00	.60
10 Matt Williams	.75	.23

1997 Fleer

'he 1997 Fleer set was issued in two series otaling 761 cards and distributed in 10-card acks with a suggested retail price of $1.49. The onts feature color action player photos with a natte finish and gold foil printing. The backs arry another player photo with player information and career statistics. Cards 491-500 are a hecklist subset of Series one and feature black-nd-white or sepia tone photos of big-name layers. Series two contains the following subets: Encore (696-720) which are redesigned ards of the big-name players from Series one, nd Checklists (721-748). Cards 749 and 750 re expansion team logo cards with the insert hecklists on the backs. Many dealers believe at cards numbered 751-761 were shortprinted. n Andruw Jones autographed Circa card numered to 200 was also randomly inserted into acks. Rookie Cards in this set include Jose Cruz :., Brian Giles and Fernando Tatis.

	Nm-Mt	Ex-Mt
OMPLETE SET (761)	110.00	33.00
OMP. SERIES 1 (500)	60.00	18.00
OMP. SERIES 2 (261)	50.00	15.00
OMMON CARD (1-750)	.30	.09
OMMON CARD (751-761)	.50	.15
Roberto Alomar	.50	.15
Brady Anderson	.30	.09
Bobby Bonilla	.30	.09
Rocky Coppinger	.30	.09
Cesar Devarez	.30	.09
Scott Erickson	.30	.09
Jeffrey Hammonds	.30	.09
Chris Hoiles	.30	.09
Eddie Murray	.75	.23
Mike Mussina	.50	.15
Randy Myers	.30	.09
Rafael Palmeiro	.50	.15
Cal Ripken	2.50	.75
B.J. Surhoff	.30	.09
David Wells	.30	.09
Todd Zeile	.30	.09
Darren Bragg	.30	.09
Jose Canseco	.75	.23
Roger Clemens	1.50	.45
Wil Cordero	.30	.09
Jeff Frye	.30	.09
Nomar Garciaparra	1.25	.35
Tom Gordon	.30	.09
Mike Greenwell	.30	.09
Reggie Jefferson	.30	.09
Jose Malave	.30	.09
27 Tim Naehring	.30	.09
28 Troy O'Leary	.30	.09
29 Heathcliff Slocumb	.30	.09
30 Mike Stanley	.30	.09
31 John Valentin	.30	.09
32 Mo Vaughn	.30	.09
33 Tim Wakefield	.30	.09
34 Garret Anderson	.30	.09
35 George Arias	.30	.09
36 Shawn Boskie	.30	.09
37 Chili Davis	.30	.09
38 Jason Dickson	.30	.09
39 Gary DiSarcina	.30	.09
40 Jim Edmonds	.30	.09
41 Darin Erstad	.30	.09
42 Jorge Fabregas	.30	.09
43 Chuck Finley	.30	.09
44 Todd Greene	.30	.09
45 Mike Holtz	.30	.09
46 Rex Hudler	.30	.09
47 Mike James	.30	.09
48 Mark Langston	.30	.09
49 Troy Percival	.30	.09
50 Tim Salmon	.50	.15
51 Jeff Schmidt	.30	.09
52 J.T. Snow	.30	.09
53 Randy Velarde	.30	.09
54 Wilson Alvarez	.30	.09
55 Harold Baines	.30	.09
56 James Baldwin	.30	.09
57 Jason Bere	.30	.09
58 Mike Cameron	.30	.09
59 Ray Durham	.30	.09
60 Alex Fernandez	.30	.09
61 Ozzie Guillen	.30	.09
62 Roberto Hernandez	.30	.09
63 Ron Karkovice	.30	.09
64 Darren Lewis	.30	.09
65 Dave Martinez	.30	.09
66 Lyle Mouton	.30	.09
67 Greg Norton	.30	.09
68 Tony Phillips	.30	.09
69 Chris Snopek	.30	.09
70 Kevin Tapani	.30	.09
71 Danny Tartabull	.30	.09
72 Frank Thomas	.75	.23
73 Robin Ventura	.30	.09
74 Sandy Alomar Jr.	.30	.09
75 Albert Belle	.30	.09
76 Mark Carreon	.30	.09
77 Julio Franco	.30	.09
78 Brian Giles RC	1.50	.45
79 Orel Hershiser	.30	.09
80 Kenny Lofton	.30	.09
81 Dennis Martinez	.30	.09
82 Jack McDowell	.30	.09
83 Jose Mesa	.30	.09
84 Charles Nagy	.30	.09
85 Chad Ogea	.30	.09
86 Eric Plunk	.30	.09
87 Manny Ramirez	.50	.15
88 Kevin Seitzer	.30	.09
89 Julian Tavarez	.30	.09
90 Jim Thome	.75	.23
91 Jose Vizcaino	.30	.09
92 Omar Vizquel	.50	.15
93 Brad Ausmus	.30	.09
94 Kimera Bartee	.30	.09
95 Raul Casanova	.30	.09
96 Tony Clark	.30	.09
97 John Cummings	.30	.09
98 Travis Fryman	.30	.09
99 Bob Higginson	.30	.09
100 Mark Lewis	.30	.09
101 Felipe Lira	.30	.09
102 Phil Nevin	.30	.09
103 Melvin Nieves	.30	.09
104 Curtis Pride	.30	.09
105 A.J. Sager	.30	.09
106 Ruben Sierra	.30	.09
107 Justin Thompson	.30	.09
108 Alan Trammell	.50	.15
109 Kevin Appier	.30	.09
110 Tim Belcher	.30	.09
111 Jaime Bluma	.30	.09
112 Johnny Damon	.50	.15
113 Tom Goodwin	.30	.09
114 Chris Haney	.30	.09
115 Keith Lockhart	.30	.09
116 Mike Macfarlane	.30	.09
117 Jeff Montgomery	.30	.09
118 Jose Offerman	.30	.09
119 Craig Paquette	.30	.09
120 Joe Randa	.30	.09
121 Bip Roberts	.30	.09
122 Jose Rosado	.30	.09
123 Mike Sweeney	.30	.09
124 Michael Tucker	.30	.09
125 Jeromy Burnitz	.30	.09
126 Jeff Cirillo	.30	.09
127 Jeff D'Amico	.30	.09
128 Mike Fetters	.30	.09
129 John Jaha	.30	.09
130 Scott Karl	.30	.09
131 Jesse Levis	.30	.09
132 Mark Loretta	.30	.09
133 Mike Matheny	.30	.09
134 Ben McDonald	.30	.09
135 Matt Mieske	.30	.09
136 Marc Newfield	.30	.09
137 Dave Nilsson	.30	.09
138 Jose Valentin	.30	.09
139 Fernando Vina	.30	.09
140 Bob Wickman	.30	.09
141 Gerald Williams	.30	.09
142 Rick Aguilera	.30	.09
143 Rich Becker	.30	.09
144 Ron Coomer	.30	.09
145 Marty Cordova	.30	.09
146 Roberto Kelly	.30	.09
147 Chuck Knoblauch	.30	.09
148 Matt Lawton	.30	.09
149 Pat Meares	.30	.09
150 Travis Miller	.30	.09
151 Paul Molitor	.50	.15
152 Greg Myers	.30	.09
153 Dan Naulty	.30	.09
154 Kirby Puckett	.75	.23
155 Brad Radke	.30	.09
156 Frank Rodriguez	.30	.09
157 Scott Stahoviak	.30	.09
158 Dave Stevens	.30	.09
159 Matt Walbeck	.30	.09
160 Todd Walker	.30	.09
161 Wade Boggs	.50	.15
162 David Cone	.30	.09
163 Mariano Duncan	.30	.09
164 Cecil Fielder	.30	.09
165 Joe Girardi	.30	.09
166 Dwight Gooden	.30	.09
167 Charlie Hayes	.30	.09
168 Derek Jeter	2.00	.60
169 Jimmy Key	.30	.09
170 Jim Leyritz	.30	.09
171 Tino Martinez	.50	.15
172 Ramiro Mendoza RC	.30	.09
173 Jeff Nelson	.30	.09
174 Paul O'Neill	.50	.15
175 Andy Pettitte	.50	.15
176 Mariano Rivera	.50	.15
177 Ruben Rivera	.30	.09
178 Kenny Rogers	.30	.09
179 Darryl Strawberry	.30	.09
180 John Wetteland	.30	.09
181 Bernie Williams	.50	.15
182 Willie Adams	.30	.09
183 Tony Batista	.30	.09
184 Geronimo Berroa	.30	.09
185 Mike Bordick	.30	.09
186 Scott Brosius	.30	.09
187 Bobby Chouinard	.30	.09
188 Jim Corsi	.30	.09
189 Brent Gates	.30	.09
190 Jason Giambi	.30	.09
191 Jose Herrera	.30	.09
192 Damon Mashore	.30	.09
193 Mark McGwire	2.00	.60
194 Mike Mohler	.30	.09
195 Scott Spiezio	.30	.09
196 Terry Steinbach	.30	.09
197 Bill Taylor	.30	.09
198 John Wasdin	.30	.09
199 Steve Wojciechowski	.30	.09
200 Ernie Young	.30	.09
201 Rich Amaral	.30	.09
202 Jay Buhner	.30	.09
203 Norm Charlton	.30	.09
204 Joey Cora	.30	.09
205 Russ Davis	.30	.09
206 Ken Griffey Jr.	1.25	.35
207 Sterling Hitchcock	.30	.09
208 Brian Hunter	.30	.09
209 Raul Ibanez	.30	.09
210 Randy Johnson	.75	.23
211 Edgar Martinez	.50	.15
212 Jamie Moyer	.30	.09
213 Alex Rodriguez	1.25	.35
214 Paul Sorrento	.30	.09
215 Matt Wagner	.30	.09
216 Bob Wells	.30	.09
217 Dan Wilson	.30	.09
218 Damon Buford	.30	.09
219 Will Clark	.75	.23
220 Kevin Elster	.30	.09
221 Juan Gonzalez	.50	.15
222 Rusty Greer	.30	.09
223 Kevin Gross	.30	.09
224 Darryl Hamilton	.30	.09
225 Mike Henneman	.30	.09
226 Ken Hill	.30	.09
227 Mark McLemore	.30	.09
228 Darren Oliver	.30	.09
229 Dean Palmer	.30	.09
230 Roger Pavlik	.30	.09
231 Ivan Rodriguez	.75	.23
232 Mickey Tettleton	.30	.09
233 Bobby Witt	.30	.09
234 Jacob Brumfield	.30	.09
235 Joe Carter	.30	.09
236 Tim Crabtree	.30	.09
237 Carlos Delgado	.30	.09
238 Huck Flener	.30	.09
239 Alex Gonzalez	.30	.09
240 Shawn Green	.30	.09
241 Juan Guzman	.30	.09
242 Pat Hentgen	.30	.09
243 Marty Janzen	.30	.09
244 Sandy Martinez	.30	.09
245 Otis Nixon	.30	.09
246 Charlie O'Brien	.30	.09
247 John Olerud	.30	.09
248 Robert Perez	.30	.09
249 Ed Sprague	.30	.09
250 Mike Timlin	.30	.09
251 Steve Avery	.30	.09
252 Jeff Blauser	.30	.09
253 Brad Clontz	.30	.09
254 Jermaine Dye	.30	.09
255 Tom Glavine	.50	.15
256 Marquis Grissom	.30	.09
257 Andruw Jones	.30	.09
258 Chipper Jones	.75	.23
259 David Justice	.30	.09
260 Ryan Klesko	.30	.09
261 Mark Lemke	.30	.09
262 Javier Lopez	.30	.09
263 Greg Maddux	1.25	.35
264 Fred McGriff	.50	.15
265 Greg McMichael	.30	.09
266 Denny Neagle	.30	.09
267 Terry Pendleton	.30	.09
268 Eddie Perez	.30	.09
269 John Smoltz	.50	.15
270 Terrell Wade	.30	.09
271 Mark Wohlers	.30	.09
272 Terry Adams	.30	.09
273 Brant Brown	.30	.09
274 Leo Gomez	.30	.09
275 Luis Gonzalez	.30	.09
276 Mark Grace	.50	.15
277 Tyler Houston	.30	.09
278 Robin Jennings	.30	.09
279 Brooks Kieschnick	.30	.09
280 Brian McRae	.30	.09
281 Jaime Navarro	.30	.09
282 Ryne Sandberg	1.25	.35
283 Scott Servais	.30	.09
284 Sammy Sosa	1.25	.35
285 Dave Swartzbaugh	.30	.09
286 Amaury Telemaco	.30	.09
287 Steve Trachsel	.30	.09
288 Pedro Valdes	.30	.09
289 Turk Wendell	.30	.09
290 Bret Boone	.30	.09
291 Jeff Branson	.30	.09
292 Jeff Brantley	.30	.09
293 Eric Davis	.30	.09
294 Willie Greene	.30	.09
295 Thomas Howard	.30	.09
296 Barry Larkin	.50	.15
297 Kevin Mitchell	.30	.09
298 Hal Morris	.30	.09
299 Chad Mottola	.30	.09
300 Joe Oliver	.30	.09
301 Mark Portugal	.30	.09
302 Roger Salkeld	.30	.09
303 Reggie Sanders	.30	.09
304 Pete Schourek	.30	.09
305 John Smiley	.30	.09
306 Eddie Taubensee	.30	.09
307 Dante Bichette	.30	.09
308 Ellis Burks	.30	.09
309 Vinny Castilla	.30	.09
310 Andres Galarraga	.30	.09
311 Curt Leskanic	.30	.09
312 Quinton McCracken	.30	.09
313 Neifi Perez	.30	.09
314 Jeff Reed	.30	.09
315 Steve Reed	.30	.09
316 Armando Reynoso	.30	.09
317 Kevin Ritz	.30	.09
318 Bruce Ruffin	.30	.09
319 Larry Walker	.50	.15
320 Walt Weiss	.30	.09
321 Jamey Wright	.30	.09
322 Eric Young	.30	.09
323 Kurt Abbott	.30	.09
324 Alex Arias	.30	.09
325 Kevin Brown	.30	.09
326 Luis Castillo	.30	.09
327 Greg Colbrunn	.30	.09
328 Jeff Conine	.30	.09
329 Andre Dawson	.30	.09
330 Charles Johnson	.30	.09
331 Al Leiter	.30	.09
332 Ralph Milliard	.30	.09
333 Robb Nen	.30	.09
334 Pat Rapp	.30	.09
335 Edgar Renteria	.30	.09
336 Gary Sheffield	.30	.09
337 Devon White	.30	.09
338 Bob Abreu	.30	.09
339 Jeff Bagwell	.50	.15
340 Derek Bell	.30	.09
341 Sean Berry	.30	.09
342 Craig Biggio	.50	.15
343 Doug Drabek	.30	.09
344 Tony Eusebio	.30	.09
345 Ricky Gutierrez	.30	.09
346 Mike Hampton	.30	.09
347 Brian Hunter	.30	.09
348 Todd Jones	.30	.09
349 Darryl Kile	.30	.09
350 Derrick May	.30	.09
351 Orlando Miller	.30	.09
352 James Mouton	.30	.09
353 Shane Reynolds	.30	.09
354 Billy Wagner	.30	.09
355 Donne Wall	.30	.09
356 Mike Blowers	.30	.09
357 Brett Butler	.30	.09
358 Roger Cedeno	.30	.09
359 Chad Curtis	.30	.09
360 Delino DeShields	.30	.09
361 Greg Gagne	.30	.09
362 Karim Garcia	.30	.09
363 Wilton Guerrero	.30	.09
364 Todd Hollandsworth	.30	.09
365 Eric Karros	.30	.09
366 Ramon Martinez	.30	.09
367 Raul Mondesi	.30	.09
368 Hideo Nomo	.75	.23
369 Antonio Osuna	.30	.09
370 Chan Ho Park	.30	.09
371 Mike Piazza	1.25	.35
372 Ismael Valdes	.30	.09
373 Todd Worrell	.30	.09
374 Moises Alou	.30	.09
375 Shane Andrews	.30	.09
376 Yamil Benitez	.30	.09
377 Jeff Fassero	.30	.09
378 Darrin Fletcher	.30	.09
379 Cliff Floyd	.30	.09
380 Mark Grudzielanek	.30	.09
381 Mike Lansing	.30	.09
382 Barry Manuel	.30	.09
383 Pedro Martinez	.75	.23
384 Henry Rodriguez	.30	.09
385 Mel Rojas	.30	.09
386 F.P. Santangelo	.30	.09
387 David Segui	.30	.09
388 Ugueth Urbina	.30	.09
389 Rondell White	.30	.09
390 Edgardo Alfonzo	.30	.09
391 Carlos Baerga	.30	.09
392 Mark Clark	.30	.09
393 Alvaro Espinoza	.30	.09
394 John Franco	.30	.09
395 Bernard Gilkey	.30	.09
396 Pete Harnisch	.30	.09
397 Todd Hundley	.30	.09
398 Butch Huskey	.30	.09
399 Jason Isringhausen	.30	.09
400 Lance Johnson	.30	.09
401 Bobby Jones	.30	.09
402 Alex Ochoa	.30	.09
403 Rey Ordonez	.30	.09
404 Robert Person	.30	.09
405 Paul Wilson	.30	.09
406 Matt Beech	.30	.09
407 Ron Blazier	.30	.09
408 Ricky Bottalico	.30	.09
409 Lenny Dykstra	.30	.09
410 Jim Eisenreich	.30	.09
411 Bobby Estalella	.30	.09
412 Mike Grace	.30	.09
413 Gregg Jefferies	.30	.09
414 Mike Lieberthal	.30	.09
415 Wendell Magee	.30	.09
416 Mickey Morandini	.30	.09
417 Ricky Otero	.30	.09
418 Scott Rolen	.75	.23
419 Ken Ryan	.30	.09
420 Benito Santiago	.30	.09
421 Curt Schilling	.30	.09
422 Kevin Sefcik	.30	.09
423 Jermaine Allensworth	.30	.09
424 Trey Beamon	.30	.09
425 Jay Bell	.30	.09
426 Francisco Cordova	.30	.09
427 Carlos Garcia	.30	.09
428 Mark Johnson	.30	.09
429 Jason Kendall	.30	.09
430 Jeff King	.30	.09
431 Jon Lieber	.30	.09
432 Al Martin	.30	.09
433 Orlando Merced	.30	.09
434 Ramon Morel	.30	.09
435 Matt Ruebel	.30	.09
436 Jason Schmidt	.30	.09
437 Marc Wilkins	.30	.09
438 Alan Benes	.30	.09
439 Andy Benes	.30	.09
440 Royce Clayton	.30	.09
441 Dennis Eckersley	.30	.09
442 Gary Gaetti	.30	.09
443 Ron Gant	.30	.09
444 Aaron Holbert	.30	.09
445 Brian Jordan	.30	.09
446 Ray Lankford	.30	.09
447 John Mabry	.30	.09
448 T.J. Mathews	.30	.09
449 Willie McGee	.30	.09
450 Donovan Osborne	.30	.09
451 Tom Pagnozzi	.30	.09
452 Ozzie Smith	1.25	.35
453 Todd Stottlemyre	.30	.09
454 Mark Sweeney	.30	.09
455 Dmitri Young	.30	.09
456 Andy Ashby	.30	.09
457 Ken Caminiti	.30	.09
458 Archi Cianfrocco	.30	.09
459 Steve Finley	.30	.09
460 John Flaherty	.30	.09
461 Chris Gomez	.30	.09
462 Tony Gwynn	1.00	.30
463 Joey Hamilton	.30	.09
464 Rickey Henderson	.75	.23
465 Trevor Hoffman	.30	.09
466 Brian Johnson	.30	.09
467 Wally Joyner	.30	.09
468 Jody Reed	.30	.09
469 Scott Sanders	.30	.09
470 Bob Tewksbury	.30	.09
471 Fernando Valenzuela	.30	.09
472 Greg Vaughn	.30	.09
473 Tim Worrell	.30	.09
474 Rich Aurilia	.30	.09
475 Rod Beck	.30	.09
476 Marvin Benard	.30	.09
477 Barry Bonds	2.00	.60
478 Jay Canizaro	.30	.09
479 Shawon Dunston	.30	.09
480 Shawn Estes	.30	.09
481 Mark Gardner	.30	.09
482 Glenallen Hill	.30	.09
483 Stan Javier	.30	.09
484 Marcus Jensen	.30	.09
485 Bill Mueller RC	3.00	.90
486 Wm. VanLandingham	.30	.09
487 Allen Watson	.30	.09
488 Rick Wilkins	.30	.09
489 Matt Williams	.30	.09
490 Desi Wilson	.30	.09
491 Albert Belle CL	.30	.09
492 Ken Griffey Jr. CL	.75	.23
493 Andruw Jones CL	.30	.09
494 Chipper Jones CL	.50	.15
495 Mark McGwire CL	1.00	.30
496 Paul Molitor CL	.30	.09
497 Mike Piazza CL	.75	.23
498 Cal Ripken CL	1.25	.35
499 Alex Rodriguez CL	.75	.23
500 Frank Thomas CL	.50	.15
501 Kenny Lofton	.30	.09
502 Carlos Perez	.30	.09
503 Tim Raines	.30	.09
504 Danny Patterson	.30	.09
505 Derrick May	.30	.09
506 Dave Hollins	.30	.09
507 Felipe Crespo	.30	.09
508 Brian Banks	.30	.09
509 Jeff Kent	.30	.09
510 Bubba Trammell RC	.40	.12
511 Robert Person	.30	.09
512 David Arias-Ortiz RC	15.00	4.50
513 Ryan Jones	.30	.09
514 David Justice	.30	.09
515 Will Cunnane	.30	.09
516 Russ Johnson	.30	.09
517 John Burkett	.30	.09
518 Robinson Checo RC	.30	.09
519 Ricardo Rincon RC	.30	.09
520 Woody Williams	.30	.09
521 Rick Helling	.30	.09
522 Jorge Posada	.50	.15
523 Kevin Orie	.30	.09
524 Fernando Tatis RC	.40	.12
525 Jermaine Dye	.30	.09
526 Brian Hunter	.30	.09
527 Greg McMichael	.30	.09
528 Matt Wagner	.30	.09
529 Richie Sexson	.30	.09
530 Scott Ruffcorn	.30	.09
531 Luis Gonzalez	.30	.09
532 Mike Johnson RC	.30	.09
533 Mark Petkovsek	.30	.09
534 Doug Drabek	.30	.09
535 Jose Canseco	.75	.23
536 Bobby Bonilla	.30	.09
537 J.T. Snow	.30	.09
538 Shawon Dunston	.30	.09
539 John Ericks	.30	.09
540 Terry Steinbach	.30	.09
541 Jay Bell	.30	.09
542 Joe Borowski RC	.30	.09

543 David Wells .30 .09
544 Justin Towle RC .30 .09
545 Mike Blowers .30 .09
546 Shannon Stewart .30 .09
547 Rudy Pemberton .30 .09
548 Bill Swift .30 .09
549 Osvaldo Fernandez .30 .09
550 Eddie Murray .75 .23
551 Don Wengert .30 .09
552 Brad Ausmus .30 .09
553 Carlos Garcia .30 .09
554 Jose Guillen .30 .09
555 Rheal Cormier .30 .09
556 Doug Brocail .30 .09
557 Rex Hudler .30 .09
558 Armando Benitez .30 .09
559 Eli Marrero .30 .09
560 Ricky Ledee RC .40 .12
561 Bartolo Colon .30 .09
562 Quilvio Veras .30 .09
563 Alex Fernandez .30 .09
564 Darren Dreifort .30 .09
565 Benji Gil .30 .09
566 Kent Mercker .30 .09
567 Glendon Rusch .30 .09
568 Ramon Tatis RC .30 .09
569 Roger Clemens 1.50 .45
570 Mark Lewis .30 .09
571 Emil Brown RC .30 .09
572 Jaime Navarro .30 .09
573 Sherman Obando .30 .09
574 John Wasdin .30 .09
575 Calvin Maduro .30 .09
576 Todd Jones .30 .09
577 Orlando Merced .30 .09
578 Cal Eldred .30 .09
579 Mark Gubicza .30 .09
580 Michael Tucker .30 .09
581 Tony Saunders RC .30 .09
582 Garvin Alston .30 .09
583 Joe Roa .30 .09
584 Brady Raggio RC .30 .09
585 Jimmy Key .30 .09
586 Marc Sagmoen RC .30 .09
587 Jim Bullinger .30 .09
588 Yorkis Perez .30 .09
589 Jose Cruz Jr. RC .50 .15
590 Mike Stanton .30 .09
591 Deivi Cruz RC .40 .12
592 Steve Karsay .30 .09
593 Mike Trombley .30 .09
594 Doug Glanville .30 .09
595 Scott Sanders .30 .09
596 Thomas Howard .30 .09
597 T.J. Staton RC .30 .09
598 Garrett Stephenson .30 .09
599 Rico Brogna .30 .09
600 Albert Belle .30 .09
601 Jose Vizcaino .30 .09
602 Chili Davis .30 .09
603 Shane Mack .30 .09
604 Jim Eisenreich .30 .09
605 Todd Zeile .30 .09
606 Brian Boehringer RC .30 .09
607 Paul Shuey .30 .09
608 Kevin Tapani .30 .09
609 John Wetteland .30 .09
610 Jim Leyritz .30 .09
611 Ray Montgomery RC .30 .09
612 Doug Bochtler .30 .09
613 Wady Almonte RC .30 .09
614 Danny Tartabull .30 .09
615 Orlando Miller .30 .09
616 Bobby Ayala .30 .09
617 Tony Graffanino .30 .09
618 Marc Valdes .30 .09
619 Ron Villone .30 .09
620 Derrek Lee .30 .09
621 Greg Colbrunn .30 .09
622 Felix Heredia RC .40 .12
623 Carl Everett .30 .09
624 Mark Thompson .30 .09
625 Jeff Granger .30 .09
626 Damian Jackson .30 .09
627 Mark Leiter .30 .09
628 Chris Holt .30 .09
629 Dario Veras RC .30 .09
630 Dave Burba .30 .09
631 Darryl Hamilton .30 .09
632 Mark Acre .30 .09
633 F.Hernandez RC .30 .09
634 Terry Mulholland .30 .09
635 Dustin Hermanson .30 .09
636 Delino DeShields .30 .09
637 Steve Avery .30 .09
638 Tony Womack RC .50 .15
639 Mark Whiten .30 .09
640 Marquis Grissom .30 .09
641 Xavier Hernandez .30 .09
642 Eric Davis .30 .09
643 Bob Tewksbury .30 .09
644 Dante Powell .30 .09
645 Carlos Castillo RC .30 .09
646 Chris Widger .30 .09
647 Moises Alou .30 .09
648 Pat Listach .30 .09
649 Edgar Ramos RC .30 .09
650 Deion Sanders .50 .15
651 John Olerud .30 .09
652 Todd Dunwoody .30 .09
653 Randall Simon RC .40 .12
654 Dan Carlson .30 .09
655 Matt Williams .30 .09
656 Jeff King .30 .09
657 Luis Alicea .30 .09
658 Brian Moehler RC .30 .09
659 Ariel Prieto .30 .09
660 Kevin Elster .30 .09
661 Mark Hutton .30 .09
662 Aaron Sele .30 .09
663 Graeme Lloyd .30 .09
664 John Burke .30 .09
665 Mel Rojas .30 .09
666 Sid Fernandez .30 .09
667 Pedro Astacio .30 .09
668 Jeff Abbott .30 .09
669 Darren Daulton .30 .09
670 Mike Bordick .30 .09
671 Sterling Hitchcock .30 .09
672 Damion Easley .30 .09
673 Armando Reynoso .30 .09
674 Pat Cline .30 .09
675 Orlando Cabrera RC 1.25 .45
676 Alan Embree .30 .09
677 Brian Bevil .30 .09
678 David Weathers .30 .09
679 Cliff Floyd .30 .09
680 Joe Randa .30 .09
681 Bill Haselman .30 .09
682 Jeff Fassero .30 .09
683 Matt Morris .30 .09
684 Mark Portugal .30 .09
685 Lee Smith .30 .09
686 Pokey Reese .30 .09
687 Benito Santiago .30 .09
688 Brian Johnson .30 .09
689 Brent Brede RC .30 .09
690 S.Hasegawa RC .75 .23
691 Julio Santana .30 .09
692 Steve Kline .30 .09
693 Julian Tavarez .30 .09
694 John Hudek .30 .09
695 Manny Alexander .30 .09
696 Roberto Alomar ENC .30 .09
697 Jeff Bagwell ENC .30 .09
698 Barry Bonds ENC .75 .23
699 Ken Caminiti ENC .30 .09
700 Juan Gonzalez ENC .30 .09
701 Ken Griffey Jr. ENC .75 .23
702 Tony Gwynn ENC .50 .15
703 Derek Jeter ENC 1.00 .30
704 Andruw Jones ENC .30 .09
705 Chipper Jones ENC .50 .15
706 Barry Larkin ENC .30 .09
707 Greg Maddux ENC .75 .23
708 Mark McGwire ENC 1.00 .30
709 Paul Molitor ENC .30 .09
710 Hideo Nomo ENC .30 .09
711 Andy Pettitte ENC .30 .09
712 Mike Piazza ENC .75 .23
713 Manny Ramirez ENC .50 .15
714 Cal Ripken ENC 1.25 .35
715 Alex Rodriguez ENC .75 .23
716 Ryne Sandberg ENC .75 .23
717 John Smoltz ENC .30 .09
718 Frank Thomas ENC .50 .15
719 Mo Vaughn ENC .30 .09
720 Bernie Williams ENC .30 .09
721 Tim Salmon CL .30 .09
722 Greg Maddux CL .75 .23
723 Cal Ripken CL 1.25 .35
724 Mo Vaughn CL .30 .09
725 Ryne Sandberg CL .75 .23
726 Frank Thomas CL .50 .15
727 Barry Larkin CL .30 .09
728 Manny Ramirez CL .30 .09
729 Andres Galarraga CL .30 .09
730 Tony Clark CL .30 .09
731 Gary Sheffield CL .30 .09
732 Jeff Bagwell CL .30 .09
733 Kevin Appier CL .30 .09
734 Mike Piazza CL .75 .23
735 Jeff Cirillo CL .30 .09
736 Paul Molitor CL .30 .09
737 Henry Rodriguez CL .30 .09
738 Todd Hundley CL .30 .09
739 Derek Jeter CL 1.00 .30
740 Mark McGwire CL 1.00 .30
741 Curt Schilling CL .30 .09
742 Jason Kendall CL .30 .09
743 Tony Gwynn CL .50 .15
744 Barry Bonds CL .75 .23
745 Ken Griffey Jr. CL .75 .23
746 Brian Jordan CL .30 .09
747 Juan Gonzalez CL .30 .09
748 Joe Carter CL .30 .09
749 Ariz. Diamondbacks .30 .09
CL Inserts
750 Tampa Bay Devil Rays .30 .09
CL Inserts
751 Hideki Irabu RC .75 .23
752 Jeremi Gonzalez RC .50 .15
753 Mario Valdez RC .50 .15
754 Aaron Boone .75 .23
755 Brett Tomko .50 .15
756 Jaret Wright RC 2.00 .60
757 Ryan McGuire .50 .15
758 Jason McDonald .50 .15
759 Adrian Brown RC .50 .15
760 Keith Foulke RC 3.00 .90
761 Bonus Checklist .50 .15
P489 M.Williams Promo 1.00 .30
NNO Andruw Jones 25.00 7.50
Circa AU/200

1997 Fleer Tiffany

Randomly inserted in series one and two packs at a rate of one in 20, this 751-card set is a parallel version of the regular set featuring a glossy holographic design, foil stamping, and UV coating.

Nm-Mt Ex-Mt
*TIFFANY 1-750: 12.5X TO 30X BASIC CARDS
*TIFFANY RC's 1-750: 6X TO 15X BASIC
*TIFFANY 751-761: 4X TO 10X BASIC
485 Bill Mueller 25.00 7.50
675 Orlando Cabrera 20.00 6.00
760 Keith Foulke 25.00 7.50

1997 Fleer Bleacher Blasters

Randomly inserted in Fleer series two retail packs only at a rate of one in 36, this 10-card set features color action photos of power hitters who reach the bleachers with great frequency.

Nm-Mt Ex-Mt
COMPLETE SET (10) 80.00 24.00
1 Albert Belle 2.50 .75
2 Barry Bonds 15.00 4.50
3 Juan Gonzalez 4.00 1.20
4 Ken Griffey Jr. 10.00 3.00
5 Mark McGwire 15.00 4.50
6 Mike Piazza 10.00 3.00
7 Alex Rodriguez 10.00 3.00
8 Frank Thomas 6.00 1.80
9 Mo Vaughn 2.50 .75
10 Matt Williams 2.50 .75

1997 Fleer Decade of Excellence

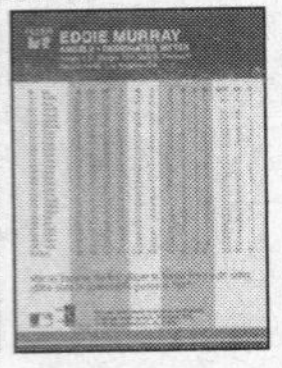

Randomly inserted in Fleer Series two hobby packs only at a rate of one in 36, this 12-card set spotlights players who started their major league careers no later than 1987. The set features photos of these players from the 1987 season in the 1987 Fleer Baseball card design.

Nm-Mt Ex-Mt
COMPLETE SET (12) 60.00 18.00
*RARE TRAD: 2X TO 5X BASIC DECADE
RARE TRAD.STATED ODDS 1:360 HOBBY
1 Wade Boggs 3.00 .90
2 Barry Bonds 12.00 3.60
3 Roger Clemens 10.00 3.00
4 Tony Gwynn 6.00 1.80
5 Rickey Henderson 5.00 1.50
6 Greg Maddux 8.00 2.40
7 Mark McGwire 12.00 3.60
8 Paul Molitor 3.00 .90
9 Eddie Murray 5.00 1.50
10 Cal Ripken 15.00 4.50
11 Ryne Sandberg 8.00 2.40
12 Matt Williams 2.00 .60

1997 Fleer Diamond Tribute

Randomly inserted in Fleer Series two packs at a rate of one in 288, this 12-card set features color action images of Baseball's top players on a dazzling foil background.

Nm-Mt Ex-Mt
1 Albert Belle 8.00 2.40
2 Barry Bonds 50.00 15.00
3 Juan Gonzalez 12.00 3.60
4 Ken Griffey Jr. 30.00 9.00
5 Tony Gwynn 25.00 7.50
6 Greg Maddux 30.00 9.00
7 Mark McGwire 50.00 15.00
8 Eddie Murray 20.00 6.00
9 Mike Piazza 30.00 9.00
10 Cal Ripken 60.00 18.00
11 Alex Rodriguez 30.00 9.00
12 Frank Thomas 20.00 6.00

1997 Fleer Golden Memories

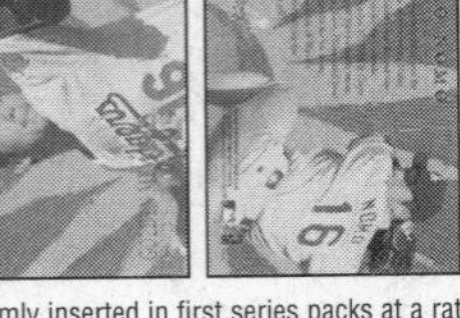

Randomly inserted in first series packs at a rate of one in 16, this ten-card set commemorates major achievements by individual players from the 1996 season. The fronts feature color player images on a background of the top portion of the sun and its rays. The backs carry player information.

Nm-Mt Ex-Mt
COMPLETE SET (10) 10.00 3.00
1 Barry Bonds 3.00 .90
2 Dwight Gooden .50 .15
3 Todd Hundley .50 .15
4 Mark McGwire 3.00 .90
5 Paul Molitor .75 .23
6 Eddie Murray 1.25 .35
7 Hideo Nomo 1.25 .35
8 Mike Piazza 2.00 .60
9 Cal Ripken 4.00 1.20
10 Ozzie Smith 2.00 .60

1997 Fleer Goudey Greats

Randomly inserted in Fleer Series two packs at a rate of one in eight, this 15-card set features color player photos of today's stars on cards styled and sized to resemble the 1933 Goudey Baseball card set.

Nm-Mt Ex-Mt
COMPLETE SET (15) 15.00 4.50
*FOIL CARDS: 6X TO 15X BASIC GOUDEY
FOIL SER.2 STATED ODDS 1:800 1.25 .35
1 Barry Bonds 3.00 .90

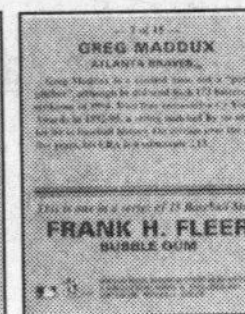

2 Ken Griffey Jr. 2.00 .60
3 Tony Gwynn 1.50 .45
4 Derek Jeter 3.00 .90
5 Chipper Jones 1.25 .35
6 Kenny Lofton .50 .15
7 Greg Maddux 2.00 .60
8 Mark McGwire 3.00 .90
9 Eddie Murray 1.25 .35
10 Mike Piazza 2.00 .60
11 Cal Ripken 4.00 1.20
12 Alex Rodriguez 2.00 .60
13 Ryne Sandberg 2.00 .60
14 Frank Thomas 1.25 .35
15 Mo Vaughn .50 .15

1997 Fleer Headliners

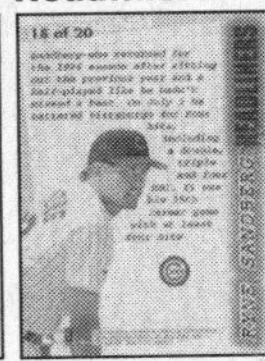

Randomly inserted in Fleer Series two packs at a rate of one in six, this 20-card set features color action photos of top players who make headlines for their teams. The backs carry player information.

Nm-Mt Ex-Mt
COMPLETE SET (20) 10.00 3.00
1 Jeff Bagwell .30 .09
2 Albert Belle .20 .06
3 Barry Bonds 1.25 .35
4 Ken Caminiti .20 .06
5 Juan Gonzalez .30 .09
6 Ken Griffey Jr. .75 .23
7 Tony Gwynn .60 .18
8 Derek Jeter 1.25 .35
9 Andruw Jones .20 .06
10 Chipper Jones .50 .15
11 Greg Maddux .75 .23
12 Mark McGwire 1.25 .35
13 Paul Molitor .30 .09
14 Eddie Murray .50 .15
15 Mike Piazza .75 .23
16 Cal Ripken 1.50 .45
17 Alex Rodriguez .75 .23
18 Ryne Sandberg .75 .23
19 John Smoltz .30 .09
20 Frank Thomas .50 .15

1997 Fleer Lumber Company

Randomly inserted exclusively in Fleer Series one retail packs, this 18-card set features a selection of the game's top sluggers. The innovative design displays pure die-cut circular borders, simulating the effect of a cut tree.

Nm-Mt Ex-Mt
COMPLETE SET (18) 120.00 36.00
1 Brady Anderson 3.00 .90
2 Jeff Bagwell 5.00 1.50
3 Albert Belle 3.00 .90
4 Barry Bonds 20.00 6.00
5 Jay Buhner 3.00 .90
6 Ellis Burks 3.00 .90
7 Andres Galarraga 3.00 .90
8 Juan Gonzalez 5.00 1.50
9 Ken Griffey Jr. 12.00 3.60
10 Todd Hundley 3.00 .90
11 Ryan Klesko 3.00 .90
12 Mark McGwire 20.00 6.00
13 Mike Piazza 12.00 3.60
14 Alex Rodriguez 12.00 3.60
15 Gary Sheffield 3.00 .90
16 Sammy Sosa 12.00 3.60
17 Frank Thomas 8.00 2.40
18 Mo Vaughn 3.00 .90

1997-98 Fleer Million Dollar Moments

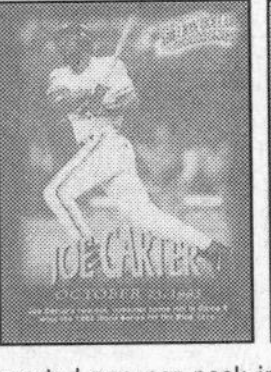

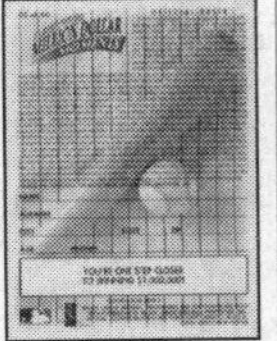

Inserted one per pack into 1997 Fleer 2, 1997 Flair Showcase, 1998 Fleer 1 and 1998 Ultra 1; these 50 cards mix a selection of retired legends with today's stars, highlighting key moments in baseball history. The first 45 cards in the set are common to find. Cards 46-50 are extremely shortprinted with each card being tougher to find than the next as you work your way up to card number 50. Prior to the July 31st, 1998 deadline, collectors could mail in their 45-card sets (plus $5.99 for postage and handling) and receive a complete 50-card exchange set. The lucky collectors that managed to obtain one or more of the shortprinted cards could receive a shopping spree at card shops nationwide selected by Fleer. Each shortprinted card had to be mailed in along with a complete 45-card set to receive the following shopping allowances: number 46/$100, number 47/$250, number 48/$500, number 49/$1000. A grand prize of $1,000,000 cash (payable in increments of $50,000 annually over 20 years) was available for one collector that could obtain and redeem all five shortprint cards (numbers 46-50). This set was actually a part of a multi-sport promotion (baseball, basketball and football) for Fleer with each sport offering a separate $1,000,000 grand prize. In addition, 10,000 instant winner cards per sport (good for an assortment of material including shopping sprees, video games and various Fleer sets) were randomly seeded into packs. We are listing cards numbered from 46-50, however no prices are assigned for these cards.

Nm-Mt Ex-Mt
COMPLETE SET (45) 8.00 2.40
1 Checklist .10 .03
2 Derek Jeter .60 .18
3 Babe Ruth 1.50 .45
4 Barry Bonds .60 .18
5 Brooks Robinson .25 .07
6 Todd Hundley .10 .03
7 Johnny Vander Meer .10 .03
8 Cal Ripken .75 .23
9 Bill Mazeroski .15 .04
10 Chipper Jones .25 .07
11 Frank Robinson .15 .04
12 Roger Clemens .50 .15
13 Bob Feller .15 .04
14 Mike Piazza .40 .12
15 Joe Nuxhall .10 .03
16 Hideo Nomo .25 .07
17 Jackie Robinson .25 .07
18 Orel Hershiser .10 .03
19 Bobby Thomson .10 .03
20 Joe Carter .10 .03
21 Al Kaline .25 .07
22 Bernie Williams .15 .04
23 Don Larsen .15 .04
24 Rickey Henderson .25 .07
25 Maury Wills .10 .03
26 Andruw Jones .10 .03
27 Bobby Richardson .10 .03
28 Alex Rodriguez .40 .12
29 Jim Bunning .15 .04
30 Ken Caminiti .10 .03
31 Bob Gibson .15 .04
32 Frank Thomas .25 .07
33 Mickey Lolich .10 .03
34 John Smoltz .15 .04
35 Ron Swoboda .10 .03
36 Albert Belle .10 .03
37 Chris Chambliss .10 .03
38 Juan Gonzalez .15 .04
39 Ron Blomberg .10 .03
40 John Wetteland .10 .03
41 Carlton Fisk .25 .07
42 Mo Vaughn .10 .03
43 Bucky Dent .10 .03
44 Greg Maddux .40 .12
45 Willie Stargell .10 .03
46 Tony Gwynn SP
47 Joel Youngblood SP
48 Andy Pettitte SP
49 Mookie Wilson SP
50 Jeff Bagwell SP

1997 Fleer New Horizons

Randomly inserted in Fleer Series two packs at a rate of one in four, this 15-card set features borderless color action photos of Rookies and prospects. The backs carry player information.

Nm-Mt Ex-Mt
COMPLETE SET (15) 8.00 2.40
1 Bob Abreu .50 .15
2 Jose Cruz Jr. .75 .23
3 Darin Erstad .50 .15
4 Nomar Garciaparra 2.00 .60
5 Vladimir Guerrero 1.25 .35
6 Wilton Guerrero .50 .15
7 Jose Guillen .50 .15
8 Hideki Irabu 1.25 .35
9 Andruw Jones .50 .15
10 Kevin Orie .50 .15
11 Scott Rolen 1.25 .35
12 Scott Spiezio .50 .15
13 Bubba Trammell .60 .18
14 Todd Walker .50 .15
15 Dmitri Young .50 .15

1997 Fleer Night and Day

Randomly inserted in Fleer Series one packs at a rate of one in 240, this ten-card set features color action player photos of superstars who excel in day games, night games, or both and are printed on lenticular 3D cards. The backs carry player information.

Nm-Mt Ex-Mt
COMPLETE SET (10) 150.00 45.00
1 Barry Bonds 30.00 9.00
2 Ellis Burks 5.00 1.50

3 Juan Gonzalez 8.00 2.40
4 Ken Griffey Jr. 20.00 6.00
5 Mark McGwire 30.00 9.00
6 Mike Piazza 20.00 6.00
7 Manny Ramirez 8.00 2.40
8 Alex Rodriguez 20.00 6.00
9 John Smoltz 8.00 2.40
10 Frank Thomas 12.00 3.60

1997 Fleer Rookie Sensations

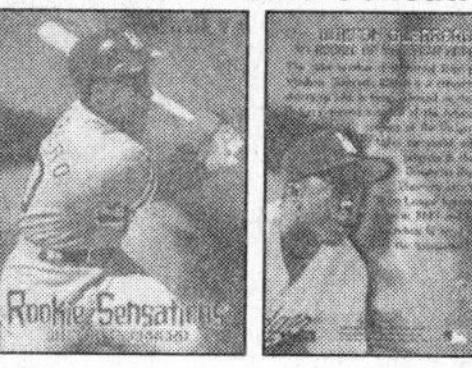
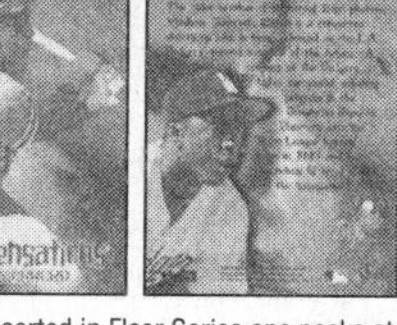

Randomly inserted in Fleer Series one packs at a rate of one in six, this 20-card set honors the top rookies from the 1996 season and the 1997 season rookies/prospects. The fronts freature color action player images on a multi-color swirling background. The backs carry a paragraph with information about the player.

Nm-Mt Ex-Mt
COMPLETE SET (20) 20.00 6.00
1 Jermaine Allensworth .75 .23
2 James Baldwin .75 .23
3 Alan Benes .75 .23
4 Jermaine Dye .75 .23
5 Darin Erstad .75 .23
6 Todd Hollandsworth .75 .23
7 Derek Jeter 5.00 1.50
8 Jason Kendall .75 .23
9 Alex Ochoa .75 .23
10 Rey Ordonez .75 .23
11 Edgar Renteria .75 .23
12 Bob Abreu .75 .23
13 Nomar Garciaparra 3.00 .90
14 Wilton Guerrero .75 .23
15 Andruw Jones .75 .23
16 Wendell Magee .75 .23
17 Neifi Perez .75 .23
18 Scott Rolen 2.00 .60
19 Scott Spiezio .75 .23
20 Todd Walker .75 .23

1997 Fleer Soaring Stars

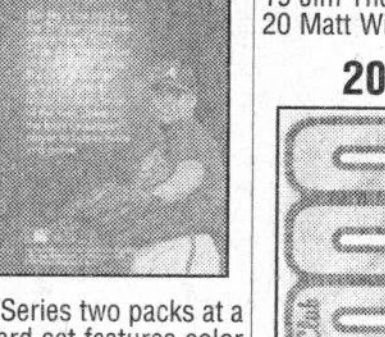

Randomly inserted in Fleer Series two packs at a rate of one in 12, this 12-card set features color action photos of players who enjoyed a meteoric rise to stardom and have all the skills to stay there. The player's image is set on a background of twinkling stars.

Nm-Mt Ex-Mt
COMPLETE SET (12) 30.00 9.00
*GLOWING: 4X TO 10X BASIC SOARING
GLOWING: RANDOM INSERTS IN SER.2 PACKS
LAST 20% OF PRINT RUN WAS GLOWING
1 Albert Belle .60 .18
2 Barry Bonds 4.00 1.20
3 Juan Gonzalez 1.00 .30
4 Ken Griffey Jr. 2.50 .75
5 Derek Jeter 4.00 1.20
6 Andruw Jones .60 .18
7 Chipper Jones 1.50 .45
8 Greg Maddux 2.50 .75
9 Mark McGwire 4.00 1.20
10 Mike Piazza 2.50 .75
11 Alex Rodriguez 2.50 .75
12 Frank Thomas 1.50 .45

1997 Fleer Team Leaders

Randomly inserted in Fleer Series one packs at a rate of one in 20, this 28-card set honors statistical or inspirational leaders from each team on a die-cut card. The fronts feature color action player images with the player's face in the background. The backs carry a paragraph with information about the player.

Nm-Mt Ex-Mt
COMPLETE SET (28) 100.00 30.00
1 Cal Ripken 15.00 4.50
2 Mo Vaughn 2.00 .60
3 Jim Edmonds 2.00 .60
4 Frank Thomas 5.00 1.50
5 Albert Belle 2.00 .60
6 Bob Higginson 2.00 .60
7 Kevin Appier 2.00 .60
8 John Jaha 2.00 .60
9 Paul Molitor 3.00 .90
10 Andy Pettitte 3.00 .90
11 Mark McGwire 12.00 3.60
12 Ken Griffey Jr. 8.00 2.40
13 Juan Gonzalez 3.00 .90
14 Pat Hentgen 2.00 .60
15 Chipper Jones 5.00 1.50
16 Mark Grace 3.00 .90
17 Barry Larkin 3.00 .90
18 Ellis Burks 2.00 .60
19 Gary Sheffield 2.00 .60
20 Jeff Bagwell 3.00 .90
21 Mike Piazza 8.00 2.40
22 Henry Rodriguez 2.00 .60
23 Todd Hundley 2.00 .60
24 Curt Schilling 2.00 .60
25 Jeff King 2.00 .60
26 Brian Jordan 2.00 .60
27 Tony Gwynn 6.00 1.80
28 Barry Bonds 12.00 3.60

1997 Fleer Zone

Randomly inserted in Fleer Series one hobby packs only at a rate of one in 80, this 20-card set features color player images of some of the 1996 season's unstoppable hitters and unhittable pitchers on a holographic card. The backs carry another color photo with a paragraph about the player.

Nm-Mt Ex-Mt
COMPLETE SET (20) 200.00 60.00
1 Jeff Bagwell 6.00 1.80
2 Albert Belle 4.00 1.20
3 Barry Bonds 25.00 7.50
4 Ken Caminiti 4.00 1.20
5 Andres Galarraga 4.00 1.20
6 Juan Gonzalez 6.00 1.80
7 Ken Griffey Jr. 15.00 4.50
8 Tony Gwynn 12.00 3.60
9 Chipper Jones 10.00 3.00
10 Greg Maddux 15.00 4.50
11 Mark McGwire 25.00 7.50
12 Dean Palmer 4.00 1.20
13 Andy Pettitte 6.00 1.80
14 Mike Piazza 15.00 4.50
15 Alex Rodriguez 15.00 4.50
16 Gary Sheffield 4.00 1.20
17 John Smoltz 6.00 1.80
18 Frank Thomas 10.00 3.00
19 Jim Thome 10.00 3.00
20 Matt Williams 4.00 1.20

2000 Fleer Club 3000

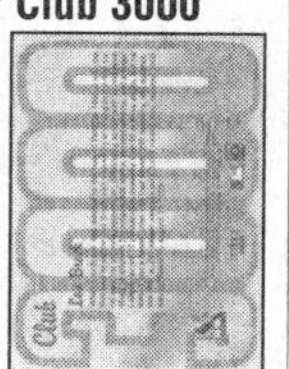

This set honors batters who have collected 3,000 hits and pitchers who have collected 3,000 strikeouts in their careers. The cards were seeded across all 2000 Fleer brands and each card in our checklist is marked with an abbreviation for the product it hails from. Pack odds are as follows - Fleer-distributed cards 1:36, Fleer Focus-distributed cards 1:36, Fleer Mystique-distributed cards 1:32, Fleer Showcase-distributed cards 1:24, and Ultra-distributed cards 1:24. These cards are unnumbered so we have sequenced them in alphabetical order by player initials.

Nm-Mt Ex-Mt
COMP.FLEER SET (3) 10.00 3.00
COMP.FOCUS SET (3) 10.00 3.00
COMP.MYSTIQUE SET (3) 12.00 3.60
COMP.SHOWCASE SET (2) 10.00 3.00
COMP.ULTRA SET (3) 10.00 3.00
BG Bob Gibson MYST 3.00 .90
CR Cal Ripken MYST 8.00 2.40
CY Carl Yastrzemski ULT 4.00 1.20
DW Dave Winfield MYST 3.00 .90
GB George Brett FLE 8.00 2.40
LB Lou Brock SHOW 3.00 .90
NR Nolan Ryan SHOW 6.00 1.80
PM Paul Molitor FOCUS 3.00 .90
RC Rod Carew FLE 3.00 .90
RY Robin Yount FLE 5.00 1.50
SC Steve Carlton FOCUS 3.00 .90
SM Stan Musial FOCUS 4.00 1.20
TG Tony Gwynn ULT 3.00 .90
WB Wade Boggs ULT 3.00 .90

2000 Fleer Club 3000 Memorabilia

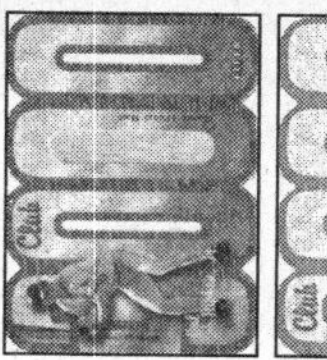

Randomly inserted into all 2000 Fleer products, these cards feature game used memorabilia from legends of the game that have either collected 3,000 hits or struck out 3,000 batters during their career. The cards (and patterns of distribution) parallel the more common Club 3000 cards that lack the memorabilia elements. Each player has five different cards: A bat, a hat, a jersey, a combo of bat and jersey and a combo of bat, hat and jersey. Each card is sequentially numbered and detailed within our checklist. Please see the Fleer Club 3000 listing for specific information on which Fleer product each card was distributed in.

Nm-Mt Ex-Mt
BG1 Bob Gibson 25.00 7.50
Bat/265
BG2 Bob Gibson 60.00 18.00
Hat/55
BG3 Bob Gibson 15.00 4.50
Jersey/825
BG4 Bob Gibson 60.00 18.00
Bat-Jersey/100
BG5 Bob Gibson
Bat-Hat-Jsy/25
CR1 Cal Ripken 80.00 24.00
Bat/265
CR2 Cal Ripken 150.00 45.00
Hat/55
CR3 Cal Ripken 40.00 12.00
Jersey/825
CR4 Cal Ripken 150.00 45.00
Bat-Jersey/100
CR5 Cal Ripken
Bat-Hat-Jsy/25
CY1 Carl Yastrzemski 50.00 15.00
Bat/250
CY2 Carl Yastrzemski 100.00 30.00
Hat/100
CY3 Carl Yastrzemski 25.00 7.50
Jersey/440
CY4 Carl Yastrzemski 150.00 45.00
Bat/Jersey/100
CY5 Carl Yastrzemski
Bat/Hat/Jersey/25
DW1 Dave Winfield 15.00 4.50
Bat/270
DW2 Dave Winfield 50.00 15.00
Hat/55
DW3 Dave Winfield 10.00 3.00
Jersey/825
DW4 Dave Winfield 50.00 15.00
Bat-Jersey/100
DW5 Dave Winfield
Bat-Hat-Jsy/25
GB1 George Brett 40.00 12.00
Bat/240
GB2 George Brett 120.00 36.00
Hat/105
GB3 George Brett 25.00 7.50
Jersey/445
GB4 George Brett 120.00 36.00
Bat-Jersey/100
GB5 George Brett
Bat-Hat-Jersey/25
LB1 Lou Brock 25.00 7.50
Bat/270
LB2 Lou Brock 60.00 18.00
Hat/60
LB3 Lou Brock 15.00 4.50
Jersey/680
LB4 Lou Brock 60.00 18.00
Bat-Jersey/100
LB5 Lou Brock
Bat-Hat-Jsy/25
NR1 Nolan Ryan 80.00 24.00
Bat/265
NR2 Nolan Ryan 150.00 45.00
Hat/65
NR3 Nolan Ryan 40.00 12.00
Jersey/780
NR4 Nolan Ryan 150.00 45.00
Bat-Jersey/100
NR5 Nolan Ryan
Bat-Hat-Jsy/25
PM1 Paul Molitor 25.00 7.50
Bat/335
PM2 Paul Molitor 60.00 18.00
Hat/65
PM3 Paul Molitor 15.00 4.50
Jersey/975
PM4 Paul Molitor 60.00 18.00
Bat-Jersey/100
PM5 Paul Molitor
Bat-Hat-Jsy/25
RC1 Rod Carew 25.00 7.50
Bat/225
RC2 Rod Carew 60.00 18.00
Hat/105
RC3 Rod Carew 15.00 4.50
Jersey/395
RC4 Rod Carew 60.00 18.00
Bat-Jersey/100
RC5 Rod Carew
Bat-Hat-Jersey/25
RY1 Robin Yount 25.00 7.50
Bat/230
RY2 Robin Yount 80.00 24.00
Hat/105
RY3 Robin Yount 15.00 4.50
Jersey/445
RY4 Robin Yount 80.00 24.00
Bat-Jersey/100
RY5 Robin Yount
Bat-Hat-Jersey/25
SC1 Steve Carlton 15.00 4.50
Bat/325
SC2 Steve Carlton 50.00 15.00
Hat/65
SC3 Steve Carlton 10.00 3.00
Jersey/750
SC4 Steve Carlton 50.00 15.00
Bat-Jersey/100
SC5 Steve Carlton
Bat-Hat-Jsy/25
SM1 Stan Musial 60.00 18.00
Bat/325
SM2 Stan Musial 150.00 45.00
Hat/65
SM3 Stan Musial 40.00 12.00
Jersey/975
SM4 Stan Musial 150.00 45.00
Bat-Jersey/100
SM5 Stan Musial
Bat-Hat-Jsy/25
TG1 Tony Gwynn 50.00 15.00
Bat/260
TG2 Tony Gwynn 100.00 30.00
Hat/115
TG3 Tony Gwynn 30.00 9.00
Jersey/450
TG4 Tony Gwynn 100.00 30.00
Bat-Jersey/100
TG5 Tony Gwynn
Bat-Hat-Jersey/25
WB1 Wade Boggs 25.00 7.50
Bat/250
WB2 Wade Boggs 60.00 18.00
Hat/100
WB3 Wade Boggs 15.00 4.50
Jersey/440
WB4 Wade Boggs 60.00 18.00
Bat-Jersey/100
WB5 Wade Boggs
Bat-Hat-Jersey/25

2001 Fleer Autographics

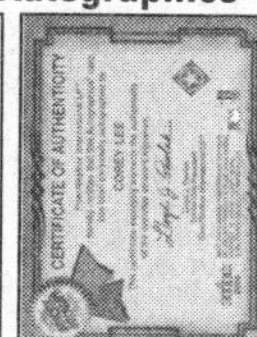

Randomly inserted into packs of Fleer Focus (1:72 w/memorabilia), Fleer Triple Crown (1:72 w/memorabilia cards), Ultra (1:48 w/memorabilia cards), 2002 Fleer Platinum Rack Packs (on average 1:6 racks contains an Autographics card) and 2002 Fleer Genuine (1:18 Hobby Direct box and 1:30 Hobby Distributor box), this insert set features authentic autographs from modern stars and prospects. The cards are designed horizontally with a full color player image at the side allowing plenty of room for the player's autograph. Card backs are unnumbered and feature Fleer's certificate of authenticity. Cards are checklisted alphabetically by player's last name and abbreviations indicating which brands each card was distributed in follows the player name. The brand legend is as follows: FC = Fleer Focus, TC = Fleer Triple Crown, UL = Ultra.

Nm-Mt Ex-Mt
FC SUFFIX ON FOCUS DISTRIBUTION
FS SUFFIX ON SHOWCASE DISTRIBUTION
FP'02 SUFFIX ON ULTRA DISTRIBUTION
GN SUFFIX ON GENUINE DISTRIBUTION
PM SUFFIX ON PREMIUM DISTRIBUTION
TC SUFFIX ON TRIPLE CROWN DISTRIBUTION
UL SUFFIX ON ULTRA DISTRIBUTION
1 Roberto Alomar 25.00 7.50
FC-FS-GN-PM-TC-UL
2 Jimmy Anderson TC-UL 10.00 3.00
3 Ryan Anderson TC 10.00 3.00
4 Rick Ankiel 10.00 3.00
FC-FS-GN-PM-TC
5 Albert Belle FC-FS-GN 15.00 4.50
6 Carlos Beltran FS-GN 40.00 12.00
7 Adrian Beltre 25.00 7.50
FC-FS-GN-PM-TC
8 Peter Bergeron 10.00 3.00
GN-PM-TC
9 Lance Berkman 25.00 7.50
FC-GN-TC-UL
10 Barry Bonds 250.00 75.00
FC-GN-TC-UL
11 Milton Bradley 15.00 4.50
FS-GN-TC
12 Ryan Bradley 10.00 3.00
GN'02
13 Dee Brown 10.00 3.00
FS-GN-PM-TC-FP'02
14 Roosevelt Brown 10.00 3.00
TC-UL
15 Jeromy Burnitz 15.00 4.50
FC-FS-GN-PM-UL
16 Pat Burrell 15.00 4.50
FC-FS-GN-PM-TC-UL
17 Alex Cabrera 10.00 3.00
UL
18 Sean Casey 15.00 4.50
FC-FS-GN-PM-TC
19 Eric Chavez 15.00 4.50
FC-GN-PM-TC-UL
20 Giuseppe Chiaramonte 10.00 3.00
TC
21 Joe Crede 10.00 3.00
FS-PM-TC-UL-FP'02
22 Jose Cruz Jr. 10.00 3.00
FS-GN-PM-TC
23 Johnny Damon 25.00 7.50
GN-PM-UL
24 Carlos Delgado 15.00 4.50
FC-GN-TC-UL
25 Ryan Dempster 10.00 3.00
FS-GN-TC-FP'02
26 J.D. Drew 25.00 7.50
FC-FS-GN-PM
27 Adam Dunn 25.00 7.50
FS-TC-UL-FP'02
28 Erubiel Durazo 10.00 3.00
FS-GN
29 Jermaine Dye 15.00 4.50
FC-FS-GN-PM
30 David Eckstein 10.00 3.00
FS-TC
31 Jim Edmonds 25.00 7.50
FC-GN-PM-TC-UL
32 Alex Escobar 10.00 3.00
FS-GN-PM
33 Seth Etherton 10.00 3.00
FS-GN
34 Adam Everett 10.00 3.00
FS-GN
35 Carlos Febles 10.00 3.00
FS-GN
36 Troy Glaus 15.00 4.50
FC-FS-GN-PM-TC
37 Chad Green 10.00 3.00
TC-UL
38 Ben Grieve 10.00 3.00
FC-FS-GN
39 Wilton Guerrero 10.00 3.00
GN'02
40 Tony Gwynn 60.00 18.00
FC-GN-PM-TC
41 Toby Hall 10.00 3.00
FS-GN
42 Todd Helton 25.00 7.50
FS-GN-PM-TC
43 Chad Hermansen 10.00 3.00
GN-PM-TC
44 Dustin Hermanson 10.00 3.00
PM-UL
45 Shea Hillenbrand 15.00 4.50
FS-GN-PM-TC
46 Aubrey Huff 15.00 4.50
FS-GN-PM-TC
47 Derek Jeter 120.00 36.00
GN-PM
48 D'Angelo Jimenez 10.00 3.00
FS
49 Randy Johnson 60.00 18.00
FC-GN-TC-UL
50 Chipper Jones 50.00 15.00
FC-GN-PMTC
51 Cesar King 10.00 3.00
GN
52 Paul Konerko 15.00 4.50
FS-GN-PM-FP'02
53 Corey Koskie 15.00 4.50
GN'02
54 Mike Lamb 10.00 3.00
FC-FS-GN-TC
55 Matt Lawton 10.00 3.00
FS-GN
56 Corey Lee 10.00 3.00
GN-TC-UL
57 Derrek Lee 15.00 4.50
FS-GN-PM-UL
58 Mike Lieberthal 15.00 4.50
FC-FS-GN-PM
59 Steve Lomasney 10.00 3.00
TC
60 Terrence Long 10.00 3.00
FC-GN-PM-TC-UL
61 Mike Lowell 15.00 4.50
FS-GN
62 Julio Lugo 10.00 3.00
FS-GN-PM-TC-UL
63 Greg Maddux 80.00 24.00
FC-GN
64 Jason Marquis 15.00 4.50
FS-GN-TC
65 Edgar Martinez 40.00 12.00
FC-FS-GN-UL
66 Justin Miller 10.00 3.00
GN-UL
67 Kevin Millwood 15.00 4.50
FC-FS-GN-PM
68 Eric Milton 10.00 3.00
FS-GN-PM
69 Bengie Molina 10.00 3.00
FS-GN-TC
70 Mike Mussina 25.00 7.50
FC-FS-GN-PM-TC
71 David Ortiz 25.00 7.50
GN'02
72 Russ Ortiz 15.00 4.50
FS-PM-UL
73 Pablo Ozuna 10.00 3.00
GN-PM-TC-UL
74 Corey Patterson 15.00 4.50
FC-FS-GN-PM-TC
75 Carl Pavano 25.00 4.50
PM
76 Jay Payton 10.00 3.00
FC-FS-GN-PM-TC
77 Wily Pena 15.00 4.50
TC
78 Josh Phelps 10.00 3.00
TC
79 Adam Piatt 10.00 3.00
FS-GN-TC-UL-FP'02
80 Juan Pierre 15.00 4.50
FC-FS-GN
81 Brad Radke 15.00 4.50
FC-FS-GN-PM-FP'02
82 Mark Redman 10.00 3.00
UL
83 Matt Riley 10.00 3.00
GN-TC
84 Cal Ripken 150.00 45.00
GN-PM
85 John Rocker 10.00 3.00
FS-GN
86 Alex Rodriguez 100.00 30.00
FS-GN-TC
87 Scott Rolen 40.00 12.00
FC-FS-GN-PM
88 Alex Sanchez 10.00 3.00
PM-TC
89 Fernando Seguignol 10.00 3.00
GN'02
90 Richie Sexson 15.00 4.50
FS-GN-PM-UL
91 Gary Sheffield 25.00 7.50
FC-FS-GN-PM-TC-UL
92 Alfonso Soriano 50.00 15.00
GN-PM-TC-UL
93 Dernell Stenson 15.00 4.50
GN-PM
94 Garrett Stephenson 10.00 3.00
PM

95 Shannon Stewart 15.00 4.50
FS-GN-PM-TC
96 Fernando Tatis 10.00 3.00
FC-GN-TC
97 Miguel Tejada 15.00 4.50
FS-FP'02
98 Jorge Toca 10.00 3.00
GN-PM
99 Robin Ventura 15.00 4.50
FC-FS-GN-PM
100 Jose Vidro 10.00 3.00
FS-GN-PM-TC-UL-FP'02
101 Billy Wagner 25.00 7.50
FS-PM
102 Kip Wells 10.00 3.00
FS-GN
103 Vernon Wells 15.00 4.50
GN-PM-UL
104 Rondell White 15.00 4.50
FS-GN
105 Bernie Williams 80.00 24.00
FP'02
106 Scott Williamson 10.00 3.00
GN
107 Preston Wilson 15.00 4.50
FS-GN-TC-UL
108 Kerry Wood 40.00 12.00
FC-FS-GN-PM-TC-FP'02
109 Jamey Wright 10.00 3.00
GN-UL
110 Julio Zuleta 10.00 3.00
FS-GN-PM-TC-UL

2001 Fleer Autographics Gold

Randomly inserted into a selection of Fleer products, this set is a complete parallel of the Autographics insert. These cards were produced with gold foil stamping on front and are individually serial numbered to 50. Corey Koskie was released exclusively in 2002 Fleer Platinum rack packs.

Nm-Mt Ex-Mt
*GOLD: 1X TO 2X BASIC AUTOS

2001 Fleer Autographics Silver

Randomly inserted into a selection of Fleer products, this set is a complete parallel of the Autographics insert. These cards were produced with silver foil stamping on front and are individually serial numbered to 250. Corey Koskie was distributed exclusively in 2002 Fleer Platinum rack packs.

Nm-Mt Ex-Mt
*SILVER: .75X TO 1.5X BASIC AUTOS

2001 Fleer Feel the Game

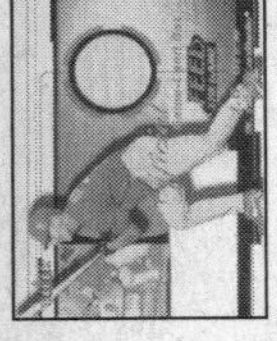

This insert set features game-used jersey cards of major league stars. The cards were distributed across several different Fleer products issued in 2001. Please note that the cards are listed below in alphabetical order for convience. Cards with "FC" listed after the players name were inserted into Fleer Focus packs (one Autographic or Feel Game in every 72 packs), "TC" listed after the players name were inserted into packs of Fleer Triple Crown (one Feel Game, Autographic or Crown of Gold in every 72 packs), while cards with "UL" after their name were inserted into Ultra packs (one Autographic or Feel Game in every 48 packs).

Nm-Mt Ex-Mt
*GOLD: 1.25X TO 2.5X BASIC FEEL GAME
1 Moises Alou FC-UL 10.00 3.00
2 Brady Anderson FC-UL 10.00 3.00
3 Adrian Beltre TC-UL 15.00 4.50
4 Dante Bichette FC-TC 10.00 3.00
5 Roger Cedeno TC 10.00 3.00
6 Ben Davis TC 10.00 3.00
7 Carlos Delgado TC-UL 10.00 3.00
8 J.D. Drew TC-UL 10.00 3.00
9 Jermaine Dye FC-UL 10.00 3.00
10 Jason Giambi TC-UL 10.00 3.00
11 Brian Giles FC-TC 10.00 3.00
12 Juan Gonzalez FC-TC 15.00 4.50
13 Rickey Henderson FC 15.00 4.50
14 Richard Hidalgo TC-UL 10.00 3.00
15 Chipper Jones TC-UL 15.00 4.50
16 Eric Karros TC-UL 10.00 3.00
17 Javy Lopez FC-TC 10.00 3.00
18 Tino Martinez FC-TC 15.00 4.50
19 Raul Mondesi TC-UL 10.00 3.00
20 Phil Nevin FC-TC 10.00 3.00
21 Chan Ho Park TC-UL 10.00 3.00
22 Ivan Rodriguez TC-UL 15.00 4.50
23 Matt Stairs FC-UL 10.00 3.00
24 Shannon Stewart FC-TC 10.00 3.00
25 Frank Thomas TC-UL 15.00 4.50
26 Jose Vidro FC-TC-UL 10.00 3.00
27 Matt Williams TC-UL 10.00 3.00
28 Preston Wilson TC-UL 10.00 3.00

2002 Fleer

This 540 card set was issued in May, 2002. These cards were issued in 10 card packs which came packed 24 packs to a box and 10 boxes to a case and had an SRP of $2 per pack. Cards number 432 through 491 featured players who switched teams in the off season while cards 492 through 531 featured leading prospects and cards numbered 532 through 540 feature photos of important ballparks along with checklists on the back.

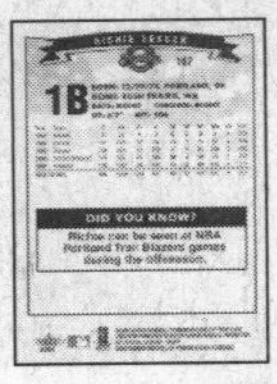

Nm-Mt Ex-Mt
COMPLETE SET (540) 100.00 30.00
COMMON CARD (1-540) .25 .07
COMMON CARD (492-531) .50 .15
1 Darin Erstad FP .25 .07
2 Randy Johnson FP .60 .18
3 Chipper Jones FP .60 .18
4 Jay Gibbons FP .25 .07
5 Nomar Garciaparra FP 1.00 .30
6 Sammy Sosa FP 1.00 .30
7 Frank Thomas FP .60 .18
8 Ken Griffey Jr. FP 1.00 .30
9 Jim Thome FP .60 .18
10 Todd Helton FP .40 .12
11 Jeff Weaver FP .25 .07
12 Cliff Floyd FP .25 .07
13 Jeff Bagwell FP .40 .12
14 Mike Sweeney FP .25 .07
15 Adrian Beltre FP .40 .12
16 Richie Sexson FP .25 .07
17 Brad Radke FP .25 .07
18 Vladimir Guerrero FP .60 .18
19 Mike Piazza FP 1.00 .30
20 Derek Jeter FP 1.25 .35
21 Eric Chavez FP .25 .07
22 Pat Burrell FP .25 .07
23 Brian Giles FP .25 .07
24 Trevor Hoffman FP .25 .07
25 Barry Bonds FP 1.00 .30
26 Ichiro Suzuki FP 1.00 .30
27 Albert Pujols FP 1.00 .30
28 Ben Grieve FP .25 .07
29 Alex Rodriguez FP 1.00 .30
30 Carlos Delgado FP .25 .07
31 Miguel Tejada .40 .12
32 Todd Hollandsworth .25 .07
33 Marlon Anderson .25 .07
34 Kerry Robinson .25 .07
35 Chris Richard .25 .07
36 Jamey Wright .25 .07
37 Ray Lankford .25 .07
38 Mike Bordick .40 .12
39 Danny Graves .25 .07
40 A.J. Pierzynski .40 .12
41 Shannon Stewart .40 .12
42 Tony Armas Jr. .25 .07
43 Brad Ausmus .25 .07
44 Alfonso Soriano .60 .18
45 Junior Spivey .25 .07
46 Brent Mayne .25 .07
47 Jim Thome 1.00 .30
48 Dan Wilson .25 .07
49 Geoff Jenkins .40 .12
50 Kris Benson .40 .12
51 Rafael Furcal .40 .12
52 Wiki Gonzalez .25 .07
53 Jeff Kent .40 .12
54 Curt Schilling .40 .12
55 Ken Harvey .25 .07
56 Roosevelt Brown .25 .07
57 David Segui .25 .07
58 Mario Valdez .25 .07
59 Adam Dunn .60 .18
60 Bob Howry .25 .07
61 Michael Barrett .25 .07
62 Garret Anderson .40 .12
63 Kelvim Escobar .25 .07
64 Ben Grieve .25 .07
65 Randy Johnson 1.00 .30
66 Jose Offerman .25 .07
67 Jason Kendall .40 .12
68 Joel Pineiro .40 .12
69 Alex Escobar .25 .07
70 Chris George .25 .07
71 Bobby Higginson .40 .12
72 Nomar Garciaparra 1.50 .45
73 Pat Burrell .40 .12
74 Lee Stevens .25 .07
75 Felipe Lopez .25 .07
76 Al Leiter .40 .12
77 Jim Edmonds .40 .12
78 Al Levine .25 .07
79 Raul Mondesi .40 .12
80 Jose Valentin .25 .07
81 Matt Clement .25 .07
82 Richard Hidalgo .25 .07
83 Jamie Moyer .40 .12
84 Brian Schneider .25 .07
85 John Franco .40 .12
86 Brian Buchanan .25 .07
87 Roy Oswalt .40 .12
88 Johnny Estrada .25 .07
89 Marcus Giles .40 .12
90 Carlos Valderrama .25 .07
91 Mark Mulder .40 .12
92 Mark Grace .60 .18
93 Andy Ashby .25 .07
94 Woody Williams .25 .07
95 Ben Petrick .25 .07
96 Roy Halladay .25 .07
97 Fred McGriff .60 .18
98 Shawn Green .40 .12
99 Todd Hundley .25 .07
100 Carlos Febles .25 .07
101 Jason Marquis .25 .07
102 Mike Redmond .25 .07
103 Shane Halter .25 .07
104 Trot Nixon .40 .12
105 Jeremy Giambi .25 .07
106 Carlos Delgado .40 .12
107 Richie Sexson .40 .12
108 Russ Ortiz .40 .12
109 David Ortiz .60 .18
110 Curtis Leskanic .25 .07
111 Jay Payton .25 .07
112 Travis Phelps .25 .07
113 J.T. Snow .40 .12
114 Edgar Renteria .40 .12
115 Freddy Garcia .40 .12
116 Cliff Floyd .40 .12
117 Charles Nagy .25 .07
118 Tony Batista .40 .12
119 Rafael Palmeiro .60 .18
120 Darren Dreifort .25 .07
121 Warren Morris .25 .07
122 Augie Ojeda .25 .07
123 Rusty Greer .40 .12
124 Esteban Yan .25 .07
125 Corey Patterson .40 .12
126 Matt Ginter .25 .07
127 Matt Lawton .25 .07
128 Miguel Batista .25 .07
129 Randy Winn .25 .07
130 Eric Milton .25 .07
131 Jack Wilson .40 .12
132 Sean Casey .40 .12
133 Mike Sweeney .40 .12
134 Jason Tyner .25 .07
135 Carlos Hernandez .25 .07
136 Shea Hillenbrand .40 .12
137 Shawn Wooten .25 .07
138 Peter Bergeron .25 .07
139 Travis Lee .25 .07
140 Craig Wilson .40 .12
141 Carlos Guillen .40 .12
142 Chipper Jones 1.00 .30
143 Gabe Kapler .25 .07
144 Raul Ibanez .25 .07
145 Eric Chavez .40 .12
146 D'Angelo Jimenez .25 .07
147 Chad Hermansen .25 .07
148 Joe Kennedy .25 .07
149 Mariano Rivera .60 .18
150 Jeff Bagwell .60 .18
151 Joe McEwing .25 .07
152 Ronnie Belliard .25 .07
153 Desi Relaford .25 .07
154 Vinny Castilla .40 .12
155 Tim Hudson .40 .12
156 Wilton Guerrero .25 .07
157 Raul Casanova .25 .07
158 Edgardo Alfonzo .25 .07
159 Derrek Lee .40 .12
160 Phil Nevin .40 .12
161 Roger Clemens 2.00 .60
162 Jason LaRue .25 .07
163 Brian Lawrence .25 .07
164 Adrian Beltre .60 .18
165 Troy Glaus .40 .12
166 Jeff Weaver .25 .07
167 B.J. Surhoff .40 .12
168 Eric Byrnes .25 .07
169 Mike Sirotka .25 .07
170 Bill Haselman .25 .07
171 Javier Vazquez .40 .12
172 Sidney Ponson .25 .07
173 Adam Everett .25 .07
174 Bubba Trammell .25 .07
175 Robb Nen .40 .12
176 Barry Larkin .60 .18
177 Tony Graffanino .25 .07
178 Rich Garces .25 .07
179 Juan Uribe .25 .07
180 Tom Glavine .60 .18
181 Eric Karros .40 .12
182 Michael Cuddyer .25 .07
183 Wade Miller .25 .07
184 Matt Williams .40 .12
185 Matt Morris .40 .12
186 Rickey Henderson 1.00 .30
187 Trevor Hoffman .40 .12
188 Wilson Betemit .25 .07
189 Steve Karsay .25 .07
190 Frank Catalanotto .25 .07
191 Jason Schmidt .40 .12
192 Roger Cedeno .25 .07
193 Magglio Ordonez .40 .12
194 Pat Hentgen .25 .07
195 Mike Lieberthal .40 .12
196 Andy Pettitte .60 .18
197 Jay Gibbons .25 .07
198 Rolando Arrojo .25 .07
199 Joe Mays .25 .07
200 Aubrey Huff .40 .12
201 Nelson Figueroa .25 .07
202 Paul Konerko .40 .12
203 Ken Griffey Jr. 1.50 .45
204 Brandon Duckworth .25 .07
205 Sammy Sosa 1.50 .45
206 Carl Everett .40 .12
207 Scott Rolen 1.00 .30
208 Orlando Hernandez .25 .07
209 Todd Helton .60 .18
210 Preston Wilson .40 .12
211 Gil Meche .25 .07
212 Bill Mueller .40 .12
213 Craig Biggio .60 .18
214 Dean Palmer .40 .12
215 Randy Wolf .25 .07
216 Jeff Suppan .25 .07
217 Jimmy Rollins .40 .12
218 Alexis Gomez .25 .07
219 Ellis Burks .40 .12
220 Ramon E. Martinez .25 .07
221 Ramiro Mendoza .25 .07
222 Einar Diaz .25 .07
223 Brent Abernathy .25 .07
224 Darin Erstad .40 .12
225 Reggie Taylor .25 .07
226 Jason Jennings .25 .07
227 Ray Durham .40 .12
228 John Parrish .25 .07
229 Kevin Young .25 .07
230 Xavier Nady .25 .07
231 Juan Cruz .25 .07
232 Greg Norton .25 .07
233 Barry Bonds 2.50 .75
234 Kip Wells .25 .07
235 Paul LoDuca .40 .12
236 Javy Lopez .40 .12
237 Luis Castillo .25 .07
238 Tom Gordon .25 .07
239 Mike Mordecai .25 .07
240 Damian Rolls .25 .07
241 Julio Lugo .25 .07
242 Ichiro Suzuki 1.50 .45
243 Tony Womack .25 .07
244 Matt Anderson .25 .07
245 Carlos Lee .40 .12
246 Alex Rodriguez 1.50 .45
247 Bernie Williams .60 .18
248 Scott Sullivan .25 .07
249 Mike Hampton .40 .12
250 Orlando Cabrera .40 .12
251 Benito Santiago .40 .12
252 Steve Finley .40 .12
253 Dave Williams .25 .07
254 Adam Kennedy .25 .07
255 Omar Vizquel .60 .18
256 Garrett Stephenson .25 .07
257 Fernando Tatis .25 .07
258 Mike Piazza 1.50 .45
259 Scott Spiezio .25 .07
260 Jacque Jones .40 .12
261 Russell Branyan .25 .07
262 Mark McLemore .25 .07
263 Mitch Meluskey .25 .07
264 Marlon Byrd .25 .07
265 Kyle Farnsworth .25 .07
266 Billy Sylvester .25 .07
267 C.C. Sabathia .40 .12
268 Mark Buehrle .40 .12
269 Geoff Blum .25 .07
270 Bret Prinz .25 .07
271 Placido Polanco .25 .07
272 John Olerud .40 .12
273 Pedro Martinez 1.00 .30
274 Doug Mientkiewicz .40 .12
275 Jason Bere .25 .07
276 Bud Smith .25 .07
277 Terrence Long .25 .07
278 Troy Percival .40 .12
279 Derek Jeter 2.50 .75
280 Eric Owens .25 .07
281 Jay Bell .40 .12
282 Mike Cameron .40 .12
283 Joe Randa .25 .07
284 Brian Roberts .25 .07
285 Ryan Klesko .40 .12
286 Ryan Dempster .25 .07
287 Cristian Guzman .25 .07
288 Tim Salmon .60 .18
289 Mark Johnson .25 .07
290 Brian Giles .40 .12
291 Jon Lieber .25 .07
292 Fernando Vina .25 .07
293 Mike Mussina .60 .18
294 Juan Pierre .40 .12
295 Carlos Beltran .60 .18
296 Vladimir Guerrero 1.00 .30
297 Orlando Merced .25 .07
298 Jose Hernandez .25 .07
299 Mike Lamb .25 .07
300 David Eckstein .25 .07
301 Mark Loretta .40 .12
302 Greg Vaughn .25 .07
303 Jose Vidro .25 .07
304 Jose Ortiz .25 .07
305 Mark Grudzielanek .25 .07
306 Rob Bell .25 .07
307 Elmer Dessens .25 .07
308 Tomas Perez .25 .07
309 Jerry Hairston Jr. .25 .07
310 Mike Stanton .25 .07
311 Todd Walker .25 .07
312 Jason Varitek .60 .18
313 Masato Yoshii .25 .07
314 Ben Sheets .40 .12
315 Roberto Hernandez .25 .07
316 Eli Marrero .25 .07
317 Josh Beckett .40 .12
318 Robert Fick .25 .07
319 Aramis Ramirez .40 .12
320 Bartolo Colon .40 .12
321 Kenny Kelly .25 .07
322 Luis Gonzalez .40 .12
323 John Smoltz .60 .18
324 Homer Bush .25 .07
325 Kevin Millwood .40 .12
326 Manny Ramirez .60 .18
327 Armando Benitez .25 .07
328 Luis Alicea .25 .07
329 Mark Kotsay .25 .07
330 Felix Rodriguez .25 .07
331 Eddie Taubensee .25 .07
332 John Burkett .25 .07
333 Ramon Ortiz .25 .07
334 Daryle Ward .25 .07
335 Jarrod Washburn .25 .07
336 Benji Gil .25 .07
337 Mike Lowell .40 .12
338 Larry Walker .60 .18
339 Andruw Jones .40 .12
340 Scott Elarton .25 .07
341 Tony McKnight .25 .07
342 Frank Thomas 1.00 .30
343 Kevin Brown .40 .12
344 Jermaine Dye .40 .12
345 Luis Rivas .25 .07
346 Jeff Conine .40 .12
347 Bobby Kielty .25 .07
348 Jeffrey Hammonds .25 .07
349 Keith Foulke .40 .12
350 Dave Martinez .25 .07
351 Adam Eaton .25 .07
352 Brandon Inge .25 .07
353 Tyler Houston .25 .07
354 Bobby Abreu .40 .12
355 Ivan Rodriguez 1.00 .30
356 Doug Glanville .25 .07
357 Jorge Julio .25 .07
358 Kerry Wood 1.00 .30
359 Eric Munson .25 .07
360 Joe Crede .25 .07
361 Denny Neagle .25 .07
362 Vance Wilson .25 .07
363 Neifi Perez .25 .07
364 Darryl Kile .40 .12
365 Jose Macias .25 .07
366 Michael Coleman .25 .07
367 Erubiel Durazo .25 .07
368 Darrin Fletcher .25 .07
369 Matt White .25 .07
370 Marvin Benard .25 .07
371 Brad Penny .25 .07
372 Chuck Finley .40 .12
373 Delino DeShields .25 .07
374 Adrian Brown .25 .07
375 Corey Koskie .40 .12
376 Kazuhiro Sasaki .40 .12
377 Brent Butler .25 .07
378 Paul Wilson .25 .07
379 Scott Williamson .25 .07
380 Mike Young 1.00 .30
381 Toby Hall .25 .07
382 Shane Reynolds .25 .07
383 Tom Goodwin .25 .07
384 Seth Etherton .25 .07
385 Billy Wagner .40 .12
386 Josh Phelps .25 .07
387 Kyle Lohse .25 .07
388 Jeremy Fikac .25 .07
389 Jorge Posada .60 .18
390 Bret Boone .40 .12
391 Angel Berroa .25 .07
392 Matt Mantei .25 .07
393 Alex Gonzalez .25 .07
394 Scott Strickland .25 .07
395 Charles Johnson .40 .12
396 Ramon Hernandez .25 .07
397 Damian Jackson .25 .07
398 Albert Pujols 2.00 .60
399 Gary Bennett .25 .07
400 Edgar Martinez .60 .18
401 Carl Pavano .40 .12
402 Chris Gomez .25 .07
403 Jaret Wright .25 .07
404 Lance Berkman .40 .12
405 Robert Person .25 .07
406 Brook Fordyce .25 .07
407 Adam Pettyjohn .25 .07
408 Chris Carpenter .25 .07
409 Rey Ordonez .25 .07
410 Eric Gagne 1.00 .30
411 Damion Easley .25 .07
412 A.J. Burnett .25 .07
413 Aaron Boone .40 .12
414 J.D. Drew .40 .12
415 Kelly Stinnett .25 .07
416 Mark Quinn .25 .07
417 Brad Radke .40 .12
418 Jose Cruz Jr. .25 .07
419 Greg Maddux 1.50 .45
420 Steve Cox .25 .07
421 Torii Hunter .40 .12
422 Sandy Alomar .25 .07
423 Barry Zito .40 .12
424 Bill Hall .25 .07
425 Marquis Grissom .40 .12
426 Rich Aurilia .25 .07
427 Royce Clayton .25 .07
428 Travis Fryman .40 .12
429 Pablo Ozuna .25 .07
430 David Dellucci .25 .07
431 Vernon Wells .40 .12
432 Gregg Zaun CP .25 .07
433 Alex Gonzalez CP .25 .07
434 Hideo Nomo CP 1.00 .30
435 Jeromy Burnitz CP .40 .12
436 Gary Sheffield CP .40 .12
437 Tino Martinez CP .60 .18
438 Tsuyoshi Shinjo CP .40 .12
439 Chan Ho Park CP .40 .12
440 Tony Clark CP .25 .07
441 Brad Fullmer CP .25 .07
442 Jason Giambi CP .60 .18
443 Billy Koch CP .25 .07
444 Mo Vaughn CP .40 .12
445 Alex Ochoa CP .25 .07
446 Darren Lewis CP .25 .07
447 John Rocker CP .25 .07
448 Scott Hatteberg CP .25 .07
449 Brady Anderson CP .40 .12
450 Chuck Knoblauch CP .40 .12
451 Pokey Reese CP .25 .07
452 Brian Jordan CP .40 .12
453 Albie Lopez CP .25 .07
454 David Bell CP .25 .07
455 Juan Gonzalez CP .60 .18
456 Terry Adams CP .25 .07
457 Kenny Lofton CP .40 .12
458 Shawn Estes CP .25 .07
459 Josh Fogg CP .25 .07
460 Dmitri Young CP .40 .12
461 Johnny Damon Sox CP 1.00 .30
462 Chris Singleton CP .25 .07
463 Ricky Ledee CP .25 .07
464 Dustin Hermanson CP .25 .07
465 Aaron Sele CP .25 .07
466 Chris Stynes CP .25 .07
467 Matt Stairs CP .25 .07
468 Kevin Appier CP .40 .12
469 Omar Daal CP .25 .07
470 Moises Alou CP .40 .12
471 Juan Encarnacion CP .25 .07
472 Robin Ventura CP .40 .12
473 Eric Hinske CP .25 .07
474 Rondell White CP .40 .12
475 Carlos Pena CP .25 .07
476 Craig Paquette CP .25 .07
477 Marty Cordova CP .25 .07
478 Brett Tomko CP .25 .07
479 Reggie Sanders CP .25 .07
480 Roberto Alomar CP .60 .18
481 Jeff Cirillo CP .25 .07
482 Todd Zeile CP .40 .12
483 John Vander Wal CP .25 .07
484 Rick Helling CP .25 .07
485 Jeff D'Amico CP .25 .07
486 David Justice CP .40 .12
487 Jason Isringhausen CP .40 .12
488 Shigetoshi Hasegawa CP .25 .07
489 Eric Young CP .25 .07
490 David Wells CP .40 .12
491 Ruben Sierra CP .25 .07
492 Aaron Cook FF RC .75 .23
493 Takahito Nomura FF RC .75 .23
494 Austin Kearns FF .75 .23
495 Kazuhisa Ishii FF RC 4.00 1.20
496 Mark Teixeira FF 1.25 .35
497 Rene Reyes FF RC .75 .23
498 Tim Spooneybarger FF .50 .15
499 Ben Broussard FF .50 .15
500 Eric Cyr FF .50 .15

501 Anastacio Martinez FF RC ...... .75 .23
502 Morgan Ensberg FF .... .75 .23
503 Steve Kent FF RC .... .75 .23
504 Franklin Nunez FF RC .... .75 .23
505 Adam Walker FF RC .... .75 .23
506 Anderson Machado FF RC .... .75 .23
507 Ryan Drese FF .... .50 .15
508 Luis Ugueto FF RC .... .75 .23
509 Jorge Nunez FF RC .... .75 .23
510 Colby Lewis FF .... .50 .15
511 Ron Calloway FF RC .... .75 .23
512 Hansel Izquierdo FF RC .... .75 .23
513 Jason Lane FF .... .50 .15
514 Rafael Soriano FF .... .50 .15
515 Jackson Melian FF .... .50 .15
516 Edwin Almonte FF RC .... .75 .23
517 Satoru Komiyama FF RC .... .75 .23
518 Corey Thurman FF RC .... .75 .23
519 Jorge De La Rosa FF RC .... .75 .23
520 Victor Martinez FF .... 2.00 .60
521 Dewon Brazelton FF .... .50 .15
522 Marlon Byrd FF .... .50 .15
523 Jae Seo FF .... .50 .15
524 Orlando Hudson FF .... .50 .15
525 Sean Burroughs FF .... .75 .23
526 Ryan Langerhans FF .... .50 .15
527 David Kelton FF .... .50 .15
528 So Taguchi FF RC .... 1.25 .35
529 Tyler Walker FF .... .50 .15
530 Hank Blalock FF .... 2.00 .60
531 Mark Prior FF 4.00 1.20
532 Yankee Stadium CL .... .40 .12
533 Fenway Park CL .... .40 .12
534 Wrigley Field CL .... .40 .12
535 Dodger Stadium CL .... .40 .12
536 Camden Yards CL .... .40 .12
537 PacBell Park CL .... .25 .07
538 Jacobs Field CL .... .25 .07
539 SAFECO Field CL .... .25 .07
540 Miller Field CL .... .25 .07
P279 Derek Jeter Promo ....

2002 Fleer Gold Backs

Randomly inserted in packs, this is a parallel to the 2002 Fleer set. These cards can be differentiated from the regular cards by either the "gold" stats or text used on the back of the cards. It was announced that 15 percent of the print run featured these gold backs.

Nm-Mt Ex-Mt
*GOLD BACK: .75X TO 2X BASIC ....
*GOLD BACK 492-531: .75X TO 2X BASIC

2002 Fleer Mini

Randomly inserted in retail packs, these cards parallel the 2002 Fleer set. They are printed to a smaller size than the regular set and also were printed to a stated print run of 50 serial numbered sets.

Nm-Mt Ex-Mt
*MINI: 10X TO 25X BASIC ....
*MINI 492-531: 5X TO 12X BASIC .....

2002 Fleer Tiffany

Randomly inserted in hobby packs, this is a parallel to the 2002 Fleer set and are printed to a stated print run of 200 serial numbered sets. These cards can be differentiated from the regular Fleer set by the glossy finish on the front.

Nm-Mt Ex-Mt
*TIFFANY: 4X TO 10X BASIC ....
*TIFFANY 492-531: 2X TO 5X BASIC..

2002 Fleer Barry Bonds Career Highlights

Issued at overall odds of one in 12 hobby packs and one in 36 retail packs, these 10 cards feature highlights from Barry Bonds career. These cards were issued in different rates depending on which card number it was.

Nm-Mt Ex-Mt
COMPLETE SET (10) 40.00 12.00
COMMON CARD (1-3) 4.00 1.20
COMMON CARD (4-6) 5.00 1.50
COMMON CARD (7-9) 8.00 2.40
COMMON CARD (10) 5.00 1.50
1-3 ODDS 1:65 HOBBY, 1:225 RETAIL
4-6 ODDS 1:125 HOBBY, 1:400 RETAIL
7-9 ODDS 1:250 HOBBY, 1:500 RETAIL
10 ODDS 1:383 HOBBY, 1:800 RETAIL
OVERALL ODDS 1:12 HOBBY, 1:36 RETAIL

2002 Fleer Barry Bonds Career Highlights Autographs

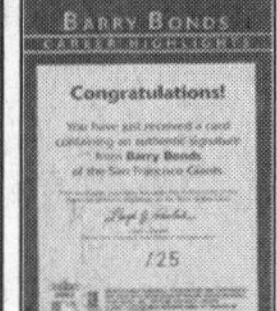

Randomly inserted in packs, these 10 cards not only parallel the Bonds Career Highlight set but also include an autograph from Barry Bonds on the card. Each card was issued to a stated print run of 25 serial numbered sets and due to market scarcity no pricing is provided.

Nm-Mt Ex-Mt
COMMON CARD (1-10) 250.00 75.00

2002 Fleer Classic Cuts Autographs

Inserted in packs at a stated rate of one in 432 hobby packs, these nine cards feature autographs from a retired legend. A few cards were issued to a smaller quantity and we have notated that information along with their stated print run next to their name in our checklist.

Nm-Mt Ex-Mt
BR-A Brooks Robinson SP/200 40.00 12.00
GP-A Gaylord Perry SP/225 .... 20.00 6.00
HK-A Harmon Killebrew 50.00 15.00
JM-A Juan Marichal 15.00 4.50
LA-A Luis Aparicio 15.00 4.50
PR-A Phil Rizzuto SP/125 .... 60.00 18.00
RC-A Ron Cey 15.00 4.50
RF-A Rollie Fingers SP/35 ....
TL-A Tommy Lasorda SP/35 ....

2002 Fleer Classic Cuts Game Used

Inserted at stated odds of one in 24, these 94 cards feature retired players along with an authentic game-used memorabilia piece of that player. Some cards were issued in shorter quantities and we have provided the stated print run next to the player's name in our checklist.

Nm-Mt Ex-Mt
YBB Yogi Berra Bat/72 .... 25.00 7.50
AD-J Andre Dawson Jsy 10.00 3.00
AT-B Alan Trammell Bat 10.00 3.00
BB-B Bobby Bonds Bat 10.00 3.00
BB-J Bobby Bonds Jsy 10.00 3.00
BD-B Bill Dickey Bat/200 .... 15.00 4.50
BJ-J Bo Jackson Jsy 15.00 4.50
BM-B Billy Martin Bat/65 .... 25.00 7.50
BR-B Brooks Robinson Bat/250 15.00 4.50
BT-B Bill Terry Bat/85 .... 25.00 7.50
CF-B Carlton Fisk Bat 15.00 4.50
CF-J Carlton Fisk Jsy/150 .... 15.00 4.50
CH-J Jim Hunter Jsy 15.00 4.50
CR-BG Cal Ripken Btg Glv/100 . 80.00 24.00
CR-FG Cal Ripken Fld Glv/60 ... 80.00 24.00
CR-J Cal Ripken Jsy 40.00 12.00
CR-P Cal Ripken Pants/200 .... 40.00 12.00
DE-B Dwight Evans Bat/250 .... 10.00 3.00
DE-J Dwight Evans Jsy 10.00 3.00
DM-B Don Mattingly Bat/200 .... 25.00 7.50
DM-J Don Mattingly Jsy 25.00 7.50
DM-P Don Mattingly Patch/50 ....
DP-B Dave Parker Bat 10.00 3.00
DR-P Dave Righetti Patch ....
DW-B Dave Winfield Bat 10.00 3.00
DW-J Dave Winfield Jsy/231 .... 10.00 3.00
DW-P Dave Winfield Pants 10.00 3.00
DW-P Dave Winfield Patch/25 ....
DZ-J Don Zimmer Jsy/90 .... 15.00 4.50
EM-B Eddie Mathews Bat/200 ... 15.00 4.50
EM-B Eddie Murray Bat 15.00 4.50
EM-J Eddie Murray Jsy 15.00 4.50
EM-P Eddie Murray Patch/45 .... 40.00 12.00
EW-J Earl Weaver Jsy 10.00 3.00
FL-B Fred Lynn Bat/25 ....
GB-B George Brett Bat/250 .... 25.00 7.50
GB-J George Brett Jsy/250 .... 25.00 7.50
GH-B Gil Hodges Bat/200 .... 15.00 4.50
GK-B George Kell Bat/150 .... 15.00 4.50
HB-B Hank Bauer Bat 10.00 3.00
HG-B Hank Greenberg Bat/13 ....
HW-B Hack Wilson Bat/8 ....
HW-P Hoyt Wilhelm Pants/150. 10.00 3.00
JB-B Johnny Bench Bat/100 .... 25.00 7.50
JB-J Johnny Bench Jsy 15.00 4.50
JM-B Joe Morgan Bat/250 .... 10.00 3.00
JP-J Jim Palmer Jsy/273 .... 10.00 3.00
JR-B Jim Rice Bat/225 .... 10.00 3.00
JR-J Jim Rice Jsy/90 .... 15.00 4.50
JT-J Joe Torre Jsy/125 .... 15.00 4.50
KG-B Kirk Gibson Bat 10.00 3.00
KP-B Kirby Puckett Bat/25 ....
KP-J Kirby Puckett Jsy 15.00 4.50
LD-B Larry Doby Bat/250 .... 10.00 3.00
LP-P Lou Piniella Pants 10.00 3.00
NF-B Nellie Fox Bat/200 .... 15.00 4.50
NR-J Nolan Ryan Jsy 40.00 12.00
NR-P Nolan Ryan Pants/200 .... 40.00 12.00
OC-B Orlando Cepeda Bat/45 .... 15.00 4.50
OC-P Orlando Cepeda Pants 10.00 3.00
OS-J Ozzie Smith Jsy/250 .... 25.00 7.50
PB-B Paul Blair Bat 10.00 3.00
PM-B Paul Molitor Bat/250 .... 15.00 4.50
PM-P Paul Molitor Patch/110 ... 25.00 7.50
PR-J Preacher Roe Jsy/19 ....
PWR-J Pee Wee Reese Jsy/20 ....
RC-B Roy Campanella Bat/7 ....
RF-J Rollie Fingers Jsy 10.00 3.00
RJ-B Reggie Jackson Bat/50 .... 25.00 7.50
RJ-P Reggie Jackson Pants 15.00 4.50
RK-B Ralph Kiner Bat/47 .... 15.00 4.50
RM-P Roger Maris Pants/200 ... 50.00 15.00
RS-B Ryne Sandberg Bat 25.00 7.50
RY-B Robin Yount Bat 15.00 4.50
SA-P Sparky Anderson Pants ... 10.00 3.00
SC-H Steve Carlton Hat/25 ....
SC-P Steve Carlton Pants 10.00 3.00
SG-B Steve Garvey Bat 10.00 3.00
TJ-J Tommy John Jsy/55 .... 15.00 4.50
TJ-P Tommy John Patch/15 ....
TK-B Ted Kluszewski Bat/200 ... 15.00 4.50
TK-P Ted Kluszewski Pants 15.00 4.50
TL-B Tony Lazzeri Bat/35 ....
TM-P Thurman Munson Pants/10 ....
TP-B Tony Perez Bat/250 .... 10.00 3.00
TP-J Tony Perez Jsy 10.00 3.00
TW-B Ted Williams Bat 80.00 24.00
TW-P Ted Williams Pants 80.00 24.00
WB-B Wade Boggs Bat/99 .... 25.00 7.50
WB-J Wade Boggs Jsy 15.00 4.50
WB-P Wade Boggs Patch/50 .... 40.00 12.00
WM-J Willie McCovey Jsy/300 . 10.00 3.00
WR-P Willie Randolph Patch/18 ....
WS-B Willie Stargell Bat/250 ... 15.00 4.50

2002 Fleer Classic Cuts Game Used Autographs

Randomly inserted in packs, these three cards feature not only a game-used piece from a retired player but also an authentic autograph. The stated print run for each player is listed next to their name in our checklist.

Nm-Mt Ex-Mt
BR-B Brooks Robinson Bat/45.. 60.00 18.00
LA-B Luis Aparicio Bat/45 .... 40.00 12.00
RF-J Rollie Fingers Jsy/35 .... 40.00 12.00

2002 Fleer Diamond Standouts

Randomly inserted in packs, these 10 cards have a stated print run of 1200 serial numbered sets. These cards feature players who most fans would consider the top 10 stars in Baseball.

Nm-Mt Ex-Mt
COMPLETE SET (10) 80.00 24.00
1 Mike Piazza 8.00 2.40
2 Derek Jeter 12.00 3.60
3 Ken Griffey Jr. 8.00 2.40
4 Barry Bonds 12.00 3.60
5 Sammy Sosa 8.00 2.40
6 Alex Rodriguez 8.00 2.40
7 Ichiro Suzuki 8.00 2.40
8 Greg Maddux 8.00 2.40
9 Jason Giambi 8.00 2.40
10 Nomar Garciaparra 8.00 2.40

2002 Fleer Golden Memories

Issued in packs at a stated rate of one in 24 packs, these 15 cards feature players who have earned many honors during their playing career.

Nm-Mt Ex-Mt
COMPLETE SET (15) 40.00 12.00
1 Frank Thomas .... 2.50 .75
2 Derek Jeter 6.00 1.80
3 Albert Pujols 5.00 1.50
4 Barry Bonds 6.00 1.80
5 Alex Rodriguez 4.00 1.20
6 Randy Johnson .... 2.50 .75
7 Jeff Bagwell .... 1.50 .45
8 Greg Maddux 4.00 1.20
9 Ivan Rodriguez .... 2.50 .75
10 Ichiro Suzuki 4.00 1.20
11 Mike Piazza 4.00 1.20
12 Pat Burrell .... 1.50 .45
13 Rickey Henderson .... 2.50 .75
14 Vladimir Guerrero .... 2.50 .75
15 Sammy Sosa 4.00 1.20

2002 Fleer Headliners

Issued at a stated rate of one in eight hobby packs and one in 12 retail packs, these 20 cards feature players who achieved noteworthy feats during the 2001 season.

Nm-Mt Ex-Mt
COMPLETE SET (20) 25.00 7.50
1 Randy Johnson .... 1.25 .35
2 Alex Rodriguez .... 2.00 .60
3 Todd Helton .... 1.00 .30
4 Pedro Martinez .... 1.25 .35

5 Ichiro Suzuki .... 2.00 .60
6 Vladimir Guerrero .... 1.25 .35
7 Derek Jeter .... 3.00 .90
8 Adam Dunn .... 1.00 .30
9 Luis Gonzalez .... 1.00 .30
10 Kazuhiro Sasaki .... 1.00 .30
11 Sammy Sosa .... 2.00 .60
12 Jason Giambi .... 1.00 .30
13 Ken Griffey Jr. .... 2.00 .60
14 Roger Clemens .... 2.50 .75
15 Brandon Duckworth .... 1.00 .30
16 Nomar Garciaparra .... 2.00 .60
17 Bud Smith .... 1.00 .30
18 Juan Gonzalez .... 1.00 .30
19 Chipper Jones .... 1.25 .35
20 Barry Bonds .... 3.00 .90

2002 Fleer Rookie Flashbacks

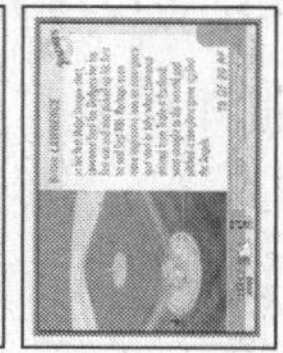

Issued at a stated rate of one in three retail packs, these 20 cards feature players who made their major league debut in 2001.

Nm-Mt Ex-Mt
COMPLETE SET (20) 25.00 7.50
1 Bret Prinz .... 1.00 .30
2 Albert Pujols 4.00 1.20
3 C.C. Sabathia .... 1.00 .30
4 Ichiro Suzuki .... 3.00 .90
5 Juan Cruz .... 1.00 .30
6 Jay Gibbons .... 1.00 .30
7 Bud Smith .... 1.00 .30
8 Johnny Estrada .... 1.00 .30
9 Roy Oswalt .... 1.00 .30
10 Tsuyoshi Shinjo .... 1.00 .30
11 Brandon Duckworth .... 1.00 .30
12 Jackson Melian .... 1.00 .30
13 Josh Beckett .... 1.00 .30
14 Morgan Ensberg .... 1.00 .30
15 Brian Lawrence .... 1.00 .30
16 Eric Hinske .... 1.00 .30
17 Juan Uribe .... 1.00 .30
18 Matt White .... 1.00 .30
19 Junior Spivey .... 1.00 .30
20 Wilson Betemit .... 1.00 .30

2002 Fleer Rookie Sensations

Randomly inserted in hobby packs and printed to a stated print run of 1500 serial numbered sets, these 20 cards feature players who made their major league debut in 2001.

Nm-Mt Ex-Mt
COMPLETE SET (20) 50.00 15.00
1 Bret Prinz 5.00 1.50
2 Albert Pujols 15.00 4.50
3 C.C. Sabathia 5.00 1.50
4 Ichiro Suzuki 12.00 3.60
5 Juan Cruz 5.00 1.50
6 Jay Gibbons 5.00 1.50
7 Bud Smith 5.00 1.50
8 Johnny Estrada 5.00 1.50
9 Roy Oswalt 5.00 1.50
10 Tsuyoshi Shinjo 5.00 1.50
11 Brandon Duckworth 5.00 1.50
12 Jackson Melian 5.00 1.50
13 Josh Beckett 5.00 1.50
14 Morgan Ensberg 5.00 1.50
15 Brian Lawrence 5.00 1.50
16 Eric Hinske 5.00 1.50
17 Juan Uribe 5.00 1.50
18 Matt White 5.00 1.50
19 Junior Spivey 5.00 1.50
20 Wilson Betemit 5.00 1.50

2002 Fleer Then and Now

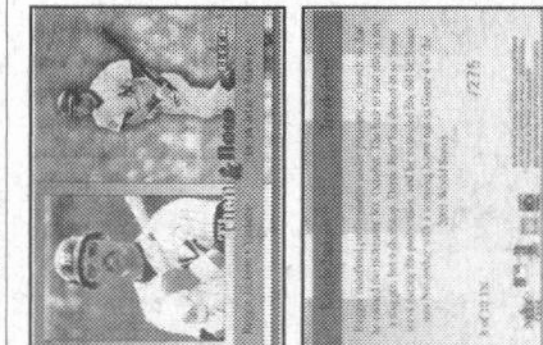

Randomly inserted in hobby packs, these 10 cards feature a player from the past who compares with one of today's stars. These cards are printed to a stated print run of 275 serial numbered sets.

Nm-Mt Ex-Mt
COMPLETE SET (10) 200.00 60.00
1 Eddie Mathews 15.00 4.50
Chipper Jones
2 Willie McCovey 30.00 9.00
Barry Bonds
3 Johnny Bench 20.00 6.00
Mika Piazza
4 Ernie Banks 20.00 6.00
Alex Rodriguez
5 Rickey Henderson 20.00 6.00
Ichiro Suzuki
6 Tom Seaver 25.00 7.50
Roger Clemens
7 Juan Marichal 15.00 4.50
Pedro Martinez
8 Reggie Jackson 30.00 9.00
Derek Jeter
9 Nolan Ryan 50.00 15.00
Kerry Wood
10 Joe Morgan 20.00 6.00
Ken Griffey Jr.

2002 Fleer Authentix

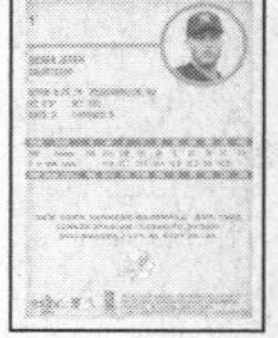

This 170-card base set features standard-size cards with a silhouetted action shot imposed over an old-school ticket design. These cards were issued in five card packs with an SRP of $3.99 with 24 packs in a box and 12 boxes in a case. Cards numbered 151 through 170 feature rookies and were randomly inserted into packs with a stated print run of 1850 serial numbered sets.

Nm-Mt Ex-Mt
COMP.SET w/o SP's (150) 40.00 12.00
COMMON CARD (1-135) .... .40 .12
COMMON CARD (136-150) .... .60 .18
COMMON CARD (151-170) 5.00 1.50
1 Derek Jeter .... 2.50 .75
2 Tim Hudson .... .40 .12
3 Robert Fick .... .40 .12
4 Javy Lopez .... .40 .12
5 Alfonso Soriano .... .60 .18
6 Ken Griffey Jr. .... 1.50 .45
7 Rafael Palmeiro .... .60 .18
8 Bernie Williams .... .60 .18
9 Adam Dunn .... .60 .18
10 Ivan Rodriguez .... 1.00 .30
11 Vladimir Guerrero .... 1.00 .30
12 Pedro Martinez .... 1.00 .30
13 Bret Boone .... .40 .12
14 Paul LoDuca .... .40 .12
15 Tony Batista .... .40 .12
16 Barry Bonds .... 2.50 .75
17 Craig Biggio .... .60 .18
18 Garret Anderson .... .40 .12
19 Mark Mulder .... .40 .12
20 Frank Thomas .... 1.00 .30
21 Alex Rodriguez .... 1.50 .45
22 Cristian Guzman .... .40 .12
23 Sammy Sosa .... 1.50 .45
24 Ichiro Suzuki .... 1.50 .45
25 Carlos Beltran .... .60 .18
26 Edgardo Alfonzo .... .40 .12
27 Josh Beckett .... .40 .12
28 Eric Chavez .... .40 .12
29 Roberto Alomar .... .60 .18
30 Raul Mondesi .... .40 .12
31 Mike Piazza .... 1.50 .45
32 Barry Larkin .... .60 .18
33 Ruben Sierra .... .40 .12
34 Tsuyoshi Shinjo .... .40 .12
35 Magglio Ordonez .... .40 .12
36 Ben Grieve .... .40 .12
37 Richie Sexson .... .40 .12
38 Manny Ramirez .... .60 .18
39 Jeff Kent .... .40 .12
40 Shawn Green .... .40 .12
41 Andruw Jones .... .40 .12
42 Aramis Ramirez .... .40 .12
43 Cliff Floyd .... .40 .12
44 Juan Pierre .... .40 .12
45 Jose Vidro .... .40 .12
46 Paul Konerko .... .40 .12
47 Greg Vaughn .... .40 .12
48 Geoff Jenkins .... .40 .12
49 Greg Maddux .... 1.50 .45
50 Ryan Klesko .... .40 .12
51 Corey Koskie .... .40 .12
52 Nomar Garciaparra .... 1.50 .45
53 Edgar Martinez .... .60 .18
54 Gary Sheffield .... .40 .12
55 Randy Johnson .... 1.00 .30
56 Bobby Abreu .... .40 .12
57 Mike Sweeney .... .40 .12
58 Chipper Jones .... 1.00 .30
59 Brian Giles .... .40 .12
60 Charles Johnson .... .40 .12
61 Ben Sheets .... .40 .12
62 Jason Giambi .... .40 .12
63 Todd Helton .... .60 .18
64 David Eckstein .... .40 .12
65 Troy Glaus .... .40 .12
66 Sean Casey .... .40 .12
67 Gabe Kapler .... .40 .12
68 Doug Mientkiewicz .... .40 .12
69 Curt Schilling .... .40 .12
70 Pat Burrell .... .40 .12
71 Albert Pujols .... 2.00 .60
72 Jermaine Dye .... .40 .12
73 Miguel Tejada .... .40 .12
74 Jim Thome .... 1.00 .30
75 Carlos Delgado .... .40 .12
76 Fred McGriff .... .60 .18
77 Mike Cameron .... .40 .12

78 Jeremy Burnitz .40 .12
79 Jay Gibbons .40 .12
80 Rich Aurilia .40 .12
81 Lance Berkman .40 .12
82 Brian Jordan .40 .12
83 Phil Nevin .40 .12
84 Moises Alou .40 .12
85 Reggie Sanders .40 .12
86 Scott Rolen 1.00 .30
87 Larry Walker .60 .18
88 Matt Williams .40 .12
89 Roger Clemens 2.00 .60
90 Juan Gonzalez .60 .18
91 Jose Cruz Jr. .40 .12
92 Tino Martinez .60 .18
93 Kerry Wood 1.00 .30
94 Freddy Garcia .40 .12
95 Jeff Bagwell .60 .18
96 Luis Gonzalez .40 .12
97 Jimmy Rollins .40 .12
98 Bobby Higginson .40 .12
99 Rondell White .40 .12
100 Jorge Posada .60 .18
101 Trot Nixon .40 .12
102 Jason Kendall .40 .12
103 Preston Wilson .40 .12
104 Corey Patterson .40 .12
105 Jose Valentin .40 .12
106 Carlos Lee .40 .12
107 Chris Richard .40 .12
108 Todd Walker .40 .12
109 Ellis Burks .40 .12
110 Brady Anderson .40 .12
111 Kazuhiro Sasaki .40 .12
112 Roy Oswalt .40 .12
113 Kevin Brown .40 .12
114 Jeff Weaver .40 .12
115 Todd Hollandsworth .40 .12
116 Joe Crede .40 .12
117 Tom Glavine .60 .18
118 Mike Lieberthal .40 .12
119 Tim Salmon .60 .18
120 Johnny Damon Sox 1.00 .30
121 Brad Fullmer .40 .12
122 Mo Vaughn .40 .12
123 Torii Hunter .40 .12
124 Jamie Moyer .40 .12
125 Terrence Long .40 .12
126 Travis Lee .40 .12
127 Jacque Jones .40 .12
128 Lee Stevens .40 .12
129 Russ Ortiz .40 .12
130 Jeremy Giambi .40 .12
131 Mike Mussina .60 .18
132 Orlando Cabrera .40 .12
133 Barry Zito .40 .12
134 Robert Person .40 .12
135 Andy Pettitte .60 .18
136 Drew Henson FS .60 .18
137 Mark Teixeira FS 1.00 .30
138 David Espinosa FS .60 .18
139 Orlando Hudson FS .60 .18
140 Colby Lewis FS .60 .18
141 Bill Hall FS .60 .18
142 Michael Restovich FS .60 .18
143 Angel Berroa FS .60 .18
144 Dewon Brazelton FS .60 .18
145 Joe Thurston FS .60 .18
146 Mark Prior FS 2.50 .75
147 Dane Sardinha FS .60 .18
148 Marlon Byrd FS .60 .18
149 Jeff Deardorff FS .60 .18
150 Austin Kearns FS .60 .18
151 Anderson Machado TM RC 5.00 1.50
152 Kazuhisa Ishii TM RC 10.00 3.00
153 Eric Junge TM RC 5.00 1.50
154 Mark Corey TM RC 5.00 1.50
155 So Taguchi TM RC 8.00 2.40
156 Jorge Padilla TM RC 5.00 1.50
157 Steve Kent TM RC 5.00 1.50
158 Jaime Cerda TM RC 5.00 1.50
159 Hansel Izquierdo TM RC 5.00 1.50
160 Rene Reyes TM RC 5.00 1.50
161 Jorge Nunez TM RC 5.00 1.50
162 Corey Thurman TM RC 5.00 1.50
163 Jorge Sosa TM RC 5.00 1.50
164 Franklin Nunez TM RC 5.00 1.50
165 Adam Walker TM RC 5.00 1.50
166 Ryan Baerlocher TM RC 5.00 1.50
167 Ron Calloway TM RC 5.00 1.50
168 Miguel Asencio TM RC 5.00 1.50
169 Luis Ugueto TM RC 5.00 1.50
170 Felix Escalona TM RC 5.00 1.50

2002 Fleer Authentix Front Row

This 170-card set is a parallel to the base set. It features standard-size cards with a silhouetted action shot imposed over an old-school ticket design.

Nm-Mt Ex-Mt
*FRONT ROW 1-135: 4X TO 10X BASIC
*FRONT ROW 136-150: 4X TO 10X BASIC
*FRONT ROW 151-170: .75X TO 2X BASIC

2002 Fleer Authentix Second Row

This 170-card set is a parallel to the base set. It features standard-size cards with a silhouetted action shot imposed over an old-school ticket design. Cards were randomly seeded into packs and 250 serial-numbered sets were produced.

Nm-Mt Ex-Mt
*2ND ROW 1-135: 2.5X TO 6X BASIC
*2ND ROW 136-150: 2.5X TO 6X BASIC
*2ND ROW 151-170: .6X TO 1.5X BASIC

2002 Fleer Authentix Autograph AuthenTIX

This eight-card insert set presents special autographed cards of current and future stars. Cards were seeded into packs at a rate of 1:780 hobby and 1:2,200 retail. The standard-size cards feature embedded team replica tickets. This Ripped version comes with the tab "torn". Exchange cards were seeded into packs for Kazuhisa Ishii

and David Espinosa with a redemption deadline of April 30th, 2003. Not all cards were printed to the same press run, we have notated these cards with an SP in our checklist and notated the stated press runs for these cards.

Nm-Mt Ex-Mt
UNRIPPED RANDOM INSERTS IN PACKS
UNRIPPED PRINT RUN 25 #'d SETS..
NO UNRIPPED PRICE DUE TO SCARCITY
AA-BR Brooks Robinson SP/145 25.00 7.50
AA-BS Ben Sheets SP/25
AA-DE David Espinosa 15.00 4.50
AA-DS Dane Sardinha 15.00 4.50
AA-KI Kazuhisa Ishii 40.00 12.00
AA-MP Mark Prior SP/145 80.00 24.00
AA-MT Mark Teixeira SP/25
AA-ST So Taguchi SP/150 25.00 7.50

2002 Fleer Authentix Ballpark Classics

This 15-card insert set highlights fifteen Major League all-time greats. The standard-size cards have a brilliant design. Cards were seeded into packs at a rate of 1:22 hobby and 1:24 retail.

Nm-Mt Ex-Mt
COMPLETE SET (15) 80.00 24.00
1 Reggie Jackson 4.00 1.20
2 Don Mattingly 10.00 3.00
3 Duke Snider 4.00 1.20
4 Carlton Fisk 4.00 1.20
5 Cal Ripken 12.00 3.60
6 Willie McCovey 4.00 1.20
7 Robin Yount 6.00 1.80
8 Paul Molitor 4.00 1.20
9 George Brett 10.00 3.00
10 Ryne Sandberg 6.00 1.80
11 Nolan Ryan 10.00 3.00
12 Thurman Munson 4.00 1.20
13 Joe Morgan 4.00 1.20
14 Jim Rice 4.00 1.20
15 Babe Ruth 15.00 4.50

2002 Fleer Authentix Ballpark Classics Memorabilia

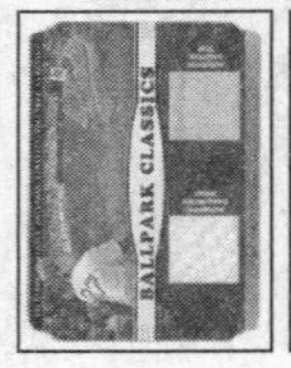

This 14-card insert set is a partial parallel to the Ballpark Classics insert. The standard-size cards feature not only a swatch of game-used memorabilia but also a piece of authentic stadium seat from either the Wrigley Field, Milwaukee County Stadium or Cleveland Stadium. Cards were seeded into hobby packs at a rate of 1:83 and retail packs at a rate of 1:440. A few cards were printed in smaller quantities and we have notated this inforrmation with an SP along with their stated print run in our checklist.

Nm-Mt Ex-Mt
CF Carlton Fisk Jsy 15.00 4.50
CR Cal Ripken Jsy 40.00 12.00
DM Don Mattingly Jsy 25.00 7.50
DS Duke Snider Bat SP/249 25.00 7.50
GB George Brett Jsy SP/482 25.00 7.50
JM Joe Morgan Bat 15.00 4.50
JR Jim Rice Jsy SP/487 15.00 4.50
NR Nolan Ryan Jsy 40.00 12.00
PM Paul Molitor Jsy 15.00 4.50
RJ Reggie Jackson Jsy SP/230 25.00 7.50
RS Ryne Sandberg Bat SP/82 60.00 18.00
RY Robin Yount Jsy SP/83 25.00 7.50
TM Thur Munson Cap SP/83 60.00 18.00
WM Willie McCovey Jsy SP/359 25.00 7.50

2002 Fleer Authentix Ballpark Classics Memorabilia Gold

This 15-card insert set is a parallel gold version to the Ballpark Classics Memorabilia insert. Babe Ruth, however, was featured only in this Gold set. Cards were randomly seeded into packs. Unlike the basic Memorabilia cards, each Gold parallel is serial-numbered to 100. The standard-size cards feature not only a swatch of game-used memorabilia but also a piece of authentic stadium seat from either the Wrigley Field, Milwaukee County Stadium or Cleveland Stadium.

Nm-Mt Ex-Mt
BR Babe Ruth Bat/Seat 200.00 60.00
CF Carlton Fisk Jsy/Seat 25.00 7.50
CR Cal Ripken Jsy/Seat 80.00 24.00
DM Don Mattingly Jsy/Seat 50.00 15.00
DS Duke Snider Bat/Seat 25.00 7.50
GB George Brett Jsy/Seat 50.00 15.00
JM Joe Morgan Bat/Seat 25.00 7.50
JR Jim Rice Jsy/Seat 25.00 7.50
NR Nolan Ryan Jsy/Seat 60.00 18.00
PM Paul Molitor Jsy/Seat 25.00 7.50
RJ Reggie Jackson Jsy/Seat 25.00 7.50
RS Ryne Sandberg Bat/Seat 50.00 15.00
RY Robin Yount Jsy/Seat 40.00 12.00
TM Thurman Munson Cap/Seat 50.00 15.00
WM Willie McCovey Jsy/Seat 25.00 7.50

2002 Fleer Authentix Bat AuthenTIX

This 14-card insert set offers a piece of bat used by fourteen of MLB's biggest stars. Each standard-size card also features an embedded team replica ticket. This Ripped version comes with the tab "torn". Cards were randomly seeded into packs at a rate of 1:68 hobby. Many cards were issued to a different print run and we have notated that information in our checklist.

Nm-Mt Ex-Mt
BA-AJ Andruw Jones SP/171 15.00 4.50
BA-BB Barry Bonds SP/437 25.00 7.50
BA-BW Bernie Williams SP/44
BA-CJ Chipper Jones SP/37
BA-DH Drew Henson 10.00 3.00
BA-DJ Derek Jeter SP/197 50.00 15.00
BA-HN Hideo Nomo SP/41
BA-JG Juan Gonzalez SP/213 15.00 4.50
BA-JR Jimmy Rollins SP/409 15.00 4.50
BA-MR Manny Ramirez 15.00 4.50
BA-NG Nomar Garciaparra 25.00 7.50
BA-OH Orlando Hernandez 10.00 3.00
BA-PB Pat Burrell SP/468 15.00 4.50
BA-RD Ray Durham SP/52

2002 Fleer Authentix Jersey AuthenTIX

This 30-card insert set features standard-size game-worn jersey cards AND embedded team replica tickets! This "ripped" version comes with the tab "torn". Cards were seeded into hobby packs at a rate of 1:27 and retail packs at a rate of 1:43. Though the cards are not serial-numbered, representatives at Fleer revealed that the following players were produced in only half the quantity of others from this set: J.D. Drew, Jim Edmonds, Darin Erstad, Nomar Garciaparra, Luis Gonzalez, Andruw Jones, Manny Ramirez, Scott Rolen, Curt Schilling, Jim Thome and Bernie Williams.

Nm-Mt Ex-Mt
JA-AJ Andruw Jones SP 15.00 4.50
JA-AR Alex Rodriguez 15.00 4.50
JA-BB Barry Bonds 25.00 7.50
JA-BW Bernie Williams SP 20.00 6.00
JA-BZ Barry Zito 10.00 3.00
JA-CJ Chipper Jones 15.00 4.50
JA-DE Darin Erstad SP 15.00 4.50
JA-DJ Derek Jeter 30.00 9.00
JA-EC Eric Chavez 10.00 3.00
JA-FG Freddy Garcia 10.00 3.00
JA-FT Frank Thomas 15.00 4.50
JA-GM Greg Maddux 15.00 4.50
JA-IR Ivan Rodriguez 15.00 4.50
JA-JB Jeff Bagwell 15.00 4.50
JA-JD J.D. Drew SP 15.00 4.50
JA-JE Jim Edmonds SP 15.00 4.50
JA-JT Jim Thome SP 20.00 6.00
JA-LG Luis Gonzalez SP 15.00 4.50
JA-MO Magglio Ordonez 10.00 3.00
JA-MP Mike Piazza 15.00 4.50
JA-MR Manny Ramirez SP 20.00 6.00
JA-NG Nomar Garciaparra SP 25.00 7.50
JA-PL Paul LoDuca 10.00 3.00
JA-PM Pedro Martinez 15.00 4.50
JA-RA Roberto Alomar 15.00 4.50
JA-RJ Randy Johnson 15.00 4.50
JA-SG Shawn Green 10.00 3.00
JA-SR Scott Rolen SP 20.00 6.00
JA-TH Todd Helton 15.00 4.50
JACS Curt Schilling SP 15.00 4.50

2002 Fleer Authentix Jersey Autograph AuthenTIX

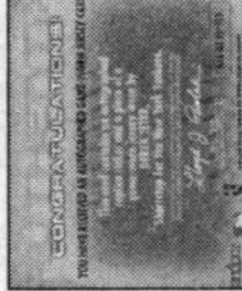

This 3-card insert set features standard-size game-worn jersey cards autographed by Derek Jeter, Chipper Jones and Greg Maddux. This Ripped version comes with the tab "torn". Cards were seeded into packs at a rate of 1:1387 hobby and 1:8,800 retail. Exchange cards were seeded into packs for Chipper Jones and Greg Maddux with a redemption deadline of April 30th, 2003. Though the cards are not serial-numbered, representatives at Fleer revealed that fifty copies of each card were produced.

Nm-Mt Ex-Mt
UNRIPPED RANDOM INSERTS IN PACKS
UNRIPPED PRINT RUN 1 SERIAL #'d SET
NO UNRIPPED PRICE DUE TO SCARCITY
AJA-CJ Chipper Jones
AJA-DJ Derek Jeter 250.00 75.00
AJA-GM Greg Maddux

2002 Fleer Authentix Derek Jeter 1996 Autographics

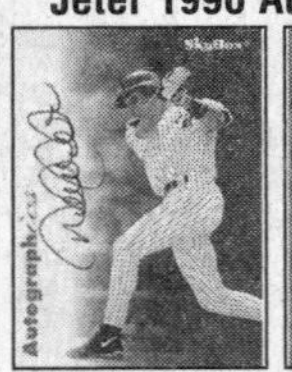

This card, which was originally supposed to be issued in 2001 as part of the Derek Jeter legacy collection, was instead inserted into the 2002 Fleer Authentix set. This card had a stated print run of 100 serial numbered sets.

Nm-Mt Ex-Mt
NNO Derek Jeter 96/100 200.00 60.00

2002 Fleer Authentix Power Alley

This 15-card insert set profiles the game's most hard-hitting sluggers. Cards were randomly seeded into packs ata a rate of 1:11.

Nm-Mt Ex-Mt
COMPLETE SET (15) 40.00 12.00
1 Sammy Sosa 4.00 1.20
2 Ken Griffey Jr. 4.00 1.20
3 Luis Gonzalez 2.00 .60
4 Alex Rodriguez 4.00 1.20
5 Shawn Green 2.00 .60
6 Barry Bonds 6.00 1.80
7 Todd Helton 2.00 .60
8 Jim Thome 2.50 .75
9 Troy Glaus 2.00 .60
10 Manny Ramirez 2.00 .60
11 Jeff Bagwell 2.00 .60
12 Jason Giambi 2.00 .60
13 Chipper Jones 2.50 .75
14 Mike Piazza 4.00 1.20
15 Albert Pujols 5.00 1.50

2003 Fleer Authentix

This 175 card set was distributed in two separate series. The primary Authentix product - containing the first 160 cards from the basic set - was issued in April, 2003. These cards were issued in five card packs with an $4 SRP. These packs were issued 24 to a box and 12 boxes to a case. Cards numbered 101 through 110 feature a Future Star subset. Cards numbered 111 through 125 featured a ticket to the majors subset and those cards were issued to a stated print run of 180 serial numbered sets. Cards numbered 126 through 160 feature Home Team extended cards. Those cards were issued in four ct home team packs where were issued one per home team box. In addition, one in 12 hobby boxes were issued as Home Team boxes. Cards 161-175 were randomly seeded within packs of Fleer Rookies and Greats of which was distributed in December, 2003. Each of these update cards was serial numbered to 1250 copies and continued the Ticket to the Majors prospect subset established in cards 111-125.

Nm-Mt Ex-Mt
COMP.LO SET w/o SP's (110) 25.00 7.50
COMMON CARD (1-100) .40 .12
COMMON CARD (101-110) .60 .18
COMMON (111-125/161-175) 4.00 1.20
COMMON CARD (126-132) 4.00 1.20
126-132 STATED PRINT RUN 1700 SETS
COMMON CARD (133-139/ 8.00 2.40
133-139 STATED PRINT RUN 210 SETS
COMMON CARD (140-153) 5.00 1.50
140-153 STATED PRINT RUN 560 SETS
COMMON CARD (154-160) 8.00 2.40
154-160 STATED PRINT RUN 280 SETS
1 Derek Jeter 2.50 .75
2 Tom Glavine .60 .18
3 Jason Jennings .40 .12
4 Craig Biggio .60 .18
5 Miguel Tejada .40 .12
6 Barry Bonds 2.50 .75
7 Juan Gonzalez .60 .18
8 Luis Gonzalez .40 .12
9 Johnny Damon 1.00 .30
10 Ellis Burks .40 .12
11 Frank Thomas 1.00 .30
12 Richie Sexson .40 .12
13 Roger Clemens 2.00 .60
14 Matt Morris .40 .12
15 Troy Glaus .40 .12
16 Tony Batista .40 .12
17 Magglio Ordonez .40 .12
18 Jose Vidro .40 .12
19 Barry Zito .40 .12
20 Chipper Jones 1.00 .30
21 Moises Alou .40 .12
22 Lance Berkman .40 .12
23 Jacque Jones .40 .12
24 Alfonso Soriano .60 .18
25 Sean Burroughs .40 .12
26 Scott Rolen 1.00 .30
27 Mark Grace .60 .18
28 Manny Ramirez .60 .18
29 Ken Griffey Jr. 1.50 .45
30 Josh Beckett .40 .12
31 Kazuhisa Ishii .40 .12
32 Pat Burrell .40 .12
33 Edgar Martinez .60 .18
34 Tim Salmon .60 .18
35 Raul Ibanez .40 .12
36 Vladimir Guerrero 1.00 .30
37 Jermaine Dye .40 .12
38 Rich Aurilia .40 .12
39 Rafael Palmeiro .60 .18
40 Kerry Wood 1.00 .30
41 Omar Vizquel .60 .18
42 Fred McGriff .60 .18
43 Ben Sheets .40 .12
44 Bernie Williams .60 .18
45 Brian Giles .40 .12
46 Jim Edmonds .40 .12
47 Garret Anderson .40 .12
48 Pedro Martinez 1.00 .30
49 Adam Dunn .60 .18
50 A.J. Burnett .40 .12
51 Eric Gagne 1.00 .30
52 Mo Vaughn .40 .12
53 Bobby Abreu .40 .12
54 Bret Boone .40 .12
55 Carlos Delgado .40 .12
56 Gary Sheffield .40 .12
57 Sammy Sosa 1.50 .45
58 Jim Thome 1.00 .30
59 Jeff Bagwell .60 .18
60 David Eckstein .40 .12
61 Jason Kendall .40 .12
62 Albert Pujols 2.00 .60
63 Curt Schilling .40 .12
64 Nomar Garciaparra 1.50 .45
65 Sean Casey .40 .12
66 Shawn Green .40 .12
67 Mike Piazza 1.50 .45
68 Ichiro Suzuki 1.50 .45
69 Eric Hinske .40 .12
70 Greg Maddux 1.50 .45
71 Larry Walker .60 .18
72 Roy Oswalt .40 .12
73 Alex Rodriguez 1.50 .45
74 Austin Kearns .40 .12
75 Cliff Floyd .40 .12
76 Kevin Brown .40 .12
77 Jason Giambi .40 .12
78 Jorge Julio .40 .12
79 Carlos Lee .40 .12
80 Mike Sweeney .40 .12
81 Edgardo Alfonzo .40 .12
82 Eric Chavez .40 .12
83 Andruw Jones .40 .12
84 Mark Prior 1.00 .30
85 Todd Helton .60 .18
86 Torii Hunter .40 .12
87 Ryan Klesko .40 .12
88 Aubrey Huff .40 .12
89 Randy Johnson 1.00 .30
90 Barry Larkin .60 .18
91 Mike Lowell .40 .12
92 Jimmy Rollins .40 .12
93 Darin Erstad .40 .12
94 Jay Gibbons .40 .12
95 Paul Konerko .40 .12
96 Bobby Higginson .40 .12
97 Carlos Beltran .60 .18
98 Bartolo Colon .40 .12
99 Jeff Kent .40 .12
100 Ivan Rodriguez 1.00 .30
101 Joe Borchard FS .60 .18
102 Mark Teixeira FS .60 .18
103 Francisco Rodriguez FS .60 .18
104 Chris Snelling FS .60 .18
105 Hee Seop Choi FS .60 .18
106 Hank Blalock FS 1.00 .30
107 Marlon Byrd FS .60 .18
108 Michael Restovich FS .60 .18
109 Victor Martinez FS 1.00 .30
110 Lyle Overbay FS .60 .18
111 Brian Stokes TM RC 4.00 1.20
112 Josh Hall TM RC 5.00 1.50
113 Chris Waters TM RC 4.00 1.20
114 Lew Ford TM RC 5.00 1.50
115 Ian Ferguson TM RC 4.00 1.20
116 Josh Willingham TM RC 5.00 1.50
117 Josh Stewart TM RC 4.00 1.20
118 Pete LaForest TM RC 5.00 1.50
119 Jose Contreras TM RC 5.00 1.50
120 Terrmel Sledge TM RC 5.00 1.50
121 Guillermo Quiroz TM RC 5.00 1.50
122 Alejandro Machado TM RC 4.00 1.20
123 Nook Logan TM RC 4.00 1.20
124 Rontrez Johnson TM RC 4.00 1.20
125 Hideki Matsui TM RC 10.00 3.00
126 Phil Rizzuto HT 5.00 1.50
127 Robin Ventura HT 5.00 1.50
128 Andy Pettitte HT 5.00 1.50
129 Mike Mussina HT 5.00 1.50
130 Mariano Rivera HT 5.00 1.50

131 Jeff Weaver HT 4.00 1.20
132 David Wells HT 4.00 1.20
133 Tommy Lasorda HT............. 8.00 2.40
134 Pee Wee Reese HT........... 10.00 3.00
135 Hideo Nomo HT 15.00 4.50
136 Adrian Beltre HT 10.00 3.00
137 Chin-Feng Chen HT............. 8.00 2.40
138 Odalis Perez HT 8.00 2.40
139 Dave Roberts HT.................. 8.00 2.40
140 Bobby Doerr HT.................... 5.00 1.50
141 Jason Varitek HT.................. 8.00 2.40
142 Trot Nixon HT....................... 5.00 1.50
143 Tim Wakefield HT................. 5.00 1.50
144 John Burkett HT.................. 5.00 1.50
145 Jeremy Giambi HT 5.00 1.50
146 Casey Fossum HT 5.00 1.50
147 Phil Niekro HT...................... 5.00 1.50
148 Warren Spahn HT 8.00 2.40
149 Rafael Furcal HT.................. 5.00 1.50
150 Vinny Castilla HT................. 5.00 1.50
151 Javy Lopez HT 5.00 1.50
152 Jason Marquis HT................ 5.00 1.50
153 Mike Hampton HT................ 5.00 1.50
154 Gaylord Perry HT 8.00 2.40
155 Ruben Sierra HT 8.00 2.40
156 Mike Cameron HT 8.00 2.40
157 Freddy Garcia HT 8.00 2.40
158 Joel Pineiro HT 8.00 2.40
159 Jamie Moyer HT.................... 8.00 2.40
160 Carlos Guillen HT................. 8.00 2.40
161 Chien-Ming Wang TM RC.... 5.00 1.50
162 Rickie Weeks TM RC........... 8.00 2.40
163 Brandon Webb TM RC......... 5.00 1.50
164 Craig Brazell TM RC............ 5.00 1.50
165 Michael Hessman TM RC..... 4.00 1.20
166 Ryan Wagner TM RC 5.00 1.50
167 Matt Kata TM RC 5.00 1.50
168 Edwin Jackson TM RC......... 8.00 2.40
169 Mike Ryan TM RC................ 5.00 1.50
170 Delmon Young TM RC 10.00 3.00
171 Bo Hart TM RC..................... 5.00 1.50
172 Jeff Duncan TM RC.............. 5.00 1.50
173 Robby Hammock TM RC 5.00 1.50
174 Jeremy Bonderman TM RC.. 5.00 1.50
175 Clint Barmes TM RC 5.00 1.50

2003 Fleer Authentix Balcony

Randomly inserted in packs, this is a parallel of the first 125 cards in the Fleer Authentix set. These cards were issued to a stated print run of 250 serial numbered sets.

Nm-Mt Ex-Mt
*BALCONY 1-100: 2X TO 5X BASIC ...
*BALCONY 101-110: 2X TO 5X BASIC
*BALCONY 111-125: .5X TO 1.2X BASIC

2003 Fleer Authentix Club Box

Randomly inserted into packs, this set parallels the first 125 cards of the Fleer Authentix set. These cards were issued to a stated print run of 100 serial numbered sets.

Nm-Mt Ex-Mt
*CLUB BOX 1-100: 4X TO 10X BASIC
*CLUB BOX 101-110: 4X TO 10X BASIC
*CLUB BOX 111-125: .6X TO 1.5X BASIC

2003 Fleer Authentix Autograph Front Row

Randomly inserted into packs, these cards feature authentic autographs of the two featured players. These cards were issued to a stated print run of 50 serial numbered sets.

Nm-Mt Ex-Mt
BB Barry Bonds 250.00 75.00
DJ Derek Jeter 200.00 60.00

2003 Fleer Authentix Autograph Second Row

Randomly inserted in packs, this card features Yankee superstar Derek Jeter. This card was issued to a stated print run of 150 serial numbered sets.

Nm-Mt Ex-Mt
DJ Derek Jeter 150.00 45.00

2003 Fleer Authentix Autograph Third Row

Randomly inserted into packs, these two cards feature authentic autographs. Each of these cards was issued to a stated print run of 250 serial numbered sets.

Nm-Mt Ex-Mt
BB Barry Bonds 250.00 75.00
DJ Derek Jeter 120.00 36.00

2003 Fleer Authentix Ballpark Classics

Issued at a stated rate of one in 12 hobby packs and one in 18 retail packs, these 10 cards feature some of the leading players in baseball.

Nm-Mt Ex-Mt
COMPLETE SET (10)................. 25.00 7.50
1 Derek Jeter............................ 6.00 1.80
2 Randy Johnson........................ 2.00 .60
3 Nomar Garciaparra.................. 4.00 1.20
4 Barry Bonds............................ 6.00 1.80
5 Alfonso Soriano .... 2.00 .60
6 Alex Rodriguez........................ 4.00 1.20
7 Jim Thome............................... 2.00 .60
8 Chipper Jones......................... 2.00 .60
9 Mike Piazza 4.00 1.20
10 Ichiro Suzuki......................... 4.00 1.20

2003 Fleer Authentix Game Bat

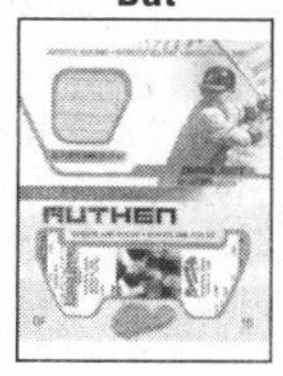

Inserted at a stated rate of one in 78 hobby packs and one in 202 retail packs, these nine cards feature a game-use bat piece. The Jason Giambi card was issued in shorter quantities and we have notated that card as an SP in our checklist.

Nm-Mt Ex-Mt
*UNRIPPED: .75X TO 2X BASIC GAME BAT
UNRIPPED RANDOM INSERTS IN PACKS
UNRIPPED PRINT RUN 50 SERIAL #'d SETS
AD Adam Dunn 10.00 3.00
CJ Chipper Jones..................... 10.00 3.00
DJ Derek Jeter 25.00 7.50
JG Jason Giambi SP 8.00 2.40
JT Jim Thome........................... 10.00 3.00
MR Manny Ramirez 10.00 3.00
NG Nomar Garciaparra............. 15.00 4.50
SS Sammy Sosa 15.00 4.50
VG Vladimir Guerrero............... 10.00 3.00

2003 Fleer Authentix Game Jersey

Issued at a stated rate of one in 10 hobby packs and one in 41 retail packs, these 24 cards feature game-used jersey pieces. The Derek Jeter and Randy Johnson cards were issued in shorter quantity and we have notated those cards with an SP in our checklist.

Nm-Mt Ex-Mt
*UNRIPPED: .75X TO 2X BASIC GAME JSY
UNRIPPED RANDOM INSERTS IN PACKS
UNRIPPED PRINT RUN 50 SERIAL #'d SETS
AD Adam Dunn 10.00 3.00
AR Alex Rodriguez 15.00 4.50
AS Alfonso Soriano.................. 10.00 3.00
CD Carlos Delgado.................... 8.00 2.40
CJ Chipper Jones..................... 10.00 3.00
DJ Derek Jeter SP.................... 30.00 9.00
EH Eric Hinske 8.00 2.40
GM Greg Maddux..................... 10.00 3.00
JB Jeff Bagwell 10.00 3.00
JB2 Josh Beckett 8.00 2.40
KW Kerry Wood 10.00 3.00
LB Lance Berkman..................... 8.00 2.40
MB Mark Buehrle 8.00 2.40
MP Mike Piazza........................ 10.00 3.00
MR Manny Ramirez 10.00 3.00
MT Miguel Tejada....................... 8.00 2.40
NG Nomar Garciaparra............. 15.00 4.50
PB Pat Burrell 8.00 2.40
RC Roger Clemens.................... 15.00 4.50
RJ Randy Johnson SP 10.00 3.00
SB Sean Burroughs.................... 8.00 2.40
SS Sammy Sosa 15.00 4.50
TH Torii Hunter........................... 8.00 2.40
VG Vladimir Guerrero............... 10.00 3.00

2003 Fleer Authentix Game Jersey All-Star

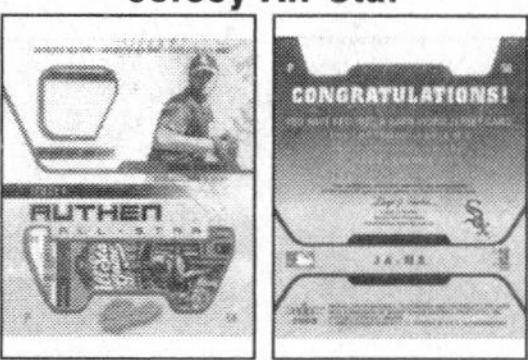

Randomly inserted in packs, these cards feature special "all-star" versions of the game jersey set. These cards are issued to varying print runs and we have notated that information next to the player's name in our checklist. Please note that for cards with a print run of 25 or fewer copies, no pricing is provided due to market scarcity.

Nm-Mt Ex-Mt
AD Adam Dunn/91 .... 25.00 7.50
AR Alex Rodriguez/111 .... 40.00 12.00
AS Alfonso Soriano/21...........................
CJ Chipper Jones/14...............................
DJ Derek Jeter/81 .... 60.00 18.00
LB Lance Berkman/103............. 15.00 4.50
MB Mark Buehrle/88 .... 15.00 4.50
MP Mike Piazza/109.................. 30.00 9.00
MR Manny Ramirez/78 .... 25.00 7.50
MT Miguel Tejada/52................. 30.00 9.00
NG Nomar Garciaparra/53......... 60.00 18.00
SS Sammy Sosa/8 ....
TH Torii Hunter/64 .... 30.00 9.00
VG Vladimir Guerrero/66........... 40.00 12.00

2003 Fleer Authentix Game Jersey Autograph Front Row

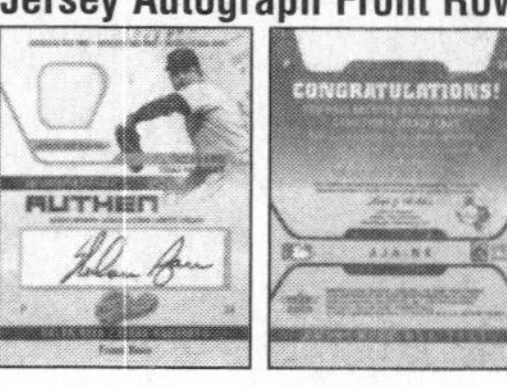

Randomly inserted into packs, these cards feature not only a game-used jersey swatch but also an authentic autograph of the featured player. These cards were issued to a stated print run of 100 serial numbered sets.

Nm-Mt Ex-Mt
DJ Derek Jeter 150.00 45.00
NR Nolan Ryan 150.00 45.00

2003 Fleer Authentix Game Jersey Autograph Second Row

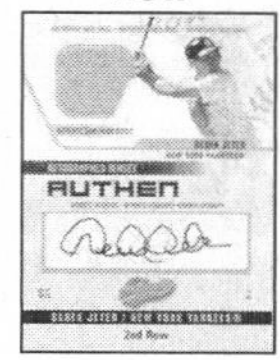

Randomly inserted into packs, these cards feature not only a game-used jersey swatch but also an authentic autograph of the featured player. These cards were issued to a stated print run of 200 serial numbered sets.

Nm-Mt Ex-Mt
DJ Derek Jeter 150.00 45.00
NR Nolan Ryan 150.00 45.00

2003 Fleer Authentix Game Jersey Autograph Third Row

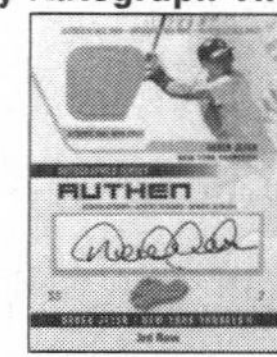

Randomly inserted into packs, this card features not only a game-used jersey swatch but also an authentic autograph of the featured player. This card was issued to a stated print run of 300 serial numbered sets.

Nm-Mt Ex-Mt
DJ Derek Jeter 120.00 36.00

2003 Fleer Authentix Game Jersey Game of the Week

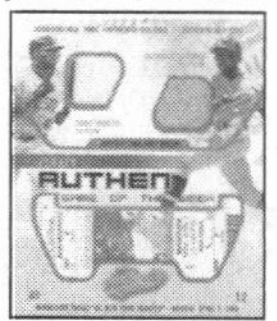

Inserted at a stated rate of one in 240 hobby packs and one in 420 retail packs, these 10 cards feature two players. These cards were issued in either group A or group B and the cards in the Group A are twice as scarce as the Group B cards. We have notated next to the card which group these cards belonged to.

Nm-Mt Ex-Mt
*UNRIPPED: 1X TO 2.5X BASIC GAME A
*UNRIPPED: .75X TO 2X BASIC GAME B
UNRIPPED RANDOM INSERTS IN PACKS
UNRIPPED PRINT RUN 50 SERIAL #'d SETS
AD-LB Adam Dunn.................... 15.00 4.50
Lance Berkman A
AR-MT Alex Rodriguez............. 30.00 9.00
Miguel Tejada A
AS-SS Alfonso Soriano 30.00 9.00
Sammy Sosa A
CJ-PB Chipper Jones............... 25.00 7.50
Pat Burrell B
DJ-MT Derek Jeter................... 40.00 12.00
Miguel Tejada A
DJ-NG Derek Jeter................... 60.00 18.00
Nomar Garciaparra A
EH-TH Eric Hinske.................... 15.00 4.50
Torii Hunter A
GM-RJ Greg Maddux 30.00 9.00
Randy Johnson B
MP-SS Mike Piazza 40.00 12.00
Sammy Sosa A
TH-AS Torii Hunter................... 15.00 4.50
Alfonso Soriano A

2003 Fleer Authentix Hometown Heroes Memorabilia

Inserted at a stated rate of one per home town hero packs, these 20 cards feature a game-used

piece from players from the most popular franchises in the game. A few cards were announced to have a stated print run of 300 or fewer cards and we have notated that information next to the player's name in our checklist.

Nm-Mt Ex-Mt
I Ichiro Suzuki Base SP/100 ..... 40.00 12.00
AJ Andruw Jones Jsy SP/150.............
AS Alfonso Soriano Jsy 15.00 4.50
BB Bret Boone Jsy SP/200 .... 15.00 4.50
CC Chin-Feng Chen Jsy SP/150 50.00 15.00
CJ Chipper Jones Jsy.........................
DJ Derek Jeter Jsy................... 40.00 12.00
EM Edgar Martinez Jsy SP/200. 25.00 7.50
FG Freddy Garcia Jsy SP/200.............
GM Greg Maddux Jsy ....
GS Gary Sheffield Jsy SP/100 .. 15.00 4.50
JD Johnny Damon Jsy SP/100 ....
JG Jason Giambi Bat SP/300.... 15.00 4.50
KB Kevin Brown Jsy SP/150..... 15.00 4.50
KI Kazuhisa Ishii Jsy SP/100 .... 15.00 4.50
MR Manny Ramirez Jsy............ 15.00 4.50
NG Nomar Garciaparra Jsy 40.00 12.00
PM Pedro Martinez Jsy SP/100 25.00 7.50
RC Roger Clemens Jsy 25.00 7.50
SG Shawn Green Jsy SP/100.... 15.00 4.50

2003 Fleer Authentix Ticket Studs

Issued at a stated rate of one in six packs, these 15 cards feature cards which look like tickets and feature some of the leading superstars in baseball.

Nm-Mt Ex-Mt
COMPLETE SET (15)................ 25.00 7.50
1 Curt Schilling .... 2.00 .60
2 Greg Maddux 4.00 1.20
3 Torii Hunter.............................. 2.00 .60
4 Mike Piazza 4.00 1.20
5 Pedro Martinez......................... 2.00 .60
6 Nomar Garciaparra.................. 4.00 1.20
7 Derek Jeter............................... 6.00 1.80
8 Alex Rodriguez......................... 4.00 1.20
9 Alfonso Soriano .... 2.00 .60
10 Pat Burrell.............................. 2.00 .60
11 Barry Bonds 6.00 1.80
12 Jason Giambi .... 2.00 .60
13 Sammy Sosa........................... 4.00 1.20
14 Vladimir Guerrero .... 2.00 .60
15 Ichiro Suzuki 4.00 1.20

2004 Fleer Authentix

This 140-card set was released in March, 2004. The set was issued in both hobby and retail format. The hobby version was issued in five-card packs with an $4 SRP which came 24 packs to a box and six boxes to a case. The retail packs were also issued in five-card packs with an $2 SRP and those packs came 24 packs to a box and six boxes to a case. In the hobby version it is important to note that one of every six boxes in an sealed case is an "Yankee" home team box. The Yankee cards are cards numbered 131 through 140 and were issued four per yankees home team pack. Those cards were issued to a stated print run of approximately 800 sets. In addition cards 101 through 130 feature leading prospect which were issued at a stated rate of one in 11 hobby packs and one in 34 retail packs. Each of those cards were issued to a stated print run of 999 serial numbered sets.

Nm-Mt Ex-Mt
COMP.SET w/o SP's (100)........ 25.00 7.50
COMMON CARD (1-100) .... .40 .12
COMMON CARD (101-130) .... 3.00 .90
COMMON CARD (131-140) 5.00 1.50
1 Albert Pujols .... 2.00 .60
2 Derek Jeter.............................. 2.00 .60
3 Jody Gerut .... .40 .12
4 Mark Teixeira............................. .40 .12
5 Tom Glavine .... .60 .18
6 Kerry Wood.............................. 1.00 .30
7 Ichiro Suzuki .... 1.50 .45
8 Jose Vidro.................................... .40 .12
9 Mark Prior................................ 1.00 .30
10 Jim Edmonds............................ .40 .12
11 Richie Sexson .... .40 .12
12 Jay Gibbons .... .40 .12
13 Jason Kendall........................... .40 .12
14 Lance Berkman .... .40 .12
15 Andruw Jones........................... .40 .12
16 Jim Thome.............................. 1.00 .30
17 Josh Beckett .... .40 .12
18 Troy Glaus................................. .40 .12
19 Jason Giambi .... .40 .12
20 Sammy Sosa........................... 1.50 .45
21 Bret Boone .... .40 .12
22 Eric Gagne .... 1.00 .30
23 Nomar Garciaparra................. 1.50 .45
24 Geoff Jenkins .... .40 .12
25 Ivan Rodriguez........................ 1.00 .30
26 Preston Wilson .... .40 .12
27 Alex Rodriguez........................ 1.50 .45
28 Jorge Posada .... .60 .18
29 Ken Griffey Jr. .... 1.50 .45
30 Rocco Baldelli .... .40 .12
31 Shannon Stewart .... .40 .12
32 Frank Thomas .... 1.00 .30
33 Edgar Renteria .... .40 .12
34 Torii Hunter .... .40 .12
35 Corey Patterson .... .40 .12
36 Edgar Martinez........................... .60 .18
37 Jeff Bagwell .... .60 .18
38 Greg Maddux .... 1.50 .45
39 Mike Lieberthal .... .40 .12
40 Craig Biggio .... .60 .18
41 Randy Johnson........................ 1.00 .30
42 Marlon Byrd................................ .40 .12
43 Jay Payton .... .40 .12
44 Carlos Delgado........................... .40 .12
45 Scott Podsednik.......................... .40 .12
46 Pedro Martinez......................... 1.00 .30
47 Carlos Beltran .... .60 .18
48 Mike Sweeney............................ .40 .12
49 Gary Sheffield .... .40 .12
50 Pat Burrell.................................. .40 .12
51 Shawn Green .... .40 .12
52 Tony Batista .... .40 .12
53 Brian Giles .... .40 .12
54 Roy Oswalt................................. .40 .12
55 Brandon Webb .... .40 .12
56 Miguel Tejada .... .40 .12
57 Miguel Cabrera........................... .60 .18
58 Luis Gonzalez............................. .40 .12
59 Billy Wagner............................... .40 .12
60 Craig Monroe .... .40 .12
61 Vernon Wells.............................. .40 .12
62 Bernie Williams.......................... .60 .18
63 Austin Kearns............................. .40 .12
64 Aubrey Huff................................ .40 .12
65 Mike Piazza .... 1.50 .45
66 Magglio Ordonez........................ .40 .12
67 Bo Hart....................................... .40 .12
68 Hideo Nomo .... 1.00 .30
69 Curt Schilling .... 1.00 .30
70 Barry Zito .... .40 .12
71 Todd Helton .... .60 .18
72 Roy Halladay.............................. .40 .12
73 Alfonso Soriano .... .60 .18
74 Roberto Alomar .... .60 .18
75 Scott Rolen .... 1.00 .30
76 Manny Ramirez.......................... .60 .18
77 Sean Burroughs .... .40 .12
78 Angel Berroa .... .40 .12
79 Javy Lopez................................. .40 .12
80 Reggie Sanders.......................... .40 .12
81 Juan Pierre................................. .40 .12
82 Chipper Jones .... 1.00 .30
83 Bobby Abreu .... .40 .12
84 Dontrelle Willis........................... .40 .12
85 Tim Salmon .... .60 .18
86 Eric Chavez .... .60 .18
87 Adam Dunn .... .60 .18
88 Rafael Palmeiro.......................... .60 .18
89 Hideki Matsui .... 1.50 .45
90 Esteban Loaiza .... .40 .12
91 Darin Erstad .... .40 .12
92 Vladimir Guerrero .... 1.00 .30
93 David Ortiz .... 1.00 .30
94 Jason Schmidt............................ .40 .12
95 Dmitri Young............................... .40 .12
96 Garret Anderson......................... .40 .12
97 Mark Mulder .... .40 .12
98 Omar Vizquel .... .60 .18
99 Hank Blalock .... .40 .12
100 Jose Reyes................................ .40 .12
101 Rickie Weeks TM .... 3.00 .90
102 Chad Gaudin TM .... 3.00 .90
103 Ryan Wagner TM .... 3.00 .90
104 Koyie Hill TM .... 3.00 .90
105 Rich Harden TM..................... 3.00 .90
106 Edwin Jackson TM................. 3.00 .90
107 Khalil Greene TM 5.00 1.50
108 Chien-Ming Wang TM .... 3.00 .90
109 Matt Kata TM .... 3.00 .90
110 Chin-Hui Tsao TM .... 3.00 .90
111 Dan Haren TM........................ 3.00 .90
112 Delmon Young TM................. 5.00 1.50
113 Mike Hessman TM................. 3.00 .90
114 Bobby Crosby TM 5.00 1.50
115 Cory Sullivan TM RC............. 3.00 .90
116 Brandon Watson TM .... 3.00 .90
117 Aaron Miles TM .... 3.00 .90
118 Jonny Gomes TM................... 3.00 .90
119 Graham Koonce TM .... 3.00 .90
120 Shawn Hill TM RC.................. 3.00 .90
121 Garrett Atkins TM.................. 3.00 .90
122 John Gall TM RC.................... 5.00 1.50
123 Chad Bentz TM RC................ 3.00 .90
124 Alfredo Simon TM RC .... 3.00 .90
125 Josh Labandeira TM RC........ 3.00 .90
126 Ryan Howard TM .... 3.00 .90
127 Jason Bartlett TM RC............ 5.00 1.50
128 Dallas McPherson TM........... 5.00 1.50
129 Greg Dobbs TM RC............... 3.00 .90
130 Jerry Gil TM RC .... 3.00 .90
131 Aaron Boone EXT.................. 5.00 1.50
132 Javier Vazquez EXT.............. 5.00 1.50
133 Mariano Rivera EXT 8.00 2.40
134 Kevin Brown EXT 5.00 1.50
135 Mike Mussina EXT 8.00 2.40
136 Ruben Sierra EXT.................. 5.00 1.50
137 Enrique Wilson EXT 5.00 1.50
138 Erick Almonte EXT 5.00 1.50
139 Jose Contreras EXT 5.00 1.50
140 Drew Henson EXT................. 5.00 1.50

2004 Fleer Authentix Balcony

Nm-Mt Ex-Mt
*BALCONY 1-100: 4X TO 10X BASIC
*BALCONY 101-130: .6X TO 1.5X BASIC
*BALCONY 101-130: .6X TO 1.5X BASIC RC
OVERALL PARALLEL ODDS 1:6 H, 1:48 R
STATED PRINT RUN 100 SERIAL #'d SETS

2004 Fleer Authentix Club Box

Nm-Mt Ex-Mt
OVERALL PARALLEL ODDS 1:6 H, 1:48 R
STATED PRINT RUN 25 SERIAL #'d SETS
NO PRICING DUE TO SCARCITY

2004 Fleer Authentix Standing Room Only

Nm-Mt Ex-Mt
OVERALL PARALLEL ODDS 1:6 H, 1:48 R
STATED PRINT RUN 5 SERIAL #'d SETS
NO PRICING DUE TO SCARCITY

2004 Fleer Authentix Ticket to the Majors Autograph Boosters

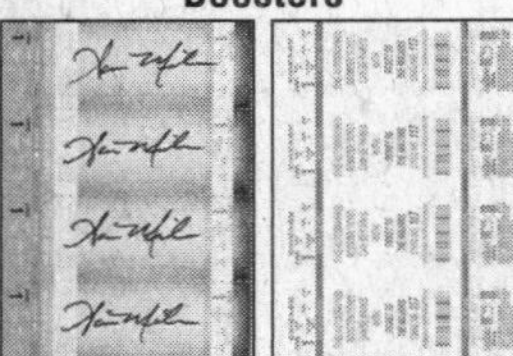

This very innovative idea was included in Authentix packs at stated rates of one in 200 hobby and one in 1560 retail packs. Each of these "non-torn" cards have four autographs on a "ticket" which the lucky collector who pulled these cards could then replace the regular card with an autograph instead of the standard ticket. A few players did not return their tickets in time for inclusion in the product and those cards could be redeemed immediately when the player's returned their tickets. In addition, there is no expiration date on those exchange cards.

Nm-Mt Ex-Mt
STATED ODDS 1:200 HOBBY, 1:1560 RETAIL
STATED PRINT RUN 50 SERIAL #'d SETS
LISTED PRICES ARE FOR NON-TORN CARDS
101 Rickie Weeks 60.00 18.00
103 Ryan Wagner 25.00 7.50
105 Rich Harden 40.00 12.00
106 Edwin Jackson 60.00 18.00
107 Khalil Greene 80.00 24.00
112 Delmon Young 80.00 24.00
114 Bobby Crosby EXCH 60.00 18.00
115 Cory Sullivan 25.00 7.50
117 Aaron Miles 40.00 12.00
118 Jonny Gomes 25.00 7.50
119 Graham Koonce 25.00 7.50
121 Garrett Atkins 25.00 7.50
122 John Gall 40.00 12.00
123 Chad Bentz 25.00 7.50
124 Alfredo Simon EXCH 25.00 7.50
125 John Labandeira 25.00 7.50
126 Ryan Howard 40.00 12.00
127 Jason Bartlett 40.00 12.00
128 Dallas McPherson 60.00 18.00
130 Jerry Gil EXCH 25.00 7.50

2004 Fleer Authentix Autograph All-Star

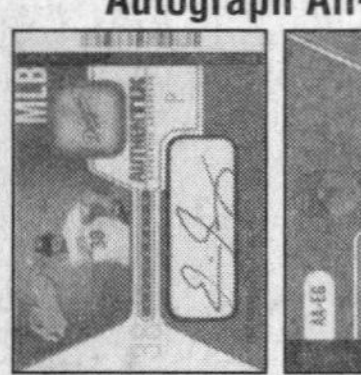

Nm-Mt Ex-Mt
STATED PRINT RUN 75 SERIAL #'d SETS
CHAMPIONSHIP PRINT RUN 25 #'d SETS
NO CHAMP.PRICING DUE TO SCARCITY
RANDOM INSERTS IN PACKS
EXCHANGE DEADLINE INDEFINITE
AB Angel Berroa EXCH 15.00 4.50
AP Albert Pujols 150.00 45.00
EG Eric Gagne 40.00 12.00
JP Juan Pierre 25.00 7.50
MB Marlon Byrd 15.00 4.50
MC Miguel Cabrera EXCH 40.00 12.00
RB Rocco Baldelli 25.00 7.50
RH Roy Halladay 15.00 4.50
TN Trot Nixon 25.00 7.50
VW Vernon Wells 25.00 7.50

2004 Fleer Authentix Ballpark Classics

Nm-Mt Ex-Mt
STATED ODDS 1:12 HOBBY, 1:18 RETAIL
1 Nomar Garciaparra 5.00 1.50
2 Alfonso Soriano 3.00 .90
3 Chipper Jones 3.00 .90
4 Albert Pujols 6.00 1.80
5 Jason Giambi 2.00 .60
6 Mark Prior 3.00 .90
7 Sammy Sosa 5.00 1.50
8 Derek Jeter 6.00 1.80
9 Greg Maddux 5.00 1.50
10 Alex Rodriguez 5.00 1.50

2004 Fleer Authentix Ballpark Classics Jersey

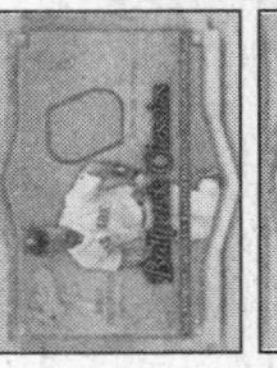

Nm-Mt Ex-Mt
STATED ODDS 1:37 HOBBY, 1:240 RETAIL
AP Albert Pujols 15.00 4.50
AR Alex Rodriguez 10.00 3.00
AS Alfonso Soriano 10.00 3.00
CJ Chipper Jones 10.00 3.00
DJ Derek Jeter 20.00 6.00
GM Greg Maddux 10.00 3.00
JG Jason Giambi 8.00 2.40
MP Mark Prior 10.00 3.00
NG Nomar Garciaparra 15.00 4.50
SS Sammy Sosa 15.00 4.50

2004 Fleer Authentix Game Jersey

Nm-Mt Ex-Mt
STATED ODDS 1:16 HOBBY, 1:71 RETAIL
*UNRIPPED: .6X TO 1.5X BASIC
UNRIPPED RANDOM INSERTS IN PACKS
UNRIPPED PRINT RUN 50 SERIAL #'d SETS
*GOLD p/r 51-89: .6X TO 1.5X BASIC
*GOLD p/r 38-44: .75X TO 2X BASIC
GOLD RANDOM INSERTS IN PACKS
GOLD PRINT B/WN 25-89 COPIES PER
NO GOLD PRICING ON QTY OF 25 OR LESS
GOLD UNRIPPED RANDOM IN HOBBY ONLY
GOLD UNRIPPED PRINT 1 SERIAL #'d SET
NO GOLD UNRIPPED PRICING AVAILABLE
AK Austin Kearns 8.00 2.40
AP Albert Pujols 15.00 4.50
AR Alex Rodriguez 10.00 3.00
AS Alfonso Soriano 10.00 3.00
BZ Barry Zito 8.00 2.40
CJ Chipper Jones 10.00 3.00
DJ Derek Jeter 20.00 6.00
DW Dontrelle Willis 8.00 2.40
GM Greg Maddux 10.00 3.00
HC Hee Seop Choi 8.00 2.40
IR Ivan Rodriguez 10.00 3.00
JB Josh Beckett 8.00 2.40
JB2 Jeff Bagwell 10.00 3.00
JG Jason Giambi 8.00 2.40
JP Juan Pierre 8.00 2.40
JR Jose Reyes 8.00 2.40
JT Jim Thome 10.00 3.00
KW Kerry Wood 10.00 3.00
MC Miguel Cabrera 10.00 3.00
MP Mark Prior 10.00 3.00
MT Mark Teixeira 8.00 2.40
NG Nomar Garciaparra 15.00 4.50
RJ Randy Johnson 10.00 3.00
SS Sammy Sosa 15.00 4.50
TH Torii Hunter 8.00 2.40

2004 Fleer Authentix Game Jersey Autograph Regular Season

Nm-Mt Ex-Mt
STATED PRINT RUN 100 SERIAL #'d SETS
*ALL-STAR: .5X TO 1.2X BASIC
ALL-STAR PRINT RUN 50 SERIAL #'d SETS
CHAMPIONSHIP PRINT 10 SERIAL #'d SETS
NO CHAMP.PRICING DUE TO SCARCITY
RANDOM INSERTS IN PACKS
EXCHANGE DEADLINE INDEFINITE
AB Angel Berroa EXCH 15.00 4.50
AP Albert Pujols 150.00 45.00
EG Eric Gagne 40.00 12.00
JP Juan Pierre 25.00 7.50
MB Marlon Byrd 15.00 4.50
MC Miguel Cabrera EXCH 40.00 12.00
RB Rocco Baldelli 25.00 7.50
RH Roy Halladay 15.00 4.50
TN Trot Nixon 25.00 7.50
VW Vernon Wells 25.00 7.50

2004 Fleer Authentix Game Jersey Dual

Nm-Mt Ex-Mt
STATED ODDS 1:120 HOBBY, 1:420 RETAIL
*UNRIPPED: .6X TO 1.5X BASIC
UNRIPPED RANDOM INSERTS IN PACKS
UNRIPPED PRINT RUN 50 SERIAL #'d SETS
ARDJ Alex Rodriguez 50.00 15.00
Derek Jeter
CJAP Chipper Jones 20.00 6.00
Albert Pujols
DWKW Dontrelle Willis 15.00 4.50
Kerry Wood
JBAK Jeff Bagwell 10.00 3.00
Austin Kearns
JBMP Josh Beckett 15.00 4.50
Mark Prior
JGBZ Jason Giambi 10.00 3.00
Barry Zito
JRJP Jose Reyes 10.00 3.00
Juan Pierre
JTIR Jim Thome 15.00 4.50
Ivan Rodriguez
MCMT Miguel Cabrera 15.00 4.50
Mark Teixeira
NGAS Nomar Garciaparra 15.00 4.50
Alfonso Soriano

2004 Fleer Authentix Ticket for Four

Nm-Mt Ex-Mt
RANDOM INSERTS IN PACKS
STATED PRINT RUN 100 SERIAL #'d SETS
GJBH Jason Giambi 25.00 7.50
Randy Johnson
Jeff Bagwell
Torii Hunter
GRJR Nomar Garciaparra 60.00 18.00
Alex Rodriguez
Derek Jeter
Jose Reyes
GSJP Nomar Garciaparra 40.00 12.00
Alfonso Soriano
Chipper Jones
Albert Pujols
GTTB Jason Giambi 25.00 7.50
Jim Thome
Mark Teixeira
Jeff Bagwell
JPSH Chipper Jones 40.00 12.00
Albert Pujols
Sammy Sosa
Torii Hunter
MJWZ Greg Maddux 30.00 9.00
Randy Johnson
Kerry Wood
Barry Zito
PMKR Mark Prior 30.00 9.00
Greg Maddux
Austin Kearns
Ivan Rodriguez
RCCP Ivan Rodriguez 25.00 7.50
Miguel Cabrera
Hee Seop Choi
Juan Pierre
SJRT Sammy Sosa 50.00 15.00
Derek Jeter
Alex Rodriguez
Jim Thome
WBPW Dontrelle Willis 25.00 7.50
Josh Beckett
Mark Prior
Kerry Wood

2004 Fleer Authentix Ticket Studs

Nm-Mt Ex-Mt
STATED ODDS 1:6 HOBBY, 1:8 RETAIL
1 Nomar Garciaparra 4.00 1.20
2 Josh Beckett 1.50 .45
3 Derek Jeter 5.00 1.50
4 Mark Prior 2.50 .75
5 Albert Pujols 5.00 1.50
6 Alfonso Soriano 2.50 .75
7 Jim Thome 2.50 .75
8 Ichiro Suzuki 4.00 1.20
9 Hideki Matsui 4.00 1.20
10 Dontrelle Willis 1.50 .45
11 Mike Schmidt 6.00 1.80
12 Nolan Ryan 8.00 2.40
13 Reggie Jackson 3.00 .90
14 Tom Seaver 3.00 .90
15 Brooks Robinson 3.00 .90

2004 Fleer Authentix Yankees Game Used Unripped

Nm-Mt Ex-Mt
ONE GU YANKS CARD PER YANKS HT PACK
*UNRIPPED 50: X TO X BASIC
UNRIPPED 50 RANDOM IN YANKS HOME TM
UNRIPPED 50 PRINT 50 SERIAL #'d SETS
DJ Derek Jeter Jsy 20.00 6.00
DM Don Mattingly Jsy 25.00 7.50
PR Phil Rizzuto Pants 15.00 4.50
RJ Reggie Jackson Jsy 15.00 4.50

2004 Fleer Authentix Yankees Game Used Dual Unripped

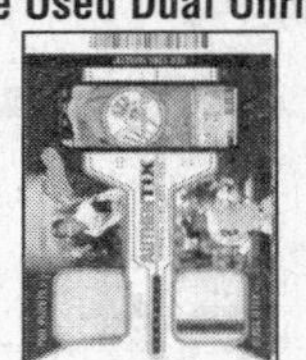

Nm-Mt Ex-Mt
ONE GU YANKS CARD PER YANKS HT PACK
STATED PRINT RUN 25 SERIAL #'d SETS
NO PRICING DUE TO SCARCITY
DMRJ Don Mattingly Jsy
Reggie Jackson Jsy
PRDJ Phil Rizzuto Pants
Derek Jeter Jsy

2001 Fleer Authority

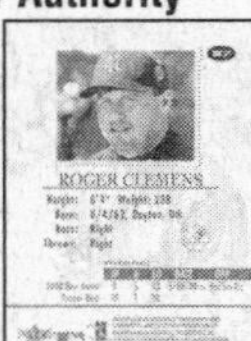

This product was released in late December 2001, and featured a 150-card base set that was broken into tiers as follows: 100 Base Veterans, and 50 Prospects (serial numbered to 2001). Each pack contained five cards.

Nm-Mt Ex-Mt
COMP.SET w/o SP's (100) 25.00 7.50
COMMON CARD (1-100) .40 .12
COMMON (101-150) 5.00 1.50
JETER MM'S RANDOM INSERTS IN PACKS
JETER 93 AU RANDOM INSERT IN PACKS
1 Mark Grace .60 .18
2 Paul Konerko .40 .12
3 Sean Casey .40 .12
4 Jim Thome 1.00 .30
5 Todd Helton .60 .18
6 Tony Clark .40 .12
7 Jeff Bagwell .60 .18
8 Mike Sweeney .40 .12
9 Eric Karros .40 .12
10 Richie Sexson .40 .12
11 Doug Mientkiewicz .40 .12
12 Ryan Klesko .40 .12
13 John Olerud .40 .12
14 Mark McGwire 2.50 .75
15 Fred McGriff .60 .18
16 Rafael Palmeiro .60 .18
17 Carlos Delgado .40 .12
18 Roberto Alomar .60 .18
19 Craig Biggio .60 .18
20 Jose Vidro .40 .12
21 Edgardo Alfonzo .40 .12
22 Jeff Kent .40 .12
23 Bret Boone .40 .12
24 Rafael Furcal .40 .12
25 Nomar Garciaparra 1.50 .45
26 Barry Larkin .60 .18
27 Cristian Guzman .40 .12
28 Derek Jeter 2.50 .75
29 Miguel Tejada .40 .12
30 Jimmy Rollins .40 .12
31 Rich Aurilia .40 .12
32 Alex Rodriguez 1.50 .45
33 Cal Ripken 3.00 .90
34 Troy Glaus .40 .12
35 Matt Williams .40 .12
36 Chipper Jones 1.00 .30
37 Jeff Cirillo .40 .12
38 Robin Ventura .40 .12
39 Eric Chavez .40 .12
40 Scott Rolen 1.00 .30
41 Phil Nevin .40 .12
42 Mike Piazza 1.50 .45
43 Jorge Posada .60 .18
44 Jason Kendall .40 .12
45 Ivan Rodriguez 1.00 .30
46 Frank Thomas 1.00 .30
47 Edgar Martinez .60 .18
48 Darin Erstad .40 .12
49 Tim Salmon .60 .18
50 Luis Gonzalez .40 .12
51 Andruw Jones .40 .12
52 Carl Everett .40 .12
53 Manny Ramirez .60 .18
54 Sammy Sosa 1.50 .45
55 Rondell White .40 .12
56 Magglio Ordonez .40 .12
57 Ken Griffey Jr. 1.50 .45
58 Juan Gonzalez .60 .18
59 Larry Walker .60 .18
60 Bobby Higginson .40 .12
61 Cliff Floyd .40 .12
62 Preston Wilson .40 .12
63 Moises Alou .40 .12
64 Lance Berkman .40 .12
65 Richard Hidalgo .40 .12
66 Jermaine Dye .40 .12
67 Mark Quinn .40 .12
68 Shawn Green .40 .12
69 Gary Sheffield .40 .12
70 Jeromy Burnitz .40 .12
71 Geoff Jenkins .40 .12
72 Vladimir Guerrero 1.00 .30
73 Bernie Williams .60 .18
74 Johnny Damon .60 .18
75 Jason Giambi .40 .12
76 Bobby Abreu .40 .12
77 Pat Burrell .40 .12
78 Brian Giles .40 .12
79 Tony Gwynn 1.25 .35
80 Barry Bonds 2.50 .75
81 J.D. Drew .40 .12
82 Jim Edmonds .40 .12
83 Greg Vaughn .40 .12
84 Raul Mondesi .40 .12
85 Shannon Stewart .40 .12
86 Randy Johnson 1.00 .30
87 Curt Schilling .40 .12
88 Tom Glavine .60 .18
89 Greg Maddux 1.50 .45
90 Pedro Martinez 1.00 .30
91 Kerry Wood 1.00 .30
92 David Wells .40 .12
93 Bartolo Colon .40 .12
94 Mike Hampton .40 .12
95 Kevin Brown .40 .12
96 Al Leiter .40 .12
97 Roger Clemens 2.00 .60
98 Mike Mussina .60 .18
99 Tim Hudson .40 .12
100 Kazuhiro Sasaki .40 .12
101 Ichiro Suzuki RC 40.00 12.00
102 Albert Pujols RC 60.00 18.00
103 Drew Henson RC 6.00 1.80
104 Adam Pettyjohn RC 5.00 1.50
105 Adrian Hernandez RC 5.00 1.50
106 Andy Morales RC 5.00 1.50
107 Tsuyoshi Shinjo RC 6.00 1.80
108 Juan Uribe RC 6.00 1.80
109 Jack Wilson RC 8.00 2.40
110 Jason Smith RC 5.00 1.50
111 Junior Spivey RC 6.00 1.80
112 Wilson Betemit RC 5.00 1.50
113 Elpidio Guzman RC 5.00 1.50
114 Esix Snead RC 5.00 1.50
115 Winston Abreu RC 5.00 1.50
116 Jeremy Owens RC 5.00 1.50
117 Jay Gibbons RC 6.00 1.80
118 Luis Lopez 5.00 1.50
119 Ryan Freel RC 5.00 1.50
120 Rafael Soriano RC 6.00 1.80
121 Johnny Estrada RC 6.00 1.80
122 Bud Smith RC 5.00 1.50
123 Jackson Melian RC 5.00 1.50
124 Matt White RC 5.00 1.50
125 Travis Hafner RC 10.00 3.00
126 Morgan Ensberg RC 6.00 1.80
127 Endy Chavez RC 5.00 1.50
128 Brett Prinz RC 5.00 1.50
129 Juan Diaz RC 5.00 1.50
130 Erick Almonte RC 5.00 1.50
131 Rob Mackowiak RC 6.00 1.80
132 Carlos Valderrama RC 5.00 1.50
133 Wilkin Ruan RC 5.00 1.50
134 Angel Berroa RC 6.00 1.80
135 Henry Mateo RC 5.00 1.50
136 Bill Ortega RC 5.00 1.50
137 Billy Sylvester RC 5.00 1.50
138 Andres Torres RC 5.00 1.50
139 Nate Frese RC 5.00 1.50
140 Casey Fossum RC 5.00 1.50
141 Ricardo Rodriguez RC 5.00 1.50
142 Brian Roberts RC 5.00 1.50
143 Carlos Garcia RC 5.00 1.50
144 Brian Lawrence RC 5.00 1.50
145 Cory Aldridge RC 5.00 1.50
146 Mark Teixeira RC 20.00 6.00
147 Juan Cruz RC 5.00 1.50
148 B. Duckworth RC 5.00 1.50
149 Dewon Brazelton RC 6.00 1.80
150 Mark Prior RC 40.00 12.00
MM4 Derek Jeter 15.00 4.50
MM/2000
MM4AU Derek Jeter 150.00 45.00
MM AU/100
NNO Derek Jeter 175.00 52.50
93 AU/500

2001 Fleer Authority Prominence 125/75

This 150-card insert is actually a parallel of the 2001 Fleer Authority base set. The set is broken into tiers as follows: 100 Base Veterans (numbered to 125), and 50 Prospects (numbered to 75).

Nm-Mt Ex-Mt
COMMON CARD (101-100) 4.00 1.20
*STARS 1-100: 5X TO 12X BASIC
COMMON CARD (101-150) 8.00 2.40
*ROOKIES 101-150: 1.25X TO 3X BASIC

2001 Fleer Authority Diamond Cuts Memorabilia

This 111-card insert set features various swatches of game-used memorabilia including shoes, hats, bats and jerseys. Overall odds on these cards were 1:10 packs. Please note that Manny Ramirez had 100 red Batting Glove cards and 100 blue Batting Glove cards. Print runs listed below.

	Nm-Mt	Ex-Mt
1 Rick Ankiel Shoes/400	8.00	2.40
2 Jeff Bagwell Jsy/1000	10.00	3.00
3 Adrian Beltre Hat/240	15.00	4.50
4 Craig Biggio Bat/800	10.00	3.00
5 Barry Bonds Hat/240	40.00	12.00
6 Barry Bonds Jsy/1000	25.00	7.50
7 Barry Bonds Pants/800	25.00	7.50
8 Barry Bonds Shoes/400	25.00	7.50
9 B.Bonds Wristband/100	40.00	12.00
10 Kevin Brown Hat/240	10.00	3.00
11 Kevin Brown Pants/800	8.00	2.40
12 Eric Byrnes Bat/800	8.00	2.40
13 Sean Casey Jsy/1000	8.00	2.40
14 Eric Chavez Hat/240	10.00	3.00
15 Bartolo Colon Hat/240	10.00	3.00
16 Erubiel Durazo Bat/800	8.00	2.40
17 Ray Durham Bat/800	8.00	2.40
18 Jim Edmonds Hat/240	10.00	3.00
19 J.Edmonds Shoes/400	8.00	2.40
20 Darin Erstad Hat/240	10.00	3.00
21 Carlos Febles Bat/800	8.00	2.40
22 Carlos Febles Shoes/400	8.00	2.40
23 Rafael Furcal Hat/240	10.00	3.00
24 Brian Giles Pants/800	8.00	2.40
25 Juan Gonzalez Btg Glv/100	15.00	4.50
26 Juan Gonzalez Hat/240	15.00	4.50
27 Luis Gonzalez Hat/240	10.00	3.00
28 Shawn Green Bat/800	8.00	2.40
29 S.Green Btg Glv/100	10.00	3.00
30 V.Guerrero Bat/800	10.00	3.00
31 Tony Gwynn Bat/975	15.00	4.50
32 J.Hairston Jr. Hat/240	10.00	3.00
33 Mike Hampton Hat/240	10.00	3.00
34 M.Hampton Shoes/400	8.00	2.40
35 Jason Hart Bat/800	8.00	2.40
36 Todd Helton Jsy/1000	10.00	3.00
37 Todd Helton Pants/800	10.00	3.00
38 O.Hernandez Bat/800	8.00	2.40
39 R.Hidalgo Bat/800	8.00	2.40
40 R.Hidalgo Btg Glv/200	10.00	3.00
41 Derek Jeter Bat/800	25.00	7.50
42 D.Jeter Btg Glv/150	40.00	12.00
43 Derek Jeter Jsy/1000	25.00	7.50
44 Derek Jeter Pants/800	25.00	7.50
45 Derek Jeter Shoes/400	40.00	12.00
46 R.Johnson Hat/240	15.00	4.50
47 Chipper Jones Bat/800	10.00	3.00
48 C. Jones Jsy/1000	10.00	3.00
49 Andruw Jones Bat/800	8.00	2.40
50 Andruw Jones Hat/240	10.00	3.00
51 Jason Kendall Hat/240	10.00	3.00
52 Jason Kendall Base/250	10.00	3.00
53 Barry Larkin Base/250	15.00	4.50
54 Barry Larkin Jsy/1000	10.00	3.00
55 Matt Lawton Hat/240	10.00	3.00
56 M.Lieberthal Btg Glv/100	10.00	3.00
57 Mike Lieberthal Wristband/25		
58 Kenny Lofton Bat/800	8.00	2.40
59 E.Martinez Btg Glv/200	15.00	4.50
60 P.Martinez Shoes/400	10.00	3.00
61 Raul Mondesi Bat/800	8.00	2.40
62 R.Mondesi Btg Glv/100	10.00	3.00
63 Hideo Nomo Bat/800	10.00	3.00
64 Hideo Nomo Hat/240	25.00	7.50
65 Magglio Ordonez Base/250	10.00	3.00
66 M.Ordonez Btg Glv/200	10.00	3.00
67 M.Ordonez Hat/240	10.00	3.00
68 David Ortiz Base/250	15.00	4.50
69 David Ortiz Bat/800	10.00	3.00
70 R.Palmeiro Bat/800	10.00	3.00
71 R.Palmeiro Hat/240	15.00	4.50
72 R.Palmeiro Hat/240	15.00	4.50
73 Chan Ho Park Hat/240	10.00	3.00
74 Mike Piazza Bat/800	15.00	4.50
75 Mike Piazza Jsy/1000	15.00	4.50
76 Mike Piazza Shoes/400	15.00	4.50
77 Albert Pujols Pants/800	40.00	12.00
78 M.Ramirez Bat/800	10.00	3.00
79 M.Ramirez Btg Glv/200	15.00	4.50
80 M.Ramirez Hat/240	15.00	4.50
81 M.Ramirez Hat/240	15.00	4.50
82 Cal Ripken Btg Glv/100	60.00	18.00
83 Cal Ripken Pants/800	40.00	12.00
84 Ivan Rodriguez Base/250	15.00	4.50
85 I.Rodriguez Btg Glv/100	15.00	4.50
86 Ivan Rodriguez Hat/240	15.00	4.50
87 I.Rodriguez Pants/800	10.00	3.00
88 I.Rodriguez Shoes/400	10.00	3.00
89 Ivan Rodriguez Wristband/50		
90 Scott Rolen Base/250	15.00	4.50
91 Scott Rolen Hat/240	15.00	4.50
92 J.Sandberg Bat/800	8.00	2.40
93 D.Sanders Jsy/1000	10.00	3.00
94 Tsuy Shinjo Bat/800	10.00	3.00
95 T.Shinjo Wristband/150	15.00	4.50
96 J.T. Snow Bat/800	8.00	2.40
97 J.T. Snow Jsy/1000	8.00	2.40
98 A.Soriano Hat/240	15.00	4.50
99 Ichiro Suzuki Bat/350	50.00	15.00
100 Ichiro Suzuki Hat/240	60.00	18.00
101 M.Sweeney Hat/240	10.00	3.00
102 Mike Sweeney Wristband/25		
103 M.Tejada Hat/240	10.00	3.00
104 Frank Thomas Base/250	15.00	4.50
105 F.Thomas Bat/800	10.00	3.00
106 F.Thomas Hat/240	15.00	4.50
107 Jim Thome Bat/800	10.00	3.00
108 Jim Thome Wristband/50		
109 Larry Walker Bat/800	10.00	3.00
110 L.Walker Jsy/1000	10.00	3.00
111 B.Williams Bat/800	10.00	3.00

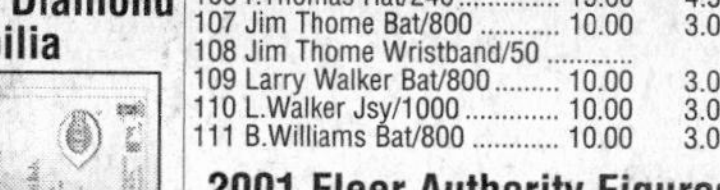

2001 Fleer Authority Figures

This 20-card insert pairs veteran players with comparable prospects. Each card is serial numbered to 1750.

	Nm-Mt	Ex-Mt
COMPLETE SET (20)	150.00	45.00
1 Mark McGwire Albert Pujols	25.00	7.50
2 Kazuhiro Sasaki Ichiro Suzuki	15.00	4.50
3 Derek Jeter Drew Henson	12.00	3.60
4 Ken Griffey Jr. Jackson Melian	10.00	3.00
5 Chipper Jones Wilson Betemit	6.00	1.80
6 Jeff Bagwell Morgan Ensberg	6.00	1.80
7 Cal Ripken Jay Gibbons	30.00	9.00
8 Mike Piazza Tsuyoshi Shinjo	8.00	2.40
9 Luis Gonzalez Junior Spivey	4.00	1.20
10 Barry Bonds Carlos Valderrama	15.00	4.50
11 Todd Helton Juan Uribe	4.00	1.20
12 Roger Clemens Adrian Hernandez	12.00	3.60
13 Alex Rodriguez Travis Hafner	10.00	3.00
14 Scott Rolen Johnny Estrada	6.00	1.80
15 Brian Giles Rob Mackowiak	4.00	1.20
16 Randy Johnson Bret Prinz	6.00	1.80
17 Carlos Delgado Luis Lopez	3.00	.90
18 Manny Ramirez Juan Diaz	4.00	1.20
19 Mike Sweeney Endy Chavez	3.00	.90
20 Sammy Sosa Jaisen Randolph	10.00	3.00

2001 Fleer Authority Seal of Approval

This 15-card insert features seasoned veterans that have received the "Seal of Approval" from fans across America. These cards were inserted into packs at a rate of 1:20.

	Nm-Mt	Ex-Mt
COMPLETE SET (15)	120.00	36.00
1 Derek Jeter	12.00	3.60
2 Alex Rodriguez	8.00	2.40
3 Nomar Garciaparra	8.00	2.40
4 Cal Ripken	15.00	4.50
5 Mike Piazza	8.00	2.40
6 Mark McGwire	12.00	3.60
7 Tony Gwynn	6.00	1.80
8 Barry Bonds	12.00	3.60
9 Greg Maddux	8.00	2.40
10 Chipper Jones	5.00	1.50
11 Roger Clemens	10.00	3.00
12 Ken Griffey Jr.	8.00	2.40
13 Vladimir Guerrero	5.00	1.50
14 Sammy Sosa	8.00	2.40
15 Todd Helton	5.00	1.50

2001 Fleer Genuine

The 2001 Fleer Genuine product was released in May, 2001 and featured a 130-card base set that was broken into tiers as follows: Base Veterans (1-100), and Rookies (100-130) featuring game-used materials and are serial numbered to 1500. Each pack contained five cards and carried a suggested retail price of $4.99. 500 exchange cards were seeded into packs for a Derek Jeter signed uncut sheet.

	Nm-Mt	Ex-Mt
COMP.SET w/o SP's (90)	25.00	7.50
COMMON CARD (1-100)	.50	.15
COMMON (101-130)	5.00	1.50
JETER AU SHEET AVAIL.VIA MAIL EXCH.		
JETER SHEET EXCH. RANDOM IN PACKS		
1 Derek Jeter	3.00	.90
2 Nomar Garciaparra	2.00	.60
3 Alex Rodriguez	2.00	.60
4 Frank Thomas	1.25	.35
5 Travis Fryman	.50	.15
6 Gary Sheffield	.50	.15
7 Jason Giambi	.50	.15
8 Trevor Hoffman	.50	.15
9 Todd Helton	.75	.23
10 Ivan Rodriguez	1.25	.35
11 Roberto Alomar	.75	.23
12 Barrry Zito	.75	.23
13 Kevin Brown	.50	.15
14 Shawn Green	.50	.15
15 Kenny Lofton	.50	.15
16 Jeff Weaver	.50	.15
17 Geoff Jenkins	.50	.15
18 Carlos Delgado	.50	.15
19 Mark Grace	.75	.23
20 Ken Griffey Jr.	2.00	.60
21 David Justice	.50	.15
22 Brian Giles	.50	.15
23 Scott Williamson	.50	.15
24 Richie Sexson	.50	.15
25 John Olerud	.50	.15
26 Sammy Sosa	2.00	.60
27 Bobby Higginson	.50	.15
28 Matt Lawton	.50	.15
29 Vinny Castilla	.50	.15
30 Alex Gonzalez	.50	.15
31 Manny Ramirez	.75	.23
32 Brad Radke	.50	.15
33 Cal Ripken	4.00	1.20
34 Richard Hidalgo	.50	.15
35 Al Leiter	.50	.15
36 Freddy Garcia	.50	.15
37 Juan Encarnacion	.50	.15
38 Corey Koskie	.50	.15
39 Greg Vaughn	.50	.15
40 Rafael Palmeiro	.75	.23
41 Vladimir Guerrero	1.25	.35
42 Troy Glaus	.50	.15
43 Mike Hampton	.50	.15
44 Jose Vidro	.50	.15
45 Ryan Rupe	.50	.15
46 Troy O'Leary	.50	.15
47 Ben Petrick	.50	.15
48 Mike Lieberthal	.50	.15
49 Mike Sweeney	.50	.15
50 Scott Rolen	1.25	.35
51 Albert Belle	.75	.23
52 Mark Quinn	.50	.15
53 Mike Piazza	2.00	.60
54 Mark McGwire	3.00	.90
55 Brady Anderson	.50	.15
56 Carlos Beltran	.75	.23
57 Michael Barrett	.50	.15
58 Jason Kendall	.50	.15
59 Jim Edmonds	.50	.15
60 Matt Williams	.50	.15
61 Pokey Reese	.50	.15
62 Bernie Williams	.75	.23
63 Barry Bonds	3.00	.90
64 David Wells	.50	.15
65 Chipper Jones	1.25	.35
66 Jim Parque	.50	.15
67 Derrek Lee	.50	.15
68 Darin Erstad	.50	.15
69 Edgar Martinez	.75	.23
70 Kerry Wood	1.25	.35
71 Omar Vizquel	.75	.23
72 Jeromy Burnitz	.50	.15
73 Warren Morris	.50	.15
74 Rick Ankiel	.50	.15
75 Andruw Jones	.50	.15
76 Paul Konerko	.50	.15
77 Mike Lowell	.50	.15
78 Roger Clemens	2.50	.75
79 Tim Hudson	.50	.15
80 Rafael Furcal	.50	.15
81 Craig Biggio	.75	.23
82 Edgardo Alfonzo	.50	.15
83 Pat Burrell	.50	.15
84 Adrian Beltre	.75	.23
85 Tony Gwynn	1.50	.45
86 J.T. Snow	.50	.15
87 Randy Johnson	1.25	.35
88 Sean Casey	.50	.15
89 Preston Wilson	.50	.15
90 Mike Mussina	.75	.23
91 Eric Chavez	.50	.15
92 Tim Salmon	.75	.23
93 Pedro Martinez	1.25	.35
94 Darryl Kile	.50	.15
95 Greg Maddux	2.00	.60
96 Magglio Ordonez	.50	.15
97 Jeff Bagwell	.75	.23
98 Timo Perez	.50	.15
99 Jeff Kent	.50	.15
100 Eric Owens	.50	.15
101 Ichiro Suzuki GU RC	40.00	12.00
102 E. Guzman GU RC	5.00	1.50
103 T. Shinjo GU RC	6.00	1.80
104 Travis Hafner GU RC	10.00	3.00
105 Larry Barnes GU	5.00	1.50
106 J. Randolph GU RC	5.00	1.50
107 Paul Phillips GU RC	5.00	1.50
108 Erick Almonte GU RC	5.00	1.50
109 Nick Punto GU RC	5.00	1.50
110 Jack Wilson GU RC	8.00	2.40
111 Jeremy Owens GU RC	5.00	1.50
112 Esix Snead GU RC	5.00	1.50
113 Jay Gibbons GU RC	6.00	1.80
114 A. Hernandez GU RC	5.00	1.50
115 Matt White GU RC	5.00	1.50
116 Ryan Freel GU RC	5.00	1.50
117 Martin Vargas GU RC	5.00	1.50
118 Winston Abreu GU RC	5.00	1.50
119 Junior Spivey GU RC	6.00	1.80
120 Paxton Crawford GU	5.00	1.50
121 Randy Keisler GU	5.00	1.50
122 Juan Diaz GU RC	5.00	1.50
123 Aaron Rowand GU	5.00	1.50
124 Toby Hall GU	5.00	1.50
125 Brian Cole GU	5.00	1.50
126 Aubrey Huff GU	5.00	1.50
127 Corey Patterson GU	5.00	1.50
128 Sun Woo Kim GU	5.00	1.50
129 Jace Brewer GU	5.00	1.50
130 Cesar Izturis GU	5.00	1.50
NNO Derek Jeter AU Sheet/500 EXCH	120.00	36.00

2001 Fleer Genuine At Large

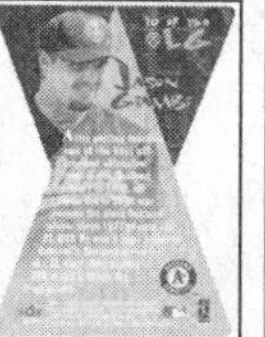

Randomly inserted into packs at one in 23, this 15-card insert features major league talents "at large". Card backs carry an "ALG" prefix.

	Nm-Mt	Ex-Mt
COMPLETE SET (15)	120.00	36.00
ALG1 Derek Jeter	12.00	3.60
ALG2 Nomar Garciaparra	8.00	2.40
ALG3 Mark McGwire	12.00	3.60
ALG4 Pedro Martinez	5.00	1.50
ALG5 Tony Gwynn	6.00	1.80
ALG6 Roger Clemens	10.00	3.00
ALG7 Ivan Rodriguez	5.00	1.50
ALG8 Sammy Sosa	8.00	2.40
ALG9 Magglio Ordonez	3.00	.90
ALG10 Jason Giambi	3.00	.90
ALG11 Carlos Delgado	3.00	.90
ALG12 Chipper Jones	5.00	1.50
ALG13 Mike Piazza	8.00	2.40
ALG14 Cal Ripken	15.00	4.50
ALG15 Ken Griffey Jr.	8.00	2.40

2001 Fleer Genuine Coverage Plus

Randomly inserted into hobby packs, this 10-card insert features jersey swatches from players like Derek Jeter and Cal Ripken. Cards are listed below in alphabetical order for convenience. Please note that there were only 150 serial numbered sets produced.

	Nm-Mt	Ex-Mt
1 Barry Bonds	50.00	15.00
2 Darin Erstad	15.00	4.50
3 Troy Glaus	15.00	4.50
4 Tony Gwynn	25.00	7.50
5 Derek Jeter	50.00	15.00
6 Randy Johnson	20.00	6.00
7 Andruw Jones	15.00	4.50
8 Chipper Jones	20.00	6.00
9 Cal Ripken	50.00	15.00
10 Frank Thomas	20.00	6.00

2001 Fleer Genuine Final Cut

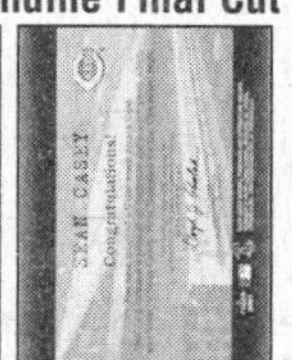

Randomly inserted into packs at one in 30, this 28-card insert features jersey swatches from players like Derek Jeter and Cal Ripken. Cards are listed below in alphabetical order for convenience. Representatives at Fleer announced specific print runs on several short-printed cards within this set, though the cards lack actual serial-numbering. Don Larsen, Ron Guidry and Reggie Jackson were not intended for public release. It's rumored that Willie Randolph and Dave Righetti were also not intended for public release. The Guidry, Larsen, Randolph and Righetti cards are extremely scarce (estimated only a few copies of each exist) as Fleer attempted to pull all of the copies they could find from production prior to shipping.

	Nm-Mt	Ex-Mt
*MULTI-COLOR PATCH: .75X TO 2X BASIC		
1 Wade Boggs	15.00	4.50
2 Barry Bonds SP/330	50.00	15.00
3 George Brett	25.00	7.50
4 Sean Casey	10.00	3.00
5 J.D. Drew SP/75	25.00	7.50
6 Bob Gibson SP/200	40.00	12.00
7 Troy Glaus	10.00	3.00
8 Ron Guidry SP		
9 Tony Gwynn	15.00	4.50
10 Reggie Jackson SP		
11 Andruw Jones SP/135	25.00	7.50
12 Chipper Jones	15.00	4.50
13 Don Larsen SP		
14 Greg Maddux	15.00	4.50
15 Edgar Martinez SP/130 UER Card says it is part of a batting glove but the pieces are game worn jersey swatches	40.00	12.00
16 Willie Randolph SP		
17 Pokey Reese	10.00	3.00
18 Dave Righetti SP		
19 Cal Ripken	40.00	12.00
20 Ivan Rodriguez SP/120	40.00	12.00
21 Scott Rolen	15.00	4.50
22 Tim Salmon	15.00	4.50
23 Miguel Tejada SP/170	25.00	7.50
24 Frank Thomas	15.00	4.50
25 Robin Ventura	10.00	3.00
26 Larry Walker	15.00	4.50
27 Matt Williams	10.00	3.00
28 Robin Yount	15.00	4.50

2001 Fleer Genuine High Interest

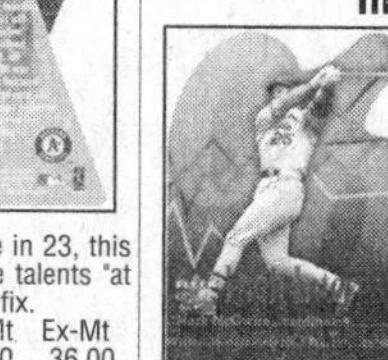
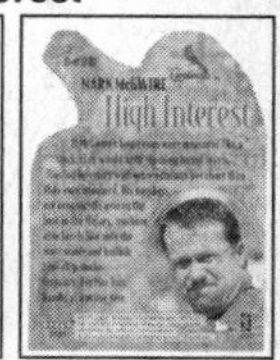

Randomly inserted into packs at one in 23, this 15-card insert features players that have earned the respect of the fans year in year out. Cards backs carry a "HI" prefix.

	Nm-Mt	Ex-Mt
COMPLETE SET (15)	100.00	30.00
HI1 Derek Jeter	12.00	3.60
HI2 Nomar Garciaparra	8.00	2.40
HI3 Greg Maddux	8.00	2.40
HI4 Todd Helton	3.00	.90
HI5 Sammy Sosa	8.00	2.40
HI6 Jeff Bagwell	3.00	.90
HI7 Jason Giambi	3.00	.90
HI8 Frank Thomas	5.00	1.50
HI9 Andruw Jones	3.00	.90
HI10 Jim Edmonds	3.00	.90
HI11 Bernie Williams	3.00	.90
HI12 Randy Johnson	5.00	1.50
HI13 Ken Griffey Jr.	8.00	2.40
HI14 Pedro Martinez	5.00	1.50
HI15 Mark McGwire	12.00	3.60

2001 Fleer Genuine Material Issue

Randomly inserted into hobby packs at one in 30, this 19-card insert features game-used jersey swatches from players like Tony Gwynn and Pedro Martinez. Cards have been listed in alphabetical order for convenience. Representatives at Fleer announced that Pedro Martinez and Curt Schilling were both shortprints. Though the cards lack actual serial-numbering, it was announced that 60 copies of the Martinez card and 120 copies of the Schilling card were produced.

	Nm-Mt	Ex-Mt
*MULTI-COLOR PATCH: 1X TO 2.5X BASIC		
1 Steve Carlton SP *	25.00	7.50
2 J.D. Drew	10.00	3.00
3 Darin Erstad	10.00	3.00
4 Troy Glaus	10.00	3.00
5 Tom Glavine	15.00	4.50
6 Tony Gwynn	15.00	4.50
7 Randy Johnson	15.00	4.50
8 Chipper Jones	15.00	4.50
9 Greg Maddux	15.00	4.50
10 Edgar Martinez SP *	30.00	9.00
11 Pedro Martinez SP/60	50.00	15.00
12 Kevin Millwood	10.00	3.00
13 Paul Molitor SP *	30.00	9.00
14 Cal Ripken	40.00	12.00
15 Scott Rolen	15.00	4.50
16 Nolan Ryan	50.00	15.00
17 Curt Schilling SP/120	25.00	7.50
18 Frank Thomas	15.00	4.50
19 Robin Ventura	10.00	3.00

2001 Fleer Genuine Names Of The Game

Randomly inserted into packs, this 34-card insert features swatches of game-used memorabilia (either bat or jersey). Cards have been listed below in alphabetical order for convenience. Please note that there were only 50 serial numbered sets produced.

	Nm-Mt	Ex-Mt
1 Yogi Berra Bat	40.00	12.00
2 Orlando Cepeda Bat	25.00	7.50
3 Rocky Colavito Bat	40.00	12.00
4 Andre Dawson Jsy	25.00	7.50
5 Bucky Dent Bat	25.00	7.50
6 Rollie Fingers Jsy	25.00	7.50

Card	Nm-Mt	Ex-Mt
7 Carlton Fisk Bat	40.00	12.00
8 Whitey Ford Jsy	40.00	12.00
9 Jimmie Foxx Bat	80.00	24.00
10 Hank Greenberg Bat	80.00	24.00
11 Catfish Hunter Jsy	40.00	12.00
12 Reggie Jackson Jsy	40.00	12.00
13 Randy Johnson Jsy	40.00	12.00
14 Chipper Jones Bat	40.00	12.00
15 Harmon Killebrew Bat	40.00	12.00
16 Tony Lazzeri Bat	25.00	7.50
17 Don Mattingly Bat	50.00	15.00
18 Willie McCovey Bat	25.00	7.50
19 Johnny Mize Bat	25.00	7.50
20 Pee Wee Reese Jsy	40.00	12.00
21 Cal Ripken Bat	60.00	18.00
22 Phil Rizzuto Bat	40.00	12.00
23 Ivan Rodriguez Bat	40.00	12.00
24 Preacher Roe Jsy	40.00	12.00
25 Babe Ruth Bat	250.00	75.00
26 Nolan Ryan Jsy	60.00	18.00
27 Tom Seaver Jsy	40.00	12.00
28 Bill Skowron Bat	40.00	12.00
29 Enos Slaughter Bat	25.00	7.50
30 Duke Snider Bat	40.00	12.00
31 Willie Stargell Bat	40.00	12.00
32 Bill Terry Bat	40.00	12.00
33 Ted Williams Bat	100.00	30.00
34 Hack Wilson Bat	80.00	24.00

2001 Fleer Genuine Names Of The Game Autographs

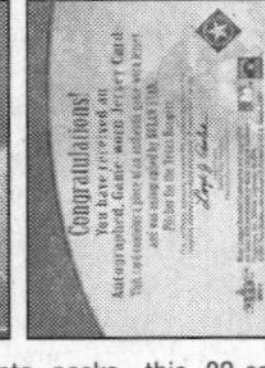

Randomly inserted into packs, this 22-card insert features swatches of game-used memorabilia (either bat or jersey) and an authentic autograph from the depicted player. Cards have been listed below in alphabetical order for convenience. Please note that there were only 100 serial numbered sets produced.

Card	Nm-Mt	Ex-Mt
1 Yogi Berra Bat	80.00	24.00
2 Orlando Cepeda Bat	40.00	12.00
3 Rocky Colavito Bat	80.00	24.00
4 Andre Dawson Jsy	40.00	12.00
5 Bucky Dent Bat	40.00	12.00
6 Rollie Fingers Jsy	40.00	12.00
7 Carlton Fisk Bat	50.00	15.00
8 Whitey Ford Jsy	50.00	15.00
9 Reggie Jackson Jsy	80.00	24.00
10 Randy Johnson Jsy	80.00	24.00
11 Chipper Jones Bat	80.00	24.00
12 Harmon Killebrew Bat	80.00	24.00
13 Don Mattingly Bat	120.00	36.00
14 Willie McCovey Bat	50.00	15.00
15 Cal Ripken Bat	200.00	60.00
16 Ivan Rodriguez Bat	80.00	24.00
17 Preacher Roe Jsy	40.00	12.00
18 Nolan Ryan Jsy	150.00	45.00
19 Tom Seaver Jsy	80.00	24.00
20 Bill Skowron Bat	40.00	12.00
21 Enos Slaughter Bat	50.00	15.00
22 Duke Snider Bat	50.00	15.00

2001 Fleer Genuine Pennant Aggression

Randomly inserted into packs at one in 23, this 10-card insert features players that play very aggressively down the stretch for the pennant. Card backs carry a "PA" prefix.

Card	Nm-Mt	Ex-Mt
COMPLETE SET (10)	60.00	18.00
PA1 Derek Jeter	10.00	3.00
PA2 Alex Rodriguez	6.00	1.80
PA3 Nomar Garciaparra	6.00	1.80
PA4 Mark McGwire	10.00	3.00
PA5 Ken Griffey Jr.	6.00	1.80
PA6 Mike Piazza	6.00	1.80
PA7 Sammy Sosa	6.00	1.80
PA8 Barry Bonds	10.00	3.00
PA9 Chipper Jones	4.00	1.20
PA10 Pedro Martinez	4.00	1.20

2001 Fleer Genuine Tip Of The Cap

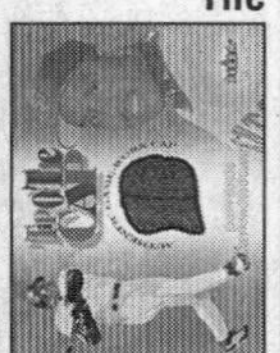
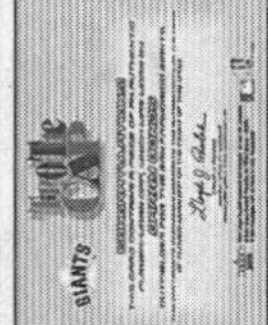

Randomly inserted into hobby packs, this 13-card insert features swatches of game-used hat. Cards have been listed below in alphabetical order for convenience. Please note that there were only 150 serial numbered sets produced.

Card	Nm-Mt	Ex-Mt
1 Roberto Alomar	25.00	7.50
2 Barry Bonds	60.00	18.00
3 Eric Chavez	15.00	4.50
4 Troy Glaus	15.00	4.50
5 Shawn Green	15.00	4.50
6 Vladimir Guerrero	25.00	7.50
7 Randy Johnson	25.00	7.50
8 Andruw Jones	15.00	4.50
9 Javy Lopez	15.00	4.50
10 Pedro Martinez	25.00	7.50
11 Rafael Palmeiro	25.00	7.50
12 Ivan Rodriguez	25.00	7.50
13 Miguel Tejada	15.00	4.50

2002 Fleer Genuine

This 140 card was released in May, 2002. These cards were issued in five card packs with an SRP of $4.99 per pack and they were issued 24 packs to a box and six boxes per case. The first 100 card feature veteran players and the final forty player feature prospect cards. Cards number 101 through 140 have a stated print run of 2002 serial numbered sets.

Card	Nm-Mt	Ex-Mt
COMP.SET w/o SP's (100)	25.00	7.50
COMMON CARD (1-100)	.50	.15
COMMON CARD (101-140)	5.00	1.50
1 Alex Rodriguez	2.00	.60
2 Manny Ramirez	.75	.23
3 Jim Thome	1.25	.35
4 Eric Milton	.50	.15
5 Todd Helton	.75	.23
6 Mike Mussina	.75	.23
7 Ichiro Suzuki	2.00	.60
8 Randy Johnson	1.25	.35
9 Mark Mulder	.50	.15
10 Johnny Damon Sox	1.25	.35
11 Sean Casey	.50	.15
12 Albert Pujols	2.50	.75
13 Mark Grace	.75	.23
14 Moises Alou	.50	.15
15 Raul Mondesi	.50	.15
16 Cliff Floyd	.50	.15
17 Vladimir Guerrero	1.25	.35
18 Pat Burrell	.50	.15
19 Ryan Klesko	.50	.15
20 Mike Hampton	.50	.15
21 Shawn Green	.50	.15
22 Rich Aurilia	.50	.15
23 Matt Morris	.50	.15
24 Curt Schilling	.50	.15
25 Kevin Brown	.50	.15
26 Adrian Beltre	.75	.23
27 Joe Mays	.50	.15
28 Luis Gonzalez	.50	.15
29 Barry Larkin	.75	.23
30 A.J. Burnett	.50	.15
31 Eric Munson	.50	.15
32 Juan Gonzalez	.75	.23
33 Lance Berkman	.50	.15
34 Fred McGriff	.75	.23
35 Paul Konerko	.50	.15
36 Pedro Martinez	1.25	.35
37 Adam Dunn	.75	.23
38 Jeromy Burnitz	.50	.15
39 Mike Sweeney	.50	.15
40 Bret Boone	.50	.15
41 Ken Griffey Jr.	2.00	.60
42 Eric Chavez	.50	.15
43 Mark Quinn	.50	.15
44 Roberto Alomar	.75	.23
45 Bobby Abreu	.50	.15
46 Bartolo Colon	.50	.15
47 Jimmy Rollins	.50	.15
48 Chipper Jones	1.25	.35
49 Ben Sheets	.50	.15
50 Freddy Garcia	.50	.15
51 Sammy Sosa	2.00	.60
52 Rafael Palmeiro	.75	.23
53 Preston Wilson	.50	.15
54 Troy Glaus	.50	.15
55 Josh Beckett	.50	.15
56 C.C. Sabathia	.50	.15
57 Magglio Ordonez	.50	.15
58 Brian Giles	.50	.15
59 Darin Erstad	.50	.15
60 Gary Sheffield	.50	.15
61 Paul LoDuca	.50	.15
62 Derek Jeter	3.00	.90
63 Greg Maddux	2.00	.60
64 Kerry Wood	1.25	.35
65 Toby Hall	.50	.15
66 Barry Bonds	3.00	.90
67 Jeff Bagwell	.75	.23
68 Jason Kendall	.50	.15
69 Richard Hidalgo	.50	.15
70 J.D. Drew	.50	.15
71 Tom Glavine	.75	.23
72 Javier Vazquez	.50	.15
73 Doug Mientkiewicz	.50	.15
74 Jason Giambi	.50	.15
75 Carlos Delgado	.50	.15
76 Aramis Ramirez	.50	.15
77 Torii Hunter	.50	.15
78 Ivan Rodriguez	1.25	.35
79 Charles Johnson	.50	.15
80 Jeff Kent	.50	.15
81 Jacque Jones	.50	.15
82 Larry Walker	.75	.23
83 Cristian Guzman	.50	.15
84 Jermaine Dye	.50	.15
85 Roger Clemens	2.50	.75
86 Mike Piazza	2.00	.60
87 Craig Biggio	.75	.23
88 Phil Nevin	.50	.15
89 Jeff Cirillo	.50	.15
90 Barry Zito	.50	.15
91 Ryan Dempster	.50	.15
92 Mark Buehrle	.50	.15
93 Nomar Garciaparra	2.00	.60
94 Frank Thomas	1.25	.35
95 Jim Edmonds	.50	.15
96 Geoff Jenkins	.50	.15
97 Scott Rolen	1.25	.35
98 Tim Hudson	.50	.15
99 Shannon Stewart	.50	.15
100 Richie Sexson	.50	.15
101 Orlando Hudson UP	5.00	1.50
102 Doug Devore UP RC	5.00	1.50
103 Rene Reyes UP RC	5.00	1.50
104 Steve Bechler UP RC	5.00	1.50
105 Jorge Nunez UP RC	5.00	1.50
106 Mitch Wylie UP RC	5.00	1.50
107 Jaime Cerda UP RC	5.00	1.50
108 Brandon Puffer UP RC	5.00	1.50
109 Tyler Yates UP RC	8.00	2.40
110 Bill Hall UP	5.00	1.50
111 Pete Zamora UP RC	5.00	1.50
112 Jeff Deardorff UP	5.00	1.50
113 J.J. Putz UP RC	5.00	1.50
114 Scotty Layfield UP RC	5.00	1.50
115 Brandon Backe UP RC	8.00	2.40
116 Andy Pratt UP RC	5.00	1.50
117 Mark Prior UP	12.00	3.60
118 Franklyn German UP RC	5.00	1.50
119 Todd Donovan UP RC	5.00	1.50
120 Franklin Nunez UP RC	5.00	1.50
121 Adam Walker UP RC	5.00	1.50
122 Ron Calloway UP RC	5.00	1.50
123 Tim Kalita UP RC	5.00	1.50
124 Kazuhisa Ishii UP RC	10.00	3.00
125 Mark Teixeira UP	8.00	2.40
126 Nate Field UP RC	5.00	1.50
127 Nelson Castro UP RC	5.00	1.50
128 So Taguchi UP RC	8.00	2.40
129 Marlon Byrd UP	5.00	1.50
130 Drew Henson UP	5.00	1.50
131 Kenny Kelly UP	5.00	1.50
132 John Ennis UP RC	5.00	1.50
133 Anastacio Martinez UP RC	5.00	1.50
134 Matt Guerrier UP	5.00	1.50
135 Tom Wilson UP RC	5.00	1.50
136 Ben Howard UP RC	5.00	1.50
137 Chris Baker UP RC	5.00	1.50
138 Kevin Frederick UP RC	5.00	1.50
139 Wilson Valdez UP RC	5.00	1.50
140 Austin Kearns UP	5.00	1.50

2002 Fleer Genuine Bats Incredible

Inserted in packs at a stated rate of one in 10 hobby and one in 20 retail, these 25 cards feature some of the leading hitters in baseball.

Card	Nm-Mt	Ex-Mt
COMPLETE SET (25)	100.00	30.00
BI1 Todd Helton	2.50	.75
BI2 Chipper Jones	4.00	1.20
BI3 Luis Gonzalez	2.50	.75
BI4 Barry Bonds	10.00	3.00
BI5 Jason Giambi	2.50	.75
BI6 Alex Rodriguez	6.00	1.80
BI7 Manny Ramirez	2.50	.75
BI8 Jeff Bagwell	2.50	.75
BI9 Shawn Green	2.50	.75
BI10 Albert Pujols	8.00	2.40
BI11 Paul LoDuca	2.50	.75
BI12 Mike Piazza	6.00	1.80
BI13 Derek Jeter	10.00	3.00
BI14 Edgar Martinez	2.50	.75
BI15 Juan Gonzalez	2.50	.75
BI16 Magglio Ordonez	2.50	.75
BI17 Jermaine Dye	2.50	.75
BI18 Larry Walker	2.50	.75
BI19 Phil Nevin	2.50	.75
BI20 Ivan Rodriguez	4.00	1.20
BI21 Ichiro Suzuki	6.00	1.80
BI22 J.D. Drew	2.50	.75
BI23 Vladimir Guerrero	4.00	1.20
BI24 Sammy Sosa	6.00	1.80
BI25 Ken Griffey Jr.	6.00	1.80

2002 Fleer Genuine Bats Incredible Game Used

Inserted at a stated rate of one in 18 hobby and one in 90 retail packs, these 12 cards partially parallel the Bats Incredible insert set. These cards have a bat chip on them in addition to the player's photo.

Card	Nm-Mt	Ex-Mt
1 Todd Helton	10.00	3.00
2 Chipper Jones	15.00	4.50
3 J.D. Drew	10.00	3.00
4 Alex Rodriguez	15.00	4.50
5 Manny Ramirez	10.00	3.00
6 Shawn Green	10.00	3.00
7 Derek Jeter	25.00	7.50
8 Edgar Martinez	10.00	3.00
9 Juan Gonzalez	10.00	3.00
10 Jermaine Dye	8.00	2.40
11 Phil Nevin	8.00	2.40
12 Ivan Rodriguez	10.00	3.00

2002 Fleer Genuine Ink

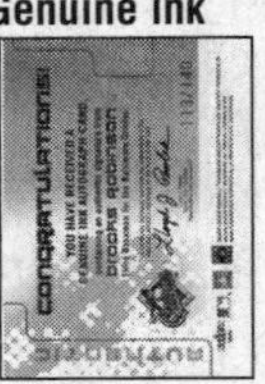

Randomly inserted in packs, these cards feature authentic autographs of the players featued. These cards all have diferent print runs and we have listed the stated print run next to the player's name. Paul Molitor did not sign his cards in time for inclusion in packs and those cards could be redeemed until June 1, 2003.

Card	Nm-Mt	Ex-Mt
1 Barry Bonds/150	250.00	75.00
2 Ron Cey/975	15.00	4.50
3 Derek Jeter/150	150.00	45.00
4 Al Kaline/300	80.00	24.00
5 Don Mattingly/50	120.00	36.00
6 Paul Molitor/365	50.00	15.00
7 Dale Murphy/700	50.00	15.00
8 Phil Rizzuto/700	30.00	9.00
9 Brooks Robinson/140	50.00	15.00
10 Maury Wills/975	15.00	4.50

2002 Fleer Genuine Leaders

Inserted into packs at a stated rate of one in six hobby and one in eight retail, these 15 cards honor some of the leading players in the game.

Card	Nm-Mt	Ex-Mt
COMPLETE SET (15)	40.00	12.00
1 Sammy Sosa	4.00	1.20
2 Todd Helton	1.50	.45
3 Alex Rodriguez	4.00	1.20
4 Roger Clemens	5.00	1.50
5 Barry Bonds	6.00	1.80
6 Randy Johnson	2.50	.75
7 Albert Pujols	5.00	1.50
8 Curt Schilling	1.50	.45
9 Bernie Williams	1.50	.45
10 Ken Griffey Jr.	4.00	1.20
11 Pedro Martinez	2.50	.75
12 Juan Gonzalez	1.50	.45
13 Hideo Nomo	2.50	.75
14 Bret Boone	1.50	.45
15 Ichiro Suzuki	4.00	1.20

2002 Fleer Genuine Leaders Game Jersey

Inserted into packs at stated odds of one in 11 hobby and one in 566 retail, these nine cards partially parallel the Leaders insert set. These cards feature a game jersey swatch on them in addition to the player's photo.

Card	Nm-Mt	Ex-Mt
1 Todd Helton	15.00	4.50
2 Alex Rodriguez	15.00	4.50
3 Roger Clemens	20.00	6.00
4 Barry Bonds	25.00	7.50
5 Randy Johnson	15.00	4.50
6 Bernie Williams	15.00	4.50
7 Curt Schilling	15.00	4.50
8 Hideo Nomo	20.00	6.00
9 Pedro Martinez	15.00	4.50

2002 Fleer Genuine Names of the Game

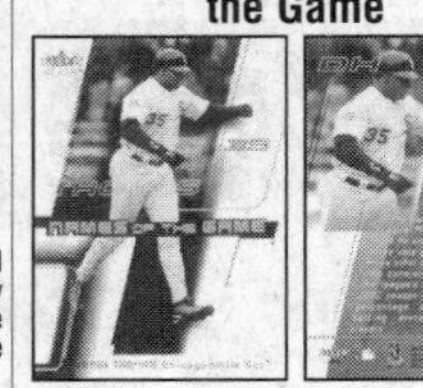

Issued in packs at stated odds of one in 10 hobby and one in 20 retail, these 30 cards feature a good mix of the leading players in baseball.

Card	Nm-Mt	Ex-Mt
COMPLETE SET (30)	120.00	36.00
1 Mike Piazza	8.00	2.40
2 Chipper Jones	5.00	1.50
3 Jim Edmonds	3.00	.90
4 Barry Larkin	3.00	.90
5 Frank Thomas	5.00	1.50
6 Manny Ramirez	3.00	.90
7 Carlos Delgado	3.00	.90
8 Brian Giles	3.00	.90
9 Kerry Wood	5.00	1.50
10 Derek Jeter	12.00	3.60
11 Adam Dunn	3.00	.90
12 Gary Sheffield	3.00	.90
13 Luis Gonzalez	3.00	.90
14 Mark Mulder	3.00	.90
15 Roberto Alomar	3.00	.90
16 Scott Rolen	5.00	1.50
17 Tom Glavine	3.00	.90
18 Bobby Abreu	3.00	.90
19 Nomar Garciaparra	8.00	2.40
20 Darin Erstad	3.00	.90
21 Cliff Floyd	3.00	.90
22 Tim Hudson	3.00	.90
23 Jim Thome	5.00	1.50
24 Nolan Ryan	12.00	3.60
25 Reggie Jackson	3.00	.90
26 Rafael Palmeiro	3.00	.90
27 Ken Griffey Jr.	8.00	2.40
28 Sammy Sosa	8.00	2.40
29 Vladimir Guerrero	5.00	1.50
30 Ichiro Suzuki	8.00	2.40

2002 Fleer Genuine Names of the Game Memorabilia

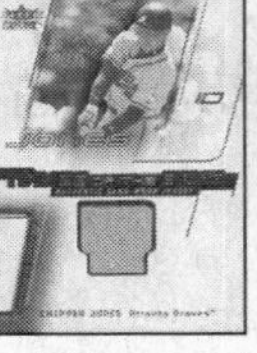
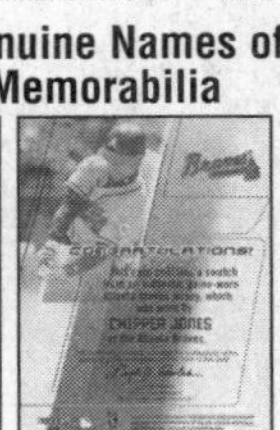

Inserted in packs at stated odds of one in 24 hobby and one in 100 retail, these 19 cards are a partial parallel of the Names of the Game memorabilia set. These cards feature a memorabilia item to go with the player's photo. The Nomar Garciaparra card was issued in shorter supply and we have notated that information along with the stated print run for that card.

Card	Nm-Mt	Ex-Mt
1 Roberto Alomar	15.00	4.50
2 Carlos Delgado	10.00	3.00
3 Jim Edmonds	10.00	3.00
4 Darin Erstad	10.00	3.00
5 Cliff Floyd	10.00	3.00
6 Nomar Garciaparra SP/90		
7 Brian Giles	10.00	3.00
8 Luis Gonzalez	10.00	3.00
9 Tim Hudson	10.00	3.00
10 Derek Jeter	30.00	9.00
11 Chipper Jones	15.00	4.50
12 Barry Larkin	15.00	4.50
13 Mark Mulder	10.00	3.00
14 Rafael Palmeiro	15.00	4.50
15 Mike Piazza	15.00	4.50
16 Manny Ramirez	15.00	4.50
17 Scott Rolen	15.00	4.50
18 Nolan Ryan	40.00	12.00
19 Jim Thome	15.00	4.50

2002 Fleer Genuine Tip of the Cap

Inserted in packs at stated odds of one in six hobby and one in eight retail, this 25 cards feature a nice mix of active and retired players.

Card	Nm-Mt	Ex-Mt
COMPLETE SET (25)	60.00	18.00
1 Alex Rodriguez	5.00	1.50
2 Derek Jeter	8.00	2.40
3 Kazuhiro Sasaki	2.00	.60
4 Barry Bonds	8.00	2.40
5 J.D. Drew	2.00	.60
6 Tsuyoshi Shinjo	2.00	.60
7 Alfonso Soriano	2.00	.60
8 Albert Pujols	6.00	1.80
9 Tom Seaver	2.00	.60
10 Drew Henson	2.00	.60
11 Dave Winfield	2.00	.60
12 Carlos Delgado	2.00	.60
13 Lou Boudreau	2.00	.60
14 Shawn Green	2.00	.60
15 Roger Clemens	6.00	1.80
16 Randy Johnson	3.00	.90
17 Sammy Sosa	5.00	1.50
18 Rafael Palmeiro	2.00	.60
19 Ken Griffey Jr.	5.00	1.50
20 Ichiro Suzuki	5.00	1.50
21 Eric Chavez	2.00	.60
22 Andruw Jones	2.00	.60
23 Miguel Tejada	2.00	.60
24 Pedro Martinez	3.00	.90
25 Tim Salmon	2.00	.60

2002 Fleer Genuine Tip of the Cap Game Used

Randomly inserted into packs, these 26 cards feature pieces of memorabilia worn by the featured player. These cards all have different stated print runs and we have listed that information next to their names in our checklist.

Card	Nm-Mt	Ex-Mt
1 Adrian Beltre/6		

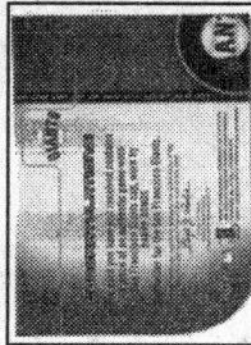

2 Barry Bonds/32
3 Lou Boudreau/303 .... 25.00 7.50
4 Kevin Brown/6
5 Eric Chavez/14
6 Bartolo Colon/16
7 Carlos Delgado/219 .... 20.00 6.00
8 J.D. Drew/8
9 Jim Edmonds/8
10 Darin Erstad/22
11 Rafael Furcal/12
12 Juan Gonzalez/6
13 Luis Gonzalez/12
14 Shawn Green/4
15 Drew Henson/361 .... 20.00 6.00
16 Randy Johnson/74
17 Andruw Jones/19
18 Jason Kendall/41
19 Pedro Martinez/2
20 Rafael Palmeiro/300 .... 25.00 7.50
21 Alex Rodriguez/670 .... 25.00 7.50
22 Tim Salmon/6
23 Tom Seaver/224 .... 25.00 7.50
24 Alfonso Soriano/4
25 Miguel Tejada/225 .... 20.00 6.00
26 Dave Winfield/363 .... 20.00 6.00

2002 Fleer Genuine Touch Em All

Inserted into packs at stated odds of one in 10 hobby and one in 20 retail, these 25 cards feature the leading sluggers in the game.

	Nm-Mt	Ex-Mt
COMPLETE SET (25)	100.00	30.00
1 Derek Jeter	10.00	3.00
2 Sammy Sosa	6.00	1.80
3 Albert Pujols	8.00	2.40
4 Vladimir Guerrero	4.00	1.20
5 Ken Griffey Jr.	6.00	1.80
6 Nomar Garciaparra	6.00	1.80
7 Luis Gonzalez	2.50	.75
8 Barry Bonds	10.00	3.00
9 Manny Ramirez	2.50	.75
10 Jason Giambi	2.50	.75
11 Chipper Jones	4.00	1.20
12 Ichiro Suzuki	6.00	1.80
13 Alex Rodriguez	6.00	1.80
14 Juan Gonzalez	2.50	.75
15 Todd Helton	2.50	.75
16 Roberto Alomar	2.50	.75
17 Jeff Bagwell	2.50	.75
18 Mike Piazza	6.00	1.80
19 Gary Sheffield	2.50	.75
20 Ivan Rodriguez	4.00	1.20
21 Frank Thomas	4.00	1.20
22 Bobby Abreu	2.50	.75
23 J.D. Drew	2.50	.75
24 Scott Rolen	4.00	1.20
25 Darin Erstad	2.50	.75

2002 Fleer Genuine Touch Em All Game Base

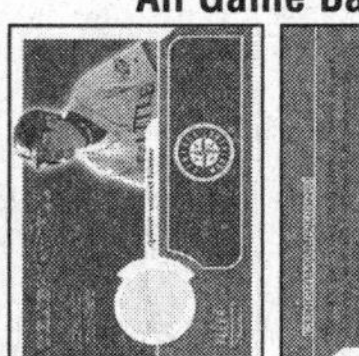

Randomly inserted into packs, these 25 cards parallel the Touch Em All insert set. These cards feature a piece of a game base used by the player in a game. These cards were issued to a stated print run of 350 serial numbered sets.

	Nm-Mt	Ex-Mt
1 Derek Jeter	25.00	7.50
2 Sammy Sosa	15.00	4.50
3 Albert Pujols	20.00	6.00
4 Vladimir Guerrero	15.00	4.50
5 Ken Griffey Jr.	15.00	4.50
6 Nomar Garciaparra	15.00	4.50
7 Luis Gonzalez	10.00	3.00
8 Barry Bonds	25.00	7.50
9 Manny Ramirez	15.00	4.50
10 Jason Giambi	10.00	3.00
11 Chipper Jones	15.00	4.50
12 Ichiro Suzuki	25.00	7.50
13 Alex Rodriguez	15.00	4.50
14 Juan Gonzalez	15.00	4.50
15 Todd Helton	15.00	4.50
16 Roberto Alomar	15.00	4.50
17 Jeff Bagwell	15.00	4.50
18 Mike Piazza	15.00	4.50
19 Gary Sheffield	10.00	3.00
20 Ivan Rodriguez	15.00	4.50
21 Frank Thomas	15.00	4.50
22 Bobby Abreu	10.00	3.00
23 J.D. Drew	10.00	3.00
24 Scott Rolen	15.00	4.50
25 Darin Erstad	10.00	3.00

2003 Fleer Genuine

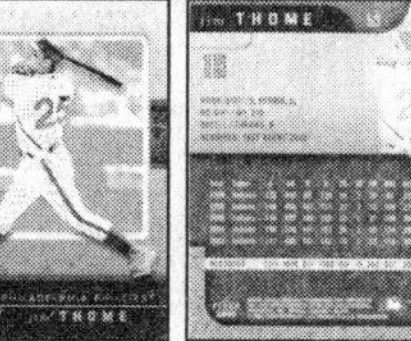

This 145-card set was distributed in two separate series. The primary Genuine product - of which contained the first 130 cards from the basic set - was released in July, 2003. This set was issued in five card packs with an $5 SRP which came 24 packs to a box and 12 boxes to a case. Cards numbered 1 through 100 feature veterans while cards numbered 101 through 130 feature a mix of rookies and prospects and those cards were issued to a stated print run of 799 serial numbered sets. Cards 131-145 were randomly seeded within packs of Fleer Rookies and Greats of which was distributed in December, 2003. These fifteen update cards continued the Genuine Upside prospect subset established with cards 101-130 from the primary "low series" set. Each update card was serial numbered to 1000 copies.

	MINT	NRMT
COMP.LO SET w/o SP's (100)	25.00	11.00
COMMON CARD (1-100)	.50	.23
COMMON CARD (101-145)	4.00	1.80
1 Derek Jeter	3.00	1.35
2 Mo Vaughn	.50	.23
3 Adam Dunn	.75	.35
4 Aubrey Huff	.50	.23
5 Jacque Jones	.50	.23
6 Kerry Wood	1.25	.55
7 Barry Bonds	3.00	1.35
8 Kevin Brown	.50	.23
9 Sammy Sosa	2.00	.90
10 Ray Durham	.50	.23
11 Carlos Beltran	.75	.35
12 Tony Batista	.50	.23
13 Bobby Abreu	.50	.23
14 Craig Biggio	.75	.35
15 Gary Sheffield	.50	.23
16 Jermaine Dye	.50	.23
17 Carlos Pena	.50	.23
18 Tim Salmon	.75	.35
19 Mike Piazza	2.00	.90
20 Moises Alou	.50	.23
21 Edgardo Alfonzo	.50	.23
22 Mike Sweeney	.50	.23
23 Jay Gibbons	.50	.23
24 Kevin Millwood	.50	.23
25 A.J. Burnett	.50	.23
26 Austin Kearns	.50	.23
27 Rafael Palmeiro	.75	.35
28 Vladimir Guerrero	1.25	.55
29 Paul Konerko	.50	.23
30 Scott Rolen	1.25	.55
31 Fred McGriff	.75	.35
32 Frank Thomas	1.25	.55
33 John Olerud	.50	.23
34 Eric Gagne	1.25	.55
35 Nomar Garciaparra	2.00	.90
36 Ryan Klesko	.50	.23
37 Lance Berkman	.50	.23
38 Andruw Jones	.50	.23
39 Pat Burrell	.50	.23
40 Juan Encarnacion	.50	.23
41 Curt Schilling	.50	.23
42 Jason Giambi	.50	.23
43 Barry Larkin	.75	.35
44 Alex Rodriguez	2.00	.90
45 Kazuhisa Ishii	.50	.23
46 Pedro Martinez	1.25	.55
47 Sean Burroughs	.50	.23
48 Roy Oswalt	.50	.23
49 Chipper Jones	1.25	.55
50 Barry Zito	.50	.23
51 Jeff Kent	.50	.23
52 Rodrigo Lopez	.50	.23
53 Jim Thome	1.25	.55
54 Ivan Rodriguez	1.25	.55
55 Luis Gonzalez	.50	.23
56 Alfonso Soriano	.75	.35
57 Josh Beckett	.50	.23
58 Junior Spivey	.50	.23
59 Bernie Williams	.75	.35
60 Omar Vizquel	.75	.35
61 Eric Hinske	.50	.23
62 Jose Vidro	.50	.23
63 Bartolo Colon	.50	.23
64 Jim Edmonds	.50	.23
65 Ben Sheets	.50	.23
66 Mark Prior	1.25	.55
67 Edgar Martinez	.75	.35
68 Raul Ibanez	.50	.23
69 Darin Erstad	.50	.23
70 Roger Clemens	2.50	1.10
71 C.C. Sabathia	.50	.23
72 Carlos Delgado	.50	.23
73 Tom Glavine	.75	.35
74 Magglio Ordonez	.50	.23
75 Ichiro Suzuki	2.00	.90
76 Johnny Damon	1.25	.55
77 Brian Giles	.50	.23
78 Jeff Bagwell	.75	.35
79 Greg Maddux	2.00	.90
80 Eric Chavez	.50	.23
81 Larry Walker	.75	.35
82 Randy Johnson	1.25	.55
83 Miguel Tejada	.50	.23
84 Todd Helton	.75	.35
85 Jarrod Washburn	.50	.23
86 Troy Glaus	.50	.23
87 Ken Griffey Jr.	2.00	.90
88 Albert Pujols	2.50	1.10
89 Torii Hunter	.50	.23
90 Joe Crede	.50	.23
91 Matt Morris	.50	.23
92 Shawn Green	.50	.23
93 Manny Ramirez	.75	.35
94 Jason Kendall	.50	.23
95 Preston Wilson	.50	.23
96 Garret Anderson	.50	.23
97 Cliff Floyd	.50	.23
98 Sean Casey	.50	.23
99 Juan Gonzalez	.75	.35
100 Richie Sexson	.50	.23
101 Joe Borchard GU	4.00	1.80
102 Josh Stewart GU RC	4.00	1.80
103 Francisco Rodriguez GU	4.00	1.80
104 Jeremy Bonderman GU RC	5.00	2.20
105 Walter Young GU	4.00	1.80
106 Brandon Webb GU RC	5.00	2.20
107 Lyle Overbay GU	4.00	1.80
108 Jose Contreras GU RC	8.00	3.60
109 Victor Martinez GU	5.00	2.20
110 Hideki Matsui GU RC	10.00	4.50
111 Brian Stokes GU RC	4.00	1.80
112 Daniel Cabrera GU RC	8.00	3.60
113 Josh Willingham GU RC	5.00	2.20
114 Mark Teixeira GU	4.00	1.80
115 Pete LaForest GU RC	5.00	2.20
116 Chris Waters GU RC	4.00	1.80
117 Chien-Ming Wang GU RC	5.00	2.20
118 Ian Ferguson GU RC	4.00	1.80
119 Rocco Baldelli GU	4.00	1.80
120 Terrmel Sledge GU RC	5.00	2.20
121 Hank Blalock GU	5.00	2.20
122 Alejandro Machado GU RC	4.00	1.80
123 Hee Seop Choi GU	4.00	1.80
124 Guillermo Quiroz GU RC	5.00	2.20
125 Chase Utley GU	4.00	1.80
126 Nook Logan GU RC	4.00	1.80
127 Josh Hall GU RC	5.00	2.20
128 Ryan Church GU	4.00	1.80
129 Lew Ford GU RC	5.00	2.20
130 Francisco Rosario GU RC	4.00	1.80
131 Dan Haren GU RC	5.00	2.20
132 Rickie Weeks GU RC	8.00	3.60
133 Prentice Redman GU RC	4.00	1.80
134 Craig Brazell GU RC	5.00	2.20
135 Jon Leicester GU RC	4.00	1.80
136 Ryan Wagner GU RC	5.00	2.20
137 Matt Kata GU RC	5.00	2.20
138 Edwin Jackson GU RC	8.00	3.60
139 Mike Ryan GU RC	5.00	2.20
140 Delmon Young GU RC	10.00	4.50
141 Bo Hart GU RC	5.00	2.20
142 Jeff Duncan GU RC	5.00	2.20
143 Robby Hammock GU RC	5.00	2.20
144 Michael Hessman GU RC	4.00	1.80
145 Clint Barmes GU RC	5.00	2.20

2003 Fleer Genuine Reflection Ascending

MINT NRMT

*1-100 PRINT RUN b/wn 26-35: 8X TO 20X
*1-100 PRINT RUN b/wn 36-50: 6X TO 15X
*1-100 PRINT RUN b/wn 51-65: 5X TO 12X
*1-100 PRINT RUN b/wn 66-80: 4X TO 10X
*1-100 PRINT RUN b/wn 81-100: 3X TO 8X
*101-130 P/R b/wn 101-130: .6X TO 1.5X
*101-130 P/R b/wn 101-130: .6X TO 1.5X RC
RANDOM INSERTS IN PACKS
PRINT RUNS B/WN 1-130 COPIES PER CARD
1-25 NOT PRICED DUE TO SCARCITY

2003 Fleer Genuine Reflection Descending

MINT NRMT

*1-100 PRINT RUN b/wn 130-101: 2.5X TO 6X
*1-100 PRINT RUN b/wn 100-81: 3X TO 8X
*1-100 PRINT RUN b/wn 80-66: 4X TO 10X
*1-100 PRINT RUN b/wn 65-51: 5X TO 12X
*1-100 PRINT RUN b/wn 50-36: 6X TO 15X
*1-100 PRINT RUN b/wn 35-31: 8X TO 20X
*101-130 P/R b/wn 80-26: 1.25X TO 3X
RANDOM INSERTS IN PACKS
PRINT RUNS B/WN 1-130 COPIES PER CARD
101-105 RC'S NOT PRICED DUE TO SCARCITY
106-130 NOT PRICED DUE TO SCARCITY

2003 Fleer Genuine Article Insider Game Jersey

Inserted into packs at a stated rate of one in 24, these 25 cards feature game-used swatches from some major league stars. Several of the cards in this set were produced in smaller quantities and we have noted the announced print run next to the player's name in our checklist.

	MINT	NRMT
AD Adam Dunn	10.00	4.50
AJ Andruw Jones SP/200	8.00	3.60
AR Alex Rodriguez SP/50		
AS Alfonso Soriano SP/300	10.00	4.50
CJ Chipper Jones	10.00	4.50
CS Curt Schilling	8.00	3.60
DJ Derek Jeter SP/450	25.00	11.00
DM Don Mattingly Pants	25.00	11.00
JB Jeff Bagwell	10.00	4.50
JG Jason Giambi SP/50		
LB Lance Berkman	8.00	3.60
MO Magglio Ordonez	8.00	3.60
MP Mike Piazza SP/100	20.00	9.00
MS Greg Maddux	10.00	4.50
MT Miguel Tejada SP/100	15.00	6.75
NG Nomar Garciaparra	15.00	6.75
PG Pat Burrell	8.00	3.60
PM Pedro Martinez	10.00	4.50
RJ Randy Johnson	10.00	4.50
SG Shawn Green	8.00	3.60
SS Sammy Sosa SP/300	15.00	6.75
TG Troy Glaus	8.00	3.60
TH Torii Hunter	8.00	3.60
TH2 Todd Helton	10.00	4.50
VG Vladimir Guerrero SP/100	20.00	9.00

2003 Fleer Genuine Article Insider Game Jersey Tag

Randomly inserted into packs, these 19 cards feature pieces of the "tags" used on uniforms. Each of these cards were issued to a stated print run of 10 serial numbered sets and no pricing is available due to market scarcity.

MINT NRMT

AJ Andruw Jones
AR Alex Rodriguez
AS Alfonso Soriano
CJ Chipper Jones
CS Curt Schilling
JB Jeff Bagwell
LB Lance Berkman
MP Mike Piazza
MT Miguel Tejada
NG Nomar Garciaparra
PB Pat Burrell
PM Pedro Martinez
RJ Randy Johnson
SG Shawn Green
SS Sammy Sosa
TG Troy Glaus
THe Todd Helton
THu Torii Hunter
VG Vladimir Guerrero

2003 Fleer Genuine Article Insider Game Jersey Autographs

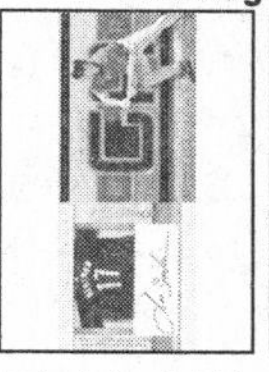
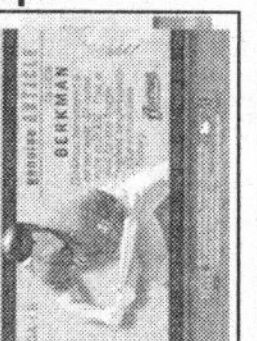

Randomly inserted into packs, these two cards parallel the Insider Game Jersey insert set but also have an autograph of the featured player.

	MINT	NRMT
RANDOM INSERTS IN PACKS		
PRINTS B/WN 165-170 COPIES PER CARD		
GA-DM Don Mattingly Pants	100.00	45.00
GA-LB Lance Berkman	30.00	13.50

2003 Fleer Genuine Article Insider Game Jersey Autographs VIP Blue

	MINT	NRMT
RANDOM INSERTS IN PACKS		
STATED PRINT RUN 50 SERIAL #'d SETS		
GA-DM Don Mattingly Pants	200.00	90.00
GA-LB Lance Berkman	60.00	27.00

2003 Fleer Genuine Article Insider Game Jersey Autographs VIP Red

	MINT	NRMT
RANDOM INSERTS IN PACKS		
STATED PRINT RUN 100 SERIAL #'d SETS		
GA-DJ Derek Jeter	150.00	70.00
GA-DM Don Mattingly Pants	150.00	70.00
GA-LB Lance Berkman	50.00	22.00

2003 Fleer Genuine Longball Threats

	MINT	NRMT
COMPLETE SET (15)	25.00	11.00
STATED ODDS 1:8		
1 Derek Jeter / Nomar Garciaparra	6.00	2.70
2 Jim Thome / Pat Burrell	2.50	1.10
3 Alex Rodriguez / Rafael Palmeiro	4.00	1.80
4 Alfonso Soriano / Hideki Matsui	5.00	2.20
5 Torii Hunter / Vladimir Guerrero	2.50	1.10
6 Mike Sweeney / Phil Nevin	1.50	.70
7 Mike Piazza / Sammy Sosa	4.00	1.80
8 Shawn Green / Jason Giambi	1.50	.70
9 Magglio Ordonez / Andruw Jones	1.50	.70
10 Eric Chavez / Carlos Delgado	1.50	.70
11 Manny Ramirez / Jeff Bagwell	1.50	.70
12 Scott Rolen / Troy Glaus	2.50	1.10
13 Barry Bonds / Miguel Tejada	6.00	2.70
14 Albert Pujols / Lance Berkman	5.00	2.20
15 Chipper Jones / Todd Helton	2.50	1.10

2003 Fleer Genuine Longball Threats Dual Patch

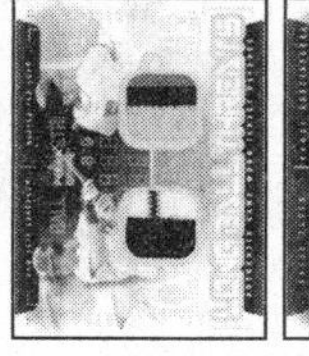

	MINT	NRMT
RANDOM INSERTS IN PACKS		
PRINT RUNS B/WN 36-100 COPIES PER CARD		
1 Derek Jeter / Nomar Garciaparra	100.00	45.00
2 Jim Thome / Pat Burrell	25.00	11.00
3 Alex Rodriguez / Rafael Palmeiro	50.00	22.00
5 Torii Hunter / Vladimir Guerrero	40.00	18.00
6 Mike Sweeney / Phil Nevin	40.00	18.00
7 Mike Piazza / Sammy Sosa	60.00	27.00
8 Shawn Green / Jason Giambi	15.00	6.75
9 Magglio Ordonez / Andruw Jones	15.00	6.75
11 Manny Ramirez / Jeff Bagwell	40.00	18.00
12 Scott Rolen / Troy Glaus	40.00	18.00
15 Chipper Jones / Todd Helton	40.00	18.00

2003 Fleer Genuine Longball Threats Dual Swatch

	MINT	NRMT
STATED ODDS 1:72		
1 Derek Jeter / Nomar Garciaparra	40.00	18.00
2 Jim Thome / Pat Burrell	15.00	6.75
3 Alex Rodriguez / Rafael Palmeiro	25.00	11.00
5 Torii Hunter / Vladimir Guerrero	15.00	6.75
6 Mike Sweeney / Phil Nevin	10.00	4.50
7 Mike Piazza / Sammy Sosa	25.00	11.00
8 Shawn Green / Jason Giambi	10.00	4.50
9 Magglio Ordonez / Andruw Jones	10.00	4.50
11 Manny Ramirez / Jeff Bagwell	15.00	6.75
12 Scott Rolen / Troy Glaus	15.00	6.75
15 Chipper Jones / Todd Helton	15.00	6.75

2003 Fleer Genuine Longball Threats Single Swatch

	MINT	NRMT
STATED ODDS 1:13		
SP PRINT RUNS PROVIDED BY FLEER		
SP'S ARE NOT SERIAL-NUMBERED		
1A Derek Jeter Jsy / Nomar Garciaparra SP/300	25.00	11.00
1B Nomar Garciaparra Jsy / Derek Jeter	15.00	6.75
2A Jim Thome Jsy / Pat Burrell	10.00	4.50
2B Pat Burrell Jsy / Jim Thome	8.00	3.60
3B Rafael Palmeiro Jsy / Alex Rodriguez	10.00	4.50
4A Alfonso Soriano Jsy / Hideki Matsui SP/250	25.00	11.00
5A Torii Hunter Jsy / Vladimir Guerrero	8.00	3.60
5B Vladimir Guerrero Jsy / Torii Hunter	10.00	4.50
6A Mike Sweeney Jsy / Phil Nevin	8.00	3.60
6B Phil Nevin Jsy / Mike Sweeney SP/300	8.00	3.60

7A Mike Piazza Jsy 15.00 6.75
Sammy Sosa
7B Sammy Sosa Jsy 25.00 11.00
Mike Piazza SP/100
8A Shawn Green Jsy 8.00 3.60
Jason Giambi
8B Jason Giambi Jsy ....
Shawn Green SP/50
9A Magglio Ordonez Jsy 8.00 3.60
Andruw Jones
9B Andruw Jones Jsy 8.00 3.60
Magglio Ordonez SP/200
10B Carlos Delgado Jsy 8.00 3.60
Eric Chavez
11A Manny Ramirez Jsy 10.00 4.50
Jeff Bagwell
11B Jeff Bagwell Jsy 10.00 4.50
Manny Ramirez SP/450
12A Scott Rolen Jsy 10.00 4.50
Troy Glaus
12B Troy Glaus Jsy 10.00 4.50
Scott Rolen
13B Miguel Tejada Jsy 8.00 3.60
Barry Bonds
14B Lance Berkman Jsy 8.00 3.60
Albert Pujols
15A Chipper Jones Jsy 10.00 4.50
Todd Helton
15B Todd Helton Jsy 10.00 4.50
Chipper Jones

2003 Fleer Genuine Tools of the Game

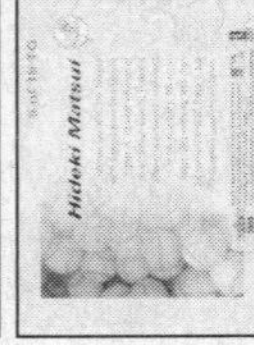

MINT NRMT
STATED ODDS 1:20..............................
1 Adam Dunn 3.00 1.35
2 Chipper Jones 5.00 2.20
3 Torii Hunter 3.00 1.35
4 Mike Piazza 8.00 3.60
5 Hideki Matsui 8.00 3.60
6 Nomar Garciaparra 8.00 3.60
7 Derek Jeter 12.00 5.50
8 Alex Rodriguez 8.00 3.60
9 Alfonso Soriano 3.00 1.35
10 Pat Burrell 3.00 1.35
11 Barry Bonds 12.00 5.50
12 Jason Giambi 3.00 1.35
13 Sammy Sosa 8.00 3.60
14 Vladimir Guerrero 5.00 2.20
15 Ichiro Suzuki 8.00 3.60

2003 Fleer Genuine Tools of the Game Bat

MINT NRMT
STATED ODDS 1:42..............................
1 Adam Dunn 8.00 3.60
4 Mike Piazza 12.00 5.50
7 Derek Jeter 20.00 9.00
8 Alex Rodriguez 12.00 5.50
9 Alfonso Soriano 8.00 3.60
12 Jason Giambi 5.00 2.20
13 Sammy Sosa 12.00 5.50
14 Vladimir Guerrero 8.00 3.60

2003 Fleer Genuine Tools of the Game Bat-Jersey

MINT NRMT
RANDOM INSERTS IN PACKS ....
STATED PRINT RUN 250 SERIAL #'d SETS
1 Adam Dunn 15.00 6.75
4 Mike Piazza 25.00 11.00
7 Derek Jeter 40.00 18.00
8 Alex Rodriguez ....
9 Alfonso Soriano 15.00 6.75
12 Jason Giambi 10.00 4.50
13 Sammy Sosa 25.00 11.00
14 Vladimir Guerrero 15.00 6.75

2003 Fleer Genuine Tools of the Game Bat-Jersey-Cap

MINT NRMT
RANDOM INSERTS IN PACKS ....
STATED PRINT RUN 100 SERIAL #'d SETS
1 Adam Dunn 30.00 13.50
4 Mike Piazza 50.00 22.00
7 Derek Jeter 80.00 36.00
8 Alex Rodriguez 50.00 22.00

9 Alfonso Soriano 30.00 13.50
12 Jason Giambi 20.00 9.00
13 Sammy Sosa 50.00 22.00
14 Vladimir Guerrero 30.00 13.50

2004 Fleer Genuine Insider

Nm-Mt Ex-Mt
COMP.SET w/o SP's (90) 25.00 7.50
COMMON CARD (1-90) .... .50 .15
COMMON CARD (91-100) 4.00 1.20
91-100 PRINT RUN 499 SERIAL #'d SETS
COMMON CARD (101-120) .... 3.00 .90
101-120 PRINT RUN 799 SERIAL #'d SETS
91-120 STATED ODDS 1:14 HOB, 1:72 RET
COMMON CARD (121-130) 5.00 1.50
121-130 SEEDED WITHIN RI 91-100 CARDS
121-130 PRINT RUN 350 SERIAL #'d SETS
121-130 ARE MINI-SIZED CARDS .....
1 Troy Glaus .... .50 .15
2 Eric Chavez .... .50 .15
3 Lance Berkman .... .50 .15
4 Pedro Martinez .... 1.25 .35
5 Jim Edmonds .... .50 .15
6 Tom Glavine .... 1.25 .35
7 Ken Griffey Jr. .... 2.00 .60
8 Vernon Wells .... .50 .15
9 Hideki Matsui .... 2.00 .60
10 Jeff Bagwell .... .75 .23
11 Rafael Palmeiro .... .75 .23
12 Edgar Martinez .... .75 .23
13 Bernie Williams .... .75 .23
14 Josh Beckett .... .50 .15
15 Javy Lopez .... .50 .15
16 Ichiro Suzuki .... 2.00 .60
17 Scott Podsednik .... .50 .15
18 Sammy Sosa .... 2.00 .60
19 Mark Teixeira .... .50 .15
20 Jorge Posada .... .75 .23
21 Miguel Cabrera .... .75 .23
22 Chipper Jones .... 1.25 .35
23 Sean Burroughs .... .50 .15
24 Dmitri Young .... .50 .15
25 Brandon Webb .... .50 .15
26 Bobby Abreu .... .50 .15
27 Hideo Nomo .... 1.25 .35
28 Frank Thomas .... 1.25 .35
29 Alex Rodriguez .... 2.00 .60
30 Derek Jeter .... 2.50 .75
31 Todd Helton .... .75 .23
32 Andruw Jones .... .50 .15
33 Jason Kendall .... .50 .15
34 Eric Gagne .... 1.25 .35
35 Omar Vizquel .... .75 .23
36 Vladimir Guerrero .... 1.25 .35
37 Jim Thome .... 1.25 .35
38 Mike Sweeney .... .50 .15
39 Manny Ramirez .... .75 .23
40 Scott Rolen .... 1.25 .35
41 Jose Vidro .... .50 .15
42 Adam Dunn .... .75 .23
43 Garret Anderson .... .50 .15
44 Mike Lieberthal .... .50 .15
45 Roy Oswalt .... .50 .15
46 Geoff Jenkins .... .50 .15
47 Magglio Ordonez .... .50 .15
48 Hank Blalock .... .50 .15
49 Barry Zito .... .50 .15
50 Dontrelle Willis .... .50 .15
51 Greg Maddux .... 2.00 .60
52 Brian Giles .... .50 .15
53 Shawn Green .... .50 .15
54 Carlos Lee .... .50 .15
55 Carlos Delgado .... .50 .15
56 Alfonso Soriano .... .75 .23
57 Angel Berroa .... .50 .15
58 Kerry Wood .... 1.25 .35
59 Rocco Baldelli .... .50 .15
60 Gary Sheffield .... .50 .15
61 Ivan Rodriguez .... 1.25 .35
62 Richie Sexson .... .50 .15
63 Marlon Byrd .... .50 .15
64 Carlos Beltran .... .75 .23
65 Mark Prior .... 1.25 .35
66 Aubrey Huff .... .50 .15
67 Jason Giambi .... .50 .15
68 Curt Schilling .... .75 .23
69 Reggie Sanders .... .50 .15
70 Mike Piazza .... 2.00 .60
71 Craig Monroe .... .50 .15
72 Randy Johnson .... 1.25 .35
73 Pat Burrell .... .50 .15
74 Craig Biggio .... .75 .23
75 Nomar Garciaparra .... 2.00 .60
76 Albert Pujols .... 2.50 .75
77 Jose Reyes .... .50 .15
78 Preston Wilson .... .50 .15
79 Miguel Tejada .... .50 .15
80 Bret Boone .... .50 .15
81 Shannon Stewart .... .50 .15
82 Jody Gerut .... .50 .15
83 Tim Salmon .... .75 .23
84 Tim Hudson .... .50 .15
85 Juan Pierre .... .50 .15
86 Jay Gibbons .... .50 .15
87 Jason Schmidt .... .50 .15
88 Torii Hunter .... .50 .15
89 Austin Kearns .... .50 .15
90 Roy Halladay .... .50 .15
91 John Gall RI RC 5.00 1.50
92 Kaz Matsui RI RC 10.00 3.00
93 Merkin Valdez RI RC 5.00 1.50
94 William Bergolla RI RC 4.00 1.20
95 Angel Chavez RI RC 4.00 1.20
96 Hector Gimenez RI RC 4.00 1.20
97 Aarom Baldiris RI RC 5.00 1.50
98 Justin Leone RI RC 5.00 1.50
99 Onil Joseph RI RC 4.00 1.20
100 Freddy Guzman RI RC 4.00 1.20
101 Rickie Weeks UP .... 3.00 .90
102 Chad Bentz UP RC .... 3.00 .90
103 Bobby Crosby UP 5.00 1.50
104 Dallas McPherson UP 5.00 1.50
105 Brandon Watson UP .... 3.00 .90
106 Garrett Atkins UP .... 3.00 .90
107 Graham Koonce UP .... 3.00 .90
108 Chien-Ming Wang UP .... 3.00 .90
109 Jonny Gomes UP .... 3.00 .90
110 Edwin Jackson UP .... 3.00 .90
111 Alfredo Simon UP RC .... 3.00 .90
112 Delmon Young UP 5.00 1.50
113 Angel Guzman UP .... 3.00 .90
114 Ryan Howard UP .... 3.00 .90
115 Scott Hairston UP .... 3.00 .90
116 Edwin Encarnacion UP .... 3.00 .90
117 Byron Gettis UP .... 3.00 .90
118 Kevin Youkilis UP .... 3.00 .90
119 Grady Sizemore UP .... 3.00 .90
120 Corey Hart UP .... 3.00 .90
121 Greg Dobbs MRI RC 5.00 1.50
122 Jerry Gil MRI RC 5.00 1.50
123 Shawn Hill MRI RC 5.00 1.50
124 John Labandeira MRI RC 5.00 1.50
125 Jason Bartlett MRI RC 8.00 2.40
126 Ronny Cedeno MRI RC 5.00 1.50
127 Don Kelly MRI RC 5.00 1.50
128 Ivan Ochoa MRI RC 5.00 1.50
129 Mariano Gomez MRI RC 5.00 1.50
130 Ruddy Yan MRI 5.00 1.50

2004 Fleer Genuine Insider Mini Masterpiece

Nm-Mt Ex-Mt
RANDOM WITHIN ROOK.INSIDER CARDS
STATED PRINT RUN 1 SERIAL #'d SET
NO PRICING DUE TO SCARCITY ....

2004 Fleer Genuine Insider Mini Parallel 137

Nm-Mt Ex-Mt
*PARA.137: .6X TO 1.5X BASIC ....
RANDOM WITHIN ROOKIE INSIDER CARDS
STATED PRINT RUN 137 SERIAL #'d SETS
92 Kaz Matsui RI 15.00 4.50

2004 Fleer Genuine Insider Reflections

Nm-Mt Ex-Mt
*REFL 1-90: 3X TO 8X BASIC ....
*REFL 101-120: .6X TO 1.5X BASIC....
STATED ODDS 1:24 HOBBY, 1:200 RETAIL
STATED PRINT RUN 99 SERIAL #'d SETS

2004 Fleer Genuine Insider Article Jersey

Nm-Mt Ex-Mt
STATED PRINT RUN 250 SERIAL #'d SETS
*ARTICLE BAT: .5X TO 1.2X BASIC ....
ARTICLE BAT PRINT RUN 100 #'d SETS
*ARTICLE BAT-JSY: 1X TO 2.5X BASIC
ARTICLE BAT-JSY PRINT RUN 50 #'d SETS
ARTICLE JSY TAG PRINT RUN 5 #'d SETS
NO ART.JSY TAG PRICE DUE TO SCARCITY
OVERALL ODDS GU 1:9 H, AU-GU 1:48 R
AD Adam Dunn 8.00 2.40
AP Albert Pujols 15.00 4.50
AR Alex Rodriguez 15.00 4.50
AS Alfonso Soriano 8.00 2.40
CD Carlos Delgado 5.00 1.50
CJ Chipper Jones 8.00 2.40
DJ Derek Jeter 20.00 6.00
GS Gary Sheffield 5.00 1.50
HB Hank Blalock 5.00 1.50
JG Jason Giambi 5.00 1.50
JR Jose Reyes 5.00 1.50
JT Jim Thome 8.00 2.40
LB Lance Berkman 5.00 1.50
MC Miguel Cabrera 8.00 2.40
MO Magglio Ordonez 5.00 1.50
MP Mike Piazza 12.00 3.60
MR Manny Ramirez 8.00 2.40
MT Mark Teixeira 5.00 1.50
NG Nomar Garciaparra 12.00 3.60
RB Rocco Baldelli 5.00 1.50
RP Rafael Palmeiro 8.00 2.40
SS Sammy Sosa 12.00 3.60
TG Troy Glaus 5.00 1.50
TH Todd Helton 8.00 2.40
VG Vladimir Guerrero 8.00 2.40

2004 Fleer Genuine Insider Autograph

Nm-Mt Ex-Mt
OVERALL ODDS AU 1:18 H, AU-GU 1:48 R
PRINT RUNS B/WN 27-550 COPIES PER

AH Aubrey Huff/550 .... 10.00 3.00
AK Austin Kearns/350 .... 10.00 3.00
BW Brandon Webb/450 .... 8.00 2.40
CJ Chipper Jones/50 ....
DE David Eckstein/350 .... 10.00 3.00
IR Ivan Rodriguez/150 .... 40.00 12.00
JG Jody Gerut/550 .... 10.00 3.00
JG2 Jay Gibbons/350 .... 8.00 2.40
JR Jose Reyes/350 .... 10.00 3.00
JR2 Jimmy Rollins/350 .... 10.00 3.00
JS Jason Schmidt/300 .... 25.00 7.50
JS2 John Smoltz/150 .... 40.00 12.00
MB Marlon Byrd/550 .... 8.00 2.40
MC Miguel Cabrera/250 .... 20.00 6.00
MO Magglio Ordonez/250 .... 12.00 3.60
MR Mariano Rivera/150 .... 50.00 15.00
MT Mark Teixeira/350 .... 15.00 4.50
OH Orlando Hudson/550 .... 8.00 2.40
RA Roberto Alomar/150 .... 20.00 6.00
RJ Randy Johnson/51 .... 80.00 24.00
RP Rafael Palmeiro/150 .... 40.00 12.00
SP Scott Podsednik/550 .... 10.00 3.00
VG Vladimir Guerrero/27 .... 60.00 18.00

2004 Fleer Genuine Insider Autograph Cuts

Nm-Mt Ex-Mt
OVERALL ODDS AU 1:18 H, AU-GU 1:48 R
PRINT RUNS B/WN 1-10 COPIES PER
NO PRICING DUE TO SCARCITY ....
BT Bill Terry/10 ....
CS Casey Stengel/3 ....
PT Pie Traynor/1 ....
RM Roger Maris/1 ....
ZW Zack Wheat/1 ....

2004 Fleer Genuine Insider Autograph-Jersey

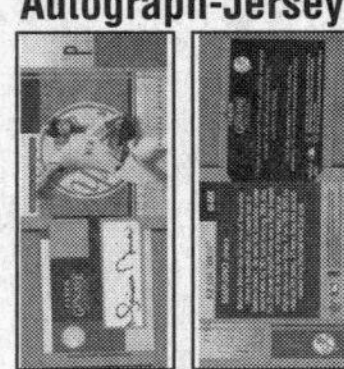

Nm-Mt Ex-Mt
STATED PRINT RUN 100 SERIAL #'d SETS
AUTO BALL PRINT RUN 10 #'d SETS.
NO AUTO BALL PRICING DUE TO SCARCITY
*AUTO BAT: .5X TO 1.2X BASIC ....
AUTO BAT PRINT RUN 50 SERIAL #'d SETS
OVERALL ODDS AU 1:18 H, AU-GU 1:48 R
AH Aubrey Huff 15.00 4.50
AK Austin Kearns 15.00 4.50
AP Albert Pujols 120.00 36.00
BW Brandon Webb 15.00 4.50
DE David Eckstein 15.00 4.50
IR Ivan Rodriguez 50.00 15.00
JG Jody Gerut 15.00 4.50
JG2 Jay Gibbons 15.00 4.50
JR Jose Reyes 15.00 4.50
JR2 Jimmy Rollins 15.00 4.50
JS Jason Schmidt 50.00 15.00
JS2 John Smoltz 50.00 15.00
MB Marlon Byrd 15.00 4.50
MC Miguel Cabrera 25.00 7.50
MO Magglio Ordonez 15.00 4.50
MR Mariano Rivera 60.00 18.00
MT Mark Teixeira 25.00 7.50
OH Orlando Hudson 15.00 4.50
RA Roberto Alomar 25.00 7.50
RP Rafael Palmeiro 50.00 15.00
SP Scott Podsednik 15.00 4.50

2004 Fleer Genuine Insider Classic Confrontations

Nm-Mt Ex-Mt
STATED ODDS 1:18 HOBBY, 1:24 RETAIL
1 Mike Piazza 8.00 2.40
Roger Clemens
2 Pedro Martinez 8.00 2.40
Derek Jeter
3 Randy Johnson 4.00 1.20
Jeff Bagwell
4 Mark Prior 8.00 2.40
Albert Pujols
5 Josh Beckett 6.00 1.80
Sammy Sosa
6 Eric Gagne 4.00 1.20
Hank Blalock
7 Mariano Rivera 6.00 1.80
Nomar Garciaparra
8 Curt Schilling 4.00 1.20
Chipper Jones
9 Kerry Wood 4.00 1.20
Jim Edmonds
10 Barry Zito 4.00 1.20
Alfonso Soriano
11 Randy Johnson 6.00 1.80
Ken Griffey Jr.
12 Derek Jeter 8.00 2.40
John Smoltz
13 Roy Oswalt 6.00 1.80
Ken Griffey Jr.
14 Dontrelle Willis 6.00 1.80
Hideki Matsui
15 Hideo Nomo 6.00 1.80
Ichiro Suzuki

2004 Fleer Genuine Insider Classic Confrontations Dual Swatch

Nm-Mt Ex-Mt
STATED PRINT RUN 100 SERIAL #'d SETS
DUAL PATCH PRINT RUN 10 #'d SETS
NO DUAL PATCH PRICE DUE TO SCARCITY
OVERALL ODDS GU 1:9 H, AU-GU 1:48 R
BZAS Barry Zito 15.00 4.50
Alfonso Soriano
CSCJ Curt Schilling 15.00 4.50
Chipper Jones
EGHB Eric Gagne 15.00 4.50
Hank Blalock
JBSS Josh Beckett 15.00 4.50
Sammy Sosa
KWJE Kerry Wood 15.00 4.50
Jim Edmonds
MPAP Mark Prior 25.00 7.50
Albert Pujols
MPRC Mike Piazza ....
Roger Clemens
MRNG Mariano Rivera 15.00 4.50
Nomar Garciaparra
PMDJ Pedro Martinez 25.00 7.50
Derek Jeter
RJJB Randy Johnson 15.00 4.50
Jeff Bagwell

2004 Fleer Genuine Insider Classic Confrontations Swatch

Nm-Mt Ex-Mt
OVERALL ODDS GU 1:9 H, AU-GU 1:48 R
STATED PRINT RUN 400 SERIAL #'d SETS
AP A.Pujols Jsy w/Prior 12.00 3.60
AS A.Soriano Jsy w/Zito 8.00 2.40
BZ B.Zito Jsy w/Soriano 5.00 1.50
CJ C.Jones Jsy w/Schilling 8.00 2.40
CS C.Schilling Jsy w/Chipper 8.00 2.40
DJ D.Jeter Jsy w/Pedro 15.00 4.50
DW D.Willis Jsy w/Matsui 5.00 1.50
EG E.Gagne Jsy w/Blalock 8.00 2.40
HB H.Blalock Jsy w/Gagne 5.00 1.50
HN H.Nomo Jsy w/Ichiro 8.00 2.40
JB J.Bagwell Jsy w/Randy 8.00 2.40
JB2 J.Beckett Jsy w/Sosa 5.00 1.50
JE J.Edmonds Jsy w/Wood 5.00 1.50
JS J.Smoltz Jsy w/Jeter 8.00 2.40
KW K.Wood Jsy w/Edmonds 8.00 2.40
MP M.Piazza Jsy w/Clemens 10.00 3.00
MP2 M.Prior Jsy w/Pujols 10.00 3.00
MR M.Rivera Jsy w/Nomar 8.00 2.40
NG N.Garciaparra Jsy w/Rivera. 10.00 3.00
PM P.Martinez Jsy w/Jeter 8.00 2.40
RC R.Clemens Jsy w/Piazza 12.00 3.60
RJ1 R.Johnson Jsy w/Bagwell 8.00 2.40
RJ2 R.Johnson Jsy w/Griffey Jr.. 8.00 2.40
RO R.Oswalt Jsy w/Griffey Jr. 5.00 1.50
SS S.Sosa Jsy w/Beckett 10.00 3.00

2004 Fleer Genuine Insider Tools of the Game

Nm-Mt Ex-Mt
STATED ODDS 1:6 HOBBY, 1:12 RETAIL
1 Jason Giambi .... 1.50 .45
2 Torii Hunter .... 1.50 .45
3 Derek Jeter 5.00 1.50
4 Nomar Garciaparra 4.00 1.20
5 Albert Pujols 5.00 1.50
6 Jim Thome .... 2.50 .75
7 Alex Rodriguez 4.00 1.20
8 Chipper Jones .... 2.50 .75

9 Sammy Sosa 4.00 1.20
10 Jose Reyes 1.50 .45
11 Pedro Martinez 2.50 .75
12 Greg Maddux 4.00 1.20
13 Randy Johnson 2.50 .75
14 Curt Schilling 2.50 .75
15 Mark Prior 2.50 .75
16 Ichiro Suzuki 4.00 1.20
17 Hideki Matsui 4.00 1.20
18 Kaz Matsui 5.00 1.50
19 Ken Griffey Jr. 4.00 1.20
20 Josh Beckett 1.50 .45

2004 Fleer Genuine Insider Tools of the Game Jersey

Nm-Mt Ex-Mt
STATED PRINT RUN 250 SERIAL #'d SETS
*TOOLS 2-PIECE: .75X TO 2X BASIC
TOOLS 2-PIECE PRINT RUN 125 #'d SETS
TOOLS 2-PIECE ARE BAT-JSY CARDS
*TOOLS 3-PIECE: 1.5X TO 4X BASIC
TOOLS 3-PIECE PRINT RUN 75 #'d SETS
TOOLS 3-PIECE ARE BAT-CAP-JSY CARDS
OVERALL ODDS GU 1:9 H, AU-GU 1:48 R
AP Albert Pujols Jsy 15.00 4.50
AR Alex Rodriguez Jsy 15.00 4.50
CJ Chipper Jones Jsy 8.00 2.40
CS Curt Schilling Jsy 8.00 2.40
DJ Derek Jeter Jsy 20.00 6.00
GM Greg Maddux Jsy 12.00 3.60
JG Jason Giambi Jsy 5.00 1.50
JR Jose Reyes Jsy 5.00 1.50
JT Jim Thome Jsy 8.00 2.40
MP Mark Prior Jsy 8.00 2.40
NG Nomar Garciaparra Jsy 12.00 3.60
PM Pedro Martinez Jsy 8.00 2.40
RJ Randy Johnson Jsy 8.00 2.40
SS Sammy Sosa Jsy 12.00 3.60
TH Torii Hunter Jsy 5.00 1.50

2002 Fleer Hot Prospects

This 125 standard-size set was released in August, 2002. It was issued in five card packs with an $3 SRP which were issued 15 packs to a box and 6 boxes to a case. Cards numbered 81-105 feature not only a rookie/prospect card but also has a game-used memorabilia piece attached to the card while cards numbered 106 through 125 just features rookies. Cards 81-105 have a stated print run of 1000 serial numbered sets and cards 106-125 have a stated print run of 1500 sets.

Nm-Mt Ex-Mt
COMP.SET w/o SP's (80) 30.00 9.00
COMMON CARD (1-80) .50 .15
COMMON CARD (81-105) 10.00 3.00
COMMON CARD (106-125) 5.00 1.50
1 Derek Jeter 3.00 .90
2 Garret Anderson .50 .15
3 Scott Rolen 1.25 .35
4 Bret Boone .50 .15
5 Lance Berkman .50 .15
6 Andruw Jones .50 .15
7 Ivan Rodriguez 1.25 .35
8 Bernie Williams .75 .23
9 Cristian Guzman .50 .15
10 Mo Vaughn .50 .15
11 Troy Glaus .50 .15
12 Tim Salmon .75 .23
13 Jason Giambi .50 .15
14 Cliff Floyd .50 .15
15 Tim Hudson .50 .15
16 Curt Schilling .50 .15
17 Sammy Sosa 2.00 .60
18 Alex Rodriguez 2.00 .60
19 Chuck Knoblauch .50 .15
20 Jason Kendall .50 .15
21 Ben Sheets .50 .15
22 Nomar Garciaparra 2.00 .60
23 Ryan Klesko .50 .15
24 Greg Vaughn .50 .15
25 Rafael Palmeiro .75 .23
26 Miguel Tejada .50 .15
27 Shea Hillenbrand .50 .15
28 Jim Thome 1.25 .35
29 Randy Johnson 1.25 .35
30 Barry Larkin .75 .23
31 Paul LoDuca .50 .15
32 Pedro Martinez 1.25 .35
33 Luis Gonzalez .50 .15
34 Carlos Delgado .50 .15
35 Richie Sexson .50 .15
36 Albert Pujols 2.50 .75
37 Bobby Abreu .50 .15
38 Gary Sheffield .50 .15
39 Magglio Ordonez .50 .15
40 Eric Chavez .50 .15
41 Jeff Bagwell .75 .23
42 Doug Mientkiewicz .50 .15
43 Moises Alou .50 .15
44 Todd Helton .75 .23
45 Ichiro Suzuki 2.00 .60
46 Jose Cruz Jr. .50 .15
47 Freddy Garcia .50 .15
48 Tino Martinez .75 .23
49 Roger Clemens 2.50 .75
50 Greg Maddux 2.00 .60
51 Mike Piazza 2.00 .60
52 Roberto Alomar .75 .23
53 Adam Dunn .75 .23
54 Kerry Wood 1.25 .35
55 Edgar Martinez .75 .23
56 Ken Griffey Jr. 2.00 .60
57 Juan Gonzalez .75 .23
58 Pat Burrell .50 .15
59 Corey Koskie .50 .15
60 Jose Vidro .50 .15
61 Ben Grieve .50 .15
62 Barry Bonds 3.00 .90
63 Raul Mondesi .50 .15
64 Jimmy Rollins .50 .15
65 Mike Sweeney .50 .15
66 Josh Beckett .50 .15
67 Chipper Jones 1.25 .35
68 Jeff Kent .50 .15
69 Tony Batista .50 .15
70 Phil Nevin .50 .15
71 Brian Jordan .50 .15
72 Rich Aurilia .50 .15
73 Brian Giles .50 .15
74 Frank Thomas 1.25 .35
75 Larry Walker .75 .23
76 Shawn Green .50 .15
77 Manny Ramirez .75 .23
78 Craig Biggio .75 .23
79 Vladimir Guerrero 1.25 .35
80 Jeromy Burnitz .50 .15
81 Mark Teixeira FS Pants 12.00 3.60
82 Corey Thurman FS Pants RC 10.00 3.00
83 Mark Prior FS Bat 20.00 6.00
84 Marlon Byrd FS Pants 10.00 3.00
85 Austin Kearns FS Pants 10.00 3.00
86 Satoru Komiyama FS Jsy RC 10.00 3.00
87 So Taguchi FS Bat RC 12.00 3.60
88 Jorge Padilla FS Pants RC 10.00 3.00
89 Rene Reyes FS Pants RC 10.00 3.00
90 Jorge Nunez FS Pants RC 10.00 3.00
91 Ron Calloway FS Pants RC 10.00 3.00
92 Kazuhisa Ishii FS Jsy RC 15.00 4.50
93 Dewon Brazelton FS Pants 10.00 3.00
94 Angel Berroa FS Pants 10.00 3.00
95 Felix Escalona FS Pants RC 10.00 3.00
96 Sean Burroughs FS Bat 10.00 3.00
97 Br. Duckworth FS Pants 10.00 3.00
98 Hank Blalock FS Pants 12.00 3.60
99 Eric Hinske FS Pants 10.00 3.00
100 Carlos Pena FS Jsy 10.00 3.00
101 Morgan Ensberg FS Pants 10.00 3.00
102 Ryan Ludwick FS Pants 10.00 3.00
103 C. Snelling FS Pants RC 10.00 3.00
104 Jason Lane FS Pants 10.00 3.00
105 Drew Henson FS Bat 10.00 3.00
106 Bobby Kielty HP 5.00 1.50
107 Earl Snyder HP RC 8.00 2.40
108 Nate Field HP RC 5.00 1.50
109 Juan Diaz HP 5.00 1.50
110 Ryan Anderson HP 5.00 1.50
111 Esteban German HP 5.00 1.50
112 Takahito Nomura HP RC 5.00 1.50
113 David Kelton HP 5.00 1.50
114 Steve Kent HP RC 5.00 1.50
115 Colby Lewis HP 5.00 1.50
116 Jason Simontacchi HP RC 5.00 1.50
117 Rodrigo Rosario HP RC 5.00 1.50
118 Ben Howard HP RC 5.00 1.50
119 Hansel Izquierdo HP RC 5.00 1.50
120 John Ennis HP RC 5.00 1.50
121 Anderson Machado HP RC 5.00 1.50
122 Luis Ugueto HP RC 5.00 1.50
123 Anastacio Martinez HP RC 5.00 1.50
124 Reed Johnson HP RC 8.00 2.40
125 Juan Cruz HP 5.00 1.50

2002 Fleer Hot Prospects Future Swatch Autographs

Randomly inserted into packs, these four cards feature autographs of the noted rookie player. Each card has a stated print run of 100 serial numbered sets. All four of these cards were issued as redemptions within packs - each with an exchange deadline of July 31, 2003.

Nm-Mt Ex-Mt
83 Mark Prior FS Bat EXCH 120.00 36.00
87 So Taguchi FS Bat EXCH 25.00 7.50
89 Rene Reyes FS Pants EXCH 15.00 4.50
105 Drew Henson FS Bat 25.00 7.50

2002 Fleer Hot Prospects Co-Stars

Inserted in hobby packs at a stated rate of one in six, these 15 cards feature two players with something in common who are either stars or upcoming prospects.

Nm-Mt Ex-Mt
COMPLETE SET (15) 50.00 15.00

1 Barry Bonds 8.00 2.40
Alex Rodriguez
2 Derek Jeter 6.00 1.80
Nomar Garciaparra
3 Andruw Jones 3.00 .90
Chipper Jones
4 Juan Gonzalez 3.00 .90
Jim Thome
5 Pedro Martinez 3.00 .90
Randy Johnson
6 Adam Dunn 2.00 .60
Pat Burrell
7 Frank Thomas 3.00 .90
Manny Ramirez
8 Jeff Bagwell 2.00 .60
Lance Berkman
9 So Taguchi 8.00 2.40
Kazuhisa Ishii
10 Jimmy Rollins 2.00 .60
Miguel Tejada
11 Morgan Ensberg 2.00 .60
Carlos Pena
12 Adam Dunn 2.00 .60
Austin Kearns
13 Vladimir Guerrero 3.00 .90
Scott Rolen
14 Drew Henson 2.00 .60
Xavier Nady
15 Mike Piazza 5.00 1.50
Ivan Rodriguez

2002 Fleer Hot Prospects Inside Barry Bonds Memorabilia

Randomly inserted into packs, these eight cards feature different Barry Bonds memorabilia. Since each card has a different stated print run, we have put that information next to the player's name in our checklist along with the specific item cut up for use on the card.

Nm-Mt Ex-Mt
1 B.Bonds Home Pants/1000 25.00 7.50
2 B.Bonds Away Pants/900 25.00 7.50
3 B.Bonds Away Jsy/800 25.00 7.50
4 B.Bonds Bat/700 25.00 7.50
5 B.Bonds Base/600 20.00 6.00
6 B.Bonds Cleats/500 30.00 9.00
7 B.Bonds Btg Glv/400 30.00 9.00
8 B.Bonds Cap/300 40.00 12.00

2002 Fleer Hot Prospects Jerseygraphs

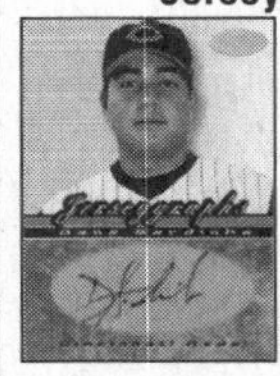
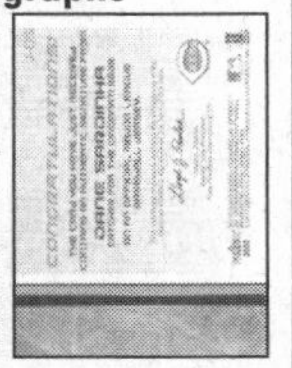

Inserted in hobby packs at stated odds of one in 186, these nine cards feature the player's signature on actual MLB jersey material. A few players were produced in shorter quantities and we have put that stated information next to their name in our checklist.

Nm-Mt Ex-Mt
J-AB Adrian Beltre SP/169 50.00 15.00
J-BB Barry Bonds SP/65 300.00 90.00
J-CJ Chipper Jones SP/100 100.00 30.00
J-DE David Espinosa 15.00 4.50
J-DH Drew Henson 40.00 12.00
J-DJ Derek Jeter SP/108 200.00 60.00
J-DS Dane Sardinha 15.00 4.50
J-GM Kazuhisa Ishii SP/40
J-ST So Taguchi SP/100 50.00 15.00

2002 Fleer Hot Prospects MLB Hot Materials

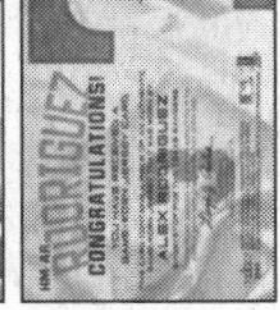

Inserted at a stated rate of one in nine, these 44 cards feature material worn and used by a variety of stars and rookies. A few players were printed in shorter quantities and we have provided the stated print run information next to their name in our checklist.

Nm-Mt Ex-Mt
AD2 Adam Dunn Jsy 15.00 4.50
AR Alex Rodriguez Jsy 15.00 4.50
BB Bret Boone Bat 10.00 3.00
BB2 Barry Bonds Pants 25.00 7.50
BD Brandon Duckworth Pants 10.00 3.00
BG Brian Giles Pants 10.00 3.00
BW Bernie Williams Jsy 15.00 4.50
CD Carlos Delgado Jsy 10.00 3.00
CG Cristian Guzman Bat SP/261 15.00 4.50
CP Carlos Pena Jsy SP/120 15.00 4.50
CP2 Corey Patterson Jsy 10.00 3.00
CS Curt Schilling Jsy 10.00 3.00
FG Freddy Garcia Jsy 10.00 3.00
FT Frank Thomas Jsy 15.00 4.50
GK Gabe Kapler Jsy 10.00 3.00
GM Greg Maddux Jsy 15.00 4.50
GS Gary Sheffield Bat 10.00 3.00
IR Ivan Rodriguez Jsy 15.00 4.50
JB Josh Beckett Jsy 10.00 3.00
JB2 Jeff Bagwell Jsy SP/108 20.00 6.00
JG Juan Gonzalez Jsy 15.00 4.50
JT Jim Thome Bat 15.00 4.50
JU Juan Uribe Bat 10.00 3.00
KI Kazuhisa Ishii Jsy SP/70
LB Lance Berkman Jsy 10.00 3.00
MM Mark Mulder Jsy 10.00 3.00
MO Moises Alou Bat 10.00 3.00
MO Magglio Ordonez Jsy 10.00 3.00
MP Mike Piazza Jsy 15.00 4.50
MS Mike Sweeney Jsy 10.00 3.00
NJ Nick Johnson Jsy 10.00 3.00
PL Paul LoDuca Jsy 10.00 3.00
PM Pedro Martinez Jsy 15.00 4.50
RF Rafael Furcal Jsy 10.00 3.00
RO Roy Oswalt Jsy 10.00 3.00
RP Rafael Palmeiro Jsy 15.00 4.50
SB Sean Burroughs Bat SP/350 15.00 4.50
SG Shawn Green Jsy 10.00 3.00
ST So Taguchi Bat 10.00 3.00
TA Tony Armas Jr. Jsy 10.00 3.00
TH Todd Helton Jsy 15.00 4.50
TH Torii Hunter Bat 10.00 3.00
TM Tino Martinez Bat 15.00 4.50
VW Vernon Wells Bat 10.00 3.00

2002 Fleer Hot Prospects MLB Red Hot Materials

Randomly inserted in packs, this is a parallel to the Hot Material insert set. Each of these cards have a stated print run of 50 serial numbered sets.

Nm-Mt Ex-Mt
*RED HOT: 1X TO 2.5X BASIC MATERIAL
*RED HOT: .75X TO 2X BASIC MATERIAL SP

2002 Fleer Hot Prospects MLB Hot Tandems

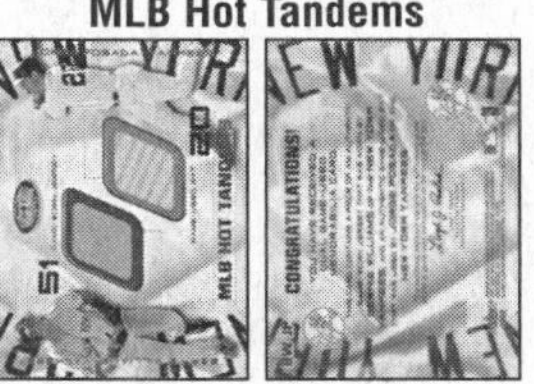

Randomly inserted in packs, these 45 cards feature dual memorabilia cards of two players who have something in common.

Nm-Mt Ex-Mt
ADCP Adam Dunn Jsy 20.00 6.00
Corey Patterson Jsy
ADLB Adam Dunn Jsy 20.00 6.00
Lance Berkman Jsy
ARIR Alex Rodriguez Jsy 40.00 12.00
Ivan Rodriguez Jsy
BBDJ Barry Bonds Pants 80.00 24.00
Derek Jeter Jsy
BBFG Bret Boone Bat 15.00 4.50
Freddy Garcia Jsy
BBKI Barry Bonds Pants 40.00 12.00
Kazuhisa Ishii Jsy
BBTH Bret Boone Bat 30.00 9.00
Torii Hunter Bat
BDJB Brandon Duckworth Pants 15.00 4.50
Josh Beckett Jsy
BDRO Brandon Duckworth Pants 15.00 4.50
Roy Oswalt Jsy
BWJP Bernie Williams Jsy 20.00 6.00
Jorge Posada Bat
BWNJ Bernie Williams Jsy 20.00 6.00
Nick Johnson Jsy
CDVW Carlos Delgado Jsy 15.00 4.50
Vernon Wells Bat
CGTH Cristian Guzman Bat 15.00 4.50
Torii Hunter Bat
CPCP Carlos Pena Jsy 15.00 4.50
Corey Patterson Jsy
CPNJ Carlos Pena Jsy 15.00 4.50
Nick Johnson Jsy
CSGM Curt Schilling Jsy 30.00 9.00
Greg Maddux Jsy
CSPM Curt Schilling Jsy 25.00 7.50
Pedro Martinez Jsy
FTMO Frank Thomas Jsy 25.00 7.50
Magglio Ordonez Jsy
GKJG Gabe Kapler Jsy 20.00 6.00
Juan Gonzalez Jsy
GKRP Gabe Kapler Jsy 20.00 6.00
Rafael Palmeiro Jsy
GMPM Greg Maddux Jsy 30.00 9.00
Pedro Martinez Jsy
GSRF Gary Sheffield Bat 15.00 4.50
Rafael Furcal Jsy
HBAK Hank Blalock Pants 25.00 7.50
Austin Kearns Pants
HBMT Hank Blalock Pants 25.00 7.50
Mark Teixeira Pants
JBLB Jeff Bagwell Jsy 20.00 6.00
Lance Berkman Jsy
JBMP Jeff Bagwell Jsy 30.00 9.00
Mike Piazza Jsy
JBRO Josh Beckett Jsy 15.00 4.50
Roy Oswalt Jsy
JGRP Juan Gonzalez Jsy 20.00 6.00
Rafael Palmeiro Jsy
JPMP Jorge Posada Bat 30.00 9.00
Mike Piazza Jsy
JTSG Jim Thome Bat 25.00 7.50
Shawn Green Jsy
JUCG Juan Uribe Bat 15.00 4.50
Cristian Guzman Bat
JUMT Juan Uribe Bat 15.00 4.50
Miguel Tejada Jsy
KIDJ Kazuhisa Ishii Jsy 40.00 12.00
Derek Jeter Jsy
KIMP Kazuhisa Ishii Jsy 25.00 7.50
Mark Prior Bat
KISK Kazuhisa Ishii Jsy 25.00 7.50
Satoru Komiyama Jsy
KIST Kazuhisa Ishii Jsy 25.00 7.50
So Taguchi Bat
MAMO Moises Alou Bat 15.00 4.50
Magglio Ordonez Jsy
MBAK Marlon Byrd Pants 15.00 4.50
Austin Kearns Pants
MBJP Marlon Byrd Pants 15.00 4.50
Jorge Padilla Pants
MMMT Mark Mulder Jsy 15.00 4.50
Miguel Tejada Jsy
MSTH Mike Sweeney Jsy 20.00 6.00
Todd Helton Jsy
PLSG Paul LoDuca Jsy 15.00 4.50
Shawn Green Jsy
SBDH Sean Burroughs Bat 15.00 4.50
Drew Henson Bat
TAFG Tony Armas Jr. Jsy 15.00 4.50
Freddy Garcia Jsy
TMTH Tino Martinez Bat 20.00 6.00
Todd Helton Jsy

2002 Fleer Hot Prospects We're Number One

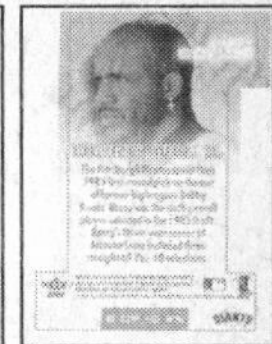

Inserted in packs at a stated rate of one in 15, these 10 cards feature players who had been drafted in the first round of the amateur draft.

Nm-Mt Ex-Mt
COMPLETE SET (10) 50.00 15.00
AR Alex Rodriguez 8.00 2.40
BB Barry Bonds 12.00 3.60
CJ Chipper Jones 4.00 1.20
DJ Derek Jeter 12.00 3.60
JD J.D. Drew 2.50 .75
KG Ken Griffey Jr. 8.00 2.40
MR Manny Ramirez 2.50 .75
NG Nomar Garciaparra 8.00 2.40
RC Roger Clemens 10.00 3.00
TH Todd Helton 2.50 .75

2002 Fleer Hot Prospects We're Number One Autographs

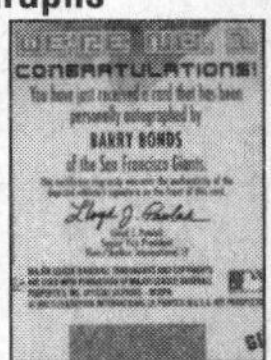

These two cards form a partial parallel to the We're Number One insert set. The two player, Bonds and Jeter each signed the number of cards numbered to the last two digits of their draft year.

Nm-Mt Ex-Mt
BB Barry Bonds/85 250.00 75.00
DJ Derek Jeter/92 150.00 45.00

2002 Fleer Hot Prospects We're Number One Memorabilia

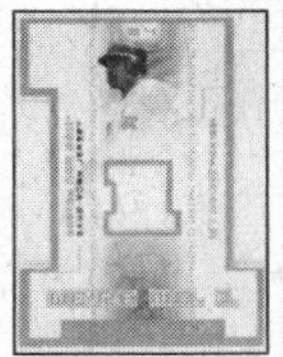

Inserted in hobby packs at stated odds, these nine cards form a partial parallel to the We're Number One insert set. With the exception of Ken Griffey Jr, each player has a game-used jersey swatch attached to it. Griffey's memorabilia piece comes from a game-used base.

Nm-Mt Ex-Mt
AR Alex Rodriguez Jsy 15.00 4.50
BB Barry Bonds Jsy 25.00 7.50
CJ Chipper Jones Jsy 15.00 4.50
DJ Derek Jeter Jsy 25.00 7.50
JD J.D. Drew Jsy 15.00 4.50
KG Ken Griffey Jr. Base SP 20.00 6.00
MR Manny Ramirez Jsy 15.00 4.50

NG Nomar Garciaparra Jsy 20.00 6.00
TH Todd Helton Jsy............... 15.00 4.50

2003 Fleer Hot Prospects

This 127-card set was distributed in two separate releases. The primary Hot Porspects product - containing the first 119 cards from the basic set - was released in August, 2003. This set was issued in five card packs with a $12 SRP which came 15 packs to a box and 12 boxes to a case. Cards numbered 1 through 80 feature veterans. Cards 81-119 feature a selection of prospects and rookies with many cards including a certified autograph or game used element (and in some cases both). One card from this run was guaranteed within each sealed box. In addition, all of these prospect cards are serial numbered to quantities ranging between 400-1250 copies per. Please note that cards 88, 96, 106 and 108 were never produced. Cards 120-127 were randomly seeded within packs of Fleer Rookies and Greats of which was distributed in December, 2003. These eight update cards (featuring a selection of top prospects) were all serial numbered to a mere 250 copies per and all included a game used element.

MINT NRMT
COMP.LO SET w/o SP's (80) 30.00 13.50
COMMON CARD (1-80) .... .50 .23
FS BAT/JSY PRINT RUN 1250 #'d SETS
CUT AU PRINT RUN 500 SERIAL #'d SETS
GG AU PRINT RUN 400 SERIAL #'d SETS
COMMON CARD (120-127) 10.00 4.50
1 Derek Jeter.......................... 3.00 1.35
2 Ryan Klesko .... .50 .23
3 Troy Glaus............................ .50 .23
4 Jeff Kent................................ .50 .23
5 Frank Thomas .... 1.25 .55
6 Gary Sheffield .... .50 .23
7 Jim Edmonds.......................... .50 .23
8 Pat Burrell.............................. .50 .23
9 Jacque Jones .... .50 .23
10 Jason Jennings...................... .50 .23
11 Pedro Martinez.................... 1.25 .55
12 Rafael Palmeiro...................... .75 .35
13 Jason Kendall.......................... .50 .23
14 Tom Glavine .... .75 .35
15 Josh Beckett .... .50 .23
16 Luis Gonzalez.......................... .50 .23
17 Edgar Martinez........................ .75 .35
18 Miguel Tejada......................... .50 .23
19 Fred McGriff............................ .75 .35
20 Adam Dunn............................. .75 .35
21 Lance Berkman .... .50 .23
22 Magglio Ordonez.................... .50 .23
23 Darin Erstad .... .50 .23
24 Rich Aurilia .... .50 .23
25 Mike Piazza .... 2.00 .90
26 Shawn Green .... .50 .23
27 Larry Walker .... .75 .35
28 Manny Ramirez....................... .75 .35
29 Juan Gonzalez......................... .75 .35
30 Eric Chavez .... .50 .23
31 Torii Hunter .... .50 .23
32 A.J. Burnett............................ .50 .23
33 Sammy Sosa........................ 2.00 .90
34 Eric Hinske............................. .50 .23
35 Brian Giles .... .50 .23
36 Mike Sweeney .... .50 .23
37 Sean Casey .... .50 .23
38 Chipper Jones...................... 1.25 .55
39 Scott Rolen .... 1.25 .55
40 Jason Giambi .... .50 .23
41 Mo Vaughn .... .50 .23
42 Roy Oswalt............................ .50 .23
43 Paul Konerko .... .50 .23
44 Tim Salmon .... .75 .35
45 Edgardo Alfonzo..................... .50 .23
46 Jermaine Dye......................... .50 .23
47 Ben Sheets............................ .50 .23
48 Todd Helton .... .75 .35
49 Greg Maddux .... 2.00 .90
50 Albert Pujols 2.50 1.10
51 Jim Thome........................... 1.25 .55
52 Vladimir Guerrero .... 1.25 .55
53 Ivan Rodriguez.................... 1.25 .55
54 Nomar Garciaparra.............. 2.00 .90
55 Alex Rodriguez.................... 2.00 .90
56 Alfonso Soriano .... .75 .35
57 Kazuhisa Ishii........................ .50 .23
58 Austin Kearns........................ .50 .23
59 Curt Schilling .... .50 .23
60 Bret Boone............................ .50 .23
61 Mark Prior .... 1.25 .55
62 Garret Anderson.................... .50 .23
63 Barry Bonds 3.00 1.35
64 Roger Clemens 2.50 1.10
65 Jeff Bagwell .... .75 .35
66 Omar Vizquel .... .75 .35
67 Jay Gibbons .... .50 .23
68 Aubrey Huff........................... .50 .23
69 Bobby Abreu .... .50 .23
70 Richie Sexson .... .50 .23
71 Bobby Higginson .... .50 .23
72 Kerry Wood........................ 1.25 .55
73 Carlos Delgado...................... .50 .23
74 Sean Burroughs..................... .50 .23
75 Jose Vidro.............................. .50 .23
76 Ken Griffey Jr. .... 2.00 .90
77 Randy Johnson................... 1.25 .55
78 Ichiro Suzuki .... 2.00 .90
79 Barry Zito .... .50 .23
80 Carlos Beltran .... .75 .35
81 Joe Borchard FS Jsy 8.00 3.60
82 Mark Teixeira FS Bat............ 8.00 3.60
83 Brandon Webb FS Jsy RC.... 10.00 4.50
84 S.Victorino Pants AU RC...... 15.00 6.75
85 Hee Seop Choi FS Jsy........... 8.00 3.60
86 Hank Blalock FS Bat........... 10.00 4.50
87 Brett Myers FS Jsy................ 8.00 3.60
88 Does Not Exist ....
89 Jesse Foppert FS Jsy............ 8.00 3.60
90 Lyle Overbay FS Jsy.............. 8.00 3.60
91 Brian Stokes Pants AU RC.... 15.00 6.75
92 Josh Hall Bat AU RC 20.00 9.00
93 Chris Waters Pants AU RC... 15.00 6.75
94 Lew Ford Pants AU RC 25.00 11.00
95 Ian Ferguson AU RC 10.00 4.50
96 Does Not Exist ....
97 Josh Stewart AU RC 10.00 4.50
98 Pete LaForest AU RC 15.00 6.75
99 Jose Contreras Jsy AU/300 RC 40.00 18.00
100 Terrmel Sledge AU RC 15.00 6.75
101 Guillermo Quiroz AU RC 15.00 6.75
102 Alejandro Machado AU RC. 10.00 4.50
103 Nook Logan Pants AU RC.. 15.00 6.75
104 R.Hammock Pants AU RC.. 20.00 9.00
105 Hideki Matsui FS Base RC . 15.00 6.75
106 Does Not Exist ....
107 Rocco Baldelli FS Jsy.......... 8.00 3.60
108 Does Not Exist ....
109 T.Wellemeyer Pants AU RC 20.00 9.00
110 Mi. Hessman Pants AU RC 15.00 6.75
111 J.Bonderman Pants AU RC 20.00 9.00
112 Craig Brazell Pants AU RC . 20.00 9.00
113 Franc Rosario Pants AU RC 15.00 6.75
114 Jeff Duncan Pants AU RC .. 20.00 9.00
115 Dan. Cabrera Pants AU RC 25.00 11.00
116 Dontrelle Willis Pants AU... 20.00 9.00
117 Cory Stewart AU RC 10.00 4.50
118 Tim Olson Pants AU RC..... 20.00 9.00
119 C.Wang Pants AU/500 RC.. 40.00 18.00
120 Josh Willingham Pants RC 10.00 4.50
121 Rickie Weeks Bat RC......... 15.00 6.75
122 Prentice Redman Pants RC 10.00 4.50
123 Mike Ryan Pants RC.......... 15.00 6.75
124 Oscar Villarreal Pants RC.... 10.00 4.50
125 Ryan Wagner Pants RC..... 10.00 4.50
126 Bo Hart Pants RC.............. 10.00 4.50
127 Edwin Jackson Pants RC ... 15.00 6.75

2003 Fleer Hot Prospects Class Of

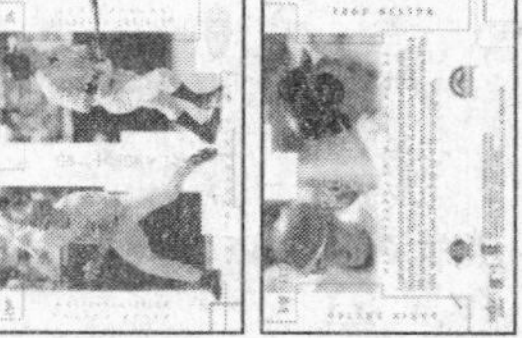

MINT NRMT
COMPLETE SET (10)............... 30.00 13.50
STATED ODDS 1:15.........................
1 Barry Zito........................... 2.50 1.10
Josh Beckett
2 Pat Burrell.......................... 2.50 1.10
J.D. Drew
3 Mark Prior.......................... 4.00 1.80
Mark Teixeira
4 Austin Kearns..................... 2.50 1.10
Sean Burroughs
5 Troy Glaus........................... 2.50 1.10
Lance Berkman
6 Darin Erstad 2.50 1.10
Todd Helton
7 Manny Ramirez.................... 2.50 1.10
Shawn Green
8 Matt Morris......................... 4.00 1.80
Kerry Wood
9 Nomar Garciaparra.............. 6.00 2.70
Paul Konerko
10 Alex Rodriguez.................. 6.00 2.70
Torii Hunter

2003 Fleer Hot Prospects Class Of Game Used

MINT NRMT
RANDOM INSERTS IN PACKS ....
STATED PRINT RUN 375 SERIAL #'d SETS
AKSB Austin Kearns Jsy 10.00 4.50
Sean Burroughs Jsy
ARTH Alex Rodriguez Jsy 20.00 9.00
Torii Hunter Jsy
BZJB Barry Zito Jsy 10.00 4.50
Josh Beckett Jsy
DETH Darin Erstad Jsy.............. 15.00 6.75
Todd Helton Jsy
MMKW Matt Morris Jsy............. 15.00 6.75
Kerry Wood Jsy
MPMT Mark Prior Jsy............... 15.00 6.75
Mark Teixeira Bat
MRSG Manny Ramirez Jsy 15.00 6.75
Shawn Green Jsy
NGPK Nomar Garciaparra Jsy... 20.00 9.00
Paul Konerko Jsy
PBJD Pat Burrell Jsy................ 10.00 4.50
J.D. Drew Jsy
TGLB Troy Glaus Jsy............... 10.00 4.50
Lance Berkman Jsy

2003 Fleer Hot Prospects Cream of the Crop

MINT NRMT
COMPLETE SET (15)................ 50.00 22.00
STATED ODDS 1:5...............................
1 Barry Bonds 6.00 2.70
2 Derek Jeter........................... 6.00 2.70
3 Ichiro Suzuki........................ 4.00 1.80
4 Nomar Garciaparra............... 4.00 1.80
5 Roger Clemens 5.00 2.20
6 Alex Rodriguez..................... 4.00 1.80
7 Greg Maddux 4.00 1.80
8 Mike Piazza 4.00 1.80
9 Sammy Sosa......................... 4.00 1.80
10 Jason Giambi 2.50 1.10
11 Hideki Matsui 8.00 3.60
12 Albert Pujols 5.00 2.20
13 Vladimir Guerrero 2.50 1.10
14 Jim Thome.......................... 2.50 1.10
15 Pedro Martinez................... 2.50 1.10

2003 Fleer Hot Prospects MLB Hot Materials

MINT NRMT
STATED PRINT RUN 499 SERIAL #'d SETS
*RED HOT: .75X TO 2X BASIC...........
RED HOT PRINT RUN 50 SERIAL #'d SETS
RANDOM INSERTS IN PACKS ....
AD Adam Dunn Jsy................. 10.00 4.50
AR Alex Rodriguez Jsy............ 15.00 6.75
AS Alfonso Soriano Jsy 10.00 4.50
BA Tom Glavine Jsy 10.00 4.50
CD Carlos Delgado Jsy 8.00 3.60
CJ Chipper Jones Jsy 10.00 4.50
DJ Derek Jeter Jsy................. 25.00 11.00
GM Greg Maddux Jsy 10.00 4.50
HC Hee Seop Choi Jsy 8.00 3.60
JB Josh Beckett Jsy 8.00 3.60
JG Jason Giambi Jsy 8.00 3.60
JT Jim Thome Jsy.................. 10.00 4.50
LB Lance Berkman Bat............. 8.00 3.60
LO Lyle Overbay Jsy 8.00 3.60
MPI Mike Piazza Jsy 10.00 4.50
MPR Mark Prior Jsy 10.00 4.50
MR Manny Ramirez Jsy.......... 10.00 4.50
MS Mike Sweeney Jsy.............. 8.00 3.60
MTJ Miguel Tejada Jsy............ 8.00 3.60
MTX Mark Teixeira Bat 8.00 3.60
NG Nomar Garciaparra Jsy 15.00 6.75
PB Pat Burrell Jsy 8.00 3.60
RJ Randy Johnson Jsy 10.00 4.50
RP Rafael Palmeiro Jsy.......... 10.00 4.50
SG Shawn Green Jsy 8.00 3.60
SS Sammy Sosa Jsy 15.00 6.75
TG Troy Glaus Jsy................... 8.00 3.60
THE Todd Helton Jsy.............. 10.00 4.50
THU Torii Hunter Jsy 8.00 3.60
VG Vladimir Guerrero Jsy 10.00 4.50

2003 Fleer Hot Prospects MLB Hot Tandems

MINT NRMT
STATED PRINT RUN 100 SERIAL #'d SETS
RED HOT PRINT RUN 10 SERIAL #'d SETS
NO RED HOT PRICING DUE TO SCARCITY
RANDOM INSERTS IN PACKS ....
ARMT Alex Rodriguez Jsy......... 25.00 11.00
Miguel Tejada Jsy
CJDJ Chipper Jones Jsy 40.00 18.00
Derek Jeter Jsy
DJMT Derek Jeter Jsy.............. 40.00 18.00
Miguel Tejada Jsy
DJNG Derek Jeter Jsy.............. 40.00 18.00
Nomar Garciaparra Jsy
HCLO Hee Seop Choi Jsy......... 10.00 4.50
Lyle Overbay Jsy
JBGM Josh Beckett Jsy............ 20.00 9.00
Greg Maddux Jsy
JGTG Jason Giambi Jsy........... 10.00 4.50
Troy Glaus Jsy
JTJG Jim Thome Jsy 15.00 6.75
Jason Giambi Jsy
LBAD Lance Berkman Bat 15.00 6.75
Adam Dunn Jsy
LORJ Lyle Overbay Jsy 15.00 6.75
Randy Johnson Jsy
MPCJ Mike Piazza Jsy 20.00 9.00
Chipper Jones Jsy
MPDJ Mike Piazza Jsy 40.00 18.00
Derek Jeter Jsy
MPJB Mark Prior Jsy................ 15.00 6.75
Josh Beckett Jsy
MPSS Mark Prior Jsy 25.00 11.00
Sammy Sosa Jsy
MTAR Mark Teixeira Bat........... 25.00 11.00
Alex Rodriguez Jsy
NGMT Nomar Garciaparra Jsy .. 25.00 11.00
Miguel Tejada Jsy
PBJT Pat Burrell Jsy 15.00 6.75
Jim Thome Jsy
RJGM Randy Johnson Jsy........ 20.00 9.00
Greg Maddux Jsy
RPAD Rafael Palmeiro Jsy 15.00 6.75
Adam Dunn Jsy
RPMT Rafael Palmeiro Jsy 15.00 6.75
Mark Teixeira Bat
SSPB Sammy Sosa Jsy 25.00 11.00
Pat Burrell Jsy
TGSG Troy Glaus Jsy.............. 10.00 4.50
Shawn Green Jsy
THAD Torii Hunter Jsy 10.00 4.50
Lance Berkman Bat
THVG Torii Hunter Jsy 15.00 6.75
Vladimir Guerrero Jsy
VGSG Vladimir Guerrero Jsy..... 15.00 6.75
Shawn Green Jsy

2003 Fleer Hot Prospects MLB Hot Triple Patch

MINT NRMT
RANDOM INSERTS IN PACKS ....
STATED PRINT RUN 50 SERIAL #'d SETS
BGJ Lance Berkman................ 50.00 22.00
Troy Glaus
Chipper Jones
BTB Pat Burrell 50.00 22.00
Jim Thome
Lance Berkman
DJB Adam Dunn 50.00 22.00
Randy Johnson
Josh Beckett
GGJ Vladimir Guerrero............. 50.00 22.00
Troy Glaus
Chipper Jones
GRT Jason Giambi 60.00 27.00
Alex Rodriguez
Miguel Tejada
GSP Nomar Garciaparra.......... 100.00 45.00
Sammy Sosa
Mike Piazza
GTD Jason Giambi 50.00 22.00
Miguel Tejada
Adam Dunn
HSG Torii Hunter ....
Sammy Sosa
Vladimir Guerrero
JGR Derek Jeter..................... 150.00 70.00
Nomar Garciaparra
Alex Rodriguez
JHP Derek Jeter..................... 100.00 45.00
Torii Hunter
Mark Prior
JSG Randy Johnson 50.00 22.00
Alfonso Soriano
Shawn Green
PBM Mark Prior...................... 100.00 45.00
Josh Beckett
Greg Maddux
PBT Mike Piazza..................... 60.00 27.00
Pat Burrell
Jim Thome
PCT Rafael Palmeiro 50.00 22.00
Hee Seop Choi
Mark Teixeira
SMG Alfonso Soriano 80.00 36.00
Greg Maddux
Shawn Green

2003 Fleer Hot Prospects PlayerGraphs

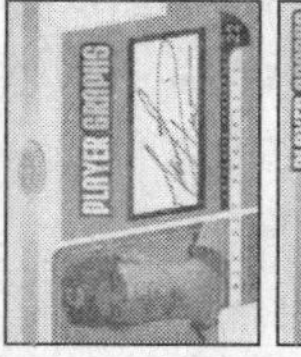

Randomly inserted in packs, these 11 cards feature authentic autographs from the featured player. Each of these cards were issued to a stated print run of 400 serial numbered sets.

MINT NRMT
*RED HOT: .6X TO 1.5X BASIC............
RED HOT PRINT RUN 100 SERIAL #'d SETS
RANDOM INSERTS IN PACKS ....
AH Aubrey Huff.................... 15.00 6.75
BM Brett Myers.................... 15.00 6.75
CZ Carlos Zambrano 25.00 11.00
FR Francisco Rodriguez 15.00 6.75
HB Hank Blalock 25.00 11.00
JR Jose Reyes 15.00 6.75
MP Mark Prior 60.00 27.00
MT Mark Teixiera 25.00 11.00
RO Roy Oswalt...................... 15.00 6.75
VW Vernon Wells 15.00 6.75
XN Xavier Nady..................... 15.00 6.75

2004 Fleer Hot Prospects Draft

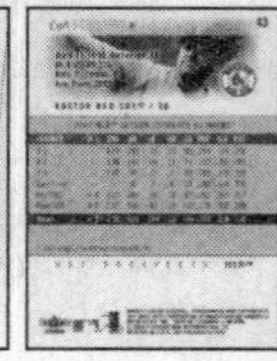

Nm-Mt Ex-Mt
COMP.SET w/o RC's (60)......... 15.00 4.50
COMMON CARD (1-60) .... .50 .15
COMMON CARD (61-70) .... 3.00 .90
61-70 ODDS 1:15 HOBBY, 1:120 RETAIL
61-70 PRINT RUN 1000 SERIAL #'d SETS
COMMON CARD (71-120) 20.00 6.00
71-120 ODDS 1:9 HOBBY, 1:990 RETAIL
71-120 PRINT RUN 299 SERIAL #'d SETS
CARDS 112 AND 113 DO NOT EXIST .
EXCHANGE DEADLINE INDEFINITE ....
1 Miguel Tejada........................ .50 .15
2 Jose Vidro............................. .50 .15
3 Hideki Matsui .... 2.00 .60
4 Roger Clemens .... 2.50 .75
5 Craig Wilson .... .50 .15
6 Bobby Crosby .... .75 .23
7 Pat Burrell............................. .50 .15
8 Mike Sweeney........................ .50 .15
9 Craig Biggio .... .75 .23
10 Scott Rolen .... 1.25 .35
11 Roy Halladay........................ .50 .15
12 Lyle Overbay .... .50 .15
13 Rocco Baldelli .... .50 .15
14 Mike Piazza .... 2.00 .60
15 Rafael Palmeiro..................... .75 .23
16 Hank Blalock .... .50 .15
17 Sammy Sosa...................... 2.00 .60
18 Dontrelle Willis...................... .50 .15
19 Alfonso Soriano .... .75 .23
20 Gary Sheffield .... .50 .15
21 Jim Thome......................... 1.25 .35
22 Ivan Rodriguez................... 1.25 .35
23 Adam Dunn.......................... .75 .23
24 Kerry Wood....................... 1.25 .35
25 Khalil Greene..................... 1.25 .35
26 Richie Sexson .... .50 .15
27 Nomar Garciaparra............. 2.00 .60
28 Andruw Jones .... .50 .15
29 Tom Glavine .... .75 .23
30 Carlos Beltran .... .75 .23
31 Chipper Jones.................... 1.25 .35
32 Jeff Bagwell .... .75 .23
33 Tim Hudson .... .50 .15
34 Alex Rodriguez................... 2.00 .60
35 Omar Vizquel .... .75 .23
36 Albert Pujols .... 2.50 .75
37 Frank Thomas .... 1.25 .35
38 Ben Sheets............................ .50 .15
39 Jason Schmidt .... .50 .15
40 Miguel Cabrera...................... .75 .23
41 Carlos Delgado...................... .50 .15
42 Ichiro Suzuki...................... 2.00 .60
43 Curt Schilling .... 1.25 .35
44 Todd Helton .... .75 .23
45 Ken Griffey Jr. .... 2.00 .60
46 Mark Prior.......................... 1.25 .35
47 Vladimir Guerrero .... 1.25 .35
48 Pedro Martinez................... 1.25 .35
49 Manny Ramirez .... .75 .23
50 Joe Mauer............................. .75 .23
51 Jorge Posada .... .75 .23
52 Troy Glaus............................ .50 .15
53 Randy Johnson................... 1.25 .35
54 Adrian Beltre .... .75 .23
55 Eric Gagne .... 1.25 .35
56 Josh Beckett .... .50 .15
57 Jason Giambi .... .50 .15
58 Barry Zito.............................. .50 .15
59 Lance Berkman .... .50 .15
60 Derek Jeter........................ 2.50 .75
61 Kaz Matsui HP RC............... 5.00 1.50
62 Jason Bartlett HP RC........... 5.00 1.50
63 John Gall HP RC.................. 5.00 1.50
64 Chris Saenz HP RC .... 3.00 .90
65 Merkin Valdez HP RC........... 5.00 1.50
66 Akinori Otsuka HP RC.......... 3.00 .90
67 Joey Gathright HP RC.......... 5.00 1.50
68 Brad Halsey HP RC.............. 5.00 1.50
69 David Aardsma HP RC .... 3.00 .90
70 Scott Kazmir HP RC........... 10.00 3.00
71 Matt Bush AU RC............... 60.00 18.00
72 John Bowker AU RC 20.00 6.00
73 Mike Ferris AU RC 25.00 7.50
74 Brian Bixler AU RC EXCH..... 20.00 6.00
75 Scott Elbert AU RC............. 40.00 12.00
76 Josh Fields AU RC.............. 50.00 15.00
77 Bill Bray AU RC.................. 20.00 6.00
78 Greg Golson AU RC 30.00 9.00
79 Neil Walker AU RC 25.00 7.50
80 Philip Hughes AU RC 25.00 7.50
81 Chris Nelson AU RC............ 60.00 18.00
82 Mark Rogers AU RC............ 60.00 18.00
83 Trevor Plouffe AU RC......... 40.00 12.00
84 Chris Garcia AU RC EXCH.... 25.00 7.50
85 Thomas Diamond AU RC..... 30.00 9.00
86 B.J. Szymanski AU RC........ 25.00 7.50
87 Richie Robnett AU RC......... 30.00 9.00
88 Seth Smith AU RC 30.00 9.00
89 Kyle Waldrop AU RC.......... 40.00 12.00
90 Curtis Thigpen AU RC......... 25.00 7.50
91 J.P. Howell AU RC EXCH..... 25.00 7.50
92 Blake DeWitt AU RC........... 50.00 15.00
93 Taylor Tankersley AU RC..... 30.00 9.00
94 Zach Jackson AU RC 25.00 7.50
95 Justin Orenduff AU RC........ 25.00 7.50
96 Tyler Lumsden AU RC......... 25.00 7.50
97 Danny Putnam AU RC......... 25.00 7.50
98 Jon Poterson AU RC........... 30.00 9.00
99 Matt Fox AU RC.................. 25.00 7.50
100 Gio Gonzalez AU RC......... 25.00 7.50
101 Huston Street AU RC 30.00 9.00
102 Jay Rainville AU RC 30.00 9.00

103 Matt Durkin AU RC 20.00 6.00
104 Brett Smith AU RC 25.00 7.50
105 Justin Hoyman AU RC 20.00 6.00
106 Erick San Pedro AU RC 20.00 6.00
107 Jeff Marquez AU RC 25.00 7.50
108 Hunter Pence AU RC 20.00 6.00
109 Dustin Pedroia AU RC 30.00 9.00
110 Kurt Suzuki AU RC 50.00 15.00
111 Billy Buckner AU RC 25.00 7.50
114 J.C. Holt AU RC EXCH 25.00 7.50
115 Homer Bailey AU RC 40.00 12.00
116 David Purcey AU RC 25.00 7.50
117 Jeremy Sowers AU RC 50.00 15.00
118 Chris Lambert AU RC EXCH 25.00 7.50
119 Eric Hurley AU RC 25.00 7.50
120 Grant Johnson AU RC 20.00 6.00

2004 Fleer Hot Prospects Draft Red Hot

Nm-Mt Ex-Mt
*RED 1-60: 2.5X TO 6X BASIC
*RED 61-70: 1X TO 2.5X BASIC
1-70 PRINT RUN 150 SERIAL #'d SETS
71-120 PRINT RUN 25 SERIAL #'d SETS
71-120 NO PRICING DUE TO SCARCITY
OVERALL PARALLEL ODDS 1:15 H, 1:120 R
CARDS 112 AND 113 DO NOT EXIST.
EXCHANGE DEADLINE INDEFINITE

2004 Fleer Hot Prospects Draft White Hot

Nm-Mt Ex-Mt
OVERALL PARALLEL ODDS 1:15 H, 1:120 R
STATED PRINT RUN 1 SERIAL #'d SET
NO PRICING DUE TO SCARCITY
CARDS 112 AND 113 DO NOT EXIST.
EXCHANGE DEADLINE INDEFINITE

2004 Fleer Hot Prospects Draft Alumni Ink

Nm-Mt Ex-Mt
STATED PRINT RUN 15 SERIAL #'d SETS
RED HOT PRINT RUN 5 SERIAL #'d SETS
WHITE HOT PRINT RUN 1 SERIAL #'d SET
OVERALL AU-GU ODDS 1:12 H, 1:24 R
NO PRICING DUE TO SCARCITY
EXCHANGE DEADLINE INDEFINITE
HS J.P. Howell
Huston Street EXCH
PJ Mark Prior
Randy Johnson
TG Mark Teixeira
Nomar Garciaparra

2004 Fleer Hot Prospects Draft Double Team Jersey

Nm-Mt Ex-Mt
STATED PRINT RUN 100 SERIAL #'d SETS
*RED HOT: .6X TO 1.5X BASIC
RED HOT PRINT RUN 25 SERIAL #'d SETS
WHITE HOT PRINT RUN 1 SERIAL #'d SET
NO WHITE HOT PRICING DUE TO SCARCITY
*PATCH: 1X TO 2.5X BASIC
PATCH PRINT RUN 50 SERIAL #'d SETS
PATCH RED HOT PRINT RUN 10 #'d SETS
NO PATCH RED HOT PRICING AVAILABLE
PATCH WHITE HOT PRINT RUN 1 #'d SET
NO PATCH WHITE HOT PRICING AVAILABLE
OVERALL AU-GU ODDS 1:12 H, 1:24 R
AS Alfonso Soriano Rgr-Yanks 15.00 4.50
CB Carlos Beltran Astros-Royals 15.00 4.50
EM Eddie Murray Mets-O's 25.00 7.50
GM Greg Maddux Braves-Cubs 20.00 6.00
HN Hideo Nomo Dgr-Sox 15.00 4.50
IR I.Rodriguez Marlins-Tigers 15.00 4.50
JG Jason Giambi A's-Yanks 10.00 3.00
MP Mike Piazza Dgr-Mets 20.00 6.00
MR Manny Ramirez Indians-Sox 15.00 4.50
MT Miguel Tejada A's-O's 10.00 3.00
NR Nolan Ryan Astros-Rgr 40.00 12.00
PM Pedro Martinez Expos-Sox 15.00 4.50
RCA Rod Carew Angels-Twins 25.00 7.50
RCL Roger Clemens Astros-Sox 20.00 6.00
RH R.Henderson A's-Padres 25.00 7.50
RJ Reggie Jackson A's-Yanks 25.00 7.50
SR Scott Rolen Cards-Phils 15.00 4.50
TG Tom Glavine Braves-Mets 15.00 4.50
VG Vlad Guerrero Angels-Expos 15.00 4.50

2004 Fleer Hot Prospects Draft Double Team Autograph Patch Red Hot

Nm-Mt Ex-Mt
STATED PRINT RUN 22 SERIAL #'d SETS
WHITE HOT PRINT RUN 1 SERIAL #'d SET
NO WHITE HOT PRICING DUE TO SCARCITY
OVERALL AU-GU ODDS 1:12 H, 1:24 R
HN Hideo Nomo Dgr-Sox

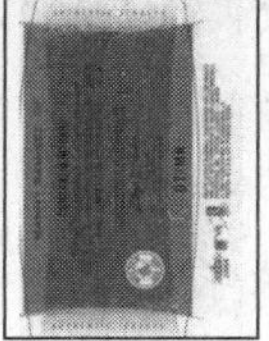

IR I.Rodriguez Marlins-Tigers 100.00 30.00
MP Mike Piazza Dgr-Mets 200.00 60.00
MR Manny Ramirez Indians-Sox 120.00 36.00
RJ Reggie Jackson A's-Yanks 100.00 30.00
SR Scott Rolen Cards-Phils 100.00 30.00
VG Vlad Guerrero Angels-Expos 100.00 30.00

2004 Fleer Hot Prospects Draft MLB Hot Materials

Nm-Mt Ex-Mt
STATED PRINT RUN 325 SERIAL #'d SETS
*RED HOT: .75X TO 2X BASIC
RED HOT PRINT RUN 50 SERIAL #'d SETS
WHITE HOT PRINT RUN 1 SERIAL #'d SET
NO WHITE HOT PRICING DUE TO SCARCITY
OVERALL AU-GU ODDS 1:12 H, 1:24 R
AD Adam Dunn Jsy 8.00 2.40
AJ Andruw Jones Jsy 5.00 1.50
APE Andy Pettitte Jsy 8.00 2.40
APU Albert Pujols Jsy 15.00 4.50
AS Alfonso Soriano Jsy 8.00 2.40
CD Carlos Delgado Jsy 5.00 1.50
CJ Chipper Jones Jsy 8.00 2.40
CS Curt Schilling Jsy 8.00 2.40
DW Dontrelle Willis Jsy 5.00 1.50
EG Eric Gagne Jsy 8.00 2.40
FT Frank Thomas Jsy 8.00 2.40
HB Hank Blalock Jsy 5.00 1.50
HM Hideki Matsui Jsy 20.00 6.00
HN Hideo Nomo Jsy 8.00 2.40
IR Ivan Rodriguez Jsy 8.00 2.40
JB Jeff Bagwell Jsy 8.00 2.40
JD J.D. Drew Jsy 5.00 1.50
JE Jim Edmonds Jsy 5.00 1.50
JM Joe Mauer Jsy 8.00 2.40
JP Jorge Posada Jsy 8.00 2.40
JS Jason Schmidt Jsy 5.00 1.50
JT Jim Thome Jsy 8.00 2.40
KM Kaz Matsui Jsy 10.00 3.00
KW Kerry Wood Jsy 8.00 2.40
LB Lance Berkman Jsy 5.00 1.50
LO Lyle Overbay Jsy 5.00 1.50
MC Miguel Cabrera Jsy 8.00 2.40
MM Mike Mussina Jsy 8.00 2.40
MPI Mike Piazza Jsy 10.00 3.00
MPR Mark Prior Jsy 8.00 2.40
MR Manny Ramirez Jsy 8.00 2.40
MTJ Miguel Tejada Jsy 5.00 1.50
MTX Mark Teixeira Jsy 5.00 1.50
RC Roger Clemens Jsy 10.00 3.00
RJ Randy Johnson Jsy 8.00 2.40
SS Sammy Sosa Jsy 10.00 3.00
THE Todd Helton Jsy 8.00 2.40
THN Torii Hunter Jsy 5.00 1.50
THU Tim Hudson Jsy 5.00 1.50
VG Vladimir Guerrero Jsy 8.00 2.40

2004 Fleer Hot Prospects Draft Past Present Future Autograph

Nm-Mt Ex-Mt
STATED PRINT RUN 33 SERIAL #'d SETS
RED HOT PRINT RUN 3 SERIAL #'d SETS
NO RED HOT PRICING DUE TO SCARCITY
WHITE HOT PRINT RUN 1 SERIAL #'d SET
NO WHITE HOT PRICING DUE TO SCARCITY
OVERALL AU-GU ODDS 1:12 H, 1:24 R
EXCHANGE DEADLINE INDEFINITE
BDB Johnny Bench 150.00 45.00
Adam Dunn
Homer Bailey
BMH Yogi Berra 100.00 30.00
Mike Mussina
Philip Hughes
BRP Bill Buckner 100.00 30.00
Manny Ramirez
Dustin Pedroia
CRP Joe Carter 60.00 18.00
Alexis Rios
David Purcey EXCH
CTG Steve Carlton 120.00 36.00
Jim Thome
Greg Golson
FMF Carlton Fisk 80.00 24.00
Ryan Meaux
Josh Fields
GGB Tony Gwynn 150.00 45.00
Khalil Greene
Matt Bush EXCH
GNE Kirk Gibson 350.00 105.00
Hideo Nomo
Scott Elbert
JCR Reggie Jackson 100.00 30.00
Eric Chavez
Richie Robnett EXCH
KBF Al Kaline
Jeremy Bonderman
TBD EXCH
KFP Harmon Killebrew 80.00 24.00
Lew Ford
Trevor Plouffe EXCH
KWW Ralph Kiner 80.00 24.00
Jack Wilson
Neil Walker
MPL Stan Musial 300.00 90.00
Albert Pujols
Chris Lambert EXCH
RYD Nolan Ryan 200.00 60.00
Michael Young
Thomas Diamond
SCT Gary Sheffield
Miguel Cabrera
Taylor Tankersley
SPJ Ryne Sandberg
Mark Prior
Grant Johnson EXCH
WPD Mookie Wilson 150.00 45.00
Mike Piazza
Matt Durkin
YWR Robin Yount
Rickie Weeks
Mark Rogers EXCH

2004 Fleer Hot Prospects Draft Rewind

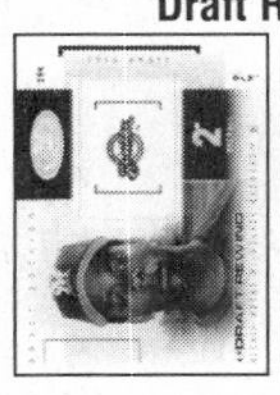
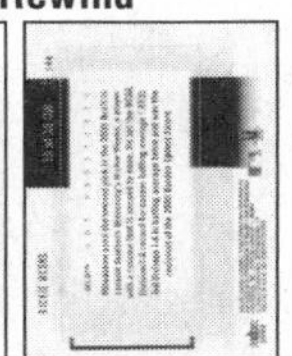

Nm-Mt Ex-Mt
STATED ODDS 1:5
1 Joe Mauer 3.00 .90
2 Derek Jeter 6.00 1.80
3 Chipper Jones 3.00 .90
4 Greg Maddux 5.00 1.50
5 Alex Rodriguez 5.00 1.50
6 Nomar Garciaparra 5.00 1.50
7 Curt Schilling 3.00 .90
8 Kerry Wood 3.00 .90
9 Troy Glaus 2.00 .60
10 Pat Burrell 2.00 .60
11 Mark Mulder 2.00 .60
12 Josh Beckett 2.00 .60
13 Barry Zito 2.00 .60
14 Mark Prior 3.00 .90
15 Rickie Weeks 2.00 .60
16 Khalil Greene 3.00 .90
17 Ken Griffey Jr. 5.00 1.50
18 Gary Sheffield 2.00 .60
19 Todd Helton 3.00 .90
20 Barry Larkin 3.00 .90
21 Kevin Brown 2.00 .60
22 Frank Thomas 3.00 .90
23 Manny Ramirez 3.00 .90
24 Roger Clemens 6.00 1.80
25 Lance Berkman 2.00 .60
26 Randy Johnson 3.00 .90
27 Jason Giambi 2.00 .60
28 Ben Sheets 2.00 .60
29 Scott Rolen 3.00 .90
30 Tom Glavine 3.00 .90

2004 Fleer Hot Prospects Draft Rewind Jersey

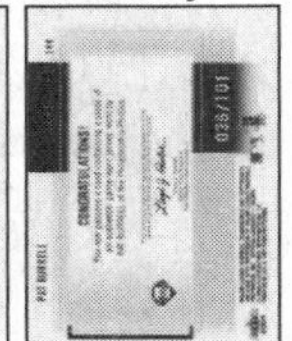

Nm-Mt Ex-Mt
PRINT RUNS B/WN 101-158 COPIES PER
RED HOT PRINT RUN 10 SERIAL #'d SETS
NO RED HOT PRICING DUE TO SCARCITY
WHITE HOT PRINT RUN 1 SERIAL #'d SET
NO WHITE HOT PRICING DUE TO SCARCITY
*PATCH p/r 68: .6X TO 1.5X BASIC
*PATCH p/r 41-57: .6X TO 1.5X BASIC
*PATCH p/r 20-29: .75X TO 2X BASIC
*PATCH p/r 16-19: 1X TO 2.5X BASIC
PATCH PRINT RUNS B/WN 10-68 PER
NO PATCH PRICING ON QTY OF 14 OR LESS
PATCH RED HOT PRINT RUN 5 #'d SETS
NO PATCH RED HOT PRICING AVAILABLE
PATCH WHITE HOT PRINT RUN 1 #'d SET
NO PATCH WHITE HOT PRICING AVAILABLE
OVERALL AU-GU ODDS 1:12 H, 1:24 R
BL Barry Larkin/104 10.00 3.00
BS Ben Sheets/110 8.00 2.40
BZ Barry Zito/109 8.00 2.40
CJ Chipper Jones/101 10.00 3.00
CK Casey Kotchman/113 15.00 4.50
CS Curt Schilling/139 10.00 3.00
EC Eric Chavez/110 8.00 2.40
FT Frank Thomas/107 10.00 3.00
GM Greg Maddux/131 15.00 4.50
GS Gary Sheffield/106 8.00 2.40
JB Josh Beckett/102 8.00 2.40
JG Jason Giambi/158 8.00 2.40
JM Joe Mauer/101 10.00 3.00
KB Kevin Brown/104 8.00 2.40
KG Khalil Greene/113 15.00 4.50
KW Kerry Wood/104 10.00 3.00
LB Lance Berkman/116 8.00 2.40
MM Mark Mulder/102 8.00 2.40
MP Mark Prior/102 10.00 3.00
MR Manny Ramirez/113 10.00 3.00
PB Pat Burrell/101 8.00 2.40
RB Rocco Baldelli/119 8.00 2.40
RC Roger Clemens/119 15.00 4.50
RJ Randy Johnson/136 10.00 3.00
RW Rickie Weeks/102 8.00 2.40
SR Scott Rolen/146 10.00 3.00
TG Troy Glaus/103 8.00 2.40
TG Tom Glavine/147 10.00 3.00
TH Todd Helton/108 10.00 3.00
ZG Zack Greinke/106 8.00 2.40

2004 Fleer Hot Prospects Draft Tandems

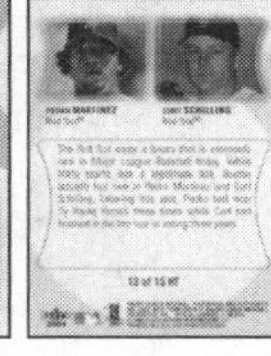

Nm-Mt Ex-Mt
STATED ODDS 1:15 H/R
1 Mark Prior 5.00 1.50
Greg Maddux
2 Jim Thome 3.00 .90
Pat Burrell
3 Ken Griffey Jr. 5.00 1.50
Adam Dunn
4 Mike Piazza 5.00 1.50
Tom Glavine
5 Alex Rodriguez 15.00 4.50
Derek Jeter
6 Roger Clemens 6.00 1.80
Andy Pettitte
7 Jason Giambi 5.00 1.50
Hideki Matsui
8 Alfonso Soriano 3.00 .90
Hank Blalock
9 Manny Ramirez 3.00 .90
David Ortiz
10 Miguel Cabrera 3.00 .90
Dontrelle Willis
11 Hideki Matsui 8.00 2.40
Ichiro Suzuki
12 Albert Pujols 6.00 1.80
Scott Rolen
13 Pedro Martinez 3.00 .90
Curt Schilling
14 Sammy Sosa 5.00 1.50
Nomar Garciaparra
15 Kaz Matsui 6.00 1.80
Derek Jeter

2004 Fleer InScribed

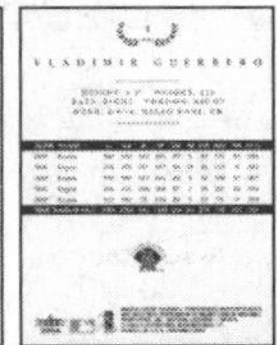

This 100 card set was released in September, 2004. The set was issued in five card hobby packs which came 12 packs to a box and six boxes to a case. The set consists of 75 veteran cards, 10 retired great cards (76-85) and 15 Rookie Cards (86-100). The retired greats cards were issued at stated odds of one in 20 hobby and one in 200 retail and were issued to a stated print run of 1000 serial numbered sets. The Rookie Cards were all serial numbered to 750 but the actual number of these cards issued are notated in our checklist. Please note that these cards were issued at a stated rate of one in 12 hobby and one in 100 retail packs. The reason that these cards all have different print runs in that many of these rookies signed cards for inclusion in this product.

Nm-Mt Ex-Mt
COMP.SET w/o SP's (75) 25.00 7.50
COMMON CARD (1-75) .40 .12
COMMON CARD (76-85) 4.00 1.20
COMMON CARD (86-100) 3.00 .90
86-100 ODDS 1:12 HOBBY, 1:100 RETAIL
86-100 W/ASTERISK = ACTUAL PRINT RUN
ACTUAL PRINT RUNS PROVIDED BY FLEER
SEE AUTO PARALLEL SETS FOR AU PRICES
1 Vladimir Guerrero 1.00 .30
2 Bartolo Colon .40 .12
3 Troy Glaus .40 .12
4 Richie Sexson .40 .12
5 Randy Johnson 1.00 .30
6 Luis Gonzalez .40 .12
7 J.D. Drew .40 .12
8 Chipper Jones 1.00 .30
9 Andruw Jones .40 .12
10 Melvin Mora .40 .12
11 Miguel Tejada .40 .12
12 Curt Schilling .60 .18
13 Pedro Martinez 1.00 .30
14 Nomar Garciaparra 1.50 .45
15 Kerry Wood 1.00 .30
16 Mark Prior 1.50 .45
17 Sammy Sosa 1.50 .45
18 Frank Thomas 1.00 .30
19 Magglio Ordonez .40 .12
20 Sean Casey .40 .12
21 Ken Griffey Jr. 1.50 .45
22 Adam Dunn .60 .18
23 Jody Gerut .40 .12
24 Omar Vizquel .60 .18
25 Todd Helton .60 .18
26 Vinny Castilla .40 .12
27 Alex Sanchez .40 .12
28 Ivan Rodriguez 1.00 .30
29 Dontrelle Willis .40 .12
30 Josh Beckett .40 .12
31 Miguel Cabrera .60 .18
32 Roger Clemens 2.00 .60
33 Andy Pettitte .60 .18
34 Jeff Bagwell .60 .18
35 Ken Harvey .40 .12
36 Carlos Beltran .60 .18
37 Shawn Green .40 .12
38 Hideo Nomo 1.00 .30
39 Scott Podsednik .40 .12
40 Ben Sheets .40 .12
41 Torii Hunter .40 .12
42 Jacque Jones .40 .12
43 Jose Vidro .40 .12
44 Mike Piazza 1.50 .45
45 Tom Glavine .60 .18
46 Derek Jeter 2.00 .60
47 Alex Rodriguez 1.50 .45
48 Jason Giambi .40 .12
49 Hideki Matsui 1.50 .45
50 Eric Chavez .40 .12
51 Barry Zito .40 .12
52 Tim Hudson .40 .12
53 Mark Mulder .40 .12
54 Jim Thome 1.00 .30
55 Pat Burrell .40 .12
56 Chase Utley .40 .12
57 Jason Kendall .40 .12
58 Jack Wilson .40 .12
59 Khalil Greene 1.00 .30
60 Brian Giles .40 .12
61 Jason Schmidt .40 .12
62 Marquis Grissom .40 .12
63 Ichiro Suzuki 1.50 .45
64 Bret Boone .40 .12
65 Albert Pujols 2.00 .60
66 Scott Rolen 1.00 .30
67 Jim Edmonds .40 .12
68 Tino Martinez .60 .18
69 Rocco Baldelli .40 .12
70 Alfonso Soriano .60 .18
71 Michael Young .40 .12
72 Hank Blalock .40 .12
73 Roy Halladay .40 .12
74 Carlos Delgado .40 .12
75 Vernon Wells .40 .12
76 Johnny Bench RET 5.00 1.50
77 Reggie Jackson RET 5.00 1.50
78 Al Kaline RET 5.00 1.50
79 Nolan Ryan RET 12.00 3.60
80 Tom Seaver RET 5.00 1.50
81 Robin Yount RET 8.00 2.40
82 Mike Schmidt RET 10.00 3.00
83 Jim Palmer RET 4.00 1.20
84 Harmon Killebrew RET 5.00 1.50
85 Joe Morgan RET 4.00 1.20
86 Kaz Matsui ROO/675 RC * 8.00 2.40
87 L.Gonzalez ROO/435 RC * 3.00 .90
88 Yadier Molina ROO/750 RC 8.00 2.40
89 Jon Knott ROO/675 RC * 3.00 .90
90 Kevin Youkilis ROO/640 * 3.00 .90
91 Chris Saenz ROO/325 RC * 3.00 .90
92 A.Blanco ROO/675 RC * 3.00 .90
93 D.Aardsma ROO/750 RC 3.00 .90
94 Merkin Valdez ROO/500 RC * 5.00 1.50
95 Jason Bartlett ROO/675 RC * 5.00 1.50
96 John Gall ROO/325 RC * 5.00 1.50
97 Zack Greinke ROO/675 * 3.00 .90
98 Scott Hairston ROO/675 * 3.00 .90
99 Matt Holliday ROO/750 3.00 .90
100 C.Kotchman ROO/375 * 5.00 1.50

2004 Fleer InScribed Autographs Purple

Randy Johnson's card is actually serial #'d to 51 copies, but according to representatives at Fleer only 40 copies were produced (skip-numbered across the print run). The card has been notated within our checklist as an uncorrected error with the erroneous and actual print runs detailed side-by-side.

Nm-Mt Ex-Mt
*PUR p/r 38-52: .5X TO 1.2X SILV p/r 235-322
*PUR p/r 38-52: .5X TO 1.2X SILV p/r 134-195
*PUR p/r 38-52: .4X TO 1X SILV p/r 55-57
*PUR p/r 38-52: .3X TO .8X SILV 20-34
*PUR p/r 20-35: .6X TO 1.5X SILV p/r 235-322
*PUR p/r 20-35: .6X TO 1.5X SILV 134-195
*PUR p/r 20-35: .5X TO 1.2X SILV p/r 55-57
*PUR p/r 15-18: .75X TO 2X SILV p/r 235-322
OVERALL AU ODDS 1:12 H, AU-GU 1:48 R
PRINT RUNS B/WN 3-52 COPIES PER
NO PRICING ON QTY OF 11 OR LESS
CARDS W/USER = ERR #ING AND ACTUAL QTY
ACTUAL R.JOHNSON QTY FROM FLEER

2004 Fleer InScribed Autographs Red

The Albert Pujols and Randy Johnson cards within this set contain erroneous serial-numbering. The Pujols cards are serial #'d to 25 but according to Fleer only 10 copies (skip-numbered across the print run) were actually printed. Similarly, the Johnson cards are serial #'d to 25 but only 15 copies were produced. Each card has been notated within our checklist as an uncorrected error with the erroneous and actual print runs detailed side-by-side.

Nm-Mt Ex-Mt
*RED: .6X TO 1.5X SILVER p/r 235-322

*RED: .6X TO 1.5X SILVER p/r 134-195
*RED: .5X TO 1.2X SILVER p/r 55-57
*RED: .4X TO 1X SILVER p/r 20-34
OVERALL AU ODDS 1:12 H, AU-GU 1:48 R
STATED PRINT RUN 25 SERIAL #'d SETS
UER'S ARE #'d OF 25 BUT 10-15 PER MADE
ACTUAL UER QTY PROVIDED BY FLEER
NO PUJOLS UER/10 PRICING AVAILABLE
AB Angel Berroa 15.00 4.50

2004 Fleer InScribed Autographs Silver

Nm-Mt Ex-Mt
OVERALL AU ODDS 1:12 H, AU-GU 1:48 R
PRINT RUNS B/WN 5-322 COPIES PER
CARDS ARE NOT SERIAL-NUMBERED
PRINT RUN INFO PROVIDED BY FLEER
NO PRICING ON QTY OF 11 OR LESS
AB Angel Berroa/11
AP Albert Pujols/5
BG Brian Giles/134 .... 10.00 3.00
BL Barry Larkin/140 .... 25.00 7.50
BR Brad Radke/168 .... 15.00 4.50
CB Carlos Beltran/296 .... 30.00 9.00
DW Dontrelle Willis/290 .... 15.00 4.50
EC Eric Chavez/322 .... 15.00 4.50
EG Eric Gagne/57 .... 40.00 12.00
JB Jeremy Bonderman/287 .... 10.00 3.00
JL Javy Lopez/257 .... 15.00 4.50
LG Luis Gonzalez/55 .... 12.00 3.60
LO Lyle Overbay/240 .... 10.00 3.00
RB Rocco Baldelli/34 .... 25.00 7.50
RHL Roy Halladay/139 .... 10.00 3.00
RHR Rich Harden/235 .... 15.00 4.50
RJ Randy Johnson/20 .... 80.00 24.00
SP Scott Podsednik/280 .... 15.00 4.50
TH Trevor Hoffman/174 .... 25.00 7.50
TN Trot Nixon/318 .... 15.00 4.50
WM Wade Miller/195 .... 10.00 3.00

2004 Fleer InScribed Rookie Autographs

Nm-Mt Ex-Mt
OVERALL AU ODDS 1:12 H, AU-GU 1:48 R
CARDS ARE SERIAL #'d TO 750
ACTUAL PRINT RUNS B/WN 34-646 PER
ACTUAL PRINT RUNS PROVIDED BY FLEER
HENN/MCPHERSON AVAIL.ONLY AS AU'S
87 Luis A. Gonzalez/240 * 8.00 2.40
90 Kevin Youkilis/34 * 40.00 12.00
91 Chris Saenz/350 * 8.00 2.40
94 Merkin Valdez/175 * 10.00 3.00
96 John Gall/350 * 10.00 3.00
100 Casey Kotchman/300 * 20.00 6.00
DM Dallas McPherson/646 * 30.00 9.00
SH Sean Henn/526 * 8.00 2.40

2004 Fleer InScribed Rookie Autographs Notation

Nm-Mt Ex-Mt
OVERALL AU ODDS 1:12 H, AU-GU 1:48 R
CARDS ARE SERIAL #'d TO 750
ACTUAL PRINT RUN 75 COPIES PER
J.GALL PRINT RUNS B/WN 25-50 PER
NOTATIONS ARE 1ST 75 #'d CARDS
NO GALL-STAR PRICING DUE TO SCARCITY
87 Luis A. Gonzalez 4/6/04 .... 15.00 4.50
89 Jon Knott 5/30/04 .... 15.00 4.50
90 Kevin Youkilis 5/15/04 .... 25.00 7.50
91 Chris Saenz 4/24/04 .... 15.00 4.50
92 Andres Blanco 4/17/04 .... 15.00 4.50
94 Merkin Valdez Go Giants 20.00 6.00
95 Jason Bartlett Go Twins 20.00 6.00
96A John Gall Gall-Star/25 *
96B John Gall Go Cards/50 * 20.00 6.00
98 Scott Hairston 5/17/04 .... 15.00 4.50
100 Casey Kotchman 5/9/04 .... 25.00 7.50

2004 Fleer InScribed Award Winners

Nm-Mt Ex-Mt
OVERALL INSERT ODDS 1:12 H, 1:12 R
STATED PRINT RUN 150 SERIAL #'d SETS
1 Alex Rodriguez 8.00 2.40
2 Eric Gagne 5.00 1.50
3 Miguel Tejada 4.00 1.20
4 Roy Halladay 4.00 1.20
5 Randy Johnson 5.00 1.50
6 Barry Zito 4.00 1.20
7 Chipper Jones 5.00 1.50
8 Ivan Rodriguez 5.00 1.50
9 Pedro Martinez 5.00 1.50
10 Barry Larkin 5.00 1.50
11 Dontrelle Willis 4.00 1.20
12 Angel Berroa 4.00 1.20
13 Kerry Wood 5.00 1.50
14 Albert Pujols 10.00 3.00
15 Hideo Nomo 5.00 1.50

2004 Fleer InScribed Award Winners Autographs

Nm-Mt Ex-Mt
OVERALL AU ODDS 1:12 H, AU-GU 1:48 R
PRINT RUNS B/WN 15-103 COPIES PER
CARDS W/UER = ERR #ING AND ACTUAL QTY
ACTUAL UER QTY PROVIDED BY FLEER
EXCHANGE DEADLINE INDEFINITE
AB Angel Berroa/103 .... 15.00 4.50
BL Barry Larkin UER 95/50 .... 40.00 12.00
BZ Barry Zito UER 99/35 .... 30.00 9.00
CJ Chipper Jones UER 99/35 .... 60.00 18.00
DW Dontrelle Willis/103 .... 25.00 7.50
HN H.Nomo UER 95/15 EXCH
IR Ivan Rodriguez UER 99/35 .... 60.00 18.00
RH Roy Halladay/102 .... 15.00 4.50

2004 Fleer InScribed Award Winners Jersey Silver

Nm-Mt Ex-Mt
STATED PRINT RUN 175 SERIAL #'d SETS
*BLUE: 1.25X TO 3X SILVER
BLUE PRINT RUN 15 SERIAL #'d SETS
*COPPER: .4X TO 1X SILVER
COPPER PRINT RUN 99 SERIAL #'d SETS
*PURPLE PATCH: 1X TO 2.5X SILVER
PURPLE PATCH PRINT RUN 49 #'d SETS
OVERALL GU ODDS 1:6 H, AU-GU 1:48 R
AB Angel Berroa 6.00 1.80
AP Albert Pujols 20.00 6.00
BL Barry Larkin 10.00 3.00
BZ Barry Zito 6.00 1.80
CJ Chipper Jones 10.00 3.00
DW Dontrelle Willis 6.00 1.80
EG Eric Gagne 10.00 3.00
HN Hideo Nomo 10.00 3.00
IR Ivan Rodriguez 10.00 3.00
KW Kerry Wood 10.00 3.00
MT Miguel Tejada 6.00 1.80
PM Pedro Martinez 10.00 3.00
RH Roy Halladay 6.00 1.80
RJ Randy Johnson 10.00 3.00

2004 Fleer InScribed Induction Ceremony

Nm-Mt Ex-Mt
OVERALL INSERT ODDS 1:12 H, 1:12 R
PRINT RUNS B/WN
1 Carlton Fisk/100 .... 10.00 3.00
2 Tony Perez/100 .... 8.00 2.40
3 Nolan Ryan/99 .... 25.00 7.50
4 Robin Yount/99 .... 15.00 4.50
5 Orlando Cepeda/99 .... 8.00 2.40
6 Bill Mazeroski/101 .... 10.00 3.00
7 Larry Doby/98 .... 8.00 2.40
8 Phil Niekro/97 .... 8.00 2.40
9 Jim Bunning/96 .... 8.00 2.40
10 Sparky Anderson/100 .... 8.00 2.40
11 Phil Rizzuto/94 .... 10.00 3.00
12 Rollie Fingers/92 .... 8.00 2.40
13 Hal Newhouser/92 .... 8.00 2.40
14 Rod Carew/91 .... 10.00 3.00
15 Reggie Jackson/93 .... 10.00 3.00
16 Tom Seaver/92 .... 10.00 3.00
17 Bob Gibson/81 .... 10.00 3.00
18 Jim Palmer/90 .... 8.00 2.40
19 Joe Morgan/90 .... 8.00 2.40
20 Al Kaline/80 .... 12.00 3.60

2004 Fleer InScribed Induction Ceremony Autographs Bronze

Though each card from this set is serial-numbered to 50, Nolan Ryan, Orlando Cepeda, Phil Niekro, Reggie Jackson, Robin Yount and Tom Seaver were all produced in smaller quantities ranging between 30-40 copies per. These cards have been tagged as UER's (uncorrected errors) in our checklist with the actual quantity listed as provided by Fleer.

Nm-Mt Ex-Mt
OVERALL AU ODDS 1:12 H, AU-GU 1:48 R
STATED PRINT RUN 50 SERIAL #'d SETS
UER'S ARE #'d OF 50 BUT 30-40 PER MADE
ACTUAL UER QTY PROVIDED BY FLEER
EXCHANGE DEADLINE INDEFINITE
AK Al Kaline 60.00 18.00
BG Bob Gibson 40.00 12.00
CF Carlton Fisk 40.00 12.00
JB Jim Bunning 25.00 7.50
JM Joe Morgan EXCH
JP Jim Palmer EXCH
NR Nolan Ryan/35 UER 120.00 36.00
OC Orlando Cepeda/40 UER 25.00 7.50
PN Phil Niekro/35 UER 50.00 15.00
RF Rollie Fingers 25.00 7.50
RJ Reggie Jackson/30 UER 80.00 24.00
RY Robin Yount/40 UER EXCH
TP Tony Perez 40.00 12.00
TS Tom Seaver/30 UER 60.00 18.00

2004 Fleer InScribed Induction Ceremony Autographs Silver

Though each card from this set is serial-numbered to 15, Carlton Fisk, Nolan Ryan, Orlando Cepeda, Phil Niekro, Reggie Jackson, Robin Yount, Tony Perez and Tom Seaver were all produced in smaller quantities ranging between 10-12 copies per. These cards have been tagged as UER's (uncorrected errors) in our checklist with the actual quantity listed as provided by Fleer.

Nm-Mt Ex-Mt
*SILVER: .6X TO 1.5X BRONZE
OVERALL AU ODDS 1:12 H, AU-GU 1:48 R
STATED PRINT RUN 15 SERIAL #'d SETS
UER'S ARE #'d OF 15 BUT 10-12 PER MADE
ACTUAL UER QTY PROVIDED BY FLEER
NO UER PRICING DUE TO SCARCITY
UER CL: CF/NR/OC/PN/RJ/RY/TP/TS
EXCHANGE DEADLINE INDEFINITE

2004 Fleer InScribed Induction Ceremony Material Silver

Nm-Mt Ex-Mt
PRINT RUNS B/WN 80-101 COPIES PER
MASTERPIECE PRINT RUN 1 #'d SET
NO M'PIECE PRICING DUE TO SCARCITY
OVERALL GU ODDS 1:6 H, AU-GU 1:48 R
AK Al Kaline Pants/80 .... 20.00 6.00
BM Bill Mazeroski Bat/101 .... 15.00 4.50
CF Carlton Fisk Jsy/100 .... 15.00 4.50
JM Joe Morgan Bat/90 .... 10.00 3.00
JP Jim Palmer Jsy/90 .... 10.00 3.00
LD Larry Doby Bat/98 .... 10.00 3.00
NR Nolan Ryan Jsy/99 .... 30.00 9.00
OC Orlando Cepeda Bat/99 .... 10.00 3.00
PN Phil Niekro Jsy/97 .... 10.00 3.00
PR Phil Rizzuto Bat/94 .... 15.00 4.50
RC Rod Carew Jsy/91 .... 15.00 4.50
RF Rollie Fingers Jsy/92 .... 10.00 3.00
RJ Reggie Jackson Pants/93 .... 15.00 4.50
RY Robin Yount Jsy/99 .... 20.00 6.00
SA Sparky Anderson Jsy/100 .... 10.00 3.00
TP Tony Perez Bat/100 .... 10.00 3.00
TS Tom Seaver Jsy/92 .... 15.00 4.50

2004 Fleer InScribed Names of the Game

Nm-Mt Ex-Mt
OVERALL INSERT ODDS 1:12 H, 1:12 R
STATED PRINT RUN 299 SERIAL #'d SETS
1 Nomar Garciaparra 8.00 2.40
2 Randy Johnson 5.00 1.50
3 Hideki Matsui 8.00 2.40
4 Frank Thomas 5.00 1.50
5 Ivan Rodriguez 5.00 1.50
6 Roger Clemens 10.00 3.00
7 Chipper Jones 5.00 1.50
8 Dontrelle Willis 4.00 1.20
9 Luis Gonzalez 4.00 1.20
10 Alex Rodriguez 8.00 2.40
11 Eric Gagne 5.00 1.50
12 Juan Gonzalez 5.00 1.50
13 Hideo Nomo 5.00 1.50
14 Sean Casey 4.00 1.20
15 Greg Maddux 8.00 2.40
16 Cal Ripken 20.00 6.00
17 Carl Yastrzemski 8.00 2.40
18 Tony Perez 5.00 1.50
19 Joe Morgan 5.00 1.50
20 Carlton Fisk 8.00 2.40
21 Willie McCovey 8.00 2.40
22 Al Kaline 8.00 2.40
23 Dennis Eckersley 5.00 1.50
24 Ted Williams 12.00 3.60
25 Willie Stargell 8.00 2.40
26 Rollie Fingers 5.00 1.50
27 Yogi Berra 8.00 2.40
28 Reggie Jackson 8.00 2.40
29 Harmon Killebrew 8.00 2.40
30 Nolan Ryan 12.00 3.60

2004 Fleer InScribed Names of the Game Autographs Silver

Nm-Mt Ex-Mt
OVERALL AU ODDS 1:12 H, AU-GU 1:48 R
CARDS ARE SERIAL #'d TO 99
UER'S ARE #'d OF 99 BUT 20-90 PER MADE
ACTUAL UER QTY PROVIDED BY FLEER
EXCHANGE DEADLINE INDEFINITE
AK Al Kaline/90 UER 50.00 15.00
CF Carlton Fisk/50 UER 40.00 12.00
CJ Chipper Jones/40 UER 60.00 18.00
CR Cal Ripken/20 UER EXCH
CY C.Yaz/30 UER EXCH
DE Dennis Eckersley/90 UER 25.00 7.50
DW Dontrelle Willis 25.00 7.50
IR Ivan Rodriguez/40 UER 60.00 18.00
JM Joe Morgan/40 UER EXCH
LG Luis Gonzalez/75 UER 15.00 4.50
NR Nolan Ryan/35 UER 150.00 45.00
RF Rollie Fingers/90 UER 25.00 7.50
RJ Reggie Jackson/35 UER 80.00 24.00
SC Sean Casey 25.00 7.50
TP Tony Perez/40 UER

2004 Fleer InScribed Names of the Game Autographs Gold

Nm-Mt Ex-Mt
*GOLD p/r 25: .6X TO 1.5X SILVER p/r 75-99
*GOLD p/r 25: .5X TO 1.2X SILVER p/r 40-50
OVERALL AU ODDS 1:12 H, AU-GU 1:48 R
CARDS ARE SERIAL #'d TO 25
UER'S ARE #'d TO 25 BUT 1-22 PER MADE
ACTUAL UER QTY PROVIDED BY FLEER
UER p/r 15's ARE NOMO, REGGIE & RYAN
NO PRICING ON UER QTY B/WN 1-10 PER
EXCHANGE DEADLINE INDEFINITE
HN Hideo Nomo/15 UER EXCH
RC Roger Clemens/22 UER
TW Ted Williams/1 UER

2004 Fleer InScribed Names of the Game Material Copper

Nm-Mt Ex-Mt
STATED PRINT RUN 250 SERIAL #'d SETS
*BLUE: 1.25X TO 3X COPPER
BLUE PRINT RUN 20 SERIAL #'d SETS
*GOLD: .4X TO 1X COPPER
GOLD PRINT RUN 150 SERIAL #'d SETS
*PURPLE BAT-PANTS: 1X TO 2.5X COPPER

*PURPLE PATCH: 1.5X TO 4X COPPER
PURPLE PRINT RUN 33 SERIAL #'d SETS
*RED: .5X TO 1.2X COPPER
RED PRINT RUN 79 SERIAL #'d SETS
*SILVER: .4X TO 1X COPPER
SILVER ODDS AU-GU 1:48 RETAIL
SILVER PRINT RUN 150 SETS
SILVER ARE NOT SERIAL-NUMBERED
SILVER PRINT RUN PROVIDED BY FLEER
OVERALL GU ODDS 1:6 H, AU-GU 1:48 R
AK Al Kaline Pants 15.00 4.50
CF Carlton Fisk Jsy 10.00 3.00
CJ Chipper Jones Jsy 8.00 2.40
CR Cal Ripken Jsy 25.00 7.50
CY Carl Yastrzemski Jsy 15.00 4.50
DE Dennis Eckersley Jsy 8.00 2.40
DW Dontrelle Willis Jsy 5.00 1.50
EG Eric Gagne Jsy 8.00 2.40
FT Frank Thomas Jsy 8.00 2.40
GM Greg Maddux Jsy 10.00 3.00
HK Harmon Killebrew Bat 15.00 4.50
HM Hideki Matsui Jsy 25.00 7.50
HN Hideo Nomo Jsy 8.00 2.40
IR Ivan Rodriguez Jsy 8.00 2.40
JG Juan Gonzalez Jsy 8.00 2.40
JM Joe Morgan Bat 8.00 2.40
LG Luis Gonzalez Jsy 5.00 1.50
NR Nolan Ryan Jsy 25.00 7.50
RC Roger Clemens Jsy 10.00 3.00
RF Rollie Fingers Jsy 8.00 2.40
RJA Reggie Jackson Pants 10.00 3.00
RJO Randy Johnson Jsy 8.00 2.40
SC Sean Casey Jsy 5.00 1.50
TP Tony Perez Bat 8.00 2.40
TW Ted Williams Bat 50.00 15.00
WM Willie McCovey Pants 10.00 3.00
WS Willie Stargell Jsy 10.00 3.00
YB Yogi Berra Bat 15.00 4.50

2001 Fleer Legacy

The 2001 Fleer Legacy product was released in mid-July, 2001 and featured a 105-card base set that was broken into tiers as follows: Base Veterans (1-90) and Prospects (91-105) that are individually serial numbered to 799. Please note that the first 300 serial-numbered cards of Albert Pujols packed out as exchange cards for a copy actually signed by Pujols. Card number 98 does not exist. Each box contained 15 packs with five cards per pack.

Nm-Mt Ex-Mt
COMP.SET w/o SP's (90) 40.00 12.00
COMMON CARD (1-90) .... 1.00 .30
COMMON AUTO (91-100) 10.00 3.00
COMMON CARD (101-105) 8.00 2.40
1 Pedro Martinez .... 2.50 .75
2 Andruw Jones .... 1.00 .30
3 Mike Hampton .... 1.00 .30
4 Gary Sheffield .... 1.00 .30
5 Barry Zito .... 1.50 .45
6 J.D. Drew .... 1.00 .30
7 Charles Johnson .... 1.00 .30
8 David Wells .... 1.00 .30
9 Kazuhiro Sasaki .... 1.00 .30
10 Vladimir Guerrero .... 2.50 .75
11 Pat Burrell .... 1.00 .30
12 Ruben Mateo .... 1.00 .30
13 Greg Maddux 4.00 1.20
14 Sean Casey .... 1.00 .30
15 Craig Biggio .... 1.50 .45
16 Bernie Williams .... 1.50 .45
17 Jeff Kent .... 1.00 .30
18 Nomar Garciaparra 4.00 1.20
19 Cal Ripken 8.00 2.40
20 Larry Walker .... 1.50 .45
21 Adrian Beltre .... 1.50 .45
22 Johnny Damon .... 1.50 .45
23 Rick Ankiel .... 1.00 .30
24 Matt Williams .... 1.00 .30
25 Magglio Ordonez .... 1.00 .30
26 Richard Hidalgo .... 1.00 .30
27 Robin Ventura .... 1.00 .30
28 Jason Kendall .... 1.00 .30
29 Tony Batista .... 1.00 .30
30 Chipper Jones .... 2.50 .75
31 Jim Thome .... 2.50 .75
32 Kevin Brown .... 1.00 .30
33 Mike Mussina .... 1.50 .45
34 Mark McGwire 6.00 1.80
35 Darin Erstad .... 1.00 .30
36 Manny Ramirez .... 1.50 .45
37 Bobby Higginson .... 1.00 .30
38 Richie Sexson .... 1.00 .30
39 Jason Giambi .... 1.00 .30
40 Alex Rodriguez 4.00 1.20
41 Mark Grace .... 1.50 .45
42 Ken Griffey Jr. 4.00 1.20
43 Moises Alou .... 1.00 .30
44 Edgardo Alfonzo .... 1.00 .30
45 Phil Nevin .... 1.00 .30
46 Rafael Palmeiro .... 1.50 .45
47 Javy Lopez .... 1.00 .30
48 Juan Gonzalez .... 1.50 .45

49 Jermaine Dye 1.00 .30
50 Roger Clemens 5.00 1.50
51 Barry Bonds 6.00 1.80
52 Carl Everett 1.00 .30
53 Ben Sheets 1.50 .45
54 Juan Encarnacion 1.00 .30
55 Jeromy Burnitz 1.00 .30
56 Miguel Tejada 1.00 .30
57 Ben Grieve 1.00 .30
58 Randy Johnson 2.50 .75
59 Frank Thomas 2.50 .75
60 Preston Wilson 1.00 .30
61 Mike Piazza 4.00 1.20
62 Brian Giles 1.00 .30
63 Carlos Delgado 1.00 .30
64 Tom Glavine 1.50 .45
65 Roberto Alomar 1.50 .45
66 Mike Sweeney 1.00 .30
67 Orlando Hernandez 1.00 .30
68 Edgar Martinez 1.50 .45
69 Tim Salmon 1.50 .45
70 Kerry Wood 2.50 .75
71 Jack Wilson RC 3.00 .90
72 Matt Lawton 1.00 .30
73 Scott Rolen 2.50 .75
74 Ivan Rodriguez 2.50 .75
75 Steve Finley 1.00 .30
76 Barry Larkin 1.50 .45
77 Jeff Bagwell 1.50 .45
78 Derek Jeter 6.00 1.80
79 Tony Gwynn 3.00 .90
80 Raul Mondesi 1.00 .30
81 Rafael Furcal 1.00 .30
82 Todd Helton 1.50 .45
83 Shawn Green 1.00 .30
84 Tim Hudson 1.00 .30
85 Jim Edmonds 1.00 .30
86 Troy Glaus 1.00 .30
87 Sammy Sosa 4.00 1.20
88 Cliff Floyd 1.00 .30
89 Jose Vidro 1.00 .30
90 Bob Abreu 1.00 .30
91 Drew Henson AU RC 40.00 12.00
92 Andy Morales AU RC 10.00 3.00
93 Wilson Betemit AU RC 10.00 3.00
94 Elpidio Guzman AU RC 10.00 3.00
95 Esix Snead AU RC 10.00 3.00
96 Winston Abreu AU RC 10.00 3.00
97 Jeremy Owens AU RC 10.00 3.00
98 Does Not Exist
99 Junior Spivey AU RC 15.00 4.50
100 J. Randolph AU RC 10.00 3.00
101 Ichiro Suzuki RC 60.00 18.00
102 Albert Pujols RC/499 120.00 36.00
102AU Albert Pujols AU/300 400.00 120.00
103 Tsuyoshi Shinjo RC 10.00 3.00
104 Jay Gibbons RC 10.00 3.00
105 Juan Uribe RC 10.00 3.00

2001 Fleer Legacy Ultimate

Randomly inserted into packs, this 105-card set is actually a complete parallel of the 2001 Fleer Legacy base set. These cards have a gold backdrop, and are serial numbered to 250.

Nm-Mt Ex-Mt
*STARS 1-90: 2.5X TO 6X BASIC CARDS
*ROOKIES 91-100: .2X TO .5X BASIC CARDS
*ROOKIES 101-105: .4X TO 1X BASIC CARDS

2001 Fleer Legacy Hit Kings

Randomly inserted into packs at one in 13, this 29-card insert features actual chips from game-used bats from the major leagues top hitters Cards have been listed in alphabetical order for convenience.

Nm-Mt Ex-Mt
1 Rick Ankiel 10.00 3.00
2 Tony Batista 10.00 3.00
3 Carlos Beltran 15.00 4.50
4 Adrian Beltre 15.00 4.50
5 Barry Bonds 30.00 9.00
6 George Brett 25.00 7.50
7 Jose Canseco 15.00 4.50
8 Roger Cedeno 10.00 3.00
9 Johnny Damon 15.00 4.50
10 Erubiel Durazo 10.00 3.00
11 Juan Encarnacion 10.00 3.00
12 Troy Glaus 10.00 3.00
13 Shawn Green 10.00 3.00
14 Vladimir Guerrero 15.00 4.50
15 Reggie Jackson 15.00 4.50
16 Andruw Jones 10.00 3.00
17 Jason Kendall 10.00 3.00
18 Ralph Kiner 15.00 4.50
19 Billy Martin 15.00 4.50
20 Ruben Mateo 10.00 3.00
21 Stan Musial 25.00 7.50
22 Troy O'Leary 10.00 3.00
23 Magglio Ordonez 10.00 3.00
24 Corey Patterson 10.00 3.00
25 Juan Pierre 10.00 3.00
26 Ivan Rodriguez 15.00 4.50
27 Tim Salmon 15.00 4.50
28 Jim Thome 15.00 4.50
29 Jose Vidro 10.00 3.00

2001 Fleer Legacy Hit Kings Short Prints

Randomly inserted into packs, this 10-card insert features actual chips from game-used bats from the major leagues top hitters Cards have been listed in alphabetical order for convenience. Please note that there were only 100 serial num

bered sets produced. These cards also have a special red-foil stamping on the card fronts.

Nm-Mt Ex-Mt
1 Johnny Bench 40.00 12.00
2 Wade Boggs 40.00 12.00
3 Roger Clemens 80.00 24.00
4 Steve Garvey 25.00 7.50
5 Tony Gwynn 50.00 15.00
6 Eddie Mathews 40.00 12.00
7 Joe Morgan 25.00 7.50
8 Scott Rolen 40.00 12.00
9 Frank Thomas 40.00 12.00
10 Robin Yount 40.00 12.00

2001 Fleer Legacy Hot Gloves

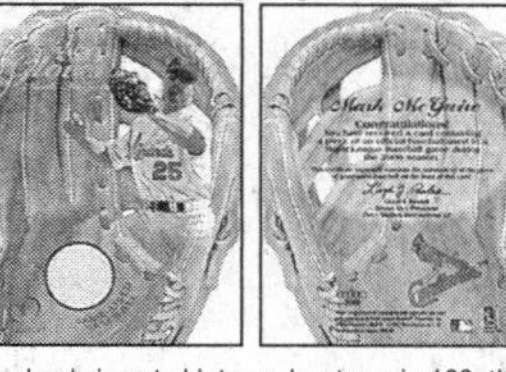

Randomly inserted into packs at one in 180, this 15-card insert featured actual swatches of game-used gloves. Unfortunately, redemption cards had to be placed into packs for all fifteen cards. The exchange deadline was 07/01/02. Prices below refer to actual memorabilia cards. The redemption cards are valued at 25 percent of listed values.

Nm-Mt Ex-Mt
*REDEMPTION CARDS: .25X VALUE..
1 Andruw Jones 25.00 7.50
2 Mike Mussina 40.00 12.00
3 Roberto Alomar 40.00 12.00
4 Tony Gwynn 50.00 15.00
5 Bernie Williams 40.00 12.00
6 Ivan Rodriguez 40.00 12.00
7 Ken Griffey Jr. 80.00 24.00
8 Robin Ventura 25.00 7.50
9 Cal Ripken 100.00 30.00
10 Jeff Bagwell 40.00 12.00
11 Mark McGwire 150.00 45.00
12 Rafael Palmeiro 40.00 12.00
13 Scott Rolen 40.00 12.00
14 Barry Bonds 100.00 30.00
15 Greg Maddux 60.00 18.00

2001 Fleer Legacy MLB Autograph Fitted Caps

Inserted at one per box (chiptopper), this collection features actual autographed hats from both modern-day and classic players. Hats have been listed in alphabetical order for convenience. Specific quantities for caps in short supply were announced by Fleer shortly after the product went live. Those figures are detailed within our checklist. According to Fleer, no more than 500 of each cap was signed. Exchange cards, with a redemption deadline of July 1st, 2002, were seeded into packs for the following players: Pat Burrell, Darin Erstad, Nomar Garciaparra, Paul Molitor, Jim Thome and Robin Yount.

Nm-Mt Ex-Mt
1 Edgardo Alfonzo 40.00 12.00
2 Roberto Alomar 50.00 15.00
3 Ernie Banks SP/100 150.00 45.00
4 Adrian Beltre 50.00 15.00
5 Johnny Bench SP/100 150.00 45.00
6 Lance Berkman 50.00 15.00
7 Yogi Berra SP/200 150.00 45.00
8 Craig Biggio 50.00 15.00
9 Barry Bonds 400.00 120.00
10 Jeromy Burnitz 40.00 12.00
11 Pat Burrell 40.00 12.00
12 Steve Carlton 50.00 15.00
13 Sean Casey 40.00 12.00
14 Orlando Cepeda 40.00 12.00
15 Eric Chavez 40.00 12.00
16 Tony Clark 40.00 12.00
17 Roger Clemens SP/100 300.00 90.00
18 Johnny Damon 50.00 15.00
19 Dom DiMaggio SP/200 100.00 30.00
20 J.D. Drew 50.00 15.00
21 Jermaine Dye 40.00 12.00
22 Darin Erstad 40.00 12.00
23 Carlton Fisk SP/150 120.00 36.00
24 Rafael Furcal 40.00 12.00
25 Nomar Garciaparra SP/150 200.00 60.00
26 Jason Giambi 40.00 12.00
27 Troy Glaus 40.00 12.00
28 Tom Glavine 80.00 24.00
29 Juan Gonzalez 50.00 15.00
30 Luis Gonzalez 40.00 12.00
31 Tony Gwynn 120.00 36.00
32 Drew Henson 50.00 15.00
33 Derek Jeter 300.00 90.00
34 Andruw Jones 40.00 12.00
35 David Justice 40.00 12.00
36 Paul Konerko 40.00 12.00
37 Don Mattingly 150.00 45.00
38 Willie McCovey 50.00 15.00
39 Paul Molitor 60.00 18.00
40 Stan Musial SP/200 150.00 45.00
41 Mike Mussina 50.00 15.00
42 Jim Palmer 40.00 12.00
43 Corey Patterson 40.00 12.00
44 Kirby Puckett SP/200 100.00 30.00
45 Cal Ripken SP/200 300.00 90.00
46 Brooks Robinson 50.00 15.00
47 Ivan Rodriguez 80.00 24.00
48 Scott Rolen 80.00 24.00
49 Nolan Ryan SP/150 250.00 75.00
50 Mike Schmidt SP/150 150.00 45.00
51 Tom Seaver SP/100 150.00 45.00
52 Ben Sheets 50.00 15.00
53 Ozzie Smith 120.00 36.00
54 Duke Snider 50.00 15.00
55 Miguel Tejada 40.00 12.00
56 Jim Thome 80.00 24.00
57 Matt Williams 40.00 12.00
58 Dave Winfield SP/150 100.00 30.00
59 C.Yastrzemski SP/150 150.00 45.00
60 Robin Yount 120.00 36.00
61 Barry Zito 50.00 15.00

2001 Fleer Legacy MLB Game Issue Base

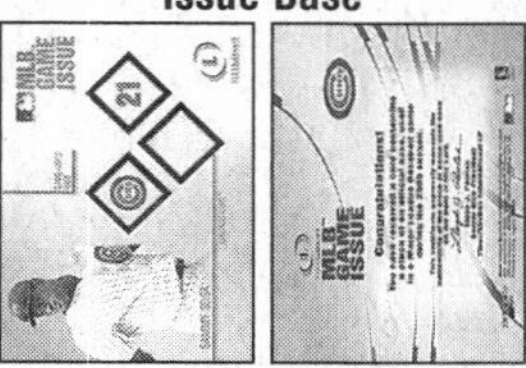

Randomly inserted into packs at one in 52, this 15-card insert features actual swatches from game-used bases from top major league talents. Cards have been listed in alphabetical order for convenience.

Nm-Mt Ex-Mt
1 Barry Bonds 30.00 9.00
2 Pat Burrell 10.00 3.00
3 Troy Glaus 10.00 3.00
4 Ken Griffey Jr. 15.00 4.50
5 Tony Gwynn 15.00 4.50
6 Todd Helton 10.00 3.00
7 Derek Jeter 30.00 9.00
8 Chipper Jones 10.00 3.00
9 Mark McGwire 50.00 15.00
10 Mike Piazza 20.00 6.00
11 Cal Ripken 40.00 12.00
12 Alex Rodriguez 25.00 7.50
13 Scott Rolen 10.00 3.00
14 Sammy Sosa 15.00 4.50
15 Frank Thomas 10.00 3.00

2001 Fleer Legacy MLB Game Issue Base-Ball

Randomly inserted into packs, this 15-card insert features actual swatches from both game-used bases and baseballs from top major league talents. Cards have been listed in alphabetical order for convenience. Please note that there were only 100 serial numbered sets produced.

Nm-Mt Ex-Mt
1 Barry Bonds 80.00 24.00
2 Pat Burrell 25.00 7.50
3 Troy Glaus 25.00 7.50
4 Ken Griffey Jr. 50.00 15.00
5 Tony Gwynn 50.00 15.00
6 Todd Helton 25.00 7.50
7 Derek Jeter 80.00 24.00
8 Chipper Jones 40.00 12.00
9 Mark McGwire 150.00 45.00
10 Mike Piazza 80.00 24.00
11 Cal Ripken 100.00 30.00
12 Scott Rolen 40.00 12.00
13 Alex Rodriguez 80.00 24.00
14 Sammy Sosa 60.00 18.00
15 Frank Thomas 40.00 12.00

2001 Fleer Legacy MLB Game Issue Base-Ball-Jersey

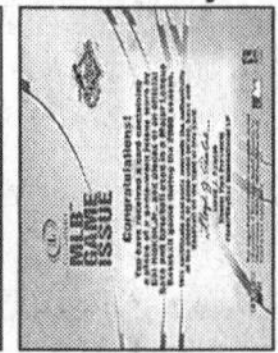

Randomly inserted into packs, this 10-card insert features actual swatches from game-used bases, baseballs, and jerseys from top major league talents. Cards have been listed in alphabetical order for convenience. Please note that there were only 50 serial numbered sets produced. Exchange cards, with a redemption deadline of July 1st, 2002, were seeded into packs for the following players: Barry Bonds, Pat Burrell, Tony Gwynn, Cal Ripken and Scott Rolen.

Nm-Mt Ex-Mt
1 Barry Bonds 150.00 45.00
2 Pat Burrell 50.00 15.00
3 Troy Glaus 50.00 15.00
4 Tony Gwynn 100.00 30.00
5 Todd Helton 50.00 15.00
6 Derek Jeter 150.00 45.00
7 Chipper Jones 80.00 24.00
8 Cal Ripken 200.00 60.00
9 Scott Rolen 80.00 24.00
10 Frank Thomas 80.00 24.00

2001 Fleer Legacy Tailor Made

Randomly inserted into packs at one in 15, this 23-card insert features actual swatches of game-used jersey from top major league talents like Barry Bonds and Reggie Jackson. Cards have been listed in alphabetical order for convenience.

Nm-Mt Ex-Mt
*MULTI-COLOR PATCH: .75X TO 2X BASIC
1 Edgardo Alfonzo 10.00 3.00
2 Rick Ankiel 10.00 3.00
3 Barry Bonds 30.00 9.00
4 Kevin Brown 10.00 3.00
5 Orlando Cepeda 10.00 3.00
6 Carlos Delgado 10.00 3.00
7 J.D. Drew 10.00 3.00
8 Shawn Green 10.00 3.00
9 Todd Helton 15.00 4.50
10 Reggie Jackson 15.00 4.50
11 Jason Kendall 10.00 3.00
12 Greg Maddux 15.00 4.50
13 Don Mattingly 50.00 15.00
14 Willie McCovey 10.00 3.00
15 Rafael Palmeiro 15.00 4.50
16 Lou Piniella 10.00 3.00
17 Manny Ramirez 15.00 4.50
18 Cal Ripken 50.00 15.00
19 Ivan Rodriguez 15.00 4.50
20 Nolan Ryan 50.00 15.00
21 Curt Schilling 10.00 3.00
22 Rondell White 10.00 3.00
23 Dave Winfield 10.00 3.00

2004 Fleer Legacy

Nm-Mt Ex-Mt
COMP.SET w/o SP's (60) 100.00 30.00
COMMON CARD (1-60) 2.00 .60
COMMON CARD (61-75) 5.00 1.50
61-75 ODDS 1:1 HOBBY, 1:96 RETAIL
61-75 PRINT RUN 599 SERIAL #'d SETS
1 Angel Berroa 2.00 .60
2 Derek Jeter 6.00 1.80
3 Jody Gerut 2.00 .60
4 Curt Schilling 3.00 .90
5 Khalil Greene 3.00 .90
6 Manny Ramirez 3.00 .90
7 Rocco Baldelli 2.00 .60
8 Sammy Sosa 5.00 1.50
9 Shawn Green 2.00 .60
10 Austin Kearns 2.00 .60
11 Frank Thomas 3.00 .90
12 Alfonso Soriano 3.00 .90
13 Alex Rodriguez 5.00 1.50
14 Carlos Delgado 2.00 .60
15 Chipper Jones 3.00 .90
16 Edgar Martinez 3.00 .90
17 Ivan Rodriguez 3.00 .90
18 Mark Prior 3.00 .90
19 Mike Piazza 5.00 1.50
20 Orlando Cabrera 3.00 .90
21 Adam Dunn 3.00 .90
22 Andruw Jones 2.00 .60
23 Eric Chavez 2.00 .60
24 Mark Teixeira 2.00 .60
25 Scott Podsednik 2.00 .60
26 Torii Hunter 2.00 .60
27 Miguel Cabrera 3.00 .90
28 Hideki Matsui 5.00 1.50
29 Jose Reyes 2.00 .60
30 Vladimir Guerrero 3.00 .90
31 Albert Pujols 6.00 1.80
32 Greg Maddux 5.00 1.50
33 Jason Giambi 2.00 .60
34 Randy Johnson 3.00 .90
35 Roger Clemens 6.00 1.80
36 Casey Kotchman 3.00 .90
37 Ken Griffey Jr. 5.00 1.50
38 Todd Helton 3.00 .90
39 Javy Lopez 2.00 .60
40 Jim Thome 3.00 .90
41 Josh Beckett 2.00 .60
42 Kerry Wood 3.00 .90
43 Scott Rolen 3.00 .90
44 Pat Burrell 2.00 .60
45 Pedro Martinez 3.00 .90
46 Barry Zito 2.00 .60
47 Hank Blalock 2.00 .60
48 Hideo Nomo 3.00 .90
49 Jeff Bagwell 3.00 .90
50 Magglio Ordonez 2.00 .60
51 Ichiro Suzuki 5.00 1.50
52 Joe Mauer 3.00 .90
53 Richie Sexson 2.00 .60
54 Shannon Stewart 2.00 .60
55 Craig Wilson 2.00 .60
56 Miguel Tejada 2.00 .60
57 Sean Casey 2.00 .60
58 Tom Glavine 3.00 .90
59 Jason Schmidt 2.00 .60
60 Nomar Garciaparra 5.00 1.50
61 Kaz Matsui FL RC 10.00 3.00
62 Justin Leone FL RC 8.00 2.40
63 Merkin Valdez FL RC 8.00 2.40
64 Shingo Takatsu FL RC 8.00 2.40
65 Andres Blanco FL RC 5.00 1.50
66 Angel Chavez FL RC 5.00 1.50
67 Hector Gimenez FL RC 5.00 1.50
68 Akinori Otsuka FL RC 5.00 1.50
69 Jason Bartlett FL RC 8.00 2.40
70 Luis Gonzalez FL RC 5.00 1.50
71 Sean Henn FL RC 5.00 1.50
72 Mike Rouse FL RC 5.00 1.50
73 Chris Aguila FL RC 5.00 1.50
74 Aarom Baldiris FL RC 8.00 2.40
75 Jerry Gil FL RC 5.00 1.50

2004 Fleer Legacy Gold

Nm-Mt Ex-Mt
*GOLD 1-60: 1.5X TO 4X BASIC
*GOLD 61-75: .75X TO 2X BASIC
OVERALL PARALLEL ODDS 1:3 H, 1:240 R
STATED PRINT RUN 50 SERIAL #'d SETS

2004 Fleer Legacy Ultimate

Nm-Mt Ex-Mt
OVERALL PARALLEL ODDS 1:3 HOBBY
STATED PRINT RUN 1 SERIAL #'d SET
NO PRICING DUE TO SCARCITY

2004 Fleer Legacy Franchise Patch 99

Nm-Mt Ex-Mt
STATED PRINT RUN 99 SERIAL #'d SETS
PATCH 1 PRINT RUN 1 SERIAL #'d SET
NO PATCH 1 PRICING DUE TO SCARCITY
OVERALL PATCH ODDS 1:1 HOBBY
PRICES BELOW REFER TO NON LOGO/TAG
LOGO/TAG CARDS COMMAND 2X-3X HI
AP Albert Pujols 40.00 12.00
CJ Chipper Jones 15.00 4.50
CR Cal Ripken 50.00 15.00
DM Don Mattingly 25.00 7.50
GM Greg Maddux 25.00 7.50
HM Hideki Matsui 50.00 15.00
HN Hideo Nomo 25.00 7.50
IR Ivan Rodriguez 15.00 4.50
JBA Jeff Bagwell 15.00 4.50
JBE Josh Beckett 10.00 3.00
JL Javy Lopez 10.00 3.00
JT Jim Thome 15.00 4.50
KM Kaz Matsui 25.00 7.50
KW Kerry Wood 15.00 4.50
MP Mike Piazza 25.00 7.50
MPR Mark Prior 15.00 4.50
MT Miguel Tejada 10.00 3.00
NR Nolan Ryan 50.00 15.00
PM Pedro Martinez 15.00 4.50
RC Roger Clemens 25.00 7.50
RJ Randy Johnson 15.00 4.50
SS Sammy Sosa 15.00 4.50
VG Vladimir Guerrero 15.00 4.50

2004 Fleer Legacy Franchise Patch 50

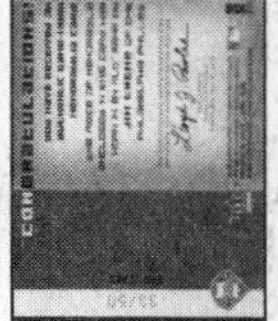

Nm-Mt Ex-Mt
*PATCH 50: .5X TO 1.2X BASIC
OVERALL PATCH ODDS 1:1 HOBBY
STATED PRINT RUN 50 SERIAL #'d SETS
PRICES BELOW REFER TO NON LOGO/TAG
LOGO/TAG CARDS COMMAND 2X-3X HI
JB Johnny Bench

2004 Fleer Legacy Franchise Patch 25

Nm-Mt Ex-Mt
*PATCH 25: .75X TO 2X BASIC
OVERALL PATCH ODDS 1:1 HOBBY
STATED PRINT RUN 25 SERIAL #'d SETS
PRICES BELOW REFER TO NON LOGO/TAG
LOGO/TAG CARDS COMMAND 2X-3X HI
JB Johnny Bench

2004 Fleer Legacy Franchise Dual Patch

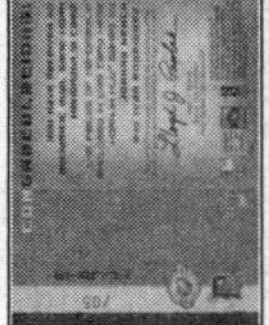

Nm-Mt Ex-Mt
OVERALL PATCH ODDS 1:1 HOBBY

PRINT RUNS B/WN 5-31 COPIES PER		
NO PRICING ON QTY OF 10 OR LESS		
HNHM Hideo Nomo		
Hideki Matsui/10		
JBIR Johnny Bench		
Ivan Rodriguez/5		
JLMT Javy Lopez		
Miguel Tejada/15		
JTJB Jim Thome	80.00	24.00
Jeff Bagwell/27		
KMMP Kaz Matsui		
Mike Piazza/7		
KWMP Kerry Wood	50.00	15.00
Mark Prior/30		
PMRJ Pedro Martinez	50.00	15.00
Randy Johnson/15		
RCNR Roger Clemens	120.00	36.00
Nolan Ryan/22		
RCRJ Roger Clemens	80.00	24.00
Randy Johnson/29		
SSAP Sammy Sosa	80.00	24.00
Albert Pujols/29		
VGCJ Vladimir Guerrero		
Chipper Jones/31		

2004 Fleer Legacy Franchise Quad Patch

	Nm-Mt	Ex-Mt
OVERALL PATCH ODDS 1:1 HOBBY		
PRINT RUNS B/WN 2-22 COPIES PER		
NO PRICING ON QTY OF 14 OR LESS		
BLRP Johnny Bench		
Javy Lopez		
Ivan Rodriguez		
Mike Piazza/2		
BRCR Johnny Bench		
Ivan Rodriguez		
Roger Clemens		
Nolan Ryan/9		
CBTR Roger Clemens		
Jeff Bagwell		
Miguel Tejada		
Cal Ripken/13		
CRJM Roger Clemens		
Nolan Ryan		
Randy Johnson		
Greg Maddux/11		
GJSP Vladimir Guerrero	120.00	36.00
Chipper Jones		
Sammy Sosa		
Albert Pujols/22		
MMMP Don Mattingly	200.00	60.00
Hideki Matsui		
Kaz Matsui		
Mike Piazza/16		
MSPG Hideki Matsui		
Sammy Sosa		
Albert Pujols		
Vladimir Guerrero/14		
MSWP Greg Maddux	100.00	30.00
Sammy Sosa		
Kerry Wood		
Mark Prior/21		
TBMP Jim Thome		
Jeff Bagwell		
Don Mattingly		
Albert Pujols/6		
WPNM Kerry Wood	120.00	36.00
Mark Prior		
Pedro Martinez		
Hideo Nomo/19		

2004 Fleer Legacy Hit Kings

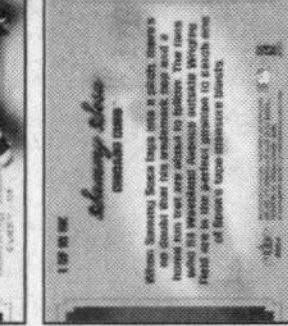

	Nm-Mt	Ex-Mt
STATED ODDS 1:8 RETAIL		
1 Sammy Sosa	4.00	1.20
2 Hideki Matsui	4.00	1.20
3 Vladimir Guerrero	2.50	.75
4 Mike Piazza	4.00	1.20
5 Jeff Bagwell	2.50	.75
6 Miguel Cabrera	2.50	.75
7 Scott Rolen	2.50	.75
8 Lance Berkman	1.50	.45
9 Jason Giambi	1.50	.45
10 Mark Teixeira	1.50	.45
11 Jim Thome	2.50	.75
12 Albert Pujols	5.00	1.50
13 Chipper Jones	2.50	.75
14 Manny Ramirez	2.50	.75
15 Adam Dunn	2.50	.75

2004 Fleer Legacy Hit Kings Jersey Copper

	Nm-Mt	Ex-Mt
STATED ODDS 1:24 RETAIL		
AD Adam Dunn	8.00	2.40
AK Austin Kearns	5.00	1.50
AP Albert Pujols	15.00	4.50
CD Carlos Delgado	5.00	1.50
CJ Chipper Jones	8.00	2.40
FT Frank Thomas	8.00	2.40
GS Gary Sheffield	5.00	1.50
HB Hank Blalock	5.00	1.50
HM Hideki Matsui	20.00	6.00
JB Jeff Bagwell	8.00	2.40
JG Jason Giambi	5.00	1.50
JT Jim Thome	8.00	2.40
LB Lance Berkman	5.00	1.50
MC Miguel Cabrera	8.00	2.40
MP Mike Piazza	10.00	3.00
MR Manny Ramirez	8.00	2.40
MS Mike Schmidt	15.00	4.50
MT Mark Teixeira	5.00	1.50
RS Richie Sexson	5.00	1.50
SR Scott Rolen	8.00	2.40
SS Sammy Sosa	10.00	3.00
VG Vladimir Guerrero	8.00	2.40

2004 Fleer Legacy Hit Kings Dual Patch

	Nm-Mt	Ex-Mt
OVERALL PATCH ODDS 1:1 HOBBY		
PRINT RUNS B/WN 7-21 COPIES PER		
NO PRICING ON QTY OF 13 OR LESS		
AKAD Austin Kearns	50.00	15.00
Adam Dunn/20		
CJMP Chipper Jones		
Mike Piazza/7		
HBMT Hank Blalock	40.00	12.00
Mark Teixeira/17		
HMJG Hideki Matsui		
Jason Giambi/15		
JBLB Jeff Bagwell	50.00	15.00
Lance Berkman/21		
JTCD Jim Thome		
Carlos Delgado/8		
JTMS Jim Thome		
Mike Schmidt/10		
MRGS Manny Ramirez	50.00	15.00
Gary Sheffield/19		
SRAB Scott Rolen	100.00	30.00
Albert Pujols/16		
SSAP Sammy Sosa		
Albert Pujols/13		
SSFT Sammy Sosa	60.00	18.00
Frank Thomas/20		
VGMC Vladimir Guerrero		
Miguel Cabrera/12		
VGMR Vladimir Guerrero		
Manny Ramirez/11		

2004 Fleer Legacy Signed Baseballs

	Nm-Mt	Ex-Mt
ONE PER HOBBY BOX		
B/WN 1-99 ACTUAL SIGNED BALLS PER		
MOST BALLS #'d B/WN 1-500 PER		
SOME #ING DOESN'T MATCH ACTUAL QTY		
SEE BECKETT.COM FOR ACTUAL QTY		
NO PRICING AVAILABLE		

2003 Fleer Mystique Diamond Dominators Memorabilia

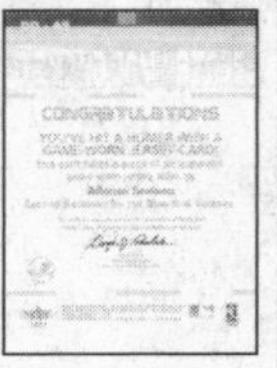

	MINT	NRMT
OVERALL #'d GU INSERT ODDS 1:20		
STATED PRINT RUN 75 SERIAL #'d SETS		
OVERALL #'d GU PARALLEL ODDS 1:350		
GOLD PRINT RUN 10 SERIAL #'d SETS		
NO GOLD PRICING DUE TO SCARCITY		
AD Adam Dunn Bat	15.00	6.75
AR Alex Rodriguez Jsy	20.00	9.00
AS Alfonso Soriano Jsy	15.00	6.75
BZ Barry Zito Jsy	12.00	5.50
GM Greg Maddux Jsy	20.00	9.00
MP Mike Piazza Jsy	20.00	9.00
PM Pedro Martinez Jsy	15.00	6.75
RC Roger Clemens Jsy	25.00	11.00
RJ Randy Johnson Jsy	15.00	6.75
SS Sammy Sosa Jsy	25.00	11.00

2003 Fleer Patchworks

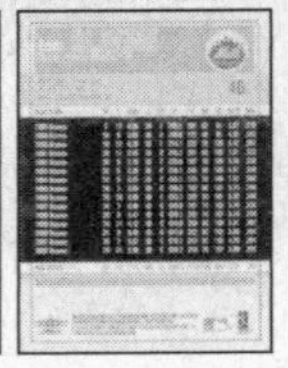

This 115 card set was released in May, 2003. This set was issued in five-card packs which were issued in five card packs with a $4.99 SRP which came 24 packs to a box and 12 boxes to a case. The set consists of 90 veterans (1-90) and 25 rookies and leading prospects (91-115). The final 25 cards were randomly inserted in packs and issued to a stated print run of 1500 serial numbered sets.

	Nm-Mt	Ex-Mt
COMP.SET w/o SP's (90)	15.00	4.50
COMMON CARD (1-90)	.40	.12
COMMON CARD (91-115)	4.00	1.20
1 Luis Castillo	.40	.12
2 Derek Jeter	2.50	.75
3 Vladimir Guerrero	1.00	.30
4 Bobby Higginson	.40	.12
5 Pat Burrell	.40	.12
6 Ivan Rodriguez	1.00	.30
7 Craig Biggio	.60	.18
8 Troy Glaus	.40	.12
9 Barry Bonds	2.50	.75
10 Hideo Nomo	1.00	.30
11 Barry Larkin	.60	.18
12 Roberto Alomar	.60	.18
13 Rodrigo Lopez	.40	.12
14 Eric Chavez	.40	.12
15 Shawn Green	.40	.12
16 Joe Randa	.40	.12
17 Mark Grace	.60	.18
18 Jason Kendall	.40	.12
19 Hee Seop Choi	.40	.12
20 Luis Gonzalez	.40	.12
21 Sammy Sosa	1.50	.45
22 Larry Walker	.60	.18
23 Phil Nevin	.40	.12
24 Manny Ramirez	.60	.18
25 Jim Thome	1.00	.30
26 Randy Johnson	1.00	.30
27 Jose Vidro	.40	.12
28 Austin Kearns	.40	.12
29 Mike Sweeney	.40	.12
30 Magglio Ordonez	.40	.12
31 Mike Piazza	1.50	.45
32 Eric Hinske	.40	.12
33 Alex Rodriguez	1.50	.45
34 Kerry Wood	1.00	.30
35 Matt Morris	.40	.12
36 Lance Berkman	.40	.12
37 Michael Cuddyer	.40	.12
38 Curt Schilling	.40	.12
39 Sean Burroughs	.40	.12
40 Ken Griffey Jr.	1.50	.45
41 Edgardo Alfonzo	.40	.12
42 Carlos Pena	.40	.12
43 Adam Dunn	.60	.18
44 Pedro Martinez	1.00	.30
45 Miguel Tejada	.40	.12
46 Tom Glavine	.60	.18
47 Torii Hunter	.40	.12
48 Jason Giambi	.40	.12
49 Tony Batista	.40	.12
50 Ben Grieve	.40	.12
51 Ichiro Suzuki	1.50	.45
52 Bobby Abreu	.40	.12
53 Todd Helton	.60	.18
54 Kazuhiro Sasaki	.40	.12
55 Nomar Garciaparra	1.50	.45
56 Francisco Rodriguez	.40	.12
57 Ellis Burks	.40	.12
58 Frank Thomas	1.00	.30
59 Greg Maddux	1.50	.45
60 Josh Beckett	.40	.12
61 Brad Wilkerson	.40	.12
62 Joe Borchard	.40	.12
63 Carlos Delgado	.40	.12
64 Alfonso Soriano	.60	.18
65 Chipper Jones	1.00	.30
66 J.D. Drew	.40	.12
67 Mark Prior	1.00	.30
68 Rafael Palmeiro	.60	.18
69 Jeff Kent	.40	.12
70 Adrian Beltre	.60	.18
71 Marlon Byrd	.40	.12
72 Orlando Hudson	.40	.12
73 Junior Spivey	.40	.12
74 Jeff Bagwell	.60	.18
75 Barry Zito	.40	.12
76 Roger Clemens	2.00	.60
77 Aubrey Huff	.40	.12
78 Geoff Jenkins	.40	.12
79 Andruw Jones	.40	.12
80 Scott Rolen	1.00	.30
81 Omar Vizquel	.60	.18
82 Darin Erstad	.40	.12
83 Bernie Williams	.60	.18
84 Freddy Garcia	.40	.12
85 Richie Sexson	.40	.12
86 Josh Phelps	.40	.12
87 Albert Pujols	2.00	.60
88 Aramis Ramirez	.40	.12
89 Shea Hillenbrand	.40	.12
90 Cristian Guzman	.40	.12
91 Adam LaRoche RR	4.00	1.20
92 David Pember RR RC	4.00	1.20
93 Terrmel Sledge RR RC	5.00	1.50
94 Hideki Matsui RR RC	10.00	3.00
95 Nook Logan RR RC	4.00	1.20
96 Jose Contreras RR RC	5.00	1.50
97 Pete LaForest RR RC	4.00	1.20
98 Rich Fischer RR RC	4.00	1.20
99 Francisco Rosario RR RC	4.00	1.20
100 Josh Willingham RR RC	5.00	1.50
101 Alejandro Machado RR RC	4.00	1.20
102 Lew Ford RR RC	5.00	1.50
103 Joe Valentine RR RC	4.00	1.20
104 Guillermo Quiroz RR RC	5.00	1.50
105 Chien-Ming Wang RR RC	5.00	1.50
106 Jhonny Peralta RR	4.00	1.20
107 Shane Victorino RR RC	4.00	1.20
108 Prentice Redman RR RC	4.00	1.20
109 Matt Bruback RR RC	4.00	1.20
110 Lance Niekro RR	4.00	1.20
111 Travis Hughes RR	4.00	1.20
112 Nic Jackson RR	4.00	1.20
113 Hector Luna RR RC	4.00	1.20
114 Cliff Lee RR	4.00	1.20
115 Tim Olson RR RC	5.00	1.50

2003 Fleer Patchworks Star Ruby

	Nm-Mt	Ex-Mt
*RUBY 1-90: 4X TO 10X BASIC		
*RUBY 91-115: .6X TO 1.5X BASIC		
RANDOM INSERTS IN PACKS		
STATED PRINT RUN 100 SERIAL #'d SETS		

2003 Fleer Patchworks Diamond Ink

Randomly inserted into packs, these six cards feature authentic signed autographs from four different players. Derek Jeter signed his cards in a mix of Black, blue and red ink. We have printed the stated print run next to the player's name in our checklist.

	Nm-Mt	Ex-Mt
DJ1 Derek Jeter Black/210	150.00	45.00
DJ2 Derek Jeter Blue/101	150.00	45.00
DJ3 Derek Jeter Red/50	200.00	60.00
MP Mark Prior/88	80.00	24.00
MS Mike Schmidt/194	80.00	24.00
TG Troy Glaus/351	25.00	7.50

2003 Fleer Patchworks Game-Worn Patch Level 1 Single

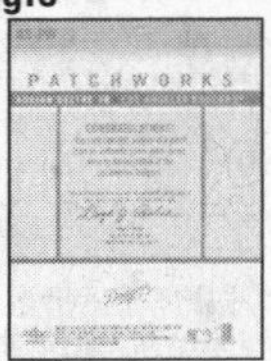

Randomly inserted into packs, these 17 cards feature a single color patch swatch. Please note that the second level cards feature dual-colored swatches and level 3 features multi-colored swatches. The level 1 patches were issued to a stated print run of 250 serial numbered sets.

	Nm-Mt	Ex-Mt
AB Adrian Beltre	15.00	4.50
AJ Andruw Jones	10.00	3.00
AR Alex Rodriguez		
BA Bob Abreu	10.00	3.00
BW Bernie Williams	15.00	4.50
CD Carlos Delgado		
EC Eric Chavez	10.00	3.00
FT Frank Thomas	15.00	4.50
GM Greg Maddux	15.00	4.50
JB Josh Beckett	10.00	3.00
KS Kazuhiro Sasaki	10.00	3.00
KW Kerry Wood	15.00	4.50
LB Lance Berkman	10.00	3.00
MG Mark Grace	15.00	4.50
RA Roberto Alomar	15.00	4.50
RO Roy Oswalt	10.00	3.00
VG Vladimir Guerrero	15.00	4.50

2003 Fleer Patchworks Game-Worn Patch Level 2 Dual

	Nm-Mt	Ex-Mt
RANDOM INSERTS IN PACKS		
STATED PRINT RUN 100 SERIAL #'d SETS		
AB Adrian Beltre	30.00	9.00
AJ Andruw Jones	25.00	7.50
AR Alex Rodriguez	50.00	15.00
BA Bob Abreu	25.00	7.50
BW Bernie Williams	30.00	9.00
CD Carlos Delgado	25.00	7.50
CS Curt Schilling	25.00	7.50
EC Eric Chavez	25.00	7.50
FT Frank Thomas	30.00	9.00
GM Greg Maddux	40.00	12.00
JB Josh Beckett	25.00	7.50
KS Kazuhiro Sasaki	25.00	7.50
KW Kerry Wood	30.00	9.00
LB Lance Berkman	25.00	7.50
MG Mark Grace	30.00	9.00
RA Roberto Alomar	30.00	9.00
RO Roy Oswalt	25.00	7.50
VG Vladimir Guerrero	30.00	9.00

2003 Fleer Patchworks Game-Worn Patch Level 3 Multi

	Nm-Mt	Ex-Mt
RANDOM INSERTS IN PACKS		
STATED PRINT RUN 50 SERIAL #'d SETS		
AB Adrian Beltre	40.00	12.00
AJ Andruw Jones	30.00	9.00
AR Alex Rodriguez	60.00	18.00
BA Bob Abreu	30.00	9.00
BW Bernie Williams	40.00	12.00
CD Carlos Delgado	30.00	9.00
CS Curt Schilling	30.00	9.00
EC Eric Chavez	30.00	9.00
FT Frank Thomas	40.00	12.00
GM Greg Maddux	50.00	15.00
JB Josh Beckett	30.00	9.00
KS Kazuhiro Sasaki	30.00	9.00
KW Kerry Wood	40.00	12.00
LB Lance Berkman	30.00	9.00
MG Mark Grace	40.00	12.00
RA Roberto Alomar	40.00	12.00
RO Roy Oswalt	30.00	9.00
VG Vladimir Guerrero	40.00	12.00

2003 Fleer Patchworks Licensed Apparel Jersey

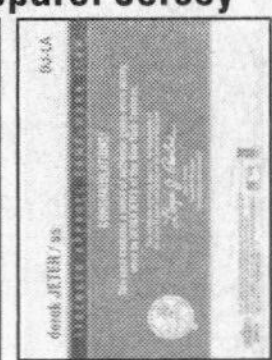

	Nm-Mt	Ex-Mt
STATED PRINT RUN 500 SERIAL #'d SETS		
*ONE-COLOR PATCH: .75X TO 2X BASIC APP		
*MULTI-COLOR PATCH: 1.25 TO 3X BASIC APP		
PATCH PRINT RUN 300 SERIAL #'d SETS		
RANDOM INSERTS IN PACKS		
AD Adam Dunn	10.00	3.00
CB Carlos Beltran	10.00	3.00
CJ Chipper Jones	10.00	3.00
DE Darin Erstad	8.00	2.40
DJ Derek Jeter	25.00	7.50
JD J.D. Drew	8.00	2.40
JR Jimmy Rollins	8.00	2.40
KB Kevin Brown	8.00	2.40
MM Mike Mussina	15.00	4.50
MO Magglio Ordonez	8.00	2.40
MP Mike Piazza	15.00	4.50
PK Paul Konerko	8.00	2.40
SG Shawn Green	8.00	2.40
SS Shannon Stewart	8.00	2.40
TH Todd Helton	10.00	3.00

2003 Fleer Patchworks Licensed Apparel Patch

	Nm-Mt	Ex-Mt
RANDOM INSERTS IN PACKS		
STATED PRINT RUN 300 SERIAL #'d SETS		

2003 Fleer Patchworks National Pastime

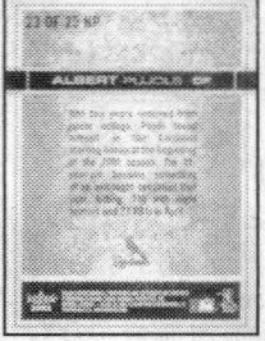

	Nm-Mt	Ex-Mt
STATED ODDS 1:12		
1 Barry Bonds	6.00	1.80
2 Kazuhiro Sasaki	2.00	.60
3 Mike Piazza	4.00	1.20
4 Barry Zito	2.00	.60
5 Sammy Sosa	4.00	1.20
6 Pedro Martinez	2.50	.75
7 Craig Biggio	2.00	.60
8 Rafael Palmeiro	2.00	.60
9 Greg Maddux	4.00	1.20
10 Manny Ramirez	2.00	.60
11 Adam Dunn	2.00	.60
12 Omar Vizquel	2.00	.60
13 Hideo Nomo	2.50	.75
14 Alex Rodriguez	4.00	1.20
15 Pat Burrell	2.00	.60
16 Nomar Garciaparra	4.00	1.20
17 Randy Johnson	2.50	.75
18 Juan Gonzalez	2.00	.60
19 Chipper Jones	2.50	.75
20 Frank Thomas	2.50	.75
21 Vladimir Guerrero	2.50	.75
22 Troy Glaus	2.00	.60
23 Albert Pujols	5.00	1.50
24 Ichiro Suzuki	4.00	1.20
25 Ken Griffey Jr.	4.00	1.20

2003 Fleer Patchworks National Patchtime Commemorative

Randomly inserted into packs, these cards feature a commemorative patch piece from the featured uniform. These cards were issued to a stated print run of 25 serial numbered sets and no pricing is available due to market scarcity.

Nm-Mt Ex-Mt
AR Alex Rodriguez
BZ Barry Zito
CB Craig Biggio
FT Frank Thomas
GM Greg Maddux
MP Mike Piazza
PM Pedro Martinez
RP Rafael Palmeiro
SS Sammy Sosa
TG Troy Glaus
VG Vladimir Guerrero

2003 Fleer Patchworks National Patchtime Nameplate

Randomly inserted into packs, these cards feature pieces from the player's uniform name. These cards were issued to a stated print run of 50 serial numbered sets.

	Nm-Mt	Ex-Mt
AR Alex Rodriguez	50.00	15.00
BZ Barry Zito	30.00	9.00
CB Craig Biggio	40.00	12.00
CJ Chipper Jones	40.00	12.00
FT Frank Thomas	40.00	12.00
GM Greg Maddux	40.00	12.00
HN Hideo Nomo	80.00	24.00
MP Mike Piazza	40.00	12.00
NG Nomar Garciaparra	60.00	18.00
PB Pat Burrell	30.00	9.00
RJ Randy Johnson	40.00	12.00
RP Rafael Palmeiro	40.00	12.00
SS Sammy Sosa	60.00	18.00
TG Troy Glaus	30.00	9.00
VG Vladimir Guerrero	40.00	12.00

2003 Fleer Patchworks National Patchtime Number

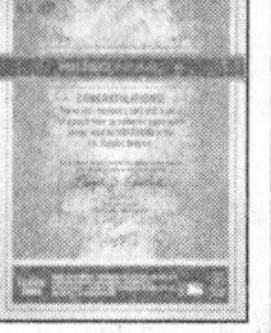

Randomly inserted into packs, these cards feature swatches of the uniform number from the game-used jersey cut up for this insert set. These cards were issued to a stated print run of 75 serial numbered sets.

	Nm-Mt	Ex-Mt
AR Alex Rodriguez	40.00	12.00
BZ Barry Zito	25.00	7.50
CB Craig Biggio	30.00	9.00
CJ Chipper Jones	30.00	9.00
FT Frank Thomas	30.00	9.00
GM Greg Maddux	30.00	9.00
HN Hideo Nomo	60.00	18.00
MP Mike Piazza	30.00	9.00
MR Manny Ramirez	30.00	9.00
NG Nomar Garciaparra	50.00	15.00
PB Pat Burrell	25.00	7.50
PM Pedro Martinez	30.00	9.00
RJ Randy Johnson	30.00	9.00
RP Rafael Palmeiro	30.00	9.00
SS Sammy Sosa	40.00	12.00
VG Vladimir Guerrero	30.00	9.00

2003 Fleer Patchworks National Patchtime Team Name

Randomly inserted into packs, these cards feature a swatch of the team name from the uniform used to create this game-used set. These cards were issued to a stated print run of 100 serial numbered sets.

	Nm-Mt	Ex-Mt
AR Alex Rodriguez	40.00	12.00
BZ Barry Zito	25.00	7.50
CJ Chipper Jones	30.00	9.00
FT Frank Thomas	30.00	9.00
GM Greg Maddux	40.00	12.00
HN Hideo Nomo	60.00	18.00
MP Mike Piazza	40.00	12.00
NG Nomar Garciaparra	50.00	15.00
OV Omar Vizquel	30.00	9.00
PB Pat Burrell	25.00	7.50
RJ Randy Johnson	30.00	9.00
RP Rafael Palmeiro	30.00	9.00
SS Sammy Sosa	40.00	12.00
TG Troy Glaus	25.00	7.50
VG Vladimir Guerrero	30.00	9.00

2003 Fleer Patchworks National Patchtime Trim

Randomly inserted into packs, these cards feature pieces cut from the uniform "trim". These cards were issued to a stated print run of 200 serial numbered sets.

	Nm-Mt	Ex-Mt
AR Alex Rodriguez	30.00	9.00
CJ Chipper Jones	25.00	7.50
FT Frank Thomas	25.00	7.50
GM Greg Maddux	30.00	9.00
HN Hideo Nomo	50.00	15.00
MP Mike Piazza	30.00	9.00
MR Manny Ramirez	25.00	7.50
NG Nomar Garciaparra	40.00	12.00
PM Pedro Martinez	25.00	7.50
RP Rafael Palmeiro	25.00	7.50
VG Vladimir Guerrero	25.00	7.50

2003 Fleer Patchworks Numbers Game

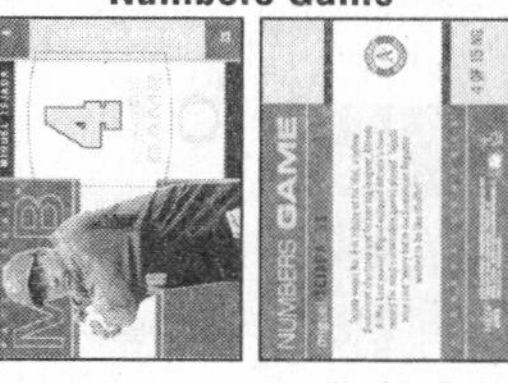

	Nm-Mt	Ex-Mt
STATED ODDS 1:24		
1 Ichiro Suzuki	5.00	1.50
2 Derek Jeter	8.00	2.40
3 Alex Rodriguez	5.00	1.50
4 Miguel Tejada	3.00	.90
5 Nomar Garciaparra	5.00	1.50
6 Jason Giambi	3.00	.90
7 J.D. Drew	3.00	.90
8 Barry Bonds	8.00	2.40
9 Alfonso Soriano	3.00	.90
10 Jeff Bagwell	3.00	.90
11 Barry Larkin	3.00	.90
12 Roberto Alomar	3.00	.90
13 Larry Walker	3.00	.90
14 Roger Clemens	6.00	1.80
15 Ken Griffey Jr.	5.00	1.50

2003 Fleer Patchworks Numbers Game Jersey

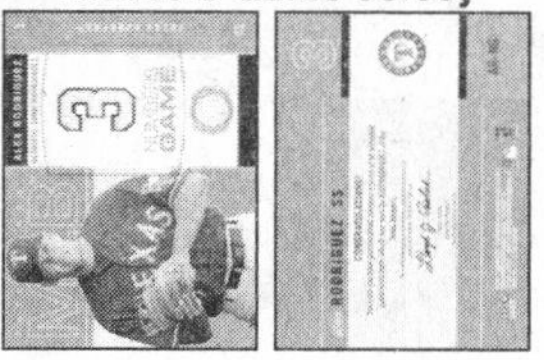

	Nm-Mt	Ex-Mt
STATED ODDS 1:33		
AR Alex Rodriguez	10.00	3.00
AS Alfonso Soriano	8.00	2.40
BL Barry Larkin	8.00	2.40
DJ Derek Jeter	12.00	3.60
JB Jeff Bagwell	8.00	2.40
JG Jason Giambi	8.00	2.40
LW Larry Walker	8.00	2.40
MT Miguel Tejada	8.00	2.40
RA Roberto Alomar	8.00	2.40
RC Roger Clemens	15.00	4.50

2003 Fleer Patchworks Numbers Game Patch

	Nm-Mt	Ex-Mt
RANDOM INSERTS IN PACKS		
STATED PRINT RUN 300 SERIAL #'d SETS		
AR Alex Rodriguez	40.00	12.00
AS Alfonso Soriano	25.00	7.50
BL Barry Larkin	25.00	7.50
DJ Derek Jeter	50.00	15.00
JB Jeff Bagwell	25.00	7.50
JG Jason Giambi	15.00	4.50
LW Larry Walker	25.00	7.50
MT Miguel Tejada	15.00	4.50
RA Roberto Alomar	25.00	7.50
RC Roger Clemens	40.00	12.00

2003 Fleer Patchworks Past Present Future

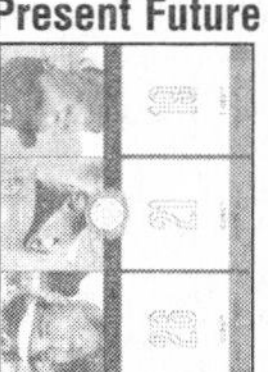

	Nm-Mt	Ex-Mt
STATED ODDS 1:72		
1 Eddie Mathews Rafael Palmeiro Alex Rodriguez	10.00	3.00
2 Phil Rizzuto Derek Jeter Alfonso Soriano	12.00	3.60
3 Reggie Jackson Barry Bonds Sammy Sosa	10.00	3.00
4 Billy Williams Sammy Sosa Hee Seop Choi	10.00	3.00
5 Joe Morgan Roberto Alomar Alfonso Soriano	10.00	3.00
6 Yogi Berra Mike Piazza Josh Phelps	10.00	3.00
7 Nolan Ryan Roger Clemens Kerry Wood	12.00	3.60
8 Mike Schmidt Scott Rolen Eric Hinske	10.00	3.00
9 Barry Bonds Alex Rodriguez Alfonso Soriano	10.00	3.00
10 Yogi Berra Derek Jeter Hideki Matsui	15.00	4.50

2003 Fleer Patchworks Patch Present Future Single

Randomly inserted into packs, these cards features three players on the card with one of the players having a game-worn swatch embedded on the card. These cards were issued to a stated print run of 200 serial numbered sets.

	Nm-Mt	Ex-Mt
AR1 Eddie Mathews Rafael Palmeiro Alex Rodriguez Patch	40.00	12.00
AR2 Barry Bonds Alex Rodriguez Patch Alfonso Soriano		
AS1 Phil Rizzuto Derek Jeter Alfonso Soriano Patch	25.00	7.50
AS2 Joe Morgan Roberto Alomar Alfonso Soriano Patch	25.00	7.50
AS3 Barry Bonds Alex Rodriguez Alfonso Soriano Patch	25.00	7.50
BB Reggie Jackson Barry Bonds Patch Sammy Sosa	50.00	15.00
DJ1 Phil Rizzuto Derek Jeter Patch Alfonso Soriano	60.00	18.00
DJ2 Yogi Berra Derek Jeter Patch Hideki Matsui	60.00	18.00
EH Mike Schmidt Scott Rolen Eric Hinske Patch	15.00	4.50
KW Nolan Ryan Roger Clemens Kerry Wood Patch	40.00	12.00
MP Yogi Berra Mike Piazza Patch Josh Phelps	40.00	12.00
RA Joe Morgan Roberto Alomar Patch Alfonso Soriano	25.00	7.50
RC Nolan Ryan Roger Clemens Patch Kerry Wood	60.00	18.00
RP Eddie Mathews Rafael Palmeiro Patch Alex Rodriguez	25.00	7.50
SR Mike Schmidt Scott Rolen Patch Eric Hinske		
SS1 Reggie Jackson Barry Bonds Sammy Sosa Patch	25.00	7.50
SS2 Billy Williams Sammy Sosa Patch Hee Seop Choi	40.00	12.00

2003 Fleer Patchworks Patch Present Future Dual

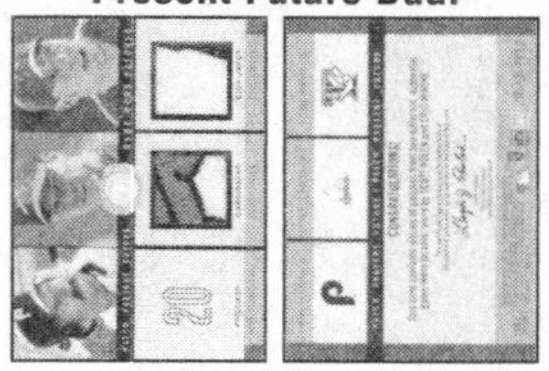

Randomly inserted into packs, this partial parallel to the Patch Present Future Set features three players on the card with the two active players having a patch piece embedded on the card. These cards were issued to a stated print run of 100 serial numbered sets.

	Nm-Mt	Ex-Mt
ARAS Barry Bonds Alex Rodriguez Patch Alfonso Soriano Patch	80.00	24.00
DJAS Phil Rizzuto Derek Jeter Patch Alfonso Soriano Patch	100.00	30.00
RAAS Joe Morgan Roberto Alomar Patch Alfonso Soriano Patch	40.00	12.00
RCKW Nolan Ryan Roger Clemens Patch Kerry Wood Patch	80.00	24.00
RPAR Eddie Mathews Rafael Palmeiro Patch Alex Rodriguez Patch	80.00	24.00
SREH Mike Schmidt Scott Rolen Patch Eric Hinske Patch	40.00	12.00

2004 Fleer Patchworks

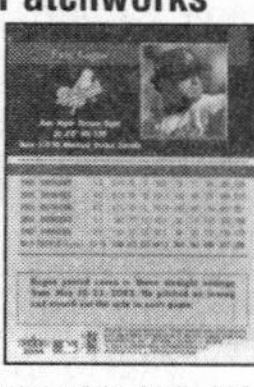

This 110-card set was released in April, 2004. The set was issued in five-card packs with an $6 SRP which came 18 packs to a box and four boxes to a case. Cards numbered 1-90 feature veterans while cards numbered 91-110 feature leading rookies and prospects. Those cards were issued at a stated rate of one in 24 hobby and one in 48 retail packs and were issued to a stated print run of 799 serial numbered sets.

	Nm-Mt	Ex-Mt
COMP.SET w/o SP's (90)	25.00	7.50
COMMON CARD (1-90)	.40	.12
COMMON CARD (91-110)	3.00	.90
91-110 ODDS 1:24 HOBBY, 1:48 RETAIL		
91-110 PRINT RUN 799 SERIAL #'d SETS		
1 Kerry Wood	1.00	.30
2 Brian Giles	.40	.12
3 Tino Martinez	.60	.18
4 Mark Mulder	.40	.12
5 Andy Pettitte	.60	.18
6 Gary Sheffield	.40	.12
7 Mark Teixeira	.40	.12
8 Garret Anderson	.40	.12
9 Craig Biggio	.60	.18
10 Alfonso Soriano	.60	.18
11 Bret Boone	.40	.12
12 Mike Piazza	1.50	.45
13 Todd Helton	.60	.18
14 Jay Gibbons	.40	.12
15 Eric Chavez	.40	.12
16 Andruw Jones	.40	.12
17 Adam Dunn	.60	.18
18 Corey Koskie	.40	.12
19 Rafael Palmeiro	.60	.18
20 Ivan Rodriguez	1.00	.30
21 Tom Glavine	.60	.18
22 Luis Gonzalez	.40	.12
23 Miguel Tejada	.40	.12
24 Jose Vidro	.40	.12
25 Richie Sexson	.40	.12
26 Roy Halladay	.40	.12
27 Vladimir Guerrero	1.00	.30
28 Randy Johnson	1.00	.30
29 Vernon Wells	.40	.12
30 Pat Burrell	.40	.12
31 Jason Schmidt	.40	.12
32 Casey Blake	.40	.12
33 Greg Maddux	1.50	.45
34 Mike Lowell	.40	.12
35 Hideo Nomo	1.00	.30
36 Carlos Delgado	.40	.12
37 Dontrelle Willis	.40	.12
38 Shawn Green	.40	.12
39 Pedro Martinez	1.00	.30
40 Josh Beckett	.40	.12
41 Eric Gagne	1.00	.30
42 Manny Ramirez	.60	.18
43 Jim Edmonds	.40	.12
44 Curt Schilling	1.00	.30
45 Mike Sweeney	.40	.12
46 Albert Pujols	2.00	.60
47 Nomar Garciaparra	1.50	.45
48 Alex Rodriguez Yanks	1.50	.45
49 Angel Berroa	.40	.12
50 Jim Thome	1.00	.30
51 Edgardo Alfonzo	.40	.12
52 Jeremy Bonderman	.40	.12
53 Miguel Cabrera	.60	.18
54 Bobby Higginson	.40	.12
55 John Smoltz	.60	.18
56 Jason Kendall	.40	.12
57 Torii Hunter	.40	.12
58 Troy Glaus	.40	.12
59 Rafael Furcal	.40	.12
60 Austin Kearns	.40	.12
61 Esteban Loaiza	.40	.12
62 Darin Erstad	.40	.12
63 Jose Reyes	.40	.12
64 Preston Wilson	.40	.12
65 Rocco Baldelli	.40	.12
66 Barry Zito	.40	.12
67 Ken Griffey Jr.	1.50	.45
68 Frank Thomas	1.00	.30
69 Roger Clemens	2.00	.60
70 Brett Myers	.40	.12
71 Billy Wagner	.40	.12
72 Scott Podsednik	.40	.12
73 Jody Gerut	.40	.12
74 Bartolo Colon	.40	.12
75 Jeff Bagwell	.60	.18
76 Jason Giambi	.40	.12
77 Edgar Martinez	.60	.18
78 Chipper Jones	1.00	.30
79 Jason Bay	.40	.12
80 Doug Mientkiewicz	.40	.12
81 Hank Blalock	.40	.12
82 Sammy Sosa	1.50	.45
83 Derek Jeter	2.00	.60
84 Ichiro Suzuki	1.50	.45
85 Ben Sheets	.40	.12
86 Magglio Ordonez	.40	.12
87 Carlos Beltran	.60	.18
88 Mark Prior	1.00	.30
89 Sean Burroughs	.40	.12
90 Tim Hudson	.40	.12
91 Hector Gimenez ROO RC	3.00	.90
92 Khalil Greene ROO	5.00	1.50
93 Rickie Weeks ROO	3.00	.90
94 Delmon Young ROO	5.00	1.50
95 Don Kelly ROO RC	3.00	.90
96 Chad Bentz ROO RC	3.00	.90
97 Greg Dobbs ROO RC	3.00	.90
98 John Gall ROO RC	5.00	1.50
99 Cory Sullivan ROO RC	3.00	.90
100 Kazuo Matsui ROO RC	8.00	2.40
101 Graham Koonce ROO	3.00	.90
102 Jason Bartlett ROO RC	5.00	1.50
103 Angel Chavez ROO RC	3.00	.90
104 Ronny Cedeno ROO RC	3.00	.90
105 Jerry Gil ROO RC	3.00	.90
106 Ivan Ochoa ROO RC	3.00	.90
107 Ruddy Yan ROO	3.00	.90
108 Mike Gosling ROO RC	3.00	.90
109 Alfredo Simon ROO RC	3.00	.90
110 Koyie Hill ROO	3.00	.90

2004 Fleer Patchworks Star Ruby

	Nm-Mt	Ex-Mt
*RUBY 1-90: 5X TO 12X BASIC		
*RUBY 91-110: .75X TO 2X BASIC		
STATED ODDS 1:48 HOBBY, 1:96 RETAIL		
STATED PRINT RUN 50 SERIAL #'d SETS		
100 Kazuo Matsui ROO	25.00	7.50

2004 Fleer Patchworks Autoworks Black

	Nm-Mt	Ex-Mt
PRINT RUNS B/WN 145-376 COPIES PER		
*BLUE: .4X TO 1X BLACK p/r 263-376		
*BLUE: .4X TO 1X BLACK p/r 145-193		
RED PATCH PRINT RUN 10 SERIAL #'d SETS		
NO RED PATCH PRICING DUE TO SCARCITY		
ALL RED PATCH ARE EXCHANGE CARDS		
RED PATCH EXCH.DEADLINE IS INDEFINITE		
OVERALL AU ODDS 1:54 HOB, 1:120 RET		
AB Angel Berroa/145	10.00	3.00
AP1 Andy Pettitte/148	40.00	12.00
AP2 Albert Pujols/193	120.00	36.00
EG Eric Gagne/193	40.00	12.00
GA Garret Anderson/145	15.00	4.50
GS Grady Sizemore/263	15.00	4.50
JB Josh Beckett/148	25.00	7.50
JG Jody Gerut/376	15.00	4.50
MM Mark Mulder/190	15.00	4.50
MT Miguel Tejada/164	25.00	7.50
RH Roy Halladay/286	10.00	3.00
SP Scott Podsednik/146	15.00	4.50

2004 Fleer Patchworks By the Numbers

	Nm-Mt	Ex-Mt
STATED ODDS 1:24 HOBBY, 1:12 RETAIL		
1 Albert Pujols	8.00	2.40
2 Derek Jeter	8.00	2.40
3 Mike Piazza	6.00	1.80
4 Nomar Garciaparra	6.00	1.80
5 Eric Gagne	4.00	1.20
6 Sammy Sosa	6.00	1.80
7 Josh Beckett	4.00	1.20
8 Vladimir Guerrero	4.00	1.20
9 Jose Reyes	4.00	1.20
10 Bret Boone	4.00	1.20
11 Alex Rodriguez Yanks	6.00	1.80
12 Randy Johnson	4.00	1.20
13 Chipper Jones	4.00	1.20
14 Tim Hudson	4.00	1.20
15 Rocco Baldelli	4.00	1.20

2004 Fleer Patchworks By the Numbers Patch

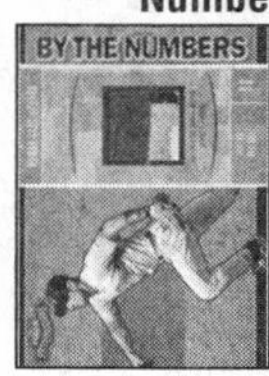

	Nm-Mt	Ex-Mt
OVERALL GU ODDS 1:6 HOBBY, 1:36 RETAIL		
STATED PRINT RUN 100 SERIAL #'d SETS		
AP Albert Pujols	30.00	9.00
AR Alex Rodriguez	25.00	7.50
BB Bret Boone	15.00	4.50
CJ Chipper Jones	25.00	7.50
DJ Derek Jeter	25.00	7.50
EG Eric Gagne	25.00	7.50
JB Josh Beckett	15.00	4.50
JR Jose Reyes	15.00	4.50
MP Mike Piazza	25.00	7.50
NG Nomar Garciaparra	25.00	7.50
RB Rocco Baldelli	15.00	4.50
RJ Randy Johnson	25.00	7.50
SS Sammy Sosa	25.00	7.50

TH Tim Hudson	15.00	4.50
VG Vladimir Guerrero	25.00	7.50

2004 Fleer Patchworks Game Used Level 1

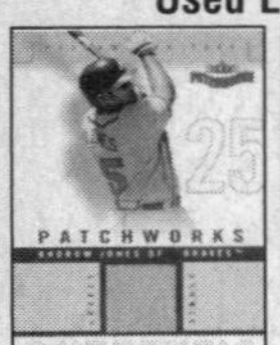
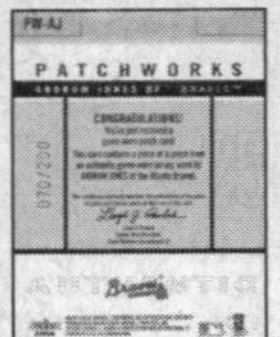

STATED PRINT RUN 200 SERIAL #'d SETS
*LEVEL 2: .5X TO 1.2X BASIC
LEVEL 2 PRINT RUN 100 SERIAL #'d SETS
*PATCH: 1.25X TO 3X BASIC
PATCH PRINT RUN 50 SERIAL #'d SETS
OVERALL GU ODDS 1:6 HOBBY, 1:36 RETAIL

	Nm-Mt	Ex-Mt
AJ Andruw Jones	8.00	2.40
AP1 Andy Pettitte	10.00	3.00
AP2 Albert Pujols	15.00	4.50
AS Alfonso Soriano	10.00	3.00
BB Bret Boone	8.00	2.40
BW Bernie Williams	10.00	3.00
BZ Barry Zito	8.00	2.40
CD Carlos Delgado	8.00	2.40
DW Dontrelle Willis	8.00	2.40
GA Garret Anderson	8.00	2.40
HB Hank Blalock	8.00	2.40
JR Jose Reyes	8.00	2.40
LW Larry Walker	10.00	3.00
MP1 Mike Piazza	12.00	3.60
MP2 Mark Prior	10.00	3.00
RH Roy Halladay	8.00	2.40
SG Shawn Green	8.00	2.40
TG Troy Glaus	8.00	2.40
TH Torii Hunter	8.00	2.40

2004 Fleer Patchworks Licensed Apparel

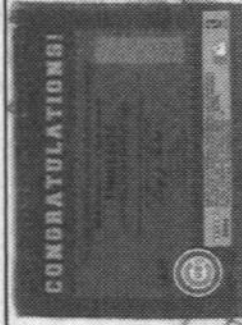

STATED PRINT RUN 300 SERIAL #'d SETS
JSY TAG PRINT RUN 10 SERIAL #'d SETS
NO JSY TAG PRICING DUE TO SCARCITY
MLB LOGO PRINT RUN 1 SERIAL #'d SET
NO MLB LOGO PRICING DUE TO SCARCITY
*NAMEPLATE: 1.25X TO 3X BASIC
NAMEPLATE PRINT RUN 50 SERIAL #'d SETS
*NUMBER: .75X TO 2X BASIC
NUMBER PRINT RUN 100 SERIAL #'d SETS
*TEAM NAME: .75X TO 2X BASIC
TEAM NAME PRINT RUN 150 SER.#'d SETS
OVERALL GU ODDS 1:6 HOBBY, 1:36 RETAIL

	Nm-Mt	Ex-Mt
AJ Andruw Jones	8.00	2.40
AK Austin Kearns	8.00	2.40
AP Albert Pujols	15.00	4.50
AR Alex Rodriguez	12.00	3.60
BB Bret Boone	8.00	2.40
DJ Derek Jeter	20.00	6.00
DW Dontrelle Willis	8.00	2.40
JB Jeff Bagwell	10.00	3.00
JT Jim Thome	10.00	3.00
MP1 Mike Piazza	12.00	3.60
MP2 Mark Prior	10.00	3.00
SS Sammy Sosa	12.00	3.60
TG Troy Glaus	8.00	2.40
TH1 Tim Hudson	8.00	2.40
TH2 Torii Hunter	8.00	2.40

2004 Fleer Patchworks National Pastime

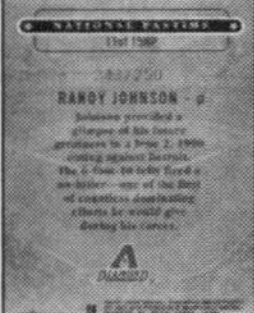

STATED ODDS 1:72 HOBBY, 1:144 RETAIL
STATED PRINT RUN 250 SERIAL #'d SETS

	Nm-Mt	Ex-Mt
1 Albert Pujols	12.00	3.60
2 Alex Rodriguez Yanks	10.00	3.00
3 Derek Jeter	15.00	4.50
4 Nomar Garciaparra	10.00	3.00
5 Jim Thome	6.00	1.80
6 Chipper Jones	6.00	1.80
7 Mark Prior	6.00	1.80
8 Ichiro Suzuki	10.00	3.00
9 Jeff Bagwell	6.00	1.80
10 Troy Glaus	5.00	1.50
11 Randy Johnson	6.00	1.80
12 Sammy Sosa	10.00	3.00
13 Austin Kearns	5.00	1.50
14 Miguel Cabrera	6.00	1.80
15 Vladimir Guerrero	6.00	1.80

2004 Fleer Patchworks National Patchtime

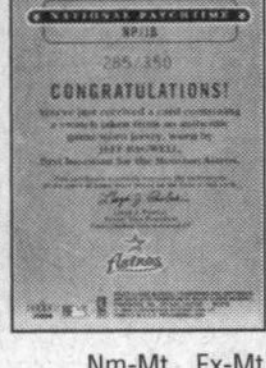

STATED PRINT RUN 350 SERIAL #'d SETS
*GOLD: .4X TO 1X BASIC
GOLD PRINT RUN 200 SERIAL #'d SETS
*PATCH: .75X TO 2X BASIC
PATCH PRINT RUN 100 SERIAL #'d SETS
OVERALL GU ODDS 1:6 HOBBY, 1:36 RETAIL

	Nm-Mt	Ex-Mt
AK Austin Kearns	8.00	2.40
AP Albert Pujols	15.00	4.50
AR Alex Rodriguez	12.00	3.60
CJ Chipper Jones	10.00	3.00
DJ Derek Jeter	20.00	6.00
JB Jeff Bagwell	10.00	3.00
JT Jim Thome	10.00	3.00
MC Miguel Cabrera	10.00	3.00
MP Mark Prior	10.00	3.00
NG Nomar Garciaparra	12.00	3.60
RJ Randy Johnson	10.00	3.00
SS Sammy Sosa	12.00	3.60
TG Troy Glaus	8.00	2.40
VG Vladimir Guerrero	10.00	3.00

2004 Fleer Patchworks Stitches In Time

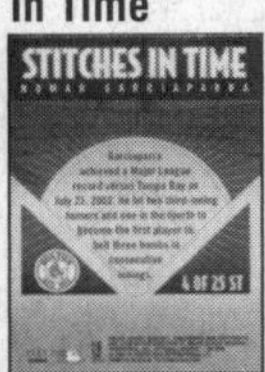

STATED ODDS 1:12 HOBBY, 1:6 RETAIL

	Nm-Mt	Ex-Mt
1 Albert Pujols	6.00	1.80
2 Alex Rodriguez Yanks	5.00	1.50
3 Derek Jeter	6.00	1.80
4 Nomar Garciaparra	5.00	1.50
5 Jim Thome	3.00	.90
6 Chipper Jones	3.00	.90
7 Mark Prior	3.00	.90
8 Eric Gagne	3.00	.90
9 Jeff Bagwell	3.00	.90
10 Troy Glaus	3.00	.90
11 Randy Johnson	3.00	.90
12 Sammy Sosa	5.00	1.50
13 Austin Kearns	3.00	.90
14 Miguel Cabrera	3.00	.90
15 Vladimir Guerrero	3.00	.90
16 Mike Piazza	5.00	1.50
17 Jason Giambi	3.00	.90
18 Tim Hudson	3.00	.90
19 Carlos Delgado	3.00	.90
20 Rocco Baldelli	3.00	.90
21 Ichiro Suzuki	5.00	1.50
22 Barry Zito	3.00	.90
23 Pedro Martinez	3.00	.90
24 Torii Hunter	3.00	.90
25 Andruw Jones	3.00	.90

2004 Fleer Patchworks Stitches in Time Jersey

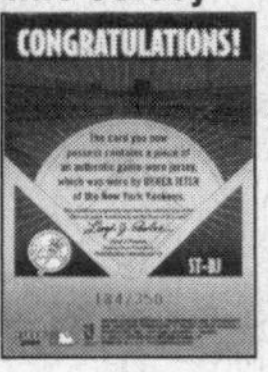

STATED PRINT RUN 350 SERIAL #'d SETS
*PATCH: .75X TO 2X BASIC
PATCH PRINT RUN 150 SERIAL #'d SETS
OVERALL GU ODDS 1:6 HOBBY, 1:36 RETAIL

	Nm-Mt	Ex-Mt
AJ Andruw Jones	8.00	2.40
AK Austin Kearns	8.00	2.40
AP Albert Pujols	15.00	4.50
AR Alex Rodriguez	12.00	3.60
BZ Barry Zito	8.00	2.40
CD Carlos Delgado	8.00	2.40
CJ Chipper Jones	10.00	3.00
DJ Derek Jeter	20.00	6.00
EG Eric Gagne	10.00	3.00
JB Jeff Bagwell	10.00	3.00
JG Jason Giambi	8.00	2.40
JT Jim Thome	10.00	3.00
MC Miguel Cabrera	10.00	3.00
MP Mike Piazza	12.00	3.60
MP Mark Prior	10.00	3.00
NG Nomar Garciaparra	12.00	3.60
PM Pedro Martinez	10.00	3.00
RB Rocco Baldelli	8.00	2.40
RJ Randy Johnson	10.00	3.00
SS Sammy Sosa	12.00	3.60
TG Troy Glaus	8.00	2.40
TH1 Tim Hudson	8.00	2.40
TH2 Torii Hunter	8.00	2.40
VG Vladimir Guerrero	10.00	3.00

2001 Fleer Platinum

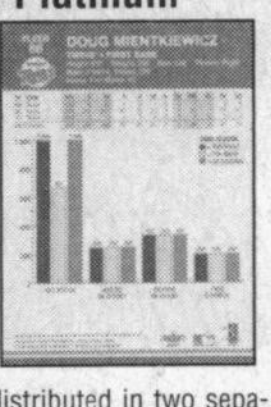

This 601-card set was distributed in two separate series. Series 1 was released in late May, 2001 with cards distributed in 10-card hobby packs with a suggested retail price of $2.99 and a 25-card jumbo pack for $9.99. Series 2 (entitled Platinum RC edition) was released in late December, 2001. The set features player photos printed in the original 1981 Fleer design. The first series contains 250 regular cards plus 31 dual short printed cards (251-280/301) and 20 All-Star cards (281-300) both with an insertion rate of 1:6 in the hobby packs and 1:2 in the jumbo packs. The second series set contains 300 cards composed of basic (302-401), Chart Toppers (402-431), Team Leaders (432-461), Franchise Futures (462-481), Postseason Glory (482-501) and Rookies (502-601), seeded at a rate of 1:3 packs). Notable Rookie Cards include Ichiro, Albert Pujols and Mark Tiexeira. According to representatives at Fleer, card 529 (Mark Prior RC) and card 402 (Freddy Garcia CT) were mistakenly switched with each other on the printing forms - thereby making card 402 a short-print (available at the same ratio as cards 502-601) and card 529 a basic card (available at the same rate as cards 302-501).

	Nm-Mt	Ex-Mt
COMP. SERIES 1 (301)	200.00	60.00
COMP. SERIES 2 (300)	200.00	60.00
COMP.SER.1 w/o SP's (250)	40.00	12.00
COMP.SER.2 w/o SP's (200)	40.00	12.00
COMMON (1-250/302-501)	.30	.09
COMMON (251-280)	2.00	.60
COMMON AS (281-300)	2.00	.60
COMMON (502-601)	2.00	.60
1 Bobby Abreu	.30	.09
2 Brad Radke	.30	.09
3 Bill Mueller	.30	.09
4 Adam Eaton	.30	.09
5 Antonio Alfonseca	.30	.09
6 Manny Ramirez	.50	.15
7 Adam Kennedy	.30	.09
8 Jose Valentin	.30	.09
9 Jaret Wright	.30	.09
10 Aramis Ramirez	.30	.09
11 Jeff Kent	.30	.09
12 Juan Encarnacion	.30	.09
13 Sandy Alomar Jr.	.30	.09
14 Joe Randa	.30	.09
15 Darryl Kile	.30	.09
16 Darren Dreifort	.30	.09
17 Matt Kinney	.30	.09
18 Pokey Reese	.30	.09
19 Ryan Klesko	.30	.09
20 Shawn Estes	.30	.09
21 Moises Alou	.30	.09
22 Edgar Renteria	.30	.09
23 Chuck Knoblauch	.30	.09
24 Carl Everett	.30	.09
25 Garret Anderson	.30	.09
26 Shane Reynolds	.30	.09
27 Billy Koch	.30	.09
28 Carlos Febles	.30	.09
29 Brian Anderson	.30	.09
30 Armando Rios	.30	.09
31 Ryan Kohlmeier	.30	.09
32 Steve Finley	.30	.09
33 Brady Anderson	.30	.09
34 Cal Ripken	2.50	.75
35 Paul Konerko	.30	.09
36 Chuck Finley	.30	.09
37 Rick Ankiel	.30	.09
38 Mariano Rivera	.50	.15
39 Corey Koskie	.30	.09
40 Cliff Floyd	.30	.09
41 Kevin Appier	.30	.09
42 Henry Rodriguez	.30	.09
43 Mark Kotsay	.30	.09
44 Brook Fordyce	.30	.09
45 Brad Ausmus	.30	.09
46 Alfonso Soriano	.50	.15
47 Ray Lankford	.30	.09
48 Keith Foulke	.30	.09
49 Rich Aurilia	.30	.09
50 Alex Rodriguez	1.50	.45
51 Eric Byrnes	.30	.09
52 Travis Fryman	.30	.09
53 Jeff Bagwell	.50	.15
54 Scott Rolen	.75	.23
55 Matt Lawton	.30	.09
56 Brad Fullmer	.30	.09
57 Tony Batista	.30	.09
58 Nate Rolison	.30	.09
59 Carlos Lee	.30	.09
60 Rafael Furcal	.30	.09
61 Jay Bell	.30	.09
62 Jimmy Rollins	.30	.09
63 Derrek Lee	.30	.09
64 Andres Galarraga	.30	.09
65 Derek Bell	.30	.09
66 Tim Salmon	.50	.15
67 Travis Lee	.30	.09
68 Kevin Millwood	.30	.09
69 Albert Belle	.30	.09
70 Kazuhiro Sasaki	.30	.09
71 Al Leiter	.30	.09
72 Britt Reames	.30	.09
73 Carlos Beltran	.50	.15
74 Curt Schilling	.30	.09
75 Curtis Leskanic	.30	.09
76 Jeremy Giambi	.30	.09
77 Adrian Beltre	.50	.15
78 David Segui	.30	.09
79 Mike Lieberthal	.30	.09
80 Brian Giles	.30	.09
81 Marvin Benard	.30	.09
82 Aaron Sele	.30	.09
83 Kenny Lofton	.30	.09
84 Doug Glanville	.30	.09
85 Kris Benson	.30	.09
86 Richie Sexson	.30	.09
87 Javy Lopez	.30	.09
88 Doug Mientkiewicz	.30	.09
89 Peter Bergeron	.30	.09
90 Gary Sheffield	.30	.09
91 Derek Lowe	.30	.09
92 Tom Glavine	.50	.15
93 Lance Berkman	.30	.09
94 Chris Singleton	.30	.09
95 Mike Lowell	.30	.09
96 Luis Gonzalez	.30	.09
97 Dante Bichette	.30	.09
98 Mike Sirotka	.30	.09
99 Julio Lugo	.30	.09
100 Juan Gonzalez	.50	.15
101 Craig Biggio	.50	.15
102 Armando Benitez	.30	.09
103 Greg Maddux	1.25	.35
104 Mark Grace	.50	.15
105 John Smoltz	.50	.15
106 J.T. Snow	.30	.09
107 Al Martin	.30	.09
108 Danny Graves	.30	.09
109 Barry Bonds	2.00	.60
110 Lee Stevens	.30	.09
111 Pedro Martinez	.75	.23
112 Shawn Green	.30	.09
113 Bret Boone	.30	.09
114 Matt Stairs	.30	.09
115 Tino Martinez	.50	.15
116 Rusty Greer	.30	.09
117 Mike Bordick	.30	.09
118 Garrett Stephenson	.30	.09
119 Edgar Martinez	.50	.15
120 Ben Grieve	.30	.09
121 Milton Bradley	.30	.09
122 Aaron Boone	.30	.09
123 Ruben Mateo	.30	.09
124 Ken Griffey Jr.	1.25	.35
125 Russell Branyan	.30	.09
126 Shannon Stewart	.30	.09
127 Fred McGriff	.50	.15
128 Ben Petrick	.30	.09
129 Kevin Brown	.30	.09
130 B.J. Surhoff	.30	.09
131 Mark McGwire	2.00	.60
132 Carlos Guillen	.30	.09
133 Adrian Brown	.30	.09
134 Mike Sweeney	.30	.09
135 Eric Milton	.30	.09
136 Cristian Guzman	.30	.09
137 Ellis Burks	.30	.09
138 Fernando Tatis	.30	.09
139 Bengie Molina	.30	.09
140 Tony Gwynn	1.00	.30
141 Jeromy Burnitz	.30	.09
142 Miguel Tejada	.30	.09
143 Raul Mondesi	.30	.09
144 Jeffrey Hammonds	.30	.09
145 Pat Burrell	.30	.09
146 Frank Thomas	.75	.23
147 Eric Munson	.30	.09
148 Mike Hampton	.30	.09
149 Mike Cameron	.30	.09
150 Jim Thome	.75	.23
151 Mike Mussina	.50	.15
152 Rick Helling	.30	.09
153 Ken Caminiti	.30	.09
154 John VanderWal	.30	.09
155 Denny Neagle	.30	.09
156 Robb Nen	.30	.09
157 Jose Canseco	.75	.23
158 Mo Vaughn	.30	.09
159 Phil Nevin	.30	.09
160 Pat Hentgen	.30	.09
161 Sean Casey	.30	.09
162 Greg Vaughn	.30	.09
163 Trot Nixon	.30	.09
164 Roberto Hernandez	.30	.09
165 Vinny Castilla	.30	.09
166 Robin Ventura	.30	.09
167 Alex Ochoa	.30	.09
168 Orlando Hernandez	.30	.09
169 Luis Castillo	.30	.09
170 Quilvio Veras	.30	.09
171 Troy O'Leary	.30	.09
172 Livan Hernandez	.30	.09
173 Roger Cedeno	.30	.09
174 Jose Vidro	.30	.09
175 John Olerud	.30	.09
176 Richard Hidalgo	.30	.09
177 Eric Chavez	.30	.09
178 Fernando Vina	.30	.09
179 Chris Stynes	.30	.09
180 Bobby Higginson	.30	.09
181 Bruce Chen	.30	.09
182 Omar Vizquel	.50	.15
183 Rey Ordonez	.30	.09
184 Trevor Hoffman	.30	.09
185 Jeff Cirillo	.30	.09
186 Billy Wagner	.30	.09
187 David Ortiz	.50	.15
188 Tim Hudson	.30	.09
189 Tony Clark	.30	.09
190 Larry Walker	.50	.15
191 Eric Owens	.30	.09
192 Aubrey Huff	.30	.09
193 Royce Clayton	.30	.09
194 Todd Walker	.30	.09
195 Rafael Palmeiro	.50	.15
196 Todd Hundley	.30	.09
197 Roger Clemens	1.50	.45
198 Jeff Weaver	.30	.09
199 Dean Palmer	.30	.09
200 Geoff Jenkins	.30	.09
201 Matt Clement	.30	.09
202 David Wells	.30	.09
203 Chan Ho Park	.30	.09
204 Hideo Nomo	.75	.23
205 Bartolo Colon	.30	.09
206 John Wetteland	.30	.09
207 Corey Patterson	.30	.09
208 Freddy Garcia	.30	.09
209 David Cone	.30	.09
210 Rondell White	.30	.09
211 Carl Pavano	.30	.09
212 Charles Johnson	.30	.09
213 Ron Coomer	.30	.09
214 Matt Williams	.30	.09
215 Jay Payton	.30	.09
216 Nick Johnson	.30	.09
217 Deivi Cruz	.30	.09
218 Scott Elarton	.30	.09
219 Neifi Perez	.30	.09
220 Jason Isringhausen	.30	.09
221 Jose Cruz Jr.	.30	.09
222 Gerald Williams	.30	.09
223 Timo Perez	.30	.09
224 Damion Easley	.30	.09
225 Jeff D'Amico	.30	.09
226 Preston Wilson	.30	.09
227 Robert Person	.30	.09
228 Jacque Jones	.30	.09
229 Johnny Damon	.50	.15
230 Tony Womack	.30	.09
231 Adam Piatt	.30	.09
232 Brian Jordan	.30	.09
233 Ben Davis	.30	.09
234 Kerry Wood	.75	.23
235 Mike Piazza	1.25	.35
236 David Justice	.30	.09
237 Dave Veres	.30	.09
238 Eric Young	.30	.09
239 Juan Pierre	.30	.09
240 Gabe Kapler	.30	.09
241 Ryan Dempster	.30	.09
242 Dmitri Young	.30	.09
243 Jorge Posada	.50	.15
244 Eric Karros	.30	.09
245 J.D. Drew	.30	.09
246 Todd Zeile	.30	.09
247 Mark Quinn	.30	.09
248 Kenny Kelly UER Listed as a Mariner on the front	.30	.09
249 Jermaine Dye	.30	.09
250 Barry Zito	.50	.15
251 Jason Hart Larry Barnes	2.00	.60
252 Ichiro Suzuki RC Elpidio Guzman RC	25.00	7.50
253 Tsuyoshi Shinjo RC Brian Cole	3.00	.90
254 John Barnes Adrian Hernandez RC	2.00	.60
255 Jason Tyner Jace Brewer	2.00	.60
256 Brian Buchanan Luis Rivas	2.00	.60
257 Brent Abernathy Jose Ortiz	2.00	.60
258 Marcus Giles Keith Ginter	2.00	.60
259 Tike Redman Jaisen Randolph RC	2.00	.60
260 Dane Sardinha David Espinosa	2.00	.60
261 Josh Beckett Craig House	2.00	.60
262 Jack Cust Hiram Bocachica	2.00	.60
263 Alex Escobar Esix Snead RC	2.00	.60
264 Chris Richard Vernon Wells	2.00	.60
265 Pedro Feliz Xavier Nady	2.00	.60
266 Brandon Inge Joe Crede	2.00	.60
267 Ben Sheets Roy Oswalt	3.00	.90
268 Drew Henson RC Andy Morales RC	4.00	1.20
269 C.C. Sabathia Justin Miller	2.00	.60
270 David Eckstein Jason Grabowski	2.00	.60
271 Dee Brown Chris Wakeland	2.00	.60
272 Junior Spivey RC Alex Cintron	2.00	.60
273 Elvis Pena Juan Uribe RC	3.00	.90
274 Carlos Pena Jason Romano	2.00	.60
275 Winston Abreu Wilson Betemit	2.00	.60
276 Jose Mieses RC Nick Neugebauer	2.00	.60
277 Shea Hillenbrand Dernell Stenson	2.00	.60
278 Jared Sandberg Toby Hall	2.00	.60
279 Jay Gibbons RC Ivanon Coffie	4.00	1.20
280 Pablo Ozuna Santiago Perez	2.00	.60
281 N.Garciaparra AS	8.00	2.40
282 Derek Jeter AS	12.00	3.60
283 Jason Giambi AS	2.00	.60
284 Magglio Ordonez AS	2.00	.60
285 Ivan Rodriguez AS	5.00	1.50
286 Troy Glaus AS	2.00	.60
287 Carlos Delgado AS	2.00	.60
288 Darin Erstad AS	2.00	.60
289 Bernie Williams AS	3.00	.90
290 Roberto Alomar AS	3.00	.90
291 Barry Larkin AS	3.00	.90
292 Chipper Jones AS	5.00	1.50
293 Vladimir Guerrero AS	5.00	1.50
294 Sammy Sosa AS	8.00	2.40
295 Todd Helton AS	3.00	.90
296 Randy Johnson AS	5.00	1.50
297 Jason Kendall AS	2.00	.60
298 Jim Edmonds AS	2.00	.60
299 Andruw Jones AS	2.00	.60
300 Edgardo Alfonzo AS	2.00	.60
301 Albert Pujols RC Donaldo Mendez RC/1500	60.00	18.00
302 Shawn Wooten	.30	.09
303 Todd Walker	.30	.09
304 Brian Buchanan	.30	.09
305 Jim Edmonds	.30	.09
306 Jarrod Washburn	.30	.09

307 Jose Rijo .30 .09
308 Tim Raines .30 .09
309 Matt Morris .30 .09
310 Troy Glaus .30 .09
311 Barry Larkin .50 .15
312 Javier Vazquez .30 .09
313 Placido Polanco .30 .09
314 Darin Erstad .30 .09
315 Marty Cordova .30 .09
316 Vladimir Guerrero .75 .23
317 Kerry Robinson .30 .09
318 Byung-Hyun Kim .30 .09
319 C.C. Sabathia .30 .09
320 Edgardo Alfonzo .30 .09
321 Jason Tyner .30 .09
322 Reggie Sanders .30 .09
323 Roberto Alomar .50 .15
324 Matt Lawton .30 .09
325 Brent Abernathy .30 .09
326 Randy Johnson .75 .23
327 Todd Helton .50 .15
328 Andy Pettitte .50 .15
329 Josh Beckett .30 .09
330 Mark DeRosa .30 .09
331 Jose Ortiz .30 .09
332 Derek Jeter 2.00 .60
333 Toby Hall .30 .09
334 Wes Helms .30 .09
335 Jose Macias .30 .09
336 Bernie Williams .50 .15
337 Ivan Rodriguez .75 .23
338 Chipper Jones .75 .23
339 Brandon Inge .30 .09
340 Jason Giambi .30 .09
341 Frank Catalanotto .30 .09
342 Andruw Jones .30 .09
343 Carlos Hernandez .30 .09
344 Jermaine Dye .30 .09
345 Mike Lamb .30 .09
346 Ken Caminiti .30 .09
347 A.J. Burnett .30 .09
348 Terrence Long .30 .09
349 Ruben Sierra .30 .09
350 Marcus Giles UER .30 .09
Listed as a pitcher on the back
351 Wade Miller .30 .09
352 Mark Mulder .30 .09
353 Carlos Delgado .30 .09
354 Chris Richard .30 .09
355 Daryle Ward .30 .09
356 Brad Penny .30 .09
357 Vernon Wells .30 .09
358 Jason Johnson .30 .09
359 Tim Redding .30 .09
360 Marlon Anderson .30 .09
361 Carlos Pena .30 .09
362 Nomar Garciaparra 1.25 .35
363 Roy Oswalt .50 .15
364 Todd Ritchie .30 .09
365 Jose Mesa .30 .09
366 Shea Hillenbrand .30 .09
367 Dee Brown .30 .09
368 Jason Kendall .30 .09
369 Vinny Castilla .30 .09
370 Fred McGriff .50 .15
371 Neifi Perez .30 .09
372 Xavier Nady .30 .09
373 Abraham Nunez .30 .09
374 Jon Lieber .30 .09
375 Paul LoDuca .30 .09
376 Bubba Trammell .30 .09
377 Brady Clark .30 .09
378 Joel Pineiro .75 .23
379 Mark Grudzielanek .30 .09
380 D'Angelo Jimenez .30 .09
381 Junior Herndon .30 .09
382 Magglio Ordonez .30 .09
383 Ben Sheets .50 .15
384 John Vander Wal .30 .09
385 Pedro Astacio .30 .09
386 Jose Canseco .75 .23
387 Jose Hernandez .30 .09
388 Eric Davis .30 .09
389 Sammy Sosa 1.25 .35
390 Mark Buehrle .30 .09
391 Mark Loretta .30 .09
392 Andres Galarraga .30 .09
393 Scott Spiezio .30 .09
394 Joe Crede .30 .09
395 Luis Rivas .30 .09
396 David Bell .30 .09
397 Einar Diaz .30 .09
398 Adam Dunn .50 .15
399 A.J. Pierzynski .30 .09
400 Jamie Moyer .30 .09
401 Nick Johnson .30 .09
402 Freddy Garcia CT SP 10.00 3.00
403 Hideo Nomo CT .30 .09
404 Mark Mulder CT .30 .09
405 Steve Sparks CT .30 .09
406 Mariano Rivera CT .30 .09
407 Mark Buehrle .30 .09
Mike Mussina CT
408 Randy Johnson CT .50 .15
409 Randy Johnson CT .50 .15
410 Curt Schilling .30 .09
Matt Morris CT
411 Greg Maddux CT .75 .23
412 Robb Nen CT .30 .09
413 Randy Johnson CT .50 .15
414 Barry Bonds CT .75 .23
415 Jason Giambi CT .30 .09
416 Ichiro Suzuki CT 5.00 1.50
417 Ichiro Suzuki CT 5.00 1.50
418 Alex Rodriguez CT .75 .23
419 Bret Boone CT .30 .09
420 Ichiro Suzuki CT 5.00 1.50
421 Alex Rodriguez CT .75 .23
422 Jason Giambi CT .30 .09
423 Alex Rodriguez CT .75 .23
424 Larry Walker CT .30 .09
425 Rich Aurilia CT .30 .09
426 Barry Bonds CT .75 .23
427 Sammy Sosa CT .75 .23
428 Jimmy Rollins .30 .09
Juan Pierre CT
429 Sammy Sosa CT .75 .23
430 Lance Berkman CT .30 .09
431 Sammy Sosa CT .75 .23
432 Carlos Delgado TL .30 .09
433 Alex Rodriguez TL .75 .23
434 Greg Vaughn TL .30 .09
435 Albert Pujols TL 15.00 4.50
436 Ichiro Suzuki TL 5.00 1.50
437 Barry Bonds TL .75 .23
438 Phil Nevin TL .30 .09
439 Brian Giles TL .30 .09
440 Bobby Abreu TL .30 .09
441 Jason Giambi TL .30 .09
442 Derek Jeter TL 1.00 .30
443 Mike Piazza TL .75 .23
444 Vladimir Guerrero TL .50 .15
445 Corey Koskie TL .30 .09
446 Richie Sexson TL .30 .09
447 Shawn Green TL .30 .09
448 Mike Sweeney TL .30 .09
449 Jeff Bagwell TL .30 .09
450 Cliff Floyd TL .30 .09
451 Roger Cedeno TL .30 .09
452 Todd Helton TL .30 .09
453 Juan Gonzalez TL .30 .09
454 Sean Casey TL .30 .09
455 Magglio Ordonez TL .30 .09
456 Sammy Sosa TL .75 .23
457 Manny Ramirez TL .30 .09
458 Jeff Conine TL .30 .09
459 Chipper Jones TL .50 .15
460 Luis Gonzalez TL .30 .09
461 Troy Glaus TL .30 .09
462 Ivan Rodriguez .50 .15
Jason Romano FF
463 Luis Gonzalez .30 .09
Jack Cust FF
464 Jim Thome .30 .09
C.C. Sabathia FF
465 Jason Giambi .30 .09
Jason Hart FF
466 Jeff Bagwell .50 .15
Roy Oswalt FF
467 Sammy Sosa .75 .23
Corey Patterson FF
468 Mike Piazza .75 .23
Alex Escobar FF
469 Ken Griffey Jr. .75 .23
Adam Dunn FF
470 Roger Clemens .75 .23
Nick Johnson FF
471 Cliff Floyd .30 .09
Josh Beckett FF
472 Cal Ripken Jr. 1.25 .35
Jerry Hairston Jr. FF
473 Phil Nevin .30 .09
Xavier Nady FF
474 Scott Rolen .50 .15
Jimmy Rollins FF
475 Barry Larkin .30 .09
David Espinosa FF
476 Larry Walker .50 .15
Jose Ortiz FF
477 Chipper Jones .50 .15
Marcus Giles FF
478 Craig Biggio .30 .09
Keith Ginter FF
479 Magglio Ordonez .30 .09
Aaron Rowand FF
480 Alex Rodriguez .75 .23
Carlos Pena FF
481 Derek Jeter 1.00 .30
Alfonso Soriano FF
482 Erubiel Durazo PG .30 .09
483 Bernie Williams PG .30 .09
484 Team Photo PG .30 .09
485 Team Photo PG .30 .09
486 Andy Pettitte PG .30 .09
487 Curt Schilling PG .30 .09
488 Randy Johnson PG .50 .15
489 Rudolph Guiliani PG .75 .23
Mayor of New York City
490 George W. Bush PG 5.00 1.50
President of United States
491 Roger Clemens PG .75 .23
492 Mariano Rivera PG .50 .15
493 Tino Martinez PG .30 .09
494 Derek Jeter PG 1.00 .30
495 Scott Brosius PG .30 .09
496 Alfonso Soriano PG .30 .09
497 Matt Williams PG .30 .09
498 Tony Womack PG .30 .09
499 Luis Gonzalez PG .30 .09
500 Arizona Diamondbacks PG .75 .23
501 Randy Johnson .50 .15
Curt Schilling
Co-MVP's PG
502 Josh Fogg RC 2.00 .60
503 Elpidio Guzman 2.00 .60
504 Corky Miller RC 2.00 .60
505 Cesar Crespo RC 2.00 .60
506 Carlos Garcia RC 2.00 .60
507 Carlos Valderrama RC 2.00 .60
508 Joe Kennedy RC 3.00 .90
509 Henry Mateo RC 2.00 .60
510 B. Duckworth RC 2.00 .60
511 Ichiro Suzuki 15.00 4.50
512 Zach Day RC 2.00 .60
513 Ryan Freel RC 2.00 .60
514 Brian Lawrence RC 2.00 .60
515 Alexis Gomez RC 2.00 .60
516 Will Ohman RC 2.00 .60
517 Juan Diaz RC 2.00 .60
518 Juan Moreno RC 2.00 .60
519 Rob Mackowiak RC 2.00 .60
520 Horacio Ramirez RC 3.00 .90
521 Albert Pujols 50.00 15.00
522 Tsuyoshi Shinjo 3.00 .90
523 Ryan Drese RC 3.00 .90
524 Angel Berroa RC 3.00 .90
525 Josh Towers RC 2.00 .60
526 Junior Spivey 3.00 .90
527 Greg Miller RC 2.00 .60
528 Esix Snead 2.00 .60
529 Mark Prior DP RC 15.00 4.50
530 Drew Henson 3.00 .90
531 Brian Reith RC 2.00 .60
532 Andres Torres RC 2.00 .60
533 Casey Fossum RC 2.00 .60
534 Wilmy Caceres RC 2.00 .60
535 Matt White RC 2.00 .60
536 Wilkin Ruan RC 2.00 .60
537 Rick Bauer RC 2.00 .60
538 Morgan Ensberg RC 3.00 .90
539 Geronimo Gil RC 2.00 .60
540 Dewon Brazelton RC 3.00 .90
541 Johnny Estrada RC 3.00 .90
542 Claudio Vargas RC 2.00 .60
543 Donaldo Mendez 2.00 .60
544 Kyle Lohse RC 3.00 .90
545 Nate Frese RC 2.00 .60
546 Christian Parker RC 2.00 .60
547 Blaine Neal RC 2.00 .60
548 Travis Hafner RC 5.00 1.50
549 Billy Sylvester RC 2.00 .60
550 Adam Pettyjohn RC 2.00 .60
551 Bill Ortega RC 2.00 .60
552 Jose Acevedo RC 2.00 .60
553 Steve Green RC 2.00 .60
554 Jay Gibbons 3.00 .90
555 Bert Snow RC 2.00 .60
556 Erick Almonte RC 2.00 .60
557 Jeremy Owens RC 2.00 .60
558 Sean Douglass RC 2.00 .60
559 Jason Smith RC 2.00 .60
560 Ricardo Rodriguez RC 2.00 .60
561 Mark Teixeira RC 12.00 3.60
562 Tyler Walker RC 2.00 .60
563 Juan Uribe 3.00 .90
564 Bud Smith RC 2.00 .60
565 Angel Santos RC 2.00 .60
566 Brandon Lyon RC 2.00 .60
567 Eric Hinske RC UER 3.00 .90
Front says he is a pitcher
568 Nick Punto RC 2.00 .60
569 Winston Abreu 2.00 .60
570 Jason Phillips RC 5.00 1.50
571 Rafael Soriano RC 3.00 .90
572 Wilson Betemit 2.00 .60
573 Endy Chavez RC 2.00 .60
574 Juan Cruz RC 2.00 .60
575 Cory Aldridge RC 2.00 .60
576 Adrian Hernandez 2.00 .60
577 Brandon Larson RC 2.00 .60
578 Bret Prinz RC 2.00 .60
579 Jackson Melian RC 2.00 .60
580 Dave Maurer RC 2.00 .60
581 Jason Michaels RC 2.00 .60
582 Travis Phelps RC 2.00 .60
583 Cody Ransom RC 2.00 .60
584 Benito Baez RC 2.00 .60
585 Brian Roberts RC 2.00 .60
586 Nate Teut RC 2.00 .60
587 Jack Wilson RC 4.00 1.20
588 Willie Harris RC 2.00 .60
589 Martin Vargas RC 2.00 .60
590 Steve Torrealba RC 2.00 .60
591 Stubby Clapp RC 2.00 .60
592 Dan Wright 2.00 .60
593 Mike Rivera RC 2.00 .60
594 Luis Pineda RC 2.00 .60
595 Lance Davis RC 2.00 .60
596 Ramon Vazquez RC 2.00 .60
597 Dustan Mohr RC 2.00 .60
598 Troy Mattes RC 2.00 .60
599 Grant Balfour RC 2.00 .60
600 Jared Fernandez RC 2.00 .60
601 Jorge Julio RC 2.00 .60

2001 Fleer Platinum Parallel

Randomly inserted in hobby packs, this 600-card set is a parallel version of the base set. Cards 1-250 and 302-501 are sequentially numbered to 201 and cards 251-300 and 502-601 to 21. Card number 300 was never produced as a Parallel.

Nm-Mt Ex-Mt
*STARS 1-250/302-501: 2.5X TO 6X BASIC
*SUBSET RC'S 402-501: 2X TO 5X BASIC

2001 Fleer Platinum 20th Anniversary Reprints

Randomly inserted in hobby packs at the rate of one in eight and in jumbo packs at the rate of one in four, this 18-card set features reprints of Fleer's best rookie cards from the past 20 years of cards.

Nm-Mt Ex-Mt
COMPLETE SET (18) 60.00 18.00
1 Cal Ripken 82F 12.00 3.60
2 Wade Boggs 83F 2.50 .75
3 Ryne Sandberg 83F 6.00 1.80
4 Tony Gwynn 83F 5.00 1.50
5 Don Mattingly 84F 10.00 3.00
6 Roger Clemens 85F 8.00 2.40
7 Kirby Puckett 85F 4.00 1.20
8 Jose Canseco 86LL 4.00 1.20
9 Barry Bonds 87F 10.00 3.00
10 Ken Griffey Jr. 89F 6.00 1.80
11 Sammy Sosa 90F 6.00 1.80
12 Ivan Rodriguez 91UU 4.00 1.20
13 Jeff Bagwell 91UU 2.50 .75
14 J.D. Drew 98UPD 2.50 .75
15 Troy Glaus 98UPD 2.50 .75
16 Rick Ankiel 99UPD 2.50 .75
17 Xavier Nady 00GL 2.50 .75
18 Jose Ortiz 00GL 2.50 .75

2001 Fleer Platinum Classic Combinations

Randomly inserted in packs, this 40-card set features dual player cards which pair some of the greatest players in the game. Cards 1-10 are serially numbered to 250, 11-20 to 500, 21-30 to 1,000, and 31-40 to 2,000.

Nm-Mt Ex-Mt
COMMON (CC1-CC10) 20.00 6.00
COMMON (CC11-CC20) 15.00 4.50
COMMON (CC21-CC30) 8.00 2.40
COMMON (CC31-CC40) 5.00 1.50
CC1 Derek Jeter 20.00 6.00
Alex Rodriguez
CC2 Willie Mays 25.00 7.50
Willie McCovey
CC3 Lou Gehrig 40.00 12.00
Babe Ruth
CC4 Mark McGwire 30.00 9.00
Ken Griffey Jr.
CC5 Johnny Bench 20.00 6.00
Roy Campanella
CC6 Ted Williams 25.00 7.50
Nomar Garciaparra
CC7 Yogi Berra 20.00 6.00
Mike Piazza
CC8 Ernie Banks 20.00 6.00
Sammy Sosa
CC9 Nolan Ryan 30.00 9.00
Randy Johnson
CC10 Roberto Clemente 25.00 7.50
Vladimir Guerrero
CC11 Stan Musial 30.00 9.00
Lou Gehrig
CC12 Bill Mazeroski 20.00 6.00
Roberto Clemente
CC13 Ernie Banks 15.00 4.50
Alex Rodriguez
CC14 Phil Rizzuto 25.00 7.50
Derek Jeter
CC15 Mike Piazza 15.00 4.50
Johnny Bench
CC16 Mark McGwire 25.00 7.50
Sammy Sosa
CC17 Ted Williams 20.00 6.00
Tony Gwynn
CC18 Eddie Mathews 20.00 6.00
Mike Schmidt
CC19 Barry Bonds 25.00 7.50
Willie Mays
CC20 Nolan Ryan 30.00 9.00
Pedro Martinez
CC21 Barry Bonds 20.00 6.00
Ken Griffey Jr.
CC22 Willie McCovey 5.00 1.50
Reggie Jackson
CC23 Roberto Clemente 15.00 4.50
Sammy Sosa
CC24 Willie Mays 15.00 4.50
Ernie Banks
CC25 Eddie Mathews 8.00 2.40
Chipper Jones
CC26 Mike Schmidt 15.00 4.50
Brooks Robinson
CC27 Stan Musial 20.00 6.00
Mark McGwire
CC28 Ted Williams 15.00 4.50
Roger Maris
CC29 Yogi Berra 5.00 1.50
Roy Campanella
CC30 Johnny Bench 8.00 2.40
Tony Perez
CC31 Bill Mazeroski 5.00 1.50
Joe Carter
CC32 Mike Piazza 8.00 2.40
Roy Campanella
CC33 Ernie Banks 5.00 1.50
Craig Biggio
CC34 Frank Robinson 5.00 1.50
Brooks Robinson
CC35 Mike Schmidt 10.00 3.00
Scott Rolen
CC36 Roger Maris 12.00 3.60
Mark McGwire
CC37 Stan Musial 8.00 2.40
Tony Gwynn
CC38 Ted Williams 10.00 3.00
Bill Terry
CC39 Derek Jeter 12.00 3.60
Reggie Jackson
CC40 Yogi Berra 5.00 1.50
Bill Dickey

2001 Fleer Platinum Classic Combinations Memorabilia

Randomly inserted in packs, this 11-card set features dual player cards which pair some of the greatest players in the game and contain pieces of game-used bats. Only 25 serially numbered sets were produced.

Nm-Mt Ex-Mt
1 Yogi Berra
Bill Dickey
2 Yogi Berra
Roy Campanella
3 Roberto Clemente Bat
Vladimir Guerrero Bat
4 Eddie Mathews
Chipper Jones
5 Willie McCovey
Reggie Jackson
6 Phil Rizzuto
Derek Jeter
7 Frank Robinson
Brooks Robinson
8 Mike Schmidt
Brooks Robinson
9 Mike Schmidt
Scott Rolen
10 Ted Williams
Bill Terry
11 Ted Williams
Tony Gwynn

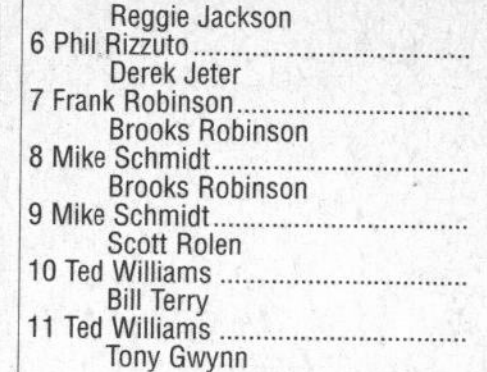

2001 Fleer Platinum Grandstand Greats

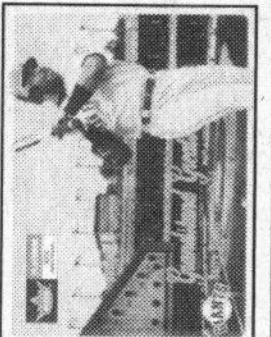

Randomly inserted in hobby packs at the rate of one in 12 and in jumbo packs at the rate of one in six, this 20-card set features color photos of the crowd-pleasers of the League.

Nm-Mt Ex-Mt
COMPLETE SET (20) 80.00 24.00
GG1 Chipper Jones 3.00 .90
GG2 Alex Rodriguez 5.00 1.50
GG3 Jeff Bagwell 2.00 .60
GG4 Troy Glaus 2.00 .60
GG5 Manny Ramirez 2.00 .60
GG6 Derek Jeter 8.00 2.40
GG7 Tony Gwynn 4.00 1.20
GG8 Greg Maddux 5.00 1.50
GG9 Nomar Garciaparra 5.00 1.50
GG10 Sammy Sosa 5.00 1.50
GG11 Mike Piazza 5.00 1.50
GG12 Barry Bonds 8.00 2.40
GG13 Mark McGwire 8.00 2.40
GG14 Vladimir Guerrero 3.00 .90
GG15 Ivan Rodriguez 3.00 .90
GG16 Ken Griffey Jr. 5.00 1.50
GG17 Todd Helton 2.00 .60
GG18 Cal Ripken 10.00 3.00
GG19 Pedro Martinez 3.00 .90
GG20 Frank Thomas 3.00 .90

2001 Fleer Platinum Lumberjacks

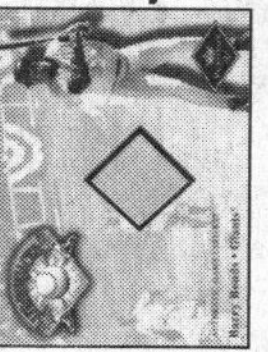

This 27-card insert set features game-used bat chips from greats like Derek Jeter and Ivan Rodriguez. These cards were inserted at a stated rate of one per rack pack

Nm-Mt Ex-Mt
1 Roberto Alomar 15.00 4.50
2 Moises Alou 10.00 3.00
3 Adrian Beltre 15.00 4.50
4 Lance Berkman 10.00 3.00
5 Barry Bonds 25.00 7.50
6 Bret Boone 10.00 3.00
7 J.D. Drew
8 Adam Dunn 15.00 4.50
9 Darin Erstad 10.00 3.00
10 Cliff Floyd 10.00 3.00
11 Brian Giles 10.00 3.00
12 Luis Gonzalez 10.00 3.00
13 Vladimir Guerrero 15.00 4.50
14 Cristian Guzman 10.00 3.00
15 Tony Gwynn 15.00 4.50
16 Todd Helton 15.00 4.50
17 Drew Henson 15.00 4.50
18 Derek Jeter 25.00 7.50
19 Chipper Jones 15.00 4.50
20 Mike Piazza 15.00 4.50
21 Albert Pujols 50.00 15.00
22 Manny Ramirez 15.00 4.50
23 Cal Ripken
24 Ivan Rodriguez 15.00 4.50
25 Gary Sheffield 10.00 3.00
26 Mike Sweeney 10.00 3.00
27 Larry Walker 15.00 4.50

2001 Fleer Platinum Lumberjacks Autographs

This eight-card set is a partial parallel to the 2001 Fleer Platinum Lumberjacks insert. Each card is autographed and individually serial numbered to 100. Not all the cards were signed in time for inclusion in packs and those exchange cards could be redeemed until November 30, 2002. The following players were seeded into packs as exchange cards: Barry Bonds, Derek

Jeter, Albert Pujols and Cal Ripken.

	Nm-Mt	Ex-Mt
6 Barry Bonds	300.00	90.00
7 J.D. Drew		
8 Adam Dunn	80.00	24.00
12 Luis Gonzalez	50.00	15.00
18 Derek Jeter	200.00	60.00
21 Albert Pujols	400.00	120.00
23 Cal Ripken	200.00	60.00
26 Mike Sweeney		

2001 Fleer Platinum Nameplates

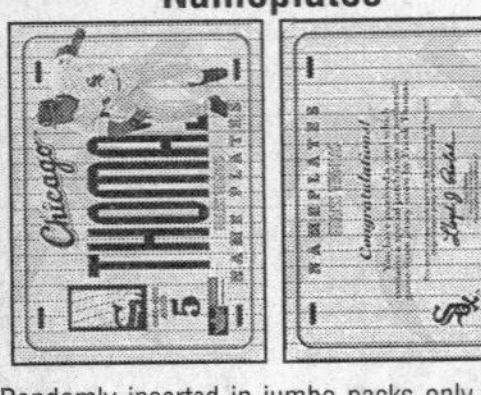

Randomly inserted in jumbo packs only at the rate of one in 12, this 42-card set features color images of top players on a license plate design background and pieces of actual name plates from players' uniforms embedded in the cards.

	Nm-Mt	Ex-Mt
1 Carlos Beltran/90	40.00	12.00
2 Adrian Beltre/55*	40.00	12.00
3 Sean Casey/21		
4 J.D. Drew/170	25.00	7.50
5 Darin Erstad/39	25.00	7.50
6 Troy Glaus/85	25.00	7.50
7 Tom Glavine/125	40.00	12.00
8 Vladimir Guerrero/80	40.00	12.00
9 Vladimir Guerrero/90	40.00	12.00
10 Tony Gwynn/35	80.00	24.00
11 Tony Gwynn/65	50.00	15.00
12 Tony Gwynn/70	50.00	15.00
13 Jeffrey Hammonds/135	25.00	7.50
14 Randy Johnson/99	40.00	12.00
15 Chipper Jones/95	40.00	12.00
16 Javy Lopez/49*	25.00	7.50
17 Greg Maddux/180	50.00	15.00
18 Edgar Martinez/87	40.00	12.00
19 Pedro Martinez/120	40.00	12.00
20 Kevin Millwood/130	25.00	7.50
21 Stan Musial/30	120.00	36.00
22 Mike Mussina/91	40.00	12.00
23 Manny Ramirez/75	40.00	12.00
24 Manny Ramirez/105	40.00	12.00
25 Cal Ripken/19		
26 Cal Ripken/21		
27 Cal Ripken/23		
28 Cal Ripken/110	100.00	30.00
29 Ivan Rodriguez/177	40.00	12.00
30 Scott Rolen/65	40.00	12.00
31 Scott Rolen/125	40.00	12.00
32 Nolan Ryan/40	150.00	45.00
33 Nolan Ryan/55	150.00	45.00
34 Curt Schilling/110*	25.00	7.50
35 Frank Thomas/35	40.00	12.00
36 Frank Thomas/75	40.00	12.00
37 Frank Thomas/80	40.00	12.00
38 Robin Ventura/99	25.00	7.50
39 Larry Walker/79	40.00	12.00
40 Larry Walker/85	40.00	12.00
41 Matt Williams/175	25.00	7.50
42 Dave Winfield/80	25.00	7.50

2001 Fleer Platinum National Patch Time

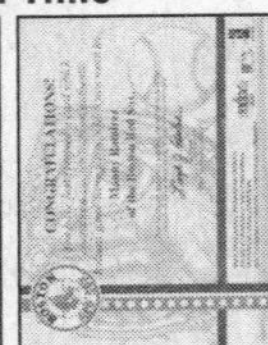

Randomly inserted in first and second series hobby packs at the rate of one in 24 and first and second series retail packs at the rate of one in 36, this set features color images of superstars of baseball with authentic game-worn jersey and pants swatches embedded in the cards. Jersey cards featuring the following players: Mo Vaughn, Kazuhiro Sasaki, Aaron Sele, Todd Walker, Jorge Posada, Vida Blue, Jim Palmer, Jim Rice, Mike Mussina, and Carl Yastrzemski were produced. However, due to MLB regulations these cards were pulled at the last minute from series one packs. Vaughn and Sasaki were eventually seeded into second series packs and a lone Mike Mussina copy was verified as coming from a second series pack, but no Mussina's or Yastrzemski's were intended for release. In late 2004 copies of the Yastrzemski card were reportedly sent out to collectors as exchange premiums for other issues Fleer could not fulfill.

	Nm-Mt	Ex-Mt
1 Edgardo Alfonzo S1	10.00	3.00
2 B.Anderson Pants S1	10.00	3.00
3 Jeff Bagwell S2	15.00	4.50
4 Adrian Beltre S2	15.00	4.50
5 Wade Boggs S1	15.00	4.50
6 Barry Bonds S2	25.00	7.50
7 George Brett S1	40.00	12.00
8 Eric Chavez S2	10.00	3.00
9 Jeff Cirillo S1	10.00	3.00
10 R.Clemens Gray S1	25.00	7.50
11 R.Clemens White S2	25.00	7.50
12 Pedro Martinez S1	15.00	4.50
12 J.D. Drew S2	10.00	3.00
13 Darin Erstad S2	10.00	3.00
14 Carl Everett S1	10.00	3.00
15 Rollie Fingers Pants S1	10.00	3.00
16 Freddy Garcia White S1	10.00	3.00
17 Freddy Garcia White S2	10.00	3.00
18 Jason Giambi SP S2	10.00	3.00
19 Juan Gonzalez SP S2	15.00	4.50
20 Mark Grace S2	15.00	4.50
21 Shawn Green S2	10.00	3.00
22 Ben Grieve S2	10.00	3.00
23 Vladimir Guerrero S2	15.00	4.50
24 Tony Gwynn White S1	15.00	4.50
25 Tony Gwynn White S2	15.00	4.50
26 Todd Helton S2	15.00	4.50
27 Randy Johnson S2	15.00	4.50
28 Chipper Jones S2	15.00	4.50
29 David Justice S2	10.00	3.00
30 Jason Kendall S1	10.00	3.00
31 Jeff Kent S2	10.00	3.00
32 Paul LoDuca S2	10.00	3.00
33 Greg Maddux White S1	15.00	4.50
34 G.Maddux Gray-White S2	15.00	4.50
36 Fred McGriff S1	15.00	4.50
37 Eddie Murray S1	15.00	4.50
38 Mike Mussina S2 SP		
39 John Olerud S2	10.00	3.00
40 M.Ordonez Gray S1	10.00	3.00
41 M.Ordonez Gray SP S2	10.00	3.00
42 Adam Piatt S1	10.00	3.00
43 Jorge Posada S2	15.00	4.50
44 Manny Ramirez S1	15.00	4.50
45 Cal Ripken Black S1	50.00	15.00
46 C.Ripken Gray-White S2	50.00	15.00
47 Mariano Rivera S2	15.00	4.50
48 Ivan Rodriguez Blue S1	15.00	4.50
49 I.Rodriguez Blue-WhiteS2	15.00	4.50
50 Scott Rolen S2	15.00	4.50
51 Nolan Ryan S1	40.00	12.00
52 Kazuhiro Sasaki S2	10.00	3.00
53 Mike Schmidt S1	25.00	7.50
54 Tom Seaver S1	15.00	4.50
55 Aaron Sele S2	10.00	3.00
56 Gary Sheffield S2	10.00	3.00
57 Ozzie Smith S1	15.00	4.50
58 John Smoltz S2	15.00	4.50
59 Frank Thomas S2	15.00	4.50
60 Mo Vaughn S2	10.00	3.00
61 Robin Ventura S2	10.00	3.00
62 Rondell White S1	10.00	3.00
63 Bernie Williams S2	15.00	4.50
64 Dave Winfield S1	10.00	3.00
65 Carl Yastrzemski SP EXCH		

2001 Fleer Platinum Prime Numbers

This 15-card insert set was issued in jumbo packs at 1:12, and features game-used jersey swatches from veteran players like Cal Ripken and Chipper Jones.

	Nm-Mt	Ex-Mt
1 Jeff Bagwell	25.00	7.50
2 Cal Ripken	100.00	30.00
3 Barry Bonds	80.00	24.00
4 Todd Helton		
5 Derek Jeter	80.00	24.00
6 Tony Gwynn	40.00	12.00
7 Kazuhiro Sasaki	15.00	4.50
8 Chan Ho Park	15.00	4.50
9 Sean Casey		
10 Chipper Jones	25.00	7.50
11 Pedro Martinez	25.00	7.50
12 Mike Piazza	50.00	15.00
13 Carlos Delgado	15.00	4.50
14 Craig Biggio		
15 Roger Clemens	60.00	18.00

2001 Fleer Platinum Rack Pack Autographs

Randomly inserted in rack packs only, this 21-card set features actual autographed player cards and autographics cards from the last 20 years. These cards were almost all originally inserted in Fleer packs and were bought back for signing for this product.

	Nm-Mt	Ex-Mt
1 H.Aaron 1997 SI/90	120.00	36.00
2 L.Brock 1998 SITN/15		
3 Roger Clemens 1998 SITN/125	100.00	30.00
4 Jose Cruz Jr. 1997 No Brand	5.00	1.50
5 J.Drew 1999 SI One's/10*		
6 S.Garvey 1987 Fleer/15*		
7 Bob Gibson 1998 SITN/300	30.00	9.00
8 B.Grieve No Brand/100*	5.00	1.50
9 T.Gwynn 1998 SITN/125	50.00	15.00
10 Wes Helms 1997 No Brand	5.00	1.50
11 Harmon Killebrew 1998 SITN/300	40.00	12.00
12 Paul Konerko No Brand/135*	15.00	4.50
13 W.Mays 1997 SI/115	150.00	45.00
14 Willie Mays 1998 SITN/120	150.00	45.00
15 K.Puckett 1997 SI/105	50.00	15.00
16 C.Ripken 1997 SI/5		
17 Brooks Robinson 1998 SITN/40	60.00	18.00
18 Frank Robinson 1997 SI/115	30.00	9.00
19 Scott Rolen 1998 SITN/150	40.00	12.00
20 Alex Rodriguez 1997 SI/94	150.00	45.00
21 Alex Rodriguez 1998 Promo/150	100.00	30.00

2001 Fleer Platinum Tickets Autographs

Randomly inserted in hobby boxes, this nine-card set is a partial parallel version of the regular insert set and is distinguished by the autographs on the tickets.

	Nm-Mt	Ex-Mt
1 George Brett 3000th Hit 9/30/92		
2 Rod Carew 3000th Hit 8/4/85		
3 Steve Carlton 300th Win 9/23/83	30.00	9.00
4 Bob Gibson 1968 WS		
5 Stan Musial Last Game 9/29/63		
6 Cal Ripken 1991 AS MVP		
7 Cal Ripken 400th HR		
8 Mike Schmidt 500th HR 4/18/87		
9 Mike Schmidt Opening Day		

2001 Fleer Platinum Winning Combinations

This 40-card insert was issued in Series two hobby packs. The set pairs players that have similar abilities. Each card is serial numbered to either 2000, 1000, 500, or 250.

	Nm-Mt	Ex-Mt
1 Derek Jeter Ozzie Smith/2000	12.00	3.60
2 Barry Bonds Mark McGwire/500	25.00	7.50
3 Ichiro Suzuki Albert Pujols/250	50.00	15.00
4 Ted Williams Manny Ramirez/1000	15.00	4.50
5 Tony Gwynn Cal Ripken/250	40.00	12.00
6 Mike Piazza Derek Jeter/500	25.00	7.50
7 Dave Winfield Tony Gwynn/2000	6.00	1.80
8 Hideo Nomo Ichiro Suzuki/2000	20.00	6.00
9 Cal Ripken Ozzie Smith/1000	25.00	7.50
10 Mark McGwire Albert Pujols/2000	15.00	4.50
11 Jeff Bagwell Craig Biggio/1000	8.00	2.40
12 Bobby Bonds Barry Bonds/250	30.00	9.00
13 Ted Williams Stan Musial/250	25.00	7.50
14 Babe Ruth Reggie Jackson/500	30.00	9.00
15 Kazuhiro Sasaki Ichiro Suzuki/500	40.00	12.00
16 Nolan Ryan Roger Clemens/500	25.00	7.50
17 Roger Clemens Derek Jeter/250	30.00	9.00
18 Mike Piazza Ivan Rodriguez/1000	12.00	3.60
19 Vladimir Guerrero Sammy Sosa/2000	8.00	2.40
20 Barry Bonds Sammy Sosa/250	30.00	9.00
21 Roger Clemens Greg Maddux/1000	15.00	4.50
22 Juan Gonzalez Manny Ramirez/2000	5.00	1.50
23 Todd Helton Jason Giambi/2000	5.00	1.50
24 Jeff Bagwell Lance Berkman/2000	5.00	1.50
25 Mike Sweeney George Brett/1000	15.00	4.50
26 Luis Gonzalez Babe Ruth/2000	15.00	4.50
27 Bill Skowron Don Mattingly/250	40.00	12.00
28 Yogi Berra Cal Ripken/2000	15.00	4.50
29 Pedro Martinez Nomar Garciaparra/500	15.00	4.50
30 Ted Kluszewski Frank Robinson/1000	8.00	2.40
31 Curt Schilling Randy Johnson/1000	8.00	2.40
32 Ken Griffey Jr. Cal Ripken/500	30.00	9.00
33 Mike Piazza Johnny Bench/1000	12.00	3.60
34 Stan Musial Albert Pujols	40.00	12.00
35 Jackie Robinson Nellie Fox	10.00	3.00
36 Lefty Grove Steve Carlton/250	15.00	4.50
37 Ty Cobb Tony Gwynn/250	20.00	6.00
38 Albert Pujols Frank Robinson/1000	25.00	7.50
39 Ryne Sandberg Sammy Sosa/500	25.00	7.50
40 Cal Ripken Lou Gehrig/250	40.00	12.00

2001 Fleer Platinum Winning Combinations Memorabilia

This 25-card set is a partial parallel of the 2001 Fleer Platinum Winning Combinations insert, each card features game-used memorabilia. These cards were inserted into Series two hobby/jumbo packs, and are individually serial numbered to 25. Due to market scarcity, no pricing is provided.

	Nm-Mt	Ex-Mt
1 Derek Jeter Ozzie Smith		
3 Ichiro Suzuki Albert Pujols		
4 Ted Williams Manny Ramirez		
5 Tony Gwynn Cal Ripken		
6 Mike Piazza Derek Jeter		
7 Dave Winfield Tony Gwynn		
8 Hideo Nomo Ichiro Suzuki		
9 Cal Ripken Ozzie Smith		
11 Jeff Bagwell Craig Biggio		
12 Bobby Bonds Barry Bonds		
14 Babe Ruth Reggie Jackson		
15 Kazuhiro Sasaki Ichiro Suzuki		
16 Nolan Ryan Roger Clemens		
17 Roger Clemens Derek Jeter		
18 Mike Piazza Ivan Rodriguez		
21 Roger Clemens Greg Maddux		
22 Juan Gonzalez Manny Ramirez		
24 Jeff Bagwell Lance Berkman		
25 Mike Sweeney George Brett		
26 Luis Gonzalez Babe Ruth		
27 Bill Skowron Don Mattingly		
30 Ted Kluszewski Frank Robinson		
33 Mike Piazza Johnny Bench		
35 Jackie Robinson Nellie Fox		
38 Albert Pujols Frank Robinson		

2002 Fleer Platinum

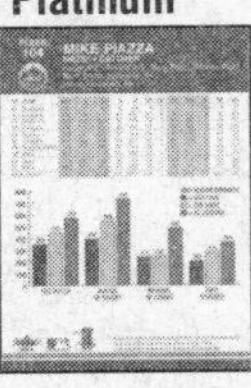

This 301 card set was issued in early Spring, 2002. These cards were issued in three different ways: 10 card hobby and retail packs. These packs were issued 24 packs to a box and six boxes to a case and had an SRP of $3. This product was also issued in 25 card jumbo packs which were packaged 12 to a box and eight boxes to a case. These cards had an SRP of $6. In addition, these cards were also issued in 45-card rack packs which were issued six packs to a box and two boxes to a case. These packs had an SRP of $10 per pack. The first 250 cards were basic cards while cards 251 through 260 are a Decade of Dominance subset, cards 261-270 feature the 10 players considered among the best young prospect and then 271-300 feature dual players prospects. Cards numbered 301 and 302 feature Japanese imports for 2002, So Taguchi and Kazuhisa Ishii. Card number 280 was not issued upon release of this set but was scheduled for release later in the 2002 season. At season's end, it was decided by the manufacturer to NOT release this card. A few copies of this card (with a large square box cut out from Satoru Komiyama's image) erroneously made their way into packs. Due to scarcity, a value has not been established. In addition, 73 redemption cards were seeded into packs whereby the holder of the card could exchange it for an actual vintage 1986 Fleer Update Bonds XRC signed and certified by Barry himself and hand-numbered "X/73". The deadline to send this card in was April 30th, 2003.

	Nm-Mt	Ex-Mt
COMPLETE SET (301)	200.00	60.00
COMP.SET w/o SP's (250)	25.00	7.50
COMMON CARD (1-250)	.30	.09
COMMON CARD (251-260)	3.00	.90
COMMON CARD (261-270)	3.00	.90
COMMON CARD (271-302)	3.00	.90
1 Garret Anderson	.30	.09
2 Randy Johnson	.75	.23
3 Chipper Jones	.75	.23
4 David Cone	.30	.09
5 Corey Patterson	.30	.09
6 Carlos Lee	.30	.09
7 Barry Larkin	.50	.15
8 Jim Thome	.75	.23
9 Larry Walker	.50	.15
10 Randall Simon	.30	.09
11 Charles Johnson	.30	.09
12 Richard Hidalgo	.30	.09
13 Mark Quinn	.30	.09
14 Paul LoDuca	.30	.09
15 Cristian Guzman	.30	.09
16 Orlando Cabrera	.30	.09
17 Al Leiter	.30	.09
18 Nick Johnson	.30	.09
19 Eric Chavez	.30	.09
20 Miguel Tejada	.30	.09
21 Mike Lieberthal	.30	.09
22 Rob Mackowiak	.30	.09
23 Ryan Klesko	.30	.09
24 Jeff Kent	.30	.09
25 Edgar Martinez	.50	.15
26 Steve Kline	.30	.09
27 Toby Hall	.30	.09
28 Rusty Greer	.30	.09
29 Jose Cruz Jr.	.30	.09
30 Darin Erstad	.30	.09
31 Reggie Sanders	.30	.09
32 Javy Lopez	.30	.09
33 Carl Everett	.30	.09
34 Sammy Sosa	1.25	.35
35 Magglio Ordonez	.30	.09
36 Todd Walker	.30	.09
37 Omar Vizquel	.50	.15
38 Matt Anderson	.30	.09
39 Jeff Weaver	.30	.09
40 Derrek Lee	.30	.09
41 Julio Lugo	.30	.09
42 Joe Randa	.30	.09
43 Chan Ho Park	.30	.09
44 Torii Hunter	.30	.09
45 Vladimir Guerrero	.75	.23
46 Rey Ordonez	.30	.09
47 Tino Martinez	.50	.15
48 Johnny Damon Sox	.75	.23
49 Barry Zito	.30	.09
50 Robert Person	.30	.09
51 Aramis Ramirez	.30	.09
52 Mark Kotsay	.30	.09
53 Jason Schmidt	.30	.09
54 Jamie Moyer	.30	.09
55 David Justice	.30	.09
56 Aubrey Huff	.30	.09
57 Rick Helling	.30	.09
58 Carlos Delgado	.30	.09
59 Troy Glaus	.30	.09
60 Curt Schilling	.30	.09
61 Greg Maddux	1.25	.35
62 Nomar Garciaparra	1.25	.35
63 Kerry Wood	.75	.23
64 Frank Thomas	.75	.23
65 Dmitri Young	.30	.09
66 Alex Ochoa	.30	.09
67 Jose Macias	.30	.09
68 Antonio Alfonseca	.30	.09
69 Mike Lowell	.30	.09
70 Wade Miller	.30	.09
71 Mike Sweeney	.30	.09
72 Gary Sheffield	.30	.09
73 Corey Koskie	.30	.09
74 Lee Stevens	.30	.09
75 Jay Payton	.30	.09
76 Mike Mussina	.50	.15
77 Jermaine Dye	.30	.09
78 Bobby Abreu	.30	.09
79 Scott Rolen	.75	.23
80 Todd Ritchie	.30	.09
81 D'Angelo Jimenez	.30	.09
82 Robb Nen	.30	.09
83 John Olerud	.30	.09
84 Matt Morris	.30	.09
85 Joe Kennedy	.30	.09
86 Gabe Kapler	.30	.09
87 Chris Carpenter	.30	.09
88 David Eckstein	.30	.09
89 Matt Williams	.30	.09
90 John Smoltz	.50	.15
91 Pedro Martinez	.75	.23
92 Eric Young	.30	.09
93 Jose Valentin	.30	.09
94 Erubiel Durazo	.30	.09
95 Jeff Cirillo	.30	.09
96 Brandon Inge	.30	.09
97 Josh Beckett	.30	.09
98 Preston Wilson	.30	.09
99 Damian Jackson	.30	.09

100 Adrian Beltre .50 .15
101 Jeromy Burnitz .30 .09
102 Joe Mays .30 .09
103 Michael Barrett .30 .09
104 Mike Piazza 1.25 .35
105 Brady Anderson .30 .09
106 Jason Giambi Yankees .30 .09
107 Marlon Anderson .30 .09
108 Jimmy Rollins .30 .09
109 Jack Wilson .30 .09
110 Brian Lawrence .30 .09
111 Russ Ortiz .30 .09
112 Kazuhiro Sasaki .30 .09
113 Placido Polanco .30 .09
114 Damian Rolls .30 .09
115 Rafael Palmeiro .50 .15
116 Brad Fullmer .30 .09
117 Tim Salmon .50 .15
118 Tony Womack .30 .09
119 Tony Batista .30 .09
120 Trot Nixon .30 .09
121 Mark Buehrle .30 .09
122 Derek Jeter 2.00 .60
123 Ellis Burks .30 .09
124 Mike Hampton .30 .09
125 Roger Cedeno .30 .09
126 A.J. Burnett .30 .09
127 Moises Alou .30 .09
128 Billy Wagner .30 .09
129 Kevin Brown .30 .09
130 Jose Hernandez .30 .09
131 Doug Mientkiewicz .30 .09
132 Javier Vazquez .30 .09
133 Tsuyoshi Shinjo .30 .09
134 Andy Pettitte .50 .15
135 Tim Hudson .30 .09
136 Pat Burrell .30 .09
137 Brian Giles .30 .09
138 Kevin Young .30 .09
139 Xavier Nady .30 .09
140 J.T. Snow .30 .09
141 Aaron Sele .30 .09
142 Albert Pujols 1.50 .45
143 Jason Tyner .30 .09
144 Ivan Rodriguez .75 .23
145 Raul Mondesi .30 .09
146 Matt Lawton .30 .09
147 Rafael Furcal .30 .09
148 Jeff Conine .30 .09
149 Hideo Nomo .75 .23
150 Jose Canseco .75 .23
151 Aaron Boone .30 .09
152 Bartolo Colon .30 .09
153 Todd Helton .50 .15
154 Tony Clark .30 .09
155 Pablo Ozuna .30 .09
156 Jeff Bagwell .50 .15
157 Carlos Beltran .50 .15
158 Shawn Green .30 .09
159 Geoff Jenkins .30 .09
160 Eric Milton .30 .09
161 Jose Vidro .30 .09
162 Robin Ventura .30 .09
163 Jorge Posada .50 .15
164 Terrence Long .30 .09
165 Brandon Duckworth .30 .09
166 Chad Hermansen .30 .09
167 Ben Davis .30 .09
168 Phil Nevin .30 .09
169 Bret Boone .30 .09
170 J.D. Drew .30 .09
171 Edgar Renteria .30 .09
172 Randy Winn .30 .09
173 Alex Rodriguez 1.25 .35
174 Shannon Stewart .30 .09
175 Steve Finley .30 .09
176 Marcus Giles .30 .09
177 Jay Gibbons .30 .09
178 Manny Ramirez .50 .15
179 Ray Durham .30 .09
180 Sean Casey .30 .09
181 Travis Fryman .30 .09
182 Denny Neagle .30 .09
183 Deivi Cruz .30 .09
184 Luis Castillo .30 .09
185 Lance Berkman .30 .09
186 Dee Brown .30 .09
187 Jeff Shaw .30 .09
188 Mark Loretta .30 .09
189 David Ortiz .50 .15
190 Edgardo Alfonzo .30 .09
191 Roger Clemens 1.50 .45
192 Mariano Rivera .50 .15
193 Jeremy Giambi .30 .09
194 Johnny Estrada .30 .09
195 Craig Wilson .30 .09
196 Adam Eaton .30 .09
197 Rich Aurilia .30 .09
198 Mike Cameron .30 .09
199 Jim Edmonds .30 .09
200 Fernando Vina .30 .09
201 Greg Vaughn .30 .09
202 Mike Young .75 .23
203 Vernon Wells .30 .09
204 Luis Gonzalez .30 .09
205 Tom Glavine .50 .15
206 Chris Richard .30 .09
207 Jon Lieber .30 .09
208 Keith Foulke .30 .09
209 Rondell White .30 .09
210 Bernie Williams .50 .15
211 Juan Pierre .30 .09
212 Juan Encarnacion .30 .09
213 Ryan Dempster .30 .09
214 Tim Redding .30 .09
215 Jeff Suppan .30 .09
216 Mark Grudzielanek .30 .09
217 Richie Sexson .30 .09
218 Brad Radke .30 .09
219 Armando Benitez .30 .09
220 Orlando Hernandez .30 .09
221 Alfonso Soriano .50 .15
222 Mark Mulder .30 .09
223 Travis Lee .30 .09
224 Jason Kendall .30 .09
225 Trevor Hoffman .30 .09
226 Barry Bonds 2.00 .60
227 Freddy Garcia .30 .09
228 Darryl Kile .30 .09
229 Ben Grieve .30 .09
230 Frank Catalanotto .30 .09
231 Ruben Sierra .30 .09
232 Homer Bush .30 .09
233 Mark Grace .50 .15
234 Andruw Jones .30 .09
235 Brian Roberts .30 .09
236 Fred McGriff .50 .15
237 Paul Konerko .30 .09
238 Ken Griffey Jr. 1.25 .35
239 John Burkett .30 .09
240 Juan Uribe .30 .09
241 Bobby Higginson .30 .09
242 Cliff Floyd .30 .09
243 Craig Biggio .50 .15
244 Neifi Perez .30 .09
245 Eric Karros .30 .09
246 Ben Sheets .30 .09
247 Tony Armas Jr. .30 .09
248 Mo Vaughn .30 .09
249 David Wells .30 .09
250 Juan Gonzalez .50 .15
251 Barry Bonds DD 8.00 2.40
252 Sammy Sosa DD 5.00 1.50
253 Ken Griffey Jr. DD 5.00 1.50
254 Roger Clemens DD 6.00 1.80
255 Greg Maddux DD 5.00 1.50
256 Chipper Jones DD 3.00 .90
257 Alex Rodriguez 6.00 1.80
Derek Jeter
Nomar Garciaparra DD
258 Roberto Alomar DD 3.00 .90
259 Jeff Bagwell DD 3.00 .90
260 Mike Piazza DD 5.00 1.50
261 Mark Teixeira BB 3.00 .90
262 Mark Prior BB 5.00 1.50
263 Alex Escobar BB 3.00 .90
264 C.C. Sabathia BB 3.00 .90
265 Drew Henson BB 3.00 .90
266 Wilson Betemit BB 3.00 .90
267 Roy Oswalt BB 3.00 .90
268 Adam Dunn BB 3.00 .90
269 Bud Smith BB 3.00 .90
270 Dewon Brazelton BB 3.00 .90
271 Brandon Backe RC 4.00 1.20
Jason Standridge
272 Wilfredo Rodriguez 3.00 .90
Carlos Hernandez
273 Geronimo Gil 3.00 .90
Luis Rivera
274 Carlos Pena 3.00 .90
Jovanny Cedeno
275 Austin Kearns 3.00 .90
Ben Broussard
276 Jorge De La RosaRC 3.00 .90
Kenny Kelly
277 Ryan Drese 4.00 1.20
Victor Martinez
278 Joel Pinero 3.00 .90
Nate Cornejo
279 David Kelton 3.00 .90
Carlos Zambrano
280 Bill Ortega
Satoru Komiyama ERR
Not intended for public release
Card features large cut out square over Komiyama image
281 Donnie Bridges 3.00 .90
Wilkin Ruan
282 Wily Mo Pena 3.00 .90
Brandon Claussen
283 Jason Jennings 3.00 .90
Rene Reyes RC
284 Steve Green 3.00 .90
Alfredo Amezaga
285 Eric Hinske 3.00 .90
Felipe Lopez
286 Anderson Machado RC 3.00 .90
Brad Baisley
287 Carlos Garcia 3.00 .90
Sean Douglass
288 Pat Strange 3.00 .90
Jae Weong Seo
289 Marcus Thames 3.00 .90
Alex Graman
290 Matt Childers RC 3.00 .90
Hansel Izquierdo RC
291 Ron Calloway RC 3.00 .90
Adam Walker RC
292 J.R. House 3.00 .90
J.J. Davis
293 Ryan Anderson 3.00 .90
Rafael Soriano
294 Mike Bynum 3.00 .90
Dennis Tankersley
295 Kurt Ainsworth 3.00 .90
Carlos Valderrama
296 Billy Hall 3.00 .90
Cristian Guerrero
297 Miguel Olivo 3.00 .90
Danny Wright
298 Marlon Byrd 3.00 .90
Jorge Padilla RC
299 Juan Cruz 3.00 .90
Ben Christensen
300 Adam Johnson 3.00 .90
Michael Restovich
301 So Taguchi SP RC 3.00 .90
302 Kazuhisa Ishii SP RC 4.00 1.20
NNO Barry Bonds 1986 AU/73 600.00 180.00

2002 Fleer Platinum Parallel

Randomly inserted into packs, this is a parallel set version of the 2002 Fleer Platinum set. These cards have a stated print run of 202 cards for cards numbered 1 through 250 and 22 for cards numbered 251-302. Please note that no pricing is provided for cards numbered 251-302 due to market scarcity.

Nm-Mt Ex-Mt
*PARALLEL 1-250: 2.5X TO 6X BASIC

2002 Fleer Platinum Clubhouse Memorabilia

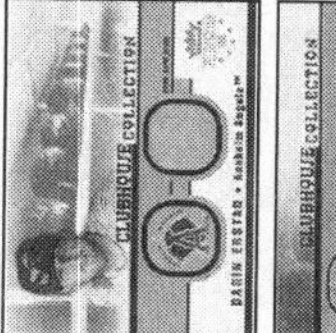

Inserted into packs at stated odds of one in 32 hobby and one in 44 retail packs, these 39 cards feature game-used memorabilia pieces. Fleer has stated the print runs for each of these cards and we have notated that information in our checklist.

	Nm-Mt	Ex-Mt
1 Edgardo Alfonzo Jsy/1000	10.00	3.00
2 Rick Ankiel Jsy/500	10.00	3.00
3 Adrian Beltre Jsy/875	15.00	4.50
4 Craig Biggio Bat/600	15.00	4.50
5 Barry Bonds Jsy/1000	30.00	9.00
6 Sean Casey Jsy/800	10.00	3.00
7 Eric Chavez Jsy/1000	10.00	3.00
8 Roger Clemens Jsy/1000	25.00	7.50
9 J.Damon Sox Bat/700	15.00	4.50
10 Carlos Delgado Jsy/750	10.00	3.00
11 J.D. Drew Jsy/1000	10.00	3.00
12 Darin Erstad Jsy/850	10.00	3.00
13 N.Garciaparra Jsy/750	20.00	6.00
14 Juan Gonzalez Bat/1000	15.00	4.50
15 Todd Helton Jsy/925	15.00	4.50
16 Tim Hudson Jsy/825	10.00	3.00
17 D.Jeter Pants/1000	30.00	9.00
18 Randy Johnson Jsy/1000	15.00	4.50
19 A.Jones Jsy/1000	10.00	3.00
20 Jason Kendall Jsy/1000	10.00	3.00
21 Paul LoDuca Jsy/1000	10.00	3.00
22 Greg Maddux Jsy/875	15.00	4.50
23 Pedro Martinez Jsy/775	15.00	4.50
24 Raul Mondesi Bat/575	10.00	3.00
25 M.Ordonez Jsy/575	10.00	3.00
26 Mike Piazza Jsy/950	15.00	4.50
27 Mike Piazza Pants/1000	15.00	4.50
28 M.Ramirez Jsy/1000	15.00	4.50
29 Mariano Rivera Jsy/725	15.00	4.50
30 Alex Rodriguez Jsy/850	20.00	6.00
31 I.Rodriguez Jsy/1000	15.00	4.50
32 Scott Rolen Jsy/120	15.00	4.50
33 K.Sasaki Jsy/1000	10.00	3.00
34 Curt Schilling Jsy/1000	10.00	3.00
35 Gary Sheffield Bat/775	10.00	3.00
36 Gary Sheffield Jsy/800	10.00	3.00
37 Frank Thomas Jsy/850	15.00	4.50
38 Jim Thome Bat/750	15.00	4.50
39 Omar Vizquel Jsy/1000	15.00	4.50

2002 Fleer Platinum Clubhouse Memorabilia Combos

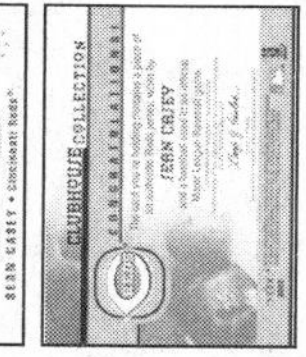

Inserted at a stated rate of one in 96 hobby packs and one in 192 retail packs, these 39 cards parallel the Clubhouse Memorabilia set. These cards can be differentiated by their having two distinct pieces of game-used memorabilia attached to the front. Since these cards have distinct press runs, we have notated that information in our checklist.

	Nm-Mt	Ex-Mt
1 Edgardo Alfonzo Ball-Jsy/125	15.00	4.50
2 Rick Ankiel Bat-Jsy/200	15.00	4.50
3 Adrian Beltre Ball-Jsy/125	25.00	7.50
4 Craig Biggio Jsy-Bat/50		
5 Barry Bonds Glove-Jsy/275	50.00	15.00
6 Sean Casey Ball-Jsy/125	15.00	4.50
7 Eric Chavez Base-Jsy/325	15.00	4.50
8 Roger Clemens Base-Jsy/325	40.00	12.00
9 J.Damon Sox Base-Bat/175	25.00	7.50
10 Carlos Delgado Bat-Jsy/325	15.00	4.50
11 J.D. Drew Ball-Jsy/125	15.00	4.50
12 Darin Erstad Bat-Jsy/125	15.00	4.50
13 N.Garciaparra Base-Jsy/275	40.00	12.00
14 Juan Gonzalez Jsy-Bat/75	25.00	7.50
15 Todd Helton Jsy-Bat/35		
16 Tim Hudson Bat-Jsy/200	15.00	4.50
17 D.Jeter Btg Glv-Pants/200	50.00	15.00
18 Randy Johnson Bat-Jsy/125	25.00	7.50
19 And Jones Btg Glv-Jsy/100	15.00	4.50
20 Jason Kendall Bat-Jsy/50		
21 Paul LoDuca Ball-Jsy/125	15.00	4.50
22 Greg Maddux Ball-Jsy/275	25.00	7.50
23 Pedro Martinez Base-Jsy/300	25.00	7.50
24 Raul Mondesi Bat-Btg Glv/75		
25 M.Ordonez Bat-Jsy/325	15.00	4.50
26 Mike Piazza Ball-Jsy/125	40.00	12.00
27 Mike Piazza Bat-Pants/125	40.00	12.00
28 M.Ramirez Base-Jsy/350	25.00	7.50
29 Mariano Rivera Base-Jsy/175	25.00	7.50
30 Alex Rodriguez Base-Jsy/300	30.00	9.00
31 I.Rodriguez Btg Glv-Glv/100	25.00	7.50
32 Scott Rolen Ball-Jsy/125	25.00	7.50
33 K.Sasaki Base-Jsy/350	15.00	4.50
34 Curt Schilling Ball-Jsy/125	15.00	4.50
35 Gary Sheffield Ball-Bat/125	15.00	4.50
36 Gary Sheffield Ball-Jsy/125	15.00	4.50
37 Frank Thomas Base-Jsy/275	25.00	7.50
38 Jim Thome Base-Bat/275	25.00	7.50
39 Omar Vizquel Base-Jsy/300	25.00	7.50

2002 Fleer Platinum Cornerstones

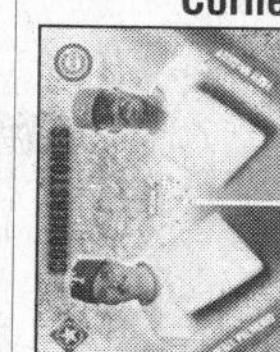

These cards were distributed in jumbo packs (1:12), rack packs (1:6) and retail packs (1:20). Each card features two prominent active and retired ballplayers paired up in a horizontal design with an image of a base floating in front of them. The cards are identical in design to the hobby-only Cornerstones Numbered except these cards lack serial-numbering, feature the word "Cornerstones" in brown lettering on front (the hobby-only versions are serial-numbered on back and feature white lettering for the "Cornerstones" moniker on front and oddly enough are entirely devoid of any checklist card number on back. The cards have been checklisted in our database using the same order as the hobby Cornerstones set.

	Nm-Mt	Ex-Mt
COMPLETE SET (40)	200.00	60.00
1 Bill Terry Johnny Mize	3.00	.90
2 Cal Ripken Eddie Murray	15.00	4.50
3 Eddie Mathews Chipper Jones	5.00	1.50
4 Albert Pujols George Sisler	10.00	3.00
5 Sean Casey Tony Perez	3.00	.90
6 Jimmie Foxx Scott Rolen	5.00	1.50
7 Wade Boggs George Brett	12.00	3.60
8 Rod Carew Troy Glaus	3.00	.90
9 Jeff Bagwell Rafael Palmeiro	3.00	.90
10 Willie Stargell Pie Traynor	3.00	.90
11 Cal Ripken Brooks Robinson	15.00	4.50
12 Tony Perez Ted Kluszewski	3.00	.90
13 Jason Giambi Don Mattingly	10.00	3.00
14 Hank Greenberg Jimmie Foxx	5.00	1.50
15 Ernie Banks Willie McCovey	5.00	1.50
16 Jim Thome Travis Fryman	5.00	1.50
17 Ted Kluszewski Sean Casey	3.00	.90
18 Gil Hodges Johnny Mize	5.00	1.50
19 Brooks Robinson Boog Powell	3.00	.90
20 Bill Terry George Sisler	3.00	.90
21 Wade Boggs Don Mattingly	12.00	3.60
22 Jason Giambi Yankees Carlos Delgado	3.00	.90
23 Willie Stargell Bill Madlock	3.00	.90
24 Mark Grace Matt Williams	3.00	.90
25 Paul Molitor George Brett	12.00	3.60
26 Carlos Delgado Mo Vaughn	3.00	.90
27 Bill Terry Willie McCovey	3.00	.90
28 Mike Sweeney George Brett	12.00	3.60
29 Eddie Mathews Ernie Banks	5.00	1.50
30 Eric Karros Gil Hodges	5.00	1.50
31 Paul Molitor Don Mattingly	12.00	3.60
32 Brooks Robinson Rod Carew	3.00	.90
33 Chipper Jones Albert Pujols	10.00	3.00
34 Harry Heilmann Hank Greenberg	5.00	1.50
35 Frank Thomas Carlos Delgado	5.00	1.50
36 Jeff Bagwell Todd Helton	3.00	.90
37 Rafael Palmeiro Fred McGriff	3.00	.90
38 Cal Ripken Wade Boggs	15.00	4.50
39 Orlando Cepeda Willie McCovey	3.00	.90
40 John Olerud Mark Grace	3.00	.90

2002 Fleer Platinum Cornerstones Memorabilia

Randomly inserted into packs, this 22-card set is a partial parallel of the Cornerstones insert set. These cards have two pieces of memorabilia and all have stated print runs of 25 serial numbered sets. Due to market scarcity, no pricing is provided for this set.

Nm-Mt Ex-Mt
1 Bill Terry Bat
Johnny Mize Bat
2 Cal Ripken Jsy
Eddie Murray Jsy

3 Eddie Mathews Bat
Chipper Jones Jsy
5 Sean Casey Jsy
Tony Perez Bat
6 Jimmie Foxx Bat
Scott Rolen Jsy
7 Wade Boggs Jsy
George Brett Jsy
9 Jeff Bagwell Bat
Rafael Palmeiro Jsy
11 Cal Ripken Jsy
Brooks Robinson Bat
12 Tony Perez Bat
Ted Kluszewski Jsy
14 Hank Greenberg Bat
Jimmie Foxx Bat
16 Jim Thome Bat
Travis Fryman Bat
17 Ted Kluszewski Jsy
Sean Casey Jsy
21 Wade Boggs Jsy
Don Mattingly Jsy
25 Paul Molitor Jsy
George Brett Jsy
27 Bill Terry Bat
Willie McCovey Jsy
28 Mike Sweeney Bat
George Brett Jsy
31 Paul Molitor Jsy
Don Mattingly Jsy
35 Frank Thomas Jsy
Carlos Delgado Jsy
36 Jeff Bagwell Bat
Todd Helton Jsy
38 Cal Ripken Jsy
Wade Boggs Jsy
39 Orlando Cepeda Jsy
Willie McCovey Jsy
40 John Olerud Jsy
Mark Grace Jsy

2002 Fleer Platinum Cornerstones Numbered

Randomly inserted into hobby packs, these 40 cards have different print runs depending on which group of cards they belong to. Cards numbered 1-10 were printed to a stated print run of 250 serial numbered sets while cards numbered 11-20 have a stated print run of 500 sets. Cards numbered 21-30 have a stated print run of 1000 sets and cards numbered 31-40 have a stated print run of 2000 sets. Other than Harry Heilmann, most of the players played a significant part of their career at either first or third base.

	Nm-Mt	Ex-Mt
COMMON CARD (1-10)	15.00	4.50
COMMON CARD (11-20)	10.00	3.00
COMMON CARD (21-30)	8.00	2.40
COMMON CARD (31-40)	5.00	1.50
1 Bill Terry Johnny Mize	15.00	4.50
2 Cal Ripken Eddie Murray	40.00	12.00
3 Eddie Mathews Chipper Jones	15.00	4.50
4 Albert Pujols George Sisler	25.00	7.50
5 Sean Casey Tony Perez	15.00	4.50
6 Jimmie Foxx Scott Rolen	15.00	4.50
7 Wade Boggs George Brett	30.00	9.00
8 Rod Carew Troy Glaus	15.00	4.50
9 Jeff Bagwell Rafael Palmeiro	15.00	4.50
10 Willie Stargell Pie Traynor	15.00	4.50
11 Cal Ripken Brooks Robinson	30.00	9.00
12 Tony Perez Ted Kluszewski	10.00	3.00
13 Jason Giambi Don Mattingly	30.00	9.00
14 Hank Greenberg Jimmie Foxx	10.00	3.00
15 Ernie Banks Willie McCovey	10.00	3.00
16 Jim Thome Travis Fryman	10.00	3.00
17 Ted Kluszewski Sean Casey	10.00	3.00
18 Gil Hodges Johnny Mize	10.00	3.00
19 Brooks Robinson Boog Powell	10.00	3.00
20 Bill Terry George Sisler	10.00	3.00
21 Wade Boggs Don Mattingly	20.00	6.00
22 Jason Giambi Yankees Carlos Delgado	8.00	2.40
23 Willie Stargell Bill Madlock	8.00	2.40
24 Mark Grace Matt Williams	8.00	2.40
25 Paul Molitor George Brett	15.00	4.50
26 Carlos Delgado Mo Vaughn	8.00	2.40
27 Bill Terry Willie McCovey	8.00	2.40
28 Mike Sweeney	15.00	4.50

George Brett
29 Eddie Mathews 8.00 2.40
Ernie Banks
30 Eric Karros 8.00 2.40
Gil Hodges
31 Paul Molitor 12.00 3.60
Don Mattingly
32 Brooks Robinson 5.00 1.50
Rod Carew
33 Chipper Jones 10.00 3.00
Albert Pujols
34 Harry Heilmann 5.00 1.50
Hank Greenberg
35 Frank Thomas 5.00 1.50
Carlos Delgado
36 Jeff Bagwell 5.00 1.50
Todd Helton
37 Rafael Palmeiro 5.00 1.50
Fred McGriff
38 Cal Ripken 15.00 4.50
Wade Boggs
39 Orlando Cepeda 5.00 1.50
Willie McCovey
40 John Olerud 5.00 1.50
Mark Grace

2002 Fleer Platinum Fence Busters

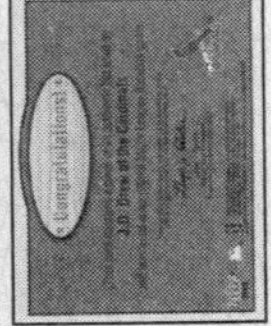

Randomly inserted into rack packs, these 22 cards feature some of the leading hitters in the game. We have provided the stated print runs for these cards in our checklist. The Jeff Bagwell card was not ready when Fleer went to press with this set and that card could be redeemed until April 30th, 2003.

	Nm-Mt	Ex-Mt
1 Roberto Alomar/800	10.00	3.00
2 Moises Alou/800	8.00	2.40
3 Jeff Bagwell/400	10.00	3.00
4 Barry Bonds/700	25.00	7.50
5 J.D. Drew/800	8.00	2.40
6 Jim Edmonds/500	8.00	2.40
7 Brian Giles/700	8.00	2.40
8 Luis Gonzalez/625	8.00	2.40
9 Shawn Green/800	8.00	2.40
10 Todd Helton/675	10.00	3.00
11 Derek Jeter/400	25.00	7.50
12 Andruw Jones/800	8.00	2.40
13 Chipper Jones/800	10.00	3.00
14 Tino Martinez/800	10.00	3.00
15 Rafael Palmeiro/800	10.00	3.00
16 Mike Piazza/800	15.00	4.50
17 Manny Ramirez/800	10.00	3.00
18 Alex Rodriguez/675	15.00	4.50
19 Miguel Tejada/700	8.00	2.40
20 Frank Thomas/800	10.00	3.00
21 Jim Thome/800	10.00	3.00
22 Larry Walker/750	10.00	3.00

2002 Fleer Platinum Fence Busters Autographs

Randomly inserted into rack packs, these four cards feature signed copies of the Fence Busters insert set. These cards were all serial numbered to the selected player's 2001 home run total. All of these cards were issued as exchange cards and could be redeemed until April 30th, 2003.

	Nm-Mt	Ex-Mt
1 Jeff Bagwell/39		
2 Barry Bonds/73	500.00	150.00
3 Derek Jeter/21		
4 Miguel Tejada/31		

2002 Fleer Platinum National Patch Time

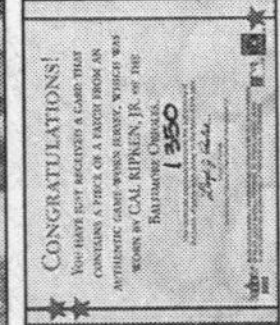

Inserted at stated odds at one in 12 jumbo packs, these 19 cards feature the selected player as well as game-worn jersey patch swatch of the featured player. The stated print runs for the players are listed next to their name in our checklist.

	Nm-Mt	Ex-Mt
1 Barry Bonds/75	120.00	36.00
2 Pat Burrell/285	40.00	12.00
3 Jose Canseco/150	60.00	18.00
4 Carlos Delgado/70	50.00	15.00
5 J.D. Drew/210	40.00	12.00
6 Adam Dunn/75	50.00	15.00
7 Darin Erstad/315	40.00	12.00
8 Juan Gonzalez/50	60.00	18.00
9 Todd Helton/110	50.00	15.00
10 Derek Jeter/65	120.00	36.00
11 Greg Maddux/775	40.00	12.00
12 Pedro Martinez/45	80.00	24.00
13 Magglio Ordonez/85	50.00	15.00
14 Manny Ramirez/100	50.00	15.00
15 Cal Ripken/350	100.00	30.00
16 Alex Rodriguez/325	60.00	18.00
17 Ivan Rodriguez/225	50.00	15.00
18 Kazuhiro Sasaki/310	40.00	12.00
19 Miguel Tejada/55	50.00	15.00

2002 Fleer Platinum Wheelhouse

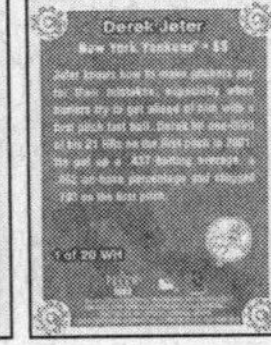

Inserted at stated odds of one in 12 hobby and one in 20 retail, these 20 cards feature some of the leading hitters in baseball.

	Nm-Mt	Ex-Mt
COMPLETE SET (20)	80.00	24.00
1 Derek Jeter	8.00	2.40
2 Barry Bonds	8.00	2.40
3 Luis Gonzalez	3.00	.90
4 Jason Giambi	3.00	.90
5 Ivan Rodriguez	3.00	.90
6 Mike Piazza	5.00	1.50
7 Troy Glaus	3.00	.90
8 Nomar Garciaparra	5.00	1.50
9 Juan Gonzalez	3.00	.90
10 Sammy Sosa	5.00	1.50
11 Albert Pujols	6.00	1.80
12 Ken Griffey Jr.	5.00	1.50
13 Scott Rolen	3.00	.90
14 Jeff Bagwell	3.00	.90
15 Ichiro Suzuki	5.00	1.50
16 Todd Helton	3.00	.90
17 Chipper Jones	3.00	.90
18 Alex Rodriguez	5.00	1.50
19 Vladimir Guerrero	3.00	.90
20 Manny Ramirez	3.00	.90

2003 Fleer Platinum

This 250 card set was release in February, 2003. These cards were issued in a variety of manners. Each box contained 14 wax packs as well as 4 jumbo packs and one rack pack. The wax packs had an SRP of $3, while the jumbos had an SRP of $5 amd the rack packs had an SRP of $10. There are several subsets in the product. Cards numbered 201 through 220 feature Unsung Heroes. Cards numbered 221 through 250 are prospects but those cards were issued in different ratios throughout the set.

	Nm-Mt	Ex-Mt
COMP.SET w/o SP's (220)	25.00	7.50
COMMON CARD (1-220)	.30	.09
COMMON CARD (221-235)	2.00	.60
221-235 ODDS 1:4 WAX, 1:2 JUM, 1:1 RACK		
COMMON CARD (236-240)	2.00	.60
236-240 ODDS 1:12 WAX		
COMMON CARD (241-245)	3.00	.90
241-245 ODDS 1:6 JUMBO		
COMMON CARD (246-250)	3.00	.90
246-250 ODDS 1:2 RACK		
1 Barry Bonds	2.00	.60
2 Sean Casey	.30	.09
3 Todd Walker	.30	.09
4 Tony Batista	.30	.09
5 Todd Zeile	.30	.09
6 Ruben Sierra	.30	.09
7 Jose Cruz Jr.	.30	.09
8 Ben Grieve	.30	.09
9 Rob Mackowiak	.30	.09
10 Gary Sheffield	.30	.09
11 Armando Benitez	.30	.09
12 Tim Hudson	.30	.09
13 Eric Milton	.30	.09
14 Andy Pettitte	.50	.15
15 Jeff Bagwell	.50	.15
16 Jeff Kent	.30	.09
17 Joe Randa	.30	.09
18 Benito Santiago	.30	.09
19 Russell Branyan	.30	.09
20 Cliff Floyd	.30	.09
21 Chris Richard	.30	.09
22 Randy Winn	.30	.09
23 Freddy Garcia	.30	.09
24 Derek Lowe	.30	.09
25 Ben Sheets	.30	.09
26 Fred McGriff	.50	.15
27 Bret Boone	.30	.09
28 Jose Hernandez	.30	.09
29 Phil Nevin	.30	.09
30 Mike Piazza	1.25	.35
31 Bobby Abreu	.30	.09
32 Darin Erstad	.30	.09
33 Andruw Jones	.30	.09
34 Brad Wilkerson	.30	.09
35 Brian Lawrence	.30	.09
36 Vladimir Nunez	.30	.09
37 Kazuhiro Sasaki	.30	.09
38 Carlos Delgado	.30	.09
39 Steve Cox	.30	.09
40 Adrian Beltre	.50	.15
41 Josh Bard	.30	.09
42 Randall Simon	.30	.09
43 Johnny Damon	.75	.23
44 Ken Griffey Jr.	1.25	.35
45 Sammy Sosa	1.25	.35
46 Kevin Brown	.30	.09
47 Kazuhisa Ishii	.30	.09
48 Matt Morris	.30	.09
49 Mark Prior	.75	.23
50 Kip Wells	.30	.09
51 Hee Seop Choi	.30	.09
52 Craig Biggio	.50	.15
53 Derek Jeter	2.00	.60
54 Albert Pujols	1.50	.45
55 Joe Borchard	.30	.09
56 Robert Fick	.30	.09
57 Jacque Jones	.30	.09
58 Juan Pierre	.30	.09
59 Bernie Williams	.50	.15
60 Elmer Dessens	.30	.09
61 Al Leiter	.30	.09
62 Curt Schilling	.30	.09
63 Carlos Pena	.30	.09
64 Tino Martinez	.50	.15
65 Fernando Vina	.30	.09
66 Aaron Boone	.30	.09
67 Michael Barrett	.30	.09
68 Frank Thomas	.75	.23
69 J.D. Drew	.30	.09
70 Vladimir Guerrero	.75	.23
71 Shannon Stewart	.30	.09
72 Mark Buehrle	.30	.09
73 Jamie Moyer	.30	.09
74 Brad Radke	.30	.09
75 Mike Williams	.30	.09
76 Ryan Klesko	.30	.09
77 Roberto Alomar	.50	.15
78 Edgardo Alfonzo	.30	.09
79 Matt Williams	.30	.09
80 Edgar Martinez	.50	.15
81 Shawn Green	.30	.09
82 Kenny Lofton	.30	.09
83 Josh Beckett	.30	.09
84 Trevor Hoffman	.30	.09
85 Kevin Millwood	.30	.09
86 Odalis Perez	.30	.09
87 Jarrod Washburn	.30	.09
88 Jason Giambi	.30	.09
89 Eric Young	.30	.09
90 Barry Larkin	.50	.15
91 Aramis Ramirez	.30	.09
92 Ivan Rodriguez	.75	.23
93 Steve Finley	.30	.09
94 Brian Jordan	.30	.09
95 Manny Ramirez	.50	.15
96 Preston Wilson	.30	.09
97 Rodrigo Lopez	.30	.09
98 Ramon Ortiz	.30	.09
99 Jim Thome	.75	.23
100 Luis Castillo	.30	.09
101 Alex Rodriguez	1.25	.35
102 Jared Sandberg	.30	.09
103 Ellis Burks	.30	.09
104 Pat Burrell	.30	.09
105 Brian Giles	.30	.09
106 Mark Kotsay	.30	.09
107 Dave Roberts	.30	.09
108 Roy Halladay	.30	.09
109 Chan Ho Park	.30	.09
110 Erubiel Durazo	.30	.09
111 Bobby Hill	.30	.09
112 Cristian Guzman	.30	.09
113 Troy Glaus	.30	.09
114 Lance Berkman	.30	.09
115 Juan Encarnacion	.30	.09
116 Chipper Jones	.75	.23
117 Corey Patterson	.30	.09
118 Vernon Wells	.30	.09
119 Matt Clement	.30	.09
120 Billy Koch	.30	.09
121 Hideo Nomo	.75	.23
122 Derrek Lee	.30	.09
123 Todd Helton	.50	.15
124 Sean Burroughs	.30	.09
125 Jason Kendall	.30	.09
126 Dmitri Young	.30	.09
127 Adam Dunn	.50	.15
128 Bobby Higginson	.30	.09
129 Raul Mondesi	.30	.09
130 Bubba Trammell	.30	.09
131 A.J. Burnett	.30	.09
132 Randy Johnson	.75	.23
133 Mark Mulder	.30	.09
134 Mariano Rivera	.50	.15
135 Kerry Wood	.75	.23
136 Mo Vaughn	.30	.09
137 Jimmy Rollins	.30	.09
138 Jose Valentin	.30	.09
139 Brad Fullmer	.30	.09
140 Mike Cameron	.30	.09
141 Luis Gonzalez	.30	.09
142 Kevin Appier	.30	.09
143 Mike Hampton	.30	.09
144 Pedro Martinez	.75	.23
145 Javier Vazquez	.30	.09
146 Doug Mientkiewicz	.30	.09
147 Adam Kennedy	.30	.09
148 Rafael Furcal	.30	.09
149 Eric Chavez	.30	.09
150 Mike Lieberthal	.30	.09
151 Moises Alou	.30	.09
152 Jermaine Dye	.30	.09
153 Torii Hunter	.30	.09
154 Trot Nixon	.30	.09
155 Larry Walker	.50	.15
156 Jorge Julio	.30	.09
157 Mike Mussina	.50	.15
158 Kirk Rueter	.30	.09
159 Rafael Palmeiro	.50	.15
160 Pokey Reese	.30	.09
161 Miguel Tejada	.30	.09
162 Robin Ventura	.30	.09
163 Raul Ibanez	.30	.09
164 Roger Cedeno	.30	.09
165 Juan Gonzalez	.50	.15
166 Carlos Lee	.30	.09
167 Tim Salmon	.50	.15
168 Orlando Hernandez	.30	.09
169 Wade Miller	.30	.09
170 Troy Percival	.30	.09
171 Billy Wagner	.30	.09
172 Jeff Conine	.30	.09
173 Junior Spivey	.30	.09
174 Edgar Renteria	.30	.09
175 Scott Rolen	.75	.23
176 Jason Varitek	.50	.15
177 Ben Broussard	.30	.09
178 Jeremy Giambi	.30	.09
179 Gabe Kapler	.30	.09
180 Armando Rios	.30	.09
181 Ichiro Suzuki	1.25	.35
182 Tom Glavine	.50	.15
183 Greg Maddux	1.25	.35
184 Roy Oswalt	.30	.09
185 John Smoltz	.50	.15
186 Eric Karros	.30	.09
187 Alfonso Soriano	.50	.15
188 Nomar Garciaparra	1.25	.35
189 Joe Crede	.30	.09
190 Javy Lopez	.30	.09
191 Carlos Beltran	.50	.15
192 Jim Edmonds	.30	.09
193 Geoff Jenkins	.30	.09
194 Magglio Ordonez	.30	.09
195 Daryle Ward	.30	.09
196 Roger Clemens	1.50	.45
197 Byung-Hyun Kim	.30	.09
198 Robb Nen	.30	.09
199 C.C. Sabathia	.30	.09
200 Barry Zito	.30	.09
201 Mark Grace UH	.30	.09
202 Paul Konerko UH	.30	.09
203 Mike Sweeney UH	.30	.09
204 John Olerud UH	.30	.09
205 Jose Vidro UH	.30	.09
206 Ray Durham UH	.30	.09
207 Omar Vizquel UH	.30	.09
208 Shea Hillenbrand UH	.30	.09
209 Mike Lowell UH	.30	.09
210 Aubrey Huff UH	.30	.09
211 Eric Hinske UH	.30	.09
212 Paul Lo Duca UH	.30	.09
213 Jay Gibbons UH	.30	.09
214 Austin Kearns UH	.30	.09
215 Richie Sexson UH	.30	.09
216 Garret Anderson UH	.30	.09
217 Eric Gagne UH	.75	.23
218 Jason Jennings UH	.30	.09
219 Damian Moss UH	.30	.09
220 David Eckstein UH	.30	.09
221 Mark Teixeira PROS	2.00	.60
222 Bill Hall PROS	2.00	.60
223 Bobby Jenks PROS	2.00	.60
224 Adam Morrissey PROS	2.00	.60
225 Rodrigo Rosario PROS	2.00	.60
226 Brett Myers PROS	2.00	.60
227 Tony Alvarez PROS	2.00	.60
228 Willie Bloomquist PROS	2.00	.60
229 Ben Howard PROS	2.00	.60
230 Nic Jackson PROS	2.00	.60
231 Carl Crawford PROS	2.00	.60
232 Omar Infante PROS	2.00	.60
233 Francisco Rodriguez PROS	2.00	.60
234 Andy Van Hekken PROS	2.00	.60
235 Kirk Saarloos PROS	2.00	.60
236 Dusty Wathan PROS RC	2.00	.60
237 Jamey Carroll PROS	2.00	.60
238 Jason Phillips PROS	2.00	.60
239 Jose Castillo PROS	2.00	.60
240 Arnaldo Munoz PROS RC	2.00	.60
241 Orlando Hudson PROS	3.00	.90
242 Drew Henson PROS	3.00	.90
243 Jason Lane PROS	3.00	.90
244 Vinny Chulk PROS	3.00	.90
245 Prentice Redman PROS RC	3.00	.90
246 Marlon Byrd PROS	3.00	.90
247 Chin-Feng Chen PROS	3.00	.90
248 Craig Brazell PROS RC	5.00	1.50
249 John Webb PROS	3.00	.90
250 Adam LaRoche PROS	3.00	.90

2003 Fleer Platinum Finish

Randomly inserted in packs, this is a parallel to the Fleer Platinum set. These cards with a "finished" type front were issued to a stated print run of 100 serial numbered sets.

	Nm-Mt	Ex-Mt
*FINISH 1-220: 3X TO 8X BASIC		
*FINISH 221-235: 1X TO 2.5X BASIC		
*FINISH 236-240: 1X TO 2.5X BASIC		
*FINISH 241-245: .6X TO 1.5X BASIC		
*FINISH 2446-250: .6X TO 1.5X BASIC		

2003 Fleer Platinum Barry Bonds Chasing History Game Used

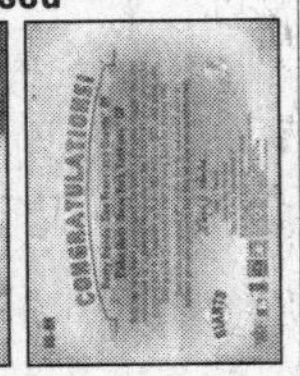

Randomly inserted in packs, these five cards feature game used swatches from both Barry Bonds and various retired players whose records he was chasing. The cards with two game-worn swatches were issued to a stated print run of 250 serial numbered sets while the five player card was issued to a stated print run of 25 serial numbered sets.

	Nm-Mt	Ex-Mt
BB Barry Bonds Bobby Bonds	40.00	12.00
BR Barry Bonds Babe Ruth	250.00	75.00
RM Barry Bonds Roger Maris	80.00	24.00
WM Barry Bonds Willie McCovey	40.00	12.00
CH Barry Bonds Bobby Bonds Roger Maris Willie McCovey Babe Ruth		

2003 Fleer Platinum Guts and Glory

Inserted at a stated rate of one in four wax packs, one in two jumbo and one per rack pack, this 20 card set features some of the leading players in baseball.

	Nm-Mt	Ex-Mt
COMPLETE SET (20)	25.00	7.50
1 Jason Giambi	1.00	.30
2 Alfonso Soriano	1.00	.30
3 Scott Rolen	1.25	.35
4 Ivan Rodriguez	1.25	.35
5 Barry Bonds	3.00	.90
6 Jim Edmonds	1.00	.30
7 Darin Erstad	1.00	.30
8 Brian Giles	1.00	.30
9 Luis Gonzalez	1.00	.30
10 Adam Dunn	1.00	.30
11 Torii Hunter	1.00	.30
12 Andruw Jones	1.00	.30
13 Sammy Sosa	2.00	.60
14 Ichiro Suzuki	2.00	.60
15 Miguel Tejada	1.00	.30
16 Roger Clemens	2.50	.75
17 Curt Schilling	1.00	.30
18 Nomar Garciaparra	2.00	.60
19 Derek Jeter	3.00	.90
20 Alex Rodriguez	2.00	.60

2003 Fleer Platinum Heart of the Order

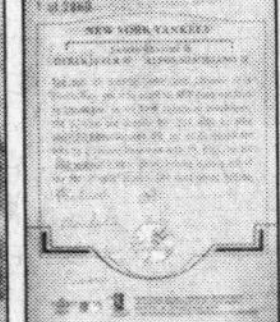

Inserted in packs at a rate of one in 12 wax, one in six jumbo and one in three rack, these cards feature three players who are the key offensive weapons for their teams.

	Nm-Mt	Ex-Mt
1 Jason Giambi Derek Jeter Alfonso Soriano	4.00	1.20
2 Todd Helton Preston Wilson Larry Walker	2.00	.60
3 Rafael Palmeiro Alex Rodriguez Ivan Rodriguez	3.00	.90
4 Adam Dunn Ken Griffey Jr. Austin Kearns	3.00	.90
5 Jeff Bagwell Craig Biggio Lance Berkman	2.00	.60
6 Eric Chavez Miguel Tejada Jermaine Dye	2.00	.60
7 Troy Glaus Garrett Anderson Darin Erstad	2.00	.60
8 Mike Piazza Mo Vaughn Roberto Alomar	3.00	.90
9 Torii Hunter Jacque Jones Corey Koskie	2.00	.60
10 Barry Bonds Jeff Kent Rich Aurilia	5.00	1.50
11 Pat Burrell Bobby Abreu Jimmy Rollins	2.00	.60
12 Shawn Green Adrian Beltre Paul Lo Duca	2.00	.60
13 Vladimir Guerrero Brad Wilkerson Jose Vidro	2.00	.60
14 Chipper Jones Andruw Jones Gary Sheffield	2.00	.60
15 Ichiro Suzuki Bret Boone Edgar Martinez	3.00	.90
16 Albert Pujols Scott Rolen J.D. Drew	4.00	1.20
17 Sammy Sosa Fred McGriff Moises Alou	3.00	.90
18 Nomar Garciaparra Shea Hillenbrand Manny Ramirez	3.00	.90
19 Frank Thomas Magglio Ordonez Paul Konerko	2.00	.60
20 Jason Kendall	2.00	.60

Brian Giles
Amaris Ramirez

2003 Fleer Platinum Heart of the Order Game Used

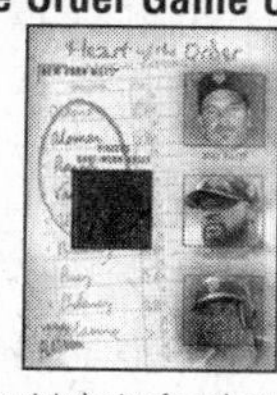

Inserted at a stated rate of one in two rack packs, this is a partial parallel to the Heart of the Order set. These cards feature a game-used memorabilia piece form one of the players on the card along with photos of the other two players. Each of these cards was issued to a stated print run of 400 serial numbered sets.

Nm-Mt Ex-Mt
AB Adrian Beltre Jsy 10.00 3.00
Shawn Green
Paul Lo Duca
AK Austin Kearns Pants 8.00 2.40
Adam Dunn
Ken Griffey Jr.
AS Alfonso Soriano Bat 10.00 3.00
Jason Giambi
Derek Jeter
BB Bret Boone Jsy 8.00 2.40
Edgar Martinez
Ichiro Suzuki
BG Brian Giles Bat 8.00 2.40
Jason Kendall
Aramis Ramirez
CJ Chipper Jones Jsy 15.00 4.50
Andruw Jones
Gary Sheffield
DE Darin Erstad Jsy 8.00 2.40
Garret Anderson
Troy Glaus
FT Frank Thomas Jsy 15.00 4.50
Paul Konerko
Magglio Ordonez
JD J.D. Drew Jsy 8.00 2.40
Albert Pujols
Scott Rolen
JK Jeff Kent Jsy 8.00 2.40
Rich Aurilia
Barry Bonds
JR Jimmy Rollins Jsy 8.00 2.40
Bob Abreu
Pat Burrell
JV Jose Vidro Jsy 8.00 2.40
Vladimir Guerrero
Brad Wilkerson
LB Lance Berkman Bat 8.00 2.40
Jeff Bagwell
Craig Biggio
MP Mike Piazza Jsy 15.00 4.50
Roberto Alomar
Mo Vaughn
MR Manny Ramirez Jsy 10.00 3.00
Nomar Garciaparra
Shea Hillenbrand
RP Rafael Palmeiro Jsy 10.00 3.00
Alex Rodriguez
Ivan Rodriguez
SS Sammy Sosa Jsy 15.00 4.50
Moises Alou
Fred McGriff
TH Todd Helton Jsy 10.00 3.00
Larry Walker
Preston Wilson

2003 Fleer Platinum MLB Scouting Report

Randomly inserted in packs, this 32 card set features information about the noted player. Each card has some scouting type information to go with some hitting charts. These cards were issued to a stated print run of 400 serial numbered sets.

Nm-Mt Ex-Mt
1 Jason Giambi 4.00 1.20
2 Paul Konerko 4.00 1.20
3 Jim Thome 4.00 1.20
4 Alfonso Soriano 4.00 1.20
5 Troy Glaus 4.00 1.20
6 Eric Hinske 4.00 1.20
7 Paul Lo Duca 4.00 1.20
8 Mike Piazza 6.00 1.80
9 Marlon Byrd 4.00 1.20
10 Garret Anderson 4.00 1.20
11 Barry Bonds 10.00 3.00
12 Pat Burrell 4.00 1.20
13 Joe Crede 4.00 1.20
14 J.D. Drew 4.00 1.20
15 Ken Griffey Jr. 6.00 1.80
16 Vladimir Guerrero 4.00 1.20
17 Torii Hunter 4.00 1.20
18 Chipper Jones 4.00 1.20
19 Austin Kearns 4.00 1.20
20 Albert Pujols 8.00 2.40
21 Manny Ramirez 4.00 1.20
22 Gary Sheffield 4.00 1.20
23 Sammy Sosa 6.00 1.80
24 Ichiro Suzuki 6.00 1.80
25 Bernie Williams 4.00 1.20
26 Randy Johnson 4.00 1.20
27 Greg Maddux 6.00 1.80
28 Hideo Nomo 4.00 1.20
29 Nomar Garciaparra 6.00 1.80
30 Derek Jeter 10.00 3.00
31 Alex Rodriguez 6.00 1.80
32 Miguel Tejada 4.00 1.20

2003 Fleer Platinum MLB Scouting Report Game Used

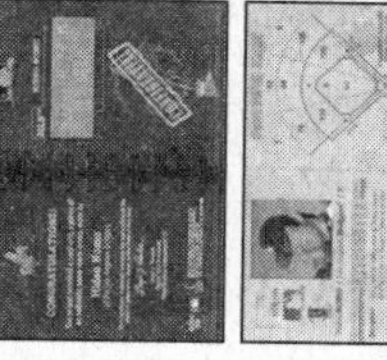

Randomly inserted in wax packs, this is a partial parallel to the Scouting Report insert set. These cards feature a game used piece to go with the scouting report information. These cards were issued to a stated print run of 250 serial numbered sets.

Nm-Mt Ex-Mt
3 Jim Thome Jsy 15.00 4.50
4 Alfonso Soriano Bat 15.00 4.50
8 Mike Piazza Jsy 15.00 4.50
11 Barry Bonds Jsy 25.00 7.50
14 J.D. Drew Jsy 10.00 3.00
18 Chipper Jones Jsy 15.00 4.50
19 Austin Kearns Pants 10.00 3.00
21 Manny Ramirez Jsy 15.00 4.50
23 Sammy Sosa Jsy 20.00 6.00
26 Randy Johnson Jsy 15.00 4.50
27 Greg Maddux Jsy 15.00 4.50
28 Hideo Nomo Jsy 30.00 9.00
30 Derek Jeter Jsy 25.00 7.50

2003 Fleer Platinum Nameplates

Inserted at a stated rate of one in eight jumbo packs, these 41 cards feature different amounts of the featured players. We have notated the print runs for the players in our checklist.

Nm-Mt Ex-Mt
AD Adam Dunn/117 25.00 7.50
AJ Andruw Jones/170 25.00 7.50
AR Alex Rodriguez/248 50.00 15.00
BB Barry Bonds/251 60.00 18.00
BL Barry Larkin/97 40.00 12.00
BZ Barry Zito/248 25.00 7.50
CB Craig Biggio/152 25.00 7.50
CC Chin-Feng Chen/110 120.00 36.00
CJ Chipper Jones/251 30.00 9.00
CK Corey Koskie/130 25.00 7.50
EH Eric Hinske/173 25.00 7.50
EM Edgar Martinez/176 25.00 7.50
FT Frank Thomas/58 50.00 15.00
FT Frank Thomas/93 50.00 15.00
GM Greg Maddux/248 40.00 12.00
HN Hideo Nomo/150
IR Ivan Rodriguez/189 40.00 12.00
JB Jeff Bagwell/121 40.00 12.00
JD Johnny Damon/35 80.00 24.00
JO John Olerud/180 25.00 7.50
JR Jimmy Rollins/74 25.00 7.50
JT Jim Thome/158 40.00 12.00
KI Kazuhisa Ishii/35 50.00 15.00
KS Kazuhiro Sasaki/82 25.00 7.50
KW Kerry Wood/49 80.00 24.00
LB Lance Berkman/176 25.00 7.50
LW Larry Walker/161 25.00 7.50
MP Mike Piazza/200 40.00 12.00
MP2 Mark Prior/123 40.00 12.00
MR Manny Ramirez/94 40.00 12.00
MS Mike Sweeney/175 25.00 7.50
MT Miguel Tejada/225 25.00 7.50
NG Nomar Garciaparra/258 40.00 12.00
PB Pat Burrell/176 25.00 7.50
PM Pedro Martinez/244 30.00 9.00
PN Phil Nevin/134
RC Roger Clemens/141 60.00 18.00
RJ Randy Johnson/142
RO Roy Oswalt/155 25.00 7.50
RP Rafael Palmeiro/245 25.00 7.50
RS Richie Sexson/160 25.00 7.50
VG Vladimir Guerrero/102 50.00 15.00

2003 Fleer Platinum Portraits

Inserted at a stated rate of one in 20 wax packs, one in 10 jumbo packs and one in five rack packs, these 20 cards feature painting like cards of the featured player.

Nm-Mt Ex-Mt
1 Josh Beckett 3.00 .90
2 Roberto Alomar 3.00 .90
3 Alfonso Soriano 3.00 .90
4 Mike Piazza 5.00 1.50
5 Ivan Rodriguez 3.00 .90
6 Edgar Martinez 3.00 .90
7 Barry Bonds 8.00 2.40
8 Adam Dunn 3.00 .90
9 Juan Gonzalez 3.00 .90
10 Chipper Jones 3.00 .90
11 Albert Pujols 6.00 1.80
12 Magglio Ordonez 3.00 .90
13 Shea Hillenbrand 3.00 .90
14 Larry Walker 3.00 .90
15 Pedro Martinez 3.00 .90
16 Kerry Wood 3.00 .90
17 Barry Zito 3.00 .90
18 Nomar Garciaparra 5.00 1.50
19 Derek Jeter 8.00 2.40
20 Alex Rodriguez 5.00 1.50

2003 Fleer Platinum Portraits Game Jersey

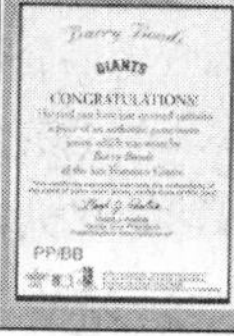

Inserted at a stated rate of one in 86 wax packs, this is a partial parallel to the Portraits insert set. These cards feature a game-worn jersey swatch on the front. The Derek Jeter card was issued in smaller quantity and we have notated that information in our data base.

Nm-Mt Ex-Mt
1 Josh Beckett 8.00 2.40
4 Mike Piazza 15.00 4.50
5 Ivan Rodriguez 10.00 3.00
7 Barry Bonds 20.00 6.00
8 Adam Dunn 10.00 3.00
10 Chipper Jones 10.00 3.00
15 Pedro Martinez 10.00 3.00
16 Kerry Wood 10.00 3.00
17 Barry Zito 8.00 2.40
18 Nomar Garciaparra 15.00 4.50
19 Derek Jeter SP/150 30.00 9.00

2003 Fleer Platinum Portraits Game Patch

Inserted at a stated rate of one in 86 wax packs, this is a partial parallel to the Portraits insert set. These cards feature a game-worn jersey swatch on the front. These cards were issued to a stated print run of 100 serial numbered sets.

Nm-Mt Ex-Mt
4 Mike Piazza 60.00 18.00
5 Ivan Rodriguez 40.00 12.00
7 Barry Bonds 60.00 18.00
8 Adam Dunn 40.00 12.00
10 Chipper Jones 40.00 12.00
15 Pedro Martinez 40.00 12.00
16 Kerry Wood 40.00 12.00
17 Barry Zito 40.00 12.00
18 Nomar Garciaparra 60.00 18.00
19 Derek Jeter

2004 Fleer Platinum

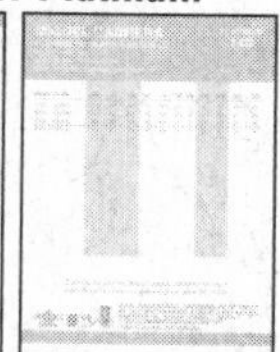

This 200-card set was released in February, 2004. The set was issued in seven-card packs with an $3 SRP which came 18 packs to a box and 16 boxes to a case. In addition, every hobby box had four jumbo packs included. Those jumbo packs had 20 cards in them. Plus rack packs were issued; those packs had 30 cards in each pack. Cards numbered 1-135 are major league veterans while cards numbered 136-143 were issued at a stated rate of one in three wax and one in 12 retail packs. Cards numbered 144-151 were issued at a stated rate of one per jumbo while cards 152 through 157 were issued exclusively in rack packs at a rate of one per and according to Fleer the stated print run of those cards was approximately 1000 cards. The set closes with the following subsets: UH (cards numbered 158 through 182 while cards numbered 183 through 200 feature multi-player prospect cards.

Nm-Mt Ex-Mt
COMP.SET w/o SP's (178) 25.00 7.50
COMMON (1-135/158-182) .30 .09
COMMON CARD (183-200) 1.00 .30
183-200 ARE NOT SHORT-PRINTS
COMMON CARD (136-143) 1.50 .45
136-143 ODDS 1:3 WAX, 1:12 RETAIL
COMMON CARD (144-151) 2.50 .75
144-151 ODDS ONE PER JUMBO
COMMON CARD (152-157) 8.00 2.40
152-157 ODDS ONE PER RACK PACK
152-157 STATED PRINT RUN APPX.1000 SETS
152-157 PRINT RUN PROVIDED BY FLEER
152-157 ARE NOT SERIAL-NUMBERED
1 Luis Castillo .30 .09
2 Preston Wilson .30 .09
3 Johan Santana .50 .15
4 Fred McGriff .50 .15
5 Albert Pujols 1.50 .45
6 Reggie Sanders .30 .09
7 Ivan Rodriguez .75 .23
8 Roy Halladay .30 .09
9 Brian Giles .30 .09
10 Bernie Williams .50 .15
11 Barry Larkin .50 .15
12 Marlon Anderson .30 .09
13 Ramon Ortiz .30 .09
14 Luis Matos .30 .09
15 Esteban Loaiza .30 .09
16 Orlando Cabrera .30 .09
17 Jamie Moyer .30 .09
18 Tino Martinez .50 .15
19 Josh Beckett .30 .09
20 Derek Jeter 1.50 .45
21 Derek Lowe .30 .09
22 Jack Wilson .30 .09
23 Bret Boone .30 .09
24 Matt Morris .30 .09
25 Javier Vazquez .30 .09
26 Joe Crede .30 .09
27 Jose Vidro .30 .09
28 Mike Piazza 1.25 .35
29 Curt Schilling .75 .23
30 Alex Rodriguez 1.25 .35
31 John Olerud .30 .09
32 Dontrelle Willis .30 .09
33 Larry Walker .50 .15
34 Joe Randa .30 .09
35 Paul Lo Duca .30 .09
36 Marlon Byrd .30 .09
37 Bo Hart .30 .09
38 Rafael Palmeiro .50 .15
39 Garret Anderson .30 .09
40 Tom Glavine .50 .15
41 Ichiro Suzuki 1.25 .35
42 Derrek Lee .30 .09
43 Lance Berkman .30 .09
44 Nomar Garciaparra 1.25 .35
45 Mike Sweeney .30 .09
46 A.J. Burnett .30 .09
47 Sean Casey .30 .09
48 Eric Gagne .75 .23
49 Joel Pineiro .30 .09
50 Russ Ortiz .30 .09
51 Placido Polanco .30 .09
52 Sammy Sosa 1.25 .35
53 Mark Teixeira .30 .09
54 Randy Wolf .30 .09
55 Vladimir Guerrero .75 .23
56 Tim Hudson .30 .09
57 Lew Ford .30 .09
58 Carlos Delgado .30 .09
59 Darin Erstad .30 .09
60 Mike Lieberthal .30 .09
61 Craig Biggio .50 .15
62 Ryan Klesko .30 .09
63 C.C. Sabathia .30 .09
64 Carlos Lee .30 .09
65 Al Leiter .30 .09
66 Brandon Webb .30 .09
67 Jacque Jones .30 .09
68 Kerry Wood .75 .23
69 Omar Vizquel .50 .15
70 Jeremy Bonderman .30 .09
71 Kevin Brown .30 .09
72 Richie Sexson .30 .09
73 Zach Day .30 .09
74 Mike Mussina .50 .15
75 Sidney Ponson .30 .09
76 Andruw Jones .30 .09
77 Woody Williams .30 .09
78 Kazuhiro Sasaki .30 .09
79 Matt Clement .30 .09
80 Shea Hillenbrand .30 .09
81 Bartolo Colon .30 .09
82 Ken Griffey Jr. 1.25 .35
83 Todd Helton .50 .15
84 Dmitri Young .30 .09
85 Richard Hidalgo .30 .09
86 Carlos Beltran .50 .15
87 Brad Wilkerson .30 .09
88 Andy Pettitte .50 .15
89 Miguel Tejada .30 .09
90 Edgar Martinez .50 .15
91 Vernon Wells .30 .09
92 Magglio Ordonez .30 .09
93 Tony Batista .30 .09
94 Jose Reyes .30 .09
95 Matt Stairs .30 .09
96 Manny Ramirez .50 .15
97 Carlos Pena .30 .09
98 A.J. Pierzynski .30 .09
99 Jim Thome .75 .23
100 Aubrey Huff .30 .09
101 Roberto Alomar .50 .15
102 Luis Gonzalez .30 .09
103 Chipper Jones .75 .23
104 Jay Gibbons .30 .09
105 Adam Dunn .50 .15
106 Jay Payton .30 .09
107 Scott Podsednik .30 .09
108 Roy Oswalt .30 .09
109 Milton Bradley .30 .09
110 Shawn Green .30 .09
111 Ryan Wagner .30 .09
112 Eric Chavez .30 .09
113 Pat Burrell .30 .09
114 Frank Thomas .75 .23
115 Jason Kendall .30 .09
116 Jake Peavy .30 .09
117 Mike Cameron .30 .09
118 Jim Edmonds .30 .09
119 Hank Blalock .30 .09
120 Troy Glaus .30 .09
121 Jeff Kent .30 .09
122 Jason Schmidt .30 .09
123 Corey Patterson .30 .09
124 Austin Kearns .30 .09
125 Edwin Jackson .30 .09
126 Alfonso Soriano .50 .15
127 Bobby Abreu .30 .09
128 Scott Rolen .75 .23
129 Jeff Bagwell .50 .15
130 Shannon Stewart .30 .09
131 Rich Aurilia .30 .09
132 Ty Wigginton .30 .09
133 Randy Johnson .75 .23
134 Rocco Baldelli .30 .09
135 Hideo Nomo .75 .23
136 Greg Maddux WE 3.00 .90
137 Johnny Damon WE 2.00 .60
138 Mark Prior WE 2.00 .60
139 Corey Koskie WE 1.50 .45
140 Miguel Cabrera WE 1.50 .45
141 Hideki Matsui WE 3.00 .90
142 Jose Cruz Jr. WE 1.50 .45
143 Barry Zito WE 1.50 .45
144 Javy Lopez JE 2.50 .75
145 Jason Varitek JE 2.50 .75
146 Moises Alou JE 2.50 .75
147 Torii Hunter JE 2.50 .75
148 Juan Encarnacion JE 2.50 .75
149 Jorge Posada JE 2.50 .75
150 Marquis Grissom JE 2.50 .75
151 Rich Harden JE 2.50 .75
152 Gary Sheffield RE 8.00 2.40
153 Pedro Martinez RE 10.00 3.00
154 Brad Radke RE 8.00 2.40
155 Mike Lowell RE 8.00 2.40
156 Jason Giambi RE 8.00 2.40
157 Mark Mulder RE 8.00 2.40
158 Ben Weber UH .30 .09
159 Mark DeRosa UH .30 .09
160 Melvin Mora UH .30 .09
161 Bill Mueller UH .30 .09
162 Jon Garland UH .30 .09
163 Jody Gerut UH .30 .09
164 Javier Lopez UH .30 .09
165 Craig Monroe UH .30 .09
166 Juan Pierre UH .30 .09
167 Morgan Ensberg UH .30 .09
168 Angel Berroa UH .30 .09
169 Geoff Jenkins UH .30 .09
170 Matt LeCroy UH .30 .09
171 Livan Hernandez UH .30 .09
172 Jason Phillips UH .30 .09
173 Mariano Rivera UH .50 .15
174 Erubiel Durazo UH .30 .09
175 Jason Michaels UH .30 .09
176 Kip Wells UH .30 .09
177 Ray Durham UH .30 .09
178 Randy Winn UH .30 .09
179 Edgar Renteria UH .30 .09
180 Carl Crawford UH .30 .09
181 Laynce Nix UH .30 .09
182 Greg Myers UH .30 .09
183 Delmon Young 1.50 .45
Chad Gaudin
184 Humberto Quintero 1.00 .30
Bernie Castro
185 Craig Brazell 1.00 .30
Danny Garcia
186 Ryan Wing RC 1.00 .30
Francisco Cruceta
187 William Bergolla RC 1.00 .30
Josh Hall
188 Clint Barmes 1.00 .30
Garrett Atkins
189 Chris Bootcheck 1.00 .30
Richard Fischer
190 Edgar Gonzalez 1.00 .30
Matt Kata
191 Andrew Brown 1.00 .30
Koyie Hill
192 John Gall RC 1.50 .45
Dan Haren
193 Chad Bentz RC 1.00 .30
Luis Ayala
194 Hector Gimenez RC 1.00 .30
Eric Bruntlett
195 Boof Bonser 1.00 .30
Rob Bowen
196 Chris Snelling 1.00 .30
Rett Johnson
197 Rickie Weeks 1.00 .30
Adam Morrissey
198 Noah Lowry 1.00 .30
Todd Linden
199 Chris Waters 1.00 .30
Brett Evert
200 Jorge De Paula 1.00 .30
Chien-Ming Wang

2004 Fleer Platinum Finish

Nm-Mt Ex-Mt
*FINISH 1-135/158-182: 3X TO 8X BASIC
*FINISH 183-200: 1X TO 2.5X BASIC.
*FINISH 136-143: 1.25X TO 3X BASIC.
*FINISH 144-151: .75X TO 2X BASIC.
*FINISH 152-157: .25X TO .6X BASIC
STATED ODDS 1:15 WAX
STATED PRINT RUN 100 SERIAL #'d SETS

2004 Fleer Platinum Big Signs

Nm-Mt Ex-Mt
ODDS 1:9 WAX, 1:2 JUMBO, 1:8 RETAIL
1 Albert Pujols 3.00 .90
2 Derek Jeter 3.00 .90
3 Mike Piazza 2.50 .75
4 Jason Giambi 1.50 .45
5 Ichiro Suzuki 2.50 .75
6 Nomar Garciaparra 2.50 .75

7 Mark Prior 1.50 .45
8 Randy Johnson 1.50 .45
9 Greg Maddux 2.50 .75
10 Sammy Sosa 2.50 .75
11 Ken Griffey Jr. 2.50 .75
12 Dontrelle Willis 1.50 .45
13 Alex Rodriguez 2.50 .75
14 Chipper Jones 1.50 .45
15 Hank Blalock 1.50 .45

2004 Fleer Platinum Big Signs Autographs

Albert Pujols and Chipper Jones did not return their cards in time for pack out. Please note there is no expiration date to return these cards by.

Nm-Mt Ex-Mt
RANDOM INSERTS IN WAX PACKS....
STATED PRINT RUN 100 SERIAL #'d SETS
EXCHANGE DEADLINE INDEFINITE ....
AP Albert Pujols EXCH 200.00 60.00
CJ Chipper Jones EXCH 50.00 15.00
DW Dontrelle Willis 15.00 4.50
HB Hank Blalock 15.00 4.50

2004 Fleer Platinum Classic Combinations

Nm-Mt Ex-Mt
STATED ODDS 1:108 WAX, 1:270 RETAIL
1 Ivan Rodriguez 12.00 3.60
Mike Piazza
2 Alex Rodriguez 12.00 3.60
Sammy Sosa
3 Dontrelle Willis 8.00 2.40
Angel Berroa
4 Nomar Garciaparra 15.00 4.50
Derek Jeter
5 Ichiro Suzuki 12.00 3.60
Hideo Nomo
6 Josh Beckett 8.00 2.40
Kerry Wood
7 Albert Pujols 15.00 4.50
Carlos Delgado
8 Alfonso Soriano 8.00 2.40
Joe Morgan
9 Jason Giambi 8.00 2.40
Reggie Jackson
10 Nolan Ryan 25.00 7.50
Tom Seaver

2004 Fleer Platinum Clubhouse Memorabilia

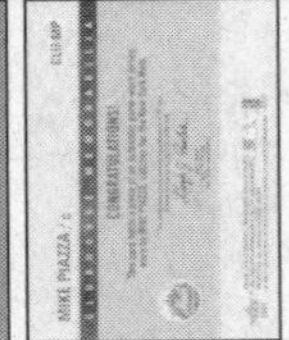

Nm-Mt Ex-Mt
STATED ODDS 1:24 WAX, 1:96 RETAIL
SP INFO PROVIDED BY FLEER
*DUAL: 1X TO 2.5X BASIC
*DUAL: .75X TO 2X BASIC SP
DUAL RANDOM IN WAX AND RETAIL
DUAL PRINT RUN 50 SERIAL #'d SETS
DUAL FEATURE TWO JSY SWATCHES
AK Austin Kearns 8.00 2.40
AP Albert Pujols SP 20.00 6.00
AR Alex Rodriguez 10.00 3.00
AS Alfonso Soriano SP 10.00 3.00
CJ Chipper Jones SP 10.00 3.00
DJ Derek Jeter 20.00 6.00
DW Dontrelle Willis 8.00 2.40
GM Greg Maddux 10.00 3.00
HB Hank Blalock 8.00 2.40
HN Hideo Nomo 15.00 4.50
JB Josh Beckett 8.00 2.40
JG Jason Giambi 8.00 2.40
JT Jim Thome 10.00 3.00
MPI Mike Piazza 10.00 3.00
MPR Mark Prior SP 10.00 3.00
MT Miguel Tejada 8.00 2.40
NG Nomar Garciaparra 10.00 3.00
RB Rocco Baldelli 8.00 2.40
RS Richie Sexson 8.00 2.40
SS Sammy Sosa 15.00 4.50
THE Todd Helton 10.00 3.00
THU Torii Hunter 8.00 2.40
VG Vladimir Guerrero 10.00 3.00

2004 Fleer Platinum Inscribed

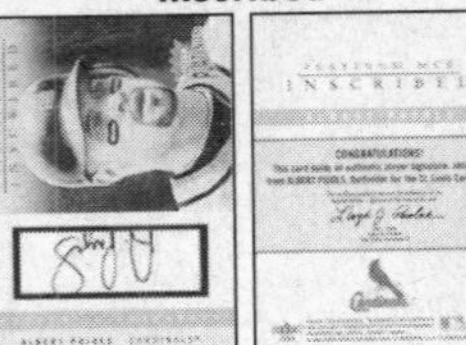

Nm-Mt Ex-Mt
ONE PER RACK PACK
PRINT RUNS B/WN 20-315 COPIES PER
EXCH PRINT RUNS PROVIDED BY FLEER
EXCHANGE DEADLINE INDEFINITE ....
NO PRICING ON QTY OF 25 OR LESS
1-CS Randy Johnson/150 EXCH
2-AS Adam LaRoche/200 EXCH 15.00 4.50
AB Angel Berroa/210 10.00 3.00
AP Albert Pujols/100 175.00 52.50
BL Barry Larkin/75 EXCH 50.00 15.00
BWA Billy Wagner/300 EXCH 25.00 7.50
BWE Brandon Webb/150 15.00 4.50
CBE Chad Bentz/310 10.00 3.00
CBO Chris Bootcheck/210 10.00 3.00
CSN Chris Snelling/310 10.00 3.00
DH Dan Haren/200 10.00 3.00
DM Dallas McPherson/160 25.00 7.50
DW Dontrelle Willis/25
DY Delmon Young/210 25.00 7.50
EG Eric Gagne/130 40.00 12.00
EJ Edwin Jackson/200 15.00 4.50
JR1 Jose Reyes/20
JR2 Jose Reyes/150 EXCH
JV Javier Vazquez/160 15.00 4.50
KG Khalil Greene/310 30.00 9.00
KH Koyie Hill/300 10.00 3.00
LN Laynce Nix/200 15.00 4.50
MB Marlon Byrd/255 10.00 3.00
MC Miguel Cabrera/200 EXCH 25.00 7.50
MK Matt Kata/315 10.00 3.00
RB Rocco Baldelli/100 25.00 7.50
RHA Rich Harden/200 15.00 4.50
RHO Ryan Howard/160 15.00 4.50
RWA Ryan Wagner/300 EXCH 10.00 3.00
RWE Rickie Weeks/200 15.00 4.50
SP Scott Podsednik/180 15.00 4.50
SR Scott Rolen/55
VW Vernon Wells/200 15.00 4.50

2004 Fleer Platinum MLB Scouting Report

Nm-Mt Ex-Mt
ODDS 1:45 WAX, 1:96 JUMBO, 1:190 RETAIL
STATED PRINT RUN 400 SERIAL #'d SETS
1 Josh Beckett 4.00 1.20
2 Todd Helton 4.00 1.20
3 Rocco Baldelli 4.00 1.20
4 Pedro Martinez 4.00 1.20
5 Jeff Bagwell 4.00 1.20
6 Mark Prior 4.00 1.20
7 Ichiro Suzuki 6.00 1.80
8 Barry Zito 4.00 1.20
9 Manny Ramirez 4.00 1.20
10 Miguel Cabrera 4.00 1.20
11 Richie Sexson 4.00 1.20
12 Hideki Matsui 6.00 1.80
13 Maggio Ordonez 4.00 1.20
14 Brandon Webb 4.00 1.20
15 Kerry Wood 4.00 1.20

2004 Fleer Platinum MLB Scouting Report Game Jersey

Nm-Mt Ex-Mt
RANDOM IN WAX AND RETAIL PACKS
STATED PRINT RUN 250 SERIAL #'d SETS
BW Brandon Webb 10.00 3.00
JB Josh Beckett 10.00 3.00
JBAG Jeff Bagwell 15.00 4.50
KW Kerry Wood 15.00 4.50
MP Mark Prior 15.00 4.50
MR Manny Ramirez 15.00 4.50
PM Pedro Martinez 15.00 4.50
RB Rocco Baldelli 10.00 3.00
TH Todd Helton 15.00 4.50

2004 Fleer Platinum Nameplates Player

Nm-Mt Ex-Mt
OVERALL NAMEPLATES ODDS 1:4 JUMBO
PRINT RUNS B/WN 25-320 COPIES PER
NO PRICING ON QTY OF 25 OR LESS
AK Austin Kearns/310 15.00 4.50
AP Albert Pujols/190 40.00 12.00
AR Alex Rodriguez/225 25.00 7.50

BZ Barry Zito/170 15.00 4.50
CJ Chipper Jones/150 25.00 7.50
CS Curt Schilling/260 20.00 6.00
GS Gary Sheffield/115 20.00 6.00
HB Hank Blalock/200 15.00 4.50
HN Hideo Nomo/85 50.00 15.00
HSC Hee Seop Choi/70 15.00 4.50
JB Josh Beckett/255 15.00 4.50
JP Juan Pierre/50 25.00 7.50
JR Jose Reyes/310 15.00 4.50
KB Kevin Brown/80 15.00 4.50
KW Kerry Wood/290 20.00 6.00
LC Luis Castillo/75 15.00 4.50
MB Marlon Byrd/75 15.00 4.50
MC Miguel Cabrera/75 25.00 7.50
MR Manny Ramirez/210 20.00 6.00
MT Mark Teixeira/250 15.00 4.50
NG Nomar Garciaparra/320 25.00 7.50
RJ Randy Johnson/200 20.00 6.00
RS Richie Sexson/165 15.00 4.50
SS Sammy Sosa/260 25.00 7.50
TG Tom Glavine/25

2004 Fleer Platinum Nameplates Team

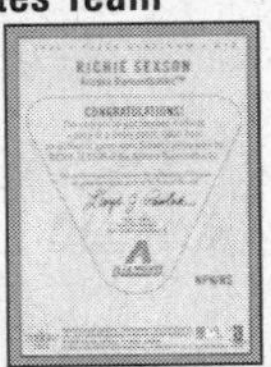

Nm-Mt Ex-Mt
OVERALL NAMEPLATES ODDS 1:4 JUMBO
PRINT RUNS B/WN 105-515 COPIES PER
AK Austin Kearns/515 10.00 3.00
AP Albert Pujols/470 30.00 9.00
AR Alex Rodriguez/510 20.00 6.00
BZ Barry Zito/515 10.00 3.00
CJ Chipper Jones/420 15.00 4.50
CS Curt Schilling/250 20.00 6.00
GS Gary Sheffield/500 10.00 3.00
HB Hank Blalock/515 10.00 3.00
HN Hideo Nomo/390 20.00 6.00
HSC Hee Seop Choi/220 10.00 3.00
JB Josh Beckett/390 10.00 3.00
JP Juan Pierre/110 20.00 6.00
JR Jose Reyes/510 10.00 3.00
KB Kevin Brown/220 10.00 3.00
KW Kerry Wood/510 15.00 4.50
LC Luis Castillo/225 10.00 3.00
MB Marlon Byrd/470 10.00 3.00
MC Miguel Cabrera/105 25.00 7.50
MR Manny Ramirez/480 15.00 4.50
MT Mark Teixeira/505 10.00 3.00
NG Nomar Garciaparra/250 25.00 7.50
RJ Randy Johnson/290 20.00 6.00
RS Richie Sexson/420 10.00 3.00
SS Sammy Sosa/490 25.00 7.50

2004 Fleer Platinum Portraits

Nm-Mt Ex-Mt
ODDS 1:18 WAX, 1:4 JUMBO, 1:24 RETAIL
1 Jason Giambi 3.00 .90
2 Nomar Garciaparra 5.00 1.50
3 Vladimir Guerrero 3.00 .90
4 Mark Prior 3.00 .90
5 Jim Thome 3.00 .90
6 Derek Jeter 6.00 1.80
7 Sammy Sosa 5.00 1.50
8 Alex Rodriguez 5.00 1.50
9 Greg Maddux 5.00 1.50
10 Albert Pujols 6.00 1.80

2004 Fleer Platinum Portraits Game Jersey

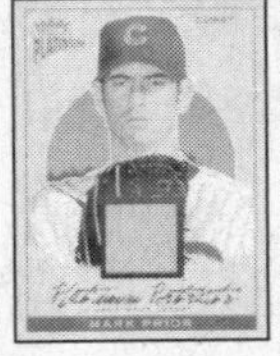
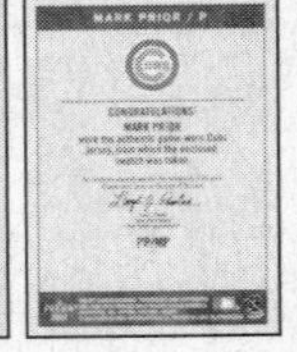

Nm-Mt Ex-Mt
STATED ODDS 1:48 WAX, 1:120 RETAIL
SP INFO PROVIDED BY FLEER
*PATCH: .75X TO 2X BASIC
*PATCH: .6X TO 1.5X BASIC SP
PATCH RANDOM IN WAX AND RETAIL
PATCH PRINT RUN 100 SERIAL #'d SETS
AP Albert Pujols 15.00 4.50
AR Alex Rodriguez 10.00 3.00
DJ Derek Jeter 20.00 6.00
GM Greg Maddux SP 15.00 4.50
JG Jason Giambi 8.00 2.40
JT Jim Thome 10.00 3.00
MP Mark Prior SP 15.00 4.50
NG Nomar Garciaparra 10.00 3.00
SS Sammy Sosa 10.00 3.00
VG Vladimir Guerrero 10.00 3.00

2001 Fleer Premium

The 2001 Fleer Premium product was released in early April, 2001 and features a 235-card base set that was broken into tiers as follows: Base Veterans (1-200), and Prospects (201-235) which were individually serial numbered to 1999. Please note that cards 231-235 all packed out as exchange cards and needed to have been exchanged to Fleer by 5/01/02. Each pack contained eight cards and carried a suggested retail price of $3.99.

Nm-Mt Ex-Mt
COMP.SET w/o SP's (200) 30.00 9.00
COMMON CARD (1-200) .40 .12
COMMON (201-230) 5.00 1.50
COMMON (231-235) 8.00 2.40
1 Cal Ripken 3.00 .90
2 Derek Jeter 2.50 .75
3 Edgardo Alfonzo .40 .12
4 Luis Castillo .40 .12
5 Mike Lieberthal .40 .12
6 Kazuhiro Sasaki .40 .12
7 Jeff Kent .40 .12
8 Eric Karros .40 .12
9 Tom Glavine .60 .18
10 Jeromy Burnitz .40 .12
11 Travis Fryman .40 .12
12 Ron Coomer .40 .12
13 Jeff D'Amico .40 .12
14 Carlos Febles .40 .12
15 Kevin Brown .40 .12
16 Deivi Cruz .40 .12
17 Tino Martinez .60 .18
18 Bobby Abreu .40 .12
19 Roger Clemens 2.00 .60
20 Jeffrey Hammonds .40 .12
21 Peter Bergeron .40 .12
22 Ray Lankford .40 .12
23 Scott Rolen 1.00 .30
24 Jermaine Dye .40 .12
25 Rusty Greer .40 .12
26 Frank Thomas 1.00 .30
27 Jeff Bagwell .60 .18
28 Cliff Floyd .40 .12
29 Chris Singleton .40 .12
30 Steve Finley .40 .12
31 Orlando Hernandez .40 .12
32 Tom Goodwin .40 .12
33 Larry Walker .60 .18
34 Mike Sweeney .40 .12
35 Tim Hudson .40 .12
36 Kerry Wood 1.00 .30
37 Mike Lowell .40 .12
38 Andruw Jones .75 .23
39 Alex Gonzalez .40 .12
40 Juan Gonzalez .75 .23
41 J.D. Drew .40 .12
42 Mark McLemore .40 .12
43 Royce Clayton .40 .12
44 Paul O'Neill .60 .18
45 Carlos Beltran .60 .18
46 Phil Nevin .40 .12
47 Rondell White .40 .12
48 Gerald Williams .40 .12
49 Geoff Jenkins .40 .12
50 Marvin Benard .40 .12
51 Alex Rodriguez 1.50 .45
52 Moises Alou .40 .12
53 Mike Lansing .40 .12
54 Omar Vizquel .60 .18
55 Eric Chavez .40 .12
56 Mark Quinn .40 .12
57 Mike Lamb .40 .12
58 Rick Ankiel .40 .12
59 Lance Berkman .40 .12
60 Jeff Conine .40 .12
61 B.J. Surhoff .40 .12
62 Todd Helton .60 .18
63 J.T. Snow .40 .12
64 John VanderWal .40 .12
65 Johnny Damon .60 .18
66 Bobby Higginson .40 .12
67 Carlos Delgado .75 .23
68 Shawn Green .40 .12
69 Mike Redmond .40 .12
70 Mike Piazza 1.50 .45
71 Adrian Beltre .40 .12
72 Juan Encarnacion .40 .12
73 Chipper Jones 1.00 .30
74 Garret Anderson .40 .12
75 Paul Konerko .40 .12
76 Barry Larkin .60 .18
77 Tony Gwynn 1.25 .35
78 Rafael Palmeiro .60 .18
79 Randy Johnson 1.00 .30
80 Mark Grace .75 .23
81 Javy Lopez .40 .12
82 Gabe Kapler .40 .12
83 Henry Rodriguez .40 .12
84 Raul Mondesi .40 .12
85 Adam Piatt .40 .12
86 Marquis Grissom .40 .12
87 Charles Johnson .40 .12
88 Sean Casey .40 .12
89 Manny Ramirez .60 .18
90 Curt Schilling .40 .12
91 Fernando Tatis .40 .12
92 Derek Bell .40 .12
93 Tony Clark .40 .12
94 Homer Bush .40 .12
95 Nomar Garciaparra 1.50 .45
96 Vinny Castilla .40 .12
97 Ben Davis .40 .12
98 Carl Everett .40 .12
99 Damion Easley .40 .12
100 Craig Biggio .60 .18
101 Todd Hollandsworth .40 .12
102 Jay Payton .40 .12
103 Gary Sheffield .40 .12
104 Sandy Alomar Jr. .40 .12
105 Doug Glanville .40 .12
106 Barry Bonds 2.50 .75
107 Tim Salmon .60 .18
108 Terrence Long .40 .12
109 Jorge Posada .60 .18
110 Jose Offerman .40 .12
111 Edgar Martinez .60 .18
112 Jeremy Giambi .40 .12
113 Dean Palmer .40 .12
114 Roberto Alomar .75 .23
115 Aaron Boone .40 .12
116 Adam Kennedy .40 .12
117 Joe Randa .40 .12
118 Jose Vidro .40 .12
119 Tony Batista .40 .12
120 Kevin Young .40 .12
121 Preston Wilson .40 .12
122 Jason Kendall .40 .12
123 Mark Kotsay .40 .12
124 Timo Perez .40 .12
125 Eric Young .40 .12
126 Greg Maddux 1.50 .45
127 Richard Hidalgo .40 .12
128 Brian Giles .40 .12
129 Fred McGriff .60 .18
130 Troy Glaus .40 .12
131 Todd Walker .40 .12
132 Brady Anderson .40 .12
133 Jim Edmonds .40 .12
134 Ben Grieve .40 .12
135 Greg Vaughn .40 .12
136 Robin Ventura .40 .12
137 Sammy Sosa 1.50 .45
138 Rich Aurilia .40 .12
139 Jose Valentin .40 .12
140 Trot Nixon .40 .12
141 Troy Percival .40 .12
142 Bernie Williams .60 .18
143 Warren Morris .40 .12
144 Jacque Jones .40 .12
145 Danny Bautista .40 .12
146 A.J. Pierzynski .40 .12
147 Mark McGwire 2.50 .75
148 Rafael Furcal .40 .12
149 Ray Durham .40 .12
150 Mike Mussina .75 .23
151 Jay Bell .40 .12
152 David Wells .40 .12
153 Ken Caminiti .40 .12
154 Jim Thome 1.00 .30
155 Ivan Rodriguez 1.00 .30
156 Milton Bradley .40 .12
157 Ken Griffey Jr. 1.50 .45
158 Al Leiter .40 .12
159 Corey Koskie .40 .12
160 Shannon Stewart .40 .12
161 Mo Vaughn .40 .12
162 Pedro Martinez 1.00 .30
163 Todd Hundley .40 .12
164 Darin Erstad .75 .23
165 Ruben Rivera .40 .12
166 Richie Sexson .40 .12
167 Andres Galarraga .40 .12
168 Darryl Kile .40 .12
169 Jose Cruz Jr. .40 .12
170 David Justice .40 .12
171 Vladimir Guerrero 1.00 .30
172 Jeff Cirillo .40 .12
173 John Olerud .40 .12
174 Devon White .40 .12
175 Ron Belliard .40 .12
176 Pokey Reese .40 .12
177 Mike Hampton .40 .12
178 David Ortiz .60 .18
179 Magglio Ordonez .40 .12
180 Ruben Mateo .40 .12
181 Carlos Lee .40 .12
182 Matt Williams .40 .12
183 Miguel Tejada .40 .12
184 Scott Elarton .40 .12
185 Bret Boone .40 .12
186 Pat Burrell .40 .12
187 Brad Radke .40 .12
188 Brian Jordan .40 .12
189 Matt Lawton .40 .12
190 Al Martin .40 .12
191 Albert Belle .40 .12
192 Tony Womack .40 .12
193 Roger Cedeno .40 .12
194 Travis Lee .40 .12
195 Dmitri Young .40 .12
196 Jay Buhner .40 .12
197 Jason Giambi .75 .23
198 Jason Tyner .40 .12
199 Ben Petrick .40 .12
200 Jose Canseco .75 .23
201 Nick Johnson 5.00 1.50
202 Jace Brewer 5.00 1.50
203 Ryan Freel RC 5.00 1.50
204 Jaisen Randolph RC 5.00 1.50
205 Marcus Giles 5.00 1.50
206 Claudio Vargas RC 5.00 1.50
207 Brian Cole 5.00 1.50
208 Scott Hodges 5.00 1.50
209 Winston Abreu RC 5.00 1.50
210 Shea Hillenbrand 5.00 1.50
211 Larry Barnes 5.00 1.50
212 Paul Phillips RC 5.00 1.50
213 Pedro Santana RC 5.00 1.50
214 Ivanon Coffie 5.00 1.50
215 Junior Spivey RC 8.00 2.40
216 Donzell McDonald 5.00 1.50
217 Vernon Wells 5.00 1.50
218 Corey Patterson 5.00 1.50

	Nm-Mt	Ex-Mt
219 Sang-Hoon Lee	5.00	1.50
220 Jack Cust	5.00	1.50
221 Jason Romano	5.00	1.50
222 Jack Wilson RC	10.00	3.00
223 Adam Everett	5.00	1.50
224 Esix Snead RC	5.00	1.50
225 Jason Hart	5.00	1.50
226 Joe Lawrence	5.00	1.50
227 Brandon Inge	5.00	1.50
228 Alex Escobar	5.00	1.50
229 Abraham Nunez	5.00	1.50
230 Jared Sandberg	5.00	1.50
231 Ichiro Suzuki RC	50.00	15.00
232 Tsuyoshi Shinjo RC	10.00	3.00
233 Albert Pujols RC	80.00	24.00
234 Wilson Betemit RC	8.00	2.40
235 Drew Henson RC	20.00	6.00
MM1 D.Jeter MM/1995	12.00	3.60
NNO D.Jeter MM AU/95 EX	120.00	36.00

2001 Fleer Premium Star Ruby

Randomly inserted into packs, this set is a parallel of the first 230 cards of the 2001 Fleer Premium base set. Each card was produced with ruby-red foil stamping and are individually serial numbered to 125.

	Nm-Mt	Ex-Mt
*RUBY 1-200: 5X TO 12X BASE HI		
*RUBY 201-230: .3X TO .8X BASE HI		

2001 Fleer Premium A Time for Heroes

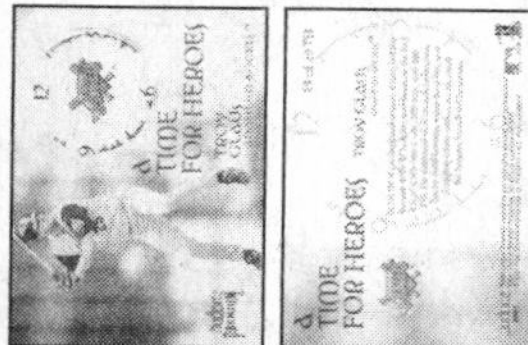

Randomly inserted into packs at one in 20, this 20-card insert set pays homage to the heroes who have emerged in the modern game Card backs carry an "ATFH" prefix.

	Nm-Mt	Ex-Mt
COMPLETE SET (20)	80.00	24.00
ATFH1 Darin Erstad	2.00	.60
ATFH2 Alex Rodriguez	6.00	1.80
ATFH3 Shawn Green	2.00	.60
ATFH4 Jeff Bagwell	2.50	.75
ATFH5 Sammy Sosa	6.00	1.80
ATFH6 Derek Jeter	10.00	3.00
ATFH7 Nomar Garciaparra	6.00	1.80
ATFH8 Carlos Delgado	2.00	.60
ATFH9 Pat Burrell	2.00	.60
ATFH10 Tony Gwynn	5.00	1.50
ATFH11 Chipper Jones	4.00	1.20
ATFH12 Jason Giambi	2.00	.60
ATFH13 Magglio Ordonez	2.00	.60
ATFH14 Troy Glaus	2.00	.60
ATFH15 Ivan Rodriguez	4.00	1.20
ATFH16 Andruw Jones	2.00	.60
ATFH17 Vladimir Guerrero	4.00	1.20
ATFH18 Ken Griffey Jr.	6.00	1.80
ATFH19 J.D. Drew	2.00	.60
ATFH20 Todd Helton	2.50	.75

2001 Fleer Premium Brother Wood

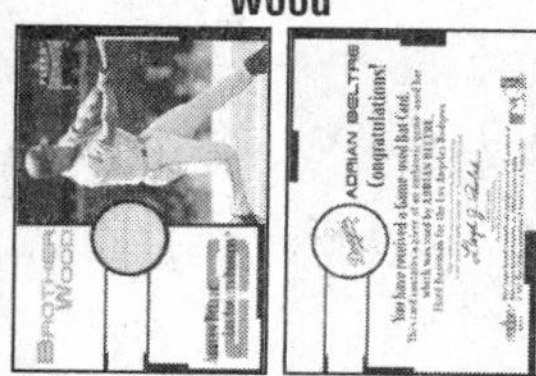

Randomly inserted into packs at one in 108, this 9-card insert set features actual pieces of game-used bats. Card backs carry a "BW" prefix.

	Nm-Mt	Ex-Mt
BW1 Vladimir Guerrero	15.00	4.50
BW2 Andruw Jones	10.00	3.00
BW3 Corey Patterson	10.00	3.00
BW4 Magglio Ordonez	10.00	3.00
BW5 Jason Giambi	10.00	3.00
BW6 Rafael Palmeiro	15.00	4.50
BW7 Eric Chavez	10.00	3.00
BW8 Pat Burrell	10.00	3.00
BW9 Adrian Beltre	15.00	4.50

2001 Fleer Premium Decades of Excellence

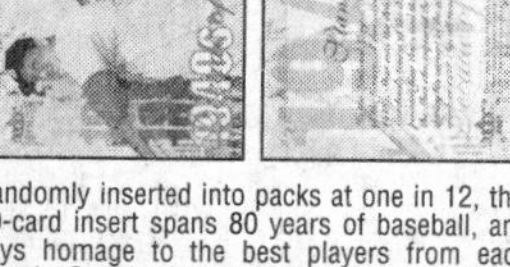

Randomly inserted into packs at one in 12, this 50-card insert spans 80 years of baseball, and pays homage to the best players from each decade. Card backs carry a "DE" prefix. The Willie Mays card was not supposed to exist but several copies have been found in packs and is tagged an SP without pricing in our checklist.

	Nm-Mt	Ex-Mt
COMPLETE SET (50)	350.00	105.00
DE1 Lou Gehrig	20.00	6.00
Babe Ruth		
DE2 Lloyd Waner	3.00	.90
DE3 Jimmie Foxx	5.00	1.50
DE4 Hank Greenberg	5.00	1.50
DE5 Ted Williams UER	12.00	3.60
DE6 Johnny Mize	3.00	.90
DE7 Enos Slaughter	3.00	.90
DE8 Jackie Robinson	5.00	1.50
DE9 Stan Musial	8.00	2.40
DE10 Duke Snider	3.00	.90
DE11 Eddie Mathews	5.00	1.50
DE12 Roy Campanella	5.00	1.50
DE13 Yogi Berra	5.00	1.50
DE14 Pee Wee Reese	5.00	1.50
DE15 Phil Rizzuto	5.00	1.50
DE16 Al Kaline	5.00	1.50
DE17 Willie Mays SP		
DE18 Frank Howard	3.00	.90
DE19 Roberto Clemente	15.00	4.50
DE20 Bob Gibson	3.00	.90
DE21 Roger Maris	5.00	1.50
DE22 Don Drysdale	5.00	1.50
DE23 Maury Wills	3.00	.90
DE24 Tom Seaver	3.00	.90
DE25 Reggie Jackson	3.00	.90
DE26 Johnny Bench	5.00	1.50
DE27 Carlton Fisk	3.00	.90
DE28 Rod Carew	3.00	.90
DE29 Steve Carlton	3.00	.90
DE30 Mike Schmidt	12.00	3.60
DE31 Nolan Ryan	15.00	4.50
DE32 Rickey Henderson	5.00	1.50
DE33 Roger Clemens	10.00	3.00
DE34 Don Mattingly	15.00	4.50
DE35 George Brett	12.00	3.60
DE36 Greg Maddux	8.00	2.40
DE37 Cal Ripken	15.00	4.50
DE38 Chipper Jones	5.00	1.50
DE39 Barry Bonds	12.00	3.60
DE40 Ivan Rodriguez	5.00	1.50
DE41 Mark McGwire	15.00	4.50
Sammy Sosa		
DE42 Ken Griffey Jr.	8.00	2.40
DE43 Tony Gwynn	6.00	1.80
DE44 Vladimir Guerrero	5.00	1.50
DE45 Shawn Green	3.00	.90
DE46 Alex Rodriguez	12.00	3.60
Derek Jeter		
Nomar Garciaparra		
DE47 Pat Burrell	3.00	.90
DE48 Rick Ankiel	3.00	.90
DE49 Eric Chavez	3.00	.90
DE50 Troy Glaus	3.00	.90

2001 Fleer Premium Decades of Excellence Autograph

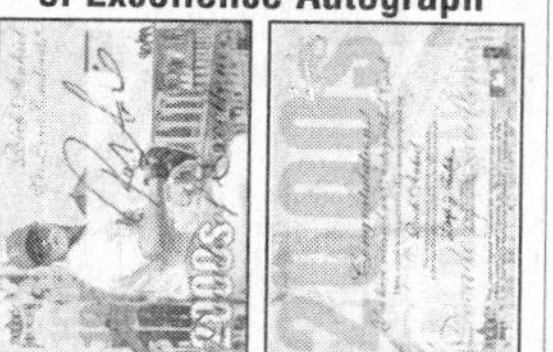

Randomly inserted into hobby packs, this 20-card insert set is a partial parallel of the 2001 Fleer Premium Decades of Excellence insert set. The set features authentic autographs from the player depicted on each card. Please note that each card is serial numbered to the year in which the player made his major league debut.

	Nm-Mt	Ex-Mt
1 Rick Ankiel/99	40.00	12.00
2 Johnny Bench/67	100.00	30.00
3 Barry Bonds/86	250.00	75.00
4 George Brett/73	150.00	45.00
5 Rod Carew/67	60.00	18.00
6 Steve Carlton/65	60.00	18.00
7 Eric Chavez/98	40.00	12.00
8 Carlton Fisk/69	60.00	18.00
9 Bob Gibson/59	60.00	18.00
10 Tony Gwynn/82	100.00	30.00
11 Reggie Jackson/67	100.00	30.00
12 Chipper Jones/93	100.00	30.00
13 Al Kaline/53	120.00	36.00
14 Don Mattingly/82	150.00	45.00
15 Cal Ripken/81	200.00	60.00
16 Nolan Ryan/66	150.00	45.00
17 Mike Schmidt/72	150.00	45.00
18 Tom Seaver/67	60.00	18.00
19 Enos Slaughter/38	60.00	18.00
20 Maury Wills/59	40.00	12.00

2001 Fleer Premium Decades of Excellence Memorabilia

Randomly inserted into hobby packs at one in 217, this 21-card insert is a partial parallel of the 2001 Fleer Premium Decades of Excellence insert. Each of these cards features either a swatch of game-used jersey or a sliver of game-used bat. Please note that the Carlton Fisk and Roger Maris cards feature swatches of game-used uniform. The cards have been listed below in alphabetical order for convenience. Though the cards lack actual serial-numbering, representatives at Fleer publicly announced specific print runs on several short-printed cards within this set. That information is detailed within our checklist.

	Nm-Mt	Ex-Mt
1 Rick Ankiel Jsy	15.00	4.50
2 Barry Bonds Jsy		
3 Pat Burrell Jsy	15.00	4.50
4 Roy Campanella	50.00	15.00
Bat SP/50		
5 Eric Chavez Bat	15.00	4.50
6 Roberto Clemente	100.00	30.00
Bat SP/50		
7 Carlton Fisk Uniform	25.00	7.50
8 Jimmie Foxx Bat SP/50	100.00	30.00
9 Shawn Green Bat	15.00	4.50
10 Tony Gwynn Jsy	25.00	7.50
11 Reggie Jackson Jsy	25.00	7.50
12 Greg Maddux Jsy	25.00	7.50
13 Roger Maris Uni		
14 Pee Wee Reese Jsy	25.00	7.50
15 Cal Ripken Jsy SP/50		
16 Ivan Rodriguez Bat	25.00	7.50
17 Nolan Ryan Jsy		
18 Mike Schmidt Jsy		
19 Tom Seaver Jsy		
20 Duke Snider Bat	25.00	7.50
21 Ted Williams	100.00	30.00
Jsy SP/50		

2001 Fleer Premium Diamond Dominators

Randomly inserted into packs at one in 51, this 14-card insert features swatches of game-used jerseys of the players depicted below. Card backs carry a "DD" prefix.

	Nm-Mt	Ex-Mt
DD1 Troy Glaus	10.00	3.00
DD2 Darin Erstad	10.00	3.00
DD3 J.D. Drew	10.00	3.00
DD4 Barry Bonds	40.00	12.00
DD5 Roger Clemens	30.00	9.00
DD6 Vladimir Guerrero	15.00	4.50
DD7 Tony Gwynn	20.00	6.00
DD8 Greg Maddux	25.00	7.50
DD9 Cal Ripken	50.00	15.00
DD10 Ivan Rodriguez	15.00	4.50
DD11 Frank Thomas	15.00	4.50
DD12 Bernie Williams	15.00	4.50
DD13 Jeromy Burnitz	10.00	3.00
DD14 Juan Gonzalez	15.00	4.50

2001 Fleer Premium Diamond Patches

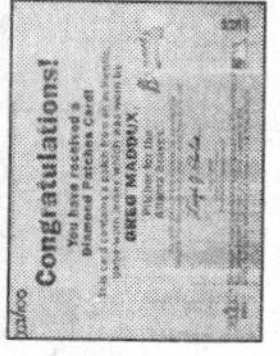

Randomly inserted into packs, this 14-card insert features swatches of jersey patches of the players depicted below. Card backs carry a "DD" prefix. Please note that there were only 100 of each card produced.

	Nm-Mt	Ex-Mt
DD1 Troy Glaus	50.00	15.00
DD2 Darin Erstad	50.00	15.00
DD3 J.D. Drew	50.00	15.00
DD4 Barry Bonds	120.00	36.00
DD5 Roger Clemens	100.00	30.00
DD6 Vladimir Guerrero	80.00	24.00
DD7 Tony Gwynn	80.00	24.00
DD8 Greg Maddux	80.00	24.00
DD9 Cal Ripken	120.00	36.00
DD10 Ivan Rodriguez	80.00	24.00
DD11 Frank Thomas	80.00	24.00
DD12 Bernie Williams	80.00	24.00
DD13 Jeromy Burnitz	50.00	15.00
DD14 Juan Gonzalez	80.00	24.00

2001 Fleer Premium Grip It and Rip It

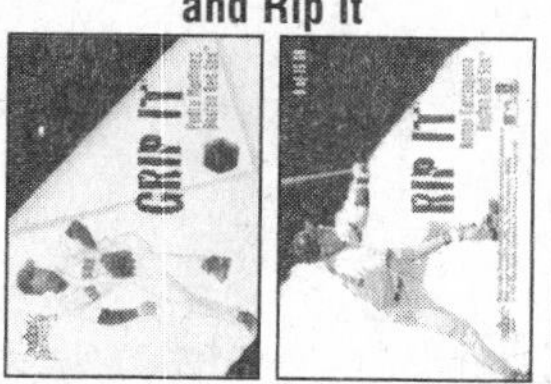

Randomly inserted into packs at one in 6, this 15-card insert pairs up teammates that get the job done with their ability to catch and hit . Card backs carry a "GRP" prefix.

	Nm-Mt	Ex-Mt
COMPLETE SET (15)	20.00	6.00
GRP1 Roger Clemens	3.00	.90
Derek Jeter		
GRP2 Scott Rolen	1.25	.35
Pat Burrell		
GRP3 Greg Maddux	2.00	.60
Andruw Jones		
GRP4 Shannon Stewart	1.00	.30
Carlos Delgado		
GRP5 Shawn Estes	3.00	.90
Barry Bonds		
GRP6 Cal Eldred	1.25	.35
Frank Thomas		
GRP7 Mark McGwire	3.00	.90
Jim Edmonds		
GRP8 Jose Vidro	1.25	.35
Vladimir Guerrero		
GRP9 Pedro Martinez	2.00	.60
Nomar Garciaparra		
GRP10 Tom Glavine	1.25	.35
Chipper Jones		
GRP11 Ken Griffey Jr.	2.00	.60
Sean Casey		
GRP12 Jeff Bagwell	1.00	.30
Moises Alou		
GRP13 Troy Glaus	1.00	.30
Darin Erstad		
GRP14 Mike Piazza	2.00	.60
Robin Ventura		
GRP15 Eric Chavez	1.00	.30
Jason Giambi		

2001 Fleer Premium Grip It and Rip It Plus

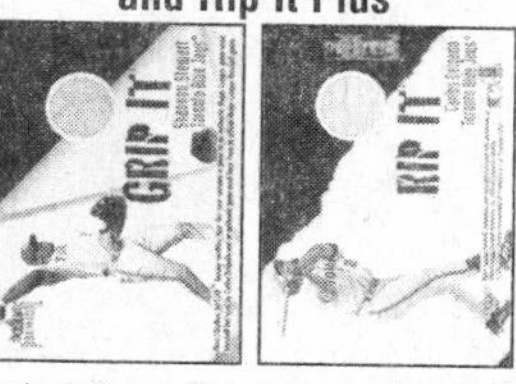

Randomly inserted into hobby packs, this 15-card set is a complete parallel of the 2001 Fleer Premium Grip It and Rip It insert. Each of these cards feature either a swatch of game-used base and bat, or a swatch of game-used ball and bat. Please note that each Base/Bat card is serial numbered to 200, while each Ball/Bat card is serial numbered to 100.

	Nm-Mt	Ex-Mt
GRP1 Roger Clemens Ball	120.00	36.00
Derek Jeter Bat		
GRP2 Scott Rolen Base	25.00	7.50
Pat Burrell Bat/200		
GRP3 Greg Maddux Ball	80.00	24.00
Andruw Jones Bat/100		
GRP4 Shan. Stewart Base	15.00	4.50
Carlos Delgado Bat		
GRP5 Shawn Estes	100.00	30.00
Barry Bonds		
GRP6 Cal Eldred	25.00	7.50
Frank Thomas		
GRP7 Mark McGwire Ball	150.00	45.00
Jim Edmonds Bat/100		
GRP8 Jose Vidro Base	25.00	7.50
Vladimir Guerrero Bat/200		
GRP9 Pedro Martinez	80.00	24.00
Nomar Garciaparra		
GRP10 Tom Glavine	25.00	7.50
Chipper Jones		
GRP11 K. Griffey Jr. Base	40.00	12.00
Sean Casey Bat/200		
GRP12 Jeff Bagwell Base	25.00	7.50
Moises Alou Bat/200		
GRP13 Troy Glaus Base	15.00	4.50
Darin Erstad Bat/200		
GRP14 Mike Piazza Ball	80.00	24.00
Robin Ventura Bat		
GRP15 Eric Chavez Base	15.00	4.50
Jason Giambi Bat/200		

2001 Fleer Premium Heroes Game Jersey

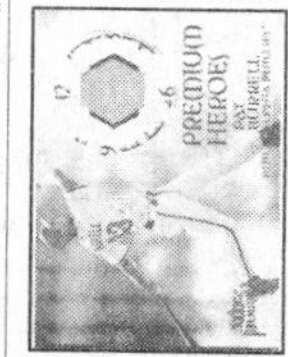

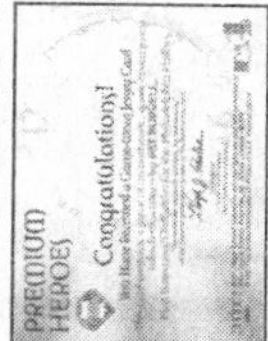

Randomly inserted into hobby packs at one in 101, this 10-card insert is a partial parallel of the 2001 Fleer Premium A Time For Heroes insert. Each of these cards features a swatch of game-used jersey. The cards are listed below in alphabetical order for convenience.

	Nm-Mt	Ex-Mt
1 Pat Burrell	10.00	3.00
2 J.D. Drew	10.00	3.00
3 Jason Giambi	10.00	3.00
4 Troy Glaus	10.00	3.00
5 Shawn Green	10.00	3.00
6 Todd Helton	15.00	4.50
7 Derek Jeter	50.00	15.00
8 Andruw Jones	10.00	3.00
9 Chipper Jones	15.00	4.50
10 Ivan Rodriguez	15.00	4.50

2001 Fleer Premium Home Field Advantage

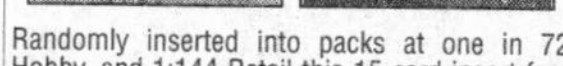

Randomly inserted into packs at one in 72 Hobby, and 1:144 Retail this 15-card insert features players with their home field in the background. Card backs carry a "HFA" prefix.

	Nm-Mt	Ex-Mt
COMPLETE SET (15)	200.00	60.00
HFA1 Mike Piazza	12.00	3.60
HFA2 Derek Jeter	20.00	6.00
HFA3 Ken Griffey Jr.	12.00	3.60
HFA4 Carlos Delgado	6.00	1.80
HFA5 Chipper Jones	8.00	2.40
HFA6 Alex Rodriguez	12.00	3.60
HFA7 Sammy Sosa	12.00	3.60
HFA8 Scott Rolen	8.00	2.40
HFA9 Nomar Garciaparra	12.00	3.60
HFA10 Todd Helton	6.00	1.80
HFA11 Vladimir Guerrero	8.00	2.40
HFA12 Jeff Bagwell	6.00	1.80
HFA13 Barry Bonds	20.00	6.00
HFA14 Cal Ripken	25.00	7.50
HFA15 Mark McGwire	20.00	6.00

2001 Fleer Premium Home Field Advantage Game Wall

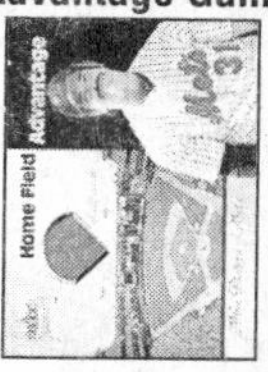

Randomly inserted into packs, this 15-card insert is a complete parallel of the 2001 Fleer Premium Home Field Advantage insert. Each of these cards feature a swatch of actual game-used wall. Card backs carry a "HFA" prefix.

	Nm-Mt	Ex-Mt
HFA1 Mike Piazza	40.00	12.00
HFA2 Derek Jeter	60.00	18.00
HFA3 Ken Griffey Jr.	40.00	12.00
HFA4 Carlos Delgado	15.00	4.50
HFA5 Chipper Jones	25.00	7.50
HFA6 Alex Rodriguez	40.00	12.00
HFA7 Sammy Sosa	40.00	12.00
HFA8 Scott Rolen	25.00	7.50
HFA9 Nomar Garciaparra	40.00	12.00
HFA10 Todd Helton	25.00	7.50
HFA11 Vladimir Guerrero	25.00	7.50
HFA12 Jeff Bagwell	25.00	7.50
HFA13 Barry Bonds	60.00	18.00
HFA14 Cal Ripken	80.00	24.00
HFA15 Mark McGwire	80.00	24.00

2001 Fleer Premium Performers Game Base

Randomly inserted into hobby packs, this 15-card insert set is a complete parallel of the 2001 Fleer Premium Solid Performers insert. Each of these cards feature a swatch of game-used base. Card backs carry a "SP" prefix. Also note that there were only 150 of each card produced.

	Nm-Mt	Ex-Mt
SP1 Mark McGwire	80.00	24.00
SP2 Alex Rodriguez	40.00	12.00
SP3 Nomar Garciaparra	30.00	9.00
SP4 Derek Jeter	50.00	15.00
SP5 Vladimir Guerrero	20.00	6.00
SP6 Todd Helton	20.00	6.00
SP7 Chipper Jones	20.00	6.00
SP8 Mike Piazza	30.00	9.00
SP9 Ivan Rodriguez	20.00	6.00
SP10 Tony Gwynn	30.00	9.00
SP11 Cal Ripken	60.00	18.00
SP12 Barry Bonds	50.00	15.00
SP13 Jeff Bagwell	20.00	6.00
SP14 Ken Griffey Jr.	30.00	9.00
SP15 Sammy Sosa	30.00	9.00

2001 Fleer Premium Solid Performers

Randomly inserted into packs at one in 20, this 15-card insert features players that ballclubs build their franchise around. Card backs carry a "SP" prefix.

	Nm-Mt	Ex-Mt
COMPLETE SET (15)	80.00	24.00
SP1 Mark McGwire	8.00	2.40
SP2 Alex Rodriguez	5.00	1.50
SP3 Nomar Garciaparra	5.00	1.50
SP4 Derek Jeter	8.00	2.40
SP5 Vladimir Guerrero	3.00	.90
SP6 Todd Helton	3.00	.90
SP7 Chipper Jones	3.00	.90
SP8 Mike Piazza	5.00	1.50
SP9 Ivan Rodriguez	3.00	.90
SP10 Tony Gwynn	4.00	1.20
SP11 Cal Ripken	10.00	3.00

SP12 Barry Bonds 8.00 2.40
SP13 Jeff Bagwell 3.00 .90
SP14 Ken Griffey Jr. 5.00 1.50
SP15 Sammy Sosa 5.00 1.50

2002 Fleer Premium

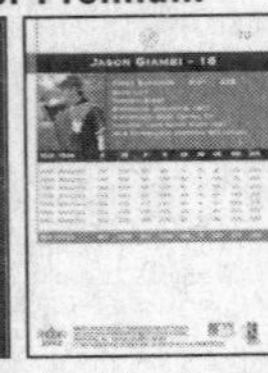

This 240 card set was released in early spring, 2002. This set was issued in 10 card packs which were issued 24 packs to a box. Cards numbered from 201 through 240 featured leading prospects entering the 2002 season and were seeded at stated odds of one in two packs. In late May, Fleer announced their "Player to be Named" program, whereby collectors could send in 10 copies of any of the short-printed prospect cards (201-240) and in turn receive ten new prospect cards (241-250) each serial numbered to 2002. The "Player to be Named" cards were actually released in October, 2002.

	Nm-Mt	Ex-Mt
COMP.MASTER SET (250)	120.00	36.00
COMPLETE SET (240)	80.00	24.00
COMP.SET w/o SP'S (200)	30.00	9.00
COMP.UPDATE SET (10)	40.00	12.00
COMMON CARD (1-200)	.40	.12
COMMON CARD (201-240)	2.00	.60
COMMON CARD (241-250)	4.00	1.20
1 Garret Anderson	.40	.12
2 Derek Jeter	2.50	.75
3 Ken Griffey Jr.	1.50	.45
4 Luis Castillo	.40	.12
5 Richie Sexson	.40	.12
6 Mike Mussina	.60	.18
7 Rickey Henderson	1.00	.30
8 Bud Smith	.40	.12
9 David Eckstein	.40	.12
10 Nomar Garciaparra	1.50	.45
11 Barry Larkin	.60	.18
12 Cliff Floyd	.40	.12
13 Ben Sheets	.40	.12
14 Jorge Posada	.60	.18
15 Phil Nevin	.40	.12
16 Fernando Vina	.40	.12
17 Darin Erstad	.40	.12
18 Shea Hillenbrand	.40	.12
19 Todd Walker	.40	.12
20 Charles Johnson	.40	.12
21 Cristian Guzman	.40	.12
22 Mariano Rivera	.60	.18
23 Bubba Trammell	.40	.12
24 Brent Abernathy	.40	.12
25 Troy Glaus	.40	.12
26 Pedro Martinez	1.00	.30
27 Dmitri Young	.40	.12
28 Derrek Lee	.40	.12
29 Torii Hunter	.40	.12
30 Alfonso Soriano	.60	.18
31 Rich Aurilia	.40	.12
32 Ben Grieve	.40	.12
33 Tim Salmon	.60	.18
34 Trot Nixon	.40	.12
35 Roberto Alomar	.60	.18
36 Mike Lowell	.40	.12
37 Jacque Jones	.40	.12
38 Bernie Williams	.60	.18
39 Barry Bonds	2.50	.75
40 Toby Hall	.40	.12
41 Mo Vaughn	.40	.12
42 Hideo Nomo	1.00	.30
43 Travis Fryman	.40	.12
44 Preston Wilson	.40	.12
45 Corey Koskie	.40	.12
46 Eric Chavez	.40	.12
47 Andres Galarraga	.40	.12
48 Greg Vaughn	.40	.12
49 Shawn Wooten	.40	.12
50 Manny Ramirez	.60	.18
51 Juan Gonzalez	.60	.18
52 Moises Alou	.40	.12
53 Joe Mays	.40	.12
54 Johnny Damon	.60	.18
55 Jeff Kent	.40	.12
56 Frank Catalanotto	.40	.12
57 Steve Finley	.40	.12
58 Jason Varitek	.60	.18
59 Kenny Lofton	.40	.12
60 Jeff Bagwell	.60	.18
61 Doug Mientkiewicz	.40	.12
62 Jermaine Dye	.40	.12
63 John Vander Wal	.40	.12
64 Gabe Kapler	.40	.12
65 Luis Gonzalez	.40	.12
66 Jon Lieber	.40	.12
67 C.C. Sabathia	.40	.12
68 Lance Berkman	.40	.12
69 Eric Milton	.40	.12
70 Jason Giambi Yankees	.40	.12
71 Ichiro Suzuki	1.50	.45
72 Rafael Palmeiro	.60	.18
73 Mark Grace	.60	.18
74 Fred McGriff	.60	.18
75 Jim Thome	1.00	.30
76 Craig Biggio	.60	.18
77 A.J. Pierzynski	.40	.12
78 Ramon Hernandez	.40	.12
79 Paul Abbott	.40	.12
80 Alex Rodriguez	1.50	.45
81 Randy Johnson	1.00	.30
82 Corey Patterson	.40	.12
83 Omar Vizquel	.60	.18
84 Richard Hidalgo	.40	.12
85 Luis Rivas	.40	.12
86 Tim Hudson	.40	.12
87 Bret Boone	.40	.12
88 Ivan Rodriguez	1.00	.30
89 Junior Spivey	.40	.12
90 Sammy Sosa	1.50	.45
91 Jeff Cirillo	.40	.12
92 Roy Oswalt	.40	.12
93 Orlando Cabrera	.40	.12
94 Terrence Long	.40	.12
95 Mike Cameron	.40	.12
96 Homer Bush	.40	.12
97 Reggie Sanders	.40	.12
98 Rondell White	.40	.12
99 Mike Hampton	.40	.12
100 Carlos Beltran	.60	.18
101 Vladimir Guerrero	1.00	.30
102 Miguel Tejada	.40	.12
103 Freddy Garcia	.40	.12
104 Jose Cruz Jr.	.40	.12
105 Curt Schilling	.40	.12
106 Kerry Wood	1.00	.30
107 Todd Helton	.60	.18
108 Neifi Perez	.40	.12
109 Javier Vazquez	.40	.12
110 Barry Zito	.40	.12
111 Edgar Martinez	.60	.18
112 Carlos Delgado	.40	.12
113 Matt Williams	.40	.12
114 Eric Young	.40	.12
115 Alex Ochoa	.40	.12
116 Mark Quinn	.40	.12
117 Jose Vidro	.40	.12
118 Bobby Abreu	.40	.12
119 David Bell	.40	.12
120 Brad Fullmer	.40	.12
121 Rafael Furcal	.40	.12
122 Ray Durham	.40	.12
123 Jose Ortiz	.40	.12
124 Joe Randa	.40	.12
125 Edgardo Alfonzo	.40	.12
126 Marlon Anderson	.40	.12
127 Jamie Moyer	.40	.12
128 Alex Gonzalez	.40	.12
129 Marcus Giles	.40	.12
130 Keith Foulke	.40	.12
131 Juan Pierre	.40	.12
132 Mike Sweeney	.40	.12
133 Matt Lawton	.40	.12
134 Pat Burrell	.40	.12
135 John Olerud	.40	.12
136 Raul Mondesi	.40	.12
137 Tom Glavine	.60	.18
138 Paul Konerko	.40	.12
139 Larry Walker	.60	.18
140 Adrian Beltre	.60	.18
141 Al Leiter	.40	.12
142 Mike Lieberthal	.40	.12
143 Kazuhiro Sasaki	.40	.12
144 Shannon Stewart	.40	.12
145 Andruw Jones	.40	.12
146 Carlos Lee	.40	.12
147 Roger Cedeno	.40	.12
148 Kevin Brown	.40	.12
149 Jay Payton	.40	.12
150 Scott Rolen	1.00	.30
151 J.D. Drew	.40	.12
152 Chipper Jones	1.00	.30
153 Magglio Ordonez	.40	.12
154 Tony Clark	.40	.12
155 Shawn Green	.40	.12
156 Mike Piazza	1.50	.45
157 Jimmy Rollins	.40	.12
158 Jim Edmonds	.40	.12
159 Javy Lopez	.40	.12
160 Chris Singleton	.40	.12
161 Juan Encarnacion	.40	.12
162 Eric Karros	.40	.12
163 Tsuyoshi Shinjo	.40	.12
164 Brian Giles	.40	.12
165 Darryl Kile	.40	.12
166 Greg Maddux	1.50	.45
167 Frank Thomas	1.00	.30
168 Shane Halter	.40	.12
169 Paul LoDuca	.40	.12
170 Robin Ventura	.40	.12
171 Jason Kendall	.40	.12
172 Jason Hart	.40	.12
173 Brady Anderson	.40	.12
174 Jose Valentin	.40	.12
175 Bobby Higginson	.40	.12
176 Gary Sheffield	.40	.12
177 Roger Clemens	2.00	.60
178 Aramis Ramirez	.40	.12
179 Matt Morris	.40	.12
180 Jeff Conine	.40	.12
181 Aaron Boone	.40	.12
182 Jose Macias	.40	.12
183 Jeromy Burnitz	.40	.12
184 Carl Everett	.40	.12
185 Trevor Hoffman	.40	.12
186 Placido Polanco	.40	.12
187 Jay Gibbons	.40	.12
188 Sean Casey	.40	.12
189 Josh Beckett	.40	.12
190 Jeffrey Hammonds	.40	.12
191 Chuck Knoblauch	.40	.12
192 Ryan Klesko	.40	.12
193 Albert Pujols	2.00	.60
194 Chris Richard	.40	.12
195 Adam Dunn	.60	.18
196 A.J. Burnett	.40	.12
197 Geoff Jenkins	.40	.12
198 Tino Martinez	.60	.18
199 Ray Lankford	.40	.12
200 Edgar Renteria	.40	.12
201 Eric Cyr PROS	2.00	.60
202 Travis Phelps PROS	2.00	.60
203 Rick Bauer PROS	2.00	.60
204 Mark Prior PROS	8.00	2.40
205 Wilson Betemit PROS	2.00	.60
206 Dewon Brazelton PROS	2.00	.60
207 Cody Ransom PROS	2.00	.60
208 Donnie Bridges PROS	2.00	.60
209 Justin Duchscherer PROS	2.00	.60
210 Nate Cornejo PROS	2.00	.60
211 Jason Romano PROS	2.00	.60
212 Juan Cruz PROS	2.00	.60
213 Pedro Santana PROS	2.00	.60
214 Ryan Drese PROS	2.00	.60
215 Bert Snow PROS	2.00	.60
216 Nate Frese PROS	2.00	.60
217 Rafael Soriano PROS	2.00	.60
218 Franklin Nunez PROS RC	2.00	.60
219 Tim Spooneybarger PROS	2.00	.60
220 Willie Harris PROS	2.00	.60
221 Billy Sylvester PROS	2.00	.60
222 Carlos Hernandez PROS	2.00	.60
223 Mark Teixeira PROS	3.00	.90
224 Adrian Hernandez PROS	2.00	.60
225 Andres Torres PROS	2.00	.60
226 Marlon Byrd PROS	2.00	.60
227 Juan Rivera PROS	2.00	.60
228 Adam Johnson PROS	2.00	.60
229 Justin Kaye PROS	2.00	.60
230 Kyle Kessel PROS	2.00	.60
231 Horacio Ramirez PROS	2.00	.60
232 Brandon Larson PROS	2.00	.60
233 Luis Lopez PROS	2.00	.60
234 Rob Mackowiak PROS	2.00	.60
235 Henry Mateo PROS	2.00	.60
236 Corky Miller PROS	2.00	.60
237 Greg Miller PROS	2.00	.60
238 Dustan Mohr PROS	2.00	.60
239 Bill Ortega PROS	2.00	.60
240 Billy Hall PROS	2.00	.60
241 Kazuhisa Ishii UPD RC	8.00	2.40
242 So Taguchi UPD RC	5.00	1.50
243 Takahito Nomura UPD RC	4.00	1.20
244 Satoru Komiyama UPD RC	4.00	1.20
245 Jorge Padilla UPD RC	4.00	1.20
246 Anastacio Martinez UPD RC	4.00	1.20
247 Rodrigo Rosario UPD RC	4.00	1.20
248 Ben Howard UPD RC	4.00	1.20
249 Reed Johnson UPD RC	5.00	1.50
250 Mike Crudale UPD RC	4.00	1.20
P2 Derek Jeter Promo	2.50	.75

2002 Fleer Premium Star Ruby

Randomly inserted into packs, this is a parallel of the 2002 Fleer Premium set. These cards were serial numbered to a stated print run of 125 sets. Cards 241-250 were available exclusively through the "Player to be Named" mail exchange program. The first 50 collectors that sent in cards for the "Player to be Named" program (of which was announced in May, 2002) received the Star Ruby parallel versions along with the basic update cards.

Nm-Mt Ex-Mt

*STARS 1-200: 5X TO 12X BASIC
*PROSPECTS 201-240: 1X TO 2.5X BASIC

2002 Fleer Premium Diamond Stars

Issued at stated odds of one in 72, these 20 cards feature some of the leading players in baseball as the 2002 season began.

	Nm-Mt	Ex-Mt
COMPLETE SET (20)	200.00	60.00
1 Pedro Martinez	8.00	2.40
2 Derek Jeter	20.00	6.00
3 Sammy Sosa	12.00	3.60
4 Ken Griffey Jr.	12.00	3.60
5 Chipper Jones	8.00	2.40
6 Roger Clemens	15.00	4.50
7 Ichiro Suzuki	12.00	3.60
8 Jeff Bagwell	5.00	1.50
9 Luis Gonzalez	5.00	1.50
10 Manny Ramirez	5.00	1.50
11 Alex Rodriguez	12.00	3.60
12 Kazuhiro Sasaki	5.00	1.50
13 Mike Piazza	12.00	3.60
14 Vladimir Guerrero	8.00	2.40
15 Randy Johnson	8.00	2.40
16 Ivan Rodriguez	8.00	2.40
17 Nomar Garciaparra	12.00	3.60
18 Barry Bonds	20.00	6.00
19 Todd Helton	5.00	1.50
20 Greg Maddux	12.00	3.60

2002 Fleer Premium Diamond Stars Autograph

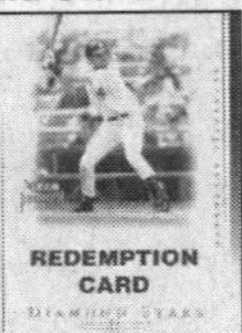

Randomly inserted in packs, and with a stated (though not serial numbered) print run of 100 copies, this card features an autograph of Derek Jeter. As Jeter did not sign these cards in time for insertion into the product, the exchange cards seeded into packs could be redeemeed until April 1, 2003.

	Nm-Mt	Ex-Mt
1 Derek Jeter	150.00	45.00

2002 Fleer Premium Diamond Stars Game Used

Issued at stated odds of one in 105, these 12 cards feature players from the Diamond Stars insert set along with a game-used memorabilia piece featuring that player.

	Nm-Mt	Ex-Mt
1 Barry Bonds Jsy	25.00	7.50
2 Manny Ramirez Jsy	15.00	4.50
3 Ivan Rodriguez Jsy	15.00	4.50
4 Kazuhiro Sasaki Jsy	15.00	4.50
5 Roger Clemens Jsy	25.00	7.50
6 Alex Rodriguez Jsy	20.00	6.00
7 Derek Jeter Bat	40.00	12.00
8 Chipper Jones Jsy	15.00	4.50
9 Todd Helton Pants	15.00	4.50
10 Luis Gonzalez Jsy	15.00	4.50
11 Mike Piazza Jsy	15.00	4.50
12 N.Garciaparra Bat SP/150	40.00	12.00

2002 Fleer Premium Diamond Stars Game Used Premium

Randomly inserted into packs and with a stated print run of 75 serial numbered cards, these 10 cards feature players from the diamond star insert set along with a game-used patch piece.

	Nm-Mt	Ex-Mt
1 Barry Bonds	100.00	30.00
2 Roger Clemens	100.00	30.00
3 Todd Helton	50.00	15.00
4 Chipper Jones	50.00	15.00
5 Manny Ramirez	50.00	15.00
6 Alex Rodriguez	80.00	24.00
7 Ivan Rodriguez	50.00	15.00
8 Luis Gonzalez	40.00	12.00
9 Mike Piazza	50.00	15.00
10 Kazuhiro Sasaki	40.00	12.00

2002 Fleer Premium Diamond Stars Dual Game Used

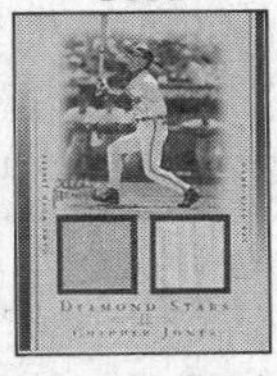

Randomly inserted into packs and with a stated print run of 100 serial numbered sets, these seven cards feature two game-used swatches of featured players from this set.

Nm-Mt Ex-Mt

PREMIUM PRINT RUN 25 #'d SETS...
NO PREMIUM PRICING DUE TO SCARCITY

	Nm-Mt	Ex-Mt
1 Barry Bonds Jsy-Pants	100.00	30.00
2 Todd Helton Jsy-Bat	50.00	15.00
3 Derek Jeter Jsy-Bat	100.00	30.00
4 Chipper Jones Jsy-Bat	50.00	15.00
5 Mike Piazza Bat-Jsy	50.00	15.00
6 Manny Ramirez Jsy-Jsy	50.00	15.00
7 Alex Rodriguez Jsy-Hat	60.00	18.00

2002 Fleer Premium International Pride

Issued at stated odds of one in six, these 15 cards feature leading players born outside the continental United States.

	Nm-Mt	Ex-Mt
COMPLETE SET (15)	25.00	7.50
1 Larry Walker	2.00	.60
2 Albert Pujols	4.00	1.20
3 Juan Gonzalez	2.00	.60
4 Ichiro Suzuki	3.00	.90
5 Rafael Palmeiro	2.00	.60
6 Carlos Delgado	2.00	.60
7 Kazuhiro Sasaki	2.00	.60
8 Vladimir Guerrero	2.00	.60
9 Bobby Abreu	2.00	.60
10 Ivan Rodriguez	2.00	.60
11 Tsuyoshi Shinjo	2.00	.60
12 Pedro Martinez	2.00	.60
13 Andruw Jones	2.00	.60
14 Sammy Sosa	3.00	.90
15 Chan Ho Park	2.00	.60

2002 Fleer Premium International Pride Game Used

Issued at stated odds of one in 90, these 10 cards feature players from the International Pride insert set along with a game-used memorabilia piece.

	Nm-Mt	Ex-Mt
1 Carlos Delgado Jsy	15.00	4.50
2 Juan Gonzalez Jsy	15.00	4.50
3 Andruw Jones Bat	15.00	4.50
4 Pedro Martinez Jsy	15.00	4.50
5 Rafael Palmeiro Jsy	15.00	4.50
6 Chan Ho Park Jsy	15.00	4.50
7 Albert Pujols Jsy	25.00	7.50
8 Ivan Rodriguez Bat	15.00	4.50
9 Kazuhiro Sasaki Jsy	15.00	4.50
10 Tsuyoshi Shinjo Jsy	15.00	4.50

2002 Fleer Premium International Pride Game Used Premium

Randomly inserted into packs and with a stated print run of 75 serial numbered sets, these 10 cards feature players from the International Pride insert set along with a game-used jersey patch of said player.

	Nm-Mt	Ex-Mt
1 Carlos Delgado	40.00	12.00
2 Juan Gonzalez	50.00	15.00
3 Andruw Jones	40.00	12.00
4 Pedro Martinez	50.00	15.00
5 Chan Ho Park	40.00	12.00
6 Ivan Rodriguez	50.00	15.00
7 Tsuyoshi Shinjo	40.00	12.00
8 Rafael Palmeiro	50.00	15.00
9 Albert Pujols	100.00	30.00
10 Kazuhiro Sasaki	40.00	12.00

2002 Fleer Premium Legendary Dynasties

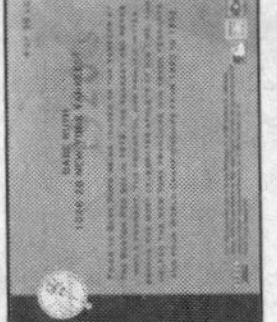

Inserted at stated odds of one in 18, these 36 cards feature players from some of the greatest past and present teams in major league history.

Nm-Mt Ex-Mt

*GOLD: .6X TO 1.5X BASIC DYNASTY
GOLD RANDOM INSERT IN PACKS
GOLD PRINT RUN 300 SERIAL #'d SETS

	Nm-Mt	Ex-Mt
1 Honus Wagner	10.00	3.00
2 Christy Mathewson	10.00	3.00
3 Lou Gehrig	12.00	3.60
4 Babe Ruth	20.00	6.00
5 Jimmie Foxx	10.00	3.00
6 Lefty Grove	8.00	2.40
7 Al Simmons	5.00	1.50
8 Bill Dickey	8.00	2.40
9 Stan Musial	10.00	3.00
10 Enos Slaughter	5.00	1.50
11 Johnny Mize	5.00	1.50
12 Yogi Berra	10.00	3.00
13 Whitey Ford	8.00	2.40
14 Jackie Robinson	5.00	1.50
15 Duke Snider	8.00	2.40
16 Roger Maris	10.00	3.00
17 Jim Palmer	5.00	1.50
18 Don Drysdale	10.00	3.00
19 Brooks Robinson	8.00	2.40
20 Rollie Fingers	5.00	1.50
21 Reggie Jackson	8.00	2.40
22 Joe Morgan	5.00	1.50
23 Johnny Bench	10.00	3.00
24 Thurman Munson	5.00	1.50
25 Jose Canseco	5.00	1.50
26 Tom Glavine	5.00	1.50
27 Chipper Jones	5.00	1.50
28 Greg Maddux	8.00	2.40
29 Roberto Alomar	5.00	1.50
30 David Cone	5.00	1.50
31 Jim Thome	5.00	1.50
32 Manny Ramirez	5.00	1.50
33 Roger Clemens	10.00	3.00
34 Derek Jeter	12.00	3.60
35 Bernie Williams	5.00	1.50
36 Alfonso Soriano	5.00	1.50

2002 Fleer Premium Legendary Dynasties Autographs

Randomly inserted into packs, these nine cards feature autographs of selected players from the legendary dynasty set. These cards are all serial numbered to a year in which the player's team won the World Series - except for Brooks Robinson's card of which honors his 1964 MVP campaign. Since all cards have different print runs, we have notated that information in our checklist. In addition, all cards were issued as exchange cards and these cards could be redeemed until April 1, 2003.

Nm-Mt Ex-Mt
1 Johnny Bench/76
2 Yogi Berra/51
3 Rollie Fingers/74
4 Tom Glavine/95
5 Reggie Jackson/73
6 Derek Jeter/96 150.00 45.00
7 Greg Maddux/95
8 Jim Palmer/70
9 Brooks Robinson/64

2002 Fleer Premium Legendary Dynasties Game Used

Issued at stated odds of one in 120, these 22 cards feature a game-worn memorabilia piece from 22 of the players featured in the Legendary Dynasty insert set. A few cards were issued in shorter supply, we have notated those cards with a SP in our checklist and their print run as well.

Nm-Mt Ex-Mt
1 Roberto Alomar Jsy 20.00 6.00
2 Johnny Bench Jsy 20.00 6.00
3 Yogi Berra Bat SP/75
4 Roger Clemens Jsy 25.00 7.50
5 Bill Dickey Bat SP/200 25.00 7.50
6 Rollie Fingers Jsy 15.00 4.50
7 Whitey Ford Jsy SP/25
8 Reggie Jackson Bat SP/250 40.00 12.00
9 Derek Jeter Bat 40.00 12.00
10 Chipper Jones Jsy 20.00 6.00
11 Roger Maris Bat SP/225 60.00 18.00
12 Johnny Mize Bat SP/225 25.00 7.50
13 Joe Morgan Bat 15.00 4.50
14 T.Munson Bat SP/250 50.00 15.00
15 Jim Palmer Jsy 15.00 4.50
16 Manny Ramirez Jsy 20.00 6.00
17 Brooks Robinson Bat SP/200 40.00 12.00
18 J.Robinson Pants SP/150 60.00 18.00
19 Babe Ruth Bat SP/60 200.00 60.00
20 Duke Snider Bat SP/250 40.00 12.00
21 Alfonso Soriano Jsy 20.00 6.00
22 Bernie Williams Jsy 20.00 6.00

2002 Fleer Premium Legendary Dynasties Game Used Premium

Randomly inserted into packs, these 12 cards feature players from the set along with a game-worn jersey patch swatch. These cards are all serial numbered to the highest win total any of their teams accomplished and we have notated that information in our checklist.

Nm-Mt Ex-Mt
1 Rollie Fingers/93 25.00 7.50
2 Roger Clemens/114 80.00 24.00
3 Roger Maris/109 100.00 30.00
4 Roberto Alomar/96 40.00 12.00
5 Reggie Jackson/93 40.00 12.00
6 Manny Ramirez/99 40.00 12.00
7 Johnny Bench/108 50.00 15.00
8 Jim Palmer/109 25.00 7.50
9 Derek Jeter/114 120.00 36.00
10 Alfonso Soriano/99 40.00 12.00
11 Chipper Jones/106 50.00 15.00
12 Bernie Williams/114 40.00 12.00

2002 Fleer Premium On Base!

Randomly inserted in packs, these 30 cards feature some of the leading offensive forces in baseball. These cards are all printed to stated print run of the player's 2002 on-base percentage. We have notated those print runs in our checklist.

Nm-Mt Ex-Mt
COMPLETE SET (30) 250.00 75.00
1 Frank Thomas/316 8.00 2.40
2 Ivan Rodriguez/347 8.00 2.40
3 Nomar Garciaparra/352 12.00 3.60
4 Ken Griffey Jr./365 12.00 3.60
5 Juan Gonzalez/370 5.00 1.50
6 Shawn Green/372 5.00 1.50
7 Vladimir Guerrero/377 8.00 2.40
8 Derek Jeter/377 20.00 6.00
9 Scott Rolen/378 8.00 2.40
10 Ichiro Suzuki/381 15.00 4.50
11 Mike Piazza/384 12.00 3.60
12 Bernie Williams/395 5.00 1.50
13 Moises Alou/396 5.00 1.50
14 Jeff Bagwell/397 5.00 1.50
15 Alex Rodriguez/399 12.00 3.60
16 Albert Pujols/403 15.00 4.50
17 Manny Ramirez/405 5.00 1.50
18 Carlos Delgado/408 5.00 1.50
19 Jim Edmonds/410 5.00 1.50
20 Roberto Alomar/415 5.00 1.50
21 Jim Thome/416 8.00 2.40
22 Gary Sheffield/417 5.00 1.50
23 Chipper Jones/427 8.00 2.40
24 Luis Gonzalez/429 5.00 1.50
25 Lance Berkman/430 5.00 1.50
26 Todd Helton/432 5.00 1.50
27 Sammy Sosa/437 12.00 3.60
28 Larry Walker/449 5.00 1.50
29 Jason Giambi/477 5.00 1.50
30 Barry Bonds/515 20.00 6.00

2002 Fleer Premium On Base! Game Used

Randomly inserted into packs, this set parallels the On Base! Insert set and was issued in a quantity of 100 serial numbered sets. These cards all feature a game-used piece of the featured player.

Nm-Mt Ex-Mt
1 Luis Gonzalez 10.00 3.00
2 Chipper Jones 15.00 4.50
3 Gary Sheffield 10.00 3.00
4 Nomar Garciaparra 25.00 7.50
5 Manny Ramirez 15.00 4.50
6 Moises Alou 10.00 3.00
7 Sammy Sosa 25.00 7.50
8 Frank Thomas 15.00 4.50
9 Ken Griffey Jr. 25.00 7.50
10 Jim Thome 15.00 4.50
11 Todd Helton 15.00 4.50
12 Larry Walker 15.00 4.50
13 Jeff Bagwell 15.00 4.50
14 Lance Berkman 10.00 3.00
15 Shawn Green 10.00 3.00
16 Vladimir Guerrero 15.00 4.50
17 Roberto Alomar 15.00 4.50
18 Mike Piazza 25.00 7.50
19 Jason Giambi 10.00 3.00
20 Derek Jeter 40.00 12.00
21 Bernie Williams 15.00 4.50
22 Scott Rolen 15.00 4.50
23 Barry Bonds 40.00 12.00
24 Ichiro Suzuki 40.00 12.00
25 Jim Edmonds 10.00 3.00
26 Albert Pujols 30.00 9.00
27 Juan Gonzalez 15.00 4.50
28 Alex Rodriguez 30.00 9.00
29 Ivan Rodriguez 15.00 4.50
30 Carlos Delgado 10.00 3.00

2003 Fleer Rookies and Greats

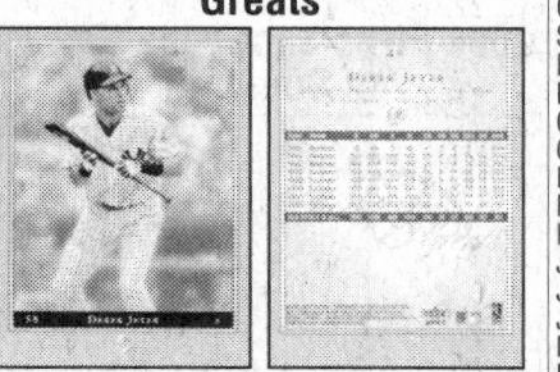

This 75-card standard-size set was released in December, 2003. The set was issued in five-card packs with an $6 SRP which came 20 packs to a box and six boxes to a case. Cards numbered 1-60 feature active stars while cards 61-75 feature a select group of retired greats. In additon, update cards for the following products: Flair, Fleer Authentix, Fleer Genuine, Fleer Hot Prospects, Fleer Showcase and Ultra were also inserted into these packs.

MINT NRMT
COMPLETE SET (75) 25.00 11.00
1 Troy Glaus .40 .18
2 Gary Sheffield .40 .18
3 Sammy Sosa 1.50 .70
4 Mark Prior 1.00 .45
5 Dontrelle Willis .60 .25
6 Shawn Green .40 .18
7 Vladimir Guerrero 1.00 .45
8 Jose Reyes .40 .18
9 Miguel Tejada .40 .18
10 Bret Boone .40 .18
11 Rocco Baldelli .40 .18
12 Rafael Palmeiro .60 .25
13 Ichiro Suzuki 1.50 .70
14 Carlos Delgado .40 .18
15 Garret Anderson .40 .18
16 Richie Sexson .40 .18
17 Roger Clemens 2.00 .90
18 Barry Zito .40 .18
19 Jim Thome 1.00 .45
20 Alex Rodriguez 1.50 .70
21 Randy Johnson 1.00 .45
22 Chipper Jones 1.00 .45
23 Kerry Wood 1.00 .45
24 Ken Griffey Jr. 1.50 .70
25 Ivan Rodriguez 1.00 .45
26 Jeff Kent .40 .18
27 Todd Helton .60 .25
28 Jeff Bagwell .60 .25
29 Hideo Nomo 1.00 .45
30 Torii Hunter .40 .18
31 Brian Giles .40 .18
32 Albert Pujols 2.00 .90
33 Vernon Wells .40 .18
34 Nomar Garciaparra 1.50 .70
35 Magglio Ordonez .40 .18
36 C.C. Sabathia .40 .18
37 Preston Wilson .40 .18
38 Mike Sweeney .40 .18
39 Jose Vidro .40 .18
40 Jason Giambi 1.00 .45
41 Derek Jeter 2.50 1.10
42 Mike Piazza 1.50 .70
43 Rich Harden .60 .25
44 Jason Kendall .40 .18
45 Barry Bonds 2.50 1.10
46 Barry Larkin .60 .25
47 Dmitri Young .40 .18
48 Craig Biggio .60 .25
49 Angel Berroa .40 .18
50 Alfonso Soriano .60 .25
51 Kevin Millwood .40 .18
52 Edgar Martinez .60 .25
53 Jim Edmonds .40 .18
54 Curt Schilling .40 .18
55 Jay Gibbons .40 .18
56 Pedro Martinez 1.00 .45
57 Greg Maddux 1.50 .70
58 Manny Ramirez .60 .25
59 Frank Thomas 1.00 .45
60 Adam Dunn .60 .25
61 Babe Ruth GR 4.00 1.80
62 Bob Gibson GR 1.50 .70
63 Willie Stargell GR 1.50 .70
64 Mike Schmidt GR 3.00 1.35
65 Nolan Ryan GR 4.00 1.80
66 Tom Seaver GR 1.50 .70
67 Brooks Robinson GR 1.50 .70
68 Willie McCovey GR 1.00 .45
69 Harmon Killebrew GR 1.50 .70
70 Al Kaline GR 1.50 .70
71 Reggie Jackson GR 1.50 .70
72 Eddie Mathews GR 1.50 .70
73 Ralph Kiner GR 1.00 .45
74 Cal Ripken GR 5.00 2.20
75 Phil Rizzuto GR 1.50 .70

2003 Fleer Rookies and Greats Blue

MINT NRMT
*BLUE 1-60: 2X TO 5X BASIC
*BLUE 61-75: 1.25X TO 3X BASIC
STATED ODDS 1:10
STATED PRINT RUN 250 SERIAL #'d SETS

2003 Fleer Rookies and Greats Boyhood Idols Game Used

MINT NRMT
OVERALL AU-GU ODDS 1:7
STATED PRINT RUN 615 SERIAL #'d SETS
BD Bucky Dent Jsy 10.00 4.50
BR Brooks Robinson Jsy 15.00 6.75
CF Carlton Fisk Jsy 15.00 6.75
CR Cal Ripken Jsy 30.00 13.50
DM Don Mattingly Jsy 25.00 11.00
FH Frank Howard Bat 10.00 4.50
HK Harmon Killebrew Pants 15.00 6.75
JC Joe Carter Bat 10.00 4.50
JM Joe Morgan Jsy 10.00 4.50
JP Jim Palmer Jsy 10.00 4.50
MS Mike Schmidt Jsy 20.00 9.00
MS2 Moose Skowron Pants 10.00 4.50
NR Nolan Ryan Jsy 25.00 11.00
RY Robin Yount Jsy 15.00 6.75

2003 Fleer Rookies and Greats Boyhood Idols Game Used Autograph

MINT NRMT
OVERALL AU-GU ODDS 1:7
PRINT RUNS B/WN 40-50 COPIES PER
BD Bucky Dent Jsy/50 30.00 13.50
BR Brooks Robinson Jsy/50 50.00 22.00
CF Carlton Fisk Jsy/50 50.00 22.00
FH Frank Howard Bat/50 30.00 13.50
HK Harmon Killebrew Pants/40 60.00 27.00
JC Joe Carter Bat/50 30.00 13.50
JP Jim Palmer Jsy/50 30.00 13.50
MS2 Moose Skowron Pants/50 30.00 13.50

2003 Fleer Rookies and Greats Dynamic Debuts

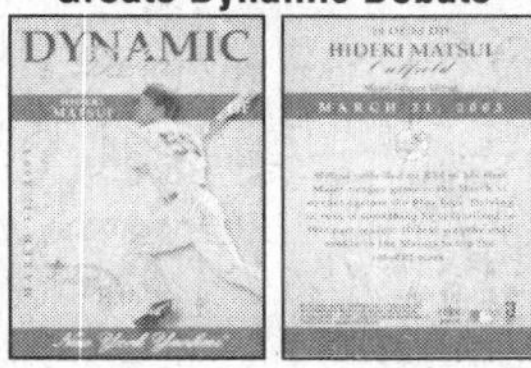

MINT NRMT
STATED ODDS 1:10
1 Rickie Weeks 5.00 2.20
2 Brandon Webb 3.00 1.35
3 Jose Reyes 2.00 .90
4 Bo Hart 3.00 1.35
5 Dontrelle Willis 3.00 1.35
6 Rich Harden 3.00 1.35
7 Ryan Wagner 3.00 1.35
8 Rocco Baldelli 2.00 .90
9 Mark Teixeira 2.00 .90
10 Hideki Matsui 6.00 2.70

2003 Fleer Rookies and Greats Dynamic Debuts Autograph

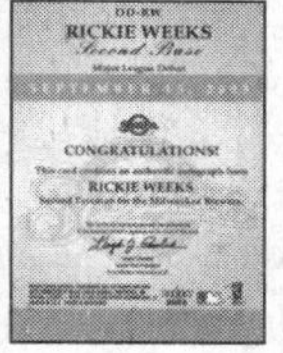

MINT NRMT
OVERALL AU-GU ODDS 1:7
STATED PRINT RUN 100 SERIAL #'d SETS
BH Bo Hart 15.00 6.75
DW Dontrelle Willis 30.00 13.50
JR Jose Reyes 25.00 11.00
RW Rickie Weeks 40.00 18.00
RW2 Ryan Wagner 15.00 6.75

2003 Fleer Rookies and Greats Looming Large

MINT NRMT
STATED PRINT RUN 500 SERIAL #'d SETS
RARE PRINT RUN 15 SERIAL #'d SETS
NO RARE PRICING DUE TO SCARCITY
*UNCOMMON: .75X TO 2X BASIC
UNCOMMON PRINT RUN 150 SERIAL #'d SETS
RANDOM INSERTS IN PACKS
BH Bo Hart 3.00 1.35
BW Brandon Webb 3.00 1.35
CB Clint Barmes 3.00 1.35
CW Chien-Ming Wang 3.00 1.35
DY Delmon Young 8.00 3.60
EJ Edwin Jackson 6.00 2.70
HM Hideki Matsui 8.00 3.60
JB Jeremy Bonderman 3.00 1.35
JC Jose Contreras 3.00 1.35
JD Jeff Duncan 3.00 1.35
MH Michael Hessman 3.00 1.35
MK Matt Kata 3.00 1.35
RH Robby Hammock 3.00 1.35
RW Rickie Weeks 6.00 2.70
RW2 Ryan Wagner 3.00 1.35

2003 Fleer Rookies and Greats Naturals

MINT NRMT
STATED ODDS 1:5
*UNCOMMON: 1.5X TO 4X BASIC
UNCOMMON RANDOM INSERTS IN PACKS
UNCOMMON PRINT RUN 75 SERIAL #'d SETS
TN1 Cal Ripken 10.00 4.50
TN2 Mike Schmidt 6.00 2.70
TN3 Derek Jeter 6.00 2.70
TN4 Joe Carter 2.00 .90
TN5 Nomar Garciaparra 4.00 1.80
TN6 Frank Howard 2.00 .90
TN7 Al Kaline 3.00 1.35
TN8 Albert Pujols 5.00 2.20
TN9 Nolan Ryan 8.00 3.60
TN10 Duke Snider 3.00 1.35
TN11 Alex Rodriguez 4.00 1.80
TN12 Brooks Robinson 3.00 1.35
TN13 Roger Clemens 5.00 2.20
TN14 Sammy Sosa 4.00 1.80
TN15 Jim Palmer 2.00 .90
TN16 Alfonso Soriano 2.50 1.10
TN17 Don Mattingly 8.00 3.60
TN18 Harmon Killebrew 3.00 1.35
TN19 Bob Feller 2.00 .90
TN20 Reggie Jackson 3.00 1.35
TN21 Ichiro Suzuki 4.00 1.80
TN22 Barry Bonds 6.00 2.70
TN23 Hideki Matsui 8.00 3.60
TN24 Willie Stargell 3.00 1.35
TN25 Pee Wee Reese 3.00 1.35

2003 Fleer Rookies and Greats Naturals Autograph

MINT NRMT
OVERALL AU-GU ODDS 1:7
STATED PRINT RUN 50 SERIAL #'d SETS
AK Al Kaline 50.00 22.00
BF Bob Feller 25.00 11.00
BR Brooks Robinson 40.00 18.00

CR Cal Ripken 150.00 70.00
DS Duke Snider 40.00 18.00
FH Frank Howard 40.00 18.00
HK Harmon Killebrew 50.00 22.00
JC Joe Carter 25.00 11.00
JP Jim Palmer 25.00 11.00
NR Nolan Ryan 120.00 55.00

2003 Fleer Rookies and Greats Naturals Game Used

MINT NRMT
PRINT RUNS B/WN 250-400 COPIES PER
PATCH PRINT RUN 25 SERIAL #'d SETS
NO PATCH PRICING DUE TO SCARCITY
OVERALL AU-GU ODDS 1:7
AK Al Kaline Bat/250 15.00 6.75
AP Albert Pujols Jsy/250 20.00 9.00
AR Alex Rodriguez Jsy/250 10.00 4.50
AS Alfonso Soriano Jsy/250 10.00 4.50
BR Brooks Robinson Jsy/400 15.00 6.75
CR Cal Ripken Jsy/250 30.00 13.50
DJ Derek Jeter Jsy/250 25.00 11.00
DM Don Mattingly Jsy/250 25.00 11.00
DS Duke Snider Jsy/250 15.00 6.75
FH Frank Howard Bat/400 10.00 4.50
HK Harmon Killebrew Pants/400 15.00 6.75
JC Joe Carter Bat/250 10.00 4.50
JP Jim Palmer Jsy/250 10.00 4.50
MS Mike Schmidt Jsy/250 20.00 9.00
NG Nomar Garciaparra Jsy/250 15.00 6.75
NR Nolan Ryan Jsy/400 25.00 11.00
RC Roger Clemens Jsy/400 15.00 6.75
RJ Reggie Jackson Jsy/400 15.00 6.75
SS Sammy Sosa Jsy/250 15.00 6.75

2003 Fleer Rookies and Greats Naturals Game Used Autograph

MINT NRMT
OVERALL AU-GU ODDS 1:7
STATED PRINT RUN 30 SERIAL #'d SETS
AU PATCH PRINT RUN 5 SERIAL #'d SETS
NO AU PATCH PRICING DUE TO SCARCITY
AK Al Kaline Bat 80.00 36.00
BR Brooks Robinson Jsy 60.00 27.00
CR Cal Ripken Jsy 200.00 90.00
DS Duke Snider Jsy 60.00 27.00
FH Frank Howard Bat 40.00 18.00
HK Harmon Killebrew Pants 80.00 36.00
JC Joe Carter Bat 40.00 18.00
JP Jim Palmer Jsy 40.00 18.00
NR Nolan Ryan Jsy 150.00 70.00

2003 Fleer Rookies and Greats Through the Years Game Used

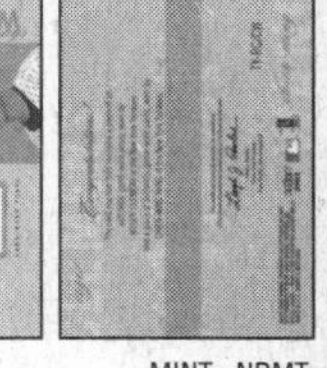

MINT NRMT
STATED PRINT RUN 360 SERIAL #'d SETS
PATCH PRINT RUN 25 SERIAL #'d SETS
NO PATCH PRICING DUE TO SCARCITY
OVERALL AU-GU ODDS 1:7
ALL ARE DUAL JSY UNLESS NOTED
ARMT Alex Rodriguez Jsy 15.00 6.75
Mark Teixeira Jsy
BHLB Bo Hart Pants 15.00 6.75
Lou Brock Jsy
BLJM Barry Larkin Jsy 15.00 6.75
Joe Morgan Jsy
DJPR Derek Jeter Jsy 40.00 18.00
Phil Rizzuto Pants
EMCJ Eddie Mathews Pants 20.00 9.00
Chipper Jones Jsy
HKTH Harmon Killebrew Pants 20.00 9.00
Torii Hunter Jsy

JCMM Jose Contreras Jsy	15.00	6.75
Mike Mussina Jsy		
JGRJ Jason Giambi Jsy	15.00	6.75
Reggie Jackson Jsy		
JTMS Jim Thome Jsy	30.00	13.50
Mike Schmidt Jsy		
MHCJ Michael Hessman Pants	15.00	6.75
Chipper Jones Jsy		
MPJR Mike Piazza Jsy	15.00	6.75
Jose Reyes Jsy		
NGBD Nomar Garciaparra Jsy	25.00	11.00
Bobby Doerr Bat		
NRHB Nolan Ryan Jsy	40.00	18.00
Hank Blalock Jsy		
PRJR Phil Rizzuto Pants	20.00	9.00
Jose Reyes Jsy		
RCCW Roger Clemens Jsy	25.00	11.00
Chien-Ming Wang Pants		
RJBW Randy Johnson Jsy	15.00	6.75
Brandon Webb Jsy		
RYSP Robin Yount Jsy	25.00	11.00
Scott Podsednik Bat		
SCKM Steve Carlton Jsy	10.00	4.50
Kevin Millwood Jsy		
SSMP Sammy Sosa Jsy	25.00	11.00
Mark Prior Jsy		
WMBB Willie McCovey Pants	25.00	11.00
Barry Bonds Base		

2000 Fleer Showcase

The 2000 Fleer Showcase product was released in October, 2000. The product featured a 140-card base set that was broken into tiers as follows: 100 Base Veterans (1-100). 40 Prospects (101-140). Please note that cards 101-115 were serial numbered to 1000, and cards 116-140 were serial numbered to 2000. Each pack contained five cards and carried a suggested retail price of $3.99.

	Nm-Mt	Ex-Mt
COMP.SET w/o SP's (100)	25.00	7.50
COMMON CARD (1-100)	.50	.15
COMMON (101-115)	8.00	2.40
COMMON (116-140)	5.00	1.50
1 Alex Rodriguez	2.00	.60
2 Derek Jeter	3.00	.90
3 Jeromy Burnitz	.50	.15
4 John Olerud	.50	.15
5 Paul Konerko	.50	.15
6 Johnny Damon	.75	.23
7 Curt Schilling	.50	.15
8 Barry Larkin	.75	.23
9 Adrian Beltre	.75	.23
10 Scott Rolen	1.25	.35
11 Carlos Delgado	.50	.15
12 Pedro Martinez	1.25	.35
13 Todd Helton	.75	.23
14 Jacque Jones	.50	.15
15 Jeff Kent	.50	.15
16 Darin Erstad	.50	.15
17 Juan Encarnacion	.50	.15
18 Roger Clemens	2.50	.75
19 Tony Gwynn	1.50	.45
20 Nomar Garciaparra	2.00	.60
21 Roberto Alomar	.75	.23
22 Matt Lawton	.50	.15
23 Rich Aurilia	.50	.15
24 Charles Johnson	.50	.15
25 Jim Thome	1.25	.35
26 Eric Milton	.50	.15
27 Barry Bonds	3.00	.90
28 Albert Belle	.50	.15
29 Travis Fryman	.50	.15
30 Ken Griffey Jr.	2.00	.60
31 Phil Nevin	.50	.15
32 Chipper Jones	1.25	.35
33 Craig Biggio	.75	.23
34 Mike Hampton	.50	.15
35 Fred McGriff	.75	.23
36 Cal Ripken	4.00	1.20
37 Manny Ramirez	.75	.23
38 Jose Vidro	.50	.15
39 Trevor Hoffman	.50	.15
40 Tom Glavine	.75	.23
41 Frank Thomas	1.25	.35
42 Chris Widger	.50	.15
43 J.D. Drew	.50	.15
44 Andres Galarraga	.50	.15
45 Pokey Reese	.50	.15
46 Mike Piazza	2.00	.60
47 Kevin Young	.50	.15
48 Sean Casey	.50	.15
49 Carlos Beltran	.75	.23
50 Jason Kendall	.50	.15
51 Vladimir Guerrero	1.25	.35
52 Jermaine Dye	.50	.15
53 Brian Giles	.50	.15
54 Andruw Jones	.50	.15
55 Richard Hidalgo	.50	.15
56 Robin Ventura	.50	.15
57 Ivan Rodriguez	1.25	.35
58 Greg Maddux	2.00	.60
59 Billy Wagner	.50	.15
60 Ruben Mateo	.50	.15
61 Troy Glaus	.50	.15
62 Dean Palmer	.50	.15
63 Eric Chavez	.50	.15
64 Edgar Martinez	.75	.23
65 Randy Johnson	1.25	.35
66 Preston Wilson	.50	.15
67 Orlando Hernandez	.50	.15
68 Jim Edmonds	.50	.15
69 Carl Everett	.50	.15
70 Larry Walker	.75	.23
71 Ron Belliard	.50	.15
72 Sammy Sosa	2.00	.60
73 Matt Williams	.50	.15
74 Cliff Floyd	.50	.15
75 Bernie Williams	.75	.23
76 Fernando Tatis	.50	.15
77 Steve Finley	.50	.15
78 Jeff Bagwell	.75	.23
79 Edgardo Alfonzo	.50	.15
80 Jose Canseco	1.25	.35
81 Magglio Ordonez	.50	.15
82 Shawn Green	.50	.15
83 Bobby Abreu	.50	.15
84 Tony Batista	.50	.15
85 Mo Vaughn	.50	.15
86 Juan Gonzalez	.75	.23
87 Paul O'Neill	.75	.23
88 Mark McGwire	3.00	.90
89 Mark Grace	.75	.23
90 Kevin Brown	.50	.15
91 Ben Grieve	.50	.15
92 Shannon Stewart	.50	.15
93 Erubiel Durazo	.50	.15
94 Antonio Alfonseca	.50	.15
95 Jeff Cirillo	.50	.15
96 Greg Vaughn	.50	.15
97 Kerry Wood	1.25	.35
98 Geoff Jenkins	.50	.15
99 Jason Giambi	.50	.15
100 Rafael Palmeiro	.75	.23
101 Rafael Furcal PROS	8.00	2.40
102 Pablo Ozuna PROS	8.00	2.40
103 Brad Penny PROS	8.00	2.40
104 Mark Mulder PROS	8.00	2.40
105 Adam Piatt PROS	8.00	2.40
106 Mike Lamb PROS RC	8.00	2.40
107 K.Sasaki PROS RC	10.00	3.00
108 A.McNeal PROS RC	8.00	2.40
109 Pat Burrell PROS	8.00	2.40
110 Rick Ankiel PROS	8.00	2.40
111 Eric Munson PROS	8.00	2.40
112 Josh Beckett PROS	8.00	2.40
113 Adam Kennedy PROS	8.00	2.40
114 Alex Escobar PROS	8.00	2.40
115 C.Hermansen PROS	8.00	2.40
116 Kip Wells PROS	5.00	1.50
117 Matt LeCroy PROS	5.00	1.50
118 Julio Ramirez PROS	5.00	1.50
119 Ben Petrick PROS	5.00	1.50
120 Nick Johnson PROS	5.00	1.50
121 G.Dawkins PROS	5.00	1.50
122 Julio Zuleta PROS RC	5.00	1.50
123 A.Soriano PROS	8.00	2.40
124 K.McDonald RC	5.00	1.50
125 Kory DeHaan PROS	5.00	1.50
126 Vernon Wells PROS	5.00	1.50
127 D.Stenson PROS	5.00	1.50
128 David Eckstein PROS	5.00	1.50
129 Robert Fick PROS	5.00	1.50
130 Cole Liniak PROS	5.00	1.50
131 Mark Quinn PROS	5.00	1.50
132 Eric Gagne PROS	15.00	4.50
133 Wily Mo Pena PROS	5.00	1.50
134 A.Thompson RC	5.00	1.50
135 Steve Sisco PROS RC	5.00	1.50
136 P.Rigdon PROS RC	5.00	1.50
137 Rob Bell PROS	5.00	1.50
138 Carlos Guillen PROS	5.00	1.50
139 Jimmy Rollins PROS	5.00	1.50
140 Jason Conti PROS	5.00	1.50

2000 Fleer Showcase Legacy Collection

Randomly inserted into packs, this 140-card set is a complete parallel of the 2000 Fleer Showcase base set. Each card in the set is individually serial numbered to 20.

	Nm-Mt	Ex-Mt
*STARS 1-100: 25X TO 60X BASIC ...		

2000 Fleer Showcase Prospect Showcase First

Randomly inserted into packs, this 40-card set features MLB's top prospects. Each card is individually serial numbered to 500.

	Nm-Mt	Ex-Mt
*PROSPECT 1-15: .4X TO 1X BASIC ..		
*PROSPECT RC 1-15: .5X TO 1.2X BASIC		
*PROSPECT 16-40: .6X TO 1.5X BASIC		
*PROSPECT RC 16-40: .75X TO 2X BASIC		

2000 Fleer Showcase Consummate Prose

Randomly inserted into packs at one in six, this 15-card die-cut set features players that perform at a higher level. Card backs carry a "CP" prefix.

	Nm-Mt	Ex-Mt
COMPLETE SET (15)	30.00	9.00
CP1 Jeff Bagwell	1.00	.30
CP2 Alex Rodriguez	2.50	.75
CP3 Chipper Jones	1.50	.45
CP4 Derek Jeter	4.00	1.20
CP5 Manny Ramirez	1.00	.30
CP6 Tony Gwynn	2.00	.60
CP7 Sammy Sosa	2.50	.75
CP8 Ivan Rodriguez	1.50	.45
CP9 Greg Maddux	2.50	.75
CP10 Ken Griffey Jr.	2.50	.75
CP11 Rick Ankiel	.60	.18
CP12 Cal Ripken	5.00	1.50
CP13 Pedro Martinez	1.50	.45
CP14 Mike Piazza	2.50	.75
CP15 Mark McGwire	4.00	1.20

2000 Fleer Showcase Feel the Game

Randomly inserted into packs at one in 72, this 10-card insert features game-used jersey cards of some of the biggest names in MLB. Card backs carry a "FG" prefix.

	Nm-Mt	Ex-Mt
FG1 Barry Bonds	40.00	12.00
FG2 Gookie Dawkins	8.00	2.40
FG3 Darin Erstad	10.00	3.00
FG4 Troy Glaus	10.00	3.00
FG5 Scott Rolen	15.00	4.50
FG6 Alex Rodriguez	25.00	7.50
FG7 Andruw Jones	10.00	3.00
FG8 Robin Ventura	10.00	3.00
FG9 Sean Casey	10.00	3.00
FG10 Cal Ripken	50.00	15.00

2000 Fleer Showcase Final Answer

Randomly inserted into packs at one in 10, this 10-card set features hitters that get the job done in clutch situations. Card backs carry a "FA" prefix.

	Nm-Mt	Ex-Mt
COMPLETE SET (10)	40.00	12.00
FA1 Alex Rodriguez	4.00	1.20
FA2 Vladimir Guerrero	2.50	.75
FA3 Cal Ripken	8.00	2.40
FA4 Sammy Sosa	4.00	1.20
FA5 Barry Bonds	6.00	1.80
FA6 Derek Jeter	6.00	1.80
FA7 Ken Griffey Jr.	4.00	1.20
FA8 Mike Piazza	4.00	1.20
FA9 Nomar Garciaparra	4.00	1.20
FA10 Mark McGwire	6.00	1.80

2000 Fleer Showcase Fresh Ink

Randomly inserted into packs at one in 24, this 38-card insert set features autographs of many of MLB's top stars and prospects. Please note that Josh Beckett and Brad Penny packed out as exchange cards and must be submited to Fleer by 07/01/01. These cards are not numbered and we have sequenced them in alphabetical order in our checklist.

	Nm-Mt	Ex-Mt
1 Rick Ankiel	15.00	4.50
2 Josh Beckett	25.00	7.50
3 Barry Bonds	250.00	75.00
4 A.J. Burnett	10.00	3.00
5 Pat Burrell	15.00	4.50
6 Ken Caminiti	25.00	7.50
7 Sean Casey	15.00	4.50
8 Jose Cruz Jr.	10.00	3.00
9 Gookie Dawkins	10.00	3.00
10 Erubiel Durazo	15.00	4.50
11 Juan Encarnacion	10.00	3.00
12 Darin Erstad	15.00	4.50
13 Rafael Furcal	15.00	4.50
14 Nomar Garciaparra	120.00	36.00
15 Jason Giambi	25.00	7.50
16 Jeremy Giambi	10.00	3.00
17 Brian Giles	15.00	4.50
18 Troy Glaus	15.00	4.50
19 Vladimir Guerrero	40.00	12.00
20 Chad Hermansen	10.00	3.00
21 Randy Johnson	60.00	18.00
22 Andruw Jones	15.00	4.50
23 Jason Kendall	15.00	4.50
24 Paul Konerko	15.00	4.50
25 Mike Lowell	15.00	4.50
26 Aaron McNeal	15.00	4.50
27 Warren Morris	10.00	3.00
28 Paul O'Neill	25.00	7.50
29 Magglio Ordonez	15.00	4.50
30 Pablo Ozuna	10.00	3.00
31 Brad Penny	15.00	4.50
32 Ben Petrick	10.00	3.00
33 Pokey Reese	15.00	4.50
34 Cal Ripken	150.00	45.00
35 Alex Rodriguez	100.00	30.00
36 Scott Rolen	40.00	12.00
37 Jose Vidro	10.00	3.00
38 Kip Wells	10.00	3.00

2000 Fleer Showcase License to Skill

Randomly inserted into packs at one in 20, this 10-card set features highly skilled players. Card backs carry a "LS" prefix.

	Nm-Mt	Ex-Mt
COMPLETE SET (10)	80.00	24.00
LS1 Vladimir Guerrero	5.00	1.50
LS2 Pedro Martinez	5.00	1.50
LS3 Nomar Garciaparra	8.00	2.40
LS4 Ivan Rodriguez	5.00	1.50
LS5 Mark McGwire	12.00	3.60
LS6 Derek Jeter	12.00	3.60
LS7 Ken Griffey Jr.	8.00	2.40
LS8 Randy Johnson	5.00	1.50
LS9 Sammy Sosa	8.00	2.40
LS10 Alex Rodriguez	8.00	2.40

2000 Fleer Showcase Long Gone

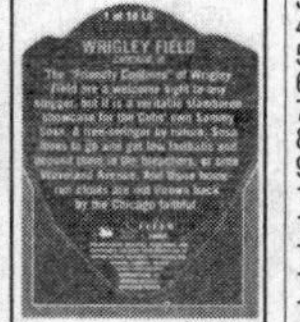

Randomly inserted into packs at one in 20, this 10-card set features hitters that are known for hitting the longball. Card backs carry a "LG" prefix.

	Nm-Mt	Ex-Mt
COMPLETE SET (10)	25.00	7.50
LG1 Sammy Sosa	3.00	.90
LG2 Derek Jeter	5.00	1.50
LG3 Nomar Garciaparra	3.00	.90
LG4 Juan Gonzalez	1.25	.35
LG5 Vladimir Guerrero	2.00	.60
LG6 Barry Bonds	5.00	1.50
LG7 Jeff Bagwell	1.25	.35
LG8 Alex Rodriguez	3.00	.90
LG9 Ken Griffey Jr.	3.00	.90
LG10 Mark McGwire	5.00	1.50

2000 Fleer Showcase Noise of Summer

Randomly inserted into packs at one in 10, this 10-card set features players that make plenty of noise during the season. Card backs carry a "NS" prefix.

	Nm-Mt	Ex-Mt
COMPLETE SET (10)	40.00	12.00
NS1 Chipper Jones	2.50	.75
NS2 Jeff Bagwell	1.50	.45
NS3 Manny Ramirez	1.50	.45
NS4 Mark McGwire	6.00	1.80
NS5 Ken Griffey Jr.	4.00	1.20
NS6 Mike Piazza	4.00	1.20
NS7 Pedro Martinez	2.50	.75
NS8 Alex Rodriguez	4.00	1.20
NS9 Derek Jeter	6.00	1.80
NS10 Randy Johnson	2.50	.75

2000 Fleer Showcase Sweet Sigs

Randomly inserted into packs at one in 250, this 10-card set features autographs of MLB players like Alex Rodriguez and Nolan Ryan. Card backs carry a "SS" prefix. A month after the product went live, representatives at Fleer publicly released print run information on three short-printed cards (Clemens, Garciaparra and A.Rodriguez). Exact amounts are provided in our checklist.

	Nm-Mt	Ex-Mt
SS1 N.Garciaparra SP/53	250.00	75.00
SS2 Alex Rodriguez SP/67	250.00	75.00
SS3 Tony Gwynn	50.00	15.00
SS4 Roger Clemens SP/79	200.00	60.00
SS5 Scott Rolen	60.00	18.00
SS6 Greg Maddux	100.00	30.00
SS7 Jose Cruz Jr.	15.00	4.50
SS8 Tony Womack	15.00	4.50
SS9 Jay Buhner	25.00	7.50
SS10 Nolan Ryan	150.00	45.00

2001 Fleer Showcase

This 160-card set was distributed in five-card packs with a suggested retail price of $4.99. The set features color player images on Satin technology and contains the following subsets: Avant (101-115), Rookie Avant (116-125), and Rookie Showcase (126-160) with the first 20 sequentially numbered to 1,500 and the next 15 to 2,000)

	Nm-Mt	Ex-Mt
COMP.SET w/o SP's (100)	30.00	9.00
COMMON CARD (1-100)	.50	.15
COMMON (101-115)	5.00	1.50
COMMON (116-125)	10.00	3.00
COMMON (126 -160)	5.00	1.50
1 Tony Gwynn	1.50	.45
2 Barry Larkin	.75	.23
3 Chan Ho Park	.50	.15
4 Darin Erstad	.50	.15
5 Rafael Furcal	.50	.15
6 Roger Cedeno	.50	.15
7 Timo Perez	.50	.15
8 Rick Ankiel	.50	.15
9 Pokey Reese	.50	.15
10 Jeromy Burnitz	.50	.15
11 Phil Nevin	.50	.15
12 Matt Williams	.50	.15
13 Mike Hampton	.50	.15
14 Fernando Tatis	.50	.15
15 Kazuhiro Sasaki	.50	.15
16 Jim Thome	1.25	.35
17 Geoff Jenkins	.50	.15
18 Jeff Kent	.50	.15
19 Tom Glavine	.75	.23
20 Dean Palmer	.50	.15
21 Todd Zeile	.50	.15
22 Edgar Renteria	.50	.15
23 Andruw Jones	.50	.15
24 Juan Encarnacion	.50	.15
25 Robin Ventura	.50	.15
26 J.D. Drew	.50	.15
27 Ray Durham	.50	.15
28 Richard Hidalgo	.50	.15
29 Eric Chavez	.50	.15
30 Rafael Palmeiro	.75	.23
31 Steve Finley	.50	.15
32 Jeff Weaver	.50	.15
33 Al Leiter	.50	.15
34 Jim Edmonds	.50	.15
35 Garret Anderson	.50	.15
36 Larry Walker	.75	.23
37 Jose Vidro	.50	.15
38 Mike Cameron	.50	.15
39 Brady Anderson	.50	.15
40 Mike Lowell	.50	.15
41 Bernie Williams	.75	.23
42 Gary Sheffield	.50	.15
43 John Smoltz	.75	.23
44 Mike Mussina	.75	.23
45 Greg Vaughn	.50	.15
46 Juan Gonzalez	.75	.23
47 Matt Lawton	.50	.15
48 Robb Nen	.50	.15
49 Brad Radke	.50	.15
50 Edgar Martinez	.75	.23
51 Mike Bordick	.50	.15
52 Shawn Green	.50	.15
53 Carl Everett	.50	.15
54 Adrian Beltre	.75	.23
55 Kerry Wood	1.25	.35
56 Kevin Brown	.50	.15
57 Brian Giles	.50	.15
58 Greg Maddux	2.00	.60
59 Preston Wilson	.50	.15
60 Orlando Hernandez	.50	.15
61 Ben Grieve	.50	.15
62 Jermaine Dye	.50	.15
63 Travis Lee	.50	.15
64 Jose Cruz Jr.	.50	.15
65 Rondell White	.50	.15
66 Carlos Beltran	.75	.23
67 Scott Rolen	1.25	.35
68 Brad Fullmer	.50	.15
69 David Wells	.50	.15
70 Mike Sweeney	.50	.15
71 Barry Zito	.75	.23
72 Tony Batista	.50	.15
73 Curt Schilling	.50	.15
74 Jeff Cirillo	.50	.15
75 Edgardo Alfonzo	.50	.15
76 John Olerud	.50	.15
77 Carlos Lee	.50	.15
78 Moises Alou	.50	.15
79 Tim Hudson	.50	.15
80 Andres Galarraga	.50	.15
81 Roberto Alomar	.75	.23
82 Richie Sexson	.50	.15
83 Trevor Hoffman	.50	.15
84 Omar Vizquel	.75	.23
85 Jacque Jones	.50	.15
86 J.T. Snow	.50	.15
87 Sean Casey	.50	.15
88 Craig Biggio	.75	.23
89 Mariano Rivera	.75	.23
90 Rusty Greer	.50	.15
91 Barry Bonds	3.00	.90
92 Pedro Martinez	1.25	.35
93 Cal Ripken	4.00	1.20
94 Pat Burrell	.50	.15
95 Chipper Jones	1.25	.35
96 Magglio Ordonez	.50	.15
97 Jeff Bagwell	.75	.23

98 Randy Johnson 1.25 .35
99 Frank Thomas 1.25 .35
100 Jason Kendall .50 .15
101 N.Garciaparra AC 12.00 3.60
102 Mark McGwire AC 20.00 6.00
103 Troy Glaus AC 5.00 1.50
104 Ivan Rodriguez AC 8.00 2.40
105 Manny Ramirez AC 5.00 1.50
106 Derek Jeter AC 20.00 6.00
107 Alex Rodriguez AC 12.00 3.60
108 Ken Griffey Jr. AC 12.00 3.60
109 Todd Helton AC 5.00 1.50
110 Sammy Sosa AC 12.00 3.60
111 Vladimir Guerrero AC 8.00 2.40
112 Mike Piazza AC 12.00 3.60
113 Roger Clemens AC 15.00 4.50
114 Jason Giambi AC 5.00 1.50
115 Carlos Delgado AC 5.00 1.50
116 Ichiro Suzuki AC RC 100.00 30.00
117 M.Ensberg AC RC 15.00 4.50
118 C. Valderrama AC RC 10.00 3.00
119 Erick Almonte AC RC 10.00 3.00
120 T.Shinjo AC RC 15.00 4.50
121 Albert Pujols AC RC 120.00 36.00
122 Wilson Betemit AC RC 10.00 3.00
123 A.Hernandez AC RC 10.00 3.00
124 J.Melian AC RC 10.00 3.00
125 Drew Henson AC RC 15.00 4.50
126 Paul Phillips RS RC 5.00 1.50
127 Esix Snead RS RC 5.00 1.50
128 Ryan Freel RS RC 5.00 1.50
129 Junior Spivey RS RC 8.00 2.40
130 E.Guzman RS RC 5.00 1.50
131 Juan Diaz RS RC 5.00 1.50
132 Andres Torres RS RC 5.00 1.50
133 Jay Gibbons RS RC 8.00 2.40
134 Bill Ortega RS RC 5.00 1.50
135 Alexis Gomez RS RC 5.00 1.50
136 Wilkin Ruan RS RC 5.00 1.50
137 Henry Mateo RS RC 5.00 1.50
138 Juan Uribe RS RC 8.00 2.40
139 J.Estrada RS RC 8.00 2.40
140 J.Randolph RS RC 5.00 1.50
141 Eric Hinske RS RC 8.00 2.40
142 Jack Wilson RS RC 10.00 3.00
143 Cody Ransom RS RC 5.00 1.50
144 Nate Frese RS RC 5.00 1.50
145 John Grabow RS RC 5.00 1.50
146 C.Parker RS RC 5.00 1.50
147 B.Lawrence RS RC 5.00 1.50
148 B. Duckworth RS RC 5.00 1.50
149 Winston Abreu RS RC 5.00 1.50
150 H.Ramirez RS RC 8.00 2.40
151 Nick Maness RS RC 5.00 1.50
152 Blaine Neal RS RC 5.00 1.50
153 Billy Sylvester RS RC 5.00 1.50
154 David Elder RS RC 5.00 1.50
155 Bert Snow RS RC 5.00 1.50
156 Claudio Vargas RS RC 5.00 1.50
157 Martin Vargas RS RC 5.00 1.50
158 Grant Balfour RS RC 5.00 1.50
159 Randy Keisler RS 5.00 1.50
160 Zach Day RS RC 5.00 1.50
P1 Tony Gwynn Promo 2.00 .60
MM3 D.Jeter MM/2000 12.00 3.60
NNO D.Jeter MM AU/100 120.00 36.00

2001 Fleer Showcase Legacy

Randomly inserted in hobby packs only, this 160-card set is a parallel version of the base set. Only 50 serially numbered sets were produced.

Nm-Mt Ex-Mt
*STARS 1-100: 8X TO 20X BASIC 1-100
*AVANT 101-115: 1.25X TO 3X BASIC 101-115
*AVANT 116-125: .75X TO 2X BASIC 116-125
*RS 126-145: 1.25X TO 3X BASIC 126-145
*RS 146-160: 1.5X TO 4X BASIC 146-160

2001 Fleer Showcase Awards Showcase

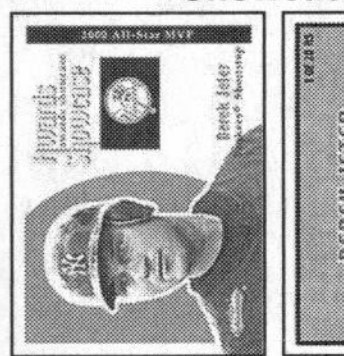
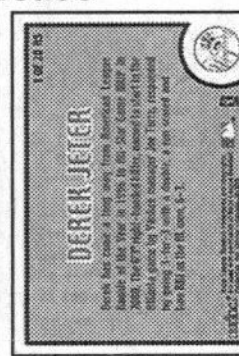

Randomly inserted in retail packs only at the rate of one in 20, this 20-card set features color photos of some of the big award winners from the 2000 season.

Nm-Mt Ex-Mt
COMPLETE SET (20) 60.00 18.00
AS1 Derek Jeter 8.00 2.40
AS2 Derek Jeter 8.00 2.40
AS3 Jason Giambi 1.25 .35
AS4 Jeff Kent 1.25 .35
AS5 Pedro Martinez 3.00 .90
AS6 Randy Johnson 3.00 .90
AS7 Kazuhiro Sasaki 1.25 .35
AS8 Rafael Furcal 1.25 .35
AS9 Carlos Delgado 1.25 .35
AS10 Todd Helton 2.00 .60
AS11 Ivan Rodriguez 3.00 .90
AS12 Darin Erstad 1.25 .35
AS13 Bernie Williams 2.00 .60
AS14 Greg Maddux 5.00 1.50
AS15 Jim Edmonds 1.25 .35
AS16 Andruw Jones 1.25 .35
AS17 Nomar Garciaparra 5.00 1.50
AS18 Todd Helton 2.00 .60
AS19 Troy Glaus 1.25 .35
AS20 Sammy Sosa 5.00 1.50

2001 Fleer Showcase Awards Showcase Memorabilia

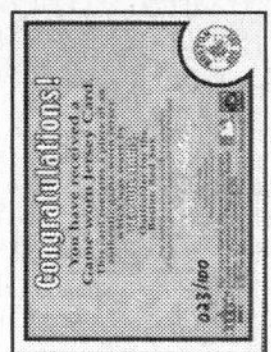

Randomly inserted in hobby packs only, this 34-card set features color photos of players who were Cy Young and MVP winners with pieces of memorabilia embedded in the cards. Only 100 serially numbered sets were produced.

Nm-Mt Ex-Mt
1 Johnny Bench Jsy 25.00 7.50
2 Yogi Berra Bat 25.00 7.50
3 George Brett Jsy 40.00 12.00
4 Lou Brock Bat 25.00 7.50
5 Roy Campanella Bat 40.00 12.00
6 Steve Carlton Jsy 15.00 4.50
7 Roger Clemens Jsy 40.00 12.00
9 Andre Dawson Jsy 15.00 4.50
10 Whitey Ford Jsy 25.00 7.50
12 Jimmie Foxx Bat 60.00 18.00
14 Kirk Gibson Bat 15.00 4.50
15 Tom Glavine Jsy 25.00 7.50
16 Juan Gonzalez Bat 25.00 7.50
17 Elston Howard Bat 25.00 7.50
18 Jim Hunter Jsy 25.00 7.50
19 Reggie Jackson Bat 25.00 7.50
20 Randy Johnson Jsy 25.00 7.50
21 Chipper Jones Bat 25.00 7.50
22 Harmon Killebrew Bat 25.00 7.50
23 Fred Lynn Bat 15.00 4.50
24 Greg Maddux Jsy 25.00 7.50
25 Don Mattingly Bat 40.00 12.00
27 Willie McCovey Jsy 15.00 4.50
28 Jim Palmer Jsy 15.00 4.50
29 Jim Rice Bat 15.00 4.50
30 Brooks Robinson Bat 25.00 7.50
31 Frank Robinson Bat 25.00 7.50
32 Jackie Robinson Pants 80.00 24.00
33 Ivan Rodriguez Jsy 25.00 7.50
34 Mike Schmidt Jsy 40.00 12.00
35 Tom Seaver Jsy 25.00 7.50
36 Willie Stargell Jsy 25.00 7.50
37 Ted Williams Jsy 100.00 30.00
38 Robin Yount Jsy 25.00 7.50

2001 Fleer Showcase Sticks

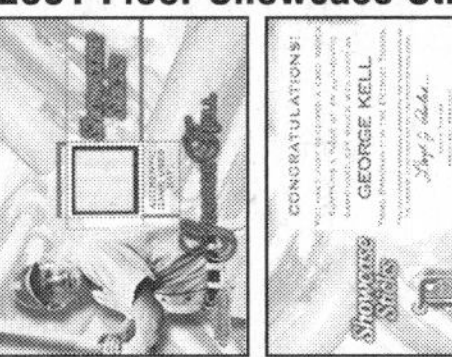

Randomly inserted into hobby packs at the rate of one in 24, this 36-card set color player photos with pieces of game-used bats embedded in the cards.

Nm-Mt Ex-Mt
1 Roberto Alomar 15.00 4.50
2 Rick Ankiel 10.00 3.00
3 Adrian Beltre 15.00 4.50
4 Barry Bonds 25.00 7.50
5 Pat Burrell 10.00 3.00
6 Roger Cedeno 10.00 3.00
7 Tony Clark 10.00 3.00
8 Roger Clemens 15.00 4.50
9 Carlos Delgado 10.00 3.00
10 J.D. Drew 10.00 3.00
11 Steve Finley 10.00 3.00
12 Rafael Furcal 10.00 3.00
13 Alex Gonzalez 10.00 3.00
14 Juan Gonzalez 15.00 4.50
15 Shawn Green 10.00 3.00
16 Vladimir Guerrero 15.00 4.50
17 Richard Hidalgo 10.00 3.00
18 Reggie Jackson 15.00 4.50
19 Randy Johnson 15.00 4.50
20 Andruw Jones 10.00 3.00
21 Chipper Jones 15.00 4.50
22 Al Kaline 15.00 4.50
23 George Kell 15.00 4.50
24 Jason Kendall 10.00 3.00
25 Magglio Ordonez 10.00 3.00
26 Adam Piatt 10.00 3.00
27 Jorge Posada 15.00 4.50
28 Ivan Rodriguez 15.00 4.50
29 Scott Rolen 15.00 4.50
30 Tsuyoshi Shinjo 15.00 4.50
31 Shannon Stewart 10.00 3.00
32 Ichiro Suzuki 40.00 12.00
33 Frank Thomas 15.00 4.50
34 Jim Thome 15.00 4.50
35 Jose Vidro 10.00 3.00
36 Preston Wilson 10.00 3.00

2001 Fleer Showcase Sweet Sigs Leather

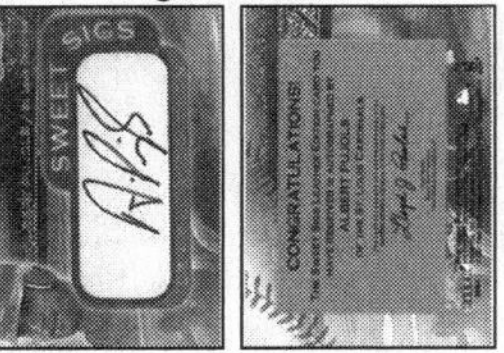

Randomly inserted in hobby packs at the rate of one in 24, this 23 card set features color player head shots with their autograph printed on a piece of simulated baseball leather. The following players cards were seeded into packs as exchange cards with a redemption deadline of 11/01/02: Bob Abreu, Wilson Betemit, Russell Branyan, Pat Burrell, Sean Casey, Eric Chavez, Rafael Furcal, Nomar Garciaparra, Juan Gonzalez, Elpidio Guzman, Brandon Inge, Willie Mays, Jackson Melian, Xavier Nady, Jose Ortiz, Ben Sheets and Mike Sweeney.

Nm-Mt Ex-Mt
1 Bob Abreu SP/100 40.00 12.00
2 Wilson Betemit 15.00 4.50
3 Russell Branyan 15.00 4.50
4 Pat Burrell SP/75 40.00 12.00
5 Sean Casey SP/75 40.00 12.00
6 E.Chavez SP/100 EXCH 40.00 12.00
7 Rafael Furcal EXCH 15.00 4.50
8 Nomar Garciaparra 200.00 60.00
SP/55 EXCH
9 Brian Giles SP/75 40.00 12.00
10 Juan Gonzalez 50.00 15.00
SP/75 EXCH
11 Elpidio Guzman 15.00 4.50
12 Drew Henson SP/75 30.00 9.00
13 Brandon Inge 15.00 4.50
14 Derek Jeter SP/75 200.00 60.00
15 Andruw Jones SP/85 40.00 12.00
16 W.Mays SP/60 EXCH 200.00 60.00
17 Jackson Melian 15.00 4.50
18 Xavier Nady 15.00 4.50
19 Jose Ortiz 15.00 4.50
20 Albert Pujols SP/75 300.00 90.00
21 Ben Sheets 20.00 6.00
22 Mike Sweeney 15.00 4.50
23 Miguel Tejada SP/75 40.00 12.00

2001 Fleer Showcase Sweet Sigs Lumber

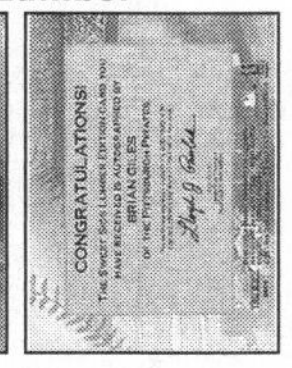

Randomly inserted in hobby packs at the rate of one in 24, this 23-card set features color player photos with their autograph printed on a piece of ash designed to look like a bat. The following players cards were seeded into packs as exchange cards with a redemption deadline of 11/01/02: Bob Abreu, Wilson Betemit, Russell Branyan, Sean Casey, Eric Chavez, Rafael Furcal, Nomar Garciaparra, Juan Gonzalez, Elpidio Guzman, Brandon Inge, Jackson Melian, Xavier Nady, Jose Ortiz, Ben Sheets and Mike Sweeney.

Nm-Mt Ex-Mt
1 Bob Abreu 15.00 4.50
2 Wilson Betemit 15.00 4.50
3 Russell Branyan 15.00 4.50
4 Pat Burrell SP/300 25.00 7.50
5 Sean Casey SP/300 25.00 7.50
6 Eric Chavez 15.00 4.50
7 Rafael Furcal 15.00 4.50
8 Nomar Garciaparra 150.00 45.00
SP/155 EXCH
9 Brian Giles SP/155 25.00 7.50
10 Juan Gonzalez 30.00 9.00
SP/300 EXCH
11 Elpidio Guzman 15.00 4.50
12 Drew Henson SP/145 25.00 7.50
13 Brandon Inge 15.00 4.50
14 Derek Jeter SP/300 150.00 45.00
15 Andruw Jones SP/300 25.00 7.50
16 Willie Mays SP/155
17 Jackson Melian 15.00 4.50
18 Xavier Nady 15.00 4.50
19 Jose Ortiz 15.00 4.50
20 Albert Pujols SP/150 250.00 75.00
21 Ben Sheets 20.00 6.00
22 Mike Sweeney 15.00 4.50
23 Miguel Tejada SP/300 25.00 7.50

2001 Fleer Showcase Sweet Sigs Wall

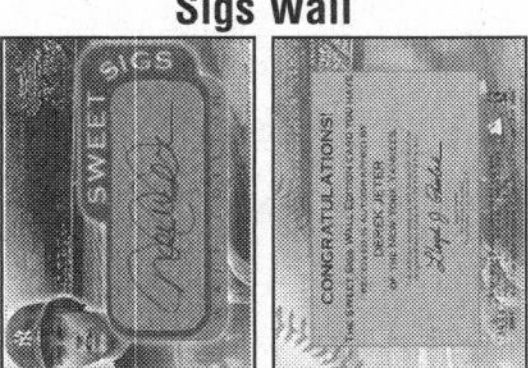

Randomly inserted in hobby packs at the rate of one in 24, this 23-card set features color player photos with their autograph printed on an actual piece of game-used outfield wall. The following players cards were seeded into packs as exchange cards with a redemption deadline of 11/01/02: Bob Abreu, Wilson Betemit, Russell Branyan, Pat Burrell, Eric Chavez, Rafael Furcal, Nomar Garciaparra, Juan Gonzalez, Elpidio Guzman, Brandon Inge, Willie Mays, Jackson Melian, Xavier Nady, Jose Ortiz and Ben Sheets.

Nm-Mt Ex-Mt
1 Bob Abreu 15.00 4.50
2 Wilson Betemit 15.00 4.50
3 Russell Branyan 15.00 4.50
4 Pat Burrell SP/93 30.00 9.00
5 Sean Casey SP/98 30.00 9.00
6 Eric Chavez 15.00 4.50
7 Rafael Furcal 15.00 4.50
8 Nomar Garciaparra 200.00 60.00
SP/80 EXCH
9 Brian Giles SP/100 30.00 9.00
10 Juan Gonzalez 60.00 18.00
SP/30 EXCH
11 Elpidio Guzman 15.00 4.50
12 Drew Henson SP/100 30.00 9.00
13 Brandon Inge 15.00 4.50
14 Derek Jeter SP/90 200.00 60.00
15 Andruw Jones SP/200 30.00 9.00
16 W.Mays SP/85 EXCH 150.00 45.00
17 Jackson Melian 15.00 4.50
18 Xavier Nady 15.00 4.50
19 Jose Ortiz 15.00 4.50
20 Albert Pujols SP/80 300.00 90.00
21 Ben Sheets 20.00 6.00
22 Mike Sweeney
23 Miguel Tejada SP/120 30.00 9.00

2002 Fleer Showcase

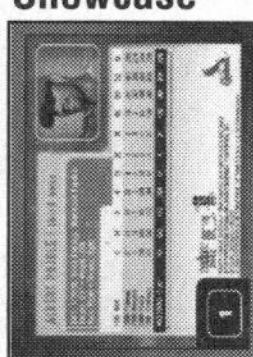

This 166 card standard-size set was released in June, 2002. It was issued in five card packs which came 24 packs to a box and four boxes to a case. Each pack had an SRP of $5. Cards numbered 1-125 featured standard cards of veterans while cards 126-135 featured special veteran "avant" cards (seeded at a rate of 1:12 packs) and cards numbered 136-166 feature rookies/prospects (randomly seeded into packs at an undisclosed rate). Those rookie/prospect cards were issued in the following way: cards 136-141 have a stated print run of 500 serial numbered sets, cards numbered 142-156 have a stated print run of 1000 serial numbered sets and cards numbered 157-166 have a stated print run of 1500 serial numbered sets.

Nm-Mt Ex-Mt
COMP.SET w/o SP's (125) 30.00 9.00
COMMON CARD (1-125) .50 .15
COMMON CARD (126-135) 8.00 2.40
COMMON CARD (136-141) 10.00 3.00
COMMON CARD (142-166) 8.00 2.40
1 Albert Pujols 2.50 .75
2 Pedro Martinez 1.25 .35
3 Frank Thomas 1.25 .35
4 Gary Sheffield .50 .15
5 Roberto Alomar .75 .23
6 Luis Gonzalez .50 .15
7 Bobby Abreu .50 .15
8 Carlos Lee .50 .15
9 Preston Wilson .50 .15
10 Todd Helton .75 .23
11 Juan Gonzalez .75 .23
12 Chuck Knoblauch .50 .15
13 Jason Kendall .50 .15
14 Aaron Sele .50 .15
15 Greg Vaughn .50 .15
16 Fred McGriff .75 .23
17 Doug Mientkiewicz .50 .15
18 Richard Hidalgo .50 .15
19 Alfonso Soriano .75 .23
20 Matt Williams .50 .15
21 Bobby Higginson .50 .15
22 Mo Vaughn .50 .15
23 Andruw Jones .50 .15
24 Omar Vizquel .75 .23
25 Bret Boone .50 .15
26 Bernie Williams .75 .23
27 Rafael Furcal .50 .15
28 Jeff Bagwell .75 .23
29 Marty Cordova .50 .15
30 Lance Berkman .50 .15
31 Vernon Wells .50 .15
32 Garret Anderson .50 .15
33 Larry Bigbie .50 .15
34 Steve Finley .50 .15
35 Barry Bonds 3.00 .90
36 Eric Chavez .50 .15
37 Tony Clark .50 .15
38 Roger Clemens 2.50 .75
39 Adam Dunn .75 .23
40 Roger Cedeno .50 .15
41 Carlos Delgado .50 .15
42 Jermaine Dye .50 .15
43 Brian Jordan .50 .15
44 Darin Erstad .50 .15
45 Paul LoDuca .50 .15
46 Jim Edmonds .50 .15
47 Tom Glavine .75 .23
48 Cliff Floyd .50 .15
49 Jon Lieber .50 .15
50 Adrian Beltre .75 .23
51 Joel Pineiro .50 .15
52 Jim Thome 1.25 .35
53 Jimmy Rollins .50 .15
54 Pat Burrell .50 .15
55 Jeromy Burnitz .50 .15
56 Larry Walker .75 .23
57 Damon Minor .50 .15
58 John Olerud .50 .15
59 Carlos Beltran .75 .23
60 Vladimir Guerrero 1.25 .35
61 David Justice .50 .15
62 Phil Nevin .50 .15
63 Tino Martinez .75 .23
64 Curt Schilling .50 .15
65 Corey Patterson .50 .15
66 Aubrey Huff .50 .15
67 Mark Grace .75 .23
68 Rafael Palmeiro .75 .23
69 Jorge Posada .75 .23
70 Craig Biggio .75 .23
71 Manny Ramirez .75 .23
72 Mark Quinn .50 .15
73 Raul Mondesi .50 .15
74 Shawn Green .50 .15
75 Brian Giles .50 .15
76 Paul Konerko .50 .15
77 Troy Glaus .50 .15
78 Mike Mussina .75 .23
79 Greg Maddux 2.00 .60
80 Edgar Martinez .75 .23
81 Jose Vidro .50 .15
82 Scott Rolen 1.25 .35
83 Ben Grieve .50 .15
84 Jeff Kent .50 .15
85 Magglio Ordonez .50 .15
86 Freddy Garcia .50 .15
87 Ivan Rodriguez 1.25 .35
88 Pokey Reese .50 .15
89 Shannon Stewart .50 .15
90 Randy Johnson 1.25 .35
91 Cristian Guzman .50 .15
92 Tsuyoshi Shinjo .50 .15
93 Steve Cox .50 .15
94 Mike Sweeney .50 .15
95 Robert Fick .50 .15
96 Sean Casey .50 .15
97 Tim Hudson .50 .15
98 Bud Smith .50 .15
99 Corey Koskie .50 .15
100 Richie Sexson .50 .15
101 Aramis Ramirez .50 .15
102 Barry Larkin .75 .23
103 Rich Aurilia .50 .15
104 Charles Johnson .50 .15
105 Ryan Klesko .50 .15
106 Ben Sheets .50 .15
107 J.D. Drew .50 .15
108 Jay Gibbons .50 .15
109 Kerry Wood 1.25 .35
110 C.C. Sabathia .50 .15
111 Eric Munson .50 .15
112 Josh Beckett .50 .15
113 Javier Vazquez .50 .15
114 Barry Zito .50 .15
115 Kazuhiro Sasaki .50 .15
116 Bubba Trammell .50 .15
117 Russell Branyan .50 .15
118 Todd Walker .50 .15
119 Mike Hampton .50 .15
120 Jeff Weaver .50 .15
121 Geoff Jenkins .50 .15
122 Edgardo Alfonzo .50 .15
123 Mike Lieberthal .50 .15
124 Mike Lowell .50 .15
125 Kevin Brown .50 .15
126 Derek Jeter AC 20.00 6.00
127 Ichiro Suzuki AC 12.00 3.60
128 Nomar Garciaparra AC 12.00 3.60
129 Ken Griffey Jr. AC 12.00 3.60
130 Jason Giambi AC 8.00 2.40
131 Alex Rodriguez AC 12.00 3.60
132 Chipper Jones AC 8.00 2.40
133 Mike Piazza AC 12.00 3.60
134 Sammy Sosa AC 12.00 3.60
135 Hideo Nomo AC 8.00 2.40
136 Kazuhisa Ishii AC RC 15.00 4.50
137 Satoru Komiyama AC RC 10.00 3.00
138 So Taguchi AC RC 15.00 4.50
139 Jorge Padilla AC RC 10.00 3.00
140 Rene Reyes AC RC 10.00 3.00
141 Jorge Nunez AC RC 10.00 3.00
142 Nelson Castro RS 8.00 2.40
143 Anderson Machado RS RC 8.00 2.40
144 Edwin Almonte RS RC 8.00 2.40
145 Luis Ugueto RS RC 8.00 2.40
146 Felix Escalona RS RC 8.00 2.40
147 Ron Calloway RS RC 8.00 2.40
148 Hansel Izquierdo RS RC 8.00 2.40
149 Mark Teixeira RS 10.00 3.00
150 Orlando Hudson RS 8.00 2.40
151 Aaron Cook RS RC 8.00 2.40
152 Aaron Taylor RS RC 8.00 2.40
153 Takahito Nomura RS RC 8.00 2.40
154 Matt Thornton RS RC 8.00 2.40
155 Mark Prior RS 15.00 4.50
156 Reed Johnson RS RC 10.00 3.00
157 Doug DeVore RS RC 8.00 2.40
158 Ben Howard RS RC 8.00 2.40
159 Francis Beltran RS RC 8.00 2.40
160 Brian Mallette RS RC 8.00 2.40
161 Sean Burroughs RS 8.00 2.40
162 Michael Restovich RS 8.00 2.40
163 Austin Kearns RS 8.00 2.40
164 Marlon Byrd RS 8.00 2.40
165 Hank Blalock RS 10.00 3.00
166 Mike Rivera RS 8.00 2.40

2002 Fleer Showcase Legacy

Issued at a stated rate of one per hobby box, this is a complete parallel of the Fleer Showcase set. Each of these cards have a stated print run of 175 serial numbered sets.

Nm-Mt Ex-Mt
*LEGACY 1-125: 2.5X TO 6X BASIC...
*LEGACY 126-135: .5X TO 1.2X BASIC
*LEGACY 136-141: .4X TO 1X BASIC.
*LEGACY 142-166: .5X TO 1.2X BASIC

2002 Fleer Showcase Baseball's Best

Issued in hobby packs at a stated rate of one in eight and retail packs at a stated rate of one in 10, these 20 cards features the leading players in the game.

Nm-Mt Ex-Mt
COMPLETE SET (20) 60.00 18.00
1 Derek Jeter 8.00 2.40
2 Barry Bonds 8.00 2.40
3 Mike Piazza 5.00 1.50
4 Alex Rodriguez 5.00 1.50
5 Pat Burrell 2.00 .60
6 Rafael Palmeiro 2.00 .60
7 Nomar Garciaparra 5.00 1.50
8 Todd Helton 2.00 .60
9 Roger Clemens 6.00 1.80
10 Shawn Green 2.00 .60
11 Chipper Jones 3.00 .90
12 Pedro Martinez 3.00 .90
13 Luis Gonzalez 2.00 .60
14 Randy Johnson 3.00 .90

15 Ichiro Suzuki 5.00 1.50
16 Ken Griffey Jr. 5.00 1.50
17 Vladimir Guerrero 3.00 .90
18 Sammy Sosa 5.00 1.50
19 Jason Giambi 2.00 .60
20 Albert Pujols 6.00 1.80

2002 Fleer Showcase Baseball's Best Memorabilia

Inserted in packs at stated odds of one in 12 hobby and one in 36 retail, these 19 cards are a partial parallel of the Baseball's Best insert set. Each of these cards have a memorabilia piece attached to them.

Nm-Mt Ex-Mt
*MULTI-COLOR PATCH: 1X TO 2.5X BASIC
*GOLD: 1X TO 2.5X BASIC
GOLD RANDOM INSERTS IN PACKS
GOLD PRINT RUN 100 SERIAL #'d SETS
1 Derek Jeter Jsy 20.00 6.00
2 Barry Bonds Jsy 20.00 6.00
3 Mike Piazza Jsy 10.00 3.00
4 Alex Rodriguez Bat 15.00 4.50
6 Rafael Palmeiro Jsy 10.00 3.00
7 Nomar Garciaparra Jsy 15.00 4.50
8 Todd Helton Bat SP/350 10.00 3.00
9 Roger Clemens Jsy 15.00 4.50
10 Shawn Green Jsy 8.00 2.40
11 Chipper Jones Jsy 10.00 3.00
12 Pedro Martinez Jsy 10.00 3.00
13 Luis Gonzalez Jsy 8.00 2.40
14 Randy Johnson Jsy 10.00 3.00
15 Ichiro Suzuki Base 20.00 6.00
16 Ken Griffey Jr. Base 15.00 4.50
17 Vladimir Guerrero Base 8.00 2.40
18 Sammy Sosa Base 15.00 4.50
19 Jason Giambi Base 8.00 2.40
20 Albert Pujols Base 15.00 4.50

2002 Fleer Showcase Baseball's Best Memorabilia Autographs Silver

Randomly inserted in packs, these two cards are a parallel of the Baseball's Best Memorabilia insert set. Each of these cards have a stated print run of 400 serial numbered sets. Each of these cards feature not only the memorabilia swatch but also the player's autograph.

Nm-Mt Ex-Mt
*GOLD: .6X TO 1.2X SILVER AU
GOLD PRINT RUN 100 SERIAL #'d SETS
1 Derek Jeter Jsy 150.00 45.00
2 Barry Bonds Jsy 250.00 75.00

2002 Fleer Showcase Derek Jeter Legacy Collection

Randomly inserted in packs, these 22 cards trace the entire career of Yankee superstar Derek Jeter who helped lead the Yankees to five pennants and four world championships in the first six years of his career.

Nm-Mt Ex-Mt
COMPLETE SET (22) 100.00 30.00
COMMON CARD (1-22) 8.00 2.40

2002 Fleer Showcase Derek Jeter Legacy Collection Memorabilia

Randomly inserted in packs, these four cards feature various memorabilia which were part of Derek Jeter's career. Each card was printed to a different stated print run and we have notated that information in our checklist.

Nm-Mt Ex-Mt
1 D.Jeter YC Jsy/300 120.00 36.00
2 Derek Jeter Combo Jsy/175 150.00 45.00
Features white NY Yankees swatch and Blue Columbus Bombers swatch
3 D.Jeter WS Ball/50 200.00 60.00
4 D.Jeter Fldg Glv/425 100.00 30.00

2002 Fleer Showcase Sweet Sigs Leather

Randomly inserted in packs, these 13 cards feature player signatures on actual non game-used leather. Since each player signed a different amount of cards we have put that stated information next to their name in our checklist. A few players signed less than 38 cards and those cards are not priced due to market scarcity.

Nm-Mt Ex-Mt
1 Bobby Abreu/10
2 Russell Branyan/90 15.00 4.50
3 Pat Burrell/35
4 Sean Casey/35
5 Eric Chavez/20
6 Rafael Furcal/92 25.00 7.50
7 Nomar Garciaparra/5
8 Brandon Inge/122 12.00 3.60
9 Jackson Melian/37
10 Xavier Nady/301 15.00 4.50
11 Jose Ortiz/50 20.00 6.00
12 Ben Sheets/60 30.00 9.00
13 Mike Sweeney/103 20.00 6.00

2002 Fleer Showcase Sweet Sigs Lumber

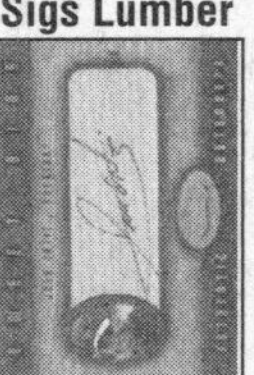

Randomly inserted in packs, these 13 cards feature player signatures on actual non game-used wood. Since each player signed a different amount of cards we have put that stated information next to their name in our checklist.

Nm-Mt Ex-Mt
1 Bobby Abreu/231 15.00 4.50
2 Russell Branyan/425 10.00 3.00
3 Pat Burrell/115 20.00 6.00
4 Sean Casey/64 30.00 9.00
5 Eric Chavez/256 15.00 4.50
6 Rafael Furcal/530 15.00 4.50
7 Nomar Garciaparra/25
8 Brandon Inge/528 10.00 3.00
9 Jackson Melian/636 10.00 3.00
10 Xavier Nady/589 10.00 3.00
11 Jose Ortiz/515 10.00 3.00
12 Ben Sheets/458 15.00 4.50
13 Mike Sweeney/495 15.00 4.50

2002 Fleer Showcase Sweet Sigs Wall

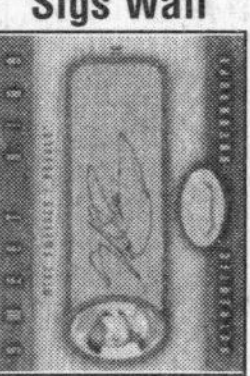

Randomly inserted in packs, these 13 cards feature player signatures on actual non game-used wall pieces. Since each player signed a different amount of cards we have put that stated information next to their name in our checklist. Cards with a print run of 35 or fewer are not priced due to market scarcity.

Nm-Mt Ex-Mt
1 Bobby Abreu/70 30.00 9.00
2 Russell Branyan/200 10.00 3.00
3 Pat Burrell/35
4 Sean Casey/35
5 Eric Chavez/108 20.00 6.00
6 Rafael Furcal/207 15.00 4.50
7 Nomar Garciaparra/25
8 Brandon Inge/187 12.00 3.60
9 Jackson Melian/146 12.00 3.60
10 Xavier Nady/286 10.00 3.00
11 Jose Ortiz/116 12.00 3.60
12 Ben Sheets/150 20.00 6.00
13 Mike Sweeney/371 15.00 4.50

2003 Fleer Showcase

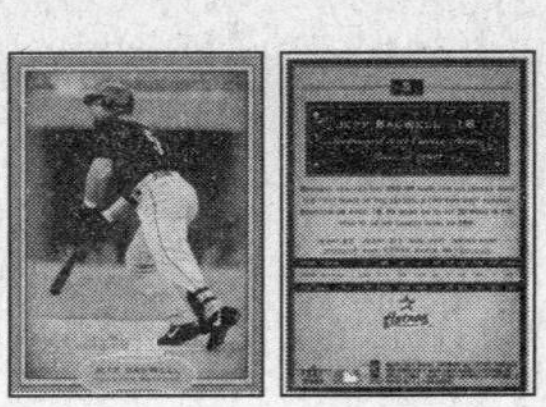

This 145-card set was issued in two separtate series. The primary Showcase product was released in March, 2003. Cards 1-95 are active ballplayers and 96- 105 feature retired players. Cards 106 through 135 are a subset entitled Showcasing Talent of which features a selection of top prospects. Three pack types were produced for this product (Jersey, Leather and Lumber) eight of each were placed into the 24-

ct sealed boxes. Each pack type contained a selection of commonly available cards plus other inserts and subsets of which were exclusive to the theme. Cards 136-145 were randomly seeded within Fleer Rookies and Greats packs of which was distributed in December, 2003. Each of these 10 update cards features a top prospect and is serial numbered to 750 copies.

Nm-Mt Ex-Mt
COMP.LO SET w/o SP's (105) 25.00 7.50
COMMON CARD (1-95) .50 .15
COMMON CARD (96-105) 1.00 .30
COMMON CARD (106-135) 3.00 .90
106-135 ODDS 1:3 HOBBY, 1:12 RETAIL
106-115 DIST IN JERSEY AND RETAIL PACKS
116-125 DIST IN LEATHER AND RETAIL PACKS
126-135 DIST IN LUMBER AND RETAIL PACKS
COMMON CARD (136-145) 4.00 1.20
1 David Eckstein .50 .15
2 Curt Schilling .50 .15
3 Jay Gibbons .50 .15
4 Kerry Wood 1.25 .35
5 Jeff Bagwell .75 .23
6 Hideo Nomo 1.25 .35
7 Tim Hudson .50 .15
8 J.D. Drew .50 .15
9 Josh Phelps .50 .15
10 Bartolo Colon .50 .15
11 Bobby Abreu .50 .15
12 Matt Morris .50 .15
13 Kazuhiro Sasaki .50 .15
14 Sean Burroughs .50 .15
15 Vicente Padilla .50 .15
16 Jorge Posada .75 .23
17 Torii Hunter .50 .15
18 Richie Sexson .50 .15
19 Lance Berkman .50 .15
20 Todd Helton .75 .23
21 Paul Konerko .50 .15
22 Pedro Martinez 1.25 .35
23 Rodrigo Lopez .50 .15
24 Gary Sheffield .50 .15
25 Darin Erstad .50 .15
26 Nomar Garciaparra 2.00 .60
27 Adam Dunn .75 .23
28 Jason Giambi .50 .15
29 Miguel Tejada .50 .15
30 Chipper Jones 1.25 .35
31 Alex Rodriguez 2.00 .60
32 Barry Bonds 3.00 .90
33 Roger Clemens 2.50 .75
34 Sammy Sosa 2.00 .60
35 Randy Johnson 1.25 .35
36 Tim Salmon .75 .23
37 Shea Hillenbrand .50 .15
38 Larry Walker .75 .23
39 A.J. Burnett .50 .15
40 Shawn Green .50 .15
41 Cristian Guzman .50 .15
42 Bernie Williams .75 .23
43 Mark Mulder .50 .15
44 Brian Giles .50 .15
45 Bret Boone .50 .15
46 Juan Gonzalez .75 .23
47 Roy Halladay .50 .15
48 Wade Miller .50 .15
49 Jeff Kent .50 .15
50 Carlos Delgado .50 .15
51 Mike Lowell .50 .15
52 Jim Edmonds .50 .15
53 Ivan Rodriguez 1.25 .35
54 Aubrey Huff .50 .15
55 Ryan Klesko .50 .15
56 Paul Lo Duca .50 .15
57 Roy Oswalt .50 .15
58 Omar Vizquel .75 .23
59 Manny Ramirez .75 .23
60 Andruw Jones .50 .15
61 Troy Glaus .75 .23
62 Ichiro Suzuki 2.00 .60
63 Albert Pujols 2.50 .75
64 Derek Jeter 3.00 .90
65 Mark Prior 1.25 .35
66 Ken Griffey Jr. 2.00 .60
67 Vladimir Guerrero 1.25 .35
68 Mike Piazza 2.00 .60
69 Alfonso Soriano .75 .23
70 Greg Maddux 2.00 .60
71 Adam Kennedy .50 .15
72 Junior Spivey .50 .15
73 Tom Glavine .75 .23
74 Derek Lowe .50 .15
75 Magglio Ordonez .50 .15
76 Jim Thome 1.25 .35
77 Robert Fick .50 .15
78 Josh Beckett .50 .15
79 Mike Sweeney .50 .15
80 Kazuhisa Ishii .50 .15
81 Roberto Alomar .75 .23
82 Barry Zito .50 .15
83 Pat Burrell .50 .15
84 Scott Rolen 1.25 .35
85 John Olerud .50 .15
86 Eric Hinske .50 .15
87 Rafael Palmeiro .75 .23
88 Edgar Martinez .75 .23
89 Eric Chavez .50 .15
90 Jose Vidro .50 .15
91 Craig Biggio .75 .23
92 Rich Aurilia .50 .15
93 Austin Kearns .50 .15
94 Luis Gonzalez .50 .15
95 Garret Anderson .50 .15
96 Yogi Berra 2.00 .60
97 Al Kaline 2.00 .60
98 Robin Yount 3.00 .90
99 Reggie Jackson 1.50 .45
100 Harmon Killebrew 2.00 .60
101 Eddie Mathews 2.00 .60
102 Willie McCovey 1.00 .30
103 Nolan Ryan 4.00 1.20
104 Mike Schmidt 2.50 .75
105 Tom Seaver 1.50 .45
106 Francisco Rodriguez ST 3.00 .90
107 Carl Crawford ST 3.00 .90
108 Ben Howard ST 3.00 .90
109 Hank Blalock ST 5.00 1.50
110 Hee Seop Choi ST 3.00 .90
111 Kirk Saarloos ST 3.00 .90
112 Lew Ford ST RC 5.00 1.50
113 Andy Van Hekken ST 3.00 .90
114 Drew Henson ST 3.00 .90
115 Marlon Byrd ST 3.00 .90
116 Jayson Werth ST 3.00 .90
117 Willie Bloomquist ST 3.00 .90
118 Joe Borchard ST 3.00 .90
119 Mark Teixeira ST 3.00 .90
120 Bobby Hill ST 3.00 .90
121 Jason Lane ST 3.00 .90
122 Omar Infante ST 3.00 .90
123 Victor Martinez ST 5.00 1.50
124 Jorge Padilla ST 3.00 .90
125 John Lackey ST 3.00 .90
126 Anderson Machado ST 3.00 .90
127 Rodrigo Rosario ST 3.00 .90
128 Freddy Sanchez ST 3.00 .90
129 Tony Alvarez ST 3.00 .90
130 Matt Thornton ST 3.00 .90
131 Joe Thurston ST 3.00 .90
132 Brett Myers ST 3.00 .90
133 Nook Logan ST RC 3.00 .90
134 Chris Snelling ST 3.00 .90
135 Terrmel Sledge ST RC 5.00 1.50
136 Chien-Ming Wang ST RC 5.00 1.50
137 Rickie Weeks ST RC 8.00 2.40
138 Brandon Webb ST RC 5.00 1.50
139 Hideki Matsui ST RC 10.00 3.00
140 Michael Hessman ST RC 4.00 1.20
141 Ryan Wagner ST RC 5.00 1.50
142 Bo Hart ST RC 5.00 1.50
143 Edwin Jackson ST RC 8.00 2.40
144 Jose Contreras ST RC 8.00 2.40
145 Delmon Young ST RC 10.00 3.00

2003 Fleer Showcase Legacy

This 135 card set was distributed exclusively in three separate forms of hobby packs. Cards 1-35 and 126-135 were available exclusively in hobby Lumber packs (signified by an orange-bar wrapper), 36-70 and 116-125 in hobby Leather packs (signified by brown-bar wrapper) and 71-105 and 106-115 in hobby Jersey packs (signified by a gray-bar wrapper). Only 150 serial numbered sets were produced. Each card is serial numbered on back in gold foil.

Nm-Mt Ex-Mt
*LEGACY 1-95: 2.5X TO 6X BASIC
*LEGACY 96-105: 3X TO 8X BASIC
*LEGACY 106-135: .6X TO 1.5X BASIC

2003 Fleer Showcase Baseball's Best

Issued at a stated rate of one in eight leather packs and one in 24 retail packs, this 15-card insert set features the best players in basbeball.

Nm-Mt Ex-Mt
1 Curt Schilling 3.00 .90
2 Barry Zito 3.00 .90
3 Torii Hunter 3.00 .90
4 Pedro Martinez 3.00 .90
5 Bernie Williams 3.00 .90
6 Magglio Ordonez 3.00 .90
7 Alfonso Soriano 3.00 .90
8 Hideo Nomo 3.00 .90
9 Jason Giambi 3.00 .90
10 Sammy Sosa 5.00 1.50
11 Vladimir Guerrero 3.00 .90
12 Ken Griffey Jr. 5.00 1.50
13 Troy Glaus 3.00 .90
14 Ichiro Suzuki 5.00 1.50
15 Albert Pujols 6.00 1.80

2003 Fleer Showcase Baseball's Best Game Jersey

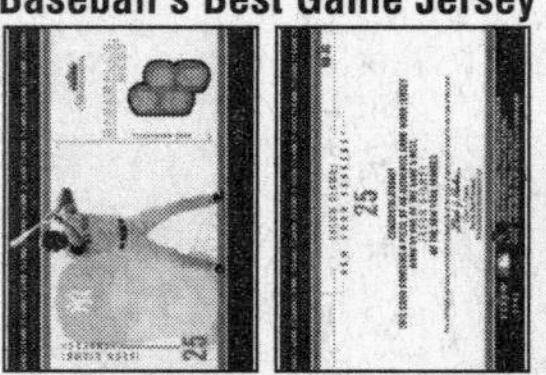

These cards parallel the Baseball's Best insert set. Although the wrappper stated odds list these cards as 1:27 Leather hobby packs - our analysis of the case breakdown, coupled with reports from dealers in the field indicates the cards were actually seeded at a rate of 1:9 Leather hobby packs.

Nm-Mt Ex-Mt
1B Curt Schilling 8.00 2.40
2 Barry Zito 8.00 2.40
3 Torii Hunter 8.00 2.40
4 Pedro Martinez 10.00 3.00
5 Bernie Williams 10.00 3.00
6 Magglio Ordonez 8.00 2.40
7 Alfonso Soriano 10.00 3.00
8 Hideo Nomo Sox 10.00 3.00
9 Jason Giambi 8.00 2.40
10 Sammy Sosa 15.00 4.50

2003 Fleer Showcase Hot Gloves

Inserted at a stated rate of one in 144 leather and one in 288 retail packs these 10 cards features some of the leading defensive players in baseball.

Nm-Mt Ex-Mt
1 Greg Maddux 25.00 7.50
2 Ivan Rodriguez 15.00 4.50
3 Derek Jeter 40.00 12.00
4 Mike Piazza 25.00 7.50
5 Nomar Garciaparra 25.00 7.50
6 Andruw Jones 15.00 4.50
7 Scott Rolen 15.00 4.50
8 Barry Bonds 40.00 12.00
9 Roger Clemens 30.00 9.00
10 Alex Rodriguez 25.00 7.50

2003 Fleer Showcase Hot Gloves Game Jersey

Randomly inserted in lumber packs, this is a parallel to the Hot Gloves insert set. These cards have a game-worn jersey card as well as the player's photo pictured.

Nm-Mt Ex-Mt
1 Greg Maddux 20.00 6.00
2 Ivan Rodriguez 15.00 4.50
3 Derek Jeter 30.00 9.00
4 Mike Piazza 20.00 6.00
5 Nomar Garciaparra 20.00 6.00
6 Andruw Jones 15.00 4.50
7 Scott Rolen 15.00 4.50
8 Barry Bonds 30.00 9.00
9 Roger Clemens 25.00 7.50
10 Alex Rodriguez 20.00 6.00

2003 Fleer Showcase Sweet Sigs

Randomly inserted in both leather and retail packs, these cards feature authentic signatures of either Barry Bonds or Derek Jeter. As these cards are issued to various print runs, we have notated that information in our checklist.

Nm-Mt Ex-Mt
BB1 Barry Bonds 90 MVP/150 250.00 75.00
BB2 Barry Bonds 92 MVP/100 250.00 75.00
BB3 Barry Bonds 93 MVP/75 250.00 75.00
BB4 Barry Bonds 01 MVP/50 300.00 90.00
BB5 Barry Bonds 02 MVP/25
BB6 Barry Bonds 5X MVP/5
DJ2 Derek Jeter Blue Ink/250 150.00 45.00
DJ3 Derek Jeter Red Ink/50 250.00 75.00

2003 Fleer Showcase Sweet Stitches

Issued at a stated rate of one in eight jersey packs and one in 24 retail packs, these 10 cards feature information about what various stars do in their off-field activities.

Nm-Mt Ex-Mt
1 Derek Jeter 8.00 2.40
2 Randy Johnson 3.00 .90
3 Jeff Bagwell 3.00 .90
4 Nomar Garciaparra 5.00 1.50
5 Roger Clemens 6.00 1.80
6 Todd Helton 3.00 .90

Barry Bonds 8.00 2.40
Alfonso Soriano 3.00 .90
Miguel Tejada 3.00 .90
0 Mark Prior 3.00 .90

2003 Fleer Showcase Sweet Stitches Game Jersey

andomly inserted in jersey packs, this is a parllel to the Sweet Stitches insert set. These cards eature game-used jersey pieces and were ssued to assorted print runs and we have notatd that information next to the player's name in ur checklist.

	Nm-Mt	Ex-Mt
Derek Jeter/599	25.00	7.50
Randy Johnson/899	10.00	3.00
Jeff Bagwell/899	10.00	3.00
Nomar Garciaparra/899	15.00	4.50
Roger Clemens/599	20.00	6.00
Todd Helton/899	10.00	3.00
Barry Bonds/899	20.00	6.00
Alfonso Soriano/599	10.00	3.00
Miguel Tejada/899	8.00	2.40
0 Mark Prior/899	10.00	3.00
1 Sammy Sosa/899	15.00	4.50
2 J.D. Drew/899	8.00	2.40
3 Alex Rodriguez/899	15.00	4.50
4 Mike Piazza/899	15.00	4.50

2003 Fleer Showcase Sweet Stitches Patch

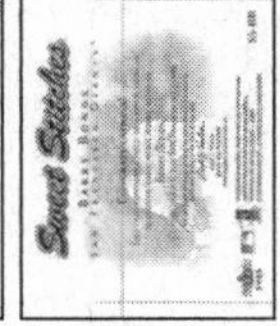

andomly inserted in jersey packs, this is a parllel to the sweet stitches insert set. These cards eature game-used jersey patch pieces and were ssued to assorted print runs and we have notatd that information next to the player's name in ur checklist.

	Nm-Mt	Ex-Mt
Derek Jeter/50		
Randy Johnson/150	40.00	12.00
Jeff Bagwell/150	40.00	12.00
Nomar Garciaparra/150	60.00	18.00
Roger Clemens/50		
Todd Helton/75	50.00	15.00
Barry Bonds/150	80.00	24.00
Alfonso Soriano/50	40.00	12.00
Miguel Tejada/150	25.00	7.50
0 Mark Prior/150	40.00	12.00
1 Sammy Sosa/150	60.00	18.00
2 J.D. Drew/150	25.00	7.50
3 Alex Rodriguez/150	60.00	18.00
4 Mike Piazza/150	60.00	18.00

2003 Fleer Showcase Thunder Sticks

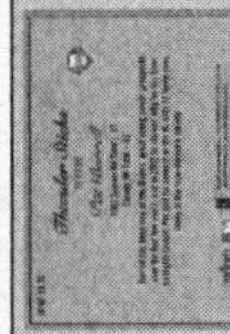

nserted in packs at a stated rate of one in eight umber and one in 24 retail, these 10 cards feaure some of the leading power hitters in baseall.

	Nm-Mt	Ex-Mt
Adam Dunn	3.00	.90
Alex Rodriguez	5.00	1.50
Barry Bonds	8.00	2.40
Jim Thome	3.00	.90
Chipper Jones	3.00	.90
Manny Ramirez	3.00	.90
Carlos Delgado	3.00	.90
Mike Piazza	5.00	1.50
Shawn Green	3.00	.90
0 Pat Burrell	3.00	.90

2003 Fleer Showcase Thunder Sticks Game Bat

andomly inserted in lumber packs, these cards arallel the Thunder Sticks insert set. These cards feature a game bat piece and were issued to a varying amount of cards. We have notated the print run information next to the player's name in our checklist.

	Nm-Mt	Ex-Mt
*GOLD: 1X TO 2.5X BASIC CARDS		
GOLD PRINT RUN 99 SERIAL #'d SETS		
1 Adam Dunn/799	10.00	3.00
2 Alex Rodriguez/799	15.00	4.50
3 Barry Bonds/899	20.00	6.00
4 Jim Thome/799	10.00	3.00
5 Chipper Jones/799	10.00	3.00
6 Manny Ramirez/799	10.00	3.00
7 Troy Glaus/799	8.00	2.40
8 Vladimir Guerrero/799	10.00	3.00
9 Shawn Green/799	8.00	2.40
10 Pat Burrell/799	8.00	2.40

2004 Fleer Showcase

	Nm-Mt	Ex-Mt
COMP.SET w/o SP's (100)	25.00	7.50
COMMON CARD (1-100)	.50	.15
COMMON CARD (101-130)	3.00	.90
101-130 ODDS 1:6 HOBBY, 1:12 RETAIL		
1 Corey Patterson	.50	.15
2 Ken Griffey Jr.	2.00	.60
3 Preston Wilson	.50	.15
4 Juan Pierre	.50	.15
5 Jose Reyes	.50	.15
6 Jason Schmidt	.50	.15
7 Rocco Baldelli	.50	.15
8 Carlos Delgado	.50	.15
9 Hideki Matsui	2.00	.60
10 Nomar Garciaparra	2.00	.60
11 Brian Giles	.50	.15
12 Darin Erstad	.50	.15
13 Larry Walker	.75	.23
14 Bernie Williams	.75	.23
15 Laynce Nix	.50	.15
16 Manny Ramirez	.75	.23
17 Magglio Ordonez	.50	.15
18 Khalil Greene	1.25	.35
19 Jim Edmonds	.50	.15
20 Troy Glaus	.50	.15
21 Curt Schilling	.50	.15
22 Chipper Jones	1.25	.35
23 Sammy Sosa	2.00	.60
24 Frank Thomas	1.25	.35
25 Todd Helton	.75	.23
26 Craig Biggio	.75	.23
27 Shannon Stewart	.50	.15
28 Mark Mulder	.50	.15
29 Mike Lieberthal	.50	.15
30 Reggie Sanders	.50	.15
31 Edgar Martinez	.75	.23
32 Bo Hart	.50	.15
33 Mark Teixeira	.50	.15
34 Jay Gibbons	.50	.15
35 Roberto Alomar	.75	.23
36 Kip Wells	.50	.15
37 J.D. Drew	.50	.15
38 Jason Varitek	.75	.23
39 Craig Monroe	.50	.15
40 Roy Oswalt	.50	.15
41 Edgardo Alfonzo	.50	.15
42 Roy Halladay	.50	.15
43 Gary Sheffield	.50	.15
44 Lance Berkman	.50	.15
45 Torii Hunter	.50	.15
46 Vladimir Guerrero	1.25	.35
47 Marlon Byrd	.50	.15
48 Austin Kearns	.50	.15
49 Angel Berroa	.50	.15
50 Geoff Jenkins	.50	.15
51 Aubrey Huff	.50	.15
52 Dontrelle Willis	.50	.15
53 Tony Batista	.50	.15
54 Shawn Green	.50	.15
55 Jason Kendall	.50	.15
56 Garret Anderson	.50	.15
57 Andruw Jones	.50	.15
58 Dmitri Young	.50	.15
59 Richie Sexson	.50	.15
60 Jorge Posada	.75	.23
61 Bobby Abreu	.50	.15
62 Vernon Wells	.50	.15
63 Javy Lopez	.50	.15
64 Josh Beckett	.50	.15
65 Eric Chavez	.50	.15
66 Tim Salmon	.75	.23
67 Brandon Webb	.50	.15
68 Pedro Martinez	1.25	.35
69 Kerry Wood	1.25	.35
70 Jose Vidro	.50	.15
71 Alfonso Soriano	.75	.23
72 Barry Zito	.50	.15
73 Sean Burroughs	.50	.15
74 Jamie Moyer	.50	.15
75 Luis Gonzalez	.50	.15
76 Adam Dunn	.75	.23
77 Mike Piazza	2.00	.60
78 Pat Burrell	.50	.15
79 Scott Rolen	1.25	.35
80 Milton Bradley	.50	.15
81 Mike Sweeney	.50	.15
82 Hank Blalock	.50	.15
83 Esteban Loaiza	.50	.15
84 Hideo Nomo	1.25	.35
85 Derek Jeter	2.50	.75
86 Albert Pujols	2.50	.75
87 Greg Maddux	2.00	.60
88 Mark Prior	1.25	.35
89 Mike Lowell	.50	.15
90 Jeff Bagwell	.75	.23
91 Scott Podsednik	.50	.15
92 Tom Glavine	.75	.23
93 Jason Giambi	.50	.15
94 Jim Thome	1.25	.35
95 Ichiro Suzuki	2.00	.60
96 Randy Johnson	1.25	.35
97 Omar Vizquel	.75	.23
98 Ivan Rodriguez	1.25	.35
99 Miguel Tejada	.50	.15
100 Alex Rodriguez	2.00	.60
101 Rickie Weeks ST	3.00	.90
102 Chad Gaudin ST	3.00	.90
103 Rich Harden ST	3.00	.90
104 Edwin Jackson ST	3.00	.90
105 Chien-Ming Wang ST	3.00	.90
106 Matt Kata ST	3.00	.90
107 Delmon Young ST	5.00	1.50
108 Ryan Wagner ST	3.00	.90
109 Jeff Duncan ST	3.00	.90
110 Prentice Redman ST	3.00	.90
111 Clint Barmes ST	3.00	.90
112 Jeremy Guthrie ST	3.00	.90
113 Brian Stokes ST	3.00	.90
114 David DeJesus ST	3.00	.90
115 Felix Sanchez ST	3.00	.90
116 Josh Stewart ST	3.00	.90
117 Daniel Garcia ST	3.00	.90
118 Jon Leicester ST	3.00	.90
119 Francisco Cruceta ST	3.00	.90
120 Oscar Villarreal ST	3.00	.90
121 Michael Hessman ST	3.00	.90
122 Michel Hernandez ST	3.00	.90
123 Richard Fischer ST	3.00	.90
124 Robby Hammock ST	3.00	.90
125 Guillermo Quiroz ST	3.00	.90
126 Craig Brazell ST	3.00	.90
127 Wilfredo Ledezma ST	3.00	.90
128 Josh Willingham ST	3.00	.90
129 Ramon Nivar ST	3.00	.90
130 Matt Diaz ST	3.00	.90

2004 Fleer Showcase Legacy

	Nm-Mt	Ex-Mt
*LEGACY 1-100: 6X TO 15X BASIC		
*LEGACY 101-130: 1.5X TO 4X BASIC		
OVERALL PARALLEL ODDS 1:24		
STATED PRINT RUN 99 SERIAL #'d SETS		

2004 Fleer Showcase Masterpiece

	Nm-Mt	Ex-Mt
OVERALL PARALLEL ODDS 1:24		
STATED PRINT RUN 1 SERIAL #'d SET		
NO PRICING DUE TO SCARCITY		

2004 Fleer Showcase Baseballs Best

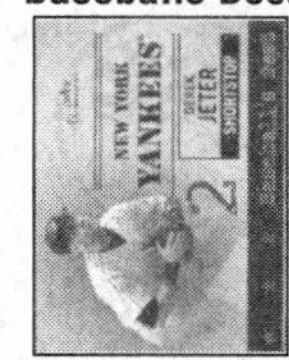

	Nm-Mt	Ex-Mt
STATED ODDS 1:24 HOBBY, 1:12 RETAIL		
1 Derek Jeter	6.00	1.80
2 Mark Prior	3.00	.90
3 Mike Piazza	5.00	1.50
4 Jeff Bagwell	3.00	.90
5 Kerry Wood	3.00	.90
6 Ivan Rodriguez	3.00	.90
7 Albert Pujols	6.00	1.80
8 Jim Thome	3.00	.90
9 Sammy Sosa	5.00	1.50
10 Vladimir Guerrero	3.00	.90
11 Eric Gagne	3.00	.90
12 Randy Johnson	3.00	.90
13 Todd Helton	3.00	.90
14 Chipper Jones	3.00	.90
15 Alex Rodriguez	5.00	1.50

2004 Fleer Showcase Baseballs Best Game Used

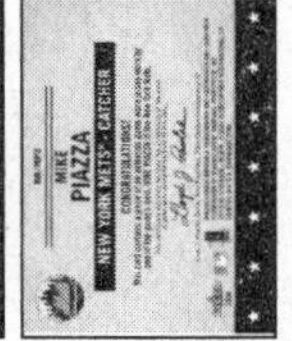

	Nm-Mt	Ex-Mt
STATED ODDS 1:72 HOBBY, 1:48 RETAIL		
*PATCH: 1.5X TO 4X BASIC		
PATCH RANDOM INSERTS IN PACKS		
PATCH PRINT RUN 50 SERIAL #'d SETS		
*GOLD: .5X TO 1.2X BASIC		
GOLD RANDOM INSERTS IN PACKS		
GOLD PRINT RUN 150 SERIAL #'d SETS		
*REWARD: 1X TO 2.5X BASIC		
REWARD ISSUED ONLY IN DEALER PACKS		
REWARD PRINTS B/WN 29-44 COPIES PER		
AP Albert Pujols Jsy	15.00	4.50
AR Alex Rodriguez Jsy	10.00	3.00
CJ Chipper Jones Jsy	10.00	3.00
DJ Derek Jeter Bat	20.00	6.00
EG Eric Gagne Jsy	10.00	3.00
IR Ivan Rodriguez Jsy	10.00	3.00
JB Jeff Bagwell Jsy	10.00	3.00
JT Jim Thome Jsy	10.00	3.00
KW Kerry Wood Jsy	10.00	3.00
MPI Mike Piazza Jsy	10.00	3.00
MPR Mark Prior Jsy	10.00	3.00
RJ Randy Johnson Jsy	10.00	3.00
SS Sammy Sosa Jsy	10.00	3.00
TH Todd Helton Jsy	10.00	3.00
VG Vladimir Guerrero Jsy	10.00	3.00

2004 Fleer Showcase Grace

	Nm-Mt	Ex-Mt
STATED ODDS 1:12 HOBBY/RETAIL		
1 Kerry Wood	3.00	.90
2 Derek Jeter	6.00	1.80
3 Nomar Garciaparra	5.00	1.50
4 Mike Piazza	5.00	1.50
5 Mark Prior	3.00	.90
6 Jose Reyes	3.00	.90
7 Dontrelle Willis	3.00	.90
8 Pedro Martinez	3.00	.90
9 Tim Hudson	3.00	.90
10 Troy Glaus	3.00	.90
11 Hank Blalock	3.00	.90
12 Albert Pujols	6.00	1.80
13 Juan Pierre	3.00	.90
14 Angel Berroa	3.00	.90
15 Rocco Baldelli	3.00	.90
16 Carlos Delgado	3.00	.90
17 Manny Ramirez	3.00	.90
18 Alex Rodriguez	5.00	1.50
19 Andruw Jones	3.00	.90
20 Luis Gonzalez	3.00	.90

2004 Fleer Showcase Grace Game Used

	Nm-Mt	Ex-Mt
STATED ODDS 1:48 HOBBY/RETAIL		
*PATCH: 1.5X TO 4X BASIC		
PATCH RANDOM INSERTS IN PACKS		
PATCH PRINT RUN 50 SERIAL #'d SETS		
*GOLD: .5X TO 1.2X BASIC		
GOLD RANDOM INSERTS IN PACKS		
GOLD PRINT RUN 150 SERIAL #'d SETS		
*REWARD p/r 44-55: 1X TO 2.5X BASIC		
REWARD ISSUED ONLY IN DEALER PACKS		
REWARD PRINTS B/WN 23-55 COPIES PER		
NO REWARD PRICING ON QTY OF 23		
AP Albert Pujols Jsy	15.00	4.50
AR Alex Rodriguez Jsy	10.00	3.00
DJ Derek Jeter Bat	20.00	6.00
DW Dontrelle Willis Jsy	8.00	2.40
MPI Mike Piazza Jsy	10.00	3.00
MPR Mark Prior Jsy	10.00	3.00
MR Manny Ramirez Jsy	10.00	3.00
NG Nomar Garciaparra Jsy	10.00	3.00
PM Pedro Martinez Jsy	10.00	3.00
RB Rocco Baldelli Jsy	8.00	2.40

2004 Fleer Showcase Hot Gloves

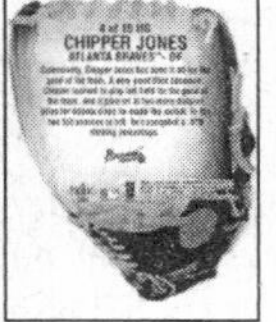

	Nm-Mt	Ex-Mt
STATED ODDS 1:288 HOBBY, 1:576 RETAIL		
NO MORE THAN 120 SETS PRODUCED		
PRINT RUN INFO PROVIDED BY FLEER		
CARDS ARE NOT SERIAL-NUMBERED		
1 Derek Jeter	40.00	12.00
2 Nomar Garciaparra	30.00	9.00
3 Alex Rodriguez	30.00	9.00
4 Chipper Jones	25.00	7.50
5 Torii Hunter	25.00	7.50
6 Ichiro Suzuki	40.00	12.00
7 Mark Prior	25.00	7.50
8 Vladimir Guerrero	25.00	7.50
9 Albert Pujols	40.00	12.00
10 Ivan Rodriguez	25.00	7.50
11 Hideki Matsui	60.00	18.00
12 Sammy Sosa	40.00	12.00
13 Jim Thome	25.00	7.50
14 Rocco Baldelli	25.00	7.50
15 Jeff Bagwell	25.00	7.50

2004 Fleer Showcase Hot Gloves Game Used

	Nm-Mt	Ex-Mt
RANDOM INSERTS IN PACKS		
STATED PRINT RUN 50 SERIAL #'d SETS		
AP Albert Pujols Jsy	60.00	18.00
AR Alex Rodriguez Jsy	50.00	15.00
CJ Chipper Jones Jsy	30.00	9.00
DJ Derek Jeter Jsy	80.00	24.00
HM Hideki Matsui Base	100.00	30.00
IR Ivan Rodriguez Jsy	30.00	9.00
IS Ichiro Suzuki Base	120.00	36.00
JB Jeff Bagwell Jsy	30.00	9.00

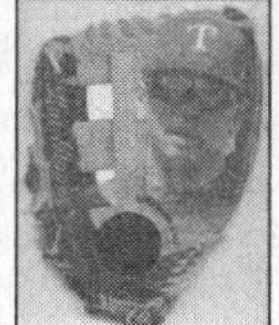

	Nm-Mt	Ex-Mt
JT Jim Thome Jsy	30.00	9.00
MP Mark Prior Jsy	30.00	9.00
NG Nomar Garciaparra Jsy	50.00	15.00
RB Rocco Baldelli Jsy	30.00	9.00
SS Sammy Sosa Jsy	50.00	15.00
TH Torii Hunter Jsy	30.00	9.00
VG Vladimir Guerrero Jsy	30.00	9.00

2004 Fleer Showcase Pujols Legacy Collection

	Nm-Mt	Ex-Mt
COMMON CARD (1-10)	8.00	2.40
STATED ODDS 1:24		
STATED PRINT RUN 1000 SERIAL #'d SETS		

2004 Fleer Showcase Pujols Legacy Collection Autograph

	Nm-Mt	Ex-Mt
OVERALL AUTOGRAPH ODDS 1:24		
PRINT RUNS B/WN 1-10 COPIES PER		
NO PRICING DUE TO SCARCITY		
1 Albert Pujols Draft 99/1		
2 Albert Pujols 01 ROY/2		
3 Albert Pujols 01 Slugger/3		
4 Albert Pujols 4 Pos/4		
5 Albert Pujols NL Records/5		
6 Albert Pujols 2X AS/6		
7 Albert Pujols HR Record/7		
8 Albert Pujols 300-100-100/8		
9 Albert Pujols 03 Btg Champ/9		
10 Albert Pujols 03 POY/10		

2004 Fleer Showcase Pujols Legacy Collection Game Jersey

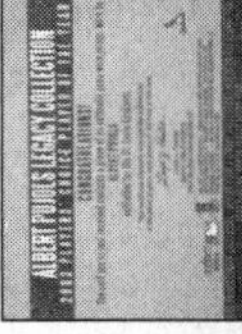

	Nm-Mt	Ex-Mt
RANDOM INSERTS IN PACKS		
PRINT RUNS B/WN 10-100 COPIES PER		
NO PRICING ON QTY OF 40 OR LESS		
1 Albert Pujols Draft 99/10		
2 Albert Pujols 01 ROY/20		
3 Albert Pujols 01 Slugger/30		
4 Albert Pujols 4 Pos/40		
5 Albert Pujols NL Records/50	30.00	9.00
6 Albert Pujols 2X AS/60	30.00	9.00
7 Albert Pujols HR Record/70	25.00	7.50
8 Albert Pujols 300-100-100/80	25.00	7.50
9 Albert Pujols 03 Btg Champ/90	25.00	7.50
10 Albert Pujols 03 POY/100	25.00	7.50

2004 Fleer Showcase Sweet Sigs

	Nm-Mt	Ex-Mt
OVERALL AUTOGRAPH ODDS 1:24		
PRINT RUNS B/WN 26-1000 COPIES PER		
EXCH.PRINT RUNS PROVIDED BY FLEER		
EXCHANGE DEADLINE INDEFINITE		
AK Austin Kearns/224	15.00	4.50
AP1 Albert Pujols/150 EXCH	200.00	60.00
AP2 A.Pujols NNO/300 EXCH	150.00	45.00
BH Bo Hart/667	10.00	3.00
BW Brandon Webb/1000	10.00	3.00
BZ Barry Zito/248	25.00	7.50
CPA Corey Patterson/176	20.00	6.00
CPE Carlos Pena/48	20.00	6.00
CW Chien Mien-Wang/35	60.00	18.00
DW Dontrelle Willis/26	40.00	12.00
DY Delmon Young/1000 EXCH	25.00	7.50
HB Hank Blalock/824	15.00	4.50
JG John Gall/900 EXCH	15.00	4.50
JR Jose Reyes/115	20.00	6.00
JW Josh Willingham/180	15.00	4.50
ML Mike Lowell/44	25.00	7.50
MR Michael Ryan/288	10.00	3.00

MT Miguel Tejada/52 25.00 7.50
RWA Ryan Wagner/700 EXCH .. 10.00 3.00
RWE Rickie Weeks/416 15.00 4.50
SR Scott Rolen/200 40.00 12.00
TB Taylor Buchholz/900 EXCH .. 10.00 3.00
TH Torii Hunter/294 15.00 4.50
WL Wilfredo Ledezma/376 10.00 3.00

2004 Fleer Showcase Sweet Sigs Game Jersey

Nm-Mt Ex-Mt
OVERALL AUTOGRAPH ODDS 1:24
STATED PRINT RUN 5 SERIAL #'d CARDS
NO PRICING DUE TO SCARCITY
AP Albert Pujols/5

2003 Fleer Splendid Splinters Wood Game Bat Dual

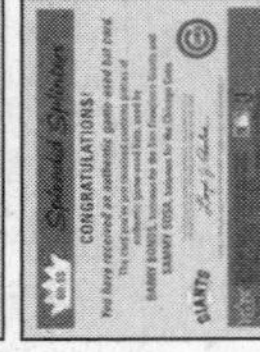

Randomly inserted into packds, these four cards feature two leading hitters as well as game-used bat chips from the featured players. Each of these cards were issued to a stated print run of 99 serial numbered sets.

Nm-Mt Ex-Mt
ARNG Alex Rodriguez 60.00 18.00
Nomar Garciaparra
BBSS Barry Bonds 80.00 24.00
Sammy Sosa
DJAS Derek Jeter 80.00 24.00
Alfonso Soriano
MPJB Mike Piazza 40.00 12.00
Jeff Bagwell

2004 Fleer Sweet Sigs

This 100-card set was released in August, 2004. The set was issued in six-card hobby packs with an $8 SRP which came 12 packs to a box and six boxes to a case. The set was also issued in five-card retail packs with an $3 SRP which came 24 packs to a box and 20 boxes to a case. The first seventy-five cards in this set feature veterans while the final 25 cards feature Rookie Cards and leading prospects. Those cards were issued to a stated print run of 999 serial numbered sets and were inserted at stated rates of one in seven hobby and one in 48 retail packs.

Nm-Mt Ex-Mt
COMP.SET w/o SP's (75) 25.00 7.50
COMMON CARD (1-75) .50 .15
COMMON CARD (76-100) 3.00 .90
76-100 ODDS 1:7 HOBBY, 1:48 RETAIL
76-100 PRINT RUN 999 SERIAL #'d SETS
1 Manny Ramirez .75 .23
2 Frank Thomas 1.25 .35
3 Josh Beckett .50 .15
4 Shawn Green .50 .15
5 Tom Glavine .75 .23
6 Marquis Grissom .50 .15
7 Nomar Garciaparra 2.00 .60
8 Magglio Ordonez .50 .15
9 Alex Rodriguez 2.00 .60
10 Chipper Jones 1.25 .35
11 Jody Gerut .50 .15
12 Dontrelle Willis .50 .15
13 Lance Berkman .50 .15
14 Jose Vidro .50 .15
15 Barry Zito .50 .15
16 Jason Kendall .50 .15
17 Scott Rolen 1.25 .35
18 Troy Glaus .50 .15
19 Brandon Webb .50 .15
20 Tim Hudson .50 .15
21 Shannon Stewart .50 .15
22 Darin Erstad .50 .15
23 Curt Schilling 1.25 .35
24 Bret Boone .50 .15
25 Richie Sexson .50 .15
26 Hideki Matsui 2.00 .60
27 Albert Pujols 2.50 .75
28 Greg Maddux 2.00 .60
29 Austin Kearns .50 .15
30 Todd Helton .75 .23
31 Miguel Cabrera .75 .23
32 Jeff Bagwell .75 .23
33 Marlon Byrd .50 .15
34 Ichiro Suzuki 2.00 .60
35 Rocco Baldelli .50 .15
36 Garret Anderson .50 .15
37 Javy Lopez .50 .15
38 Kerry Wood 1.25 .35
39 Adam Dunn .75 .23
40 Geoff Jenkins .50 .15
41 Derek Jeter 2.50 .75
42 Rich Harden .50 .15
43 Alfonso Soriano .75 .23
44 Ken Griffey Jr. 2.00 .60
45 Ivan Rodriguez 1.25 .35
46 Pedro Martinez 1.25 .35
47 Andy Pettitte .75 .23
48 Gary Sheffield .50 .15
49 Brian Giles .50 .15

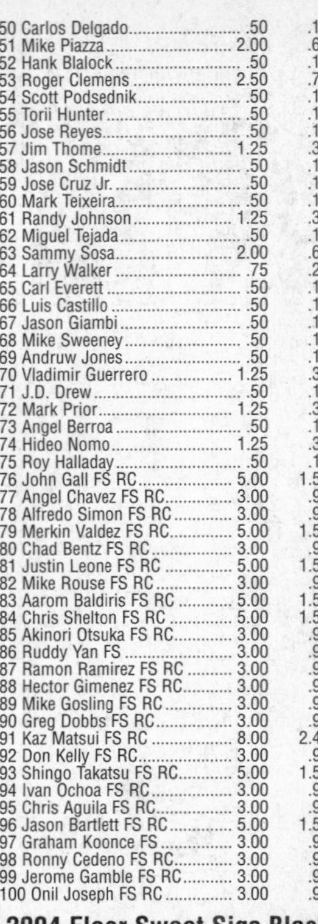

50 Carlos Delgado .50 .15
51 Mike Piazza 2.00 .60
52 Hank Blalock .50 .15
53 Roger Clemens 2.50 .75
54 Scott Podsednik .50 .15
55 Torii Hunter .50 .15
56 Jose Reyes .50 .15
57 Jim Thome 1.25 .35
58 Jason Schmidt .50 .15
59 Jose Cruz Jr. .50 .15
60 Mark Teixeira .50 .15
61 Randy Johnson 1.25 .35
62 Miguel Tejada .50 .15
63 Sammy Sosa 2.00 .60
64 Larry Walker .75 .23
65 Carl Everett .50 .15
66 Luis Castillo .50 .15
67 Jason Giambi .50 .15
68 Mike Sweeney .50 .15
69 Andruw Jones .50 .15
70 Vladimir Guerrero 1.25 .35
71 J.D. Drew .50 .15
72 Mark Prior 1.25 .35
73 Angel Berroa .50 .15
74 Hideo Nomo 1.25 .35
75 Roy Halladay .50 .15
76 John Gall FS RC 5.00 1.50
77 Angel Chavez FS RC 3.00 .90
78 Alfredo Simon FS RC 3.00 .90
79 Merkin Valdez FS RC 5.00 1.50
80 Chad Bentz FS RC 3.00 .90
81 Justin Leone FS RC 5.00 1.50
82 Mike Rouse FS RC 3.00 .90
83 Aarom Baldiris FS RC 5.00 1.50
84 Chris Shelton FS RC 5.00 1.50
85 Akinori Otsuka FS RC 3.00 .90
86 Ruddy Yan FS 3.00 .90
87 Ramon Ramirez FS RC 3.00 .90
88 Hector Gimenez FS RC 3.00 .90
89 Mike Gosling FS RC 3.00 .90
90 Greg Dobbs FS RC 3.00 .90
91 Kaz Matsui FS RC 8.00 2.40
92 Don Kelly FS RC 3.00 .90
93 Shingo Takatsu FS RC 5.00 1.50
94 Ivan Ochoa FS RC 3.00 .90
95 Chris Aguila FS RC 3.00 .90
96 Jason Bartlett FS RC 5.00 1.50
97 Graham Koonce FS 3.00 .90
98 Ronny Cedeno FS RC 3.00 .90
99 Jerome Gamble FS RC 3.00 .90
100 Onil Joseph FS RC 3.00 .90

2004 Fleer Sweet Sigs Black

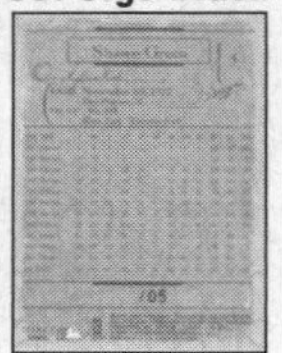

Nm-Mt Ex-Mt
OVERALL PARALLEL ODDS 1:18 H, 1:96 R
STATED PRINT RUN 5 SERIAL #'d SETS
NO PRICING DUE TO SCARCITY

2004 Fleer Sweet Sigs Gold

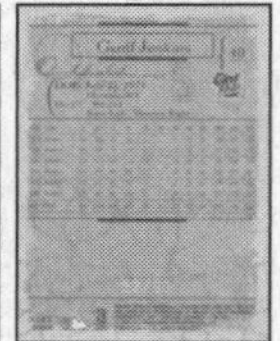

Nm-Mt Ex-Mt
*GOLD 1-75: 2X TO 5X BASIC
*GOLD 76-100: .6X TO 1.5X BASIC
OVERALL PARALLEL ODDS 1:18 H, 1:96 R
STATED PRINT RUN 99 SERIAL #'d SETS

2004 Fleer Sweet Sigs Autograph Gold

Nm-Mt Ex-Mt
*GOLD: .6X TO 1.5X RED p/r 150-163
*GOLD: .6X TO 1.5X RED p/r 73-100
*GOLD: .5X TO 1.2X RED p/r 44-52
*GOLD: .4X TO 1X RED p/r 28
*GOLD: .4X TO 1X RED p/r 25
OVERALL AU ODDS 1:12 H, AU-GU 1:24 R
STATED PRINT RUN 30 SERIAL #'d SETS
EXCHANGE DEADLINE INDEFINITE
HN Hideo Nomo 400.00 120.00

2004 Fleer Sweet Sigs Autograph Platinum

Nm-Mt Ex-Mt
*PLAT p/r 75: .3X TO .8X RED p/r 44
*PLAT p/r 38-61: .3X TO .8X RED p/r 28
*PLAT p/r 38-61: .4X TO 1X RED p/r 50
*PLAT p/r 38-61: .5X TO 1.2X RED p/r 75-100
*PLAT p/r 38-61: .5X TO 1.2X RED p/r 150
*PLAT p/r 27-35: .5X TO 1.2X RED p/r 50
*PLAT p/r 27-35: .6X TO 1.5X RED p/r 75-100

*PLAT p/r 27-35: .6X TO 1.5X RED p/r 150
*PLAT p/r 20-24: .5X TO 1.2X RED p/r 50-52
*PLAT p/r 20-24: .6X TO 1.5X RED p/r 75-100
*PLAT p/r 20-24: .6X TO 1.5X RED p/r 150
*PLAT p/r 15-18: .75X TO 2X RED p/r 75-100
*PLAT p/r 15-18: .75X TO 2X RED p/r 150
OVERALL AU ODDS 1:12 H, AU-GU 1:24 R
PRINT RUNS B/WN 3-75 COPIES PER
NO PRICING ON QTY OF 14 OR LESS
EXCHANGE DEADLINE INDEFINITE

2004 Fleer Sweet Sigs Autograph Red

Nm-Mt Ex-Mt
OVERALL AU ODDS 1:12 H, AU-GU 1:24 R
PRINT RUNS B/WN 5-163 COPIES PER
NO PRICING ON QTY OF 5 OR LESS
MASTERPIECE PRINT RUN 1 #'d SET
NO M'PIECE PRICING DUE TO SCARCITY
EXCHANGE DEADLINE INDEFINITE
AB Angel Berroa/75 15.00 4.50
AE Adam Everett/150 15.00 4.50
AL Al Leiter/75 EXCH 25.00 7.50
AO Akinori Otsuka/150 EXCH 25.00 7.50
AP1 Andy Pettitte/50 50.00 15.00
AP2 Albert Pujols/73 175.00 52.50
AR Alexis Rios/150 EXCH 25.00 7.50
BL Barry Larkin/50 50.00 15.00
BP Brad Penny/150 15.00 4.50
BR Brad Radke/100 EXCH 15.00 4.50
BW Bernie Williams/50 80.00 24.00
BZ Barry Zito/44 40.00 12.00
CB Carlos Beltran/75 EXCH 40.00 12.00
CC Carl Crawford/150 EXCH 15.00 4.50
CJ Chipper Jones/50 60.00 18.00
CL Carlos Lee/150 15.00 4.50
CS C.C. Sabathia/150 EXCH 15.00 4.50
CY Carl Yastrzemski/50 80.00 24.00
DE Dennis Eckersley/75 25.00 7.50
DS Deion Sanders/50 EXCH 60.00 18.00
DW Dontrelle Willis/150 25.00 7.50
EJ Edwin Jackson/75 15.00 4.50
FT Frank Thomas/75 EXCH 60.00 18.00
GA Garret Anderson/100 25.00 7.50
GM Greg Maddux/50 EXCH 80.00 24.00
HN Hideo Nomo/5
JB1 Josh Beckett/75 25.00 7.50
JB2 J.Bonderman/150 EXCH 15.00 4.50
JD1 Johnny Damon/100 60.00 18.00
JD2 J.D. Drew/75 40.00 12.00
JF Julio Franco/150 25.00 7.50
JL Javy Lopez/75 EXCH 25.00 7.50
JM Joe Mauer/150 EXCH 40.00 12.00
JO John Olerud/75 40.00 12.00
JR Jose Reyes/163 EXCH 15.00 4.50
JS Johan Santana/150 40.00 12.00
JV Jason Varitek/75 40.00 12.00
KG Khalil Greene/150 50.00 15.00
KL Kenny Lofton/50 40.00 12.00
KM Kevin Millwood/100 EXCH 15.00 4.50
KW Kerry Wood/75 40.00 12.00
LB Lance Berkman/150 25.00 7.50
LG Luis Gonzalez/150 15.00 4.50
LN Lance Niekro/150 15.00 4.50
MC1 Miguel Cabrera/150 25.00 7.50
MC2 Mike Cameron/150 15.00 4.50
MK Matt Kata/150 15.00 4.50
MM Mike Mussina/50 40.00 12.00
MO Magglio Ordonez/150 25.00 7.50
MP Mike Piazza/50 150.00 45.00
MS Mike Schmidt/50 EXCH 60.00 18.00
MV Merkin Valdez/150 EXCH 15.00 4.50
NR Nolan Ryan/50 EXCH 150.00 45.00
OV Omar Vizquel/100 EXCH 40.00 12.00
PM1 Pedro Martinez/75 100.00 30.00
PM2 Paul Molitor/75 40.00 12.00
RB Rocco Baldelli/75 15.00 4.50
RC Roger Clemens/52 EXCH 120.00 36.00
RJ Randy Johnson/28 100.00 30.00
RO1 Russ Ortiz/150 15.00 4.50
RO2 Roy Oswalt/150 15.00 4.50
SM Stan Musial/25 100.00 30.00
SS Shannon Stewart/75 EXCH 15.00 4.50
TH Torii Hunter/150 EXCH 15.00 4.50
TS Tim Salmon/100 40.00 12.00
TW1 Tim Wakefield/150 50.00 15.00
VG Vladimir Guerrero/75 60.00 18.00
VW Vernon Wells/150 15.00 4.50
WM Wade Miller/150 15.00 4.50

2004 Fleer Sweet Sigs Ballpark Heroes

Nm-Mt Ex-Mt
STATED ODDS 1:6 HOBBY/RETAIL
1 Rocco Baldelli 2.00 .60
2 Adam Dunn 2.00 .60
3 Nomar Garciaparra 5.00 1.50
4 Ken Griffey Jr. 5.00 1.50
5 Vladimir Guerrero 3.00 .90
6 Torii Hunter 2.00 .60
7 Andruw Jones 2.00 .60
8 Mike Piazza 5.00 1.50

9 Alfonso Soriano 2.00 .60
10 Frank Thomas 3.00 .90
11 Dontrelle Willis 2.00 .60
12 Barry Zito 2.00 .60
13 Javy Lopez 2.00 .60
14 Miguel Cabrera 2.00 .60
15 Kaz Matsui 4.00 1.20
16 Josh Beckett 2.00 .60
17 Derek Jeter 6.00 1.80
18 Greg Maddux 5.00 1.50
19 Pedro Martinez 3.00 .90
20 Hideo Nomo 3.00 .90
21 Mark Prior 3.00 .90
22 Albert Pujols 6.00 1.80
23 Alex Rodriguez 5.00 1.50
24 Scott Rolen 3.00 .90
25 Ichiro Suzuki 5.00 1.50

2004 Fleer Sweet Sigs Ballpark Heroes Jersey Red

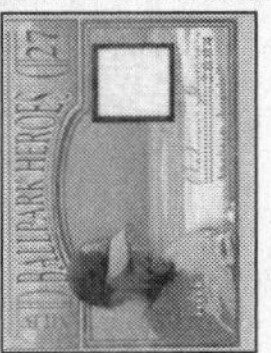

Nm-Mt Ex-Mt
STATED ODDS 1:108 RETAIL
LOGO M'PIECE RANDOM IN HOBBY PACKS
LOGO MASTERPIECE PRINT RUN 1 #'d SET
OVERALL GU ODDS 1:8 H, AU-GU 1:24 R
AD Adam Dunn 10.00 3.00
AP Albert Pujols 20.00 6.00
AR Alex Rodriguez 12.00 3.60
AS Alfonso Soriano 10.00 3.00
BZ Barry Zito 6.00 1.80
DW Dontrelle Willis 6.00 1.80
FT Frank Thomas 10.00 3.00
GM Greg Maddux 15.00 4.50
HN Hideo Nomo 10.00 3.00
JB Josh Beckett 6.00 1.80
KM Kaz Matsui 15.00 4.50
MC Miguel Cabrera 10.00 3.00
MP1 Mike Piazza 15.00 4.50
MP2 Mark Prior 10.00 3.00
PM Pedro Martinez 10.00 3.00
RB Rocco Baldelli 6.00 1.80
SR Scott Rolen 10.00 3.00
VG Vladimir Guerrero 10.00 3.00

2004 Fleer Sweet Sigs Ballpark Heroes Quad Patch

Nm-Mt Ex-Mt
OVERALL GU ODDS 1:8 H, AU-GU 1:24 R
PRINT RUNS B/WN 9-42 COPIES PER
NO PRICING ON QTY OF 9 OR LESS
BDGC Rocco Baldelli
Adam Dunn
Vladimir Guerrero
Miguel Cabrera/9
BMMP Josh Beckett 60.00 18.00
Greg Maddux
Pedro Martinez
Mark Prior/42
PGPR Albert Pujols 100.00 30.00
Vladimir Guerrero
Mike Piazza
Alex Rodriguez/37
WBJR Dontrelle Willis 100.00 30.00
Josh Beckett
Derek Jeter
Alex Rodriguez/32
WMCB Dontrelle Willis 50.00 15.00
Kaz Matsui
Miguel Cabrera
Rocco Baldelli/26

2004 Fleer Sweet Sigs Sweet Stitches Jersey Red

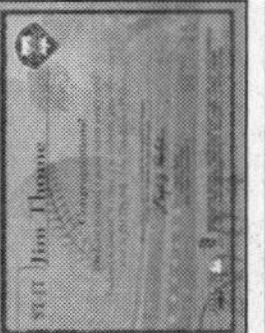

Nm-Mt Ex-Mt
STATED ODDS 1:108 RETAIL
STATED PRINT RUN 125 SERIAL #'d SETS
LOGO M'PIECE RANDOM IN HOBBY PACKS
LOGO MASTERPIECE PRINT RUN 1 #'d SET
NO LOGO M'PIECE PRICE DUE TO SCARCITY
OVERALL GU ODDS 1:8 H, AU-GU 1:24 R
AJ Andruw Jones 6.00 1.80
AP Albert Pujols 20.00 6.00
AR Alex Rodriguez 12.00 3.60
AS Alfonso Soriano 10.00 3.00
FT Frank Thomas 10.00 3.00
GM Greg Maddux 15.00 4.50
GS Gary Sheffield 6.00 1.80
HB Hank Blalock 6.00 1.80
HN Hideo Nomo 10.00 3.00
JB Josh Beckett 6.00 1.80
JG Jason Giambi 6.00 1.80
JR Jose Reyes 6.00 1.80
JT Jim Thome 10.00 3.00
KM Kaz Matsui 15.00 4.50
KW Kerry Wood 10.00 3.00
MC Miguel Cabrera 10.00 3.00
MO Magglio Ordonez 6.00 1.80
MP1 Mike Piazza 15.00 4.50
MP2 Mark Prior 10.00 3.00
MR Manny Ramirez 10.00 3.00
MT1 Mark Teixeira 6.00 1.80
MT2 Miguel Tejada 6.00 1.80
RB Rocco Baldelli 6.00 1.80
RC Roger Clemens 15.00 4.50
RJ Randy Johnson 10.00 3.00
SR Scott Rolen 10.00 3.00
SS Sammy Sosa 15.00 4.50
VG Vladimir Guerrero 10.00 3.00

2004 Fleer Sweet Sigs Sweet Stitches Quad Patch

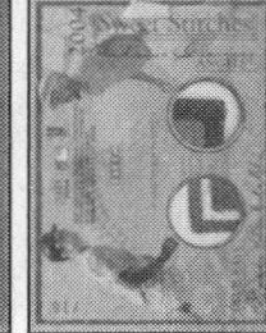

Nm-Mt Ex-Mt
OVERALL GU ODDS 1:8 H, AU-GU 1:24 R
PRINT RUNS B/WN 2-33 COPIES PER
NO PRICING ON QTY OF 10 OR LESS
CPBW Roger Clemens 80.00 24.00
Mark Prior
Josh Beckett
Kerry Wood/24
GRPR Jason Giambi 60.00 18.00
Alex Rodriguez
Mike Piazza
Jose Reyes/22
GSCR Jason Giambi 60.00 18.00
Alfonso Soriano
Miguel Cabrera
Alex Rodriguez/29
JCPS Andruw Jones 80.00 24.00
Miguel Cabrera
Albert Pujols
Sammy Sosa/31
MSPW Greg Maddux 120.00 36.00
Sammy Sosa
Mark Prior
Kerry Wood/33
PNPB Mike Piazza
Hideo Nomo
Albert Pujols
Angel Berroa/10
RSBG Manny Ramirez 50.00 15.00
Gary Sheffield
Rocco Baldelli
Vladimir Guerrero/16
SRTM Alfonso Soriano 60.00 18.00
Jose Reyes
Miguel Tejada
Kaz Matsui/26
TOSP Frank Thomas
Magglio Ordonez
Sammy Sosa
Mark Prior/2
TRMR Jim Thome 60.00 18.00
Jose Reyes
Kaz Matsui
Scott Rolen/32

2004 Fleer Sweet Sigs Sweet Swing

Nm-Mt Ex-Mt
STATED ODDS 1:12 HOBBY/RETAIL
1 Sammy Sosa 5.00 1.50
2 Vladimir Guerrero 3.00 .90
3 Jason Giambi 2.00 .60
4 Chipper Jones 3.00 .90
5 Alfonso Soriano 2.00 .60
6 Manny Ramirez 2.00 .60
7 Todd Helton 2.00 .60
8 Alex Rodriguez 5.00 1.50
9 Albert Pujols 6.00 1.80
10 Jeff Bagwell 2.00 .60
11 Mike Piazza 5.00 1.50
12 Hank Blalock 2.00 .60
13 Jim Thome 3.00 .90
14 Carlos Delgado 2.00 .60
15 Nomar Garciaparra 5.00 1.50

2004 Fleer Sweet Sigs Sweet Swing Jersey Red

Nm-Mt Ex-Mt
STATED ODDS 1:108 RETAIL
STATED PRINT RUN 200 SERIAL #'d SETS
*BAT SILVER p/r 213-250: .4X TO 1X RED
*BAT SILVER p/r 15: 1.5X TO 4X RED
BAT SILVER PRINT RUNS B/WN 15-250 PER
*BAT-JSY GOLD: .75X TO 2X RED
BAT-JSY GOLD PRINT RUN 50 #'d SETS
BAT LOGO M'PIECE PRINT RUN 1 #'d SET
NO BAT LOGO MP PRICE DUE TO SCARCITY
*BAT-PATCH BLK p/r 66: 1X TO 2.5X RED
*BAT-PATCH BLK p/r 39-57: 1.25X TO 3X RED
*BAT-PATCH BLK p/r 29: 1.5X TO 4X RED
BAT-PATCH BLACK PRINT B/WN 29-66 PER
OVERALL GU ODDS 1:8 H, AU-GU 1:24 R
AP Albert Pujols 15.00 4.50
AR Alex Rodriguez 10.00 3.00
AS Alfonso Soriano 8.00 2.40
CJ Chipper Jones 8.00 2.40
HB Hank Blalock 5.00 1.50
JG Jason Giambi 5.00 1.50
JT Jim Thome 8.00 2.40
MP Mike Piazza 12.00 3.60
MR Manny Ramirez 8.00 2.40
SS Sammy Sosa 12.00 3.60
VG Vladimir Guerrero 8.00 2.40

2004 Fleer Sweet Sigs Sweet Swing Quad Patch

Nm-Mt Ex-Mt
OVERALL GU ODDS 1:8 H, AU-GU 1:24 R
PRINT RUNS B/WN 12-35 COPIES PER
NO PRICING ON QTY OF 12 OR LESS
GHBT Jason Giambi
Todd Helton
Jeff Bagwell
Jim Thome/12
GPJS Vladimir Guerrero 100.00 30.00
Albert Pujols
Chipper Jones
Sammy Sosa/27
GRBR Jason Giambi 80.00 24.00
Alex Rodriguez
Jeff Bagwell
Manny Ramirez/35
PSHB Mike Piazza 80.00 24.00
Alfonso Soriano
Todd Helton
Hank Blalock/32
RDTP Alex Rodriguez 100.00 30.00
Carlos Delgado
Jim Thome
Albert Pujols/22

1998 Fleer Tradition

The 600-card 1998 Fleer set was issued in two series. Series one consists of 350 cards and Series two consists of 250 cards. The packs for either series consisted of 12 cards and had a SRP of $1.49. Card fronts feature borderless color action player photos with UV-coating and foil stamping. The backs display player information and career statistics. The set contains the following topical subsets: Smoke 'N Heat (301-310), Golden Memories (311-320), Tale of the Tape (321-340) and Unforgettable Moments (576-600). The Golden Memories (1:6 packs), Tale of the Tape (1:4 packs) and Unforgettable Moments (1:4 packs) cards are shortprinted. An Alex Rodriguez Promo card was distributed to dealers along with their 1998 Fleer series one order forms. The card can be readily distinguished by the "Promotional Sample" text running diagonally across both the front and back of the card. 50 Fleer Flashback Exchange cards were hand-numbered and randomly inserted into packs. Each of these cards could be exchanged for a framed, uncut press sheet from one of Fleer's baseball sets dating anywhere from 1981 to 1993.

Nm-Mt Ex-Mt
COMPLETE SET (600) 150.00 45.00
COMP. SERIES 1 (350) 90.00 27.00
COMP. SERIES 2 (250) 60.00 18.00
COMMON CARD (1-600) .30 .09
COMMON GM (311-320) .50 .15
COMMON TT (321-340) .60 .18
COMMON UM (576-600) .75 .23
1 Ken Griffey Jr. 1.25 .35
2 Derek Jeter 2.00 .60
3 Gerald Williams .30 .09
4 Carlos Delgado .30 .09
5 Nomar Garciaparra 1.25 .35
6 Gary Sheffield .30 .09
7 Jeff King .30 .09
8 Cal Ripken 2.50 .75
9 Matt Williams .30 .09
10 Chipper Jones .75 .23
11 Chuck Knoblauch .30 .09
12 Mark Grudzielanek .30 .09
13 Edgardo Alfonzo .30 .09
14 Andres Galarraga .30 .09
15 Tim Salmon .50 .15
16 Reggie Sanders .30 .09
17 Tony Clark .30 .09
18 Jason Kendall .30 .09
19 Juan Gonzalez .50 .15
20 Ben Grieve .30 .09
21 Roger Clemens 1.50 .45
22 Raul Mondesi .30 .09
23 Robin Ventura .30 .09
24 Derrek Lee .30 .09
25 Mark McGwire 2.00 .60
26 Luis Gonzalez .30 .09
27 Kevin Brown .50 .15
28 Kirk Rueter .30 .09
29 Bobby Estalella .30 .09
30 Shawn Green .30 .09
31 Greg Maddux 1.25 .35
32 Jorge Velandia .30 .09
33 Larry Walker .50 .15
34 Joey Cora .30 .09
35 Frank Thomas .75 .23
36 Curtis King RC .30 .09
37 Aaron Boone .30 .09
38 Curt Schilling .30 .09
39 Bruce Aven .30 .09
40 Ben McDonald .30 .09
41 Andy Ashby .30 .09
42 Jason McDonald .30 .09
43 Eric Davis .30 .09
44 Mark Grace .50 .15
45 Pedro Martinez .75 .23
46 Lou Collier .30 .09
47 Chan Ho Park .30 .09
48 Shane Halter .30 .09
49 Brian Hunter .30 .09
50 Jeff Bagwell .50 .15
51 Bernie Williams .50 .15
52 J.T. Snow .30 .09
53 Todd Greene .30 .09
54 Shannon Stewart .30 .09
55 Darren Bragg .30 .09
56 Fernando Tatis .30 .09
57 Darryl Kile .30 .09
58 Chris Stynes .30 .09
59 Javier Valentin .30 .09
60 Brian McRae .30 .09
61 Tom Evans .30 .09
62 Randall Simon .30 .09
63 Darrin Fletcher .30 .09
64 Jaret Wright .30 .09
65 Luis Ordaz .30 .09
66 Jose Canseco .75 .23
67 Edgar Renteria .30 .09
68 Jay Buhner .30 .09
69 Paul Konerko .30 .09
70 Adrian Brown .30 .09
71 Chris Carpenter .30 .09
72 Mike Lieberthal .30 .09
73 Dean Palmer .30 .09
74 Jorge Fabregas .30 .09
75 Stan Javier .30 .09
76 Damion Easley .30 .09
77 David Cone .30 .09
78 Aaron Sele .30 .09
79 Antonio Alfonseca .30 .09
80 Bobby Jones .30 .09
81 David Justice .30 .09
82 Jeffrey Hammonds .30 .09
83 Doug Glanville .30 .09
84 Jason Dickson .30 .09
85 Brad Radke .30 .09
86 David Segui .30 .09
87 Greg Vaughn .30 .09
88 Mike Cather RC .30 .09
89 Alex Fernandez .30 .09
90 Billy Taylor .30 .09
91 Jason Schmidt .30 .09
92 Mike DeJean RC .30 .09
93 Domingo Cedeno .30 .09
94 Jeff Cirillo .30 .09
95 Manny Aybar RC .30 .09
96 Jaime Navarro .30 .09
97 Dennis Reyes .30 .09
98 Barry Larkin .50 .15
99 Troy O'Leary .30 .09
100 Alex Rodriguez 1.25 .35
101 Pat Hentgen .30 .09
102 Bubba Trammell .30 .09
103 Glendon Rusch .30 .09
104 Kenny Lofton .30 .09
105 Craig Biggio .50 .15
106 Kelvim Escobar .30 .09
107 Mark Kotsay .30 .09
108 Rondell White .30 .09
109 Darren Oliver .30 .09
110 Jim Thome .75 .23
111 Rich Becker .30 .09
112 Chad Curtis .30 .09
113 Dave Hollins .30 .09
114 Bill Mueller .30 .09
115 Antone Williamson .30 .09
116 Tony Womack .30 .09
117 Randy Myers .30 .09
118 Rico Brogna .30 .09
119 Pat Watkins .30 .09
120 Eli Marrero .30 .09
121 Jay Bell .30 .09
122 Kevin Tapani .30 .09
123 Todd Erdos RC .30 .09
124 Neifi Perez .30 .09
125 Todd Hundley .30 .09
126 Jeff Abbott .30 .09
127 Todd Zeile .30 .09
128 Travis Fryman .30 .09
129 Sandy Alomar Jr. .30 .09
130 Fred McGriff .50 .15
131 Richard Hidalgo .30 .09
132 Scott Spiezio .30 .09
133 John Valentin .30 .09
134 Quilvio Veras .30 .09
135 Mike Lansing .30 .09
136 Paul Molitor .50 .15
137 Randy Johnson .75 .23
138 Harold Baines .30 .09
139 Doug Jones .30 .09
140 Abraham Nunez .30 .09
141 Alan Benes .30 .09
142 Matt Perisho .30 .09
143 Chris Clemons .30 .09
144 Andy Pettitte .50 .15
145 Jason Giambi .30 .09
146 Moises Alou .30 .09
147 Chad Fox RC .30 .09
148 Felix Martinez .30 .09
149 Carlos Mendoza RC .30 .09
150 Scott Rolen .75 .23
151 Jose Cabrera RC .30 .09
152 Justin Thompson .30 .09
153 Ellis Burks .30 .09
154 Pokey Reese .30 .09
155 Bartolo Colon .30 .09
156 Ray Durham .30 .09
157 Ugueth Urbina .30 .09
158 Tom Goodwin .30 .09
159 Dave Dellucci RC .50 .15
160 Rod Beck .30 .09
161 Ramon Martinez .30 .09
162 Joe Carter .30 .09
163 Kevin Orie .30 .09
164 Trevor Hoffman .30 .09
165 Emil Brown .30 .09
166 Robb Nen .30 .09
167 Paul O'Neill .50 .15
168 Ryan Long .30 .09
169 Ray Lankford .30 .09
170 Ivan Rodriguez .75 .23
171 Rick Aguilera .30 .09
172 Deivi Cruz .30 .09
173 Ricky Bottalico .30 .09
174 Garret Anderson .30 .09
175 Jose Vizcaino .30 .09
176 Omar Vizquel .50 .15
177 Jeff Blauser .30 .09
178 Orlando Cabrera .30 .09
179 Russ Johnson .30 .09
180 Matt Stairs .30 .09
181 Will Cunnane .30 .09
182 Adam Riggs .30 .09
183 Matt Morris .30 .09
184 Mario Valdez .30 .09
185 Larry Sutton .30 .09
186 Marc Pisciotta RC .30 .09
187 Dan Wilson .30 .09
188 John Franco .30 .09
189 Darren Daulton .30 .09
190 Todd Helton .50 .15
191 Brady Anderson .30 .09
192 Ricardo Rincon .30 .09
193 Kevin Stocker .30 .09
194 Jose Valentin .30 .09
195 Ed Sprague .30 .09
196 Ryan McGuire .30 .09
197 Scott Eyre .30 .09
198 Steve Finley .30 .09
199 T.J. Mathews .30 .09
200 Mike Piazza 1.25 .35
201 Mark Wohlers .30 .09
202 Brian Giles .30 .09
203 Eduardo Perez .30 .09
204 Shigetoshi Hasegawa .30 .09
205 Mariano Rivera .50 .15
206 Jose Rosado .30 .09
207 Michael Coleman .30 .09
208 James Baldwin .30 .09
209 Russ Davis .30 .09
210 Billy Wagner .30 .09
211 Sammy Sosa 1.25 .35
212 Frank Catalanotto RC .50 .15
213 Delino DeShields .30 .09
214 John Olerud .30 .09
215 Heath Murray .30 .09
216 Jose Vidro .30 .09
217 Jim Edmonds .30 .09
218 Shawon Dunston .30 .09
219 Homer Bush .30 .09
220 Midre Cummings .30 .09
221 Tony Saunders .30 .09
222 Jeromy Burnitz .30 .09
223 Enrique Wilson .30 .09
224 Chili Davis .30 .09
225 Jerry DiPoto .30 .09
226 Dante Powell .30 .09
227 Javier Lopez .30 .09
228 Kevin Polcovich .30 .09
229 Deion Sanders .50 .15
230 Jimmy Key .30 .09
231 Rusty Greer .30 .09
232 Reggie Jefferson .30 .09
233 Ron Coomer .30 .09
234 Bobby Higginson .50 .15
235 Magglio Ordonez RC 2.00 .60
236 Miguel Tejada .30 .09
237 Rick Gorecki .30 .09
238 Charles Johnson .30 .09
239 Lance Johnson .30 .09
240 Derek Bell .30 .09
241 Will Clark .75 .23
242 Brady Raggio .30 .09
243 Orel Hershiser .30 .09
244 Vladimir Guerrero .75 .23
245 John LeRoy .30 .09
246 Shawn Estes .30 .09
247 Brett Tomko .30 .09
248 Dave Nilsson .30 .09
249 Edgar Martinez .50 .15
250 Tony Gwynn 1.00 .30
251 Mark Bellhorn .30 .09
252 Jed Hansen .30 .09
253 Butch Huskey .30 .09
254 Eric Young .30 .09
255 Vinny Castilla .30 .09
256 Hideki Irabu .30 .09
257 Mike Cameron .30 .09
258 Juan Encarnacion .30 .09
259 Brian Rose .30 .09
260 Brad Ausmus .30 .09
261 Dan Serafini .30 .09
262 Willie Greene .30 .09
263 Troy Percival .30 .09
264 Jeff Wallace .30 .09
265 Richie Sexson .30 .09
266 Rafael Palmeiro .50 .15
267 Brad Fullmer .30 .09
268 Jeremi Gonzalez .30 .09
269 Rob Stanifer RC .30 .09
270 Mickey Morandini .30 .09
271 Andruw Jones .30 .09
272 Royce Clayton .30 .09
273 T.Kashiwada RC .30 .09
274 Steve Woodard .30 .09
275 Jose Cruz Jr. .30 .09
276 Keith Foulke .30 .09
277 Brad Rigby .30 .09
278 Tino Martinez .50 .15
279 Todd Jones .30 .09
280 John Wetteland .30 .09
281 Alex Gonzalez .30 .09
282 Ken Cloude .30 .09
283 Jose Guillen .30 .09
284 Danny Clyburn .30 .09
285 David Ortiz .75 .23
286 John Thomson .30 .09
287 Kevin Appier .30 .09
288 Ismael Valdes .30 .09
289 Gary DiSarcina .30 .09
290 Todd Dunwoody .30 .09
291 Wally Joyner .30 .09
292 Charles Nagy .30 .09
293 Jeff Shaw .30 .09
294 Kevin Millwood RC 1.00 .30
295 Rigo Beltran RC .30 .09
296 Jeff Frye .30 .09
297 Oscar Henriquez .30 .09
298 Mike Thurman .30 .09
299 Garrett Stephenson .30 .09
300 Barry Bonds 2.00 .60
301 Roger Clemens SH .75 .23
302 David Cone SH .30 .09
303 Hideki Irabu SH .30 .09
304 Randy Johnson SH .50 .15
305 Greg Maddux SH .75 .23
306 Pedro Martinez SH .50 .15
307 Mike Mussina SH .30 .09
308 Andy Pettitte SH .30 .09
309 Curt Schilling SH .30 .09
310 John Smoltz SH .30 .09
311 Roger Clemens GM 2.50 .75
312 Jose Cruz JR. GM .50 .15
313 N.Garciaparra GM 2.00 .60
314 Ken Griffey Jr. GM 2.00 .60
315 Tony Gwynn GM 1.50 .45
316 Hideki Irabu GM .50 .15
317 Randy Johnson GM 1.25 .35
318 Mark McGwire GM 3.00 .90
319 Curt Schilling GM .50 .15
320 Larry Walker GM .75 .23
321 Jeff Bagwell TT 1.00 .30
322 Albert Belle TT .60 .18
323 Barry Bonds TT 4.00 1.20
324 Jay Buhner TT .60 .18
325 Tony Clark TT .60 .18
326 Jose Cruz Jr. TT .60 .18
327 Andres Galarraga TT .60 .18
328 Juan Gonzalez TT 1.00 .30
329 Ken Griffey Jr. TT 2.50 .75
330 Andruw Jones TT .60 .18
331 Tino Martinez TT 1.00 .30
332 Mark McGwire TT 4.00 1.20
333 Rafael Palmeiro TT 1.00 .30
334 Mike Piazza TT 2.50 .75
335 Manny Ramirez TT 1.00 .30
336 Alex Rodriguez TT 2.50 .75
337 Frank Thomas TT 1.50 .45
338 Jim Thome TT 1.50 .45
339 Mo Vaughn TT .60 .18
340 Larry Walker TT 1.00 .30
341 Jose Cruz Jr. CL .30 .09
342 Ken Griffey Jr. CL .75 .23
343 Derek Jeter CL 1.00 .30
344 Andruw Jones CL .30 .09
345 Chipper Jones CL .50 .15
346 Greg Maddux CL .75 .23
347 Mike Piazza CL .75 .23
348 Cal Ripken CL 1.25 .35
349 Alex Rodriguez CL .75 .23
350 Frank Thomas CL .50 .15
351 Mo Vaughn .30 .09
352 Andres Galarraga .30 .09
353 Roberto Alomar .50 .15
354 Darin Erstad .30 .09
355 Albert Belle .30 .09
356 Matt Williams .30 .09
357 Darryl Kile .30 .09
358 Kenny Lofton .50 .15
359 Orel Hershiser .30 .09
360 Bob Abreu .30 .09
361 Chris Widger .30 .09
362 Glenallen Hill .30 .09
363 Chili Davis .30 .09
364 Kevin Brown .50 .15
365 Marquis Grissom .30 .09
366 Livan Hernandez .30 .09
367 Moises Alou .30 .09
368 Matt Lawton .30 .09
369 Rey Ordonez .30 .09
370 Kenny Rogers .30 .09
371 Lee Stevens .30 .09
372 Wade Boggs .50 .15
373 Luis Gonzalez .30 .09
374 Jeff Conine .30 .09
375 Esteban Loaiza .30 .09
376 Jose Canseco .75 .23
377 Henry Rodriguez .30 .09
378 Dave Burba .30 .09
379 Todd Hollandsworth .30 .09
380 Ron Gant .30 .09
381 Pedro Martinez .75 .23
382 Ryan Klesko .30 .09
383 Derrek Lee .30 .09
384 Doug Glanville .30 .09
385 David Wells .30 .09
386 Ken Caminiti .30 .09
387 Damon Hollins .30 .09
388 Manny Ramirez .50 .15
389 Mike Mussina .50 .15
390 Jay Bell .30 .09
391 Mike Piazza 1.25 .35
392 Mike Lansing .30 .09
393 Mike Hampton .30 .09
394 Geoff Jenkins .30 .09
395 Jimmy Haynes .30 .09
396 Scott Servais .30 .09
397 Kent Mercker .30 .09
398 Jeff Kent .30 .09
399 Kevin Elster .30 .09
400 Masato Yoshii RC .50 .15
401 Jose Vizcaino .30 .09
402 Javier Martinez RC .30 .09
403 David Segui .30 .09
404 Tony Saunders .30 .09
405 Karim Garcia .30 .09
406 Armando Benitez .30 .09
407 Joe Randa .30 .09
408 Vic Darensbourg .30 .09
409 Sean Casey .30 .09
410 Eric Milton .30 .09
411 Trey Moore .30 .09
412 Mike Stanley .30 .09
413 Tom Gordon .30 .09
414 Hal Morris .30 .09
415 Braden Looper .30 .09
416 Mike Kelly .30 .09
417 John Smoltz .50 .15
418 Roger Cedeno .30 .09
419 Al Leiter .30 .09
420 Chuck Knoblauch .30 .09
421 Felix Rodriguez .30 .09
422 Bip Roberts .30 .09
423 Ken Hill .30 .09
424 Jermaine Allensworth .30 .09
425 Esteban Yan RC .30 .09
426 Scott Karl .30 .09
427 Sean Berry .30 .09
428 Rafael Medina .30 .09
429 Javier Vazquez .30 .09
430 Rickey Henderson .75 .23
431 Adam Butler .30 .09
432 Todd Stottlemyre .30 .09
433 Yamil Benitez .30 .09
434 Sterling Hitchcock .30 .09
435 Paul Sorrento .30 .09
436 Bobby Ayala .30 .09
437 Tim Raines .30 .09
438 Chris Hoiles .30 .09
439 Rod Beck .30 .09
440 Donnie Sadler .30 .09
441 Charles Johnson .30 .09
442 Russ Ortiz .30 .09
443 Pedro Astacio .30 .09
444 Wilson Alvarez .30 .09
445 Mike Blowers .30 .09
446 Todd Zeile .30 .09
447 Mel Rojas .30 .09
448 F.P. Santangelo .30 .09
449 Dmitri Young .30 .09
450 Brian Anderson .30 .09
451 Cecil Fielder .30 .09
452 Roberto Hernandez .30 .09
453 Todd Walker .30 .09
454 Tyler Green .30 .09
455 Jorge Posada .50 .15
456 Geronimo Berroa .30 .09
457 Jose Silva .30 .09
458 Bobby Bonilla .30 .09
459 Walt Weiss .30 .09
460 Darren Dreifort .30 .09
461 B.J. Surhoff .30 .09
462 Quinton McCracken .30 .09
463 Derek Lowe .30 .09
464 Jorge Fabregas .30 .09
465 Joey Hamilton .30 .09
466 Brian Jordan .30 .09
467 Allen Watson .30 .09
468 John Jaha .30 .09
469 Heathcliff Slocumb .30 .09
470 Gregg Jefferies .30 .09
471 Scott Brosius .30 .09
472 Chad Ogea .30 .09
473 A.J. Hinch .30 .09
474 Bobby Smith .30 .09
475 Brian Moehler .30 .09
476 DaRond Stovall .30 .09
477 Kevin Young .30 .09
478 Jeff Suppan .30 .09
479 Marty Cordova .30 .09
480 John Halama RC .30 .09
481 Bubba Trammell .30 .09
482 Mike Caruso .30 .09
483 Eric Karros .30 .09
484 Jamey Wright .30 .09
485 Mike Sweeney .30 .09
486 Aaron Sele .30 .09
487 Cliff Floyd .30 .09
488 Jeff Brantley .30 .09
489 Jim Leyritz .30 .09
490 Denny Neagle .30 .09
491 Travis Fryman .30 .09
492 Carlos Baerga .30 .09
493 Eddie Taubensee .30 .09
494 Darryl Strawberry .30 .09
495 Brian Johnson .30 .09
496 Randy Myers .30 .09
497 Jeff Blauser .30 .09
498 Jason Wood .30 .09
499 Rolando Arrojo RC .30 .09
500 Johnny Damon .50 .15
501 Jose Mercedes .30 .09
502 Tony Batista .30 .09
503 Mike Piazza Mets 1.25 .35
504 Hideo Nomo .75 .23
505 Chris Gomez .30 .09
506 Jesus Sanchez RC .30 .09
507 Al Martin .30 .09
508 Brian Edmondson .30 .09
509 Joe Girardi .30 .09
510 Shayne Bennett .30 .09
511 Joe Carter .30 .09
512 Dave Mlicki .30 .09
513 Rich Butler RC .30 .09
514 Dennis Eckersley .30 .09

515 Travis Lee	.30	.09
516 John Mabry	.30	.09
517 Jose Mesa	.30	.09
518 Phil Nevin	.30	.09
519 Raul Casanova	.30	.09
520 Mike Fetters	.30	.09
521 Gary Sheffield	.30	.09
522 Terry Steinbach	.30	.09
523 Steve Trachsel	.30	.09
524 Josh Booty	.30	.09
525 Darryl Hamilton	.30	.09
526 Mark McLemore	.30	.09
527 Kevin Stocker	.30	.09
528 Bret Boone	.30	.09
529 Shane Andrews	.30	.09
530 Robb Nen	.30	.09
531 Carl Everett	.30	.09
532 LaTroy Hawkins	.30	.09
533 Fernando Vina	.30	.09
534 Michael Tucker	.30	.09
535 Mark Langston	.30	.09
536 Mickey Mantle	5.00	1.50
537 Bernard Gilkey	.30	.09
538 Francisco Cordova	.30	.09
539 Mike Bordick	.30	.09
540 Fred McGriff	.50	.15
541 Cliff Politte	.30	.09
542 Jason Varitek	.75	.23
543 Shawon Dunston	.30	.09
544 Brian Meadows	.30	.09
545 Pat Meares	.30	.09
546 Carlos Perez	.30	.09
547 Desi Relaford	.30	.09
548 Antonio Osuna	.30	.09
549 Devon White	.30	.09
550 Sean Runyan	.30	.09
551 Mickey Morandini	.30	.09
552 Dave Martinez	.30	.09
553 Jeff Fassero	.30	.09
554 Ryan Jackson RC	.30	.09
555 Stan Javier	.30	.09
556 Jaime Navarro	.30	.09
557 Jose Offerman	.30	.09
558 Mike Lowell RC	1.50	.45
559 Darrin Fletcher	.30	.09
560 Mark Lewis	.30	.09
561 Dante Bichette	.30	.09
562 Chuck Finley	.30	.09
563 Kerry Wood	.75	.23
564 Andy Benes	.30	.09
565 Freddy Garcia	.30	.09
566 Tom Glavine	.50	.15
567 Jon Nunnally	.30	.09
568 Miguel Cairo	.30	.09
569 Shane Reynolds	.30	.09
570 Roberto Kelly	.30	.09
571 Jose Cruz Jr. CL	.30	.09
572 Ken Griffey Jr. CL	.75	.23
573 Mark McGwire CL	1.00	.30
574 Cal Ripken CL	1.25	.35
575 Frank Thomas CL	.50	.15
576 Jeff Bagwell UM	1.25	.35
577 Barry Bonds UM	5.00	1.50
578 Tony Clark UM	.75	.23
579 Roger Clemens UM	4.00	1.20
580 Jose Cruz Jr. UM	.75	.23
581 N.Garciaparra UM	3.00	.90
582 Juan Gonzalez UM	1.25	.35
583 Ben Grieve UM	.75	.23
584 Ken Griffey Jr. UM	3.00	.90
585 Tony Gwynn UM	2.50	.75
586 Derek Jeter UM	5.00	1.50
587 Randy Johnson UM	2.00	.60
588 Chipper Jones UM	2.00	.60
589 Greg Maddux UM	3.00	.90
590 Mark McGwire UM	5.00	1.50
591 Andy Pettitte UM	1.25	.35
592 Paul Molitor UM	1.25	.35
593 Cal Ripken UM	6.00	1.80
594 Alex Rodriguez UM	3.00	.90
595 Scott Rolen UM	2.00	.60
596 Curt Schilling UM	.75	.23
597 Frank Thomas UM	2.00	.60
598 Jim Thome UM	2.00	.60
599 Larry Walker UM	1.25	.35
600 Bernie Williams UM	1.25	.35
P100 A.Rodriguez Promo	1.50	.45

1998 Fleer Tradition Vintage '63

Randomly inserted one in every first and second series hobby pack, this 128-card set commemorates the 35th anniversary of the Fleer set and features color photos of top players printed in the 1963 Fleer Baseball card design.

	Nm-Mt	Ex-Mt
*'63 CLASSIC STARS: 30X TO 80X BASIC VINTAGE		
63 CLASSIC RANDOM INS.IN HOBBY PACKS		
63 CLASSIC PRINT RUN 63 SERIAL #'d SETS		
1 Jason Dickson	.40	.12
2 Tim Salmon	.60	.18
3 Andruw Jones	.40	.12
4 Chipper Jones	1.00	.30
5 Kenny Lofton	.40	.12
6 Greg Maddux	1.50	.45
7 Rafael Palmeiro	.60	.18
8 Cal Ripken	3.00	.90
9 Nomar Garciaparra	1.50	.45
10 Mark Grace	.60	.18
11 Sammy Sosa	1.50	.45
12 Frank Thomas	1.00	.30
13 Deion Sanders	.60	.18
14 Sandy Alomar Jr.	.40	.12
15 David Justice	.40	.12
16 Jim Thome	1.00	.30
17 Matt Williams	.40	.12
18 Jaret Wright	.40	.12
19 Vinny Castilla	.40	.12
20 Andres Galarraga	.40	.12
21 Todd Helton	.60	.18
22 Larry Walker	.60	.18
23 Tony Clark	.40	.12
24 Moises Alou	.40	.12
25 Kevin Brown	.60	.18
26 Charles Johnson	.40	.12
27 Edgar Renteria	.40	.12
28 Gary Sheffield	.40	.12
29 Jeff Bagwell	.60	.18
30 Craig Biggio	.60	.18
31 Raul Mondesi	.40	.12
32 Mike Piazza	1.50	.45
33 Chuck Knoblauch	.40	.12
34 Paul Molitor	.60	.18
35 Vladimir Guerrero	1.00	.30
36 Pedro Martinez	1.00	.30
37 Todd Hundley	.40	.12
38 Derek Jeter	2.50	.75
39 Tino Martinez	.60	.18
40 Paul O'Neill	.60	.18
41 Andy Pettitte	.60	.18
42 Mariano Rivera	.60	.18
43 Bernie Williams	.60	.18
44 Ben Grieve	.40	.12
45 Scott Rolen	1.00	.30
46 Curt Schilling	.40	.12
47 Jason Kendall	.40	.12
48 Tony Womack	.40	.12
49 Ray Lankford	.40	.12
50 Mark McGwire	2.50	.75
51 Matt Morris	.40	.12
52 Tony Gwynn	1.25	.35
53 Barry Bonds	2.50	.75
54 Jay Buhner	.40	.12
55 Ken Griffey Jr.	1.50	.45
56 Randy Johnson	1.00	.30
57 Edgar Martinez	.60	.18
58 Alex Rodriguez	1.50	.45
59 Juan Gonzalez	.60	.18
60 Rusty Greer	.40	.12
61 Ivan Rodriguez	1.00	.30
62 Roger Clemens	2.00	.60
63 Jose Cruz Jr.	.40	.12
64 Darin Erstad	.40	.12
65 Jay Bell	.40	.12
66 Andy Benes	.40	.12
67 Mickey Mantle	6.00	1.80
68 Karim Garcia	.40	.12
69 Travis Lee	.40	.12
70 Matt Williams	.40	.12
71 Andres Galarraga	.40	.12
72 Tom Glavine	.60	.18
73 Ryan Klesko	.40	.12
74 Denny Neagle	.40	.12
75 John Smoltz	.60	.18
76 Roberto Alomar	.60	.18
77 Joe Carter	.40	.12
78 Mike Mussina	.60	.18
79 B.J. Surhoff	.40	.12
80 Dennis Eckersley	.40	.12
81 Pedro Martinez	1.00	.30
82 Mo Vaughn	.40	.12
83 Henry Rodriguez	.40	.12
84 Kerry Wood	1.00	.30
85 Albert Belle	.40	.12
86 Sean Casey	.40	.12
87 Travis Fryman	.40	.12
88 Kenny Lofton	.40	.12
89 Darryl Kile	.40	.12
90 Mike Lansing	.40	.12
91 Bobby Bonilla	.40	.12
92 Cliff Floyd	.40	.12
93 Livan Hernandez	.40	.12
94 Derrek Lee	.40	.12
95 Moises Alou	.40	.12
96 Shane Reynolds	.40	.12
97 Mike Piazza	1.50	.45
98 Johnny Damon	.60	.18
99 Eric Karros	.40	.12
100 Hideo Nomo	1.00	.30
101 Marquis Grissom	.40	.12
102 Matt Lawton	.40	.12
103 Todd Walker	.40	.12
104 Gary Sheffield	.40	.12
105 Bernard Gilkey	.40	.12
106 Rey Ordonez	.40	.12
107 Chili Davis	.40	.12
108 Chuck Knoblauch	.40	.12
109 Charles Johnson	.40	.12
110 Rickey Henderson	1.00	.30
111 Bob Abreu	.40	.12
112 Doug Glanville	.40	.12
113 Gregg Jefferies	.40	.12
114 Al Martin	.40	.12
115 Kevin Young	.40	.12
116 Ron Gant	.40	.12
117 Kevin Brown	.60	.18
118 Ken Caminiti	.40	.12
119 Joey Hamilton	.40	.12
120 Jeff Kent	.40	.12
121 Wade Boggs	.60	.18
122 Quinton McCracken	.40	.12
123 Fred McGriff	.60	.18
124 Paul Sorrento	.40	.12
125 Jose Canseco	1.00	.30
126 Randy Myers	.40	.12
NNO Checklist 1	.40	.12
NNO Checklist 2	.40	.12

1998 Fleer Tradition Decade of Excellence

Randomly inserted in hobby packs only at the rate of one in 72, this 12-card set features 1988 season photos in Fleer's 1988 card design of current players who have been in playing major league baseball for ten years or more.

	Nm-Mt	Ex-Mt
COMPLETE SET (12)	120.00	36.00
*RARE TRAD: 2X TO 5X BASIC DECADES		
RARE TRAD. STATED ODDS 1:720 HOBBY		
1 Roberto Alomar	4.00	1.20
2 Barry Bonds	15.00	4.50
3 Roger Clemens	12.00	3.60
4 David Cone	2.50	.75
5 Andres Galarraga	2.50	.75
6 Mark Grace	4.00	1.20
7 Tony Gwynn	8.00	2.40
8 Randy Johnson	6.00	1.80
9 Greg Maddux	10.00	3.00
10 Mark McGwire	15.00	4.50
11 Paul O'Neill	4.00	1.20
12 Cal Ripken	20.00	6.00

1998 Fleer Tradition Diamond Standouts

Randomly inserted in packs at the rate of one in 12, this 20-card set features color photos of great players on a diamond design silver foil background. The backs display detailed player information.

	Nm-Mt	Ex-Mt
COMPLETE SET (20)	50.00	15.00
1 Jeff Bagwell	1.25	.35
2 Barry Bonds	5.00	1.50
3 Roger Clemens	4.00	1.20
4 Jose Cruz Jr.	.75	.23
5 Andres Galarraga	.75	.23
6 Nomar Garciaparra	3.00	.90
7 Juan Gonzalez	1.25	.35
8 Ken Griffey Jr.	3.00	.90
9 Derek Jeter	5.00	1.50
10 Randy Johnson	2.00	.60
11 Chipper Jones	2.00	.60
12 Kenny Lofton	.75	.23
13 Greg Maddux	3.00	.90
14 Pedro Martinez	2.00	.60
15 Mark McGwire	5.00	1.50
16 Mike Piazza	3.00	.90
17 Alex Rodriguez	3.00	.90
18 Curt Schilling	.75	.23
19 Frank Thomas	2.00	.60
20 Larry Walker	1.25	.35

1998 Fleer Tradition Diamond Tribute

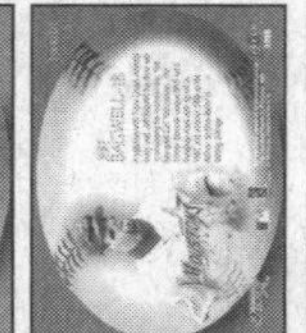

Randomly inserted in packs at a rate of one in 300, this 10-card insert set features color action photos printed on leatherette laminated stock with silver holofoil stamping.

	Nm-Mt	Ex-Mt
COMPLETE SET (10)	200.00	60.00
DT1 Jeff Bagwell	10.00	3.00
DT2 Roger Clemens	30.00	9.00
DT3 Nomar Garciaparra	25.00	7.50
DT4 Juan Gonzalez	10.00	3.00
DT5 Ken Griffey Jr.	25.00	7.50
DT6 Mark McGwire	40.00	12.00
DT7 Mike Piazza	25.00	7.50
DT8 Cal Ripken	50.00	15.00
DT9 Alex Rodriguez	25.00	7.50
DT10 Frank Thomas	15.00	4.50

1998 Fleer Tradition In The Clutch

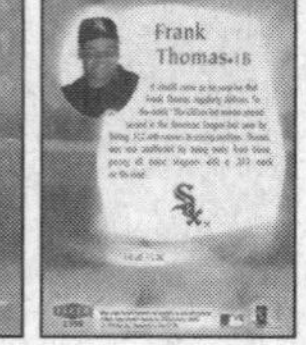

Randomly inserted in packs at a rate of one in 20, this 15-card insert offers color action photos on a green holofoil background.

	Nm-Mt	Ex-Mt
COMPLETE SET (15)	80.00	24.00
IC1 Jeff Bagwell	2.50	.75
IC2 Barry Bonds	10.00	3.00
IC3 Roger Clemens	8.00	2.40
IC4 Jose Cruz Jr.	1.50	.45
IC5 Nomar Garciaparra	6.00	1.80
IC6 Juan Gonzalez	2.50	.75
IC7 Ken Griffey Jr.	6.00	1.80
IC8 Tony Gwynn	5.00	1.50
IC9 Derek Jeter	10.00	3.00
IC10 Chipper Jones	4.00	1.20
IC11 Greg Maddux	6.00	1.80
IC12 Mark McGwire	10.00	3.00
IC13 Mike Piazza	6.00	1.80
IC14 Frank Thomas	4.00	1.20
IC15 Larry Walker	2.50	.75

1998 Fleer Tradition Lumber Company

Randomly inserted in retail packs only at the rate of one in 36, this 15-card set features color photos of high-powered offensive players.

	Nm-Mt	Ex-Mt
COMPLETE SET (15)	120.00	36.00
1 Jeff Bagwell	4.00	1.20
2 Barry Bonds	15.00	4.50
3 Jose Cruz Jr.	2.50	.75
4 Nomar Garciaparra	10.00	3.00
5 Juan Gonzalez	4.00	1.20
6 Ken Griffey Jr.	10.00	3.00
7 Tony Gwynn	8.00	2.40
8 Chipper Jones	6.00	1.80
9 Tino Martinez	4.00	1.20
10 Mark McGwire	15.00	4.50
11 Mike Piazza	10.00	3.00
12 Cal Ripken	20.00	6.00
13 Alex Rodriguez	10.00	3.00
14 Frank Thomas	6.00	1.80
15 Larry Walker	4.00	1.20

1998 Fleer Tradition Mickey Mantle Monumental Moments

This 10 card set features highlights from Mickey Mantle's long and illustrious career with the New York Yankees. Mantle, who hit 536 Homers in his career and 18 more in the World Series is honored with these cards which were inserted one every 68 packs.

	Nm-Mt	Ex-Mt
COMPLETE SET (10)	150.00	45.00
COMMON CARD (1-10)	25.00	7.50
*GOLD: 1.5X TO 4X BASIC MANTLE ..		
GOLD: RANDOM INSERTS IN SER.2 PACKS		
GOLD PRINT RUN 51 SERIAL #'d SETS		

1998 Fleer Tradition Power Game

Randomly inserted in packs at the rate of one in 36, this 20-card set features color action player photos of great pitchers and hitters highlighted with purple metallic foil and glossy UV coating. The backs display player statistics.

	Nm-Mt	Ex-Mt
COMPLETE SET (20)	120.00	36.00
1 Jeff Bagwell	4.00	1.20
2 Albert Belle	2.50	.75
3 Barry Bonds	15.00	4.50
4 Tony Clark	2.50	.75
5 Roger Clemens	12.00	3.60
6 Jose Cruz Jr.	2.50	.75
7 Andres Galarraga	2.50	.75
8 Nomar Garciaparra	10.00	3.00
9 Juan Gonzalez	4.00	1.20
10 Ken Griffey Jr.	10.00	3.00
11 Randy Johnson	6.00	1.80
12 Greg Maddux	10.00	3.00
13 Pedro Martinez	6.00	1.80
14 Tino Martinez	4.00	1.20
15 Mark McGwire	15.00	4.50
16 Mike Piazza	10.00	3.00
17 Curt Schilling	2.50	.75
18 Frank Thomas	6.00	1.80
19 Jim Thome	6.00	1.80
20 Larry Walker	4.00	1.20

1998 Fleer Tradition Promising Forecast

Randomly inserted in packs at a rate of one in 12, this 20-card insert features color action photos on cards with flood aqueous coating, silver foil stamping and a white glow around the player's UV coated image.

	Nm-Mt	Ex-Mt
COMPLETE SET (20)	15.00	4.50
PF1 Rolando Arrojo	1.00	.30
PF2 Sean Casey	1.00	.30
PF3 Brad Fullmer	1.00	.30
PF4 Karim Garcia	1.00	.30
PF5 Ben Grieve	1.00	.30
PF6 Todd Helton	1.50	.45
PF7 Richard Hidalgo	1.00	.30
PF8 A.J. Hinch	1.00	.30
PF9 Paul Konerko	1.00	.30
PF10 Mark Kotsay	1.00	.30
PF11 Derrek Lee	1.00	.30
PF12 Travis Lee	1.00	.30
PF13 Eric Milton	1.00	.30
PF14 Magglio Ordonez	3.00	.90
PF15 David Ortiz	2.50	.75
PF16 Brian Rose	1.00	.30
PF17 Miguel Tejada	1.00	.30
PF18 Jason Varitek	2.50	.75
PF19 Enrique Wilson	1.00	.30
PF20 Kerry Wood	2.50	.75

1998 Fleer Tradition Rookie Sensations

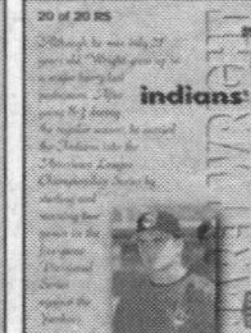

Randomly inserted in packs at the rate of one in 18, this 20-card set features gray-bordered action color images of the 1997 most promising players who were eligible for Rookie of the Year honors on multi-colored backgrounds.

	Nm-Mt	Ex-Mt
COMPLETE SET (20)	40.00	12.00
1 Mike Cameron	1.50	.45
2 Jose Cruz Jr.	1.50	.45
3 Jason Dickson	1.50	.45
4 Kelvim Escobar	1.50	.45
5 Nomar Garciaparra	6.00	1.80
6 Ben Grieve	1.50	.45
7 Vladimir Guerrero	4.00	1.20
8 Wilton Guerrero	1.50	.45
9 Jose Guillen	1.50	.45
10 Todd Helton	2.50	.75
11 Livan Hernandez	1.50	.45
12 Hideki Irabu	1.50	.45
13 Andruw Jones	1.50	.45
14 Matt Morris	1.50	.45
15 Magglio Ordonez	10.00	3.00
16 Neifi Perez	1.50	.45
17 Scott Rolen	4.00	1.20
18 Fernando Tatis	1.50	.45
19 Brett Tomko	1.50	.45
20 Jaret Wright	1.50	.45

1998 Fleer Tradition Zone

Randomly inserted in packs at the rate of one in 288, this 15-card set features color photos of unstoppable players printed on cards with custom pattern rainbow foil and etching.

	Nm-Mt	Ex-Mt
COMPLETE SET (15)	250.00	75.00
1 Jeff Bagwell	10.00	3.00
2 Barry Bonds	40.00	12.00
3 Roger Clemens	30.00	9.00
4 Jose Cruz Jr.	6.00	1.80
5 Nomar Garciaparra	25.00	7.50
6 Juan Gonzalez	10.00	3.00
7 Ken Griffey Jr.	25.00	7.50
8 Tony Gwynn	20.00	6.00
9 Chipper Jones	15.00	4.50
10 Greg Maddux	25.00	7.50
11 Mark McGwire	40.00	12.00
12 Mike Piazza	25.00	7.50
13 Alex Rodriguez	25.00	7.50
14 Frank Thomas	15.00	4.50
15 Larry Walker	10.00	3.00

1998 Fleer Tradition Update

The 1998 Fleer Update set was issued exclusively in factory set form. This set, issued in November, 1998, was created in large part to get the first J.D. Drew Rookie Card on the market. The set also took advantage of the "retro" themes that were popular in 1998 and represented the return of Fleer Update factory sets that had a rich history from 1984 through 1994. In addition to the aforementioned Drew, other notable RC's in this set include Troy Glaus, Orlando Hernandez and Gabe Kapler.

	Nm-Mt	Ex-Mt
COMP.FACT.SET (100)	20.00	6.00
U1 Mark McGwire HL	1.25	.35
U2 Sammy Sosa HL	.75	.23
U3 Roger Clemens HL	1.00	.30
U4 Barry Bonds HL	1.25	.35
U5 Kerry Wood HL	.50	.15
U6 Paul Molitor HL	.30	.09
U7 Ken Griffey Jr. HL	.75	.23
U8 Cal Ripken HL	1.50	.45
U9 David Wells HL	.20	.06
U10 Alex Rodriguez HL	.75	.23
U11 Angel Pena RC	.25	.07
U12 Bruce Chen	.20	.06
U13 Craig Wilson	.20	.06
U14 O.Hernandez RC	1.00	.30
U15 Aramis Ramirez	.20	.06
U16 Aaron Boone	.20	.06
U17 Bob Henley	.20	.06
U18 Juan Guzman	.20	.06
U19 Darryl Hamilton	.20	.06
U20 Jay Payton	.20	.06
U21 Jeremy Powell	.20	.06
U22 Ben Davis	.20	.06
U23 Preston Wilson	.20	.06
U24 Jim Parque RC	.40	.12
U25 Odalis Perez RC	1.00	.30
U26 Ronnie Belliard	.20	.06
U27 Royce Clayton	.20	.06
U28 George Lombard	.20	.06
U29 Tony Phillips	.20	.06
U30 F.Seguignol RC	.25	.07
U31 Armando Rios RC	.40	.12
U32 Jerry Hairston Jr. RC	.40	.12
U33 Justin Baughman RC	.25	.07
U34 Seth Greisinger	.20	.06
U35 Alex Gonzalez	.20	.06
U36 Michael Barrett	.20	.06
U37 Carlos Beltran	.75	.23
U38 Ellis Burks	.20	.06
U39 Jose Jimenez RC	.60	.18
U40 Carlos Guillen	.20	.06
U41 Marlon Anderson	.20	.06
U42 Scott Elarton	.20	.06
U43 Glenallen Hill	.20	.06
U44 Shane Monahan	.20	.06
U45 Dennis Martinez	.20	.06
U46 Carlos Febles RC	.40	.12
U47 Carlos Perez	.20	.06
U48 Wilton Guerrero	.20	.06
U49 Randy Johnson	.50	.15
U50 Brian Simmons RC	.25	.07
U51 Carlton Loewer	.20	.06
U52 Mark DeRosa RC	.40	.12
U53 Tim Young RC	.25	.07
U54 Gary Gaetti	.20	.06
U55 Eric Chavez	.20	.06
U56 Carl Pavano	.30	.06
U57 Mike Stanley	.20	.06
U58 Todd Stottlemyre	.20	.06
U59 Gabe Kapler RC	.60	.18
U60 Mike Jerzembeck RC	.25	.07
U61 Mitch Meluskey RC	.40	.12
U62 Bill Pulsipher	.20	.06
U63 Derrick Gibson	.20	.06
U64 John Rocker RC	.40	.12
U65 Calvin Pickering	.20	.06
U66 Blake Stein	.20	.06
U67 Fernando Tatis	.20	.06
U68 Gabe Alvarez	.20	.06
U69 Jeffrey Hammonds	.20	.06
U70 Adrian Beltre	.50	.15
U71 Ryan Bradley RC	.25	.07
U72 Edgard Clemente	.20	.06
U73 Rick Croushore RC	.25	.07
U74 Matt Clement	.20	.06
U75 Dermal Brown	.20	.06
U76 Paul Bako	.20	.06
U77 Placido Polanco RC	.40	.12
U78 Jay Tessmer	.20	.06
U79 Jarrod Washburn	.20	.06
U80 Kevin Witt	.20	.06
U81 Mike Metcalfe	.20	.06
U82 Daryle Ward	.20	.06
U83 Benj Sampson RC	.25	.07
U84 Mike Kinkade RC	.25	.07
U85 Randy Winn	.20	.06
U86 Jeff Shaw	.20	.06
U87 Troy Glaus RC	3.00	.90
U88 Hideo Nomo	.50	.15
U89 Mark Grudzielanek	.20	.06
U90 Mike Frank RC	.25	.07
U91 Bobby Howry RC	.40	.12
U92 Ryan Minor RC	.25	.07
U93 Corey Koskie RC	1.00	.30
U94 Matt Anderson RC	.40	.12
U95 Joe Carter	.20	.06
U96 Paul Konerko	.20	.06
U97 Sidney Ponson	.20	.06
U98 Jeremy Giambi RC	.40	.12
U99 Jeff Kubenka RC	.25	.07
U100 J.D. Drew RC	3.00	.90

1999 Fleer Tradition

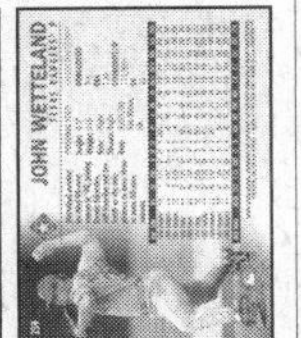

The 1999 Fleer set was issued in one series totalling 600 cards and was distributed in 10-card packs with a suggested retail price of $1.59. The fronts feature color action photos with gold foil player names. The backs carry another player photo with biographical information and career statistics. The set includes the following subsets: Franchise Futures (576-590) and Checklists (591-600).

	Nm-Mt	Ex-Mt
COMPLETE SET (600)	60.00	18.00
1 Mark McGwire	2.00	.60
2 Sammy Sosa	1.25	.35
3 Ken Griffey Jr.	1.25	.35
4 Kerry Wood	.75	.23
5 Derek Jeter	2.00	.60
6 Stan Musial	1.50	.45
7 J.D. Drew	.30	.09
8 Cal Ripken	2.50	.75
9 Alex Rodriguez	1.25	.35
10 Travis Lee	.20	.06
11 Andres Galarraga	.30	.09
12 Nomar Garciaparra	1.25	.35
13 Albert Belle	.30	.09
14 Barry Larkin	.50	.15
15 Dante Bichette	.30	.09
16 Tony Clark	.20	.06
17 Moises Alou	.30	.09
18 Rafael Palmeiro	.50	.15
19 Raul Mondesi	.30	.09
20 Vladimir Guerrero	.75	.23
21 John Olerud	.30	.09
22 Bernie Williams	.50	.15
23 Ben Grieve	.20	.06
24 Scott Rolen	.75	.23
25 Jeromy Burnitz	.30	.09
26 Ken Caminiti	.30	.09
27 Barry Bonds	2.00	.60
28 Todd Helton	.50	.15
29 Juan Gonzalez	.50	.15
30 Roger Clemens	1.50	.45
31 Andruw Jones	.30	.09
32 Mo Vaughn	.30	.09
33 Larry Walker	.50	.15
34 Frank Thomas	.75	.23
35 Manny Ramirez	.50	.15
36 Randy Johnson	.75	.23
37 Vinny Castilla	.30	.09
38 Juan Encarnacion	.20	.06
39 Jeff Bagwell	.50	.15
40 Gary Sheffield	.30	.09
41 Mike Piazza	1.25	.35
42 Richie Sexson	.30	.09
43 Tony Gwynn	1.00	.30
44 Chipper Jones	.75	.23
45 Jim Thome	.75	.23
46 Craig Biggio	.50	.15
47 Carlos Delgado	.30	.09
48 Greg Vaughn	.20	.06
49 Greg Maddux	1.25	.35
50 Troy Glaus	.30	.09
51 Roberto Alomar	.50	.15
52 Dennis Eckersley	.30	.09
53 Mike Caruso	.20	.06
54 Bruce Chen	.20	.06
55 Aaron Boone	.30	.09
56 Bartolo Colon	.30	.09
57 Derrick Gibson	.20	.06
58 Brian Anderson	.20	.06
59 Gabe Alvarez	.20	.06
60 Todd Dunwoody	.20	.06
61 Rod Beck	.20	.06
62 Derek Bell	.20	.06
63 Francisco Cordova	.20	.06
64 Johnny Damon	.50	.15
65 Adrian Beltre	.50	.15
66 Garret Anderson	.30	.09
67 Armando Benitez	.20	.06
68 Edgardo Alfonzo	.20	.06
69 Ryan Bradley	.20	.06
70 Eric Chavez	.30	.09
71 Bobby Abreu	.30	.09
72 Andy Ashby	.20	.06
73 Ellis Burks	.30	.09
74 Jeff Cirillo	.20	.06
75 Jay Buhner	.30	.09
76 Ron Gant	.30	.09
77 Rolando Arrojo	.20	.06
78 Will Clark	.75	.23
79 Chris Carpenter	.20	.06
80 Jim Edmonds	.30	.09
81 Tony Batista	.30	.09
82 Shane Andrews	.20	.06
83 Mark DeRosa	.20	.06
84 Brady Anderson	.30	.09
85 Tom Gordon	.20	.06
86 Brant Brown	.20	.06
87 Ray Durham	.30	.09
88 Ron Coomer	.20	.06
89 Bret Boone	.30	.09
90 Travis Fryman	.30	.09
91 Darryl Kile	.30	.09
92 Paul Bako	.20	.06
93 Cliff Floyd	.30	.09
94 Scott Elarton	.20	.06
95 Jeremy Giambi	.20	.06
96 Darren Dreifort	.20	.06
97 Marquis Grissom	.30	.09
98 Marty Cordova	.20	.06
99 Fernando Seguignol	.20	.06
100 Orlando Hernandez	.20	.06
101 Jose Cruz Jr.	.30	.09
102 Jason Giambi	.30	.09
103 Damion Easley	.20	.06
104 Freddy Garcia	.20	.06
105 Marlon Anderson	.20	.06
106 Kevin Brown	.50	.15
107 Joe Carter	.30	.09
108 Russ Davis	.20	.06
109 Brian Jordan	.30	.09
110 Wade Boggs	.50	.15
111 Tom Goodwin	.20	.06
112 Scott Brosius	.30	.09
113 Darin Erstad	.30	.09
114 Jay Bell	.30	.09
115 Tom Glavine	.50	.15
116 Pedro Martinez	.75	.23
117 Mark Grace	.50	.15
118 Russ Ortiz	.30	.09
119 Magglio Ordonez	.30	.09
120 Sean Casey	.30	.09
121 Rafael Roque RC	.20	.06
122 Brian Giles	.30	.09
123 Mike Lansing	.20	.06
124 David Cone	.30	.09
125 Alex Gonzalez	.20	.06
126 Carl Everett	.30	.09
127 Jeff King	.20	.06
128 Charles Johnson	.30	.09
129 Geoff Jenkins	.30	.09
130 Corey Koskie	.30	.09
131 Brad Fullmer	.20	.06
132 Al Leiter	.30	.09
133 Rickey Henderson	.75	.23
134 Rico Brogna	.20	.06
135 Jose Guillen	.30	.09
136 Matt Clement	.20	.06
137 Carlos Guillen	.30	.09
138 Orel Hershiser	.30	.09
139 Ray Lankford	.20	.06
140 Miguel Cairo	.20	.06
141 Chuck Finley	.30	.09
142 Rusty Greer	.30	.09
143 Kelvim Escobar	.20	.06
144 Ryan Klesko	.30	.09
145 Andy Benes	.20	.06
146 Eric Davis	.30	.09
147 David Wells	.30	.09
148 Trot Nixon	.30	.09
149 Jose Hernandez	.20	.06
150 Mark Johnson	.20	.06
151 Mike Frank	.20	.06
152 Joey Hamilton	.20	.06
153 David Justice	.30	.09
154 Mike Mussina	.50	.15
155 Neifi Perez	.20	.06
156 Luis Gonzalez	.30	.09
157 Livan Hernandez	.20	.06
158 Dermal Brown	.20	.06
159 Jose Lima	.20	.06
160 Eric Karros	.30	.09
161 Ronnie Belliard	.20	.06
162 Matt Lawton	.20	.06
163 Dustin Hermanson	.20	.06
164 Brian McRae	.20	.06
165 Mike Kinkade	.20	.06
166 A.J. Hinch	.20	.06
167 Doug Glanville	.20	.06
168 Hideo Nomo	.75	.23
169 Jason Kendall	.30	.09
170 Steve Finley	.30	.09
171 Jeff Kent	.30	.09
172 Ben Davis	.20	.06
173 Edgar Martinez	.50	.15
174 Eli Marrero	.20	.06
175 Quinton McCracken	.20	.06
176 Rick Helling	.20	.06
177 Tom Evans	.20	.06
178 Carl Pavano	.30	.09
179 Todd Greene	.20	.06
180 Omar Daal	.20	.06
181 George Lombard	.20	.06
182 Ryan Minor	.20	.06
183 Troy O'Leary	.20	.06
184 Robb Nen	.30	.09
185 Mickey Morandini	.20	.06
186 Robin Ventura	.30	.09
187 Pete Harnisch	.20	.06
188 Kenny Lofton	.30	.09
189 Eric Milton	.20	.06
190 Bobby Higginson	.30	.09
191 Jamie Moyer	.30	.09
192 Mark Kotsay	.20	.06
193 Shane Reynolds	.20	.06
194 Carlos Febles	.20	.06
195 Jeff Kubenka	.20	.06
196 Chuck Knoblauch	.30	.09
197 Kenny Rogers	.30	.09
198 Bill Mueller	.30	.09
199 Shane Monahan	.20	.06
200 Matt Morris	.30	.09
201 Fred McGriff	.50	.15
202 Ivan Rodriguez	.75	.23
203 Kevin Witt	.20	.06
204 Troy Percival	.30	.09
205 David Dellucci	.30	.09
206 Kevin Millwood	.30	.09
207 Jerry Hairston Jr.	.30	.09
208 Mike Stanley	.20	.06
209 Henry Rodriguez	.20	.06
210 Trevor Hoffman	.30	.09
211 Craig Wilson	.20	.06
212 Reggie Sanders	.20	.06
213 Carlton Loewer	.20	.06
214 Omar Vizquel	.50	.15
215 Gabe Kapler	.20	.06
216 Derrek Lee	.20	.06
217 Billy Wagner	.30	.09
218 Dean Palmer	.30	.09
219 Chan Ho Park	.30	.09
220 Fernando Vina	.20	.06
221 Roy Halladay	.30	.09
222 Paul Molitor	.50	.15
223 Ugueth Urbina	.20	.06
224 Rey Ordonez	.20	.06
225 Ricky Ledee	.20	.06
226 Scott Spiezio	.20	.06
227 Wendell Magee	.20	.06
228 Aramis Ramirez	.30	.09
229 Brian Simmons	.20	.06
230 Fernando Tatis	.20	.06
231 Bobby Smith	.20	.06
232 Aaron Sele	.20	.06
233 Shawn Green	.30	.09
234 Mariano Rivera	.50	.15
235 Tim Salmon	.50	.15
236 Andy Fox	.20	.06
237 Denny Neagle	.20	.06
238 John Valentin	.20	.06
239 Kevin Tapani	.20	.06
240 Paul Konerko	.30	.09
241 Robert Fick	.20	.06
242 Edgar Renteria	.30	.09
243 Brett Tomko	.20	.06
244 Daryle Ward	.20	.06
245 Carlos Beltran	.50	.15
246 Angel Pena	.20	.06
247 Steve Woodard	.20	.06
248 David Ortiz	.50	.15
249 Justin Thompson	.20	.06
250 Rondell White	.30	.09
251 Jaret Wright	.20	.06
252 Ed Sprague	.20	.06
253 Jay Payton	.20	.06
254 Mike Lowell	.30	.09
255 Orlando Cabrera	.30	.09
256 Jason Schmidt	.30	.09
257 David Segui	.20	.06
258 Paul Sorrento	.20	.06
259 John Wetteland	.30	.09
260 Devon White	.30	.09
261 Odalis Perez	.20	.06
262 Calvin Pickering	.20	.06
263 Tyler Green	.20	.06
264 Preston Wilson	.30	.09
265 Brad Radke	.30	.09
266 Walt Weiss	.20	.06
267 Tim Young	.20	.06
268 Tino Martinez	.50	.15
269 Matt Stairs	.20	.06
270 Curt Schilling	.30	.09
271 Tony Womack	.20	.06
272 Ismael Valdes	.20	.06
273 Wally Joyner	.30	.09
274 Armando Rios	.20	.06
275 Andy Pettitte	.50	.15
276 Bubba Trammell	.20	.06
277 Todd Zeile	.30	.09
278 Shannon Stewart	.30	.09
279 Matt Williams	.30	.09
280 John Rocker	.20	.06
281 B.J. Surhoff	.30	.09
282 Eric Young	.20	.06
283 Dmitri Young	.30	.09
284 John Smoltz	.50	.15
285 Todd Walker	.20	.06
286 Paul O'Neill	.50	.15
287 Blake Stein	.20	.06
288 Kevin Young	.30	.09
289 Quilvio Veras	.20	.06
290 Kirk Rueter	.20	.06
291 Randy Winn	.20	.06
292 Miguel Tejada	.30	.09
293 J.T. Snow	.30	.09
294 Michael Tucker	.20	.06
295 Jay Tessmer	.20	.06
296 Scott Erickson	.20	.06
297 Tim Wakefield	.30	.09
298 Jeff Abbott	.20	.06
299 Eddie Taubensee	.20	.06
300 Darryl Hamilton	.20	.06
301 Kevin Orie	.20	.06
302 Jose Offerman	.20	.06
303 Scott Karl	.20	.06
304 Chris Widger	.20	.06
305 Todd Hundley	.20	.06
306 Desi Relaford	.20	.06
307 Sterling Hitchcock	.20	.06
308 Delino DeShields	.20	.06
309 Alex Gonzalez	.20	.06
310 Justin Baughman	.20	.06
311 Jamey Wright	.20	.06
312 Wes Helms	.20	.06
313 Dante Powell	.20	.06
314 Jim Abbott	.50	.15
315 Manny Alexander	.20	.06
316 Harold Baines	.30	.09
317 Danny Graves	.20	.06
318 Sandy Alomar Jr.	.20	.06
319 Pedro Astacio	.20	.06
320 Jermaine Allensworth	.20	.06
321 Matt Anderson	.20	.06
322 Chad Curtis	.20	.06
323 Antonio Osuna	.20	.06
324 Brad Ausmus	.20	.06
325 Steve Trachsel	.20	.06
326 Mike Blowers	.20	.06
327 Brian Bohanon	.20	.06
328 Chris Gomez	.20	.06
329 Valerio De Los Santos	.20	.06
330 Rich Aurilia	.20	.06
331 Michael Barrett	.20	.06
332 Rick Aguilera	.20	.06
333 Adrian Brown	.20	.06
334 Bill Spiers	.20	.06
335 Matt Beech	.20	.06
336 David Bell	.20	.06
337 Juan Acevedo	.20	.06
338 Jose Canseco	.75	.23
339 Wilson Alvarez	.20	.06
340 Luis Alicea	.20	.06
341 Jason Dickson	.20	.06
342 Mike Bordick	.20	.06
343 Ben Ford	.20	.06
344 Javy Lopez	.30	.09
345 Jason Christiansen	.20	.06
346 Darren Bragg	.20	.06
347 Doug Brocail	.20	.06
348 Jeff Blauser	.20	.06
349 James Baldwin	.20	.06
350 Jeffrey Hammonds	.20	.06
351 Ricky Bottalico	.20	.06
352 Russ Branyan	.20	.06
353 Mark Brownson RC	.20	.06
354 Dave Berg	.20	.06
355 Sean Bergman	.20	.06
356 Jeff Conine	.30	.09
357 Shayne Bennett	.20	.06
358 Bobby Bonilla	.30	.09
359 Bob Wickman	.20	.06
360 Carlos Baerga	.20	.06
361 Chris Fussell	.20	.06
362 Chili Davis	.30	.09
363 Jerry Spradlin	.20	.06
364 Carlos Hernandez	.20	.06
365 Roberto Hernandez	.20	.06
366 Marvin Benard	.20	.06
367 Ken Cloude	.20	.06
368 Tony Fernandez	.20	.06
369 John Burkett	.20	.06
370 Gary DiSarcina	.20	.06
371 Alan Benes	.20	.06
372 Karim Garcia	.20	.06
373 Carlos Perez	.20	.06
374 Damon Buford	.20	.06
375 Mark Clark	.20	.06
376 Edgard Clemente	.20	.06
377 Chad Bradford RC	.20	.06
378 Frank Catalanotto	.20	.06
379 Vic Darensbourg	.20	.06
380 Sean Berry	.20	.06
381 Dave Burba	.20	.06
382 Sal Fasano	.20	.06
383 Steve Parris	.20	.06
384 Roger Cedeno	.20	.06
385 Chad Fox	.20	.06
386 Wilton Guerrero	.20	.06
387 Dennis Cook	.20	.06
388 Joe Girardi	.20	.06
389 LaTroy Hawkins	.20	.06
390 Ryan Christenson	.20	.06
391 Paul Byrd	.20	.06
392 Lou Collier	.20	.06
393 Jeff Fassero	.20	.06
394 Jim Leyritz	.20	.06
395 Shawn Estes	.20	.06
396 Mike Kelly	.20	.06
397 Rich Croushore	.20	.06
398 Royce Clayton	.20	.06
399 Rudy Seanez	.20	.06
400 Darrin Fletcher	.20	.06
401 Shigetoshi Hasegawa	.30	.09
402 Bernard Gilkey	.20	.06
403 Juan Guzman	.20	.06
404 Jeff Frye	.20	.06
405 Donovan Osborne	.20	.06
406 Alex Fernandez	.20	.06
407 Gary Gaetti	.20	.06
408 Dan Miceli	.20	.06
409 Mike Cameron	.30	.09
410 Mike Remlinger	.20	.06
411 Joey Cora	.20	.06
412 Mark Gardner	.20	.06
413 Aaron Ledesma	.20	.06
414 Jerry Dipoto	.20	.06
415 Ricky Gutierrez	.20	.06
416 John Franco	.30	.09
417 Mendy Lopez	.20	.06
418 Hideki Irabu	.20	.06
419 Mark Grudzielanek	.20	.06
420 Bobby Hughes	.20	.06
421 Pat Meares	.20	.06
422 Jimmy Haynes	.20	.06
423 Bob Henley	.20	.06
424 Bobby Estalella	.20	.06
425 Jon Lieber	.20	.06
426 Giomar Guevara RC	.20	.06
427 Jose Jimenez	.20	.06
428 Deivi Cruz	.20	.06
429 Jonathan Johnson	.20	.06
430 Ken Hill	.20	.06
431 Craig Grebeck	.20	.06
432 Jose Rosado	.20	.06
433 Danny Klassen	.20	.06
434 Bobby Howry	.20	.06
435 Gerald Williams	.20	.06
436 Omar Olivares	.20	.06
437 Chris Hoiles	.20	.06
438 Seth Greisinger	.20	.06
439 Scott Hatteberg	.20	.06
440 Jeremi Gonzalez	.20	.06
441 Wil Cordero	.20	.06
442 Jeff Montgomery	.20	.06
443 Chris Stynes	.20	.06
444 Tony Saunders	.20	.06
445 Einar Diaz	.20	.06
446 Lariel Gonzalez	.20	.06
447 Ryan Jackson	.20	.06
448 Mike Hampton	.30	.09
449 Todd Hollandsworth	.20	.06
450 Gabe White	.20	.06
451 John Jaha	.20	.06
452 Bret Saberhagen	.30	.09
453 Otis Nixon	.20	.06
454 Steve Kline	.20	.06
455 Butch Huskey	.20	.06
456 Mike Jerzembeck	.20	.06
457 Wayne Gomes	.20	.06
458 Mike Macfarlane	.20	.06
459 Jesus Sanchez	.20	.06
460 Al Martin	.20	.06
461 Dwight Gooden	.30	.09
462 Ruben Rivera	.20	.06
463 Pat Hentgen	.20	.06
464 Jose Valentin	.20	.06
465 Vladimir Nunez	.20	.06
466 Charlie Hayes	.20	.06
467 Jay Powell	.20	.06
468 Raul Ibanez	.20	.06
469 Kent Mercker	.20	.06
470 John Mabry	.20	.06
471 Woody Williams	.20	.06
472 Roberto Kelly	.20	.06
473 Jim Mecir	.20	.06
474 Dave Hollins	.20	.06
475 Rafael Medina	.20	.06
476 Darren Lewis	.20	.06
477 Felix Heredia	.20	.06
478 Brian Hunter	.20	.06
479 Matt Mantei	.20	.06
480 Richard Hidalgo	.20	.06
481 Bobby Jones	.20	.06
482 Hal Morris	.20	.06
483 Ramiro Mendoza	.20	.06
484 Matt Luke	.20	.06
485 Esteban Loaiza	.20	.06
486 Mark Loretta	.30	.09
487 A.J. Pierzynski	.30	.09
488 Charles Nagy	.20	.06
489 Kevin Sefcik	.20	.06
490 Jason McDonald	.20	.06
491 Jeremy Powell	.20	.06
492 Scott Servais	.20	.06
493 Abraham Nunez	.20	.06
494 Stan Spencer	.20	.06
495 Stan Javier	.20	.06
496 Jose Paniagua	.20	.06
497 Gregg Jefferies	.20	.06
498 Gregg Olson	.20	.06
499 Derek Lowe	.30	.09
500 Willis Otanez	.20	.06
501 Brian Moehler	.20	.06
502 Glenallen Hill	.20	.06
503 Bobby M. Jones	.20	.06
504 Greg Norton	.20	.06
505 Mike Jackson	.20	.06
506 Kirt Manwaring	.20	.06
507 Eric Weaver RC	.20	.06
508 Mitch Meluskey	.20	.06
509 Todd Jones	.20	.06

Card	Nm-Mt	Ex-Mt
510 Mike Matheny	.30	.09
511 Benj Sampson	.20	.06
512 Tony Phillips	.20	.06
513 Mike Thurman	.20	.06
514 Jorge Posada	.50	.15
515 Bill Taylor	.20	.06
516 Mike Sweeney	.30	.09
517 Jose Silva	.20	.06
518 Mark Lewis	.20	.06
519 Chris Peters	.20	.06
520 Brian Johnson	.20	.06
521 Mike Timlin	.20	.06
522 Mark McLemore	.20	.06
523 Dan Plesac	.20	.06
524 Kelly Stinnett	.20	.06
525 Sidney Ponson	.20	.06
526 Jim Parque	.20	.06
527 Tyler Houston	.20	.06
528 John Thomson	.20	.06
529 Reggie Jefferson	.20	.06
530 Robert Person	.20	.06
531 Marc Newfield	.20	.06
532 Javier Vazquez	.30	.09
533 Terry Steinbach	.20	.06
534 Turk Wendell	.20	.06
535 Tim Raines	.30	.09
536 Brian Meadows	.20	.06
537 Mike Lieberthal	.30	.09
538 Ricardo Rincon	.20	.06
539 Dan Wilson	.20	.06
540 John Johnstone	.20	.06
541 Todd Stottlemyre	.20	.06
542 Kevin Stocker	.20	.06
543 Ramon Martinez	.20	.06
544 Mike Simms	.20	.06
545 Paul Quantrill	.20	.06
546 Matt Walbeck	.20	.06
547 Turner Ward	.20	.06
548 Bill Pulsipher	.20	.06
549 Donnie Sadler	.20	.06
550 Lance Johnson	.20	.06
551 Bill Simas	.20	.06
552 Jeff Reed	.20	.06
553 Jeff Shaw	.20	.06
554 Joe Randa	.20	.06
555 Paul Shuey	.20	.06
556 Mike Redmond RC	.20	.06
557 Sean Runyan	.20	.06
558 Enrique Wilson	.20	.06
559 Scott Radinsky	.20	.06
560 Larry Sutton	.20	.06
561 Masato Yoshii	.20	.06
562 David Nilsson	.20	.06
563 Mike Trombley	.20	.06
564 Darryl Strawberry	.30	.09
565 Dave Mlicki	.20	.06
566 Placido Polanco	.20	.06
567 Yorkis Perez	.20	.06
568 Esteban Yan	.20	.06
569 Lee Stevens	.20	.06
570 Steve Sinclair	.20	.06
571 Jarrod Washburn	.20	.06
572 Lenny Webster	.20	.06
573 Mike Sirotka	.20	.06
574 Jason Varitek	.50	.15
575 Terry Mulholland	.20	.06
576 Adrian Beltre FF	.30	.09
577 Eric Chavez FF	.20	.06
578 J.D. Drew FF	.20	.06
579 Juan Encarnacion FF	.20	.06
580 Nomar Garciaparra FF	.75	.23
581 Troy Glaus FF	.20	.06
582 Ben Grieve FF	.20	.06
583 Vladimir Guerrero FF	.50	.15
584 Todd Helton FF	.30	.09
585 Derek Jeter FF	1.00	.30
586 Travis Lee FF	.20	.06
587 Alex Rodriguez FF	.75	.23
588 Scott Rolen FF	.50	.15
589 Richie Sexson FF	.20	.06
590 Kerry Wood FF	.50	.15
591 Ken Griffey Jr. CL	.75	.23
592 Chipper Jones CL	.50	.15
593 Alex Rodriguez CL	.75	.23
594 Sammy Sosa CL	.75	.23
595 Mark McGwire CL	1.00	.30
596 Cal Ripken CL	1.25	.35
597 Nomar Garciaparra CL	.75	.23
598 Derek Jeter CL	1.00	.30
599 Kerry Wood CL	.50	.15
600 J.D. Drew CL	.20	.06
P7 J.D. Drew Promo	1.00	.30

1999 Fleer Tradition Millenium

Fleer printed 5,000 Millenium factory sets, primarily intended for sale on Shop at Home at the end of the 1999 calendar year. Each set came shrink-wrapped in an attractive factory box, of which is sealed with a gold sticker serial numbered of 5,000. Each set contains 620 cards consisting of the 600-card basic issue set plus 20 cards from the Fleer Update set (rookies U1-U10 and highlights U141-U150). The cards hailing from the Update set have been renumbered. The Update rookies are numbered 601-610 and the Update highlights are numbered 611-620. All 620 cards contain a special gold foil "Year 2000" logo.

	Nm-Mt	Ex-Mt
COMP.FACT.SET (620)	100.00	30.00
*STARS 1-600: 1X TO 2.5X BASIC CARDS		
*ROOKIES 1-600: 1X TO 2.5X BASIC CARDS		
601 Rick Ankiel	10.00	3.00
602 Peter Bergeron	1.50	.45
603 Pat Burrell	5.00	1.50
604 Eric Munson	2.50	.75
605 Alfonso Soriano	15.00	4.50
606 Tim Hudson	10.00	3.00
607 Erubiel Durazo	2.50	.75
608 Chad Hermansen	.75	.23
609 Jeff Zimmerman	1.50	.45
610 Jesus Pena	.75	.23
611 Wade Boggs HL	1.25	.35
612 Jose Canseco HL	2.00	.60
613 Roger Clemens HL	4.00	1.20
614 David Cone HL	.75	.23
615 Tony Gwynn HL	2.50	.75
616 Mark McGwire HL	5.00	1.50
617 Cal Ripken HL	6.00	1.80
618 Alex Rodriguez HL	3.00	.90
619 Fernando Tatis HL	.50	.15
620 Robin Ventura HL	.75	.23

1999 Fleer Tradition Warning Track

Cards from this parallel set were seeded at a rate of one per retail pack. Warning Track cards can be easily identified by the red foil "Warning Track Collection" logo at the base of the card front and the W suffix numbering on the card backs.

	Nm-Mt	Ex-Mt
*STARS: 2.5X TO 6X BASIC CARDS...		

1999 Fleer Tradition Vintage '61

Inserted one in every hobby pack only, this 50-card set features the first 50 cards of the 1999 Fleer Tradition set in cards designed similar to the 1961 Fleer Baseball Greats set.

	Nm-Mt	Ex-Mt
COMPLETE SET (50)	25.00	7.50
*SINGLES: .4X TO 1X BASE CARD HI		

1999 Fleer Tradition Date With Destiny

These attractive bronze foil cards are designed to mimic the famous plaques on display at the Hall of Fame. Fleer selected ten of the games greatest active players, all of whom are well on their way to the Hall of Fame. Only 100 sets were printed (each card is serial numbered "X/100" on front) and the cards were randomly seeded into packs at an unannounced rate. Suffice to say, they're not easy to pull from packs.

	Nm-Mt	Ex-Mt
1 Barry Bonds	60.00	18.00
2 Roger Clemens	50.00	15.00
3 Ken Griffey Jr.	40.00	12.00
4 Tony Gwynn	30.00	9.00
5 Greg Maddux	40.00	12.00
6 Mark McGwire	60.00	18.00
7 Mike Piazza	40.00	12.00
8 Cal Ripken	80.00	24.00
9 Alex Rodriguez	40.00	12.00
10 Frank Thomas	25.00	7.50

1999 Fleer Tradition Diamond Magic

Randomly inserted in packs at the rate of one in 96, this 15-card set features color action player images printed with a special die-cut treatment on a multi-layer card for a kaleidoscope effect behind the player image.

	Nm-Mt	Ex-Mt
COMPLETE SET (15)	250.00	75.00
1 Barry Bonds	25.00	7.50
2 Roger Clemens	20.00	6.00
3 Nomar Garciaparra	15.00	4.50
4 Ken Griffey Jr.	15.00	4.50
5 Tony Gwynn	12.00	3.60
6 Orlando Hernandez	2.50	.75
7 Derek Jeter	25.00	7.50
8 Randy Johnson	10.00	3.00
9 Chipper Jones	10.00	3.00
10 Greg Maddux	15.00	4.50
11 Mark McGwire	25.00	7.50
12 Alex Rodriguez	15.00	4.50
13 Sammy Sosa	15.00	4.50
14 Bernie Williams	6.00	1.80
15 Kerry Wood	10.00	3.00

1999 Fleer Tradition Going Yard

Randomly inserted in packs at the rate of one in 18, this 15-card set features color action photos of players who hit the longest home runs printed on extra wide cards to illustrate the greatness of their feats.

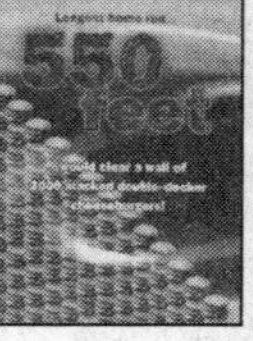

	Nm-Mt	Ex-Mt
COMPLETE SET (15)	40.00	12.00
1 Moises Alou	1.00	.30
2 Albert Belle	1.00	.30
3 Jose Canseco	2.50	.75
4 Vinny Castilla	1.00	.30
5 Andres Galarraga	1.00	.30
6 Juan Gonzalez	1.50	.45
7 Ken Griffey Jr.	4.00	1.20
8 Chipper Jones	2.50	.75
9 Mark McGwire	6.00	1.80
10 Rafael Palmeiro	1.50	.45
11 Mike Piazza	4.00	1.20
12 Alex Rodriguez	4.00	1.20
13 Sammy Sosa	4.00	1.20
14 Greg Vaughn	.60	.18
15 Mo Vaughn	1.00	.30

1999 Fleer Tradition Golden Memories

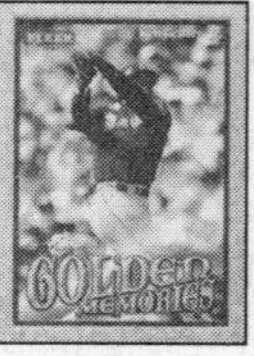

Randomly inserted in packs at the rate of one in 54, this 15-card set features color action player photos with an embossed frame design.

	Nm-Mt	Ex-Mt
COMPLETE SET (15)	150.00	45.00
1 Albert Belle	2.50	.75
2 Barry Bonds	15.00	4.50
3 Roger Clemens	12.00	3.60
4 Nomar Garciaparra	10.00	3.00
5 Juan Gonzalez	4.00	1.20
6 Ken Griffey Jr.	10.00	3.00
7 Randy Johnson	6.00	1.80
8 Greg Maddux	10.00	3.00
9 Mark McGwire	15.00	4.50
10 Mike Piazza	10.00	3.00
11 Cal Ripken	20.00	6.00
12 Alex Rodriguez	10.00	3.00
13 Sammy Sosa	10.00	3.00
14 David Wells	2.50	.75
15 Kerry Wood	6.00	1.80

1999 Fleer Tradition Stan Musial Monumental Moments

Randomly inserted in packs at the rate of one in 36, this 10-card set features photos of Stan Musial during his legendary career. As a bonus to collectors, Stan signed 50 of each of these cards in this set.

	Nm-Mt	Ex-Mt
COMPLETE SET (10)	25.00	7.50
COMMON CARD (1-10)	2.50	.75

1999 Fleer Tradition Rookie Flashback

Randomly inserted in packs at the rate of one in six, this 15-card set features color action photos of players who were rookies during the 1998 season printed on sculpture embossed cards.

	Nm-Mt	Ex-Mt
COMPLETE SET (15)	10.00	3.00
1 Matt Anderson	.50	.15
2 Rolando Arrojo	.50	.15
3 Adrian Beltre	1.25	.35
4 Mike Caruso	.50	.15
5 Eric Chavez	.75	.23
6 J.D. Drew	.75	.23
7 Juan Encarnacion	.50	.15
8 Brad Fullmer	.50	.15
9 Troy Glaus	.75	.23
10 Ben Grieve	.50	.15
11 Todd Helton	1.25	.35
12 Orlando Hernandez	.50	.15
13 Travis Lee	.50	.15
14 Richie Sexson	.75	.23
15 Kerry Wood	2.00	.60

1999 Fleer Tradition Update

The 1999 Fleer Update set was issued in one series totalling 150 cards and distributed only as a factory boxed set. The fronts feature color action player photos. The backs carry player information. The set features the Season Highlights subset (Cards 141-150). Over 100 Rookie Cards are featured in this set. Among these Rookie Cards are Rick Ankiel, Josh Beckett, Pat Burrell, Tim Hudson, Eric Munson, Wily Mo Pena and Alfonso Soriano.

	Nm-Mt	Ex-Mt
COMP.FACT.SET (150)	30.00	9.00
U1 Rick Ankiel RC	2.00	.60
U2 Peter Bergeron RC	.30	.09
U3 Pat Burrell RC	1.25	.35
U4 Eric Munson RC	.50	.15
U5 Alfonso Soriano RC	4.00	1.20
U6 Tim Hudson RC	1.50	.45
U7 Erubiel Durazo RC	.50	.15
U8 Chad Hermansen	.20	.06
U9 Jeff Zimmerman RC	.30	.09
U10 Jesus Pena RC	.30	.09
U11 Ramon Hernandez	.20	.06
U12 Trent Durrington RC	.30	.09
U13 Tony Armas Jr.	.20	.06
U14 Mike Fyhrie RC	.30	.09
U15 Danny Kolb RC	.75	.23
U16 Mike Porzio RC	.30	.09
U17 Will Brunson RC	.30	.09
U18 Mike Duvall RC	.30	.09
U19 D.Mientkiewicz RC	.60	.18
U20 Gabe Molina RC	.30	.09
U21 Luis Vizcaino RC	.30	.09
U22 Robinson Cancel RC	.30	.09
U23 Brett Laxton RC	.30	.09
U24 Joe McEwing RC	.30	.09
U25 Justin Speier RC	.30	.09
U26 Kip Wells RC	.50	.15
U27 Armando Almanza RC	.30	.09
U28 Joe Davenport RC	.30	.09
U29 Yamid Haad RC	.30	.09
U30 John Halama	.20	.06
U31 Adam Kennedy	.20	.06
U32 Micah Bowie RC	.30	.09
U33 Gookie Dawkins RC	.30	.09
U34 Ryan Rupe RC	.30	.09
U35 B.J. Ryan RC	.30	.09
U36 Chance Sanford RC	.30	.09
U37 A.Shumaker RC	.30	.09
U38 Ryan Glynn RC	.30	.09
U39 Roosevelt Brown RC	.30	.09
U40 Ben Molina RC	.50	.15
U41 Scott Williamson	.20	.06
U42 Eric Gagne RC	15.00	4.50
U43 John McDonald RC	.30	.09
U44 Scott Sauerbeck RC	.30	.09
U45 Mike Venafro RC	.30	.09
U46 Edwards Guzman RC	.30	.09
U47 Richard Barker RC	.30	.09
U48 Braden Looper	.20	.06
U49 Chad Meyers RC	.30	.09
U50 Scott Strickland RC	.30	.09
U51 Billy Koch	.20	.06
U52 David Newhan RC	2.00	.60
U53 David Riske RC	.30	.09
U54 Jose Santiago RC	.30	.09
U55 Miguel Del Toro RC	.30	.09
U56 Orber Moreno RC	.30	.09
U57 Dave Roberts RC	.50	.15
U58 Tim Byrdak RC	.30	.09
U59 David Lee RC	.30	.09
U60 Guillermo Mota RC	.30	.09
U61 Wilton Veras RC	.30	.09
U62 Joe Mays RC	.30	.09
U63 Jose Fernandez RC	.30	.09
U64 Ray King RC	.30	.09
U65 Chris Petersen RC	.30	.09
U66 Vernon Wells	.20	.06
U67 Ruben Mateo	.20	.06
U68 Ben Petrick	.20	.06
U69 Chris Tremie RC	.30	.09
U70 Lance Berkman	.20	.06
U71 Dan Smith RC	.30	.09
U72 Carlos E. Hernandez RC	.30	.09
U73 Chad Harville RC	.30	.09
U74 Damaso Marte RC	.30	.09
U75 Aaron Myette RC	.30	.09
U76 Willis Roberts RC	.30	.09
U77 Erik Sabel RC	.30	.09
U78 Hector Almonte RC	.30	.09
U79 Kris Benson	.20	.06
U80 Pat Daneker RC	.30	.09
U81 Freddy Garcia RC	.60	.18
U82 Byung-Hyun Kim RC	.60	.18
U83 Wily Pena RC	1.50	.45
U84 Dan Wheeler RC	.30	.09
U85 Tim Harikkala RC	.30	.09
U86 Derrin Ebert RC	.30	.09
U87 Horacio Estrada RC	.30	.09
U88 Liu Rodriguez RC	.30	.09
U89 J.Zimmerman RC	.30	.09
U90 A.J. Burnett RC	.60	.18
U91 Doug Davis RC	.30	.09
U92 Rob Ramsay RC	.30	.09
U93 Clay Bellinger RC	.30	.09
U94 Charlie Greene RC	.30	.09
U95 Bo Porter RC	.30	.09
U96 Jorge Toca RC	.30	.09
U97 Casey Blake RC	2.00	.60
U98 Amaury Garcia RC	.30	.09
U99 Jose Molina RC	.30	.09
U100 Melvin Mora RC	3.00	.90
U101 Joe Nathan RC	.60	.18
U102 Juan Pena RC	.30	.09
U103 Dave Borkowski RC	.30	.09
U104 Eddie Gaillard RC	.30	.09
U105 Glen Barker RC	.30	.09
U106 Brett Hinchliffe RC	.30	.09
U107 Carlos Lee	.20	.06
U108 Rob Ryan RC	.30	.09
U109 Jeff Weaver RC	.50	.15
U110 Ed Yarnall	.20	.06
U111 Nelson Cruz RC	.30	.09
U112 C.Davidson RC	.30	.09
U113 Tim Kubinski RC	.30	.09
U114 Sean Spencer RC	.30	.09
U115 Joe Winkelsas RC	.30	.09
U116 Mike Colangelo RC	.30	.09
U117 Tom Davey RC	.30	.09
U118 Warren Morris	.20	.06
U119 Dan Murray RC	.30	.09
U120 Jose Nieves RC	.30	.09
U121 Mark Quinn RC	.30	.09
U122 Josh Beckett RC	5.00	1.50
U123 Chad Allen RC	.30	.09
U124 Mike Figga	.30	.09
U125 Beiker Graterol RC	.30	.09
U126 Aaron Scheffer RC	.30	.09
U127 Wiki Gonzalez RC	.30	.09
U128 Ramon E.Martinez RC	.30	.09
U129 Matt Riley RC	1.00	.30
U130 Chris Woodward RC	.30	.09
U131 Albert Belle	.20	.06
U132 Roger Cedeno	.20	.06
U133 Roger Clemens	1.00	.30
U134 Brian Giles	.20	.06
U135 Rickey Henderson	.50	.15
U136 Randy Johnson	.50	.15
U137 Brian Jordan	.20	.06
U138 Paul Konerko	.20	.06
U139 Hideo Nomo	.50	.15
U140 Kenny Rogers	.20	.06
U141 Wade Boggs HL	.30	.09
U142 Jose Canseco HL	.20	.06
U143 Roger Clemens HL	1.00	.30
U144 David Cone HL	.20	.06
U145 Tony Gwynn HL	.60	.18
U146 Mark McGwire HL	1.25	.35
U147 Cal Ripken HL	1.50	.45
U148 Alex Rodriguez HL	.75	.23
U149 Fernando Tatis HL	.20	.06
U150 Robin Ventura HL	.20	.06

2000 Fleer Tradition

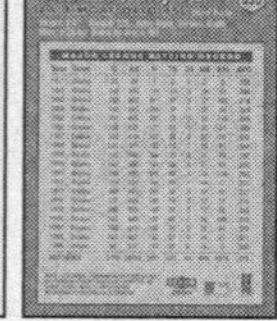

This 450-card single series set was released in February, 2000. Ten-card hobby and retail packs carried an SRP of $1.59. The basic cards are somewhat reminiscent of the 1954 Topps baseball set featuring a large headshot set against a flat color background and a small, cut-out action shot. Subsets are as follows: League Leaders (1-10), Award Winners (435-440), Division Playoffs-World Series Highlights (441-450). Dual-player prospect cards, team cards and six checklist cards (featuring a floating head image of several of the game's top stars) are also sprinkled throughout the set. In addition, a Cal Ripken promotional card was distributed to dealers and hobby media several weeks prior to the product's release. The card is easy to identify by the "PROMOTIONAL SAMPLE" text running diagonally across the front and back.

	Nm-Mt	Ex-Mt
COMPLETE SET (450)	50.00	15.00
1 Ken Griffey Jr / Rafael Palmeiro / Carlos Delgado LL	.75	.23
2 Mark McGwire / Sammy Sosa / Chipper Jones LL	.50	.15
3 Manny Ramirez / Rafael Palmeiro / Ken Griffey Jr. LL	.30	.09
4 Mark McGwire / Matt Williams / Sammy Sosa LL	.75	.23
5 Nomar Garciaparra / Derek Jeter / Bernie Williams LL	.75	.23
6 Larry Walker / Luis Gonzalez / Bob Abreu LL	.30	.09
7 Pedro Martinez / Bartolo Colon / Mike Mussina LL	.30	.09
8 Mike Hampton / Jose Lima / Greg Maddux LL	.30	.09
9 Pedro Martinez / David Cone / Mike Mussina LL	.30	.09
10 Randy Johnson / Kevin Millwood / Mike Hampton LL	.50	.15
11 Matt Mantei	.30	.09
12 John Rocker	.30	.09
13 Kyle Farnsworth	.30	.09
14 Juan Guzman	.30	.09
15 Manny Ramirez	.50	.15
16 Matt Riley / Calvin Pickering	.30	.09
17 Tony Clark	.30	.09
18 Brian Meadows	.30	.09
19 Orber Moreno	.30	.09
20 Eric Karros	.30	.09
21 Steve Woodard	.30	.09
22 Scott Brosius	.30	.09
23 Gary Bennett	.30	.09
24 Jason Wood / Dave Borkowski	.30	.09
25 Joe McEwing	.30	.09

Juan Gonzalez .50 .15
Roy Halladay .30 .09
Trevor Hoffman .30 .09
Arizona Diamondbacks .30 .09
Domingo Guzman RC .30 .09
Wiki Gonzalez
Bret Boone .30 .09
Nomar Garciaparra 1.25 .35
Bo Porter .30 .09
Eddie Taubensee .30 .09
Pedro Astacio .30 .09
Derek Bell .30 .09
Jacque Jones .30 .09
Ricky Ledee .30 .09
Jeff Kent .30 .09
Matt Williams .30 .09
Alfonso Soriano .75 .23
D'Angelo Jimenez
B.J. Surhoff .30 .09
Denny Neagle .30 .09
Omar Vizquel .50 .15
Jeff Bagwell .50 .15
Mark Grudzielanek .30 .09
LaTroy Hawkins .30 .09
Orlando Hernandez .30 .09
Ken Griffey Jr. CL .75 .23
Fernando Tatis .30 .09
Quilvio Veras .30 .09
Wayne Gomes .30 .09
Rick Helling .30 .09
Shannon Stewart .30 .09
Dermal Brown .30 .09
Mark Quinn
Randy Johnson .75 .23
Greg Maddux 1.25 .35
Mike Cameron .30 .09
Matt Anderson .30 .09
Milwaukee Brewers .30 .09
Derrek Lee .30 .09
Mike Sweeney .30 .09
Fernando Vina .30 .09
Orlando Cabrera .30 .09
Doug Glanville .30 .09
Stan Spencer .30 .09
Ray Lankford .30 .09
Kelly Dransfeldt .30 .09
Alex Gonzalez .30 .09
Russ Branyan .30 .09
Danny Peoples
Jim Edmonds .30 .09
Brady Anderson .30 .09
Mike Stanley .30 .09
Travis Fryman .30 .09
Carlos Febles .30 .09
Bobby Higginson .30 .09
Carlos Perez .30 .09
Steve Cox .30 .09
Alex Sanchez
Dustin Hermanson .30 .09
Kenny Rogers .30 .09
Miguel Tejada .30 .09
Ben Davis .30 .09
Reggie Sanders .30 .09
Eric Davis .30 .09
J.D. Drew .30 .09
Ryan Rupe .30 .09
Bobby Smith .30 .09
Jose Cruz Jr. .30 .09
Carlos Delgado .30 .09
Toronto Blue Jays .30 .09
Denny Stark RC .30 .09
Gil Meche
Randy Velarde .30 .09
Aaron Boone .30 .09
Javy Lopez .30 .09
Johnny Damon .50 .15
Jon Lieber .30 .09
Montreal Expos .30 .09
Mark Kotsay .30 .09
Luis Gonzalez .30 .09
00 Larry Walker .50 .15
01 Adrian Beltre .50 .15
02 Alex Ochoa .30 .09
03 Michael Barrett .30 .09
04 Tampa Bay Devil Rays .30 .09
05 Rey Ordonez .30 .09
06 Derek Jeter 1.50 .45
07 Mike Lieberthal .30 .09
08 Ellis Burks .30 .09
09 Steve Finley .30 .09
10 Ryan Klesko .30 .09
11 Steve Avery .30 .09
12 Dave Veres .30 .09
13 Cliff Floyd .30 .09
14 Shane Reynolds .30 .09
15 Kevin Brown .50 .15
16 Dave Nilsson .30 .09
17 Mike Trombley .30 .09
18 Todd Walker .30 .09
19 John Olerud .30 .09
20 Chuck Knoblauch .30 .09
21 Nomar Garciaparra CL .75 .23
22 Trot Nixon .30 .09
23 Erubiel Durazo .30 .09
24 Edwards Guzman .30 .09
25 Curt Schilling .30 .09
26 Brian Jordan .30 .09
27 Cleveland Indians .30 .09
28 Benito Santiago .30 .09
29 Frank Thomas .75 .23
30 Neifi Perez .30 .09
31 Alex Fernandez .30 .09
32 Jose Lima .30 .09
33 Jorge Toca .30 .09
Melvin Mora
34 Scott Karl .30 .09
35 Brad Radke .30 .09
36 Paul O'Neill .50 .15
37 Kris Benson .30 .09
38 Colorado Rockies .30 .09
39 Jason Phillips .30 .09
40 Robb Nen .30 .09
41 Ken Hill .30 .09
42 Charles Johnson .30 .09
43 Paul Konerko .30 .09
44 Dmitri Young .30 .09
45 Justin Thompson .30 .09
46 Mark Loretta .30 .09
47 Edgardo Alfonzo .30 .09
148 Armando Benitez .30 .09
149 Octavio Dotel .30 .09
150 Wade Boggs .50 .15
151 Ramon Hernandez .30 .09
152 Freddy Garcia .30 .09
153 Edgar Martinez .50 .15
154 Ivan Rodriguez .75 .23
155 Kansas City Royals .30 .09
156 Cleatus Davidson .30 .09
Cristian Guzman
157 Andy Benes .30 .09
158 Todd Dunwoody .30 .09
159 Pedro Martinez .75 .23
160 Mike Caruso .30 .09
161 Mike Sirotka .30 .09
162 Houston Astros .30 .09
163 Darryl Kile .30 .09
164 Chipper Jones .75 .23
165 Carl Everett .30 .09
166 Geoff Jenkins .30 .09
167 Dan Perkins .30 .09
168 Andy Pettitte .50 .15
169 Francisco Cordova .30 .09
170 Jay Buhner .30 .09
171 Jay Bell .30 .09
172 Andruw Jones .30 .09
173 Bobby Howry .30 .09
174 Chris Singleton .30 .09
175 Todd Helton .50 .15
176 A.J. Burnett .30 .09
177 Marquis Grissom .30 .09
178 Eric Milton .30 .09
179 Los Angeles Dodgers .30 .09
180 Kevin Appier .30 .09
181 Brian Giles .30 .09
182 Tom Davey .30 .09
183 Mo Vaughn .30 .09
184 Jose Hernandez .30 .09
185 Jim Parque .30 .09
186 Derrick Gibson .30 .09
187 Bruce Aven .30 .09
188 Jeff Cirillo .30 .09
189 Doug Mientkiewicz .30 .09
190 Eric Chavez .30 .09
191 Al Martin .30 .09
192 Tom Glavine .50 .15
193 Butch Huskey .30 .09
194 Ray Durham .30 .09
195 Greg Vaughn .30 .09
196 Vinny Castilla .30 .09
197 Ken Caminiti .30 .09
198 Joe Mays .30 .09
199 Chicago White Sox .30 .09
200 Mariano Rivera .50 .15
201 Mark McGwire CL 1.00 .30
202 Pat Meares .30 .09
203 Andres Galarraga .30 .09
204 Tom Gordon .30 .09
205 Henry Rodriguez .30 .09
206 Brett Tomko .30 .09
207 Dante Bichette .30 .09
208 Craig Biggio .50 .15
209 Matt Lawton .30 .09
210 Tino Martinez .50 .15
211 Aaron Myette .30 .09
Josh Paul
212 Warren Morris .30 .09
213 San Diego Padres .30 .09
214 Ramon E. Martinez .30 .09
215 Troy Percival .30 .09
216 Jason Johnson .30 .09
217 Carlos Lee .30 .09
218 Scott Williamson .30 .09
219 Jeff Weaver .30 .09
220 Ronnie Belliard .30 .09
221 Jason Giambi .30 .09
222 Ken Griffey Jr. 1.25 .35
223 John Halama .30 .09
224 Brett Hinchliffe .30 .09
225 Wilson Alvarez .30 .09
226 Rolando Arrojo .30 .09
227 Ruben Mateo .30 .09
228 Rafael Palmeiro .50 .15
229 David Wells .30 .09
230 Eric Gagne 1.25 .35
Jeff Williams RC
231 Tim Salmon .50 .15
232 Mike Mussina .50 .15
233 Magglio Ordonez .30 .09
234 Ron Villone .30 .09
235 Antonio Alfonseca .30 .09
236 Jeromy Burnitz .30 .09
237 Ben Grieve .30 .09
238 Giomar Guevara .30 .09
239 Garret Anderson .30 .09
240 John Smoltz .50 .15
241 Mark Grace .50 .15
242 Cole Liniak .30 .09
Jose Molina
243 Damion Easley .30 .09
244 Jeff Montgomery .30 .09
245 Kenny Lofton .30 .09
246 Masato Yoshii .30 .09
247 Philadelphia Phillies .30 .09
248 Raul Mondesi .30 .09
249 Marlon Anderson .30 .09
250 Shawn Green .30 .09
251 Sterling Hitchcock .30 .09
252 Randy Wolf .30 .09
Anthony Shumaker
253 Jeff Fassero .30 .09
254 Eli Marrero .30 .09
255 Cincinnati Reds .30 .09
256 Rick Ankiel .30 .09
Adam Kennedy
257 Darin Erstad .30 .09
258 Albert Belle .30 .09
259 Bartolo Colon .30 .09
260 Bret Saberhagen .30 .09
261 Carlos Beltran .50 .15
262 Glenallen Hill .30 .09
263 Gregg Jefferies .30 .09
264 Matt Clement .30 .09
265 Miguel Del Toro .30 .09
266 Robinson Cancel .30 .09
Kevin Barker
267 San Francisco Giants .30 .09
268 Kent Bottenfield .30 .09
269 Fred McGriff .50 .15
270 Chris Carpenter .30 .09
271 Atlanta Braves .30 .09
272 Wilton Veras .30 .09
Tomo Ohka RC
273 Will Clark .75 .23
274 Troy O'Leary .30 .09
275 Sammy Sosa CL .75 .23
276 Travis Lee .30 .09
277 Sean Casey .30 .09
278 Ron Gant .30 .09
279 Roger Clemens 1.50 .45
280 Phil Nevin .30 .09
281 Mike Piazza 1.25 .35
282 Mike Lowell .30 .09
283 Kevin Millwood .30 .09
284 Joe Randa .30 .09
285 Jeff Shaw .30 .09
286 Jason Varitek .50 .15
287 Harold Baines .30 .09
288 Gabe Kapler .30 .09
289 Chuck Finley .30 .09
290 Carl Pavano .30 .09
291 Brad Ausmus .30 .09
292 Brad Fullmer .30 .09
293 Boston Red Sox .30 .09
294 Bob Wickman .30 .09
295 Billy Wagner .30 .09
296 Shawn Estes .30 .09
297 Gary Sheffield .30 .09
298 Fernando Seguignol .30 .09
299 Omar Olivares .30 .09
300 Baltimore Orioles .30 .09
301 Matt Stairs .30 .09
302 Andy Ashby .30 .09
303 Todd Greene .30 .09
304 Jesse Garcia .30 .09
305 Kerry Wood .75 .23
306 Roberto Alomar .50 .15
307 New York Mets .30 .09
308 Dean Palmer .30 .09
309 Mike Hampton .30 .09
310 Devon White .30 .09
311 Chad Hermansen .30 .09
Mike Garcia RC
312 Tim Hudson .30 .09
313 John Franco .30 .09
314 Jason Schmidt .30 .09
315 J.T. Snow .30 .09
316 Ed Sprague .30 .09
317 Chris Widger .30 .09
318 Ben Petrick .30 .09
Luther Hackman RC
319 Jose Mesa .30 .09
320 Jose Canseco .75 .23
321 John Wetteland .30 .09
322 Minnesota Twins .30 .09
323 Jeff DaVanon RC .40 .12
Brian Cooper
324 Tony Womack .30 .09
325 Rod Beck .30 .09
326 Mickey Morandini .30 .09
327 Pokey Reese .30 .09
328 Jaret Wright .30 .09
329 Glen Barker .30 .09
330 Darren Dreifort .30 .09
331 Torii Hunter .30 .09
332 Tony Armas .30 .09
Peter Bergeron
333 Hideki Irabu .30 .09
334 Desi Relaford .30 .09
335 Barry Bonds 2.00 .60
336 Gary DiSarcina .30 .09
337 Gerald Williams .30 .09
338 John Valentin .30 .09
339 David Justice .30 .09
340 Juan Encarnacion .30 .09
341 Jeremy Giambi .30 .09
342 Chan Ho Park .30 .09
343 Vladimir Guerrero .75 .23
344 Robin Ventura .50 .15
345 Bob Abreu .30 .09
346 Tony Gwynn 1.00 .30
347 Jose Jimenez .30 .09
348 Royce Clayton .30 .09
349 Kelvim Escobar .30 .09
350 Chicago Cubs .30 .09
351 Travis Dawkins .30 .09
Jason LaRue
352 Barry Larkin .50 .15
353 Cal Ripken 2.50 .75
354 Alex Rodriguez CL .75 .23
355 Todd Stottlemyre .30 .09
356 Terry Adams .30 .09
357 Pittsburgh Pirates .30 .09
358 Jim Thome .75 .23
359 Corey Lee .30 .09
Doug Davis
360 Moises Alou .30 .09
361 Todd Hollandsworth .30 .09
362 Marty Cordova .30 .09
363 David Cone .30 .09
364 Joe Nathan .30 .09
Wilson Delgado
365 Paul Byrd .30 .09
366 Edgar Renteria .30 .09
367 Rusty Greer .30 .09
368 David Segui .30 .09
369 New York Yankees .50 .15
370 Daryle Ward .30 .09
Carlos Hernandez
371 Troy Glaus .30 .09
372 Delino DeShields .30 .09
373 Jose Offerman .30 .09
374 Sammy Sosa 1.25 .35
375 Sandy Alomar Jr. .30 .09
376 Masao Kida .30 .09
377 Richard Hidalgo .30 .09
378 Ismael Valdes .30 .09
379 Ugueth Urbina .30 .09
380 Darryl Hamilton .30 .09
381 John Jaha .30 .09
382 St. Louis Cardinals .30 .09
383 Scott Sauerbeck .30 .09
384 Russ Ortiz .30 .09
385 Jamie Moyer .30 .09
386 Dave Martinez .30 .09
387 Todd Zeile .30 .09
388 Anaheim Angels .30 .09
389 Rob Ryan .30 .09
Nick Bierbrodt
390 Rickey Henderson .75 .23
391 Alex Rodriguez 1.25 .35
392 Texas Rangers .30 .09
393 Roberto Hernandez .30 .09
394 Tony Batista .30 .09
395 Oakland Athletics .30 .09
396 Randall Simon .30 .09
Dave Cortes RC
397 Gregg Olson .30 .09
398 Sidney Ponson .30 .09
399 Micah Bowie .30 .09
400 Mark McGwire 2.00 .60
401 Florida Marlins .30 .09
402 Chad Allen .30 .09
403 Casey Blake .30 .09
Vernon Wells
404 Pete Harnisch .30 .09
405 Preston Wilson .30 .09
406 Richie Sexson .30 .09
407 Rico Brogna .30 .09
408 Todd Hundley .30 .09
409 Wally Joyner .30 .09
410 Tom Goodwin .30 .09
411 Joey Hamilton .30 .09
412 Detroit Tigers .30 .09
413 Michael Tejera RC .30 .09
Ramon Castro
414 Alex Gonzalez .30 .09
415 Jermaine Dye .30 .09
416 Jose Rosado .30 .09
417 Wilton Guerrero .30 .09
418 Rondell White .30 .09
419 Al Leiter .30 .09
420 Bernie Williams .50 .15
421 A.J. Hinch .30 .09
422 Pat Burrell .30 .09
423 Scott Rolen .75 .23
424 Jason Kendall .30 .09
425 Kevin Young .30 .09
426 Eric Owens .30 .09
427 Derek Jeter CL .75 .23
428 Livan Hernandez .30 .09
429 Russ Davis .30 .09
430 Dan Wilson .30 .09
431 Quinton McCracken .30 .09
432 Homer Bush .30 .09
433 Seattle Mariners .30 .09
434 Chad Harville .30 .09
Luis Vizcaino
435 Carlos Beltran AW .50 .15
436 Scott Williamson AW .30 .09
437 Pedro Martinez AW .50 .15
438 Randy Johnson AW .50 .15
439 Ivan Rodriguez AW .50 .15
440 Chipper Jones AW .50 .15
441 Bernie Williams DIV .30 .09
442 Pedro Martinez DIV .50 .15
443 Derek Jeter DIV 1.00 .30
444 Brian Jordan DIV .30 .09
445 Todd Pratt DIV .30 .09
446 Kevin Millwood DIV .30 .09
447 Orl.Hernandez WS .30 .09
448 Derek Jeter WS 1.00 .30
449 Chad Curtis WS .30 .09
450 Roger Clemens WS .75 .23
P353 Cal Ripken Promo 3.00 .90

2000 Fleer Tradition Glossy

The 2000 Fleer Glossy set was released in early December, 2000 and features a 500-card base set. Please note that you only receive 455 of the 500 total cards that make up this set per sealed factory set. Card 451-500 are short-printed and are inserted into sets at five per factory sealed set. Cards 451-500 are serial numbered to 1000.

	Nm-Mt	Ex-Mt
COMP.FACT.SET (455)	60.00	18.00
*STARS 1-450: .75X TO 2X BASIC		
*ROOKIES 1-450: .75X TO 2X BASIC		
451 Carlos Casimiro RC	10.00	3.00
452 Adam Melhuse RC	10.00	3.00
453 Adam Bernero RC	10.00	3.00
454 Dusty Allen RC	10.00	3.00
455 Chan Perry RC	10.00	3.00
456 Damian Rolls RC	10.00	3.00
457 Josh Phelps RC	15.00	4.50
458 Barry Zito	20.00	6.00
459 Hector Ortiz RC	10.00	3.00
460 Juan Pierre RC	15.00	4.50
461 Jose Ortiz RC	10.00	3.00
462 Chad Zerbe RC	15.00	4.50
463 Julio Zuleta RC	10.00	3.00
464 Eric Byrnes	15.00	4.50
465 Wilf. Rodriguez RC	10.00	3.00
466 Wascar Serrano RC	10.00	3.00
467 Aaron McNeal RC	10.00	3.00
468 Paul Rigdon RC	10.00	3.00
469 John Snyder RC	10.00	3.00
470 J.C. Romero RC	10.00	3.00
471 Talmadge Nunnari RC	10.00	3.00
472 Mike Lamb	10.00	3.00
473 Ryan Kohlmeier RC	10.00	3.00
474 Rodney Lindsey RC	10.00	3.00
475 Elvis Pena RC	10.00	3.00
476 Alex Cabrera	10.00	3.00
477 Chris Richard	10.00	3.00
478 Pedro Feliz RC	15.00	4.50
479 Ross Gload RC	10.00	3.00
480 Timo Perez RC	10.00	3.00
481 Jason Woolf RC	10.00	3.00
482 Kenny Kelly RC	10.00	3.00
483 Sang-Hoon Lee	10.00	3.00
484 John Riedling RC	10.00	3.00
485 Chris Wakeland RC	10.00	3.00
486 Britt Reames RC	10.00	3.00
487 Greg LaRocca RC	10.00	3.00
488 Randy Keisler RC	10.00	3.00
489 Xavier Nady RC	15.00	4.50
490 Keith Ginter RC	10.00	3.00
491 Joey Nation RC	10.00	3.00
492 Kazuhiro Sasaki	15.00	4.50
493 Lesli Brea RC	10.00	3.00
494 Jace Brewer	10.00	3.00
495 Yohanny Valera RC	10.00	3.00
496 Adam Piatt	10.00	3.00
497 Nate Rolison	10.00	3.00
498 Aubrey Huff	10.00	3.00
499 Jason Tyner	10.00	3.00
500 Corey Patterson	10.00	3.00

2000 Fleer Tradition Dividends

Inserted at a rate of one in six packs, these 15 cards feature some of the best players in the game.

	Nm-Mt	Ex-Mt
COMPLETE SET (15)	15.00	4.50
D1 Alex Rodriguez	1.25	.35
D2 Ben Grieve	.30	.09
D3 Cal Ripken	2.50	.75
D4 Chipper Jones	.75	.23
D5 Derek Jeter	1.50	.45
D6 Frank Thomas	.75	.23
D7 Jeff Bagwell	.50	.15
D8 Sammy Sosa	1.25	.35
D9 Tony Gwynn	1.00	.30
D10 Scott Rolen	.75	.23
D11 Nomar Garciaparra	1.25	.35
D12 Mike Piazza	1.25	.35
D13 Mark McGwire	2.00	.60
D14 Ken Griffey Jr.	1.25	.35
D15 Juan Gonzalez	.50	.15

2000 Fleer Tradition Fresh Ink

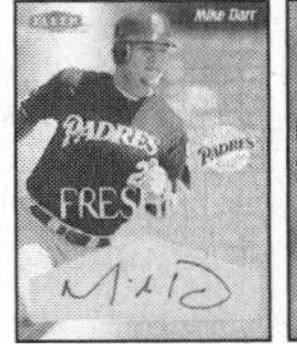

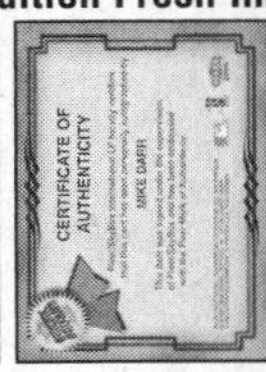

Randomly inserted into packs at one in 144 packs, this insert set features autographed cards of players such as Rick Ankiel, Sean Casey and J.D. Drew.

	Nm-Mt	Ex-Mt
1 Rick Ankiel	10.00	3.00
2 Carlos Beltran	40.00	12.00
3 Pat Burrell	10.00	3.00
4 Miguel Cairo	10.00	3.00
5 Sean Casey	15.00	4.50
6 Will Clark	40.00	12.00
7 Mike Darr	10.00	3.00
8 J.D. Drew	25.00	7.50
9 Erubiel Durazo	10.00	3.00
10 Carlos Febles	10.00	3.00
11 Freddy Garcia	10.00	3.00
12 Jason Grilli	10.00	3.00
13 Vladimir Guerrero	40.00	12.00
14 Tony Gwynn	50.00	15.00
15 Jerry Hairston Jr.	10.00	3.00
16 Tim Hudson	15.00	4.50
17 John Jaha	10.00	3.00
18 D'Angelo Jimenez	10.00	3.00
19 Andruw Jones	15.00	4.50
20 Gabe Kapler	10.00	3.00
21 Cesar King	10.00	3.00
22 Jason LaRue	10.00	3.00
23 Mike Lieberthal	15.00	4.50
24 Greg Maddux	120.00	36.00
25 Pedro Martinez	80.00	24.00
26 Gary Matthews Jr.	10.00	3.00
27 Orber Moreno	10.00	3.00
28 Eric Munson	10.00	3.00
29 Rafael Palmeiro	40.00	12.00
30 Jim Parque	10.00	3.00
31 Wily Pena	15.00	4.50
32 Cal Ripken	150.00	45.00
33 Alex Rodriguez	120.00	36.00
34 Tim Salmon	25.00	7.50
35 Chris Singleton	10.00	3.00
36 Alfonso Soriano	40.00	12.00
37 Ed Yarnall	10.00	3.00

2000 Fleer Tradition Grasskickers

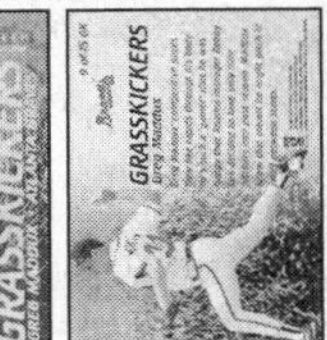

Inserted at a rate of one in 30 packs, these 15 cards printed on rainbow holofoil feature players who put fear into their opponents.

	Nm-Mt	Ex-Mt
COMPLETE SET (15)	60.00	18.00
GK1 Tony Gwynn	5.00	1.50
GK2 Scott Rolen	4.00	1.20
GK3 Nomar Garciaparra	6.00	1.80
GK4 Mike Piazza	6.00	1.80
GK5 Mark McGwire	10.00	3.00
GK6 Frank Thomas	4.00	1.20
GK7 Cal Ripken	12.00	3.60
GK8 Chipper Jones	4.00	1.20
GK9 Greg Maddux	6.00	1.80
GK10 Ken Griffey Jr.	6.00	1.80
GK11 Juan Gonzalez	2.50	.75
GK12 Derek Jeter	8.00	2.40
GK13 Sammy Sosa	6.00	1.80
GK14 Roger Clemens	8.00	2.40
GK15 Alex Rodriguez	6.00	1.80

2000 Fleer Tradition Hall's Well

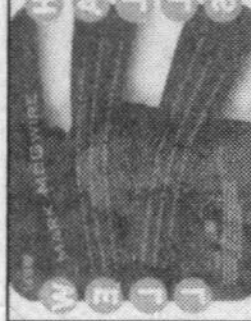

Inserted at a rate of one in 30 packs, these 15 cards feature players on their path to the Hall of Fame. The cards were printed on a combination of transparent plastic stock with overlays of silver foil stamping.

Nm-Mt Ex-Mt
COMPLETE SET (15) 50.00 15.00
HW1 Mark McGwire 10.00 3.00
HW2 Alex Rodriguez 6.00 1.80
HW3 Cal Ripken 12.00 3.60
HW4 Chipper Jones 4.00 1.20
HW5 Derek Jeter 8.00 2.40
HW6 Frank Thomas 4.00 1.20
HW7 Greg Maddux 6.00 1.80
HW8 Juan Gonzalez 2.50 .75
HW9 Ken Griffey Jr. 6.00 1.80
HW10 Mike Piazza 6.00 1.80
HW11 Nomar Garciaparra 6.00 1.80
HW12 Sammy Sosa 6.00 1.80
HW13 Roger Clemens 8.00 2.40
HW14 Ivan Rodriguez 4.00 1.20
HW15 Tony Gwynn 5.00 1.50

2000 Fleer Tradition Ripken Collection

Inserted at a rate of one in 30 packs, these 10 cards feature photos of Cal Ripken Jr. in the style of vintage Fleer cards. We have identified the style of the card and the sport next to Ripken's name.

Nm-Mt Ex-Mt
COMMON CARD (1-10) 10.00 3.00

2000 Fleer Tradition Ten-4

Issued at a rate of one in 18 packs, these 10 cards feature the best home run hitters highlighted on a die-cut card with silver foil stamping.

Nm-Mt Ex-Mt
COMPLETE SET (10) 25.00 7.50
TF1 Sammy Sosa 3.00 .90
TF2 Nomar Garciaparra 3.00 .90
TF3 Mike Piazza 3.00 .90
TF4 Mark McGwire 5.00 1.50
TF5 Ken Griffey Jr. 3.00 .90
TF6 Juan Gonzalez 1.25 .35
TF7 Derek Jeter 4.00 1.20
TF8 Chipper Jones 2.00 .60
TF9 Cal Ripken 6.00 1.80
TF10 Alex Rodriguez 3.00 .90

2000 Fleer Tradition Who To Watch

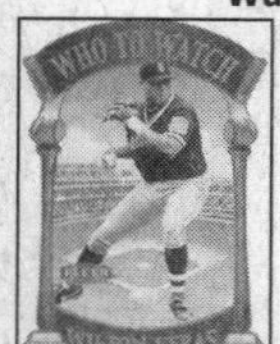

Inserted at a rate of one in three, these 15 cards feature leading prospects against a nostalgic die-cut background.

Nm-Mt Ex-Mt
COMPLETE SET (15) 5.00 1.50
WW1 Rick Ankiel .50 .15
WW2 Matt Riley .50 .15
WW3 Wilton Veras .50 .15
WW4 Ben Petrick .50 .15
WW5 Chad Hermansen .50 .15
WW6 Peter Bergeron .50 .15
WW7 Mark Quinn .50 .15
WW8 Russell Branyan .50 .15
WW9 Alfonso Soriano 1.00 .30
WW10 Randy Wolf .50 .15
WW11 Ben Davis .50 .15
WW12 Jeff DaVanon .50 .15
WW13 D'Angelo Jimenez .50 .15
WW14 Vernon Wells .50 .15
WW15 Adam Kennedy .50 .15

2000 Fleer Tradition Glossy Lumberjacks

Inserted into Fleer Glossy sets at one per set, this 45-card insert set features game-used bat pieces from some of the top players in baseball. Print runs are listed below.

Nm-Mt Ex-Mt
1 Edgardo Alfonzo/145 12.00 3.60
2 Roberto Alomar/627 15.00 4.50
3 Moises Alou/529 10.00 3.00
4 Carlos Beltran/489 15.00 4.50
5 Adrian Beltre/127 20.00 6.00
6 Wade Boggs/30
7 Barry Bonds/305 40.00 12.00
8 Jeromy Burnitz/34
9 Pat Burrell/45
10 Sean Casey/50
11 Eric Chavez/259 10.00 3.00
12 Tony Clark/70 15.00 4.50
13 Carlos Delgado/70 15.00 4.50
14 J.D. Drew/135 12.00 3.60
15 Erubiel Durazo/70 15.00 4.50
16 Ray Durham/35
17 Carlos Febles/120 12.00 3.60
18 Jason Giambi/220 10.00 3.00
19 Shawn Green/429 10.00 3.00
20 Vladimir Guerrero/809 15.00 4.50
21 Derek Jeter/180 60.00 18.00
22 Chipper Jones/725 15.00 4.50
23 Gabe Kapler/160 12.00 3.60
24 Jason Kendall/34
25 Paul Konerko/70 15.00 4.50
26 Ray Lankford/35
27 Mike Lieberthal/45
28 Edgar Martinez/211 15.00 4.50
29 Raul Mondesi/458 10.00 3.00
30 Warren Morris/35
31 Magglio Ordonez/190 12.00 3.60
32 Rafael Palmeiro/49
33 Pokey Reese/110 12.00 3.60
34 Cal Ripken/235 80.00 24.00
35 Alex Rodriguez/292 40.00 12.00
36 Ivan Rodriguez/602 15.00 4.50
37 Scott Rolen/502 15.00 4.50
38 Chris Singleton/68 15.00 4.50
39 Alfonso Soriano/285 15.00 4.50
40 Frank Thomas/489 15.00 4.50
41 Jim Thome/479 15.00 4.50
42 Robin Ventura/114 12.00 3.60
43 Jose Vidro/60 15.00 4.50
44 Bernie Williams/215 15.00 4.50
45 Matt Williams/152 12.00 3.60

2000 Fleer Tradition Update

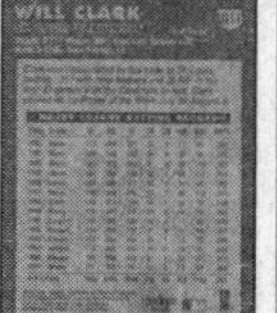

The 2000 Fleer Tradition Update set was released in October, 2000 as a 150-card factory set. The set includes 10 Season Highlight cards (1-10), and 140 cards of players that were either traded during the season or who made their major league debut (cards 11-150). Each set originally carried a suggested retail price of $29.99. Please note that card number 50 does not exist. All cards have a "U" prefix. Notable Rookie Cards include Kazuhiro Sasaki and Barry Zito. Finally, one in every 80 sets contained a Mickey Mantle game-worn jersey memorabilia card.

Nm-Mt Ex-Mt
COMP.FACT.SET (149) 20.00 6.00
1 Ken Griffey Jr. SH .75 .23
2 Cal Ripken SH 1.00 .30
3 Randy Velarde SH .30 .09
4 Fred McGriff SH .30 .09
5 Derek Jeter SH .75 .23
6 Tom Glavine SH .30 .09
7 Brent Mayne SH .30 .09
8 Alex Ochoa SH .30 .09
9 Scott Sheldon SH .30 .09
10 Randy Johnson SH .50 .15
11 Daniel Garibay RC .30 .09
12 Brad Fullmer .30 .09
13 Kazuhiro Sasaki RC 1.00 .30
14 Andy Tracy RC .30 .09
15 Bret Boone .30 .09
16 Chad Durbin RC .40 .12
17 Mark Buehrle RC 1.25 .35
18 Julio Zuleta RC .30 .09
19 Jeremy Giambi .30 .09
20 Gene Stechschulte RC .30 .09
21 Lou Pote .30 .09
Bengie Molina
22 Darrell Einertson RC .30 .09
23 Ken Griffey Jr. 1.25 .35
24 Jeff Sparks RC .30 .09
Dan Wheeler
25 Aaron Fultz RC .30 .09
26 Derek Bell .30 .09
27 Rob Bell .30 .09
D.T. Cromer
28 Robert Fick .30 .09
29 Darryl Kile .30 .09
30 Clayton Andrews .30 .09
John Bale RC
31 Dave Veres .30 .09
32 Hector Mercado RC .30 .09
33 Willie Morales RC .30 .09
34 Kelly Wunsch .30 .09
Kip Wells
35 Hideki Irabu .30 .09
36 Sean DePaula RC .30 .09
37 DeWayne Wise .30 .09
Chris Woodward
38 Curt Schilling .30 .09
39 Mark Johnson .30 .09
40 Mike Cameron .30 .09
41 Scott Sheldon .30 .09
Tom Evans
42 Brett Tomko .30 .09
43 Johan Santana RC 10.00 3.00
44 Andy Benes .30 .09
45 Matt LeCroy .30 .09
Mark Redman
46 Ryan Klesko .30 .09
47 Andy Ashby .30 .09
48 Octavio Dotel .30 .09
49 Eric Byrnes RC 1.00 .30
50 Does Not Exist
51 Kenny Rogers .30 .09
52 Ben Weber RC .40 .12
53 Matt Blank .30 .09
Scott Strickland
54 Tom Goodwin .30 .09
55 Jim Edmonds Cards .30 .09
56 Derrick Turnbow RC .30 .09
57 Mark Mulder .30 .09
58 Tarrick Brock .30 .09
Ruben Quevedo
59 Danny Young RC .30 .09
60 Fernando Vina .30 .09
61 Justin Brunette RC .30 .09
62 Jimmy Anderson .30 .09
63 Reggie Sanders .30 .09
64 Adam Kennedy .30 .09
65 Jesse Garcia .30 .09
B.J. Ryan
66 Al Martin .30 .09
67 Kevin Walker RC .30 .09
68 Brad Penny .30 .09
69 B.J. Surhoff .30 .09
70 Geoff Blum .30 .09
Trace Coquillette RC
71 Jose Jimenez .30 .09
72 Chuck Finley .30 .09
73 Valerio De Los Santos .30 .09
Everett Stull
74 Terry Adams .30 .09
75 Rafael Furcal .30 .09
76 John Roskos .30 .09
Mike Darr
77 Quilvio Veras .30 .09
78 Armando Almanza .30 .09
Nate Rolison
79 Greg Vaughn .30 .09
80 Keith McDonald RC .30 .09
81 Eric Cammack RC .30 .09
82 Horacio Estrada .30 .09
Ray King
83 Kory DeHaan .30 .09
84 Kevin Hodges RC .30 .09
85 Mike Lamb RC .40 .12
86 Shawn Green .30 .09
87 Dan Reichert .30 .09
Jason Rakers
88 Adam Piatt .30 .09
89 Mike Garcia .30 .09
90 Rodrigo Lopez RC .60 .18
91 John Olerud .30 .09
92 Barry Zito RC 2.00 .60
Terrence Long
93 Jimmy Rollins .30 .09
94 Denny Neagle .30 .09
95 Rickey Henderson .75 .23
96 Adam Eaton .30 .09
Buddy Carlyle
97 Brian O'Connor RC .30 .09
98 Andy Thompson RC .30 .09
99 Jason Boyd RC .30 .09
100 Joel Pineiro RC 2.00 .60
Carlos Guillen
101 Raul Gonzalez RC .30 .09
102 Brandon Kolb RC .30 .09
103 Jason Maxwell .30 .09
Mike Lincoln
104 Luis Matos RC .40 .12
105 Morgan Burkhart RC .30 .09
106 Ismael Villegas RC .30 .09
Steve Sisco RC
107 David Justice Yankees .30 .09
108 Pablo Ozuna .30 .09
109 Jose Canseco .75 .23
110 Alex Cora .30 .09
Shawn Gilbert
111 Will Clark Cardinals .75 .23
112 Keith Luuloa .30 .09
Eric Weaver
113 Bruce Chen .30 .09
114 Adam Hyzdu .30 .09
115 Scott Forster RC .30 .09
Yovanny Lara RC
116 Allen McDill RC .30 .09
Jose Macias
117 Kevin Nicholson .30 .09
118 Israel Alcantara .30 .09
Tim Young
119 Juan Alvarez RC .30 .09
120 Julio Lugo .30 .09
Mitch Meluskey
121 B.J. Waszgis RC .30 .09
122 Jeff M. D'Amico RC .30 .09
Brett Laxton
123 Ricky Ledee .30 .09
124 Mark DeRosa .30 .09
Jason Marquis
125 Alex Cabrera RC .40 .12
126 Augie Ojeda RC .30 .09
Gary Matthews Jr.
127 Richie Sexson .30 .09
128 Santiago Perez RC .30 .09
Hector Ramirez RC
129 Rondell White .30 .09
130 Craig House RC .30 .09
131 Kevin Beirne .30 .09
Jon Garland
132 Wayne Franklin RC .30 .09
133 Henry Rodriguez .30 .09
134 Jay Payton .30 .09
Jim Mann
135 Ron Gant .30 .09
136 Paxton Crawford RC .30 .09
Sang-Hoon Lee RC
137 Kent Bottenfield .30 .09
138 Rocky Biddle RC .30 .09
139 Travis Lee .30 .09
140 Ryan Vogelsong RC .40 .12
141 Jason Conti .30 .09
Geraldo Guzman RC
142 Tim Drew .30 .09
Mark Watson RC
143 John Parrish RC .30 .09
Chris Richard RC
144 Javier Cardona RC .30 .09
Brandon Villafuerte RC
145 Tike Redman RC .60 .18
Steve Sparks RC
146 Brian Schneider .30 .09
Matt Skrmetta RC
147 Pasqual Coco RC .30 .09
148 Lorenzo Barcelo RC .30 .09
Joe Crede
149 Jace Brewer RC .30 .09
150 Milton Bradley .40 .12
Tomas De La Rosa RC
MP1 Mickey Mantle Jsy 200.00 60.00

2001 Fleer Tradition

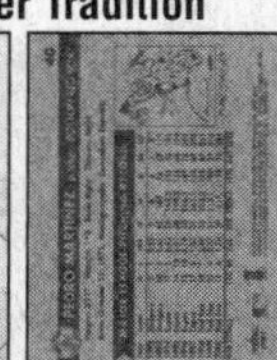

The 2001 Fleer Tradition product was released in early February, 2001 and initially featured a 450-card base set that was broken into tiers as follows: Base Veterans (1-350), Prospects (351-380), League Leaders (381-410), World Series Highlights (411-420), and Team Checklists (421-450). Each pack contained 10 cards and carried a suggested retail price of $1.99 per pack. In late October, 2001, a 485-card factory set carrying a $42.99 SRP was released. Each factory set contained the basic 450-card set plus 35 new cards (451-485) featuring a selection of rookies and prospects. Please note that there was also 100 exchange cards inserted into packs in which lucky collectors received an uncut sheet of 2001 Fleer.

Nm-Mt Ex-Mt
COMP.FACT.SET (485) 60.00 18.00
COMPLETE SET (450) 25.00 7.50
COMMON CARD (1-450) .30 .09
COMMON (451-485) .50 .15
1 Andres Galarraga .30 .09
2 Armando Rios .30 .09
3 Julio Lugo .30 .09
4 Darryl Hamilton .30 .09
5 Dave Veres .30 .09
6 Edgardo Alfonzo .30 .09
7 Brook Fordyce .30 .09
8 Eric Karros .30 .09
9 Neifi Perez .30 .09
10 Jim Edmonds .30 .09
11 Barry Larkin .50 .15
12 Trot Nixon .30 .09
13 Andy Pettitte .50 .15
14 Jose Guillen .30 .09
15 David Wells .30 .09
16 Magglio Ordonez .30 .09
17 David Segui .30 .09
17A David Segui ERR .30 .09
Card has no number on the back
18 Juan Encarnacion .30 .09
19 Robert Person .30 .09
20 Quilvio Veras .30 .09
21 Mo Vaughn .30 .09
22 B.J. Surhoff .30 .09
23 Ken Caminiti .30 .09
24 Frank Catalanotto .30 .09
25 Luis Gonzalez .30 .09
26 Pete Harnisch .30 .09
27 Alex Gonzalez .30 .09
28 Mark Quinn .30 .09
29 Luis Castillo .30 .09
30 Rick Helling .30 .09
31 Barry Bonds 2.00 .60
32 Warren Morris .30 .09
33 Aaron Boone .30 .09
34 Ricky Gutierrez .30 .09
35 Preston Wilson .30 .09
36 Erubiel Durazo .30 .09
37 Jermaine Dye .30 .09
38 John Rocker .30 .09
39 Mark Grudzielanek .30 .09
40 Pedro Martinez .75 .23
41 Phil Nevin .30 .09
42 Luis Matos .30 .09
43 Orlando Hernandez .30 .09
44 Steve Cox .30 .09
45 James Baldwin .30 .09
46 Rafael Furcal .30 .09
47 Todd Zeile .30 .09
48 Elmer Dessens .30 .09
49 Russell Branyan .30 .09
50 Juan Gonzalez .50 .15
51 Mac Suzuki .30 .09
52 Adam Kennedy .30 .09
53 Randy Velarde .30 .09
54 David Bell .30 .09
55 Royce Clayton .30 .09
56 Greg Colbrunn .30 .09
57 Rey Ordonez .30 .09
58 Kevin Millwood .30 .09
59 Fernando Vina .30 .09
60 Eddie Taubensee .30 .09
61 Enrique Wilson .30 .09
62 Jay Bell .30 .09
63 Brian Moehler .30 .09
64 Brad Fullmer .30 .09
65 Ben Petrick .30 .09
66 Orlando Cabrera .30 .09
67 Shane Reynolds .30 .09
68 Mitch Meluskey .30 .09
69 Jeff Shaw .30 .09
70 Chipper Jones .75 .23
71 Tomo Ohka .30 .09
72 Ruben Rivera .30 .09
73 Mike Sirotka .30 .09
74 Scott Rolen .75 .23
75 Glendon Rusch .30 .09
76 Miguel Tejada .30 .09
77 Brady Anderson .30 .09
78 Bartolo Colon .30 .09
79 Ron Coomer .30 .09
80 Gary DiSarcina .30 .09
81 Geoff Jenkins .30 .09
82 Billy Koch .30 .09
83 Mike Lamb .30 .09
84 Alex Rodriguez 1.25 .35
85 Denny Neagle .30 .09
86 Michael Tucker .30 .09
87 Edgar Renteria .30 .09
88 Brian Anderson .30 .09
89 Glenallen Hill .30 .09
90 Aramis Ramirez .30 .09
91 Rondell White .30 .09
92 Tony Womack .30 .09
93 Jeffrey Hammonds .30 .09
94 Freddy Garcia .30 .09
95 Bill Mueller .30 .09
96 Mike Lieberthal .30 .09
97 Michael Barrett .30 .09
98 Derrek Lee .30 .09
99 Bill Spiers .30 .09
100 Derek Lowe .30 .09
101 Javy Lopez .30 .09
102 Adrian Beltre .50 .15
103 Jim Parque .30 .09
104 Marquis Grissom .30 .09
105 Eric Chavez .30 .09
106 Todd Jones .30 .09
107 Eric Owens .30 .09
108 Roger Clemens 1.50 .45
109 Denny Hocking .30 .09
110 Roberto Hernandez .30 .09
111 Albert Belle .30 .09
112 Troy Glaus .30 .09
113 Ivan Rodriguez .75 .23
114 Carlos Guillen .30 .09
115 Chuck Finley .30 .09
116 Dmitri Young .30 .09
117 Paul Konerko .30 .09
118 Damon Buford .30 .09
119 Fernando Tatis .30 .09
120 Larry Walker .50 .15
121 Jason Kendall .30 .09
122 Matt Williams .30 .09
123 Henry Rodriguez .30 .09
124 Placido Polanco .30 .09
125 Bobby Estalella .30 .09
126 Pat Burrell .30 .09
127 Mark Loretta .30 .09
128 Moises Alou .30 .09
129 Tino Martinez .50 .15
130 Milton Bradley .30 .09
131 Todd Hundley .30 .09
132 Keith Foulke .30 .09
133 Robert Fick .30 .09
134 Cristian Guzman .30 .09
135 Rusty Greer .30 .09
136 John Olerud .30 .09
137 Mariano Rivera .50 .15
138 Jeromy Burnitz .30 .09
139 Dave Burba .30 .09
140 Ken Griffey Jr. 1.25 .35
141 Tony Gwynn 1.00 .30
142 Carlos Delgado .30 .09
143 Edgar Martinez .50 .15
144 Ramon Hernandez .30 .09
145 Pedro Astacio .30 .09
146 Ray Lankford .30 .09
147 Mike Mussina .50 .15
148 Ray Durham .30 .09
149 Lee Stevens .30 .09
150 Jay Canizaro .30 .09
151 Adrian Brown .30 .09
152 Mike Piazza 1.25 .35
153 Cliff Floyd .30 .09
154 Jose Vidro .30 .09
155 Jason Giambi .30 .09
156 Andruw Jones .30 .09
157 Robin Ventura .30 .09
158 Gary Sheffield .30 .09
159 Jeff D'Amico .30 .09
160 Chuck Knoblauch .30 .09
161 Roger Cedeno .30 .09
162 Jim Thome .75 .23
163 Peter Bergeron .30 .09
164 Kerry Wood .75 .23
165 Gabe Kapler .30 .09
166 Corey Koskie .30 .09
167 Doug Glanville .30 .09
168 Brent Mayne .30 .09
169 Scott Spiezio .30 .09
170 Steve Karsay .30 .09
171 Al Martin .30 .09
172 Fred McGriff .50 .15
173 Gabe White .30 .09
174 Alex Gonzalez .30 .09
175 Mike Darr .30 .09
176 Bengie Molina .30 .09
177 Ben Grieve .30 .09
178 Marlon Anderson .30 .09
179 Brian Giles .30 .09
180 Jose Valentin .30 .09
181 Brian Jordan .30 .09
182 Randy Johnson .75 .23
183 Ricky Ledee .30 .09
184 Russ Ortiz .30 .09
185 Mike Lowell .30 .09
186 Curtis Leskanic .30 .09
187 Bob Abreu .30 .09
188 Derek Jeter 2.00 .60

89 Lance Berkman .30 .09
90 Roberto Alomar .50 .15
91 Darin Erstad .30 .09
92 Richie Sexson .30 .09
93 Alex Ochoa .30 .09
94 Carlos Febles .30 .09
95 David Ortiz .50 .15
96 Shawn Green .30 .09
97 Mike Sweeney .30 .09
98 Vladimir Guerrero .75 .23
99 Jose Jimenez .30 .09
00 Travis Lee .30 .09
01 Rickey Henderson .75 .23
02 Bob Wickman .30 .09
03 Miguel Cairo .30 .09
04 Steve Finley .30 .09
05 Tony Batista .30 .09
06 Jamey Wright .30 .09
07 Terrence Long .30 .09
08 Trevor Hoffman .30 .09
09 John VanderWal .30 .09
10 Greg Maddux 1.25 .35
11 Tim Salmon .50 .15
12 Herbert Perry .30 .09
13 Marvin Benard .30 .09
14 Jose Offerman .30 .09
15 Jay Payton .30 .09
16 Jon Lieber .30 .09
17 Mark Kotsay .30 .09
18 Scott Brosius .30 .09
19 Scott Williamson .30 .09
20 Omar Vizquel .50 .15
21 Mike Hampton .30 .09
22 Richard Hidalgo .30 .09
23 Rey Sanchez .30 .09
24 Matt Lawton .30 .09
25 Bruce Chen .30 .09
26 Ryan Klesko .30 .09
27 Garret Anderson .30 .09
28 Kevin Brown .30 .09
29 Mike Cameron .30 .09
30 Tony Clark .30 .09
31 Curt Schilling .30 .09
32 Vinny Castilla .30 .09
33 Carl Pavano .30 .09
34 Eric Davis .30 .09
35 Darrin Fletcher .30 .09
36 Matt Stairs .30 .09
37 Octavio Dotel .30 .09
38 Mark Grace .50 .15
39 John Smoltz .50 .15
40 Matt Clement .30 .09
41 Ellis Burks .30 .09
42 Charles Johnson .30 .09
43 Jeff Bagwell .50 .15
44 Derek Bell .30 .09
45 Nomar Garciaparra 1.25 .35
46 Jorge Posada .50 .15
47 Ryan Dempster .30 .09
48 J.T. Snow .30 .09
49 Eric Young .30 .09
50 Daryle Ward .30 .09
51 Joe Randa .30 .09
52 Travis Fryman .30 .09
53 Mike Williams .30 .09
54 Jacque Jones .30 .09
55 Scott Elarton .30 .09
56 Mark McGwire 2.00 .60
57 Jay Buhner .30 .09
58 Randy Wolf .30 .09
59 Sammy Sosa 1.25 .35
60 Chan Ho Park .30 .09
61 Damion Easley .30 .09
62 Rick Ankiel .30 .09
63 Frank Thomas .75 .23
64 Kris Benson .30 .09
65 Luis Alicea .30 .09
66 Jeromy Burnitz .30 .09
67 Geoff Blum .30 .09
68 Joe Girardi .30 .09
69 Livan Hernandez .30 .09
70 Jeff Conine .30 .09
71 Danny Graves .30 .09
72 Craig Biggio .50 .15
73 Jose Canseco .75 .23
74 Tom Glavine .50 .15
75 Ruben Mateo .30 .09
76 Jeff Kent .30 .09
77 Kevin Young .30 .09
78 A.J. Burnett .30 .09
79 Dante Bichette .30 .09
80 Sandy Alomar Jr. .30 .09
81 John Wetteland .30 .09
82 Torii Hunter .30 .09
83 Jarrod Washburn .30 .09
84 Rich Aurilia .30 .09
85 Jeff Cirillo .30 .09
86 Fernando Seguignol .30 .09
87 Darren Dreifort .30 .09
88 Deivi Cruz .30 .09
89 Pokey Reese .30 .09
90 Garrett Stephenson .30 .09
91 Bret Boone .30 .09
92 Tim Hudson .30 .09
93 John Flaherty .30 .09
94 Shannon Stewart .30 .09
95 Shawn Estes .30 .09
96 Wilton Guerrero .30 .09
97 Delino DeShields .30 .09
98 David Justice .30 .09
99 Harold Baines .30 .09
00 Al Leiter .30 .09
01 Wil Cordero .30 .09
02 Antonio Alfonseca .30 .09
03 Sean Casey .30 .09
04 Carlos Beltran .50 .15
05 Brad Radke .30 .09
06 Jason Varitek .50 .15
07 Shigetoshi Hasegawa .30 .09
08 Todd Stottlemyre .30 .09
09 Raul Mondesi .30 .09
10 Mike Bordick .30 .09
11 Darryl Kile .30 .09
12 Dean Palmer .30 .09
13 Johnny Damon .50 .15
14 Todd Helton .50 .15
15 Chad Hermansen .30 .09
16 Kevin Appier .30 .09
17 Greg Vaughn .30 .09
318 Robb Nen .30 .09
319 Jose Cruz Jr. .30 .09
320 Ron Belliard .30 .09
321 Bernie Williams .50 .15
322 Melvin Mora .30 .09
323 Kenny Lofton .30 .09
324 Armando Benitez .30 .09
325 Carlos Lee .30 .09
326 Damian Jackson .30 .09
327 Eric Milton .30 .09
328 J.D. Drew .30 .09
329 Byung-Hyun Kim .30 .09
330 Chris Stynes .30 .09
331 Kazuhiro Sasaki .30 .09
332 Troy O'Leary .30 .09
333 Pat Hentgen .30 .09
334 Brad Ausmus .30 .09
335 Todd Walker .30 .09
336 Jason Isringhausen .30 .09
337 Gerald Williams .30 .09
338 Aaron Sele .30 .09
339 Paul O'Neill .50 .15
340 Cal Ripken 2.50 .75
341 Manny Ramirez .50 .15
342 Will Clark .75 .23
343 Mark Redman .30 .09
344 Bubba Trammell .30 .09
345 Troy Percival .30 .09
346 Chris Singleton .30 .09
347 Rafael Palmeiro .50 .15
348 Carl Everett .30 .09
349 Andy Benes .30 .09
350 Bobby Higginson .30 .09
351 Alex Cabrera .30 .09
352 Barry Zito .50 .15
353 Jace Brewer .30 .09
354 Paxton Crawford .30 .09
355 Oswaldo Mairena .30 .09
356 Joe Crede .30 .09
357 A.J. Pierzynski .30 .09
358 Daniel Garibay .30 .09
359 Jason Tyner .30 .09
360 Nate Rolison .30 .09
361 Scott Downs .30 .09
362 Keith Ginter .30 .09
363 Juan Pierre .30 .09
364 Adam Bernero .30 .09
365 Chris Richard .30 .09
366 Joey Nation .30 .09
367 Aubrey Huff .30 .09
368 Adam Eaton .30 .09
369 Jose Ortiz .30 .09
370 Eric Munson .30 .09
371 Matt Kinney .30 .09
372 Eric Byrnes .30 .09
373 Keith McDonald .30 .09
374 Matt Wise .30 .09
375 Timo Perez .30 .09
376 Julio Zuleta .30 .09
377 Jimmy Rollins .30 .09
378 Xavier Nady .30 .09
379 Ryan Kohlmeier .30 .09
380 Corey Patterson .30 .09
381 Todd Helton LL .30 .09
382 Moises Alou LL .30 .09
383 Vladimir Guerrero LL .50 .15
384 Luis Castillo LL .30 .09
385 Jeffrey Hammonds LL .30 .09
386 Nomar Garciaparra LL .75 .23
387 Carlos Delgado LL .30 .09
388 Darin Erstad LL .30 .09
389 Manny Ramirez LL .30 .09
390 Mike Sweeney LL .30 .09
391 Sammy Sosa LL .75 .23
392 Barry Bonds LL .75 .23
393 Jeff Bagwell LL .30 .09
394 Richard Hidalgo LL .30 .09
395 Vladimir Guerrero LL .50 .15
396 Troy Glaus LL .30 .09
397 Frank Thomas LL .50 .15
398 Carlos Delgado LL .30 .09
399 David Justice LL .30 .09
400 Jason Giambi LL .30 .09
401 Randy Johnson LL .50 .15
402 Kevin Brown LL .30 .09
403 Greg Maddux LL .75 .23
404 Al Leiter LL .30 .09
405 Mike Hampton LL .30 .09
406 Pedro Martinez LL .50 .15
407 Roger Clemens LL .75 .23
408 Mike Sirotka LL .30 .09
409 Mike Mussina LL .30 .09
410 Bartolo Colon LL .30 .09
411 Subway Series WS .50 .15
412 Jose Vizcaino WS .50 .15
413 Jose Vizcaino WS .50 .15
414 Roger Clemens WS .75 .23
415 Armando Benitez .30 .09
Edgardo Alfonzo
Timo Perez WS
416 Al Leiter WS .50 .15
417 Luis Sojo WS .50 .15
418 Yankees 3-Peat WS .75 .23
419 Derek Jeter WS 1.00 .30
420 Toast of the Town WS .50 .15
421 Rafael Furcal .30 .09
Chipper Jones
Greg Maddux
John Rocker
Tom Glavine CL
422 Armando Benitez .75 .23
Mike Piazza
Mike Hampton
Al Leiter CL
423 Ryan Dempster .30 .09
Luis Castillo
Antonio Alfonseca
Preston Wilson CL
424 Robert Person .30 .09
Scott Rolen
Randy Wolf
Bob Abreu
Doug Glanville CL
425 Vladimir Guerrero .50 .15
Peter Bergeron CL
426 Fernando Vina .30 .09
Dave Veres
Jim Edmonds
Rick Ankiel
Edgar Renteria
Darryl Kile CL
427 Danny Graves .30 .09
Ken Griffey Jr.
Sean Casey
Pokey Reese CL
428 Jon Lieber .50 .15
Sammy Sosa
Eric Young CL
429 Curtis Leskanic .50 .15
Geoff Jenkins
Jeff D'Amico
Jeromy Burnitz
Marquis Grissom CL
430 Scott Elarton .30 .09
Jeff Bagwell
Octavio Dotel
Moises Alou
Roger Cedeno CL
431 Mike Williams .50 .15
Jason Kendall
Kris Benson
Brian Giles CL
432 Livan Hernandez .30 .09
Jeff Kent
Robb Nen
Barry Bonds
Marvin Benard CL
433 Luis Gonzalez .30 .09
Steve Finley
Tony Womack
Randy Johnson CL
434 Jeff Shaw .30 .09
Gary Sheffield
Kevin Brown
Shawn Green
Chan Ho Park CL UER
B.Shaw should be J.Shaw
435 Jose Jimenez .30 .09
Todd Helton
Brian Bohanon
Tom Goodwin CL UER
C.Goodwin should be T.Goodwin
436 Trevor Hoffman .30 .09
Phil Nevin
Matt Clement
Eric Owens CL
437 Mariano Rivera .75 .23
Derek Jeter
Roger Clemens
Bernie Williams
Andy Pettitte CL
438 Pedro Martinez .50 .15
Nomar Garciaparra
Derek Lowe
Carl Everett CL
439 Ryan Kohlmeier .30 .09
Delino DeShields
Mike Mussina
Albert Belle CL
440 David Wells .30 .09
Carlos Delgado
Billy Koch
Raul Mondesi CL
441 Ramon Hernandez .30 .09
Fred McGriff
Miguel Cairo
Greg Vaughn CL
442 Mike Sirotka .50 .15
Frank Thomas
Keith Foulke
Ray Durham CL
443 Steve Karsay .30 .09
Manny Ramirez
Bartolo Colon
Roberto Alomar CL
444 Brian Moehler .30 .09
Deivi Cruz
Juan Encarnacion
Todd Jones
Bobby Higginson CL
445 Mac Suzuki .30 .09
Mike Sweeney
Johnny Damon
Jermaine Dye CL
446 Brad Radke .30 .09
Matt Lawton
Eric Milton
Jacque Jones
Cristian Guzman CL
447 Kazuhiro Sasaki .30 .09
Edgar Martinez
Aaron Sele
Rickey Henderson CL
448 Jason Isringhausen .30 .09
Jason Giambi
Tim Hudson
Randy Velarde CL
449 Shigetoshi Hasegawa .30 .09
Darin Erstad
Troy Percival
Troy Glaus CL
450 Rick Helling .30 .09
Rafael Palmeiro
John Wetteland
Luis Alicea CL
451 Albert Pujols RC 30.00 9.00
452 Ichiro Suzuki RC 15.00 4.50
453 Tsuyoshi Shinjo RC .75 .23
454 Johnny Estrada RC 1.25 .35
455 Elpidio Guzman RC .50 .15
456 Adrian Hernandez RC .50 .15
457 Rafael Soriano RC .75 .23
458 Drew Henson RC 1.25 .35
459 Juan Uribe RC .75 .23
460 Matt White RC .50 .15
461 Endy Chavez RC .50 .15
462 Bud Smith RC .50 .15
463 Morgan Ensberg RC 1.25 .35
464 Jay Gibbons RC 1.25 .35
465 Jackson Melian RC .50 .15
466 Junior Spivey RC .75 .23
467 Juan Cruz RC .50 .15
468 Wilson Betemit RC .50 .15
469 Alexis Gomez RC .50 .15
470 Mark Teixeira RC 6.00 1.80
471 Erick Almonte RC .50 .15
472 Travis Hafner RC 2.50 .75
473 Carlos Valderrama RC .50 .15
474 Brandon Duckworth RC .50 .15
475 Ryan Freel RC .50 .15
476 Wilkin Ruan RC .50 .15
477 Andres Torres RC .50 .15
478 Josh Towers RC .50 .15
479 Kyle Lohse RC .75 .23
480 Jason Michaels RC .50 .15
481 Alfonso Soriano .75 .23
482 C.C. Sabathia .50 .15
483 Roy Oswalt .75 .23
484 Ben Sheets UER .75 .23
Wrong team logo on the front
485 Adam Dunn .75 .23
NNO Uncut Sheet EXCH/100 2.00 .60

2001 Fleer Tradition Diamond Tributes

Randomly inserted into packs at one in seven, this 30-card insert is a tribute to some of the most classic players to ever step foot onto a playing field. Card backs carry a "DT" prefix.

	Nm-Mt	Ex-Mt
COMPLETE SET (30)	60.00	18.00
DT1 Jackie Robinson	1.50	.45
DT2 Mike Piazza	2.50	.75
DT3 Alex Rodriguez	2.50	.75
DT4 Barry Bonds	4.00	1.20
DT5 Nomar Garciaparra	2.50	.75
DT6 Roger Clemens	3.00	.90
DT7 Ivan Rodriguez	1.50	.45
DT8 Cal Ripken	5.00	1.50
DT9 Manny Ramirez	1.00	.30
DT10 Chipper Jones	1.50	.45
DT11 Barry Larkin	1.00	.30
DT12 Carlos Delgado	1.00	.30
DT13 J.D. Drew	1.00	.30
DT14 Carl Everett	1.00	.30
DT15 Todd Helton	1.00	.30
DT16 Greg Maddux	2.50	.75
DT17 Scott Rolen	1.50	.45
DT18 Troy Glaus	1.00	.30
DT19 Brian Giles	1.00	.30
DT20 Jeff Bagwell	1.00	.30
DT21 Sammy Sosa	2.50	.75
DT22 Randy Johnson	1.50	.45
DT23 Andruw Jones	1.00	.30
DT24 Ken Griffey Jr.	2.50	.75
DT25 Mark McGwire	4.00	1.20
DT26 Derek Jeter	4.00	1.20
DT27 Vladimir Guerrero	1.50	.45
DT28 Frank Thomas	1.50	.45
DT29 Pedro Martinez	1.50	.45
DT30 Bernie Williams	1.00	.30

2001 Fleer Tradition Grass Roots

Inserted at a rate of one every 18 packs, this 15 card set describes some of the early moments of these star players careers.

	Nm-Mt	Ex-Mt
COMPLETE SET (15)	60.00	18.00
GR1 Derek Jeter	6.00	1.80
GR2 Greg Maddux	4.00	1.20
GR3 Sammy Sosa	4.00	1.20
GR4 Alex Rodriguez	4.00	1.20
GR5 Vladimir Guerrero	2.50	.75
GR6 Scott Rolen	2.50	.75
GR7 Frank Thomas	2.50	.75
GR8 Nomar Garciaparra	4.00	1.20
GR9 Cal Ripken	8.00	2.40
GR10 Mike Piazza	4.00	1.20
GR11 Ivan Rodriguez	2.50	.75
GR12 Chipper Jones	2.50	.75
GR13 Tony Gwynn	3.00	.90
GR14 Ken Griffey Jr.	4.00	1.20
GR15 Mark McGwire	6.00	1.80

2001 Fleer Tradition Lumber Company

Randomly inserted into packs at one in 12, this 20-card insert set features players that are capable of breaking the game wide open with one swing of the bat. Card backs carry a "LC" prefix.

	Nm-Mt	Ex-Mt
COMPLETE SET (20)	50.00	15.00
LC1 Vladimir Guerrero	2.00	.60
LC2 Mo Vaughn	1.00	.30
LC3 Ken Griffey Jr.	3.00	.90
LC4 Juan Gonzalez	1.25	.35
LC5 Tony Gwynn	2.50	.75
LC6 Jim Edmonds	1.00	.30
LC7 Jason Giambi	1.00	.30
LC8 Alex Rodriguez	3.00	.90
LC9 Derek Jeter	5.00	1.50
LC10 Darin Erstad	1.00	.30
LC11 Andruw Jones	1.00	.30
LC12 Cal Ripken	6.00	1.80
LC13 Magglio Ordonez	1.00	.30
LC14 Nomar Garciaparra	3.00	.90
LC15 Chipper Jones	2.00	.60
LC16 Sean Casey	1.00	.30
LC17 Shawn Green	1.00	.30
LC18 Mike Piazza	3.00	.90
LC19 Sammy Sosa	3.00	.90
LC20 Barry Bonds	5.00	1.50

2001 Fleer Tradition Stitches in Time

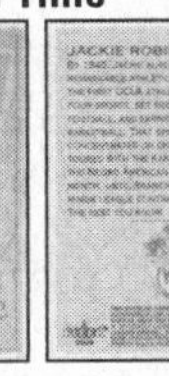

Randomly inserted into packs at one in 18, this 24-card insert features Negro League greats like Josh Gibson and Satchel Paige. Card backs carry a "ST" prefix. Please note that cards ST1 and ST3 do not exist, and the card of Henry Kimbro is unnumbered.

	Nm-Mt	Ex-Mt
COMPLETE SET (24)	100.00	30.00
ST1 Does Not Exist		
ST2 Ernie Banks	5.00	1.50
ST3 Does Not Exist		
ST4 Joe Black	3.00	.90
ST5 Roy Campanella	6.00	1.80
ST6 Ray Dandridge	3.00	.90
ST7 Leon Day	3.00	.90
ST8 Larry Doby	3.00	.90
ST9 Josh Gibson	5.00	1.50
ST10 Elston Howard	3.00	.90
ST11 Monte Irvin	3.00	.90
ST12 Buck Leonard	3.00	.90
ST13 Max Manning	3.00	.90
ST14 Willie Mays	10.00	3.00
ST15 Buck O'Neil	3.00	.90
ST16 Satchel Paige	5.00	1.50
ST17 Ted Radcliffe	3.00	.90
ST18 Jackie Robinson	5.00	1.50
ST19 Bill Perkins	3.00	.90
ST20 Rube Foster	5.00	1.50
ST21 Judy Johnson	3.00	.90
ST22 Oscar Charleston	3.00	.90
ST23 Pop Lloyd	3.00	.90
ST24 Artie Wilson	3.00	.90
ST25 Sam Jethroe	3.00	.90
NNO Henry Kimbro	3.00	.90

2001 Fleer Tradition Stitches in Time Autographs

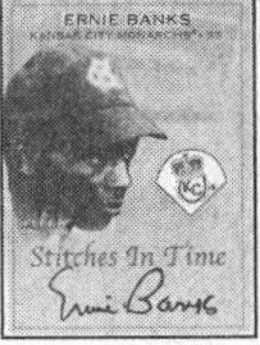
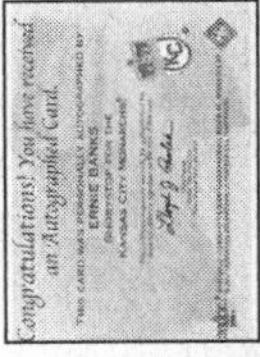

Randomly inserted at one in four boxes, this seven-card insert set features authentic autographs from players like Willie Mays and Ernie Banks. Please note that these cards are not numbered and are listed below in alphabetical order. Also note that Willie Mays and Artie Wilson packed out as exchange cards with a redemption deadline of 02/01/02.

	Nm-Mt	Ex-Mt
1 Ernie Banks	60.00	18.00
2 Joe Black	30.00	9.00
3 Monte Irvin	40.00	12.00
4 Willie Mays	200.00	60.00
5 Buck O'Neil	40.00	12.00
6 Ted Radcliffe	30.00	9.00
7 Artie Wilson	30.00	9.00

2001 Fleer Tradition Stitches in Time Memorabilia

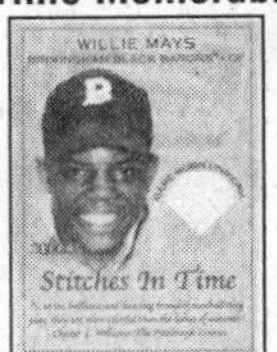

Randomly inserted at one in four boxes, this five-card insert set features actual swatches from game-used Bats or Pants from players like Willie Mays and Jackie Robinson. Please note that these cards are not numbered and are listed below in alphabetical order.

	Nm-Mt	Ex-Mt
1 Roy Campanella Bat	80.00	24.00
2 Larry Doby Bat	40.00	12.00
3 Elston Howard Bat	50.00	15.00
4 Willie Mays Pants	200.00	60.00
5 Jackie Robinson Pants	150.00	45.00

2001 Fleer Tradition Turn Back the Clock

Randomly inserted at one in four boxes, this 21-card insert set features swatches from actual game-used jerseys from players like Cal Ripken and Chipper Jones. Card backs carry a "TBC" prefix.

	Nm-Mt	Ex-Mt
TBC1 Tom Glavine	15.00	4.50
TBC2 Greg Maddux	40.00	12.00
TBC3 Sean Casey	10.00	3.00
TBC4 Pokey Reese	10.00	3.00
TBC5 Jason Giambi	10.00	3.00
TBC6 Tim Hudson	10.00	3.00
TBC7 Larry Walker	15.00	4.50
TBC8 Jeffrey Hammonds	10.00	3.00
TBC9 Scott Rolen	15.00	4.50
TBC10 Pat Burrell	10.00	3.00
TBC11 Chipper Jones	15.00	4.50
TBC12 Greg Maddux	40.00	12.00
TBC13 Troy Glaus	10.00	3.00
TBC14 Tony Gwynn	25.00	7.50
TBC15 Cal Ripken	60.00	18.00
TBC16 Tom Glavine Greg Maddux	80.00	24.00
TBC17 Sean Casey Pokey Reese	40.00	12.00
TBC18 Chipper Jones Greg Maddux	100.00	30.00
TBC19 Larry Walker Jeffrey Hammonds	40.00	12.00
TBC20 Scott Rolen Pat Burrell	50.00	15.00
TBC21 Jason Giambi Tim Hudson	40.00	12.00

2001 Fleer Tradition Warning Track

Randomly inserted into packs at one in 72, this 23-card insert takes a look at how today's power hitters stack up to yesterdays greats. Card backs carry a "WT" prefix. Please note, cards 2 and 5 (originally intended for Hank Aaron and Ernie Banks) were never produced, thus though numbered 1-25, the set is complete at 23 cards.

	Nm-Mt	Ex-Mt
COMPLETE SET (23)	250.00	75.00
WT1 Josh Gibson	10.00	3.00
WT2 Does Not Exist		
WT3 Willie Mays	15.00	4.50
WT4 Mark McGwire	20.00	6.00
WT5 Does Not Exist		
WT6 Barry Bonds	20.00	6.00
WT7 Jose Canseco	8.00	2.40
WT8 Ken Griffey Jr.	12.00	3.60
WT9 Cal Ripken	25.00	7.50
WT10 Rafael Palmeiro	5.00	1.50
WT11 Sammy Sosa	12.00	3.60
WT12 Juan Gonzalez	5.00	1.50
WT13 Frank Thomas	8.00	2.40
WT14 Jeff Bagwell	5.00	1.50
WT15 Gary Sheffield	5.00	1.50
WT16 Larry Walker	5.00	1.50
WT17 Mike Piazza	12.00	3.60
WT18 Larry Doby	5.00	1.50
WT19 Roy Campanella	10.00	3.00
WT20 Manny Ramirez	5.00	1.50
WT21 Chipper Jones	8.00	2.40
WT22 Alex Rodriguez	12.00	3.60
WT23 Ivan Rodriguez	8.00	2.40
WT24 Vladimir Guerrero	8.00	2.40
WT25 Nomar Garciaparra	12.00	3.60

2002 Fleer Tradition

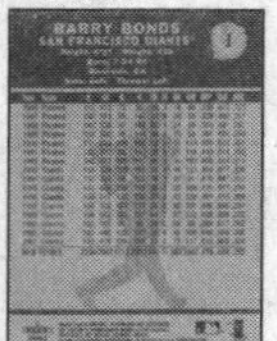

This 500 card set was issued early in 2002. This set was issued in 10 card packs and 36 packs to a box with a SRP of $1.49 per pack. The first 100 cards in this set were issued at an overall rate of one in two. In addition, cards numbered 436 through 470 featured leading prospects and cards numbered 471 through 500 featured players who had noteworthy seasons in 2001. These cards feature the 1934 Goudey-style design.

	Nm-Mt	Ex-Mt
COMPLETE SET (500)	200.00	60.00
COMP.SET w/o SP's (400)	50.00	15.00
COMMON CARD (101-500)	.30	.09
COMMON SP (1-100)	3.00	.90
COMMON CARD (436-470)	.50	.15
1 Barry Bonds SP	12.00	3.60
2 Cal Ripken SP	15.00	4.50
3 Tony Gwynn SP	6.00	1.80
4 Brad Radke SP	3.00	.90
5 Jose Ortiz SP	3.00	.90
6 Mark Mulder SP	3.00	.90
7 Jon Lieber SP	3.00	.90
8 John Olerud SP	3.00	.90
9 Phil Nevin SP	3.00	.90
10 Craig Biggio SP	3.00	.90
11 Pedro Martinez SP	5.00	1.50
12 Fred McGriff SP	3.00	.90
13 Vladimir Guerrero SP	5.00	1.50
14 Jason Giambi SP	3.00	.90
15 Mark Kotsay SP	3.00	.90
16 Bud Smith SP	3.00	.90
17 Kevin Brown SP	3.00	.90
18 Darin Erstad SP	3.00	.90
19 Julio Franco SP	3.00	.90
20 C.C. Sabathia SP	3.00	.90
21 Larry Walker SP	3.00	.90
22 Doug Mientkiewicz SP	3.00	.90
23 Luis Gonzalez SP	3.00	.90
24 Albert Pujols SP	10.00	3.00
25 Brian Lawrence SP	3.00	.90
26 Al Leiter SP	3.00	.90
27 Mike Sweeney SP	3.00	.90
28 Jeff Weaver SP	3.00	.90
29 Matt Morris SP	3.00	.90
30 Hideo Nomo SP	5.00	1.50
31 Tom Glavine SP	3.00	.90
32 Magglio Ordonez SP	3.00	.90
33 Roberto Alomar SP	3.00	.90
34 Roger Cedeno SP	3.00	.90
35 Greg Vaughn SP	3.00	.90
36 Chan Ho Park SP	3.00	.90
37 Rich Aurilia SP	3.00	.90
38 Tsuyoshi Shinjo SP	3.00	.90
39 Eric Young SP	3.00	.90
40 Bobby Higginson SP	3.00	.90
41 Marlon Anderson SP	3.00	.90
42 Mark Grace SP	3.00	.90
43 Steve Cox SP	3.00	.90
44 Cliff Floyd SP	3.00	.90
45 Brian Roberts SP	3.00	.90
46 Paul Konerko SP	3.00	.90
47 Brandon Duckworth SP	3.00	.90
48 Josh Beckett SP	3.00	.90
49 David Ortiz SP	3.00	.90
50 Geoff Jenkins SP	3.00	.90
51 Ruben Sierra SP	3.00	.90
52 John Franco SP	3.00	.90
53 Einar Diaz SP	3.00	.90
54 Luis Castillo SP	3.00	.90
55 Mark Quinn SP	3.00	.90
56 Shea Hillenbrand SP	3.00	.90
57 Rafael Palmeiro SP	3.00	.90
58 Paul O'Neill SP	3.00	.90
59 Andruw Jones SP	3.00	.90
60 Lance Berkman SP	3.00	.90
61 Jimmy Rollins SP	3.00	.90
62 Jose Hernandez SP	3.00	.90
63 Rusty Greer SP	3.00	.90
64 Wade Miller SP	3.00	.90
65 David Eckstein SP	3.00	.90
66 Jose Valentin SP	3.00	.90
67 Javier Vazquez SP	3.00	.90
68 Roger Clemens SP	10.00	3.00
69 Omar Vizquel SP	3.00	.90
70 Roy Oswalt SP	3.00	.90
71 Shannon Stewart SP	3.00	.90
72 Byung-Hyun Kim SP	3.00	.90
73 Jay Gibbons SP	3.00	.90
74 Barry Larkin SP	3.00	.90
75 Brian Giles SP	3.00	.90
76 Andres Galarraga SP	3.00	.90
77 Sammy Sosa SP	8.00	2.40
78 Manny Ramirez SP	3.00	.90
79 Carlos Delgado SP	3.00	.90
80 Jorge Posada SP	3.00	.90
81 Todd Ritchie SP	3.00	.90
82 Russ Ortiz SP	3.00	.90
83 Brent Mayne SP	3.00	.90
84 Mike Mussina SP	3.00	.90
85 Raul Mondesi SP	3.00	.90
86 Mark Loretta SP	3.00	.90
87 Tim Raines SP	3.00	.90
88 Ichiro Suzuki SP	8.00	2.40
89 Juan Pierre SP	3.00	.90
90 Adam Dunn SP	3.00	.90
91 Jason Tyner SP	3.00	.90
92 Miguel Tejada SP	3.00	.90
93 Elpidio Guzman SP	3.00	.90
94 Freddy Garcia SP	3.00	.90
95 Marcus Giles SP	3.00	.90
96 Junior Spivey SP	3.00	.90
97 Aramis Ramirez SP	3.00	.90
98 Jose Rijo SP	3.00	.90
99 Paul LoDuca SP	3.00	.90
100 Mike Cameron SP	3.00	.90
101 Alex Hernandez	.30	.09
102 Benji Gil	.30	.09
103 Benito Santiago	.30	.09
104 Bobby Abreu	.30	.09
105 Brad Penny	.30	.09
106 Calvin Murray	.30	.09
107 Chad Durbin	.30	.09
108 Chris Singleton	.30	.09
109 Chris Carpenter	.30	.09
110 David Justice	.30	.09
111 Eric Chavez	.30	.09
112 Fernando Tatis	.30	.09
113 Frank Castillo	.30	.09
114 Jason LaRue	.30	.09
115 Jim Edmonds	.30	.09
116 Joe Kennedy	.30	.09
117 Jose Jimenez	.30	.09
118 Josh Towers	.30	.09
119 Junior Herndon	.30	.09
120 Luke Prokopec	.30	.09
121 Mac Suzuki	.30	.09
122 Mark DeRosa	.30	.09
123 Marty Cordova	.30	.09
124 Michael Tucker	.30	.09
125 Michael Young	.75	.23
126 Robin Ventura	.30	.09
127 Shane Halter	.30	.09
128 Shane Reynolds	.30	.09
129 Tony Womack	.30	.09
130 A.J. Pierzynski	.30	.09
131 Aaron Rowand	.30	.09
132 Antonio Alfonseca	.30	.09
133 Arthur Rhodes	.30	.09
134 Bob Wickman	.30	.09
135 Brady Clark	.30	.09
136 Chad Hermansen	.30	.09
137 Marlon Byrd	.30	.09
138 Dan Wilson	.30	.09
139 David Cone	.30	.09
140 Dean Palmer	.30	.09
141 Denny Neagle	.30	.09
142 Derek Jeter	2.00	.60
143 Erubiel Durazo	.30	.09
144 Felix Rodriguez	.30	.09
145 Jason Hart	.30	.09
146 Jay Bell	.30	.09
147 Jeff Suppan	.30	.09
148 Jeff Zimmerman	.30	.09
149 Kerry Wood	.75	.23
150 Kerry Robinson	.30	.09
151 Kevin Appier	.30	.09
152 Michael Barrett	.30	.09
153 Mo Vaughn	.30	.09
154 Rafael Furcal	.30	.09
155 Sidney Ponson	.30	.09
156 Terry Adams	.30	.09
157 Tim Redding	.30	.09
158 Toby Hall	.30	.09
159 Aaron Sele	.30	.09
160 Bartolo Colon	.30	.09
161 Brad Ausmus	.30	.09
162 Carlos Pena	.30	.09
163 Jace Brewer	.30	.09
164 David Wells	.30	.09
165 David Segui	.30	.09
166 Derek Lowe	.30	.09
167 Derek Bell	.30	.09
168 Jason Grabowski	.30	.09
169 Johnny Damon	.50	.15
170 Jose Mesa	.30	.09
171 Juan Encarnacion	.30	.09
172 Ken Caminiti	.30	.09
173 Ken Griffey Jr.	1.25	.35
174 Luis Rivas	.30	.09
175 Mariano Rivera	.50	.15
176 Mark Grudzielanek	.30	.09
177 Mark McGwire	2.00	.60
178 Mike Bordick	.30	.09
179 Mike Hampton	.30	.09
180 Nick Bierbrodt	.30	.09
181 Paul Byrd	.30	.09
182 Robb Nen	.30	.09
183 Ryan Dempster	.30	.09
184 Ryan Klesko	.30	.09
185 Scott Spiezio	.30	.09
186 Scott Strickland	.30	.09
187 Todd Zeile	.30	.09
188 Tom Gordon	.30	.09
189 Troy Glaus	.30	.09
190 Matt Williams	.30	.09
191 Wes Helms	.30	.09
192 Jerry Hairston Jr.	.30	.09
193 Brook Fordyce	.30	.09
194 Nomar Garciaparra	1.25	.35
195 Kevin Tapani	.30	.09
196 Mark Buehrle	.30	.09
197 Dmitri Young	.30	.09
198 John Rocker	.30	.09
199 Juan Uribe	.30	.09
200 Matt Anderson	.30	.09
201 Alex Gonzalez	.30	.09
202 Julio Lugo	.30	.09
203 Roberto Hernandez	.30	.09
204 Richie Sexson	.30	.09
205 Corey Koskie	.30	.09
206 Tony Armas Jr.	.30	.09
207 Rey Ordonez	.30	.09
208 Orlando Hernandez	.30	.09
209 Pokey Reese	.30	.09
210 Mike Lieberthal	.30	.09
211 Kris Benson	.30	.09
212 Jermaine Dye	.30	.09
213 Livan Hernandez	.30	.09
214 Bret Boone	.30	.09
215 Dustin Hermanson	.30	.09
216 Placido Polanco	.30	.09
217 Jesus Colome	.30	.09
218 Alex Gonzalez	.30	.09
219 Adam Everett	.30	.09
220 Adam Piatt	.30	.09
221 Brad Fullmer	.30	.09
222 Brian Buchanan	.30	.09
223 Chipper Jones	.75	.23
224 Chuck Finley	.30	.09
225 David Bell	.30	.09
226 Jack Wilson	.30	.09
227 Jason Bere	.30	.09
228 Jeff Conine	.30	.09
229 Jeff Bagwell	.50	.15
230 Joe McEwing	.30	.09
231 Kip Wells	.30	.09
232 Mike Lansing	.30	.09
233 Neifi Perez	.30	.09
234 Omar Daal	.30	.09
235 Reggie Sanders	.30	.09
236 Shawn Wooten	.30	.09
237 Shawn Chacon	.30	.09
238 Shawn Estes	.30	.09
239 Steve Sparks	.30	.09
240 Steve Kline	.30	.09
241 Tino Martinez	.50	.15
242 Tyler Houston	.30	.09
243 Xavier Nady	.30	.09
244 Bengie Molina	.30	.09
245 Ben Davis	.30	.09
246 Casey Fossum	.30	.09
247 Chris Stynes	.30	.09
248 Danny Graves	.30	.09
249 Pedro Feliz	.30	.09
250 Darren Oliver	.30	.09
251 Dave Veres	.30	.09
252 Deivi Cruz	.30	.09
253 Desi Relaford	.30	.09
254 Devon White	.30	.09
255 Edgar Martinez	.50	.15
256 Eric Munson	.30	.09
257 Eric Karros	.30	.09
258 Homer Bush	.30	.09
259 Jason Kendall	.30	.09
260 Javy Lopez	.30	.09
261 Keith Foulke	.30	.09
262 Keith Ginter	.30	.09
263 Nick Johnson	.30	.09
264 Pat Burrell	.30	.09
265 Ricky Gutierrez	.30	.09
266 Russ Johnson	.30	.09
267 Steve Finley	.30	.09
268 Terrence Long	.30	.09
269 Tony Batista	.30	.09
270 Torii Hunter	.30	.09
271 Vinny Castilla	.30	.09
272 A.J. Burnett	.30	.09
273 Adrian Beltre	.50	.15
274 Alex Rodriguez	1.25	.35
275 Armando Benitez	.30	.09
276 Billy Koch	.30	.09
277 Brady Anderson	.30	.09
278 Brian Jordan	.30	.09
279 Carlos Febles	.30	.09
280 Daryle Ward	.30	.09
281 Eli Marrero	.30	.09
282 Garret Anderson	.30	.09
283 Jack Cust	.30	.09
284 Jacque Jones	.30	.09
285 Jamie Moyer	.30	.09
286 Jeffrey Hammonds	.30	.09
287 Jim Thome	.75	.23
288 Jon Garland	.30	.09
289 Jose Offerman	.30	.09
290 Matt Stairs	.30	.09
291 Orlando Cabrera	.30	.09
292 Ramiro Mendoza	.30	.09
293 Ray Durham	.30	.09
294 Rickey Henderson	.75	.23
295 Rob Mackowiak	.30	.09
296 Scott Rolen	.75	.23
297 Tim Hudson	.30	.09
298 Todd Helton	.50	.15
299 Tony Clark	.30	.09
300 B.J. Surhoff	.30	.09
301 Bernie Williams	.50	.15
302 Bill Mueller	.30	.09
303 Chris Richard	.30	.09
304 Craig Paquette	.30	.09
305 Curt Schilling	.30	.09
306 Damian Jackson	.30	.09
307 Derrek Lee	.30	.09
308 Eric Milton	.30	.09
309 Frank Catalanotto	.30	.09
310 J.T. Snow	.30	.09
311 Jared Sandberg	.30	.09
312 Jason Varitek	.50	.15
313 Jeff Cirillo	.30	.09
314 Jeromy Burnitz	.30	.09
315 Joe Crede	.30	.09
316 Joel Pineiro	.30	.09
317 Jose Cruz Jr.	.30	.09
318 Kevin Young	.30	.09
319 Marquis Grissom	.30	.09
320 Moises Alou	.30	.09
321 Randall Simon	.30	.09
322 Royce Clayton	.30	.09
323 Tim Salmon	.50	.15
324 Travis Fryman	.30	.09
325 Travis Lee	.30	.09
326 Vance Wilson	.30	.09
327 Jarrod Washburn	.30	.09
328 Ben Petrick	.30	.09
329 Ben Grieve	.30	.09
330 Carl Everett	.30	.09
331 Eric Byrnes	.30	.09
332 Doug Glanville	.30	.09
333 Edgardo Alfonzo	.30	.09
334 Ellis Burks	.30	.09
335 Gabe Kapler	.30	.09
336 Gary Sheffield	.30	.09
337 Greg Maddux	1.25	.35
338 J.D. Drew	.30	.09
339 Jamey Wright	.30	.09
340 Jeff Kent	.30	.09
341 Jeremy Giambi	.30	.09
342 Joe Randa	.30	.09
343 Joe Mays	.30	.09
344 Jose Macias	.30	.09
345 Kazuhiro Sasaki	.30	.09
346 Mike Kinkade	.30	.09
347 Mike Lowell	.30	.09
348 Randy Johnson	.75	.23
349 Randy Wolf	.30	.09
350 Richard Hidalgo	.30	.09
351 Ron Coomer	.30	.09
352 Sandy Alomar Jr.	.30	.09
353 Sean Casey	.30	.09
354 Trevor Hoffman	.30	.09
355 Adam Eaton	.30	.09
356 Alfonso Soriano	.50	.15
357 Barry Zito	.50	.15
358 Billy Wagner	.30	.09
359 Brent Abernathy	.30	.09
360 Bret Prinz	.30	.09
361 Carlos Beltran	.50	.15
362 Carlos Guillen	.30	.09
363 Charles Johnson	.30	.09
364 Cristian Guzman	.30	.09
365 Damion Easley	.30	.09
366 Darryl Kile	.30	.09
367 Delino DeShields	.30	.09
368 Eric Davis	.30	.09
369 Frank Thomas	.75	.23
370 Ivan Rodriguez	.75	.23
371 Jay Payton	.30	.09
372 Jeff D'Amico	.30	.09
373 John Burkett	.30	.09
374 Melvin Mora	.30	.09
375 Ramon Ortiz	.30	.09
376 Robert Person	.30	.09
377 Russell Branyan	.30	.09
378 Shawn Green	.30	.09
379 Todd Hollandsworth	.30	.09
380 Tony McKnight	.30	.09
381 Trot Nixon	.30	.09
382 Vernon Wells	.30	.09
383 Troy Percival	.30	.09
384 Albie Lopez	.30	.09
385 Alex Ochoa	.30	.09
386 Andy Pettitte	.50	.15
387 Brandon Inge	.30	.09
388 Bubba Trammell	.30	.09
389 Corey Patterson	.30	.09
390 Damian Rolls	.30	.09
391 Dee Brown	.30	.09
392 Edgar Renteria	.30	.09
393 Eric Gagne	.75	.23
394 Jason Johnson	.30	.09
395 Jeff Nelson	.30	.09
396 John Vander Wal	.30	.09
397 Johnny Estrada	.30	.09
398 Jose Canseco	.75	.23
399 Juan Gonzalez	.50	.15
400 Kevin Millwood	.30	.09
401 Lee Stevens	.30	.09
402 Matt Lawton	.30	.09
403 Mike Lamb	.30	.09
404 Octavio Dotel	.30	.09
405 Ramon Hernandez	.30	.09
406 Ruben Quevedo	.30	.09
407 Todd Walker	.30	.09
408 Troy O'Leary	.30	.09
409 Wascar Serrano	.30	.09
410 Aaron Boone	.30	.09
411 Aubrey Huff	.30	.09
412 Ben Sheets	.30	.09
413 Carlos Lee	.30	.09
414 Chuck Knoblauch	.30	.09
415 Steve Karsay	.30	.09
416 Dante Bichette	.30	.09
417 David Dellucci	.30	.09
418 Esteban Loaiza	.30	.09
419 Fernando Vina	.30	.09
420 Ismael Valdes	.30	.09
421 Jason Isringhausen	.30	.09
422 Jeff Shaw	.30	.09
423 John Smoltz	.50	.15
424 Jose Vidro	.30	.09
425 Kenny Lofton	.30	.09
426 Mark Little	.30	.09
427 Mark McLemore	.30	.09
428 Marvin Benard	.30	.09
429 Mike Piazza	1.25	.35
430 Pat Hentgen	.30	.09
431 Preston Wilson	.30	.09
432 Rick Helling	.30	.09
433 Robert Fick	.30	.09
434 Rondell White	.30	.09
435 Adam Kennedy	.30	.09
436 David Espinosa PROS	.50	.15
437 Dewon Brazelton PROS	.50	.15
438 Drew Henson PROS	.50	.15
439 Juan Cruz PROS	.50	.15
440 Jason Jennings PROS	.50	.15
441 Carlos Garcia PROS	.50	.15
442 Carlos Hernandez PROS	.50	.15
443 Wilkin Ruan PROS	.50	.15
444 Wilson Betemit PROS	.50	.15
445 Horacio Ramirez PROS	.50	.15
446 Danys Baez PROS	.50	.15
447 Abraham Nunez PROS	.50	.15
448 Josh Hamilton PROS	.50	.15
449 Chris George PROS	.50	.15
450 Rick Bauer PROS	.50	.15
451 Donnie Bridges PROS	.50	.15
452 Erick Almonte PROS	.50	.15
453 Cory Aldridge PROS	.50	.15
454 Ryan Drese PROS	.50	.15
455 Jason Romano PROS	.50	.15
456 Corky Miller PROS	.50	.15
457 Rafael Soriano PROS	.50	.15
458 Mark Prior PROS	2.00	.60
459 Mark Teixeira PROS	.75	.23
460 Adrian Hernandez PROS	.50	.15
461 Tim Spooneybarger PROS	.50	.15
462 Bill Ortega PROS	.50	.15
463 D'Angelo Jimenez PROS	.50	.15
464 Andres Torres PROS	.50	.15
465 Alexis Gomez PROS	.50	.15
466 Angel Berroa PROS	.50	.15
467 Henry Mateo PROS	.50	.15
468 Endy Chavez PROS	.50	.15
469 Billy Sylvester PROS	.50	.15
470 Nate Frese PROS	.50	.15
471 Luis Gonzalez BNR	.30	.09
472 Barry Bonds BNR	2.00	.60
473 Rich Aurilia BNR	.30	.09
474 Albert Pujols BNR	1.50	.45
475 Todd Helton BNR	.50	.15
476 Moises Alou BNR	.30	.09
477 Lance Berkman BNR	.30	.09
478 Brian Giles BNR	.30	.09
479 Cliff Floyd BNR	.30	.09
480 Sammy Sosa BNR	1.25	.35
481 Shawn Green BNR	.30	.09
482 Jon Lieber BNR	.30	.09
483 Matt Morris BNR	.30	.09
484 Curt Schilling BNR	.30	.09
485 Randy Johnson BNR	.50	.15
486 Manny Ramirez BNR	.30	.09
487 Ichiro Suzuki BNR	1.25	.35
488 Juan Gonzalez BNR	.50	.15
489 Derek Jeter BNR	2.00	.60
490 Alex Rodriguez BNR	1.25	.35
491 Bret Boone BNR	.30	.09
492 Roberto Alomar BNR	.50	.15
493 Jason Giambi BNR	.50	.15
494 Rafael Palmeiro BNR	.50	.15
495 Doug Mientkiewicz BNR	.30	.09
496 Jim Thome BNR	.50	.15
497 Freddy Garcia BNR	.30	.09
498 Mark Buehrle BNR	.30	.09
499 Mark Mulder BNR	.30	.09
500 Roger Clemens BNR	1.50	.45

2002 Fleer Tradition Glossy

Randomly inserted into Fleer Tradition Update packs, this is a parallel of the basic Fleer Tradition set. These cards can be differentiated from the regular Fleer cards by their "glossy" sheen and have a stated print run of 200 serial numbered sets.

Nm-Mt Ex-Mt

*GLOSSY 1-100: .5X TO 1.2X BASIC
*GLOSSY 101-435/471-500: 3X TO 8X BASIC
*GLOSSY 436-470: 2X TO 5X BASIC

2002 Fleer Tradition Diamond Tributes

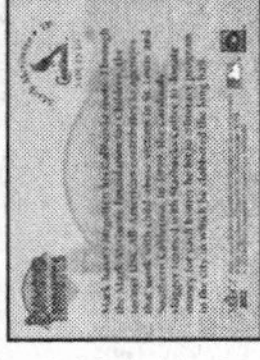

nserted into hobby packs at stated odds of one n six and retail packs at stated odds of one in 10, these 15 cards feature players who have per- formed on the field of play but have also had a positive impact on the community.

	Nm-Mt	Ex-Mt
COMPLETE SET (15)	20.00	6.00
1 Cal Ripken	4.00	1.20
2 Tony Gwynn	1.50	.45
3 Derek Jeter	3.00	.90
4 Pedro Martinez	1.25	.35
5 Mark McGwire	3.00	.90
6 Sammy Sosa	2.00	.60
7 Barry Bonds	3.00	.90
8 Roger Clemens	2.50	.75
9 Mike Piazza	2.00	.60
10 Alex Rodriguez	2.00	.60
11 Randy Johnson	1.25	.35
12 Chipper Jones	1.25	.35
13 Nomar Garciaparra	2.00	.60
14 Ichiro Suzuki	2.00	.60
15 Jason Giambi	1.25	.35

2002 Fleer Tradition Grass Patch

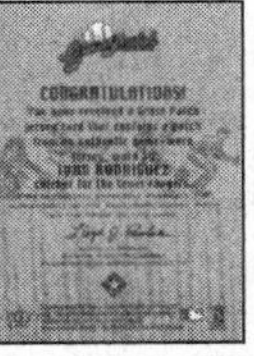

This 10 card set is a parallel to the Grass Roots insert set. Each card in this set features not only the defensive whiz pictured but also a special game-worn jersey swatch. According to repre- sentatives at Fleer, each cards has a stated print run of 50 copies (though the cards lack any form of serial-numbering).

	Nm-Mt	Ex-Mt
1 Jeff Bagwell	40.00	12.00
2 Barry Bonds	80.00	24.00
3 Derek Jeter		
4 Greg Maddux	60.00	18.00
5 Cal Ripken	150.00	45.00
6 Alex Rodriguez	60.00	18.00
7 Ivan Rodriguez	50.00	15.00
8 Scott Rolen	50.00	15.00
9 Larry Walker	40.00	12.00
10 Bernie Williams	40.00	12.00

2002 Fleer Tradition Grass Roots

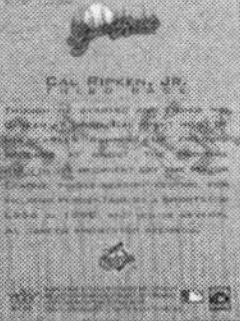

Inserted into hobby packs at stated odds of one in 18 and retail packs at stated odds of one in 20, these 10 cards feature leading defensive players.

	Nm-Mt	Ex-Mt
COMPLETE SET (10)	30.00	9.00
1 Barry Bonds	6.00	1.80
2 Alex Rodriguez	4.00	1.20
3 Derek Jeter	6.00	1.80
4 Greg Maddux	4.00	1.20
5 Ivan Rodriguez	2.50	.75
6 Cal Ripken	8.00	2.40
7 Bernie Williams	1.50	.45
8 Jeff Bagwell	1.50	.45
9 Scott Rolen	2.50	.75
10 Larry Walker	1.50	.45

2002 Fleer Tradition Heads Up

Inserted into hobby packs at stated odds of one in 36 and retail packs at stated odds of one in 40, these 10 cards feature leading players as they would look as bobbleheads.

	Nm-Mt	Ex-Mt
COMPLETE SET (10)	80.00	24.00
1 Derek Jeter	10.00	3.00
2 Ichiro Suzuki	6.00	1.80
3 Sammy Sosa	6.00	1.80
4 Mike Piazza	6.00	1.80
5 Ken Griffey Jr.	6.00	1.80
6 Alex Rodriguez	6.00	1.80
7 Barry Bonds	10.00	3.00
8 Nomar Garciaparra	6.00	1.80
9 Mark McGwire	10.00	3.00
10 Cal Ripken	12.00	3.60

2002 Fleer Tradition Lumber Company

Inserted into packs at stated odds of one in 12 hobby and one in 20 retail, these 30 cards fea- ture superstars who can hit the ball with above average skills.

	Nm-Mt	Ex-Mt
COMPLETE SET (30)	60.00	18.00
1 Moises Alou	1.50	.45
2 Luis Gonzalez	1.50	.45
3 Todd Helton	1.50	.45
4 Mike Piazza	4.00	1.20
5 J.D. Drew	1.50	.45
6 Albert Pujols	5.00	1.50
7 Chipper Jones	2.50	.75
8 Manny Ramirez	1.50	.45
9 Miguel Tejada	1.50	.45
10 Curt Schilling	1.50	.45
11 Alex Rodriguez	4.00	1.20
12 Barry Larkin	1.50	.45
13 Nomar Garciaparra	4.00	1.20
14 Cliff Floyd	1.50	.45
15 Alfonso Soriano	1.50	.45
16 Sean Casey	1.50	.45
17 Scott Rolen	2.50	.75
18 Jose Ortiz	1.50	.45
19 Corey Patterson	1.50	.45
20 Joe Crede	1.50	.45
21 Jace Brewer	1.50	.45
22 Derek Jeter	6.00	1.80
23 Jim Thome	2.50	.75
24 Frank Thomas	2.50	.75
25 Shawn Green	1.50	.45
26 Drew Henson	1.50	.45
27 Jimmy Rollins	1.50	.45
28 David Justice	1.50	.45
29 Roberto Alomar	1.50	.45
30 Bernie Williams	1.50	.45

2002 Fleer Tradition Lumber Company Game Bat

This parallel to the Lumber Company insert set was inserted in packs at a rate of one in 72 packs. These cards feature not only the player pictured but a bat piece swatch related to that player. Jace Brewer, Sean Casey, Joe Crede, Derek Jeter, Corey Patterson and Scott Rolen were all short-prints according to representa- tives at Fleer.

	Nm-Mt	Ex-Mt
1 Roberto Alomar	15.00	4.50
2 Moises Alou	10.00	3.00
3 Jace Brewer SP/250	10.00	3.00
4 Sean Casey SP/250	10.00	3.00
5 Joe Crede SP/250	10.00	3.00
6 J.D. Drew	10.00	3.00
7 Cliff Floyd	10.00	3.00
8 Nomar Garciaparra	20.00	6.00
9 Luis Gonzalez	10.00	3.00
10 Shawn Green	10.00	3.00
11 Todd Helton	15.00	4.50
12 Drew Henson	10.00	3.00
13 Derek Jeter SP/250	40.00	12.00
14 Chipper Jones	15.00	4.50
15 David Justice	10.00	3.00
16 Barry Larkin	15.00	4.50
17 Jose Ortiz SP/250	10.00	3.00
18 Corey Patterson SP/250	10.00	3.00
19 Mike Piazza	15.00	4.50
20 Albert Pujols	25.00	7.50
21 Manny Ramirez	15.00	4.50
22 Alex Rodriguez	20.00	6.00
23 Scott Rolen SP/250	15.00	4.50
24 Jimmy Rollins	10.00	3.00
25 Curt Schilling	10.00	3.00
26 Alfonso Soriano	15.00	4.50
27 Miguel Tejada	10.00	3.00
28 Frank Thomas	15.00	4.50
29 Jim Thome	15.00	4.50
30 Bernie Williams	15.00	4.50

2002 Fleer Tradition This Day in History

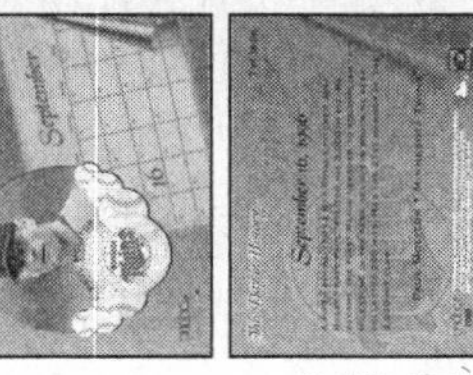

Inserted into hobby packs at stated odds of one in 18 and retail packs at stated odds of one in 24, these 29 cards feature highlights of some of the greatest days in baseball history. Please note that card number 24 (originally intended to fea- ture Orel Hershiser) was pulled from production, thus the set is complete at 29 cards.

	Nm-Mt	Ex-Mt
COMPLETE SET (29)	150.00	45.00
1 Cal Ripken	15.00	4.50
2 Barry Bonds	12.00	3.60
3 George Brett	12.00	3.60
4 Tony Gwynn	6.00	1.80
5 Nolan Ryan	12.00	3.60
6 Reggie Jackson	3.00	.90
7 Paul Molitor	3.00	.90
8 Ichiro Suzuki	8.00	2.40
9 Alex Rodriguez	8.00	2.40
10 Don Mattingly	12.00	3.60
11 Sammy Sosa	8.00	2.40
12 Mark McGwire	12.00	3.60
13 Derek Jeter	12.00	3.60
14 Roger Clemens	10.00	3.00
15 Jim Hunter	3.00	.90
16 Greg Maddux	8.00	2.40
17 Ken Griffey Jr.	8.00	2.40
18 Gil Hodges	5.00	1.50
19 Edgar Martinez	3.00	.90
20 Mike Piazza	8.00	2.40
21 Jimmie Foxx	5.00	1.50
22 Albert Pujols	10.00	3.00
23 Chipper Jones	5.00	1.50
24 Does Not Exist		
25 Jeff Bagwell	3.00	.90
26 Nomar Garciaparra	8.00	2.40
27 Randy Johnson	5.00	1.50
28 Todd Helton	3.00	.90
29 Ted Kluszewski	3.00	.90
30 Ivan Rodriguez	5.00	1.50

2002 Fleer Tradition This Day in History Autographs

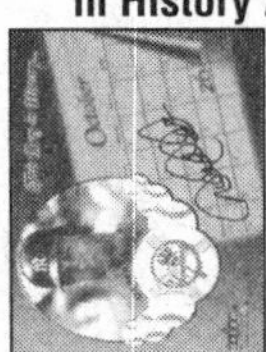
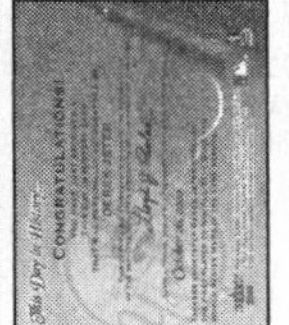

Randomly inserted into packs, these eight cards feature autographs of the player notated. Most of the players did not sign their cards in time for inclusion in this product so they were available as exchange cards. Please note that Fleer pro- vided print run information for these cards but they are not serial numbered. Exchange cards with a redemption deadline of 01/31/03 were seeded into packs for the following players: Gwynn, R.Jackson, R.Johnson, Mattingly, Molitor and Ripken.

	Nm-Mt	Ex-Mt
1 Tony Gwynn/50		
2 Reggie Jackson/50		
3 Derek Jeter/100	120.00	36.00
4 Randy Johnson/75	80.00	24.00
5 Don Mattingly/50	120.00	36.00
6 Paul Molitor/50		
7 Albert Pujols/50	150.00	45.00
8 Cal Ripken/50	150.00	45.00

2002 Fleer Tradition This Day in History Game Used

Randomly inserted into packs, these 22 cards feature memorabilia pieces from the noted play- er. As these cards are printed to different amounts, we have notated that information in our checklist.

	Nm-Mt	Ex-Mt
1 Jeff Bagwell Bat/100	25.00	7.50
2 Barry Bonds Jsy/250	50.00	15.00
3 George Brett Jsy/50		
4 Roger Clemens Jsy/150	40.00	12.00
5 Jimmie Foxx Bat/250	50.00	15.00
6 Todd Helton Bat/150	25.00	7.50
7 Gil Hodges Bat/50		
8 Jim Hunter Jsy/250	25.00	7.50
10 Reggie Jackson Bat/50		
11 Derek Jeter Jsy/250	60.00	18.00
12 Randy Johnson Jsy/50		
13 Chipper Jones Bat/50		
14 Ted Kluszewski Jsy/50		
15 Greg Maddux Jsy/100	30.00	9.00
16 Don Mattingly Jsy/50		
17 Paul Molitor Bat/50		
18 Mike Piazza Bat/150	25.00	7.50
19 Albert Pujols Jsy/50		
20 Cal Ripken Jsy/50		
21 Alex Rodriguez Hat/250	40.00	12.00
22 Ivan Rodriguez Jsy/50		
23 Nolan Ryan Pants/50		

2002 Fleer Tradition Update

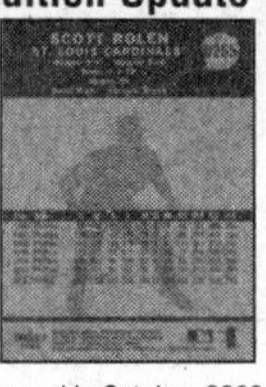

This 400 card set was released in October, 2003. This set was issued in 10 card packs which came 28 packs to a box and six boxes to a case with the packs having an SRP of $2. Cards numbered U1 through U100, which feature a mix of rookies and prospects, were issued at a stated rate of one per pack and are in shorter supply than the rest of the set. Other subsets include Diamond Standouts (U276-U297), All-Stars (U298-U360), Curtain Call (U361-U385) and Tale of the Tape (U386-U400).

	Nm-Mt	Ex-Mt
COMPLETE SET (400)	120.00	36.00
COMP.SET w/o SP's (300)	40.00	12.00
COMMON CARD (U101-U400)	.30	.09
COMMON CARD (U1-U100)	1.00	.30
U1 P.J. Bevis SP RC	1.00	.30
U2 Mike Crudale SP RC	1.00	.30
U3 Ben Howard SP RC	1.00	.30
U4 Travis Driskill SP RC	1.00	.30
U5 Reed Johnson SP RC	1.25	.35
U6 Kyle Kane SP RC	1.00	.30
U7 Deivis Santos SP	1.00	.30
U8 Tim Kalita SP RC	1.00	.30
U9 Brandon Puffer SP RC	1.00	.30
U10 Chris Snelling SP RC	1.00	.30
U11 Juan Brito SP RC	1.00	.30
U12 Tyler Yates SP RC	1.25	.35
U13 Victor Alvarez SP RC	1.00	.30
U14 Takahito Nomura SP RC	1.00	.30
U15 Ron Calloway SP RC	1.00	.30
U16 Satoru Komiyama SP RC	1.00	.30
U17 Julius Matos SP RC	1.00	.30
U18 Jorge Nunez SP RC	1.00	.30
U19 Anderson Machado SP RC	1.00	.30
U20 Scott Layfield SP RC	1.00	.30
U21 Aaron Cook SP RC	1.00	.30
U22 Alex Pelaez SP RC	1.00	.30
U23 Corey Thurman SP RC	1.00	.30
U24 Nelson Castro SP RC	1.00	.30
U25 Jeff Austin SP RC	1.00	.30
U26 Felix Escalona SP RC	1.00	.30
U27 Luis Ugueto SP RC	1.00	.30
U28 Jaime Cerda SP RC	1.00	.30
U29 J.J. Trujillo SP RC	1.00	.30
U30 Rodrigo Rosario SP RC	1.00	.30
U31 Jorge Padilla SP RC	1.00	.30
U32 Shawn Sedlacek SP RC	1.00	.30
U33 Nate Field SP RC	1.00	.30
U34 Earl Snyder SP RC	1.25	.35
U35 Miguel Asencio SP RC	1.00	.30
U36 Ken Huckaby SP RC	1.00	.30
U37 Valentino Pascucci SP	1.00	.30
U38 So Taguchi SP RC	1.25	.35
U39 Brian Mallette SP RC	1.00	.30
U40 Kazuhisa Ishii SP RC	3.00	.90
U41 Matt Thornton SP RC	1.00	.30
U42 Mark Corey SP RC	1.00	.30
U43 Kirk Saarloos SP RC	1.00	.30
U44 Josh Bard SP RC	1.00	.30
U45 Hansel Izquierdo SP RC	1.00	.30
U46 Rene Reyes SP RC	1.00	.30
U47 Luis Garcia SP	1.00	.30
U48 Jason Simontacchi SP RC	1.00	.30
U49 John Ennis SP RC	1.00	.30
U50 Franklyn German SP RC	1.00	.30
U51 Aaron Guiel SP RC	1.00	.30
U52 Howie Clark SP RC	1.00	.30
U53 David Ross SP RC	1.00	.30
U54 Jason Davis SP RC	2.00	.60
U55 Francis Beltran SP RC	1.00	.30
U56 Barry Wesson SP RC	1.00	.30
U57 Run. Hernandez SP RC	1.00	.30
U58 Oliver Perez SP RC	8.00	2.40
U59 Ryan Bukvich SP RC	1.00	.30
U60 Steve Kent SP RC	1.00	.30
U61 Julio Mateo SP RC	1.00	.30
U62 Jason Jimenez SP RC	1.00	.30
U63 Jayson Durocher SP RC	1.00	.30
U64 Kevin Frederick SP RC	1.00	.30
U65 Kevin Gryboski SP RC	1.00	.30
U66 Edwin Almonte SP RC	1.00	.30
U67 John Foster SP RC	1.00	.30
U68 Doug Devore SP RC	1.00	.30
U69 Tom Shearn SP RC	1.00	.30
U70 Colin Young SP RC	1.00	.30
U71 Jon Adkins SP RC	1.00	.30
U72 Wilbert Nieves SP RC	1.00	.30
U73 Matt Duff SP RC	1.00	.30
U74 Carl Sadler SP RC	1.00	.30
U75 Jason Kershner SP RC	1.00	.30
U76 Brandon Backe SP RC	2.00	.60
U77 Josh Hancock SP RC	1.00	.30
U78 Chris Baker SP RC	1.00	.30
U79 Travis Hughes SP RC	1.00	.30
U80 Steve Bechler SP RC	1.00	.30
U81 Allan Simpson SP RC	1.00	.30
U82 Aaron Taylor SP RC	1.00	.30
U83 Kevin Cash SP RC	1.00	.30
U84 Chone Figgins SP RC	2.00	.60
U85 Clay Condrey SP RC	1.00	.30
U86 Shane Nance SP RC	1.00	.30
U87 Freddy Sanchez SP RC	1.00	.30
U88 Jim Rushford SP RC	1.00	.30
U89 Jeriome Robertson SP RC	1.00	.30
U90 Trey Lunsford SP RC	1.00	.30
U91 Cody McKay SP RC	1.00	.30
U92 Trey Hodges SP RC	1.00	.30
U93 Hee Seop Choi SP	1.00	.30
U94 Joe Borchard SP	1.00	.30
U95 Orlando Hudson SP	1.00	.30
U96 Carl Crawford SP	1.00	.30
U97 Mark Prior SP	4.00	1.20
U98 Brett Myers SP	1.00	.30
U99 Kenny Lofton SP	1.00	.30
U100 Cliff Floyd SP	1.00	.30
U101 Randy Winn	.30	.09
U102 Ryan Dempster	.30	.09
U103 Josh Phelps	.30	.09
U104 Marcus Giles	.30	.09
U105 Rickey Henderson	.75	.23
U106 Jose Leon	.30	.09
U107 Tino Martinez	.50	.15
U108 Greg Norton	.30	.09
U109 Odalis Perez	.30	.09
U110 J.C. Romero	.30	.09
U111 Gary Sheffield	.30	.09
U112 Ismael Valdes	.30	.09
U113 Juan Acevedo	.30	.09
U114 Ben Broussard	.30	.09
U115 Deivi Cruz	.30	.09
U116 Geronimo Gil	.30	.09
U117 Eric Hinske	.30	.09
U118 Ted Lilly	.30	.09
U119 Quinton McCracken	.30	.09
U120 Antonio Alfonseca	.30	.09
U121 Brent Abernathy	.30	.09
U122 Johnny Damon Sox	.75	.23
U123 Francisco Cordero	.30	.09
U124 Sterling Hitchcock	.30	.09
U125 Vladimir Nunez	.30	.09
U126 Andres Galarraga	.30	.09
U127 Timo Perez	.30	.09
U128 Tsuyoshi Shinjo	.30	.09
U129 Joe Girardi	.30	.09
U130 Roberto Alomar	.50	.15
U131 Ellis Burks	.30	.09
U132 Mike DeJean	.30	.09
U133 Alex Gonzalez	.30	.09
U134 Johan Santana	1.00	.30
U135 Kenny Lofton	.30	.09
U136 Juan Encarnacion	.30	.09
U137 Dewon Brazelton	.30	.09
U138 Jeromy Burnitz	.30	.09
U139 Elmer Dessens	.30	.09
U140 Juan Gonzalez	.50	.15
U141 Todd Hundley	.30	.09
U142 Tomo Ohka	.30	.09
U143 Robin Ventura	.30	.09
U144 Rodrigo Lopez	.30	.09
U145 Ruben Sierra	.30	.09
U146 Jason Phillips	.30	.09
U147 Ryan Rupe	.30	.09
U148 Kevin Appier	.30	.09
U149 Sean Burroughs	.30	.09
U150 Masato Yoshii	.30	.09
U151 Juan Diaz	.30	.09
U152 Tony Graffanino	.30	.09
U153 Raul Ibanez	.30	.09
U154 Kevin Mench	.30	.09
U155 Pedro Astacio	.30	.09
U156 Brent Butler	.30	.09
U157 Kirk Rueter	.30	.09
U158 Eddie Guardado	.30	.09
U159 Hideki Irabu	.30	.09
U160 Wendell Magee	.30	.09
U161 Antonio Osuna	.30	.09
U162 Jose Vizcaino	.30	.09
U163 Danny Bautista	.30	.09
U164 Vinny Castilla	.30	.09
U165 Chris Singleton	.30	.09
U166 Mark Redman	.30	.09
U167 Olmedo Saenz	.30	.09
U168 Scott Erickson	.30	.09
U169 Ty Wigginton	.30	.09
U170 Jason Isringhausen	.30	.09
U171 Andy Van Hekken	.30	.09
U172 Chris Magruder	.30	.09
U173 Brandon Berger	.30	.09
U174 Roger Cedeno	.30	.09
U175 Kelvim Escobar	.30	.09
U176 Jose Guillen	.30	.09
U177 Damian Jackson	.30	.09
U178 Eric Owens	.30	.09
U179 Angel Berroa	.30	.09
U180 Alex Cintron	.30	.09
U181 Jeff Weaver	.30	.09
U182 Damon Minor	.30	.09
U183 Bobby Estalella	.30	.09
U184 David Justice	.30	.09
U185 Roy Halladay	.30	.09
U186 Brian Jordan	.30	.09
U187 Mike Maroth	.30	.09
U188 Pokey Reese	.30	.09
U189 Rey Sanchez	.30	.09
U190 Hank Blalock	.75	.23
U191 Jeff Cirillo	.30	.09
U192 Dmitri Young	.30	.09
U193 Carl Everett	.30	.09
U194 Joey Hamilton	.30	.09
U195 Jorge Julio	.30	.09
U196 Pablo Ozuna	.30	.09
U197 Jason Marquis	.30	.09
U198 Dustan Mohr	.30	.09
U199 Joe Borowski	.30	.09
U200 Tony Clark	.30	.09
U201 David Wells	.30	.09
U202 Josh Fogg	.30	.09
U203 Aaron Harang	.30	.09
U204 John McDonald	.30	.09
U205 John Stephens	.30	.09
U206 Chris Reitsma	.30	.09
U207 Alex Sanchez	.30	.09
U208 Milton Bradley	.30	.09
U209 Matt Clement	.30	.09
U210 Brad Fullmer	.30	.09
U211 Shigetoshi Hasegawa	.30	.09
U212 Austin Kearns	.30	.09
U213 Damaso Marte	.30	.09
U214 Vicente Padilla	.30	.09
U215 Raul Mondesi	.30	.09
U216 Russell Branyan	.30	.09
U217 Bartolo Colon	.30	.09
U218 Moises Alou	.30	.09
U219 Scott Hatteberg	.30	.09
U220 Bobby Kielty	.30	.09
U221 Kip Wells	.30	.09
U222 Scott Stewart	.30	.09
U223 Victor Martinez	.75	.23
U224 Marty Cordova	.30	.09
U225 Desi Relaford	.30	.09
U226 Reggie Sanders	.30	.09
U227 Jason Giambi	.30	.09
U228 Jimmy Haynes	.30	.09

U229 Billy Koch .30 .09
U230 Damian Moss .30 .09
U231 Chan Ho Park .30 .09
U232 Cliff Floyd .30 .09
U233 Todd Zeile .30 .09
U234 Jeremy Giambi .30 .09
U235 Rick Helling .30 .09
U236 Matt Lawton .30 .09
U237 Ramon Martinez .30 .09
U238 Rondell White .30 .09
U239 Scott Sullivan .30 .09
U240 Hideo Nomo .75 .23
U241 Todd Ritchie .30 .09
U242 Ramon Santiago .30 .09
U243 Jake Peavy .30 .09
U244 Brad Wilkerson .30 .09
U245 Reggie Taylor .30 .09
U246 Carlos Pena .30 .09
U247 Willis Roberts UER .30 .09
No U in front of card number
U248 Jason Schmidt .30 .09
U249 Mike Williams .30 .09
U250 Alan Zinter .30 .09
U251 Michael Tejera .30 .09
U252 Dave Roberts .30 .09
U253 Scott Schoeneweis .30 .09
U254 Woody Williams .30 .09
U255 John Thomson .30 .09
U256 Ricardo Rodriguez .30 .09
U257 Aaron Sele .30 .09
U258 Paul Wilson .30 .09
U259 Brett Tomko .30 .09
U260 Kenny Rogers .30 .09
U261 Mo Vaughn .30 .09
U262 John Burkett .30 .09
U263 Dennis Stark .30 .09
U264 Ray Durham .30 .09
U265 Scott Rolen .75 .23
U266 Gabe Kapler .30 .09
U267 Todd Hollandsworth .30 .09
U268 Bud Smith .30 .09
U269 Jay Payton .30 .09
U270 Tyler Houston .30 .09
U271 Brian Moehler .30 .09
U272 David Espinosa .30 .09
U273 Placido Polanco .30 .09
U274 John Patterson .30 .09
U275 Adam Hyzdu .30 .09
U276 Albert Pujols DS .75 .23
U277 Larry Walker DS .30 .09
U278 Magglio Ordonez DS .30 .09
U279 Ryan Klesko DS .30 .09
U280 Darin Erstad DS .30 .09
U281 Jeff Kent DS .30 .09
U282 Paul Lo Duca DS .30 .09
U283 Jim Edmonds DS .30 .09
U284 Chipper Jones DS .50 .15
U285 Bernie Williams DS .30 .09
U286 Pat Burrell DS .30 .09
U287 Cliff Floyd DS .30 .09
U288 Troy Glaus DS .30 .09
U289 Brian Giles DS .30 .09
U290 Jim Thome DS .50 .15
U291 Greg Maddux DS .75 .23
U292 Roberto Alomar DS .30 .09
U293 Jeff Bagwell DS .30 .09
U294 Rafael Furcal DS .30 .09
U295 Josh Beckett DS .30 .09
U296 Carlos Delgado DS .30 .09
U297 Ken Griffey Jr. DS .75 .23
U298 Jason Giambi AS .30 .09
U299 Paul Konerko AS .30 .09
U300 Mike Sweeney AS .30 .09
U301 Alfonso Soriano AS .30 .09
U302 Shea Hillenbrand AS .30 .09
U303 Tony Batista AS .30 .09
U304 Robin Ventura AS .30 .09
U305 Alex Rodriguez AS .75 .23
U306 Nomar Garciaparra AS .75 .23
U307 Derek Jeter AS 1.00 .30
U308 Miguel Tejada AS .30 .09
U309 Omar Vizquel AS .30 .09
U310 Jorge Posada AS .30 .09
U311 A.J. Pierzynski AS .30 .09
U312 Ichiro Suzuki AS .75 .23
U313 Manny Ramirez AS .30 .09
U314 Torii Hunter AS .30 .09
U315 Garret Anderson AS .30 .09
U316 Robert Fick AS .30 .09
U317 Randy Winn AS .30 .09
U318 Mark Buehrle AS .30 .09
U319 Freddy Garcia AS .30 .09
U320 Eddie Guardado AS .30 .09
U321 Roy Halladay AS .30 .09
U322 Derek Lowe AS .30 .09
U323 Pedro Martinez AS .50 .15
U324 Mariano Rivera AS .30 .09
U325 Kazuhiro Sasaki AS .30 .09
U326 Barry Zito AS .30 .09
U327 Johnny Damon Sox AS .50 .15
U328 Ugueth Urbina AS .30 .09
U329 Todd Helton AS .30 .09
U330 Richie Sexson AS .30 .09
U331 Jose Vidro AS .30 .09
U332 Luis Castillo AS .30 .09
U333 Junior Spivey AS .30 .09
U334 Scott Rolen AS .50 .15
U335 Mike Lowell AS .30 .09
U336 Jimmy Rollins AS .30 .09
U337 Jose Hernandez AS .30 .09
U338 Mike Piazza AS .75 .23
U339 Benito Santiago AS .30 .09
U340 Sammy Sosa AS .75 .23
U341 Barry Bonds AS 1.00 .30
U342 Vladimir Guerrero AS .50 .15
U343 Lance Berkman AS .30 .09
U344 Adam Dunn AS .30 .09
U345 Shawn Green AS .30 .09
U346 Luis Gonzalez AS .30 .09
U347 Eric Gagne AS .50 .15
U348 Tom Glavine AS .30 .09
U349 Trevor Hoffman AS .30 .09
U350 Randy Johnson AS .50 .15
U351 Byung-Hyun Kim AS .30 .09
U352 Matt Morris AS .30 .09
U353 Odalis Perez AS .30 .09
U354 Curt Schilling AS .30 .09
U355 John Smoltz AS .30 .09
U356 Mike Williams AS .30 .09
U357 Andruw Jones AS .30 .09
U358 Vicente Padilla AS .30 .09
U359 Mike Remlinger AS .30 .09
U360 Robb Nen AS .30 .09
U361 Shawn Green CC .30 .09
U362 Derek Jeter CC 1.00 .30
U363 Troy Glaus CC .30 .09
U364 Ken Griffey Jr. CC .75 .23
U365 Mike Piazza CC .75 .23
U366 Jason Giambi CC .30 .09
U367 Greg Maddux CC .75 .23
U368 Albert Pujols CC .75 .23
U369 Pedro Martinez CC .50 .15
U370 Barry Zito CC .30 .09
U371 Ichiro Suzuki CC .75 .23
U372 Nomar Garciaparra CC .75 .23
U373 Vladimir Guerrero CC .50 .15
U374 Randy Johnson CC .50 .15
U375 Barry Bonds CC 1.00 .30
U376 Sammy Sosa CC .75 .23
U377 Hideo Nomo CC .50 .15
U378 Jeff Bagwell CC .30 .09
U379 Curt Schilling CC .30 .09
U380 Jim Thome CC .50 .15
U381 Todd Helton CC .30 .09
U382 Roger Clemens CC .75 .23
U383 Chipper Jones CC .50 .15
U384 Alex Rodriguez CC .75 .23
U385 Manny Ramirez CC .30 .09
U386 Barry Bonds TT 1.00 .30
U387 Jim Thome TT .50 .15
U388 Adam Dunn TT .30 .09
U389 Alex Rodriguez TT .75 .23
U390 Shawn Green TT .30 .09
U391 Jason Giambi TT .30 .09
U392 Lance Berkman TT .30 .09
U393 Pat Burrell TT .30 .09
U394 Eric Chavez TT .30 .09
U395 Mike Piazza TT .75 .23
U396 Vladimir Guerrero TT .50 .15
U397 Paul Konerko TT .30 .09
U398 Sammy Sosa TT .75 .23
U399 Richie Sexson TT .30 .09
U400 Torii Hunter TT .30 .09

2002 Fleer Tradition Update Glossy

Randomly inserted into packs, this is a parallel to the basic Fleer Tradition Update set. These cards can be differentiated from the regular cards by their "glossy" sheen on the front and each card has a stated print run of 200 serial numbered sets.

Nm-Mt Ex-Mt
*GLOSSY 1-100: 1X TO 2.5X BASIC
*GLOSSY 101-275: 3X TO 8X BASIC
*GLOSSY 276-400: 6X TO 15X BASIC

2002 Fleer Tradition Update Diamond Debuts

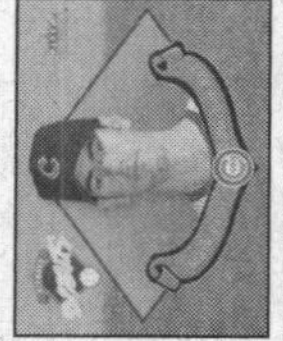

Inserted into packs at a stated rate of one in six, these 15 cards feature players who made their major league debut during the 2002 season.

Nm-Mt Ex-Mt
COMPLETE SET (15) 15.00 4.50
U1 Mark Prior 3.00 .90
U2 Eric Hinske 1.00 .30
U3 Kazuhisa Ishii 3.00 .90
U4 Ben Broussard 1.00 .30
U5 Sean Burroughs 1.00 .30
U6 Austin Kearns 1.00 .30
U7 Hee Seop Choi 1.00 .30
U8 Kirk Saarloos 1.00 .30
U9 Orlando Hudson 1.00 .30
U10 So Taguchi 1.25 .35
U11 Kevin Mench 1.00 .30
U12 Carl Crawford 1.00 .30
U13 Marlon Byrd 1.00 .30
U14 Hank Blalock 2.00 .60
U15 Brett Myers 1.00 .30

2002 Fleer Tradition Update Grass Patch

Randomly inserted into packs, these seven cards feature some of the leading fielders in the game. Each card not only has a game-used memorabilia swatch on it but also has a stated print run of 50 serial numbered sets.

Nm-Mt Ex-Mt
1 Roberto Alomar 40.00 12.00
2 Jim Edmonds 25.00 7.50
3 Nomar Garciaparra 80.00 24.00
4 Shawn Green 25.00 7.50
5 Torii Hunter 25.00 7.50
6 Andruw Jones 25.00 7.50
7 Alfonso Soriano 40.00 12.00

2002 Fleer Tradition Update Grass Roots

Inserted into packs at a stated rate of one in 18, this 10 card set honors some of the most excit

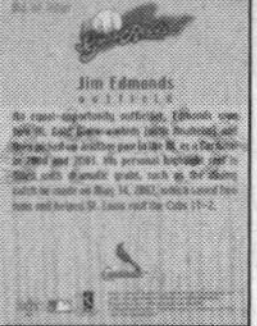

ing fielders in baseball.

Nm-Mt Ex-Mt
COMPLETE SET (10) 15.00 4.50
U1 Alfonso Soriano 2.00 .60
U2 Torii Hunter 2.00 .60
U3 Andruw Jones 2.00 .60
U4 Jim Edmonds 2.00 .60
U5 Shawn Green 2.00 .60
U6 Todd Helton 2.00 .60
U7 Nomar Garciaparra 4.00 1.20
U8 Roberto Alomar 2.00 .60
U9 Vladimir Guerrero 2.50 .75
U10 Ichiro Suzuki 4.00 1.20

2002 Fleer Tradition Update Heads Up

Inserted at a stated rate of one in 36, this 10 card set is designed in the style of the old Heads Up set of the 1930's.

Nm-Mt Ex-Mt
U1 Roger Clemens 8.00 2.40
U2 Adam Dunn 3.00 .90
U3 Kazuhisa Ishii 5.00 1.50
U4 Barry Zito 3.00 .90
U5 Pedro Martinez 4.00 1.20
U6 Alfonso Soriano 3.00 .90
U7 Mark Prior 6.00 1.80
U8 Chipper Jones 4.00 1.20
U9 Randy Johnson 4.00 1.20
U10 Lance Berkman 3.00 .90

2002 Fleer Tradition Update Heads Up Game Used Caps

Randomly inserted in packs, these cards are designed in the style of the old Heads Up cards from the 1930's. However, they are different from the regular insert set as a piece of a game-used cap is also part of the card. Each card is also printed to a stated print run of 150.

Nm-Mt Ex-Mt
1 Lance Berkman 20.00 6.00
2 Barry Bonds 60.00 18.00
3 Roger Clemens 50.00 15.00
4 Adam Dunn 25.00 7.50
5 Kazuhisa Ishii 25.00 7.50
6 Randy Johnson 25.00 7.50
7 Chipper Jones 25.00 7.50
8 Mike Piazza 30.00 9.00
9 Mark Prior 30.00 9.00
10 Alfonso Soriano 25.00 7.50
11 Barry Zito 20.00 6.00

2002 Fleer Tradition Update New York's Finest

Inserted into packs at stated odds of one in 83, these 15 cards honor some of the best players for either the New York Yankees or the New York Mets.

Nm-Mt Ex-Mt
1 Edgardo Alfonzo 8.00 2.40
2 Roberto Alomar 8.00 2.40
3 Jeromy Burnitz 8.00 2.40
4 Satoru Komiyama 8.00 2.40
5 Rey Ordonez 8.00 2.40
6 Mike Piazza 12.00 3.60
7 Mo Vaughn 8.00 2.40
8 Roger Clemens 15.00 4.50
9 Jason Giambi 8.00 2.40
10 Derek Jeter 20.00 6.00
11 Mike Mussina 8.00 2.40
12 Jorge Posada 8.00 2.40
13 Alfonso Soriano 8.00 2.40
14 Robin Ventura 8.00 2.40
15 Bernie Williams 8.00 2.40

2002 Fleer Tradition Update New York's Finest Dual Swatch

Randomly inserted into packs, these six cards feature two leading players from New York along with a game-used memorabilia piece for both players.

Nm-Mt Ex-Mt
1 Derek Jeter 100.00 30.00
Rey Ordonez
2 Alfonso Soriano 40.00 12.00
Roberto Alomar
3 Roger Clemens 120.00 36.00
Mike Piazza
4 Mike Mussina 40.00 12.00
Mo Vaughn
5 Bernie Williams 40.00 12.00
Jeromy Burnitz
6 Robin Ventura 25.00 7.50
Edgardo Alfonzo

2002 Fleer Tradition Update New York's Finest Single Swatch

Inserted into packs at stated odds of one in 112, these cards feature two star players from New York but only one memorabilia piece on each card. The player who has a memorabilia piece is listed first in our checklist along with what type of memorabilia piece is used.

Nm-Mt Ex-Mt
1 Derek Jeter Jsy 30.00 9.00
Rey Ordonez
2 Alfonso Soriano Jsy 15.00 4.50
Roberto Alomar
3 Roger Clemens Jsy 20.00 6.00
Mike Piazza
4 Mike Mussina Jsy 15.00 4.50
Mo Vaughn
5 Bernie Williams Jsy 15.00 4.50
Jeromy Burnitz
6 Derek Jeter Jsy 30.00 9.00
Satoru Komiyama
7 Robin Ventura Jsy 10.00 3.00
Edgardo Alfonzo
8 Jorge Posada Jsy 15.00 4.50
Mike Piazza
9 Jason Giambi Base SP 10.00 3.00
Mo Vaughn
10 Alfonso Soriano Jsy 15.00 4.50
Edgardo Alfonzo
11 Rey Ordonez Jsy 10.00 3.00
Derek Jeter
12 Roberto Alomar Jsy 15.00 4.50
Alfonso Soriano
13 Mike Piazza Jsy 15.00 4.50
Roger Clemens
14 Mo Vaughn Jsy 10.00 3.00
Mike Mussina
15 Jeromy Burnitz Jsy 10.00 3.00
Bernie Williams
16 Satoru Komiyama Bat 15.00 4.50
Derek Jeter
17 Edgardo Alfonzo Jsy 10.00 3.00
Robin Ventura
18 Mike Piazza Jsy 15.00 4.50
Jorge Posada
19 Mo Vaughn Jsy 10.00 3.00
Jason Giambi
20 Edgardo Alfonzo Jsy 10.00 3.00
Alfonso Soriano

2002 Fleer Tradition Update Plays of the Week

Inserted at stated odds of one in 12, these 30 cards feature some of the leading players of the 2002 season along with their highlight play of the season.

Nm-Mt Ex-Mt
1 Troy Glaus 1.50 .45
2 Andruw Jones 1.50 .45
3 Curt Schilling 1.50 .45
4 Manny Ramirez 1.50 .45
5 Sammy Sosa 4.00 1.20
6 Magglio Ordonez 1.50 .45
7 Ken Griffey Jr. 4.00 1.20
8 Jim Thome 2.50 .75
9 Larry Walker 1.50 .45
10 Robert Fick 1.50 .45
11 Josh Beckett 1.50 .45
12 Roy Oswalt 1.50 .45
13 Mike Sweeney 1.50 .45
14 Shawn Green 1.50 .45
15 Torii Hunter 1.50 .45
16 Vladimir Guerrero 2.50 .75
17 Mike Piazza 4.00 1.20
18 Jason Giambi 1.50 .45
19 Eric Chavez 1.50 .45
20 Pat Burrell 1.50 .45
21 Brian Giles 1.50 .45
22 Ryan Klesko 1.50 .45
23 Barry Bonds 6.00 1.80
24 Mike Cameron 1.50 .45
25 Albert Pujols 5.00 1.50
26 Alex Rodriguez 4.00 1.20
27 Carlos Delgado 1.50 .45
28 Richie Sexson 1.50 .45
29 Jay Gibbons 1.50 .45
30 Randy Winn 1.50 .45

2002 Fleer Tradition Update This Day In History

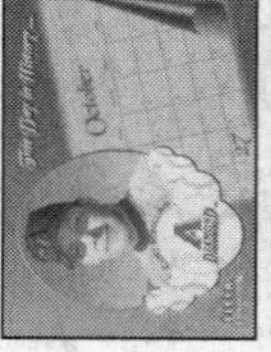

Inserted into packs at stated odds of one in 12, this 25 card set feature a mix of active and retired players along with an historical highlight that the player was involved with.

Nm-Mt Ex-Mt
U1 Shawn Green 1.50 .45
U2 Ozzie Smith 3.00 .90
U3 Derek Lowe 1.50 .45
U4 Ken Griffey Jr. 4.00 1.20
U5 Barry Bonds 6.00 1.80
U6 Juan Gonzalez 1.50 .45
U7 Wade Boggs 2.00 .60
U8 Mark Prior 4.00 1.20
U9 Thurman Munson 3.00 .90
U10 Curt Schilling 1.50 .45
U11 Jason Giambi 1.50 .45
U12 Cal Ripken 10.00 3.00
U13 Craig Biggio 1.50 .45
U14 Drew Henson 1.50 .45
U15 Steve Carlton 2.00 .60
U16 Greg Maddux 4.00 1.20
U17 Adam Dunn 1.50 .45
U18 Vladimir Guerrero 2.50 .75
U19 Alex Rodriguez 4.00 1.20
U20 Carlton Fisk 2.00 .60
U21 Ichiro Suzuki 4.00 1.20
U22 Johnny Bench 3.00 .90
U23 Kazuhisa Ishii 3.00 .90
U24 Derek Jeter 6.00 1.80
U25 Jim Thome 2.50 .75

2002 Fleer Tradition Update This Day In History Autographs

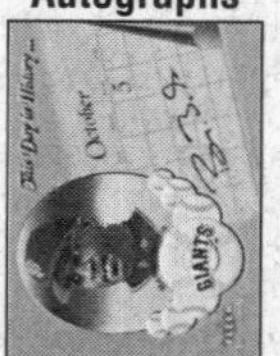

Inserted into packs at a stated rate of one in 582, this is a partial parallel to the This Day in History insert set. A few players signed an amount of cards in much shorter supply than others. Fortunately, Fleer provided the specific quantities signed for the short prints and the information is detailed in full within our checklist. In addition, an exchange card with a redemption deadline of October 31st, 2003 was seeded into packs for the Greg Maddux card.

Nm-Mt Ex-Mt
1 Barry Bonds SP/150 250.00 75.00
2 Mark Prior SP/64 120.00 36.00
3 Cal Ripken SP/35
4 Drew Henson 25.00 7.50
5 Greg Maddux SP/99
6 Derek Jeter 120.00 36.00

2002 Fleer Tradition Update This Day In History Game Used

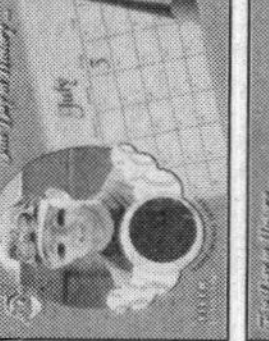
 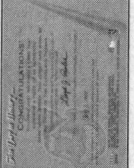

Inserted into packs at a stated rate of one in 28, these 20 cards form a partial parallel to the This Day in History insert set. These cards feature a game-used memorabilia piece of the featured player. A couple players are featured on more than one memorabilia card and we have notated that information in our checklist as well as the

:ated print run for the cards which were issued notably shorter supply.

	Nm-Mt	Ex-Mt
Craig Biggio Bat SP/80		
Craig Biggio Jsy	15.00	4.50
Wade Boggs Jsy	15.00	4.50
Wade Boggs Pants	15.00	4.50
Barry Bonds Bat	20.00	6.00
Barry Bonds Jsy	20.00	6.00
Adam Dunn Jsy	15.00	4.50
Carlton Fisk Bat	15.00	4.50
Juan Gonzalez Bat	15.00	4.50
0 Shawn Green Jsy	10.00	3.00
1 Kazuhisa Ishii Bat	15.00	4.50
2 Derek Jeter Pants	25.00	7.50
3 Greg Maddux Jsy	15.00	4.50
4 Thurman Munson Jsy SP/40		
5 Alex Rodriguez Bat	15.00	4.50
6 Alex Rodriguez Jsy	15.00	4.50
7 Curt Schilling Jsy	10.00	3.00
8 Ozzie Smith Jsy	20.00	6.00
9 Jim Thome Bat SP/120		
0 Jim Thome Jsy	15.00	4.50

2003 Fleer Tradition

his 485 card set, deisgned in the style of 1963 leer, was released in January, 2003. These ards were issued in 10 card packs which were acked 40 packs to a box and 20 boxes to a case with an SRP of $1.49 per pack. The following ubsets are part of the set: Cards numbered 1 hrough 30 are Team Leader cards, cards number 67 through 85 are Missing Link (featuring layers active but not on Fleer cards in 1963) ards, cards number 417 rhrough 425 are Award Winner cards, cards number 426 through 460 re Prospect cards and cards numbered 461 hrough 485 are Banner Season cards. All cards umbered 1 through 100 were short printed and nserted at an rate of one per hobby pack and ne per 12 retail pack. In addition, retail boxes ad a special Barry Bonds pin as a box topper nd a Derek Jeter promo card was issued a few weeks before this product became live so media nd dealers could see what this set look like.

	Nm-Mt	Ex-Mt
COMPLETE SET (485)	150.00	45.00
COMP.SET w/o SP's (385)	40.00	12.00
COMMON CARD (1-30)	1.00	.30
COMM.SP (31-66/86-100)	1.00	.30
COMMON ML (67-85)	1.50	.45
COMMON CARD (	.30	.09
COMMON PR (426-460)	.30	.09
Jarrod Washburn / Troy Glaus / Garret Anderson / Ramon Ortiz TL SP	1.00	.30
2 Luis Gonzalez / Randy Johnson TL SP	1.50	.45
3 Andruw Jones / Chipper Jones / Tom Glavine / Kevin Millwood TL SP	1.50	.45
4 Tony Batista / Rodrigo Lopez TL SP	1.00	.30
5 Manny Ramirez / Nomar Garciaparra / Derek Lowe / Pedro Martinez TL SP	2.50	.75
6 Sammy Sosa / Matt Clement / Kerry Wood TL SP	2.50	.75
7 Matt Buehrle / Magglio Ordonez / Danny Wright TL SP	1.00	.30
8 Adam Dunn / Aaron Boone / Jimmy Haynes TL SP	1.00	.30
9 C.C. Sabathia / Jim Thome TL SP	1.50	.45
10 Todd Helton / Jason Jennings TL SP	1.00	.30
11 Randall Simon / Steve Sparks / Mark Redman TL SP	1.00	.30
12 Derrek Lee / Mike Lowell / A.J. Burnett TL SP	1.00	.30
13 Lance Berkman / Roy Oswalt TL SP	1.00	.30
14 Paul Byrd / Carlos Beltran TL SP	1.00	.30
15 Shawn Green / Hideo Nomo TL SP	1.50	.45
16 Richie Sexson / Ben Sheets TL SP	1.00	.30
17 Torii Hunter / Kyle Lohse / Johan Santana TL SP	1.50	.45
18 Vladimir Guerrrero / Tomo Ohka / Javier Vazquez TL SP	1.50	.45
19 Mike Piazza / Al Leiter TL SP	2.50	.75
20 Jason Giambi / David Wells / Roger Clemens TL SP	2.50	.75
21 Eric Chavez / Miguel Tejada / Barry Zito TL SP	1.00	.30
22 Pat Burrell / Vicente Padilla / Randy Wolf TL SP	1.00	.30
23 Brian Giles / Josh Fogg / Kip Wells TL SP	1.00	.30
24 Ryan Klesko / Brian Lawrence TL SP	1.00	.30
25 Barry Bonds / Russ Ortiz / Jason Schmidt TL SP	2.50	.75
26 Mike Cameron / Bret Boone / Freddy Garcia TL SP	1.00	.30
27 Albert Pujols / Matt Morris TL SP	2.50	.75
28 Aubry Huff / Randy Winn / Joe Kennedy / Tanyon Sturtze TL SP	1.00	.30
29 Alex Rodriguez / Kenny Rogers / Chan Ho Park TL SP	2.50	.75
30 Carlos Delgado / Roy Halladay TL SP	1.00	.30
31 Greg Maddux SP	4.00	1.20
32 Nick Neugebauer SP	1.00	.30
33 Larry Walker SP	1.50	.45
34 Freddy Garcia SP	1.00	.30
35 Rich Aurilia SP	1.00	.30
36 Craig Wilson SP	1.00	.30
37 Jeff Suppan SP	1.00	.30
38 Joel Pineiro SP	1.00	.30
39 Pedro Feliz SP	1.00	.30
40 Bartolo Colon SP	1.00	.30
41 Pete Walker SP	1.00	.30
42 Mo Vaughn SP	1.00	.30
43 Sidney Ponson SP	1.00	.30
44 Jason Isringhausen SP	1.00	.30
45 Hideki Irabu SP	1.00	.30
46 Pedro Martinez SP	2.50	.75
47 Tom Glavine SP	1.50	.45
48 Matt Lawton SP	1.00	.30
49 Kyle Lohse SP	1.00	.30
50 Corey Patterson SP	1.00	.30
51 Ichiro Suzuki SP UER / RBI total for 2002 incorrect	4.00	1.20
52 Wade Miller SP	1.00	.30
53 Ben Diggins SP	1.00	.30
54 Jayson Werth SP	1.00	.30
55 Masato Yoshii SP	1.00	.30
56 Mark Buehrle SP	1.00	.30
57 Drew Henson SP	1.00	.30
58 Dave Williams SP	1.00	.30
59 Juan Rivera SP	1.00	.30
60 Scott Schoenewels SP	1.00	.30
61 Josh Beckett SP	1.00	.30
62 Vinny Castilla SP	1.00	.30
63 Barry Zito SP	1.00	.30
64 Jose Valentin SP	1.00	.30
65 Jon Lieber SP	1.00	.30
66 Jorge Padilla SP	1.00	.30
67 Luis Aparicio ML SP	1.50	.45
68 Boog Powell ML SP	2.50	.75
69 Dick Radatz ML SP	1.50	.45
70 Frank Malzone ML SP	1.50	.45
71 Lou Brock ML SP	2.50	.75
72 Billy Williams ML SP	1.50	.45
73 Early Wynn ML SP	1.50	.45
74 Jim Bunning ML SP	2.50	.75
75 Al Kaline ML SP	4.00	1.20
76 Eddie Mathews ML SP	4.00	1.20
77 Harmon Killebrew ML SP	4.00	1.20
78 Gil Hodges ML SP	2.50	.75
79 Duke Snider ML SP	2.50	.75
80 Yogi Berra ML SP	4.00	1.20
81 Whitey Ford ML SP	2.50	.75
82 Willie Stargell ML SP	2.50	.75
83 Willie McCovey ML SP	1.50	.45
84 Gaylord Perry ML SP	1.50	.45
85 Red Schoendienst ML SP	1.50	.45
86 Luis Castillo SP	1.00	.30
87 Derek Jeter SP	6.00	1.80
88 Orlando Hudson SP	1.00	.30
89 Bobby Higginson SP	1.00	.30
90 Brent Butler SP	1.00	.30
91 Brad Wilkerson SP	1.00	.30
92 Craig Biggio SP	1.50	.45
93 Marlon Anderson SP	1.00	.30
94 Ty Wigginton SP	1.00	.30
95 Hideo Nomo SP	2.50	.75
96 Barry Larkin SP	1.50	.45
97 Roberto Alomar SP	1.50	.45
98 Omar Vizquel SP	1.50	.45
99 Andres Galarraga SP	1.00	.30
100 Shawn Green SP	1.00	.30
101 Rafael Furcal	.30	.09
102 Bill Selby	.30	.09
103 Brent Abernathy	.30	.09
104 Nomar Garciaparra	1.25	.35
105 Michael Barrett	.30	.09
106 Travis Hafner	.30	.09
107 Carl Crawford	.30	.09
108 Jeff Cirillo	.30	.09
109 Mike Hampton	.30	.09
110 Kip Wells	.30	.09
111 Luis Alicea	.30	.09
112 Ellis Burks	.30	.09
113 Matt Anderson	.30	.09
114 Carlos Beltran	.50	.15
115 Paul Lo Duca	.30	.09
116 Lance Berkman	.30	.09
117 Moises Alou	.30	.09
118 Roger Cedeno	.30	.09
119 Brad Fullmer	.30	.09
120 Sean Burroughs	.30	.09
121 Eric Byrnes	.30	.09
122 Milton Bradley	.30	.09
123 Jason Giambi	.30	.09
124 Brook Fordyce	.30	.09
125 Kevin Appier	.30	.09
126 Steve Cox	.30	.09
127 Danny Bautista	.30	.09
128 Edgardo Alfonzo	.30	.09
129 Matt Clement	.30	.09
130 Robb Nen	.30	.09
131 Roy Halladay	.30	.09
132 Brian Jordan	.30	.09
133 A.J. Burnett	.30	.09
134 Aaron Cook	.30	.09
135 Paul Byrd	.30	.09
136 Ramon Ortiz	.30	.09
137 Adam Hyzdu	.30	.09
138 Rafael Soriano	.30	.09
139 Marty Cordova	.30	.09
140 Nelson Cruz	.30	.09
141 Jamie Moyer	.30	.09
142 Raul Mondesi	.30	.09
143 Josh Bard	.30	.09
144 Elmer Dessens	.30	.09
145 Rickey Henderson	.75	.23
146 Joe McEwing	.30	.09
147 Luis Rivas	.30	.09
148 Armando Benitez	.30	.09
149 Keith Foulke	.30	.09
150 Zach Day	.30	.09
151 Trey Lunsford	.30	.09
152 Bobby Abreu	.30	.09
153 Juan Cruz	.30	.09
154 Ramon Hernandez	.30	.09
155 Brandon Duckworth	.30	.09
156 Matt Ginter	.30	.09
157 Rob Mackowiak	.30	.09
158 Josh Pearce	.30	.09
159 Marlon Byrd	.30	.09
160 Todd Walker	.30	.09
161 Chad Hermansen	.30	.09
162 Felix Escalona	.30	.09
163 Ruben Mateo	.30	.09
164 Mark Johnson	.30	.09
165 Juan Pierre	.30	.09
166 Gary Sheffield	.30	.09
167 Edgar Martinez	.50	.15
168 Randy Winn	.30	.09
169 Pokey Reese	.30	.09
170 Kevin Mench	.30	.09
171 Albert Pujols	1.50	.45
172 J.T. Snow	.30	.09
173 Dean Palmer	.30	.09
174 Jay Payton	.30	.09
175 Abraham Nunez	.30	.09
176 Richie Sexson	.30	.09
177 Jose Vidro	.30	.09
178 Geoff Jenkins	.30	.09
179 Dan Wilson	.30	.09
180 John Olerud	.30	.09
181 Javy Lopez	.30	.09
182 Carl Everett	.30	.09
183 Vernon Wells	.30	.09
184 Juan Gonzalez	.50	.15
185 Jorge Posada	.50	.15
186 Mike Sweeney	.30	.09
187 Cesar Izturis	.30	.09
188 Jason Schmidt	.30	.09
189 Chris Richard	.30	.09
190 Jason Phillips	.30	.09
191 Fred McGriff	.50	.15
192 Shea Hillenbrand	.30	.09
193 Ivan Rodriguez	.75	.23
194 Mike Lowell	.30	.09
195 Neifi Perez	.30	.09
196 Kenny Lofton	.30	.09
197 A.J. Pierzynski	.30	.09
198 Larry Bigbie	.30	.09
199 Juan Uribe	.30	.09
200 Jeff Bagwell	.50	.15
201 Timo Perez	.30	.09
202 Jeremy Giambi	.30	.09
203 Deivi Cruz	.30	.09
204 Marquis Grissom	.30	.09
205 Chipper Jones	.75	.23
206 Alex Gonzalez	.30	.09
207 Steve Finley	.30	.09
208 Ben Davis	.30	.09
209 Mike Bordick	.30	.09
210 Casey Fossum	.30	.09
211 Aramis Ramirez	.30	.09
212 Aaron Boone	.30	.09
213 Orlando Cabrera	.30	.09
214 Hee Seop Choi	.30	.09
215 Jeromy Burnitz	.30	.09
216 Todd Hollandsworth	.30	.09
217 Rey Sanchez	.30	.09
218 Jose Cruz	.30	.09
219 Roosevelt Brown	.30	.09
220 Odalis Perez	.30	.09
221 Carlos Delgado	.30	.09
222 Orlando Hernandez	.30	.09
223 Adam Everett	.30	.09
224 Adrian Beltre	.50	.15
225 Ken Griffey Jr.	1.25	.35
226 Brad Penny	.30	.09
227 Carlos Lee	.30	.09
228 J.C. Romero	.30	.09
229 Ramon Martinez	.30	.09
230 Matt Morris	.30	.09
231 Ben Howard	.30	.09
232 Damon Minor	.30	.09
233 Jason Marquis	.30	.09
234 Paul Wilson	.30	.09
235 Ryan Dempster	.30	.09
236 Jeffrey Hammonds	.30	.09
237 Jaret Wright	.30	.09
238 Carlos Pena	.30	.09
239 Toby Hall	.30	.09
240 Rick Helling	.30	.09
241 Alex Escobar	.30	.09
242 Trevor Hoffman	.30	.09
243 Bernie Williams	.50	.15
244 Jorge Julio	.30	.09
245 Byung-Hyun Kim	.30	.09
246 Mike Redmond	.30	.09
247 Tony Armas	.30	.09
248 Aaron Rowand	.30	.09
249 Rusty Greer	.30	.09
250 Aaron Harang	.30	.09
251 Jeremy Fikac	.30	.09
252 Jay Gibbons	.30	.09
253 Brandon Puffer	.30	.09
254 Dewayne Wise	.30	.09
255 Chan Ho Park	.30	.09
256 David Bell	.30	.09
257 Kenny Rogers	.30	.09
258 Mark Quinn	.30	.09
259 Greg LaRocca	.30	.09
260 Reggie Taylor	.30	.09
261 Brett Tomko	.30	.09
262 Jack Wilson	.30	.09
263 Billy Wagner	.30	.09
264 Greg Norton	.30	.09
265 Tim Salmon	.50	.15
266 Joe Randa	.30	.09
267 Geronimo Gil	.30	.09
268 Johnny Damon	.75	.23
269 Robin Ventura	.30	.09
270 Frank Thomas	.75	.23
271 Terrence Long	.30	.09
272 Mark Redman	.30	.09
273 Mark Kotsay	.30	.09
274 Ben Sheets	.30	.09
275 Reggie Sanders	.30	.09
276 Mark Grace	.50	.15
277 Eddie Guardado	.30	.09
278 Julio Mateo	.30	.09
279 Bengie Molina	.30	.09
280 Bill Hall	.30	.09
281 Eric Chavez	.30	.09
282 Joe Kennedy	.30	.09
283 John Valentin	.30	.09
284 Ray Durham	.30	.09
285 Trot Nixon	.30	.09
286 Rondell White	.30	.09
287 Alex Gonzalez	.30	.09
288 Tomas Perez	.30	.09
289 Jared Sandberg	.30	.09
290 Jacque Jones	.30	.09
291 Cliff Floyd	.30	.09
292 Ryan Klesko	.30	.09
293 Morgan Ensberg	.30	.09
294 Jerry Hairston	.30	.09
295 Doug Mientkiewicz	.30	.09
296 Darin Erstad	.30	.09
297 Jeff Conine	.30	.09
298 Johnny Estrada	.30	.09
299 Mark Mulder	.30	.09
300 Jeff Kent	.30	.09
301 Roger Clemens	1.50	.45
302 Endy Chavez	.30	.09
303 Joe Crede	.30	.09
304 J.D. Drew	.30	.09
305 David Dellucci	.30	.09
306 Eli Marrero	.30	.09
307 Josh Fogg	.30	.09
308 Mike Crudale	.30	.09
309 Bret Boone	.30	.09
310 Mariano Rivera	.50	.15
311 Mike Piazza	1.25	.35
312 Jason Jennings	.30	.09
313 Jason Varitek	.50	.15
314 Vicente Padilla	.30	.09
315 Kevin Millwood	.30	.09
316 Nick Johnson	.30	.09
317 Shane Reynolds	.30	.09
318 Joe Thurston	.30	.09
319 Mike Lamb	.30	.09
320 Aaron Sele	.30	.09
321 Fernando Tatis	.30	.09
322 Randy Wolf	.30	.09
323 David Justice	.30	.09
324 Andy Pettitte	.50	.15
325 Freddy Sanchez	.30	.09
326 Scott Spiezio	.30	.09
327 Randy Johnson	.75	.23
328 Karim Garcia	.30	.09
329 Eric Milton	.30	.09
330 Jermaine Dye	.30	.09
331 Kevin Brown	.30	.09
332 Adam Pettyjohn	.30	.09
333 Jason Lane	.30	.09
334 Mark Prior	.75	.23
335 Mike Lieberthal	.30	.09
336 Matt White	.30	.09
337 John Patterson	.30	.09
338 Marcus Giles	.30	.09
339 Kazuhisa Ishii	.30	.09
340 Willie Harris	.30	.09
341 Travis Phelps	.30	.09
342 Randall Simon	.30	.09
343 Manny Ramirez	.50	.15
344 Kerry Wood	.75	.23
345 Shannon Stewart	.30	.09
346 Mike Mussina	.50	.15
347 Joe Borchard	.30	.09
348 Tyler Walker	.30	.09
349 Preston Wilson	.30	.09
350 Damian Moss	.30	.09
351 Eric Karros	.30	.09
352 Bobby Kielty	.30	.09
353 Jason LaRue	.30	.09
354 Phil Nevin	.30	.09
355 Tony Graffanino	.30	.09
356 Antonio Alfonseca	.30	.09
357 Eddie Taubensee	.30	.09
358 Luis Ugueto	.30	.09
359 Greg Vaughn	.30	.09
360 Corey Thurman	.30	.09
361 Omar Infante	.30	.09
362 Alex Cintron	.30	.09
363 Esteban Loaiza	.30	.09
364 Tino Martinez	.50	.15
365 David Eckstein	.30	.09
366 Dave Pember RC	.30	.09
367 Damian Rolls	.30	.09
368 Richard Hidalgo	.30	.09
369 Brad Radke	.30	.09
370 Alex Sanchez	.30	.09
371 Ben Grieve	.30	.09
372 Brandon Inge	.30	.09
373 Adam Piatt	.30	.09
374 Charles Johnson	.30	.09
375 Rafael Palmeiro	.50	.15
376 Joe Mays	.30	.09
377 Derrek Lee	.30	.09
378 Fernando Vina	.30	.09
379 Andruw Jones	.30	.09
380 Troy Glaus	.30	.09
381 Bobby Hill	.30	.09
382 C.C. Sabathia	.30	.09
383 Jose Hernandez	.30	.09
384 Al Leiter	.30	.09
385 Jarrod Washburn	.30	.09
386 Cody Ransom	.30	.09
387 Matt Stairs	.30	.09
388 Edgar Renteria	.30	.09
389 Tsuyoshi Shinjo	.30	.09
390 Matt Williams	.30	.09
391 Bubba Trammell	.30	.09
392 Jason Kendall	.30	.09
393 Scott Rolen	.75	.23
394 Chuck Knoblauch	.30	.09
395 Jimmy Rollins	.30	.09
396 Gary Bennett	.30	.09
397 David Wells	.30	.09
398 Ronnie Belliard	.30	.09
399 Austin Kearns	.30	.09
400 Tim Hudson	.30	.09
401 Andy Van Hekken	.30	.09
402 Ray Lankford	.30	.09
403 Todd Helton	.50	.15
404 Jeff Weaver	.30	.09
405 Gabe Kapler	.30	.09
406 Luis Gonzalez	.30	.09
407 Sean Casey	.30	.09
408 Kazuhiro Sasaki	.30	.09
409 Mark Teixeira	.30	.09
410 Brian Giles	.30	.09
411 Robert Fick	.30	.09
412 Wilkin Ruan	.30	.09
413 Jose Rijo	.30	.09
414 Ben Broussard	.30	.09
415 Aubrey Huff	.30	.09
416 Magglio Ordonez	.30	.09
417 Barry Bonds AW	1.00	.30
418 Miguel Tejada AW	.30	.09
419 Randy Johnson AW	.50	.15
420 Barry Zito AW	.30	.09
421 Jason Jennings AW	.30	.09
422 Eric Hinske AW	.30	.09
423 Benito Santiago AW	.30	.09
424 Adam Kennedy AW	.30	.09
425 Troy Glaus AW	.30	.09
426 Brandon Phillips PR	.30	.09
427 Jake Peavy PR	.30	.09
428 Jason Romano PR	.30	.09
429 Jeriome Robertson PR	.30	.09
430 Aaron Guiel PR	.30	.09
431 Hank Blalock PR	.50	.15
432 Brad Lidge PR	.30	.09
433 Francisco Rodriguez PR	.30	.09
434 Jaime Cerda PR	.30	.09
435 Jung Bong PR	.30	.09
436 Reed Johnson PR	.30	.09
437 Rene Reyes PR	.30	.09
438 Chris Snelling PR	.30	.09
439 Miguel Olivo PR	.30	.09
440 Brian Banks PR	.30	.09
441 Eric Junge PR	.30	.09
442 Kirk Saarloos PR	.30	.09
443 Jamey Carroll PR	.30	.09
444 Josh Hancock PR	.30	.09
445 Michael Restovich PR	.30	.09
446 Willie Bloomquist PR	.30	.09
447 John Lackey PR	.30	.09
448 Marcus Thames PR	.30	.09
449 Victor Martinez PR	.50	.15
450 Brett Myers PR	.30	.09
451 Wes Obermueller PR	.30	.09
452 Hansel Izquierdo PR	.30	.09
453 Brian Tallet PR	.30	.09
454 Craig Monroe PR	.30	.09
455 Doug Devore PR	.30	.09
456 John Buck PR	.30	.09
457 Tony Alvarez PR	.30	.09
458 Wily Mo Pena PR	.30	.09
459 John Stephens PR	.30	.09
460 Tony Torcato PR	.30	.09
461 Adam Kennedy BNR	.30	.09
462 Alex Rodriguez BNR	.75	.23
463 Derek Lowe BNR	.30	.09
464 Garret Anderson BNR	.30	.09
465 Pat Burrell BNR	.30	.09
466 Eric Gagne BNR	.50	.15
467 Tomo Ohka BNR	.30	.09
468 Josh Phelps BNR	.30	.09
469 Sammy Sosa BNR	.75	.23
470 Jim Thome BNR	.50	.15
471 Vladimir Guerrero BNR	.50	.15
472 Jason Simontacchi BNR	.30	.09
473 Adam Dunn BNR	.50	.15
474 Jim Edmonds BNR	.30	.09
475 Barry Bonds BNR	1.00	.30
476 Paul Konerko BNR	.30	.09
477 Alfonso Soriano BNR	.50	.15
478 Curt Schilling BNR	.30	.09
479 John Smoltz BNR	.30	.09
480 Torii Hunter BNR	.30	.09
481 Rodrigo Lopez BNR	.30	.09
482 Miguel Tejada BNR	.30	.09
483 Eric Hinske BNR	.30	.09
484 Roy Oswalt BNR	.30	.09
485 Junior Spivey BNR	.30	.09
P1 Barry Bonds Pin	8.00	2.40
P87 Derek Jeter Promo	2.00	.60

2003 Fleer Tradition Glossy

MINT NRMT

*GLOSSY 1-100: 1.5X TO 4X BASIC
*GLOSSY 101-485: 5X TO 12X BASIC
RANDOM IN HOBBY UPDATE PACKS
STATED ODDS 1:24 RETAIL
STATED PRINT RUN 100 SERIAL #'d SETS

2003 Fleer Tradition Game Used

Inserted in packs at a stated rate of one in 35 hobby and one in 90 retail; these cards partially parallel the regular Fleer Tradition set. Some of these cards were issued to a shorter print run and we have notated that information next to the player's name in our checklist.

	Nm-Mt	Ex-Mt
*GOLD: .75X TO 2X BASIC GU		
*GOLD: .6X TO 1.5X GU p/r 150-200		
*GOLD ML: .6X TO 1.5X GU p/r 150-200		
*GOLD: .4X TO 1X GU p/r 50-60		
GOLD RANDOM INSERTS IN PACKS		
GOLD PRINT RUN 100 SERIAL #'d SETS		
2 Derek Jeter Jsy SP/150	30.00	9.00

7 Craig Biggio Bat 10.00 3.00
10 Hideo Nomo Jsy SP/200 25.00 7.50
11 Barry Larkin Jsy SP/200 15.00 4.50
22 Kazuhiro Sasaki Jsy SP/200 10.00 3.00
31 Greg Maddux Jsy 15.00 4.50
42 Mo Vaughn Jsy SP/60 15.00 4.50
46 Pedro Martinez Jsy SP/200 15.00 4.50
63 Barry Zito Jsy 8.00 2.40
67 Luis Aparicio ML Jsy SP/150 15.00 4.50
97 W.Stargell ML Pants SP/150 15.00 4.50
104 N.Garciaparra Jsy SP/200 25.00 7.50
128 Edg Alfonzo Jsy SP/200 10.00 3.00
180 John Olerud Jsy 8.00 2.40
184 Juan Gonzalez Bat SP/200 15.00 4.50
185 Jorge Posada Bat 10.00 3.00
192 Shea Hillenbrand Bat 8.00 2.40
193 Ivan Rodriguez Jsy 15.00 4.50
194 Mike Lowell Bat 8.00 2.40
200 Jeff Bagwell Jsy SP/200 15.00 4.50
205 Chipper Jones Jsy 15.00 4.50
215 Jeromy Burnitz Jsy SP/200 10.00 3.00
224 Adrian Beltre Jsy 10.00 3.00
269 Robin Ventura Jsy 8.00 2.40
270 Frank Thomas Jsy 15.00 4.50
276 Mark Grace Jsy 10.00 3.00
296 Darin Erstad Jsy 8.00 2.40
301 Roger Clemens Jsy SP/150 25.00 7.50
304 J.D. Drew Jsy 8.00 2.40
311 Mike Piazza Jsy SP/150 25.00 7.50
327 Randy Johnson Jsy SP/150 15.00 4.50
334 Mark Prior Jsy SP/200 15.00 4.50
339 Kazuhisa Ishii Jsy 8.00 2.40
343 Manny Ramirez Jsy SP/150 15.00 4.50
344 Kerry Wood Jsy SP/200 15.00 4.50
346 Mike Mussina Jsy 10.00 3.00
351 Eric Karros Jsy 8.00 2.40
375 Rafael Palmeiro Jsy 10.00 3.00
379 Andruw Jones Bat SP/150 10.00 3.00
392 Jason Kendall Pants 8.00 2.40
395 Jimmy Rollins Jsy 8.00 2.40
402 Barry Bonds AW Jsy SP/50 50.00 15.00
403 M.Tejada AW Bat SP/150 10.00 3.00
406 Jason Jennings AW Pants 8.00 2.40

2003 Fleer Tradition Black-White Goudey

Inserted randomly into hobby packs, these cards were issued in the design of the 1936 Goudey Black and White set. To honor the 1936 set further each of these cards were issued to a stated print run of 1936 serial numbered sets.

Nm-Mt Ex-Mt
*GOLD: 2.5X TO 6X BASIC B/W GOUDEY
GOLD RANDOM INSERTS IN HOBBY PACKS
GOLD PRINT RUN 36 SERIAL #'d SETS
*RED: X TO X BASIC B/W GOUDEY....
RED RANDOM INSERTS IN RETAIL PACKS
RED PRINT RUN 500 SERIAL #'d SETS
1 Jim Thome 4.00 1.20
2 Derek Jeter 10.00 3.00
3 Alex Rodriguez 6.00 1.80
4 Mark Prior 4.00 1.20
5 Nomar Garciaparra 6.00 1.80
6 Curt Schilling 4.00 1.20
7 Pat Burrell 4.00 1.20
8 Frank Thomas 4.00 1.20
9 Roger Clemens 8.00 2.40
10 Chipper Jones 4.00 1.20
11 Barry Larkin 4.00 1.20
12 Hideo Nomo 4.00 1.20
13 Pedro Martinez 4.00 1.20
14 Jeff Bagwell 4.00 1.20
15 Greg Maddux 6.00 1.80
16 Vladimir Guerrero 4.00 1.20
17 Ichiro Suzuki 6.00 1.80
18 Mike Piazza 6.00 1.80
19 Drew Henson 4.00 1.20
20 Albert Pujols 8.00 2.40
21 Sammy Sosa 6.00 1.80
22 Jason Giambi 4.00 1.20
23 Randy Johnson 4.00 1.20
24 Ken Griffey Jr. 6.00 1.80
25 Barry Bonds 10.00 3.00

2003 Fleer Tradition Checklists

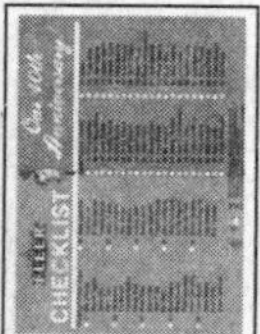

Inserted in packs at a stated rate of one in four, these 18 cards feature either Derek Jeter or Barry Bonds. These cards when matched together make up a puzzle of the featured players

Nm-Mt Ex-Mt
COMP.JETER PUZZLE (9) 8.00 2.40
COMMON JETER 1.00 .30
COMP.BONDS PUZZLE (9) 6.00 1.80
COMMON BONDS .75 .23

2003 Fleer Tradition Hardball Preview

Inserted into packs at a stated rate of one in 400 hobby and one in 480 retail, this 10 card set was

issued to preview what the new Hardball set that Fleer would be releasing slightly later in 2003.

Nm-Mt Ex-Mt
1 Miguel Tejada 20.00 6.00
2 Derek Jeter 40.00 12.00
3 Mike Piazza 25.00 7.50
4 Barry Bonds 40.00 12.00
5 Mark Prior 20.00 6.00
6 Ichiro Suzuki 25.00 7.50
7 Alex Rodriguez 25.00 7.50
8 Nomar Garciaparra 25.00 7.50
9 Alfonso Soriano 20.00 6.00
10 Ken Griffey Jr. 25.00 7.50

2003 Fleer Tradition Lumber Company

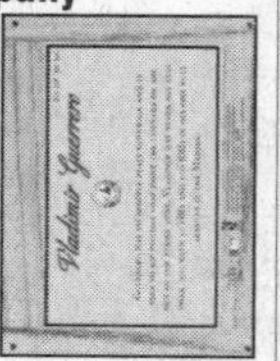

Issued at a stated rate of one in 10 hobby and one in 12 retail, these 30 cards focus on players known for the prowess with the bat.

Nm-Mt Ex-Mt
COMPLETE SET (30) 60.00 18.00
1 Mike Piazza 4.00 1.20
2 Derek Jeter 6.00 1.80
3 Alex Rodriguez 4.00 1.20
4 Miguel Tejada 1.50 .45
5 Nomar Garciaparra 4.00 1.20
6 Andruw Jones 1.50 .45
7 Pat Burrell 1.50 .45
8 Albert Pujols 5.00 1.50
9 Jeff Bagwell 1.50 .45
10 Chipper Jones 2.50 .75
11 Ichiro Suzuki 4.00 1.20
12 Alfonso Soriano 1.50 .45
13 Eric Chavez 1.50 .45
14 Brian Giles 1.50 .45
15 Shawn Green 1.50 .45
16 Jim Thome 2.50 .75
17 Lance Berkman 1.50 .45
18 Bernie Williams 1.50 .45
19 Manny Ramirez 1.50 .45
20 Vladimir Guerrero 2.50 .75
21 Carlos Delgado 1.50 .45
22 Scott Rolen 2.50 .75
23 Sammy Sosa 4.00 1.20
24 Ken Griffey Jr. 4.00 1.20
25 Barry Bonds 6.00 1.80
26 Todd Helton 1.50 .45
27 Jason Giambi 1.50 .45
28 Austin Kearns 1.50 .45
29 Jeff Kent 1.50 .45
30 Magglio Ordonez 1.50 .45

2003 Fleer Tradition Lumber Company Game Used

Inserted at a stated rate of one in 108 hobby and one in 195 retail, this is a partial parallel to the Lumber Company insert set. A few cards were issued in shorter supply and we have notated the print run information in our checklist.

Nm-Mt Ex-Mt
1 Jeff Bagwell SP/200 15.00 4.50
2 Lance Berkman SP/200 10.00 3.00
3 Barry Bonds SP/150 30.00 9.00
4 Pat Burrell SP/75 15.00 4.50
5 Eric Chavez SP/125 10.00 3.00
6 Carlos Delgado SP/200 10.00 3.00
7 Nomar Garciaparra SP/200 20.00 6.00
8 Brian Giles SP/200 10.00 3.00
9 Shawn Green SP/200 10.00 3.00
10 Todd Helton 10.00 3.00
11 Derek Jeter SP/96 40.00 12.00
12 Andruw Jones 8.00 2.40
13 Chipper Jones 15.00 4.50
14 Austin Kearns SP/75 15.00 4.50
15 Jeff Kent SP/200 10.00 3.00
16 Magglio Ordonez 8.00 2.40
17 Mike Piazza SP/200 25.00 7.50
18 Manny Ramirez 10.00 3.00
19 Alex Rodriguez 15.00 4.50
20 Scott Rolen SP/80 25.00 7.50
21 Alfonso Soriano SP/200 15.00 4.50
22 Miguel Tejada 8.00 2.40
23 Jim Thome SP/200 15.00 4.50
24 Bernie Williams 10.00 3.00

2003 Fleer Tradition Lumber Company Game Used Gold

Randomly inserted in packs, this is a parallel to the Lumber Company Game Used insert set.

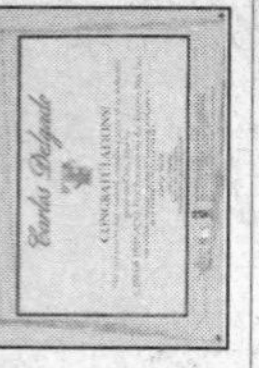

These cards were printed to a stated print run matching the number of homers the featured player hit in 2002. If the card was issued to a stated print run of 25 or fewer, no pricing is provided due to market scarcity.

Nm-Mt Ex-Mt
1 Jeff Bagwell/31
2 Lance Berkman/42 25.00 7.50
3 Barry Bonds/46 80.00 24.00
4 Pat Burrell/37 25.00 7.50
5 Eric Chavez/34 25.00 7.50
6 Carlos Delgado/33 25.00 7.50
7 Nomar Garciaparra/24
8 Brian Giles/38 25.00 7.50
9 Shawn Green/42 25.00 7.50
10 Todd Helton/30 40.00 12.00
11 Derek Jeter/18
12 Andruw Jones/35 25.00 7.50
13 Chipper Jones/26 40.00 12.00
14 Austin Kearns/13
15 Jeff Kent/37 25.00 7.50
16 Magglio Ordonez/38 25.00 7.50
17 Mike Piazza/33 80.00 24.00
18 Manny Ramirez/33 40.00 12.00
19 Alex Rodriguez/57 50.00 15.00
20 Scott Rolen/31 40.00 12.00
21 Alfonso Soriano/39 40.00 12.00
22 Miguel Tejada/34 25.00 7.50
23 Jim Thome/52 40.00 12.00
24 Bernie Williams/19

2003 Fleer Tradition Milestones

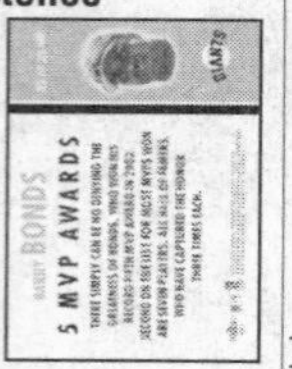

Inserted in packs at a stated rate of one in five hobby and one in four retail, these 25 cards feature either milestones passed by active players in the 2002 season or by retired players in past seasons.

Nm-Mt Ex-Mt
COMPLETE SET (25) 30.00 9.00
1 Eddie Mathews 2.00 .60
2 Rickey Henderson 1.25 .35
3 Harmon Killebrew 2.00 .60
4 Al Kaline 2.00 .60
5 Willie McCovey 2.00 .60
6 Tom Seaver 2.00 .60
7 Reggie Jackson 2.00 .60
8 Mike Schmidt 3.00 .90
9 Nolan Ryan 4.00 1.20
10 Mike Piazza 2.00 .60
11 Randy Johnson 1.25 .35
12 Bernie Williams 1.00 .30
13 Rafael Palmeiro 1.00 .30
14 Juan Gonzalez 1.00 .30
15 Ken Griffey Jr. 2.00 .60
16 Derek Jeter 3.00 .90
17 Roger Clemens 2.50 .75
18 Roberto Alomar 1.00 .30
19 Manny Ramirez 1.00 .30
20 Luis Gonzalez 1.00 .30
21 Barry Bonds 3.00 .90
22 Nomar Garciaparra 2.00 .60
23 Fred McGriff 1.00 .30
24 Greg Maddux 2.00 .60
25 Barry Bonds 3.00 .90

2003 Fleer Tradition Milestones Game Used

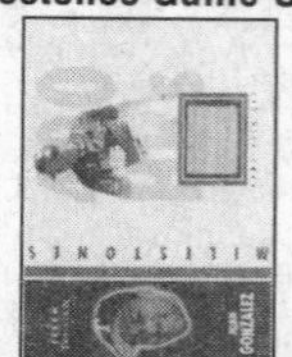

Inserted at a stated rate of one in 143 hobby and one in 270 retail these 14 cards feature memorabilia cards from the some of the featured players in the Milestone set. A few of these cards were issued to a smaller print run and we have notated that information along with the print run information provided in our checklist.

Nm-Mt Ex-Mt
*GOLD: .75X TO 2X BASIC MILE
*GOLD: .6X TO 1.5X MILE SP/150-200
*GOLD: .5X TO 1.2X MILE SP/100
GOLD RANDOM INSERTS IN PACKS
GOLD PRINT RUN 100 SERIAL #'d SETS
1 B.Bonds 5 MVP Jsy SP/200 30.00 9.00
2 B.Bonds 600 HR Bat SP/100 40.00 12.00
3 Derek Jeter Jsy SP/150 30.00 9.00
4 Greg Maddux Jsy 15.00 4.50
5 Rafael Palmeiro Jsy SP/200 15.00 4.50
6 Mike Piazza Jsy SP/100 25.00 7.50
7 Randy Johnson Jsy SP/100 15.00 4.50
8 Roberto Alomar Bat SP/200 15.00 4.50
9 Roger Clemens Jsy SP/150 25.00 7.50
10 Manny Ramirez Jsy SP/150 15.00 4.50
11 N.Garciaparra Jsy SP/200 20.00 6.00
12 Juan Gonzalez Bat SP/250 15.00 4.50
13 Fred McGriff Bat 10.00 3.00
14 Bernie Williams Jsy SP/200 15.00 4.50

2003 Fleer Tradition Standouts

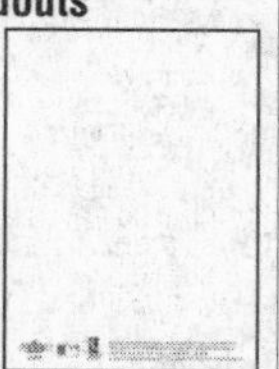

Inserted in packs at a stated rate of one in 40 hobby and one in 72 retail, these 15 cards become mini-standees when the player's photo is "popped-out" of the card.

Nm-Mt Ex-Mt
1 Barry Bonds 10.00 3.00
2 Pat Burrell 5.00 1.50
3 Roger Clemens 8.00 2.40
4 Adam Dunn 5.00 1.50
5 Nomar Garciaparra 6.00 1.80
6 Ken Griffey Jr. 6.00 1.80
7 Vladimir Guerrero 5.00 1.50
8 Derek Jeter 10.00 3.00
9 Greg Maddux 6.00 1.80
10 Mike Piazza 6.00 1.80
11 Alex Rodriguez 6.00 1.80
12 Alfonso Soriano 5.00 1.50
13 Sammy Sosa 6.00 1.80
14 Ichiro Suzuki 6.00 1.80
15 Miguel Tejada 5.00 1.50

2003 Fleer Tradition Update

This 398 card set was released in October, 2003. The set was issued in 10-card packs with an $2 SRP which came 32 packs to a box and 20 boxes to a case. In addition, each sealed box contained a 25 card "mini-box". Cards numbered 1-200 featured veterans, cards numbered 201 through 259 featured all stars, cards 260 through 275 feature interleague match-up cards while cards numbered 276 through 285 is a Tale of the Tape subset. Cards numbered 286 through 299 feature 2003 rookies and those cards were inserted at a stated rate of one in four. Cards numbered 300 through 398 feature 2003 rookies and those cards were issued as part of the 25 card mini-boxes.

MINT NRMT
COMP.SET w/o SP's (285) 40.00 18.00
COMMON CARD (1-285) .30 .14
COMMON CARD (286-299) 1.00 .45
COMMON RC (286-299) 1.00 .45
286-299 STATED ODDS 1:4 HOB/RET
COMMON CARD (300-398) 1.00 .45
COMMON RC (300-398) 1.00 .45
300-398 ISSUED IN MINI-BOXES
ONE MINI-BOX PER UPDATE BOX
25 CARDS PER MINI-BOX
1 Aaron Boone .30 .14
2 Carl Everett .30 .14
3 Eduardo Perez .30 .14
4 Jason Michaels .30 .14
5 Karim Garcia .30 .14
6 Rainer Olmedo .30 .14
7 Scott Williamson .30 .14
8 Adam Kennedy .30 .14
9 Carl Pavano .30 .14
10 Eli Marrero .30 .14
11 Jason Simontacchi .30 .14
12 Keith Foulke .30 .14
13 Preston Wilson .30 .14
14 Scott Hatteberg .30 .14
15 Adam Dunn .50 .23
16 Carlos Baerga .30 .14
17 Elmer Dessens .30 .14
18 Javier Vazquez .30 .14
19 Kenny Rogers .30 .14
20 Quinton McCracken .30 .14
21 Shane Reynolds .30 .14
22 Adam Eaton .30 .14
23 Carlos Zambrano .30 .14
24 Enrique Wilson .30 .14
25 Jeff DaVanon .30 .14
26 Kenny Lofton .30 .14
27 Ramon Castro .30 .14
28 Shannon Stewart .30 .14
29 Al Martin .30 .14
30 Carlos Guillen .30 .14
31 Eric Karros .30 .14
32 Tim Worrell .30 .14
33 Kevin Millwood .30 .14
34 Randall Simon .30 .14
35 Shawn Chacon .30 .14
36 Alex Rodriguez 1.25 .55
37 Casey Blake .30 .14
38 Eric Munson .30 .14
39 Jeff Kent .30 .14
40 Kris Benson .30 .14
41 Randy Winn .30 .14
42 Shea Hillenbrand .30 .14
43 Alfonso Soriano .50 .23
44 Chris George .30 .14
45 Eric Bruntlett .30 .14
46 Jeromy Burnitz .30 .14
47 Kyle Farnsworth .30 .14
48 Torii Hunter .30 .14
49 Sidney Ponson .30 .14
50 Andres Galarraga .30 .14
51 Chris Singleton .30 .14
52 Eric Gagne .75 .35
53 Jesse Foppert .30 .14
54 Lance Carter .30 .14
55 Ray Durham .30 .14
56 Tanyon Sturtze .30 .14
57 Andy Ashby .30 .14
58 Cliff Floyd .30 .14
59 Eric Young .30 .14
60 Jhonny Peralta .50 .23
61 Livan Hernandez .30 .14
62 Reggie Sanders .30 .14
63 Tim Spooneybarger .30 .14
64 Angel Berroa .30 .14
65 Coco Crisp .30 .14
66 Eric Hinske .30 .14
67 Jim Edmonds .30 .14
68 Luis Matos .30 .14
69 Rickey Henderson .75 .35
70 Todd Walker .30 .14
71 Antonio Alfonseca .30 .14
72 Corey Koskie .30 .14
73 Erubiel Durazo .30 .14
74 Jim Thome .75 .35
75 Lyle Overbay .30 .14
76 Robert Fick .30 .14
77 Todd Hollandsworth .30 .14
78 Aramis Ramirez .30 .14
79 Cristian Guzman .30 .14
80 Esteban Loaiza .30 .14
81 Jody Gerut .30 .14
82 Mark Grudzielanek .30 .14
83 Roberto Alomar .50 .23
84 Todd Hundley .30 .14
85 Mike Hampton .30 .14
86 Curt Schilling .30 .14
87 Francisco Rodriguez .30 .14
88 John Lackey .30 .14
89 Mark Redman .30 .14
90 Robin Ventura .30 .14
91 Todd Zeile .30 .14
92 B.J. Surhoff .30 .14
93 Raul Mondesi .30 .14
94 Frank Catalanotto .30 .14
95 John Smoltz .50 .23
96 Mark Ellis .30 .14
97 Rocco Baldelli .30 .14
98 Todd Pratt .30 .14
99 Barry Bonds 2.00 .90
100 Danny Graves .30 .14
101 Fred McGriff .50 .23
102 John Burkett .30 .14
103 Marquis Grissom .30 .14
104 Rocky Biddle .30 .14
105 Tom Glavine .50 .23
106 Bartolo Colon .30 .14
107 Darren Bragg .30 .14
108 Gabe Kapler .30 .14
109 John Franco .30 .14
110 Matt Mantei .30 .14
111 Rod Beck .30 .14
112 Tomo Ohka .30 .14
113 Ben Petrick .30 .14
114 Darren Dreifort .30 .14
115 Garret Anderson .30 .14
116 John Vander Wal .30 .14
117 Melvin Mora .30 .14
118 Rodrigo Lopez .30 .14
119 Raul Ibanez .30 .14
120 Benito Santiago .30 .14
121 David Ortiz Sox .75 .35
122 Gary Bennett .30 .14
123 Jon Garland .30 .14
124 Michael Young .50 .23
125 Rodrigo Rosario .30 .14
126 Travis Lee .30 .14
127 Bill Mueller .30 .14
128 Derek Lowe .30 .14
129 Gil Meche .30 .14
130 Jose Guillen .30 .14
131 Miguel Cabrera .75 .35
132 Ron Calloway .30 .14
133 Troy Percival .30 .14
134 Billy Koch .30 .14
135 Dmitri Young .30 .14
136 Glendon Rusch .30 .14
137 Jose Jimenez .30 .14
138 Miguel Tejada .30 .14
139 John Thomson .30 .14
140 Troy O'Leary .30 .14
141 Bobby Kielty .30 .14
142 Dontrelle Willis .50 .23
143 Greg Myers .30 .14
144 Jose Vizcaino .30 .14
145 Mike MacDougal .30 .14
146 Ronnie Belliard .30 .14
147 Tyler Houston .30 .14
148 Brady Clark .30 .14
149 Edgardo Alfonzo .30 .14
150 Guillermo Mota .30 .14
151 Jose Lima .30 .14
152 Mike Williams .30 .14
153 Roy Oswalt .30 .14
154 Scott Podsednik 5.00 2.20
155 Brandon Lyon .30 .14
156 Henry Mateo .30 .14
157 Jose Macias .30 .14
158 Mike Bordick .30 .14
159 Royce Clayton .30 .14
160 Vance Wilson .30 .14
161 Brent Abernathy .30 .14
162 Horacio Ramirez .30 .14
163 Jose Reyes .30 .14
164 Nick Punto .30 .14
165 Ruben Sierra .30 .14
166 Victor Zambrano .30 .14
167 Brett Tomko .30 .14
168 Ivan Rodriguez .75 .35
169 Jose Mesa .30 .14
170 Octavio Dotel .30 .14
171 Russ Ortiz .30 .14
172 Vladimir Guerrero .75 .35
173 Brian Lawrence .30 .14
174 Jae Weong Seo .30 .14
175 Jose Cruz Jr. .30 .14

176 Pat Burrell .30 .14
177 Russell Branyan .30 .14
178 Warren Morris .30 .14
179 Brian Boehringer .30 .14
180 Jason Johnson .30 .14
181 Josh Phelps .30 .14
182 Paul Konerko .30 .14
183 Ryan Franklin .30 .14
184 Wes Helms .30 .14
185 Brooks Kieschnick .30 .14
186 Jason Davis .30 .14
187 Juan Pierre .30 .14
188 Paul Wilson .30 .14
189 Sammy Sosa 1.25 .55
190 Wil Cordero .30 .14
191 Byung-Hyun Kim .30 .14
192 Juan Encarnacion .30 .14
193 Placido Polanco .30 .14
194 Sandy Alomar Jr. .30 .14
195 Julio Lugo .30 .14
196 Junior Spivey .30 .14
197 Woody Williams .30 .14
198 Xavier Nady .30 .14
199 Mark Loretta .30 .14
200 Deivi Cruz .30 .14
201 Jorge Posada AS .30 .14
202 Carlos Delgado AS .30 .14
203 Alfonso Soriano AS .30 .14
204 Alex Rodriguez AS .75 .35
205 Troy Glaus AS .30 .14
206 Garret Anderson AS .30 .14
207 Hideki Matsui AS 2.00 .90
208 Ichiro Suzuki AS .75 .35
209 Esteban Loaiza AS .30 .14
210 Manny Ramirez AS .30 .14
211 Roger Clemens AS .75 .35
212 Roy Halladay AS .30 .14
213 Jason Giambi AS .30 .14
214 Edgar Martinez AS .30 .14
215 Bret Boone AS .30 .14
216 Hank Blalock AS .50 .23
217 Nomar Garciaparra AS .75 .35
218 Vernon Wells AS .30 .14
219 Melvin Mora AS .30 .14
220 Magglio Ordonez AS .30 .14
221 Mike Sweeney AS .30 .14
222 Barry Zito AS .30 .14
223 Carl Everett AS .30 .14
224 Shigetoshi Hasegawa AS .30 .14
225 Jamie Moyer AS .30 .14
226 Mark Mulder AS .30 .14
227 Eddie Guardado AS .30 .14
228 Ramon Hernandez AS .30 .14
229 Keith Foulke AS .30 .14
230 Javy Lopez AS .30 .14
231 Todd Helton AS .30 .14
232 Marcus Giles AS .30 .14
233 Edgar Renteria AS .30 .14
234 Scott Rolen AS .50 .23
235 Barry Bonds AS 1.00 .45
236 Albert Pujols AS .75 .35
237 Gary Sheffield AS .30 .14
238 Jim Edmonds AS .30 .14
239 Jason Schmidt AS .30 .14
240 Mark Prior AS .50 .23
241 Dontrelle Willis AS .30 .14
242 Kerry Wood AS .50 .23
243 Kevin Brown AS .30 .14
244 Woody Williams AS .30 .14
245 Paul Lo Duca AS .30 .14
246 Richie Sexson AS .30 .14
247 Jose Vidro AS .30 .14
248 Luis Castillo AS .30 .14
249 Aaron Boone AS .30 .14
250 Mike Lowell AS .30 .14
251 Rafael Furcal AS .30 .14
252 Andruw Jones AS .30 .14
253 Preston Wilson AS .30 .14
254 John Smoltz AS .30 .14
255 Eric Gagne AS .50 .23
256 Randy Wolf AS .30 .14
257 Billy Wagner AS .30 .14
258 Luis Gonzalez AS .30 .14
259 Russ Ortiz AS .30 .14
260 Jim Thome .50 .23
Pedro Martinez IL
261 Alfonso Soriano .50 .23
Jeff Bagwell IL
262 Dontrelle Willis .30 .14
Rocco Baldelli IL
263 Carlos Delgado .50 .23
Vladimir Guerrero IL
264 Sammy Sosa .75 .35
Magglio Ordonez IL
265 Jason Giambi .30 .14
Adam Dunn IL
266 Mike Sweeney .75 .35
Albert Pujols IL
267 Barry Bonds 1.00 .45
Torii Hunter IL
268 Ichiro Suzuki .75 .35
Andruw Jones IL
269 Chipper Jones .50 .23
Hank Blalock IL
270 Mark Prior .50 .23
Vernon Wells IL
271 Nomar Garciaparra .75 .35
Scott Rolen IL
272 Alex Rodriguez .75 .35
Lance Berkman IL
273 Roger Clemens .75 .35
Kerry Wood IL
274 Derek Jeter 1.00 .45
Jose Reyes IL
275 Greg Maddux .75 .35
Barry Zito IL
276 Carlos Delgado TT .30 .14
277 J.D. Drew TT .30 .14
278 Barry Bonds TT 1.00 .45
279 Albert Pujols TT .75 .35
280 Jim Thome TT .50 .23
281 Sammy Sosa TT .75 .35
282 Alfonso Soriano TT .30 .14
283 Hideki Matsui TT 2.00 .90
284 Mike Piazza TT .75 .35
285 Vladimir Guerrero TT .50 .23
286 Rich Harden ROO 1.50 .70
287 Chin-Hui Tsao ROO 1.00 .45
288 Edwin Jackson ROO RC 5.00 2.20
289 Chien-Ming Wang ROO RC 2.50 1.10
290 Josh Willingham ROO RC 1.50 .70
291 Matt Kata ROO RC 2.50 1.10
292 Jose Contreras ROO RC 2.50 1.10
293 Chris Bootcheck ROO 1.00 .45
294 Javier Lopez ROO RC 1.00 .45
295 Delmon Young ROO RC 8.00 3.60
296 Pedro Liriano ROO 1.00 .45
297 Noah Lowry ROO 1.50 .70
298 Khalil Greene ROO 5.00 2.20
299 Rob Bowen ROO 1.00 .45
300 Bo Hart ROO RC 1.50 .70
301 Beau Kemp ROO RC 1.00 .45
302 Gerald Laird ROO 1.00 .45
303 Miguel Ojeda ROO RC 1.00 .45
304 Todd Wellemeyer ROO RC 1.50 .70
305 Ryan Wagner ROO RC 1.50 .70
306 Jeff Duncan ROO RC 1.50 .70
307 Wilfredo Ledezma ROO RC 1.50 .70
308 Wes Obermueller ROO 1.00 .45
309 Bernie Castro ROO RC 1.00 .45
310 Tim Olson ROO RC 1.50 .70
311 Colin Porter ROO RC 1.00 .45
312 Francisco Cruceta ROO RC 1.00 .45
313 Guillermo Quiroz ROO RC 2.00 .90
314 Brian Stokes ROO RC 1.00 .45
315 Robby Hammock ROO RC 1.50 .70
316 Lew Ford ROO RC 3.00 1.35
317 Todd Linden ROO 1.00 .45
318 Mike Gallo ROO RC 1.00 .45
319 Francisco Rosario ROO RC 1.00 .45
320 Rosman Garcia ROO RC 1.00 .45
321 Felix Sanchez ROO RC 1.00 .45
322 Chad Gaudin ROO RC 1.00 .45
323 Phil Seibel ROO RC 1.00 .45
324 Jason Gilfillan ROO RC 1.00 .45
325 Terrmel Sledge ROO RC 1.50 .70
326 Alfredo Gonzalez ROO RC 1.00 .45
327 Josh Stewart ROO RC 1.00 .45
328 Jeremy Griffiths ROO RC 1.50 .70
329 Cory Stewart ROO RC 1.00 .45
330 Josh Hall ROO RC 1.50 .70
331 Arnie Munoz ROO RC 1.00 .45
332 Garrett Atkins ROO 1.00 .45
333 Neal Cotts ROO 1.00 .45
334 Dan Haren ROO RC 2.00 .90
335 Shane Victorino ROO RC 1.00 .45
336 David Sanders ROO RC 1.00 .45
337 Oscar Villarreal ROO RC 1.00 .45
338 Michael Hessman ROO RC 1.00 .45
339 Andrew Brown ROO RC 1.50 .70
340 Kevin Hooper ROO 1.00 .45
341 Prentice Redman ROO RC 1.00 .45
342 Brandon Webb ROO RC 2.50 1.10
343 Jimmy Gobble ROO 1.00 .45
344 Pete LaForest ROO RC 1.50 .70
345 Chris Waters ROO RC 1.00 .45
346 Hideki Matsui ROO RC 8.00 3.60
347 Chris Capuano ROO RC 1.00 .45
348 Jon Leicester ROO RC 1.00 .45
349 Mike Nicolas ROO RC 1.00 .45
350 Nook Logan ROO RC 1.00 .45
351 Craig Brazell ROO RC 1.50 .70
352 Aaron Looper ROO RC 1.00 .45
353 D.J. Carrasco ROO RC 1.00 .45
354 Clint Barmes ROO RC 1.50 .70
355 Doug Waechter ROO RC 1.50 .70
356 Julio Manon ROO RC 1.00 .45
357 Jer. Bonderman ROO RC 2.00 .90
358 D. Markwell ROO RC 1.00 .45
359 Dave Matranga ROO RC 1.00 .45
360 Luis Ayala ROO RC 1.00 .45
361 Jason Stanford ROO 1.00 .45
362 Roger Deago ROO RC 1.00 .45
363 Geoff Geary ROO RC 1.00 .45
364 Edgar Gonzalez ROO RC 1.00 .45
365 Michel Hernandez ROO RC 1.00 .45
366 Aquilino Lopez ROO RC 1.00 .45
367 David Manning ROO 1.00 .45
368 Carlos Mendez ROO RC 1.00 .45
369 Matt Miller ROO RC 1.00 .45
370 Mi. Nakamura ROO RC 1.00 .45
371 Mike Neu ROO RC 1.00 .45
372 Ramon Nivar ROO RC 2.00 .90
373 Kevin Ohme ROO RC 1.00 .45
374 Alex Prieto ROO RC 1.00 .45
375 Stephen Randolph ROO RC 1.00 .45
376 Brian Sweeney ROO RC 1.00 .45
377 Matt Diaz ROO RC 1.50 .70
378 Mike Gonzalez ROO 1.00 .45
379 Daniel Cabrera ROO RC 2.50 1.10
380 Fernando Cabrera ROO RC 1.00 .45
381 David DeJesus ROO RC 1.50 .70
382 Mike Ryan ROO RC 1.50 .70
383 Rick Roberts ROO RC 1.00 .45
384 Seung Song ROO 1.00 .45
385 Rickie Weeks ROO RC 6.00 2.70
386 Hum. Quintero ROO RC 1.00 .45
387 Alexis Rios ROO 1.50 .70
388 Aaron Miles ROO RC 2.50 1.10
389 Tom Gregorio ROO RC 1.00 .45
390 Anthony Ferrari ROO RC 1.00 .45
391 Kevin Correia ROO RC 1.00 .45
392 Rafael Betancourt ROO RC 1.50 .70
393 Rett Johnson ROO RC 1.50 .70
394 Richard Fischer ROO RC 1.00 .45
395 Greg Aquino ROO RC 1.00 .45
396 Daniel Garcia ROO RC 1.00 .45
397 Sergio Mitre ROO RC 1.50 .70
398 Edwin Almonte ROO 1.00 .45

2003 Fleer Tradition Update Glossy

MINT NRMT
*GLOSSY 1-285: 5X TO 12X BASIC
*GLOSSY 1-285: 3X TO 8X BASIC RC's
*GLOSSY MATSUI 207/283: 2.5X TO 6X BASIC
*GLOSSY 286-299: 1.5X TO 4X BASIC
*GLOSSY 286-299: 1.5X TO 4X BASIC RC's
*GLOSSY 300-398: 1.5X TO 4X BASIC
*GLOSSY 300-398: 1.5X TO 4X BASIC RC's
RANDOM INSERTS IN HOBBY PACKS
STATED ODDS 1:24 RETAIL
STATED PRINT RUN 100 SERIAL #'d SETS

2003 Fleer Tradition Update Diamond Debuts

MINT NRMT
STATED ODDS 1:10 HOBBY, 1:8 RETAIL
1 Dontrelle Willis 1.50 .70
2 Bo Hart 1.50 .70
3 Jose Reyes 1.00 .45

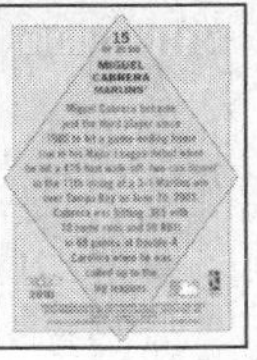

4 Chin-Hui Tsao 1.00 .45
5 Brandon Webb 2.00 .90
6 Rich Harden 1.50 .70
7 Jesse Foppert 1.00 .45
8 Rocco Baldelli 1.00 .45
9 Hideki Matsui 8.00 3.60
10 Ron Calloway 1.00 .45
11 Jeremy Bonderman 2.00 .90
12 Mark Teixeira 1.00 .45
13 Ryan Wagner 1.50 .70
14 Jose Contreras 2.50 1.10
15 Miguel Cabrera 2.50 1.10
16 Lew Ford 2.50 1.10
17 Jeff Duncan 1.50 .70
18 Matt Kata 2.00 .90
19 Jeremy Griffiths 1.50 .70
20 Todd Wellemeyer 1.50 .70
21 Robby Hammock 1.50 .70
22 Dave Matranga 1.00 .45
23 Laynce Nix 1.00 .45
24 Jhonny Peralta 1.00 .45
25 Oscar Villareal 1.00 .45

2003 Fleer Tradition Update Long Gone!

MINT NRMT
RANDOM INSERTS IN HOBBY PACKS
STATED ODDS 1:72 RETAIL
1 Barry Bonds/475 12.00 5.50
2 Jason Giambi/440 5.00 2.20
3 Albert Pujols/452 10.00 4.50
4 Chipper Jones/420 5.00 2.20
5 Manny Ramirez/430 5.00 2.20
6 Sammy Sosa/536 8.00 3.60
7 Alfonso Soriano/440 5.00 2.20
8 Alex Rodriguez/430 8.00 3.60
9 Jim Thome/445 5.00 2.20
10 Vladimir Guerrero/502 5.00 2.20
11 Austin Kearns/430 5.00 2.20
12 Jeff Bagwell/420 5.00 2.20
13 Andruw Jones/430 5.00 2.20
14 Carlos Delgado/451 5.00 2.20
15 Nomar Garciaparra/440 8.00 3.60
16 Adam Dunn/464 5.00 2.20
17 Mike Piazza/450 8.00 3.60
18 Derek Jeter/410 12.00 5.50
19 Ken Griffey Jr./430 8.00 3.60
20 Hank Blalock/424 5.00 2.20

2003 Fleer Tradition Update Milestones

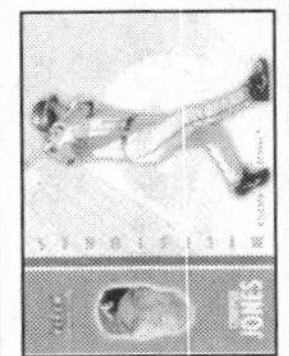

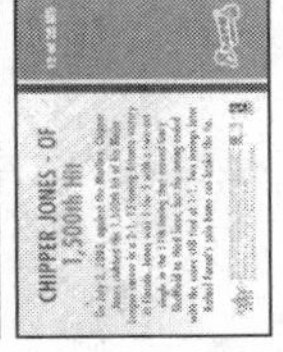

MINT NRMT
STATED ODDS 1:8 HOBBY, 1:6 RETAIL
1 Roger Clemens 4.00 1.80
2 Rafael Palmeiro 1.25 .55
3 Jeff Bagwell 1.25 .55
4 Barry Bonds 5.00 2.20
5 Sammy Sosa 3.00 1.35
6 Albert Pujols 4.00 1.80
7 Ichiro Suzuki 3.00 1.35
8 Alfonso Soriano 1.25 .55
9 Alex Rodriguez 3.00 1.35
10 Randy Johnson 2.00 .90
11 Manny Ramirez 1.25 .55
12 Chipper Jones 2.00 .90
13 Todd Helton 1.25 .55
14 Ken Griffey Jr. 3.00 1.35
15 Jim Thome 2.00 .90
16 Frank Thomas 2.00 .90
17 Pedro Martinez 2.00 .90
18 Hideo Nomo 2.00 .90
19 Jason Schmidt .75 .35
20 Carlos Delgado .75 .35

2003 Fleer Tradition Update Milestones Game Jersey

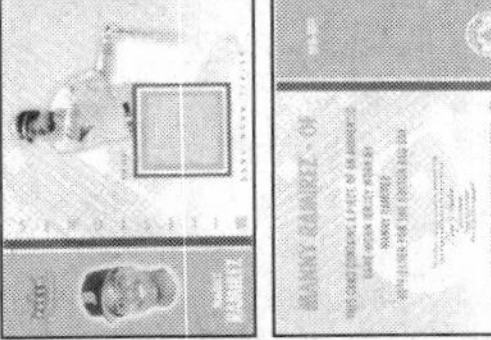

MINT NRMT
STATED ODDS 1:20 HOBBY, 1:96 RETAIL
*GOLD: .75X TO 2X BASIC
GOLD RANDOM IN HOB/RET PACKS
GOLD PRINT RUN 100 SERIAL #'d SETS
AR Alex Rodriguez 10.00 4.50
AS Alfonso Soriano 10.00 4.50
CD Carlos Delgado 8.00 3.60
CJ Chipper Jones 10.00 4.50
FT Frank Thomas 10.00 4.50
HN Hideo Nomo 10.00 4.50
JB Jeff Bagwell 10.00 4.50
JS Jason Schmidt 8.00 3.60
JT Jim Thome 10.00 4.50
MR Manny Ramirez 10.00 4.50
PM Pedro Martinez 10.00 4.50
RC Roger Clemens 15.00 6.75
RJ Randy Johnson 10.00 4.50
RP Rafael Palmeiro 10.00 4.50
SS Sammy Sosa 15.00 6.75
TH Todd Helton 10.00 4.50

2003 Fleer Tradition Update Throwback Threads

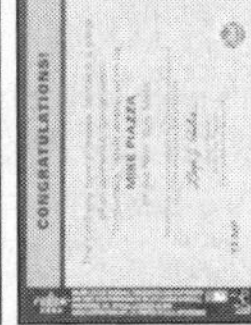

MINT NRMT
STATED ODDS 1:64 HOBBY, 1:288 RETAIL
*PATCH: 1X TO 2.5X BASIC
PATCH RANDOM INSERTS IN PACKS.
PATCH PRINT RUN 100 SERIAL #'d SETS
AL Al Leiter 8.00 3.60
KM Kevin Millwood 8.00 3.60
MP Mike Piazza 15.00 6.75
TG Troy Glaus 8.00 3.60
VG Vladimir Guerrero 10.00 4.50

2003 Fleer Tradition Update Throwback Threads Dual

MINT NRMT
RANDOM INSERTS IN HOB/RET PACKS
STATED PRINT RUN 100 SERIAL #'d SETS
MP-AL Mike Piazza 25.00 11.00
Al Leiter
VG-TG Vladimir Guerrero 20.00 9.00
Troy Glaus

2003 Fleer Tradition Update Turn Back the Clock

MINT NRMT
STATED ODDS 1:160 HOBBY, 1:288 RETAIL
1 Yogi Berra 15.00 6.75
2 Mike Schmidt 20.00 9.00
3 Tom Seaver 10.00 4.50
4 Reggie Jackson 10.00 4.50
5 Pee Wee Reese 10.00 4.50
6 Phil Rizzuto 10.00 4.50
7 Jim Palmer 10.00 4.50
8 Robin Yount 15.00 6.75
9 Nolan Ryan 20.00 9.00
10 Al Kaline 15.00 6.75

2004 Fleer Tradition

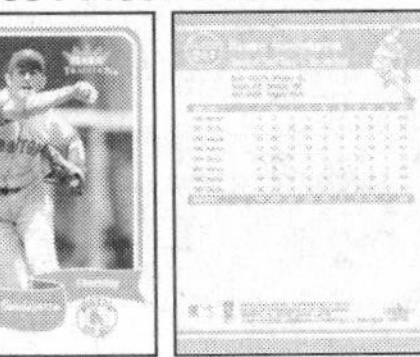

This 500-card standard-size set was released in January, 2004. The set was issued in 10 card packs which came 36 packs to a box and six boxes to a case. Cards numbered 401 through 500 were printed in lesser quantity than the first 400 cards in this set. This set has these topical subsets: Cards 1 through 10 feature World Series highlights, Cards 11-40 feature Team Leaders. In the higher numbers cards 446 through 462 feature young players in an "Standout" subset which cards 462 through 471 feature players who won major awards in 2003. The set concludes with a 30-card three player prospect set which features leading prospects for each of the major league teams.

Nm-Mt Ex-Mt
COMPLETE SET (500) 150.00 45.00
COMP.SET w/o SP's (400) 40.00 12.00
COMMON CARD (1-400) .30 .09
COMMON CARD (401-470) 1.00 .30
COMMON CARD (471-500) 1.00 .30
401-445 STATED ODDS 1:2
446-461 STATED ODDS 1:6
462-470 STATED ODDS 1:9
471-500 STATED ODDS 1:3
1 Juan Pierre WS .30 .09
2 Josh Beckett WS .30 .09
3 Ivan Rodriguez WS .75 .23
4 Miguel Cabrera WS .50 .15
5 Dontrelle Willis WS .30 .09
6 Derek Jeter WS 1.50 .45
7 Jason Giambi WS .30 .09
8 Bernie Williams WS .50 .15
9 Alfonso Soriano WS .50 .15
10 Hideki Matsui WS 1.25 .35
11 Garret Anderson .30 .09
Garret Anderson
Ramon Ortiz
John Lackey TL
12 Luis Gonzalez .30 .09
Luis Gonzalez
Brandon Webb
Curt Schilling TL
13 Javy Lopez .30 .09
Gary Sheffield
Russ Ortiz
Russ Ortiz TL
14 Tony Batista .30 .09
Jay Gibbons
Sidney Ponson
Jason Johnson TL
15 Manny Ramirez .75 .23
Nomar Garciaparra
Derek Lowe
Pedro Martinez TL
16 Sammy Sosa .75 .23
Sammy Sosa
Mark Prior
Kerry Wood TL
17 Frank Thomas .50 .15
Carlos Lee
Esteban Loaiza
Esteban Loaiza TL
18 Adam Dunn .30 .09
Sean Casey
Chris Reitsma
Paul Wilson TL
19 Jody Gerut .30 .09
Jody Gerut
C.C. Sabathia
C.C. Sabathia TL
20 Preston Wilson .30 .09
Preston Wilson
Darren Oliver
Jason Jennings TL
21 Dmitri Young .30 .09
Dmitri Young
Mike Maroth
Jeremy Bonderman TL
22 Mike Lowell .30 .09
Mike Lowell
Dontrelle Willis
Josh Beckett TL
23 Jeff Bagwell .30 .09
Jeff Bagwell
Jeriome Robertson
Wade Miller TL
24 Carlos Beltran .30 .09
Carlos Beltran
Darrell May
Darrell May TL
25 Adrian Beltre .30 .09
Shawn Green
Hideo Nomo
Kevin Brown TL
26 Richie Sexson .30 .09
Richie Sexson
Ben Sheets
Ben Sheets TL
27 Torii Hunter .50 .15
Torii Hunter
Brad Radke
Johan Santana TL
28 Vladimir Guerrero .50 .15
Orlando Cabrera
Livan Hernandez
Javier Vazquez TL
29 Cliff Floyd .30 .09
Ty Wigginton
Steve Trachsel
Al Leiter TL
30 Jason Giambi .50 .15
Jason Giambi
Andy Pettitte
Mike Mussina TL
31 Eric Chavez .30 .09
Miguel Tejada
Tim Hudson
Tim Hudson TL
32 Jim Thome .50 .15
Jim Thome
Randy Wolf
Randy Wolf TL
33 Reggie Sanders .30 .09
Reggie Sanders
Josh Fogg
Kip Wells TL
34 Ryan Klesko .30 .09
Mark Loretta
Jake Peavy
Jake Peavy TL
35 Jose Cruz Jr. .30 .09
Edgardo Alfonzo
Jason Schmidt
Jason Schmidt TL
36 Bret Boone .30 .09
Bret Boone
Jamie Moyer
Joel Pineiro TL
37 Albert Pujols .75 .23
Albert Pujols
Woody Williams
Woody Williams TL

38 Aubrey Huff .30 .09
Aubrey Huff
Victor Zambrano
Victor Zambrano TL
39 Alex Rodriguez .75 .23
Alex Rodriguez
John Thomson
John Thomson TL
40 Carlos Delgado .30 .09
Carlos Delgado
Roy Halladay
Roy Halladay TL
41 Greg Maddux 1.25 .35
42 Ben Grieve .30 .09
43 Darin Erstad .30 .09
44 Ruben Sierra .30 .09
45 Byung-Hyung Kim .30 .09
46 Freddy Garcia .30 .09
47 Richard Hidalgo .30 .09
48 Tike Redman .30 .09
49 Kevin Millwood .30 .09
50 Marquis Grissom .30 .09
51 Jae Weong Seo .30 .09
52 Wil Cordero .30 .09
53 LaTroy Hawkins .30 .09
54 Jolbert Cabrera .30 .09
55 Kevin Appier .30 .09
56 John Lackey .30 .09
57 Garret Anderson .30 .09
58 R.A. Dickey .30 .09
59 David Segui .30 .09
60 Erubiel Durazo .30 .09
61 Bobby Abreu .30 .09
62 Travis Hafner .30 .09
63 Victor Zambrano .30 .09
64 Randy Johnson .75 .23
65 Bernie Williams .50 .15
66 J.T. Snow .30 .09
67 Sammy Sosa 1.25 .35
68 Al Leiter .30 .09
69 Jason Jennings .30 .09
70 Matt Morris .30 .09
71 Mike Hampton .30 .09
72 Juan Encarnacion .30 .09
73 Alex Gonzalez .30 .09
74 Bartolo Colon .30 .09
75 Brett Myers .30 .09
76 Michael Young .30 .09
77 Ichiro Suzuki 1.25 .35
78 Jason Johnson .30 .09
79 Brad Ausmus .30 .09
80 Ted Lilly .30 .09
81 Ken Griffey Jr. 1.25 .35
82 Chone Figgins .30 .09
83 Edgar Martinez .50 .15
84 Adam Eaton .30 .09
85 Ken Harvey .30 .09
86 Francisco Rodriguez .30 .09
87 Bill Mueller .30 .09
88 Mike Maroth .30 .09
89 Charles Johnson .30 .09
90 Jhonny Peralta .30 .09
91 Kip Wells .30 .09
92 Cesar Izturis .30 .09
93 Matt Clement .30 .09
94 Lyle Overbay .30 .09
95 Kirk Rueter .30 .09
96 Cristian Guzman .30 .09
97 Garrett Stephenson .30 .09
98 Lance Berkman .30 .09
99 Brett Tomko .30 .09
100 Chris Stynes .30 .09
101 Nate Cornejo .30 .09
102 Aaron Rowand .30 .09
103 Javier Vazquez .30 .09
104 Jason Kendall .30 .09
105 Mark Redman .30 .09
106 Benito Santiago .30 .09
107 C.C. Sabathia .30 .09
108 David Wells .30 .09
109 Mark Ellis .30 .09
110 Casey Blake .30 .09
111 Sean Burroughs .30 .09
112 Carlos Beltran .50 .15
113 Ramon Hernandez .30 .09
114 Eric Hinske .30 .09
115 Luis Gonzalez .30 .09
116 Jarrod Washburn .30 .09
117 Ronnie Belliard .30 .09
118 Troy Percival .30 .09
119 Jose Valentin .30 .09
120 Chase Utley .30 .09
121 Odalis Perez .30 .09
122 Steve Finley .30 .09
123 Bret Boone .30 .09
124 Jeff Conine .30 .09
125 Josh Fogg .30 .09
126 Neifi Perez .30 .09
127 Ben Sheets .30 .09
128 Randy Winn .30 .09
129 Matt Stairs .30 .09
130 Carlos Delgado .30 .09
131 Morgan Ensberg .30 .09
132 Vinny Castilla .30 .09
133 Matt Mantei .30 .09
134 Alex Rodriguez 1.25 .35
135 Matthew LeCroy .30 .09
136 Woody Williams .30 .09
137 Frank Catalanotto .30 .09
138 Rondell White .30 .09
139 Scott Rolen .75 .23
140 Cliff Floyd .30 .09
141 Chipper Jones .75 .23
142 Robin Ventura .30 .09
143 Mariano Rivera .50 .15
144 Brady Clark .30 .09
145 Ramon Ortiz .30 .09
146 Omar Infante .30 .09
147 Mike Matheny .30 .09
148 Pedro Martinez .75 .23
149 Carlos Baerga .30 .09
150 Shannon Stewart .30 .09
151 Travis Lee .30 .09
152 Eric Byrnes .30 .09
153 Rafael Furcal .30 .09
154 B.J. Surhoff .30 .09
155 Zach Day .30 .09
156 Marlon Anderson .30 .09
157 Mark Hendrickson .30 .09
158 Mike Mussina .50 .15
159 Randall Simon .30 .09
160 Jeff DaVanon .30 .09
161 Joel Pineiro .30 .09
162 Vernon Wells .30 .09
163 Adam Kennedy .30 .09
164 Trot Nixon .30 .09
165 Rodrigo Lopez .30 .09
166 Curt Schilling .30 .09
167 Horacio Ramirez .30 .09
168 Jason Marquis .30 .09
169 Magglio Ordonez .30 .09
170 Scott Schoeneweis .30 .09
171 Andruw Jones .30 .09
172 Tino Martinez .50 .15
173 Moises Alou .30 .09
174 Kelvim Escobar .30 .09
175 Xavier Nady .30 .09
176 Ramon Martinez .30 .09
177 Pat Hentgen .30 .09
178 Austin Kearns .30 .09
179 D'Angelo Jimenez .30 .09
180 Deivi Cruz .30 .09
181 John Smoltz .50 .15
182 Toby Hall .30 .09
183 Mark Buehrle .30 .09
184 Howie Clark .30 .09
185 David Ortiz .75 .23
186 Raul Mondesi .30 .09
187 Milton Bradley .30 .09
188 Jorge Julio .30 .09
189 Victor Martinez .30 .09
190 Gabe Kapler .30 .09
191 Julio Franco .30 .09
192 Ryan Freel .30 .09
193 Brad Fullmer .30 .09
194 Joe Borowski .30 .09
195 Darren Oliver .30 .09
196 Jason Varitek .50 .15
197 Greg Myers .30 .09
198 Eric Munson .30 .09
199 Tim Wakefield .30 .09
200 Kyle Farnsworth .30 .09
201 Johnny Vander Wal .30 .09
202 Alex Escobar .30 .09
203 Sean Casey .30 .09
204 John Thomson .30 .09
205 Carlos Zambrano .30 .09
206 Kenny Lofton .30 .09
207 Marcus Giles .30 .09
208 Wade Miller .30 .09
209 Geoff Blum .30 .09
210 Jason LaRue .30 .09
211 Omar Vizquel .50 .15
212 Carlos Pena .30 .09
213 Adam Dunn .50 .15
214 Oscar Villarreal .30 .09
215 Paul Konerko .30 .09
216 Hideo Nomo .75 .23
217 Mike Sweeney .30 .09
218 Coco Crisp .30 .09
219 Shawn Chacon .30 .09
220 Brook Fordyce .30 .09
221 Josh Beckett .30 .09
222 Paul Wilson .30 .09
223 Josh Towers .30 .09
224 Geoff Jenkins .30 .09
225 Shawn Green .30 .09
226 Derrek Lee .30 .09
227 Karim Garcia .30 .09
228 Preston Wilson .30 .09
229 Dane Sardinha .30 .09
230 Aramis Ramirez .30 .09
231 Doug Mientkiewicz .30 .09
232 Jay Gibbons .30 .09
233 Adam Everett .30 .09
234 Brooks Kieschnick .30 .09
235 Dmitri Young .30 .09
236 Brad Penny .30 .09
237 Todd Zeile .30 .09
238 Eric Gagne .75 .23
239 Esteban Loaiza .30 .09
240 Billy Wagner .30 .09
241 Nomar Garciaparra 1.25 .35
242 Desi Relaford .30 .09
243 Luis Rivas .30 .09
244 Andy Pettitte .50 .15
245 Ty Wigginton .30 .09
246 Edgar Gonzalez .30 .09
247 Brian Anderson .30 .09
248 Richie Sexson .30 .09
249 Russell Branyan .30 .09
250 Jose Guillen .30 .09
251 Chin-Hui Tsao .30 .09
252 Jose Hernandez .30 .09
253 Kevin Brown .30 .09
254 Pete LaForest .30 .09
255 Adrian Beltre .50 .15
256 Jacque Jones .30 .09
257 Jimmy Rollins .30 .09
258 Brandon Phillips .30 .09
259 Derek Jeter 1.50 .45
260 Carl Everett .30 .09
261 Wes Helms .30 .09
262 Kyle Lohse .30 .09
263 Jason Phillips .30 .09
264 Jake Peavy .30 .09
265 Orlando Hernandez .30 .09
266 Keith Foulke .30 .09
267 Brad Wilkerson .30 .09
268 Corey Koskie .30 .09
269 Josh Hall .30 .09
270 Bobby Higginson .30 .09
271 Andres Galarraga .30 .09
272 Alfonso Soriano .50 .15
273 Carlos Rivera .30 .09
274 Steve Trachsel .30 .09
275 David Bell .30 .09
276 Endy Chavez .30 .09
277 Jay Payton .30 .09
278 Mark Mulder .30 .09
279 Terrence Long .30 .09
280 A.J. Burnett .30 .09
281 Pokey Reese .30 .09
282 Phil Nevin .30 .09
283 Jose Contreras .30 .09
284 Jim Thome .75 .23
285 Pat Burrell .30 .09
286 Luis Castillo .30 .09
287 Juan Uribe .30 .09
288 Raul Ibanez .30 .09
289 Sidney Ponson .30 .09
290 Scott Hatteberg .30 .09
291 Jack Wilson .30 .09
292 Reggie Sanders .30 .09
293 Brian Giles .30 .09
294 Craig Biggio .50 .15
295 Kazuhisa Ishii .30 .09
296 Jim Edmonds .30 .09
297 Trevor Hoffman .30 .09
298 Ray Durham .30 .09
299 Mike Lieberthal .30 .09
300 Tim Worrell .30 .09
301 Chris George .30 .09
302 Jamie Moyer .30 .09
303 Mike Cameron .30 .09
304 Matt Kinney .30 .09
305 Aubrey Huff .30 .09
306 Brian Lawrence .30 .09
307 Carlos Guillen .30 .09
308 J.D. Drew .30 .09
309 Paul Lo Duca .30 .09
310 Tim Salmon .50 .15
311 Jason Schmidt .30 .09
312 A.J. Pierzynski .30 .09
313 Lance Carter .30 .09
314 Julio Lugo .30 .09
315 Johan Santana .50 .15
316 Laynce Nix .30 .09
317 John Olerud .30 .09
318 Robb Quinlan .30 .09
319 Scott Spiezio .30 .09
320 Tony Clark .30 .09
321 Jose Vidro .30 .09
322 Shea Hillenbrand .30 .09
323 Doug Glanville .30 .09
324 Orlando Palmeiro .30 .09
325 Juan Gonzalez .50 .15
326 Jason Giambi .30 .09
327 Junior Spivey .30 .09
328 Tom Glavine .50 .15
329 Reed Johnson .30 .09
330 David Eckstein .30 .09
331 Damian Jackson .30 .09
332 Orlando Hudson .30 .09
333 Barry Zito .30 .09
334 Robert Fick .30 .09
335 Aaron Boone .30 .09
336 Rafael Palmeiro .50 .15
337 Bobby Kielty .30 .09
338 Tony Batista .30 .09
339 Ryan Dempster .30 .09
340 Derek Lowe .30 .09
341 Alex Cintron .30 .09
342 Jermaine Dye .30 .09
343 John Burkett .30 .09
344 Javy Lopez .30 .09
345 Eric Karros .30 .09
346 Corey Patterson .30 .09
347 Josh Phelps .30 .09
348 Ryan Klesko .30 .09
349 Craig Wilson .30 .09
350 Brian Roberts .30 .09
351 Roberto Alomar .50 .15
352 Frank Thomas .75 .23
353 Gary Sheffield .30 .09
354 Alex Gonzalez .30 .09
355 Jose Cruz Jr. .30 .09
356 Jerome Williams .30 .09
357 Mark Kotsay .30 .09
358 Chris Reitsma .30 .09
359 Carlos Lee .30 .09
360 Todd Helton .50 .15
361 Gil Meche .30 .09
362 Ryan Franklin .30 .09
363 Josh Bard .30 .09
364 Juan Pierre .30 .09
365 Barry Larkin .50 .15
366 Edgar Renteria .30 .09
367 Alex Sanchez .30 .09
368 Jeff Bagwell .50 .15
369 Ben Broussard .30 .09
370 Chan-Ho Park .30 .09
371 Darrell May .30 .09
372 Roy Oswalt .30 .09
373 Craig Monroe .30 .09
374 Fred McGriff .50 .15
375 Bengie Molina .30 .09
376 Aaron Guiel .30 .09
377 Jeriome Robertson .30 .09
378 Kenny Rogers .30 .09
379 Colby Lewis .30 .09
380 Jeromy Burnitz .30 .09
381 Orlando Cabrera .30 .09
382 Joe Randa .30 .09
383 Miguel Batista .30 .09
384 Brad Radke .30 .09
385 Jeremy Giambi .30 .09
386 Vladimir Guerrero .75 .23
387 Melvin Mora .30 .09
388 Royce Clayton .30 .09
389 Danny Garcia .30 .09
390 Manny Ramirez .75 .23
391 Dave McCarty .30 .09
392 Mark Grudzielanek .30 .09
393 Mike Piazza 1.25 .35
394 Jorge Posada .50 .15
395 Tim Hudson .30 .09
396 Placido Polanco .30 .09
397 Mark Loretta .30 .09
398 Jesse Foppert .30 .09
399 Albert Pujols 1.50 .45
400 Jeremi Gonzalez .30 .09
401 Paul Bako SP 1.00 .30
402 Luis Matos SP 1.00 .30
403 Johnny Damon SP 2.50 .75
404 Kerry Wood SP 2.50 .75
405 Joe Crede SP 1.00 .30
406 Jason Davis SP 1.00 .30
407 Larry Walker SP 1.50 .45
408 Ivan Rodriguez SP 2.50 .75
409 Nick Johnson SP 1.00 .30
410 Jose Lima SP 1.00 .30
411 Brian Jordan SP 1.00 .30
412 Eddie Guardado SP 1.00 .30
413 Ron Calloway SP 1.00 .30
414 Aaron Heilman SP 1.00 .30
415 Eric Chavez SP 1.00 .30
416 Randy Wolf SP 1.00 .30
417 Jason Bay SP 1.00 .30
418 Edgardo Alfonzo SP 1.00 .30
419 Kazuhiro Sasaki SP 1.00 .30
420 Eduardo Perez SP 1.00 .30
421 Carl Crawford SP 1.00 .30
422 Troy Glaus SP 1.00 .30
423 Joaquin Benoit SP 1.00 .30
424 Russ Ortiz SP 1.00 .30
425 Larry Bigbie SP 1.00 .30
426 Todd Walker SP 1.00 .30
427 Kris Benson SP 1.00 .30
428 Sandy Alomar Jr. SP 1.00 .30
429 Jody Gerut SP 1.00 .30
430 Rene Reyes SP 1.00 .30
431 Mike Lowell SP 1.00 .30
432 Jeff Kent SP 1.00 .30
433 Mike MacDougal SP 1.00 .30
434 Dave Roberts SP 1.00 .30
435 Torii Hunter SP 1.00 .30
436 Tomo Ohka SP 1.00 .30
437 Jeremy Griffiths SP 1.00 .30
438 Miguel Tejada SP 1.00 .30
439 Vicente Padilla SP 1.00 .30
440 Bobby Hill SP 1.00 .30
441 Rich Aurilia SP 1.00 .30
442 Shigetoshi Hasegawa SP 1.00 .30
443 So Taguchi SP 1.00 .30
444 Damian Rolls SP 1.00 .30
445 Roy Halladay SP 1.00 .30
446 Rocco Baldelli SO SP 1.00 .30
447 Dontrelle Willis SO SP 1.00 .30
448 Mark Prior SO SP 2.50 .75
449 Jason Lane SO SP 1.00 .30
450 Angel Berroa SO SP 1.00 .30
451 Jose Reyes SO SP 1.00 .30
452 Ryan Wagner SO SP 1.00 .30
453 Marlon Byrd SO SP 1.00 .30
454 Hee Seop Choi SO SP 1.00 .30
455 Brandon Webb SO SP 1.00 .30
456 Bo Hart SO SP 1.00 .30
457 Hank Blalock SO SP 1.00 .30
458 Mark Teixeira SO SP 1.00 .30
459 Hideki Matsui SO SP 4.00 1.20
460 Scott Podsednik SO SP 1.00 .30
461 Miguel Cabrera SO SP 1.50 .45
462 Josh Beckett AW SP 1.00 .30
463 Mariano Rivera AW SP 1.50 .45
464 Ivan Rodriguez AW SP 2.50 .75
465 Alex Rodriguez AW SP 4.00 1.20
466 Albert Pujols AW SP 5.00 1.50
467 Roy Halladay AW SP 1.00 .30
468 Eric Gagne AW SP 2.50 .75
469 Angel Berroa AW SP 1.00 .30
470 Dontrelle Willis AW SP 1.00 .30
471 Chris Bootcheck 1.00 .30
Tom Gregorio
Richard Fischer SP
472 Matt Kata 1.00 .30
Tim Olson
Robby Hammock SP
473 Michael Hessman 1.00 .30
Chris Waters
Greg Aquino SP
474 Carlos Mendez 1.50 .45
Daniel Cabrera
Jeremy Guthrie SP
475 Edwin Almonte 1.00 .30
Phil Seibel
Felix Sanchez SP
476 Todd Wellemeyer 1.00 .30
Jon Leicester
Sergio Mitre SP
477 Josh Stewart 1.50 .45
Neal Cotts
Aaron Miles SP
478 Terrmel Sledge 1.00 .30
Josh Hall
Brandon Claussen SP
479 Francisco Cruceta 1.00 .30
Jason Stanford
Rafael Betancourt SP
480 Javier A.Lopez 1.00 .30
Garrett Atkins
Clint Barmes SP
481 Wilfredo Ledezma 1.00 .30
Nook Logan
Jeremy Bonderman SP
482 Josh Willingham 1.00 .30
Kevin Hooper
Rick Roberts SP
483 Colin Porter 1.00 .30
Mike Gallo
Dave Matranga SP
484 David DeJesus 1.00 .30
Jason Gilfillan
Jimmy Gobble SP
485 Koyie Hill 1.00 .30
Alfredo Gonzalez
Andrew Brown SP
486 Rickie Weeks 1.50 .45
Pedro Liriano
Wes Obermueller SP
487 Alex Prieto 1.50 .45
Mike Ryan
Lew Ford SP
488 Julio Manon 1.00 .30
Luis Ayala
Seung Song SP
489 Jeff Duncan 1.50 .45
Prentice Redman
Craig Brazell SP
490 Chien-Ming Wang 1.50 .45
Michel Hernandez
Mike Gonzalez SP
491 Rich Harden 1.50 .45
Mike Neu
Geoff Geary SP
492 Diegomar Markwell 1.00 .30
Chad Gaudin
David Sanders SP
493 Beau Kemp 1.00 .30
Micheal Nakamura
D.J. Carrasco SP
494 Khalil Greene 4.00 1.20
Miguel Ojeda
Bernie Castro SP
495 Noah Lowry 1.50 .45
Todd Linden
Kevin Correia SP
496 Aaron Looper 1.00 .30
Brian Sweeney
Rett Johnson SP
497 John Gall RC 2.50 .75
Dan Haren
Kevin Ohme SP
498 Delmon Young 2.50 .75
Doug Waechter
Matt Diaz SP
499 Gerald Laird 1.00 .30
Rosman Garcia
Ramon Nivar SP
500 Alexis Rios 1.50 .45
Guillermo Quiroz
Francisco Rosario SP

2004 Fleer Tradition Career Tributes

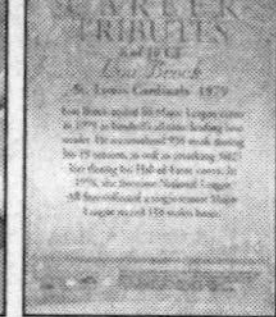

	Nm-Mt	Ex-Mt
PRINT RUNS B/WN 1956-1993 COPIES PER		
*DIE CUT: 1.25X TO 3X BASIC		
DIE CUT PRINTS B/WN 56-93 COPIES PER		
OVERALL CAREER TRIBUTE ODDS 1:36		
1 Mike Schmidt/1989	10.00	3.00
2 Nolan Ryan/1993	12.00	3.60
3 Tom Seaver/1986	5.00	1.50
4 Reggie Jackson/1987	5.00	1.50
5 Bob Gibson/1975	5.00	1.50
6 Harmon Killebrew/1975	8.00	2.40
7 Phil Rizzuto/1956	5.00	1.50
8 Lou Brock/1979	5.00	1.50
9 Eddie Mathews/1968	8.00	2.40
10 Al Kaline/1974	8.00	2.40

2004 Fleer Tradition Diamond Tributes

	Nm-Mt	Ex-Mt
COMPLETE SET (20)	20.00	6.00
STATED ODDS 1:6		
1 Derek Jeter	3.00	.90
2 Chipper Jones	1.50	.45
3 Vladimir Guerrero	1.50	.45
4 Kerry Wood	1.50	.45
5 Jim Thome	1.50	.45
6 Nomar Garciaparra	2.50	.75
7 Alex Rodriguez	2.50	.75
8 Mike Piazza	2.50	.75
9 Jason Giambi	1.00	.30
10 Barry Zito	1.00	.30
11 Dontrelle Willis	1.00	.30
12 Albert Pujols	3.00	.90
13 Todd Helton	1.00	.30
14 Richie Sexson	1.00	.30
15 Randy Johnson	1.50	.45
16 Pedro Martinez	1.50	.45
17 Josh Beckett	1.00	.30
18 Manny Ramirez	1.00	.30
19 Roy Halladay	1.00	.30
20 Mark Prior	1.50	.45

2004 Fleer Tradition Diamond Tributes Game Jersey

	Nm-Mt	Ex-Mt
STATED ODDS 1:36		
*PATCH: 1X TO 2.5X BASIC		
PATCH RANDOM INSERTS IN PACKS		
PATCH PRINT RUN 50 SERIAL #'d SETS		
AP Albert Pujols	15.00	4.50
AR Alex Rodriguez	10.00	3.00
BZ Barry Zito	8.00	2.40
CJ Chipper Jones	10.00	3.00
DJ Derek Jeter	20.00	6.00
DW Dontrelle Willis	8.00	2.40
JB Josh Beckett	8.00	2.40
JG Jason Giambi	8.00	2.40
JT Jim Thome	10.00	3.00
KW Kerry Wood	10.00	3.00
MP Mike Piazza	10.00	3.00
MP2 Mark Prior	10.00	3.00
MR Manny Ramirez	10.00	3.00
NG Nomar Garciaparra	10.00	3.00
PM Pedro Martinez	10.00	3.00
RH Roy Halladay	8.00	2.40
RJ Randy Johnson	10.00	3.00
RS Richie Sexson	8.00	2.40
TH Todd Helton	10.00	3.00
VG Vladimir Guerrero	10.00	3.00

2004 Fleer Tradition Retrospection

	Nm-Mt	Ex-Mt
STATED ODDS 1:360		
1 Rickie Weeks	15.00	4.50
2 Delmon Young	20.00	6.00
3 Torii Hunter	15.00	4.50
4 Aubrey Huff	15.00	4.50
5 Rocco Baldelli	15.00	4.50
6 Mike Lowell	15.00	4.50

Card	Nm-Mt	Ex-Mt
7 Dontrelle Willis	15.00	4.50
8 Albert Pujols	30.00	9.00
9 Bo Hart	15.00	4.50
10 Brandon Webb	15.00	4.50

2004 Fleer Tradition Retrospection Autographs

Please note that a few players did not return their autographs in time for inclusion in this product and no expiration date was set for redeeming those cards.

Card	Nm-Mt	Ex-Mt
OVERALL AUTO ODDS 1:720		
STATED PRINT RUN 60 SERIAL #'d SETS		
AH Aubrey Huff	25.00	7.50
AK Austin Kearns	25.00	7.50
AP Albert Pujols EXCH	120.00	36.00
BO Bo Hart	25.00	7.50
BW Brandon Webb	25.00	7.50
CP Corey Patterson	25.00	7.50
DW Dontrelle Willis	25.00	7.50
DY Delmon Young EXCH	40.00	12.00
HB Hank Blalock	25.00	7.50
JR Jose Reyes	25.00	7.50
JW Josh Willingham	25.00	7.50
MR Mike Ryan	25.00	7.50
RW Ryan Wagner EXCH	25.00	7.50
RW Rickie Weeks	40.00	12.00
SR Scott Rolen	40.00	12.00
TH Torii Hunter	25.00	7.50

2004 Fleer Tradition Retrospection Autographs Dual

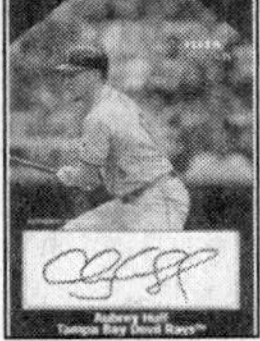

Card	Nm-Mt	Ex-Mt
OVERALL AUTO ODDS 1:720		
STATED PRINT RUN 19 SERIAL #'d SETS		
NO PRICING DUE TO SCARCITY		
EXCHANGE DEADLINE INDEFINITE		
AHAK Aubrey Huff / Austin Kearns		
APBH Albert Pujols / Bo Hart EXCH		
BWRW Brandon Webb / Ryan Wagner EXCH		
CPJR Corey Patterson / Jose Reyes		
HBSR Hank Blalock / Scott Rolen		
JWDW Josh Willingham / Dontrelle Willis		
RWDY Rickie Weeks / Delmon Young EXCH		
THMR Torii Hunter / Mike Ryan		

2004 Fleer Tradition Stand Outs Game Used

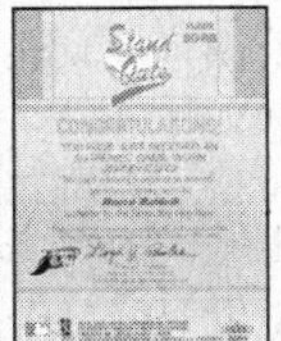

Card	Nm-Mt	Ex-Mt
STATED ODDS 1:41		
GOLD RANDOM INSERTS IN PACKS		
GOLD PRINTS B/WN 20-27 COPIES PER		
NO GOLD PRICING DUE TO SCARCITY		
AB Angel Berroa Pants	8.00	2.40
BH Bo Hart Jsy	8.00	2.40
BW Brandon Webb Pants	8.00	2.40
DW Dontrelle Willis Jsy	8.00	2.40
HB Hank Blalock Jsy	8.00	2.40
HC Hee Seop Choi Jsy	8.00	2.40
JR Jose Reyes Jsy	8.00	2.40
MB Marlon Byrd Jsy	8.00	2.40
MC Miguel Cabrera Jsy	10.00	3.00
MT Mark Teixeira Jsy	8.00	2.40
RB Rocco Baldelli Jsy	8.00	2.40

2004 Fleer Tradition This Day in History

Card	Nm-Mt	Ex-Mt
STATED ODDS 1:18		
1 Josh Beckett	1.50	.45
2 Carlos Delgado	1.50	.45
3 Javy Lopez	1.50	.45
4 Greg Maddux	4.00	1.20
5 Rafael Palmeiro	1.50	.45
6 Sammy Sosa	4.00	1.20
7 Jeff Bagwell	1.50	.45
8 Frank Thomas	2.50	.75
9 Kevin Millwood	1.50	.45
10 Jose Reyes	1.50	.45
11 Rafael Furcal	1.50	.45
12 Alfonso Soriano	1.50	.45
13 Eric Gagne	2.50	.75
14 Hideki Matsui	4.00	1.20
15 Hank Blalock	1.50	.45

2004 Fleer Tradition This Day in History Game Used

Card	Nm-Mt	Ex-Mt
STATED ODDS 1:288		
AS Alfonso Soriano Jsy	15.00	4.50
CD Carlos Delgado Jsy	10.00	3.00
FT Frank Thomas Jsy	15.00	4.50
GM Greg Maddux Jsy	15.00	4.50
JB Josh Beckett Jsy	10.00	3.00
JB Jeff Bagwell Jsy	15.00	4.50
JL Javy Lopez Jsy	10.00	3.00
JR Jose Reyes Jsy	10.00	3.00
RP Rafael Palmeiro Jsy	15.00	4.50
SS Sammy Sosa Bat	20.00	6.00

2004 Fleer Tradition This Day in History Game Used Dual

Card	Nm-Mt	Ex-Mt
RANDOM INSERTS IN PACKS		
STATED PRINT RUN 25 SERIAL #'d SETS		
NO PRICING DUE TO SCARCITY		
CDJR Carlos Delgado Jsy / Jose Reyes Jsy		
FTJB Frank Thomas Jsy / Jeff Bagwell Jsy		
JBGM Josh Beckett Jsy / Greg Maddux Jsy		
JLAS Javy Lopez Jsy / Alfonso Soriano Jsy		
RPSS Rafael Palmeiro Jsy / Sammy Sosa Bat		

1933 Goudey

The cards in this 240-card set measure approximately 2 3/8" by 2 7/8". The 1933 Goudey set, was that company's first baseball issue. The four Babe Ruth and two Lou Gehrig cards in the set are extremely popular with collectors. Card number 106, Napoleon Lajoie, was not printed in 1933, and was circulated to a limited number of collectors in 1934 upon request (it was printed along with the 1934 Goudey cards). An album was offered to house the 1933 set. Several minor leaguers are depicted. Card number 1 (Bengough) is very rarely found in mint condition; in fact, as a general rule all the first series cards are more difficult to find in Mint condition. Players with more than one card are also sometimes differentiated below by their pose: BAT (Batting), FIELD (Fielding), PIT (Pitching), THROW (Throwing). One of the Babe Ruth cards was double printed (DP) apparently in place of the Lajoie and hence is easier to obtain than the others. Due to the scarcity of the Lajoie card, the set is considered complete at 239 cards and is priced as such below. One copy of card number 106 as Leo Durocher is known to exist. The card was apparently cut from a proof sheet and is the only known copy to exist. A large window display poster which measured 5 3/8" by 11 1/4" was sent to stores and used the same Babe Ruth photo as in the Goudey Premium set. The gum used was approximately the same dimension as the actual card. At the factory each piece was scored twice so it could be snapped into three pieces. The gum had a spearmint flavor and according to collectors who remember chewing said gum, the flavor did not last very long.

	Ex-Mt	VG
COMPLETE SET (239)	40000.00	20000.00
COMMON CARD (1-52)	75.00	38.00
COMMON (41/43/53-240)	60.00	30.00
WRAP.(1-CENT, BATTER)	100.00	50.00
WRAP.(1-CENT, AD FRONT)	175.00	90.00
1 Benny Bengough	1500.00	450.00
2 Dazzy Vance	200.00	100.00
3 Hugh Critz	75.00	38.00
4 Heinie Schuble	75.00	38.00
5 Babe Herman	75.00	38.00
6 Jimmy Dykes	75.00	38.00
7 Ted Lyons	150.00	75.00
8 Roy Johnson	75.00	38.00
9 Dave Harris	75.00	38.00
10 Glenn Myatt	75.00	38.00
11 Billy Rogell	75.00	38.00
12 George Pipgras	75.00	38.00
13 Fresco Thompson	75.00	38.00
14 Henry Johnson	75.00	38.00
15 Victor Sorrell	75.00	38.00
16 George Blaeholder	75.00	38.00
17 Watson Clark	75.00	38.00
18 Muddy Ruel	75.00	38.00
19 Bill Dickey	350.00	180.00
20 Bill Terry THROW	250.00	125.00
21 Phil Collins	75.00	38.00
22 Pie Traynor	250.00	125.00
23 Kiki Cuyler	200.00	100.00
24 Horace Ford	75.00	38.00
25 Paul Waner	200.00	100.00
26 Chalmer Cissell	75.00	38.00
27 George Connally	75.00	38.00
28 Dick Bartell	75.00	38.00
29 Jimmie Foxx	600.00	300.00
30 Frank Hogan	75.00	38.00
31 Tony Lazzeri	400.00	200.00
32 Bud Clancy	75.00	38.00
33 Ralph Kress	75.00	38.00
34 Bob O'Farrell	75.00	38.00
35 Al Simmons	350.00	180.00
36 Tommy Thevenow	75.00	38.00
37 Jimmy Wilson	75.00	38.00
38 Fred Brickell	75.00	38.00
39 Mark Koenig	75.00	38.00
40 Taylor Douthit	75.00	38.00
41 Gus Mancuso	60.00	30.00
42 Eddie Collins	150.00	75.00
43 Lew Fonseca	60.00	30.00
44 Jim Bottomley	150.00	75.00
45 Larry Benton	75.00	38.00
46 Ethan Allen	75.00	38.00
47 Heinie Manush BAT	175.00	90.00
48 Marty McManus	75.00	38.00
49 Frankie Frisch	300.00	150.00
50 Ed Brandt	75.00	38.00
51 Charlie Grimm	75.00	38.00
52 Andy Cohen	75.00	38.00
53 Babe Ruth	6000.00	3000.00
54 Ray Kremer	60.00	30.00
55 Pat Malone	60.00	30.00
56 Red Ruffing	175.00	90.00
57 Earl Clark	60.00	30.00
58 Lefty O'Doul	125.00	60.00
59 Bing Miller	60.00	30.00
60 Waite Hoyt	125.00	60.00
61 Max Bishop	60.00	30.00
62 Pepper Martin	125.00	60.00
63 Joe Cronin BAT	150.00	75.00
64 Burleigh Grimes	250.00	125.00
65 Milt Gaston	60.00	30.00
66 George Grantham	60.00	30.00
67 Guy Bush	60.00	30.00
68 Horace Lisenbee	60.00	30.00
69 Randy Moore	60.00	30.00
70 Floyd (Pete) Scott	60.00	30.00
71 Robert J. Burke	60.00	30.00
72 Owen Carroll	60.00	30.00
73 Jesse Haines	125.00	60.00
74 Eppa Rixey	150.00	75.00
75 Willie Kamm	60.00	30.00
76 Mickey Cochrane	250.00	125.00
77 Adam Comorosky	60.00	30.00
78 Jack Quinn	60.00	30.00
79 Red Faber	125.00	60.00
80 Clyde Manion	60.00	30.00
81 Sam Jones	60.00	30.00
82 Dib Williams	60.00	30.00
83 Pete Jablonowski	60.00	30.00
84 Glenn Spencer	60.00	30.00
85 Heinie Sand	60.00	30.00
86 Phil Todt	60.00	30.00
87 Frank O'Rourke	60.00	30.00
88 Russell Rollings	60.00	30.00
89 Tris Speaker RET	300.00	150.00
90 Jess Petty	60.00	30.00
91 Tom Zachary	60.00	30.00
92 Lou Gehrig	2500.00	1250.00
93 John Welch	60.00	30.00
94 Bill Walker	60.00	30.00
95 Alvin Crowder	60.00	30.00
96 Willis Hudlin	60.00	30.00
97 Joe Morrissey	60.00	30.00
98 Wally Berger	75.00	38.00
99 Tony Cuccinello	75.00	38.00
100 George Uhle	60.00	30.00
101 Richard Coffman	60.00	30.00
102 Travis Jackson	150.00	75.00
103 Earle Combs	125.00	60.00
104 Fred Marberry	60.00	30.00
105 Bernie Friberg	60.00	30.00
106 Napoleon Lajoie SP (Not issued until 1934)	25000.00	12500.00
107 Heinie Manush	125.00	60.00
108 Joe Kuhel	60.00	30.00
109 Joe Cronin	300.00	150.00
110 Goose Goslin	250.00	125.00
111 Monte Weaver	60.00	30.00
112 Fred Schulte	60.00	30.00
113 Oswald Bluege	60.00	30.00
114 Luke Sewell	75.00	38.00
115 Cliff Heathcote	60.00	30.00
116 Eddie Morgan	60.00	30.00
117 Rabbit Maranville	125.00	60.00
118 Val Picinich	60.00	30.00
119 R. Hornsby FIELD	600.00	250.00
120 Carl Reynolds	60.00	30.00
121 Walter Stewart	60.00	30.00
122 Alvin Crowder	60.00	30.00
123 Jack Russell	60.00	30.00
124 Earl Whitehill	60.00	30.00
125 Bill Terry	250.00	125.00
126 Joe Moore	60.00	30.00
127 Mel Ott	400.00	200.00
128 Chuck Klein	175.00	90.00
129 Hal Schumacher PIT	60.00	30.00
130 Fred Fitzsimmons	60.00	30.00
131 Fred Frankhouse	60.00	30.00
132 Jim Elliott	60.00	30.00
133 Fred Lindstrom	125.00	60.00
134 Sam Rice	200.00	100.00
135 Woody English	60.00	30.00
136 Flint Rhem	60.00	30.00
137 Fred(Red) Lucas	60.00	30.00
138 Herb Pennock	175.00	90.00
139 Ben Cantwell	60.00	30.00
140 Bump Hadley	60.00	30.00
141 Ray Benge	60.00	30.00
142 Paul Richards	75.00	38.00
143 Glenn Wright	60.00	30.00
144 Babe Ruth Bat DP	4000.00	2000.00
145 Rube Walberg	60.00	30.00
146 Walter Stewart PIT	60.00	30.00
147 Leo Durocher	200.00	100.00
148 Eddie Farrell	60.00	30.00
149 Babe Ruth	5000.00	2500.00
150 Ray Kolp	60.00	30.00
151 Jake Flowers	60.00	30.00
152 Zack Taylor	60.00	30.00
153 Buddy Myer	60.00	30.00
154 Jimmie Foxx	600.00	300.00
155 Joe Judge	60.00	30.00
156 Danny MacFayden	60.00	30.00
157 Sam Byrd	60.00	30.00
158 Moe Berg	400.00	200.00
159 Oswald Bluege	60.00	30.00
160 Lou Gehrig	3000.00	1500.00
161 Al Spohrer	60.00	30.00
162 Leo Mangum	60.00	30.00
163 Luke Sewell	75.00	38.00
164 Lloyd Waner	250.00	125.00
165 Joe Sewell	125.00	60.00
166 Sam West	60.00	30.00
167 Jack Russell	60.00	30.00
168 Goose Goslin	200.00	100.00
169 Al Thomas	60.00	30.00
170 Harry McCurdy	60.00	30.00
171 Charlie Jamieson	60.00	30.00
172 Billy Hargrave	60.00	30.00
173 Roscoe Holm	60.00	30.00
174 Warren(Curly) Ogden	60.00	30.00
175 Dan Howley MG	60.00	30.00
176 John Ogden	60.00	30.00
177 Walter French	60.00	30.00
178 Jackie Warner	60.00	30.00
179 Fred Leach	60.00	30.00
180 Eddie Moore	60.00	30.00
181 Babe Ruth	4000.00	2000.00
182 Andy High	60.00	30.00
183 Rube Walberg	60.00	30.00
184 Charley Berry	60.00	30.00
185 Bob Smith	60.00	30.00
186 John Schulte	60.00	30.00
187 Heinie Manush	150.00	75.00
188 Rogers Hornsby	600.00	300.00
189 Joe Cronin	200.00	100.00
190 Fred Schulte	60.00	30.00
191 Ben Chapman	75.00	38.00
192 Walter Brown	60.00	30.00
193 Lynford Lary	60.00	30.00
194 Earl Averill	200.00	100.00
195 Evar Swanson	60.00	30.00
196 Leroy Mahaffey	60.00	30.00
197 Rick Ferrell	125.00	60.00
198 Jack Burns	60.00	30.00
199 Tom Bridges	60.00	30.00
200 Bill Hallahan	60.00	30.00
201 Ernie Orsatti	60.00	30.00
202 Gabby Hartnett	250.00	125.00
203 Lon Warneke	60.00	30.00
204 Riggs Stephenson	60.00	30.00
205 Heinie Meine	60.00	30.00
206 Gus Suhr	60.00	30.00
207 Mel Ott Bat	400.00	200.00
208 Bernie James	60.00	30.00
209 Adolfo Luque	75.00	38.00
210 Spud Davis	60.00	30.00
211 Hack Wilson	400.00	200.00
212 Billy Urbanski	60.00	30.00
213 Earl Adams	60.00	30.00
214 John Kerr	60.00	30.00
215 Russ Van Atta	60.00	30.00
216 Lefty Gomez	300.00	150.00
217 Frank Crosetti	150.00	75.00
218 Wes Ferrell	75.00	38.00
219 Mule Haas UER (Name spelled Hass on front)	60.00	30.00
220 Lefty Grove	500.00	250.00
221 Dale Alexander	60.00	30.00
222 Charley Gehringer	400.00	200.00
223 Dizzy Dean	800.00	300.00
224 Frank Demaree	60.00	30.00
225 Bill Jurges	60.00	30.00
226 Charley Root	60.00	30.00
227 Billy Herman	150.00	75.00
228 Tony Piet	60.00	30.00
229 Arky Vaughan	150.00	75.00
230 Carl Hubbell PIT	400.00	150.00
231 Joe Moore FIELD	60.00	30.00
232 Lefty O'Doul	125.00	60.00
233 Johnny Vergez	60.00	30.00
234 Carl Hubbell	400.00	150.00
235 Fred Fitzsimmons	60.00	30.00
236 George Davis	60.00	30.00
237 Gus Mancuso	60.00	30.00
238 Hugh Critz	60.00	30.00
239 Leroy Parmelee	60.00	30.00
240 Hal Schumacher	125.00	60.00

1934 Goudey

The cards in this 96-card color set measure approximately 2 3/8" by 2 7/8". Cards 1-48 are

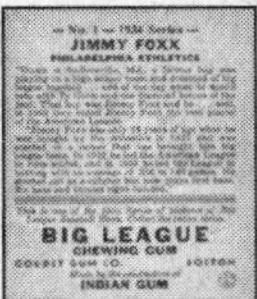

considered to be the easiest to find (although card number 1, Foxx, is very scarce in mint condition) while 73-96 are much more difficult to find. Cards of this 1934 Goudey series are slightly less abundant than cards of the 1933 Goudey set. Of the 96 cards, 84 contain a "Lou Gehrig Says" line on the front in a blue design, while 12 of the high series (80-91) contain a "Chuck Klein Says" line in a red design. These Chuck Klein cards are indicated in the checklist below by CK and are in fact the 12 National Leaguers in the high series.

	Ex-Mt	VG
COMPLETE SET (96)	16000.00	8000.00
COMMON CARD (1-48)	50.00	25.00
COMMON CARD (49-72)	75.00	38.00
COMMON CARD (73-96)	175.00	90.00
WRAP.(1-CENT, WHITE)	100.00	50.00
WRAP.(1-CENT, CLEAR)	100.00	50.00
1 Jimmie Foxx	750.00	220.00
2 Mickey Cochrane	175.00	90.00
3 Charlie Grimm	60.00	30.00
4 Woody English	50.00	25.00
5 Ed Brandt	50.00	25.00
6 Dizzy Dean	700.00	300.00
7 Leo Durocher	175.00	90.00
8 Tony Piet	50.00	25.00
9 Ben Chapman	60.00	30.00
10 Chuck Klein	150.00	75.00
11 Paul Waner	150.00	75.00
12 Carl Hubbell	175.00	90.00
13 Frankie Frisch	175.00	90.00
14 Willie Kamm	50.00	25.00
15 Alvin Crowder	50.00	25.00
16 Joe Kuhel	50.00	25.00
17 Hugh Critz	50.00	25.00
18 Heinie Manush	125.00	60.00
19 Lefty Grove	300.00	150.00
20 Frank Hogan	50.00	25.00
21 Bill Terry	200.00	100.00
22 Arky Vaughan	125.00	60.00
23 Charley Gehringer	200.00	100.00
24 Ray Benge	50.00	25.00
25 Roger Cramer	60.00	30.00
26 Gerald Walker	50.00	25.00
27 Luke Appling	150.00	75.00
28 Ed Coleman	50.00	25.00
29 Larry French	50.00	25.00
30 Julius Solters	50.00	25.00
31 Buck Jordan	50.00	25.00
32 Blondy Ryan	50.00	25.00
33 Frank Hurst	50.00	25.00
34 Chick Hafey	125.00	60.00
35 Ernie Lombardi	150.00	75.00
36 Walter Betts	50.00	25.00
37 Lou Gehrig	3000.00	1500.00
38 Oral Hildebrand	50.00	25.00
39 Fred Walker	50.00	25.00
40 John Stone	50.00	25.00
41 George Earnshaw	50.00	25.00
42 John Allen	50.00	25.00
43 Dick Porter	50.00	25.00
44 Tom Bridges	60.00	30.00
45 Oscar Melillo	50.00	25.00
46 Joe Stripp	50.00	25.00
47 John Frederick	50.00	25.00
48 Tex Carleton	50.00	25.00
49 Sam Leslie	75.00	38.00
50 Walter Beck	75.00	38.00
51 Rip Collins	75.00	38.00
52 Herman Bell	75.00	38.00
53 George Watkins	75.00	38.00
54 Wesley Schulmerich	75.00	38.00
55 Ed Holley	75.00	38.00
56 Mark Koenig	100.00	50.00
57 Bill Swift	75.00	38.00
58 Earl Grace	75.00	38.00
59 Joe Mowry	75.00	38.00
60 Lynn Nelson	75.00	38.00
61 Lou Gehrig	3000.00	1500.00
62 Hank Greenberg	700.00	300.00
63 Minter Hayes	75.00	38.00
64 Frank Grube	75.00	38.00
65 Cliff Bolton	75.00	38.00
66 Mel Harder	100.00	50.00
67 Bob Weiland	75.00	38.00
68 Bob Johnson	100.00	50.00
69 John Marcum	75.00	38.00
70 Pete Fox	75.00	38.00
71 Lyle Tinning	75.00	38.00
72 Arndt Jorgens	75.00	38.00
73 Ed Wells	175.00	90.00
74 Bob Boken	175.00	90.00
75 Bill Werber	175.00	90.00
76 Hal Trosky	200.00	100.00
77 Joe Vosmik	175.00	90.00
78 Pinky Higgins	200.00	100.00
79 Eddie Durham	175.00	90.00
80 Marty McManus CK	175.00	90.00
81 Bob Brown CK	175.00	90.00
82 Bill Hallahan CK	175.00	90.00
83 Jim Mooney CK	175.00	90.00
84 Paul Derringer CK	225.00	110.00
85 Adam Comorosky CK	175.00	90.00
86 Lloyd Johnson CK	175.00	90.00
87 George Darrow CK	175.00	90.00
88 Homer Peel CK	175.00	90.00
89 Linus Frey CK	175.00	90.00
90 KiKi Cuyler CK	350.00	180.00
91 Dolph Camilli CK	200.00	100.00
92 Steve Larkin	175.00	90.00
93 Fred Ostermueller	175.00	90.00
94 Red Rolfe	200.00	100.00
95 Myril Hoag	175.00	90.00
96 James DeShong	500.00	200.00

1936 Goudey B/W

The cards in this 25-card black and white set measure approximately 2 3/8" by 2 7/8". In contrast to the color artwork of its previous sets, the 1936 Goudey set contained a simple black and white player photograph. A facsimile autograph appeared within the picture area. Each card was issued with a number of different "game situation" backs, and there may be as many as 200 different front/back combinations. This unnumbered set is checklisted and numbered below in alphabetical order for convenience. The cards were issued in penny packs which came 100 to a box.

	Ex-Mt	VG
COMPLETE SET (25)	1800.00	900.00
WRAPPER (1-CENT)	200.00	100.00
1 Wally Berger	50.00	25.00
2 Zeke Bonura	40.00	20.00
3 Frenchy Bordagaray	40.00	20.00
4 Bill Brubaker	40.00	20.00
5 Dolph Camilli	50.00	25.00
6 Clyde Castleman	40.00	20.00
7 Mickey Cochrane	200.00	100.00
8 Joe Coscarart	40.00	20.00
9 Frank Crosetti	60.00	30.00
10 Kiki Cuyler	80.00	40.00
11 Paul Derringer	50.00	25.00
12 Jimmy Dykes	50.00	25.00
13 Rick Ferrell	80.00	40.00
14 Lefty Gomez	200.00	100.00
15 Hank Greenberg	250.00	125.00
16 Bucky Harris	80.00	40.00
17 Rollie Hemsley	40.00	20.00
18 Pinky Higgins	50.00	25.00
19 Oral Hildebrand	40.00	20.00
20 Chuck Klein	120.00	60.00
21 Pepper Martin	60.00	30.00
22 Bobo Newsom	50.00	25.00
23 Joe Vosmik	40.00	20.00
24 Paul Waner	120.00	60.00
25 Bill Werber	40.00	20.00

1938 Goudey Heads Up

The cards in this 48-card set measure approximately 2 3/8" by 2 7/8". The 1938 Goudey set is commonly referred to as the Heads-Up set. These very popular but difficult to obtain cards came in two series of the same 24 players. The first series, numbers 241-264, is distinguished from the second series, numbers 265-288, in that the second contains etched cartoons and comments surrounding the player picture. Although the set starts with number 241, it is not a continuation of the 1933 Goudey set, but a separate set in its own right.

	Ex-Mt	VG
COMPLETE SET (48)	15000.00	7500.00
COMMON (241-264)	100.00	50.00
COMMON (265-288)	100.00	50.00
WRAP.(1-CENT, 6-FIGURE)	800.00	400.00
241 Charley Gehringer	300.00	150.00
242 Pete Fox	100.00	50.00
243 Joe Kuhel	100.00	50.00
244 Frank Demaree	100.00	50.00
245 Frank Pytlak	100.00	50.00
246 Ernie Lombardi	175.00	90.00
247 Joe Vosmik	100.00	50.00
248 Dick Bartell	100.00	50.00
249 Jimmie Foxx	400.00	200.00
250 Joe DiMaggio	3500.00	1800.00
251 Bump Hadley	100.00	50.00
252 Zeke Bonura	100.00	50.00
253 Hank Greenberg	400.00	200.00
254 Van Lingle Mungo	125.00	60.00
255 Moose Solters	100.00	50.00
256 Vernon Kennedy	100.00	50.00
257 Al Lopez	200.00	100.00
258 Bobby Doerr	250.00	125.00
259 Billy Werber	100.00	50.00
260 Rudy York	125.00	60.00
261 Rip Radcliff	100.00	50.00
262 Joe Medwick	250.00	125.00
263 Marvin Owen	100.00	50.00
264 Bob Feller	600.00	300.00
265 Charley Gehringer	300.00	150.00
266 Pete Fox	100.00	50.00
267 Joe Kuhel	100.00	50.00
268 Frank Demaree	100.00	50.00
269 Frank Pytlak	100.00	50.00
270 Ernie Lombardi	200.00	100.00
271 Joe Vosmik	100.00	50.00
272 Dick Bartell	100.00	50.00
273 Jimmie Foxx	400.00	200.00
274 Joe DiMaggio	3500.00	1800.00
275 Bump Hadley	100.00	50.00
276 Zeke Bonura	100.00	50.00
277 Hank Greenberg	400.00	200.00
278 Van Lingle Mungo	125.00	60.00
279 Moose Solters	100.00	50.00
280 Vernon Kennedy	100.00	50.00
281 Al Lopez	250.00	125.00
282 Bobby Doerr	250.00	125.00
283 Billy Werber	100.00	50.00
284 Rudy York	125.00	60.00
285 Rip Radcliff	100.00	50.00
286 Joe Medwick	250.00	125.00
287 Marvin Owen	100.00	50.00
288 Bob Feller	750.00	375.00

1941 Goudey

The cards in this 33-card set measure 2 3/8" by 2 7/8". The 1941 Series of blank backed baseball cards was the last baseball issue marketed by Goudey before the war closed the door on that company for good. Each black and white player photo comes with four color backgrounds (blue, green, red, or yellow). Cards without numbers are probably miscut. Cards 21-25 are especially scarce in relation to the rest of the set. In fact the eight hardest to find cards in the set are, in order, 22, 24, 23, 25, 21, 27, 29 and 32.

	Ex-Mt	VG
COMPLETE SET (33)	2000.00	1000.00
WRAPPER (1-CENT)	200.00	100.00
1 Hugh Mulcahy	30.00	15.00
2 Harland Clift	30.00	15.00
3 Louis Chiozza	30.00	15.00
4 Buddy Rosar	30.00	15.00
5 George McQuinn	30.00	15.00
6 George Dickman	30.00	15.00
7 Wayne Ambler	30.00	15.00
8 Bob Muncrief	30.00	15.00
9 Bill Dietrich	30.00	15.00
10 Taft Wright	30.00	15.00
11 Don Heffner	30.00	15.00
12 Fritz Ostermueller	30.00	15.00
13 Frank Hayes	30.00	15.00
14 John Kramer	30.00	15.00
15 Dario Lodigiani	30.00	15.00
16 George Case	30.00	15.00
17 Vito Tamulis	30.00	15.00
18 Whitlow Wyatt	40.00	20.00
19 Bill Posedel	30.00	15.00
20 Carl Hubbell	80.00	40.00
21 Harold Warstler SP	120.00	60.00
22 Joe Sullivan SP	300.00	150.00
23 Norman Young SP	200.00	100.00
24 Stanley Andrews SP	250.00	125.00
25 Morris Arnovich SP	120.00	60.00
26 Elbert Fletcher	30.00	15.00
27 Bill Crouch	60.00	30.00
28 Al Todd	30.00	15.00
29 Debs Garms	50.00	25.00
30 Jim Tobin	30.00	15.00
31 Chester Ross	30.00	15.00
32 George Coffman	40.00	20.00
33 Mel Ott	125.00	60.00

2000 Greats of the Game

The 2000 Fleer Greats of the Game set was released in late March, 2000 as a 107-card set that features some of the greatest players to ever play the game. There was only one series offered. Each pack contained six cards and carried a suggested retail price of 4.99. A promotional sample card featuring Nolan Ryan was distributed to dealers and hobby media several weeks before the product went live. Card fronts featured an attractive burgundy frame with (in most cases) a full color player image. Fueled by a great selection of autographs, the popular Yankee Clippings game-used jersey inserts and the aforementioned superior design of the base set, the product turned out to be one of the most popular releases of the 2000 calendar.

	Nm-Mt	Ex-Mt
COMPLETE SET (107)	40.00	12.00
1 Mickey Mantle	10.00	3.00
2 Gil Hodges	1.50	.45
3 Monte Irvin	1.00	.30
4 Satchel Paige	1.50	.45
5 Roy Campanella	1.50	.45
6 Richie Ashburn	1.00	.30
7 Roger Maris	1.50	.45
8 Ozzie Smith	2.50	.75
9 Reggie Jackson	1.00	.30
10 Eddie Mathews	1.50	.45
11 Dave Righetti	.60	.18
12 Dave Winfield	.60	.18
13 Lou Whitaker	.60	.18
14 Phil Garner	.60	.18
15 Ron Cey	.60	.18
16 Brooks Robinson	1.00	.30
17 Bruce Sutter	.60	.18
18 Dave Parker	.60	.18
19 Johnny Bench	1.50	.45
20 Fernando Valenzuela	.60	.18
21 George Brett	4.00	1.20
22 Paul Molitor	1.00	.30
23 Hoyt Wilhelm	.60	.18
24 Luis Aparicio	.60	.18
25 Frank White	.60	.18
26 Herb Score	.60	.18
27 Kirk Gibson	.60	.18
28 Mike Schmidt	3.00	.90
29 Don Baylor	.60	.18
30 Joe Pepitone	.60	.18
31 Hal McRae	.60	.18
32 Lee Smith	.60	.18
33 Nolan Ryan	4.00	1.20
34 Bill Mazeroski	1.00	.30
35 Bobby Doerr	1.00	.30
36 Duke Snider	1.00	.30
37 Dick Groat	.60	.18
38 Larry Doby	.60	.18
39 Kirby Puckett	1.50	.45
40 Steve Carlton	.60	.18
41 Dennis Eckersley	.60	.18
42 Jim Bunning	1.00	.30
43 Ron Guidry	.60	.18
44 Alan Trammell	.60	.18
45 Bob Feller	.60	.18
46 Dave Concepcion	.60	.18
47 Dwight Evans	.60	.18
48 Enos Slaughter	.60	.18
49 Tom Seaver	1.00	.30
50 Tony Oliva	.60	.18
51 Mel Stottlemyre	.60	.18
52 Tommy John	.60	.18
53 Willie McCovey	.60	.18
54 Red Schoendienst	.60	.18
55 Gorman Thomas	.60	.18
56 Ralph Kiner	.60	.18
57 Robin Yount	2.50	.75
58 Andre Dawson	.60	.18
59 Al Kaline	1.50	.45
60 Dom DiMaggio	1.00	.30
61 Juan Marichal	.60	.18
62 Jack Morris	.60	.18
63 Warren Spahn	1.00	.30
64 Preacher Roe	.60	.18
65 Darrell Evans	.60	.18
66 Jim Bouton	.60	.18
67 Rocky Colavito	1.00	.30
68 Bob Gibson	1.00	.30
69 Whitey Ford	1.00	.30
70 Moose Skowron	.60	.18
71 Boog Powell	.60	.18
72 Al Lopez	1.00	.30
73 Lou Brock	1.00	.30
74 Mickey Lolich	.60	.18
75 Rod Carew	1.00	.30
76 Bob Lemon	1.00	.30
77 Frank Howard	.60	.18
78 Phil Rizzuto	1.50	.45
79 Carl Yastrzemski	2.50	.75
80 Rico Carty	.60	.18
81 Jim Kaat	.60	.18
82 Bert Blyleven	.60	.18
83 George Kell	1.00	.30
84 Jim Palmer	.60	.18
85 Maury Wills	.60	.18
86 Jim Rice	.60	.18
87 Joe Carter	.60	.18
88 Clete Boyer	.60	.18
89 Yogi Berra	1.50	.45
90 Cecil Cooper	.60	.18
91 Davey Johnson	.60	.18
92 Lou Boudreau	1.00	.30
93 Orlando Cepeda	.60	.18
94 Tommy Henrich	.60	.18
95 Hank Bauer	.60	.18
96 Don Larsen	.60	.18
97 Vida Blue	.60	.18
98 Ben Oglivie	.60	.18
99 Don Mattingly	4.00	1.20
100 Dale Murphy	1.50	.45
101 Ferguson Jenkins	.60	.18
102 Bobby Bonds	.60	.18
103 Dick Allen	.60	.18
104 Stan Musial	2.50	.75
105 Gaylord Perry	.60	.18
106 Willie Randolph	.60	.18
107 Willie Stargell	1.00	.30
P33 Nolan Ryan Promo	1.50	.45

2000 Greats of the Game Autographs

Randomly inserted in packs at one in six, this 90-card insert features autographed cards of some of the greatest players in major league history. The card design closely parallels the attractive basic issue cards, except of course for the player's singature. Representatives at Fleer eventually released cryptic details on a few cards confirming widespread belief on suspected shortprints within the set. It's known that the scarcest cards are Johnny Bench and Mike Schmidt. Several other cards from this set experienced amazing surges iin value throughout the course of the year 2000 as collectors scrambled to complete their sets in the midst of heavy demand and rumours of additional short prints. Also, Herb Score mistakenly signed several of his basic autographs with an "ROY 55" notation. Score was supposed so sign only 55 purple-bordered Memorable Moments variations. Finally, a Derek Jeter card was released in early 2004. It's believed that the card was only made available as a redemption to collectors for autograph exchange cards of other players that they could not fulfill. Please note that these cards are unnumbered and we have sequenced them in alphabetical order.

	Nm-Mt	Ex-Mt
JETER EXCH PRINT RUN 150 CARDS		
JETER EXCH IS NOT SERIAL #'d		
JETER PRINT RUN PROVIDED BY FLEER		
1 Luis Aparicio	15.00	4.50
2 Hank Bauer	15.00	4.50
3 Don Baylor	15.00	4.50
4 Johnny Bench SP	200.00	60.00
5 Yogi Berra SP	200.00	60.00
6 Vida Blue	15.00	4.50
7 Bert Blyleven	15.00	4.50
8 Bobby Bonds	25.00	7.50
9 Lou Boudreau	120.00	36.00
10 Jim Bouton	25.00	7.50
11 Clete Boyer	15.00	4.50
12 George Brett SP	200.00	60.00
13 Lou Brock	25.00	7.50
14 Jim Bunning	40.00	12.00
15 Rod Carew	60.00	18.00
16 Steve Carlton	25.00	7.50
17 Joe Carter SP	120.00	36.00
18 Orlando Cepeda	15.00	4.50
19 Ron Cey	10.00	3.00
20 Rocky Colavito	50.00	15.00
21 Dave Concepcion	15.00	4.50
21A Dave Concepcion	15.00	4.50
Signed in Red Ink		
22 Cecil Cooper	10.00	3.00
23 Andre Dawson	10.00	3.00
24 Dom DiMaggio	120.00	36.00
25 Bobby Doerr	15.00	4.50
26 Darrell Evans	10.00	3.00
27 Bob Feller	25.00	7.50
28 Whitey Ford SP	150.00	45.00
29 Phil Garner	10.00	3.00
30 Bob Gibson	25.00	7.50
31 Kirk Gibson	25.00	7.50
32 Dick Groat	15.00	4.50
33 Ron Guidry	25.00	7.50
34 Tommy Henrich SP	200.00	60.00
35 Frank Howard	15.00	4.50
36 Reggie Jackson SP	150.00	45.00
37 Ferguson Jenkins	15.00	4.50
38 Derek Jeter/150 EXCH	200.00	60.00
39 Tommy John	15.00	4.50
40 Davey Johnson	10.00	3.00
41 Jim Kaat	15.00	4.50
42 Al Kaline	40.00	12.00
43 George Kell	15.00	4.50
44 Ralph Kiner	25.00	7.50
45 Don Larsen	25.00	7.50
46 Mickey Lolich	15.00	4.50
47 Juan Marichal	60.00	18.00
48 Eddie Mathews	100.00	30.00
49 Don Mattingly SP	300.00	90.00
50 Bill Mazeroski	25.00	7.50
51 Willie McCovey SP	120.00	36.00
52 Hal McRae	10.00	3.00
53 Paul Molitor	50.00	15.00
54 Jack Morris	15.00	4.50
55 Dale Murphy	40.00	12.00
56 Stan Musial SP	100.00	30.00
57 Ben Oglivie	10.00	3.00
58 Tony Oliva	15.00	4.50
59 Jim Palmer SP	120.00	36.00
60 Dave Parker	15.00	4.50
61 Joe Pepitone	15.00	4.50
62 Gaylord Perry	15.00	4.50
63 Boog Powell	15.00	4.50
64 Kirby Puckett SP	175.00	52.50
65 Willie Randolph	25.00	7.50
66 Jim Rice	15.00	4.50
67 Dave Righetti	15.00	4.50
68 Phil Rizzuto SP	175.00	52.50
69 Brooks Robinson	25.00	7.50
70 Preacher Roe	15.00	4.50
71 Nolan Ryan	175.00	52.50
72 Mike Schmidt SP	300.00	90.00
73 Red Schoendienst	25.00	7.50
74 Herb Score	15.00	4.50
Card has no ROY 55 on signature		
75 Herb Score	40.00	12.00
ROY 55 in signature		
76 Tom Seaver	100.00	30.00
77 Moose Skowron	15.00	4.50
78 Enos Slaughter	25.00	7.50
79 Lee Smith	15.00	4.50
80 Ozzie Smith SP	200.00	60.00
81 Duke Snider SP	200.00	60.00
82 Warren Spahn SP	100.00	30.00
83 Willie Stargell	60.00	18.00
84 Bruce Sutter	15.00	4.50
85 Gorman Thomas	10.00	3.00
86 Alan Trammell	15.00	4.50
87 Frank White	15.00	4.50
88 Hoyt Wilhelm	25.00	7.50
89 Maury Wills	15.00	4.50
90 Carl Yastrzemski	60.00	18.00
91 Robin Yount SP	175.00	52.50

2000 Greats of the Game Autographs Memorable Moments

Randomly inserted in packs, this insert features autographs of Ron Guidry, Nolan Ryan, Herb Score and Tom Seaver. Each card is autographed and contains a notion by the player related to a career achievement. Each card is serial-numbered to the year of that achievement. The fronts of these cards are purple-bordered instead of burgandy-bordered. Please note that Herb Score signed some of his regular burgandy-bordered autograph cards with the "HOF 55" notation. Please refer to the basic autograph set for price listings on that card.

	Nm-Mt	Ex-Mt
1 Ron Guidry/CY 78	150.00	45.00
2 Nolan Ryan/HOF 99	400.00	120.00
3 Herb Score/ROY 55	120.00	36.00
4 Tom Seaver/CY 69	300.00	90.00

2000 Greats of the Game Retrospection

Randomly inserted in packs at one in six, this insert set pays tribute to 15 truly legendary players. Card backs carry a "R" prefix.

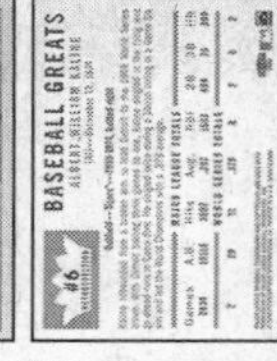

	Nm-Mt	Ex-Mt
COMPLETE SET (15)	100.00	30.00
R1 Rod Carew	3.00	.90
R2 Stan Musial	8.00	2.40
R3 Nolan Ryan	12.00	3.60
R4 Tom Seaver	3.00	.90
R5 Brooks Robinson	3.00	.90
R6 Al Kaline	5.00	1.50
R7 Mike Schmidt	10.00	3.00
R8 Thurman Munson	5.00	1.50
R9 Steve Carlton	2.00	.60
R10 Roger Maris	5.00	1.50
R11 Duke Snider	3.00	.90
R12 Yogi Berra	5.00	1.50
R13 Carl Yastrzemski	8.00	2.40
R14 Reggie Jackson	3.00	.90
R15 Johnny Bench	5.00	1.50

2000 Greats of the Game Yankees Clippings

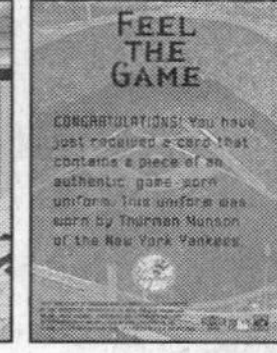

Randomly inserted in packs at one in 48, this insert set features 15 cards that contain pieces of game-used jerseys of legendary New York Yankee players. Card backs carry a "YC" prefix. This set represents one of the earliest attempts by manufacturers to incorporate a theme into a memorabilia-based insert.

	Nm-Mt	Ex-Mt
YC1 Mickey Mantle	250.00	75.00
YC2 Ron Guidry	50.00	15.00
YC3 Don Larsen	50.00	15.00
YC4 Elston Howard	50.00	15.00
YC5 Mel Stottlemyre	40.00	12.00
YC6 Don Mattingly	100.00	30.00
YC7 Reggie Jackson	60.00	18.00
YC8 Tommy John	40.00	12.00
YC9 Dave Winfield	40.00	12.00
YC10 Willie Randolph	40.00	12.00
Uniform is home pinstripes		
YC10A Willie Randolph	40.00	12.00
Grey Uniform		
YC11 Tommy Henrich	40.00	12.00
YC12 Billy Martin	80.00	24.00
YC13 Dave Righetti	40.00	12.00
YC14 Joe Pepitone	40.00	12.00
YC15 Thurman Munson	100.00	30.00

2001 Greats of the Game

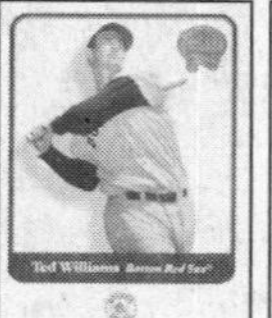

The 2001 Fleer Greats of the Game product was released in March, 2001 and features a 137-card base set that includes many players that are in the Major League Hall of Fame. Each pack contains five cards and carried a suggested retail price of $4.99.

	Nm-Mt	Ex-Mt
COMPLETE SET (137)	50.00	15.00
1 Roberto Clemente	6.00	1.80
2 George Anderson	1.00	.30
3 Babe Ruth	8.00	2.40
4 Paul Molitor	1.50	.45
5 Don Larsen	1.00	.30
6 Cy Young	2.50	.75
7 Billy Martin	1.50	.45
8 Lou Brock	1.50	.45
9 Fred Lynn	1.00	.30
10 Johnny VanderMeer	1.00	.30
11 Harmon Killebrew	2.50	.75
12 Dave Winfield	1.00	.30
13 Orlando Cepeda	1.00	.30
14 Johnny Mize	1.50	.45
15 Walter Johnson	2.50	.75
16 Roy Campanella	2.50	.75
17 Monte Irvin	1.50	.45
18 Mookie Wilson	1.00	.30
19 Elston Howard	1.50	.45
20 Walter Alston	1.00	.30
21 Rollie Fingers	1.00	.30
22 Brooks Robinson	1.50	.45
23 Hank Greenberg	2.50	.75
24 Maury Wills	1.00	.30
25 Rich Gossage	1.00	.30
26 Leon Day	1.00	.30
27 Jimmie Foxx	2.50	.75
28 Alan Trammell	1.00	.30
29 Dennis Martinez	1.00	.30
30 Don Drysdale	2.50	.75
31 Bob Feller	1.00	.30
32 Jackie Robinson	2.50	.75
33 Whitey Ford	1.50	.45

34 Enos Slaughter	1.00	.30
35 Rod Carew	1.50	.45
36 Eddie Mathews	2.50	.75
37 Ron Cey	1.00	.30
38 Thurman Munson	2.50	.75
39 Henry Kimbro	1.00	.30
40 Ty Cobb	4.00	1.20
41 Rocky Colavito	2.50	.75
42 Satchel Paige	2.50	.75
43 Andre Dawson	1.00	.30
44 Phil Rizzuto	2.50	.75
45 Roger Maris	2.50	.75
46 Bobby Bonds	1.00	.30
47 Joe Carter	1.00	.30
48 Christy Mathewson	2.50	.75
49 Tony Lazzeri	1.00	.30
50 Gil Hodges	2.50	.75
51 Ray Dandridge	1.00	.30
52 Gaylord Perry	1.00	.30
53 Ernie Banks	2.50	.75
54 Lou Gehrig	5.00	1.50
55 George Kell	1.50	.45
56 Wes Parker	1.00	.30
57 Sam Jethroe	1.00	.30
58 Joe Morgan	1.00	.30
59 Steve Garvey	1.00	.30
60 Joe Torre	1.00	.30
61 Roger Craig	1.00	.30
62 Warren Spahn	1.50	.45
63 Willie McCovey	1.00	.30
64 Cool Papa Bell	1.00	.30
65 Frank Robinson	1.50	.45
66 Richie Allen	1.00	.30
67 Bucky Dent	1.00	.30
68 George Foster	1.00	.30
69 Hoyt Wilhelm	1.00	.30
70 Phil Niekro	1.00	.30
71 Buck Leonard	1.00	.30
72 Preacher Roe	1.00	.30
73 Yogi Berra	2.50	.75
74 Joe Black	1.00	.30
75 Nolan Ryan	6.00	1.80
76 Pop Lloyd	1.00	.30
77 Lester Lockett	1.00	.30
78 Paul Blair	1.00	.30
79 Ryne Sandberg	4.00	1.20
80 Bill Perkins	1.00	.30
81 Frank Howard	1.00	.30
82 Hack Wilson	1.50	.45
83 Robin Yount	4.00	1.20
84 Harry Heilmann	1.00	.30
85 Mike Schmidt	5.00	1.50
86 Vida Blue	1.00	.30
87 George Brett	6.00	1.80
88 Juan Marichal	1.00	.30
89 Tom Seaver	1.50	.45
90 Bill Skowron	1.00	.30
91 Don Mattingly	6.00	1.80
92 Jim Bunning	1.50	.45
93 Eddie Murray	2.50	.75
94 Tommy Lasorda	1.00	.30
95 Pee Wee Reese	2.50	.75
96 Bill Dickey	1.50	.45
97 Ozzie Smith	4.00	1.20
98 Dale Murphy	2.50	.75
99 Artie Wilson	1.00	.30
100 Bill Terry	1.00	.30
101 Jim Hunter	1.50	.45
102 Don Sutton	1.00	.30
103 Luis Aparicio	1.00	.30
104 Reggie Jackson	1.50	.45
105 Ted Radcliffe	1.00	.30
106 Carl Erskine	1.00	.30
107 Johnny Bench	2.50	.75
108 Carl Furillo	1.00	.30
109 Stan Musial	4.00	1.20
110 Carlton Fisk	1.50	.45
111 Rube Foster	1.00	.30
112 Tony Oliva	1.00	.30
113 Hank Bauer	1.00	.30
114 Jim Rice	1.00	.30
115 Willie Mays	5.00	1.50
116 Ralph Kiner	1.00	.30
117 Al Kaline	2.50	.75
118 Billy Williams	1.00	.30
119 Buck O'Neil	1.00	.30
120 Tony Perez	1.00	.30
121 Dave Parker	1.00	.30
122 Kirk Gibson	1.00	.30
123 Lou Piniella	1.00	.30
124 Ted Williams	5.00	1.50
125 Steve Carlton	1.00	.30
126 Dizzy Dean	2.50	.75
127 Willie Stargell	1.50	.45
128 Joe Niekro	1.00	.30
129 Lloyd Waner	1.50	.45
130 Wade Boggs	1.50	.45
131 Wilmer Fields	1.00	.30
132 Bill Mazeroski	1.50	.45
133 Duke Snider	1.50	.45
134 Joe Williams	1.00	.30
135 Bob Gibson	1.50	.45
136 Jim Palmer	1.00	.30
137 Oscar Charleston	1.00	.30

2001 Greats of the Game Autographs

Randomly inserted into packs at one in eight Hobby, and one in 20 Retail, this 93-card insert set features authentic autographs from legendary players such as Nolan Ryan, Mike Schmidt, and recently inducted Hall of Famer Dave Winfield. Please note, the following players packed out as exchange cards with a redemption deadline of March 1st, 2002: Luis Aparicio, Sam Jethroe, Tommy Lasorda, Juan Marichal, Willie Mays, Phil Rizzuto and Willie Stargell. In addition, the following players had about 50 percent actual signed cards and 50 percent exchange cards seeded into packs: Jim Bunning, Ron Cey, Rollie Fingers, Carlton Fisk, Harmon Killebrew, Gaylord Perry and Brooks Robinson. Also, representatives at Fleer announced specific print runs for several short-printed cards within this set. Though the cards lack actual serial-numbering, the announced quantities for these SP's have been added to our checklist. Willie Stargell passed on before he could sign his card and Fleer used various redemption cards to send to those collectors who had pulled one of those cards from packs.

	Nm-Mt	Ex-Mt
1 Richie Allen	15.00	4.50
2 Sparky Anderson	15.00	4.50
3 Luis Aparicio	15.00	4.50
4 Ernie Banks SP/250	120.00	36.00
5 Hank Bauer	15.00	4.50
6 Johnny Bench SP/400	120.00	36.00
7 Yogi Berra SP/500	80.00	24.00
8 Joe Black	15.00	4.50
9 Paul Blair	15.00	4.50
9A Paul Blair	15.00	4.50
Double-Signed		
10 Vida Blue	15.00	4.50
11 Wade Boggs	50.00	15.00
12 Bobby Bonds	25.00	7.50
13 George Brett SP/247	150.00	45.00
14 Lou Brock SP/500	50.00	15.00
15 Jim Bunning	40.00	12.00
16 Rod Carew	25.00	7.50
17 Steve Carlton	30.00	9.00
18 Joe Carter	15.00	4.50
19 Orlando Cepeda	15.00	4.50
20 Ron Cey	15.00	4.50
21 Rocky Colavito	25.00	7.50
22 Roger Craig	15.00	4.50
23 Andre Dawson	15.00	4.50
24 Bucky Dent	15.00	4.50
25 Carl Erskine	15.00	4.50
26 Bob Feller	15.00	4.50
27 Wilmer Fields	15.00	4.50
28 Rollie Fingers	15.00	4.50
29 Carlton Fisk	50.00	15.00
30 Whitey Ford	40.00	12.00
31 George Foster	15.00	4.50
32 Steve Garvey SP/400	50.00	15.00
33 Bob Gibson	30.00	9.00
34 Kirk Gibson	15.00	4.50
35 Rich Gossage	15.00	4.50
36 Frank Howard	15.00	4.50
37 Monte Irvin	25.00	7.50
38 Reg. Jackson SP/400	80.00	24.00
39 Sam Jethroe	15.00	4.50
40 Al Kaline	40.00	12.00
41 George Kell	25.00	7.50
42 H. Killebrew EXCH*	30.00	9.00
43 Ralph Kiner	25.00	7.50
44 Don Larsen	25.00	7.50
45 Tommy Lasorda SP/400	60.00	18.00
46 Lester Lockett	15.00	4.50
47 Fred Lynn	15.00	4.50
48 Juan Marichal	15.00	4.50
49 Dennis Martinez	15.00	4.50
50 Don Mattingly	80.00	24.00
51 Willie Mays SP/100	600.00	180.00
52 Bill Mazeroski UER	25.00	7.50
Baltimore Elite Giants logo on card back		
53 Willie McCovey	25.00	7.50
54 Paul Molitor	25.00	7.50
55 Joe Morgan	15.00	4.50
56 Dale Murphy	40.00	12.00
57 Eddie Murray SP/140	250.00	75.00
58 Stan Musial SP/525	100.00	30.00
59 Joe Niekro	15.00	4.50
60 Phil Niekro	15.00	4.50
61 Tony Oliva	15.00	4.50
62 Buck O'Neil	25.00	7.50
63 Jim Palmer SP/600	25.00	7.50
64 Dave Parker	15.00	4.50
65 Tony Perez	25.00	7.50
66 Gaylord Perry	15.00	4.50
67 Lou Piniella	15.00	4.50
68 Ted Radcliffe	15.00	4.50
69 Jim Rice	15.00	4.50
70 Phil Rizzuto	100.00	30.00
EXCH SP/425		
71 Brooks Robinson	25.00	7.50
72 Frank Robinson	30.00	9.00
73 Preacher Roe	15.00	4.50
74 Nolan Ryan SP/650	200.00	60.00
75 Ryne Sandberg	60.00	18.00
76 Mike Schmidt SP/213	200.00	60.00
77 Tom Seaver	50.00	15.00
78 Bill Skowron	15.00	4.50
79 Enos Slaughter	25.00	7.50
80 Ozzie Smith	60.00	18.00
81 Duke Snider SP/600	80.00	24.00
82 Warren Spahn	40.00	12.00
83 Willie Stargell NO AU	25.00	7.50
84 Don Sutton	15.00	4.50
85 Joe Torre SP/500	60.00	18.00
86 Alan Trammell	15.00	4.50
87 Hoyt Wilhelm	15.00	4.50
88 Billy Williams	15.00	4.50
89 Maury Wills	15.00	4.50
90 Artie Wilson	15.00	4.50
91 Mookie Wilson	15.00	4.50
92 Dave Winfield SP/370	80.00	24.00
93 Robin Yount SP/400	100.00	30.00

2001 Greats of the Game Dodger Blues

Randomly inserted into packs at one in 36 Hobby, this 15-card insert set features swatches from actual game-used Jerseys, Uniforms, and Bats from legendary Dodger players. The cards have been listed below in alphabetical order for convenience. Please note, according to representatives at Fleer less than 200 of each SP was produced.

	Nm-Mt	Ex-Mt
1 Walter Alston Jsy	15.00	4.50
2 Walter Alston Uni	15.00	4.50
3 Roy Campanella Bat SP	120.00	36.00
4 Roger Craig Jsy	15.00	4.50
5 Don Drysdale Jsy	25.00	7.50
6 Carl Furillo Jsy	15.00	4.50
7 Steve Garvey Jsy	15.00	4.50
8 Gil Hodges Uni	25.00	7.50
9 Wes Parker Bat	15.00	4.50
10 Wes Parker Jsy	15.00	4.50
11 Pee Wee Reese Jsy	25.00	7.50
12 Jackie Robinson	200.00	60.00
Uniform SP		
13 Preacher Roe Jsy	25.00	7.50
14 Duke Snider Bat SP	120.00	36.00
15 Don Sutton Jsy	15.00	4.50

2001 Greats of the Game Feel the Game Classics

Randomly inserted into packs at one in 72 Hobby, and one in 400 Retail, this 24-card insert features swatches of actual game-used Bats or Jerseys from legendary players like Babe Ruth and Roger Maris. Please note that the cards are listed below in alphabetical order. Though the cards lack actual serial-numbering, specific print runs for several short-printed cards was publicly announced by representativces at Fleer. These figures are detailed in our checklist.

	Nm-Mt	Ex-Mt
1 L. Aparicio Bat SP/200	25.00	7.50
2 George Brett Jsy SP/300	50.00	15.00
3 Lou Brock Jsy	15.00	4.50
4 O. Cepeda Bat SP/300	25.00	7.50
5 Whitey Ford Jsy	15.00	4.50
6 Hank Greenberg Bat SP/300	80.00	24.00
7 Elston Howard Bat SP/300	25.00	7.50
8 Jim Hunter Jsy	15.00	4.50
9 Harmon Killebrew Bat	15.00	4.50
10 Roger Maris Bat	50.00	15.00
11 Eddie Mathews Bat	15.00	4.50
12 Willie McCovey	25.00	7.50
Bat SP/200		
13 Johnny Mize Bat	15.00	4.50
14 Paul Molitor Jsy	15.00	4.50
15 Jim Palmer Jsy	10.00	3.00
16 Tony Perez Bat	10.00	3.00
17 B.Robinson Bat SP/144	25.00	7.50
18 Babe Ruth Bat SP/250	250.00	75.00
19 Mike Schmidt Jsy	40.00	12.00
20 Tom Seaver Jsy	15.00	4.50
21 Enos Slaughter	25.00	7.50
Bat SP/200		
22 Willie Stargell Jsy	15.00	4.50
23 Hack Wilson Bat	80.00	24.00
24 Harry Heilmann Bat	10.00	3.00

2001 Greats of the Game Retrospection

Randomly inserted into hobby and retail packs at one in six, this 10-card insert set takes a look at the careers of some of the best players to have ever played the game. Card backs carry a "RC' prefix.

	Nm-Mt	Ex-Mt
COMPLETE SET (10)	30.00	9.00
RC1 Babe Ruth	15.00	4.50
RC2 Stan Musial	6.00	1.80
RC3 Jimmie Foxx	5.00	1.50
RC4 Roberto Clemente	12.00	3.60
RC5 Ted Williams	10.00	3.00
RC6 Mike Schmidt	8.00	2.40
RC7 Cy Young	5.00	1.50
RC8 Satchel Paige	5.00	1.50
RC9 Hank Greenberg	5.00	1.50
RC10 Jim Bunning	3.00	.90

2002 Greats of the Game Autographs

Randomly inserted into packs at one in 24, this insert set features authentic autographs from legendary players such as Nolan Ryan, Bob Gibson, and recently inducted Hall of Famer Ozzie Smith. Please note that a few of the players were short-printed and are listed below with an "SP" after their name. A number of exchange cards with a redemption deadline of 12/01/02 were seeded into packs. The following players were available via redemption: Al Kaline, Alan Trammell, Bobby Bonds, Bob Feller, Carlton Fisk, Rocky Colavito, Cal Ripken, Dave Winfield, Eddie Murray, Enos Slaughter, Harmon Killebrew, Juan Marichal, Kirby Puckett, Luis Aparicio, Lou Brock, Mike Schmidt, Dale Murphy, Maury Wills, Nolan Ryan, Ozzie Smith, Phil Rizzuto, Rod Carew, Rollie Fingers, Rich Gossage, Ralph Kiner, Robin Yount, Steve Garvey, Whitey Ford, Willie McCovey and Yogi Berra.

	Nm-Mt	Ex-Mt
AD Andre Dawson	15.00	4.50
AK Al Kaline	40.00	12.00
AT Alan Trammell	15.00	4.50
BB Bobby Bonds	25.00	7.50
BF Bob Feller	15.00	4.50
BG Bob Gibson SP/200	30.00	9.00
BM Bill Mazeroski SP/200	30.00	9.00
BR Brooks Robinson	25.00	7.50
BS Bill Skowron	15.00	4.50
BW Billy Williams	15.00	4.50
CE Ron Cey	10.00	3.00
CF C.Fisk SP/100 EXCH	80.00	24.00
CO Rocky Colavito	40.00	12.00
CR C.Ripken SP/100 EXCH	200.00	60.00
CY C.Yastrzemski SP/200	80.00	24.00
DM Don Mattingly SP/300	80.00	24.00
DP Dave Parker	15.00	4.50
DS Duke Snider	25.00	7.50
DW D.Winfield SP/250 EXCH	30.00	9.00
EM E.Murray SP/250 EXCH	80.00	24.00
ES Enos Slaughter	25.00	7.50
FH Frank Howard	15.00	4.50
FL Fred Lynn	15.00	4.50
FR F.Robinson SP/250	30.00	9.00
GB George Brett SP/150	150.00	45.00
GK George Kell	25.00	7.50
GP Gaylord Perry	15.00	4.50
HB Hank Bauer	15.00	4.50
HK H.Killebrew EXCH	30.00	9.00
HW Hoyt Wilhelm	15.00	4.50
JB Johnny Bench	60.00	18.00
JC Joe Carter	15.00	4.50
JM Juan Marichal	15.00	4.50
JM Joe Morgan	15.00	4.50
JP Jim Palmer	25.00	7.50
JR Jim Rice	15.00	4.50
KP K.Puckett SP/250 EXCH	80.00	24.00
LA Luis Aparicio	15.00	4.50
LB L.Brock SP/250 EXCH	30.00	9.00
MS M.Schmidt SP/150 EXCH	120.00	36.00
MU Dale Murphy	40.00	12.00
MW Maury Wills	15.00	4.50
NR N.Ryan SP/150 EXCH	120.00	36.00
OC Orlando Cepeda	15.00	4.50
OS Ozzie Smith SP/300	80.00	24.00
PB Paul Blair	10.00	3.00
PM Paul Molitor	25.00	7.50
PR P.Rizzuto SP/300 EXCH	60.00	18.00
PR Preacher Roe	15.00	4.50
RC R.Carew SP/250 EXCH	50.00	15.00
RF Rollie Fingers	15.00	4.50
RG Rich Gossage	15.00	4.50
RJ R.Jackson SP/150	80.00	24.00
RK R.Kiner SP/250 EXCH	25.00	7.50
RS R.Sandberg SP/200	80.00	24.00
RY R.Yount SP/250 EXCH	80.00	24.00
SA Sparky Anderson	15.00	4.50
SC Steve Carlton	30.00	9.00
SG Steve Garvey	15.00	4.50
SM Stan Musial SP/200	80.00	24.00
TO Tony Oliva	15.00	4.50
TP Tony Perez	15.00	4.50
TS Tom Seaver SP/150	60.00	18.00
VB Vida Blue	15.00	4.50
WB Wade Boggs	25.00	7.50
WF Whitey Ford	40.00	12.00
WM Willie McCovey	25.00	7.50
WS Warren Spahn	40.00	12.00
YB Yogi Berra	50.00	15.00

2002 Greats of the Game Dueling Duos

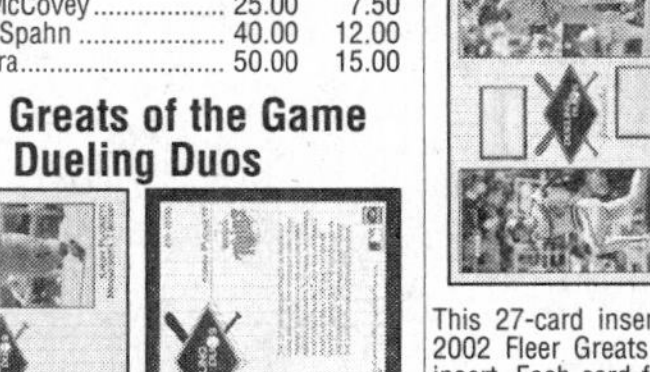

This 29-card insert pairs contemporaries that competed against each other in their respective eras. These cards were inserted into packs at one in six.

	Nm-Mt	Ex-Mt
1 Johnny Bench	4.00	1.20
Carlton Fisk		
2 Roy Campanella	5.00	1.50
Yogi Berra		
3 Stan Musial	6.00	1.80
Ted Williams		
4 Carl Yastrzemski	5.00	1.50
Reggie Jackson		
5 Babe Ruth	10.00	3.00
Jimmie Foxx		
6 Kirby Puckett	8.00	2.40
Don Mattingly		
7 Steve Carlton	8.00	2.40
Nolan Ryan		
8 Wade Boggs	10.00	3.00
Don Mattingly		
9 Brooks Robinson	4.00	1.20
Roger Maris		
10 Paul Molitor	10.00	3.00
Don Mattingly		
11 Sparky Anderson	3.00	.90
Earl Weaver		
12 Bob Gibson	3.00	.90
Duke Snider		
13 Yogi Berra	5.00	1.50
Gil Hodges		
14 Joe Morgan	6.00	1.80
Ryne Sandberg		
15 Tony Perez	5.00	1.50
Carl Yastrzemski		
16 Jimmie Foxx	4.00	1.20
Bill Dickey		
17 Ralph Kiner	3.00	.90
Duke Snider		
18 Nellie Fox	3.00	.90
Rocky Colavito		
19 Willie McCovey	4.00	1.20
Johnny Bench		
20 Duke Snider	3.00	.90
Eddie Mathews		
21 Reggie Jackson	3.00	.90
Jim Rice		
22 Eddie Murray	4.00	1.20
Jim Rice		
23 Paul Molitor	3.00	.90
Dave Winfield		
24 Robin Yount	5.00	1.50
Dave Winfield		
25 Enos Slaughter	3.00	.90
Ted Kluszewski		
26 Wade Boggs	10.00	3.00
George Brett		
27 George Brett	10.00	3.00
Mike Schmidt		
28 George Brett	10.00	3.00
Eddie Murray		
29 George Brett	12.00	3.60
Cal Ripken		

2002 Greats of the Game Dueling Duos Autographs

This six-card insert set is a partial parallel of the 2002 Fleer Greats of the Game Dueling Duos insert, and features dual autographs from greats like Bench/Fisk. Each card is individually serial numbered to 25. Due to market scarcity, no pricing is provided. The following cards were distributed in packs as exchange cards with a redemption deadline of 12/01/02: Bench/Fisk, Boggs/Mattingly, Brett/Schmidt and Puckett/Mattingly.

	Nm-Mt	Ex-Mt
1 Johnny Bench		
Carlton Fisk		
2 Wade Boggs		
Don Mattingly		
3 George Brett		
Mike Schmidt		
4 Kirby Puckett		
Don Mattingly		
5 Duke Snider		
Bob Gibson		
6 Carl Yastrzemski		
Reggie Jackson		

2002 Greats of the Game Dueling Duos Game Used Double

This 27-card insert is a partial parallel of the 2002 Fleer Greats of the Game Dueling Duos insert. Each card features dual jersey swatches from greats like Boggs/Brett, and is individually serial numbered to 25. Due to market scarcity, no pricing is provided.

	Nm-Mt	Ex-Mt
1 Sparky Anderson		
Earl Weaver		
2 Johnny Bench		
Carlton Fisk		
3 Yogi Berra		
Gil Hodges		
4 Wade Boggs		
George Brett		
5 Wade Boggs		
Don Mattingly		
6 George Brett		
Eddie Murray		
7 George Brett		
Cal Ripken		
8 Roy Campanella		
Yogi Berra		
9 Steve Carlton		
Nolan Ryan		
10 Nellie Fox		
Rocky Colavito		
11 Jimmie Foxx		
Bill Dickey		
12 Bob Gibson		
Duke Snider		
13 Reggie Jackson		
Jim Rice		

14 Ralph Kiner
Duke Snider
15 Willie McCovey
Johnny Bench
16 Paul Molitor
Don Mattingly
17 Paul Molitor
Dave Winfield
18 Joe Morgan
Ryne Sandberg
19 Eddie Murray
Jim Rice
20 Tony Perez
Carl Yastrzemski
21 Kirby Puckett
Don Mattingly
22 Brooks Robinson
Roger Maris
23 Babe Ruth
Jimmie Foxx
24 Enos Slaughter
Ted Kluszewski
25 Duke Snider
Eddie Mathews
26 Carl Yastrzemski
Reggie Jackson
27 Robin Yount
Dave Winfield

2002 Greats of the Game Dueling Duos Game Used Single

This 54-card insert features a single swatch of game-used jersey, and was inserted into packs at 1:24. Please note that a few of the players were short-printed and are notated as such in our checklist.

	Nm-Mt	Ex-Mt
BD1 Jimmie Foxx / Bill Dickey Bat	20.00	6.00
BG1 Bob Gibson Jsy / Duke Snider SP/200	20.00	6.00
BR1 Brooks Robinson Bat / Roger Maris	20.00	6.00
BR1 Babe Ruth Bat / Jimmie Foxx SP/75		
CF1 Johnny Bench / Carlton Fisk Bat	20.00	6.00
CR1 George Brett / Cal Ripken Bat	40.00	12.00
CY1 Carl Yastrzemski Bat / Reggie Jackson	30.00	9.00
CY2 Tony Perez / Carl Yastrzemski Bat	30.00	9.00
DM1 Kirby Puckett / Don Mattingly Bat	25.00	7.50
DM2 Wade Boggs / Don Mattingly Bat	25.00	7.50
DM3 Paul Molitor / Don Mattingly Bat	25.00	7.50
DS1 Bob Gibson / Duke Snider Bat SP/200	20.00	6.00
DS2 Ralph Kiner / Duke Snider Bat	20.00	6.00
DS3 Duke Snider Bat / Eddie Mathews	20.00	6.00
DW1 Paul Molitor / Dave Winfield Bat	15.00	4.50
DW2 Robin Yount / Dave Winfield Bat	15.00	4.50
EM1 Duke Snider / Eddie Mathews Bat	25.00	7.50
EM1 Eddie Murray Bat / Jim Rice	25.00	7.50
EM2 George Brett / Eddie Murray Bat	25.00	7.50
ES1 Enos Slaughter Bat / Ted Kluszewski	15.00	4.50
EW1 Sparky Anderson / Earl Weaver Pants SP/400	15.00	4.50
GB1 Wade Boggs / George Brett Bat	25.00	7.50
GB2 George Brett Bat / Eddie Murray	25.00	7.50
GB3 George Brett Bat / Cal Ripken	25.00	7.50
GH1 Yogi Berra / Gil Hodges Bat	20.00	6.00
JB1 Johnny Bench Bat / Carlton Fisk	25.00	7.50
JB2 Willie McCovey / Johnny Bench Bat	25.00	7.50
JF1 Babe Ruth / Jimmie Foxx Bat SP/75		
JF2 Jimmie Foxx Bat / Bill Dickey SP/400	30.00	9.00
JM1 Joe Morgan Bat / Ryne Sandberg	15.00	4.50
JR1 Reggie Jackson / Jim Rice Bat	15.00	4.50
JR2 Eddie Murray / Jim Rice Bat	20.00	6.00
KP1 Kirby Puckett Bat / Don Mattingly	25.00	7.50
NF1 Nellie Fox Bat / Rocky Colavito	25.00	7.50
NR1 Steve Carlton / Nolan Ryan Jsy SP/100		
PM1 Paul Molitor Bat / Don Mattingly	20.00	6.00
PM2 Paul Molitor Bat / Dave Winfield	20.00	6.00
RC1 Roy Campanella / Yogi Berra Glove	25.00	7.50
RC1 Nellie Fox / Rocky Colavito Bat	20.00	6.00
RJ1 Carl Yastrzemski / Reggie Jackson Bat	20.00	6.00
RJ2 Reggie Jackson Bat / Jim Rice	20.00	6.00
RK1 Ralph Kiner Bat / Duke Snider	20.00	6.00
RM1 Brooks Robinson / Roger Maris Pants	50.00	15.00
RS1 Joe Morgan / Ryne Sandberg Bat	25.00	7.50
RY1 Robin Yount Bat / Dave Winfield	20.00	6.00
SA1 Sparky Anderson / Earl Weaver Pants SP/400	15.00	4.50
SC1 Steve Carlton Jersey / Nolan Ryan SP/100		
TK1 Enos Slaughter / Ted Kluszewski Bat	20.00	6.00
TP1 Tony Perez Bat / Carl Yastrzemski	15.00	4.50
WB1 Wade Boggs Bat / Don Mattingly	20.00	6.00
WB2 Wade Boggs Bat / George Brett	20.00	6.00
WM1 Willie McCovey Bat / Johnny Bench	25.00	7.50
YB1 Roy Campanella / Yogi Berra Bat	25.00	7.50
YB2 Yogi Berra Bat / Gil Hodges	25.00	7.50

2002 Greats of the Game Through the Years Level 1

This 31-card insert features swatches of authentic game-used jersey on a silver-foil based card. These cards were inserted into packs at a rate of 1:24.

	Nm-Mt	Ex-Mt
1 Johnny Bench Pants	20.00	6.00
2 Vida Blue	15.00	4.50
3 Wade Boggs	15.00	4.50
4 George Brett	25.00	7.50
5 Carlton Fisk Hitting	15.00	4.50
6 Carlton Fisk Fielding	15.00	4.50
7 Bo Jackson Royals	20.00	6.00
8 Bo Jackson White Sox	20.00	6.00
9 Reggie Jackson A's	15.00	4.50
10 Reggie Jackson Angels	15.00	4.50
11 Ted Kluszewski	15.00	4.50
12 Don Mattingly	25.00	7.50
13 Willie McCovey	15.00	4.50
14 Paul Molitor Blue Jays	15.00	4.50
15 Paul Molitor Brewers	15.00	4.50
16 Eddie Murray	20.00	6.00
17 Jim Palmer	15.00	4.50
18 Tony Perez	15.00	4.50
19 J.Rice Red Sox Home	15.00	4.50
20 Jim Rice Red Sox Road	15.00	4.50
21 C.Ripken Orioles Hitting	40.00	12.00
22 Cal Ripken Orioles Fielding	40.00	12.00
23 Brooks Robinson Bat	15.00	4.50
24 Frank Robinson	15.00	4.50
25 J.Robinson Pants SP/200	60.00	18.00
26 Nolan Ryan	40.00	12.00
27 Hoyt Wilhelm	15.00	4.50
28 Ted Williams SP/350	100.00	30.00
29 Dave Winfield	15.00	4.50
30 Carl Yastrzemski	25.00	7.50
31 Robin Yount	20.00	6.00

2002 Greats of the Game Through the Years Level 1 Patch

This 27-card insert features swatches of authentic jersey patch on a gold-foil based card. Each card is also individually serial numbered to 100.

	Nm-Mt	Ex-Mt
1 Johnny Bench	50.00	15.00
2 Wade Boggs	40.00	12.00
3 George Brett	80.00	24.00
4 Carlton Fisk Hitting	40.00	12.00
5 Carlton Fisk Fielding	40.00	12.00
6 Bo Jackson Royals	50.00	15.00
7 Bo Jackson White Sox	50.00	15.00
8 Reggie Jackson A's	40.00	12.00
9 Reggie Jackson Angels	40.00	12.00
10 Ted Kluszewski	40.00	12.00
11 Don Mattingly	80.00	24.00
12 Willie McCovey	40.00	12.00
13 Paul Molitor Blue Jays	40.00	12.00
14 Paul Molitor Brewers	40.00	12.00
15 Eddie Murray	50.00	15.00
16 Jim Palmer	40.00	12.00
17 Tony Perez	40.00	12.00
18 Jim Rice Red Sox	40.00	12.00
19 Jim Rice Red Sox	40.00	12.00
20 Cal Ripken Hitting	100.00	30.00
21 Cal Ripken Fielding	100.00	30.00
22 Frank Robinson	40.00	12.00
23 Nolan Ryan	80.00	24.00
24 Ted Williams	150.00	45.00
25 Dave Winfield	40.00	12.00
26 Carl Yastrzemski	80.00	24.00
27 Robin Yount	60.00	18.00

2002 Greats of the Game Through the Years Level 2

This 22-card insert features swatches of authentic game-used jersey on a silver-foil based card. These cards were individually serial numbered to 100.

	Nm-Mt	Ex-Mt
1 Johnny Bench	50.00	15.00
2 Wade Boggs	40.00	12.00
3 George Brett	80.00	24.00
4 Carlton Fisk White Sox	40.00	12.00
5 Bo Jackson Royals	50.00	15.00
6 Bo Jackson White Sox	50.00	15.00
7 Reggie Jackson A's	40.00	12.00
8 Ted Kluszewski	40.00	12.00
9 Don Mattingly	80.00	24.00
10 Willie McCovey	40.00	12.00
11 Paul Molitor Brewers	40.00	12.00
12 Eddie Murray	50.00	15.00
13 Jim Palmer	40.00	12.00
14 Jim Rice Home	40.00	12.00
15 Jim Rice Road	40.00	12.00
16 Cal Ripken Hitting	100.00	30.00
17 Cal Ripken Fielding	100.00	30.00
18 Nolan Ryan	80.00	24.00
19 Ted Williams	150.00	45.00
20 Dave Winfield	40.00	12.00
21 Carl Yastrzemski	80.00	24.00
22 Robin Yount	60.00	18.00

2002 Greats of the Game Through the Years Level 3

This 19-card insert features swatches of authentic game-used jersey on a silver-foil based card. These cards were individually serial numbered to 25. Due to market scarcity, no pricing is provided for these cards.

	Nm-Mt	Ex-Mt
1 Johnny Bench		
2 Wade Boggs		
3 George Brett		
4 Carlton Fisk White Sox		
5 Reggie Jackson A's		
6 Ted Kluszewski		
7 Don Mattingly		
8 Willie McCovey		
9 Paul Molitor Brewers		
10 Eddie Murray		
11 Jim Rice Home		
12 Jim Rice Road		
13 Cal Ripken Hitting		
14 Cal Ripken Batting		
15 Nolan Ryan		
16 Ted Williams		
17 Dave Winfield		
18 Carl Yastrzemski		
19 Robin Yount		

2004 Greats of the Game

This 80-card set was released in June, 2004. The set was issued in five card packs with an $10 SRP which came packed 15 packs to a box and 12 boxes to a case.

	Nm-Mt	Ex-Mt
COMPLETE SET (80)	40.00	12.00
1 Lou Gehrig	3.00	.90
2 Ty Cobb	2.50	.75
3 Dizzy Dean	2.00	.60
4 Jimmie Foxx	2.00	.60
5 Hank Greenberg	2.00	.60
6 Babe Ruth	5.00	1.50
7 Honus Wagner	2.00	.60
8 Mickey Cochrane	.75	.23
9 Pepper Martin	.75	.23
10 Charlie Gehringer	.75	.23
11 Carl Hubbell	1.25	.35
12 Bill Terry	.75	.23
13 Mel Ott	2.00	.60
14 Bill Dickey	1.25	.35
15 Ted Williams	4.00	1.20
16 Roger Maris	2.00	.60
17 Thurman Munson	2.00	.60
18 Phil Rizzuto	1.25	.35
19 Stan Musial	3.00	.90
20 Duke Snider	1.25	.35
21 Reggie Jackson	1.25	.35
22 Don Mattingly	4.00	1.20
23 Vida Blue	.75	.23
24 Harmon Killebrew	2.00	.60
25 Lou Brock	1.25	.35
26 Al Kaline	2.00	.60
27 Dave Parker	.75	.23
28 Nolan Ryan	5.00	1.50
29 Jim Rice	.75	.23
30 Paul Molitor	1.25	.35
31 Dwight Evans	1.25	.35
32 Brooks Robinson	1.25	.35
33 Jose Canseco	2.00	.60
34 Alan Trammell	.75	.23
35 Johnny Bench	2.00	.60
36 Carlton Fisk	1.25	.35
37 Jim Palmer	.75	.23
38 George Brett	5.00	1.50
39 Mike Schmidt	4.00	1.20
40 Tony Perez	.75	.23
41 Paul Blair	.50	.15
42 Fred Lynn	.75	.23
43 Carl Yastrzemski	3.00	.90
44 Steve Carlton	.75	.23
45 Dennis Eckersley	1.25	.35
46 Tom Seaver	1.25	.35
47 Juan Marichal	.75	.23
48 Tony Gwynn	2.50	.75
49 Moose Skowron	.75	.23
50 Bob Gibson	1.25	.35
51 Luis Tiant	.75	.23
52 Eddie Murray	2.00	.60
53 Frank Robinson	.75	.23
54 Rocky Colavito	1.25	.35
55 Bobby Shantz	.50	.15
56 Ernie Banks	2.00	.60
57 Rod Carew	1.25	.35
58 Gorman Thomas	.75	.23
59 Bernie Carbo	.50	.15
60 Joe Rudi	.50	.15
61 Graig Nettles	.75	.23
62 Ron Guidry	.75	.23
63 Whitey Ford	1.25	.35
64 George Kell	.75	.23
65 Cal Ripken	6.00	1.80
66 Willie McCovey	1.25	.35
67 Bo Jackson	2.00	.60
68 Kirby Puckett	2.00	.60
69 Ted Kluszewski	1.25	.35
70 Johnny Podres	.75	.23
71 Davey Lopes	.75	.23
72 Chris Short	.50	.15
73 Jeff Torborg	.50	.15
74 Bill Freehan	.75	.23
75 Frank Tanana	.75	.23
76 Jack Morris	.75	.23
77 Rick Dempsey	.50	.15
78 Yogi Berra	2.00	.60
79 Tim McCarver	.75	.23
80 Rusty Staub	.75	.23

2004 Greats of the Game Blue

Nm-Mt Ex-Mt

*SILVER POST-WAR: 1.25X TO 3X BASIC
*SILVER PRE-WAR: 1X TO 2.5X BASIC
STATED ODDS 1:7.5 HOBBY, 1:24 RETAIL
STATED PRINT RUN 500 SERIAL #'d SETS

2004 Greats of the Game Autographs

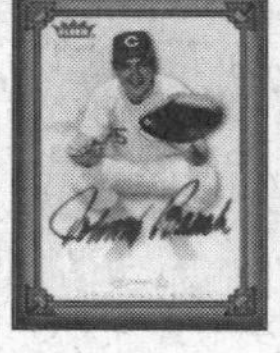
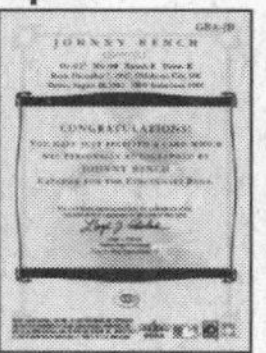

Nm-Mt Ex-Mt

OVERALL AUTO ODDS 1:5 HOB, 1:960 RET
GROUP A PRINT RUN 150 SETS
GROUP B PRINT RUN 250 SETS
GROUP C PRINT RUN 300 SETS
CARDS ARE NOT SERIAL-NUMBERED
PRINT RUN INFO PROVIDED BY FLEER
EXCHANGE DEADLINE INDEFINITE

	Nm-Mt	Ex-Mt
AK Al Kaline D	40.00	12.00
AT Alan Trammell F	15.00	4.50
BC Bernie Carbo G	10.00	3.00
BF Bill Freehan G	15.00	4.50
BG Bob Gibson F	20.00	6.00
BJ Bo Jackson C	60.00	18.00
BR Brooks Robinson F	20.00	6.00
BS Bobby Shantz G	10.00	3.00
CF Carlton Fisk D	40.00	12.00
CR Cal Ripken A	150.00	45.00
CY Carl Yastrzemski D	60.00	18.00
DE1 Dennis Eckersley B	40.00	12.00
DE2 Dwight Evans F	15.00	4.50
DL Davey Lopes G	10.00	3.00
DM1 Don Mattingly A	100.00	30.00
DM2 Denny McLain G EXCH	40.00	12.00
DP Dave Parker G	10.00	3.00
DS Duke Snider D	40.00	12.00
EB Ernie Banks A	60.00	18.00
EM Eddie Murray B	80.00	24.00
FL Fred Lynn F	10.00	3.00
FR Frank Robinson E	25.00	7.50
FT Frank Tanana G	10.00	3.00
GB George Brett A	80.00	24.00
GK George Kell F	15.00	4.50
GN Graig Nettles G	15.00	4.50
GT Gorman Thomas G	10.00	3.00
HK Harmon Killebrew F	25.00	7.50
JB Johnny Bench D	60.00	18.00
JC Jose Canseco D	40.00	12.00
JM1 Juan Marichal F	15.00	4.50
JM2 Jack Morris F	10.00	3.00
JP1 Jim Palmer F	15.00	4.50
JP2 Johnny Podres G	10.00	3.00
JR1 Jim Rice F	15.00	4.50
JR2 Joe Rudi G	10.00	3.00
JT Jeff Torborg G	10.00	3.00
KP Kirby Puckett A EXCH	100.00	30.00
LB Lou Brock F	20.00	6.00
LT Luis Tiant G	10.00	3.00
MM Marty Marion G EXCH	15.00	4.50
MS1 Mike Schmidt B	60.00	18.00
MS2 Moose Skowron G	15.00	4.50
NR Nolan Ryan A	120.00	36.00
PB Paul Blair G	10.00	3.00
PM Paul Molitor B	40.00	12.00
PR Phil Rizzuto E EXCH	50.00	15.00
RC1 Rod Carew D	25.00	7.50
RC2 Rocky Colavito D	120.00	36.00
RD Rick Dempsey A	25.00	7.50
RG Ron Guidry F	20.00	6.00
RJ Reggie Jackson A	100.00	30.00
RS Rusty Staub G	15.00	4.50
SC Steve Carlton D	25.00	7.50
SM Stan Musial A	120.00	36.00
TG Tony Gwynn E	40.00	12.00
TM Tim McCarver F	15.00	4.50
TP Tony Perez F	40.00	12.00
TS Tom Seaver A	60.00	18.00
VB Vida Blue G	10.00	3.00
WF Whitey Ford D	40.00	12.00
WM Willie McCovey E	25.00	7.50
YB Yogi Berra B	80.00	24.00

2004 Greats of the Game Battery Mates

Nm-Mt Ex-Mt

RANDOM INSERTS IN PACKS
PRINT RUNS B/WN 1934-1979 COPIES PER

	Nm-Mt	Ex-Mt
1 Steve Carlton / Tim McCarver/1972	4.00	1.20
2 Don Drysdale / Roy Campanella/1957	5.00	1.50
3 Tom Seaver / Johnny Bench/1979	5.00	1.50
4 Whitey Ford / Yogi Berra/1956	5.00	1.50
5 Ron Guidry / Thurman Munson/1978	5.00	1.50
6 Nolan Ryan / Jeff Torborg/1973	10.00	3.00
7 Denny McLain / Bill Freehan/1968	5.00	1.50
8 Lefty Gomez / Bill Dickey/1934	5.00	1.50
9 Jim Palmer / Rick Dempsey/1977	4.00	1.20
10 Luis Tiant / Carlton Fisk/1973	5.00	1.50

2004 Greats of the Game Battery Mates Autograph

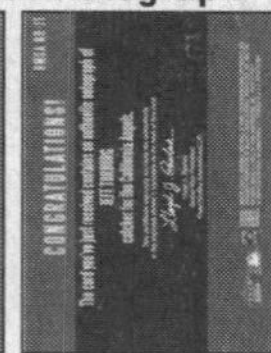

Nm-Mt Ex-Mt

OVERALL AUTO ODDS 1:5 HOB, 1:960 RET
PRINT RUNS B/WN 56-79 COPIES PER
AUTO IS ONLY FOR 1ST PLAYER LISTED

	Nm-Mt	Ex-Mt
DMBF Denny McLain w/Freehan/68		
JPRD Jim Palmer w/Dempsey/77	20.00	6.00
NRJT Jeff Torborg w/Ryan/73	15.00	4.50
RGTM Ron Guidry w/Munson/78	25.00	7.50
SCTM Steve Carlton w/McCarver/72	25.00	7.50
TSJB Johnny Bench w/Seaver/79	50.00	15.00
WFYB Whitey Ford w/Berra/56	40.00	12.00

2004 Greats of the Game Battery Mates Autograph Dual

Nm-Mt Ex-Mt

OVERALL AUTO ODDS 1:5 HOB, 1:960 RET
STATED PRINT RUN 10 SERIAL #'d SETS
NO PRICING DUE TO SCARCITY

2004 Greats of the Game Comparison Cuts

An innovative pairing of Wally Pipp and the guy who replaced him at 1st for the Yankees; Lou Gehrig, was a highlight of this set.

Nm-Mt Ex-Mt

OVERALL AUTO ODDS 1:5 HOB, 1:960 RET
STATED PRINT RUN 1 SERIAL #'d SET
NO PRICING DUE TO SCARCITY

BRRM Babe Ruth
Roger Maris
JRLD Jackie Robinson
Larry Doby
LGCR Lou Gehrig
Cal Ripken
LGWP Lou Gehrig
Wally Pipp
LWPW Lloyd Waner
Paul Waner
TWCY Ted Williams
Carl Yastrzemski

2004 Greats of the Game Etched in Time Cuts

	Nm-Mt	Ex-Mt
OVERALL AUTO ODDS 1:5 HOB, 1:960 RET		
PRINT RUNS B/WN 1-3 COPIES PER		
NO PRICING DUE TO SCARCITY		
BD Bill Dickey/1		
BT Bill Terry/3		
CG Charlie Gehringer/1		
CH Carl Hubbell/3		
DD Dizzy Dean/1		
HG Hank Greenberg/1		
HW Honus Wagner/1		
JF Jimmie Foxx/1		
MC Mickey Cochrane/1		
MO Mel Ott/1		
RC1 Roy Campanella/1		
RC2 Roberto Clemente/1		
TC Ty Cobb/1		
TM Thurman Munson/1		
TW Ted Williams/1		

2004 Greats of the Game Glory of Their Time

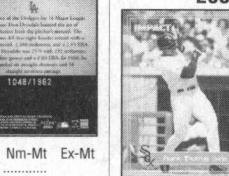

	Nm-Mt	Ex-Mt
RANDOM INSERTS IN PACKS		
PRINT RUNS B/WN		
1 Harmon Killebrew/1961	5.00	1.50
2 Johnny Bench/1974	5.00	1.50
3 George Brett/1980	10.00	3.00
4 Tony Gwynn/1987	5.00	1.50
5 Paul Molitor/1987	5.00	1.50
6 Don Mattingly/1986	8.00	2.40
7 Reggie Jackson/1980	5.00	1.50
8 Carlton Fisk/1985	5.00	1.50
9 Cal Ripken/1983	12.00	3.60
10 Brooks Robinson/1964	5.00	1.50
11 Eddie Murray/1980	5.00	1.50
12 Moose Skowron/1960	4.00	1.20
13 Lou Brock/1974	5.00	1.50
14 Don Drysdale/1962	5.00	1.50
15 Tony Gwynn/1997	5.00	1.50
16 Mike Schmidt/1980	8.00	2.40
17 Carl Yastrzemski/1967	6.00	1.80
18 Babe Ruth/1927	8.00	2.40
19 Nolan Ryan/1989	10.00	3.00
20 Yogi Berra/1950	5.00	1.50
21 Al Kaline/1955	5.00	1.50
22 Ty Cobb/1911	5.00	1.50
23 Duke Snider/1955	5.00	1.50
24 Stan Musial/1948	6.00	1.80
25 Jose Canseco/1988	5.00	1.50
26 Rocky Colavito/1958	5.00	1.50
27 Dave Winfield/1979	4.00	1.20
28 Nolan Ryan/1982	10.00	3.00
29 Thurman Munson/1977	5.00	1.50
30 Jackie Robinson/1949	5.00	1.50
31 Kirby Puckett/1988	5.00	1.50
32 Ted Kluszewski/1954	5.00	1.50
33 Warren Spahn/1953	5.00	1.50
34 Willie McCovey/1969	5.00	1.50
35 Phil Rizzuto/1950	5.00	1.50

2004 Greats of the Game Glory of Their Time Game Used

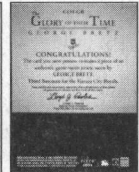

	Nm-Mt	Ex-Mt
STATED PRINT RUN 250 SERIAL #'d SETS		
GOLD: .4X TO 1X BASIC		
GOLD STATED ODDS 1:24 RETAIL		
OVERALL GU ODDS 1:30 HOB, 1:24 RET		
AK Al Kaline Pants	15.00	4.50
BR Brooks Robinson Jsy	15.00	4.50
CF1 Carlton Fisk Jsy	15.00	4.50
CF2 Carlton Fisk Bat	15.00	4.50
CR Cal Ripken Jsy	25.00	7.50
CY Carl Yastrzemski Jsy	20.00	6.00
DD Don Drysdale Jsy	15.00	4.50
DM Don Mattingly Pants	20.00	6.00
DW Dave Winfield Jsy	10.00	3.00
EM Eddie Murray Jsy	15.00	4.50
GB George Brett Jsy	20.00	6.00
HK Harmon Killebrew Bat	15.00	4.50
JB Johnny Bench Jsy	15.00	4.50
JC1 Jose Canseco Jsy	15.00	4.50
JC2 Jose Canseco Bat	15.00	4.50
KP Kirby Puckett Bat	15.00	4.50
LB Lou Brock Jsy	15.00	4.50
MS Mike Schmidt Jsy	20.00	6.00
MS Moose Skowron Pants	10.00	3.00
NR1 Nolan Ryan Jsy	25.00	7.50
NR2 Nolan Ryan Bat	25.00	7.50
PM Paul Molitor Jsy	15.00	4.50
PR Phil Rizzuto Pants	15.00	4.50
RC Rocky Colavito Bat	30.00	9.00
RJ Reggie Jackson Pants	15.00	4.50
TG1 Tony Gwynn White Jsy	15.00	4.50
TG2 Tony Gwynn Grey Jsy	15.00	4.50
TK Ted Kluszewski Pants	15.00	4.50
TM Thurman Munson Pants	25.00	7.50
WM Willie McCovey Pants	15.00	4.50
WS Warren Spahn Jsy	15.00	4.50
YB Yogi Berra Pants	15.00	4.50

2004 Greats of the Game Personality Cuts

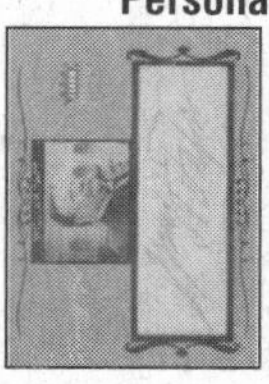
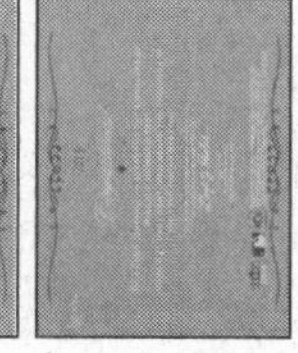

	Nm-Mt	Ex-Mt
OVERALL AUTO ODDS 1:5 HOB, 1:960 RET		
STATED PRINT RUN 1 SERIAL #'d SET		
NO PRICING DUE TO SCARCITY		
CM Connie Mack		
HC Happy Chandler		
WT William Taft		

2000 Impact

The 2000 Impact product (produced by Fleer) was released in July, 2000 as a 200-card set. The set features 175 veteran players and 25 prospect cards. Each pack contained 10 cards, and carried a suggested retail price of $.99. Despite the obvious need for the hobby to offer affordable packs to children and other newer collectors, this product was largely met with indifference in the secondary market.

	Nm-Mt	Ex-Mt
COMPLETE SET (200)	15.00	4.50
1 Cal Ripken	1.50	.45
2 Jose Canseco	.50	.15
3 Manny Ramirez	.30	.09
4 Bernie Williams	.30	.09
5 Troy Glaus	.20	.06
6 Jeff Bagwell	.30	.09
7 Corey Koskie	.20	.06
8 Barry Larkin	.30	.09
9 Mark Quinn	.20	.06
10 Russ Ortiz	.20	.06
11 Tim Salmon	.30	.09
12 Preston Wilson	.20	.06
13 Mo Vaughn	.20	.06
14 Ray Lankford	.20	.06
15 Sterling Hitchcock	.20	.06
16 Al Leiter	.20	.06
17 Jim Morris	.50	.15
18 Freddy Garcia	.20	.06
19 Adrian Beltre	.30	.09
20 Eric Chavez	.20	.06
21 Robinson Cancel	.20	.06
22 Edgar Renteria	.20	.06
23 John Jaha	.20	.06
24 Chuck Finley	.20	.06
25 Andres Galarraga	.20	.06
26 Paul Byrd	.20	.06
27 John Halama	.20	.06
28 Eric Karros	.20	.06
29 Mike Piazza	.75	.23
30 Ryan Rupe	.20	.06
31 Frank Thomas	.50	.15
32 Randy Velarde	.20	.06
33 Bobby Abreu	.20	.06
34 Randy Johnson	.50	.15
35 Matt Williams	.20	.06
36 Tony Gwynn	.60	.18
37 Dean Palmer	.20	.06
38 Aaron Sele	.20	.06
39 Rondell White	.20	.06
40 Erubiel Durazo	.20	.06
41 Curt Schilling	.20	.06
42 Kip Wells	.20	.06
43 Craig Biggio	.30	.09
44 Tom Glavine	.30	.09
45 Trevor Hoffman	.20	.06
46 Greg Vaughn	.20	.06
47 Edgar Martinez	.30	.09
48 Magglio Ordonez	.20	.06
49 Mark Mulder	.20	.06
50 John Rocker	.20	.06
51 Kenny Rogers	.20	.06
52 Gary Sheffield	.20	.06
53 Brian Simmons	.20	.06
54 Tony Womack	.20	.06
55 Ken Caminiti	.20	.06
56 Jeff Cirillo	.20	.06
57 Ray Durham	.20	.06
58 Mike Lieberthal	.20	.06
59 Ruben Mateo	.20	.06
60 Mike Cameron	.20	.06
61 Rusty Greer	.20	.06
62 Alex Rodriguez	.75	.23
63 Robin Ventura	.20	.06
64 Pokey Reese	.20	.06
65 Jose Lima	.20	.06
66 Neifi Perez	.20	.06
67 Rafael Palmeiro	.30	.09
68 Scott Rolen	.50	.15
69 Mike Hampton	.20	.06
70 Sammy Sosa	.75	.23
71 Mike Stanley	.20	.06
72 Dan Wilson	.20	.06
73 Kerry Wood	.50	.15
74 Mike Mussina	.30	.09
75 Masato Yoshii	.20	.06
76 Peter Bergeron	.20	.06
77 Carlos Delgado	.20	.06
78 Juan Encarnacion	.20	.06
79 Nomar Garciaparra	.75	.23
80 Jason Kendall	.20	.06
81 Pedro Martinez	.50	.15
82 Darin Erstad	.20	.06
83 Larry Walker	.30	.09
84 Rick Ankiel	.20	.06
85 Scott Erickson	.20	.06
86 Roger Clemens	1.00	.30
87 Matt Lawton	.20	.06
88 Jon Lieber	.20	.06
89 Shane Reynolds	.20	.06
90 Ivan Rodriguez	.50	.15
91 Pat Burrell	.20	.06
92 Kent Bottenfield	.20	.06
93 David Cone	.20	.06
94 Mark Grace	.30	.09
95 Paul Konerko	.20	.06
96 Eric Milton	.20	.06
97 Lee Stevens	.20	.06
98 B.J. Surhoff	.20	.06
99 Billy Wagner	.20	.06
100 Ken Griffey Jr.	.75	.23
101 Randy Wolf	.20	.06
102 Henry Rodriguez	.20	.06
103 Carlos Beltran	.30	.09
104 Rich Aurilia	.20	.06
105 Chipper Jones	.50	.15
106 Homer Bush	.20	.06
107 Johnny Damon	.30	.09
108 J.D. Drew	.20	.06
109 Orlando Hernandez	.20	.06
110 Brad Radke	.20	.06
111 Wilton Veras	.20	.06
112 Dmitri Young	.20	.06
113 Jermaine Dye	.20	.06
114 Kris Benson	.20	.06
115 Derek Jeter	1.25	.35
116 Cole Liniak	.20	.06
117 Jim Thome	.50	.15
118 Pedro Astacio	.20	.06
119 Carlos Febles	.20	.06
120 Darryl Kile	.20	.06
121 Alfonso Soriano	.50	.15
122 Michael Barrett	.20	.06
123 Ellis Burks	.20	.06
124 Chad Hermansen	.20	.06
125 Trot Nixon	.20	.06
126 Bobby Higginson	.20	.06
127 Rick Helling	.20	.06
128 Chris Carpenter	.20	.06
129 Vinny Castilla	.20	.06
130 Brian Giles	.20	.06
131 Todd Helton	.30	.09
132 Jason Varitek	.30	.09
133 Rob Ducey	.20	.06
134 Octavio Dotel	.20	.06
135 Adam Kennedy	.20	.06
136 Jeff Kent	.20	.06
137 Aaron Boone	.20	.06
138 Todd Walker	.20	.06
139 Jeromy Burnitz	.20	.06
140 Roberto Hernandez	.20	.06
141 Matt LeCroy	.20	.06
142 Ugueth Urbina	.20	.06
143 David Wells	.20	.06
144 Luis Gonzalez	.20	.06
145 Andruw Jones	.20	.06
146 Juan Gonzalez	.30	.09
147 Moises Alou	.20	.06
148 Michael Tejera	.20	.06
149 Brian Jordan	.20	.06
150 Mark McGwire	1.25	.35
151 Shawn Green	.20	.06
152 Jay Bell	.20	.06
153 Fred McGriff	.30	.09
154 Rey Ordonez	.20	.06
155 Matt Stairs	.20	.06
156 A.J. Burnett	.20	.06
157 Omar Vizquel	.30	.09
158 Damion Easley	.20	.06
159 Dante Bichette	.20	.06
160 Javy Lopez	.20	.06
161 Fernando Seguignol	.20	.06
162 Richie Sexson	.20	.06
163 Vladimir Guerrero	.50	.15
164 Kevin Young	.20	.06
165 Josh Beckett	.30	.09
166 Albert Belle	.20	.06
167 Cliff Floyd	.20	.06
168 Gabe Kapler	.20	.06
169 Nick Johnson	.20	.06
170 Raul Mondesi	.20	.06
171 Warren Morris	.20	.06
172 Kenny Lofton	.20	.06
173 Reggie Sanders	.20	.06
174 Mike Sweeney	.20	.06
175 Robert Fick	.20	.06
176 Barry Bonds	1.25	.35
177 Luis Castillo	.20	.06
178 Roger Cedeno	.20	.06
179 Jim Edmonds	.20	.06
180 Geoff Jenkins	.20	.06
181 Adam Piatt	.20	.06
182 Phil Nevin	.20	.06
183 Roberto Alomar	.30	.09
184 Kevin Brown	.20	.06
185 D.T. Cromer	.20	.06
186 Jason Giambi	.20	.06
187 Fernando Tatis	.20	.06
188 Brady Anderson	.20	.06
189 Tony Clark	.20	.06
190 Alex Fernandez	.20	.06
191 Matt Blank	.20	.06
192 Greg Maddux	.75	.23
193 Kevin Millwood	.20	.06
194 Jason Schmidt	.20	.06
195 Shannon Stewart	.20	.06
196 Rolando Arrojo	.20	.06
197 Darren Dreifort	.20	.06
198 Ben Grieve	.20	.06
199 Bartolo Colon	.20	.06
200 Sean Casey	.20	.06

2000 Impact Genuine Coverage

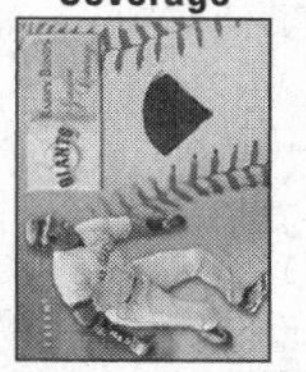

Randomly inserted into packs at a rate of one in 720 hobby and one in 2500 retail, this insert set features swatches of game-used batting gloves incorporated directly into the card. They are some of the toughest memorabilia cards to located on the secondary market and share a very similar design to other Genuine Coverage memorabilia cards issued in 2000 SkyBox packs.

	Nm-Mt	Ex-Mt
1 Bob Abreu	15.00	4.50
2 Glen Barker	15.00	4.50
3 Barry Bonds	80.00	24.00
4 Jose Cruz Jr.	15.00	4.50
5 Ben Davis	15.00	4.50
6 Jason Giambi	15.00	4.50
7 Trevor Hoffman	15.00	4.50
8 Jacque Jones	15.00	4.50
9 Jason LaRue	15.00	4.50
10 Matt Lawton	15.00	4.50
11 Carlos Lee	15.00	4.50
12 Cole Liniak	15.00	4.50
13 Joe Nathan	15.00	4.50
14 Maggio Ordonez	15.00	4.50
15 Rafael Palmeiro	25.00	7.50
16 Alex Rodriguez	60.00	18.00
17 Shannon Stewart	15.00	4.50
18 Mike Sweeney	15.00	4.50

2000 Impact Mighty Fine in '99

Inserted at one per pack, this 40-card insert set features players that had outstanding seasons in 1999. The first 25 cards from this set feature members of the World Champion 1999 New York Yankees squad. Card backs carry a "MF" prefix.

	Nm-Mt	Ex-Mt
COMPLETE SET (40)	15.00	4.50
MF1 Clay Bellinger	.30	.09
MF2 Scott Brosius	.30	.09
MF3 Roger Clemens	1.50	.45
MF4 David Cone	.30	.09
MF5 Chad Curtis	.30	.09
MF6 Chili Davis	.30	.09
MF7 Joe Girardi	.30	.09
MF8 Jason Grimsley	.30	.09
MF9 Orlando Hernandez	.30	.09
MF10 Hideki Irabu	.30	.09
MF11 Derek Jeter	2.00	.60
MF12 Chuck Knoblauch	.30	.09
MF13 Ricky Ledee	.30	.09
MF14 Jim Leyritz	.30	.09
MF15 Tino Martinez	.30	.09
MF16 Ramiro Mendoza	.30	.09
MF17 Jeff Nelson	.30	.09
MF18 Paul O'Neill	.30	.09
MF19 Andy Pettitte	.30	.09
MF20 Jorge Posada	.30	.09
MF21 Mariano Rivera	.30	.09
MF22 Luis Sojo	.30	.09
MF23 Mike Stanton	.30	.09
MF24 Allen Watson	.30	.09
MF25 Bernie Williams	.50	.15
MF26 Chipper Jones	.75	.23
MF27 Ivan Rodriguez	.75	.23
MF28 Randy Johnson	.75	.23
MF29 Pedro Martinez	.75	.23
MF30 Scott Williamson	.30	.09
MF31 Carlos Beltran	.50	.15
MF32 Mark McGwire	2.00	.60
MF33 Ken Griffey Jr.	1.25	.35
MF34 Robin Ventura	.30	.09
MF35 Tony Gwynn	1.00	.30
MF36 Wade Boggs	.75	.23
MF37 Cal Ripken	2.50	.75
MF38 Jose Canseco	.75	.23
MF39 Alex Rodriguez	1.25	.35
MF40 Fernando Tatis	.30	.09

2000 Impact Point of Impact

Randomly inserted into packs at one in 30, this insert set features 10 of the major league's top homerun hitters. Card backs carry a "PI" prefix.

	Nm-Mt	Ex-Mt
COMPLETE SET (10)	50.00	15.00
PI1 Ken Griffey Jr.	4.00	1.20
PI2 Mark McGwire	6.00	1.80
PI3 Sammy Sosa	4.00	1.20
PI4 Jeff Bagwell	1.50	.45
PI5 Derek Jeter	6.00	1.80
PI6 Chipper Jones	2.50	.75
PI7 Nomar Garciaparra	4.00	1.20
PI8 Cal Ripken	8.00	2.40
PI9 Barry Bonds	6.00	1.80
PI10 Alex Rodriguez	4.00	1.20

1949 Leaf

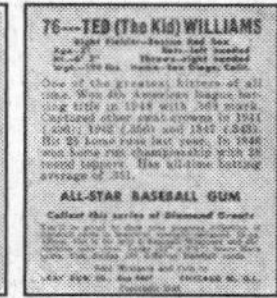

The cards in this 98-card set measure 2 3/8" by 2 7/8". The 1949 Leaf set was the first post-war baseball series issued in color. This effort was not entirely successful due to a lack of refinement which resulted in many color variations and cards out of register. In addition, the set was skip numbered from 1-168, with 49 of the 98 cards printed in limited quantities (marked with SP in the checklist). Cards 102 and 136 have variations, and cards are sometimes found with overprinted, incorrect or blank backs. Some cards were produced with a 1948 copyright date but overwhelming evidence seemed to indicate that this set was not actually released until early in 1949. An album to hold these cards was available as a premium. The album could only be obtained by sending in five wrappers and 25 cents. Since so few albums appear on the secondary market, no value is attached to them. Notable Rookie Cards in this set include Stan Musial, Satchel Paige, and Jackie Robinson.

	NM	Ex
COMPLETE SET (98)	30000.00	15000.00
COMMON CARD (1-168)	25.00	12.50
COMMON SP's	300.00	150.00
WRAPPER (1-CENT)	160.00	80.00
1 Joe DiMaggio	3000.00	1200.00
3 Babe Ruth	2500.00	1250.00
4 Stan Musial	1000.00	500.00
5 Virgil Trucks SP RC	400.00	200.00
8 S.Paige SP RC	12000.00	6000.00
10 Dizzy Trout	40.00	20.00
11 Phil Rizzuto	350.00	180.00
13 Cass Michaels SP	300.00	150.00
14 Billy Johnson	40.00	20.00
17 Frank Overmire	25.00	12.50
19 Johnny Wyrostek SP	300.00	150.00
20 Hank Sauer SP	400.00	200.00
22 Al Evans	25.00	12.50
26 Sam Chapman	40.00	20.00
27 Mickey Harris	25.00	12.50
28 Jim Hegan RC	40.00	20.00
29 Elmer Valo RC	40.00	20.00
30 Billy Goodman SP RC	400.00	200.00
31 Lou Brissie	25.00	12.50
32 Warren Spahn	350.00	180.00
33 Peanuts Lowrey SP	300.00	150.00
36 Al Zarilla SP	300.00	150.00
38 Ted Kluszewski RC	200.00	100.00
39 Ewell Blackwell	60.00	30.00
42 Kent Peterson	25.00	12.50
43 Ed Stevens SP	300.00	150.00
45 Ken Keltner SP	300.00	150.00
46 Johnny Mize	100.00	50.00
47 George Vico	25.00	12.50
48 Johnny Schmitz SP	300.00	150.00
49 Del Ennis RC	60.00	30.00
50 Dick Wakefield	25.00	12.50
51 Al Dark SP RC	500.00	250.00
53 Johnny VanderMeer	100.00	50.00
54 Bobby Adams SP	300.00	150.00
55 Tommy Henrich SP	500.00	250.00
56 Larry Jansen RC UER (Misspelled Jensen)	40.00	20.00
57 Bob McCall	25.00	12.50
59 Luke Appling	100.00	50.00
61 Jake Early	25.00	12.50
62 Eddie Joost SP	300.00	150.00
63 Barney McCosky SP	300.00	150.00
65 Robert Elliott RC UER (Misspelled Elliot on card front)	100.00	50.00
66 Orval Grove SP	300.00	150.00
68 Eddie Miller SP	300.00	150.00
70 Honus Wagner CO	350.00	180.00
72 Hank Edwards	25.00	12.50
73 Pat Seerey	25.00	12.50
75 Dom DiMaggio SP	600.00	300.00
76 Ted Williams	1200.00	600.00
77 Roy Smalley RC	25.00	12.50
78 Hoot Evers SP	300.00	150.00
79 Jackie Robinson RC	1500.00	750.00
81 Whitey Kurowski SP	300.00	150.00
82 Johnny Lindell	40.00	20.00
83 Bobby Doerr	100.00	50.00
84 Sid Hudson	25.00	12.50
85 Dave Philley SP RC	400.00	200.00
86 Ralph Weigel	25.00	12.50
88 Frank Gustine SP	300.00	150.00
91 Ralph Kiner	200.00	100.00
93 Bob Feller SP	2000.00	1000.00
95 George Stirnweiss RC	40.00	20.00
97 Marty Marion	60.00	30.00
98 Hal Newhouser SP RC	600.00	300.00
102A Gene Hermansk ERR	250.00	125.00
102B G.Hermanski COR	40.00	20.00
104 Eddie Stewart SP	300.00	150.00
106 Lou Boudreau	100.00	50.00

108 Matt Batts SP 300.00 150.00
111 Jerry Priddy 25.00 12.50
113 Dutch Leonard SP 300.00 150.00
117 Joe Gordon 40.00 20.00
120 George Kell SP RC 600.00 300.00
121 Johnny Pesky SP RC 400.00 200.00
123 Cliff Fannin SP 300.00 150.00
125 Andy Pafko RC 25.00 12.50
127 Enos Slaughter SP 800.00 400.00
128 Buddy Rosar 25.00 12.50
129 Kirby Higbe SP 300.00 150.00
131 Sid Gordon SP 300.00 150.00
133 Tommy Holmes SP 500.00 250.00
136A Cliff Aberson 25.00 12.50
(Full sleeve)
136B Cliff Aberson 250.00 125.00
(Short sleeve)
137 Harry Walker SP 400.00 200.00
138 Larry Doby SP RC 700.00 350.00
139 Johnny Hopp RC 25.00 12.50
142 D.Murtaugh SP RC 400.00 200.00
143 Dick Sisler SP 300.00 150.00
144 Bob Dillinger SP 300.00 150.00
146 Pete Reiser SP 500.00 250.00
149 Hank Majeski SP 300.00 150.00
153 Floyd Baker SP 300.00 150.00
158 H. Brecheen SP RC 400.00 200.00
159 Mizell Platt 25.00 12.50
160 Bob Scheffing SP 300.00 150.00
161 Vern Stephens SP RC 400.00 200.00
163 F.Hutchinson SP RC 400.00 200.00
165 Dale Mitchell SP RC 400.00 200.00
168 P.Cavarretta SP UER 500.00 200.00
Name spelled Cavaretta
NNO Album

1960 Leaf

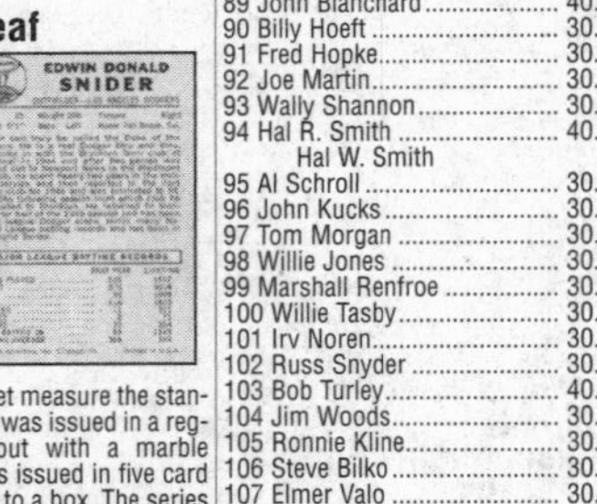

The cards in this 144-card set measure the standard size. The 1960 Leaf set was issued in a regular gum package style but with a marble instead of gum. This set was issued in five card nickel packs which came 24 to a box. The series was a joint production by Sports Novelties, Inc., and Leaf, two Chicago-based companies. Cards 73-144 are more difficult to find than the lower numbers. Photo variations exist (probably proof cards) for the seven cards listed with an asterisk and there is a well-known error card, number 25 showing Brooks Lawrence (in a Reds uniform) with Jim Grant's name on front, and Grant's biography and record on back. The corrected version with Grant's photo is the more difficult variety. The only notable Rookie Card in this set is Dallas Green. The complete set price below includes both versions of Jim Grant.

NM Ex
COMPLETE SET (144) 1750.00 700.00
COMMON CARD (1-72) 3.00 1.20
COMMON CARD (73-144) 30.00 12.00
WRAPPER 50.00 20.00
1 Luis Aparicio * 25.00 6.25
2 Woody Held 3.00 1.20
3 Frank Lary 4.00 1.60
4 Camilo Pascual 5.00 2.00
5 Pancho Herrera 3.00 1.20
6 Felipe Alou 8.00 3.20
7 Benjamin Daniels 3.00 1.20
8 Roger Craig 5.00 2.00
9 Eddie Kasko 3.00 1.20
10 Bob Grim 4.00 1.60
11 Jim Busby 4.00 1.60
12 Ken Boyer 8.00 3.20
13 Bob Boyd 3.00 1.20
14 Sam Jones 4.00 1.60
15 Larry Jackson 4.00 1.60
16 Elroy Face 4.00 1.60
17 Walt Moryn * 3.00 1.20
18 Jim Gilliam 5.00 2.00
19 Don Newcombe 5.00 2.00
20 Glen Hobbie 3.00 1.20
21 Pedro Ramos 4.00 1.60
22 Ryne Duren 3.00 1.20
23 Joey Jay * 4.00 1.60
24 Lou Berberet 3.00 1.20
25A Jim Grant ERR 15.00 6.00
(Photo actually
Brooks Lawrence)
25B Jim Grant COR 25.00 10.00
26 Tom Borland 3.00 1.20
27 Brooks Robinson 40.00 16.00
28 Jerry Adair 3.00 1.20
29 Ron Jackson 3.00 1.20
30 George Strickland 3.00 1.20
31 Rocky Bridges 3.00 1.20
32 Bill Tuttle 4.00 1.60
33 Ken Hunt 3.00 1.20
34 Hal Griggs 3.00 1.20
35 Jim Coates * 3.00 1.20
36 Brooks Lawrence 3.00 1.20
37 Duke Snider 40.00 16.00
38 Al Spangler 3.00 1.20
39 Jim Owens 3.00 1.20
40 Bill Virdon 5.00 2.00
41 Ernie Broglio 3.00 1.20
42 Andre Rodgers 3.00 1.20
43 Julio Becquer 4.00 1.60
44 Tony Taylor 4.00 1.60
45 Jerry Lynch 4.00 1.60
46 Cletis Boyer 8.00 3.20
47 Jerry Lumpe 4.00 1.60
48 Charlie Maxwell 4.00 1.60
49 Jim Perry 4.00 1.60
50 Danny McDevitt 3.00 1.20
51 Juan Pizarro 3.00 1.20
52 Dallas Green RC 8.00 3.20
53 Bob Friend 4.00 1.60
54 Jack Sanford 4.00 1.60
55 Jim Rivera 3.00 1.20
56 Ted Wills 3.00 1.20
57 Milt Pappas 4.00 1.60
58 Hal Smith * 3.00 1.20
59 Bobby Avila 3.00 1.20
60 Clem Labine 5.00 2.00
61 Norman Rehm * 3.00 1.20
62 John Gabler 4.00 1.60
63 John Tsitouris 3.00 1.20
64 Dave Sisler 3.00 1.20
65 Vic Power 4.00 1.60
66 Earl Battey 3.00 1.20
67 Bob Purkey 3.00 1.20
68 Moe Drabowsky 4.00 1.60
69 Hoyt Wilhelm 15.00 6.00
70 Humberto Robinson 3.00 1.20
71 Whitey Herzog 8.00 3.20
72 Dick Donovan * 3.00 1.20
73 Gordon Jones 30.00 12.00
74 Joe Hicks 30.00 12.00
75 Ray Culp RC 40.00 16.00
76 Dick Drott 30.00 12.00
77 Bob Duliba 30.00 12.00
78 Art Ditmar 30.00 12.00
79 Steve Korcheck 30.00 12.00
80 Henry Mason 30.00 12.00
81 Harry Simpson 30.00 12.00
82 Gene Green 30.00 12.00
83 Bob Shaw 30.00 12.00
84 Howard Reed 30.00 12.00
85 Dick Stigman 30.00 12.00
86 Rip Repulski 30.00 12.00
87 Seth Morehead 30.00 12.00
88 Camilo Carreon 30.00 12.00
89 John Blanchard 40.00 16.00
90 Billy Hoeft 30.00 12.00
91 Fred Hopke 30.00 12.00
92 Joe Martin 30.00 12.00
93 Wally Shannon 30.00 12.00
94 Hal R. Smith 40.00 16.00
Hal W. Smith
95 Al Schroll 30.00 12.00
96 John Kucks 30.00 12.00
97 Tom Morgan 30.00 12.00
98 Willie Jones 30.00 12.00
99 Marshall Renfroe 30.00 12.00
100 Willie Tasby 30.00 12.00
101 Irv Noren 30.00 12.00
102 Russ Snyder 30.00 12.00
103 Bob Turley 40.00 16.00
104 Jim Woods 30.00 12.00
105 Ronnie Kline 30.00 12.00
106 Steve Bilko 30.00 12.00
107 Elmer Valo 30.00 12.00
108 Tom McAvoy 30.00 12.00
109 Stan Williams 30.00 12.00
110 Earl Averill Jr. 30.00 12.00
111 Lee Walls 30.00 12.00
112 Paul Richards MG 30.00 12.00
113 Ed Sadowski 30.00 12.00
114 Stover McIlwain 30.00 12.00
115 Chuck Tanner UER 40.00 16.00
(Photo actually
Ken Kuhn)
116 Lou Klimchock 30.00 12.00
117 Neil Chrisley 30.00 12.00
118 John Callison 50.00 20.00
119 Hal Smith 30.00 12.00
120 Carl Sawatski 30.00 12.00
121 Frank Leja 30.00 12.00
122 Earl Torgeson 30.00 12.00
123 Art Schult 30.00 12.00
124 Jim Brosnan 30.00 12.00
125 Sparky Anderson 60.00 24.00
126 Joe Pignatano 30.00 12.00
127 Rocky Nelson 30.00 12.00
128 Orlando Cepeda 80.00 32.00
129 Daryl Spencer 30.00 12.00
130 Ralph Lumenti 30.00 12.00
131 Sam Taylor 30.00 12.00
132 Harry Brecheen CO 40.00 16.00
133 Johnny Groth 30.00 12.00
134 Wayne Terwilliger 30.00 12.00
135 Kent Hadley 30.00 12.00
136 Faye Throneberry 30.00 12.00
137 Jack Meyer 30.00 12.00
138 Chuck Cottier RC 30.00 12.00
139 Joe DeMaestri 30.00 12.00
140 Gene Freese 30.00 12.00
141 Curt Flood 50.00 20.00
142 Gino Cimoli 30.00 12.00
143 Clay Dalrymple 30.00 12.00
144 Jim Bunning 80.00 20.00

1985 Leaf/Donruss

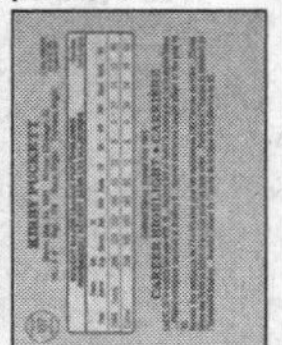

This standard-size set of cards was produced in an effort to establish a Canadian baseball card market much as Topps' affiliate O-Pee-Chee had done. The Donruss Company in conjunction with its new parent Leaf Company issued this set to the Canadian market. The set was later released in the United States through hobby dealer channels. The cards were issued in wax packs. A piece of a large Lou Gehrig puzzle was inserted in each pack. Aside from card number differences the cards are essentially the same as the Donruss U.S. regular issue of the cards of the same players; however the backs are in both French and English. Two cards, Dick Perez artwork of Tim Raines (252) and Dave Stieb (251), are called Canadian Greats (CG) and are not contained in the Donruss U.S. set. As in most Canadian sets, the players featured are heavily biased towards Canadian teams and those American teams closest to the Canadian border. Diamond Kings (numbers 1-26 denoted DK) and Rated Rookies (number 27 denoted RR) are included just as in the American set. Those players selected for and included as Diamond Kings do not have a regular card in the set. The player cards are numbered on the back. The checklist cards (listed at the end of the list below) are numbered one, two and three (but are not given a traditional card number); the Diamond Kings checklist card is unnumbered; and the Lou Gehrig puzzle card is mistakenly numbered 635. Key cards in this set include Roger Clemens and Dwight Gooden in their Rookie Card year.

Nm-Mt Ex-Mt
COMPLETE SET (264) 50.00 20.00
1 Ryne Sandberg DK 2.00 .80
2 Doug DeCinces DK .05 .02
3 Richard Dotson DK .05 .02
4 Bert Blyleven DK .10 .04
5 Lou Whitaker DK .15 .06
6 Dan Quisenberry DK .05 .02
7 Don Mattingly DK 3.00 1.20
8 Carney Lansford DK .05 .02
9 Frank Tanana DK .05 .02
10 Willie Upshaw DK .05 .02
11 C.Washington DK .05 .02
12 Mike Marshall DK .05 .02
13 Joaquin Andujar DK .05 .02
14 Cal Ripken DK 4.00 1.60
15 Jim Rice DK .10 .04
16 Don Sutton DK .40 .16
17 Frank Viola DK .10 .04
18 Alvin Davis DK .05 .02
19 Mario Soto DK .05 .02
20 Jose Cruz DK .10 .04
21 Charlie Lea DK .05 .02
22 Jesse Orosco DK .10 .04
23 Juan Samuel DK .05 .02
24 Tony Pena DK .10 .04
25 Tony Gwynn DK 5.00 2.00
26 Bob Brenly DK .10 .04
27 Steve Kiefer RR .05 .02
28 Joe Morgan .50 .20
29 Luis Leal .05 .02
30 Dan Gladden .10 .04
31 Shane Rawley .05 .02
32 Mark Clear .05 .02
33 Terry Kennedy .05 .02
34 Hal McRae .10 .04
35 Mickey Rivers .05 .02
36 Tom Brunansky .05 .02
37 LaMarr Hoyt .05 .02
38 Orel Hershiser 1.50 .60
39 Chris Bando .05 .02
40 Lee Lacy .05 .02
41 Lance Parrish .10 .04
42 George Foster .10 .04
43 Kevin McReynolds .10 .04
44 Robin Yount .50 .20
45 Craig McMurtry .05 .02
46 Mike Witt .05 .02
47 Gary Redus .05 .02
48 Dennis Rasmussen .05 .02
49 Gary Woods .05 .02
50 Phil Bradley .10 .04
51 Steve Bedrosian .05 .02
52 Duane Walker .05 .02
53 Geoff Zahn .05 .02
54 Dave Stieb .05 .02
55 Pascual Perez .05 .02
56 Mark Langston .20 .08
57 Bob Dernier .05 .02
58 Joe Cowley .05 .02
59 Dan Schatzeder .05 .02
60 Ozzie Smith 1.50 .60
61 Bob Knepper .05 .02
62 Keith Hernandez .10 .04
63 Rick Rhoden .05 .02
64 Alejandro Pena .05 .02
65 Damaso Garcia .05 .02
66 Chili Davis .10 .04
67 Al Oliver .10 .04
68 Alan Wiggins .05 .02
69 Darryl Motley .05 .02
70 Gary Ward .05 .02
71 John Butcher .05 .02
72 Scott McGregor .05 .02
73 Bruce Hurst .05 .02
74 Dwayne Murphy .05 .02
75 Greg Luzinski .10 .04
76 Pat Tabler .05 .02
77 Chet Lemon .05 .02
78 Jim Sundberg .05 .02
79 Wally Backman .05 .02
80 Terry Puhl .05 .02
81 Storm Davis .05 .02
82 Jim Wohlford .05 .02
83 Willie Randolph .10 .04
84 Ron Cey .10 .04
85 Jim Beattie .05 .02
86 Rafael Ramirez .05 .02
87 Cesar Cedeno .10 .04
88 Bobby Grich .10 .04
89 Jason Thompson .05 .02
90 Steve Sax .05 .02
91 Tony Fernandez .20 .08
92 Jeff Leonard .05 .02
93 Von Hayes .05 .02
94 Steve Garvey .20 .08
95 Steve Balboni .05 .02
96 Larry Parrish .05 .02
97 Tim Teufel .05 .02
98 Sammy Stewart .05 .02
99 Roger Clemens RC 20.00 8.00
100 Steve Kemp .05 .02
101 Tom Seaver .75 .30
102 Andre Thornton .05 .02
103 Kirk Gibson .15 .06
104 Ted Simmons .10 .04
105 David Palmer .05 .02
106 Roy Lee Jackson .05 .02
107 Kirby Puckett RC 5.00 2.00
108 Charlie Hough .10 .04
109 Mike Boddicker .05 .02
110 Willie Wilson .05 .02
111 Tim Lollar .05 .02
112 Tony Armas .05 .02
113 Steve Carlton .50 .20
114 Gary Lavelle .05 .02
115 Cliff Johnson .05 .02
116 Ray Burris .05 .02
117 Rudy Law .05 .02
118 Mike Scioscia .15 .06
119 Kent Tekulve UER .10 .04
(Telukve on back)
120 George Vukovich .05 .02
121 Barbaro Garbey .05 .02
122 Mookie Wilson .10 .04
123 Ben Oglivie .05 .02
124 Jerry Mumphrey .05 .02
125 Willie McGee .10 .04
126 Jeff Reardon .10 .04
127 Dave Winfield .75 .30
128 Lee Smith .15 .06
129 Ken Phelps .05 .02
130 Rick Camp .05 .02
131 Dave Concepcion .10 .04
132 Rod Carew .50 .20
133 Andre Dawson .20 .08
134 Doyle Alexander .05 .02
135 Miguel Dilone .05 .02
136 Jim Gott .05 .02
137 Eric Show .05 .02
138 Phil Niekro .20 .08
139 Rick Sutcliffe .05 .02
140 Dave Winfield 1.50 .60
Don Mattingly
141 Ken Oberkfell .05 .02
142 Jack Morris .10 .04
143 Lloyd Moseby .05 .02
144 Pete Rose 1.25 .50
145 Gary Gaetti .10 .04
146 Don Baylor .10 .04
147 Bobby Meacham .05 .02
148 Frank White .10 .04
149 Mark Thurmond .05 .02
150 Dwight Evans .10 .04
151 Al Holland .05 .02
152 Joel Youngblood .05 .02
153 Rance Mulliniks .05 .02
154 Bill Caudill .05 .02
155 Carlton Fisk .75 .30
156 Rick Honeycutt .05 .02
157 John Candelaria .05 .02
158 Alan Trammell .15 .06
159 Darryl Strawberry .20 .08
160 Aurelio Lopez .05 .02
161 Enos Cabell .05 .02
162 Dion James .05 .02
163 Bruce Sutter .10 .04
164 Razor Shines .05 .02
165 Butch Wynegar .05 .02
166 Rich Bordi .05 .02
167 Spike Owen .05 .02
168 Chris Chambliss .05 .02
169 Dave Parker .10 .04
170 Reggie Jackson .75 .30
171 Bryn Smith .05 .02
172 Dave Collins .05 .02
173 Dave Engle .05 .02
174 Buddy Bell .05 .02
175 Mike Flanagan .05 .02
176 George Brett 2.50 1.00
177 Graig Nettles .10 .04
178 Jerry Koosman .05 .02
179 Wade Boggs 1.50 .60
180 Jody Davis .05 .02
181 Ernie Whitt .05 .02
182 Dave Kingman .10 .04
183 Vance Law .05 .02
184 Fernando Valenzuela .10 .04
185 Bill Madlock .05 .02
186 Brett Butler .10 .04
187 Doug Sisk .05 .02
188 Dan Petry .05 .02
189 Joe Niekro .05 .02
190 Rollie Fingers .20 .08
191 David Green .05 .02
192 Steve Rogers .05 .02
193 Ken Griffey .10 .04
194 Scott Sanderson .05 .02
195 Barry Bonnell .05 .02
196 Bruce Benedict .05 .02
197 Keith Moreland .05 .02
198 Fred Lynn .10 .04
199 Tim Wallach .05 .02
200 Kent Hrbek .10 .04
201 Pete O'Brien .05 .02
202 Bud Black .05 .02
203 Eddie Murray 1.50 .60
204 Goose Gossage .10 .04
205 Mike Schmidt 1.25 .50
206 Mike Easler .05 .02
207 Jack Clark .10 .04
208 Rickey Henderson 1.25 .50
209 Jesse Barfield .05 .02
210 Ron Kittle .05 .02
211 Pedro Guerrero .05 .02
212 Johnny Ray .05 .02
213 Julio Franco .10 .04
214 Hubie Brooks .05 .02
215 Darrell Evans .10 .04
216 Nolan Ryan 5.00 2.00
217 Jim Gantner .05 .02
218 Tim Raines .10 .04
219 Dave Righetti .05 .02
220 Gary Matthews .05 .02
221 Jack Perconte .05 .02
222 Dale Murphy .20 .08
223 Brian Downing .05 .02
224 Mickey Hatcher .05 .02
225 Lonnie Smith .05 .02
226 Jorge Orta .05 .02
227 Milt Wilcox .05 .02
228 John Denny .05 .02
229 Marty Barrett .05 .02
230 Alfredo Griffin .05 .02
231 Harold Baines .15 .06
232 Bill Russell .05 .02
233 Marvell Wynne .05 .02
234 Dwight Gooden 1.50 .60
235 Willie Hernandez .05 .02
236 Bill Gullickson .05 .02
237 Ron Guidry .10 .04
238 Leon Durham .05 .02
239 Al Cowens .05 .02
240 Bob Horner .05 .02
241 Gary Carter .50 .20
242 Glenn Hubbard .05 .02
243 Steve Trout .05 .02
244 Jay Howell .05 .02
245 Terry Francona .10 .04
246 Cecil Cooper .10 .04
247 Larry McWilliams .05 .02
248 George Bell .05 .02
249 Larry Herndon .05 .02
250 Ozzie Virgil .05 .02
251 Dave Stieb CG .10 .04
252 Tim Raines CG .20 .08
253 Ricky Horton .05 .02
254 Bill Buckner .10 .04
255 Dan Driessen .05 .02
256 Ron Darling .05 .02
257 Doug Flynn .05 .02
258 Darrell Porter .05 .02
259 George Hendrick .05 .02
260 Checklist DK 1-26 .05 .02
(Unnumbered)
261 Checklist 27-106 .05 .02
(Unnumbered)
262 Checklist 107-178 .05 .02
(Unnumbered)
263 Checklist 179-259 .05 .02
(Unnumbered)
635 Lou Gehrig .20 .08
Puzzle Card UER
(Misnumbered)

1986 Leaf/Donruss

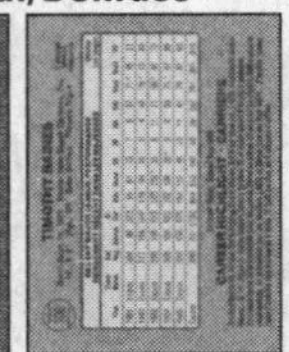

This 264-card standard-size set was issued with a puzzle of Hank Aaron. Except for the numbering, the company logo and the bilingual backs, the cards are essentially the same as the Donruss U.S. regular issue cards of the same players. On a light blue background, the horizontal backs carry player biography, statistics and career highlights in French and English. Two cards, Dick Perez artwork of Jesse Barfield (254) and Jeff Reardon (214), are called Canadian Greats (CG) and are not contained in the Donruss U.S. set. Diamond Kings (numbers 1-26, denoted DK) and Rated Rookies (numbers 27-29, denoted RR) are included just as in the American set. The cards are numbered on the back. As in most Canadian sets, the players featured are heavily biased toward Canadian teams and those American teams closest to the Canadian border. Those players selected for and included as Diamond Kings do not have a regular card in the set. The checklist cards (listed at the end of the list below) are numbered one, two and three (but are not given a traditional card number); the Diamond Kings checklist card is also unnumbered. Two key cards in this set are Andres Galarraga and Fred McGriff, who are Rookie Cards in the 1986 Donruss set.

Nm-Mt Ex-Mt
COMPLETE SET (264) 20.00 8.00
1 Kirk Gibson DK .20 .08
2 Goose Gossage DK .15 .06
3 Willie McGee DK .10 .04
4 George Bell DK .05 .02
5 Tony Armas DK .05 .02
6 Chili Davis DK .10 .04
7 Cecil Cooper DK .10 .04
8 Mike Boddicker DK .05 .02
9 Davey Lopes DK .05 .02
10 Bill Doran DK .05 .02
11 Bret Saberhagen DK .10 .04
12 Brett Butler DK .10 .04
13 Harold Baines DK .15 .06
14 Mike Davis DK .05 .02
15 Tony Perez DK .40 .16
16 Willie Randolph DK .10 .04
17 Bob Boone DK .10 .04
18 Orel Hershiser DK .15 .06
19 Johnny Ray DK .05 .02
20 Gary Ward DK .05 .02
21 Rick Mahler DK .05 .02
22 Phil Bradley DK .05 .02
23 Jerry Koosman DK .10 .04
24 Tom Brunansky DK .05 .02
25 Andre Dawson DK .20 .08
26 Dwight Gooden DK .20 .08
27 A.Galarraga RR RC 5.00 2.00
28 Fred McGriff RR RC 5.00 2.00
29 Dave Shipanoff RR .05 .02
30 Danny Jackson .05 .02
31 Robin Yount .40 .16
32 Mike Fitzgerald .05 .02
33 Lou Whitaker .10 .04
34 Alfredo Griffin .05 .02
35 Oil Can Boyd .05 .02
36 Ron Guidry .10 .04
37 Rickey Henderson .75 .30
38 Jack Morris .10 .04
39 Brian Downing .05 .02
40 Mike Marshall .05 .02
41 Tony Gwynn 1.50 .60
42 George Brett 1.25 .50
43 Jim Gantner .05 .02
44 Hubie Brooks .05 .02
45 Tony Fernandez .10 .04
46 Oddibe McDowell .05 .02
47 Ozzie Smith 1.00 .40
48 Ken Griffey .10 .04
49 Jose Cruz .10 .04
50 Mariano Duncan .10 .04
51 Mike Schmidt .60 .24
52 Pat Tabler .05 .02
53 Pete Rose .60 .24
54 Frank White .10 .04
55 Carney Lansford .05 .02
56 Steve Garvey .20 .08

57 Vance Law .05 .02
58 Tony Pena .10 .04
59 Wayne Tolleson .05 .02
60 Dale Murphy .20 .08
61 LaMarr Hoyt .05 .02
62 Ryne Sandberg 1.00 .40
63 Gary Carter .50 .20
64 Lee Smith .15 .06
65 Alvin Davis .05 .02
66 Edwin Nunez .05 .02
67 Kent Hrbek .10 .04
68 Dave Stieb .10 .04
69 Kirby Puckett 1.25 .50
70 Paul Molitor .60 .24
71 Glenn Hubbard .05 .02
72 Lloyd Moseby .05 .02
73 Mike Smithson .05 .02
74 Jeff Leonard .05 .02
75 Danny Darwin .05 .02
76 Kevin McReynolds .05 .02
77 Bill Buckner .10 .04
78 Ron Oester .05 .02
79 Tommy Herr .05 .02
80 Mike Pagliarulo .05 .02
81 Ron Romanick .05 .02
82 Brook Jacoby .05 .02
83 Eddie Murray .75 .30
84 Gary Pettis .05 .02
85 Chet Lemon .05 .02
86 Toby Harrah .05 .02
87 Mike Scioscia .15 .06
88 Bert Blyleven .10 .04
89 Dave Righetti .05 .02
90 Bob Knepper .05 .02
91 Fernando Valenzuela .10 .04
92 Dave Dravecky .10 .04
93 Julio Franco .10 .04
94 Keith Moreland .05 .02
95 Darryl Motley .05 .02
96 Jack Clark .10 .04
97 Tim Wallach .05 .02
98 Steve Balboni .05 .02
99 Storm Davis .05 .02
100 Jay Howell .05 .02
101 Alan Trammell .15 .06
102 Willie Hernandez .05 .02
103 Don Mattingly 1.50 .60
104 Lee Lacy .05 .02
105 Pedro Guerrero .05 .02
106 Willie Wilson .05 .02
107 Craig Reynolds .05 .02
108 Tim Raines .10 .04
109 Shane Rawley .05 .02
110 Larry Parrish .05 .02
111 Eric Show .05 .02
112 Mike Witt .05 .02
113 Dennis Eckersley .50 .20
114 Mike Moore .05 .02
115 Vince Coleman .10 .04
116 Damaso Garcia .05 .02
117 Steve Carlton .40 .16
118 Floyd Bannister .05 .02
119 Mario Soto .05 .02
120 Fred Lynn .10 .04
121 Bob Horner .05 .02
122 Rick Sutcliffe .05 .02
123 Walt Terrell .05 .02
124 Keith Hernandez .10 .04
125 Dave Winfield .50 .20
126 Frank Viola .10 .04
127 Dwight Evans .10 .04
128 Willie Upshaw .05 .02
129 Andre Thornton .05 .02
130 Donnie Moore .05 .02
131 Darryl Strawberry .10 .04
132 Nolan Ryan 2.50 1.00
133 Garry Templeton .05 .02
134 John Tudor .05 .02
135 Dave Parker .10 .04
136 Larry McWilliams .05 .02
137 Terry Pendleton .10 .04
138 Terry Puhl .05 .02
139 Bob Dernier .05 .02
140 Ozzie Guillen RC* .20 .08
141 Jim Clancy .05 .02
142 Cal Ripken 2.50 1.00
143 Mickey Hatcher .05 .02
144 Dan Petry .05 .02
145 Rich Gedman .05 .02
146 Jim Rice .10 .04
147 Butch Wynegar .05 .02
148 Donnie Hill .05 .02
149 Jim Sundberg .05 .02
150 Joe Hesketh .05 .02
151 Chris Codiroli .05 .02
152 Charlie Hough .10 .04
153 Herm Winningham .05 .02
154 Dave Rozema .05 .02
155 Don Slaught .05 .02
156 Juan Beniquez .05 .02
157 Ted Higuera .05 .02
158 Andy Hawkins .05 .02
159 Don Robinson .05 .02
160 Glenn Wilson .05 .02
161 Earnest Riles .05 .02
162 Nick Esasky .05 .02
163 Carlton Fisk .40 .16
164 Claudell Washington .05 .02
165 Scott McGregor .05 .02
166 Nate Snell .05 .02
167 Ted Simmons .10 .04
168 Wade Boggs .50 .20
169 Marty Barrett .05 .02
170 Bud Black .05 .02
171 Charlie Leibrandt .05 .02
172 Charlie Lea .05 .02
173 Reggie Jackson .50 .20
174 Bryn Smith .05 .02
175 Glenn Davis .05 .02
176 Von Hayes .05 .02
177 Danny Cox .05 .02
178 Sammy Khalifa .05 .02
179 Tom Browning .05 .02
180 Scott Garrelts .05 .02
181 Shawon Dunston .10 .04
182 Doyle Alexander .05 .02
183 Jim Presley .05 .02
184 Al Cowens .05 .02
185 Mark Salas .05 .02
186 Tom Niedenfuer .05 .02
187 Dave Henderson .05 .02
188 Lonnie Smith .05 .02
189 Bruce Bochte .05 .02
190 Leon Durham .05 .02
191 Terry Francona .05 .02
192 Bruce Sutter .10 .04
193 Steve Crawford .05 .02
194 Bob Brenly .10 .04
195 Dan Pasqua .05 .02
196 Juan Samuel .05 .02
197 Floyd Rayford .05 .02
198 Tim Burke .05 .02
199 Ben Oglivie .05 .02
200 Don Carman .05 .02
201 Lance Parrish .10 .04
202 Terry Forster .05 .02
203 Neal Heaton .05 .02
204 Ivan Calderon .05 .02
205 Jorge Orta .05 .02
206 Tom Henke .05 .02
207 Rick Reuschel .10 .04
208 Dan Quisenberry .10 .04
209 Pete Rose HL 1.25 .50
210 Floyd Youmans .05 .02
211 Tom Filer .05 .02
212 R.J. Reynolds .05 .02
213 Gorman Thomas .05 .02
214 Jeff Reardon CG .10 .04
215 Chris Brown .05 .02
216 Rick Aguilera .15 .06
217 Ernie Whitt .05 .02
218 Joe Orsulak .05 .02
219 Jimmy Key .15 .06
220 Atlee Hammaker .05 .02
221 Ron Darling .05 .02
222 Zane Smith .05 .02
223 Bob Welch .05 .02
224 Reid Nichols .05 .02
225 Vince Coleman .10 .04
Willie McGee
226 Mark Gubicza .05 .02
227 Tim Birtsas .05 .02
228 Mike Hargrove .10 .04
229 Randy St. Claire .05 .02
230 Larry Herndon .05 .02
231 Dusty Baker .10 .04
232 Mookie Wilson .10 .04
233 Jeff Lahti .05 .02
234 Tom Seaver .50 .20
235 Mike Scott .05 .02
236 Don Sutton .40 .16
237 Roy Smalley .05 .02
238 Bill Madlock .10 .04
239 Charlie Hudson .05 .02
Charles on both sides
240 John Franco .20 .08
241 Frank Tanana .10 .04
242 Sid Fernandez .05 .02
243 Phil Niekro .20 .08
Joe Niekro
244 Dennis Lamp .05 .02
245 Gene Nelson .05 .02
246 Terry Harper .05 .02
247 Vida Blue .10 .04
248 Roger McDowell .20 .08
249 Tony Bernazard .05 .02
250 Cliff Johnson .05 .02
251 Hal McRae .05 .02
252 Garth Iorg .05 .02
253 Mitch Webster .05 .02
254 Jesse Barfield CG .10 .04
255 Dan Driessen .05 .02
256 Mike Brown .05 .02
257 Ron Kittle .05 .02
258 Bo Diaz .05 .02
259 Hank Aaron Puzzle .20 .08
260 Pete Rose KING 1.25 .50
261 Checklist DK 1-26 .05 .02
Unnumbered
262 Checklist 27-106 .05 .02
Unnumbered
263 Checklist 107-186 .05 .02
Unnumbered
264 Checklist 187-260 .05 .02
Unnumbered

1987 Leaf/Donruss

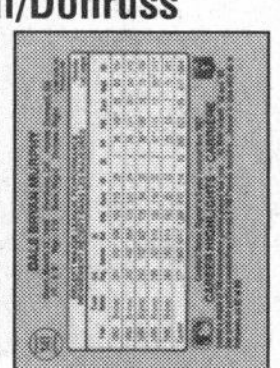

This 264-card standard-size set was issued with a puzzle of Roberto Clemente. Except for the numbering, the company logo and the bilingual backs, the cards are essentially the same as the Donruss U.S. regular issue cards of the same players. On a golden background, the horizontal backs carry player biography, statistics and career hightlights in French and English. Two cards, Dick Perez artwork of Floyd Youmans (65) and Mark Eichhorn (173), are called Canadian Greats (CG) and are not contained in the Donruss U.S. set. Diamond Kings (numbers 1-26, denoted DK) and Rated Rookies (numbers 28-47, denoted RR) are included just as in the American set. The players featured in this set are heavily biased toward Canadian teams and those American teams closest to the Canadian border. Players appearing in their Rookie Card year include Will Clark, Wally Joyner and Greg Maddux. There is also a early Mark McGwire card in this set.

Nm-Mt Ex-Mt
COMPLETE SET (264) 50.00 20.00
1 Wally Joyner DK .20 .08
2 Roger Clemens DK 1.00 .40
3 Dale Murphy DK .20 .08
4 Darryl Strawberry DK .10 .04
5 Ozzie Smith DK .50 .20
6 Jose Canseco DK .60 .24
7 Charlie Hough DK .05 .02
8 Brook Jacoby DK .05 .02
9 Fred Lynn DK .10 .04
10 Rick Rhoden DK .05 .02
11 Chris Brown DK .05 .02
12 Von Hayes DK .05 .02
13 Jack Morris DK .10 .04
14 Kevin McReynolds DK .05 .02
15 George Brett DK .60 .24
16 Ted Higuera DK .05 .02
17 Hubie Brooks DK .05 .02
18 Mike Scott DK .05 .02
19 Kirby Puckett DK .25 .10
20 Dave Winfield DK .30 .12
21 Lloyd Moseby DK .05 .02
22 Eric Davis DK .15 .06
23 Jim Presley DK .05 .02
24 Keith Moreland DK .05 .02
25 Greg Walker DK .05 .02
26 Steve Sax DK .05 .02
27 DK Checklist 1-26 .05 .02
28 B.J. Surhoff RR RC .50 .20
29 Randy Myers RR RC .20 .08
30 Ken Gerhart RR .05 .02
31 Benito Santiago RR .15 .06
32 Greg Swindell RR RC .10 .04
33 Mike Birkbeck RR .05 .02
34 Terry Steinbach RR RC .20 .08
35 Bo Jackson RR RC 1.50 .60
36 Greg Maddux RR RC 10.00 4.00
37 Jim Lindeman RR .05 .02
38 Devon White RR RC .30 .12
39 Eric Bell RR .05 .02
40 Will Fraser RR .05 .02
41 Jerry Browne RR .05 .02
42 Chris James RR .05 .02
43 Rafael Palmeiro RR RC 5.00 2.00
44 Pat Dodson RR .05 .02
45 Duane Ward RR .10 .04
46 Mark McGwire RR 10.00 4.00
47 Bruce Fields RR .05 .02
48 Jody Davis .05 .02
49 Roger McDowell .05 .02
50 Jose Guzman .05 .02
51 Oddibe McDowell .05 .02
52 Harold Baines .15 .06
53 Dave Righetti .05 .02
54 Moose Haas .05 .02
55 Mark Langston .05 .02
56 Kirby Puckett .50 .20
57 Dwight Evans .10 .04
58 Willie Randolph .10 .04
59 Wally Backman .05 .02
60 Bryn Smith .05 .02
61 Tim Wallach .05 .02
62 Joe Hesketh .05 .02
63 Garry Templeton .05 .02
64 Robby Thompson .10 .04
65 Floyd Youmans CG .10 .04
66 Ernest Riles .05 .02
67 Robin Yount .40 .16
68 Darryl Strawberry .10 .04
69 Ernie Whitt .05 .02
70 Dave Winfield .40 .16
71 Paul Molitor .40 .16
72 Dave Stieb .10 .04
73 Tom Henke .05 .02
74 Frank Viola .05 .02
75 Scott Garrelts .05 .02
76 Mike Boddicker .05 .02
77 Keith Moreland .05 .02
78 Lou Whitaker .10 .04
79 Dave Parker .10 .04
80 Lee Smith .15 .06
81 Tom Candiotti .05 .02
82 Greg A. Harris .05 .02
83 Fred Lynn .10 .04
84 Dwight Gooden .10 .04
85 Ron Darling .05 .02
86 Mike Krukow .05 .02
87 Spike Owen .05 .02
88 Len Dykstra .15 .06
89 Rick Aguilera .10 .04
90 Jim Clancy .05 .02
91 Joe Johnson .05 .02
92 Damaso Garcia .05 .02
93 Sid Fernandez .05 .02
94 Bob Ojeda .05 .02
95 Ted Higuera .05 .02
96 George Brett 1.00 .40
97 Willie Wilson .10 .04
98 Cal Ripken 2.50 1.00
99 Kent Hrbek .10 .04
100 Bert Blyleven .10 .04
101 Ron Guidry .10 .04
102 Andy Allanson .05 .02
103 Dave Henderson .05 .02
104 Kirk Gibson .10 .04
105 Lloyd Moseby .05 .02
106 Tony Fernandez .10 .04
107 Lance Parrish .10 .04
108 Ozzie Smith .60 .24
109 Gary Carter .50 .20
110 Eddie Murray .50 .20
111 Mike Witt .05 .02
112 Bobby Witt .05 .02
113 Willie McGee .10 .04
114 Steve Garvey .15 .06
115 Glenn Davis .05 .02
116 Jose Cruz .05 .02
117 Ozzie Guillen .10 .04
118 Alvin Davis .05 .02
119 Jose Rijo .05 .02
120 Bill Madlock .10 .04
121 Tommy Herr .05 .02
122 Mike Schmidt .60 .24
123 Mike Scioscia .15 .06
124 Terry Pendleton .10 .04
125 Leon Durham .05 .02
126 Alan Trammell .15 .06
127 Jesse Barfield .05 .02
128 Shawon Dunston .05 .02
129 Pete Rose .60 .24
130 Von Hayes .05 .02
131 Julio Franco .10 .04
132 Juan Samuel .05 .02
133 Joe Carter .20 .08
134 Brook Jacoby .05 .02
135 Jack Morris .10 .04
136 Bob Horner .05 .02
137 Calvin Schiraldi .05 .02
138 Tom Browning .05 .02
139 Shane Rawley .05 .02
140 Mario Soto .05 .02
141 Dale Murphy .20 .08
142 Hubie Brooks .05 .02
143 Jeff Reardon .10 .04
144 Will Clark 2.00 .80
145 Ed Correa .05 .02
146 Glenn Wilson .05 .02
147 Johnny Ray .05 .02
148 Fernando Valenzuela .10 .04
149 Tim Raines .10 .04
150 Don Mattingly 1.25 .50
151 Jose Canseco .60 .24
152 Gary Pettis .05 .02
153 Don Sutton .40 .16
154 Jim Presley .05 .02
155 Checklist 28-105 .05 .02
156 Dale Sveum .05 .02
157 Cory Snyder .05 .02
158 Jeff Sellers .05 .02
159 Denny Walling .05 .02
160 Danny Cox .05 .02
161 Bob Forsch .05 .02
162 Joaquin Andujar .05 .02
163 Roberto Clemente .20 .08
Puzzle Card
164 Paul Assenmacher .10 .04
165 Marty Barrett .05 .02
166 Ray Knight .05 .02
167 Rafael Santana .05 .02
168 Bruce Ruffin .05 .02
169 Buddy Bell .10 .04
170 Kevin Mitchell .20 .08
171 Ken Oberkfell .05 .02
172 Gene Garber .05 .02
173 Mark Eichhorn CG .10 .04
174 Don Carman .05 .02
175 Jesse Orosco .10 .04
176 Mookie Wilson .10 .04
177 Gary Ward .05 .02
178 John Franco .10 .04
179 Eric Davis .15 .06
180 Walt Terrell .05 .02
181 Phil Niekro .40 .16
182 Pat Tabler .05 .02
183 Brett Butler .10 .04
184 George Bell .05 .02
185 Pete Incaviglia .10 .04
186 Pete O'Brien .05 .02
187 Jimmy Key .15 .06
188 Frank White .10 .04
189 Mike Pagliarulo .05 .02
190 Roger Clemens 1.25 .50
191 Rickey Henderson .75 .30
192 Mike Easler .05 .02
193 Wade Boggs .40 .16
194 Vince Coleman .05 .02
195 Charlie Kerfeld .05 .02
196 Dickie Thon .05 .02
197 Bill Doran .05 .02
198 Alfredo Griffin .05 .02
199 Carlton Fisk .40 .16
200 Phil Bradley .05 .02
201 Reggie Jackson .50 .20
202 Bob Boone .05 .02
203 Steve Sax .05 .02
204 Tom Niedenfuer .05 .02
205 Tim Burke .05 .02
206 Floyd Youmans .05 .02
207 Jay Tibbs .05 .02
208 Chili Davis .15 .06
209 Larry Parrish .05 .02
210 John Cerutti .05 .02
211 Kevin Bass .05 .02
212 Andre Dawson .20 .08
213 Bob Sebra .05 .02
214 Kevin McReynolds .05 .02
215 Jim Morrison .05 .02
216 Candy Maldonado .05 .02
217 John Kruk .20 .08
218 Todd Worrell .10 .04
219 Barry Bonds RC* 20.00 8.00
220 Andy McGaffigan .05 .02
221 Andres Galarraga .40 .16
222 Mike Fitzgerald .05 .02
223 Kirk McCaskill .05 .02
224 Dave Smith .05 .02
225 Ruben Sierra RC .50 .20
226 Scott Fletcher .05 .02
227 Chet Lemon .05 .02
228 Dan Petry .05 .02
229 Mark Eichhorn .05 .02
230 Cecil Cooper .10 .04
231 Willie Upshaw .05 .02
232 Don Baylor .10 .04
233 Keith Hernandez .10 .04
234 Ryne Sandberg .75 .30
235 Tony Gwynn 1.25 .50
236 Chris Brown .05 .02
237 Pedro Guerrero .05 .02
238 Mark Gubicza .05 .02
239 Sid Bream .05 .02
240 Joe Cowley .05 .02
241 Bill Buckner .10 .04
242 John Candelaria .05 .02
243 Scott McGregor .05 .02
244 Tom Brunansky .05 .02
245 Gary Gaetti .10 .04
246 Orel Hershiser .10 .04
247 Jim Rice .10 .04
248 Oil Can Boyd .05 .02
249 Bob Knepper .05 .02
250 Danny Tartabull .05 .02
251 John Cangelosi .05 .02
252 Wally Joyner RC* .50 .20
253 Bruce Hurst .05 .02
254 Rich Gedman .05 .02
255 Jim Deshaies .05 .02
256 Tony Pena .10 .04
257 Nolan Ryan 2.50 1.00
258 Mike Scott .05 .02
259 Checklist 106-183 .05 .02
260 Dennis Rasmussen .05 .02
261 Bret Saberhagen .10 .04
262 Steve Balboni .05 .02
263 Tom Seaver .40 .16
264 Checklist 184-264 .05 .02

1988 Leaf/Donruss

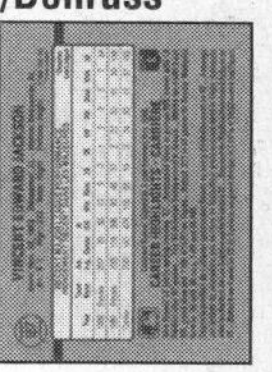

This 264-card standard-size set was issued with a puzzle of Stan Musial. Except for the numbering, the company logo and the bilingual backs, the cards are essentially the same as the Donruss U.S. regular issue cards of the same players. On a light blue background, the horizontal backs carry player biography, statistics, and career hightlights in French and English. Two cards, Dick Perez artwork of George Bell (213) and Tim Wallach (255), are called Canadian Greats (CG) and are not contained in the Donruss U.S. set. Diamond Kings (numbers 1-26, denoted DK) and Rated Rookies (numbers 28-47, denoted RR) are included just as in the American set. There are also bonus cards of the the two Canadian teams' MVP's, George Bell and Tim Raines, as in the Donruss American set. The players featured are heavily biased toward Canadian teams and those American teams closest to the Canadian border. Players appearing in their Rookie Card year include Roberto Alomar and Mark Grace.

Nm-Mt Ex-Mt
COMPLETE SET (264) 15.00 6.00
1 Mark McGwire DK 2.00 .80
2 Tim Raines DK .10 .04
3 Benito Santiago DK .10 .04
4 Alan Trammell DK .15 .06
5 Danny Tartabull DK .05 .02
6 Ron Darling DK .05 .02
7 Paul Molitor DK .40 .16
8 Devon White DK .05 .02
9 Andre Dawson DK .20 .08
10 Julio Franco DK .10 .04
11 Scott Fletcher DK .05 .02
12 Tony Fernandez DK .10 .04
13 Shane Rawley DK .05 .02
14 Kal Daniels DK .05 .02
15 Jack Clark DK .10 .04
16 Dwight Evans DK .05 .02
17 Tommy John DK .10 .04
18 Andy Van Slyke DK .05 .02
19 Gary Gaetti DK .10 .04
20 Mark Langston DK .05 .02
21 Will Clark DK .40 .16
22 Glenn Hubbard DK .05 .02
23 Billy Hatcher DK .05 .02
24 Bob Welch DK .05 .02
25 Ivan Calderon DK .05 .02
26 Cal Ripken DK 1.50 .60
27 DK Checklist 1-26 .05 .02
28 Mackey Sasser RR RC .05 .02
29 Jeff Treadway RR .05 .02
30 Mike Campbell RR .05 .02
31 Lance Johnson RR RC .15 .06
32 Nelson Liriano RR .05 .02
33 Shawn Abner RR .05 .02
34 Roberto Alomar RR RC 2.00 .80
35 Shawn Hillegas RR .05 .02
36 Joey Meyer RR .05 .02
37 Kevin Elster RR .05 .02
38 Jose Lind RR RC .05 .02
39 Kirt Manwaring RR RC .05 .02
40 Mark Grace RR RC 2.00 .80
41 Jody Reed RR RC .05 .02
42 John Farrell RR .05 .02
43 Al Leiter RR RC .40 .16
44 Gary Thurman RR .05 .02
45 Vicente Palacios RR .05 .02
46 Eddie Williams RR .05 .02
47 Jack McDowell RR RC .20 .08
48 Dwight Gooden .10 .04
49 Mike Witt .05 .02
50 Wally Joyner .15 .06
51 Brook Jacoby .05 .02
52 Bert Blyleven .10 .04
53 Ted Higuera .05 .02
54 Mike Scott .05 .02
55 Jose Guzman .05 .02
56 Roger Clemens .75 .30
57 Dave Righetti .05 .02
58 Benito Santiago .10 .04
59 Ozzie Guillen .10 .04
60 Matt Nokes .05 .02
61 Fernando Valenzuela .10 .04
62 Orel Hershiser .10 .04
63 Sid Fernandez .05 .02
64 Ozzie Virgil .05 .02
65 Wade Boggs .40 .16
66 Floyd Youmans .05 .02
67 Jimmy Key .10 .04
68 Bret Saberhagen .10 .04
69 Jody Davis .05 .02
70 Shawon Dunston .10 .04
71 Julio Franco .10 .04
72 Danny Cox .05 .02
73 Jim Clancy .05 .02
74 Mark Eichhorn .05 .02
75 Scott Bradley .05 .02
76 Charlie Leibrandt .05 .02
77 Nolan Ryan 1.50 .60
78 Ron Darling .05 .02
79 John Franco .10 .04
80 Dave Stieb .10 .04
81 Mike Fitzgerald .05 .02
82 Steve Bedrosian .05 .02
83 Dale Murphy .20 .08
84 Tim Burke .05 .02
85 Jack Morris .10 .04
86 Greg Walker .05 .02
87 Kevin Mitchell .10 .04
88 Doug Drabek .05 .02

89 Charlie Hough .10 .04
90 Tony Gwynn .75 .30
91 Rick Sutcliffe .05 .02
92 Shane Rawley .05 .02
93 George Brett .60 .24
94 Frank Viola .05 .02
95 Tony Pena .10 .04
96 Jim Deshaies .05 .02
97 Mike Scioscia .10 .04
98 Rick Rhoden .05 .02
99 Terry Kennedy .05 .02
100 Cal Ripken 1.50 .60
101 Pedro Guerrero .05 .02
102 Andy Van Slyke .10 .04
103 Willie McGee .10 .04
104 Mike Kingery .05 .02
105 Kevin Seitzer .05 .02
106 Robin Yount .40 .16
107 Tracy Jones .05 .02
108 Dave Magadan .05 .02
109 Mel Hall .05 .02
110 Billy Hatcher .05 .02
111 Todd Benzinger .05 .02
112 Mike LaValliere .05 .02
113 Barry Bonds 1.00 .40
114 Tim Raines .10 .04
115 Ozzie Smith .50 .20
116 Dave Winfield .40 .16
117 Keith Hernandez .10 .04
118 Jeffrey Leonard .05 .02
119 Larry Parrish .05 .02
120 Robby Thompson .05 .02
121 Andres Galarraga .20 .08
122 Mickey Hatcher .05 .02
123 Mark Langston .05 .02
124 Mike Schmidt .60 .24
125 Cory Snyder .05 .02
126 Andre Dawson .20 .08
127 Devon White .05 .02
128 Vince Coleman .05 .02
129 Bryn Smith .05 .02
130 Lance Parrish .05 .02
131 Willie Upshaw .05 .02
132 Pete O'Brien .05 .02
133 Tony Fernandez .10 .04
134 Billy Ripken .05 .02
135 Len Dykstra .10 .04
136 Kirk Gibson .10 .04
137 Kevin Bass .05 .02
138 Jose Canseco .50 .20
139 Kent Hrbek .10 .04
140 Lloyd Moseby .05 .02
141 Marty Barrett .05 .02
142 Carmelo Martinez .05 .02
143 Tom Foley .05 .02
144 Kirby Puckett .30 .12
145 Rickey Henderson .60 .24
146 Juan Samuel .05 .02
147 Pete Incaviglia .05 .02
148 Greg Brock .05 .02
149 Eric Davis .10 .04
150 Kal Daniels .05 .02
151 Bob Boone .10 .04
152 John Cerutti .05 .02
153 Mike Greenwell .05 .02
154 Oddibe McDowell .05 .02
155 Scott Fletcher .05 .02
156 Gary Carter .40 .16
157 Harold Baines .10 .04
158 Greg Swindell .05 .02
159 Mark McLemore .10 .04
160 Keith Moreland .05 .02
161 Jim Gantner .05 .02
162 Willie Randolph .10 .04
163 Fred Lynn .05 .02
164 B.J. Surhoff .10 .04
165 Ken Griffey .10 .04
166 Chet Lemon .05 .02
167 Alan Trammell .15 .06
168 Paul Molitor .40 .16
169 Lou Whitaker .10 .04
170 Will Clark .40 .16
171 Dwight Evans .10 .04
172 Eddie Murray .40 .16
173 Darrell Evans .10 .04
174 Ellis Burks .40 .16
175 Ivan Calderon .05 .02
176 John Kruk .10 .04
177 Don Mattingly .75 .30
178 Dick Schofield .05 .02
179 Bruce Hurst .05 .02
180 Ron Guidry .10 .04
181 Jack Clark .10 .04
182 Franklin Stubbs .05 .02
183 Bill Doran .05 .02
184 Joe Carter .20 .08
185 Steve Sax .05 .02
186 Glenn Davis .05 .02
187 Bo Jackson .40 .16
188 Bobby Bonilla .05 .02
189 Willie Wilson .05 .02
190 Danny Tartabull .05 .02
191 Bo Diaz .05 .02
192 Buddy Bell .10 .04
193 Tim Wallach .05 .02
194 Mark McGwire 1.50 .60
195 Carney Lansford .10 .04
196 Alvin Davis .05 .02
197 Von Hayes .05 .02
198 Mitch Webster .05 .02
199 Casey Candaele .05 .02
200 Gary Gaetti .10 .04
201 Tommy Herr .05 .02
202 Wally Backman .05 .02
203 Brian Downing .05 .02
204 Rance Mulliniks .05 .02
205 Craig Reynolds .05 .02
206 Ruben Sierra .10 .04
207 Ryne Sandberg .60 .24
208 Carlton Fisk .40 .16
209 Checklist 28-107 .05 .02
210 Gerald Young .05 .02
211 Tim Raines MVP .15 .06
(Bonus card pose)
212 John Tudor .05 .02
213 George Bell CG .10 .04
214 George Bell MVP .10 .04
(Bonus card pose)
215 Jim Rice .10 .04
216 Gerald Perry .05 .02
217 Dave Stewart .10 .04
218 Jose Uribe .05 .02
219 Rick Reuschel .10 .04
220 Darryl Strawberry .10 .04
221 Chris Brown .05 .02
222 Ted Simmons .10 .04
223 Lee Mazzilli .05 .02
224 Denny Walling .05 .02
225 Jesse Barfield .05 .02
226 Barry Larkin .50 .20
227 Harold Reynolds .10 .04
228 Kevin McReynolds .05 .02
229 Todd Worrell .10 .04
230 Tommy John .10 .04
231 Rick Aguilera .05 .02
232 Bill Madlock .10 .04
233 Roy Smalley .05 .02
234 Jeff Musselman .05 .02
235 Mike Dunne .05 .02
236 Jerry Browne .05 .02
237 Sam Horn .05 .02
238 Howard Johnson .05 .02
239 Candy Maldonado .05 .02
240 Nick Esasky .05 .02
241 Geno Petralli .05 .02
242 Herm Winningham .05 .02
243 Roger McDowell .05 .02
244 Brian Fisher .05 .02
245 John Marzano .05 .02
246 Terry Pendleton .10 .04
247 Rick Leach .05 .02
248 Pascual Perez .05 .02
249 Mookie Wilson .10 .04
250 Ernie Whitt .05 .02
251 Ron Kittle .05 .02
252 Oil Can Boyd .05 .02
253 Jim Gott .05 .02
254 George Bell .05 .02
255 Tim Wallach CG .10 .04
256 Luis Polonia .05 .02
257 Hubie Brooks .05 .02
258 Mickey Brantley .05 .02
259 Gregg Jefferies RC .10 .04
260 Johnny Ray .05 .02
261 Checklist 108-187 .05 .02
262 Dennis Martinez .10 .04
263 Stan Musial .20 .08
Puzzle Card
264 Checklist 188-264 .05 .02

1990 Leaf

The 1990 Leaf set was the first premium set introduced by Donruss and represents one of the more significant products issued in the 1990's. The cards were issued in 15-card foil wrapped packs and were not available in factory sets. Each pack also contained one three-piece puzzle panel of a 63-piece Yogi Berra "Donruss Hall of Fame Diamond King" puzzle. This set, which was produced on high quality paper stock, was issued in two separate series of 264 standard-size cards each. The second series was issued approximately six weeks after the release of the first series. The cards feature full-color photos on both the front and back. Rookie Cards in the set include David Justice, John Olerud, Sammy Sosa, Frank Thomas and Larry Walker.

	Nm-Mt	Ex-Mt
COMPLETE SET (528)	100.00	30.00
COMPLETE SERIES 1 (264)	60.00	18.00
COMPLETE SERIES 2 (264)	40.00	12.00
COMP. BERRA PUZZLE	1.00	.30

1 Introductory Card .40 .12
2 Mike Henneman .40 .12
3 Steve Bedrosian .40 .12
4 Mike Scott .40 .12
5 Allan Anderson .40 .12
6 Rick Sutcliffe .60 .18
7 Gregg Olson .60 .18
8 Kevin Elster .40 .12
9 Pete O'Brien .40 .12
10 Carlton Fisk 1.00 .30
11 Joe Magrane .40 .12
12 Roger Clemens 3.00 .90
13 Tom Glavine 1.00 .30
14 Tom Gordon .60 .18
15 Todd Benzinger .40 .12
16 Hubie Brooks .40 .12
17 Roberto Kelly .40 .12
18 Barry Larkin 1.00 .30
19 Mike Boddicker .40 .12
20 Roger McDowell .40 .12
21 Nolan Ryan 5.00 1.50
22 John Farrell .40 .12
23 Bruce Hurst .40 .12
24 Wally Joyner .60 .18
25 Greg Maddux 5.00 1.50
26 Chris Bosio .40 .12
27 John Cerutti .40 .12
28 Tim Burke .40 .12
29 Dennis Eckersley .60 .18
30 Glenn Davis .40 .12
31 Jim Abbott 1.00 .30
32 Mike LaValliere .40 .12
33 Andres Thomas .40 .12
34 Lou Whitaker .60 .18
35 Alvin Davis .40 .12
36 Melido Perez .40 .12
37 Craig Biggio 1.00 .30
38 Rick Aguilera .60 .18
39 Pete Harnisch .40 .12
40 David Cone .60 .18
41 Scott Garrelts .40 .12
42 Jay Howell .40 .12
43 Eric King .40 .12
44 Pedro Guerrero .40 .12
45 Mike Bielecki .40 .12
46 Bob Boone .60 .18
47 Kevin Brown .60 .18
48 Jerry Browne .40 .12
49 Mike Scioscia .40 .12
50 Chuck Cary .40 .12
51 Wade Boggs 1.00 .30
52 Von Hayes .40 .12
53 Tony Fernandez .40 .12
54 Dennis Martinez .60 .18
55 Tom Candiotti .40 .12
56 Andy Benes .60 .18
57 Rob Dibble .60 .18
58 Chuck Crim .40 .12
59 John Smoltz 1.50 .45
60 Mike Heath .40 .12
61 Kevin Gross .40 .12
62 Mark McGwire 4.00 1.20
63 Bert Blyleven .60 .18
64 Bob Walk .40 .12
65 Mickey Tettleton .40 .12
66 Sid Fernandez .40 .12
67 Terry Kennedy .40 .12
68 Fernando Valenzuela .60 .18
69 Don Mattingly 4.00 1.20
70 Paul O'Neill 1.00 .30
71 Robin Yount 2.50 .75
72 Bret Saberhagen .60 .18
73 Geno Petralli .40 .12
74 Brook Jacoby .40 .12
75 Roberto Alomar 1.00 .30
76 Devon White .60 .18
77 Jose Lind .40 .12
78 Pat Combs .40 .12
79 Dave Stieb .60 .18
80 Tim Wallach .40 .12
81 Dave Stewart .60 .18
82 Eric Anthony RC .40 .12
83 Randy Bush .40 .12
84 Rickey Henderson CL .60 .18
85 Jaime Navarro .40 .12
86 Tommy Gregg .40 .12
87 Frank Tanana .40 .12
88 Omar Vizquel 1.50 .45
89 Ivan Calderon .40 .12
90 Vince Coleman .40 .12
91 Barry Bonds 4.00 1.20
92 Randy Milligan .40 .12
93 Frank Viola .40 .12
94 Matt Williams .60 .18
95 Alfredo Griffin .40 .12
96 Steve Sax .40 .12
97 Gary Gaetti .60 .18
98 Ryne Sandberg 3.00 .90
99 Danny Tartabull .40 .12
100 Rafael Palmeiro 1.00 .30
101 Jesse Orosco .40 .12
102 Garry Templeton .40 .12
103 Frank DiPino .40 .12
104 Tony Pena .40 .12
105 Dickie Thon .40 .12
106 Kelly Gruber .40 .12
107 Marquis Grissom RC 2.00 .60
108 Jose Canseco 1.50 .45
109 Mike Blowers RC .40 .12
110 Tom Browning .40 .12
111 Greg Vaughn .40 .12
112 Oddibe McDowell .40 .12
113 Gary Ward .40 .12
114 Jay Buhner .60 .18
115 Eric Show .40 .12
116 Bryan Harvey .40 .12
117 Andy Van Slyke .60 .18
118 Jeff Ballard .40 .12
119 Barry Lyons .40 .12
120 Kevin Mitchell .40 .12
121 Mike Gallego .40 .12
122 Dave Smith .40 .12
123 Kirby Puckett 1.50 .45
124 Jerome Walton .40 .12
125 Bo Jackson 1.50 .45
126 Harold Baines .60 .18
127 Scott Bankhead .40 .12
128 Ozzie Guillen .40 .12
129 Jose Oquendo UER .40 .12
(League misspelled
as Legue)
130 John Dopson .40 .12
131 Charlie Hayes .40 .12
132 Fred McGriff 1.50 .45
133 Chet Lemon .40 .12
134 Gary Carter .60 .18
135 Rafael Ramirez .40 .12
136 Shane Mack .40 .12
137 Mark Grace UER 1.00 .30
(Card back has OB:L,
should be B:L)
138 Phil Bradley .40 .12
139 Dwight Gooden .60 .18
140 Harold Reynolds .60 .18
141 Scott Fletcher .40 .12
142 Ozzie Smith 2.50 .75
143 Mike Greenwell .40 .12
144 Pete Smith .40 .12
145 Mark Gubicza .40 .12
146 Chris Sabo .40 .12
147 Ramon Martinez .40 .12
148 Tim Leary .40 .12
149 Randy Myers .60 .18
150 Jody Reed .40 .12
151 Bruce Ruffin .40 .12
152 Jeff Russell .40 .12
153 Doug Jones .40 .12
154 Tony Gwynn 2.00 .60
155 Mark Langston .40 .12
156 Mitch Williams .40 .12
157 Gary Sheffield 1.50 .45
158 Tom Henke .40 .12
159 Oil Can Boyd .40 .12
160 Rickey Henderson 1.50 .45
161 Bill Doran .40 .12
162 Chuck Finley .60 .18
163 Jeff King .40 .12
164 Nick Esasky .40 .12
165 Cecil Fielder .60 .18
166 Dave Valle .40 .12
167 Robin Ventura 1.50 .45
168 Jim Deshaies .40 .12
169 Juan Berenguer .40 .12
170 Craig Worthington .40 .12
171 Gregg Jefferies .60 .18
172 Will Clark 1.50 .45
173 Kirk Gibson .60 .18
174 Carlton Fisk CL .60 .18
175 Bobby Thigpen .40 .12
176 John Tudor .40 .12
177 Andre Dawson .60 .18
178 George Brett 4.00 1.20
179 Steve Buechele .40 .12
180 Joey Belle 1.50 .45
181 Eddie Murray 1.50 .45
182 Bob Geren .40 .12
183 Rob Murphy .40 .12
184 Tom Herr .40 .12
185 George Bell .40 .12
186 Spike Owen .40 .12
187 Cory Snyder .40 .12
188 Fred Lynn .40 .12
189 Eric Davis .60 .18
190 Dave Parker .60 .18
191 Jeff Blauser .40 .12
192 Matt Nokes .40 .12
193 Delino DeShields RC 1.00 .30
194 Scott Sanderson .40 .12
195 Lance Parrish .40 .12
196 Bobby Bonilla .60 .18
197 Cal Ripken UER 5.00 1.50
(Reistertown, should
be Reisterstown)
198 Kevin McReynolds .40 .12
199 Robby Thompson .40 .12
200 Tim Belcher .40 .12
201 Jesse Barfield .40 .12
202 Mariano Duncan .40 .12
203 Bill Spiers .40 .12
204 Frank White .60 .18
205 Julio Franco .60 .18
206 Greg Swindell .40 .12
207 Benito Santiago .60 .18
208 Johnny Ray .40 .12
209 Gary Redus .40 .12
210 Jeff Parrett .40 .12
211 Jimmy Key .60 .18
212 Tim Raines .60 .18
213 Carney Lansford .60 .18
214 Gerald Young .40 .12
215 Gene Larkin .40 .12
216 Dan Plesac .40 .12
217 Lonnie Smith .40 .12
218 Alan Trammell .60 .18
219 Jeffrey Leonard .40 .12
220 Sammy Sosa RC 40.00 12.00
221 Todd Zeile .60 .18
222 Bill Landrum .40 .12
223 Mike Devereaux .40 .12
224 Mike Marshall .40 .12
225 Jose Uribe .40 .12
226 Juan Samuel .40 .12
227 Mel Hall .40 .12
228 Kent Hrbek .60 .18
229 Shawon Dunston .40 .12
230 Kevin Seitzer .40 .12
231 Pete Incaviglia .40 .12
232 Sandy Alomar Jr. .60 .18
233 Bip Roberts .40 .12
234 Scott Terry .40 .12
235 Dwight Evans .60 .18
236 Ricky Jordan .40 .12
237 John Olerud RC 3.00 .90
238 Zane Smith .40 .12
239 Walt Weiss .40 .12
240 Alvaro Espinoza .40 .12
241 Billy Hatcher .40 .12
242 Paul Molitor 1.00 .30
243 Dale Murphy 1.50 .45
244 Dave Bergman .40 .12
245 Ken Griffey Jr. 5.00 1.50
246 Ed Whitson .40 .12
247 Kirk McCaskill .40 .12
248 Jay Bell .60 .18
249 Ben McDonald RC 1.00 .30
250 Darryl Strawberry .60 .18
251 Brett Butler .60 .18
252 Terry Steinbach .60 .18
253 Ken Caminiti .60 .18
254 Dan Gladden .40 .12
255 Dwight Smith .40 .12
256 Kurt Stillwell .40 .12
257 Ruben Sierra .40 .12
258 Mike Schooler .40 .12
259 Lance Johnson .40 .12
260 Terry Pendleton .60 .18
261 Ellis Burks 1.00 .30
262 Len Dykstra .60 .18
263 Mookie Wilson .60 .18
264 Nolan Ryan CL UER 1.50 .45
No TM after Ranger logo
265 Nolan Ryan 2.50 .75
No Hit King
266 Brian DuBois .40 .12
267 Don Robinson .40 .12
268 Glenn Wilson .40 .12
269 Kevin Tapani RC 1.00 .30
270 Marvell Wynne .40 .12
271 Bill Ripken .40 .12
272 Howard Johnson .40 .12
273 Brian Holman .40 .12
274 Dan Pasqua .40 .12
275 Ken Dayley .40 .12
276 Jeff Reardon .60 .18
277 Jim Presley .40 .12
278 Jim Eisenreich .40 .12
279 Danny Jackson .40 .12
280 Orel Hershiser .60 .18
281 Andy Hawkins .40 .12
282 Jose Rijo .40 .12
283 Luis Rivera .40 .12
284 John Kruk .60 .18
285 Jeff Huson RC .40 .12
286 Joel Skinner .40 .12
287 Jack Clark .60 .18
288 Chili Davis .60 .18
289 Joe Girardi 1.00 .30
290 B.J. Surhoff .60 .18
291 Luis Sojo .40 .12
292 Tom Foley .40 .12
293 Mike Moore .40 .12
294 Ken Oberkfell .40 .12
295 Luis Polonia .40 .12
296 Doug Drabek .40 .12
297 Dave Justice RC 3.00 .90
298 Paul Gibson .40 .12
299 Edgar Martinez 1.00 .30
300 F.Thomas RC UER 20.00 6.00
No B in front
of birthdate
301 Eric Yelding .40 .12
302 Greg Gagne .40 .12
303 Brad Komminsk .40 .12
304 Ron Darling .40 .12
305 Kevin Bass .40 .12
306 Jeff Hamilton .40 .12
307 Ron Karkovice .40 .12
308 Milt Thompson UER .60 .18
(Ray Lankford pictured
on card back)
309 Mike Harkey .40 .12
310 Mel Stottlemyre Jr. .40 .12
311 Kenny Rogers .60 .18
312 Mitch Webster .40 .12
313 Kal Daniels .40 .12
314 Matt Nokes .40 .12
315 Dennis Lamp .40 .12
316 Ken Howell .40 .12
317 Glenallen Hill .40 .12
318 Dave Martinez .40 .12
319 Chris James .40 .12
320 Mike Pagliarulo .40 .12
321 Hal Morris .40 .12
322 Rob Deer .40 .12
323 Greg Olson .40 .12
324 Tony Phillips .40 .12
325 Larry Walker RC 8.00 2.40
326 Ron Hassey .40 .12
327 Jack Howell .40 .12
328 John Smiley .40 .12
329 Steve Finley .60 .18
330 Dave Magadan .40 .12
331 Greg Litton .40 .12
332 Mickey Hatcher .40 .12
333 Lee Guetterman .40 .12
334 Norm Charlton .40 .12
335 Edgar Diaz .40 .12
336 Willie Wilson .40 .12
337 Bobby Witt .40 .12
338 Candy Maldonado .40 .12
339 Craig Lefferts .40 .12
340 Dante Bichette 1.50 .45
341 Wally Backman .40 .12
342 Dennis Cook .40 .12
343 Pat Borders .40 .12
344 Wallace Johnson .40 .12
345 Willie Randolph .60 .18
346 Danny Darwin .40 .12
347 Al Newman .40 .12
348 Mark Knudson .40 .12
349 Joe Boever .40 .12
350 Larry Sheets .40 .12
351 Mike Jackson .40 .12
352 Wayne Edwards .40 .12
353 Bernard Gilkey RC 1.00 .30
354 Don Slaught .40 .12
355 Joe Orsulak .40 .12
356 John Franco .60 .18
357 Jeff Brantley .40 .12
358 Mike Morgan .40 .12
359 Deion Sanders 1.50 .45
360 Terry Leach .40 .12
361 Les Lancaster .40 .12
362 Storm Davis .40 .12
363 Scott Coolbaugh .40 .12
364 Ozzie Smith CL 1.00 .30
365 Cecilio Guante .40 .12
366 Joey Cora .60 .18
367 Willie McGee .60 .18
368 Jerry Reed .40 .12
369 Darren Daulton .60 .18
370 Manny Lee .40 .12
371 Mark Gardner .40 .12
372 Rick Honeycutt .40 .12
373 Steve Balboni .40 .12
374 Jack Armstrong .40 .12
375 Charlie O'Brien .40 .12
376 Ron Gant .60 .18
377 Lloyd Moseby .40 .12
378 Gene Harris .40 .12
379 Joe Carter .60 .18
380 Scott Bailes .40 .12
381 R.J. Reynolds .40 .12
382 Bob Melvin .40 .12
383 Tim Teufel .40 .12
384 John Burkett .40 .12
385 Felix Jose .40 .12
386 Larry Andersen .40 .12
387 David West .40 .12
388 Luis Salazar .40 .12
389 Mike Macfarlane .40 .12
390 Charlie Hough .60 .18
391 Greg Briley .40 .12
392 Donn Pall .40 .12
393 Bryn Smith .40 .12
394 Carlos Quintana .40 .12
395 Steve Lake .40 .12
396 Mark Whiten RC 1.00 .30
397 Edwin Nunez .40 .12
398 Rick Parker .40 .12
399 Mark Portugal .40 .12
400 Roy Smith .40 .12
401 Hector Villanueva .40 .12
402 Bob Milacki .40 .12
403 Alejandro Pena .40 .12
404 Scott Bradley .40 .12
405 Ron Kittle .40 .12
406 Bob Tewksbury .40 .12
407 Wes Gardner .40 .12
408 Ernie Whitt .40 .12
409 Terry Shumpert .40 .12
410 Tim Layana .40 .12
411 Chris Gwynn .40 .12
412 Jeff D. Robinson .40 .12
413 Scott Scudder .40 .12
414 Kevin Romine .40 .12
415 Jose DeJesus .40 .12
416 Mike Jeffcoat .40 .12
417 Rudy Seanez .40 .12

418 Mike Dunne .40 .12
419 Dick Schofield .40 .12
420 Steve Wilson .40 .12
421 Bill Krueger .40 .12
422 Junior Felix .40 .12
423 Drew Hall .40 .12
424 Curt Young .40 .12
425 Franklin Stubbs .40 .12
426 Dave Winfield .60 .18
427 Rick Reed RC 1.00 .30
428 Charlie Leibrandt .40 .12
429 Jeff M. Robinson .40 .12
430 Erik Hanson .40 .12
431 Barry Jones .40 .12
432 Alex Trevino .40 .12
433 John Moses .40 .12
434 Dave Johnson .40 .12
435 Mackey Sasser .40 .12
436 Rick Leach .40 .12
437 Lenny Harris .40 .12
438 Carlos Martinez .40 .12
439 Rex Hudler .40 .12
440 Domingo Ramos .40 .12
441 Gerald Perry .40 .12
442 Jeff Russell .40 .12
443 Carlos Baerga RC 1.00 .30
444 Will Clark CL .60 .18
445 Stan Javier .40 .12
446 Kevin Maas RC 1.00 .30
447 Tom Brunansky .40 .12
448 Carmelo Martinez .40 .12
449 Willie Blair RC .40 .12
450 Andres Galarraga .60 .18
451 Bud Black .40 .12
452 Greg W. Harris .40 .12
453 Joe Oliver .40 .12
454 Greg Brock .40 .12
455 Jeff Treadway .40 .12
456 Lance McCullers .40 .12
457 Dave Schmidt .40 .12
458 Todd Burns .40 .12
459 Max Venable .40 .12
460 Neal Heaton .40 .12
461 Mark Williamson .40 .12
462 Keith Miller .40 .12
463 Mike LaCoss .40 .12
464 Jose Offerman RC 1.00 .30
465 Jim Leyritz RC 1.00 .30
466 Glenn Braggs .40 .12
467 Ron Robinson .40 .12
468 Mark Davis .40 .12
469 Gary Pettis .40 .12
470 Keith Hernandez .60 .18
471 Dennis Rasmussen .40 .12
472 Mark Eichhorn .40 .12
473 Ted Power .40 .12
474 Terry Mulholland .40 .12
475 Todd Stottlemyre .60 .18
476 Jerry Goff .40 .12
477 Gene Nelson .40 .12
478 Rich Gedman .40 .12
479 Brian Harper .40 .12
480 Mike Felder .40 .12
481 Steve Avery .40 .12
482 Jack Morris .60 .18
483 Randy Johnson 3.00 .75
484 Scott Radinsky RC .40 .12
485 Jose DeLeon .40 .12
486 Stan Belinda RC .40 .12
487 Brian Holton .40 .12
488 Mark Carreon .40 .12
489 Trevor Wilson .40 .12
490 Mike Sharperson .40 .12
491 Alan Mills RC .40 .12
492 John Candelaria .40 .12
493 Paul Assenmacher .40 .12
494 Steve Crawford .40 .12
495 Brad Arnsberg .40 .12
496 Sergio Valdez .40 .12
497 Mark Parent .40 .12
498 Tom Pagnozzi .40 .12
499 Greg A. Harris .40 .12
500 Randy Ready .40 .12
501 Duane Ward .40 .12
502 Nelson Santovenia .40 .12
503 Joe Klink .40 .12
504 Eric Plunk .40 .12
505 Jeff Reed .40 .12
506 Ted Higuera .40 .12
507 Joe Hesketh .40 .12
508 Dan Petry .40 .12
509 Matt Young .40 .12
510 Jerald Clark .40 .12
511 John Orton .40 .12
512 Scott Ruskin .40 .12
513 Chris Hoiles RC 1.00 .30
514 Daryl Boston .40 .12
515 Francisco Oliveras .40 .12
516 Ozzie Canseco .40 .12
517 Xavier Hernandez RC .40 .12
518 Fred Manrique .40 .12
519 Shawn Boskie RC .40 .12
520 Jeff Montgomery .60 .18
521 Jack Daugherty .40 .12
522 Keith Comstock .40 .12
523 Greg Hibbard RC .40 .12
524 Lee Smith .60 .18
525 Dana Kiecker .40 .12
526 Darrel Akerfelds .40 .12
527 Greg Myers .40 .12
528 Ryne Sandberg CL 1.50 .45

1991 Leaf Previews

The 1991 Leaf Previews set consists of 26 standard-size cards. Cards from this set were issued as inserts (four at a time) inside specially marked 1991 Donruss hobby factory sets. The front design has color action player photos, with white and silver borders.

	Nm-Mt	Ex-Mt
COMPLETE SET (26)	40.00	12.00
1 Dave Justice	1.00	.30
2 Ryne Sandberg	4.00	1.20
3 Barry Larkin	1.50	.45
4 Craig Biggio	1.50	.45
5 Ramon Martinez	.50	.15
6 Tim Wallach	.50	.15
7 Dwight Gooden	1.00	.30
8 Len Dykstra	1.00	.30
9 Barry Bonds	6.00	1.80
10 Ray Lankford	.50	.15
11 Tony Gwynn	3.00	.90
12 Will Clark	2.50	.75
13 Leo Gomez	.50	.15
14 Wade Boggs	1.50	.45
15 Chuck Finley UER (Position on card back is First Base)	1.00	.30
16 Carlton Fisk	1.50	.45
17 Sandy Alomar Jr.	.50	.15
18 Cecil Fielder	1.00	.30
19 Bo Jackson	1.00	.30
20 Paul Molitor	1.50	.45
21 Kirby Puckett	2.50	.75
22 Don Mattingly	6.00	1.80
23 Rickey Henderson	2.50	.75
24 Tino Martinez	1.00	.30
25 Nolan Ryan	10.00	3.00
26 Dave Stieb	.50	.15

1991 Leaf

This 528-card standard size set was issued by Donruss in two separate series of 264 cards. Cards were exclusively issued in foil packs. The front design has color action player photos, with white and silver borders. A thicker stock was used for these (then) premium level cards. Production for the 1991 set was greatly increased due to the huge demand for the benchmark 1990 Leaf set. However, the 1991 cards were met with modest enthusiasm due to a weak selection of Rookie Cards and superior competition from brands like 1991 Stadium Club.

	Nm-Mt	Ex-Mt
COMPLETE SET (528)	15.00	4.50
COMP. SERIES 1 (264)	5.00	1.50
COMP. SERIES 2 (264)	10.00	3.00
COMP. KILLEBREW PUZZLE	1.00	.30

1 The Leaf Card .10 .03
2 Kurt Stillwell .10 .03
3 Bobby Witt .10 .03
4 Tony Phillips .10 .03
5 Scott Garrelts .10 .03
6 Greg Swindell .10 .03
7 Billy Ripken .10 .03
8 Dave Martinez .10 .03
9 Kelly Gruber .10 .03
10 Juan Samuel .10 .03
11 Brian Holman .10 .03
12 Craig Biggio .30 .09
13 Lonnie Smith .10 .03
14 Ron Robinson .10 .03
15 Mike LaValliere .10 .03
16 Mark Davis .10 .03
17 Jack Daugherty .10 .03
18 Mike Henneman .10 .03
19 Mike Greenwell .10 .03
20 Dave Magadan .10 .03
21 Mark Williamson .10 .03
22 Marquis Grissom .20 .06
23 Pat Borders .10 .03
24 Mike Scioscia .10 .03
25 Shawon Dunston .10 .03
26 Randy Bush .10 .03
27 John Smoltz .30 .09
28 Chuck Crim .10 .03
29 Don Slaught .10 .03
30 Mike Macfarlane .10 .03
31 Wally Joyner .20 .06
32 Pat Combs .10 .03
33 Tony Pena .10 .03
34 Howard Johnson .10 .03
35 Leo Gomez .10 .03
36 Spike Owen .10 .03
37 Eric Davis .20 .06
38 Roberto Kelly .10 .03
39 Jerome Walton .10 .03
40 Shane Mack .10 .03
41 Kent Mercker .10 .03
42 B.J. Surhoff .20 .06
43 Jerry Browne .10 .03
44 Lee Smith .20 .06
45 Chuck Finley .20 .06
46 Terry Mulholland .10 .03
47 Tom Bolton .10 .03
48 Tom Herr .10 .03
49 Jim Deshaies .10 .03
50 Walt Weiss .10 .03
51 Hal Morris .10 .03
52 Lee Guetterman .10 .03
53 Paul Assenmacher .10 .03
54 Brian Harper .10 .03
55 Paul Gibson .10 .03
56 John Burkett .10 .03
57 Doug Jones .10 .03
58 Jose Oquendo .10 .03
59 Dick Schofield .10 .03
60 Dickie Thon .10 .03
61 Ramon Martinez .10 .03
62 Jay Buhner .20 .06
63 Mark Portugal .10 .03
64 Bob Welch .10 .03
65 Chris Sabo .10 .03
66 Chuck Cary .10 .03
67 Mark Langston .10 .03
68 Joe Boever .10 .03
69 Jody Reed .10 .03
70 Alejandro Pena .10 .03
71 Jeff King .10 .03
72 Tom Pagnozzi .10 .03
73 Joe Oliver .10 .03
74 Mike Witt .10 .03
75 Hector Villanueva .10 .03
76 Dan Gladden .10 .03
77 Dave Justice .20 .06
78 Mike Gallego .10 .03
79 Tom Candiotti .10 .03
80 Ozzie Smith .75 .23
81 Luis Polonia .10 .03
82 Randy Ready .10 .03
83 Greg A. Harris .10 .03
84 David Justice CL .10 .03
85 Kevin Mitchell .10 .03
86 Mark McLemore .10 .03
87 Terry Steinbach .10 .03
88 Tom Browning .10 .03
89 Matt Nokes .10 .03
90 Mike Harkey .10 .03
91 Omar Vizquel .30 .09
92 Dave Bergman .10 .03
93 Matt Williams .20 .06
94 Steve Olin .10 .03
95 Craig Wilson .10 .03
96 Dave Stieb .10 .03
97 Ruben Sierra .10 .03
98 Jay Howell .10 .03
99 Scott Bradley .10 .03
100 Eric Yelding .10 .03
101 Rickey Henderson .50 .15
102 Jeff Reed .10 .03
103 Jimmy Key .20 .06
104 Terry Shumpert .10 .03
105 Kenny Rogers .20 .06
106 Cecil Fielder .20 .06
107 Robby Thompson .10 .03
108 Alex Cole .10 .03
109 Randy Milligan .10 .03
110 Andres Galarraga .20 .06
111 Bill Spiers .10 .03
112 Kal Daniels .10 .03
113 Henry Cotto .10 .03
114 Casey Candaele .10 .03
115 Jeff Blauser .10 .03
116 Robin Yount .75 .23
117 Ben McDonald .10 .03
118 Bret Saberhagen .20 .06
119 Juan Gonzalez .30 .09
120 Lou Whitaker .20 .06
121 Ellis Burks .20 .06
122 Charlie O'Brien .10 .03
123 John Smiley .10 .03
124 Tim Burke .10 .03
125 John Olerud .20 .06
126 Eddie Murray .50 .15
127 Greg Maddux .75 .23
128 Kevin Tapani .10 .03
129 Ron Gant .20 .06
130 Jay Bell .20 .06
131 Chris Hoiles .10 .03
132 Tom Gordon .10 .03
133 Kevin Seitzer .10 .03
134 Jeff Huson .10 .03
135 Jerry Don Gleaton .10 .03
136 Jeff Brantley UER .10 .03
(Photo actually Rick Leach on back)
137 Felix Fermin .10 .03
138 Mike Devereaux .10 .03
139 Delino DeShields .20 .06
140 David Wells .20 .06
141 Tim Crews .10 .03
142 Erik Hanson .10 .03
143 Mark Davidson .10 .03
144 Tommy Gregg .10 .03
145 Jim Gantner .10 .03
146 Jose Lind .10 .03
147 Danny Tartabull .10 .03
148 Geno Petralli .10 .03
149 Travis Fryman .20 .06
150 Tim Naehring .10 .03
151 Kevin McReynolds .10 .03
152 Joe Orsulak .10 .03
153 Steve Frey .10 .03
154 Duane Ward .10 .03
155 Stan Javier .10 .03
156 Damon Berryhill .10 .03
157 Gene Larkin .10 .03
158 Greg Olson .10 .03
159 Mark Knudson .10 .03
160 Carmelo Martinez .10 .03
161 Storm Davis .10 .03
162 Jim Abbott .30 .09
163 Len Dykstra .20 .06
164 Tom Brunansky .10 .03
165 Dwight Gooden .20 .06
166 Jose Mesa .10 .03
167 Oil Can Boyd .10 .03
168 Barry Larkin .30 .09
169 Scott Sanderson .10 .03
170 Mark Grace .30 .09
171 Mark Guthrie .10 .03
172 Tom Glavine .30 .09
173 Gary Sheffield .20 .06
174 Roger Clemens CL .50 .15
175 Chris James .10 .03
176 Milt Thompson .10 .03
177 Donnie Hill .10 .03
178 Wes Chamberlain RC .10 .03
179 John Marzano .10 .03
180 Frank Viola .20 .06
181 Eric Anthony .10 .03
182 Jose Canseco .50 .15
183 Scott Scudder .10 .03
184 Dave Eiland .10 .03
185 Luis Salazar .10 .03
186 Pedro Munoz RC .10 .03
187 Steve Searcy .10 .03
188 Don Robinson .10 .03
189 Sandy Alomar Jr. .10 .03
190 Jose DeLeon .10 .03
191 John Orton .10 .03
192 Darren Daulton .20 .06
193 Mike Morgan .10 .03
194 Greg Briley .10 .03
195 Karl Rhodes .10 .03
196 Harold Baines .20 .06
197 Bill Doran .10 .03
198 Alvaro Espinoza .10 .03
199 Kirk McCaskill .10 .03
200 Jose DeJesus .10 .03
201 Jack Clark .20 .06
202 Daryl Boston .10 .03
203 Randy Tomlin RC .10 .03
204 Pedro Guerrero .20 .06
205 Billy Hatcher .10 .03
206 Tim Leary .10 .03
207 Ryne Sandberg .75 .23
208 Kirby Puckett .50 .15
209 Charlie Leibrandt .10 .03
210 Rick Honeycutt .10 .03
211 Joel Skinner .10 .03
212 Rex Hudler .10 .03
213 Bryan Harvey .10 .03
214 Charlie Hayes .10 .03
215 Matt Young .10 .03
216 Terry Kennedy .10 .03
217 Carl Nichols .10 .03
218 Mike Moore .10 .03
219 Paul O'Neill .30 .09
220 Steve Sax .10 .03
221 Shawn Boskie .10 .03
222 Rich DeLucia .10 .03
223 Lloyd Moseby .10 .03
224 Mike Kingery .10 .03
225 Carlos Baerga .10 .03
226 Bryn Smith .10 .03
227 Todd Stottlemyre .10 .03
228 Julio Franco .20 .06
229 Jim Gott .10 .03
230 Mike Schooler .10 .03
231 Steve Finley .20 .06
232 Dave Henderson .10 .03
233 Luis Quinones .10 .03
234 Mark Whiten .10 .03
235 Brian McRae RC .20 .06
236 Rich Gossage .20 .06
237 Rob Deer .10 .03
238 Will Clark .50 .15
239 Albert Belle .20 .06
240 Bob Melvin .10 .03
241 Larry Walker .50 .15
242 Dante Bichette .20 .06
243 Orel Hershiser .20 .06
244 Pete O'Brien .10 .03
245 Pete Harnisch .10 .03
246 Jeff Treadway .10 .03
247 Julio Machado .10 .03
248 Dave Johnson .10 .03
249 Kirk Gibson .20 .06
250 Kevin Brown .20 .06
251 Milt Cuyler .10 .03
252 Jeff Reardon .20 .06
253 David Cone .20 .06
254 Gary Redus .10 .03
255 Junior Noboa .10 .03
256 Greg Myers .10 .03
257 Dennis Cook .10 .03
258 Joe Girardi .10 .03
259 Allan Anderson .10 .03
260 Paul Marak .10 .03
261 Barry Bonds 1.25 .35
262 Juan Bell .10 .03
263 Russ Morman .10 .03
264 George Brett CL .50 .15
265 Jerald Clark .10 .03
266 Dwight Evans .20 .06
267 Roberto Alomar .30 .09
268 Danny Jackson .10 .03
269 Brian Downing .10 .03
270 John Cerutti .10 .03
271 Robin Ventura .20 .06
272 Gerald Perry .10 .03
273 Wade Boggs .30 .09
274 Dennis Martinez .20 .06
275 Andy Benes .10 .03
276 Tony Fossas .10 .03
277 Franklin Stubbs .10 .03
278 John Kruk .20 .06
279 Kevin Gross .10 .03
280 Von Hayes .10 .03
281 Frank Thomas .50 .15
282 Rob Dibble .20 .06
283 Mel Hall .10 .03
284 Rick Mahler .10 .03
285 Dennis Eckersley .20 .06
286 Bernard Gilkey .10 .03
287 Dan Plesac .10 .03
288 Jason Grimsley .10 .03
289 Mark Lewis .10 .03
290 Tony Gwynn .60 .18
291 Jeff Russell .10 .03
292 Curt Schilling .50 .15
293 Pascual Perez .10 .03
294 Jack Morris .20 .06
295 Hubie Brooks .10 .03
296 Alex Fernandez .10 .03
297 Harold Reynolds .20 .06
298 Craig Worthington .10 .03
299 Willie Wilson .10 .03
300 Mike Maddux .10 .03
301 Dave Righetti .20 .06
302 Paul Molitor .30 .09
303 Gary Gaetti .20 .06
304 Terry Pendleton .20 .06
305 Kevin Elster .10 .03
306 Scott Fletcher .10 .03
307 Jeff Robinson .10 .03
308 Jesse Barfield .10 .03
309 Mike LaCoss .10 .03
310 Andy Van Slyke .20 .06
311 Glenallen Hill .10 .03
312 Bud Black .10 .03
313 Kent Hrbek .20 .06
314 Tim Teufel .10 .03
315 Tony Fernandez .10 .03
316 Beau Allred .10 .03
317 Curtis Wilkerson .10 .03
318 Bill Sampen .10 .03
319 Randy Johnson .60 .18
320 Mike Heath .10 .03
321 Sammy Sosa 1.00 .30
322 Mickey Tettleton .10 .03
323 Jose Vizcaino .10 .03
324 John Candelaria .10 .03
325 Dave Howard .10 .03
326 Jose Rijo .10 .03
327 Todd Zeile .10 .03
328 Gene Nelson .10 .03
329 Dwayne Henry .10 .03
330 Mike Boddicker .10 .03
331 Ozzie Guillen .10 .03
332 Sam Horn .10 .03
333 Wally Whitehurst .10 .03
334 Dave Parker .20 .06
335 George Brett 1.25 .35
336 Bobby Thigpen .10 .03
337 Ed Whitson .10 .03
338 Ivan Calderon .10 .03
339 Mike Pagliarulo .10 .03
340 Jack McDowell .10 .03
341 Dana Kiecker .10 .03
342 Fred McGriff .30 .09
343 Mark Lee RC .10 .03
344 Alfredo Griffin .10 .03
345 Scott Bankhead .10 .03
346 Darrin Jackson .10 .03
347 Rafael Palmeiro .30 .09
348 Steve Farr .10 .03
349 Hensley Meulens .10 .03
350 Danny Cox .10 .03
351 Alan Trammell .20 .06
352 Edwin Nunez .10 .03
353 Joe Carter .20 .06
354 Eric Show .10 .03
355 Vance Law .10 .03
356 Jeff Gray .10 .03
357 Bobby Bonilla .20 .06
358 Ernest Riles .10 .03
359 Ron Hassey .10 .03
360 Willie McGee .20 .06
361 Mackey Sasser .10 .03
362 Glenn Braggs .10 .03
363 Mario Diaz .10 .03
364 Barry Bonds CL .60 .18
365 Kevin Bass .10 .03
366 Pete Incaviglia .10 .03
367 Luis Sojo UER .10 .03
(1989 stats interspersed with 1990's)
368 Lance Parrish .20 .06
369 Mark Leonard .10 .03
370 Heath. Slocumb RC .20 .06
371 Jimmy Jones .10 .03
372 Ken Griffey Jr. 1.00 .30
373 Chris Hammond .10 .03
374 Chili Davis .20 .06
375 Joey Cora .10 .03
376 Ken Hill .10 .03
377 Darryl Strawberry .20 .06
378 Ron Darling .10 .03
379 Sid Bream .10 .03
380 Bill Swift .10 .03
381 Shawn Abner .10 .03
382 Eric King .10 .03
383 Mickey Morandini .10 .03
384 Carlton Fisk .30 .09
385 Steve Lake .10 .03
386 Mike Jeffcoat .10 .03
387 Darren Holmes RC .20 .06
388 Tim Wallach .10 .03
389 George Bell .10 .03
390 Craig Lefferts .10 .03
391 Ernie Whitt .10 .03
392 Felix Jose .10 .03
393 Kevin Maas .10 .03
394 Devon White .20 .06
395 Otis Nixon .10 .03
396 Chuck Knoblauch .20 .06
397 Scott Coolbaugh .10 .03
398 Glenn Davis .10 .03
399 Manny Lee .10 .03
400 Andre Dawson .20 .06
401 Scott Chiamparino .10 .03
402 Bill Gullickson .10 .03
403 Lance Johnson .10 .03
404 Juan Agosto .10 .03
405 Danny Darwin .10 .03
406 Barry Jones .10 .03
407 Larry Andersen .10 .03
408 Luis Rivera .10 .03
409 Jaime Navarro .10 .03
410 Roger McDowell .10 .03
411 Brett Butler .20 .06
412 Dale Murphy .50 .15
413 Tim Raines UER .20 .06
(Listed as hitting .500 in 1980, should be .050)
414 Norm Charlton .10 .03
415 Greg Cadaret .10 .03
416 Chris Nabholz .10 .03
417 Dave Stewart .20 .06
418 Rich Gedman .10 .03
419 Willie Randolph .20 .06
420 Mitch Williams .10 .03
421 Brook Jacoby .10 .03
422 Greg W. Harris .10 .03
423 Nolan Ryan 2.00 .60
424 Dave Rohde .10 .03
425 Don Mattingly 1.25 .35
426 Greg Gagne .10 .03
427 Vince Coleman .10 .03
428 Dan Pasqua .10 .03
429 Alvin Davis .10 .03
430 Cal Ripken 1.50 .45
431 Jamie Quirk .10 .03
432 Benito Santiago .20 .06
433 Jose Uribe .10 .03
434 Candy Maldonado .10 .03
435 Junior Felix .10 .03
436 Deion Sanders .30 .09
437 John Franco .20 .06
438 Greg Hibbard .10 .03
439 Floyd Bannister .10 .03
440 Steve Howe .10 .03
441 Steve Decker .10 .03
442 Vicente Palacios .10 .03
443 Pat Tabler .10 .03
444 Darryl Strawberry CL .10 .03
445 Mike Felder .10 .03
446 Al Newman .10 .03
447 Chris Donnels .10 .03
448 Rich Rodriguez .10 .03
449 Turner Ward RC .20 .06
450 Bob Walk .10 .03
451 Gilberto Reyes .10 .03
452 Mike Jackson .10 .03
453 Rafael Belliard .10 .03
454 Wayne Edwards .10 .03
455 Andy Allanson .10 .03
456 Dave Smith .10 .03
457 Gary Carter .20 .06

458 Warren Cromartie .10 .03
459 Jack Armstrong .10 .03
460 Bob Tewksbury .10 .03
461 Joe Klink .10 .03
462 Xavier Hernandez .10 .03
463 Scott Radinsky .10 .03
464 Jeff Robinson .10 .03
465 Gregg Jefferies .10 .03
466 Denny Neagle RC .50 .15
467 Carmelo Martinez .10 .03
468 Donn Pall .10 .03
469 Bruce Hurst .10 .03
470 Eric Bullock .10 .03
471 Rick Aguilera .20 .06
472 Charlie Hough .20 .06
473 Carlos Quintana .10 .03
474 Marty Barrett .10 .03
475 Kevin D. Brown .10 .03
476 Bobby Ojeda .10 .03
477 Edgar Martinez .30 .09
478 Bip Roberts .10 .03
479 Mike Flanagan .10 .03
480 John Habyan .10 .03
481 Larry Casian .10 .03
482 Wally Backman .10 .03
483 Doug Dascenzo .10 .03
484 Rick Dempsey .10 .03
485 Ed Sprague .10 .03
486 Steve Chitren .10 .03
487 Mark McGwire 1.25 .35
488 Roger Clemens 1.00 .30
489 Orlando Merced RC .10 .03
490 Rene Gonzales .10 .03
491 Mike Stanton .10 .03
492 Al Osuna RC .10 .03
493 Rick Cerone .10 .03
494 Mariano Duncan .10 .03
495 Zane Smith .10 .03
496 John Morris .10 .03
497 Frank Tanana .10 .03
498 Junior Ortiz .10 .03
499 Dave Winfield .20 .06
500 Gary Varsho .10 .03
501 Chico Walker .10 .03
502 Ken Caminiti .20 .06
503 Ken Griffey Sr. .20 .06
504 Randy Myers .10 .03
505 Steve Bedrosian .10 .03
506 Cory Snyder .10 .03
507 Cris Carpenter .10 .03
508 Tim Belcher .10 .03
509 Jeff Hamilton .10 .03
510 Steve Avery .10 .03
511 Dave Valle .10 .03
512 Tom Lampkin .10 .03
513 Shawn Hillegas .10 .03
514 Reggie Jefferson .10 .03
515 Ron Karkovice .10 .03
516 Doug Drabek .10 .03
517 Tom Henke .10 .03
518 Chris Bosio .10 .03
519 Gregg Olson .10 .03
520 Bob Scanlan .10 .03
521 Alonzo Powell .10 .03
522 Jeff Ballard .10 .03
523 Ray Lankford .10 .03
524 Tommy Greene .10 .03
525 Mike Timlin RC .30 .09
526 Juan Berenguer .10 .03
527 Scott Erickson .10 .03
528 Sandy Alomar Jr. CL .10 .03

1991 Leaf Gold Rookies

This 26-card standard size set was issued by Leaf as an insert to their 1991 Leaf regular issue. The first twelve cards were issued as random inserts in with the first series of 1991 Leaf foil packs. The rest were issued as random inserts in with the second series. The set features a selection of rookie prospects. The earliest Leaf Gold Rookie cards issued with the first series can sometimes be found with erroneous regular numbered backs 265 through 276 instead of the correct BC1 through BC12. These numbered variations are very tough to find.

Nm-Mt Ex-Mt
COMPLETE SET (26) 15.00 4.50
*265-276 ERR: 4X TO 10X BASIC GR
265-276 ERR RANDOM IN EARLY PACKS
BC1 Scott Leius 1.00 .30
BC2 Luis Gonzalez 1.50 .45
BC3 Wil Cordero 1.00 .30
BC4 Gary Scott 1.00 .30
BC5 Willie Banks 1.00 .30
BC6 Arthur Rhodes 1.00 .30
BC7 Mo Vaughn 1.00 .30
BC8 Henry Rodriguez 1.00 .30
BC9 Todd Van Poppel 1.00 .30
BC10 Reggie Sanders 1.00 .30
BC11 Rico Brogna 1.00 .30
BC12 Mike Mussina 2.50 .75
BC13 Kirk Dressendorfer 1.00 .30
BC14 Jeff Bagwell 4.00 1.20
BC15 Pete Schourek 1.00 .30
BC16 Wade Taylor 1.00 .30
BC17 Pat Kelly 1.00 .30
BC18 Tim Costo 1.00 .30
BC19 Roger Salkeld 1.00 .30
BC20 Andujar Cedeno 1.00 .30
BC21 Ryan Klesko UER 2.00 .60
(1990 Sumter BA .289; should be .368)
BC22 Mike Huff 1.00 .30
BC23 Anthony Young 1.00 .30
BC24 Eddie Zosky 1.00 .30
BC25 Nolan Ryan DP UER 2.00 .60
No Hitter 7
(Word other repeated in 7th line)
BC26 R.Henderson DP 1.50 .45
Record Steal

1992 Leaf Previews

Four Leaf Preview standard-size cards were included in each 1992 Donruss hobby factory set. The cards were intended to show collectors and dealers the style of the 1992 Leaf set. The fronts carry glossy color player photos framed by silver borders.

Nm-Mt Ex-Mt
COMPLETE SET (26) 50.00 15.00
1 Steve Avery .30 .09
2 Ryne Sandberg 4.00 1.20
3 Chris Sabo .30 .09
4 Jeff Bagwell 2.50 .75
5 Darryl Strawberry 1.00 .30
6 Bret Barberie .30 .09
7 Howard Johnson .30 .09
8 John Kruk 1.00 .30
9 Andy Van Slyke 1.00 .30
10 Felix Jose .30 .09
11 Fred McGriff 1.50 .45
12 Will Clark 2.50 .75
13 Cal Ripken 8.00 2.40
14 Phil Plantier .30 .09
15 Lee Stevens .30 .09
16 Frank Thomas 2.50 .75
17 Mark Whiten .30 .09
18 Cecil Fielder 1.00 .30
19 George Brett 6.00 1.80
20 Robin Yount 4.00 1.20
21 Scott Erickson .30 .09
22 Don Mattingly 6.00 1.80
23 Jose Canseco 2.50 .75
24 Ken Griffey Jr. 4.00 1.20
25 Nolan Ryan 10.00 3.00
26 Joe Carter 1.00 .30

1992 Leaf

The 1992 Leaf set consists of 528 cards, issued in two separate 264-card series. Cards were distributed in first and second series 15-card foil packs. Each pack contained a selection of basic cards and one black gold parallel card. The basic card fronts feature color action player photos on a silver card face. The player's name appears in a black bar edged at the bottom by a thin red stripe. The team logo overlaps the bar at the right corner. Rookie Cards in this set include Brian Jordan and Jeff Kent.

Nm-Mt Ex-Mt
COMPLETE SET (528) 15.00 4.50
COMP. SERIES 1 (264) 5.00 1.50
COMP. SERIES 2 (264) 10.00 3.00
1 Jim Abbott .25 .07
2 Cal Eldred .05 .02
3 Bud Black .05 .02
4 Dave Howard .05 .02
5 Luis Sojo .05 .02
6 Gary Scott .05 .02
7 Joe Oliver .05 .02
8 Chris Gardner .05 .02
9 Sandy Alomar Jr. .05 .02
10 Greg W. Harris .05 .02
11 Doug Drabek .05 .02
12 Darryl Hamilton .05 .02
13 Mike Mussina .40 .12
14 Kevin Tapani .05 .02
15 Ron Gant .15 .04
16 Mark McGwire 1.00 .30
17 Robin Ventura .15 .04
18 Pedro Guerrero .15 .04
19 Roger Clemens .75 .23
20 Steve Farr .05 .02
21 Frank Tanana .05 .02
22 Joe Hesketh .05 .02
23 Erik Hanson .05 .02
24 Greg Cadaret .05 .02
25 Rex Hudler .05 .02
26 Mark Grace .25 .07
27 Kelly Gruber .05 .02
28 Jeff Bagwell .40 .12
29 Darryl Strawberry .15 .04
30 Dave Smith .05 .02
31 Kevin Appier .15 .04
32 Steve Chitren .05 .02
33 Kevin Gross .05 .02
34 Rick Aguilera .15 .04
35 Juan Guzman .05 .02
36 Joe Orsulak .05 .02
37 Tim Raines .15 .04
38 Harold Reynolds .15 .04
39 Charlie Hough .15 .04
40 Tony Phillips .05 .02
41 Nolan Ryan 1.50 .45
42 Vince Coleman .05 .02
43 Andy Van Slyke .15 .04
44 Tim Burke .05 .02
45 Luis Polonia .05 .02
46 Tom Browning .05 .02
47 Willie McGee .15 .04
48 Gary DiSarcina .05 .02
49 Mark Lewis .05 .02
50 Phil Plantier .05 .02
51 Doug Dascenzo .05 .02
52 Cal Ripken 1.25 .35
53 Pedro Munoz .05 .02
54 Carlos Hernandez .05 .02
55 Jerald Clark .05 .02
56 Jeff Brantley .05 .02
57 Don Mattingly 1.00 .30
58 Roger McDowell .05 .02
59 Steve Avery .05 .02
60 John Olerud .15 .04
61 Bill Gullickson .05 .02
62 Juan Gonzalez .25 .07
63 Felix Jose .05 .02
64 Robin Yount .60 .18
65 Greg Briley .05 .02
66 Steve Finley .15 .04
67 Frank Thomas CL .25 .07
68 Tom Gordon .05 .02
69 Rob Dibble .15 .04
70 Glenallen Hill .05 .02
71 Calvin Jones .05 .02
72 Joe Girardi .05 .02
73 Barry Larkin .25 .07
74 Andy Benes .05 .02
75 Milt Cuyler .05 .02
76 Kevin Bass .05 .02
77 Pete Harnisch .05 .02
78 Wilson Alvarez .05 .02
79 Mike Devereaux .05 .02
80 Doug Henry RC .10 .03
81 Orel Hershiser .15 .04
82 Shane Mack .05 .02
83 Mike Macfarlane .05 .02
84 Thomas Howard .05 .02
85 Alex Fernandez .05 .02
86 Reggie Jefferson .05 .02
87 Leo Gomez .05 .02
88 Mel Hall .05 .02
89 Mike Greenwell .05 .02
90 Jeff Russell .05 .02
91 Steve Buechele .05 .02
92 David Cone .15 .04
93 Kevin Reimer .05 .02
94 Mark Lemke .05 .02
95 Bob Tewksbury .05 .02
96 Zane Smith .05 .02
97 Mark Eichhorn .05 .02
98 Kirby Puckett .40 .12
99 Paul O'Neill .25 .07
100 Dennis Eckersley .15 .04
101 Duane Ward .05 .02
102 Matt Nokes .05 .02
103 Mo Vaughn .15 .04
104 Pat Kelly .05 .02
105 Ron Karkovice .05 .02
106 Bill Spiers .05 .02
107 Gary Gaetti .15 .04
108 Mackey Sasser .05 .02
109 Robby Thompson .05 .02
110 Marvin Freeman .05 .02
111 Jimmy Key .15 .04
112 Dwight Gooden .15 .04
113 Charlie Leibrandt .05 .02
114 Devon White .15 .04
115 Charles Nagy .05 .02
116 Rickey Henderson .40 .12
117 Paul Assenmacher .05 .02
118 Junior Felix .05 .02
119 Julio Franco .15 .04
120 Norm Charlton .05 .02
121 Scott Servais .05 .02
122 Gerald Perry .05 .02
123 Brian McRae .05 .02
124 Don Slaught .05 .02
125 Juan Samuel .05 .02
126 Harold Baines .15 .04
127 Scott Livingstone .05 .02
128 Jay Buhner .15 .04
129 Darrin Jackson .05 .02
130 Luis Mercedes .05 .02
131 Brian Harper .05 .02
132 Howard Johnson .05 .02
133 Nolan Ryan CL .40 .12
134 Dante Bichette .15 .04
135 Dave Righetti .15 .04
136 Jeff Montgomery .05 .02
137 Joe Grahe .05 .02
138 Delino DeShields .05 .02
139 Jose Rijo .05 .02
140 Ken Caminiti .15 .04
141 Steve Olin .05 .02
142 Kurt Stillwell .05 .02
143 Jay Bell .15 .04
144 Jaime Navarro .05 .02
145 Ben McDonald .05 .02
146 Greg Gagne .05 .02
147 Jeff Blauser .15 .04
148 Carney Lansford .15 .04
149 Ozzie Guillen .05 .02
150 Milt Thompson .05 .02
151 Jeff Reardon .15 .04
152 Scott Sanderson .05 .02
153 Cecil Fielder .15 .04
154 Greg A. Harris .05 .02
155 Rich DeLucia .05 .02
156 Roberto Kelly .05 .02
157 Bryn Smith .05 .02
158 Chuck McElroy .05 .02
159 Tom Henke .05 .02
160 Luis Gonzalez .15 .04
161 Steve Wilson .05 .02
162 Shawn Boskie .05 .02
163 Mark Davis .05 .02
164 Mike Moore .05 .02
165 Mike Scioscia .05 .02
166 Scott Erickson .05 .02
167 Todd Stottlemyre .05 .02
168 Alvin Davis .05 .02
169 Greg Hibbard .05 .02
170 David Valle .05 .02
171 Dave Winfield .15 .04
172 Alan Trammell .15 .04
173 Kenny Rogers .15 .04
174 John Franco .15 .04
175 Jose Lind .05 .02
176 Pete Schourek .05 .02
177 Von Hayes .05 .02
178 Chris Hammond .05 .02
179 John Burkett .05 .02
180 Dickie Thon .05 .02
181 Joel Skinner .05 .02
182 Scott Cooper .05 .02
183 Andre Dawson .15 .04
184 Billy Ripken .05 .02
185 Kevin Mitchell .05 .02
186 Brett Butler .15 .04
187 Tony Fernandez .05 .02
188 Cory Snyder .05 .02
189 John Habyan .05 .02
190 Dennis Martinez .15 .04
191 John Smoltz .25 .07
192 Greg Myers .05 .02
193 Rob Deer .05 .02
194 Ivan Rodriguez .40 .12
195 Ray Lankford .05 .02
196 Bill Wegman .05 .02
197 Edgar Martinez .25 .07
198 Darryl Kile .15 .04
199 Cal Ripken CL .40 .12
200 Brent Mayne .05 .02
201 Larry Walker .25 .07
202 Carlos Baerga .05 .02
203 Russ Swan .05 .02
204 Mike Morgan .05 .02
205 Hal Morris .05 .02
206 Tony Gwynn .50 .15
207 Mark Leiter .05 .02
208 Kirt Manwaring .05 .02
209 Al Osuna .05 .02
210 Bobby Thigpen .05 .02
211 Chris Hoiles .05 .02
212 B.J. Surhoff .15 .04
213 Lenny Harris .05 .02
214 Scott Leius .05 .02
215 Gregg Jefferies .05 .02
216 Bruce Hurst .05 .02
217 Steve Sax .05 .02
218 Dave Otto .05 .02
219 Sam Horn .05 .02
220 Charlie Hayes .05 .02
221 Frank Viola .15 .04
222 Jose Guzman .05 .02
223 Gary Redus .05 .02
224 Dave Gallagher .05 .02
225 Dean Palmer .15 .04
226 Greg Olson .05 .02
227 Jose DeLeon .05 .02
228 Mike LaValliere .05 .02
229 Mark Langston .05 .02
230 Chuck Knoblauch .15 .04
231 Bill Doran .05 .02
232 Dave Henderson .05 .02
233 Roberto Alomar .25 .07
234 Scott Fletcher .05 .02
235 Tim Naehring .05 .02
236 Mike Gallego .05 .02
237 Lance Johnson .05 .02
238 Paul Molitor .25 .07
239 Dan Gladden .05 .02
240 Willie Randolph .15 .04
241 Will Clark .40 .12
242 Sid Bream .05 .02
243 Derek Bell .15 .04
244 Bill Pecota .05 .02
245 Terry Pendleton .15 .04
246 Randy Ready .05 .02
247 Jack Armstrong .05 .02
248 Todd Van Poppel .05 .02
249 Shawon Dunston .05 .02
250 Bobby Rose .05 .02
251 Jeff Huson .05 .02
252 Bip Roberts .05 .02
253 Doug Jones .05 .02
254 Lee Smith .15 .04
255 George Brett 1.00 .30
256 Randy Tomlin .05 .02
257 Todd Benzinger .05 .02
258 Dave Stewart .15 .04
259 Mark Carreon .05 .02
260 Pete O'Brien .05 .02
261 Tim Teufel .05 .02
262 Bob Milacki .05 .02
263 Mark Guthrie .05 .02
264 Darrin Fletcher .05 .02
265 Omar Vizquel .25 .07
266 Chris Bosio .05 .02
267 Jose Canseco .40 .12
268 Mike Boddicker .05 .02
269 Lance Parrish .15 .04
270 Jose Vizcaino .05 .02
271 Chris Sabo .05 .02
272 Royce Clayton .05 .02
273 Marquis Grissom .15 .04
274 Fred McGriff .25 .07
275 Barry Bonds 1.00 .30
276 Greg Vaughn .05 .02
277 Gregg Olson .05 .02
278 Dave Hollins .05 .02
279 Tom Glavine .25 .07
280 Bryan Hickerson UER .05 .02
Name spelled Brian on front
281 Scott Radinsky .05 .02
282 Omar Olivares .05 .02
283 Ivan Calderon .05 .02
284 Kevin Maas .05 .02
285 Mickey Tettleton .05 .02
286 Wade Boggs .25 .07
287 Stan Belinda .05 .02
288 Bret Barberie .05 .02
289 Jose Oquendo .05 .02
290 Frank Castillo .05 .02
291 Dave Stieb .05 .02
292 Tommy Greene .05 .02
293 Eric Karros .15 .04
294 Greg Maddux .60 .18
295 Jim Eisenreich .05 .02
296 Rafael Palmeiro .25 .07
297 Ramon Martinez .05 .02
298 Tim Wallach .05 .02
299 Jim Thome .40 .12
300 Chito Martinez .05 .02
301 Mitch Williams .05 .02
302 Randy Johnson .40 .12
303 Carlton Fisk .25 .07
304 Travis Fryman .15 .04
305 Bobby Witt .05 .02
306 Dave Magadan .05 .02
307 Alex Cole .05 .02
308 Bobby Bonilla .15 .04
309 Bryan Harvey .05 .02
310 Rafael Belliard .05 .02
311 Mariano Duncan .05 .02
312 Chuck Crim .05 .02
313 John Kruk .15 .04
314 Ellis Burks .15 .04
315 Craig Biggio .25 .07
316 Glenn Davis .05 .02
317 Ryne Sandberg .60 .18
318 Mike Sharperson .05 .02
319 Rich Rodriguez .05 .02
320 Lee Guetterman .05 .02
321 Benito Santiago .15 .04
322 Jose Offerman .05 .02
323 Tony Pena .05 .02
324 Pat Borders .05 .02
325 Mike Henneman .05 .02
326 Kevin Brown .15 .04
327 Chris Nabholz .05 .02
328 Franklin Stubbs .05 .02
329 Tino Martinez .25 .07
330 Mickey Morandini .05 .02
331 Ryne Sandberg CL .40 .12
332 Mark Gubicza .05 .02
333 Bill Landrum .05 .02
334 Mark Whiten .05 .02
335 Darren Daulton .15 .04
336 Rick Wilkins .05 .02
337 Brian Jordan RC .50 .15
338 Kevin Ward .05 .02
339 Ruben Amaro .05 .02
340 Trevor Wilson .05 .02
341 Andujar Cedeno .05 .02
342 Michael Huff .05 .02
343 Brady Anderson .15 .04
344 Craig Grebeck .05 .02
345 Bob Ojeda .05 .02
346 Mike Pagliarulo .05 .02
347 Terry Shumpert .05 .02
348 Dann Bilardello .05 .02
349 Frank Thomas .40 .12
350 Albert Belle .15 .04
351 Jose Mesa .05 .02
352 Rich Monteleone .05 .02
353 Bob Walk .05 .02
354 Monty Fariss .05 .02
355 Luis Rivera .05 .02
356 Anthony Young .05 .02
357 Geno Petralli .05 .02
358 Otis Nixon .05 .02
359 Tom Pagnozzi .05 .02
360 Reggie Sanders .05 .02
361 Lee Stevens .05 .02
362 Kent Hrbek .15 .04
363 Orlando Merced .05 .02
364 Mike Bordick .05 .02
365 Dion James UER .05 .02
(Blue Jays logo on card back)
366 Jack Clark .15 .04
367 Mike Stanley .05 .02
368 Randy Velarde .05 .02
369 Dan Pasqua .05 .02
370 Pat Listach RC .25 .07
371 Mike Fitzgerald .05 .02
372 Tom Foley .05 .02
373 Matt Williams .15 .04
374 Brian Hunter .05 .02
375 Joe Carter .15 .04
376 Bret Saberhagen .15 .04
377 Mike Stanton .05 .02
378 Hubie Brooks .05 .02
379 Eric Bell .05 .02
380 Walt Weiss .05 .02
381 Danny Jackson .05 .02
382 Manuel Lee .05 .02
383 Ruben Sierra .05 .02
384 Greg Swindell .05 .02
385 Ryan Bowen .05 .02
386 Kevin Ritz .05 .02
387 Curtis Wilkerson .05 .02
388 Gary Varsho .05 .02
389 Dave Hansen .05 .02
390 Bob Welch .05 .02
391 Lou Whitaker .15 .04
392 Ken Griffey Jr. .60 .18
393 Mike Maddux .05 .02
394 Arthur Rhodes .05 .02
395 Chili Davis .15 .04
396 Eddie Murray .40 .12
397 Robin Yount CL .25 .07
398 Dave Cochrane .05 .02
399 Kevin Seitzer .05 .02
400 Ozzie Smith .60 .18
401 Paul Sorrento .05 .02
402 Les Lancaster .05 .02
403 Junior Noboa .05 .02
404 David Justice .15 .04
405 Andy Ashby .05 .02
406 Danny Tartabull .05 .02
407 Bill Swift .05 .02
408 Craig Lefferts .05 .02
409 Tom Candiotti .05 .02
410 Lance Blankenship .05 .02
411 Jeff Tackett .05 .02
412 Sammy Sosa .60 .18
413 Jody Reed .05 .02
414 Bruce Ruffin .05 .02
415 Gene Larkin .05 .02
416 John Vander Wal RC .25 .07
417 Tim Belcher .05 .02
418 Steve Frey .05 .02
419 Dick Schofield .05 .02
420 Jeff King .05 .02
421 Kim Batiste .05 .02
422 Jack McDowell .05 .02
423 Damon Berryhill .05 .02
424 Gary Wayne .05 .02
425 Jack Morris .15 .04
426 Moises Alou .15 .04
427 Mark McLemore .05 .02
428 Juan Guerrero .05 .02
429 Scott Scudder .05 .02
430 Eric Davis .15 .04
431 Joe Slusarski .05 .02
432 Todd Zeile .05 .02
433 Dwayne Henry .05 .02
434 Cliff Brantley .05 .02
435 Butch Henry RC .10 .03
436 Todd Worrell .05 .02
437 Bob Scanlan .05 .02
438 Wally Joyner .15 .04
439 John Flaherty .05 .02
440 Brian Downing .05 .02
441 Darren Lewis .05 .02
442 Gary Carter .15 .04

443 Wally Ritchie .05 .02
444 Chris Jones .05 .02
445 Jeff Kent RC 1.50 .45
446 Gary Sheffield .15 .04
447 Ron Darling .05 .02
448 Deion Sanders .25 .07
449 Andres Galarraga .15 .04
450 Chuck Finley .15 .04
451 Derek Lilliquist .05 .02
452 Carl Willis .05 .02
453 Wes Chamberlain .05 .02
454 Roger Mason .05 .02
455 Spike Owen .05 .02
456 Thomas Howard .05 .02
457 Dave Martinez .05 .02
458 Pete Incaviglia .05 .02
459 Keith A. Miller .05 .02
460 Mike Fetters .05 .02
461 Paul Gibson .05 .02
462 George Bell .05 .02
463 Bobby Bonilla CL .05 .02
464 Terry Mulholland .05 .02
465 Storm Davis .05 .02
466 Gary Pettis .05 .02
467 Randy Bush .05 .02
468 Ken Hill .05 .02
469 Rheal Cormier .05 .02
470 Andy Stankiewicz .05 .02
471 Dave Burba .05 .02
472 Henry Cotto .05 .02
473 Dale Sveum .05 .02
474 Rich Gossage .15 .04
475 William Suero .05 .02
476 Doug Strange .05 .02
477 Bill Krueger .05 .02
478 John Wetteland .15 .04
479 Melido Perez .05 .02
480 Lonnie Smith .05 .02
481 Mike Jackson .05 .02
482 Mike Gardiner .05 .02
483 David Wells .15 .04
484 Barry Jones .05 .02
485 Scott Bankhead .05 .02
486 Terry Leach .05 .02
487 Vince Horsman .05 .02
488 Dave Eiland .05 .02
489 Alejandro Pena .05 .02
490 Julio Valera .05 .02
491 Joe Boever .05 .02
492 Paul Miller RC .05 .02
493 Archi Cianfrocco RC .10 .03
494 Dave Fleming .05 .02
495 Kyle Abbott .05 .02
496 Chad Kreuter .05 .02
497 Chris James .05 .02
498 Donnie Hill .05 .02
499 Jacob Brumfield .05 .02
500 Ricky Bones .05 .02
501 Terry Steinbach .05 .02
502 Bernard Gilkey .05 .02
503 Dennis Cook .05 .02
504 Len Dykstra .15 .04
505 Mike Bielecki .05 .02
506 Bob Kipper .05 .02
507 Jose Melendez .05 .02
508 Rick Sutcliffe .15 .04
509 Ken Patterson .05 .02
510 Andy Allanson .05 .02
511 Al Newman .05 .02
512 Mark Gardner .05 .02
513 Jeff Schaefer .05 .02
514 Jim McNamara .05 .02
515 Peter Hoy .05 .02
516 Curt Schilling .25 .07
517 Kirk McCaskill .05 .02
518 Chris Gwynn .05 .02
519 Sid Fernandez .05 .02
520 Jeff Parrett .05 .02
521 Scott Ruskin .05 .02
522 Kevin McReynolds .05 .02
523 Rick Cerone .05 .02
524 Jesse Orosco .05 .02
525 Troy Afenir .05 .02
526 John Smiley .05 .02
527 Dale Murphy .40 .12
528 Leaf Set Card .05 .02

1992 Leaf Black Gold

his 528-card standard-size set was issued in wo 264-card series. These Black Gold cards ere inserted one per foil pack. The cards are imilar to the regular issue Leaf cards, except hat the card face is black rather than silver and ccented by a gold foil inner border. Likewise, he horizontal backs have a gold rather than a siler background. The set is noteworthy as one of he earliest pack-distributed parallel issues in the obby.

	Nm-Mt	Ex-Mt
OMPLETE SET (528)	60.00	18.00
OMP. SERIES 1 (264)	20.00	6.00
OMP. SERIES 2 (264)	40.00	12.00

B.GOLD STARS: 2X TO 5X BASIC CARDS
B.GOLD RC'S: 1.25X TO 3X BASIC CARDS

1992 Leaf Gold Rookies

his 24-card standard-size set honors 1992's ost promising newcomers. The first 12 cards ere randomly inserted in Leaf series I foil acks, while the second 12 cards were featured nly in series II packs. The fronts display fulleed color action photos highlighted by gold foil order stripes. A gold foil diamond appears at he corners of the picture frame, and the player's ame appears in a black bar that extends etween the bottom two diamonds. An early Pedro Martinez insert is the key card in this set.

	Nm-Mt	Ex-Mt
COMPLETE SET (24)	15.00	4.50
COMPLETE SERIES 1 (12)	10.00	3.00
COMPLETE SERIES 2 (12)	5.00	1.50
BC1 Chad Curtis	1.00	.30
BC2 Brent Gates	1.00	.30
BC3 Pedro Martinez	8.00	2.40
BC4 Kenny Lofton	1.50	.45
BC5 Turk Wendell	1.00	.30
BC6 Mark Hutton	1.00	.30
BC7 Todd Hundley	1.00	.30
BC8 Matt Stairs	1.00	.30
BC9 Eddie Taubensee	1.00	.30
BC10 David Nied	1.00	.30
BC11 Salomon Torres	1.00	.30
BC12 Bret Boone	2.00	.60
BC13 Johnny Ruffin	1.00	.30
BC14 Ed Martel	1.00	.30
BC15 Rick Trlicek	1.00	.30
BC16 Raul Mondesi	1.00	.30
BC17 Pat Mahomes	1.00	.30
BC18 Dan Wilson	1.00	.30
BC19 Donovan Osborne	1.00	.30
BC20 Dave Silvestri	1.00	.30
BC21 Gary DiSarcina	1.00	.30
BC22 Denny Neagle	1.00	.30
BC23 Steve Hosey	1.00	.30
BC24 John Doherty	1.00	.30

1993 Leaf

The 1993 Leaf baseball set consists of three series of 220, 220, and 110 standard-size cards, respectively. Cards were distributed in 14-card foil packs, jumbo packs and magazine packs. Rookie Cards in this set include J.T. Snow. White Sox slugger (and at that time, Leaf Representative) Frank Thomas signed 3,500 cards, which were randomly seeded into packs. In addition, a special card commemorating Dave Winfield's 3,000 hit was also seeded into packs. Both cards are listed at the end of our checklist but are not considered part of the 550-card basic set.

	Nm-Mt	Ex-Mt
COMPLETE SET (550)	35.00	10.50
COMP. SERIES 1 (220)	15.00	4.50
COMP. SERIES 2 (220)	15.00	4.50
COMPLETE UPDATE (110)	5.00	1.50

1 Ben McDonald .15 .04
2 Sid Fernandez .15 .04
3 Juan Guzman .15 .04
4 Curt Schilling .30 .09
5 Ivan Rodriguez .75 .23
6 Don Slaught .15 .04
7 Terry Steinbach .15 .04
8 Todd Zeile .15 .04
9 Andy Stankiewicz .15 .04
10 Tim Teufel .15 .04
11 Marvin Freeman .15 .04
12 Jim Austin .15 .04
13 Bob Scanlan .15 .04
14 Rusty Meacham .15 .04
15 Casey Candaele .15 .04
16 Travis Fryman .30 .09
17 Jose Offerman .15 .04
18 Albert Belle .30 .09
19 John Vander Wal .15 .04
20 Dan Pasqua .15 .04
21 Frank Viola .30 .09
22 Terry Mulholland .15 .04
23 Gregg Olson .15 .04
24 Randy Tomlin .15 .04
25 Todd Stottlemyre .15 .04
26 Jose Oquendo .15 .04
27 Julio Franco .30 .09
28 Tony Gwynn 1.00 .30
29 Ruben Sierra .15 .04
30 Robby Thompson .15 .04
31 Jim Bullinger .15 .04
32 Rick Aguilera .15 .04
33 Scott Servais .15 .04
34 Cal Eldred .15 .04
35 Mike Piazza 2.00 .60
36 Brent Mayne .15 .04
37 Wil Cordero .15 .04
38 Milt Cuyler .15 .04
39 Howard Johnson .15 .04
40 Kenny Lofton .30 .09
41 Alex Fernandez .15 .04
42 Denny Neagle .30 .09
43 Tony Pena .15 .04
44 Bob Tewksbury .15 .04
45 Glenn Davis .15 .04
46 Fred McGriff .50 .15
47 John Olerud .30 .09
48 Steve Hosey .15 .04
49 Rafael Palmeiro .50 .15
50 David Justice .30 .09
51 Pete Harnisch .15 .04
52 Sam Militello .15 .04
53 Orel Hershiser .30 .09
54 Pat Mahomes .15 .04
55 Greg Colbrunn .15 .04
56 Greg Vaughn .15 .04
57 Vince Coleman .15 .04
58 Brian McRae .15 .04
59 Len Dykstra .30 .09
60 Dan Gladden .15 .04
61 Ted Power .15 .04
62 Donovan Osborne .15 .04
63 Ron Karkovice .15 .04
64 Frank Seminara .15 .04
65 Bob Zupcic .15 .04
66 Kirt Manwaring .15 .04
67 Mike Devereaux .15 .04
68 Mark Lemke .15 .04
69 Devon White .30 .09
70 Sammy Sosa 1.25 .35
71 Pedro Astacio .15 .04
72 Dennis Eckersley .30 .09
73 Chris Nabholz .15 .04
74 Melido Perez .15 .04
75 Todd Hundley .15 .04
76 Kent Hrbek .30 .09
77 Mickey Morandini .15 .04
78 Tim McIntosh .15 .04
79 Andy Van Slyke .30 .09
80 Kevin McReynolds .15 .04
81 Mike Henneman .15 .04
82 Greg W. Harris .15 .04
83 Sandy Alomar Jr. .15 .04
84 Mike Jackson .15 .04
85 Ozzie Guillen .15 .04
86 Jeff Blauser .15 .04
87 John Valentin .15 .04
88 Rey Sanchez .15 .04
89 Rick Sutcliffe .30 .09
90 Luis Gonzalez .30 .09
91 Jeff Fassero .15 .04
92 Kenny Rogers .30 .09
93 Bret Saberhagen .30 .09
94 Bob Welch .15 .04
95 Darren Daulton .30 .09
96 Mike Gallego .15 .04
97 Orlando Merced .15 .04
98 Chuck Knoblauch .30 .09
99 Bernard Gilkey .15 .04
100 Billy Ashley .15 .04
101 Kevin Appier .30 .09
102 Jeff Brantley .15 .04
103 Bill Gullickson .15 .04
104 John Smoltz .50 .15
105 Paul Sorrento .15 .04
106 Steve Buechele .15 .04
107 Steve Sax .15 .04
108 Andujar Cedeno .15 .04
109 Billy Hatcher .15 .04
110 Checklist .15 .04
111 Alan Mills .15 .04
112 John Franco .30 .09
113 Jack Morris .30 .09
114 Mitch Williams .15 .04
115 Nolan Ryan 3.00 .90
116 Jay Bell .30 .09
117 Mike Bordick .15 .04
118 Geronimo Pena .15 .04
119 Danny Tartabull .15 .04
120 Checklist .15 .04
121 Steve Avery .15 .04
122 Ricky Bones .15 .04
123 Mike Morgan .15 .04
124 Jeff Montgomery .15 .04
125 Jeff Bagwell .50 .15
126 Tony Phillips .15 .04
127 Lenny Harris .15 .04
128 Glenallen Hill .15 .04
129 Marquis Grissom .30 .09
130 Gerald Williams UER .15 .04
(Bernie Williams picture and stats)
131 Greg A. Harris .15 .04
132 Tommy Greene .15 .04
133 Chris Hoiles .15 .04
134 Bob Walk .15 .04
135 Duane Ward .15 .04
136 Tom Pagnozzi .15 .04
137 Jeff Huson .15 .04
138 Kurt Stillwell .15 .04
139 Dave Henderson .15 .04
140 Darrin Jackson .15 .04
141 Frank Castillo .15 .04
142 Scott Erickson .15 .04
143 Darryl Kile .30 .09
144 Bill Wegman .15 .04
145 Steve Wilson .15 .04
146 George Brett 2.00 .60
147 Moises Alou .30 .09
148 Lou Whitaker .30 .09
149 Chico Walker .15 .04
150 Jerry Browne .15 .04
151 Kirk McCaskill .15 .04
152 Zane Smith .15 .04
153 Matt Young .15 .04
154 Lee Smith .30 .09
155 Leo Gomez .15 .04
156 Dan Walters .15 .04
157 Pat Borders .15 .04
158 Matt Williams .30 .09
159 Dean Palmer .30 .09
160 John Patterson .15 .04
161 Doug Jones .15 .04
162 John Habyan .15 .04
163 Pedro Martinez 1.50 .45
164 Carl Willis .15 .04
165 Darrin Fletcher .15 .04
166 B.J. Surhoff .30 .09
167 Eddie Murray .75 .23
168 Keith Miller .15 .04
169 Ricky Jordan .15 .04
170 Juan Gonzalez .50 .15
171 Charles Nagy .15 .04
172 Mark Clark .15 .04
173 Bobby Thigpen .15 .04
174 Tim Scott .15 .04
175 Scott Cooper .15 .04
176 Royce Clayton .15 .04
177 Brady Anderson .30 .09
178 Sid Bream .15 .04
179 Derek Bell .15 .04
180 Otis Nixon .15 .04
181 Kevin Gross .15 .04
182 Ron Darling .15 .04
183 John Wetteland .30 .09
184 Mike Stanley .15 .04
185 Jeff Kent .75 .23
186 Brian Harper .15 .04
187 Mariano Duncan .15 .04
188 Robin Yount 1.25 .35
189 Al Martin .15 .04
190 Eddie Zosky .15 .04
191 Mike Munoz .15 .04
192 Andy Benes .15 .04
193 Dennis Cook .15 .04
194 Bill Swift .15 .04
195 Frank Thomas .75 .23
195A Frank Thomas 1.25 .35
Franklin visible on batting glove
196 Damon Berryhill .15 .04
197 Mike Greenwell .15 .04
198 Mark Grace .50 .15
199 Darryl Hamilton .15 .04
200 Derrick May .15 .04
201 Ken Hill .15 .04
202 Kevin Brown .30 .09
203 Dwight Gooden .30 .09
204 Bobby Witt .15 .04
205 Juan Bell .15 .04
206 Kevin Maas .15 .04
207 Jeff King .15 .04
208 Scott Leius .15 .04
209 Rheal Cormier .15 .04
210 Darryl Strawberry .30 .09
211 Tom Gordon .15 .04
212 Bud Black .15 .04
213 Mickey Tettleton .15 .04
214 Pete Smith .15 .04
215 Felix Fermin .15 .04
216 Rick Wilkins .15 .04
217 George Bell .15 .04
218 Eric Anthony .15 .04
219 Pedro Munoz .15 .04
220 Checklist .15 .04
221 Lance Blankenship .15 .04
222 Deion Sanders .50 .15
223 Craig Biggio .50 .15
224 Ryne Sandberg 1.25 .35
225 Ron Gant .30 .09
226 Tom Brunansky .15 .04
227 Chad Curtis .15 .04
228 Joe Carter .30 .09
229 Brian Jordan .30 .09
230 Brett Butler .30 .09
231 Frank Bolick .15 .04
232 Rod Beck .15 .04
233 Carlos Baerga .15 .04
234 Eric Karros .30 .09
235 Jack Armstrong .15 .04
236 Bobby Bonilla .30 .09
237 Don Mattingly 2.00 .60
238 Jeff Gardner .15 .04
239 Dave Hollins .15 .04
240 Steve Cooke .15 .04
241 Jose Canseco .75 .23
242 Ivan Calderon .15 .04
243 Tim Belcher .15 .04
244 Freddie Benavides .15 .04
245 Roberto Alomar .50 .15
246 Rob Deer .15 .04
247 Will Clark .75 .23
248 Mike Felder .15 .04
249 Harold Baines .30 .09
250 David Cone .30 .09
251 Mark Guthrie .15 .04
252 Ellis Burks .30 .09
253 Jim Abbott .50 .15
254 Chili Davis .30 .09
255 Chris Bosio .15 .04
256 Bret Barberie .15 .04
257 Hal Morris .15 .04
258 Dante Bichette .30 .09
259 Storm Davis .15 .04
260 Gary DiSarcina .15 .04
261 Ken Caminiti .30 .09
262 Paul Molitor .50 .15
263 Joe Oliver .15 .04
264 Pat Listach .15 .04
265 Gregg Jefferies .15 .04
266 Jose Guzman .15 .04
267 Eric Davis .30 .09
268 Delino DeShields .15 .04
269 Barry Bonds 2.00 .60
270 Mike Bielecki .15 .04
271 Jay Buhner .30 .09
272 Scott Pose RC .15 .04
273 Tony Fernandez .15 .04
274 Chito Martinez .15 .04
275 Phil Plantier .15 .04
276 Pete Incaviglia .15 .04
277 Carlos Garcia .15 .04
278 Tom Henke .15 .04
279 Roger Clemens 1.50 .45
280 Rob Dibble .30 .09
281 Daryl Boston .15 .04
282 Greg Gagne .15 .04
283 Cecil Fielder .30 .09
284 Carlton Fisk .50 .15
285 Wade Boggs .50 .15
286 Damion Easley .15 .04
287 Norm Charlton .15 .04
288 Jeff Conine .30 .09
289 Roberto Kelly .15 .04
290 Jerald Clark .15 .04
291 Rickey Henderson .75 .23
292 Chuck Finley .30 .09
293 Doug Drabek .15 .04
294 Dave Stewart .30 .09
295 Tom Glavine .50 .15
296 Jaime Navarro .15 .04
297 Ray Lankford .15 .04
298 Greg Hibbard .15 .04
299 Jody Reed .15 .04
300 Dennis Martinez .30 .09
301 Dave Martinez .15 .04
302 Reggie Jefferson .15 .04
303 John Cummings RC .15 .04
304 Orestes Destrade .15 .04
305 Mike Maddux .15 .04
306 David Segui .15 .04
307 Gary Sheffield .30 .09
308 Danny Jackson .15 .04
309 Craig Lefferts .15 .04
310 Andre Dawson .30 .09
311 Barry Larkin .50 .15
312 Alex Cole .15 .04
313 Mark Gardner .15 .04
314 Kirk Gibson .30 .09
315 Shane Mack .15 .04
316 Bo Jackson .75 .23
317 Jimmy Key .30 .09
318 Greg Myers .15 .04
319 Ken Griffey Jr. 1.25 .35
320 Monty Fariss .15 .04
321 Kevin Mitchell .15 .04
322 Andres Galarraga .30 .09
323 Mark McGwire 2.00 .60
324 Mark Langston .15 .04
325 Steve Finley .30 .09
326 Greg Maddux 1.25 .35
327 Dave Nilsson .15 .04
328 Ozzie Smith 1.25 .35
329 Candy Maldonado .15 .04
330 Checklist .15 .04
331 Tim Pugh RC .15 .04
332 Joe Girardi .15 .04
333 Junior Felix .15 .04
334 Greg Swindell .15 .04
335 Ramon Martinez .15 .04
336 Sean Berry .15 .04
337 Joe Orsulak .15 .04
338 Wes Chamberlain .15 .04
339 Stan Belinda .15 .04
340 Checklist UER .15 .04
(306 Luis Mercedes)
341 Bruce Hurst .15 .04
342 John Burkett .15 .04
343 Mike Mussina .50 .15
344 Scott Fletcher .15 .04
345 Rene Gonzales .15 .04
346 Roberto Hernandez .15 .04
347 Carlos Martinez .15 .04
348 Bill Krueger .15 .04
349 Felix Jose .15 .04
350 John Jaha .15 .04
351 Willie Banks .15 .04
352 Matt Nokes .15 .04
353 Kevin Seitzer .15 .04
354 Erik Hanson .15 .04
355 David Hulse RC .15 .04
356 Domingo Martinez RC .15 .04
357 Greg Olson .15 .04
358 Randy Myers .15 .04
359 Tom Browning .15 .04
360 Charlie Hayes .15 .04
361 Bryan Harvey .15 .04
362 Eddie Taubensee .15 .04
363 Tim Wallach .15 .04
364 Mel Rojas .15 .04
365 Frank Tanana .15 .04
366 John Kruk .30 .09
367 Tim Laker RC .15 .04
368 Rich Rodriguez .15 .04
369 Darren Lewis .15 .04
370 Harold Reynolds .30 .09
371 Jose Melendez .15 .04
372 Joe Grahe .15 .04
373 Lance Johnson .15 .04
374 Jose Mesa .15 .04
375 Scott Livingstone .15 .04
376 Wally Joyner .30 .09
377 Kevin Reimer .15 .04
378 Kirby Puckett .75 .23
379 Paul O'Neill .50 .15
380 Randy Johnson .75 .23
381 Manuel Lee .15 .04
382 Dick Schofield .15 .04
383 Darren Holmes .15 .04
384 Charlie Hough .30 .09
385 John Orton .15 .04
386 Edgar Martinez .50 .15
387 Terry Pendleton .30 .09
388 Dan Plesac .15 .04
389 Jeff Reardon .30 .09
390 David Nied .15 .04
391 Dave Magadan .15 .04
392 Larry Walker .50 .15
393 Ben Rivera .15 .04
394 Lonnie Smith .15 .04
395 Craig Shipley .15 .04
396 Willie McGee .30 .09
397 Arthur Rhodes .15 .04
398 Mike Stanton .15 .04
399 Luis Polonia .15 .04
400 Jack McDowell .15 .04
401 Mike Moore .15 .04
402 Jose Lind .15 .04
403 Bill Spiers .15 .04
404 Kevin Tapani .15 .04
405 Spike Owen .15 .04
406 Tino Martinez .50 .15
407 Charlie Leibrandt .15 .04
408 Ed Sprague .15 .04
409 Bryn Smith .15 .04
410 Benito Santiago .30 .09
411 Jose Rijo .15 .04
412 Pete O'Brien .15 .04
413 Willie Wilson .15 .04
414 Bip Roberts .15 .04
415 Eric Young .15 .04
416 Walt Weiss .15 .04
417 Milt Thompson .15 .04
418 Chris Sabo .15 .04
419 Scott Sanderson .15 .04
420 Tim Raines .30 .09
421 Alan Trammell .30 .09
422 Mike Macfarlane .15 .04
423 Dave Winfield .30 .09
424 Bob Wickman .15 .04
425 David Valle .15 .04
426 Gary Redus .15 .04
427 Turner Ward .15 .04
428 Reggie Sanders .15 .04
429 Todd Worrell .15 .04
430 Julio Valera .15 .04
431 Cal Ripken Jr. 2.50 .75
432 Mo Vaughn .30 .09
433 John Smiley .15 .04
434 Omar Vizquel .50 .15
435 Billy Ripken .15 .04
436 Cory Snyder .15 .04
437 Carlos Quintana .15 .04
438 Omar Olivares .15 .04
439 Robin Ventura .30 .09
440 Checklist .15 .04
441 Kevin Higgins .15 .04
442 Carlos Hernandez .15 .04
443 Dan Peltier .15 .04
444 Derek Lilliquist .15 .04
445 Tim Salmon .50 .15
446 Sherman Obando RC .15 .04
447 Pat Kelly .15 .04
448 Todd Van Poppel .15 .04
449 Mark Whiten .15 .04

450 Checklist .15 .04
451 Pat Meares RC .30 .09
452 Tony Tarasco RC .15 .04
453 Chris Gwynn .15 .04
454 Armando Reynoso .15 .04
455 Danny Darwin .15 .04
456 Willie Greene .15 .04
457 Mike Blowers .15 .04
458 Kevin Roberson RC .15 .04
459 Graeme Lloyd RC .30 .09
460 David West .15 .04
461 Joey Cora .15 .04
462 Alex Arias .15 .04
463 Chad Kreuter .15 .04
464 Mike Lansing RC .30 .09
465 Mike Timlin .15 .04
466 Paul Wagner .15 .04
467 Mark Portugal .15 .04
468 Jim Leyritz .15 .04
469 Ryan Klesko .30 .09
470 Mario Diaz .15 .04
471 Guillermo Velasquez .15 .04
472 Fernando Valenzuela .30 .09
473 Raul Mondesi .30 .09
474 Mike Pagliarulo .15 .04
475 Chris Hammond .15 .04
476 Torey Lovullo .15 .04
477 Trevor Wilson .15 .04
478 Marcos Armas RC .15 .04
479 Dave Gallagher .15 .04
480 Jeff Treadway .15 .04
481 Jeff Branson .15 .04
482 Dickie Thon .15 .04
483 Eduardo Perez .15 .04
484 David Wells .30 .09
485 Brian Williams .15 .04
486 Domingo Cedeno RC .15 .04
487 Tom Candiotti .15 .04
488 Steve Frey .15 .04
489 Greg McMichael RC .15 .04
490 Marc Newfield .15 .04
491 Larry Andersen .15 .04
492 Damon Buford .15 .04
493 Ricky Gutierrez .15 .04
494 Jeff Russell .15 .04
495 Vinny Castilla .30 .09
496 Wilson Alvarez .15 .04
497 Scott Bullett .15 .04
498 Larry Casian .15 .04
499 Jose Vizcaino .15 .04
500 J.T. Snow RC .50 .15
501 Bryan Hickerson .15 .04
502 Jeremy Hernandez .15 .04
503 Jeromy Burnitz .30 .09
504 Steve Farr .15 .04
505 J. Owens RC .15 .04
506 Craig Paquette .15 .04
507 Jim Eisenreich .15 .04
508 Matt Whiteside RC .15 .04
509 Luis Aquino .15 .04
510 Mike LaValliere .15 .04
511 Jim Gott .15 .04
512 Mark McLemore .15 .04
513 Randy Milligan .15 .04
514 Gary Gaetti .30 .09
515 Lou Frazier RC .15 .04
516 Rich Amaral .15 .04
517 Gene Harris .15 .04
518 Aaron Sele .15 .04
519 Mark Wohlers .15 .04
520 Scott Kamieniecki .15 .04
521 Kent Mercker .15 .04
522 Jim Deshaies .15 .04
523 Kevin Stocker .15 .04
524 Jason Bere .15 .04
525 Tim Bogar RC .15 .04
526 Brad Pennington .15 .04
527 Curt Leskanic RC .15 .04
528 Wayne Kirby .15 .04
529 Tim Costo .15 .04
530 Doug Henry .15 .04
531 Trevor Hoffman .30 .09
532 Kelly Gruber .15 .04
533 Mike Harkey .15 .04
534 John Doherty .15 .04
535 Erik Pappas .15 .04
536 Brent Gates .15 .04
537 Roger McDowell .15 .04
538 Chris Haney .15 .04
539 Blas Minor .15 .04
540 Pat Hentgen .15 .04
541 Chuck Carr .15 .04
542 Doug Strange .15 .04
543 Xavier Hernandez .15 .04
544 Paul Quantrill .15 .04
545 Anthony Young .15 .04
546 Bret Boone .50 .15
547 Dwight Smith .15 .04
548 Bobby Munoz .15 .04
549 Russ Springer .15 .04
550 Roger Pavlik .15 .04
DW Dave Winfield 1.00 .30
3000 Hits
FT Frank Thomas AU/3500 50.00 15.00
(Certified autograph)

1993 Leaf Fasttrack

These 20 standard-size cards, featuring a selection of talented young stars, were randomly inserted into 1993 Leaf retail packs; the first ten were series I inserts, the second ten were series II inserts.

	Nm-Mt	Ex-Mt
COMPLETE SET (20)	60.00	18.00
COMPLETE SERIES 1 (10)	40.00	12.00
COMPLETE SERIES 2 (10)	30.00	9.00

1 Frank Thomas 10.00 3.00
2 Tim Wakefield 2.00 .60
3 Kenny Lofton 4.00 1.20
4 Mike Mussina 6.00 1.80
5 Juan Gonzalez 6.00 1.80
6 Chuck Knoblauch 4.00 1.20
7 Eric Karros 4.00 1.20
8 Ray Lankford 2.00 .60
9 Juan Guzman 2.00 .60
10 Pat Listach 2.00 .60
11 Carlos Baerga 2.00 .60
12 Felix Jose 2.00 .60
13 Steve Avery 2.00 .60
14 Robin Ventura 4.00 1.20
15 Ivan Rodriguez 10.00 3.00
16 Cal Eldred 2.00 .60
17 Jeff Bagwell 6.00 1.80
18 David Justice 4.00 1.20
19 Travis Fryman 4.00 1.20
20 Marquis Grissom 4.00 1.20

1993 Leaf Gold All-Stars

These 30 standard-size dual-sided cards feature members of the American and National league All-Star squads. The first 20 were inserted one per 1993 Leaf jumbo packs; the first ten were series I inserts, the second ten were series II inserts. The final ten cards were randomly inserted in 1993 Leaf Update packs.

	Nm-Mt	Ex-Mt
COMPLETE REG.SET (20)	40.00	12.00
COMP. UPDATE SET (10)	12.00	3.60

R1 Ivan Rodriguez 1.25 .35
Darren Daulton
R2 Don Mattingly 3.00 .90
Fred McGriff
R3 Cecil Fielder .75 .23
Jeff Bagwell
R4 Carlos Baerga 2.00 .60
Ryne Sandberg
R5 Chuck Knoblauch .50 .15
Delino DeShields
R6 Robin Ventura .50 .15
Terry Pendleton
R7 Ken Griffey Jr. 2.00 .60
Andy Van Slyke
R8 Joe Carter .50 .15
Dave Justice
R9 Jose Canseco 1.50 .45
Tony Gwynn
R10 Dennis Eckersley .50 .15
Rob Dibble
R11 Mark McGwire 3.00 .90
Will Clark
R12 Frank Thomas 1.25 .35
Mark Grace
R13 Roberto Alomar .75 .23
Craig Biggio
R14 Cal Ripken 4.00 1.20
Barry Larkin
R15 Edgar Martinez .75 .23
Gary Sheffield
R16 Juan Gonzalez 3.00 .90
Barry Bonds
R17 Kirby Puckett 1.25 .35
Marquis Grissom
R18 Jim Abbott .75 .23
Tom Glavine
R19 Nolan Ryan 5.00 1.50
Greg Maddux
R20 Roger Clemens 2.50 .75
Doug Drabek
U1 Mark Langston .25 .07
Terry Mulholland
U2 Ivan Rodriguez 1.25 .35
Darren Daulton
U3 John Olerud .50 .15
John Kruk
U4 Roberto Alomar 2.00 .60
Ryne Sandberg
U5 Wade Boggs .75 .23
Gary Sheffield
U6 Cal Ripken 4.00 1.20
Barry Larkin
U7 Kirby Puckett 1.25 .35
Barry Bonds
U8 Ken Griffey Jr. 2.00 .60
Marquis Grissom
U9 Joe Carter .50 .15
David Justice
U10 Paul Molitor .75 .23
Mark Grace

1993 Leaf Gold Rookies

These cards of promising newcomers were randomly inserted into 1993 Leaf packs; the first ten in series I, the last ten in series II, and five in the Update product. Leaf produced jumbo (3 1/2 by 5 inch) versions for retail repacks; they are valued at approximately double the prices below.

	Nm-Mt	Ex-Mt
COMPLETE REG.SET (20)	30.00	9.00
COMP. UPDATE SET (5)	20.00	6.00

*JUMBOS:2X BASIC GOLD ROOKIES.
JUMBOS DIST.IN RETAIL PACKS

R1 Kevin Young 2.00 .60
R2 Wil Cordero 1.00 .30
R3 Mark Kiefer 1.00 .30
R4 Gerald Williams 1.00 .30
R5 Brandon Wilson 1.00 .30
R6 Greg Gohr 1.00 .30
R7 Ryan Thompson 1.00 .30
R8 Tim Wakefield 5.00 1.50
R9 Troy Neel 1.00 .30
R10 Tim Salmon 3.00 .90
R11 Kevin Rogers 1.00 .30
R12 Rod Bolton 1.00 .30
R13 Ken Ryan 1.00 .30
R14 Phil Hiatt 1.00 .30
R15 Rene Arocha 2.00 .60
R16 Nigel Wilson 1.00 .30
R17 J.T. Snow 3.00 .90
R18 Benji Gil 1.00 .30
R19 Chipper Jones 5.00 1.50
R20 Darrell Sherman 1.00 .30
U1 Allen Watson 1.00 .30
U2 Jeffrey Hammonds 1.00 .30
U3 David McCarty 1.00 .30
U4 Mike Piazza 8.00 2.40
U5 Roberto Mejia 1.00 .30

1993 Leaf Heading for the Hall

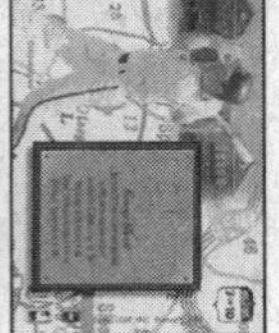

Randomly inserted into 1993 Leaf series 1 and 2 packs, this ten-card standard-size set features potential Hall of Famers. Cards 1-5 were series I inserts and cards 6-10 were series II inserts.

	Nm-Mt	Ex-Mt
COMPLETE SET (10)	30.00	9.00
COMPLETE SERIES 1 (5)	20.00	6.00
COMPLETE SERIES 2 (5)	10.00	3.00

1 Nolan Ryan 12.00 3.60
2 Tony Gwynn 4.00 1.20
3 Robin Yount 5.00 1.50
4 Eddie Murray 3.00 .90
5 Cal Ripken 10.00 3.00
6 Roger Clemens 6.00 1.80
7 George Brett 8.00 2.40
8 Ryne Sandberg 5.00 1.50
9 Kirby Puckett 3.00 .90
10 Ozzie Smith 5.00 1.50

1993 Leaf Thomas

This ten-card standard-size set spotlights Chicago White Sox slugger and Donruss/Leaf spokesperson Frank Thomas and were randomly inserted into all forms of Leaf packs. Five cards were inserted in each of the two series. Jumbo (5" by 7") versions of these cards were issued one per box of Leaf Update. The Jumbos are individually numbered out of 7,500.

	Nm-Mt	Ex-Mt
COMMON (1-10)	2.00	.60

*JUMBOS: .6X TO 1.5X BASIC THOMAS
ONE JUMBO CARD PER UPDATE BOX

1994 Leaf

The 1994 Leaf baseball set consists of two series of 220 standard-size cards for a total of 440. Randomly seeded "Super Packs" contained complete insert sets. Cards featuring players from the Texas Rangers, Cleveland Indians, Milwaukee Brewers and Houston Astros were held out of the first series in order to have up-to-date photography in each team's new uniforms. A limited number of players from the San Francisco Giants are featured in the first series because of minor modifications to the team's uniforms. Randomly inserted in hobby packs at a rate of one in 36 was a stamped version of Frank Thomas' 1990 Leaf rookie card.

	Nm-Mt	Ex-Mt
COMPLETE SET (440)	24.00	7.25
COMP. SERIES 1 (220)	12.00	3.60
COMP. SERIES 2 (220)	12.00	3.60

1 Cal Ripken Jr. 2.50 .75
2 Tony Tarasco .15 .04
3 Joe Girardi .15 .04
4 Bernie Williams .50 .15
5 Chad Kreuter .15 .04
6 Troy Neel .15 .04
7 Tom Pagnozzi .15 .04
8 Kirk Rueter .30 .09
9 Chris Bosio .15 .04
10 Dwight Gooden .30 .09
11 Mariano Duncan .15 .04
12 Jay Bell .30 .09
13 Lance Johnson .15 .04
14 Richie Lewis .15 .04
15 Dave Martinez .15 .04
16 Orel Hershiser .30 .09
17 Rob Butler .15 .04
18 Glenallen Hill .15 .04
19 Chad Curtis .15 .04
20 Mike Stanton .15 .04
21 Tim Wallach .15 .04
22 Milt Thompson .15 .04
23 Kevin Young .15 .04
24 John Smiley .15 .04
25 Jeff Montgomery .15 .04
26 Robin Ventura .30 .09
27 Scott Lydy .15 .04
28 Todd Stottlemyre .15 .04
29 Mark Whiten .15 .04
30 Robby Thompson .15 .04
31 Bobby Bonilla .30 .09
32 Andy Ashby .15 .04
33 Greg Myers .15 .04
34 Billy Hatcher .15 .04
35 Brad Holman .15 .04
36 Mark McLemore .15 .04
37 Scott Sanders .15 .04
38 Jim Abbott .50 .15
39 David Wells .30 .09
40 Roberto Kelly .15 .04
41 Jeff Conine .30 .09
42 Sean Berry .15 .04
43 Mark Grace .50 .15
44 Eric Young .15 .04
45 Rick Aguilera .15 .04
46 Chipper Jones .75 .23
47 Mel Rojas .15 .04
48 Ryan Thompson .15 .04
49 Al Martin .15 .04
50 Cecil Fielder .30 .09
51 Pat Kelly .15 .04
52 Kevin Tapani .15 .04
53 Tim Costo .15 .04
54 Dave Hollins .15 .04
55 Kirt Manwaring .15 .04
56 Gregg Jefferies .15 .04
57 Ron Darling .15 .04
58 Bill Haselman .15 .04
59 Phil Plantier .15 .04
60 Frank Viola .30 .09
61 Todd Zeile .15 .04
62 Bret Barberie .15 .04
63 Roberto Mejia .15 .04
64 Chuck Knoblauch .30 .09
65 Jose Lind .15 .04
66 Brady Anderson .30 .09
67 Ruben Sierra .15 .04
68 Jose Vizcaino .15 .04
69 Joe Grahe .15 .04
70 Kevin Appier .30 .09
71 Wilson Alvarez .15 .04
72 Tom Candiotti .15 .04
73 John Burkett .15 .04
74 Anthony Young .15 .04
75 Scott Cooper .15 .04
76 Nigel Wilson .15 .04
77 John Valentin .15 .04
78 David McCarty .15 .04
79 Archi Cianfrocco .15 .04
80 Lou Whitaker .30 .09
81 Dante Bichette .30 .09
82 Mark Dewey .15 .04
83 Danny Jackson .15 .04
84 Harold Baines .30 .09
85 Todd Benzinger .15 .04
86 Damion Easley .15 .04
87 Danny Cox .15 .04
88 Jose Bautista .15 .04
89 Mike Lansing .15 .04
90 Phil Hiatt .15 .04
91 Tim Pugh .15 .04
92 Tino Martinez .50 .15
93 Raul Mondesi .30 .09
94 Greg Maddux 1.25 .35
95 Al Leiter .30 .09
96 Benito Santiago .30 .09
97 Lenny Dykstra .30 .09
98 Sammy Sosa 1.50 .45
99 Tim Bogar .15 .04
100 Checklist .15 .04
101 Deion Sanders .50 .15
102 Bobby Witt .15 .04
103 Wil Cordero .15 .04
104 Rich Amaral .15 .04
105 Mike Mussina .50 .15
106 Reggie Sanders .30 .09
107 Ozzie Guillen .15 .04
108 Paul O'Neill .50 .15
109 Tim Salmon .50 .15
110 Rheal Cormier .15 .04
111 Billy Ashley .15 .04
112 Jeff Kent .30 .09
113 Derek Bell .15 .04
114 Danny Darwin .15 .04
115 Chip Hale .15 .04
116 Tim Raines .30 .09
117 Ed Sprague .15 .04
118 Darrin Fletcher .15 .04
119 Darren Holmes .15 .04
120 Alan Trammell .30 .09
121 Don Mattingly 2.00 .60
122 Greg Gagne .15 .04
123 Jose Offerman .15 .04
124 Joe Orsulak .15 .04
125 Jack McDowell .15 .04
126 Barry Larkin .50 .15
127 Ben McDonald .15 .04
128 Mike Bordick .15 .04
129 Devon White .30 .09
130 Mike Perez .15 .04
131 Jay Buhner .30 .09
132 Phil Leftwich RC .15 .04
133 Tommy Greene .15 .04
134 Charlie Hayes .15 .04
135 Don Slaught .15 .04
136 Mike Gallego .15 .04
137 Dave Winfield .30 .09
138 Steve Avery .15 .04
139 Derrick May .15 .04
140 Bryan Harvey .15 .04
141 Wally Joyner .30 .09
142 Andre Dawson .30 .09
143 Andy Benes .15 .04
144 John Franco .30 .09
145 Jeff King .15 .04
146 Joe Oliver .15 .04
147 Bill Gullickson .15 .04
148 Armando Reynoso .15 .04
149 Dave Fleming .15 .04
150 Checklist .15 .04
151 Todd Van Poppel .15 .04
152 Bernard Gilkey .15 .04
153 Kevin Gross .15 .04
154 Mike Devereaux .15 .04
155 Tim Wakefield .30 .09
156 Andres Galarraga .30 .09
157 Pat Meares .15 .04
158 Jim Leyritz .15 .04
159 Mike Macfarlane .15 .04
160 Tony Phillips .15 .04
161 Brent Gates .15 .04
162 Mark Langston .15 .04
163 Allen Watson .15 .04
164 Randy Johnson .75 .23
165 Doug Brocail .15 .04
166 Rob Dibble .30 .09
167 Roberto Hernandez .15 .04
168 Felix Jose .15 .04
169 Steve Cooke .15 .04
170 Darren Daulton .30 .09
171 Eric Karros .30 .09
172 Geronimo Pena .15 .04
173 Gary DiSarcina .15 .04
174 Marquis Grissom .30 .09
175 Joey Cora .15 .04
176 Jim Eisenreich .15 .04
177 Brad Pennington .15 .04
178 Terry Steinbach .15 .04
179 Pat Borders .15 .04
180 Steve Buechele .15 .04
181 Jeff Fassero .15 .04
182 Mike Greenwell .15 .04
183 Mike Henneman .15 .04
184 Ron Karkovice .15 .04
185 Pat Hentgen .15 .04
186 Jose Guzman .15 .04
187 Brett Butler .30 .09
188 Charlie Hough .30 .09
189 Terry Pendleton .30 .09
190 Melido Perez .15 .04
191 Orestes Destrade .15 .04
192 Mike Morgan .15 .04
193 Joe Carter .30 .09
194 Jeff Blauser .15 .04
195 Chris Hoiles .15 .04
196 Ricky Gutierrez .15 .04
197 Mike Moore .15 .04
198 Carl Willis .15 .04
199 Aaron Sele .15 .04
200 Checklist .15 .04
201 Tim Naehring .15 .04
202 Scott Livingstone .15 .04
203 Luis Alicea .15 .04
204 Torey Lovullo .15 .04
205 Jim Gott .15 .04
206 Bob Wickman .15 .04
207 Greg McMichael .15 .04
208 Scott Brosius .30 .09
209 Chris Gwynn .15 .04
210 Steve Sax .15 .04
211 Dick Schofield .15 .04
212 Robb Nen .30 .09
213 Ben Rivera .15 .04
214 Vinny Castilla .30 .09
215 Jamie Moyer .30 .09
216 Wally Whitehurst .15 .04
217 Frank Castillo .15 .04
218 Mike Blowers .15 .04
219 Tim Scott .15 .04
220 Paul Wagner .15 .04
221 Jeff Bagwell .50 .15
222 Ricky Bones .15 .04
223 Sandy Alomar Jr. .15 .04
224 Rod Beck .15 .04
225 Roberto Alomar .50 .15
226 Jack Armstrong .15 .04
227 Scott Erickson .15 .04
228 Rene Arocha .15 .04
229 Eric Anthony .15 .04
230 Jeromy Burnitz .30 .09
231 Kevin Brown .30 .09
232 Tim Belcher .15 .04
233 Bret Boone .30 .09
234 Dennis Eckersley .30 .09
235 Tom Glavine .50 .15
236 Craig Biggio .50 .15
237 Pedro Astacio .15 .04
238 Ryan Bowen .15 .04
239 Brad Ausmus .15 .04
240 Vince Coleman .15 .04
241 Jason Bere .15 .04
242 Ellis Burks .30 .09
243 Wes Chamberlain .15 .04
244 Ken Caminiti .30 .09
245 Willie Banks .15 .04
246 Sid Fernandez .15 .04
247 Carlos Baerga .15 .04
248 Carlos Garcia .15 .04
249 Jose Canseco .75 .23
250 Alex Diaz .15 .04
251 Albert Belle .30 .09
252 Moises Alou .30 .09
253 Bobby Ayala .15 .04
254 Tony Gwynn 1.00 .30
255 Roger Clemens 1.50 .45
256 Eric Davis .30 .09
257 Wade Boggs .50 .15
258 Chili Davis .30 .09
259 Rickey Henderson .75 .23
260 Andujar Cedeno .15 .04
261 Cris Carpenter .15 .04
262 Juan Guzman .15 .04
263 David Justice .30 .09
264 Barry Bonds 2.00 .60

265 Pete Incaviglia .15 .04
266 Tony Fernandez .15 .04
267 Cal Eldred .15 .04
268 Alex Fernandez .15 .04
269 Kent Hrbek .30 .09
270 Steve Farr .15 .04
271 Doug Drabek .15 .04
272 Brian Jordan .30 .09
273 Xavier Hernandez .15 .04
274 David Cone .30 .09
275 Brian Hunter .15 .04
276 Mike Harkey .15 .04
277 Delino DeShields .15 .04
278 David Hulse .15 .04
279 Mickey Tettleton .15 .04
280 Kevin McReynolds .15 .04
281 Darryl Hamilton .15 .04
282 Ken Hill .15 .04
283 Wayne Kirby .15 .04
284 Chris Hammond .15 .04
285 Mo Vaughn .30 .09
286 Ryan Klesko .30 .09
287 Rick Wilkins .15 .04
288 Bill Swift .15 .04
289 Rafael Palmeiro .50 .15
290 Brian Harper .15 .04
291 Chris Turner .15 .04
292 Luis Gonzalez .30 .09
293 Kenny Rogers .30 .09
294 Kirby Puckett .75 .23
295 Mickey Stanley .15 .04
296 Carlos Reyes RC .15 .04
297 Charles Nagy .15 .04
298 Reggie Jefferson .15 .04
299 Bip Roberts .15 .04
300 Darrin Jackson .15 .04
301 Mike Jackson .15 .04
302 Dave Nilsson .15 .04
303 Ramon Martinez .15 .04
304 Bobby Jones .15 .04
305 Johnny Ruffin .15 .04
306 Brian McRae .15 .04
307 Bo Jackson .75 .23
308 Dave Stewart .30 .09
309 John Smoltz .50 .15
310 Dennis Martinez .30 .09
311 Dean Palmer .30 .09
312 David Nied .15 .04
313 Eddie Murray .75 .23
314 Darryl Kile .30 .09
315 Rick Sutcliffe .30 .09
316 Shawon Dunston .15 .04
317 John Jaha .15 .04
318 Salomon Torres .15 .04
319 Gary Sheffield .30 .09
320 Curt Schilling .30 .09
321 Greg Vaughn .15 .04
322 Jay Howell .15 .04
323 Todd Hundley .15 .04
324 Chris Sabo .15 .04
325 Stan Javier .15 .04
326 Willie Greene .15 .04
327 Hipolito Pichardo .15 .04
328 Doug Strange .15 .04
329 Dan Wilson .15 .04
330 Checklist .15 .04
331 Omar Vizquel .50 .15
332 Scott Servais .15 .04
333 Bob Tewksbury .15 .04
334 Matt Williams .30 .09
335 Tom Foley .15 .04
336 Jeff Russell .15 .04
337 Scott Leius .15 .04
338 Ivan Rodriguez .75 .23
339 Kevin Seitzer .15 .04
340 Jose Rijo .15 .04
341 Eduardo Perez .15 .04
342 Kirk Gibson .30 .09
343 Randy Milligan .15 .04
344 Edgar Martinez .50 .15
345 Fred McGriff .50 .15
346 Kurt Abbott RC .30 .09
347 John Kruk .30 .09
348 Mike Felder .15 .04
349 Dave Staton .15 .04
350 Kenny Lofton .30 .09
351 Graeme Lloyd .15 .04
352 David Segui .15 .04
353 Danny Tartabull .15 .04
354 Bob Welch .15 .04
355 Duane Ward .15 .04
356 Karl Rhodes .15 .04
357 Lee Smith .30 .09
358 Chris James .15 .04
359 Walt Weiss .15 .04
360 Pedro Munoz .15 .04
361 Paul Sorrento .15 .04
362 Todd Worrell .15 .04
363 Bob Hamelin .15 .04
364 Julio Franco .30 .09
365 Roberto Petagine .15 .04
366 Willie McGee .30 .09
367 Pedro Martinez .75 .23
368 Ken Griffey Jr. 1.25 .35
369 B.J. Surhoff .30 .09
370 Kevin Mitchell .15 .04
371 John Doherty .15 .04
372 Manuel Lee .15 .04
373 Terry Mulholland .15 .04
374 Zane Smith .15 .04
375 Otis Nixon .15 .04
376 Jody Reed .15 .04
377 Doug Jones .15 .04
378 John Olerud .30 .09
379 Greg Swindell .15 .04
380 Checklist .15 .04
381 Royce Clayton .15 .04
382 Jim Thome .75 .23
383 Steve Finley .30 .09
384 Ray Lankford .15 .04
385 Henry Rodriguez .15 .04
386 Dave Magadan .15 .04
387 Gary Redus .15 .04
388 Orlando Merced .15 .04
389 Tom Gordon .15 .04
390 Luis Polonia .15 .04
391 Mark McGwire 2.00 .60
392 Mark Lemke .15 .04
393 Doug Henry .15 .04
394 Chuck Finley .30 .09
395 Paul Molitor .50 .15
396 Randy Myers .15 .04
397 Larry Walker .50 .15
398 Pete Harnisch .15 .04
399 Darren Lewis .15 .04
400 Frank Thomas .75 .23
401 Jack Morris .30 .09
402 Greg Hibbard .15 .04
403 Jeffrey Hammonds .15 .04
404 Will Clark .75 .23
405 Travis Fryman .30 .09
406 Scott Sanderson .15 .04
407 Gene Harris .15 .04
408 Chuck Carr .15 .04
409 Ozzie Smith 1.25 .35
410 Kent Mercker .15 .04
411 Andy Van Slyke .30 .09
412 Jimmy Key .30 .09
413 Pat Mahomes .15 .04
414 John Wetteland .30 .09
415 Todd Jones .15 .04
416 Greg Harris .15 .04
417 Kevin Stocker .15 .04
418 Juan Gonzalez .50 .15
419 Pete Smith .15 .04
420 Pat Listach .15 .04
421 Trevor Hoffman .30 .09
422 Scott Fletcher .15 .04
423 Mark Lewis .15 .04
424 Mickey Morandini .15 .04
425 Ryne Sandberg 1.25 .35
426 Erik Hanson .15 .04
427 Gary Gaetti .30 .09
428 Harold Reynolds .30 .09
429 Mark Portugal .15 .04
430 David Valle .15 .04
431 Mitch Williams .15 .04
432 Howard Johnson .15 .04
433 Hal Morris .15 .04
434 Tom Henke .15 .04
435 Shane Mack .15 .04
436 Mike Piazza 1.50 .45
437 Bret Saberhagen .30 .09
438 Jose Mesa .15 .04
439 Jaime Navarro .15 .04
440 Checklist .15 .04
A300 Frank Thomas .75 .23
Leaf 5th Anniversary

1994 Leaf Clean-Up Crew

Inserted in magazine jumbo packs at a rate of one in 12, this 12-card set was issued in two series of six.

Nm-Mt Ex-Mt
COMPLETE SET (12) 30.00 9.00
COMPLETE SERIES 1 (6) 10.00 3.00
COMPLETE SERIES 2 (6) 20.00 6.00
1 Larry Walker 5.00 1.50
2 Andres Galarraga 3.00 .90
3 Dave Hollins 1.50 .45
4 Bobby Bonilla 3.00 .90
5 Cecil Fielder 3.00 .90
6 Danny Tartabull 1.50 .45
7 Juan Gonzalez 5.00 1.50
8 Joe Carter 3.00 .90
9 Fred McGriff 5.00 1.50
10 Matt Williams 3.00 .90
11 Albert Belle 3.00 .90
12 Harold Baines 3.00 .90

1994 Leaf Gamers

A close-up photo of the player highlights this 12-card standard-size set that was issued in two series of six. They were randomly inserted in jumbo packs at a rate of one in eight.

Nm-Mt Ex-Mt
COMPLETE SET (12) 80.00 24.00
COMPLETE SERIES 1 (6) 40.00 12.00
COMPLETE SERIES 2 (6) 40.00 12.00
1 Ken Griffey Jr. 10.00 3.00
2 Lenny Dykstra 2.50 .75
3 Juan Gonzalez 4.00 1.20
4 Don Mattingly 15.00 4.50
5 David Justice 2.50 .75
6 Mark Grace 4.00 1.20
7 Frank Thomas 6.00 1.80
8 Barry Bonds 15.00 4.50
9 Kirby Puckett 6.00 1.80
10 Will Clark 6.00 1.80
11 John Kruk 2.50 .75
12 Mike Piazza 12.00 3.60

1994 Leaf Gold Rookies

This set, which was randomly inserted in first series packs at a rate of one in 18 and second series packs at a rate of one in twelve, features 20 of the hottest young stars in the majors.

Nm-Mt Ex-Mt
COMPLETE SERIES 1 (10) 10.00 3.00
COMPLETE SERIES 2 (10) 5.00 1.50
1 Javier Lopez 1.50 .45

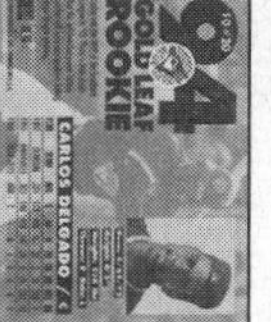

2 Rondell White 1.50 .45
3 Butch Huskey 1.00 .30
4 Midre Cummings 1.00 .30
5 Scott Ruffcorn 1.00 .30
6 Manny Ramirez 2.50 .75
7 Danny Bautista 1.00 .30
8 Russ Davis 1.00 .30
9 Steve Karsay 1.00 .30
10 Carlos Delgado 2.50 .75
11 Bob Hamelin 1.00 .30
12 Marcus Moore 1.00 .30
13 Miguel Jimenez 1.00 .30
14 Matt Walbeck 1.00 .30
15 James Mouton 1.00 .30
16 Rich Becker 1.00 .30
17 Brian Anderson 1.50 .45
18 Cliff Floyd 1.50 .45
19 Steve Trachsel 1.00 .30
20 Hector Carrasco 1.00 .30

1994 Leaf Gold Stars

Randomly inserted in all packs at a rate of one in 90, the 15 standard-size cards in this set are individually numbered and limited to 10,000 per player. The cards were issued in two series with eight cards in series one and seven in series two. They are numbered "X/10,000".

Nm-Mt Ex-Mt
COMPLETE SET (15) 150.00 45.00
COMPLETE SERIES 1 (8) 100.00 30.00
COMPLETE SERIES 2 (7) 50.00 15.00
1 Roberto Alomar 8.00 2.40
2 Barry Bonds 30.00 9.00
3 David Justice 5.00 1.50
4 Ken Griffey Jr. 20.00 6.00
5 Lenny Dykstra 5.00 1.50
6 Don Mattingly 30.00 9.00
7 Andres Galarraga 5.00 1.50
8 Greg Maddux 20.00 6.00
9 Carlos Baerga 2.50 .75
10 Paul Molitor 8.00 2.40
11 Frank Thomas 12.00 3.60
12 John Olerud 5.00 1.50
13 Juan Gonzalez 8.00 2.40
14 Fred McGriff 8.00 2.40
15 Jack McDowell 2.50 .75

1994 Leaf MVP Contenders

This 30-card standard-size set contains 15 players from each league who were projected to be 1994 MVP hopefuls. These unnumbered cards were randomly inserted in all second series packs at a rate of one in 36. If the player appearing on the card was named his league's MVP (Frank Thomas American League and Jeff Bagwell National League), the card could be redeemed for a 5" x 7" Frank Thomas card individually numbered out of 20,000. The backs contain all the rules and read "1 of 10,000". The expiration for redeeming Thomas and Bagwell cards was Jan. 19, 1995.

Nm-Mt Ex-Mt
COMPLETE SET (30) 150.00 45.00
*GOLD: SAME PRICE AS BASIC MVPS
ONE GOLD SET PER A12 OR N2 VIA MAIL
ONE THOMAS J400 PER A12 OR N2 VIA MAIL
THOMAS J400 PRINT RUN 20,000 #'d CARDS
A1 Albert Belle 3.00 .90
A2 Jose Canseco 8.00 2.40
A3 Joe Carter 3.00 .90
A4 Will Clark 8.00 2.40
A5 Cecil Fielder 3.00 .90
A6 Juan Gonzalez 5.00 1.50
A7 Ken Griffey Jr. 12.00 3.60
A8 Paul Molitor 5.00 1.50
A9 Rafael Palmeiro 5.00 1.50
A10 Kirby Puckett 8.00 2.40
A11 Cal Ripken Jr. 25.00 7.50
A12 Frank Thomas W 6.00 1.80
A13 Mo Vaughn 3.00 .90
A14 Carlos Baerga 1.50 .45
A15 AL Bonus Card 1.50 .45
N1 Gary Sheffield 3.00 .90
N2 Jeff Bagwell W 5.00 1.50
N3 Dante Bichette 3.00 .90
N4 Barry Bonds 20.00 6.00
N5 Darren Daulton 3.00 .90
N6 Andres Galarraga 3.00 .90
N7 Gregg Jefferies 1.50 .45
N8 David Justice 3.00 .90
N9 Ray Lankford 1.50 .45
N10 Fred McGriff 5.00 1.50
N11 Barry Larkin 5.00 1.50
N12 Mike Piazza 15.00 4.50
N13 Deion Sanders 5.00 1.50
N14 Matt Williams 3.00 .90
N15 NL Bonus Card 1.50 .45
J400 F.Thomas Jumbo 6.00 1.80

1994 Leaf Power Brokers

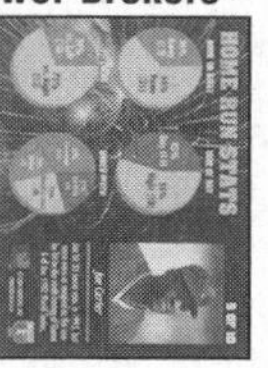

Inserted in second series retail and hobby foil packs at a rate of one in 12, this 10-card standard-size set spotlights top sluggers.

Nm-Mt Ex-Mt
COMPLETE SET (10) 20.00 6.00
1 Frank Thomas 2.00 .60
2 David Justice .75 .23
3 Barry Bonds 5.00 1.50
4 Juan Gonzalez 1.25 .35
5 Ken Griffey Jr. 3.00 .90
6 Mike Piazza 4.00 1.20
7 Cecil Fielder .75 .23
8 Fred McGriff 1.25 .35
9 Joe Carter .75 .23
10 Albert Belle .75 .23

1994 Leaf Slideshow

Randomly inserted in first and second series packs at a rate of one in 54, these ten standard-size cards simulate mounted photographic slides, but the images of the players are actually printed on acetate.

Nm-Mt Ex-Mt
COMPLETE SET (10) 50.00 15.00
COMPLETE SERIES 1 (5) 25.00 7.50
COMPLETE SERIES 2 (5) 25.00 7.50
1 Frank Thomas 5.00 1.50
2 Mike Piazza 10.00 3.00
3 Darren Daulton 2.00 .60
4 Ryne Sandberg 8.00 2.40
5 Roberto Alomar 3.00 .90
6 Barry Bonds 12.00 3.60
7 Juan Gonzalez 3.00 .90
8 Tim Salmon 3.00 .90
9 Ken Griffey Jr. 8.00 2.40
10 David Justice 2.00 .60

1994 Leaf Statistical Standouts

Inserted in retail and hobby foil packs at a rate of one in 12, this 10-card standard-size set features players that had significant statistical achievements in 1993. For example: Cal Ripken's home run record for a shortstop.

Nm-Mt Ex-Mt
COMPLETE SET (10) 15.00 4.50
1 Frank Thomas 1.25 .35
2 Barry Bonds 3.00 .90
3 Juan Gonzalez .75 .23
4 Mike Piazza 2.50 .75
5 Greg Maddux 2.00 .60
6 Ken Griffey Jr. 2.00 .60
7 Joe Carter .50 .15
8 Dave Winfield .50 .15
9 Tony Gwynn 1.50 .45
10 Cal Ripken 4.00 1.20

1995 Leaf

The 1995 Leaf set was issued in two series of 200 standard-size cards for a total of 400. Full-bleed fronts contain diamond-shaped player hologram in the upper left. The team name is done in silver foil up the left side. Peculiar backs contain two photos, the card number within a stamp or seal like emblem in the upper right and '94 and career stats graph toward bottom left. Hideo Nomo is the only key Rookie Card in this set.

Nm-Mt Ex-Mt
COMPLETE SET (400) 40.00 12.00
COMP. SERIES 1 (200) 15.00 4.50
COMP. SERIES 2 (200) 25.00 7.50
1 Frank Thomas .75 .23
2 Carlos Garcia .15 .04
3 Todd Hundley .15 .04
4 Damion Easley .15 .04
5 Roberto Mejia .15 .04
6 John Mabry .15 .04
7 Aaron Sele .15 .04
8 Kenny Lofton .30 .09
9 John Doherty .15 .04
10 Joe Carter .30 .09
11 Mike Lansing .15 .04
12 John Valentin .15 .04
13 Ismael Valdes .15 .04
14 Dave McCarty .15 .04
15 Melvin Nieves .15 .04
16 Bobby Jones .15 .04
17 Trevor Hoffman .30 .09
18 John Smoltz .50 .15
19 Leo Gomez .15 .04
20 Roger Pavlik .15 .04
21 Dean Palmer .30 .09
22 Rickey Henderson .75 .23
23 Eddie Taubensee .15 .04
24 Damon Buford .15 .04
25 Mark Wohlers .15 .04
26 Jim Edmonds .50 .15
27 Wilson Alvarez .15 .04
28 Matt Williams .30 .09
29 Jeff Montgomery .15 .04
30 Shawon Dunston .15 .04
31 Tom Pagnozzi .15 .04
32 Jose Lind .15 .04
33 Royce Clayton .15 .04
34 Cal Eldred .15 .04
35 Chris Gomez .15 .04
36 Henry Rodriguez .15 .04
37 Dave Fleming .15 .04
38 Jon Lieber .15 .04
39 Scott Servais .15 .04
40 Wade Boggs .50 .15
41 John Olerud .30 .09
42 Eddie Williams .15 .04
43 Paul Sorrento .15 .04
44 Ron Karkovice .15 .04
45 Kevin Foster .15 .04
46 Miguel Jimenez .15 .04
47 Reggie Sanders .15 .04
48 Rondell White .30 .09
49 Scott Leius .15 .04
50 Jose Valentin .15 .04
51 Wm. VanLandingham .15 .04
52 Denny Hocking .15 .04
53 Jeff Fassero .15 .04
54 Chris Hoiles .15 .04
55 Walt Weiss .15 .04
56 Geronimo Berroa .15 .04
57 Rich Rowland .15 .04
58 Dave Weathers .15 .04
59 Sterling Hitchcock .15 .04
60 Raul Mondesi .30 .09
61 Rusty Greer .30 .09
62 David Justice .30 .09
63 Cecil Fielder .30 .09
64 Brian Jordan .30 .09
65 Mike Lieberthal .30 .09
66 Rick Aguilera .15 .04
67 Chuck Finley .30 .09
68 Andy Ashby .15 .04
69 Alex Fernandez .15 .04
70 Ed Sprague .15 .04
71 Steve Buechele .15 .04
72 Willie Greene .15 .04
73 Dave Nilsson .15 .04
74 Bret Saberhagen .30 .09
75 Jimmy Key .30 .09
76 Darren Lewis .15 .04
77 Steve Cooke .15 .04
78 Kirk Gibson .30 .09
79 Ray Lankford .15 .04
80 Paul O'Neill .50 .15
81 Mike Bordick .15 .04
82 Wes Chamberlain .15 .04
83 Rico Brogna .15 .04
84 Kevin Appier .30 .09
85 Juan Guzman .15 .04
86 Kevin Seitzer .15 .04
87 Mickey Morandini .15 .04
88 Pedro Martinez .75 .23
89 Matt Mieske .15 .04
90 Tino Martinez .50 .15
91 Paul Shuey .15 .04
92 Bip Roberts .15 .04
93 Chili Davis .30 .09
94 Deion Sanders .50 .15
95 Darrell Whitmore .15 .04
96 Joe Orsulak .15 .04
97 Bret Boone .30 .09
98 Kent Mercker .15 .04
99 Scott Livingstone .15 .04
100 Brady Anderson .30 .09
101 James Mouton .15 .04
102 Jose Rijo .15 .04
103 Bobby Munoz .15 .04
104 Ramon Martinez .15 .04
105 Bernie Williams .50 .15
106 Troy Neel .15 .04
107 Ivan Rodriguez .75 .23
108 Salomon Torres .15 .04
109 Johnny Ruffin .15 .04
110 Darryl Kile .30 .09
111 Bobby Ayala .15 .04
112 Ron Darling .15 .04
113 Jose Lima .15 .04
114 Joey Hamilton .15 .04
115 Greg Maddux 1.25 .35
116 Greg Colbrunn .15 .04
117 Ozzie Guillen .15 .04
118 Brian Anderson .15 .04
119 Jeff Bagwell .50 .15
120 Pat Listach .15 .04
121 Sandy Alomar Jr. .15 .04
122 Jose Vizcaino .15 .04
123 Rick Helling .15 .04

124 Allen Watson .15 .04
125 Pedro Munoz .15 .04
126 Craig Biggio .50 .15
127 Kevin Stocker .15 .04
128 Wil Cordero .15 .04
129 Rafael Palmeiro .50 .15
130 Gar Finnvold .15 .04
131 Darren Hall .15 .04
132 Heathcliff Slocumb .15 .04
133 Darrin Fletcher .15 .04
134 Cal Ripken 2.50 .75
135 Dante Bichette .30 .09
136 Don Slaught .15 .04
137 Pedro Astacio .15 .04
138 Ryan Thompson .15 .04
139 Greg Gohr .15 .04
140 Javier Lopez .30 .09
141 Lenny Dykstra .30 .09
142 Pat Rapp .15 .04
143 Mark Kiefer .15 .04
144 Greg Gagne .15 .04
145 Eduardo Perez .15 .04
146 Felix Fermin .15 .04
147 Jeff Frye .15 .04
148 Terry Steinbach .15 .04
149 Jim Eisenreich .15 .04
150 Brad Ausmus .15 .04
151 Randy Myers .15 .04
152 Rick White .15 .04
153 Mark Portugal .15 .04
154 Delino DeShields .15 .04
155 Scott Cooper .15 .04
156 Pat Hentgen .15 .04
157 Mark Gubicza .15 .04
158 Carlos Baerga .15 .04
159 Joe Girardi .15 .04
160 Rey Sanchez .15 .04
161 Todd Jones .15 .04
162 Luis Polonia .15 .04
163 Steve Trachsel .15 .04
164 Roberto Hernandez .15 .04
165 John Patterson .15 .04
166 Rene Arocha .15 .04
167 Will Clark .75 .23
168 Jim Leyritz .15 .04
169 Todd Van Poppel .15 .04
170 Robb Nen .30 .09
171 Midre Cummings .15 .04
172 Jay Buhner .30 .09
173 Kevin Tapani .15 .04
174 Mark Lemke .15 .04
175 Marcus Moore .15 .04
176 Wayne Kirby .15 .04
177 Rich Amaral .15 .04
178 Lou Whitaker .30 .09
179 Jay Bell .30 .09
180 Rick Wilkins .15 .04
181 Paul Molitor .50 .15
182 Gary Sheffield .30 .09
183 Kirby Puckett .75 .23
184 Cliff Floyd .30 .09
185 Darren Oliver .15 .04
186 Tim Naehring .15 .04
187 John Hudek .15 .04
188 Eric Young .15 .04
189 Roger Salkeld .15 .04
190 Kirt Manwaring .15 .04
191 Kurt Abbott .15 .04
192 David Nied .15 .04
193 Todd Zeile .15 .04
194 Wally Joyner .30 .09
195 Dennis Martinez .30 .09
196 Billy Ashley .15 .04
197 Ben McDonald .15 .04
198 Bob Hamelin .15 .04
199 Chris Turner .15 .04
200 Lance Johnson .15 .04
201 Willie Banks .15 .04
202 Juan Gonzalez .50 .15
203 Scott Sanders .15 .04
204 Scott Brosius .30 .09
205 Curt Schilling .30 .09
206 Alex Gonzalez .15 .04
207 Travis Fryman .30 .09
208 Tim Raines .30 .09
209 Steve Avery .15 .04
210 Hal Morris .15 .04
211 Ken Griffey Jr. 1.25 .35
212 Ozzie Smith 1.25 .35
213 Chuck Carr .15 .04
214 Ryan Klesko .30 .09
215 Robin Ventura .30 .09
216 Luis Gonzalez .30 .09
217 Ken Ryan .15 .04
218 Mike Piazza 1.25 .35
219 Matt Walbeck .15 .04
220 Jeff Kent .30 .09
221 Orlando Miller .15 .04
222 Kenny Rogers .30 .09
223 J.T. Snow .30 .09
224 Alan Trammell .30 .09
225 John Franco .30 .09
226 Gerald Williams .15 .04
227 Andy Benes .15 .04
228 Dan Wilson .15 .04
229 Dave Hollins .15 .04
230 Vinny Castilla .30 .09
231 Devon White .30 .09
232 Fred McGriff .50 .15
233 Quilvio Veras .15 .04
234 Tom Candiotti .15 .04
235 Jason Bere .15 .04
236 Mark Langston .15 .04
237 Mel Rojas .15 .04
238 Chuck Knoblauch .30 .09
239 Bernard Gilkey .15 .04
240 Mark McGwire 2.00 .60
241 Kirk Rueter .15 .04
242 Pat Kelly .15 .04
243 Ruben Sierra .15 .04
244 Randy Johnson .75 .23
245 Shane Reynolds .15 .04
246 Danny Tartabull .15 .04
247 Darryl Hamilton .15 .04
248 Danny Bautista .15 .04
249 Tom Gordon .15 .04
250 Tom Glavine .50 .15
251 Orlando Merced .15 .04
252 Eric Karros .30 .09
253 Benji Gil .15 .04
254 Sean Bergman .15 .04
255 Roger Clemens 1.50 .45
256 Roberto Alomar .50 .15
257 Benito Santiago .30 .09
258 Robby Thompson .15 .04
259 Marvin Freeman .15 .04
260 Jose Offerman .15 .04
261 Greg Vaughn .15 .04
262 David Segui .15 .04
263 Geronimo Pena .15 .04
264 Tim Salmon .50 .15
265 Eddie Murray .75 .23
266 Mariano Duncan .15 .04
267 Hideo Nomo RC 1.50 .45
268 Derek Bell .15 .04
269 Mo Vaughn .30 .09
270 Jeff King .15 .04
271 Edgar Martinez .50 .15
272 Sammy Sosa 1.25 .35
273 Scott Ruffcorn .15 .04
274 Darren Daulton .30 .09
275 John Jaha .15 .04
276 Andres Galarraga .30 .09
277 Mark Grace .50 .15
278 Mike Moore .15 .04
279 Barry Bonds 2.00 .60
280 Manny Ramirez .50 .15
281 Ellis Burks .30 .09
282 Greg Swindell .15 .04
283 Barry Larkin .50 .15
284 Albert Belle .30 .09
285 Shawn Green .30 .09
286 John Roper .15 .04
287 Scott Erickson .15 .04
288 Moises Alou .30 .09
289 Mike Blowers .15 .04
290 Brent Gates .15 .04
291 Sean Berry .15 .04
292 Mike Stanley .15 .04
293 Jeff Conine .30 .09
294 Tim Wallach .15 .04
295 Bobby Bonilla .30 .09
296 Bruce Ruffin .15 .04
297 Chad Curtis .15 .04
298 Mike Greenwell .15 .04
299 Tony Gwynn 1.00 .30
300 Russ Davis .15 .04
301 Danny Jackson .15 .04
302 Pete Harnisch .15 .04
303 Don Mattingly 2.00 .60
304 Rheal Cormier .15 .04
305 Larry Walker .50 .15
306 Hector Carrasco .15 .04
307 Jason Jacome .15 .04
308 Phil Plantier .15 .04
309 Harold Baines .30 .09
310 Mitch Williams .15 .04
311 Charles Nagy .15 .04
312 Ken Caminiti .30 .09
313 Alex Rodriguez 2.00 .60
314 Chris Sabo .15 .04
315 Gary Gaetti .30 .09
316 Andre Dawson .30 .09
317 Mark Clark .15 .04
318 Vince Coleman .15 .04
319 Brad Clontz .15 .04
320 Steve Finley .30 .09
321 Doug Drabek .15 .04
322 Mark McLemore .15 .04
323 Stan Javier .15 .04
324 Ron Gant .30 .09
325 Charlie Hayes .15 .04
326 Carlos Delgado .30 .09
327 Ricky Bottalico .15 .04
328 Rod Beck .15 .04
329 Mark Acre .15 .04
330 Chris Bosio .15 .04
331 Tony Phillips .15 .04
332 Garret Anderson .30 .09
333 Pat Meares .15 .04
334 Todd Worrell .15 .04
335 Marquis Grissom .30 .09
336 Brent Mayne .15 .04
337 Lee Tinsley .15 .04
338 Terry Pendleton .30 .09
339 David Cone .30 .09
340 Tony Fernandez .15 .04
341 Jim Bullinger .15 .04
342 Armando Benitez .30 .09
343 John Smiley .15 .04
344 Dan Miceli .15 .04
345 Charles Johnson .30 .09
346 Lee Smith .30 .09
347 Brian McRae .15 .04
348 Jim Thome .75 .23
349 Jose Oliva .15 .04
350 Terry Mulholland .15 .04
351 Tom Henke .15 .04
352 Dennis Eckersley .30 .09
353 Sid Fernandez .15 .04
354 Paul Wagner .15 .04
355 John Dettmer .15 .04
356 John Wetteland .30 .09
357 John Burkett .15 .04
358 Marty Cordova .15 .04
359 Norm Charlton .15 .04
360 Mike Devereaux .15 .04
361 Alex Cole .15 .04
362 Brett Butler .30 .09
363 Mickey Tettleton .15 .04
364 Al Martin .15 .04
365 Tony Tarasco .15 .04
366 Pat Mahomes .15 .04
367 Gary DiSarcina .15 .04
368 Bill Swift .15 .04
369 Chipper Jones .75 .23
370 Orel Hershiser .30 .09
371 Kevin Gross .15 .04
372 Dave Winfield .30 .09
373 Andujar Cedeno .15 .04
374 Jim Abbott .50 .15
375 Glenallen Hill .15 .04
376 Otis Nixon .15 .04
377 Roberto Kelly .15 .04
378 Chris Hammond .15 .04
379 Mike Macfarlane .15 .04
380 J.R. Phillips .15 .04
381 Luis Alicea .15 .04
382 Bret Barberie .15 .04
383 Tom Goodwin .15 .04
384 Mark Whiten .15 .04
385 Jeffrey Hammonds .15 .04
386 Omar Vizquel .50 .15
387 Mike Mussina .50 .15
388 Ricky Bones .15 .04
389 Steve Ontiveros .15 .04
390 Jeff Blauser .15 .04
391 Jose Canseco .75 .23
392 Bob Tewksbury .15 .04
393 Jacob Brumfield .15 .04
394 Doug Jones .15 .04
395 Ken Hill .15 .04
396 Pat Borders .15 .04
397 Carl Everett .30 .09
398 Gregg Jefferies .15 .04
399 Jack McDowell .15 .04
400 Denny Neagle .30 .09

1995 Leaf 300 Club

Randomly inserted in first and second series mini and retail packs at a rate of one every 12 packs, this set depicts all 18 players who had a career average of .300 or better entering the 1995 campaign. Full-bleed backs list the 18 players and their averages to that point.

	Nm-Mt	Ex-Mt
COMPLETE SET (18)	100.00	30.00
COMPLETE SERIES 1 (9)	35.00	10.50
COMPLETE SERIES 2 (9)	65.00	19.50
1 Frank Thomas	6.00	1.80
2 Paul Molitor	4.00	1.20
3 Mike Piazza	10.00	3.00
4 Moises Alou	2.50	.75
5 Mike Greenwell	1.25	.35
6 Will Clark	6.00	1.80
7 Hal Morris	1.25	.35
8 Edgar Martinez	4.00	1.20
9 Carlos Baerga	1.25	.35
10 Ken Griffey Jr.	10.00	3.00
11 Wade Boggs	4.00	1.20
12 Jeff Bagwell	4.00	1.20
13 Tony Gwynn	8.00	2.40
14 John Kruk	1.25	.35
15 Don Mattingly	15.00	4.50
16 Mark Grace	4.00	1.20
17 Kirby Puckett	6.00	1.80
18 Kenny Lofton	2.50	.75

1995 Leaf Checklists

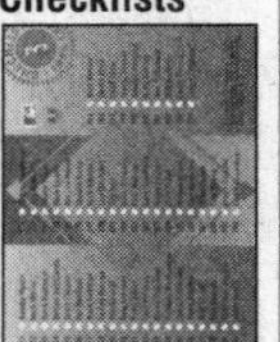

Four checklist cards were randomly inserted in either series for a total of eight standard-size cards. The set was composed of major award winners from the 1994 season.

	Nm-Mt	Ex-Mt
COMPLETE SERIES 1 (4)	1.50	.45
COMPLETE SERIES 2 (4)	3.00	.90
1 Bob Hamelin UER (Name spelled Hamlin)	.15	.04
2 David Cone	.30	.09
3 Frank Thomas	.75	.23
4 Paul O'Neill	.50	.15
5 Raul Mondesi	.30	.09
6 Greg Maddux	1.25	.35
7 Tony Gwynn	1.00	.30
8 Jeff Bagwell	.50	.15

1995 Leaf Cornerstones

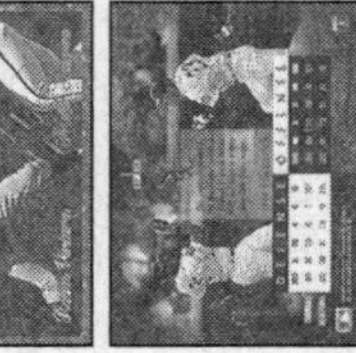

Cards from this six-card standard-size set were randomly inserted in first series packs. Horizontally designed, leading first and thrid basemen from the same team are featured.

	Nm-Mt	Ex-Mt
COMPLETE SET (6)	8.00	2.40
1 Frank Thomas / Robin Ventura	1.50	.45
2 Cecil Fielder / Travis Fryman	.60	.18
3 Don Mattingly / Wade Boggs	4.00	1.20
4 Jeff Bagwell / Ken Caminiti	1.00	.30
5 Will Clark / Dean Palmer	1.50	.45
6 J.R. Phillips / Matt Williams	.60	.18

1995 Leaf Gold Rookies

Inserted in every other first series pack, this 16-card standard-size set showcases those that were expected to have an impact in 1995.

	Nm-Mt	Ex-Mt
COMPLETE SET (16)	6.00	1.80
1 Alex Rodriguez	3.00	.90
2 Garret Anderson	.50	.15
3 Shawn Green	.50	.15
4 Armando Benitez	.50	.15
5 Darren Dreifort	.25	.07
6 Orlando Miller	.25	.07
7 Jose Oliva	.25	.07
8 Ricky Bottalico	.25	.07
9 Charles Johnson	.50	.15
10 Brian L.Hunter	.50	.15
11 Ray McDavid	.25	.07
12 Chan Ho Park	.25	.07
13 Mike Kelly	.25	.07
14 Cory Bailey	.25	.07
15 Alex Gonzalez	.25	.07
16 Andrew Lorraine	.25	.07

1995 Leaf Gold Stars

Randomly inserted in first and second series packs at a rate of one in 110, this 14-card standard-size set (eight first series, six second series) showcases some of the game's superstars.Individually numbered on back out of 10,000, the cards feature fronts that have a player photo superimposed metallic, refractive background.

	Nm-Mt	Ex-Mt
COMPLETE SET (14)	160.00	47.50
COMPLETE SERIES 1 (8)	80.00	24.00
COMPLETE SERIES 2 (6)	80.00	24.00
1 Jeff Bagwell	6.00	1.80
2 Albert Belle	4.00	1.20
3 Tony Gwynn	12.00	3.60
4 Ken Griffey Jr.	15.00	4.50
5 Barry Bonds	25.00	7.50
6 Don Mattingly	25.00	7.50
7 Raul Mondesi	4.00	1.20
8 Joe Carter	4.00	1.20
9 Greg Maddux	15.00	4.50
10 Frank Thomas	10.00	3.00
11 Mike Piazza	15.00	4.50
12 Jose Canseco	10.00	3.00
13 Kirby Puckett	10.00	3.00
14 Matt Williams	4.00	1.20

1995 Leaf Great Gloves

This 16-card standard-size set was randomly inserted in series two packs at a rate of one every two packs. The cards are numbered "X" of 16 in the upper right.

	Nm-Mt	Ex-Mt
COMPLETE SET (16)	10.00	3.00
1 Jeff Bagwell	.50	.15
2 Roberto Alomar	.50	.15
3 Barry Bonds	2.00	.60
4 Wade Boggs	.50	.15
5 Andres Galarraga	.30	.09
6 Ken Griffey Jr.	1.25	.35
7 Marquis Grissom	.30	.09
8 Kenny Lofton	.30	.09
9 Barry Larkin	.50	.15
10 Don Mattingly	2.00	.60
11 Greg Maddux	1.25	.35
12 Kirby Puckett	.75	.23
13 Ozzie Smith	1.25	.35
14 Cal Ripken Jr.	2.50	.75
15 Matt Williams	.30	.09
16 Ivan Rodriguez	.75	.23

1995 Leaf Heading for the Hall

This eight-card standard-size set was randomly inserted into series two hobby packs. The cards are individually numbered out of 5,000 as well.

	Nm-Mt	Ex-Mt
COMPLETE SET (8)	150.00	45.00
1 Frank Thomas	12.00	3.60
2 Ken Griffey Jr.	20.00	6.00
3 Jeff Bagwell	8.00	2.40
4 Barry Bonds	30.00	9.00
5 Kirby Puckett	12.00	3.60
6 Cal Ripken	40.00	12.00

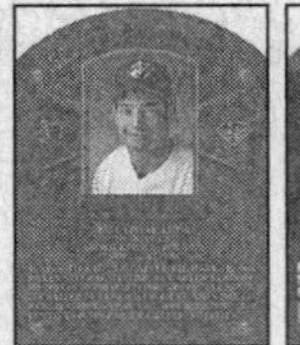

7 Tony Gwynn	15.00	4.50
8 Paul Molitor	8.00	2.40

1995 Leaf Slideshow

This 16-card standard-size set was issued eight per series and randomly inserted at a rate of one per 30 hobby packs and one per 36 retail packs. The eight cards in the first series are numbered 1A-8A and repeated with different photos in the second series as 1B-8B. Both versions carry the same value.

	Nm-Mt	Ex-Mt
COMPLETE SET (16)	80.00	24.00
COMPLETE SERIES 1 (8)	40.00	12.00
COMPLETE SERIES 2 (8)	40.00	12.00
1A Raul Mondesi	1.50	.45
2A Frank Thomas	4.00	1.20
3A Fred McGriff	2.50	.75
4A Cal Ripken	12.00	3.60
5A Jeff Bagwell	2.50	.75
6A Will Clark	4.00	1.20
7A Matt Williams	1.50	.45
8A Ken Griffey Jr.	6.00	1.80

1995 Leaf Statistical Standouts

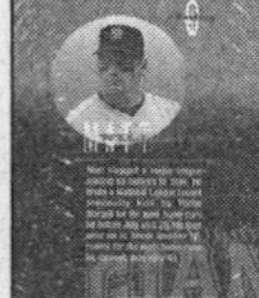

Randomly inserted in first series hobby packs at a rate of one in 70, this set features nine players who stood out from the rest statistically.

	Nm-Mt	Ex-Mt
COMPLETE SET (9)	150.00	45.00
1 Joe Carter	8.00	2.40
2 Ken Griffey Jr.	25.00	7.50
3 Don Mattingly	40.00	12.00
4 Fred McGriff	10.00	3.00
5 Paul Molitor	10.00	3.00
6 Kirby Puckett	15.00	4.50
7 Cal Ripken	50.00	15.00
8 Frank Thomas	15.00	4.50
9 Matt Williams	8.00	2.40

1995 Leaf Thomas

This six-card standard-size set was randomly inserted into series two packs at a rate of one in eighteen.

	Nm-Mt	Ex-Mt
COMPLETE SET (6)	10.00	3.00
COMMON CARD (1-6)	2.00	.60

1996 Leaf

The 1996 Leaf set was issued in one series totalling 220 cards. The fronts feature color action player photos with silver foil printing and lines forming a border on the left and bottom. The backs display another player photo with 1995 season and career statistics. Card number 210 is a checklist for the insert sets and cards number 211-220 feature rookies. The fronts of these 10 cards are different in design from the first 200 with a color action player cut-out over a green-shadow background of the same picture and gold lettering.

	Nm-Mt	Ex-Mt
COMPLETE SET (220)	20.00	6.00
1 John Smoltz	.50	.15
2 Dennis Eckersley	.30	.09
3 Delino DeShields	.30	.09
4 Cliff Floyd	.30	.09
5 Chuck Finley	.30	.09
6 Cecil Fielder	.30	.09
7 Tim Naehring	.30	.09
8 Carlos Perez	.30	.09
9 Brad Ausmus	.30	.09
10 Matt Lawton RC	.50	.15
11 Alan Trammell	.30	.09
12 Steve Finley	.30	.09
13 Paul O'Neill	.50	.15
14 Gary Sheffield	.30	.09
15 Mark McGwire	2.00	.60
16 Bernie Williams	.50	.15
17 Jeff Montgomery	.30	.09
18 Chan Ho Park	.30	.09
19 Greg Vaughn	.30	.09
20 Jeff Kent	.30	.09
21 Cal Ripken	2.50	.75
22 Charles Johnson	.30	.09
23 Eric Karros	.30	.09
24 Alex Rodriguez	1.50	.45
25 Chris Snopek	.30	.09
26 Jason Isringhausen	.30	.09
27 Chili Davis	.30	.09
28 Chipper Jones	.75	.23
29 Bret Saberhagen	.30	.09
30 Tony Clark	.30	.09
31 Marty Cordova	.30	.09
32 Dwayne Hosey	.30	.09
33 Fred McGriff	.50	.15
34 Deion Sanders	.50	.15
35 Orlando Merced	.30	.09
36 Brady Anderson	.30	.09
37 Ray Lankford	.30	.09
38 Manny Ramirez	.50	.15
39 Alex Fernandez	.30	.09
40 Greg Colbrunn	.30	.09
41 Ken Griffey, Jr.	1.25	.35
42 Mickey Morandini	.30	.09
43 Chuck Knoblauch	.30	.09
44 Quinton McCracken	.30	.09
45 Tim Salmon	.50	.15
46 Jose Mesa	.30	.09
47 Marquis Grissom	.30	.09
48 Greg Maddux Randy Johnson CL	.30	.09
49 Raul Mondesi	.30	.09
50 Mark Grudzielanek	.30	.09
51 Ray Durham	.30	.09
52 Matt Williams	.30	.09
53 Bob Hamelin	.30	.09
54 Lenny Dykstra	.30	.09
55 Jeff King	.30	.09
56 LaTroy Hawkins	.30	.09
57 Terry Pendleton	.30	.09
58 Kevin Stocker	.30	.09
59 Ozzie Timmons	.30	.09
60 David Justice	.30	.09
61 Ricky Bottalico	.30	.09
62 Andy Ashby	.30	.09
63 Larry Walker	.50	.15
64 Jose Canseco	.75	.23
65 Bret Boone	.30	.09
66 Shawn Green	.30	.09
67 Chad Curtis	.30	.09
68 Travis Fryman	.30	.09
69 Roger Clemens	1.50	.45
70 David Bell	.30	.09
71 Rusty Greer	.30	.09
72 Bob Higginson	.30	.09
73 Joey Hamilton	.30	.09
74 Kevin Seitzer	.30	.09
75 Julian Tavarez	.30	.09
76 Troy Percival	.30	.09
77 Kirby Puckett	.75	.23
78 Barry Bonds	2.00	.60
79 Michael Tucker	.30	.09
80 Paul Molitor	.50	.15
81 Carlos Garcia	.30	.09
82 Johnny Damon	.50	.15
83 Mike Hampton	.30	.09
84 Ariel Prieto	.30	.09
85 Tony Tarasco	.30	.09
86 Pete Schourek	.30	.09
87 Tom Glavine	.50	.15
88 Rondell White	.30	.09
89 Jim Edmonds	.30	.09
90 Robby Thompson	.30	.09
91 Wade Boggs	.50	.15
92 Pedro Martinez	.75	.23
93 Gregg Jefferies	.30	.09
94 Albert Belle	.30	.09
95 Benji Gil	.30	.09
96 Denny Neagle	.30	.09
97 Mark Langston	.30	.09
98 Sandy Alomar Jr.	.30	.09
99 Tony Gwynn	1.00	.30
100 Todd Hundley	.30	.09
101 Dante Bichette	.30	.09
102 Eddie Murray	.75	.23
103 Lyle Mouton	.30	.09
104 John Jaha	.30	.09
105 Barry Larkin Mo Vaughn CL	.30	.09
106 Jon Nunnally	.30	.09
107 Juan Gonzalez	.50	.15
108 Kevin Appier	.30	.09
109 Brian McRae	.30	.09
110 Lee Smith	.30	.09
111 Tim Wakefield	.30	.09
112 Sammy Sosa	1.25	.35
113 Jay Buhner	.30	.09
114 Garret Anderson	.30	.09
115 Edgar Martinez	.50	.15
116 Edgardo Alfonzo	.30	.09
117 Billy Ashley	.30	.09
118 Joe Carter	.30	.09
119 Javy Lopez	.30	.09
120 Bobby Bonilla	.30	.09
121 Ken Caminiti	.30	.09
122 Barry Larkin	.50	.15
123 Shannon Stewart	.30	.09
124 Orel Hershiser	.30	.09
125 Jeff Conine	.30	.09
126 Mark Grace	.50	.15
127 Kenny Lofton	.30	.09
128 Luis Gonzalez	.30	.09
129 Rico Brogna	.30	.09
130 Mo Vaughn	.30	.09
131 Brad Radke	.30	.09
132 Jose Herrera	.30	.09
133 Rick Aguilera	.30	.09
134 Gary DiSarcina	.30	.09
135 Andres Galarraga	.30	.09
136 Carl Everett	.30	.09
137 Steve Avery	.30	.09
138 Vinny Castilla	.30	.09
139 Dennis Martinez	.30	.09
140 John Wetteland	.30	.09
141 Alex Gonzalez	.30	.09
142 Brian Jordan	.30	.09
143 Todd Hollandsworth	.30	.09
144 Terrell Wade	.30	.09
145 Wilson Alvarez	.30	.09
146 Reggie Sanders	.30	.09
147 Will Clark	.75	.23
148 Hideo Nomo	.75	.23
149 J.T.Snow	.30	.09
150 Frank Thomas	.75	.23
151 Ivan Rodriguez	.75	.23
152 Jay Bell	.30	.09
153 Hideo Nomo CL Marty Cordova	.30	.09
154 David Cone	.30	.09
155 Roberto Alomar	.50	.15
156 Carlos Delgado	.30	.09
157 Carlos Baerga	.30	.09
158 Geronimo Berroa	.30	.09
159 Joe Vitiello	.30	.09
160 Terry Steinbach	.30	.09
161 Doug Drabek	.30	.09
162 David Segui	.30	.09
163 Ozzie Smith	1.25	.35
164 Kurt Abbott	.30	.09
165 Randy Johnson	.75	.23
166 John Valentin	.30	.09
167 Mickey Tettleton	.30	.09
168 Ruben Sierra	.30	.09
169 Jim Thome	.75	.23
170 Mike Greenwell	.30	.09
171 Quilvio Veras	.30	.09
172 Robin Ventura	.30	.09
173 Bill Pulsipher	.30	.09
174 Rafael Palmeiro	.50	.15
175 Hal Morris	.30	.09
176 Ryan Klesko	.30	.09
177 Eric Young	.30	.09
178 Shane Andrews	.30	.09
179 Brian L.Hunter	.30	.09
180 Brett Butler	.30	.09
181 John Olerud	.30	.09
182 Moises Alou	.30	.09
183 Glenallen Hill	.30	.09
184 Ismael Valdes	.30	.09
185 Andy Pettitte	.50	.15
186 Yamil Benitez	.30	.09
187 Jason Bere	.30	.09
188 Dean Palmer	.30	.09
189 Jimmy Haynes	.30	.09
190 Trevor Hoffman	.30	.09
191 Mike Mussina	.50	.15
192 Greg Maddux	1.25	.35
193 Ozzie Guillen	.30	.09
194 Pat Listach	.30	.09
195 Derek Bell	.30	.09
196 Darren Daulton	.30	.09
197 John Mabry	.30	.09
198 Ramon Martinez	.30	.09
199 Jeff Bagwell	.50	.15
200 Mike Piazza	1.25	.35
201 Al Martin	.30	.09
202 Aaron Sele	.30	.09
203 Ed Sprague	.30	.09
204 Rod Beck	.30	.09
205 Tony Gwynn Edgar Martinez CL	.30	.09
206 Mike Lansing	.30	.09
207 Craig Biggio	.50	.15
208 Jeffrey Hammonds	.30	.09
209 Dave Nilsson	.30	.09
210 Dante Bichette Albert Belle CL	.30	.09
211 Derek Jeter	2.00	.60
212 Alan Benes	.30	.09
213 Jason Schmidt	.50	.15
214 Alex Ochoa	.30	.09
215 Ruben Rivera	.30	.09
216 Roger Cedeno	.30	.09
217 Jeff Suppan	.30	.09
218 Billy Wagner	.30	.09
219 Mark Loretta	.30	.09
220 Karim Garcia	.30	.09

1996 Leaf Bronze Press Proofs

This 220-card Bronze set is parallel to the regular Leaf set and between the three types of press proofs were inserted at a rate of one in 10 packs. Similar in design to the regular set, 2,000 non-serial numbered Bronze sets were produced and feature a special holographic foil.

Nm-Mt Ex-Mt
*STARS: 4X TO 10X BASIC CARDS....
*ROOKIES: 2.5X TO 6X BASIC CARDS

1996 Leaf Gold Press Proofs

This 220-card Gold set is parallel to the regular Leaf set. Only five hundred sets were produced and they were randomly inserted into packs. One in every ten packs contained either a Bronze, Gold or Silver Press Proof. Collectors need to be careful as the Bronze and the Gold press proofs look very similar. 500 non-serial numbered sets were produced.

Nm-Mt Ex-Mt
*STARS: 12.5X TO 30X BASIC CARDS
*ROOKIES: 8X TO 20X BASIC CARDS

1996 Leaf Silver Press Proofs

This 220-card Silver set is also a parallel to the regular Leaf issue. One thousand sets were produced and the cards were randomly inserted into packs. One in every 10 packs contains either a bronze, gold or silver press proof. 1,000 non-serial numbered sets were produced.

Nm-Mt Ex-Mt
*STARS: 8X TO 20X BASIC CARDS....
*ROOKIES: 5X TO 12X BASIC CARDS

1996 Leaf All-Star Game MVP Contenders

This 20 card set features possible contenders for the MVP at the 1996 All-Star Game held in Philadelphia. The cards were randomly inserted into packs. If the player on the front of the card won the MVP Award (which turned out to be Mike Piazza), the holder could send it in for a special Gold MVP Contenders set of which only 5,000 were produced. The fronts display a color action player photo. The backs carry the instructions on how to redeem the card. The expiration date for the redemption was August 15th, 1996. The Piazza card when returned with the redemption set had a hole in it to indicate the set had been redeemed.

	Nm-Mt	Ex-Mt
COMPLETE SET (20	40.00	12.00
1 Frank Thomas	1.50	.45
2 Mike Piazza W	4.00	1.20
3 Sammy Sosa	2.50	.75
4 Cal Ripken	5.00	1.50
5 Jeff Bagwell	1.00	.30
6 Reggie Sanders	.60	.18
7 Mo Vaughn	.60	.18
8 Tony Gwynn	2.00	.60
9 Dante Bichette	.60	.18
10 Tim Salmon	1.00	.30
11 Chipper Jones	1.50	.45
12 Kenny Lofton	.60	.18
13 Manny Ramirez	1.00	.30
14 Barry Bonds	4.00	1.20
15 Raul Mondesi	.60	.18
16 Kirby Puckett	1.50	.45
17 Albert Belle	.60	.18
18 Ken Griffey Jr.	2.50	.75
19 Greg Maddux	2.50	.75
20 Bonus Card	.60	.18

1996 Leaf Gold Stars

Randomly inserted in hobby and retail packs at a rate of one in 190, this 15-card set honors some of the games great players on 22 karat gold trim cards. Only 2,500 cards of each player were printed and are individually numbered.

	Nm-Mt	Ex-Mt
COMPLETE SET (15)	300.00	90.00
1 Frank Thomas	20.00	6.00
2 Dante Bichette	8.00	2.40
3 Sammy Sosa	30.00	9.00
4 Ken Griffey Jr.	30.00	9.00
5 Mike Piazza	30.00	9.00
6 Tim Salmon	12.00	3.60
7 Hideo Nomo	20.00	6.00
8 Cal Ripken	60.00	18.00
9 Chipper Jones	20.00	6.00
10 Albert Belle	8.00	2.40
11 Tony Gwynn	25.00	7.50
12 Mo Vaughn	8.00	2.40
13 Barry Larkin	12.00	3.60
14 Manny Ramirez	12.00	3.60
15 Greg Maddux	30.00	9.00

1996 Leaf Hats Off

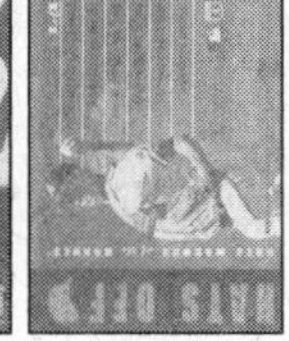

Randomly inserted in retail packs only at a rate of one in 72, this eight-card set was printed and embossed on a wool-like material with the feel of a Major League ball cap. Only 5,000 of each player was produced and is individually numbered.

	Nm-Mt	Ex-Mt
COMPLETE SET (8)	100.00	30.00
1 Cal Ripken	30.00	9.00
2 Barry Larkin	6.00	1.80
3 Frank Thomas	10.00	3.00
4 Mo Vaughn	4.00	1.20
5 Ken Griffey Jr.	15.00	4.50
6 Hideo Nomo	10.00	3.00
7 Albert Belle	4.00	1.20
8 Greg Maddux	15.00	4.50

1996 Leaf Picture Perfect

Randomly inserted in hobby (1-6) and retail (7-12) packs at a rate of one in 140, this 12-card set is printed on real wood with gold foil trim. The fronts feature a color player action framed photo. The backs carry another player photo with player information. Only 5,000 of each card were printed and each is individually numbered.

	Nm-Mt	Ex-Mt
COMPLETE SET (12)	150.00	45.00
1 Frank Thomas	10.00	3.00
2 Cal Ripken	30.00	9.00
3 Greg Maddux	15.00	4.50
4 Manny Ramirez	6.00	1.80
5 Chipper Jones	10.00	3.00
6 Tony Gwynn	12.00	3.60
7 Ken Griffey Jr.	15.00	4.50
8 Albert Belle	4.00	1.20
9 Jeff Bagwell	6.00	1.80
10 Mike Piazza	15.00	4.50
11 Mo Vaughn	4.00	1.20
12 Barry Bonds	25.00	7.50

1996 Leaf Statistical Standouts

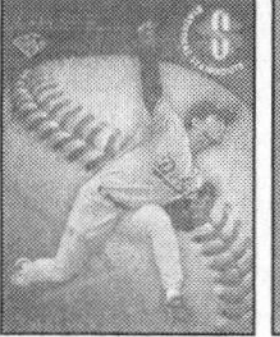

Randomly inserted in hobby packs only at a rate of one in 210, this eight-card set features players who stood out statistically. The cards were printed on a material with the feel of the leather that's between the seams or stitches of a baseball. Only 2,500 of each card was printed and each is numbered individually on the back.

	Nm-Mt	Ex-Mt
COMPLETE SET (8)	150.00	45.00
1 Cal Ripken	50.00	15.00
2 Tony Gwynn	20.00	6.00
3 Frank Thomas	15.00	4.50
4 Ken Griffey Jr.	25.00	7.50
5 Hideo Nomo	15.00	4.50
6 Greg Maddux	25.00	7.50
7 Albert Belle	6.00	1.80
8 Chipper Jones	15.00	4.50

1996 Leaf Thomas Greatest Hits

Randomly inserted in hobby (1-4) and retail (5-7) packs at a rate of one in 210, this eight-card set was printed on die-cut plastic to simulate a compact disc. The cards feature the statistical highlights of Frank Thomas. The wrapper displays the details for the special mail-in offer to obtain card number 8. Five thousand sets were printed.

	Nm-Mt	Ex-Mt
COMMON CARD (1-7)	12.00	3.60
COMMON EXCHANGE (8)	15.00	4.50

1996 Leaf Total Bases

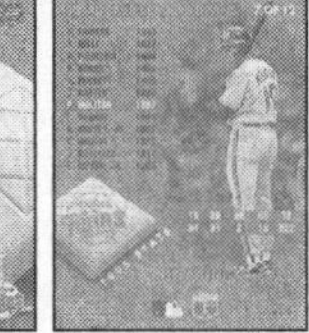

Randomly inserted in hobby packs only at a rate of one in 72, this 12-card set is printed on canvas and features the top offensive stars. Only 5,000 of each card was printed and are individually numbered. The fronts carry a color action player cut-out over a base background. The backs display another player photo and 1995 stats.

	Nm-Mt	Ex-Mt
COMPLETE SET (12)	100.00	30.00
1 Frank Thomas	8.00	2.40
2 Albert Belle	3.00	.90
3 Rafael Palmeiro	5.00	1.50
4 Barry Bonds	20.00	6.00
5 Kirby Puckett	8.00	2.40
6 Joe Carter	3.00	.90
7 Paul Molitor	5.00	1.50
8 Fred McGriff	5.00	1.50
9 Ken Griffey Jr.	12.00	3.60
10 Carlos Baerga	3.00	.90
11 Juan Gonzalez	5.00	1.50
12 Cal Ripken	25.00	7.50

1997 Leaf

The 400-card Leaf set was issued in two separate 200-card series. 10-card packs carried a suggested retail of $2.99. Each card features color action player photos with foil enhancement. The backs carry another player photo and season and career statistics. The set contains the following subsets: Legacy (188-197/348-367), Checklists (198-200/398-400) and Gamers (368-397). Rookie Cards in this set include Jose Cruz Jr., Brian Giles and Hideki Irabu. In a tie in with the 50th anniversary of Jackie Robinson's major league debut, Donruss/Leaf also issued some collectible items. They made 42 all-leather jackets (issued to match Robinson's uniform number). There were also 311 leather jackets produced (to match Robinson's career batting average). 1,500 lithographs were also produced of which Rachel Robinson (Jackie's widow) signed 500 of them.

	Nm-Mt	Ex-Mt
COMPLETE SET (400)	40.00	12.00
COMP. SERIES 1 (200)	20.00	6.00
COMP. SERIES 2 (200)	20.00	6.00
1 Wade Boggs	.50	.15
2 Brian McRae	.30	.09
3 Jeff D'Amico	.30	.09
4 George Arias	.30	.09
5 Billy Wagner	.30	.09
6 Ray Lankford	.30	.09
7 Will Clark	.75	.23
8 Edgar Renteria	.30	.09
9 Alex Ochoa	.30	.09
10 Roberto Hernandez	.30	.09
11 Joe Carter	.30	.09
12 Gregg Jefferies	.30	.09
13 Mark Grace	.50	.15
14 Roberto Alomar	.50	.15
15 Joe Randa	.30	.09
16 Alex Rodriguez	1.25	.35
17 Tony Gwynn	1.00	.30
18 Steve Gibralter	.30	.09
19 Scott Stahoviak	.30	.09
20 Matt Williams	.30	.09
21 Quinton McCracken	.30	.09
22 Ugueth Urbina	.30	.09
23 Jermaine Allensworth	.30	.09
24 Paul Molitor	.50	.15
25 Carlos Delgado	.30	.09
26 Bob Abreu	.30	.09
27 John Jaha	.30	.09
28 Rusty Greer	.30	.09
29 Kimera Bartee	.30	.09
30 Ruben Rivera	.30	.09
31 Jason Kendall	.30	.09
32 Lance Johnson	.30	.09
33 Robin Ventura	.30	.09
34 Kevin Appier	.30	.09
35 John Mabry	.30	.09
36 Ricky Otero	.30	.09
37 Mike Lansing	.30	.09
38 Mark McGwire	2.00	.60
39 Tim Naehring	.30	.09
40 Tom Glavine	.50	.15
41 Rey Ordonez	.30	.09
42 Tony Clark	.30	.09
43 Rafael Palmeiro	.50	.15
44 Pedro Martinez	.75	.23
45 Keith Lockhart	.30	.09
46 Dan Wilson	.30	.09
47 John Wetteland	.30	.09
48 Chan Ho Park	.30	.09
49 Gary Sheffield	.30	.09
50 Shawn Estes	.30	.09
51 Royce Clayton	.30	.09
52 Jaime Navarro	.30	.09
53 Raul Casanova	.30	.09
54 Jeff Bagwell	.50	.15
55 Barry Larkin	.50	.15
56 Charles Nagy	.30	.09
57 Ken Caminiti	.30	.09
58 Todd Hollandsworth	.30	.09
59 Pat Hentgen	.30	.09
60 Jose Valentin	.30	.09
61 Frank Rodriguez	.30	.09
62 Mickey Tettleton	.30	.09
63 Marty Cordova	.30	.09
64 Cecil Fielder	.30	.09
65 Barry Bonds	2.00	.60
66 Scott Servais	.30	.09
67 Ernie Young	.30	.09
68 Wilson Alvarez	.30	.09
69 Mike Grace	.30	.09
70 Shane Reynolds	.30	.09
71 Henry Rodriguez	.30	.09
72 Eric Karros	.30	.09
73 Mark Langston	.30	.09
74 Scott Karl	.30	.09
75 Trevor Hoffman	.30	.09
76 Orel Hershiser	.30	.09
77 John Smoltz	.50	.15
78 Raul Mondesi	.30	.09
79 Jeff Brantley	.30	.09
80 Donne Wall	.30	.09
81 Joey Cora	.30	.09
82 Mel Rojas	.30	.09
83 Chad Mottola	.30	.09
84 Omar Vizquel	.50	.15
85 Greg Maddux	1.25	.35
86 Jamey Wright	.30	.09

87 Chuck Finley .30 .09
88 Brady Anderson .30 .09
89 Alex Gonzalez .30 .09
90 Andy Benes .30 .09
91 Reggie Jefferson .30 .09
92 Paul O'Neill .50 .15
93 Javier Lopez .30 .09
94 Mark Grudzielanek .30 .09
95 Marc Newfield .30 .09
96 Kevin Ritz .30 .09
97 Fred McGriff .50 .15
98 Dwight Gooden .30 .09
99 Hideo Nomo .75 .23
100 Steve Finley .30 .09
101 Juan Gonzalez .50 .15
102 Jay Buhner .30 .09
103 Paul Wilson .30 .09
104 Alan Benes .30 .09
105 Manny Ramirez .50 .15
106 Kevin Elster .30 .09
107 Frank Thomas .75 .23
108 Orlando Miller .30 .09
109 Ramon Martinez .30 .09
110 Kenny Lofton .30 .09
111 Bernie Williams .50 .15
112 Robby Thompson .30 .09
113 Bernard Gilkey .30 .09
114 Ray Durham .30 .09
115 Jeff Cirillo .30 .09
116 Brian Jordan .30 .09
117 Rich Becker .30 .09
118 Al Leiter .30 .09
119 Mark Johnson .30 .09
120 Ellis Burks .30 .09
121 Sammy Sosa 1.25 .35
122 Willie Greene .30 .09
123 Michael Tucker .30 .09
124 Eddie Murray .75 .23
125 Joey Hamilton .30 .09
126 Antonio Osuna .30 .09
127 Bobby Higginson .30 .09
128 Tomas Perez .30 .09
129 Tim Salmon .50 .15
130 Mark Wohlers .30 .09
131 Charles Johnson .30 .09
132 Randy Johnson .75 .23
133 Brooks Kieschnick .30 .09
134 Al Martin .30 .09
135 Dante Bichette .30 .09
136 Andy Pettitte .50 .15
137 Jason Giambi .30 .09
138 James Baldwin .30 .09
139 Ben McDonald .30 .09
140 Shawn Green .30 .09
141 Geronimo Berroa .30 .09
142 Jose Offerman .30 .09
143 Curtis Pride .30 .09
144 Terrell Wade .30 .09
145 Ismael Valdes .30 .09
146 Mike Mussina .50 .15
147 Mariano Rivera .50 .15
148 Ken Hill .30 .09
149 Darin Erstad .30 .09
150 Jay Bell .30 .09
151 Mo Vaughn .30 .09
152 Ozzie Smith 1.25 .35
153 Jose Mesa .30 .09
154 Osvaldo Fernandez .30 .09
155 Vinny Castilla .30 .09
156 Jason Isringhausen .30 .09
157 B.J. Surhoff .30 .09
158 Robert Perez .30 .09
159 Ron Coomer .30 .09
160 Darren Oliver .30 .09
161 Mike Mohler .30 .09
162 Russ Davis .30 .09
163 Bret Boone .30 .09
164 Ricky Bottalico .30 .09
165 Derek Jeter 2.00 .60
166 Orlando Merced .30 .09
167 John Valentin .30 .09
168 Andruw Jones .30 .09
169 Angel Echevarria .30 .09
170 Todd Walker .30 .09
171 Desi Relaford .30 .09
172 Trey Beamon .30 .09
173 Brian Giles RC 1.50 .45
174 Scott Rolen .75 .23
175 Shannon Stewart .30 .09
176 Dmitri Young .30 .09
177 Justin Thompson .30 .09
178 Trot Nixon .30 .09
179 Josh Booty .30 .09
180 Robin Jennings .30 .09
181 Marvin Benard .30 .09
182 Luis Castillo .30 .09
183 Wendell Magee .30 .09
184 Vladimir Guerrero .75 .23
185 Nomar Garciaparra 1.25 .35
186 Ryan Hancock .30 .09
187 Mike Cameron .30 .09
188 Cal Ripken LG 1.25 .35
189 Chipper Jones LG .50 .15
190 Albert Belle LG .30 .09
191 Mike Piazza LG .75 .23
192 Chuck Knoblauch LG .30 .09
193 Ken Griffey Jr. LG .75 .23
194 Ivan Rodriguez LG .50 .15
195 Jose Canseco LG .30 .09
196 Ryne Sandberg LG .75 .23
197 Jim Thome LG .30 .09
198 Andy Pettitte CL .30 .09
199 Andruw Jones CL .30 .09
200 Derek Jeter CL 1.00 .30
201 Chipper Jones .75 .23
202 Albert Belle .30 .09
203 Mike Piazza 1.25 .35
204 Ken Griffey Jr. 1.25 .35
205 Ryne Sandberg 1.25 .35
206 Jose Canseco .75 .23
207 Chili Davis .30 .09
208 Roger Clemens 1.50 .45
209 Deion Sanders .50 .15
210 Darryl Hamilton .30 .09
211 Jermaine Dye .30 .09
212 Matt Williams .30 .09
213 Kevin Elster .30 .09
214 John Wetteland .30 .09
215 Garret Anderson .30 .09
216 Kevin Brown .30 .09
217 Matt Lawton .30 .09
218 Cal Ripken 2.50 .75
219 Moises Alou .30 .09
220 Chuck Knoblauch .30 .09
221 Ivan Rodriguez .75 .23
222 Travis Fryman .30 .09
223 Jim Thome .75 .23
224 Eddie Murray .75 .23
225 Eric Young .30 .09
226 Ron Gant .30 .09
227 Tony Phillips .30 .09
228 Reggie Sanders .30 .09
229 Johnny Damon .50 .15
230 Bill Pulsipher .30 .09
231 Jim Edmonds .30 .09
232 Melvin Nieves .30 .09
233 Ryan Klesko .30 .09
234 David Cone .30 .09
235 Derek Bell .30 .09
236 Julio Franco .30 .09
237 Juan Guzman .30 .09
238 Larry Walker .50 .15
239 Delino DeShields .30 .09
240 Troy Percival .30 .09
241 Andres Galarraga .30 .09
242 Rondell White .30 .09
243 John Burkett .30 .09
244 J.T. Snow .30 .09
245 Alex Fernandez .30 .09
246 Edgar Martinez .50 .15
247 Craig Biggio .50 .15
248 Todd Hundley .30 .09
249 Jimmy Key .30 .09
250 Cliff Floyd .30 .09
251 Jeff Conine .30 .09
252 Curt Schilling .30 .09
253 Jeff King .30 .09
254 Tino Martinez .50 .15
255 Carlos Baerga .30 .09
256 Jeff Fassero .30 .09
257 Dean Palmer .30 .09
258 Robb Nen .30 .09
259 Sandy Alomar Jr. .30 .09
260 Carlos Perez .30 .09
261 Rickey Henderson .75 .23
262 Bobby Bonilla .30 .09
263 Darren Daulton .30 .09
264 Jim Leyritz .30 .09
265 Dennis Martinez .30 .09
266 Butch Huskey .30 .09
267 Joe Vitiello .30 .09
268 Steve Trachsel .30 .09
269 Glenallen Hill .30 .09
270 Terry Steinbach .30 .09
271 Mark McLemore .30 .09
272 Devon White .30 .09
273 Jeff Kent .30 .09
274 Tim Raines .30 .09
275 Carlos Garcia .30 .09
276 Hal Morris .30 .09
277 Gary Gaetti .30 .09
278 John Olerud .30 .09
279 Wally Joyner .30 .09
280 Brian Hunter .30 .09
281 Steve Karsay .30 .09
282 Denny Neagle .30 .09
283 Jose Herrera .30 .09
284 Todd Stottlemyre .30 .09
285 Bip Roberts .30 .09
286 Kevin Seitzer .30 .09
287 Benji Gil .30 .09
288 Dennis Eckersley .30 .09
289 Brad Ausmus .30 .09
290 Otis Nixon .30 .09
291 Darryl Strawberry .30 .09
292 Marquis Grissom .30 .09
293 Darryl Kile .30 .09
294 Quilvio Veras .30 .09
295 Tom Goodwin .30 .09
296 Benito Santiago .30 .09
297 Mike Bordick .30 .09
298 Roberto Kelly .30 .09
299 David Justice .30 .09
300 Carl Everett .30 .09
301 Mark Whiten .30 .09
302 Aaron Sele .30 .09
303 Darren Dreifort .30 .09
304 Bobby Jones .30 .09
305 Fernando Vina .30 .09
306 Ed Sprague .30 .09
307 Andy Ashby .30 .09
308 Tony Fernandez .30 .09
309 Roger Pavlik .30 .09
310 Mark Clark .30 .09
311 Mariano Duncan .30 .09
312 Tyler Houston .30 .09
313 Eric Davis .30 .09
314 Greg Vaughn .30 .09
315 David Segui .30 .09
316 Dave Nilsson .30 .09
317 F.P. Santangelo .30 .09
318 Wilton Guerrero .30 .09
319 Jose Guillen .30 .09
320 Kevin Orie .30 .09
321 Derrek Lee .30 .09
322 Bubba Trammell RC .40 .12
323 Pokey Reese .30 .09
324 Hideki Irabu RC .40 .12
325 Scott Spiezio .30 .09
326 Bartolo Colon .30 .09
327 Damon Mashore .30 .09
328 Ryan McGuire .30 .09
329 Chris Carpenter .30 .09
330 Jose Cruz Jr. RC .50 .15
331 Todd Greene .30 .09
332 Brian Moehler .30 .09
333 Mike Sweeney .30 .09
334 Neifi Perez .30 .09
335 Matt Morris .30 .09
336 Marvin Benard .30 .09
337 Karim Garcia .30 .09
338 Jason Dickson .30 .09
339 Brant Brown .30 .09
340 Jeff Suppan .30 .09
341 Deivi Cruz RC .40 .12
342 Antone Williamson .30 .09
343 Curtis Goodwin .30 .09
344 Brooks Kieschnick .30 .09
345 Tony Womack RC .50 .15
346 Rudy Pemberton .30 .09
347 Todd Dunwoody .30 .09
348 Frank Thomas LG .50 .15
349 Andruw Jones LG .30 .09
350 Alex Rodriguez LG .75 .23
351 Greg Maddux LG .75 .23
352 Jeff Bagwell LG .30 .09
353 Juan Gonzalez LG .30 .09
354 Barry Bonds LG .75 .23
355 Mark McGwire LG 1.00 .30
356 Tony Gwynn LG .50 .15
357 Gary Sheffield LG .30 .09
358 Derek Jeter LG 1.00 .30
359 Manny Ramirez LG .30 .09
360 Hideo Nomo LG .30 .09
361 Sammy Sosa LG .75 .23
362 Paul Molitor LG .30 .09
363 Kenny Lofton LG .30 .09
364 Eddie Murray LG .50 .15
365 Barry Larkin LG .30 .09
366 Roger Clemens LG .75 .23
367 John Smoltz LG .30 .09
368 Alex Rodriguez GM .75 .23
369 Frank Thomas GM .50 .15
370 Cal Ripken GM 1.25 .35
371 Ken Griffey Jr. GM .75 .23
372 Greg Maddux GM .75 .23
373 Mike Piazza GM .75 .23
374 Chipper Jones GM .50 .15
375 Albert Belle GM .30 .09
376 Chuck Knoblauch GM .30 .09
377 Brady Anderson GM .30 .09
378 David Justice GM .30 .09
379 Randy Johnson GM .50 .15
380 Wade Boggs GM .30 .09
381 Kevin Brown GM .30 .09
382 Tom Glavine GM .30 .09
383 Raul Mondesi GM .30 .09
384 Ivan Rodriguez GM .50 .15
385 Larry Walker GM .30 .09
386 Bernie Williams GM .30 .09
387 Rusty Greer GM .30 .09
388 Rafael Palmeiro GM .30 .09
389 Matt Williams GM .30 .09
390 Eric Young GM .30 .09
391 Fred McGriff GM .30 .09
392 Ken Caminiti GM .30 .09
393 Roberto Alomar GM .30 .09
394 Brian Jordan GM .30 .09
395 Mark Grace GM .30 .09
396 Jim Edmonds GM .30 .09
397 Deion Sanders GM .30 .09
398 Vladimir Guerrero CL .50 .15
399 Darin Erstad CL .30 .09
400 N. Garciaparra CL .30 .09
NNO J.Robinson Reprint 25.00 7.50

1997 Leaf Fractal Matrix

Randomly inserted in packs, this 400-card set is parallel to the regular Leaf issue and features color player photos with either a bronze, silver or gold finish. Only 200 cards are bronze, 120 cards are silver, and 80 cards are gold. No card is available in more than one of the colors. In a convoluted effort, the fractal matrix parallel concept split the 400 card set into nine different tiered levels of parallels, each with print runs that varied from as many of several thousand of some cards (mostly the Bronze cards) to less than a few hundred of other cards (In the Gold X subset). Cards were split into colors (Bronze, Gold and Silver) and axis (X, Y and Z). Cards are listed in our checklist with color and axis designation. Unfortunately, the designers at Leaf failed to create any notable markings to differentiate the X, Y and Z axis for all the cards in this set. Leaf did issue an axis schematic on the back of the 1997 boxes and we've carefully incorporated that information into our checklist for accurate reference.

Nm-Mt Ex-Mt
*BRONZE: 1.5X TO 4X BASIC CARDS
*SILVER: 2X TO 5X BASIC CARDS
*SILVER ROOKIES: .6X TO 1.5X BASIC
*GOLD Y/Z: 3X TO 8X BASIC CARDS
*GOLD X: 6X TO 15X BASIC CARDS
*GOLD X RC's: 2X TO 5X BASIC CARDS
RANDOM INSERTS IN PACKS
SEE WEBSITE FOR AXIS SCHEMATIC

1997 Leaf Fractal Matrix Die Cuts

This 400-card set is parallel to the regular set and features three different die-cut versions in three different finishes. 200 of the 400-card set are produced in the X-Axis cut with 150 of those bronze, 40 of those silver, and 10 of those gold. 120 of the 400-card set are available in type Y-Axis cut with 40 of those bronze, 60 silver, and 20 gold. Eighty of the 200-card set are produced in the Z-Axis cut with 10 of those bronze, 20 of those silver and 50 of those gold. No card was available in more than one color nor in more than one die-cut version. Unlike the non die-cut Fractal Matrix cards, these Die Cut parallels have distinguishable axis groupings based on the shape of the die cut edges.

Nm-Mt Ex-Mt
*X-AXIS: 2X TO 5X BASIC CARDS
*X-AXIS ROOKIES: 1.25X TO 3X BASIC
*Y-AXIS: 3X TO 8X BASIC CARDS
*Y-AXIS ROOKIES: .75X TO 2X BASIC
*Z-AXIS: 2.5X TO 6X BASIC CARDS
RANDOM INSERTS IN PACKS
SEE WEBSITE FOR AXIS SCHEMATIC

1997 Leaf Banner Season

Randomly inserted in series one magazine packs, this 15-card set features color action player photos on die-cut cards and is printed on canvas card stock. Only 2500 of each card was produced and are sequentially numbered.

Nm-Mt Ex-Mt
COMPLETE SET (15) 120.00 36.00
1 Jeff Bagwell 8.00 2.40
2 Ken Griffey Jr. 20.00 6.00

3 Juan Gonzalez 8.00 2.40
4 Frank Thomas 12.00 3.60
5 Alex Rodriguez 20.00 6.00
6 Kenny Lofton 5.00 1.50
7 Chuck Knoblauch 5.00 1.50
8 Mo Vaughn 5.00 1.50
9 Chipper Jones 12.00 3.60
10 Ken Caminiti 5.00 1.50
11 Craig Biggio 8.00 2.40
12 John Smoltz 8.00 2.40
13 Pat Hentgen 5.00 1.50
14 Derek Jeter 30.00 9.00
15 Todd Hollandsworth 5.00 1.50

1997 Leaf Dress for Success

Randomly inserted in series one retail packs, this 18-card retail only set features color player photos prined on a jersey-simulated, nylon card stock and is accented with flocking on the team logo and gold-foil stamping. Only 3,500 of each card were produced and are sequentially numbered.

Nm-Mt Ex-Mt
COMPLETE SET (18) 40.00 12.00
1 Greg Maddux 3.00 .90
2 Cal Ripken 6.00 1.80
3 Albert Belle .75 .23
4 Frank Thomas 2.00 .60
5 Dante Bichette .75 .23
6 Gary Sheffield .75 .23
7 Jeff Bagwell 1.25 .35
8 Mike Piazza 3.00 .90
9 Mark McGwire 5.00 1.50
10 Ken Caminiti .75 .23
11 Alex Rodriguez 3.00 .90
12 Ken Griffey Jr. 3.00 .90
13 Juan Gonzalez 1.25 .35
14 Brian Jordan .75 .23
15 Mo Vaughn .75 .23
16 Ivan Rodriguez 2.00 .60
17 Andruw Jones .75 .23
18 Chipper Jones 2.00 .60

1997 Leaf Get-A-Grip

Randomly inserted in series one hobby packs, this 16-card double player insert set features color player photos of some of the current top pitchers matched against some of the league's current power hitters. The set is printed on full-silver, ploy-laminated card stock with gold-foil stamping. Only 3,500 of each card was produced and are sequentially numbered.

Nm-Mt Ex-Mt
COMPLETE SET (16) 150.00 45.00
1 Ken Griffey Jr. 12.00 3.60
Greg Maddux
2 John Smoltz 8.00 2.40
Frank Thomas
3 Mike Piazza 12.00 3.60
Andy Pettitte
4 Randy Johnson 8.00 2.40
Chipper Jones
5 Tom Glavine 12.00 3.60
Alex Rodriguez
6 Pat Hentgen 5.00 1.50
Jeff Bagwell
7 Kevin Brown 5.00 1.50
Juan Gonzalez
8 Barry Bonds 20.00 6.00
Mike Mussina
9 Hideo Nomo 8.00 2.40
Albert Belle
10 Troy Percival 3.00 .90
Andruw Jones
11 Roger Clemens 15.00 4.50
Brian Jordan
12 Paul Wilson 8.00 2.40
Ivan Rodriguez
13 Andy Benes 3.00 .90
Mo Vaughn
14 Al Leiter 20.00 6.00
Derek Jeter
15 Bill Pulsipher 25.00 7.50
Cal Ripken
16 Mariano Rivera 5.00 1.50
Ken Caminiti

1997 Leaf Gold Stars

Randomly inserted in all series two packs, this 36-card set features color action images of some of Baseball's hottest names with actual 24kt. gold foil stamping. Only 2,500 of each card were produced and are sequentially numbered.

Nm-Mt Ex-Mt
1 Frank Thomas 8.00 2.40
2 Alex Rodriguez 12.00 3.60
3 Ken Griffey Jr. 12.00 3.60
4 Andruw Jones 3.00 .90
5 Chipper Jones 8.00 2.40
6 Jeff Bagwell 5.00 1.50
7 Derek Jeter 20.00 6.00
8 Deion Sanders 5.00 1.50
9 Ivan Rodriguez 8.00 2.40
10 Juan Gonzalez 5.00 1.50
11 Greg Maddux 12.00 3.60
12 Andy Pettitte 5.00 1.50
13 Roger Clemens 15.00 4.50
14 Hideo Nomo 8.00 2.40
15 Tony Gwynn 10.00 3.00
16 Barry Bonds 20.00 6.00
17 Kenny Lofton 3.00 .90
18 Paul Molitor 5.00 1.50
19 Jim Thome 8.00 2.40
20 Albert Belle 3.00 .90
21 Cal Ripken 25.00 7.50
22 Mark McGwire 20.00 6.00
23 Barry Larkin 5.00 1.50
24 Mike Piazza 12.00 3.60
25 Darin Erstad 3.00 .90
26 Chuck Knoblauch 3.00 .90
27 Vladimir Guerrero 8.00 2.40
28 Tony Clark 3.00 .90
29 Scott Rolen 8.00 2.40
30 Nomar Garciaparra 12.00 3.60
31 Eric Young 3.00 .90
32 Ryne Sandberg 12.00 3.60
33 Roberto Alomar 5.00 1.50
34 Eddie Murray 8.00 2.40
35 Rafael Palmeiro 5.00 1.50
36 Jose Guillen 3.00 .90

1997 Leaf Knot-Hole Gang

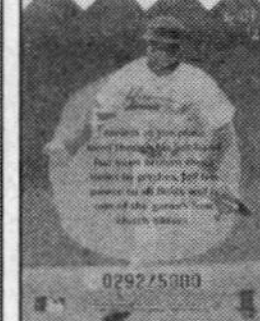

This 12-card insert set, randomly seeded into first series hobby packs, features color action player photos printed on wooden card stock. The die-cut card resembles a wooden fence with the player being seen in action through a knot hole. Only 5,000 of this set was produced and is sequentially numbered.

Nm-Mt Ex-Mt
COMPLETE SET (12) 50.00 15.00
1 Chuck Knoblauch 1.50 .45
2 Ken Griffey Jr. 6.00 1.80
3 Frank Thomas 4.00 1.20
4 Tony Gwynn 5.00 1.50
5 Mike Piazza 6.00 1.80
6 Jeff Bagwell 2.50 .75
7 Rusty Greer 1.50 .45
8 Cal Ripken 12.00 3.60
9 Chipper Jones 4.00 1.20
10 Ryan Klesko 1.50 .45
11 Barry Larkin 2.50 .75
12 Paul Molitor 2.50 .75

1997 Leaf Leagues of the Nation

Randomly inserted in all series two packs, this 15-card set celebrates the first season of interleague play with double-sided, die-cut cards that highlight some of the best interleague matchups. Using flocking technology, the cards display color action player photos with the place and date of the game where the match-up between the pictured players took place. Only 2,500 of each card were produced and are sequentially numbered.

Nm-Mt Ex-Mt
COMPLETE SET (15) 300.00 90.00
1 Juan Gonzalez 30.00 9.00
Barry Bonds
2 Cal Ripken 40.00 12.00
Chipper Jones
3 Mark McGwire 30.00 9.00
Ken Caminiti
4 Derek Jeter 30.00 9.00

Card	Nm-Mt	Ex-Mt
Kenny Lofton		
Ivan Rodriguez	20.00	6.00
Mike Piazza		
Ken Griffey Jr.	20.00	6.00
Larry Walker		
Frank Thomas	20.00	6.00
Sammy Sosa		
Paul Molitor	8.00	2.40
Barry Larkin		
Albert Belle	5.00	1.50
Deion Sanders		
0 Matt Williams	8.00	2.40
Jeff Bagwell		
1 Mo Vaughn	5.00	1.50
Gary Sheffield		
2 Alex Rodriguez	20.00	6.00
Tony Gwynn		
3 Tino Martinez	12.00	3.60
Scott Rolen		
4 Darin Erstad	5.00	1.50
Wilton Guerrero		
5 Tony Clark	12.00	3.60
Vladimir Guerrero		

1997 Leaf Statistical Standouts

his 15-card insert set, randomly seeded into all rst series packs, showcases some of the eague's statistical leaders and is printed on full-eather, die-cut, foil-stamped card stock. The layer's statistics are displayed beside a color layer photo. Only 1,000 of this set were produced and are sequentially numbered.

	Nm-Mt	Ex-Mt
OMPLETE SET (15)	400.00	120.00
Albert Belle	8.00	2.40
Juan Gonzalez	12.00	3.60
Ken Griffey Jr.	30.00	9.00
Alex Rodriguez	30.00	9.00
Frank Thomas	20.00	6.00
Chipper Jones	20.00	6.00
Greg Maddux	30.00	9.00
Mike Piazza	30.00	9.00
Cal Ripken	60.00	18.00
0 Mark McGwire	50.00	15.00
1 Barry Bonds	50.00	15.00
2 Derek Jeter	50.00	15.00
3 Ken Caminiti	8.00	2.40
4 John Smoltz	12.00	3.60
5 Paul Molitor	12.00	3.60

1997 Leaf Thomas Collection

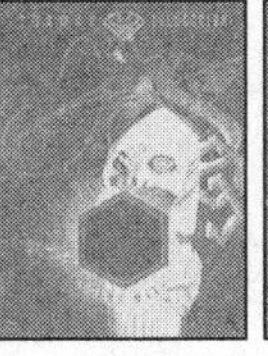

landomly inserted in all series two packs, this ix-card set commemorates the multi-faceted alents of first baseman and at the time, Leaf ompany spokesman, Frank Thomas with actual ieces of his game-used hats, jerseys (home and way), sweatbands, batting gloves or bats mbedded in the cards. Only 100 of each card vere produced and are sequentially numbered. his set, along with the 1997 Upper Deck Game ersey inserts, represents one of the earliest forays by an mlb-licensed manufactuer into game-sed memorabilia inserts.

	Nm-Mt	Ex-Mt
Frank Thomas	150.00	45.00
Game Hat/Blue Text		
Frank Thomas	150.00	45.00
Home Jersey/Orange Text		
Frank Thomas	150.00	45.00
Batting Glove/Yellow Text		
Frank Thomas	150.00	45.00
Bat/Green Text		
Frank Thomas	150.00	45.00
Sweatband/Purple Text		
Frank Thomas	150.00	45.00
Away Jersey/Red Text		

1997 Leaf Warning Track

landomly inserted in all series two packs, this 8-card set features color action photos of outstanding outfielders printed on embossed can-as card stock. Only 3,500 of each card were roduced and are sequentially numbered.

	Nm-Mt	Ex-Mt
OMPLETE SET (18)	100.00	30.00
Ken Griffey Jr.	12.00	3.60
Albert Belle	3.00	.90
Barry Bonds	20.00	6.00
4 Andruw Jones	3.00	.90
5 Kenny Lofton	3.00	.90
6 Tony Gwynn	10.00	3.00
7 Manny Ramirez	5.00	1.50
8 Rusty Greer	3.00	.90
9 Bernie Williams	5.00	1.50
10 Gary Sheffield	3.00	.90
11 Juan Gonzalez	5.00	1.50
12 Raul Mondesi	3.00	.90
13 Brady Anderson	3.00	.90
14 Rondell White	3.00	.90
15 Sammy Sosa	12.00	3.60
16 Deion Sanders	5.00	1.50
17 Dave Justice	3.00	.90
18 Jim Edmonds	3.00	.90

1998 Leaf

The 1998 Leaf set was issued in one series totalling 200 cards. The 10-card packs carried a suggested retail price of $2.99. The set contains the topical subsets: Curtain Calls (148-157), Gold Leaf Stars (158-177), and Gold Leaf Rookies (178-197). All three subsets are short-printed in relation to cards from 1-147 and 201. Those short prints represent one of the early efforts by a manufacturer to incorporate short-print subsets cards into a basic issue set. The product went live in mid-March, 1998. Card number 42 does not exist as Leaf retired the number in honor of Jackie Robinson.

	Nm-Mt	Ex-Mt
COMPLETE SET (200)	60.00	18.00
COMP.SET w/o SP's (147)	15.00	4.50
COMMON CARD (1-201)	.30	.09
COMMON SP (148-197)	1.50	.45
1 Rusty Greer	.30	.09
2 Tino Martinez	.50	.15
3 Bobby Bonilla	.30	.09
4 Jason Giambi	.30	.09
5 Matt Morris	.30	.09
6 Craig Counsell	.30	.09
7 Reggie Jefferson	.30	.09
8 Brian Rose	.30	.09
9 Ruben Rivera	.30	.09
10 Shawn Estes	.30	.09
11 Tony Gwynn	1.00	.30
12 Jeff Abbott	.30	.09
13 Jose Cruz Jr.	.30	.09
14 Francisco Cordova	.30	.09
15 Ryan Klesko	.30	.09
16 Tim Salmon	.50	.15
17 Brett Tomko	.30	.09
18 Matt Williams	.30	.09
19 Joe Carter	.30	.09
20 Harold Baines	.30	.09
21 Gary Sheffield	.30	.09
22 Charles Johnson	.30	.09
23 Aaron Boone	.30	.09
24 Eddie Murray	.75	.23
25 Matt Stairs	.30	.09
26 David Cone	.30	.09
27 Jon Nunnally	.30	.09
28 Chris Stynes	.30	.09
29 Enrique Wilson	.30	.09
30 Randy Johnson	.75	.23
31 Garret Anderson	.30	.09
32 Manny Ramirez	.50	.15
33 Jeff Suppan	.30	.09
34 Rickey Henderson	.75	.23
35 Scott Spiezio	.30	.09
36 Rondell White	.30	.09
37 Todd Greene	.30	.09
38 Delino DeShields	.30	.09
39 Kevin Brown	.50	.15
40 Chili Davis	.30	.09
41 Jimmy Key	.30	.09
43 Mike Mussina	.50	.15
44 Joe Randa	.30	.09
45 Chan Ho Park	.30	.09
46 Brad Radke	.30	.09
47 Geronimo Berroa	.30	.09
48 Wade Boggs	.50	.15
49 Kevin Appier	.30	.09
50 Moises Alou	.30	.09
51 David Justice	.30	.09
52 Ivan Rodriguez	.75	.23
53 J.T. Snow	.30	.09
54 Brian Giles	.30	.09
55 Will Clark	.75	.23
56 Justin Thompson	.30	.09
57 Javier Lopez	.30	.09
58 Hideki Irabu	.30	.09
59 Mark Grudzielanek	.30	.09
60 Abraham Nunez	.30	.09
61 Todd Hollandsworth	.30	.09
62 Jay Bell	.30	.09
63 Nomar Garciaparra	1.25	.35
64 Vinny Castilla	.30	.09
65 Lou Collier	.30	.09
66 Kevin Orie	.30	.09
67 John Valentin	.30	.09
68 Robin Ventura	.30	.09
69 Denny Neagle	.30	.09
70 Tony Womack	.30	.09
71 Dennis Reyes	.30	.09
72 Wally Joyner	.30	.09
73 Kevin Brown	.50	.15
74 Ray Durham	.30	.09
75 Mike Cameron	.30	.09
76 Dante Bichette	.30	.09
77 Jose Guillen	.30	.09
78 Carlos Delgado	.30	.09
79 Paul Molitor	.50	.15
80 Jason Kendall	.30	.09
81 Mark Bellhorn	.30	.09
82 Damian Jackson	.30	.09
83 Bill Mueller	.30	.09
84 Kevin Young	.30	.09
85 Curt Schilling	.30	.09
86 Jeffrey Hammonds	.30	.09
87 Sandy Alomar Jr.	.30	.09
88 Bartolo Colon	.30	.09
89 Wilton Guerrero	.30	.09
90 Bernie Williams	.50	.15
91 Deion Sanders	.50	.15
92 Mike Piazza	1.25	.35
93 Butch Huskey	.30	.09
94 Edgardo Alfonzo	.30	.09
95 Alan Benes	.30	.09
96 Craig Biggio	.50	.15
97 Mark Grace	.50	.15
98 Shawn Green	.30	.09
99 Derrek Lee	.30	.09
100 Ken Griffey Jr.	1.25	.35
101 Tim Raines	.30	.09
102 Pokey Reese	.30	.09
103 Lee Stevens	.30	.09
104 Shannon Stewart	.30	.09
105 John Smoltz	.50	.15
106 Frank Thomas	.75	.23
107 Jeff Fassero	.30	.09
108 Jay Buhner	.30	.09
109 Jose Canseco	.75	.23
110 Omar Vizquel	.50	.15
111 Travis Fryman	.30	.09
112 Dave Nilsson	.30	.09
113 John Olerud	.30	.09
114 Larry Walker	.50	.15
115 Jim Edmonds	.30	.09
116 Bobby Higginson	.30	.09
117 Todd Hundley	.30	.09
118 Paul O'Neill	.50	.15
119 Bip Roberts	.30	.09
120 Ismael Valdes	.30	.09
121 Pedro Martinez	.75	.23
122 Jeff Cirillo	.30	.09
123 Andy Benes	.30	.09
124 Bobby Jones	.30	.09
125 Brian Hunter	.30	.09
126 Darryl Kile	.30	.09
127 Pat Hentgen	.30	.09
128 Marquis Grissom	.30	.09
129 Eric Davis	.30	.09
130 Chipper Jones	.75	.23
131 Edgar Martinez	.50	.15
132 Andy Pettitte	.50	.15
133 Cal Ripken	2.50	.75
134 Scott Rolen	.75	.23
135 Ron Coomer	.30	.09
136 Luis Castillo	.30	.09
137 Fred McGriff	.50	.15
138 Neifi Perez	.30	.09
139 Eric Karros	.30	.09
140 Alex Fernandez	.30	.09
141 Jason Dickson	.30	.09
142 Lance Johnson	.30	.09
143 Ray Lankford	.30	.09
144 Sammy Sosa	1.25	.35
145 Eric Young	.30	.09
146 Bubba Trammell	.30	.09
147 Todd Walker	.30	.09
148 Mo Vaughn CC	1.50	.45
149 Jeff Bagwell CC	2.50	.75
150 Kenny Lofton CC	1.50	.45
151 Raul Mondesi CC	1.50	.45
152 Mike Piazza CC	6.00	1.80
153 Chipper Jones CC	4.00	1.20
154 Larry Walker CC	2.50	.75
155 Greg Maddux CC	6.00	1.80
156 Ken Griffey Jr. CC	6.00	1.80
157 Frank Thomas CC	4.00	1.20
158 Darin Erstad GLS	1.50	.45
159 Roberto Alomar GLS	2.50	.75
160 Albert Belle GLS	1.50	.45
161 Jim Thome GLS	4.00	1.20
162 Tony Clark GLS	1.50	.45
163 Chuck Knoblauch GLS	1.50	.45
164 Derek Jeter GLS	10.00	3.00
165 Alex Rodriguez GLS	6.00	1.80
166 Tony Gwynn GLS	5.00	1.50
167 Roger Clemens GLS	8.00	2.40
168 Barry Larkin GLS	2.50	.75
169 Andres Galarraga GLS	1.50	.45
170 Vlad. Guerrero GLS	4.00	1.20
171 Mark McGwire GLS	10.00	3.00
172 Barry Bonds GLS	10.00	3.00
173 Juan Gonzalez GLS	2.50	.75
174 Andruw Jones GLS	1.50	.45
175 Paul Molitor GLS	2.50	.75
176 Hideo Nomo GLS	4.00	1.20
177 Cal Ripken GLS	12.00	3.60
178 Brad Fullmer GLR	1.50	.45
179 Jaret Wright GLR	1.50	.45
180 Bobby Estalella GLR	1.50	.45
181 Ben Grieve GLR	1.50	.45
182 Paul Konerko GLR	1.50	.45
183 David Ortiz GLR	4.00	1.20
184 Todd Helton GLR	2.50	.75
185 J.Encarnacion GLR	1.50	.45
186 Miguel Tejada GLR	1.50	.45
187 Jacob Cruz GLR	1.50	.45
188 Mark Kotsay GLR	1.50	.45
189 Fernando Tatis GLR	1.50	.45
190 Ricky Ledee GLR	1.50	.45
191 Richard Hidalgo GLR	1.50	.45
192 Richie Sexson GLR	1.50	.45
193 Luis Ordaz GLR	1.50	.45
194 Eli Marrero GLR	1.50	.45
195 Livan Hernandez GLR	1.50	.45
196 Homer Bush GLR	1.50	.45
197 Raul Ibanez GLR	1.50	.45
198 Nomar Garciaparra CL	.75	.23
199 Scott Rolen CL	.50	.15
200 Jose Cruz Jr. CL	.30	.09
201 Al Martin	.30	.09

1998 Leaf Fractal Diamond Axis

Randomly inserted in packs, this 200-card set is parallel to the Leaf base set. Each card features die cut edges and blue foil fronts. Only 50 serially numbered sets were produced. Card number 42 does not exist.

Nm-Mt Ex-Mt

*STARS 1-147/198-201: 15X TO 40X BASIC
*SP STARS 148-197: 3X TO 8X BASIC SP'S

1998 Leaf Fractal Matrix

Randomly inserted in packs, this 200-card set is parallel to the Leaf base set and features color player photos with either a bronze, silver or gold finish. Only 100 cards are bronze, 60 are silver, and 40 are gold. No card is available in more than one of the colors. The set is broken into nine tiers based on three colors (Bronze, Gold and Silver) and three axis (X, Y and Z). Unlike the previous year, the 1998 cards carry an axis-logo on the card front, allowing collectors to identify the specific tier. It's estimated that print runs range from as few as 50 to as many of 2000 of each card.

Nm-Mt Ex-Mt

*BRONZE 1-147/198-201: 1.5X TO 4X BASIC
*BRONZE 148-197: .3X TO .8X BASIC
BRONZE X STATED PRINT RUN 1600 SETS
BRONZE Y STATED PRINT RUN 1800 SETS
BRONZE Z STATED PRINT RUN 1900 SETS
*SILVER 1-147/198-201: 3X TO 8X BASIC
*SILVER: 148-197: .6X TO 1.5X BASIC
SILVER X STATED PRINT RUN 600 SETS
SILVER Y STATED PRINT RUN 800 SETS
SILVER Z STATED PRINT RUN 900 SETS
*GOLD 1-147/198-201: 5X TO 12X BASIC
*GOLD: 148-197: 1X TO 2.5X BASIC..
GOLD X STATED PRINT RUN 100 SETS
GOLD Y STATED PRINT RUN 300 SETS
GOLD Z STATED PRINT RUN 400 SETS
RANDOM INSERTS IN PACKS ....
CARD NUMBER 42 DOES NOT EXIST.

1998 Leaf Fractal Matrix Die Cuts

Randomly inserted in packs, this 200-card set is parallel to the regular set and features three different die-cut versions in three different finishes. Only 100 of the set are produced in the x-axis cut with 75 of those bronze, 20 silver, and five gold. Only 60 are available in the type y-axis cut with 20 of those bronze, 30 silver, and 10 gold. Only 40 are produced in the z-axis cut with five bronze, 10 silver and 25 gold. No card is available in more than one color nor in more than one die-cut version. Card number 42 does not exist.

Nm-Mt Ex-Mt

*X-AXIS 1-147/198-201: 5X TO 12X BASIC
*X-AXIS 148-197: 1X TO 2.5X BASIC.
X-AXIS STATED PRINT RUN 400 SETS
*Y-AXIS 1-147/198-201: 8X TO 20X BASIC
*Y-AXIS 148-197: 1.5X TO 4X BASIC.
Y-AXIS STATED PRINT RUN 200 SETS
*Z-AXIS 1-147/198-201: 12.5X TO 30X BASIC
*Z-AXIS 148-197: 2.5X TO 6X BASIC.
Z-AXIS STATED PRINT RUN 100 SETS
RANDOM INSERTS IN PACKS ....
CARD NUMBER 42 DOES NOT EXIST.
SEE WEBSITE FOR AXIS SCHEMATIC

1998 Leaf Heading for the Hall

This 20 card set was randomly inserted into 1998 Leaf packs. The fronts have a design similar to the Hall of Fame packs. The player's name and team is at top. The back has another photo along with a brief blurb. The cards are numbered "X of 3500" on the back as well.

	Nm-Mt	Ex-Mt
COMPLETE SET (20)	150.00	45.00
1 Roberto Alomar	5.00	1.50
2 Jeff Bagwell	5.00	1.50
3 Albert Belle	3.00	.90
4 Wade Boggs	5.00	1.50
5 Barry Bonds	20.00	6.00
6 Roger Clemens	15.00	4.50
7 Juan Gonzalez	5.00	1.50
8 Ken Griffey Jr.	12.00	3.60
9 Tony Gwynn	10.00	3.00
10 Barry Larkin	5.00	1.50
11 Kenny Lofton	3.00	.90
12 Greg Maddux	12.00	3.60
13 Mark McGwire	20.00	6.00
14 Paul Molitor	5.00	1.50
15 Eddie Murray	8.00	2.40
16 Mike Piazza	12.00	3.60
17 Cal Ripken	25.00	7.50
18 Ivan Rodriguez	8.00	2.40
19 Ryne Sandberg	12.00	3.60
20 Frank Thomas	8.00	2.40

1998 Leaf State Representatives

This 30 card set was randomly inserted into packs. The fronts have the words 'State Representatives' on the top with the player's name and team on the bottom. The player's photo has a metallic sheen to it as he is pictured against a state outline. The back has a small player portrait along with some information about the player. The cards are serial numbered "X of 5,000" on the back.

	Nm-Mt	Ex-Mt
COMPLETE SET (30)	150.00	45.00
1 Ken Griffey Jr.	10.00	3.00
2 Frank Thomas	6.00	1.80
3 Alex Rodriguez	10.00	3.00
4 Cal Ripken	20.00	6.00
5 Chipper Jones	6.00	1.80
6 Andruw Jones	2.50	.75
7 Scott Rolen	6.00	1.80
8 Nomar Garciaparra	10.00	3.00
9 Tim Salmon	4.00	1.20
10 Manny Ramirez	4.00	1.20
11 Jose Cruz Jr.	2.50	.75
12 Vladimir Guerrero	6.00	1.80
13 Tino Martinez	4.00	1.20
14 Larry Walker	4.00	1.20
15 Mo Vaughn	2.50	.75
16 Jim Thome	6.00	1.80
17 Tony Clark	2.50	.75
18 Derek Jeter	15.00	4.50
19 Juan Gonzalez	4.00	1.20
20 Jeff Bagwell	4.00	1.20
21 Ivan Rodriguez	6.00	1.80
22 Mark McGwire	15.00	4.50
23 David Justice	2.50	.75
24 Chuck Knoblauch	2.50	.75
25 Andy Pettitte	4.00	1.20
26 Raul Mondesi	2.50	.75
27 Randy Johnson	6.00	1.80
28 Greg Maddux	10.00	3.00
29 Bernie Williams	4.00	1.20
30 Rusty Greer	2.50	.75

1998 Leaf Statistical Standouts

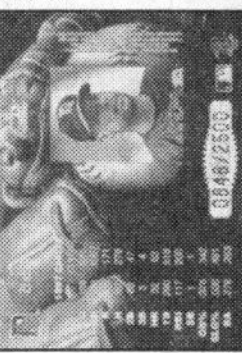

These 24 horizontal cards feature leading players. The front of the card has the players photo against a background of a glove and ball. The ball has been signed by that player. The card's front feels like leather and the words "Statistical Standouts" is printed on the side. The backs have year and career stats on the back along with another player photo. The cards are serial numbered "X of 2500" on the back.

	Nm-Mt	Ex-Mt
COMPLETE SET (24)	250.00	75.00
*DIE CUTS: .75X TO 2X BASIC STAT.STAND.		
DIE CUT PRINT RUN 250 SERIAL #'d SETS		
RANDOM INSERTS IN PACKS		
1 Frank Thomas	10.00	3.00
2 Ken Griffey Jr.	15.00	4.50
3 Alex Rodriguez	15.00	4.50
4 Mike Piazza	15.00	4.50
5 Greg Maddux	15.00	4.50
6 Cal Ripken	30.00	9.00
7 Chipper Jones	10.00	3.00
8 Juan Gonzalez	6.00	1.80
9 Jeff Bagwell	6.00	1.80
10 Mark McGwire	25.00	7.50
11 Tony Gwynn	12.00	3.60
12 Mo Vaughn	4.00	1.20
13 Nomar Garciaparra	15.00	4.50
14 Jose Cruz Jr.	4.00	1.20
15 Vladimir Guerrero	10.00	3.00
16 Scott Rolen	10.00	3.00
17 Andy Pettitte	6.00	1.80
18 Randy Johnson	10.00	3.00
19 Larry Walker	6.00	1.80
20 Kenny Lofton	4.00	1.20
21 Tony Clark	4.00	1.20
22 David Justice	4.00	1.20
23 Derek Jeter	25.00	7.50
24 Barry Bonds	25.00	7.50

2002 Leaf

This 200 card set was issued in late winter, 2002. This set was distributed in four card packs with an SRP of $3 which were sent in 24 packs to a box with 20 boxes to a case. Cards numbered from 151-200, which were inserted at a stated rate of one in six, featured 50 of the leading rookie prospects entering the 2002 season. Card number 42, which Leaf had previously retired in honor of Jackie Robinson, was originally intended to feature a short-print card honoring the sensational rookie season of Ichiro Suzuki. However, Leaf decided to continue honoring Robinson and never went through with printing card 42. Cards numbered 201 and 202 feature Japanese imports So Taguchi and Kazuhisa Ishii, both of which were short-printed in relation to the other prospect cards 151-200. The cards production runs were announced by the manufacturer as 250 copies for Ishii and 500 for Taguchi.

	Nm-Mt	Ex-Mt
COMP.SET w/o SP's (149)	25.00	7.50
COMMON (1-41/43-150)	.30	.09

COMMON CARD (151-200) 4.00 1.20
1 Tim Salmon .50 .15
2 Troy Glaus .30 .09
3 Curt Schilling .30 .09
4 Luis Gonzalez .30 .09
5 Mark Grace .50 .15
6 Matt Williams .30 .09
7 Randy Johnson .75 .23
8 Tom Glavine .50 .15
9 Brady Anderson .30 .09
10 Hideo Nomo .75 .23
11 Pedro Martinez .75 .23
12 Corey Patterson .30 .09
13 Paul Konerko .30 .09
14 Jon Lieber .30 .09
15 Carlos Lee .30 .09
16 Magglio Ordonez .30 .09
17 Adam Dunn .50 .15
18 Ken Griffey Jr. 1.25 .35
19 C.C. Sabathia .30 .09
20 Jim Thome .75 .23
21 Juan Gonzalez .50 .15
22 Kenny Lofton .30 .09
23 Juan Encarnacion .30 .09
24 Tony Clark .30 .09
25 A.J. Burnett .30 .09
26 Josh Beckett .30 .09
27 Lance Berkman .30 .09
28 Eric Karros .30 .09
29 Shawn Green .30 .09
30 Brad Radke .30 .09
31 Joe Mays .30 .09
32 Javier Vazquez .30 .09
33 Alfonso Soriano .50 .15
34 Jorge Posada .50 .15
35 Eric Chavez .30 .09
36 Mark Mulder .30 .09
37 Miguel Tejada .30 .09
38 Tim Hudson .30 .09
39 Bob Abreu .30 .09
40 Pat Burrell .30 .09
41 Ryan Klesko .30 .09
43 John Olerud .30 .09
44 Ellis Burks .30 .09
45 Mike Cameron .30 .09
46 Jim Edmonds .30 .09
47 Ben Grieve .30 .09
48 Carlos Pena .30 .09
49 Alex Rodriguez 1.25 .35
50 Raul Mondesi .30 .09
51 Billy Koch .30 .09
52 Manny Ramirez .50 .15
53 Darin Erstad .30 .09
54 Troy Percival .30 .09
55 Andruw Jones .30 .09
56 Chipper Jones .75 .23
57 David Segui .30 .09
58 Chris Stynes .30 .09
59 Trot Nixon .30 .09
60 Sammy Sosa 1.25 .35
61 Kerry Wood .75 .23
62 Frank Thomas .75 .23
63 Barry Larkin .50 .15
64 Bartolo Colon .30 .09
65 Kazuhiro Sasaki .30 .09
66 Roberto Alomar .50 .15
67 Mike Hampton .30 .09
68 Roger Cedeno .30 .09
69 Cliff Floyd .30 .09
70 Mike Lowell .30 .09
71 Billy Wagner .30 .09
72 Craig Biggio .50 .15
73 Jeff Bagwell .50 .15
74 Carlos Beltran .50 .15
75 Mark Quinn .30 .09
76 Mike Sweeney .30 .09
77 Gary Sheffield .30 .09
78 Kevin Brown .30 .09
79 Paul LoDuca .30 .09
80 Ben Sheets .30 .09
81 Jeromy Burnitz .30 .09
82 Richie Sexson .30 .09
83 Corey Koskie .30 .09
84 Eric Milton .30 .09
85 Jose Vidro .30 .09
86 Mike Piazza 1.25 .35
87 Robin Ventura .30 .09
88 Andy Pettitte .50 .15
89 Mike Mussina .50 .15
90 Orlando Hernandez .30 .09
91 Roger Clemens 1.50 .45
92 Barry Zito .30 .09
93 Jermaine Dye .30 .09
94 Jimmy Rollins .30 .09
95 Jason Kendall .30 .09
96 Rickey Henderson .75 .23
97 Andres Galarraga .30 .09
98 Bret Boone .30 .09
99 Freddy Garcia .30 .09
100 J.D. Drew .30 .09
101 Jose Cruz Jr. .30 .09
102 Greg Maddux 1.25 .35
103 Javy Lopez .30 .09
104 Nomar Garciaparra 1.25 .35
105 Fred McGriff .50 .15
106 Keith Foulke .30 .09
107 Ray Durham .30 .09
108 Sean Casey .30 .09
109 Todd Walker .30 .09
110 Omar Vizquel .50 .15
111 Travis Fryman .30 .09
112 Larry Walker .50 .15
113 Todd Helton .50 .15
114 Bobby Higginson .30 .09
115 Charles Johnson .30 .09
116 Moises Alou .30 .09
117 Richard Hidalgo .30 .09
118 Roy Oswalt .30 .09
119 Neifi Perez .30 .09
120 Adrian Beltre .50 .15
121 Chan Ho Park .30 .09
122 Geoff Jenkins .30 .09
123 Doug Mientkiewicz .30 .09
124 Torii Hunter .30 .09
125 Vladimir Guerrero .75 .23
126 Matt Lawton .30 .09
127 Tsuyoshi Shinjo .30 .09
128 Bernie Williams .50 .15
129 Derek Jeter 2.00 .60
130 Mariano Rivera .50 .15
131 Tino Martinez .50 .15
132 Jason Giambi .30 .09
133 Scott Rolen .75 .23
134 Brian Giles .30 .09
135 Phil Nevin .30 .09
136 Trevor Hoffman .30 .09
137 Barry Bonds 2.00 .60
138 Jeff Kent .30 .09
139 Shannon Stewart .30 .09
140 Shawn Estes .30 .09
141 Edgar Martinez .50 .15
142 Ichiro Suzuki 1.25 .35
143 Albert Pujols 1.50 .45
144 Bud Smith .30 .09
145 Matt Morris .30 .09
146 Frank Catalanotto .30 .09
147 Gabe Kapler .30 .09
148 Ivan Rodriguez .75 .23
149 Rafael Palmeiro .50 .15
150 Carlos Delgado .30 .09
151 Marlon Byrd ROO 4.00 1.20
152 Alex Herrera ROO 4.00 1.20
153 Brandon Backe ROO RC 8.00 2.40
154 Jorge De La Rosa ROO RC 4.00 1.20
155 Corky Miller ROO 4.00 1.20
156 Dennis Tankersley ROO 4.00 1.20
157 Kyle Kane ROO RC 4.00 1.20
158 Justin Duchscherer ROO 4.00 1.20
159 Brian Mallette ROO RC 4.00 1.20
160 Eric Hinske ROO 4.00 1.20
161 Jason Lane ROO 4.00 1.20
162 Hee Seop Choi ROO 4.00 1.20
163 Juan Cruz ROO 4.00 1.20
164 Rodrigo Rosario ROO RC 4.00 1.20
165 Matt Guerrier ROO 4.00 1.20
166 And. Machado ROO RC 4.00 1.20
167 Geronimo Gil ROO 4.00 1.20
168 Dewon Brazelton ROO 4.00 1.20
169 Mark Prior ROO 12.00 3.60
170 Bill Hall ROO 4.00 1.20
171 Jorge Padilla ROO RC 4.00 1.20
172 Josh Pearce ROO 4.00 1.20
173 Allan Simpson ROO RC 4.00 1.20
174 Doug Devore ROO RC 4.00 1.20
175 Luis Garcia ROO 4.00 1.20
176 Angel Berroa ROO 4.00 1.20
177 Steve Bechler ROO RC 4.00 1.20
178 Antonio Perez ROO 4.00 1.20
179 Mark Teixeira ROO 5.00 1.50
180 Mark Ellis ROO 4.00 1.20
181 Michael Cuddyer ROO 4.00 1.20
182 Michael Rivera ROO 4.00 1.20
183 Raul Chavez ROO RC 4.00 1.20
184 Juan Pena ROO 4.00 1.20
185 Austin Kearns ROO 4.00 1.20
186 Ryan Ludwick ROO 4.00 1.20
187 Ed Rogers ROO 4.00 1.20
188 Wilson Betemit ROO 4.00 1.20
189 Nick Neugebauer ROO 4.00 1.20
190 Tom Shearn ROO RC 4.00 1.20
191 Eric Cyr ROO 4.00 1.20
192 Victor Martinez ROO 8.00 2.40
193 Brandon Berger ROO 4.00 1.20
194 Erik Bedard ROO 4.00 1.20
195 Franklyn German ROO RC 4.00 1.20
196 Joe Thurston ROO 4.00 1.20
197 John Buck ROO 4.00 1.20
198 Jeff Deardorff ROO 4.00 1.20
199 Ryan Jamison ROO 4.00 1.20
200 Alfredo Amezaga ROO 4.00 1.20
201 So Taguchi ROO/500 RC 15.00 4.50
202 Kazuhisa Ishii ROO/250 RC 25.00 7.50

2002 Leaf Autographs

Taguchi signed 50 serial numbered cards and Ishii signed 25 serial numbered cards. The Taguchi autographs were distributed in packs but an exchange card with a deadline of October 1st, 2003 was seeded into packs for the Ishii autographs. Each card is a straight parallel of the basic RC's except for a signed silver foil sticker placed over the front and foil serial-numbering on back.

Nm-Mt Ex-Mt
201 So Taguchi /50
202 Kazuhisa Ishii/25

2002 Leaf Lineage

Inserted in hobby packs at stated odds of one in 12, this is a mini-parallel of the 2002 Leaf set. Only the first 150 cards from this set are featured and the set is split up into three sections: Cards numbered 1-50 feature 1999 replicas, while cards numbered from 51-100 feature 2000 replicas and cards numbered from 101-150 feature 2001 replicas.

Nm-Mt Ex-Mt
*LINEAGE: 3X TO 8X BASIC CARDS

2002 Leaf Lineage Century

Randomly Iserted in hobby packs, this is a mini-parallel of the 2002 Leaf set. Only the first 150 cards from this set are featured and the set is split up into three sections: Cards numbered 1-50 feature 1999 replicas, while cards numbered from 51-100 feature 2000 replicas and cards numbered from 101-150 feature 2001 replicas. These cards are serial numbered to 100.

Nm-Mt Ex-Mt
*CENTURY: 8X TO 20X BASIC CARDS

2002 Leaf Press Proofs Blue

Inserted at stated odds of one in 24 retail packs, this is a partial parallel of the 2002 Leaf set and featured the first 150 cards from that set.

Nm-Mt Ex-Mt
*BLUE: 6X TO 15X BASIC CARDS

2002 Leaf Press Proofs Platinum

Randomly inserted in hobby packs, this is a mini-parallel of the 2002 Leaf set. Only the first 150 cards from the basic Leaf set and cards 201 and 202 are featured in this parallel. All cards except for card 202 are serial numbered to 25. Only ten serial-numbered copies of card number 202 (featuring Japanese pitcher Kazuhisa Ishii) were produced.

Nm-Mt Ex-Mt
*PLATINUM: 30X TO 80X BASIC CARDS
201-202 NOT PRICED DUE TO SCARCITY

2002 Leaf Press Proofs Red

Issued at stated odds of one in 12 retail packs, this set parallels the first 150 cards of the 2002 Leaf set. In addition, the two cards of Japanese imports So Taguchi and Kazuhisa Ishii are printed to stated print runs of 500 and 250 respectively.

Nm-Mt Ex-Mt
*RED 1-150: 3X TO 8X BASIC CARDS
201 So Taguchi/500 15.00 4.50
202 Kazuhisa Ishii/250 25.00 7.50

2002 Leaf Burn and Turn

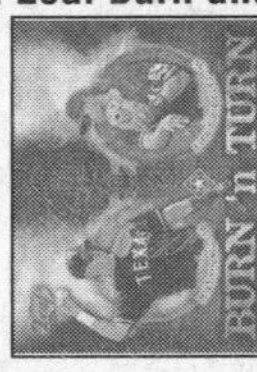

Issued at stated odds of one in 96 hobby and one in 120 retail packs, these 10 cards feature most of the leading double play duos in major league baseball.

Nm-Mt Ex-Mt
COMPLETE SET (10) 100.00 30.00
1 Fernando Vina 8.00 2.40
Edgar Renteria
2 Alex Rodriguez 15.00 4.50
Mike Young
3 Derek Jeter 25.00 7.50
Alfonso Soriano
4 Carlos Guillen 8.00 2.40
Bret Boone
5 Jose Vidro 8.00 2.40
Orlando Cabrera
6 Barry Larkin 8.00 2.40
Todd Walker
7 Carlos Febles 8.00 2.40
Neifi Perez
8 Jeff Kent 8.00 2.40
Rich Aurilia
9 Craig Biggio 8.00 2.40
Julio Lugo
10 Miguel Tejada 8.00 2.40
Mark Ellis

2002 Leaf Clean Up Crew

Issued at stated odds of one in 192 hobby and one in 240 retail packs, these 15 cards feature leading sluggers of the game. The cards are set on conventional cardboard with silver foil stamping.

Nm-Mt Ex-Mt
COMPLETE SET (15) 200.00 60.00
1 Barry Bonds 30.00 9.00
2 Sammy Sosa 20.00 6.00
3 Luis Gonzalez 10.00 3.00
4 Richie Sexson 10.00 3.00
5 Jim Thome 12.00 3.60
6 Chipper Jones 12.00 3.60
7 Alex Rodriguez 20.00 6.00
8 Troy Glaus 10.00 3.00
9 Rafael Palmeiro 10.00 3.00
10 Lance Berkman 10.00 3.00
11 Mike Piazza 20.00 6.00
12 Jason Giambi 10.00 3.00
13 Todd Helton 10.00 3.00
14 Shawn Green 10.00 3.00
15 Carlos Delgado 10.00 3.00

2002 Leaf Clubhouse Signatures Bronze

Randomly inserted in packs, these 33 cards feature a mix of signed cards of retired legends, superstar veterans and future stars. Each of these cards is serial numbered and we have listed the print run in our checklist. Cards with a print run of 100 or fewer are not priced due to market scarcity.

Nm-Mt Ex-Mt
1 Adam Dunn/200 25.00 7.50
2 Alan Trammell/75 15.00 4.50
3 Alfonso Soriano/75
4 Andre Dawson/100
5 Aramis Ramirez/250 15.00 4.50
6 Austin Kearns/300 15.00 4.50
7 Barry Zito/100 30.00 9.00
8 Billy Williams/150 15.00 4.50
9 Bob Feller/250 15.00 4.50
10 Bud Smith/200 10.00 3.00
11 Don Mattingly/25
12 Edgar Martinez/50
13 J.D. Drew/25
14 Jason Lane/250 10.00 3.00
15 Jermaine Dye/125 20.00 6.00
16 Joe Crede/200 10.00 3.00
17 Joe Mays/200 10.00 3.00
18 Johnny Estrada/250 15.00 4.50
19 Mark Ellis/300 10.00 3.00
20 Mark Mulder/50
21 Marlon Byrd/200 10.00 3.00
22 Ozzie Smith/25
23 Paul LoDuca/300 15.00 4.50
24 Phil Rizzuto/25
25 Robert Fick/300 10.00 3.00
26 Ron Santo/300 25.00 7.50
27 Roy Oswalt/300 15.00 4.50
28 Ryne Sandberg/25
29 Steve Garvey/200 15.00 4.50
30 Terrence Long/250 10.00 3.00
31 Tim Redding/300 10.00 3.00
32 Wilson Betemit/150 10.00 3.00
33 Xavier Nady/200 10.00 3.00

2002 Leaf Clubhouse Signatures Gold

Randomly inserted in packs, these 48 cards feature a mix of signed cards of retired legends, superstar veterans and future stars. Each of these cards is serial numbered to 25. An exchange card with a redemption deadline of October 1st, 2003 was seeded into packs for the Ozzie Smith card. Due to market scarcity, no pricing is provided for these cards.

Nm-Mt Ex-Mt
1 Adam Dunn
2 Alan Trammell
3 Alfonso Soriano
4 Andre Dawson
5 Aramis Ramirez
6 Austin Kearns
7 Barry Zito
8 Billy Williams
9 Bob Feller
10 Bud Smith
11 Cal Ripken
12 Chan Ho Park
13 Don Mattingly
14 Edgar Martinez
15 Eric Chavez
16 J.D. Drew
17 Jason Lane
18 Javier Vazquez
19 Jermaine Dye
20 Joe Crede
21 Joe Mays
22 Johnny Estrada
23 Josh Beckett
24 Kirby Puckett
25 Luis Gonzalez
26 Mark Ellis
27 Mark Mulder
28 Marlon Byrd
29 Miguel Tejada
30 Mike Schmidt
31 Orel Hershiser
32 Ozzie Smith
33 Paul LoDuca
34 Phil Rizzuto
35 Rich Aurilia
36 Robert Fick
37 Roger Clemens
38 Ron Santo
39 Roy Oswalt
40 Ryne Sandberg
41 Sean Casey
42 Steve Garvey
43 Terrence Long
44 Tim Redding
45 Todd Helton
46 Vladimir Guerrero
47 Wilson Betemit
48 Xavier Nady

2002 Leaf Clubhouse Signatures Silver

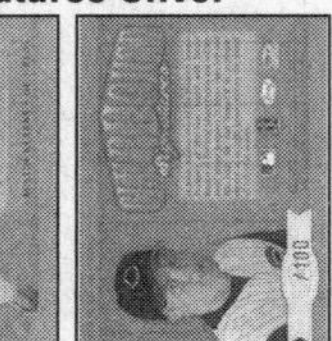

Randomly inserted in packs, these 37 cards feature a mix of signed cards of retired legends, superstar veterans and future stars. Each of these cards is serial numbered and we have listed the print run in our checklist. Cards with a stated print run of 25 or fewer are not priced due to market scarcity.

Nm-Mt Ex-Mt
1 Adam Dunn/75 30.00 9.00
2 Andre Dawson/100
3 Aramis Ramirez/100 20.00 6.00
4 Austin Kearns/100 20.00 6.00
5 Barry Zito/100 30.00 9.00
6 Billy Williams/100 20.00 6.00
7 Bob Feller/100 20.00 6.00
8 Bud Smith/100 15.00 4.50
9 Cal Ripken/25
10 Edgar Martinez/100 40.00 12.00
11 Eric Chavez/100 20.00 6.00
12 Jason Lane/100 15.00 4.50
13 Jermaine Dye/100 20.00 6.00
14 Joe Crede/50 15.00 4.50
15 Joe Mays/50 15.00 4.50
16 Johnny Estrada/100 20.00 6.00
17 Javier Vazquez/100 20.00 6.00
18 Mark Ellis/100 15.00 4.50
19 Mark Mulder/100 20.00 6.00
20 Marlon Byrd/100 15.00 4.50
21 Miguel Tejada/100 20.00 6.00
22 Mike Schmidt/75
23 Paul LoDuca/100
24 Phil Rizzuto/25
25 Rich Aurilia/100 15.00 4.50
26 Robert Fick/100 15.00 4.50
27 Roger Clemens/25
28 Ron Santo/100 30.00 9.00
29 Roy Oswalt/100 20.00 6.00
30 Sean Casey/50
31 Steve Garvey/100 20.00 6.00
32 Terrence Long/100 15.00 4.50
33 Tim Redding/100 15.00 4.50
34 Todd Helton/25
35 Vladimir Guerrero/25
36 Wilson Betemit/100 15.00 4.50
37 Xavier Nady/100 15.00 4.50

2002 Leaf Cornerstones

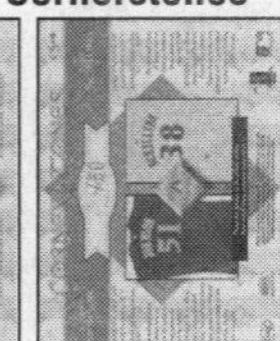

Randomly inserted in packs, these 10 cards feature some of the elite perfomers with dual-player game-worn jersey swatches. These cards are serial numbered to 50. Due to market scarcity, no pricing is provided for these cards.

Nm-Mt Ex-Mt
1 Andruw Jones
Chipper Jones
2 Craig Biggio
Jeff Bagwell
3 Ivan Rodriguez
Rafael Palmeiro
4 Curt Schilling
Randy Johnson
5 Gary Sheffield
Shawn Green
6 Larry Walker
Todd Helton
7 Carlos Delgado
Shannon Stewart
8 Omar Vizquel
Jim Thome
9 Vladimir Guerrero
Jose Vidro
10 Bernie Williams
Roger Clemens

2002 Leaf Future 500 Club

Inserted at stated odds of one in 64 hobby and one in 103 retail, these 10 cards honor players who appear to have good chances of reaching the 500 career homer mark. These cards have holo-foil stamping as well as the year that the player is projected to arrive at the 500 homer club.

Nm-Mt Ex-Mt
COMPLETE SET (10) 80.00 24.00
1 Sammy Sosa 10.00 3.00
2 Mike Piazza 10.00 3.00
3 Alex Rodriguez 10.00 3.00
4 Chipper Jones 6.00 1.80
5 Jeff Bagwell 5.00 1.50
6 Carlos Delgado 5.00 1.50
7 Shawn Green 5.00 1.50
8 Ken Griffey Jr. 10.00 3.00
9 Rafael Palmeiro 5.00 1.50
10 Vladimir Guerrero 6.00 1.80

2002 Leaf Game Collection

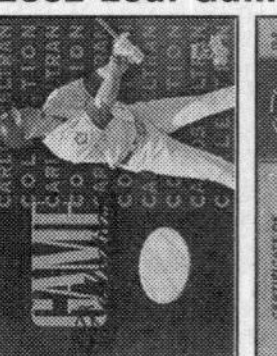

Inserted into retail packs at stated odds of one in 62, these 46 cards feature game-used memorabilia from the featured player. Some cards were printed in shorter quantities and we have provided those stated print runs in our checklist. For cards with a stated print run of 25 or fewer, no pricing is provided due to market scarcity.

Nm-Mt Ex-Mt
AB-B Adrian Beltre Bat 15.00 4.50
AD-BG Adam Dunn Btg Glv SP/25
AG-B Andres Galarraga Bat 10.00 3.00
AJ-B Andruw Jones Bat SP/300 15.00 4.50
BG-B Brian Giles Bat 10.00 3.00
BH-B Bobby Higginson Bat 10.00 3.00
BS-H Ben Sheets Hat SP/25
BW-S Bernie Williams Shoes SP/25
BZ-FG Barry Zito Fld Glv SP/25
CB-B Carlos Beltran Bat 15.00 4.50
CB-IB Craig Biggio Bat 15.00 4.50
CF-B Carlton Fisk Bat 15.00 4.50
CK-B Chuck Knoblauch Bat 10.00 3.00
CP-S Corey Patterson Shoes SP/25
EM-B Eddie Murray Bat SP/250 25.00 7.50
GJ-P Geoff Jenkins Pants 10.00 3.00
IR-BG Ivan Rodriguez Btg Glv SP/25
JB-B Jeff Bagwell Bat SP/100
JD-H Johnny Damon Hat SP/25
JE-B Juan Encarnacion Bat 10.00 3.00
JG-B Juan Gonzalez Bat 15.00 4.50
KL-B Kenny Lofton Bat 10.00 3.00
KW-S Kerry Wood Shoes SP/25
LB-BG Lance Berkman Btg Glv SP/25
LW-B Larry Walker Bat SP/50
MB-BG Marlon Byrd Btg Glv SP/25
MG-B Mark Grace Bat SP/200 25.00 7.50
MM-FG Mike Mussina Fld Glv SP/25
MO-B Magglio Ordonez Bat SP/150 15.00 4.50
MP-B Mike Piazza Bat SP/100
PB-B Pat Burrell Bat SP/100
RA-B Roberto Alomar Bat 15.00 4.50
RD-B Ray Durham Bat 10.00 3.00
RG-B Rusty Greer Bat 10.00 3.00
RJ-FG Randy Johnson Fld Glv SP/25
RP-B Rafael Palmeiro Bat 15.00 4.50
RP-BG Rafael Palmeiro Btg Glv SP/25
RV-B Robin Ventura Bat 10.00 3.00
SC-B Sean Casey Bat 10.00 3.00
SR-B Scott Rolen Bat SP/250 25.00 7.50
SS-H Shannon Stewart Hat SP/25
TC-B Tony Clark Bat 10.00 3.00
TG-BG Tony Gwynn Btg Glv SP/25
TH-B Todd Helton Bat 15.00 4.50
TN-B Trot Nixon Bat 10.00 3.00
WB-B Wade Boggs Bat 15.00 4.50

2002 Leaf Gold Rookies

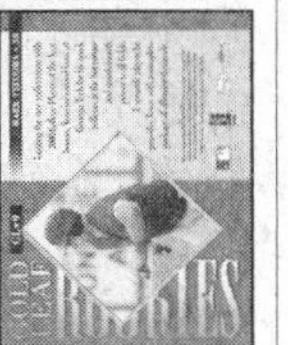

Inserted at stated rate of one in 24 hobby or retail packs, these 10 cards feature the leading prospects entering the 2002 season. These cards are spotlighted on mirror board with gold foil.

Nm-Mt Ex-Mt
COMPLETE SET (10) 50.00 15.00
1 Josh Beckett 4.00 1.20
2 Marlon Byrd 4.00 1.20
3 Dennis Tankersley 4.00 1.20
4 Jason Lane 4.00 1.20
5 Dewon Brazelton 4.00 1.20
6 Mark Prior 10.00 3.00
7 Bill Hall 4.00 1.20
8 Angel Berroa 4.00 1.20
9 Mark Teixeira 4.00 1.20
10 John Buck 4.00 1.20

2002 Leaf Heading for the Hall

Inserted at stated odds of one in 64 hobby and one in 240 retail, these 10 cards feature active or retired players who are virtually insured enshirement in the Baseball Hall of Fame.

Nm-Mt Ex-Mt
COMPLETE SET (10) 80.00 24.00
1 Greg Maddux 10.00 3.00
2 Ozzie Smith 10.00 3.00
3 Andre Dawson 5.00 1.50
4 Dennis Eckersley 5.00 1.50
5 Roberto Alomar 5.00 1.50
6 Cal Ripken 20.00 6.00
7 Roger Clemens 12.00 3.60
8 Tony Gwynn 8.00 2.40
9 Alex Rodriguez 10.00 3.00
10 Jeff Bagwell 5.00 1.50

2002 Leaf Heading for the Hall Autographs

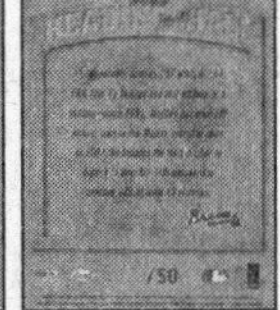

Randomly inserted in hobby packs, these cards parallel the Leaf Heading to the Hall insert set. Each player signed 50 cards for this product. These cards can also be differentiated from the regular cards as these cards are also die cut. No pricing is provided due to market scarcity.

Nm-Mt Ex-Mt
1 Greg Maddux
2 Ozzie Smith
3 Andre Dawson
4 Dennis Eckersley
5 Roberto Alomar
6 Cal Ripken
7 Roger Clemens
8 Tony Gwynn
9 Alex Rodriguez
10 Jeff Bagwell

2002 Leaf League of Nations

Inserted at stated odds of one in 60, these 10 cards feature players from foreign countries. These cards are highlighted with holo-foil and color tint relating to their homeland colors.

Nm-Mt Ex-Mt
1 Ichiro Suzuki 10.00 3.00
2 Tsuyoshi Shinjo 5.00 1.50
3 Chan Ho Park 5.00 1.50
4 Larry Walker 5.00 1.50
5 Andruw Jones 5.00 1.50
6 Hideo Nomo 12.00 3.60
7 Byung-Hyun Kim 5.00 1.50
8 Sun-Woo Kim 5.00 1.50
9 Orlando Hernandez 5.00 1.50
10 Luke Prokopec 5.00 1.50

2002 Leaf Retired Number Jerseys

Randomly inserted in packs, these five cards feature jersey swatches from players who have had their uniform numbers retired. This insert set is sequentially numbered to the player's jersey number. We have listed each print run in our checklist below. Please note that these cards are not priced due to market scarcity.

Nm-Mt Ex-Mt
RN1 Mike Schmidt/20
RN2 Tom Seaver/41
RN3 Rod Carew/29
RN4 Ted Williams/9
RN5 Johnny Bench/5

2002 Leaf Rookie Reprints

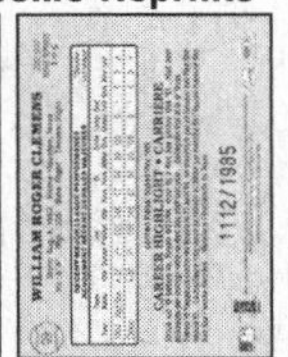

Randomly inserted in packs, these six cards feature reprints sequentially numbered to the card's original year of issue. We have listed those print runs in our checklist.

Nm-Mt Ex-Mt
1 Roger Clemens/1985 15.00 4.50
2 Kirby Puckett/1985 8.00 2.40
3 Andres Galarraga/1986 5.00 1.50
4 Fred McGriff/1986 5.00 1.50
5 Sammy Sosa/1990 12.00 3.60
6 Frank Thomas/1990 8.00 2.40

2002 Leaf Shirt Off My Back

Inserted at stated odds of one in 29 hobby packs, these 60 cards feature a game-worn jersey swatch from either an active or retired star. Some cards were printed in shorter quantity than others, we have noted those cards with their stated print runs in our checklist. Cards with a stated print run of 50 or fewer are not priced due to market scarcity.

Nm-Mt Ex-Mt
*MULTI-COLOR PATCH 1.25X TO 3X HI
AB A.J. Burnett 10.00 3.00
AK Al Kaline SP/100 40.00 12.00
AP Andy Pettitte SP/50 50.00 15.00
AR Alex Rodriguez SP/150 40.00 12.00
BJA Bo Jackson SP/25
BL Barry Larkin 15.00 4.50
BR Brad Radke 10.00 3.00
CB Carlos Beltran 15.00 4.50
CD Carlos Delgado 10.00 3.00
CF Cliff Floyd 10.00 3.00
CHP Chan Ho Park SP/100 25.00 7.50
CJ Chipper Jones SP/100 40.00 12.00
CL Carlos Lee 10.00 3.00
CR Cal Ripken SP/50 150.00 45.00
CS Curt Schilling SP/150 25.00 7.50
DE Darin Erstad SP/100 25.00 7.50
DM Don Mattingly SP/100 60.00 18.00
DW Dave Winfield SP/150 25.00 7.50
EK Eric Karros 10.00 3.00
EM Edgar Martinez SP/150 40.00 12.00
FG Freddy Garcia SP/100 25.00 7.50
GB George Brett SP/100 60.00 18.00
GM Greg Maddux SP/100 40.00 12.00
HN Hideo Nomo SP/100 40.00 12.00
JB Jeff Bagwell SP/100 40.00 12.00
JBU Jeromy Burnitz 10.00 3.00
JL Javy Lopez 10.00 3.00
JO John Olerud 10.00 3.00
JS John Smoltz 15.00 4.50
KB Kevin Brown SP/100 25.00 7.50
KM Kevin Millwood 10.00 3.00
KP Kirby Puckett SP/100 40.00 12.00
KS Kazuhiro Sasaki SP/100 25.00 7.50
LB Lance Berkman SP/300 25.00 7.50
LG Luis Gonzalez 10.00 3.00
LW Larry Walker SP/50 50.00 15.00
MB Michael Barrett 10.00 3.00
MBU Mark Buehrle 10.00 3.00
MH Mike Hampton 10.00 3.00
MO Magglio Ordonez 10.00 3.00
MP Mike Piazza SP/150 40.00 12.00
MR Manny Ramirez SP/100 40.00 12.00
MS Mike Sweeney 10.00 3.00
MT Miguel Tejada 10.00 3.00
MW Matt Williams 10.00 3.00
NG Nomar Garciaparra SP/25
PM Pedro Martinez SP/100 40.00 12.00
RA Roberto Alomar SP/250 15.00 4.50
RD Ryan Dempster 10.00 3.00
RJ Randy Johnson SP/100 40.00 12.00
RP Rafael Palmeiro 15.00 4.50
RS Richie Sexson 10.00 3.00
SR Scott Rolen SP/250 40.00 12.00
TG Tony Gwynn SP/100 40.00 12.00
TG Tom Glavine 15.00 4.50
TGL Troy Glaus SP/275 25.00 7.50
TH Todd Helton 15.00 4.50
TH Tim Hudson 10.00 3.00
TP Troy Percival 10.00 3.00
TS Tsuyoshi Shinjo SP/100 25.00 7.50

2003 Leaf

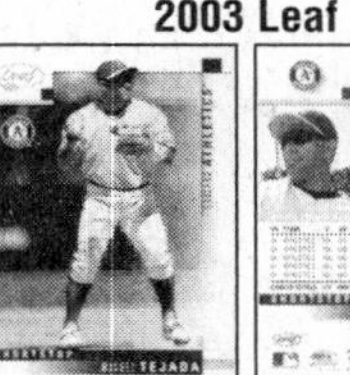
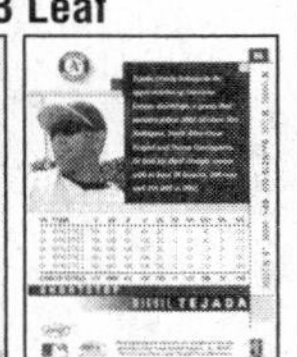

This 329-card set was issued in two separate releases. The primary Leaf product - containing cards 1-320 from the basic set - was released in February, 2003. This product was issued in 10-card packs with an SRP of $3 per pack. These packs were issued in 24 pack boxes which came 20 boxes to a case. This set includes the following subsets: Passing the Torch (251 to 270) and a Rookies subset (271-320). Jose Contreras, the cuban refugee signed to a large free-agent contract, had his very first card in this set. Cards 321-329 were issued within packs of DLP Rookies and Traded in December, 2003. There is no card number 42 as both Bobby Higginson and Carlos Pena share card number 41.

Nm-Mt Ex-Mt
COMP.LO SET (320) 40.00 12.00
COMP.UPDATE SET (9) 8.00 2.40
COMMON CARD (1-270) .30 .09
COMMON CARD (271-320) .50 .15
COMMON CARD (321-329) .50 .15
1 Brad Fullmer .30 .09
2 Darin Erstad .30 .09
3 David Eckstein .30 .09
4 Garret Anderson .30 .09
5 Jarrod Washburn .30 .09
6 Kevin Appier .30 .09
7 Tim Salmon .50 .15
8 Troy Glaus .30 .09
9 Troy Percival .30 .09
10 Buddy Groom .30 .09
11 Jay Gibbons .30 .09
12 Jeff Conine .30 .09
13 Marty Cordova .30 .09
14 Melvin Mora .30 .09
15 Rodrigo Lopez .30 .09
16 Tony Batista .30 .09
17 Jorge Julio .30 .09
18 Cliff Floyd .30 .09
19 Derek Lowe .30 .09
20 Jason Varitek .50 .15
21 Johnny Damon .75 .23
22 Manny Ramirez .50 .15
23 Nomar Garciaparra 1.25 .35
24 Pedro Martinez .75 .23
25 Rickey Henderson .75 .23
26 Shea Hillenbrand .30 .09
27 Trot Nixon .30 .09
28 Carlos Lee .30 .09
29 Frank Thomas .75 .23
30 Jose Valentin .30 .09
31 Magglio Ordonez .30 .09
32 Mark Buehrle .30 .09
33 Paul Konerko .30 .09
34 C.C. Sabathia .30 .09
35 Danys Baez .30 .09
36 Ellis Burks .30 .09
37 Jim Thome .75 .23
38 Omar Vizquel .50 .15
39 Ricky Gutierrez .30 .09
40 Travis Fryman .30 .09
41A Bobby Higginson .30 .09
41B Carlos Pena .30 .09
43 Juan Acevedo .30 .09
44 Mark Redman .30 .09
45 Randall Simon .30 .09
46 Robert Fick .30 .09
47 Steve Sparks .30 .09
48 Carlos Beltran .50 .15
49 Joe Randa .30 .09
50 Michael Tucker .30 .09
51 Mike Sweeney .30 .09
52 Paul Byrd .30 .09
53 Raul Ibanez .30 .09
54 Runelvys Hernandez .30 .09
55 A.J. Pierzynski .30 .09
56 Brad Radke .30 .09
57 Corey Koskie .30 .09
58 Cristian Guzman .30 .09
59 David Ortiz .50 .15
60 Doug Mientkiewicz .30 .09
61 Dustan Mohr .30 .09
62 Eddie Guardado .30 .09
63 Jacque Jones .30 .09
64 Torii Hunter .30 .09
65 Alfonso Soriano .50 .15
66 Andy Pettitte .50 .15
67 Bernie Williams .50 .15
68 David Wells .30 .09
69 Derek Jeter 2.00 .60
70 Jason Giambi .30 .09
71 Jeff Weaver .30 .09
72 Jorge Posada .50 .15
73 Mike Mussina .50 .15
74 Nick Johnson .30 .09
75 Raul Mondesi .30 .09
76 Robin Ventura .30 .09
77 Roger Clemens 1.50 .45
78 Barry Zito .30 .09
79 Billy Koch .30 .09
80 David Justice .30 .09
81 Eric Chavez .30 .09
82 Jermaine Dye .30 .09
83 Mark Mulder .30 .09
84 Miguel Tejada .30 .09
85 Ray Durham .30 .09
86 Scott Hatteberg .30 .09
87 Ted Lilly .30 .09
88 Tim Hudson .30 .09
89 Bret Boone .30 .09
90 Carlos Guillen .30 .09
91 Chris Snelling .30 .09
92 Dan Wilson .30 .09
93 Edgar Martinez .50 .15
94 Freddy Garcia .30 .09
95 Ichiro Suzuki 1.25 .35
96 Jamie Moyer .30 .09
97 Joel Pineiro .30 .09
98 John Olerud .30 .09
99 Mark McLemore .30 .09
100 Mike Cameron .30 .09
101 Kazuhiro Sasaki .30 .09
102 Aubrey Huff .30 .09
103 Ben Grieve .30 .09
104 Joe Kennedy .30 .09
105 Paul Wilson .30 .09
106 Randy Winn .30 .09
107 Steve Cox .30 .09
108 Alex Rodriguez 1.25 .35
109 Chan Ho Park .30 .09
110 Hank Blalock .50 .15
111 Herbert Perry .30 .09
112 Ivan Rodriguez .75 .23
113 Juan Gonzalez .50 .15
114 Kenny Rogers .30 .09
115 Kevin Mench .30 .09
116 Rafael Palmeiro .50 .15
117 Carlos Delgado .30 .09
118 Eric Hinske .30 .09
119 Jose Cruz .30 .09
120 Josh Phelps .30 .09
121 Roy Halladay .30 .09
122 Shannon Stewart .30 .09
123 Vernon Wells .30 .09
124 Curt Schilling .30 .09
125 Junior Spivey .30 .09
126 Luis Gonzalez .30 .09
127 Mark Grace .50 .15
128 Randy Johnson .75 .23
129 Steve Finley .30 .09
130 Tony Womack .30 .09
131 Andruw Jones .30 .09
132 Chipper Jones .75 .23
133 Gary Sheffield .30 .09
134 Greg Maddux 1.25 .35
135 John Smoltz .50 .15
136 Kevin Millwood .30 .09
137 Rafael Furcal .30 .09
138 Tom Glavine .50 .15
139 Alex Gonzalez .30 .09
140 Corey Patterson .30 .09
141 Fred McGriff .50 .15
142 Jon Lieber .30 .09
143 Kerry Wood .75 .23
144 Mark Prior .75 .23
145 Matt Clement .30 .09
146 Moises Alou .30 .09
147 Sammy Sosa 1.25 .35
148 Aaron Boone .30 .09
149 Adam Dunn .50 .15
150 Austin Kearns .30 .09
151 Barry Larkin .50 .15
152 Danny Graves .30 .09
153 Elmer Dessens .30 .09
154 Ken Griffey Jr. 1.25 .35
155 Sean Casey .30 .09
156 Todd Walker .30 .09
157 Gabe Kapler .30 .09
158 Jason Jennings .30 .09
159 Jay Payton .30 .09
160 Larry Walker .50 .15
161 Mike Hampton .30 .09
162 Todd Helton .50 .15
163 Todd Zeile .30 .09
164 A.J. Burnett .30 .09
165 Derrek Lee .30 .09
166 Josh Beckett .30 .09
167 Juan Encarnacion .30 .09
168 Luis Castillo .30 .09
169 Mike Lowell .30 .09
170 Preston Wilson .30 .09
171 Billy Wagner .30 .09
172 Craig Biggio .50 .15
173 Daryle Ward .30 .09
174 Jeff Bagwell .50 .15
175 Lance Berkman .30 .09
176 Octavio Dotel .30 .09
177 Richard Hidalgo .30 .09
178 Roy Oswalt .30 .09
179 Adrian Beltre .50 .15
180 Eric Gagne .75 .23
181 Eric Karros .30 .09
182 Hideo Nomo .75 .23
183 Kazuhisa Ishii .30 .09
184 Kevin Brown .30 .09
185 Mark Grudzielanek .30 .09
186 Odalis Perez .30 .09
187 Paul Lo Duca .30 .09
188 Shawn Green .30 .09
189 Alex Sanchez .30 .09
190 Ben Sheets .30 .09
191 Jeffrey Hammonds .30 .09
192 Jose Hernandez .30 .09
193 Takahito Nomura .30 .09
194 Richie Sexson .30 .09
195 Andres Galarraga .30 .09
196 Bartolo Colon .30 .09
197 Brad Wilkerson .30 .09
198 Javier Vazquez .30 .09
199 Jose Vidro .30 .09
200 Michael Barrett .30 .09
201 Tomo Ohka .30 .09
202 Vladimir Guerrero .75 .23
203 Al Leiter .30 .09
204 Armando Benitez .30 .09
205 Edgardo Alfonzo .30 .09
206 Mike Piazza 1.25 .35
207 Mo Vaughn .30 .09
208 Pedro Astacio .30 .09
209 Roberto Alomar .50 .15
210 Roger Cedeno .30 .09
211 Timo Perez .30 .09
212 Bobby Abreu .30 .09
213 Jimmy Rollins .30 .09
214 Mike Lieberthal .30 .09
215 Pat Burrell .30 .09
216 Randy Wolf .30 .09
217 Travis Lee .30 .09
218 Vicente Padilla .30 .09
219 Aramis Ramirez .30 .09
220 Brian Giles .30 .09
221 Craig Wilson .30 .09
222 Jason Kendall .30 .09
223 Josh Fogg .30 .09
224 Kevin Young .30 .09
225 Kip Wells .30 .09
226 Mike Williams .30 .09
227 Brett Tomko .30 .09
228 Brian Lawrence .30 .09
229 Mark Kotsay .30 .09
230 Oliver Perez .30 .09
231 Phil Nevin .30 .09
232 Ryan Klesko .30 .09
233 Sean Burroughs .30 .09
234 Trevor Hoffman .30 .09
235 Barry Bonds 2.00 .60
236 Benito Santiago .30 .09
237 Jeff Kent .30 .09
238 Kirk Rueter .30 .09
239 Livan Hernandez .30 .09
240 Kenny Lofton .30 .09
241 Rich Aurilia .30 .09
242 Russ Ortiz .30 .09
243 Albert Pujols 1.50 .45
244 Edgar Renteria .30 .09
245 J.D. Drew .30 .09
246 Jason Isringhausen .30 .09
247 Jim Edmonds .30 .09
248 Matt Morris .30 .09
249 Tino Martinez .50 .15
250 Scott Rolen .75 .23
251 Curt Schilling PT .30 .09
252 Ivan Rodriguez PT .50 .15
253 Mike Piazza PT .75 .23
254 Sammy Sosa PT .75 .23
255 Matt Williams PT .30 .09
256 Frank Thomas PT .50 .15
257 Barry Bonds PT 1.00 .30
258 Roger Clemens PT .75 .23
259 Rickey Henderson PT .75 .23
260 Ken Griffey Jr. PT .75 .23
261 Greg Maddux PT .75 .23
262 Randy Johnson PT .50 .15
263 Jeff Bagwell PT .30 .09
264 Roberto Alomar PT .30 .09
265 Tom Glavine PT .30 .09
266 Juan Gonzalez PT .30 .09
267 Mark Grace PT .30 .09
268 Mike Mussina PT .30 .09
269 Ryan Klesko PT .30 .09
270 Fred McGriff PT .50 .15
271 Joe Borchard ROO .50 .15
272 Chris Snelling ROO .50 .15
273 Brian Tallet ROO .50 .15
274 Cliff Lee ROO .50 .15
275 Freddy Sanchez ROO .50 .15
276 Chone Figgins ROO .50 .15
277 Kevin Cash ROO .50 .15
278 Josh Bard ROO .50 .15
279 Jeriome Robertson ROO .50 .15
280 Jeremy Hill ROO .50 .15
281 Shane Nance ROO .50 .15
282 Jeff Baker ROO .50 .15
283 Trey Hodges ROO .50 .15
284 Eric Eckenstahler ROO .50 .15
285 Jim Rushford ROO .50 .15
286 Carlos Rivera ROO .50 .15
287 Josh Bonifay ROO .40 .12
288 Garrett Atkins ROO .50 .15
289 Nic Jackson ROO .50 .15
290 Corwin Malone ROO .50 .15
291 Jimmy Gobble ROO .50 .15
292 Josh Wilson ROO .50 .15

293 Clint Barmes ROO RC .60 .18
294 Jon Adkins ROO .50 .15
295 Tim Kalita ROO .50 .15
296 Nelson Castro ROO .50 .15
297 Colin Young ROO .50 .15
298 Adrian Burnside ROO .50 .15
299 Luis Martinez ROO .50 .15
300 Terrmel Sledge ROO RC .60 .18
301 Todd Donovan ROO .50 .15
302 Jeremy Ward ROO .50 .15
303 Wilson Valdez ROO .50 .15
304 Jose Contreras ROO RC 1.00 .30
305 Marshall McDougall ROO .50 .15
306 Mitch Wylie ROO .50 .15
307 Ron Calloway ROO .50 .15
308 Jose Valverde ROO .50 .15
309 Jason Davis ROO .40 .12
310 Scotty Layfield ROO .50 .15
311 Matt Thornton ROO .50 .15
312 Adam Walker ROO .50 .15
313 Gustavo Chacin ROO .50 .15
314 Ron Chiavacci ROO .50 .15
315 Wilbert Nieves ROO .50 .15
316 Cliff Bartosh ROO .50 .15
317 Mike Gonzalez ROO .50 .15
318 Jeremy Guthrie ROO .50 .15
319 Eric Junge ROO .50 .15
320 Ben Kozlowski ROO .50 .15
321 Hideki Matsui ROO RC 2.00 .60
322 Ramon Nivar ROO RC .50 .15
323 Adam Loewen ROO RC .60 .18
324 Brandon Webb ROO RC .60 .18
325 Chien-Ming Wang ROO RC .60 .18
326 Delmon Young ROO RC 2.00 .60
327 Ryan Wagner ROO RC .50 .15
328 Dan Haren ROO RC .50 .15
329 Rickie Weeks ROO RC 1.50 .45

2003 Leaf Autographs

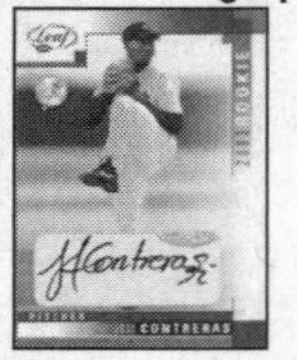

This nine card set was issued in two separate series. Card 304 features Yankees rookie Jose Contreras and was distrbuted within standard 2003 Leaf packs. The remaining eight cards from this set were randomly seeded into packs of 2003 DLP Rookies and Traded. Print runs range from 10-100 copies per and all cards are serial numbered.

Nm-Mt Ex-Mt
304 Jose Contreras ROO/100 25.00 7.50
322 Ramon Nivar ROO/100 20.00 6.00
323 Adam Loewen ROO/100 25.00 7.50
324 Brandon Webb ROO/100 25.00 7.50
325 Chien-Ming Wang ROO/50 50.00 15.00
326 Delmon Young ROO/25
327 Ryan Wagner ROO/100 15.00 4.50
328 Dan Haren ROO/100 20.00 6.00
329 Rickie Weeks ROO/10

2003 Leaf Press Proofs Blue

Randomly inserted into packs, this is a parallel to the Leaf Set. Cards 321-329 were randomly seeded into packs of DLP Rookies and Traded. These cards feature a blue foil logo and were issued to a stated print run of 50 serial numbered sets.

Nm-Mt Ex-Mt
*BLUE 1-250: 6X TO 15X BASIC
*BLUE 251-270: 10X TO 25X BASIC
*BLUE 271-320: 4X TO 10X BASIC
*BLUE 271-320: 4X TO 10X BASIC RC's
*BLUE 321-329: 6X TO 15X BASIC

2003 Leaf Press Proofs Red

Inserted in packs at a stated rate of one in 12, this is a complete parallel to the Leaf Set. Cards 321-329 were randomly seeded into packs of DLP Rookies and Traded - and unlike the first 320 cards - are serial numbered to 100 copies per. These cards feature the words Press Proof printed in red foil on each card front.

Nm-Mt Ex-Mt
*RED 1-250: 2.5X TO 6X BASIC
*RED 251-270: 4X TO 10X BASIC
*RED 271-320: 2.5X TO 6X BASIC
*RED 271-320: 2X TO 5X BASIC RC's
*RED 321-329: 4X TO 10X BASIC RC's

2003 Leaf 60

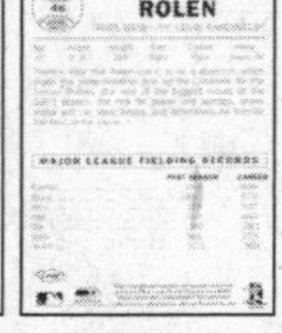

This 50 card insert set was issued at a stated rate of one in eight packs. These cards were designed in the style of the 1960 Leaf set and feature black and white photos.

Nm-Mt Ex-Mt
*FOIL: 2X TO 5X BASIC CARDS
FOIL RANDOM INSERTS IN PACKS
FOIL PRINT RUN 60 SERIAL #'d SETS
1 Troy Glaus 3.00 .90
2 Curt Schilling 3.00 .90
3 Randy Johnson 4.00 1.20
4 Andruw Jones 3.00 .90
5 Chipper Jones 4.00 1.20
6 Greg Maddux 6.00 1.80
7 Tom Glavine 3.00 .90
8 Manny Ramirez 3.00 .90
9 Nomar Garciaparra 6.00 1.80
10 Pedro Martinez 4.00 1.20
11 Rickey Henderson 4.00 1.20
12 Sammy Sosa 6.00 1.80
13 Frank Thomas 4.00 1.20
14 Magglio Ordonez 3.00 .90
15 Mark Buehrle 3.00 .90
16 Adam Dunn 3.00 .90
17 Ken Griffey Jr. 6.00 1.80
18 Jim Thome 4.00 1.20
19 Omar Vizquel 3.00 .90
20 Larry Walker 3.00 .90
21 Todd Helton 3.00 .90
22 Lance Berkman 3.00 .90
23 Roy Oswalt 3.00 .90
24 Mike Sweeney 3.00 .90
25 Hideo Nomo 4.00 1.20
26 Kazuhisa Ishii 3.00 .90
27 Shawn Green 3.00 .90
28 Torii Hunter 3.00 .90
29 Vladimir Guerrero 4.00 1.20
30 Mike Piazza 6.00 1.80
31 Alfonso Soriano 3.00 .90
32 Bernie Williams 3.00 .90
33 Derek Jeter 10.00 3.00
34 Jason Giambi 3.00 .90
35 Roger Clemens 8.00 2.40
36 Barry Zito 3.00 .90
37 Miguel Tejada 3.00 .90
38 Pat Burrell 3.00 .90
39 Ryan Klesko 3.00 .90
40 Barry Bonds 10.00 3.00
41 Jeff Kent 3.00 .90
42 Ichiro Suzuki 6.00 1.80
43 John Olerud 3.00 .90
44 Albert Pujols 8.00 2.40
45 Jim Edmonds 3.00 .90
46 Scott Rolen 4.00 1.20
47 Alex Rodriguez 6.00 1.80
48 Ivan Rodriguez 4.00 1.20
49 Rafael Palmeiro 3.00 .90
50 Roy Halladay 3.00 .90

2003 Leaf Certified Samples

Inserted in packs at a stated rate of one in 23, this 15-card insert set previews the upcoming Leaf Certified set. These cards were printed on metalized film board.

Nm-Mt Ex-Mt
*MIRROR RED: 1.5X TO 4X BASIC
MIRROR RED PRINT RUN 150 #'d SETS
*MIRROR BLUE: 1X TO 2.5X BASIC
MIRROR BLUE PRINT RUN 75 #'d SETS
MIRROR GOLD PRINT RUN 25 #'d SETS
MIRROR GOLD TOO SCARCE TO PRICE
MIRROR CARDS RANDOM INSERTS IN PACKS
1 Derek Jeter 10.00 3.00
2 Greg Maddux 6.00 1.80
3 Mike Piazza 6.00 1.80
4 Barry Bonds 10.00 3.00
5 Lance Berkman 3.00 .90
6 Alex Rodriguez 6.00 1.80
7 Alfonso Soriano 3.00 .90
8 Ichiro Suzuki 6.00 1.80
9 Sammy Sosa 6.00 1.80
10 Vladimir Guerrero 4.00 1.20
11 Albert Pujols 8.00 2.40
12 Pedro Martinez 4.00 1.20
13 Randy Johnson 4.00 1.20
14 Nomar Garciaparra 6.00 1.80
15 Barry Zito 3.00 .90

2003 Leaf Clean Up Crew

Inserted in packs at a stated rate of one in 49, these ten cards feature the middle of the lineup for ten different major league teams.

Nm-Mt Ex-Mt
1 Alex Rodriguez 6.00 1.80
Rafael Palmeiro
Ivan Rodriguez
2 Nomar Garciaparra 6.00 1.80
Manny Ramirez
Cliff Floyd
3 Jason Giambi 4.00 1.20
Bernie Williams
Jorge Posada
4 Rich Aurilla 10.00 3.00
Jeff Kent
Barry Bonds
5 Larry Walker 4.00 1.20
Todd Helton
Jay Payton
6 Lance Berkman 4.00 1.20
Jeff Bagwell
Darryl Ward
7 Scott Rolen 8.00 2.40
Albert Pujols
Jim Edmonds
8 Gary Sheffield 4.00 1.20
Chipper Jones
Andruw Jones
9 Miguel Tejada 4.00 1.20
Eric Chavez
Jermaine Dye
10 Sammy Sosa 6.00 1.80
Moises Alou
Fred McGriff

2003 Leaf Clean Up Crew Materials

Randomly inserted into packs, this is a parallel to the Clean Up Crew set. These cards feature a memorabilia piece from each of the three players featured and these cards were issued to a stated print run of 25 serial numbered sets.

Nm-Mt Ex-Mt
1 Alex Rodriguez Jsy 40.00 12.00
Rafael Palmeiro Jsy
Ivan Rodriguez Jsy
2 Nomar Garciaparra Jsy 40.00 12.00
Manny Ramirez Jsy
Cliff Floyd Bat
3 Jason Giambi Ball 40.00 12.00
Bernie Williams Ball
Jorge Posada Ball
4 Rich Aurilla Ball 60.00 18.00
Jeff Kent Ball
Barry Bonds Ball
5 Larry Walker Jsy 40.00 12.00
Todd Helton Jsy
Jay Payton Jsy
6 Lance Berkman Jsy 40.00 12.00
Jeff Bagwell Jsy
Daryle Ward Bat
7 Scott Rolen Ball 60.00 18.00
Albert Pujols Ball
Jim Edmonds Base
8 Gary Sheffield Bat 40.00 12.00
Chipper Jones Jsy
Andruw Jones Jsy
9 Miguel Tejada Jsy 25.00 7.50
Eric Chavez Jsy
Jermaine Dye Bat
10 Sammy Sosa Ball 40.00 12.00
Moises Alou Ball
Fred McGriff Ball

2003 Leaf Clubhouse Signatures Bronze

Randomly inserted into packs, these 24 cards feature authentic signatures of the players. Some of these cards were issued to a smaller quantity and we have notated that information and the stated print run information next to the player's name in our checklist. Please note that for cards with a print run of 25 or fewer, no pricing is provided due to market scarcity.

Nm-Mt Ex-Mt
1 Edwin Almonte 10.00 3.00
2 Jeff Baker SP/100 10.00 3.00
3 Josh Bard 10.00 3.00
4 Angel Berroa SP/100 10.00 3.00
5 Joe Crede SP/25
6 Andre Dawson SP/50 40.00 12.00
7 Bobby Doerr SP/100 25.00 7.50
8 Adam Dunn SP/10
9 Doc Gooden SP/100 25.00 7.50
10 Drew Henson SP/50 50.00 15.00
11 Eric Hinske 10.00 3.00
12 Torii Hunter SP/75 40.00 12.00
13 Omar Infante 10.00 3.00
14 Brian Lawrence 10.00 3.00
15 Kevin Mench 10.00 3.00
16 Jack Morris SP/100 25.00 7.50
17 Franklin Nunez 10.00 3.00
18 Magglio Ordonez SP/50 40.00 12.00
19 Corey Patterson SP/100 15.00 4.50
20 Jhonny Peralta 15.00 4.50
21 J.C. Romero 10.00 3.00
22 Chris Snelling SP/100 10.00 3.00
23 Alfonso Soriano SP/25
24 Brian Tallet SP/100 10.00 3.00

2003 Leaf Clubhouse Signatures Gold

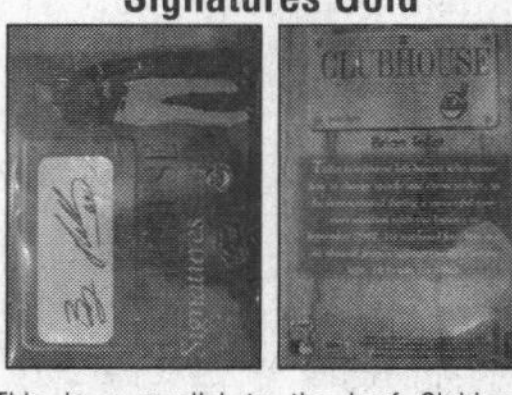

This is a parallel to the Leaf Clubhouse Signatures set. These cards were issued to a stated print run of 25 serial numbered sets and no pricing is provided due to market scarcity.

Nm-Mt Ex-Mt
1 Edwin Almonte
2 Jeff Baker
3 Josh Bard
4 Angel Berroa
5 Joe Crede
6 Andre Dawson
7 Bobby Doerr
8 Adam Dunn
9 Doc Gooden
10 Vladimir Guerrero
11 Drew Henson
12 Eric Hinske
13 Torii Hunter
14 Omar Infante
15 Brian Lawrence
16 Kevin Mench
17 Jack Morris
18 Franklin Nunez
19 Magglio Ordonez
20 Corey Patterson
21 Jhonny Peralta
22 J.C. Romero
23 Chris Snelling
24 Alfonso Soriano
25 Brian Tallet

2003 Leaf Clubhouse Signatures Silver

Randomly inserted into packs, this is a parallel to the Leaf Clubhouse Signatures set. These cards were issued to a stated print run of 100 serial numbered sets except for Andre Dawson who was issued to a stated print run of 25 serial numbered sets.

Nm-Mt Ex-Mt
1 Edwin Almonte 10.00 3.00
2 Jeff Baker 10.00 3.00
3 Josh Bard 10.00 3.00
4 Angel Berroa 10.00 3.00
5 Andre Dawson SP/25
6 Bobby Doerr 25.00 7.50
7 Doc Gooden 25.00 7.50
8 Drew Henson 25.00 7.50
9 Eric Hinske 10.00 3.00
10 Torii Hunter 50.00 15.00
11 Omar Infante 10.00 3.00
12 Brian Lawrence 10.00 3.00
13 Kevin Mench 10.00 3.00
14 Jack Morris 25.00 7.50
15 Franklin Nunez 10.00 3.00
16 Magglio Ordonez 25.00 7.50
17 Jhonny Peralta 15.00 4.50
18 J.C. Romero 10.00 3.00
19 Chris Snelling 10.00 3.00
20 Brian Tallet 10.00 3.00

2003 Leaf Game Collection

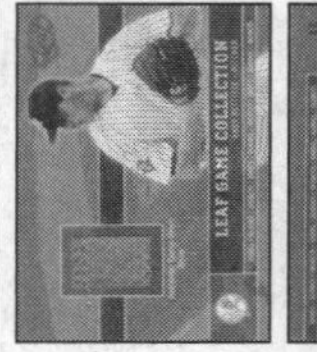

Randomly inserted into packs, this set displays one swatch of game-used materials. These cards were issued to a stated print run of 150 serial numbered sets.

Nm-Mt Ex-Mt
1 Miguel Tejada Hat 10.00 3.00
2 Shannon Stewart Hat 10.00 3.00
3 Mike Schmidt Jacket 50.00 15.00
4 Nolan Ryan Jacket 80.00 24.00
5 Rafael Palmeiro Fld Glv 25.00 7.50
6 Andruw Jones Shoe 10.00 3.00
7 Bernie Williams Shoe 15.00 4.50
8 Ivan Rodriguez Shoe 15.00 4.50
9 Lance Berkman Shoe 10.00 3.00
10 Magglio Ordonez Shoe 10.00 3.00
11 Roy Oswalt Fld Glv 15.00 4.50
12 Andy Pettitte Shoe 15.00 4.50
13 Vladimir Guerrero Fld Glv 40.00 12.00
14 Jason Jennings Fld Glv 15.00 4.50
15 Mike Sweeney Shoe 10.00 3.00
16 Joe Borchard Shoe 10.00 3.00
17 Mark Prior Shoe 15.00 4.50
18 Gary Carter Jacket 10.00 3.00
19 Austin Kearns Fld Glv 15.00 4.50
20 Ryan Klesko Fld Glv 15.00 4.50

2003 Leaf Gold Rookies

Issued at a stated rate of one in 24, this 10 card set features some of the leading candidates for Rookie of the Year. These cards were issued on a special foil board.

Nm-Mt Ex-Mt
MIRROR GOLD RANDOM INSERTS IN PACKS
MIRROR GOLD PRINT RUN 25 #'d SETS
MIRROR GOLD TOO SCARCE TO PRICE
1 Joe Borchard 3.00 .90
2 Chone Figgins 3.00 .90
3 Alexis Gomez 3.00 .90
4 Chris Snelling 3.00 .90
5 Cliff Lee 3.00 .90
6 Victor Martinez 5.00 1.50
7 Hee Seop Choi 3.00 .90
8 Michael Restovich 3.00 .90
9 Anderson Machado 3.00 .90
10 Drew Henson 3.00 .90

2003 Leaf Hard Hats

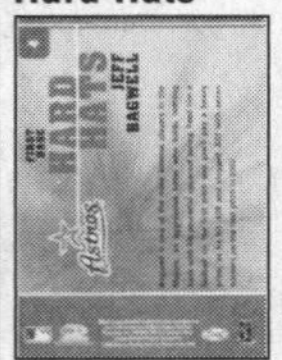

Issued at a stated rate of one in 13, these 12 cards feature the 1997 Studio design set against a rainbow board.

Nm-Mt Ex-Mt
1 Alex Rodriguez 4.00 1.20
2 Bernie Williams 2.00 .60
3 Ivan Rodriguez 2.50 .75
4 Jeff Bagwell 2.00 .60
5 Rafael Furcal 2.00 .60
6 Rafael Palmeiro 2.00 .60
7 Tony Gwynn 3.00 .90
8 Vladimir Guerrero 2.50 .75
9 Adrian Beltre 2.00 .60
10 Shawn Green 2.00 .60
11 Andruw Jones 2.00 .60
12 George Brett 6.00 1.80

2003 Leaf Hard Hats Batting Helmets

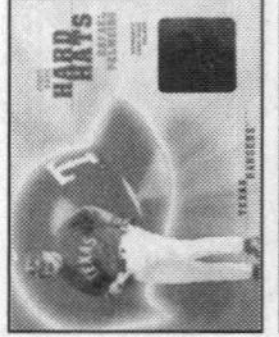

Randomly inserted into packs, this is a parallel to the Hard Hats insert set. These cards feature a swatch of a game-worn batting helmet embedded on the card and these cards were issued to a stated print run of 100 serial numbered sets.

Nm-Mt Ex-Mt
1 Alex Rodriguez 60.00 18.00
2 Bernie Williams 40.00 12.00
3 Ivan Rodriguez 40.00 12.00
4 Jeff Bagwell 40.00 12.00
5 Rafael Furcal 25.00 7.50
6 Rafael Palmeiro 40.00 12.00
7 Tony Gwynn 50.00 15.00
8 Vladimir Guerrero 40.00 12.00
9 Adrian Beltre 40.00 12.00
10 Shawn Green 25.00 7.50
11 Andruw Jones 25.00 7.50
12 George Brett 120.00 36.00

2003 Leaf Home/Away

Issued at a stated rate of one in 34, these 20 cards feature either home or away stats for these 10 featured players. The last three year of stats are featured on the cards.

Nm-Mt Ex-Mt
1A Andruw Jones A 4.00 1.20
1H Andruw Jones H 4.00 1.20
2A Cal Ripken A 15.00 4.50
2H Cal Ripken H 15.00 4.50
3A Edgar Martinez A 4.00 1.20
3H Edgar Martinez H 4.00 1.20
4A Jim Thome A 5.00 1.50
4H Jim Thome H 5.00 1.50
5A Larry Walker A 4.00 1.20
5H Larry Walker H 4.00 1.20
6A Nomar Garciaparra A 8.00 2.40
6H Nomar Garciaparra H 8.00 2.40
7A Mark Prior A 5.00 1.50
7H Mark Prior H 5.00 1.50
8A Mike Piazza A 8.00 2.40
8H Mike Piazza H 8.00 2.40
9A Vladimir Guerrero A 5.00 1.50
9H Vladimir Guerrero H 5.00 1.50
10A Chipper Jones A 5.00 1.50
10H Chipper Jones H 5.00 1.50

2003 Leaf Home/Away Materials

Randomly inserted into packs, this is a parallel to the Home/Away set. These cards feature jersey swatches displayed on the front and these cards were issued to a stated print run of 250

serial numbered sets.

	Nm-Mt	Ex-Mt
1A Andruw Jones A	10.00	3.00
1H Andruw Jones H	10.00	3.00
2A Cal Ripken A	60.00	18.00
2H Cal Ripken H	60.00	18.00
3A Edgar Martinez A	15.00	4.50
3H Edgar Martinez H	15.00	4.50
4A Jim Thome A	15.00	4.50
4H Jim Thome H	15.00	4.50
5A Larry Walker A	15.00	4.50
5H Larry Walker H	15.00	4.50
6A Nomar Garciaparra A	20.00	6.00
6H Nomar Garciaparra H	20.00	6.00
7A Mark Prior A	15.00	4.50
7H Mark Prior H	15.00	4.50
8A Mike Piazza A	20.00	6.00
8H Mike Piazza H	20.00	6.00
9A Vladimir Guerrero A	15.00	4.50
9H Vladimir Guerrero H	15.00	4.50
10A Chipper Jones A	15.00	4.50
10H Chipper Jones H	15.00	4.50

2003 Leaf Maple and Ash

Randomly inserted into packs, these cards feature faux wood grain and also have a game-used bat piece. These cards were issued to a stated print run of 400 serial numbered sets.

	Nm-Mt	Ex-Mt
1 Jorge Posada	15.00	4.50
2 Mike Piazza	20.00	6.00
3 Alex Rodriguez	20.00	6.00
4 Jeff Bagwell	15.00	4.50
5 Joe Borchard	10.00	3.00
6 Miguel Tejada	10.00	3.00
7 Adam Dunn	15.00	4.50
8 Jim Thome	15.00	4.50
9 Lance Berkman	10.00	3.00
10 Torii Hunter	10.00	3.00
11 Carlos Delgado	10.00	3.00
12 Reggie Jackson	15.00	4.50
13 Juan Gonzalez	15.00	4.50
14 Vladimir Guerrero	15.00	4.50
15 Richie Sexson	10.00	3.00

2003 Leaf Number Off My Back

Randomly inserted in packs, these cards feature a swatch from a game-worn jersey number. These cards were issued to a stated print run of 50 serial numbered sets.

	Nm-Mt	Ex-Mt
1 Carlos Delgado	25.00	7.50
2 Don Mattingly	150.00	45.00
3 Todd Helton	40.00	12.00
4 Vernon Wells	25.00	7.50
5 Bernie Williams	40.00	12.00
6 Luis Gonzalez	25.00	7.50
7 Kerry Wood	40.00	12.00
8 Eric Chavez	25.00	7.50
9 Shawn Green	25.00	7.50
10 Roy Oswalt	25.00	7.50
11 Nomar Garciaparra	60.00	18.00
12 Robin Yount	100.00	30.00
13 Troy Glaus	25.00	7.50
14 C.C. Sabathia	25.00	7.50
15 Alex Rodriguez	60.00	18.00
16 Mark Mulder	25.00	7.50
17 Will Clark	100.00	30.00
18 Alfonso Soriano	40.00	12.00
19 Andy Pettitte	40.00	12.00
20 Curt Schilling	25.00	7.50

2003 Leaf Shirt Off My Back

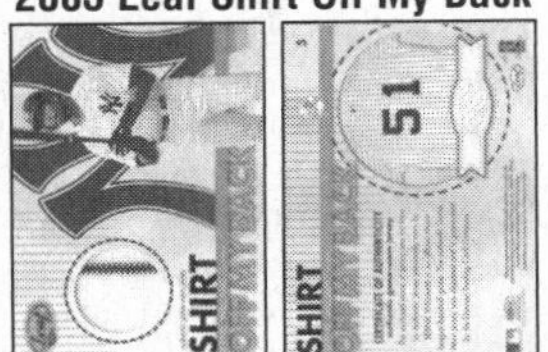

Randomly inserted into packs, this 20-card insert set features one swatch of game-worn jersey of the featured player. These cards were issued to a stated print run of 500 serial numbered sets.

	Nm-Mt	Ex-Mt
1 Carlos Delgado	8.00	2.40
2 Don Mattingly	25.00	7.50
3 Todd Helton	10.00	3.00
4 Vernon Wells	8.00	2.40
5 Bernie Williams	10.00	3.00
6 Luis Gonzalez	8.00	2.40
7 Kerry Wood	10.00	3.00
8 Eric Chavez	8.00	2.40
9 Shawn Green	8.00	2.40
10 Roy Oswalt	8.00	2.40
11 Nomar Garciaparra	15.00	4.50
12 Robin Yount	15.00	4.50
13 Troy Glaus	8.00	2.40
14 C.C. Sabathia	8.00	2.40
15 Alex Rodriguez	10.00	3.00
16 Mark Mulder	8.00	2.40
17 Will Clark	15.00	4.50
18 Alfonso Soriano	10.00	3.00
19 Andy Pettitte	10.00	3.00
20 Curt Schilling	8.00	2.40

2003 Leaf Slick Leather

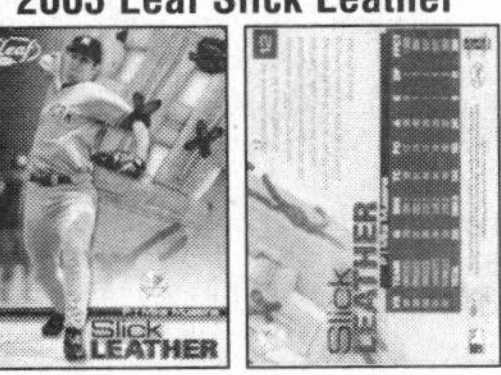

Issued at a stated rate of one in 21, this 15-card insert set features the most skilled fielders on cards featuring faux leather grain.

	Nm-Mt	Ex-Mt
1 Omar Vizquel	3.00	.90
2 Roberto Alomar	3.00	.90
3 Ivan Rodriguez	4.00	1.20
4 Greg Maddux	6.00	1.80
5 Scott Rolen	4.00	1.20
6 Todd Helton	3.00	.90
7 Andruw Jones	3.00	.90
8 Jim Edmonds	3.00	.90
9 Barry Bonds	10.00	3.00
10 Eric Chavez	3.00	.90
11 Ichiro Suzuki	6.00	1.80
12 Mike Mussina	3.00	.90
13 John Olerud	3.00	.90
14 Torii Hunter	3.00	.90
15 Larry Walker	3.00	.90

2004 Leaf

This 301-card standard-size set was released in January, 2004. The set was issued in six-card packs with an $3 SRP which came 24 packs to a box and six boxes to a case. The first 200 cards were printed in higher quantities than the last 101 cards in this set. Cards numbered 201 through 251 feature 50 of the leading prospects. Cards numbered 252 through 271 feature 20 players in a Passing Through Time subset while the final 30 cards of the set feature team checklists. Card number 42 was not issued as this product does not use that number in honor of Jackie Robinson.

	Nm-Mt	Ex-Mt
COMPLETE SET (301)	100.00	30.00
COMP.SETw/o SP's (200)	25.00	7.50
COMMON CARD (1-201)	.30	.09
COMMON CARD (202-251)	1.00	.30
COMMON CARD (252-301)	1.00	.30
202-301 RANDOM INSERTS IN PACKS		
CARD 42 DOES NOT EXIST		
1 Darin Erstad	.30	.09
2 Garret Anderson	.30	.09
3 Jarrod Washburn	.30	.09
4 Kevin Appier	.30	.09
5 Tim Salmon	.50	.15
6 Troy Glaus	.30	.09
7 Troy Percival	.30	.09
8 Jason Johnson	.30	.09
9 Jay Gibbons	.30	.09
10 Melvin Mora	.30	.09
11 Sidney Ponson	.30	.09
12 Tony Batista	.30	.09
13 Derek Lowe	.30	.09
14 Robert Person	.30	.09
15 Manny Ramirez	.50	.15
16 Nomar Garciaparra	1.25	.35
17 Pedro Martinez	.75	.23
18 Jorge De La Rosa	.30	.09
19 Bartolo Colon	.30	.09
20 Carlos Lee	.30	.09
21 Esteban Loaiza	.30	.09
22 Frank Thomas	.75	.23
23 Joe Crede	.30	.09
24 Magglio Ordonez	.30	.09
25 Ryan Ludwick	.30	.09
26 Luis Garcia	.30	.09
27 Brandon Phillips	.30	.09
28 C.C Sabathia	.30	.09
29 Jhonny Peralta	.30	.09
30 Josh Bard	.30	.09
31 Omar Vizquel	.50	.15
32 Fernando Rodney	.30	.09
33 Mike Maroth	.30	.09
34 Bobby Higginson	.30	.09
35 Omar Infante	.30	.09
36 Dmitri Young	.30	.09
37 Eric Munson	.30	.09
38 Jeremy Bonderman	.30	.09
39 Carlos Beltran	.50	.15
40 Jeremy Affeldt	.30	.09
41 Dee Brown	.30	.09
42 Does Not Exist		
43 Mike Sweeney	.30	.09
44 Brent Abernathy	.30	.09
45 Runelvys Hernandez	.30	.09
46 A.J. Pierzynski	.30	.09
47 Corey Koskie	.30	.09
48 Cristian Guzman	.30	.09
49 Jacque Jones	.30	.09
50 Kenny Rogers	.30	.09
51 J.C. Romero	.30	.09
52 Torii Hunter	.30	.09
53 Alfonso Soriano	.50	.15
54 Bernie Williams	.50	.15
55 David Wells	.30	.09
56 Derek Jeter	1.50	.45
57 Hideki Matsui	1.25	.35
58 Jason Giambi	.30	.09
59 Jorge Posada	.50	.15
60 Jose Contreras	.30	.09
61 Mike Mussina	.50	.15
62 Nick Johnson	.30	.09
63 Roger Clemens	1.50	.45
64 Barry Zito	.30	.09
65 Justin Duchscherer	.30	.09
66 Eric Chavez	.30	.09
67 Erubial Durazo	.30	.09
68 Miguel Tejada	.30	.09
69 Mark Mulder	.30	.09
70 Terrence Long	.30	.09
71 Tim Hudson	.30	.09
72 Bret Boone	.30	.09
73 Dan Wilson	.30	.09
74 Edgar Martinez	.50	.15
75 Freddy Garcia	.30	.09
76 Rafael Soriano	.30	.09
77 Ichiro Suzuki	1.25	.35
78 Jamie Moyer	.30	.09
79 John Olerud	.30	.09
80 Kazuhiro Sasaki	.30	.09
81 Aubrey Huff	.30	.09
82 Carl Crawford	.30	.09
83 Joe Kennedy	.30	.09
84 Rocco Baldelli	.30	.09
85 Toby Hall	.30	.09
86 Alex Rodriguez	1.25	.35
87 Kevin Mench	.30	.09
88 Hank Blalock	.30	.09
89 Juan Gonzalez	.50	.15
90 Mark Teixeira	.30	.09
91 Rafael Palmeiro	.50	.15
92 Carlos Delgado	.30	.09
93 Eric Hinske	.30	.09
94 Josh Phelps	.30	.09
95 Brian Bowles	.30	.09
96 Roy Halladay	.30	.09
97 Shannon Stewart	.30	.09
98 Vernon Wells	.30	.09
99 Curt Schilling	.30	.09
100 Junior Spivey	.30	.09
101 Luis Gonzalez	.30	.09
102 Lyle Overbay	.30	.09
103 Mark Grace	.50	.15
104 Randy Johnson	.75	.23
105 Shea Hillenbrand	.30	.09
106 Andruw Jones	.30	.09
107 Chipper Jones	.75	.23
108 Gary Sheffield	.30	.09
109 Greg Maddux	1.25	.35
110 Javy Lopez	.30	.09
111 John Smoltz	.50	.15
112 Marcus Giles	.30	.09
113 Rafael Furcal	.30	.09
114 Corey Patterson	.30	.09
115 Juan Cruz	.30	.09
116 Kerry Wood	.75	.23
117 Mark Prior	.75	.23
118 Moises Alou	.30	.09
119 Sammy Sosa	1.25	.35
120 Aaron Boone	.30	.09
121 Adam Dunn	.50	.15
122 Austin Kearns	.30	.09
123 Barry Larkin	.50	.15
124 Ken Griffey Jr.	1.25	.35
125 Brian Reith	.30	.09
126 Wily Mo Pena	.30	.09
127 Jason Jennings	.30	.09
128 Jay Payton	.30	.09
129 Larry Walker	.50	.15
130 Preston Wilson	.30	.09
131 Todd Helton	.50	.15
132 Dontrelle Willis	.30	.09
133 Ivan Rodriguez	.75	.23
134 Josh Beckett	.30	.09
135 Juan Encarnacion	.30	.09
136 Mike Lowell	.30	.09
137 Craig Biggio	.50	.15
138 Jeff Bagwell	.50	.15
139 Jeff Kent	.30	.09
140 Lance Berkman	.30	.09
141 Richard Hidalgo	.30	.09
142 Roy Oswalt	.30	.09
143 Eric Gagne	.75	.23
144 Fred McGriff	.50	.15
145 Hideo Nomo	.75	.23
146 Kazuhisa Ishii	.30	.09
147 Kevin Brown	.30	.09
148 Paul Lo Duca	.30	.09
149 Shawn Green	.30	.09
150 Ben Sheets	.30	.09
151 Geoff Jenkins	.30	.09
152 Rey Sanchez	.30	.09
153 Richie Sexson	.30	.09
154 Wes Helms	.30	.09
155 Shane Nance	.30	.09
156 Fernando Tatis	.30	.09
157 Javier Vazquez	.30	.09
158 Jose Vidro	.30	.09
159 Orlando Cabrera	.30	.09
160 Henry Mateo	.30	.09
161 Vladimir Guerrero	.75	.23
162 Zach Day	.30	.09
163 Edwin Almonte	.30	.09
164 Al Leiter	.30	.09
165 Cliff Floyd	.30	.09
166 Jae Weong Seo	.30	.09
167 Mike Piazza	1.25	.35
168 Roberto Alomar	.50	.15
169 Tom Glavine	.50	.15
170 Bobby Abreu	.30	.09
171 Brandon Duckworth	.30	.09
172 Jim Thome	.75	.23
173 Kevin Millwood	.30	.09
174 Pat Burrell	.30	.09
175 Aramis Ramirez	.30	.09
176 Jack Wilson	.30	.09
177 Brian Giles	.30	.09
178 Jason Kendall	.30	.09
179 Kenny Lofton	.30	.09
180 Kip Wells	.30	.09
181 Kris Benson	.30	.09
182 Albert Pujols	1.50	.45
183 J.D. Drew	.30	.09
184 Jim Edmonds	.30	.09
185 Matt Morris	.30	.09
186 Scott Rolen	.75	.23
187 Woody Williams	.30	.09
188 Cliff Bartosh	.30	.09
189 Brian Lawrence	.30	.09
190 Ryan Klesko	.30	.09
191 Sean Burroughs	.30	.09
192 Xavier Nady	.30	.09
193 Dennis Tankersley	.30	.09
194 Donaldo Mendez	.30	.09
195 Barry Bonds	2.00	.60
196 Benito Santiago	.30	.09
197 Edgardo Alfonzo	.30	.09
198 Cody Ransom	.30	.09
199 Jason Schmidt	.30	.09
200 Rich Aurilia	.30	.09
201 Ken Harvey	.30	.09
202 Adam Loewen ROO	1.00	.30
203 Alfredo Gonzalez ROO	1.00	.30
204 Arnie Munoz ROO	1.00	.30
205 Andrew Brown ROO	1.00	.30
206 Josh Hall ROO	1.00	.30
207 Josh Stewart PROS	1.00	.30
208 Clint Barmes PROS	1.00	.30
209 Brandon Webb PROS	1.00	.30
210 Chien-Ming Wang PROS	2.00	.60
211 Edgar Gonzalez PROS	1.00	.30
212 Alejandro Machado PROS	1.00	.30
213 Jeremy Griffiths PROS	1.00	.30
214 Craig Brazell PROS	1.00	.30
215 Daniel Cabrera PROS	2.00	.60
216 Fernando Cabrera PROS	1.00	.30
217 Terrmel Sledge PROS	1.00	.30
218 Rob Hammock PROS	1.00	.30
219 Francisco Rosario PROS	1.00	.30
220 Francisco Cruceta PROS	1.00	.30
221 Rett Johnson PROS	1.00	.30
222 Guillermo Quiroz PROS	1.00	.30
223 Hong-Chih Kuo PROS	2.00	.60
224 Ian Ferguson PROS	1.00	.30
225 Tim Olson PROS	1.00	.30
226 Todd Wellemeyer PROS	1.00	.30
227 Rich Fischer PROS	1.00	.30
228 Phil Seibel PROS	1.00	.30
229 Joe Valentine PROS	1.00	.30
230 Matt Kata PROS	1.00	.30
231 Michael Hessman PROS	1.00	.30
232 Michel Hernandez PROS	1.00	.30
233 Doug Waechter PROS	1.00	.30
234 Prentice Redman PROS	1.00	.30
235 Nook Logan PROS	1.00	.30
236 Oscar Villarreal PROS	1.00	.30
237 Pete LaForest PROS	1.00	.30
238 Matt Bruback PROS	1.00	.30
239 Josh Willingham PROS	1.00	.30
240 Greg Aquino PROS	1.00	.30
241 Lew Ford PROS	2.00	.60
242 Jeff Duncan PROS	1.00	.30
243 Chris Waters PROS	1.00	.30
244 Miguel Ojeda PROS	1.00	.30
245 Rosman Garcia PROS	1.00	.30
246 Felix Sanchez PROS	1.00	.30
247 Jon Leicester PROS	1.00	.30
248 Roger Deago PROS	1.00	.30
249 Mike Ryan PROS	1.00	.30
250 Chris Capuano PROS	1.00	.30
251 Matt White PROS	1.00	.30
252 Bernie Williams PTT	1.00	.30
253 Mark Grace PTT	1.00	.30
254 Chipper Jones PTT	1.50	.45
255 Greg Maddux PTT	2.50	.75
256 Sammy Sosa PTT	2.50	.75
257 Mike Mussina PTT	1.00	.30
258 Tim Salmon PTT	1.00	.30
259 Barry Larkin PTT	1.00	.30
260 Randy Johnson PTT	1.50	.45
261 Jeff Bagwell PTT	1.00	.30
262 Roberto Alomar PTT	1.00	.30
263 Tom Glavine PTT	1.00	.30
264 Roger Clemens PTT	3.00	.90
265 Barry Bonds PTT	4.00	1.20
266 Ivan Rodriguez PTT	1.50	.45
267 Pedro Martinez PTT	1.50	.45
268 Ken Griffey Jr. PTT	2.50	.75
269 Jim Thome PTT	1.50	.45
270 Frank Thomas PTT	1.50	.45
271 Mike Piazza PTT	2.50	.75
272 Troy Glaus TC	1.00	.30
273 Melvin Mora TC	1.00	.30
274 Nomar Garciaparra TC	2.50	.75
275 Magglio Ordonez TC	1.00	.30
276 Omar Vizquel TC	1.00	.30
277 Dmitri Young TC	1.00	.30
278 Mike Sweeney TC	1.00	.30
279 Torii Hunter TC	1.00	.30
280 Derek Jeter TC	3.00	.90
281 Barry Zito TC	1.00	.30
282 Ichiro Suzuki TC	2.50	.75
283 Rocco Baldelli TC	1.00	.30
284 Alex Rodriguez TC	2.50	.75
285 Carlos Delgado TC	1.00	.30
286 Randy Johnson TC	1.50	.45
287 Greg Maddux TC	2.50	.75
288 Sammy Sosa TC	2.50	.75
289 Ken Griffey Jr. TC	2.50	.75
290 Todd Helton TC	1.00	.30
291 Ivan Rodriguez TC	1.50	.45
292 Jeff Bagwell TC	1.00	.30
293 Hideo Nomo TC	1.50	.45
294 Richie Sexson TC	1.00	.30
295 Vladimir Guerrero TC	1.50	.45
296 Mike Piazza TC	2.50	.75
297 Jim Thome TC	1.50	.45
298 Jason Kendall TC	1.00	.30
299 Albert Pujols TC	3.00	.90
300 Ryan Klesko TC	1.00	.30
301 Barry Bonds TC	4.00	1.20

2004 Leaf Second Edition

	Nm-Mt	Ex-Mt
*2ND ED 1-201: .4X TO 1X BASIC		
*2ND ED 202-301: .4X TO 1X BASIC		
ISSUED IN SECOND EDITION PACKS		

2004 Leaf Autographs

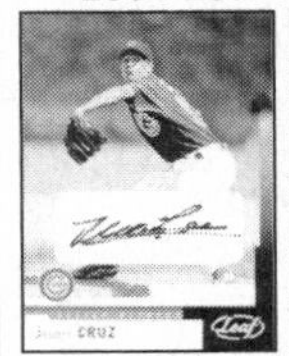

	Nm-Mt	Ex-Mt
RANDOM INSERTS IN PACKS		
SP INFO PROVIDED BY DONRUSS		
SP'S ARE NOT SERIAL-NUMBERED		
14 Robert Person	10.00	3.00
18 Jorge De La Rosa	10.00	3.00
25 Ryan Ludwick	10.00	3.00
26 Luis Garcia	10.00	3.00
29 Jhonny Peralta	15.00	4.50
30 Josh Bard	10.00	3.00
32 Fernando Rodney	10.00	3.00
33 Mike Maroth	10.00	3.00
35 Omar Infante	10.00	3.00
37 Eric Munson SP/9		
41 Dee Brown	10.00	3.00
44 Brent Abernathy SP	15.00	4.50
51 J.C. Romero	10.00	3.00
65 Justin Duchscherer	15.00	4.50
70 Terrence Long SP	15.00	4.50
76 Rafael Soriano	10.00	3.00
85 Toby Hall SP	15.00	4.50
87 Kevin Mench	10.00	3.00
95 Brian Bowles	10.00	3.00
115 Juan Cruz	10.00	3.00
125 Brian Reith	10.00	3.00
126 Wily Mo Pena	15.00	4.50
127 Jason Jennings	10.00	3.00
150 Ben Sheets SP/17		
155 Shane Nance	10.00	3.00
160 Henry Mateo SP	15.00	4.50
163 Edwin Almonte	10.00	3.00
171 Brandon Duckworth	10.00	3.00
176 Jack Wilson	15.00	4.50
180 Kip Wells	10.00	3.00
188 Cliff Bartosh	10.00	3.00
189 Brian Lawrence	10.00	3.00
193 Dennis Tankersley	10.00	3.00
194 Donaldo Mendez	10.00	3.00
198 Cody Ransom SP	15.00	4.50
247 Jon Leicester PROS SP	15.00	4.50

2004 Leaf Press Proofs Blue

	Nm-Mt	Ex-Mt
*BLUE 1-201: 4X TO 10X BASIC		
*BLUE 202-251: 1.25X TO 3X BASIC		
*BLUE 252-301: 2X TO 5X BASIC		
RANDOM INSERTS IN PACKS		
STATED PRINT RUN 100 SERIAL #'d SETS		

2004 Leaf Press Proofs Gold

	Nm-Mt	Ex-Mt
RANDOM INSERTS IN PACKS		
STATED PRINT RUN 25 SERIAL #'d SETS		
NO PRICING DUE TO SCARCITY		

2004 Leaf Press Proofs Red

	Nm-Mt	Ex-Mt
*RED 1-201: 2X TO 5X BASIC		
*RED 202-251: .6X TO 1.5X BASIC		
*RED 252-301: 1X TO 2.5X BASIC		
STATED ODDS 1:8		

2004 Leaf Press Proofs Silver

	Nm-Mt	Ex-Mt
*SILVER 1-201: 6X TO 15X BASIC		
*SILVER 202-251: 2X TO 5X BASIC		
*SILVER 252-301: 3X TO 8X BASIC		
RANDOM INSERTS IN PACKS		
STATED PRINT RUN 50 SERIAL #'d SETS		

2004 Leaf Clean Up Crew

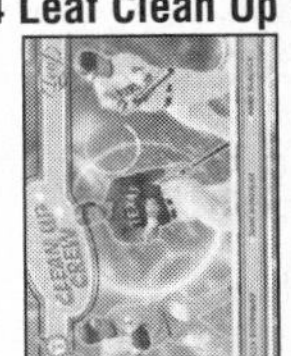

	Nm-Mt	Ex-Mt
STATED ODDS 1:49		
*2ND ED: .4X TO 1X BASIC		
2ND ED.ODDS 1:72 2ND ED.PACKS		
1 Sammy Sosa Moises Alou Hee Seop Choi	6.00	1.80
2 Jason Giambi Alfonso Soriano Hideki Matsui	6.00	1.80
3 Vernon Wells Carlos Delgado Josh Phelps	4.00	1.20

4 Alex Rodriguez 6.00 1.80
Juan Gonzalez
Hank Blalock
5 Gary Sheffield 4.00 1.20
Chipper Jones
Andruw Jones
6 Ken Griffey Jr. 6.00 1.80
Austin Kearns
Aaron Boone
7 Albert Pujols 8.00 2.40
Jim Edmonds
Scott Rolen
8 Jeff Bagwell 4.00 1.20
Lance Berkman
Jeff Kent
9 Todd Helton 4.00 1.20
Preston Wilson
Larry Walker
10 Miguel Tejada 4.00 1.20
Erubial Durazo
Eric Chavez

2004 Leaf Clean Up Crew Materials

Nm-Mt Ex-Mt
RANDOM INSERTS IN PACKS
STATED PRINT RUN 50 SERIAL #'d SETS
2ND ED.RANDOM IN 2ND ED.PACKS
2ND ED.PRINT RUNS 5 SERIAL #'d SETS
NO 2ND ED.PRICING DUE TO SCARCITY
1 Sammy Sosa Bat 40.00 12.00
Moises Alou Bat
Hee Seop Choi Jsy
2 Alfonso Soriano Base 60.00 18.00
Jason Giambi Base
Hideki Matsui Base
3 Vernon Wells Jsy 25.00 7.50
Carlos Delgado Jsy
Josh Phelps Jsy
4 Alex Rodriguez Bat 40.00 12.00
Juan Gonzalez Bat
Hank Blalock Bat
5 Gary Sheffield Jsy 40.00 12.00
Chipper Jones Jsy
Andruw Jones Bat
6 Ken Griffey Jr. Base 40.00 12.00
Austin Kearns Base
Aaron Boone Base
7 Albert Pujols Bat 50.00 15.00
Jim Edmonds Jsy
Scott Rolen Bat
8 Jeff Bagwell Bat 40.00 12.00
Lance Berkman Bat
Jeff Kent Jsy
9 Todd Helton Bat 40.00 12.00
Preston Wilson Bat
Larry Walker Jsy
10 Miguel Tejada Jsy 25.00 7.50
Erubial Durazo Bat
Eric Chavez Jsy

2004 Leaf Cornerstones

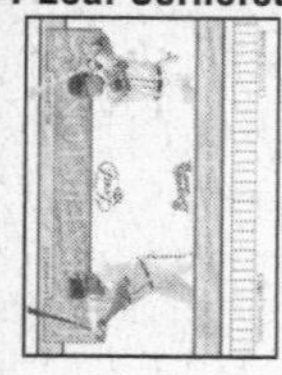

Nm-Mt Ex-Mt
STATED ODDS 1:78
*2ND ED: .4X TO 1X BASIC
2ND ED.ODDS 1:90 2ND ED.PACKS
1 Alex Rodriguez 8.00 2.40
Hank Blalock
2 Kerry Wood 5.00 1.50
Mark Prior
3 Roger Clemens 10.00 3.00
Alfonso Soriano
4 Nomar Garicaparra 8.00 2.40
Manny Ramirez
5 Austin Kearns 5.00 1.50
Adam Dunn
6 Tom Glavine 8.00 2.40
Mike Piazza
7 Andruw Jones 5.00 1.50
Chipper Jones
8 Albert Pujols 10.00 3.00
Scott Rolen
9 Curt Schilling 5.00 1.50
Randy Johnson
10 Hideo Nomo 5.00 1.50
Kazuhisa Ishii

2004 Leaf Cornerstones Materials

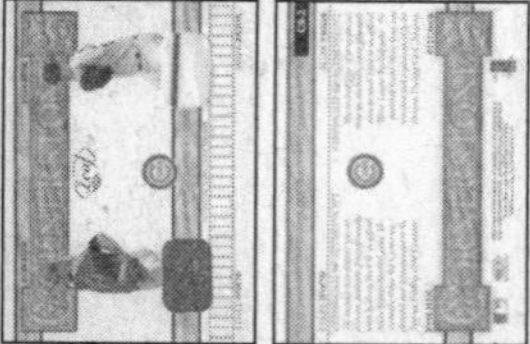

Nm-Mt Ex-Mt
RANDOM INSERTS IN PACKS
STATED PRINT RUN 50 SERIAL #'d SETS
2ND ED.RANDOM IN 2ND ED.PACKS
2ND ED.PRINT RUN 10 SERIAL #'d SETS
NO 2ND ED.PRICING DUE TO SCARCITY
1 Alex Rodriguez Bat 25.00 7.50
Hank Blalock Bat
2 Kerry Wood Jsy 25.00 7.50
Mark Prior Jsy
3 Roger Clemens Jsy 30.00 9.00
Alfonso Soriano Bat
4 Nomar Garicaparra Bat 25.00 7.50
Manny Ramirez Jsy
5 Austin Kearns Bat 15.00 4.50
Adam Dunn Jsy
6 Tom Glavine Jsy 25.00 7.50
Mike Piazza Bat
7 Andruw Jones Bat 25.00 7.50
Chipper Jones Jsy
8 Albert Pujols Bat 50.00 15.00
Scott Rolen Bat
9 Curt Schilling Jsy 25.00 7.50
Randy Johnson Jsy
10 Hideo Nomo Jsy 25.00 7.50
Kazuhisa Ishii Jsy

2004 Leaf Exhibits 1947-66 Made by Donruss-Playoff Print

This 51-card set features players in the design of the old exhibit company cards issued from 1921 through 1964. Please note that there were more than 40 varieties for each of these cards issued and we have notated what the multipier is for each card.

MINT NRMT
STATED PRINT RUN 66 SERIAL #'d SETS
*1921 ACTIVE: .75X TO 2X
*1921 RETIRED: 1X TO 2.5X
1921 PRINT RUN 21 #'d SETS
*1921 AML ACTIVE: .75X TO 2X
*1921 AML RETIRED: 1X TO 2.5X
1921 AL P.RUN 21 #'d SETS
*1925 L ACTIVE: .75X TO 2X
*1925 L RETIRED: 1X TO 2.5X
1925 L PRINT RUN 25 #'d SETS
*1925 R ACTIVE: .75X TO 2X
*1925 R RETIRED: 1X TO 2.5X
1925 R PRINT RUN25 #'d SETS
*1926 B ACTIVE: .75X TO 2X
*1926 B RETIRED: 1X TO 2.5X
1926 B PRINT RUN 26 #'d SETS
*1926 BDP ACTIVE: .75X TO 2X
*1926 BDP RETIRED: 1X TO 2.5X
1926 BDP PRINT RUN 26 #'d SETS
*1926 U ACTIVE: .75X TO 2X
*1926 U RETIRED: 1X TO 2.5X
1926 U PRINT RUN 26 #'d SETS
*1926 UDP ACTIVE: .75X TO 2X
*1926 UDP RETIRED: 1X TO 2.5X
1926 UDP PRINT RUN 26 #'d SETS
*1927 ACTIVE: .75X TO 2X
*1927 RETIRED: 1X TO 2.5X
1927 PRINT RUN 27 #'d SETS
*1927 DP ACTIVE: .75X TO 2X
*1927 DP RETIRED: 1X TO 2.5X
1927 DP PRINT RUN 27 #'d SETS
*1939-46 BOLL: .5X TO 1.2X
1939-46 BOLL PRINT RUN 46 #'d SETS
*1939-46 BOLR: .5X TO 1.2X
1939-46 BOLR PRINT RUN 46 #'d SETS
*1939-46 BWL: .5X TO 1.2X
1939-46 BWL PRINT RUN 46 #'d SETS
*1939-46 BWR: .5X TO 1.2X
1939-46 BWR PRINT RUN 46 #'d SETS
*1939-46 CL: .5X TO 1.2X
1939-46 CL PRINT RUN 46 #'d SETS.
*1939-46 CR: .5X TO 1.2X
1939-46 CR PRINT RUN 46 #'d SETS
*1939-46 CYL: .5X TO 1.2X
1939-46 CYL PRINT RUN 46 #'d SETS
*1939-46 CYR: .5X TO 1.2X
1939-46 CYR PRINT RUN 46 #'d SETS
*1939-46 SL: .5X TO 1.2X
1939-46 SL PRINT RUN 46 #'d SETS.
*1939-46 SR: .5X TO 1.2X
1939-46 SR PRINT RUN 46 #'d SETS
*1939-46 SYL: .5X TO 1.2X
1939-46 SYL PRINT RUN 46 #'d SETS
*1939-46 SYR: .5X TO 1.2X
1939-46 SYR PRINT RUN 46 #'d SETS
*1939-46 TYL: .5X TO 1.2X
1939-46 TYL PRINT RUN 46 #'d SETS
*1939-46 TYR: .5X TO 1.2X
1939-46 TYR PRINT RUN 46 #'d SETS
*1939-46 VBWL: .5X TO 1.2X
1939-46 VBWL PRINT RUN 46 #'d SETS
*1939-46 VBWR: .5X TO 1.2X
1939-46 VBWR PRINT RUN 46 #'d SETS
*1939-46 VTYL: .5X TO 1.2X
1939-46 VTYL PRINT RUN 46 #'d SETS
*1939-46 VTYR: .5X TO 1.2X
1939-46 VTYR PRINT RUN 46 #'d SETS
*1939-46 YTL: .5X TO 1.2X
1939-46 YTL PRINT RUN 46 #'d SETS
*1939-46 YTR: .5X TO 1.2X
1939-46 YTR PRINT RUN 46 #'d SETS
*1947-66 DP SIG: .4X TO 1X
1947-66 DP SIG PRINT RUN 66 #'d SETS
*1947-66 MPRI: .4X TO 1X
1947-66 MPRI PRINT RUN 66 #'d SETS
*1947-66 MSIG: .4X TO 1X
1947-66 MSIG PRINT RUN 66 #'d SETS
*1947-66 PDPPRI: .4X TO 1X
1947-66 PDPPRI PRINT RUN 66 #'d SETS
*1947-66 PDPSIG: .4X TO 1X
1947-66 PDPSIG PRINT RUN 66 #'d SETS
*1947-66 PPRI: .4X TO 1X
1947-66 PPRI PRINT RUN 66 #'d SETS
*1947-66 PSIG: .4X TO 1X
1947-66 PSIG PRINT RUN 66 #'d SETS
*1962-63 NSNL: .4X TO 1X
1962-63 NSNL PRINT RUN 63 #'d SETS
*1962-63 NSNR: .4X TO 1X
1962-63 NSNR PRINT RUN 63 #'d SETS
*1962-63 SBNL: .4X TO 1X
1962-63 SBNL PRINT RUN 63 #'d SETS
*1962-63 SBNR: .4X TO 1X
1962-63 SBNR PRINT RUN 63 #'d SETS
*1962-63 SRNL: .4X TO 1X
1962-63 SRNL PRINT RUN 63 #'d SETS
*1962-63 SRNR: .4X TO 1X
1962-63 SRNR PRINT RUN 63 #'d SETS
RANDOM INSERTS IN PACKS
*ALL 2ND ED: .4X TO 1X
ALL 2ND ED.RANDOM IN 2ND ED.PACKS
SEE CARD BACKS FOR ABBREV.LEGEND
1 Adam Dunn 5.00 2.20
2 Albert Pujols 10.00 4.50
3 Alex Rodriguez 8.00 3.60
4 Alfonso Soriano 5.00 2.20
5 Andruw Jones 4.00 1.80
6 Barry Bonds 12.00 5.50
7 Barry Larkin 5.00 2.20
8 Barry Zito 4.00 1.80
9 Cal Ripken 15.00 6.75
10 Chipper Jones 5.00 2.20
11 Dale Murphy 5.00 2.20
12 Derek Jeter 10.00 4.50
13 Don Mattingly 12.00 5.50
14 Ernie Banks 5.00 2.20
15 Frank Thomas 5.00 2.20
16 George Brett 12.00 5.50
17 Greg Maddux 8.00 3.60
18 Hank Blalock 4.00 1.80
19 Hideo Nomo 5.00 2.20
20 Ichiro Suzuki 8.00 3.60
21 Jason Giambi 4.00 1.80
22 Jim Thome 5.00 2.20
23 Juan Gonzalez 5.00 2.20
24 Ken Griffey Jr. 8.00 3.60
25 Kirby Puckett 5.00 2.20
26 Mark Prior 5.00 2.20
27 Mike Mussina 5.00 2.20
28 Mike Piazza 8.00 3.60
29 Mike Schmidt 10.00 4.50
30 Nolan Ryan Angels 10.00 4.50
31 Nolan Ryan Astros 10.00 4.50
32 Nolan Ryan Rangers 10.00 4.50
33 Nomar Garciaparra 8.00 3.60
34 Ozzie Smith 8.00 3.60
35 Pedro Martinez 5.00 2.20
36 Randy Johnson 5.00 2.20
37 Reggie Jackson Yanks 5.00 2.20
38 Reggie Jackson A's 5.00 2.20
39 Rickey Henderson 5.00 2.20
40 Roberto Alomar 5.00 2.20
41 Roberto Clemente 10.00 4.50
42 Rod Carew 5.00 2.20
43 Roger Clemens 10.00 4.50
44 Sammy Sosa 8.00 3.60
45 Stan Musial 8.00 3.60
46 Tom Glavine 5.00 2.20
47 Tom Seaver 5.00 2.20
48 Tony Gwynn 6.00 2.70
49 Vladimir Guerrero 5.00 2.20
50 Yogi Berra 5.00 2.20

2004 Leaf Gamers

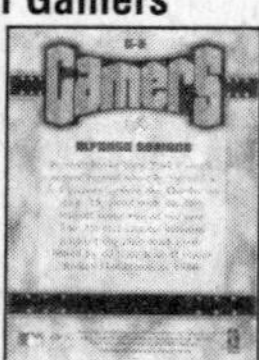

MINT NRMT
STATED ODDS 1:19
*QUANTUM: 1X TO 2.5X BASIC
QUANTUM RANDOM INSERTS IN PACKS
QUANTUM PRINT RUN 100 #'d SETS
*2ND ED: .4X TO 1X BASIC
2ND ED.ODDS 1:22 2ND ED.PACKS
2ND ED.QUAN.RANDOM IN 2ND ED.PACKS
2ND ED.QUANTUM PRINT RUN 10 #'d SETS
NO 2ND ED.QUAN.PRICE DUE TO SCARCITY
1 Albert Pujols 6.00 2.70
2 Alex Rodriguez 5.00 2.20
3 Alfonso Soriano 3.00 1.35
4 Barry Bonds 8.00 3.60
5 Barry Zito 2.00 .90
6 Chipper Jones 3.00 1.35
7 Derek Jeter 6.00 2.70
8 Greg Maddux 5.00 2.20
9 Ichiro Suzuki 5.00 2.20
10 Jason Giambi 2.00 .90
11 Jeff Bagwell 3.00 1.35
12 Ken Griffey Jr. 5.00 2.20
13 Manny Ramirez 3.00 1.35
14 Mark Prior 3.00 1.35
15 Mike Piazza 5.00 2.20
16 Nomar Garciaparra 5.00 2.20
17 Pedro Martinez 3.00 1.35
18 Randy Johnson 3.00 1.35
19 Roger Clemens 6.00 2.70
20 Sammy Sosa 5.00 2.20

2004 Leaf Gold Rookies

MINT NRMT
STATED ODDS 1:23
MIRROR RANDOM INSERTS IN PACKS
MIRROR PRINT RUN 25 SERIAL #'d SETS
NO MIRROR PRICING DUE TO SCARCITY
*2ND ED: .4X TO 1X BASIC
2ND ED.ODDS 1:24 2ND ED.PACKS
2ND ED.MIRR.RANDOM IN 2ND ED.PACKS
2ND ED.MIRROR PRINT RUN 5 #'d SETS

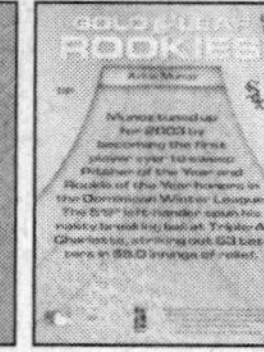

NO 2ND ED.MIRR.PRICE DUE TO SCARCITY
1 Adam Loewen 3.00 1.35
2 Rickie Weeks 3.00 1.35
3 Khalil Greene 5.00 2.20
4 Chad Tracy 3.00 1.35
5 Alexis Rios 3.00 1.35
6 Craig Brazell 3.00 1.35
7 Clint Barmes 3.00 1.35
8 Pete LaForest 3.00 1.35
9 Alfredo Gonzalez 3.00 1.35
10 Arnie Munoz 3.00 1.35

2004 Leaf Home/Away

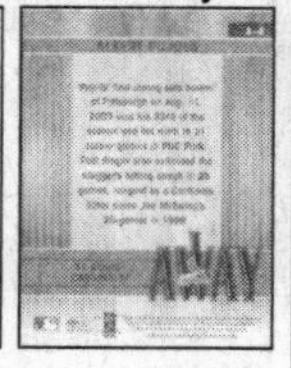

MINT NRMT
STATED ODDS 1:35
*2ND ED: .4X TO 1X BASIC
2ND ED.ODDS 1:35 2ND ED.PACKS
1A Greg Maddux A 8.00 3.60
1H Greg Maddux H 8.00 3.60
2A Sammy Sosa A 8.00 3.60
2H Sammy Sosa H 8.00 3.60
3A Alex Rodriguez A 8.00 3.60
3H Alex Rodriguez H 8.00 3.60
4A Albert Pujols A 10.00 4.50
4H Albert Pujols H 10.00 4.50
5A Jason Giambi A 4.00 1.80
5H Jason Giambi H 4.00 1.80
6A Chipper Jones A 5.00 2.20
6H Chipper Jones H 5.00 2.20
7A Vladimir Guerrero A 5.00 2.20
7H Vladimir Guerrero H 5.00 2.20
8A Mike Piazza A 8.00 3.60
8H Mike Piazza H 8.00 3.60
9A Nomar Garciaparra A 8.00 3.60
9H Nomar Garciaparra H 8.00 3.60
10A Austin Kearns A 4.00 1.80
10H Austin Kearns H 4.00 1.80

2004 Leaf Home/Away Jerseys

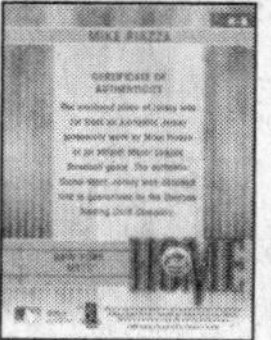

MINT NRMT
STATED ODDS 1:119
*PRIME: 1.25X TO 3X BASIC
PRIME RANDOM INSERTS IN PACKS
PRIME PRINT RUN 50 #'d SETS
*2ND ED: .4X TO 1X BASIC
2ND ED.RANDOM IN 2ND.ED PACKS
2ND ED.PRIME RANDOM IN 2ND ED.PACKS
2ND ED.PRIME PRINT RUN 5 #'d SETS
NO 2ND ED.PRIME PRICE DUE SCARCITY
1A Greg Maddux A 10.00 4.50
1H Greg Maddux H 10.00 4.50
2A Sammy Sosa A 10.00 4.50
2H Sammy Sosa H 10.00 4.50
3A Alex Rodriguez A 10.00 4.50
3H Alex Rodriguez H 10.00 4.50
4A Albert Pujols A 15.00 6.75
4H Albert Pujols H 15.00 6.75
5A Jason Giambi A 5.00 2.20
5H Jason Giambi H 5.00 2.20
6A Chipper Jones A 8.00 3.60
6H Chipper Jones H 8.00 3.60
7A Vladimir Guerrero A 8.00 3.60
7H Vladimir Guerrero H 8.00 3.60
8A Mike Piazza A 10.00 4.50
8H Mike Piazza H 10.00 4.50
9A Nomar Garciaparra A 10.00 4.50
9H Nomar Garciaparra H 10.00 4.50
10A Austin Kearns A 5.00 2.20
10H Austin Kearns H 5.00 2.20

2004 Leaf Limited Previews

MINT NRMT
*GOLD: 1.25X TO 3X BASIC
GOLD PRINT RUN 50 SERIAL #'d SETS
*SILVER: .75X TO 2X BASIC
SILVER PRINT RUN 100 SERIAL #'d SETS
RANDOM INSERTS IN PACKS
1 Derek Jeter 8.00 3.60
2 Barry Zito 4.00 1.80
3 Ichiro Suzuki 6.00 2.70
4 Pedro Martinez 4.00 1.80
5 Alfonso Soriano 4.00 1.80
6 Alex Rodriguez 6.00 2.70
7 Greg Maddux 6.00 2.70
8 Mike Piazza 6.00 2.70
9 Mark Prior 4.00 1.80
10 Albert Pujols 8.00 3.60
11 Sammy Sosa 6.00 2.70
12 Ken Griffey Jr. 6.00 2.70
13 Nomar Garciaparra 6.00 2.70
14 Randy Johnson 4.00 1.80
15 Jason Giambi 4.00 1.80
16 Barry Bonds 10.00 4.50
17 Manny Ramirez 4.00 1.80
18 Chipper Jones 4.00 1.80
19 Jeff Bagwell 4.00 1.80
20 Roger Clemens 8.00 3.60

2004 Leaf MVP Winners

Nm-Mt Ex-Mt
STATED ODDS 1:11
*GOLD: .6X TO 1.5X BASIC
GOLD RANDOM INSERTS IN PACKS
GOLD PRINT RUN 500 SERIAL #'d SETS
*2ND ED: .4X TO 1X BASIC
2ND ED.ODDS 1:12 2ND ED.PACKS
2ND ED.GOLD RANDOM IN 2ND ED.PACKS
2ND ED.GOLD PRINT RUN 25 #'d SETS
NO 2ND ED.GOLD PRICE DUE TO SCARCITY
1 Stan Musial 4.00 1.20
2 Ernie Banks 3.00 .90
3 Roberto Clemente 5.00 1.50
4 George Brett 6.00 1.80
5 Mike Schmidt 5.00 1.50
6 Cal Ripken 83 8.00 2.40
7 Dale Murphy 3.00 .90
8 Ryne Sandberg 5.00 1.50
9 Don Mattingly 6.00 1.80
10 Roger Clemens 5.00 1.50
11 Rickey Henderson 3.00 .90
12 Cal Ripken 91 8.00 2.40
13 Barry Bonds 92 6.00 1.80
14 Barry Bonds 93 6.00 1.80
15 Frank Thomas 3.00 .90
16 Ken Griffey Jr. 4.00 1.20
17 Sammy Sosa 4.00 1.20
18 Chipper Jones 3.00 .90
19 Jason Giambi 3.00 .90
20 Ichiro Suzuki 4.00 1.20

2004 Leaf Picture Perfect

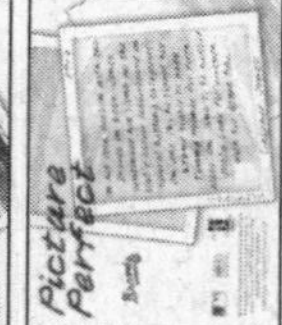

MINT NRMT
STATED ODDS 1:37
*2ND ED: .4X TO 1X BASIC
2ND ED.ODDS 1:45 2ND ED.PACKS
1 Albert Pujols 10.00 4.50
2 Alex Rodriguez 8.00 3.60
3 Alfonso Soriano 5.00 2.20
4 Austin Kearns 3.00 1.35
5 Carlos Delgado 3.00 1.35
6 Chipper Jones 5.00 2.20
7 Hank Blalock 3.00 1.35
8 Jason Giambi 3.00 1.35
9 Jeff Bagwell 5.00 2.20
10 Jim Thome 5.00 2.20
11 Manny Ramirez 5.00 2.20
12 Mike Piazza 8.00 3.60
13 Nomar Garciaparra 8.00 3.60
14 Sammy Sosa 8.00 3.60
15 Todd Helton 5.00 2.20

2004 Leaf Picture Perfect Bats

MINT NRMT
STATED ODDS 1:437
*2ND ED: .4X TO 1X BASIC
2ND ED.RANDOM IN 2ND ED.PACKS
1 Albert Pujols 15.00 6.75
2 Alex Rodriguez 10.00 4.50
3 Alfonso Soriano 8.00 3.60
4 Austin Kearns 5.00 2.20
5 Carlos Delgado 5.00 2.20
6 Chipper Jones 8.00 3.60
7 Hank Blalock 5.00 2.20

ason Giambi 5.00 2.20
eff Bagwell 8.00 3.60
Jim Thome 8.00 3.60
Manny Ramirez 8.00 3.60
Mike Piazza 10.00 4.50
Nomar Garciaparra 10.00 4.50
Sammy Sosa 10.00 4.50
Todd Helton 8.00 3.60

2004 Leaf Recollection Autographs

MINT NRMT
NDOM INSERTS IN PACKS
INT RUNS B/WN 1-31 COPIES PER
) PRICING ON QTY OF 25 OR LESS
.L CARDS ARE 1990 LEAF BUYBACKS
Jesse Barfield 90/29 30.00 13.50
Charlie Hough 90/31 20.00 9.00

2004 Leaf Shirt Off My Back

MINT NRMT
TATED ODDS 1:47
2ND ED: .4X TO 1X BASIC
ND ED.RANDOM IN 2ND ED.PACKS.
Shawn Green 5.00 2.20
Andruw Jones 5.00 2.20
Ivan Rodriguez 8.00 3.60
Hideo Nomo 8.00 3.60
Don Mattingly 15.00 6.75
Mark Prior 8.00 3.60
Alfonso Soriano 8.00 3.60
Richie Sexson 5.00 2.20
Vernon Wells 5.00 2.20
) Nomar Garciaparra 10.00 4.50
1 Jason Giambi 5.00 2.20
2 Austin Kearns 5.00 2.20
3 Chipper Jones 8.00 3.60
4 Rickey Henderson 8.00 3.60
5 Alex Rodriguez 10.00 4.50
6 Garret Anderson 5.00 2.20
7 Vladimir Guerrero 8.00 3.60
8 Sammy Sosa 10.00 4.50
9 Mike Piazza 10.00 4.50
0 David Wells 5.00 2.20
1 Scott Rolen 8.00 3.60
2 Adam Dunn 8.00 3.60
3 Carlos Delgado 5.00 2.20
4 Greg Maddux 10.00 4.50
5 Hank Blalock 5.00 2.20

2004 Leaf Shirt Off My Back Jersey Number Patch

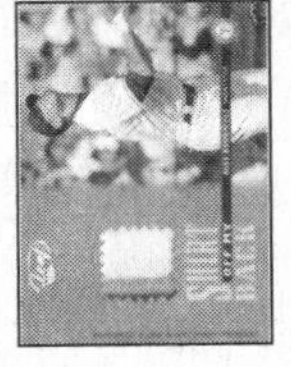

MINT NRMT
RANDOM INSERTS IN PACKS
STATED PRINT RUN 50 SERIAL #'d SETS
BLALOCK PRINT RUN 32 SERIAL #'d CARDS
SOSA PRINT RUN 42 SERIAL #'d CARDS
2ND ED.RANDOM IN 2ND.ED PACKS.
2ND ED.PRINT RUN SERIAL 5 #'d SETS
NO 2ND ED.PRICING DUE TO SCARCITY
Shawn Green 15.00 6.75
Andruw Jones 15.00 6.75
Ivan Rodriguez 25.00 11.00
Hideo Nomo 25.00 11.00
Don Mattingly 40.00 18.00
Mark Prior 25.00 11.00
Alfonso Soriano 25.00 11.00
Richie Sexson 15.00 6.75
Vernon Wells 15.00 6.75
10 Nomar Garciaparra 30.00 13.50
11 Jason Giambi 15.00 6.75
12 Austin Kearns 15.00 6.75
13 Chipper Jones 25.00 11.00
14 Rickey Henderson 25.00 11.00
15 Alex Rodriguez 30.00 13.50
16 Garret Anderson 15.00 6.75
17 Vladimir Guerrero 25.00 11.00
18 Sammy Sosa/42 40.00 18.00
19 Mike Piazza 30.00 13.50
20 David Wells 15.00 6.75
21 Scott Rolen 25.00 11.00
22 Adam Dunn 25.00 11.00
23 Carlos Delgado 15.00 6.75
24 Greg Maddux 30.00 13.50
25 Hank Blalock/32 15.00 6.75

2004 Leaf Shirt Off My Back Jersey Number Patch Autographs

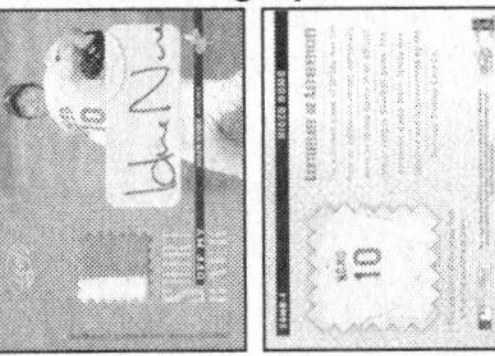

MINT NRMT
RANDOM INSERTS IN PACKS
STATED PRINT RUN 5 SERIAL #'d SETS
2ND ED.RANDOM IN 2ND.ED PACKS.
2ND ED.PRINT RUN 5 SERIAL #'d SETS
NO PRICING DUE TO SCARCITY

2004 Leaf Shirt Off My Back Team Logo Patch

Nm-Mt Ex-Mt
RANDOM INSERTS IN PACKS
PRINT RUNS B/WN 7-75 COPIES PER
NO PRICING ON QTY OF 25 OR LESS
2ND ED.RANDOM IN 2ND ED.PACKS.
2ND ED.PRINT RUN 5 SERIAL #'d SETS
NO 2ND ED.PRICING DUE TO SCARCITY
1 Shawn Green/41 15.00 4.50
2 Andruw Jones/75 15.00 4.50
3 Ivan Rodriguez/75 25.00 7.50
4 Hideo Nomo/74 30.00 9.00
5 Don Mattingly/7
6 Mark Prior/46 25.00 7.50
7 Alfonso Soriano/28 30.00 9.00
8 Richie Sexson/38 15.00 4.50
9 Vernon Wells/74 15.00 4.50
10 Nomar Garciaparra/75 30.00 9.00
11 Jason Giambi/26 20.00 6.00
12 Austin Kearns/32 20.00 6.00
13 Chipper Jones/75 25.00 7.50
14 Rickey Henderson/40 25.00 7.50
15 Alex Rodriguez/75 30.00 9.00
16 Garret Anderson/71 15.00 4.50
17 Vladimir Guerrero/55 25.00 7.50
18 Sammy Sosa/39 40.00 12.00
19 Mike Piazza/75 30.00 9.00
20 David Wells/74 15.00 4.50
21 Scott Rolen/29 30.00 9.00
22 Adam Dunn/32 30.00 9.00
23 Carlos Delgado/56 15.00 4.50
24 Greg Maddux/75 30.00 9.00
25 Hank Blalock/62 15.00 4.50

2004 Leaf Shirt Off My Back Team Logo Patch Autographs

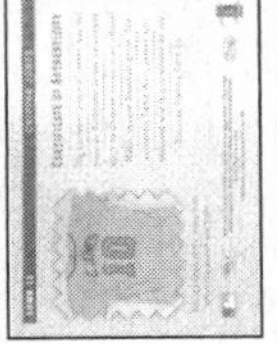

Nm-Mt Ex-Mt
RANDOM INSERTS IN PACKS
STATED PRINT RUN 5 SERIAL #'d SETS
2ND ED.RANDOM IN 2ND ED.PACKS.
2ND ED.PRINT RUN 5 SERIAL #'d SETS
NO PRICING DUE TO SCARCITY

2004 Leaf Sunday Dress

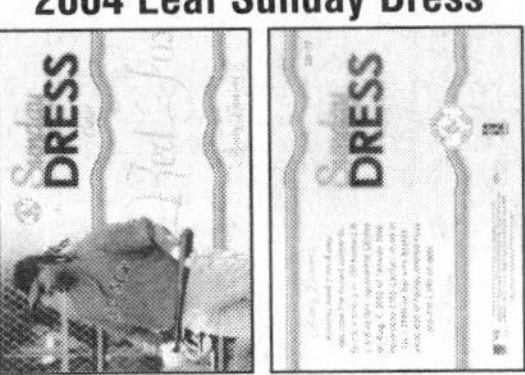

Nm-Mt Ex-Mt
STATED ODDS 1:17
*2ND ED: .4X TO 1X BASIC
2ND ED.ODDS 1:20 2ND ED.PACKS
1 Frank Thomas 2.50 .75
2 Barry Zito 2.00 .60
3 Mike Piazza 4.00 1.20
4 Mark Prior 2.50 .75
5 Jeff Bagwell 2.00 .60
6 Roy Oswalt 2.00 .60
7 Todd Helton 2.00 .60
8 Magglio Ordonez 2.00 .60
9 Alex Rodriguez 4.00 1.20
10 Manny Ramirez 2.00 .60

2004 Leaf Sunday Dress Jerseys

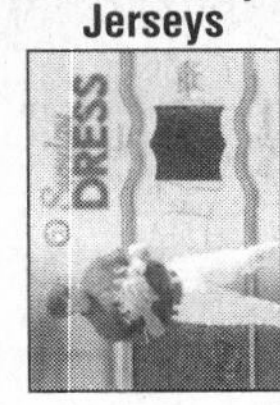

Nm-Mt Ex-Mt
STATED ODDS 1:119
*PRIME: .75X TO 2X BASIC
PRIME RANDOM INSERTS IN PACKS
PRIME PRINT RUN 100 SERIAL #'d SETS
*2ND ED: .4X TO 1X BASIC
2ND ED.RANDOM IN 2ND ED.PACKS.
2ND ED.PRIME RANDOM IN 2ND ED.PACKS
2ND ED.PRIME PRINT RUN 15 #'d SETS
NO 2ND ED.PRIME PRICE DUE SCARCITY
1 Frank Thomas 8.00 2.40
2 Barry Zito 5.00 1.50
3 Mike Piazza 10.00 3.00
4 Mark Prior 8.00 2.40
5 Jeff Bagwell 8.00 2.40
6 Roy Oswalt 5.00 1.50
7 Todd Helton 8.00 2.40
8 Magglio Ordonez 5.00 1.50
9 Alex Rodriguez 10.00 3.00
10 Manny Ramirez 8.00 2.40

2004 Leaf Certified Cuts

This 300-card set was released in September, 2004. The first 200 cards in this set consist of veteran players. Cards 201-221 consists of players who switched teams in the off-season while cards 221-250 are retired legends of baseball and cards 251-300 all feature Rookie Cards. Cards numbered 201 through 250 were randomly inserted into packs and were issued to a stated print run of 599 serial numbered sets. Most cards from 251 through 300 were issued to a stated print run of 499 serial numbered sets and those cards were all autographed by the featured player except fo Kazuo Matsui.

Nm-Mt Ex-Mt
COMP.SET w/o SP's (200) 50.00 15.00
COMMON CARD (1-200) .75 .23
COMMON CARD (201-221) 3.00 .90
COMMON CARD (222-250) 3.00 .90
201-250 RANDOM INSERTS IN PACKS
201-250 PRNT RUN 599 SERIAL #'d SETS
COMMON CARD (251-300) 5.00 1.50
251-300 RANDOM INSERTS IN PACKS
251-300 PRINT RUN 499 SERIAL #'d SETS
OVERALL AU ODDS THREE PER BOX
AUTO PRINT RUNS B/WN 99-499 #'d PER
*OTSUKA JAPANESE SIG: .75X TO 2X HI
1 Vladimir Guerrero 2.00 .60
2 Garret Anderson .75 .23
3 John Lackey .75 .23
4 Bartolo Colon .75 .23
5 Troy Glaus .75 .23
6 Tim Salmon 1.25 .35
7 Shea Hillenbrand .75 .23
8 Brandon Webb .75 .23
9 Roberto Alomar 1.25 .35
10 Randy Johnson 2.00 .60
11 Alex Cintron .75 .23
12 Richie Sexson .75 .23
13 Luis Gonzalez .75 .23
14 Adam LaRoche .75 .23
15 Rafael Furcal .75 .23
16 Chipper Jones 2.00 .60
17 Marcus Giles .75 .23
18 Andruw Jones .75 .23
19 Russ Ortiz .75 .23
20 Rafael Palmeiro 1.25 .35
21 Melvin Mora .75 .23
22 Luis Matos .75 .23
23 Jay Gibbons .75 .23
24 Adam Loewen .75 .23
25 Larry Bigbie .75 .23
26 Rodrigo Lopez .75 .23
27 Javy Lopez .75 .23
28 Miguel Tejada .75 .23
29 Trot Nixon .75 .23
30 Curt Schilling 2.00 .60
31 Jason Varitek 1.25 .35
32 Manny Ramirez 1.25 .35
33 Keith Foulke Sox 1.25 .35
34 Derek Lowe .75 .23
35 Pedro Martinez 2.00 .60
36 Nomar Garciaparra 3.00 .90
37 Bill Mueller .75 .23
38 Johnny Damon 2.00 .60
39 David Ortiz 2.00 .60
40 Mark Prior 2.00 .60
41 Kerry Wood 2.00 .60
42 Sammy Sosa 3.00 .90
43 Derrek Lee .75 .23
44 Greg Maddux 3.00 .90
45 Aramis Ramirez .75 .23
46 Matt Clement .75 .23
47 Carlos Zambrano .75 .23
48 Todd Walker .75 .23
49 Moises Alou .75 .23
50 Corey Patterson .75 .23
51 Frank Thomas 2.00 .60
52 Magglio Ordonez .75 .23
53 Carlos Lee .75 .23
54 Mark Buehrle .75 .23
55 Esteban Loaiza .75 .23
56 Joe Crede .75 .23
57 Paul Konerko .75 .23
58 Adam Dunn 1.25 .35
59 Austin Kearns .75 .23
60 Barry Larkin 1.25 .35
61 Ryan Wagner .75 .23
62 Danny Graves .75 .23
63 Sean Casey .75 .23
64 Ken Griffey Jr. 3.00 .90
65 Jody Gerut .75 .23
66 Cliff Lee .75 .23
67 Victor Martinez .75 .23
68 C.C. Sabathia .75 .23
69 Omar Vizquel 1.25 .35
70 Travis Hafner .75 .23
71 Todd Helton 1.25 .35
72 Preston Wilson .75 .23
73 Jeromy Burnitz .75 .23
74 Larry Walker 1.25 .35
75 Ivan Rodriguez 2.00 .60
76 Rondell White .75 .23
77 Miguel Cabrera 1.25 .35
78 Luis Castillo .75 .23
79 Josh Beckett .75 .23
80 Mike Lowell .75 .23
81 Dontrelle Willis .75 .23
82 Brad Penny .75 .23
83 Hee Seop Choi .75 .23
84 Juan Pierre .75 .23
85 Andy Pettitte 1.25 .35
86 Jeff Bagwell 1.25 .35
87 Roy Oswalt .75 .23
88 Lance Berkman .75 .23
89 Morgan Ensberg .75 .23
90 Craig Biggio 1.25 .35
91 Octavio Dotel .75 .23
92 Wade Miller .75 .23
93 Jeff Kent .75 .23
94 Richard Hidalgo .75 .23
95 Roger Clemens 4.00 1.20
96 Carlos Beltran 1.25 .35
97 Angel Berroa .75 .23
98 Jeremy Affeldt .75 .23
99 Juan Gonzalez 1.25 .35
100 Mike Sweeney .75 .23
101 Kazuhisa Ishii .75 .23
102 Shawn Green .75 .23
103 Milton Bradley .75 .23
104 Paul Lo Duca .75 .23
105 Hideo Nomo 2.00 .60
106 Eric Gagne 2.00 .60
107 Adrian Beltre 1.25 .35
108 Scott Podsednik .75 .23
109 Rickie Weeks .75 .23
110 Ben Sheets .75 .23
111 Geoff Jenkins .75 .23
112 Jacque Jones .75 .23
113 Johan Santana 1.25 .35
114 Shannon Stewart .75 .23
115 Corey Koskie .75 .23
116 Lew Ford .75 .23
117 Torii Hunter .75 .23
118 Chad Cordero .75 .23
119 Orlando Cabrera .75 .23
120 Jose Vidro .75 .23
121 Nick Johnson .75 .23
122 Brad Wilkerson .75 .23
123 Mike Piazza 3.00 .90
124 Jae Weong Seo .75 .23
125 Jose Reyes .75 .23
126 Tom Glavine 1.25 .35
127 Jorge Posada 1.25 .35
128 Gary Sheffield .75 .23
129 Bernie Williams 1.25 .35
130 Mike Mussina 1.25 .35
131 Mariano Rivera 1.25 .35
132 Bubba Crosby .75 .23
133 Kevin Brown .75 .23
134 Javier Vazquez .75 .23
135 Jason Giambi .75 .23
136 Derek Jeter 4.00 1.20
137 Alex Rodriguez 3.00 .90
138 Hideki Matsui 3.00 .90
139 Mark Mulder .75 .23
140 Jermaine Dye .75 .23
141 Tim Hudson .75 .23
142 Barry Zito .75 .23
143 Eric Chavez .75 .23
144 Bobby Crosby 1.25 .35
145 Eric Byrnes .75 .23
146 Marlon Byrd .75 .23
147 Billy Wagner .75 .23
148 Mike Lieberthal .75 .23
149 Jimmy Rollins .75 .23
150 Jim Thome 2.00 .60
151 Bobby Abreu .75 .23
152 Pat Burrell .75 .23
153 Jose Castillo .75 .23
154 Craig Wilson .75 .23
155 Jason Bay .75 .23
156 Jason Kendall .75 .23
157 Raul Mondesi .75 .23
158 Jay Payton .75 .23
159 Trevor Hoffman .75 .23
160 Jake Peavy .75 .23
161 Sean Burroughs .75 .23
162 Phil Nevin .75 .23
163 Brian Giles .75 .23
164 Ryan Klesko .75 .23
165 Todd Linden .75 .23
166 Jerome Williams .75 .23
167 Jason Schmidt .75 .23
168 Ray Durham .75 .23
169 Marquis Grissom .75 .23
170 Shigetoshi Hasegawa .75 .23
171 Edgar Martinez 1.25 .35
172 Freddy Garcia .75 .23
173 Bret Boone .75 .23
174 Raul Ibanez .75 .23
175 Ichiro Suzuki 3.00 .90
176 Randy Winn .75 .23
177 Scott Rolen 2.00 .60
178 Jim Edmonds .75 .23
179 Albert Pujols 4.00 1.20
180 Matt Morris .75 .23
181 Edgar Renteria .75 .23
182 Aubrey Huff .75 .23
183 Delmon Young .75 .23
184 Dewon Brazelton .75 .23
185 Rocco Baldelli .75 .23
186 Carl Crawford .75 .23
187 Mark Teixeira .75 .23
188 Hank Blalock .75 .23
189 Michael Young .75 .23
190 Laynce Nix .75 .23
191 Alfonso Soriano 1.25 .35
192 Kevin Mench .75 .23
193 Adrian Gonzalez .75 .23
194 Alexis Rios .75 .23
195 Roy Halladay .75 .23
196 Vernon Wells .75 .23
197 Carlos Delgado .75 .23
198 Bill Hall .75 .23
199 Jose Guillen .75 .23
200 Jeremy Bonderman .75 .23
201 Roger Clemens Yanks SP 8.00 2.40
202 Alex Rodriguez Rgr SP 8.00 2.40
203 Greg Maddux Braves SP 8.00 2.40
204 Miguel Tejada A's SP 3.00 .90
205 Alfonso Soriano Yanks SP 5.00 1.50
206 Andy Pettitte Yanks SP 5.00 1.50
207 Curt Schilling D'backs SP 3.00 .90
208 Gary Sheffield Braves SP 5.00 1.50
209 Ivan Rodriguez Marlins SP 5.00 1.50
210 Jim Thome Indians SP 5.00 1.50
211 Mike Mussina O's SP 5.00 1.50
212 Mike Piazza Dodgers SP 8.00 2.40
213 Randy Johnson M's SP 5.00 1.50
214 Roger Clemens Sox SP 8.00 2.40
215 Sammy Sosa Sox SP 8.00 2.40
216 Alex Rodriguez M's SP 8.00 2.40
217 Randy Johnson Astros SP 5.00 1.50
218 Vladimir Guerrero Expos SP 5.00 1.50
219 Rafael Palmeiro Rgr SP 5.00 1.50
220 Manny Ramirez Indians SP 5.00 1.50
221 Mike Piazza Marlins SP 8.00 2.40
222 Cal Ripken LGD 15.00 4.50
223 Ted Williams LGD 10.00 3.00
224 Duke Snider LGD 5.00 1.50
225 Ernie Banks LGD 5.00 1.50
226 Ryne Sandberg LGD 10.00 3.00
227 Mark Grace LGD 5.00 1.50
228 Andre Dawson LGD 3.00 .90
229 Bob Feller LGD 5.00 1.50
230 Ty Cobb LGD 8.00 2.40
231 George Brett LGD 10.00 3.00
232 Bo Jackson LGD 5.00 1.50
233 Robin Yount LGD 8.00 2.40
234 Harmon Killebrew LGD 5.00 1.50
235 Gary Carter LGD 3.00 .90
236 Don Mattingly LGD 10.00 3.00
237 Phil Rizzuto LGD 5.00 1.50
238 Babe Ruth LGD 10.00 3.00
239 Lou Gehrig LGD 8.00 2.40
240 Reggie Jackson LGD 5.00 1.50
241 Rickey Henderson LGD 5.00 1.50
242 Mike Schmidt LGD 10.00 3.00
243 Roberto Clemente LGD 10.00 3.00
244 Tony Gwynn LGD 8.00 2.40
245 Will Clark LGD 5.00 1.50
246 Lou Brock LGD 5.00 1.50
247 Bob Gibson LGD 5.00 1.50
248 Stan Musial LGD 8.00 2.40
249 Nolan Ryan LGD 12.00 3.60
250 Dale Murphy LGD 5.00 1.50
251 A.Baldiris ROO AU/499 RC 10.00 3.00
252 A.Otsuka ROO AU/99 RC 40.00 12.00
253 A.Blanco ROO AU/499 RC 8.00 2.40
254 A.Chavez ROO AU/499 RC 8.00 2.40
255 C.Hines ROO AU/199 RC 10.00 3.00
256 C.Vasquez ROO AU/499 RC 10.00 3.00
257 Casey Daigle ROO/499 RC 5.00 1.50
258 C.Oxspring ROO AU/499 RC 10.00 3.00
259 C.Miller ROO AU/499 RC 8.00 2.40
260 D.Crouthers ROO AU/199 RC 10.00 3.00
261 D.Kelly ROO AU/499 RC 8.00 2.40
262 E.Rodriguez ROO AU/499 RC 10.00 3.00
263 E.Sierra ROO AU/299 RC 10.00 3.00
264 E.Moreno ROO AU/499 RC 10.00 3.00
265 F.Nieve ROO AU/499 RC 8.00 2.40
266 F.Guzman ROO AU/499 RC 8.00 2.40
267 G.Dobbs ROO AU/499 RC 8.00 2.40
268 B.Halsey ROO AU/499 RC 10.00 3.00
269 H.Gimenez ROO AU/499 RC 8.00 2.40
270 I.Ochoa ROO AU/499 RC 8.00 2.40
271 J.Woods ROO AU/499 RC 8.00 2.40
272 J.Brown ROO AU/499 RC 8.00 2.40
273 J.Bartlett ROO AU/499 RC 10.00 3.00
274 J.Szuminski ROO AU/499 RC 8.00 2.40
275 John Gall ROO/499 RC 8.00 2.40
276 J.Vasquez ROO AU/499 RC 8.00 2.40
277 J.Labandeira ROO AU/499 RC 8.00 2.40
278 J.Hampson ROO AU/499 RC 8.00 2.40
279 Kazuo Matsui ROO/499 RC 15.00 4.50
280 K.Cave ROO AU/499 RC 10.00 3.00
281 L.Cormier ROO AU/499 RC 8.00 2.40
282 L.Holdzkom ROO AU/199 RC 10.00 3.00
283 M.Valdez ROO AU/199 RC 15.00 4.50
284 M.Wuertz ROO AU/499 RC 10.00 3.00
285 M.Johnston ROO AU/499 RC 8.00 2.40
286 M.Rouse ROO AU/329 RC 8.00 2.40
287 O.Joseph ROO AU/499 RC 8.00 2.40
288 P.Stockman ROO AU/499 RC 8.00 2.40
289 R.Novoa ROO AU/499 RC 10.00 3.00
290 R.Belisario ROO AU/499 RC 8.00 2.40
291 R.Cedeno ROO AU/499 RC 8.00 2.40
292 R.Meaux ROO AU/499 RC 8.00 2.40
293 Scott Proctor ROO/499 RC 8.00 2.40
294 S.Henn ROO AU/199 RC 10.00 3.00
295 S.Camp ROO AU/499 RC 8.00 2.40
296 S.Hill ROO AU/499 RC 8.00 2.40
297 S.Takatsu ROO AU/99 RC 50.00 15.00
298 T.Bittner ROO AU/199 RC 10.00 3.00
299 William Bergolla ROO/499 RC 5.00 1.50
300 Y.Molina ROO AU/499 RC 20.00 6.00

2004 Leaf Certified Cuts Marble Black

Nm-Mt Ex-Mt
RANDOM INSERTS IN PACKS
STATED PRINT RUN 1 SERIAL #'d SET
NO PRICING DUE TO SCARCITY

2004 Leaf Certified Cuts Marble Blue

Nm-Mt Ex-Mt
*BLUE 1-200: 2.5X TO 6X BASIC
*BLUE 201-221: 1.25X TO 3X BASIC
*BLUE 222-250: 1.25X TO 3X BASIC
*BLUE 251-300: .6X TO 1.5X BASIC
*BLUE 251-300: .3X TO .8X AU p/r 299-499
*BLUE 251-300: .25X TO .6X AU p/r 199
*BLUE 251-300: .15X TO .4X AU p/r 99
RANDOM INSERTS IN PACKS
STATED PRINT RUN 50 SERIAL #'d SETS

2004 Leaf Certified Cuts Marble Emerald

Nm-Mt Ex-Mt
RANDOM INSERTS IN PACKS
STATED PRINT RUN 5 SERIAL #'d SETS
NO PRICING DUE TO SCARCITY

2004 Leaf Certified Cuts Marble Gold

Nm-Mt Ex-Mt
*GOLD 1-200: 4X TO 10X BASIC
*GOLD 201-221: 2X TO 5X BASIC
*GOLD 222-250: 2X TO 5X BASIC
RANDOM INSERTS IN PACKS
STATED PRINT RUN 25 SERIAL #'d SETS
251-300 NO PRICING DUE TO SCARCITY

2004 Leaf Certified Cuts Marble Red

Nm-Mt Ex-Mt
*RED 1-200: 1.5X TO 4X BASIC
*RED 201-221: .75X TO 2X BASIC
*RED 222-250: .75X TO 2X BASIC
*RED 251-300: .4X TO 1X BASIC
*RED 251-300: .2X TO .5X AU p/r 299-499
*RED 251-300: .15X TO .4X AU p/r 199
*RED 251-300: .1X TO .25X AU p/r 99
RANDOM INSERTS IN PACKS
STATED PRINT RUN 100 SERIAL #'d SETS

2004 Leaf Certified Cuts Marble Material Blue Number

Nm-Mt Ex-Mt
*BLUE p/r 66-100: .4X TO 1X RED p/r 66-100
*BLUE p/r 36-65: .6X TO 1.5X RED p/r 66-100
*BLUE p/r 36-65: .25X TO .6X RED p/r 20-35
*BLUE p/r 36-65: .2X TO .5X RED p/r 15-19
*BLUE p/r 20-35: 1X TO 2.5X RED p/r 66-100
*BLUE p/r 20-35: .6X TO 1.5X RED p/r 36-65
*BLUE p/r 20-35: .4X TO 1X RED p/r 20-35
*BLUE p/r 20-35: .3X TO .8X RED p/r 15-19
*BLUE p/r 15-19: 1.25X TO 3X RED p/r 66-100
*BLUE p/r 15-19: .75X TO 2X RED p/r 36-65
*BLUE p/r 15-19: .5X TO 1.2X RED p/r 20-35
*BLUE p/r 15-19: .4X TO 1X RED p/r 15-19
OVERALL GU ODDS ONE PER BOX
PRINT RUNS B/WN 1-75 COPIES PER
NO PRICING ON QTY OF 14 OR LESS

2004 Leaf Certified Cuts Marble Material Red Position

Nm-Mt Ex-Mt
OVERALL GU ODDS ONE PER BOX
PRINT RUNS B/WN 1-100 COPIES PER
NO PRICING ON QTY OF 10 OR LESS
1 Vladimir Guerrero Jsy/100 10.00 3.00
2 Garret Anderson Jsy/100 5.00 1.50
5 Troy Glaus Jsy/75 5.00 1.50
6 Tim Salmon Jsy/75 8.00 2.40
8 Brandon Webb Jsy/10
10 Randy Johnson Jsy/100 10.00 3.00
12 Richie Sexson Jsy/10
13 Luis Gonzalez Jsy/100 5.00 1.50
15 Rafael Furcal Jsy/100 5.00 1.50
16 Chipper Jones Jsy/100 10.00 3.00
17 Marcus Giles Jsy/100 5.00 1.50
18 Andruw Jones Jsy/100 5.00 1.50
20 Rafael Palmeiro Jsy/100 8.00 2.40
21 Melvin Mora Jsy/50 8.00 2.40
22 Luis Matos Jsy/50 8.00 2.40
23 Jay Gibbons Jsy/100 5.00 1.50
25 Larry Bigbie Jsy/50 8.00 2.40
26 Rodrigo Lopez Jsy/50 8.00 2.40
27 Javy Lopez Jsy/25 12.00 3.60
28 Miguel Tejada Jsy/100 5.00 1.50
30 Curt Schilling Jsy/50 15.00 4.50
31 Jason Varitek Jsy/100 8.00 2.40
32 Manny Ramirez Jsy/100 8.00 2.40
35 Pedro Martinez Jsy/100 10.00 3.00
39 David Ortiz Jsy/100 10.00 3.00
40 Mark Prior Jsy/100 10.00 3.00
41 Kerry Wood Pants/100 10.00 3.00
42 Sammy Sosa Jsy/100 12.00 3.60
44 Greg Maddux Jsy/50 20.00 6.00
45 Aramis Ramirez Jsy/100 5.00 1.50
49 Moises Alou Jsy/10
51 Frank Thomas Jsy/100 10.00 3.00
52 Magglio Ordonez Jsy/100 5.00 1.50
53 Carlos Lee Jsy/100 5.00 1.50
54 Mark Buehrle Jsy/100 5.00 1.50
57 Paul Konerko Jsy/50 8.00 2.40
58 Adam Dunn Jsy/100 8.00 2.40
59 Austin Kearns Jsy/100 5.00 1.50
60 Barry Larkin Jsy/100 5.00 1.50
63 Sean Casey Jsy/10
65 Jody Gerut Jsy/100 5.00 1.50
66 Cliff Lee Jsy/100 5.00 1.50
67 Victor Martinez Jsy/100 5.00 1.50
68 C.C. Sabathia Jsy/100 5.00 1.50
69 Omar Vizquel Jsy/100 8.00 2.40
70 Travis Hafner Jsy/100 5.00 1.50
71 Todd Helton Jsy/100 8.00 2.40
72 Preston Wilson Jsy/100 5.00 1.50
73 Jeromy Burnitz Jsy/10
74 Larry Walker Jsy/10
75 Ivan Rodriguez Jsy/50 15.00 4.50
77 Miguel Cabrera Jsy/100 8.00 2.40
79 Josh Beckett Jsy/100 5.00 1.50
81 Dontrelle Willis Jsy/100 5.00 1.50
82 Brad Penny Jsy/100 5.00 1.50
85 Andy Pettitte Jsy/10
86 Jeff Bagwell Jsy/100 8.00 2.40
87 Roy Oswalt Jsy/100 5.00 1.50
88 Lance Berkman Jsy/100 5.00 1.50
89 Morgan Ensberg Jsy/100 5.00 1.50
90 Craig Biggio Jsy/100 8.00 2.40
93 Jeff Kent Jsy/100 5.00 1.50
94 Richard Hidalgo Pants/100 5.00 1.50
95 Roger Clemens Jsy/25 30.00 9.00
96 Carlos Beltran Jsy/100 8.00 2.40
97 Angel Berroa Pants/100 5.00 1.50
100 Mike Sweeney Jsy/100 5.00 1.50
101 Kazuhisa Ishii Jsy/100 5.00 1.50
102 Shawn Green Jsy/100 5.00 1.50
104 Paul Lo Duca Jsy/100 5.00 1.50
105 Hideo Nomo Jsy/100 10.00 3.00
107 Adrian Beltre Jsy/100 8.00 2.40
110 Ben Sheets Jsy/100 5.00 1.50
111 Geoff Jenkins Jsy/100 5.00 1.50
112 Jacque Jones Jsy/100 5.00 1.50
113 Johan Santana Jsy/100 8.00 2.40
114 Shannon Stewart Jsy/100 5.00 1.50
117 Torii Hunter Jsy/75 5.00 1.50
119 Orlando Cabrera Jsy/10
120 Jose Vidro Jsy/10
123 Mike Piazza Jsy/100 12.00 3.60
124 Jae Weong Seo Jsy/10
125 Jose Reyes Jsy/75 5.00 1.50
126 Tom Glavine Jsy/75 8.00 2.40
127 Jorge Posada Jsy/100 8.00 2.40
129 Bernie Williams Jsy/100 8.00 2.40
130 Mike Mussina Jsy/25 20.00 6.00
131 Mariano Rivera Jsy/100 8.00 2.40
135 Jason Giambi Jsy/10
138 Hideki Matsui Jsy/100 30.00 9.00
139 Mark Mulder Jsy/100 5.00 1.50
141 Tim Hudson Jsy/10
142 Barry Zito Jsy/100 5.00 1.50
143 Eric Chavez Jsy/100 5.00 1.50
146 Marlon Byrd Jsy/100 5.00 1.50
150 Jim Thome Jsy/100 10.00 3.00
151 Bobby Abreu Jsy/100 5.00 1.50
152 Pat Burrell Jsy/100 5.00 1.50
154 Craig Wilson Jsy/100 5.00 1.50
156 Jason Kendall Jsy/100 5.00 1.50
161 Sean Burroughs Jsy/100 5.00 1.50
163 Brian Giles Jsy/10
164 Ryan Klesko Jsy/100 5.00 1.50
166 Jerome Williams Jsy/25 12.00 3.60
171 Edgar Martinez Jsy/100 8.00 2.40
172 Freddy Garcia Jsy/100 5.00 1.50
177 Scott Rolen Jsy/100 10.00 3.00
178 Jim Edmonds Jsy/100 5.00 1.50
179 Albert Pujols Jsy/100 25.00 7.50
180 Matt Morris Jsy/75 5.00 1.50
181 Edgar Renteria Jsy/25 12.00 3.60
182 Aubrey Huff Jsy/100 5.00 1.50
184 Dewon Brazelton Jsy/100 5.00 1.50
185 Rocco Baldelli Jsy/100 5.00 1.50
186 Carl Crawford Jsy/100 5.00 1.50
187 Mark Teixeira Jsy/25 12.00 3.60
188 Hank Blalock Jsy/100 5.00 1.50
191 Alfonso Soriano Jsy/100 8.00 2.40
192 Kevin Mench Jsy/100 5.00 1.50
195 Roy Halladay Jsy/100 5.00 1.50
196 Vernon Wells Jsy/100 5.00 1.50
197 Carlos Delgado Jsy/100 5.00 1.50
200 Jeremy Bonderman Jsy/100 5.00 1.50
201 R.Clemens Yanks Jsy/100 12.00 3.60
202 Alex Rodriguez Rgr Jsy/100 12.00 3.60
203 G.Maddux Braves Jsy/100 12.00 3.60
204 Miguel Tejada A's Jsy/100 5.00 1.50
205 Alf Soriano Yanks Jsy/100 8.00 2.40
206 A.Pettitte Yanks Jsy/100 8.00 2.40
207 C.Schilling D'backs Jsy/100 5.00 1.50
208 G.Sheffield Braves Jsy/50 8.00 2.40
209 I.Rodriguez Marlins Jsy/100 10.00 3.00
210 Jim Thome Indians Jsy/25 25.00 7.50
211 Mike Mussina O's Jsy/50 12.00 3.60
212 M.Piazza Dodgers Jsy/100 12.00 3.60
213 R.Johnson M's Jsy/100 10.00 3.00
214 R.Clemens Sox Jsy/100 12.00 3.60
215 Sammy Sosa Sox Jsy/50 20.00 6.00
216 A.Rodriguez M's Jsy/100 12.00 3.60
217 R.Johnson Astros Jsy/100 10.00 3.00
218 V.Guerrero Expos Jsy/100 10.00 3.00
219 R.Palmeiro Rgr Jsy/100 8.00 2.40
221 M.Piazza Marlins Jsy/100 12.00 3.60
222 Cal Ripken LGD Jsy/50 60.00 18.00
223 Ted Williams LGD Jsy/25 120.00 36.00
225 Ernie Banks LGD Jsy/50 20.00 6.00
226 R.Sandberg LGD Jsy/100 20.00 6.00
227 Mark Grace LGD Jsy/25 25.00 7.50
228 Andre Dawson LGD Jsy/100 8.00 2.40
229 Bob Feller LGD Jsy/25 25.00 7.50
230 Ty Cobb LGD Pants/1
231 George Brett LGD Jsy/100 20.00 6.00
232 Bo Jackson LGD Jsy/100 15.00 4.50
233 Robin Yount LGD Jsy/100 15.00 4.50
234 H.Killebrew LGD Jsy/25 30.00 9.00
235 Gary Carter LGD Jkt/100 8.00 2.40
236 Don Mattingly LGD Jsy/50 30.00 9.00
237 Phil Rizzuto LGD Pants/25 25.00 7.50
238 Babe Ruth LGD Pants/50 200.00 60.00
239 Lou Gehrig LGD Pants/50 150.00 45.00
240 R.Jackson LGD Jsy/100 12.00 3.60
241 R.Henderson LGD Jsy/100 15.00 4.50
242 Mike Schmidt LGD Jsy/50 30.00 9.00
243 R.Clemente LGD Jsy/50 100.00 30.00
244 Tony Gwynn LGD Jsy/100 15.00 4.50
245 Will Clark LGD Jsy/100 15.00 4.50
246 Lou Brock LGD Jsy/25 25.00 7.50
247 Bob Gibson LGD Jsy/25 25.00 7.50
248 Stan Musial LGD Jsy/25 50.00 15.00
249 Nolan Ryan LGD Jsy/50 40.00 12.00
250 Dale Murphy LGD Jsy/100 12.00 3.60

2004 Leaf Certified Cuts Marble Signature Blue

Nm-Mt Ex-Mt
*1-250 p/r 75: .4X TO 1X RED p/r 66-100
*1-250 p/r 50: .5X TO 1.2X RED p/r 66-100
*1-250 p/r 50: .4X TO 1X RED p/r 36-65
*1-250 p/r 50: .3X TO .8X RED p/r 20-35
*1-250 p/r 50: .25X TO .6X RED p/r 15-19
*1-250 p/r 25: .6X TO 1.5X RED p/r 66-100
*1-250 p/r 25: .5X TO 1.2X RED p/r 36-65
*1-250 p/r 25: .4X TO 1X RED p/r 20-35
*251-300 p/r 65-75: .4X TO 1X RED p/r 66-100
OVERALL AU ODDS THREE PER BOX
PRINT RUNS B/WN 1-75 COPIES PER
1-250 NO PRICING ON QTY OF 10 OR LESS
251-300 NO PRICING ON QTY 25 OR LESS

2004 Leaf Certified Cuts Marble Signature Gold

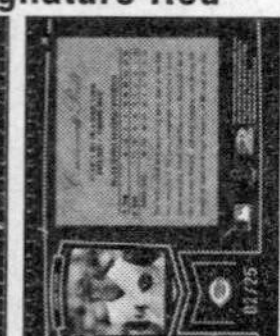

Nm-Mt Ex-Mt
*1-250 p/r 25: .6X TO 1.5X RED p/r 66-100
*1-250 p/r 25: .5X TO 1.2X RED p/r 36-65
*1-250 p/r 25: .4X TO 1X RED p/r 20-35
*1-250 p/r 25: .3X TO .8X RED p/r 15-19
OVERALL AU ODDS THREE PER BOX
PRINT RUNS B/WN 1-25 COPIES PER
1-250 NO PRICING ON QTY OF 10 OR LESS
251-300 NO PRICING DUE TO SCARCITY
33 Keith Foulke Sox/25 60.00 18.00

2004 Leaf Certified Cuts Marble Signature Red

Nm-Mt Ex-Mt
OVERALL AU ODDS THREE PER BOX
PRINT RUNS B/WN 1-100 COPIES PER
1-250 NO PRICING ON QTY OF 10 OR LESS
251-300 NO PRICING ON QTY 25 OR LESS
2 Garret Anderson/50 20.00 6.00
3 John Lackey/100 15.00 4.50
7 Shea Hillenbrand/100 15.00 4.50
8 Brandon Webb/100 10.00 3.00
9 Roberto Alomar/1
11 Alex Cintron/100 10.00 3.00
14 Adam LaRoche/100 10.00 3.00
15 Rafael Furcal/50 20.00 6.00
16 Chipper Jones/1
17 Marcus Giles/50 20.00 6.00
18 Andruw Jones/1
19 Russ Ortiz/100 15.00 4.50
20 Rafael Palmeiro/1
21 Melvin Mora/100 15.00 4.50
22 Luis Matos/100 10.00 3.00
23 Jay Gibbons/100 15.00 4.50
24 Adam Loewen/17 20.00 6.00
25 Larry Bigbie/100 15.00 4.50
26 Rodrigo Lopez/100 10.00 3.00
29 Trot Nixon/50 20.00 6.00
32 Manny Ramirez/1
33 Keith Foulke Sox/100 50.00 15.00
39 David Ortiz/50 50.00 15.00
40 Mark Prior/25 60.00 18.00
41 Kerry Wood/10
42 Sammy Sosa/10
43 Derrek Lee/50 20.00 6.00
44 Greg Maddux/1
45 Aramis Ramirez/100 15.00 4.50
46 Matt Clement/25 25.00 4.50
47 Carlos Zambrano/100 25.00 7.50
48 Todd Walker/100 10.00 3.00
51 Frank Thomas/5
53 Carlos Lee/100 15.00 4.50
54 Mark Buehrle/50 20.00 6.00
55 Esteban Loaiza/100 10.00 3.00
58 Adam Dunn/25 40.00 12.00
59 Austin Kearns/25 25.00 7.50
60 Barry Larkin/5
63 Sean Casey/25 25.00 7.50
65 Jody Gerut/100 10.00 3.00
66 Cliff Lee/100 10.00 3.00
67 Victor Martinez/100 15.00 4.50
68 C.C. Sabathia/100 15.00 4.50
70 Travis Hafner/100 15.00 4.50
71 Todd Helton/1
72 Preston Wilson/100 15.00 4.50
77 Miguel Cabrera/50 30.00 9.00
80 Mike Lowell/25 25.00 7.50
81 Dontrelle Willis/5
82 Brad Penny/100 10.00 3.00
85 Andy Pettitte/1
86 Jeff Bagwell/10
88 Lance Berkman/5
89 Morgan Ensberg/100 10.00 3.00
90 Craig Biggio/25 40.00 12.00
91 Octavio Dotel/100 10.00 3.00
92 Wade Miller/100 10.00 3.00
95 Roger Clemens/1
96 Carlos Beltran/50 40.00 12.00
97 Angel Berroa/50 12.00 3.60
98 Jeremy Affeldt/100 10.00 3.00
99 Juan Gonzalez/5
101 Kazuhisa Ishii/1
102 Shawn Green/1
103 Milton Bradley/100 15.00 4.50
104 Paul Lo Duca/50 20.00 6.00
105 Hideo Nomo/1
108 Scott Podsednik/100 15.00 4.50
109 Rickie Weeks/25 25.00 7.50
112 Jacque Jones/100 15.00 4.50
113 Johan Santana/50 40.00 12.00
114 Shannon Stewart/50 20.00 6.00
116 Lew Ford/100 15.00 4.50
117 Torii Hunter/25 25.00 7.50
118 Chad Cordero/100 10.00 3.00
119 Orlando Cabrera/100 15.00 4.50
120 Jose Vidro/50 12.00 3.60
123 Mike Piazza/5
124 Jae Weong Seo/5
127 Jorge Posada/5
128 Gary Sheffield/10
129 Bernie Williams/1
130 Mike Mussina/5
131 Mariano Rivera/1
132 Bubba Crosby/100 10.00 3.00
139 Mark Mulder/25 25.00 7.50
140 Jermaine Dye/100 15.00 4.50
141 Tim Hudson/1
142 Barry Zito/1
144 Bobby Crosby/100 25.00 7.50
145 Eric Byrnes/100 15.00 4.50
146 Marlon Byrd/100 10.00 3.00
148 Mike Lieberthal/100 15.00 4.50
153 Jose Castillo/100 10.00 3.00
154 Craig Wilson/100 15.00 4.50
155 Jason Bay/100 15.00 4.50
158 Jay Payton/100 10.00 3.00
161 Sean Burroughs/25 25.00 7.50
165 Todd Linden/100 10.00 3.00
170 Shigetoshi Hasegawa/50 50.00 15.00
171 Edgar Martinez/25 50.00 15.00
174 Raul Ibanez/100 10.00 3.00
177 Scott Rolen/50 40.00 12.00
178 Jim Edmonds/5
179 Albert Pujols/10
182 Aubrey Huff/100 15.00 4.50
183 Delmon Young/25 25.00 7.50
184 Dewon Brazelton/100 10.00 3.00
186 Carl Crawford/100 15.00 4.50
187 Mark Teixeira/25 40.00 12.00
188 Hank Blalock/50 20.00 6.00
189 Michael Young/100 15.00 4.50
190 Laynce Nix/100 15.00 4.50
191 Alfonso Soriano/25 50.00 15.00
193 Adrian Gonzalez/100 10.00 3.00
194 Alexis Rios/100 15.00 4.50
195 Roy Halladay/5
196 Vernon Wells/50 20.00 6.00
198 Bill Hall/100 10.00 3.00
199 Jose Guillen/100 15.00 4.50
200 Jeremy Bonderman/100 10.00 3.00
201 Roger Clemens Yanks/1
203 Greg Maddux Braves/1
205 Alfonso Soriano Yanks/25 50.00 15.00
206 Andy Pettitte Yanks/1
208 Gary Sheffield Braves/10
211 Mike Mussina O's/1
212 Mike Piazza Dodgers/5
215 Sammy Sosa Sox/5
220 Manny Ramirez Indians/1
221 Mike Piazza Marlins/5
222 Cal Ripken LGD/25 200.00 60.00
224 Duke Snider LGD/25 40.00 12.00
226 Ryne Sandberg LGD/5
227 Mark Grace LGD/5
228 Andre Dawson LGD/100 15.00 4.50
229 Bob Feller LGD/100 25.00 7.50
231 George Brett LGD/10
232 Bo Jackson LGD/5
234 Harmon Killebrew LGD/10
235 Gary Carter LGD/25 25.00 7.50
236 Don Mattingly LGD/5
237 Phil Rizzuto LGD/25 40.00 12.00
240 Reggie Jackson LGD/10
241 Rickey Henderson LGD/1
242 Mike Schmidt LGD/1
244 Tony Gwynn LGD/5
245 Will Clark LGD/25 60.00 18.00
246 Lou Brock LGD/10
247 Bob Gibson LGD/25 40.00 12.00
248 Stan Musial LGD/25 80.00 24.00
249 Nolan Ryan LGD/25 150.00 45.00
250 Dale Murphy LGD/50 30.00 9.00
251 Aarom Baldiris ROO/100 12.00 3.60
252 Akinori Otsuka ROO/25
253 Andres Blanco ROO/100 8.00 2.40
254 Angel Chavez ROO/100 8.00 2.40
255 Carlos Hines ROO/100 8.00 2.40
256 Carlos Vasquez ROO/100 12.00 3.60
258 Chris Oxspring ROO/100 12.00 3.60
259 Colby Miller ROO/100 8.00 2.40
260 Dave Crouthers ROO/50 10.00 3.00
261 Don Kelly ROO/100 8.00 2.40
262 Eddy Rodriguez ROO/100 12.00 3.60
263 Edwardo Sierra ROO/100 12.00 3.60
264 Edwin Moreno ROO/100 12.00 3.60
266 Freddy Guzman ROO/100 8.00 2.40
267 Greg Dobbs ROO/100 8.00 2.40
268 Brad Halsey ROO/100 12.00 3.60
269 Hector Gimenez ROO/100 8.00 2.40
270 Ivan Ochoa ROO/100 8.00 2.40
271 Jake Woods ROO/100 8.00 2.40
272 Jamie Brown ROO/100 8.00 2.40
273 Jason Bartlett ROO/100 12.00 3.60
274 Jason Szuminski ROO/100 8.00 2.40
275 John Gall ROO/100 12.00 3.60
276 Jorge Vasquez ROO/100 8.00 2.40
277 Josh Labandeira ROO/100 8.00 2.40
280 Kevin Cave ROO/100 12.00 3.60
281 Lance Cormier ROO/100 8.00 2.40
283 Merkin Valdez ROO/100 15.00 4.50
284 Michael Wuertz ROO/100 12.00 3.60
285 Mike Johnston ROO/100 8.00 2.40
287 Onil Joseph ROO/100 8.00 2.40
288 Phil Stockman ROO/100 8.00 2.40
289 Roberto Novoa ROO/100 12.00 3.60
291 Ronny Cedeno ROO/100 8.00 2.40
292 Ryan Meaux ROO/100 8.00 2.40
293 Scott Proctor ROO/100 12.00 3.60
295 Shawn Camp ROO/100 8.00 2.40
297 Shingo Takatsu ROO/25
299 William Bergolla ROO/100 8.00 2.40
300 Yadier Molina ROO/100 20.00 6.00

2004 Leaf Certified Cuts Marble Signature Material Gold Number

Nm-Mt Ex-Mt
*1-221 p/r 35-65: .6X TO 1.5X RED p/r 66-100
*1-221 p/r 35-65: .5X TO 1.2X RED p/r 36-65
*1-221 p/r 35-65: .4X TO 1X RED p/r 20-35
*1-221 p/r 20-35: .75X TO 2X RED p/r 66-100
*1-221 p/r 20-35: .6X TO 1.5X RED p/r 36-65
*1-221 p/r 20-35: .5X TO 1.2X RED p/r 20-35
*1-221 p/r 15-19: 1X TO 2.5X RED p/r 66-100
*1-221 p/r 15-19: .75X TO 2X RED p/r 36-65
*222-250 p/r 36-65: .4X TO 1X RED p/r 20-35
*222-250p/r20-35: .5X TO 1.2X REDp/r20-35
*222-250p/r15-19: 1X TO 2.5X REDp/r66-100
OVERALL AU ODDS THREE PER BOX
PRINT RUNS B/WN 1-57 COPIES PER
NO PRICING ON QTY OF 13 OR LESS
18 Andruw Jones Jsy/25 50.00 15.00
32 Manny Ramirez Jsy/24 80.00 24.00
41 Kerry Wood Pants/34 60.00 18.00
42 Sammy Sosa Jsy/21 150.00 45.00
44 Greg Maddux Jsy/31 120.00 36.00
51 Frank Thomas Jsy/35 60.00 18.00
52 Magglio Ordonez Jsy/30 30.00 9.00
71 Todd Helton Jsy/17 60.00 18.00
81 Dontrelle Willis Jsy/35 30.00 9.00
85 Andy Pettitte Jsy/21 60.00 18.00
88 Lance Berkman Jsy/17 60.00 18.00
101 Kazuhisa Ishii Jsy/17 60.00 18.00
102 Shawn Green Jsy/15 40.00 12.00
123 Mike Piazza Jsy/31 150.00 45.00
124 Jae Weong Seo Jsy/26 30.00 9.00
127 Jorge Posada Jsy/20 60.00 18.00
130 Mike Mussina Jsy/35 50.00 15.00
141 Tim Hudson Jsy/15 40.00 12.00
178 Jim Edmonds Jsy/15 60.00 18.00
195 Roy Halladay Jsy/32 20.00 6.00
227 Mark Grace LGD Jsy/17 60.00 18.00
232 Bo Jackson LGD Jsy/16 150.00 45.00
236 D.Mattingly LGD Jsy/23 100.00 30.00
240 R.Jackson LGD Jsy/44 60.00 18.00
241 R.Henderson LGD Jsy/35 80.00 24.00
242 M.Schmidt LGD Pants/20 100.00 30.00
244 Tony Gwynn LGD Jsy/19 100.00 30.00
246 Lou Brock LGD Jsy/20 50.00 15.00

2004 Leaf Certified Cuts Marble Signature Material Gold Position

Nm-Mt Ex-Mt
*1-221 p/r 50: .6X TO 1.5X RED p/r 66-100
*1-221 p/r 50: .5X TO 1.2X RED p/r 36-65
*1-221 p/r 50: .4X TO 1X RED p/r 20-35
*1-221 p/r 25: .6X TO 1.5X RED p/r 36-65
*1-221 p/r 25: .5X TO 1.2X RED p/r 20-35
*222-250 p/r 50: .6X TO 1.5X RED p/r 66-100
*222-250 p/r 25: .6X TO 1.5X RED p/r 36-65
OVERALL AU ODDS THREE PER BOX
PRINT RUNS B/WN 1-50 COPIES PER
NO PRICING ON QTY OF 10 OR LESS
234 H.Killebrew LGD Jsy/25 80.00 24.00

2004 Leaf Certified Cuts Check Signature Blue

Nm-Mt Ex-Mt
OVERALL AU ODDS THREE PER BOX
PRINT RUNS B/WN 2-60 COPIES PER
NO PRICING ON QTY OF 10 OR LESS
ALL CARDS FEATURE BLUE CHECKS.

Al Kaline/22 80.00 24.00
Andre Dawson/22 30.00 9.00
Bob Gibson/10
Bobby Doerr/10
Brooks Robinson/10
Cal Ripken/5
Cal Ripken/5
Cal Ripken/5
) Cal Ripken/5
1 Carl Yastrzemski/3
2 Carl Yastrzemski/3
3 Carlton Fisk W.Sox/10
4 Carlton Fisk R.Sox/10
5 Dale Murphy/10
7 Dale Murphy/10
8 Don Mattingly/5
9 Don Mattingly/5
0 Don Mattingly/5
1 Don Mattingly/5
2 Duke Snider/20 50.00 15.00
3 Ozzie Smith Padres/4
4 Ozzie Smith Cards/4
5 Ozzie Smith Cards/4
6 Frank Robinson/10
7 George Brett/10
8 George Brett/10
9 George Brett/10
1 George Kell/60 40.00 12.00
3 Harmon Killebrew/10
4 Harmon Killebrew/10
5 Honus Wagner/2
8 Kirby Puckett/5
9 Kirby Puckett/5
1 Lou Brock/10
3 Luis Aparicio/10
4 Mark Grace/10
6 Mike Schmidt/5
7 Mike Schmidt/5
8 Mike Schmidt/5
9 Mike Schmidt/5
0 Nolan Ryan Astros/10
1 Nolan Ryan Rgr/10
2 Nolan Ryan Angels/10
3 Paul Molitor/10
7 Red Schoendienst/10
3 Ron Santo/5
5 Ryne Sandberg/10
7 Stan Musial/8
8 Stan Musial/8
9 Stan Musial/8
0 Steve Carlton Phils/5
1 Steve Carlton W.Sox/5
3 Tony Gwynn/10
4 Tony Gwynn/10
7 Whitey Ford/16 60.00 18.00
8 Will Clark/10
9 Will Clark/10

2004 Leaf Certified Cuts Check Signature Green

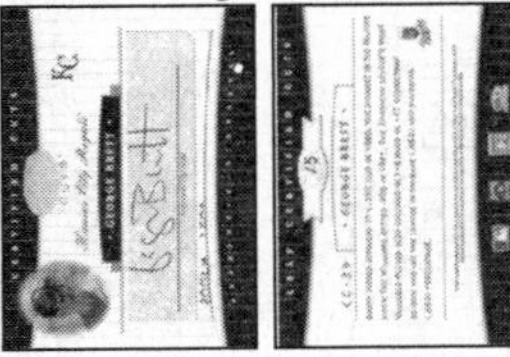

Nm-Mt Ex-Mt
*GREEN p/r 15-18: .6X TO 1.5X BLUE p/r 60
*GREEN p/r 15-18: .4X TO 1X BLUE p/r 16
OVERALL AU ODDS THREE PER BOX
PRINT RUNS B/WN 1-18 COPIES PER
NO PRICING ON QTY OF 5 OR LESS
ALL BUT RYAN FEATURE GREEN CHECKS
RYAN IS BLUE CHECK W/GREEN HOF LOGO

2004 Leaf Certified Cuts Check Signature Red

Nm-Mt Ex-Mt
*RED p/r 36: .4X TO 1X BLUE p/r 60
*RED p/r 16-17: .5X TO 1.2X BLUE p/r 20
*RED p/r 16-17: .4X TO 1X BLUE p/r 16
OVERALL AU ODDS THREE PER BOX
PRINT RUNS B/WN 3-36 COPIES PER
NO PRICING ON QTY OF 11 OR LESS
ALL BUT RYAN FEATURE RED CHECKS
RYAN IS BLUE CHECK W/RED 34 LOGO

2004 Leaf Certified Cuts Check Signature Material Blue

Nm-Mt Ex-Mt
OVERALL AU ODDS THREE PER BOX
PRINT RUNS B/WN 1-100 COPIES PER

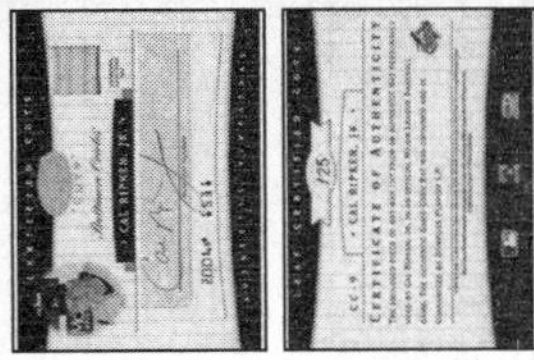

NO PRICING ON QTY OF 6 OR LESS
1 Al Kaline Bat/50 60.00 18.00
2 Andre Dawson Jsy/50 25.00 7.50
3 Babe Ruth Jsy/2
4 Bob Gibson Hat/50 40.00 12.00
5 Bobby Doerr Jsy/50 25.00 7.50
6 Brooks Robinson Bat/50 40.00 12.00
7 Cal Ripken White Jsy/25 250.00 75.00
8 Cal Ripken Orange Jsy/25 250.00 75.00
9 Cal Ripken Bat/25 250.00 75.00
10 Cal Ripken Jkt/25 250.00 75.00
11 Carl Yastrzemski Jsy/6
12 Carl Yastrzemski Bat/6
13 Carlton Fisk Jkt/35 50.00 15.00
14 Carlton Fisk Jsy/35 50.00 15.00
15 Catfish Hunter Jsy/2
16 Dale Murphy White Jsy/50 40.00 12.00
17 Dale Murphy Gray Jsy/50 40.00 12.00
18 Don Mattingly White Jsy/25 100.00 30.00
19 Don Mattingly Gray Jsy/25 100.00 30.00
20 Don Mattingly Bat/25 100.00 30.00
21 Don Mattingly Jkt/25 100.00 30.00
22 Duke Snider Pants/100 40.00 12.00
23 Ozzie Smith Padres Jsy/40 80.00 24.00
24 Ozzie Smith Cards Jsy/40 80.00 24.00
25 Ozzie Smith Bat/40 80.00 24.00
26 Frank Robinson Bat/50 40.00 12.00
27 George Brett White Jsy/30 100.00 30.00
28 George Brett Blue Jsy/30 100.00 30.00
29 George Brett Bat/30 100.00 30.00
30 Hack Wilson Bat/2
32 Hal Newhouser Jsy/15 40.00 12.00
33 Harmon Killebrew Shoe/35 80.00 24.00
34 Harmon Killebrew Bat/35 80.00 24.00
36 Jackie Robinson Jkt/1
37 Jimmie Foxx Bat/3
38 Kirby Puckett Fld Glv/25 80.00 24.00
39 Kirby Puckett Bat/25 80.00 24.00
40 Lou Boudreau Jsy/15 120.00 36.00
41 Lou Brock Jsy/50 40.00 12.00
42 Lou Gehrig Pants/2
43 Luis Aparicio Pants/50 25.00 7.50
44 Mark Grace Fld Glv/50 40.00 12.00
45 Mel Ott Bat/1
46 Mike Schmidt Fld Glv/25 100.00 30.00
47 Mike Schmidt Jsy/25 100.00 30.00
48 Mike Schmidt Jkt/25 100.00 30.00
49 Mike Schmidt Bat/25 100.00 30.00
50 Nolan Ryan Astros Jkt/30 150.00 45.00
51 Nolan Ryan Rgr Pants/30 150.00 45.00
52 Nolan Ryan Angels Jkt/30 150.00 45.00
53 Paul Molitor Bat/50 40.00 12.00
54 Pee Wee Reese Bat/5
57 Red Schoendienst Bat/50 25.00 7.50
58 Roberto Clemente Bat/2
61 Roger Maris Pants/1
62 Rogers Hornsby Bat/2
63 Ron Santo Bat/25 50.00 15.00
64 Roy Campanella Pants/1
65 Ryne Sandberg Jsy/50 80.00 24.00
66 Satchel Paige CO Jsy/1
67 Stan Musial White Jsy/30 100.00 30.00
68 Stan Musial Gray Jsy/30 100.00 30.00
69 Stan Musial Bat/30 100.00 30.00
70 Steve Carlton Pants/25 50.00 15.00
71 Steve Carlton Jsy/25 50.00 15.00
72 Ted Williams Jsy/2
73 Tony Gwynn White Jsy/50 60.00 18.00
74 Tony Gwynn Navy Jsy/50 60.00 18.00
75 Ty Cobb Pants/2
77 Whitey Ford Pants/50 40.00 12.00
78 Will Clark Jsy/50 60.00 18.00
79 Will Clark Bat/50 60.00 18.00
80 Willie Stargell Jsy/2

2004 Leaf Certified Cuts Check Signature Material Green

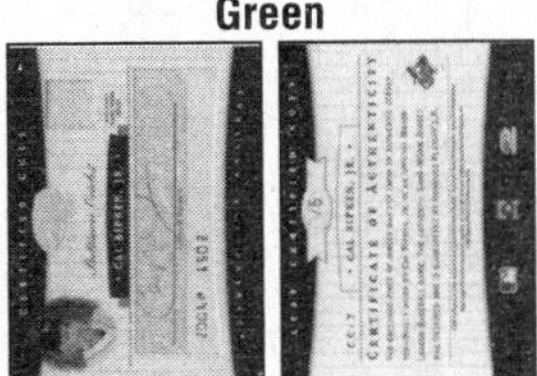

Nm-Mt Ex-Mt
*GREEN p/r 25-33: .6X TO 1.5X BLUE p/r 100
*GREEN p/r 25-33: .5X TO 1.2X BLUE p/r 50
*GREEN p/r 15: .6X TO 1.5X BLUE p/r 50
OVERALL AU ODDS THREE PER BOX
PRINT RUNS B/WN 5-33 COPIES PER
NO PRICING ON QTY OF 10 OR LESS

2004 Leaf Certified Cuts Check Signature Material Red

Nm-Mt Ex-Mt
*RED p/r 50: .5X TO 1.2X BLUE p/r 100
*RED p/r 25: .5X TO 1.2X BLUE p/r 36-65
*RED p/r 25: .4X TO 1X BLUE p/r 20-35
*RED p/r 15: .5X TO 1.2X BLUE p/r 20-35
OVERALL AU ODDS THREE PER BOX
PRINT RUNS B/WN 6-50 COPIES PER
NO PRICING ON QTY OF 14 OR LESS

2004 Leaf Certified Cuts Hall of Fame Souvenirs

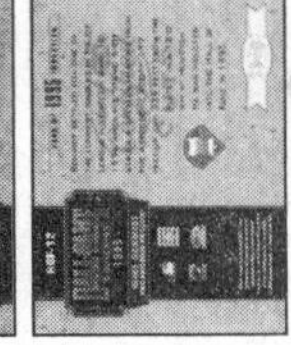

Nm-Mt Ex-Mt
RANDOM INSERTS IN PACKS
PRINT RUNS B/WN 75-100 COPIES PER
1 Ernie Banks/84 10.00 3.00
2 Stan Musial/93 15.00 4.50
3 Nolan Ryan/99 25.00 7.50
4 Duke Snider/87 8.00 2.40
5 Bob Feller/94 8.00 2.40
6 George Brett/98 20.00 6.00
7 Robin Yount/78 15.00 4.50
8 Harmon Killebrew/83 10.00 3.00
9 Gary Carter/78 5.00 1.50
10 Phil Rizzuto/75 8.00 2.40
11 Reggie Jackson/94 8.00 2.40
12 Mike Schmidt/97 20.00 6.00
13 Lou Brock/80 8.00 2.40
14 Bob Gibson/84 8.00 2.40
15 Bobby Doerr/75 5.00 1.50
16 Tony Perez/77 5.00 1.50
17 Whitey Ford/78 8.00 2.40
18 Juan Marichal/84 5.00 1.50
19 Monte Irvin/75 5.00 1.50
20 Fergie Jenkins/75 5.00 1.50
21 Ralph Kiner/75 8.00 2.40
22 Eddie Murray/85 10.00 3.00
23 George Kell/75 5.00 1.50
24 Hoyt Wilhelm/84 5.00 1.50
25 Carlton Fisk/80 8.00 2.40
26 Rod Carew/91 8.00 2.40
27 Frank Robinson/89 5.00 1.50
28 Gaylord Perry/77 5.00 1.50
29 Red Schoendienst/75 5.00 1.50
30 Brooks Robinson/92 8.00 2.40
31 Al Kaline/88 10.00 3.00
32 Orlando Cepeda/75 5.00 1.50
33 Steve Carlton/96 5.00 1.50
34 Luis Aparicio/85 5.00 1.50
35 Warren Spahn/83 8.00 2.40
36 Kirby Puckett/82 10.00 3.00
37 Phil Niekro/80 5.00 1.50
38 Jim Bunning/75 5.00 1.50
39 Tom Seaver/99 8.00 2.40
40 Paul Molitor/85 8.00 2.40
41 Johnny Bench/96 10.00 3.00
42 Don Sutton/82 5.00 1.50
43 Robin Roberts/87 5.00 1.50
44 Jim Palmer/93 5.00 1.50
45 Joe Morgan/82 5.00 1.50
46 Roberto Clemente/93 25.00 7.50
47 Lou Gehrig/100 12.00 3.60
48 Babe Ruth/95 20.00 6.00
49 Ty Cobb/98 10.00 3.00
50 Ted Williams/94 25.00 7.50

2004 Leaf Certified Cuts Hall of Fame Souvenirs Material

Nm-Mt Ex-Mt
OVERALL GU ODDS ONE PER BOX
STATED PRINT RUN 25 SERIAL #'d SETS
1 Ernie Banks Jsy 30.00 9.00
2 Stan Musial Jsy 50.00 15.00
3 Nolan Ryan Jsy 60.00 18.00
4 Duke Snider Pants 25.00 7.50
5 Bob Feller Jsy 25.00 7.50
6 George Brett Jsy 50.00 15.00
7 Robin Yount Jsy 40.00 12.00
8 Harmon Killebrew Jsy 30.00 9.00
9 Gary Carter Jkt 15.00 4.50
10 Phil Rizzuto Pants 25.00 7.50
11 Reggie Jackson Jsy 25.00 7.50
12 Mike Schmidt Jsy 50.00 15.00
13 Lou Brock Jsy 25.00 7.50
14 Bob Gibson Jsy 25.00 7.50
15 Bobby Doerr Jsy 15.00 4.50
16 Tony Perez Bat 15.00 4.50
17 Whitey Ford Pants 25.00 7.50
18 Juan Marichal Jsy 15.00 4.50
20 Fergie Jenkins Pants 15.00 4.50
21 Ralph Kiner Bat 25.00 7.50
22 Eddie Murray Jsy 30.00 9.00
24 Hoyt Wilhelm Jsy 15.00 4.50
25 Carlton Fisk Jsy 25.00 7.50
26 Rod Carew Jsy 25.00 7.50
27 Frank Robinson Jsy 15.00 4.50
29 Red Schoendienst Jsy 15.00 4.50
30 Brooks Robinson Bat 25.00 7.50
31 Al Kaline Pants 30.00 9.00
32 Orlando Cepeda Bat 15.00 4.50
33 Steve Carlton Pants 15.00 4.50
34 Luis Aparicio Pants 15.00 4.50
35 Warren Spahn Pants 25.00 7.50
36 Kirby Puckett Jsy 30.00 9.00
37 Phil Niekro Jsy 15.00 4.50
39 Tom Seaver Jsy 25.00 7.50
40 Paul Molitor Bat 25.00 7.50
41 Johnny Bench Jsy 30.00 9.00
42 Don Sutton Jsy 15.00 4.50
43 Robin Roberts Hat 15.00 4.50
44 Jim Palmer Jsy 15.00 4.50
45 Joe Morgan Jsy 15.00 4.50
46 Roberto Clemente Jsy 100.00 30.00
47 Lou Gehrig Pants 150.00 45.00
48 Babe Ruth Pants 250.00 75.00
49 Ty Cobb Pants 120.00 36.00
50 Ted Williams Jsy 120.00 36.00

2004 Leaf Certified Cuts Hall of Fame Souvenirs Signature

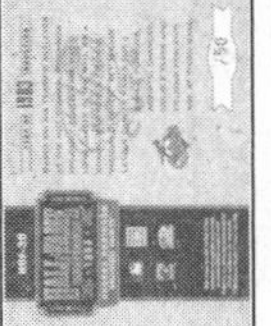

Nm-Mt Ex-Mt
OVERALL AU ODDS THREE PER BOX
PRINT RUNS B/WN 5-50 COPIES PER
NO PRICING ON QTY OF 10 OR LESS
2 Stan Musial/10
3 Nolan Ryan/34 150.00 45.00
4 Duke Snider/50 30.00 9.00
5 Bob Feller/50 30.00 9.00
6 George Brett/5
8 Harmon Killebrew/25 60.00 18.00
9 Gary Carter/50 20.00 6.00
10 Phil Rizzuto/50 30.00 9.00
11 Reggie Jackson/9
12 Mike Schmidt/20 80.00 24.00
13 Lou Brock/50 30.00 9.00
14 Bob Gibson/45 30.00 9.00
15 Bobby Doerr/50 20.00 6.00
16 Tony Perez/50 20.00 6.00
17 Whitey Ford/16 50.00 15.00
18 Juan Marichal/50 20.00 6.00
19 Monte Irvin/50 30.00 9.00
20 Fergie Jenkins/50 20.00 6.00
21 Ralph Kiner/50 30.00 9.00
22 Eddie Murray/33 80.00 24.00
23 George Kell/50 20.00 6.00
24 Hoyt Wilhelm/49 20.00 6.00
25 Carlton Fisk/27 40.00 12.00
26 Rod Carew/29 40.00 12.00
28 Gaylord Perry/50 20.00 6.00
29 Red Schoendienst/50 20.00 6.00
30 Brooks Robinson/50 30.00 9.00
31 Al Kaline/50 50.00 15.00
32 Orlando Cepeda/50 20.00 6.00
33 Steve Carlton/50 30.00 9.00
34 Luis Aparicio/50 20.00 6.00
35 Warren Spahn/21 60.00 18.00
36 Kirby Puckett/34 60.00 18.00
37 Phil Niekro/50 20.00 6.00
38 Jim Bunning/50 20.00 6.00
40 Paul Molitor/25 40.00 12.00
41 Johnny Bench/5
42 Don Sutton/50 20.00 6.00
43 Robin Roberts/50 20.00 6.00
44 Jim Palmer/22 25.00 7.50
45 Joe Morgan/25 25.00 7.50

2004 Leaf Certified Cuts Hall of Fame Souvenirs Signature Material

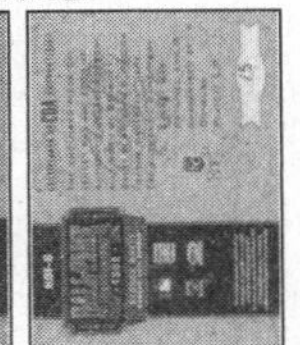

Nm-Mt Ex-Mt
*MTL AU p/r 36-45: .5X TO 1.2X AU p/r 36-50
*MTL AU p/r 20-35: .6X TO 1.5X AU p/r 36-50
*MTL AU p/r 20-35: .5X TO 1.2X AU p/r 20-35
*MTL AU p/r 16-19: .75X TO 2X AU p/r 36-50
*MTL AU p/r 16-19: .6X TO 1.5X AU p/r 20-35
*MTL AU p/r 16-19: .5X TO 1.2X AU p/r 15-19
OVERALL AU ODDS THREE PER BOX
PRINT RUNS B/WN 1-45 COPIES PER
NO PRICING ON QTY OF 11 OR LESS

2004 Leaf Certified Cuts K-Force

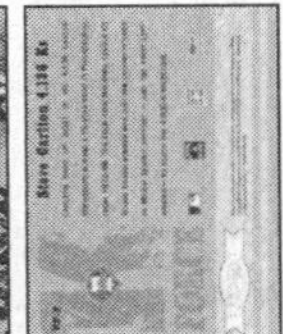

Nm-Mt Ex-Mt
1-44 PRINT RUNS B/WN 17-500 #'d PER
45-50 PRINT RUNS B/WN 20-500 #'d PER
RANDOM INSERTS IN PACKS
1 Nolan Ryan Rgr/500 10.00 3.00
2 Steve Carlton/500 3.00 .90
3 Roger Clemens Astros/500 8.00 2.40
4 Randy Johnson D'backs/500 3.00 .90
5 Bert Blyleven/500 3.00 .90
6 Tom Seaver Reds/500 4.00 1.20
7 Don Sutton/500 3.00 .90
8 Gaylord Perry/500 3.00 .90
9 Phil Niekro/500 3.00 .90
10 Fergie Jenkins/500 3.00 .90
11 Bob Gibson/500 4.00 1.20
12 Nolan Ryan Angels/383 10.00 3.00
13 Randy Johnson M's/308 3.00 .90
14 Bob Feller/348 4.00 1.20
15 Curt Schilling Phils/319 3.00 .90
16 Pedro Martinez Sox/313 3.00 .90
17 Dwight Gooden/276 3.00 .90
18 John Smoltz/276 3.00 .90
19 Curt Schilling D'backs/316 3.00 .90
20 Randy Johnson Astros/329 3.00 .90
21 Pedro Martinez Expos/305 3.00 .90
22 Roger Clemens Sox/291 8.00 2.40
23 Roger Clemens Jays/292 8.00 2.40
24 Tom Seaver Mets/289 4.00 1.20
25 Hal Newhouser/275 3.00 .90
26 Jim Bunning/201 4.00 1.20
27 Robin Roberts/198 4.00 1.20
28 Warren Spahn/191 5.00 1.50
29 Jack Morris/232 4.00 1.20
30 Nolan Ryan Astros/270 10.00 3.00
31 Hideo Nomo/236 4.00 1.20
32 Barry Zito/205 4.00 1.20
33 Mike Mussina/214 4.00 1.20
34 Roy Oswalt/208 4.00 1.20
35 Mark Prior/245 4.00 1.20
36 Kerry Wood/266 3.00 .90
37 Roy Halladay/204 4.00 1.20
38 Esteban Loaiza/207 4.00 1.20
39 Whitey Ford/94 8.00 2.40
40 Bob Gibson/17 15.00 4.50
41 Ben Sheets/18 10.00 3.00
42 Hoyt Wilhelm/139 4.00 1.20
43 Satchel Paige/91 10.00 3.00
44 Burleigh Grimes/136 4.00 1.20
45 Mark Prior 4.00 1.20
Kerry Wood/500
46 Nolan Ryan 10.00 3.00
Roger Clemens/500
47 Steve Carlton 4.00 1.20
Randy Johnson/500
48 Nolan Ryan 10.00 3.00
Roger Clemens/500
49 Nolan Ryan 10.00 3.00
Steve Carlton/500
50 Kerry Wood 40.00 12.00
Roger Clemens/20

2004 Leaf Certified Cuts K-Force Material

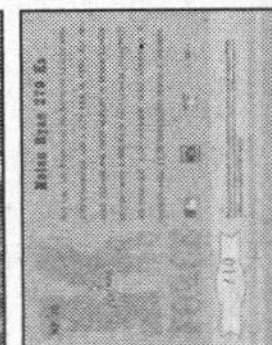

Nm-Mt Ex-Mt
1-44 PRINT RUNS B/WN 2-100 #'d PER
1-44 NO PRICING ON QTY OF 5 OR LESS
45-50 PRINT RUN 50 SERIAL #'d SETS
OVERALL GU ODDS ONE PER BOX
1 Nolan Ryan Rgr Jsy/100 25.00 7.50
2 Steve Carlton Jsy/32 15.00 4.50
3 R.Clemens Astros Jsy/25 30.00 9.00
4 R.Johnson D'backs Jsy/51 15.00 4.50
5 Bert Blyleven Jsy/28 15.00 4.50
6 Tom Seaver Reds Jsy/25 25.00 7.50
7 Don Sutton Jsy/2
8 Gaylord Perry Jsy/36 10.00 3.00
9 Phil Niekro Jsy/35 15.00 4.50
10 Fergie Jenkins Pants/31 15.00 4.50
11 Bob Gibson Jsy/45 15.00 4.50
12 Nolan Ryan Angels Jkt/100 25.00 7.50
13 Randy Johnson M's Jsy/51 15.00 4.50
14 Bob Feller Jsy/25 25.00 7.50
15 Curt Schilling Phils Jsy/25 12.00 3.60
16 Pedro Martinez Sox Jsy/45 15.00 4.50
17 Dwight Gooden Jsy/25 15.00 4.50
18 John Smoltz Jsy/25 20.00 6.00
19 C.Schilling D'backs Jsy/25 12.00 3.60
20 R.Johnson Astros Jsy/51 15.00 4.50
21 P.Martinez Expos Jsy/45 15.00 4.50
22 R.Clemens Sox Jsy/100 12.00 3.60
25 Hal Newhouser Jsy/25 25.00 7.50
28 Warren Spahn Jsy/50 15.00 4.50
29 Jack Morris Jsy/47 10.00 3.00
30 N.Ryan Astros Jkt/100 25.00 7.50
31 Hideo Nomo Jsy/25 25.00 7.50
32 Barry Zito Jsy/25 12.00 3.60
33 Mike Mussina Jsy/25 20.00 6.00
34 Roy Oswalt Jsy/44 8.00 2.40
35 Mark Prior Jsy/50 15.00 4.50
36 Kerry Wood Jsy/34 25.00 7.50
37 Roy Halladay Jsy/5
39 Whitey Ford Jsy/50 15.00 4.50
40 Bob Gibson Jsy/50 15.00 4.50
41 Ben Sheets Jsy/25 12.00 3.60
43 Satchel Paige CO Jsy/100 60.00 18.00
44 Burleigh Grimes Pants/100 60.00 18.00
45 Mark Prior Jsy 25.00 7.50
Kerry Wood Pants/50
46 Nolan Ryan Jsy 50.00 15.00
Roger Clemens Astros Jsy/50
47 Steve Carlton Jsy 25.00 7.50
Randy Johnson Jsy/50
48 Nolan Ryan Pants 50.00 15.00
Roger Clemens Yanks Jsy/50
49 Nolan Ryan Jsy 40.00 12.00
Steve Carlton Pants/50
50 Kerry Wood Jsy 25.00 7.50
Roger Clemens Jsy/50

2004 Leaf Certified Cuts K-Force Signature

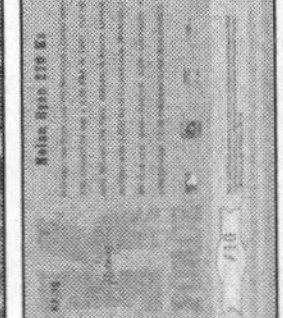

Nm-Mt Ex-Mt
OVERALL AU ODDS THREE PER BOX

PRINT RUNS B/WN 1-50 COPIES PER
NO PRICING ON QTY OF 10 OR LESS
1 Nolan Ryan Rgr/10
2 Steve Carlton/50 .... 30.00 9.00
3 Roger Clemens Astros/1
5 Bert Blyleven/50 .... 20.00 6.00
6 Tom Seaver Reds/5
7 Don Sutton/50 .... 20.00 6.00
8 Gaylord Perry/50 .... 20.00 6.00
9 Phil Niekro/50 .... 30.00 9.00
10 Fergie Jenkins/50 .... 20.00 6.00
11 Bob Gibson/10
12 Nolan Ryan Angels/10
14 Bob Feller/50 .... 30.00 9.00
15 Curt Schilling Phils/1
16 Pedro Martinez Sox/1
17 Dwight Gooden/50 .... 20.00 6.00
19 Curt Schilling D'backs/1
21 Pedro Martinez Expos/1
22 Roger Clemens Sox/1
23 Roger Clemens Jays/1
24 Tom Seaver Mets/5
26 Jim Bunning/50 .... 30.00 9.00
27 Robin Roberts/50 .... 20.00 6.00
28 Warren Spahn/10
29 Jack Morris/50 .... 20.00 6.00
30 Nolan Ryan Astros/10
31 Hideo Nomo/1
32 Barry Zito/1
33 Mike Mussina/1
34 Roy Oswalt/50 .... 20.00 6.00
35 Mark Prior/10
36 Kerry Wood/5
37 Roy Halladay/10
38 Esteban Loaiza/50 .... 12.00 3.60
39 Whitey Ford/5
40 Bob Gibson/10
45 Mark Prior
Kerry Wood/10
46 Nolan Ryan
Roger Clemens Astros/1
48 Nolan Ryan
Roger Clemens Yanks/1
49 Nolan Ryan
Steve Carlton/5
50 Kerry Wood
Roger Clemens/1

2004 Leaf Certified Cuts K-Force Signature Material

Nm-Mt Ex-Mt
*A.MTL AU p/r 36-50: .5X TO 1.2X AU p/r 50
*R.MTL AU p/r 36-50: .5X TO 1.2X AU p/r 50
*R.MTL AU p/r 20-35: .6X TO 1.5X AU p/r 50
*R.MTL AU p/r 15-19: .75X TO 2X AU p/r 50
PRINT RUNS B/WN 1-47 COPIES PER
NO PRICING ON QTY OF 5 OR LESS
PRIME PRINT RUN 1 SERIAL #'d SET
NO PRIME PRICING DUE TO SCARCITY
OVERALL AU ODDS THREE PER BOX
1 Nolan Ryan Rgr Jsy/34 .... 150.00 45.00
11 Bob Gibson Jsy/45 .... 40.00 12.00
12 Nolan Ryan Angels Jkt/34 .. 150.00 45.00
28 Warren Spahn Jsy/21 .... 80.00 24.00
30 Nolan Ryan Astros Jkt/34 .. 150.00 45.00
36 Kerry Wood Jsy/34 .... 60.00 18.00
37 Roy Halladay Jsy/32 .... 20.00 6.00
39 Whitey Ford Jsy/16 .... 60.00 18.00
40 Bob Gibson Jsy/45 .... 40.00 12.00

2004 Leaf Certified Cuts Stars

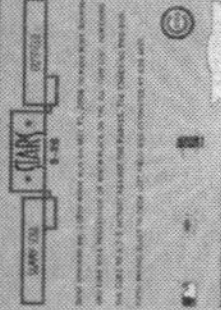

Nm-Mt Ex-Mt
RANDOM INSERTS IN PACKS
STATED PRINT RUN 599 SERIAL #'d SETS
1 Ryne Sandberg 8.00 2.40
2 Mark Prior .... 3.00 .90
3 Andre Dawson .... 3.00 .90
4 Don Mattingly 8.00 2.40
5 Vladimir Guerrero .... 3.00 .90
6 Garret Anderson .... 3.00 .90
7 Dale Murphy 4.00 1.20
8 Cal Ripken 15.00 4.50
9 Mark Grace 4.00 1.20
10 Kerry Wood .... 3.00 .90
11 Frank Thomas .... 3.00 .90
12 Magglio Ordonez .... 3.00 .90
13 Adam Dunn .... 3.00 .90
14 Preston Wilson .... 3.00 .90
15 Bo Jackson 4.00 1.20
16 Carlos Beltran .... 3.00 .90
17 Tony Gwynn 6.00 1.80
18 Will Clark 4.00 1.20
19 Edgar Martinez .... 3.00 .90
20 Scott Rolen .... 3.00 .90
21 Alfonso Soriano .... 3.00 .90
22 Randy Johnson .... 3.00 .90
23 Chipper Jones .... 3.00 .90
24 Andruw Jones .... 3.00 .90
25 Javy Lopez .... 3.00 .90
26 Curt Schilling .... 3.00 .90
27 Manny Ramirez .... 3.00 .90
28 Sammy Sosa 5.00 1.50
29 Greg Maddux 5.00 1.50
30 Todd Helton .... 3.00 .90
31 Jeff Bagwell .... 3.00 .90
32 Shawn Green .... 3.00 .90
33 Mike Piazza 5.00 1.50
34 Jorge Posada .... 3.00 .90
35 Gary Sheffield .... 3.00 .90
36 Mike Mussina .... 3.00 .90
37 Miguel Cabrera .... 3.00 .90
38 Rickey Henderson 4.00 1.20
39 Albert Pujols 6.00 1.80
40 Vernon Wells .... 3.00 .90
41 Fred Lynn .... 3.00 .90
42 Alan Trammell .... 3.00 .90
43 Lenny Dykstra .... 3.00 .90
44 Dwight Gooden .... 3.00 .90
45 Keith Hernandez .... 3.00 .90
46 Luis Tiant .... 3.00 .90
47 Orel Hershiser .... 3.00 .90
48 George Foster .... 3.00 .90
49 Darryl Strawberry .... 3.00 .90
50 Marty Marion .... 3.00 .90

2004 Leaf Certified Cuts Stars Signature

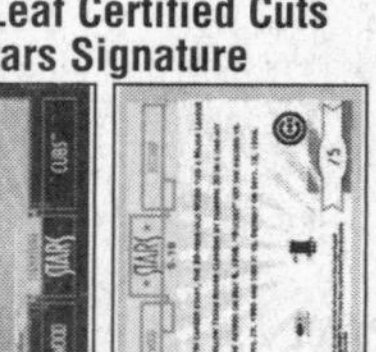

Nm-Mt Ex-Mt
OVERALL AU ODDS THREE PER BOX
PRINT RUNS B/WN 1-50 COPIES PER
NO PRICING ON QTY OF 10 OR LESS
1 Ryne Sandberg/5
2 Mark Prior/5
3 Andre Dawson/50 .... 20.00 6.00
4 Don Mattingly/25 .... 80.00 24.00
5 Vladimir Guerrero/5
6 Garret Anderson/50 .... 20.00 6.00
7 Dale Murphy/50 .... 30.00 9.00
8 Cal Ripken/5
9 Mark Grace/5
10 Kerry Wood/5
11 Frank Thomas/10
12 Magglio Ordonez/25 .... 25.00 7.50
13 Adam Dunn/25 .... 40.00 12.00
14 Preston Wilson/50 .... 20.00 6.00
15 Bo Jackson/5
16 Carlos Beltran/50 .... 40.00 12.00
17 Tony Gwynn/5
18 Will Clark/25 .... 60.00 18.00
19 Edgar Martinez/25 .... 50.00 15.00
20 Scott Rolen/25 .... 50.00 15.00
21 Alfonso Soriano/5
23 Chipper Jones/5
24 Andruw Jones/5
26 Curt Schilling/5
27 Manny Ramirez/5
28 Sammy Sosa/5
29 Greg Maddux/5
30 Todd Helton/5
31 Jeff Bagwell/5
32 Shawn Green/5
33 Mike Piazza/5
34 Jorge Posada/10
35 Gary Sheffield/10
36 Mike Mussina/5
37 Miguel Cabrera/50 .... 30.00 9.00
38 Rickey Henderson/5
39 Albert Pujols/5
40 Vernon Wells/25 .... 25.00 7.50
41 Fred Lynn/50 .... 12.00 3.60
42 Alan Trammell/50 .... 20.00 6.00
43 Lenny Dykstra/50 .... 20.00 6.00
44 Dwight Gooden/50 .... 20.00 6.00
45 Keith Hernandez/50 .... 20.00 6.00
46 Luis Tiant/50 .... 20.00 6.00
47 Orel Hershiser/50 .... 30.00 9.00
48 George Foster/50 .... 12.00 3.60
49 Darryl Strawberry/50 .... 20.00 6.00

2004 Leaf Certified Cuts Stars Signature Jersey

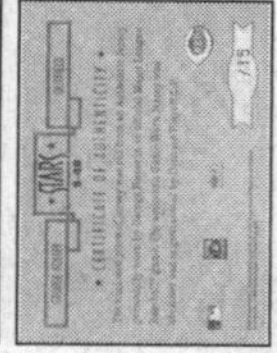

Nm-Mt Ex-Mt
*JSY AU p/r 36-50: .5X TO 1.2X AU p/r 36-50
*JSY AU p/r 36-50: .6X TO 1.5X AU p/r 20-35
*JSY AU p/r 20-35: .6X TO 1.5X AU p/r 36-50
*JSY AU p/r 20-35: .5X TO 1.2X AU p/r 20-35
*JSY AU p/r 15-19: .75X TO 2X AU p/r 36-50
PRINT RUNS B/WN 1-44 COPIES PER
NO PRICING ON QTY OF 12 OR LESS
PRIME PRINT RUN 1 SERIAL #'d SET
NO PRIME PRICING DUE TO SCARCITY
OVERALL AU ODDS THREE PER BOX
1 Ryne Sandberg/23 .... 100.00 30.00
2 Mark Prior/22 .... 60.00 18.00
5 Vladimir Guerrero/27 .... 60.00 18.00
9 Mark Grace/17 .... 60.00 18.00
10 Kerry Wood/34 .... 60.00 18.00
11 Frank Thomas/35 .... 60.00 18.00
15 Bo Jackson/16 .... 150.00 45.00
17 Tony Gwynn/19 .... 100.00 30.00
24 Andruw Jones/25 .... 50.00 15.00
28 Sammy Sosa/21 .... 150.00 45.00
29 Greg Maddux/31 .... 120.00 36.00
30 Todd Helton/17 .... 60.00 18.00
32 Shawn Green/15 .... 40.00 12.00
34 Jorge Posada/20 .... 60.00 18.00
50 Marty Marion/25 .... 30.00 9.00

2001 Leaf Certified Materials

This 160 card set was issued in five card packs. Cards numbered 111-160 feature young players along with a piece of game-used memorabilia. These cards are serial numbered to 200.

Nm-Mt Ex-Mt
COMP.SET w/o SP's (110) 40.00 12.00
COMMON CARD (1-110) .... 1.00 .30
COMMON (111-160) 15.00 4.50
1 Alex Rodriguez 4.00 1.20
2 Barry Bonds 6.00 1.80
3 Cal Ripken 8.00 2.40
4 Chipper Jones .... 2.50 .75
5 Derek Jeter 6.00 1.80
6 Troy Glaus .... 1.00 .30
7 Frank Thomas .... 2.50 .75
8 Greg Maddux 4.00 1.20
9 Ivan Rodriguez .... 2.50 .75
10 Jeff Bagwell .... 1.50 .45
11 Eric Karros .... 1.00 .30
12 Todd Helton .... 1.50 .45
13 Ken Griffey Jr. 4.00 1.20
14 Manny Ramirez .... 1.50 .45
15 Mark McGwire 6.00 1.80
16 Mike Piazza 4.00 1.20
17 Nomar Garciaparra 4.00 1.20
18 Pedro Martinez .... 2.50 .75
19 Randy Johnson .... 2.50 .75
20 Rick Ankiel .... 1.00 .30
21 Rickey Henderson .... 2.50 .75
22 Roger Clemens 5.00 1.50
23 Sammy Sosa 4.00 1.20
24 Tony Gwynn .... 3.00 .90
25 Vladimir Guerrero .... 2.50 .75
26 Kazuhiro Sasaki .... 1.00 .30
27 Roberto Alomar .... 1.50 .45
28 Barry Zito .... 1.50 .45
29 Pat Burrell .... 1.00 .30
30 Harold Baines .... 1.00 .30
31 Carlos Delgado .... 1.00 .30
32 J.D. Drew .... 1.00 .30
33 Jim Edmonds .... 1.00 .30
34 Darin Erstad .... 1.00 .30
35 Jason Giambi .... 1.00 .30
36 Tom Glavine .... 1.50 .45
37 Juan Gonzalez .... 1.50 .45
38 Mark Grace .... 1.50 .45
39 Shawn Green .... 1.00 .30
40 Tim Hudson .... 1.00 .30
41 Andruw Jones .... 1.00 .30
42 Jeff Kent .... 1.00 .30
43 Barry Larkin .... 1.50 .45
44 Rafael Furcal .... 1.00 .30
45 Mike Mussina .... 1.50 .45
46 Hideo Nomo .... 2.50 .75
47 Rafael Palmeiro .... 1.50 .45
48 Scott Rolen .... 2.50 .75
49 Gary Sheffield .... 1.00 .30
50 Bernie Williams .... 1.50 .45
51 Bob Abreu .... 1.00 .30
52 Edgardo Alfonzo .... 1.00 .30
53 Edgar Martinez .... 1.50 .45
54 Magglio Ordonez .... 1.00 .30
55 Kerry Wood .... 2.50 .75
56 Adrian Beltre .... 1.50 .45
57 Lance Berkman .... 1.00 .30
58 Kevin Brown .... 1.00 .30
59 Sean Casey .... 1.00 .30
60 Eric Chavez .... 1.00 .30
61 Bartolo Colon .... 1.00 .30
62 Johnny Damon .... 1.50 .45
63 Jermaine Dye .... 1.00 .30
64 Juan Encarnacion UER .... 1.00 .30
Card has him playing for Detroit Lions
65 Carl Everett .... 1.00 .30
66 Brian Giles .... 1.00 .30
67 Mike Hampton .... 1.00 .30
68 Richard Hidalgo .... 1.00 .30
69 Geoff Jenkins .... 1.00 .30
70 Jacque Jones .... 1.00 .30
71 Jason Kendall .... 1.00 .30
72 Ryan Klesko .... 1.00 .30
73 Chan Ho Park .... 1.00 .30
74 Richie Sexson .... 1.00 .30
75 Mike Sweeney .... 1.00 .30
76 Fernando Tatis .... 1.00 .30
77 Miguel Tejada .... 1.00 .30
78 Jose Vidro .... 1.00 .30
79 Larry Walker .... 1.50 .45
80 Preston Wilson .... 1.00 .30
81 Craig Biggio .... 1.50 .45
82 Fred McGriff .... 1.50 .45
83 Jim Thome .... 2.50 .75
84 Garret Anderson .... 1.00 .30
85 Russell Branyan .... 1.00 .30
86 Tony Batista .... 1.00 .30
87 Terrence Long .... 1.00 .30
88 Deion Sanders .... 1.50 .45
89 Rusty Greer .... 1.00 .30
90 Orlando Hernandez .... 1.00 .30
91 Gabe Kapler .... 1.00 .30
92 Paul Konerko .... 1.00 .30
93 Carlos Lee .... 1.00 .30
94 Kenny Lofton .... 1.00 .30
95 Raul Mondesi .... 1.00 .30
96 Jorge Posada .... 1.50 .45
97 Tim Salmon .... 1.50 .45
98 Greg Vaughn .... 1.00 .30
99 Mo Vaughn .... 1.00 .30
100 Omar Vizquel .... 1.50 .45
101 Ray Durham .... 1.00 .30
102 Jeff Cirillo .... 1.00 .30
103 Dean Palmer .... 1.00 .30
104 Ryan Dempster .... 1.00 .30
105 Carlos Beltran .... 1.50 .45
106 Timo Perez .... 1.00 .30
107 Robin Ventura .... 1.00 .30
108 Andy Pettitte .... 1.50 .45
109 Aramis Ramirez .... 1.00 .30
110 Phil Nevin .... 1.00 .30
111 Alex Escobar FF 15.00 4.50
112 Johnny Estrada FF RC 20.00 6.00
113 Pedro Feliz FF 15.00 4.50
114 Nate Frese FF RC 15.00 4.50
115 Joe Kennedy FF RC 20.00 6.00
116 B. Larson FF RC 15.00 4.50
117 Alexis Gomez FF RC 15.00 4.50
118 Jason Hart FF 15.00 4.50
119 Jason Michaels FF RC 15.00 4.50
120 Marcus Giles FF 15.00 4.50
121 C. Parker FF RC 15.00 4.50
122 Jackson Melian FF RC 15.00 4.50
123 D. Mendez FF RC 15.00 4.50
124 A. Hernandez FF RC 15.00 4.50
125 Bud Smith FF RC 15.00 4.50
126 Jose Mieses FF RC 15.00 4.50
127 Roy Oswalt FF 20.00 6.00
128 Eric Munson FF 15.00 4.50
129 Xavier Nady FF 15.00 4.50
130 H. Ramirez FF RC 20.00 6.00
131 Abraham Nunez FF 15.00 4.50
132 Jose Ortiz FF 15.00 4.50
133 Jeremy Owens FF RC 15.00 4.50
134 Claudio Vargas FF RC 15.00 4.50
135 R. Rodriguez FF RC 15.00 4.50
136 Aubrey Huff FF 15.00 4.50
137 Ben Sheets FF 20.00 6.00
138 Adam Dunn FF 20.00 6.00
139 Andres Torres FF RC 15.00 4.50
140 Elpidio Guzman FF RC 15.00 4.50
141 Jay Gibbons FF RC 20.00 6.00
142 Wilkin Ruan FF RC 15.00 4.50
143 T. Shinjo FF RC 20.00 6.00
144 Alfonso Soriano FF 20.00 6.00
145 Josh Towers FF RC 15.00 4.50
146 Ichiro Suzuki FF RC 150.00 45.00
147 Juan Uribe FF RC 20.00 6.00
148 Joe Crede FF 15.00 4.50
149 C. Valderrama FF RC 15.00 4.50
150 Matt White FF RC 15.00 4.50
151 Dee Brown FF 15.00 4.50
152 Juan Cruz FF RC 15.00 4.50
153 Cory Aldridge FF RC 15.00 4.50
154 Wilmy Caceres FF RC 15.00 4.50
155 Josh Beckett FF 20.00 6.00
156 Wilson Betemit FF RC 15.00 4.50
157 Corey Patterson FF 15.00 4.50
158 Albert Pujols FF RC 150.00 45.00
159 Rafael Soriano FF RC 20.00 6.00
160 Jack Wilson FF RC 25.00 7.50

2001 Leaf Certified Materials Mirror Gold

Randomly inserted into packs, these 160 cards parallel the basic Leaf Certified Material set. Each card is serial numbered to 25.

Nm-Mt Ex-Mt
*STARS 1-110: 10X TO 25X BASIC CARDS

2001 Leaf Certified Materials Mirror Red

Randomly inserted into packs, these 160 cards parallel the basic Leaf Certified Material set. Each card is serial numbered to 75. An exchange card with a redemption deadline of November 1st, 2003 was seeded into packs for card 125 Bud Smith.

Nm-Mt Ex-Mt
*STARS 1-110: 4X TO 10X BASIC CARDS
111 Alex Escobar FF AU 20.00 6.00
112 Johnny Estrada FF AU 40.00 12.00
113 Pedro Feliz FF AU 20.00 6.00
114 Nate Frese FF AU 20.00 6.00
115 Joe Kennedy FF 20.00 6.00
116 B. Larson FF AU 20.00 6.00
117 Alexis Gomez FF AU 20.00 6.00
118 Jason Hart FF AU 20.00 6.00
119 Jason Michaels FF AU 20.00 6.00
120 Marcus Giles FF AU 20.00 6.00
121 C. Parker FF AU 20.00 6.00
122 Jackson Melian FF 15.00 4.50
123 D. Mendez FF AU 20.00 6.00
124 A. Hernandez FF AU 20.00 6.00
125 B. Smith FF AU EXCH 20.00 6.00
126 Jose Mieses FF AU 20.00 6.00
127 Roy Oswalt FF AU 25.00 7.50
128 Eric Munson FF 15.00 4.50
129 Xavier Nady FF AU 20.00 6.00
130 H. Ramirez FF AU 25.00 7.50
131 A. Nunez FF AU 20.00 6.00
132 Jose Ortiz FF AU 20.00 6.00
133 Jeremy Owens FF AU 20.00 6.00
134 Claudio Vargas FF AU 20.00 6.00
135 R. Rodriguez FF AU 20.00 6.00
136 Aubrey Huff FF AU 20.00 6.00
137 Ben Sheets FF AU 25.00 7.50
138 Adam Dunn FF AU 25.00 7.50
139 Andres Torres FF AU 20.00 6.00
140 Elpidio Guzman FF AU 20.00 6.00
141 Jay Gibbons FF AU 40.00 12.00
142 Wilkin Ruan FF AU 20.00 6.00
143 Tsuyoshi Shinjo FF 20.00 6.00
144 A. Soriano FF AU 80.00 24.00
145 Josh Towers FF AU 20.00 6.00
146 Ichiro Suzuki FF 200.00 60.00
147 Juan Uribe FF AU 25.00 7.50
148 Joe Crede FF AU 20.00 6.00
149 C. Valderrama FF AU 20.00 6.00
150 Matt White FF AU 20.00 6.00
151 Dee Brown FF AU 20.00 6.00
152 Juan Cruz FF AU 20.00 6.00
153 Cory Aldridge FF AU 20.00 6.00
154 Wilmy Caceres FF AU 20.00 6.00
155 Josh Beckett FF AU 40.00 12.00
156 Wilson Betemit FF AU 20.00 6.00
157 C. Patterson FF AU 20.00 6.00
158 Albert Pujols FF AU 400.00 120.00
159 Rafael Soriano FF AU 25.00 7.50
160 Jack Wilson FF AU 50.00 15.00

2001 Leaf Certified Materials Fabric of the Game

Randomly inserted into packs, 118 players are featured in this set. Each player has a base card as well as cards serial numbered to a key career stat, jersey number, a key seasonal stat or a Century card. All the Century cards are serial numbered to 21. Certain players had less basic cards issued, these cards are notated with an SP and according to the manufacturer less than 100 of these cards were produced. In addition, exchange cards with a redemption deadline of November 1st, 2003 were seeded into packs for the following: Jeff Bagwell CE AU, Ernie Banks JN AU, Roger Clemens JN AU, Vladimir Guerrero JN AU, Tony Gwynn CE AU, Don Mattingly CE AU, Kirby Puckett JN AU, Nolan Ryan CE AU, Ryne Sandberg CE AU and Mike Schmidt JN AU.

Nm-Mt Ex-Mt
1BA Lou Gehrig SP
1CE Lou Gehrig/21
1CR Lou Gehrig/23
1JN Lou Gehrig/4
1SN Lou Gehrig/184 .... 250.00 75.00
2BA Babe Ruth SP
2CE Babe Ruth/21
2CR Babe Ruth/136 .... 300.00 90.00
2JN Babe Ruth/3
2SN Babe Ruth/60 .... 500.00 150.00
3BA Stan Musial SP 80.00 24.00
3CE Stan Musial/21
3CR Stan Musial/177 .... 50.00 15.00
3JN Stan Musial/6
3SN Stan Musial/39 .... 100.00 30.00
4BA Nolan Ryan 50.00 15.00
4CE Nolan Ryan AU/21
4CR Nolan Ryan/61 .... 100.00 30.00
4JN Nolan Ryan/34 .... 120.00 36.00
4SN Nolan Ryan/22
5BA Roberto Clemente SP
5CE Roberto Clemente/21
5CR R. Clemente/166 .... 120.00 36.00
5JN Roberto Clemente/21
5SN Roberto Clemente/29 .... 250.00 75.00
6BA Al Kaline SP 40.00 12.00
6CE Al Kaline/21
6CR Al Kaline/137 .... 40.00 12.00
6JN Al Kaline/6
6SN Al Kaline/29 .... 80.00 24.00
7BA Brooks Robinson 25.00 7.50
7CE Brooks Robinson/21
7CR Brooks Robinson/68 .... 40.00 12.00
7JN Brooks Robinson/5
7SN Brooks Robinson/28 .... 80.00 24.00
8BA Mel Ott 50.00 15.00
8CE Mel Ott/21
8CR Mel Ott/72 .... 60.00 18.00
8JN Mel Ott/4
8SN Mel Ott/42 .... 80.00 24.00
9BA Dave Winfield SP 25.00 7.50
9CE Dave Winfield/21
9CR Dave Winfield/88 .... 25.00 7.50
9JN Dave Winfield/31 .... 40.00 12.00
9SN Dave Winfield/37 .... 40.00 12.00
10BA Eddie Mathews SP 40.00 12.00
10CE Eddie Mathews/21
10CR Eddie Mathews/72 .... 40.00 12.00
10JN Eddie Mathews/41 .... 60.00 18.00
10SN Eddie Mathews/47 .... 60.00 18.00
11BA Ernie Banks 25.00 7.50
11CE Ernie Banks/21
11CR Ernie Banks/50 .... 40.00 12.00
11JN Ernie Banks AU/14
11SN Ernie Banks/47 .... 60.00 18.00
12BA Frank Robinson SP 40.00 12.00
12CE Frank Robinson/21
12CR Frank Robinson/72 .... 40.00 12.00
12JN Frank Robinson/20
12SN Frank Robinson/49 .... 60.00 18.00
13BA George Brett SP 80.00 24.00
13CE George Brett/21
13CR George Brett/137 .... 50.00 15.00
13JN George Brett/5
13SN George Brett/30 .... 120.00 36.00
14BA Hank Aaron SP 120.00 36.00
14CE Hank Aaron/21
14CR Hank Aaron/98 .... 80.00 24.00
14JN Hank Aaron/44 .... 200.00 60.00
14SN Hank Aaron/47 .... 150.00 45.00
15BA Harmon Killebrew 25.00 7.50
15CE Harmon Killebrew/21
15CR Harmon Killebrew/24
15JN Harmon Killebrew/3
15SN H. Killebrew/49 .... 60.00 18.00
16BA Joe Morgan SP 25.00 7.50
16CE Joe Morgan/21
16CR Joe Morgan/96 .... 25.00 7.50
16JN Joe Morgan/8
16SN Joe Morgan/27 .... 50.00 15.00
17BA Johnny Bench 25.00 7.50
17CE Johnny Bench/21
17CR Johnny Bench/68 .... 40.00 12.00
17JN Johnny Bench/5
17SN Johnny Bench/45 .... 60.00 18.00
18BA Kirby Puckett SP 40.00 12.00
18CE Kirby Puckett/21
18CR Kirby Puckett/134 .... 40.00 12.00
18JN Kirby Puckett AU/34 .... 150.00 45.00
18SN Kirby Puckett/31 .... 80.00 24.00
19BA Mike Schmidt SP 50.00 15.00
19CE Mike Schmidt/21
19CR Mike Schmidt/59 .... 60.00 18.00

JN Mike Schmidt AU/20
SN Mike Schmidt/48 80.00 24.00
BA Phil Rizzuto SP 40.00 12.00
CE Phil Rizzuto/21
CR Phil Rizzuto/149 40.00 12.00
JN Phil Rizzuto/10
SN Phil Rizzuto/7
BA Reggie Jackson SP 40.00 12.00
CE Reggie Jackson/21
CR Reggie Jackson/49 60.00 18.00
JN Reggie Jackson/44 60.00 18.00
SN Reggie Jackson/47 60.00 18.00
BA Jim Hunter 25.00 7.50
CE Jim Hunter/21
CR Jim Hunter/42 60.00 18.00
JN Jim Hunter/27 80.00 24.00
SN Jim Hunter/25
BA Rod Carew SP 40.00 12.00
CE Rod Carew/21
CR Rod Carew/92 40.00 12.00
JN Rod Carew/29 80.00 24.00
SN Rod Carew/100 40.00 12.00
BA Bob Feller 15.00 4.50
CE Bob Feller/21
CR Bob Feller/44 40.00 12.00
JN Bob Feller/19
SN Bob Feller/36 40.00 12.00
BA Lou Brock SP 40.00 12.00
CE Lou Brock/21
CR Lou Brock/141 40.00 12.00
JN Lou Brock/20
SN Lou Brock/21
BA Tom Seaver SP 40.00 12.00
CE Tom Seaver/21
CR Tom Seaver/61 40.00 12.00
JN Tom Seaver/41 60.00 18.00
SN Tom Seaver/25
BA Paul Molitor SP 40.00 12.00
CE Paul Molitor/21
CR Paul Molitor/114 40.00 12.00
JN Paul Molitor/4
SN Paul Molitor/41 60.00 18.00
BA Willie McCovey SP 25.00 7.50
CE Willie McCovey/21
CR Willie McCovey/18
JN Willie McCovey/44 40.00 12.00
SN Willie McCovey/126 25.00 7.50
BA Yogi Berra 25.00 7.50
CE Yogi Berra/21
CR Yogi Berra/49 60.00 18.00
JN Yogi Berra/35 80.00 24.00
SN Yogi Berra/30 80.00 24.00
BA Don Drysdale SP 40.00 12.00
CE Don Drysdale/21
CR Don Drysdale/49 60.00 18.00
JN Don Drysdale/53 40.00 12.00
SN Don Drysdale/25
1BA Duke Snider SP 40.00 12.00
1CE Duke Snider/21
1CR Duke Snider/99 40.00 12.00
1JN Duke Snider/4
1SN Duke Snider/43 60.00 18.00
2BA Does Not Exist
2CE Does Not Exist
2CR Does Not Exist
2JN Does Not Exist
2SN Does Not Exist
3BA Orlando Cepeda 15.00 4.50
3CE Orlando Cepeda/21
3CR Orlando Cepeda/27 50.00 15.00
3JN Orlando Cepeda/30 50.00 15.00
3SN Orlando Cepeda/46 40.00 12.00
4BA Casey Stengel SP 40.00 12.00
4CE Casey Stengel/21
4CR Casey Stengel/10
4JN Casey Stengel/37 60.00 18.00
4SN Casey Stengel/103 40.00 12.00
5BA Robin Yount SP 40.00 12.00
5CE Robin Yount/21
5CR Robin Yount/126 40.00 12.00
5JN Robin Yount/19
5SN Robin Yount/29 80.00 24.00
6BA Eddie Murray 25.00 7.50
6CE Eddie Murray/21
6CR Eddie Murray/35 80.00 24.00
6JN Eddie Murray/22
6SN Eddie Murray/33 80.00 24.00
7BA Jim Palmer 15.00 4.50
7CE Jim Palmer/21
7CR Jim Palmer/53 25.00 7.50
7JN Jim Palmer/22
7SN Jim Palmer/23
8BA Juan Marichal 15.00 4.50
8CE Juan Marichal/21
8CR Juan Marichal/52 25.00 7.50
8JN Juan Marichal/27 50.00 15.00
8SN Juan Marichal/26 50.00 15.00
9BA Willie Stargell 25.00 7.50
9CE Willie Stargell/21
9CR Willie Stargell/55 40.00 12.00
9JN Willie Stargell/8
9SN Willie Stargell/48 60.00 18.00
0BA Ted Williams SP 100.00 30.00
0CE Ted Williams/21
0CR Ted Williams/71 100.00 30.00
0JN Ted Williams/9
0SN Ted Williams/43 150.00 45.00
1BA Cal Ripken 40.00 12.00
1CE Cal Ripken/21
1CR Cal Ripken/277 50.00 15.00
1JN Cal Ripken/8
1SN Cal Ripken/114 100.00 30.00
2BA V. Guerrero SP 25.00 7.50
2CE Vladimir Guerrero/21
2CR V. Guerrero/322 15.00 4.50
2JN Vladimir Guerrero AU/27 EXCH
2SN V. Guerrero/44 50.00 15.00
3BA Greg Maddux 25.00 7.50
3CE Greg Maddux/21
3CR Greg Maddux/240 25.00 7.50
3JN Greg Maddux/31 80.00 24.00
3SN Greg Maddux/20
4BA Barry Bonds 30.00 9.00
4CE Barry Bonds/21
4CR Barry Bonds/289 40.00 12.00
4JN Barry Bonds/25
4SN Barry Bonds/49 100.00 30.00
5BA Pedro Martinez 15.00 4.50
5CE Pedro Martinez/21
45CR Pedro Martinez/268 15.00 4.50
45JN Pedro Martinez/45 50.00 15.00
45SN Pedro Martinez/23
46BA Ivan Rodriguez 15.00 4.50
46CE Ivan Rodriguez/21
46CR Ivan Rodriguez/304 15.00 4.50
46JN Ivan Rodriguez/7
46SN Ivan Rodriguez/35 60.00 18.00
47BA Roger Maris 50.00 15.00
47CE Roger Maris/21
47CR Roger Maris/275 50.00 15.00
47JN Roger Maris/23
47SN Roger Maris/61 100.00 30.00
48BA Randy Johnson 15.00 4.50
48CE Randy Johnson/21
48CR Randy Johnson/179 15.00 4.50
48JN Randy Johnson/51 40.00 12.00
48SN Randy Johnson/20
49BA Roger Clemens 25.00 7.50
49CE Roger Clemens/21
49CR Roger Clemens/260 30.00 9.00
49JN Roger Clemens AU/22
49SN Roger Clemens/24
50BA Todd Helton 15.00 4.50
50CE Todd Helton/21
50CR Todd Helton/334 15.00 4.50
50JN Todd Helton/17
50SN Todd Helton/42 50.00 15.00
51BA Tony Gwynn 15.00 4.50
51CE Tony Gwynn AU/21
51CR Tony Gwynn/134 40.00 12.00
51JN Tony Gwynn/19
51SN Tony Gwynn/119 40.00 12.00
52BA Troy Glaus 10.00 3.00
52CE Troy Glaus/21
52CR Troy Glaus/256 10.00 3.00
52JN Troy Glaus/25
52SN Troy Glaus/47 30.00 9.00
53BA Phil Niekro 15.00 4.50
53CE Phil Niekro/21
53CR Phil Niekro/245 15.00 4.50
53JN Phil Niekro/35 50.00 15.00
53SN Phil Niekro/23
54BA Don Sutton 15.00 4.50
54CE Don Sutton/21
54CR Don Sutton/178 15.00 4.50
54JN Don Sutton/20
54SN Don Sutton/21
55BA Frank Thomas 15.00 4.50
55CE Frank Thomas/21
55CR Frank Thomas/321 15.00 4.50
55JN Frank Thomas/35 60.00 18.00
55SN Frank Thomas/43 50.00 15.00
56BA Jeff Bagwell 15.00 4.50
56CE Jeff Bagwell AU/21
56CR Jeff Bagwell/305 15.00 4.50
56JN Jeff Bagwell/5
56SN Jeff Bagwell/135 25.00 7.50
57BA Rickey Henderson 15.00 4.50
57CE Rickey Henderson/21
57CR R. Henderson/282 15.00 4.50
57JN R. Henderson/35 60.00 18.00
57SN R. Henderson/28 60.00 18.00
58BA Darin Erstad SP 15.00 4.50
58CE Darin Erstad/21
58CR Darin Erstad/301 10.00 3.00
58JN Darin Erstad/17
58SN Darin Erstad/100 15.00 4.50
59BA Andruw Jones 10.00 3.00
59CE Andruw Jones/21
59CR Andruw Jones/272 10.00 3.00
59JN Andruw Jones/25
59SN Andruw Jones/36 30.00 9.00
60BA Roberto Alomar 15.00 4.50
60CE Roberto Alomar/21
60CR Roberto Alomar/170 15.00 4.50
60JN Roberto Alomar/12
60SN Roberto Alomar/120 25.00 7.50
61BA Mike Piazza SP 40.00 12.00
61CE Mike Piazza/21
61CR Mike Piazza/328 25.00 7.50
61JN Mike Piazza/31 80.00 24.00
61SN Mike Piazza/40 80.00 24.00
62BA Chipper Jones 15.00 4.50
62CE Chipper Jones/21
62CR Chipper Jones/189 15.00 4.50
62JN Chipper Jones/10
62SN Chipper Jones/45 50.00 15.00
63BA Shawn Green 10.00 3.00
63CE Shawn Green/21
63CR Shawn Green/143 15.00 4.50
63JN Shawn Green/15
63SN Shawn Green/123 15.00 4.50
64BA Don Mattingly SP 80.00 24.00
64CE Don Mattingly AU/21
64CR Don Mattingly/222 40.00 12.00
64JN Don Mattingly/23
64SN Don Mattingly/145 60.00 18.00
65BA Rafael Palmeiro 15.00 4.50
65CE Rafael Palmeiro/21
65CR Rafael Palmeiro/296 15.00 4.50
65JN Rafael Palmeiro/25
65SN Rafael Palmeiro/47 50.00 15.00
66BA Wade Boggs 25.00 7.50
66CE Wade Boggs/21
66CR Wade Boggs/116 40.00 12.00
66JN Wade Boggs/26 80.00 24.00
66SN Wade Boggs/89 40.00 12.00
67BA Hoyt Wilhelm 15.00 4.50
67CE Hoyt Wilhelm/21
67CR Hoyt Wilhelm/143 25.00 7.50
67JN Hoyt Wilhelm/31 50.00 15.00
67SN Hoyt Wilhelm/27 50.00 15.00
68BA Andre Dawson 15.00 4.50
68CE Andre Dawson/21
68CR Andre Dawson/314 15.00 4.50
68JN Andre Dawson/8
68SN Andre Dawson/49 40.00 12.00
69BA Ryne Sandberg 40.00 12.00
69CE Ryne Sandberg AU/21
69CR Ryne Sandberg/282 25.00 7.50
69JN Ryne Sandberg/23
69SN Ryne Sandberg/40 80.00 24.00
70BA N.Garciaparra SP 40.00 12.00
70CE Nomar Garciaparra/21
70CR N.Garciaparra/333 25.00 7.50
70JN Nomar Garciaparra/5
70SN N.Garciaparra/35 100.00 30.00
71BA Tom Glavine 15.00 4.50
71CE Tom Glavine/21
71CR Tom Glavine/208 15.00 4.50
71JN Tom Glavine/47 50.00 15.00
71SN Tom Glavine/247 15.00 4.50
72BA Magglio Ordonez 10.00 3.00
72CE Magglio Ordonez/21
72CR M.Ordonez/301 10.00 3.00
72JN Magglio Ordonez/30 40.00 12.00
72SN Magglio Ordonez/126 15.00 4.50
73BA Bernie Williams 15.00 4.50
73CE Bernie Williams/21
73CR Bernie Williams/304 15.00 4.50
73JN Bernie Williams/51 40.00 12.00
73SN Bernie Williams/30 60.00 18.00
74BA Jim Edmonds 10.00 3.00
74CE Jim Edmonds/21
74CR Jim Edmonds/291 10.00 3.00
74JN Jim Edmonds/15
74SN Jim Edmonds/108 15.00 4.50
75BA Hideo Nomo 50.00 15.00
75CE Hideo Nomo/21
75CR Hideo Nomo/69 100.00 30.00
75JN Hideo Nomo/11
75SN Hideo Nomo/16
76BA Barry Larkin 15.00 4.50
76CE Barry Larkin/21
76CR Barry Larkin/300 15.00 4.50
76JN Barry Larkin/11
76SN Barry Larkin/33 60.00 18.00
77BA Scott Rolen 15.00 4.50
77CE Scott Rolen/21
77CR Scott Rolen/284 15.00 4.50
77JN Scott Rolen/17
77SN Scott Rolen/31 60.00 18.00
78BA Miguel Tejada 10.00 3.00
78CE Miguel Tejada/21
78CR Miguel Tejada/253 10.00 3.00
78JN Miguel Tejada/4
78SN Miguel Tejada/30 40.00 12.00
79BA Freddy Garcia 10.00 3.00
79CE Freddy Garcia/21
79CR Freddy Garcia/249 10.00 3.00
79JN Freddy Garcia/34 40.00 12.00
79SN Freddy Garcia/170 10.00 3.00
80BA Edgar Martinez 15.00 4.50
80CE Edgar Martinez/21
80CR Edgar Martinez/320 15.00 4.50
80JN Edgar Martinez/11
80SN Edgar Martinez/37 50.00 15.00
81BA Edgardo Alfonzo 10.00 3.00
81CE Edgardo Alfonzo/21
81CR E. Alfonzo/296 10.00 3.00
81JN Edgardo Alfonzo/13
81SN E. Alfonzo/108 15.00 4.50
82BA Steve Garvey 15.00 4.50
82CE Steve Garvey/21
82CR Steve Garvey/272 15.00 4.50
82JN Steve Garvey/6
82SN Steve Garvey/33 50.00 15.00
83BA Larry Walker 15.00 4.50
83CE Larry Walker/21
83CR Larry Walker/311 15.00 4.50
83JN Larry Walker/12
83SN Larry Walker/49 50.00 15.00
84BA A.J. Burnett 10.00 3.00
84CE A.J. Burnett/21
84CR A.J. Burnett/90 15.00 4.50
84JN A.J. Burnett/43 30.00 9.00
84SN A.J. Burnett/57 25.00 7.50
85BA Richie Sexson 10.00 3.00
85CE Richie Sexson/21
85CR Richie Sexson/242 10.00 3.00
85JN Richie Sexson/11
85SN Richie Sexson/116 15.00 4.50
86BA Mark Mulder 10.00 3.00
86CE Mark Mulder/21
86CR Mark Mulder/88 15.00 4.50
86JN Mark Mulder/20
86SN Mark Mulder/9
87BA Kerry Wood 15.00 4.50
87CE Kerry Wood/21
87CR Kerry Wood/21
87JN Kerry Wood/34 60.00 18.00
87SN Kerry Wood/233 15.00 4.50
88BA Sean Casey 10.00 3.00
88CE Sean Casey/21
88CR Sean Casey/312 10.00 3.00
88JN Sean Casey/21
88SN Sean Casey/25
89BA Jermaine Dye SP 15.00 4.50
89CE Jermaine Dye/21
89CR Jermaine Dye/286 10.00 3.00
89JN Jermaine Dye/24
89SN Jermaine Dye/118 15.00 4.50
90BA Kevin Brown SP 15.00 4.50
90CE Kevin Brown/21
90CR Kevin Brown/170 10.00 3.00
90JN Kevin Brown/27 40.00 12.00
90SN Kevin Brown/257 10.00 3.00
91BA Craig Biggio 15.00 4.50
91CE Craig Biggio/21
91CR Craig Biggio/291 15.00 4.50
91JN Craig Biggio/7
91SN Craig Biggio/88 25.00 7.50
92BA Mike Sweeney SP 15.00 4.50
92CE Mike Sweeney/21
92CR Mike Sweeney/302 10.00 3.00
92JN Mike Sweeney/29 40.00 12.00
92SN Mike Sweeney/144 15.00 4.50
93BA Jim Thome 15.00 4.50
93CE Jim Thome/21
93CR Jim Thome/233 15.00 4.50
93JN Jim Thome/25
93SN Jim Thome/40 50.00 15.00
94BA Al Leiter 10.00 3.00
94CE Al Leiter/21
94CR Al Leiter/106 15.00 4.50
94JN Al Leiter/22
94SN Al Leiter/247 10.00 3.00
95BA Barry Zito 15.00 4.50
95CE Barry Zito/21
95CR Barry Zito/272 15.00 4.50
95JN Barry Zito/75 25.00 7.50
95SN Barry Zito/78 25.00 7.50
96BA Rafael Furcal 10.00 3.00
96CE Rafael Furcal/21
96CR Rafael Furcal/295 10.00 3.00
96JN Rafael Furcal/1
96SN Rafael Furcal/37 30.00 9.00
97BA J.D. Drew 10.00 3.00
97CE J.D. Drew/21
97CR J.D. Drew/276 10.00 3.00
97JN J.D. Drew/7
97SN J.D. Drew/18
98BA Andres Galarraga 10.00 3.00
98CE Andres Galarraga/21
98CR A. Galarraga/291 10.00 3.00
98JN Andres Galarraga/14
98SN A. Galarraga/150 10.00 3.00
99BA Kazuhiro Sasaki 10.00 3.00
99CE Kazuhiro Sasaki/21
99CR Kazuhiro Sasaki/266 10.00 3.00
99JN Kazuhiro Sasaki/22
99SN Kazuhiro Sasaki/45 30.00 9.00
100BA Chan Ho Park 10.00 3.00
100CE Chan Ho Park/21
100CR Chan Ho Park/65 25.00 7.50
100JN Chan Ho Park/61 25.00 7.50
100SN Chan Ho Park/217 10.00 3.00
101BA Eric Milton 10.00 3.00
101CE Eric Milton/21
101CR Eric Milton/28 40.00 12.00
101JN Eric Milton/21
101SN Eric Milton/163 10.00 3.00
102BA Carlos Lee 10.00 3.00
102CE Carlos Lee/21
102CR Carlos Lee/297 10.00 3.00
102JN Carlos Lee/45 30.00 9.00
102SN Carlos Lee/24
103BA Preston Wilson 10.00 3.00
103CE Preston Wilson/21
103CR P. Wilson/266 10.00 3.00
103JN Preston Wilson/44 30.00 9.00
103SN Preston Wilson/31 40.00 12.00
104BA Adrian Beltre 15.00 4.50
104CE Adrian Beltre/21
104CR Adrian Beltre/272 15.00 4.50
104JN Adrian Beltre/29 60.00 18.00
104SN Adrian Beltre/85 25.00 7.50
105BA Luis Gonzalez 10.00 3.00
105CE Luis Gonzalez/21
105CR Luis Gonzalez/281 10.00 3.00
105JN Luis Gonzalez/20
105SN Luis Gonzalez/114 15.00 4.50
106BA Kenny Lofton 10.00 3.00
106CE Kenny Lofton/21
106CR Kenny Lofton/306 10.00 3.00
106JN Kenny Lofton/7
106SN Kenny Lofton/15
107BA Shannon Stewart 10.00 3.00
107CE Shannon Stewart/21
107CR S. Stewart/297 10.00 3.00
107JN Shannon Stewart/24
107SN Shannon Stewart/21
108BA Javy Lopez 10.00 3.00
108CE Javy Lopez/21
108CR Javy Lopez/290 10.00 3.00
108JN Javy Lopez/8
108SN Javy Lopez/106 15.00 4.50
109BA Raul Mondesi 10.00 3.00
109CE Raul Mondesi/21
109CR Raul Mondesi/286 10.00 3.00
109JN Raul Mondesi/43 30.00 9.00
109SN Raul Mondesi/33 40.00 12.00
110BA Mark Grace 15.00 4.50
110CE Mark Grace/21
110CR Mark Grace/308 15.00 4.50
110JN Mark Grace/17
110SN Mark Grace/51 40.00 12.00
111BA Curt Schilling 10.00 3.00
111CE Curt Schilling/21
111CR Curt Schilling/110 15.00 4.50
111JN Curt Schilling/38 30.00 9.00
111SN Curt Schilling/235 10.00 3.00
112BA Cliff Floyd 10.00 3.00
112CE Cliff Floyd/21
112CR Cliff Floyd/275 10.00 3.00
112JN Cliff Floyd/30 40.00 12.00
112SN Cliff Floyd/22
113BA Moises Alou 10.00 3.00
113CE Moises Alou/21
113CR Moises Alou/303 10.00 3.00
113JN Moises Alou/18
113SN Moises Alou/124 15.00 4.50
114BA Aaron Sele 10.00 3.00
114CE Aaron Sele/21
114CR Aaron Sele/92 15.00 4.50
114JN Aaron Sele/30 40.00 12.00
114SN Aaron Sele/19
115BA Jose Cruz Jr. 10.00 3.00
115CE Jose Cruz Jr./21
115CR Jose Cruz Jr./245 10.00 3.00
115JN Jose Cruz Jr./23
115SN Jose Cruz Jr./31 40.00 12.00
116BA John Olerud 10.00 3.00
116CE John Olerud/21
116CR John Olerud/186 10.00 3.00
116JN John Olerud/5
116SN John Olerud/107 15.00 4.50
117BA Jose Vidro 10.00 3.00
117CE Jose Vidro/21
117CR Jose Vidro/296 10.00 3.00
117JN Jose Vidro/3
117SN Jose Vidro/24
118BA John Smoltz 15.00 4.50
118CE John Smoltz/21
118CR John Smoltz/335 15.00 4.50
118JN John Smoltz/29 60.00 18.00
118SN John Smoltz/24

2002 Leaf Certified

This 200-card set was released in early September, 2002. It was issued in five card packs which came 12 packs to a box and six boxes to a case. The first 150 card featured veteran stars while the final 50 cards features rookies and prospects along with a game-used memorabilia piece for each of them. Those final fifty cards have a stated print run of 500 serial numbered sets.

	Nm-Mt	Ex-Mt
COMP.SET w/o SP's (150)	80.00	24.00
COMMON CARD (1-150)	1.00	.30
COMMON CARD (151-200)	10.00	3.00
1 Alex Rodriguez	4.00	1.20
2 Luis Gonzalez	1.00	.30
3 Javier Vazquez	1.00	.30
4 Juan Uribe	1.00	.30
5 Ben Sheets	1.00	.30
6 George Brett	6.00	1.80
7 Magglio Ordonez	1.00	.30
8 Randy Johnson	2.50	.75
9 Joe Kennedy	1.00	.30
10 Richie Sexson	1.00	.30
11 Larry Walker	1.50	.45
12 Lance Berkman	1.00	.30
13 Jose Cruz Jr.	1.00	.30
14 Doug Davis	1.00	.30
15 Cliff Floyd	1.00	.30
16 Ryan Klesko	1.00	.30
17 Troy Glaus	1.00	.30
18 Robert Person	1.00	.30
19 Bartolo Colon	1.00	.30
20 Adam Dunn	1.50	.45
21 Kevin Brown	1.00	.30
22 John Smoltz	1.50	.45
23 Edgar Martinez	1.50	.45
24 Eric Karros	1.00	.30
25 Tony Gwynn	3.00	.90
26 Mark Mulder	1.00	.30
27 Don Mattingly	6.00	1.80
28 Brandon Duckworth	1.00	.30
29 C.C. Sabathia	1.00	.30
30 Nomar Garciaparra	4.00	1.20
31 Adam Johnson	1.00	.30
32 Miguel Tejada	1.00	.30
33 Ryne Sandberg	5.00	1.50
34 Roger Clemens	5.00	1.50
35 Edgardo Alfonzo	1.00	.30
36 Jason Jennings	1.00	.30
37 Todd Helton	1.50	.45
38 Nolan Ryan	6.00	1.80
39 Paul LoDuca	1.00	.30
40 Cal Ripken	8.00	2.40
41 Terrence Long	1.00	.30
42 Mike Sweeney	1.00	.30
43 Carlos Lee	1.00	.30
44 Ben Grieve	1.00	.30
45 Tony Armas Jr.	1.00	.30
46 Joe Mays	1.00	.30
47 Jeff Kent	1.00	.30
48 Andy Pettitte	1.50	.45
49 Kirby Puckett	2.50	.75
50 Aramis Ramirez	1.00	.30
51 Tim Redding	1.00	.30
52 Freddy Garcia	1.00	.30
53 Javy Lopez	1.00	.30
54 Mike Schmidt	6.00	1.80
55 Wade Miller	1.00	.30
56 Ramon Ortiz	1.00	.30
57 Ray Durham	1.00	.30
58 J.D. Drew	1.00	.30
59 Bret Boone	1.00	.30
60 Mark Buehrle	1.00	.30
61 Geoff Jenkins	1.00	.30
62 Greg Maddux	4.00	1.20
63 Mark Grace	1.50	.45
64 Toby Hall	1.00	.30
65 A.J. Burnett	1.00	.30
66 Bernie Williams	1.50	.45
67 Roy Oswalt	1.00	.30
68 Shannon Stewart	1.00	.30
69 Barry Zito	1.00	.30
70 Juan Pierre	1.00	.30
71 Preston Wilson	1.00	.30
72 Rafael Furcal	1.00	.30
73 Sean Casey	1.00	.30
74 John Olerud	1.00	.30
75 Paul Konerko	1.00	.30
76 Vernon Wells	1.00	.30
77 Juan Gonzalez	1.50	.45
78 Ellis Burks	1.00	.30
79 Jim Edmonds	1.00	.30
80 Robert Fick	1.00	.30
81 Michael Cuddyer	1.00	.30
82 Tim Hudson	1.00	.30
83 Phil Nevin	1.00	.30
84 Curt Schilling	1.00	.30
85 Juan Cruz	1.00	.30
86 Jeff Bagwell	1.50	.45
87 Raul Mondesi	1.00	.30
88 Bud Smith	1.00	.30
89 Omar Vizquel	1.50	.45
90 Vladimir Guerrero	2.50	.75
91 Garret Anderson	1.00	.30
92 Mike Piazza	4.00	1.20
93 Josh Beckett	1.00	.30
94 Carlos Delgado	1.00	.30
95 Kazuhiro Sasaki	1.00	.30
96 Chipper Jones	2.50	.75
97 Jacque Jones	1.00	.30
98 Pedro Martinez	2.50	.75
99 Marcus Giles	1.00	.30
100 Craig Biggio	1.50	.45
101 Orlando Cabrera	1.00	.30
102 Al Leiter	1.00	.30
103 Michael Barrett	1.00	.30
104 Hideo Nomo	2.50	.75
105 Mike Mussina	1.50	.45
106 Jeremy Giambi	1.00	.30
107 Cristian Guzman	1.00	.30
108 Frank Thomas	2.50	.75
109 Carlos Beltran	1.50	.45
110 Jorge Posada	1.50	.45
111 Roberto Alomar	1.50	.45
112 Bob Abreu	1.00	.30
113 Robin Ventura	1.00	.30
114 Pat Burrell	1.00	.30
115 Kenny Lofton	1.00	.30
116 Adrian Beltre	1.50	.45
117 Gary Sheffield	1.00	.30
118 Jermaine Dye	1.00	.30
119 Manny Ramirez	1.50	.45
120 Brian Giles	1.00	.30

121 Tsuyoshi Shinjo.................. 1.00 .30
122 Rafael Palmeiro.................. 1.50 .45
123 Mo Vaughn UER.................. 1.00 .30
Yankee Logo on back
124 Kerry Wood.................. 2.50 .75
125 Moises Alou.................. 1.00 .30
126 Rickey Henderson.................. 2.50 .75
127 Corey Patterson.................. 1.00 .30
128 Jim Thome.................. 2.50 .75
129 Richard Hidalgo.................. 1.00 .30
130 Darin Erstad.................. 1.00 .30
131 Johnny Damon Sox.................. 2.50 .75
132 Juan Encarnacion.................. 1.00 .30
133 Scott Rolen.................. 2.50 .75
134 Tom Glavine.................. 1.50 .45
135 Ivan Rodriguez.................. 2.50 .75
136 Jay Gibbons.................. 1.00 .30
137 Trot Nixon.................. 1.00 .30
138 Nick Neugebauer.................. 1.00 .30
139 Barry Larkin.................. 1.50 .45
140 Andruw Jones.................. 1.00 .30
141 Shawn Green.................. 1.00 .30
142 Jose Vidro.................. 1.00 .30
143 Derek Jeter.................. 6.00 1.80
144 Ichiro Suzuki.................. 4.00 1.20
145 Ken Griffey Jr.................. 4.00 1.20
146 Barry Bonds.................. 6.00 1.80
147 Albert Pujols.................. 5.00 1.50
148 Sammy Sosa.................. 4.00 1.20
149 Jason Giambi.................. 1.00 .30
150 Alfonso Soriano.................. 1.50 .45
151 Drew Henson NG Bat.......... 10.00 3.00
152 Luis Garcia NG Bat.......... 10.00 3.00
153 Geronimo Gil NG Jsy.......... 10.00 3.00
154 Corky Miller NG Jsy.......... 10.00 3.00
155 Mike Rivera NG Bat.......... 10.00 3.00
156 Mark Ellis NG Jsy.......... 10.00 3.00
157 Josh Pearce NG Bat.......... 10.00 3.00
158 Ryan Ludwick NG Bat.......... 10.00 3.00
159 So Taguchi NG Bat RC.......... 15.00 4.50
160 Cody Ransom NG Jsy.......... 10.00 3.00
161 Jeff Deardorff NG Bat.......... 10.00 3.00
162 Fr. German NG Bat RC.......... 10.00 3.00
163 Ed Rogers NG Jsy.......... 10.00 3.00
164 Eric Cyr NG Jsy.......... 10.00 3.00
165 Victor Alvarez NG Jsy RC... 10.00 3.00
166 Victor Martinez NG Jsy.......... 15.00 4.50
167 Brandon Berger NG Jsy.......... 10.00 3.00
168 Juan Diaz NG Jsy.......... 10.00 3.00
169 Kevin Frederick NG Jsy RC 10.00 3.00
170 Earl Snyder NG Bat RC.......... 15.00 4.50
171 Morgan Ensberg NG Bat.......... 10.00 3.00
172 Ryan Jamison NG Jsy.......... 10.00 3.00
173 Rod. Rosario NG Jsy RC.......... 10.00 3.00
174 Willie Harris NG Bat.......... 10.00 3.00
175 Ramon Vazquez NG Bat.......... 10.00 3.00
176 Kazuhisa Ishii NG Bat RC... 20.00 6.00
177 Hank Blalock NG Jsy.......... 15.00 4.50
178 Mark Prior NG Bat.......... 20.00 6.00
179 Dewon Brazelton NG Jsy.......... 10.00 3.00
180 Doug Devore NG Jsy RC.......... 10.00 3.00
181 Jorge Padilla NG Jsy RC.......... 10.00 3.00
182 Mark Teixeira NG Jsy.......... 15.00 4.50
183 Orlando Hudson NG Bat.......... 10.00 3.00
184 John Buck NG Jsy.......... 10.00 3.00
185 Erik Bedard NG Jsy.......... 10.00 3.00
186 Allan Simpson NG Jsy RC.......... 10.00 3.00
187 Travis Hafner NG Jsy.......... 10.00 3.00
188 Jason Lane NG Jsy.......... 10.00 3.00
189 Marlon Byrd NG Jsy.......... 10.00 3.00
190 Joe Thurston NG Jsy.......... 10.00 3.00
191 Brandon Backe NG Jsy RC. 15.00 4.50
192 Josh Phelps NG Jsy.......... 10.00 3.00
193 Bill Hall NG Bat.......... 10.00 3.00
194 Chris Snelling NG Bat RC... 10.00 3.00
195 Austin Kearns NG Jsy.......... 10.00 3.00
196 Antonio Perez NG Bat.......... 10.00 3.00
197 Angel Berroa NG Bat.......... 10.00 3.00
198 Andy Machado NG Jsy RC. 10.00 3.00
199 Alfredo Amezaga NG Jsy.......... 10.00 3.00
200 Eric Hinske NG Bat.......... 10.00 3.00

2002 Leaf Certified Mirror Blue

Randomly inserted in packs, this is a parallel to the Leaf Certified set. These cards used blue tint and foil and are printed to a stated print run of 75 serial numbered set.

Nm-Mt Ex-Mt
*MIRROR BLUE 1-150: .6X TO 1.5X MIR.RED
*MIRROR BLUE 151-200: .6X TO 1.5X MIR.RED..........

2002 Leaf Certified Mirror Red

Randomly inserted in packs, this is a parallel to the Leaf Certified set. These cards used red tint and foil and are printed to a stated print run of 150 serial numbered set.

Nm-Mt Ex-Mt
1 Alex Rodriguez Jsy.......... 25.00 7.50
2 Luis Gonzalez Jsy.......... 10.00 3.00
3 Javier Vazquez Jsy.......... 10.00 3.00
4 Juan Uribe Jsy.......... 10.00 3.00
5 Ben Sheets Jsy.......... 10.00 3.00
6 George Brett Jsy.......... 60.00 18.00
7 Magglio Ordonez Jsy.......... 10.00 3.00
8 Randy Johnson Jsy.......... 20.00 6.00
9 Joe Kennedy Jsy.......... 10.00 3.00
10 Richie Sexson Jsy.......... 10.00 3.00
11 Larry Walker Jsy.......... 15.00 4.50
12 Lance Berkman Jsy.......... 10.00 3.00
13 Jose Cruz Jr. Jsy.......... 10.00 3.00
14 Doug Davis Jsy.......... 10.00 3.00
15 Cliff Floyd Jsy.......... 10.00 3.00
16 Ryan Klesko Bat SP/100.......... 10.00 3.00
17 Troy Glaus Jsy.......... 10.00 3.00
18 Robert Person Jsy.......... 10.00 3.00
19 Bartolo Colon Jsy.......... 10.00 3.00
20 Adam Dunn Jsy.......... 15.00 4.50
21 Kevin Brown Jsy.......... 10.00 3.00
22 John Smoltz Jsy.......... 15.00 4.50
23 Edgar Martinez Jsy.......... 15.00 4.50
24 Eric Karros Jsy.......... 10.00 3.00
25 Tony Gwynn Jsy.......... 25.00 7.50
26 Mark Mulder Jsy.......... 10.00 3.00
27 Don Mattingly Jsy.......... 60.00 18.00
28 Brandon Duckworth Jsy.......... 10.00 3.00
29 C.C. Sabathia Jsy.......... 10.00 3.00
30 Nomar Garciaparra Jsy.......... 25.00 7.50
31 Adam Johnson Jsy.......... 10.00 3.00
32 Miguel Tejada Jsy.......... 10.00 3.00
33 Ryne Sandberg Jsy.......... 50.00 15.00
34 Roger Clemens Jsy.......... 40.00 12.00
35 Edgardo Alfonzo Jsy.......... 10.00 3.00
36 Jason Jennings Jsy.......... 10.00 3.00
37 Todd Helton Jsy.......... 15.00 4.50
38 Nolan Ryan Jsy.......... 80.00 24.00
39 Paul LoDuca Jsy.......... 10.00 3.00
40 Cal Ripken Jsy.......... 80.00 24.00
41 Terrence Long Jsy.......... 10.00 3.00
42 Mike Sweeney Jsy.......... 10.00 3.00
43 Carlos Lee Jsy.......... 10.00 3.00
44 Ben Grieve Jsy.......... 10.00 3.00
45 Tony Armas Jr. Jsy.......... 10.00 3.00
46 Joe Mays Jsy.......... 10.00 3.00
47 Jeff Kent Jsy.......... 10.00 3.00
48 Andy Pettitte Jsy.......... 15.00 4.50
49 Kirby Puckett Jsy.......... 20.00 6.00
50 Aramis Ramirez Jsy.......... 10.00 3.00
51 Tim Redding Jsy.......... 10.00 3.00
52 Freddy Garcia Jsy.......... 10.00 3.00
53 Javy Lopez Jsy.......... 10.00 3.00
54 Mike Schmidt Jsy.......... 50.00 15.00
55 Wade Miller Jsy.......... 10.00 3.00
56 Ramon Ortiz Jsy.......... 10.00 3.00
57 Ray Durham Jsy.......... 10.00 3.00
58 J.D. Drew Jsy.......... 10.00 3.00
59 Bret Boone Jsy.......... 10.00 3.00
60 Mark Buehrle Jsy.......... 10.00 3.00
61 Geoff Jenkins Jsy.......... 10.00 3.00
62 Greg Maddux Jsy.......... 25.00 7.50
63 Mark Grace Jsy.......... 15.00 4.50
64 Toby Hall Jsy.......... 10.00 3.00
65 A.J. Burnett Jsy.......... 10.00 3.00
66 Bernie Williams Jsy.......... 15.00 4.50
67 Roy Oswalt Jsy.......... 10.00 3.00
68 Shannon Stewart Jsy.......... 10.00 3.00
69 Barry Zito Jsy.......... 10.00 3.00
70 Juan Pierre Jsy.......... 10.00 3.00
71 Preston Wilson Jsy.......... 10.00 3.00
72 Rafael Furcal Jsy.......... 10.00 3.00
73 Sean Casey Jsy.......... 10.00 3.00
74 John Olerud Jsy.......... 10.00 3.00
75 Paul Konerko Jsy.......... 15.00 4.50
76 Vernon Wells Jsy.......... 10.00 3.00
77 Juan Gonzalez Jsy.......... 15.00 4.50
78 Ellis Burks Jsy.......... 10.00 3.00
79 Jim Edmonds Jsy.......... 10.00 3.00
80 Robert Fick Jsy.......... 10.00 3.00
81 Michael Cuddyer Jsy.......... 10.00 3.00
82 Tim Hudson Jsy.......... 10.00 3.00
83 Phil Nevin Jsy.......... 10.00 3.00
84 Curt Schilling Jsy.......... 10.00 3.00
85 Juan Cruz Jsy.......... 10.00 3.00
86 Jeff Bagwell Jsy.......... 15.00 4.50
87 Raul Mondesi Jsy.......... 10.00 3.00
88 Bud Smith Jsy.......... 10.00 3.00
89 Omar Vizquel Jsy.......... 15.00 4.50
90 Vladimir Guerrero Jsy.......... 20.00 6.00
91 Garret Anderson Jsy.......... 10.00 3.00
92 Mike Piazza Jsy.......... 25.00 7.50
93 Josh Beckett Jsy.......... 10.00 3.00
94 Carlos Delgado Jsy.......... 10.00 3.00
95 Kazuhiro Sasaki Jsy.......... 10.00 3.00
96 Chipper Jones Jsy.......... 20.00 6.00
97 Jacque Jones Jsy.......... 10.00 3.00
98 Pedro Martinez Jsy.......... 20.00 6.00
99 Marcus Giles Jsy.......... 10.00 3.00
100 Craig Biggio Jsy.......... 15.00 4.50
101 Orlando Cabrera Jsy.......... 10.00 3.00
102 Al Leiter Jsy.......... 10.00 3.00
103 Michael Barrett Jsy.......... 10.00 3.00
104 Hideo Nomo Jsy.......... 20.00 6.00
105 Mike Mussina Jsy.......... 15.00 4.50
106 Jeremy Giambi Jsy.......... 10.00 3.00
107 Cristian Guzman Jsy.......... 10.00 3.00
108 Frank Thomas Jsy.......... 20.00 6.00
109 Carlos Beltran Bat.......... 15.00 4.50
110 Jorge Posada Bat.......... 15.00 4.50
111 Roberto Alomar Bat.......... 15.00 4.50
112 Bob Abreu Bat.......... 10.00 3.00
113 Robin Ventura Bat.......... 10.00 3.00
114 Pat Burrell Bat.......... 10.00 3.00
115 Kenny Lofton Bat.......... 10.00 3.00
116 Adrian Beltre Bat.......... 15.00 4.50
117 Gary Sheffield Bat.......... 10.00 3.00
118 Jermaine Dye Bat.......... 10.00 3.00
119 Manny Ramirez Bat.......... 15.00 4.50
120 Brian Giles Bat.......... 10.00 3.00
121 Tsuyoshi Shinjo Bat.......... 10.00 3.00
122 Rafael Palmeiro Bat.......... 15.00 4.50
123 Mo Vaughn Bat.......... 10.00 3.00
124 Kerry Wood Bat.......... 20.00 6.00
125 Moises Alou Bat.......... 10.00 3.00
126 Rickey Henderson Bat.......... 20.00 6.00
127 Corey Patterson Bat.......... 10.00 3.00
128 Jim Thome Bat.......... 20.00 6.00
129 Richard Hidalgo Bat.......... 10.00 3.00
130 Darin Erstad Bat.......... 10.00 3.00
131 Johnny Damon Sox Bat.......... 20.00 6.00
132 Juan Encarnacion Bat.......... 10.00 3.00
133 Scott Rolen Bat.......... 20.00 6.00
134 Tom Glavine Bat.......... 15.00 4.50
135 Ivan Rodriguez Bat.......... 20.00 6.00
136 Jay Gibbons Bat.......... 10.00 3.00
137 Trot Nixon Bat.......... 10.00 3.00
138 Nick Neugebauer Bat.......... 10.00 3.00
139 Barry Larkin Bat.......... 15.00 4.50
140 Andruw Jones Bat.......... 10.00 3.00
141 Shawn Green Bat.......... 10.00 3.00
142 Jose Vidro Jsy.......... 10.00 3.00
143 Derek Jeter Base.......... 30.00 9.00
144 Ichiro Suzuki Base.......... 25.00 7.50
145 Ken Griffey Jr. Base.......... 20.00 6.00
146 Barry Bonds Base.......... 30.00 9.00
147 Albert Pujols Base.......... 20.00 6.00
148 Sammy Sosa Base.......... 15.00 4.50
149 Jason Giambi Base.......... 10.00 3.00
150 Alfonso Soriano Jsy.......... 15.00 4.50
151 Drew Henson NG Bat.......... 10.00 3.00
152 Luis Garcia NG Bat.......... 10.00 3.00
153 Geronimo Gil NG Jsy.......... 10.00 3.00
154 Corky Miller NG Jsy.......... 10.00 3.00
155 Mike Rivera NG Bat.......... 10.00 3.00
156 Mark Ellis NG Jsy.......... 10.00 3.00
157 Josh Pearce NG Bat.......... 10.00 3.00
158 Ryan Ludwick NG Bat.......... 10.00 3.00
159 So Taguchi NG Bat.......... 15.00 4.50
160 Cody Ransom NG Jsy.......... 10.00 3.00
161 Jeff Deardorff NG Bat.......... 10.00 3.00
162 Franklyn German NG Bat.......... 10.00 3.00
163 Ed Rogers NG Jsy.......... 10.00 3.00
164 Eric Cyr NG Jsy.......... 10.00 3.00
165 Victor Alvarez NG Jsy.......... 10.00 3.00
166 Victor Martinez NG Jsy.......... 15.00 4.50
167 Brandon Berger NG Jsy.......... 10.00 3.00
168 Juan Diaz NG Jsy.......... 10.00 3.00
169 Kevin Frederick NG Jsy.......... 10.00 3.00
170 Earl Snyder NG Bat.......... 15.00 4.50
171 Morgan Ensberg NG Bat.......... 10.00 3.00
172 Ryan Jamison NG Jsy.......... 10.00 3.00
173 Rodrigo Rosario NG Jsy.......... 10.00 3.00
174 Willie Harris NG Bat.......... 10.00 3.00
175 Ramon Vazquez NG Bat.......... 10.00 3.00
176 Kazuhisa Ishii NG Bat.......... 20.00 6.00
177 Hank Blalock NG Jsy.......... 15.00 4.50
178 Mark Prior NG Bat.......... 20.00 6.00
179 Dewon Brazelton NG Jsy.......... 10.00 3.00
180 Doug Devore NG Jsy.......... 10.00 3.00
181 Jorge Padilla NG Jsy.......... 10.00 3.00
182 Mark Teixeira NG Jsy.......... 15.00 4.50
183 Orlando Hudson NG Bat.......... 10.00 3.00
184 John Buck NG Jsy.......... 10.00 3.00
185 Erik Bedard NG Jsy.......... 10.00 3.00
186 Allan Simpson NG Jsy.......... 10.00 3.00
187 Travis Hafner NG Jsy.......... 10.00 3.00
188 Jason Lane NG Jsy.......... 10.00 3.00
189 Marlon Byrd NG Jsy.......... 10.00 3.00
190 Joe Thurston NG Jsy.......... 10.00 3.00
191 Brandon Backe NG Jsy.......... 15.00 4.50
192 Josh Phelps NG Jsy.......... 10.00 3.00
193 Bill Hall NG Bat.......... 10.00 3.00
194 Chris Snelling NG Bat.......... 10.00 3.00
195 Austin Kearns NG Jsy.......... 10.00 3.00
196 Antonio Perez NG Bat.......... 10.00 3.00
197 Angel Berroa NG Bat.......... 10.00 3.00
198 Anderson Machado NG Jsy 10.00 3.00
199 Alfredo Amezaga NG Jsy.......... 10.00 3.00
200 Eric Hinske NG Bat.......... 10.00 3.00

2002 Leaf Certified All-Certified Team

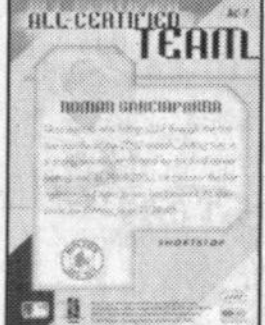

Inserted at stated odds of one in 17, these 25 card feature major stars using mirror board and gold foil stamping.

Nm-Mt Ex-Mt
COMPLETE SET (25).......... 100.00 30.00
*BLUE: 2X TO 5X BASIC ALL-CERT.TEAM
BLUE: RANDOM INSERTS IN PACKS..
BLUE PRINT RUN 50 SERIAL #'d SETS
GOLD: RANDOM INSERTS IN PACKS..
GOLD PRINT RUN 25 SERIAL #'d SETS
NO GOLD PRICING DUE TO SCARCITY
*RED: 1.25X TO 3X BASIC ALL-CERT.TEAM
RED: RANDOM INSERTS IN PACKS...
RED PRINT RUN 75 SERIAL #'d SETS
1 Ichiro Suzuki.......... 6.00 1.80
2 Alex Rodriguez.......... 6.00 1.80
3 Sammy Sosa.......... 6.00 1.80
4 Jeff Bagwell.......... 3.00 .90
5 Greg Maddux.......... 6.00 1.80
6 Todd Helton.......... 3.00 .90
7 Nomar Garciaparra.......... 6.00 1.80
8 Ken Griffey Jr.......... 6.00 1.80
9 Roger Clemens.......... 8.00 2.40
10 Adam Dunn.......... 3.00 .90
11 Chipper Jones.......... 4.00 1.20
12 Hideo Nomo.......... 4.00 1.20
13 Lance Berkman.......... 3.00 .90
14 Barry Bonds.......... 10.00 3.00
15 Manny Ramirez.......... 3.00 .90
16 Jason Giambi.......... 3.00 .90
17 Rickey Henderson.......... 4.00 1.20
18 Randy Johnson.......... 4.00 1.20
19 Derek Jeter.......... 10.00 3.00
20 Kazuhisa Ishii.......... 5.00 1.50
21 Frank Thomas.......... 4.00 1.20
22 Mike Piazza.......... 6.00 1.80
23 Albert Pujols.......... 8.00 2.40
24 Pedro Martinez.......... 4.00 1.20
25 Vladimir Guerrero.......... 4.00 1.20

2002 Leaf Certified Fabric of the Game

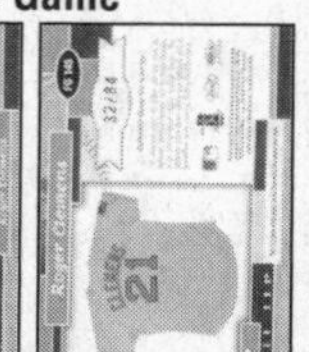

Randomly inserted in packs, these 703 cards feature a game-used swatch and are broken up into the following categories. There is a base card which has a stated print run of anywhere from five to 100 copies and cut into a design of a base. There is also pattern which have a stated print run of five to 50 copies with the swatch cut into the shape of the player's position. There is also a jersey subset which is cut into the shape of the player's uniform number. These cards range anywhere from a stated print run to anywhere from one to 75 serial numbered cards. There is also the debut year subset which has a stated print run of anywhere from 14 to 101 serial numbered cards. In addition, an unnannounced subset featured either information about the player's induction into the Hall of Fame or their nickname. These cards mostly have stated print runs of 25 or less and therefore are not priced due to market scarcity.

Nm-Mt Ex-Mt
1BA Bobby Doerr/10..........
1DY Bobby Doerr/37.......... 30.00 9.00
1IN Bobby Doerr HOF 86/4..........
1JN Bobby Doerr/1..........
1PS Bobby Doerr/25..........
1INA Bobby Doerr HOF 86 AU/1..........
2BA Ozzie Smith/15..........
2DY Ozzie Smith/78.......... 40.00 12.00
2JN Ozzie Smith/1..........
2PS Ozzie Smith/15..........
2INA Ozzie Smith HOF 02 AU/5..........
3BA Pee Wee Reese/5..........
3DY Pee Wee Reese/40.......... 50.00 15.00
3IN Pee Wee Reese HOF 84/5..........
3JN Pee Wee Reese/1..........
3PS Pee Wee Reese/10..........
4BA Tommy Lasorda/80.......... 15.00 4.50
4DY Tommy Lasorda/54.......... 25.00 7.50
4IN Tommy Lasorda HOF 97/20..........
4JN Tommy Lasorda/2..........
4PS Tommy Lasorda/50.......... 25.00 7.50
5BA Red Schoendienst/5..........
5DY Red Schoendienst/45.......... 30.00 9.00
5IN Red Schoendienst HOF 89/5..........
5JN Red Schoendienst/2..........
5PS Red Schoendienst/10..........
6BA Lou Gehrig/5..........
6DY Lou Gehrig/23..........
6IN Lou Gehrig HOF 39/5..........
6JN Lou Gehrig/4..........
6PS Lou Gehrig/10..........
7BA Harmon Killebrew/10..........
7DY Harmon Killebrew/54.......... 40.00 12.00
7JN Harmon Killebrew/3..........
7PS Harmon Killebrew/20..........
7INA Harmon Killebrew HOF 84 AU/5..........
8BA Roger Maris A's/10..........
8DY Roger Maris A's/57.......... 80.00 24.00
8JN Roger Maris A's/3..........
8PS Roger Maris A's/10..........
9BA Babe Ruth/5..........
9DY Babe Ruth/15..........
9IN Babe Ruth HOF 36/5..........
9JN Babe Ruth/3..........
9PS Babe Ruth/10..........
10BA Mel Ott/5..........
10DY Mel Ott/26.......... 100.00 30.00
10IN Mel Ott HOF 51/5..........
10JN Mel Ott/4..........
10PS Mel Ott/10..........
11BA Paul Molitor/100.......... 25.00 7.50
11DY Paul Molitor/78.......... 25.00 7.50
11JN Paul Molitor/4..........
11PS Paul Molitor/50.......... 40.00 12.00
12BA Duke Snider/5..........
12DY Duke Snider/47.......... 50.00 15.00
12JN Duke Snider/4..........
12PS Duke Snider/10..........
12INA Duke Snider HOF 80 AU/5..........
13BA Brooks Robinson/5..........
13DY Brooks Robinson/55.......... 40.00 12.00
13JN Brooks Robinson/5..........
13PS Brooks Robinson/10..........
13INA Brooks Robinson HOF 83 AU/5
14BA George Brett/40.......... 80.00 24.00
14DY George Brett/73.......... 60.00 18.00
14IN George Brett HOF 99/5..........
14JN George Brett/5..........
14PS George Brett/25..........
14INA George Brett HOF 99 AU/5..........
15BA Johnny Bench/80.......... 25.00 7.50
15DY Johnny Bench/67.......... 40.00 12.00
15IN Johnny Bench HOF 89/15..........
15JN Johnny Bench/5..........
15PS Johnny Bench/50.......... 40.00 12.00
15INA Johnny Bench HOF 89 AU/5..........
16BA Lou Boudreau/5..........
16DY Lou Boudreau/38.......... 30.00 9.00
16IN Lou Boudreau HOF 70/5..........
16JN Lou Boudreau/5..........
16PS Lou Boudreau/10..........
17BA Stan Musial/5..........
17DY Stan Musial/41.......... 80.00 24.00
17JN Stan Musial/6..........
17PS Stan Musial/10..........
17INA Stan Musial HOF 69 AU/5..........
18BA Al Kaline/5..........
18DY Al Kaline/53.......... 40.00 12.00
18JN Al Kaline/6..........
18PS Al Kaline/10..........
18INA Al Kaline HOF 80 AU/5..........
19BA Steve Garvey/100.......... 15.00 4.50
19DY Steve Garvey/69.......... 25.00 7.50
19JN Steve Garvey/6..........
19PS Steve Garvey/45.......... 30.00 9.00
20BA Nomar Garciaparra/100... 30.00 9.00
20DY Nomar Garciaparra/96.......... 30.00 9.00
20PS Nomar Garciaparra/50.......... 40.00 12.00
20JNA Nomar Garciaparra AU /5..........
21BA Joe Morgan/80.......... 15.00 4.50
21DY Joe Morgan/63.......... 25.00 7.50
21IN Joe Morgan HOF 90/15..........
21JN Joe Morgan/8..........
21PS Joe Morgan/50.......... 25.00 7.50
21INA Joe Morgan HOF 90 AU/5..........
22BA Willie Stargell/5..........
22DY Willie Stargell/62.......... 40.00 12.00
22IN Willie Stargell HOF 88/5..........
22JN Willie Stargell/8..........
22PS Willie Stargell/10..........
23BA Andre Dawson/80.......... 15.00 4.50
23DY Andre Dawson/76.......... 15.00 4.50
23IN Andre Dawson Hawk/15..........
23JN Andre Dawson/8..........
23PS Andre Dawson/50.......... 25.00 7.50
23INA Andre Dawson Hawk AU/5..........
24BA Gary Carter/100.......... 15.00 4.50
24DY Gary Carter/74.......... 25.00 7.50
24JN Gary Carter/8..........
24PS Gary Carter/50.......... 25.00 7.50
25BA Reggie Jackson A's/10..........
25DY Reggie Jackson A's/67.......... 40.00 12.00
25JN Reggie Jackson A's/9..........
25PS Reggie Jackson A's/25..........
25INA Reggie Jackson A's HOF 93 AU/5
26BA Ted Williams/5..........
26DY Ted Williams/39..........
26IN Ted Williams HOF 66/5..........
26JN Ted Williams/9..........
26PS Ted Williams/10..........
27BA Phil Rizzuto/5..........
27DY Phil Rizzuto/41.......... 50.00 15.00
27JN Phil Rizzuto/10..........
27PS Phil Rizzuto/10..........
27INA Phil Rizzuto HOF 94 AU/5..........
28BA Luis Aparicio/5..........
28DY Luis Aparicio/56.......... 25.00 7.50
28JN Luis Aparicio/11..........
28PS Luis Aparicio/10..........
28INA Luis Aparicio HOF 84 AU/5..........
29BA Robin Yount/80.......... 40.00 12.00
29DY Robin Yount/74.......... 40.00 12.00
29IN Robin Yount HOF 99/15..........
29JN Robin Yount/19..........
29PS Robin Yount/50.......... 40.00 12.00
29INA Robin Yount HOF 99 AU/5..........
30BA Tony Gwynn/100.......... 25.00 7.50
30DY Tony Gwynn/82.......... 25.00 7.50
30JN Tony Gwynn/14..........
30PS Tony Gwynn/50.......... 40.00 12.00
30JNA Tony Gwynn AU/5..........
31BA Ernie Banks/5..........
31DY Ernie Banks/53.......... 40.00 12.00
31JN Ernie Banks/14..........
31PS Ernie Banks/10..........
31INA Ernie Banks HOF 77 AU/5..........
32BA Joe Torre/50.......... 25.00 7.50
32DY Joe Torre/60.......... 25.00 7.50
32JN Joe Torre/15..........
32PS Joe Torre/25..........
33BA Bo Jackson/100.......... 25.00 7.50
33DY Bo Jackson/86.......... 25.00 7.50
33JN Bo Jackson/16..........
33PS Bo Jackson/35.......... 60.00 18.00
34BA Alfonso Soriano/80.......... 25.00 7.50
34DY Alfonso Soriano/99.......... 25.00 7.50
34JN Alfonso Soriano/12..........
34PS Alfonso Soriano/50.......... 40.00 12.00
35BA Cal Ripken/80.......... 80.00 24.00
35DY Cal Ripken/81.......... 80.00 24.00
35IN Cal Ripken Iron Man/15..........
35JN Cal Ripken/8..........
35PS Cal Ripken/50.......... 100.00 30.00
35INA Cal Ripken Iron Man AU/5..........
36BA Miguel Tejada/100.......... 15.00 4.50
36DY Miguel Tejada/97.......... 15.00 4.50
36JN Miguel Tejada/4..........
36PS Miguel Tejada/50.......... 25.00 7.50
37BA Alex Rodriguez M's/100.. 25.00 7.50
37DY Alex Rodriguez M's/94.......... 25.00 7.50
37JN Alex Rodriguez M's/3..........
37PS Alex Rodriguez M's/50.......... 40.00 12.00
38BA Mike Schmidt/80.......... 50.00 15.00
38DY Mike Schmidt/72.......... 50.00 15.00
38IN Mike Schmidt HOF 95/15..........
38JN Mike Schmidt/20..........
38PS Mike Schmidt/50.......... 60.00 18.00
38INA Mike Schmidt HOF 95 AU/5..........
39BA Lou Brock/5..........
39DY Lou Brock/61.......... 40.00 12.00
39JN Lou Brock/20..........
39PS Lou Brock/10..........
39INA Lou Brock HOF 85 AU/5..........
40BA Don Sutton/80.......... 15.00 4.50
40DY Don Sutton/66.......... 25.00 7.50
40IN Don Sutton HOF 98/15..........
40JN Don Sutton/20..........
40PS Don Sutton/50.......... 25.00 7.50
40INA Don Sutton HOF 98 AU/5..........
41BA Roberto Clemente/5..........
41DY Roberto Clemente/55.......... 150.00 45.00
41IN Roberto Clemente HOF 73/5..........
41JN Roberto Clemente/21..........
41PS Roberto Clemente/10..........
42BA Jim Palmer/20..........
42DY Jim Palmer/65.......... 25.00 7.50
42JN Jim Palmer/22..........
42PS Jim Palmer/15..........
42INA Jim Palmer HOF 90 AU/5..........
43BA Don Mattingly/40.......... 100.00 30.00
43DY Don Mattingly/82.......... 60.00 18.00
43IN Don Mattingly Donnie BB/5..........
43JN Don Mattingly/23..........
43PS Don Mattingly/25..........
43INA Don Mattingly Donnie BB AU/5
44BA Ryne Sandberg 40.......... 80.00 24.00
44DY Ryne Sandberg/81.......... 60.00 18.00
44IN Ryne Sandberg Ryno/5..........
44JN Ryne Sandberg/23..........
44PS Ryne Sandberg/25..........
44INA Ryne Sandberg Ryno AU/5..........
45BA Early Wynn/5..........
45DY Early Wynn/39.......... 30.00 9.00
45IN Early Wynn HOF 72/5..........
45JN Early Wynn/24..........
45PS Early Wynn/10..........
46BA Mike Piazza Dodgers/100 25.00 7.50
46DY Mike Piazza Dodgers/92.. 25.00 7.50
46JN Mike Piazza Dodgers/31.. 50.00 15.00
46PS Mike Piazza Dodgers/50.. 30.00 9.00
47BA Wade Boggs/100.......... 25.00 7.50
47DY Wade Boggs/82.......... 25.00 7.50
47JN Wade Boggs/26.......... 60.00 18.00
47PS Wade Boggs/45.......... 50.00 15.00
48BA Catfish Hunter/10..........
48DY Catfish Hunter/65.......... 40.00 12.00
48IN Catfish Hunter HOF 87/5..........
48JN Catfish Hunter/27.......... 60.00 18.00
48PS Catfish Hunter/25..........
49BA Juan Marichal/20..........
49DY Juan Marichal/60.......... 25.00 7.50
49JN Juan Marichal/27.......... 40.00 12.00
49PS Juan Marichal/15..........
49INA Juan Marichal HOF 83 AU/5..........
50BA Carlton Fisk Red Sox/80.. 25.00 7.50
50DY Carlton Fisk Red Sox/69.. 40.00 12.00
50IN Carlton Fisk Red Sox/00/15
50JN Carlton Fisk Red Sox/27.. 60.00 18.00
50PS Carlton Fisk Red Sox/50.. 40.00 12.00
50INA Carlton Fisk Red Sox HOF 00 AU/5

51BA Curt Schilling/100 ... 15.00 4.50
51DY Curt Schilling/88 ... 15.00 4.50
51JN Curt Schilling/38 ... 30.00 9.00
51PS Curt Schilling/50 ... 25.00 7.50
52BA Rod Carew Angels/80 ... 25.00 7.50
52DY Rod Carew Angels/67 ... 40.00 12.00
52IN Rod Carew Angels HOF 91/15 ...
52JN Rod Carew Angels/29 ...
52PS Rod Carew Angels/50 ... 40.00 12.00
52INA Rod Carew Angels HOF 91 AU/5
53BA Rod Carew Twins/10 ...
53DY Rod Carew Twins/67 ... 40.00 12.00
53JN Rod Carew Twins/29 ...
53PS Rod Carew Twins/25 ...
53INA Rod Carew Twins HOF 91 AU/5
54BA Joe Carter/100 ... 15.00 4.50
54DY Joe Carter/83 ... 15.00 4.50
54JN Joe Carter/29 ... 40.00 12.00
54PS Joe Carter/50 ... 25.00 7.50
55BA Nolan Ryan Angels/5 ...
55DY Nolan Ryan Angels/66 ... 80.00 24.00
55IN Nolan Ryan Angels HOF 99/5 ...
55JN Nolan Ryan Angels/30 ...
55PS Nolan Ryan Angels/10 ...
55INA Nolan Ryan Angels HOF 99 AU/5
56BA Orlando Cepeda/80 ... 15.00 4.50
56DY Orlando Cepeda/58 ... 25.00 7.50
56IN Orlando Cepeda HOF 99/15 ...
56JN Orlando Cepeda/30 ... 40.00 12.00
56PS Orlando Cepeda/50 ... 25.00 7.50
56INA Orlando Cepeda HOF 99 AU/5 ..
57BA Dave Winfield/80 ... 15.00 4.50
57DY Dave Winfield/73 ... 25.00 7.50
57IN Dave Winfield HOF 01/15 ...
57JN Dave Winfield/31 ... 40.00 12.00
57PS Dave Winfield/50 ... 25.00 7.50
57INA Dave Winfield HOF 01 AU/5 ...
58BA Hoyt Wilhelm/80 ... 15.00 4.50
58DY Hoyt Wilhelm/52 ... 25.00 7.50
58IN Hoyt Wilhelm HOF 85/15 ...
58JN Hoyt Wilhelm/31 ... 40.00 12.00
58PS Hoyt Wilhelm/50 ... 25.00 7.50
58INA Hoyt Wilhelm HOF 85 AU/5 ...
59BA Steve Carlton/80 ... 15.00 4.50
59DY Steve Carlton/65 ... 25.00 7.50
59IN Steve Carlton HOF 94/15 ...
59JN Steve Carlton/32 ... 40.00 12.00
59PS Steve Carlton/50 ... 25.00 7.50
59INA Steve Carlton HOF 94 AU/5 ...
60BA Eddie Murray/100 ... 25.00 7.50
60DY Eddie Murray/77 ... 25.00 7.50
60JN Eddie Murray/33 ... 60.00 18.00
60PS Eddie Murray/50 ... 40.00 12.00
61BA Nolan Ryan Rangers/40. 100.00 30.00
61DY Nolan Ryan Rangers/66 .. 80.00 24.00
61IN Nolan Ryan Rangers HOF 99/5 ...
61JN Nolan Ryan Rangers/34. 100.00 30.00
61PS Nolan Ryan Rangers/25 ...
61INA Nolan Ryan Rangers HOF 99 AU/5
62BA Nolan Ryan Astros/40 ... 100.00 30.00
62DY Nolan Ryan Astros/66 ... 80.00 24.00
62IN Nolan Ryan Astros HOF 99/5 ...
62JN Nolan Ryan Astros/34 ... 100.00 30.00
62PS Nolan Ryan Astros/25 ...
62INA Nolan Ryan Astros HOF 99 AU/5
63BA Kirby Puckett/40 ... 50.00 15.00
63DY Kirby Puckett/84 ... 25.00 7.50
63IN Kirby Puckett HOF 01/5 ...
63JN Kirby Puckett/34 ... 60.00 18.00
63PS Kirby Puckett/25 ...
63INA Kirby Puckett HOF 01 AU/5 ...
64BA Yogi Berra/5 ...
64DY Yogi Berra/46 ... 50.00 15.00
64JN Yogi Berra/35 ... 60.00 18.00
64PS Yogi Berra/10 ...
64INA Yogi Berra HOF 72 AU/5 ...
65BA Phil Niekro/80 ... 15.00 4.50
65DY Phil Niekro/64 ... 25.00 7.50
65IN Phil Niekro HOF 97/15 ...
65JN Phil Niekro/35 ... 40.00 12.00
65PS Phil Niekro/50 ... 25.00 7.50
65INA Phil Niekro HOF 97 AU/5 ...
66BA Gaylord Perry/80 ... 15.00 4.50
66DY Gaylord Perry/62 ... 25.00 7.50
66IN Gaylord Perry HOF 91/20 ...
66JN Gaylord Perry/36 ... 30.00 9.00
66PS Gaylord Perry/50 ... 25.00 7.50
67BA Pedro Martinez Expos/100 25.00 7.50
67DY Pedro Martinez Expos/92 25.00 7.50
67JN Pedro Martinez Expos/45. 50.00 15.00
67PS Pedro Martinez Expos/50 40.00 12.00
68BA Alex Rodriguez Rgr/100 .. 25.00 7.50
68DY Alex Rodriguez Rgr/94 ... 25.00 7.50
68PS Alex Rodriguez Rgr/50 ... 40.00 12.00
68JNA Alex Rodriguez Rgr AU/3 ...
69BA Dave Parker/100 ... 15.00 4.50
69DY Dave Parker/73 ... 25.00 7.50
69JN Dave Parker/39 ... 30.00 9.00
69PS Dave Parker/50 ... 25.00 7.50
70BA Darin Erstad/100 ... 15.00 4.50
70DY Darin Erstad/96 ... 15.00 4.50
70JN Darin Erstad 17 ...
70PS Darin Erstad/50 ... 25.00 7.50
71BA Eddie Mathews/5 ...
71DY Eddie Mathews/52 ... 40.00 12.00
71IN Eddie Mathews HOF 78/5 ...
71JN Eddie Mathews/41 ... 50.00 15.00
71PS Eddie Mathews/10 ...
72BA Tom Seaver Mets/5 ...
72DY Tom Seaver Mets/67 ... 40.00 12.00
72JN Tom Seaver Mets/41 ... 50.00 15.00
72PS Tom Seaver Mets/10 ...
72INA Tom Seaver Mets HOF 92 AU/5
73BA Tom Seaver Reds/10 ...
73DY Tom Seaver Reds/67 ... 40.00 12.00
73JN Tom Seaver Reds/41 ... 50.00 15.00
73PS Tom Seaver Reds/25 ...
73INA Tom Seaver Reds HOF 92 AU/5
74BA Jackie Robinson/5 ...
74DY Jackie Robinson/47 ... 100.00 30.00
74IN Jackie Robinson HOF 62/5 ...
74JN Jackie Robinson/42 ... 100.00 30.00
74PS Jackie Robinson/10 ...
75BA Randy Johnson M's/80 ... 25.00 7.50
75DY Randy Johnson M's/88 ... 25.00 7.50
75IN Randy Johnson M's Big Unit/20.
75JN Randy Johnson M's/51 ... 40.00 12.00
75PS Randy Johnson M's/50 ... 40.00 12.00
76BA Reggie Jackson Yanks/10 ...
76DY Reggie Jackson Yanks/67 40.00 12.00
76JN Reggie Jackson Yanks/44 50.00 15.00
76PS Reggie Jackson Yanks/25 ...
76INA Reggie Jackson Yanks HOF 93 AU/5
77BA Reggie Jackson Angels/80 25.00 7.50
77DY Reggie Jackson Angels/67 40.00 12.00
77IN Reggie Jackson Angels HOF 93/15
77JN Reggie Jackson Angels/44 50.00 15.00
77PS Reggie Jackson Angels/50 40.00 12.00
77INA Reggie Jackson Angels HOF 93 AU/5
78BA Willie McCovey/80 ... 15.00 4.50
78DY Willie McCovey/59 ... 25.00 7.50
78IN Willie McCovey HOF 86/15 ...
78JN Willie McCovey/44 ... 30.00 9.00
78PS Willie McCovey/50 ... 25.00 7.50
78INA Willie McCovey HOF 86 AU/5 ...
79BA Eric Davis/100 ... 15.00 4.50
79DY Eric Davis/84 ... 15.00 4.50
79JN Eric Davis/34 ... 40.00 12.00
79PS Eric Davis/50 ... 25.00 7.50
79JNA Eric Davis AU/10 ...
80BA Carlos Delgado/95 ... 15.00 4.50
80DY Carlos Delgado/93 ... 15.00 4.50
80JN Carlos Delgado/25 ...
80PS Carlos Delgado/25 ...
81BA Dale Murphy/100 ... 25.00 7.50
81DY Dale Murphy/76 ... 25.00 7.50
81PS Dale Murphy/50 ... 40.00 12.00
81JNA Dale Murphy AU/3 ...
82BA Brian Giles/100 ... 15.00 4.50
82DY Brian Giles/95 ... 15.00 4.50
82JN Brian Giles/24 ...
82PS Brian Giles/50 ... 25.00 7.50
83BA Kazuhiro Sasaki/100 ... 15.00 4.50
83DY Kazuhiro Sasaki/100 ... 15.00 4.50
83JN Kazuhiro Sasaki/22 ...
83PS Kazuhiro Sasaki 50 ... 25.00 7.50
84BA Phil Nevin/100 ... 15.00 4.50
84DY Phil Nevin/95 ... 15.00 4.50
84JN Phil Nevin/23 ...
84PS Phil Nevin/50 ... 25.00 7.50
85BA Frank Thomas/80 ... 25.00 7.50
85DY Frank Thomas/90 ... 25.00 7.50
85IN Frank Thomas Big Hurt/15 ...
85JN Frank Thomas/35 ... 60.00 18.00
85PS Frank Thomas/50 ... 40.00 12.00
85INA Frank Thomas Big Hurt AU/5 ...
86BA Raul Mondesi/100 ... 15.00 4.50
86DY Raul Mondesi/93 ... 15.00 4.50
86JN Raul Mondesi/43 ... 30.00 9.00
86PS Raul Mondesi/50 ... 25.00 7.50
87BA Don Drysdale/5 ...
87DY Don Drysdale/56 ... 40.00 12.00
87IN Don Drysdale HOF 84/5 ...
87JN Don Drysdale/53 ... 40.00 12.00
87PS Don Drysdale/10 ...
88BA Gary Sheffield/100 ... 15.00 4.50
88DY Gary Sheffield/88 ... 15.00 4.50
88JN Gary Sheffield/10 ...
88PS Gary Sheffield/50 ... 25.00 7.50
89BA Andy Pettitte/100 ... 25.00 7.50
89DY Andy Pettitte/95 ... 25.00 7.50
89JN Andy Pettitte/46 ... 50.00 15.00
89PS Andy Pettitte/50 ... 40.00 12.00
90BA Lance Berkman/45 ... 30.00 9.00
90DY Lance Berkman/99 ... 15.00 4.50
90JN Lance Berkman/12 ...
90PS Lance Berkman/25 ...
90JNA Lance Berkman AU/5 ...
91BA Paul Lo Duca/100 ... 15.00 4.50
91DY Paul Lo Duca/98 ... 15.00 4.50
91JN Paul Lo Duca/16 ...
91PS Paul Lo Duca/50 ... 25.00 7.50
92BA Kevin Brown/25 ...
92DY Kevin Brown/86 ... 15.00 4.50
92JN Kevin Brown/27 ... 40.00 12.00
92PS Kevin Brown/25 ...
93BA Jim Thome/100 ... 25.00 7.50
93DY Jim Thome/91 ... 25.00 7.50
93JN Jim Thome/20 ...
93PS Jim Thome/50 ... 40.00 12.00
93JNA Jim Thome AU/5 ...
94BA Mike Sweeney/100 ... 15.00 4.50
94DY Mike Sweeney/95 ... 15.00 4.50
94JN Mike Sweeney/29 ... 40.00 12.00
94PS Mike Sweeney/50 ... 25.00 7.50
95BA Pedro Martinez Red Sox/100 25.00 7.50
95DY Pedro Martinez Red Sox/92 25.00 7.50
95JN Pedro Martinez Red Sox/45 50.00 15.00
95PS Pedro Martinez Red Sox/45 50.00 15.00
96BA Cliff Floyd/100 ... 15.00 4.50
96DY Cliff Floyd/93 ... 15.00 4.50
96JN Cliff Floyd/30 ... 40.00 12.00
96PS Cliff Floyd/50 ... 25.00 7.50
97BA Larry Walker/100 ... 25.00 7.50
97DY Larry Walker/89 ... 25.00 7.50
97JN Larry Walker/33 ... 60.00 18.00
97PS Larry Walker/50 ... 40.00 12.00
98BA Ivan Rodriguez/80 ... 25.00 7.50
98DY Ivan Rodriguez/91 ... 25.00 7.50
98IN Ivan Rodriguez Pudge/15 ...
98JN Ivan Rodriguez/7 ...
98PS Ivan Rodriguez/50 ... 40.00 12.00
98INA Ivan Rodriguez Pudge AU/5 ...
99BA Aramis Ramirez/100 ... 15.00 4.50
99DY Aramis Ramirez/98 ... 15.00 4.50
99JN Aramis Ramirez/16 ...
99PS Aramis Ramirez/50 ... 25.00 7.50
100BA Roberto Alomar/100 ... 25.00 7.50
100DY Roberto Alomar/88 ... 25.00 7.50
100JN Roberto Alomar/12 ...
100PS Roberto Alomar/50 ... 40.00 12.00
101BA Ben Sheets/100 ... 15.00 4.50
101DY Ben Sheets/101 ... 15.00 4.50
101JN Ben Sheets/15 ...
101PS Ben Sheets/50 ... 25.00 7.50
102BA Adam Dunn/5 ...
102DY Adam Dunn/101 ... 25.00 7.50
102JN Adam Dunn/39 ... 50.00 15.00
102PS Adam Dunn/5 ...
102JNA Adam Dunn AU/5 ...
103BA Hideo Nomo/15 ...
103DY Hideo Nomo/95 ... 40.00 12.00
103JN Hideo Nomo/11 ...
103PS Hideo Nomo/20 ...
104BA C.C. Sabathia/50 ... 25.00 7.50
104DY C.C. Sabathia/101 ... 15.00 4.50
104JN C.C. Sabathia/52 ... 25.00 7.50
104PS C.C. Sabathia/50 ... 25.00 7.50
105BA R.Henderson A's/100 ... 25.00 7.50
105DY Rickey Henderson A's/79 25.00 7.50
105JN R.Henderson A's/30 ... 60.00 18.00
105PS Rickey Henderson A's/50 40.00 12.00
105JNA Rickey Henderson A's AU/5 ...
106BA Carlton Fisk W.Sox/80 ... 25.00 7.50
106DY Carlton Fisk W.Sox/69 ... 40.00 12.00
106IN Carlton Fisk W.Sox HOF 00/15 .
106JN Carlton Fisk W.Sox/72 ... 40.00 12.00
106PS Carlton Fisk W.Sox/50 ... 40.00 12.00
106INA Carlton Fisk W.Sox HOF 00 AU/5
107BA Chan Ho Park/100 ... 15.00 4.50
107DY Chan Ho Park/94 ... 15.00 4.50
107JN Chan Ho Park/61 ... 25.00 7.50
107PS Chan Ho Park/50 ... 25.00 7.50
108BA Mike Mussina/100 ... 25.00 7.50
108DY Mike Mussina/91 ... 25.00 7.50
108JN Mike Mussina 35 ... 60.00 18.00
108PS Mike Mussina/50 ... 40.00 12.00
109BA Mark Mulder/100 ... 15.00 4.50
109DY Mark Mulder/100 ... 15.00 4.50
109JN Mark Mulder/20 ...
109PS Mark Mulder/35 ... 40.00 12.00
110BA Tsuyoshi Shinjo/100 ... 15.00 4.50
110DY Tsuyoshi Shinjo/101 ... 15.00 4.50
110JN Tsuyoshi Shinjo/5 ...
110PS Tsuyoshi Shinjo/30 ... 40.00 12.00
111BA Pat Burrell/100 ... 15.00 4.50
111DY Pat Burrell/100 ... 15.00 4.50
111JN Pat Burrell/5 ...
111PS Pat Burrell/50 ... 25.00 7.50
112BA Edgar Martinez/100 ... 25.00 7.50
112DY Edgar Martinez/87 ... 25.00 7.50
112JN Edgar Martinez/11 ...
112PS Edgar Martinez/50 ... 40.00 12.00
113BA Barry Larkin/100 ... 25.00 7.50
113DY Barry Larkin/86 ... 25.00 7.50
113JN Barry Larkin/11 ...
113PS Barry Larkin/50 ... 40.00 12.00
114BA Jeff Kent/100 ... 15.00 4.50
114DY Jeff Kent/92 ... 15.00 4.50
114JN Jeff Kent/21 ...
114PS Jeff Kent/50 ... 25.00 7.50
115BA Chipper Jones/100 ... 25.00 7.50
115DY Chipper Jones/93 ... 25.00 7.50
115JN Chipper Jones/10 ...
115PS Chipper Jones/50 ... 40.00 12.00
116BA Magglio Ordonez/100 ... 15.00 4.50
116DY Magglio Ordonez/97 ... 15.00 4.50
116JN Magglio Ordonez/30 ... 40.00 12.00
116PS Magglio Ordonez/50 ... 25.00 7.50
117BA Jim Edmonds/100 ... 15.00 4.50
117DY Jim Edmonds/93 ... 15.00 4.50
117JN Jim Edmonds/15 ...
117PS Jim Edmonds/50 ... 25.00 7.50
118BA Andruw Jones/100 ... 15.00 4.50
118DY Andruw Jones/96 ... 15.00 4.50
118JN Andruw Jones/25 ...
118PS Andruw Jones/45 ... 30.00 9.00
119BA Jose Canseco/100 ... 25.00 7.50
119DY Jose Canseco/85 ... 25.00 7.50
119JN Jose Canseco/23 ...
119PS Jose Canseco/50 ... 40.00 12.00
119JNA Jose Canseco AU/10 ...
120BA Manny Ramirez/100 ... 25.00 7.50
120DY Manny Ramirez/93 ... 25.00 7.50
120JN Manny Ramirez/24 ...
120PS Manny Ramirez/50 ... 40.00 12.00
121BA Sean Casey/100 ... 15.00 4.50
121DY Sean Casey/97 ... 15.00 4.50
121JN Sean Casey/21 ...
121PS Sean Casey/50 ... 25.00 7.50
122BA Bret Boone/100 ... 15.00 4.50
122DY Bret Boone/92 ... 15.00 4.50
122JN Bret Boone/29 ... 40.00 12.00
122PS Bret Boone/50 ... 25.00 7.50
123BA Tim Hudson/100 ... 15.00 4.50
123DY Tim Hudson/99 ... 15.00 4.50
123JN Tim Hudson/15 ...
123PS Tim Hudson/50 ... 25.00 7.50
124BA Craig Biggio/100 ... 25.00 7.50
124DY Craig Biggio/88 ... 25.00 7.50
124JN Craig Biggio/7 ...
124PS Craig Biggio/50 ... 40.00 12.00
125BA Mike Piazza Mets/100 ... 25.00 7.50
125DY Mike Piazza Mets/92 ... 25.00 7.50
125JN Mike Piazza Mets/31 ... 50.00 15.00
125PS Mike Piazza Mets/50 ... 30.00 9.00
126BA Jack Morris/100 ... 15.00 4.50
126DY Jack Morris/77 ... 15.00 4.50
126JN Jack Morris/47 ... 30.00 9.00
126PS Jack Morris/25 ...
127BA Roy Oswalt/100 ... 15.00 4.50
127DY Roy Oswalt/101 ... 15.00 4.50
127JN Roy Oswalt/39 ... 30.00 9.00
127PS Roy Oswalt/50 ... 25.00 7.50
127JNA Roy Oswalt AU/5
128BA Shawn Green/100 ... 15.00 4.50
128DY Shawn Green/93 ... 15.00 4.50
128JN Shawn Green/15 ...
128PS Shawn Green/50 ... 25.00 7.50
129BA Carlos Beltran/100 ... 25.00 7.50
129DY Carlos Beltran/98 ... 25.00 7.50
129JN Carlos Beltran/15 ...
129PS Carlos Beltran/50 ... 40.00 12.00
130BA Todd Helton/100 ... 25.00 7.50
130DY Todd Helton/97 ... 25.00 7.50
130JN Todd Helton/17 ...
130PS Todd Helton/50 ... 40.00 12.00
131BA Barry Zito/75 ... 15.00 4.50
131DY Barry Zito/100 ... 15.00 4.50
131JN Barry Zito/75 ... 15.00 4.50
131PS Barry Zito/30 ... 40.00 12.00
132BA J.D. Drew/100 ... 15.00 4.50
132DY J.D. Drew/98 ... 15.00 4.50
132JN J.D. Drew/7 ...
132PS J.D. Drew/50 ... 25.00 7.50
133BA Mark Grace/100 ... 25.00 7.50
133DY Mark Grace 88 ... 25.00 7.50
133JN Mark Grace/17 ...
133PS Mark Grace/50 ... 40.00 12.00
134BA R.Henderson Mets/100 .. 25.00 7.50
134DY R.Henderson Mets/79 .. 25.00 7.50
134JN Rickey Henderson Mets/24 ...
134PS R.Henderson Mets/50 ... 40.00 12.00
135BA Greg Maddux/100 ... 25.00 7.50
135DY Greg Maddux/86 ... 25.00 7.50
135JN Greg Maddux/31 ...
135PS Greg Maddux/50 ... 30.00 9.00

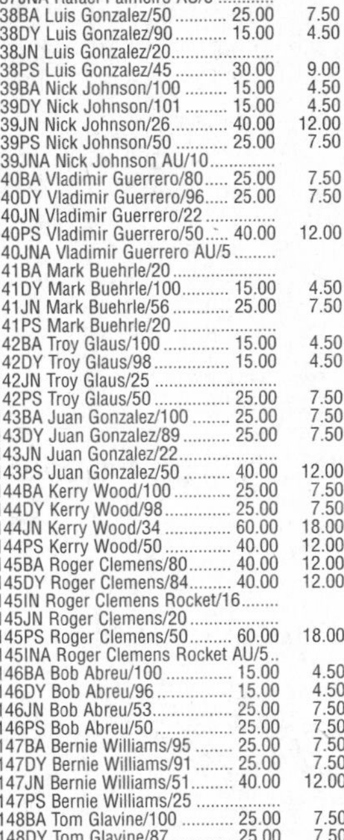

136BA Garret Anderson/100 ... 15.00 4.50
136DY Garret Anderson/94 ... 15.00 4.50
136JN Garret Anderson/16 ...
136PS Garret Anderson/50 ... 25.00 7.50
137BA Rafael Palmeiro/100 ... 25.00 7.50
137DY Rafael Palmeiro/86 ... 25.00 7.50
137JN Rafael Palmeiro/20 ...
137PS Rafael Palmeiro/50 ... 40.00 12.00
137JNA Rafael Palmeiro AU/5 ...
138BA Luis Gonzalez/50 ... 25.00 7.50
138DY Luis Gonzalez/90 ... 15.00 4.50
138JN Luis Gonzalez/20 ...
138PS Luis Gonzalez/45 ... 30.00 9.00
139BA Nick Johnson/100 ... 15.00 4.50
139DY Nick Johnson/101 ... 15.00 4.50
139JN Nick Johnson/26 ... 40.00 12.00
139PS Nick Johnson/50 ... 25.00 7.50
139JNA Nick Johnson AU/10 ...
140BA Vladimir Guerrero/80 ... 25.00 7.50
140DY Vladimir Guerrero/96 ... 25.00 7.50
140JN Vladimir Guerrero/22 ...
140PS Vladimir Guerrero/50 ... 40.00 12.00
140JNA Vladimir Guerrero AU/5 ...
141BA Mark Buehrle/20 ...
141DY Mark Buehrle/100 ... 15.00 4.50
141JN Mark Buehrle/56 ... 25.00 7.50
141PS Mark Buehrle/20 ...
142BA Troy Glaus/100 ... 15.00 4.50
142DY Troy Glaus/98 ... 15.00 4.50
142JN Troy Glaus/25 ...
142PS Troy Glaus/50 ... 25.00 7.50
143BA Juan Gonzalez/100 ... 25.00 7.50
143DY Juan Gonzalez/89 ... 25.00 7.50
143JN Juan Gonzalez/22 ...
143PS Juan Gonzalez/50 ... 40.00 12.00
144BA Kerry Wood/100 ... 25.00 7.50
144DY Kerry Wood/98 ... 25.00 7.50
144JN Kerry Wood/34 ... 60.00 18.00
144PS Kerry Wood/50 ... 40.00 12.00
145BA Roger Clemens/80 ... 40.00 12.00
145DY Roger Clemens/84 ... 40.00 12.00
145IN Roger Clemens Rocket/16 ...
145JN Roger Clemens/20 ...
145PS Roger Clemens/50 ... 60.00 18.00
145INA Roger Clemens Rocket AU/5 ..
146BA Bob Abreu/100 ... 15.00 4.50
146DY Bob Abreu/96 ... 15.00 4.50
146JN Bob Abreu/53 ... 25.00 7.50
146PS Bob Abreu/50 ... 25.00 7.50
147BA Bernie Williams/95 ... 25.00 7.50
147DY Bernie Williams/91 ... 25.00 7.50
147JN Bernie Williams/51 ... 40.00 12.00
147PS Bernie Williams/25 ...
148BA Tom Glavine/100 ... 25.00 7.50
148DY Tom Glavine/87 ... 25.00 7.50
148JN Tom Glavine/47 ... 50.00 15.00
148PS Tom Glavine/50 ... 40.00 12.00
149BA Jorge Posada/100 ... 25.00 7.50
149DY Jorge Posada/95 ... 25.00 7.50
149JN Jorge Posada/20 ...
149PS Jorge Posada/50 ... 40.00 12.00
150BA R.Johnson D'Backs/80 .. 25.00 7.50
150DY R.Johnson D'Backs/88 .. 25.00 7.50
150IN Randy Johnson D'Backs Big Unit/20
150JN R.Johnson D'Backs/51 .. 40.00 12.00
150PS R.Johnson D'Backs/50 .. 40.00 12.00

2002 Leaf Certified Skills

Inserted at stated odds of one in 17, these 20 cards feature players who have have already established excellent stats be it for a game, season or career. These cards are produced on mirror board with silver foil stamping.

	Nm-Mt	Ex-Mt
COMPLETE SET (20)	120.00	36.00
*BLUE: 1.25X TO 3X BASIC SKILLS...		
BLUE: RANDOM INSERTS IN PACKS...		
BLUE PRINT RUN 75 SERIAL #'d SETS		
GOLD: RANDOM INSERTS IN PACKS.		
GOLD PRINT RUN 25 SERIAL #'d SETS		
NO GOLD PRICING DUE TO SCARCITY		
*RED: .75X TO 2X BASIC SKILLS...		
RED: RANDOM INSERTS IN PACKS ...		
RED PRINT RUN 150 SERIAL #'d SETS		
1 Barry Bonds	10.00	3.00
2 Greg Maddux	6.00	1.80
3 Rickey Henderson	4.00	1.20
4 Ichiro Suzuki	6.00	1.80
5 Pedro Martinez	4.00	1.20
6 Kazuhisa Ishii	5.00	1.50
7 Alex Rodriguez	6.00	1.80
8 Mike Piazza	6.00	1.80
9 Sammy Sosa	6.00	1.80
10 Derek Jeter	10.00	3.00
11 Albert Pujols	8.00	2.40
12 Roger Clemens	8.00	2.40
13 Mark Prior	6.00	1.80
14 Chipper Jones	4.00	1.20
15 Ken Griffey Jr.	6.00	1.80
16 Frank Thomas	4.00	1.20
17 Randy Johnson	4.00	1.20
18 Vladimir Guerrero	4.00	1.20
19 Nomar Garciaparra	6.00	1.80
20 Jeff Bagwell	3.00	.90

2003 Leaf Certified Materials

This 259-card set was issued in two separate series. The primary Leaf Certified Materials brand - containing cards 1-250 from the basic set - was released in August, 2003. The set was issued in seven card packs with an $10 SRP which were packaged 10 to a box and 20 boxes to a case. Cards numbered 1 through 200 feature veterans. Cards numbered 201 through 205 featured some baseball legends while cards numbered 206 through 250 are entitled New Generation and feature top prospects and rookies. Those cards, with the exception of card 220 were issued to a stated print run of 400 serial numbered sets. Card 220, featuring Jose Contreras, was issued to a stated print run of 100 serial numbered sets. Cards 251-259 were randomly seeded into packs of DLP Rookies and Traded of which was distributed in December, 2003. The nine update cards carry on the New Generation subset featuring top prospects, and like the earlier cards feature certified autographs. Serial numbered print runs for these update cards range from 100-250 copies per.

	MINT	NRMT
COMP.LO SET w/o SP's (200)	50.00	22.00
COMMON CARD (1-200)	1.00	.45
COMMON CARD (201-205)	10.00	4.50
COMMON CARD (206-250)	10.00	4.50
201-250 RANDOM INSERTS IN PACKS		
COM.(251-259) p/r 150-250	10.00	4.50
1 Troy Glaus	1.00	.45
2 Alfredo Amezaga	1.00	.45
3 Garret Anderson	1.00	.45
4 Nolan Ryan Angels	6.00	2.70
5 Darin Erstad	1.00	.45
6 Junior Spivey	1.00	.45
7 Randy Johnson	2.50	1.10
8 Curt Schilling	1.00	.45
9 Luis Gonzalez	1.00	.45
10 Steve Finley	1.00	.45
11 Matt Williams	1.00	.45
12 Greg Maddux	4.00	1.80
13 Chipper Jones	2.50	1.10
14 Gary Sheffield	1.00	.45
15 Adam LaRoche	1.00	.45
16 Andruw Jones	1.00	.45
17 Robert Fick	1.00	.45
18 John Smoltz	1.50	.70
19 Javy Lopez	1.00	.45
20 Jay Gibbons	1.00	.45
21 Geronimo Gil	1.00	.45
22 Cal Ripken	8.00	3.60
23 Nomar Garciaparra	4.00	1.80
24 Pedro Martinez	2.50	1.10
25 Freddy Sanchez	1.00	.45
26 Rickey Henderson	2.50	1.10
27 Manny Ramirez	1.50	.70
28 Casey Fossum	1.00	.45
29 Sammy Sosa	4.00	1.80
30 Kerry Wood	2.50	1.10
31 Corey Patterson	1.00	.45
32 Nic Jackson	1.00	.45
33 Mark Prior	2.50	1.10
34 Juan Cruz	1.00	.45
35 Steve Smyth	1.00	.45
36 Magglio Ordonez	1.00	.45
37 Joe Borchard	1.00	.45
38 Frank Thomas	2.50	1.10
39 Mark Buehrle	1.00	.45
40 Joe Crede	1.00	.45
41 Carlos Lee	1.00	.45
42 Paul Konerko	1.00	.45
43 Adam Dunn	1.50	.70
44 Corky Miller	1.00	.45
45 Brandon Larson	1.00	.45
46 Ken Griffey Jr.	4.00	1.80
47 Barry Larkin	1.50	.70
48 Sean Casey	1.00	.45
49 Wily Mo Pena	1.00	.45
50 Austin Kearns	1.00	.45
51 Victor Martinez	1.50	.70
52 Brian Tallet	1.00	.45
53 Cliff Lee	1.00	.45
54 Jeremy Guthrie	1.00	.45
55 C.C. Sabathia	1.00	.45
56 Ricardo Rodriguez	1.00	.45
57 Omar Vizquel	1.50	.70
58 Travis Hafner	1.00	.45
59 Todd Helton	1.50	.70
60 Jason Jennings	1.00	.45
61 Jeff Baker	1.00	.45
62 Larry Walker	1.50	.70
63 Travis Chapman	1.00	.45
64 Mike Maroth	1.00	.45
65 Josh Beckett	1.00	.45
66 Ivan Rodriguez	2.50	1.10
67 Brad Penny	1.00	.45
68 A.J. Burnett	1.00	.45
69 Craig Biggio	1.50	.70
70 Roy Oswalt	1.00	.45
71 Jason Lane	1.00	.45
72 Nolan Ryan Astros	6.00	2.70
73 Wade Miller	1.00	.45
74 Richard Hidalgo	1.00	.45
75 Jeff Bagwell	1.50	.70
76 Lance Berkman	1.00	.45
77 Rodrigo Rosario	1.00	.45
78 Jeff Kent	1.00	.45
79 John Buck	1.00	.45
80 Angel Berroa	1.00	.45
81 Mike Sweeney	1.00	.45
82 Mac Suzuki	1.00	.45
83 Alexis Gomez	1.00	.45
84 Carlos Beltran	1.50	.70
85 Runelvys Hernandez	1.00	.45
86 Hideo Nomo	2.50	1.10
87 Paul Lo Duca	1.00	.45
88 Cesar Izturis	1.00	.45
89 Kazuhisa Ishii	1.00	.45
90 Shawn Green	1.00	.45
91 Joe Thurston	1.00	.45
92 Adrian Beltre	1.50	.70
93 Kevin Brown	1.00	.45
94 Richie Sexson	1.00	.45
95 Ben Sheets	1.00	.45
96 Takahito Nomura	1.00	.45
97 Geoff Jenkins	1.00	.45

98 Bill Hall 1.00 .45
99 Torii Hunter 1.00 .45
100 A.J. Pierzynski 1.00 .45
101 Michael Cuddyer 1.00 .45
102 Jose Morban 1.00 .45
103 Brad Radke 1.00 .45
104 Jacque Jones 1.00 .45
105 Eric Milton 1.00 .45
106 Joe Mays 1.00 .45
107 Adam Johnson 1.00 .45
108 Javier Vazquez 1.00 .45
109 Vladimir Guerrero 2.50 1.10
110 Jose Vidro 1.00 .45
111 Michael Barrett 1.00 .45
112 Orlando Cabrera 1.00 .45
113 Tom Glavine 1.50 .70
114 Roberto Alomar 1.50 .70
115 Tsuyoshi Shinjo 1.50 .70
116 Cliff Floyd 1.00 .45
117 Mike Piazza 4.00 1.80
118 Al Leiter 1.00 .45
119 Don Mattingly 6.00 2.70
120 Roger Clemens 5.00 2.20
121 Derek Jeter 6.00 2.70
122 Alfonso Soriano 1.50 .70
123 Drew Henson 1.00 .45
124 Brandon Claussen 1.00 .45
125 Christian Parker 1.00 .45
126 Jason Giambi 1.00 .45
127 Mike Mussina 1.50 .70
128 Bernie Williams 1.50 .70
129 Jason Anderson 1.00 .45
130 Nick Johnson 1.00 .45
131 Jorge Posada 1.50 .70
132 Andy Pettitte 1.50 .70
133 Barry Zito 1.00 .45
134 Miguel Tejada 1.00 .45
135 Eric Chavez 1.00 .45
136 Tim Hudson 1.00 .45
137 Mark Mulder 1.00 .45
138 Terrence Long 1.00 .45
139 Mark Ellis 1.00 .45
140 Jim Thome 2.50 1.10
141 Pat Burrell 1.00 .45
142 Marlon Byrd 1.00 .45
143 Bobby Abreu 1.00 .45
144 Brandon Duckworth 1.00 .45
145 Robert Person 1.00 .45
146 Anderson Machado 1.00 .45
147 Aramis Ramirez 1.00 .45
148 Jack Wilson 1.00 .45
149 Carlos Rivera 1.00 .45
150 Jose Castillo 1.00 .45
151 Walter Young 1.00 .45
152 Brian Giles 1.00 .45
153 Jason Kendall 1.00 .45
154 Ryan Klesko 1.00 .45
155 Mike Rivera 1.00 .45
156 Sean Burroughs 1.00 .45
157 Brian Lawrence 1.00 .45
158 Xavier Nady 1.00 .45
159 Dennis Tankersley 1.00 .45
160 Phil Nevin 1.00 .45
161 Barry Bonds 6.00 2.70
162 Kenny Lofton 1.00 .45
163 Rich Aurilia 1.00 .45
164 Ichiro Suzuki 4.00 1.80
165 Edgar Martinez 1.50 .70
166 Chris Snelling 1.00 .45
167 Rafael Soriano 1.00 .45
168 John Olerud 1.00 .45
169 Bret Boone 1.00 .45
170 Freddy Garcia 1.00 .45
171 Aaron Sele 1.00 .45
172 Kazuhiro Sasaki 1.00 .45
173 Albert Pujols 5.00 2.20
174 Scott Rolen 2.50 1.10
175 So Taguchi 1.00 .45
176 Jim Edmonds 1.00 .45
177 Edgar Renteria 1.00 .45
178 J.D. Drew 1.00 .45
179 Antonio Perez 1.00 .45
180 Dewon Brazelton 1.00 .45
181 Aubrey Huff 1.00 .45
182 Toby Hall 1.00 .45
183 Ben Grieve 1.00 .45
184 Joe Kennedy 1.00 .45
185 Alex Rodriguez 4.00 1.80
186 Rafael Palmeiro 1.50 .70
187 Hank Blalock 1.50 .70
188 Mark Teixeira 1.00 .45
189 Juan Gonzalez 1.00 .45
190 Kevin Mench 1.00 .45
191 Nolan Ryan Rgr 6.00 2.70
192 Doug Davis 1.00 .45
193 Eric Hinske 1.00 .45
194 Vinny Chulk 1.00 .45
195 Alexis Rios 1.50 .70
196 Carlos Delgado 1.00 .45
197 Shannon Stewart 1.00 .45
198 Josh Phelps 1.00 .45
199 Vernon Wells 1.00 .45
200 Roy Halladay 1.00 .45
201 Babe Ruth RET 20.00 9.00
202 Lou Gehrig RET 12.00 5.50
203 Jackie Robinson RET 10.00 4.50
204 Ty Cobb RET 15.00 6.75
205 Thurman Munson RET 10.00 4.50
206 Pr. Redman NG AU RC 10.00 4.50
207 Craig Brazell NG AU RC 15.00 6.75
208 Nook Logan NG AU RC 10.00 4.50
209 Hong-Chih Kuo NG AU RC 25.00 11.00
210 Matt Kata NG AU RC 15.00 6.75
211 C.Wang NG AU RC 40.00 18.00
212 Alej Machado NG AU RC 10.00 4.50
213 Mike Hessman NG AU RC 10.00 4.50
214 Franc Rosario NG AU RC 10.00 4.50
215 Pedro Liriano NG AU 10.00 4.50
216 J.Bonderman NG AU RC 15.00 6.75
217 Oscar Villarreal NG AU RC 10.00 4.50
218 Arnie Munoz NG AU RC 10.00 4.50
219 Tim Olson NG AU RC 15.00 6.75
220 J.Contreras NG AU/100 RC 40.00 18.00
221 Franc Cruceta NG AU RC 10.00 4.50
222 John Webb NG AU 10.00 4.50
223 Phil Seibel NG AU RC 10.00 4.50
224 Aaron Looper NG AU RC 10.00 4.50
225 Brian Stokes NG AU RC 10.00 4.50
226 G.Quiroz NG AU RC 15.00 6.75
227 Fern Cabrera NG AU RC 10.00 4.50
228 Josh Hall NG AU RC 15.00 6.75
229 Diego Markwell NG AU RC 10.00 4.50
230 Andrew Brown NG AU RC 15.00 6.75
231 Doug Waechter NG AU RC 15.00 6.75
232 Felix Sanchez NG AU RC 10.00 4.50
233 Gerardo Garcia NG AU 10.00 4.50
234 Matt Bruback NG AU RC 10.00 4.50
235 Mi. Hernandez NG AU RC 10.00 4.50
236 Rett Johnson NG AU RC 15.00 6.75
237 Ryan Cameron NG AU RC 10.00 4.50
238 Rob Hammock NG AU RC 15.00 6.75
239 Clint Barmes NG AU RC 15.00 6.75
240 Brandon Webb NG AU RC 20.00 9.00
241 Jon Leicester NG AU RC 10.00 4.50
242 Shane Bazzell NG AU RC 10.00 4.50
243 Joe Valentine NG AU RC 10.00 4.50
244 Josh Stewart NG AU RC 10.00 4.50
245 Pete LaForest NG AU RC 15.00 6.75
246 Shane Victorino NG AU RC 10.00 4.50
247 Terrmel Sledge NG AU RC 15.00 6.75
248 Lew Ford NG AU RC 25.00 11.00
249 T.Wellemeyer NG AU RC 15.00 6.75
250 Hideki Matsui NG RC 15.00 6.75
251 A.Loewen NG AU/250 RC 25.00 11.00
252 Dan Haren NG AU/250 RC 20.00 9.00
253 Dontrelle Willis NG AU/150 15.00 6.75
254 Ramon Nivar NG AU/250 RC 20.00 9.00
255 Chad Gaudin NG AU/250 RC 10.00 4.50
256 Kevin Correia NG AU/150 RC 10.00 4.50
257 R.Weeks NG AU/100 RC 80.00 36.00
258 R.Wagner NG AU/250 RC 15.00 6.75
259 Del.Young NG AU/100 RC 150.00 70.00

2003 Leaf Certified Materials Mirror Black

MINT NRMT
1-250 RANDOM INSERTS IN PACKS
251-259 RANDOM IN DLP R/T PACKS
STATED PRINT RUN 1 SERIAL #'d SET
NO PRICING DUE TO SCARCITY

2003 Leaf Certified Materials Mirror Black Autographs

MINT NRMT
1-250 RANDOM INSERTS IN PACKS
251-259 RANDOM IN DLP R/T PACKS
STATED PRINT RUN 1 SERIAL #'d SET
NO PRICING DUE TO SCARCITY

2003 Leaf Certified Materials Mirror Black Materials

MINT NRMT
RANDOM INSERTS IN PACKS
STATED PRINT RUN 1 SERIAL #'d SET
NO PRICING DUE TO SCARCITY

2003 Leaf Certified Materials Mirror Blue

MINT NRMT
*BLUE 1-200: 3X TO 8X BASIC
*BLUE 201-205: 1X TO 2.5X BASIC
*BLUE 206-219/221-249: .3X TO .8X BASIC
*BLUE 220: .2X TO .5X BASIC 220
*BLUE 250: .75X TO 2X BASIC 250
*BLUE 251-259: .3X TO .8X BASIC p/r 250
*BLUE 251-259: .2X TO .5X BASIC p/r 100-150
1-250 RANDOM INSERTS IN PACKS
251-259 RANDOM IN DLP R/T PACKS
STATED PRINT RUN 50 SERIAL #'d SETS

2003 Leaf Certified Materials Mirror Blue Autographs

MINT NRMT
1-250 RANDOM INSERTS IN PACKS
251-259 RANDOM IN DLP R/T PACKS
PRINT RUNS B/WN 5-50 COPIES PER
NO PRICING ON QTY OF 25 OR LESS
2 Alfredo Amezaga/50 15.00 6.75
3 Garret Anderson/10
4 Nolan Ryan Angels/5
6 Junior Spivey/50 15.00 6.75
15 Adam LaRoche/50 15.00 6.75
17 Robert Fick/10
20 Jay Gibbons/50 15.00 6.75
21 Geronimo Gil/50 15.00 6.75
22 Cal Ripken/5
25 Freddy Sanchez/17
28 Casey Fossum/50 15.00 6.75
31 Corey Patterson/5
32 Nic Jackson/50 15.00 6.75
33 Mark Prior/50 80.00 36.00
34 Juan Cruz/50 15.00 6.75
35 Steve Smyth/50 15.00 6.75
37 Joe Borchard/50 15.00 6.75
39 Mark Buehrle/50 25.00 11.00
40 Joe Crede/30 15.00 6.75
41 Carlos Lee/5
45 Brandon Larson/50 15.00 6.75
49 Wily Mo Pena/50 25.00 11.00
51 Victor Martinez/50 40.00 18.00
52 Brian Tallet/50 15.00 6.75
53 Cliff Lee/50 15.00 6.75
54 Jeremy Guthrie/50 15.00 6.75
55 C.C. Sabathia/4
56 Ricardo Rodriguez/50 15.00 6.75
60 Jason Jennings/50 15.00 6.75
61 Jeff Baker/50 15.00 6.75
63 Travis Chapman/50 15.00 6.75
64 Mike Maroth/50 15.00 6.75
70 Roy Oswalt/50 25.00 11.00
71 Jason Lane/50 15.00 6.75
72 Nolan Ryan Astros/5
73 Wade Miller/50 15.00 6.75
74 Richard Hidalgo/5
77 Rodrigo Rosario/50 15.00 6.75
79 John Buck/10
80 Angel Berroa/50 15.00 6.75
81 Mike Sweeney/5
82 Mac Suzuki/50 25.00 11.00
83 Alexis Gomez/10
85 Runelvys Hernandez/50 15.00 6.75
86 Hideo Nomo/15
87 Paul Lo Duca/10
88 Cesar Izturis/50 15.00 6.75
89 Kazuhisa Ishii/5
91 Joe Thurston/50 15.00 6.75
94 Richie Sexson/5
95 Ben Sheets/5
96 Takahito Nomura/10
98 Bill Hall/30 15.00 6.75
100 A.J. Pierzynski/5
102 Jose Morban/50 15.00 6.75
107 Adam Johnson/50 15.00 6.75
108 Javier Vazquez/10
110 Jose Vidro/10
116 Cliff Floyd/5
117 Mike Piazza/15
119 Don Mattingly/5
122 Alfonso Soriano/10
123 Drew Henson/5
124 Brandon Claussen/50 15.00 6.75
125 Christian Parker/50 15.00 6.75
129 Jason Anderson/50 15.00 6.75
130 Nick Johnson/10
133 Barry Zito/5
134 Miguel Tejada/5
135 Eric Chavez/5
136 Tim Hudson/5
138 Terrence Long/50 15.00 6.75
142 Marlon Byrd/50 15.00 6.75
143 Bobby Abreu/5
144 Brandon Duckworth/50 15.00 6.75
145 Robert Person/50 15.00 6.75
146 Anderson Machado/50 15.00 6.75
147 Aramis Ramirez/8
148 Jack Wilson/50 25.00 11.00
149 Carlos Rivera/50 15.00 6.75
150 Jose Castillo/50 15.00 6.75
151 Walter Young/50 15.00 6.75
154 Ryan Klesko/5
155 Mike Rivera/50 15.00 6.75
157 Brian Lawrence/50 15.00 6.75
158 Xavier Nady/50 15.00 6.75
159 Dennis Tankersley/50 15.00 6.75
165 Edgar Martinez/5
166 Chris Snelling/50 15.00 6.75
167 Rafael Soriano/50 15.00 6.75
170 Freddy Garcia/5
173 Albert Pujols/5
176 Jim Edmonds/10
179 Antonio Perez/50 15.00 6.75
180 Dewon Brazelton/50 15.00 6.75
181 Aubrey Huff/50 25.00 11.00
182 Toby Hall/50 15.00 6.75
184 Joe Kennedy/50 15.00 6.75
187 Hank Blalock/50 40.00 18.00
188 Mark Teixeira/50 40.00 18.00
189 Juan Gonzalez/10
190 Kevin Mench/50 15.00 6.75
191 Nolan Ryan Rgr/5
193 Eric Hinske/50 15.00 6.75
194 Vinny Chulk/50 15.00 6.75
195 Alexis Rios/50 40.00 18.00
197 Shannon Stewart/10
206 Prentice Redman NG/50 15.00 6.75
207 Craig Brazell NG/50 25.00 11.00
208 Nook Logan NG/50 15.00 6.75
209 Hong-Chih Kuo NG/40 50.00 22.00
210 Matt Kata NG/50 40.00 18.00
211 Chien-Ming Wang NG/40 60.00 27.00
212 Alejandro Machado NG/50 15.00 6.75
213 Michael Hessman NG/50 15.00 6.75
214 Francisco Rosario NG/50 15.00 6.75
215 Pedro Liriano NG/50 15.00 6.75
216 Jeremy Bonderman NG/50 40.00 18.00
217 Oscar Villarreal NG/50 15.00 6.75
218 Arnie Munoz NG/50 15.00 6.75
219 Tim Olson NG/50 25.00 11.00
220 Jose Contreras NG/15
221 Francisco Cruceta NG/50 15.00 6.75
222 John Webb NG/50 15.00 6.75
223 Phil Seibel NG/50 15.00 6.75
224 Aaron Looper NG/50 15.00 6.75
225 Brian Stokes NG/50 15.00 6.75
226 Guillermo Quiroz NG/50 40.00 18.00
227 Fernando Cabrera NG/50 15.00 6.75
228 Josh Hall NG/50 25.00 11.00
229 Diegomar Markwell NG/50 15.00 6.75
230 Andrew Brown NG/50 25.00 11.00
231 Doug Waechter NG/50 25.00 11.00
232 Felix Sanchez NG/50 15.00 6.75
233 Gerardo Garcia NG/50 15.00 6.75
234 Matt Bruback NG/50 15.00 6.75
235 Michel Hernandez NG/50 15.00 6.75
236 Rett Johnson NG/50 25.00 11.00
237 Ryan Cameron NG/50 15.00 6.75
238 Rob Hammock NG/50 25.00 11.00
239 Clint Barmes NG/50 25.00 11.00
240 Brandon Webb NG/50 50.00 22.00
241 Jon Leicester NG/50 15.00 6.75
242 Shane Bazzell NG/50 15.00 6.75
243 Joe Valentine NG/50 15.00 6.75
244 Josh Stewart NG/50 15.00 6.75
245 Pete LaForest NG/50 25.00 11.00
246 Shane Victorino NG/50 15.00 6.75
247 Terrmel Sledge NG/50 25.00 11.00
248 Lew Ford NG/50 50.00 22.00
249 Todd Wellemeyer NG/50 25.00 11.00
251 Adam Loewen NG/50 50.00 22.00
252 Dan Haren NG/50 40.00 18.00
253 Dontrelle Willis NG/25
254 Ramon Nivar NG/50 40.00 18.00
255 Chad Gaudin NG/50 15.00 6.75
256 Kevin Correia NG/25
257 Rickie Weeks NG/15
258 Ryan Wagner NG/50 25.00 11.00
259 Delmon Young NG/25

2003 Leaf Certified Materials Mirror Blue Materials

MINT NRMT
RANDOM INSERTS IN PACKS
PRINT RUNS B/WN 10-100 COPIES PER
NO PRICING ON QTY OF 25 OR FEWER
1 Troy Glaus Jsy/100 10.00 4.50
2 Alfredo Amezaga Jsy/100 10.00 4.50
3 Garret Anderson Bat/100 10.00 4.50
4 Nolan Ryan Angels Jsy/15
5 Darin Erstad Bat/100 10.00 4.50
6 Junior Spivey Bat/100 10.00 4.50
7 Randy Johnson Jsy/100 15.00 6.75
8 Curt Schilling Jsy/100 10.00 4.50
9 Luis Gonzalez Jsy/100 10.00 4.50
10 Steve Finley Jsy/100 10.00 4.50
11 Matt Williams Jsy/100 10.00 4.50
12 Greg Maddux Jsy/100 25.00 11.00
13 Chipper Jones Jsy/50 25.00 11.00
14 Gary Sheffield Bat/100 10.00 4.50
15 Adam LaRoche Bat/100 10.00 4.50
16 Andruw Jones Jsy/100 10.00 4.50
17 Robert Fick Bat/100 10.00 4.50
18 John Smoltz Jsy/100 15.00 6.75
19 Javy Lopez Jsy/100 10.00 4.50
20 Jay Gibbons Jsy/100 10.00 4.50
21 Geronimo Gil Jsy/100 10.00 4.50
22 Cal Ripken Jsy/15
23 Nomar Garciaparra Jsy/100 30.00 13.50
24 Pedro Martinez Jsy/100 15.00 6.75
25 Freddy Sanchez Bat/100 10.00 4.50
26 Rickey Henderson Bat/100 15.00 6.75
27 Manny Ramirez Jsy/100 15.00 6.75
28 Casey Fossum Jsy/100 10.00 4.50
29 Sammy Sosa Jsy/100 30.00 13.50
30 Kerry Wood Jsy/100 15.00 6.75
31 Corey Patterson Bat/100 10.00 4.50
32 Nic Jackson Bat/100 10.00 4.50
33 Mark Prior Jsy/100 15.00 6.75
34 Juan Cruz Jsy/100 10.00 4.50
35 Steve Smyth Jsy/100 10.00 4.50
36 Magglio Ordonez Jsy/100 10.00 4.50
37 Joe Borchard Jsy/100 10.00 4.50
38 Frank Thomas Jsy/100 15.00 6.75
39 Mark Buehrle Jsy/100 10.00 4.50
40 Joe Crede Hat/100 10.00 4.50
41 Carlos Lee Jsy/100 10.00 4.50
42 Paul Konerko Jsy/100 10.00 4.50
43 Adam Dunn Jsy/100 15.00 6.75
45 Brandon Larson Spikes/40 15.00 6.75
46 Ken Griffey Jr. Base/100 25.00 11.00
47 Barry Larkin Jsy/100 15.00 6.75
48 Sean Casey Bat/100 10.00 4.50
49 Wily Mo Pena Bat/100 10.00 4.50
50 Austin Kearns Jsy/100 10.00 4.50
51 Victor Martinez Jsy/100 15.00 6.75
55 C.C. Sabathia Jsy/100 10.00 4.50
56 Ricardo Rodriguez Bat/100 10.00 4.50
57 Omar Vizquel Jsy/100 15.00 6.75
58 Travis Hafner Bat/100 10.00 4.50
59 Todd Helton Jsy/100 15.00 6.75
60 Jason Jennings Jsy/100 10.00 4.50
62 Larry Walker Jsy/100 15.00 6.75
63 Travis Chapman Bat/100 10.00 4.50
64 Mike Maroth Jsy/100 10.00 4.50
65 Josh Beckett Jsy/100 10.00 4.50
66 Ivan Rodriguez Bat/100 15.00 6.75
67 Brad Penny Jsy/100 10.00 4.50
68 A.J. Burnett Jsy/100 10.00 4.50
69 Craig Biggio Jsy/100 15.00 6.75
70 Roy Oswalt Jsy/100 10.00 4.50
71 Jason Lane Jsy/100 10.00 4.50
72 Nolan Ryan Astros Jsy/15
73 Wade Miller Jsy/100 10.00 4.50
74 Richard Hidalgo Pants/100 10.00 4.50
75 Jeff Bagwell Jsy/100 15.00 6.75
76 Lance Berkman Jsy/100 10.00 4.50
77 Rodrigo Rosario Jsy/100 10.00 4.50
78 Jeff Kent Bat/100 10.00 4.50
79 John Buck Jsy/100 10.00 4.50
80 Angel Berroa Bat/100 10.00 4.50
81 Mike Sweeney Jsy/100 10.00 4.50
84 Carlos Beltran Jsy/100 15.00 6.75
86 Hideo Nomo Jsy/100 40.00 18.00
87 Paul Lo Duca Jsy/100 10.00 4.50
88 Cesar Izturis Pants/100 10.00 4.50
89 Kazuhisa Ishii Jsy/100 10.00 4.50
90 Shawn Green Jsy/100 10.00 4.50
91 Joe Thurston Jsy/100 10.00 4.50
92 Adrian Beltre Bat/100 15.00 6.75
93 Kevin Brown Jsy/100 10.00 4.50
94 Richie Sexson Jsy/100 10.00 4.50
95 Ben Sheets Jsy/100 10.00 4.50
97 Geoff Jenkins Jsy/100 10.00 4.50
98 Bill Hall Bat/100 10.00 4.50
99 Torii Hunter Jsy/100 10.00 4.50
101 Michael Cuddyer Jsy/100 10.00 4.50
102 Jose Morban Bat/100 10.00 4.50
103 Brad Radke Jsy/100 10.00 4.50
104 Jacque Jones Jsy/100 10.00 4.50
105 Eric Milton Jsy/100 10.00 4.50
106 Joe Mays Jsy/100 10.00 4.50
107 Adam Johnson Jsy/100 10.00 4.50
108 Javier Vazquez Jsy/100 10.00 4.50
109 Vladimir Guerrero Jsy/100 15.00 6.75
110 Jose Vidro Jsy/100 10.00 4.50
111 Michael Barrett Jsy/40 15.00 6.75
112 Orlando Cabrera Jsy/100 10.00 4.50
113 Tom Glavine Bat/100 15.00 6.75
114 Roberto Alomar Bat/100 15.00 6.75
115 Tsuyoshi Shinjo Jsy/100 10.00 4.50
116 Cliff Floyd Bat/100 10.00 4.50
117 Mike Piazza Jsy/100 25.00 11.00
118 Al Leiter Jsy/100 10.00 4.50
119 Don Mattingly Jsy/15
120 Roger Clemens Jsy/100 30.00 13.50
121 Derek Jeter Base/100 30.00 13.50
122 Alfonso Soriano Jsy/100 15.00 6.75
123 Drew Henson Bat/100 10.00 4.50
124 Brandon Claussen Hat/40 15.00 6.75
125 Christian Parker Pants/100 10.00 4.50
126 Jason Giambi Jsy/100 10.00 4.50
127 Mike Mussina Jsy/40 25.00 11.00
128 Bernie Williams Jsy/100 15.00 6.75
130 Nick Johnson Jsy/100 10.00 4.50
131 Jorge Posada Jsy/100 15.00 6.75
132 Andy Pettitte Jsy/100 15.00 6.75
133 Barry Zito Jsy/100 10.00 4.50
134 Miguel Tejada Jsy/100 10.00 4.50
135 Eric Chavez Jsy/100 10.00 4.50
136 Tim Hudson Jsy/100 10.00 4.50
137 Mark Mulder Jsy/100 10.00 4.50
138 Terrence Long Jsy/100 10.00 4.50
139 Mark Ellis Jsy/100 10.00 4.50
140 Jim Thome Bat/100 15.00 6.75
141 Pat Burrell Bat/100 10.00 4.50
142 Marlon Byrd Jsy/100 10.00 4.50
143 Bobby Abreu Jsy/100 10.00 4.50
144 Brandon Duckworth Jsy/100 10.00 4.50
145 Robert Person Jsy/100 10.00 4.50
146 Anderson Machado Jsy/100 10.00 4.50
147 Aramis Ramirez Jsy/100 10.00 4.50
148 Jack Wilson Bat/100 10.00 4.50
150 Jose Castillo Bat/100 10.00 4.50
151 Walter Young Bat/100 10.00 4.50
152 Brian Giles Bat/100 10.00 4.50
153 Jason Kendall Jsy/100 10.00 4.50
154 Ryan Klesko Jsy/50 15.00 6.75
155 Mike Rivera Bat/100 10.00 4.50
157 Brian Lawrence Bat/100 10.00 4.50
158 Xavier Nady Hat/40 15.00 6.75
159 Dennis Tankersley Jsy/100 10.00 4.50
160 Phil Nevin Jsy/100 10.00 4.50
161 Barry Bonds Base/100 30.00 13.50
162 Kenny Lofton Bat/100 10.00 4.50
163 Rich Aurilia Jsy/100 10.00 4.50
164 Ichiro Suzuki Base/100 30.00 13.50
165 Edgar Martinez Jsy/100 15.00 6.75
166 Chris Snelling Bat/100 10.00 4.50
167 Rafael Soriano Jsy/100 10.00 4.50
168 John Olerud Jsy/100 10.00 4.50
169 Bret Boone Jsy/100 10.00 4.50
170 Freddy Garcia Jsy/100 10.00 4.50
171 Aaron Sele Jsy/100 10.00 4.50
172 Kazuhiro Sasaki Jsy/100 10.00 4.50
173 Albert Pujols Jsy/100 40.00 18.00
174 Scott Rolen Bat/100 15.00 6.75
175 So Taguchi Jsy/100 10.00 4.50
176 Jim Edmonds Jsy/100 10.00 4.50
177 Edgar Renteria Jsy/100 10.00 4.50
178 J.D. Drew Jsy/100 10.00 4.50
179 Antonio Perez Bat/100 10.00 4.50
180 Dewon Brazelton Jsy/100 10.00 4.50
181 Aubrey Huff Jsy/50 15.00 6.75
182 Toby Hall Jsy/100 10.00 4.50
183 Ben Grieve Jsy/100 10.00 4.50
184 Joe Kennedy Jsy/100 10.00 4.50
185 Alex Rodriguez Jsy/100 30.00 13.50
186 Rafael Palmeiro Jsy/100 15.00 6.75
187 Hank Blalock Jsy/100 15.00 6.75
188 Mark Teixeira Jsy/100 10.00 4.50
189 Juan Gonzalez Bat/100 15.00 6.75
190 Kevin Mench Jsy/100 10.00 4.50
191 Nolan Ryan Rgr Jsy/15
192 Doug Davis Jsy/100 10.00 4.50
193 Eric Hinske Jsy/100 10.00 4.50
196 Carlos Delgado Jsy/100 10.00 4.50
197 Shannon Stewart Jsy/100 10.00 4.50
198 Josh Phelps Jsy/100 10.00 4.50
199 Vernon Wells Jsy/100 10.00 4.50
200 Roy Halladay Jsy/100 10.00 4.50
201 Babe Ruth RET Pants/10
202 Lou Gehrig RET Pants/10
203 Jackie Robinson RET Jsy/10
204 Ty Cobb RET Pants/10
205 Thurman Munson RET Jsy/10

2003 Leaf Certified Materials Mirror Emerald

MINT NRMT
1-250 RANDOM INSERTS IN PACKS
251-259 RANDOM IN DLP R/T PACKS
STATED PRINT RUN 5 SERIAL #'d SETS
NO PRICING DUE TO SCARCITY

2003 Leaf Certified Materials Mirror Emerald Autographs

MINT NRMT
1-250 RANDOM INSERTS IN PACKS
251-259 RANDOM IN DLP R/T PACKS
STATED PRINT RUN 5 SERIAL #'d SETS
NO PRICING DUE TO SCARCITY

2003 Leaf Certified Materials Mirror Emerald Materials

MINT NRMT
RANDOM INSERTS IN PACKS
STATED PRINT RUN 5 SERIAL #'d SETS
NO PRICING DUE TO SCARCITY

2003 Leaf Certified Materials Mirror Gold

MINT NRMT
1-250 RANDOM INSERTS IN PACKS
251-259 RANDOM IN DLP R/T PACKS
STATED PRINT RUN 25 SERIAL #'d SETS
NO PRICING DUE TO SCARCITY

2003 Leaf Certified Materials Mirror Gold Autographs

MINT NRMT
1-250 RANDOM INSERTS IN PACKS..
251-259 RANDOM IN DLP R/T PACKS
PRINT RUNS B/WN 5-25 COPIES PER
NO PRICING DUE TO SCARCITY ....

2003 Leaf Certified Materials Mirror Gold Materials

MINT NRMT
RANDOM INSERTS IN PACKS ....
PRINT RUNS B/WN 5-25 COPIES PER
NO PRICING DUE TO SCARCITY ....

2003 Leaf Certified Materials Mirror Red

MINT NRMT
*ACTIVE RED 1-200: 2X TO 5X BASIC
*RETIRED RED 1-200: 2.5X TO 6X BASIC
*RED 201-205: .75X TO 2X BASIC ....
*RED 206-219/221-250: .2X TO .5X BASIC
*RED 220: .12X TO .3X BASIC 220 ....
*RED 250: .5X TO 1.2X BASIC 250 ....
*RED 251-259: .2X TO .5X BASIC p/r 250
*RED 251-259: .15X TO .4X BASIC p/r 100-150
1-250 RANDOM INSERTS IN PACKS..
251-259 RANDOM IN DLP R/T PACKS
STATED PRINT RUN 100 SERIAL #'d SETS

2003 Leaf Certified Materials Mirror Red Autographs

MINT NRMT
1-250 RANDOM INSERTS IN PACKS..
251-259 RANDOM IN DLP R/T PACKS
PRINT RUNS B/WN 5-100 COPIES PER
NO PRICING ON QTY OF 25 OR LESS
2 Alfredo Amezaga/100 .... 15.00 6.75
3 Garret Anderson/10....................
4 Nolan Ryan Angels/5....................
6 Junior Spivey/15....................
15 Adam LaRoche/100 .... 15.00 6.75
17 Robert Fick/15....................
20 Jay Gibbons/100 .... 15.00 6.75
21 Geronimo Gil/15....................
22 Cal Ripken/5....................
25 Freddy Sanchez/100............ 15.00 6.75
28 Casey Fossum/50............ 15.00 6.75
31 Corey Patterson/6....................
32 Nic Jackson/100 .... 15.00 6.75
33 Mark Prior/15....................
34 Juan Cruz/15....................
35 Steve Smyth/94 .... 15.00 6.75
37 Joe Borchard/15....................
39 Mark Buehrle/15....................
40 Joe Crede/15....................
45 Brandon Larson/100 .... 15.00 6.75
49 Wily Mo Pena/100 .... 25.00 11.00
51 Victor Martinez/15....................
52 Brian Tallet/15....................
53 Cliff Lee/15....................
54 Jeremy Guthrie/15....................
56 Ricardo Rodriguez/100 .... 15.00 6.75
60 Jason Jennings/15....................
61 Jeff Baker/15....................
63 Travis Chapman/100 .... 15.00 6.75
64 Mike Maroth/100 .... 15.00 6.75
70 Roy Oswalt/15....................
71 Jason Lane/100 .... 15.00 6.75
72 Nolan Ryan Astros/5....................
73 Wade Miller/15....................
74 Richard Hidalgo/10....................
77 Rodrigo Rosario/100 .... 15.00 6.75
79 John Buck/15....................
80 Angel Berroa/15....................
81 Mike Sweeney/10....................
82 Mac Suzuki/15....................
83 Alexis Gomez/15....................
85 Runelvys Hernandez/100 .... 15.00 6.75
86 Hideo Nomo/16....................
87 Paul Lo Duca/15....................
88 Cesar Izturis/100............ 15.00 6.75
89 Kazuhisa Ishii/5....................
91 Joe Thurston/100............ 15.00 6.75
94 Richie Sexson/10....................
95 Ben Sheets/10....................
96 Takahito Nomura/15....................
98 Bill Hall/100 .... 15.00 6.75
100 A.J. Pierzynski/10....................
102 Jose Morban/100............ 15.00 6.75
106 Joe Mays/9....................
107 Adam Johnson/15....................
108 Javier Vazquez/15....................
110 Jose Vidro/15....................
116 Cliff Floyd/10....................
117 Mike Piazza/20....................
119 Don Mattingly/5....................
122 Alfonso Soriano/15....................
123 Drew Henson/10....................
124 Brandon Claussen/60......... 15.00 6.75
125 Christian Parker/15....................
129 Jason Anderson/100......... 15.00 6.75
130 Nick Johnson/15....................
133 Barry Zito/10....................
134 Miguel Tejada/10....................
135 Eric Chavez/10....................
136 Tim Hudson/10....................
138 Terrence Long/15....................
141 Pat Burrell/6....................
142 Marlon Byrd/100......... 15.00 6.75
143 Bobby Abreu/10....................
144 Brandon Duckworth/15....................
145 Robert Person/15....................
146 Anderson Machado/100...... 15.00 6.75
148 Jack Wilson/15....................
149 Carlos Rivera/100 .... 15.00 6.75
150 Jose Castillo/100 .... 15.00 6.75
151 Walter Young/100 .... 15.00 6.75
152 Brian Giles/15....................
154 Ryan Klesko/10....................
155 Mike Rivera/100......... 15.00 6.75
157 Brian Lawrence/100......... 15.00 6.75
158 Xavier Nady Hat/15....................
159 Dennis Tankersley/15....................
165 Edgar Martinez/10....................
166 Chris Snelling/100 .... 15.00 6.75
167 Rafael Soriano/15....................
170 Freddy Garcia/15....................
173 Albert Pujols/10....................
176 Jim Edmonds/10....................
179 Antonio Perez/15....................
180 Dewon Brazelton/15....................
181 Aubrey Huff/15....................
182 Toby Hall/15....................
184 Joe Kennedy/15....................
187 Hank Blalock/15....................
188 Mark Teixeira/15....................
189 Juan Gonzalez/10....................
190 Kevin Mench/100......... 15.00 6.75
191 Nolan Ryan Rgr/5....................
193 Eric Hinske/100......... 15.00 6.75
194 Vinny Chulk/100......... 15.00 6.75
195 Alexis Rios/100......... 40.00 18.00
197 Shannon Stewart/15....................
206 Prentice Redman NG/100 .. 10.00 4.50
207 Craig Brazell NG/100......... 15.00 6.75
208 Nook Logan NG/100 .... 10.00 4.50
209 Hong-Chih Kuo NG/50 .... 40.00 18.00
210 Matt Kata NG/100 .... 25.00 11.00
211 Chien-Ming Wang NG/50... 60.00 27.00
212 Alejandro Machado NG/100 10.00 4.50
213 Michael Hessman NG/100 . 10.00 4.50
214 Francisco Rosario NG/100. 10.00 4.50
215 Pedro Liriano NG/100 .... 10.00 4.50
216 Jeremy Bonderman NG/100 25.00 11.00
217 Oscar Villarreal NG/100 ..... 10.00 4.50
218 Arnie Munoz NG/100 .... 10.00 4.50
219 Tim Olson NG/100 .... 15.00 6.75
220 Jose Contreras NG/5....................
221 Francisco Cruceta NG/100. 10.00 4.50
222 John Webb NG/100......... 10.00 4.50
223 Phil Seibel NG/100......... 10.00 4.50
224 Aaron Looper NG/100......... 10.00 4.50
225 Brian Stokes NG/100......... 10.00 4.50
226 Guillermo Quiroz NG/100... 25.00 11.00
227 Fernando Cabrera NG/100 . 10.00 4.50
228 Josh Hall NG/100......... 15.00 6.75
229 Diegomar Markwell NG/100 10.00 4.50
230 Andrew Brown NG/100...... 15.00 6.75
231 Doug Waechter NG/100...... 15.00 6.75
232 Felix Sanchez NG/100......... 10.00 4.50
233 Gerardo Garcia NG/100...... 10.00 4.50
234 Matt Bruback NG/100 .... 10.00 4.50
235 Michel Hernandez NG/100 . 10.00 4.50
236 Rett Johnson NG/100 .... 15.00 6.75
237 Ryan Cameron NG/100...... 10.00 4.50
238 Rob Hammock NG/100...... 15.00 6.75
239 Clint Barmes NG/100......... 15.00 6.75
240 Brandon Webb NG/100...... 30.00 13.50
241 Jon Leicester NG/100......... 10.00 4.50
242 Shane Bazzell NG/100......... 10.00 4.50
243 Joe Valentine NG/100......... 10.00 4.50
244 Josh Stewart NG/100......... 10.00 4.50
245 Pete LaForest NG/100......... 15.00 6.75
246 Shane Victorino NG/100 ..... 10.00 4.50
247 Termel Sledge NG/100......... 15.00 6.75
248 Lew Ford NG/100......... 30.00 13.50
249 Todd Wellemeyer NG/100.. 15.00 6.75
251 Adam Loewen NG/100......... 30.00 13.50
252 Dan Haren NG/100......... 25.00 11.00
253 Dontrelle Willis NG/50 ...... 25.00 11.00
254 Ramon Nivar NG/100......... 25.00 11.00
255 Chad Gaudin NG/100......... 10.00 4.50
256 Kevin Correia NG/100 .... 10.00 4.50
257 Rickie Weeks NG/25....................
258 Ryan Wagner NG/100......... 15.00 6.75
259 Delmon Young NG/50 ...... 150.00 70.00

2003 Leaf Certified Materials Mirror Red Materials

MINT NRMT
RANDOM INSERTS IN PACKS ....
PRINT RUNS B/WN 15-250 COPIES PER
NO PRICING ON QTY OF 25 OR LESS
1 Troy Glaus Jsy/250 .... 8.00 3.60
2 Alfredo Amezaga Jsy/100 ...... 10.00 4.50
3 Garret Anderson Bat/250 ...... 8.00 3.60
4 Nolan Ryan Angels Jsy/35 ..... 80.00 36.00
5 Darin Erstad Bat/250......... 8.00 3.60
6 Junior Spivey Bat/250......... 8.00 3.60
7 Randy Johnson Jsy/250 ...... 10.00 4.50
8 Curt Schilling Jsy/250......... 8.00 3.60
9 Luis Gonzalez Jsy/250 .... 8.00 3.60
10 Steve Finley Jsy/250 .... 8.00 3.60
11 Matt Williams Jsy/100 .... 10.00 4.50
12 Greg Maddux Jsy/250......... 20.00 9.00
13 Chipper Jones Jsy/250 ...... 10.00 4.50
14 Gary Sheffield Bat/125 ...... 10.00 4.50
15 Adam LaRoche Bat/250 .... 8.00 3.60
16 Andruw Jones Jsy/250 .... 8.00 3.60
17 Robert Fick Bat/250......... 8.00 3.60
18 John Smoltz Jsy/250......... 10.00 4.50
19 Javy Lopez Jsy/250......... 8.00 3.60
20 Jay Gibbons Jsy/250 .... 8.00 3.60
21 Geronimo Gil Jsy/250......... 8.00 3.60
22 Cal Ripken Jsy/35 .... 120.00 55.00
23 Nomar Garciaparra Jsy/250. 25.00 11.00
24 Pedro Martinez Jsy/250 .... 10.00 4.50
25 Freddy Sanchez Bat/250 .... 8.00 3.60
26 Rickey Henderson Bat/250... 10.00 4.50
27 Manny Ramirez Jsy/250 ...... 10.00 4.50
28 Casey Fossum Jsy/250 .... 8.00 3.60
29 Sammy Sosa Jsy/250 .... 25.00 11.00
30 Kerry Wood Jsy/250......... 10.00 4.50
31 Corey Patterson Bat/250......... 8.00 3.60
32 Nic Jackson Bat/250 .... 8.00 3.60
33 Mark Prior Jsy/250 .... 10.00 4.50
34 Juan Cruz Jsy/250 .... 8.00 3.60
35 Steve Smyth Jsy/250 .... 8.00 3.60
36 Magglio Ordonez Jsy/250 ...... 8.00 3.60
37 Joe Borchard Jsy/250 .... 8.00 3.60
38 Frank Thomas Jsy/250......... 10.00 4.50
39 Mark Buehrle Jsy/250......... 8.00 3.60
40 Joe Crede Hat/100 .... 10.00 4.50
41 Carlos Lee Jsy/250 .... 8.00 3.60
42 Paul Konerko Jsy/250......... 8.00 3.60
43 Adam Dunn Jsy/250 .... 10.00 4.50
45 Brandon Larson Spikes/150... 8.00 3.60
46 Ken Griffey Jr. Base/250 ...... 20.00 9.00
47 Barry Larkin Jsy/250 .... 10.00 4.50
48 Sean Casey Bat/250......... 8.00 3.60
49 Wily Mo Pena Bat/250 .... 8.00 3.60
50 Austin Kearns Jsy/250......... 8.00 3.60
51 Victor Martinez Jsy/100 ...... 15.00 6.75
55 C.C. Sabathia Jsy/250......... 8.00 3.60
56 Ricardo Rodriguez Bat/250.... 8.00 3.60
57 Omar Vizquel Jsy/250 .... 10.00 4.50
58 Travis Hafner Bat/250 .... 8.00 3.60
59 Todd Helton Jsy/250 .... 10.00 4.50
60 Jason Jennings Jsy/250 .... 8.00 3.60
62 Larry Walker Jsy/250......... 10.00 4.50
63 Travis Chapman Bat/250......... 8.00 3.60
64 Mike Maroth Jsy/250......... 8.00 3.60
65 Josh Beckett Jsy/250 .... 8.00 3.60
66 Ivan Rodriguez Bat/250 ...... 10.00 4.50
67 Brad Penny Jsy/250......... 8.00 3.60
68 A.J. Burnett Jsy/250......... 8.00 3.60
69 Craig Biggio Jsy/250......... 10.00 4.50
70 Roy Oswalt Jsy/250 .... 8.00 3.60
71 Jason Lane Jsy/250 .... 8.00 3.60
72 Nolan Ryan Astros Jsy/35 ... 80.00 36.00
73 Wade Miller Jsy/250 .... 8.00 3.60
74 Richard Hidalgo Pants/250 .... 8.00 3.60
75 Jeff Bagwell Jsy/250 .... 10.00 4.50
76 Lance Berkman Jsy/250......... 8.00 3.60
77 Rodrigo Rosario Jsy/250......... 8.00 3.60
78 Jeff Kent Bat/250 .... 8.00 3.60
79 John Buck Jsy/250 .... 8.00 3.60
80 Angel Berroa Jsy/250......... 10.00 4.50
81 Mike Sweeney Jsy/250 .... 8.00 3.60
84 Carlos Beltran Jsy/250......... 10.00 4.50
86 Hideo Nomo Jsy/250......... 30.00 13.50
87 Paul Lo Duca Jsy/250......... 8.00 3.60
88 Cesar Izturis Pants/250......... 8.00 3.60
89 Kazuhisa Ishii Jsy/250 .... 8.00 3.60
90 Shawn Green Jsy/250......... 8.00 3.60
91 Joe Thurston Jsy/250 .... 8.00 3.60
92 Adrian Beltre Bat/250......... 10.00 4.50
93 Kevin Brown Jsy/250 .... 8.00 3.60
94 Richie Sexson Jsy/250......... 8.00 3.60
95 Ben Sheets Jsy/250 .... 8.00 3.60
97 Geoff Jenkins Jsy/250 .... 8.00 3.60
98 Bill Hall Bat/250 .... 8.00 3.60
99 Torii Hunter Jsy/250 .... 8.00 3.60
101 Michael Cuddyer Jsy/250..... 8.00 3.60
102 Jose Morban Bat/250 .... 8.00 3.60
103 Brad Radke Jsy/250......... 8.00 3.60
104 Jacque Jones Jsy/250 .... 8.00 3.60
105 Eric Milton Jsy/250......... 8.00 3.60
106 Joe Mays Jsy/250......... 8.00 3.60
107 Adam Johnson Jsy/250 .... 8.00 3.60
108 Javier Vazquez Jsy/250 .... 8.00 3.60
109 Vladimir Guerrero Jsy/250. 10.00 4.50
110 Jose Vidro Jsy/250 .... 8.00 3.60
111 Michael Barrett Jsy/50 ...... 15.00 6.75
112 Orlando Cabrera Jsy/250 ...... 8.00 3.60
113 Tom Glavine Bat/250......... 10.00 4.50
114 Roberto Alomar Bat/250 .... 10.00 4.50
115 Tsuyoshi Shinjo Jsy/250...... 8.00 3.60
116 Cliff Floyd Bat/250 .... 8.00 3.60
117 Mike Piazza Jsy/250......... 20.00 9.00
118 Al Leiter Jsy/250 .... 8.00 3.60
119 Don Mattingly Jsy/35 .... 80.00 36.00
120 Roger Clemens Jsy/250...... 25.00 11.00
121 Derek Jeter Base/250......... 25.00 11.00
122 Alfonso Soriano Jsy/250..... 10.00 4.50
123 Drew Henson Bat/250......... 8.00 3.60
124 Brandon Claussen Hat/50 .. 15.00 6.75
125 Christian Parker Pants/250.. 8.00 3.60
126 Jason Giambi Jsy/250 .... 8.00 3.60
127 Mike Mussina Jsy/250 ...... 10.00 4.50
128 Bernie Williams Jsy/250 ..... 10.00 4.50
130 Nick Johnson Jsy/250 .... 8.00 3.60
131 Jorge Posada Jsy/250 .... 10.00 4.50
132 Andy Pettitte Jsy/250......... 10.00 4.50
133 Barry Zito Jsy/250 .... 8.00 3.60
134 Miguel Tejada Jsy/250 .... 8.00 3.60
135 Eric Chavez Jsy/250......... 8.00 3.60
136 Tim Hudson Jsy/250......... 8.00 3.60
137 Mark Mulder Jsy/250......... 8.00 3.60
138 Terrence Long Jsy/250 .... 8.00 3.60
139 Mark Ellis Jsy/250......... 8.00 3.60
140 Jim Thome Bat/250......... 10.00 4.50
141 Pat Burrell Bat/250......... 8.00 3.60
142 Marlon Byrd Jsy/250 .... 8.00 3.60
143 Bobby Abreu Jsy/250......... 8.00 3.60
144 Brandon Duckworth Jsy/250 8.00 3.60
145 Robert Person Jsy/250......... 8.00 3.60
146 Anderson Machado Jsy/250 8.00 3.60
147 Aramis Ramirez Jsy/250....... 8.00 3.60
148 Jack Wilson Bat/250 .... 8.00 3.60
150 Jose Castillo Bat/250 .... 8.00 3.60
151 Walter Young Bat/250 .... 8.00 3.60
152 Brian Giles Bat/250......... 8.00 3.60
153 Jason Kendall Jsy/250 .... 8.00 3.60
154 Ryan Klesko Jsy/25....................
155 Mike Rivera Bat/250......... 8.00 3.60
157 Brian Lawrence Bat/250......... 8.00 3.60
158 Xavier Nady Hat/60......... 15.00 6.75
159 Dennis Tankersley Jsy/250 .. 8.00 3.60
160 Phil Nevin Jsy/250......... 8.00 3.60
161 Barry Bonds Base/250 ...... 25.00 11.00
162 Kenny Lofton Bat/250 .... 8.00 3.60
163 Rich Aurilia Jsy/250......... 8.00 3.60
164 Ichiro Suzuki Base/250 ...... 25.00 11.00
165 Edgar Martinez Jsy/100 ...... 15.00 6.75
166 Chris Snelling Bat/250......... 8.00 3.60
167 Rafael Soriano Jsy/250......... 8.00 3.60
168 John Olerud Jsy/250......... 8.00 3.60
169 Bret Boone Jsy/250 .... 8.00 3.60
170 Freddy Garcia Jsy/250 .... 8.00 3.60
171 Aaron Sele Jsy/250......... 8.00 3.60
172 Kazuhiro Sasaki Jsy/250...... 8.00 3.60
173 Albert Pujols Jsy/250......... 30.00 13.50
174 Scott Rolen Bat/250......... 10.00 4.50
175 So Taguchi Jsy/250......... 8.00 3.60
176 Jim Edmonds Jsy/250 .... 8.00 3.60
177 Edgar Renteria Jsy/250......... 8.00 3.60
178 J.D. Drew Jsy/250 .... 8.00 3.60
179 Antonio Perez Bat/250 .... 8.00 3.60
180 Dewon Brazelton Jsy/250 ... 8.00 3.60
181 Aubrey Huff Jsy/50 .... 15.00 6.75
182 Toby Hall Jsy/250 .... 8.00 3.60
183 Ben Grieve Jsy/100......... 10.00 4.50
184 Joe Kennedy Jsy/250......... 8.00 3.60
185 Alex Rodriguez Jsy/250 ..... 25.00 11.00
186 Rafael Palmeiro Jsy/250 .... 10.00 4.50
187 Hank Blalock Jsy/250......... 10.00 4.50
188 Mark Teixeira Jsy/250 .... 8.00 3.60
189 Juan Gonzalez Bat/250...... 10.00 4.50
190 Kevin Mench Jsy/250......... 8.00 3.60
191 Nolan Ryan Rgr Jsy/35 ...... 80.00 36.00
192 Doug Davis Jsy/250......... 8.00 3.60
193 Eric Hinske Jsy/250 .... 8.00 3.60
196 Carlos Delgado Jsy/250 ...... 8.00 3.60
197 Shannon Stewart Jsy/250.... 8.00 3.60
198 Josh Phelps Jsy/250......... 8.00 3.60
199 Vernon Wells Jsy/250 .... 8.00 3.60
200 Roy Halladay Jsy/250 .... 8.00 3.60
201 Babe Ruth RET Pants/15....................
202 Lou Gehrig RET Pants/15....................
203 Jackie Robinson RET Jsy/15.......
204 Ty Cobb RET Pants/15....................
205 Thurman Munson RET Jsy/15 .....

2003 Leaf Certified Materials Fabric of the Game

Randomly inserted into packs, these 900 cards feature six versions of 150 different cards. The set is broken down into BA (designed like a Base); DY (indicating the year the team was 1st known by their current nomenclature); IN (inscription; JN (Jersey Number); JY (Jersey Year that this jersey was used in) and PS (Position). We have put the stated print run next to the player's name in our checklist.

MINT NRMT
PRINT RUNS BETWEEN 1-102 COPIES PER
NO PRICING ON QTY OF 25 OR LESS
1BA Bobby Doerr BA/50 .... 10.00 4.50
1DY Bobby Doerr DY/7....................
1IN Bobby Doerr IN/25....................
1JN Bobby Doerr JN/1....................
1JY Bobby Doerr JY/39 .... 15.00 6.75
1PS Bobby Doerr PS/50 .... 10.00 4.50
2BA Ozzie Smith BA/100......... 25.00 11.00
2DY Ozzie Smith DY/1....................
2IN Ozzie Smith IN/50......... 30.00 13.50
2JN Ozzie Smith JN/1....................
2JY Ozzie Smith JY/88......... 25.00 11.00
2PS Ozzie Smith PS/50......... 30.00 13.50
3BA Pee Wee Reese BA/20....................
3DY Pee Wee Reese DY/32......... 30.00 13.50
3IN Pee Wee Reese IN/15....................
3JN Pee Wee Reese JN/1....................
3JY Pee Wee Reese JY/58 .... 15.00 6.75
3PS Pee Wee Reese PS/20....................
4BA Jeff Bagwell Pants BA/100 10.00 4.50
4DY Jeff Bagwell Pants DY/65.. 15.00 6.75
4IN Jeff Bagwell Pants IN/50 .... 15.00 6.75
4JN Jeff Bagwell Pants JN/5....................
4JY Jeff Bagwell Pants JY/98 .... 10.00 4.50
4PS Jeff Bagwell Pants PS/50 .. 15.00 6.75
5BA Tommy Lasorda BA/100 ...... 10.00 4.50
5DY Tommy Lasorda DY/58...... 10.00 4.50
5IN Tommy Lasorda IN/25....................
5JN Tommy Lasorda JN/2....................
5JY Tommy Lasorda JY/84 ...... 10.00 4.50
5PS Tommy Lasorda PS/50...... 10.00 4.50
6BA Red Schoendienst BA/25....................
6DY Red Schoendienst DY/1....................
6IN Red Schoendienst IN/15....................
6JN Red Schoendienst JN/2....................
6JY Red Schoendienst JY/55.... 10.00 4.50
6PS Red Schoendienst PS/50... 10.00 4.50
7BA Harmon Killebrew BA/50 ... 15.00 6.75
7DY Harmon Killebrew DY/61 ... 15.00 6.75
7IN Harmon Killebrew IN/50...... 15.00 6.75
7JN Harmon Killebrew JN/3....................
7JY Harmon Killebrew JY/71 .... 15.00 6.75
7PS Harmon Killebrew PS/50 ... 15.00 6.75
8BA Roger Maris BA/25....................
8DY Roger Maris DY/55 .... 40.00 18.00
8IN Roger Maris IN/20....................
8JN Roger Maris JN/3....................
8JY Roger Maris JY/58......... 40.00 18.00
8PS Roger Maris PS/50......... 40.00 18.00
9BA Alex Rodriguez M's BA/100 15.00 6.75
9DY Alex Rodriguez M's DY/77 15.00 6.75
9IN Alex Rodriguez M's IN/50 .. 25.00 11.00
9JN Alex Rodriguez M's JN/3....................
9JY Alex Rodriguez M's JY/99.. 15.00 6.75
9PS Alex Rodriguez M's PS/50. 25.00 11.00
10BA Alex Rodriguez Rgr BA/100 15.00 6.75
10DY Alex Rodriguez Rgr DY/72 25.00 11.00
10IN Alex Rodriguez Rgr IN/50. 25.00 11.00
10JN Alex Rodriguez Rgr JN/3....................
10JY Alex Rodriguez Rgr JY/101 15.00 6.75
10PS Alex Rodriguez Rgr PS/50 25.00 11.00
11BA Dale Murphy BA/50 .... 15.00 6.75
11DY Dale Murphy DY/66......... 15.00 6.75
11IN Dale Murphy IN/50......... 15.00 6.75
11JN Dale Murphy JN/3....................
11JY Dale Murphy JY/85 .... 15.00 6.75
11PS Dale Murphy PS/50......... 15.00 6.75
12BA Alan Trammell BA/100..... 10.00 4.50
12DY Alan Trammell DY/1....................
12IN Alan Trammell IN/50 .... 10.00 4.50
12JN Alan Trammell JN/3....................
12JY Alan Trammell JY/90......... 10.00 4.50
12PS Alan Trammell PS/50 ...... 10.00 4.50
13BA Babe Ruth Pants BA/10....................
13DY Babe Ruth Pants DY/13....................
13IN Babe Ruth Pants IN/10....................
13JN Babe Ruth Pants JN/3....................
13JY Babe Ruth Pants JY/30.. 350.00 160.00
13PS Babe Ruth Pants PS/10....................
14BA Lou Gehrig BA/10....................
14DY Lou Gehrig DY/13....................
14IN Lou Gehrig IN/10....................
14JN Lou Gehrig JN/4....................
14JY Lou Gehrig JY/38......... 300.00 135.00
14PS Lou Gehrig PS/10....................
15BA Babe Ruth BA/10....................
15DY Babe Ruth DY/13....................
15IN Babe Ruth IN/10....................
15JN Babe Ruth JN/3....................
15JY Babe Ruth JY/30......... 400.00 180.00
15PS Babe Ruth PS/10....................
16BA Mel Ott BA/10....................
16DY Mel Ott DY/1....................
16IN Mel Ott IN/10....................
16JN Mel Ott JN/4....................
16JY Mel Ott JY/46......... 40.00 18.00
16PS Mel Ott PS/10....................
17BA Paul Molitor BA/100 .... 15.00 6.75
17DY Paul Molitor DY/70......... 15.00 6.75
17IN Paul Molitor IN/50......... 15.00 6.75
17JN Paul Molitor JN/4....................
17JY Paul Molitor JY/84 .... 15.00 6.75
17PS Paul Molitor PS/50......... 15.00 6.75
18BA Duke Snider BA/15....................
18DY Duke Snider DY/58......... 15.00 6.75
18IN Duke Snider IN/15....................
18JN Duke Snider JN/4....................
18JY Duke Snider JY/62......... 15.00 6.75
18PS Duke Snider PS/15....................
19BA Miguel Tejada BA/50...... 10.00 4.50
19DY Miguel Tejada DY/68 ...... 10.00 4.50
19IN Miguel Tejada IN/50...... 10.00 4.50
19JN Miguel Tejada JN/4....................
19JY Miguel Tejada JY/99......... 8.00 3.60
19PS Miguel Tejada PS/50...... 10.00 4.50
20BA Lou Gehrig Pants BA/10....................
20DY Lou Gehrig Pants DY/13....................
20IN Lou Gehrig Pants IN/10....................
20JN Lou Gehrig Pants JN/4....................
20JY Lou Gehrig Pants JY/38. 250.00 110.00
20PS Lou Gehrig Pants PS/10....................
21BA Brooks Robinson BA/15....................
21DY Brooks Robinson DY/54.. 15.00 6.75
21IN Brooks Robinson IN/15....................
21JN Brooks Robinson JN/5....................
21JY Brooks Robinson JY/66... 15.00 6.75
21PS Brooks Robinson PS/15....................
22BA George Brett BA/50 ...... 40.00 18.00
22DY George Brett DY/69 ...... 40.00 18.00
22IN George Brett IN/50 ...... 40.00 18.00
22JN George Brett JN/5....................
22JY George Brett JY/91 ...... 30.00 13.50
22PS George Brett PS/50 ...... 40.00 18.00
23BA Johnny Bench BA/50...... 15.00 6.75
23DY Johnny Bench DY/59...... 15.00 6.75
23IN Johnny Bench IN/50...... 15.00 6.75
23JN Johnny Bench JN/5....................
23JY Johnny Bench JY/81...... 15.00 6.75
23PS Johnny Bench PS/50...... 15.00 6.75
24BA Lou Boudreau BA/15....................
24DY Lou Boudreau DY/15....................
24IN Lou Boudreau IN/15....................
24JN Lou Boudreau JN/5....................
24JY Lou Boudreau JY/48 ...... 15.00 6.75
24PS Lou Boudreau PS/15....................
25BA Nomar Garciaparra BA/100 25.00 11.00
25DY Nomar Garciaparra DY/7....................
25IN Nomar Garciaparra IN/50 . 25.00 11.00
25JN Nomar Garciaparra JN/5....................
25JY Nomar Garciaparra JY/100 25.00 11.00
25PS Nomar Garciaparra PS/50 25.00 11.00
26BA Tsuyoshi Shinjo BA/50 .... 10.00 4.50
26DY Tsuyoshi Shinjo DY/62 .... 10.00 4.50
26IN Tsuyoshi Shinjo IN/25....................
26JN Tsuyoshi Shinjo JN/5....................
26JY Tsuyoshi Shinjo JY/101 ..... 8.00 3.60
26PS Tsuyoshi Shinjo PS/25....................
27BA Pat Burrell BA/100......... 8.00 3.60
27DY Pat Burrell DY/46 .... 12.00 5.50
27IN Pat Burrell IN/25....................
27JN Pat Burrell JN/5....................
27JY Pat Burrell JY/101......... 8.00 3.60
27PS Pat Burrell PS/25....................
28BA Albert Pujols BA/100 ...... 25.00 11.00
28DY Albert Pujols DY/1....................
28IN Albert Pujols IN/50......... 30.00 13.50
28JN Albert Pujols JN/5....................
28JY Albert Pujols JY/101 ...... 25.00 11.00
28PS Albert Pujols PS/50 ...... 30.00 13.50
29BA Stan Musial BA/10....................
29DY Stan Musial DY/1....................
29IN Stan Musial IN/10....................
29JN Stan Musial JN/6....................
29JY Stan Musial JY/43......... 40.00 18.00
29PS Stan Musial PS/10....................
30BA Al Kaline BA/20....................
30DY Al Kaline DY/1....................
30IN Al Kaline IN/15....................
30JN Al Kaline JN/6....................
30JY Al Kaline JY/64......... 15.00 6.75
30PS Al Kaline PS/15....................
31BA Ivan Rodriguez BA/100.... 10.00 4.50
31DY Ivan Rodriguez DY/72 .... 15.00 6.75
31IN Ivan Rodriguez IN/50 ...... 15.00 6.75
31JN Ivan Rodriguez JN/7....................
31JY Ivan Rodriguez JY/101.... 10.00 4.50
31PS Ivan Rodriguez PS/50...... 15.00 6.75
32BA Craig Biggio BA/100...... 10.00 4.50
32DY Craig Biggio DY/65......... 15.00 6.75
32IN Craig Biggio IN/25....................
32JN Craig Biggio JN/7....................
32JY Craig Biggio JY/101...... 10.00 4.50
32PS Craig Biggio PS/50 ...... 15.00 6.75

33BA Joe Morgan BA/10
33DY Joe Morgan DY/59 10.00 4.50
33IN Joe Morgan IN/10
33JN Joe Morgan JN/8
33JY Joe Morgan JY/74 10.00 4.50
33PS Joe Morgan PS/10
34BA Willie Stargell BA/50 15.00 6.75
34DY Willie Stargell DY/1
34IN Willie Stargell IN/15
34JN Willie Stargell JN/8
34JY Willie Stargell JY/68 15.00 6.75
34PS Willie Stargell PS/50 15.00 6.75
35BA Andre Dawson BA/100 10.00 4.50
35DY Andre Dawson DY/7
35IN Andre Dawson IN/50 10.00 4.50
35JN Andre Dawson JN/8
35JY Andre Dawson JY/87 10.00 4.50
35PS Andre Dawson PS/50 10.00 4.50
36BA Gary Carter BA/100 10.00 4.50
36DY Gary Carter DY/62 10.00 4.50
36IN Gary Carter IN/50 10.00 4.50
36JN Gary Carter JN/8
36JY Gary Carter JY/85 10.00 4.50
36PS Gary Carter PS/50 10.00 4.50
37BA Cal Ripken BA/50 60.00 27.00
37DY Cal Ripken DY/54 60.00 27.00
37IN Cal Ripken IN/50 60.00 27.00
37JN Cal Ripken JN/8
37JY Cal Ripken JY/101 50.00 22.00
37PS Cal Ripken PS/50 60.00 27.00
38BA Enos Slaughter BA/15
38DY Enos Slaughter DY/1
38IN Enos Slaughter IN/15
38JN Enos Slaughter JN/9
38JY Enos Slaughter JY/53 10.00 4.50
38PS Enos Slaughter PS/25
39BA Reggie Jackson A's BA/50 15.00 6.75
39DY Reggie Jackson A's DY/68 15.00 6.75
39IN Reggie Jackson A's IN/25
39JN Reggie Jackson A's JN/9
39JY Reggie Jackson A's JY/75 15.00 6.75
39PS Reggie Jackson A's PS/50 15.00 6.75
40BA Phil Rizzuto BA/20
40DY Phil Rizzuto DY/13
40IN Phil Rizzuto IN/15
40JN Phil Rizzuto JN/10
40JY Phil Rizzuto JY/47 25.00 11.00
40PS Phil Rizzuto PS/15
41BA Chipper Jones BA/100 10.00 4.50
41DY Chipper Jones DY/66 15.00 6.75
41IN Chipper Jones IN/50 15.00 6.75
41JN Chipper Jones JN/10
41JY Chipper Jones JY/101 10.00 4.50
41PS Chipper Jones PS/50 15.00 6.75
42BA H.Nomo Dodgers BA/100 10.00 4.50
42DY H.Nomo Dodgers DY/58 15.00 6.75
42IN H.Nomo Dodgers IN/50 15.00 6.75
42JN H.Nomo Dodgers JN/16
42JY H.Nomo Dodgers JY/95 10.00 4.50
42PS H.Nomo Dodgers PS/50 15.00 6.75
43BA Luis Aparicio BA/25
43DY Luis Aparicio DY/4
43IN Luis Aparicio IN/15
43JN Luis Aparicio JN/11
43JY Luis Aparicio JY/69 10.00 4.50
43PS Luis Aparicio PS/20
44BA H.Nomo R.Sox BA/100 10.00 4.50
44DY H.Nomo R.Sox DY/7
44IN H.Nomo R.Sox IN/50 15.00 6.75
44JN H.Nomo R.Sox JN/11
44JY H.Nomo R.Sox JY/101 10.00 4.50
44PS H.Nomo R.Sox PS/50 15.00 6.75
45BA Edgar Martinez BA/100 10.00 4.50
45DY Edgar Martinez DY/77 10.00 4.50
45IN Edgar Martinez IN/25
45JN Edgar Martinez JN/11
45JY Edgar Martinez JY/100 10.00 4.50
45PS Edgar Martinez PS/50 15.00 6.75
46BA Barry Larkin BA/100 10.00 4.50
46DY Barry Larkin DY/59 15.00 6.75
46IN Barry Larkin IN/25
46JN Barry Larkin JN/11
46JY Barry Larkin JY/100 10.00 4.50
46PS Barry Larkin PS/50 15.00 6.75
47BA Alfonso Soriano BA/100 10.00 4.50
47DY Alfonso Soriano DY/13
47IN Alfonso Soriano IN/50 15.00 6.75
47JN Alfonso Soriano JN/12
47JY Alfonso Soriano JY/102 10.00 4.50
47PS Alfonso Soriano PS/50 15.00 6.75
48BA Wade Boggs Rays BA/100 15.00 6.75
48DY Wade Boggs Rays DY/98 15.00 6.75
48IN Wade Boggs Rays IN/50 15.00 6.75
48JN Wade Boggs Rays JN/12
48JY Wade Boggs Rays JY/99 15.00 6.75
48PS Wade Boggs Rays PS/50 15.00 6.75
49BA Wade Boggs Yanks BA/50 15.00 6.75
49DY Wade Boggs Yanks DY/13
49IN Wade Boggs Yanks IN/50 15.00 6.75
49JN Wade Boggs Yanks JN/12
49JY Wade Boggs Yanks JY/94 15.00 6.75
49PS Wade Boggs Yanks PS/50 15.00 6.75
50BA Ernie Banks BA/15
50DY Ernie Banks DY/7
50IN Ernie Banks IN/15
50JN Ernie Banks JN/14
50JY Ernie Banks JY/68 15.00 6.75
50PS Ernie Banks PS/15
51BA Joe Torre BA/50 15.00 6.75
51DY Joe Torre DY/66 15.00 6.75
51IN Joe Torre IN/50 15.00 6.75
51JN Joe Torre JN/15
51JY Joe Torre JY/66 15.00 6.75
51PS Joe Torre PS/50 15.00 6.75
52BA Tim Hudson BA/100 8.00 3.60
52DY Tim Hudson DY/68 10.00 4.50
52IN Tim Hudson IN/25
52JN Tim Hudson JN/15
52JY Tim Hudson JY/101 8.00 3.60
52PS Tim Hudson PS/50 10.00 4.50
53BA Shawn Green BA/100 8.00 3.60
53DY Shawn Green DY/58 10.00 4.50
53IN Shawn Green IN/25
53JN Shawn Green JN/15
53JY Shawn Green JY/102 8.00 3.60
53PS Shawn Green PS/50 10.00 4.50
54BA Carlos Beltran BA/100 10.00 4.50
54DY Carlos Beltran DY/69 15.00 6.75
54IN Carlos Beltran IN/25
54JN Carlos Beltran JN/15
54JY Carlos Beltran JY/101 10.00 4.50
54PS Carlos Beltran PS/50 15.00 6.75
55BA Bo Jackson BA/50 15.00 6.75
55DY Bo Jackson DY/69 15.00 6.75
55IN Bo Jackson IN/25
55JN Bo Jackson JN/16
55JY Bo Jackson JY/90 15.00 6.75
55PS Bo Jackson PS/50 15.00 6.75
56BA Hal Newhouser BA/50 10.00 4.50
56DY Hal Newhouser DY/15
56IN Hal Newhouser IN/25
56JN Hal Newhouser JN/16
56JY Hal Newhouser JY/55 10.00 4.50
56PS Hal Newhouser PS/50 10.00 4.50
57BA Jason Giambi A's BA/100 8.00 3.60
57DY Jason Giambi A's DY/68 10.00 4.50
57IN Jason Giambi A's IN/50 10.00 4.50
57JN Jason Giambi A's JN/16
57JY Jason Giambi A's JY/101 8.00 3.60
57PS Jason Giambi A's PS/50 10.00 4.50
58BA Lance Berkman BA/100 8.00 3.60
58DY Lance Berkman DY/65 10.00 4.50
58IN Lance Berkman IN/50 10.00 4.50
58JN Lance Berkman JN/17
58JY Lance Berkman JY/102 8.00 3.60
58PS Lance Berkman PS/50 10.00 4.50
59BA Todd Helton BA/100 10.00 4.50
59DY Todd Helton DY/93 10.00 4.50
59IN Todd Helton IN/25
59JN Todd Helton JN/17
59JY Todd Helton JY/100 10.00 4.50
59PS Todd Helton PS/50 15.00 6.75
60BA Mark Grace BA/100 10.00 4.50
60DY Mark Grace DY/7
60IN Mark Grace IN/25
60JN Mark Grace JN/17
60JY Mark Grace JY/95 10.00 4.50
60PS Mark Grace PS/50 15.00 6.75
61BA Fred Lynn BA/100 10.00 4.50
61DY Fred Lynn DY/7
61IN Fred Lynn IN/25
61JN Fred Lynn JN/19
61JY Fred Lynn JY/75 10.00 4.50
61PS Fred Lynn PS/50 10.00 4.50
62BA Bob Feller BA/10
62DY Bob Feller DY/15
62IN Bob Feller IN/10
62JN Bob Feller JN/19
62JY Bob Feller JY/52 15.00 6.75
62PS Bob Feller PS/10
63BA Robin Yount BA/100 25.00 11.00
63DY Robin Yount DY/70 30.00 13.50
63IN Robin Yount IN/50 30.00 13.50
63JN Robin Yount JN/19
63JY Robin Yount JY/88 25.00 11.00
63PS Robin Yount PS/50 30.00 13.50
64BA Tony Gwynn BA/100 20.00 9.00
64DY Tony Gwynn DY/69 25.00 11.00
64IN Tony Gwynn IN/50 25.00 11.00
64JN Tony Gwynn JN/19
64JY Tony Gwynn JY/99 25.00 11.00
64PS Tony Gwynn PS/50 20.00 9.00
65BA Tony Gwynn Pants BA/100 20.00 9.00
65DY Tony Gwynn Pants DY/69 25.00 11.00
65IN Tony Gwynn Pants IN/50 25.00 11.00
65JN Tony Gwynn Pants JN/19
65JY Tony Gwynn Pants JY/99 20.00 9.00
65PS Tony Gwynn Pants PS/50 25.00 11.00
66BA Frank Robinson BA/10
66DY Frank Robinson DY/54 15.00 6.75
66IN Frank Robinson IN/10
66JN Frank Robinson JN/20
66JY Frank Robinson JY/70 15.00 6.75
66PS Frank Robinson PS/10
67BA Mike Schmidt BA/50 40.00 18.00
67DY Mike Schmidt DY/46 40.00 18.00
67IN Mike Schmidt IN/50 40.00 18.00
67JN Mike Schmidt JN/20
67JY Mike Schmidt JY/81 30.00 13.50
67PS Mike Schmidt PS/50 40.00 18.00
68BA Lou Brock BA/20
68DY Lou Brock DY/1
68IN Lou Brock IN/15
68JN Lou Brock JN/20
68JY Lou Brock JY/66 15.00 6.75
68PS Lou Brock PS/15
69BA Don Sutton BA/50 10.00 4.50
69DY Don Sutton DY/58 10.00 4.50
69IN Don Sutton IN/25
69JN Don Sutton JN/20
69JY Don Sutton JY/72 10.00 4.50
69PS Don Sutton PS/25
70BA Mark Mulder BA/100 8.00 3.60
70DY Mark Mulder DY/68 10.00 4.50
70IN Mark Mulder IN/25
70JN Mark Mulder JN/20
70JY Mark Mulder JY/101 8.00 3.60
70PS Mark Mulder PS/50 10.00 4.50
71BA Luis Gonzalez BA/100 8.00 3.60
71DY Luis Gonzalez DY/98 8.00 3.60
71IN Luis Gonzalez IN/25
71JN Luis Gonzalez JN/20
71JY Luis Gonzalez JY/101 8.00 3.60
71PS Luis Gonzalez PS/50 10.00 4.50
72BA Jorge Posada BA/100 10.00 4.50
72DY Jorge Posada DY/13
72IN Jorge Posada IN/25
72JN Jorge Posada JN/20
72JY Jorge Posada JY/101 10.00 4.50
72PS Jorge Posada PS/50 15.00 6.75
73BA Sammy Sosa BA/100 25.00 11.00
73DY Sammy Sosa DY/7
73IN Sammy Sosa IN/50 25.00 11.00
73JN Sammy Sosa JN/21
73JY Sammy Sosa JY/101 25.00 11.00
73PS Sammy Sosa PS/50 25.00 11.00
74BA Roberto Alomar BA/100 10.00 4.50
74DY Roberto Alomar DY/62 15.00 6.75
74IN Roberto Alomar IN/25
74JN Roberto Alomar JN/12
74JY Roberto Alomar JY/102 10.00 4.50
74PS Roberto Alomar PS/50 15.00 6.75
75BA Roberto Clemente BA/10
75DY Roberto Clemente DY/1
75IN Roberto Clemente IN/10
75JN Roberto Clemente JN/21
75JY Roberto Clemente JY/69 120.00 55.00
75PS Roberto Clemente PS/10
76BA Jeff Kent BA/100 8.00 3.60
76DY Jeff Kent DY/58 10.00 4.50
76IN Jeff Kent IN/25
76JN Jeff Kent JN/21
76JY Jeff Kent JY/101 8.00 3.60
76PS Jeff Kent PS/50 10.00 4.50
77BA Sean Casey BA/20
77DY Sean Casey DY/59 10.00 4.50
77IN Sean Casey IN/25
77JN Sean Casey JN/21
77JY Sean Casey JY/100 8.00 3.60
77PS Sean Casey PS/25
78BA R.Clemens R.Sox BA/50 25.00 11.00
78DY R.Clemens R.Sox DY/7
78IN R.Clemens R.Sox IN/50 25.00 11.00
78JN R.Clemens R.Sox JN/21
78JY R.Clemens R.Sox JY/95 25.00 11.00
78PS R.Clemens R.Sox PS/50 25.00 11.00
79BA Warren Spahn BA/20
79DY Warren Spahn DY/53 15.00 6.75
79IN Warren Spahn IN/15
79JN Warren Spahn JN/21
79JY Warren Spahn JY/58 15.00 6.75
79PS Warren Spahn PS/15
80BA R.Clemens Yanks BA/100 25.00 11.00
80DY R.Clemens Yanks DY/13
80IN R.Clemens Yanks IN/50 25.00 11.00
80JN R.Clemens Yanks JN/22
80JY R.Clemens Yanks JY/102 25.00 11.00
80PS R.Clemens Yanks PS/50 25.00 11.00
81BA Jim Palmer BA/50 15.00 6.75
81DY Jim Palmer DY/54 15.00 6.75
81IN Jim Palmer IN/25
81JN Jim Palmer JN/22
81JY Jim Palmer JY/69 15.00 6.75
81PS Jim Palmer PS/50 15.00 6.75
82BA Juan Gonzalez BA/50 15.00 6.75
82DY Juan Gonzalez DY/15
82IN Juan Gonzalez IN/25
82JN Juan Gonzalez JN/22
82JY Juan Gonzalez JY/101 10.00 4.50
82PS Juan Gonzalez PS/50 15.00 6.75
83BA Will Clark BA/100 15.00 6.75
83DY Will Clark DY/58 15.00 6.75
83IN Will Clark IN/25
83JN Will Clark JN/22
83JY Will Clark JY/88 15.00 6.75
83PS Will Clark PS/50 15.00 6.75
84BA Don Mattingly BA/50 30.00 13.50
84DY Don Mattingly DY/13
84IN Don Mattingly IN/50 30.00 13.50
84JN Don Mattingly JN/23
84JY Don Mattingly JY/93 30.00 13.50
84PS Don Mattingly PS/50 30.00 13.50
85BA Ryne Sandberg BA/40 40.00 18.00
85DY Ryne Sandberg DY/7
85IN Ryne Sandberg IN/50 40.00 18.00
85JN Ryne Sandberg JN/23
85JY Ryne Sandberg JY/85 30.00 13.50
85PS Ryne Sandberg PS/50 40.00 18.00
86BA Early Wynn BA/20
86DY Early Wynn DY/15
86IN Early Wynn IN/15
86JN Early Wynn JN/24
86JY Early Wynn JY/55 10.00 4.50
86PS Early Wynn PS/15
87BA Manny Ramirez BA/50 15.00 6.75
87DY Manny Ramirez DY/7
87IN Manny Ramirez IN/25
87JN Manny Ramirez JN/24
87JY Manny Ramirez JY/102 10.00 4.50
87PS Manny Ramirez PS/50 15.00 6.75
88BA R.Henderson Mets BA/100 10.00 4.50
88DY R.Henderson Mets DY/62 15.00 6.75
88IN R.Henderson Mets IN/50 15.00 6.75
88JN R.Henderson Mets JN/24
88JY R.Henderson Mets JY/99 10.00 4.50
88PS R.Henderson Mets PS/50 15.00 6.75
89BA R.Henderson Padres BA/100 10.00 4.50
89DY R.Henderson Padres DY/69 15.00 6.75
89IN R.Henderson Padres IN/25
89JN R.Henderson Padres JN/24
89JY R.Henderson Padres JY/102 10.00 4.50
89PS R.Henderson Padres PS/50 15.00 6.75
90BA Jason Giambi Yanks BA/100 8.00 3.60
90DY Jason Giambi Yanks DY/13
90IN Jason Giambi Yanks IN/50 10.00 4.50
90JN Jason Giambi Yanks JN/25
90JY Jason Giambi Yanks JY/102 8.00 3.60
90PS Jason Giambi Yanks PS/50 10.00 4.50
91BA Carlos Delgado BA/100 8.00 3.60
91DY Carlos Delgado DY/77 8.00 3.60
91IN Carlos Delgado IN/25
91JN Carlos Delgado JN/25
91JY Carlos Delgado JY/100 8.00 3.60
91PS Carlos Delgado PS/50 10.00 4.50
92BA Jim Thome BA/100 10.00 4.50
92DY Jim Thome DY/15
92IN Jim Thome IN/25
92JN Jim Thome JN/25
92JY Jim Thome JY/102 10.00 4.50
92PS Jim Thome PS/50 15.00 6.75
93BA Andruw Jones BA/100 8.00 3.60
93DY Andruw Jones DY/66 10.00 4.50
93IN Andruw Jones IN/25
93JN Andruw Jones JN/25
93JY Andruw Jones JY/101 8.00 3.60
93PS Andruw Jones PS/50 10.00 4.50
94BA Rafael Palmeiro BA/100 10.00 4.50
94DY Rafael Palmeiro DY/72 15.00 6.75
94IN Rafael Palmeiro IN/25
94JN Rafael Palmeiro JN/25
94JY Rafael Palmeiro JY/102 10.00 4.50
94PS Rafael Palmeiro PS/50 15.00 6.75
95BA Troy Glaus BA/100 8.00 3.60
95DY Troy Glaus DY/97 8.00 3.60
95IN Troy Glaus IN/50 10.00 4.50
95JN Troy Glaus JN/25
95JY Troy Glaus JY/100 8.00 3.60
95PS Troy Glaus PS/50 10.00 4.50
96BA Wade Boggs R.Sox BA/100 15.00 6.75
96DY Wade Boggs R.Sox DY/7
96IN Wade Boggs R.Sox IN/50 15.00 6.75
96JN Wade Boggs R.Sox JN/26 30.00 13.50
96JY Wade Boggs R.Sox JY/86 15.00 6.75
96PS Wade Boggs R.Sox PS/50 15.00 6.75
97BA Catfish Hunter BA/50 15.00 6.75
97DY Catfish Hunter DY/68 15.00 6.75
97IN Catfish Hunter IN/25
97JN Catfish Hunter JN/27 30.00 13.50
97JY Catfish Hunter JY/68 15.00 6.75
97PS Catfish Hunter PS/50 15.00 6.75
98BA Juan Marichal BA/50 10.00 4.50
98DY Juan Marichal DY/58 10.00 4.50
98IN Juan Marichal IN/25
98JN Juan Marichal JN/27 20.00 9.00
98JY Juan Marichal JY/67 10.00 4.50
98PS Juan Marichal PS/50 10.00 4.50
99BA Carlton Fisk R.Sox BA/50 15.00 6.75
99DY Carlton Fisk R.Sox DY/7
99IN Carlton Fisk R.Sox IN/25
99JN Carlton Fisk R.Sox JN/27 30.00 13.50
99JY Carlton Fisk R.Sox JY/80 15.00 6.75
99PS Carlton Fisk R.Sox PS/50 15.00 6.75
100BA Vladimir Guerrero BA/100 10.00 4.50
100DY Vladimir Guerrero DY/69 15.00 6.75
100IN Vladimir Guerrero IN/25
100JN Vladimir Guerrero JN/27 25.00 11.00
100JY Vladimir Guerrero JY/101 10.00 4.50
100PS Vladimir Guerrero PS/50 15.00 6.75
101BA Rod Carew Angels BA/50 15.00 6.75
101DY Rod Carew Angels DY/65 15.00 6.75
101IN Rod Carew Angels IN/25
101JN Rod Carew Angels JN/29 30.00 13.50
101JY Rod Carew Angels JY/85 15.00 6.75
101PS Rod Carew Angels PS/50 15.00 6.75
102BA Rod Carew Twins BA/50 15.00 6.75
102DY Rod Carew Twins DY/61 15.00 6.75
102IN Rod Carew Twins IN/25
102JN Rod Carew Twins JN/29 30.00 13.50
102JY Rod Carew Twins JY/71 15.00 6.75
102PS Rod Carew Twins PS/50 15.00 6.75
103BA Joe Carter BA/50 10.00 4.50
103DY Joe Carter DY/77 10.00 4.50
103IN Joe Carter IN/25
103JN Joe Carter JN/29 20.00 9.00
103JY Joe Carter JY/94 10.00 4.50
103PS Joe Carter PS/25
104BA Mike Sweeney BA/100 8.00 3.60
104DY Mike Sweeney DY/69 10.00 4.50
104IN Mike Sweeney IN/25
104JN Mike Sweeney JN/29 15.00 6.75
104JY Mike Sweeney JY/101 8.00 3.60
104PS Mike Sweeney PS/50 10.00 4.50
105BA Nolan Ryan Angels BA/25
105DY Nolan Ryan Angels DY/65 40.00 18.00
105IN Nolan Ryan Angels IN/25
105JN Nolan Ryan Angels JN/30 50.00 22.00
105JY N.Ryan Angels JY/70 UER 40.00 18.00
Jersey year is credited to 1970; Ryan did not arrive in California till 1972
105PS Nolan Ryan Angels PS/50 40.00 18.00
106BA Orlando Cepeda BA/50 10.00 4.50
106DY Orlando Cepeda DY/58 10.00 4.50
106IN Orlando Cepeda IN/50 10.00 4.50
106JN Orlando Cepeda JN/30 20.00 9.00
106JY Orlando Cepeda JY/65 10.00 4.50
106PS Orlando Cepeda PS/50 10.00 4.50
107BA Magglio Ordonez BA/100 8.00 3.60
107DY Magglio Ordonez DY/4
107IN Magglio Ordonez IN/25
107JN Magglio Ordonez JN/30 15.00 6.75
107JY Magglio Ordonez JY/102 8.00 3.60
107PS Magglio Ordonez PS/50 10.00 4.50
108BA Hoyt Wilhelm BA/50 10.00 4.50
108DY Hoyt Wilhelm DY/4
108IN Hoyt Wilhelm IN/25
108JN Hoyt Wilhelm JN/31 20.00 9.00
108JY Hoyt Wilhelm JY/68 10.00 4.50
108PS Hoyt Wilhelm PS/50 10.00 4.50
109BA Mike Piazza BA/100 15.00 6.75
109DY Mike Piazza DY/62 25.00 11.00
109IN Mike Piazza IN/50 25.00 11.00
109JN Mike Piazza JN/31 40.00 18.00
109JY Mike Piazza JY/100 15.00 6.75
109PS Mike Piazza PS/50 25.00 11.00
110BA Greg Maddux BA/100 15.00 6.75
110DY Greg Maddux DY/66 25.00 11.00
110IN Greg Maddux IN/50 25.00 11.00
110JN Greg Maddux JN/31 40.00 18.00
110JY Greg Maddux JY/102 15.00 6.75
110PS Greg Maddux PS/50 25.00 11.00
111BA Mark Prior BA/100 10.00 4.50
111DY Mark Prior DY/7
111IN Mark Prior IN/50 15.00 6.75
111JN Mark Prior JN/22
111JY Mark Prior JY/102 10.00 4.50
111PS Mark Prior PS/50 15.00 6.75
112BA Torii Hunter BA/100 8.00 3.60
112DY Torii Hunter DY/61 10.00 4.50
112IN Torii Hunter IN/50 10.00 4.50
112JN Torii Hunter JN/48 12.00 5.50
112JY Torii Hunter JY/101 8.00 3.60
112PS Torii Hunter PS/50 10.00 4.50
113BA Steve Carlton BA/100 10.00 4.50
113DY Steve Carlton DY/46 15.00 6.75
113IN Steve Carlton IN/50 10.00 4.50
113JN Steve Carlton JN/32 20.00 9.00
113JY Steve Carlton JY/81 10.00 4.50
113PS Steve Carlton PS/50 10.00 4.50
114BA Jose Canseco BA/100 15.00 6.75
114DY Jose Canseco DY/68 15.00 6.75
114IN Jose Canseco IN/50 15.00 6.75
114JN Jose Canseco JN/33 15.00 6.75
114JY Jose Canseco JY/89 15.00 6.75
114PS Jose Canseco PS/50 15.00 6.75
115BA Nolan Ryan Rgr BA/50 40.00 18.00
115DY Nolan Ryan Rgr DY/72 40.00 18.00
115IN Nolan Ryan Rgr IN/50 40.00 18.00
115JN Nolan Ryan Rgr JN/34 50.00 22.00
115JY Nolan Ryan Rgr JY/90 40.00 18.00
115PS Nolan Ryan Rgr PS/50 40.00 18.00
116BA Nolan Ryan Astros BA/50 40.00 18.00
116DY Nolan Ryan Astros DY/65 40.00 18.00
116IN Nolan Ryan Astros IN/25
116JN Nolan Ryan Astros JN/34 50.00 22.00
116JY Nolan Ryan Astros JY/84 40.00 18.00
116PS Nolan Ryan Astros PS/50 40.00 18.00
117BA Ty Cobb Pants BA/25
117DY Ty Cobb Pants DY/1
117IN Ty Cobb Pants IN/25
117JN Ty Cobb Pants JN/1
117JY Ty Cobb Pants JY/27 150.00 70.00
117PS Ty Cobb Pants PS/10
118BA Kerry Wood BA/100 10.00 4.50
118DY Kerry Wood DY/7
118IN Kerry Wood IN/25
118JN Kerry Wood JN/34 25.00 11.00
118JY Kerry Wood JY/101 10.00 4.50
118PS Kerry Wood PS/50 15.00 6.75
119BA M.Mussina Yanks BA/50 15.00 6.75
119DY M.Mussina Yanks DY/13
119IN M.Mussina Yanks IN/25
119JN M.Mussina Yanks JN/35 25.00 11.00
119JY M.Mussina Yanks JY/101 10.00 4.50
119PS M.Mussina Yanks PS/50 15.00 6.75
120BA Yogi Berra BA/10
120DY Yogi Berra DY/13
120IN Yogi Berra IN/10
120JN Yogi Berra JN/35 30.00 13.50
120JY Yogi Berra JY/47 25.00 11.00
120PS Yogi Berra PS/10
121BA Thurman Munson BA/25
121DY Thurman Munson DY/13
121IN Thurman Munson IN/25
121JN Thurman Munson JN/15
121JY Thurman Munson JY/79 40.00 18.00
121PS Thurman Munson PS/5
122BA Frank Thomas BA/100 10.00 4.50
122DY Frank Thomas DY/4
122IN Frank Thomas IN/25
122JN Frank Thomas JN/35 25.00 11.00
122JY Frank Thomas JY/94 10.00 4.50
122PS Frank Thomas PS/50 15.00 6.75
123BA R.Henderson A's BA/50 15.00 6.75
123DY R.Henderson A's DY/68 15.00 6.75
123IN R.Henderson A's IN/25
123JN R.Henderson A's JN/35 25.00 11.00
123JY R.Henderson A's JY/80 10.00 4.50
123PS R.Henderson A's PS/50 15.00 6.75
124BA M.Muss O's Pants BA/100 10.00 4.50
124DY M.Muss O's Pants DY/54 15.00 6.75
124IN M.Muss O's Pants IN/25
124JN M.Muss O's Pants JN/35 25.00 11.00
124JY M.Muss O's Pants JY/97 10.00 4.50
124PS M.Muss O's Pants PS/50 15.00 6.75
125BA Gaylord Perry BA/100 10.00 4.50
125DY Gaylord Perry DY/77 10.00 4.50
125IN Gaylord Perry IN/25
125JN Gaylord Perry JN/36 15.00 6.75
125JY Gaylord Perry JY/82 10.00 4.50
125PS Gaylord Perry PS/50 10.00 4.50
126BA Nick Johnson BA/100 8.00 3.60
126DY Nick Johnson DY/13
126IN Nick Johnson IN/25
126JN Nick Johnson JN/36 12.00 5.50
126JY Nick Johnson JY/102 8.00 3.60
126PS Nick Johnson PS/50 10.00 4.50
127BA Curt Schilling BA/100 8.00 3.60
127DY Curt Schilling DY/98 8.00 3.60
127IN Curt Schilling IN/25
127JN Curt Schilling JN/38 12.00 5.50
127JY Curt Schilling JY/102 8.00 3.60
127PS Curt Schilling PS/50 10.00 4.50
128BA Dave Parker BA/100 10.00 4.50
128DY Dave Parker DY/1
128IN Dave Parker IN/25
128JN Dave Parker JN/39 15.00 6.75
128JY Dave Parker JY/80 10.00 4.50
128PS Dave Parker PS/50 10.00 4.50
129BA Eddie Mathews BA/15
129DY Eddie Mathews DY/53 15.00 6.75
129IN Eddie Mathews IN/15
129JN Eddie Mathews JN/41 25.00 11.00
129JY Eddie Mathews JY/59 15.00 6.75
129PS Eddie Mathews PS/15
130BA Tom Seaver Mets BA/10
130DY Tom Seaver Mets DY/62 15.00 6.75
130IN Tom Seaver Mets IN/10
130JN Tom Seaver Mets JN/41 25.00 11.00
130JY Tom Seaver Mets JY/69 15.00 6.75
130PS Tom Seaver Mets PS/10
131BA Tom Seaver Reds BA/10
131DY Tom Seaver Reds DY/59 15.00 6.75
131IN Tom Seaver Reds IN/10
131JN Tom Seaver Reds JN/41 25.00 11.00
131JY Tom Seaver Reds JY/78 15.00 6.75
131PS Tom Seaver Reds PS/22
132BA Jackie Robinson BA/10
132DY Jackie Robinson DY/32
132IN Jackie Robinson IN/10
132JN Jackie Robinson JN/42 80.00 36.00
132JY Jackie Robinson JY/52 80.00 36.00
132PS Jackie Robinson PS/10
133BA R.Jackson Angels BA/100 15.00 6.75
133DY R.Jackson Angels DY/65 15.00 6.75
133IN R.Jackson Angels IN/50 15.00 6.75
133JN R.Jackson Angels JN/44 25.00 11.00
133JY R.Jackson Angels JY/80 15.00 6.75
133PS R.Jackson Angels PS/50 15.00 6.75
134BA Willie McCovey BA/100 10.00 4.50
134DY Willie McCovey DY/58 10.00 4.50
134IN Willie McCovey IN/25
134JN Willie McCovey JN/44 15.00 6.75
134JY Willie McCovey JY/77 10.00 4.50
134PS Willie McCovey PS/50 10.00 4.50
135BA Eric Davis BA/100 10.00 4.50
135DY Eric Davis DY/59 10.00 4.50
135IN Eric Davis IN/25
135JN Eric Davis JN/44 15.00 6.75
135JY Eric Davis JY/89 10.00 4.50
135PS Eric Davis PS/50 10.00 4.50
136BA Adam Dunn BA/100 10.00 4.50
136DY Adam Dunn DY/59 15.00 6.75
136IN Adam Dunn IN/25
136JN Adam Dunn JN/44 20.00 9.00
136JY Adam Dunn JY/102 10.00 4.50
136PS Adam Dunn PS/50 15.00 6.75
137BA Roy Oswalt BA/100 8.00 3.60
137DY Roy Oswalt DY/65 10.00 4.50
137IN Roy Oswalt IN/50 10.00 4.50
137JN Roy Oswalt JN/44 12.00 5.50
137JY Roy Oswalt JY/102 8.00 3.60
137PS Roy Oswalt PS/50 10.00 4.50
138BA P.Martinez Expos BA/50 15.00 6.75
138DY P.Martinez Expos DY/69 15.00 6.75
138IN P.Martinez Expos IN/25
138JN P.Martinez Expos JN/45 20.00 9.00
138JY P.Martinez Expos JY/95 10.00 4.50
138PS P.Martinez Expos PS/50 15.00 6.75
139BA P.Martinez R.Sox BA/100 10.00 4.50
139DY P.Martinez R.Sox DY/7
139IN P.Martinez R.Sox IN/50 15.00 6.75
139JN P.Martinez R.Sox JN/45 20.00 9.00
139JY P.Martinez R.Sox JY/102 10.00 4.50
139PS P.Martinez R.Sox PS/50 15.00 6.75
140BA Andy Pettitte BA/100 10.00 4.50

140DY Andy Pettitte DY/13
140IN Andy Pettitte IN/25
140JN Andy Pettitte JN/46........ 20.00 9.00
140JY Andy Pettitte JY/97........ 10.00 4.50
140PS Andy Pettitte PS/50........ 15.00 6.75
141BA Jack Morris BA/100....... 10.00 4.50
141DY Jack Morris DY/1
141IN Jack Morris IN/50.......... 10.00 4.50
141JN Jack Morris JN/47.......... 15.00 6.75
141JY Jack Morris JY/85.......... 10.00 4.50
141PS Jack Morris PS/50.......... 10.00 4.50
142BA Tom Glavine BA/100....... 10.00 4.50
142DY Tom Glavine DY/66........ 15.00 6.75
142IN Tom Glavine IN/25
142JN Tom Glavine JN/47 .... 20.00 9.00
142JY Tom Glavine JY/100....... 10.00 4.50
142PS Tom Glavine PS/50........ 15.00 6.75
143BA R.Johnson M's BA/100 . 10.00 4.50
143DY R.Johnson M's DY/77 ... 10.00 4.50
143IN R.Johnson M's IN/50...... 15.00 6.75
143JN R.Johnson M's JN/51 .... 15.00 6.75
143JY R.Johnson M's JY/98 ..... 10.00 4.50
143PS R.Johnson M's PS/50 .... 15.00 6.75
144BA Bernie Williams BA/100. 10.00 4.50
144DY Bernie Williams DY/13
144IN Bernie Williams IN/50..... 15.00 6.75
144JN Bernie Williams JN/51 .... 15.00 6.75
144JY Bernie Williams JY/100.. 10.00 4.50
144PS Bernie Williams PS/50.... 15.00 6.75
145BA R.Johnson D'backs BA/50 15.00 6.75
145DY R.Johnson D'backs DY/98 10.00 4.50
145IN R.Johnson D'backs IN/50 15.00 6.75
145JN R.Johnson D'backs JN/51 15.00 6.75
145JY R.Johnson D'backs JY/102 10.00 4.50
145PS R.Johnson D'backs PS/50 15.00 6.75
146BA Don Drysdale BA/15
146DY Don Drysdale DY/58...... 15.00 6.75
146IN Don Drysdale IN/25
146JN Don Drysdale JN/53 ...... 15.00 6.75
146JY Don Drysdale JY/64...... 15.00 6.75
146PS Don Drysdale PS/25
147BA Mark Buehrle BA/100 ...... 8.00 3.60
147DY Mark Buehrle DY/4
147IN Mark Buehrle IN/25
147JN Mark Buehrle JN/56....... 10.00 4.50
147JY Mark Buehrle JY/101 .... 8.00 3.60
147PS Mark Buehrle PS/50....... 10.00 4.50
148BA Chan Ho Park BA/100.... 10.00 4.50
148DY Chan Ho Park DY/58 ..... 15.00 6.75
148IN Chan Ho Park IN/25
148JN Chan Ho Park JN/61 ...... 15.00 6.75
148JY Chan Ho Park JY/101..... 10.00 4.50
148PS Chan Ho Park PS/50...... 15.00 6.75
149BA Carlton Fisk W.Sox BA/100 15.00 6.75
149DY Carlton Fisk W.Sox DY/4
149IN Carlton Fisk W.Sox IN/50 15.00 6.75
149JN Carlton Fisk W.Sox JN/72 15.00 6.75
149JY Carlton Fisk W.Sox JY/92 15.00 6.75
149PS Carlton Fisk W.Sox PS/50 15.00 6.75
150BA Barry Zito BA/100........... 8.00 3.60
150DY Barry Zito DY/68 .... 10.00 4.50
150IN Barry Zito IN/25
150JN Barry Zito JN/75 .... 10.00 4.50
150JY Barry Zito JY/101............ 8.00 3.60
150PS Barry Zito PS/50............ 10.00 4.50

2003 Leaf Certified Materials Fabric of the Game Autographs

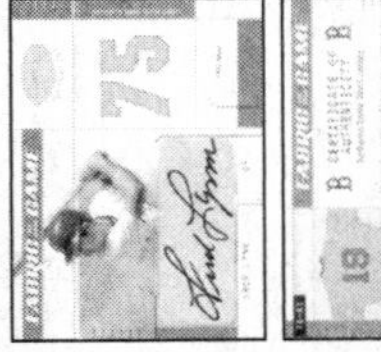

This is a partial parallel to the Fabric of the Game insert set. Each of these cards were signed, using Donruss/Playoff "band-aid" autographs to a stated print run of five or fewer cards. We have put the announced print run next to the player's name in our checklist and please note there is no pricing due to market scarcity. In addition, because of the use of stickered autographs, please note that autographs of deceased players such as Enos Slaughter and Hoyt Wilhelm are included in this set.

MINT NRMT
RANDOM INSERTS IN PACKS
CARDS DISPLAY CUMULATIVE PRINT RUNS
ACTUAL PRINT RUNS B/WN 1-5 COPIES PER
SKIP-NUMBERED 302-CARD SET
NO PRICING DUE TO SCARCITY

2004 Leaf Certified Materials

This 300-card set was released in July, 2004. The set was issued in five-card packs with an $10 SRP which were issued 10 packs per box and 24 boxes per case. The first 200 cards featured active players while cards numbered 201-211 feature players who moved teams in the off-season in their old uniform. Cards numbered 201-211 were inserted at a stated rate of one in 120. Cards 212 through 240 featured retired legends while cards 241-300 featured signed Rookie Cards (except for Kaz Matsui). Cards 212-240 were issued to a stated print run of 500 serial numbered sets and cards numbered 241-300 were issued to a stated print run of 1000 serial numbered sets unless noted in our checklist.

Nm-Mt Ex-Mt
COMP.SET w/o SP's (200)........ 40.00 12.00
COMMON CARD (1-200) .... .75 .23
COMMON CARD (201-211) .... 3.00 .90
201-211 STATED ODDS 1:120
COMMON CARD (212 .... 3.00 .90
212-240 PRINT RUN 500 SERIAL #'d SETS
COMMON NO AU (241-300) 5.00 1.50
241-300 NO AU PRINT RUN 500 #'d PER
OVERALL AU ODDS 1:10
AU PRINT RUNS B/WN 100-1000 PER
AU PRINT RUN 500 #'d PER UNLESS NOTED
1 A.J. Burnett .75 .23
2 Adam Dunn 1.25 .35
3 Adam LaRoche .75 .23
4 Adam Loewen .75 .23
5 Adrian Beltre 1.25 .35
6 Al Leiter .75 .23
7 Albert Pujols 4.00 1.20
8 Alex Rodriguez Yanks 3.00 .90
9 Alexis Rios .75 .23
10 Alfonso Soriano Rgr 1.25 .35
11 Andruw Jones .75 .23
12 Andy Pettitte 1.25 .35
13 Angel Berroa .75 .23
14 Aramis Ramirez .75 .23
15 Aubrey Huff .75 .23
16 Austin Kearns .75 .23
17 Barry Larkin 1.25 .35
18 Barry Zito .75 .23
19 Ben Sheets .75 .23
20 Bernie Williams 1.25 .35
21 Bobby Abreu .75 .23
22 Brad Penny .75 .23
23 Brad Wilkerson .75 .23
24 Brandon Webb .75 .23
25 Brendan Harris .75 .23
26 Bret Boone .75 .23
27 Brett Myers .75 .23
28 Bubba Crosby .75 .23
29 Brian Giles .75 .23
30 Chad Cordero .75 .23
31 Bubba Nelson .75 .23
32 Byron Gettis .75 .23
33 C.C. Sabathia .75 .23
34 Carl Crawford .75 .23
35 Carl Everett .75 .23
36 Carlos Beltran 1.25 .35
37 Carlos Delgado .75 .23
38 Carlos Lee .75 .23
39 Chad Gaudin .75 .23
40 Cliff Lee .75 .23
41 Chipper Jones 2.00 .60
42 Cliff Floyd .75 .23
43 Clint Barmes .75 .23
44 Corey Patterson .75 .23
45 Craig Biggio 1.25 .35
46 Curt Schilling Sox 2.00 .60
47 Dan Haren .75 .23
48 Darin Erstad .75 .23
49 David Ortiz 2.00 .60
50 Delmon Young 1.25 .35
51 Derek Jeter 4.00 1.20
52 Dewon Brazelton .75 .23
53 Dontrelle Willis .75 .23
54 Edgar Martinez 1.25 .35
55 Edgar Renteria .75 .23
56 Edwin Almonte .75 .23
57 Edwin Jackson .75 .23
58 Eric Chavez .75 .23
59 Eric Hinske .75 .23
60 Eric Munson .75 .23
61 Erubial Durazo .75 .23
62 Frank Thomas 2.00 .60
63 Fred McGriff 1.25 .35
64 Freddy Garcia .75 .23
65 Garret Anderson .75 .23
66 Garrett Atkins .75 .23
67 Gary Sheffield .75 .23
68 Geoff Jenkins .75 .23
69 Greg Maddux Cubs 3.00 .90
70 Hank Blalock .75 .23
71 Hee Seop Choi .75 .23
72 Hideki Matsui 3.00 .90
73 Hideo Nomo 2.00 .60
74 Craig Wilson .75 .23
75 Ichiro Suzuki 3.00 .90
76 Ivan Rodriguez Tigers 2.00 .60
77 J.D. Drew .75 .23
78 John Lackey .75 .23
79 Jacque Jones .75 .23
80 Jae Weong Seo .75 .23
81 Jamie Moyer .75 .23
82 Jason Giambi Yanks .75 .23
83 Jason Jennings .75 .23
84 Jason Kendall .75 .23
85 Melvin Mora .75 .23
86 Jason Varitek 1.25 .35
87 Javier Vazquez .75 .23
88 Javy Lopez .75 .23
89 Jay Gibbons .75 .23
90 Jay Payton .75 .23
91 Jeff Bagwell 1.25 .35
92 Jeff Baker .75 .23
93 Jeff Kent .75 .23
94 Jeremy Bonderman .75 .23
95 Milton Bradley .75 .23
96 Jerome Williams .75 .23
97 Jim Edmonds .75 .23
98 Jim Thome 2.00 .60
99 Jody Gerut .75 .23
100 Joe Borchard .75 .23
101 Joe Crede .75 .23
102 Johan Santana 1.25 .35
103 John Olerud .75 .23
104 John Smoltz 1.25 .35
105 Johnny Damon 2.00 .60
106 Jorge Posada 1.25 .35
107 Jose Castillo .75 .23
108 Jose Reyes .75 .23
109 Jose Vidro .75 .23
110 Josh Beckett .75 .23
111 Josh Phelps .75 .23
112 Juan Encarnacion .75 .23
113 Juan Gonzalez 1.25 .35
114 Junior Spivey .75 .23
115 Kazuhisa Ishii .75 .23
116 Kenny Lofton .75 .23
117 Kerry Wood 2.00 .60
118 Kevin Millwood .75 .23
119 Kevin Youkilis .75 .23
120 Lance Berkman .75 .23
121 Larry Bigbie .75 .23
122 Larry Walker 1.25 .35
123 Luis Castillo .75 .23
124 Luis Gonzalez .75 .23
125 Luis Matos .75 .23
126 Lyle Overbay .75 .23
127 Magglio Ordonez .75 .23
128 Manny Ramirez 1.25 .35
129 Marcus Giles .75 .23
130 Mariano Rivera 1.25 .35
131 Mark Buehrle .75 .23
132 Mark Mulder .75 .23
133 Mark Prior 2.00 .60
134 Mark Teixeira .75 .23
135 Marlon Byrd .75 .23
136 Matt Morris .75 .23
137 Miguel Cabrera 1.25 .35
138 Mike Lowell .75 .23
139 Mike Mussina 1.25 .35
140 Mike Piazza 3.00 .90
141 Mike Sweeney .75 .23
142 Morgan Ensberg .75 .23
143 Nick Johnson .75 .23
144 Nomar Garciaparra 3.00 .90
145 Omar Vizquel 1.25 .35
146 Orlando Cabrera .75 .23
147 Orlando Hudson .75 .23
148 Pat Burrell .75 .23
149 Paul Konerko .75 .23
150 Paul Lo Duca .75 .23
151 Pedro Martinez 2.00 .60
152 Jermaine Dye .75 .23
153 Preston Wilson .75 .23
154 Rafael Furcal .75 .23
155 Rafael Palmeiro O's 1.25 .35
156 Randy Johnson 2.00 .60
157 Rich Aurilia .75 .23
158 Rich Harden .75 .23
159 Richard Hidalgo .75 .23
160 Richie Sexson .75 .23
161 Rickie Weeks .75 .23
162 Roberto Alomar 1.25 .35
163 Rocco Baldelli .75 .23
164 Roger Clemens Astros 4.00 1.20
165 Roy Halladay .75 .23
166 Roy Oswalt .75 .23
167 Ryan Howard .75 .23
168 Ryan Klesko .75 .23
169 Rodrigo Lopez .75 .23
170 Sammy Sosa 3.00 .90
171 Scott Podsednik .75 .23
172 Scott Rolen 2.00 .60
173 Sean Burroughs .75 .23
174 Sean Casey .75 .23
175 Shannon Stewart .75 .23
176 Shawn Green .75 .23
177 Shea Hillenbrand .75 .23
178 Shigetoshi Hasegawa .75 .23
179 Steve Finley .75 .23
180 Tim Hudson .75 .23
181 Todd Helton 1.25 .35
182 Tom Glavine 1.25 .35
183 Torii Hunter .75 .23
184 Trot Nixon .75 .23
185 Troy Glaus .75 .23
186 Vernon Wells .75 .23
187 Victor Martinez .75 .23
188 Vladimir Guerrero Angels 2.00 .60
189 Wade Miller .75 .23
190 Brandon Larson .75 .23
191 Travis Hafner .75 .23
192 Tim Salmon 1.25 .35
193 Tim Redding .75 .23
194 Runelvys Hernandez .75 .23
195 Ramon Nivar .75 .23
196 Moises Alou .75 .23
197 Michael Young .75 .23
198 Laynce Nix .75 .23
199 Tino Martinez 1.25 .35
200 Randall Simon .75 .23
201 Roger Clemens Yanks SP 8.00 2.40
202 Greg Maddux Braves SP 8.00 2.40
203 Vladimir Guerrero Expos SP 5.00 1.50
204 Miguel Tejada SP 3.00 .90
205 Kevin Brown SP 3.00 .90
206 Jason Giambi A's SP 3.00 .90
207 Curt Schilling D'backs SP 3.00 .90
208 Alex Rodriguez Rgr SP 8.00 2.40
209 Alfonso Soriano Yanks SP 5.00 1.50
210 Ivan Rodriguez Marlins SP 5.00 1.50
211 Rafael Palmeiro Rgr SP 5.00 1.50
212 Gary Carter LGD 3.00 .90
213 Duke Snider LGD 5.00 1.50
214 Whitey Ford LGD 5.00 1.50
215 Bob Feller LGD 3.00 .90
216 Reggie Jackson LGD 5.00 1.50
217 Ryne Sandberg LGD 10.00 3.00
218 Dale Murphy LGD 5.00 1.50
219 Tony Gwynn LGD 8.00 2.40
220 Don Mattingly LGD 10.00 3.00
221 Mike Schmidt LGD 10.00 3.00
222 Rickey Henderson LGD 5.00 1.50
223 Cal Ripken LGD 15.00 4.50
224 Nolan Ryan LGD 12.00 3.60
225 George Brett LGD 10.00 3.00
226 Bob Gibson LGD 5.00 1.50
227 Lou Brock LGD 5.00 1.50
228 Andre Dawson LGD 3.00 .90
229 Rod Carew LGD 5.00 1.50
230 Wade Boggs LGD 5.00 1.50
231 Roberto Clemente LGD 10.00 3.00
232 Roy Campanella LGD 5.00 1.50
233 Babe Ruth LGD 10.00 3.00
234 Lou Gehrig LGD 8.00 2.40
235 Ty Cobb LGD 8.00 2.40
236 Roger Maris LGD 5.00 1.50
237 Satchel Paige LGD 5.00 1.50
238 Ernie Banks LGD 5.00 1.50
239 Ted Williams LGD 10.00 3.00
240 Stan Musial LGD 8.00 2.40
241 Hector Gimenez NG AU RC 8.00 2.40
242 Justin Germano NG AU RC 8.00 2.40
243 Ian Snell NG AU RC 10.00 3.00
244 Graham Koonce NG AU 8.00 2.40
245 Jose Capellan NG AU RC 25.00 7.50
246 Onil Joseph NG AU RC 8.00 2.40
247 S.Takatsu NG AU/200 RC 40.00 12.00
248 Carlos Hines NG AU RC 8.00 2.40
249 Linc Holdzkom NG AU RC 8.00 2.40
250 Mike Gosling NG AU RC 8.00 2.40
251 Eduardo Sierra NG AU RC 10.00 3.00
252 Renyel Pinto NG AU RC 10.00 3.00
253 Merkin Valdez NG AU RC 15.00 4.50
254 Angel Chavez NG AU RC 8.00 2.40
255 I.Ochoa NG AU/1000 RC 8.00 2.40
256 G.Dobbs NG AU/300 RC 8.00 2.40
257 William Bergolla NG AU RC 8.00 2.40
258 Aarom Baldiris NG AU RC 10.00 3.00
259 Kazuo Matsui NG RC 15.00 4.50
260 Carlos Vasquez NG AU RC 10.00 3.00
261 Freddy Guzman NG AU RC 8.00 2.40
262 Aki Otsuka NG AU/200 RC 40.00 12.00
263 M.Gomez NG AU/200 RC 10.00 3.00
264 Nick Regilio NG AU RC 8.00 2.40
265 Jamie Brown NG AU RC 8.00 2.40
266 Shawn Hill NG AU RC 8.00 2.40
267 Roberto Novoa NG AU RC 10.00 3.00
268 Sean Henn NG AU RC 8.00 2.40
269 Ramon Ramirez NG AU RC 8.00 2.40
270 R.Cedeno NG AU/1000 RC 8.00 2.40
271 Ryan Wing NG AU/400 RC 8.00 2.40
272 Ruddy Yan NG AU 8.00 2.40
273 Fernando Nieve NG AU RC 8.00 2.40
274 Rusty Tucker NG AU RC 10.00 3.00
275 Jason Bartlett NG AU RC 10.00 3.00
276 Mike Rouse NG AU RC 8.00 2.40
277 Dennis Sarfate NG AU RC 8.00 2.40
278 Cory Sullivan NG AU RC 8.00 2.40
279 C.Daigle NG AU/250 RC 10.00 3.00
280 C.Shelton NG AU/400 RC 10.00 3.00
281 J.Harper NG AU/400 RC 8.00 2.40
282 Michael Wuertz NG AU RC 10.00 3.00
283 T.Bausher NG AU/400 RC 8.00 2.40
284 Jorge Sequea NG AU RC 8.00 2.40
285 J.Labandeira NG AU/100 RC 15.00 4.50
286 Justin Leone NG AU RC 10.00 3.00
287 Tim Bittner NG AU RC 8.00 2.40
288 Andres Blanco NG AU RC 8.00 2.40
289 K.Cave NG AU/1000 RC 10.00 3.00
290 M.Johnston NG AU/1000 RC 8.00 2.40
291 J.Szuminski NG AU RC 8.00 2.40
292 Shawn Camp NG RC 5.00 1.50
293 Colby Miller NG AU RC 8.00 2.40
294 Jake Woods NG AU RC 8.00 2.40
295 Ryan Meaux NG AU RC 8.00 2.40
296 Don Kelly NG AU RC 8.00 2.40
297 Edwin Moreno NG AU RC 8.00 2.40
298 Phil Stockman NG AU RC 8.00 2.40
299 Jorge Vasquez NG RC 8.00 2.40
300 Kaz Tadano NG AU RC 25.00 7.50

2004 Leaf Certified Materials Mirror Black

Nm-Mt Ex-Mt
RANDOM INSERTS IN PACKS
STATED PRINT RUN 1 SERIAL #'d SET
NO PRICING DUE TO SCARCITY

2004 Leaf Certified Materials Mirror Blue

Nm-Mt Ex-Mt
*1-200: 2.5X TO 6X BASIC
*BLUE 201-211: 1.25X TO 3X BASIC
*BLUE 212-240: 1.25X TO 3X BASIC
*241-300: .6X TO 1.5X BASIC NO AU
*241-300: .3X TO .8X BASIC AU/1000
*241-300: .3X TO .8X BASIC AU/300-500
*241-300: .25X TO .6X BASIC AU/200-250
*BLUE 241-300: .15X TO .4X BASIC AU/100
RANDOM INSERTS IN PACKS
STATED PRINT RUN 50 SERIAL #'d SETS

2004 Leaf Certified Materials Mirror Emerald

Nm-Mt Ex-Mt
RANDOM INSERTS IN PACKS
STATED PRINT RUN 5 SERIAL #'d SETS
NO PRICING DUE TO SCARCITY

2004 Leaf Certified Materials Mirror Gold

Nm-Mt Ex-Mt
*GOLD 1-200: 4X TO 10X BASIC
*GOLD 201-211: 2X TO 5X BASIC
*GOLD 212-240: 2X TO 5X BASIC
RANDOM INSERTS IN PACKS
STATED PRINT RUN 25 SERIAL #'d SETS
241-300 NO PRICING DUE TO SCARCITY

2004 Leaf Certified Materials Mirror Red

Nm-Mt Ex-Mt
*RED 1-200: 1.5X TO 4X BASIC
*RED 201-211: .75X TO 2X BASIC
*RED 212-240: .75X TO 2X BASIC
*RED 241-300: .4X TO 1X BASIC NO AU
*RED 241-300: .2X TO .5X BASIC AU/1000
*RED 241-300: .2X TO .5X BASIC AU/300-500
*RED 241-300: .15X TO .4X BASIC AU/200-250
*RED 241-300: .1X TO .25X BASIC AU/100
RANDOM INSERTS IN PACKS
STATED PRINT RUN 100 SERIAL #'d SETS

2004 Leaf Certified Materials Mirror White

Nm-Mt Ex-Mt
*WHITE 1-200: 1.5X TO 4X BASIC
*WHITE 201-211: .75X TO 2X BASIC
*WHITE 212-240: .75X TO 2X BASIC
*WHITE 241-300: .4X TO 1X BASIC NO AU
*WHITE 241-300: .2X TO .5X AU/1000
*WHITE 241-300: .2X TO .5X AU/400-500
*WHITE 241-300: .15X TO .4X AU/200-300
*WHITE 241-300: .12X TO .3X AU/100
RANDOM INSERTS IN PACKS
PRINT RUN 100 SERIAL #'d SETS

2004 Leaf Certified Materials Mirror Autograph Blue

Nm-Mt Ex-Mt
*1-240 p/r 100: .5X TO 1.2X RED p/r 200-250
*1-240 p/r 100: .4X TO 1X RED p/r 100
*1-240 p/r 50: .6X TO 1.5X RED p/r 200-250
*1-240 p/r 50: .5X TO 1.2X RED p/r 100
*1-240 p/r 50: .4X TO 1X RED p/r 50
*1-240 p/r 25: 1X TO 2.5X RED p/r 250
*1-240 p/r 25: .6X TO 1.5X RED p/r 50
*1-240 p/r 25: .4X TO 1X RED p/r 25
*241-300 p/r 100: .5X TO 1.2X RED p/r 200-250
*241-300 p/r 100: .4X TO 1X RED p/r 100
*241-300 p/r 50: .4X TO 1X RED p/r 50
OVERALL AU ODDS 1:10
PRINT RUNS B/WN 1-100 COPIES PER
NO PRICING ON QTY OF 10 OR LESS
2 Adam Dunn/47 30.00 9.00

2004 Leaf Certified Materials Mirror Autograph Gold

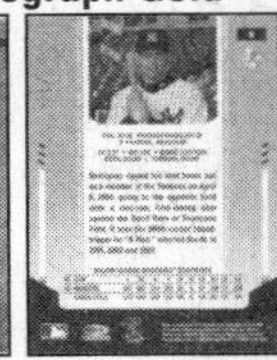

Nm-Mt Ex-Mt
*1-240 p/r 25: 1X TO 2.5X RED p/r 200-250
*1-240 p/r 25: .75X TO 2X RED p/r 100
*1-240 p/r 25: .6X TO 1.5X RED p/r 50
*1-240 p/r 25: .4X TO 1X RED p/r 25
OVERALL AU ODDS 1:10
PRINT RUNS B/WN 1-25 COPIES PER
1-240 NO PRICING ON QTY OF 10 OR LESS
241-300 NO PRICING ON QTY OF 25 OR LESS

2004 Leaf Certified Materials Mirror Autograph Red

Nm-Mt Ex-Mt
OVERALL AU ODDS 1:10
PRINT RUNS B/WN 1-250 COPIES PER
NO PRICING ON QTY OF 10 OR LESS
3 Adam LaRoche/250 8.00 2.40
4 Adam Loewen/250 8.00 2.40
7 Albert Pujols/25
8 Alex Rodriguez Yanks/1
9 Alexis Rios/250 12.00 3.60
10 Alfonso Soriano Rgr/25 50.00 15.00
11 Andruw Jones/25 30.00 9.00
12 Andy Pettitte/25 50.00 15.00
13 Angel Berroa/100 10.00 3.00
14 Aramis Ramirez/100 25.00 7.50
15 Aubrey Huff/250 12.00 3.60
16 Austin Kearns/200 12.00 3.60
17 Barry Larkin/25 50.00 15.00
18 Barry Zito/10
20 Bernie Williams/5
22 Brad Penny/25 20.00 6.00
24 Brandon Webb/250 8.00 2.40
25 Brendan Harris/50 12.00 3.60
27 Brett Myers/100 10.00 3.00
28 Bubba Crosby/250 8.00 2.40
30 Chad Cordero/250 8.00 2.40
31 Bubba Nelson/250 8.00 2.40
32 Byron Gettis/250 8.00 2.40
36 Carlos Beltran/100 40.00 12.00
38 Carlos Lee/250 12.00 3.60
39 Chad Gaudin/100 10.00 3.00
40 Cliff Lee/250 8.00 2.40
41 Chipper Jones/5
43 Clint Barmes/100 10.00 3.00
45 Craig Biggio/1
46 Curt Schilling Sox/5
47 Dan Haren/250 8.00 2.40
49 David Ortiz/250 40.00 12.00
50 Delmon Young/50 30.00 9.00
52 Dewon Brazelton/250 8.00 2.40
53 Dontrelle Willis/100 15.00 4.50
56 Edwin Almonte/250 8.00 2.40
57 Edwin Jackson/250 12.00 3.60
58 Eric Chavez/25 30.00 9.00
59 Eric Hinske/5
62 Frank Thomas/50 50.00 15.00
63 Fred McGriff/10
65 Garret Anderson/250 12.00 3.60
67 Gary Sheffield/50 30.00 9.00
70 Hank Blalock/100 15.00 4.50
73 Hideo Nomo/1
74 Craig Wilson/250 12.00 3.60
77 J.D. Drew/1
78 John Lackey/250 12.00 3.60
79 Jacque Jones/250 12.00 3.60
80 Jae Weong Seo/100 15.00 4.50

85 Melvin Mora/250 12.00 3.60
86 Jason Varitek/100 40.00 12.00
87 Javier Vazquez/5
89 Jay Gibbons/250 8.00 2.40
90 Jay Payton/250 8.00 2.40
91 Jeff Bagwell/50 50.00 15.00
92 Jeff Baker/25 20.00 6.00
96 Jerome Williams/100 25.00 7.50
97 Jim Edmonds/25 50.00 15.00
99 Jody Gerut/250 12.00 3.60
100 Joe Borchard/250 8.00 2.40
101 Joe Crede/50 12.00 3.60
102 Johan Santana/250 30.00 9.00
106 Jorge Posada/25 50.00 15.00
107 Jose Castillo/250 8.00 2.40
108 Jose Reyes/10
109 Jose Vidro/250 8.00 2.40
110 Josh Beckett/25 50.00 15.00
111 Josh Phelps/10
113 Juan Gonzalez/25 50.00 15.00
114 Junior Spivey/25 20.00 6.00
115 Kazuhisa Ishii/10
117 Kerry Wood/50 50.00 15.00
119 Kevin Youkilis/250 12.00 3.60
120 Lance Berkman/25 30.00 9.00
121 Larry Bigbie/250 12.00 3.60
123 Luis Castillo/25 20.00 6.00
125 Luis Matos/250 8.00 2.40
127 Magglio Ordonez/250 12.00 3.60
128 Manny Ramirez/1
129 Marcus Giles/250 12.00 3.60
130 Mariano Rivera/1
131 Mark Buehrle/250 12.00 3.60
132 Mark Mulder/250 12.00 3.60
133 Mark Prior/100 60.00 18.00
134 Mark Teixeira/100 25.00 7.50
135 Marlon Byrd/250 8.00 2.40
137 Miguel Cabrera/250 20.00 6.00
138 Mike Lowell/5
139 Mike Mussina/1
140 Mike Piazza/25 150.00 45.00
142 Morgan Ensberg/250 8.00 2.40
143 Nick Johnson/1
146 Orlando Cabrera/25 30.00 9.00
147 Orlando Hudson/10
150 Paul Lo Duca/25 30.00 9.00
151 Pedro Martinez/1
152 Jermaine Dye/250 12.00 3.60
153 Preston Wilson/250 12.00 3.60
154 Rafael Furcal/100 15.00 4.50
155 Rafael Palmeiro O's/5
156 Randy Johnson/5
157 Rich Aurilia/25 20.00 6.00
158 Rich Harden/203 12.00 3.60
160 Richie Sexson/1
161 Rickie Weeks/4
162 Roberto Alomar/10
163 Rocco Baldelli/5
165 Roy Halladay/50 12.00 3.60
166 Roy Oswalt/50 20.00 6.00
167 Ryan Howard/100 25.00 7.50
169 Rodrigo Lopez/250 8.00 2.40
170 Sammy Sosa/50 120.00 36.00
171 Scott Podsednik/250 12.00 3.60
172 Scott Rolen/100 40.00 12.00
175 Shannon Stewart/100 15.00 4.50
176 Shawn Green/25 30.00 9.00
177 Shea Hillenbrand/250 12.00 3.60
178 Shigetoshi Hasegawa/250 40.00 12.00
179 Steve Finley/100 15.00 4.50
180 Tim Hudson/1
181 Todd Helton/1
182 Tom Glavine/5
183 Torii Hunter/250 12.00 3.60
184 Trot Nixon/250 12.00 3.60
185 Troy Glaus/1
186 Vernon Wells/5
187 Victor Martinez/250 12.00 3.60
188 Vlad Guerrero Angels/50 50.00 15.00
189 Wade Miller/5
190 Brandon Larson/200 8.00 2.40
191 Travis Hafner/250 12.00 3.60
195 Ramon Nivar/10
197 Michael Young/250 20.00 6.00
203 Vladimir Guerrero Expos/5
204 Miguel Tejada/1
207 Curt Schilling D'backs/1
208 Alex Rodriguez Rgr/1
209 Alfonso Soriano Yanks/5
211 Rafael Palmeiro Rgr/1
212 Gary Carter LGD/250 12.00 3.60
213 Duke Snider LGD/250 20.00 6.00
214 Whitey Ford LGD/50 50.00 15.00
215 Bob Feller LGD/250 20.00 6.00
216 Reggie Jackson LGD/50 50.00 15.00
217 Ryne Sandberg LGD/50 80.00 24.00
218 Dale Murphy LGD/50 30.00 9.00
219 Tony Gwynn LGD/50 60.00 18.00
220 Don Mattingly LGD/50 80.00 24.00
221 Mike Schmidt LGD/50 80.00 24.00
222 Rickey Henderson LGD/50 80.00 24.00
223 Cal Ripken LGD/50 200.00 60.00
224 Nolan Ryan LGD/50 120.00 36.00
225 George Brett LGD/50 100.00 30.00
226 Bob Gibson LGD/100 25.00 7.50
227 Lou Brock LGD/100 25.00 7.50
228 Andre Dawson LGD/250 12.00 3.60
229 Rod Carew LGD/50 30.00 9.00
230 Wade Boggs LGD/50 30.00 9.00
238 Ernie Banks LGD/50 60.00 18.00
240 Stan Musial LGD/100 50.00 15.00
241 Hector Gimenez NG/200 8.00 2.40
242 Justin Germano NG/100 10.00 3.00
243 Ian Snell NG/100 12.00 3.60
244 Graham Koonce NG/200 8.00 2.40
245 Jose Capellan NG/100 30.00 9.00
246 Onil Joseph NG/200 8.00 2.40
247 Shingo Takatsu NG/50 50.00 15.00
248 Carlos Hines NG/200 8.00 2.40
249 Lincoln Holdzkom NG/100 10.00 3.00
250 Mike Gosling NG/100 10.00 3.00
251 Eduardo Sierra NG/200 10.00 3.00
252 Renyel Pinto NG/100 12.00 3.60
253 Merkin Valdez NG/200 15.00 4.50
254 Angel Chavez NG/200 8.00 2.40
255 Ivan Ochoa NG/200 8.00 2.40
257 William Bergolla NG/200 8.00 2.40
258 Aarom Baldiris NG/100 12.00 3.60
260 Carlos Vasquez NG/200 10.00 3.00
261 Freddy Guzman NG/200 8.00 2.40
262 Akinori Otsuka NG/50 50.00 15.00
264 Nick Regilio NG/200 8.00 2.40
266 Shawn Hill NG/200 8.00 2.40
268 Sean Henn NG/200 8.00 2.40
269 Ramon Ramirez NG/200 8.00 2.40
270 Ronny Cedeno NG/100 10.00 3.00
273 Fernando Nieve NG/200 8.00 2.40
274 Rusty Tucker NG/200 10.00 3.00
275 Jason Bartlett NG/200 10.00 3.00
276 Mike Rouse NG/200 8.00 2.40
277 Dennis Sarfate NG/200 8.00 2.40
278 Cory Sullivan NG/200 8.00 2.40
282 Michael Wuertz NG/200 10.00 3.00
284 Jorge Sequea NG/100 10.00 3.00
287 Tim Bittner NG/250 8.00 2.40
288 Andres Blanco NG/100 10.00 3.00
289 Kevin Cave NG/100 12.00 3.60
290 Mike Johnston NG/100 10.00 3.00
293 Colby Miller NG/100 10.00 3.00
294 Jake Woods NG/100 10.00 3.00
295 Ryan Meaux NG/200 8.00 2.40
296 Don Kelly NG/100 10.00 3.00
297 Edwin Moreno NG/100 10.00 3.00
298 Phil Stockman NG/100 10.00 3.00

2004 Leaf Certified Materials Mirror Autograph White

Nm-Mt Ex-Mt
*1-240 p/r 100: .5X TO 1.2X RED p/r 250
*1-240 p/r 100: .4X TO 1X RED p/r 100
*1-240 p/r 50: .6X TO 1.5X RED p/r 200-250
*1-240 p/r 50: .5X TO 1.2X RED p/r 100
*1-240 p/r 50: .4X TO 1X RED p/r 50
*1-240 p/r 25: 1X TO 2.5X RED p/r 203
*1-240 p/r 25: .75X TO 2X RED p/r 100
*1-240 p/r 25: .6X TO 1.5X RED p/r 50
*1-240 p/r 25: .4X TO 1X RED p/r 25
*241-300 p/r 100: .5X TO 1.2X RED p/r 200
*241-300 p/r 100: .4X TO 1X RED p/r 100
*241-300 p/r 50: .6X TO 1.5X RED p/r 200-250
*241-300 p/r 50: .5X TO 1.2X RED p/r 100
OVERALL AU ODDS 1:10
PRINT RUNS B/WN 1-100 COPIES PER
NO PRICING ON QTY OF 10 OR LESS
2 Adam Dunn/24 50.00 15.00

2004 Leaf Certified Materials Mirror Bat Blue

Nm-Mt Ex-Mt
*BLUE p/r 100: .5X TO 1.2X RED p/r 175-250
*BLUE p/r 50: .75X TO 2X RED p/r 150-250
*BLUE p/r 25: 1X TO 2.5X RED p/r 100
RANDOM INSERTS IN PACKS
PRINT RUNS B/WN 25-100 COPIES PER
23 Brad Wilkerson/100 5.00 1.50
58 Eric Chavez/50 8.00 2.40
142 Morgan Ensberg/50 8.00 2.40
151 Pedro Martinez/50 15.00 4.50
156 Randy Johnson/50 15.00 4.50
166 Roy Oswalt/50 8.00 2.40
172 Scott Rolen/50 15.00 4.50
180 Tim Hudson/50 8.00 2.40
182 Tom Glavine/50 12.00 3.60
207 Curt Schilling D'backs/50 8.00 2.40
217 Ryne Sandberg LGD/50 30.00 9.00
218 Dale Murphy LGD/50 15.00 4.50
219 Tony Gwynn LGD/50 25.00 7.50
221 Mike Schmidt LGD/50 30.00 9.00
223 Cal Ripken LGD/50 60.00 18.00
224 Nolan Ryan LGD/50 40.00 12.00
225 George Brett LGD/50 30.00 9.00

2004 Leaf Certified Materials Mirror Bat Gold

Nm-Mt Ex-Mt
*GOLD p/r 25: 1.25X TO 3X RED p/r 150-250
*GOLD p/r 25: 1X TO 2.5X RED p/r 100
RANDOM INSERTS IN PACKS
207 SCHILLING PRINT RUN 20 COPIES
18 Barry Zito 12.00 3.60
19 Ben Sheets 12.00 3.60
22 Brad Penny 12.00 3.60
23 Brad Wilkerson 12.00 3.60
46 Curt Schilling Sox 25.00 7.50
58 Eric Chavez 12.00 3.60
69 Greg Maddux Cubs 30.00 9.00
142 Morgan Ensberg 12.00 3.60
151 Pedro Martinez 25.00 7.50
156 Randy Johnson 25.00 7.50
166 Roy Oswalt 12.00 3.60
172 Scott Rolen 25.00 7.50
180 Tim Hudson 12.00 3.60
182 Tom Glavine 20.00 6.00
207 Curt Schilling D'backs 12.00 3.60
213 Duke Snider LGD 25.00 7.50
217 Ryne Sandberg LGD 50.00 15.00
218 Dale Murphy LGD 25.00 7.50
219 Tony Gwynn LGD 40.00 12.00
221 Mike Schmidt LGD 50.00 15.00
223 Cal Ripken LGD 100.00 30.00
224 Nolan Ryan LGD 60.00 18.00
225 George Brett LGD 50.00 15.00
231 Roberto Clemente LGD 100.00 30.00
232 Roy Campanella LGD 30.00 9.00
233 Babe Ruth LGD 250.00 75.00
234 Lou Gehrig LGD 150.00 45.00
235 Ty Cobb LGD 120.00 36.00
236 Roger Maris LGD 50.00 15.00
238 Ernie Banks LGD 30.00 9.00
239 Ted Williams LGD 100.00 30.00

2004 Leaf Certified Materials Mirror Bat Red

Nm-Mt Ex-Mt
PRINT RUNS B/WN 100-250 COPIES PER
BLACK PRINT RUN 1 SERIAL #'d SET
NO BLACK PRICING DUE TO SCARCITY
EMERALD PRINT RUN 5 SERIAL #'d SETS
NO EMERALD PRICING DUE TO SCARCITY
RANDOM INSERTS IN PACKS
2 Adam Dunn/150 8.00 2.40
3 Adam LaRoche/250 5.00 1.50
5 Adrian Beltre/150 8.00 2.40
7 Albert Pujols/150 15.00 4.50
8 Alex Rodriguez Yanks/250 10.00 3.00
9 Alexis Rios/250 5.00 1.50
10 Alfonso Soriano Rgr/150 8.00 2.40
11 Andruw Jones/150 5.00 1.50
12 Andy Pettitte/250 8.00 2.40
13 Angel Berroa/150 5.00 1.50
15 Aubrey Huff/150 5.00 1.50
16 Austin Kearns/150 5.00 1.50
17 Barry Larkin/150 8.00 2.40
20 Bernie Williams/150 8.00 2.40
21 Bobby Abreu/150 5.00 1.50
24 Brandon Webb/150 5.00 1.50
25 Brendan Harris/250 5.00 1.50
26 Bret Boone/150 5.00 1.50
29 Brian Giles/250 5.00 1.50
35 Carl Everett/250 5.00 1.50
36 Carlos Beltran/150 8.00 2.40
37 Carlos Delgado/150 5.00 1.50
38 Carlos Lee/150 5.00 1.50
41 Chipper Jones/150 8.00 2.40
42 Cliff Floyd/250 5.00 1.50
43 Clint Barmes/250 5.00 1.50
44 Corey Patterson/250 5.00 1.50
45 Craig Biggio/150 8.00 2.40
47 Dan Haren/150 5.00 1.50
48 Darin Erstad/150 5.00 1.50
49 David Ortiz/250 8.00 2.40
50 Delmon Young/250 8.00 2.40
51 Derek Jeter/150 20.00 6.00
54 Edgar Martinez/150 8.00 2.40
55 Edgar Renteria/150 8.00 2.40
58 Eric Chavez/150 5.00 1.50
59 Eric Hinske/150 5.00 1.50
60 Eric Munson/250 5.00 1.50
61 Erubiel Durazo/250 5.00 1.50
62 Frank Thomas/150 8.00 2.40
63 Fred McGriff/150 8.00 2.40
65 Garret Anderson/150 5.00 1.50
67 Gary Sheffield/250 5.00 1.50
68 Geoff Jenkins/150 5.00 1.50
70 Hank Blalock/150 5.00 1.50
71 Hee Seop Choi/250 5.00 1.50
73 Hideo Nomo/150 8.00 2.40
76 Ivan Rodriguez Tigers/250 8.00 2.40
77 J.D. Drew/250 5.00 1.50
79 Jacque Jones/150 5.00 1.50
82 Jason Giambi Yanks/150 5.00 1.50
83 Jason Jennings/150 5.00 1.50
86 Jason Varitek/150 8.00 2.40
88 Javy Lopez/250 5.00 1.50
89 Jay Gibbons/150 5.00 1.50
91 Jeff Bagwell/150 8.00 2.40
92 Jeff Baker/250 5.00 1.50
93 Jeff Kent/150 5.00 1.50
97 Jim Edmonds/150 5.00 1.50
98 Jim Thome/150 8.00 2.40
100 Joe Borchard/150 5.00 1.50
101 Joe Crede/250 5.00 1.50
103 John Olerud/150 5.00 1.50
105 Johnny Damon/250 8.00 2.40
106 Jorge Posada/150 8.00 2.40
107 Jose Castillo/250 5.00 1.50
108 Jose Reyes/150 5.00 1.50
109 Jose Vidro/150 5.00 1.50
110 Josh Beckett/150 5.00 1.50
111 Josh Phelps/150 5.00 1.50
112 Juan Encarnacion/250 5.00 1.50
113 Juan Gonzalez/250 8.00 2.40
114 Junior Spivey/250 5.00 1.50
115 Kazuhisa Ishii/150 5.00 1.50
116 Kenny Lofton/250 5.00 1.50
117 Kerry Wood/150 8.00 2.40
119 Kevin Youkilis/250 5.00 1.50
120 Lance Berkman/150 5.00 1.50
122 Larry Walker/150 8.00 2.40
123 Luis Castillo/150 5.00 1.50
124 Luis Gonzalez/150 5.00 1.50
126 Lyle Overbay/250 5.00 1.50
127 Magglio Ordonez/150 5.00 1.50
128 Manny Ramirez/150 8.00 2.40
129 Marcus Giles/250 5.00 1.50
131 Mark Buehrle/150 5.00 1.50
132 Mark Mulder/150 5.00 1.50
133 Mark Prior/150 8.00 2.40
134 Mark Teixeira/150 5.00 1.50
135 Marlon Byrd/150 5.00 1.50
137 Miguel Cabrera/250 8.00 2.40
138 Mike Lowell/150 5.00 1.50
140 Mike Piazza/150 10.00 3.00
141 Mike Sweeney/150 5.00 1.50
143 Nick Johnson/250 5.00 1.50
144 Nomar Garciaparra/150 12.00 3.60
145 Omar Vizquel/150 8.00 2.40
146 Orlando Cabrera/250 5.00 1.50
147 Orlando Hudson/150 5.00 1.50
148 Pat Burrell/150 5.00 1.50
149 Paul Konerko/150 5.00 1.50
150 Paul Lo Duca/150 5.00 1.50
152 Jermaine Dye/250 5.00 1.50
153 Preston Wilson/150 5.00 1.50
154 Rafael Furcal/150 5.00 1.50
155 Rafael Palmeiro O's/150 8.00 2.40
157 Rich Aurilia/250 5.00 1.50
159 Richard Hidalgo/150 5.00 1.50
160 Richie Sexson/250 5.00 1.50
161 Rickie Weeks/250 5.00 1.50
162 Roberto Alomar/250 8.00 2.40
163 Rocco Baldelli/150 5.00 1.50
164 Roger Clemens Astros/250 10.00 3.00
168 Ryan Klesko/150 5.00 1.50
170 Sammy Sosa/150 10.00 3.00
174 Sean Casey/250 5.00 1.50
175 Shannon Stewart/150 5.00 1.50
176 Shawn Green/150 5.00 1.50
181 Todd Helton/150 8.00 2.40
183 Torii Hunter/150 5.00 1.50
184 Trot Nixon/150 5.00 1.50
185 Troy Glaus/150 5.00 1.50
186 Vernon Wells/150 5.00 1.50
187 Victor Martinez/250 5.00 1.50
188 Vladimir Guerrero Angels/250 8.00 2.40
189 Wade Miller/250 5.00 1.50
190 Brandon Larson/175 5.00 1.50
191 Travis Hafner/250 5.00 1.50
192 Tim Salmon/150 8.00 2.40
195 Ramon Nivar/150 5.00 1.50
196 Moises Alou/250 5.00 1.50
197 Michael Young/250 5.00 1.50
198 Laynce Nix/150 5.00 1.50
199 Tino Martinez/250 8.00 2.40
200 Randall Simon/250 5.00 1.50
201 Roger Clemens Yanks/150 10.00 3.00
203 Vladimir Guerrero Expos/150 8.00 2.40
204 Miguel Tejada/150 5.00 1.50
206 Jason Giambi A's/150 5.00 1.50
208 Alex Rodriguez Rgr/150 10.00 3.00
209 Alfonso Soriano Yanks/150 8.00 2.40
210 Ivan Rodriguez Marlins/150 8.00 2.40
211 Rafael Palmeiro Rgr/150 8.00 2.40
212 Gary Carter LGD/150 8.00 2.40
216 Reggie Jackson LGD/150 10.00 3.00
220 Don Mattingly LGD/150 15.00 4.50
222 Rickey Henderson LGD/150 10.00 3.00
227 Lou Brock LGD/150 10.00 3.00
228 Andre Dawson LGD/150 8.00 2.40
229 Rod Carew LGD/150 10.00 3.00
230 Wade Boggs LGD/150 10.00 3.00
240 Stan Musial LGD/100 25.00 7.50

2004 Leaf Certified Materials Mirror Bat White

Nm-Mt Ex-Mt
*WHITE p/r 200: .4X TO 1X RED p/r 250
*WHITE p/r 100: .5X TO 1.2X RED p/r 150
*WHITE p/r 50: .6X TO 1.5X RED p/r 100
RANDOM INSERTS IN PACKS
PRINT RUNS B/WN 25-200 COPIES PER
14 Aramis Ramirez/100 5.00 1.50
23 Brad Wilkerson/200 5.00 1.50
156 Randy Johnson/100 10.00 3.00
166 Roy Oswalt/100 5.00 1.50
180 Tim Hudson/100 5.00 1.50
182 Tom Glavine/100 8.00 2.40
205 Kevin Brown/100 5.00 1.50
218 Dale Murphy LGD/100 12.00 3.60
219 Tony Gwynn LGD/100 15.00 4.50
221 Mike Schmidt LGD/100 20.00 6.00
223 Cal Ripken LGD/100 40.00 12.00
224 Nolan Ryan LGD/100 25.00 7.50
225 George Brett LGD/100 20.00 6.00
231 Roberto Clemente LGD/50 80.00 24.00
232 Roy Campanella LGD/50 20.00 6.00
233 Babe Ruth LGD/25 250.00 75.00
234 Lou Gehrig LGD/25 150.00 45.00
235 Ty Cobb LGD/25 120.00 36.00
236 Roger Maris LGD/25 50.00 15.00
238 Ernie Banks LGD/25 20.00 6.00
239 Ted Williams LGD/25 100.00 30.00

2004 Leaf Certified Materials Mirror Combo Red

Nm-Mt Ex-Mt
2-211 PRINT RUN 250 SERIAL #'d SETS
212-239 PRINT RUNS B/WN 50-250 PER
BLACK PRIME PRINT RUN 1 SERIAL #'d SET
NO BLACK PRIME PRICING AVAILABLE
RANDOM INSERTS IN PACKS
2 Adam Dunn Bat-Jsy 12.00 3.60
5 Adrian Beltre Bat-Jsy 12.00 3.60
7 Albert Pujols Bat-Jsy 25.00 7.50
11 Andruw Jones Bat-Jsy 8.00 2.40
13 Angel Berroa Bat-Pants 8.00 2.40
15 Aubrey Huff Bat-Jsy 8.00 2.40
16 Austin Kearns Bat-Jsy 8.00 2.40
17 Barry Larkin Bat-Jsy 12.00 3.60
18 Barry Zito Bat-Jsy 8.00 2.40
19 Ben Sheets Bat-Jsy 8.00 2.40
20 Bernie Williams Bat-Jsy 12.00 3.60
21 Bobby Abreu Bat-Jsy 8.00 2.40
22 Brad Penny Bat-Jsy 8.00 2.40
24 Brandon Webb Bat-Jsy 8.00 2.40
26 Bret Boone Bat-Jsy 8.00 2.40
36 Carlos Beltran Bat-Jsy 12.00 3.60
37 Carlos Delgado Bat-Jsy 8.00 2.40
38 Carlos Lee Bat-Jsy 8.00 2.40
41 Chipper Jones Bat-Jsy 12.00 3.60
45 Craig Biggio Bat-Pants 12.00 3.60
47 Dan Haren Bat-Jsy 8.00 2.40
51 Derek Jeter Bat-Jsy 30.00 9.00
52 Dewon Brazelton Fld Glv-Jsy 8.00 2.40
54 Edgar Martinez Bat-Jsy 12.00 3.60
55 Edgar Renteria Bat-Jsy 8.00 2.40
58 Eric Chavez Bat-Jsy 8.00 2.40
59 Eric Hinske Bat-Jsy 8.00 2.40
62 Frank Thomas Bat-Jsy 12.00 3.60
63 Fred McGriff Bat-Jsy 12.00 3.60
65 Garret Anderson Bat-Jsy 8.00 2.40
68 Geoff Jenkins Bat-Jsy 8.00 2.40
70 Hank Blalock Bat-Jsy 8.00 2.40
73 Hideo Nomo Bat-Jsy 12.00 3.60
79 Jacque Jones Bat-Jsy 8.00 2.40
82 Jason Giambi Yanks Bat-Jsy 8.00 2.40
83 Jason Jennings Bat-Jsy 8.00 2.40
86 Jason Varitek Bat-Jsy 12.00 3.60
89 Jay Gibbons Bat-Jsy 8.00 2.40
91 Jeff Bagwell Bat-Jsy 12.00 3.60
93 Jeff Kent Bat-Jsy 8.00 2.40
97 Jim Edmonds Bat-Jsy 8.00 2.40
98 Jim Thome Bat-Jsy 12.00 3.60
100 Joe Borchard Bat-Jsy 8.00 2.40
103 John Olerud Bat-Jsy 8.00 2.40
106 Jorge Posada Bat-Jsy 12.00 3.60
108 Jose Reyes Bat-Jsy 8.00 2.40
109 Jose Vidro Bat-Jsy 8.00 2.40
110 Josh Beckett Bat-Jsy 8.00 2.40
111 Josh Phelps Bat-Jsy 8.00 2.40
115 Kazuhisa Ishii Bat-Jsy 8.00 2.40
117 Kerry Wood Bat-Jsy 12.00 3.60
120 Lance Berkman Bat-Jsy 8.00 2.40
122 Larry Walker Bat-Jsy 12.00 3.60
123 Luis Castillo Bat-Jsy 8.00 2.40
124 Luis Gonzalez Bat-Jsy 8.00 2.40
127 Magglio Ordonez Bat-Jsy 8.00 2.40
128 Manny Ramirez Bat-Jsy 12.00 3.60
131 Mark Buehrle Bat-Jsy 8.00 2.40
132 Mark Mulder Bat-Jsy 8.00 2.40
133 Mark Prior Bat-Jsy 12.00 3.60
134 Mark Teixeira Bat-Jsy 8.00 2.40
135 Marlon Byrd Bat-Jsy 8.00 2.40
138 Mike Lowell Bat-Jsy 8.00 2.40
140 Mike Piazza Bat-Jsy 15.00 4.50
141 Mike Sweeney Bat-Jsy 8.00 2.40
142 Morgan Ensberg Bat-Jsy 8.00 2.40
144 Nomar Garciaparra Bat-Jsy 15.00 4.50
145 Omar Vizquel Bat-Jsy 12.00 3.60
147 Orlando Hudson Bat-Jsy 8.00 2.40
148 Pat Burrell Bat-Jsy 8.00 2.40
149 Paul Konerko Bat-Jsy 8.00 2.40
150 Paul Lo Duca Bat-Jsy 8.00 2.40
151 Pedro Martinez Bat-Jsy 12.00 3.60
153 Preston Wilson Bat-Jsy 8.00 2.40
154 Rafael Furcal Bat-Jsy 8.00 2.40
155 Rafael Palmeiro O's Bat-Jsy 12.00 3.60
156 Randy Johnson Bat-Jsy 12.00 3.60
159 Richard Hidalgo Bat-Pants 8.00 2.40
163 Rocco Baldelli Bat-Jsy 8.00 2.40
166 Roy Oswalt Bat-Jsy 8.00 2.40
168 Ryan Klesko Bat-Jsy 8.00 2.40
170 Sammy Sosa Bat-Jsy 15.00 4.50
172 Scott Rolen Bat-Jsy 12.00 3.60
175 Shannon Stewart Bat-Jsy 8.00 2.40
176 Shawn Green Bat-Jsy 8.00 2.40
180 Tim Hudson Bat-Jsy 8.00 2.40
181 Todd Helton Bat-Jsy 12.00 3.60
182 Tom Glavine Bat-Jsy 12.00 3.60
183 Torii Hunter Bat-Jsy 8.00 2.40
184 Trot Nixon Bat-Jsy 8.00 2.40
185 Troy Glaus Bat-Jsy 8.00 2.40
186 Vernon Wells Bat-Jsy 8.00 2.40
191 Travis Hafner Bat-Jsy 8.00 2.40
192 Tim Salmon Bat-Jsy 12.00 3.60
195 Ramon Nivar Bat-Jsy 8.00 2.40
201 R.Clemens Yanks Bat-Jsy 15.00 4.50
203 Vlad Guerrero Expos Bat-Jsy 12.00 3.60
204 Miguel Tejada Bat-Jsy 8.00 2.40
206 Jason Giambi A's Bat-Jsy 8.00 2.40
207 Curt Schilling D'backs Bat-Jsy 8.00 2.40
208 Alex Rodriguez Rgr Bat-Jsy 15.00 4.50
209 Alf Soriano Yanks Bat-Jsy 12.00 3.60
210 Ivan Rod Marlins Bat-Jsy 12.00 3.60
211 Rafael Palmeiro Rgr Bat-Jsy 12.00 3.60
212 G.Carter LGD Bat-Pants/250 10.00 3.00
216 R.Jackson LGD Bat-Jsy/250 15.00 4.50
217 R.Sandberg LGD Bat-Jsy/250 25.00 7.50
218 D.Murphy LGD Bat-Jsy/250 15.00 4.50
219 T.Gwynn LGD Bat-Jsy/250 15.00 4.50
220 D.Mattingly LGD Bat-Jsy/250 25.00 7.50
221 M.Schm LGD Bat-Pants/250 25.00 7.50
222 R.Hend LGD Bat-Jsy/250 15.00 4.50
223 C.Ripken LGD Bat-Jsy/250 40.00 12.00
224 N.Ryan LGD Bat-Jsy/250 40.00 12.00
225 G.Brett LGD Bat-Jsy/250 25.00 7.50
227 L.Brock LGD Bat-Jsy/250 15.00 4.50
228 A.Dawson LGD Bat-Jsy/250 10.00 3.00
229 R.Carew LGD Bat-Jkt/250 15.00 4.50
230 W.Boggs LGD Bat-Jsy/250 15.00 4.50
231 R.Clemente LGD Bat-Jsy/100 120.00 36.00
232 R.Campy LGD Bat-Pants/100 20.00 6.00
233 B.Ruth LGD Bat-Pants/50 400.00 120.00
234 L.Gehrig LGD Bat-Pants/50 200.00 60.00

35 T.Cobb LGD Bat-Pants/50 200.00 60.00
36 R.Maris LGD Bat-Pants/100 50.00 15.00
38 E.Banks LGD Bat-Pants/100 20.00 6.00
39 T.Williams LGD Bat-Jkt/100 100.00 30.00

2004 Leaf Certified Materials Mirror Fabric Blue Position

Nm-Mt Ex-Mt
*1-211 p/r 100: .5X TO 1.2X RED p/r 150-250
1-211 PRINT RUN 100 SERIAL #'d SETS
212-239 p/r 100: .5X TO 1.2X REDp/r150-250
212-239 p/r 25: 1X TO 2.5X RED p/r 100
212-239 PRINT RUN 25-100 #'d COPIES PER
RANDOM INSERTS IN PACKS
4 Brandon Webb Jsy 5.00 1.50
5 Bret Boone Jsy 5.00 1.50
7 Carlos Delgado Jsy 5.00 1.50
2 Dewon Brazelton Jsy 5.00 1.50
5 Garret Anderson Jsy 5.00 1.50
0 Jae Weong Seo Jsy 5.00 1.50
00 Joe Borchard Jsy 5.00 1.50
06 Jorge Posada Jsy 8.00 2.40
27 Magglio Ordonez Jsy 5.00 1.50
28 Manny Ramirez Jsy 8.00 2.40
32 Mark Mulder Jsy 5.00 1.50
34 Mark Teixeira Jsy 5.00 1.50
38 Mike Lowell Jsy 5.00 1.50
49 Paul Konerko Jsy 5.00 1.50
50 Paul Lo Duca Jsy 5.00 1.50
55 Rafael Palmeiro O's Jsy 8.00 2.40
66 Roy Oswalt Jsy 5.00 1.50
83 Torii Hunter Jsy 5.00 1.50
84 Trot Nixon Jsy 5.00 1.50
11 Rafael Palmeiro Rgr Jsy 8.00 2.40
14 W.Ford LGD Jsy/100 12.00 3.60
16 R.Jackson LGD Jsy/100 12.00 3.60
17 R.Sandberg LGD Jsy/100 20.00 6.00
18 D.Murphy LGD Jsy/100 12.00 3.60
19 T.Gwynn LGD Jsy/100 15.00 4.50
20 Don Mattingly LGD Jsy/100 20.00 6.00
21 M.Schmidt LGD Pants/100 20.00 6.00
22 R.Henderson LGD Jsy/100 15.00 4.50
23 Cal Ripken LGD Jsy/100 40.00 12.00
24 Nolan Ryan LGD Jsy/100 25.00 7.50
25 George Brett LGD Jsy/100 20.00 6.00
27 L.Brock LGD Jsy/100 12.00 3.60
28 A.Dawson LGD Jsy/100 8.00 2.40
29 R.Carew LGD Jkt/100 12.00 3.60
30 W.Boggs LGD Jsy/100 12.00 3.60
31 R.Clemente LGD Jsy/25 100.00 30.00
32 R.Campy LGD Pants/25 30.00 9.00
33 Babe Ruth LGD Pants/25 250.00 75.00
34 Lou Gehrig LGD Pants/25 150.00 45.00
35 Ty Cobb LGD Pants/25 120.00 36.00
36 Roger Maris LGD Pants/25 50.00 15.00
38 E.Banks LGD Pants/25 30.00 9.00
39 Ted Williams LGD Jkt/25 100.00 30.00

2004 Leaf Certified Materials Mirror Fabric Gold Number

Nm-Mt Ex-Mt
1-211 p/r 25: 1.25X TO 3X RED p/r 150-250
1-211 PRINT RUN 25 SERIAL #'d SETS
212-239 p/r 25: 1.25X TO 3X RED p/r 150-250
212-239 PRINT RUNS B/WN 10-25 #'d PER
212-239 NO PRICING ON QTY OF 10 OR LESS
RANDOM INSERTS IN PACKS
4 Brandon Webb Jsy 12.00 3.60
6 Bret Boone Jsy 12.00 3.60
7 Carlos Delgado Jsy 12.00 3.60
2 Dewon Brazelton Jsy 12.00 3.60
3 Fred McGriff Jsy 20.00 6.00
5 Garret Anderson Jsy 12.00 3.60
0 Jae Weong Seo Jsy 12.00 3.60
00 Joe Borchard Jsy 12.00 3.60
06 Jorge Posada Jsy 20.00 6.00
27 Magglio Ordonez Jsy 12.00 3.60
28 Manny Ramirez Jsy 20.00 6.00
32 Mark Mulder Jsy 12.00 3.60
34 Mark Teixeira Jsy 12.00 3.60
38 Mike Lowell Jsy 12.00 3.60
49 Paul Konerko Jsy 12.00 3.60
50 Paul Lo Duca Jsy 12.00 3.60
55 Rafael Palmeiro O's Jsy 20.00 6.00
66 Roy Oswalt Jsy 12.00 3.60
83 Torii Hunter Jsy 12.00 3.60
84 Trot Nixon Jsy 12.00 3.60
11 Rafael Palmeiro Rgr Jsy 20.00 6.00
14 Whitey Ford LGD Jsy/25 25.00 7.50
15 B.Feller LGD Jsy/25 15.00 4.50
16 R.Jackson LGD Jsy/25 25.00 7.50
17 Ryne Sandberg LGD Jsy/25 50.00 15.00
18 D.Murphy LGD Jsy/25 25.00 7.50
19 Tony Gwynn LGD Jsy/25 40.00 12.00
20 Don Mattingly LGD Jsy/25 50.00 15.00
21 Mike Schmidt LGD Pants/25 50.00 15.00
22 R.Henderson LGD Jsy/25 30.00 9.00
23 Cal Ripken LGD Jsy/25 100.00 30.00
24 Nolan Ryan LGD Jsy/25 60.00 18.00
25 George Brett LGD Jsy/25 50.00 15.00
27 L.Brock LGD Jsy/25 25.00 7.50
28 A.Dawson LGD Jsy/25 15.00 4.50
229 R.Carew LGD Jkt/25 25.00 7.50
230 W.Boggs LGD Jsy/25 25.00 7.50
231 R.Clemente LGD Jsy/10
232 R.Campy LGD Pants/10
233 B.Ruth LGD Pants/10
234 L.Gehrig LGD Pants/10
235 T.Cobb LGD Pants/10
236 R.Maris LGD Pants/10
238 E.Banks LGD Pants/10
239 Ted Williams LGD Jkt/10

2004 Leaf Certified Materials Mirror Fabric Red

Nm-Mt Ex-Mt
PRINT RUNS B/WN 100-250 COPIES PER
BLACK AL/NL PRINT RUN 1 SERIAL #'d SET
NO BLK AL/NL PRICING DUE TO SCARCITY
BLACK NUMBER PRINT RUN 1 #'d SET
NO BLACK NBR.PRICING DUE TO SCARCITY
BLACK POSITION PRINT RUN 1 #'d SET
NO BLACK POS.PRICING DUE TO SCARCITY
BLACK PRIME PRINT RUN 1 SERIAL #'d SET
NO BLK PRIME PRICING DUE TO SCARCITY
EMERALD PRINT RUN 1-5 COPIES PER
NO EMERALD PRICING DUE TO SCARCITY
RANDOM INSERTS IN PACKS
1 A.J. Burnett Jsy/250 5.00 1.50
2 Adam Dunn Jsy/150 8.00 2.40
5 Adrian Beltre Jsy/150 8.00 2.40
6 Al Leiter Jsy/250 5.00 1.50
7 Albert Pujols Jsy/150 15.00 4.50
11 Andruw Jones Jsy/150 5.00 1.50
13 Angel Berroa Pants/150 5.00 1.50
15 Aubrey Huff Jsy/150 5.00 1.50
16 Austin Kearns Jsy/150 5.00 1.50
17 Barry Larkin Jsy/150 8.00 2.40
18 Barry Zito Jsy/150 5.00 1.50
19 Ben Sheets Jsy/150 5.00 1.50
20 Bernie Williams Jsy/150 8.00 2.40
21 Bobby Abreu Jsy/150 5.00 1.50
22 Brad Penny Jsy/150 5.00 1.50
27 Brett Myers Jsy/250 5.00 1.50
33 C.C. Sabathia Jsy/250 5.00 1.50
34 Carl Crawford Jsy/250 5.00 1.50
36 Carlos Beltran Jsy/150 8.00 2.40
38 Carlos Lee Jsy/150 5.00 1.50
40 Chad Gaudin Jsy/250 5.00 1.50
41 Chipper Jones Jsy/150 8.00 2.40
45 Craig Biggio Pants/150 8.00 2.40
47 Dan Haren Jsy/150 5.00 1.50
48 Darin Erstad Jsy/250 5.00 1.50
51 Derek Jeter Jsy/150 20.00 6.00
53 Dontrelle Willis Jsy/250 5.00 1.50
54 Edgar Martinez Jsy/150 8.00 2.40
55 Edgar Renteria Jsy/150 5.00 1.50
58 Eric Chavez Jsy/150 5.00 1.50
59 Eric Hinske Jsy/150 5.00 1.50
62 Frank Thomas Jsy/150 8.00 2.40
64 Freddy Garcia Jsy/150 5.00 1.50
66 Garrett Atkins Jsy/250 5.00 1.50
68 Geoff Jenkins Jsy/150 5.00 1.50
70 Hank Blalock Jsy/150 5.00 1.50
72 Hideki Matsui Base/250 15.00 4.50
73 Hideo Nomo Jsy/150 8.00 2.40
75 Ichiro Suzuki Base/250 15.00 4.50
79 Jacque Jones Jsy/150 5.00 1.50
81 Jamie Moyer Jsy/250 5.00 1.50
82 Jason Giambi Yanks Jsy/150 5.00 1.50
83 Jason Jennings Jsy/150 5.00 1.50
84 Jason Kendall Jsy/250 5.00 1.50
86 Jason Varitek Jsy/150 8.00 2.40
89 Jay Gibbons Jsy/150 5.00 1.50
91 Jeff Bagwell Jsy/150 8.00 2.40
93 Jeff Kent Jsy/150 5.00 1.50
96 Jerome Williams Jsy/250 5.00 1.50
97 Jim Edmonds Jsy/150 5.00 1.50
98 Jim Thome Jsy/150 8.00 2.40
102 Johan Santana Jsy/250 8.00 2.40
103 John Olerud Jsy/150 5.00 1.50
104 John Smoltz Jsy/250 8.00 2.40
108 Jose Reyes Jsy/150 5.00 1.50
109 Jose Vidro Jsy/150 5.00 1.50
110 Josh Beckett Jsy/150 5.00 1.50
111 Josh Phelps Jsy/150 5.00 1.50
115 Kazuhisa Ishii Jsy/150 5.00 1.50
117 Kerry Wood Jsy/150 8.00 2.40
118 Kevin Millwood Jsy/250 5.00 1.50
120 Lance Berkman Jsy/150 5.00 1.50
121 Larry Bigbie Jsy/250 5.00 1.50
122 Larry Walker Jsy/150 8.00 2.40
123 Luis Castillo Jsy/150 5.00 1.50
124 Luis Gonzalez Jsy/150 5.00 1.50
130 Mariano Rivera Jsy/250 8.00 2.40
131 Mark Buehrle Jsy/150 5.00 1.50
133 Mark Prior Jsy/150 8.00 2.40
135 Marlon Byrd Jsy/150 5.00 1.50
136 Matt Morris Jsy/250 5.00 1.50
139 Mike Mussina Jsy/250 8.00 2.40
140 Mike Piazza Jsy/150 10.00 3.00
141 Mike Sweeney Jsy/150 5.00 1.50
142 Morgan Ensberg Jsy/150 5.00 1.50
144 Nomar Garciaparra Jsy/150 12.00 3.60
145 Omar Vizquel Jsy/150 8.00 2.40
147 Orlando Hudson Jsy/150 5.00 1.50
148 Pat Burrell Jsy/150 5.00 1.50
151 Pedro Martinez Jsy/150 8.00 2.40
153 Preston Wilson Jsy/150 5.00 1.50
154 Rafael Furcal Jsy/150 5.00 1.50
156 Randy Johnson Jsy/150 8.00 2.40
158 Rich Harden Jsy/250 5.00 1.50
159 Richard Hidalgo Pants/150 5.00 1.50
163 Rocco Baldelli Jsy/150 5.00 1.50
165 Roy Halladay Jsy/250 5.00 1.50
168 Ryan Klesko Jsy/150 5.00 1.50
170 Sammy Sosa Jsy/150 10.00 3.00
172 Scott Rolen Jsy/150 8.00 2.40
173 Sean Burroughs Jsy/250 5.00 1.50
175 Shannon Stewart Jsy/150 5.00 1.50
176 Shawn Green Jsy/150 5.00 1.50
179 Steve Finley Jsy/250 5.00 1.50
180 Tim Hudson Jsy/150 5.00 1.50
181 Todd Helton Jsy/150 8.00 2.40
182 Tom Glavine Jsy/150 8.00 2.40
185 Troy Glaus Jsy/150 5.00 1.50
186 Vernon Wells Jsy/150 5.00 1.50
191 Travis Hafner Jsy/150 5.00 1.50
192 Tim Salmon Jsy/150 8.00 2.40
193 Tim Redding Jsy/250 5.00 1.50
194 Runelvys Hernandez Jsy/250 5.00 1.50
195 Ramon Nivar Jsy/150 5.00 1.50
201 R.Clemens Yanks Jsy/150 10.00 3.00
202 G.Maddux Braves Jsy/250 12.00 3.60
203 V.Guerrero Expos Jsy/150 8.00 2.40
204 Miguel Tejada Jsy/150 5.00 1.50
205 Kevin Brown Jsy/250 5.00 1.50
206 Jason Giambi A's Jsy/150 5.00 1.50
207 C.Schilling D'backs Jsy/150 5.00 1.50
208 Alex Rodriguez Rgr Jsy/150 10.00 3.00
209 Alf Soriano Yanks Jsy/150 8.00 2.40
210 Ivan Rod Marlins Jsy/150 8.00 2.40
212 Gary Carter LGD Pants/150 8.00 2.40
226 Bob Gibson LGD Jsy/250 10.00 3.00
237 S.Paige LGD CO Jsy/100 60.00 18.00

2004 Leaf Certified Materials Mirror Fabric White

Nm-Mt Ex-Mt
*1-211 p/r 200-215: .4X TO 1X REDp/r150-250
*1-211 p/r 100: .5X TO 1.2X RED p/r 150-250
*1-211 p/r 50: .75X TO 2X RED p/r 250
*212-239 p/r 200: .4X TO 1X RED p/r 150
*212-239 p/r 25: 1.25X TO 3X RED p/r 250
*212-239 p/r 25: 1X TO 2.5X RED p/r 100
212-239 PRINT RUNS B/WN 25-200 #'d PER
RANDOM INSERTS IN PACKS
24 Brandon Webb Pants/200 5.00 1.50
37 Carlos Delgado Jsy/200 5.00 1.50
52 Dewon Brazelton Jsy/200 5.00 1.50
65 Garret Anderson Jsy/200 5.00 1.50
106 Jorge Posada Jsy/200 8.00 2.40
127 Magglio Ordonez Jsy/200 5.00 1.50
128 Manny Ramirez Jsy/200 8.00 2.40
132 Mark Mulder Jsy/200 5.00 1.50
134 Mark Teixeira Jsy/200 5.00 1.50
138 Mike Lowell Jsy/75 5.00 1.50
149 Paul Konerko Jsy/100 5.00 1.50
150 Paul Lo Duca Jsy/200 5.00 1.50
155 Rafael Palmeiro O's Jsy/50 12.00 3.60
166 Roy Oswalt Jsy/100 5.00 1.50
183 Torii Hunter Jsy/200 5.00 1.50
184 Trot Nixon Jsy/50 8.00 2.40
211 Rafael Palmeiro Rgr Jsy/200 8.00 2.40
216 Reggie Jackson LGD Jsy/25 25.00 7.50
217 Ryne Sandberg LGD Jsy/25 50.00 15.00
219 Tony Gwynn LGD Jsy/25 40.00 12.00
220 Don Mattingly LGD Jsy/25 50.00 15.00
221 Mike Schmidt LGD Pants/25 50.00 15.00
222 R.Henderson LGD Jsy/25 30.00 9.00
223 Cal Ripken LGD Jsy/25 100.00 30.00
224 Nolan Ryan LGD Jsy/25 60.00 18.00
225 George Brett LGD Jsy/25 50.00 15.00
227 Lou Brock LGD Jsy/25 25.00 7.50
228 Andre Dawson LGD Jsy/25 15.00 4.50
229 Rod Carew LGD Jkt/25 25.00 7.50
230 Wade Boggs LGD Jsy/25 25.00 7.50
231 R.Clemente LGD Jsy/25 100.00 30.00
232 R.Campy LGD Pants/25 30.00 9.00
233 Babe Ruth LGD Pants/25 250.00 75.00
234 Lou Gehrig LGD Pants/25 150.00 45.00
235 Ty Cobb LGD Pants/25 120.00 36.00
236 Roger Maris LGD Pants/25 50.00 15.00
238 Ernie Banks LGD Pants/25 30.00 9.00
239 Ted Williams LGD Jkt/25 100.00 30.00

2004 Leaf Certified Materials Fabric of the Game

This set was highlighted by the debut of swatches cut from a 1968 Atlanta Braves jersey of Negro League legend Satchel Paige who was serving as a coach for the Braves at that time so he could qualify for a baseball pension.

Nm-Mt Ex-Mt
RANDOM INSERTS IN PACKS
PRINT RUNS B/WN 1-100 COPIES PER
NO PRICING ON QTY OF 10 OR LESS
1 Ozzie Smith Padres Jsy/100 15.00 4.50
2 Al Kaline Pants/100 15.00 4.50
3 Alan Trammell Jsy/100 8.00 2.40
4 Albert Pujols Grey Jsy/100 25.00 7.50
5 Alex Rodriguez M's Jsy/100 12.00 3.60
6 Alex Rodriguez Rgr Jsy/100 12.00 3.60
7 A.Dawson Cubs Jsy/100 8.00 2.40
8 A.Dawson Cubs Pants/100 8.00 2.40
9 Babe Ruth Jsy/10
10 Babe Ruth Pants/10
11 Billy Williams Jsy/100 8.00 2.40
12 Bo Jackson Royals Jsy/100 15.00 4.50
13 Bob Feller Jsy/50 15.00 4.50
14 Bob Gibson Jsy/50 15.00 4.50
15 Bobby Doerr Jsy/100 8.00 2.40
16 Brooks Robinson Jsy/25 25.00 7.50
17 Cal Ripken Jsy/100 40.00 12.00
18 Carl Yastrzemski Jsy/100 20.00 6.00
19 Carlton Fisk R.Sox Jsy/100 12.00 3.60
20 Dale Murphy Jsy/100 12.00 3.60
21 D.Strawberry Mets Pants/100 8.00 2.40
22 D.Strawberry Dgr Jsy/100 8.00 2.40
23 Dave Parker Reds Jsy/100 8.00 2.40
24 Dave Parker Pirates Jsy/100 8.00 2.40
25 D.Winfield Yanks Jsy/50 10.00 3.00
26 D.Winfield Padres Jsy/100 8.00 2.40
27 Deion Sanders Jsy/25 25.00 7.50
28 Derek Jeter Jsy/100 25.00 7.50
29 Don Drysdale Jsy/100 12.00 3.60
30 Don Mattingly Jsy/100 20.00 6.00
31 Don Mattingly Jkt/100 20.00 6.00
32 Don Sutton Jsy/100 8.00 2.40
33 Duke Snider Jsy/100 12.00 3.60
34 Dwight Gooden Jsy/100 8.00 2.40
35 Early Wynn Jsy/100 8.00 2.40
36 Eddie Mathews Jsy/50 20.00 6.00
37 Eddie Murray Dgr Jsy/100 12.00 3.60
38 Eddie Murray O's Jsy/100 12.00 3.60
39 Enos Slaughter Jsy/100 8.00 2.40
40 Eric Davis Jsy/50 10.00 3.00
41 Ernie Banks Jsy/100 15.00 4.50
42 Fergie Jenkins Pants/100 8.00 2.40
43 Frank Robinson Jsy/100 8.00 2.40
44 Fred Lynn Jsy/10
45 Gary Carter Jsy/100 8.00 2.40
46 Gaylord Perry Jsy/25 15.00 4.50
47 George Brett White Jsy/100 20.00 6.00
48 George Foster Jsy/100 8.00 2.40
49 Hal Newhouser Jsy/100 8.00 2.40
50 Harmon Killebrew Jsy/25 30.00 9.00
51 Harmon Killebrew Pants/25 30.00 9.00
52 Harold Baines Jsy/100 8.00 2.40
53 Hoyt Wilhelm Jsy/50 10.00 3.00
54 Jack Morris Jsy/100 8.00 2.40
55 Jackie Robinson Jsy/10
56 Catfish Hunter Jsy/100 12.00 3.60
57 Jim Palmer Jsy/100 8.00 2.40
58 Jim Rice Jsy/100 8.00 2.40
59 Joe Carter Jsy/100 8.00 2.40
60 Joe Morgan Reds Jsy/100 8.00 2.40
61 Tommy Lasorda Jsy/100 8.00 2.40
62 Johnny Mize Pants/100 12.00 3.60
63 Johnny Bench Jsy/100 15.00 4.50
64 Jose Canseco Grey Jsy/100 15.00 4.50
65 Juan Marichal Jsy/100 8.00 2.40
66 Kirby Puckett Jsy/100 15.00 4.50
67 Lou Boudreau Jsy/100 8.00 2.40
68 Lou Brock Jsy/100 12.00 3.60
69 Lou Gehrig Jsy/10
70 Lou Gehrig Pants/10
71 Luis Aparicio Jsy/100 8.00 2.40
72 Luis Aparicio Pants/100 8.00 2.40
73 Mariano Rivera Jsy/100 8.00 2.40
74 Mark Grace Cubs Jsy/100 12.00 3.60
75 Mark Prior Jsy/100 10.00 3.00
76 Mel Ott Jsy/25 50.00 15.00
77 Mel Ott Pants/25 50.00 15.00
78 Mike Schmidt Jsy/100 20.00 6.00
79 Mike Schmidt Pants/100 20.00 6.00
80 Mike Schmidt Jkt/100 20.00 6.00
81 Nolan Ryan Angels Jsy/100 25.00 7.50
82 Nolan Ryan Angels Jkt/100 25.00 7.50
83 Nolan Ryan Astros Jsy/100 25.00 7.50
84 Nolan Ryan Astros Jkt/100 25.00 7.50
85 Nolan Ryan Rgr Jsy/100 25.00 7.50
86 Nolan Ryan Rgr Pants/100 25.00 7.50
87 Ty Cobb Pants/10
88 Ozzie Smith Cards Jsy/100 15.00 4.50
89 Paul Molitor Jsy/100 12.00 3.60
90 Pee Wee Reese Jsy/100 12.00 3.60
91 Phil Niekro Jsy/100 8.00 2.40
92 Phil Rizzuto Jsy/100 12.00 3.60
93 Phil Rizzuto Pants/100 12.00 3.60
94 Red Schoendienst Jsy/100 8.00 2.40
95 R.Jackson A's Jkt/100 12.00 3.60
96 R.Jackson Angels Jsy/100 12.00 3.60
97 Richie Ashburn Jsy/100 25.00 7.50
98 R.Henderson Yanks Jsy/50 15.00 4.50
99 Roberto Clemente Jsy/50 80.00 24.00
100 Robin Yount Jsy/100 15.00 4.50
101 R.Carew Angels Jsy/100 12.00 3.60
102 R.Carew Angels Pants/100 12.00 3.60
103 R.Carew Angels Jkt/100 12.00 3.60
104 R.Carew Twins Jsy/100 12.00 3.60
105 R.Clemens Sox Jsy/100 12.00 3.60
106 R.Clemens Yanks Jsy/100 12.00 3.60
107 Roger Maris A's Jsy/100 40.00 12.00
108 Roger Maris A's Pants/100 30.00 9.00
109 Roger Maris Yanks Jsy/100 40.00 12.00
110 Roy Campanella Pants/100 15.00 4.50
111 Ryne Sandberg Jsy/100 20.00 6.00
112 Stan Musial White Jsy/50 30.00 9.00
113 Steve Carlton Phils Jsy/100 8.00 2.40
114 Ted Williams Jsy/100 80.00 24.00
115 Ted Williams Jkt/100 60.00 18.00
116 Thurman Munson Jsy/100 25.00 7.50
117 T.Munson Pants/100 25.00 7.50
118 Tony Gwynn Jsy/100 15.00 4.50
119 Wade Boggs Yanks Jsy/100 12.00 3.60
120 Wade Boggs Sox Jsy/100 12.00 3.60
121 Warren Spahn Jsy/100 12.00 3.60
122 Warren Spahn Pants/100 12.00 3.60
123 Whitey Ford Jsy/100 12.00 3.60
124 Whitey Ford Pants/100 12.00 3.60
125 Will Clark Jsy/100 15.00 4.50
126 Willie McCovey Jsy/100 12.00 3.60
127 W.Stargell Black Jsy/100 12.00 3.60
128 Yogi Berra Jsy/25 30.00 9.00
129 Frankie Frisch Jkt/100 20.00 6.00
130 Marty Marion Jsy/100 8.00 2.40
131 Tommy John Pants/100 8.00 2.40
132 Chipper Jones Jsy/100 10.00 3.00
133 S.Sosa White Jsy/100 12.00 3.60
134 R.Henderson Dgr Jsy/100 10.00 3.00
135 Mike Piazza Dgr Jsy/100 12.00 3.60
136 Mike Piazza Mets Jsy/100 12.00 3.60
137 N.Garciaparra Grey Jsy/100 12.00 3.60
138 Hideo Nomo Dgr Jsy/100 10.00 3.00
139 Hideo Nomo Mets Jsy/50 15.00 4.50
140 R.Johnson M's Jsy/100 10.00 3.00
141 R.Johnson D'backs Jsy/100 10.00 3.00
142 R.Johnson Astros Jsy/100 10.00 3.00
143 J.Giambi Yanks Jsy/100 5.00 1.50
144 Jason Giambi A's Jsy/100 5.00 1.50
145 C.Schilling Phils Jsy/100 5.00 1.50
146 Dennis Eckersley Jsy/100 12.00 3.60
147 Carlton Fisk W.Sox Jkt/100 12.00 3.60
148 Tom Seaver Mets Jsy/25 25.00 7.50
149 Joe Torre Jsy/100 12.00 3.60
150 P.Martinez Sox Jsy/100 10.00 3.00
151 A.Pujols White Jsy/100 25.00 7.50
152 Andre Dawson Sox Jsy/50 10.00 3.00
153 Bert Blyleven Jsy/100 8.00 2.40
154 Bo Jackson Sox Jsy/100 15.00 4.50
155 Cal Ripken Pants/100 40.00 12.00
156 C.Fisk W.Sox Jsy/100 12.00 3.60
157 C.Schill D'backs Jsy/100 5.00 1.50
158 D.Strawberry Yanks Jsy/100 8.00 2.40
159 Dave Concepcion Jsy/100 8.00 2.40
160 Dwight Evans Jsy/100 8.00 2.40
161 Ernie Banks Pants/100 15.00 4.50
162 Fred McGriff Jsy/1
163 Gary Carter Pants/100 8.00 2.40
164 Gary Sheffield Jsy/100 5.00 1.50
165 George Brett Blue Jsy/100 20.00 6.00
166 Greg Maddux Jsy/100 12.00 3.60
167 Ivan Rodriguez Jsy/100 10.00 3.00
168 Joe Morgan Giants Jsy/100 8.00 2.40
169 J.Canseco White Jsy/100 15.00 4.50
170 J.Gonzalez Rgr Jsy/100 8.00 2.40
171 J.Gonzalez Indians Jsy/100 8.00 2.40
172 Keith Hernandez Jsy/100 8.00 2.40
173 Ken Boyer Jsy/100 20.00 6.00
174 Kerry Wood Jsy/100 10.00 3.00
175 Lee Smith Jsy/100 8.00 2.40
176 Luis Tiant Jsy/100 8.00 2.40
177 Manny Ramirez Jsy/100 8.00 2.40
178 M.Grace D'backs Jsy/100 12.00 3.60
179 Matt Williams Jsy/100 8.00 2.40
180 Miguel Tejada Jsy/100 5.00 1.50
181 Mike Mussina Jsy/100 8.00 2.40
182 M.Piazza Marlins Jsy/100 12.00 3.60
183 N.Garc White Jsy/100 12.00 3.60
184 P.Martinez Dgr Jsy/100 10.00 3.00
185 Rafael Palmeiro Jsy/100 8.00 2.40
186 R.Jackson Yanks Pants/100 12.00 3.60
187 R.Henderson M's Jsy/100 10.00 3.00
188 R.Hend Mets Pants/100 10.00 3.00
189 R.Henderson A's Jsy/100 10.00 3.00
190 Sammy Sosa Blue Jsy/100 12.00 3.60
191 Satchel Paige CO Jsy/100 60.00 18.00
192 Shawn Green Jsy/100 5.00 1.50
193 Stan Musial Grey Jsy/50 30.00 9.00
194 Steve Carlton Sox Jsy/100 8.00 2.40
195 Steve Garvey Jsy/100 8.00 2.40
196 Tom Seaver Reds Jsy/100 12.00 3.60
197 Tony Gwynn Pants/100 15.00 4.50
198 Vladimir Guerrero Jsy/100 10.00 3.00
199 Wade Boggs Rays Jsy/100 12.00 3.60
200 W.Stargell Grey Jsy/100 12.00 3.60

2004 Leaf Certified Materials Fabric of the Game AL/NL

Nm-Mt Ex-Mt
*AL/NL p/r 100: 4X TO 1X FOTG p/r 100
*AL/NL p/r 50: .6X TO 1.5X FOTG p/r 100
*AL/NL p/r 50: .4X TO 1X FOTG p/r 50
*AL/NL p/r 25: 1X TO 2.5X FOTG p/r 100
*AL/NL p/r 25: .6X TO 1.5X FOTG p/r 50
*AL/NL p/r 25: .4X TO 1X FOTG p/r 25
RANDOM INSERTS IN PACKS
PRINT RUNS B/WN 1-100 #'d COPIES PER
NO PRICING ON QTY OF 10 OR LESS

2004 Leaf Certified Materials Fabric of the Game Jersey Number

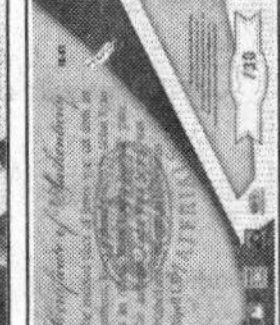

Nm-Mt Ex-Mt
*JSY # p/r 72: .4X TO 1X FOTG p/r 100
*JSY # p/r 36-53: .6X TO 1.5X FOTG p/r 100
*JSY # p/r 36-53: .4X TO 1X FOTG p/r 50
*JSY # p/r 36-53: .25X TO .6X FOTG p/r 25
*JSY # p/r 20-35: 1X TO 2.5X FOTG p/r 100
*JSY # p/r 20-35: .6X TO 1.5X FOTG p/r 50
*JSY # p/r 20-35: .4X TO 1X FOTG p/r 25
*JSY # p/r 15-19: 1.25X TO 3X FOTG p/r 100
*JSY # p/r 15-19: .75X TO 2X FOTG p/r 50
RANDOM INSERTS IN PACKS
PRINT RUNS B/WN 1-72 #'d COPIES PER
NO PRICING ON QTY OF 14 OR LESS
44 Fred Lynn Jsy/19 20.00 6.00
55 Jackie Robinson Jsy/42 60.00 18.00

2004 Leaf Certified Materials Fabric of the Game Jersey Year

Nm-Mt Ex-Mt
*JSY YR p/r 66-99: .4X TO 1X FOTG p/r 100
*JSY YR p/r 66-99: .25X TO .6X FOTG p/r 50
*JSY YR p/r 66-99: .15X TO .4X FOTG p/r 25
*JSY YR p/r 38-65: .6X TO 1.5X FOTG p/r 100

*JSY YR p/r 38-65: .4X TO 1X FOTG p/r 50
*JSY YR p/r 38-65: .25X TO .6X FOTG p/r 25
*JSY YR p/r 20-34: 1X TO 2.5X FOTG p/r 100
*JSY YR p/r 19: 1.25X TO 3X FOTG p/r 100
*JSY YR p/r 19: .75X TO 2X FOTG p/r 50
*JSY YR p/r 19: .5X TO 1.2X FOTG p/r 25
RANDOM INSERTS IN PACKS
PRINT RUNS B/WN 1-99 COPIES PER
NO PRICING ON QTY OF 1 CARD
9 Babe Ruth Jsy/25 500.00 150.00
10 Babe Ruth Pants/30 300.00 90.00
44 Fred Lynn Jsy/19 20.00 6.00
55 Jackie Robinson Jsy/19 100.00 30.00
69 Lou Gehrig Jsy/19 300.00 90.00
70 Lou Gehrig Pants/38 200.00 60.00
87 Ty Cobb Pants/25 120.00 36.00

2004 Leaf Certified Materials Fabric of the Game Position

Nm-Mt Ex-Mt
*POS p/r 100: .4X TO 1X FOTG p/r 100
*POS p/r 50: .6X TO 1.5X FOTG p/r 100
*POS p/r 50: .4X TO 1X FOTG p/r 50..
*POS p/r 25: 1X TO 2.5X FOTG p/r 100
*POS p/r 25: .6X TO 1.5X FOTG p/r 50
*POS p/r 25: .4X TO 1X FOTG p/r 25..
RANDOM INSERTS IN PACKS
PRINT RUNS B/WN 1-100 COPIES PER
NO PRICING ON QTY OF 10 OR LESS

2004 Leaf Certified Materials Fabric of the Game Reward

Nm-Mt Ex-Mt
*RWD p/r 50: .6X TO 1.5X FOTG p/r 100
*RWD p/r 50: .4X TO 1X FOTG p/r 50
*RWD p/r 25: 1X TO 2.5X FOTG p/r 100
*RWD p/r 25: .6X TO 1.5X FOTG p/r 50
*RWD p/r 25: .4X TO 1X FOTG p/r 25
RANDOM INSERTS IN PACKS
PRINT RUNS B/WN 1-50 #'d COPIES PER
NO PRICING ON QTY OF 10 OR LESS
87 Ty Cobb Pants/50 100.00 30.00

2004 Leaf Certified Materials Fabric of the Game Stats

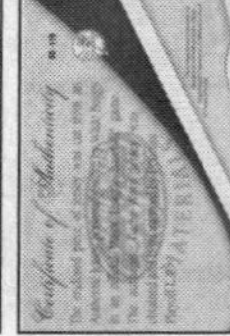

Nm-Mt Ex-Mt
*STAT p/r 66: .4X TO 1X FOTG p/r 100
*STAT p/r 36-57: .6X TO 1.5X FOTG p/r 100
*STAT p/r 36-57: .4X TO 1X FOTG p/r 50
*STAT p/r 36-57: .25X TO .6X FOTG p/r 25
*STAT p/r 20-35: 1X TO 2.5X FOTG p/r 100
*STAT p/r 20-35: .6X TO 1.5X FOTG p/r 50
*STAT p/r 20-35: .4X TO 1X FOTG p/r 25
*STAT p/r 15-19: 1.25X TO 3X FOTG p/r 100
*STAT p/r 15-19: .75X TO 2X FOTG p/r 50
RANDOM INSERTS IN PACKS
PRINT RUNS B/WN 1-66 #'d COPIES PER
NO PRICING ON QTY OF 14 OR LESS
55 Jackie Robinson Jsy/19 100.00 30.00

1998 Leaf Fractal Foundations

The 1998 Leaf Fractal Foundations set was issued in one series totalling 200 cards. The cards are an upgraded parallel from the 1998 leaf set and the fronts feature color player photos printed on foil board. Each card is sequentially numbered to 3,999. Card number 42 does not exist.

Nm-Mt Ex-Mt
COMPLETE SET (200) 150.00 45.00
1 Rusty Greer 2.00 .60
2 Tino Martinez 3.00 .90
3 Bobby Bonilla 2.00 .60
4 Jason Giambi 2.00 .60
5 Matt Morris 2.00 .60
6 Craig Counsell 2.00 .60
7 Reggie Jefferson 2.00 .60
8 Brian Rose 2.00 .60
9 Ruben Rivera 2.00 .60
10 Shawn Estes 2.00 .60
11 Tony Gwynn 6.00 1.80
12 Jeff Abbott 2.00 .60
13 Jose Cruz Jr. 2.00 .60
14 Francisco Cordova 2.00 .60
15 Ryan Klesko 2.00 .60
16 Tim Salmon 3.00 .90
17 Brett Tomko 2.00 .60
18 Matt Williams 2.00 .60
19 Joe Carter 2.00 .60
20 Harold Baines 2.00 .60
21 Gary Sheffield 2.00 .60
22 Charles Johnson 2.00 .60
23 Aaron Boone 2.00 .60
24 Eddie Murray 5.00 1.50
25 Matt Stairs 2.00 .60
26 David Cone 2.00 .60
27 Jon Nunnally 2.00 .60
28 Chris Stynes 2.00 .60
29 Enrique Wilson 2.00 .60
30 Randy Johnson 5.00 1.50
31 Garret Anderson 2.00 .60
32 Manny Ramirez 3.00 .90
33 Jeff Suppan 2.00 .60
34 Rickey Henderson 5.00 1.50
35 Scott Spiezio 2.00 .60
36 Rondell White 2.00 .60
37 Todd Greene 2.00 .60
38 Delino DeShields 2.00 .60
39 Kevin Brown 3.00 .90
40 Chili Davis 2.00 .60
41 Jimmy Key 2.00 .60
43 Mike Mussina 3.00 .90
44 Joe Randa 2.00 .60
45 Chan Ho Park 2.00 .60
46 Brad Radke 2.00 .60
47 Geronimo Berroa 2.00 .60
48 Wade Boggs 3.00 .90
49 Kevin Appier 2.00 .60
50 Moises Alou 2.00 .60
51 David Justice 2.00 .60
52 Ivan Rodriguez 5.00 1.50
53 J.T. Snow 2.00 .60
54 Brian Giles 2.00 .60
55 Will Clark 5.00 1.50
56 Justin Thompson 2.00 .60
57 Javier Lopez 2.00 .60
58 Hideki Irabu 2.00 .60
59 Mark Grudzielanek 2.00 .60
60 Abraham Nunez 2.00 .60
61 Todd Hollandsworth 2.00 .60
62 Jay Bell 2.00 .60
63 Nomar Garciaparra 8.00 2.40
64 Vinny Castilla 2.00 .60
65 Lou Collier 2.00 .60
66 Kevin Orie 2.00 .60
67 John Valentin 2.00 .60
68 Robin Ventura 2.00 .60
69 Denny Neagle 2.00 .60
70 Tony Womack 2.00 .60
71 Dennis Reyes 2.00 .60
72 Wally Joyner 2.00 .60
73 Kevin Brown 3.00 .90
74 Ray Durham 2.00 .60
75 Mike Cameron 2.00 .60
76 Dante Bichette 2.00 .60
77 Jose Guillen 2.00 .60
78 Carlos Delgado 2.00 .60
79 Paul Molitor 3.00 .90
80 Jason Kendall 2.00 .60
81 Mark Bellhorn 2.00 .60
82 Damian Jackson 2.00 .60
83 Bill Mueller 2.00 .60
84 Kevin Young 2.00 .60
85 Curt Schilling 2.00 .60
86 Jeffrey Hammonds 2.00 .60
87 Sandy Alomar Jr. 2.00 .60
88 Bartolo Colon 2.00 .60
89 Wilton Guerrero 2.00 .60
90 Bernie Williams 3.00 .90
91 Deion Sanders 3.00 .90
92 Mike Piazza 8.00 2.40
93 Butch Huskey 2.00 .60
94 Edgardo Alfonzo 2.00 .60
95 Alan Benes 2.00 .60
96 Craig Biggio 3.00 .90
97 Mark Grace 3.00 .90
98 Shawn Green 2.00 .60
99 Derrek Lee 2.00 .60
100 Ken Griffey Jr. 8.00 2.40
101 Tim Raines 2.00 .60
102 Pokey Reese 2.00 .60
103 Lee Stevens 2.00 .60
104 Shannon Stewart 2.00 .60
105 John Smoltz 3.00 .90
106 Frank Thomas 5.00 1.50
107 Jeff Fassero 2.00 .60
108 Jay Buhner 2.00 .60
109 Jose Canseco 5.00 1.50
110 Omar Vizquel 3.00 .90
111 Travis Fryman 2.00 .60
112 Dave Nilsson 2.00 .60
113 John Olerud 2.00 .60
114 Larry Walker 3.00 .90
115 Jim Edmonds 2.00 .60
116 Bobby Higginson 2.00 .60
117 Todd Hundley 2.00 .60
118 Paul O'Neill 3.00 .90
119 Bip Roberts 2.00 .60
120 Ismael Valdes 2.00 .60
121 Pedro Martinez 5.00 1.50
122 Jeff Cirillo 2.00 .60
123 Andy Benes 2.00 .60
124 Bobby Jones 2.00 .60
125 Brian Hunter 2.00 .60
126 Darryl Kile 2.00 .60
127 Pat Hentgen 2.00 .60
128 Marquis Grissom 2.00 .60
129 Eric Davis 2.00 .60
130 Chipper Jones 5.00 1.50
131 Edgar Martinez 3.00 .90
132 Andy Pettitte 3.00 .90
133 Cal Ripken 15.00 4.50
134 Scott Rolen 5.00 1.50
135 Ron Coomer 2.00 .60
136 Luis Castillo 2.00 .60
137 Fred McGriff 3.00 .90
138 Neifi Perez 2.00 .60
139 Eric Karros 2.00 .60
140 Alex Fernandez 2.00 .60
141 Jason Dickson 2.00 .60
142 Lance Johnson 2.00 .60
143 Ray Lankford 2.00 .60
144 Sammy Sosa 8.00 2.40
145 Eric Young 2.00 .60
146 Bubba Trammell 2.00 .60
147 Todd Walker 2.00 .60
148 Mo Vaughn CC 2.00 .60
149 Jeff Bagwell CC 3.00 .90
150 Kenny Lofton CC 2.00 .60
151 Raul Mondesi CC 2.00 .60
152 Mike Piazza CC 8.00 2.40
153 Chipper Jones CC 5.00 1.50
154 Larry Walker CC 3.00 .90
155 Greg Maddux CC 8.00 2.40
156 Ken Griffey Jr. CC 8.00 2.40
157 Frank Thomas CC 5.00 1.50
158 Darin Erstad GLS 2.00 .60
159 Roberto Alomar GLS 3.00 .90
160 Albert Belle GLS 2.00 .60
161 Jim Thome GLS 5.00 1.50
162 Tony Clark GLS 2.00 .60
163 Chuck Knoblauch GLS 2.00 .60
164 Derek Jeter GLS 12.00 3.60
165 Alex Rodriguez GLS 8.00 2.40
166 Tony Gwynn GLS 6.00 1.80
167 Roger Clemens GLS 10.00 3.00
168 Barry Larkin GLS 3.00 .90
169 A. Galarraga GLS 2.00 .60
170 Vlad. Guerrero GLS 5.00 1.50
171 Mark McGwire GLS 12.50 3.70
172 Barry Bonds GLS 12.00 3.60
173 Juan Gonzalez GLS 3.00 .90
174 Andruw Jones GLS 2.00 .60
175 Paul Molitor GLS 3.00 .90
176 Hideo Nomo GLS 5.00 1.50
177 Cal Ripken GLS 15.00 4.50
178 Brad Fullmer GLR 2.00 .60
179 Jaret Wright GLR 2.00 .60
180 Bobby Estalella GLR 2.00 .60
181 Ben Grieve GLR 2.00 .60
182 Paul Konerko GLR 2.00 .60
183 David Ortiz GLR 5.00 1.50
184 Todd Helton GLR 3.00 .90
185 J.Encarnacion GLR 2.00 .60
186 Miguel Tejada GLR 2.00 .60
187 Jacob Cruz GLR 2.00 .60
188 Mark Kotsay GLR 2.00 .60
189 Fernando Tatis GLR 2.00 .60
190 Ricky Ledee GLR 2.00 .60
191 Richard Hidalgo GLR 2.00 .60
192 Richie Sexson GLR 2.00 .60
193 Luis Ordaz GLR 2.00 .60
194 Eli Marrero GLR 2.00 .60
195 Livan Hernandez GLR 2.00 .60
196 Homer Bush GLR 2.00 .60
197 Raul Ibanez GLR 2.00 .60
198 N. Garciaparra CL 5.00 1.50
199 Scott Rolen CL 3.00 .90
200 Jose Cruz Jr. CL 2.00 .60
201 Al Martin 2.00 .60

1998 Leaf Fractal Materials

Inserted at a rate of one per pack, cards from this 200-card set parallel the base Leaf Fractal Foundation set. The cards are printed on real "feel of the game" materials including wood, nylon, plastic and leather. Of the 100 cards printed on plastic, only 3,250 of each card was made; of the 50 on leather, 1000 were made; only 500 of the 30 printed on nylon were made; and of the 20 printed on wood, only 250 of each were made. All the cards are sequentially numbered. Card number 42 does not exist.

Nm-Mt Ex-Mt
*PLASTIC: .25X TO .6X BASIC CARDS
PLASTIC X PRINT RUN 3050 SERIAL #'d SETS
PLASTIC Y PRINT RUN 3150 SERIAL #'d SETS
PLASTIC Z PRINT RUN 3200 SERIAL #'d SETS
*LEATHER: .5X TO 1.25X BASIC CARDS
LEATHER X PRINT RUN 800 SERIAL #'d SETS
LEATHER Y PRINT RUN 900 SERIAL #'d SETS
LEATHER Z PRINT RUN 950 SERIAL #'d SETS
*NYLON: 1X TO 2.5X BASIC CARDS ..
NYLON X PRINT RUN 300 SERIAL #'d SETS
NYLON Y PRINT RUN 400 SERIAL #'d SETS
NYLON Z PRINT RUN 450 SERIAL #'d SETS
*WOOD Y/Z: 1.25X TO 3X BASIC CARDS
*WOOD X: 6X TO 15X BASIC CARDS.
WOOD X PRINT RUN 50 SERIAL #'d SETS
WOOD Y PRINT RUN 150 SERIAL #'d SETS
WOOD Z PRINT RUN 200 SERIAL #'d SETS
CARD NUMBER 42 DOES NOT EXIST.

1998 Leaf Fractal Materials Die Cuts

This 200-card set is a die-cut parallel version of the Leaf Fractal Materials set. The first 200 cards of 75 players printed on plastic, 15 printed on leather, five printed on nylon, and five printed on wood have a die-cut x-axis background. The first 100 cards of 20 players printed on plastic, 25 printed on leather, 10 printed on nylon and five printed on wood have a die-cut y-axis background. The first 50 cards of five players printed on plastic, 10 printed on leather, 15 printed on nylon, and 10 printed on wood have a die-cut z-axis background. Each card is sequentially numbered. Card number 42 does not exist. Only 200 of each x-axis were produced, 100 of each y-axis and 50 of each z-axis were produced. Serial numbering on the actual cards is misleading because the non die cut Fractal Materials and the Die-Cut Fractal Materials were numbered prior to being die cut.

Nm-Mt Ex-Mt
*X-AXIS: 1.25X TO 3X BASIC CARDS
X-AXIS PRINT RUN 200 SERIAL #'d SETS
*Y-AXIS: 2X TO 5X BASIC CARDS
Y-AXIS PRINT RUN 100 SERIAL #'d SETS
*Z-AXIS: 2.5X TO 6X BASIC CARDS...
Z-AXIS PRINT RUN 50 SERIAL #'d SETS

1998 Leaf Fractal Materials Z2 Axis

This 200-card set is parallel to the base set and features full die-cut cards. Each card is sequentially numbered to 20. Card number 42 does not exist.

Nm-Mt Ex-Mt
*STARS: 6X TO 15X BASIC FOUNDATION

1994 Leaf Limited

This 160-card standard-size set was issued exclusively to hobby dealers. The set is organized alphabetically within teams with AL preceding NL.

Nm-Mt Ex-Mt
COMPLETE SET (160) 80.00 24.00
1 Jeffrey Hammonds .50 .15
2 Ben McDonald .50 .15
3 Mike Mussina 1.50 .45
4 Rafael Palmeiro 1.50 .45
5 Cal Ripken Jr. 8.00 2.40
6 Lee Smith 1.00 .30
7 Roger Clemens 5.00 1.50
8 Scott Cooper .50 .15
9 Andre Dawson 1.00 .30
10 Mike Greenwell .50 .15
11 Aaron Sele .50 .15
12 Mo Vaughn 1.00 .30
13 Brian Anderson RC 1.00 .30
14 Chad Curtis .50 .15
15 Chili Davis 1.00 .30
16 Gary DiSarcina .50 .15
17 Mark Langston .50 .15
18 Tim Salmon 1.50 .45
19 Wilson Alvarez .50 .15
20 Jason Bere .50 .15
21 Julio Franco 1.00 .30
22 Jack McDowell .50 .15
23 Tim Raines 1.00 .30
24 Frank Thomas 2.50 .75
25 Robin Ventura 1.00 .30
26 Carlos Baerga .50 .15
27 Albert Belle 1.00 .30
28 Kenny Lofton 1.00 .30
29 Eddie Murray 2.50 .75
30 Manny Ramirez 1.50 .45
31 Cecil Fielder 1.00 .30
32 Travis Fryman 1.00 .30
33 Mickey Tettleton .50 .15
34 Alan Trammell 1.00 .30
35 Lou Whitaker 1.00 .30
36 David Cone 1.00 .30
37 Gary Gaetti 1.00 .30
38 Greg Gagne .50 .15
39 Bob Hamelin .50 .15
40 Wally Joyner 1.00 .30
41 Brian McRae .50 .15
42 Ricky Bones .50 .15
43 Brian Harper .50 .15
44 John Jaha .50 .15
45 Pat Listach .50 .15
46 Dave Nilsson .50 .15
47 Greg Vaughn .50 .15
48 Kent Hrbek 1.00 .30
49 Chuck Knoblauch 1.00 .30
50 Shane Mack .50 .15
51 Kirby Puckett 2.50 .75
52 Dave Winfield 1.00 .30
53 Jim Abbott 1.50 .45
54 Wade Boggs 1.50 .45
55 Jimmy Key 1.00 .30
56 Don Mattingly 6.00 1.80
57 Paul O'Neill 1.50 .45
58 Danny Tartabull .50 .15
59 Dennis Eckersley 1.00 .30
60 Rickey Henderson 2.50 .75
61 Mark McGwire 6.00 1.80
62 Troy Neel .50 .15
63 Ruben Sierra .50 .15
64 Eric Anthony .50 .15
65 Jay Buhner 1.00 .30
66 Ken Griffey Jr. 4.00 1.20
67 Randy Johnson 2.50 .75
68 Edgar Martinez 1.50 .45
69 Tino Martinez 1.50 .45
70 Jose Canseco 2.50 .75
71 Will Clark 2.50 .75
72 Juan Gonzalez 1.50 .45
73 Dean Palmer 1.00 .30
74 Ivan Rodriguez 2.50 .75
75 Roberto Alomar 1.50 .45
76 Joe Carter 1.00 .30
77 Carlos Delgado 1.50 .45
78 Paul Molitor 1.50 .45
79 John Olerud 1.00 .30
80 Devon White 1.00 .30
81 Steve Avery .50 .15
82 Tom Glavine 1.50 .45
83 David Justice 1.00 .30
84 Roberto Kelly .50 .15
85 Ryan Klesko 1.00 .30
86 Javier Lopez 1.00 .30
87 Greg Maddux 4.00 1.20
88 Fred McGriff 1.50 .45
89 Shawon Dunston .50 .15
90 Mark Grace 1.50 .45
91 Derrick May .50 .15
92 Sammy Sosa 4.00 1.20
93 Rick Wilkins .50 .15
94 Bret Boone 1.00 .30
95 Barry Larkin 1.50 .45
96 Kevin Mitchell .50 .15
97 Hal Morris .50 .15
98 Deion Sanders 1.50 .45
99 Reggie Sanders .50 .15
100 Dante Bichette 1.00 .30
101 Ellis Burks 1.00 .30
102 Andres Galarraga 1.00 .30
103 Joe Girardi .50 .15
104 Charlie Hayes .50 .15
105 Chuck Carr .50 .15
106 Jeff Conine 1.00 .30
107 Bryan Harvey .50 .15
108 Benito Santiago 1.00 .30
109 Gary Sheffield 1.00 .30
110 Jeff Bagwell 1.50 .45
111 Craig Biggio 1.50 .45
112 Ken Caminiti 1.00 .30
113 Andujar Cedeno .50 .15
114 Doug Drabek .50 .15
115 Luis Gonzalez 1.00 .30
116 Brett Butler 1.00 .30
117 Delino DeShields .50 .15
118 Eric Karros 1.00 .30
119 Raul Mondesi 1.00 .30
120 Mike Piazza 5.00 1.50
121 Henry Rodriguez .50 .15
122 Tim Wallach .50 .15
123 Moises Alou 1.00 .30
124 Cliff Floyd 1.00 .30
125 Marquis Grissom 1.00 .30
126 Ken Hill .50 .15
127 Larry Walker 1.50 .45
128 John Wetteland 1.00 .30
129 Bobby Bonilla 1.00 .30
130 John Franco 1.00 .30
131 Jeff Kent 1.00 .30
132 Bret Saberhagen 1.00 .30
133 Ryan Thompson .50 .15
134 Darren Daulton 1.00 .30
135 Mariano Duncan .50 .15
136 Lenny Dykstra 1.00 .30
137 Danny Jackson .50 .15
138 John Kruk 1.00 .30
139 Jay Bell 1.00 .30
140 Jeff King .50 .15
141 Al Martin .50 .15
142 Orlando Merced .50 .15
143 Andy Van Slyke 1.00 .30
144 Bernard Gilkey .50 .15
145 Gregg Jefferies .50 .15
146 Ray Lankford .50 .15
147 Ozzie Smith 4.00 1.20
148 Mark Whiten .50 .15
149 Todd Zeile .50 .15
150 Derek Bell .50 .15
151 Andy Benes .50 .15
152 Tony Gwynn 3.00 .90
153 Phil Plantier .50 .15
154 Bip Roberts .50 .15
155 Rod Beck .50 .15
156 Barry Bonds 6.00 1.80
157 John Burkett .50 .15
158 Royce Clayton .50 .15
159 Bill Swift .50 .15
160 Matt Williams 1.00 .30

1994 Leaf Limited Gold All-Stars

Randomly inserted in packs at a rate of one in seven, this 18-card standard-size set features the starting players at each position in both the National and American leagues for the 1994 All-Star Game. They are identical in design to the basic Limited product except for being gold and individually numbered out of 10,000.

Nm-Mt Ex-Mt
COMPLETE SET (18) 40.00 12.00
1 Frank Thomas 2.00 .60
2 Gregg Jefferies .40 .12
3 Roberto Alomar 1.25 .35
4 Mariano Duncan .40 .12
5 Wade Boggs 1.25 .35
6 Matt Williams .75 .23
7 Cal Ripken Jr. 6.00 1.80
8 Ozzie Smith 3.00 .90
9 Kirby Puckett 2.00 .60
10 Barry Bonds 5.00 1.50
11 Ken Griffey Jr. 3.00 .90
12 Tony Gwynn 2.50 .75
13 Joe Carter .75 .23
14 David Justice .75 .23
15 Ivan Rodriguez 2.00 .60
16 Mike Piazza 4.00 1.20
17 Jimmy Key .75 .23
18 Greg Maddux 3.00 .90

1994 Leaf Limited Rookies

This 80-card standard-size premium set was issued by Donruss exclusively to hobby dealers. The set showcases top rookies and prospects of 1994. Rookie Cards in this set include Armando Benitez, Rusty Greer and Chan Ho Park.

Nm-Mt Ex-Mt
COMPLETE SET (80) 25.00 7.50
1 Charles Johnson .75 .23

Rico Brogna	.40	.12
Melvin Nieves	.40	.12
Rich Becker	.40	.12
Russ Davis	.40	.12
Matt Mieske	.40	.12
Paul Shuey	.40	.12
Hector Carrasco	.40	.12
J.R. Phillips	.40	.12
) Scott Ruffcorn	.40	.12
1 Kurt Abbott RC	.75	.23
2 Danny Bautista	.40	.12
3 Rick White	.40	.12
4 Steve Dunn	.40	.12
5 Joe Ausanio	.40	.12
6 Salomon Torres	.40	.12
7 Ricky Bottalico RC	.75	.23
3 Johnny Ruffin	.40	.12
9 Kevin Foster RC	.40	.12
) W.VanLandingham RC	.40	.12
1 Troy O'Leary	.40	.12
2 Mark Acre RC	.40	.12
3 Norberto Martin	.40	.12
4 Jason Jacome RC	.40	.12
5 Steve Trachsel	.40	.12
6 Denny Hocking	.40	.12
7 Mike Lieberthal	.75	.23
3 Gerald Williams	.40	.12
9 John Mabry RC	.75	.23
) Greg Blosser	.40	.12
1 Carl Everett	.75	.23
2 Steve Karsay	.40	.12
3 Jose Valentin	.40	.12
4 Jon Lieber	.40	.12
5 Chris Gomez	.40	.12
5 Jesus Tavarez RC	.40	.12
7 Tony Longmire	.40	.12
3 Luis Lopez	.40	.12
9 Matt Walbeck	.40	.12
) Rikkert Faneyte RC	.40	.12
1 Shane Reynolds	.40	.12
2 Joey Hamilton	.40	.12
3 Ismael Valdes RC	.75	.23
4 Danny Miceli	.40	.12
5 Darren Bragg RC	.40	.12
5 Alex Gonzalez	.40	.12
7 Rick Helling	.40	.12
3 Jose Oliva	.40	.12
3 Jim Edmonds	2.00	.60
) Miguel Jimenez	.40	.12
1 Tony Eusebio	.40	.12
2 Shawn Green	2.00	.60
3 Billy Ashley	.40	.12
4 Rondell White	.75	.23
5 Cory Bailey RC	.40	.12
5 Tim Davis	.40	.12
7 John Hudek RC	.40	.12
3 Darren Hall	.40	.12
9 Darren Dreifort	.40	.12
) Mike Kelly	.40	.12
1 Marcus Moore	.40	.12
2 Garret Anderson	2.00	.60
3 Brian L. Hunter	.40	.12
4 Mark Smith	.40	.12
5 Garey Ingram RC	.40	.12
5 Rusty Greer RC	1.25	.35
7 Marc Newfield	.40	.12
3 Gar Finnvold	.40	.12
9 Paul Spoljaric	.40	.12
) Ray McDavid	.40	.12
1 Orlando Miller	.40	.12
2 Jorge Fabregas	.40	.12
3 Ray Holbert	.40	.12
4 Armando Benitez RC	2.00	.60
5 Ernie Young RC	.75	.23
5 James Mouton	.40	.12
7 Robert Perez RC	.40	.12
3 Chan Ho Park RC	1.25	.35
9 Roger Salkeld	.40	.12
) Tony Tarasco	.40	.12

1994 Leaf Limited Rookies Phenoms

his 10-card standard-size set was randomly serted in Leaf Limited Rookies packs at a rate approximately of one in twelve. This set show-ases top 1994 rookies especially Alex odriguez. The fronts are designed much like e Limited Rookies basic set cards except the ard is comprised of gold foil instead of silver on e front. Gold backs are also virtually identical the Limited Rookies in terms of content and yout. The cards are individually numbered on ack out of 5,000. The Rodriguez card, primari- because of it's status as one of A-Rod's earli-st serial-numbered MLB-liscensed issues (cou-led with high-end production qualities and a nown print run) has become one of the more esirable cards issued in the 1990's. Collectors hould take caution of trimmed copies when urchasing this card in "raw" form.

	Nm-Mt	Ex-Mt
Raul Mondesi	8.00	2.40
Bob Hamelin	5.00	1.50
3 Midre Cummings	5.00	1.50
4 Carlos Delgado	10.00	3.00
5 Cliff Floyd	8.00	2.40
6 Jeffrey Hammonds	5.00	1.50
7 Ryan Klesko	8.00	2.40
8 Javier Lopez	8.00	2.40
9 Manny Ramirez	10.00	3.00
10 Alex Rodriguez	200.00	60.00

1995 Leaf Limited

This 192 standard-size card set was issued in two series. Each series contained 96 cards. These cards were issued in six-box cases with 20 packs per box and five cards per pack. Forty-five thousand boxes of each series was produced. Rookie Cards in this set include Bob Higginson and Hideo Nomo.

	Nm-Mt	Ex-Mt
COMPLETE SET (192)	40.00	12.00
COMPLETE SERIES 1 (96)	20.00	6.00
COMPLETE SERIES 2 (96)	20.00	6.00
1 Frank Thomas	1.25	.35
2 Geronimo Berroa	.25	.07
3 Tony Phillips	.25	.07
4 Roberto Alomar	.75	.23
5 Steve Avery	.25	.07
6 Darryl Hamilton	.25	.07
7 Scott Cooper	.25	.07
8 Mark Grace	.75	.23
9 Billy Ashley	.25	.07
10 Wil Cordero	.25	.07
11 Barry Bonds	3.00	.90
12 Kenny Lofton	.50	.15
13 Jay Buhner	.50	.15
14 Alex Rodriguez	3.00	.90
15 Bobby Bonilla	.50	.15
16 Brady Anderson	.50	.15
17 Ken Caminiti	.50	.15
18 Charlie Hayes	.25	.07
19 Jay Bell	.50	.15
20 Will Clark	1.25	.35
21 Jose Canseco	1.25	.35
22 Bret Boone	.50	.15
23 Dante Bichette	.50	.15
24 Kevin Appier	.50	.15
25 Chad Curtis	.25	.07
26 Marty Cordova	.25	.07
27 Jason Bere	.25	.07
28 Jimmy Key	.50	.15
29 Rickey Henderson	1.25	.35
30 Tim Salmon	.75	.23
31 Joe Carter	.50	.15
32 Tom Glavine	.75	.23
33 Pat Listach	.25	.07
34 Brian Jordan	.50	.15
35 Brian McRae	.25	.07
36 Eric Karros	.50	.15
37 Pedro Martinez	1.25	.35
38 Royce Clayton	.25	.07
39 Eddie Murray	1.25	.35
40 Randy Johnson	1.25	.35
41 Jeff Conine	.50	.15
42 Brett Butler	.50	.15
43 Jeffrey Hammonds	.25	.07
44 Andujar Cedeno	.25	.07
45 Dave Hollins	.25	.07
46 Jeff King	.25	.07
47 Benji Gil	.25	.07
48 Roger Clemens	2.50	.75
49 Barry Larkin	.75	.23
50 Joe Girardi	.25	.07
51 Bob Hamelin	.25	.07
52 Travis Fryman	.50	.15
53 Chuck Knoblauch	.50	.15
54 Ray Durham	.50	.15
55 Don Mattingly	3.00	.90
56 Ruben Sierra	.25	.07
57 J.T. Snow	.50	.15
58 Derek Bell	.25	.07
59 David Cone	.50	.15
60 Marquis Grissom	.50	.15
61 Kevin Seitzer	.25	.07
62 Ozzie Smith	2.00	.60
63 Rick Wilkins	.25	.07
64 Hideo Nomo RC	2.50	.75
65 Tony Tarasco	.25	.07
66 Manny Ramirez	.75	.23
67 Charles Johnson	.50	.15
68 Craig Biggio	.75	.23
69 Bobby Jones	.25	.07
70 Mike Mussina	.75	.23
71 Alex Gonzalez	.25	.07
72 Gregg Jefferies	.25	.07
73 Rusty Greer	.50	.15
74 Mike Greenwell	.25	.07
75 Hal Morris	.25	.07
76 Paul O'Neill	.75	.23
77 Luis Gonzalez	.50	.15
78 Chipper Jones	1.25	.35
79 Mike Piazza	2.00	.60
80 Rondell White	.50	.15
81 Glenallen Hill	.25	.07
82 Shawn Green	.50	.15
83 Bernie Williams	.75	.23
84 Jim Thome	1.25	.35
85 Terry Pendleton	.50	.15
86 Rafael Palmeiro	.75	.23
87 Tony Gwynn	1.50	.45
88 Mickey Tettleton	.25	.07
89 John Valentin	.25	.07
90 Deion Sanders	.75	.23
91 Larry Walker	.75	.23
92 Michael Tucker	.25	.07
93 Alan Trammell	.50	.15
94 Tim Raines	.50	.15
95 David Justice	.50	.15
96 Tino Martinez	.75	.23
97 Cal Ripken Jr.	4.00	1.20
98 Deion Sanders	.75	.23
99 Darren Daulton	.50	.15
100 Paul Molitor	.75	.23
101 Randy Myers	.25	.07
102 Wally Joyner	.50	.15
103 Carlos Perez RC	.50	.15
104 Brian Hunter	.25	.07
105 Wade Boggs	.75	.23
106 Bob Higginson RC	.75	.23
107 Jeff Kent	.50	.15
108 Jose Offerman	.25	.07
109 Dennis Eckersley	.50	.15
110 Dave Nilsson	.25	.07
111 Chuck Finley	.50	.15
112 Devon White	.50	.15
113 Bip Roberts	.25	.07
114 Ramon Martinez	.25	.07
115 Greg Maddux	2.00	.60
116 Curtis Goodwin	.25	.07
117 John Jaha	.25	.07
118 Ken Griffey Jr.	2.00	.60
119 Geronimo Pena	.25	.07
120 Shawon Dunston	.25	.07
121 Ariel Prieto RC	.25	.07
122 Kirby Puckett	1.25	.35
123 Carlos Baerga	.25	.07
124 Todd Hundley	.25	.07
125 Tim Naehring	.25	.07
126 Gary Sheffield	.50	.15
127 Dean Palmer	.50	.15
128 Rondell White	.50	.15
129 Greg Gagne	.25	.07
130 Jose Rijo	.25	.07
131 Ivan Rodriguez	1.25	.35
132 Jeff Bagwell	.75	.23
133 Greg Vaughn	.25	.07
134 Chili Davis	.50	.15
135 Al Martin	.25	.07
136 Kenny Rogers	.50	.15
137 Aaron Sele	.25	.07
138 Raul Mondesi	.50	.15
139 Cecil Fielder	.50	.15
140 Tim Wallach	.25	.07
141 Andres Galarraga	.50	.15
142 Lou Whitaker	.50	.15
143 Jack McDowell	.25	.07
144 Matt Williams	.50	.15
145 Ryan Klesko	.50	.15
146 Carlos Garcia	.25	.07
147 Albert Belle	.50	.15
148 Ryan Thompson	.25	.07
149 Roberto Kelly	.25	.07
150 Edgar Martinez	.75	.23
151 Robby Thompson	.25	.07
152 Mo Vaughn	.50	.15
153 Todd Zeile	.25	.07
154 Harold Baines	.50	.15
155 Phil Plantier	.25	.07
156 Mike Stanley	.25	.07
157 Ed Sprague	.25	.07
158 Moises Alou	.50	.15
159 Quilvio Veras	.25	.07
160 Reggie Sanders	.25	.07
161 Delino DeShields	.25	.07
162 Rico Brogna	.25	.07
163 Greg Colbrunn	.25	.07
164 Steve Finley	.50	.15
165 Orlando Merced	.25	.07
166 Mark McGwire	3.00	.90
167 Garret Anderson	.50	.15
168 Paul Sorrento	.25	.07
169 Mark Langston	.25	.07
170 Danny Tartabull	.25	.07
171 Vinny Castilla	.50	.15
172 Javier Lopez	.50	.15
173 Bret Saberhagen	.50	.15
174 Eddie Williams	.25	.07
175 Scott Leius	.25	.07
176 Juan Gonzalez	.75	.23
177 Gary Gaetti	.50	.15
178 Jim Edmonds	.75	.23
179 John Olerud	.50	.15
180 Lenny Dykstra	.50	.15
181 Ray Lankford	.25	.07
182 Ron Gant	.50	.15
183 Doug Drabek	.25	.07
184 Fred McGriff	.75	.23
185 Andy Benes	.25	.07
186 Kurt Abbott	.25	.07
187 Bernard Gilkey	.25	.07
188 Sammy Sosa	2.00	.60
189 Lee Smith	.50	.15
190 Dennis Martinez	.50	.15
191 Ozzie Guillen	.25	.07
192 Robin Ventura	.50	.15

1995 Leaf Limited Gold

These 24 standard-size quasi-parallel cards were inserted one per series one pack. Players from both series were included in this set. While using the same design as the regular issue, they are distinguished by different photos, different numbers and gold holographic foil.

	Nm-Mt	Ex-Mt
1 Frank Thomas	1.25	.35
2 Jeff Bagwell	.75	.23
3 Raul Mondesi	.50	.15
4 Barry Bonds	3.00	.90
5 Albert Belle	.50	.15
6 Ken Griffey Jr.	2.00	.60
7 Cal Ripken UER Name spelled Ripkin on card	4.00	1.20
8 Will Clark	1.25	.35
9 Jose Canseco	1.25	.35
10 Larry Walker	.75	.23
11 Kirby Puckett	1.25	.35
12 Don Mattingly	3.00	.90
13 Tim Salmon	.75	.23
14 Roberto Alomar	.75	.23
15 Greg Maddux	2.00	.60
16 Mike Piazza	2.00	.60
17 Matt Williams	.50	.15
18 Kenny Lofton	.50	.15
19 Alex Rodriguez UER Name spelled Rodriquez on card	3.00	.90
20 Tony Gwynn	1.50	.45
21 Mo Vaughn	.50	.15
22 Chipper Jones	1.25	.35
23 Manny Ramirez	.75	.23
24 Deion Sanders	.75	.23

1995 Leaf Limited Bat Patrol

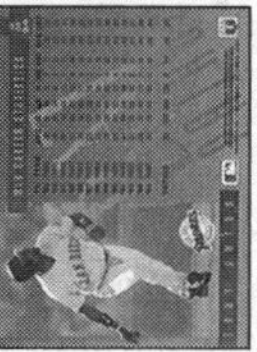

These 24 standard-size cards were inserted one per series two pack. The cards are numbered in the upper right corner as "X" of 24.

	Nm-Mt	Ex-Mt
COMPLETE SET (24)	25.00	7.50
1 Frank Thomas	1.25	.35
2 Tony Gwynn	1.50	.45
3 Wade Boggs	.75	.23
4 Larry Walker	.75	.23
5 Ken Griffey, Jr.	2.00	.60
6 Jeff Bagwell	.75	.23
7 Manny Ramirez	.75	.23
8 Mark Grace	.75	.23
9 Kenny Lofton	.50	.15
10 Mike Piazza	2.00	.60
11 Will Clark	1.25	.35
12 Mo Vaughn	.50	.15
13 Carlos Baerga	.25	.07
14 Rafael Palmeiro	.75	.23
15 Barry Bonds	3.00	.90
16 Kirby Puckett	1.25	.35
17 Roberto Alomar	.75	.23
18 Barry Larkin	.75	.23
19 Eddie Murray	1.25	.35
20 Tim Salmon	.75	.23
21 Don Mattingly	3.00	.90
22 Fred McGriff	.75	.23
23 Albert Belle	.50	.15
24 Dante Bichette	.50	.15

1995 Leaf Limited Lumberjacks

These eight standard-size cards were randomly inserted into second series packs. The cards are individually numbered out of 5,000. The fronts feature a player photo surrounded by his name, the word "Lumberjacks" and "Handcrafted" in a semi-circular pattern on a simulated wood grain stock. Please note, these cards do not feature elements of game-used material.

	Nm-Mt	Ex-Mt
COMPLETE SET (16)	200.00	60.00
COMPLETE SERIES 1 (8)	100.00	30.00
COMPLETE SERIES 2 (8)	100.00	30.00
1 Albert Belle	4.00	1.20
2 Barry Bonds	25.00	7.50
3 Juan Gonzalez	6.00	1.80
4 Ken Griffey Jr.	15.00	4.50
5 Fred McGriff	6.00	1.80
6 Mike Piazza	15.00	4.50
7 Kirby Puckett	10.00	3.00
8 Mo Vaughn	4.00	1.20
9 Frank Thomas	10.00	3.00
10 Jeff Bagwell	6.00	1.80
11 Matt Williams	4.00	1.20
12 Jose Canseco	10.00	3.00
13 Raul Mondesi	4.00	1.20
14 Manny Ramirez	6.00	1.80
15 Cecil Fielder	4.00	1.20
16 Cal Ripken	30.00	9.00

1996 Leaf Limited

The 1996 Leaf Limited set was issued exclusively to hobby outlets with a maximum production run of 45,000 boxes. Each box contained two smaller mini-boxes, enabling the dealer to use his imagination in the marketing of this product. The five-card packs carried a suggested retail price of $3.24. Each Master Box was sequentially- numbered via a box topper. If this number matched the 1996 year-ending stats, the collector and the dealer both had a chance to win prizes such as a Frank Thomas game-used bat, autographed batting glove, or a "Two Biggest Weapons" poster. The collector would return the winning box number to the hobby shop, and the dealer would mail it to Donruss with both receiving the same prize. The card fronts displayed color player photos with another photo and player information on the backs.

	Nm-Mt	Ex-Mt
COMPLETE SET (90)	50.00	15.00
1 Ivan Rodriguez	1.50	.45
2 Roger Clemens	3.00	.90
3 Gary Sheffield	.60	.18
4 Tino Martinez	1.00	.30
5 Sammy Sosa	2.50	.75
6 Reggie Sanders	.60	.18
7 Ray Lankford	.60	.18
8 Manny Ramirez	1.00	.30
9 Jeff Bagwell	1.00	.30
10 Greg Maddux	2.50	.75
11 Ken Griffey Jr.	2.50	.75
12 Rondell White	.60	.18
13 Mike Piazza	2.50	.75
14 Marc Newfield	.60	.18
15 Cal Ripken	5.00	1.50
16 Carlos Delgado	.60	.18
17 Tim Salmon	1.00	.30
18 Andres Galarraga	.60	.18
19 Chuck Knoblauch	.60	.18
20 Matt Williams	.60	.18
21 Mark McGwire	4.00	1.20
22 Ben McDonald	.60	.18
23 Frank Thomas	1.50	.45
24 Johnny Damon	1.00	.30
25 Gregg Jefferies	.60	.18
26 Travis Fryman	.60	.18
27 Chipper Jones	1.50	.45
28 David Cone	.60	.18
29 Kenny Lofton	.60	.18
30 Mike Mussina	1.00	.30
31 Alex Rodriguez	3.00	.90
32 Carlos Baerga	.60	.18
33 Brian Hunter	.60	.18
34 Juan Gonzalez	1.00	.30
35 Bernie Williams	1.00	.30
36 Wally Joyner	.60	.18
37 Fred McGriff	1.00	.30
38 Randy Johnson	1.50	.45
39 Marty Cordova	.60	.18
40 Garret Anderson	.60	.18
41 Albert Belle	.60	.18
42 Edgar Martinez	1.00	.30
43 Barry Larkin	1.00	.30
44 Paul O'Neill	1.00	.30
45 Cecil Fielder	.60	.18
46 Rusty Greer	.60	.18
47 Mo Vaughn	.60	.18
48 Dante Bichette	.60	.18
49 Ryan Klesko	.60	.18
50 Roberto Alomar	1.00	.30
51 Raul Mondesi	.60	.18
52 Robin Ventura	.60	.18
53 Tony Gwynn	2.00	.60
54 Mark Grace	1.00	.30
55 Jim Thome	1.50	.45
56 Jason Giambi	.60	.18
57 Tom Glavine	1.00	.30
58 Jim Edmonds	.60	.18
59 Pedro Martinez	1.50	.45
60 Charles Johnson	.60	.18
61 Wade Boggs	1.00	.30
62 Orlando Merced	.60	.18
63 Craig Biggio	1.00	.30
64 Brady Anderson	.60	.18
65 Hideo Nomo	1.50	.45
66 Ozzie Smith	2.50	.75
67 Eddie Murray	1.50	.45
68 Will Clark	1.50	.45
69 Jay Buhner	.60	.18
70 Kirby Puckett	1.50	.45
71 Barry Bonds	4.00	1.20
72 Ray Durham	.60	.18
73 Sterling Hitchcock	.60	.18
74 John Smoltz	1.00	.30
75 Andre Dawson	.60	.18
76 Joe Carter	.60	.18
77 Ryne Sandberg	2.50	.75
78 Rickey Henderson	1.50	.45
79 Brian Jordan	.60	.18
80 Greg Vaughn	.60	.18
81 Andy Pettitte	1.00	.30
82 Dean Palmer	.60	.18
83 Paul Molitor	1.00	.30
84 Rafael Palmeiro	1.00	.30
85 Henry Rodriguez	.60	.18
86 Larry Walker	1.00	.30
87 Ismael Valdes	.60	.18
88 Derek Bell	.60	.18
89 J.T. Snow	.60	.18
90 Jack McDowell	.60	.18

1996 Leaf Limited Gold

Randomly inserted into one in every 11 packs, cards from this 90-card insert set parallel the regular Leaf Limited issue. Similar in design, it differs from the regular set with its gold holographic foil treatment.

	Nm-Mt	Ex-Mt
*STARS: 2.5X TO 6X BASIC CARDS...		

1996 Leaf Limited Lumberjacks

Printed with maple stock that puts wood grains on both sides (but does not incorporate game-used bat chips), this 10-card insert set features the league's top sluggers. The fronts carry color player photos with player information and statistics on the backs. Only 5,000 sets were produced and each card is individually numbered.

	Nm-Mt	Ex-Mt
COMPLETE SET (10)	120.00	36.00
*BLACK: 1.5X TO 4X BASIC LUMBERJACK		
BLACK PRINT RUN 500 SERIAL #'d SETS		
1 Ken Griffey Jr.	12.00	3.60
2 Sammy Sosa	12.00	3.60
3 Cal Ripken	25.00	7.50
4 Frank Thomas	8.00	2.40

5 Alex Rodriguez 15.00 4.50
6 Mo Vaughn 3.00 .90
7 Chipper Jones 8.00 2.40
8 Mike Piazza 12.00 3.60
9 Jeff Bagwell 5.00 1.50
10 Mark McGwire 20.00 6.00

1996 Leaf Limited Pennant Craze

This 10-card insert set features 10 superstars who have a thirst for the pennant. A special flocking technique puts the felt feel of a pennant on a die cut card. Only 2,500 sets were produced and are individually numbered.

Nm-Mt Ex-Mt
COMPLETE SET (10) 200.00 60.00
1 Juan Gonzalez 10.00 3.00
2 Cal Ripken 50.00 15.00
3 Frank Thomas 15.00 4.50
4 Ken Griffey Jr. 25.00 7.50
5 Albert Belle 6.00 1.80
6 Greg Maddux 25.00 7.50
7 Paul Molitor 10.00 3.00
8 Alex Rodriguez 30.00 9.00
9 Barry Bonds 40.00 12.00
10 Chipper Jones 15.00 4.50

1996 Leaf Limited Rookies

Randomly inserted in packs at a rate of one in seven, this 10-card set printed in silver holographic foil features some of the hottest rookies of the year. A first year card of Darin Erstad is in this set.

Nm-Mt Ex-Mt
COMPLETE SET (10) 40.00 12.00
*GOLD: 1X TO 2.5X BASIC ROOKIES
GOLD: RANDOM INSERTS IN PACKS.
1 Alex Ochoa 1.00 .30
2 Darin Erstad 4.00 1.20
3 Ruben Rivera 1.00 .30
4 Derek Jeter 15.00 4.50
5 Jermaine Dye 2.00 .60
6 Jason Kendall 2.00 .60
7 Mike Grace 1.00 .30
8 Andruw Jones 2.00 .60
9 Rey Ordonez 1.00 .30
10 George Arias 1.00 .30

2001 Leaf Limited

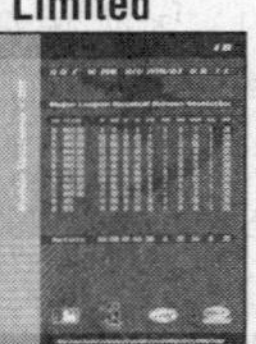

This hobby-exclusive product was released in mid-December 2001, and featured a 375-card base set that was broken into tiers as follows: 150 Base Veterans, 50 Lumberjacks (numbered to either 500, 250, or 100), 100 Rookies (numbered to either 1500 or 1000), 25 Autographed Rookies (numbered to 1000, 750, or 500), and 50 Memorabilia Rookies (see print runs below). Each pack contained three cards, and carried a $6.99 S.R.P.

Nm-Mt Ex-Mt
COMP.SET w/o SP'S (150) 100.00 30.00
COMMON CARD (1-150) 1.00 .30
COMMON HAT (326-375) 25.00 7.50
COMMON LUM/500 (151-200) 8.00 2.40
COMMON LUM/250 (151-200) 10.00 3.00
COMMON LUM/100 (151-200) 15.00 4.50
COMMON (201-250) 5.00 1.50
COMMON (251-300) 5.00 1.50
COMMON (301-325) 10.00 3.00
COMMON BASE (326-375) 15.00 4.50
COMMON BAT (326-375) 8.00 2.40
COMMON JSY (326-375) 8.00 2.40
COMMON PANTS (326-375) 8.00 2.40
COMMON SPIKES (326-375) 25.00 7.50
1 Curt Schilling 1.00 .30
2 Craig Biggio 1.50 .45
3 Brian Giles 1.00 .30
4 Scott Brosius 1.00 .30
5 Barry Larkin 1.50 .45
6 Bartolo Colon 1.00 .30
7 John Olerud 1.00 .30
8 Cal Ripken 8.00 2.40
9 Moises Alou 1.00 .30
10 Barry Zito 1.50 .45
11 Ken Griffey Jr. 4.00 1.20
12 Garret Anderson 1.00 .30
13 Andy Pettitte 1.50 .45
14 Jim Edmonds 1.00 .30
15 Tom Glavine 1.50 .45
16 Jose Canseco 2.50 .75
17 Fred McGriff 1.50 .45
18 Robin Ventura 1.00 .30
19 Tony Gwynn 3.00 .90
20 Jeff Cirillo 1.00 .30
21 Brad Radke 1.00 .30
22 Ellis Burks 1.00 .30
23 Scott Rolen 2.50 .75
24 Rickey Henderson 2.50 .75
25 Edgar Martinez 1.50 .45
26 Kerry Wood 2.50 .75
27 Al Leiter 1.00 .30
28 Jose Cruz Jr. 1.00 .30
29 Sean Casey 1.00 .30
30 Eric Chavez 1.00 .30
31 Jarrod Washburn 1.00 .30
32 Gary Sheffield 1.00 .30
33 Jermaine Dye 1.00 .30
34 Bernie Williams 1.50 .45
35 Tony Armas Jr. 1.00 .30
36 Carlos Beltran 1.50 .45
37 Geoff Jenkins 1.00 .30
38 Shawn Green 1.00 .30
39 Ryan Klesko 1.00 .30
40 Richie Sexson 1.00 .30
41 Pat Burrell 1.00 .30
42 J.D. Drew 1.00 .30
43 Larry Walker 1.50 .45
44 Andres Galarraga 1.00 .30
45 Tino Martinez 1.50 .45
46 Rafael Furcal 1.00 .30
47 Cristian Guzman 1.00 .30
48 Omar Vizquel 1.50 .45
49 Bret Boone 1.00 .30
50 Wade Miller 1.00 .30
51 Eric Milton 1.00 .30
52 Gabe Kapler 1.00 .30
53 Johnny Damon 1.50 .45
54 Shannon Stewart 1.00 .30
55 Kenny Lofton 1.00 .30
56 Raul Mondesi 1.00 .30
57 Jorge Posada 1.50 .45
58 Mark Grace 1.50 .45
59 Robert Fick 1.00 .30
60 Phil Nevin 1.00 .30
61 Mike Mussina 1.50 .45
62 Joe Mays 1.00 .30
63 Todd Helton 1.50 .45
64 Tim Hudson 1.00 .30
65 Manny Ramirez 1.50 .45
66 Sammy Sosa 4.00 1.20
67 Darin Erstad 1.00 .30
68 Roberto Alomar 1.50 .45
69 Jeff Bagwell 1.50 .45
70 Mark McGwire 6.00 1.80
71 Jason Giambi 1.00 .30
72 Cliff Floyd 1.00 .30
73 Barry Bonds 6.00 1.80
74 Juan Gonzalez 1.50 .45
75 Jeremy Giambi 1.00 .30
76 Carlos Lee 1.00 .30
77 Randy Johnson 2.50 .75
78 Frank Thomas 2.50 .75
79 Carlos Delgado 1.00 .30
80 Pedro Martinez 2.50 .75
81 Rusty Greer 1.00 .30
82 Brian Jordan 1.00 .30
83 Vladimir Guerrero 2.50 .75
84 Mike Sweeney 1.00 .30
85 Jose Vidro 1.00 .30
86 Paul LoDuca 1.00 .30
87 Matt Morris 1.00 .30
88 Adrian Beltre 1.50 .45
89 Aramis Ramirez 1.00 .30
90 Derek Jeter 6.00 1.80
91 Rich Aurilia 1.00 .30
92 Freddy Garcia 1.00 .30
93 Preston Wilson 1.00 .30
94 Greg Maddux 4.00 1.20
95 Miguel Tejada 1.00 .30
96 Luis Gonzalez 1.00 .30
97 Torii Hunter 1.00 .30
98 Nomar Garciaparra 4.00 1.20
99 Jamie Moyer 1.00 .30
100 Javier Vazquez 1.00 .30
101 Ben Grieve 1.00 .30
102 Mike Piazza 4.00 1.20
103 Paul O'Neill 1.50 .45
104 Terrence Long 1.00 .30
105 Charles Johnson 1.00 .30
106 Rafael Palmeiro 1.50 .45
107 David Cone 1.00 .30
108 Alex Rodriguez 4.00 1.20
109 John Burkett 1.00 .30
110 Chipper Jones 2.50 .75
111 Ryan Dempster 1.00 .30
112 Bobby Abreu 1.00 .30
113 Brad Fullmer 1.00 .30
114 Kazuhiro Sasaki 1.00 .30
115 Mariano Rivera 1.50 .45
116 Edgardo Alfonzo 1.00 .30
117 Ray Durham 1.00 .30
118 Richard Hidalgo 1.00 .30
119 Jeff Weaver 1.00 .30
120 Paul Konerko 1.00 .30
121 Jon Lieber 1.00 .30
122 Mike Hampton 1.00 .30
123 Mike Cameron 1.00 .30
124 Kevin Brown 1.00 .30
125 Doug Mientkiewicz 1.00 .30
126 Jim Thome 2.50 .75
127 Corey Koskie 1.00 .30
128 Trot Nixon 1.00 .30
129 Darryl Kile 1.00 .30
130 Ivan Rodriguez 2.50 .75
131 Carl Everett 1.00 .30
132 Jeff Kent 1.00 .30
133 Rondell White 1.00 .30
134 Chan Ho Park 1.00 .30
135 Robert Person 1.00 .30
136 Troy Glaus 1.00 .30
137 Aaron Sele 1.00 .30
138 Roger Clemens 5.00 1.50
139 Tony Clark 1.00 .30
140 Mark Buehrle 1.00 .30
141 David Justice 1.00 .30
142 Magglio Ordonez 1.00 .30
143 Bobby Higginson 1.00 .30
144 Hideo Nomo 2.50 .75
145 Tim Salmon 1.50 .45
146 Mark Mulder 1.00 .30
147 Troy Percival 1.00 .30
148 Lance Berkman 1.00 .30
149 Russ Ortiz 1.00 .30
150 Andruw Jones 1.00 .30
151 Mike Piazza LUM/500 15.00 4.50
152 M.Ramirez LUM/500 10.00 3.00
153 B.Williams LUM/500 10.00 3.00
154 N.Garciaparra LUM/500 15.00 4.50
155 A.Galarraga LUM/500 8.00 2.40
156 K.Lofton LUM/500 8.00 2.40
157 Scott Rolen LUM/250 15.00 4.50
158 Jim Thome LUM/500 10.00 3.00
159 Darin Erstad LUM/500 8.00 2.40
160 G.Anderson LUM/500 8.00 2.40
161 A.Jones LUM/500 8.00 2.40
162 J.Gonzalez LUM/500 10.00 3.00
163 R.Palmeiro LUM/500 10.00 3.00
164 M.Ordonez LUM/500 8.00 2.40
165 Jeff Bagwell LUM/250 15.00 4.50
166 Eric Chavez LUM/500 8.00 2.40
167 Brian Giles LUM/500 8.00 2.40
168 A.Beltre LUM/500 10.00 3.00
169 T.Gwynn LUM/500 15.00 4.50
170 S.Green LUM/500 8.00 2.40
171 Todd Helton LUM/500 10.00 3.00
172 Troy Glaus LUM/100 15.00 4.50
173 L.Berkman LUM/500 8.00 2.40
174 I.Rodriguez LUM/500 10.00 3.00
175 Sean Casey LUM/500 8.00 2.40
176 A.Ramirez LUM/100 15.00 4.50
177 J.D. Drew LUM/500 8.00 2.40
178 Barry Bonds LUM/250 30.00 9.00
179 Barry Larkin LUM/500 10.00 3.00
180 Cal Ripken LUM/500 40.00 12.00
181 F.Thomas LUM/500 10.00 3.00
182 Craig Biggio LUM/250 15.00 4.50
183 Carlos Lee LUM/500 8.00 2.40
184 C. Jones LUM/500 10.00 3.00
185 Miguel Tejada LUM/250 10.00 3.00
186 Jose Vidro LUM/500 8.00 2.40
187 T.Long LUM/500 8.00 2.40
188 Moises Alou LUM/500 8.00 2.40
189 Trot Nixon LUM/500 8.00 2.40
190 S.Stewart LUM/500 8.00 2.40
191 Ryan Klesko LUM/500 8.00 2.40
192 C.Beltran LUM/500 10.00 3.00
193 V.Guerrero LUM/500 10.00 3.00
194 E.Martinez LUM/500 10.00 3.00
195 L.Gonzalez LUM/500 8.00 2.40
196 R.Hidalgo LUM/500 8.00 2.40
197 R.Alomar LUM/500 10.00 3.00
198 M.Sweeney LUM/100 15.00 4.50
199 B.Abreu LUM/250 10.00 3.00
200 Cliff Floyd LUM/500 8.00 2.40
201 Jackson Melian RC 5.00 1.50
202 Jason Jennings 5.00 1.50
203 Toby Hall 5.00 1.50
204 Jason Karnuth RC 5.00 1.50
205 Jason Smith RC 5.00 1.50
206 Mike Maroth RC 5.00 1.50
207 Sean Douglass RC 5.00 1.50
208 Adam Johnson 5.00 1.50
209 Luke Hudson RC 5.00 1.50
210 Nick Maness RC 5.00 1.50
211 Les Walrond RC 5.00 1.50
212 Travis Phelps RC 5.00 1.50
213 Carlos Garcia RC 5.00 1.50
214 Bill Ortega RC 5.00 1.50
215 Gene Altman RC 5.00 1.50
216 Nate Frese RC 5.00 1.50
217 Bob File RC 5.00 1.50
218 Steve Green RC 5.00 1.50
219 Kris Keller RC 5.00 1.50
220 Matt White RC 5.00 1.50
221 Nate Teut RC 5.00 1.50
222 Nick Johnson 5.00 1.50
223 Jeremy Fikac RC 5.00 1.50
224 Abraham Nunez 5.00 1.50
225 Mike Penney RC 5.00 1.50
226 Roy Smith RC 5.00 1.50
227 Tim Christman RC 5.00 1.50
228 Carlos Pena 5.00 1.50
229 Joe Beimel RC 5.00 1.50
230 Mike Koplove RC 5.00 1.50
231 Scott MacRae RC 5.00 1.50
232 Kyle Lohse RC 8.00 2.40
233 Jerrod Riggan RC 5.00 1.50
234 Scott Podsednik RC 15.00 4.50
235 Winston Abreu RC 5.00 1.50
236 Ryan Freel RC 5.00 1.50
237 Ken Vining RC 5.00 1.50
238 Bret Prinz RC 5.00 1.50
239 Paul Phillips RC 5.00 1.50
240 Josh Fogg RC 5.00 1.50
241 Saul Rivera RC 5.00 1.50
242 Esix Snead RC 5.00 1.50
243 John Grabow RC 5.00 1.50
244 Tony Cogan RC 5.00 1.50
245 Pedro Santana RC 5.00 1.50
246 Jack Cust 5.00 1.50
247 Joe Crede 5.00 1.50
248 Juan Moreno RC 5.00 1.50
249 Kevin Joseph RC 5.00 1.50
250 Scott Stewart RC 5.00 1.50
251 Rob Mackowiak RC 8.00 2.40
252 Luis Pineda RC 5.00 1.50
253 Bert Snow RC 5.00 1.50
254 Dustan Mohr RC 5.00 1.50
255 Justin Kaye RC 5.00 1.50
256 Chad Paronto RC 5.00 1.50
257 Nick Punto RC 5.00 1.50
258 Brian Roberts RC 5.00 1.50
259 Eric Hinske RC 8.00 2.40
260 Victor Zambrano RC 8.00 2.40
261 Juan Pena RC 5.00 1.50
262 Rick Bauer RC 5.00 1.50
263 Jorge Julio RC 5.00 1.50
264 Craig Monroe RC 5.00 1.50
265 Stubby Clapp RC 5.00 1.50
266 Martin Vargas RC 5.00 1.50
267 Josue Perez RC 5.00 1.50
268 Cody Ransom RC 5.00 1.50
269 Will Ohman RC 5.00 1.50
270 Juan Diaz RC 5.00 1.50
271 Ramon Vazquez RC 5.00 1.50
272 Grant Balfour RC 5.00 1.50
273 Ryan Jensen RC 5.00 1.50
274 Benito Baez RC 5.00 1.50
275 Angel Santos RC 5.00 1.50
276 Brian Reith RC 5.00 1.50
277 Brandon Lyon RC 5.00 1.50
278 Erik Hiljus RC 5.00 1.50
279 Brandon Knight RC 5.00 1.50
280 Jose Acevedo RC 5.00 1.50
281 Cesar Crespo RC 5.00 1.50
282 Kevin Olsen RC 5.00 1.50
283 Duaner Sanchez RC 5.00 1.50
284 Endy Chavez RC 5.00 1.50
285 Blaine Neal RC 5.00 1.50
286 Brett Jodie RC 5.00 1.50
287 Brad Voyles RC 5.00 1.50
288 Doug Nickle RC 5.00 1.50
289 Junior Spivey RC 8.00 2.40
290 Henry Mateo RC 5.00 1.50
291 Xavier Nady 5.00 1.50
292 Lance Davis RC 5.00 1.50
293 Willie Harris RC 5.00 1.50
294 Mark Lukasiewicz RC 5.00 1.50
295 Ryan Drese RC 8.00 2.40
296 Morgan Ensberg RC 8.00 2.40
297 Jose Mieses RC 5.00 1.50
298 Jason Michaels RC 5.00 1.50
299 Kris Foster RC 5.00 1.50
300 J.Duchscherer RC 5.00 1.50
301 Elpidio Guzman AU RC 10.00 3.00
302 Cory Aldridge AU RC 10.00 3.00
303 A.Berroa AU/500 RC 15.00 4.50
304 Travis Hafner AU RC 30.00 9.00
305 H.Ramirez AU RC 15.00 4.50
306 Juan Uribe AU RC 15.00 4.50
307 M.Prior AU/500 RC 175.00 52.50
308 B.Larson AU RC 10.00 3.00
309 N.Neugebauer AU/750 10.00 3.00
310 Zach Day AU/750 RC 10.00 3.00
311 Jeremy Owens AU RC 10.00 3.00
312 D.Brazelton AU/500 RC 15.00 4.50
313 B.Duckworth AU/750 RC 10.00 3.00
314 A.Hernandez AU RC 10.00 3.00
315 M.Teixeira AU/500 RC 100.00 30.00
316 Brian Rogers AU RC 10.00 3.00
317 D.Brous AU/750 RC 10.00 3.00
318 Geronimo Gil AU RC 10.00 3.00
319 Erick Almonte AU RC 10.00 3.00
320 Claudio Vargas AU RC 10.00 3.00
321 Wilkin Ruan AU RC 10.00 3.00
322 David Williams AU RC 10.00 3.00
323 Alexis Gomez AU RC 10.00 3.00
324 Mike Rivera AU RC 10.00 3.00
325 B.Berger AU RC 10.00 3.00
326 Keith Ginter Bat/125 25.00 7.50
327 Brandon Inge Bat/700 8.00 2.40
328 B.Abernathy Bat/700 8.00 2.40
329 B.Sylvester Bat/700 RC 8.00 2.40
330 B.Miadich Jsy/500 RC 8.00 2.40
331 T.Shinjo Jsy/500 RC 10.00 3.00
332 E.Valent Spikes/125 25.00 7.50
333 Dee Brown Jsy/500 8.00 2.40
334 A.Torres Spikes/125 RC 25.00 7.50
335 Timo Perez Bat/700 8.00 2.40
336 C.Izturis Pants/650 8.00 2.40
337 P.Feliz Spikes/125 25.00 7.50
338 Jason Hart Bat/200 10.00 3.00
339 G.Miller Bat/700 RC 8.00 2.40
340 Eric Munson Bat/700 8.00 2.40
341 Aubrey Huff Jsy/450 8.00 2.40
342 W.Caceres Bat/700 RC 8.00 2.40
343 A.Escobar Pants/650 8.00 2.40
344 B.Lawrence Bat/700 RC 8.00 2.40
345 Adam Pettyjohn Pants/650 RC 8.00 2.40
346 D.Mendez Bat/700 RC 8.00 2.40
347 Carlos Valderrama Jsy/250 RC 10.00 3.00
348 C.Parker Pants/650 RC 8.00 2.40
349 C.Miller Jsy/500 RC 8.00 2.40
350 M.Cuddyer Jsy/500 8.00 2.40
351 Adam Dunn Bat/500 10.00 3.00
352 J.Beckett Pants/650 8.00 2.40
353 Juan Cruz Jsy/500 RC 8.00 2.40
354 Ben Sheets Jsy/400 10.00 3.00
355 Roy Oswalt Bat/100 40.00 12.00
356 R.Soriano Pants/650 RC 10.00 3.00
357 R.Rodriguez Pants/650 RC 8.00 2.40
358 J.Rollins Base/300 15.00 4.50
359 C.C. Sabathia Jsy/500 8.00 2.40
360 B.Smith Jsy/500 RC 8.00 2.40
361 Jose Ortiz Hat/100 25.00 7.50
362 Marcus Giles Jsy/400 8.00 2.40
363 J.Wilson Hat/100 RC 40.00 12.00
364 W.Betemit Hat/100 RC 25.00 7.50
365 C.Patterson Pants/650 8.00 2.40
366 J.Gibbons Spikes/125 RC 40.00 12.00
367 A.Pujols Jsy/250 RC 150.00 45.00
368 J.Kennedy Hat/100 RC 40.00 12.00
369 A.Soriano Hat/100 40.00 12.00
370 D.James Pants/650 RC 8.00 2.40
371 J.Towers Pants/650 RC 8.00 2.40
372 J.Affeldt Pants/650 RC 10.00 3.00
373 Tim Redding Jsy/500 8.00 2.40
374 I.Suzuki Base/100 RC 500.00 150.00
375 J.Estrada Bat/100 RC 40.00 12.00

2003 Leaf Limited

This 204 card set was issued in two separate series. The primary Leaf Limited product - containing cards 1-200 from the basic set - was released in September, 2003. The set was issued in four card packs with an $70 SRP which came four packs to a box and 10 boxes to a case. The first 150 cards feature active veteran players and were issued to a stated print run of 999 serial numbered sets. Cards numbered 151 through 170 feature retired greats and were randomly inserted into packs and issued to a stated print run of 399 serial numbered sets. Cards numbered 171 through 200 are entitled Phenoms and feature rookie players, most of whom signed their cards and most of those cards were issued to a stated print run of 99 serial numbered sets. Cards number 174 and 199 are not autographed and those cards just feature game-used pieces of memorabilia. Cards 201-204 were randomly seeded within packs of DLP Rookies and Traded released in December, 2003. Each of these Update cards was signed by the featured athlete, serial-numbered to 99 copies and continued the Phenoms subset established in cards 171-200.

MINT NRMT
COMMON CARD (1-151) 3.00 1.35
1-151 PRINT RUN 999 SERIAL #'d SETS
COMMON CARD (151-170) 4.00 1.80
151-170 RANDOM INSERTS IN PACKS
151-170 PRINT RUN 399 SERIAL #'d SETS
COMMON AU GU (171-200) 20.00 9.00
AU GU 171-200 PRINT 99 SERIAL #'d SETS
GU 174/199 PRINT RUN 99 SERIAL #'d SETS
COMMON AU (171-204) p/r 99 15.00 6.75
AU 171-204 PRINT B/WN 49-99 COPIES PER
171-200 RANDOM INSERTS IN PACKS
201-204 RANDOM IN DLP R/T PACKS
A EQUALS AWAY UNIFORM IMAGE...
H EQUALS HOME UNIFORM IMAGE...
1 Derek Jeter Btg 8.00 3.60
2 Eric Chavez 3.00 1.35
3 Alex Rodriguez Rgr A 6.00 2.70
4 Miguel Tejada Fldg 3.00 1.35
5 Nomar Garciaparra H 6.00 2.70
6 Jeff Bagwell H 3.00 1.35
7 Jim Thome Phils A 4.00 1.80
8 Pat Burrell w/Bat 3.00 1.35
9 Albert Pujols H 8.00 3.60
10 Juan Gonzalez Rgr Btg 3.00 1.35
11 Shawn Green Jays 3.00 1.35
12 Craig Biggio H 3.00 1.35
13 Chipper Jones H 4.00 1.80
14 H.Nomo Dodgers 4.00 1.80
15 Vernon Wells 3.00 1.35
16 Gary Sheffield 3.00 1.35
17 Barry Larkin 3.00 1.35
18 Josh Beckett White 3.00 1.35
19 Edgar Martinez A 3.00 1.35
20 I.Rodriguez Marlins 4.00 1.80
21 Jeff Kent Astros 3.00 1.35
22 Roberto Alomar Mets A 3.00 1.35
23 Alfonso Soriano A 3.00 1.35
24 Jim Thome Indians H 4.00 1.80
25 J.Gonzalez Indians Btg 3.00 1.35
26 Carlos Beltran 3.00 1.35
27 S.Green Dodgers H 3.00 1.35
28 Tim Hudson H 3.00 1.35
29 Deion Sanders 3.00 1.35
30 Rafael Palmeiro O's 3.00 1.35
31 Todd Helton H 3.00 1.35
32 L.Berkman No Socks 3.00 1.35
33 M.Mussina Yanks H 3.00 1.35
34 Kazuhisa Ishii H 3.00 1.35
35 Pat Burrell Run 3.00 1.35
36 Miguel Tejada Btg 3.00 1.35
37 J.Gonzalez Rgr Stand 3.00 1.35
38 Roberto Alomar Mets H 3.00 1.35
39 R.Alom Indians Bunt 3.00 1.35
40 Luis Gonzalez 3.00 1.35
41 Jorge Posada 3.00 1.35
42 Mark Mulder Leg 3.00 1.35
43 Sammy Sosa H 6.00 2.70
44 Mark Prior H 4.00 1.80
45 R.Clemens Yanks H 8.00 3.60
46 Tom Glavine Mets H 3.00 1.35
47 Mark Teixeira A 3.00 1.35
48 Manny Ramirez H 3.00 1.35
49 Frank Thomas Swing 4.00 1.80
50 Troy Glaus White 3.00 1.35
51 Andruw Jones H 3.00 1.35
52 J.Giambi Yanks H 3.00 1.35
53 Jim Thome Phils H 4.00 1.80
54 Barry Bonds H 10.00 4.50
55 R.Palmeiro Rgr A 3.00 1.35
56 Edgar Martinez H 3.00 1.35
57 Vladimir Guerrero H 4.00 1.80
58 Roberto Alomar O's 3.00 1.35
59 Mike Sweeney 3.00 1.35
60 Magglio Ordonez A 3.00 1.35
61 Ken Griffey Jr. Btg 6.00 2.70
62 Craig Biggio A 3.00 1.35
63 Greg Maddux H 6.00 2.70
64 Mike Piazza Mets H 6.00 2.70
65 T.Glavine Braves A 3.00 1.35
66 Kerry Wood H 4.00 1.80
67 Frank Thomas Arms 4.00 1.80
68 M.Mussina Yanks A 3.00 1.35
69 Nick Johnson H 3.00 1.35
70 Bernie Williams H 3.00 1.35
71 Scott Rolen 4.00 1.80
72 C.Schill D'backs Leg 3.00 1.35
73 Adam Dunn A 3.00 1.35
74 Roy Oswalt A 3.00 1.35
75 P.Martinez Sox H 4.00 1.80
76 Tom Glavine Mets A 3.00 1.35
77 Torii Hunter Swing 3.00 1.35
78 Austin Kearns 3.00 1.35
79 R.Johnson D'backs A 4.00 1.80
80 Bernie Williams A 3.00 1.35
81 Ichiro Suzuki Btg 6.00 2.70
82 Kerry Wood A 4.00 1.80
83 Kazuhisa Ishii A 3.00 1.35
84 R.Johnson Astros 4.00 1.80
85 Nick Johnson A 3.00 1.35
86 J.Beckett Pinstripe 3.00 1.35
87 Curt Schilling Phils 3.00 1.35
88 Mike Mussina O's 3.00 1.35
89 P.Martinez Dodgers 4.00 1.80
90 Barry Zito A 3.00 1.35
91 Jim Edmonds 3.00 1.35
92 R.Henderson Sox 4.00 1.80
93 R.Henderson Padres 4.00 1.80
94 R.Henderson M's 4.00 1.80
95 R.Henderson Mets 4.00 1.80
96 R.Henderson Jays 4.00 1.80
97 R.Johnson M's Arm Up 4.00 1.80
98 Mark Grace 3.00 1.35
99 P.Martinez Expos 4.00 1.80

100 Hee Seop Choi 3.00 1.35
101 Ivan Rodriguez Rgr.............. 4.00 1.80
102 Jeff Kent Giants 3.00 1.35
103 Hideo Nomo Sox.................. 4.00 1.80
104 Hideo Nomo Mets................. 4.00 1.80
105 Mike Piazza Dodgers............ 6.00 2.70
106 T.Glavine Braves H.............. 3.00 1.35
107 R.Alom Indians Swing 3.00 1.35
108 Roger Clemens Sox............. 8.00 3.60
109 Jason Giambi A's A............. 3.00 1.35
110 Jim Thome Indians A............ 4.00 1.80
111 Alex Rodriguez M's H.......... 6.00 2.70
112 J.Gonz Indians Hands.......... 3.00 1.35
113 Torii Hunter Crouch.............. 3.00 1.35
114 Roy Oswalt H........................ 3.00 1.35
115 C.Schill D'backs Throw........ 3.00 1.35
116 Magglio Ordonez H.............. 3.00 1.35
117 R.Palmeiro Rgr H................. 3.00 1.35
118 Andruw Jones A................... 3.00 1.35
119 Manny Ramirez A................. 3.00 1.35
120 Mark Teixeira H.................... 3.00 1.35
121 Mark Mulder Stance............. 3.00 1.35
122 Garret Anderson.................. 3.00 1.35
123 Tim Hudson A....................... 3.00 1.35
124 Todd Helton A...................... 3.00 1.35
125 Troy Glaus Pinstripe............ 3.00 1.35
126 Derek Jeter Run.................. 8.00 3.60
127 Barry Bonds A.................... 10.00 4.50
128 Greg Maddux A..................... 6.00 2.70
129 R.Clemens Yanks A............. 8.00 3.60
130 Nomar Garciaparra A........... 6.00 2.70
131 Mike Piazza Mets A.............. 6.00 2.70
132 Alex Rodriguez Rgr H.......... 6.00 2.70
133 Ichiro Suzuki Run................. 6.00 2.70
134 R.Johnson D'backs H........... 4.00 1.80
135 Sammy Sosa A..................... 6.00 2.70
136 Ken Griffey Jr. Fldg.............. 6.00 2.70
137 Alfonso Soriano H................ 3.00 1.35
138 J.Giambi Yanks A................. 3.00 1.35
139 Albert Pujols A..................... 8.00 3.60
140 Chipper Jones A.................. 4.00 1.80
141 Adam Dunn H....................... 3.00 1.35
142 P.Martinez Sox A.................. 4.00 1.80
143 Vladimir Guerrero A............. 4.00 1.80
144 Mark Prior A......................... 4.00 1.80
145 Barry Zito H.......................... 3.00 1.35
146 Jeff Bagwell A...................... 3.00 1.35
147 Lance Berkman Socks......... 3.00 1.35
148 S.Green Dodgers A.............. 3.00 1.35
149 Jason Giambi A's A.............. 3.00 1.35
150 R.Johnson M's Arm Out...... 4.00 1.80
151 Alex Rodriguez M's A.......... 6.00 2.70
152 Babe Ruth.......................... 10.00 4.50
153 Ty Cobb................................ 6.00 2.70
154 Jackie Robinson.................. 5.00 2.20
155 Lou Gehrig........................... 8.00 3.60
156 Thurman Munson................. 5.00 2.20
157 Roberto Clemente............... 12.00 5.50
158 Nolan Ryan Rgr.................. 10.00 4.50
159 Nolan Ryan Angels.............. 10.00 4.50
160 Nolan Ryan Astros.............. 10.00 4.50
161 Cal Ripken.......................... 20.00 9.00
162 Don Mattingly...................... 10.00 4.50
163 Stan Musial........................... 8.00 3.60
164 Tony Gwynn.......................... 8.00 3.60
165 Yogi Berra............................ 5.00 2.20
166 Johnny Bench....................... 5.00 2.20
167 Mike Schmidt....................... 10.00 4.50
168 George Brett....................... 10.00 4.50
169 Ryne Sandberg................... 10.00 4.50
170 Ernie Banks........................... 5.00 2.20
171 J.Bonder A PH AU Jsy RC . 25.00 11.00
172 J.Contreras A PH AU RC.... 40.00 18.00
173 C.Wang PH AU RC............. 50.00 22.00
174 H.Matsui H PH Base RC..... 40.00 18.00
175 Hong-Chih Kuo 40.00 18.00
PH AU Bat RC
176 B.Webb A PH AU Bat RC ... 40.00 18.00
177 Rich Fischer PH AU RC...... 15.00 6.75
178 R.Hammock PH AU Bat RC 25.00 11.00
179 T.Welle Stance PH AU/49 RC 25.00 11.00
180 P.Redman PH AU Bat RC ... 20.00 9.00
181 Nook Logan PH AU RC....... 15.00 6.75
182 Craig Brazell PH AU RC 15.00 6.75
183 Tim Olson PH AU Bat RC.... 25.00 11.00
184 Matt Kata PH AU Bat RC.... 25.00 11.00
185 Alej Machado PH AU RC..... 15.00 6.75
186 Mike Hessman PH AU RC.. 15.00 6.75
187 Oscar Villarreal PH AU RC . 15.00 6.75
188 G.Quiroz PH AU Bat RC..... 25.00 11.00
189 M.Hernandez PH AU RC 15.00 6.75
190 C.Barmes H PH AU Bat RC 25.00 11.00
191 P.LaForest PH AU Bat RC... 25.00 11.00
192 Adam Loewen PH AU RC... 60.00 27.00
193 T.Sledge PH AU Bat RC..... 25.00 11.00
194 Lew Ford PH AU Bat RC 50.00 22.00
195 T.Welle Throw PH AU/49 RC 25.00 11.00
196 C.Barmes A PH AU Bat RC 25.00 11.00
197 J.Bonder H PH AU Jsy RC . 25.00 11.00
198 B.Webb H PH AU Jsy RC... 40.00 18.00
199 H.Matsui A PH Base RC..... 40.00 18.00
200 J.Contreras H PH AU RC.... 40.00 18.00
201 Delmon Young PH AU RC 150.00 70.00
202 Rickie Weeks PH AU RC.. 100.00 45.00
203 Edwin Jackson PH AU RC.. 80.00 36.00
204 Dan Haren PH AU RC......... 20.00 9.00

2003 Leaf Limited Gold Spotlight

MINT NRMT
*GOLD 1-151: 1.25X TO 3X BASIC.....
*GOLD 152-170: 1.25X TO 3X BASIC.
1-170 PRINT RUN 50 SERIAL #'d SETS
171-204 PRINT RUN 25 SERIAL #'d SETS
179/195/202 PRINT RUN 10 SERIAL #'d PER
171-204 NO PRICING DUE TO SCARCITY
1-200 RANDOM INSERTS IN PACKS..
201-204 RANDOM IN DLP R/T PACKS

2003 Leaf Limited Silver Spotlight

MINT NRMT
*SILVER 1-151: .75X TO 2X BASIC....
*SILVER 152-170: .75X TO 2X BASIC
1-170 PRINT RUN 100 SERIAL #'d SETS
*SILVER AU GU 171-200: .5X TO 1.2X
*SILVER GU 174/199: .6X TO 1.5X.....
*SILVER AU 171-204 p/r 50: .5X TO 1.2X
171-204 PRINT RUN 50 SERIAL #'d SETS
179/195 PRINT 29 SERIAL #'d COPIES PER
CARD 202 PRINT RUN 25 SERIAL #'d COPIES
NO PRICING ON QTY OF 29 OR LESS
1-200 RANDOM INSERTS IN PACKS..
201-204 RANDOM IN DLP R/T PACKS

2003 Leaf Limited Moniker

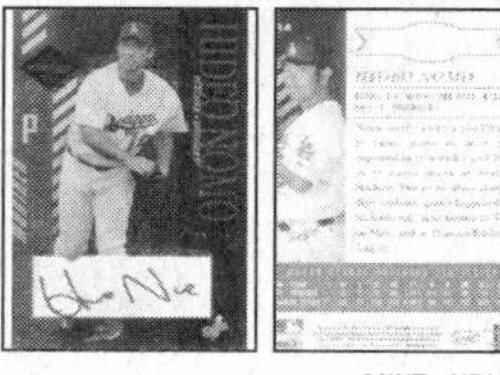

MINT NRMT
RANDOM INSERTS IN PACKS ....
PRINT RUNS B/WN 1-10 COPIES PER
NO PRICING DUE TO SCARCITY ....

2003 Leaf Limited Moniker Bat

MINT NRMT
RANDOM INSERTS IN PACKS ....
PRINT RUNS B/WN 1-25 COPIES PER
NO PRICING ON QTY OF 10 OR LESS

2003 Leaf Limited Moniker Jersey

MINT NRMT
RANDOM INSERTS IN PACKS ....
PRINT RUNS B/WN 1-25 COPIES PER
NO PRICING ON QTY OF 10 OR LESS

2003 Leaf Limited Moniker Jersey Number

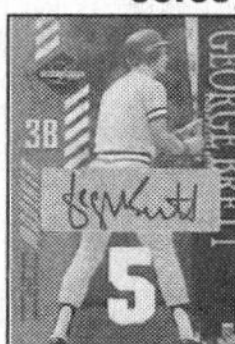
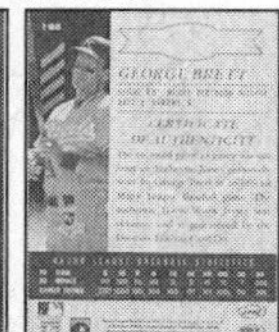

MINT NRMT
RANDOM INSERTS IN PACKS ....
PRINT RUNS B/WN 1-25 COPIES PER
NO PRICING ON QTY OF 10 OR LESS

2003 Leaf Limited Moniker Jersey Position

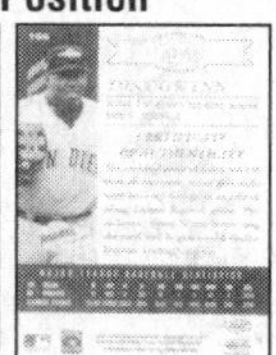

MINT NRMT
RANDOM INSERTS IN PACKS ....
PRINT RUNS B/WN 1-25 COPIES PER
NO PRICING ON QTY OF 10 OR LESS

2003 Leaf Limited Threads

MINT NRMT
RANDOM INSERTS IN PACKS ....
PRINT RUNS B/WN 5-100 COPIES PER
NO PRICING ON QTY OF 10 OR LESS
1 Derek Jeter Btg Base/50 .... 40.00 18.00
2 Eric Chavez/25 .... 15.00 6.75
3 Alex Rodriguez Rgr A/100 ..... 15.00 6.75
4 Miguel Tejada Fldg/50............ 10.00 4.50
5 Nomar Garciaparra H/100...... 15.00 6.75
6 Jeff Bagwell H/50.................. 15.00 6.75
7 Jim Thome Phils A/50 .... 15.00 6.75
8 Pat Burrell w/Bat/25............. 15.00 6.75
9 Albert Pujols H/100.............. 25.00 11.00
10 Juan Gonzalez Rgr Btg/25 ... 25.00 11.00
11 Shawn Green Jays/25.......... 15.00 6.75
12 Craig Biggio H/25................ 25.00 11.00
13 Chipper Jones H/50............. 15.00 6.75
14 H.Nomo Dodgers/100.......... 20.00 9.00
15 Vernon Wells/25 .... 15.00 6.75
16 Gary Sheffield/25................. 15.00 6.75
17 Barry Larkin/25.................... 25.00 11.00
18 Josh Beckett White/25......... 15.00 6.75
19 Edgar Martinez A/25............ 25.00 11.00
20 I.Rodriguez Marlins/25........ 25.00 11.00
21 Jeff Kent Astros/25.............. 15.00 6.75
22 Roberto Alomar Mets A/25 .. 25.00 11.00
23 Alfonso Soriano A/100......... 10.00 4.50
24 Jim Thome Indians H/25 ..... 25.00 11.00
25 J.Gonzalez Indians Btg/25.... 25.00 11.00
26 Carlos Beltran/25................. 25.00 11.00
27 S.Green Dodgers H/50......... 10.00 4.50
28 Tim Hudson H/25.................. 15.00 6.75
29 Deion Sanders/25................ 25.00 11.00
30 Rafael Palmeiro O's/25........ 25.00 11.00
31 Todd Helton H/50................. 15.00 6.75
32 L.Berkman No Socks/25...... 15.00 6.75
33 M.Mussina Yanks H/50........ 15.00 6.75
34 Kazuhisa Ishii H/50............. 10.00 4.50
35 Pat Burrell Run/25............... 15.00 6.75
36 Miguel Tejada Btg/50........... 10.00 4.50
37 J.Gonzalez Rgr Stand/25...... 25.00 11.00
38 Roberto Alomar Mets H/25 .. 25.00 11.00
39 R.Alom Indians Bunt/25....... 25.00 11.00
40 Luis Gonzalez/25................. 15.00 6.75
41 Jorge Posada/50.................. 15.00 6.75
42 Mark Mulder Leg/25............ 15.00 6.75
43 Sammy Sosa H/100............ 20.00 9.00
44 Mark Prior H/50.................... 15.00 6.75
45 R.Clemens Yanks H/100...... 15.00 6.75
46 Tom Glavine Mets H/25........ 25.00 11.00
47 Mark Teixeira A/25............... 15.00 6.75
48 Manny Ramirez H/50............ 15.00 6.75
49 Frank Thomas Swing/25...... 25.00 11.00
50 Troy Glaus White/50............ 10.00 4.50
51 Andruw Jones H/50............. 10.00 4.50
52 J.Giambi Yanks H/100........... 8.00 3.60
53 Jim Thome Phils H/50.......... 15.00 6.75
54 Barry Bonds H Base/50........ 40.00 18.00
55 R.Palmeiro Rgr A/25............ 25.00 11.00
56 Edgar Martinez H/25............ 25.00 11.00
57 Vladimir Guerrero H/50........ 15.00 6.75
58 Roberto Alomar O's/25........ 25.00 11.00
59 Mike Sweeney/25................. 15.00 6.75
60 Magglio Ordonez A/25......... 15.00 6.75
62 Craig Biggio A/25................ 25.00 11.00
63 Greg Maddux H/100............. 15.00 6.75
64 Mike Piazza Mets H/100....... 15.00 6.75
65 T.Glavine Braves A/25......... 25.00 11.00
66 Kerry Wood H/25................. 25.00 11.00
67 Frank Thomas Arms/25........ 25.00 11.00
68 M.Mussina Yanks A/50......... 15.00 6.75
69 Nick Johnson H/25.............. 15.00 6.75
70 Bernie Williams H/50............ 15.00 6.75
71 Scott Rolen/25..................... 25.00 11.00
72 C.Schill D'backs Leg/25....... 15.00 6.75
73 Adam Dunn A/50.................. 15.00 6.75
74 Roy Oswalt A/25.................. 15.00 6.75
75 P.Martinez Sox H/50............ 15.00 6.75
76 Tom Glavine Mets A/25........ 25.00 11.00
77 Torii Hunter Swing/25.......... 15.00 6.75
78 Austin Kearns/25................. 15.00 6.75
79 R.Johnson D'backs A/100 ... 10.00 4.50
80 Bernie Williams A/50............ 15.00 6.75
81 Ichiro Suzuki Btg Base/50.... 40.00 18.00
82 Kerry Wood A/25................. 25.00 11.00
83 Kazuhisa Ishii A/50.............. 10.00 4.50
84 R.Johnson Astros/50........... 15.00 6.75
85 Nick Johnson A/25............... 15.00 6.75
86 J.Beckett Pinstripe/25......... 15.00 6.75
87 Curt Schilling Phils/25......... 15.00 6.75
88 Mike Mussina O's/50............ 15.00 6.75
89 P.Martinez Dodgers/25......... 25.00 11.00
90 Barry Zito A/50..................... 10.00 4.50
91 Jim Edmonds/100.................. 8.00 3.60
92 R.Henderson Sox/100.......... 10.00 4.50
93 R.Henderson Padres/50....... 15.00 6.75
94 R.Henderson M's/50............ 15.00 6.75
95 R.Henderson Mets/50.......... 15.00 6.75
96 R.Henderson Jays/50........... 15.00 6.75
97 R.Johnson M's Arm Up/50.. 15.00 6.75
98 Mark Grace/50..................... 15.00 6.75
99 P.Martinez Expos/25............ 25.00 11.00
100 Hee Seop Choi/25.............. 15.00 6.75
101 Ivan Rodriguez Rgr/25........ 25.00 11.00
102 Jeff Kent Giants/25............ 15.00 6.75
103 Hideo Nomo Sox/5......................
104 Hideo Nomo Mets/50.......... 20.00 9.00
105 Mike Piazza Dodgers/100.... 15.00 6.75
106 T.Glavine Braves H/25........ 25.00 11.00
107 R.Alom Indians Swing/25 .. 25.00 11.00
108 Roger Clemens Sox/100 .... 15.00 6.75
109 Jason Giambi A's H/25 .... 15.00 6.75
110 Jim Thome Indians A/25..... 25.00 11.00
111 Alex Rodriguez M's H/100. 15.00 6.75
112 J.Gonz Indians Hands/25... 25.00 11.00
113 Torii Hunter Crouch/25 ...... 15.00 6.75
114 Roy Oswalt H/25................. 15.00 6.75
115 C.Schill D'backs Throw/25. 15.00 6.75
116 Magglio Ordonez H/25....... 15.00 6.75
117 R.Palmeiro Rgr H/25.......... 25.00 11.00
118 Andruw Jones A/50............ 10.00 4.50
119 Manny Ramirez A/50.......... 15.00 6.75
120 Mark Teixeira H/25............. 15.00 6.75
121 Mark Mulder Stance/25 ..... 15.00 6.75
123 Tim Hudson A/25................ 15.00 6.75
124 Todd Helton A/50............... 15.00 6.75
125 Troy Glaus Pinstripe/50...... 10.00 4.50
126 Derek Jeter Run Base/50 ... 40.00 18.00
127 Barry Bonds A Base/50...... 40.00 18.00
128 Greg Maddux A/100........... 15.00 6.75
129 R.Clemens Yanks A/100..... 15.00 6.75
130 Nomar Garciaparra A/100 .. 15.00 6.75
131 Mike Piazza Mets A/100..... 15.00 6.75
132 Alex Rodriguez Rgr H/100 . 15.00 6.75
133 Ichiro Suzuki Run Base/50. 40.00 18.00
134 R.Johnson D'backs H/100 . 10.00 4.50
135 Sammy Sosa A/100........... 20.00 9.00
137 Alfonso Soriano H/100....... 10.00 4.50
138 J.Giambi Yanks A/100......... 8.00 3.60
139 Albert Pujols A/100............ 25.00 11.00
140 Chipper Jones A/25 .... 25.00 11.00
141 Adam Dunn H/50................ 15.00 6.75
142 P.Martinez Sox A/50........... 15.00 6.75
143 Vladimir Guerrero A/50...... 15.00 6.75
144 Mark Prior A/50.................. 15.00 6.75
145 Barry Zito H/50................... 10.00 4.50
146 Jeff Bagwell A/50............... 15.00 6.75
147 Lance Berkman Socks/25 .. 15.00 6.75
148 S.Green Dodgers A/25....... 15.00 6.75
149 Jason Giambi A's A/25 ...... 15.00 6.75
150 R.Johnson M's Arm Out/25 25.00 11.00
151 Alex Rodriguez M's A/100 . 15.00 6.75
152 Babe Ruth/5.................................
153 Ty Cobb Pants/100.......... 120.00 55.00
154 Jackie Robinson/50 .... 80.00 36.00
155 Lou Gehrig/5.................................
156 Thurman Munson/100 .... 25.00 11.00
157 Roberto Clemente/10...................
158 Nolan Ryan Rgr/100 .... 50.00 22.00
159 Nolan Ryan Angels/100 ..... 50.00 22.00
160 Nolan Ryan Astros/100....... 50.00 22.00
161 Cal Ripken/100.................. 60.00 27.00
162 Don Mattingly/100 .... 40.00 18.00
163 Stan Musial/100................. 40.00 18.00
164 Tony Gwynn/100................ 20.00 9.00
165 Yogi Berra/100................... 20.00 9.00
166 Johnny Bench/100.............. 20.00 9.00
167 Mike Schmidt/100.............. 40.00 18.00
168 George Brett/100............... 40.00 18.00
169 Ryne Sandberg/100 .... 40.00 18.00
170 Ernie Banks/50.................. 50.00 22.00

2003 Leaf Limited Threads Button

MINT NRMT
RANDOM INSERTS IN PACKS ....
PRINT RUNS B/WN 2-6 COPIES PER .
NO PRICING DUE TO SCARCITY ....

2003 Leaf Limited Threads Double

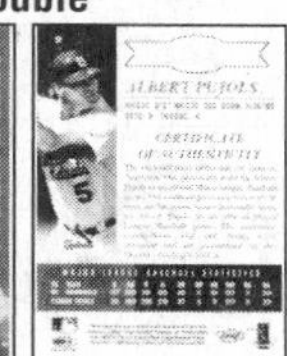

MINT NRMT
RANDOM INSERTS IN PACKS ....
PRINT RUNS B/WN 5-25 COPIES PER
NO PRICING ON QTY 15 OR LESS .....
3 A.Rod Rgr A Hat-Jsy/25 .... 60.00 27.00
4 M.Tejada Fldg Hat-Jsy/25...... 25.00 11.00
9 Albert Pujols H Hat-Jsy/15..............
10 J.Gonz Rgr Btg Hat-Jsy/25 .. 40.00 18.00
12 Craig Biggio H Hat-Jsy/25 ... 40.00 18.00
14 H.Nomo Dgr Jsy-Pants/25... 80.00 36.00
15 Vernon Wells Hat-Jsy/25 ..... 25.00 11.00
26 Carlos Beltran Hat-Jsy/25.... 40.00 18.00
28 Tim Hudson H Hat-Jsy/25..... 25.00 11.00
31 Todd Helton H Hat-Jsy/25.... 40.00 18.00
32 L.Berk No Socks Hat-Jsy/25 25.00 11.00
34 Kazuhisa Ishii H Hat-Jsy/25 . 25.00 11.00
37 J.Gonz Rgr Stand Hat-Jsy/25 40.00 18.00
43 Sammy Sosa H Hat-Jsy/25.. 80.00 36.00
44 Mark Prior H Hat-Jsy/25...... 40.00 18.00
47 Mark Teixeira A Hat-Jsy/25.. 25.00 11.00
51 Andruw Jones H Hat-Jsy/25 25.00 11.00
54 Barry Bonds H Ball-Base/25. 80.00 36.00
55 R.Palmeiro Rgr A Hat-Jsy/25 40.00 18.00
60 M.Ordonez A Hat-Jsy/25...... 25.00 11.00
66 Kerry Wood H Hat-Jsy/5..................
73 Adam Dunn A Hat-Jsy/25 .... 40.00 18.00
75 P.Martinez Sox H Hat-Jsy/25 40.00 18.00
78 Austin Kearns Hat-Jsy/25 .... 25.00 11.00
81 I.Suzuki Btg Ball-Base/25.... 80.00 36.00
90 Barry Zito A Hat-Jsy/25 .... 25.00 11.00
94 R.Hend M's Hat-Jsy/25........ 40.00 18.00
101 I.Rodriguez Rgr Hat-Jsy/25 40.00 18.00
109 J.Giambi A's H Hat-Jsy/25. 25.00 11.00
116 M.Ordonez H Hat-Jsy/25... 25.00 11.00
117 R.Palmeiro Rgr H Hat-Jsy/25 40.00 18.00
118 Andruw Jones A Hat-Jsy/25 25.00 11.00
120 Mark Teixeira H Hat-Jsy/25 25.00 11.00
123 Tim Hudson A Hat-Jsy/25.. 25.00 11.00
124 Todd Helton A Hat-Jsy/25.. 40.00 18.00
127 Barry Bonds A Ball-Base/25 80.00 36.00
132 A.Rod Rgr H Hat-Jsy/25 .... 60.00 27.00
133 I.Suzuki Run Ball-Base/25.. 80.00 36.00
135 Sammy Sosa A Hat-Jsy/25 80.00 36.00
141 Adam Dunn H Hat-Jsy/25 .. 40.00 18.00
142 P.Martinez Sox A Hat-Jsy/25 40.00 18.00
144 Mark Prior A Hat-Jsy/25 .... 40.00 18.00
145 Barry Zito H Hat-Jsy/25 ..... 25.00 11.00
146 Jeff Bagwell A Jsy-Pants/25 40.00 18.00
147 L.Berkman Socks Hat-Jsy/25 25.00 11.00
149 J.Giambi A's A Hat-Jsy/25 . 25.00 11.00
152 Babe Ruth Jsy-Pants/5 ....
155 Lou Gehrig Jsy-Pants/5 ....
157 Roberto Clemente Hat-Jsy/5........
158 N.Ryan Rgr Jsy-Pants/25 120.00 55.00
162 D.Mattingly Btg Glv-Jsy/25 120.00 55.00
164 Tony Gwynn Btg Glv-Jsy/25 60.00 27.00
167 Mike Schmidt Hat-Jsy/25. 120.00 55.00
168 George Brett Hat-Jsy/25 .. 120.00 55.00
169 Ryne Sandberg Hat-Jsy/25 120.00 55.00

2003 Leaf Limited Threads Double Prime

MINT NRMT
RANDOM INSERTS IN PACKS ....
PRINT RUNS B/WN 1-10 COPIES PER
NO PRICING DUE TO SCARCITY ....

2003 Leaf Limited Threads Number

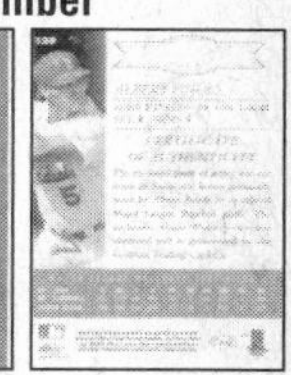

MINT NRMT
RANDOM INSERTS IN PACKS ....
PRINT RUNS B/WN 1-75 COPIES PER
NO PRICING ON QTY OF 19 OR LESS
7 Jim Thome Phils A/25 .... 25.00 11.00
18 Josh Beckett White/61 .... 10.00 4.50
24 Jim Thome Indians H/25 ..... 25.00 11.00
25 J.Gonzalez Indians Btg/22.... 40.00 18.00
29 Deion Sanders/21 .... 40.00 18.00
30 Rafael Palmeiro O's/25 .... 25.00 11.00
33 M.Mussina Yanks H/35 .... 25.00 11.00
40 Luis Gonzalez/20................. 25.00 11.00
41 Jorge Posada/20 .... 40.00 18.00
42 Mark Mulder Leg/20 .... 25.00 11.00
43 Sammy Sosa H/21 .... 80.00 36.00
44 Mark Prior H/22 .... 40.00 18.00
45 R.Clemens Yanks H/22 .... 60.00 27.00
46 Tom Glavine Mets H/47........ 15.00 6.75
47 Mark Teixeira A/23 .... 25.00 11.00
48 Manny Ramirez H/24 .... 40.00 18.00
49 Frank Thomas Swing/35...... 25.00 11.00
50 Troy Glaus White/25............ 15.00 6.75
51 Andruw Jones H/25 .... 15.00 6.75
52 J.Giambi Yanks H/25........... 15.00 6.75
53 Jim Thome Phils H/25.......... 25.00 11.00
55 R.Palmeiro Rgr A/25............ 25.00 11.00
57 Vladimir Guerrero H/27........ 25.00 11.00
59 Mike Sweeney/29................. 15.00 6.75
60 Magglio Ordonez A/30......... 15.00 6.75
63 Greg Maddux H/31.............. 40.00 18.00
64 Mike Piazza Mets H/31........ 40.00 18.00
65 T.Glavine Braves A/47 .... 15.00 6.75
66 Kerry Wood H/52................. 15.00 6.75
67 Frank Thomas Arms/35........ 25.00 11.00
68 M.Mussina Yanks A/35........ 25.00 11.00
69 Nick Johnson H/36 .... 10.00 4.50
70 Bernie Williams H/51 .... 15.00 6.75
71 Scott Rolen/27..................... 25.00 11.00
72 C.Schill D'backs Leg/38....... 10.00 4.50
73 Adam Dunn A/44 .... 15.00 6.75
74 Roy Oswalt A/44 .... 10.00 4.50
75 P.Martinez Sox H/45............ 15.00 6.75
76 Tom Glavine Mets A/47........ 15.00 6.75
77 Torii Hunter Swing/48.......... 10.00 4.50
78 Austin Kearns/28 .... 15.00 6.75
79 R.Johnson D'backs A/51 ..... 15.00 6.75
80 Bernie Williams A/51 .... 15.00 6.75
82 Kerry Wood A/34 .... 25.00 11.00
84 R.Johnson Astros/51 .... 15.00 6.75
85 Nick Johnson A/36.............. 10.00 4.50
86 J.Beckett Pinstripe/61.......... 10.00 4.50
87 Curt Schilling Phils/38 .... 10.00 4.50
88 Mike Mussina O's/35 .... 25.00 11.00
89 P.Martinez Dodgers/45......... 15.00 6.75
90 Barry Zito A/75 .... 10.00 4.50
92 R.Henderson Sox/35............ 25.00 11.00
93 R.Henderson Padres/24....... 40.00 18.00
94 R.Henderson M's/35........... 25.00 11.00
95 R.Henderson Mets/24.......... 40.00 18.00
96 R.Henderson Jays/24........... 40.00 18.00
97 R.Johnson M's Arm Up/51 .. 15.00 6.75
99 P.Martinez Expos/45............ 15.00 6.75
102 Jeff Kent Giants/21 .... 25.00 11.00
105 Mike Piazza Dodgers/31..... 40.00 18.00
106 T.Glavine Braves H/47 .... 15.00 6.75
108 Roger Clemens Sox/21 ...... 60.00 27.00
110 Jim Thome Indians A/25..... 25.00 11.00
112 J.Gonz Indians Hands/22... 40.00 18.00
113 Torii Hunter Crouch/48 ...... 10.00 4.50
114 Roy Oswalt H/44 .... 10.00 4.50
115 C.Schill D'backs Throw/38. 10.00 4.50
116 Magglio Ordonez H/30....... 15.00 6.75
117 R.Palmeiro Rgr H/25.......... 25.00 11.00
118 Andruw Jones A/25 .... 15.00 6.75
119 Manny Ramirez A/24 .... 40.00 18.00
120 Mark Teixeira H/23............. 25.00 11.00
121 Mark Mulder Stance/20 ..... 25.00 11.00
125 Troy Glaus Pinstripe/25...... 15.00 6.75
128 Greg Maddux A/31............. 40.00 18.00
129 R.Clemens Yanks A/22....... 60.00 27.00
131 Mike Piazza Mets A/31....... 40.00 18.00
134 R.Johnson D'backs H/51 ... 15.00 6.75
135 Sammy Sosa A/21 .... 80.00 36.00
138 J.Giambi Yanks A/25.......... 15.00 6.75
141 Adam Dunn H/44 .... 15.00 6.75
142 P.Martinez Sox A/45........... 15.00 6.75
143 Vladimir Guerrero A/27....... 25.00 11.00
145 Barry Zito H/75 .... 10.00 4.50
150 R.Johnson M's Arm Out/51 15.00 6.75
154 Jackie Robinson/42 .... 80.00 36.00
157 Roberto Clemente/21 .... 150.00 70.00
158 Nolan Ryan Rgr/34 .... 80.00 36.00
159 Nolan Ryan Angels/30 .... 80.00 36.00
160 Nolan Ryan Astros/34........ 80.00 36.00
162 Don Mattingly/23 .... 80.00 36.00
165 Yogi Berra/42..................... 25.00 11.00
167 Mike Schmidt/20................ 80.00 36.00
169 Ryne Sandberg/23 .... 80.00 36.00

2003 Leaf Limited Threads Position

MINT NRMT
RANDOM INSERTS IN PACKS
2-151 PRINT RUNS 25 SERIAL #'d SETS
152-170 PRINTS B/WN 5-25 COPIES PER
NO PRICING ON QTY OF 10 OR LESS
2 Eric Chavez 15.00 6.75
3 Alex Rodriguez Rgr A 40.00 18.00
4 Miguel Tejada Fldg 15.00 6.75
5 Nomar Garciaparra H 40.00 18.00
6 Jeff Bagwell H 25.00 11.00
7 Jim Thome Phils A 25.00 11.00
8 Pat Burrell w/Bat 15.00 6.75
9 Albert Pujols H 60.00 27.00
10 Juan Gonzalez Rgr Btg 25.00 11.00
11 Shawn Green Jays 15.00 6.75
12 Craig Biggio H 25.00 11.00
13 Chipper Jones H 25.00 11.00
14 Hideo Nomo Dodgers 50.00 22.00
15 Vernon Wells 15.00 6.75
16 Gary Sheffield 15.00 6.75
17 Barry Larkin 25.00 11.00
18 Josh Beckett White 15.00 6.75
19 Edgar Martinez A 25.00 11.00
20 Ivan Rodriguez Marlins 25.00 11.00
21 Jeff Kent Astros 15.00 6.75
22 Roberto Alomar Mets A 25.00 11.00
23 Alfonso Soriano A 25.00 11.00
24 Jim Thome Indians H 25.00 11.00
25 J.Gonzalez Indians Btg 25.00 11.00
26 Carlos Beltran 25.00 11.00
27 S.Green Dodgers H 15.00 6.75
28 Tim Hudson H 15.00 6.75
29 Deion Sanders 25.00 11.00
30 Rafael Palmeiro O's 25.00 11.00
31 Todd Helton H 25.00 11.00
32 L.Berkman No Socks 15.00 6.75
33 Mike Mussina Yanks H 25.00 11.00
34 Kazuhisa Ishii H 15.00 6.75
35 Pat Burrell Run 15.00 6.75
36 Miguel Tejada Btg 15.00 6.75
37 J.Gonzalez Rgr Stand 25.00 11.00
38 Roberto Alomar Mets H 25.00 11.00
39 R.Alomar Indians Bunt 25.00 11.00
40 Luis Gonzalez 15.00 6.75
41 Jorge Posada 25.00 11.00
42 Mark Mulder Leg 15.00 6.75
43 Sammy Sosa H 50.00 22.00
44 Mark Prior H 25.00 11.00
45 R.Clemens Yanks H 40.00 18.00
46 Tom Glavine Mets H 25.00 11.00
47 Mark Teixeira A 15.00 6.75
48 Manny Ramirez H 25.00 11.00
49 Frank Thomas Swing 25.00 11.00
50 Troy Glaus White 15.00 6.75
51 Andruw Jones H 15.00 6.75
52 Jason Giambi Yanks H 25.00 11.00
53 Jim Thome Phils H 25.00 11.00
55 Rafael Palmeiro Rgr A 25.00 11.00
56 Edgar Martinez H 25.00 11.00
57 Vladimir Guerrero H 25.00 11.00
58 Roberto Alomar O's 25.00 11.00
59 Mike Sweeney 15.00 6.75
60 Magglio Ordonez A 15.00 6.75
62 Craig Biggio A 25.00 11.00
63 Greg Maddux H 40.00 18.00
64 Mike Piazza Mets H 40.00 18.00
65 T.Glavine Braves A 25.00 11.00
66 Kerry Wood H 25.00 11.00
67 Frank Thomas Arms 25.00 11.00
68 Mike Mussina Yanks A 25.00 11.00
69 Nick Johnson H 15.00 6.75
70 Bernie Williams H 25.00 11.00
71 Scott Rolen 25.00 11.00
72 C.Schilling D'backs Leg 15.00 6.75
73 Adam Dunn A 25.00 11.00
74 Roy Oswalt A 15.00 6.75
75 Pedro Martinez Sox H 25.00 11.00
76 Tom Glavine Mets A 25.00 11.00
77 Torii Hunter Swing 15.00 6.75
78 Austin Kearns 15.00 6.75
79 R.Johnson D'backs A 25.00 11.00
80 Bernie Williams A 25.00 11.00
82 Kerry Wood A 25.00 11.00
83 Kazuhisa Ishii A 15.00 6.75
84 Randy Johnson Astros 25.00 11.00
85 Nick Johnson A 15.00 6.75
86 J.Beckett Pinstripe 15.00 6.75
87 Curt Schilling Phils 15.00 6.75
88 Mike Mussina O's 25.00 11.00
89 P.Martinez Dodgers 25.00 11.00
90 Barry Zito A 15.00 6.75
91 Jim Edmonds 15.00 6.75
92 R.Henderson Sox 25.00 11.00
93 R.Henderson Padres 25.00 11.00
94 R.Henderson M's 25.00 11.00
95 R.Henderson Mets 25.00 11.00
96 R.Henderson Jays 25.00 11.00
97 R.Johnson M's Arm Up 25.00 11.00
98 Mark Grace 25.00 11.00
99 Pedro Martinez Expos 25.00 11.00
100 Hee Seop Choi 15.00 6.75
101 Ivan Rodriguez Rgr 25.00 11.00
102 Jeff Kent Giants 15.00 6.75
103 Hideo Nomo Sox 50.00 22.00
104 Hideo Nomo Mets 50.00 22.00
105 Mike Piazza Dodgers 40.00 18.00
106 Tom Glavine Braves H 25.00 11.00
107 R.Alomar Indians Swing 25.00 11.00
108 Roger Clemens Sox 40.00 18.00
109 Jason Giambi A's H 15.00 6.75
110 Jim Thome Indians A 25.00 11.00
111 Alex Rodriguez M's H 40.00 18.00
112 J.Gonz Indians Hands 25.00 11.00
113 Torii Hunter Crouch 15.00 6.75
114 Roy Oswalt H 15.00 6.75
115 C.Schilling D'backs Throw 15.00 6.75
116 Magglio Ordonez H 15.00 6.75
117 Rafael Palmeiro Rgr H 25.00 11.00
118 Andruw Jones A 15.00 6.75
119 Manny Ramirez A 25.00 11.00
120 Mark Teixeira H 15.00 6.75
121 Mark Mulder Stance 15.00 6.75
123 Tim Hudson A 15.00 6.75
124 Todd Helton A 25.00 11.00
125 Troy Glaus Pinstripe 15.00 6.75
128 Greg Maddux A 40.00 18.00
129 Roger Clemens Yanks A 40.00 18.00
130 Nomar Garciaparra A 40.00 18.00
131 Mike Piazza Mets A 40.00 18.00
132 Alex Rodriguez Rgr H 40.00 18.00
134 R.Johnson D'backs H 25.00 11.00
135 Sammy Sosa A 50.00 22.00
137 Alfonso Soriano H 25.00 11.00
138 J.Giambi Yanks A 25.00 11.00
139 Albert Pujols A 60.00 27.00
140 Chipper Jones A 25.00 11.00
141 Adam Dunn H 25.00 11.00
142 Pedro Martinez Sox A 25.00 11.00
143 Vladimir Guerrero A 25.00 11.00
144 Mark Prior A 25.00 11.00
145 Barry Zito H 15.00 6.75
146 Jeff Bagwell A 25.00 11.00
147 Lance Berkman Socks 15.00 6.75
148 S.Green Dodgers A 15.00 6.75
149 Jason Giambi A's A 15.00 6.75
150 R.Johnson M's Arm Out 25.00 11.00
151 Alex Rodriguez M's A 40.00 18.00
152 Babe Ruth/5
153 Ty Cobb Pants 150.00 70.00
154 Jackie Robinson/10
155 Lou Gehrig/5
156 Thurman Munson 50.00 22.00
157 Roberto Clemente/5
158 Nolan Ryan Rgr 80.00 36.00
159 Nolan Ryan Angels 80.00 36.00
160 Nolan Ryan Astros 80.00 36.00
161 Cal Ripken 120.00 55.00
162 Don Mattingly 80.00 36.00
163 Stan Musial 80.00 36.00
164 Tony Gwynn 40.00 18.00
165 Yogi Berra 30.00 13.50
166 Johnny Bench 30.00 13.50
167 Mike Schmidt 80.00 36.00
168 George Brett 80.00 36.00
169 Ryne Sandberg 80.00 36.00
170 Ernie Banks/5

2003 Leaf Limited Threads Prime

MINT NRMT
RANDOM INSERTS IN PACKS
2-151 PRINTS 25 #'d PER UNLESS NOTED
152-170 PRINTS B/WN 3-25 COPIES PER
NO PRICING ON QTY OF 10 OR LESS
2 Eric Chavez 25.00 11.00
3 Alex Rodriguez Rgr A 60.00 27.00
4 Miguel Tejada Fldg 25.00 11.00
5 Nomar Garciaparra H 60.00 27.00
6 Jeff Bagwell H 40.00 18.00
7 Jim Thome Phils A/20 50.00 22.00
8 Pat Burrell w/Bat 25.00 11.00
9 Albert Pujols H 100.00 45.00
10 Juan Gonzalez Rgr Btg 40.00 18.00
11 Shawn Green Jays 25.00 11.00
12 Craig Biggio H 40.00 18.00
13 Chipper Jones H 40.00 18.00
14 Hideo Nomo Dodgers 80.00 36.00
15 Vernon Wells 25.00 11.00
16 Gary Sheffield 25.00 11.00
17 Barry Larkin 40.00 18.00
18 Josh Beckett White 25.00 11.00
19 Edgar Martinez A 40.00 18.00
20 Ivan Rodriguez Marlins 40.00 18.00
21 Jeff Kent Astros 25.00 11.00
22 Roberto Alomar Mets A 40.00 18.00
23 Alfonso Soriano A 40.00 18.00
24 Jim Thome Indians H 40.00 18.00
25 J.Gonzalez Indians Btg 40.00 18.00
26 Carlos Beltran 40.00 18.00
27 S.Green Dodgers H 25.00 11.00
28 Tim Hudson H 25.00 11.00
29 Deion Sanders 40.00 18.00
30 Rafael Palmeiro O's 40.00 18.00
31 Todd Helton H 40.00 18.00
32 L.Berkman No Socks 25.00 11.00
33 Mike Mussina Yanks H 40.00 18.00
34 Kazuhisa Ishii H 25.00 11.00
35 Pat Burrell Run 25.00 11.00
36 Miguel Tejada Btg 25.00 11.00
37 J.Gonzalez Rgr Stand 40.00 18.00
38 Roberto Alomar Mets H 40.00 18.00
39 R.Alomar Indians Bunt 40.00 18.00
40 Luis Gonzalez 25.00 11.00
41 Jorge Posada 40.00 18.00
42 Mark Mulder Leg 25.00 11.00
43 Sammy Sosa H 80.00 36.00
44 Mark Prior H 40.00 18.00
45 Roger Clemens Yanks H 60.00 27.00
46 Tom Glavine Mets H 40.00 18.00
47 Mark Teixeira A 25.00 11.00
48 Manny Ramirez H 40.00 18.00
49 Frank Thomas Swing 40.00 18.00
50 Troy Glaus White 25.00 11.00
51 Andruw Jones H 25.00 11.00
52 Jason Giambi Yanks H 25.00 11.00
53 Jim Thome Phils H 40.00 18.00
55 Rafael Palmeiro Rgr A 40.00 18.00
56 Edgar Martinez H 40.00 18.00
57 Vladimir Guerrero H 40.00 18.00
58 Roberto Alomar O's 40.00 18.00
59 Mike Sweeney 25.00 11.00
60 Magglio Ordonez A 25.00 11.00
62 Craig Biggio A 40.00 18.00
63 Greg Maddux H 60.00 27.00
64 Mike Piazza Mets H 60.00 27.00
65 Tom Glavine Braves A 40.00 18.00
66 Kerry Wood H 40.00 18.00
67 Frank Thomas Arms 40.00 18.00
68 Mike Mussina Yanks A 40.00 18.00
69 Nick Johnson H 25.00 11.00
70 Bernie Williams H 40.00 18.00
71 Scott Rolen 40.00 18.00
72 C.Schilling D'backs Leg 25.00 11.00
73 Adam Dunn A 40.00 18.00
74 Roy Oswalt A 25.00 11.00
75 Pedro Martinez Sox H 40.00 18.00
76 Tom Glavine Mets A 40.00 18.00
77 Torii Hunter Swing 25.00 11.00
78 Austin Kearns 25.00 11.00
79 R.Johnson D'backs A 40.00 18.00
80 Bernie Williams A 40.00 18.00
82 Kerry Wood A 40.00 18.00
83 Kazuhisa Ishii A 25.00 11.00
84 Randy Johnson Astros 40.00 18.00
85 Nick Johnson A 25.00 11.00
86 J.Beckett Pinstripe 25.00 11.00
87 Curt Schilling Phils 25.00 11.00
88 Mike Mussina O's 40.00 18.00
89 P.Martinez Dodgers 40.00 18.00
90 Barry Zito A 25.00 11.00
91 Jim Edmonds 25.00 11.00
92 R.Henderson Sox 40.00 18.00
93 R.Henderson Padres 40.00 18.00
94 R.Henderson M's 40.00 18.00
95 R.Henderson Mets 40.00 18.00
96 R.Henderson Jays 40.00 18.00
97 R.Johnson M's Arm Up 40.00 18.00
98 Mark Grace 40.00 18.00
99 Pedro Martinez Expos 40.00 18.00
100 Hee Seop Choi 25.00 11.00
101 Ivan Rodriguez Rgr 40.00 18.00
102 Jeff Kent Giants 25.00 11.00
104 Hideo Nomo Mets 80.00 36.00
105 Mike Piazza Dodgers 60.00 27.00
106 Tom Glavine Braves H 40.00 18.00
107 R.Alomar Indians Swing 40.00 18.00
108 Roger Clemens Sox 60.00 27.00
109 Jason Giambi A's H 25.00 11.00
110 Jim Thome Indians A 40.00 18.00
111 Alex Rodriguez M's H 60.00 27.00
112 J.Gonz Indians Hands 40.00 18.00
113 Torii Hunter Crouch 25.00 11.00
114 Roy Oswalt H 25.00 11.00
115 C.Schilling D'backs Throw 25.00 11.00
116 Magglio Ordonez H 25.00 11.00
117 Rafael Palmeiro Rgr H 40.00 18.00
118 Andruw Jones A 25.00 11.00
119 Manny Ramirez A 40.00 18.00
120 Mark Teixeira H 25.00 11.00
121 Mark Mulder Stance 25.00 11.00
123 Tim Hudson A 25.00 11.00
124 Todd Helton A 40.00 18.00
125 Troy Glaus Pinstripe 25.00 11.00
128 Greg Maddux A 60.00 27.00
129 Roger Clemens Yanks A 60.00 27.00
130 Nomar Garciaparra A 60.00 27.00
131 Mike Piazza Mets A 60.00 27.00
132 Alex Rodriguez Rgr H 60.00 27.00
134 R.Johnson D'backs H 40.00 18.00
135 Sammy Sosa A 80.00 36.00
137 Alfonso Soriano H 40.00 18.00
138 J.Giambi Yanks A 25.00 11.00
139 Albert Pujols A 100.00 45.00
140 Chipper Jones A 40.00 18.00
141 Adam Dunn H 40.00 18.00
142 P.Martinez Sox A 40.00 18.00
143 Vladimir Guerrero A 40.00 18.00
144 Mark Prior A 40.00 18.00
145 Barry Zito H 25.00 11.00
146 Jeff Bagwell A 40.00 18.00
147 Lance Berkman Socks 25.00 11.00
148 S.Green Dodgers A 25.00 11.00
149 Jason Giambi A's A 25.00 11.00
150 R.Johnson M's Arm Out 40.00 18.00
151 Alex Rodriguez M's A 60.00 27.00
152 Babe Ruth/3
153 Ty Cobb Pants 200.00 90.00
154 Jackie Robinson/10
155 Lou Gehrig/5
156 Thurman Munson 80.00 36.00
157 Roberto Clemente/5
158 Nolan Ryan Rgr 120.00 55.00
159 Nolan Ryan Angels 120.00 55.00
160 Nolan Ryan Astros 120.00 55.00
161 Cal Ripken 150.00 70.00
162 Don Mattingly 120.00 55.00
163 Stan Musial 150.00 70.00
164 Tony Gwynn 60.00 27.00
165 Yogi Berra 50.00 22.00
166 Johnny Bench 50.00 22.00
167 Mike Schmidt 120.00 55.00
168 George Brett 120.00 55.00
169 Ryne Sandberg 120.00 55.00
170 Ernie Banks/10

2003 Leaf Limited Timber

MINT NRMT
RANDOM INSERTS IN PACKS
STATED PRINT RUN 25 SERIAL #'d SETS
CARD 170 PRINT RUN 1 SERIAL #'d CARD
NO 170 PRICING DUE TO SCARCITY
2 Eric Chavez 15.00 6.75
3 Alex Rodriguez Rgr A 40.00 18.00
4 Miguel Tejada Fldg 15.00 6.75
5 Nomar Garciaparra H 40.00 18.00
6 Jeff Bagwell H 25.00 11.00
7 Jim Thome Phils A 25.00 11.00
8 Pat Burrell w/Bat 15.00 6.75
9 Albert Pujols H 60.00 27.00
10 Juan Gonzalez Rgr Btg 25.00 11.00
11 Shawn Green Jays 15.00 6.75
12 Craig Biggio H 25.00 11.00
13 Chipper Jones H 25.00 11.00
14 Hideo Nomo Dodgers 50.00 22.00
15 Vernon Wells 15.00 6.75
16 Gary Sheffield 15.00 6.75
17 Barry Larkin 25.00 11.00
18 Josh Beckett White 15.00 6.75
19 Edgar Martinez A 25.00 11.00
20 Ivan Rodriguez Marlins 25.00 11.00
21 Jeff Kent Astros 15.00 6.75
22 Roberto Alomar Mets A 25.00 11.00
23 Alfonso Soriano A 25.00 11.00
24 Jim Thome Indians H 25.00 11.00
25 J.Gonzalez Indians Btg 25.00 11.00
26 Carlos Beltran 25.00 11.00
27 S.Green Dodgers H 15.00 6.75
28 Tim Hudson H 15.00 6.75
30 Rafael Palmeiro O's 25.00 11.00
31 Todd Helton H 25.00 11.00
32 L.Berkman No Socks 15.00 6.75
33 Mike Mussina Yanks H 25.00 11.00
34 Kazuhisa Ishii H 15.00 6.75
35 Pat Burrell Run 15.00 6.75
36 Miguel Tejada Btg 15.00 6.75
37 J.Gonzalez Rgr Stand 25.00 11.00
38 Roberto Alomar Mets H 25.00 11.00
39 R.Alomar Indians Bunt 25.00 11.00
40 Luis Gonzalez 15.00 6.75
41 Jorge Posada 25.00 11.00
42 Mark Mulder Leg 15.00 6.75
43 Sammy Sosa H 50.00 22.00
44 Mark Prior H 25.00 11.00
45 R.Clemens Yanks H 40.00 18.00
46 Tom Glavine Mets H 25.00 11.00
47 Mark Teixeira A 15.00 6.75
48 Manny Ramirez H 25.00 11.00
49 Frank Thomas Swing 25.00 11.00
50 Troy Glaus White 15.00 6.75
51 Andruw Jones H 15.00 6.75
52 Jason Giambi Yanks H 15.00 6.75
53 Jim Thome Phils H 25.00 11.00
55 Rafael Palmeiro Rgr A 25.00 11.00
56 Edgar Martinez H 25.00 11.00
57 Vladimir Guerrero H 25.00 11.00
58 Roberto Alomar O's 25.00 11.00
59 Mike Sweeney 15.00 6.75
60 Magglio Ordonez A 15.00 6.75
62 Craig Biggio A 25.00 11.00
63 Greg Maddux H 40.00 18.00
64 Mike Piazza Mets H 40.00 18.00
65 T.Glavine Braves A 25.00 11.00
66 Kerry Wood H 25.00 11.00
67 Frank Thomas Arms 25.00 11.00
68 Mike Mussina Yanks A 25.00 11.00
69 Nick Johnson H 15.00 6.75
70 Bernie Williams H 25.00 11.00
71 Scott Rolen 25.00 11.00
72 C.Schilling D'backs Leg 15.00 6.75
73 Adam Dunn A 25.00 11.00
74 Roy Oswalt A 15.00 6.75
75 Pedro Martinez Sox H 25.00 11.00
76 Tom Glavine Mets A 25.00 11.00
77 Torii Hunter Swing 15.00 6.75
78 Austin Kearns 15.00 6.75
79 R.Johnson D'backs A 25.00 11.00
80 Bernie Williams A 25.00 11.00
82 Kerry Wood A 25.00 11.00
83 Kazuhisa Ishii A 15.00 6.75
84 Randy Johnson Astros 25.00 11.00
85 Nick Johnson A 15.00 6.75
86 J.Beckett Pinstripe 15.00 6.75
87 Curt Schilling Phils 15.00 6.75
88 Mike Mussina O's 25.00 11.00
89 P.Martinez Dodgers 25.00 11.00
90 Barry Zito A 15.00 6.75
91 Jim Edmonds 15.00 6.75
92 R.Henderson Sox 25.00 11.00
93 R.Henderson Padres 25.00 11.00
94 R.Henderson M's 25.00 11.00
95 R.Henderson Mets 25.00 11.00
96 R.Henderson Jays 25.00 11.00
97 R.Johnson M's Arm Up 25.00 11.00
98 Mark Grace 25.00 11.00
99 Pedro Martinez Expos 25.00 11.00
101 Ivan Rodriguez Rgr 25.00 11.00
102 Jeff Kent Giants 15.00 6.75
103 Hideo Nomo Sox 50.00 22.00
104 Hideo Nomo Mets 50.00 22.00
105 Mike Piazza Dodgers 40.00 18.00
106 Tom Glavine Braves H 25.00 11.00
107 R.Alomar Indians Swing 25.00 11.00
108 Roger Clemens Sox 40.00 18.00
109 Jason Giambi A's H 15.00 6.75
110 Jim Thome Indians A 25.00 11.00
111 Alex Rodriguez M's H 40.00 18.00
112 J.Gonz Indians Hands 25.00 11.00
113 Torii Hunter Crouch 15.00 6.75
114 Roy Oswalt H 15.00 6.75
115 C.Schilling D'backs Throw 15.00 6.75
116 Magglio Ordonez H 15.00 6.75
117 Rafael Palmeiro Rgr H 25.00 11.00
118 Andruw Jones A 15.00 6.75
119 Manny Ramirez A 25.00 11.00
120 Mark Teixeira H 15.00 6.75
121 Mark Mulder Stance 15.00 6.75
122 Garret Anderson 15.00 6.75
123 Tim Hudson A 15.00 6.75
124 Todd Helton A 25.00 11.00
125 Troy Glaus Pinstripe 15.00 6.75
128 Greg Maddux A 40.00 18.00
129 Roger Clemens Yanks A 40.00 18.00
130 Nomar Garciaparra A 40.00 18.00
131 Mike Piazza Mets A 40.00 18.00
132 Alex Rodriguez Rgr H 40.00 18.00
134 R.Johnson D'backs H 25.00 11.00
135 Sammy Sosa A 50.00 22.00
137 Alfonso Soriano H 25.00 11.00
138 J.Giambi Yanks A 15.00 6.75
139 Albert Pujols A 60.00 27.00
140 Chipper Jones A 25.00 11.00
141 Adam Dunn H 25.00 11.00
142 Pedro Martinez Sox A 25.00 11.00
143 Vladimir Guerrero A 25.00 11.00
144 Mark Prior A 25.00 11.00
145 Barry Zito H 15.00 6.75
146 Jeff Bagwell A 25.00 11.00
147 Lance Berkman Socks 15.00 6.75
148 S.Green Dodgers A 15.00 6.75
149 Jason Giambi A's A 15.00 6.75
150 R.Johnson M's Arm Out 25.00 11.00
151 Alex Rodriguez M's A 40.00 18.00
152 Babe Ruth 300.00 135.00
153 Ty Cobb 150.00 70.00
155 Lou Gehrig 200.00 90.00
156 Thurman Munson 50.00 22.00
157 Roberto Clemente 150.00 70.00
158 Nolan Ryan Rgr 80.00 36.00
159 Nolan Ryan Angels 80.00 36.00
160 Nolan Ryan Astros 80.00 36.00
161 Cal Ripken 120.00 55.00
162 Don Mattingly 80.00 36.00
163 Stan Musial 60.00 27.00
164 Tony Gwynn 40.00 18.00
165 Yogi Berra 30.00 13.50
166 Johnny Bench 30.00 13.50
167 Mike Schmidt 80.00 36.00
168 George Brett 80.00 36.00
169 Ryne Sandberg 80.00 36.00
170 Ernie Banks/1

2003 Leaf Limited TNT

MINT NRMT
RANDOM INSERTS IN PACKS
PRINT RUNS B/WN 1-25 COPIES PER
NO PRICING ON QTY OF 10 OR LESS
2 Eric Chavez Bat-Jsy 25.00 11.00
3 A.Rod Rgr A Bat-Jsy 50.00 22.00
4 M.Tejada Fldg Bat-Jsy/10
5 N.Garciaparra H Bat-Jsy 50.00 22.00
6 Jeff Bagwell H Bat-Jsy 40.00 18.00
7 J.Thome Phils A Bat-Jsy 40.00 18.00
8 P.Burrell w/Bat Bat-Jsy 25.00 11.00
9 Albert Pujols H Bat-Jsy 60.00 27.00
10 J.Gonz Rgr Btg Bat-Jsy 40.00 18.00
11 S.Green Jays Bat-Jsy 25.00 11.00
12 Craig Biggio H Bat-Jsy 40.00 18.00
13 C.Jones H Bat-Jsy 40.00 18.00
14 H.Nomo Dodgers Bat-Jsy 50.00 22.00
15 Vernon Wells Bat-Jsy 25.00 11.00
16 G.Sheffield Bat-Jsy 25.00 11.00
17 Barry Larkin Bat-Jsy 40.00 18.00
18 J.Beckett White Bat-Jsy 25.00 11.00
19 E.Martinez A Bat-Jsy 40.00 18.00
20 I.Rodriguez Marlins Bat-Jsy 40.00 18.00
21 Jeff Kent Astros Bat-Jsy 25.00 11.00
22 R.Alomar Mets A Bat-Jsy 40.00 18.00
23 A.Soriano A Bat-Jsy 40.00 18.00
24 J.Thome Indians H Bat-Jsy 40.00 18.00
25 J.Gonz Indians Btg Bat-Jsy 40.00 18.00
26 Carlos Beltran Bat-Jsy 40.00 18.00
27 S.Green Dodgers H Bat-Jsy 25.00 11.00
28 Tim Hudson H Bat-Jsy 25.00 11.00
30 R.Palmeiro O's Bat-Jsy 40.00 18.00
31 Todd Helton H Bat-Jsy 40.00 18.00
32 L.Berk No Socks Bat-Jsy 25.00 11.00
33 M.Mussina Yanks H Bat-Jsy 40.00 18.00
34 Kazuhisa Ishii H Bat-Jsy 25.00 11.00
35 Pat Burrell Run Bat-Jsy 25.00 11.00
36 M.Tejada Btg Bat-Jsy/10
37 J.Gonz Rgr Stand Bat-Jsy 40.00 18.00
38 R.Alomar Mets H Bat-Jsy 40.00 18.00
39 R.Alom Indian Bunt Bat-Jsy 40.00 18.00
40 Luis Gonzalez Bat-Jsy 25.00 11.00
41 Jorge Posada Bat-Jsy 40.00 18.00
42 M.Mulder Leg Bat-Jsy 25.00 11.00
43 Sammy Sosa H Bat-Jsy 50.00 22.00
44 Mark Prior H Bat-Jsy 40.00 18.00
45 R.Clemens Yanks H Bat-Jsy 50.00 22.00
46 T.Glavine Mets H Bat-Jsy 40.00 18.00
47 Mark Teixeira A Bat-Jsy 25.00 11.00
48 Manny Ramirez H Bat-Jsy 40.00 18.00
49 F.Thomas Swing Bat-Jsy 40.00 18.00
50 Troy Glaus White Bat-Jsy 25.00 11.00
51 Andruw Jones H Bat-Jsy 25.00 11.00
52 J.Giambi Yanks H Bat-Jsy 25.00 11.00
53 J.Thome Phils H Bat-Jsy 40.00 18.00
55 R.Palmeiro Rgr A Bat-Jsy 40.00 18.00
56 E.Martinez H Bat-Jsy 40.00 18.00
57 V.Guerrero H Bat-Jsy 40.00 18.00
59 Mike Sweeney Bat-Jsy 25.00 11.00
60 M.Ordonez A Bat-Jsy 25.00 11.00
62 Craig Biggio A Bat-Jsy 40.00 18.00
63 Greg Maddux H Bat-Jsy 50.00 22.00
64 M.Piazza Mets H Bat-Jsy 50.00 22.00
65 T.Glavine Braves A Bat-Jsy 40.00 18.00
66 Kerry Wood H Bat-Jsy 40.00 18.00
67 F.Thomas Arms Bat-Jsy 40.00 18.00
68 M.Mussina Yanks A Bat-Jsy 40.00 18.00
69 Nick Johnson H Bat-Jsy 25.00 11.00
70 Bernie Williams H Bat-Jsy 40.00 18.00
71 Scott Rolen Bat-Jsy 40.00 18.00
72 C.Schill D'backs Leg Bat-Jsy 25.00 11.00
73 Adam Dunn A Bat-Jsy 40.00 18.00
74 Roy Oswalt A Bat-Jsy 25.00 11.00
75 P.Martinez Sox H Bat-Jsy 40.00 18.00
76 T.Glavine Mets A Bat-Jsy 40.00 18.00
77 T.Hunter Swing Bat-Jsy 25.00 11.00
78 Austin Kearns Bat-Jsy 25.00 11.00
79 R.John D'backs A Bat-Jsy 40.00 18.00
80 Bernie Williams A Bat-Jsy 40.00 18.00
82 Kerry Wood A Bat-Jsy 40.00 18.00
83 Kazuhisa Ishii A Bat-Jsy 25.00 11.00
84 R.Johnson Astros Bat-Jsy 40.00 18.00
85 Nick Johnson A Bat-Jsy 25.00 11.00
86 J.Beckett Pinstripe Bat-Jsy 25.00 11.00
87 C.Schilling Phils Bat-Jsy 25.00 11.00
88 Mike Mussina O's Bat-Jsy 40.00 18.00
89 P.Martinez Dgr Bat-Jsy 40.00 18.00
90 Barry Zito A Bat-Jsy 25.00 11.00
91 Jim Edmonds Bat-Jsy 25.00 11.00
92 R.Henderson Sox Bat-Jsy 40.00 18.00
93 R.Hend Padres Bat-Jsy 40.00 18.00
94 R.Henderson M's Bat-Jsy 40.00 18.00
95 R.Hend Mets Bat-Jsy 40.00 18.00
96 R.Hend Jays Bat-Jsy 40.00 18.00
97 R.John M's Arm Up Bat-Jsy 40.00 18.00
98 Mark Grace Bat-Jsy 40.00 18.00
99 P.Martinez Expos Bat-Jsy 40.00 18.00
101 I.Rodriguez Rgr Bat-Jsy 40.00 18.00
102 Jeff Kent Giants Bat-Jsy 25.00 11.00
103 Hideo Nomo Sox Bat-Jsy 50.00 22.00

104 Hideo Nomo Mets Bat-Jsy . 50.00 22.00
105 M.Piazza Dodgers Bat-Jsy . 50.00 22.00
106 T.Glav Braves H Bat-Jsy 40.00 18.00
107 R.Alom Ind Swing Bat-Jsy . 40.00 18.00
108 R.Clemens Sox Bat-Jsy 50.00 22.00
109 J.Giambi A's H Bat-Jsy 25.00 11.00
110 J.Thome Indians A Bat-Jsy 40.00 18.00
111 A.Rod M's H Bat-Jsy 50.00 22.00
112 J.Gonz Ind Hands Bat-Jsy.. 40.00 18.00
113 T.Hunter Crouch Bat-Jsy.... 25.00 11.00
114 Roy Oswalt H Bat-Jsy 25.00 11.00
115 C.Schill D'b Throw Bat-Jsy 25.00 11.00
116 M.Ordonez H Bat-Jsy 25.00 11.00
117 R.Palmeiro Rgr H Bat-Jsy.. 40.00 18.00
118 Andruw Jones A Bat-Jsy.... 25.00 11.00
119 Manny Ramirez A Bat-Jsy.. 40.00 18.00
120 Mark Teixeira H Bat-Jsy 25.00 11.00
121 M.Mulder Stance Bat-Jsy... 25.00 11.00
123 Tim Hudson A Bat-Jsy 25.00 11.00
124 Todd Helton A Bat-Jsy 40.00 18.00
125 T.Glaus Pinstripe Bat-Jsy ... 25.00 11.00
128 Greg Maddux A Bat-Jsy 50.00 22.00
129 R.Clemens Yanks A Bat-Jsy 50.00 22.00
130 N.Garciaparra A Bat-Jsy..... 50.00 22.00
131 M.Piazza Mets A Bat-Jsy..... 50.00 22.00
132 A.Rod Rgr H Bat-Jsy.......... 50.00 22.00
134 R.John D'backs H Bat-Jsy . 40.00 18.00
135 Sammy Sosa A Bat-Jsy 50.00 22.00
137 A.Soriano H Bat-Jsy........... 40.00 18.00
138 J.Giambi Yanks A Bat-Jsy .. 25.00 11.00
139 Albert Pujols A Bat-Jsy 60.00 27.00
140 Chipper Jones A Bat-Jsy..... 40.00 18.00
141 Adam Dunn H Bat-Jsy 40.00 18.00
142 P.Martinez Sox A Bat-Jsy... 40.00 18.00
143 V.Guerrero A Bat-Jsy 40.00 18.00
144 Mark Prior A Bat-Jsy 40.00 18.00
145 Barry Zito H Bat-Jsy.......... 25.00 11.00
146 Jeff Bagwell A Bat-Jsy 40.00 18.00
147 L.Berkman Socks Bat-Jsy .. 25.00 11.00
148 S.Green Dgr A Bat-Jsy 25.00 11.00
149 J.Giambi A's A Bat-Jsy 25.00 11.00
150 R.John M's Arm Out Bat-Jsy 40.00 18.00
151 A.Rod M's A Bat-Jsy........... 50.00 22.00
152 Babe Ruth Bat-Jsy/5
153 Ty Cobb Bat-Pants/10
155 Lou Gehrig Bat-Jsy/5
156 Thurman Munson Bat-Jsy . 80.00 36.00
157 Roberto Clemente Bat-Jsy/5
158 Nolan Ryan Rgr Bat-Jsy... 100.00 45.00
159 N.Ryan Angels Bat-Jsy 100.00 45.00
160 N.Ryan Astros Bat-Jsy 100.00 45.00
161 Cal Ripken Bat-Jsy 120.00 55.00
162 Don Mattingly Bat-Jsy 100.00 45.00
163 Stan Musial Bat-Jsy 100.00 45.00
164 Tony Gwynn Bat-Jsy 50.00 22.00
165 Yogi Berra Bat-Jsy 60.00 27.00
166 Johnny Bench Bat-Jsy 60.00 27.00
167 Mike Schmidt Bat-Jsy...... 100.00 45.00
168 George Brett Bat-Jsy....... 100.00 45.00
169 Ryne Sandberg Bat-Jsy ... 100.00 45.00
170 Ernie Banks Bat-Jsy/1

2003 Leaf Limited TNT Prime

MINT NRMT
*TNT PRIME: .5X TO 1.2X BASIC TNT
RANDOM INSERTS PACKS
PRINT RUNS B/WN 1-25 COPIES PER
NO PRICING ON QTY OF 10 OR LESS

2003 Leaf Limited 7th Inning Stretch Jersey

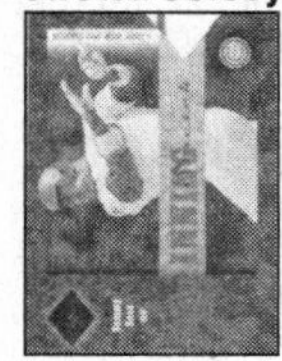

MINT NRMT
RANDOM INSERTS IN PACKS
PRINT RUNS B/WN 40-50 COPIES PER
1 Alex Rodriguez 25.00 11.00
3 Sammy Sosa......................... 30.00 13.50
4 Juan Gonzalez 15.00 6.75
5 Albert Pujols 40.00 18.00
6 Chipper Jones 15.00 6.75
7 Alfonso Soriano/40 .... 15.00 6.75
8 Jim Thome............................ 15.00 6.75
9 Mike Piazza 25.00 11.00
10 Rafael Palmeiro................... 15.00 6.75

2003 Leaf Limited Jersey Numbers

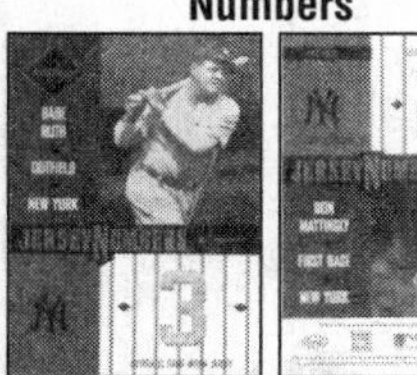

MINT NRMT
1-54 PRINT RUNS B/WN 5-100 COPIES PER
55-100 PRINT RUNS B/WN 5-25 COPIES PER
NO PRICING ON QTY OF 10 OR LESS
RANDOM INSERTS IN PACKS
1 Rod Carew Angels/50 .... 25.00 11.00
2 Nolan Ryan Angels/50 .... 60.00 27.00
3 Reggie Jackson Angels/50..... 25.00 11.00
4 Brooks Robinson/50 .... 25.00 11.00
5 Frank Robinson/25............... 25.00 11.00
6 Cal Ripken/100..................... 60.00 27.00
7 Carlton Fisk W.Sox/50........... 25.00 11.00
8 Roger Clemens/100 .... 20.00 9.00
9 Carlton Fisk R.Sox/5
10 Lou Boudreau/50 .... 15.00 6.75
11 Bob Feller/25....................... 25.00 11.00
12 Al Kaline/10
13 Alan Trammell/50 .... 15.00 6.75
14 Harmon Killebrew/50 .... 40.00 18.00
15 Rod Carew Twins/50 .... 25.00 11.00
16 Kirby Puckett/50 .... 40.00 18.00
17 Babe Ruth/5
18 Lou Gehrig/5
19 Yogi Berra/50 .... 40.00 18.00
20 Thurman Munson/50 .... 40.00 18.00
21 Don Mattingly/100 .... 40.00 18.00
22 Roger Maris Pants/10
23 Rickey Henderson/5
24 Reggie Jackson A's/5
25 Alex Rodriguez/100............... 20.00 9.00
26 Randy Johnson M's/50.......... 15.00 6.75
27 Nolan Ryan Rgr/100 .... 50.00 22.00
28 Dale Murphy/50 .... 40.00 18.00
29 Warren Spahn/50................. 25.00 11.00
30 Eddie Mathews/50 .... 40.00 18.00
31 Ernie Banks/5
32 Ryne Sandberg/100 .... 40.00 18.00
33 Johnny Bench/50.................. 40.00 18.00
34 Joe Morgan/50...................... 15.00 6.75
35 Randy Johnson Astros/50 .... 15.00 6.75
36 Nolan Ryan Astros/100 .... 50.00 22.00
37 Pee Wee Reese/50 .... 25.00 11.00
38 Duke Snider/50 .... 25.00 11.00
39 Jackie Robinson/25 .... 100.00 45.00
40 Robin Yount/50..................... 50.00 22.00
41 Paul Molitor/50 .... 25.00 11.00
42 Pedro Martinez/50 .... 15.00 6.75
43 Randy Johnson Expos/50 ..... 15.00 6.75
44 Tom Seaver/25..................... 40.00 18.00
45 Gary Carter/50 .... 15.00 6.75
46 Mike Schmidt/50................... 50.00 22.00
47 Steve Carlton/50 .... 15.00 6.75
48 Willie Stargell/50................... 25.00 11.00
49 Roberto Clemente/5
50 Ozzie Smith/50...................... 50.00 22.00
51 Stan Musial/100.................... 40.00 18.00
52 Enos Slaughter/50 .... 15.00 6.75
53 Orlando Cepeda/50 .... 15.00 6.75
54 Willie McCovey/50 .... 15.00 6.75
55 Brooks Robinson
Frank Robinson/10
56 Lou Boudreau
Bob Feller/10
57 Harmon Killebrew 100.00 45.00
Rod Carew/25
58 Harmon Killebrew 100.00 45.00
Kirby Puckett/25
59 Babe Ruth
Lou Gehrig/5
60 Babe Ruth
Yogi Berra/5
61 Babe Ruth
Thurman Munson/5
62 Babe Ruth
Don Mattingly/5
63 Babe Ruth
Roger Maris Pants/5
64 Lou Gehrig
Yogi Berra/5
65 Lou Gehrig
Thurman Munson/5
66 Lou Gehrig
Don Mattingly/5
67 Lou Gehrig
Roger Maris Pants/5
68 Yogi Berra 80.00 36.00
Thurman Munson/25
69 Yogi Berra 100.00 45.00
Don Mattingly/25
70 Yogi Berra
Roger Maris/5
71 Dale Murphy 80.00 36.00
Warren Spahn/25
72 Dale Murphy 80.00 36.00
Eddie Mathews/25
73 Warren Spahn 80.00 36.00
Eddie Mathews/25
74 Johnny Bench 60.00 27.00
Joe Morgan/25
75 Pee Wee Reese 60.00 27.00
Duke Snider/25
76 Pee Wee Reese
Jackie Robinson/10
77 Duke Snider
Jackie Robinson/10
78 Robin Yount 100.00 45.00
Paul Molitor/25
79 Mike Schmidt
Steve Carlton/25
80 Willie Stargell
Roberto Clemente/5
81 Ozzie Smith 100.00 45.00
Stan Musial/25
82 Stan Musial.......................... 100.00 45.00
Enos Slaughter/25
83 Orlando Cepeda 60.00 27.00
Willie McCovey/25
84 Nolan Ryan 100.00 45.00
Reggie Jackson/25
85 Brooks Robinson
Cal Ripken/25
86 Frank Robinson
Cal Ripken/10
87 Carlton Fisk
Roger Clemens/5
88 Al Kaline
Alan Trammell/10
89 Rickey Henderson
Reggie Jackson/5
90 Alex Rodriguez 50.00 22.00
Randy Johnson/25
91 Pedro Martinez...................... 50.00 22.00
Randy Johnson/25
92 Tom Seaver
Gary Carter/10
93 Ernie Banks
Ryne Sandberg/10
94 Reggie Jackson A's................ 60.00 27.00
Reggie Jackson Angels/25
95 Nolan Ryan Angels.............. 100.00 45.00
Nolan Ryan Rgr/25
96 Nolan Ryan Rgr 100.00 45.00
Nolan Ryan Astros/25
97 Nolan Ryan Astros 100.00 45.00
Nolan Ryan Angels/25
98 Nolan Ryan 100.00 45.00
Randy Johnson/25
99 Cal Ripken........................... 150.00 70.00
Rafael Palmeiro/25
100 Dale Murphy 80.00 36.00
Deion Sanders/25

2003 Leaf Limited Jersey Numbers Retired

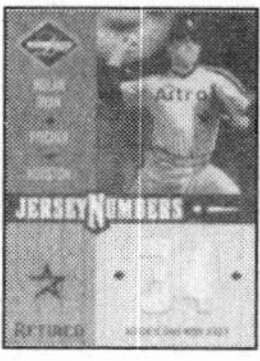

MINT NRMT
RANDOM INSERTS IN PACKS
PRINT RUNS B/WN 1-72 COPIES PER
NO PRICING ON QTY OF 19 OR LESS
1 Rod Carew Angels/29 .... 40.00 18.00
2 Nolan Ryan Angels/30 .... 80.00 36.00
4 Brooks Robinson/5
5 Frank Robinson/20................ 30.00 13.50
7 Carlton Fisk R.Sox/27 .... 40.00 18.00
9 Carlton Fisk W.Sox/72........... 25.00 11.00
10 Lou Boudreau/5
11 Bob Feller/19
12 Al Kaline/6
14 Harmon Killebrew/3
15 Rod Carew Twins/29........... 40.00 18.00
16 Kirby Puckett/34 .... 50.00 22.00
17 Babe Ruth/3
18 Lou Gehrig/4
19 Yogi Berra/8
20 Thurman Munson/15
21 Don Mattingly/23 .... 80.00 36.00
22 R.Maris Pants/9
27 Nolan Ryan Rgr/34 .... 80.00 36.00
28 Dale Murphy/3
29 Warren Spahn/21 .... 50.00 22.00
30 Eddie Mathews/41 .... 25.00 11.00
31 Ernie Banks/14
33 Johnny Bench/5
34 Joe Morgan/8
36 Nolan Ryan Astros/34.......... 80.00 36.00
37 Pee Wee Reese/1
38 Duke Snider/4
39 Jackie Robinson/42 .... 80.00 36.00
40 Robin Yount/19
41 Paul Molitor/4
44 Tom Seaver/41 .... 25.00 11.00
46 Mike Schmidt/20.................. 80.00 36.00
47 Steve Carlton/32 .... 25.00 11.00
48 Willie Stargell/8
49 Roberto Clemente/21 .... 150.00 70.00
50 Ozzie Smith/1
51 Stan Musial/6
52 Enos Slaughter/9
53 Orlando Cepeda/30 .... 25.00 11.00
54 Willie McCovey/44 .... 15.00 6.75

2003 Leaf Limited Leather

MINT NRMT
RANDOM INSERTS IN PACKS
PRINT RUNS B/WN 10-25 COPIES PER
NO PRICNG ON QTY OF 10 OR LESS
1 Alex Rodriguez/25................ 60.00 27.00
2 Chipper Jones/25.................. 40.00 18.00
3 Jimmie Foxx/25 .... 100.00 45.00
4 Kirby Puckett/25 .... 40.00 18.00
5 Mike Schmidt/25................ 120.00 55.00
6 Roger Clemens/25 .... 60.00 27.00
7 Steve Carlton/25 .... 40.00 18.00
8 Tony Gywnn/25.................... 60.00 27.00
9 Nolan Ryan/10
10 Vladimir Guerrero/25 .... 40.00 18.00
11 Adam Dunn/25.................... 40.00 18.00
12 Andruw Jones/25 .... 40.00 18.00
13 Curt Schilling/25 .... 40.00 18.00
14 Randy Johnson/25............... 40.00 18.00
15 Mark Prior/25....................... 40.00 18.00

2003 Leaf Limited Leather Gold

MINT NRMT
RANDOM INSERTS IN PACKS
PRINT RUNS B/WN 5-10 COPIES PER
NO PRICING DUE TO SCARCITY

2003 Leaf Limited Leather and Lace

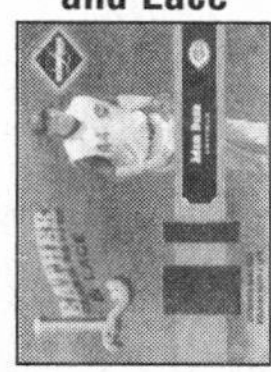

MINT NRMT
RANDOM INSERTS IN PACKS
STATED PRINT RUN 10 SERIAL #'d SETS
N.RYAN PRINT RUN 5 SERIAL #'d CARDS
NO PRICING DUE TO SCARCITY

2003 Leaf Limited Leather and Lace Gold

MINT NRMT
RANDOM INSERTS IN PACKS
STATED PRINT RUN 5 SERIAL #'d SETS
NO PRICING DUE TO SCARCITY

2003 Leaf Limited Lineups Bat

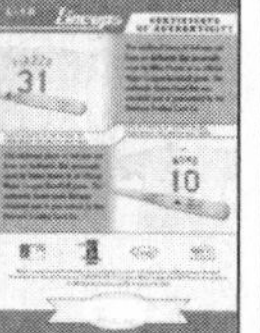

MINT NRMT
RANDOM INSERTS IN PACKS
PRINT RUNS B/WN 25-50 COPIES PER
ALL ARE DUAL BAT CARDS UNLESS NOTED
CARD NUMBER 3 DOES NOT EXIST
1 Paul Molitor 50.00 22.00
Robin Yount/50
2 Don Mattingly 50.00 22.00
Bernie Williams/50
4 Hideki Matsui Ball 80.00 36.00
Derek Jeter Ball/25
5 Ryne Sandberg 50.00 22.00
Andre Dawson/50
6 George Brett......................... 80.00 36.00
Bo Jackson/50
7 Reggie Jackson 40.00 18.00
Jose Canseco/50
8 Mark Grace 50.00 22.00
Ryne Sandberg/50
9 Rickey Henderson 40.00 18.00
Jose Canseco/50
10 Mike Piazza 40.00 18.00
Hideo Nomo/50

2003 Leaf Limited Lineups Button

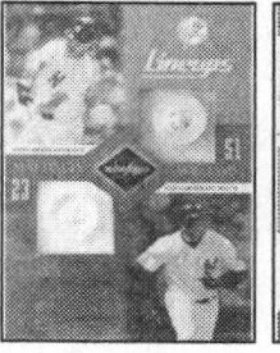

MINT NRMT
RANDOM INSERTS IN PACKS
STATED PRINT RUN 1 SERIAL #'d SET
NO PRICING DUE TO SCARCITY
2 Don Mattingly
Bernie Williams
3 Sammy Sosa
Hee Seop Choi
6 George Brett
Bo Jackson
10 Mike Piazza
Hideo Nomo

2003 Leaf Limited Lineups Jersey

MINT NRMT
RANDOM INSERTS IN PACKS
PRINT RUNS B/WN 25
NO PRICING ON QTY OF 5 OR LESS
ALL ARE DUAL JSY CARDS UNLESS NOTED
1 Paul Molitor 50.00 22.00
Robin Yount/50
2 Don Mattingly 50.00 22.00
Bernie Williams/50
3 Sammy Sosa......................... 40.00 18.00
Hee Seop Choi/50
4 Hideki Matsui Base 40.00 18.00
Derek Jeter Base/50
5 Ryne Sandberg 50.00 22.00
Andre Dawson/50
6 George Brett......................... 80.00 36.00
Bo Jackson/50
7 Reggie Jackson
Jose Canseco/5
8 Mark Grace 50.00 22.00
Ryne Sandberg/50
9 Rickey Henderson
Jose Canseco/5
10 Mike Piazza 40.00 18.00
Hideo Nomo/50

2003 Leaf Limited Lineups Jersey Tag

MINT NRMT
RANDOM INSERTS IN PACKS
PRINT RUNS B/WN 4-5 COPIES PER
NO PRICING DUE TO SCARCITY

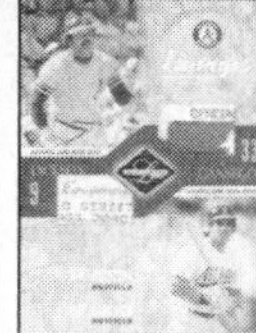

1 Paul Molitor
Robin Yount/5
2 Don Mattingly
Bernie Williams/5
3 Sammy Sosa
Hee Seop Choi/5
6 George Brett
Bo Jackson/5
7 Reggie Jackson
Jose Canseco/4
8 Mark Grace
Ryne Sandberg/5
9 Rickey Henderson
Jose Canseco/4
10 Mike Piazza
Hideo Nomo/5

2003 Leaf Limited Lumberjacks Barrel

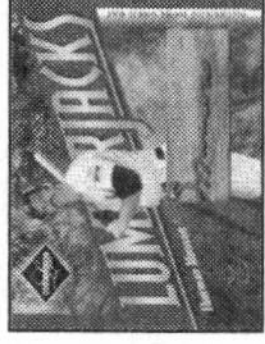

MINT NRMT
RANDOM INSERTS IN PACKS
PRINT RUNS B/WN 1-2 COPIES PER
NO PRICING DUE TO SCARCITY
1 Babe Ruth/2
2 Lou Gehrig/1
3 Roberto Clemente/1
4 Stan Musial/1
5 Rogers Hornsby/1
6 Don Mattingly/1
7 Rickey Henderson/2
8 Cal Ripken/1
9 Yogi Berra/1
10 Reggie Jackson/1
11 George Brett/1
12 Mel Ott/1
13 Roger Maris/1
14 Ryne Sandberg/1
15 Eddie Mathews/1
16 Richie Ashburn/1
17 Mike Schmidt/1
18 Tony Gwynn/1
19 Ty Cobb/1
20 Thurman Munson/2
21 Jimmie Foxx/1
22 Duke Snider/1
23 Ernie Banks/2
24 Alex Rodriguez/1
25 Nomar Garciaparra/2
29 Mike Piazza/1
30 Alfonso Soriano/2
31 Al Kaline/1
32 Harmon Killebrew/2
33 Dale Murphy/1
34 Orlando Cepeda/1
35 Willie McCovey/1
36 Willie Stargell/1
37 Brooks Robinson/1

2003 Leaf Limited Lumberjacks Bat

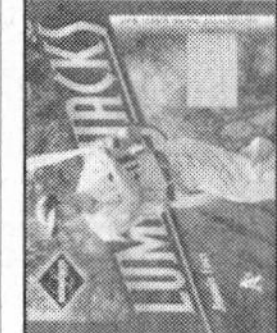

MINT NRMT
1-37 PRINT RUNS B/WN 1-25 COPIES PER
38-45 PRINT RUNS B/WN 1-25 COPIES PER
NO PRICING ON QTY OF 15 OR LESS
RANDOM INSERTS IN PACKS
1 Babe Ruth/25...................... 300.00 135.00
2 Lou Gehrig/25..................... 200.00 90.00
3 Roberto Clemente/25.......... 150.00 70.00
4 Stan Musial/25..................... 60.00 27.00
5 Rogers Hornsby/25............... 80.00 36.00
6 Don Mattingly/25 .... 80.00 36.00
7 Rickey Henderson/25............ 25.00 11.00
8 Cal Ripken/25..................... 120.00 55.00
9 Yogi Berra/25....................... 50.00 22.00
10 Reggie Jackson/25............... 40.00 18.00
11 George Brett/25 .... 80.00 36.00
12 Mel Ott/25........................... 60.00 27.00
13 Roger Maris/25.................. 100.00 45.00
14 Ryne Sandberg/25 .... 80.00 36.00
15 Eddie Mathews/15
16 Richie Ashburn/25 .... 40.00 18.00
17 Mike Schmidt/25.................. 80.00 36.00
18 Tony Gwynn/25.................... 40.00 18.00
19 Ty Cobb/25........................ 150.00 70.00
20 Thurman Munson/25 .... 50.00 22.00
21 Jimmie Foxx/25 .... 80.00 36.00
22 Duke Snider/25 .... 40.00 18.00
23 Ernie Banks/1
24 Alex Rodriguez/25............... 40.00 18.00

25 Nomar Garciaparra/25 40.00 18.00
26 Hideki Matsui Base/25 80.00 36.00
27 Ichiro Suzuki Base/25 60.00 27.00
28 Barry Bonds Base/25 60.00 27.00
29 Mike Piazza/25 40.00 18.00
30 Alfonso Soriano/25 25.00 11.00
31 Al Kaline/25 50.00 22.00
32 Harmon Killebrew/5
33 Dale Murphy/25 50.00 22.00
34 Orlando Cepeda/5
35 Willie McCovey/25 25.00 11.00
36 Willie Stargell/5
37 Brooks Robinson/25 40.00 18.00
38 Hideki Matsui Base 120.00 55.00
Ichiro Suzuki Base/25
39 Ryne Sandberg
Ernie Banks/1
40 Don Mattingly 250.00 110.00
Lou Gehrig/25
41 Yogi Berra 80.00 36.00
Thurman Munson/25
42 Mike Schmidt 100.00 45.00
Richie Ashburn/25
43 Stan Musial 120.00 55.00
Rogers Hornsby/25
44 Don Mattingly 150.00 70.00
Roger Maris/25
45 Babe Ruth
Lou Gehrig/15

2003 Leaf Limited Lumberjacks Bat Black

MINT NRMT
RANDOM INSERTS IN PACKS
PRINT RUNS B/WN 1-5 COPIES PER
NO PRICING DUE TO SCARCITY

2003 Leaf Limited Lumberjacks Bat Silver

MINT NRMT
RANDOM INSERTS IN PACKS
PRINT RUNS B/WN 1-10 COPIES PER
NO PRICING DUE TO SCARCITY

2003 Leaf Limited Lumberjacks Bat-Jersey

MINT NRMT
1-37 PRINT RUNS B/WN 1-25 COPIES PER
38-45 PRINT RUNS B/WN 1-25 COPIES PER
NO PRICING ON QTY OF 15 OR LESS
RANDOM INSERTS IN PACKS
ALL ARE BAT-JSY COMBOS UNLESS NOTED
1 Babe Ruth/5
2 Lou Gehrig/10
3 Roberto Clemente/10
4 Stan Musial/25 100.00 45.00
6 Don Mattingly/25 120.00 55.00
7 Rickey Henderson/5
8 Cal Ripken/25 150.00 70.00
9 Yogi Berra/25 60.00 27.00
10 Reggie Jackson/5
11 George Brett/25 120.00 55.00
12 Mel Ott/15
13 Roger Maris Bat-Pants/25 150.00 70.00
14 Ryne Sandberg/25 120.00 55.00
15 Eddie Mathews/25 60.00 27.00
17 Mike Schmidt/25 120.00 55.00
18 Tony Gwynn/25 60.00 27.00
19 Ty Cobb Bat-Pants/15
20 Thurman Munson/25 80.00 36.00
22 Duke Snider/15
23 Ernie Banks/1
24 Alex Rodriguez/25 60.00 27.00
25 Nomar Garciaparra/25 60.00 27.00
26 Hideki Matsui Base-Ball/25 120.00 55.00
27 Ichiro Suzuki Base-Ball/25 80.00 36.00
28 Barry Bonds Base-Ball/25 80.00 36.00
29 Mike Piazza/25 60.00 27.00
30 Alfonso Soriano/25 40.00 18.00
31 Al Kaline/10
32 Harmon Killebrew/10
33 Dale Murphy/25 60.00 27.00
34 Orlando Cepeda/5
35 Willie McCovey/25 30.00 13.50
36 Willie Stargell/25 50.00 22.00
37 Brooks Robinson/25 50.00 22.00
38A Hideki Matsui Base 120.00 55.00
Ichiro Suzuki Ball/25
38B Hideki Matsui Ball 120.00 55.00
Ichiro Suzuki Base/25
39A Ryne Sandberg Bat
Ernie Banks Jsy/5
39B Ryne Sandberg Jsy
Ernie Banks Bat/1
40A Don Mattingly Jsy
Lou Gehrig Bat/10
40B Don Mattingly Bat
Lou Gehrig Jsy/5
41A Yogi Berra Jsy 80.00 36.00
Thurman Munson Bat/25
41B Yogi Berra Bat 80.00 36.00
Thurman Munson Jsy/25
42 Mike Schmidt Jsy 100.00 45.00
Richie Ashburn Bat/25
43 Stan Musial Jsy 120.00 55.00
Rogers Hornsby Bat/25
44 Don Mattingly Bat
Roger Maris Pants/5
45A Babe Ruth Jsy
Lou Gehrig Bat/5
45B Babe Ruth Bat
Lou Gehrig Jsy/5

2003 Leaf Limited Lumberjacks Bat-Jersey Black

MINT NRMT
RANDOM INSERTS IN PACKS
PRINT RUNS B/WN 1-5 COPIES PER
NO PRICING DUE TO SCARCITY

2003 Leaf Limited Lumberjacks Bat-Jersey Silver

MINT NRMT
RANDOM INSERTS IN PACKS
PRINT RUNS B/WN 1-10 COPIES PER
NO PRICING DUE TO SCARCITY

2003 Leaf Limited Lumberjacks Jersey

MINT NRMT
1-37 PRINT RUNS B/WN 1-25 COPIES PER
38-45 PRINT RUNS B/WN 1-25 COPIES PER
NO PRICING ON QTY OF 15 OR LESS
RANDOM INSERTS IN PACKS
1 Babe Ruth/5
2 Lou Gehrig/10
3 Roberto Clemente/10
4 Stan Musial/25 60.00 27.00
6 Don Mattingly/25 80.00 36.00
7 Rickey Henderson/10
8 Cal Ripken/25 120.00 55.00
9 Yogi Berra/25 40.00 18.00
10 Reggie Jackson/10
11 George Brett/25 80.00 36.00
12 Mel Ott/25 60.00 27.00
13 Roger Maris Pants/10
14 Ryne Sandberg/25 80.00 36.00
15 Eddie Mathews/25 40.00 18.00
17 Mike Schmidt/25 80.00 36.00
18 Tony Gwynn/25 40.00 18.00
19 Ty Cobb Pants/5
20 Thurman Munson/25 50.00 22.00
22 Duke Snider/25 30.00 13.50
23 Ernie Banks/5
24 Alex Rodriguez/25 40.00 18.00
25 Nomar Garciaparra/25 40.00 18.00
26 Hideki Matsui Ball/25 80.00 36.00
27 Ichiro Suzuki Ball/25 60.00 27.00
28 Barry Bonds Ball/25 60.00 27.00
29 Mike Piazza/25 40.00 18.00
30 Alfonso Soriano/25 25.00 11.00
31 Al Kaline/10
32 Harmon Killebrew/25 40.00 18.00
33 Dale Murphy/25 40.00 18.00
34 Orlando Cepeda/25 20.00 9.00
35 Willie McCovey/25 20.00 9.00
36 Willie Stargell/25 30.00 13.50
37 Brooks Robinson/25 30.00 13.50
38 Hideki Matsui Ball 120.00 55.00
Ichiro Suzuki Ball/25
39 Ryne Sandberg
Ernie Banks/5
40 Don Mattingly
Lou Gehrig/15
41 Yogi Berra 80.00 36.00
Thurman Munson/25
44 Don Mattingly
Roger Maris Pants/5
45 Babe Ruth
Lou Gehrig/5

2003 Leaf Limited Lumberjacks Jersey Black

MINT NRMT
RANDOM INSERTS IN PACKS
PRINT RUNS B/WN 1-5 COPIES PER
NO PRICING DUE TO SCARCITY

2003 Leaf Limited Lumberjacks Jersey Silver

MINT NRMT
RANDOM INSERTS IN PACKS
PRINT RUNS B/WN 3-10 COPIES PER
NO PRICING DUE TO SCARCITY

2003 Leaf Limited Player Threads

MINT NRMT
RANDOM INSERTS IN PACKS
PRINT RUNS B/WN 5-50 COPIES PER
NO PRICING ON QTY OF 5 OR LESS
1 Roger Clemens/50 25.00 11.00
2 Alex Rodriguez/50 25.00 11.00
3 Pedro Martinez/50 15.00 6.75
4 Randy Johnson/50 15.00 6.75
5 Curt Schilling/50 10.00 4.50
6 Reggie Jackson/5
7 Nolan Ryan/50 60.00 27.00
8 Hideo Nomo/50 40.00 18.00
9 Mike Piazza/50 25.00 11.00
10 Rickey Henderson Padres/5
11 Rickey Henderson Mets/50 15.00 6.75
12 Ivan Rodriguez/50 15.00 6.75
13 Gary Sheffield/50 10.00 4.50
14 Jeff Kent/50 10.00 4.50
15 Roberto Alomar/50 15.00 6.75
16 Rafael Palmeiro/50 15.00 6.75
17 Juan Gonzalez/50 15.00 6.75
18 Shawn Green/50 10.00 4.50
19 Jason Giambi/50 10.00 4.50
20 Jim Thome/50 15.00 6.75
21 Scott Rolen/50 15.00 6.75
22 Mike Mussina/50 15.00 6.75
23 Tom Glavine/50 15.00 6.75
24 Sammy Sosa/50 25.00 11.00

2003 Leaf Limited Player Threads Prime

MINT NRMT
RANDOM INSERTS IN PACKS
PRINT RUNS B/WN 5-10 COPIES PER
NO PRICING DUE TO SCARCITY

2003 Leaf Limited Player Threads Double

MINT NRMT
RANDOM INSERTS IN PACKS
STATED PRINT RUN 50 SERIAL #'d SETS
CARD 6/10 PRINT RUN 5 SERIAL #'d SETS
1 R.Clemens Yanks-Sox 40.00 18.00
2 Alex Rodriguez Rgr-M's 40.00 18.00
3 P.Martinez Sox-Dodgers 25.00 11.00
4 Randy Johnson D'backs-Astros 25.00 11.00
5 C.Schilling D'backs-Phils 15.00 6.75
6 R.Jackson A's-Angels/5
7 Nolan Ryan Rgr-Astros 80.00 36.00
8 H.Nomo Dodgers-Sox 60.00 27.00
9 M.Piazza Mets-Dodgers 40.00 18.00
10 R.Henderson Padres-Sox/5
11 R.Henderson Mets-M's 25.00 11.00
12 I.Rodriguez Marlins-Rgr 25.00 11.00
13 G.Sheffield Braves-Dodgers 15.00 6.75
14 Jeff Kent Astros-Giants 15.00 6.75
15 R.Alomar Mets-Indians 25.00 11.00
16 Rafael Palmeiro Rgr-O's 25.00 11.00
17 J.Gonzalez Rgr-Indians 25.00 11.00
18 S.Green Dodgers-Jays 15.00 6.75
19 Jason Giambi Yanks-A's 15.00 6.75
20 Jim Thome Phils-Indians 25.00 11.00
21 Scott Rolen Cards-Phils 25.00 11.00
22 Mike Mussina Yanks-O's 25.00 11.00
23 Tom Glavine Mets-Braves 25.00 11.00
24 Sammy Sosa Cubs-Sox 40.00 18.00

2003 Leaf Limited Player Threads Double Prime

MINT NRMT
RANDOM INSERTS IN PACKS
PRINT RUNS B/WN 5-10 COPIES PER
NO PRICING DUE TO SCARCITY

2003 Leaf Limited Player Threads Triple

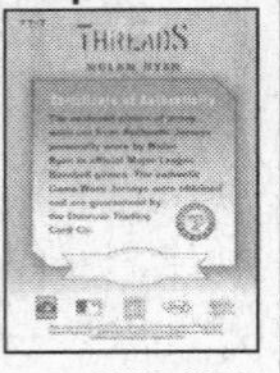

MINT NRMT
RANDOM INSERTS IN PACKS
STATED PRINT RUN 50 SERIAL #'d SETS
HENDERSON PADRES-SOX-A'S 5 #'d CARDS
NO HENDERSON PADRES-SOX-A'S PRICING
4 R.John D'backs-Astros-M's 40.00 18.00
7 N.Ryan Rgr-Astros-Angels 120.00 55.00
8 H.Nomo Dodgers-Sox-Mets 100.00 45.00
10 R.Henderson Padres-Sox-A's/5
11 R.Henderson Mets-M's-Jays 40.00 18.00
13 G.Sheffield Braves-Dgr-Brew 25.00 11.00
14 J.Kent Astros-Giants-Jays 25.00 11.00
15 R.Alomar Mets-Indians-O's 40.00 18.00

2003 Leaf Limited Player Threads Triple Prime

MINT NRMT
RANDOM INSERTS IN PACKS
PRINT RUNS B/WN 5-10 COPIES PER
NO PRICING DUE TO SCARCITY

2003 Leaf Limited Team Threads

MINT NRMT
RANDOM INSERTS IN PACKS
PRINT RUNS B/WN 10-50 COPIES PER
NO PRICING ON QTY OF 10 OR LESS
25 Jackie Robinson
Duke Snider/10
26 Alex Rodriguez 80.00 36.00
Nolan Ryan/50

27 Mike Piazza 40.00 18.00
Hideo Nomo/50
28 Cal Ripken 100.00 45.00
Mike Mussina/50
29 Hideo Nomo 40.00 18.00
Kazuhisa Ishii/50
30 Nolan Ryan 50.00 22.00
Randy Johnson/50

2003 Leaf Limited Team Threads Prime

MINT NRMT
RANDOM INSERTS IN PACKS
PRINT RUNS B/WN 5-10 COPIES PER
NO PRICING DUE TO SCARCITY

2003 Leaf Limited Team Trademarks Autographs

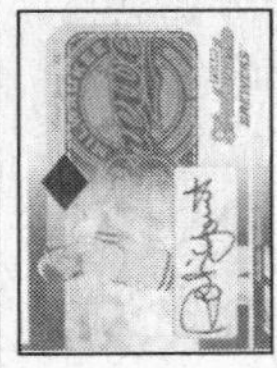
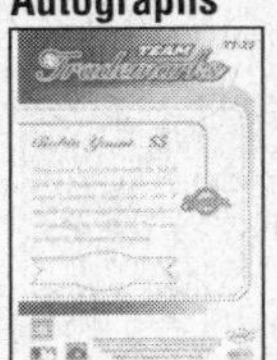

MINT NRMT
RANDOM INSERTS IN PACKS
PRINT RUNS B/WN 5-25 COPIES PER
NO PRICING ON QTY OF 10 OR LESS
1 Alan Trammell/25 50.00 22.00
2 Joe Morgan/5
3 Jim Palmer/25 50.00 22.00
4 Bob Feller/5
5 Gary Carter/25 50.00 22.00
6 Andre Dawson/25 50.00 22.00
7 Duke Snider/5
8 Dale Murphy/25 60.00 27.00
9 Bo Jackson/5
10 Bobby Doerr/25 40.00 18.00
11 Brooks Robinson/25 60.00 27.00
12 Eric Davis/25 50.00 22.00
13 Fred Lynn/25 40.00 18.00
14 Harmon Killebrew/10
15 Jack Morris/25 40.00 18.00
16 Al Kaline/25 80.00 36.00
17 Deion Sanders/25 120.00 55.00
18 Luis Aparicio/25 40.00 18.00
19 Orlando Cepeda/5
20 Phil Rizzuto/25 60.00 27.00
21 Reggie Jackson/5
22 Robin Yount/5
23 Rod Carew Twins/5
24 Will Clark/25 120.00 55.00
25 Willie McCovey/5
26 Tony Gwynn/5
27 Nolan Ryan Astros/5
28 Cal Ripken/5
29 Stan Musial/5
30 Mike Schmidt/5
31 Rod Carew Angels/5
32 Nolan Ryan Rgr/5
33 George Brett/5
34 Nolan Ryan Angels/5
35 Alex Rodriguez/5
36 Roger Clemens/5
37 Greg Maddux/5
38 Albert Pujols/5
39 Alfonso Soriano/5
40 Mark Grace/5

2003 Leaf Limited Team Trademarks Autographs Jersey

MINT NRMT
RANDOM INSERTS IN PACKS
PRINT RUNS B/WN 1-47 COPIES PER
NO PRICING ON QTY OF 24 OR LESS
1 Alan Trammell/3
2 Joe Morgan/8
3 Jim Palmer/22
4 Bob Feller/19
5 Gary Carter/8
6 Andre Dawson/8
7 Duke Snider/4
8 Dale Murphy/3
9 Bo Jackson/16
10 Bobby Doerr/1
11 Brooks Robinson/5
12 Eric Davis/44 50.00 22.00
13 Fred Lynn/19
14 Harmon Killebrew/3
15 Jack Morris/47 40.00 18.00
16 Al Kaline/6
17 Deion Sanders/24
18 Luis Aparicio/11
19 Orlando Cepeda/30 50.00 22.00
20 Phil Rizzuto/10
21 Reggie Jackson/9
22 Robin Yount/19
23 Rod Carew Twins/29 80.00 36.00
24 Will Clark/22
25 Willie McCovey/44 60.00 27.00
26 Tony Gwynn/19
27 Nolan Ryan Astros/34 150.00 70.00
28 Cal Ripken/8
29 Stan Musial/6
30 Mike Schmidt/20
31 Rod Carew Angels/29 80.00 36.00
32 Nolan Ryan Rgr/34 150.00 70.00
33 George Brett/5
34 Nolan Ryan Angels/30 150.00 70.00
35 Alex Rodriguez/3
36 Roger Clemens/22
37 Greg Maddux/31 150.00 70.00
38 Albert Pujols/5
39 Alfonso Soriano/12
40 Mark Grace/17

2003 Leaf Limited Team Trademarks Threads Number

MINT NRMT
RANDOM INSERTS IN PACKS
PRINT RUNS B/WN 1-47 COPIES PER
NO PRICING ON QTY OF 19 OR LESS
1 Alan Trammell/3
2 Joe Morgan/8
3 Jim Palmer/22 30.00 13.50
4 Bob Feller/19
5 Gary Carter/8
6 Andre Dawson/8
7 Duke Snider/4
8 Dale Murphy/3
9 Bo Jackson/16
10 Bobby Doerr/1
11 Brooks Robinson/5
12 Eric Davis/44 15.00 6.75
13 Fred Lynn/19
14 Harmon Killebrew/3
15 Jack Morris/47 15.00 6.75
16 Al Kaline/6
17 Deion Sanders/24 50.00 22.00
18 Luis Aparicio/11
19 Orlando Cepeda/30 25.00 11.00
20 Phil Rizzuto/10
21 Reggie Jackson/9
22 Robin Yount/19
23 Rod Carew Twins/29 40.00 18.00
24 Will Clark/22 100.00 45.00
25 Willie McCovey/44 15.00 6.75
26 Tony Gwynn/19
27 Nolan Ryan Astros/34 80.00 36.00
28 Cal Ripken/8
29 Stan Musial/6
30 Mike Schmidt/20 80.00 36.00
31 Rod Carew Angels/29 40.00 18.00
32 Nolan Ryan Rgr/34 80.00 36.00
33 George Brett/5
34 Nolan Ryan Angels/30 80.00 36.00
35 Alex Rodriguez/3
36 Roger Clemens/22 60.00 27.00
37 Greg Maddux/31 40.00 18.00
38 Albert Pujols/5
39 Alfonso Soriano/12
40 Mark Grace/17

2003 Leaf Limited Team Trademarks Threads Prime

MINT NRMT
RANDOM INSERTS IN PACKS
PRINT RUNS B/WN 5-25 COPIES PER
NO PRICING ON QTY OF 10 OR LESS
1 Alan Trammell/25 40.00 18.00
2 Joe Morgan/25 40.00 18.00
3 Jim Palmer/25 40.00 18.00
4 Bob Feller/10
5 Gary Carter/25 40.00 18.00
6 Andre Dawson/25 40.00 18.00
7 Duke Snider/25 60.00 27.00
8 Dale Murphy/25 60.00 27.00
9 Bo Jackson/25 60.00 27.00
10 Bobby Doerr/20 50.00 22.00
11 Brooks Robinson/25 60.00 27.00
12 Eric Davis/25 40.00 18.00
13 Fred Lynn/25 25.00 11.00
14 Harmon Killebrew/25 80.00 36.00
15 Jack Morris/25 25.00 11.00
16 Al Kaline/5
17 Deion Sanders/25 60.00 27.00
18 Luis Aparicio/25 40.00 18.00
19 Orlando Cepeda/25 40.00 18.00
20 Phil Rizzuto/10
21 Reggie Jackson/5
22 Robin Yount/25 80.00 36.00
23 Rod Carew Twins/25 60.00 27.00
24 Will Clark/25 120.00 55.00
25 Willie McCovey/25 40.00 18.00
26 Tony Gwynn/25 60.00 27.00
27 Nolan Ryan Astros/25 120.00 55.00
28 Cal Ripken/25 150.00 70.00
29 Stan Musial/25 150.00 70.00
30 Mike Schmidt/25 120.00 55.00
31 Rod Carew Angels/25 60.00 27.00
32 Nolan Ryan Rgr/25 120.00 55.00
33 George Brett/25 120.00 55.00
34 Nolan Ryan Angels/25 120.00 55.00
35 Alex Rodriguez/25 60.00 27.00
36 Roger Clemens/20 80.00 36.00
37 Greg Maddux/25 60.00 27.00
38 Albert Pujols/25 100.00 45.00
39 Alfonso Soriano/25 40.00 18.00
40 Mark Grace/25 60.00 27.00

2004 Leaf Limited

This 275-card set was relased in October, 2004. The set was issued in four-card packs with an $70 SRP which came four packs to a box and 10 boxes to a case. The first 200 cards in this set and cards numbered 230 through 250 comprise the basic set. Cards numbered 201 through 229 feature retired greats that were issued to a stated print run of 499 serial numbered sets and

cards numbered 251 through 275 are autographed rookie cards which were issued to a stated print run of 99 serial numbered sets.

Nm-Mt Ex-Mt
COMMON CARD (1-200/230-250) 3.00 .90
COMMON CARD (201-229) 4.00 1.20
201-229 PRINT RUN 499 SERIAL #'d SETS
COMMON AUTO (251-275)........ 15.00 4.50
251-275: OVERALL AU-GU ONE PER PACK
251-275 AUTO PRINT RUN 99 #'d SETS
1 Adam Dunn A.......................... 3.00 .90
2 Adrian Beltre.......................... 3.00 .90
3 Albert Pujols H........................ 8.00 2.40
4 Alex Rodriguez Yanks 6.00 1.80
5 Alfonso Soriano Rgr .... 3.00 .90
6 Andruw Jones.......................... 3.00 .90
7 Andy Pettitte Astros................ 3.00 .90
8 Angel Berroa .... 3.00 .90
9 Aramis Ramirez .... 3.00 .90
10 Aubrey Huff.......................... 3.00 .90
11 Austin Kearns........................ 3.00 .90
12 Barry Larkin .... 3.00 .90
13 Barry Zito H .... 3.00 .90
14 Bartolo Colon .... 3.00 .90
15 Ben Sheets............................ 3.00 .90
16 Bernie Williams...................... 3.00 .90
17 Bobby Abreu .... 3.00 .90
18 Brandon Webb........................ 3.00 .90
19 Brian Giles .... 3.00 .90
20 C.C. Sabathia .... 3.00 .90
21 Carlos Beltran Royals A .... 3.00 .90
22 Carlos Delgado...................... 3.00 .90
23 Chipper Jones H 4.00 1.20
24 Craig Biggio .... 3.00 .90
25 Curt Schilling Sox................... 4.00 1.20
26 Darin Erstad .... 3.00 .90
27 Delmon Young .... 3.00 .90
28 Derek Jeter............................ 8.00 2.40
29 Derrek Lee .... 3.00 .90
30 Dontrelle Willis...................... 3.00 .90
31 Edgar Renteria .... 3.00 .90
32 Eric Chavez .... 3.00 .90
33 Esteban Loaiza .... 3.00 .90
34 Frank Thomas 4.00 1.20
35 Fred McGriff........................... 3.00 .90
36 Garret Anderson H.................. 3.00 .90
37 Gary Sheffield Yanks .... 3.00 .90
38 Geoff Jenkins .... 3.00 .90
39 Greg Maddux Cubs................. 6.00 1.80
40 Hank Blalock H....................... 3.00 .90
41 Hideki Matsui 6.00 1.80
42 Hideo Nomo Dodgers 4.00 1.20
43 Ichiro Suzuki.......................... 6.00 1.80
44 Ivan Rodriguez Tigers............. 4.00 1.20
45 J.D. Drew .... 3.00 .90
46 Jacque Jones .... 3.00 .90
47 Jae Weong Seo...................... 3.00 .90
48 Jake Peavy .... 3.00 .90
49 Jamie Moyer .... 3.00 .90
50 Jason Giambi Yanks............... 3.00 .90
51 Jason Kendall......................... 3.00 .90
52 Jason Schmidt........................ 3.00 .90
53 Jason Varitek .... 3.00 .90
54 Javier Vazquez .... 3.00 .90
55 Javy Lopez .... 3.00 .90
56 Jay Gibbons .... 3.00 .90
57 Jay Payton .... 3.00 .90
58 Jeff Bagwell H........................ 3.00 .90
59 Jeff Kent................................ 3.00 .90
60 Jeremy Bonderman................ 3.00 .90
61 Jermaine Dye......................... 3.00 .90
62 Jeromy Burnitz....................... 3.00 .90
63 Jim Edmonds.......................... 3.00 .90
64 Jim Thome Phils..................... 4.00 1.20
65 Jimmy Rollins......................... 3.00 .90
66 Jody Gerut .... 3.00 .90
67 Johan Santana .... 3.00 .90
68 John Olerud .... 3.00 .90
69 John Smoltz........................... 3.00 .90
70 Johnny Damon........................ 4.00 1.20
71 Jorge Posada .... 3.00 .90
72 Jose Contreras....................... 3.00 .90
73 Jose Reyes............................. 3.00 .90
74 Jose Vidro.............................. 3.00 .90
75 Josh Beckett H....................... 3.00 .90
76 Juan Gonzalez Royals .... 3.00 .90
77 Juan Pierre............................. 3.00 .90
78 Junior Spivey .... 3.00 .90
79 Kazuhisa Ishii......................... 3.00 .90
80 Keith Foulke Sox .... 3.00 .90
81 Ken Griffey Jr. Reds............... 6.00 1.80
82 Ken Harvey .... 3.00 .90
83 Kenny Rogers .... 3.00 .90
84 Kerry Wood............................ 4.00 1.20
85 Kevin Brown Yanks................. 3.00 .90
86 Kevin Millwood .... 3.00 .90
87 Kip Wells................................ 3.00 .90
88 Lance Berkman .... 3.00 .90
89 Larry Bigbie .... 3.00 .90
90 Larry Walker .... 3.00 .90
91 Laynce Nix .... 3.00 .90
92 Luis Castillo .... 3.00 .90
93 Luis Gonzalez......................... 3.00 .90
94 Luis Matos .... 3.00 .90
95 Lyle Overbay.......................... 3.00 .90
96 Magglio Ordonez H................. 3.00 .90
97 Manny Ramirez Sox................ 3.00 .90
98 Marcus Giles.......................... 3.00 .90
99 Mark Buehrle.......................... 3.00 .90
100 Mark Mulder .... 3.00 .90
101 Mark Prior H 4.00 1.20
102 Mark Teixeira........................ 3.00 .90
103 Marlon Byrd .... 3.00 .90
104 Matt Morris........................... 3.00 .90
105 Melvin Mora.......................... 3.00 .90
106 Michael Young .... 3.00 .90
107 Miguel Cabrera Batting .... 3.00 .90
108 Miguel Tejada O's................. 3.00 .90
109 Mike Lowell........................... 3.00 .90
110 Mike Mussina Yanks .... 3.00 .90
111 Mike Piazza Mets 6.00 1.80
112 Mike Sweeney....................... 3.00 .90
113 Milton Bradley....................... 3.00 .90
114 Moises Alou .... 3.00 .90
115 Morgan Ensberg .... 3.00 .90
116 Nick Johnson........................ 3.00 .90
117 Nomar Garciaparra............... 6.00 1.80
118 Omar Vizquel .... 3.00 .90
119 Orlando Cabrera................... 3.00 .90
120 Pat Burrell............................ 3.00 .90
121 Paul Konerko .... 3.00 .90
122 Paul Lo Duca .... 3.00 .90
123 Pedro Martinez Sox 4.00 1.20
124 Preston Wilson H.................. 3.00 .90
125 Rafael Furcal .... 3.00 .90
126 Rafael Palmeiro O's .... 3.00 .90
127 Randy Johnson D'backs 4.00 1.20
128 Rich Harden......................... 3.00 .90
129 Richard Hidalgo .... 3.00 .90
130 Richie Sexson .... 3.00 .90
131 Rickie Weeks........................ 3.00 .90
132 Roberto Alomar .... 3.00 .90
133 Robin Ventura....................... 3.00 .90
134 Rocco Baldelli .... 3.00 .90
135 Roger Clemens Astros 8.00 2.40
136 Roy Halladay .... 3.00 .90
137 Roy Oswalt A .... 3.00 .90
138 Russ Ortiz .... 3.00 .90
139 Ryan Klesko .... 3.00 .90
140 Sammy Sosa H 6.00 1.80
141 Scott Podsednik.................... 3.00 .90
142 Scott Rolen Cards A............. 4.00 1.20
143 Sean Burroughs .... 3.00 .90
144 Sean Casey .... 3.00 .90
145 Shannon Stewart .... 3.00 .90
146 Shawn Green Dodgers .... 3.00 .90
147 Shigetoshi Hasegawa........... 3.00 .90
148 Sidney Ponson...................... 3.00 .90
149 Steve Finley.......................... 3.00 .90
150 Tim Hudson .... 3.00 .90
151 Tim Salmon .... 3.00 .90
152 Tino Martinez .... 3.00 .90
153 Todd Helton H .... 3.00 .90
154 Tom Glavine Mets .... 3.00 .90
155 Torii Hunter .... 3.00 .90
156 Trot Nixon .... 3.00 .90
157 Troy Glaus............................ 3.00 .90
158 Vernon Wells H .... 3.00 .90
159 Victor Martinez A .... 3.00 .90
160 Vinny Castilla .... 3.00 .90
161 Vladimir Guerrero Angels...... 4.00 1.20
162 Alex Rodriguez Rgr 6.00 1.80
163 Alfonso Soriano Yanks......... 3.00 .90
164 Andy Pettitte Yanks .... 3.00 .90
165 Curt Schilling D'backs........... 3.00 .90
166 Gary Sheffield Braves .... 3.00 .90
167 Greg Maddux Braves 6.00 1.80
168 Hideo Nomo Sox.................. 4.00 1.20
169 Ivan Rodriguez Marlins......... 4.00 1.20
170 Jason Giambi A's................. 3.00 .90
171 Jim Thome Indians 4.00 1.20
172 Juan Gonzalez Rgr .... 3.00 .90
173 Ken Griffey Jr. M's 6.00 1.80
174 Kevin Brown Dodgers .... 3.00 .90
175 Manny Ramirez Indians .... 3.00 .90
176 Miguel Tejada A's................. 3.00 .90
177 Mike Mussina O's .... 3.00 .90
178 Mike Piazza Dodgers............ 6.00 1.80
179 Pedro Martinez Expos.......... 4.00 1.20
180 Rafael Palmeiro Rgr............. 3.00 .90
181 Randy Johnson Astros......... 4.00 1.20
182 Roger Clemens Sox 8.00 2.40
183 Scott Rolen Phils 4.00 1.20
184 Shawn Green Jays .... 3.00 .90
185 Tom Glavine Braves .... 3.00 .90
186 Vladimir Guerrero Expos...... 4.00 1.20
187 Alex Rodriguez M's.............. 6.00 1.80
188 Mike Piazza Marlins 6.00 1.80
189 Randy Johnson M's............. 4.00 1.20
190 Roger Clemens Yanks......... 8.00 2.40
191 Albert Pujols A 8.00 2.40
192 Barry Zito A......................... 3.00 .90
193 Chipper Jones A.................. 4.00 1.20
194 Garret Anderson A .... 3.00 .90
195 Jeff Bagwell A .... 3.00 .90
196 Josh Beckett A..................... 3.00 .90
197 Magglio Ordonez A .... 3.00 .90
198 Mark Prior A 4.00 1.20
199 Sammy Sosa A 6.00 1.80
200 Todd Helton A .... 3.00 .90
201 Andre Dawson RET 4.00 1.20
202 Babe Ruth RET.................. 10.00 3.00
203 Bob Feller RET..................... 5.00 1.50
204 Bob Gibson RET................... 5.00 1.50
205 Bobby Doerr RET 4.00 1.20
206 Cal Ripken RET 20.00 6.00
207 Dale Murphy RET................. 5.00 1.50
208 Don Mattingly RET............ 10.00 3.00
209 Gary Carter RET 4.00 1.20
210 George Brett RET 10.00 3.00
211 Jackie Robinson RET 5.00 1.50
212 Lou Brock RET 5.00 1.50
213 Lou Gehrig RET 8.00 2.40
214 Mark Grace RET................... 5.00 1.50
215 Maury Wills RET 4.00 1.20
216 Mike Schmidt RET 10.00 3.00
217 Nolan Ryan RET 10.00 3.00
218 Orel Hershiser RET 4.00 1.20
219 Paul Molitor RET.................. 5.00 1.50
220 Roberto Clemente RET....... 12.00 3.60
221 Rod Carew RET.................... 5.00 1.50
222 Roy Campanella RET 5.00 1.50
223 Ryne Sandberg RET 10.00 3.00
224 Stan Musial RET 8.00 2.40
225 Ted Williams RET 10.00 3.00
226 Tony Gwynn RET.................. 8.00 2.40
227 Ty Cobb RET 6.00 1.80
228 Whitey Ford RET................... 5.00 1.50
229 Yogi Berra RET..................... 5.00 1.50
230 Carlos Beltran Astros H .... 3.00 .90
231 David Ortiz H........................ 4.00 1.20
232 David Ortiz A 4.00 1.20
233 Carlos Zambrano .... 3.00 .90
234 Carlos Lee............................ 3.00 .90
235 Travis Hafner........................ 3.00 .90
236 Brad Penny .... 3.00 .90
237 Wade Miller.......................... 3.00 .90
238 Edgar Martinez..................... 3.00 .90
239 Carl Crawford....................... 3.00 .90
240 Roy Oswalt H .... 3.00 .90
241 Kazuo Matsui RC 10.00 3.00
242 Carlos Beltran Astros A........ 3.00 .90
243 Carlos Beltran Royals H....... 3.00 .90
244 Miguel Cabrera Fielding .... 3.00 .90
245 Scott Rolen Cards H 4.00 1.20
246 Hank Blalock A..................... 3.00 .90
247 Vernon Wells A .... 3.00 .90
248 Adam Dunn H .... 3.00 .90
249 Preston Wilson A .... 3.00 .90
250 Victor Martinez H .... 3.00 .90
251 Aarom Baldiris PH AU RC.. 15.00 4.50
252 Akinori Otsuka PH AU RC .. 40.00 12.00
253 Andres Blanco PH AU RC .. 15.00 4.50
254 Brad Halsey PH AU RC 15.00 4.50
255 Joey Gathright PH AU RC .. 30.00 9.00
256 Colby Miller PH AU RC 15.00 4.50
257 Fernando Nieve PH AU RC. 15.00 4.50
258 Freddy Guzman PH AU RC. 15.00 4.50
259 Hector Gimenez PH AU RC 15.00 4.50
260 Jake Woods PH AU RC...... 15.00 4.50
261 Jason Bartlett PH AU RC ... 15.00 4.50
262 John Gall PH AU RC 15.00 4.50
263 Jose Capellan PH AU RC ... 40.00 12.00
264 Josh Labandeira PH AU RC 15.00 4.50
265 Justin Germano PH AU RC 15.00 4.50
266 Kazuhito Tadano PH AU RC 40.00 12.00
267 Lance Cormier PH AU RC... 15.00 4.50
268 Merkin Valdez PH AU RC... 25.00 7.50
269 Mike Gosling PH AU RC..... 15.00 4.50
270 Ramon Ramirez PH AU RC 15.00 4.50
271 Rusty Tucker PH AU RC..... 15.00 4.50
272 Shawn Hill PH AU RC......... 15.00 4.50
273 Shingo Takatsu PH AU RC . 50.00 15.00
274 William Bergolla PH AU RC 15.00 4.50
275 Yadier Molina PH AU RC.... 30.00 9.00

2004 Leaf Limited Bronze Spotlight

Nm-Mt Ex-Mt
*BRONZE 1-200/230-250: .75X TO 2X
*BRONZE 201-229: .75X TO 2X..........
*BRONZE RC'S 1-200/230-250: .6X TO 1.5X
RANDOM INSERTS IN PACKS
STATED PRINT RUN 100 SERIAL #'d SETS

2004 Leaf Limited Gold Spotlight

Nm-Mt Ex-Mt
*GOLD 1-200/230-250: 2X TO 5X......
*GOLD 201-229: 2X TO 5X..........
RANDOM INSERTS IN PACKS
STATED PRINT RUN 25 SERIAL #'d SETS
NO RC YR PRICING DUE TO SCARCITY

2004 Leaf Limited Platinum Spotlight

Nm-Mt Ex-Mt
RANDOM INSERTS IN PACKS ....
STATED PRINT RUN 1 SERIAL #'d SET
NO PRICING DUE TO SCARCITY

2004 Leaf Limited Silver Spotlight

Nm-Mt Ex-Mt
*SILVER 1-200/230-250: 1.25X TO 3X
*SILVER 201-229: 1.25X TO 3X ....
*SILVER RC'S 1-200/230-250: 1X TO 2.5X
RANDOM INSERTS IN PACKS ....
STATED PRINT RUN 50 SERIAL #'d SETS

2004 Leaf Limited Barrels

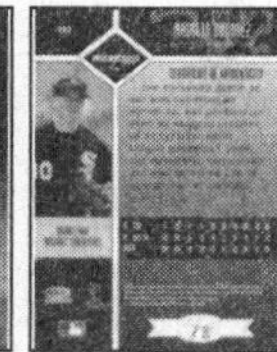

Nm-Mt Ex-Mt
OVERALL AU-GU ODDS ONE PER PACK
PRINT RUNS B/WN 1-5 COPIES PER .
NO PRICING DUE TO SCARCITY ....

2004 Leaf Limited Moniker Bronze

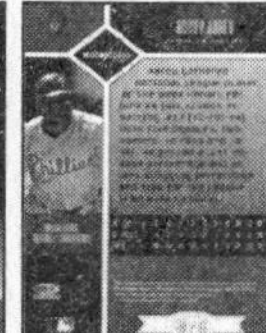

Nm-Mt Ex-Mt
OVERALL AU-GU ODDS ONE PER PACK
PRINT RUNS B/WN 1-100 COPIES PER
NO PRICING ON QTY OF 10 OR LESS
1 Adam Dunn A/50 .... 30.00 9.00
3 Albert Pujols H/25............... 200.00 60.00
5 Alfonso Soriano Rgr/100 .... 30.00 9.00
6 Andruw Jones/50................... 30.00 9.00
7 Andy Pettitte Astros/10..................
8 Angel Berroa/25 .... 15.00 4.50
9 Aramis Ramirez/10 ....
10 Aubrey Huff/10.........................
11 Austin Kearns/50 .... 20.00 6.00
12 Barry Larkin/1 ....
13 Barry Zito H/10 ....
15 Ben Sheets/10..........................
16 Bernie Williams/10.......................
17 Bobby Abreu/9 ....
18 Brandon Webb/21 .... 15.00 4.50
20 C.C. Sabathia/10 ....
21 Carlos Beltran Royals A/50 .. 40.00 12.00
23 Chipper Jones H/25 .... 60.00 18.00
24 Craig Biggio/25 .... 40.00 12.00
27 Delmon Young/10 ....
29 Derrek Lee/10 ....
30 Dontrelle Willis/25 .... 25.00 7.50
31 Edgar Renteria/25 .... 40.00 7.50
32 Eric Chavez/10 ....
33 Esteban Loaiza/10.......................
34 Frank Thomas/50................. 50.00 15.00
35 Fred McGriff/10..........................
36 Garret Anderson H/50.......... 20.00 6.00
37 Gary Sheffield Yanks/50........ 30.00 9.00
39 Greg Maddux Cubs/25 .... 100.00 30.00
40 Hank Blalock H/50 .... 20.00 6.00
42 Hideo Nomo Dodgers/1 ....
46 Jacque Jones/25 .... 25.00 7.50
48 Jake Peavy/10 ....
53 Jason Varitek/3 ....
54 Javier Vazquez/10.......................
56 Jay Gibbons/10...........................
57 Jay Payton/10 ....
58 Jeff Bagwell H/25................ 80.00 24.00
60 Jeremy Bonderman/10................
61 Jermaine Dye/10.........................
66 Jody Gerut/10 ....
67 Johan Santana/10 ....
71 Jorge Posada/25 .... 50.00 15.00
72 Jose Contreras/10.......................
73 Jose Reyes/10............................
74 Jose Vidro/10.............................
76 Juan Gonzalez Royals/25 ..... 40.00 12.00
79 Kazuhisa Ishii/25................. 40.00 12.00
80 Keith Foulke Sox/10....................
82 Ken Harvey/10 ....
84 Kerry Wood/25.................... 50.00 15.00
88 Lance Berkman/50.............. 30.00 9.00
89 Larry Bigbie/10 ....
91 Laynce Nix/10.............................
94 Luis Matos/10.............................
95 Lyle Overbay/10..........................
97 Manny Ramirez Sox/10................
98 Marcus Giles/25.................. 25.00 7.50
99 Mark Buehrle/10..........................
100 Mark Mulder/100 .... 15.00 4.50
101 Mark Prior H/50 .... 50.00 15.00
102 Mark Teixeira/50 .... 30.00 9.00
105 Melvin Mora/10.........................
106 Michael Young/50............. 20.00 6.00
107 Miguel Cabrera Batting/50 . 30.00 9.00
109 Mike Lowell/25.................. 25.00 7.50
110 Mike Mussina Yanks/10 ....
111 Mike Piazza Mets/1 ....
113 Milton Bradley/10......................
115 Morgan Ensberg/10...................
122 Paul Lo Duca/25 .... 25.00 7.50
123 Pedro Martinez Sox/5 ....
125 Rafael Furcal/10........................
127 Randy Johnson D'backs/10 ....
128 Rich Harden/10.........................
131 Rickie Weeks/25 .... 25.00 7.50
132 Roberto Alomar/10....................
133 Robin Ventura/10......................
135 Roger Clemens Astros/5............
136 Roy Halladay/10........................
137 Roy Oswalt A/50 .... 20.00 6.00
140 Sammy Sosa H/25.......... 100.00 30.00
141 Scott Podsednik/10...................
142 Scott Rolen Cards A/25 .... 50.00 15.00
143 Sean Burroughs/10...................
144 Sean Casey/25 .... 25.00 7.50
145 Shannon Stewart/25 .... 25.00 7.50
146 Shawn Green Dodgers/10..........
149 Steve Finley/5...........................
153 Todd Helton H/25.............. 40.00 12.00
154 Tom Glavine Mets/10 ....
155 Torii Hunter/50 .... 20.00 6.00
156 Trot Nixon/25................... 25.00 7.50
158 Vernon Wells H/25 .... 25.00 7.50
159 Victor Martinez A/10 ....
163 Alfonso Soriano Yanks/100 30.00 9.00
164 Andy Pettitte Yanks/10 ....
166 Gary Sheffield Braves/50 ... 30.00 9.00
167 Greg Maddux Braves/25 .. 100.00 30.00
168 Hideo Nomo Sox/1...................
172 Juan Gonzalez Rgr/25........ 40.00 12.00
175 Manny Ramirez Indians/10........
177 Mike Mussina O's/10 ....
178 Mike Piazza Dodgers/1..............
179 Pedro Martinez Expos/5............
181 Randy Johnson Astros/10.........
182 Roger Clemens Sox/5...............
183 Scott Rolen Phils/25 .... 50.00 15.00
184 Shawn Green Jays/10 ....
185 Tom Glavine Braves/10.............
188 Mike Piazza Marlins/1 ....
189 Randy Johnson M's/10.............
190 Roger Clemens Yanks/5...........
191 Albert Pujols A/25........... 200.00 60.00
192 Barry Zito A/10........................
193 Chipper Jones A/25 .... 60.00 18.00
194 Garret Anderson A/50 .... 20.00 6.00
195 Jeff Bagwell A/25.............. 80.00 24.00
198 Mark Prior A/50 .... 50.00 15.00
199 Sammy Sosa A/25 .... 100.00 30.00
200 Todd Helton A/25 .... 40.00 12.00
201 Andre Dawson RET/100..... 15.00 4.50
203 Bob Feller RET/100........... 25.00 7.50
204 Bob Gibson RET/100 .... 25.00 7.50
205 Bobby Doerr RET/100........ 15.00 4.50
206 Cal Ripken RET/25 .... 200.00 60.00
207 Dale Murphy RET/100........ 25.00 7.50
208 Don Mattingly RET/100...... 60.00 18.00
209 Gary Carter RET/100......... 15.00 4.50
210 George Brett RET/25 .... 80.00 24.00
212 Lou Brock RET/100............ 25.00 7.50
214 Mark Grace RET/100 .... 25.00 7.50
215 Maury Wills RET/100 .... 15.00 4.50
216 Mike Schmidt RET/100 ...... 60.00 18.00
217 Nolan Ryan RET/100........ 100.00 30.00
218 Orel Hershiser RET/25 .... 40.00 12.00
219 Paul Molitor RET/100......... 25.00 7.50
221 Rod Carew RET/100........... 25.00 7.50
223 Ryne Sandberg RET/100..... 50.00 15.00
224 Stan Musial RET/100 .... 60.00 18.00
226 Tony Gwynn RET/100 .... 40.00 12.00
228 Whitey Ford RET/10 ....
229 Yogi Berra RET/10......................
230 Carlos Beltran Astros H/50 40.00 12.00
231 David Ortiz H/50 .... 50.00 15.00
232 David Ortiz A/50 .... 50.00 15.00
233 Carlos Zambrano/25 .... 40.00 12.00
234 Carlos Lee/25.................... 25.00 7.50
235 Travis Hafner/10........................
236 Brad Penny/10 ....
237 Wade Miller/10...........................
238 Edgar Martinez/25............. 50.00 15.00
239 Carl Crawford/10........................
240 Roy Oswalt H/50 .... 20.00 6.00
242 Carlos Beltran Astros A/50. 40.00 12.00
243 Carlos Beltran Royals H/50 40.00 12.00
244 Miguel Cabrera Fielding/50 30.00 9.00
245 Scott Rolen Cards H/25 ..... 50.00 15.00
246 Hank Blalock A/50............. 20.00 6.00
247 Vernon Wells A/25 .... 25.00 7.50
248 Adam Dunn H/50 .... 30.00 9.00
250 Victor Martinez H/10...................

2004 Leaf Limited Moniker Gold

Nm-Mt Ex-Mt
*1-220/230-250 p/r 25: .6X TO 1.5X p/r 100
*1-220/230-250 p/r 25: .5X TO 1.2X p/r 50
*201-229 p/r 25: .6X TO 1.5X p/r 100
OVERALL AU-GU ODDS ONE PER PACK
PRINT RUNS B/WN 1-25 COPIES PER
NO PRICING ON QTY OF 10 OR LESS

2004 Leaf Limited Moniker Silver

Nm-Mt Ex-Mt
*1-200/230-250 p/r 50: .5X TO 1.2X p/r 100
*1-200/230-250 p/r 25: .5X TO 1.2X p/r 50
*201-229 p/r 50: .5X TO 1.2X p/r 100
OVERALL AU-GU ODDS ONE PER PACK
PRINT RUNS B/WN 1-50 COPIES PER
NO PRICING ON QTY OF 10 OR LESS

2004 Leaf Limited Moniker Bat

Nm-Mt Ex-Mt
*1-200/230-250 p/r 40-50: .5X TO 1.2X Jsy/75
*1-200/230-250p/r40-50: .4X TO 1X Jsy/38-50
*1-200/230-250 p/r 40-50: .3X TO .8X Jsy/25
*1-200/230-250 p/r 25: .5X TO 1.2X Jsy/50
*1-200/230-250 p/r 25: .4X TO 1X Jsy/25
*1-200/230-250 p/r 15: .6X TO 1.5X Jsy/50
*1-200/230-250 p/r 15: .5X TO 1.2X Jsy/25
*201-229 p/r 100: .4X TO 1X Jsy/100
*201-229 p/r 50: .5X TO 1.2X Jsy/100
*201-229 p/r 50: .4X TO 1X Jsy/50....
*201-229 p/r 50: .3X TO .8X Jsy/25....
*201-229 p/r 25: .5X TO 1.2X Jsy/50....
*201-229 p/r 25: .4X TO 1X Jsy/25....
OVERALL AU-GU ODDS ONE PER PACK
PRINT RUNS B/WN 1-100 COPIES PER
NO PRICING ON QTY OF 10 OR LESS
27 Delmon Young/50 .... 40.00 12.00
31 Edgar Renteria/25 .... 50.00 9.00
37 Gary Sheffield Yanks/25....... 50.00 15.00
61 Jermaine Dye/25................. 30.00 9.00
106 Michael Young/50.............. 25.00 7.50
131 Rickie Weeks/25 .... 30.00 9.00
212 Lou Brock RET/50.............. 40.00 12.00
214 Mark Grace RET/25............ 50.00 15.00
250 Victor Martinez H/25........... 30.00 9.00

2004 Leaf Limited Moniker Jersey

Nm-Mt Ex-Mt
OVERALL AU-GU ODDS ONE PER PACK
PRINT RUNS B/WN 1-100 COPIES PER
NO PRICING ON QTY OF 10 OR LESS
1 Adam Dunn A/50 40.00 12.00
3 Albert Pujols H/10
5 Alfonso Soriano Rgr/50 50.00 15.00
6 Andruw Jones/25 50.00 15.00
7 Andy Pettitte Astros/10
8 Angel Berroa Pants/25 20.00 6.00
9 Aramis Ramirez/25 30.00 9.00
10 Aubrey Huff/25 30.00 9.00
11 Austin Kearns/25 30.00 9.00
12 Barry Larkin/1
13 Barry Zito H/10
15 Ben Sheets/25 30.00 9.00
16 Bernie Williams/10
17 Bobby Abreu/5
18 Brandon Webb/25 20.00 6.00
20 C.C. Sabathia/25 30.00 9.00
21 Carlos Beltran Royals A/50 50.00 15.00
23 Chipper Jones H/25 80.00 24.00
24 Craig Biggio/25 50.00 15.00
30 Dontrelle Willis/25 30.00 9.00
31 Edgar Renteria/10
32 Eric Chavez/50 25.00 7.50
34 Frank Thomas/25 80.00 24.00
35 Fred McGriff/25 50.00 15.00
36 Garret Anderson H/50 25.00 7.50
39 Greg Maddux Cubs/10
40 Hank Blalock H/50 25.00 7.50
42 Hideo Nomo Dodgers/1
46 Jacque Jones/25 30.00 9.00
53 Jason Varitek/1
56 Jay Gibbons/5
58 Jeff Bagwell H/10
60 Jeremy Bonderman/5
63 Jim Edmonds/25 50.00 15.00
66 Jody Gerut/25 20.00 6.00
67 Johan Santana/25 50.00 15.00
71 Jorge Posada/25 60.00 18.00
73 Jose Reyes/5
74 Jose Vidro/25 20.00 6.00
76 Juan Gonzalez Royals/10
78 Junior Spivey/1
79 Kazuhisa Ishii/10
84 Kerry Wood/25 60.00 18.00
88 Lance Berkman/25 50.00 15.00
89 Larry Bigbie/25 30.00 9.00
94 Luis Matos/10
97 Manny Ramirez Sox/10
98 Marcus Giles/25 30.00 9.00
99 Mark Buehrle/25 30.00 9.00
100 Mark Mulder/75 20.00 6.00
101 Mark Prior H/50 60.00 18.00
102 Mark Teixeira/25 50.00 15.00
103 Marlon Byrd/1
105 Melvin Mora/25 30.00 9.00
107 Miguel Cabrera Batting/38 40.00 12.00
109 Mike Lowell/25 30.00 9.00
110 Mike Mussina Yanks/5
111 Mike Piazza Mets/5
115 Morgan Ensberg/25 20.00 6.00
122 Paul Lo Duca/25 30.00 9.00
123 Pedro Martinez Sox/10
124 Preston Wilson H/25 30.00 9.00
125 Rafael Furcal/10
127 Randy Johnson D'backs/10
128 Rich Harden/1
135 Roger Clemens Astros/10
137 Roy Oswalt A/25 30.00 9.00
140 Sammy Sosa H/10
142 Scott Rolen Cards A/50 50.00 15.00
143 Sean Burroughs/25 30.00 9.00
144 Sean Casey/25 30.00 9.00
145 Shannon Stewart/25 30.00 9.00
146 Shawn Green Dodgers/10
149 Steve Finley/25 30.00 9.00
153 Todd Helton H/25 50.00 15.00
154 Tom Glavine Mets/25 50.00 15.00
155 Torii Hunter/25 30.00 9.00
156 Trot Nixon/25 30.00 9.00
158 Vernon Wells H/50 25.00 7.50
159 Victor Martinez A/50 25.00 7.50
162 Alex Rodriguez Rgr/1
163 Alfonso Soriano Yanks/50 50.00 15.00
164 Andy Pettitte Yanks/10
166 Gary Sheffield Braves/25 50.00 15.00
167 Greg Maddux Braves/10
168 Hideo Nomo Sox/1
172 Juan Gonzalez Rgr/25 50.00 15.00
177 Mike Mussina O's/5
178 Mike Piazza Dodgers/5
179 Pedro Martinez Expos/10
181 Randy Johnson Astros/10
182 Roger Clemens Sox/10
183 Scott Rolen Phils/50 50.00 15.00
184 Shawn Green Jays/10
185 Tom Glavine Braves/25 50.00 15.00
187 Alex Rodriguez M's/1
188 Mike Piazza Marlins/5
189 Randy Johnson M's/10
190 Roger Clemens Yanks/10
191 Albert Pujols A/10
192 Barry Zito A/10
193 Chipper Jones A/25 80.00 24.00
194 Garret Anderson A/50 25.00 7.50
195 Jeff Bagwell A/10
198 Mark Prior A/50 60.00 18.00
199 Sammy Sosa A/10
200 Todd Helton A/25 50.00 15.00
201 Andre Dawson RET/50 25.00 7.50
203 Bob Feller RET/5
204 Bob Gibson RET/50 40.00 12.00
205 Bobby Doerr RET/50 25.00 7.50
206 Cal Ripken RET/10
207 Dale Murphy RET/100 30.00 9.00
208 Don Mattingly RET/50 80.00 24.00
209 Gary Carter RET/100 20.00 6.00
210 George Brett RET/10
212 Lou Brock RET/5
214 Mark Grace RET/10
216 Mike Schmidt RET/50 80.00 24.00
217 Nolan Ryan RET/100 120.00 36.00
218 Orel Hershiser RET/50 40.00 12.00
219 Paul Molitor RET/50 40.00 12.00
221 Rod Carew RET/50 40.00 12.00
223 Ryne Sandberg RET/25 100.00 30.00
224 Stan Musial RET/25 100.00 30.00
226 Tony Gwynn RET/100 50.00 15.00
228 Whitey Ford RET Pants/25 50.00 15.00
229 Yogi Berra RET/25 80.00 24.00
230 Carlos Beltran Astros H/50 50.00 15.00
231 David Ortiz H/50 60.00 18.00
232 David Ortiz A/50 60.00 18.00
234 Carlos Lee/50 25.00 7.50
235 Travis Hafner/25 30.00 9.00
236 Brad Penny/25 20.00 6.00
237 Wade Miller/25 20.00 6.00
238 Edgar Martinez/50 50.00 15.00
239 Carl Crawford/25 30.00 9.00
240 Roy Oswalt H/25 30.00 9.00
242 Carlos Beltran Astros A/50 50.00 15.00
243 Carlos Beltran Royals H/50 50.00 15.00
244 Miguel Cabrera Fielding/50 40.00 12.00
245 Scott Rolen Cards H/50 50.00 15.00
246 Hank Blalock A/50 25.00 7.50
247 Vernon Wells A/50 25.00 7.50
248 Adam Dunn H/50 40.00 12.00
249 Preston Wilson A/25 30.00 9.00

2004 Leaf Limited Moniker Jersey Number

Nm-Mt Ex-Mt
*1-200/230-250 p/r 75: .4X TO 1X Jsy/75
*1-200/230-250 p/r 50: .4X TO 1X Jsy/38-50
*1-200/230-250 p/r 25: .5X TO 1.2X Jsy/50
*1-200/230-250 p/r 25: .4X TO 1X Jsy/25
*201-229 p/r 100: .4X TO 1X Jsy/100
*201-229 p/r 50: .4X TO 1X Jsy/50
*201-229 p/r 25: .5X TO 1.2X Jsy/50
*201-229 p/r 25: .4X TO 1X Jsy/25
OVERALL AU-GU ODDS ONE PER PACK
PRINT RUNS B/WN 1-100 COPIES PER
NO PRICING ON QTY OF 10 OR LESS
140 Sammy Sosa H/25 120.00 36.00
199 Sammy Sosa A/25 120.00 36.00

2004 Leaf Limited Threads Button

Nm-Mt Ex-Mt
OVERALL AU-GU ODDS ONE PER PACK
PRINT RUNS B/WN 1-6 COPIES PER
NO PRICING DUE TO SCARCITY

2004 Leaf Limited Threads Jersey

Nm-Mt Ex-Mt
OVERALL AU-GU ODDS ONE PER PACK
PRINT RUNS B/WN 1-100 COPIES PER
NO PRICING ON QTY OF 10 OR LESS
NO RC YR PRICING DUE TO SCARCITY
1 Adam Dunn A/25 20.00 6.00
2 Adrian Beltre/5
3 Albert Pujols H/50 25.00 7.50
5 Alfonso Soriano Rgr/25 20.00 6.00
6 Andruw Jones/25 12.00 3.60
7 Andy Pettitte Astros/5
8 Angel Berroa Pants/5
9 Aramis Ramirez/5
10 Aubrey Huff/5
11 Austin Kearns/25 12.00 3.60
12 Barry Larkin/25 20.00 6.00
13 Barry Zito H/25 12.00 3.60
15 Ben Sheets/5
16 Bernie Williams/50 12.00 3.60
17 Bobby Abreu/5
18 Brandon Webb/5
19 Brian Giles/5
20 C.C. Sabathia/5
21 Carlos Beltran Royals A/25 20.00 6.00
22 Carlos Delgado/25 12.00 3.60
23 Chipper Jones H/50 15.00 4.50
24 Craig Biggio/25 20.00 6.00
25 Curt Schilling Sox/25 25.00 7.50
26 Darin Erstad/10
30 Dontrelle Willis/25 12.00 3.60
31 Edgar Renteria/25 12.00 3.60
32 Eric Chavez/25 12.00 3.60
34 Frank Thomas/25 25.00 7.50
35 Fred McGriff/10
36 Garret Anderson H/25 12.00 3.60
38 Geoff Jenkins/5
39 Greg Maddux Cubs/50 20.00 6.00
40 Hank Blalock H/25 12.00 3.60
41 Hideki Matsui/50 50.00 15.00
42 Hideo Nomo Dodgers/50 15.00 4.50
44 Ivan Rodriguez Tigers/25 25.00 7.50
46 Jacque Jones/10
47 Jae Weong Seo/5
49 Jamie Moyer/5
50 Jason Giambi Yanks/25 8.00 2.40
51 Jason Kendall/5
53 Jason Varitek/5
55 Javy Lopez/25 12.00 3.60
56 Jay Gibbons/5
58 Jeff Bagwell H/50 12.00 3.60
59 Jeff Kent/50 8.00 2.40
60 Jeremy Bonderman/5
62 Jeromy Burnitz/1
63 Jim Edmonds/25 12.00 3.60
64 Jim Thome Phils/50 15.00 4.50
65 Jimmy Rollins/5
66 Jody Gerut/5
67 Johan Santana/5
68 John Olerud/10
69 John Smoltz/25 20.00 6.00
71 Jorge Posada/25 20.00 6.00
73 Jose Reyes/5
74 Jose Vidro/5
75 Josh Beckett H/25 12.00 3.60
76 Juan Gonzalez Royals/25 20.00 6.00
78 Junior Spivey/1
79 Kazuhisa Ishii/10
84 Kerry Wood/50 15.00 4.50
86 Kevin Millwood/10
88 Lance Berkman/50 8.00 2.40
89 Larry Bigbie/5
90 Larry Walker/25 20.00 6.00
92 Luis Castillo/5
93 Luis Gonzalez/25 12.00 3.60
94 Luis Matos/5
96 Magglio Ordonez H/25 12.00 3.60
97 Manny Ramirez Sox/50 12.00 3.60
98 Marcus Giles/5
99 Mark Buehrle/10
100 Mark Mulder/25 12.00 3.60
101 Mark Prior H/50 15.00 4.50
102 Mark Teixeira/10
103 Marlon Byrd/5
104 Matt Morris/10
105 Melvin Mora/5
107 Miguel Cabrera Batting/25 20.00 6.00
108 Miguel Tejada O's/25 12.00 3.60
109 Mike Lowell/1
110 Mike Mussina Yanks/50 12.00 3.60
111 Mike Piazza Mets/50 20.00 6.00
112 Mike Sweeney/25 12.00 3.60
115 Morgan Ensberg/5
118 Omar Vizquel/5
119 Orlando Cabrera/5
120 Pat Burrell/5
121 Paul Konerko/10
122 Paul Lo Duca/10
123 Pedro Martinez Sox/50 15.00 4.50
124 Preston Wilson H/5
125 Rafael Furcal/5
126 Rafael Palmeiro O's/25 20.00 6.00
127 Randy Johnson D'backs/25 25.00 7.50
128 Rich Harden/1
129 Richard Hidalgo Pants/5
130 Richie Sexson/10
134 Rocco Baldelli/10
135 Roger Clemens Astros/5
136 Roy Halladay/1
137 Roy Oswalt A/25 12.00 3.60
139 Ryan Klesko/5
140 Sammy Sosa H/50 20.00 6.00
142 Scott Rolen Cards A/25 25.00 7.50
143 Sean Burroughs/5
144 Sean Casey/5
145 Shannon Stewart/10
146 Shawn Green Dodgers/25 12.00 3.60
149 Steve Finley/5
150 Tim Hudson/25 12.00 3.60
151 Tim Salmon/5
152 Tino Martinez/5
153 Todd Helton H/50 12.00 3.60
154 Tom Glavine Mets/25 20.00 6.00
155 Torii Hunter/25 12.00 3.60
156 Trot Nixon/1
157 Troy Glaus/25 12.00 3.60
158 Vernon Wells H/25 12.00 3.60
159 Victor Martinez A/5
160 Vinny Castilla/5
161 Vladimir Guerrero Angels/25 25.00 7.50
162 Alex Rodriguez Rgr/100 12.00 3.60
163 Alfonso Soriano Yanks/50 12.00 3.60
164 Andy Pettitte Yanks/25 20.00 6.00
165 Curt Schilling D'backs/25 12.00 3.60
166 Gary Sheffield Braves/25 12.00 3.60
167 Greg Maddux Braves/50 20.00 6.00
168 Hideo Nomo Sox/25 25.00 7.50
169 Ivan Rodriguez Marlins/50 15.00 4.50
170 Jason Giambi A's/25 12.00 3.60
171 Jim Thome Indians/10
172 Juan Gonzalez Rgr/25 20.00 6.00
174 Kevin Brown Dodgers/25 12.00 3.60
176 Miguel Tejada A's/25 12.00 3.60
177 Mike Mussina O's/50 12.00 3.60
178 Mike Piazza Dodgers/25 30.00 9.00
179 Pedro Martinez Expos/25 25.00 7.50
180 Rafael Palmeiro Rgr/25 20.00 6.00
181 Randy Johnson Astros/50 15.00 4.50
182 Roger Clemens Sox/100 12.00 3.60
183 Scott Rolen Phils/25 25.00 7.50
184 Shawn Green Jays/25 12.00 3.60
185 Tom Glavine Braves/25 20.00 6.00
186 Vladimir Guerrero Expos/25 25.00 7.50
187 Alex Rodriguez M's/100 12.00 3.60
188 Mike Piazza Marlins/10
189 Randy Johnson M's/50 15.00 4.50
190 Roger Clemens Yanks/100 12.00 3.60
191 Albert Pujols A/50 25.00 7.50
192 Barry Zito A/25 12.00 3.60
193 Chipper Jones A/50 15.00 4.50
194 Garret Anderson A/25 12.00 3.60
195 Jeff Bagwell A/50 12.00 3.60
196 Josh Beckett A/25 12.00 3.60
197 Magglio Ordonez A/25 12.00 3.60
198 Mark Prior A/50 15.00 4.50
199 Sammy Sosa A/50 20.00 6.00
200 Todd Helton A/50 12.00 3.60
201 Andre Dawson RET/50 10.00 3.00
202 Babe Ruth RET/25 400.00 120.00
203 Bob Feller RET/25 25.00 7.50
204 Bob Gibson RET/1
205 Bobby Doerr RET/50 10.00 3.00
206 Cal Ripken RET/100 50.00 15.00
207 Dale Murphy RET/100 12.00 3.60
208 Don Mattingly RET/50 30.00 9.00
209 Gary Carter RET/50 10.00 3.00
210 George Brett RET/100 20.00 6.00
211 J.Robinson RET Jkt/50 50.00 15.00
212 Lou Brock RET/25 25.00 7.50
213 Lou Gehrig RET/25 175.00 52.50
214 Mark Grace RET/25 25.00 7.50
215 Maury Wills RET/50 10.00 3.00
216 Mike Schmidt RET/100 20.00 6.00
217 Nolan Ryan RET/100 25.00 7.50
218 Orel Hershiser RET/25 25.00 7.50
219 Paul Molitor RET/50 15.00 4.50
220 Roberto Clemente RET/25 100.00 30.00
221 Rod Carew RET/100 12.00 3.60
222 R.Campanella RET Pants/50 20.00 6.00
223 Ryne Sandberg RET/50 30.00 9.00
224 Stan Musial RET/25 50.00 15.00
225 Ted Williams RET/50 80.00 24.00
226 Tony Gwynn RET/100 15.00 4.50
227 Ty Cobb RET Pants/100 80.00 24.00
228 Whitey Ford RET Pants/25 25.00 7.50
229 Yogi Berra RET/25 30.00 9.00
230 Carlos Beltran Astros H/25 20.00 6.00
231 David Ortiz H/25 25.00 7.50
232 David Ortiz A/25 25.00 7.50
234 Carlos Lee/10
235 Travis Hafner/5
236 Brad Penny/5
237 Wade Miller/5
238 Edgar Martinez/25 20.00 6.00
239 Carl Crawford/5
240 Roy Oswalt H/25 12.00 3.60
241 Kazuo Matsui/25
242 Carlos Beltran Astros A/25 20.00 6.00
243 Carlos Beltran Royals H/25 20.00 6.00
244 Miguel Cabrera Fielding/25 20.00 6.00
245 Scott Rolen Cards H/25 25.00 7.50
246 Hank Blalock A/25 12.00 3.60
247 Vernon Wells A/25 12.00 3.60
248 Adam Dunn H/25 20.00 6.00
249 Preston Wilson A/5

2004 Leaf Limited Threads Jersey Number

Nm-Mt Ex-Mt
*1-200/230-250 p/r 100: .4X TO 1X Thrd/100
*1-200/230-250 p/r 50: .4X TO 1X Thrd/50
*1-200/230-250 p/r 25: .6X TO 1.5X Thrd/50
*1-200/230-250 p/r 25: .4X TO 1X Thrd/25
*201-229 p/r 100: .4X TO 1X Thrd/100
*201-229 p/r 100: .3X TO .8X Thrd/50
*201-229 p/r 50: .4X TO 1X Thrd/50
*201-229 p/r 25: .4X TO 1X Thrd/25
OVERALL AU-GU ODDS ONE PER PACK
PRINT RUNS B/WN 1-100 COPIES PER
NO PRICING ON QTY OF 10 OR LESS

2004 Leaf Limited Threads MLB Logo

Nm-Mt Ex-Mt
OVERALL AU-GU ODDS ONE PER PACK
STATED PRINT RUN 1 SERIAL #'d SET
NO PRICING DUE TO SCARCITY

2004 Leaf Limited Timber

Nm-Mt Ex-Mt
*1-200/230-250 p/r 100: .4X TO 1X Thrd/100
*1-200/230-250 p/r 50: .4X TO 1X Thrd/50
*1-200/230-250 p/r 25: 1X TO 2.5X Thrd/100
*1-200/230-250 p/r 25: .6X TO 1.5X Thrd/50
*1-200/230-250 p/r 25: .4X TO 1X Thrd/25
*201-229 p/r 100: .4X TO 1X Thrd/100
*201-229 p/r 100: .25X TO .6X Thrd/50
*201-229 p/r 100: .15X TO .4X Thrd/25
*201-229 p/r 50: .6X TO 1.5X Thrd/100
*201-229 p/r 50: .4X TO 1X Thrd/50
*201-229 p/r 25: 1X TO 2.5X Thrd/100
*201-229 p/r 25: .6X TO 1.5X Thrd/50
*201-229 p/r 25: .4X TO 1X Thrd/25
OVERALL AU-GU ODDS ONE PER PACK
PRINT RUNS B/WN 1-100 COPIES PER
NO PRICING ON QTY OF 10 OR LESS
4 Alex Rodriguez Yanks/100 12.00 3.60
7 Andy Pettitte Astros/25 20.00 6.00
35 Fred McGriff/25 20.00 6.00
37 Gary Sheffield Yanks/25 12.00 3.60
85 Kevin Brown Yanks/25 12.00 3.60
102 Mark Teixeira/25 12.00 3.60
106 Michael Young/25 12.00 3.60
109 Mike Lowell/25 12.00 3.60
116 Nick Johnson/25 12.00 3.60
117 Nomar Garciaparra/25 30.00 9.00
122 Paul Lo Duca/25 12.00 3.60
130 Richie Sexson/25 12.00 3.60
134 Rocco Baldelli/25 12.00 3.60
135 Roger Clemens Astros/25 30.00 9.00
156 Trot Nixon/25 12.00 3.60
171 Jim Thome Indians/25 25.00 7.50
175 Manny Ramirez Indians/25 20.00 6.00
188 Mike Piazza Marlins/25 30.00 9.00
202 Babe Ruth RET/100 150.00 45.00
213 Lou Gehrig RET/100 120.00 36.00
220 Roberto Clemente RET/100 80.00 24.00
225 Ted Williams RET/100 60.00 18.00

2004 Leaf Limited TNT

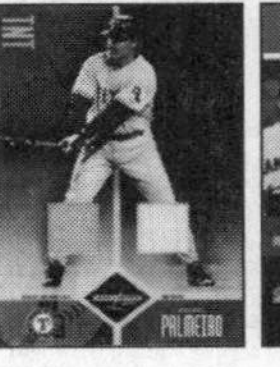

Nm-Mt Ex-Mt
*1-200/230-250 p/r 100: .5X TO 1.2X Thrd/100
*1-200/230-250 p/r 100: .3X TO .8X Thrd/50
*1-200/230-250 p/r 50: .5X TO 1.2X Thrd/50
*1-200/230-250 p/r 50: .3X TO .8X Thrd/25
*1-200/230-250 p/r 25: .75X TO 2X Thrd/50
*1-200/230-250 p/r 25: .5X TO 1.2X Thrd/25
*201-229 p/r 100: .5X TO 1.2X Thrd/100
*201-229 p/r 100: .3X TO .8X Thrd/50
*201-229 p/r 50: .75X TO 2X Thrd/100
*201-229 p/r 50: .5X TO 1.2X Thrd/50
*201-229 p/r 25: .75X TO 2X Thrd/50
*201-229 p/r 25: .5X TO 1.2X Thrd/25
OVERALL AU-GU ODDS ONE PER PACK
PRINT RUNS B/WN 5-100 COPIES PER
NO PRICING ON QTY OF 10 OR LESS
102 Mark Teixeira Bat-Jsy/25 15.00 4.50
109 Mike Lowell Bat-Jsy/25 15.00 4.50

2004 Leaf Limited Cuts

Nm-Mt Ex-Mt
OVERALL AU-GU ODDS ONE PER PACK
PRINT RUNS B/WN 50-100 COPIES PER
CUTS FABRIC IS NOT GAME-USED
1 Nolan Ryan/100 150.00 45.00
2 Bob Gibson/50 50.00 15.00
3 Harmon Killebrew/100 50.00 15.00
4 Duke Snider/100 40.00 12.00
5 George Brett/100 80.00 24.00
6 Stan Musial/100 100.00 30.00
7 Alan Trammell/100 25.00 7.50
8 Cal Ripken/100 200.00 60.00
9 Steve Carlton/50 50.00 15.00
10 Phil Rizzuto/100 40.00 12.00
11 Mark Prior/50 80.00 24.00
12 Will Clark/100 50.00 15.00
13 Lou Brock/100 40.00 12.00
14 Ozzie Smith/100 60.00 18.00
15 Bob Feller/100 40.00 12.00
16 Gary Carter/50 30.00 9.00
17 Al Kaline/100 50.00 15.00
18 Brooks Robinson/100 40.00 12.00
19 Tony Gwynn/100 60.00 18.00
20 Mike Schmidt/100 80.00 24.00
21 Ralph Kiner/50 50.00 15.00
22 Jim Palmer/50 50.00 15.00
23 Don Mattingly/100 80.00 24.00
24 Paul Molitor/50 50.00 15.00
25 Dale Murphy/100 40.00 12.00

2004 Leaf Limited Cuts Gold

Nm-Mt Ex-Mt
*GOLD p/r 45: .4X TO 1X BASIC p/r 50
*GOLD p/r 20-35: .6X TO 1.5X BASIC p/r 100
*GOLD p/r 20-35: .5X TO 1.2X BASIC p/r 50
*GOLD p/r 19: .75X TO 2X BASIC p/r 100
OVERALL AU-GU ODDS ONE PER PACK
PRINT RUNS B/WN 1-45 COPIES PER
NO PRICING ON QTY OF 10 OR LESS
CUTS FABRIC IS NOT GAME-USED

2004 Leaf Limited Legends Material Number

Nm-Mt Ex-Mt
PRINT RUNS B/WN 5-100 COPIES PER
*POSITION: .4X TO 1X NUMBER
POSITION PRINT RUNS B/WN 5-100 PER
OVERALL AU-GU ODDS ONE PER PACK

NO PRICING ON QTY OF 5 OR LESS..
1 Al Kaline Pants/50 .... 20.00 6.00
2 Babe Ruth Pants/50 .... 200.00 60.00
3 Bob Feller Jsy/50 .... 15.00 4.50
4 Bob Gibson Jsy/50 .... 15.00 4.50
5 Brooks Robinson Jsy/5 ....
6 Burleigh Grimes Pants/100 .... 50.00 15.00
7 Carl Yastrzemski Jsy/100 .... 20.00 6.00
8 Harmon Killebrew Jsy/25 .... 30.00 9.00
9 Hoyt Wilhelm Jsy/100 .... 8.00 2.40
10 Johnny Mize Pants/100 .... 12.00 3.60
11 Ernie Banks Pants/50 .... 20.00 6.00
12 Lou Brock Jsy/50 .... 15.00 4.50
13 Luis Aparicio Pants/100 .... 8.00 2.40
14 Pee Wee Reese Jsy/50 .... 15.00 4.50
15 Reggie Jackson Jsy/100 .... 12.00 3.60
16 Red Schoendienst Jsy/50 .... 10.00 3.00
17 Roberto Clemente Jsy/25 .... 100.00 30.00
18 Roger Maris Pants/100 .... 30.00 9.00
19 Stan Musial Jsy/100 .... 25.00 7.50
20 Ted Williams Jsy/50 .... 80.00 24.00
21 Ty Cobb Pants/50 .... 100.00 30.00
22 Warren Spahn Jsy/100 .... 12.00 3.60
23 Whitey Ford Pants/100 .... 12.00 3.60
24 Yogi Berra Jsy/50 .... 20.00 6.00
25 Satchel Paige CO Jsy/100 .... 60.00 18.00

2004 Leaf Limited Legends Material Autographs Number

Nm-Mt Ex-Mt
PRINT RUNS B/WN 5-50 COPIES PER
*POSITION: .4X TO 1X NUMBER
POSITION PRINT RUNS B/WN 5-100 PER
OVERALL AU-GU ODDS ONE PER PACK
NO PRICING ON QTY OF 10 OR LESS
1 Al Kaline Pants/50 .... 60.00 18.00
3 Bob Feller Jsy/50 .... 40.00 12.00
4 Bob Gibson Jsy/50 .... 40.00 12.00
5 Brooks Robinson Jsy/5 ....
7 Carl Yastrzemski Jsy/25 .... 100.00 30.00
8 Harmon Killebrew Jsy/25 .... 80.00 24.00
9 Hoyt Wilhelm Jsy/25 .... 50.00 15.00
12 Lou Brock Jsy/50 .... 40.00 12.00
13 Luis Aparicio Pants/50 .... 25.00 7.50
15 Reggie Jackson Jsy/50 .... 60.00 18.00
16 Red Schoendienst Jsy/50 .... 40.00 12.00
19 Stan Musial Jsy/50 .... 80.00 24.00
22 Warren Spahn Jsy/10 ....
23 Whitey Ford Pants/25 .... 50.00 15.00
24 Yogi Berra Jsy/25 .... 80.00 24.00

2004 Leaf Limited Lumberjacks

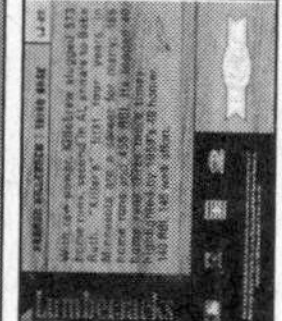

Nm-Mt Ex-Mt
1-40 PRINT RUNS B/WN 16-714 PER
41-50 PRINT RUN 500 #'d SETS
RANDOM INSERTS IN PACKS
1 Al Kaline/399 .... 5.00 1.50
2 Albert Pujols/114 .... 15.00 4.50
3 Andre Dawson/438 .... 3.00 .90
4 Babe Ruth/714 .... 8.00 2.40
5 Bo Jackson/141 .... 6.00 1.80
6 Bobby Doerr/223 .... 4.00 1.20
7 Brooks Robinson/268 .... 4.00 1.20
8 Cal Ripken/431 .... 15.00 4.50
9 Carlton Fisk/376 .... 4.00 1.20
10 Dale Murphy/398 .... 4.00 1.20
11 Darryl Strawberry/335 .... 3.00 .90
12 Don Mattingly/222 .... 10.00 3.00
13 Duke Snider/407 .... 4.00 1.20
14 Eddie Mathews/512 .... 5.00 1.50
15 Eddie Murray/504 .... 5.00 1.50
16 Frank Robinson/586 .... 3.00 .90
17 Frank Thomas/418 .... 5.00 1.50
18 Gary Carter/324 .... 3.00 .90
19 George Brett/317 .... 8.00 2.40
20 Harmon Killebrew/573 .... 5.00 1.50
21 Hideki Matsui/16 .... 60.00 18.00
22 Lou Gehrig/493 .... 6.00 1.80
23 Mark Grace/173 .... 5.00 1.50
24 Mike Piazza/358 .... 5.00 1.50
25 Mike Schmidt/548 .... 8.00 2.40
26 Orlando Cepeda/379 .... 3.00 .90
27 Rafael Palmeiro/528 .... 3.00 .90
28 Ralph Kiner/369 .... 3.00 .90
29 Reggie Jackson/563 .... 4.00 1.20
30 Rickey Henderson/297 .... 5.00 1.50
31 Roger Maris/275 .... 5.00 1.50
32 Ryne Sandberg/282 .... 8.00 2.40
33 Sammy Sosa/539 .... 5.00 1.50
34 Scott Rolen/192 .... 6.00 1.80
35 Stan Musial/475 .... 6.00 1.80
36 Ted Williams/521 .... 8.00 2.40
37 Thurman Munson/113 .... 8.00 2.40
38 Vladimir Guerrero/234 .... 6.00 1.80
39 Willie McCovey/521 .... 4.00 1.20
40 Willie Stargell/475 .... 4.00 1.20
41 Roberto Clemente 8.00 2.40
Stan Musial
42 Cal Ripken 15.00 4.50
Ernie Banks
43 Babe Ruth 8.00 2.40
Lou Gehrig
44 George Brett 8.00 2.40
Mike Schmidt
45 Frank Robinson 5.00 1.50
Jackie Robinson
46 Don Mattingly 8.00 2.40
Roger Maris
47 Nomar Garciaparra 8.00 2.40
Ted Williams
48 Johnny Bench 5.00 1.50
Mike Piazza
49 Reggie Jackson 5.00 1.50
Sammy Sosa
50 Mel Ott 5.00 1.50
Willie McCovey

2004 Leaf Limited Lumberjacks Black

Nm-Mt Ex-Mt
*1-40 p/r 66: 1.5X TO 4X LJ p/r 251+
*1-40 p/r 37-61: 1.5X TO 4X LJ p/r 251+
*1-40 p/r 37-61: .75X TO 2X LJ p/r 126-250
*1-40 p/r 37-61: .6X TO 1.5X LJ p/r 66-125
*1-40 p/r 20-35: 2X TO 5X LJ p/r 251+
*1-40 p/r 20-35: 1.5X TO 4X LJ p/r 126-250
*1-40 p/r 20-35: 1.25X TO 3X LJ p/r 66-125
*1-40 p/r 16-17: 2X TO 5X LJ p/r 126-250
*1-40 p/r 16-17: .4X TO 1X LJ p/r 16
1-40 PRINT RUNS B/WN 16-66 COPIES PER
*BLACK 41-50: 1X TO 2.5X LJ 41-50
41-50 PRINT RUN 100 SERIAL #'d SETS
RANDOM INSERTS IN PACKS

2004 Leaf Limited Lumberjacks Autographs

Nm-Mt Ex-Mt
OVERALL AU-GU ODDS ONE PER PACK
PRINT RUNS B/WN 1-100 COPIES PER
NO PRICING ON QTY OF 10 OR LESS
1 Al Kaline/100 .... 40.00 12.00
2 Albert Pujols/10 ....
3 Andre Dawson/100 .... 15.00 4.50
5 Bo Jackson/25 .... 60.00 18.00
6 Bobby Doerr/100 .... 15.00 4.50
7 Brooks Robinson/100 .... 25.00 7.50
8 Cal Ripken/25 .... 200.00 60.00
9 Carlton Fisk/25 .... 40.00 12.00
10 Dale Murphy/100 .... 25.00 7.50
11 Darryl Strawberry/100 .... 15.00 4.50
12 Don Mattingly/25 .... 80.00 24.00
13 Duke Snider/100 .... 25.00 7.50
15 Eddie Murray/10 ....
16 Frank Robinson/100 .... 25.00 7.50
17 Frank Thomas/50 .... 50.00 15.00
18 Gary Carter/100 .... 15.00 4.50
19 George Brett/25 .... 80.00 24.00
20 Harmon Killebrew/100 .... 40.00 12.00
23 Mark Grace/25 .... 40.00 12.00
24 Mike Piazza/10 ....
25 Mike Schmidt/50 .... 60.00 18.00
26 Orlando Cepeda/1 ....
27 Rafael Palmeiro/1 ....
28 Ralph Kiner/100 .... 25.00 7.50
29 Reggie Jackson/25 .... 60.00 18.00
30 Rickey Henderson/25 .... 60.00 18.00
32 Ryne Sandberg/25 .... 80.00 24.00
33 Sammy Sosa/10 ....
34 Scott Rolen/25 .... 50.00 15.00
35 Stan Musial/50 .... 60.00 18.00
39 Willie McCovey/25 .... 40.00 12.00

2004 Leaf Limited Lumberjacks Autographs Bat

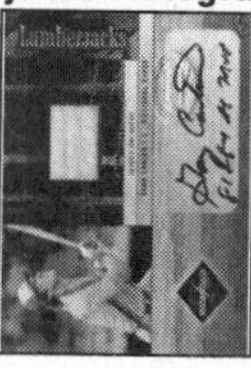

Nm-Mt Ex-Mt
*BAT p/r 100: .5X TO1.2X AU p/r 100
*BAT p/r 50: .6X TO1.5X AU p/r 100 ..
*BAT p/r 50: .5X TO1.2X AU p/r 50 ....
*BAT p/r 25: .75X TO2X AU p/r 100 ...
*BAT p/r 25: .6X TO1.5X AU p/r 50 ....
*BAT p/r 25: .5X TO1.2X AU p/r 25 ....
*BAT p/r 17: .6X TO1.5X AU p/r 25 ....
OVERALL AU-GU ODDS ONE PER PACK
PRINT RUNS B/WN 1-100 COPIES PER
NO PRICING ON QTY OF 10 OR LESS

2004 Leaf Limited Lumberjacks Autographs Jersey

Nm-Mt Ex-Mt
*JSY p/r 100: .5X TO 1.2X AU p/r 100
*JSY p/r 50: .6X TO 1.5X AU p/r 100 .
*JSY p/r 50: .5X TO 1.2X AU p/r 50 ...
*JSY p/r 50: .4X TO 1X AU p/r 25 ....
*JSY p/r 25: .75X TO 2X AU p/r 100 ...
*JSY p/r 25: .6X TO 1.5X AU p/r 50 ...
*JSY p/r 25: .5X TO 1.2X AU p/r 25 ...
*JSY p/r 17: .6X TO 1.5X AU p/r 25 ...
OVERALL AU-GU ODDS ONE PER PACK
PRINT RUNS B/WN 5-100 COPIES PER
NO PRICING ON QTY OF 10 OR LESS
15 Eddie Murray/25 .... 80.00 24.00
26 Orlando Cepeda Pants/50 .... 25.00 7.50

2004 Leaf Limited Lumberjacks Barrel

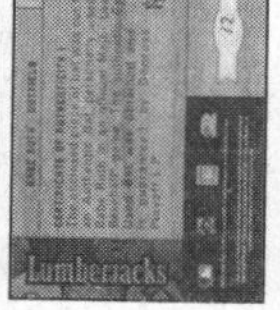

Nm-Mt Ex-Mt
OVERALL AU-GU ODDS ONE PER PACK
PRINT RUNS B/WN 1-5 COPIES PER
NO PRICING DUE TO SCARCITY ......

2004 Leaf Limited Lumberjacks Bat

Nm-Mt Ex-Mt
OVERALL AU-GU ODDS ONE PER PACK
PRINT RUNS B/WN 25-100 COPIES PER
1 Al Kaline/100 .... 15.00 4.50
2 Albert Pujols/100 .... 15.00 4.50
3 Andre Dawson/25 .... 15.00 4.50
4 Babe Ruth/100 .... 150.00 45.00
5 Bo Jackson/100 .... 20.00 6.00
6 Bobby Doerr/25 .... 15.00 4.50
7 Brooks Robinson/100 .... 12.00 3.60
8 Cal Ripken/100 .... 50.00 15.00
9 Carlton Fisk/100 .... 12.00 3.60
10 Dale Murphy/50 .... 15.00 4.50
11 Darryl Strawberry/25 .... 15.00 4.50
12 Don Mattingly/100 .... 20.00 6.00
14 Eddie Mathews/100 .... 15.00 4.50
15 Eddie Murray/100 .... 15.00 4.50
16 Frank Robinson/100 .... 8.00 2.40
17 Frank Thomas/25 .... 25.00 7.50
18 Gary Carter/50 .... 10.00 3.00
19 George Brett/100 .... 20.00 6.00
20 Harmon Killebrew/100 .... 15.00 4.50
21 Hideki Matsui/100 .... 30.00 9.00
22 Lou Gehrig/100 .... 120.00 36.00
23 Mark Grace/25 .... 25.00 7.50
24 Mike Piazza/50 .... 20.00 6.00
25 Mike Schmidt/100 .... 20.00 6.00
26 Orlando Cepeda/50 .... 10.00 3.00
27 Rafael Palmeiro/50 .... 12.00 3.60
28 Ralph Kiner/100 .... 8.00 2.40
29 Reggie Jackson/100 .... 12.00 3.60
30 Rickey Henderson/100 .... 15.00 4.50
31 Roger Maris/100 .... 30.00 9.00
32 Ryne Sandberg/100 .... 20.00 6.00
33 Sammy Sosa/100 .... 12.00 3.60
34 Scott Rolen/25 .... 25.00 7.50
35 Stan Musial/100 .... 25.00 7.50
36 Ted Williams/100 .... 60.00 18.00
37 Thurman Munson/100 .... 25.00 7.50
38 Vladimir Guerrero/25 .... 25.00 7.50
39 Willie McCovey/100 .... 12.00 3.60
40 Willie Stargell/50 .... 15.00 4.50
41 Roberto Clemente 100.00 30.00
Stan Musial /100
42 Cal Ripken 100.00 30.00
Ernie Banks /50
43 Babe Ruth 300.00 90.00
Lou Gehrig /25
44 George Brett 50.00 15.00
Mike Schmidt /50
46 Don Mattingly 50.00 15.00
Roger Maris /50
47 Nomar Garciaparra 80.00 24.00
Ted Williams /100
48 Johnny Bench 40.00 12.00
Mike Piazza /25
49 Reggie Jackson 25.00 7.50
Sammy Sosa /50
50 Mel Ott 40.00 12.00
Willie McCovey /100

2004 Leaf Limited Lumberjacks Jersey

Nm-Mt Ex-Mt
*1-40 p/r 100: .4X TO 1X BAT p/r 100
*1-40 p/r 100: .25X TO .6X BAT p/r 50
*1-40 p/r 100: .15X TO .4X BAT p/r 25
*1-40 p/r 50: .6X TO 1.5X BAT p/r 100
*1-40 p/r 50: .4X TO 1X BAT p/r 50....
*1-40 p/r 50: .25X TO .6X BAT p/r 25.
*1-40 p/r 25: 1X TO 2.5X BAT p/r 100
*1-40 p/r 25: .4X TO 1X BAT p/r 25....
*41-50 p/r 100: .25X TO .6X BAT p/r 50
*41-50 p/r 100: .15X TO .4X BAT p/r 25
*41-50 p/r 50: .6X TO 1.5X BAT p/r 100
*41-50 p/r 25: 1X TO 2.5X BAT p/r 100
*41-50 p/r 25: .4X TO 1X BAT p/r 25..
OVERALL AU-GU ODDS ONE PER PACK
PRINT RUNS B/WN 4-100 COPIES PER
NO PRICING ON QTY OF 4 OR LESS..

2004 Leaf Limited Lumberjacks Combos

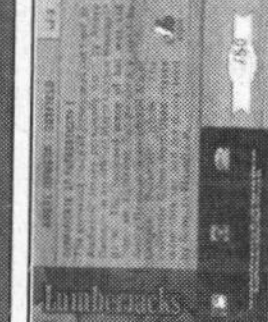

Nm-Mt Ex-Mt
*COMBO p/r 100: .5X TO 1.2X BAT p/r 100
*COMBO p/r 100: .3X TO .8X BAT p/r 50
*COMBO p/r 50: .75X TO 2X BAT p/r 100
*COMBO p/r 50: .5X TO 1.2X BAT p/r 50
*COMBO p/r 50: .3X TO .8X BAT p/r 25
*COMBO p/r 25: 1.25X TO 3X BAT p/r 100
*COMBO p/r 25: .5X TO 1.2X BAT p/r 25
*COMBO p/r 17: .6X TO 1.5X BAT p/r 25
OVERALL AU-GU ODDS ONE PER PACK
PRINT RUNS B/WN 17-100 COPIES PER

2004 Leaf Limited Matching Numbers

Nm-Mt Ex-Mt
PRINT RUNS B/WN 25-100 COPIES PER
PRIME PRINT RUN 1 SERIAL #'d SET
NO PRIME PRICING DUE TO SCARCITY
OVERALL AU-GU ODDS ONE PER PACK
1 Bobby Doerr Jsy 15.00 4.50
Pee Wee Reese Jsy/100
2 Lou Gehrig Pants 200.00 60.00
Mel Ott Jsy/50
3 Albert Pujols Jsy 40.00 12.00
George Brett Jsy/100
4 Cal Ripken Jsy 60.00 18.00
Carl Yastrzemski Jsy/100
5 Dwight Gooden Jsy 20.00 6.00
Whitey Ford Pants/50
6 Mark Grace Jsy 30.00 9.00
Todd Helton Jsy/25
7 Robin Yount Jsy 50.00 15.00
Tony Gwynn Jsy/50
8 Frank Robinson Jsy 30.00 9.00
Mike Schmidt Jsy/100
9 Roberto Clemente Jsy 80.00 24.00
Sammy Sosa Jsy/100
10 Roger Clemens Jsy 30.00 9.00
Warren Spahn Pants/100
11 Mark Prior Jsy 30.00 9.00
Roger Clemens Jsy/50
12 Don Mattingly Jkt 40.00 12.00
Ryne Sandberg Jsy/100
13 Billy Williams Jsy 15.00 4.50
Wade Boggs Jsy/100
14 Catfish Hunter Jsy 15.00 4.50
Juan Marichal Jsy/50
15 Fergie Jenkins Pants 25.00 7.50
Greg Maddux Jsy/50
16 Kerry Wood Pants 40.00 12.00
Nolan Ryan Jsy/100
17 Rickey Henderson Jsy 40.00 12.00
Roger Maris Pants/100
18 Dontrelle Willis Jsy 20.00 6.00
Mike Mussina Jsy/50
19 Reggie Jackson Jsy 15.00 4.50
Willie McCovey Jsy/100
20 Bob Gibson Jsy 20.00 6.00
Pedro Martinez Jsy/50
21 Duke Snider Jsy 15.00 4.50
Paul Molitor Jsy/100
22 Johnny Bench Jsy 20.00 6.00
Lou Boudreau Jsy/100
23 Andre Dawson Jsy 20.00 6.00
Chipper Jones Jsy/100
24 Ernie Banks Jsy 20.00 6.00
Ken Boyer Jsy/100
25 Manny Ramirez Jsy 20.00 6.00
Rickey Henderson Jsy/100
26 Carlton Fisk Jsy 20.00 6.00
Scott Rolen Jsy/100
27 Nolan Ryan Jsy 30.00 9.00
Orlando Cepeda Pants/100
28 Roy Halladay Jsy 10.00 3.00
Steve Carlton Jsy/100
29 Eddie Mathews Jsy 20.00 6.00
Tom Seaver Jsy/100
30 Brandon Webb Jsy 15.00 4.50
Orel Hershiser Jsy/100

2004 Leaf Limited Player Threads Jersey Number

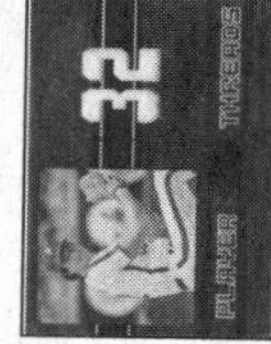

Nm-Mt Ex-Mt
PRINT RUNS B/WN 10-100 COPIES PER
NO PRICING ON QTY OF 10 OR LESS
PRIME PRINT RUN 1 SERIAL #'d SET
NO PRIME PRICING DUE TO SCARCITY
OVERALL AU-GU ODDS ONE PER PACK
1 Mike Piazza/100 .... 12.00 3.60
2 Roger Clemens/10 ....
3 Nolan Ryan Jkt/100 .... 25.00 7.50
4 Reggie Jackson/100 .... 12.00 3.60
5 Wade Boggs/50 .... 15.00 4.50
6 Steve Carlton Pants/100 .... 8.00 2.40
7 Ivan Rodriguez/25 .... 25.00 7.50
8 Pedro Martinez/50 .... 15.00 4.50
9 R.Henderson Yanks/10 ....
10 R.Hend Mets Pants/100 .... 15.00 4.50
11 Randy Johnson/50 .... 15.00 4.50
12 Curt Schilling/25 .... 25.00 7.50
13 Roger Maris/50 .... 50.00 15.00
14 Sammy Sosa/100 .... 12.00 3.60
15 Gary Carter Pants/50 .... 10.00 3.00
16 Gary Sheffield/25 .... 12.00 3.60
17 Eddie Murray/50 .... 20.00 6.00
18 Hideo Nomo/50 .... 15.00 4.50
19 Rafael Palmeiro/50 .... 12.00 3.60
20 Andre Dawson/50 .... 10.00 3.00

2004 Leaf Limited Player Threads Double

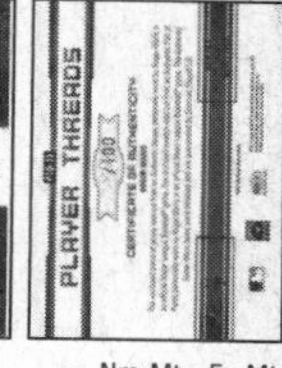

Nm-Mt Ex-Mt
*DBL p/r 100: .6X TO 1.5X PT p/r 100
*DBL p/r 100: .4X TO 1X PT p/r 50 ...
*DBL p/r 100: .25X TO .6X PT p/r 25 .
*DBL p/r 50: .6X TO 1.5X PT p/r 50 ...
*DBL p/r 50: .4X TO 1X PT p/r 25 ......
OVERALL AU-GU ODDS ONE PER PACK
PRINT RUNS B/WN 50-100 COPIES PER
2 R.Clemens Sox-Yanks/100 .... 25.00 7.50
9 R.Henderson A's-Jays/50 .... 30.00 9.00

2004 Leaf Limited Player Threads Triple

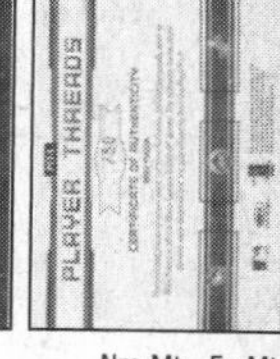

Nm-Mt Ex-Mt
*TRIPLE p/r 50: 1.25X TO 3X PT p/r 100
*TRIPLE p/r 50: .75X TO 2X PT p/r 50
*TRIPLE p/r 25: 1.5X TO 4X PT p/r 100
*TRIPLE p/r 25: 1X TO 2.5X PT p/r 50
*TRIPLE p/r 25: .6X TO 1.5X PT p/r 25
OVERALL AU-GU ODDS ONE PER PACK
PRINT RUNS B/WN 10-50 COPIES PER
NO PRICING ON QTY OF 10 OR LESS
2 R.Clem Astros-Sox-Yanks/25. 60.00 18.00
13 Roger Maris 150.00 45.00
A's Pants-Cards Bat-Yanks Jsy/25

2004 Leaf Limited Team Threads Jersey Number

Nm-Mt Ex-Mt
STATED PRINT RUN 100 SERIAL #'d SETS
PRIME PRINT RUN 1 SERIAL #'d SET
NO PRIME PRICING DUE TO SCARCITY
OVERALL AU-GU ODDS ONE PER PACK
ALL ARE DUAL JSY CARDS UNLESS NOTED
1 Stan Musial 50.00 15.00
Albert Pujols
2 Cal Ripken Jkt 50.00 15.00
Mike Mussina
3 Carlton Fisk 30.00 9.00
Roger Clemens
4 Dale Murphy 20.00 6.00
Chipper Jones
5 Tony Gwynn 30.00 9.00

Dave Winfield
6 Don Mattingly 60.00 18.00
Hideki Matsui
7 Lou Boudreau 20.00 6.00
Early Wynn
8 Ernie Banks 40.00 12.00
Sammy Sosa
9 Nolan Ryan Jkt 60.00 18.00
Jeff Bagwell
10 Mike Schmidt 30.00 9.00
Jim Thome

2004 Leaf Limited Team Trademarks

Nm-Mt Ex-Mt
STATED PRINT RUN 100 SERIAL #'d SETS
GOLD PRINT RUN 10 SERIAL #'d SETS
NO GOLD PRICING DUE TO SCARCITY
RANDOM INSERTS IN PACKS
1 Bob Gibson 10.00 3.00
2 Cal Ripken 40.00 12.00
3 Carl Yastrzemski 15.00 4.50
4 Dale Murphy 10.00 3.00
5 Gary Carter 8.00 2.40
6 George Brett 20.00 6.00
7 Tom Seaver 10.00 3.00
8 Kerry Wood 8.00 2.40
9 Lou Brock 10.00 3.00
10 Luis Aparicio 8.00 2.40
11 Mike Piazza 12.00 3.60
12 Nolan Ryan Astros 20.00 6.00
13 Nolan Ryan Rgr 20.00 6.00
14 Randy Johnson 8.00 2.40
15 Reggie Jackson 10.00 3.00
16 Rickey Henderson 10.00 3.00
17 Robin Yount 15.00 4.50
18 Rod Carew 10.00 3.00
19 Ryne Sandberg 20.00 6.00
20 Steve Carlton 8.00 2.40
21 Steve Garvey 8.00 2.40
22 Johnny Bench 10.00 3.00
23 Tony Gwynn 15.00 4.50
24 Whitey Ford 10.00 3.00
25 Will Clark 10.00 3.00

2004 Leaf Limited Team Trademarks Autographs

Nm-Mt Ex-Mt
OVERALL AU-GU ODDS ONE PER PACK
PRINT RUNS B/WN 5-100 COPIES PER
NO PRICING ON QTY OF 10 OR LESS
1 Bob Gibson/100 25.00 7.50
2 Cal Ripken/25 200.00 60.00
3 Carl Yastrzemski/25 80.00 24.00
4 Dale Murphy/100 25.00 7.50
5 Gary Carter/100 15.00 4.50
6 George Brett/25 80.00 24.00
7 Tom Seaver/25 60.00 18.00
8 Kerry Wood/25 50.00 15.00
9 Lou Brock/100 25.00 7.50
10 Luis Aparicio/100 15.00 4.50
11 Mike Piazza/5
12 Nolan Ryan Astros/25 120.00 36.00
13 Nolan Ryan Rgr/25 120.00 36.00
14 Randy Johnson/5
15 Reggie Jackson/25 60.00 18.00
16 Rickey Henderson/10
17 Robin Yount/50 60.00 18.00
18 Rod Carew/50 30.00 9.00
19 Ryne Sandberg/25 80.00 24.00
20 Steve Carlton/100 25.00 7.50
21 Steve Garvey/50 20.00 6.00
22 Johnny Bench/25 60.00 18.00
23 Tony Gwynn/100 40.00 12.00
24 Whitey Ford/25 40.00 12.00
25 Will Clark/34 60.00 18.00

2004 Leaf Limited Team Trademarks Autographs Jersey Number

Nm-Mt Ex-Mt
*JSY NBR p/r 84-100: .5X TO 1.2X AU p/r 100
*JSY NBR p/r 84-100: .3X TO .8X AU p/r 25-34
*JSY NBR p/r 50: .6X TO 1.5X AU p/r 100
*JSY NBR p/r 50: .5X TO 1.2X AU p/r 50
*JSY NBR p/r 50: .4X TO 1X AU p/r 25-34
*JSY NBR p/r 25: .75X TO 2X AU p/r 100
*JSY NBR p/r 25: .5X TO 1.2X AU p/r 25-34

PRINT RUNS B/WN 5-100 COPIES PER
NO PRICING ON QTY OF 10 OR LESS
PRIME PRINT RUN 1 SERIAL #'d SET
NO PRIME PRICING DUE TO SCARCITY
OVERALL AU-GU ODDS ONE PER PACK

2004 Leaf Limited Team Trademarks Jersey Number

Nm-Mt Ex-Mt
PRINT RUNS B/WN 6-100 COPIES PER
NO PRICING ON QTY OF 6 OR LESS
PRIME PRINT RUN 1 SERIAL #'d SET
NO PRIME PRICING DUE TO SCARCITY
OVERALL AU-GU ODDS ONE PER PACK
1 Bob Gibson/100 12.00 3.60
2 Cal Ripken Pants/100 50.00 15.00
3 Carl Yastrzemski/100 20.00 6.00
4 Dale Murphy/100 12.00 3.60
5 Gary Carter/100 8.00 2.40
6 George Brett/100 20.00 6.00
7 Tom Seaver/100 12.00 3.60
8 Kerry Wood Pants/50 15.00 4.50
9 Lou Brock/100 12.00 3.60
10 Luis Aparicio Pants/100 8.00 2.40
11 Mike Piazza/50 20.00 6.00
12 Nolan Ryan Astros/100 25.00 7.50
13 Nolan Ryan Rgr/100 25.00 7.50
14 Randy Johnson/50 15.00 4.50
15 Reggie Jackson Pants/100 12.00 3.60
16 Rickey Henderson/100 15.00 4.50
17 Robin Yount/100 15.00 4.50
18 Rod Carew Jkt/100 12.00 3.60
19 Ryne Sandberg/100 20.00 6.00
20 Steve Carlton/50 10.00 3.00
21 Steve Garvey/6
22 Johnny Bench/100 15.00 4.50
23 Tony Gwynn/100 15.00 4.50
24 Whitey Ford/100 12.00 3.60
25 Will Clark/50 20.00 6.00

1998 Leaf Rookies and Stars

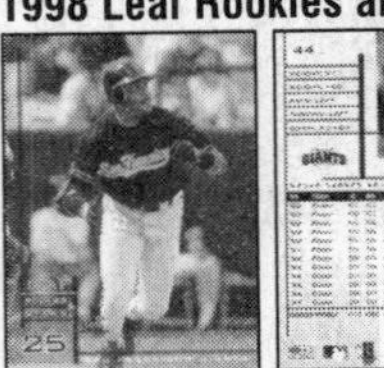

The 1998 Leaf Rookies and Stars set was issued in one series totalling 339 cards. The nine-card packs retailed for $2.99 each. The product was released very late in the year going live in December, 1998. This late release allowed for the inclusion of several rookies added to the 40 man roster at the end of the 1998 season. The set contains the topical subsets: Power Tools (131-160), Team Line-Up (161-190), and Rookies (191-300). Cards 131-230 were short-printed, being seeded at a rate of 1:2 packs. In addition, 39 cards were tacked on to the end of the set (301-339) just prior to release. These cards were seeded at noticeably shorter rates (approximately 1:8 packs) than other subsets. Several key Rookie Cards, including J.D. Drew, Troy Glaus, Gabe Kapler and Ruben Mateo appear within this run of "high series" cards. Though not confirmed by the manufacturer, it is believed that card number 317 Ryan Minor was printed in a lesser amount than the other cards in the high series. All card fronts feature full-bleed color action photos. The featured player's name lines the bottom of the card with his jersey number in the lower left corner. This product was originally created by Pinnacle in their final days as a card manufacturer. After Playoff went out of business, Playoff paid for the right to distribute this product and release it late in 1998 as much of the product had already been created. Because of the especially strong selection of Rookie Cards and an large number of shortprints, this set endured to become one of the more popular and notable base brand issues of the late 1990's.

Nm-Mt Ex-Mt
COMPLETE SET (339) 300.00 90.00
COMP.SET w/o SP's (200) 25.00 7.50
COMMON (1-130/231-300) .30 .09
COMMON (131-190) 1.00 .30
COMMON (191-230) 2.00 .60
COMMON RC (191-230) 2.50 .75
COMMON (301-339) 2.50 .75
COMMON RC (301-339) 4.00 1.20
2 Roberto Alomar .50 .15
3 Randy Johnson .75 .23
4 Manny Ramirez .50 .15
5 Paul Molitor .50 .15
6 Mike Mussina .50 .15
7 Jim Thome .75 .23
8 Tino Martinez .50 .15
9 Gary Sheffield .30 .09
10 Chuck Knoblauch .30 .09
11 Bernie Williams .50 .15
12 Tim Salmon .50 .15
13 Sammy Sosa 1.25 .35
14 Wade Boggs .50 .15
15 Andres Galarraga .30 .09
16 Pedro Martinez .75 .23
17 David Justice .30 .09
18 Chan Ho Park .30 .09
19 Jay Buhner .30 .09
20 Ryan Klesko .30 .09
21 Barry Larkin .50 .15
22 Will Clark .75 .23
23 Raul Mondesi .30 .09
24 Rickey Henderson .75 .23
25 Jim Edmonds .30 .09
26 Ken Griffey Jr. 1.25 .35
27 Frank Thomas .75 .23
28 Cal Ripken 2.50 .75
29 Alex Rodriguez 1.25 .35
30 Mike Piazza 1.25 .35
31 Greg Maddux 1.25 .35
32 Chipper Jones .75 .23
33 Tony Gwynn 1.00 .30
34 Derek Jeter 2.00 .60
35 Jeff Bagwell .50 .15
36 Juan Gonzalez .50 .15
37 Nomar Garciaparra 1.25 .35
38 Andruw Jones .30 .09
39 Hideo Nomo .75 .23
40 Roger Clemens 1.50 .45
41 Mark McGwire 2.00 .60
42 Scott Rolen .75 .23
43 Vladimir Guerrero .75 .23
44 Barry Bonds 2.00 .60
45 Darin Erstad .30 .09
46 Albert Belle .30 .09
47 Kenny Lofton .30 .09
48 Mo Vaughn .30 .09
49 Ivan Rodriguez .75 .23
50 Jose Cruz Jr. .30 .09
51 Tony Clark .30 .09
52 Larry Walker .50 .15
53 Mark Grace .50 .15
54 Edgar Martinez .50 .15
55 Fred McGriff .50 .15
56 Rafael Palmeiro .50 .15
57 Matt Williams .30 .09
58 Craig Biggio .50 .15
59 Ken Caminiti .30 .09
60 Jose Canseco .75 .23
61 Brady Anderson .30 .09
62 Moises Alou .30 .09
63 Justin Thompson .30 .09
64 John Smoltz .50 .15
65 Carlos Delgado .30 .09
66 J.T. Snow .30 .09
67 Jason Giambi .30 .09
68 Garret Anderson .30 .09
69 Rondell White .30 .09
70 Eric Karros .30 .09
71 Javier Lopez .30 .09
72 Pat Hentgen .30 .09
73 Dante Bichette .30 .09
74 Charles Johnson .30 .09
75 Tom Glavine .50 .15
76 Rusty Greer .30 .09
77 Travis Fryman .30 .09
78 Todd Hundley .30 .09
79 Ray Lankford .30 .09
80 Denny Neagle .30 .09
81 Henry Rodriguez .30 .09
82 Sandy Alomar Jr. .30 .09
83 Robin Ventura .30 .09
84 John Olerud .30 .09
85 Omar Vizquel .50 .15
86 Darren Dreifort .30 .09
87 Kevin Brown .50 .15
88 Curt Schilling .30 .09
89 Francisco Cordova .30 .09
90 Brad Radke .30 .09
91 David Cone .30 .09
92 Paul O'Neill .50 .15
93 Vinny Castilla .30 .09
94 Marquis Grissom .30 .09
95 Brian L.Hunter .30 .09
96 Kevin Appier .30 .09
97 Bobby Bonilla .30 .09
98 Eric Young .30 .09
99 Jason Kendall .30 .09
100 Shawn Green .30 .09
101 Edgardo Alfonzo .30 .09
102 Alan Benes .30 .09
103 Bobby Higginson .30 .09
104 Todd Greene .30 .09
105 Jose Guillen .30 .09
106 Neifi Perez .30 .09
107 Edgar Renteria .30 .09
108 Chris Stynes .30 .09
109 Todd Walker .30 .09
110 Brian Jordan .30 .09
111 Joe Carter .30 .09
112 Ellis Burks .30 .09
113 Brett Tomko .30 .09
114 Mike Cameron .30 .09
115 Shannon Stewart .30 .09
116 Kevin Orie .30 .09
117 Brian Giles .30 .09
118 Hideki Irabu .30 .09
119 Delino DeShields .30 .09
120 David Segui .30 .09
121 Dustin Hermanson .30 .09
122 Kevin Young .30 .09
123 Jay Bell .30 .09
124 Doug Glanville .30 .09
125 John Roskos RC .30 .09
126 Damon Hollins .30 .09
127 Matt Stairs .30 .09
128 Cliff Floyd .30 .09
129 Derek Bell .30 .09
130 Darryl Strawberry .30 .09
131 Ken Griffey Jr. PT SP 4.00 1.20
132 Tim Salmon PT SP 1.50 .45
133 M.Ramirez PT SP 1.50 .45
134 Paul Konerko PT SP 1.00 .30
135 Frank Thomas PT SP 2.50 .75
136 Todd Helton PT SP 1.50 .45
137 Larry Walker PT SP 1.50 .45
138 Mo Vaughn PT SP 1.00 .30
139 Travis Lee PT SP 1.00 .30
140 Ivan Rodriguez PT SP 2.50 .75
141 Ben Grieve PT SP 1.00 .30
142 Brad Fullmer PT SP 1.00 .30
143 Alex Rodriguez PT SP 4.00 1.20
144 Mike Piazza PT SP 4.00 1.20
145 Greg Maddux PT SP 4.00 1.20
146 Chipper Jones PT SP 2.50 .75
147 Kenny Lofton PT SP 1.00 .30
148 Albert Belle PT SP 1.00 .30
149 Barry Bonds PT SP 6.00 1.80
150 V.Guerrero PT SP 2.50 .75
151 Tony Gwynn PT SP 3.00 .90
152 Derek Jeter PT SP 6.00 1.80
153 Jeff Bagwell PT SP 1.50 .45
154 Juan Gonzalez PT SP 1.50 .45
155 N.Garciaparra PT SP 4.00 1.20
156 Andruw Jones PT SP 1.00 .30
157 Hideo Nomo PT SP 2.50 .75
158 Roger Clemens PT SP 5.00 1.50
159 Mark McGwire PT SP 6.00 1.80
160 Scott Rolen PT SP 2.50 .75
161 Travis Lee TLU SP 1.00 .30
162 Ben Grieve TLU SP 1.00 .30
163 Jose Guillen TLU SP 1.00 .30
164 Mike Piazza TLU SP 4.00 1.20
165 Kevin Appier TLU SP 1.00 .30
166 M.Grissom TLU SP 1.00 .30
167 Rusty Greer TLU SP 1.00 .30
168 Ken Caminiti TLU SP 1.00 .30
169 Craig Biggio TLU SP 1.50 .45
170 K.Griffey Jr. TLU SP 4.00 1.20
171 Larry Walker TLU SP 1.50 .45
172 Barry Larkin TLU SP 1.50 .45
173 A.Galarraga TLU SP 1.00 .30
174 Wade Boggs TLU SP 1.50 .45
175 Sammy Sosa TLU SP 4.00 1.20
176 T.Dunwoody TLU SP 1.00 .30
177 Jim Thome TLU SP 2.50 .75
178 Paul Molitor TLU SP 1.50 .45
179 Tony Clark TLU SP 1.00 .30
180 Jose Cruz Jr. TLU SP 1.00 .30
181 Darin Erstad TLU SP 1.00 .30
182 Barry Bonds TLU SP 6.00 1.80
183 Vlad.Guerrero TLU SP 2.50 .75
184 Scott Rolen TLU SP 2.50 .75
185 M.McGwire TLU SP 6.00 1.80
186 N.Garciaparra TLU SP 4.00 1.20
187 Gary Sheffield TLU SP 1.00 .30
188 Cal Ripken TLU SP 8.00 2.40
189 F.Thomas TLU SP 2.50 .75
190 Andy Pettitte TLU SP 1.50 .45
191 Paul Konerko SP 2.00 .60
192 Todd Helton SP 3.00 .90
193 Mark Kotsay SP 2.00 .60
194 Brad Fullmer SP 2.00 .60
195 K.Millwood SP RC 10.00 3.00
196 David Ortiz SP 8.00 2.40
197 Kerry Wood SP 5.00 1.50
198 Miguel Tejada SP 2.00 .60
199 Fernando Tatis SP 2.00 .60
200 Jaret Wright SP 2.00 .60
201 Ben Grieve SP 2.00 .60
202 Travis Lee SP 2.00 .60
203 Wes Helms SP 2.00 .60
204 Geoff Jenkins SP 10.00 3.00
205 Russell Branyan SP 2.00 .60
206 Esteban Yan SP RC 4.00 1.20
207 Ben Ford SP RC 2.50 .75
208 Rich Butler SP RC 2.50 .75
209 Ryan Jackson SP RC 2.50 .75
210 A.J. Hinch SP 2.00 .60
211 M.Ordonez SP RC 40.00 12.00
212 Dave Dellucci SP RC 6.00 1.80
213 Billy McMillon SP 2.00 .60
214 Mike Lowell SP RC 15.00 4.50
215 Todd Erdos SP RC 2.50 .75
216 C.Mendoza SP RC 2.50 .75
217 F.Catalanotto SP RC 6.00 1.80
218 Julio Ramirez SP RC 4.00 1.20
219 John Halama SP RC 4.00 1.20
220 Wilson Delgado SP 2.00 .60
221 Mike Judd SP RC 4.00 1.20
222 Rolando Arrojo SP RC 4.00 1.20
223 Jason LaRue SP RC 4.00 1.20
224 Manny Aybar SP RC 4.00 1.20
225 Jorge Velandia SP 2.00 .60
226 Mike Kinkade SP RC 4.00 1.20
227 Carlos Lee SP RC 10.00 3.00
228 Bobby Hughes SP 2.00 .60
229 R.Christenson SP RC 2.50 .75
230 Masato Yoshii SP RC 6.00 1.80
231 Richard Hidalgo .30 .09
232 Rafael Medina .30 .09
233 Damian Jackson .30 .09
234 Derek Lowe .30 .09
235 Mario Valdez .30 .09
236 Eli Marrero .30 .09
237 Juan Encarnacion .30 .09
238 Livan Hernandez .30 .09
239 Bruce Chen .30 .09
240 Eric Milton .30 .09
241 Jason Varitek .75 .23
242 Scott Elarton .30 .09
243 Manuel Barrios RC .30 .09
244 Mike Caruso .30 .09
245 Tom Evans .30 .09
246 Pat Cline .30 .09
247 Matt Clement .30 .09
248 Karim Garcia .30 .09
249 Richie Sexson .30 .09
250 Sidney Ponson .30 .09
251 Randall Simon .30 .09
252 Tony Saunders .30 .09
253 Javier Valentin .30 .09
254 Danny Clyburn .30 .09
255 Michael Coleman .30 .09
256 Hanley Frias RC .30 .09
257 Miguel Cairo .30 .09
258 Rob Stanifer RC .30 .09
259 Lou Collier .30 .09
260 Abraham Nunez .30 .09
261 Ricky Ledee .30 .09
262 Carl Pavano .50 .15
263 Derrek Lee .30 .09
264 Jeff Abbott .30 .09
265 Bob Abreu .30 .09
266 Bartolo Colon .30 .09
267 Mike Drumright .30 .09
268 Daryle Ward .30 .09
269 Gabe Alvarez .30 .09
270 Josh Booty .30 .09
271 Damian Moss .30 .09
272 Brian Rose .30 .09
273 Jarrod Washburn .30 .09
274 Bobby Estalella .30 .09
275 Enrique Wilson .30 .09
276 Derrick Gibson .30 .09
277 Ken Cloude .30 .09
278 Kevin Witt .30 .09
279 Donnie Sadler .30 .09
280 Sean Casey .30 .09
281 Jacob Cruz .30 .09
282 Ron Wright .30 .09
283 Jeremi Gonzalez .30 .09
284 Desi Relaford .30 .09
285 Bobby Smith .30 .09
286 Javier Vazquez .30 .09
287 Steve Woodard .30 .09
288 Greg Norton .30 .09
289 Cliff Politte .30 .09
290 Felix Heredia .30 .09
291 Braden Looper .30 .09
292 Felix Martinez .30 .09
293 Brian Meadows .30 .09
294 Edwin Diaz .30 .09
295 Pat Watkins .30 .09
296 Marc Pisciotta RC .30 .09
297 Rick Gorecki .30 .09
298 DaRond Stovall .30 .09
299 Andy Larkin .30 .09
300 Felix Rodriguez .30 .09
301 Blake Stein SP 2.50 .75
302 John Rocker SP RC 6.00 1.80
303 J.Baughman SP RC 4.00 1.20
304 Jesus Sanchez SP RC 6.00 1.80
305 Randy Winn SP 2.50 .75
306 Lou Merloni SP 2.50 .75
307 Jim Parque SP RC 6.00 1.80
308 Dennis Reyes SP 2.50 .75
309 O.Hernandez SP RC 15.00 4.50
310 Jason Johnson SP 2.50 .75
311 Torii Hunter SP 2.50 .75
312 M.Piazza Marlins SP 10.00 3.00
313 Mike Frank SP RC 4.00 1.20
314 Troy Glaus SP RC 80.00 24.00
315 Jin Ho Cho SP RC 6.00 1.80
316 Ruben Mateo SP RC 6.00 1.80
317 Ryan Minor SP RC 6.00 1.80
318 Aramis Ramirez SP 2.50 .75
319 Adrian Beltre SP 6.00 1.80
320 Matt Anderson SP RC 6.00 1.80
321 Gabe Kapler SP RC 10.00 3.00
322 Jeremy Giambi SP RC 6.00 1.80
323 Carlos Beltran SP 8.00 2.40
324 Dermal Brown SP 2.50 .75
325 Ben Davis SP 2.50 .75
326 Eric Chavez SP 2.50 .75
327 Bobby Howry SP RC 6.00 1.80
328 Roy Halladay SP 2.50 .75
329 George Lombard SP 2.50 .75
330 Michael Barrett SP 2.50 .75
331 F. Seguignol SP RC 4.00 1.20
332 J.D. Drew SP RC 50.00 15.00
333 Odalis Perez SP RC 15.00 4.50
334 Alex Cora SP RC 6.00 1.80
335 P.Polanco SP RC 6.00 1.80
336 Armando Rios SP RC 6.00 1.80
337 Sammy Sosa HR SP 10.00 3.00
338 Mark McGwire HR SP 15.00 4.50
339 Sammy Sosa 12.00 3.60
Mark McGwire CL SP

1998 Leaf Rookies and Stars Longevity

Randomly inserted in packs, this 339-card set is a parallel to the Leaf Rookies and Stars base set. The set is serially numbered to 50 (although only 49 sets were actually produced because the first set - cards numbered "1/50" were given a holographic foil coating) and printed on foil board with foil stamping.

Nm-Mt Ex-Mt
*STARS 1-130/231-300: 15X TO 40X BASIC
*ROOKIES 1-130/231-300: 20X TO 50X BASIC
*STARS 131-190: 3X TO 8X BASIC
*STARS 191-230: 3X TO 8X BASIC
*ROOKIES 191-230: 1.5X TO 4X BASIC
*STARS 301-339: 2.5X TO 6X BASIC
*ROOKIES 301-339: 1.25X TO 3X BASIC

1998 Leaf Rookies and Stars True Blue

Randomly inserted in packs, this 339-card set is a parallel to the Leaf Rookies and Stars base set. Only 500 sets were printed (though the cards are not serial numbered - instead, they say "1 of 500" on back) and each card features blue foil stamping accents.

Nm-Mt Ex-Mt
*STARS 1-130/231-300: 6X TO 15X BASIC
*ROOKIES 1-130/231-300: 3X TO 8X BASIC CARDS
*LO SP STARS 131-190: 1X TO 2.5X BASIC
*LO SP STARS 191-230: 2X TO 5X BASIC
*ROOKIES 191-230: .5X TO 1.2X BASIC
*STARS 301-339: .75X TO 2X BASIC
*ROOKIES 301-339: .4X TO 1X BASIC

1998 Leaf Rookies and Stars Crosstraining

Randomly inserted in packs, this 10-card set is an insert to the Leaf Rookies and Stars brand. The set is sequentially numbered to 1000. The cards are printed on foil board. Each card front highlights a color action player photo surrounded by a crosstraining shoe sole design. The same player is highlighted on the back with information on his different skills.

Nm-Mt Ex-Mt
COMPLETE SET (10) 120.00 36.00
1 Kenny Lofton 4.00 1.20

2 Ken Griffey Jr. 15.00 4.50
3 Alex Rodriguez 15.00 4.50
4 Greg Maddux 15.00 4.50
5 Barry Bonds 25.00 7.50
6 Ivan Rodriguez 10.00 3.00
7 Chipper Jones 10.00 3.00
8 Jeff Bagwell 6.00 1.80
9 Nomar Garciaparra 15.00 4.50
10 Derek Jeter 25.00 7.50

1998 Leaf Rookies and Stars Crusade Update Green

Randomly inserted in packs, this 30-card set is an insert to the Leaf Rookies and Stars brand and was intended as an update to the 100 Crusade insert cards seeded in 1998 Donruss Update, 1998 Leaf and 1998 Donruss packs (thus the numbering 101-130). The set is sequentially numbered to 250. The fronts feature color action photos placed on a background of a Crusade shield design. The set features three parallel versions printed with a "Spectra-tech" holographic technology. First year serial-numbered cards of Kevin Millwood and Magglio Ordonez are featured in this set.

	Nm-Mt	Ex-Mt
COMPLETE SET (30)	300.00	90.00
101 Richard Hidalgo	10.00	3.00
102 Paul Konerko	15.00	4.50
103 Miguel Tejada	15.00	4.50
104 Fernando Tatis	10.00	3.00
105 Travis Lee	10.00	3.00
106 Wes Helms	10.00	3.00
107 Rich Butler	10.00	3.00
108 Mark Kotsay	10.00	3.00
109 Eli Marrero	10.00	3.00
110 David Ortiz	25.00	7.50
111 Juan Encarnacion	10.00	3.00
112 Jaret Wright	10.00	3.00
113 Livan Hernandez	10.00	3.00
114 Ron Wright	10.00	3.00
115 Ryan Christenson	10.00	3.00
116 Eric Milton	10.00	3.00
117 Brad Fullmer	10.00	3.00
118 Karim Garcia	10.00	3.00
119 Abraham Nunez	10.00	3.00
120 Ricky Ledee	10.00	3.00
121 Carl Pavano	20.00	4.50
122 Derrek Lee	15.00	4.50
123 A.J. Hinch	10.00	3.00
124 Brian Rose	10.00	3.00
125 Bobby Estalella	10.00	3.00
126 Kevin Millwood	25.00	7.50
127 Kerry Wood	25.00	7.50
128 Sean Casey	15.00	4.50
129 Russell Branyan	10.00	3.00
130 Magglio Ordonez	40.00	12.00

1998 Leaf Rookies and Stars Extreme Measures

Randomly inserted in packs, this 10-card set is an insert to the Leaf Rookies and Stars brand. The cards are printed on foil board and sequentially numbered to 1000. However, a parallel version was created wherby a specific amount of each card was die cut to a featured statistic. The result, was varying print runs of the non-die cut cards. Specific print runs for each card are provided in our checklist after the player's name. Card fronts feature color action photos and highlights the featured player's extreme statistics.

	Nm-Mt	Ex-Mt
COMPLETE SET (10)	120.00	36.00
1 Ken Griffey Jr./944	15.00	4.50
2 Frank Thomas/653	10.00	3.00
3 Tony Gwynn/628	12.00	3.60
4 Mark McGwire/942	25.00	7.50
5 Larry Walker/280	6.00	1.80
6 Mike Piazza/960	15.00	4.50
7 Roger Clemens/708	20.00	6.00
8 Greg Maddux/980	15.00	4.50
9 Jeff Bagwell/873	6.00	1.80
10 Nomar Garciaparra/989	15.00	4.50

1998 Leaf Rookies and Stars Extreme Measures Die Cuts

Randomly inserted in packs, this 10-card set is a parallel insert to the Leaf Rookies and Stars Extreme Measures set. The set is sequentially numbered to 1000. The low serial numbered cards are die-cut to showcase a specific statistic for each player. For example, Ken Griffey hit 56 home runs last year, so the 1st 56 of his cards are die-cut and cards serial numbered from 57 through 1000 are not.

	Nm-Mt	Ex-Mt
NO PRICING ON 11 OR LESS		
1 Ken Griffey Jr./56	50.00	15.00
2 Frank Thomas/347	15.00	4.50
3 Tony Gwynn/372	15.00	4.50
4 Mark McGwire/58	80.00	24.00
5 Larry Walker/720	10.00	3.00
6 Mike Piazza/40	50.00	15.00
7 Roger Clemens/292	25.00	7.50
8 Greg Maddux/20		
9 Jeff Bagwell/127	20.00	6.00
10 Nomar Garciaparra/11		

1998 Leaf Rookies and Stars Freshman Orientation

Randomly inserted in packs, this 20-card set is an insert to the Leaf Rookies and Stars brand. The set is sequentially numbered to 5000 and printed with holographic foil. The fronts feature color photos of the top up and coming stars in the game today surrounded by a background of banners and baseballs. The backs highlight the date of the featured player's Major League debut.

	Nm-Mt	Ex-Mt
COMPLETE SET (20)	25.00	7.50
1 Todd Helton	2.00	.60
2 Ben Grieve	1.00	.30
3 Travis Lee	1.00	.30
4 Paul Konerko	1.50	.45
5 Jaret Wright	1.00	.30
6 Livan Hernandez	1.00	.30
7 Brad Fullmer	1.00	.30
8 Carl Pavano	2.00	.45
9 Richard Hidalgo	1.00	.30
10 Miguel Tejada	1.50	.45
11 Mark Kotsay	1.00	.30
12 David Ortiz	3.00	.90
13 Juan Encarnacion	1.00	.30
14 Fernando Tatis	1.00	.30
15 Kevin Millwood	3.00	.90
16 Kerry Wood	3.00	.90
17 Magglio Ordonez	5.00	1.50
18 Derrek Lee	1.50	.45
19 Jose Cruz Jr.	1.00	.30
20 A.J. Hinch	1.00	.30

1998 Leaf Rookies and Stars Great American Heroes

Randomly inserted in packs, this 20-card set is an insert to the Leaf Rookies and Stars brand. The set is sequentially numbered to 2500 and stamped with holographic foil. The fronts feature color player photos placed in an open star with "Great American Heroes" written in the upper right corner. In remembrance of his turbulent 1998 season, Mike Piazza is featured on three different versions (pictured separately as a Dodger, Marlin and Met).

	Nm-Mt	Ex-Mt
COMPLETE SET (20)	150.00	45.00
1 Frank Thomas	6.00	1.80
2 Cal Ripken	20.00	6.00
3 Ken Griffey Jr.	10.00	3.00
4 Alex Rodriguez	10.00	3.00
5 Greg Maddux	10.00	3.00
6 Mike Piazza Dodgers	10.00	3.00
6B Mike Piazza Marlins	10.00	3.00
6C Mike Piazza Mets	10.00	3.00
7 Chipper Jones	6.00	1.80
8 Tony Gwynn	8.00	2.40
9 Jeff Bagwell	4.00	1.20
10 Juan Gonzalez	4.00	1.20
11 Hideo Nomo	6.00	1.80
12 Roger Clemens	12.00	3.60
13 Mark McGwire	15.00	4.50
14 Barry Bonds	15.00	4.50
15 Kenny Lofton	2.50	.75
16 Larry Walker	4.00	1.20
17 Paul Molitor	4.00	1.20
18 Wade Boggs	4.00	1.20
19 Barry Larkin	4.00	1.20
20 Andres Galarraga	2.50	.75

1998 Leaf Rookies and Stars Greatest Hits

Randomly inserted in packs, this 20-card set features color photos of the season's great rookies as well as stars of the game. The backs carry player information. Only 2500 serially numbered sets were produced.

	Nm-Mt	Ex-Mt
COMPLETE SET (20)	120.00	36.00
1 Ken Griffey Jr.	10.00	3.00
2 Frank Thomas	6.00	1.80
3 Cal Ripken	20.00	6.00
4 Alex Rodriguez	10.00	3.00
5 Ben Grieve	6.00	1.80
6 Mike Piazza	10.00	3.00
7 Chipper Jones	6.00	1.80
8 Tony Gwynn	8.00	2.40
9 Derek Jeter	15.00	4.50
10 Jeff Bagwell	4.00	1.20
11 Tino Martinez	4.00	1.20
12 Juan Gonzalez	4.00	1.20
13 Nomar Garciaparra	10.00	3.00
14 Mark McGwire	15.00	4.50
15 Scott Rolen	6.00	1.80
16 David Justice	2.50	.75
17 Darin Erstad	2.50	.75
18 Mo Vaughn	2.50	.75
19 Ivan Rodriguez	6.00	1.80
20 Travis Lee	4.00	1.20

1998 Leaf Rookies and Stars Home Run Derby

Randomly inserted in packs, this 20-card set is an insert to the Leaf Rookies and Stars brand. The set is sequentially numbered to 2500 and printed on foil board. The card fronts feature color player photos of today's top homerun hitters surrounded by a nostalgic bordered background that takes a look at the TV show from the 50's with the same name.

	Nm-Mt	Ex-Mt
COMPLETE SET (20)	100.00	30.00
1 Tino Martinez	4.00	1.20
2 Jim Thome	6.00	1.80
3 Larry Walker	4.00	1.20
4 Tony Clark	2.50	.75
5 Jose Cruz Jr.	2.50	.75
6 Barry Bonds	15.00	4.50
7 Scott Rolen	6.00	1.80
8 Paul Konerko	2.50	.75
9 Travis Lee	2.50	.75
10 Todd Helton	6.00	1.80
11 Mark McGwire	15.00	4.50
12 Andruw Jones	2.50	.75
13 Nomar Garciaparra	10.00	3.00
14 Juan Gonzalez	4.00	1.20
15 Jeff Bagwell	4.00	1.20
16 Chipper Jones	6.00	1.80
17 Mike Piazza	10.00	3.00
18 Frank Thomas	6.00	1.80
19 Ken Griffey Jr.	10.00	3.00
20 Albert Belle	2.50	.75

1998 Leaf Rookies and Stars Leaf MVP's

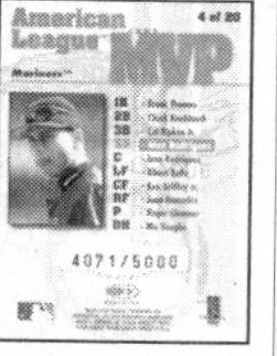

Randomly inserted in packs, this 20-card set is an insert to the Leaf Rookies and Stars brand. Each card is printed on foil board, with a red background and sequentially numbered to 5000 - although the first 500 of each card was die cut for a parallel set. Thus, only cards serial numbered from 501 through 5000 are featured in this set. The fronts feature color action photos on top of an "MVP" logo in the background.

	Nm-Mt	Ex-Mt
COMPLETE SET (20)	80.00	24.00
*PENNANT ED: 1.5X TO 4X BASIC LEAF MVP		
PENNANT ED.1ST 500 SERIAL #'d SETS		
RANDOM INSERTS IN PACKS		
1 Frank Thomas	4.00	1.20
2 Chuck Knoblauch	1.50	.45
3 Cal Ripken	12.00	3.60
4 Alex Rodriguez	6.00	1.80
5 Ivan Rodriguez	4.00	1.20
6 Albert Belle	1.50	.45
7 Ken Griffey Jr.	6.00	1.80
8 Juan Gonzalez	2.50	.75
9 Roger Clemens	8.00	2.40
10 Mo Vaughn	1.50	.45
11 Jeff Bagwell	2.50	.75
12 Craig Biggio	2.50	.75
13 Chipper Jones	4.00	1.20
14 Barry Larkin	2.50	.75
15 Mike Piazza	6.00	1.80
16 Barry Bonds	10.00	3.00
17 Andruw Jones	1.50	.45
18 Tony Gwynn	5.00	1.50
19 Greg Maddux	6.00	1.80
20 Mark McGwire	10.00	3.00

1998 Leaf Rookies and Stars Major League Hard Drives

Randomly inserted in packs, this 20-card set is an insert to the Leaf Rookies and Stars brand. The set is printed with holographic foil stamping and sequentially numbered to 2500. The fronts feature color action photos of some of today's hottest hitting machines placed in a baseball diamond background. In remembrance of his turbulent 1998 season, Mike Piazza is featured on three different versions (pictured separately as a Dodger, Marlin and Met). All three versions of

the Piazza card had 2500 cards printed.

	Nm-Mt	Ex-Mt
COMPLETE SET (20)	150.00	45.00
1 Jeff Bagwell	4.00	1.20
2 Juan Gonzalez	4.00	1.20
3 Nomar Garciaparra	10.00	3.00
4 Ken Griffey Jr.	10.00	3.00
5 Frank Thomas	6.00	1.80
6 Cal Ripken	20.00	6.00
7 Alex Rodriguez	10.00	3.00
8 Mike Piazza Dodgers	10.00	3.00
8B Mike Piazza Marlins	10.00	3.00
8C Mike Piazza Mets	10.00	3.00
9 Chipper Jones	6.00	1.80
10 Tony Gwynn	8.00	2.40
11 Derek Jeter	15.00	4.50
12 Mo Vaughn	2.50	.75
13 Ben Grieve	6.00	1.80
14 Manny Ramirez	4.00	1.20
15 Vladimir Guerrero	6.00	1.80
16 Scott Rolen	6.00	1.80
17 Darin Erstad	2.50	.75
18 Kenny Lofton	2.50	.75
19 Brad Fullmer	2.50	.75
20 David Justice	2.50	.75

1998 Leaf Rookies and Stars Standing Ovations

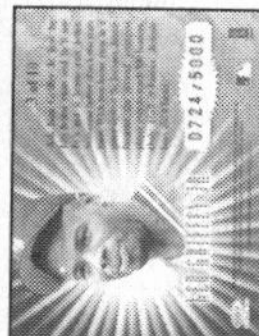

Randomly inserted in packs, this 10-card set is an insert to the Leaf Rookies and Stars brand set. The set is sequentially numbered to 5000 and printed with holographic foil stamping. The fronts feature full-bleed color photos. The featured player's ovation deserved accomplishments are found lining the bottom of the card along with his name and team.

	Nm-Mt	Ex-Mt
COMPLETE SET (10)	50.00	15.00
1 Barry Bonds	10.00	3.00
2 Mark McGwire	10.00	3.00
3 Ken Griffey Jr.	6.00	1.80
4 Frank Thomas	4.00	1.20
5 Tony Gwynn	5.00	1.50
6 Cal Ripken	12.00	3.60
7 Greg Maddux	6.00	1.80
8 Roger Clemens	8.00	2.40
9 Paul Molitor	2.50	.75
10 Ivan Rodriguez	4.00	1.20

1998 Leaf Rookies and Stars Ticket Masters

Randomly inserted in packs, this 20-card set is an insert to the Leaf Rookies and Stars base set. The set is sequentially numbered to 2500, but the first 250 cards were die cut for a parallel set. This double-sided set is printed on foil board and features color photos of players from the same team.

	Nm-Mt	Ex-Mt
COMPLETE SET (20)	150.00	45.00
*DIE CUTS: 1.25X TO 3X BASIC TICKET		
DIE CUTS 1ST 250 SERIAL #'d SETS		
RANDOM INSERTS IN PACKS		
1 Ken Griffey Jr. Alex Rodriguez	12.00	3.60
2 Frank Thomas Albert Belle	8.00	2.40
3 Cal Ripken Roberto Alomar	25.00	7.50
4 Greg Maddux Chipper Jones	12.00	3.60
5 Tony Gwynn Ken Caminiti	10.00	3.00
6 Derek Jeter Andy Pettitte	20.00	6.00
7 Jeff Bagwell Craig Biggio	5.00	1.50
8 Juan Gonzalez Ivan Rodriguez	8.00	2.40
9 Nomar Garciaparra Mo Vaughn	12.00	3.60
10 Vladimir Guerrero Brad Fullmer	8.00	2.40
11 Andruw Jones Andres Galarraga	3.00	.90
12 Tino Martinez Chuck Knoblauch	5.00	1.50
13 Raul Mondesi Paul Konerko	3.00	.90
14 Roger Clemens Jose Cruz Jr.	15.00	4.50
15 Mark McGwire Brian Jordan	20.00	6.00
16 Kenny Lofton Manny Ramirez	5.00	1.50
17 Larry Walker Todd Helton	5.00	1.50
18 Darin Erstad Tim Salmon	3.00	.90
19 Travis Lee Matt Williams	3.00	.90
20 Ben Grieve Jason Giambi	3.00	.90

2001 Leaf Rookies and Stars

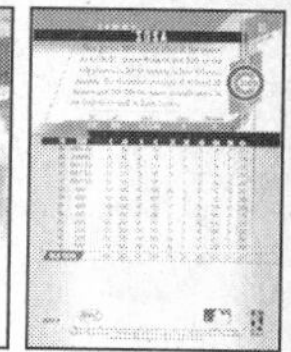

This 300 card set was issued in five card packs. All cards numbered over 100 were shortprinted. Cards numbered 101-200 were inserted at a rate of one in four while cards numbered 201-300 were inserted at a rate of one in 24.

	Nm-Mt	Ex-Mt
COMP.SET w/o SP'S (100)	20.00	6.00
COMMON CARD (1-100)	.30	.09
COMMON (101-200)	3.00	.90
COMMON (201-300)	8.00	2.40
1 Alex Rodriguez	1.25	.35
2 Derek Jeter	2.00	.60
3 Aramis Ramirez	.30	.09
4 Cliff Floyd	.30	.09
5 Nomar Garciaparra	1.25	.35
6 Craig Biggio	.50	.15
7 Ivan Rodriguez	.75	.23
8 Cal Ripken	2.50	.75
9 Fred McGriff	.50	.15
10 Chipper Jones	.75	.23
11 Roberto Alomar	.50	.15
12 Moises Alou	.30	.09
13 Freddy Garcia	.30	.09
14 Bobby Abreu	.30	.09
15 Shawn Green	.30	.09
16 Jason Giambi	.30	.09
17 Todd Helton	.50	.15
18 Robert Fick	.30	.09
19 Tony Gwynn	1.00	.30
20 Luis Gonzalez	.30	.09
21 Sean Casey	.30	.09
22 Roger Clemens	1.50	.45
23 Brian Giles	.30	.09
24 Manny Ramirez	.50	.15
25 Barry Bonds	2.00	.60
26 Richard Hidalgo	.30	.09
27 Vladimir Guerrero	.75	.23
28 Kevin Brown UER Batting headers for stats	.30	.09
29 Mike Sweeney	.30	.09
30 Ken Griffey Jr.	1.25	.35
31 Mike Piazza	1.25	.35
32 Richie Sexson	.30	.09
33 Matt Morris	.30	.09
34 Jorge Posada	.50	.15
35 Eric Chavez	.30	.09
36 Mark Buehrle	.30	.09
37 Jeff Bagwell	.50	.15
38 Curt Schilling	.30	.09
39 Bartolo Colon	.30	.09
40 Mark Quinn	.30	.09
41 Tony Clark	.30	.09
42 Brad Radke	.30	.09
43 Gary Sheffield	.30	.09
44 Doug Mientkiewicz	.30	.09
45 Pedro Martinez	.75	.23
46 Carlos Lee	.30	.09
47 Troy Glaus	.30	.09
48 Preston Wilson	.30	.09
49 Phil Nevin	.30	.09
50 Chan Ho Park	.30	.09
51 Randy Johnson	.75	.23
52 Jermaine Dye	.30	.09
53 Terrence Long	.30	.09
54 Joe Mays	.30	.09
55 Scott Rolen	.75	.23
56 Miguel Tejada	.30	.09
57 Jim Thome	.75	.23
58 Jose Vidro	.30	.09
59 Gabe Kapler	.30	.09
60 Darin Erstad	.30	.09
61 Jim Edmonds	.30	.09
62 Jarrod Washburn	.30	.09
63 Tom Glavine	.50	.15
64 Adrian Beltre	.50	.15
65 Sammy Sosa	1.25	.35
66 Juan Gonzalez	.50	.15
67 Rafael Furcal	.30	.09
68 Mike Mussina	.50	.15
69 Mark McGwire	2.00	.60
70 Ryan Klesko	.30	.09
71 Raul Mondesi	.30	.09
72 Trot Nixon	.30	.09
73 Barry Larkin	.50	.15
74 Rafael Palmeiro	.50	.15
75 Mark Mulder	.30	.09
76 Carlos Delgado	.30	.09
77 Mike Hampton	.30	.09
78 Carl Everett	.30	.09
79 Paul Konerko	.30	.09
80 Larry Walker	.50	.15
81 Kerry Wood	.75	.23
82 Frank Thomas	.75	.23
83 Andruw Jones	.30	.09
84 Eric Milton	.30	.09
85 Ben Grieve	.30	.09
86 Carlos Beltran	.50	.15
87 Tim Hudson	.30	.09
88 Hideo Nomo	.75	.23
89 Greg Maddux	1.25	.35

90 Edgar Martinez .50 .15
91 Lance Berkman .30 .09
92 Pat Burrell .30 .09
93 Jeff Kent .30 .09
94 Magglio Ordonez .30 .09
95 Cristian Guzman .30 .09
96 Jose Canseco .75 .23
97 J.D. Drew .30 .09
98 Bernie Williams .50 .15
99 Kazuhiro Sasaki .30 .09
100 Rickey Henderson .75 .23
101 Wilson Guzman RC 3.00 .90
102 Nick Neugebauer 3.00 .90
103 Lance Davis RC 3.00 .90
104 Felipe Lopez 3.00 .90
105 Toby Hall 3.00 .90
106 Jack Cust 3.00 .90
107 Jason Karnuth RC 3.00 .90
108 Bart Miadich RC 3.00 .90
109 Brian Roberts RC 3.00 .90
110 Brandon Larson RC 3.00 .90
111 Sean Douglass RC 3.00 .90
112 Joe Crede 3.00 .90
113 Tim Redding 3.00 .90
114 Adam Johnson 3.00 .90
115 Marcus Giles 3.00 .90
116 Jose Ortiz 3.00 .90
117 Jose Mieses RC 3.00 .90
118 Nick Maness RC 3.00 .90
119 Les Walrond RC 3.00 .90
120 Travis Phelps RC 3.00 .90
121 Troy Mattes RC 3.00 .90
122 Carlos Garcia RC 3.00 .90
123 Bill Ortega RC 3.00 .90
124 Gene Altman RC 3.00 .90
125 Nate Frese RC 3.00 .90
126 Alfonso Soriano 5.00 1.50
127 Jose Nunez RC 3.00 .90
128 Bob File RC 3.00 .90
129 Dan Wright 3.00 .90
130 Nick Johnson 3.00 .90
131 Brent Abernathy 3.00 .90
132 Steve Green RC 3.00 .90
133 Billy Sylvester RC 3.00 .90
134 Scott MacRae RC 3.00 .90
135 Kris Keller RC 3.00 .90
136 Scott Stewart RC 3.00 .90
137 Henry Mateo RC 3.00 .90
138 Timo Perez 3.00 .90
139 Nate Teut RC 3.00 .90
140 Jason Michaels RC 3.00 .90
141 Junior Spivey RC 5.00 1.50
142 Carlos Pena 3.00 .90
143 Wilmy Caceres RC 3.00 .90
144 David Lundquist 3.00 .90
145 Jack Wilson RC 8.00 2.40
146 Jeremy Fikac RC 3.00 .90
147 Alex Escobar 3.00 .90
148 Abraham Nunez 3.00 .90
149 Xavier Nady 3.00 .90
150 Michael Cuddyer 3.00 .90
151 Greg Miller RC 3.00 .90
152 Eric Munson 3.00 .90
153 Aubrey Huff 3.00 .90
154 Tim Christman RC 3.00 .90
155 Erick Almonte RC 3.00 .90
156 Mike Penney RC 3.00 .90
157 Delvin James RC 3.00 .90
158 Ben Sheets 5.00 1.50
159 Jason Hart 3.00 .90
160 Jose Acevedo RC 3.00 .90
161 Will Ohman RC 3.00 .90
162 Erik Hiljus RC 3.00 .90
163 Juan Moreno RC 3.00 .90
164 Mike Koplove RC 3.00 .90
165 Pedro Santana RC 3.00 .90
166 Jimmy Rollins 3.00 .90
167 Matt White RC 3.00 .90
168 Cesar Crespo RC 3.00 .90
169 Carlos Hernandez 3.00 .90
170 Chris George 3.00 .90
171 Brad Voyles RC 3.00 .90
172 Luis Pineda RC 3.00 .90
173 Carlos Zambrano RC 5.00 1.50
174 Nate Cornejo 3.00 .90
175 Jason Smith RC 3.00 .90
176 Craig Monroe RC 3.00 .90
177 Cody Ransom RC 3.00 .90
178 John Grabow RC 3.00 .90
179 Pedro Feliz 3.00 .90
180 Jeremy Owens RC 3.00 .90
181 Kurt Ainsworth 3.00 .90
182 Luis Lopez 3.00 .90
183 Stubby Clapp RC 3.00 .90
184 Ryan Freel RC 3.00 .90
185 Duaner Sanchez RC 3.00 .90
186 Jason Jennings 3.00 .90
187 Kyle Lohse RC 5.00 1.50
188 Jerrod Riggan RC 3.00 .90
189 Joe Beimel RC 3.00 .90
190 Nick Punto RC 3.00 .90
191 Willie Harris RC 3.00 .90
192 Ryan Jensen RC 3.00 .90
193 Adam Pettyjohn RC 3.00 .90
194 Donaldo Mendez RC 3.00 .90
195 Bret Prinz RC 3.00 .90
196 Paul Phillips RC 3.00 .90
197 Brian Lawrence RC 3.00 .90
198 Cesar Izturis 3.00 .90
199 Blaine Neal RC 3.00 .90
200 Josh Fogg RC 8.00 2.40
201 Josh Towers RC 8.00 2.40
202 T.Spooneybarger RC 8.00 2.40
203 Michael Rivera RC 8.00 2.40
204 Juan Cruz RC 8.00 2.40
205 Albert Pujols RC 125.00 38.00
206 Josh Beckett 8.00 2.40
207 Roy Oswalt 10.00 3.00
208 Elpidio Guzman RC 8.00 2.40
209 Horacio Ramirez RC 10.00 3.00
210 Corey Patterson 8.00 2.40
211 Geronimo Gil RC 8.00 2.40
212 Jay Gibbons RC 10.00 3.00
213 O.Woodards RC 8.00 2.40
214 David Espinosa 8.00 2.40
215 Angel Berroa RC 10.00 3.00
216 B.Duckworth RC 8.00 2.40
217 Brian Reith RC 8.00 2.40
218 David Brous RC 8.00 2.40
219 Bud Smith RC 8.00 2.40
220 Ramon Vazquez RC 8.00 2.40
221 Mark Teixeira RC 50.00 15.00
222 Justin Atchley RC 8.00 2.40
223 Tony Cogan RC 8.00 2.40
224 Grant Balfour RC 8.00 2.40
225 Ricardo Rodriguez RC 8.00 2.40
226 Brian Rogers RC 8.00 2.40
227 Adam Dunn 10.00 3.00
228 Wilson Betemit RC 8.00 2.40
229 Juan Diaz RC 8.00 2.40
230 Jackson Melian RC 8.00 2.40
231 Claudio Vargas RC 8.00 2.40
232 Wilkin Ruan RC 8.00 2.40
233 J.Duchscherer RC 8.00 2.40
234 Kevin Olsen RC 8.00 2.40
235 Tony Fiore RC 8.00 2.40
236 Jeremy Affeldt RC 10.00 3.00
237 Mike Maroth RC 8.00 2.40
238 C.C. Sabathia 8.00 2.40
239 Cory Aldridge RC 8.00 2.40
240 Zach Day RC 8.00 2.40
241 Brett Jodie RC 8.00 2.40
242 Winston Abreu RC 8.00 2.40
243 Travis Hafner RC 15.00 4.50
244 Joe Kennedy RC 10.00 3.00
245 Rick Bauer RC 8.00 2.40
246 Mike Young 10.00 3.00
247 Ken Vining RC 8.00 2.40
248 Doug Nickle RC 8.00 2.40
249 Pablo Ozuna 8.00 2.40
250 Dustan Mohr RC 8.00 2.40
251 Ichiro Suzuki RC 60.00 18.00
252 Ryan Drese RC 10.00 3.00
253 Morgan Ensberg RC 10.00 3.00
254 George Perez RC 8.00 2.40
255 Roy Smith RC 8.00 2.40
256 Juan Uribe RC 10.00 3.00
257 Dewon Brazelton RC 10.00 3.00
258 Endy Chavez RC 8.00 2.40
259 Kris Foster 8.00 2.40
260 Eric Knott RC 8.00 2.40
261 Corky Miller RC 8.00 2.40
262 Larry Bigbie 8.00 2.40
263 Andres Torres RC 8.00 2.40
264 Adrian Hernandez RC 8.00 2.40
265 Johnny Estrada RC 15.00 4.50
266 David Williams RC 8.00 2.40
267 Steve Lomasney 8.00 2.40
268 Victor Zambrano RC 10.00 3.00
269 Keith Ginter 8.00 2.40
270 Casey Fossum RC 8.00 2.40
271 Josue Perez RC 8.00 2.40
272 Josh Phelps 8.00 2.40
273 Mark Prior RC 60.00 18.00
274 Brandon Berger RC 8.00 2.40
275 Scott Podsednik RC 20.00 6.00
276 Jorge Julio RC 8.00 2.40
277 Esix Snead RC 8.00 2.40
278 Brandon Knight RC 8.00 2.40
279 Saul Rivera RC 8.00 2.40
280 Benito Baez RC 8.00 2.40
281 Rob MacKowiak RC 10.00 3.00
282 Eric Hinske RC 10.00 3.00
283 Juan Rivera 8.00 2.40
284 Kevin Joseph RC 8.00 2.40
285 Juan A. Pena RC 8.00 2.40
286 Brandon Lyon RC 8.00 2.40
287 Adam Everett 8.00 2.40
288 Eric Valent 8.00 2.40
289 Ken Harvey 8.00 2.40
290 Bert Snow RC 8.00 2.40
291 Wily Mo Pena 8.00 2.40
292 Rafael Soriano RC 10.00 3.00
293 Carlos Valderrama RC 8.00 2.40
294 Christian Parker RC 8.00 2.40
295 Tsuyoshi Shinjo RC 10.00 3.00
296 Martin Vargas RC 8.00 2.40
297 Luke Hudson RC 8.00 2.40
298 Dee Brown 8.00 2.40
299 Alexis Gomez RC 8.00 2.40
300 Angel Santos RC 8.00 2.40

2001 Leaf Rookies and Stars Autographs

Randomly inserted in packs, these 76 cards feature signed cards of some of the prospects and rookies included in the Leaf Rookie and Stars set. According to Donruss/Playoff most players signed 250 cards for inclusion in this product. A few signed 100 cards so we have included that information in our checklist next to the player's name.

Nm-Mt Ex-Mt
107 Jason Karnuth 10.00 3.00
110 Brandon Larson/100 15.00 4.50
117 Jose Mieses 10.00 3.00
118 Nick Maness 10.00 3.00
119 Les Walrond 10.00 3.00
122 Carlos Garcia 10.00 3.00
123 Bill Ortega 10.00 3.00
124 Gene Altman 10.00 3.00
125 Nate Frese 10.00 3.00
130 Nick Johnson/100 25.00 7.50
133 Billy Sylvester 10.00 3.00
135 Kris Keller 10.00 3.00
139 Nate Teut 10.00 3.00
140 Jason Michaels 10.00 3.00
143 Wilmy Caceres 10.00 3.00
145 Jack Wilson/100 50.00 15.00
151 Greg Miller 10.00 3.00
155 Erick Almonte 10.00 3.00
156 Mike Penney 10.00 3.00
157 Delvin James 10.00 3.00
161 Will Ohman 10.00 3.00
167 Matt White 10.00 3.00
180 Jeremy Owens 10.00 3.00
184 Ryan Freel 10.00 3.00
185 Duaner Sanchez 10.00 3.00
193 Adam Pettyjohn/100 25.00 7.50
194 Donaldo Mendez/100 15.00 4.50
196 Paul Phillips 10.00 3.00
197 Brian Lawrence/100 15.00 4.50
199 Blaine Neal 10.00 3.00
201 Josh Towers/100 15.00 4.50
203 Michael Rivera 10.00 3.00
204 Juan Cruz/100 15.00 4.50
205 Albert Pujols SP
207 Roy Oswalt SP 50.00 15.00
208 Elpidio Guzman/100 15.00 4.50
209 Horacio Ramirez 15.00 4.50
210 Corey Patterson SP 30.00 9.00
211 Geronimo Gil 10.00 3.00
212 Jay Gibbons/100 40.00 12.00
213 Orlando Woodards 10.00 3.00
215 Angel Berroa/100 40.00 12.00
216 B. Duckworth/100 15.00 4.50
218 David Brous 10.00 3.00
219 Bud Smith SP 25.00 7.50
221 Mark Teixeira/100 250.00 75.00
223 Tony Cogan 10.00 3.00
225 Ricardo Rodriguez 10.00 3.00
226 Brian Rogers 10.00 3.00
227 Adam Dunn SP 50.00 15.00
228 Wilson Betemit/100 15.00 4.50
231 Claudio Vargas 10.00 3.00
232 Wilkin Ruan 10.00 3.00
234 Kevin Olsen 10.00 3.00
236 Jeremy Affeldt 15.00 4.50
237 Mike Maroth 10.00 3.00
238 C.C. Sabathia SP 30.00 9.00
239 Cory Aldridge 10.00 3.00
240 Zach Day 10.00 3.00
243 Travis Hafner 50.00 15.00
244 Joe Kennedy/100 25.00 7.50
254 George Perez 10.00 3.00
256 Juan Uribe 15.00 4.50
257 Dewon Brazelton/100 40.00 12.00
261 Corky Miller/100 15.00 4.50
263 Andres Torres/100 15.00 4.50
265 Johnny Estrada/100 40.00 12.00
266 David Williams 10.00 3.00
270 Casey Fossum 10.00 3.00
273 Mark Prior/100 400.00 120.00
274 Brandon Berger 10.00 3.00
277 Esix Snead 10.00 3.00
282 Eric Hinske 15.00 4.50
292 Rafael Soriano 15.00 4.50
293 Carlos Valderrama 10.00 3.00
299 Alexis Gomez 10.00 3.00

2001 Leaf Rookies and Stars Longevity

Randomly inserted into packs, these cards parallel the Leaf Rookie and Stars set. Cards numbered 1-100 are serial numbered to 50 while cards numbered 101-300 are serial numbered to 25.

Nm-Mt Ex-Mt
*LONGEVITY: 1-100: 12.5X TO 30X BASIC CARDS

2001 Leaf Rookies and Stars Dress for Success

Inserted one per 96 packs, these 25 cards feature two swatches of game-used memorabilia on each card.

	Nm-Mt	Ex-Mt
DFS-1 Cal Ripken	50.00	15.00
DFS-2 Mike Piazza	25.00	7.50
DFS-3 Barry Bonds	50.00	15.00
DFS-4 Frank Thomas	20.00	6.00
DFS-5 Nomar Garciaparra	30.00	9.00
DFS-6 Richie Sexson	15.00	4.50
DFS-7 Brian Giles	15.00	4.50
DFS-8 Todd Helton	20.00	6.00
DFS-9 Ivan Rodriguez	20.00	6.00
DFS-10 Andruw Jones	15.00	4.50
DFS-11 Juan Gonzalez	20.00	6.00
DFS-12 Vladimir Guerrero	20.00	6.00
DFS-13 Greg Maddux	25.00	7.50
DFS-14 Tony Gwynn	25.00	7.50
DFS-15 Randy Johnson	20.00	6.00
DFS-16 Jeff Bagwell	20.00	6.00
DFS-17 Kerry Wood SP		
DFS-18 Roberto Alomar	20.00	6.00
DFS-19 Chipper Jones	20.00	6.00
DFS-20 Pedro Martinez	20.00	6.00
DFS-21 Shawn Green	15.00	4.50
DFS-22 Magglio Ordonez	15.00	4.50
DFS-23 Darin Erstad SP		
DFS-24 Rafael Palmeiro SP		
DFS-25 Edgar Martinez	20.00	6.00

2001 Leaf Rookies and Stars Dress for Success Prime Cuts

Randomly inserted into packs, these cards parallel the Dress for Success insert set. Each card had a stated print run of 50 serial numbered sets.

	Nm-Mt	Ex-Mt
*PRIME CUTS: 1.25X TO 3X BASIC DRESS		
DFS-17 Kerry Wood	80.00	24.00
DFS-23 Darin Erstad	40.00	12.00
DFS-24 Rafael Palmeiro	50.00	15.00

2001 Leaf Rookies and Stars Freshman Orientation

Inserted into packs at odds of one in 96, these 25 cards feature leading prospects along with a piece of game-used memorabilia. The Dunn, Pujols and Gibbons cards are shortprinted compared to the rest of the set.

	Nm-Mt	Ex-Mt
FO-1 Adam Dunn Bat SP		
FO-2 Josh Towers Pants	10.00	3.00
FO-3 Vernon Wells Jsy	10.00	3.00
FO-4 Corey Patterson Pants	10.00	3.00
FO-5 Albert Pujols Bat SP		
FO-6 Ben Sheets Jsy	15.00	4.50
FO-7 Pedro Feliz Bat	10.00	3.00
FO-8 Keith Ginter Bat	10.00	3.00
FO-9 Luis Rivas Bat	10.00	3.00
FO-10 Andres Torres Bat	10.00	3.00
FO-11 Carlos Valderrama Jsy	10.00	3.00
FO-12 Brandon Inge Jsy	10.00	3.00
FO-13 Jay Gibbons Cap SP		
FO-14 Cesar Izturis Bat	10.00	3.00
FO-15 Marcus Giles Jsy	10.00	3.00
FO-16 Tsuyoshi Shinjo Jsy	15.00	4.50
FO-17 Eric Valent Bat	10.00	3.00
FO-18 David Espinosa Bat	10.00	3.00
FO-19 Aubrey Huff Jsy	10.00	3.00
FO-20 Wilmy Caceres Jsy	10.00	3.00
FO-21 Bud Smith Jsy	10.00	3.00
FO-22 Ricardo Rodriguez Pants	10.00	3.00
FO-23 Wes Helms Jsy	10.00	3.00
FO-24 Jason Hart Bat	10.00	3.00
FO-25 Dee Brown Jsy	10.00	3.00

2001 Leaf Rookies and Stars Freshman Orientation Autographs

Randomly inserted into packs, these 21 cards parallel the Freshman Orientation insert set. Each of these players signed 100 cards or less for this product. If the player signed less than 100 cards we have notated that with an SP in our checklist.

	Nm-Mt	Ex-Mt
FO-1 Adam Dunn Bat SP		
FO-2 Josh Towers Pants SP		
FO-4 Corey Patterson Pants SP		
FO-5 Albert Pujols Bat SP		
FO-6 Ben Sheets Jsy SP		
FO-7 Pedro Feliz Bat	20.00	6.00
FO-8 Keith Ginter Bat	20.00	6.00
FO-9 Luis Rivas Bat	20.00	6.00
FO-10 Andres Torres Bat	20.00	6.00
FO-11 Carlos Valderrama Jsy	20.00	6.00
FO-13 Jay Gibbons Cap	25.00	7.50
FO-14 Cesar Izturis Bat	20.00	6.00
FO-15 Marcus Giles Jsy	20.00	6.00
FO-17 Eric Valent Bat	20.00	6.00
FO-18 David Espinosa Bat	20.00	6.00
FO-19 Aubrey Huff Jsy	20.00	6.00
FO-20 Wilmy Caceres Jsy	20.00	6.00
FO-21 Bud Smith Jsy SP		
FO-22 Ricardo Rodriguez Pants	20.00	6.00
FO-24 Jason Hart Bat	20.00	6.00
FO-25 Dee Brown Jsy	20.00	6.00

2001 Leaf Rookies and Stars Freshman Orientation Class Officers

Randomly inserted into packs, these cards parallel the Freshman Orientation insert set. Each card had a stated print run of 50 serial numbered sets.

	Nm-Mt	Ex-Mt
*CLASS OFFICER: .75X TO 2X BASIC FRESH		
FO-1 Adam Dunn Bat	20.00	6.00
FO-5 Albert Pujols Bat	150.00	45.00
FO-13 Jay Gibbons Cap	20.00	6.00

2001 Leaf Rookies and Stars Great American Treasures

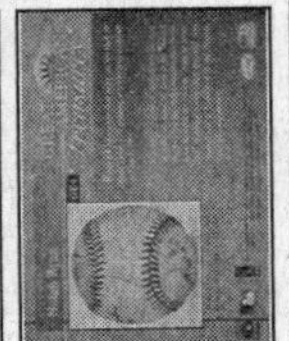

Inserted at a rate of one in 1,120 packs, these 20 cards feature pieces of memorabilia from key moments in a players career.

	Nm-Mt	Ex-Mt
PRINT RUN INFO PROVIDED BY DONRUSS		
CARDS ARE NOT SERIAL-NUMBERED		
NO PRICING ON QTY OF 25 DUE TO SCARCITY		
GT1 B.Bonds HR Jsy/50 *		
GT2 M.Ordonez HR Bat/200 *	25.00	7.50
GT3 D.Jeter 1st Game Ball/25 *		
GT4 N.Ryan 7th No-Hit Ball/25 *		
GT5 S.Sosa June HR Ball/25 *		
GT6 T.Glavine 96 WS Jsy/100 *	50.00	15.00
GT7 I.Rod 99 MVP Bat/200 *	40.00	12.00
GT8 P.Martinez 300 K Ball/25 *		
GT9 M.McGwire 60 HR Ball/25 *		
GT10 T.Williams 517 HR Ball/25 *		
GT11 R.Sandberg 91 AS Bat/200 *	60.00	18.00
GT12 B.Bonds 500 HR Ball/25 *		
GT13 H.Nomo No-Hit Ball/25 *		
GT14 R.Maris 61 HR Ball/25 *		
GT15 T.Cobb 09 WS Ball/25 *		
GT16 H.Killebrew 570 HR Bat/50 *		
GT17 M.Ordonez 00 AS Cap/100 *	40.00	12.00
GT18 W.Boggs WS Bat/200 *	40.00	12.00
GT19 H.Aaron 755 HR Cap/25 *		
GT20 D.Cone Perfect Ball-Ticket/25 *		

2001 Leaf Rookies and Stars Great American Treasures Autograph

This four card parallel to the Great American Treasure set features signed cards by these players on cards relating to a key event in their career. Due to scarcity, no pricing information is provided.

Nm-Mt Ex-Mt
GT6 Tom Glavine 96 WS Jsy
GT11 Ryne Sandberg 91 AS Bat
GT16 Harmon Killebrew 570 HR Bat
GT18 Wade Boggs WS Bat

2001 Leaf Rookies and Stars Players Collection Autographs

Randomly inserted into packs, these three cards feature signed cards of the players along with a memorabilia piece. Due to market scarcity, no pricing is provided.

Nm-Mt Ex-Mt
PC-1 Tony Gwynn Bat
PC-6 Cal Ripken Jsy
PC-7 Cal Ripken Bat

2001 Leaf Rookies and Stars Slideshow

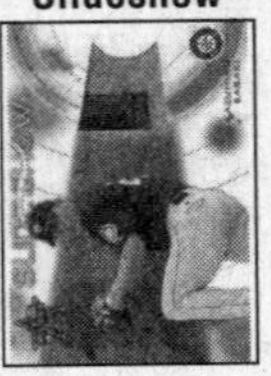

Randomly inserted into packs, each card features a jersey swatch along with a snapshot of major league action. Most players have 100 serial numbered cards but a few have less and we have notated those players with an SP.

	Nm-Mt	Ex-Mt
VIEW MASTER PRINT RUN 25 #'d SETS		
NO V'MASTER PRICING DUE TO SCARCITY		
S-1 Cal Ripken	50.00	15.00
S-2 Chipper Jones SP	25.00	7.50
S-3 Jeff Bagwell	25.00	7.50
S-4 Larry Walker	25.00	7.50
S-5 Greg Maddux SP	25.00	7.50
S-6 Ivan Rodriguez	25.00	7.50
S-7 Andruw Jones SP	15.00	4.50
S-8 Lance Berkman SP	15.00	4.50
S-9 Luis Gonzalez SP	15.00	4.50
S-10 Tony Gwynn	25.00	7.50
S-11 Troy Glaus SP	15.00	4.50
S-12 Todd Helton	25.00	7.50
S-13 Roberto Alomar	25.00	7.50
S-14 Barry Bonds	50.00	15.00
S-15 Vladimir Guerrero SP	25.00	7.50
S-16 Sean Casey SP	15.00	4.50
S-17 Curt Schilling SP	15.00	4.50
S-18 Frank Thomas	25.00	7.50
S-19 Pedro Martinez	25.00	7.50
S-20 Juan Gonzalez	25.00	7.50
S-21 Randy Johnson	25.00	7.50
S-22 Kerry Wood SP	25.00	7.50
S-23 Mike Sweeney	15.00	4.50
S-24 Magglio Ordonez	15.00	4.50
S-25 Kazuhiro Sasaki	15.00	4.50
S-26 Manny Ramirez	25.00	7.50
S-27 Roger Clemens	40.00	12.00
S-28 Albert Pujols SP	100.00	30.00

S-29 Hideo Nomo 25.00 7.50
S-30 Miguel Tejada SP 15.00 4.50

2001 Leaf Rookies and Stars Statistical Standouts

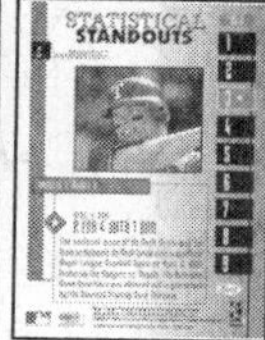

Inserted at packs at a rate of one in 96, these 25 cards feature star players along with a swatch of game-used materials. A few of these cards were printed in shorter quantites than the others and we have notated those with an SP.

Nm-Mt Ex-Mt
*SUPER: 1X TO 2.5X BASIC STAT. STANDOUT
SUPER STATED PRINT RUN 50 SERIAL #'D SETS
RANDOM INSERTS IN PACKS
SS-1 Ichiro Suzuki 40.00 12.00
SS-2 Barry Bonds SP
SS-3 Ivan Rodriguez 15.00 4.50
SS-4 Jeff Bagwell 15.00 4.50
SS-5 Vladimir Guerrero SP
SS-6 Mike Sweeney 10.00 3.00
SS-7 Miguel Tejada 10.00 3.00
SS-8 Mike Piazza SP
SS-9 Darin Erstad 10.00 3.00
SS-10 Alex Rodriguez 25.00 7.50
SS-11 Jason Giambi 10.00 3.00
SS-12 Cal Ripken 40.00 12.00
SS-13 Albert Pujols 60.00 18.00
SS-14 Carlos Delgado 10.00 3.00
SS-15 Rafael Palmeiro 15.00 4.50
SS-16 Lance Berkman 10.00 3.00
SS-17 Luis Gonzalez SP
SS-18 Sammy Sosa SP
SS-19 Andruw Jones SP
SS-20 Derek Jeter 40.00 12.00
SS-21 Edgar Martinez 15.00 4.50
SS-22 Troy Glaus 10.00 3.00
SS-23 Magglio Ordonez 10.00 3.00
SS-24 Mark McGwire 40.00 12.00
SS-25 Manny Ramirez 15.00 4.50

2001 Leaf Rookies and Stars Statistical Standouts Super

This parallel to the Statistical Standout set was randomly inserted into packs. Each of these cards are serial numbered to 50.

Nm-Mt Ex-Mt
*SUPER: 1X TO 2.5X BASIC STAT.STAND

2001 Leaf Rookies and Stars Triple Threads

Randomly inserted into packs, each of these cards feature three swatches of game-worn jerseys from players of the same franchise. Each of these cards are serial numbered to 100.

Nm-Mt Ex-Mt
T1 Pedro Martinez 100.00 30.00
Manny Ramirez
Nomar Garciaparra
T2 Frank Robinson 150.00 45.00
Cal Ripken
Brooks Robinson
T3 Yogi Berra 800.00 240.00
Lou Gehrig
Babe Ruth
T4 Andre Dawson 150.00 45.00
Ryne Sandberg
Ernie Banks
T5 Warren Spahn 150.00 45.00
Hank Aaron
Eddie Mathews
T6 Greg Maddux 100.00 30.00
Chipper Jones
Andruw Jones
T7 Nolan Ryan 150.00 45.00
Ivan Rodriguez
Juan Gonzalez
T8 Lance Berkman 80.00 24.00
Jeff Bagwell
Craig Biggio
T9 Rod Carew 150.00 45.00
Harmon Killebrew
Kirby Puckett
T10 Luis Gonzalez 80.00 24.00
Curt Schilling
Randy Johnson

2002 Leaf Rookies and Stars

This 502 card set was issued in November, 2002. This set was issued in six card packs which came 24 packs to a box and 20 boxes to a case with an SRP of $3 per pack. Originally designed as a 400 card set, this set mushroomed to 501 when 101 variations of some of the basic cards were discovered upon release. These cards feature some of the players who have been on more than one team with cards from their time with that earlier team. Those variation cards were inserted at stated odds of one in four. In addition, cards numbered 301 through 400, which featured a mix of rookies and prospects, were issued at stated odds of one in two. Another subset, which was not printed in shorter supply, was an award winner group from cards numbered 251 through 300.

Nm-Mt Ex-Mt
COMP.SET w/o SP's (300) 40.00 12.00
COMMON CARD (1-300) .30 .09
COMMON SP (1-300) 2.00 .60
COMMON CARD (301-400) 1.00 .30
1 Darin Erstad .30 .09
2 Garret Anderson .30 .09
3 Troy Glaus .30 .09
4 David Eckstein .30 .09
5 Adam Kennedy .30 .09
6 Kevin Appier Angels .30 .09
6A Kevin Appier Mets SP 2.00 .60
6B Kevin Appier Royals SP 2.00 .60
7 Jarrod Washburn .30 .09
8 David Segui .30 .09
9 Jay Gibbons .30 .09
10 Tony Batista .30 .09
11 Scott Erickson .30 .09
12 Jeff Conine .30 .09
13 Melvin Mora .30 .09
14 Shea Hillenbrand .30 .09
15 Manny Ramirez Red Sox .50 .15
15A Manny Ramirez Indians SP . 2.50 .75
16 Pedro Martinez Red Sox .75 .23
16A Ped. Martinez Dodgers SP 4.00 1.20
16B Pedro Martinez Expos SP 4.00 1.20
17 Nomar Garciaparra 1.25 .35
18 Rickey Henderson Red Sox .75 .23
18A Ri. Henderson Angels SP 4.00 1.20
18B Rickey Henderson A's SP 4.00 1.20
18C Ri. Henderson Bl.Jays SP 4.00 1.20
18D Rickey Henderson M's SP 4.00 1.20
18E Rickey Henderson Mets SP . 4.00 1.20
18F Ri. Henderson Padres SP 4.00 1.20
18G Ri. Henderson Yanks SP 4.00 1.20
19 Johnny Damon Red Sox .75 .23
19A Johnny Damon A's SP 2.50 .75
19B Johnny Damon Royals SP 2.50 .75
20 Trot Nixon .30 .09
21 Derek Lowe .30 .09
22 Jason Varitek .50 .15
23 Tim Wakefield .30 .09
24 Frank Thomas .75 .23
25 Kenny Lofton White Sox .30 .09
25A Kenny Lofton Indians SP 2.00 .60
25B Kenny Lofton Giants SP 2.00 .60
26 Magglio Ordonez .30 .09
27 Ray Durham .30 .09
28 Mark Buehrle .30 .09
29 Paul Konerko White Sox .30 .09
29A Paul Konerko Dodgers SP 2.00 .60
29B Paul Konerko Reds SP 2.00 .60
30 Jose Valentin .30 .09
31 C.C. Sabathia .30 .09
32 Ellis Burks Indians .30 .09
32A Ellis Burks Giants SP 2.00 .60
32B Ellis Burks Red Sox SP 2.00 .60
32C Ellis Burks Rockies SP 2.00 .60
33 Omar Vizquel Indians .50 .15
33A Omar Vizquel Mariners SP 2.50 .75
34 Jim Thome .75 .23
35 Matt Lawton .30 .09
36 Travis Fryman Indians .30 .09
36A Travis Fryman Tigers SP 2.00 .60
37 Robert Fick .30 .09
38 Bobby Higginson .30 .09
39 Steve Sparks .30 .09
40 Mike Rivera .30 .09
41 Wendell Magee .30 .09
42 Randall Simon .30 .09
43 Carlos Pena Yankees .30 .09
43A Carlos Pena A's SP 2.00 .60
43B Carlos Pena Rangers SP 2.00 .60
44 Mike Sweeney .30 .09
45 Chuck Knoblauch .30 .09
46 Carlos Beltran .50 .15
47 Joe Randa .30 .09
48 Paul Byrd .30 .09
49 Mac Suzuki .30 .09
50 Torii Hunter .30 .09
51 Jacque Jones .30 .09
52 David Ortiz .50 .15
53 Corey Koskie .30 .09
54 Brad Radke .30 .09
55 Doug Mientkiewicz .30 .09
56 A.J. Pierzynski .30 .09
57 Dustan Mohr .30 .09
58 Derek Jeter 2.00 .60
59 Bernie Williams .50 .15
60 Roger Clemens Yankees 1.50 .45
60A R.Clemens Blue Jays SP 8.00 2.40
60B R.Clemens Red Sox SP 8.00 2.40
61 Mike Mussina Yankees .50 .15
61A Mike Mussina Orioles SP 2.50 .75
62 Jorge Posada .50 .15
63 Alfonso Soriano .50 .15
64 Jason Giambi Yankees .30 .09
64A Jason Giambi A's SP 2.00 .60
65 Robin Ventura Yankees .30 .09
65A Robin Ventura Mets SP 2.00 .60
65B Robin Ventura White Sox SP 2.00 .60
66 Andy Pettitte .50 .15
67 David Wells Yankees .30 .09
67A David Wells Blue Jays SP 2.00 .60
67B David Wells Tigers SP 2.00 .60
68 Nick Johnson .30 .09
69 Jeff Weaver Yankees .30 .09
69A Jeff Weaver Tigers SP 2.00 .60
70 Raul Mondesi Yankees .30 .09
70A R.Mondesi Blue Jays SP 2.00 .60
70B Raul Mondesi Dodgers SP 2.00 .60
71 Tim Hudson .30 .09
72 Barry Zito .30 .09
73 Mark Mulder .30 .09
74 Miguel Tejada .30 .09
75 Eric Chavez .30 .09
76 Billy Koch A's .30 .09
76A Billy Koch Blue Jays SP 2.00 .60
77 Jermaine Dye A's .30 .09
77A Jermaine Dye Royals SP 2.00 .60
78 Scott Hatteberg .30 .09
79 Ichiro Suzuki 1.25 .35
80 Edgar Martinez .50 .15
81 Mike Cameron Mariners .30 .09
81A M.Cameron White Sox SP 2.00 .60
82 John Olerud Mariners .30 .09
82A John Olerud Blue Jays SP 2.00 .60
82B John Olerud Mets SP 2.00 .60
83 Bret Boone .30 .09
84 Dan Wilson .30 .09
85 Freddy Garcia .30 .09
86 Jamie Moyer .30 .09
87 Carlos Guillen .30 .09
88 Ruben Sierra .30 .09
89 Kazuhiro Sasaki .30 .09
90 Mark McLemore .30 .09
91 Ben Grieve .30 .09
92 Aubrey Huff .30 .09
93 Steve Cox .30 .09
94 Toby Hall .30 .09
95 Randy Winn .30 .09
96 Brent Abernathy .30 .09
97 Chan Ho Park Rangers .30 .09
97A Chan Ho Park Dodgers SP 2.00 .60
98 Alex Rodriguez Rangers 1.25 .35
98A A.Rodriguez Mariners SP 6.00 1.80
99 Juan Gonzalez Rangers .50 .15
99A Juan Gonzalez Indians SP 2.50 .75
99B Juan Gonzalez Tigers SP 2.50 .75
100 Rafael Palmeiro Rangers .50 .15
100A Rafael Palmeiro Cubs SP 2.50 .75
100B Raf. Palmeiro Orioles SP 2.50 .75
101 Ivan Rodriguez .75 .23
102 Rusty Greer .30 .09
103 Kenny Rogers Rangers .30 .09
103A Kenny Rogers A's SP 2.00 .60
103B Ken. Rogers Yankees SP 2.00 .60
104 Hank Blalock .75 .23
105 Mark Teixeira .50 .15
106 Carlos Delgado .30 .09
107 Shannon Stewart .30 .09
108 Eric Hinske .30 .09
109 Roy Halladay .30 .09
110 Felipe Lopez .30 .09
111 Vernon Wells .30 .09
112 Curt Schilling D'backs .30 .09
112A Curt Schilling Phillies SP 2.00 .60
113 Randy Johnson D'backs .75 .23
113A Randy Johnson Astros SP 4.00 1.20
113B Randy Johnson Expos SP 4.00 1.20
113C R.Johnson Mariners SP 4.00 1.20
114 Luis Gonzalez D'backs .30 .09
114A Luis Gonzalez Astros SP 2.00 .60
114B Luis Gonzalez Cubs SP 2.00 .60
115 Mark Grace D'backs .50 .15
115A Mark Grace Cubs SP 2.50 .75
116 Junior Spivey .30 .09
117 Tony Womack .30 .09
118 Matt Williams D'backs .30 .09
118A Matt Williams Giants SP 2.00 .60
118B Matt Williams Indians SP 2.00 .60
119 Danny Bautista .30 .09
120 Byung-Hyun Kim .30 .09
121 Craig Counsell .30 .09
122 Greg Maddux Braves 1.25 .35
122A Greg Maddux Cubs SP 6.00 1.80
123 Tom Glavine .50 .15
124 John Smoltz Braves .50 .15
124A John Smoltz Tigers SP 2.50 .75
125 Chipper Jones .75 .23
126 Gary Sheffield .30 .09
127 Andruw Jones .30 .09
128 Vinny Castilla .30 .09
129 Damian Moss .30 .09
130 Rafael Furcal .30 .09
131 Kerry Wood .75 .23
132 Fred McGriff Cubs .50 .15
132A F.McGriff Blue Jays SP 2.50 .75
132B Fred McGriff Braves SP 2.50 .75
132C F.McGriff Devil Rays SP 2.50 .75
132D Fred McGriff Padres SP 2.50 .75
133 Sammy Sosa Cubs 1.25 .35
133A Sammy Sosa Rangers SP 6.00 1.80
133B S.Sosa White Sox SP 6.00 1.80
134 Alex Gonzalez .30 .09
135 Corey Patterson .30 .09
136 Moises Alou .30 .09
137 Mark Prior 1.25 .35
138 Jon Lieber .30 .09
139 Matt Clement .30 .09
140 Ken Griffey Jr. Reds 1.25 .35
140A K.Griffey Jr. Mariners SP 6.00 1.80
141 Barry Larkin .50 .15
142 Adam Dunn .50 .15
143 Sean Casey Reds .30 .09
143A Sean Casey Indians SP 2.00 .60
144 Jose Rijo .30 .09
145 Elmer Dessens .30 .09
146 Austin Kearns .30 .09
147 Corky Miller .30 .09
148 Todd Walker Reds .30 .09
148A Todd Walker Rockies SP 2.00 .60
149 Chris Reitsma .30 .09
150 Ryan Dempster .30 .09
151 Larry Walker Rockies .50 .15
151A Larry Walker Expos SP 2.50 .75
152 Todd Helton .50 .15
153 Juan Uribe .30 .09
154 Juan Pierre .30 .09
155 Mike Hampton .30 .09
156 Todd Zeile .30 .09
157 Josh Beckett .30 .09
158 Mike Lowell Marlins .30 .09
158A Mike Lowell Yankees SP 2.00 .60
159 Derrek Lee .30 .09
160 A.J. Burnett .30 .09
161 Luis Castillo .30 .09
162 Tim Raines .30 .09
163 Preston Wilson .30 .09
164 Juan Encarnacion .30 .09
165 Jeff Bagwell .50 .15
166 Craig Biggio .50 .15
167 Lance Berkman .30 .09
168 Wade Miller .30 .09
169 Roy Oswalt .30 .09
170 Richard Hidalgo .30 .09
171 Carlos Hernandez .30 .09
172 Daryle Ward .30 .09
173 Shawn Green Dodgers .30 .09
173A S.Green Blue Jays SP 2.00 .60
174 Adrian Beltre .50 .15
175 Paul Lo Duca .30 .09
176 Eric Karros .30 .09
177 Kevin Brown .30 .09
178 Hideo Nomo Dodgers .75 .23
178A Hideo Nomo Brewers SP 4.00 1.20
178B Hideo Nomo Mets SP 4.00 1.20
178C Hideo Nomo Red Sox SP 4.00 1.20
178D Hideo Nomo Tigers SP 4.00 1.20
179 Odalis Perez .30 .09
180 Eric Gagne .75 .23
181 Brian Jordan .30 .09
182 Cesar Izturis .30 .09
183 Geoff Jenkins .30 .09
184 Richie Sexson Brewers .30 .09
184A Richie Sexson Indians SP 2.00 .60
185 Jose Hernandez .30 .09
186 Ben Sheets .30 .09
187 Ruben Quevedo .30 .09
188 Jeffrey Hammonds .30 .09
189 Alex Sanchez .30 .09
190 Vladimir Guerrero .75 .23
191 Jose Vidro .30 .09
192 Orlando Cabrera .30 .09
193 Michael Barrett .30 .09
194 Javier Vazquez .30 .09
195 Tony Armas Jr. .30 .09
196 Andres Galarraga .30 .09
197 Tomo Ohka .30 .09
198 Bartolo Colon Expos .30 .09
198A Bartolo Colon Indians SP 2.00 .60
199 Cliff Floyd Expos .30 .09
199A Cliff Floyd Marlins SP 2.00 .60
199B Cliff Floyd Red Sox SP 2.00 .60
200 Mike Piazza Mets 1.25 .35
200A Mike Piazza Dodgers SP 6.00 1.80
200B Mike Piazza Marlins SP 6.00 1.80
201 Jeromy Burnitz .30 .09
202 Roberto Alomar Mets .50 .15
202A Rob. Alomar Bl.Jays SP 2.50 .75
202B Ro. Alomar Indians SP 2.50 .75
202C Ro. Alomar Orioles SP 2.50 .75
202D Ro. Alomar Padres SP 2.50 .75
203 Mo Vaughn Mets .30 .09
203A Mo Vaughn Angels SP 2.00 .60
203B Mo Vaughn Red Sox SP 2.00 .60
204 Al Leiter Mets .30 .09
204A Al Leiter Blue Jays SP 2.00 .60
205 Pedro Astacio .30 .09
206 Edgardo Alfonzo .30 .09
207 Armando Benitez .30 .09
208 Scott Rolen .75 .23
209 Pat Burrell .30 .09
210 Bobby Abreu Phillies .30 .09
210A Bobby Abreu Astros SP 2.00 .60
211 Mike Lieberthal .30 .09
212 Brandon Duckworth .30 .09
213 Jimmy Rollins .30 .09
214 Jeremy Giambi .30 .09
215 Vicente Padilla .30 .09
216 Travis Lee .30 .09
217 Jason Kendall .30 .09
218 Brian Giles Pirates .30 .09
218A Brian Giles Indians SP 2.00 .60
219 Aramis Ramirez .30 .09
220 Pokey Reese .30 .09
221 Kip Wells .30 .09
222 Josh Fogg Pirates .30 .09
222A Josh Fogg White Sox SP 2.00 .60
223 Mike Williams .30 .09
224 Ryan Klesko Padres .30 .09
224A Ryan Klesko Braves SP 2.00 .60
225 Phil Nevin Padres .30 .09
225A Phil Nevin Tigers SP 2.00 .60
226 Brian Lawrence .30 .09
227 Mark Kotsay .30 .09
228 Brett Tomko .30 .09
229 Trevor Hoffman Padres .30 .09
229A Tr. Hoffman Marlins SP 2.00 .60
230 Barry Bonds Giants 2.00 .60
230A Barry Bonds Pirates SP 10.00 3.00
231 Jeff Kent Giants .30 .09
231A Jeff Kent Blue Jays SP 2.00 .60
232 Rich Aurilia .30 .09
233 Tsuyoshi Shinjo Giants .30 .09
233A Tsuyoshi Shinjo Mets SP 2.00 .60
234 Benito Santiago Giants .30 .09
234A Ben. Santiago Padres SP 2.00 .60
235 Kirk Rueter .30 .09
236 Kurt Ainsworth .30 .09
237 Livan Hernandez .30 .09
238 Russ Ortiz .30 .09
239 David Bell .30 .09
240 Jason Schmidt .30 .09
241 Reggie Sanders .30 .09
242 Jim Edmonds Cardinals .30 .09
242A Jim Edmonds Angels SP 2.00 .60
243 J.D. Drew .30 .09
244 Albert Pujols 1.50 .45
245 Fernando Vina .30 .09
246 Tino Martinez Cardinals .50 .15
246A T.Martinez Mariners SP 2.50 .75
246B T.Martinez Yankees SP 2.50 .75
247 Edgar Renteria .30 .09
248 Matt Morris .30 .09
249 Woody Williams .30 .09
250 Jason Isringhausen Cards .30 .09
250A J.Isringhausen A's SP 2.00 .60
251 Cal Ripken 82 ROY 2.50 .75
252 Cal Ripken 83 MVP 2.50 .75
253 Cal Ripken 91 MVP 2.50 .75
254 Cal Ripken 91 AS 2.50 .75
255 Ryne Sandberg 84 MVP 1.50 .45
256 Don Mattingly 85 MVP 2.00 .60
257 Don Mattingly 85-94 GLV 2.00 .60
258 Roger Clemens 01 CY 1.50 .45
259 Roger Clemens 87 CY 1.50 .45
260 Roger Clemens 91 CY 1.50 .45
261 Roger Clemens 97 CY 1.50 .45
262 Roger Clemens 98 CY 1.50 .45
263 Roger Clemens 86 CY 1.50 .45
264 Roger Clemens 86 MVP 1.50 .45
265 Rickey Henderson 90 MVP .75 .23
266 Rickey Henderson 81 GLV .75 .23
267 Jose Canseco 88 MVP .50 .15
268 Barry Bonds 01 MVP 2.00 .60
269 Barry Bonds 90 MVP 2.00 .60
270 Barry Bonds 92 MVP 2.00 .60
271 Barry Bonds 93 MVP 2.00 .60
272 Jeff Bagwell 94 MVP .30 .09
273 Kirby Puckett 91 ALCS .75 .23
274 Kirby Puckett 93 AS .75 .23
275 Greg Maddux 95 CY 1.25 .35
276 Greg Maddux 92 CY 1.25 .35
277 Greg Maddux 93 CY 1.25 .35
278 Greg Maddux 94 CY 1.25 .35
279 Ken Griffey Jr. 97 MVP 1.25 .35
280 Mike Piazza 93 ROY 1.25 .35
281 Kirby Puckett 86-89 GLV .75 .23
282 Mike Piazza 96 AS 1.25 .35
283 Frank Thomas 93 MVP .50 .15
284 Hideo Nomo 95 ROY .50 .15
285 Randy Johnson 01 CY .50 .15
286 Juan Gonzalez 96 MVP .30 .09
287 Derek Jeter 96 ROY 2.00 .60
288 Derek Jeter 00 WS 2.00 .60
289 Derek Jeter 00 AS 2.00 .60
290 Nomar Garciaparra 97 ROY . 1.25 .35
291 Pedro Martinez 00 CY .50 .15
292 Kerry Wood 98 ROY .50 .15
293 Sammy Sosa 98 MVP 1.25 .35
294 Chipper Jones 99 MVP .50 .15
295 Ivan Rodriguez 99 MVP .50 .15
296 Ivan Rodriguez 92-01 GLV .50 .15
297 Albert Pujols 01 ROY 1.50 .45
298 Ichiro Suzuki 01 ROY 1.25 .35
299 Ichiro Suzuki 01 MVP 1.25 .35
300 Ichiro Suzuki 01 GLV 1.25 .35
301 So Taguchi RS RC 1.25 .35
302 Kazuhisa Ishii RS RC 3.00 .90
303 Jeremy Lambert RS RC 1.00 .30
304 Sean Burroughs RS 1.00 .30
305 P.J. Bevis RS RC 1.00 .30
306 Jon Rauch RS 1.00 .30
307 Scotty Layfield RS RC 1.00 .30
308 Miguel Asencio RS RC 1.00 .30
309 Franklyn German RS RC 1.00 .30
310 Luis Ugueto RS RC 1.00 .30
311 Jorge Sosa RS RC 1.00 .30
312 Felix Escalona RS RC 1.00 .30
313 Jose Valverde RS RC 1.25 .35
314 Jeremy Ward RS RC 1.00 .30
315 Kevin Gryboski RS RC 1.00 .30
316 Francis Beltran RS RC 1.00 .30
317 Joe Thurston RS 1.00 .30
318 Cliff Lee RS RC 2.00 .60
319 Takahito Nomura RS RC 1.00 .30
320 Bill Hall RS 1.00 .30
321 Marlon Byrd RS 1.00 .30
322 Andy Shibilo RS RC 1.00 .30
323 Edwin Almonte RS RC 1.00 .30
324 Brandon Backe RS RC 2.00 .60
325 Chone Figgins RS RC 2.00 .60
326 Brian Mallette RS RC 1.00 .30
327 Rodrigo Rosario RS RC 1.00 .30
328 Anderson Machado RS RC 1.00 .30
329 Jorge Padilla RS RC 1.00 .30
330 Allan Simpson RS RC 1.00 .30
331 Doug Devore RS RC 1.00 .30
332 Drew Henson RS 1.00 .30
333 Raul Chavez RS RC 1.00 .30
334 Tom Shearn RS RC 1.00 .30
335 Ben Howard RS RC 1.00 .30
336 Chris Baker RS RC 1.00 .30
337 Travis Hughes RS RC 1.00 .30
338 Kevin Mench RS 1.00 .30
339 Brian Tallet RS RC 1.00 .30
340 Mike Moriarty RS RC 1.00 .30
341 Corey Thurman RS RC 1.00 .30
342 Terry Pearson RS RC 1.00 .30
343 Steve Kent RS RC 1.00 .30
344 Satoru Komiyama RS RC 1.00 .30
345 Jason Lane RS 1.00 .30
346 Freddy Sanchez RS RC 1.00 .30
347 Brandon Puffer RS RC 1.00 .30
348 Clay Condrey RS RC 1.00 .30
349 Rene Reyes RS RC 1.00 .30
350 Hee Seop Choi RS 1.00 .30
351 Rodrigo Lopez RS 1.00 .30
352 Colin Young RS RC 1.00 .30
353 Jason Simontacchi RS RC 1.00 .30
354 Oliver Perez RS RC 8.00 2.40
355 Kirk Saarloos RS RC 1.00 .30
356 Marcus Thames RS 1.00 .30
357 Jeff Austin RS RC 1.00 .30
358 Justin Kaye RS 1.00 .30
359 Julio Mateo RS RC 1.00 .30
360 Mike A. Smith RS RC 1.00 .30
361 Chris Snelling RS RC 1.00 .30
362 Dennis Tankersley RS 1.00 .30
363 Runelvys Hernandez RS RC 1.00 .30
364 Aaron Cook RS RC 1.00 .30
365 Joe Borchard RS 1.00 .30
366 Earl Snyder RS RC 1.25 .35
367 Shane Nance RS RC 1.00 .30
368 Aaron Guiel RS RC 1.00 .30
369 Steve Bechler RS RC 1.00 .30
370 Tim Kalita RS RC 1.00 .30
371 Shawn Sedlacek RS RC 1.00 .30
372 Eric Good RS RC 1.00 .30
373 Eric Junge RS RC 1.00 .30
374 Matt Thornton RS RC 1.00 .30
375 Travis Driskill RS RC 1.00 .30
376 Mitch Wylie RS RC 1.00 .30
377 John Ennis RS RC 1.00 .30
378 Reed Johnson RS RC 1.25 .35
379 Juan Brito RS RC 1.00 .30
380 Ron Calloway RS RC 1.00 .30
381 Adrian Burnside RS RC 1.00 .30
382 Josh Bard RS RC 1.00 .30
383 Matt Childers RS RC 1.00 .30
384 Gustavo Chacin RS RC 1.25 .35
385 Luis Martinez RS RC 1.00 .30
386 Trey Hodges RS RC 1.00 .30
387 Hansel Izquierdo RS RC 1.00 .30
388 Jeriome Robertson RS RC 1.00 .30
389 Victor Alvarez RS RC 1.00 .30
390 David Ross RS RC 1.00 .30
391 Ron Chiavacci RS 1.00 .30

392 Adam Walker RS RC 1.00 .30
393 Mike Gonzalez RS RC 1.00 .30
394 John Foster RS RC 1.00 .30
395 Kyle Kane RS RC 1.00 .30
396 Cam Esslinger RS RC 1.00 .30
397 Kevin Frederick RS RC 1.00 .30
398 Franklin Nunez RS RC 1.00 .30
399 Todd Donovan RS RC 1.00 .30
400 Kevin Cash RS RC 1.00 .30

2002 Leaf Rookies and Stars Great American Signings

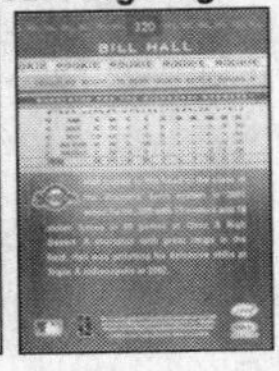

Randomly inserted into packs, this is a partial parallel to the basic Leaf Rookies and Stars set. These cards feature the basic card along with the attached "sticker" autograph. Since cards were issued to different stated print runs, we have notated that information next to the player's name in our checklist. If a card has a stated print run of 25 or fewer it is not printed due to market scarcity.

Nm-Mt Ex-Mt
9 Jay Gibbons/150 10.00 3.00
18 Rickey Henderson/20
40 Mike Rivera/175 10.00 3.00
49 Mac Suzuki/100 40.00 12.00
59 Bernie Williams/15
60 Roger Clemens/10
63 Alfonso Soriano/25
68 Nick Johnson/175 15.00 4.50
92 Aubrey Huff/175 15.00 4.50
96 Brent Abernathy/175 10.00 3.00
108 Eric Hinske/175 10.00 3.00
131 Kerry Wood/25
141 Barry Larkin/25
142 Adam Dunn/25
146 Austin Kearns/75 15.00 4.50
169 Roy Oswalt/100 15.00 4.50
182 Cesar Izturis/175 10.00 3.00
190 Vladimir Guerrero/15
210 Bobby Abreu/25
221 Kip Wells/175 10.00 3.00
226 Brian Lawrence/175 10.00 3.00
244 Albert Pujols/25
256 Don Mattingly/25
301 So Taguchi/50
302 Kazuhisa Ishii/25
309 Franklyn German/175 10.00 3.00
310 Luis Ugueto/175 10.00 3.00
312 Felix Escalona/100 15.00 4.50
316 Francis Beltran/175 10.00 3.00
320 Bill Hall/175 10.00 3.00
324 Brandon Backe/175 25.00 7.50
327 Rodrigo Rosario/175 10.00 3.00
328 Anderson Machado/175 10.00 3.00
329 Jorge Padilla/175 10.00 3.00
331 Doug Devore/175 10.00 3.00
332 Drew Henson/50 40.00 12.00
333 Raul Chavez/175 10.00 3.00
334 Tom Shearn/175 10.00 3.00
335 Ben Howard/175 10.00 3.00
336 Chris Baker/175 10.00 3.00
337 Travis Hughes/175 10.00 3.00
341 Corey Thurman/175 10.00 3.00
344 Satoru Komiyama/75 25.00 7.50
345 Jason Lane/150 10.00 3.00
349 Rene Reyes/175 10.00 3.00
354 Oliver Perez/175 80.00 24.00
361 Chris Snelling/175 10.00 3.00
362 Dennis Tankersley/175 10.00 3.00

2002 Leaf Rookies and Stars Longevity

Randomly inserted into packs, this is a parallel to the basic Leaf Rookie and Stars set. Cards numbered between 1-300 (and including all of the variations) were printed to a stated print run of 100 serial numbered sets while cards 301 through 400 were printed to a stated print run of 25 serial numbered sets.

Nm-Mt Ex-Mt
*LONGEVITY 1-300: 6X TO 15X BASIC
*LONGEVITY 1-300: 1.25X TO 3X BASIC SP'S
*RETIRED STARS 251-300: 12.5X TO 30X

2002 Leaf Rookies and Stars BLC Homers

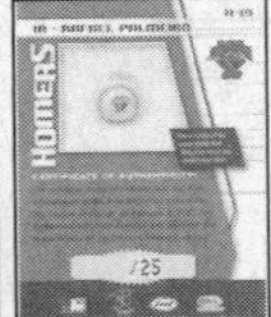

Randomly inserted into packs, these 30 cards feature pieces of baseball's used during the Big League Challenge held in Las Vegas before the 2002 season began. Each card has a stated print run of 25 serial numbered sets.

Nm-Mt Ex-Mt
LUIS GONZALEZ (1-3) 25.00 7.50
TODD HELTON (4-11) 40.00 12.00
JIM THOME (12-14) 40.00 12.00
RAFAEL PALMEIRO (15-19) 40.00 12.00
TROY GLAUS (20-22) 40.00 12.00
GARY SHEFFIELD (23-25) 25.00 7.50
MIKE PIAZZA (26-30) 60.00 18.00

2002 Leaf Rookies and Stars Dress for Success

Randomly inserted into packs, these 15 cards feature two game-used memorabilia pieces from the featured players. Each card was also issued to a stated print run of 250 serial numbered sets.

Nm-Mt Ex-Mt
1 Mike Piazza Jsy-Jsy 25.00 7.50
2 Cal Ripken Jsy-Jsy 60.00 18.00
3 Carlos Delgado Jsy-Jsy 20.00 6.00
4 Chipper Jones Jsy-Jsy 25.00 7.50
5 Bernie Williams Jsy-Shoe 25.00 7.50
6 Carlos Beltran Jsy-Shoe 25.00 7.50
7 Curt Schilling Jsy-Jsy 20.00 6.00
8 Greg Maddux Jsy-Jsy 25.00 7.50
9 Ivan Rodriguez Jsy-Jsy 25.00 7.50
10 Alex Rodriguez Jsy-Jsy 40.00 12.00
11 Roger Clemens Jsy-Jsy 40.00 12.00
12 Todd Helton Jsy-Jsy 25.00 7.50
13 Jim Edmonds Shoe-Jsy 20.00 6.00
14 Manny Ramirez Jsy-Fld Glv 25.00 7.50
15 Mark Buehrle Jsy-Shoe 20.00 6.00

2002 Leaf Rookies and Stars Freshman Orientation

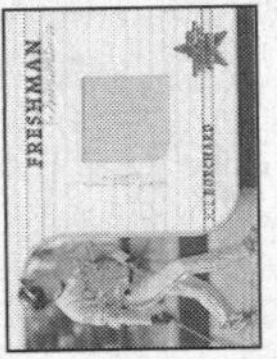

Inserted in packs at a stated rate of one in 142, these 20 cards feature not only players who debuted during the 2002 season but also a game-used memorabilia piece from that player.

Nm-Mt Ex-Mt
*CLASS OFFICERS: .6X TO 1.5X BASIC
CLASS OFFICERS RANDOM IN PACKS
CLASS OFFICERS PRINT RUN 50 #'d SETS
1 Andres Torres Bat 15.00 4.50
2 Mark Ellis Jsy 15.00 4.50
3 Erik Bedard Bat 15.00 4.50
4 Delvin James Jsy 15.00 4.50
5 Austin Kearns Bat 15.00 4.50
6 Josh Pearce Bat 15.00 4.50
7 Rafael Soriano Jsy 15.00 4.50
8 Jason Lane Bat 15.00 4.50
9 Mark Prior Jsy 25.00 7.50
10 Alfredo Amezaga Bat 15.00 4.50
11 Ryan Ludwick Bat 15.00 4.50
12 So Taguchi Bat 25.00 7.50
13 Duaner Sanchez Bat 15.00 4.50
14 Kazuhisa Ishii Jsy 20.00 6.00
15 Zach Day Pants 15.00 4.50
16 Eric Cyr Bat 15.00 4.50
17 Francis Beltran Jsy 15.00 4.50
18 Joe Borchard Jsy 15.00 4.50
19 Jeremy Affeldt Shoe 15.00 4.50
20 Alexis Gomez Shoe 15.00 4.50

2002 Leaf Rookies and Stars Statistical Standouts

Issued at stated odds of one in 12, these 50 cards feature some of the leading players in baseball.

Nm-Mt Ex-Mt
1 Adam Dunn 4.00 1.20
2 Alex Rodriguez 10.00 3.00
3 Andruw Jones 2.50 .75
4 Brian Giles 2.50 .75
5 Chipper Jones 6.00 1.80
6 Cliff Floyd 2.50 .75
7 Craig Biggio 4.00 1.20
8 Frank Thomas 6.00 1.80
9 Fred McGriff 4.00 1.20
10 Garret Anderson 2.50 .75
11 Greg Maddux 10.00 3.00
12 Luis Gonzalez 2.50 .75
13 Magglio Ordonez 2.50 .75
14 Ivan Rodriguez 6.00 1.80
15 Ken Griffey Jr. 10.00 3.00
16 Ichiro Suzuki 10.00 3.00
17 Jason Giambi 2.50 .75
18 Derek Jeter 15.00 4.50
19 Sammy Sosa 10.00 3.00
20 Albert Pujols 12.00 3.60
21 J.D. Drew 2.50 .75
22 Jeff Bagwell 4.00 1.20
23 Jim Edmonds 2.50 .75
24 Jose Vidro 2.50 .75
25 Juan Encarnacion 2.50 .75
26 Kerry Wood 6.00 1.80
27 Al Leiter 2.50 .75
28 Curt Schilling 2.50 .75
29 Manny Ramirez 4.00 1.20
30 Lance Berkman 2.50 .75
31 Miguel Tejada 2.50 .75
32 Mike Piazza 10.00 3.00
33 Nomar Garciaparra 10.00 3.00
34 Omar Vizquel 4.00 1.20
35 Pat Burrell 2.50 .75
36 Paul Konerko 2.50 .75
37 Rafael Palmeiro 4.00 1.20
38 Randy Johnson 6.00 1.80
39 Richie Sexson 2.50 .75
40 Roger Clemens 12.00 3.60
41 Shawn Green 2.50 .75
42 Todd Helton 4.00 1.20
43 Tom Glavine 4.00 1.20
44 Troy Glaus 2.50 .75
45 Vladimir Guerrero 6.00 1.80
46 Mike Sweeney 2.50 .75
47 Alfonso Soriano 4.00 1.20
48 Barry Zito 2.50 .75
49 John Smoltz 4.00 1.20
50 Ellis Burks 2.50 .75

2002 Leaf Rookies and Stars Statistical Standouts Materials

Randomly inserted into packs, this is a parallel to the basic Statistical Standouts insert set. These cards feature a game-used memorabilia piece from each player. Please note that some cards were issued in shorter supply and we have notated that information along with the stated print run information next to the player's name in our checklist.

Nm-Mt Ex-Mt
SUPER: RANDOM INSERTS IN PACKS
SUPER PRINT RUN 25 SERIAL #'d SETS
SUPER: NO PRICING DUE TO SCARCITY
1 Adam Dunn Bat/200 20.00 6.00
2 Alex Rodriguez Bat/200 20.00 6.00
3 Andruw Jones Bat/200 15.00 4.50
4 Brian Giles Bat 15.00 4.50
5 Chipper Jones Bat/200 20.00 6.00
6 Cliff Floyd Jsy 15.00 4.50
7 Craig Biggio Pants 20.00 6.00
8 Frank Thomas Jsy/125 20.00 6.00
9 Fred McGriff Bat 20.00 6.00
10 Garret Anderson Bat
11 Greg Maddux Jsy/200 20.00 6.00
12 Luis Gonzalez Jsy 15.00 4.50
13 Magglio Ordonez Bat/150 15.00 4.50
14 Ivan Rodriguez Jsy/100
15 Ken Griffey Jr. Base/100 25.00 7.50
16 Ichiro Suzuki Base/100
17 Jason Giambi Base 15.00 4.50
18 Derek Jeter Base/100
19 Sammy Sosa Base/100 25.00 7.50
20 Albert Pujols Base/100
21 J.D. Drew Bat/150 15.00 4.50
22 Jeff Bagwell Pants/150
23 Jim Edmonds Bat 15.00 4.50
24 Jose Vidro Bat 10.00 3.00
25 Juan Encarnacion Bat 10.00 3.00
26 Kerry Wood Jsy/200 20.00 6.00
27 Al Leiter Jsy 15.00 4.50
28 Curt Schilling Jsy/225
29 Manny Ramirez Bat/100
30 Lance Berkman Bat/150
31 Miguel Tejada Jsy 15.00 4.50
32 Mike Piazza Bat/200 20.00 6.00
33 Nomar Garciaparra Bat/200 25.00 7.50
34 Omar Vizquel Jsy 20.00 6.00
35 Pat Burrell Bat 15.00 4.50
36 Paul Konerko Jsy 15.00 4.50
37 Rafael Palmeiro Bat 20.00 6.00
38 Randy Johnson Jsy/200 20.00 6.00
39 Richie Sexson Jsy 15.00 4.50
40 Roger Clemens Jsy/200 30.00 9.00
41 Shawn Green Jsy 15.00 4.50
42 Todd Helton Jsy/175 20.00 6.00
43 Tom Glavine Jsy/125 20.00 6.00
44 Troy Glaus Jsy 15.00 4.50
45 Vladimir Guerrero Jsy 20.00 6.00
46 Mike Sweeney Bat 15.00 4.50
47 Alfonso Soriano Jsy/200 20.00 6.00
48 Barry Zito Jsy/100 15.00 4.50
49 John Smoltz Jsy
50 Ellis Burks Jsy/50 15.00 4.50

2002 Leaf Rookies and Stars Triple Threads

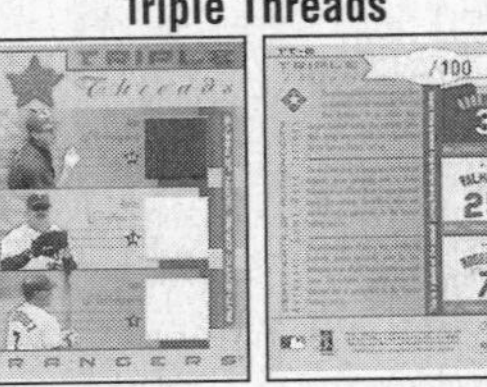

Randomly inserted into packs, this 10 card set featured three players who have something in common along with a memorabilia piece of each player featured on the card. Each card was also issued to a stated print run of 100 serial numbered sets.

Nm-Mt Ex-Mt
1 Reggie Jackson 100.00 30.00
Alfonso Soriano
Don Mattingly
2 Alex Rodriguez 60.00 18.00
Rafael Palmeiro
Ivan Rodriguez
3 Mike Piazza 60.00 18.00
Gary Carter
Rickey Henderson
4 Dale Murphy 50.00 15.00
Andruw Jones
Chipper Jones
5 Mike Schmidt 100.00 30.00
Steve Carlton
Scott Rolen
6 Rickey Henderson 50.00 15.00
Rickey Henderson
Rickey Henderson
7 Johnny Bench 100.00 30.00
Joe Morgan
Tom Seaver
8 Randy Johnson 50.00 15.00
Pedro Martinez
Vladimir Guerrero
9 Nolan Ryan 100.00 30.00
Rod Carew
Troy Glaus
10 Lou Brock 100.00 30.00
J.D Drew
Stan Musial

2002 Leaf Rookies and Stars View Masters

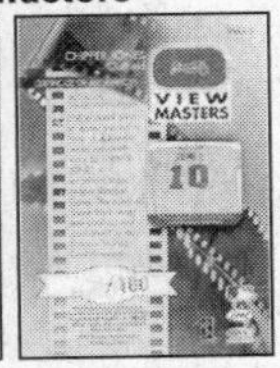

Randomly inserted into packs, these 20 cards feature some of the leading players in the game in a style reminiscent of the old "View Masters" which became popular in the 1950's. Each of these cards were printed to a stated print run of 100 serial numbered sets and have a game used-memorabilia piece attached to them.

Nm-Mt Ex-Mt
SLIDESHOW: RANDOM INSERTS IN PACKS
SLIDESHOW PRINT 25 SERIAL #'d SETS
SLIDESHOW: NO PRICE DUE TO SCARCITY
1 Carlos Delgado 25.00 7.50
2 Todd Helton 25.00 7.50
3 Tony Gwynn 40.00 12.00
4 Bernie Williams 25.00 7.50
5 Luis Gonzalez 25.00 7.50
6 Larry Walker 25.00 7.50
7 Troy Glaus 25.00 7.50
8 Alfonso Soriano 25.00 7.50
9 Curt Schilling 25.00 7.50
10 Chipper Jones 40.00 12.00
11 Vladimir Guerrero 40.00 12.00
12 Adam Dunn 25.00 7.50
13 Rickey Henderson 40.00 12.00
14 Miguel Tejada 25.00 7.50
15 Kazuhisa Ishii 40.00 12.00
16 Greg Maddux 40.00 12.00
17 Pedro Martinez 40.00 12.00
18 Nomar Garciaparra 50.00 15.00
19 Mike Piazza 40.00 12.00
20 Lance Berkman 25.00 7.50

1996 Leaf Signature

The 1996 Leaf Signature Set was issued by Donruss in two series totalling 150 cards. The four-card packs carried a suggested retail price of $9.99 each. It's interesting to note that the Extended Series was the last of the 1996 releases. In fact, it was released in January, 1997 - so late in the year that it's categorization as a 1996 issue was a bit of a stretch at that time. Production for the Extended Series was only 40 percent that of the regular issue. Extended Series packs actually contained a mix of both series cards, thus the Extended Series cards are somewhat scarcer. Card fronts feature borderless color action player photos with the card name printed in a silver foil emblem. The backs carry player information. Rookie Cards include Darin Erstad. This product was a benchmark release in hobby history due to it's inclusion of one or more autograph cards per pack (explaining it's high suggested retail pack price). The product was highly successful upon release and opened the doors for wide incorporation of autograph cards into a wide array of brands from that point forward.

Nm-Mt Ex-Mt
COMPLETE SET (150) 100.00 30.00
COMP. SERIES 1 (100) 60.00 18.00
COMPLETE SERIES 2 (50) 40.00 12.00
COMMON CARD (1-100) .50 .15
COMMON (101-150) .30 .09
1 Mike Piazza 2.00 .60
2 Juan Gonzalez .75 .23
3 Greg Maddux 2.00 .60
4 Marc Newfield .50 .15
5 Wade Boggs .75 .23
6 Ray Lankford .50 .15
7 Frank Thomas 1.25 .35
8 Rico Brogna .50 .15
9 Tim Salmon .75 .23
10 Ken Griffey Jr. 2.00 .60
11 Manny Ramirez .75 .23
12 Cecil Fielder .50 .15
13 Gregg Jefferies .50 .15
14 Rondell White .50 .15
15 Cal Ripken 4.00 1.20
16 Alex Rodriguez 2.50 .75
17 Bernie Williams .75 .23
18 Andres Galarraga .50 .15
19 Mike Mussina .75 .23
20 Chuck Knoblauch .50 .15
21 Joe Carter .50 .15
22 Jeff Bagwell .75 .23
23 Mark McGwire 3.00 .90
24 Sammy Sosa 2.00 .60
25 Reggie Sanders .50 .15
26 Chipper Jones 1.25 .35
27 Jeff Cirillo .50 .15
28 Roger Clemens 2.50 .75
29 Craig Biggio .75 .23
30 Gary Sheffield .50 .15
31 Paul O'Neill .75 .23
32 Johnny Damon .75 .23
33 Jason Isringhausen .50 .15
34 Jay Bell .50 .15
35 Henry Rodriguez .50 .15
36 Matt Williams .50 .15
37 Randy Johnson 1.25 .35
38 Fred McGriff .75 .23
39 Jason Giambi .50 .15
40 Ivan Rodriguez 1.25 .35
41 Raul Mondesi .50 .15
42 Barry Larkin .75 .23
43 Ryan Klesko .50 .15
44 Joey Hamilton .50 .15
45 Todd Hundley .50 .15
46 Jim Edmonds .50 .15
47 Dante Bichette .50 .15
48 Roberto Alomar .75 .23
49 Mark Grace .75 .23
50 Brady Anderson .50 .15
51 Hideo Nomo 1.25 .35
52 Ozzie Smith 2.00 .60
53 Robin Ventura .50 .15
54 Andy Pettitte .75 .23
55 Kenny Lofton .50 .15
56 John Mabry .50 .15
57 Paul Molitor .75 .23
58 Rey Ordonez .50 .15
59 Albert Belle .50 .15
60 Charles Johnson .50 .15
61 Edgar Martinez .75 .23
62 Derek Bell .50 .15
63 Carlos Delgado .50 .15
64 Raul Casanova .50 .15
65 Ismael Valdes .50 .15
66 J.T. Snow .50 .15
67 Derek Jeter 3.00 .90
68 Jason Kendall .50 .15
69 John Smoltz .75 .23
70 Chad Mottola .50 .15
71 Jim Thome 1.25 .35
72 Will Clark 1.25 .35
73 Mo Vaughn .50 .15
74 John Wasdin .50 .15
75 Rafael Palmeiro .75 .23
76 Mark Grudzielanek .50 .15
77 Larry Walker .75 .23
78 Alan Benes .50 .15
79 Michael Tucker .50 .15
80 Billy Wagner .50 .15
81 Paul Wilson .50 .15
82 Greg Vaughn .50 .15
83 Dean Palmer .50 .15
84 Ryne Sandberg 2.00 .60
85 Eric Young .50 .15
86 Jay Buhner .50 .15
87 Tony Clark .50 .15
88 Jermaine Dye .50 .15
89 Barry Bonds 3.00 .90
90 Ugueth Urbina .50 .15
91 Charles Nagy .50 .15
92 Ruben Rivera .50 .15
93 Todd Hollandsworth .50 .15
94 Darin Erstad RC 4.00 1.20
95 Brooks Kieschnick .50 .15
96 Edgar Renteria .50 .15
97 Lenny Dykstra .50 .15
98 Tony Gwynn 1.50 .45
99 Kirby Puckett 1.25 .35
100 Checklist .50 .15
101 Andruw Jones 1.25 .35
102 Alex Ochoa .30 .09
103 David Cone .50 .15
104 Rusty Greer .50 .15
105 Jose Canseco 1.25 .35
106 Ken Caminiti .50 .15
107 Mariano Rivera .75 .23
108 Ron Gant .50 .15
109 Darryl Strawberry .50 .15
110 Vladimir Guerrero 3.00 .90
111 George Arias .30 .09
112 Jeff Conine .50 .15
113 Bobby Higginson .50 .15
114 Eric Karros .50 .15
115 Brian Hunter .30 .09
116 Eddie Murray 1.25 .35
117 Todd Walker .30 .09
118 Chan Ho Park .50 .15
119 John Jaha .30 .09
120 Dave Justice .50 .15
121 Makoto Suzuki .30 .09
122 Scott Rolen 1.25 .35
123 Tino Martinez .75 .23
124 Kimera Bartee .30 .09
125 Garret Anderson .50 .15
126 Brian Jordan .50 .15
127 Andre Dawson .50 .15
128 Javier Lopez .50 .15
129 Bill Pulsipher .30 .09
130 Dwight Gooden .50 .15
131 Al Martin .30 .09
132 Terrell Wade .30 .09
133 Steve Gibralter .30 .09
134 Tom Glavine .75 .23
135 Kevin Appier .50 .15
136 Tim Raines .50 .15
137 Curtis Pride .30 .09
138 Todd Greene .30 .09

139 Bobby Bonilla	.50	.15
140 Trey Beamon	.30	.09
141 Marty Cordova	.30	.09
142 Rickey Henderson	1.25	.35
143 Ellis Burks	.50	.15
144 Dennis Eckersley	.50	.15
145 Kevin Brown	.50	.15
146 Carlos Baerga	.30	.09
147 Brett Butler	.50	.15
148 Marquis Grissom	.50	.15
149 Karim Garcia	.30	.09
150 Frank Thomas CL	.75	.23

1996 Leaf Signature Gold Press Proofs

Randomly inserted in first series packs at an approximate rate of one in 12 and second series packs at an approximate rate of one in 8, this 150-card set is parallel to the regular version. The design is similar to the regular card with the exception of the card name being printed in a gold foil emblem and the words "Press Proof" printed in gold foil vertically down the side.

Nm-Mt Ex-Mt
*SER.1 STARS: 4X TO 10X BASIC CARDS
*SER.1 ROOKIES: 1.25X TO 3X BASIC CARDS
*SER.2 STARS: 3X TO 8X BASIC CARDS

1996 Leaf Signature Platinum Press Proofs

Randomly inserted exclusively into Extended Series packs at the rate of one in 24, this 150-card set is parallel to the regular Leaf Signature Set. Only 150 sets were produced. Unlike the multi-series base set and Gold Press Proofs, these scarce Platinum cards were issued in one comprehensive series. The cards are similar in design to the regular set with the exception of holographic platinum foil stamping.

Nm-Mt Ex-Mt
*SER.1 STARS: 10X TO 25X BASIC CARDS
*SER. 1 ROOKIES: 2.5X TO 6X BASIC CARDS
*SER.2 STARS: 8X TO 20X BASIC CARDS

1996 Leaf Signature Autographs

Inserted into 1996 Leaf Signature Series first series packs, these unnumbered cards were one of the first major autograph issues featured in an MLB-licensed trading card set. First series packs contained at least one autograph, with the chance of getting more. Donruss/Leaf reports that all but 10 players in the Leaf Signature Series signed close to 5,000 total autographs (3,500 bronze, 1,000 silver, 500 gold). The 10 players who signed 1,000 (700 bronze, 200 silver, 100 gold) are: Roberto Alomar, Wade Boggs, Derek Jeter, Kenny Lofton, Paul Molitor, Raul Mondesi, Manny Ramirez, Alex Rodriguez, Frank Thomas and Mo Vaughn. It's also important to note that six additional players did not submit their cards in time to be included in first series packs. Thus, their cards were thrown into Extended series packs. Those six players are as follows: Brian L.Hunter, Carlos Delgado, Phil Plantier, Jim Thome, Terrell Wade and Ernie Young. Thome signed only silver and gold foil cards, thus the Bronze set is considered complete at 251 cards. Prices below refer exclusively to Bronze versions. Blue and black ink variations have been found for Carlos Delgado, Alex Rodriguez and Michael Tucker. No consistent premiums for these variations has been tracked. Finally, an autographed jumbo silver foil version of the Frank Thomas card was distributed to dealers in March, 1997. Dealers received either this first series or the Extended Series jumbo Thomas for every Extended Series case ordered. Each Thomas jumbo is individually serial numbered to 1,500. A standard-size promo card of Frank Thomas with a fascimile signature was also created and released several weeks before this set's release.

	Nm-Mt	Ex-Mt
1 Kurt Abbott	5.00	1.50
2 Juan Acevedo	5.00	1.50
3 Terry Adams	5.00	1.50
4 Manny Alexander	5.00	1.50
5 Roberto Alomar SP	40.00	12.00
6 Moises Alou	10.00	3.00
7 Wilson Alvarez	5.00	1.50
8 Garret Anderson	15.00	4.50
9 Shane Andrews	5.00	1.50
10 Andy Ashby	5.00	1.50
11 Pedro Astacio	5.00	1.50
12 Brad Ausmus	5.00	1.50
13 Bobby Ayala	5.00	1.50
14 Carlos Baerga	5.00	1.50
15 Harold Baines	15.00	4.50
16 Jason Bates	5.00	1.50
17 Allen Battle	5.00	1.50
18 Rich Becker	5.00	1.50
19 David Bell	5.00	1.50
20 Rafael Belliard	5.00	1.50
21 Andy Benes	5.00	1.50
22 Armando Benitez	10.00	3.00
23 Jason Bere	5.00	1.50
24 Geronimo Berroa	5.00	1.50
25 Willie Blair	5.00	1.50
26 Mike Blowers	5.00	1.50
27 Wade Boggs SP	50.00	15.00
28 Ricky Bones	5.00	1.50
29 Mike Bordick	10.00	3.00
30 Toby Borland	5.00	1.50
31 Ricky Bottalico	5.00	1.50
32 Darren Bragg	5.00	1.50
33 Jeff Branson	5.00	1.50
34 Tilson Brito	5.00	1.50
35 Rico Brogna	5.00	1.50
36 Scott Brosius	15.00	4.50
37 Damon Buford	5.00	1.50
38 Mike Busby	5.00	1.50
39 Tom Candiotti	5.00	1.50
40 Frank Castillo	5.00	1.50
41 Andujar Cedeno	5.00	1.50
42 Domingo Cedeno	5.00	1.50
43 Roger Cedeno	5.00	1.50
44 Norm Charlton	5.00	1.50
45 Jeff Cirillo	5.00	1.50
46 Will Clark	25.00	7.50
47 Jeff Conine	10.00	3.00
48 Steve Cooke	5.00	1.50
49 Joey Cora	5.00	1.50
50 Marty Cordova	5.00	1.50
51 Rheal Cormier	5.00	1.50
52 Felipe Crespo	5.00	1.50
53 Chad Curtis	5.00	1.50
54 Johnny Damon	15.00	4.50
55 Russ Davis	5.00	1.50
56 Andre Dawson	15.00	4.50
57 Carlos Delgado	15.00	4.50
58 Doug Drabek	5.00	1.50
59 Darren Dreifort	5.00	1.50
60 Shawon Dunston	5.00	1.50
61 Ray Durham	10.00	3.00
62 Jim Edmonds	15.00	4.50
63 Joey Eischen	5.00	1.50
64 Jim Eisenreich	5.00	1.50
65 Sal Fasano	5.00	1.50
66 Jeff Fassero	5.00	1.50
67 Alex Fernandez	5.00	1.50
68 Darrin Fletcher	5.00	1.50
69 Chad Fonville	5.00	1.50
70 Kevin Foster	5.00	1.50
71 John Franco	10.00	3.00
72 Julio Franco	10.00	3.00
73 Marvin Freeman	5.00	1.50
74 Travis Fryman	10.00	3.00
75 Gary Gaetti	10.00	3.00
76 Carlos Garcia	5.00	1.50
77 Jason Giambi	15.00	4.50
78 Benji Gil	5.00	1.50
79 Greg Gohr	5.00	1.50
80 Chris Gomez	5.00	1.50
81 Leo Gomez	5.00	1.50
82 Tom Goodwin	5.00	1.50
83 Mike Grace	5.00	1.50
84 Mike Greenwell	5.00	1.50
85 Rusty Greer	10.00	3.00
86 Mark Grudzielanek	5.00	1.50
87 Mark Gubicza	5.00	1.50
88 Juan Guzman	5.00	1.50
89 Darryl Hamilton	5.00	1.50
90 Joey Hamilton	5.00	1.50
91 Chris Hammond	5.00	1.50
92 Mike Hampton	10.00	3.00
93 Chris Haney	5.00	1.50
94 Todd Haney	5.00	1.50
95 Erik Hanson	5.00	1.50
96 Pete Harnisch	5.00	1.50
97 LaTroy Hawkins	5.00	1.50
98 Charlie Hayes	5.00	1.50
99 Jimmy Haynes	5.00	1.50
100 Roberto Hernandez	5.00	1.50
101 Bobby Higginson	10.00	3.00
102 Glenallen Hill	5.00	1.50
103 Ken Hill	5.00	1.50
104 Sterling Hitchcock	5.00	1.50
105 Trevor Hoffman	15.00	4.50
106 Dave Hollins	5.00	1.50
107 Dwayne Hosey	5.00	1.50
108 Thomas Howard	5.00	1.50
109 Steve Howe	5.00	1.50
110 John Hudek	5.00	1.50
111 Rex Hudler	5.00	1.50
112 Brian L.Hunter	5.00	1.50
113 Butch Huskey	5.00	1.50
114 Mark Hutton	5.00	1.50
115 Jason Jacome	5.00	1.50
116 John Jaha	5.00	1.50
117 Reggie Jefferson	5.00	1.50
118 Derek Jeter SP	150.00	45.00
119 Bobby Jones	5.00	1.50
120 Todd Jones	5.00	1.50
121 Brian Jordan	10.00	3.00
122 Kevin Jordan	5.00	1.50
123 Jeff Juden	5.00	1.50
124 Ron Karkovice	5.00	1.50
125 Roberto Kelly	5.00	1.50
126 Mark Kiefer	5.00	1.50
127 Brooks Kieschnick	5.00	1.50
128 Jeff King	5.00	1.50
129 Mike Lansing	5.00	1.50
130 Matt Lawton	10.00	3.00
131 Al Leiter	10.00	3.00
132 Mark Leiter	5.00	1.50
133 Curtis Leskanic	5.00	1.50
134 Darren Lewis	5.00	1.50
135 Mark Lewis	5.00	1.50
136 Felipe Lira	5.00	1.50
137 Pat Listach	5.00	1.50
138 Keith Lockhart	5.00	1.50
139 Kenny Lofton SP	40.00	12.00
140 John Mabry	5.00	1.50
141 Mike Macfarlane	5.00	1.50
142 Kirt Manwaring	5.00	1.50
143 Al Martin	5.00	1.50
144 Norberto Martin	5.00	1.50
145 Dennis Martinez	10.00	3.00
146 Pedro Martinez	50.00	15.00
147 Sandy Martinez	5.00	1.50
148 Mike Matheny	10.00	3.00
149 T.J. Mathews	5.00	1.50
150 David McCarty	5.00	1.50
151 Ben McDonald	5.00	1.50
152 Pat Meares	5.00	1.50
153 Orlando Merced	5.00	1.50
154 Jose Mesa	5.00	1.50
155 Matt Mieske	5.00	1.50
156 Orlando Miller	5.00	1.50
157 Mike Mimbs	5.00	1.50
158 Paul Molitor SP	50.00	15.00
159 Raul Mondesi SP	25.00	7.50
160 Jeff Montgomery	5.00	1.50
161 Mickey Morandini	5.00	1.50
162 Lyle Mouton	5.00	1.50
163 James Mouton	5.00	1.50
164 Jamie Moyer	10.00	3.00
165 Rodney Myers	5.00	1.50
166 Denny Neagle	5.00	1.50
167 Robb Nen	10.00	3.00
168 Marc Newfield	5.00	1.50
169 Dave Nilsson	5.00	1.50
170 Jon Nunnally	5.00	1.50
171 Chad Ogea	5.00	1.50
172 Troy O'Leary	5.00	1.50
173 Rey Ordonez	5.00	1.50
174 Jayhawk Owens	5.00	1.50
175 Tom Pagnozzi	5.00	1.50
176 Dean Palmer	5.00	1.50
177 Roger Pavlik	5.00	1.50
178 Troy Percival	10.00	3.00
179 Carlos Perez	5.00	1.50
180 Robert Perez	5.00	1.50
181 Andy Pettitte	40.00	12.00
182 Phil Plantier	5.00	1.50
183 Mike Potts	5.00	1.50
184 Curtis Pride	5.00	1.50
185 Ariel Prieto	5.00	1.50
186 Bill Pulsipher	5.00	1.50
187 Brad Radke	10.00	3.00
188 Manny Ramirez SP	50.00	15.00
189 Joe Randa	5.00	1.50
190 Pat Rapp	5.00	1.50
191 Bryan Rekar	5.00	1.50
192 Shane Reynolds	5.00	1.50
193 Arthur Rhodes	5.00	1.50
194 Mariano Rivera	40.00	12.00
195 Alex Rodriguez SP	120.00	36.00
196 Frank Rodriguez	5.00	1.50
197 Mel Rojas	5.00	1.50
198 Ken Ryan	5.00	1.50
199 Bret Saberhagen	10.00	3.00
200 Tim Salmon	15.00	4.50
201 Rey Sanchez	5.00	1.50
202 Scott Sanders	5.00	1.50
203 Steve Scarsone	5.00	1.50
204 Curt Schilling	40.00	12.00
205 Jason Schmidt	15.00	4.50
206 David Segui	5.00	1.50
207 Kevin Seitzer	5.00	1.50
208 Scott Servais	5.00	1.50
209 Don Slaught	5.00	1.50
210 Zane Smith	5.00	1.50
211 Paul Sorrento	5.00	1.50
212 Scott Stahoviak	5.00	1.50
213 Mike Stanley	5.00	1.50
214 Terry Steinbach	5.00	1.50
215 Kevin Stocker	5.00	1.50
216 Jeff Suppan	5.00	1.50
217 Bill Swift	5.00	1.50
218 Greg Swindell	5.00	1.50
219 Kevin Tapani	5.00	1.50
220 Danny Tartabull	5.00	1.50
221 Julian Tavarez	5.00	1.50
222 Frank Thomas SP	60.00	18.00
223 Ozzie Timmons	5.00	1.50
224 Michael Tucker	5.00	1.50
225 Ismael Valdes	5.00	1.50
226 Jose Valentin	5.00	1.50
227 Todd Van Poppel	5.00	1.50
228 Mo Vaughn SP	25.00	7.50
229 Quilvio Veras	5.00	1.50
230 Fernando Vina	5.00	1.50
231 Joe Vitiello	5.00	1.50
232 Jose Vizcaino	5.00	1.50
233 Omar Vizquel	15.00	4.50
234 Terrell Wade	5.00	1.50
235 Paul Wagner	5.00	1.50
236 Matt Walbeck	5.00	1.50
237 Jerome Walton	5.00	1.50
238 Turner Ward	5.00	1.50
239 Allen Watson	5.00	1.50
240 David Weathers	5.00	1.50
241 Walt Weiss	5.00	1.50
242 Turk Wendell	5.00	1.50
243 Rondell White	10.00	3.00
244 Brian Williams	5.00	1.50
245 George Williams	5.00	1.50
246 Paul Wilson	5.00	1.50
247 Bobby Witt	5.00	1.50
248 Bob Wolcott	5.00	1.50
249 Eric Young	5.00	1.50
250 Ernie Young	5.00	1.50
251 Greg Zaun	5.00	1.50
NNO F.Thomas Jumbo AU	40.00	12.00
NNO Frank Thomas Sample Fascimile Auto	2.00	.60

1996 Leaf Signature Autographs Gold

Randomly inserted primarily in first series packs, this 252-card set is parallel to the regular set and is similar in design with the exception of the gold foil printing on each card front. Each player signed 500 cards, except for the SP's of which only 100 of each are signed. Jim Thome erroneously signed 514 Gold cards.

	Nm-Mt	Ex-Mt
*GOLD: .6X TO 1.5X BRONZE CARDS		
223 Jim Thome SP/514	50.00	15.00

1996 Leaf Signature Autographs Silver

Randomly inserted primarily in first series packs, this 252-card set is parallel to the regular set and is similar in design with the exception of the silver foil printing on each card front. Each player signed 1000 silver cards, except for the SP's of which only 200 are signed. Jim Thome erroneously signed 410 Silver cards.

	Nm-Mt	Ex-Mt
*SILVER: .4X TO 1X BRONZE CARDS.		
223 Jim Thome SP/410	50.00	15.00

1996 Leaf Signature Extended Autographs

At least two autographed cards from this 217-card set were inserted in every Extended Series pack. Super Packs with four autographed cards were seeded one in every 12 packs. Most players signed 5000 cards, but short prints (500-2500 of each) do exist. On average, one in every nine packs contains a short print. All short print cards are individually noted in our checklist. By mistake, Andruw Jones, Ryan Klesko, Andy Pettitte, Kirby Puckett and Frank Thomas signed a few hundred of each of their cards in blue ink instead of black. No difference in price has been noted. Also, the Juan Gonzalez, Andruw Jones and Alex Rodriguez cards available in packs were not signed. All three cards had information on the back on how to mail them into Donruss/Leaf for an actual signed version. The deadline to exchange these cards was December 31st, 1998. In addition, middle relievers Doug Creek and Steve Parris failed to sign all 5000 of their cards. Creek submitted 1,950 cards and Parris submitted 1,800. Finally, an autographed jumbo version of the Extended Series Frank Thomas card was distributed to dealers in March, 1997. Dealers received either this card or the first series jumbo Thomas for every Extended Series case ordered. Each Extended Thomas jumbo is individually serial numbered to 1,500. A very popular Sammy Sosa card, one of his only certified autographs, is the key card in the set.

	Nm-Mt	Ex-Mt
1 Scott Aldred	5.00	1.50
2 Mike Aldrete	5.00	1.50
3 Rich Amaral	5.00	1.50
4 Alex Arias	5.00	1.50
5 Paul Assenmacher	5.00	1.50
6 Roger Bailey	5.00	1.50
7 Erik Bennett	5.00	1.50
8 Sean Bergman	5.00	1.50
9 Doug Bochtler	5.00	1.50
10 Tim Bogar	5.00	1.50
11 Pat Borders	5.00	1.50
12 Pedro Borbon	5.00	1.50
13 Shawn Boskie	5.00	1.50
14 Rafael Bournigal	5.00	1.50
15 Mark Brandenburg	5.00	1.50
16 John Briscoe	5.00	1.50
17 Jorge Brito	5.00	1.50
18 Doug Brocail	5.00	1.50
19 Jay Buhner SP/1000	25.00	7.50
20 Scott Bullett	5.00	1.50
21 Dave Burba	5.00	1.50
22 Ken Caminiti SP/1000	40.00	12.00
23 John Cangelosi	5.00	1.50
24 Cris Carpenter	5.00	1.50
25 Chuck Carr	5.00	1.50
26 Larry Casian	5.00	1.50
27 Tony Castillo	5.00	1.50
28 Jason Christiansen	5.00	1.50
29 Archi Cianfrocco	5.00	1.50
30 Mark Clark	5.00	1.50
31 Terry Clark	5.00	1.50
32 R. Clemens SP1000	150.00	45.00
33 Jim Converse	5.00	1.50
34 Dennis Cook	5.00	1.50
35 Francisco Cordova	5.00	1.50
36 Jim Corsi	5.00	1.50
37 Tim Crabtree	5.00	1.50
38 Doug Creek SP/1950	15.00	4.50
39 John Cummings	5.00	1.50
40 Omar Daal	5.00	1.50
41 Rich DeLucia	5.00	1.50
42 Mark Dewey	5.00	1.50
43 Alex Diaz	5.00	1.50
44 Jermaine Dye SP/2500	25.00	7.50
45 Ken Edenfield	5.00	1.50
46 Mark Eichhorn	5.00	1.50
47 John Ericks	5.00	1.50
48 Darin Erstad	15.00	4.50
49 Alvaro Espinoza	5.00	1.50
50 Jorge Fabregas	5.00	1.50
51 Mike Fetters	5.00	1.50
52 John Flaherty	5.00	1.50
53 Bryce Florie	5.00	1.50
54 Tony Fossas	5.00	1.50
55 Lou Frazier	5.00	1.50
56 Mike Gallego	5.00	1.50
57 Karim Garcia SP/2500	15.00	4.50
58 Jason Giambi	15.00	4.50
59 Ed Giovanola	5.00	1.50
60 Tom Glavine SP/1250	50.00	15.00
61 Juan Gonzalez SP/1000	40.00	12.00
62 Craig Grebeck	5.00	1.50
63 Buddy Groom	5.00	1.50
64 Kevin Gross	5.00	1.50
65 Eddie Guardado	5.00	1.50
66 Mark Guthrie	5.00	1.50
67 Tony Gwynn SP/1000	60.00	18.00
68 Chip Hale	5.00	1.50
69 Darren Hall	5.00	1.50
70 Lee Hancock	5.00	1.50
71 Dave Hansen	5.00	1.50
72 Bryan Harvey	5.00	1.50
73 Bill Haselman	5.00	1.50
74 Mike Henneman	5.00	1.50
75 Doug Henry	5.00	1.50
76 Gil Heredia	5.00	1.50
77 Carlos Hernandez	5.00	1.50
78 Jose Hernandez	5.00	1.50
79 Darren Holmes	5.00	1.50
80 Mark Holzemer	5.00	1.50
81 Rick Honeycutt	5.00	1.50
82 Chris Hook	5.00	1.50
83 Chris Howard	5.00	1.50
84 Jack Howell	5.00	1.50
85 David Hulse	5.00	1.50
86 Edwin Hurtado	5.00	1.50
87 Jeff Huson	5.00	1.50
88 Mike James	5.00	1.50
89 Derek Jeter SP/1000	150.00	45.00
90 Brian Johnson	5.00	1.50
91 R. Johnson SP1000	120.00	36.00
92 Mark Johnson	5.00	1.50
93 Andruw Jones SP/2000	40.00	12.00
94 Chris Jones	5.00	1.50
95 Ricky Jordan	5.00	1.50
96 Matt Karchner	5.00	1.50
97 Scott Karl	5.00	1.50
98 Jason Kendall SP/2500	25.00	7.50
99 Brian Keyser	5.00	1.50
100 Mike Kingery	5.00	1.50
101 Wayne Kirby	5.00	1.50
102 Ryan Klesko SP/1000	25.00	7.50
103 C. Knoblauch SP1000	25.00	7.50
104 Chad Kreuter	5.00	1.50
105 Tom Lampkin	5.00	1.50
106 Scott Leius	5.00	1.50
107 Jon Lieber	5.00	1.50
108 Nelson Liriano	5.00	1.50
109 Scott Livingstone	5.00	1.50
110 Graeme Lloyd	5.00	1.50
111 Kenny Lofton SP/1000	40.00	12.00
112 Luis Lopez	5.00	1.50
113 Torey Lovullo	5.00	1.50
114 Greg Maddux SP/500	250.00	75.00
115 Mike Maddux	5.00	1.50
116 Dave Magadan	5.00	1.50
117 Mike Magnante	5.00	1.50
118 Joe Magrane	5.00	1.50
119 Pat Mahomes	5.00	1.50
120 Matt Mantei	5.00	1.50
121 John Marzano	5.00	1.50
122 Terry Mathews	5.00	1.50
123 Chuck McElroy	5.00	1.50
124 Fred McGriff SP/1000	60.00	18.00
125 Mark McLemore	5.00	1.50
126 Greg McMichael	5.00	1.50
127 Blas Minor	5.00	1.50
128 Dave Mlicki	5.00	1.50
129 Mike Mohler	5.00	1.50
130 Paul Molitor SP/1000	40.00	12.00
131 Steve Montgomery	5.00	1.50
132 Mike Mordecai	5.00	1.50
133 Mike Morgan	5.00	1.50
134 Mike Munoz	5.00	1.50
135 Greg Myers	5.00	1.50
136 Jimmy Myers	5.00	1.50
137 Mike Myers	5.00	1.50
138 Bob Natal	5.00	1.50
139 Dan Naulty	5.00	1.50
140 Jeff Nelson	10.00	3.00
141 Warren Newson	5.00	1.50
142 Chris Nichting	5.00	1.50
143 Melvin Nieves	5.00	1.50
144 Charlie O'Brien	5.00	1.50
145 Alex Ochoa	5.00	1.50
146 Omar Olivares	5.00	1.50
147 Joe Oliver	5.00	1.50
148 Lance Painter	5.00	1.50
149 R. Palmeiro SP2000	50.00	15.00
150 Mark Parent	5.00	1.50
151 Steve Parris SP/1800	15.00	4.50
152 Bob Patterson	5.00	1.50
153 Tony Pena	5.00	1.50
154 Eddie Perez	5.00	1.50
155 Yorkis Perez	5.00	1.50
156 Robert Person	5.00	1.50
157 Mark Petkovsek	5.00	1.50
158 Andy Pettitte SP/1000	80.00	24.00
159 J.R. Phillips	5.00	1.50
160 Hipolito Pichardo	5.00	1.50
161 Eric Plunk	5.00	1.50
162 Jimmy Poole	5.00	1.50
163 K. Puckett SP/1000	80.00	24.00
164 Paul Quantrill	5.00	1.50
165 Tom Quinlan	5.00	1.50
166 Jeff Reboulet	5.00	1.50
167 Jeff Reed	5.00	1.50
168 Steve Reed	5.00	1.50
169 Carlos Reyes	5.00	1.50
170 Bill Risley	5.00	1.50
171 Kevin Ritz	5.00	1.50
172 Kevin Roberson	5.00	1.50
173 Rich Robertson	5.00	1.50
174 A. Rodriguez SP/500	150.00	45.00
175 I. Rodriguez SP1250	50.00	15.00
176 Bruce Ruffin	5.00	1.50
177 Juan Samuel	5.00	1.50
178 Tim Scott	5.00	1.50
179 Kevin Sefcik	5.00	1.50
180 Jeff Shaw	5.00	1.50
181 Danny Sheaffer	5.00	1.50
182 Craig Shipley	5.00	1.50
183 Dave Silvestri	5.00	1.50
184 Aaron Small	5.00	1.50
185 John Smoltz SP/1000	100.00	30.00
186 Luis Sojo	5.00	1.50
187 S. Sosa SP/1000	250.00	75.00
188 Steve Sparks	5.00	1.50
189 Tim Spehr	5.00	1.50
190 Russ Springer	5.00	1.50
191 Matt Stairs	5.00	1.50

192 Andy Stankiewicz 5.00 1.50
193 Mike Stanton 5.00 1.50
194 Kelly Stinnett 5.00 1.50
195 Doug Strange 5.00 1.50
196 Mark Sweeney 5.00 1.50
197 Jeff Tabaka 5.00 1.50
198 Jesus Tavarez 5.00 1.50
199 F. Thomas SP1000 60.00 18.00
200 Larry Thomas 5.00 1.50
201 Mark Thompson 5.00 1.50
202 Mike Timlin 15.00 4.50
203 Steve Trachsel 5.00 1.50
204 Tom Urbani 5.00 1.50
205 Julio Valera 5.00 1.50
206 Dave Valle 5.00 1.50
207 Wm. VanLandingham 5.00 1.50
208 Mo Vaughn SP/1000 25.00 7.50
209 Dave Veres 5.00 1.50
210 Ed Vosberg 5.00 1.50
211 Don Wengert 5.00 1.50
212 Matt Whiteside 5.00 1.50
213 Bob Wickman 5.00 1.50
214 M.Williams SP/1250 25.00 7.50
215 Mike Williams 5.00 1.50
216 Woody Williams 15.00 4.50
217 Craig Worthington 5.00 1.50
NNO F.Thomas Jumbo AU 40.00 12.00

1996 Leaf Signature Extended Autographs Century Marks

Randomly inserted exclusively into Extended Series packs, cards from this 31-card parallel set feature a selection of star and rising young prospect players taken from the more comprehensive 217-card Extended Autograph set. The cards differ by a special blue holographic foil treatment. Only 100 of each card exists. In addition, Juan Gonzalez, Derek Jeter, Andruw Jones, Rafael Palmeiro and Alex Rodriguez did not sign the cards distributed in packs. All of these players cards had information on the back on how to mail them into Leaf/Donruss to receive a signed version.

Nm-Mt Ex-Mt
1 Jay Buhner 60.00 18.00
2 Ken Caminiti 100.00 30.00
3 Roger Clemens 250.00 75.00
4 Jermaine Dye 60.00 18.00
5 Darin Erstad 50.00 15.00
6 Karim Garcia 25.00 7.50
7 Jason Giambi 100.00 30.00
8 Tom Glavine 150.00 45.00
9 Juan Gonzalez 100.00 30.00
10 Tony Gwynn 150.00 45.00
11 Derek Jeter 350.00 105.00
12 Randy Johnson 150.00 45.00
13 Andruw Jones 100.00 30.00
14 Jason Kendall 60.00 18.00
15 Ryan Klesko 60.00 18.00
16 Chuck Knoblauch 60.00 18.00
17 Kenny Lofton 100.00 30.00
18 Greg Maddux 250.00 75.00
19 Fred McGriff 100.00 30.00
20 Paul Molitor 100.00 30.00
21 Alex Ochoa 25.00 7.50
22 Rafael Palmeiro 150.00 45.00
23 Andy Pettitte 150.00 45.00
24 Kirby Puckett 150.00 45.00
25 Alex Rodriguez 300.00 90.00
26 Ivan Rodriguez 150.00 45.00
27 John Smoltz 100.00 30.00
28 Sammy Sosa 400.00 120.00
29 Frank Thomas 150.00 45.00
30 Mo Vaughn 60.00 18.00
31 Matt Williams 100.00 30.00

2004 Leather and Lumber

This 175-card set was released in September, 2004. The set was issued in five card packs with an $6 SRP which were issued 24 packs to a box and 12 boxes to a case. The first 150 cards of this set feature a mix of veterans and retired players while cards numbered 151 through 173 feature autographed Rookie Cards and cards numbers 174 and 175 are unsigned Rookie Cards. All cards numbered 151 through 175 were issued to a stated print run of 500 serial numbered sets.

Nm-Mt Ex-Mt
COMP.SET w/o SP's (150) 40.00 12.00
COMMON CARD (1-150) .40 .12
COMMON RETIRED (1-150) .50 .15
COMMON AUTO (151-175) 8.00 2.40
COMMON CARD (151-175) 4.00 1.20
1 Bartolo Colon .40 .12
2 Garret Anderson .40 .12
3 Tim Salmon .60 .18
4 Troy Glaus .40 .12
5 Vladimir Guerrero 1.00 .30
6 Brandon Webb .40 .12
7 Luis Gonzalez .40 .12
8 Randy Johnson 1.00 .30
9 Richie Sexson .40 .12
10 Shea Hillenbrand .40 .12
11 Adam LaRoche .40 .12
12 Andruw Jones .40 .12
13 Chipper Jones 1.00 .30
14 Dale Murphy .75 .23
15 J.D. Drew .40 .12
16 Marcus Giles .40 .12
17 Rafael Furcal .40 .12
18 Cal Ripken 5.00 1.50
19 Javy Lopez .40 .12
20 Jay Gibbons .40 .12
21 Luis Matos .40 .12
22 Miguel Tejada .40 .12
23 Rafael Palmeiro .60 .18
24 Curt Schilling 1.00 .30
25 Jason Varitek .60 .18
26 Manny Ramirez .60 .18
27 Nomar Garciaparra 1.50 .45
28 Pedro Martinez 1.00 .30
29 Trot Nixon .40 .12
30 Greg Maddux 1.50 .45
31 Kerry Wood 1.00 .30
32 Mark Prior 1.00 .30
33 Ryne Sandberg UER 2.50 .75
Hit 267th career homer in 1977
34 Sammy Sosa 1.50 .45
35 Carlos Lee .40 .12
36 Frank Thomas 1.00 .30
37 Magglio Ordonez .40 .12
38 Paul Konerko .40 .12
39 Adam Dunn .60 .18
40 Austin Kearns .40 .12
41 Barry Larkin .60 .18
42 Ken Griffey Jr. 1.50 .45
43 Ryan Wagner .40 .12
44 C.C. Sabathia .40 .12
45 Jody Gerut .40 .12
46 Omar Vizquel .60 .18
47 Larry Walker .60 .18
48 Preston Wilson .40 .12
49 Todd Helton .60 .18
50 Alan Trammell .50 .15
51 Ivan Rodriguez 1.00 .30
52 Jeremy Bonderman .40 .12
53 Dontrelle Willis .40 .12
54 Josh Beckett .40 .12
55 Luis Castillo .40 .12
56 Miguel Cabrera .60 .18
57 Mike Lowell .60 .18
58 Andy Pettitte .60 .18
59 Craig Biggio .60 .18
60 Jeff Bagwell .60 .18
61 Jeff Kent .40 .12
62 Lance Berkman .40 .12
63 Roger Clemens 2.00 .60
64 Roy Oswalt .40 .12
65 Angel Berroa .40 .12
66 Carlos Beltran .60 .18
67 George Brett 2.50 .75
68 Juan Gonzalez .60 .18
69 Mike Sweeney .40 .12
70 Eric Gagne 1.00 .30
71 Hideo Nomo 1.00 .30
72 Kazuhisa Ishii .40 .12
73 Paul Lo Duca .40 .12
74 Shawn Green .40 .12
75 Geoff Jenkins .40 .12
76 Junior Spivey .40 .12
77 Rickie Weeks 1.50 .45
78 Robin Yount 2.00 .60
79 Scott Podsednik .40 .12
80 Jacque Jones .40 .12
81 Johan Santana .60 .18
82 Shannon Stewart .40 .12
83 Torii Hunter .40 .12
84 Andre Dawson .50 .15
85 Chad Cordero .40 .12
86 Jose Vidro .40 .12
87 Nick Johnson .40 .12
88 Orlando Cabrera .40 .12
89 Gary Carter .50 .15
90 Jae Weong Seo .40 .12
91 Jose Reyes .40 .12
92 Mike Piazza 1.50 .45
93 Tom Glavine .60 .18
94 Alex Rodriguez 1.50 .45
95 Bernie Williams .60 .18
96 Derek Jeter 2.00 .60
97 Don Mattingly 2.50 .75
98 Gary Sheffield .40 .12
99 Hideki Matsui 1.50 .45
100 Jason Giambi .40 .12
101 Jorge Posada .60 .18
102 Mike Mussina .60 .18
103 Barry Zito .40 .12
104 Bobby Crosby .60 .18
105 Eric Chavez .40 .12
106 Jermaine Dye .40 .12
107 Mark Mulder .40 .12
108 Rich Harden .40 .12
109 Rickey Henderson 1.25 .35
110 Tim Hudson .40 .12
111 Bobby Abreu .40 .12
112 Brett Myers .40 .12
113 Jim Thome 1.00 .30
114 Kevin Millwood .40 .12
115 Marlon Byrd .40 .12
116 Mike Schmidt 2.50 .75
117 Pat Burrell .40 .12
118 Dave Parker .50 .15
119 Jason Bay .40 .12
120 Jason Kendall .40 .12
121 Brian Giles .40 .12
122 Jay Payton .40 .12
123 Ryan Klesko .40 .12
124 Tony Gwynn 2.00 .60
125 Edgardo Alfonzo .40 .12
126 Jason Schmidt .40 .12
127 Jerome Williams .40 .12
128 Bret Boone .40 .12
129 Edgar Martinez .60 .18
130 Ichiro Suzuki 1.50 .45
131 Jamie Moyer .40 .12
132 John Olerud .40 .12
133 Albert Pujols 2.00 .60
134 Edgar Renteria .40 .12
135 Jim Edmonds .40 .12
136 Matt Morris .40 .12
137 Scott Rolen 1.00 .30
138 Aubrey Huff .40 .12
139 Carl Crawford .40 .12
140 Delmon Young .60 .18
141 Rocco Baldelli .40 .12
142 Alfonso Soriano .60 .18
143 Hank Blalock .40 .12
144 Mark Teixeira .40 .12
145 Michael Young .40 .12
146 Nolan Ryan 3.00 .90
147 Carlos Delgado .40 .12
148 Eric Hinske .40 .12
149 Roy Halladay .40 .12
150 Vernon Wells .40 .12
151 Andres Blanco ROO AU RC 8.00 2.40
152 Kevin Cave ROO AU RC 10.00 3.00
153 Ryan Meaux ROO AU RC 8.00 2.40
154 Tim Bausher ROO AU RC 8.00 2.40
155 Jesse Harper ROO AU RC 8.00 2.40
156 Mike Wuertz ROO AU RC 10.00 3.00
157 Colby Miller ROO AU RC 8.00 2.40
158 Don Kelly ROO AU RC 8.00 2.40
159 Edwin Moreno ROO AU RC 10.00 3.00
160 Mike Johnston ROO AU RC 8.00 2.40
161 O.Rodriguez ROO AU RC 8.00 2.40
162 Phil Stockman ROO AU RC 8.00 2.40
163 Yadier Molina ROO RC 6.00 1.80
164 Jorge Vasquez ROO AU RC 8.00 2.40
165 Scott Proctor ROO AU RC 10.00 3.00
166 Jake Woods ROO AU RC 8.00 2.40
167 Aarom Baldiris ROO AU RC 10.00 3.00
168 Jason Bartlett ROO AU RC 10.00 3.00
169 Casey Daigle ROO AU RC 8.00 2.40
170 Dennis Sarfate ROO AU RC 8.00 2.40
171 E.Sierra ROO AU RC 10.00 3.00
172 Merkin Valdez ROO AU RC 10.00 3.00
173 E.Rodriguez ROO AU RC 10.00 3.00
174 Kazuo Matsui ROO RC 10.00 3.00
175 David Aardsma ROO RC 4.00 1.20

2004 Leather and Lumber B/W

Nm-Mt Ex-Mt
*B/W: 1X TO 2.5X BASIC
*B/W ROO: .4X TO 1X BASIC ROO
RANDOM INSERTS IN PACKS
STATED PRINT RUN 1000 SERIAL #'d SETS
SKIP-NUMBERED 25-CARD SET
CL: 13-14/18/27/30/32-34/63/67/78/89/92
CL: 94/96-97/99/109/116/124/130/133/142
CL: 146/174

2004 Leather and Lumber Gold

Nm-Mt Ex-Mt
*GOLD 1-150: 8X TO 20X BASIC
*GOLD RETIRED 1-150: 6X TO 15X BASIC
RANDOM INSERTS IN PACKS
STATED PRINT RUN 25 SERIAL #'d SETS
NO PRICING ON 151-175 DUE TO SCARCITY

2004 Leather and Lumber Gold B/W

Nm-Mt Ex-Mt
*GOLD B/W: 8X TO 20X BASIC
*GOLD RETIRED B/W: 6X TO 15X BASIC
RANDOM INSERTS IN PACKS
STATED PRINT RUN 25 SERIAL #'d SETS
NO CARD 174 PRICING DUE TO SCARCITY

2004 Leather and Lumber Platinum

Nm-Mt Ex-Mt
RANDOM INSERTS IN HOBBY PACKS
STATED PRINT RUN 1 SERIAL #'d SET
NO PRICING DUE TO SCARCITY

2004 Leather and Lumber Platinum B/W

Nm-Mt Ex-Mt
RANDOM INSERTS IN HOBBY PACKS
STATED PRINT RUN 1 SERIAL #'d SET
NO PRICING DUE TO SCARCITY

2004 Leather and Lumber Silver

Nm-Mt Ex-Mt
*SILVER 1-150: 3X TO 8X BASIC
*SILVER RETIRED 1-150: 3X TO 8X BASIC
*SILVER 151-173: .2X TO .5X BASIC AUTO
*SILVER 174-175: .4X TO 1X BASIC
RANDOM INSERTS IN PACKS
STATED PRINT RUN 100 SERIAL #'d SETS
174 Kazuo Matsui ROO 15.00 4.50

2004 Leather and Lumber Silver B/W

Nm-Mt Ex-Mt
*SILV.RETIRED B/W 1-150: 3X TO 8X BASIC
*SILV.B/W 174: .6X TO 1.5X BASIC
RANDOM INSERTS IN PACKS
STATED PRINT RUN 100 SERIAL #'d SETS

2004 Leather and Lumber Materials Barrel

Nm-Mt Ex-Mt
PRINT RUNS B/WN 1-5 COPIES PER
B/W PRINT RUNS B/WN 2-5 COPIES PER
OVERALL AU-GU ODDS 1:6 HOBBY
BARRELS ISSUED ONLY IN HOBBY PACKS
NO PRICING DUE TO SCARCITY

2004 Leather and Lumber Materials Bat

Nm-Mt Ex-Mt
*BAT p/r 100: .5X TO 1.2X JSY p/r 150-250
*BAT p/r 100: .4X TO 1X JSY p/r 100
*BAT p/r 100: .25X TO .6X JSY p/r 50
*BAT p/r 100: .15X TO .4X JSY p/r 25
*BAT p/r 50: .6X TO 1.5X JSY p/r 100
*BAT p/r 25: 1.25X TO 3X JSY p/r 150-250
OVERALL AU-GU ODDS 1:6 HOBBY
PRINT RUNS B/WN 1-100 COPIES PER
NO PRICING ON QTY OF 10 OR LESS
5 Vladimir Guerrero/100 10.00 3.00
6 Brandon Webb/10
9 Richie Sexson/10
11 Adam LaRoche/100 5.00 1.50
15 J.D. Drew/100 5.00 1.50
24 Curt Schilling/100 10.00 3.00
27 Nomar Garciaparra/100 12.00 3.60
53 Dontrelle Willis/1
63 Roger Clemens/50 20.00 6.00
68 Juan Gonzalez/100 8.00 2.40
76 Junior Spivey/100 5.00 1.50
77 Rickie Weeks/25 12.00 3.60
87 Nick Johnson/100 5.00 1.50
94 Alex Rodriguez/100 12.00 3.60
98 Gary Sheffield/100 5.00 1.50
105 Eric Chavez/3
121 Brian Giles/100 5.00 1.50
125 Edgardo Alfonzo/100 5.00 1.50
128 Bret Boone/100 5.00 1.50
137 Scott Rolen/5
140 Delmon Young/100 8.00 2.40
142 Alfonso Soriano/100 8.00 2.40
144 Mark Teixeira/100 5.00 1.50
145 Michael Young/100 5.00 1.50
148 Eric Hinske/1

2004 Leather and Lumber Materials Jersey

Nm-Mt Ex-Mt
OVERALL AU-GU ODDS 1:6 HOBBY
PRINT RUNS B/WN 1-250 COPIES PER
NO PRICING ON QTY OF 10 OR LESS
2 Garret Anderson/50 8.00 2.40
3 Tim Salmon/250 8.00 2.40
4 Troy Glaus/200 5.00 1.50
6 Brandon Webb/100 5.00 1.50
7 Luis Gonzalez/250 5.00 1.50
8 Randy Johnson/100 10.00 3.00
12 Andruw Jones/250 5.00 1.50
13 Chipper Jones/250 8.00 2.40
14 Dale Murphy/250 10.00 3.00
16 Marcus Giles/250 5.00 1.50
17 Rafael Furcal/250 5.00 1.50
18 Cal Ripken/100 40.00 12.00
19 Javy Lopez/150 5.00 1.50
20 Jay Gibbons/250 5.00 1.50
21 Luis Matos/250 5.00 1.50
22 Miguel Tejada/250 5.00 1.50
23 Rafael Palmeiro/250 8.00 2.40
25 Jason Varitek/250 8.00 2.40
26 Manny Ramirez/250 8.00 2.40
28 Pedro Martinez/250 8.00 2.40
29 Trot Nixon/25 12.00 3.60
30 Greg Maddux/100 12.00 3.60
31 Kerry Wood/250 8.00 2.40
32 Mark Prior/250 8.00 2.40
33 Ryne Sandberg/50 40.00 12.00
34 Sammy Sosa/250 10.00 3.00
35 Carlos Lee/250 5.00 1.50
36 Frank Thomas/250 8.00 2.40
37 Magglio Ordonez/250 5.00 1.50
38 Paul Konerko/250 5.00 1.50
39 Adam Dunn/250 8.00 2.40
40 Austin Kearns/250 5.00 1.50
41 Barry Larkin/250 8.00 2.40
44 C.C. Sabathia/250 5.00 1.50
45 Jody Gerut/250 5.00 1.50
46 Omar Vizquel/250 8.00 2.40
47 Larry Walker/250 8.00 2.40
48 Preston Wilson/250 5.00 1.50
49 Todd Helton/250 8.00 2.40
50 Alan Trammell/50 10.00 3.00
51 Ivan Rodriguez/100 10.00 3.00
52 Jeremy Bonderman/150 5.00 1.50
53 Dontrelle Willis/100 5.00 1.50
54 Josh Beckett/250 5.00 1.50
55 Luis Castillo/250 5.00 1.50
56 Miguel Cabrera/50 12.00 3.60
57 Mike Lowell/25 12.00 3.60
58 Andy Pettitte/25 20.00 6.00
59 Craig Biggio/250 8.00 2.40
60 Jeff Bagwell/250 8.00 2.40
61 Jeff Kent/250 5.00 1.50
62 Lance Berkman/250 5.00 1.50
64 Roy Oswalt/250 5.00 1.50
65 Angel Berroa/50 8.00 2.40
66 Carlos Beltran/250 8.00 2.40
67 George Brett/250 15.00 4.50
69 Mike Sweeney/100 5.00 1.50
71 Hideo Nomo/250 8.00 2.40
72 Kazuhisa Ishii/250 5.00 1.50
73 Paul Lo Duca/250 5.00 1.50
74 Shawn Green/250 5.00 1.50
75 Geoff Jenkins/250 5.00 1.50
78 Robin Yount/250 10.00 3.00
80 Jacque Jones/250 5.00 1.50
81 Johan Santana/250 8.00 2.40
82 Shannon Stewart/250 5.00 1.50
83 Torii Hunter/250 5.00 1.50
84 Andre Dawson/50 10.00 3.00
86 Jose Vidro/100 5.00 1.50
88 Orlando Cabrera/100 5.00 1.50
89 Gary Carter/250 8.00 2.40
90 Jae Weong Seo/100 5.00 1.50
91 Jose Reyes/250 5.00 1.50
92 Mike Piazza/250 10.00 3.00
93 Tom Glavine/250 8.00 2.40
95 Bernie Williams/250 8.00 2.40
96 Derek Jeter/150 20.00 6.00
97 Don Mattingly/250 15.00 4.50
99 Hideki Matsui/250 20.00 6.00
100 Jason Giambi/250 5.00 1.50
101 Jorge Posada/50 12.00 3.60
102 Mike Mussina/100 8.00 2.40
103 Barry Zito/250 5.00 1.50
105 Eric Chavez/100 5.00 1.50
107 Mark Mulder/250 5.00 1.50
108 Rich Harden/50 8.00 2.40
109 Rickey Henderson/100 15.00 4.50
110 Tim Hudson/250 5.00 1.50
111 Bobby Abreu/250 5.00 1.50
112 Brett Myers/250 5.00 1.50
113 Jim Thome/250 8.00 2.40
114 Kevin Millwood/250 5.00 1.50
115 Marlon Byrd/250 5.00 1.50
116 Mike Schmidt/50 25.00 7.50
117 Pat Burrell/250 5.00 1.50
118 Dave Parker/250 8.00 2.40
120 Jason Kendall/50 8.00 2.40
123 Ryan Klesko/250 5.00 1.50
124 Tony Gwynn/100 15.00 4.50
127 Jerome Williams/200 5.00 1.50
128 Bret Boone/10
129 Edgar Martinez/250 8.00 2.40
131 Jamie Moyer/250 5.00 1.50
132 John Olerud/150 5.00 1.50
133 Albert Pujols/250 15.00 4.50
134 Edgar Renteria/100 5.00 1.50
135 Jim Edmonds/250 5.00 1.50
136 Matt Morris/250 5.00 1.50
137 Scott Rolen/250 8.00 2.40
138 Aubrey Huff/100 5.00 1.50
139 Carl Crawford/250 5.00 1.50
141 Rocco Baldelli/250 5.00 1.50
143 Hank Blalock/250 5.00 1.50
144 Mark Teixeira/1
146 Nolan Ryan/100 30.00 9.00
147 Carlos Delgado/250 5.00 1.50
148 Eric Hinske/250 5.00 1.50
149 Roy Halladay/100 5.00 1.50
150 Vernon Wells/250 5.00 1.50

2004 Leather and Lumber Materials MLB Logo

Nm-Mt Ex-Mt
STATED PRINT RUN 1 SERIAL #'d SET
B/W PRINT RUN 1 SERIAL #'d SET
OVERALL AU-GU ODDS 1:6 HOBBY
LOGOS ISSUED ONLY IN HOBBY PACKS
NO PRICING DUE TO SCARCITY

2004 Leather and Lumber Signatures Bronze

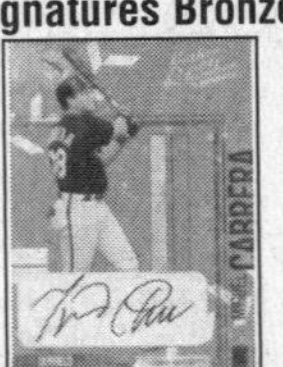

Nm-Mt Ex-Mt
OVERALL AU-GU ODDS 1:6 HOBBY
PRINT RUNS B/WN 1-100 COPIES PER
NO PRICING ON QTY OF 10 OR LESS
2 Garret Anderson/25 25.00 7.50
6 Brandon Webb/10
10 Shea Hillenbrand/100 15.00 4.50
11 Adam LaRoche/100 10.00 3.00
12 Andruw Jones/1
13 Chipper Jones/1
14 Dale Murphy/25 40.00 12.00
16 Marcus Giles/50 20.00 6.00
17 Rafael Furcal/25 25.00 7.50
18 Cal Ripken/1
20 Jay Gibbons/100 10.00 3.00
21 Luis Matos/100 10.00 3.00
26 Manny Ramirez/1
28 Pedro Martinez/1
29 Trot Nixon/10
31 Kerry Wood/1
32 Mark Prior/10
34 Sammy Sosa/5

35 Carlos Lee/100 10.00 3.00
36 Frank Thomas/5
37 Magglio Ordonez/1
39 Adam Dunn/25 40.00 12.00
40 Austin Kearns/10
41 Barry Larkin/1
43 Ryan Wagner/5
44 C.C. Sabathia/100 15.00 4.50
45 Jody Gerut/100 15.00 4.50
48 Preston Wilson/50 20.00 6.00
50 Alan Trammell/50 20.00 6.00
52 Jeremy Bonderman/100 10.00 3.00
56 Miguel Cabrera/50 30.00 9.00
57 Mike Lowell/5
58 Andy Pettitte/1
59 Craig Biggio/1
60 Jeff Bagwell/1
63 Roger Clemens/1
65 Angel Berroa/100 10.00 3.00
66 Carlos Beltran/100 30.00 9.00
67 George Brett/1
71 Hideo Nomo/1
73 Paul Lo Duca/10
77 Rickie Weeks/1
79 Scott Podsednik/100 15.00 4.50
80 Jacque Jones/100 15.00 4.50
81 Johan Santana/100 30.00 9.00
82 Shannon Stewart/100 15.00 4.50
83 Torii Hunter/50 20.00 6.00
84 Andre Dawson/100 15.00 4.50
85 Chad Cordero/100 10.00 3.00
86 Jose Vidro/100 10.00 3.00
88 Orlando Cabrera/100 15.00 4.50
89 Gary Carter/5
91 Jose Reyes/1
92 Mike Piazza/1
95 Bernie Williams/1
97 Don Mattingly/10
98 Gary Sheffield/5
101 Jorge Posada/5
102 Mike Mussina/1
104 Bobby Crosby/100 25.00 7.50
106 Jermaine Dye/100 15.00 4.50
107 Mark Mulder/10
108 Rich Harden/50 20.00 6.00
109 Rickey Henderson/1
110 Tim Hudson/1
112 Brett Myers/5
115 Marlon Byrd/25 15.00 4.50
119 Jason Bay/100 15.00 4.50
122 Jay Payton/50 12.00 3.60
124 Tony Gwynn/1
127 Jerome Williams/1
129 Edgar Martinez/1
133 Albert Pujols/1
135 Jim Edmonds/1
137 Scott Rolen/5
138 Aubrey Huff/50 20.00 6.00
139 Carl Crawford/50 20.00 6.00
140 Delmon Young/5
142 Alfonso Soriano/5
143 Hank Blalock/10
144 Mark Teixeira/5
145 Michael Young/100 20.00 6.00
146 Nolan Ryan/1
149 Roy Halladay/1
150 Vernon Wells/10
151 Andres Blanco ROO/50 10.00 3.00
152 Kevin Cave ROO/50 15.00 4.50
153 Ryan Meaux ROO/50 10.00 3.00
154 Tim Bausher ROO/50 10.00 3.00
155 Jesse Harper ROO/50 10.00 3.00
156 Michael Wuertz ROO/50 15.00 4.50
158 Don Kelly ROO/50 10.00 3.00
159 Edwin Moreno ROO/50 15.00 4.50
160 Mike Johnston ROO/50 10.00 3.00
161 Orlando Rodriguez ROO/50 10.00 3.00
164 Jorge Vasquez ROO/50 10.00 3.00
166 Jake Woods ROO/50 10.00 3.00
167 Aarom Baldiris ROO/50 15.00 4.50
170 Dennis Sarfate ROO/50 10.00 3.00
173 Eddy Rodriguez ROO/50 15.00 4.50

2004 Leather and Lumber Signatures Bronze B/W

Nm-Mt Ex-Mt
*BRONZE B/W p/r 25: .4X TO 1X p/r 25
OVERALL AU-GU ODDS 1:6 HOBBY
PRINT RUNS B/WN 1-25 COPIES PER
NO PRICING ON QTY OF 10 OR LESS

2004 Leather and Lumber Signatures Gold

Nm-Mt Ex-Mt
*GOLD 1-150 p/r 25: .6X TO 1.5X p/r 100
*GOLD 1-150 p/r 25: .5X TO 1.2X p/r 50
*GOLD 1-150 p/r 25: .4X TO 1X p/r 25
*GOLD 151-175 p/r 50: .4X TO 1X p/r 50
OVERALL AU-GU ODDS 1:6 HOBBY
GOLD SIGS ISSUED ONLY IN HOBBY PACKS
PRINT RUNS B/WN 1-25 COPIES PER
NO PRICING ON QTY OF 10 OR LESS
168 Jason Bartlett ROO/50 15.00 4.50

2004 Leather and Lumber Signatures Gold B/W

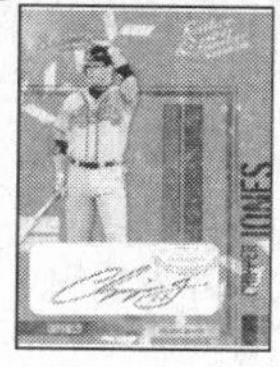

Nm-Mt Ex-Mt
*GOLD B/W p/r 25: .4X TO 1X p/r 25
OVERALL AU-GU ODDS 1:6 HOBBY
GOLD SIGS ISSUED ONLY IN HOBBY PACKS
PRINT RUNS B/WN 1-25 COPIES PER
NO PRICING ON QTY OF 10 OR LESS

2004 Leather and Lumber Signatures Silver

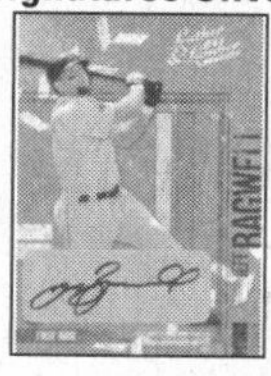

Nm-Mt Ex-Mt
*SILV 1-150 p/r 50: .5X TO 1.2X p/r 100
*SILV 1-150 p/r 50: .4X TO 1X p/r 50
*SILV 1-150 p/r 50: .3X TO .8X p/r 25
*SILV 1-150 p/r 25: .4X TO 1X p/r 25
*SILV 151-175 p/r 100: .3X TO .8X p/r 50
OVERALL AU-GU ODDS 1:6 HOBBY
PRINT RUNS B/WN 1-100 COPIES PER
NO PRICING ON QTY OF 14 OR LESS
29 Trot Nixon/25 25.00 7.50
32 Mark Prior/25 80.00 24.00
40 Austin Kearns/25 25.00 7.50
43 Ryan Wagner/50 12.00 3.60
73 Paul Lo Duca/25 25.00 7.50
107 Mark Mulder/25 25.00 7.50
143 Hank Blalock/50 20.00 6.00
150 Vernon Wells/50 20.00 6.00

2004 Leather and Lumber Signatures Silver B/W

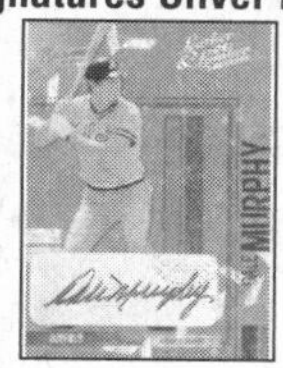

Nm-Mt Ex-Mt
*SILV B/W p/r 25: .4X TO 1X p/r 25
OVERALL AU-GU ODDS 1:6 HOBBY
PRINT RUNS B/WN 1-25 COPIES PER
NO PRICING ON QTY OF 10 OR LESS
32 Mark Prior/25 80.00 24.00

2004 Leather and Lumber Fans of the Game

Nm-Mt Ex-Mt
STATED ODDS 1:24
1 John Travolta 5.00 1.50
2 Dennis Haysbert 2.00 .60
3 Chris O'Donnell 2.00 .60
4 Abby Wambach 5.00 1.50
5 Jules Asner 3.00 .90

2004 Leather and Lumber Fans of the Game Signatures

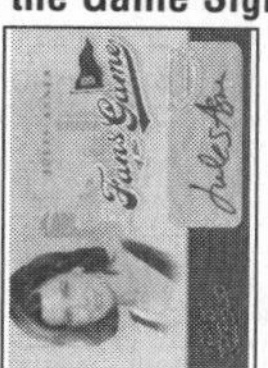

Nm-Mt Ex-Mt
OVERALL AU-GU ODDS 1:6 HOBBY
EXCHANGE DEADLINE 03/01/06
1 John Travolta SP EXCH 250.00 75.00
2 Dennis Haysbert 40.00 12.00
3 Chris O'Donnell 40.00 12.00
4 Abby Wambach 60.00 18.00
5 Jules Asner 60.00 18.00

2004 Leather and Lumber Hall of Fame

Nm-Mt Ex-Mt
RANDOM INSERTS IN PACKS
PRINT RUNS B/WN 1989-2002 COPIES PER
*SILVER: 1.25X TO 3X BASIC
SILVER RANDOM IN HOBBY PACKS
SILVER PRINT RUN 100 SERIAL #'d SETS
1 Carl Yastrzemski/1989 5.00 1.50
2 Carlton Fisk/2000 3.00 .90
3 George Brett/1999 6.00 1.80
4 Johnny Bench/1989 3.00 .90
5 Mike Schmidt/1995 6.00 1.80
6 Nolan Ryan/1999 8.00 2.40
7 Ozzie Smith/2002 5.00 1.50
8 Robin Yount/1999 5.00 1.50
9 Rod Carew/1991 3.00 .90
10 Tom Seaver/1992 3.00 .90

2004 Leather and Lumber Hall of Fame Materials

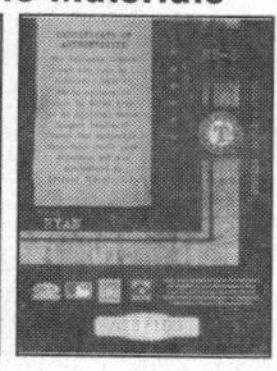

Nm-Mt Ex-Mt
OVERALL AU-GU ODDS 1:6 HOBBY
PRINT RUNS B/WN 100-250 COPIES PER
1 Carl Yastrzemski Jsy/250 15.00 4.50
2 Carlton Fisk Jsy/250 10.00 3.00
3 George Brett Jsy/250 15.00 4.50
4 Johnny Bench Jsy/100 15.00 4.50
5 Mike Schmidt Jkt/250 15.00 4.50
6 Nolan Ryan Pants/100 30.00 9.00
7 Ozzie Smith Jsy/100 20.00 6.00
8 Robin Yount Jsy/250 15.00 4.50
9 Rod Carew Jkt/250 10.00 3.00
10 Tom Seaver Jsy/200 10.00 3.00

2004 Leather and Lumber Leather Cuts Glove

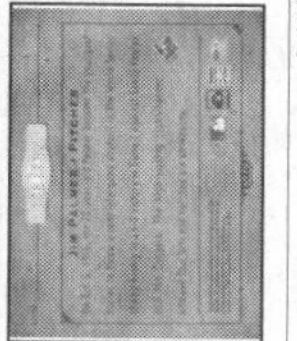

Nm-Mt Ex-Mt
PRINT RUNS B/WN 32-224 COPIES PER
BALL PRINT RUNS B/WN 5-10 COPIES PER
NO BALL PRICING DUE TO SCARCITY
*LUMBER: .4X TO 1X BASIC
LUMBER PRINT B/WN 32-224 COPIES PER
OVERALL AU-GU ODDS 1:6 HOBBY
CUTS ISSUED ONLY IN HOBBY PACKS
1 Adam Dunn/192 25.00 7.50
2 Al Kaline/192 40.00 12.00
3 Alfonso Soriano/160 40.00 12.00
4 Andre Dawson/224 15.00 4.50
5 Angel Berroa/224 10.00 3.00
6 Harmon Killebrew/192 40.00 12.00
7 Bob Gibson/96 25.00 7.50
8 Brooks Robinson/192 25.00 7.50
9 Cal Ripken/32 250.00 75.00
10 Dale Murphy/224 25.00 7.50
11 Darryl Strawberry/224 15.00 4.50
12 Delmon Young/192 25.00 7.50
13 Don Mattingly/96 60.00 18.00
14 Duke Snider/96 40.00 12.00
15 Dwight Gooden/224 15.00 4.50
16 Ozzie Smith/96 60.00 18.00
18 Garret Anderson/224 15.00 4.50
19 Gary Carter/160 15.00 4.50
20 George Kell/224 15.00 4.50
21 Hank Blalock/224 15.00 4.50
22 Jim Palmer/192 15.00 4.50
23 Kirk Gibson/160 15.00 4.50
24 Lou Brock/192 25.00 7.50
25 Ryne Sandberg/160 60.00 18.00
26 Mark Prior/160 50.00 15.00
27 Miguel Cabrera/224 25.00 7.50
28 Mike Lowell/160 15.00 4.50
29 Nolan Ryan/96 120.00 36.00
30 Luis Aparicio/224 15.00 4.50
31 Paul Molitor/160 40.00 12.00
32 Red Schoendienst/224 25.00 7.50
33 Rickie Weeks/224 15.00 4.50
34 Ron Santo/224 25.00 7.50
35 Roy Oswalt/224 15.00 4.50
36 Stan Musial/96 60.00 18.00
37 Steve Carlton/192 25.00 7.50
38 Tony Gwynn/192 40.00 12.00
39 Vernon Wells/160 15.00 4.50
40 Will Clark/192 40.00 12.00
41 Bob Feller/224 25.00 7.50
42 Bobby Doerr/224 15.00 4.50
44 Ralph Kiner/224 25.00 7.50
45 Torii Hunter/224 15.00 4.50
46 Rollie Fingers/224 15.00 4.50
47 Steve Garvey/224 15.00 4.50
48 Alan Trammell/224 15.00 4.50
49 Maury Wills/224 15.00 4.50
50 Gaylord Perry/224 15.00 4.50

2004 Leather and Lumber Leather in Leather

Nm-Mt Ex-Mt
RANDOM INSERTS IN PACKS
STATED PRINT RUN 2499 SERIAL #'d SETS
*SILVER ACTIVE: 1X TO 2.5X BASIC
*SILVER RETIRED: 1.25X TO 3X BASIC
SILVER RANDOM IN HOBBY PACKS
SILVER PRINT RUN 100 SERIAL #'d SETS
1 Garret Anderson BB 2.00 .60
2 Albert Pujols BB 6.00 1.80
3 John Smoltz BB 3.00 .90
4 Cal Ripken BB 10.00 3.00
5 Ichiro Suzuki BB 5.00 1.50
6 Pedro Martinez BB 3.00 .90
7 Shawn Green BB 2.00 .60
8 Juan Gonzalez BB 3.00 .90
9 Mariano Rivera BB 3.00 .90
10 Jason Giambi BB 2.00 .60
11 Dave Parker BG 2.00 .60
12 Dwight Gooden BG 2.00 .60
13 Eric Munson BG 2.00 .60
14 Frank Thomas BG 3.00 .90
15 Joe Carter BG 2.00 .60
16 Jose Canseco BG 3.00 .90
17 Paul O'Neill BG 3.00 .90
18 Tony Gwynn BG 5.00 1.50
19 Wade Boggs BG 3.00 .90
20 Xavier Nady BG 2.00 .60
21 Albert Pujols FG 6.00 1.80
22 Alex Rodriguez FG 6.00 1.80
23 Chipper Jones FG 3.00 .90
24 Derek Jeter FG 6.00 1.80
25 Jack Wilson FG 2.00 .60
26 Lenny Dykstra FG 2.00 .60
27 Mark Grace FG 3.00 .90
28 Steve Carlton FG 2.00 .60
29 Tony Perez FG 2.00 .60
30 Vladimir Guerrero FG 3.00 .90
31 Bernie Williams SH 3.00 .90
32 Eddie Murray SH 3.00 .90
33 Frank Robinson SH 2.00 .60
34 Greg Maddux SH 5.00 1.50
35 Harmon Killebrew SH 3.00 .90
36 Manny Ramirez SH 3.00 .90
37 Mike Piazza SH 5.00 1.50
38 Paul Molitor SH 3.00 .90
39 Sammy Sosa SH 5.00 1.50
40 Tim Hudson SH 2.00 .60

2004 Leather and Lumber Leather in Leather Materials

Nm-Mt Ex-Mt
OVERALL AU-GU ODDS 1:6 HOBBY
L IN L MATERIAL ISSUED ONLY IN HOBBY
PRINT RUNS B/WN 10-50 COPIES PER
NO PRICING ON QTY OF 10 OR LESS
1 Garret Anderson Ball/50 10.00 3.00
2 Albert Pujols Ball/50 40.00 12.00
3 John Smoltz Ball/50 40.00 12.00
4 Cal Ripken Ball/50 80.00 24.00
5 Ichiro Suzuki Ball/50 60.00 18.00
6 Pedro Martinez Ball/50 20.00 6.00
7 Shawn Green Ball/50 10.00 3.00
8 Juan Gonzalez Ball/50 15.00 4.50
9 Mariano Rivera Ball/50 15.00 4.50
10 Jason Giambi Ball/50 10.00 3.00
11 Dave Parker Btg Glv/25 20.00 6.00
12 Dwight Gooden Btg Glv/25 20.00 6.00
13 Eric Munson Btg Glv/50 10.00 3.00
14 Frank Thomas Btg Glv/25 30.00 9.00
15 Joe Carter Btg Glv/50 15.00 4.50
16 Jose Canseco Btg Glv/50 25.00 7.50
17 Paul O'Neill Btg Glv/50 25.00 7.50
18 Tony Gwynn Btg Glv/50 40.00 12.00
19 Wade Boggs Btg Glv/25 30.00 9.00
20 Xavier Nady Btg Glv/50 10.00 3.00
21 Albert Pujols Fld Glv/10
22 Alex Rodriguez Fld Glv/25 40.00 12.00
23 Chipper Jones Fld Glv/25 30.00 9.00
24 Derek Jeter Fld Glv/25 50.00 15.00
25 Jack Wilson Fld Glv/50 10.00 3.00
26 Lenny Dykstra Fld Glv/50 15.00 4.50
27 Mark Grace Fld Glv/50 20.00 6.00
28 Steve Carlton Fld Glv/50 15.00 4.50
29 Tony Perez Fld Glv/25 20.00 6.00
30 Vladimir Guerrero Fld Glv/10
31 Bernie Williams Spikes/50 15.00 4.50
32 Eddie Murray Spikes/50 40.00 12.00
33 Frank Robinson Spikes/50 15.00 4.50
34 Greg Maddux Spikes/25 40.00 12.00
35 Harmon Killebrew Spikes/25 40.00 12.00
36 Manny Ramirez Spikes/50 15.00 4.50
37 Mike Piazza Spikes/25 40.00 12.00
38 Paul Molitor Spikes/25 30.00 9.00
39 Sammy Sosa Spikes/25 40.00 12.00
40 Tim Hudson Spikes/50 10.00 3.00

2004 Leather and Lumber Lumber/Leather Barrel

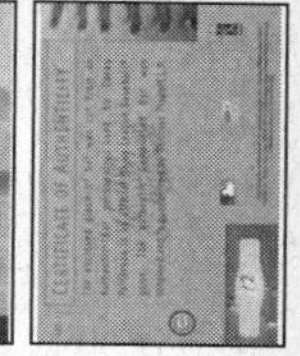

Nm-Mt Ex-Mt
OVERALL AU-GU ODDS 1:6 HOBBY
BARRELS ISSUED ONLY IN HOBBY PACKS
PRINT RUNS B/WN 1-5 COPIES PER
NO PRICING DUE TO SCARCITY

2004 Leather and Lumber Lumber/Leather Barrel-Jersey

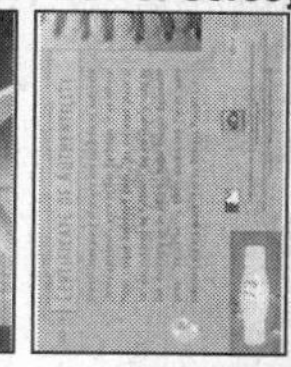

Nm-Mt Ex-Mt
OVERALL AU-GU ODDS 1:6 HOBBY
BARRELS ISSUED ONLY IN HOBBY PACKS
PRINT RUNS B/WN 1-5 COPIES PER
NO PRICING DUE TO SCARCITY

2004 Leather and Lumber Lumber/Leather Barrel-Jersey Prime

Nm-Mt Ex-Mt
OVERALL AU-GU ODDS 1:6 HOBBY
BARRELS ISSUED ONLY IN HOBBY PACKS
STATED PRINT RUN 1 SERIAL #'d SET
NO PRICING DUE TO SCARCITY

2004 Leather and Lumber Lumber/Leather Bat-Ball

Nm-Mt Ex-Mt
*BALL p/r 25: .6X TO 1.5X SPIKE p/r 50
*BALL p/r 25: .4X TO 1X SPIKE p/r 25
OVERALL AU-GU ODDS 1:6 HOBBY
L/L BAT COMBOS ISSUED ONLY IN HOBBY
PRINT RUNS B/WN 5-25 COPIES PER
NO PRICING ON QTY OF 10 OR LESS
4 Aubrey Huff/25 15.00 4.50
5 Austin Kearns/25 15.00 4.50
16 Gary Sheffield/25 15.00 4.50
42 Richie Sexson/25 15.00 4.50
47 Tony Gwynn/25 40.00 12.00

2004 Leather and Lumber Lumber/Leather Bat-Btg Glove

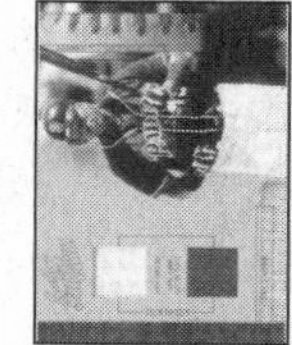

Nm-Mt Ex-Mt
*BTG GLV p/r 25: .6X TO 1.5X SPIKE p/r 50
*BTG GLV p/r 25: .4X TO 1X SPIKE p/r 25
OVERALL AU-GU ODDS 1:6 HOBBY
L/L BAT COMBOS ISSUED ONLY IN HOBBY
PRINT RUNS B/WN 1-25 COPIES PER
NO PRICING ON QTY OF 10 OR LESS
4 Aubrey Huff/25 15.00 4.50
16 Gary Sheffield/25 15.00 4.50
28 Kirby Puckett/25 50.00 15.00
42 Richie Sexson/25 15.00 4.50
47 Tony Gwynn/25 40.00 12.00

2004 Leather and Lumber Lumber/Leather Bat-Fld Glove

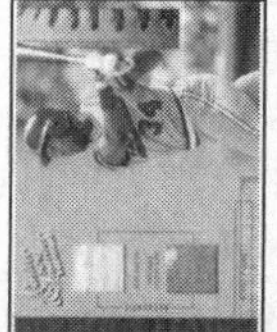

Nm-Mt Ex-Mt
*FLD.GLV p/r 50: .4X TO 1X SPIKE p/r 50
*FLD.GLV p/r 50: .25X TO .6X SPIKE p/r 25
*FLD.GLV p/r 25: .6X TO 1.5X SPIKE p/r 50
*FLD.GLV p/r 25: .4X TO 1X SPIKE p/r 25
OVERALL AU-GU ODDS 1:6 HOBBY
L/L BAT COMBOS ISSUED ONLY IN HOBBY
PRINT RUNS B/WN 1-50 COPIES PER
NO PRICING ON QTY OF 10 OR LESS
12 Derek Jeter/25 60.00 18.00
16 Gary Sheffield/25 15.00 4.50
28 Kirby Puckett/25 50.00 15.00
45 Ryne Sandberg/25 60.00 18.00
47 Tony Gwynn/25 40.00 12.00

2004 Leather and Lumber Lumber/Leather Bat-Spikes

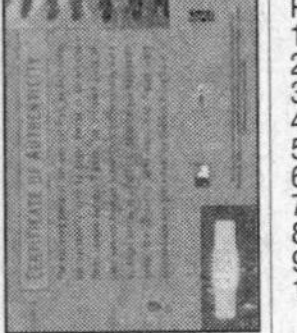

Nm-Mt Ex-Mt
OVERALL AU-GU ODDS 1:6 HOBBY
L/L BAT COMBOS ISSUED ONLY IN HOBBY
PRINT RUNS B/WN 1-50 COPIES PER
NO PRICING ON QTY OF 10 OR LESS
1 Andruw Jones/25 15.00 4.50
2 Andy Pettitte/5
3 Angel Berroa/25 15.00 4.50
4 Aubrey Huff/5
5 Austin Kearns/1
6 Barry Zito/25 15.00 4.50
7 Ben Sheets/50 10.00 3.00
8 Brad Penny/50 10.00 3.00
9 Brian Giles/50 10.00 3.00
10 Carlos Lee/50 10.00 3.00
11 Corey Patterson/50 10.00 3.00
12 Derek Jeter/10
13 Don Mattingly/25 50.00 15.00
14 Eric Hinske/5
15 Gary Carter/50 15.00 4.50
17 Ivan Rodriguez/50 20.00 6.00
18 Jack Cust/50 10.00 3.00
19 Jason Jennings/50 10.00 3.00
21 Jim Edmonds/50 10.00 3.00
22 Joe Borchard/50 10.00 3.00
23 Joe Crede/50 10.00 3.00
24 Josh Beckett/25 15.00 4.50
25 Josh Phelps/50 10.00 3.00
26 Juan Pierre/50 10.00 3.00
27 Kenny Lofton/50 10.00 3.00
28 Kirby Puckett/1
29 Lance Berkman/25 15.00 4.50
30 Magglio Ordonez/25 15.00 4.50
31 Marcus Giles/50 10.00 3.00
32 Mark Buehrle/50 10.00 3.00
33 Mark Prior/25 30.00 9.00
34 Mark Teixeira/25 15.00 4.50
35 Marlon Byrd/50 10.00 3.00
36 Mike Sweeney/10
37 Morgan Ensberg/10
38 Nick Johnson/25 15.00 4.50
39 Orlando Hudson/50 10.00 3.00
40 Paul Lo Duca/25 15.00 4.50
41 Rafael Palmeiro/25 25.00 7.50
42 Richie Sexson/5
43 Roy Oswalt/25 15.00 4.50
44 Ryan Klesko/50 10.00 3.00
46 Sean Casey/50 10.00 3.00
47 Tony Gwynn/10
48 Travis Hafner/50 10.00 3.00
49 Victor Martinez/50 10.00 3.00
50 Wade Miller/50 10.00 3.00

2004 Leather and Lumber Naturals

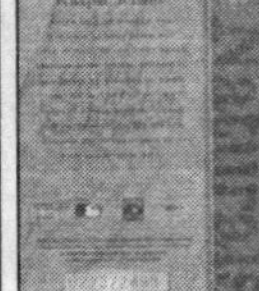

Nm-Mt Ex-Mt
RANDOM INSERTS IN PACKS
STATED PRINT RUN 2499 SERIAL #'d SETS
*SILVER ACTIVE: 1X TO 2.5X BASIC
*SILVER RETIRED: 1.25X TO 3X BASIC
SILVER RANDOM IN HOBBY PACKS
SILVER PRINT RUN 100 SERIAL #'d SETS
1 Eric Chavez 2.00 .60
2 Garret Anderson 2.00 .60
3 Lance Berkman 2.00 .60
4 Paul Molitor 3.00 .90
5 Rafael Palmeiro 3.00 .90
6 Ralph Kiner 2.00 .60
7 Todd Helton 3.00 .90
8 Tony Gwynn 5.00 1.50
9 Wade Boggs 3.00 .90
10 Will Clark 3.00 .90

2004 Leather and Lumber Naturals Materials Barrel

Nm-Mt Ex-Mt
OVERALL AU-GU ODDS 1:6
BARRELS ISSUED ONLY IN HOBBY PACKS
PRINT RUNS B/WN 1-5 COPIES PER
NO PRICING DUE TO SCARCITY

2004 Leather and Lumber Naturals Materials Bat

Nm-Mt Ex-Mt
OVERALL AU-GU ODDS 1:6 HOBBY
PRINT RUNS B/WN 20-250 COPIES PER
1 Eric Chavez/20 12.00 3.60
2 Garret Anderson/250 5.00 1.50
3 Lance Berkman/250 5.00 1.50
4 Paul Molitor/250 10.00 3.00
5 Rafael Palmeiro/250 8.00 2.40
6 Ralph Kiner/250 10.00 3.00
7 Todd Helton/250 8.00 2.40
8 Tony Gwynn/250 15.00 4.50
9 Wade Boggs/250 10.00 3.00
10 Will Clark/250 10.00 3.00

2004 Leather and Lumber Pennants/Pinstripes

Nm-Mt Ex-Mt
RANDOM INSERTS IN PACKS
STATED PRINT RUN 2499 SERIAL #'d SETS
*GOLD ACTIVE: 1X TO 2.5X BASIC
*GOLD RETIRED: 1.25X TO 3X BASIC
GOLD RANDOM IN HOBBY PACKS
GOLD PRINT RUN 100 SERIAL #'d SETS
1 Reggie Jackson 3.00 .90
2 Mike Schmidt 6.00 1.80
3 Steve Carlton 2.00 .60
4 Dwight Gooden 2.00 .60
5 Darryl Strawberry 2.00 .60
6 Roger Clemens 6.00 1.80
7 Curt Schilling 2.00 .60
8 Mark Grace 3.00 .90
9 Ivan Rodriguez 3.00 .90
10 Josh Beckett 2.00 .60

2004 Leather and Lumber Pennants/Pinstripes Materials

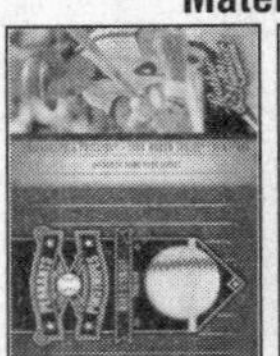

Nm-Mt Ex-Mt
OVERALL AU-GU ODDS 1:6 HOBBY
PRINT RUNS B/WN 25-250 COPIES PER
1 Reggie Jackson Pants/100 12.00 3.60
2 Mike Schmidt Jsy/25 40.00 12.00
3 Steve Carlton Jsy/100 8.00 2.40
4 Dwight Gooden Jsy/250 8.00 2.40
5 Darryl Strawberry Pants/250 8.00 2.40
6 Roger Clemens Jsy/250 10.00 3.00
7 Curt Schilling Jsy/250 5.00 1.50
8 Mark Grace Jsy/250 10.00 3.00
9 Ivan Rodriguez Jsy/250 8.00 2.40
10 Josh Beckett Jsy/100 5.00 1.50

2004 Leather and Lumber Rivals

Nm-Mt Ex-Mt
RANDOM INSERTS IN PACKS
STATED PRINT RUN 2499 SERIAL #'d SETS
SILVER RANDOM IN HOBBY PACKS
SILVER PRINT RUN 100 SERIAL #'d SETS
1 Derek Jeter 6.00 1.80
Nomar Garciaparra
2 Mark Prior 6.00 1.80
Albert Pujols
3 Warren Spahn 5.00 1.50
Stan Musial
4 Don Sutton 3.00 .90
Reggie Jackson
5 Roger Clemens 6.00 1.80
Mike Piazza
6 Dennis Eckersley 3.00 .90
Matt Williams
7 Kerry Wood 3.00 .90
Frank Thomas
8 Jim Palmer 3.00 .90
Willie Stargell
9 Tom Seaver 6.00 1.80
Mike Schmidt
10 Jack Morris 6.00 1.80
George Brett
11 Randy Johnson 3.00 .90
Todd Helton
12 Tommy John 3.00 .90
Rod Carew
13 Pedro Martinez 3.00 .90
Jason Giambi
14 Dwight Gooden 3.00 .90
Wade Boggs
15 Bob Gibson 3.00 .90
Ernie Banks
16 Hideo Nomo 3.00 .90
Barry Larkin
17 Roy Halladay 3.00 .90
Vladimir Guerrero
18 Greg Maddux 5.00 1.50
Jeff Bagwell
19 Barry Zito 5.00 1.50
Alex Rodriguez
20 Steve Carlton 2.00 .60
Andre Dawson
21 Mariano Rivera 3.00 .90
Chipper Jones
22 Tom Glavine 3.00 .90
Manny Ramirez
23 Whitey Ford 3.00 .90
Harmon Killebrew
24 Carl Yastrzemski 5.00 1.50
Catfish Hunter
25 Nolan Ryan 8.00 2.40
Robin Ventura
26 Carlton Fisk 3.00 .90
Joe Morgan
27 Phil Rizzuto 3.00 .90
Duke Snider
28 Fergie Jenkins 3.00 .90
Lou Brock
29 Jose Canseco 3.00 .90
Will Clark
30 Mike Mussina 3.00 .90
Josh Beckett
31 Rickey Henderson 3.00 .90
Ivan Rodriguez
32 Don Mattingly 6.00 1.80
Eddie Murray
33 Troy Glaus 2.00 .60
Eric Chavez
34 Ryne Sandberg 6.00 1.80
Steve Garvey
35 Bob Gibson 3.00 .90
Roger Maris
36 Roger Clemens 10.00 3.00
Cal Ripken
37 Orel Hershiser 2.00 .60
Darryl Strawberry
38 Curt Schilling 3.00 .90
Paul Molitor
39 Ichiro Suzuki 5.00 1.50
Hideki Matsui
40 Sammy Sosa 5.00 1.50
Jim Thome

2004 Leather and Lumber Rivals Materials

Nm-Mt Ex-Mt
OVERALL AU-GU ODDS 1:6 HOBBY
PRINT RUNS B/WN 5-250 COPIES PER
NO PRICING ON QTY OF 10 OR LESS
1 Derek Jeter Jsy 25.00 7.50
Nomar Garciaparra Bat/250
2 Mark Prior Jsy 25.00 7.50
Albert Pujols Jsy/250
3 Warren Spahn Pants 40.00 12.00
Stan Musial Jsy/100
4 Don Sutton Jsy
Reggie Jackson Jsy/10
5 Roger Clemens Jsy 25.00 7.50
Mike Piazza Jsy/250
7 Kerry Wood Jsy 15.00 4.50
Frank Thomas Jsy/250
8 Jim Palmer Jsy 15.00 4.50
Willie Stargell Jsy/250
9 Tom Seaver Jsy 20.00 6.00
Mike Schmidt Jsy/250
10 Jack Morris Jsy 15.00 4.50
George Brett Jsy/250
11 Randy Johnson Jsy 10.00 3.00
Todd Helton Jsy/250
12 Tommy John Pants 15.00 4.50
Rod Carew Jkt/250
13 Pedro Martinez Jsy 10.00 3.00
Jason Giambi Jsy/250
14 Dwight Gooden Jsy 15.00 4.50
Wade Boggs Jsy/250
15 Bob Gibson Jsy 25.00 7.50
Ernie Banks Pants/100
16 Hideo Nomo Jsy 15.00 4.50
Barry Larkin Jsy/250
17 Roy Halladay Jsy 10.00 3.00
Vladimir Guerrero Jsy/250
18 Greg Maddux Jsy 15.00 4.50
Jeff Bagwell Jsy/250
19 Barry Zito Jsy 15.00 4.50
Alex Rodriguez Jsy/250
20 Steve Carlton Jsy 10.00 3.00
Andre Dawson Jsy/250
21 Mariano Rivera Jsy
Chipper Jones Jsy/10
22 Tom Glavine Jsy 10.00 3.00
Manny Ramirez Jsy/250
23 Whitey Ford Pants 40.00 12.00
Harmon Killebrew Jsy/100
24 Carl Yastrzemski Jsy 25.00 7.50
Catfish Hunter Jsy/250
25 Nolan Ryan Pants 25.00 7.50
Robin Ventura Jsy/250
26 Carlton Fisk Jsy 15.00 4.50
Joe Morgan Jsy/250
27 Phil Rizzuto Jsy
Duke Snider Jsy/5
28 Fergie Jenkins Pants 25.00 7.50
Lou Brock Jsy/100
29 Jose Canseco Bat 20.00 6.00
Will Clark Bat/250
30 Mike Mussina Jsy 10.00 3.00
Josh Beckett Jsy/250
31 Rickey Henderson Jsy 15.00 4.50
Ivan Rodriguez Jsy/250
32 Don Mattingly Pants 25.00 7.50
Eddie Murray Jsy/250
33 Troy Glaus Jsy 8.00 2.40
Eric Chavez Jsy/250
34 Ryne Sandberg Jsy 25.00 7.50
Steve Garvey Jsy/250
35 Bob Gibson Jsy 50.00 15.00
Roger Maris Jsy/100
36 Roger Clemens Jsy 40.00 12.00
Cal Ripken Pants/250
38 Curt Schilling Jsy 15.00 4.50
Paul Molitor Bat/250
39 Ichiro Suzuki Base 50.00 15.00
Hideki Matsui Base/250
40 Sammy Sosa Jsy 15.00 4.50
Jim Thome Jsy/250

1996 Metal Universe

The Metal Universe set (created by Fleer) was issued in one series totalling 250 standard-size cards. The cards were issued in foil-wrapped packs. The theme for the set was based on intermingling fantasy comic book elements with baseball, thus each card features a player set against a wide variety of bizarre backgrounds. The cards are grouped alphabetically within teams below.

Nm-Mt Ex-Mt
COMPLETE SET (250) 40.00 12.00
1 Roberto Alomar .50 .15
2 Brady Anderson .30 .09
3 Bobby Bonilla .30 .09
4 Chris Hoiles .30 .09
5 Ben McDonald .30 .09
6 Mike Mussina .50 .15
7 Randy Myers .30 .09
8 Rafael Palmeiro .50 .15
9 Cal Ripken 2.50 .75
10 B.J. Surhoff .30 .09
11 Luis Alicea .30 .09
12 Jose Canseco .75 .23
13 Roger Clemens 1.50 .45
14 Wil Cordero .30 .09
15 Tom Gordon .30 .09
16 Mike Greenwall .30 .09
17 Tim Naehring .30 .09
18 Troy O'Leary .30 .09
19 Mike Stanley .30 .09
20 John Valentin .30 .09
21 Mo Vaughn .30 .09
22 Tim Wakefield .30 .09
23 Garret Anderson .30 .09
24 Chili Davis .30 .09
25 Gary DiSarcina .30 .09
26 Jim Edmonds .30 .09
27 Chuck Finley .30 .09
28 Todd Greene .30 .09
29 Mark Langston .30 .09
30 Troy Percival .30 .09
31 Tony Phillips .30 .09
32 Tim Salmon .50 .15
33 Lee Smith .30 .09
34 J.T. Snow .30 .09
35 Ray Durham .30 .09
36 Alex Fernandez .30 .09
37 Ozzie Guillen .30 .09
38 Roberto Hernandez .30 .09
39 Lyle Mouton .30 .09
40 Frank Thomas .75 .23
41 Robin Ventura .30 .09
42 Sandy Alomar Jr. .30 .09
43 Carlos Baerga .30 .09
44 Albert Belle .30 .09
45 Orel Hershiser .30 .09
46 Kenny Lofton .30 .09
47 Dennis Martinez .30 .09
48 Jack McDowell .30 .09
49 Jose Mesa .30 .09
50 Eddie Murray .75 .23
51 Charles Nagy .30 .09
52 Manny Ramirez .50 .15
53 Julian Tavarez .30 .09
54 Jim Thome .75 .23
55 Omar Vizquel .50 .15
56 Chad Curtis .30 .09
57 Cecil Fielder .30 .09
58 John Flaherty .30 .09
59 Travis Fryman .30 .09
60 Chris Gomez .30 .09
61 Felipe Lira .30 .09
62 Kevin Appier .30 .09
63 Johnny Damon .50 .15
64 Tom Goodwin .30 .09
65 Mark Gubicza .30 .09
66 Jeff Montgomery .30 .09
67 Jon Nunnally .30 .09
68 Ricky Bones .30 .09
69 Jeff Cirillo .30 .09
70 John Jaha .30 .09
71 Dave Nilsson .30 .09
72 Joe Oliver .30 .09
73 Kevin Seitzer .30 .09
74 Greg Vaughn .30 .09
75 Marty Cordova .30 .09
76 Chuck Knoblauch .30 .09
77 Pat Meares .30 .09
78 Paul Molitor .50 .15
79 Pedro Munoz .30 .09
80 Kirby Puckett .75 .23
81 Brad Radke .30 .09
82 Scott Stahoviak .30 .09
83 Matt Walbeck .30 .09
84 Wade Boggs .50 .15
85 David Cone .30 .09
86 Joe Girardi .30 .09
87 Derek Jeter 2.00 .60
88 Jim Leyritz .30 .09
89 Tino Martinez .50 .15
90 Don Mattingly 2.00 .60
91 Paul O'Neill .50 .15
92 Andy Pettitte .50 .15
93 Tim Raines .30 .09
94 Kenny Rogers .30 .09
95 Ruben Sierra .30 .09
96 John Wetteland .30 .09
97 Bernie Williams .50 .15
98 Geronimo Berroa .30 .09
99 Dennis Eckersley .30 .09
100 Brent Gates .30 .09
101 Mark McGwire 2.00 .60
102 Steve Ontiveros .30 .09
103 Terry Steinbach .30 .09
104 Jay Buhner .30 .09
105 Vince Coleman .30 .09
106 Joey Cora .30 .09
107 Ken Griffey, Jr. 1.25 .35
108 Randy Johnson .75 .23
109 Edgar Martinez .50 .15
110 Alex Rodriguez 1.50 .45
111 Paul Sorrento .30 .09
112 Will Clark .75 .23
113 Juan Gonzalez .50 .15
114 Rusty Greer .30 .09
115 Dean Palmer .30 .09
116 Ivan Rodriguez .75 .23
117 Mickey Tettleton .30 .09
118 Joe Carter .30 .09
119 Alex Gonzalez .30 .09
120 Shawn Green .30 .09
121 Erik Hanson .30 .09
122 Pat Hentgen .30 .09
123 Sandy Martinez .30 .09
124 Otis Nixon .30 .09
125 John Olerud .30 .09
126 Steve Avery .30 .09
127 Tom Glavine .50 .15
128 Marquis Grissom .30 .09
129 Chipper Jones .75 .23
130 David Justice .30 .09
131 Ryan Klesko .30 .09
132 Mark Lemke .30 .09
133 Javier Lopez .30 .09
134 Greg Maddux 1.25 .35
135 Fred McGriff .50 .15
136 John Smoltz .50 .15
137 Mark Wohlers .30 .09
138 Frank Castillo .30 .09
139 Shawon Dunston .30 .09
140 Luis Gonzalez .30 .09
141 Mark Grace .50 .15
142 Brian McRae .30 .09
143 Jaime Navarro .30 .09
144 Rey Sanchez .30 .09
145 Ryne Sandberg 1.25 .35
146 Sammy Sosa 1.25 .35
147 Bret Boone .30 .09
148 Curtis Goodwin .30 .09
149 Barry Larkin .50 .15
150 Hal Morris .30 .09
151 Reggie Sanders .30 .09
152 Pete Schourek .30 .09
153 John Smiley .30 .09
154 Dante Bichette .30 .09
155 Vinny Castilla .30 .09
156 Andres Galarraga .30 .09
157 Bret Saberhagen .30 .09
158 Bill Swift .30 .09
159 Larry Walker .50 .15
160 Walt Weiss .30 .09
161 Kurt Abbott .30 .09
162 John Burkett .30 .09
163 Greg Colbrunn .30 .09
164 Jeff Conine .30 .09
165 Chris Hammond .30 .09
166 Charles Johnson .30 .09
167 Al Leiter .30 .09
168 Pat Rapp .30 .09
169 Gary Sheffield .30 .09
170 Quilvio Veras .30 .09
171 Devon White .30 .09
172 Jeff Bagwell .50 .15
173 Derek Bell .30 .09
174 Sean Berry .30 .09
175 Craig Biggio .50 .15
176 Doug Drabek .30 .09
177 Tony Eusebio .30 .09
178 Brian L.Hunter .30 .09
179 Orlando Miller .30 .09
180 Shane Reynolds .30 .09
181 Mike Blowers .30 .09
182 Roger Cedeno .30 .09
183 Eric Karros .30 .09
184 Ramon Martinez .30 .09
185 Raul Mondesi .30 .09
186 Hideo Nomo .75 .23
187 Mike Piazza 1.25 .35
188 Moises Alou .30 .09
189 Yamil Benitez .30 .09
190 Darrin Fletcher .30 .09
191 Cliff Floyd .30 .09
192 Pedro Martinez .75 .23
193 Carlos Perez .30 .09
194 David Segui .30 .09
195 Tony Tarasco .30 .09
196 Rondell White .30 .09
197 Edgardo Alfonzo .30 .09

198 Rico Brogna .30 .09
199 Carl Everett .30 .09
200 Todd Hundley .30 .09
201 Jason Isringhausen .30 .09
202 Lance Johnson .30 .09
203 Bobby Jones .30 .09
204 Jeff Kent .30 .09
205 Bill Pulsipher .30 .09
206 Jose Vizcaino .30 .09
207 Ricky Bottalico .30 .09
208 Darren Daulton .30 .09
209 Lenny Dykstra .30 .09
210 Jim Eisenreich .30 .09
211 Gregg Jefferies .30 .09
212 Mickey Morandini .30 .09
213 Heathcliff Slocumb .30 .09
214 Jay Bell .30 .09
215 Carlos Garcia .30 .09
216 Jeff King .30 .09
217 Al Martin .30 .09
218 Orlando Merced .30 .09
219 Dan Miceli .30 .09
220 Denny Neagle .30 .09
221 Andy Benes .30 .09
222 Royce Clayton .30 .09
223 Gary Gaetti .30 .09
224 Ron Gant .30 .09
225 Bernard Gilkey .30 .09
226 Brian Jordan .30 .09
227 Ray Lankford .30 .09
228 John Mabry .30 .09
229 Ozzie Smith 1.25 .35
230 Todd Stottlemyre .30 .09
231 Andy Ashby .30 .09
232 Brad Ausmus .30 .09
233 Ken Caminiti .30 .09
234 Steve Finley .30 .09
235 Tony Gwynn 1.00 .30
236 Joey Hamilton .30 .09
237 Rickey Henderson .75 .23
238 Trevor Hoffman .30 .09
239 Wally Joyner .30 .09
240 Rod Beck .30 .09
241 Barry Bonds 2.00 .60
242 Glenallen Hill .30 .09
243 Stan Javier .30 .09
244 Mark Leiter .30 .09
245 Deion Sanders .50 .15
246 Wm. Van Landingham .30 .09
247 Matt Williams .30 .09
248 Checklist .30 .09
249 Checklist .30 .09
250 Checklist .30 .09

1996 Metal Universe Platinum

'he 1996 Fleer Metal Universe Platinum is a 50-card parallel version of the regular series and were inserted one per pack. The silver foil backgrounds differentiate these from the regular cards.

Nm-Mt Ex-Mt
COMPLETE SET (250) 120.00 36.00
STARS: 1.25X TO 3X BASIC CARDS.
ROOKIES: 1.25X TO 3X BASIC CARDS

1996 Metal Universe Heavy Metal

andomly inserted in packs at a rate of one in ght this 10-card set features the Power Hitters f Baseball. The fronts feature a color action layer cut-out over a silver foil background. The acks carry a player portrait and information bout the player.

Nm-Mt Ex-Mt
OMPLETE SET (10) 25.00 7.50
Albert Belle 1.00 .30
Barry Bonds 6.00 1.80
Juan Gonzalez 1.50 .45
Ken Griffey Jr. 4.00 1.20
Mark McGwire 6.00 1.80
Mike Piazza 4.00 1.20
Sammy Sosa 4.00 1.20
Frank Thomas 2.50 .75
Mo Vaughn 1.00 .30
) Matt Williams 1.00 .30

1996 Metal Universe Mining For Gold

andomly inserted in retail packs only at a rate one in 12, this 12-card set highlights major ospects and rookies. The fronts feature a play- photo on the top half with the words "Mining r Gold" on the bottom. The backs feature other player photo along with a brief blurb.

Nm-Mt Ex-Mt
)MPLETE SET (12) 60.00 18.00
Yamil Benitez 3.00 .90
Marty Cordova 3.00 .90
Shawn Green 3.00 .90
Todd Greene 3.00 .90

5 Brian Hunter 3.00 .90
6 Derek Jeter 20.00 6.00
7 Charles Johnson 3.00 .90
8 Chipper Jones 8.00 2.40
9 Hideo Nomo 8.00 2.40
10 Alex Ochoa 3.00 .90
11 Andy Pettitte 5.00 1.50
12 Quilvio Veras 3.00 .90

1996 Metal Universe Mother Lode

Randomly inserted in hobby packs only at a rate of one in 12, this 12-card set features multi-tool players. The fronts carry a color action player cut-out over a silver-foil, scroll-design background. The backs display another player photo and information about the player.

Nm-Mt Ex-Mt
COMPLETE SET (12) 50.00 15.00
1 Barry Bonds 10.00 3.00
2 Jim Edmonds 1.50 .45
3 Ken Griffey Jr. 6.00 1.80
4 Kenny Lofton 1.50 .45
5 Raul Mondesi 1.50 .45
6 Rafael Palmeiro 2.50 .17
7 Manny Ramirez 2.50 .75
8 Cal Ripken 12.00 3.60
9 Tim Salmon 2.50 .75
10 Ryne Sandberg 6.00 1.80
11 Frank Thomas 4.00 1.20
12 Matt Williams 1.50 .45

1996 Metal Universe Platinum Portraits

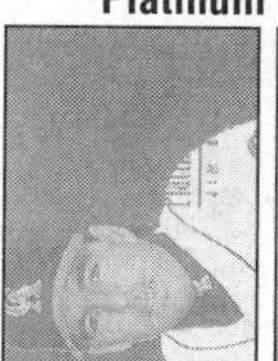

Randomly inserted in packs at a rate of one in four, this 10-card set features ten of the hottest young stars. The fronts display a player portrait on a platinum foil background. The backs carry a color action player photo and why the player is hot.

Nm-Mt Ex-Mt
COMPLETE SET (10) 10.00 3.00
1 Garret Anderson .75 .23
2 Marty Cordova .75 .23
3 Jim Edmonds .75 .23
4 Jason Isringhausen .75 .23
5 Chipper Jones 2.00 .60
6 Ryan Klesko .75 .23
7 Hideo Nomo 2.00 .60
8 Carlos Perez .75 .23
9 Manny Ramirez 1.25 .35
10 Rondell White .75 .23

1996 Metal Universe Titanium

Randomly inserted in packs at a rate of one in 24, this 10-card set features ten of the fans' favorite players. The fronts feature an action color player cut-out on a foil baseball background. The backs display a player portrait and why the player is liked by the fans.

Nm-Mt Ex-Mt
COMPLETE SET (10) 80.00 24.00
1 Albert Belle 2.50 .75
2 Barry Bonds 15.00 4.50
3 Ken Griffey Jr. 10.00 3.00
4 Tony Gwynn 8.00 2.40
5 Greg Maddux 10.00 3.00
6 Mike Piazza 10.00 3.00
7 Cal Ripken 20.00 6.00
8 Frank Thomas 6.00 1.80
9 Mo Vaughn 2.50 .75
10 Matt Williams 2.50 .75

1997 Metal Universe

The 1997 Metal Universe set, (produced by Fleer), was issued in one series totalling 250 cards and distributed in eight-card foil packs with a suggested retail price of $2.49. Printed in 100 percent etched foil with UV-coating, the fronts features color photos of star players on full-bleed backgrounds of comic book art with the player's name, team, position and card logo printed near the bottom of the card. The backs carry another player photo and statistics. An Alex Rodriguez promo card was distributed to dealers and hobby media several weekd prior to the product's release.

Nm-Mt Ex-Mt
COMPLETE SET (250) 30.00 9.00
1 Roberto Alomar .50 .15
2 Brady Anderson .30 .09
3 Rocky Coppinger .30 .09
4 Chris Hoiles .30 .09
5 Eddie Murray .75 .23
6 Mike Mussina .50 .15
7 Rafael Palmeiro .50 .15
8 Cal Ripken 2.50 .75
9 B.J. Surhoff .30 .09
10 Brant Brown .30 .09
11 Mark Grace .50 .15
12 Brian McRae .30 .09
13 Jaime Navarro .30 .09
14 Ryne Sandberg 1.25 .35
15 Sammy Sosa 1.25 .35
16 Amaury Telemaco .30 .09
17 Steve Trachsel .30 .09
18 Darren Bragg .30 .09
19 Jose Canseco .75 .23
20 Roger Clemens 1.50 .45
21 Nomar Garciaparra 1.25 .35
22 Tom Gordon .30 .09
23 Tim Naehring .30 .09
24 Mike Stanley .30 .09
25 John Valentin .30 .09
26 Mo Vaughn .30 .09
27 Jermaine Dye .30 .09
28 Tom Glavine .50 .15
29 Marquis Grissom .30 .09
30 Andruw Jones .30 .09
31 Chipper Jones .75 .23
32 Ryan Klesko .30 .09
33 Greg Maddux 1.25 .35
34 Fred McGriff .50 .15
35 John Smoltz .50 .15
36 Garret Anderson .30 .09
37 George Arias .30 .09
38 Gary DiSarcina .30 .09
39 Jim Edmonds .30 .09
40 Darin Erstad .30 .09
41 Chuck Finley .30 .09
42 Troy Percival .30 .09
43 Tim Salmon .50 .15
44 Bret Boone .30 .09
45 Jeff Brantley .30 .09
46 Eric Davis .30 .09
47 Barry Larkin .50 .15
48 Hal Morris .30 .09
49 Mark Portugal .30 .09
50 Reggie Sanders .30 .09
51 John Smiley .30 .09
52 Wilson Alvarez .30 .09
53 Harold Baines .30 .09
54 James Baldwin .30 .09
55 Albert Belle .30 .09
56 Mike Cameron .30 .09
57 Ray Durham .30 .09
58 Alex Fernandez .30 .09
59 Roberto Hernandez .30 .09
60 Tony Phillips .30 .09
61 Frank Thomas .75 .23
62 Robin Ventura .30 .09
63 Jeff Cirillo .30 .09
64 Jeff D'Amico .30 .09
65 John Jaha .30 .09
66 Scott Karl .30 .09
67 Ben McDonald .30 .09
68 Marc Newfield .30 .09
69 Dave Nilsson .30 .09
70 Jose Valentin .30 .09
71 Dante Bichette .30 .09
72 Ellis Burks .30 .09
73 Vinny Castilla .30 .09
74 Andres Galarraga .30 .09
75 Kevin Ritz .30 .09
76 Larry Walker .50 .15
77 Walt Weiss .30 .09
78 Jamey Wright .30 .09
79 Eric Young .30 .09
80 Julio Franco .30 .09
81 Orel Hershiser .30 .09
82 Kenny Lofton .30 .09
83 Jack McDowell .30 .09
84 Jose Mesa .30 .09
85 Charles Nagy .30 .09
86 Manny Ramirez .50 .15
87 Jim Thome .75 .23
88 Omar Vizquel .50 .15
89 Matt Williams .30 .09
90 Kevin Appier .30 .09
91 Johnny Damon .50 .15
92 Chili Davis .30 .09
93 Tom Goodwin .30 .09
94 Keith Lockhart .30 .09
95 Jeff Montgomery .30 .09
96 Craig Paquette .30 .09
97 Jose Rosado .30 .09
98 Michael Tucker .30 .09
99 Wilton Guerrero .30 .09
100 Todd Hollandsworth .30 .09
101 Eric Karros .30 .09
102 Ramon Martinez .30 .09
103 Raul Mondesi .30 .09
104 Hideo Nomo .75 .23
105 Mike Piazza 1.25 .35
106 Ismael Valdes .30 .09
107 Todd Worrell .30 .09
108 Tony Clark .30 .09
109 Travis Fryman .30 .09
110 Bob Higginson .30 .09
111 Mark Lewis .30 .09
112 Melvin Nieves .30 .09
113 Justin Thompson .30 .09
114 Wade Boggs .50 .15
115 David Cone .30 .09
116 Cecil Fielder .30 .09
117 Dwight Gooden .30 .09
118 Derek Jeter 2.00 .60
119 Tino Martinez .50 .15
120 Paul O'Neill .50 .15
121 Andy Pettitte .50 .15
122 Mariano Rivera .50 .15
123 Darryl Strawberry .30 .09
124 John Wetteland .30 .09
125 Bernie Williams .50 .15
126 Tony Batista .30 .09
127 Geronimo Berroa .30 .09
128 Scott Brosius .30 .09
129 Jason Giambi .30 .09
130 Jose Herrera .30 .09
131 Mark McGwire 2.00 .60
132 John Wasdin .30 .09
133 Bob Abreu .30 .09
134 Jeff Bagwell .50 .15
135 Derek Bell .30 .09
136 Craig Biggio .50 .15
137 Brian Hunter .30 .09
138 Darryl Kile .30 .09
139 Orlando Miller .30 .09
140 Shane Reynolds .30 .09
141 Billy Wagner .30 .09
142 Donne Wall .30 .09
143 Jay Buhner .30 .09
144 Jeff Fassero .30 .09
145 Ken Griffey Jr. 1.25 .35
146 Sterling Hitchcock .30 .09
147 Randy Johnson .75 .23
148 Edgar Martinez .50 .15
149 Alex Rodriguez 1.25 .35
150 Paul Sorrento .30 .09
151 Dan Wilson .30 .09
152 Moises Alou .30 .09
153 Darrin Fletcher .30 .09
154 Cliff Floyd .30 .09
155 Mark Grudzielanek .30 .09
156 Vladimir Guerrero .75 .23
157 Mike Lansing .30 .09
158 Pedro Martinez .75 .23
159 Henry Rodriguez .30 .09
160 Rondell White .30 .09
161 Will Clark .75 .23
162 Juan Gonzalez .50 .15
163 Rusty Greer .30 .09
164 Ken Hill .30 .09
165 Mark McLemore .30 .09
166 Dean Palmer .30 .09
167 Roger Pavlik .30 .09
168 Ivan Rodriguez .75 .23
169 Mickey Tettleton .30 .09
170 Bobby Bonilla .30 .09
171 Kevin Brown .30 .09
172 Greg Colbrunn .30 .09
173 Jeff Conine .30 .09
174 Jim Eisenreich .30 .09
175 Charles Johnson .30 .09
176 Al Leiter .30 .09
177 Robb Nen .30 .09
178 Edgar Renteria .30 .09
179 Gary Sheffield .30 .09
180 Devon White .30 .09
181 Joe Carter .30 .09
182 Carlos Delgado .30 .09
183 Alex Gonzalez .30 .09
184 Shawn Green .30 .09
185 Juan Guzman .30 .09
186 Pat Hentgen .30 .09
187 Orlando Merced .30 .09
188 John Olerud .30 .09
189 Robert Perez .30 .09
190 Ed Sprague .30 .09
191 Mark Clark .30 .09
192 John Franco .30 .09
193 Bernard Gilkey .30 .09
194 Todd Hundley .30 .09
195 Lance Johnson .30 .09
196 Bobby Jones .30 .09
197 Alex Ochoa .30 .09
198 Rey Ordonez .30 .09
199 Paul Wilson .30 .09
200 Ricky Bottalico .30 .09
201 Gregg Jefferies .30 .09
202 Wendell Magee .30 .09
203 Mickey Morandini .30 .09
204 Ricky Otero .30 .09
205 Scott Rolen .75 .23
206 Benito Santiago .30 .09
207 Curt Schilling .30 .09
208 Rich Becker .30 .09
209 Marty Cordova .30 .09
210 Chuck Knoblauch .30 .09
211 Pat Meares .30 .09
212 Paul Molitor .50 .15
213 Frank Rodriguez .30 .09
214 Terry Steinbach .30 .09
215 Todd Walker .30 .09
216 Andy Ashby .30 .09
217 Ken Caminiti .30 .09
218 Steve Finley .30 .09
219 Tony Gwynn 1.00 .30
220 Joey Hamilton .30 .09
221 Rickey Henderson .75 .23
222 Trevor Hoffman .30 .09
223 Wally Joyner .30 .09
224 Scott Sanders .30 .09
225 Fernando Valenzuela .30 .09
226 Greg Vaughn .30 .09
227 Alan Benes .30 .09
228 Andy Benes .30 .09
229 Dennis Eckersley .30 .09
230 Ron Gant .30 .09
231 Brian Jordan .30 .09
232 Ray Lankford .30 .09
233 John Mabry .30 .09
234 Tom Pagnozzi .30 .09
235 Todd Stottlemyre .30 .09
236 Jermaine Allensworth .30 .09
237 Francisco Cordova .30 .09
238 Jason Kendall .30 .09
239 Jeff King .30 .09
240 Al Martin .30 .09
241 Rod Beck .30 .09
242 Barry Bonds 2.00 .60
243 Shawn Estes .30 .09
244 Mark Gardner .30 .09
245 Glenallen Hill .30 .09
246 Bill Mueller RC 3.00 .90
247 J.T. Snow .30 .09
248 Checklist 1-107 .30 .09
249 Checklist 108-207 .30 .09
250 CL 208-250/inserts .30 .09
P149 A. Rodriguez Promo 1.50 .45

1997 Metal Universe Blast Furnace

Randomly inserted in hobby packs only at a rate of one in 48, this 12-card set features color photos of some of baseball's biggest sluggers.

Nm-Mt Ex-Mt
COMPLETE SET (12) 100.00 30.00
1 Jeff Bagwell 5.00 1.50
2 Albert Belle 3.00 .90
3 Barry Bonds 20.00 6.00
4 Andres Galarraga 3.00 .90
5 Juan Gonzalez 5.00 1.50
6 Ken Griffey Jr. 12.00 3.60
7 Todd Hundley 3.00 .90
8 Mark McGwire 20.00 6.00
9 Mike Piazza 12.00 3.60
10 Alex Rodriguez 12.00 3.60
11 Frank Thomas 8.00 2.40
12 Mo Vaughn 3.00 .90

1997 Metal Universe Emerald Autographs

These autographed cards were distributed via mail to lucky collectors that sent in an Emerald Autograph Exchange card seeded at a rate of one in 20 boxes. The autographed cards parallel the corresponding basic cards except of course for the signature on front, coupled with special emerald foil and an embossed Fleer/SkyBox stamp. In addition, the area used for the card number on back of the regular issue card is replaced by a logo stating "certified emerald autograph". These autographed cards are unnumbered and have been assigned numbers based upon alphabetical order of each player's last name.

Nm-Mt Ex-Mt
*EXCH.CARDS: .1X TO .25X BASIC CARDS
AU1 Darin Erstad 15.00 4.50
AU2 Todd Hollandsworth 10.00 3.00
AU3 Alex Ochoa 10.00 3.00
AU4 Alex Rodriguez 100.00 30.00
AU5 Scott Rolen 30.00 9.00
AU6 Todd Walker 15.00 4.50

1997 Metal Universe Magnetic Field

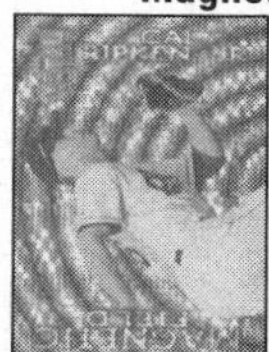

Randomly inserted in packs at a rate of one in 12, this ten-card set honors "Gold Glovers" who appear to have a special attraction to the ball. The fronts feature color player photos on refractive foil backgrounds.

Nm-Mt Ex-Mt
COMPLETE SET (10) 25.00 7.50
1 Roberto Alomar 1.50 .45
2 Jeff Bagwell 1.50 .45
3 Barry Bonds 6.00 1.80
4 Ken Griffey Jr. 4.00 1.20
5 Derek Jeter 6.00 1.80
6 Kenny Lofton 1.00 .30
7 Edgar Renteria 1.00 .30
8 Cal Ripken 8.00 2.40
9 Alex Rodriguez 4.00 1.20
10 Matt Williams 1.00 .30

1997 Metal Universe Mining for Gold

Randomly inserted in packs at a rate of one in nine, this 10-card set features some of baseball's brightest young stars on die-cut "ingot" cards with pearlized gold coating.

	Nm-Mt	Ex-Mt
COMPLETE SET (10)	15.00	4.50
1 Bob Abreu	1.00	.30
2 Kevin Brown C	1.00	.30
3 Nomar Garciaparra	4.00	1.20
4 Vladimir Guerrero	2.50	.75
5 Wilton Guerrero	1.00	.30
6 Andruw Jones	1.00	.30
7 Curt Lyons	1.00	.30
8 Neifi Perez	1.00	.30
9 Scott Rolen	2.50	.75
10 Todd Walker	1.00	.30

1997 Metal Universe Mother Lode

Randomly inserted in packs at a rate of one in 288, this 12-card set features color player photos on die-cut cards in 100 percent etched foil.

	Nm-Mt	Ex-Mt
COMPLETE SET (12)	300.00	90.00
1 Roberto Alomar	12.00	3.60
2 Jeff Bagwell	12.00	3.60
3 Barry Bonds	50.00	15.00
4 Ken Griffey Jr.	30.00	9.00
5 Andruw Jones	8.00	2.40
6 Chipper Jones	20.00	6.00
7 Kenny Lofton	8.00	2.40
8 Mike Piazza	30.00	9.00
9 Cal Ripken	60.00	18.00
10 Alex Rodriguez	30.00	9.00
11 Frank Thomas	20.00	6.00
12 Matt Williams	8.00	2.40

1997 Metal Universe Platinum Portraits

Randomly inserted in packs at a rate of one in 36, this 10-card set features color photos of some of Baseball's rising stars with backgrounds of platinum-colored etched foil.

	Nm-Mt	Ex-Mt
COMPLETE SET (10)	50.00	15.00
1 James Baldwin	3.00	.90
2 Jermaine Dye	3.00	.90
3 Todd Hollandsworth	3.00	.90
4 Derek Jeter	20.00	6.00
5 Chipper Jones	8.00	2.40
6 Jason Kendall	3.00	.90
7 Rey Ordonez	3.00	.90
8 Andy Pettitte	5.00	1.50
9 Edgar Renteria	3.00	.90
10 Alex Rodriguez	12.00	3.60

1997 Metal Universe Titanium

Randomly inserted in packs at a rate of one in 24, this 10-card set honors some of baseball's favorite superstars. The fronts feature color player photos printed on die-cut embossed cards and sculpted on 100 percent etched foil.

	Nm-Mt	Ex-Mt
COMPLETE SET (10)	80.00	24.00
1 Jeff Bagwell	3.00	.90
2 Albert Belle	2.00	.60
3 Ken Griffey Jr.	8.00	2.40
4 Chipper Jones	5.00	1.50
5 Greg Maddux	8.00	2.40
6 Mark McGwire	12.00	3.60
7 Mike Piazza	8.00	2.40
8 Cal Ripken	15.00	4.50
9 Alex Rodriguez	8.00	2.40
10 Frank Thomas	5.00	1.50

1998 Metal Universe

The 1998 Metal Universe set, produced by Fleer, was issued in one series totalling 220 cards. The fronts feature color player photos with metal etching. The backs carry player information. The set contains the topical subset: Hardball Galaxy (203-217). An Alex Rodriguez promo card was distributed along with all dealer order forms. The card is identical to the regular issue Rodriguez card except for the text "PROMOTIONAL SAMPLE" written diagonally along the card back.

	Nm-Mt	Ex-Mt
COMPLETE SET (220)	40.00	12.00
1 Jose Cruz Jr.	.30	.09
2 Jeff Abbott	.30	.09
3 Rafael Palmeiro	.50	.15
4 Ivan Rodriguez	.75	.23
5 Jaret Wright	.30	.09
6 Derek Bell	.30	.09
7 Chuck Finley	.30	.09
8 Travis Fryman	.30	.09
9 Randy Johnson	.75	.23
10 Derrek Lee	.30	.09
11 Bernie Williams	.50	.15
12 Carlos Baerga	.30	.09
13 Ricky Bottalico	.30	.09
14 Ellis Burks	.30	.09
15 Russ Davis	.30	.09
16 Nomar Garciaparra	1.25	.35
17 Joey Hamilton	.30	.09
18 Jason Kendall	.30	.09
19 Darryl Kile	.30	.09
20 Edgardo Alfonzo	.30	.09
21 Moises Alou	.30	.09
22 Bobby Bonilla	.30	.09
23 Jim Edmonds	.30	.09
24 Jose Guillen	.30	.09
25 Chuck Knoblauch	.30	.09
26 Javy Lopez	.30	.09
27 Billy Wagner	.30	.09
28 Kevin Appier	.30	.09
29 Joe Carter	.30	.09
30 Todd Dunwoody	.30	.09
31 Gary Gaetti	.30	.09
32 Juan Gonzalez	.50	.15
33 Jeffrey Hammonds	.30	.09
34 Roberto Hernandez	.30	.09
35 Dave Nilsson	.30	.09
36 Manny Ramirez	.50	.15
37 Robin Ventura	.30	.09
38 Rondell White	.30	.09
39 Vinny Castilla	.30	.09
40 Will Clark	.75	.23
41 Scott Hatteberg	.30	.09
42 Russ Johnson	.30	.09
43 Ricky Ledee	.30	.09
44 Kenny Lofton	.30	.09
45 Paul Molitor	.50	.15
46 Justin Thompson	.30	.09
47 Craig Biggio	.50	.15
48 Damion Easley	.30	.09
49 Brad Radke	.30	.09
50 Ben Grieve	.30	.09
51 Mark Bellhorn	.30	.09
52 Henry Blanco	.30	.09
53 Mariano Rivera	.50	.15
54 Reggie Sanders	.30	.09
55 Paul Sorrento	.30	.09
56 Terry Steinbach	.30	.09
57 Mo Vaughn	.30	.09
58 Brady Anderson	.30	.09
59 Tom Glavine	.50	.15
60 Sammy Sosa	1.25	.35
61 Larry Walker	.50	.15
62 Rod Beck	.30	.09
63 Jose Canseco	.75	.23
64 Steve Finley	.30	.09
65 Pedro Martinez	.75	.23
66 John Olerud	.30	.09
67 Scott Rolen	.75	.23
68 Ismael Valdes	.30	.09
69 Andrew Vessel	.30	.09
70 Mark Grudzielanek	.30	.09
71 Eric Karros	.30	.09
72 Jeff Shaw	.30	.09
73 Lou Collier	.30	.09
74 Edgar Martinez	.50	.15
75 Vladimir Guerrero	.75	.23
76 Paul Konerko	.30	.09
77 Kevin Orie	.30	.09
78 Kevin Polcovich	.30	.09
79 Brett Tomko	.30	.09
80 Jeff Bagwell	.50	.15
81 Barry Bonds	2.00	.60
82 David Justice	.30	.09
83 Hideo Nomo	.75	.23
84 Ryne Sandberg	1.25	.35
85 Shannon Stewart	.30	.09
86 Derek Wallace	.30	.09
87 Tony Womack	.30	.09
88 Jason Giambi	.30	.09
89 Mark Grace	.50	.15
90 Pat Hentgen	.30	.09
91 Raul Mondesi	.30	.09
92 Matt Morris	.30	.09
93 Matt Perisho	.30	.09
94 Tim Salmon	.50	.15
95 Jeremi Gonzalez	.30	.09
96 Shawn Green	.30	.09
97 Todd Greene	.30	.09
98 Ruben Rivera	.30	.09
99 Deion Sanders	.50	.15
100 Alex Rodriguez	1.25	.35
101 Will Cunnane	.30	.09
102 Ray Lankford	.30	.09
103 Ryan McGuire	.30	.09
104 Charles Nagy	.30	.09
105 Rey Ordonez	.30	.09
106 Mike Piazza	1.25	.35
107 Tony Saunders	.30	.09
108 Curt Schilling	.30	.09
109 Fernando Tatis	.30	.09
110 Mark McGwire	2.00	.60
111 Dave Dellucci RC	.50	.15
112 Garret Anderson	.30	.09
113 Shane Bowers RC	.30	.09
114 David Cone	.30	.09
115 Jeff King	.30	.09
116 Matt Williams	.30	.09
117 Aaron Boone	.30	.09
118 Dennis Eckersley	.30	.09
119 Livan Hernandez	.30	.09
120 Richard Hidalgo	.30	.09
121 Bobby Higginson	.30	.09
122 Tino Martinez	.50	.15
123 Tim Naehring	.30	.09
124 Jose Vidro	.30	.09
125 John Wetteland	.30	.09
126 Jay Bell	.30	.09
127 Albert Belle	.30	.09
128 Marty Cordova	.30	.09
129 Chili Davis	.30	.09
130 Jason Dickson	.30	.09
131 Rusty Greer	.30	.09
132 Hideki Irabu	.30	.09
133 Greg Maddux	1.25	.35
134 Billy Taylor	.30	.09
135 Jim Thome	.75	.23
136 Gerald Williams	.30	.09
137 Jeff Cirillo	.30	.09
138 Delino DeShields	.30	.09
139 Andres Galarraga	.30	.09
140 Willie Greene	.30	.09
141 John Jaha	.30	.09
142 Charles Johnson	.30	.09
143 Ryan Klesko	.30	.09
144 Paul O'Neill	.50	.15
145 Robinson Checo	.30	.09
146 Roberto Alomar	.50	.15
147 Wilson Alvarez	.30	.09
148 Bobby Jones	.30	.09
149 Raul Casanova	.30	.09
150 Andruw Jones	.30	.09
151 Mike Lansing	.30	.09
152 Mickey Morandini	.30	.09
153 Neifi Perez	.30	.09
154 Pokey Reese	.30	.09
155 Edgar Renteria	.30	.09
156 Eric Young	.30	.09
157 Darin Erstad	.30	.09
158 Kelvim Escobar	.30	.09
159 Carl Everett	.30	.09
160 Tom Gordon	.30	.09
161 Ken Griffey Jr.	1.25	.35
162 Al Martin	.30	.09
163 Bubba Trammell	.30	.09
164 Carlos Delgado	.30	.09
165 Kevin Brown	.50	.15
166 Ken Caminiti	.30	.09
167 Roger Clemens	1.50	.45
168 Ron Gant	.30	.09
169 Jeff Kent	.30	.09
170 Mike Mussina	.50	.15
171 Dean Palmer	.30	.09
172 Henry Rodriguez	.30	.09
173 Matt Stairs	.30	.09
174 Jay Buhner	.30	.09
175 Frank Thomas	.75	.23
176 Mike Cameron	.30	.09
177 Johnny Damon	.50	.15
178 Tony Gwynn	1.00	.30
179 John Smoltz	.50	.15
180 B.J. Surhoff	.30	.09
181 Antone Williamson	.30	.09
182 Alan Benes	.30	.09
183 Jeromy Burnitz	.30	.09
184 Tony Clark	.30	.09
185 Shawn Estes	.30	.09
186 Todd Helton	.50	.15
187 Todd Hundley	.30	.09
188 Chipper Jones	.75	.23
189 Mark Kotsay	.30	.09
190 Barry Larkin	.50	.15
191 Mike Lieberthal	.30	.09
192 Andy Pettitte	.50	.15
193 Gary Sheffield	.30	.09
194 Jeff Suppan	.30	.09
195 Mark Wohlers	.30	.09
196 Dante Bichette	.30	.09
197 Trevor Hoffman	.30	.09
198 J.T. Snow	.30	.09
199 Derek Jeter	2.00	.60
200 Cal Ripken	2.50	.75
201 Steve Woodard	.30	.09
202 Ray Durham	.30	.09
203 Barry Bonds HG	.75	.23
204 Tony Clark HG	.30	.09
205 Roger Clemens HG	.75	.23
206 Ken Griffey Jr. HG	.75	.23
207 Deion Sanders HG	.30	.09
208 Derek Jeter HG	1.00	.30
209 Randy Johnson HG	.50	.15
210 Brady Anderson HG	.30	.09
211 Hideo Nomo HG	.50	.15
212 Mike Piazza HG	.75	.23
213 Cal Ripken HG	1.25	.35
214 Alex Rodriguez HG	.75	.23
215 Frank Thomas HG	.50	.15
216 Mo Vaughn HG	.30	.09
217 Larry Walker HG	.30	.09
218 Ken Griffey Jr. CL	.75	.23
219 Alex Rodriguez CL	.75	.23
220 Frank Thomas CL	.50	.15
P100 A. Rodriguez Promo	1.50	.45

1998 Metal Universe Precious Metal Gems

Randomly inserted only in hobby packs, cards from this 217-card set parallel the base set (except for the last three checklists cards in the set). Only 50 of these sets were produced and each card is serial numbered on back. In addition, five "Ultimate Gems" exchange cards (good for one complete Precious Gems set) were randomly seeded into packs. Due to this promotion, cards from only the first 45 serial numbered sets were seeded into packs. Sets serial numbered between 46-50 were held back for the Ultimate Gems exchange program.

Nm-Mt Ex-Mt

*STARS: 12.5X TO 30X BASIC CARDS
*ROOKIES: 12.5X TO 30X BASIC CARDS

1998 Metal Universe All-Galactic Team

Randomly inserted in packs at the rate of one in 192, this 18-card set features color player photos on backgrounds of planets. The backs carry player information.

	Nm-Mt	Ex-Mt
COMPLETE SET (18)	300.00	90.00
1 Ken Griffey Jr.	20.00	6.00
2 Frank Thomas	12.00	3.60
3 Chipper Jones	12.00	3.60
4 Albert Belle	5.00	1.50
5 Juan Gonzalez	8.00	2.40
6 Jeff Bagwell	8.00	2.40
7 Andruw Jones	5.00	1.50
8 Cal Ripken	40.00	12.00
9 Derek Jeter	30.00	9.00
10 Nomar Garciaparra	20.00	6.00
11 Darin Erstad	5.00	1.50
12 Greg Maddux	20.00	6.00
13 Alex Rodriguez	20.00	6.00
14 Mike Piazza	20.00	6.00
15 Vladimir Guerrero	12.00	3.60
16 Jose Cruz Jr.	5.00	1.50
17 Mark McGwire	30.00	9.00
18 Scott Rolen	12.00	3.60

1998 Metal Universe Diamond Heroes

Randomly inserted in packs at the rate of one in 18, this six-card set features color photos of five top players in a mini-comic book form.

	Nm-Mt	Ex-Mt
COMPLETE SET (6)	12.00	3.60
1 Ken Griffey Jr.	2.50	.75
2 Frank Thomas	1.50	.45
3 Andruw Jones	.60	.18
4 Alex Rodriguez	2.50	.75
5 Jose Cruz Jr.	.60	.18
6 Cal Ripken	5.00	1.50

1998 Metal Universe Platinum Portraits

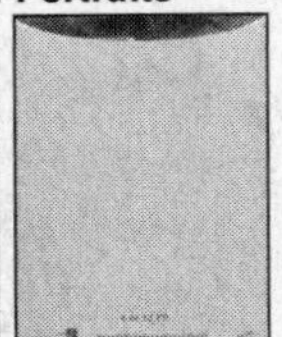

Randomly inserted in packs at the rate of one in 360, this 12-card set features color portraits of top players highlighted with platinum-colored etched foil.

	Nm-Mt	Ex-Mt
COMPLETE SET (12)	200.00	60.00
1 Ken Griffey Jr.	25.00	7.50
2 Frank Thomas	15.00	4.50
3 Chipper Jones	15.00	4.50
4 Jose Cruz Jr.	6.00	1.80
5 Andruw Jones	6.00	1.80
6 Cal Ripken	50.00	15.00
7 Derek Jeter	40.00	12.00
8 Darin Erstad	6.00	1.80
9 Greg Maddux	25.00	7.50
10 Alex Rodriguez	25.00	7.50
11 Mike Piazza	25.00	7.50
12 Vladimir Guerrero	15.00	4.50

1998 Metal Universe Titanium

Randomly inserted in packs at the rate of one in 96, this 15-card set features color photos of top stars printed on die-cut embossed cards and sculpted on etched foil.

	Nm-Mt	Ex-Mt
COMPLETE SET (15)	150.00	45.00
1 Ken Griffey Jr.	15.00	4.50
2 Frank Thomas	10.00	3.00
3 Chipper Jones	10.00	3.00
4 Jose Cruz Jr.	4.00	1.20
5 Juan Gonzalez	6.00	1.80
6 Scott Rolen	10.00	3.00
7 Andruw Jones	4.00	1.20
8 Cal Ripken	30.00	9.00
9 Derek Jeter	25.00	7.50
10 Nomar Garciaparra	15.00	4.50
11 Darin Erstad	4.00	1.20
12 Greg Maddux	15.00	4.50
13 Alex Rodriguez	15.00	4.50
14 Mike Piazza	15.00	4.50
15 Vladimir Guerrero	10.00	3.00

1998 Metal Universe Universal Language

Randomly inserted in packs at the rate of one in six, this 20-card set features color player photos of players whose culture provides illustration and copy is done in the player's native language.

	Nm-Mt	Ex-Mt
COMPLETE SET (20)	50.00	15.00
1 Ken Griffey Jr.	3.00	.90
2 Frank Thomas	2.00	.60
3 Chipper Jones	2.00	.60
4 Albert Belle	.75	.23
5 Juan Gonzalez	1.25	.35
6 Jeff Bagwell	1.25	.35
7 Andruw Jones	.75	.23
8 Cal Ripken	6.00	1.80
9 Derek Jeter	5.00	1.50
10 Nomar Garciaparra	3.00	.90
11 Darin Erstad	.75	.23
12 Greg Maddux	3.00	.90
13 Alex Rodriguez	3.00	.90
14 Mike Piazza	3.00	.90
15 Vladimir Guerrero	2.00	.60
16 Jose Cruz Jr.	.75	.23
17 Hideo Nomo	2.00	.60
18 Kenny Lofton	.75	.23
19 Tony Gwynn	2.50	.75
20 Scott Rolen	2.00	.60

1999 Metal Universe

This 300-card set, produced by Fleer, was distributed in eight-card hobby and retail packs carrying a suggested retail price of $2.69. The product was released in January, 1999. Card fronts feature color action player photos with brushed metal backgrounds in 100 percent etched silver foil and an embossed nameplate with the look of forged steel. The backs carry player information. The set includes the following subsets: Caught on the Fly (233-247), Building Blocks (248-272), and M.L.P.D. (273-300) which features prominent and dominant stars. In an unannounced promotion, thirty-five hand-numbered J.D. Drew Building Blocks subset sample cards were signed by the athlete and randomly seeded into packs. Each of these cards has an embossed authentication seal and the word SAMPLE replaces the card number on back.

	Nm-Mt	Ex-Mt
COMPLETE SET (300)	50.00	15.00
1 Mark McGwire	2.00	.60
2 Jim Edmonds	.30	.09
3 Travis Fryman	.30	.09
4 Tom Gordon	.30	.09
5 Jeff Bagwell	.50	.15
6 Rico Brogna	.30	.09
7 Tom Evans	.30	.09
8 John Franco	.30	.09
9 Juan Gonzalez	.50	.15
10 Paul Molitor	.50	.15
11 Roberto Alomar	.50	.15
12 Mike Hampton	.30	.09
13 Orel Hershiser	.30	.09
14 Todd Stottlemyre	.30	.09
15 Robin Ventura	.30	.09
16 Todd Walker	.30	.09
17 Bernie Williams	.50	.15
18 Shawn Estes	.30	.09
19 Richie Sexson	.30	.09
20 Kevin Millwood	.30	.09
21 David Ortiz	.50	.15
22 Mariano Rivera	.50	.15
23 Ivan Rodriguez	.75	.23
24 Mike Sirotka	.30	.09
25 David Justice	.30	.09
26 Carl Pavano	.30	.09
27 Albert Belle	.30	.09
28 Will Clark	.75	.23
29 Jose Cruz Jr.	.30	.09
30 Trevor Hoffman	.30	.09
31 Dean Palmer	.30	.09
32 Edgar Renteria	.30	.09
33 David Segui	.30	.09
34 B.J. Surhoff	.30	.09
35 Miguel Tejada	.30	.09
36 Bob Wickman	.30	.09
37 Charles Johnson	.30	.09
38 Andruw Jones	.30	.09
39 Mike Lieberthal	.30	.09
40 Eli Marrero	.30	.09
41 Neifi Perez	.30	.09
42 Jim Thome	.75	.23

43 Barry Bonds 2.00 .60
44 Carlos Delgado .30 .09
45 Chuck Finley .30 .09
46 Brian Meadows .30 .09
47 Tony Gwynn 1.00 .30
48 Jose Offerman .30 .09
49 Cal Ripken 2.50 .75
50 Alex Rodriguez 1.25 .35
51 Esteban Yan .30 .09
52 Matt Stairs .30 .09
53 Fernando Vina .30 .09
54 Rondell White .30 .09
55 Kerry Wood .75 .23
56 Dmitri Young .30 .09
57 Ken Caminiti .30 .09
58 Alex Gonzalez .30 .09
59 Matt Mantei .30 .09
60 Tino Martinez .50 .15
61 Hal Morris .30 .09
62 Rafael Palmeiro .50 .15
63 Troy Percival .30 .09
64 Bobby Smith .30 .09
65 Ed Sprague .30 .09
66 Brett Tomko .30 .09
67 Steve Trachsel .30 .09
68 Ugueth Urbina .30 .09
69 Jose Valentin .30 .09
70 Kevin Brown .50 .15
71 Shawn Green .30 .09
72 Dustin Hermanson .30 .09
73 Livan Hernandez .30 .09
74 Geoff Jenkins .30 .09
75 Jeff King .30 .09
76 Chuck Knoblauch .30 .09
77 Edgar Martinez .50 .15
78 Fred McGriff .50 .15
79 Mike Mussina .50 .15
80 Dave Nilsson .30 .09
81 Kenny Rogers .30 .09
82 Tim Salmon .50 .15
83 Reggie Sanders .30 .09
84 Wilson Alvarez .30 .09
85 Rod Beck .30 .09
86 Jose Guillen .30 .09
87 Bob Higginson .30 .09
88 Gregg Olson .30 .09
89 Jeff Shaw .30 .09
90 Masato Yoshii .30 .09
91 Todd Helton .50 .15
92 David Dellucci .30 .09
93 Johnny Damon .50 .15
94 Cliff Floyd .30 .09
95 Ken Griffey Jr. 1.25 .35
96 Juan Guzman .30 .09
97 Derek Jeter 2.00 .60
98 Barry Larkin .50 .15
99 Quinton McCracken .30 .09
100 Sammy Sosa 1.25 .35
101 Kevin Young .30 .09
102 Jay Bell .30 .09
103 Jay Buhner .30 .09
104 Jeff Conine .30 .09
105 Ryan Jackson .30 .09
106 Sidney Ponson .30 .09
107 Jeromy Burnitz .30 .09
108 Roberto Hernandez .30 .09
109 A.J. Hinch .30 .09
110 Hideki Irabu .30 .09
111 Paul Konerko .30 .09
112 Henry Rodriguez .30 .09
113 Shannon Stewart .30 .09
114 Tony Womack .30 .09
115 Wilton Guerrero .30 .09
116 Andy Benes .30 .09
117 Jeff Cirillo .30 .09
118 Chili Davis .30 .09
119 Eric Davis .30 .09
120 Vladimir Guerrero .75 .23
121 Dennis Reyes .30 .09
122 Rickey Henderson .75 .23
123 Mickey Morandini .30 .09
124 Jason Schmidt .30 .09
125 J.T. Snow .30 .09
126 Justin Thompson .30 .09
127 Billy Wagner .30 .09
128 Armando Benitez .30 .09
129 Sean Casey .30 .09
130 Brad Fullmer .30 .09
131 Ben Grieve .30 .09
132 Robb Nen .30 .09
133 Shane Reynolds .30 .09
134 Todd Zeile .30 .09
135 Brady Anderson .30 .09
136 Aaron Boone .30 .09
137 Orlando Cabrera .30 .09
138 Jason Giambi .30 .09
139 Randy Johnson .75 .23
140 Jeff Kent .30 .09
141 John Wetteland .30 .09
142 Rolando Arrojo .30 .09
143 Scott Brosius .30 .09
144 Mark Grace .50 .15
145 Jason Kendall .30 .09
146 Travis Lee .30 .09
147 Gary Sheffield .30 .09
148 David Cone .30 .09
149 Jose Hernandez .30 .09
150 Todd Jones .30 .09
151 Al Martin .30 .09
152 Ismael Valdes .30 .09
153 Wade Boggs .50 .15
154 Garret Anderson .30 .09
155 Bobby Bonilla .30 .09
156 Darryl Kile .30 .09
157 Ryan Klesko .30 .09
158 Tim Wakefield .30 .09
159 Kenny Lofton .30 .09
160 Jose Canseco .75 .23
161 Doug Glanville .30 .09
162 Todd Hundley .30 .09
163 Brian Jordan .30 .09
164 Steve Finley .30 .09
165 Tom Glavine .50 .15
166 Al Leiter .30 .09
167 Raul Mondesi .30 .09
168 Desi Relaford .30 .09
169 Bret Saberhagen .30 .09
170 Omar Vizquel .50 .15
171 Larry Walker .50 .15
172 Bobby Abreu .30 .09
173 Moises Alou .30 .09
174 Mike Caruso .30 .09
175 Royce Clayton .30 .09
176 Bartolo Colon .30 .09
177 Marty Cordova .30 .09
178 Darin Erstad .30 .09
179 Nomar Garciaparra 1.25 .35
180 Andy Ashby .30 .09
181 Dan Wilson .30 .09
182 Larry Sutton .30 .09
183 Tony Clark .30 .09
184 Andres Galarraga .30 .09
185 Ray Durham .30 .09
186 Hideo Nomo .75 .23
187 Steve Woodard .30 .09
188 Scott Rolen .75 .23
189 Mike Stanley .30 .09
190 Jaret Wright .30 .09
191 Vinny Castilla .30 .09
192 Jason Christiansen .30 .09
193 Paul Bako .30 .09
194 Carlos Perez .30 .09
195 Mike Piazza 1.25 .35
196 Fernando Tatis .30 .09
197 Mo Vaughn .30 .09
198 Devon White .30 .09
199 Ricky Gutierrez .30 .09
200 Charlie Hayes .30 .09
201 Brad Radke .30 .09
202 Rick Helling .30 .09
203 John Smoltz .50 .15
204 Frank Thomas .75 .23
205 David Wells .30 .09
206 Roger Clemens 1.50 .45
207 Mark Grudzielanek .30 .09
208 Chipper Jones .75 .23
209 Ray Lankford .30 .09
210 Pedro Martinez .75 .23
211 Manny Ramirez .50 .15
212 Greg Vaughn .30 .09
213 Craig Biggio .50 .15
214 Rusty Greer .30 .09
215 Greg Maddux 1.25 .35
216 Rick Aguilera .30 .09
217 Andy Pettitte .50 .15
218 Dante Bichette .30 .09
219 Damion Easley .30 .09
220 Matt Morris .30 .09
221 John Olerud .30 .09
222 Chan Ho Park .30 .09
223 Curt Schilling .30 .09
224 John Valentin .30 .09
225 Matt Williams .30 .09
226 Ellis Burks .30 .09
227 Tom Goodwin .30 .09
228 Javy Lopez .30 .09
229 Eric Milton .30 .09
230 Paul O'Neill .50 .15
231 Magglio Ordonez .30 .09
232 Derrek Lee .30 .09
233 Ken Griffey Jr. FLY .75 .23
234 Randy Johnson FLY .50 .15
235 Alex Rodriguez FLY .75 .23
236 Darin Erstad FLY .30 .09
237 Juan Gonzalez FLY .30 .09
238 Derek Jeter FLY 1.00 .30
239 Tony Gwynn FLY .50 .15
240 Kerry Wood FLY .50 .15
241 Cal Ripken FLY 1.25 .35
242 Sammy Sosa FLY .75 .23
243 Greg Maddux FLY .75 .23
244 Mark McGwire FLY 1.00 .30
245 Chipper Jones FLY .50 .15
246 Barry Bonds FLY .75 .23
247 Ben Grieve FLY .30 .09
248 Ben Davis BB .30 .09
249 Robert Fick BB .30 .09
250 Carlos Guillen BB .30 .09
251 Mike Frank BB .30 .09
252 Ryan Minor BB .30 .09
253 Troy Glaus BB .30 .09
254 Matt Anderson BB .30 .09
255 Josh Booty BB .30 .09
256 Gabe Alvarez BB .30 .09
257 Gabe Kapler BB .30 .09
258 Enrique Wilson BB .30 .09
259 Alex Gonzalez BB .30 .09
260 Preston Wilson BB .30 .09
261 Eric Chavez BB .30 .09
262 Adrian Beltre BB .50 .15
263 Corey Koskie BB .30 .09
264 Robert Machado BB .30 .09
265 Orl. Hernandez BB .30 .09
266 Matt Clement BB .30 .09
267 Luis Ordaz BB .30 .09
268 Jeremy Giambi BB .30 .09
269 J.D. Drew BB .30 .09
270 Cliff Politte BB .30 .09
271 Carlton Loewer BB .30 .09
272 Aramis Ramirez BB .30 .09
273 Ken Griffey Jr. MLPD .75 .23
274 Ra. Johnson MLPD .50 .15
275 Alex Rodriguez MLPD .75 .23
276 Darin Erstad MLPD .30 .09
277 Scott Rolen MLPD .50 .15
278 Juan Gonzalez MLPD .30 .09
279 Jeff Bagwell MLPD .30 .09
280 Mike Piazza MLPD .75 .23
281 Derek Jeter MLPD 1.00 .30
282 Travis Lee MLPD .30 .09
283 Tony Gwynn MLPD .50 .15
284 Kerry Wood MLPD .50 .15
285 Albert Belle MLPD .30 .09
286 Sammy Sosa MLPD .75 .23
287 Mo Vaughn MLPD .30 .09
288 N. Garciaparra MLPD .75 .23
289 FrankThomas MLPD .50 .15
290 Cal Ripken MLPD 1.25 .35
291 Greg Maddux MLPD .75 .23
292 Chipper Jones MLPD .50 .15
293 Ben Grieve MLPD .30 .09
294 Andruw Jones MLPD .30 .09
295 Mark McGwire MLPD 1.00 .30
296 Roger Clemens MLPD .75 .23
297 Barry Bonds MLPD .75 .23
298 Ken Griffey Jr. CL .75 .23
299 Kerry Wood CL .50 .15
300 Alex Rodriguez CL .75 .23
SAMP J.D. Drew AU/35 40.00 12.00

1999 Metal Universe Precious Metal Gems

Randomly inserted in hobby packs only, this 300-card set is a parallel version of the base set printed on etched gold holographic foil cards. Only 50 serially numbered sets were produced.

Nm-Mt Ex-Mt
*STARS: 20X TO 50X BASIC CARDS..

1999 Metal Universe Boyz With The Wood

Randomly inserted in packs at the rate of one in 18, this 15-card set features color action photos of the game's most prolific hitters printed on special four-sided cards with a copyrighted design by Intervisual.

	Nm-Mt	Ex-Mt
COMPLETE SET (15)	60.00	18.00
1 Ken Griffey Jr.	5.00	1.50
2 Frank Thomas	3.00	.90
3 Jeff Bagwell	2.00	.60
4 Juan Gonzalez	2.00	.60
5 Mark McGwire	8.00	2.40
6 Scott Rolen	3.00	.90
7 Travis Lee	1.25	.35
8 Tony Gwynn	4.00	1.20
9 Mike Piazza	5.00	1.50
10 Chipper Jones	3.00	.90
11 Nomar Garciaparra	5.00	1.50
12 Derek Jeter	8.00	2.40
13 Cal Ripken	10.00	3.00
14 Andruw Jones	1.25	.35
15 Alex Rodriguez	5.00	1.50

1999 Metal Universe Diamond Soul

Randomly inserted in packs at the rate of one in 72, this 15-card set features color action player images printed on sturdy "Galactic" patterned Lenticular card stock with gold foil stamping.

	Nm-Mt	Ex-Mt
COMPLETE SET (15)	250.00	75.00
1 Cal Ripken	30.00	9.00
2 Alex Rodriguez	15.00	4.50
3 Chipper Jones	10.00	3.00
4 Derek Jeter	25.00	7.50
5 Frank Thomas	10.00	3.00
6 Greg Maddux	15.00	4.50
7 Juan Gonzalez	6.00	1.80
8 Ken Griffey Jr.	15.00	4.50
9 Kerry Wood	10.00	3.00
10 Mark McGwire	25.00	7.50
11 Mike Piazza	15.00	4.50
12 Nomar Garciaparra	15.00	4.50
13 Scott Rolen	10.00	3.00
14 Tony Gwynn	12.00	3.60
15 Travis Lee	4.00	1.20

1999 Metal Universe Linchpins

Randomly inserted in packs at the rate of one in 360, this 10-card set features color action images of clubhouse and field leaders silhouetted on a card with a multitude of laser die-cut pins in the background.

	Nm-Mt	Ex-Mt
COMPLETE SET (10)	300.00	90.00
1 Mike Piazza	25.00	7.50
2 Mark McGwire	40.00	12.00
3 Kerry Wood	15.00	4.50
4 Ken Griffey Jr.	25.00	7.50
5 Greg Maddux	25.00	7.50
6 Frank Thomas	15.00	4.50
7 Derek Jeter	40.00	12.00
8 Chipper Jones	15.00	4.50
9 Cal Ripken	50.00	15.00
10 Alex Rodriguez	25.00	7.50

1999 Metal Universe Neophytes

Randomly inserted in packs at the rate of one in six, this 15-card set features color photos of top young stars printed on horizontal, silver-foil stamped cards.

	Nm-Mt	Ex-Mt
COMPLETE SET (15)	10.00	3.00
1 Troy Glaus	.75	.23
2 Travis Lee	.75	.23
3 Scott Elarton	.75	.23
4 Ricky Ledee	.75	.23
5 Richard Hidalgo	.75	.23
6 J.D. Drew	.75	.23
7 Paul Konerko	.75	.23
8 Orlando Hernandez	.75	.23
9 Mike Caruso	.75	.23
10 Mike Frank	.75	.23
11 Miguel Tejada	.75	.23
12 Matt Anderson	.75	.23
13 Kerry Wood	2.00	.60
14 Gabe Alvarez	.75	.23
15 Adrian Beltre	1.25	.35

1999 Metal Universe Planet Metal

Randomly inserted in packs at the rate of one in 36, this 15-card set features color images of some of the best players of the game printed on die-cut cards that feature a metallic view of Earth in the background.

	Nm-Mt	Ex-Mt
COMPLETE SET (15)	120.00	36.00
1 Alex Rodriguez	10.00	3.00
2 Andruw Jones	2.50	.75
3 Cal Ripken	20.00	6.00
4 Chipper Jones	6.00	1.80
5 Darin Erstad	2.50	.75
6 Derek Jeter	15.00	4.50
7 Frank Thomas	6.00	1.80
8 Travis Lee	2.50	.75
9 Scott Rolen	6.00	1.80
10 Nomar Garciaparra	10.00	3.00
11 Mike Piazza	10.00	3.00
12 Mark McGwire	15.00	4.50
13 Ken Griffey Jr.	10.00	3.00
14 Juan Gonzalez	4.00	1.20
15 Jeff Bagwell	4.00	1.20

2000 Metal

The 2000 Metal set, produced by Fleer, was released in late March, 2000 as a 250-card set. The set features 200 player cards and 50 prospect cards (numbers 201 through 250) that are short printed at one in two packs. Each pack contained 10-cards and carried a suggested retail price of 1.99. A promotional sample card featuring Alex Rodriguez was distributed to dealers and hobby media several weeks before the product went live.

	Nm-Mt	Ex-Mt
COMPLETE SET (250)	60.00	18.00
COMP.SET w/o SP's (200)	20.00	6.00
COMMON CARD (1-200)	.25	.07
COMMON (201-250)	.50	.15
1 Tony Gwynn	.75	.23
2 Derek Jeter	1.50	.45
3 Johnny Damon	.40	.12
4 Javy Lopez	.25	.07
5 Preston Wilson	.25	.07
6 Derek Bell	.25	.07
7 Richie Sexson	.25	.07
8 Vinny Castilla	.25	.07
9 Billy Wagner	.25	.07
10 Carlos Beltran	.40	.12
11 Chris Singleton	.25	.07
12 Nomar Garciaparra	1.00	.30
13 Carlos Febles	.25	.07
14 Jason Varitek	.40	.12
15 Luis Gonzalez	.25	.07
16 Jon Lieber	.25	.07
17 Mo Vaughn	.25	.07
18 Dave Burba	.25	.07
19 Brady Anderson	.25	.07
20 Carlos Lee	.25	.07
21 Chuck Finley	.25	.07
22 Alex Gonzalez	.25	.07
23 Matt Williams	.25	.07
24 Chipper Jones	.60	.18
25 Pokey Reese	.25	.07
26 Todd Helton	.40	.12
27 Mike Mussina	.40	.12
28 Butch Huskey	.25	.07
29 Jeff Bagwell	.40	.12
30 Juan Encarnacion	.25	.07
31 A.J. Burnett	.25	.07
32 Micah Bowie	.25	.07
33 Brian Jordan	.25	.07
34 Scott Erickson	.25	.07
35 Sean Casey	.25	.07
36 John Smoltz	.40	.12
37 Edgard Clemente	.25	.07
38 Mike Hampton	.25	.07
39 Tom Glavine	.40	.12
40 Albert Belle	.25	.07
41 Jim Thome	.60	.18
42 Jermaine Dye	.25	.07
43 Sammy Sosa	1.00	.30
44 Pedro Martinez	.60	.18
45 Paul Konerko	.25	.07
46 Damion Easley	.25	.07
47 Cal Ripken	2.00	.60
48 Jose Lima	.25	.07
49 Mike Lowell	.25	.07
50 Randy Johnson	.60	.18
51 Dean Palmer	.25	.07
52 Tim Salmon	.40	.12
53 Kevin Millwood	.25	.07
54 Mark Grace	.40	.12
55 Aaron Boone	.25	.07
56 Omar Vizquel	.40	.12
57 Moises Alou	.25	.07
58 Travis Fryman	.25	.07
59 Erubiel Durazo	.25	.07
60 Carl Everett	.25	.07
61 Charles Johnson	.25	.07
62 Trot Nixon	.25	.07
63 Andres Galarraga	.25	.07
64 Magglio Ordonez	.25	.07
65 Pedro Astacio	.25	.07
66 Roberto Alomar	.40	.12
67 Pete Harnisch	.25	.07
68 Scott Williamson	.25	.07
69 Alex Fernandez	.25	.07
70 Robin Ventura	.40	.12
71 Chad Allen	.25	.07
72 Darin Erstad	.25	.07
73 Ron Coomer	.25	.07
74 Ellis Burks	.25	.07
75 Kent Bottenfield	.25	.07
76 Ken Griffey Jr.	1.00	.30
77 Mike Piazza	1.00	.30
78 Jorge Posada	.40	.12
79 Dante Bichette	.25	.07
80 Adrian Beltre	.40	.12
81 Andruw Jones	.25	.07
82 Wilson Alvarez	.25	.07
83 Edgardo Alfonzo	.25	.07
84 Brian Giles	.25	.07
85 Gary Sheffield	.25	.07
86 Matt Stairs	.25	.07
87 Bret Boone	.25	.07
88 Kenny Rogers	.25	.07
89 Barry Bonds	1.50	.45
90 Scott Rolen	.60	.18
91 Edgar Renteria	.25	.07
92 Larry Walker	.40	.12
93 Roger Cedeno	.25	.07
94 Kevin Brown	.40	.12
95 Lee Stevens	.25	.07
96 Brad Radke	.25	.07
97 Andy Pettitte	.40	.12
98 Bobby Higginson	.25	.07
99 Eric Chavez	.25	.07
100 Alex Rodriguez	1.00	.30
101 Shannon Stewart	.25	.07
102 Ryan Rupe	.25	.07
103 Freddy Garcia	.25	.07
104 John Jaha	.25	.07
105 Greg Maddux	1.00	.30
106 Hideki Irabu	.25	.07
107 Rey Ordonez	.25	.07
108 Troy O'Leary	.25	.07
109 Frank Thomas	.60	.18
110 Corey Koskie	.25	.07
111 Bernie Williams	.40	.12
112 Barry Larkin	.40	.12
113 Kevin Appier	.25	.07
114 Curt Schilling	.25	.07
115 Bartolo Colon	.25	.07
116 Edgar Martinez	.40	.12
117 Ray Lankford	.25	.07
118 Todd Walker	.25	.07
119 John Wetteland	.25	.07
120 David Nilsson	.25	.07
121 Tino Martinez	.40	.12
122 Phil Nevin	.25	.07
123 Ben Grieve	.25	.07
124 Ron Gant	.25	.07
125 Jeff Kent	.25	.07
126 Rick Helling	.25	.07
127 Russ Ortiz	.25	.07
128 Troy Glaus	.25	.07
129 Chan Ho Park	.25	.07
130 Jeromy Burnitz	.25	.07
131 Aaron Sele	.25	.07
132 Mike Sirotka	.25	.07
133 Brad Ausmus	.25	.07
134 Jose Rosado	.25	.07
135 Mariano Rivera	.40	.12
136 Jason Giambi	.25	.07
137 Mike Lieberthal	.25	.07
138 Chris Carpenter	.25	.07
139 Henry Rodriguez	.25	.07
140 Mike Sweeney	.25	.07
141 Vladimir Guerrero	.60	.18
142 Charles Nagy	.25	.07
143 Jason Kendall	.25	.07
144 Matt Lawton	.25	.07
145 Michael Barrett	.25	.07
146 David Cone	.25	.07
147 Bobby Abreu	.25	.07
148 Fernando Tatis	.25	.07
149 Jose Canseco	.60	.18
150 Craig Biggio	.40	.12
151 Matt Mantei	.25	.07
152 Jacque Jones	.25	.07
153 John Halama	.25	.07
154 Trevor Hoffman	.25	.07
155 Rondell White	.25	.07
156 Reggie Sanders	.25	.07
157 Steve Finley	.25	.07
158 Roberto Hernandez	.25	.07
159 Geoff Jenkins	.25	.07
160 Chris Widger	.25	.07
161 Orel Hershiser	.25	.07
162 Tim Hudson	.25	.07
163 Kris Benson	.25	.07

164 Kevin Young .25 .07
165 Rafael Palmeiro .40 .12
166 David Wells .25 .07
167 Ben Davis .25 .07
168 Jamie Moyer .25 .07
169 Randy Wolf .25 .07
170 Jeff Cirillo .25 .07
171 Warren Morris .25 .07
172 Billy Koch .25 .07
173 Marquis Grissom .25 .07
174 Geoff Blum .25 .07
175 Octavio Dotel .25 .07
176 Orlando Hernandez .25 .07
177 J.D. Drew .25 .07
178 Carlos Delgado .25 .07
179 Sterling Hitchcock .25 .07
180 Shawn Green .25 .07
181 Tony Clark .25 .07
182 Joe McEwing .25 .07
183 Fred McGriff .40 .12
184 Tony Batista .25 .07
185 Al Leiter .25 .07
186 Roger Clemens 1.25 .35
187 Al Martin .25 .07
188 Eric Milton .25 .07
189 Bobby Smith .25 .07
190 Rusty Greer .25 .07
191 Shawn Estes .25 .07
192 Ken Caminiti .25 .07
193 Eric Karros .25 .07
194 Manny Ramirez .40 .12
195 Jim Edmonds .25 .07
196 Paul O'Neill .40 .12
197 Rico Brogna .25 .07
198 Ivan Rodriguez .60 .18
199 Doug Glanville .25 .07
200 Mark McGwire 1.50 .45
201 Mark Quinn PROS .50 .15
202 Norm Hutchins PROS .50 .15
203 Ramon Ortiz PROS .50 .15
204 Brett Laxton PROS .50 .15
205 J.Anderson PROS .50 .15
206 Calvin Murray PROS .50 .15
207 Wilton Veras PROS .50 .15
208 C.Hermansen PROS .50 .15
209 Nick Johnson PROS .50 .15
210 Kevin Barker PROS .50 .15
211 Casey Blake PROS .50 .15
212 Chad Meyers PROS .50 .15
213 Kip Wells PROS .50 .15
214 Eric Munson PROS .50 .15
215 Lance Berkman PROS .50 .15
216 Wily Pena PROS .50 .15
217 G.Matthews Jr. PROS .50 .15
218 Travis Dawkins PROS .50 .15
219 Josh Beckett PROS .75 .23
220 Tony Armas Jr. PROS .50 .15
221 A.Soriano PROS 1.25 .35
222 Pat Burrell PROS .50 .15
223 Danys Baez PROS RC .50 .15
224 Adam Kennedy PROS .50 .15
225 Ruben Mateo PROS .50 .15
226 Vernon Wells PROS .50 .15
227 Brian Cooper PROS .50 .15
228 Jeff DaVanon PROS RC .50 .15
229 Glen Barker PROS .50 .15
230 R.Cancel PROS .50 .15
231 D.Jimenez PROS .50 .15
232 Adam Piatt PROS .50 .15
233 Buddy Carlyle PROS .50 .15
234 C.Hutchinson PROS .50 .15
235 Matt Riley PROS .50 .15
236 Cole Liniak PROS .50 .15
237 Ben Petrick PROS .50 .15
238 Peter Bergeron PROS .50 .15
239 Cesar King PROS .50 .15
240 Aaron Myette PROS .50 .15
241 Eric Gagne PROS 2.00 .60
242 Joe Nathan PROS .50 .15
243 Bruce Chen PROS .50 .15
244 Rob Bell PROS .50 .15
245 Juan Sosa PROS RC .50 .15
246 Julio Ramirez PROS .50 .15
247 Wade Miller PROS .50 .15
248 T.Coquillette RC .50 .15
249 Rob Ramsay PROS .50 .15
250 Rick Ankiel PROS .50 .15
P100 A.Rodriguez Promo 2.00 .60

2000 Metal Emerald

Randomly inserted in packs, this insert is a complete parallel of the 2000 Metal base set. The cards feature an emerald green foil background. Cards 1-200 are inserted at a rate of one in four, while cards 201-250 are inserted at a rate of one in eight.

Nm-Mt Ex-Mt
COMPLETE SET (250) 300.00 90.00
*STARS 1-200: 6X TO 15X BASIC
*PROSPECTS 201-250: .75X TO 2X BASIC

2000 Metal Base Shredders

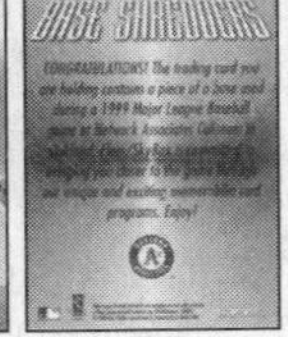

Randomly inserted in packs at one in 288, this 18-card insert set features a swatch from an actual game-used base.

Nm-Mt Ex-Mt
1 Roberto Alomar 10.00 3.00
2 Manny Ramirez 10.00 3.00
3 Tony Gwynn 15.00 4.50
4 Ben Davis 8.00 2.40
5 Vladimir Guerrero 10.00 3.00
6 Michael Barrett 8.00 2.40
7 Eric Munson 8.00 2.40
8 Tony Clark 8.00 2.40
9 Ben Grieve 8.00 2.40
10 Miguel Tejada 8.00 2.40
11 Rafael Palmeiro 10.00 3.00
12 Ivan Rodriguez 10.00 3.00
13 Matt Williams 8.00 2.40
14 Erubiel Durazo 8.00 2.40
15 Mo Vaughn 8.00 2.40
16 Troy Glaus 8.00 2.40
17 Larry Walker 10.00 3.00
18 Todd Helton 10.00 3.00

2000 Metal Fusion

Randomly inserted in packs at one in four, this 15-card insert set features dual-player cards of some of the greatest teammates in the game. Card backs carry a "F" prefix.

Nm-Mt Ex-Mt
COMPLETE SET (15) 25.00 7.50
F1 Ken Griffey Jr. 1.50 .45
Alex Rodriguez
F2 Mark McGwire 2.50 .75
Rick Ankiel
F3 Scott Rolen 1.00 .30
Curt Schilling
F4 Pedro Martinez 1.50 .45
Nomar Garciaparra
F5 Carlos Beltran .60 .18
Carlos Febles
F6 Sammy Sosa 1.50 .45
Mark Grace
F7 Vladimir Guerrero 1.00 .30
Ugueth Urbina
F8 Roger Clemens 2.50 .75
Derek Jeter
F9 Jeff Bagwell .60 .18
Craig Biggio
F10 Chipper Jones 1.00 .30
Andruw Jones
F11 Cal Ripken 3.00 .90
Mike Mussina
F12 Manny Ramirez .60 .18
Roberto Alomar
F13 Sean Casey .60 .18
Barry Larkin
F14 Ivan Rodriguez 1.00 .30
Rafael Palmeiro
F15 Mike Piazza 1.50 .45
Robin Ventura

2000 Metal Heavy Metal

Randomly inserted in packs at one in 20, this insert set features 10 of the leagues most powerful players. Card backs carry a "GS" prefix.

Nm-Mt Ex-Mt
COMPLETE SET (10) 40.00 12.00
GS1 Sammy Sosa 3.00 .90
GS2 Mark McGwire 5.00 1.50
GS3 Ken Griffey Jr. 3.00 .90
GS4 Mike Piazza 3.00 .90
GS5 Nomar Garciaparra 3.00 .90
GS6 Alex Rodriguez 3.00 .90
GS7 Manny Ramirez 1.25 .35
GS8 Jeff Bagwell 1.25 .35
GS9 Chipper Jones 2.00 .60
GS10 Vladimir Guerrero 2.00 .60

2000 Metal Hitting Machines

Randomly inserted in packs at one in 20, this insert set features 10 of the greatest hitters in the league. Card backs carry a "H" prefix.

Nm-Mt Ex-Mt
COMPLETE SET (10) 30.00 9.00
H1 Ken Griffey Jr. 3.00 .90
H2 Mark McGwire 5.00 1.50
H3 Frank Thomas 2.00 .60
H4 Tony Gwynn 2.50 .75
H5 Rafael Palmeiro 1.25 .35
H6 Bernie Williams 1.25 .35
H7 Derek Jeter 5.00 1.50
H8 Sammy Sosa 3.00 .90
H9 Mike Piazza 3.00 .90
H10 Chipper Jones 2.00 .60

2000 Metal Platinum Portraits

Randomly inserted in packs at one in eight, this insert set features 10 portrait shots of players on silver foiled cards. Card backs carry a "PP" prefix.

Nm-Mt Ex-Mt
COMPLETE SET (10) 20.00 6.00

PP1 Carlos Beltran 1.00 .30
PP2 Vladimir Guerrero 1.50 .45
PP3 Manny Ramirez 1.00 .30
PP4 Ivan Rodriguez 1.50 .45
PP5 Sean Casey .60 .18
PP6 Alex Rodriguez 2.50 .75
PP7 Derek Jeter 4.00 1.20
PP8 Nomar Garciaparra 2.50 .75
PP9 Vernon Wells .60 .18
PP10 Shawn Green .60 .18

2000 Metal Talent Show

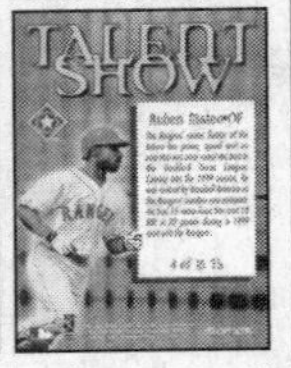

Randomly inserted in packs at one in four, this insert set features 15 of the major leagues top prospects. Card backs carry a "TS" prefix.

Nm-Mt Ex-Mt
COMPLETE SET (15) 8.00 2.40
TS1 Rick Ankiel .50 .15
TS2 Matt Riley .50 .15
TS3 Chad Hermansen .50 .15
TS4 Ruben Mateo .50 .15
TS5 Eric Munson .50 .15
TS6 Alfonso Soriano 1.00 .30
TS7 Wilton Veras .50 .15
TS8 Vernon Wells .50 .15
TS9 Erubiel Durazo .50 .15
TS10 Pat Burrell .50 .15
TS11 Ben Davis .50 .15
TS12 A.J. Burnett .50 .15
TS13 Peter Bergeron .50 .15
TS14 Mark Quinn .50 .15
TS15 Ben Petrick .50 .15

2000 MLB Showdown 1st Edition

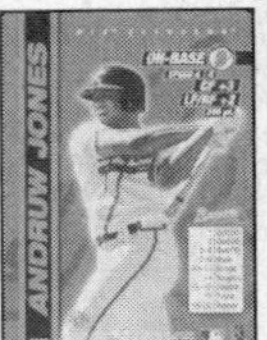

The 2000 MLB Showdown product was released in late April, 2000 as a 462-card baseball game. The 1st Edition cards were released with a silver stamp on front of the card indicating the first print run. The set features 400-player cards and 62 foil superstar cards that were short printed at one in three packs. The 1st Edition packs were released as nine-card packs and carried a suggested retail price of 2.99. Please note that the 1st Edition Greg Maddux and David Cone foil cards were released in starter sets, as well as in packs. Also note that Dennis Cook, Al Leiter, and Kenny Rogers were printed as RHP, but are actually LHP in real life.

Nm-Mt Ex-Mt
COMPLETE SET (462) 200.00 60.00
COMP.SET w/o FOIL (400) 80.00 24.00
COMMON CARD (1-462) .25 .07
COMMON FOIL 3.00 .90
1 Garret Anderson .75 .23
2 Tim Belcher .25 .07
3 Gary DiSarcina UER .25 .07
Tim Salmon incorrectly pictured
4 Darin Erstad .75 .23
5 Chuck Finley FOIL 5.00 1.50
6 Troy Glaus .75 .23
7 Todd Greene .25 .07
8 Jeff Huson .25 .07
9 Orlando Palmeiro .25 .07
10 Troy Percival .75 .23
11 Mark Petkovsek .25 .07
12 Tim Salmon 1.25 .35
13 Steve Sparks .25 .07
14 Mo Vaughn .75 .23
15 Matt Walbeck .25 .07
16 Jay Bell FOIL 5.00 1.50
17 Andy Benes .25 .07
18 Omar Daal .25 .07
19 Steve Finley .75 .23
20 Andy Fox .25 .07
21 Hanley Frias .25 .07
22 Bernard Gilkey .25 .07
23 Luis Gonzalez FOIL 5.00 1.50
24 Randy Johnson FOIL 8.00 2.40
25 Travis Lee .25 .07
26 Matt Mantei .25 .07
27 Dan Plesac .25 .07
28 Kelly Stinnett .25 .07
29 Greg Swindell .25 .07
30 Matt Williams FOIL 5.00 1.50
31 Tony Womack .25 .07
32 Bret Boone .75 .23
33 Tom Glavine 1.25 .35
34 Jose Hernandez .25 .07
35 Brian Hunter .25 .07
36 Andruw Jones .75 .23
37 Chipper Jones FOIL 8.00 2.40
38 Brian Jordan .25 .07
39 Ryan Klesko .75 .23
40 Keith Lockhart .25 .07
41 Greg Maddux FOIL * 3.00 .90
42 Kevin Millwood FOIL 5.00 1.50
43 Eddie Perez .25 .07
44 Mike Remlinger .25 .07
45 John Rocker .25 .07
46 John Smoltz 1.25 .35
47 Walt Weiss .25 .07
48 Gerald Williams .25 .07
49 Rich Amaral .25 .07
50 Brady Anderson .75 .23
51 Albert Belle .75 .23
52 Mike Bordick .25 .07
53 Jeff Conine .75 .23
54 Delino DeShields .75 .23
55 Scott Erickson .25 .07
56 Charles Johnson .75 .23
57 Mike Mussina 1.25 .35
58 Jesse Orosco .25 .07
59 Sidney Ponson .25 .07
60 Jeff Reboulet .25 .07
61 Cal Ripken FOIL 20.00 6.00
62 B.J. Surhoff .75 .23
63 Mike Timlin .25 .07
64 Rod Beck .25 .07
65 Damon Buford .25 .07
66 Rheal Cormier .25 .07
67 N.Garciaparra FOIL 12.00 3.60
68 Butch Huskey .25 .07
69 Darren Lewis .25 .07
70 Derek Lowe .75 .23
71 Pedro Martinez FOIL 8.00 2.40
72 Trot Nixon .75 .23
73 Jose Offerman .25 .07
74 Troy O'Leary .25 .07
75 Mark Portugal .25 .07
76 Pat Rapp .25 .07
77 Mike Stanley .25 .07
78 John Valentin .25 .07
79 Jason Varitek 1.25 .35
80 Tim Wakefield .75 .23
81 Rick Aguilera .75 .23
82 Jeff Blauser .25 .07
83 Kyle Farnsworth .25 .07
84 Gary Gaetti .75 .23
85 Mark Grace 1.25 .35
86 Lance Johnson .25 .07
87 Jon Lieber .25 .07
88 Mickey Morandini .25 .07
89 Jose Nieves .25 .07
90 Jeff Reed .25 .07
91 Henry Rodriguez .25 .07
92 Scott Sanders .25 .07
93 Benito Santiago .75 .23
94 Sammy Sosa FOIL 20.00 6.00
95 Steve Trachsel .25 .07
96 James Baldwin .25 .07
97 Mike Caruso .25 .07
98 Ray Durham .75 .23
99 Brook Fordyce .25 .07
100 Bob Howry .25 .07
101 Paul Konerko .75 .23
102 Carlos Lee .75 .23
103 Greg Norton .25 .07
104 Maggilo Ordonez .75 .23
105 Jim Parque .25 .07
106 Bill Simas .25 .07
107 Chris Singleton .25 .07
108 Mike Sirotka .25 .07
109 Frank Thomas FOIL 8.00 2.40
110 Craig Wilson .25 .07
111 Aaron Boone .75 .23
112 Mike Cameron .75 .23
113 Sean Casey FOIL 5.00 1.50
114 Danny Graves .25 .07
115 Pete Harnisch .25 .07
116 Barry Larkin FOIL 5.00 1.50
117 Pokey Reese .25 .07
118 Scott Sullivan .25 .07
119 Eddie Taubensee .25 .07
120 Brett Tomko .25 .07
121 Michael Tucker .25 .07
122 Greg Vaughn .25 .07
123 Ron Villone .25 .07
124 Scott Williamson FOIL 3.00 .90
125 Dmitri Young .75 .23
126 Roberto Alomar FOIL 5.00 1.50
127 Harold Baines .75 .23
128 Dave Burba .25 .07
129 Bartolo Colon .75 .23
130 Einar Diaz .25 .07
131 Travis Fryman .75 .23
132 Mike Jackson .25 .07
133 David Justice .75 .23
134 Kenny Lofton FOIL 5.00 1.50
135 Charles Nagy .25 .07
136 Manny Ramirez FOIL 5.00 1.50
137 Richie Sexson .75 .23
138 Paul Shuey .25 .07
139 Jim Thome FOIL 8.00 2.40
140 Omar Vizquel 1.25 .35
141 Enrique Wilson .25 .07
142 Kurt Abbott .25 .07
143 Pedro Astacio .25 .07
144 Jeff Barry .25 .07
145 Dante Bichette .75 .23
146 Henry Blanco .25 .07
147 Brian Bohanon .25 .07
148 Vinny Castilla .75 .23
149 Jerry Dipoto .25 .07
150 Todd Helton 1.25 .35
151 Darryl Kile .25 .07
152 Curtis Leskanic .25 .07
153 Neifi Perez .25 .07
154 Terry Shumpert .25 .07
155 Dave Veres .25 .07
156 Larry Walker FOIL 5.00 1.50
157 Brad Ausmus .25 .07
158 Frank Catalanotto .25 .07
159 Tony Clark .25 .07
160 Deivi Cruz .25 .07
161 Damion Easley .25 .07
162 Juan Encarnacion .25 .07
163 Karim Garcia .25 .07
164 Bobby Higginson .25 .07
165 Todd Jones .25 .07
166 Gabe Kapler .25 .07
167 Dave Mlicki .25 .07
168 Brian Moehler .25 .07
169 C.J. Nitkowski .25 .07
170 Dean Palmer FOIL 5.00 1.50
171 Jeff Weaver .25 .07
172 Antonio Alfonseca .25 .07
173 Bruce Aven .25 .07
174 Dave Berg .25 .07
175 Luis Castillo FOIL 3.00 .90
176 Ryan Dempster .25 .07
177 Brian Edmondson .25 .07
178 Alex Gonzalez .25 .07
179 Mark Kotsay .25 .07
180 Derrek Lee .75 .23
181 Braden Looper .25 .07
182 Mike Lowell .75 .23
183 Brian Meadows .25 .07
184 Mike Redmond .25 .07
185 Dennis Springer .25 .07
186 Preston Wilson .75 .23
187 Jeff Bagwell FOIL 5.00 1.50
188 Derek Bell .25 .07
189 Craig Biggio 1.25 .35
190 Tim Bogar .25 .07
191 Ken Caminiti .75 .23
192 Scott Elarton .25 .07
193 Tony Eusebio .25 .07
194 Carl Everett FOIL 5.00 1.50
195 Mike Hampton FOIL 5.00 1.50
196 Richard Hidalgo .25 .07
197 Stan Javier .25 .07
198 Jose Lima .25 .07
199 Jay Powell .25 .07
200 Shane Reynolds .25 .07
201 Bill Spiers .25 .07
202 Billy Wagner FOIL 5.00 1.50
203 Carlos Beltran FOIL 5.00 1.50
204 Johnny Damon 1.25 .35
205 Jermaine Dye .25 .07
206 Carlos Febles .25 .07
207 Jeremy Giambi .25 .07
208 Chad Kreuter .25 .07
209 Jeff Montgomery .25 .07
210 Joe Randa .75 .23
211 Jose Rosado .25 .07
212 Rey Sanchez .25 .07
213 Scott Service .25 .07
214 Tim Spehr .25 .07
215 Jeff Suppan .25 .07
216 Mike Sweeney .75 .23
217 Jay Witasick .25 .07
218 Adrian Beltre 1.25 .35
219 Pedro Borbon .25 .07
220 Kevin Brown FOIL 5.00 1.50
221 Mark Grudzielanek .25 .07
222 Dave Hansen .25 .07
223 Todd Hundley .25 .07
224 Eric Karros .75 .23
225 Raul Mondesi .75 .23
226 Chan Ho Park .75 .23
227 Jeff Shaw .25 .07
228 Gary Sheffield FOIL 5.00 1.50
229 Ismael Valdes .25 .07
230 Jose Vizcaino .25 .07
231 Devon White .75 .23
232 Eric Young .25 .07
233 Ron Belliard .25 .07
234 Sean Berry .25 .07
235 Jeromy Burnitz FOIL 5.00 1.50
236 Jeff Cirillo .25 .07
237 Marquis Grissom .75 .23
238 Geoff Jenkins .75 .23
239 Scott Karl .25 .07
240 Mark Loretta .75 .23
241 Mike Myers .25 .07
242 David Nilsson FOIL 3.00 .90
243 Hideo Nomo 2.00 .60
244 Alex Ochoa .25 .07
245 Jose Valentin .25 .07
246 Bob Wickman .25 .07
247 Steve Woodard .25 .07
248 Chad Allen .25 .07
249 Ron Coomer .25 .07
250 Cristian Guzman .25 .07
251 Denny Hocking .25 .07
252 Torii Hunter .75 .23
253 Corey Koskie .75 .23
254 Matt Lawton .25 .07
255 Joe Mays .25 .07
256 Doug Mientkiewicz .75 .23
257 Eric Milton .25 .07
258 Brad Radke FOIL 5.00 1.50
259 Terry Steinbach .25 .07
260 Mike Trombley .25 .07
261 Todd Walker .25 .07
262 Bob Wells .25 .07
263 Shane Andrews .25 .07
264 Michael Barrett .25 .07
265 Orlando Cabrera .25 .07
266 Brad Fullmer .25 .07
267 Vlad. Guerrero FOIL 8.00 2.40
268 Wilton Guerrero .25 .07
269 Dustin Hermanson .25 .07
270 Steve Kline .25 .07
271 Manny Martinez .25 .07
272 Mike Thurman .25 .07
273 Ugueth Urbina .25 .07
274 Javier Vazquez .75 .23
275 Jose Vidro .25 .07
276 Rondell White .75 .23
277 Chris Widger .25 .07
278 Edgardo Alfonzo FOIL 3.00 .90
279 Armando Benitez .75 .23
280 Roger Cedeno .25 .07
281 Dennis Cook UER .25 .07
Mistakenly printed as a RHP
282 Shawon Dunston .25 .07
283 Matt Franco .25 .07
284 Darryl Hamilton .25 .07
285 R. Henderson FOIL 8.00 2.40
286 Orel Hershiser .75 .23
287 Al Leiter UER .75 .23
Mistakenly printed as a RHP
288 John Olerud .75 .23
289 Rey Ordonez .25 .07
290 Mike Piazza FOIL 10.00 3.00
291 Kenny Rogers UER .75 .23
Mistakenly printed as a RHP
292 Robin Ventura 1.25 .35

293 Turk Wendell .25 .07
294 Masato Yoshii .25 .07
295 Scott Brosius .25 .07
296 Roger Clemens FOIL 12.00 3.60
297 David Cone FOIL * 2.00 .60
298 Chad Curtis .25 .07
299 Chili Davis .75 .23
300 Orlando Hernandez .25 .07
301 Derek Jeter FOIL 12.00 3.60
302 Chuck Knoblauch .75 .23
303 Ricky Ledee .25 .07
304 Tino Martinez 1.25 .35
305 Ramiro Mendoza .25 .07
306 Paul O'Neill 1.25 .35
307 Andy Pettitte 1.25 .35
308 Jorge Posada 1.25 .35
309 Mariano Rivera FOIL 5.00 1.50
310 Mike Stanton .25 .07
311 Bernie Williams FOIL 5.00 1.50
312 Kevin Appier .75 .23
313 Eric Chavez .75 .23
314 Ryan Christenson .25 .07
315 Jason Giambi FOIL 5.00 1.50
316 Ben Grieve .25 .07
317 Buddy Groom .25 .07
318 Gil Heredia .25 .07
319 A.J. Hinch .25 .07
320 John Jaha .25 .07
321 Doug Jones .25 .07
322 Omar Olivares .25 .07
323 Tony Phillips .25 .07
324 Matt Stairs .25 .07
325 Miguel Tejada .75 .23
326 Randy Velarde FOIL 3.00 .90
327 Bobby Abreu FOIL 5.00 1.50
328 Marlon Anderson .25 .07
329 Alex Arias .25 .07
330 Rico Brogna .25 .07
331 Paul Byrd .25 .07
332 Ron Gant .75 .23
333 Doug Glanville .25 .07
334 Wayne Gomes .25 .07
335 Kevin Jordan .25 .07
336 Mike Lieberthal .75 .23
337 Steve Montgomery .25 .07
338 Chad Ogea .25 .07
339 Scott Rolen 2.00 .60
340 Curt Schilling FOIL 5.00 1.50
341 Kevin Sefcik .25 .07
342 Mike Benjamin .25 .07
343 Kris Benson .25 .07
344 Adrian Brown .25 .07
345 Brant Brown .25 .07
345 Tom Goodwin .25 .07
346 Brad Clontz .25 .07
347 Brian Giles FOIL 5.00 1.50
348 Jason Kendall FOIL 5.00 1.50
349 Al Martin .25 .07
350 Warren Morris .25 .07
351 Todd Ritchie .25 .07
352 Scott Sauerbeck .25 .07
353 Jason Schmidt .75 .23
354 Ed Sprague .25 .07
355 Mike Williams .25 .07
356 Kevin Young .25 .07
357 Andy Ashby .25 .07
358 Ben Davis .25 .07
359 Tony Gwynn FOIL 8.00 2.40
360 Sterling Hitchcock .25 .07
361 Trevor Hoffman FOIL 5.00 1.50
362 Damian Jackson .25 .07
363 Wally Joyner .75 .23
364 Phil Nevin .75 .23
365 Eric Owens .25 .07
366 Ruben Rivera .25 .07
367 Reggie Sanders .25 .07
368 John Vander Wal .25 .07
369 Quilvio Veras .25 .07
370 Matt Whisenant .25 .07
371 Woody Williams .25 .07
372 Rich Aurilia .25 .07
373 Marvin Benard .25 .07
374 Barry Bonds FOIL 20.00 6.00
375 Ellis Burks .25 .07
376 Alan Embree .25 .07
377 Shawn Estes .25 .07
378 John Johnstone .25 .07
379 Jeff Kent .25 .07
380 Brent Mayne .25 .07
381 Bill Mueller .75 .23
382 Robb Nen .75 .23
383 Russ Ortiz .75 .23
384 Kirk Rueter .25 .07
385 F.P. Santangelo .25 .07
386 J.T. Snow .75 .23
387 David Bell .25 .07
388 Jay Buhner .75 .23
389 Russ Davis .25 .07
390 Freddy Garcia .75 .23
391 Ken Griffey Jr. FOIL 12.00 3.60
392 John Halama .25 .07
393 Brian Hunter .25 .07
394 Raul Ibanez .25 .07
395 Tom Lampkin .25 .07
396 Edgar Martinez FOIL 5.00 1.50
397 Jose Mesa .25 .07
398 Jamie Moyer .75 .23
399 Jose Paniagua .25 .07
400 Alex Rodriguez FOIL 10.00 3.00
401 Dan Wilson .25 .07
402 Manny Aybar .25 .07
403 Ricky Bottalico .25 .07
404 Kent Bottenfield .25 .07
405 Darren Bragg .25 .07
406 Alberto Castillo .25 .07
407 J.D. Drew .75 .23
408 Jose Jimenez .25 .07
409 Ray Lankford .25 .07
410 Joe McEwing .25 .07
411 Willie McGee .75 .23
412 Mark McGwire FOIL 25.00 7.50
413 Darren Oliver .25 .07
414 Lance Painter .25 .07
415 Edgar Renteria .75 .23
416 Fernando Tatis FOIL 3.00 .90
417 Wilson Alvarez .25 .07
418 Rolando Arrojo .25 .07
419 Wade Boggs 1.25 .35
420 Miguel Cairo .25 .07
421 Jose Canseco FOIL 8.00 2.40
422 John Flaherty .25 .07
423 Roberto Hernandez .25 .07
424 Dave Martinez .25 .07
425 Fred McGriff 1.25 .35
426 Paul Sorrento .25 .07
427 Kevin Stocker .25 .07
428 Bubba Trammell .25 .07
429 Rick White .25 .07
430 Randy Winn .25 .07
431 Bobby Witt .25 .07
432 Royce Clayton .25 .07
433 Tim Crabtree .25 .07
434 Juan Gonzalez 1.25 .35
436 Rusty Greer .25 .07
437 Rick Helling .25 .07
438 Mark McLemore .25 .07
439 Mike Morgan .25 .07
440 Rafael Palmeiro FOIL 5.00 1.50
441 Ivan Rodriguez FOIL 8.00 2.40
442 Aaron Sele .25 .07
443 Lee Stevens .25 .07
444 Mike Venafro .25 .07
445 John Wetteland .25 .07
446 Todd Zeile .75 .23
447 Jeff Zimmerman FOIL 3.00 .90
448 Tony Batista .75 .23
449 Homer Bush .25 .07
450 Jose Cruz Jr. .25 .07
451 Carlos Delgado .75 .23
452 Kelvim Escobar .25 .07
453 Tony Fernandez FOIL 3.00 .90
454 Darrin Fletcher .25 .07
455 Shawn Green FOIL 5.00 1.50
456 Pat Hentgen .25 .07
457 Billy Koch .25 .07
458 Graeme Lloyd .25 .07
459 Brian McRae .25 .07
460 David Segui .25 .07
461 Shannon Stewart .75 .23
462 David Wells .25 .07

2000 MLB Showdown Unlimited

Randomly inserted into starter sets, this 462-card set is a partial parallel of the MLB Showdown 1st Edition set. This set does not have the silver 1st edition stamp. The starter sets carried a suggested retail price of $9.99.

Nm-Mt Ex-Mt
COMPLETE SET (462) 200.00 60.00
COMP.SET w/o FOIL (400) 50.00 15.00
*UNLIMITED: .2X TO .5X 1ST EDITION
*UNL.FOIL: .2X TO .5X BASIC FOIL

2000 MLB Showdown Strategy

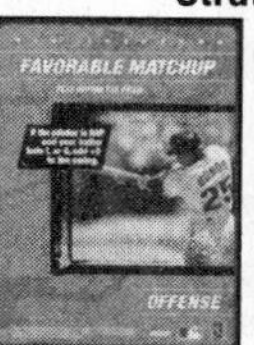

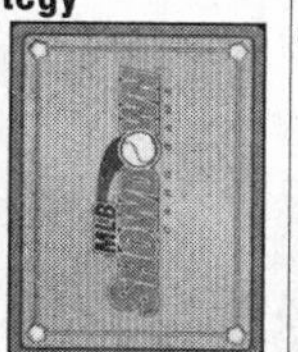

Inserted into packs at a rate of two per pack, and starter sets at 40 per starter set, this 55-card insert set features the strategy cards necessary for playing the MLB Showdown game. Cards carry an "S" prefix.

Nm-Mt Ex-Mt
COMPLETE SET (55) 20.00 6.00
S1 Umpire .25 .07
Bad Call
S2 Mike Stanley .25 .07
Big Inning
S3 Tony Phillips .25 .07
Bobbled in Outfield
S4 Manny Ramirez .30 .09
Clutch Hitting
S5 Chuck Knoblauch .25 .07
Do or Die
S6 Dodgers Outfielder .25 .07
Down the Middle
S7 Carl Everett .25 .07
Ducks on Pond
S8 Barry Bonds 1.25 .35
Favorable Matchup
S9 Deivi Cruz .25 .07
Free Steal
S10 Jose Offerman .25 .07
Get Under It
S11 Rickey Henderson .50 .15
Great Lead
S12 Damian Jackson .25 .07
Hard Slide
S13 Derek Jeter 1.25 .35
High Fives
S14 Paul O' Neill .30 .09
Last Chance
S15 Derek Jeter 1.25 .35
Long Single
S16 Rangers Pitcher .25 .07
Out of Gas
S17 Rickey Henderson .50 .15
Out of Position
S18 Chipper Jones .50 .15
Play the Percentages
S19 Omar Vizquel .30 .09
Rally Cap
S20 Mike Henneman .25 .07
Rattled
S21 Miguel Tejada .25 .07
Runner Not Held
S22 Rockies Pitcher .25 .07
Slow Roller
S23 Braves Pitcher .25 .07
Stick a Fork in Him
S24 Sammy Sosa .75 .23
Swing for Fences
S25 Bernie Williams .30 .09
To the Warning Track
S26 Mark McGwire 1.25 .35
Whiplash
S27 Will Clark .50 .15
Wide Throw
S28 Eddie Taubensee .25 .07
Wild Pitch
S29 Walt Weiss .25 .07
By the Book
S30 Billy Wagner .25 .07
Dominating
S31 Orlando Hernandez .25 .07
Full Windup
S32 Rey Ordonez .25 .07
Ryan Klesko
Good Fielding
S33 Jason Kendall .25 .07
Gun 'Em Down!
S34 Sammy Sosa .75 .23
He's Got a Gun
S35 David Cone .25 .07
In the Groove
S36 Pedro Martinez .50 .15
In the Zone
S37 S.F. Giants .25 .07
Infield In
S38 Randy Johnson .50 .15
Intimidation
S39 Ken Griffey Jr. .75 .23
Just Over Wall
S40 Padres Pitcher .25 .07
Knock Down
S41 Jesse Orosco .25 .07
Lefty Specialist
S42 Mariano Rivera .30 .09
Nerves of Steel
S43 Randy Johnson .50 .15
Nothing but Heat
S44 Bobby Hughes .25 .07
Pitchout
S45 John Rocker .25 .07
Pumped Up
S46 Greg Maddux .75 .23
Quick Pitch
S47 Carlos Baerga .25 .07
Ryan Klesko
Rally Killer
S48 Chuck Knoblauch .25 .07
Short Fly
S49 Pedro Martinez .50 .15
Three Up, Three Down
S50 Derek Jeter 1.25 .35
Trick Pitch
S51 Sammy Sosa .75 .23
Belt-High
S52 Joe Torre .25 .07
Change in Strategy
S53 Pokey Reese .25 .07
Grounder to Second
S54 Mark Grace .30 .09
Stealing Signals
S55 Cal Ripken 1.50 .45
Swing at Anything

2001 MLB Showdown 1st Edition

The 2001 MLB Showdown product was released in mid-April, 2001 as a 462-card baseball game. The 1st Edition cards were released with a silver stamp on front of the card indicating the first print run. The set features 400-player cards and 62 foil superstar cards that were short printed at one in three packs. The 1st Edition packs were released as nine-card packs and carried a suggested retail price of 2.99.

Nm-Mt Ex-Mt
COMPLETE SET (462) 400.00 120.00
COMP.SET w/o FOIL (400) 100.00 30.00
COMMON CARD (1-462) .25 .07
COMMON FOIL 3.00 .90
STATED FOIL ODDS: 1:3
ERSTAD/VLADDIE IN EVERY STARTER DECK
1 Garret Anderson .75 .23
2 Darin Erstad FOIL * 3.00 .90
3 Ron Gant .75 .23
4 Troy Glaus FOIL 3.00 .90
5 Shigetoshi Hasegawa .25 .07
6 Adam Kennedy .25 .07
7 Al Levine RC .25 .07
8 Ben Molina .25 .07
9 Troy Percival .75 .23
10 Mark Petkovsek .25 .07
11 Tim Salmon 1.50 .45
12 Scott Schoeneweis .25 .07
13 Scott Spiezio .25 .07
14 Mo Vaughn .75 .23
15 Jarrod Washburn .25 .07
16 Brian Anderson .25 .07
17 Danny Bautista .25 .07
18 Jay Bell .75 .23
19 Greg Colbrunn .25 .07
20 Steve Finley .75 .23
21 Luis Gonzalez 3.00 .90
22 Randy Johnson FOIL 8.00 2.40
23 Byung-Hyun Kim .75 .23
24 Matt Mantei .25 .07
25 Mike Morgan .25 .07
26 Curt Schilling .75 .23
27 Kelly Stinnett .25 .07
28 Greg Swindell .25 .07
29 Matt Williams .75 .23
30 Tony Womack .25 .07
31 Andy Ashby .25 .07
32 Bobby Bonilla .75 .23
33 Rafael Furcal FOIL 3.00 .90
34 Andres Galarraga .75 .23
35 Tom Glavine FOIL 5.00 1.50
36 Andruw Jones .75 .23
37 Chipper Jones FOIL 8.00 2.40
38 Brian Jordan .75 .23
39 Wally Joyner .75 .23
40 Keith Lockhart .25 .07
41 Javy Lopez .75 .23
42 Greg Maddux FOIL 10.00 3.00
43 Kevin Millwood .75 .23
44 Mike Remlinger .25 .07
45 John Rocker .25 .07
46 B.J. Surhoff .75 .23
47 Quilvio Veras .25 .07
48 Brady Anderson .75 .23
49 Albert Belle .75 .23
50 Jeff Conine .75 .23
51 Delino DeShields .25 .07
52 Buddy Groom .25 .07
53 Trenidad Hubbard .25 .07
54 Luis Matos .25 .07
55 Jose Mercedes .25 .07
56 Melvin Mora .75 .23
57 Mike Mussina FOIL 5.00 1.50
58 Sidney Ponson .25 .07
59 Pat Rapp .25 .07
60 Chris Richard .25 .07
61 Cal Ripken FOIL 15.00 4.50
62 Mike Trombley .25 .07
63 Rolando Arrojo .25 .07
64 Dante Bichette .75 .23
65 Rheal Cormier .25 .07
66 Carl Everett .75 .23
67 Rich Garces .25 .07
68 N. Garciaparra FOIL 12.00 3.60
69 Mike Lansing .25 .07
70 Darren Lewis .25 .07
71 Derek Lowe .75 .23
72 Pedro Martinez FOIL 8.00 2.40
73 Ramon Martinez .25 .07
74 Trot Nixon .75 .23
75 Jose Offerman .25 .07
76 Troy O'Leary .25 .07
77 Jason Varitek 1.50 .45
78 Rick Aguilera .25 .07
79 Damon Buford .25 .07
80 Joe Girardi .25 .07
81 Mark Grace 1.50 .45
82 Willie Greene .25 .07
83 Ricky Gutierrez .25 .07
84 Felix Heredia .25 .07
85 Jon Lieber .25 .07
86 Jeff Reed .25 .07
87 Sammy Sosa FOIL 15.00 4.50
88 Kevin Tapani .25 .07
89 Todd Van Poppel .25 .07
90 Rondell White .75 .23
91 Kerry Wood 2.50 .75
92 Eric Young .25 .07
93 James Baldwin .25 .07
94 Ray Durham .75 .23
95 Keith Foulke FOIL 3.00 .90
96 Bob Howry .25 .07
97 Charles Johnson FOIL 3.00 .90
98 Mark Johnson .25 .07
99 Paul Konerko .75 .23
100 Carlos Lee .75 .23
101 Magglio Ordonez .75 .23
102 Jim Parque .25 .07
103 Herbert Perry .25 .07
104 Bill Simas .25 .07
105 Chris Singleton .25 .07
106 Mike Sirotka .25 .07
107 Frank Thomas FOIL 8.00 2.40
108 Jose Valentin .25 .07
109 Kelly Wunsch .25 .07
110 Aaron Boone .75 .23
111 Sean Casey .75 .23
112 Danny Graves .25 .07
113 Ken Griffey Jr. FOIL 12.00 3.60
114 Pete Harnisch .25 .07
115 Barry Larkin FOIL 5.00 1.50
116 Alex Ochoa .25 .07
117 Steve Parris .25 .07
118 Pokey Reese .25 .07
119 Chris Stynes .25 .07
120 Scott Sullivan .25 .07
121 Eddie Taubensee .25 .07
122 Michael Tucker .25 .07
123 Ron Villone .25 .07
124 Dmitri Young .75 .23
125 Roberto Alomar FOIL 5.00 1.50
126 Sandy Alomar Jr. .25 .07
127 Jason Bere .25 .07
128 Dave Burba .25 .07
129 Bartolo Colon .75 .23
130 Wil Cordero .25 .07
131 Chuck Finley .75 .23
132 Travis Fryman .75 .23
133 Steve Karsay .25 .07
134 Kenny Lofton .75 .23
135 Manny Ramirez FOIL 5.00 1.50
136 David Segui .25 .07
137 Jim Thome 2.50 .75
138 Omar Vizquel 1.50 .45
139 Bob Wickman .25 .07
140 Pedro Astacio .25 .07
141 Brian Bohanon .25 .07
142 Jeff Cirillo .25 .07
143 Jeff Frye .25 .07
144 Jeffrey Hammonds .25 .07
145 Todd Helton FOIL 5.00 1.50
146 Todd Hollandsworth .25 .07
147 Butch Huskey .25 .07
148 Jose Jimenez .25 .07
149 Brent Mayne .25 .07
150 Neifi Perez .25 .07
151 Terry Shumpert .25 .07
152 Larry Walker 1.50 .45
153 Gabe White FOIL 3.00 .90
154 Masato Yoshii .25 .07
155 Matt Anderson .25 .07
156 Brad Ausmus .25 .07
157 Rich Becker .25 .07
158 Tony Clark .25 .07
159 Deivi Cruz .25 .07
160 Damion Easley .25 .07
161 Juan Encarnacion .25 .07
162 Juan Gonzalez 1.50 .45
163 Shane Halter .25 .07
164 Bobby Higginson .75 .23
165 Todd Jones FOIL 3.00 .90
166 Brian Moehler .25 .07
167 Hideo Nomo 2.50 .75
168 Dean Palmer .75 .23
169 Jeff Weaver .25 .07
170 Antonio Alfonseca .25 .07
171 Luis Castillo FOIL 3.00 .90
172 Ryan Dempster FOIL 3.00 .90
173 Cliff Floyd .75 .23
174 Alex Gonzalez .25 .07
175 Mark Kotsay .25 .07
176 Derrek Lee .75 .23
177 Braden Looper .25 .07
178 Mike Lowell .75 .23
179 Brad Penny .25 .07
180 Mike Redmond .25 .07
181 Henry Rodriguez .25 .07
182 Jesus Sanchez .25 .07
183 Mark Smith .25 .07
184 Preston Wilson .75 .23
185 Moises Alou .75 .23
186 Jeff Bagwell FOIL 5.00 1.50
187 Lance Berkman .75 .23
188 Craig Biggio 1.50 .45
189 Tim Bogar .25 .07
190 Jose Cabrera .25 .07
191 Octavio Dotel .25 .07
192 Scott Elarton FOIL 3.00 .90
193 Richard Hidalgo .25 .07
194 Chris Holt .25 .07
195 Jose Lima .25 .07
196 Julio Lugo .25 .07
197 Mitch Meluskey .25 .07
198 Bill Spiers .25 .07
199 Daryle Ward .25 .07
200 Carlos Beltran 1.50 .45
201 Ricky Bottalico .25 .07
202 Johnny Damon FOIL 5.00 1.50
203 Jermaine Dye .75 .23
204 Carlos Febles .25 .07
205 Dave McCarty .25 .07
206 Mark Quinn .25 .07
207 Joe Randa .25 .07
208 Dan Reichert .25 .07
209 Rey Sanchez .25 .07
210 Jose Santiago .25 .07
211 Jeff Suppan .25 .07
212 Mac Suzuki .75 .23
213 Mike Sweeney .75 .23
214 Gregg Zaun .25 .07
215 Terry Adams .25 .07
216 Adrian Beltre 1.50 .45
217 Kevin Brown FOIL 3.00 .90
218 Alex Cora .25 .07
219 Darren Dreifort .25 .07
220 Tom Goodwin .25 .07
221 Shawn Green .75 .23
222 Mark Grudzielanek .25 .07
223 Dave Hansen .25 .07
224 Todd Hundley .25 .07
225 Eric Karros .75 .23
226 Chad Kreuter .25 .07
227 Chan Ho Park .75 .23
228 Jeff Shaw .25 .07
229 Gary Sheffield FOIL 3.00 .90
230 Juan Acevedo .25 .07
231 Ron Belliard .25 .07
232 Henry Blanco .25 .07
233 Jeromy Burnitz .75 .23
234 Jeff D'Amico FOIL 3.00 .90
235 Valerio De Los Santos .25 .07
236 Marquis Grissom .75 .23
237 Charlie Hayes .25 .07
238 Jimmy Haynes .25 .07
239 Jose Hernandez .25 .07
240 Geoff Jenkins .75 .23
241 Curtis Leskanic .25 .07
242 Mark Loretta .25 .07
243 Richie Sexson .75 .23
244 Dave Weathers .25 .07
245 Jay Canizaro .25 .07
246 Ron Coomer .25 .07
247 Cristian Guzman .25 .07
248 LaTroy Hawkins .25 .07
249 Denny Hocking .25 .07
250 Torii Hunter .75 .23
251 Jacque Jones .75 .23
252 Corey Koskie .75 .23
253 Matt Lawton .75 .23
254 Matt LeCroy .75 .23
255 Eric Milton .25 .07
256 David Ortiz 1.50 .45
257 Brad Radke FOIL 3.00 .90
258 Mark Redman .25 .07
259 Bob Wells .25 .07
260 Michael Barrett .25 .07
261 Peter Bergeron .25 .07
262 Milton Bradley .75 .23
263 Orlando Cabrera .75 .23
264 Vladimir Guerrero FOIL * 8.00 2.40
265 Wilton Guerrero .25 .07
266 Dustin Hermanson .25 .07
267 Terry Jones .25 .07
268 Steve Kline .25 .07
269 Felipe Lira .25 .07
270 Mike Mordecai .25 .07
271 Lee Stevens .25 .07
272 Anthony Telford .25 .07
273 Javier Vazquez .75 .23
274 Jose Vidro FOIL 3.00 .90
275 Edgardo Alfonzo FOIL 3.00 .90
276 Derek Bell .25 .07
277 Armando Benitez .75 .23
278 Mike Bordick .25 .07
279 Mike Hampton FOIL 3.00 .90
280 Lenny Harris .25 .07
281 Al Leiter .75 .23
282 Jay Payton .25 .07
283 Mike Piazza FOIL 10.00 3.00
284 Todd Pratt .25 .07
285 Glendon Rusch .25 .07
286 Bubba Trammell .25 .07
287 Robin Ventura .75 .23
288 Turk Wendell .25 .07
289 Rick White .25 .07
290 Todd Zeile .75 .23
291 Scott Brosius .75 .23
292 Roger Clemens FOIL 12.00 3.60
293 Jason Grimsley .25 .07
294 Orlando Hernandez .25 .07
295 Derek Jeter FOIL 12.00 3.60
296 Dave Justice .75 .23
297 Chuck Knoblauch .75 .23

298 Tino Martinez 1.50 .45
299 Denny Neagle .25 .07
300 Jeff Nelson .25 .07
301 Paul O'Neill 1.50 .45
302 Andy Pettitte 1.50 .45
303 Jorge Posada 1.50 .45
304 Mariano Rivera FOIL 5.00 1.50
305 Jose Vizcaino .25 .07
306 Bernie Williams FOIL 5.00 1.50
307 Kevin Appier .75 .23
308 Eric Chavez .75 .23
309 Ryan Christenson .25 .07
310 Jason Giambi FOIL 3.00 .90
311 Jeremy Giambi .25 .07
312 Ben Grieve .25 .07
313 Gil Heredia .25 .07
314 Ramon Hernandez .25 .07
315 Tim Hudson FOIL 3.00 .90
316 Jason Isringhausen .75 .23
317 Terrence Long FOIL 3.00 .90
318 Jim Mecir .25 .07
319 Mark Mulder .75 .23
320 Matt Stairs .25 .07
321 Miguel Tejada .75 .23
322 Randy Velarde .25 .07
323 Bobby Abreu .75 .23
324 Jeff Brantley .25 .07
325 Pat Burrell .75 .23
326 Omar Daal .25 .07
327 Rob Ducey .25 .07
328 Doug Glanville .25 .07
329 Wayne Gomes .25 .07
330 Kevin Jordan .25 .07
331 Travis Lee .25 .07
332 Mike Lieberthal .75 .23
333 Vicente Padilla .25 .07
334 Robert Person .25 .07
335 Scott Rolen FOIL 8.00 2.40
336 Kevin Sefcik .25 .07
337 Randy Wolf .25 .07
338 Jimmy Anderson .25 .07
339 Mike Benjamin .25 .07
340 Kris Benson .25 .07
341 Adrian Brown .25 .07
342 Brian Giles FOIL 3.00 .90
343 Jason Kendall FOIL 3.00 .90
344 Pat Meares .25 .07
345 Warren Morris .25 .07
346 Aramis Ramirez .75 .23
347 Todd Ritchie .25 .07
348 Scott Sauerbeck .25 .07
349 Jose Silva .25 .07
350 John VanderWal .25 .07
351 Mike Williams .25 .07
352 Kevin Young .25 .07
353 Carlos Almanzar .25 .07
354 Bret Boone .75 .23
355 Matt Clement .25 .07
356 Adam Eaton .25 .07
357 Wiki Gonzalez .25 .07
358 Trevor Hoffman FOIL 3.00 .90
359 Damian Jackson .25 .07
360 Ryan Klesko .75 .23
361 Phil Nevin FOIL 3.00 .90
362 Eric Owens .25 .07
363 Desi Relaford .25 .07
364 Ruben Rivera .25 .07
365 Kevin Walker .25 .07
366 Woody Williams .25 .07
367 Jay Witasick .25 .07
368 Rich Aurilia .25 .07
369 Marvin Benard .25 .07
370 Barry Bonds FOIL 20.00 6.00
371 Ellis Burks .75 .23
372 Bobby Estalella .25 .07
373 Doug Henry .25 .07
374 Livan Hernandez .25 .07
375 Jeff Kent FOIL 3.00 .90
376 Doug Mirabelli .25 .07
377 Bill Mueller .75 .23
378 Calvin Murray .25 .07
379 Robb Nen FOIL 3.00 .90
380 Russ Ortiz .75 .23
381 Armando Rios .25 .07
382 Felix Rodriguez .25 .07
383 Kirk Rueter .25 .07
384 J.T. Snow .75 .23
385 Paul Abbott .25 .07
386 David Bell .25 .07
387 Jay Buhner .75 .23
388 Mike Cameron .75 .23
389 John Halama .25 .07
390 Rickey Henderson 2.50 .75
391 Al Martin .25 .07
392 Edgar Martinez FOIL 5.00 1.50
393 Mark McLemore .25 .07
394 John Olerud .75 .23
395 Jose Paniagua .25 .07
396 Arthur Rhodes .25 .07
397 Alex Rodriguez FOIL 10.00 3.00
398 Kazuhiro Sasaki FOIL 3.00 .90
399 Aaron Sele .25 .07
400 Dan Wilson .25 .07
401 Rick Ankiel FOIL 3.00 .90
402 Will Clark 2.50 .75
403 J.D. Drew .75 .23
404 Jim Edmonds FOIL 3.00 .90
405 Pat Hentgen .25 .07
406 Darryl Kile .75 .23
407 Ray Lankford .25 .07
408 Mike Matheny .75 .23
409 Mark McGwire FOIL 20.00 6.00
410 Craig Paquette .25 .07
411 Placido Polanco .25 .07
412 Edgar Renteria .75 .23
413 Garrett Stephenson .25 .07
414 Fernando Tatis .25 .07
415 Mike Timlin .25 .07
416 Dave Veres .25 .07
417 Fernando Vina .25 .07
418 Miguel Cairo .25 .07
419 Vinny Castilla .75 .23
420 Steve Cox .25 .07
421 Doug Creek .25 .07
422 John Flaherty .25 .07
423 Jose Guillen .25 .07
424 Roberto Hernandez FOIL 3.00 .90
425 Russ Johnson .25 .07
426 Albie Lopez .25 .07
427 Felix Martinez .25 .07
428 Fred McGriff 1.50 .45
429 Bryan Rekar .25 .07
430 Greg Vaughn .25 .07
431 Gerald Williams .25 .07
432 Esteban Yan .25 .07
433 Luis Alicea .25 .07
434 Frank Catalanotto .25 .07
435 Royce Clayton .25 .07
436 Tim Crabtree .25 .07
437 Chad Curtis .25 .07
438 Rusty Greer .75 .23
439 Rick Helling .25 .07
440 Gabe Kapler .25 .07
441 Mike Lamb .25 .07
442 Ricky Ledee .25 .07
443 Rafael Palmeiro 1.50 .45
444 Ivan Rodriguez FOIL 8.00 2.40
445 Kenny Rogers .75 .23
446 Mike Venafro .25 .07
447 John Wetteland .75 .23
448 Tony Batista FOIL 3.00 .90
449 Jose Cruz Jr. .25 .07
450 Carlos Delgado FOIL 3.00 .90
451 Kelvim Escobar .25 .07
452 Darrin Fletcher .25 .07
453 Brad Fullmer .25 .07
454 Alex Gonzalez .25 .07
455 Mark Guthrie .25 .07
456 Billy Koch .25 .07
457 Esteban Loaiza .25 .07
458 Raul Mondesi .75 .23
459 Mickey Morandini .25 .07
460 Paul Quantrill .25 .07
461 Shannon Stewart .75 .23
462 David Wells FOIL 3.00 .90

2001 MLB Showdown Unlimited

Randomly inserted into starter sets, this 462-card set is a partial parallel of the MLB Showdown 1st Edition set. This set does not have the silver 1st edition stamp.

	Nm-Mt	Ex-Mt
COMPLETE SET (462)	200.00	60.00
COMP.SET w/o FOIL (400)	50.00	15.00

*UNLIMITED: .2X TO .5X 1ST EDITION
*UNL.FOIL: .2X TO .5X IST ED.FOIL...

2001 MLB Showdown Strategy

Inserted into packs at a rate of two per pack, and starter sets at 40 per starter set, this 75-card insert set features the strategy cards necessary for playing the MLB Showdown game. Card numbers carry an "S" prefix.

	Nm-Mt	Ex-Mt
COMPLETE SET (75)	15.00	4.50

S1 Jorge Posada .40 .12
Change Sides
S2 Nomar Garciaparra .75 .23
Clutch Hitter
S3 Manny Ramirez .40 .12
Clutch Hitting
S4 Bernie Williams .60 .18
Derek Jeter
Contact Hitter
S5 Sammy Sosa .75 .23
Deep in the Gap
S6 Brian Buchanon .25 .07
Dog Meat
S7 Jay Canizaro .25 .07
Double Steal
S8 Michael Tucker .25 .07
Down the Middle
S9 Drag Bunt .25 .07
Phillies Player
S10 Luis Castillo .25 .07
Drained
S11 Carl Everett .25 .07
Ducks on the Pond
S12 Carlos Delgado .25 .07
Favorable Matchup
S13 Fight it Off .25 .07
S14 Benji Molina .25 .07
Free Swinger
S15 Eric Young .25 .07
Fuel on the Fire
S16 Hiding an Injury .25 .07
S17 Nomar Garciaparra .75 .23
In Motion
S18 Alex Ochoa .25 .07
Last Chance
S19 Reds Player .25 .07
Lean Into It
S20 Rickey Henderson .50 .15
Nuisance
S21 Alex Gonzalez .25 .07
Off Balance
S22 Hideo Nomo .50 .15
Out of Gas
S23 Sean Casey .25 .07
Overthrow
S24 Angels Player .25 .07
Play the Percentages
S25 Power Hitter .25 .07
S26 Chuch Knoblauch .25 .07
Protect the Runner
S27 Todd Helton .40 .12
Pull The Ball
S28 Tim Salmon .40 .12
Rally Cap
S29 Randy Johnson .50 .15
Rough Outing
S30 Johnny Damon .40 .12
Runner not Held
S31 Cincinnati Reds .25 .07
Running On Fumes
S32 Alex Rodriguez .75 .23
Ruptured Duck
S33 Pokey Reese .25 .07
Sail Into Center
S34 Mark McGwire 1.25 .35
Say The Magic Word
S35 Pirates Pitcher .25 .07
Shell Shocked
S36 Homer Bush .25 .07
Singles Hitter
S37 Smash Up the Middle .25 .07
Cubs Player
S38 Twins Pitcher .25 .07
Stick a Fork in Him
S39 Take What's Given .25 .07
S40 Brian Giles .25 .07
To The Warning Track
S41 Shawn Dunston .25 .07
Turn On It
S42 Curtis Leskanic .25 .07
Anointed Closer
S43 By the Book .25 .07
S44 Bobby Higginson .25 .07
Cannon
S45 Orioles Player .25 .07
Choke
S46 Greg Maddux .75 .23
Fast Worker
S47 Fans .25 .07
Flamethrower
S48 Kevin Brown .25 .07
Full Windup
S49 Omar Vizquel .40 .12
Goose Egg
S50 Tom Glavine .40 .12
Great Start
S51 Neifi Perez .25 .07
Great Throw
S52 Mike Lamb .25 .07
Gutsy Play
S53 Pokey Reese .25 .07
Highlight Reel
S54 Insult to Injury .25 .07
S55 Randy Johnson .50 .15
In the Groove
S56 Job Well Done .25 .07
S57 Fans .25 .07
Just Foul
S58 Bernie Williams .40 .12
Just Over the Wall
S59 Barry Bonds 1.25 .35
Leaping Catch
S60 Jason Christiansen .25 .07
Lefty Specialist
S61 Eddie Taubensee .25 .07
Low and Away
S62 Chicago White Sox .25 .07
Mound Conference
S63 Todd Jones .25 .07
Nerves of Steel
S64 Pitchout .25 .07
S65 Brian Moehler .25 .07
Scuff the Ball
S66 Livan Hernandez .25 .07
Sloppy Bunt
S67 Omar Vizquel .40 .12
Soft Hands
S68 Byung-Hyun Kim .25 .07
Submarine Pitch
S69 Visibly Upset .25 .07
S70 Benito Santiago .25 .07
What Were You Thinking
S71 Kevin Brown .25 .07
Air it Out
S72 Pedro Martinez .50 .15
Bear Down
S73 Bobby Cox .25 .07
Brainstorm
S74 Dmitri Young .25 .07
Game of Inches
S75 Moises Alou .25 .07
Second Look

2002 MLB Showdown

The 2002 MLB Showdown product was released in mid-April, 2002 as a 356-card baseball game. The set features 300-player cards and 56 foil superstar cards that were short printed at one in three booster packs.

	Nm-Mt	Ex-Mt
COMP.SET w/o FOIL (300)	60.00	18.00
COMMON CARD (1-356)	.50	.15
COMMON FOIL	3.00	.90

1 Garret Anderson 1.00 .30
2 David Eckstein .50 .15
3 Darin Erstad 1.00 .30
4 Troy Glaus FOIL 5.00 1.50
5 Adam Kennedy .50 .15
6 Ben Molina .50 .15
7 Ramon Ortiz .50 .15
8 Troy Percival 1.00 .30
9 Tim Salmon 1.50 .45
10 Scott Schoeneweis .50 .15
11 Scott Spiezio .50 .15
12 Jarrod Washburn .50 .15
13 Miguel Batista .50 .15
14 Jay Bell 1.00 .30
15 Craig Counsell .50 .15
16 David Dellucci .50 .15
17 Erubiel Durazo .50 .15
18 Steve Finley 1.00 .30
19 Luis Gonzalez FOIL 5.00 1.50
20 Mark Grace 1.50 .45
21 Randy Johnson FOIL 10.00 3.00
22 Byung-Hyun Kim 1.00 .30
23 Albie Lopez .50 .15
24 Curt Schilling FOIL 5.00 1.50
25 Matt Williams 1.00 .30
26 Tony Womack .50 .15
27 Marcus Giles FOIL 5.00 1.50
28 Tom Glavine 1.50 .45
29 Andruw Jones 1.00 .30
30 Chipper Jones FOIL 10.00 3.00
31 Brian Jordan 1.00 .30
32 Steve Karsay .50 .15
33 Javy Lopez 1.00 .30
34 Greg Maddux FOIL 10.00 3.00
35 Jason Marquis .50 .15
36 Mike Remlinger .50 .15
37 Rey Sanchez .50 .15
38 B. J. Surhoff 1.00 .30
39 Brady Anderson 1.00 .30
40 Tony Batista FOIL 5.00 1.50
41 Mike Bordick 1.00 .30
42 Jeff Conine 1.00 .30
43 Buddy Groom .50 .15
44 Jerry Hairston Jr. .50 .15
45 Jason Johnson .50 .15
46 Melvin Mora 1.00 .30
47 Chris Richard .50 .15
48 B. J. Ryan .50 .15
49 Josh Towers .50 .15
50 Rolando Arrojo .50 .15
51 Rod Beck .50 .15
52 Dante Bichette 1.00 .30
53 David Cone 1.00 .30
54 Carl Everett 1.00 .30
55 Rich Garces .50 .15
56 Derek Lowe 1.00 .30
57 Trot Nixon 1.00 .30
58 Hideo Nomo 2.50 .75
59 Jose Offerman .50 .15
60 Troy O'Leary .50 .15
61 Manny Ramirez FOIL 8.00 2.40
62 Delino DeShields .50 .15
63 Kyle Farnsworth .50 .15
64 Jeff Fassero .50 .15
65 Ricky Gutierrez .50 .15
66 Todd Hundley .50 .15
67 Jon Lieber .50 .15
68 Fred McGriff 1.50 .45
69 Bill Mueller 1.00 .30
70 Corey Patterson 1.00 .30
71 Sammy Sosa FOIL 15.00 4.50
72 Julian Tavarez .50 .15
73 Kerry Wood 2.50 .75
74 Eric Young .50 .15
75 Mark Buehrle FOIL 5.00 1.50
76 Royce Clayton .50 .15
77 Joe Crede .50 .15
78 Ray Durham 1.00 .30
79 Keith Foulke 1.00 .30
80 Bob Howry .50 .15
81 Mark Johnson .50 .15
82 Paul Konerko 1.00 .30
83 Carlos Lee 1.00 .30
84 Sean Lowe .50 .15
85 Magglio Ordonez 1.00 .30
86 Jose Valentin 1.00 .30
87 Aaron Boone 1.00 .30
88 Jim Brower .50 .15
89 Sean Casey 1.00 .30
90 Brady Clark .50 .15
91 Adam Dunn FOIL 8.00 2.40
92 Danny Graves .50 .15
93 Ken Griffey Jr. FOIL 10.00 3.00
94 Pokey Reese .50 .15
95 Chris Reitsma .50 .15
96 Kelly Stinnett .50 .15
97 Dmitri Young .50 .15
98 Roberto Alomar FOIL 8.00 2.40
99 Danys Baez .50 .15
100 Russell Branyan .50 .15
101 Ellis Burks 1.00 .30
102 Bartolo Colon 1.00 .30
103 Marty Cordova .50 .15
104 Einar Diaz .50 .15
105 Juan Gonzalez 1.50 .45
106 Ricardo Rincon .50 .15
107 C. C. Sabathia FOIL 5.00 1.50
108 Paul Shuey .50 .15
109 Jim Thome FOIL 10.00 3.00
110 Omar Vizquel 1.50 .45
111 Bob Wickman .50 .15
112 Shawn Chacon .50 .15
113 Jeff Cirillo .50 .15
114 Mike Hampton 1.00 .30
115 Todd Helton FOIL 8.00 2.40
116 Greg Norton .50 .15
117 Ben Petrick .50 .15
118 Juan Pierre .50 .30
119 Terry Shumpert .50 .15
120 Larry Walker FOIL 8.00 2.40
121 Matt Anderson .50 .15
122 Roger Cedeno .50 .15
123 Tony Clark .50 .15
124 Deivi Cruz .50 .15
125 Damion Easley .50 .15
126 Shane Halter .50 .15
127 Bobby Higginson FOIL 5.00 1.50
128 Jose Macias .50 .15
129 Steve Sparks .50 .15
130 Jeff Weaver .50 .15
131 Antonio Alfonseca .50 .15
132 Josh Beckett FOIL 5.00 1.50
133 A. J. Burnett .50 .15
134 Luis Castillo .50 .15
135 Ryan Dempster .50 .15
136 Cliff Floyd 1.00 .30
137 Alex Gonzalez .50 .15
138 Braden Looper .50 .15
139 Mike Lowell 1.00 .30
140 Eric Owens .50 .15
141 Brad Penny .50 .15
142 Preston Wilson 1.00 .30
143 Moises Alou 1.00 .30
144 Brad Ausmus .50 .15
145 Jeff Bagwell FOIL 8.00 2.40
146 Lance Berkman FOIL 5.00 1.50
147 Craig Biggio 1.50 .45
148 Octavio Dotel .50 .15
149 Richard Hidalgo .50 .15
150 Julio Lugo .50 .15
151 Wade Miller .50 .15
152 Roy Oswalt FOIL 5.00 1.50
153 Shane Reynolds .50 .15
154 Jose Vizcaino .50 .15
155 Daryle Ward .50 .15
156 Carlos Beltran FOIL 8.00 2.40
157 Dee Brown .50 .15
158 Roberto Hernandez .50 .15
159 Mark Quinn .50 .15
160 Joe Randa .50 .15
161 Dan Reichert .50 .15
162 Jeff Suppan .50 .15
163 Mike Sweeney 1.00 .30
164 Kris Wilson .50 .15
165 Terry Adams .50 .15
166 Adrian Beltre 1.50 .45
167 Alex Cora .50 .15
168 Tom Goodwin .50 .15
169 Shawn Green 1.00 .30
170 Marquis Grissom 1.00 .30
171 Mark Grudzielanek .50 .15
172 Eric Karros 1.00 .30
173 Paul LoDuca FOIL 5.00 1.50
174 Chan Ho Park 1.00 .30
175 Luke Prokopec .50 .15
176 Gary Sheffield 1.00 .30
177 Ronnie Belliard .50 .15
178 Henry Blanco .50 .15
179 Jeromy Burnitz 1.00 .30
180 Mike DeJean .50 .15
181 Chad Fox .50 .15
182 Jose Hernandez .50 .15
183 Geoff Jenkins 1.00 .30
184 Mark Loretta 1.00 .30
185 Nick Neugebauer .50 .15
186 Richie Sexson 1.00 .30
187 Ben Sheets FOIL 5.00 1.50
188 Devon White 1.00 .30
189 Cristian Guzman FOIL 3.00 .90
190 Torii Hunter 1.00 .30
191 Jacque Jones 1.00 .30
192 Corey Koskie 1.00 .30
193 Joe Mays .50 .15
194 Doug Mientkiewicz 1.00 .30
195 Eric Milton .50 .15
196 David Ortiz 1.50 .45
197 A. J. Pierzynski 1.00 .30
198 Brad Radke 1.00 .30
199 Luis Rivas .50 .15
200 Tony Armas Jr. .50 .15
201 Michael Barrett .50 .15
202 Peter Bergeron .50 .15
203 Orlando Cabrera 1.00 .30
204 Vladimir Guerrero FOIL 10.00 3.00
205 Graeme Lloyd .50 .15
206 Scott Strickland .50 .15
207 Fernando Tatis .50 .15
208 Mike Thurman .50 .15
209 Javier Vazquez 1.00 .30
210 Jose Vidro .50 .15
211 Brad Wilkerson .50 .15
212 Edgardo Alfonzo .50 .15
213 Kevin Appier 1.00 .30
214 Armando Benitez 1.00 .30
215 Alex Escobar .50 .15
216 John Franco 1.00 .30
217 Al Leiter 1.00 .30
218 Rey Ordonez .50 .15
219 Mike Piazza FOIL 10.00 3.00
220 Glendon Rusch .50 .15
221 Tsuyoshi Shinjo 1.00 .30
222 Steve Trachsel .50 .15
223 Todd Zeile 1.00 .30
224 Roger Clemens FOIL 15.00 4.50
225 Derek Jeter FOIL 15.00 4.50
226 Nick Johnson .50 .15
227 David Justice 1.00 .30
228 Tino Martinez 1.50 .45
229 Ramiro Mendoza .50 .15
230 Mike Mussina FOIL 8.00 2.40
231 Andy Pettitte 1.50 .45
232 Jorge Posada 1.50 .45
233 Mariano Rivera FOIL 8.00 2.40
234 Alfonso Soriano 1.50 .45
235 Mike Stanton .50 .15
236 Bernie Williams FOIL 8.00 2.40
237 Eric Chavez 1.00 .30
238 Johnny Damon Sox 2.50 .75
239 Jermaine Dye 1.00 .30
240 Jason Giambi FOIL 5.00 1.50
241 Jeremy Giambi .50 .15
242 Ramon Hernandez .50 .15
243 Tim Hudson FOIL 5.00 1.50
244 Jason Isringhausen 1.00 .30
245 Terrence Long .50 .15
246 Mark Mulder FOIL 5.00 1.50
247 Olmedo Saenz .50 .15
248 Miguel Tejada 1.00 .30
249 Barry Zito 1.00 .30
250 Bobby Abreu 1.00 .30
251 Marlon Anderson .50 .15
252 Ricky Bottalico .50 .15
253 Pat Burrell 1.00 .30
254 Omar Daal .50 .15
255 Johnny Estrada .50 .15
256 Nelson Figueroa .50 .15
257 Travis Lee .50 .15
258 Robert Person .50 .15
259 Scott Rolen FOIL 10.00 3.00
260 Jimmy Rollins FOIL 5.00 1.50
261 Randy Wolf .50 .15
262 Brian Giles FOIL 5.00 1.50
263 Jason Kendall 1.00 .30
264 Josias Manzanillo .50 .15
265 Warren Morris .50 .15
266 Aramis Ramirez 1.00 .30
267 Todd Ritchie .50 .15
268 Craig Wilson 1.00 .30
269 Jack Wilson 1.00 .30
270 Kevin Young .50 .15
271 Ben Davis .50 .15
272 Wiki Gonzalez .50 .15
273 Rickey Henderson 2.50 .75
274 Junior Herndon .50 .15
275 Trevor Hoffman 1.00 .30
276 Damian Jackson .50 .15
277 D'Angelo Jimenez .50 .15
278 Mark Kotsay .50 .15
279 Phil Nevin FOIL 5.00 1.50
280 Bubba Trammell .50 .15
281 Rich Aurilia FOIL 3.00 .90
282 Marvin Benard .50 .15

283 Barry Bonds FOIL 40.00 12.00
284 Shawn Estes .50 .15
285 Pedro Feliz .50 .15
286 Jeff Kent FOIL 5.00 1.50
287 Robb Nen 1.00 .30
288 Russ Ortiz 1.00 .30
289 Felix Rodriguez .50 .15
290 Kirk Rueter .50 .15
291 Benito Santiago 1.00 .30
292 J.T. Snow 1.00 .30
293 John Vander Wal .50 .15
294 Bret Boone FOIL 5.00 1.50
295 Mike Cameron 1.00 .30
296 Freddy Garcia FOIL 5.00 1.50
297 Carlos Guillen 1.00 .30
298 Edgar Martinez FOIL 8.00 2.40
299 Mark McLemore .50 .15
300 Jamie Moyer 1.00 .30
301 Jeff Nelson .50 .15
302 John Olerud 1.00 .30
303 Arthur Rhodes .50 .15
304 Kazuhiro Sasaki FOIL 5.00 1.50
305 Aaron Sele .50 .15
306 Ichiro Suzuki FOIL 10.00 3.00
307 Dan Wilson .50 .15
308 J.D. Drew FOIL 5.00 1.50
309 Jim Edmonds FOIL 5.00 1.50
310 Dustin Hermanson .50 .15
311 Darryl Kile 1.00 .30
312 Steve Kline .50 .15
313 Mike Matheny 1.00 .30
314 Matt Morris 1.00 .30
315 Craig Paquette .50 .15
316 Placido Polanco .50 .15
317 Albert Pujols FOIL 12.00 3.60
318 Edgar Renteria 1.00 .30
319 Bud Smith .50 .15
320 Dave Veres .50 .15
321 Fernando Vina .50 .15
322 Brent Abernathy .50 .15
323 Steve Cox .50 .15
324 Ben Grieve .50 .15
325 Aubrey Huff 1.00 .30
326 Joe Kennedy FOIL 3.00 .90
327 Tanyon Sturtze .50 .15
328 Jason Tyner .50 .15
329 Greg Vaughn .50 .15
330 Paul Wilson .50 .15
331 Esteban Yan .50 .15
332 Frank Catalanotto .50 .15
333 Chad Curtis .50 .15
334 Doug Davis .50 .15
335 Gabe Kapler .50 .15
336 Mike Lamb .50 .15
337 Darren Oliver .50 .15
338 Rafael Palmeiro 1.50 .45
339 Alex Rodriguez FOIL 15.00 4.50
340 Ivan Rodriguez FOIL 10.00 3.00
341 Mike Venafro .50 .15
342 Michael Young 2.50 .75
343 Jeff Zimmerman .50 .15
344 Chris Carpenter .50 .15
345 Jose Cruz Jr. .50 .15
346 Carlos Delgado FOIL 5.00 1.50
347 Kelvim Escobar .50 .15
348 Darrin Fletcher .50 .15
349 Brad Fullmer .50 .15
350 Alex S.Gonzalez .50 .15
351 Billy Koch .50 .15
352 Esteban Loaiza .50 .15
353 Raul Mondesi 1.00 .30
354 Paul Quantrill .50 .15
355 Shannon Stewart 1.00 .30
356 Vernon Wells 1.00 .30

2002 MLB Showdown Strategy

Inserted into packs at a rate of two per pack, this 50-card insert set features the strategy cards necessary for playing the MLB Showdown game. Card numbers carry an "S" prefix.

Nm-Mt Ex-Mt
COMPLETE SET (50) 10.00 3.00
S1 Bernie Williams .40 .12
Bad Call
S2 Mike Piazza .75 .23
Clutch Hitting
S3 Troy Glaus .25 .07
Crowd the Plate
S4 Down the Middle SP .50 .15
S5 Corey Patterson .50 .15
Drag Bunt SP
S6 Ducks on the Pond .25 .07
S7 Barry Bonds 1.25 .35
Fuel on the Fire
S8 Craig Biggio .40 .12
Last Chance
S9 Nuisance/Mets SP .50 .15
S10 Out of Gas/Cubs .25 .07
S11 Manny Ramirez .75 .23
Payoff Pitch SP
S12 Pro Baserunner/Phillies SP .50 .15
S13 Protect the Runner SP .50 .15
S14 Rafael Palmeiro .40 .12
Pull the Ball
S15 Tom Goodwin .25 .07
Rally Cap
S16 Rough Outing .25 .07
S17 Runner Not Held/Cardinals .25 .07
S18 Run on Fumes/Giants SP .50 .15
S19 Ruptured Duck SP .50 .15
S20 Jose Cruz Jr. .25 .07
Sit on the Fastball
S21 Kevin Appier .25 .07
Stick a Fork in Him
S22 Barry Bonds 1.25 .35
Sweet Swing
S23 Johnny Damon 1.25 .35
Take Given SP
S24 Warning Track/Pirates .25 .07
S25 Lance Berkman .25 .07
Turn On It
S26 Brad Radke .25 .07
By the Book
S27 Cut Off in the Gap SP .50 .15
S28 Andy Pettitte .40 .12
Full Windup
S29 Barry Zito .25 .07
Great Start
S30 Ichiro Suzuki .75 .23
Great Throw
S31 Brent Abernathy .50 .15
HL Reel SP
S32 Curt Schilling .25 .07
Insult to Injury
S33 Mark Mulder .25 .07
In the Groove
S34 Mariano Rivera .40 .12
Intimidation
S35 Arthur Rhodes .50 .15
Job Well Done SP
S36 Just Over the Wall SP .50 .15
S37 Abraham Nunez .25 .07
Knock Ball Down
S38 Billy Wagner .25 .07
Lefty Specialist
S39 Randy Johnson .50 .15
Low and Away
S40 Trevor Hoffman .25 .07
Nerves of Steel
S41 Pitchout SP .50 .15
S42 Pumped Up .25 .07
S43 Kazuhiro Sasaki .25 .07
Put Out the Fire
S44 Rally Killer SP .50 .15
S45 Sloppy Bunt/Indians SP .50 .15
S46 Byung-Hyun Kim .50 .15
Submarine Pitch SP
S47 Change in Strategy .25 .07
S48 Grounder to 2nd/Reds SP .50 .15
S49 Crunch Time/Dodgers SP .50 .15
S50 Sean Casey .25 .07
Second Look

2002 MLB Showdown All-Star Game

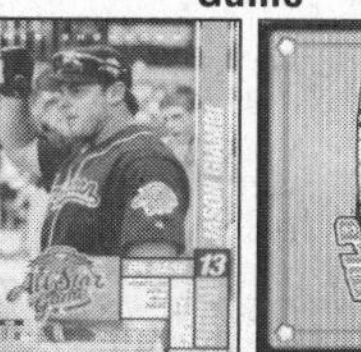

This set was distributed exclusively in an attractive sealed All-Star Game box of which carried a suggested retail price of $29.99. Each box contained the 50 All-Star Game cards plus an additional 50 Strategy cards (all of which were reissued from the basic Strategy card set initially distributed in the basic 2002 MLB Showdown product earlier that year. Interestingly, the 50 Strategy cards are NOT a full run of cards 1-50. Rather, each box contains two separate stacks of 25 Strategy cards (one for each game player) of which include a skip-numbered selection of cards (including several duplicates) designed especially for game play. The box also contains 30 team tab checklists, a rulebook, an All-Star theme playmat and one 20-sided die. The fifty new All-Star cards feature a similar design that runs throughout all of the 2002 MLB Showdown brands - attractive full bleed images on cards shaped like playing cards (with rounded edges). The All-Star Game logo is prominently placed on the lower left front corner (along with the checklist number in a tiny black box) with various statistics to play the game on the lower right corner. The card backs simply feature the brand logo.

Nm-Mt Ex-Mt
COMP.FACT.SET (100) 40.00 12.00
COMPLETE SET (50) 30.00 9.00
1 Garret Anderson 1.00 .30
2 Tony Batista 1.00 .30
3 Mark Buehrle 1.00 .30
4 Johnny Damon Sox 2.50 .75
5 Robert Fick 1.00 .30
6 Freddy Garcia 1.00 .30
7 Nomar Garciaparra 4.00 1.20
8 Jason Giambi 1.00 .30
9 Roy Halladay 1.00 .30
10 Shea Hillenbrand 1.00 .30
11 Torii Hunter 1.00 .30
12 Ichiro Suzuki 4.00 1.20
13 Derek Jeter 6.00 1.80
14 Paul Konerko 1.00 .30
15 Derek Lowe 1.00 .30
16 Jorge Posada 1.50 .45
17 Manny Ramirez 1.50 .45
18 Mariano Rivera 1.50 .45
19 Alex Rodriguez 4.00 1.20
20 Kazuhiro Sasaki 1.00 .30
21 Alfonso Soriano 1.50 .45
22 Mike Sweeney 1.00 .30
23 Robin Ventura 1.00 .30
24 Omar Vizquel 1.50 .45
25 Barry Zito 1.00 .30
26 Lance Berkman 1.00 .30
27 Barry Bonds 6.00 1.80
28 Luis Castillo 1.00 .30
29 Adam Dunn 1.50 .45
30 Eric Gagne 2.50 .75
31 Luis Gonzalez 1.00 .30
32 Shawn Green 1.00 .30
33 Vladimir Guerrero 2.50 .75
34 Todd Helton 2.50 .75
35 Jose Hernandez 1.00 .30
36 Andruw Jones 1.00 .30
37 Mike Lowell 1.00 .30
38 Robb Nen 1.00 .30
39 Vicente Padilla 1.00 .30
40 Odalis Perez 1.00 .30
41 Mike Piazza 4.00 1.20
42 Scott Rolen 2.50 .75
43 Jimmy Rollins 1.00 .30
44 Benito Santiago 1.00 .30
45 Curt Schilling 1.00 .30
46 John Smoltz 1.50 .45
47 Sammy Sosa 4.00 1.20
48 Junior Spivey 1.00 .30
49 Jose Vidro 1.00 .30
50 Mike Williams 1.00 .30

2003 MLB Showdown

This 304 card set was issued in April, 2003. Fifty two cards in this set are foil cards and those cards were issued at a stated rate of one in three. A promo card featuring Pee Wee Reese was issued to dealers to preview the product. The promo card can be differentiated from Reese's basic card by the fact that it's numbered on back as "P51".

Nm-Mt Ex-Mt
COMP.SET w/o FOIL (252) 60.00 18.00
COMMON CARD (1-304) .50 .15
COMMON FOIL 3.00 .90
1 Garret Anderson FOIL 5.00 1.50
2 David Eckstein FOIL 3.00 .90
3 Darin Erstad 1.00 .30
4 Brad Fullmer .50 .15
5 Troy Glaus 1.00 .30
6 Adam Kennedy .50 .15
7 Bengie Molina .50 .15
8 Ramon Ortiz .50 .15
9 Orlando Palmeiro .50 .15
10 Troy Percival 1.00 .30
11 Tim Salmon 1.50 .45
12 Jarrod Washburn FOIL 3.00 .90
13 Miguel Batista .50 .15
14 Danny Bautista .50 .15
15 Craig Counsell .50 .15
16 Steve Finley 1.00 .30
17 Luis Gonzalez FOIL 5.00 1.50
18 Mark Grace 1.50 .45
19 Randy Johnson FOIL 10.00 3.00
20 Byung-Hyun Kim 1.00 .30
21 Quinton McCracken .50 .15
22 Curt Schilling FOIL 15.00 4.50
23 Junior Spivey FOIL 3.00 .90
24 Tony Womack .50 .15
25 Vinny Castilla 1.00 .30
26 Julio Franco 1.00 .30
27 Rafael Furcal FOIL 5.00 1.50
28 Marcus Giles 1.00 .30
29 Tom Glavine FOIL 8.00 2.40
30 Andruw Jones FOIL 5.00 1.50
31 Keith Lockhart .50 .15
32 Javy Lopez 1.00 .30
33 Greg Maddux FOIL 10.00 3.00
34 Kevin Millwood 1.00 .30
35 Gary Sheffield 1.00 .30
36 John Smoltz FOIL 8.00 2.40
37 Tony Batista 1.00 .30
38 Mike Bordick 1.00 .30
39 Jeff Conine 1.00 .30
40 Marty Cordova .50 .15
41 Jay Gibbons .50 .15
42 Geronimo Gil .50 .15
43 Jerry Hairston .50 .15
44 Jorge Julio .50 .15
45 Rodrigo Lopez .50 .15
46 Gary Matthews Jr. .50 .15
47 Melvin Mora 1.00 .30
48 Sidney Ponson .50 .15
49 Chris Singleton .50 .15
50 John Burkett .50 .15
51 Tony Clark .50 .15
52 Johnny Damon 2.50 .75
53 Alan Embree .50 .15
54 Nomar Garciaparra FOIL 10.00 3.00
55 Shea Hillenbrand 1.00 .30
56 Derek Lowe FOIL 5.00 1.50
57 Pedro Martinez FOIL 10.00 3.00
58 Trot Nixon 1.00 .30
59 Manny Ramirez 1.50 .45
60 Rey Sanchez .50 .15
61 Ugueth Urbina .50 .15
62 Jason Varitek 1.50 .45
63 Moises Alou 1.00 .30
64 Mark Bellhorn 1.00 .30
65 Roosevelt Brown .50 .15
66 Matt Clement .50 .15
67 Joe Girardi .50 .15
68 Alex Gonzalez .50 .15
69 Todd Hundley .50 .15
70 Jon Lieber .50 .15
71 Fred McGriff 1.50 .45
72 Bill Mueller 1.00 .30
73 Corey Patterson 1.00 .30
74 Mark Prior FOIL 10.00 3.00
75 Sammy Sosa FOIL 15.00 4.50
76 Mark Buehrle FOIL 5.00 1.50
77 Jon Garland .50 .15
78 Tony Graffanino .50 .15
79 Paul Konerko FOIL 5.00 1.50
80 Carlos Lee 1.00 .30
81 Magglio Ordonez FOIL 5.00 1.50
82 Frank Thomas 2.50 .75
83 Dan Wright .50 .15
84 Aaron Boone 1.00 .30
85 Sean Casey 1.00 .30
86 Elmer Dessens .50 .15
87 Adam Dunn 1.50 .45
88 Danny Graves .50 .15
89 Joey Hamilton .50 .15
90 Jimmy Haynes .50 .15
91 Austin Kearns FOIL 5.00 1.50
92 Barry Larkin 1.50 .45
93 Jason LaRue .50 .15
94 Reggie Taylor .50 .15
95 Todd Walker .50 .15
96 Danys Baez .50 .15
97 Milton Bradley 1.00 .30
98 Ellis Burks 1.00 .30
99 Einar Diaz .50 .15
100 Ricky Gutierrez .50 .15
101 Matt Lawton .50 .15
102 Chris Magruder .50 .15
103 C. C. Sabathia 1.00 .30
104 Lee Stevens .50 .15
105 Jim Thome FOIL 10.00 3.00
106 Omar Vizquel 1.50 .45
107 Bob Wickman .50 .15
108 Gary Bennett .50 .15
109 Mike Hampton 1.00 .30
110 Todd Helton 1.50 .45
111 Jose Jimenez .50 .15
112 Denny Neagle .50 .15
113 Jose Ortiz .50 .15
114 Juan Pierre 1.00 .30
115 Juan Uribe .50 .15
116 Larry Walker FOIL 1.50 .45
117 Todd Zeile 1.00 .30
118 Juan Acevedo .50 .15
119 Robert Fick .50 .15
120 Bobby Higginson 1.00 .30
121 Damian Jackson .50 .15
122 Craig Paquette .50 .15
123 Carlos Pena .50 .15
124 Mark Redman .50 .15
125 Randall Simon .50 .15
126 Steve Sparks .50 .15
127 Dmitri Young 1.00 .30
128 A. J. Burnett .50 .15
129 Luis Castillo .50 .15
130 Juan Encarnacion .50 .15
131 Alex Gonzalez .50 .15
132 Charles Johnson 1.00 .30
133 Derrek Lee 1.00 .30
134 Mike Lowell 1.00 .30
135 Vladimir Nunez .50 .15
136 Eric Owens .50 .15
137 Preston Wilson 1.00 .30
138 Brad Ausmus .50 .15
139 Lance Berkman FOIL 5.00 1.50
140 Craig Biggio 1.50 .45
141 Geoff Blum .50 .15
142 Richard Hidalgo .50 .15
143 Julio Lugo .50 .15
144 Orlando Merced .50 .15
145 Billy Wagner 1.00 .30
146 Carlos Beltran 1.50 .45
147 Paul Byrd .50 .15
148 Raul Ibanez .50 .15
149 Chuck Knoblauch 1.00 .30
150 Brent Mayne .50 .15
151 Neifi Perez .50 .15
152 Joe Randa .50 .15
153 Mike Sweeney 1.00 .30
154 Adrian Beltre 1.50 .45
155 Eric Gagne FOIL 10.00 3.00
156 Shawn Green 1.00 .30
157 Marquis Grissom 1.00 .30
158 Mark Grudzielanek .50 .15
159 Kazuhisa Ishii FOIL 5.00 1.50
160 Cesar Izturis .50 .15
161 Brian Jordan 1.00 .30
162 Eric Karros 1.00 .30
163 Paul Lo Duca FOIL 5.00 1.50
164 Hideo Nomo 2.50 .75
165 Jesse Orosco .50 .15
166 Odalis Perez .50 .15
167 Mike DeJean .50 .15
168 Jose Hernandez .50 .15
169 Geoff Jenkins 1.00 .30
170 Alex Sanchez .50 .15
171 Richie Sexson 1.00 .30
172 Ben Sheets 1.00 .30
173 Eric Young .50 .15
174 Eddie Guardado .50 .15
175 Cristian Guzman .50 .15
176 Torii Hunter FOIL 5.00 1.50
177 Jacque Jones 1.00 .30
178 Corey Koskie 1.00 .30
179 Doug Mientkiewicz 1.00 .30
180 Eric Milton .50 .15
181 A. J. Pierzynski 1.00 .30
182 Michael Barrett .50 .15
183 Orlando Cabrera 1.00 .30
184 Cliff Floyd 1.00 .30
185 Vladimir Guerrero FOIL 15.00 4.50
186 Tomo Ohka .50 .15
187 Fernando Tatis .50 .15
188 Javier Vazquez 1.00 .30
189 Jose Vidro FOIL 3.00 .90
190 Brad Wilkerson .50 .15
191 Edgardo Alfonzo .50 .15
192 Roberto Alomar 1.50 .45
193 Pedro Astacio .50 .15
194 Armando Benitez 1.00 .30
195 Jeromy Burnitz 1.00 .30
196 Al Leiter 1.00 .30
197 Rey Ordonez .50 .15
198 Timo Perez .50 .15
199 Mike Piazza FOIL 12.00 3.60
200 Steve Trachsel .50 .15
201 Mo Vaughn 1.00 .30
202 Roger Clemens 5.00 1.50
203 Jason Giambi FOIL 5.00 1.50
204 Derek Jeter 6.00 1.80
205 Nick Johnson .50 .15
206 Steve Karsay .50 .15
207 Mike Mussina FOIL 8.00 2.40
208 Jorge Posada 1.50 .45
209 Mariano Rivera FOIL 8.00 2.40
210 Alfonso Soriano FOIL 8.00 2.40
211 Mike Stanton .50 .15
212 Robin Ventura 1.00 .30
213 Jeff Weaver .50 .15
214 Rondell White 1.00 .30
215 Bernie Williams FOIL 8.00 2.40
216 Eric Chavez 1.00 .30
217 Jermaine Dye 1.00 .30
218 Scott Hatteberg .50 .15
219 Tim Hudson 1.00 .30
220 Billy Koch 1.00 .30
221 Terrence Long .50 .15
222 Mark Mulder 1.00 .30
223 Miguel Tejada FOIL 5.00 1.50
224 Barry Zito FOIL 5.00 1.50
225 Bobby Abreu 1.00 .30
226 Marlon Anderson .50 .15
227 Pat Burrell 1.00 .30
228 Brandon Duckworth .50 .15
229 Jeremy Giambi .50 .15
230 Doug Glanville .50 .15
231 Mike Lieberthal 1.00 .30
232 Jose Mesa .50 .15
233 Vicente Padilla .50 .15
234 Jimmy Rollins 1.00 .30
235 Adrian Brown .50 .15
236 Josh Fogg .50 .15
237 Brian Giles 1.00 .30
238 Jason Kendall 1.00 .30
239 Pokey Reese .50 .15
240 Kip Wells .50 .15
241 Mike Williams FOIL 3.00 .90
242 Craig Wilson 1.00 .30
243 Jack Wilson 1.00 .30
244 Kevin Young .50 .15
245 Trevor Hoffman FOIL 5.00 1.50
246 Mark Kotsay .50 .15
247 Ray Lankford .50 .15
248 Brian Lawrence .50 .15
249 Phil Nevin 1.00 .30
250 Kurt Ainsworth .50 .15
251 David Bell .50 .15
252 Barry Bonds FOIL 30.00 9.00
253 Ryan Jensen .50 .15
254 Jeff Kent FOIL 5.00 1.50
255 Robb Nen 1.00 .30
256 Reggie Sanders .50 .15
257 Benito Santiago 1.00 .30
258 Tsuyoshi Shinjo 1.00 .30
259 J. T. Snow 1.00 .30
260 Bret Boone 1.00 .30
261 Mike Cameron 1.00 .30
262 Jeff Cirillo .50 .15
263 Freddy Garcia 1.00 .30
264 Carlos Guillen 1.00 .30
265 Mark McLemore .50 .15
266 Jamie Moyer 1.00 .30
267 John Olerud 1.00 .30
268 Joel Pineiro FOIL 5.00 1.50
269 Kazuhiro Sasaki FOIL 5.00 1.50
270 Ruben Sierra .50 .15
271 Dan Wilson .50 .15
272 Ichiro Suzuki FOIL 10.00 3.00
273 J.D. Drew 1.00 .30
274 Jim Edmonds FOIL 5.00 1.50
275 Jason Isringhausen 1.00 .30
276 Matt Morris FOIL 5.00 1.50
277 Albert Pujols FOIL 12.00 3.60
278 Edgar Renteria 1.00 .30
279 Scott Rolen FOIL 10.00 3.00
280 Jason Simontacchi .50 .15
281 Fernando Vina .50 .15
282 Brent Abernathy .50 .15
283 Steve Cox .50 .15
284 Chris Gomez .50 .15
285 Ben Grieve .50 .15
286 Joe Kennedy .50 .15
287 Tanyon Sturtze .50 .15
288 Paul Wilson .50 .15
289 Randy Winn FOIL 3.00 .90
290 Juan Gonzalez 1.50 .45
291 Hideki Irabu .50 .15
292 Rafael Palmeiro FOIL 8.00 2.40
293 Herbert Perry .50 .15
294 Alex Rodriguez FOIL 15.00 4.50
295 Ivan Rodriguez 2.50 .75
296 Kenny Rogers 1.00 .30
297 Ismael Valdes .50 .15
298 Mike Young 1.50 .45
299 Dave Berg .50 .15
300 Carlos Delgado 1.00 .30
301 Kelvim Escobar .50 .15
302 Roy Halladay FOIL 3.00 .90
303 Eric Hinske FOIL 3.00 .90
304 Shannon Stewart 1.00 .30
P51 Pee Wee Reese Promo

2003 MLB Showdown Strategy

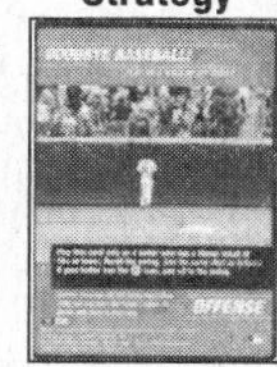

Issued at a stated rate of two per pack, these 50 cards feature various known terms as well as a photo to go with the caption. Whenever possible, we have notated who the player is before the caption in our data base.

Nm-Mt Ex-Mt
COMPLETE SET (50) 8.00 2.40
S1 Sean Casey .25 .07
Bad Call
S2 Ellis Burks .25 .07
Clutch Hitting
S3 Danny Graves .25 .07
Down Middle
S4 Mark Mulder .25 .07
Drag Bunt
S5 Ducks on the Pond .25 .07
S6 Benito Santiago .25 .07
Fuel on Fire
S7 Ichiro Suzuki .75 .23
Goodbye BB
S8 Ichiro Suzuki .75 .23
Great Addition
S9 Ichiro Suzuki .75 .23
Last Chance
S10 Barry Larkin .40 .12
Nuisance
S11 Jacque Jones .25 .07
Protect Runner
S12 Jim Thome .50 .15

Pull the Ball
S13 Tino Martinez .40 .12
Rally Cap
S14 Eric Hinske .25 .07
Rookie's Chance
S15 Runner Not Held .25 .07
S16 Vladimir Guerrero .50 .15
See Clearly
S17 Deivi Cruz .25 .07
Serious Wheels
S18 Carlos Guillen .25 .07
Sit on Fastball
S19 David Eckstein .25 .07
Take Given
S20 Derek Jeter 1.25 .35
Turn On It
S21 Barry Bonds 1.25 .35
Valuable Asset
S22 Mark Mulder .25 .07
Aces Up
S23 Dan Reichert .25 .07
By the Book
S24 Denny Neagle .25 .07
Change It Up
S25 Juan Encarnacion .25 .07
Cut Off Gap
S26 Chris Reitsma .25 .07
Full Windup
S27 Juan Encarnacion .25 .07
Good Leather
S28 Mark Mulder .25 .07
Great Start
S29 Danny Bautista .25 .07
Great Throw
S30 Jose Hernandez .25 .07
Highlight Reel
S31 In the Groove .25 .07
S32 David Eckstein .25 .07
Insult to Injury
S33 Job Well Done .25 .07
S34 David Justice .25 .07
Just Over Wall
S35 Luis Gonzalez .25 .07
Knock Ball Down
S36 Ricardo Rincon .25 .07
Lefty Specialist
S37 Eric Gagne .50 .15
Nerves of Steel
S38 Carlos Febles .25 .07
Paint Corner
S39 Raul Ibanez .25 .07
Pumped Up
S40 Mark Wohlers .25 .07
Put Out Fire
S41 Abraham Nunez .25 .07
Rally Killer
S42 Byung-Hyun Kim .25 .07
Submarine Pitch
S43 Dave Roberts .25 .07
Throwing Heat
S44 What a Relief! .25 .07
S45 Change in Strategy .25 .07
S46 Giovanni Carrara .25 .07
Feast or Famine
S47 Barry Larkin .40 .12
Grounder to 2nd
S48 It's Crunch Time .25 .07
S49 Shane Halter .25 .07
Just Over Rail
S50 Art Howe .25 .07
Ray Knight
Outmanaged

2004 MLB Showdown

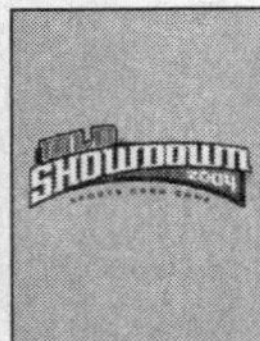

This 348 card set was released in March 2004. The set featured a wide assortment of stars and common players and was issued both in "Starter decks" as well as in booster packs. Many cards were issued with "foil" and those cards are notated in our checklist.

Nm-Mt Ex-Mt
COMP.SET w/o FOIL (298) 60.00 18.00
COMMON CARD .50 .15
COMMON FOIL 3.00 .90
FOIL STATED ODDS 1:3
1 Garret Anderson FOIL UER 5.00 1.50
Name Spelled Garrett
2 David Eckstein .50 .15
3 Darin Erstad 1.00 .30
4 Troy Glaus 1.00 .30
5 Bengie Molina .50 .15
6 Ramon Ortiz .50 .15
7 Eric Owens .50 .15
8 Tim Salmon 1.50 .45
9 Scot Shields .50 .15
10 Scott Spiezio .50 .15
11 Jarrod Washburn .50 .15
12 Rod Barajas .50 .15
13 Alex Cintron .50 .15
14 Elmer Dessens .50 .15
15 Steve Finley 1.00 .30
16 Luis Gonzalez FOIL 5.00 1.50
17 Mark Grace 1.50 .45
18 Shea Hillenbrand 1.00 .30
19 Matt Kata .50 .15
20 Quinton McCracken .50 .15
21 Curt Schilling FOIL 5.00 1.50
22 Vinny Castilla 1.00 .30
23 Robert Fick .50 .15
24 Rafael Furcal 1.00 .30
25 Marcus Giles 1.00 .30
26 Andruw Jones 1.00 .30
27 Chipper Jones FOIL 10.00 3.00
28 Ray King .50 .15
29 Javy Lopez FOIL 5.00 1.50
30 Greg Maddux 4.00 1.20
31 Russ Ortiz 1.00 .30
32 Gary Sheffield FOIL 5.00 1.50
33 Tony Batista 1.00 .30
34 Deivi Cruz .50 .15
35 Travis Driskill .50 .15
36 Brook Fordyce .50 .15
37 Jay Gibbons .50 .15
38 Pat Hentgen .50 .15
39 Jorge Julio .50 .15
40 Rodrigo Lopez .50 .15
41 Luis Matos FOIL 3.00 .90
42 Melvin Mora 1.00 .30
43 Brian Roberts .50 .15
44 B.J. Surhoff 1.00 .30
45 Johnny Damon 2.50 .75
46 Alan Embree .50 .15
47 Nomar Garciaparra FOIL 10.00 3.00
48 Byung-Hyun Kim 1.00 .30
49 Derek Lowe 1.00 .30
50 Pedro Martinez FOIL 15.00 4.50
51 Bill Mueller FOIL 5.00 1.50
52 Trot Nixon 1.00 .30
53 David Ortiz 2.50 .75
54 Manny Ramirez 1.50 .45
55 Jason Varitek 1.50 .45
56 Tim Wakefield 1.00 .30
57 Todd Walker .50 .15
58 Antonio Alfonseca .50 .15
59 Moises Alou 1.00 .30
60 Paul Bako .50 .15
61 Alex Gonzalez .50 .15
62 Tom Goodwin .50 .15
63 Mark Grudzielanek .50 .15
64 Eric Karros 1.00 .30
65 Kenny Lofton 1.00 .30
66 Ramon E. Martinez .50 .15
67 Corey Patterson 1.00 .30
68 Mark Prior FOIL 10.00 3.00
69 Aramis Ramirez 1.00 .30
70 Mike Remlinger .50 .15
71 Sammy Sosa FOIL 10.00 3.00
72 Kerry Wood FOIL 10.00 3.00
73 Carlos Zambrano 1.00 .30
74 Mark Buehrle 1.00 .30
75 Bartolo Colon 1.00 .30
76 Joe Crede 1.00 .30
77 Tom Gordon .50 .15
78 Paul Konerko 1.00 .30
79 Carlos Lee 1.00 .30
80 Damaso Marte .50 .15
81 Miguel Olivo .50 .15
82 Magglio Ordonez FOIL 5.00 1.50
83 Frank Thomas 2.50 .75
84 Jose Valentin .50 .15
85 Sean Casey 1.00 .30
86 Juan Castro .50 .15
87 Adam Dunn 1.50 .45
88 Danny Graves .50 .15
89 Ken Griffey Jr. 4.00 1.20
90 D'Angelo Jimenez .50 .15
91 Austin Kearns 1.00 .30
92 Barry Larkin 1.50 .45
93 Jason LaRue .50 .15
94 Chris Reitsma .50 .15
95 Reggie Taylor .50 .15
96 Paul Wilson .50 .15
97 Danys Baez .50 .15
98 Josh Bard .50 .15
99 Casey Blake .50 .15
100 Jason Boyd .50 .15
101 Milton Bradley FOIL 5.00 1.50
102 Ellis Burks 1.00 .30
103 Coco Crisp .50 .15
104 Jody Gerut .50 .15
105 Travis Hafner 1.00 .30
106 Matt Lawton .50 .15
107 John McDonald .50 .15
108 Terry Mulholland .50 .15
109 C.C. Sabathia 1.00 .30
110 Omar Vizquel 1.50 .45
111 Ronnie Belliard .50 .15
112 Shawn Chacon .50 .15
113 Todd Helton FOIL 10.00 3.00
114 Charles Johnson 1.00 .30
115 Darren Oliver .50 .15
116 Jay Payton 1.00 .30
117 Justin Speier .50 .15
118 Chris Stynes .50 .15
119 Larry Walker 1.50 .45
120 Preston Wilson 1.00 .30
121 Jeremy Bonderman .50 .15
122 Shane Halter .50 .15
123 Bobby Higginson 1.00 .30
124 Brandon Inge .50 .15
125 Wilfredo Ledezma .50 .15
126 Chris Mears .50 .15
127 Warren Morris .50 .15
128 Carlos Pena .50 .15
129 Ramon Santiago .50 .15
130 Andres Torres .50 .15
131 Dmitri Young 1.00 .30
132 Josh Beckett 1.00 .30
133 Miguel Cabrera 1.50 .45
134 Luis Castillo .50 .15
135 Juan Encarnacion .50 .15
136 Alex Gonzalez .50 .15
137 Derrek Lee 1.00 .30
138 Braden Looper .50 .15
139 Mike Lowell 1.00 .30
140 Juan Pierre 1.00 .30
141 Mark Redman .50 .15
142 Ivan Rodriguez FOIL 10.00 3.00
143 Tim Spooneybarger .50 .15
144 Dontrelle Willis FOIL 5.00 1.50
145 Brad Ausmus .50 .15
146 Jeff Bagwell 1.50 .45
147 Lance Berkman 1.00 .30
148 Craig Biggio 1.50 .45
149 Geoff Blum .50 .15
150 Octavio Dotel FOIL 8.00 2.40
151 Morgan Ensberg .50 .15
152 Adam Everett .50 .15
153 Richard Hidalgo FOIL 3.00 .90
154 Jeff Kent 1.00 .30
155 Brad Lidge 1.00 .30
156 Roy Oswalt 1.00 .30
157 Jeriome Robertson .50 .15
158 Billy Wagner FOIL 8.00 2.40
159 Carlos Beltran FOIL 8.00 2.40
160 Angel Berroa .50 .15
161 Jason Grimsley .50 .15
162 Aaron Guiel .50 .15
163 Runelvys Hernandez .50 .15
164 Raul Ibanez .50 .15
165 Curtis Leskanic .50 .15
166 Jose Lima .50 .15
167 Mike MacDougal .50 .15
168 Brent Mayne .50 .15
169 Joe Randa .50 .15
170 Desi Relaford .50 .15
171 Mike Sweeney 1.00 .30
172 Michael Tucker .50 .15
173 Adrian Beltre 1.50 .45
174 Kevin Brown FOIL 5.00 1.50
175 Ron Coomer .50 .15
176 Alex Cora .50 .15
177 Eric Gagne FOIL 20.00 6.00
178 Shawn Green 1.00 .30
179 Cesar Izturis .50 .15
180 Brian Jordan 1.00 .30
181 Paul Lo Duca 1.00 .30
182 Fred McGriff 1.50 .45
183 Hideo Nomo 2.50 .75
184 Paul Quantrill .50 .15
185 Dave Roberts .50 .15
186 Royce Clayton .50 .15
187 Keith Ginter .50 .15
188 Wes Helms .50 .15
189 Geoff Jenkins 1.00 .30
190 Brooks Kieschnick .50 .15
191 Eddie Perez .50 .15
192 Scott Podsednik FOIL 5.00 1.50
193 Richie Sexson FOIL 5.00 1.50
194 Ben Sheets 1.00 .30
195 John Vander Wal .50 .15
196 Chris Gomez .50 .15
197 Cristian Guzman .50 .15
198 LaTroy Hawkins .50 .15
199 Torii Hunter 1.00 .30
200 Jacque Jones 1.00 .30
201 Corey Koskie 1.00 .30
202 Doug Mientkiewicz 1.00 .30
203 A.J. Pierzynski 1.00 .30
204 Brad Radke 1.00 .30
205 Shannon Stewart FOIL 5.00 1.50
206 Michael Barrett .50 .15
207 Orlando Cabrera FOIL 5.00 1.50
208 Endy Chavez .50 .15
209 Zach Day .50 .15
210 Vladimir Guerrero FOIL 10.00 3.00
211 Fernando Tatis .50 .15
212 Javier Vazquez 1.00 .30
213 Jose Vidro .50 .15
214 Brad Wilkerson .50 .15
215 Tony Clark .50 .15
216 Cliff Floyd 1.00 .30
217 John Franco 1.00 .30
218 Joe McEwing .50 .15
219 Timo Perez .50 .15
220 Jason Phillips .50 .15
221 Mike Piazza 4.00 1.20
222 Jose Reyes FOIL 5.00 1.50
223 Steve Trachsel .50 .15
224 Dave Weathers .50 .15
225 Ty Wigginton .50 .15
226 Roger Clemens FOIL 15.00 4.50
227 Chris Hammond .50 .15
228 Derek Jeter FOIL 15.00 4.50
229 Nick Johnson .50 .15
230 Hideki Matsui 4.00 1.20
231 Mike Mussina FOIL 8.00 2.40
232 Andy Pettitte 1.50 .45
233 Jorge Posada 1.50 .45
234 Mariano Rivera 1.50 .45
235 Alfonso Soriano 1.50 .45
236 Jeff Weaver .50 .15
237 Bernie Williams 1.50 .45
238 Enrique Wilson .50 .15
239 Chad Bradford .50 .15
240 Eric Byrnes .50 .15
241 Mark Ellis .50 .15
242 Keith Foulke FOIL 5.00 1.50
243 Scott Hatteberg .50 .15
244 Ramon Hernandez .50 .15
245 Tim Hudson FOIL 8.00 2.40
246 Terrence Long .50 .15
247 Mark Mulder FOIL 5.00 1.50
248 Ricardo Rincon .50 .15
249 Chris Singleton .50 .15
250 Miguel Tejada 1.00 .30
251 Barry Zito 1.00 .30
252 Bobby Abreu 1.00 .30
253 David Bell .50 .15
254 Pat Burrell 1.00 .30
255 Marlon Byrd .50 .15
256 Rheal Cormier .50 .15
257 Vicente Padilla .50 .15
258 Tomas Perez .50 .15
259 Placido Polanco .50 .15
260 Jimmy Rollins 1.00 .30
261 Carlos Silva .50 .15
262 Jim Thome FOIL 10.00 3.00
263 Randy Wolf FOIL 3.00 .90
264 Kris Benson .50 .15
265 Jeff D'Amico .50 .15
266 Adam Hyzdu .50 .15
267 Jason Kendall FOIL 5.00 1.50
268 Brian Meadows .50 .15
269 Abraham Nunez .50 .15
270 Reggie Sanders .50 .15
271 Matt Stairs .50 .15
272 Jack Wilson 1.00 .30
273 Gary Bennett .50 .15
274 Sean Burroughs 1.00 .30
275 Adam Eaton .50 .15
276 Luther Hackman .50 .15
277 Ryan Klesko 1.00 .30
278 Brian Lawrence .50 .15
279 Mark Loretta 1.00 .30
280 Phil Nevin 1.00 .30
281 Ramon Vazquez .50 .15
282 Edgardo Alfonzo .50 .15
283 Rich Aurilia .50 .15
284 Jim Brower .50 .15
285 Jose Cruz Jr. .50 .15
286 Ray Durham 1.00 .30
287 Andres Galarraga 1.00 .30
288 Marquis Grissom 1.00 .30
289 Neifi Perez .50 .15
290 Felix Rodriguez .50 .15
291 Benito Santiago 1.00 .30
292 Jason Schmidt FOIL 5.00 1.50
293 J.T. Snow 1.00 .30
294 Tim Worrell .50 .15
295 Bret Boone FOIL 8.00 2.40
296 Mike Cameron 1.00 .30
297 Ryan Franklin .50 .15
298 Carlos Guillen 1.00 .30
299 Shigetoshi Hasegawa 1.00 .30
300 Edgar Martinez 1.50 .45
301 Mark McLemore .50 .15
302 Jamie Moyer FOIL 5.00 1.50
303 John Olerud 1.00 .30
304 Ichiro Suzuki FOIL 10.00 3.00
305 Dan Wilson .50 .15
306 Randy Winn .50 .15
307 J.D. Drew 1.00 .30
308 Jeff Fassero .50 .15
309 Bo Hart .50 .15
310 Jason Isringhausen 1.00 .30
311 Tino Martinez 1.50 .45
312 Mike Matheny 1.00 .30
313 Orlando Palmeiro .50 .15
314 Albert Pujols FOIL 20.00 6.00
315 Edgar Renteria FOIL 8.00 2.40
316 Garrett Stephenson .50 .15
317 Woody Williams FOIL 3.00 .90
318 Rocco Baldelli 1.00 .30
319 Lance Carter .50 .15
320 Carl Crawford 1.00 .30
321 Toby Hall .50 .15
322 Travis Harper .50 .15
323 Aubrey Huff FOIL 5.00 1.50
324 Travis Lee .50 .15
325 Julio Lugo .50 .15
326 Damian Rolls .50 .15
327 Jorge Sosa .50 .15
328 Hank Blalock 1.00 .30
329 Francisco Cordero .50 .15
330 Aaron Fultz .50 .15
331 Juan Gonzalez 1.50 .45
332 Rafael Palmeiro 1.50 .45
333 Alex Rodriguez FOIL 25.00 7.50
334 Mark Teixeira 1.00 .30
335 John Thomson .50 .15
336 Ismael Valdes .50 .15
337 Michael Young 1.00 .30
338 Frank Catalanotto .50 .15
339 Carlos Delgado 1.00 .30
340 Kelvim Escobar .50 .15
341 Roy Halladay FOIL 3.00 .90
342 Eric Hinske .50 .15
343 Orlando Hudson .50 .15
344 Greg Myers .50 .15
345 Josh Phelps .50 .15
346 Cliff Politte .50 .15
347 Vernon Wells FOIL 5.00 1.50
348 Chris Woodward .50 .15

2004 MLB Showdown Strategy

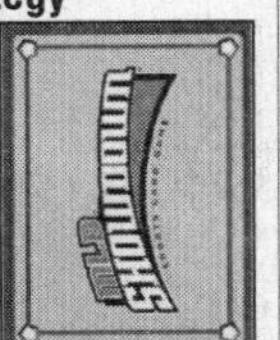

Nm-Mt Ex-Mt
COMPLETE SET (50) 8.00 2.40
TWO PER BOOSTER PACK
S1 Lenny Harris .25 .07
Bad Call
S2 Adam Dunn .40 .12
Burned
S3 Alex Rodriguez .75 .23
Check Swing
S4 Manny Ramirez .40 .12
Deep in Gap
S5 Pokey Reese .25 .07
Drained
S6 Ducks on Pond/Wrigley Field .25 .07
S7 Ichiro Suzuki .75 .23
Great Addition
S8 Alex Gonzalez .25 .07
Hard Slide
S9 Juan Pierre .25 .07
Inside Park HR
S10 Sean Casey .25 .07
Options
S11 Steve Trachsel .25 .07
Frying Pan
S12 Dontrelle Willis .25 .07
Play the Percentages
S13 Albert Pujols 1.00 .30
Pointers
S14 Jeff Cirillo .25 .07
Poor Positioning
S15 Carlos Delgado .25 .07
Pull the Ball
S16 Tony LaRussa MG .25 .07
Rough Outing
S17 Nomar Garciaparra .75 .23
Slow Roller
S18 Bob Cluck CO .25 .07
Stick a Fork
S19 Bernie Williams .40 .12
Sweet Swing
S20 Adam Dunn .40 .12
Take What's Given
S21 Larry Bowa MG .25 .07
Think Again
S22 Jeff Bagwell .40 .12
Turn on It
S23 Russ Ortiz .25 .07
Aces Up
S24 Ben Broussard .25 .07
Caught Leaning
S25 Mark Prior .50 .15
Caught Corner
S26 Michael Cuddyer .25 .07
Choke
S27 Jack Wilson .25 .07
Cover Second
S28 Roy Halladay .25 .07
Dominating
S29 Frank Thomas .50 .15
Foul Ball
S30 Rafael Furcal .25 .07
Good Leather
S31 Jason Giambi .25 .07
Hooking Foul
S32 A.J.Burnett .25 .07
In the Zone
S33 Omar Vizquel .40 .12
Infield In
S34 Lined Out Play/Foul Pole .25 .07
S35 Curt Schilling .25 .07
Locate
S36 Locked In/Padres Catcher .25 .07
S37 Nerves Steel/Marlins Pitcher .25 .07
S38 Curt Schilling .25 .07
Paint Corner
S39 Kerry Wood .50 .15
Power Pitching
S40 Alex Cora .25 .07
Short Fly
S41 Nomar Garciaparra .75 .23
Sloppy Bunt
S42 Kazuhiro Sasaki .25 .07
Split-Finger
S43 Mike Scioscia MG .25 .07
Top-Level
S44 Chris Hammond .25 .07
Tough Nails
S45 Jamie Moyer .25 .07
Change Strategy
S46 Orlando Cabrera .25 .07
Close Call
S47 Art Howe MG .25 .07
New Strategies
S48 Rob Mackowiak .25 .07
Second Look
S49 Michael Cuddyer .25 .07
Swing Anything
S50 Jason Schmidt .25 .07
Think Twice

2000 MLB Showdown Pennant Run 1st Edition

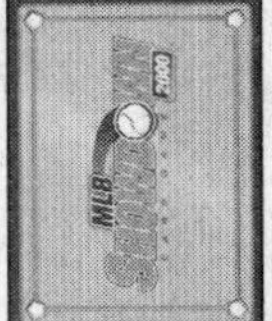

The 2000 MLB Showdown Pennant Run product was released in late August, 2000 as a 150-card set. The 1st Edition cards were released with a silver stamp on front of the card indicating the first print run. The set features 130-player cards and 20 foil superstar cards that were short printed at one in three packs. The 1st Edition packs were released as nine-card packs and carried a suggested retail price of 2.99. Please note that these cards were only released in pack form, there were no starters sets produced of Pennant Run.

Nm-Mt Ex-Mt
COMPLETE SET (150) 100.00 30.00
COMP.SET w/o FOIL (130) 25.00 7.50
COMMON CARD (1-150) .25 .07
COMMON FOIL 3.00 .90
1 Kent Bottenfield .25 .07
2 Ken Hill .25 .07
3 Adam Kennedy .25 .07
4 Ben Molina .25 .07
5 Scott Spiezio .25 .07
6 Brian Anderson .25 .07
7 Erubiel Durazo FOIL 3.00 .90
8 Armando Reynoso .25 .07
9 Russ Springer .25 .07
10 Todd Stottlemyre .25 .07
11 Tony Womack .25 .07
12 Andres Galarraga FOIL 3.00 .90
13 Javy Lopez FOIL 3.00 .90
14 Kevin McGlinchy .25 .07
15 Terry Mulholland .25 .07
16 Reggie Sanders .25 .07
17 Harold Baines .75 .23
18 Will Clark 2.00 .60
19 Mike Trombley .25 .07
20 Manny Alexander .25 .07
21 Carl Everett FOIL 3.00 .90
22 Ramon Martinez FOIL 3.00 .90
23 Bret Saberhagen .75 .23
24 John Wasdin .25 .07
25 Joe Girardi .25 .07
26 Ricky Gutierrez .25 .07
27 Glenallen Hill .25 .07
28 Kevin Tapani .25 .07
29 Kerry Wood FOIL 8.00 2.40
30 Eric Young .25 .07
31 Keith Foulke FOIL 3.00 .90
32 Mark Johnson .25 .07
33 Sean Lowe .25 .07
34 Jose Valentin .25 .07
35 Dante Bichette .75 .23
36 Ken Griffey Jr. FOIL 12.00 3.60
37 Denny Neagle .25 .07
38 Steve Parris .25 .07
39 Dennys Reyes .25 .07
40 Sandy Alomar Jr. .25 .07
41 Chuck Finley FOIL 3.00 .90
42 Steve Karsay .25 .07
43 Steve Reed .25 .07
44 Jaret Wright .25 .07
45 Jeff Cirillo .25 .07
46 Tom Goodwin .25 .07
47 Jeffrey Hammonds .25 .07
48 Mike Lansing .25 .07
49 Aaron Ledesma .25 .07
50 Brent Mayne .25 .07
51 Doug Brocail .25 .07
52 Robert Fick .25 .07
53 Juan Gonzalez 1.25 .35

54 Hideo Nomo 2.00 .60
55 Luis Polonia .25 .07
56 Brant Brown .25 .07
57 Alex Fernandez .25 .07
58 Cliff Floyd .75 .23
59 Dan Miceli .25 .07
60 Vladimir Nunez .25 .07
61 Moises Alou FOIL 3.00 .90
62 Roger Cedeno FOIL 3.00 .90
63 Octavio Dotel .25 .07
64 Mitch Meluskey .25 .07
65 Daryle Ward .25 .07
66 Mark Quinn FOIL 3.00 .90
67 Brad Rigby .25 .07
68 Blake Stein .25 .07
69 Mac Suzuki .25 .07
70 Terry Adams .25 .07
71 Darren Dreifort .25 .07
72 Kevin Elster .25 .07
73 Shawn Green FOIL 3.00 .90
74 Todd Hollandsworth .25 .07
75 Gregg Olson .25 .07
76 Kevin Barker .25 .07
77 Jose Hernandez .25 .07
78 Dave Weathers .25 .07
79 Hector Carrasco .25 .07
80 Eddie Guardado .25 .07
81 Jacque Jones .75 .23
82 David Ortiz 1.25 .35
83 Peter Bergeron .25 .07
84 Hideki Irabu .25 .07
85 Lee Stevens .25 .07
86 Anthony Telford .25 .07
87 Derek Bell .25 .07
88 John Franco .75 .23
89 Mike Hampton FOIL 3.00 .90
90 Bobby Jones .25 .07
91 Todd Pratt .25 .07
92 Todd Zeile .75 .23
93 Jason Grimsley .25 .07
94 Roberto Kelly .25 .07
95 Jim Leyritz .25 .07
96 Ramiro Mendoza .25 .07
97 Rich Becker .25 .07
98 Ramon Hernandez .25 .07
99 Tim Hudson FOIL 3.00 .90
100 Jason Isringhausen .75 .23
101 Mike Magnante .25 .07
102 Olmedo Saenz .25 .07
103 Mickey Morandini .25 .07
104 Robert Person .25 .07
105 Desi Relaford .25 .07
106 Jason Christiansen .25 .07
107 Wil Cordero .25 .07
108 Francisco Cordova .25 .07
109 Chad Hermansen .25 .07
110 Pat Meares .25 .07
111 Aramis Ramirez .75 .23
112 Bret Boone .75 .23
113 Matt Clement .25 .07
114 Carlos Hernandez .25 .07
115 Ryan Klesko .75 .23
116 Dave Magadan .25 .07
117 Al Martin .25 .07
118 Bobby Estalella .25 .07
119 Livan Hernandez .25 .07
120 Doug Mirabelli .25 .07
121 Joe Nathan .25 .07
122 Mike Cameron .75 .23
123 Mark McLemore .25 .07
124 Gil Meche .25 .07
125 John Olerud .75 .23
126 Arthur Rhodes .25 .07
127 Aaron Sele FOIL 3.00 .90
128 Jim Edmonds FOIL 3.00 .90
129 Pat Hentgen .25 .07
130 Darryl Kile .75 .23
131 Eli Marrero .25 .07
132 Dave Veres .25 .07
133 Fernando Vina .25 .07
134 Vinny Castilla .75 .23
135 Juan Guzman .25 .07
136 Ryan Rupe .25 .07
137 Greg Vaughn FOIL 3.00 .90
138 Gerald Williams .25 .07
139 Esteban Yan .25 .07
140 Tom Evans .25 .07
141 Gabe Kapler .25 .07
142 Ruben Mateo FOIL 3.00 .90
143 Kenny Rogers .75 .23
144 David Segui .25 .07
145 Tony Batista .75 .23
146 Chris Carpenter .25 .07
147 Brad Fullmer .25 .07
148 Alex Gonzalez .25 .07
149 Roy Halladay .25 .07
150 Raul Mondesi FOIL 3.00 .90

2000 MLB Showdown Pennant Run Strategy

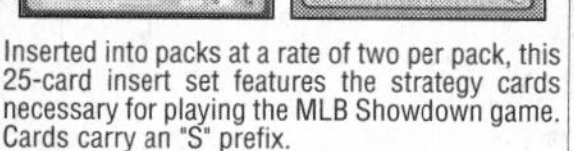

Inserted into packs at a rate of two per pack, this 25-card insert set features the strategy cards necessary for playing the MLB Showdown game. Cards carry an "S" prefix.

Nm-Mt Ex-Mt
COMPLETE SET (25) 10.00 3.00
S1 Aaron Boone .25 .07
S2 Chipper Jones .50 .15
S3 Bob Abreu .25 .07
S4 Fernando Tatis .25 .07
S5 Rod Carew .30 .09
S6 J.D. Drew .25 .07
S7 John Vander Wal .25 .07
S8 Pokey Reese .25 .07
S9 Greg Maddux .75 .23
S10 Cincinnati Reds .25 .07
S11 Larry Walker .30 .09
S12 Alex Rodriguez .75 .23
S13 Alex Rodriguez .75 .23
S14 New York Mets .25 .07
S15 Kevin Brown .30 .09
S16 Paul O'Neill .30 .09
S17 Scott Williamson .25 .07
S18 Jamie Moyer .25 .07
S19 Bernie Williams .30 .09
S20 John Franco .25 .07
S21 Pittsburgh Pirates .25 .07
S22 John Rocker .25 .07
S23 Mike Lansing .25 .07
S24 Roger Clemens .75 .23
Joe Torre
S25 Derek Jeter 1.25 .35

2001 MLB Showdown Pennant Run

The 2001 MLB Showdown Pennant Run product was released in mid-July, 2001 as a 175-card baseball game. The 1st Edition cards were released with a silver stamp on front of the card indicating the first print run. The set features 148-player cards and 27 foil superstar cards that were short printed at one in three packs. The 1st Edition packs were released as nine-card packs and carried a suggested retail price of 2.99.

Nm-Mt Ex-Mt
COMPLETE SET (175) 200.00 60.00
COMP.SET w/o FOIL (150) 40.00 12.00
COMMON CARD (1-175) .25 .07
COMMON FOIL 5.00 1.50
1 Randy Velarde .25 .07
2 Dustin Hermanson .25 .07
3 Jamie Moyer .75 .23
4 Aaron Fultz .25 .07
5 Barry Zito FOIL 8.00 2.40
6 Adam Piatt .25 .07
7 Ben Grieve .25 .07
8 C.C. Sabathia FOIL 5.00 1.50
9 Eddie Guardado .25 .07
10 Matt Kinney .25 .07
11 Blake Stein .25 .07
12 Billy Wagner FOIL 5.00 1.50
13 Chris Holt .25 .07
14 Homer Bush .25 .07
15 Vladimir Nunez .25 .07
16 C.J. Nitkowski .25 .07
17 Juan Pierre .75 .23
18 Jose Valentin .25 .07
19 Juan Gonzalez 1.50 .45
20 Derek Bell .25 .07
21 Wade Miller .25 .07
22 Shawn Estes .25 .07
23 Enrique Wilson .25 .07
24 Dave Magadan .25 .07
25 Jason Christiansen .25 .07
26 Paul Shuey .25 .07
27 Mark Wohlers .25 .07
28 John Riedling .25 .07
29 Francisco Cordova .25 .07
30 Craig House .25 .07
31 Scott Strickland .25 .07
32 Octavio Dotel .25 .07
33 Jimmy Rollins FOIL 5.00 1.50
34 Carl Pavano .75 .23
35 Sandy Alomar Jr. .25 .07
36 Hideki Irabu .25 .07
37 Tom Gordon .25 .07
38 Roosevelt Brown .25 .07
39 Alex Rodriguez FOIL 15.00 4.50
40 Andres Galarraga .75 .23
41 Rob Bell .25 .07
42 Jason Schmidt .75 .23
43 Rod Beck .25 .07
44 Paul Rigdon .25 .07
45 Dan Miceli .25 .07
46 Ricky Bones .25 .07
47 Mike Hampton FOIL 8.00 2.40
48 Cliff Politte .25 .07
49 Chris Stynes .25 .07
50 Ramiro Mendoza .25 .07
51 Todd Walker .25 .07
52 Fernando Seguignol .25 .07
53 Mark Guthrie .25 .07
54 Tony Armas Jr. .25 .07
55 Billy McMillon .25 .07
56 Gary Bennett .25 .07
57 Corey Patterson FOIL 5.00 1.50
58 Juan Guzman .25 .07
59 Joe Crede .25 .07
60 A.J. Pierzynski .75 .23
61 Ben Davis .25 .07
62 Alan Embree .25 .07
63 Jon Garland FOIL 5.00 1.50
64 Ryan Kohlmeier .25 .07
65 Andy Benes .25 .07
66 Ron Gant .75 .23
67 Jerry Hairston Jr. .25 .07
68 Odalis Perez .25 .07
69 Lance Painter .25 .07
70 David Segui .25 .07
71 Russ Davis .25 .07
72 Jeff Zimmerman .25 .07
73 Dennys Reyes .25 .07
74 Jamey Wright .25 .07
75 Rico Brogna .25 .07
76 Geraldo Guzman .25 .07
77 Eric Gagne 2.50 .75
78 Bruce Chen .25 .07
79 Justin Speier .25 .07
80 Randy Keisler .25 .07
81 Ellis Burks FOIL 8.00 2.40
82 Alfonso Soriano 1.50 .45
83 Jeff Nelson .25 .07
84 Wes Helms .25 .07
85 Freddy Garcia FOIL 5.00 1.50
86 Erubiel Durazo .25 .07
87 Ben Sheets FOIL 8.00 2.40
88 Jose Ortiz FOIL 5.00 1.50
89 Paul Wilson .25 .07
90 Onan Masaoka .25 .07
91 Jose Rosado .25 .07
92 A.J. Burnett .25 .07
93 Bubba Trammell .25 .07
94 Mike Fetters .25 .07
95 Jacob Cruz .25 .07
96 John Franco .75 .23
97 Armando Reynoso .75 .23
98 Lou Pote .25 .07
99 D'Angelo Jimenez FOIL 5.00 1.50
100 Julio Zuleta .25 .07
101 Charles Johnson FOIL 8.00 2.40
102 Tsuyoshi Shinjo RC 1.50 .45
103 Brett Tomko .25 .07
104 Marcus Giles .75 .23
105 Craig Counsell .25 .07
106 Ruben Mateo .25 .07
107 Andy Ashby .25 .07
108 Marlon Anderson .25 .07
109 Mark Grace 1.50 .45
110 Russ Branyan .25 .07
111 Julian Tavarez .25 .07
112 Joey Hamilton .25 .07
113 Jason LaRue .25 .07
114 Benji Gil .25 .07
115 Bill Mueller .75 .23
116 Mike Stanton .25 .07
117 Ray King .25 .07
118 Timo Perez .25 .07
119 Johnny Damon FOIL 8.00 2.40
120 Matt Morris .75 .23
121 Kevin Appier .75 .23
122 Frank Castillo .25 .07
123 Mike Darr .25 .07
124 Felipe Crespo .25 .07
125 John Smoltz FOIL 8.00 2.40
126 Ben Weber .25 .07
127 Luis Rivas .25 .07
128 Travis Harper .25 .07
129 Aubrey Huff .75 .23
130 Paul LoDuca .75 .23
131 Eric Davis .75 .23
132 Fernando Tatis .25 .07
133 Ugueth Urbina .25 .07
134 Steve Kline .25 .07
135 Tanyon Sturtze .25 .07
136 Scott Hatteberg .25 .07
137 Tomokazu Ohka FOIL 5.00 1.50
138 Melvin Mora .75 .23
139 Kip Wells .25 .07
140 Ken Caminiti .75 .23
141 Dave Martinez .25 .07
142 Robert Fick .25 .07
143 Mike Bordick .75 .23
144 Doug Mientkiewicz .75 .23
145 Darryl Hamilton .25 .07
146 Shane Reynolds .25 .07
147 Vernon Wells FOIL 5.00 1.50
148 Rey Ordonez .25 .07
149 Brad Ausmus .25 .07
150 Jay Powell .25 .07
151 Todd Hundley .25 .07
152 Travis Miller .25 .07
153 Tyler Houston .25 .07
154 Nelson Cruz .25 .07
155 Manny Ramirez FOIL 8.00 2.40
156 Luis Lopez .25 .07
157 Luis Sojo .25 .07
158 Tony Gwynn FOIL 8.00 2.40
159 Roger Cedeno .25 .07
160 Royce Clayton .25 .07
161 Olmedo Saenz .25 .07
162 Brook Fordyce .25 .07
163 Dee Brown .25 .07
164 David Wells FOIL 5.00 1.50
165 Jack Wilson RC 3.00 .90
166 Pedro Feliz .25 .07
167 Hideo Nomo 2.50 .75
168 Albert Pujols FOIL RC 25.00 7.50
169 Ichiro Suzuki FOIL RC 20.00 6.00
170 Ramon Ortiz .75 .23
171 Mike Holtz .25 .07
172 Chris Woodward .25 .07
173 Mike Mussina FOIL 8.00 2.40
174 Carlos Guillen .75 .23
175 Ben Petrick FOIL 5.00 1.50

2001 MLB Showdown Pennant Run Strategy

Inserted into packs at a rate of two per pack, this 75-card insert set features the strategy cards necessary for playing the MLB Showdown Pennant Run game. Card numbers carry an "S" prefix.

Nm-Mt Ex-Mt
COMPLETE SET (25) 5.00 1.50
S1 Johnny Damon .40 .12
Advance on Throw
S2 Ruben Mateo .25 .07
Ball in the Dirt
S3 Mark McGwire 1.25 .35
Sammy Sosa
Constant Pressure
S4 Jeff Liefer .25 .07
Emergency Bunt
S5 Cal Ripken 1.50 .45
1st-Pitch Swinging
S6 Mike Piazza .75 .23
Go Up Hacking
S7 Derek Jeter 1.25 .35
Speedster
S8 Jose Valentin .25 .07
Sprint to Second
S9 Benito Santiago .25 .07
Wild Thing
S10 Pokey Reese .25 .07
Wipeout
S11 Tony Gwynn .60 .18
Caught Napping
S12 Greg Maddux .75 .23
Comebacker
S13 Julio Zuleta .25 .07
Confusion
S14 Ray Durham .25 .07
Double-Play
S15 Abraham Nunez .25 .07
Fired Up
S16 Rey Ordonez .25 .07
Focused
S17 Roger Clemens 1.00 .30
Going the Distance
S18 Rick Ankiel .25 .07
Great Pickoff Move
S19 Greg Maddux .75 .23
Groundball Pitcher
S20 Danny Graves .25 .07
Hung It
S21 Mark McGwire 1.25 .35
Pitch Around
S22 Al Leiter .25 .07
Pour It On
S23 Barry Bonds 1.25 .35
Clutch Performance
S24 Mascot .25 .07
Dot Racing
S25 Dennys Reyes .25 .07
It's Crunch Time

2002 MLB Showdown Pennant Run

This 125 card set was issued in October, 2002 and feauted many players who would be important to their teams during the late part of the 2002 season. The 25 foil cards were issued at a stated rate of one in three.

Nm-Mt Ex-Mt
COMP.SET w/o SP's (100) 40.00 12.00
COMMON CARD (1-125) .40 .12
COMMON FOIL 3.00 .90
1 J.C. Romero .40 .12
2 Robb Nen .60 .18
3 Raul Mondesi .60 .18
4 Mike Piazza 2.50 .75
5 Scott Rolen 1.50 .45
6 Shigetoshi Hasegawa .60 .18
7 Shannon Stewart .60 .18
8 David Eckstein FOIL 3.00 .90
9 Melvin Mora .60 .18
10 Jose Rijo .60 .18
11 Einar Diaz .40 .12
12 A.J. Burnett .40 .12
13 Mike Sweeney .60 .18
14 Jorge Posada FOIL 8.00 2.40
15 Mark Kotsay .40 .12
16 Doug Davis .40 .12
17 Steve Woodard .40 .12
18 Sun Woo Kim .40 .12
19 Sean Casey .60 .18
20 Juan Acevedo .40 .12
21 Dustan Mohr .40 .12
22 Mariano Rivera 1.00 .30
23 Kip Wells .40 .12
24 Kenny Lofton FOIL 5.00 1.50
25 Steve Cox .40 .12
26 Josh Fogg FOIL 3.00 .90
27 Ruben Sierra .40 .12
28 Sandy Alomar Jr. .40 .12
29 Vicente Padilla FOIL 3.00 .90
30 Carlos Beltran 1.00 .30
31 Mike Lowell .60 .18
32 Omar Vizquel 1.00 .30
33 Ricky Stone RC .60 .18
34 Geoff Jenkins .60 .18
35 Eric Karros .60 .18
36 Ryan Drese .40 .12
37 Adam Dunn 1.00 .30
38 Hank Blalock 1.50 .45
39 Marcus Giles .60 .18
40 Joe Randa .40 .12
41 Bob Wickman .40 .12
42 Roy Halladay .40 .12
43 Craig Counsell .40 .12
44 Derek Lowe .60 .18
45 Ray Durham .60 .18
46 Paul Shuey .40 .12
47 Cliff Floyd .60 .18
48 Shawn Green .60 .18
49 Torii Hunter FOIL 5.00 1.50
50 Edgardo Alfonzo .40 .12
51 Carlos Pena .40 .12
52 Sean Burroughs .60 .18
53 Placido Polanco .40 .12
54 Rafael Palmeiro 1.00 .30
55 Nate Cornejo .40 .12
56 Tim Salmon 1.00 .30
57 Craig Biggio 1.00 .30
58 Eric Hinske FOIL 3.00 .90
59 Rickey Henderson 1.50 .45
60 Nick Johnson .40 .12
61 Rey Ordonez .40 .12
62 Jose Hernandez .40 .12
63 Antonio Alfonseca .40 .12
64 Alfonso Soriano FOIL 8.00 2.40
65 Eric Chavez .60 .18
66 B.J. Surhoff FOIL 5.00 1.50
67 Austin Kearns FOIL 5.00 1.50
68 Jacob Cruz .40 .12
69 Armando Benitez .60 .18
70 Derek Jeter 4.00 1.20
71 Ryan Jensen .40 .12
72 Kevin Mench .40 .12
73 Mike Remlinger .40 .12
74 Luis Castillo .40 .12
75 Kazuhisa Ishii FOIL RC 8.00 2.40
76 Bobby Abreu .60 .18
77 Dave Veres .40 .12
78 Tony Batista .60 .18
79 Rey Sanchez .40 .12
80 Jason Grimsley .40 .12
81 Al Leiter FOIL 5.00 1.50
82 Kerry Wood FOIL 10.00 3.00
83 Ellis Burks .60 .18
84 Corey Patterson .60 .18
85 Adrian Beltre 1.00 .30
86 Barry Zito .60 .18
87 Doug Mientkiewicz .60 .18
88 Jeffrey Hammonds .40 .12
89 Jeremy Giambi .40 .12
90 Tsuyoshi Shinjo .60 .18
91 Roger Clemens SS FOIL 12.00 3.60
92 John Franco SS .60 .18
93 Alex Rodriguez SS FOIL 15.00 4.50
94 Barry Bonds SS FOIL 30.00 9.00
95 Fred McGriff SS 1.00 .30
96 Chuck Finley SS .60 .18
97 Jose Rijo SS .40 .12
98 Jeff Bagwell SS FOIL 8.00 2.40
99 Ron Gant SS .60 .18
100 Tom Glavine SS 1.00 .30
101 Mike Mussina SS 1.00 .30
102 Gary Sheffield SS .60 .18
103 Barry Larkin SS 1.00 .30
104 Jim Thome SS 1.50 .45
105 Chipper Jones SS FOIL 10.00 3.00
106 Rickey Henderson SS 1.50 .45
107 Randy Johnson SS FOIL 10.00 3.00
108 Mike Piazza SS FOIL 10.00 3.00
109 John Smoltz SS 1.00 .30
110 Edgar Martinez SS 1.00 .30
111 Larry Walker SS 1.00 .30
112 Pedro Martinez SS FOIL 10.00 3.00
113 Sammy Sosa SS FOIL 20.00 6.00
114 Roberto Alomar SS FOIL 8.00 2.40
115 Curt Schilling SS FOIL 5.00 1.50
116 Chuck Knoblauch SS .60 .18
117 Frank Thomas SS 1.50 .45
118 Jeff Kent SS .60 .18
119 Kenny Lofton SS .60 .18
120 Ken Griffey Jr. SS 2.50 .75
121 Trevor Hoffman SS FOIL 5.00 1.50
122 Mo Vaughn SS .60 .18
123 Robin Ventura SS .60 .18
124 Ellis Burks SS .60 .18
125 Tim Raines SS .60 .18

2002 MLB Showdown Pennant Run Strategy

Issued at a stated rate of two per pack, these 23 cards feature "strategy" insert cards. Cards numbered 19 and 24 were actually issued in the trade deadline packs.

Nm-Mt Ex-Mt
COMPLETE SET (23) 5.00 1.50
S1 Bernie Williams .40 .12
Bad Call
S2 Mike Piazza .75 .23
Clutch Hitting
S3 Troy Glaus .25 .07
Crowd Plate
S4 Down the Middle .25 .07
S5 Ducks on the Pond .25 .07
S6 Alex Rodriguez .75 .23
Free Steal
S7 Overthrow .25 .07
S8 Payoff Pitch .25 .07
S9 Tom Goodwin .25 .07
Rally Cap
S10 Nate Cornejo .25 .07
Rattled
S11 Rick Ankiel .25 .07
Shell-Shocked
S12 Scott Sullivan .25 .07
Shelled
S13 Dave Williams .25 .07
Comebacker
S14 Fast Worker .25 .07
S15 Andy Pettitte .40 .12
Full Windup
S16 Ichiro Suzuki .75 .23
Great Throw
S17 Hung It .25 .07
S18 Mark Mulder .25 .07
In Groove
S20 Curt Schilling .25 .07
Insult Injury
S21 Trevor Hoffman .25 .07
Nerves Steel
S22 Pitchout .25 .07
S23 Brian Moehler .25 .07
Scuff Ball
S25 Change in Strategy .25 .07

2003 MLB Showdown Pennant Run

This 125 card set was released in August, 2003 season. Interspersed throughout the set is 25 foil cards. Those foil cards were inserted at a stated rate of one per three. Cards numbered 106 through 115 feature players from early in their career while cards numbered 116 through 125 feature Hall of Famers.

	MINT	NRMT
COMP.SET w/o SP's (100)	40.00	18.00
COMMON CARD (1-125)	.50	.23
COMMON FOIL	3.00	1.35
1 Jeremy Bonderman RC	2.50	1.10
2 Tom Goodwin	.50	.23
3 Terry Mulholland	.50	.23
4 Jake Westbrook	.50	.23
5 Jake Peavy	1.00	.45
6 Felix Rodriguez	.50	.23
7 Marlon Byrd	.50	.23
8 Toby Hall	.50	.23
9 Roberto Hernandez	.50	.23
10 Carlos Silva	.50	.23
11 Chris Hammond	.50	.23
12 David Dellucci	.50	.23
13 R.A. Dickey	.50	.23
14 Cliff Politte	.50	.23
15 Russ Springer	.50	.23
16 Vance Wilson	.50	.23
17 Scott Williamson	.50	.23
18 Ryan Franklin	.50	.23
19 Juan Castro	.50	.23
20 Craig Monroe	.50	.23
21 Joe Beimel	.50	.23
22 John Halama	.50	.23
23 Eli Marrero	.50	.23
24 Felipe Lopez	.50	.23
25 Mike MacDougal	.50	.23
26 Kris Benson	.50	.23
27 Josh Beckett	1.00	.45
28 Carlos Febles	.50	.23
29 Luis Rivas	.50	.23
30 Scott Sullivan	.50	.23
31 John Thomson	.50	.23
32 Lance Carter	.50	.23
33 Chris George	.50	.23
34 Rocky Biddle	.50	.23
35 Brandon Lyon	.50	.23
36 Eric Munson	.50	.23
37 Kirk Rueter	.50	.23
38 Scott Schoeneweis	.50	.23
39 Casey Blake	.50	.23
40 Francisco Cordero	.50	.23
41 Tom Gordon	.50	.23
42 Neifi Perez	.50	.23
43 Chad Bradford	.50	.23
44 Miguel Cairo	.50	.23
45 Mike Matheny	1.00	.45
46 Mike Timlin	.50	.23
47 D.J. Carrasco RC	.50	.23
48 Eddie Perez	.50	.23
49 Gregg Zaun	.50	.23
50 Ronnie Belliard	.50	.23
51 Ricardo Rodriguez	.50	.23
52 B.J. Ryan	.50	.23
53 Michael Tucker	.50	.23
54 Rheal Cormier	.50	.23
55 Felix Heredia	.50	.23
56 Alex Cora	.50	.23
57 Travis Lee	.50	.23
58 Ted Lilly	.50	.23
59 Tom Wilson	.50	.23
60 Jeff D'Amico	.50	.23
61 Adam Eaton	.50	.23
62 Travis Harper	.50	.23
63 Mark Loretta	1.00	.45
64 Ricky Stone	.50	.23
65 Wil Cordero	.50	.23
66 Cliff Floyd	1.00	.45
67 Livan Hernandez	.50	.23
68 Paul Quantrill	.50	.23
69 Ben Davis	.50	.23
70 Shawn Estes	.50	.23
71 Chris Stynes	.50	.23
72 Jay Payton	.50	.23
73 Ramon Hernandez	.50	.23
74 Jason Johnson	.50	.23
75 John Vander Wal	.50	.23
76 Shawn Chacon FOIL	3.00	1.35
77 D'Angelo Jimenez	.50	.23
78 Desi Relaford	.50	.23
79 Rich Aurilia	.50	.23
80 Rod Barajas	.50	.23
81 Jose Cruz FOIL	3.00	1.35
82 Kyle Lohse	.50	.23
83 Rondell White	1.00	.45
84 Gil Meche FOIL	3.00	1.35
85 Jose Guillen	1.00	.45
86 Kenny Lofton	1.00	.45
87 Zach Day FOIL	3.00	1.35
88 Mark Redman	.50	.23
89 Melvin Mora FOIL	5.00	2.20
90 Todd Walker	.50	.23
91 Torii Hunter	1.00	.45
92 Frank Catalanotto	.50	.23
93 Andres Galarraga	1.00	.45
94 Jason Schmidt	1.00	.45
95 Eric Byrnes	.50	.23
96 Hank Blalock FOIL	8.00	3.60
97 Jacque Jones FOIL	5.00	2.20
98 Michael Young	1.50	.70
99 Carl Everett	1.00	.45
100 Preston Wilson	1.00	.45
101 Esteban Loaiza	.50	.23
102 Raul Mondesi FOIL	5.00	2.20
103 Carlos Delgado FOIL	5.00	2.20
104 Gary Sheffield FOIL	5.00	2.20
105 Kevin Appier	1.00	.45
106 Jesse Orosco SS	.50	.23
107 Pat Hentgen SS	.50	.23
108 Matt Williams SS	1.00	.45
109 David Cone SS FOIL	5.00	2.20
110 Mark Grace SS FOIL	8.00	3.60
111 Carlos Baerga SS FOIL	3.00	1.35
112 Greg Maddux SS FOIL	10.00	4.50
113 Kevin Brown SS FOIL	8.00	3.60
114 Ivan Rodriguez SS FOIL	15.00	6.75
115 John Olerud SS FOIL	5.00	2.20
116 Larry Doby CC	1.00	.45
117 Yogi Berra CC FOIL	10.00	4.50
118 Hoyt Wilhelm CC FOIL	15.00	6.75
119 Pee Wee Reese CC	1.50	.70
120 Br. Robinson CC FOIL	8.00	3.60
121 Robin Yount CC FOIL	12.00	5.50
122 Reggie Jackson CC FOIL	15.00	6.75
123 Har. Killebrew CC FOIL	15.00	6.75
124 Rod Carew CC FOIL	15.00	6.75
125 Nolan Ryan CC FOIL	15.00	6.75

2003 MLB Showdown Pennant Run Strategy

Issued at a stated rate of two per pack, these 25 cards feature various known terms as well as a photo to go with the caption. Whenever possible, we have notated who the player is before the caption in our data base.

	MINT	NRMT
COMPLETE SET (25)	5.00	2.20
1 Omar Vizquel	.40	.18
Change Sides		
2 Jerry Hairston Jr.	.25	.11
Emergency Bunt		
3 Bret Boone	.25	.11
Get Under It		
4 Dave Hansen	.25	.11
In Motion		
5 Out of Position	.25	.11
6 Einar Diaz	.25	.11
Passed Ball		
7 Jack McKeon	.25	.11
Say the Magic Word		
8 Suicide Squeeze	.25	.11
9 Brian Giles	.25	.11
To the Warning Track		
10 Keith Osik	.25	.11
Block the Plate		
11 Curt Schilling	.25	.11
Brent Butler		
Comebacker		
12 Kazuhisa Ishii	.25	.11
Good Matchup		
13 Austin Kearns	.25	.11
Ground Rule Double		
14 Pedro Martinez	.50	.23
In the Zone		
15 Infield In	.25	.11
16 Wilkin Ruan	.25	.11
Pickoff Attempt		
17 Roger Clemens		
Play the Odds		
18 Austin Kearns	.25	.11
Playing Shallow		
19 Quick Pitch	.25	.11
20 Jason Jennings	.25	.11
Sinker		
21 Jay Bell	.25	.11
Up and In		
22 Dee Brown	.25	.11
Good Scouting		
23 Buck Showalter	.25	.11
Looking Ahead		
24 Old Tricks	.25	.11
25 Buck Showalter MG	.75	.35
Alex Rodriguez		
Think Twice		

2004 MLB Showdown Pennant Run

This 125 card set was released in Spetember, 2004. The set featured a wide assortment of stars and common players. Many cards were issued with "foil" and those cards are notated in our checklist.

	Nm-Mt	Ex-Mt
COMP.SET w/o FOIL (100)	40.00	12.00
COMMON CARD	.50	.15
COMMON FOIL	3.00	.90
FOIL STATED ODDS 1:3		
1 Shawn Chacon	.50	.15
2 Bobby Crosby	1.50	.45
3 Russ Ortiz	1.00	.30
4 Jason Simontacchi	.50	.15
5 Oscar Villarreal	.50	.15
6 Rocky Biddle	.50	.15
7 Joe Borowski	.50	.15
8 Shawn Estes	.50	.15
9 Adam LaRoche	.50	.15
10 Carl Everett	1.00	.30
11 Willie Harris	.50	.15
12 Carlos Silva	.50	.15
13 Aaron Rowand	1.00	.30
14 Francisco Cordero	1.00	.30
15 Ryan Freel	.50	.15
16 Trevor Hoffman	1.00	.30
17 Edgar Renteria AS	1.00	.30
18 Mike Maroth	.50	.15
19 Carlos Pena	.50	.15
20 John Smoltz	1.50	.45
21 Carlos Guillen	1.00	.30
22 Buddy Groom	.50	.15
23 Aaron Miles	.50	.15
24 Jason Schmidt AS FOIL	5.00	1.50
25 Danny Kolb AS	.50	.15
26 Marcos Scutaro	.50	.15
27 Gary Sheffield AS	1.00	.30
28 Eric Gagne AS FOIL	10.00	3.00
29 Kazuhisa Ishii	1.00	.30
30 B.J. Ryan	.50	.15
31 Mark Mulder AS FOIL	5.00	1.50
32 Gerald Laird	.50	.15
33 Joe Mauer	1.50	.45
34 Nate Robertson	.50	.15
35 Hideki Matsui AS	4.00	1.20
36 Ray Lankford	.50	.15
37 Jake Peavy	1.00	.30
38 Esteban Loaiza AS	.50	.15
39 Mike Stanton	.50	.15
40 Kevin Gregg	.50	.15
41 Steve Trachsel	.50	.15
42 Albert Pujols AS FOIL	15.00	4.50
43 Shingo Takatsu RC	2.50	.75
44 Ichiro Suzuki AS FOIL	10.00	3.00
45 Milton Bradley	1.00	.30
46 Eric Chavez	1.00	.30
47 Paul Lo Duca AS FOIL	5.00	1.50
48 Kip Wells	.50	.15
49 Miguel Cabrera AS FOIL	8.00	2.40
50 Johnny Estrada AS	1.00	.30
51 Pedro Martinez FOIL	10.00	3.00
52 Jason Giambi AS	1.00	.30
53 Kenny Rogers AS	1.00	.30
54 Alex Rodriguez AS FOIL	15.00	4.50
55 Chone Figgins	.50	.15
56 Ken Harvey AS	.50	.15
57 Todd Helton AS	1.50	.45
58 Javy Lopez	1.00	.30
59 R.A. Dickey	.50	.15
60 J.D. Drew	1.00	.30
61 Melvin Mora	1.00	.30
62 Danny Bautista	.50	.15
63 Kerry Wood	2.50	.75
64 Randy Johnson AS	2.50	.75
65 Scott Rolen AS FOIL	10.00	3.00
66 Roger Clemens AS FOIL	10.00	3.00
67 Brad Penny	.50	.15
68 Matt Clement	.50	.15
69 Ronnie Belliard AS FOIL	.50	.15
70 Alfonso Soriano AS FOIL	8.00	2.40
71 Lew Ford	1.00	.30
72 Sean Casey AS FOIL	5.00	1.50
73 Troy Glaus	1.00	.30
74 Mike Lowell AS	1.00	.30
75 Juan Uribe	.50	.15
76 Adrian Beltre	1.50	.45
77 Jack Wilson AS	1.00	.30
78 Craig Wilson	.50	.15
79 Lyle Overbay FOIL	5.00	1.50
80 Jose Contreras	1.00	.30
81 Jason Jennings	.50	.15
82 Matt Mantei	.50	.15
83 Luis Vizcaino	.50	.15
84 Luis Ayala	.50	.15
85 Danny Patterson	.50	.15
86 C.J. Nitkowski	.50	.15
87 Larry Bigbie	1.00	.30
88 Mike Lieberthal	1.00	.30
89 Mike Timlin	.50	.15
90 Rob Mackowiak	.50	.15
91 Kevin Cash	.50	.15
92 Danys Baez	.50	.15
93 J.C. Romero	.50	.15
94 Dan Miceli	.50	.15
95 Armando Benitez AS	.50	.15
96 Hank Blalock AS	1.00	.30
97 Vinny Castilla	1.00	.30
98 Danny Graves AS FOIL	3.00	.90
99 Derek Jeter AS	5.00	1.50
100 Jim Thome AS FOIL	10.00	3.00
101 Mark Loretta AS	1.00	.30
102 Victor Martinez AS	1.00	.30
103 Ken Griffey Jr. AS	4.00	1.20
104 Miguel Tejada AS	1.00	.30
105 Mike Piazza AS	4.00	1.20
106 Ivan Rodriguez AS	2.50	.75
107 Tom Glavine AS	1.50	.45
108 Carl Crawford AS FOIL	5.00	1.50
109 Jeff Kent AS	1.00	.30
110 Ben Sheets AS	1.00	.30
111 Sammy Sosa AS	4.00	1.20
112 Vladimir Guerrero AS	2.50	.75
113 Curt Schilling AS	2.50	.75
114 Carl Pavano AS	1.00	.30
115 Manny Ramirez AS FOIL	8.00	2.40
116 Billy Williams HOF	1.00	.30
117 Ralph Kiner HOF	1.50	.45
118 Whitey Ford HOF FOIL	10.00	3.00
119 Jim Palmer HOF FOIL	8.00	2.40
120 Willie McCovey HOF FOIL	10.00	3.00
121 Phil Rizzuto HOF	1.50	.45
122 Orlando Cepeda HOF	8.00	2.40
123 Eddie Mathews HOF FOIL	15.00	4.50
124 Tom Seaver HOF FOIL	10.00	3.00
125 Bob Feller HOF FOIL	10.00	3.00

2004 MLB Showdown Pennant Run Strategy

	Nm-Mt	Ex-Mt
COMPLETE SET (25)	5.00	1.50
TWO PER BOOSTER PACK		
S1 Ivan Rodriguez	.50	.15
Down the Middle		
S2 Carlos Pena	.25	.07
Grooved		
S3 Alfredo Amezaga	.25	.07
Lost in the Sun		
S4 Protect the Runner	.25	.07
S5 M.Herges/Y.Torrealba	.25	.07
Running on Fumes		
S6 Neifi Perez	.25	.07
Serious Wheels		
S7 Craig Counsell	.25	.07
Smash up the Middle		
S8 Scott Rolen	.50	.15
Superior Talent		
S9 J.T. Snow	.25	.07
Swat!		
S10 Shigetoshi Hasegawa	.25	.07
Timing		
S11 Sean Casey	.25	.07
Calculated Risk		
S12 Reggie Sanders	.25	.07
Chin Music		
S13 Randy Johnson	.50	.15
Great Start		
S14 Frank Thomas	.50	.15
High and Tight		
S15 Roger Clemens	1.00	.30
Intimidation		
S16 Jose Valentin	.25	.07
On Your Toes		
S17 Ryan Klesko	.25	.07
Rally Killer		
S18 Chad Bradford	.25	.07
Setup Man		
S19 Darin Erstad	.25	.07
Whiff!		
S20 B.Showalter MG/M.Alexander	.25	.07
Dugout General		
S21 Jose Molina	.25	.07
Old Tricks		
S22 Out of Sync	.25	.07
S23 Barry Larkin	.40	.12
Revelation		
S24 Mark Teixeira	.25	.07
Stealing Signals		
S25 Alex Rodriguez	1.00	.30
Superstar		

2002 MLB Showdown Trading Deadline

The 2002 MLB Showdown product was released in mid summer, 2002 as a 150-card baseball game which updated the regular MLB Showdown set. The set features 125-player cards and 25 foil superstar cards that were short printed at one in three booster packs.

	Nm-Mt	Ex-Mt
COMP.SET w/o SP'S (125)	40.00	12.00
COMMON CARD (1-150)	.50	.15
COMMON FOIL	3.00	.90
1 Jason Giambi FOIL	5.00	1.50
2 Chris Singleton	.50	.15
3 Ben Davis	.50	.15
4 Tsuyoshi Shinjo	1.00	.30
5 Brian Jordan	1.00	.30
6 Tony Clark	.50	.15
7 Moises Alou FOIL	5.00	1.50
8 Todd Walker	.50	.15
9 Ricky Gutierrez	.50	.15
10 Brad Fullmer	.50	.15
11 Jeromy Burnitz	1.00	.30
12 Gary Sheffield FOIL	8.00	2.40
13 Marty Cordova FOIL	3.00	.90
14 Todd Zeile	1.00	.30
15 Alex Gonzalez	.50	.15
16 Kenny Lofton	1.00	.30
17 Vinny Castilla	1.00	.30
18 Craig Paquette	.50	.15
19 Michael Tucker	.50	.15
20 Cesar Izturis	.50	.15
21 Eric Young	.50	.15
22 Chuck Knoblauch	1.00	.30
23 Roberto Alomar FOIL	8.00	2.40
24 David Bell	.50	.15
25 Johnny Damon Sox	2.50	.75
26 Roger Cedeno	.50	.15
27 Robin Ventura	1.00	.30
28 David Justice FOIL	5.00	1.50
29 Brady Anderson	1.00	.30
30 Pokey Reese	.50	.15
31 Reggie Sanders FOIL	3.00	.90
32 Jeff Cirillo FOIL	3.00	.90
33 Juan Encarnacion	.50	.15
34 Tino Martinez FOIL	8.00	2.40
35 Carl Everett FOIL	5.00	1.50
36 Danny Bautista	.50	.15
37 Rafael Furcal	1.00	.30
38 Dmitri Young FOIL	5.00	1.50
39 Jay Gibbons	.50	.15
40 Brian Buchanan	.50	.15
41 David Segui	.50	.15
42 Barry Larkin FOIL	8.00	2.40
43 John Vander Wal	.50	.15
44 Brent Mayne	.50	.15
45 Neifi Perez	.50	.15
46 Lenny Harris	.50	.15
47 Jason LaRue	.50	.15
48 Travis Fryman	1.00	.30
49 Juan Uribe	1.00	.30
50 Shea Hillenbrand	1.00	.30
51 Aaron Rowand	1.00	.30
52 Jose Ortiz	.50	.15
53 Robert Fick	.50	.15
54 Doug Glanville	.50	.15
55 Charles Johnson FOIL	5.00	1.50
56 Derrek Lee	1.00	.30
57 Carlos Febles	.50	.15
58 Luis Rivas	.50	.15
59 Lee Stevens	.50	.15
60 Mike Lieberthal	1.00	.30
61 Ryan Klesko FOIL	8.00	2.40
62 Chris Gomez	.50	.15
63 Randy Winn	.50	.15
64 Rusty Greer	1.00	.30
65 Felipe Lopez	.50	.15
66 Carlos Pena	.50	.15
67 Toby Hall	.50	.15
68 Milton Bradley	1.00	.30
69 Matt Lawton	.50	.15
70 Gregg Zaun	.50	.15
71 Eric Hinske	.50	.15
72 Alex Ochoa	.50	.15
73 Rondell White	1.00	.30
74 Armando Rios	.50	.15
75 Desi Relaford	.50	.15
76 Nomar Garciaparra FOIL	10.00	3.00
77 Frank Thomas FOIL	10.00	3.00
78 Mitch Meluskey	.50	.15
79 Morgan Ensberg	1.00	.30
80 Mo Vaughn FOIL	5.00	1.50
81 Adrian Brown	.50	.15
82 Juan Gonzalez FOIL	8.00	2.40
83 Tom Wilson RC	1.00	.30
84 Matt Stairs	.50	.15
85 Andres Galarraga	1.00	.30
86 Sidney Ponson	.50	.15
87 Jesus Colome	.50	.15
88 Juan Cruz	.50	.15
89 Eddie Guardado	.50	.15
90 Jon Garland	.50	.15
91 Denny Neagle	.50	.15
92 Chad Durbin	.50	.15
93 Kevin Brown FOIL	5.00	1.50
94 Elmer Dessens	.50	.15
95 Eric Gagne	2.50	.75
96 Jamey Wright	.50	.15
97 Pedro Martinez FOIL	2.50	.75
98 Jason Bere	.50	.15
99 Ugueth Urbina	.50	.15
100 Carl Pavano	1.00	.30
101 Kip Wells	.50	.15
102 Paul Abbott	.50	.15
103 Billy Wagner FOIL	5.00	1.50
104 Erik Hiljus	.50	.15
105 Brandon Duckworth	.50	.15
106 Ruben Quevedo	.50	.15
107 Jimmy Anderson	.50	.15
108 Bobby Jones	.50	.15
109 Livan Hernandez	.50	.15
110 Curtis Leskanic	.50	.15
111 Tom Gordon	.50	.15
112 Jeff Austin RC	1.00	.30
113 Joel Pineiro	1.00	.30
114 Chad Bradford	.50	.15
115 Woody Williams	.50	.15
116 Victor Zambrano FOIL	3.00	.90
117 Jose Mesa	.50	.15
118 Roy Halladay	.50	.15
119 Steve Karsay	.50	.15
120 Hideo Nomo	2.50	.75
121 Jeff Farnsworth	.50	.15
122 Dave Weathers	.50	.15
123 Sean Lowe	.50	.15
124 Mike Myers	.50	.15
125 Jason Schmidt	1.00	.30
126 Mike Williams	.50	.15
127 Terry Adams	.50	.15
128 Chan Ho Park FOIL	5.00	1.50
129 Jeff D'Amico	.50	.15
130 Kevin Appier FOIL	5.00	1.50
131 Glendon Rusch	.50	.15
132 Jason Isringhausen	1.00	.30
133 Todd Ritchie	.50	.15
134 Shawn Estes	.50	.15
135 Kevin Millwood	1.00	.30
136 Aaron Sele	.50	.15
137 Rick Helling	.50	.15
138 Billy Koch	.50	.15
139 Paul Quantrill	.50	.15
140 Tim Spooneybarger	.50	.15
141 Jorge Julio	.50	.15
142 Carlos Hernandez	.50	.15
143 Rick Ankiel	.50	.15
144 Scott Erickson	.50	.15
145 Denny Hocking	.50	.15
146 Kazuhisa Ishii RC	5.00	1.50
147 Pedro Astacio	.50	.15
148 Satoru Komiyama RC	1.00	.30
149 Kurt Ainsworth	.50	.15
150 John Smoltz FOIL	8.00	2.40

2002 MLB Showdown Trading Deadline Strategy

Inserted into packs at a rate of two per pack, this 25-card insert set features the strategy cards necessary for playing the MLB Showdown game. Card numbers carry an "S" prefix.

	Nm-Mt	Ex-Mt
COMPLETE SET (25)	5.00	1.50
S1 Luis Gonzalez	.25	.07
Big Inning		
S2 Jeff Cirillo	.25	.07
Do or Die		
S3 Alex Rodriguez	.75	.23
Free Steal		
S4 Tsuyoshi Shinjo	.25	.07
Lean Into It		
S5 Overthrow/Cubs-Mets	.25	.07
S6 Corey Patterson	.25	.07
Pointers		
S7 David Justice	.25	.07
Pro Hitter		
S8 Nate Cornejo	.25	.07
Rattled		
S9 Scott Sullivan	.25	.07
Shelled		

S10 Rick Ankiel .25 .07
Shell-Shocked
S11 Swing Fences/Cubs .25 .07
S12 Marlon Anderson .25 .07
Tricky Hop
S13 Whiplash .25 .07
S14 Aaron Boone .25 .07
Choke
S15 Dave Williams .25 .07
Comebacker
S16 Takahito Nomura .25 .07
Fast Worker
S17 Paul Abbott .25 .07
Focused
S18 Hung It .25 .07
S19 Rick Helling .25 .07
In the Zone
S20 Brian Moehler .25 .07
Scuff Ball
S21 Joel Pineiro .25 .07
Swiss Army
S22 What Were You Thinking? .25 .07
S23 Alex Gonzalez .25 .07
Whoops
S24 Brian Giles .25 .07
Bear Down
S25 Rich Aurilia .25 .07
Game Inches

2003 MLB Showdown Trading Deadline

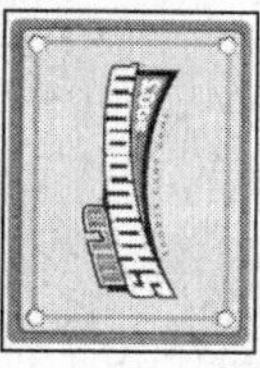

This 145 card set was released during the 2003 season. Interspersed throughout the set is 25 foil cards. Those foil cards were inserted at a stated rate of one per three. Please note there is no card number 140. Kerry Wood's foil card was mistakenly numbered as number 60 and thus we have created a 60A and a 60B listing.

MINT NRMT
COMP.SET w/o SP's (120) 40.00 18.00
COMMON CARD (1-145) .50 .23
COMMON FOIL 3.00 1.35
1 So Taguchi 1.00 .45
2 Ryan Drese .50 .23
3 Mike Hampton 1.00 .45
4 Sandy Alomar Jr. .50 .23
5 Steve Sparks .50 .23
6 Chan Ho Park 1.00 .45
7 Roger Cedeno .50 .23
8 Antonio Osuna .50 .23
9 Ryan Dempster .50 .23
10 Jesse Orosco .50 .23
11 Angel Berroa .50 .23
12 Sean Burroughs 1.00 .45
13 Matt Mantei .50 .23
14 Einar Diaz .50 .23
15 Ken Griffey Jr. 4.00 1.80
16 Rey Sanchez .50 .23
17 Antonio Alfonseca .50 .23
18 Carl Crawford 1.00 .45
19 Rey Ordonez .50 .23
20 Brandon Inge .50 .23
21 Hank Blalock 1.50 .70
22 Albie Lopez .50 .23
23 Aaron Sele .50 .23
24 Willie Bloomquist 1.00 .45
25 Shigetoshi Hasegawa 1.00 .45
26 Steve Kline .50 .23
27 Ramiro Mendoza .50 .23
28 Mike Stanton .50 .23
29 Carlos Zambrano 1.00 .45
30 Dean Palmer .50 .23
31 Mark Grudzielanek .50 .23
32 Matt Williams 1.00 .45
33 Michael Cuddyer .50 .23
34 Glendon Rusch .50 .23
35 Hee Seop Choi .50 .23
36 Mike Bordick 1.00 .45
37 Ray King .50 .23
38 Bill Mueller 1.00 .45
39 John McDonald .50 .23
40 Brent Butler .50 .23
41 Josh Bard .50 .23
42 Xavier Nady .50 .23
43 J.C. Romero .50 .23
44 Paul Shuey .50 .23
45 Eric Karros 1.00 .45
46 Runelvys Hernandez .50 .23
47 Braden Looper .50 .23
48 Dave Roberts .50 .23
49 Deivi Cruz .50 .23
50 Todd Hollandsworth .50 .23
51 Billy Koch .50 .23
52 Brandon Villafuerte .50 .23
53 Ricardo Rincon .50 .23
54 Joe Crede .50 .23
55 Juan Pierre 1.00 .45
56 Tsuyoshi Shinjo 1.00 .45
57 Ugueth Urbina .50 .23
58 Luis Vizcaino FOIL 3.00 1.35
59 Ben Weber .50 .23
60A Kerry Wood 2.50 1.10
60B Kerry Wood FOIL 10.00 4.50
61 Tim Worrell .50 .23
62 Royce Clayton .50 .23
63 Chone Figgins .50 .23
64 Ken Huckaby .50 .23
65 Brian Anderson .50 .23
66 Aramis Ramirez 1.00 .45
67 Edgar Martinez 1.50 .70
68 Keith Foulke 1.00 .45
69 LaTroy Hawkins .50 .23
70 Mike Remlinger .50 .23
71 Lyle Overbay 1.00 .45
72 Buddy Groom .50 .23
73 Orlando Hudson .50 .23
74 Francisco Rodriguez FOIL 5.00 2.20
75 Craig Biggio 1.50 .70
76 Todd Zeile 1.00 .45
77 Vernon Wells 1.00 .45
78 Casey Fossum .50 .23
79 Wes Helms .50 .23
80 Robert Fick .50 .23
81 Scott Spiezio .50 .23
82 Ty Wigginton .50 .23
83 Elmer Dessens .50 .23
84 Arthur Rhodes .50 .23
85 Matt Stairs .50 .23
86 Miguel Olivo .50 .23
87 Tino Martinez 1.50 .70
88 Travis Hafner 1.00 .45
89 Octavio Dotel .50 .23
90 Jimmy Rollins 1.00 .45
91 Placido Polanco .50 .23
92 Kevin Brown 1.00 .45
93 John Patterson .50 .23
94 Andy Pettitte 1.50 .70
95 Bobby Kielty .50 .23
96 Jeremy Giambi .50 .23
97 Brandon Phillips .50 .23
98 Fred McGriff 1.50 .70
99 Damian Moss .50 .23
100 Russ Ortiz 1.00 .45
101 Mark Teixeira 1.00 .45
102 Tom Glavine FOIL 8.00 3.60
103 Chris Woodward .50 .23
104 Brad Radke 1.00 .45
105 Edgardo Alfonzo .50 .23
106 Jose Contreras FOIL RC 8.00 3.60
107 Josh Beckett 1.00 .45
108 Johan Santana 1.50 .70
109 Brandon Larson .50 .23
110 Randall Simon .50 .23
111 Randy Winn FOIL 3.00 1.35
112 Ray Durham 1.00 .45
113 Omar Daal FOIL 3.00 1.35
114 David Wells FOIL 5.00 2.20
115 Wade Miller .50 .23
116 Bartolo Colon FOIL 5.00 2.20
117 Ryan Klesko FOIL 5.00 2.20
118 Jeff Bagwell 1.50 .70
119 Roy Oswalt FOIL 5.00 2.20
120 Orlando Hernandez FOIL 3.00 1.35
121 Ivan Rodriguez FOIL 10.00 4.50
122 Tim Wakefield 1.00 .45
123 Josh Phelps .50 .23
124 Woody Williams .50 .23
125 Chipper Jones FOIL 10.00 4.50
126 Randy Wolf .50 .23
127 Kevin Millwood FOIL 5.00 2.20
128 Jeff Kent FOIL 5.00 2.20
129 Rocco Baldelli FOIL 5.00 2.20
130 Hideki Matsui FOIL RC 15.00 6.75
131 Jim Thome FOIL 10.00 4.50
132 Kazuhiro Sasaki RS 1.00 .45
133 Jason Jennings RS FOIL 3.00 1.35
134 Rafael Furcal RS 1.00 .45
135 Derek Jeter RS FOIL 15.00 6.75
136 Benito Santiago RS 1.00 .45
137 Jeff Bagwell RS 1.50 .70
138 Carlos Beltran RS 1.50 .70
139 Scott Rolen RS FOIL 10.00 4.50
141 Tim Salmon RS 1.00 .45
142 Ichiro Suzuki RS FOIL 10.00 4.50
143 Mike Piazza RS FOIL 10.00 4.50
144 Albert Pujols RS 5.00 2.20
145 Nomar Garciaparra RS FOIL 10.00 4.50

2003 MLB Showdown Trading Deadline Strategy

Issued at a stated rate of two per pack, these 25 cards feature various known terms as well as a photo to go with the caption. Whenever possible, we have notated who the player is before the caption in our data base.

MINT NRMT
COMPLETE SET (25) 5.00 2.20
S1 Sammy Sosa .75 .35
Clutch Hitting
S2 Brad Wilkerson .25 .11
Clutch Rookie
S3 Hideki Matsui 2.00 .90
Great Addition
S4 Brent Mayne .25 .11
Headed Home
S5 Jose Vizcaino .40 .18
Jeff Bagwell
High Fives
S6 Barry Bonds 1.25 .55
Long Gone!
S7 On the Move .25 .11
S8 Edgar Martinez .40 .18
Take What's Given
S9 Eric Hinske .25 .11
Who Is This Guy
S10 Jason Jennings .25 .11
Add by Subtrac
S11 Orlando Hudson .25 .11
De-nied!
S12 Roger Clemens 1.00 .45
Digging Deep
S13 Randy Johnson .50 .23
Lock It Down
S14 Matt Herges .25 .11
New Arrival
S15 Einar Diaz .25 .11
Not So Fast
S16 Ichiro Suzuki .75 .35
Pitch Around
S17 Francisco Rodriguez .25 .11
Rookie Fireballer
S18 John Smoltz .25 .11
Split-Finger Fastball
S19 Brian Buchanan .25 .11
Still Learning
S20 Barry Zito .25 .11
3 up 3 Down
S21 Brent Butler .25 .11
Triple Dip
S22 Brainstorm .25 .11
S23 Gary Varsho .25 .11
Outmanaged
S24 Mark McLemore .25 .11
Stealing Signals
S25 Mike Cameron .25 .11
Swing at Anything

2004 MLB Showdown Trading Deadline

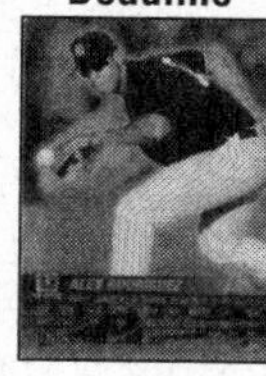

This 125 card set was released during the 2004 season. Interspersed throughout the set is 25 foil cards. Those foil cards were inserted at a stated rate of one per three.

Nm-Mt Ex-Mt
COMP.SET w/o SP's (100) 40.00 12.00
COMMON CARD (1-125) .50 .15
COMMON FOIL (1-115) 3.00 .90
COMMON FOIL (116-125) 8.00 2.40
FOIL STATED ODDS 1:3 BOOSTER
1 Jose Mesa .50 .15
2 Pokey Reese .50 .15
3 Rey Sanchez .50 .15
4 Jeff Weaver .50 .15
5 Todd Zeile 1.00 .30
6 Carlos Rivera .50 .15
7 Orlando Palmeiro .50 .15
8 Roberto Alomar 1.50 .45
9 Doug Glanville .50 .15
10 Khalil Greene 2.50 .75
11 Victor Martinez 1.00 .30
12 Jeffrey Hammonds .50 .15
13 Bobby Kielty .50 .15
14 Brian Schneider .50 .15
15 Arthur Rhodes .50 .15
16 David Dellucci .50 .15
17 Eric Young .50 .15
18 Grant Balfour .50 .15
19 Javier A. Lopez 1.00 .30
20 Jeff Nelson .50 .15
21 Kelvim Escobar .50 .15
22 Braden Looper .50 .15
23 Tino Martinez 1.50 .45
24 Laynce Nix 1.00 .30
25 Horacio Ramirez .50 .15
26 Hideki Matsui 4.00 1.20
27 Kevin Mench .50 .15
28 Scott Sullivan .50 .15
29 Michael Barrett .50 .15
30 Jose Cruz Jr. .50 .15
31 Robert Fick .50 .15
32 Brad Fullmer .50 .15
33 Eric Karros 1.00 .30
34 Mark Kotsay 1.00 .30
35 Fernando Vina .50 .15
36 Tim Worrell .50 .15
37 Mike Cameron 1.00 .30
38 Howie Clark .50 .15
39 Tom Gordon .50 .15
40 Adam Kennedy .50 .15
41 Rafael Palmeiro 1.50 .45
42 Reed Johnson .50 .15
43 Aquilino Lopez .50 .15
44 Julian Tavarez .50 .15
45 Ben Broussard .50 .15
46 Miguel Cabrera 1.50 .45
47 Raul Ibanez .50 .15
48 Randall Simon .50 .15
49 Ronnie Belliard .50 .15
50 Scott Spiezio .50 .15
51 Ellis Burks 1.00 .30
52 LaTroy Hawkins .50 .15
53 Pat Hentgen .50 .15
54 Eddie Guardado .50 .15
55 Todd Walker .50 .15
56 Ivan Rodriguez 2.50 .75
57 Raul Mondesi 1.00 .30
58 Jeromy Burnitz 1.00 .30
59 Rich Aurilia .50 .15
60 Keith Foulke Sox 1.50 .45
61 Ramon Hernandez .50 .15
62 Kenny Lofton 1.00 .30
63 Rafael Soriano FOIL 3.00 .90
64 Jody Gerut .50 .15
65 Randy Johnson 2.50 .75
66 John Burkett .50 .15
67 Brian Giles FOIL 5.00 1.50
68 Matt Morris 1.00 .30
69 Derrek Lee 1.00 .30
70 Miguel Tejada 1.00 .30
71 Ted Lilly .50 .15
72 David Wells 1.00 .30
73 Carl Everett 1.00 .30
74 A.J. Pierzynski 1.00 .30
75 Gary Sheffield 1.00 .30
76 Juan Gonzalez 1.50 .45
77 Brandon Webb .50 .15
78 Joel Pineiro 1.00 .30
79 Scott Rolen FOIL 10.00 3.00
80 Jim Edmonds FOIL 5.00 1.50
81 Curt Schilling FOIL 10.00 3.00
82 Kevin Brown FOIL 5.00 1.50
83 Chad Cordero .50 .15
84 Rich Harden 1.00 .30
85 Lyle Overbay 1.00 .30
86 Paul Quantrill .50 .15
87 Rondell White 1.00 .30
88 Joe Nathan 1.00 .30
89 Jose Valverde .50 .15
90 Francisco Rodriguez 1.00 .30
91 Billy Wagner 1.00 .30
92 Jason Giambi 1.00 .30
93 Jason Lane .50 .15
94 Frank Thomas 2.50 .75
95 Greg Maddux 4.00 1.20
96 Andy Pettitte 1.50 .45
97 Jay Payton .50 .15
98 Roger Clemens 5.00 1.50
99 Bartolo Colon FOIL 5.00 1.50
100 Vladimir Guerrero 2.50 .75
101 Kazuo Matsui FOIL RC 10.00 3.00
102 Javier Vazquez 1.00 .30
103 Esteban Loaiza FOIL 3.00 .90
104 Alex Rodriguez FOIL 15.00 4.50
105 Javy Lopez FOIL 5.00 1.50
106 Tino Martinez SS 1.50 .45
107 Vladimir Guerrero SS FOIL 10.00 3.00
108 Derek Jeter SS FOIL 10.00 3.00
109 Craig Biggio SS 1.50 .45
110 Tom Glavine SS 1.50 .45
111 Nomar Garciaparra SS FOIL 10.00 3.00
112 Mike Mussina SS FOIL 8.00 2.40
113 Todd Helton SS FOIL 8.00 2.40
114 Greg Maddux SS FOIL 10.00 3.00
115 Roger Clemens SS FOIL 15.00 4.50
116 Rollie Fingers CC FOIL
117 Luis Aparicio CC 8.00 2.40
118 Lou Brock CC 10.00 3.00
119 Joe Morgan CC FOIL
120 Richie Ashburn CC FOIL
121 Al Kaline CC FOIL
122 Bob Gibson CC FOIL
123 Willie Stargell CC 10.00 3.00
124 Warren Spahn CC FOIL
125 Mike Schmidt CC FOIL 15.00 4.50

2004 MLB Showdown Trading Deadline Strategy

Nm-Mt Ex-Mt
COMPLETE SET (25) 5.00 1.50
COMMON CARD (S1-S25) .25 .07
STATED ODDS 2:1
S1 D.Wells/Dialed-In .25 .07
S2 A.Pujols/En Fuego! 1.00 .30
S3 S.Casey/Last Chance .25 .07
S4 On the Move .25 .07
S5 Opposite Field Power .25 .07
S6 L.Rothschild CO/Out of Gas .25 .07
S7 A.Soriano/Quick Thinking .40 .12
S8 R.Sexson/Swing for Fences .25 .07
S9 Wheelhouse .25 .07
S10 Beaned .25 .07
S11 M.Alou/M.Giles/Broken Bat .25 .07
S12 C.Everett/Caught Napping .25 .07
S13 R.Simon/Chopper .25 .07
S14 J.Pierre/Dying Quail .25 .07
S15 K.Matsui/Great Reactions 1.00 .30
S16 M.Piazza/J.Seo .75 .23
Insult to Injury
S17 T.Helton/Lefty Shift .40 .12
S18 A.Huff/T.Hall/Pumped Up .25 .07
S19 S.Sosa/Punched Out .75 .23
S20 Robbed! .25 .07
S21 F.Alou MG/Feast or Famine .25 .07
S22 Pac Bell Park/Home Field .25 .07
S23 Just Over the Rail .25 .07
S24 Umpires/Late Call .25 .07
S25 B.Melvin MG/Outmanaged .25 .07

2004 National Pastime

This 90-card set was released in July, 2004. The set was issued in five-card hobby and retail packs. The hobby packs, which were issued without an suggested SRP, were packed 10 packs to a box and six boxes to a case. The retail packs, which were issued with an $3 SRP were issued 24 packs to a box and 20 boxes to a case. Cards number 1-60 feature veterans while cards numbered 61-90 featured rookies which were issued at a stated rate of one in seven hobby and one in 48 retail and were issued to a stated print run of 699 serial numbered sets.

Nm-Mt Ex-Mt
COMP.SET w/o SP's (60) 25.00 7.50
COMMON CARD (1-60) .40 .12
COMMON CARD (61-90) 4.00 1.20
61-90 ODDS 1:7 HOBBY, 1:48 RETAIL
61-90 PRINT RUN 699 SERIAL #'d SETS
1 Hideki Matsui 1.50 .45
2 Khalil Greene 1.00 .30
3 Pedro Martinez 1.00 .30
4 Sammy Sosa 1.50 .45
5 Mark Teixeira .40 .12
6 Orlando Cabrera .40 .12
7 Scott Podsednik .40 .12
8 Miguel Tejada .40 .12
9 Andruw Jones .40 .12
10 Manny Ramirez .60 .18
11 Jose Reyes .40 .12
12 Bobby Abreu .40 .12
13 Alex Rodriguez 1.50 .45
14 Ivan Rodriguez 1.00 .30
15 Jason Schmidt .40 .12
16 Mike Piazza 1.50 .45
17 Eric Chavez .40 .12
18 Mark Prior 1.00 .30
19 Adam Dunn .60 .18
20 Richard Hidalgo .40 .12
21 Todd Helton .60 .18
22 Rocco Baldelli .40 .12
23 Roy Oswalt .40 .12
24 Angel Berroa .40 .12
25 Jason Giambi .40 .12
26 Jim Thome 1.00 .30
27 Javy Lopez .40 .12
28 Derek Jeter 2.00 .60
29 Tom Glavine .60 .18
30 Magglio Ordonez .40 .12
31 Austin Kearns .40 .12
32 Scott Rolen 1.00 .30
33 Miguel Cabrera .60 .18
34 Vernon Wells .40 .12
35 Frank Thomas 1.00 .30
36 Jeff Bagwell .60 .18
37 Shannon Stewart .40 .12
38 Richie Sexson .40 .12
39 Hideo Nomo 1.00 .30
40 Nomar Garciaparra 1.50 .45
41 C.C. Sabathia .40 .12
42 Albert Pujols 2.00 .60
43 Barry Zito .40 .12
44 Hank Blalock .40 .12
45 Carlos Delgado .40 .12
46 Greg Maddux 1.50 .45
47 Randy Johnson 1.00 .30
48 Josh Beckett .40 .12
49 Kerry Wood 1.00 .30
50 Roger Clemens 2.00 .60
51 Garret Anderson .40 .12
52 Ichiro Suzuki 1.50 .45
53 Kip Wells .40 .12
54 Vladimir Guerrero 1.00 .30
55 Shawn Green .40 .12
56 Chipper Jones 1.00 .30
57 Aubrey Huff .40 .12
58 Ken Griffey Jr. 1.50 .45
59 Torii Hunter .40 .12
60 Alfonso Soriano .60 .18
61 Chris Shelton ROO RC 5.00 1.50
62 Graham Koonce ROO 4.00 1.20
63 Kaz Matsui ROO RC 8.00 2.40
64 Alfredo Simon ROO RC 4.00 1.20
65 Mike Gosling ROO RC 4.00 1.20
66 Mike Rouse ROO RC 4.00 1.20
67 Mariano Gomez ROO RC 4.00 1.20
68 Justin Leone ROO RC 5.00 1.50
69 Jose Capellan ROO RC 6.00 1.80
70 Donnie Kelly ROO RC 4.00 1.20
71 Merkin Valdez ROO RC 5.00 1.50
72 Greg Dobbs ROO RC 4.00 1.20
73 Shingo Takatsu ROO RC 5.00 1.50
74 Chris Aguila ROO RC 4.00 1.20
75 Jerome Gamble ROO RC 4.00 1.20
76 Onil Joseph ROO RC 4.00 1.20
77 Ramon Ramirez ROO RC 4.00 1.20
78 Angel Chavez ROO RC 4.00 1.20
79 Hector Gimenez ROO RC 4.00 1.20
80 Ivan Ochoa ROO RC 4.00 1.20
81 Aarom Baldiris ROO RC 5.00 1.50
82 Akinori Otsuka ROO RC 4.00 1.20
83 Ruddy Yan ROO 4.00 1.20
84 Jerry Gil ROO RC 4.00 1.20
85 Shawn Hill ROO RC 4.00 1.20
86 John Gall ROO RC 5.00 1.50
87 Jason Bartlett ROO RC 5.00 1.50
88 Jorge Sequea ROO RC 4.00 1.20
89 Luis A. Gonzalez ROO RC 5.00 1.50
90 Sean Henn ROO RC 4.00 1.20

2004 National Pastime Blue Foil

Nm-Mt Ex-Mt
OVERALL PARALLEL ODDS 1:10 HOBBY
STATED PRINT RUN 1 SERIAL #'d SET
NO PRICING DUE TO SCARCITY

2004 National Pastime Red Foil

Nm-Mt Ex-Mt
*RED 1-60: 2X TO 5X BASIC
*RED 61-90: .4X TO 1X BASIC
OVERALL PARALLEL ODDS 1:10 H, 1:48 R
STATED PRINT RUN 150 SERIAL #'d SETS

2004 National Pastime White Foil

Nm-Mt Ex-Mt
*WHITE 1-60: 4X TO 10X BASIC
*WHITE 61-90: .6X TO 1.5X BASIC
OVERALL PARALLEL ODDS 1:10 H, 1:48 R
STATED PRINT RUN 50 SERIAL #'d SETS

2004 National Pastime 1959 Ted Williams Reprint

Nm-Mt Ex-Mt
COMMON CARD (1-80) 5.00 1.50
STATED PRINT RUN 406 SERIAL #'d SETS
59 SET EXCH.PRINT RUN 1 #'d CARD
COMMON M'PIECE (1-80) 100.00 30.00
MASTERPIECE RANDOM IN HOBBY PACKS
MASTERPIECE PRINT RUN 1 #'d SET
OVERALL T.WILLIAMS ODDS 1:3 HOBBY
NNO Complete 59 Set EXCH/1

2004 National Pastime 1959 Ted Williams Reprint Bat

Nm-Mt Ex-Mt
COMMON CARD (1-40) 100.00 30.00
OVERALL GAME-USED ODDS 1:60 HOBBY
STATED PRINT RUN 9 SERIAL #'d SETS

2004 National Pastime American Flag Patch

Nm-Mt Ex-Mt
STATED ODDS 1:240 HOBBY BOXES..
PRINT RUNS B/WN 1-3 COPIES PER .
NO PRICING DUE TO SCARCITY ....
AP Albert Pujols/3
AR Alex Rodriguez/2
BZ Barry Zito/3
CJ Chipper Jones/2
DJ Derek Jeter/2
EC Eric Chavez/1
EM Edgar Martinez/1
GM Greg Maddux/2
HN Hideo Nomo/3
JB Josh Beckett/2
JG Jason Giambi/2
JK Jeff Kent/1
JT Jim Thome/2
KW Kerry Wood/2
MP Mike Piazza/3
MT Miguel Tejada/2
PM Pedro Martinez/2
RC Roger Clemens/2
RJ Randy Johnson/2
RM Manny Ramirez/2
SG Shawn Green/1
SR Scott Rolen/3
SS Sammy Sosa/2
TH Tim Hudson/1
VG Vladimir Guerrero/2

2004 National Pastime American Game

Nm-Mt Ex-Mt
STATED ODDS 1:10 HOBBY; 1:12 RETAIL
1 Greg Maddux 3.00 .90
2 Randy Johnson 1.50 .45
3 Roger Clemens 4.00 1.20
4 Mark Prior 1.50 .45
5 Mike Piazza 3.00 .90
6 Alex Rodriguez 2.50 .75
7 Adam Dunn 1.50 .45
8 Jim Thome 1.50 .45
9 Derek Jeter 4.00 1.20
10 Scott Rolen 1.50 .45
11 Nomar Garciaparra 3.00 .90
12 Kerry Wood 1.50 .45
13 Chipper Jones 1.50 .45
14 Frank Thomas 1.50 .45
15 Jeff Bagwell 1.50 .45

2004 National Pastime American Game Jersey

Nm-Mt Ex-Mt
STATED ODDS 1:96 RETAIL
SP PRINT RUNS PROVIDED BY FLEER
SP'S ARE NOT SERIAL-NUMBERED
*PATCH p/r 37-50: 1.25X TO 3X JSY .
*PATCH p/r 46: 1.25X TO 3X JSY SP .
*PATCH p/r 30: 1.5X TO 4X JSY
*PATCH p/r 29-35: 1.5X TO 4X JSY SP
PATCH PRINTS B/WN 10-50 COPIES PER
NO PATCH PRICING ON QTY OF 13 OR LESS
PATCH M'PIECE PRINT RUN 1 #'d SET
NO PATCH MP PRICING DUE TO SCARCITY
OVERALL GU ODDS 1:60 H, AU-GU 1:24 R
PATCH MP ISSUED ONLY IN HOBBY PACKS
AD Adam Dunn 8.00 2.40
AR Alex Rodriguez 10.00 3.00
CJ Chipper Jones 8.00 2.40
DJ Derek Jeter 20.00 6.00
FT Frank Thomas SP/150 10.00 3.00
GM Greg Maddux SP/150 12.00 3.60
JB Jeff Bagwell 8.00 2.40
JT Jim Thome 8.00 2.40
KW Kerry Wood 8.00 2.40
MP Mike Piazza SP/200 12.00 3.60
MPR Mark Prior 8.00 2.40
RCL Roger Clemens 12.00 3.60
RJO Randy Johnson 8.00 2.40
SR Scott Rolen 8.00 2.40

2004 National Pastime American Game Retired GU

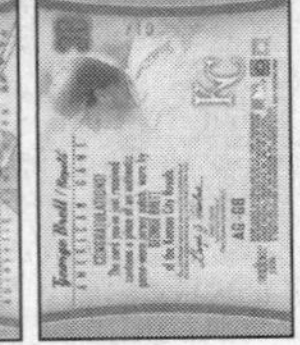

Nm-Mt Ex-Mt
OVERALL GAME USED ODDS 1:60 HOBBY
PRINT RUNS B/WN 6-31 COPIES PER
NO PRICING ON QTY OF 10 OR LESS
AK Al Kaline Pants/6
BR Babe Ruth Bat/25 250.00 75.00
CF Carlton Fisk Patch/25 40.00 12.00
CR Cal Ripken Patch/25 120.00 36.00
DM Don Mattingly Pants/23 50.00 15.00
DW Dave Winfield Patch/31 50.00 15.00
GB George Brett Patch/10
MS Mike Schmidt Patch/25 100.00 30.00
RC Roberto Clemente Bat/25 120.00 36.00
TM Thurman Munson Bat/25 40.00 12.00

2004 National Pastime American Game Retired GU Autograph

Nm-Mt Ex-Mt
OVERALL GAME USED ODDS 1:60 HOBBY
PRINT RUNS B/WN 5-25 COPIES PER
NO PRICING ON QTY OF 8 OR LESS ..
CF Carlton Fisk Patch/5
CR Cal Ripken Patch/8
DM Don Mattingly Pants/5
JB Johnny Bench Patch/5
MS Mike Schmidt Patch/5
RJ Reggie Jackson Pants/5
WM Willie McCovey Jsy/22 80.00 24.00
WS Warren Spahn Patch/25

2004 National Pastime American Game Retired GU Dual

Nm-Mt Ex-Mt
OVERALL GAME USED ODDS 1:60 HOBBY
PRINT RUNS B/WN 5-25 COPIES PER
NO PRICING ON QTY OF 10 OR LESS
DM Don Mattingly Bat-Pants/5
DW Dave Winfield Bat-Patch/10
JB Johnny Bench Bat-Patch/20. 80.00 24.00
NR Nolan Ryan Bat-Jsy/25 80.00 24.00
RJ Reg Jackson Bat-Pants/25 40.00 12.00

2004 National Pastime Buyback Autographs

Nm-Mt Ex-Mt
OVERALL AUTO ODDS 1:5 HOBBY
PRINT RUNS B/WN 1-174 #'d COPIES PER
L.DOBY PRINT RUN 447 COPIES
L.DOBY IS NOT SERIAL-NUMBERED .
L.DOBY PRINT RUN PROVIDED BY FLEER
NO PRICING ON QTY OF 12 OR LESS
AD Andre Dawson 02 GG/130 15.00 4.50
AK Al Kaline 00 GG/6
BBL Bert Blyleven 00 GG/57 15.00 4.50
BBO1 Bobby Bonds 00 GG/24 25.00 7.50
BBO2 Bobby Bonds 01 GG/3
BF Bob Feller 00 GG/36 25.00 7.50
BG1 Bob Gibson 01 PREM DE/3
BG2 B.Gibson 02 ULT FC/125 20.00 6.00
BM B.Maz 02 ULT FC/167 20.00 6.00
BP Boog Powell 00 GG/1
BR Brooks Robinson 02 GG/64 25.00 7.50
BS Bruce Sutter 00 GG/83 15.00 4.50
BW Billy Williams 02 GG/126 15.00 4.50
CB Clete Boyer 00 GG/65 15.00 4.50
CC Cecil Cooper 00 GG/28 12.00 3.60
CF1 C.Fisk 01 FOC ROY/15 40.00 12.00
CF2 Carlton Fisk 01 PREM DE/3
CF3 Carlton Fisk 02 GG/7
CF4 Carlton Fisk 02 ULT FC/9
DB Don Baylor 00 GG/24 15.00 4.50
DC1 D.Conc 00 GG Black/11
DC2 D.Conc 00 GG Red/12
DE Darrell Evans 00 GG/67 10.00 3.00
DG Dick Groat 00 GG/70 15.00 4.50
DJ Davey Johnson 00 GG/5
DL Don Larsen 00 GG/27 30.00 9.00
DM Don Mattingly 01 PREM DE/3
DP1 Dave Parker 00 GG/3
DP2 Dave Parker 02 GG/61 15.00 4.50
DR Dave Righetti 00 GG/1
DS Duke Snider 02 GG/71 20.00 6.00
DW Dave Winfield 02 GG/64 15.00 4.50
EM1 Eddie Murray 02 GG/33 40.00 12.00
EM2 Eddie Murray 02 ULT FC/13
ES Enos Slaughter 00 GG/52 25.00 7.50
FH Frank Howard 00 GG/104 15.00 4.50
FJ Fergie Jenkins 00 GG/61 15.00 4.50
FL Fred Lynn 02 GG/126 10.00 3.00
FR F.Robinson 02 ULT FC/20 40.00 12.00
FW Frank White 00 GG/30 12.00 3.60
GB George Brett 02 GG/2
GK1 George Kell 00 GG/30 20.00 6.00
GK2 George Kell 02 GG Black/10
GK3 George Kell 02 GG Blue/40 15.00 4.50
GP1 Gaylord Perry 00 GG/70 15.00 4.50
GP2 Gaylord Perry 02 GG/52 15.00 4.50
GT Gorman Thomas 00 GG/85 10.00 3.00
HB1 Hank Bauer 00 GG/4
HB2 Hank Bauer 02 GG/65 15.00 4.50
HM Hal McRae 00 GG/25 15.00 4.50
HS1 Herb Score 00 GG/56 15.00 4.50
HS2 Herb Score 00 GG ROY/46 15.00 4.50
HW1 Hoyt Wilhelm 02 GG/12
HW2 H.Wilhelm 02 GG Black/36 15.00 4.50
HW3 H.Wilhelm 02 GG Blue/20 25.00 7.50
JB Jim Bouton 00 GG/71 10.00 3.00
JB1 Johnny Bench 02 GG/140 50.00 15.00
JB2 Johnny Bench 02 ULT FC/5
JK Jim Kaat 00 GG/58 15.00 4.50
JM Jack Morris 00 GG/81 15.00 4.50
JP Joe Pepitone 00 GG/82 15.00 4.50
JP1 Jim Palmer 02 GG/62 15.00 4.50
JP2 Jim Palmer 02 ULT FC/18 25.00 7.50
JR Jim Rice 00 GG/14
LA Luis Aparicio 00 GG/16 25.00 7.50
LBO Lou Boudreau 00 GG/12
LBR Lou Brock 02 GG/18 40.00 12.00
LD Larry Doby 01 GG/447 * 30.00 9.00
LS Lee Smith 00 GG/24 25.00 7.50
ML Mickey Lolich 00 GG/40 25.00 7.50
MS Moose Skowron 00 GG/58 15.00 4.50
MW Maury Wills 01 GG/12
OC1 Orlando Cepeda 00 GG/31 20.00 6.00
OC2 O.Cepeda 02 GG/174 15.00 4.50
PB Paul Blair 02 GG/67 10.00 3.00
PG Phil Garner 00 GG/55 10.00 3.00
PRI1 Phil Rizzuto 02 GG/49 30.00 9.00
PRO1 Preacher Roe 00 GG/52 25.00 7.50
PRO2 Preacher Roe 02 GG/68 20.00 6.00
RCA Rod Carew 01 PREM DE/2
RCE Ron Cey 00 GG/22 25.00 7.50
RCO Rocky Colavito 02 GG/72 40.00 12.00
RG Ron Guidry 00 GG/2
RJ1 Reggie Jackson 01 PREM DE/1
RJ2 Reggie Jackson 02 GG/5
RK Ralph Kiner 00 GG/17 40.00 12.00
RS Ryne Sandberg 02 GG/49 60.00 18.00
RY Robin Yount 02 ULT FC/24 80.00 24.00
SA S.Anderson 02 GG/112 15.00 4.50
SC Steve Carlton 02 GG/99 20.00 6.00
TG Tony Gwynn 02 TRAD TDH/5
TL Tommy Lasorda 01 GG/7
TO1 Tony Oliva 00 GG/110 15.00 4.50
TO2 Tony Oliva 01 GG/3
TO3 Tony Oliva 02 GG/58 15.00 4.50
TP Tony Perez 02 ULT FC/160 20.00 6.00
TS Tom Seaver 02 ULT FC/7
VB1 Vida Blue 00 GG/124 10.00 3.00
VB2 Vida Blue 02 GG/60 10.00 3.00
WB Wade Boggs 01 GG/1
WF Whitey Ford 02 GG/67 30.00 9.00
WM1 W.McCovey 01 GG/92 40.00 12.00
WM2 W.McCovey 02 GG/142 25.00 7.50
WM3 W.McCov 02 ULT FC/27 60.00 18.00
WR Willie Randolph 00 GG/8
WS Warren Spahn 02 GG/63 30.00 9.00
YB Yogi Berra 02 GG/43 40.00 12.00

2004 National Pastime Buyback Game Used

Nm-Mt Ex-Mt
OVERALL GAME USED ODDS 1:60 HOBBY
PRINT RUNS B/WN 1-32 COPIES PER
NO PRICING ON QTY OF 14 OR LESS
BD Bill Dickey 02 PREM LD Bat/2
BG Bob Gibson 02 GG DD Jsy/17 25.00 7.50
w/Duke Snider
BJ B.Jackson 02 GG TY Jsy/24 40.00 12.00
BR1 Brooks Robinson 01 GG FGC Bat/13
BR2 B.Rob 02 GG TY Bat/24 20.00 6.00
CF1 C.Fisk 02 GG TY Fld Jsy/25 20.00 6.00
CF2 C.Fisk 02 GG TY Hit Jsy/29 20.00 6.00
CH Catfish Hunter 01 GG FGC Jsy/4
CR1 Cal Ripken 00 GAM LUM Bat/8
CR2 Cal Ripken 00 SHOW FG Jsy/8
CR3 Cal Ripken 01 AUTH DC Pants/8
CR4 Cal Ripken 01 AUTH DC Btg Glv/1
CR5 C.Rip 01 FUT BL Base/15 120.00 36.00
CR6 Cal Ripken 01 LEG GI Base/4
CR7 Cal Ripken 01 LEG HG Fld Glv/3
CR8 Cal Ripken 01 TRAD TBC Jsy/10
CR9 Cal Ripken 02 GG DD Bat/17 120.00 36.00
w/George Brett
CY C.Yaz 02 GG TY Jsy/22 40.00 12.00
DE D.Eckersley 02 FC OL Jsy/3
DM1 Don Mattingly 01 FUT BF Bat/5
DM2 Don Mattingly 02 GG DD Bat/10
w/Wade Boggs
DM3 Don Mattingly 02 GG DD Bat/23 40.00 12.00
w/Paul Molitor
DM4 Don Mattingly 02 GG DD Bat/10
w/Kirby Puckett
DM5 Don Matt 02 GG TY Jsy/23 40.00 12.00
DP Dave Parker 01 FUT BF Bat/12
DS D.Sand 01 Auth DC Jsy/21 40.00 12.00
EH1 Elston Howard 01 GG FGC Bat/13
EH2 Elston Howard 01 TRAD ST Jsy/3
EMU E.Murray 02 GG TY Jsy/23 25.00 7.50
EMA1 Eddie Mathews 01 GG FGC Bat/9
EMA2 Eddie Mathews 02 GG DD Bat/19 40.00 12.00
w/Duke Snider
ES1 Enos Slaughter 01 GG FGC Bat/14
ES2 Enos Slaughter 02 GG DD Bat/15 25.00 7.50
w/Ted Kluszewski
EW Earl Weaver 02 GG DD Jsy/4
w/Sparky Anderson
FF Frankie Frisch 02 FC OL Pants/5
GB1 George Brett 01 GG FGC Jsy/1
GB2 George Brett 02 GG DD Bat/18 50.00 15.00
w/Cal Ripken
GB3 G.Brett 02 GG TY Jsy/21 50.00 15.00
GC Gary Carter 02 FC OL Jsy/8
HG Hank Greenberg 01 GG FGC Bat/11
HH Harry Heilmann 01 GG FGC Bat/12
HK Harmon Killebrew 01 GG FGC Bat/13
HW Hack Wilson 01 GG FGC Bat/12
JM Johnny Mize 01 GG FGC Bat/13
JP1 Jim Palmer 01 GG FGC Jsy/13
JP2 Jim Palmer 02 GG TY Jsy/14
JRO Jackie Robinson 02 GG TY Pants/3
JRI1 Jim Rice 01 FUT BF Bat/14
JRI2 Jim Rice 02 GG DD Bat/14
w/Reggie Jackson
KH K.Hernandez 02 FC OL Bat/2
KP Kirby Puckett 02 GG DD Bat/15 50.00 15.00
w/Don Mattingly
LA Luis Aparicio 01 GG FGC Bat/12
LB Lou Brock 01 GG FGC Jsy/6
LD Larry Doby 01 TRAD ST Bat/2
LP L.Pin 01 LEG TM Jsy/29 15.00 4.50
MM1 M.McGw 01 Fut BL Base/18 60.00 18.00
MM2 Mark McGwire 01 LEG GI Base/10
MS M.Schm 01 FUT BF Bat/20 40.00 12.00
NF Nellie Fox GG DD Bat/15 40.00 12.00
w/Rocky Colavito
NR1 N.Ryan 01 LEG TM Jsy/34 60.00 18.00
NR2 N.Ryan 02 GG TY Jsy/20 60.00 18.00
OC1 O.Cep 01 GG FGC Bat/16 25.00 7.50
OC2 O.Cep 01 LEG TM Jsy/32 15.00 4.50
PM1 Paul Molitor 01 GG FGC Jsy/11
PM2 Paul Molitor 02 FC OL Bat/2
PM3 Paul Molitor 02 GG DD Bat/16 25.00 7.50
w/Dave Winfield
PM4 P.Mol 02 GG TY Brw Jsy/18 25.00 7.50
PM5 P.Mol 02 GG TY Jays Jsy/23 20.00 6.00
RC1 Roy Campanella 01 TRAD ST Jsy/2
RC2 R.Camp 02 GG DD F.Glv/15 40.00 12.00
RF Rollie Fingers 02 PREM LD Jsy/4
RJ1 Reggie Jackson 02 GG DD Bat/15 25.00 7.50
w/Jim Rice
RJ2 R.Jack 02 GG TY A's Jsy/25 20.00 6.00
RJ3 Reggie Jackson 02 GG TY Angels Jsy/12
RM Roger Maris 01 GG FGC Bat/1
RY1 R.Yount 01 FUT BF Bat/19 40.00 12.00
RY2 R.Yount 02 GG TY Jsy/18 40.00 12.00
TG1 T.Gwy 01 AUTH DC Bat/32 40.00 12.00
TG2 T.Gwy 01 FUT BL Base/19 40.00 12.00
TG3 Tony Gwynn 01 LEG HG Fld Glv/3
TG4 Tony Gwynn 01 TRAD TBC Jsy/11
TK T.Klusz 02 GG TY Jsy/18 25.00 7.50
TP1 Tony Perez 01 GG FGC Bat/12
TP2 Tony Perez 02 GG DD Bat/5
w/Carl Yastrzemski
TP3 T.Perez 02 GG TY Jsy/22 20.00 6.00
TS Tom Seaver 01 GG FGC Jsy/6
WB W.Boggs 02 GG TY Jsy/26 20.00 6.00
WF Whitey Ford 01 GG FGC Jsy/4
WM1 Willie McCovey 01 GG FGC Bat/13
WM2 Willie McCovey 01 LEG TM Jsy/1
WM3 W.McCov 02 GG TY Jsy/15 25.00 7.50
YB1 Y.Berra 02 GG DD Bat/15 25.00 7.50
YB2 Y.Berra 02 GG DD Bat/15 25.00 7.50

2004 National Pastime History in the Making

Nm-Mt Ex-Mt
STATED ODDS 1:5 HOBBY, 1:4 RETAIL
1 Pedro Martinez 1.50 .45
2 Alex Rodriguez 2.50 .75
3 Sammy Sosa 3.00 .90
4 Mike Piazza 3.00 .90
5 Jason Giambi 1.00 .30
6 Jim Thome 1.50 .45
7 Derek Jeter 4.00 1.20
8 Hideo Nomo 1.50 .45
9 Nomar Garciaparra 3.00 .90
10 Albert Pujols 4.00 1.20
11 Greg Maddux 3.00 .90
12 Randy Johnson 1.50 .45
13 Roger Clemens 4.00 1.20
14 Ichiro Suzuki 3.00 .90
15 Vladimir Guerrero 1.50 .45
16 Chipper Jones 1.50 .45
17 Ken Griffey 3.00 .90
18 Manny Ramirez 1.50 .45
19 Ivan Rodriguez 1.50 .45
20 Mark Prior 1.50 .45
21 Austin Kearns 1.00 .30
22 Alfonso Soriano 1.50 .45
23 Barry Zito 1.00 .30
24 Josh Beckett 1.00 .30
25 Angel Berroa 1.00 .30
26 Jose Reyes 1.00 .30
27 Adam Dunn 1.50 .45
28 Todd Helton 1.50 .45
29 Hank Blalock 1.00 .30
30 Kaz Matsui 4.00 1.20

2004 National Pastime History in the Making Dual Bat

Nm-Mt Ex-Mt
OVERALL GAME USED ODDS 1:60 HOBBY
STATED PRINT RUN 5 SERIAL #'d CARDS
NO PRICING DUE TO SCARCITY
BRJF Babe Ruth Bat
Jimmie Foxx Bat/5

2004 National Pastime History in the Making Jersey

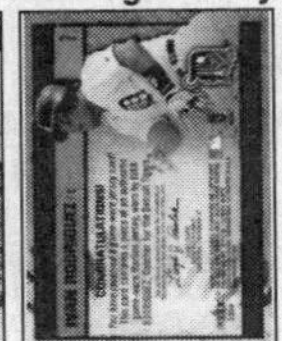

Nm-Mt Ex-Mt
STATED ODDS 1:36 RETAIL
SP INFO PROVIDED BY FLEER
SP'S ARE NOT SERIAL-NUMBERED
*PATCH p/r 37-50: 1.25X TO 3X JSY .
*PATCHp/r42-50: 1.2X TO 3X JSY SP 150-200
*PATCH p/r 41-49: 1X TO 2.5X JSY SP 75-100
*PATCH p/r 32: 1.5X TO 4X JSY SP 150-200
*PATCH p/r 26: 1.25X TO 3X JSY SP 75-100
*PATCH p/r 20-24: 2X TO 5X JSY
PATCH PRINTS B/WN 20-50 COPIES PER
K.MATSUI PATCH TOO VOLATILE TO PRICE
PATCH MASTERPIECE PRINT RUN 1 #'d SET
NO PATCH MP PRICING DUE TO SCARCITY
OVERALL GU ODDS 1:60 H, AU-GU 1:24 R
PATCH MP ISSUED ONLY IN HOBBY PACKS
AB Angel Berroa 5.00 1.50
AD Adam Dunn SP/100 10.00 3.00
AK Austin Kearns SP/100 8.00 2.40
AP Albert Pujols 15.00 4.50
AR Alex Rodriguez 10.00 3.00
AS Alfonso Soriano 8.00 2.40
BZ Barry Zito 5.00 1.50
CJ Chipper Jones 8.00 2.40
DJ Derek Jeter 20.00 6.00
GM Greg Maddux SP/150 12.00 3.60
HB Hank Blalock 5.00 1.50
HN Hideo Nomo 8.00 2.40
IR Ivan Rodriguez SP/150 10.00 3.00
JB Josh Beckett 5.00 1.50
JG Jason Giambi 5.00 1.50
JR Jose Reyes 5.00 1.50
JT Jim Thome 8.00 2.40
KM Kaz Matsui 25.00 7.50
MP Mike Piazza SP/200 12.00 3.60
MPR Mark Prior 8.00 2.40
MR Manny Ramirez 8.00 2.40
PM Pedro Martinez 8.00 2.40
RC Roger Clemens SP/75 15.00 4.50
RJ Randy Johnson 8.00 2.40
SS Sammy Sosa 10.00 3.00
TH Todd Helton SP/200 10.00 3.00
VG Vladimir Guerrero 8.00 2.40

2004 National Pastime National Treasures

Nm-Mt Ex-Mt
STATED PRINT RUN 500 SERIAL #'d SETS
*GOLD p/r 75-94: .75X TO 2X BASIC .
*GOLD p/r 49: 1X TO 2.5X BASIC
*GOLD p/r 19: 2X TO 5X BASIC
GOLD PRINT RUNS B/WN 2-94 COPIES PER
NO GOLD PRICING ON QTY OF 2 OR LESS
OVERALL NAT'L.TREA.ODDS 1:12 H, 1:240 R
GOLD ISSUED ONLY IN HOBBY PACKS
2 Kenesaw Landis 2.00 .60
5 Leo Durocher 2.00 .60
9 Peter Gammons 2.00 .60
10 Ernie Harwell 3.00 .90
11 Billy Martin 3.00 .90
12 John McGraw 3.00 .90
13 Red Barber 2.00 .60
15 Casey Stengel 3.00 .90

16 Sparky Anderson 2.00 .60
17 Harry Caray 3.00 .90
18 Ban Johnson 2.00 .60
20 Ralph Kiner 3.00 .90

2004 National Pastime National Treasures Autograph Red

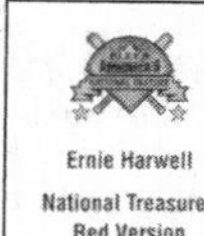

Ernie Harwell
National Treasures
Red Version
Autograph
Redemption Card

Nm-Mt Ex-Mt
STATED PRINT RUN 50 SERIAL #'d SETS
BLUE PRINT RUN 6 SERIAL #'d SETS
NO BLUE PRICING DUE TO SCARCITY
M'PIECE PRINT RUN 1 SERIAL #'d SET
NO M'PIECE PRICING DUE TO SCARCITY
*WHITE p/r 22-30: .6X TO 1.5X RED..
WHITE PRINT RUNS B/WN 1-30 COPIES PER
NO WHITE PRICING ON QTY OF 2 OR LESS
OVERALL AUTO ODDS 1:5 HOBBY....
EXCHANGE DEADLINE INDEFINITE ....
EH Ernie Harwell EXCH 25.00 7.50
PG Peter Gammons EXCH 25.00 7.50
RK Ralph Kiner EXCH 25.00 7.50

2004 National Pastime Signature Swings Gold

Nm-Mt Ex-Mt
OVERALL AU ODDS 1:5 HOBBY, 1:24 RETAIL
PRINT RUNS B/WN 3-265 COPIES PER
NO PRICING ON QTY OF 10 OR LESS
EXCHANGE DEADLINE INDEFINITE ....
AJ Andruw Jones/23 25.00 7.50
AK1 Al Kaline/79 40.00 12.00
AK2 Austin Kearns/20 25.00 7.50
AP Albert Pujols/110 EXCH 150.00 45.00
AT Alan Trammell/138 15.00 4.50
BD Bucky Dent/21 25.00 7.50
BM Bill Mazeroski/61 30.00 9.00
CB Carlos Beltran/176 EXCH 25.00 7.50
CF Carlton Fisk/36 30.00 9.00
CJ Chipper Jones/109 40.00 12.00
CP Corey Patterson/8
CR Cal Ripken/6
DE David Eckstein/161 15.00 4.50
DJ Derek Jeter/35 150.00 45.00
DM Don Mattingly/15 100.00 30.00
DP Dave Parker/57 20.00 6.00
EC Eric Chavez/138 EXCH 15.00 4.50
EM Edgar Martinez/85 25.00 7.50
FH Frank Howard/60 20.00 6.00
GS Gary Sheffield/25 40.00 12.00
HB Hank Blalock/265 15.00 4.50
JC Joe Carter/95 15.00 4.50
JE Jim Edmonds/10
JL Javy Lopez/220 EXCH 15.00 4.50
JP1 Jim Palmer/33 EXCH 25.00 7.50
LB Lance Berkman/172 15.00 4.50
LF Lew Ford/183 15.00 4.50
LG Luis Gonzalez/61 20.00 6.00
MP Mike Piazza/64 EXCH 120.00 36.00
MT Miguel Tejada/3
SC Sean Casey/169 15.00 4.50
SM Stan Musial/15 100.00 30.00
VG Vladimir Guerrero/4
WS Warren Spahn/188 EXCH 25.00 7.50

2004 National Pastime Signature Swings Red

Nm-Mt Ex-Mt
REDp/r106-109:.5X TO 1.2X GOLDp/r169-265
RED p/r 106-109: .25X TO .6X GOLD p/r 61
RED p/r 73-98: .6X TO 1.5X GOLDp/r161-173
RED p/r 73-98: .5X TO 1.2X GOLDp/r109-138
RED p/r 73-98: .3X TO .8X GOLD p/r 57
RED p/r 73-98: .25X TO .6X GOLD p/r 15
RED p/r 36-65: .75X TO 2X GOLD p/r 220
RED p/r 36-65: .5X TO 1.2X GOLD p/r 79
RED p/r 36-65: .4X TO 1X GOLD p/r 36-61
RED p/r 36-65: .2X TO .5X GOLD p/r 15
RED p/r 26-35: .5X TO 1.2X GOLD p/r 64
RED p/r 26-35: .3X TO .8X GOLD p/r 21-25
RED p/r 22-25: .75X TO 2X GOLD p/r 85-95
RED p/r 22-25: .6X TO 1.5X GOLD p/r 60
RED p/r 22-25: .5X TO 1.2X GOLD p/r 33-35
VERALL AU ODDS 1:5 H, AU-GU 1:24 R
RINT RUNS B/WN 22-109 COPIES PER
XCHANGE DEADLINE INDEFINITE ....
B George Brett/42 100.00 30.00
E Jim Edmonds/22 50.00 15.00

JG2 Jay Gibbons/33 15.00 4.50
JP2 Juan Pierre/52
MS2 Moose Skowron/59 20.00 6.00

2004 National Pastime Signature Swings White

Nm-Mt Ex-Mt
*WHITEp/r36-65: .75X TO 2X GOLDp/r173-220
*WHITEp/r36-65:.6X TO 1.5X GOLDp/r109-110
*WHITE p/r 36-65: .5X TO 1.2X GOLD p/r 85
*WHITE p/r 36-65: .4X TO 1X GOLD p/r 36-64
*WHITE p/r 36-65: .25X TO .6X GOLD p/r 25
*WHITE p/r 36-65: .2X TO .5X GOLD p/r 15
*WHITEp/r28-35:1X TO 2.5X GOLDp/r176-265
*WHITE p/r 28-35: .75X TO 2X GOLD p/r 138
*WHITE p/r 28-35: .6X TO 1.5X GOLDp/r79-95
*WHITE p/r 28-35: .5X TO 1.2X GOLD p/r 57
*WHITE p/r 28-35: .3X TO .8X GOLD p/r 15
*WHITE p/r 24-25: 1.25X TO 3X GOLD p/r 169
*WHITE p/r 24-25: .5X TO 1.2X GOLD p/r 35
*WHITE p/r 19: .75X TO 2X GOLD p/r 61
OVERALL AU ODDS 1:5 H, AU-GU 1:24 R
PRINT RUNS B/WN 1-57 COPIES PER
NO PRICING ON QTY OF 14 OR LESS
EXCHANGE DEADLINE INDEFINITE ....
AH Aubrey Huff/34 25.00 7.50
CR Cal Ripken/25 200.00 60.00
FT Frank Thomas/43 50.00 15.00
GB George Brett/30 120.00 36.00
IR Ivan Rodriguez/35 60.00 18.00
JE Jim Edmonds/42 30.00 9.00
JG2 Jay Gibbons/28 15.00 4.50
MS2 Moose Skowron/28 25.00 7.50
RP Rafael Palmeiro/47 50.00 15.00
SR Scott Rolen/28 60.00 18.00
VG Vladimir Guerrero/44 50.00 15.00

2004 National Pastime Signature Swings Bat Blue

Nm-Mt Ex-Mt
PRINT RUNS B/WN 2-44 COPIES PER
NO PRICING ON QTY OF 14 OR LESS
M'PIECE PRINT RUN 1 SERIAL #'d SET
NO M'PIECE PRICING DUE TO SCARCITY
OVERALL AU ODDS 1:5 H, AU-GU 1:24 R
EXCHANGE DEADLINE INDEFINITE ....
AD Adam Dunn/31 40.00 12.00
AK1 Al Kaline/5
AP Albert Pujols/10 EXCH
AT Alan Trammell/19 40.00 12.00
BD Bucky Dent/15 40.00 12.00
BM Bill Mazeroski/39 40.00 12.00
CB Carlos Beltran/19 EXCH 80.00 24.00
CF Carlton Fisk/17 60.00 18.00
CJ Chipper Jones/7
CP Corey Patterson/5
CR Cal Ripken/8
DE David Eckstein/44 25.00 7.50
DJ Derek Jeter/2
DM Don Mattingly/23 120.00 36.00
DP Dave Parker/29 25.00 7.50
EC Eric Chavez/21 EXCH 30.00 9.00
EM Edgar Martinez/11
FH Frank Howard/7
GB George Brett/6
GS Gary Sheffield/5
HB Hank Blalock/16 40.00 12.00
IR Ivan Rodriguez/19 80.00 24.00
JC Joe Carter/11
JE Jim Edmonds/37 40.00 12.00
JG2 Jay Gibbons/6
JL Javy Lopez/12 EXCH
JP1 Jim Palmer/44 EXCH 25.00 7.50
JP2 Juan Pierre/9
LB Lance Berkman/11
LF Lew Ford/44 25.00 7.50
MP Mike Piazza/14 EXCH
MS2 Moose Skowron/11
RP Rafael Palmeiro/19 80.00 24.00
SC Sean Casey/37 25.00 7.50
SM Stan Musial/9 EXCH
SP Scott Podsednik/38 25.00 7.50
VG Vladimir Guerrero/7
WS Warren Spahn/26 EXCH 50.00 15.00

2004 National Pastime Signs of the Future Blue

Nm-Mt Ex-Mt
*BLUE p/r 98: .2X TO .5X GOLD p/r 21
OVERALL AU ODDS 1:5 H, AU-GU 1:24 R
PRINT RUNS B/WN 1-98 COPIES PER
NO PRICING ON QTY OF 4 OR LESS
EXCHANGE DEADLINE INDEFINITE ....
KW Kerry Wood/98 40.00 12.00

2004 National Pastime Signs of the Future Gold

Nm-Mt Ex-Mt
OVERALL AU ODDS 1:5 H, AU-GU 1:24 R
PRINT RUNS B/WN 21-340 COPIES PER
EXCHANGE DEADLINE INDEFINITE ....
AE Adam Everett/285 8.00 2.40
AL Adam LaRoche/78 10.00 3.00
AR Alexis Rios/45 15.00 4.50
AS Alfredo Simon/258 8.00 2.40
BC Bobby Crosby/299 20.00 6.00
DW Dontrelle Willis/47 15.00 4.50
JB Jeremy Bonderman/300 EXCH 8.00 2.40
JV Javier Vazquez/21 25.00 7.50
KG Khalil Greene/300 30.00 9.00
KH Koyie Hill/340 8.00 2.40
KY Kevin Youkilis/317 10.00 3.00
LG Luis A. Gonzalez/264 EXCH 8.00 2.40
MC Miguel Cabrera/300 15.00 4.50
MG Mike Gosling/195 8.00 2.40
MN Michael Nakamura/231 8.00 2.40
RH1 Rich Harden/304 10.00 3.00
RH2 Ryan Howard/53 25.00 7.50
RW1 Ryan Wagner/251 8.00 2.40
SH Sean Henn/300 8.00 2.40
TH Tim Hudson/72 25.00 7.50

2004 National Pastime Signs of the Future Red

Nm-Mt Ex-Mt
*REDp/r106-133: .5X TO 1.2X GOLDp/r195-317
*RED p/r 106-133: .3X TO .8X GOLD p/r 78
*RED p/r 98: .6X TO 1.5X GOLD p/r 251
*RED p/r 58: .75X TO 2X GOLD p/r 340
OVERALL AU ODDS 1:5 H, AU-GU 1:24 R
PRINT RUNS B/WN 52-133 COPIES PER
EXCHANGE DEADLINE INDEFINITE ....
AB1 Aarom Baldiris/64 15.00 4.50
AB2 A.J. Burnett/58 10.00 3.00
BN Bubba Nelson/99 10.00 3.00
CS Chris Shelton/55 25.00 7.50
EJ Edwin Jackson/52 15.00 4.50
GK Graham Koonce/55 10.00 3.00
JL1 Josh Labandeira/55 10.00 3.00
JL2 Justin Leone/68 15.00 4.50
JR Jose Reyes/93 15.00 4.50
KW Kerry Wood/55 40.00 12.00
MR Michael Rouse/124 8.00 2.40

2004 National Pastime Signs of the Future White

Nm-Mt Ex-Mt
*WHITEp/r36-65: .75X TO 2X GOLDp/r195-317
*WHITE p/r 36-65: .5X TO 1.2X GOLD p/r 78
*WHITE p/r 36-65: .4X TO 1X GOLD p/r 45
*WHITEp/r26-35: 1X TO 2.5X GOLDp/r231-340
*WHITE p/r 26-35: .6X TO 1.5X GOLD p/r 72
*WHITE p/r 26-35: .3X TO .8X GOLD p/r 21
*WHITE p/r 20-21: 1.25X TO 3X GOLD p/r 300
*WHITE p/r 20-21: .6X TO 1.5X GOLD p/r 47
*WHITE p/r 15: .75X TO 2X GOLD p/r 53
OVERALL AU ODDS 1:5 H, AU-GU 1:24 R
PRINT RUNS B/WN 10-52 COPIES PER
NO PRICING ON QTY OF 10 OR LESS
NO RC YR PRICING ON QTY OF 25 OR LESS
EXCHANGE DEADLINE INDEFINITE ....
AB2 A.J. Burnett/22 15.00 4.50
EJ Edwin Jackson/24 25.00 7.50
GA Garrett Atkins/25 15.00 4.50
JR Jose Reyes/52 15.00 4.50
KW Kerry Wood/19 50.00 15.00
MR Michael Rouse/40 10.00 3.00
RW2 Rickie Weeks/17 25.00 7.50

1984 Nestle 792

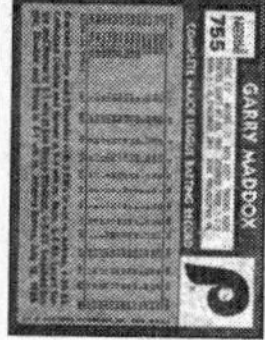

The cards in this 792-card standard-size set are extremely similar to the 1984 Topps regular issue (except for the Nestle logo instead of Topps logo on the front). In conjunction with Topps, the Nestle Company issued this set as six sheets available as a premium. The set was (as detailed on the back of the checklist card for the Nestle Dream Team cards) originally available from the Nestle Company in full sheets of 132 cards, 24" by 48", for 4.95 plus five Nestle candy wrappers per sheet. The backs are virtually identical to the Topps cards of this year, i.e., same player-number correspondence. These sheets have been cut up into individual cards and are available from a few dealers around the country. This is one of the few instances in this hobby where the complete uncut sheet is worth considerably less than the sum of the individual cards due to the expense required in having the sheet cut professionally (and precisely) into individual cards. Supposedly less than 5000 sets were printed. Since the checklist is exactly the same as that of the 1984 Topps, these Nestle cards are generally priced as a multiple of the corresponding Topps card. Individual Nestle cards are priced at up to eight times the corresponding 1984 Topps price. Please see multiplication tables below. Beware also on this set to look for fakes and forgeries. Cards billed as Nestle proofs in black and white are fakes; there are even a few counterfeits in color.

Nm-Mt Ex-Mt
COMP. CUT SET (792) 350.00 140.00
*STARS:4X to 8X BASIC CARDS ....
*ROOKIES: 3X to 6X BASIC CARDS ...

1994 Pacific

The 660 standard-size cards comprising this set feature color player action shots on their fronts that are borderless, except at the bottom, where a team color-coded marbleized border set off by a gold-foil line carries the team color-coded player's name. The cards are grouped alphabetically within teams. The set closes with an Award Winners subset (655-660). There are no key Rookie Cards in this set.

Nm-Mt Ex-Mt
COMPLETE SET (660) 50.00 15.00
1 Steve Avery .10 .03
2 Steve Bedrosian .10 .03
3 Damon Berryhill .10 .03
4 Jeff Blauser .10 .03
5 Sid Bream .10 .03
6 Francisco Cabrera .10 .03
7 Ramon Caraballo .10 .03
8 Ron Gant .20 .06
9 Tom Glavine .30 .09
10 Chipper Jones .50 .15
11 Dave Justice .20 .06
12 Ryan Klesko .20 .06
13 Mark Lemke .10 .03
14 Javier Lopez .20 .06
15 Greg Maddux .75 .23
16 Fred McGriff .30 .09
17 Greg McMichael .10 .03
18 Kent Mercker .10 .03
19 Otis Nixon .10 .03
20 Terry Pendleton .20 .06
21 Deion Sanders .30 .09
22 John Smoltz .30 .09
23 Tony Tarasco .10 .03
24 Manny Alexander .10 .03
25 Brady Anderson .20 .06
26 Harold Baines .20 .06
27 Damon Buford .10 .03
28 Paul Carey .10 .03
29 Mike Devereaux .10 .03
30 Todd Frohwirth .10 .03
31 Leo Gomez .10 .03
32 Jeffrey Hammonds .10 .03
33 Chris Hoiles .10 .03
34 Tim Hulett .10 .03
35 Ben McDonald .10 .03
36 Mark McLemore .10 .03
37 Alan Mills .10 .03
38 Mike Mussina .30 .09
39 Sherman Obando .10 .03
40 Gregg Olson .10 .03
41 Mike Pagliarulo .10 .03
42 Jim Poole .10 .03
43 Harold Reynolds .20 .06
44 Cal Ripken 1.50 .45
45 David Segui .10 .03
46 Fernando Valenzuela .20 .06
47 Jack Voigt .10 .03
48 Scott Bankhead .10 .03
49 Roger Clemens 1.00 .30
50 Scott Cooper .10 .03
51 Danny Darwin .10 .03
52 Andre Dawson .20 .06
53 John Dopson .10 .03
54 Scott Fletcher .10 .03
55 Tony Fossas .10 .03
56 Mike Greenwell .10 .03
57 Billy Hatcher .10 .03
58 Jeff McNeely .10 .03
59 Jose Melendez .10 .03
60 Tim Naehring .10 .03
61 Tony Pena .10 .03
62 Paul Quantrill .10 .03
63 Carlos Quintana .10 .03
64 Luis Rivera .10 .03
65 Jeff Russell .10 .03
66 Aaron Sele .10 .03
67 John Valentin .10 .03
68 Mo Vaughn .20 .06
69 Frank Viola .20 .06
70 Bob Zupcic .10 .03
71 Mike Butcher .10 .03
72 Rod Correia .10 .03
73 Chad Curtis .10 .03
74 Chili Davis .20 .06
75 Gary DiSarcina .10 .03
76 Damion Easley .10 .03
77 John Farrell .10 .03
78 Chuck Finley .20 .06
79 Joe Grahe .10 .03
80 Stan Javier .10 .03
81 Mark Langston .10 .03
82 Phil Leftwich RC .10 .03
83 Torey Lovullo .10 .03
84 Joe Magrane .10 .03
85 Greg Myers .10 .03
86 Eduardo Perez .10 .03
87 Luis Polonia .10 .03
88 Tim Salmon .30 .09
89 J.T. Snow .20 .06
90 Kurt Stillwell .10 .03
91 Ron Tingley .10 .03
92 Chris Turner .10 .03
93 Julio Valera .10 .03
94 Jose Bautista .10 .03
95 Shawn Boskie .10 .03
96 Steve Buechele .10 .03
97 Frank Castillo .10 .03
98 Mark Grace UER .30 .09
(stats have 98 home runs in 1993; should be 14)
99 Jose Guzman .10 .03
100 Mike Harkey .10 .03
101 Greg Hibbard .10 .03
102 Doug Jennings .10 .03
103 Derrick May .10 .03
104 Mike Morgan .10 .03
105 Randy Myers .10 .03
106 Karl Rhodes .10 .03
107 Kevin Roberson .10 .03
108 Rey Sanchez .10 .03
109 Ryne Sandberg .75 .23
110 Tommy Shields .10 .03
111 Dwight Smith .10 .03
112 Sammy Sosa .75 .23
113 Jose Vizcaino .10 .03
114 Turk Wendell .10 .03
115 Rick Wilkins .10 .03
116 Willie Wilson .10 .03
117 Ed. Zambrano RC .10 .03
118 Wilson Alvarez .10 .03
119 Tim Belcher .10 .03
120 Jason Bere .10 .03
121 Rodney Bolton .10 .03
122 Ellis Burks .20 .06
123 Joey Cora .10 .03
124 Alex Fernandez .10 .03
125 Ozzie Guillen .10 .03
126 Craig Grebeck .10 .03
127 Roberto Hernandez .10 .03
128 Bo Jackson .50 .15
129 Lance Johnson .10 .03
130 Ron Karkovice .10 .03
131 Mike LaValliere .10 .03
132 Norberto Martin .10 .03
133 Kirk McCaskill .10 .03
134 Jack McDowell .10 .03
135 Scott Radinsky .10 .03
136 Tim Raines .20 .06
137 Steve Sax .10 .03
138 Frank Thomas .50 .15
139 Dan Pasqua .10 .03
140 Robin Ventura .20 .06
141 Jeff Branson .10 .03
142 Tom Browning .10 .03
143 Jacob Brumfield .10 .03
144 Tim Costo .10 .03
145 Rob Dibble .20 .06
146 Brian Dorsett .10 .03
147 Steve Foster .10 .03
148 Cesar Hernandez .10 .03
149 Roberto Kelly .10 .03
150 Barry Larkin .30 .09
151 Larry Luebbers .10 .03
152 Kevin Mitchell .10 .03
153 Joe Oliver .10 .03
154 Tim Pugh .10 .03
155 Jeff Reardon .20 .06
156 Jose Rijo .10 .03
157 Bip Roberts .10 .03
158 Chris Sabo .10 .03
159 Juan Samuel .10 .03
160 Reggie Sanders .10 .03
161 John Smiley .10 .03
162 Jerry Spradlin .10 .03
163 Gary Varsho .10 .03
164 Sandy Alomar Jr. .10 .03
165 Albert Belle .20 .06
166 Carlos Baerga .10 .03
167 Mark Clark .10 .03
168 Alvaro Espinoza .10 .03
169 Felix Fermin .10 .03
170 Reggie Jefferson .10 .03
171 Wayne Kirby .10 .03
172 Tom Kramer .10 .03
173 Kenny Lofton .20 .06
174 Jesse Levis .10 .03
175 Candy Maldonado .10 .03
176 Carlos Martinez .10 .03
177 Jose Mesa .10 .03
178 Jeff Mutis .10 .03
179 Charles Nagy .10 .03
180 Bob Ojeda .10 .03
181 Junior Ortiz .10 .03
182 Eric Plunk .10 .03
183 Manny Ramirez .30 .09
184 Jeff Treadway .10 .03
185 Bill Wertz .10 .03
186 Paul Sorrento .10 .03
187 Freddie Benavides .10 .03
188 Dante Bichette .20 .06
189 Willie Blair .10 .03
190 Daryl Boston .10 .03
191 Pedro Castellano .10 .03

192 Vinny Castilla .20 .06
193 Jerald Clark .10 .03
194 Alex Cole .10 .03
195 Andres Galarraga .20 .06
196 Joe Girardi .10 .03
197 Charlie Hayes .10 .03
198 Darren Holmes .10 .03
199 Chris Jones .10 .03
200 Curt Leskanic .10 .03
201 Roberto Mejia .10 .03
202 David Nied .10 .03
203 Jayhawk Owens .10 .03
204 Steve Reed .10 .03
205 Armando Reynoso .10 .03
206 Bruce Ruffin .10 .03
207 Keith Shepherd .10 .03
208 Jim Tatum .10 .03
209 Eric Young .10 .03
210 Skeeter Barnes .10 .03
211 Danny Bautista .10 .03
212 Tom Bolton .10 .03
213 Eric Davis .20 .06
214 Storm Davis .10 .03
215 Cecil Fielder .20 .06
216 Travis Fryman .20 .06
217 Kirk Gibson .20 .06
218 Dan Gladden .10 .03
219 John Doherty .10 .03
220 Chris Gomez .10 .03
221 David Haas .10 .03
222 Bill Krueger .10 .03
223 Chad Kreuter .10 .03
224 Mark Leiter .10 .03
225 Bob MacDonald .10 .03
226 Mike Moore .10 .03
227 Tony Phillips .10 .03
228 Rich Rowland .10 .03
229 Mickey Tettleton .10 .03
230 Alan Trammell .20 .06
231 Lou Whitaker .20 .06
232 David Wells .20 .06
233 Luis Aquino .10 .03
234 Alex Arias .10 .03
235 Jack Armstrong .10 .03
236 Ryan Bowen .10 .03
237 Chuck Carr .10 .03
238 Matias Carrillo .10 .03
239 Jeff Conine .20 .06
240 Henry Cotto .10 .03
241 Orestes Destrade .10 .03
242 Chris Hammond .10 .03
243 Bryan Harvey .10 .03
244 Charlie Hough .20 .06
245 Richie Lewis .10 .03
246 Mitch Lyden .10 .03
247 Dave Magadan .10 .03
248 Bob Natal .10 .03
249 Benito Santiago .20 .06
250 Gary Sheffield .20 .06
251 Matt Turner .10 .03
252 David Weathers .10 .03
253 Walt Weiss .10 .03
254 Darrell Whitmore .10 .03
255 Nigel Wilson .10 .03
256 Eric Anthony .10 .03
257 Jeff Bagwell .30 .09
258 Kevin Bass .10 .03
259 Craig Biggio .30 .09
260 Ken Caminiti .20 .06
261 Andujar Cedeno .10 .03
262 Chris Donnels .10 .03
263 Doug Drabek .10 .03
264 Tom Edens .10 .03
265 Steve Finley .20 .06
266 Luis Gonzalez .20 .06
267 Pete Harnisch .10 .03
268 Xavier Hernandez .10 .03
269 Todd Jones .10 .03
270 Darryl Kile .20 .06
271 Al Osuna .10 .03
272 Rick Parker .10 .03
273 Mark Portugal .10 .03
274 Scott Servais .10 .03
275 Greg Swindell .10 .03
276 Eddie Taubensee .10 .03
277 Jose Uribe .10 .03
278 Brian Williams .10 .03
279 Kevin Appier .20 .06
280 Billy Brewer .10 .03
281 David Cone .20 .06
282 Greg Gagne .10 .03
283 Tom Gordon .10 .03
284 Chris Gwynn .10 .03
285 John Habyan .10 .03
286 Chris Haney .10 .03
287 Phil Hiatt .10 .03
288 David Howard .10 .03
289 Felix Jose .10 .03
290 Wally Joyner .20 .06
291 Kevin Koslofski .10 .03
292 Jose Lind .10 .03
293 Brent Mayne .10 .03
294 Mike Macfarlane .10 .03
295 Brian McRae .10 .03
296 Kevin McReynolds .10 .03
297 Keith Miller .10 .03
298 Jeff Montgomery .10 .03
299 Hipolito Pichardo .10 .03
300 Rico Rossy .10 .03
301 Curtis Wilkerson .10 .03
302 Pedro Astacio .10 .03
303 Rafael Bournigal .10 .03
304 Brett Butler .20 .06
305 Tom Candiotti .10 .03
306 Omar Daal .10 .03
307 Jim Gott .10 .03
308 Kevin Gross .10 .03
309 Dave Hansen .10 .03
310 Carlos Hernandez .10 .03
311 Orel Hershiser .20 .06
312 Eric Karros .20 .06
313 Pedro Martinez .50 .15
314 Ramon Martinez .10 .03
315 Roger McDowell .10 .03
316 Raul Mondesi .20 .06
317 Jose Offerman .10 .03
318 Mike Piazza 1.00 .30
319 Jody Reed .10 .03
320 Henry Rodriguez .10 .03
321 Cory Snyder .10 .03
322 Darryl Strawberry .20 .06
323 Tim Wallach .10 .03
324 Steve Wilson .10 .03
325 Juan Bell .10 .03
326 Ricky Bones .10 .03
327 Alex Diaz RC .10 .03
328 Cal Eldred .10 .03
329 Darryl Hamilton .10 .03
330 Doug Henry .10 .03
331 John Jaha .10 .03
332 Pat Listach .10 .03
333 Graeme Lloyd .10 .03
334 Carlos Maldonado .10 .03
335 Angel Miranda .10 .03
336 Jaime Navarro .10 .03
337 Dave Nilsson .10 .03
338 Rafael Novoa .10 .03
339 Troy O'Leary .10 .03
340 Jesse Orosco .10 .03
341 Kevin Seitzer .10 .03
342 Bill Spiers .10 .03
343 William Suero .10 .03
344 B.J. Surhoff .20 .06
345 Dickie Thon .10 .03
346 Jose Valentin .10 .03
347 Greg Vaughn .10 .03
348 Robin Yount .75 .23
349 Willie Banks .10 .03
350 Bernardo Brito .10 .03
351 Scott Erickson .10 .03
352 Mark Guthrie .10 .03
353 Chip Hale .10 .03
354 Brian Harper .10 .03
355 Kent Hrbek .20 .06
356 Terry Jorgensen .10 .03
357 Chuck Knoblauch .20 .06
358 Gene Larkin .10 .03
359 Scott Leius .10 .03
360 Shane Mack .10 .03
361 David McCarty .10 .03
362 Pat Meares .10 .03
363 Pedro Munoz .10 .03
364 Derek Parks .10 .03
365 Kirby Puckett .50 .15
366 Jeff Reboulet .10 .03
367 Kevin Tapani .10 .03
368 Mike Trombley .10 .03
369 George Tsamis .10 .03
370 Carl Willis .10 .03
371 Dave Winfield .20 .06
372 Moises Alou .20 .06
373 Brian Barnes .10 .03
374 Sean Berry .10 .03
375 Frank Bolick .10 .03
376 Wil Cordero .10 .03
377 Delino DeShields .10 .03
378 Jeff Fassero .10 .03
379 Darrin Fletcher .10 .03
380 Cliff Floyd .20 .06
381 Lou Frazier .10 .03
382 Marquis Grissom .20 .06
383 Gil Heredia .10 .03
384 Mike Lansing .10 .03
385 Oreste Marrero RC .10 .03
386 Dennis Martinez .20 .06
387 Curtis Pride RC .20 .06
388 Mel Rojas .10 .03
389 Kirk Rueter .20 .06
390 Joe Siddall .10 .03
391 John Vander Wal .10 .03
392 Larry Walker .30 .09
393 John Wetteland .20 .06
394 Rondell White .20 .06
395 Tim Bogar .10 .03
396 Bobby Bonilla .20 .06
397 Jeromy Burnitz .20 .06
398 Mike Draper .10 .03
399 Sid Fernandez .10 .03
400 John Franco .20 .06
401 Dave Gallagher .10 .03
402 Dwight Gooden .20 .06
403 Eric Hillman .10 .03
404 Todd Hundley .10 .03
405 Butch Huskey .10 .03
406 Jeff Innis .10 .03
407 Howard Johnson .10 .03
408 Jeff Kent .20 .06
409 Ced Landrum .10 .03
410 Mike Maddux .10 .03
411 Josias Manzanillo .10 .03
412 Jeff McKnight .10 .03
413 Eddie Murray .50 .15
414 Tito Navarro .10 .03
415 Joe Orsulak .10 .03
416 Bret Saberhagen .20 .06
417 Dave Telgheder .10 .03
418 Ryan Thompson .10 .03
419 Chico Walker .10 .03
420 Jim Abbott .30 .09
421 Wade Boggs .30 .09
422 Mike Gallego .10 .03
423 Mark Hutton .10 .03
424 Dion James .10 .03
425 Domingo Jean .10 .03
426 Pat Kelly .10 .03
427 Jimmy Key .20 .06
428 Jim Leyritz .10 .03
429 Kevin Maas .10 .03
430 Don Mattingly 1.25 .35
431 Bobby Munoz .10 .03
432 Matt Nokes .10 .03
433 Paul O'Neill .30 .09
434 Spike Owen .10 .03
435 Melido Perez .10 .03
436 Lee Smith .20 .06
437 Andy Stankiewicz .10 .03
438 Mike Stanley .10 .03
439 Danny Tartabull .10 .03
440 Randy Velarde .10 .03
441 Bernie Williams .30 .09
442 Gerald Williams .10 .03
443 Mike Witt .10 .03
444 Marcos Armas .10 .03
445 Lance Blankenship .10 .03
446 Mike Bordick .20 .06
447 Ron Darling UER .10 .03
Reversed negative on front
448 Dennis Eckersley .20 .06
449 Brent Gates .10 .03
450 Rich Gossage .20 .06
451 Scott Hemond .10 .03
452 Dave Henderson .10 .03
453 Shawn Hillegas .10 .03
454 Rick Honeycutt .10 .03
455 Scott Lydy .10 .03
456 Mark McGwire 1.25 .35
457 Henry Mercedes .10 .03
458 Mike Mohler .10 .03
459 Troy Neel .10 .03
460 Edwin Nunez .10 .03
461 Craig Paquette .10 .03
462 Ruben Sierra .10 .03
463 Terry Steinbach .10 .03
464 Todd Van Poppel .10 .03
465 Bob Welch .10 .03
466 Bobby Witt .10 .03
467 Ruben Amaro .10 .03
468 Larry Andersen .10 .03
469 Kim Batiste .10 .03
470 Wes Chamberlain .10 .03
471 Darren Daulton .20 .06
472 Mariano Duncan .10 .03
473 Len Dykstra .20 .06
474 Jim Eisenreich .10 .03
475 Tommy Greene .10 .03
476 Dave Hollins .10 .03
477 Pete Incaviglia .10 .03
478 Danny Jackson .10 .03
479 John Kruk .20 .06
480 Tony Longmire .10 .03
481 Jeff Manto .10 .03
482 Mickey Morandini .10 .03
483 Terry Mulholland .10 .03
484 Todd Pratt .10 .03
485 Ben Rivera .10 .03
486 Curt Schilling .20 .06
487 Kevin Stocker .10 .03
488 Milt Thompson .10 .03
489 David West .10 .03
490 Mitch Williams .10 .03
491 Jeff Ballard .10 .03
492 Jay Bell .20 .06
493 Scott Bullett .10 .03
494 Dave Clark .10 .03
495 Steve Cooke .10 .03
496 Midre Cummings .10 .03
497 Mark Dewey .10 .03
498 Carlos Garcia .10 .03
499 Jeff King .10 .03
500 Al Martin .10 .03
501 Lloyd McClendon .10 .03
502 Orlando Merced .10 .03
503 Blas Minor .10 .03
504 Denny Neagle .20 .06
505 Tom Prince .10 .03
506 Don Slaught .10 .03
507 Zane Smith .10 .03
508 Randy Tomlin .10 .03
509 Andy Van Slyke .20 .06
510 Paul Wagner .10 .03
511 Tim Wakefield .20 .06
512 Bob Walk .10 .03
513 John Wehner .10 .03
514 Kevin Young .10 .03
515 Billy Bean .10 .03
516 Andy Benes .10 .03
517 Derek Bell .10 .03
518 Doug Brocail .10 .03
519 Jarvis Brown .10 .03
520 Phil Clark .10 .03
521 Mark Davis .10 .03
522 Jeff Gardner .10 .03
523 Pat Gomez .10 .03
524 Ricky Gutierrez .10 .03
525 Tony Gwynn .60 .18
526 Gene Harris .10 .03
527 Kevin Higgins .10 .03
528 Trevor Hoffman .20 .06
529 Luis Lopez .10 .03
530 Pedro A.Martinez RC .10 .03
531 Melvin Nieves .10 .03
532 Phil Plantier .10 .03
533 Frank Seminara .10 .03
534 Craig Shipley .10 .03
535 Tim Teufel .10 .03
536 Guillermo Velasquez .10 .03
537 Wally Whitehurst .10 .03
538 Rod Beck .10 .03
539 Todd Benzinger .10 .03
540 Barry Bonds 1.25 .35
541 Jeff Brantley .10 .03
542 Dave Burba .10 .03
543 John Burkett .10 .03
544 Will Clark .50 .15
545 Royce Clayton .10 .03
546 Bryan Hickerson .10 .03
547 Mike Jackson .10 .03
548 Darren Lewis .10 .03
549 Kirt Manwaring .10 .03
550 Dave Martinez .10 .03
551 Willie McGee .20 .06
552 Jeff Reed .10 .03
553 Dave Righetti .20 .06
554 Kevin Rogers .10 .03
555 Steve Scarsone .10 .03
556 Bill Swift .10 .03
557 Robby Thompson .10 .03
558 Salomon Torres .10 .03
559 Matt Williams .20 .06
560 Trevor Wilson .10 .03
561 Rich Amaral .10 .03
562 Mike Blowers .10 .03
563 Chris Bosio .10 .03
564 Jay Buhner .20 .06
565 Norm Charlton .10 .03
566 Jim Converse .10 .03
567 Rich DeLucia .10 .03
568 Mike Felder .10 .03
569 Dave Fleming .10 .03
570 Ken Griffey Jr. .75 .23
571 Bill Haselman .10 .03
572 Dwayne Henry .10 .03
573 Brad Holman .10 .03
574 Randy Johnson .50 .15
575 Greg Litton .10 .03
576 Edgar Martinez .30 .09
577 Tino Martinez .30 .09
578 Jeff Nelson .10 .03
579 Marc Newfield .10 .03
580 Roger Salkeld .10 .03
581 Mackey Sasser .10 .03
582 Brian Turang RC .10 .03
583 Omar Vizquel .30 .09
584 Dave Valle .10 .03
585 Luis Alicea .10 .03
586 Rene Arocha .10 .03
587 Rheal Cormier .10 .03
588 Tripp Cromer .10 .03
589 Bernard Gilkey .10 .03
590 Lee Guetterman .10 .03
591 Gregg Jefferies .10 .03
592 Tim Jones .10 .03
593 Paul Kilgus .10 .03
594 Les Lancaster .10 .03
595 Omar Olivares .10 .03
596 Jose Oquendo .10 .03
597 Donovan Osborne .10 .03
598 Tom Pagnozzi .10 .03
599 Erik Pappas .10 .03
600 Geronimo Pena .10 .03
601 Mike Perez .10 .03
602 Gerald Perry .10 .03
603 Stan Royer .10 .03
604 Ozzie Smith .75 .23
605 Bob Tewksbury .10 .03
606 Allen Watson .10 .03
607 Mark Whiten .10 .03
608 Todd Zeile .10 .03
609 Jeff Bronkey .10 .03
610 Kevin Brown .20 .06
611 Jose Canseco .50 .15
612 Doug Dascenzo .10 .03
613 Butch Davis .10 .03
614 Mario Diaz .10 .03
615 Julio Franco .20 .06
616 Benji Gil .10 .03
617 Juan Gonzalez .30 .09
618 Tom Henke .10 .03
619 Jeff Huson .10 .03
620 David Hulse .10 .03
621 Craig Lefferts .10 .03
622 Rafael Palmeiro .30 .09
623 Dean Palmer .20 .06
624 Bob Patterson .10 .03
625 Roger Pavlik .10 .03
626 Gary Redus .10 .03
627 Ivan Rodriguez .50 .15
628 Kenny Rogers .20 .06
629 Jon Shave .10 .03
630 Doug Strange .10 .03
631 Matt Whiteside .10 .03
632 Roberto Alomar .30 .09
633 Pat Borders .10 .03
634 Scott Brow .10 .03
635 Rob Butler .10 .03
636 Joe Carter .20 .06
637 Tony Castillo .10 .03
638 Mark Eichhorn .10 .03
639 Tony Fernandez .10 .03
640 Huck Flener RC .10 .03
641 Alfredo Griffin .10 .03
642 Juan Guzman .10 .03
643 Rickey Henderson .50 .15
644 Pat Hentgen .10 .03
645 Randy Knorr .10 .03
646 Al Leiter .20 .06
647 Domingo Martinez .10 .03
648 Paul Molitor .30 .09
649 Jack Morris .20 .06
650 John Olerud .20 .06
651 Ed Sprague .10 .03
652 Dave Stewart .20 .06
653 Devon White .20 .06
654 Woody Williams .20 .06
655 Barry Bonds MVP .60 .18
656 Greg Maddux CY .50 .15
657 Jack McDowell CY .10 .03
658 Mike Piazza ROY .50 .15
659 Tim Salmon ROY .20 .06
660 Frank Thomas MVP .30 .09

1994 Pacific All-Latino

Randomly inserted in Pacific purple foil packs at a rate of one in 25, this 20-card standard-size set spotlights the greatest Latin players chosen by the Pacific staff. Print run was limited to 8,000 sets. The set subdivides into National League (1-10) and American League (11-20) players.

	Nm-Mt	Ex-Mt
COMPLETE SET (20)	25.00	7.50
1 Benito Santiago	1.25	.35
2 Dave Magadan	1.25	.35
3 Andres Galarraga	2.50	.75
4 Luis Gonzalez	2.50	.75
5 Jose Offerman	1.25	.35
6 Bobby Bonilla	2.50	.75
7 Dennis Martinez	2.50	.75
8 Mariano Duncan	1.25	.35
9 Orlando Merced	1.25	.35
10 Jose Rijo	1.25	.35
11 Danny Tartabull	1.25	.35
12 Ruben Sierra	1.25	.35
13 Ivan Rodriguez	6.00	1.80
14 Juan Gonzalez	4.00	1.20
15 Jose Canseco	6.00	1.80
16 Rafael Palmeiro	4.00	1.20
17 Roberto Alomar	4.00	1.20
18 Eduardo Perez	1.25	.35
19 Alex Fernandez	1.25	.35
20 Omar Vizquel	4.00	1.20

1994 Pacific Gold Prisms

Randomly inserted in Pacific purple foil packs at a rate of one in 25, this 20-card standard-size prismatic "Home Run Leaders" set honors the top 1993 home run leaders. Print run was

reportedly limited to 8,000 sets. The set subdivides into American League (1-10) and National League (11-20) players.

	Nm-Mt	Ex-Mt
COMPLETE SET (20)	80.00	24.00
1 Juan Gonzalez	4.00	1.20
2 Ken Griffey Jr.	10.00	3.00
3 Frank Thomas	6.00	1.80
4 Albert Belle	2.50	.75
5 Rafael Palmeiro	4.00	1.20
6 Joe Carter	2.50	.75
7 Dean Palmer	2.50	.75
8 Mickey Tettleton	1.25	.35
9 Tim Salmon	4.00	1.20
10 Danny Tartabull	1.25	.35
11 Barry Bonds	15.00	4.50
12 Dave Justice	2.50	.75
13 Matt Williams	2.50	.75
14 Fred McGriff	4.00	1.20
15 Ron Gant	2.50	.75
16 Mike Piazza	12.00	3.60
17 Bobby Bonilla	2.50	.75
18 Phil Plantier	1.25	.35
19 Sammy Sosa	10.00	3.00
20 Rick Wilkins	1.25	.35

1994 Pacific Silver Prisms

Randomly inserted in Pacific foil packs, this 36-card standard-size set is also known as "Jewels of the Crown". The triangular versions were randomly inserted in purple packs and the more common circular one per black retail pack. The print run was reportedly limited to 8,000 sets. The set divides into American League (1-18) and National League (19-36) players.

	Nm-Mt	Ex-Mt
COMPLETE SET (36)	120.00	36.00
*CIRCULAR: .2X TO .5X SILVER PRISM.		
ONE CIRCULAR PER BLACK RETAIL PACK		
1 Robin Yount	8.00	2.40
2 Juan Gonzalez	3.00	.90
3 Rafael Palmeiro	3.00	.90
4 Paul Molitor	3.00	.90
5 Roberto Alomar	3.00	.90
6 John Olerud	2.00	.60
7 Randy Johnson	5.00	1.50
8 Ken Griffey Jr.	8.00	2.40
9 Wade Boggs	3.00	.90
10 Don Mattingly	12.00	3.60
11 Kirby Puckett	5.00	1.50
12 Tim Salmon	3.00	.90
13 Frank Thomas	5.00	1.50
14 Fernando Valenzuela	2.00	.60
15 Cal Ripken	15.00	4.50
16 Carlos Baerga	1.00	.30
17 Kenny Lofton	2.00	.60
18 Cecil Fielder	2.00	.60
19 John Burkett	1.00	.30
20 Andres Galarraga	2.00	.60
21 Charlie Hayes	1.00	.30
22 Orestes Destrade	1.00	.30
23 Jeff Conine	2.00	.60
24 Jeff Bagwell	3.00	.90
25 Mark Grace	3.00	.90
26 Ryne Sandberg	8.00	2.40
27 Gregg Jefferies	1.00	.30
28 Barry Bonds	12.00	3.60
29 Mike Piazza	10.00	3.00
30 Greg Maddux	8.00	2.40
31 Darren Daulton	2.00	.60
32 John Kruk	2.00	.60
33 Lenny Dykstra	2.00	.60
34 Orlando Merced	1.00	.30
35 Tony Gwynn	6.00	1.80
36 Robby Thompson	1.00	.30

1995 Pacific

This 450-card standard-size set was issued in one series. The full-bleed fronts have action photos; the "Pacific Collection" logo is on the upper left and the player's name is at the bottom. The horizontal backs have a player photo on the left with 1994 stats and some career highlights on the right. The career highlights are in both English and Spanish. The cards are numbered in the lower right corner. The cards are grouped alphabetically within teams and checklisted below alphabetically according to teams for each league. There are no key Rookie Cards in this set.

	Nm-Mt	Ex-Mt
COMPLETE SET (450)	50.00	15.00
1 Steve Avery	.10	.03
2 Rafael Belliard	.10	.03
3 Jeff Blauser	.10	.03
4 Tom Glavine	.30	.09
5 David Justice	.20	.06
6 Mike Kelly	.10	.03
7 Roberto Kelly	.10	.03
8 Ryan Klesko	.20	.06
9 Mark Lemke	.10	.03
10 Javier Lopez	.20	.06
11 Greg Maddux	.75	.23
12 Fred McGriff	.30	.09
13 Greg McMichael	.10	.03
14 Jose Oliva	.10	.03
15 John Smoltz	.30	.09
16 Tony Tarasco	.10	.03
17 Brady Anderson	.20	.06
18 Harold Baines	.20	.06
19 Armando Benitez	.20	.06
20 Mike Devereaux	.10	.03
21 Leo Gomez	.10	.03
22 Jeffrey Hammonds	.10	.03
23 Chris Hoiles	.10	.03
24 Ben McDonald	.10	.03
25 Mark McLemore	.10	.03
26 Jamie Moyer	.20	.06
27 Mike Mussina	.30	.09
28 Rafael Palmeiro	.30	.09
29 Jim Poole	.10	.03
30 Cal Ripken Jr.	1.50	.45
31 Lee Smith	.20	.06
32 Mark Smith	.10	.03
33 Jose Canseco	.50	.15
34 Roger Clemens	1.00	.30
35 Scott Cooper	.10	.03
36 Andre Dawson	.20	.06
37 Tony Fossas	.10	.03
38 Mike Greenwell	.10	.03
39 Chris Howard	.10	.03
40 Jose Melendez	.10	.03
41 Nate Minchey	.10	.03
42 Tim Naehring	.10	.03
43 Otis Nixon	.10	.03
44 Carlos Rodriguez	.10	.03
45 Aaron Sele	.10	.03
46 Lee Tinsley	.10	.03
47 Sergio Valdez	.10	.03
48 John Valentin	.10	.03
49 Mo Vaughn	.20	.06
50 Brian Anderson	.10	.03
51 Garret Anderson	.20	.06
52 Rod Correia	.10	.03
53 Chad Curtis	.10	.03
54 Mark Dalesandro	.10	.03
55 Chili Davis	.20	.06
56 Gary DiSarcina	.10	.03
57 Damion Easley	.10	.03
58 Jim Edmonds	.30	.09
59 Jorge Fabregas	.10	.03
60 Chuck Finley	.20	.06
61 Bo Jackson	.50	.15
62 Mark Langston	.10	.03
63 Eduardo Perez	.10	.03
64 Tim Salmon	.30	.09
65 J.T. Snow	.20	.06
66 Willie Banks	.10	.03
67 Jose Bautista	.10	.03
68 Shawon Dunston	.10	.03
69 Kevin Foster	.10	.03
70 Mark Grace	.30	.09
71 Jose Guzman	.10	.03
72 Jose Hernandez	.10	.03
73 Blaise Ilsley	.10	.03
74 Derrick May	.10	.03
75 Randy Myers	.10	.03
76 Karl Rhodes	.10	.03
77 Kevin Roberson	.10	.03
78 Rey Sanchez	.10	.03
79 Sammy Sosa	.75	.23
80 Steve Trachsel	.10	.03
81 Eddie Zambrano	.10	.03
82 Wilson Alvarez	.10	.03
83 Jason Bere	.10	.03
84 Joey Cora	.10	.03
85 Jose DeLeon	.10	.03
86 Alex Fernandez	.10	.03
87 Julio Franco	.20	.06
88 Ozzie Guillen	.10	.03
89 Joe Hall	.10	.03
90 Roberto Hernandez	.10	.03
91 Darrin Jackson	.10	.03
92 Lance Johnson	.10	.03
93 Norberto Martin	.10	.03
94 Jack McDowell	.10	.03
95 Tim Raines	.20	.06
96 Olmedo Saenz	.10	.03
97 Frank Thomas	.50	.15
98 Robin Ventura	.20	.06
99 Bret Boone	.20	.06
100 Jeff Brantley	.10	.03
101 Jacob Brumfield	.10	.03
102 Hector Carrasco	.10	.03
103 Brian Dorsett	.10	.03
104 Tony Fernandez	.10	.03
105 Willie Greene	.10	.03
106 Erik Hanson	.10	.03
107 Kevin Jarvis	.10	.03
108 Barry Larkin	.30	.09
109 Kevin Mitchell	.10	.03
110 Hal Morris	.10	.03
111 Jose Rijo	.10	.03
112 Johnny Ruffin	.10	.03
113 Deion Sanders	.30	.09
114 Reggie Sanders	.10	.03
115 Sandy Alomar Jr.	.10	.03
116 Ruben Amaro	.10	.03
117 Carlos Baerga	.10	.03
118 Albert Belle	.20	.06
119 Alvaro Espinoza	.10	.03
120 Rene Gonzales	.10	.03
121 Wayne Kirby	.10	.03
122 Kenny Lofton	.20	.06
123 Candy Maldonado	.10	.03
124 Dennis Martinez	.20	.06
125 Eddie Murray	.50	.15
126 Charles Nagy	.10	.03
127 Tony Pena	.10	.03
128 Manny Ramirez	.30	.09
129 Paul Sorrento	.10	.03
130 Jim Thome	.50	.15
131 Omar Vizquel	.30	.09
132 Dante Bichette	.20	.06
133 Ellis Burks	.20	.06
134 Vinny Castilla	.20	.06
135 Marvin Freeman	.10	.03
136 Andres Galarraga	.20	.06
137 Joe Girardi	.10	.03
138 Charlie Hayes	.10	.03
139 Mike Kingery	.10	.03
140 Nelson Liriano	.10	.03
141 Roberto Mejia	.10	.03
142 David Nied	.10	.03
143 Steve Reed	.10	.03
144 Armando Reynoso	.10	.03
145 Bruce Ruffin	.10	.03
146 John Vander Wal	.10	.03
147 Walt Weiss	.10	.03
148 Skeeter Barnes	.10	.03
149 Tim Belcher	.10	.03
150 Junior Felix	.10	.03
151 Cecil Fielder	.20	.06
152 Travis Fryman	.20	.06
153 Kirk Gibson	.20	.06
154 Chris Gomez	.10	.03
155 Buddy Groom	.10	.03
156 Chad Kreuter	.10	.03
157 Mike Moore	.10	.03
158 Tony Phillips	.10	.03
159 Juan Samuel	.10	.03
160 Mickey Tettleton	.10	.03
161 Alan Trammell	.20	.06
162 David Wells	.20	.06
163 Lou Whitaker	.20	.06
164 Kurt Abbott	.10	.03
165 Luis Aquino	.10	.03
166 Alex Arias	.10	.03
167 Bret Barberie	.10	.03
168 Jerry Browne	.10	.03
169 Chuck Carr	.10	.03
170 Matias Carrillo	.10	.03
171 Greg Colbrunn	.10	.03
172 Jeff Conine	.20	.06
173 Carl Everett	.20	.06
174 Robb Nen	.20	.06
175 Yorkis Perez	.10	.03
176 Pat Rapp	.10	.03
177 Benito Santiago	.20	.06
178 Gary Sheffield	.20	.06
179 Darrell Whitmore	.10	.03
180 Jeff Bagwell	.30	.09
181 Kevin Bass	.10	.03
182 Craig Biggio	.30	.09
183 Andujar Cedeno	.10	.03
184 Doug Drabek	.10	.03
185 Tony Eusebio	.10	.03
186 Steve Finley	.20	.06
187 Luis Gonzalez	.20	.06
188 Pete Harnisch	.10	.03
189 John Hudek	.10	.03
190 Orlando Miller	.10	.03
191 James Mouton	.10	.03
192 Roberto Petagine	.10	.03
193 Shane Reynolds	.10	.03
194 Greg Swindell	.10	.03
195 Dave Veres	.10	.03
196 Kevin Appier	.20	.06
197 Stan Belinda	.10	.03
198 Vince Coleman	.10	.03
199 David Cone	.20	.06
200 Gary Gaetti	.20	.06
201 Greg Gagne	.10	.03
202 Mark Gubicza	.10	.03
203 Bob Hamelin	.10	.03
204 Dave Henderson	.10	.03
205 Felix Jose	.10	.03
206 Wally Joyner	.20	.06
207 Jose Lind	.10	.03
208 Mike Macfarlane	.10	.03
209 Brian McRae	.10	.03
210 Jeff Montgomery	.10	.03
211 Hipolito Pichardo	.10	.03
212 Pedro Astacio	.10	.03
213 Brett Butler	.20	.06
214 Omar Daal	.10	.03
215 Delino DeShields	.10	.03
216 Darren Dreifort	.10	.03
217 Carlos Hernandez	.10	.03
218 Orel Hershiser	.20	.06
219 Garey Ingram	.10	.03
220 Eric Karros	.20	.06
221 Ramon Martinez	.10	.03
222 Raul Mondesi	.20	.06
223 Jose Offerman	.10	.03
224 Mike Piazza	.75	.23
225 Henry Rodriguez	.10	.03
226 Ismael Valdes	.10	.03
227 Tim Wallach	.10	.03
228 Jeff Cirillo	.10	.03
229 Alex Diaz	.10	.03
230 Cal Eldred	.10	.03
231 Mike Fetters	.10	.03
232 Brian Harper	.10	.03
233 Ted Higuera	.10	.03
234 John Jaha	.10	.03
235 Graeme Lloyd	.10	.03
236 Jose Mercedes	.10	.03
237 Jaime Navarro	.10	.03
238 Dave Nilsson	.10	.03
239 Jesse Orosco	.10	.03
240 Jody Reed	.10	.03
241 Jose Valentin	.10	.03
242 Greg Vaughn	.10	.03
243 Turner Ward	.10	.03
244 Rick Aguilera	.10	.03
245 Rich Becker	.10	.03
246 Jim Deshaies	.10	.03
247 Steve Dunn	.10	.03
248 Scott Erickson	.10	.03
249 Kent Hrbek	.20	.06
250 Chuck Knoblauch	.20	.06
251 Scott Leius	.10	.03
252 David McCarty	.10	.03
253 Pat Meares	.10	.03
254 Pedro Munoz	.10	.03
255 Kirby Puckett	.50	.15
256 Carlos Pulido	.10	.03
257 Kevin Tapani	.10	.03
258 Matt Walbeck	.10	.03
259 Dave Winfield	.20	.06
260 Moises Alou	.20	.06
261 Juan Bell	.10	.03
262 Freddie Benavides	.10	.03
263 Sean Berry	.10	.03
264 Wil Cordero	.10	.03
265 Jeff Fassero	.10	.03
266 Darrin Fletcher	.10	.03
267 Cliff Floyd	.20	.06
268 Marquis Grissom	.20	.06
269 Gil Heredia	.10	.03
270 Ken Hill	.10	.03
271 Pedro Martinez	.50	.15
272 Mel Rojas	.10	.03
273 Larry Walker	.30	.09
274 John Wetteland	.20	.06
275 Rondell White	.20	.06
276 Tim Bogar	.10	.03
277 Bobby Bonilla	.20	.06
278 Rico Brogna	.10	.03
279 Jeromy Burnitz	.20	.06
280 John Franco	.20	.06
281 Eric Hillman	.10	.03
282 Todd Hundley	.10	.03
283 Jeff Kent	.20	.06
284 Mike Maddux	.10	.03
285 Joe Orsulak	.10	.03
286 Luis Rivera	.10	.03
287 Bret Saberhagen	.20	.06
288 David Segui	.10	.03
289 Ryan Thompson	.10	.03
290 Fernando Vina	.10	.03
291 Jose Vizcaino	.10	.03
292 Jim Abbott	.30	.09
293 Wade Boggs	.30	.09
294 Russ Davis	.10	.03
295 Mike Gallego	.10	.03
296 Xavier Hernandez	.10	.03
297 Steve Howe	.10	.03
298 Jimmy Key	.20	.06
299 Don Mattingly	1.25	.35
300 Terry Mulholland	.10	.03
301 Paul O'Neill	.30	.09
302 Luis Polonia	.10	.03
303 Mike Stanley	.10	.03
304 Danny Tartabull	.10	.03
305 Randy Velarde	.10	.03
306 Bob Wickman	.10	.03
307 Bernie Williams	.30	.09
308 Mark Acre	.10	.03
309 Geronimo Berroa	.10	.03
310 Mike Bordick	.10	.03
311 Dennis Eckersley	.20	.06
312 Rickey Henderson	.50	.15
313 Stan Javier	.10	.03
314 Miguel Jimenez	.10	.03
315 Francisco Matos RC	.10	.03
316 Mark McGwire	1.25	.35
317 Troy Neel	.10	.03
318 Steve Ontiveros	.10	.03
319 Carlos Reyes	.10	.03
320 Ruben Sierra	.10	.03
321 Terry Steinbach	.10	.03
322 Bob Welch	.10	.03
323 Bobby Witt	.10	.03
324 Larry Andersen	.10	.03
325 Kim Batiste	.10	.03
326 Darren Daulton	.20	.06
327 Mariano Duncan	.10	.03
328 Lenny Dykstra	.20	.06
329 Jim Eisenreich	.10	.03
330 Danny Jackson	.10	.03
331 John Kruk	.20	.06
332 Tony Longmire	.10	.03
333 Tom Marsh	.10	.03
334 Mickey Morandini	.10	.03
335 Bobby Munoz	.10	.03
336 Todd Pratt	.10	.03
337 Tom Quinlan	.10	.03
338 Kevin Stocker	.10	.03
339 Fernando Valenzuela	.20	.06
340 Jay Bell	.20	.06
341 Dave Clark	.10	.03
342 Steve Cooke	.10	.03
343 Carlos Garcia	.10	.03
344 Jeff King	.10	.03
345 Jon Lieber	.10	.03
346 Ravelo Manzanillo	.10	.03
347 Al Martin	.10	.03
348 Orlando Merced	.10	.03
349 Denny Neagle	.20	.06
350 Alejandro Pena	.10	.03
351 Don Slaught	.10	.03
352 Zane Smith	.10	.03
353 Andy Van Slyke	.20	.06
354 Rick White	.10	.03
355 Kevin Young	.10	.03
356 Andy Ashby	.10	.03
357 Derek Bell	.10	.03
358 Andy Benes	.10	.03
359 Phil Clark	.10	.03
360 Donnie Elliott	.10	.03
361 Ricky Gutierrez	.10	.03
362 Tony Gwynn	.60	.18
363 Trevor Hoffman	.20	.06
364 Tim Hyers	.10	.03
365 Luis Lopez	.10	.03
366 Jose Martinez	.10	.03
367 Pedro A. Martinez	.10	.03
368 Phil Plantier	.10	.03
369 Bip Roberts	.10	.03
370 A.J. Sager	.10	.03
371 Jeff Tabaka	.10	.03
372 Todd Benzinger	.10	.03
373 Barry Bonds	.75	.23
374 John Burkett	.10	.03
375 Mark Carreon	.10	.03
376 Royce Clayton	.10	.03
377 Pat Gomez	.10	.03
378 Erik Johnson	.10	.03
379 Darren Lewis	.10	.03
380 Kirt Manwaring	.10	.03
381 Dave Martinez	.10	.03
382 John Patterson	.10	.03
383 Mark Portugal	.10	.03
384 Darryl Strawberry	.20	.06
385 Salomon Torres	.10	.03
386 W. VanLandingham	.10	.03
387 Matt Williams	.20	.06
388 Rich Amaral	.10	.03
389 Bobby Ayala	.10	.03
390 Mike Blowers	.10	.03
391 Chris Bosio	.10	.03
392 Jay Buhner	.20	.06
393 Jim Converse	.10	.03
394 Tim Davis	.10	.03
395 Felix Fermin	.10	.03
396 Dave Fleming	.10	.03
397 Goose Gossage	.20	.06
398 Ken Griffey Jr.	.75	.23
399 Randy Johnson	.50	.15
400 Edgar Martinez	.30	.09
401 Tino Martinez	.30	.09
402 Alex Rodriguez	1.25	.35
403 Dan Wilson	.10	.03
404 Luis Alicea	.10	.03
405 Rene Arocha	.10	.03
406 Bernard Gilkey	.10	.03
407 Gregg Jefferies	.10	.03
408 Ray Lankford	.10	.03
409 Terry McGriff	.10	.03
410 Omar Olivares	.10	.03
411 Jose Oquendo	.10	.03
412 Vicente Palacios	.10	.03
413 Geronimo Pena	.10	.03
414 Mike Perez	.10	.03
415 Gerald Perry	.10	.03
416 Ozzie Smith	.75	.23
417 Bob Tewksbury	.10	.03
418 Mark Whiten	.10	.03
419 Todd Zeile	.10	.03
420 Esteban Beltre	.10	.03
421 Kevin Brown	.20	.06
422 Cris Carpenter	.10	.03
423 Will Clark	.50	.15
424 Hector Fajardo	.10	.03
425 Jeff Frye	.10	.03
426 Juan Gonzalez	.30	.09
427 Rusty Greer	.20	.06
428 Rick Honeycutt	.10	.03
429 David Hulse	.10	.03
430 Manny Lee	.10	.03
431 Junior Ortiz	.10	.03
432 Dean Palmer	.20	.06
433 Ivan Rodriguez	.50	.15
434 Dan Smith	.10	.03
435 Roberto Alomar	.30	.09
436 Pat Borders	.10	.03
437 Scott Brow	.10	.03
438 Rob Butler	.10	.03
439 Joe Carter	.20	.06
440 Tony Castillo	.10	.03
441 Domingo Cedeno	.10	.03
442 Brad Cornett	.10	.03
443 Carlos Delgado	.20	.06
444 Alex Gonzalez	.10	.03
445 Juan Guzman	.10	.03
446 Darren Hall	.10	.03
447 Paul Molitor	.30	.09
448 John Olerud	.20	.06
449 Robert Perez	.10	.03
450 Devon White	.20	.06

1995 Pacific Gold Crown Die Cuts

Inserted approximately one in every 18 packs, these cards are in a diecut design. The cards are sequenced in alphabetical order according to team name.

	Nm-Mt	Ex-Mt
COMPLETE SET (20)	150.00	45.00
1 Greg Maddux	12.00	3.60
2 Fred McGriff	5.00	1.50
3 Rafael Palmeiro	5.00	1.50
4 Cal Ripken Jr.	25.00	7.50
5 Jose Canseco	8.00	2.40
6 Frank Thomas	8.00	2.40
7 Albert Belle	3.00	.90
8 Manny Ramirez	5.00	1.50
9 Andres Galarraga	3.00	.90
10 Jeff Bagwell	5.00	1.50
11 Chan Ho Park	1.50	.45
12 Raul Mondesi	3.00	.90
13 Mike Piazza	12.00	3.60
14 Kirby Puckett	8.00	2.40
15 Barry Bonds	12.00	3.60
16 Ken Griffey Jr.	12.00	3.60
17 Alex Rodriguez	20.00	6.00
18 Juan Gonzalez	5.00	1.50
19 Roberto Alomar	5.00	1.50
20 Carlos Delgado	3.00	.90

1995 Pacific Gold Prisms

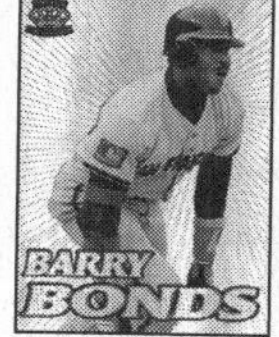

This 36-card standard-size set was inserted approximately one in every 12 packs.

	Nm-Mt	Ex-Mt
COMPLETE SET (36)	120.00	36.00
1 Jose Canseco	6.00	1.80
2 Gregg Jefferies	1.25	.35
3 Fred McGriff	4.00	1.20
4 Joe Carter	2.50	.75
5 Tim Salmon	4.00	1.20
6 Wade Boggs	4.00	1.20
7 Dave Winfield	2.50	.75
8 Bob Hamelin	1.25	.35
9 Cal Ripken Jr.	20.00	6.00
10 Don Mattingly	15.00	4.50
11 Juan Gonzalez	4.00	1.20
12 Carlos Delgado	2.50	.75
13 Barry Bonds	10.00	3.00
14 Albert Belle	2.50	.75
15 Raul Mondesi	2.50	.75
16 Jeff Bagwell	4.00	1.20
17 Mike Piazza	10.00	3.00
18 Rafael Palmeiro	4.00	1.20
19 Frank Thomas	6.00	1.80
20 Matt Williams	2.50	.75
21 Ken Griffey Jr.	10.00	3.00
22 Will Clark	6.00	1.80
23 Bobby Bonilla	2.50	.75
24 Kenny Lofton	2.50	.75
25 Paul Molitor	4.00	1.20
26 Kirby Puckett	6.00	1.80
27 David Justice	2.50	.75
28 Jeff Conine	2.50	.75
29 Bret Boone	2.50	.75
30 Larry Walker	4.00	1.20
31 Cecil Fielder	2.50	.75
32 Manny Ramirez	4.00	1.20
33 Javier Lopez	2.50	.75
34 Jimmy Key	2.50	.75
35 Andres Galarraga	2.50	.75
36 Tony Gwynn	8.00	2.40

1995 Pacific Latinos Destacados

This 36-card standard size set was inserted approximately one in every nine packs. A literal translation for this set is Hot Hispanics and features only Spanish players. The cards are numbered and arranged in alphabetical order.

	Nm-Mt	Ex-Mt
COMPLETE SET (36)	50.00	15.00
1 Roberto Alomar	3.00	.90
2 Moises Alou	2.00	.60
3 Wilson Alvarez	1.00	.30
4 Carlos Baerga	1.00	.30
5 Geronimo Berroa	1.00	.30
6 Jose Canseco	5.00	1.50
7 Hector Carrasco	1.00	.30
8 Wil Cordero	1.00	.30
9 Carlos Delgado	2.00	.60
10 Damion Easley	1.00	.30
11 Tony Eusebio	1.00	.30
12 Hector Fajardo	1.00	.30
13 Andres Galarraga	2.00	.60
14 Carlos Garcia	1.00	.30
15 Chris Gomez	1.00	.30
16 Alex Gonzalez	1.00	.30
17 Juan Gonzalez	3.00	.90
18 Luis Gonzalez	2.00	.60
19 Felix Jose	1.00	.30
20 Javier Lopez	2.00	.60
21 Luis Lopez	1.00	.30
22 Dennis Martinez	2.00	.60
23 Orlando Miller	1.00	.30
24 Raul Mondesi	2.00	.60
25 Jose Oliva	1.00	.30
26 Rafael Palmeiro	3.00	.90
27 Yorkis Perez	1.00	.30
28 Manny Ramirez	3.00	.90
29 Jose Rijo	1.00	.30
30 Alex Rodriguez	12.00	3.60
31 Ivan Rodriguez	5.00	1.50
32 Carlos Rodriguez	1.00	.30
33 Sammy Sosa	8.00	2.40
34 Tony Tarasco	1.00	.30
35 Ismael Valdes	1.00	.30
36 Bernie Williams	3.00	.90

1996 Pacific

This 450-card set was issued in 12-card packs. The fronts feature borderless color action player photos with double-etched gold foil printing. The horizontal backs carry a color player portrait with player information in both English and Spanish and 1995 season player statistics.

	Nm-Mt	Ex-Mt
COMPLETE SET (450)	40.00	12.00
1 Steve Avery	.20	.06
2 Ryan Klesko	.20	.06
3 Pedro Borbon	.20	.06
4 Chipper Jones	.50	.15
5 Kent Mercker	.20	.06
6 Greg Maddux	.75	.23
7 Greg McMichael	.20	.06
8 Mark Wohlers	.20	.06
9 Fred McGriff	.30	.09
10 John Smoltz	.30	.09
11 Rafael Belliard	.20	.06
12 Mark Lemke	.20	.06
13 Tom Glavine	.30	.09
14 Javier Lopez	.20	.06
15 Jeff Blauser	.20	.06
16 David Justice	.20	.06
17 Marquis Grissom	.20	.06

18 Greg Maddux CY	.50	.15
19 Randy Myers	.20	.06
20 Scott Servais	.20	.06
21 Sammy Sosa	.75	.23
22 Kevin Foster	.20	.06
23 Jose Hernandez	.20	.06
24 Jim Bullinger	.20	.06
25 Mike Perez	.20	.06
26 Shawon Dunston	.20	.06
27 Rey Sanchez	.20	.06
28 Frank Castillo	.20	.06
29 Jaime Navarro	.20	.06
30 Brian McRae	.20	.06
31 Mark Grace	.30	.09
32 Roberto Rivera	.20	.06
33 Luis Gonzalez	.20	.06
34 Hector Carrasco	.20	.06
35 Bret Boone	.20	.06
36 Thomas Howard	.20	.06
37 Hal Morris	.20	.06
38 John Smiley	.20	.06
39 Jeff Brantley	.20	.06
40 Barry Larkin	.30	.09
41 Mariano Duncan	.20	.06
42 Xavier Hernandez	.20	.06
43 Pete Schourek	.20	.06
44 Reggie Sanders	.20	.06
45 Dave Burba	.20	.06
46 Jeff Branson	.20	.06
47 Mark Portugal	.20	.06
48 Ron Gant	.20	.06
49 Benito Santiago	.20	.06
50 Barry Larkin MVP	.20	.06
51 Steve Reed	.20	.06
52 Kevin Ritz	.20	.06
53 Dante Bichette	.20	.06
54 Darren Holmes	.20	.06
55 Ellis Burks	.20	.06
56 Walt Weiss	.20	.06
57 Armando Reynoso	.20	.06
58 Vinny Castilla	.20	.06
59 Jason Bates	.20	.06
60 Mike Kingery	.20	.06
61 Bryan Rekar	.20	.06
62 Curtis Leskanic	.20	.06
63 Bret Saberhagen	.20	.06
64 Andres Galarraga	.20	.06
65 Larry Walker	.30	.09
66 Joe Girardi	.20	.06
67 Quilvio Veras	.20	.06
68 Robb Nen	.20	.06
69 Mario Diaz	.20	.06
70 Chuck Carr	.20	.06
71 Alex Arias	.20	.06
72 Pat Rapp	.20	.06
73 Rich Garces	.20	.06
74 Kurt Abbott	.20	.06
75 Andre Dawson	.20	.06
76 Greg Colbrunn	.20	.06
77 John Burkett	.20	.06
78 Terry Pendleton	.20	.06
79 Jesus Tavarez	.20	.06
80 Charles Johnson	.20	.06
81 Yorkis Perez	.20	.06
82 Jeff Conine	.20	.06
83 Gary Sheffield	.20	.06
84 Brian L. Hunter	.20	.06
85 Derrick May	.20	.06
86 Greg Swindell	.20	.06
87 Derek Bell	.20	.06
88 Dave Veres	.20	.06
89 Jeff Bagwell	.30	.09
90 Todd Jones	.20	.06
91 Orlando Miller	.20	.06
92 Pedro A. Martinez	.20	.06
93 Tony Eusebio	.20	.06
94 Craig Biggio	.30	.09
95 Shane Reynolds	.20	.06
96 James Mouton	.20	.06
97 Doug Drabek	.20	.06
98 Dave Magadan	.20	.06
99 Ricky Gutierrez	.20	.06
100 Hideo Nomo	.50	.15
101 Delino DeShields	.20	.06
102 Tom Candiotti	.20	.06
103 Mike Piazza	.75	.23
104 Ramon Martinez	.20	.06
105 Pedro Astacio	.20	.06
106 Chad Fonville	.20	.06
107 Raul Mondesi	.20	.06
108 Ismael Valdes	.20	.06
109 Jose Offerman	.20	.06
110 Todd Worrell	.20	.06
111 Eric Karros	.20	.06
112 Brett Butler	.20	.06
113 Juan Castro	.20	.06
114 Roberto Kelly	.20	.06
115 Omar Daal	.20	.06
116 Antonio Osuna	.20	.06
117 Hideo Nomo ROY	.30	.09
118 Mike Lansing	.20	.06
119 Mel Rojas	.20	.06
120 Sean Berry	.20	.06
121 David Segui	.20	.06
122 Tavo Alvarez	.20	.06
123 Pedro J.Martinez	.50	.15
124 F.P. Santangelo	.20	.06
125 Rondell White	.20	.06
126 Cliff Floyd	.20	.06
127 Henry Rodriguez	.20	.06
128 Tony Tarasco	.20	.06
129 Yamil Benitez	.20	.06
130 Carlos Perez	.20	.06
131 Wil Cordero	.20	.06
132 Jeff Fassero	.20	.06
133 Moises Alou	.20	.06
134 John Franco	.20	.06
135 Rico Brogna	.20	.06
136 Dave Mlicki	.20	.06
137 Bill Pulsipher	.20	.06
138 Jose Vizcaino	.20	.06
139 Carl Everett	.20	.06
140 Edgardo Alfonzo	.20	.06
141 Bobby Jones	.20	.06
142 Alberto Castillo	.20	.06
143 Joe Orsulak	.20	.06
144 Jeff Kent	.20	.06
145 Ryan Thompson	.20	.06
146 Jason Isringhausen	.20	.06
147 Todd Hundley	.20	.06
148 Alex Ochoa	.20	.06
149 Charlie Hayes	.20	.06
150 Michael Mimbs	.20	.06
151 Darren Daulton	.20	.06
152 Toby Borland	.20	.06
153 Andy Van Slyke	.20	.06
154 Mickey Morandini	.20	.06
155 Sid Fernandez	.20	.06
156 Tom Marsh	.20	.06
157 Kevin Stocker	.20	.06
158 Paul Quantrill	.20	.06
159 Gregg Jefferies	.20	.06
160 Ricky Bottalico	.20	.06
161 Lenny Dykstra	.20	.06
162 Mark Whiten	.20	.06
163 Tyler Green	.20	.06
164 Jim Eisenreich	.20	.06
165 Heathcliff Slocumb	.20	.06
166 Esteban Loaiza	.20	.06
167 Rich Aude	.20	.06
168 Jason Christiansen	.20	.06
169 Ramon Morel	.20	.06
170 Orlando Merced	.20	.06
171 Paul Wagner	.20	.06
172 Jeff King	.20	.06
173 Jay Bell	.20	.06
174 Jacob Brumfield	.20	.06
175 Nelson Liriano	.20	.06
176 Dan Miceli	.20	.06
177 Carlos Garcia	.20	.06
178 Denny Neagle	.20	.06
179 Angelo Encarnacion	.20	.06
180 Al Martin	.20	.06
181 Midre Cummings	.20	.06
182 Eddie Williams	.20	.06
183 Roberto Petagine	.20	.06
184 Tony Gwynn	.60	.18
185 Andy Ashby	.20	.06
186 Melvin Nieves	.20	.06
187 Phil Clark	.20	.06
188 Brad Ausmus	.20	.06
189 Bip Roberts	.20	.06
190 Fernando Valenzuela	.20	.06
191 Marc Newfield	.20	.06
192 Steve Finley	.20	.06
193 Trevor Hoffman	.20	.06
194 Andujar Cedeno	.20	.06
195 Jody Reed	.20	.06
196 Ken Caminiti	.20	.06
197 Joey Hamilton	.20	.06
198 Tony Gwynn BAC	.30	.09
199 Shawn Barton	.20	.06
200 Deion Sanders	.30	.09
201 Rikkert Faneyte	.20	.06
202 Barry Bonds	1.25	.35
203 Matt Williams	.20	.06
204 Jose Bautista	.20	.06
205 Mark Leiter	.20	.06
206 Mark Carreon	.20	.06
207 Robby Thompson	.20	.06
208 Terry Mulholland	.20	.06
209 Rod Beck	.20	.06
210 Royce Clayton	.20	.06
211 J.R. Phillips	.20	.06
212 Kirt Manwaring	.20	.06
213 Glenallen Hill	.20	.06
214 W.VanLandingham	.20	.06
215 Scott Cooper	.20	.06
216 Bernard Gilkey	.20	.06
217 Allen Watson	.20	.06
218 Donovan Osborne	.20	.06
219 Ray Lankford	.20	.06
220 Tony Fossas	.20	.06
221 Tom Pagnozzi	.20	.06
222 John Mabry	.20	.06
223 Tripp Cromer	.20	.06
224 Mark Petkovsek	.20	.06
225 Mike Morgan	.20	.06
226 Ozzie Smith	.75	.23
227 Tom Henke	.20	.06
228 Jose Oquendo	.20	.06
229 Brian Jordan	.20	.06
230 Cal Ripken	1.50	.45
231 Scott Erickson	.20	.06
232 Harold Baines	.20	.06
233 Jeff Manto	.20	.06
234 Jesse Orosco	.20	.06
235 Jeffrey Hammonds	.20	.06
236 Brady Anderson	.20	.06
237 Manny Alexander	.20	.06
238 Chris Hoiles	.20	.06
239 Rafael Palmeiro	.30	.09
240 Ben McDonald	.20	.06
241 Curtis Goodwin	.20	.06
242 Bobby Bonilla	.20	.06
243 Mike Mussina	.30	.09
244 Kevin Brown	.20	.06
245 Armando Benitez	.20	.06
246 Jose Canseco	.50	.15
247 Erik Hanson	.20	.06
248 Mo Vaughn	.20	.06
249 Tim Naehring	.20	.06
250 Vaughn Eshelman	.20	.06
251 Mike Greenwell	.20	.06
252 Troy O'Leary	.20	.06
253 Tim Wakefield	.20	.06
254 Dwayne Hosey	.20	.06
255 John Valentin	.20	.06
256 Rick Aguilera	.20	.06
257 Mike Macfarlane	.20	.06
258 Roger Clemens	1.00	.30
259 Luis Alicea	.20	.06
260 Mo Vaughn MVP	.20	.06
261 Mark Langston	.20	.06
262 Jim Edmonds	.20	.06
263 Rod Correia	.20	.06
264 Tim Salmon	.30	.09
265 J.T. Snow	.20	.06
266 Orlando Palmeiro	.20	.06
267 Jorge Fabregas	.20	.06
268 Jim Abbott	.30	.09
269 Eduardo Perez	.20	.06
270 Lee Smith	.20	.06
271 Gary DiSarcina	.20	.06
272 Damion Easley	.20	.06
273 Tony Phillips	.20	.06
274 Garret Anderson	.20	.06
275 Chuck Finley	.20	.06
276 Chili Davis	.20	.06
277 Lance Johnson	.20	.06
278 Alex Fernandez	.20	.06
279 Robin Ventura	.20	.06
280 Chris Snopek	.20	.06
281 Brian Keyser	.20	.06
282 Lyle Mouton	.20	.06
283 Luis Andujar	.20	.06
284 Tim Raines	.20	.06
285 Larry Thomas	.20	.06
286 Ozzie Guillen	.20	.06
287 Frank Thomas	.50	.15
288 Roberto Hernandez	.20	.06
289 Dave Martinez	.20	.06
290 Ray Durham	.20	.06
291 Ron Karkovice	.20	.06
292 Wilson Alvarez	.20	.06
293 Omar Vizquel	.30	.09
294 Eddie Murray	.50	.15
295 Sandy Alomar Jr.	.20	.06
296 Orel Hershiser	.20	.06
297 Jose Mesa	.20	.06
298 Julian Tavarez	.20	.06
299 Dennis Martinez	.20	.06
300 Carlos Baerga	.20	.06
301 Manny Ramirez	.30	.09
302 Jim Thome	.50	.15
303 Kenny Lofton	.20	.06
304 Tony Pena	.20	.06
305 Alvaro Espinoza	.20	.06
306 Paul Sorrento	.20	.06
307 Albert Belle	.20	.06
308 Danny Bautista	.20	.06
309 Chris Gomez	.20	.06
310 Jose Lima	.20	.06
311 Phil Nevin	.20	.06
312 Alan Trammell	.20	.06
313 Chad Curtis	.20	.06
314 John Flaherty	.20	.06
315 Travis Fryman	.20	.06
316 Todd Steverson	.20	.06
317 Brian Bohanon	.20	.06
318 Lou Whitaker	.20	.06
319 Bobby Higginson	.20	.06
320 Steve Rodriguez	.20	.06
321 Cecil Fielder	.20	.06
322 Felipe Lira	.20	.06
323 Juan Samuel	.20	.06
324 Bob Hamelin	.20	.06
325 Tom Goodwin	.20	.06
326 Johnny Damon	.30	.09
327 Hipolito Pichardo	.20	.06
328 Dilson Torres	.20	.06
329 Kevin Appier	.20	.06
330 Mark Gubicza	.20	.06
331 Jon Nunnally	.20	.06
332 Gary Gaetti	.20	.06
333 Brent Mayne	.20	.06
334 Brent Cookson	.20	.06
335 Tom Gordon	.20	.06
336 Wally Joyner	.20	.06
337 Greg Gagne	.20	.06
338 Fernando Vina	.20	.06
339 Joe Oliver	.20	.06
340 John Jaha	.20	.06
341 Jeff Cirillo	.20	.06
342 Pat Listach	.20	.06
343 Dave Nilsson	.20	.06
344 Steve Sparks	.20	.06
345 Ricky Bones	.20	.06
346 David Hulse	.20	.06
347 Scott Karl	.20	.06
348 Darryl Hamilton	.20	.06
349 B.J. Surhoff	.20	.06
350 Angel Miranda	.20	.06
351 Sid Roberson	.20	.06
352 Matt Mieske	.20	.06
353 Jose Valentin	.20	.06
354 Matt Lawton RC	.50	.15
355 Eddie Guardado	.20	.06
356 Brad Radke	.20	.06
357 Pedro Munoz	.20	.06
358 Scott Stahoviak	.20	.06
359 Erik Schullstrom	.20	.06
360 Pat Meares	.20	.06
361 Marty Cordova	.20	.06
362 Scott Leius	.20	.06
363 Matt Walbeck	.20	.06
364 Rich Becker	.20	.06
365 Kirby Puckett	.50	.15
366 Oscar Munoz	.20	.06
367 Chuck Knoblauch	.20	.06
368 Marty Cordova ROY	.20	.06
369 Bernie Williams	.30	.09
370 Mike Stanley	.20	.06
371 Andy Pettitte	.30	.09
372 Jack McDowell	.20	.06
373 Sterling Hitchcock	.20	.06
374 David Cone	.20	.06
375 Randy Velarde	.20	.06
376 Don Mattingly	1.25	.35
377 Melido Perez	.20	.06
378 Wade Boggs	.30	.09
379 Ruben Sierra	.20	.06
380 Tony Fernandez	.20	.06
381 John Wetteland	.20	.06
382 Mariano Rivera	.30	.09
383 Derek Jeter	1.25	.35
384 Paul O'Neill	.30	.09
385 Mark McGwire	1.25	.35
386 Scott Brosius	.20	.06
387 Don Wengert	.20	.06
388 Terry Steinbach	.20	.06
389 Brent Gates	.20	.06
390 Craig Paquette	.20	.06
391 Mike Bordick	.20	.06
392 Ariel Prieto	.20	.06
393 Dennis Eckersley	.20	.06
394 Carlos Reyes	.20	.06
395 Todd Stottleymyre	.20	.06
396 Rickey Henderson	.50	.15
397 Geronimo Berroa	.20	.06
398 Steve Ontiveros	.20	.06
399 Mike Gallego	.20	.06
400 Stan Javier	.20	.06
401 Randy Johnson	.50	.15
402 Norm Charlton	.20	.06
403 Mike Blowers	.20	.06
404 Tino Martinez	.30	.09
405 Dan Wilson	.20	.06
406 Andy Benes	.20	.06
407 Alex Diaz	.20	.06
408 Edgar Martinez	.30	.09
409 Chris Bosio	.20	.06
410 Ken Griffey Jr.	.75	.23
411 Luis Sojo	.20	.06
412 Bob Wolcott	.20	.06
413 Vince Coleman	.20	.06
414 Rich Amaral	.20	.06
415 Jay Buhner	.20	.06
416 Alex Rodriguez	1.00	.30
417 Joey Cora	.20	.06
418 Randy Johnson CY	.30	.09
419 Edgar Martinez BAC	.20	.06
420 Ivan Rodriguez	.50	.15
421 Mark McLemore	.20	.06
422 Mickey Tettleton	.20	.06
423 Juan Gonzalez	.30	.09
424 Will Clark	.50	.15
425 Kevin Gross	.20	.06
426 Dean Palmer	.20	.06
427 Kenny Rogers	.20	.06
428 Bob Tewksbury	.20	.06
429 Benji Gil	.20	.06
430 Jeff Russell	.20	.06
431 Rusty Greer	.20	.06
432 Roger Pavlik	.20	.06
433 Esteban Beltre	.20	.06
434 Otis Nixon	.20	.06
435 Paul Molitor	.30	.09
436 Carlos Delgado	.20	.06
437 Ed Sprague	.20	.06
438 Juan Guzman	.20	.06
439 Domingo Cedeno	.20	.06
440 Pat Hentgen	.20	.06
441 Tomas Perez	.20	.06
442 John Olerud	.20	.06
443 Shawn Green	.20	.06
444 Al Leiter	.20	.06
445 Joe Carter	.20	.06
446 Robert Perez	.20	.06
447 Devon White	.20	.06
448 Tony Castillo	.20	.06
449 Alex Gonzalez	.20	.06
450 Roberto Alomar	.30	.09

1996 Pacific Cramer's Choice

Randomly inserted in packs at a rate of one in 721, this 10-card set features the top Major League Baseball players as chosen by Pacific President and CEO, Michael Cramer. The fronts display a color player cut-out on a pyramid diecut shaped background. The backs carry information about why the player was selected for this set in both English and Spanish.

	Nm-Mt	Ex-Mt
COMPLETE SET (10)	300.00	90.00
CC1 Roberto Alomar	20.00	6.00
CC2 Wade Boggs	20.00	6.00
CC3 Cal Ripken	100.00	30.00
CC4 Greg Maddux	50.00	15.00
CC5 Frank Thomas	30.00	9.00
CC6 Tony Gwynn	40.00	12.00
CC7 Mike Piazza	50.00	15.00
CC8 Ken Griffey Jr.	50.00	15.00
CC9 Manny Ramirez	20.00	6.00
CC10 Edgar Martinez	20.00	6.00

1996 Pacific Estrellas Latinas

Randomly inserted in packs at a rate of four in 37, this 36-card set salutes the great Latino players in the major leagues today. The fronts feature color player action cut-outs on a black and gold foil background. The horizontal backs carry a player portrait with information about the player in both English and Spanish.

	Nm-Mt	Ex-Mt
COMPLETE SET (36)	40.00	12.00
EL1 Roberto Alomar	2.00	.60
EL2 Moises Alou	1.25	.35
EL3 Carlos Baerga	1.25	.35
EL4 Geronimo Berroa	1.25	.35
EL5 Ricky Bones	1.25	.35
EL6 Bobby Bonilla	1.25	.35
EL7 Jose Canseco	3.00	.90
EL8 Vinny Castilla	1.25	.35
EL9 Pedro Martinez	3.00	.90
EL10 John Valentin	1.25	.35
EL11 Andres Galarraga	1.25	.35
EL12 Juan Gonzalez	2.00	.60
EL13 Ozzie Guillen	1.25	.35
EL14 Esteban Loaiza	1.25	.35
EL15 Javier Lopez	1.25	.35
EL16 Dennis Martinez	1.25	.35
EL17 Edgar Martinez	2.00	.60
EL18 Tino Martinez	2.00	.60
EL19 Orlando Merced	1.25	.35
EL20 Jose Mesa	1.25	.35
EL21 Raul Mondesi	1.25	.35
EL22 Jaime Navarro	1.25	.35
EL23 Rafael Palmeiro	2.00	.60
EL24 Carlos Perez	1.25	.35
EL25 Manny Ramirez	2.00	.60
EL26 Alex Rodriguez	6.00	1.80
EL27 Ivan Rodriguez	3.00	.90
EL28 David Segui	1.25	.35
EL29 Ruben Sierra	1.25	.35
EL30 Sammy Sosa	5.00	1.50
EL31 Julian Tavarez	1.25	.35
EL32 Ismael Valdes	1.25	.35
EL33 Fernando Valenzuela	1.25	.35
EL34 Quilvio Veras	1.25	.35
EL35 Omar Vizquel	2.00	.60
EL36 Bernie Williams	2.00	.60

1996 Pacific Gold Crown Die Cuts

Randomly inserted in packs at a rate of one in 37, this 36-card set features 1996 Major League Baseball Super Stars. The fronts display color action player photos with a diecut gold crown at the top and gold foil printing. The backs carry a color player portrait and information about the player in English and Spanish.

	Nm-Mt	Ex-Mt
COMPLETE SET (36)	150.00	45.00
DC1 Roberto Alomar	5.00	1.50
DC2 Will Clark	8.00	2.40
DC3 Johnny Damon	5.00	1.50
DC4 Don Mattingly	20.00	6.00
DC5 Edgar Martinez	5.00	1.50
DC6 Manny Ramirez	5.00	1.50
DC7 Mike Piazza	12.00	3.60
DC8 Quilvio Veras	3.00	.90
DC9 Rickey Henderson	8.00	2.40
DC10 Jeff Bagwell	5.00	1.50
DC11 Andres Galarraga	3.00	.90
DC12 Tim Salmon	5.00	1.50
DC13 Ken Griffey Jr.	12.00	3.60
DC14 Sammy Sosa	12.00	3.60
DC15 Cal Ripken	25.00	7.50
DC16 Raul Mondesi	3.00	.90
DC17 Jose Canseco	8.00	2.40
DC18 Frank Thomas	8.00	2.40
DC19 Hideo Nomo	8.00	2.40
DC20 Wade Boggs	5.00	1.50
DC21 Reggie Sanders	3.00	.90
DC22 Carlos Baerga	3.00	.90
DC23 Mo Vaughn	3.00	.90
DC24 Ivan Rodriguez	8.00	2.40
DC25 Kirby Puckett	8.00	2.40
DC26 Albert Belle	3.00	.90
DC27 Vinny Castilla	3.00	.90
DC28 Greg Maddux	12.00	3.60
DC29 Dante Bichette	3.00	.90
DC30 Deion Sanders	5.00	1.50
DC31 Chipper Jones	8.00	2.40
DC32 Cecil Fielder	3.00	.90
DC33 Randy Johnson	8.00	2.40
DC34 Mark McGwire	20.00	6.00
DC35 Tony Gwynn	10.00	3.00
DC36 Barry Bonds	20.00	6.00

1996 Pacific Hometowns

Randomly inserted in packs at a rate of two in 37, this 20-card set features color action player photos with a gold foil border on the left and gold foil printing. The backs carry a player portrait with the player's hometown or city and country and player information printed in both English and Spanish.

	Nm-Mt	Ex-Mt
COMPLETE SET (20)	60.00	18.00
HP1 Mike Piazza	6.00	1.80
HP2 Greg Maddux	6.00	1.80
HP3 Tony Gwynn	5.00	1.50
HP4 Carlos Baerga	1.50	.45
HP5 Don Mattingly	10.00	3.00
HP6 Cal Ripken	12.00	3.60
HP7 Chipper Jones	4.00	1.20
HP8 Andres Galarraga	1.50	.45
HP9 Manny Ramirez	2.50	.75
HP10 Roberto Alomar	2.50	.75
HP11 Ken Griffey Jr.	6.00	1.80
HP12 Jose Canseco	4.00	1.20
HP13 Frank Thomas	4.00	1.20
HP14 Vinny Castilla	1.50	.45
HP15 Roberto Kelly	1.50	.45
HP16 Dennis Martinez	1.50	.45
HP17 Kirby Puckett	4.00	1.20
HP18 Raul Mondesi	1.50	.45
HP19 Hideo Nomo	4.00	1.20
HP20 Edgar Martinez	2.50	.75

1996 Pacific Milestones

Randomly inserted in packs at a rate of one in 37, this 10-card set denotes the outstanding milestone and record-breaking achievements of baseball's superstars in 1995. The fronts feature a color action player cut-out on a blue foil background with embossed symbols representing the team logo, baseball, and the milestone or achievement. The backs carry a player portrait with the milestone or achievement printed in both English and Spanish.

	Nm-Mt	Ex-Mt
COMPLETE SET (10)	50.00	15.00
M1 Albert Belle	1.50	.45
M2 Don Mattingly	10.00	3.00
M3 Tony Gwynn	5.00	1.50
M4 Jose Canseco	4.00	1.20
M5 Marty Cordova	1.50	.45
M6 Wade Boggs	2.50	.75
M7 Greg Maddux	6.00	1.80
M8 Eddie Murray	4.00	1.20
M9 Ken Griffey Jr.	6.00	1.80
M10 Cal Ripken	12.00	3.60

1996 Pacific October Moments

Randomly inserted in packs at a rate of one in 37, this 20-card set highlights 1995 postseason heroics and the players involved. The fronts feature borderless color player action photos with a bronze foil background and printing. The backs carry a player portrait with the heroic action printed in both English and Spanish.

	Nm-Mt	Ex-Mt
COMPLETE SET (20)	80.00	24.00
OM1 Carlos Baerga	2.50	.75
OM2 Albert Belle	2.50	.75
OM3 Dante Bichette	2.50	.75
OM4 Jose Canseco	6.00	1.80
OM5 Tom Glavine	4.00	1.20
OM6 Ken Griffey Jr.	10.00	3.00
OM7 Randy Johnson	6.00	1.80
OM8 Chipper Jones	6.00	1.80
OM9 David Justice	2.50	.75
OM10 Ryan Klesko	2.50	.75
OM11 Kenny Lofton	2.50	.75
OM12 Javier Lopez	2.50	.75
OM13 Greg Maddux	10.00	3.00
OM14 Edgar Martinez	4.00	1.20
OM15 Don Mattingly	15.00	4.50
OM16 Hideo Nomo	6.00	1.80
OM17 Mike Piazza	10.00	3.00
OM18 Manny Ramirez	4.00	1.20
OM19 Reggie Sanders	2.50	.75
OM20 Jim Thome	6.00	1.80

1997 Pacific

This 450-card set was issued in one series and distributed in 12-card packs. The fronts feature color action player photos foiled in gold. The backs carry player information in both English and Spanish with player statistics. No subsets are featured as the manufacturer focused on providing collectors with the most comprehensive selection of major league players as possible. Rookie Cards include Brian Giles.

	Nm-Mt	Ex-Mt
COMPLETE SET (450)	50.00	15.00
1 Garret Anderson	.30	.09
2 George Arias	.30	.09
3 Chili Davis	.30	.09
4 Gary DiSarcina	.30	.09
5 Jim Edmonds	.30	.09
6 Darin Erstad	.30	.09
7 Jorge Fabregas	.30	.09
8 Chuck Finley	.30	.09
9 Rex Hudler	.30	.09
10 Mark Langston	.30	.09
11 Orlando Palmeiro	.30	.09
12 Troy Percival	.30	.09
13 Tim Salmon	.50	.15
14 J.T. Snow	.30	.09
15 Randy Velarde	.30	.09
16 Manny Alexander	.30	.09
17 Roberto Alomar	.50	.15
18 Brady Anderson	.30	.09
19 Armando Benitez	.30	.09
20 Bobby Bonilla	.30	.09
21 Rocky Coppinger	.30	.09
22 Scott Erickson	.30	.09
23 Jeffrey Hammonds	.30	.09
24 Chris Hoiles	.30	.09
25 Eddie Murray	.75	.23
26 Mike Mussina	.50	.15
27 Randy Myers	.30	.09
28 Rafael Palmeiro	.50	.15
29 Cal Ripken	2.50	.75
30 B.J. Surhoff	.30	.09
31 Tony Tarasco	.30	.09
32 Esteban Beltre	.30	.09
33 Darren Bragg	.30	.09
34 Jose Canseco	.75	.23
35 Roger Clemens	1.50	.45
36 Wil Cordero	.30	.09
37 Alex Delgado	.30	.09
38 Jeff Frye	.30	.09
39 Nomar Garciaparra	1.25	.35
40 Tom Gordon	.30	.09
41 Mike Greenwell	.30	.09
42 Reggie Jefferson	.30	.09
43 Tim Naehring	.30	.09
44 Troy O'Leary	.30	.09
45 Heathcliff Slocumb	.30	.09
46 Lee Tinsley	.30	.09
47 John Valentin	.30	.09
48 Mo Vaughn	.30	.09
49 Wilson Alvarez	.30	.09
50 Harold Baines	.30	.09
51 Ray Durham	.30	.09
52 Alex Fernandez	.30	.09
53 Ozzie Guillen	.30	.09
54 Roberto Hernandez	.30	.09
55 Ron Karkovice	.30	.09
56 Darren Lewis	.30	.09
57 Norberto Martin	.30	.09
58 Dave Martinez	.30	.09
59 Lyle Mouton	.30	.09
60 Jose Munoz	.30	.09
61 Tony Phillips	.30	.09
62 Kevin Tapani	.30	.09
63 Danny Tartabull	.30	.09
64 Frank Thomas	.75	.23
65 Robin Ventura	.30	.09
66 Sandy Alomar Jr.	.30	.09
67 Albert Belle	.30	.09
68 Julio Franco	.30	.09
69 Brian Giles RC	1.50	.45
70 Danny Graves	.30	.09
71 Orel Hershiser	.30	.09
72 Jeff Kent	.30	.09
73 Kenny Lofton	.30	.09
74 Dennis Martinez	.30	.09
75 Jack McDowell	.30	.09
76 Jose Mesa	.30	.09
77 Charles Nagy	.30	.09
78 Manny Ramirez	.50	.15
79 Julian Tavarez	.30	.09
80 Jim Thome	.75	.23
81 Jose Vizcaino	.30	.09
82 Omar Vizquel	.50	.15
83 Brad Ausmus	.30	.09
84 Kimera Bartee	.30	.09
85 Raul Casanova	.30	.09
86 Tony Clark	.30	.09
87 Travis Fryman	.30	.09
88 Bobby Higginson	.30	.09
89 Mark Lewis	.30	.09
90 Jose Lima	.30	.09
91 Felipe Lira	.30	.09
92 Phil Nevin	.30	.09
93 Melvin Nieves	.30	.09
94 Curtis Pride	.30	.09
95 Ruben Sierra	.30	.09
96 Alan Trammell	.30	.09
97 Kevin Appier	.30	.09
98 Tim Belcher	.30	.09
99 Johnny Damon	.50	.15
100 Tom Goodwin	.30	.09
101 Bob Hamelin	.30	.09
102 David Howard	.30	.09
103 Jason Jacome	.30	.09
104 Keith Lockhart	.30	.09
105 Mike Macfarlane	.30	.09
106 Jeff Montgomery	.30	.09
107 Jose Offerman	.30	.09
108 Hipolito Pichardo	.30	.09
109 Joe Randa	.30	.09
110 Bip Roberts	.30	.09
111 Chris Stynes	.30	.09
112 Mike Sweeney	.30	.09
113 Joe Vitiello	.30	.09
114 Jeromy Burnitz	.30	.09
115 Chuck Carr	.30	.09
116 Jeff Cirillo	.30	.09
117 Mike Fetters	.30	.09
118 David Hulse	.30	.09
119 John Jaha	.30	.09
120 Scott Karl	.30	.09
121 Jesse Levis	.30	.09
122 Mark Loretta	.30	.09
123 Mike Matheny	.30	.09
124 Ben McDonald	.30	.09
125 Matt Mieske	.30	.09
126 Angel Miranda	.30	.09
127 Dave Nilsson	.30	.09
128 Jose Valentin	.30	.09
129 Fernando Vina	.30	.09
130 Ron Villone	.30	.09
131 Gerald Williams	.30	.09
132 Rick Aguilera	.30	.09
133 Rich Becker	.30	.09
134 Ron Coomer	.30	.09
135 Marty Cordova	.30	.09
136 Eddie Guardado	.30	.09
137 Denny Hocking	.30	.09
138 Roberto Kelly	.30	.09
139 Chuck Knoblauch	.30	.09
140 Matt Lawton	.30	.09
141 Pat Meares	.30	.09
142 Paul Molitor	.50	.15
143 Greg Myers	.30	.09
144 Jeff Reboulet	.30	.09
145 Scott Stahoviak	.30	.09
146 Todd Walker	.30	.09
147 Wade Boggs	.50	.15
148 David Cone	.30	.09
149 Mariano Duncan	.30	.09
150 Cecil Fielder	.30	.09
151 Dwight Gooden	.30	.09
152 Derek Jeter	2.00	.60
153 Jim Leyritz	.30	.09
154 Tino Martinez	.50	.15
155 Paul O'Neill	.50	.15
156 Andy Pettitte	.50	.15
157 Tim Raines	.30	.09
158 Mariano Rivera	.50	.15
159 Ruben Rivera	.30	.09
160 Kenny Rogers	.30	.09
161 Darryl Strawberry	.30	.09
162 John Wetteland	.30	.09
163 Bernie Williams	.50	.15
164 Tony Batista	.30	.09
165 Geronimo Berroa	.30	.09
166 Mike Bordick	.30	.09
167 Scott Brosius	.30	.09
168 Brent Gates	.30	.09
169 Jason Giambi	.30	.09
170 Jose Herrera	.30	.09
171 Brian Lesher RC	.30	.09
172 Damon Mashore	.30	.09
173 Mark McGwire	2.00	.60
174 Ariel Prieto	.30	.09
175 Carlos Reyes	.30	.09
176 Matt Stairs	.30	.09
177 Terry Steinbach	.30	.09
178 John Wasdin	.30	.09
179 Ernie Young	.30	.09
180 Rich Amaral	.30	.09
181 Bobby Ayala	.30	.09
182 Jay Buhner	.30	.09
183 Rafael Carmona	.30	.09
184 Norm Charlton	.30	.09
185 Joey Cora	.30	.09
186 Ken Griffey Jr.	1.25	.35
187 Sterling Hitchcock	.30	.09
188 Dave Hollins	.30	.09
189 Randy Johnson	.75	.23
190 Edgar Martinez	.50	.15
191 Jamie Moyer	.30	.09
192 Alex Rodriguez	1.25	.35
193 Paul Sorrento	.30	.09
194 Salomon Torres	.30	.09
195 Bob Wells	.30	.09
196 Dan Wilson	.30	.09
197 Will Clark	.75	.23
198 Kevin Elster	.30	.09
199 Rene Gonzales	.30	.09
200 Juan Gonzalez	.50	.15
201 Rusty Greer	.30	.09
202 Darryl Hamilton	.30	.09
203 Mike Henneman	.30	.09
204 Ken Hill	.30	.09
205 Mark McLemore	.30	.09
206 Darren Oliver	.30	.09
207 Dean Palmer	.30	.09
208 Roger Pavlik	.30	.09
209 Ivan Rodriguez	.75	.23
210 Kurt Stillwell	.30	.09
211 Mickey Tettleton	.30	.09
212 Bobby Witt	.30	.09
213 Tilson Brito	.30	.09
214 Jacob Brumfield	.30	.09
215 Miguel Cairo	.30	.09
216 Joe Carter	.30	.09
217 Felipe Crespo	.30	.09
218 Carlos Delgado	.30	.09
219 Alex Gonzalez	.30	.09
220 Shawn Green	.30	.09
221 Juan Guzman	.30	.09
222 Pat Hentgen	.30	.09
223 Charlie O'Brien	.30	.09
224 John Olerud	.30	.09
225 Robert Perez	.30	.09
226 Tomas Perez	.30	.09
227 Juan Samuel	.30	.09
228 Ed Sprague	.30	.09
229 Mike Timlin	.30	.09
230 Rafael Belliard	.30	.09
231 Jermaine Dye	.30	.09
232 Tom Glavine	.50	.15
233 Marquis Grissom	.30	.09
234 Andruw Jones	.30	.09
235 Chipper Jones	.75	.23
236 David Justice	.30	.09
237 Ryan Klesko	.30	.09
238 Mark Lemke	.30	.09
239 Javier Lopez	.30	.09
240 Greg Maddux	1.25	.35
241 Fred McGriff	.50	.15
242 Denny Neagle	.30	.09
243 Eddie Perez	.30	.09
244 John Smoltz	.50	.15
245 Mark Wohlers	.30	.09
246 Brant Brown	.30	.09
247 Scott Bullett	.30	.09
248 Leo Gomez	.30	.09
249 Luis Gonzalez	.30	.09
250 Mark Grace	.50	.15
251 Jose Hernandez	.30	.09
252 Brooks Kieschnick	.30	.09
253 Brian McRae	.30	.09
254 Jaime Navarro	.30	.09
255 Mike Perez	.30	.09
256 Rey Sanchez	.30	.09
257 Ryne Sandberg	1.25	.35
258 Scott Servais	.30	.09
259 Sammy Sosa	1.25	.35
260 Pedro Valdes	.30	.09
261 Turk Wendell	.30	.09
262 Bret Boone	.30	.09
263 Jeff Branson	.30	.09
264 Jeff Brantley	.30	.09
265 Dave Burba	.30	.09
266 Hector Carrasco	.30	.09
267 Eric Davis	.30	.09
268 Willie Greene	.30	.09
269 Lenny Harris	.30	.09
270 Thomas Howard	.30	.09
271 Barry Larkin	.50	.15
272 Hal Morris	.30	.09
273 Joe Oliver	.30	.09
274 Eric Owens	.30	.09
275 Jose Rijo	.30	.09
276 Reggie Sanders	.30	.09
277 Eddie Taubensee	.30	.09
278 Jason Bates	.30	.09
279 Dante Bichette	.30	.09
280 Ellis Burks	.30	.09
281 Vinny Castilla	.30	.09
282 Andres Galarraga	.30	.09
283 Quinton McCracken	.30	.09
284 Jayhawk Owens	.30	.09
285 Jeff Reed	.30	.09
286 Bryan Rekar	.30	.09
287 Armando Reynoso	.30	.09
288 Kevin Ritz	.30	.09
289 Bruce Ruffin	.30	.09
290 John Vander Wal	.30	.09
291 Larry Walker	.50	.15
292 Walt Weiss	.30	.09
293 Eric Young	.30	.09
294 Kurt Abbott	.30	.09
295 Alex Arias	.30	.09
296 Miguel Batista	.30	.09
297 Kevin Brown	.30	.09
298 Luis Castillo	.30	.09
299 Greg Colbrunn	.30	.09
300 Jeff Conine	.30	.09
301 Charles Johnson	.30	.09
302 Al Leiter	.30	.09
303 Robb Nen	.30	.09
304 Joe Orsulak	.30	.09
305 Yorkis Perez	.30	.09
306 Edgar Renteria	.30	.09
307 Gary Sheffield	.30	.09
308 Jesus Tavarez	.30	.09
309 Quilvio Veras	.30	.09
310 Devon White	.30	.09
311 Jeff Bagwell	.50	.15
312 Derek Bell	.30	.09
313 Sean Berry	.30	.09
314 Craig Biggio	.50	.15
315 Doug Drabek	.30	.09
316 Tony Eusebio	.30	.09
317 Ricky Gutierrez	.30	.09
318 Xavier Hernandez	.30	.09
319 Brian L. Hunter	.30	.09
320 Darryl Kile	.30	.09
321 Derrick May	.30	.09
322 Orlando Miller	.30	.09
323 James Mouton	.30	.09
324 Bill Spiers	.30	.09
325 Pedro Astacio	.30	.09
326 Brett Butler	.30	.09
327 Juan Castro	.30	.09
328 Roger Cedeno	.30	.09
329 Delino DeShields	.30	.09
330 Karim Garcia	.30	.09
331 Todd Hollandsworth	.30	.09
332 Eric Karros	.30	.09
333 Oreste Marrero	.30	.09
334 Ramon Martinez	.30	.09
335 Raul Mondesi	.30	.09
336 Hideo Nomo	.75	.23
337 Antonio Osuna	.30	.09
338 Chan Ho Park	.30	.09
339 Mike Piazza	1.25	.35
340 Ismael Valdes	.30	.09
341 Moises Alou	.30	.09
342 Omar Daal	.30	.09
343 Jeff Fassero	.30	.09
344 Cliff Floyd	.30	.09
345 Mark Grudzielanek	.30	.09
346 Mike Lansing	.30	.09
347 Pedro Martinez	.75	.23
348 Sherman Obando	.30	.09
349 Jose Paniagua	.30	.09
350 Henry Rodriguez	.30	.09
351 Mel Rojas	.30	.09
352 F.P. Santangelo	.30	.09
353 David Segui	.30	.09
354 Dave Silvestri	.30	.09
355 Ugueth Urbina	.30	.09
356 Rondell White	.30	.09
357 Edgardo Alfonzo	.30	.09
358 Carlos Baerga	.30	.09
359 Tim Bogar	.30	.09
360 Rico Brogna	.30	.09
361 Alvaro Espinoza	.30	.09
362 Carl Everett	.30	.09
363 John Franco	.30	.09
364 Bernard Gilkey	.30	.09
365 Todd Hundley	.30	.09
366 Butch Huskey	.30	.09
367 Jason Isringhausen	.30	.09
368 Bobby Jones	.30	.09
369 Lance Johnson	.30	.09
370 Brent Mayne	.30	.09
371 Alex Ochoa	.30	.09
372 Rey Ordonez	.30	.09
373 Ron Blazier	.30	.09
374 Ricky Bottalico	.30	.09
375 David Doster	.30	.09
376 Lenny Dykstra	.30	.09
377 Jim Eisenreich	.30	.09
378 Bobby Estalella	.30	.09
379 Gregg Jefferies	.30	.09
380 Kevin Jordan	.30	.09
381 Ricardo Jordan	.30	.09
382 Mickey Morandini	.30	.09
383 Ricky Otero	.30	.09
384 Benito Santiago	.30	.09
385 Gene Schall	.30	.09
386 Curt Schilling	.30	.09
387 Kevin Sefcik	.30	.09
388 Kevin Stocker	.30	.09
389 Jermaine Allensworth	.30	.09
390 Jay Bell	.30	.09
391 Jason Christiansen	.30	.09
392 Francisco Cordova	.30	.09
393 Mark Johnson	.30	.09
394 Jason Kendall	.30	.09
395 Jeff King	.30	.09
396 Jon Lieber	.30	.09
397 Nelson Liriano	.30	.09
398 Esteban Loaiza	.30	.09
399 Al Martin	.30	.09
400 Orlando Merced	.30	.09
401 Ramon Morel	.30	.09
402 Luis Alicea	.30	.09
403 Alan Benes	.30	.09
404 Andy Benes	.30	.09
405 Terry Bradshaw	.30	.09
406 Royce Clayton	.30	.09
407 Dennis Eckersley	.30	.09
408 Gary Gaetti	.30	.09
409 Mike Gallego	.30	.09
410 Ron Gant	.30	.09
411 Brian Jordan	.30	.09
412 Ray Lankford	.30	.09
413 John Mabry	.30	.09
414 Willie McGee	.30	.09
415 Tom Pagnozzi	.30	.09
416 Ozzie Smith	1.25	.35
417 Todd Stottlemyre	.30	.09
418 Mark Sweeney	.30	.09
419 Andy Ashby	.30	.09
420 Ken Caminiti	.30	.09
421 Archi Cianfrocco	.30	.09
422 Steve Finley	.30	.09
423 Chris Gomez	.30	.09
424 Tony Gwynn	1.00	.30
425 Joey Hamilton	.30	.09
426 Rickey Henderson	.75	.23
427 Trevor Hoffman	.30	.09
428 Brian Johnson	.30	.09
429 Wally Joyner	.30	.09
430 Scott Livingstone	.30	.09
431 Jody Reed	.30	.09
432 Craig Shipley	.30	.09
433 Fernando Valenzuela	.30	.09
434 Greg Vaughn	.30	.09
435 Rich Aurilia	.30	.09
436 Kim Batiste	.30	.09
437 Jose Bautista	.30	.09
438 Rod Beck	.30	.09
439 Marvin Benard	.30	.09
440 Barry Bonds	2.00	.60
441 Shawon Dunston	.30	.09
442 Shawn Estes	.30	.09
443 Osvaldo Fernandez	.30	.09
444 Stan Javier	.30	.09
445 David McCarty	.30	.09
446 Bill Mueller RC	3.00	.90
447 Steve Scarsone	.30	.09
448 Robby Thompson	.30	.09
449 Rick Wilkins	.30	.09
450 Matt Williams	.30	.09

1997 Pacific Light Blue

These Light Blue parallel foil cards were found one per pack exclusively in Wal-Mart and Sam's 14-card retail packs. The cards are very similar in design to the scarce Silver parallels randomly seeded in basic packs resulting in a source of confusion for dealers and collectors alike. The Light Blue parallels are not as reflective as the Silvers. Collectors should take extreme caution when purchasing Silver or Light Blue cards.

	Nm-Mt	Ex-Mt
*STARS: 2.5X TO 6X BASIC CARDS...		
*ROOKIES: 1.25X TO 3X BASIC CARDS		

1997 Pacific Silver

Randomly inserted in packs at a rate of one in 73, this 450-card set is a silver foil parallel version of the regular set and is similar in design. Only 67 of these sets were produced.

	Nm-Mt	Ex-Mt
*STARS: 20X TO 50X BASIC CARDS..		
*ROOKIES: 6X TO 15X BASIC CARDS		
446 Bill Mueller	25.00	7.50

1997 Pacific Card-Supials

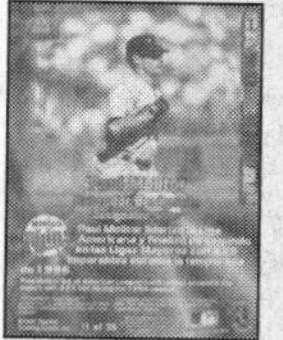

Randomly inserted in packs at a rate of one in 37, this 36-paired-card insert set features color action player photos of some of the greatest players in the Major Leagues. A smaller card was made to pair with the regular size card of the same player. The backs carry a slot for insertion of the small card.

	Nm-Mt	Ex-Mt
COMP.LARGE SET (36)	100.00	30.00
*MINIS: .25X TO .6X LARGE SUPIALS		
1 Roberto Alomar	4.00	1.20
2 Brady Anderson	2.50	.75
3 Eddie Murray	6.00	1.80
4 Cal Ripken	20.00	6.00
5 Jose Canseco	6.00	1.80
6 Mo Vaughn	2.50	.75
7 Frank Thomas	6.00	1.80
8 Albert Belle	2.50	.75
9 Omar Vizquel	4.00	1.20
10 Chuck Knoblauch	2.50	.75
11 Paul Molitor	4.00	1.20
12 Wade Boggs	4.00	1.20
13 Derek Jeter	15.00	4.50
14 Andy Pettitte	4.00	1.20
15 Mark McGwire	15.00	4.50
16 Jay Buhner	2.50	.75
17 Ken Griffey Jr.	10.00	3.00
18 Alex Rodriguez	10.00	3.00
19 Juan Gonzalez	4.00	1.20
20 Ivan Rodriguez	6.00	1.80
21 Andruw Jones	2.50	.75
22 Chipper Jones	6.00	1.80
23 Ryan Klesko	2.50	.75
24 Greg Maddux	10.00	3.00
25 Ryne Sandberg	10.00	3.00
26 Andres Galarraga	2.50	.75
27 Gary Sheffield	2.50	.75
28 Jeff Bagwell	4.00	1.20
29 Todd Hollandsworth	2.50	.75
30 Hideo Nomo	6.00	1.80
31 Mike Piazza	10.00	3.00
32 Todd Hundley	2.50	.75
33 Dennis Eckersley	2.50	.75
34 Ken Caminiti	2.50	.75
35 Tony Gwynn	8.00	2.40
36 Barry Bonds	15.00	4.50

1997 Pacific Cramer's Choice

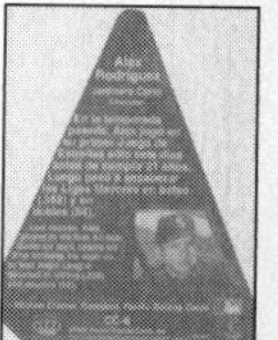

Randomly inserted in packs at a rate of one in 721, this 10-card set features the top Major League Baseball players as chosen by Pacific

President and CEO, Michael Cramer. The fronts display a color player cut-out on a pyramid die-cut shaped background. The backs carry information about why the player was selected for this set in both English and Spanish.

	Nm-Mt	Ex-Mt
1 Roberto Alomar	15.00	4.50
2 Frank Thomas	25.00	7.50
3 Albert Belle	10.00	3.00
4 Andy Pettitte	15.00	4.50
5 Ken Griffey Jr.	40.00	12.00
6 Alex Rodriguez	40.00	12.00
7 Chipper Jones	25.00	7.50
8 John Smoltz	15.00	4.50
9 Mike Piazza	40.00	12.00
10 Tony Gwynn	30.00	9.00

1997 Pacific Fireworks Die Cuts

Randomly inserted in packs at a rate of one in 73, this 20-card set features color action player photos on a fireworks die-cut background. The backs carry player information in both English and Spanish.

	Nm-Mt	Ex-Mt
COMPLETE SET (20)	150.00	45.00
1 Roberto Alomar	5.00	1.50
2 Brady Anderson	3.00	.90
3 Eddie Murray	8.00	2.40
4 Cal Ripken	25.00	7.50
5 Frank Thomas	8.00	2.40
6 Albert Belle	3.00	.90
7 Derek Jeter	20.00	6.00
8 Andy Pettitte	5.00	1.50
9 Bernie Williams	5.00	1.50
10 Mark McGwire	20.00	6.00
11 Ken Griffey Jr.	12.00	3.60
12 Alex Rodriguez	12.00	3.60
13 Juan Gonzalez	5.00	1.50
14 Andruw Jones	3.00	.90
15 Chipper Jones	8.00	2.40
16 Hideo Nomo	8.00	2.40
17 Mike Piazza	12.00	3.60
18 Henry Rodriguez	3.00	.90
19 Tony Gwynn	10.00	3.00
20 Barry Bonds	20.00	6.00

1997 Pacific Gold Crown Die Cuts

Randomly inserted in packs at a rate of one in 37, this 36-card set honors some of Major League Baseball's Super Stars of today. The fronts feature color action player photos with a die-cut gold crown at the top and gold foil printing. The backs carry player information in both English and Spanish.

	Nm-Mt	Ex-Mt
COMPLETE SET (36)	200.00	60.00
1 Roberto Alomar	5.00	1.50
2 Brady Anderson	3.00	.90
3 Mike Mussina	5.00	1.50
4 Eddie Murray	8.00	2.40
5 Cal Ripken	25.00	7.50
6 Jose Canseco	8.00	2.40
7 Frank Thomas	8.00	2.40
8 Albert Belle	3.00	.90
9 Omar Vizquel	5.00	1.50
10 Wade Boggs	5.00	1.50
11 Derek Jeter	20.00	6.00
12 Andy Pettitte	5.00	1.50
13 Mariano Rivera	5.00	1.50
14 Bernie Williams	5.00	1.50
15 Mark McGwire	20.00	6.00
16 Ken Griffey Jr.	12.00	3.60
17 Edgar Martinez	5.00	1.50
18 Alex Rodriguez	12.00	3.60
19 Juan Gonzalez	5.00	1.50
20 Ivan Rodriguez	8.00	2.40
21 Andruw Jones	3.00	.90
22 Chipper Jones	8.00	2.40
23 Ryan Klesko	3.00	.90
24 John Smoltz	5.00	1.50
25 Ryne Sandberg	12.00	3.60
26 Andres Galarraga	3.00	.90
27 Edgar Renteria	3.00	.90
28 Jeff Bagwell	5.00	1.50
29 Todd Hollandsworth	3.00	.90
30 Hideo Nomo	8.00	2.40
31 Mike Piazza	12.00	3.60
32 Todd Hundley	3.00	.90
33 Brian Jordan	3.00	.90
34 Ken Caminiti	3.00	.90
35 Tony Gwynn	10.00	3.00
36 Barry Bonds	20.00	6.00

1997 Pacific Latinos of the Major Leagues

Randomly inserted in packs at a rate of two in 37, this 36-card set salutes the great Latino players in the Major Leagues today. The fronts feature color player action images on a gold foil background of their name. The backs carry player information in both English and Spanish.

	Nm-Mt	Ex-Mt
COMPLETE SET (36)	50.00	15.00
1 George Arias	1.50	.45
2 Roberto Alomar	2.50	.75
3 Rafael Palmeiro	2.50	.75
4 Bobby Bonilla	1.50	.45
5 Jose Canseco	4.00	1.20
6 Wilson Alvarez	1.50	.45
7 Dave Martinez	1.50	.45
8 Julio Franco	1.50	.45
9 Manny Ramirez	2.50	.75
10 Omar Vizquel	2.50	.75
11 Marty Cordova	1.50	.45
12 Roberto Kelly	1.50	.45
13 Tino Martinez	2.50	.75
14 Mariano Rivera	2.50	.75
15 Ruben Rivera	1.50	.45
16 Bernie Williams	2.50	.75
17 Geronimo Berroa	1.50	.45
18 Joey Cora	1.50	.45
19 Edgar Martinez	2.50	.75
20 Alex Rodriguez	6.00	1.80
21 Juan Gonzalez	2.50	.75
22 Ivan Rodriguez	4.00	1.20
23 Andruw Jones	1.50	.45
24 Javier Lopez	1.50	.45
25 Sammy Sosa	6.00	1.80
26 Vinny Castilla	1.50	.45
27 Andres Galarraga	1.50	.45
28 Ramon Martinez	1.50	.45
29 Raul Mondesi	1.50	.45
30 Ismael Valdes	1.50	.45
31 Pedro Martinez	4.00	1.20
32 Henry Rodriguez	1.50	.45
33 Carlos Baerga	1.50	.45
34 Rey Ordonez	1.50	.45
35 Fernando Valenzuela	1.50	.45
36 Osvaldo Fernandez	1.50	.45

1997 Pacific Triple Crown Die Cuts

Randomly inserted in packs at a rate of one in 145, this 20-card set features color player images over a gold foil diamond-shaped background with a die-cut gold crown at the top. The backs carry player information in both English and Spanish.

	Nm-Mt	Ex-Mt
COMPLETE SET (20)	200.00	60.00
1 Brady Anderson	6.00	1.80
2 Rafael Palmeiro	10.00	3.00
3 Mo Vaughn	6.00	1.80
4 Frank Thomas	15.00	4.50
5 Albert Belle	6.00	1.80
6 Jim Thome	15.00	4.50
7 Cecil Fielder	6.00	1.80
8 Mark McGwire	40.00	12.00
9 Ken Griffey Jr.	25.00	7.50
10 Alex Rodriguez	25.00	7.50
11 Juan Gonzalez	10.00	3.00
12 Andruw Jones	6.00	1.80
13 Chipper Jones	15.00	4.50
14 Dante Bichette	6.00	1.80
15 Ellis Burks	6.00	1.80
16 Andres Galarraga	6.00	1.80
17 Jeff Bagwell	10.00	3.00
18 Mike Piazza	25.00	7.50
19 Ken Caminiti	6.00	1.80
20 Barry Bonds	40.00	12.00

1998 Pacific

The 1998 Pacific set was issued in one series totalling 450 cards and distributed in 12-card packs with a suggested retail price of $2.49. The fronts features borderless color player photos with gold foil highlights. The backs carry player information in both Spanish and English. As is standard with base-brand Pacific, the entire set is devoid of subset cards, instead focusing on a comprehensive selection of major league players.

	Nm-Mt	Ex-Mt
COMPLETE SET (450)	60.00	18.00
1 Luis Alicea	.30	.09
2 Garret Anderson	.30	.09
3 Jason Dickson	.30	.09
4 Gary DiSarcina	.30	.09
5 Jim Edmonds	.30	.09
6 Darin Erstad	.30	.09
7 Chuck Finley	.30	.09
8 Shigetoshi Hasegawa	.30	.09
9 Rickey Henderson	.75	.23
10 Dave Hollins	.30	.09
11 Mark Langston	.30	.09
12 Orlando Palmeiro	.30	.09
13 Troy Percival	.30	.09
14 Tony Phillips	.30	.09
15 Tim Salmon	.50	.15
16 Allen Watson	.30	.09
17 Roberto Alomar	.50	.15
18 Brady Anderson	.30	.09
19 Harold Baines	.30	.09
20 Armando Benitez	.30	.09
21 Geronimo Berroa	.30	.09
22 Mike Bordick	.30	.09
23 Eric Davis	.30	.09
24 Scott Erickson	.30	.09
25 Chris Hoiles	.30	.09
26 Jimmy Key	.30	.09
27 Aaron Ledesma	.30	.09
28 Mike Mussina	.50	.15
29 Randy Myers	.30	.09
30 Jesse Orosco	.30	.09
31 Rafael Palmeiro	.50	.15
32 Jeff Reboulet	.30	.09
33 Cal Ripken	2.50	.75
34 B.J. Surhoff	.30	.09
35 Steve Avery	.30	.09
36 Darren Bragg	.30	.09
37 Wil Cordero	.30	.09
38 Jeff Frye	.30	.09
39 Nomar Garciaparra	1.25	.35
40 Tom Gordon	.30	.09
41 Bill Haselman	.30	.09
42 Scott Hatteberg	.30	.09
43 Butch Henry	.30	.09
44 Reggie Jefferson	.30	.09
45 Tim Naehring	.30	.09
46 Troy O'Leary	.30	.09
47 Jeff Suppan	.30	.09
48 John Valentin	.30	.09
49 Mo Vaughn	.30	.09
50 Tim Wakefield	.30	.09
51 James Baldwin	.30	.09
52 Albert Belle	.30	.09
53 Tony Castillo	.30	.09
54 Doug Drabek	.30	.09
55 Ray Durham	.30	.09
56 Jorge Fabregas	.30	.09
57 Ozzie Guillen	.30	.09
58 Matt Karchner	.30	.09
59 Norberto Martin	.30	.09
60 Dave Martinez	.30	.09
61 Lyle Mouton	.30	.09
62 Jaime Navarro	.30	.09
63 Frank Thomas	.75	.23
64 Mario Valdez	.30	.09
65 Robin Ventura	.30	.09
66 Sandy Alomar Jr.	.30	.09
67 Paul Assenmacher	.30	.09
68 Tony Fernandez	.30	.09
69 Brian Giles	.30	.09
70 Marquis Grissom	.30	.09
71 Orel Hershiser	.30	.09
72 Mike Jackson	.30	.09
73 David Justice	.30	.09
74 Albie Lopez	.30	.09
75 Jose Mesa	.30	.09
76 Charles Nagy	.30	.09
77 Chad Ogea	.30	.09
78 Manny Ramirez	.50	.15
79 Jim Thome	.75	.23
80 Omar Vizquel	.50	.15
81 Matt Williams	.30	.09
82 Jaret Wright	.30	.09
83 Willie Blair	.30	.09
84 Raul Casanova	.30	.09
85 Tony Clark	.30	.09
86 Deivi Cruz	.30	.09
87 Damion Easley	.30	.09
88 Travis Fryman	.30	.09
89 Bobby Higginson	.30	.09
90 Brian L. Hunter	.30	.09
91 Todd Jones	.30	.09
92 Dan Miceli	.30	.09
93 Brian Moehler	.30	.09
94 Mel Nieves	.30	.09
95 Jody Reed	.30	.09
96 Justin Thompson	.30	.09
97 Bubba Trammell	.30	.09
98 Kevin Appier	.30	.09
99 Jay Bell	.30	.09
100 Yamil Benitez	.30	.09
101 Johnny Damon	.50	.15
102 Chili Davis	.30	.09
103 Jermaine Dye	.30	.09
104 Jed Hansen	.30	.09
105 Jeff King	.30	.09
106 Mike Macfarlane	.30	.09
107 Felix Martinez	.30	.09
108 Jeff Montgomery	.30	.09
109 Jose Offerman	.30	.09
110 Dean Palmer	.30	.09
111 Hipolito Pichardo	.30	.09
112 Jose Rosado	.30	.09
113 Jeromy Burnitz	.30	.09
114 Jeff Cirillo	.30	.09
115 Cal Eldred	.30	.09
116 John Jaha	.30	.09
117 Doug Jones	.30	.09
118 Scott Karl	.30	.09
119 Jesse Levis	.30	.09
120 Mark Loretta	.30	.09
121 Ben McDonald	.30	.09
122 Jose Mercedes	.30	.09
123 Matt Mieske	.30	.09
124 Dave Nilsson	.30	.09
125 Jose Valentin	.30	.09
126 Fernando Vina	.30	.09
127 Gerald Williams	.30	.09
128 Rick Aguilera	.30	.09
129 Rich Becker	.30	.09
130 Ron Coomer	.30	.09
131 Marty Cordova	.30	.09
132 Eddie Guardado	.30	.09
133 LaTroy Hawkins	.30	.09
134 Denny Hocking	.30	.09
135 Chuck Knoblauch	.30	.09
136 Matt Lawton	.30	.09
137 Pat Meares	.30	.09
138 Paul Molitor	.50	.15
139 David Ortiz	.75	.23
140 Brad Radke	.30	.09
141 Terry Steinbach	.30	.09
142 Bob Tewksbury	.30	.09
143 Javier Valentin	.30	.09
144 Wade Boggs	.50	.15
145 David Cone	.30	.09
146 Chad Curtis	.30	.09
147 Cecil Fielder	.30	.09
148 Joe Girardi	.30	.09
149 Dwight Gooden	.30	.09
150 Hideki Irabu	.30	.09
151 Derek Jeter	2.00	.60
152 Tino Martinez	.50	.15
153 Ramiro Mendoza	.30	.09
154 Paul O'Neill	.50	.15
155 Andy Pettitte	.50	.15
156 Jorge Posada	.50	.15
157 Mariano Rivera	.50	.15
158 Rey Sanchez	.30	.09
159 Luis Sojo	.30	.09
160 David Wells	.30	.09
161 Bernie Williams	.50	.15
162 Rafael Bournigal	.30	.09
163 Scott Brosius	.30	.09
164 Jose Canseco	.75	.23
165 Jason Giambi	.30	.09
166 Ben Grieve	.30	.09
167 Dave Magadan	.30	.09
168 Brent Mayne	.30	.09
169 Jason McDonald	.30	.09
170 Izzy Molina	.30	.09
171 Ariel Prieto	.30	.09
172 Carlos Reyes	.30	.09
173 Scott Spiezio	.30	.09
174 Matt Stairs	.30	.09
175 Bill Taylor	.30	.09
176 Dave Telgheder	.30	.09
177 Steve Wojciechowski	.30	.09
178 Rich Amaral	.30	.09
179 Bobby Ayala	.30	.09
180 Jay Buhner	.30	.09
181 Rafael Carmona	.30	.09
182 Ken Cloude	.30	.09
183 Joey Cora	.30	.09
184 Russ Davis	.30	.09
185 Jeff Fassero	.30	.09
186 Ken Griffey Jr.	1.25	.35
187 Raul Ibanez	.30	.09
188 Randy Johnson	.75	.23
189 Roberto Kelly	.30	.09
190 Edgar Martinez	.50	.15
191 Jamie Moyer	.30	.09
192 Omar Olivares	.30	.09
193 Alex Rodriguez	1.25	.35
194 Heathcliff Slocumb	.30	.09
195 Paul Sorrento	.30	.09
196 Dan Wilson	.30	.09
197 Scott Bailes	.30	.09
198 John Burkett	.30	.09
199 Domingo Cedeno	.30	.09
200 Will Clark	.75	.23
201 Hanley Frias RC	.30	.09
202 Juan Gonzalez	.50	.15
203 Tom Goodwin	.30	.09
204 Rusty Greer	.30	.09
205 Wilson Heredia	.30	.09
206 Darren Oliver	.30	.09
207 Bill Ripken	.30	.09
208 Ivan Rodriguez	.75	.23
209 Lee Stevens	.30	.09
210 Fernando Tatis	.30	.09
211 John Wetteland	.30	.09
212 Bobby Witt	.30	.09
213 Jacob Brumfield	.30	.09
214 Joe Carter	.30	.09
215 Roger Clemens	1.50	.45
216 Felipe Crespo	.30	.09
217 Jose Cruz Jr.	.30	.09
218 Carlos Delgado	.30	.09
219 Mariano Duncan	.30	.09
220 Carlos Garcia	.30	.09
221 Alex Gonzalez	.30	.09
222 Juan Guzman	.30	.09
223 Pat Hentgen	.30	.09
224 Orlando Merced	.30	.09
225 Tomas Perez	.30	.09
226 Paul Quantrill	.30	.09
227 Benito Santiago	.30	.09
228 Woody Williams	.30	.09
229 Rafael Belliard	.30	.09
230 Jeff Blauser	.30	.09
231 Pedro Borbon	.30	.09
232 Tom Glavine	.50	.15
233 Tony Graffanino	.30	.09
234 Andruw Jones	.30	.09
235 Chipper Jones	.75	.23
236 Ryan Klesko	.30	.09
237 Mark Lemke	.30	.09
238 Kenny Lofton	.30	.09
239 Javier Lopez	.30	.09
240 Fred McGriff	.50	.15
241 Greg Maddux	1.25	.35
242 Denny Neagle	.30	.09
243 John Smoltz	.50	.15
244 Michael Tucker	.30	.09
245 Mark Wohlers	.30	.09
246 Manny Alexander	.30	.09
247 Miguel Batista	.30	.09
248 Mark Clark	.30	.09
249 Doug Glanville	.30	.09
250 Jeremi Gonzalez	.30	.09
251 Mark Grace	.50	.15
252 Jose Hernandez	.30	.09
253 Lance Johnson	.30	.09
254 Brooks Kieschnick	.30	.09
255 Kevin Orie	.30	.09
256 Ryne Sandberg	1.25	.35
257 Scott Servais	.30	.09
258 Sammy Sosa	1.25	.35
259 Kevin Tapani	.30	.09
260 Ramon Tatis	.30	.09
261 Bret Boone	.30	.09
262 Dave Burba	.30	.09
263 Brook Fordyce	.30	.09
264 Willie Greene	.30	.09
265 Barry Larkin	.50	.15
266 Pedro A. Martinez	.30	.09
267 Hal Morris	.30	.09
268 Joe Oliver	.30	.09
269 Eduardo Perez	.30	.09
270 Pokey Reese	.30	.09
271 Felix Rodriguez	.30	.09
272 Deion Sanders	.50	.15
273 Reggie Sanders	.30	.09
274 Jeff Shaw	.30	.09
275 Scott Sullivan	.30	.09
276 Brett Tomko	.30	.09
277 Roger Bailey	.30	.09
278 Dante Bichette	.30	.09
279 Ellis Burks	.30	.09
280 Vinny Castilla	.30	.09
281 Frank Castillo	.30	.09
282 Mike DeJean RC	.30	.09
283 Andres Galarraga	.30	.09
284 Darren Holmes	.30	.09
285 Kirt Manwaring	.30	.09
286 Quinton McCracken	.30	.09
287 Neifi Perez	.30	.09
288 Steve Reed	.30	.09
289 John Thomson	.30	.09
290 Larry Walker	.50	.15
291 Walt Weiss	.30	.09
292 Kurt Abbott	.30	.09
293 Antonio Alfonseca	.30	.09
294 Moises Alou	.30	.09
295 Alex Arias	.30	.09
296 Bobby Bonilla	.30	.09
297 Kevin Brown	.50	.15
298 Craig Counsell	.30	.09
299 Darren Daulton	.30	.09
300 Jim Eisenreich	.30	.09
301 Alex Fernandez	.30	.09
302 Felix Heredia	.30	.09
303 Livan Hernandez	.30	.09
304 Charles Johnson	.30	.09
305 Al Leiter	.30	.09
306 Robb Nen	.30	.09
307 Edgar Renteria	.30	.09
308 Gary Sheffield	.30	.09
309 Devon White	.30	.09
310 Bob Abreu	.30	.09
311 Brad Ausmus	.30	.09
312 Jeff Bagwell	.50	.15
313 Derek Bell	.30	.09
314 Sean Berry	.30	.09
315 Craig Biggio	.50	.15
316 Ramon Garcia	.30	.09
317 Luis Gonzalez	.30	.09
318 Ricky Gutierrez	.30	.09
319 Mike Hampton	.30	.09
320 Richard Hidalgo	.30	.09
321 Thomas Howard	.30	.09
322 Darryl Kile	.30	.09
323 Jose Lima	.30	.09
324 Shane Reynolds	.30	.09
325 Bill Spiers	.30	.09
326 Tom Candiotti	.30	.09
327 Roger Cedeno	.30	.09
328 Greg Gagne	.30	.09
329 Karim Garcia	.30	.09
330 Wilton Guerrero	.30	.09
331 Todd Hollandsworth	.30	.09
332 Eric Karros	.30	.09
333 Ramon Martinez	.30	.09
334 Raul Mondesi	.30	.09
335 Otis Nixon	.30	.09
336 Hideo Nomo	.75	.23
337 Antonio Osuna	.30	.09
338 Chan Ho Park	.30	.09
339 Mike Piazza	1.25	.35
340 Dennis Reyes	.30	.09
341 Ismael Valdes	.30	.09
342 Todd Worrell	.30	.09
343 Todd Zeile	.30	.09
344 Darrin Fletcher	.30	.09
345 Mark Grudzielanek	.30	.09
346 Vladimir Guerrero	.75	.23
347 Dustin Hermanson	.30	.09
348 Mike Lansing	.30	.09
349 Pedro Martinez	.75	.23
350 Ryan McGuire	.30	.09
351 Jose Paniagua	.30	.09
352 Carlos Perez	.30	.09
353 Henry Rodriguez	.30	.09
354 F.P. Santangelo	.30	.09
355 David Segui	.30	.09
356 Ugueth Urbina	.30	.09
357 Marc Valdes	.30	.09
358 Jose Vidro	.30	.09
359 Rondell White	.30	.09
360 Juan Acevedo	.30	.09
361 Edgardo Alfonzo	.30	.09
362 Carlos Baerga	.30	.09
363 Carl Everett	.30	.09
364 John Franco	.30	.09
365 Bernard Gilkey	.30	.09
366 Todd Hundley	.30	.09
367 Butch Huskey	.30	.09
368 Bobby Jones	.30	.09
369 T.Kashiwada RC	.30	.09
370 Greg McMichael	.30	.09
371 Brian McRae	.30	.09
372 Alex Ochoa	.30	.09
373 John Olerud	.30	.09
374 Rey Ordonez	.30	.09
375 Turk Wendell	.30	.09
376 Ricky Bottalico	.30	.09
377 Rico Brogna	.30	.09
378 Len Dykstra	.30	.09
379 Bobby Estalella	.30	.09
380 Wayne Gomes	.30	.09
381 Tyler Green	.30	.09
382 Gregg Jefferies	.30	.09
383 Mark Leiter	.30	.09
384 Mike Lieberthal	.30	.09
385 Mickey Morandini	.30	.09
386 Scott Rolen	.75	.23
387 Curt Schilling	.30	.09
388 Kevin Stocker	.30	.09
389 Danny Tartabull	.30	.09
390 Jermaine Allensworth	.30	.09
391 Adrian Brown	.30	.09
392 Jason Christiansen	.30	.09
393 Steve Cooke	.30	.09
394 Francisco Cordova	.30	.09
395 Jose Guillen	.30	.09

396 Jason Kendall .30 .09
397 Jon Lieber .30 .09
398 Esteban Loaiza .30 .09
399 Al Martin .30 .09
400 Kevin Polcovich .30 .09
401 Joe Randa .30 .09
402 Ricardo Rincon .30 .09
403 Tony Womack .30 .09
404 Kevin Young .30 .09
405 Andy Benes .30 .09
406 Royce Clayton .30 .09
407 Delino DeShields .30 .09
408 Mike Difelice RC .30 .09
409 Dennis Eckersley .30 .09
410 John Frascatore .30 .09
411 Gary Gaetti .30 .09
412 Ron Gant .30 .09
413 Brian Jordan .30 .09
414 Ray Lankford .30 .09
415 Willie McGee .30 .09
416 Mark McGwire 2.00 .60
417 Matt Morris .30 .09
418 Luis Ordaz .30 .09
419 Todd Stottlemyre .30 .09
420 Andy Ashby .30 .09
421 Jim Bruske .30 .09
422 Ken Caminiti .30 .09
423 Will Cunnane .30 .09
424 Steve Finley .30 .09
425 John Flaherty .30 .09
426 Chris Gomez .30 .09
427 Tony Gwynn 1.00 .30
428 Joey Hamilton .30 .09
429 Carlos Hernandez .30 .09
430 Sterling Hitchcock .30 .09
431 Trevor Hoffman .30 .09
432 Wally Joyner .30 .09
433 Greg Vaughn .30 .09
434 Quilvio Veras .30 .09
435 Wilson Alvarez .30 .09
436 Rod Beck .30 .09
437 Barry Bonds 2.00 .60
438 Jacob Cruz .30 .09
439 Shawn Estes .30 .09
440 Darryl Hamilton .30 .09
441 Roberto Hernandez .30 .09
442 Glenallen Hill .30 .09
443 Stan Javier .30 .09
444 Brian Johnson .30 .09
445 Jeff Kent .30 .09
446 Bill Mueller .30 .09
447 Kirk Rueter .30 .09
448 J.T. Snow .30 .09
449 Julian Tavarez .30 .09
450 Jose Vizcaino .30 .09

1998 Pacific Platinum Blue

Randomly inserted in packs at the rate of one in 73, this 450 card set is parallel to the base set and is similar in design. The difference is found in the platinum blue foil highlights. According to the manufacturer, only 67 sets were produced.

Nm-Mt Ex-Mt
*STARS: 8X TO 20X BASIC CARDS....

1998 Pacific Red Threatt

Inserted one per Wal-Mart pack, this 450-card set is parallel to the base set and is similar in design. The difference is found in the red foil highlights.

Nm-Mt Ex-Mt
*STARS: 2.5X TO 6X BASIC CARDS...

1998 Pacific Silver

Inserted one per pack, this 450-card set is parallel to the base set and is similar in design. The difference is found in the silver foil highlights.

Nm-Mt Ex-Mt
*STARS: 2X TO 5X BASIC CARDS......

1998 Pacific Cramer's Choice

Randomly inserted in packs at the rate of one in 721, this 10-card set features top Major League players as chosen by Michael Cramer. The fronts display a color player cut-out on a pyramid die-cut shaped background. The backs carry information about why the player was selected for this set in both Spanish and English.

Nm-Mt Ex-Mt
1 Greg Maddux 50.00 15.00
2 Roberto Alomar 20.00 6.00
3 Cal Ripken 100.00 30.00
4 Nomar Garciaparra 50.00 15.00
5 Larry Walker 20.00 6.00
6 Mike Piazza 50.00 15.00
7 Mark McGwire 80.00 24.00
8 Tony Gwynn 40.00 12.00
9 Ken Griffey Jr. 50.00 15.00
10 Roger Clemens 60.00 18.00

1998 Pacific Gold Crown Die Cuts

Randomly inserted in packs at the rate of one in 37, this 36-card set features color action player photos with a die-cut crown at the top printed on a holographic silver foil background and gold etching on the trim. The backs carry player information in both Spanish and English.

Nm-Mt Ex-Mt
COMPLETE SET (36) 250.00 75.00
1 Chipper Jones 10.00 3.00
2 Greg Maddux 15.00 4.50
3 Denny Neagle 4.00 1.20
4 Roberto Alomar 6.00 1.80

5 Rafael Palmeiro 6.00 1.80
6 Cal Ripken 30.00 9.00
7 Nomar Garciaparra 15.00 4.50
8 Mo Vaughn 4.00 1.20
9 Frank Thomas 10.00 3.00
10 Sandy Alomar Jr. 4.00 1.20
11 David Justice 4.00 1.20
12 Manny Ramirez 6.00 1.80
13 Andres Galarraga 4.00 1.20
14 Larry Walker 6.00 1.80
15 Moises Alou 4.00 1.20
16 Livan Hernandez 4.00 1.20
17 Gary Sheffield 4.00 1.20
18 Jeff Bagwell 6.00 1.80
19 Raul Mondesi 4.00 1.20
20 Hideo Nomo 10.00 3.00
21 Mike Piazza 15.00 4.50
22 Derek Jeter 25.00 7.50
23 Tino Martinez 6.00 1.80
24 Bernie Williams 6.00 1.80
25 Ben Grieve 4.00 1.20
26 Mark McGwire 25.00 7.50
27 Tony Gwynn 12.00 3.60
28 Barry Bonds 25.00 7.50
29 Ken Griffey Jr. 15.00 4.50
30 Randy Johnson 10.00 3.00
31 Edgar Martinez 6.00 1.80
32 Alex Rodriguez 15.00 4.50
33 Juan Gonzalez 6.00 1.80
34 Ivan Rodriguez 10.00 3.00
35 Roger Clemens 20.00 6.00
36 Jose Cruz Jr. 4.00 1.20

1998 Pacific Home Run Hitters

Randomly inserted in packs at the rate of one in 73, this 20-card set features color player cut-outs of top home run hitters printed on full-foil cards with the number of home runs they hit in 1997 embossed in the background. The backs carry player information in both Spanish and English.

Nm-Mt Ex-Mt
COMPLETE SET (20) 150.00 45.00
1 Rafael Palmeiro 8.00 2.40
2 Mo Vaughn 5.00 1.50
3 Sammy Sosa 20.00 6.00
4 Albert Belle 5.00 1.50
5 Frank Thomas 12.00 3.60
6 David Justice 5.00 1.50
7 Jim Thome 12.00 3.60
8 Matt Williams 5.00 1.50
9 Vinny Castilla 5.00 1.50
10 Andres Galarraga 5.00 1.50
11 Larry Walker 8.00 2.40
12 Jeff Bagwell 8.00 2.40
13 Mike Piazza 20.00 6.00
14 Tino Martinez 8.00 2.40
15 Mark McGwire 30.00 9.00
16 Barry Bonds 30.00 9.00
17 Jay Buhner 5.00 1.50
18 Ken Griffey Jr. 20.00 6.00
19 Alex Rodriguez 20.00 6.00
20 Juan Gonzalez 8.00 2.40

1998 Pacific In The Cage

Randomly inserted in packs at the rate of one in 145, this 20-card set features color player cut-outs of the league's best hitters printed on a die-cut card with a laser-cut batting cage as the background. The backs carry player information in both Spanish and English.

Nm-Mt Ex-Mt
COMPLETE SET (20) 150.00 45.00
1 Chipper Jones 12.00 3.60
2 Roberto Alomar 8.00 2.40
3 Cal Ripken 40.00 12.00
4 Nomar Garciaparra 20.00 6.00
5 Frank Thomas 12.00 3.60
6 Sandy Alomar Jr. 5.00 1.50
7 David Justice 5.00 1.50
8 Larry Walker 8.00 2.40
9 Bobby Bonilla 5.00 1.50
10 Mike Piazza 20.00 6.00
11 Tino Martinez 8.00 2.40
12 Bernie Williams 8.00 2.40
13 Mark McGwire 30.00 9.00
14 Tony Gwynn 15.00 4.50
15 Barry Bonds 30.00 9.00
16 Ken Griffey Jr. 20.00 6.00
17 Edgar Martinez 8.00 2.40
18 Alex Rodriguez 20.00 6.00
19 Juan Gonzalez 8.00 2.40
20 Ivan Rodriguez 12.00 3.60

1998 Pacific Latinos of the Major Leagues

Randomly inserted in packs at the rate of two in 37, this 36-card set features color action photos of top players of Hispanic decent printed on foil cards with images of South and North America, the player's team logo, and the United States Flag in the background. The backs carry player information in both Spanish and English.

Nm-Mt Ex-Mt
COMPLETE SET (36) 80.00 24.00
1 Andruw Jones 2.00 .60
2 Javier Lopez 2.00 .60
3 Roberto Alomar 3.00 .90
4 Geronimo Berroa 2.00 .60
5 Rafael Palmeiro 3.00 .90
6 Nomar Garciaparra 8.00 2.40
7 Sammy Sosa 8.00 2.40
8 Ozzie Guillen 2.00 .60
9 Sandy Alomar Jr. 2.00 .60
10 Manny Ramirez 3.00 .90
11 Omar Vizquel 3.00 .90
12 Vinny Castilla 2.00 .60
13 Andres Galarraga 2.00 .60
14 Moises Alou 2.00 .60
15 Bobby Bonilla 2.00 .60
16 Livan Hernandez 2.00 .60
17 Edgar Renteria 2.00 .60
18 Wilton Guerrero 2.00 .60
19 Raul Mondesi 2.00 .60
20 Ismael Valdes 2.00 .60
21 Fernando Vina 2.00 .60
22 Pedro Martinez 5.00 1.50
23 Edgardo Alfonzo 2.00 .60
24 Carlos Baerga 2.00 .60
25 Rey Ordonez 2.00 .60
26 Tino Martinez 3.00 .90
27 Mariano Rivera 3.00 .90
28 Bernie Williams 3.00 .90
29 Jose Canseco 5.00 1.50
30 Joey Cora 2.00 .60
31 Roberto Kelly 2.00 .60
32 Edgar Martinez 3.00 .90
33 Alex Rodriguez 8.00 2.40
34 Juan Gonzalez 3.00 .90
35 Ivan Rodriguez 5.00 1.50
36 Jose Cruz Jr. 2.00 .60

1998 Pacific Team Checklists

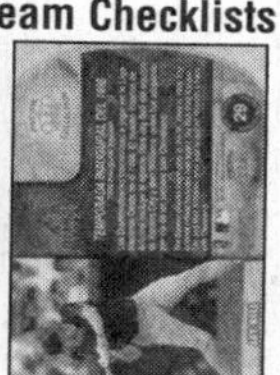

Randomly inserted in packs at the rate of one in 37, this 30-card set features color player photos printed on a die-cut card in the shape of the end of a baseball bat with a laser cut team logo. The two 1998 expansion teams, the Arizona Diamondbacks and the Tampa Bay Devil Rays, are included in these checklists.

Nm-Mt Ex-Mt
COMPLETE SET (30) 150.00 45.00
1 Tim Salmon 3.00 .90
Jim Edmonds
2 Cal Ripken 25.00 7.50
Roberto Alomar
3 Nomar Garciaparra 12.00 3.60
Mo Vaughn
4 Frank Thomas 8.00 2.40
Albert Belle
5 Sandy Alomar Jr. 5.00 1.50
Manny Ramirez
6 Justin Thompson 3.00 .90
Tony Clark
7 Johnny Damon 5.00 1.50
Jermaine Dye
8 Dave Nilsson 3.00 .90
Jeff Cirillo
9 Paul Molitor 5.00 1.50
Chuck Knoblauch
10 Tino Martinez 20.00 6.00
Derek Jeter
11 Ben Grieve 8.00 2.40
Jose Canseco
12 Ken Griffey Jr. 12.00 3.60
Alex Rodriguez
13 Juan Gonzalez 8.00 2.40
Ivan Rodriguez
14 Jose Cruz Jr. 15.00 4.50
Roger Clemens
15 Greg Maddux 12.00 3.60
Chipper Jones
16 Sammy Sosa 12.00 3.60
Mark Grace
17 Barry Larkin 5.00 1.50
Deion Sanders
18 Larry Walker 3.00 .90
Andres Galarraga
19 Moises Alou 3.00 .90
Bobby Bonilla
20 Jeff Bagwell 5.00 1.50
Craig Biggio
21 Mike Piazza 12.00 3.60
Hideo Nomo
22 Pedro Martinez 8.00 2.40
Henry Rodriguez
23 Rey Ordonez 3.00 .90
Carlos Baerga
24 Curt Schilling 8.00 2.40
Scott Rolen
25 Al Martin 3.00 .90
Tony Womack
26 Mark McGwire 20.00 6.00
Dennis Eckersley
27 Tony Gwynn 10.00 3.00
Wally Joyner
28 Barry Bonds 20.00 6.00
J.T.Snow
29 Matt Williams 3.00 .90
Jay Bell
30 Fred McGriff 5.00 1.50
Roberto Hernandez

1999 Pacific

This 500 card standard-size set was issued in 10 card packs that had a SRP of $2.19 per pack. Each Box containted 36 packs and each case had 20 boxes. Continuing the trend begun in 1998 with Pacific On-Line, Pacific issued two versions of 50 of the star or leading prospect players in the set with both an action version as well as a head shot. Thus the cards are actually numbered from 1 through 450, but the 50 additional head-shot cards (carrying identical numbering to the action cards) bring the total number of cards in the set to 500. The complete set includes both versions of each player. The head shots were inserted one per pack. An unnumbered Tony Gwynn sample card was distributed to dealers and hobby media prior to the product's release. The card is easy to recognize by the bold, diagonal "SAMPLE" text running across the back.

Nm-Mt Ex-Mt
COMPLETE SET (500) 80.00 24.00
1 Garret Anderson .30 .09
2 Jason Dickson .30 .09
3 Gary DiSarcina .30 .09
4 Jim Edmonds .30 .09
5 Darin Erstad .30 .09
6 Chuck Finley .30 .09
7 Shigetoshi Hasegawa .30 .09
8 Ken Hill .30 .09
9 Dave Hollins .30 .09
10 Phil Nevin .30 .09
11 Troy Percival .30 .09
12 Tim Salmon * .50 .15
12A Tim Salmon Headshot .50 .15
13 Brian Anderson .30 .09
14 Tony Batista .30 .09
15 Jay Bell .30 .09
16 Andy Benes .30 .09
17 Yamil Benitez .30 .09
18 Omar Daal .30 .09
19 David Dellucci .30 .09
20 Karim Garcia .30 .09
21 Bernard Gilkey .30 .09
22 Travis Lee * .30 .09
22A Travis Lee Headshot .30 .09
23 Aaron Small .30 .09
24 Kelly Stinnett .30 .09
25 Devon White .30 .09
26 Matt Williams .30 .09
27 Bruce Chen * .30 .09
27A Bruce Chen Headshot .30 .09
28 Andres Galarraga * .30 .09
28A A.Galarraga Headshot .30 .09
29 Tom Glavine .50 .15
30 Ozzie Guillen .30 .09
31 Andruw Jones .30 .09
32 Chipper Jones * .75 .23
32A C.Jones Headshot .75 .23
33 Ryan Klesko .30 .09
34 George Lombard .30 .09
35 Javy Lopez .30 .09
36 Greg Maddux * 1.25 .35
36A G.Maddux Headshot 1.25 .35
37 Marty Malloy * .30 .09
37A M.Malloy Headshot .30 .09
38 Dennis Martinez .30 .09
39 Kevin Millwood .30 .09
40 Alex Rodriguez * 1.25 .35
40A Alex Rodriguez Headshot 1.25 .35
41 Denny Neagle .30 .09
42 John Smoltz .50 .15
43 Michael Tucker .30 .09
44 Walt Weiss .30 .09
45 Roberto Alomar * .50 .15
45A R.Alomar Headshot .50 .15
46 Brady Anderson .30 .09
47 Harold Baines .30 .09
48 Mike Bordick .30 .09
49 Danny Clyburn * .30 .09
49A D.Clyburn Headshot .30 .09
50 Eric Davis .30 .09
51 Scott Erickson .30 .09
52 Chris Hoiles .30 .09
53 Jimmy Key .30 .09
54 Ryan Minor * .30 .09
54A Ryan Minor Headshot .30 .09
55 Mike Mussina .50 .15
56 Jesse Orosco .30 .09
57 Rafael Palmeiro * .50 .15
57A R.Palmeiro Headshot .50 .15
58 Sidney Ponson .30 .09
59 Arthur Rhodes .30 .09
60 Cal Ripken * 2.50 .75
60A Cal Ripken Headshot 2.50 .75
61 B.J. Surhoff .30 .09
62 Steve Avery .30 .09
63 Darren Bragg .30 .09
64 Dennis Eckersley .30 .09
65 Nomar Garciaparra * 1.25 .35
65A Nomar Garciaparra Headshot 1.25 .35
66 Sammy Sosa * 1.25 .35
66A S.Sosa Headshot 1.25 .35
67 Tom Gordon .30 .09
68 Reggie Jefferson .30 .09
69 Darren Lewis .30 .09
70 Mark McGwire * 2.00 .60
70A M.McGwire Headshot 2.00 .60
71 Pedro Martinez .75 .23
72 Troy O'Leary .30 .09
73 Bret Saberhagen .30 .09
74 Mike Stanley .30 .09
75 John Valentin .30 .09
76 Jason Varitek .50 .15
77 Mo Vaughn .30 .09
78 Tim Wakefield .30 .09
79 Manny Alexander .30 .09
80 Rod Beck .30 .09
81 Brant Brown .30 .09
82 Mark Clark .30 .09
83 Gary Gaetti .30 .09
84 Mark Grace .50 .15
85 Jose Hernandez .30 .09
86 Lance Johnson .30 .09
87 Jason Maxwell * .30 .09
87A J.Maxwell Headshot .30 .09
88 Mickey Morandini .30 .09
89 Terry Mulholland .30 .09
90 Henry Rodriguez .30 .09
91 Scott Servais .30 .09
92 Kevin Tapani .30 .09
93 Pedro Valdes .30 .09
94 Kerry Wood .75 .23
95 Jeff Abbott .30 .09
96 James Baldwin .30 .09
97 Albert Belle .30 .09
98 Mike Cameron .30 .09
99 Mike Caruso .30 .09
100 Wil Cordero .30 .09
101 Ray Durham .30 .09
102 Jaime Navarro .30 .09
103 Greg Norton .30 .09
104 Magglio Ordonez .30 .09
105 Mike Sirotka .30 .09
106 Frank Thomas * .75 .23
106A F.Thomas Headshot .75 .23
107 Robin Ventura .30 .09
108 Craig Wilson .30 .09
109 Aaron Boone .30 .09
110 Bret Boone .30 .09
111 Sean Casey .30 .09
112 Pete Harnisch .30 .09
113 John Hudek .30 .09
114 Barry Larkin .50 .15
115 Eduardo Perez .30 .09
116 Mike Remlinger .30 .09
117 Reggie Sanders .30 .09
118 Chris Stynes .30 .09
119 Eddie Taubensee .30 .09
120 Brett Tomko .30 .09
121 Pat Watkins .30 .09
122 Dmitri Young .30 .09
123 Sandy Alomar Jr. .30 .09
124 Dave Burba .30 .09
125 Bartolo Colon .30 .09
126 Joey Cora .30 .09
127 Brian Giles .30 .09
128 Dwight Gooden .50 .15
129 Mike Jackson .30 .09
130 David Justice .30 .09
131 Kenny Lofton .30 .09
132 Charles Nagy .30 .09
133 Chad Ogea .30 .09
134 Manny Ramirez * .50 .15
134A M.Ramirez Headshot .50 .15
135 Richie Sexson .30 .09
136 Jim Thome * .75 .23
136A J.Thome Headshot .75 .23
137 Omar Vizquel .50 .15
138 Jaret Wright .30 .09
139 Pedro Astacio .30 .09
140 Jason Bates .30 .09
141 Dante Bichette * .30 .09
141A Dante Bichette Headshot .30 .09
142 Vinny Castilla * .30 .09
142A V.Castilla Headshot .30 .09
143 Edgard Clemente * .30 .09
143A Edgard Clemente Headshot .30 .09
144 Derrick Gibson * .30 .09
144A D. Gibson Headshot .30 .09
145 Curtis Goodwin .30 .09
146 Todd Helton * .50 .15
146A T.Helton Headshot .50 .15
147 Bobby Jones .30 .09
148 Darryl Kile .30 .09
149 Mike Lansing .30 .09
150 Chuck McElroy .30 .09
151 Neifi Perez .30 .09
152 Jeff Reed .30 .09
153 John Thomson .30 .09
154 Larry Walker * .50 .15
154A L.Walker Headshot .50 .15
155 Jamey Wright .30 .09
156 Kimera Bartee .30 .09
157 Geronimo Berroa .30 .09
158 Raul Casanova .30 .09
159 Frank Catalanotto .30 .09
160 Tony Clark .30 .09
161 Deivi Cruz .30 .09
162 Damion Easley .30 .09
163 Juan Encarnacion .30 .09
164 Luis Gonzalez .30 .09
165 Seth Greisinger .30 .09
166 Bob Higginson .30 .09
167 Brian L.Hunter .30 .09
168 Todd Jones .30 .09
169 Justin Thompson .30 .09
170 Antonio Alfonseca .30 .09
171 Dave Berg .30 .09
172 John Cangelosi .30 .09
173 Craig Counsell .30 .09
174 Todd Dunwoody .30 .09
175 Cliff Floyd .30 .09

176 Alex Gonzalez .30 .09
177 Livan Hernandez .30 .09
178 Ryan Jackson .30 .09
179 Mark Kotsay .30 .09
180 Derrek Lee .30 .09
181 Matt Mantei .30 .09
182 Brian Meadows .30 .09
183 Edgar Renteria .30 .09
184 Moises Alou * .30 .09
184A M.Alou Headshot .30 .09
185 Brad Ausmus .30 .09
186 Jeff Bagwell * .50 .15
186A J.Bagwell Headshot .50 .15
187 Derek Bell .30 .09
188 Sean Berry .30 .09
189 Craig Biggio .50 .15
190 Carl Everett .30 .09
191 Ricky Gutierrez .30 .09
192 Mike Hampton .30 .09
193 Doug Henry .30 .09
194 Richard Hidalgo .30 .09
195 Randy Johnson .75 .23
196 Russ Johnson * .30 .09
196A R.Johnson Headshot .30 .09
197 Shane Reynolds .30 .09
198 Bill Spiers .30 .09
199 Kevin Appier .30 .09
200 Tim Belcher .30 .09
201 Jeff Conine .30 .09
202 Johnny Damon .50 .15
203 Jermaine Dye .30 .09
204 Jeremy Giambi * .30 .09
204A Je. Giambi Headshot .30 .09
205 Jeff King .30 .09
206 Shane Mack .30 .09
207 Jeff Montgomery .30 .09
208 Hal Morris .30 .09
209 Jose Offerman .30 .09
210 Dean Palmer .30 .09
211 Jose Rosado .30 .09
212 Glendon Rusch .30 .09
213 Larry Sutton .30 .09
214 Mike Sweeney .30 .09
215 Bobby Bonilla .30 .09
216 Alex Cora .30 .09
217 Darren Dreifort .30 .09
218 Mark Grudzielanek .30 .09
219 Todd Hollandsworth .30 .09
220 Trenidad Hubbard .30 .09
221 Charles Johnson .30 .09
222 Eric Karros .30 .09
223 Matt Luke .30 .09
224 Ramon Martinez .30 .09
225 Raul Mondesi .30 .09
226 Chan Ho Park .30 .09
227 Jeff Shaw .30 .09
228 Gary Sheffield .30 .09
229 Eric Young .30 .09
230 Jeromy Burnitz .30 .09
231 Jeff Cirillo .30 .09
232 Marquis Grissom .30 .09
233 Bobby Hughes .30 .09
234 John Jaha .30 .09
235 Geoff Jenkins .30 .09
236 Scott Karl .30 .09
237 Mark Loretta .30 .09
238 Mike Matheny .30 .09
239 Mike Myers .30 .09
240 Dave Nilsson .30 .09
241 Bob Wickman .30 .09
242 Jose Valentin .30 .09
243 Fernando Vina .30 .09
244 Rick Aguilera .30 .09
245 Ron Coomer .30 .09
246 Marty Cordova .30 .09
247 Denny Hocking .30 .09
248 Matt Lawton .30 .09
249 Pat Meares .30 .09
250 Paul Molitor * .50 .15
250A P.Molitor Headshot .50 .15
251 Otis Nixon .30 .09
252 Alex Ochoa .30 .09
253 David Ortiz .50 .15
254 A.J. Pierzynski .30 .09
255 Brad Radke .30 .09
256 Terry Steinbach .30 .09
257 Bob Tewksbury .30 .09
258 Todd Walker .30 .09
259 Shane Andrews .30 .09
260 Shayne Bennett .30 .09
261 Orlando Cabrera .30 .09
262 Brad Fullmer .30 .09
263 Vladimir Guerrero .75 .23
264 Wilton Guerrero .30 .09
265 Dustin Hermanson .30 .09
266 Terry Jones RC .30 .09
267 Steve Kline .30 .09
268 Carl Pavano .30 .09
269 F.P. Santangelo .30 .09
270 Fernando Seguignol * .30 .09
270A Fernando Seguignol Headshot .30 .09
271 Ugueth Urbina .30 .09
272 Jose Vidro .30 .09
273 Chris Widger .30 .09
274 Edgardo Alfonzo .30 .09
275 Carlos Baerga .30 .09
276 John Franco .30 .09
277 Todd Hundley .30 .09
278 Butch Huskey .30 .09
279 Bobby Jones .30 .09
280 Al Leiter .30 .09
281 Greg McMichael .30 .09
282 Brian McRae .30 .09
283 Hideo Nomo .75 .23
284 John Olerud .30 .09
285 Rey Ordonez .30 .09
286 Mike Piazza * 1.25 .35
286A M.Piazza Headshot 1.25 .35
287 Turk Wendell .30 .09
288 Masato Yoshii .30 .09
289 David Cone .30 .09
290 Chad Curtis .30 .09
291 Joe Girardi .30 .09
292 Orlando Hernandez .30 .09
293 Hideki Irabu * .30 .09
293A H.Irabu Headshot .30 .09
294 Derek Jeter * 2.00 .60
294A D.Jeter Headshot 2.00 .60
295 Chuck Knoblauch .30 .09
296 Mike Lowell * .30 .09
296A M.Lowell Headshot .30 .09
297 Tino Martinez .50 .15
298 Ramiro Mendoza .30 .09
299 Paul O'Neill .50 .15
300 Andy Pettitte .50 .15
301 Jorge Posada .50 .15
302 Tim Raines .30 .09
303 Mariano Rivera .50 .15
304 David Wells .30 .09
305 Bernie Williams * .50 .15
305A Bernie Williams Headshot .50 .15
306 Mike Blowers .30 .09
307 Tom Candiotti .30 .09
308 Eric Chavez * .30 .09
308A E.Chavez Headshot .30 .09
309 Ryan Christenson .30 .09
310 Jason Giambi .30 .09
311 Ben Grieve * .30 .09
311A Ben Grieve Headshot .30 .09
312 Rickey Henderson .75 .23
313 A.J. Hinch .30 .09
314 Jason McDonald .30 .09
315 Bip Roberts .30 .09
316 Kenny Rogers .30 .09
317 Scott Spiezio .30 .09
318 Matt Stairs .30 .09
319 Miguel Tejada .30 .09
320 Bob Abreu .30 .09
321 Alex Arias .30 .09
322 Gary Bennett RC .30 .09
322A Gary Bennett RC Headshot .30 .09
323 Ricky Bottalico .30 .09
324 Rico Brogna .30 .09
325 Bobby Estalella .30 .09
326 Doug Glanville .30 .09
327 Kevin Jordan .30 .09
328 Mark Leiter .30 .09
329 Wendell Magee .30 .09
330 Mark Portugal .30 .09
331 Desi Relaford .30 .09
332 Scott Rolen .75 .23
333 Curt Schilling .30 .09
334 Kevin Sefcik .30 .09
335 Adrian Brown .30 .09
336 Emil Brown .30 .09
337 Lou Collier .30 .09
338 Francisco Cordova .30 .09
339 Freddy Garcia .30 .09
340 Jose Guillen .30 .09
341 Jason Kendall .30 .09
342 Al Martin .30 .09
343 Abraham Nunez .30 .09
344 Aramis Ramirez .30 .09
345 Ricardo Rincon .30 .09
346 Jason Schmidt .30 .09
347 Turner Ward .30 .09
348 Tony Womack .30 .09
349 Kevin Young .30 .09
350 Juan Acevedo .30 .09
351 Delino DeShields .30 .09
352 J.D. Drew * .30 .09
352A J.D. Drew Headshot .30 .09
353 Ron Gant .30 .09
354 Brian Jordan .30 .09
355 Ray Lankford .30 .09
356 Eli Marrero .30 .09
357 Kent Mercker .30 .09
358 Matt Morris .30 .09
359 Luis Ordaz .30 .09
360 Donovan Osborne .30 .09
361 Placido Polanco .30 .09
362 Fernando Tatis .30 .09
363 Andy Ashby .30 .09
364 Kevin Brown .50 .15
365 Ken Caminiti .30 .09
366 Steve Finley .30 .09
367 Chris Gomez .30 .09
368 Tony Gwynn * 1.00 .30
368A T.Gwynn Headshot 1.00 .30
369 Joey Hamilton .30 .09
370 Carlos Hernandez .30 .09
371 Trevor Hoffman .30 .09
372 Wally Joyner .30 .09
373 Jim Leyritz .30 .09
374 Ruben Rivera .30 .09
375 Greg Vaughn .30 .09
376 Quilvio Veras .30 .09
377 Rich Aurilia .30 .09
378 Barry Bonds * 2.00 .60
378A B.Bonds Headshot 1.50 .45
379 Ellis Burks .30 .09
380 Joe Carter .30 .09
381 Stan Javier .30 .09
382 Brian Johnson .30 .09
383 Jeff Kent .30 .09
384 Jose Mesa .30 .09
385 Bill Mueller .30 .09
386 Robb Nen .30 .09
387 Armando Rios * .30 .09
387A A.Rios Headshot .30 .09
388 Kirk Rueter .30 .09
389 Rey Sanchez .30 .09
390 J.T. Snow .30 .09
391 David Bell .30 .09
392 Jay Buhner .30 .09
393 Ken Cloude .30 .09
394 Russ Davis .30 .09
395 Jeff Fassero .30 .09
396 Ken Griffey Jr. * 1.25 .35
396A Ken Griffey Jr. Headshot 1.25 .35
397 Giomar Guevara RC .30 .09
398 Carlos Guillen .30 .09
399 Edgar Martinez .50 .15
400 Shane Monahan .30 .09
401 Jamie Moyer .30 .09
402 David Segui .30 .09
403 Makoto Suzuki .30 .09
404 Mike Timlin .30 .09
405 Dan Wilson .30 .09
406 Wilson Alvarez .30 .09
407 Rolando Arrojo .30 .09
408 Wade Boggs .50 .15
409 Miguel Cairo .30 .09
410 Roberto Hernandez .30 .09
411 Mike Kelly .30 .09
412 Aaron Ledesma .30 .09
413 Albie Lopez .30 .09
414 Dave Martinez .30 .09
415 Quinton McCracken .30 .09
416 Fred McGriff .50 .15
417 Bryan Rekar .30 .09
418 Paul Sorrento .30 .09
419 Randy Winn .30 .09
420 John Burkett .30 .09
421 Will Clark .75 .23
422 Royce Clayton .30 .09
423 Juan Gonzalez * .50 .15
423A Juan Gonzalez Headshot .50 .15
424 Tom Goodwin .30 .09
425 Rusty Greer .30 .09
426 Rick Helling .30 .09
427 Roberto Kelly .30 .09
428 Mark McLemore .30 .09
429 Ivan Rodriguez * .75 .23
429A Ivan Rodriguez Headshot .75 .23
430 Aaron Sele .30 .09
431 Lee Stevens .30 .09
432 Todd Stottlemyre .30 .09
433 John Wetteland .30 .09
434 Todd Zeile .30 .09
435 Jose Canseco * .75 .23
435A J.Canseco Headshot .75 .23
436 Roger Clemens * 1.50 .45
436A R.Clemens Headshot 1.50 .45
437 Felipe Crespo .30 .09
438 Jose Cruz Jr. .30 .09
439 Carlos Delgado .30 .09
440 Tom Evans * .30 .09
440A T.Evans Headshot .30 .09
441 Tony Fernandez .30 .09
442 Darrin Fletcher .30 .09
443 Alex Gonzalez .30 .09
444 Shawn Green .30 .09
445 Roy Halladay .30 .09
446 Pat Hentgen .30 .09
447 Juan Samuel .30 .09
448 Benito Santiago .30 .09
449 Shannon Stewart .30 .09
450 Woody Williams .30 .09
NNO Tony Gwynn Sample 1.00 .30

1999 Pacific Platinum Blue

This 500 card set is a parallel version to the basic 1999 Pacific set. Each card front features platinum-blue foil accents. These cards were issued one every 73 packs.

Nm-Mt Ex-Mt
*STARS: 10X TO 25X BASIC CARDS..

1999 Pacific Red

This parallel to the regular Pacific set was issued one per retail pack. Each card front features red foil accents.

Nm-Mt Ex-Mt
*STARS: 2X TO 5X BASIC CARDS.....

1999 Pacific Cramer's Choice

This 10 card set continues the Pacific tradition of having their President/CEO/Founder Mike Cramer select 10 players for the honor of being included in this set to honor the leading players in baseball. The die-cut design features the players photo on the front to go with back commentary on why they deserve the honor. 299 serial numbered sets were produced (of which card is stamped in black ink on back).

	Nm-Mt	Ex-Mt
COMPLETE SET (10)	400.00	120.00
1 Cal Ripken	80.00	24.00
2 Nomar Garciaparra	40.00	12.00
3 Frank Thomas	25.00	7.50
4 Ken Griffey Jr.	40.00	12.00
5 Alex Rodriguez	40.00	12.00
6 Greg Maddux	40.00	12.00
7 Sammy Sosa	40.00	12.00
8 Kerry Wood	25.00	7.50
9 Mark McGwire	60.00	18.00
10 Tony Gwynn	30.00	9.00

1999 Pacific Dynagon Diamond

This 20 card set, seeded at a rate of four in 37 packs, contains some of baseball biggest stars in action against a mirror patterned full-foil background. The fronts feature a little baseball diamond design in the lower left corner.

	Nm-Mt	Ex-Mt
COMPLETE SET (20)	80.00	24.00
*TITANIUM: 4X TO 10X BASIC DYN.DIAM.		
TITANIUM: RANDOM INS.IN HOBBY PACKS		
TITANIUM PRINT RUN 99 SERIAL #'d SETS		
1 Cal Ripken	10.00	3.00
2 Nomar Garciaparra	5.00	1.50
3 Frank Thomas	3.00	.90
4 Derek Jeter	8.00	2.40
5 Ben Grieve	1.25	.35
6 Ken Griffey Jr.	5.00	1.50
7 Alex Rodriguez	5.00	1.50
8 Juan Gonzalez	2.00	.60
9 Travis Lee	1.25	.35
10 Chipper Jones	3.00	.90
11 Greg Maddux	5.00	1.50
12 Sammy Sosa	5.00	1.50
13 Kerry Wood	3.00	.90
14 Jeff Bagwell	2.00	.60
15 Hideo Nomo	3.00	.90
16 Mike Piazza	5.00	1.50
17 J.D. Drew	1.25	.35
18 Mark McGwire	8.00	2.40
19 Tony Gwynn	4.00	1.20
20 Barry Bonds	8.00	2.40

1999 Pacific Gold Crown Die Cuts

This die-cut set featuring Pacific's popular Gold Crown design were inserted one every 37 packs. Thirty-six of baseball's leading players are featured in this set which contains dual foiling and were printed on 24 point stock.

	Nm-Mt	Ex-Mt
COMPLETE SET (36)	250.00	75.00
1 Darin Erstad	4.00	1.20
2 Cal Ripken	30.00	9.00
3 Nomar Garciaparra	15.00	4.50
4 Pedro Martinez	10.00	3.00
5 Mo Vaughn	4.00	1.20
6 Frank Thomas	10.00	3.00
7 Kenny Lofton	4.00	1.20
8 Manny Ramirez	6.00	1.80
9 Paul Molitor	6.00	1.80
10 Derek Jeter	25.00	7.50
11 Bernie Williams	6.00	1.80
12 Ben Grieve	4.00	1.20
13 Ken Griffey Jr.	15.00	4.50
14 Alex Rodriguez	15.00	4.50
15 Wade Boggs	6.00	1.80
16 Juan Gonzalez	6.00	1.80
17 Ivan Rodriguez	10.00	3.00
18 Jose Canseco	10.00	3.00
19 Roger Clemens	20.00	6.00
20 Travis Lee	4.00	1.20
21 Chipper Jones	10.00	3.00
22 Greg Maddux	15.00	4.50
23 Sammy Sosa	15.00	4.50
24 Kerry Wood	10.00	3.00
25 Todd Helton	6.00	1.80
26 Larry Walker	6.00	1.80
27 Jeff Bagwell	6.00	1.80
28 Craig Biggio	6.00	1.80
29 Raul Mondesi	4.00	1.20
30 Vladimir Guerrero	10.00	3.00
31 Mike Piazza	15.00	4.50
32 Scott Rolen	10.00	3.00
33 J.D. Drew	4.00	1.20
34 Mark McGwire	25.00	7.50
35 Tony Gwynn	12.00	3.60
36 Barry Bonds	25.00	7.50

1999 Pacific Hot Cards

This ten card set features a selection of top stars. Only 500 serial numbered sets were produced. Hot Cards were distributed at year's end to dealers that applied for the Hot Card registry program. Each pacific product issued in 1999 had an insert set designated as a Hot Card registry set. Shop owners that had customers pull a card from the designated Hot Card registry set could then report the find to Pacific and register the card online. For their efforts, the dealers were rewarded with these special exchange cards. These were the products which were noted as eligible for the "Hot Card Registry": 1999 Private Stock Exclusive, 1999 Prism Holographic Blue, 1999 Aurora signed cards of Tony Gwynn, 1999 Paramount Cooperstown Bound Pacific Proofs, 1999 Invincible Giants of the Game, 1999 Crown Royale Cramer's Choice Red, 1999 Revolution Tier 1, 1999 Omega 5-Tool Talents Tier 1, 2000 Pacific Premire Date, 2000 Private Stock PS-2000 Rookies, 2000 Paramount Fielder's Choice Gold Glove and 2000 Crown Collection Platinum Blue. No dealer was eligible for more than five sets per product.

	Nm-Mt	Ex-Mt
COMPLETE SET (10)	120.00	36.00
1 Alex Rodriguez	12.00	3.60
2 Tony Gwynn	10.00	3.00
3 Ken Griffey Jr.	12.00	3.60
4 Sammy Sosa	12.00	3.60
5 Ivan Rodriguez	8.00	2.40
6 Derek Jeter	20.00	6.00
7 Cal Ripken	25.00	7.50
8 Mark McGwire	20.00	6.00
9 J.D. Drew	3.00	.90
10 Bernie Williams	5.00	1.50

1999 Pacific Team Checklists

The old tradtion of knowing which players one needs to collect for all the cards of their favorite team is resurrected on these cards. Each card, which was inserted two per 37 packs has a photo of a star player for that team on the front and the complete team checklist on the back. Another photo of the featured player is included on the back as well.

	Nm-Mt	Ex-Mt
COMPLETE SET (30)	150.00	45.00
1 Darin Erstad	2.00	.60
2 Cal Ripken	15.00	4.50
3 Nomar Garciaparra	8.00	2.40
4 Frank Thomas	5.00	1.50
5 Manny Ramirez	3.00	.90
6 Damion Easley	2.00	.60
7 Jeff King	2.00	.60
8 Paul Molitor	3.00	.90
9 Derek Jeter	12.00	3.60
10 Ben Grieve	2.00	.60
11 Ken Griffey Jr.	8.00	2.40
12 Wade Boggs	3.00	.90
13 Juan Gonzalez	3.00	.90
14 Roger Clemens	10.00	3.00
15 Travis Lee	2.00	.60
16 Chipper Jones	5.00	1.50
17 Sammy Sosa	8.00	2.40
18 Barry Larkin	3.00	.90
19 Todd Helton	3.00	.90
20 Mark Kotsay	2.00	.60
21 Jeff Bagwell	3.00	.90
22 Raul Mondesi	2.00	.60
23 Jeff Cirillo	2.00	.60
24 Vladimir Guerrero	5.00	1.50
25 Mike Piazza	8.00	2.40
26 Scott Rolen	5.00	1.50
27 Jason Kendall	2.00	.60
28 Mark McGwire	12.00	3.60
29 Tony Gwynn	6.00	1.80
30 Barry Bonds	12.00	3.60

1999 Pacific Timelines

This hobby only set features 20 leading players. Three photos of each player are featured on the front, including many with these players original teams. These cards give a chronological history of each players career. This inserted was limited to 199 serial numbered sets.

	Nm-Mt	Ex-Mt
1 Cal Ripken	80.00	24.00
2 Frank Thomas	25.00	7.50
3 Jim Thome	25.00	7.50
4 Paul Molitor	15.00	4.50
5 Bernie Williams	15.00	4.50
6 Derek Jeter	60.00	18.00
7 Ken Griffey Jr.	40.00	12.00
8 Alex Rodriguez	40.00	12.00
9 Wade Boggs	15.00	4.50
10 Jose Canseco	25.00	7.50
11 Roger Clemens	50.00	15.00
12 Andres Galarraga	10.00	3.00
13 Chipper Jones	25.00	7.50
14 Greg Maddux	40.00	12.00
15 Sammy Sosa	40.00	12.00
16 Larry Walker	15.00	4.50
17 Randy Johnson	25.00	7.50
18 Mike Piazza	40.00	12.00
19 Mark McGwire	60.00	18.00
20 Tony Gwynn	30.00	9.00

2000 Pacific

Though numbered 1-450, fifty supertsars were featured in both action and portrait variations on the card front photos. Therefore the set is considered complete at 500 cards. The product was issued in 12 card packs with 24 packs in each box and 20 boxes per case. The packs carried a suggested retail price of $2.49 each. Special Jewel Collection packs were issued for the 7/11 convenience store chain and they contained 12 cards with an SRP of $2.99. A Tony Gwynn Sample card was distributed to dealers and hobby media several weeks prior to the release of the product. The Gwynn card is readily identifiable by the bold "SAMPLE" text running diagonally across the card back.

	Nm-Mt	Ex-Mt
COMPLETE SET (500)	50.00	15.00
1 Garret Anderson	.30	.09

2 Tim Belcher .30 .09
3 Gary DiSarcina .30 .09
4 Trent Durrington .30 .09
5 Jim Edmonds .30 .09
6 Darin Erstad ACTION .30 .09
6A Darin Erstad POR .30 .09
7 Chuck Finley .30 .09
8 Troy Glaus .30 .09
9 Todd Greene .30 .09
10 Bret Hemphill .30 .09
11 Ken Hill .30 .09
12 Ramon Ortiz .30 .09
13 Troy Percival .30 .09
14 Mark Petkovsek .30 .09
15 Tim Salmon .50 .15
16 Mo Vaughn ACTION .30 .09
16A Mo Vaughn POR .30 .09
17 Jay Bell .30 .09
18 Omar Daal .30 .09
19 Erubiel Durazo .30 .09
20 Steve Finley .30 .09
21 Bernard Gilkey .30 .09
22 Luis Gonzalez .30 .09
23 Randy Johnson .75 .23
24 Byung-Hyun Kim .30 .09
25 Travis Lee .30 .09
26 Matt Mantei .30 .09
27 Armando Reynoso .30 .09
28 Rob Ryan .30 .09
29 Kelly Stinnett .30 .09
30 Todd Stottlemyre .30 .09
31 Matt Williams ACTION .30 .09
31A Matt Williams POR .30 .09
32 Tony Womack .30 .09
33 Bret Boone .30 .09
34 Andres Galarraga .30 .09
35 Tom Glavine .50 .15
36 Ozzie Guillen .30 .09
37 Andruw Jones ACTION .30 .09
37A Andruw Jones POR .30 .09
38 Chipper Jones ACTION .75 .23
38A Chipper Jones POR .75 .23
39 Brian Jordan .30 .09
40 Ryan Klesko .30 .09
41 Javy Lopez .30 .09
42 Greg Maddux ACTION 1.25 .35
42A Greg Maddux POR 1.25 .35
43 Kevin Millwood .30 .09
44 John Rocker .30 .09
45 Randall Simon .30 .09
46 John Smoltz .50 .15
47 Gerald Williams .30 .09
48 Brady Anderson .30 .09
49 Albert Belle ACTION .30 .09
49A Albert Belle POR .30 .09
50 Mike Bordick .30 .09
51 Will Clark .75 .23
52 Jeff Conine .30 .09
53 Delino DeShields .30 .09
54 Jerry Hairston Jr. .30 .09
55 Charles Johnson .30 .09
56 Eugene Kingsale .30 .09
57 Ryan Minor .30 .09
58 Mike Mussina .50 .15
59 Sidney Ponson .30 .09
60 Cal Ripken ACTION 2.50 .75
60A Cal Ripken POR 2.50 .75
61 B.J. Surhoff .30 .09
62 Mike Timlin .30 .09
63 Rod Beck .30 .09
64 N.Garciaparra ACTION 1.25 .35
64A N.Garciaparra POR 1.25 .35
65 Tom Gordon .30 .09
66 Butch Huskey .30 .09
67 Derek Lowe .30 .09
68 P.Martinez ACTION .75 .23
68A Pedro Martinez POR .75 .23
69 Trot Nixon .30 .09
70 Jose Offerman .30 .09
71 Troy O'Leary .30 .09
72 Pat Rapp .30 .09
73 Donnie Sadler .30 .09
74 Mike Stanley .30 .09
75 John Valentin .30 .09
76 Jason Varitek .50 .15
77 Wilton Veras .30 .09
78 Tim Wakefield .30 .09
79 Rick Aguilera .30 .09
80 Manny Alexander .30 .09
81 Roosevelt Brown .30 .09
82 Mark Grace .50 .15
83 Glenallen Hill .30 .09
84 Lance Johnson .30 .09
85 Jon Lieber .30 .09
86 Cole Liniak .30 .09
87 Chad Meyers .30 .09
88 Mickey Morandini .30 .09
89 Jose Nieves .30 .09
90 Henry Rodriguez .30 .09
91 Sammy Sosa ACTION 1.25 .35
91A Sammy Sosa POR 1.25 .35
92 Kevin Tapani .30 .09
93 Kerry Wood .75 .23
94 Mike Caruso .30 .09
95 Ray Durham .30 .09
96 Brook Fordyce .30 .09
97 Bobby Howry .30 .09
98 Paul Konerko .30 .09
99 Carlos Lee .30 .09
100 Aaron Myette .30 .09
101 Greg Norton .30 .09
102 Magglio Ordonez .30 .09
103 Jim Parque .30 .09
104 Liu Rodriguez .30 .09
105 Chris Singleton .30 .09
106 Mike Sirotka .30 .09
107 F.Thomas ACTION .75 .23
107A Frank Thomas POR .75 .23
108 Kip Wells .30 .09
109 Aaron Boone .30 .09
110 Mike Cameron .30 .09
111 Sean Casey ACTION .30 .09
111A Sean Casey POR .30 .09
112 Jeffrey Hammonds .30 .09
113 Pete Harnisch .30 .09
114 Barry Larkin ACTION .50 .15
114A Barry Larkin POR .50 .15
115 Jason LaRue .30 .09
116 Denny Neagle .30 .09
117 Pokey Reese .30 .09
118 Scott Sullivan .30 .09
119 Eddie Taubensee .30 .09
120 Greg Vaughn .30 .09
121 Scott Williamson .30 .09
122 Dmitri Young .30 .09
123 R.Alomar ACTION .50 .15
123A R.Alomar POR .50 .15
124 Sandy Alomar Jr. .30 .09
125 Harold Baines .30 .09
126 Russell Branyan .30 .09
127 Dave Burba .30 .09
128 Bartolo Colon .30 .09
129 Travis Fryman .30 .09
130 Mike Jackson .30 .09
131 David Justice .30 .09
132 Kenny Lofton ACTION .30 .09
132A Kenny Lofton POR .30 .09
133 Charles Nagy .30 .09
134 M.Ramirez ACTION .50 .15
134A Manny Ramirez POR .50 .15
135 Dave Roberts .30 .09
136 Richie Sexson .30 .09
137 Jim Thome .75 .23
138 Omar Vizquel .50 .15
139 Jaret Wright .30 .09
140 Pedro Astacio .30 .09
141 Dante Bichette .30 .09
142 Brian Bohanon .30 .09
143 Vinny Castilla ACTION .30 .09
143A Vinny Castilla POR .30 .09
144 Edgard Clemente .30 .09
145 Derrick Gibson .30 .09
146 Todd Helton .50 .15
147 Darryl Kile .30 .09
148 Mike Lansing .30 .09
149 Kirt Manwaring .30 .09
150 Neifi Perez .30 .09
151 Ben Petrick .30 .09
152 Juan Sosa RC .30 .09
153 Dave Veres .30 .09
154 Larry Walker ACTION .50 .15
154A Larry Walker POR .50 .15
155 Brad Ausmus .30 .09
156 Dave Borkowski .30 .09
157 Tony Clark .30 .09
158 Francisco Cordero .30 .09
159 Deivi Cruz .30 .09
160 Damion Easley .30 .09
161 Juan Encarnacion .30 .09
162 Robert Fick .30 .09
163 Bobby Higginson .30 .09
164 Gabe Kapler .30 .09
165 Brian Moehler .30 .09
166 Dean Palmer .30 .09
167 Luis Polonia .30 .09
168 Justin Thompson .30 .09
169 Jeff Weaver .30 .09
170 Antonio Alfonseca .30 .09
171 Bruce Aven .30 .09
172 A.J. Burnett .30 .09
173 Luis Castillo .30 .09
174 Ramon Castro .30 .09
175 Ryan Dempster .30 .09
176 Alex Fernandez .30 .09
177 Cliff Floyd .30 .09
178 Amaury Garcia .30 .09
179 Alex Gonzalez .30 .09
180 Mark Kotsay .30 .09
181 Mike Lowell .30 .09
182 Brian Meadows .30 .09
183 Kevin Orie .30 .09
184 Julio Ramirez .30 .09
185 Preston Wilson .30 .09
186 Moises Alou .30 .09
187 Jeff Bagwell ACTION .50 .15
187A Jeff Bagwell POR .50 .15
188 Glen Barker .30 .09
189 Derek Bell .30 .09
190 Craig Biggio ACTION .50 .15
190A Craig Biggio POR .50 .15
191 Ken Caminiti .30 .09
192 Scott Elarton .30 .09
193 Carl Everett .30 .09
194 Mike Hampton .30 .09
195 Carlos E. Hernandez .30 .09
196 Richard Hidalgo .30 .09
197 Jose Lima .30 .09
198 Shane Reynolds .30 .09
199 Bill Spiers .30 .09
200 Billy Wagner .30 .09
201 C. Beltran ACTION .50 .15
201A Carlos Beltran POR .50 .15
202 Dermal Brown .30 .09
203 Johnny Damon .50 .15
204 Jermaine Dye .30 .09
205 Carlos Febles .30 .09
206 Jeremy Giambi .30 .09
207 Mark Quinn .30 .09
208 Joe Randa .30 .09
209 Dan Reichert .30 .09
210 Jose Rosado .30 .09
211 Rey Sanchez .30 .09
212 Jeff Suppan .30 .09
213 Mike Sweeney .30 .09
214 Kevin Brown ACTION .30 .09
214A Kevin Brown POR .30 .09
215 Darren Dreifort .30 .09
216 Eric Gagne 1.25 .35
217 Mark Grudzielanek .30 .09
218 Todd Hollandsworth .30 .09
219 Todd Hundley .30 .09
220 Eric Karros .30 .09
221 Raul Mondesi .30 .09
222 Chan Ho Park .30 .09
223 Jeff Shaw .30 .09
224 G.Sheffield ACTION .30 .09
224A Gary Sheffield POR .30 .09
225 Ismael Valdes .30 .09
226 Devon White .30 .09
227 Eric Young .30 .09
228 Kevin Barker .30 .09
229 Ron Belliard .30 .09
230 J.Burnitz ACTION .30 .09
230A Jeromy Burnitz POR .30 .09
231 Jeff Cirillo .30 .09
232 Marquis Grissom .30 .09
233 Geoff Jenkins .30 .09
234 Mark Loretta .30 .09
235 David Nilsson .30 .09
236 Hideo Nomo .75 .23
237 Alex Ochoa .30 .09
238 Kyle Peterson .30 .09
239 Fernando Vina .30 .09
240 Bob Wickman .30 .09
241 Steve Woodard .30 .09
242 Chad Allen .30 .09
243 Ron Coomer .30 .09
244 Marty Cordova .30 .09
245 Cristian Guzman .30 .09
246 Denny Hocking .30 .09
247 Jacque Jones .30 .09
248 Corey Koskie .30 .09
249 Matt Lawton .30 .09
250 Joe Mays .30 .09
251 Eric Milton .30 .09
252 Brad Radke .30 .09
253 Mark Redman .30 .09
254 Terry Steinbach .30 .09
255 Todd Walker .30 .09
256 Tony Armas Jr. .30 .09
257 Michael Barrett .30 .09
258 Peter Bergeron .30 .09
259 Geoff Blum .30 .09
260 Orlando Cabrera .30 .09
261 Trace Coquillette RC .30 .09
262 Brad Fullmer .30 .09
263 V.Guerrero ACTION .75 .23
263A V.Guerrero POR .75 .23
264 Wilton Guerrero .30 .09
265 Dustin Hermanson .30 .09
266 Manny Martinez RC .30 .09
267 Ryan McGuire .30 .09
268 Ugueth Urbina .30 .09
269 Jose Vidro .30 .09
270 Rondell White .30 .09
271 Chris Widger .30 .09
272 Edgardo Alfonzo .30 .09
273 Armando Benitez .30 .09
274 Roger Cedeno .30 .09
275 Dennis Cook .30 .09
276 Octavio Dotel .30 .09
277 John Franco .30 .09
278 Darryl Hamilton .30 .09
279 Rickey Henderson .75 .23
280 Orel Hershiser .30 .09
281 Al Leiter .30 .09
282 John Olerud ACTION .30 .09
282A John Olerud POR .30 .09
283 Rey Ordonez .30 .09
284 Mike Piazza ACTION 1.25 .35
284A Mike Piazza POR 1.25 .35
285 Kenny Rogers .30 .09
286 Jorge Toca .30 .09
287 Robin Ventura .50 .15
288 Scott Brosius .30 .09
289 R.Clemens ACTION 1.50 .45
289A Roger Clemens POR 1.50 .45
290 David Cone .30 .09
291 Chili Davis .30 .09
292 Orlando Hernandez .30 .09
293 Hideki Irabu .30 .09
294 Derek Jeter ACTION 2.00 .60
294A Derek Jeter POR 2.00 .60
295 Chuck Knoblauch .30 .09
296 Ricky Ledee .30 .09
297 Jim Leyritz .30 .09
298 Tino Martinez .50 .15
299 Paul O'Neill .50 .15
300 Andy Pettitte .50 .15
301 Jorge Posada .50 .15
302 Mariano Rivera .50 .15
303 Alfonso Soriano .75 .23
304 B.Williams ACTION .50 .15
304A Bernie Williams POR .50 .15
305 Ed Yarnall .30 .09
306 Kevin Appier .30 .09
307 Rich Becker .30 .09
308 Eric Chavez .30 .09
309 Jason Giambi .30 .09
310 Ben Grieve .30 .09
311 Ramon Hernandez .30 .09
312 Tim Hudson .30 .09
313 John Jaha .30 .09
314 Doug Jones .30 .09
315 Omar Olivares .30 .09
316 Mike Oquist .30 .09
317 Matt Stairs .30 .09
318 Miguel Tejada .30 .09
319 Randy Velarde .30 .09
320 Bob Abreu .30 .09
321 Marlon Anderson .30 .09
322 Alex Arias .30 .09
323 Rico Brogna .30 .09
324 Paul Byrd .30 .09
325 Ron Gant .30 .09
326 Doug Glanville .30 .09
327 Wayne Gomes .30 .09
328 Mike Lieberthal .30 .09
329 Robert Person .30 .09
330 Desi Relaford .30 .09
331 Scott Rolen ACTION .75 .23
331A Scott Rolen POR .75 .23
332 Curt Schilling ACTION .30 .09
332A Curt Schilling POR .30 .09
333 Kris Benson .30 .09
334 Adrian Brown .30 .09
335 Brant Brown .30 .09
336 Brian Giles .30 .09
337 Chad Hermansen .30 .09
338 Jason Kendall .30 .09
339 Al Martin .30 .09
340 Pat Meares .30 .09
341 W.Morris ACTION .30 .09
341A Warren Morris POR .30 .09
342 Todd Ritchie .30 .09
343 Jason Schmidt .30 .09
344 Ed Sprague .30 .09
345 Mike Williams .30 .09
346 Kevin Young .30 .09
347 Rick Ankiel .30 .09
348 Ricky Bottalico .30 .09
349 Kent Bottenfield .30 .09
350 Darren Bragg .30 .09
351 Eric Davis .30 .09
352 J.D. Drew ACTION .30 .09
352A J.D. Drew POR .30 .09
353 Adam Kennedy .30 .09
354 Ray Lankford .30 .09
355 Joe McEwing .30 .09
356 M.McGwire ACTION 2.00 .60
356A Mark McGwire POR 2.00 .60
357 Matt Morris .30 .09
358 Darren Oliver .30 .09
359 Edgar Renteria .30 .09
360 Fernando Tatis .30 .09
361 Andy Ashby .30 .09
362 Ben Davis .30 .09
363 Tony Gwynn ACTION 1.00 .30
363A Tony Gwynn POR 1.00 .30
364 Sterling Hitchcock .30 .09
365 Trevor Hoffman .30 .09
366 Damian Jackson .30 .09
367 Wally Joyner .30 .09
368 Dave Magadan .30 .09
369 Gary Matthews Jr. .30 .09
370 Phil Nevin .30 .09
371 Eric Owens .30 .09
372 Ruben Rivera .30 .09
373 R.Sanders ACTION .30 .09
373A Reggie Sanders POR .30 .09
374 Quilvio Veras .30 .09
375 Rich Aurilia .30 .09
376 Marvin Benard .30 .09
377 Barry Bonds ACTION 2.00 .60
377A Barry Bonds POR 2.00 .60
378 Ellis Burks .30 .09
379 Shawn Estes .30 .09
380 Livan Hernandez .30 .09
381 Jeff Kent ACTION .30 .09
381A Jeff Kent POR .30 .09
382 Brent Mayne .30 .09
383 Bill Mueller .30 .09
384 Calvin Murray .30 .09
385 Robb Nen .30 .09
386 Russ Ortiz .30 .09
387 Kirk Rueter .30 .09
388 J.T. Snow .30 .09
389 David Bell .30 .09
390 Jay Buhner .30 .09
391 Russ Davis .30 .09
392 Freddy Garcia ACTION .30 .09
392A Freddy Garcia POR .30 .09
393 K.Griffey Jr. ACTION 1.25 .35
393A Ken Griffey Jr. POR 1.25 .35
394 Carlos Guillen .30 .09
395 John Halama .30 .09
396 Brian L.Hunter .30 .09
397 Ryan Jackson .30 .09
398 Edgar Martinez .50 .15
399 Gil Meche .30 .09
400 Jose Mesa .30 .09
401 Jamie Moyer .30 .09
402 A.Rodriguez ACTION 1.25 .35
402A Alex Rodriguez POR 1.25 .35
403 Dan Wilson .30 .09
404 Wilson Alvarez .30 .09
405 Rolando Arrojo .30 .09
406 Wade Boggs ACTION .50 .15
406A Wade Boggs POR .50 .15
407 Miguel Cairo .30 .09
408 Jose Canseco ACTION .75 .23
408A Jose Canseco POR .75 .23
409 John Flaherty .30 .09
410 Jose Guillen .30 .09
411 Roberto Hernandez .30 .09
412 Terrell Lowery .30 .09
413 Dave Martinez .30 .09
414 Quinton McCracken .30 .09
415 Fred McGriff ACTION .50 .15
415A Fred McGriff POR .50 .15
416 Ryan Rupe .30 .09
417 Kevin Stocker .30 .09
418 Bubba Trammell .30 .09
419 Royce Clayton .30 .09
420 J.Gonzalez ACTION .50 .15
420A Juan Gonzalez POR .50 .15
421 Tom Goodwin .30 .09
422 Rusty Greer .30 .09
423 Rick Helling .30 .09
424 Roberto Kelly .30 .09
425 Ruben Mateo .30 .09
426 Mark McLemore .30 .09
427 Mike Morgan .30 .09
428 Rafael Palmeiro .50 .15
429 I.Rodriguez ACTION .75 .23
429A Ivan Rodriguez POR .75 .23
430 Aaron Sele .30 .09
431 Lee Stevens .30 .09
432 John Wetteland .30 .09
433 Todd Zeile .30 .09
434 Jeff Zimmerman .30 .09
435 Tony Batista .30 .09
436 Casey Blake .30 .09
437 Homer Bush .30 .09
438 Chris Carpenter .30 .09
439 Jose Cruz Jr. .30 .09
440 C.Delgado ACTION .30 .09
440A Carlos Delgado POR .30 .09
441 Tony Fernandez .30 .09
442 Darrin Fletcher .30 .09
443 Alex Gonzalez .30 .09
444 Shawn Green ACTION .30 .09
444A Shawn Green POR .30 .09
445 Roy Halladay .30 .09
446 Billy Koch .30 .09
447 David Segui .30 .09
448 Shannon Stewart .30 .09
449 David Wells .30 .09
450 Vernon Wells .30 .09
SAMP T.Gwynn Sample 1.00 .30

2000 Pacific Copper

Randomly inserted in hobby packs, these parallel cards feature copper foil and are serial numbered to 99 cards.

Nm-Mt Ex-Mt
*STARS: 8X TO 20X BASIC CARDS
*ROOKIES: 5X TO 12X BASIC CARDS

2000 Pacific Emerald Green

Randomly inserted exclusively into Jewel Collection retail packs, this set parallels the regular Pacific set and is serial numbered to 99 cards. This set is printed in green foil which is how it can be differentiated from the regular cards.

Nm-Mt Ex-Mt
*STARS: 8X TO 20X BASIC CARDS
*ROOKIES: 5X TO 12X BASIC CARDS

2000 Pacific Gold

Randomly inserted in retail packs, this is a parallel of the regular Pacific Set. These cards are printed in gold foil and are serial numbered to 199 which are two ways of differentiating them from the regular Pacific cards.

Nm-Mt Ex-Mt
*STARS: 5X TO 12X BASIC CARDS
*ROOKIES: 3X TO 8X BASIC CARDS

2000 Pacific Platinum Blue

Randomly inserted in all Pacific packs, these cards parallel the basic Pacific set. The cards have blue foil accents on them and are serial numbered to 75.

Nm-Mt Ex-Mt
*STARS: 10X TO 25X BASIC CARDS
*ROOKIES: 6X TO 15X BASIC CARDS

2000 Pacific Premiere Date

Issued one per 24 pack hobby box, this set parallels the regular Pacific set. These cards are serial numbered to 37 and feature a large "Premiere Date" logo on front.

Nm-Mt Ex-Mt
*STARS: 20X TO 50X BASIC CARDS
*ROOKIES: 12.5X TO 30X BASIC CARDS

2000 Pacific Ruby

Issued 12 cards per Jewel Collection retail pack, this set parallels the regular 2000 Pacific set. The ruby-colored foil on the player's name and team make it easy to differentiate from the silver-foil standard cards.

Nm-Mt Ex-Mt
COMPLETE SET (500) 250.00 75.00
*STARS: 1.25X TO 3X BASIC CARDS
*ROOKIES: .75X TO 2X BASIC CARDS

2000 Pacific Command Performers

These cards were inserted one in every 24 Jewel Collection special retail (7/11) packs. The 20-card set features some of the leading players in baseball.

	Nm-Mt	Ex-Mt
COMPLETE SET (20)	100.00	30.00
PROOFS RANDOM IN JEWEL RETAIL PACKS		
PROOFS PRINT RUN 10 SERIAL #'d SETS		
PROOFS: NO PRICING DUE TO SCARCITY		
1 Chipper Jones	5.00	1.50
2 Greg Maddux	8.00	2.40
3 Cal Ripken	15.00	4.50
4 Nomar Garciaparra	8.00	2.40
5 Sammy Sosa	8.00	2.40
6 Sean Casey	2.00	.60
7 Manny Ramirez	3.00	.90
8 Larry Walker	3.00	.90
9 Jeff Bagwell	3.00	.90
10 Vladimir Guerrero	5.00	1.50
11 Mike Piazza	8.00	2.40
12 Roger Clemens	10.00	3.00
13 Derek Jeter	12.00	3.60
14 Mark McGwire	12.00	3.60
15 Tony Gwynn	6.00	1.80
16 Barry Bonds	12.00	3.60
17 Ken Griffey Jr.	8.00	2.40
18 Alex Rodriguez	8.00	2.40
19 Ivan Rodriguez	5.00	1.50
20 Shawn Green	2.00	.60

2000 Pacific Cramer's Choice

Inserted at a rate of one in every 721 packs, these die-cut cards feature 10 players Pacific founder Mike Cramer considers to be among the very best players in baseball.

	Nm-Mt	Ex-Mt
1 Chipper Jones	25.00	7.50
2 Cal Ripken	80.00	24.00
3 Nomar Garciaparra	40.00	12.00
4 Sammy Sosa	40.00	12.00
5 Mike Piazza	40.00	12.00
6 Derek Jeter	60.00	18.00
7 Mark McGwire	60.00	18.00
8 Tony Gwynn	30.00	9.00
9 Ken Griffey Jr.	40.00	12.00
10 Alex Rodriguez	40.00	12.00

2000 Pacific Diamond Leaders

Inserted two every 25 packs, this 30 card set features three or more leaders from each team in various statistical categories. The cards are printed in holographic silver foil and are sequenced in alphabetical order by league.

	Nm-Mt	Ex-Mt
COMPLETE SET (30)	60.00	18.00
1 Garret Anderson Chuck Finley	1.25	.35

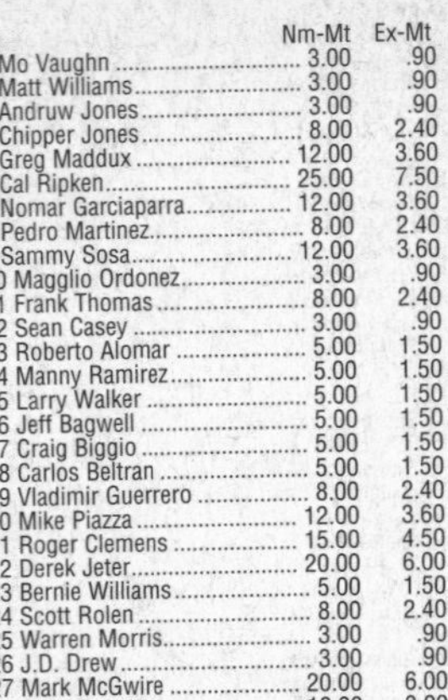

Troy Percival
Mo Vaughn
2 Albert Belle 2.00 .60
Mike Mussina
B.J. Surhoff
3 Nomar Garciaparra 5.00 1.50
Pedro Martinez
Troy O'Leary
4 Ray Durham 3.00 .90
Magglio Ordonez
Frank Thomas
5 Bartolo Colon 2.00 .60
Manny Ramirez
Omar Vizquel
6 Deivi Cruz 1.25 .35
Dave Mlicki
Dean Palmer
7 Johnny Damon 1.25 .35
Jermaine Dye
Jose Rosado
Mike Sweeney
8 Corey Koskie 1.25 .35
Eric Milton
Brad Radke
9 Orlando Hernandez 8.00 2.40
Derek Jeter
Mariano Rivera
Bernie Williams
10 Jason Giambi 1.25 .35
Tim Hudson
Matt Stairs
11 Freddy Garcia 5.00 1.50
Ken Griffey Jr.
Edgar Martinez
12 Jose Canseco 3.00 .90
Roberto Hernandez
Fred McGriff
13 Rafael Palmeiro 3.00 .90
Ivan Rodriguez
John Wetteland
14 Carlos Delgado 1.25 .35
Shannon Stewart
David Wells
15 Luis Gonzalez 3.00 .90
Randy Johnson
Matt Williams
16 Chipper Jones 5.00 1.50
Brian Jordan
Greg Maddux
17 Mark Grace 5.00 1.50
Jon Lieber
Sammy Sosa
18 Sean Casey 1.25 .35
Pete Harnisch
Greg Vaughn
19 Pedro Astacio 2.00 .60
Dante Bichette
Larry Walker
20 Luis Castillo 1.25 .35
Alex Fernandez
Preston Wilson
21 Jeff Bagwell 2.00 .60
Mike Hampton
Billy Wagner
22 Kevin Brown 1.25 .35
Mark Grudzielanek
Eric Karros
23 Jeromy Burnitz 3.00 .90
Jeff Cirillo
Marquis Grissom
Hideo Nomo
24 Vladimir Guerrero 3.00 .90
Dustin Hermanson
Ugueth Urbina
25 Roger Cedeno 5.00 1.50
Rickey Henderson
Mike Piazza
26 Bob Abreu 1.25 .35
Mike Lieberthal
Curt Schilling
27 Brian Giles 1.25 .35
Jason Kendall
Kevin Young
28 Kent Bottenfield 8.00 2.40
Ray Lankford
Mark McGwire
29 Tony Gwynn 4.00 1.20
Trevor Hoffman
Reggie Sanders
30 Barry Bonds 8.00 2.40
Jeff Kent
Russ Ortiz

2000 Pacific Gold Crown Die Cuts

Inserted one every 25 packs, this 36 card set features a selection of baseball's top stars. This set uses the Gold Crown Die Cut style used on many Pacific products and has a dual foil design utilizing both holographic gold and holographic silver. In addition the cards are printed on extra sturdy 24 point stock.

	Nm-Mt	Ex-Mt
1 Mo Vaughn	3.00	.90
2 Matt Williams	3.00	.90
3 Andruw Jones	3.00	.90
4 Chipper Jones	8.00	2.40
5 Greg Maddux	12.00	3.60
6 Cal Ripken	25.00	7.50
7 Nomar Garciaparra	12.00	3.60
8 Pedro Martinez	8.00	2.40
9 Sammy Sosa	12.00	3.60
10 Magglio Ordonez	3.00	.90
11 Frank Thomas	8.00	2.40
12 Sean Casey	3.00	.90
13 Roberto Alomar	5.00	1.50
14 Manny Ramirez	5.00	1.50
15 Larry Walker	5.00	1.50
16 Jeff Bagwell	5.00	1.50
17 Craig Biggio	5.00	1.50
18 Carlos Beltran	5.00	1.50
19 Vladimir Guerrero	8.00	2.40
20 Mike Piazza	12.00	3.60
21 Roger Clemens	15.00	4.50
22 Derek Jeter	20.00	6.00
23 Bernie Williams	5.00	1.50
24 Scott Rolen	8.00	2.40
25 Warren Morris	3.00	.90
26 J.D. Drew	3.00	.90
27 Mark McGwire	20.00	6.00
28 Tony Gwynn	10.00	3.00
29 Barry Bonds	20.00	6.00
30 Ken Griffey Jr.	12.00	3.60
31 Alex Rodriguez	12.00	3.60
32 Jose Canseco	8.00	2.40
33 Juan Gonzalez	5.00	1.50
34 Rafael Palmeiro	5.00	1.50
35 Ivan Rodriguez	8.00	2.40
36 Shawn Green	3.00	.90

2000 Pacific Ornaments

Inserted two every 25 packs, these 20 cards are designed in the shape of Christmas ornaments. The cards have full custom holographic patterned silver foil and a string loop on top so they can be hung on a tree. Five different holiday shapes were featured.

	Nm-Mt	Ex-Mt
COMPLETE SET (20)	80.00	24.00
1 Mo Vaughn	2.00	.60
2 Chipper Jones	5.00	1.50
3 Greg Maddux	8.00	2.40
4 Cal Ripken	15.00	4.50
5 Nomar Garciaparra	8.00	2.40
6 Sammy Sosa	8.00	2.40
7 Frank Thomas	5.00	1.50
8 Manny Ramirez	3.00	.90
9 Larry Walker	3.00	.90
10 Jeff Bagwell	3.00	.90
11 Mike Piazza	8.00	2.40
12 Roger Clemens	10.00	3.00
13 Derek Jeter	12.00	3.60
14 Scott Rolen	5.00	1.50
15 J.D. Drew	2.00	.60
16 Mark McGwire	12.00	3.60
17 Tony Gwynn	6.00	1.80
18 Ken Griffey Jr.	8.00	2.40
19 Alex Rodriguez	8.00	2.40
20 Ivan Rodriguez	5.00	1.50

2000 Pacific Past and Present

These 20 stars were inserted at a rate of one every 24 packs. The cards have a laminated full foil front featuring a current photo and a photo-engraved-style back featuring a photo early in the player's career.

	Nm-Mt	Ex-Mt
COMPLETE SET (20)	150.00	45.00
PROOFS RANDOM INSERTS IN PACKS		
PROOFS PRINT RUN 1 SERIAL #'d SET		
PROOFS NOT PRICED DUE TO SCARCITY		
1 Chipper Jones	8.00	2.40
2 Greg Maddux	12.00	3.60
3 Cal Ripken	25.00	7.50
4 Nomar Garciaparra	12.00	3.60
5 Pedro Martinez	8.00	2.40
6 Sammy Sosa	12.00	3.60
7 Frank Thomas	8.00	2.40
8 Manny Ramirez	5.00	1.50
9 Larry Walker	5.00	1.50
10 Jeff Bagwell	5.00	1.50
11 Mike Piazza	12.00	3.60
12 Roger Clemens	15.00	4.50
13 Derek Jeter	20.00	6.00
14 Mark McGwire	20.00	6.00
15 Tony Gwynn	10.00	3.00
16 Barry Bonds	20.00	6.00
17 Ken Griffey Jr.	12.00	3.60
18 Alex Rodriguez	12.00	3.60
19 Wade Boggs	5.00	1.50
20 Ivan Rodriguez	8.00	2.40

2000 Pacific Reflections

Inserted one every 97 packs, these 20 cards feature some of the leading baseball stars. The

cards mere produced using a special cel sun glasses on cap design. The player's headshot photo is seen on one side of the sunglasses.

	Nm-Mt	Ex-Mt
COMPLETE SET (20)	250.00	75.00
1 Andruw Jones	6.00	1.80
2 Chipper Jones	15.00	4.50
3 Cal Ripken	50.00	15.00
4 Nomar Garciaparra	25.00	7.50
5 Sammy Sosa	25.00	7.50
6 Frank Thomas	15.00	4.50
7 Manny Ramirez	10.00	3.00
8 Jeff Bagwell	10.00	3.00
9 Vladimir Guerrero	15.00	4.50
10 Mike Piazza	25.00	7.50
11 Derek Jeter	40.00	12.00
12 Bernie Williams	10.00	3.00
13 Scott Rolen	15.00	4.50
14 J.D. Drew	6.00	1.80
15 Mark McGwire	40.00	12.00
16 Tony Gwynn	20.00	6.00
17 Ken Griffey Jr.	25.00	7.50
18 Alex Rodriguez	25.00	7.50
19 Juan Gonzalez	10.00	3.00
20 Ivan Rodriguez	15.00	4.50

2001 Pacific

The 2001 Pacific product was released in December, 2000 and features a 500-card base set. Each pack contained 12 cards, and carried a suggested retail price of 2.99.

	Nm-Mt	Ex-Mt
COMPLETE SET (500)	100.00	30.00
1 Garret Anderson	.30	.09
2 Gary DiSarcina	.30	.09
3 Darin Erstad	.30	.09
4 Seth Etherton	.30	.09
5 Ron Gant	.30	.09
6 Troy Glaus	.30	.09
7 Shigetoshi Hasegawa	.30	.09
8 Adam Kennedy	.30	.09
9 Ben Molina	.30	.09
10 Ramon Ortiz	.30	.09
11 Troy Percival	.30	.09
12 Tim Salmon	.50	.15
13 Scott Schoeneweis	.30	.09
14 Mo Vaughn	.30	.09
15 Jarrod Washburn	.30	.09
16 Brian Anderson	.30	.09
17 Danny Bautista	.30	.09
18 Jay Bell	.30	.09
19 Greg Colbrunn	.30	.09
20 Erubiel Durazo	.30	.09
21 Steve Finley	.30	.09
22 Luis Gonzalez	.30	.09
23 Randy Johnson	.75	.23
24 Byung-Hyun Kim	.30	.09
25 Matt Mantei	.30	.09
26 Armando Reynoso	.30	.09
27 Todd Stottlemyre	.30	.09
28 Matt Williams	.30	.09
29 Tony Womack	.30	.09
30 Andy Ashby	.30	.09
31 Bobby Bonilla	.30	.09
32 Rafael Furcal	.30	.09
33 Andres Galarraga	.30	.09
34 Tom Glavine	.50	.15
35 Andruw Jones	.30	.09
36 Chipper Jones	.75	.23
37 Brian Jordan	.30	.09
38 Wally Joyner	.30	.09
39 Keith Lockhart	.30	.09
40 Javy Lopez	.30	.09
41 Greg Maddux	1.25	.35
42 Kevin Millwood	.30	.09
43 John Rocker	.30	.09
44 Reggie Sanders	.30	.09
45 John Smoltz	.50	.15
46 B.J. Surhoff	.30	.09
47 Quilvio Veras	.30	.09
48 Walt Weiss	.30	.09
49 Brady Anderson	.30	.09
50 Albert Belle	.30	.09
51 Jeff Conine	.30	.09
52 Delino DeShields	.30	.09
53 Brook Fordyce	.30	.09
54 Jerry Hairston Jr.	.30	.09
55 Mark Lewis	.30	.09
56 Luis Matos	.30	.09
57 Melvin Mora	.30	.09
58 Mike Mussina	.50	.15
59 Chris Richard	.30	.09
60 Cal Ripken	2.50	.75
61 Manny Alexander	.30	.09
62 Rolando Arrojo	.30	.09
63 Midre Cummings	.30	.09
64 Carl Everett	.30	.09
65 Nomar Garciaparra	1.25	.35
66 Mike Lansing	.30	.09
67 Darren Lewis	.30	.09
68 Derek Lowe	.30	.09
69 Pedro Martinez	.75	.23
70 Ramon Martinez	.30	.09
71 Trot Nixon	.30	.09
72 Troy O'Leary	.30	.09
73 Jose Offerman	.30	.09
74 Tomo Ohka	.30	.09
75 Jason Varitek	.50	.15
76 Rick Aguilera	.30	.09
77 Shane Andrews	.30	.09
78 Brant Brown	.30	.09
79 Damon Buford	.30	.09
80 Joe Girardi	.30	.09
81 Mark Grace	.50	.15
82 Willie Greene	.30	.09
83 Ricky Gutierrez	.30	.09
84 Jon Lieber	.30	.09
85 Sammy Sosa	1.25	.35
86 Kevin Tapani	.30	.09
87 Rondell White	.30	.09
88 Kerry Wood	.75	.23
89 Eric Young	.30	.09
90 Harold Baines	.30	.09
91 James Baldwin	.30	.09
92 Ray Durham	.30	.09
93 Cal Eldred	.30	.09
94 Keith Foulke	.30	.09
95 Charles Johnson	.30	.09
96 Paul Konerko	.30	.09
97 Carlos Lee	.30	.09
98 Magglio Ordonez	.30	.09
99 Jim Parque	.30	.09
100 Herbert Perry	.30	.09
101 Chris Singleton	.30	.09
102 Mike Sirotka	.30	.09
103 Frank Thomas	.75	.23
104 Jose Valentin	.30	.09
105 Rob Bell	.30	.09
106 Aaron Boone	.30	.09
107 Sean Casey	.30	.09
108 Danny Graves	.30	.09
109 Ken Griffey Jr.	1.25	.35
110 Pete Harnisch	.30	.09
111 Brian Hunter	.30	.09
112 Barry Larkin	.50	.15
113 Pokey Reese	.30	.09
114 Benito Santiago	.30	.09
115 Chris Stynes	.30	.09
116 Michael Tucker	.30	.09
117 Ron Villone	.30	.09
118 Scott Williamson	.30	.09
119 Dmitri Young	.30	.09
120 Roberto Alomar	.50	.15
121 Sandy Alomar Jr.	.30	.09
122 Russell Branyan	.30	.09
123 Dave Burba	.30	.09
124 Bartolo Colon	.30	.09
125 Wil Cordero	.30	.09
126 Einar Diaz	.30	.09
127 Chuck Finley	.30	.09
128 Travis Fryman	.30	.09
129 Kenny Lofton	.30	.09
130 Charles Nagy	.30	.09
131 Manny Ramirez	.50	.15
132 David Segui	.30	.09
133 Jim Thome	.75	.23
134 Omar Vizquel	.50	.15
135 Brian Bohanon	.30	.09
136 Jeff Cirillo	.30	.09
137 Jeff Frye	.30	.09
138 Jeffrey Hammonds	.30	.09
139 Todd Helton	.50	.15
140 Todd Hollandsworth	.30	.09
141 Jose Jimenez	.30	.09
142 Brent Mayne	.30	.09
143 Neifi Perez	.30	.09
144 Ben Petrick	.30	.09
145 Juan Pierre	.30	.09
146 Larry Walker	.50	.15
147 Todd Walker	.30	.09
148 Masato Yoshii	.30	.09
149 Brad Ausmus	.30	.09
150 Rich Becker	.30	.09
151 Tony Clark	.30	.09
152 Deivi Cruz	.30	.09
153 Damion Easley	.30	.09
154 Juan Encarnacion	.30	.09
155 Robert Fick	.30	.09
156 Juan Gonzalez	.50	.15
157 Bobby Higginson	.30	.09
158 Todd Jones	.30	.09
159 Wendell Magee Jr.	.30	.09
160 Brian Moehler	.30	.09
161 Hideo Nomo	.75	.23
162 Dean Palmer	.30	.09
163 Jeff Weaver	.30	.09
164 Antonio Alfonseca	.30	.09
165 Dave Berg	.30	.09
166 A.J. Burnett	.30	.09
167 Luis Castillo	.30	.09
168 Ryan Dempster	.30	.09
169 Cliff Floyd	.30	.09
170 Alex Gonzalez	.30	.09
171 Mark Kotsay	.30	.09
172 Derrek Lee	.30	.09
173 Mike Lowell	.30	.09
174 Mike Redmond	.30	.09
175 Henry Rodriguez	.30	.09
176 Jesus Sanchez	.30	.09
177 Preston Wilson	.30	.09
178 Moises Alou	.30	.09
179 Jeff Bagwell	.50	.15
180 Glen Barker	.30	.09
181 Lance Berkman	.30	.09
182 Craig Biggio	.50	.15
183 Tim Bogar	.30	.09
184 Ken Caminiti	.30	.09
185 Roger Cedeno	.30	.09
186 Scott Elarton	.30	.09
187 Tony Eusebio	.30	.09
188 Richard Hidalgo	.30	.09
189 Jose Lima	.30	.09
190 Mitch Meluskey	.30	.09
191 Shane Reynolds	.30	.09
192 Bill Spiers	.30	.09
193 Billy Wagner	.30	.09
194 Daryle Ward	.30	.09
195 Carlos Beltran	.50	.15
196 Ricky Bottalico	.30	.09
197 Johnny Damon	.50	.15
198 Jermaine Dye	.30	.09
199 Jorge Fabregas	.30	.09
200 David McCarty	.30	.09
201 Mark Quinn	.30	.09
202 Joe Randa	.30	.09
203 Jeff Reboulet	.30	.09
204 Rey Sanchez	.30	.09
205 Blake Stein	.30	.09
206 Jeff Suppan	.30	.09
207 Mac Suzuki	.30	.09
208 Mike Sweeney	.30	.09
209 Greg Zaun	.30	.09
210 Adrian Beltre	.50	.15
211 Kevin Brown	.30	.09
212 Alex Cora	.30	.09
213 Darren Dreifort	.30	.09
214 Tom Goodwin	.30	.09
215 Shawn Green	.30	.09
216 Mark Grudzielanek	.30	.09
217 Todd Hundley	.30	.09
218 Eric Karros	.30	.09
219 Chad Kreuter	.30	.09
220 Jim Leyritz	.30	.09
221 Chan Ho Park	.30	.09
222 Jeff Shaw	.30	.09
223 Gary Sheffield	.30	.09
224 Devon White	.30	.09
225 Ron Belliard	.30	.09
226 Henry Blanco	.30	.09
227 Jeromy Burnitz	.30	.09
228 Jeff D'Amico	.30	.09
229 Marquis Grissom	.30	.09
230 Charlie Hayes	.30	.09
231 Jimmy Haynes	.30	.09
232 Tyler Houston	.30	.09
233 Geoff Jenkins	.30	.09
234 Mark Loretta	.30	.09
235 James Mouton	.30	.09
236 Richie Sexson	.30	.09
237 Jamey Wright	.30	.09
238 Jay Canizaro	.30	.09
239 Ron Coomer	.30	.09
240 Cristian Guzman	.30	.09
241 Denny Hocking	.30	.09
242 Torii Hunter	.30	.09
243 Jacque Jones	.30	.09
244 Corey Koskie	.30	.09
245 Matt Lawton	.30	.09
246 Matt LeCroy	.30	.09
247 Eric Milton	.30	.09
248 David Ortiz	.50	.15
249 Brad Radke	.30	.09
250 Mark Redman	.30	.09
251 Michael Barrett	.30	.09
252 Peter Bergeron	.30	.09
253 Milton Bradley	.30	.09
254 Orlando Cabrera	.30	.09
255 Vladimir Guerrero	.75	.23
256 Wilton Guerrero	.30	.09
257 Dustin Hermanson	.30	.09
258 Hideki Irabu	.30	.09
259 Fernando Seguignol	.30	.09
260 Lee Stevens	.30	.09
261 Andy Tracy	.30	.09
262 Javier Vazquez	.30	.09
263 Jose Vidro	.30	.09
264 Edgardo Alfonzo	.30	.09
265 Derek Bell	.30	.09
266 Armando Benitez	.30	.09
267 Mike Bordick	.30	.09
268 John Franco	.30	.09
269 Darryl Hamilton	.30	.09
270 Mike Hampton	.30	.09
271 Lenny Harris	.30	.09
272 Al Leiter	.30	.09
273 Joe McEwing	.30	.09
274 Rey Ordonez	.30	.09
275 Jay Payton	.30	.09
276 Mike Piazza	1.25	.35
277 Glendon Rusch	.30	.09
278 Bubba Trammell	.30	.09
279 Robin Ventura	.30	.09
280 Todd Zeile	.30	.09
281 Scott Brosius	.30	.09
282 Jose Canseco	.75	.23
283 Roger Clemens	1.50	.45
284 David Cone	.30	.09
285 Dwight Gooden	.30	.09
286 Orlando Hernandez	.30	.09
287 Glenallen Hill	.30	.09
288 Derek Jeter	2.00	.60
289 David Justice	.30	.09
290 Chuck Knoblauch	.30	.09
291 Tino Martinez	.50	.15
292 Denny Neagle	.30	.09
293 Paul O'Neill	.50	.15
294 Andy Pettitte	.50	.15
295 Jorge Posada	.50	.15
296 Mariano Rivera	.50	.15
297 Luis Sojo	.30	.09
298 Jose Vizcaino	.30	.09
299 Bernie Williams	.50	.15
300 Kevin Appier	.30	.09
301 Eric Chavez	.30	.09
302 Ryan Christenson	.30	.09
303 Jason Giambi	.30	.09
304 Jeremy Giambi	.30	.09
305 Ben Grieve	.30	.09
306 Gil Heredia	.30	.09
307 Ramon Hernandez	.30	.09
308 Tim Hudson	.30	.09
309 Jason Isringhausen	.30	.09
310 Terrence Long	.30	.09
311 Mark Mulder	.30	.09
312 Adam Piatt	.30	.09
313 Matt Stairs	.30	.09
314 Miguel Tejada	.30	.09
315 Randy Velarde	.30	.09
316 Alex Arias	.30	.09
317 Pat Burrell	.30	.09
318 Omar Daal	.30	.09
319 Travis Lee	.30	.09
320 Mike Lieberthal	.30	.09
321 Randy Wolf	.30	.09
322 Bobby Abreu	.30	.09
323 Jeff Brantley	.30	.09
324 Bruce Chen	.30	.09
325 Doug Glanville	.30	.09
326 Kevin Jordan	.30	.09
327 Robert Person	.30	.09
328 Scott Rolen	.75	.23
329 Jimmy Anderson	.30	.09
330 Mike Benjamin	.30	.09
331 Kris Benson	.30	.09

332 Adrian Brown .30 .09
333 Brian Giles .30 .09
334 Jason Kendall .30 .09
335 Pat Meares .30 .09
336 Warren Morris .30 .09
337 Aramis Ramirez .30 .09
338 Todd Ritchie .30 .09
339 Jason Schmidt .30 .09
340 John VanderWal .30 .09
341 Mike Williams .30 .09
342 Enrique Wilson .30 .09
343 Kevin Young .30 .09
344 Rick Ankiel .30 .09
345 Andy Benes .30 .09
346 Will Clark .75 .23
347 Eric Davis .30 .09
348 J.D. Drew .30 .09
349 Shawon Dunston .30 .09
350 Jim Edmonds .30 .09
351 Pat Hentgen .30 .09
352 Darryl Kile .30 .09
353 Ray Lankford .30 .09
354 Mike Matheny .30 .09
355 Mark McGwire 2.00 .60
356 Craig Paquette .30 .09
357 Edgar Renteria .30 .09
358 Garrett Stephenson .30 .09
359 Fernando Tatis .30 .09
360 Dave Veres .30 .09
361 Fernando Vina .30 .09
362 Bret Boone .30 .09
363 Matt Clement .30 .09
364 Ben Davis .30 .09
365 Adam Eaton .30 .09
366 Wiki Gonzalez .30 .09
367 Tony Gwynn 1.00 .30
368 Damian Jackson .30 .09
369 Ryan Klesko .30 .09
370 John Mabry .30 .09
371 Dave Magadan .30 .09
372 Phil Nevin .30 .09
373 Eric Owens .30 .09
374 Desi Relaford .30 .09
375 Ruben Rivera .30 .09
376 Woody Williams .30 .09
377 Rich Aurilia .30 .09
378 Marvin Benard .30 .09
379 Barry Bonds 2.00 .60
380 Ellis Burks .30 .09
381 Bobby Estalella .30 .09
382 Shawn Estes .30 .09
383 Mark Gardner .30 .09
384 Livan Hernandez .30 .09
385 Jeff Kent .30 .09
386 Bill Mueller .30 .09
387 Robb Nen .30 .09
388 Russ Ortiz .30 .09
389 Armando Rios .30 .09
390 Kirk Rueter .30 .09
391 J.T. Snow .30 .09
392 David Bell .30 .09
393 Jay Buhner .30 .09
394 Mike Cameron .30 .09
395 Freddy Garcia .30 .09
396 Carlos Guillen .30 .09
397 John Halama .30 .09
398 Rickey Henderson .75 .23
399 Al Martin .30 .09
400 Edgar Martinez .50 .15
401 Mark McLemore .30 .09
402 Jamie Moyer .30 .09
403 John Olerud .30 .09
404 Joe Oliver .30 .09
405 Alex Rodriguez 1.25 .35
406 Kazuhiro Sasaki .30 .09
407 Aaron Sele .30 .09
408 Dan Wilson .30 .09
409 Miguel Cairo .30 .09
410 Vinny Castilla .30 .09
411 Steve Cox .30 .09
412 John Flaherty .30 .09
413 Jose Guillen .30 .09
414 Roberto Hernandez .30 .09
415 Russ Johnson .30 .09
416 Felix Martinez .30 .09
417 Fred McGriff .50 .15
418 Greg Vaughn .30 .09
419 Gerald Williams .30 .09
420 Luis Alicea .30 .09
421 Frank Catalanotto .30 .09
422 Royce Clayton .30 .09
423 Chad Curtis .30 .09
424 Rusty Greer .30 .09
425 Bill Haselman .30 .09
426 Rick Helling .30 .09
427 Gabe Kapler .30 .09
428 Mike Lamb .30 .09
429 Ricky Ledee .30 .09
430 Ruben Mateo .30 .09
431 Rafael Palmeiro .50 .15
432 Ivan Rodriguez .75 .23
433 Kenny Rogers .30 .09
434 John Wetteland .30 .09
435 Jeff Zimmerman .30 .09
436 Tony Batista .30 .09
437 Homer Bush .30 .09
438 Chris Carpenter .30 .09
439 Marty Cordova .30 .09
440 Jose Cruz Jr. .30 .09
441 Carlos Delgado .30 .09
442 Darrin Fletcher .30 .09
443 Brad Fullmer .30 .09
444 Alex Gonzalez .30 .09
445 Billy Koch .30 .09
446 Raul Mondesi .30 .09
447 Mickey Morandini .30 .09
448 Shannon Stewart .30 .09
449 Steve Trachsel .30 .09
450 David Wells .30 .09
451 Juan Alvarez .30 .09
452 Shawn Wooten .30 .09
453 Ismael Villegas .30 .09
454 Carlos Casimiro .30 .09
455 Morgan Burkhart .30 .09
456 Paxton Crawford .30 .09
457 Dernell Stenson .30 .09
458 Ross Gload .30 .09
459 Raul Gonzalez .30 .09
460 Corey Patterson .30 .09
461 Julio Zuleta .30 .09
462 Rocky Biddle .30 .09
463 Joe Crede .30 .09
464 Matt Ginter .30 .09
465 Aaron Myette .30 .09
466 Mike Bell .30 .09
467 Travis Dawkins .30 .09
468 Mark Watson .30 .09
469 Elvis Pena .30 .09
470 Eric Munson .30 .09
471 Pablo Ozuna .30 .09
472 Frank Charles .30 .09
473 Mike Judd .30 .09
474 Hector Ramirez .30 .09
475 Jack Cressend .30 .09
476 Talmadge Nunnari .30 .09
477 Jorge Toca .30 .09
478 Alfonso Soriano .50 .15
479 Jay Tessmer .30 .09
480 Jake Westbrook .30 .09
481 Eric Byrnes .30 .09
482 Jose Ortiz .30 .09
483 Tike Redman .30 .09
484 Domingo Guzman .30 .09
485 Rodrigo Lopez .30 .09
486 Xavier Nady .30 .09
487 Pedro Feliz .30 .09
488 Damon Minor .30 .09
489 Ryan Vogelsong .30 .09
490 Joel Pineiro .75 .23
491 Justin Brunette .30 .09
492 Keith McDonald .30 .09
493 Aubrey Huff .30 .09
494 Kenny Kelly .30 .09
495 Damian Rolls .30 .09
496 John Bale UER .30 .09
1999 ERA is in save column
497 Pasqual Coco .30 .09
498 Matt DeWitt .30 .09
499 Leo Estrella .30 .09
500 Josh Phelps .30 .09

2001 Pacific Extreme LTD

Randomly inserted into packs, this 500-card set is a complete parallel of the 2001 Pacific base set. Each card in this set features the words "Extreme LTD" printed diagonally across front of each card. Every card in this set is individually serial numbered to 45.

Nm-Mt Ex-Mt
*STARS: 20X TO 50X BASIC CARDS..

2001 Pacific Hobby LTD

Randomly inserted into hobby packs, this 500-card set is a complete parallel of the 2001 Pacific base set. Each card in this set features the words "Hobby LTD" printed diagonally across front of each card. Every card in this set is individually serial numbered to 70.

Nm-Mt Ex-Mt
*STARS: 12.5X TO 30X BASIC CARDS

2001 Pacific Premiere Date

Randomly inserted into hobby packs (approx. one per box), this 500-card set is a complete parallel of the 2001 Pacific base set. Each card in this set features the words "Premiere Date" printed diagonally across front of each card. Every card in this set is individually serial numbered to 36.

Nm-Mt Ex-Mt
*STARS: 25X TO 60X BASIC CARDS..

2001 Pacific Retail LTD

Randomly inserted into retail packs, this 500-card set is a complete parallel of the 2001 Pacific base set. Each card in this set features the words "Retail LTD" printed diagonally across front of each card. Every card in this set is individually serial numbered to 85.

Nm-Mt Ex-Mt
*STARS: 10X TO 25X BASIC CARDS..

2001 Pacific Cramer's Choice

Inserted at a rate of one in every 721 packs, these die-cut cards feature 10 players Pacific founder Mike Cramer considers to be among the very best players in baseball.

Nm-Mt Ex-Mt
*CANVAS: .75X TO 2X BASIC CRAMER
CANVAS RANDOM INSERTS IN PACKS
*STYRENE: .6X TO 1.5X BASIC CRAMER
STYRENE RANDOM INSERTS IN PACKS
1 Cal Ripken 80.00 24.00
2 Nomar Garciaparra 40.00 12.00
3 Sammy Sosa 40.00 12.00
4 Frank Thomas 25.00 7.50
5 Ken Griffey Jr. 40.00 12.00
6 Mike Piazza 40.00 12.00
7 Derek Jeter 60.00 18.00
8 Mark McGwire 60.00 18.00
9 Barry Bonds 50.00 15.00
10 Alex Rodriguez 40.00 12.00

2001 Pacific Decade's Best

Randomly inserted into packs at two in 37, this 36-card insert features some of the most productive players in the 90's. Please note that we have included an "A" and "N" prefix below to differentiate the National and American league players.

Nm-Mt Ex-Mt
COMPLETE SET (36) 120.00 36.00
A1 Rickey Henderson 3.00 .90

A2 Rafael Palmeiro 2.00 .60
A3 Cal Ripken 10.00 3.00
A4 Jose Canseco 3.00 .90
A5 Juan Gonzalez 2.00 .60
A6 Frank Thomas 3.00 .90
A7 Albert Belle 1.25 .35
A8 Edgar Martinez 2.00 .60
A9 Mo Vaughn 1.25 .35
A10 Derek Jeter 8.00 2.40
A11 Mark McGwire 8.00 2.40
A12 Alex Rodriguez 5.00 1.50
A13 Ken Griffey Jr. 5.00 1.50
A14 Nomar Garciaparra 5.00 1.50
A15 Roger Clemens 6.00 1.80
A16 Bernie Williams 2.00 .60
A17 Ivan Rodriguez 3.00 .90
A18 Pedro Martinez 3.00 .90
N1 Barry Bonds 8.00 2.40
N2 Jeff Bagwell 2.00 .60
N3 Tom Glavine 2.00 .60
N4 Gary Sheffield 1.25 .35
N5 Fred McGriff 2.00 .60
N6 Greg Maddux 5.00 1.50
N7 Mike Piazza 5.00 1.50
N8 Tony Gwynn 4.00 1.20
N9 Hideo Nomo 3.00 .90
N10 Andres Galarraga 1.25 .35
N11 Larry Walker 2.00 .60
N12 Scott Rolen 3.00 .90
N13 Pedro Martinez 3.00 .90
N14 Sammy Sosa 5.00 1.50
N15 Mark McGwire 8.00 2.40
N16 Kerry Wood 3.00 .90
N17 Chipper Jones 3.00 .90
N18 Mark Grace 2.00 .60

2001 Pacific Game Jersey

Randomly inserted into packs, this five-card insert features game-used jersey cards of players like Tony Gwynn and Alex Rodriguez. Please note that this is a skip-numbered set.

Nm-Mt Ex-Mt
3 Gary Sheffield 10.00 3.00
5 Scott Rolen 15.00 4.50
7 Tony Gwynn 20.00 6.00
8 Alex Rodriguez 25.00 7.50
9 Rafael Palmeiro 15.00 4.50

2001 Pacific Game Jersey Patch

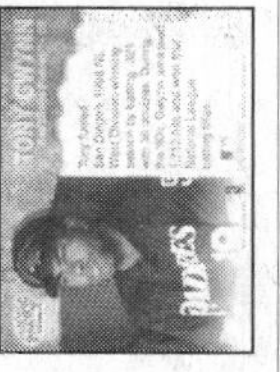

Randomly inserted into packs, this five-card insert is a complete parallel of the Game Jersey insert. These cards feature a swatch from the patch portion of these jerseys. The individual print runs are listed below. Please note that this is a skip-numbered set.

Nm-Mt Ex-Mt
3 Gary Sheffield/226 25.00 7.50
5 Scott Rolen/157 50.00 15.00
7 Tony Gwynn/183 60.00 18.00
8 Alex Rodriguez/221 100.00 30.00
9 Rafael Palmeiro/154 40.00 12.00

2001 Pacific Gold Crown Die Cuts

Inserted one every 73 packs, this 36 card set features a selection of baseball's top stars. This set uses the Gold Crown Die Cut style used on many Pacific products. Please note that there is also a Blue and Purple parallel of this insert. Also note that autographed versions exist of six players.

Nm-Mt Ex-Mt
*BLUE: .6X TO 1.5X BASIC CROWN...
BLUE RANDOM INSERTS IN PACKS...
BLUE PRINT RUN 100 SERIAL #'d SETS
*PURPLE: 1X TO 2.5X BASIC CROWN
PURPLE RANDOM INSERTS IN PACKS
PURPLE PRINT RUN 50 SERIAL #'d SETS
CARD NUMBER 27 DOES NOT EXIST.
ANKIEL/BURRELL BOTH NUMBERED 26
1 Darin Erstad 4.00 1.20
2 Troy Glaus 4.00 1.20
3 Randy Johnson 4.00 1.20
4 Rafael Furcal 4.00 1.20
5 Andruw Jones 4.00 1.20
6 Chipper Jones 4.00 1.20
7 Greg Maddux 6.00 1.80
8 Cal Ripken 12.00 3.60
9 Nomar Garciaparra 6.00 1.80
10 Pedro Martinez 4.00 1.20
11 Corey Patterson 4.00 1.20
12 Sammy Sosa 6.00 1.80
13 Frank Thomas 4.00 1.20
14 Ken Griffey Jr. 6.00 1.80
15 Manny Ramirez 4.00 1.20
16 Todd Helton 4.00 1.20
17 Jeff Bagwell 4.00 1.20
18 Shawn Green 4.00 1.20
19 Gary Sheffield 4.00 1.20
20 Vladimir Guerrero 4.00 1.20
21 Mike Piazza 6.00 1.80
22 Jose Canseco 4.00 1.20
23 Roger Clemens 8.00 2.40
24 Derek Jeter 10.00 3.00
25 Jason Giambi 4.00 1.20
26 Rick Ankiel 4.00 1.20
26 Pat Burrell 4.00 1.20
28 Jim Edmonds 4.00 1.20
29 Mark McGwire 10.00 3.00
30 Tony Gwynn 5.00 1.50
31 Barry Bonds 10.00 3.00
32 Rickey Henderson 4.00 1.20
33 Edgar Martinez 4.00 1.20
34 Alex Rodriguez 6.00 1.80
35 Ivan Rodriguez 4.00 1.20
36 Carlos Delgado 4.00 1.20

2001 Pacific Gold Crown Die Cuts Autograph

Randomly inserted into packs, this six-card insert features autographed Gold Crown Die Cuts of players like Barry Bonds and Chipper Jones. Please note that this is a partial parallel of the Gold Crown Die Cuts, and that the crown portion of these cards is stamped with green foil.

Nm-Mt Ex-Mt
6 Chipper Jones 80.00 24.00
11 Corey Patterson 25.00 7.50
13 Frank Thomas 80.00 24.00
19 Gary Sheffield 40.00 12.00
28 Jim Edmonds 40.00 12.00
31 Barry Bonds 250.00 75.00

2001 Pacific On the Horizon

Randomly inserted into packs at one in 145, this 10-card insert features players that are on the verge of stardom.

Nm-Mt Ex-Mt
COMPLETE SET (10) 100.00 30.00
1 Rafael Furcal 10.00 3.00
2 Corey Patterson 10.00 3.00
3 Russell Branyan 10.00 3.00
4 Juan Pierre 10.00 3.00
5 Mark Quinn 10.00 3.00
6 Alfonso Soriano 15.00 4.50
7 Adam Piatt 10.00 3.00
8 Pat Burrell 10.00 3.00
9 Kazuhiro Sasaki 10.00 3.00
10 Aubrey Huff 10.00 3.00

2001 Pacific Ornaments

Inserted two every 37 packs, these 24 cards are designed in the shape of Christmas ornaments. The cards have full custom holographic patterned silver foil and a string loop on top so they can be hung on a tree. Please note that cards 21-24 were inserted into retail packs only.

Nm-Mt Ex-Mt
COMPLETE SET (24) 150.00 45.00
1 Rafael Furcal 4.00 1.20
2 Chipper Jones 5.00 1.50
3 Greg Maddux 8.00 2.40
4 Cal Ripken 15.00 4.50
5 Nomar Garciaparra 8.00 2.40
6 Pedro Martinez 5.00 1.50
7 Sammy Sosa 8.00 2.40
8 Frank Thomas 5.00 1.50
9 Ken Griffey Jr. 8.00 2.40
10 Manny Ramirez 4.00 1.20
11 Todd Helton 4.00 1.20
12 Vladimir Guerrero 5.00 1.50
13 Mike Piazza 8.00 2.40
14 Roger Clemens 10.00 3.00
15 Derek Jeter 12.00 3.60
16 Pat Burrell 4.00 1.20
17 Rick Ankiel 4.00 1.20
18 Mark McGwire 12.00 3.60
19 Barry Bonds 12.00 3.60
20 Alex Rodriguez 8.00 2.40
21 Troy Glaus 4.00 1.20
22 Tom Glavine 4.00 1.20
23 Jim Edmonds 4.00 1.20
24 Ivan Rodriguez 5.00 1.50

1998 Pacific Invincible

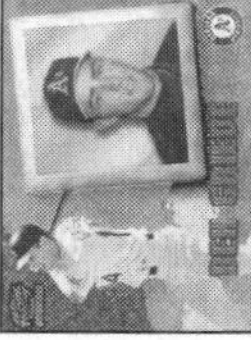

The 1998 Pacific Invincible set was issued in one series totalling 150 cards and was distributed in five-card packs with an SRP of $2.99. The fronts feature a color action player photo as well as a head shot printed on an inlaid cel window with gold foil printing. The backs carry another player photo with a paragraph highlighting the player's career accomplishments.

Nm-Mt Ex-Mt
COMPLETE SET (150) 100.00 30.00
1 Garret Anderson 1.50 .45
2 Jim Edmonds 1.50 .45
3 Darin Erstad 1.50 .45
4 Chuck Finley 1.50 .45
5 Tim Salmon 2.50 .75
6 Roberto Alomar 2.50 .75
7 Brady Anderson 1.50 .45
8 Geronimo Berroa 1.00 .30
9 Eric Davis 1.50 .45
10 Mike Mussina 2.50 .75
11 Rafael Palmeiro 2.50 .75
12 Cal Ripken 12.00 3.60
13 Steve Avery 1.00 .30
14 Nomar Garciaparra 6.00 1.80
15 John Valentin 1.00 .30
16 Mo Vaughn 1.50 .45
17 Albert Belle 1.50 .45
18 Ozzie Guillen 1.00 .30
19 Norberto Martin 1.00 .30
20 Frank Thomas 4.00 1.20
21 Robin Ventura 1.50 .45
22 Sandy Alomar Jr. 1.00 .30
23 David Justice 1.50 .45
24 Kenny Lofton 1.50 .45
25 Manny Ramirez 2.50 .75
26 Jim Thome 4.00 1.20
27 Omar Vizquel 2.50 .75
28 Matt Williams 1.50 .45
29 Jaret Wright 1.00 .30
30 Raul Casanova 1.00 .30
31 Tony Clark 1.00 .30
32 Deivi Cruz 1.00 .30
33 Bobby Higginson 1.50 .45
34 Justin Thompson 1.00 .30
35 Yamil Benitez 1.00 .30
36 Johnny Damon 2.50 .75
37 Jermaine Dye 1.50 .45
38 Jed Hansen 1.00 .30
39 Larry Sutton 1.00 .30
40 Jeromy Burnitz 1.50 .45
41 Jeff Cirillo 1.00 .30
42 Dave Nilsson 1.00 .30
43 Jose Valentin 1.00 .30
44 Fernando Vina 1.00 .30
45 Marty Cordova 1.00 .30
46 Chuck Knoblauch 1.50 .45
47 Paul Molitor 2.50 .75
48 Brad Radke 1.50 .45
49 Terry Steinbach 1.00 .30
50 Wade Boggs 2.50 .75
51 Hideki Irabu 1.00 .30
52 Derek Jeter 10.00 3.00
53 Tino Martinez 2.50 .75
54 Andy Pettitte 2.50 .75
55 Mariano Rivera 2.50 .75
56 Bernie Williams 2.50 .75
57 Jose Canseco 4.00 1.20
58 Jason Giambi 1.50 .45
59 Ben Grieve 1.00 .30
60 Aaron Small 1.00 .30
61 Jay Buhner 1.50 .45
62 Ken Cloude 1.00 .30
63 Joey Cora 1.00 .30
64 Ken Griffey Jr. 6.00 1.80
65 Randy Johnson 4.00 1.20
66 Edgar Martinez 2.50 .75
67 Alex Rodriguez 6.00 1.80
68 Will Clark 4.00 1.20
69 Juan Gonzalez 2.50 .75
70 Rusty Greer 1.50 .45
71 Ivan Rodriguez 4.00 1.20
72 Joe Carter 1.50 .45
73 Roger Clemens 8.00 2.40
74 Jose Cruz Jr. 1.00 .30
75 Carlos Delgado 1.50 .45
76 Andruw Jones 1.50 .45
77 Chipper Jones 4.00 1.20
78 Ryan Klesko 1.50 .45
79 Javier Lopez 1.50 .45
80 Greg Maddux 6.00 1.80
81 Miguel Batista 1.00 .30
82 Jeremi Gonzalez 1.00 .30
83 Mark Grace 2.50 .75
84 Kevin Orie 1.00 .30
85 Sammy Sosa 6.00 1.80
86 Barry Larkin 2.50 .75
87 Deion Sanders 2.50 .75

88 Reggie Sanders 1.00 .30
89 Chris Stynes 1.00 .30
90 Dante Bichette 1.50 .45
91 Vinny Castilla 1.50 .45
92 Andres Galarraga 1.50 .45
93 Neifi Perez 1.00 .30
94 Larry Walker 2.50 .75
95 Moises Alou 1.50 .45
96 Bobby Bonilla 1.50 .45
97 Kevin Brown 2.50 .75
98 Craig Counsell 1.00 .30
99 Livan Hernandez 1.00 .30
100 Edgar Renteria 1.50 .45
101 Gary Sheffield 1.50 .45
102 Jeff Bagwell 2.50 .75
103 Craig Biggio 2.50 .75
104 Luis Gonzalez 1.50 .45
105 Darryl Kile 1.50 .45
106 Wilton Guerrero 1.00 .30
107 Eric Karros 1.50 .45
108 Ramon Martinez 1.00 .30
109 Raul Mondesi 1.50 .45
110 Hideo Nomo 4.00 1.20
111 Chan Ho Park 1.50 .45
112 Mike Piazza 6.00 1.80
113 Mark Grudzielanek 1.00 .30
114 Vladimir Guerrero 4.00 1.20
115 Pedro Martinez 4.00 1.20
116 Henry Rodriguez 1.00 .30
117 David Segui 1.00 .30
118 Edgardo Alfonzo 1.00 .30
119 Carlos Baerga 1.00 .30
120 John Franco 1.50 .45
121 John Olerud 1.50 .45
122 Rey Ordonez 1.00 .30
123 Ricky Bottalico 1.00 .30
124 Gregg Jefferies 1.00 .30
125 Mickey Morandini 1.00 .30
126 Scott Rolen 4.00 1.20
127 Curt Schilling 1.50 .45
128 Jose Guillen 1.50 .45
129 Esteban Loaiza 1.00 .30
130 Al Martin 1.00 .30
131 Tony Womack 1.00 .30
132 Dennis Eckersley 1.50 .45
133 Gary Gaetti 1.50 .45
134 Curtis King 1.00 .30
135 Ray Lankford 1.00 .30
136 Mark McGwire 10.00 3.00
137 Ken Caminiti 1.50 .45
138 Steve Finley 1.50 .45
139 Tony Gwynn 5.00 1.50
140 Carlos Hernandez 1.00 .30
141 Wally Joyner 1.50 .45
142 Barry Bonds 10.00 3.00
143 Jacob Cruz 1.00 .30
144 Shawn Estes 1.00 .30
145 Stan Javier 1.00 .30
146 J.T. Snow 1.50 .45
147 N.Garciaparra ROY 4.00 1.20
148 Scott Rolen ROY 4.00 1.20
149 Ken Griffey Jr. MVP 4.00 1.20
150 Larry Walker MVP 1.50 .45

1998 Pacific Invincible Platinum Blue

Randomly inserted in packs at the rate of one in 73, this 150-card set is parallel to the base set with platinum blue foil highlighting.

Nm-Mt Ex-Mt
*STARS: 2X TO 5X BASIC CARDS

1998 Pacific Invincible Silver

Randomly seeded into hobby and retail packs at a rate of 2:37, cards from this 150-card set are parallel to the base set. Silver foil highlighting differentiates them.

Nm-Mt Ex-Mt
*STARS: 1X TO 2.5X BASIC CARDS

1998 Pacific Invincible Gems of the Diamond

Inserted in packs at the rate of four per pack, this 220-card set features color action player photos with gold foil printing.

Nm-Mt Ex-Mt
COMPLETE SET (220) 50.00 15.00
1 Jim Edmonds .30 .09
2 Todd Greene .30 .09
3 Ken Hill .30 .09
4 Mike Holtz .30 .09
5 Mike James .30 .09
6 Chad Kreuter .30 .09
7 Tim Salmon .50 .15
8 Roberto Alomar .50 .15
9 Brady Anderson .50 .15
10 Dave Dellucci .50 .15
11 Jeffrey Hammonds .30 .09
12 Mike Mussina .50 .15
13 Rafael Palmeiro .50 .15
14 Arthur Rhodes .30 .09
15 Cal Ripken 2.50 .75
16 Nerio Rodriguez .30 .09
17 Tony Tarasco .30 .09
18 Lenny Webster .30 .09
19 Mike Benjamin .30 .09
20 Rich Garces .30 .09
21 Nomar Garciaparra 1.25 .35
22 Shane Mack .30 .09
23 Jose Malave .30 .09
24 Jesus Tavarez .30 .09
25 Mo Vaughn .30 .09
26 John Wasdin .30 .09
27 Jeff Abbott .30 .09
28 Albert Belle .30 .09
29 Mike Cameron .30 .09
30 Al Levine .30 .09
31 Robert Machado .30 .09
32 Greg Norton .30 .09
33 Magglio Ordonez 2.00 .60
34 Mike Sirotka .30 .09
35 Frank Thomas .75 .23
36 Mario Valdez .30 .09
37 Sandy Alomar Jr. .30 .09
38 David Justice .30 .09
39 Jack McDowell .30 .09
40 Eric Plunk .30 .09
41 Manny Ramirez .50 .15
42 Kevin Seitzer .30 .09
43 Paul Shuey .30 .09
44 Omar Vizquel .50 .15
45 Kimera Bartee .30 .09
46 Glenn Dishman .30 .09
47 Orlando Miller .30 .09
48 Mike Myers .30 .09
49 Phil Nevin .30 .09
50 A.J. Sager .30 .09
51 Ricky Bones .30 .09
52 Scott Cooper .30 .09
53 Shane Halter .30 .09
54 David Howard .30 .09
55 Glendon Rusch .30 .09
56 Joe Vitiello .30 .09
57 Jeff D'Amico .30 .09
58 Mike Fetters .30 .09
59 Mike Matheny .30 .09
60 Jose Mercedes .30 .09
61 Ron Villone .30 .09
62 Jack Voigt .30 .09
63 Brent Brede .30 .09
64 Chuck Knoblauch .30 .09
65 Paul Molitor .50 .15
66 Todd Ritchie .30 .09
67 Frankie Rodriguez .30 .09
68 Scott Stahoviak .30 .09
69 Greg Swindell .30 .09
70 Todd Walker .30 .09
71 Wade Boggs .50 .15
72 Hideki Irabu .30 .09
73 Derek Jeter 2.00 .60
74 Pat Kelly .30 .09
75 Graeme Lloyd .30 .09
76 Tino Martinez .50 .15
77 Jeff Nelson .30 .09
78 Scott Pose .30 .09
79 Mike Stanton .30 .09
80 Darryl Strawberry .30 .09
81 Bernie Williams .50 .15
82 Tony Batista .30 .09
83 Mark Bellhorn .30 .09
84 Ben Grieve .30 .09
85 Pat Lennon .30 .09
86 Brian Lesher .30 .09
87 Miguel Tejada .30 .09
88 George Williams .30 .09
89 Joey Cora .30 .09
90 Rob Ducey .30 .09
91 Ken Griffey Jr. 1.25 .35
92 Randy Johnson .75 .23
93 Edgar Martinez .50 .15
94 John Marzano .30 .09
95 Greg McCarthy .30 .09
96 Alex Rodriguez 1.25 .35
97 Andy Sheets .30 .09
98 Mike Timlin .30 .09
99 Lee Tinsley .30 .09
100 Damon Buford .30 .09
101 Alex Diaz .30 .09
102 Benji Gil .30 .09
103 Juan Gonzalez .50 .15
104 Eric Gunderson .30 .09
105 Danny Patterson .30 .09
106 Ivan Rodriguez .75 .23
107 Mike Simms .30 .09
108 Luis Andujar .30 .09
109 Joe Carter .30 .09
110 Roger Clemens 1.50 .45
111 Jose Cruz Jr. .30 .09
112 Shawn Green .30 .09
113 Robert Perez .30 .09
114 Juan Samuel .30 .09
115 Ed Sprague .30 .09
116 Shannon Stewart .30 .09
117 Danny Bautista .30 .09
118 Chipper Jones .75 .23
119 Ryan Klesko .30 .09
120 Keith Lockhart .30 .09
121 Javier Lopez .30 .09
122 Greg Maddux 1.25 .35
123 Kevin Millwood 1.00 .30
124 Mike Mordecai .30 .09
125 Eddie Perez .30 .09
126 Randall Simon .30 .09
127 Miguel Cairo .30 .09
128 Dave Clark .30 .09
129 Kevin Foster .30 .09
130 Mark Grace .50 .15
131 Tyler Houston .30 .09
132 Mike Hubbard .30 .09
133 Kevin Orie .30 .09
134 Ryne Sandberg 1.25 .35
135 Sammy Sosa 1.25 .35
136 Lenny Harris .30 .09
137 Kent Mercker .30 .09
138 Mike Morgan .30 .09
139 Deion Sanders .50 .15
140 Chris Stynes .30 .09
141 Gabe White .30 .09
142 Jason Bates .30 .09
143 Vinny Castilla .30 .09
144 Andres Galarraga .30 .09
145 Curtis Leskanic .30 .09
146 Jeff McCurry .30 .09
147 Mike Munoz .30 .09
148 Larry Walker .50 .15
149 Jamey Wright .30 .09
150 Moises Alou .30 .09
151 Bobby Bonilla .30 .09
152 Kevin Brown .50 .15
153 John Cangelosi .30 .09
154 Jeff Conine .30 .09
155 Cliff Floyd .30 .09
156 Jay Powell .30 .09
157 Edgar Renteria .30 .09
158 Tony Saunders .30 .09
159 Gary Sheffield .30 .09
160 Jeff Bagwell .50 .15
161 Tim Bogar .30 .09
162 Tony Eusebio .30 .09
163 Chris Holt .30 .09
164 Ray Montgomery .30 .09
165 Luis Rivera .30 .09
166 Eric Anthony .30 .09
167 Brett Butler .30 .09
168 Juan Castro .30 .09
169 Tripp Cromer .30 .09
170 Raul Mondesi .30 .09
171 Hideo Nomo .75 .23
172 Mike Piazza 1.25 .35
173 Tom Prince .30 .09
174 Adam Riggs .30 .09
175 Shane Andrews .30 .09
176 Shayne Bennett .30 .09
177 Raul Chavez .30 .09
178 Pedro Martinez .75 .23
179 Sherman Obando .30 .09
180 Andy Stankiewicz .30 .09
181 Alberto Castillo .30 .09
182 Shawn Gilbert .30 .09
183 Luis Lopez .30 .09
184 Roberto Petagine .30 .09
185 Armando Reynoso .30 .09
186 Midre Cummings .30 .09
187 Kevin Jordan .30 .09
188 Desi Relaford .30 .09
189 Scott Rolen .75 .23
190 Ken Ryan .30 .09
191 Kevin Sefcik .30 .09
192 Emil Brown .30 .09
193 Lou Collier .30 .09
194 Francisco Cordova .30 .09
195 Kevin Elster .30 .09
196 Mark Smith .30 .09
197 Marc Wilkins .30 .09
198 Manny Aybar .30 .09
199 Jose Bautista .30 .09
200 David Bell .30 .09
201 Rigo Beltran .30 .09
202 Delino DeShields .30 .09
203 Dennis Eckersley .30 .09
204 John Mabry .30 .09
205 Eli Marrero .30 .09
206 Willie McGee .30 .09
207 Mark McGwire 2.00 .60
208 Ken Caminiti .30 .09
209 Tony Gwynn 1.00 .30
210 Chris Jones .30 .09
211 Craig Shipley .30 .09
212 Pete Smith .30 .09
213 Jorge Velandia .30 .09
214 Dario Veras .30 .09
215 Rich Aurilia .30 .09
216 Damon Berryhill .30 .09
217 Barry Bonds 2.00 .60
218 Osvaldo Fernandez .30 .09
219 Dante Powell .30 .09
220 Rich Rodriguez .30 .09

1998 Pacific Invincible Interleague Players

Randomly inserted one in every 73 packs, this 30-card set features color player photos which when placed side by side form the MLB Interleague log in the center. Each card is bordered with white leather-like material.

Nm-Mt Ex-Mt
COMPLETE SET (30) 400.00 120.00
1A Roberto Alomar 10.00 3.00
1N Craig Biggio 10.00 3.00
2A Cal Ripken 50.00 15.00
2N Chipper Jones 15.00 4.50
3A Nomar Garciaparra 25.00 7.50
3N Scott Rolen 15.00 4.50
4A Mo Vaughn 6.00 1.80
4N Andres Galarraga 6.00 1.80
5A Frank Thomas 15.00 4.50
5N Tony Gwynn 20.00 6.00
6A Albert Belle 6.00 1.80
6N Barry Bonds 40.00 12.00
7A Hideki Irabu 4.00 1.20
7N Hideo Nomo 15.00 4.50
8A Derek Jeter 40.00 12.00
8N Rey Ordonez 4.00 1.20
9A Tino Martinez 10.00 3.00
9N Mark McGwire 40.00 12.00
10A Alex Rodriguez 25.00 7.50
10N Edgar Renteria 6.00 1.80
11A Ken Griffey Jr. 25.00 7.50
11N Larry Walker 10.00 3.00
12A Randy Johnson 15.00 4.50
12N Greg Maddux 25.00 7.50
13A Ivan Rodriguez 15.00 4.50
13N Mike Piazza 25.00 7.50
14A Roger Clemens 30.00 9.00
14N Pedro Martinez 15.00 4.50
15A Jose Cruz Jr. 4.00 1.20
15N Wilton Guerrero 4.00 1.20

1998 Pacific Invincible Moments in Time

Randonly inserted in packs at the rate of one in 145, this 20-card set features color player photos with full foil coverage printed on a scoreboard screen with laser-cut stadium scoreboard features defining categories for a special game in the player's career.

Nm-Mt Ex-Mt
COMPLETE SET (20) 300.00 90.00
1 Chipper Jones 20.00 6.00

2 Cal Ripken 60.00 18.00
3 Frank Thomas 20.00 6.00
4 David Justice 8.00 2.40
5 Andres Galarraga 8.00 2.40
6 Larry Walker 12.00 3.60
7 Livan Hernandez 5.00 1.50
8 Wilton Guerrero 5.00 1.50
9 Hideo Nomo 20.00 6.00
10 Mike Piazza 30.00 9.00
11 Pedro Martinez 20.00 6.00
12 Bernie Williams 12.00 3.60
13 Ben Grieve 5.00 1.50
14 Scott Rolen 20.00 6.00
15 Mark McGwire 50.00 15.00
16 Tony Gwynn 25.00 7.50
17 Ken Griffey Jr. 30.00 9.00
18 Alex Rodriguez 30.00 9.00
19 Juan Gonzalez 12.00 3.60
20 Jose Cruz Jr. 5.00 1.50

1998 Pacific Invincible Photoengravings

Randomly inserted in packs at the rate of one in 37, this 18-card set features filtered photos with clear facial player shots with unique old-style design elements artwork.

Nm-Mt Ex-Mt
COMPLETE SET (18) 100.00 30.00
1 Greg Maddux 10.00 3.00
2 Cal Ripken 20.00 6.00
3 Nomar Garciaparra 10.00 3.00
4 Frank Thomas 6.00 1.80
5 Larry Walker 4.00 1.20
6 Mike Piazza 10.00 3.00
7 Hideo Nomo 6.00 1.80
8 Pedro Martinez 6.00 1.80
9 Derek Jeter 15.00 4.50
10 Tino Martinez 4.00 1.20
11 Mark McGwire 15.00 4.50
12 Tony Gwynn 8.00 2.40
13 Barry Bonds 15.00 4.50
14 Ken Griffey Jr. 10.00 3.00
15 Alex Rodriguez 10.00 3.00
16 Ivan Rodriguez 6.00 1.80
17 Roger Clemens 12.00 3.60
18 Jose Cruz Jr. 1.50 .45

1998 Pacific Invincible Team Checklists

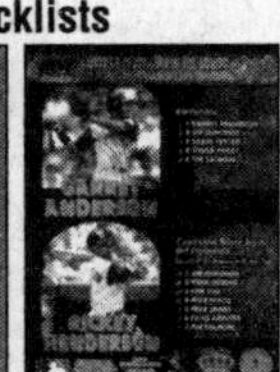

Randomly inserted two in 37 packs, this 30-card set features a collage of action player images printed with full foil coverage with an etching pattern and the team logo in the background. The backs carry player checklists for the entire 1998 Pacific Prisms Invincible product.

Nm-Mt Ex-Mt
COMPLETE SET (30) 120.00 36.00
1 Jim Edmonds 6.00 1.80
Tim Salmon
Darin Erstad
Garret Anderson
Rickey Henderson
2 Greg Maddux 8.00 2.40
Chipper Jones
Javier Lopez
Ryan Klesko
Andruw Jones
3 Cal Ripken 20.00 6.00
Roberto Alomar
Brady Anderson
Mike Mussina
Rafael Palmeiro
4 Nomar Garciaparra 10.00 3.00
Mo Vaughn
Steve Avery
John Valentin
5 Sammy Sosa 10.00 3.00
Mark Grace
Ryne Sandberg
Jeremi Gonzalez
6 Frank Thomas 6.00 1.80
Albert Belle
Robin Ventura
Ozzie Guillen
7 Barry Larkin 4.00 1.20
Deion Sanders
Reggie Sanders
Brett Tomko
8 Sandy Alomar 6.00 1.80

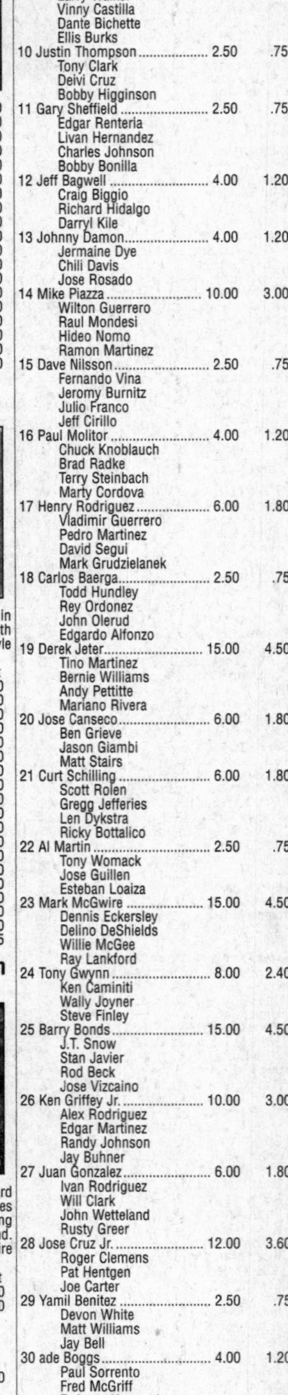

Manny Ramirez
David Justice
Jim Thome
Omar Vizquel
9 Andres Galarraga 4.00 1.20
Larry Walker
Vinny Castilla
Dante Bichette
Ellis Burks
10 Justin Thompson 2.50 .75
Tony Clark
Deivi Cruz
Bobby Higginson
11 Gary Sheffield 2.50 .75
Edgar Renteria
Livan Hernandez
Charles Johnson
Bobby Bonilla
12 Jeff Bagwell 4.00 1.20
Craig Biggio
Richard Hidalgo
Darryl Kile
13 Johnny Damon 4.00 1.20
Jermaine Dye
Chili Davis
Jose Rosado
14 Mike Piazza 10.00 3.00
Wilton Guerrero
Raul Mondesi
Hideo Nomo
Ramon Martinez
15 Dave Nilsson 2.50 .75
Fernando Vina
Jeromy Burnitz
Julio Franco
Jeff Cirillo
16 Paul Molitor 4.00 1.20
Chuck Knoblauch
Brad Radke
Terry Steinbach
Marty Cordova
17 Henry Rodriguez 6.00 1.80
Vladimir Guerrero
Pedro Martinez
David Segui
Mark Grudzielanek
18 Carlos Baerga 2.50 .75
Todd Hundley
Rey Ordonez
John Olerud
Edgardo Alfonzo
19 Derek Jeter 15.00 4.50
Tino Martinez
Bernie Williams
Andy Pettitte
Mariano Rivera
20 Jose Canseco 6.00 1.80
Ben Grieve
Jason Giambi
Matt Stairs
21 Curt Schilling 6.00 1.80
Scott Rolen
Gregg Jefferies
Len Dykstra
Ricky Bottalico
22 Al Martin 2.50 .75
Tony Womack
Jose Guillen
Esteban Loaiza
23 Mark McGwire 15.00 4.50
Dennis Eckersley
Delino DeShields
Willie McGee
Ray Lankford
24 Tony Gwynn 8.00 2.40
Ken Caminiti
Wally Joyner
Steve Finley
25 Barry Bonds 15.00 4.50
J.T. Snow
Stan Javier
Rod Beck
Jose Vizcaino
26 Ken Griffey Jr. 10.00 3.00
Alex Rodriguez
Edgar Martinez
Randy Johnson
Jay Buhner
27 Juan Gonzalez 6.00 1.80
Ivan Rodriguez
Will Clark
John Wetteland
Rusty Greer
28 Jose Cruz Jr. 12.00 3.60
Roger Clemens
Pat Hentgen
Joe Carter
29 Yamil Benitez 2.50 .75
Devon White
Matt Williams
Jay Bell
30 ade Boggs 4.00 1.20
Paul Sorrento
Fred McGriff
Roberto Hernandez

1999 Pacific Invincible

The 1999 Pacific Invincible set was issued in one series totalling 150 cards and was distributed in three-card packs with an SRP of $2.99. The fronts feature a color action player photo as well as a head shot printed on an inlaid cel window with gold foil printing. The backs carry information about the player.

Nm-Mt Ex-Mt
COMPLETE SET (150) 180.00 55.00
1 Jim Edmonds 1.25 .35

2 Darin Erstad	1.25	.35
3 Troy Glaus	1.25	.35
4 Tim Salmon	2.00	.60
5 Mo Vaughn	1.25	.35
6 Steve Finley	1.25	.35
7 Randy Johnson	3.00	.90
8 Travis Lee	.75	.23
9 Dante Powell	.75	.23
10 Matt Williams	1.25	.35
11 Bret Boone	1.25	.35
12 Andruw Jones	1.25	.35
13 Chipper Jones	3.00	.90
14 Brian Jordan	1.25	.35
15 Ryan Klesko	1.25	.35
16 Javy Lopez	1.25	.35
17 Greg Maddux	5.00	1.50
18 Brady Anderson	1.25	.35
19 Albert Belle	1.25	.35
20 Will Clark	3.00	.90
21 Mike Mussina	2.00	.60
22 Cal Ripken	10.00	3.00
23 Nomar Garciaparra	5.00	1.50
24 Pedro Martinez	3.00	.90
25 Trot Nixon	1.25	.35
26 Jose Offerman	.75	.23
27 Donnie Sadler	.75	.23
28 John Valentin	.75	.23
29 Mark Grace	2.00	.60
30 Lance Johnson	.75	.23
31 Henry Rodriguez	.75	.23
32 Sammy Sosa	5.00	1.50
33 Kerry Wood	3.00	.90
34 McKay Christensen	.75	.23
35 Ray Durham	1.25	.35
36 Jeff Liefer	.75	.23
37 Frank Thomas	3.00	.90
38 Mike Cameron	1.25	.35
39 Barry Larkin	2.00	.60
40 Greg Vaughn	.75	.23
41 Dmitri Young	1.25	.35
42 Roberto Alomar	2.00	.60
43 Sandy Alomar Jr.	.75	.23
44 David Justice	1.25	.35
45 Kenny Lofton	1.25	.35
46 Manny Ramirez	2.00	.60
47 Jim Thome	3.00	.90
48 Dante Bichette	1.25	.35
49 Vinny Castilla	1.25	.35
50 Darryl Hamilton	.75	.23
51 Todd Helton	2.00	.60
52 Neifi Perez	.75	.23
53 Larry Walker	2.00	.60
54 Tony Clark	.75	.23
55 Damion Easley	.75	.23
56 Bob Higginson	1.25	.35
57 Brian L.Hunter	.75	.23
58 Gabe Kapler	.75	.23
59 Cliff Floyd	1.25	.35
60 Alex Gonzalez	.75	.23
61 Mark Kotsay	.75	.23
62 Derrek Lee	1.25	.35
63 Braden Looper	.75	.23
64 Moises Alou	1.25	.35
65 Jeff Bagwell	2.00	.60
66 Craig Biggio	2.00	.60
67 Ken Caminiti	1.25	.35
68 Scott Elarton	.75	.23
69 Mitch Meluskey	.75	.23
70 Carlos Beltran	2.00	.60
71 Johnny Damon	2.00	.60
72 Carlos Febles	.75	.23
73 Jeremy Giambi	.75	.23
74 Kevin Brown	2.00	.60
75 Todd Hundley	.75	.23
76 Paul LoDuca	1.25	.35
77 Raul Mondesi	1.25	.35
78 Gary Sheffield	1.25	.35
79 Geoff Jenkins	1.25	.35
80 Jeromy Burnitz	1.25	.35
81 Marquis Grissom	1.25	.35
82 Jose Valentin	.75	.23
83 Fernando Vina	.75	.23
84 Corey Koskie	1.25	.35
85 Matt Lawton	.75	.23
86 Christian Guzman	.75	.23
87 Torii Hunter	.75	.23
88 Doug Mientkiewicz RC	3.00	.90
89 Michael Barrett	.75	.23
90 Brad Fullmer	.75	.23
91 Vladimir Guerrero	3.00	.90
92 Fernando Seguignol	.75	.23
93 Ugueth Urbina	.75	.23
94 Bobby Bonilla	1.25	.35
95 Rickey Henderson	3.00	.90
96 Rey Ordonez	.75	.23
97 Mike Piazza	5.00	1.50
98 Robin Ventura	1.25	.35
99 Roger Clemens	6.00	1.80
100 Derek Jeter	8.00	2.40
101 Chuck Knoblauch	1.25	.35
102 Tino Martinez	2.00	.60
103 Paul O'Neill	2.00	.60
104 Bernie Williams	2.00	.60
105 Eric Chavez	1.25	.35
106 Ryan Christenson	.75	.23
107 Jason Giambi	1.25	.35
108 Ben Grieve	.75	.23
109 Miguel Tejada	1.25	.35
110 Marlon Anderson	.75	.23
111 Doug Glanville	.75	.23
112 Scott Rolen	3.00	.90
113 Curt Schilling	1.25	.35
114 Brian Giles	1.25	.35
115 Warren Morris	.75	.23
116 Jason Kendall	1.25	.35
117 Kris Benson	.75	.23
118 J.D. Drew	1.25	.35
119 Ray Lankford	.75	.23
120 Mark McGwire	8.00	2.40
121 Matt Clement	.75	.23
122 Tony Gwynn	4.00	1.20
123 Trevor Hoffman	1.25	.35
124 Wally Joyner	1.25	.35
125 Reggie Sanders	.75	.23
126 Barry Bonds	8.00	2.40
127 Ellis Burks	1.25	.35
128 Jeff Kent	1.25	.35
129 Stan Javier	.75	.23
130 J.T. Snow	1.25	.35
131 Jay Buhner	1.25	.35
132 Freddy Garcia RC	3.00	.90
133 Ken Griffey Jr.	5.00	1.50
134 Russ Davis	.75	.23
135 Edgar Martinez	2.00	.60
136 Alex Rodriguez	5.00	1.50
137 David Segui	.75	.23
138 Rolando Arrojo	.75	.23
139 Wade Boggs	2.00	.60
140 Jose Canseco	3.00	.90
141 Quinton McCracken	.75	.23
142 Fred McGriff	2.00	.60
143 Juan Gonzalez	2.00	.60
144 Tom Goodwin	.75	.23
145 Rusty Greer	1.25	.35
146 Ivan Rodriguez	3.00	.90
147 Jose Cruz Jr.	.75	.23
148 Carlos Delgado	1.25	.35
149 Shawn Green	1.25	.35
150 Roy Halladay	.75	.23

1999 Pacific Invincible Opening Day

Randomly inserted in hobby packs only at the rate of one in 25 (basically one per box), this 150-card set is parallel to the Pacific Invincible base set. Only 69 serial-numbered sets were produced. Each card carries a large sunburst gold-foil "Opening Day" logo on the front with the serial numbering in the center.

	Nm-Mt	Ex-Mt
*STARS: 4X TO 10X BASIC CARDS		
*ROOKIES: 2.5X TO 6X BASIC CARDS		

1999 Pacific Invincible Platinum Blue

Randomly inserted into packs, this 150-card set is parallel to the base set with platinum blue foil highlighting. Only 67 serial-numbered sets were produced.

	Nm-Mt	Ex-Mt
*STARS: 4X TO 10X BASIC CARDS		
*ROOKIES: 2.5X TO 6X BASIC CARDS		

1999 Pacific Invincible Diamond Magic

Randomly inserted into packs at the rate of one in 49, this 10-card set features color action photos of top players with silver and gold foil highlights.

	Nm-Mt	Ex-Mt
COMPLETE SET (10)	80.00	24.00
1 Cal Ripken	25.00	7.50
2 Nomar Garciaparra	12.00	3.60
3 Sammy Sosa	12.00	3.60
4 Frank Thomas	8.00	2.40
5 Mike Piazza	12.00	3.60
6 J.D. Drew	3.00	.90
7 Mark McGwire	20.00	6.00
8 Tony Gwynn	10.00	3.00
9 Ken Griffey Jr.	12.00	3.60
10 Alex Rodriguez	12.00	3.60

1999 Pacific Invincible Flash Point

Randomly inserted into packs at the rate of one in 25, this 20-card set features color photos of top players with gold foil highlights.

	Nm-Mt	Ex-Mt
COMPLETE SET (20)	100.00	30.00
1 Mo Vaughn	2.50	.75
2 Chipper Jones	6.00	1.80
3 Greg Maddux	10.00	3.00
4 Cal Ripken	20.00	6.00
5 Nomar Garciaparra	10.00	3.00
6 Sammy Sosa	10.00	3.00
7 Frank Thomas	6.00	1.80
8 Manny Ramirez	4.00	1.20
9 Vladimir Guerrero	6.00	1.80
10 Mike Piazza	10.00	3.00
11 Roger Clemens	12.00	3.60
12 Derek Jeter	15.00	4.50
13 Ben Grieve	1.50	.45
14 Scott Rolen	6.00	1.80
15 J.D. Drew	2.50	.75
16 Mark McGwire	15.00	4.50
17 Tony Gwynn	8.00	2.40
18 Ken Griffey Jr.	10.00	3.00
19 Alex Rodriguez	10.00	3.00
20 Juan Gonzalez	4.00	1.20

1999 Pacific Invincible Giants of the Game

These jumbo cards, which measure approximately 35" by 51" were available exclusively through obtaining one of the scarce exchange cards randomly seeded into packs. The lucky collector who pulled one of these exchange cards not only got the large card but his exchange card back. The jumbo cards features

color cut-outs of top players silhouetted on a background of city buildings. Only 10 serial-numbered sets were produced. No pricing is available due to scarcity, but a checklist is provided.

	Nm-Mt	Ex-Mt
1 Cal Ripken		
2 Nomar Garciaparra		
3 Sammy Sosa		
4 Frank Thomas		
5 Mike Piazza		
6 J.D. Drew		
7 Mark McGwire		
8 Tony Gwynn		
9 Ken Griffey Jr.		
10 Alex Rodriguez		

1999 Pacific Invincible Sandlot Heroes

Inserted one per pack, this 40-card set features color photos of 20 top players. Each player has two versions of his card.

	Nm-Mt	Ex-Mt
COMPLETE SET (40)	25.00	7.50
1 Mo Vaughn	.25	.07
2 Chipper Jones	.60	.18
3 Greg Maddux	1.00	.30
4 Cal Ripken	2.00	.60
5 Nomar Garciaparra	1.00	.30
6 Sammy Sosa	1.00	.30
7 Frank Thomas	.60	.18
8 Manny Ramirez	.40	.12
9 Vladimir Guerrero	.60	.18
10 Mike Piazza	1.00	.30
11 Roger Clemens	1.25	.35
12 Derek Jeter	1.50	.45
13 Eric Chavez	.25	.07
14 Ben Grieve	.15	.04
15 J.D. Drew	.25	.07
16 Mark McGwire	1.50	.45
17 Tony Gwynn	.75	.23
18 Ken Griffey Jr.	1.00	.30
19 Alex Rodriguez	1.00	.30
20 Juan Gonzalez	.40	.12

1999 Pacific Invincible Seismic Force

Inserted one per pack, this 40-card set features color portraits of 20 top players. Each player has two versions of his card.

	Nm-Mt	Ex-Mt
COMPLETE SET (40)	25.00	7.50
1 Mo Vaughn	.25	.07
2 Chipper Jones	.60	.18
3 Greg Maddux	1.00	.30
4 Cal Ripken	2.00	.60
5 Nomar Garciaparra	1.00	.30
6 Sammy Sosa	1.00	.30
7 Frank Thomas	.60	.18
8 Manny Ramirez	.40	.12
9 Vladimir Guerrero	.60	.18
10 Mike Piazza	1.00	.30
11 Bernie Williams	.40	.12
12 Derek Jeter	1.50	.45
13 Ben Grieve	.15	.04
14 J.D. Drew	.25	.07
15 Mark McGwire	1.50	.45
16 Tony Gwynn	.75	.23
17 Ken Griffey Jr.	1.00	.30
18 Alex Rodriguez	1.00	.30
19 Juan Gonzalez	.40	.12
20 Ivan Rodriguez	.60	.18

1999 Pacific Invincible Thunder Alley

Randomly inserted in packs at the rate of one in 121, this 20-card set features color images of powerful top players silhouetted on a background of the player's team logo.

	Nm-Mt	Ex-Mt
1 Mo Vaughn	6.00	1.80
2 Chipper Jones	15.00	4.50
3 Cal Ripken	50.00	15.00
4 Nomar Garciaparra	25.00	7.50
5 Sammy Sosa	25.00	7.50
6 Frank Thomas	15.00	4.50
7 Manny Ramirez	10.00	3.00
8 Todd Helton	10.00	3.00
9 Vladimir Guerrero	15.00	4.50
10 Mike Piazza	25.00	7.50
11 Derek Jeter	40.00	12.00
12 Ben Grieve	4.00	1.20
13 Scott Rolen	15.00	4.50
14 J.D. Drew	6.00	1.80
15 Mark McGwire	40.00	12.00
16 Tony Gwynn	20.00	6.00
17 Ken Griffey Jr.	25.00	7.50
18 Alex Rodriguez	25.00	7.50
19 Juan Gonzalez	10.00	3.00
20 Ivan Rodriguez	15.00	4.50

2000 Pacific Invincible

The 2000 Pacific Invincible product was originally intended for release in August, 2000 but was delayed to mid-October in an effort to incorporate game-used equipment insert cards into the product. The base set features 150 veteran and prospect cards. Each pack contained three cards and carried a suggested retail price of $2.99. Notable Rookie Cards include Kazuhiro Sasaki.

	Nm-Mt	Ex-Mt
COMPLETE SET (150)	100.00	30.00
1 Darin Erstad	1.25	.35
2 Troy Glaus	1.25	.35
3 Ramon Ortiz	.75	.23
4 Tim Salmon	2.00	.60
5 Mo Vaughn	1.25	.35
6 Erubiel Durazo	.75	.23
7 Luis Gonzalez	1.25	.35
8 Randy Johnson	3.00	.90
9 Matt Williams	.75	.23
10 Rafael Furcal	1.25	.35
11 Andres Galarraga	1.25	.35
12 Tom Glavine	2.00	.60
13 Andruw Jones	1.25	.35
14 Chipper Jones	3.00	.90
15 Greg Maddux	5.00	1.50
16 Kevin Millwood	1.25	.35
17 Albert Belle	1.25	.35
18 Will Clark	3.00	.90
19 Mike Mussina	2.00	.60
20 Matt Riley	.75	.23
21 Cal Ripken	10.00	3.00
22 Carl Everett	1.25	.35
23 Nomar Garciaparra	5.00	1.50
24 Steve Lomasney	.75	.23
25 Pedro Martinez	3.00	.90
26 Tomo Ohka RC	1.25	.35
27 Wilton Veras	.75	.23
28 Mark Grace	2.00	.60
29 Sammy Sosa	5.00	1.50
30 Kerry Wood	3.00	.90
31 Eric Young	.75	.23
32 Julio Zuleta RC	.75	.23
33 Paul Konerko	1.25	.35
34 Carlos Lee	1.25	.35
35 Magglio Ordonez	1.25	.35
36 Josh Paul	.75	.23
37 Frank Thomas	3.00	.90
38 Rob Bell	.75	.23
39 Dante Bichette	1.25	.35
40 Sean Casey	1.25	.35
41 Ken Griffey Jr.	5.00	1.50
42 Barry Larkin	2.00	.60
43 Pokey Reese	.75	.23
44 Roberto Alomar	2.00	.60
45 Manny Ramirez	2.00	.60
46 Richie Sexson	1.25	.35
47 Jim Thome	3.00	.90
48 Omar Vizquel	2.00	.60
49 Jeff Cirillo	.75	.23
50 Todd Helton	2.00	.60
51 Neifi Perez	.75	.23
52 Larry Walker	2.00	.60
53 Tony Clark	.75	.23
54 Juan Encarnacion	.75	.23
55 Juan Gonzalez	2.00	.60
56 Hideo Nomo	3.00	.90
57 Luis Castillo	.75	.23
58 Alex Gonzalez	.75	.23
59 Brad Penny	.75	.23
60 Preston Wilson	1.25	.35
61 Moises Alou	1.25	.35
62 Jeff Bagwell	2.00	.60
63 Lance Berkman	1.25	.35
64 Craig Biggio	2.00	.60
65 Roger Cedeno	.75	.23
66 Jose Lima	.75	.23
67 Carlos Beltran	2.00	.60
68 Johnny Damon	2.00	.60
69 Chad Durbin RC	.75	.23
70 Jermaine Dye	1.25	.35
71 Carlos Febles	.75	.23
72 Mark Quinn	.75	.23
73 Kevin Brown	1.25	.35
74 Eric Gagne	5.00	1.50
75 Shawn Green	1.25	.35
76 Eric Karros	1.25	.35
77 Gary Sheffield	1.25	.35
78 Kevin Barker	.75	.23
79 Ron Belliard	.75	.23
80 Jeromy Burnitz	1.25	.35
81 Geoff Jenkins	1.25	.35
82 Jacque Jones	1.25	.35
83 Corey Koskie	1.25	.35
84 Matt LeCroy	.75	.23
85 David Ortiz	2.00	.60
86 Johan Santana RC	15.00	4.50
87 Todd Walker	.75	.23
88 Peter Bergeron	.75	.23
89 Vladimir Guerrero	3.00	.90
90 Jose Vidro	.75	.23
91 Rondell White	1.25	.35
92 Edgardo Alfonzo	.75	.23
93 Derek Bell	.75	.23
94 Mike Hampton	1.25	.35
95 Rey Ordonez	.75	.23
96 Mike Piazza	5.00	1.50
97 Robin Ventura	1.25	.35
98 Roger Clemens	6.00	1.80
99 Orlando Hernandez	.75	.23
100 Derek Jeter	8.00	2.40
101 Alfonso Soriano	3.00	.90
102 Bernie Williams	2.00	.60
103 Eric Chavez	1.25	.35
104 Jason Giambi	1.25	.35
105 Ben Grieve	.75	.23
106 Tim Hudson	1.25	.35
107 Miguel Tejada	1.25	.35
108 Bob Abreu	1.25	.35
109 Doug Glanville	.75	.23
110 Mike Lieberthal	1.25	.35
111 Scott Rolen	3.00	.90
112 Brian Giles	1.25	.35
113 Chad Hermansen	.75	.23
114 Jason Kendall	1.25	.35
115 Warren Morris	.75	.23
116 Aramis Ramirez	1.25	.35
117 Rick Ankiel	1.25	.35
118 J.D. Drew	1.25	.35
119 Mark McGwire	8.00	2.40
120 Fernando Tatis	.75	.23
121 Fernando Vina	.75	.23
122 Bret Boone	1.25	.35
123 Ben Davis	.75	.23
124 Tony Gwynn	4.00	1.20
125 Trevor Hoffman	1.25	.35
126 Ryan Klesko	1.25	.35
127 Rich Aurilia	.75	.23
128 Barry Bonds	8.00	2.40
129 Ellis Burks	1.25	.35
130 Jeff Kent	1.25	.35
131 Freddy Garcia	1.25	.35
132 Carlos Guillen	1.25	.35
133 Edgar Martinez	2.00	.60
134 John Olerud	1.25	.35
135 Rob Ramsay	.75	.23
136 Alex Rodriguez	5.00	1.50
137 Kazuhiro Sasaki RC	3.00	.90
138 Jose Canseco	3.00	.90
139 Vinny Castilla	1.25	.35
140 Fred McGriff	2.00	.60
141 Greg Vaughn UER	.75	.23
Mo Vaughn is pictured		
142 Dan Wheeler	.75	.23
143 Gabe Kapler	.75	.23
144 Ruben Mateo	.75	.23
145 Rafael Palmeiro	2.00	.60
146 Ivan Rodriguez	3.00	.90
147 Tony Batista	1.25	.35
148 Carlos Delgado	1.25	.35
149 Raul Mondesi	1.25	.35
150 Vernon Wells	1.25	.35

2000 Pacific Invincible Holographic Purple

Randomly inserted into packs, this 150-card set is a complete parallel of the Pacific Invincible base set. Each card in the set feature purple foil and are individually serial numbered to 299.

	Nm-Mt	Ex-Mt
*STARS: 1X TO 2.5X BASIC CARDS		
*ROOKIES: 1.25X TO 3X BASIC CARDS		

2000 Pacific Invincible Platinum Blue

Randomly inserted into packs, this 150-card set is a complete parallel of the Pacific Invincible base set. Each card in the set feature blue foil, and are individually serial numbered to 67.

	Nm-Mt	Ex-Mt
*STARS: 3X TO 8X BASIC CARDS		
*ROOKIES: 4X TO 10X BASIC CARDS		

2000 Pacific Invincible Diamond Aces

Inserted at one per pack, this 20-card insert features some of the best pitchers in the major leagues.

	Nm-Mt	Ex-Mt
COMPLETE SET (20)	8.00	2.40
*ACES 399: 3X TO 8X BASIC ACES		
ACES 399 RANDOM INSERTS IN PACKS		
ACES 399 PRINT RUN 399 SERIAL #'d SETS		
1 Randy Johnson	.75	.23
2 Greg Maddux	1.25	.35
3 Tom Glavine	.50	.15
4 John Smoltz	.30	.09
5 Mike Mussina	.50	.15
6 Pedro Martinez	.75	.23
7 Kerry Wood	.75	.23
8 Bartolo Colon	.20	.06
9 Brad Penny	.20	.06
10 Billy Wagner	.20	.06
11 Kevin Brown	.30	.09
12 Mike Hampton	.30	.09

Card	Nm-Mt	Ex-Mt
13 Roger Clemens	1.50	.45
14 David Cone	.20	.06
15 Orlando Hernandez	.20	.06
16 Mariano Rivera	.30	.09
17 Tim Hudson	.30	.09
18 Trevor Hoffman	.30	.09
19 Rick Ankiel	.30	.09
20 Freddy Garcia	.30	.09

2000 Pacific Invincible Eyes of the World

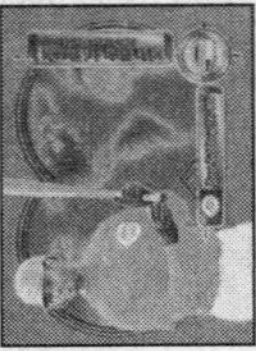

Randomly inserted into packs at one in 37, this 20-card insert features some of the league's top stars and a map showing where they are from.

Card	Nm-Mt	Ex-Mt
COMPLETE SET (20)	100.00	30.00
1 Erubiel Durazo	1.50	.45
2 Andruw Jones	2.50	.75
3 Cal Ripken	20.00	6.00
4 Nomar Garciaparra	10.00	3.00
5 Pedro Martinez	6.00	1.80
6 Sammy Sosa	10.00	3.00
7 Ken Griffey Jr.	10.00	3.00
8 Manny Ramirez	4.00	1.20
9 Larry Walker	4.00	1.20
10 Juan Gonzalez	4.00	1.20
11 Carlos Beltran	4.00	1.20
12 Vladimir Guerrero	6.00	1.80
13 Orlando Hernandez	1.50	.45
14 Derek Jeter	15.00	4.50
15 Mark McGwire	15.00	4.50
16 Tony Gwynn	8.00	2.40
17 Freddy Garcia	2.50	.75
18 Alex Rodriguez	10.00	3.00
19 Jose Canseco	6.00	1.80
20 Ivan Rodriguez	6.00	1.80

2000 Pacific Invincible Game Gear

Randomly inserted into packs, this 32-card insert features game-used memorabilia cards from some of the biggest names in MLB. The set features game-used jersey, bat-jersey, and jersey patch cards. Each card is serial numbered on the front in gold foil. Stated print runs are provided in our checklist.

Card	Nm-Mt	Ex-Mt
1 Jeff Bagwell Jsy/1000	10.00	3.00
2 Tom Glavine Jsy/1000	10.00	3.00
3 Mark Grace Jsy/1000	10.00	3.00
4 Eric Karros Jsy/1000	8.00	2.40
5 Edgar Martinez Jsy/800	10.00	3.00
6 Manny Ramirez Jsy/975	10.00	3.00
7 Cal Ripken Jsy/1000	25.00	7.50
8 Alex Rodriguez Jsy/900	15.00	4.50
9 Ivan Rodriguez Jsy/675	10.00	3.00
10 Mo Vaughn Jsy/1000	8.00	2.40
11 Edgar Martinez Bat-Jsy/200	20.00	6.00
12 Manny Ramirez Bat-Jsy/145	20.00	6.00
13 Alex Rodriguez Bat-Jsy/200	25.00	7.50
14 Ivan Rodriguez Bat-Jsy/200	20.00	6.00
15 Edgar Martinez Bat/200	15.00	4.50
16 Manny Ramirez Bat/200	15.00	4.50
17 Ivan Rodriguez Bat/200	15.00	4.50
18 Alex Rodriguez Bat/200	20.00	6.00
19 Jeff Bagwell Patch/125	40.00	12.00
20 Tom Glavine Patch/110	40.00	12.00
21 Mark Grace Patch/125	40.00	12.00
22 Tony Gwynn Patch/65	50.00	15.00
23 Chipper Jones Patch/	40.00	12.00
24 Eric Karros Patch/125	25.00	7.50
25 Greg Maddux Patch/80	80.00	24.00
26 Edgar Martinez Patch/125	40.00	12.00
27 Manny Ramirez Patch/125	40.00	12.00
28 Cal Ripken Patch/125	100.00	30.00
29 Alex Rodriguez Patch/125	60.00	18.00
30 Ivan Rodriguez Patch/125	40.00	12.00
31 Frank Thomas Patch/125	40.00	12.00
32 Mo Vaughn Patch/125	25.00	7.50

2000 Pacific Invincible Kings of the Diamond

Inserted at one per pack, this 30-card insert features some of the top hitters in the major leagues.

Card	Nm-Mt	Ex-Mt
COMPLETE SET (30)	15.00	4.50
*KINGS 299: 4X TO 10X BASIC KINGS		
KINGS 299 RANDOM INSERTS IN PACKS		
KINGS 299 PRINT RUN 299 SERIAL #'d SETS		
1 Mo Vaughn	.30	.09

Card	Nm-Mt	Ex-Mt
2 Erubiel Durazo	.20	.06
3 Andruw Jones	.30	.09
4 Chipper Jones	.75	.23
5 Cal Ripken	2.50	.75
6 Nomar Garciaparra	1.25	.35
7 Sammy Sosa	1.25	.35
8 Frank Thomas	.75	.23
9 Sean Casey	.30	.09
10 Ken Griffey Jr.	1.25	.35
11 Manny Ramirez	.50	.15
12 Larry Walker	.50	.15
13 Juan Gonzalez	.50	.15
14 Jeff Bagwell	.50	.15
15 Craig Biggio	.50	.15
16 Carlos Beltran	.50	.15
17 Shawn Green	.30	.09
18 Vladimir Guerrero	.75	.23
19 Mike Piazza	1.25	.35
20 Derek Jeter	2.00	.60
21 Bernie Williams	.50	.15
22 Ben Grieve	.20	.06
23 Scott Rolen	.75	.23
24 Mark McGwire	2.00	.60
25 Tony Gwynn	1.00	.30
26 Barry Bonds	2.00	.60
27 Alex Rodriguez	1.25	.35
28 Jose Canseco	.75	.23
29 Rafael Palmeiro	.50	.15
30 Ivan Rodriguez	.75	.23

2000 Pacific Invincible Lighting the Fire

Randomly inserted into packs at one in 73, this 20-card die-cut insert features players that can catch fire at any point during the season.

Card	Nm-Mt	Ex-Mt
COMPLETE SET (20)	200.00	60.00
1 Chipper Jones	10.00	3.00
2 Greg Maddux	15.00	4.50
3 Cal Ripken	30.00	9.00
4 Nomar Garciaparra	15.00	4.50
5 Pedro Martinez	10.00	3.00
6 Ken Griffey Jr.	15.00	4.50
7 Sammy Sosa	15.00	4.50
8 Manny Ramirez	6.00	1.80
9 Juan Gonzalez	6.00	1.80
10 Jeff Bagwell	6.00	1.80
11 Shawn Green	4.00	1.20
12 Vladimir Guerrero	10.00	3.00
13 Mike Piazza	15.00	4.50
14 Roger Clemens	20.00	6.00
15 Derek Jeter	25.00	7.50
16 Mark McGwire	25.00	7.50
17 Tony Gwynn	12.00	3.60
18 Alex Rodriguez	15.00	4.50
19 Jose Canseco	10.00	3.00
20 Ivan Rodriguez	10.00	3.00

2000 Pacific Invincible Ticket to Stardom

Randomly inserted into packs at one in 181, this 20-card set features some of the major league's best players on cards that resemble ticket stubs.

Card	Nm-Mt	Ex-Mt
1 Andruw Jones	8.00	2.40
2 Chipper Jones	20.00	6.00
3 Cal Ripken	60.00	18.00
4 Nomar Garciaparra	30.00	9.00
5 Pedro Martinez	20.00	6.00
6 Ken Griffey Jr.	30.00	9.00
7 Sammy Sosa	30.00	9.00
8 Manny Ramirez	12.00	3.60
9 Jeff Bagwell	12.00	3.60
10 Shawn Green	8.00	2.40
11 Vladimir Guerrero	20.00	6.00
12 Mike Piazza	30.00	9.00
13 Derek Jeter	50.00	15.00
14 Alfonso Soriano	20.00	6.00
15 Scott Rolen	20.00	6.00
16 Rick Ankiel	8.00	2.40
17 Mark McGwire	50.00	15.00
18 Tony Gwynn	25.00	7.50
19 Alex Rodriguez	30.00	9.00
20 Ivan Rodriguez	20.00	6.00

2000 Pacific Invincible Wild Vinyl

Randomly inserted into packs, this 10-card insert features the league's top hitters on a vinyl based card. Please note that each card is individually serial numbered to 10. Pricing in not available due to scarcity.

Card	Nm-Mt	Ex-Mt
1 Chipper Jones		
2 Cal Ripken		
3 Nomar Garciaparra		
4 Ken Griffey Jr.		
5 Sammy Sosa		
6 Mike Piazza		
7 Derek Jeter		
8 Mark McGwire		
9 Tony Gwynn		
10 Alex Rodriguez		

1998 Pacific Omega

The 1998 Pacific Omega set was issued in one series totalling 250 cards. The cards were issued in eight-card packs with an SRP of $1.99. In addition, a Tony Gwynn sample card was issued prior to the product's release. The card was distributed to dealers and hobby media to preview the product. It's identical in design to a standard Aurora card except for the word "SAMPLE" printed diagonally against the back of the card coupled with a large MLB "Genuine Merchandise" sticker. Notable Rookie Cards include Kevin Millwood and Magglio Ordonez.

Card	Nm-Mt	Ex-Mt
COMPLETE SET (250)	40.00	12.00
1 Garret Anderson	.30	.09
2 Gary DiSarcina	.30	.09
3 Jim Edmonds	.30	.09
4 Darin Erstad	.30	.09
5 Cecil Fielder	.30	.09
6 Chuck Finley	.30	.09
7 Shigetoshi Hasegawa	.30	.09
8 Tim Salmon	.50	.15
9 Brian Anderson	.30	.09
10 Jay Bell	.30	.09
11 Andy Benes	.30	.09
12 Yamil Benitez	.30	.09
13 Jorge Fabregas	.30	.09
14 Travis Lee	.30	.09
15 Devon White	.30	.09
16 Matt Williams	.30	.09
17 Andres Galarraga	.30	.09
18 Tom Glavine	.50	.15
19 Andruw Jones	.30	.09
20 Chipper Jones	.75	.23
21 Ryan Klesko	.30	.09
22 Javy Lopez	.30	.09
23 Greg Maddux	1.25	.35
24 Kevin Millwood RC	1.00	.30
25 Denny Neagle	.30	.09
26 John Smoltz	.50	.15
27 Roberto Alomar	.50	.15
28 Brady Anderson	.30	.09
29 Joe Carter	.30	.09
30 Eric Davis	.30	.09
31 Jimmy Key	.30	.09
32 Mike Mussina	.50	.15
33 Rafael Palmeiro	.50	.15
34 Cal Ripken	2.50	.75
35 B.J. Surhoff	.30	.09
36 Dennis Eckersley	.30	.09
37 Nomar Garciaparra	1.25	.35
38 Reggie Jefferson	.30	.09
39 Derek Lowe	.30	.09
40 Pedro Martinez	.75	.23
41 Brian Rose	.30	.09
42 John Valentin	.30	.09
43 Jason Varitek	.75	.23
44 Mo Vaughn	.30	.09
45 Jeff Blauser	.30	.09
46 Jeremi Gonzalez	.30	.09
47 Mark Grace	.50	.15
48 Lance Johnson	.30	.09
49 Kevin Orie	.30	.09
50 Henry Rodriguez	.30	.09
51 Sammy Sosa	1.25	.35
52 Kerry Wood	.75	.23
53 Albert Belle	.30	.09
54 Mike Cameron	.30	.09
55 Mike Caruso	.30	.09
56 Ray Durham	.30	.09
57 Jaime Navarro	.30	.09
58 Greg Norton	.30	.09
59 Maggio Ordonez RC	2.00	.60
60 Frank Thomas	.75	.23
61 Robin Ventura	.30	.09
62 Bret Boone	.30	.09
63 Willie Greene	.30	.09
64 Barry Larkin	.50	.15
65 Jon Nunnally	.30	.09
66 Eduardo Perez	.30	.09
67 Reggie Sanders	.30	.09
68 Brett Tomko	.30	.09
69 Sandy Alomar Jr.	.30	.09
70 Travis Fryman	.30	.09
71 David Justice	.30	.09
72 Kenny Lofton	.30	.09
73 Charles Nagy	.30	.09
74 Manny Ramirez	.50	.15
75 Jim Thome	.75	.23
76 Omar Vizquel	.50	.15
77 Enrique Wilson	.30	.09
78 Jaret Wright	.30	.09
79 Dante Bichette	.30	.09
80 Ellis Burks	.30	.09
81 Vinny Castilla	.30	.09
82 Todd Helton	.50	.15
83 Darryl Kile	.30	.09
84 Mike Lansing	.30	.09
85 Neifi Perez	.30	.09
86 Larry Walker	.50	.15
87 Raul Casanova	.30	.09
88 Tony Clark	.30	.09
89 Luis Gonzalez	.30	.09
90 Bobby Higginson	.30	.09
91 Brian Hunter	.30	.09
92 Bip Roberts	.30	.09
93 Justin Thompson	.30	.09
94 Josh Booty	.30	.09
95 Craig Counsell	.30	.09
96 Livan Hernandez	.30	.09
97 Ryan Jackson RC	.30	.09
98 Mark Kotsay	.30	.09
99 Derrek Lee	.30	.09
100 Mike Piazza	1.25	.35
101 Edgar Renteria	.30	.09
102 Cliff Floyd	.30	.09
103 Moises Alou	.30	.09
104 Jeff Bagwell	.50	.15
105 Derek Bell	.30	.09
106 Sean Berry	.30	.09
107 Craig Biggio	.50	.15
108 John Halama RC	.30	.09
109 Richard Hidalgo	.30	.09
110 Shane Reynolds	.30	.09
111 Tim Belcher	.30	.09
112 Brian Bevil	.30	.09
113 Jeff Conine	.30	.09
114 Johnny Damon	.50	.15
115 Jeff King	.30	.09
116 Jeff Montgomery	.30	.09
117 Dean Palmer	.30	.09
118 Terry Pendleton	.30	.09
119 Bobby Bonilla	.30	.09
120 Wilton Guerrero	.30	.09
121 Todd Hollandsworth	.30	.09
122 Charles Johnson	.30	.09
123 Eric Karros	.30	.09
124 Paul Konerko	.30	.09
125 Ramon Martinez	.30	.09
126 Raul Mondesi	.30	.09
127 Hideo Nomo	.75	.23
128 Gary Sheffield	.30	.09
129 Ismael Valdes	.30	.09
130 Jeromy Burnitz	.30	.09
131 Jeff Cirillo	.30	.09
132 Todd Dunn	.30	.09
133 Marquis Grissom	.30	.09
134 John Jaha	.30	.09
135 Scott Karl	.30	.09
136 Dave Nilsson	.30	.09
137 Jose Valentin	.30	.09
138 Fernando Vina	.30	.09
139 Rick Aguilera	.30	.09
140 Marty Cordova	.30	.09
141 Pat Meares	.30	.09
142 Paul Molitor	.50	.15
143 David Ortiz	.75	.23
144 Brad Radke	.30	.09
145 Terry Steinbach	.30	.09
146 Todd Walker	.30	.09
147 Shane Andrews	.30	.09
148 Brad Fullmer	.30	.09
149 Mark Grudzielanek	.30	.09
150 Vladimir Guerrero	.75	.23
151 F.P. Santangelo	.30	.09
152 Jose Vidro	.30	.09
153 Rondell White	.30	.09
154 Carlos Baerga	.30	.09
155 Bernard Gilkey	.30	.09
156 Todd Hundley	.30	.09
157 Butch Huskey	.30	.09
158 Bobby Jones	.30	.09
159 Brian McRae	.30	.09
160 John Olerud	.30	.09
161 Rey Ordonez	.30	.09
162 Masato Yoshii RC	.50	.15
163 David Cone	.30	.09
164 Hideki Irabu	.30	.09
165 Derek Jeter	2.00	.60
166 Chuck Knoblauch	.30	.09
167 Tino Martinez	.50	.15
168 Paul O'Neill	.50	.15
169 Andy Pettitte	.50	.15
170 Mariano Rivera	.50	.15
171 Darryl Strawberry	.50	.15
172 David Wells	.30	.09
173 Bernie Williams	.50	.15
174 Ryan Christenson RC	.30	.09
175 Jason Giambi	.30	.09
176 Ben Grieve	.30	.09
177 Rickey Henderson	.75	.23
178 A.J. Hinch	.30	.09
179 Kenny Rogers	.30	.09
180 Ricky Bottalico	.30	.09
181 Rico Brogna	.30	.09
182 Doug Glanville	.30	.09
183 Gregg Jefferies	.30	.09
184 Mike Lieberthal	.30	.09
185 Scott Rolen	.75	.23
186 Curt Schilling	.30	.09
187 Jermaine Allensworth	.30	.09
188 Lou Collier	.30	.09
189 Jose Guillen	.30	.09
190 Jason Kendall	.30	.09
191 Al Martin	.30	.09
192 Tony Womack	.30	.09
193 Kevin Young	.30	.09
194 Royce Clayton	.30	.09
195 Delino DeShields	.30	.09
196 Gary Gaetti	.30	.09
197 Ron Gant	.30	.09
198 Brian Jordan	.30	.09
199 Ray Lankford	.30	.09
200 Mark McGwire	2.00	.60
201 Todd Stottlemyre	.30	.09
202 Kevin Brown	.50	.15
203 Ken Caminiti	.30	.09
204 Steve Finley	.30	.09
205 Tony Gwynn	1.00	.30
206 Carlos Hernandez	.30	.09
207 Wally Joyner	.30	.09
208 Greg Vaughn	.30	.09
209 Barry Bonds	2.00	.60
210 Shawn Estes	.30	.09
211 Orel Hershiser	.30	.09
212 Stan Javier	.30	.09
213 Jeff Kent	.30	.09
214 Bill Mueller	.30	.09
215 Robb Nen	.30	.09
216 J.T. Snow	.30	.09
217 Jay Buhner	.30	.09
218 Ken Cloude	.30	.09
219 Joey Cora	.30	.09
220 Ken Griffey Jr.	1.25	.35
221 Glenallen Hill	.30	.09
222 Randy Johnson	.75	.23
223 Edgar Martinez	.50	.15
224 Jamie Moyer	.30	.09
225 Alex Rodriguez	1.25	.35
226 David Segui	.30	.09
227 Dan Wilson	.30	.09
228 Rolando Arrojo RC	.30	.09
229 Wade Boggs	.50	.15
230 Miguel Cairo	.30	.09
231 Roberto Hernandez	.30	.09
232 Quinton McCracken	.30	.09
233 Fred McGriff	.50	.15
234 Paul Sorrento	.30	.09
235 Kevin Stocker	.30	.09
236 Will Clark	.75	.23
237 Juan Gonzalez	.50	.15
238 Rusty Greer	.30	.09
239 Rick Helling	.30	.09
240 Roberto Kelly	.30	.09
241 Ivan Rodriguez	.75	.23
242 Aaron Sele	.30	.09
243 John Wetteland	.30	.09
244 Jose Canseco	.75	.23
245 Roger Clemens	1.50	.45
246 Jose Cruz Jr.	.30	.09
247 Carlos Delgado	.30	.09
248 Alex Gonzalez	.30	.09
249 Ed Sprague	.30	.09
250 Shannon Stewart	.30	.09
NNO Tony Gwynn Sample	1.00	.30

1998 Pacific Omega EO Portraits

Randomly inserted in packs at a rate of one in 73, this 20-card set is an insert to the Pacific Omega base set. The fronts feature 20 exciting player photos on exclusive Electro-Optical technology. The featured player's name and team run across the bottom border. The Omega logo sits in the upper left corner.

Card	Nm-Mt	Ex-Mt
COMPLETE SET (20)	150.00	45.00
PORTRAIT 1 OF 1 PRINT RUN 1 #'d SET		
PORT.1/1 NOT PRICED DUE TO SCARCITY		
1 Cal Ripken	40.00	12.00
2 Nomar Garciaparra	20.00	6.00
3 Mo Vaughn	5.00	1.50
4 Frank Thomas	12.00	3.60
5 Manny Ramirez	8.00	2.40
6 Ben Grieve	5.00	1.50
7 Ken Griffey Jr.	20.00	6.00
8 Alex Rodriguez	20.00	6.00
9 Juan Gonzalez	8.00	2.40
10 Ivan Rodriguez	12.00	3.60
11 Travis Lee	5.00	1.50
12 Greg Maddux	20.00	6.00
13 Chipper Jones	12.00	3.60
14 Kerry Wood	12.00	3.60
15 Larry Walker	8.00	2.40
16 Jeff Bagwell	8.00	2.40
17 Mike Piazza	20.00	6.00
18 Mark McGwire	30.00	9.00
19 Tony Gwynn	15.00	4.50
20 Barry Bonds	30.00	9.00

1998 Pacific Omega Face To Face

Randomly inserted in packs at a rate of one in 145, this 10-card set is an insert to the Pacific Omega base set. Each card front features a background of "brick wall" design and salutes two superstars. The featured player's names run across the bottom border separated by the Omega logo.

Card	Nm-Mt	Ex-Mt
COMPLETE SET (10)	150.00	45.00
1 Alex Rodriguez / Nomar Garciaparra	20.00	6.00
2 Mark McGwire / Ken Griffey Jr.	30.00	9.00
3 Mike Piazza / Sandy Alomar Jr.	20.00	6.00
4 Kerry Wood / Roger Clemens	25.00	7.50
5 Cal Ripken / Paul Molitor	40.00	12.00
6 Tony Gwynn / Wade Boggs	15.00	4.50
7 Frank Thomas / Chipper Jones	12.00	3.60
8 Travis Lee / Ben Grieve	5.00	1.50
9 Hideo Nomo	12.00	3.60

Hideki Irabu
10 Juan Gonzalez 8.00 2.40
Manny Ramirez

1998 Pacific Omega Online Inserts

Randomly inserted in packs at a rate of four in 37, this 36-card set is an insert to the Pacific Omega base set. The card fronts feature a color game action photo on a fully foiled hi-tech web designed card. With this card, you can log on to bigleaguers.com and majorleaguebaseball.com and keep track of your favorite players.

Nm-Mt Ex-Mt
COMPLETE SET (36) 120.00 36.00
1 Cal Ripken 15.00 4.50
2 Nomar Garciaparra 8.00 2.40
3 Pedro Martinez 5.00 1.50
4 Mo Vaughn 2.00 .60
5 Frank Thomas 5.00 1.50
6 Sandy Alomar Jr. 2.00 .60
7 Manny Ramirez 3.00 .90
8 Jaret Wright 2.00 .60
9 Paul Molitor 3.00 .90
10 Derek Jeter 12.00 3.60
11 Bernie Williams 3.00 .90
12 Ben Grieve 2.00 .60
13 Ken Griffey Jr. 8.00 2.40
14 Edgar Martinez 3.00 .90
15 Alex Rodriguez 8.00 2.40
16 Wade Boggs 3.00 .90
17 Juan Gonzalez 3.00 .90
18 Ivan Rodriguez 5.00 1.50
19 Roger Clemens 10.00 3.00
20 Travis Lee 2.00 .60
21 Matt Williams 2.00 .60
22 Andres Galarraga 2.00 .60
23 Chipper Jones 5.00 1.50
24 Greg Maddux 8.00 2.40
25 Sammy Sosa 8.00 2.40
26 Kerry Wood 5.00 1.50
27 Barry Larkin 3.00 .90
28 Larry Walker 3.00 .90
29 Derrek Lee 2.00 .60
30 Jeff Bagwell 3.00 .90
31 Hideo Nomo 5.00 1.50
32 Mike Piazza 8.00 2.40
33 Scott Rolen 5.00 1.50
34 Mark McGwire 12.00 3.60
35 Tony Gwynn 6.00 1.80
36 Barry Bonds 12.00 3.60

1998 Pacific Omega Prisms

Randomly inserted in packs at a rate of one in 37, this 20-card set is an insert to the Pacific Omega base set. The fronts feature a background of Omega's patented prismatic foil to help showcase 20 of the game's top players. The featured player's name is found in the lower right corner with his team logo in the lower left corner.

Nm-Mt Ex-Mt
COMPLETE SET (20) 150.00 45.00
1 Cal Ripken 20.00 6.00
2 Nomar Garciaparra 10.00 3.00
3 Pedro Martinez 6.00 1.80
4 Frank Thomas 6.00 1.80
5 Manny Ramirez 4.00 1.20
6 Brian Giles 6.00 1.80
7 Derek Jeter 15.00 4.50
8 Ben Grieve 2.50 .75
9 Ken Griffey Jr. 10.00 3.00
10 Alex Rodriguez 10.00 3.00
11 Juan Gonzalez 4.00 1.20
12 Travis Lee 2.50 .75
13 Chipper Jones 6.00 1.80
14 Greg Maddux 10.00 3.00
15 Kerry Wood 6.00 1.80
16 Larry Walker 4.00 1.20
17 Hideo Nomo 6.00 1.80
18 Mike Piazza 10.00 3.00
19 Mark McGwire 15.00 4.50
20 Tony Gwynn 8.00 2.40

1998 Pacific Omega Rising Stars

Randomly inserted in packs at a rate of four in 37, this 30-card hobby only set is an insert to the Pacific Omega base set. Each card features several prospects from the team featured.

Nm-Mt Ex-Mt
*TIER 1: 4X TO 10X BASIC RISING STARS
TIER 1 PRINT RUN 100 SERIAL #'d SETS
TIER 1 CARDS ARE 2/10/16/19/20/25
*TIER 2: 5X TO 12X BASIC RISING STARS
TIER 2 PRINT RUN 75 SERIAL #'d SETS
TIER 2 CARDS ARE 3/12/18/23/26/27
*TIER 3: 6X TO 15X BASIC RISING STARS
TIER 3 PRINT RUN 50 SERIAL #'d SETS
TIER 3 CARDS ARE 1/7/15/17/22/28..
*TIER 4: 12.5X TO 30X BASIC RISING STARS
TIER 4 PRINT RUN 25 SERIAL #'d SETS
TIER 4 CARDS ARE 6/9/11/14/21/29..
TIER 5 STATED PRINT RUN 1 SET .....
TIER 5 CARDS ARE 4/5/8/13/24/30....
TIER 5 NOT PRICED DUE TO SCARCITY
TIER 1-5: RANDOM INSERTS IN PACKS
1 Nerio Rodriguez 2.00 .60
Sidney Ponson
2 Frank Catalanotto 3.00 .90
Roberto Duran
Sean Runyan
3 Kevin L.Brown 2.00 .60
Carlos Almanzar
4 Aaron Boone 2.00 .60
Pat Watkins
Scott Winchester
5 Brian Meadows 2.00 .60
Andy Larkin
Antonio Alfonseca
6 DaRond Stovall 2.00 .60
Trey Moore
Shayne Bennett
7 Felix Martinez 2.00 .60
Larry Sutton
Brian Bevil
8 Homer Bush 2.00 .60
Mike Buddie
9 Rich Butler 2.00 .60
Esteban Yan
10 Dave Hollins 2.00 .60
Brian Edmondson
11 Lou Collier 2.00 .60
Jose Silva
Javier Martinez
12 Steve Sinclair 2.00 .60
Mark Dalesandro
13 Jason Varitek 5.00 1.50
Brian Rose
Brian Shouse
14 Mike Caruso 2.00 .60
Jeff Abbott
Tom Fordham
15 Jason Johnson 2.00 .60
Bobby Smith
16 Dave Berg 2.00 .60
Mark Kotsay
Jesus Sanchez
17 Richard Hidalgo 2.00 .60
John Halama
Trever Miller
18 Geoff Jenkins 2.00 .60
Bobby Hughes
Steve Woodard
19 Eli Marrero 2.00 .60
Cliff Politte
Mike Busby
20 Desi Relaford 2.00 .60
Darrin Winston
21 Todd Helton 3.00 .90
Bobby Jones
22 Rolando Arrojo 5.00 1.50
Miguel Cairo
Dan Carlson
23 David Ortiz 5.00 1.50
Jose Valentin
Eric Milton
24 Magglio Ordonez 6.00 1.80
Greg Norton
25 Brad Fullmer 2.00 .60
Javier Vazquez
Rick DeHart
26 Paul Konerko 2.00 .60
Matt Luke
27 Derrek Lee 2.00 .60
Ryan Jackson
John Roskos
28 Ben Grieve 2.00 .60
A.J.Hinch
Ryan Christenson
29 Travis Lee 3.00 .90
Karim Garcia
Dave Dellucci
30 Kerry Wood 5.00 1.50
Marc Pisciotta

1999 Pacific Omega

The 1999 Pacific Omega set was issued in one series for a total of 250 cards and distributed in six-card packs. The set features color player photos printed on silver foiled cards in a three-panel horizontal design. A Tony Gwynn Sample card was distributed to dealers and hobby media several weeks prior to the release of the product. The card can be readily identified by the bold "SAMPLE" text running across the back. An embossed stamped version of this same sample card was distributed exclusively at the 1999 Chicago Sportsfest card at the Pacific booth.

Nm-Mt Ex-Mt
COMPLETE SET (250) 40.00 12.00
COMMON CARD (1-250) .30 .09
COMMON DUAL-PLAYER .40 .12
1 Garret Anderson .30 .09
2 Jim Edmonds .30 .09
3 Darin Erstad .30 .09
4 Chuck Finley .30 .09
5 Troy Glaus .30 .09
6 Troy Percival .30 .09
7 Chris Pritchett .30 .09
8 Tim Salmon .50 .15
9 Mo Vaughn .30 .09
10 Jay Bell .30 .09
11 Steve Finley .30 .09
12 Luis Gonzalez .30 .09
13 Randy Johnson .75 .23
14 Byung-Hyun Kim RC 1.00 .30
15 Travis Lee .30 .09
16 Matt Williams .30 .09
17 Tony Womack .30 .09
18 Bret Boone .30 .09
19 Mark DeRosa .30 .09
20 Tom Glavine .50 .15
21 Andruw Jones .30 .09
22 Chipper Jones .75 .23
23 Brian Jordan .30 .09
24 Ryan Klesko .30 .09
25 Javy Lopez .30 .09
26 Greg Maddux 1.25 .35
27 John Smoltz .50 .15
28 Bruce Chen .40 .12
Odalis Perez
29 Brady Anderson .30 .09
30 Harold Baines .30 .09
31 Albert Belle .30 .09
32 Will Clark .75 .23
33 Delino DeShields .30 .09
34 Jerry Hairston Jr. .30 .09
35 Charles Johnson .30 .09
36 Mike Mussina .50 .15
37 Cal Ripken 2.50 .75
38 B.J. Surhoff .30 .09
39 Jin Ho Cho .30 .09
40 Nomar Garciaparra 1.25 .35
41 Pedro Martinez .75 .23
42 Jose Offerman .30 .09
43 Troy O'Leary .30 .09
44 John Valentin .30 .09
45 Jason Varitek .50 .15
46 Juan Pena RC .40 .12
Brian Rose
47 Mark Grace .50 .15
48 Glenallen Hill .30 .09
49 Tyler Houston .30 .09
50 Mickey Morandini .30 .09
51 Henry Rodriguez .30 .09
52 Sammy Sosa 1.25 .35
53 Kevin Tapani .30 .09
54 Mike Caruso .30 .09
55 Ray Durham .30 .09
56 Paul Konerko .30 .09
57 Carlos Lee .30 .09
58 Magglio Ordonez .30 .09
59 Mike Sirotka .30 .09
60 Frank Thomas .75 .23
61 Mark Johnson .40 .12
Chris Singleton
62 Mike Cameron .30 .09
63 Sean Casey .30 .09
64 Pete Harnisch .30 .09
65 Barry Larkin .50 .15
66 Pokey Reese .30 .09
67 Greg Vaughn .30 .09
68 Scott Williamson .30 .09
69 Dmitri Young .30 .09
70 Roberto Alomar .50 .15
71 Sandy Alomar Jr. .30 .09
72 Travis Fryman .30 .09
73 David Justice .30 .09
74 Kenny Lofton .30 .09
75 Manny Ramirez .50 .15
76 Richie Sexson .30 .09
77 Jim Thome .75 .23
78 Omar Vizquel .50 .15
79 Jaret Wright .30 .09
80 Dante Bichette .30 .09
81 Vinny Castilla .30 .09
82 Todd Helton .50 .15
83 Darryl Hamilton .30 .09
84 Darryl Kile .30 .09
85 Neifi Perez .30 .09
86 Larry Walker .50 .15
87 Tony Clark .30 .09
88 Damion Easley .30 .09
89 Juan Encarnacion .30 .09
90 Bobby Higginson .30 .09
91 Gabe Kapler .30 .09
92 Dean Palmer .30 .09
93 Justin Thompson .30 .09
94 Jeff Weaver .60 .18
Masao Kida RC
95 Bruce Aven .30 .09
96 Luis Castillo .30 .09
97 Alex Fernandez .30 .09
98 Cliff Floyd .30 .09
99 Alex Gonzalez .30 .09
100 Mark Kotsay .30 .09
101 Preston Wilson .30 .09
102 Moises Alou .30 .09
103 Jeff Bagwell .50 .15
104 Craig Biggio .50 .15
105 Derek Bell .30 .09
106 Mike Hampton .30 .09
107 Richard Hidalgo .30 .09
108 Jose Lima .30 .09
109 Billy Wagner .30 .09
110 Russ Johnson .40 .12
Daryle Ward
111 Carlos Beltran .50 .15
112 Johnny Damon .50 .15
113 Jermaine Dye .30 .09
114 Carlos Febles .30 .09
115 Jeremy Giambi .30 .09
116 Joe Randa .30 .09
117 Mike Sweeney .30 .09
118 Orber Moreno .40 .12
Jose Santiago RC
119 Kevin Brown .50 .15
120 Todd Hundley .30 .09
121 Eric Karros .30 .09
122 Raul Mondesi .30 .09
123 Chan Ho Park .30 .09
124 Angel Pena .30 .09
125 Gary Sheffield .30 .09
126 Devon White .30 .09
127 Eric Young .30 .09
128 Ron Belliard .30 .09
129 Jeromy Burnitz .30 .09
130 Jeff Cirillo .30 .09
131 Marquis Grissom .30 .09
132 Geoff Jenkins .30 .09
133 David Nilsson .30 .09
134 Hideo Nomo .75 .23
135 Fernando Vina .30 .09
136 Ron Coomer .30 .09
137 Marty Cordova .30 .09
138 Corey Koskie .30 .09
139 Brad Radke .30 .09
140 Todd Walker .30 .09
141 Chad Allen RC .40 .12
Torii Hunter
142 Cristian Guzman .40 .12
Jacque Jones
143 Michael Barrett .30 .09
144 Orlando Cabrera .30 .09
145 Vladimir Guerrero .75 .23
146 Wilton Guerrero .30 .09
147 Ugueth Urbina .30 .09
148 Rondell White .30 .09
149 Chris Widger .30 .09
150 Edgardo Alfonzo .30 .09
151 Roger Cedeno .30 .09
152 Octavio Dotel .30 .09
153 Rickey Henderson .75 .23
154 John Olerud .30 .09
155 Rey Ordonez .30 .09
156 Mike Piazza 1.25 .35
157 Robin Ventura .30 .09
158 Scott Brosius .30 .09
159 Roger Clemens 1.50 .45
160 David Cone .30 .09
161 Chili Davis .30 .09
162 Orlando Hernandez .30 .09
163 Derek Jeter 2.00 .60
164 Chuck Knoblauch .30 .09
165 Tino Martinez .50 .15
166 Paul O'Neill .50 .15
167 Bernie Williams .50 .15
168 Jason Giambi .30 .09
169 Ben Grieve .30 .09
170 Chad Harville RC .30 .09
171 Tim Hudson RC 2.00 .60
172 Tony Phillips .30 .09
173 Kenny Rogers .30 .09
174 Matt Stairs .30 .09
175 Miguel Tejada .30 .09
176 Eric Chavez .40 .12
Olmedo Saenz
177 Bobby Abreu .30 .09
178 Ron Gant .30 .09
179 Doug Glanville .30 .09
180 Mike Lieberthal .30 .09
181 Desi Relaford .30 .09
182 Scott Rolen .75 .23
183 Curt Schilling .30 .09
184 Marlon Anderson .40 .12
Randy Wolf
185 Brant Brown .30 .09
186 Brian Giles .30 .09
187 Jason Kendall .30 .09
188 Al Martin .30 .09
189 Ed Sprague .30 .09
190 Kevin Young .30 .09
191 Kris Benson .40 .12
Warren Morris
192 Kent Bottenfield .30 .09
193 Eric Davis .30 .09
194 J.D. Drew .30 .09
195 Ray Lankford .30 .09
196 Joe McEwing RC .30 .09
197 Mark McGwire 2.00 .60
198 Edgar Renteria .30 .09
199 Fernando Tatis .30 .09
200 Andy Ashby .30 .09
201 Ben Davis .30 .09
202 Tony Gwynn 1.00 .30
203 Trevor Hoffman .30 .09
204 Wally Joyner .30 .09
205 Gary Matthews Jr. .30 .09
206 Ruben Rivera .30 .09
207 Reggie Sanders .30 .09
208 Rich Aurilia .50 .15
209 Marvin Benard .30 .09
210 Barry Bonds 2.00 .60
211 Ellis Burks .30 .09
212 Stan Javier .30 .09
213 Jeff Kent .30 .09
214 Robb Nen .30 .09
215 J.T. Snow .30 .09
216 Gil Meche .30 .09
217 David Bell .30 .09
218 Freddy Garcia RC .75 .23
219 Ken Griffey Jr. 1.25 .35
220 Brian L.Hunter .30 .09
221 John Halama .30 .09
222 Edgar Martinez .50 .15
223 Jamie Moyer .30 .09
224 Alex Rodriguez 1.25 .35
225 Jay Buhner .30 .09
226 Rolando Arrojo .30 .09
227 Wade Boggs .50 .15
228 Miguel Cairo .30 .09
229 Jose Canseco .75 .23
230 Dave Martinez .30 .09
231 Fred McGriff .50 .15
232 Kevin Stocker .30 .09
233 Michael Duvall RC .40 .12
David Lamb
234 Royce Clayton .30 .09
235 Juan Gonzalez .50 .15
236 Rusty Greer .30 .09
237 Ruben Mateo .30 .09
238 Rafael Palmeiro .50 .15
239 Ivan Rodriguez .75 .23
240 John Wetteland .30 .09
241 Todd Zeile .30 .09
242 Jeff Zimmerman RC .30 .09
243 Homer Bush .30 .09
244 Jose Cruz Jr. .30 .09
245 Carlos Delgado .30 .09
246 Tony Fernandez .30 .09
247 Shawn Green .30 .09
248 Shannon Stewart .30 .09
249 David Wells .30 .09
250 Roy Halladay .40 .12
Billy Koch
S1 Tony Gwynn Sample 2.00 .60
S1A T.Gwynn Samp. Stamp 5.00 1.50

1999 Pacific Omega Copper

Randomly inserted in hobby packs only, this 250-card set is a copper foil parallel version of the base set. Only 99 serial-numbered sets were produced.

Nm-Mt Ex-Mt
*STARS: 8X TO 20X BASIC CARDS....
*RC'S/DUAL: 5X TO 12X BASIC CARDS

1999 Pacific Omega Gold

Randomly inserted in retail packs, this 250-card set is a gold foil parallel version of the base set. Only 299 serial-numbered sets were produced.

Nm-Mt Ex-Mt
*STARS: 4X TO 10X BASIC CARDS....
*RC'S/DUAL: 2X TO 5X BASIC CARDS

1999 Pacific Omega Platinum Blue

Randomly inserted in all packs, this 250-card set is a platinum blue foil parallel version of the base set. Only 75 serial-numbered sets were produced.

Nm-Mt Ex-Mt
*STARS: 10X TO 25X BASIC CARDS..
*RC'S/DUAL: 6X TO 15X BASIC CARDS

1999 Pacific Omega Premiere Date

Inserted one per 24-pack hobby box, this 250-card set is parallel to the base set. Only 50 serial-numbered sets were produced.

Nm-Mt Ex-Mt
*STARS: 12.5X TO 30X BASIC CARDS
*RC'S/DUAL: 8X TO 20X BASIC CARDS

1999 Pacific Omega 5-Tool Talents

Randomly inserted in packs only at the rate of four in 37, this 30-card set features color action photos of some of the best players of the League.

Nm-Mt Ex-Mt
COMPLETE SET (30) 80.00 24.00
1 Randy Johnson 3.00 .90
2 Greg Maddux 5.00 1.50
3 Pedro Martinez 3.00 .90
4 Kevin Brown 2.00 .60
5 Roger Clemens 6.00 1.80
6 Carlos Lee 1.25 .35
7 Gabe Kapler 1.25 .35
8 Carlos Beltran 2.00 .60
9 J.D. Drew 1.25 .35
10 Ruben Mateo 1.25 .35
11 Chipper Jones 3.00 .90
12 Sammy Sosa 5.00 1.50
13 Manny Ramirez 2.00 .60
14 Vladimir Guerrero 3.00 .90
15 Mark McGwire 8.00 2.40
16 Ken Griffey Jr. 5.00 1.50
17 Jose Canseco 3.00 .90
18 Nomar Garciaparra 5.00 1.50
19 Frank Thomas 3.00 .90
20 Larry Walker 2.00 .60
21 Jeff Bagwell 2.00 .60
22 Mike Piazza 5.00 1.50
23 Tony Gwynn 4.00 1.20
24 Juan Gonzalez 2.00 .60
25 Cal Ripken 10.00 3.00
26 Derek Jeter 8.00 2.40
27 Scott Rolen 3.00 .90
28 Barry Bonds 8.00 2.40
29 Alex Rodriguez 5.00 1.50
30 Ivan Rodriguez 3.00 .90

1999 Pacific Omega Debut Duos

Randomly inserted in packs at the rate of one in 145, this 10-card set features color action photos of two MLB stars from the same debut year. The backs track each player's career development.

Nm-Mt Ex-Mt
COMPLETE SET (10) 120.00 36.00
1 Nomar Garciaparra 20.00 6.00
Vladimir Guerrero
2 Derek Jeter 30.00 9.00
Andy Pettitte
3 Garrett Anderson 20.00 6.00
Alex Rodriguez
4 Chipper Jones 12.00 3.60
Raul Mondesi
5 Pedro Martinez 20.00 6.00
Mike Piazza
6 Mo Vaughn 8.00 2.40
Bernie Williams

7 Juan Gonzalez 20.00 6.00
Ken Griffey Jr.
8 Sammy Sosa 20.00 6.00
Larry Walker
9 Barry Bonds 30.00 9.00
Mark McGwire
10 Wade Boggs 15.00 4.50
Tony Gwynn

1999 Pacific Omega Diamond Masters

Randomly inserted in packs at the rate of four in 37, this 36-card set features color action photos of top players printed on ink-on-foil cards.

	Nm-Mt	Ex-Mt
COMPLETE SET (36)	100.00	30.00
1 Darin Erstad	1.50	.45
2 Mo Vaughn	1.50	.45
3 Matt Williams	1.50	.45
4 Andruw Jones	1.50	.45
5 Chipper Jones	4.00	1.20
6 Greg Maddux	6.00	1.80
7 Cal Ripken	12.00	3.60
8 Nomar Garciaparra	6.00	1.80
9 Pedro Martinez	4.00	1.20
10 Sammy Sosa	6.00	1.80
11 Frank Thomas	4.00	1.20
12 Kenny Lofton	1.50	.45
13 Manny Ramirez	2.50	.75
14 Larry Walker	2.50	.75
15 Gabe Kapler	1.50	.45
16 Jeff Bagwell	2.50	.75
17 Craig Biggio	2.50	.75
18 Raul Mondesi	1.50	.45
19 Vladimir Guerrero	4.00	1.20
20 Mike Piazza	6.00	1.80
21 Roger Clemens	8.00	2.40
22 Derek Jeter	10.00	3.00
23 Bernie Williams	2.50	.75
24 Scott Rolen	4.00	1.20
25 J.D. Drew	1.50	.45
26 Mark McGwire	10.00	3.00
27 Fernando Tatis	1.50	.45
28 Tony Gwynn	5.00	1.50
29 Barry Bonds	10.00	3.00
30 Ken Griffey Jr.	6.00	1.80
31 Alex Rodriguez	6.00	1.80
32 Jose Canseco	4.00	1.20
33 Juan Gonzalez	2.50	.75
34 Ruben Mateo	1.50	.45
35 Ivan Rodriguez	4.00	1.20
36 Shawn Green	1.50	.45

1999 Pacific Omega EO Portraits

Randomly inserted in packs at the rate of one in 73, this 20-card set features color action photos of top players printed with exclusive Electro-Optical technology. A close-up silhouette of the player appears in the background. A very scare "1 of 1" parallel set was also produced.

	Nm-Mt	Ex-Mt
COMPLETE SET (20)	250.00	75.00
EO PORTRAIT 1 OF 1 PARALLELS EXIST		
EO PORT.1 OF 1'S TOO SCARCE TO PRICE		
1 Mo Vaughn	5.00	1.50
2 Chipper Jones	12.00	3.60
3 Greg Maddux	20.00	6.00
4 Cal Ripken	40.00	12.00
5 Nomar Garciaparra	20.00	6.00
6 Sammy Sosa	20.00	6.00
7 Frank Thomas	12.00	3.60
8 Manny Ramirez	8.00	2.40
9 Jeff Bagwell	8.00	2.40
10 Mike Piazza	20.00	6.00
11 Roger Clemens	25.00	7.50
12 Derek Jeter	30.00	9.00
13 Scott Rolen	12.00	3.60
14 Mark McGwire	30.00	9.00
15 Tony Gwynn	15.00	4.50
16 Barry Bonds	30.00	9.00
17 Ken Griffey Jr.	20.00	6.00
18 Alex Rodriguez	20.00	6.00
19 Jose Canseco	12.00	3.60
20 Juan Gonzalez	8.00	2.40

1999 Pacific Omega Hit Machine 3000

Randomly inserted in packs, this 21-card set features color action photos of Tony Gwynn as he heads towards his 3,000th hit. Only 3,000 serial-numbered sets were produced. Card number 21 was available only at SportsFest collectibles show in Philadelphia.

	Nm-Mt	Ex-Mt
COMPLETE SET (20)	120.00	36.00
COMMON CARD (1-20)	10.00	3.00
21 Tony Gwynn SportsFest	15.00	4.50

1999 Pacific Omega HR 99

Randomly inserted in packs at the rate of one in 37, this 20-card set features color action photos of some of baseball's most powerful hitters printed on holographic prism-style foil cards.

	Nm-Mt	Ex-Mt
COMPLETE SET (20)	100.00	30.00
1 Mo Vaughn	2.50	.75
2 Matt Williams	2.50	.75
3 Chipper Jones	6.00	1.80
4 Albert Belle	2.50	.75
5 Nomar Garciaparra	10.00	3.00
6 Sammy Sosa	10.00	3.00
7 Frank Thomas	6.00	1.80
8 Manny Ramirez	4.00	1.20
9 Jeff Bagwell	4.00	1.20
10 Raul Mondesi	2.50	.75
11 Vladimir Guerrero	6.00	1.80
12 Mike Piazza	10.00	3.00
13 Derek Jeter	15.00	4.50
14 Mark McGwire	15.00	4.50
15 Fernando Tatis	2.50	.75
16 Barry Bonds	15.00	4.50
17 Ken Griffey Jr.	10.00	3.00
18 Alex Rodriguez	10.00	3.00
19 Jose Canseco	6.00	1.80
20 Juan Gonzalez	4.00	1.20

2000 Pacific Omega

The 2000 Pacific Omega product was released in late November, 2000. Each pack contained six cards, and carried a suggested retail price of $2.99. The product features a 255-card base set broken into tiers as follows: 150 Base Veterans (1-150), and 105 Prospects (151-255) that are serial numbered to 999. Notable Rookie Cards include Xavier Nady, Jose Ortiz, Kazuhiro Sasaki and Barry Zito.

	Nm-Mt	Ex-Mt
COMP.SET w/o SP's (150)	20.00	6.00
COMMON CARD (1-150)	.30	.09
COMMON (151-255)	5.00	1.50
1 Garret Anderson	.30	.09
2 Darin Erstad	.30	.09
3 Troy Glaus	.30	.09
4 Tim Salmon	.50	.15
5 Mo Vaughn	.30	.09
6 Jay Bell	.30	.09
7 Steve Finley	.30	.09
8 Luis Gonzalez	.30	.09
9 Randy Johnson	.75	.23
10 Matt Williams	.30	.09
11 Andres Galarraga	.30	.09
12 Andruw Jones	.30	.09
13 Chipper Jones	.75	.23
14 Brian Jordan	.30	.09
15 Greg Maddux	1.25	.35
16 B.J. Surhoff	.30	.09
17 Brady Anderson	.30	.09
18 Albert Belle	.30	.09
19 Mike Mussina	.50	.15
20 Cal Ripken	2.50	.75
21 Carl Everett	.30	.09
22 Nomar Garciaparra	1.25	.35
23 Pedro Martinez	.75	.23
24 Jason Varitek	.50	.15
25 Mark Grace	.50	.15
26 Sammy Sosa	1.25	.35
27 Rondell White	.30	.09
28 Kerry Wood	.75	.23
29 Eric Young	.30	.09
30 Ray Durham	.30	.09
31 Carlos Lee	.30	.09
32 Magglio Ordonez	.30	.09
33 Frank Thomas	.75	.23
34 Sean Casey	.30	.09
35 Ken Griffey Jr.	1.25	.35
36 Barry Larkin	.50	.15
37 Pokey Reese	.30	.09
38 Roberto Alomar	.50	.15
39 Kenny Lofton	.30	.09
40 Manny Ramirez	.50	.15
41 David Segui	.30	.09
42 Jim Thome	.75	.23
43 Omar Vizquel	.50	.15
44 Jeff Cirillo	.30	.09
45 Jeffrey Hammonds	.30	.09
46 Todd Helton	.50	.15
47 Todd Hollandsworth	.30	.09
48 Larry Walker	.50	.15
49 Tony Clark	.30	.09
50 Juan Encarnacion	.30	.09
51 Juan Gonzalez	.50	.15
52 Bobby Higginson	.30	.09
53 Hideo Nomo	.75	.23
54 Dean Palmer	.30	.09
55 Luis Castillo	.30	.09
56 Cliff Floyd	.30	.09
57 Derrek Lee	.30	.09
58 Mike Lowell	.30	.09
59 Henry Rodriguez	.30	.09
60 Preston Wilson	.30	.09
61 Moises Alou	.30	.09
62 Jeff Bagwell	.50	.15
63 Craig Biggio	.50	.15
64 Ken Caminiti	.30	.09
65 Richard Hidalgo	.30	.09
66 Carlos Beltran	.50	.15
67 Johnny Damon	.50	.15
68 Jermaine Dye	.30	.09
69 Joe Randa	.30	.09
70 Mike Sweeney	.30	.09
71 Adrian Beltre	.50	.15
72 Kevin Brown	.30	.09
73 Shawn Green	.30	.09
74 Eric Karros	.30	.09
75 Chan Ho Park	.30	.09
76 Gary Sheffield	.30	.09
77 Ron Belliard	.30	.09
78 Jeromy Burnitz	.30	.09
79 Geoff Jenkins	.30	.09
80 Richie Sexson	.30	.09
81 Ron Coomer	.30	.09
82 Jacque Jones	.30	.09
83 Corey Koskie	.30	.09
84 Matt Lawton	.30	.09
85 Vladimir Guerrero	.75	.23
86 Lee Stevens	.30	.09
87 Jose Vidro	.30	.09
88 Edgardo Alfonzo	.30	.09
89 Derek Bell	.30	.09
90 Mike Bordick	.30	.09
91 Mike Piazza	1.25	.35
92 Robin Ventura	.30	.09
93 Jose Canseco	.75	.23
94 Roger Clemens	1.50	.45
95 Orlando Hernandez	.30	.09
96 Derek Jeter	2.00	.60
97 David Justice	.30	.09
98 Tino Martinez	.50	.15
99 Jorge Posada	.50	.15
100 Bernie Williams	.50	.15
101 Eric Chavez	.30	.09
102 Jason Giambi	.30	.09
103 Ben Grieve	.30	.09
104 Miguel Tejada	.30	.09
105 Bobby Abreu	.30	.09
106 Doug Glanville	.30	.09
107 Travis Lee	.30	.09
108 Mike Lieberthal	.30	.09
109 Scott Rolen	.75	.23
110 Brian Giles	.30	.09
111 Jason Kendall	.30	.09
112 Warren Morris	.30	.09
113 Kevin Young	.30	.09
114 Will Clark	.75	.23
115 J.D. Drew	.30	.09
116 Jim Edmonds	.30	.09
117 Mark McGwire	2.00	.60
118 Edgar Renteria	.30	.09
119 Fernando Tatis	.30	.09
120 Fernando Vina	.30	.09
121 Bret Boone	.30	.09
122 Tony Gwynn	1.00	.30
123 Trevor Hoffman	.30	.09
124 Phil Nevin	.30	.09
125 Eric Owens	.30	.09
126 Barry Bonds	2.00	.60
127 Ellis Burks	.30	.09
128 Jeff Kent	.30	.09
129 J.T. Snow	.30	.09
130 Jay Buhner	.30	.09
131 Mike Cameron	.30	.09
132 Rickey Henderson	.75	.23
133 Edgar Martinez	.50	.15
134 John Olerud	.30	.09
135 Alex Rodriguez	1.25	.35
136 Kazuhiro Sasaki RC	.75	.23
137 Fred McGriff	.50	.15
138 Greg Vaughn	.30	.09
139 Gerald Williams	.30	.09
140 Rusty Greer	.30	.09
141 Gabe Kapler	.30	.09
142 Ricky Ledee	.30	.09
143 Rafael Palmeiro	.50	.15
144 Ivan Rodriguez	.75	.23
145 Tony Batista	.30	.09
146 Jose Cruz Jr.	.30	.09
147 Carlos Delgado	.30	.09
148 Brad Fullmer	.30	.09
149 Shannon Stewart	.30	.09
150 David Wells	.30	.09
151 Juan Alvarez RC / Jeff DaVanon RC	5.00	1.50
152 Seth Etherton / Adam Kennedy	5.00	1.50
153 Ramon Ortiz / Lou Pote	5.00	1.50
154 Derrick Turnbow RC / Eric Weaver	5.00	1.50
155 Rod Barajas / Jason Conti	5.00	1.50
156 Byung-Hyun Kim / Rob Ryan	.30	.09
157 David Cortes RC / George Lombard	5.00	1.50
158 Ivanon Coffie / Melvin Mora	5.00	1.50
159 Ryan Kohlmeier RC / Luis Matos RC	5.00	1.50
160 Willie Morales RC / John Parrish RC	5.00	1.50
161 Chris Richard RC / Jay Spurgeon RC	5.00	1.50
162 Israel Alcantara / Tomokazu Ohka RC	5.00	1.50
163 Paxton Crawford RC / Sang-Hoon Lee RC	5.00	1.50
164 Mike Mahoney RC / Wilton Veras	5.00	1.50
165 Daniel Garibay RC / Ross Gload RC	5.00	1.50
166 Gary Matthews Jr. / Phil Norton	5.00	1.50
167 Roosevelt Brown / Ruben Quevedo	5.00	1.50
168 Lorenzo Barcelo RC / Rocky Biddle RC	5.00	1.50
169 Mark Buehrle / John Garland	10.00	3.00
170 Aaron Myette / Josh Paul	5.00	1.50
171 Kip Wells / Kelly Wunsch	5.00	1.50
172 Rob Bell / Travis Dawkins	5.00	1.50
173 Hector Mercado RC / John Riedling RC	5.00	1.50
174 Russell Branyan / Sean DePaula RC	5.00	1.50
175 Tim Drew / Mark Watson RC	5.00	1.50
176 Craig House RC / Ben Petrick	5.00	1.50
177 Robert Fick / Jose Macias	5.00	1.50
178 Javier Cardona RC / Brandon Villafuerte RC	5.00	1.50
179 Armando Almanza / A.J. Burnett	5.00	1.50
180 Ramon Castro / Pablo Ozuna	5.00	1.50
181 Lance Berkman / Jason Green	5.00	1.50
182 Julio Lugo / Tony McKnight	5.00	1.50
183 Mitch Meluskey / Wade Miller	5.00	1.50
184 Chad Durbin RC / Hector Ortiz RC	5.00	1.50
185 Dermal Brown / Mark Quinn	5.00	1.50
186 Eric Gagne / Mike Judd	10.00	3.00
187 Kane Davis RC / Valerio De Los Santos	5.00	1.50
188 Santiago Perez RC / Paul Rigdon RC	5.00	1.50
189 Matt Kinney / Matt LeCroy	5.00	1.50
190 Jason Maxwell / A.J. Pierzynski	5.00	1.50
191 J.C. Romero RC / Johan Santana RC	50.00	15.00
192 Tony Armas Jr. / Peter Bergeron	5.00	1.50
193 Matt Blank / Milton Bradley	5.00	1.50
194 T.De La Rosa RC / Scott Forster RC	5.00	1.50
195 Yovanny Lara RC / Talmadge Nunnari RC	5.00	1.50
196 Brian Schneider / Andy Tracy RC	5.00	1.50
197 Scott Strickland / T.J. Tucker	5.00	1.50
198 Eric Cammack RC / Jim Mann RC	5.00	1.50
199 Grant Roberts / Jorge Toca	5.00	1.50
200 Alfonso Soriano / Jay Tessmer	8.00	2.40
201 Terrence Long / Mark Mulder	5.00	1.50
202 Pat Burrell / Cliff Politte	5.00	1.50
203 Jimmy Anderson / Bronson Arroyo	8.00	2.40
204 Mike Darr / Kory DeHaan	5.00	1.50
205 Adam Eaton / Wiki Gonzalez	5.00	1.50
206 Brandon Kolb RC / Kevin Walker RC	5.00	1.50
207 Damon Minor / Calvin Murray	5.00	1.50
208 Kevin Hodges RC / Joel Pineiro RC	100.00	30.00
209 Rob Ramsay / Kazuhiro Sasaki	8.00	2.40
210 Rick Ankiel / Mike Matthews	5.00	1.50
211 Steve Cox / Travis Harper	5.00	1.50
212 Kenny Kelly RC / Damian Rolls RC	5.00	1.50
213 Doug Davis / Scott Sheldon	5.00	1.50
214 Brian Sikorski / Pedro Valdes	5.00	1.50
215 Francisco Cordero / B.J. Waszgis RC	5.00	1.50
216 Matt DeWitt RC / Josh Phelps RC	8.00	2.40
217 Vernon Wells / Dewayne Wise	5.00	1.50
218 Geraldo Guzman RC / Jason Marquis	5.00	1.50
219 Rafael Furcal / Steve Sisco RC	5.00	1.50
220 B.J. Ryan / Kevin Beirne	5.00	1.50
221 Matt Ginter RC / Brad Penny	5.00	1.50
222 Julio Zuleta RC / Eric Munson	5.00	1.50
223 Dan Reichert / Jeff Williams RC	5.00	1.50
224 Jason LaRue / Danny Ardoin RC	5.00	1.50
225 Ray King / Mark Redman	5.00	1.50
226 Joe Crede / Mike Bell	5.00	1.50
227 Juan Pierre RC / Jay Payton	8.00	2.40
228 Wayne Franklin RC / Randy Choate RC	5.00	1.50
229 Chris Truby / Adam Piatt	5.00	1.50
230 Kevin Nicholson / Chris Woodward	5.00	1.50
231 Barry Zito RC / Jason Boyd RC	15.00	4.50
232 Brian O'Connor RC / Miguel Del Toro	5.00	1.50
233 Carlos Guillen / Aubrey Huff	5.00	1.50
234 Chad Hermansen / Jason Tyner	5.00	1.50
235 Aaron Fultz RC / Ryan Vogelsong RC	5.00	1.50
236 Shawn Wooten / Vance Wilson	5.00	1.50
237 Danny Klassen / Mike Lamb RC	5.00	1.50
238 Chad Bradford / Gene Stechshulte RC	5.00	1.50
239 Ismael Villegas RC / Hector Ramirez RC / Matt T.Williams RC / Luis Vizcaino	5.00	1.50
240 Mike Garcia RC / Domingo Guzman RC / Justin Brunette RC / Pasqual Coco RC	5.00	1.50
241 Frank Charles RC / Keith McDonald RC	5.00	1.50
242 Carlos Casimiro RC / Morgan Burkhart RC	5.00	1.50
243 Raul Gonzalez RC / Shawn Gilbert	5.00	1.50
244 Darrell Einertson RC / Jeff Sparks RC	5.00	1.50
245 Augie Ojeda RC / Brady Clark / Todd Belitz / Eric Byrnes RC	8.00	2.40
246 Leo Estrella RC / Charlie Greene	5.00	1.50
247 Trace Coquillette RC / Pedro Feliz RC	8.00	2.40
248 Tike Redman RC / David Newhan	8.00	2.40
249 Rodrigo Lopez RC / John Bale RC	8.00	2.40
250 Corey Patterson / Jose Ortiz RC	5.00	1.50
251 Britt Reames RC / Oswaldo Mairena RC	5.00	1.50
252 Xavier Nady RC / Timo Perez RC	8.00	2.40
253 Tom Jacquez RC / Vicente Padilla RC	5.00	1.50
254 Elvis Pena RC / Adam Melhuse RC	5.00	1.50
255 Ben Weber RC / Alex Cabrera RC	5.00	1.50

2000 Pacific Omega Copper

Randomly inserted into hobby packs at one in 73, this 150-card set is a partial parallel of the Omega base set. These cards were produced with copper foil stamping, and each card is individually serial numbered to 45.

	Nm-Mt	Ex-Mt
*STARS: 15X TO 30X BASIC CARDS		
*ROOKIES: 15X TO 40X BASIC		

2000 Pacific Omega Gold

Randomly inserted into retail packs at one in 37, this 150-card set is a partial parallel of the Omega base set. These cards were produced with gold foil stamping, and each card is individually serial numbered to 77.

	Nm-Mt	Ex-Mt
*STARS 1-150: 8X TO 20X BASIC		
*ROOKIES 1-150: 10X TO 25X BASIC		

2000 Pacific Omega Platinum Blue

Randomly inserted into packs at one in 145, this 150-card set is a partial parallel of the Omega base set. These cards were produced with platinum blue foil stamping, and each card is individually serial numbered to 55.

	Nm-Mt	Ex-Mt
*STARS 1-150: 15X TO 30X BASIC		
*ROOKIES 1-150: 15X TO 40X BASIC		

2000 Pacific Omega Premiere Date

Randomly inserted into hobby packs at one in 37, this 150-card set is a partial parallel of the Omega base set. These cards were produced with a premiere date stamp, and each card is individually serial numbered to 77.

	Nm-Mt	Ex-Mt
*STARS 1-150: 15X TO 30X BASIC CARDS		
*ROOKIES 1-150: 12.5X TO 30X BASIC		

2000 Pacific Omega AL/NL Contenders

Randomly inserted into packs at 2:37, this 36 card set features superstar caliber players that are on contending teams. Please note that this set is broken into 18 AL contenders, and 18 NL contenders. We have labeled them AL and NL below to help differentiate.

	Nm-Mt	Ex-Mt
COMPLETE AL SET (18)	60.00	18.00
COMPLETE NL SET (18)	60.00	18.00
AL1 Darin Erstad	2.00	.60

Card	Nm-Mt	Ex-Mt
AL2 Troy Glaus	2.00	.60
AL3 Mo Vaughn	2.00	.60
AL4 Albert Belle	2.00	.60
AL5 Cal Ripken	15.00	4.50
AL6 Nomar Garciaparra	8.00	2.40
AL7 Pedro Martinez	5.00	1.50
AL8 Frank Thomas	5.00	1.50
AL9 Manny Ramirez	3.00	.90
AL10 Jim Thome	5.00	1.50
AL11 Juan Gonzalez	3.00	.90
AL12 Roger Clemens	10.00	3.00
AL13 Derek Jeter	12.00	3.60
AL14 Bernie Williams	3.00	.90
AL15 Jason Giambi	2.00	.60
AL16 Alex Rodriguez	8.00	2.40
AL17 Edgar Martinez	3.00	.90
AL18 Carlos Delgado	2.00	.60
NL1 Randy Johnson	5.00	1.50
NL2 Chipper Jones	5.00	1.50
NL3 Greg Maddux	8.00	2.40
NL4 Sammy Sosa	8.00	2.40
NL5 Sean Casey	2.00	.60
NL6 Ken Griffey Jr.	8.00	2.40
NL7 Todd Helton	3.00	.90
NL8 Jeff Bagwell	3.00	.90
NL9 Shawn Green	2.00	.60
NL10 Gary Sheffield	2.00	.60
NL11 Vladimir Guerrero	5.00	1.50
NL12 Mike Piazza	8.00	2.40
NL13 Scott Rolen	5.00	1.50
NL14 Rick Ankiel	2.50	.75
NL15 J.D. Drew	2.00	.60
NL16 Jim Edmonds	2.00	.60
NL17 Mark McGwire	12.00	3.60
NL18 Barry Bonds	12.00	3.60

2000 Pacific Omega EO Portraits

Randomly inserted into packs at one in 73, this 20-card insert features a special die-cut photo of the corresponding player's face.

Card	Nm-Mt	Ex-Mt
COMPLETE SET (20)	200.00	60.00
ONE OF ONE PARALLEL RANDOM IN PACKS		
ONE OF ONE PRINT RUN 1 SERIAL #'d SET		
NO ONE OF ONE PRICING AVAILABLE		
1 Chipper Jones	12.00	3.60
2 Greg Maddux	20.00	6.00
3 Cal Ripken	40.00	12.00
4 Pedro Martinez	12.00	3.60
5 Nomar Garciaparra	20.00	6.00
6 Sammy Sosa	20.00	6.00
7 Frank Thomas	12.00	3.60
8 Ken Griffey Jr.	20.00	6.00
9 Gary Sheffield	5.00	1.50
10 Vladimir Guerrero	12.00	3.60
11 Mike Piazza	20.00	6.00
12 Roger Clemens	25.00	7.50
13 Derek Jeter	30.00	9.00
14 Pat Burrell	6.00	1.80
15 Rick Ankiel	6.00	1.80
16 Mark McGwire	30.00	9.00
17 Tony Gwynn	15.00	4.50
18 Barry Bonds	30.00	9.00
19 Alex Rodriguez	20.00	6.00
20 Ivan Rodriguez	12.00	3.60

2000 Pacific Omega Full Count

Randomly inserted into hobby packs at 4:37, this 36-card insert features the Major League's RBI, Slugging Percent, Strikeout, and Home Run leaders. Please note that a serial-numbered parallel exists of this insert.

Card	Nm-Mt	Ex-Mt
COMPLETE SET (36)	80.00	24.00
1 Magglio Ordonez	1.25	.35
2 Manny Ramirez	2.00	.60
4 David Justice	1.25	.35
5 Bernie Williams	2.00	.60
6 Jason Giambi	1.25	.35
7 Scott Rolen	3.00	.90
8 Jeff Kent	1.25	.35
9 Edgar Martinez	2.00	.60
10 Randy Johnson	3.00	.90
11 Greg Maddux	5.00	1.50
12 Mike Mussina	2.00	.60
13 Pedro Martinez	3.00	.90
14 Chuck Finley	1.25	.35
15 Kevin Brown	1.25	.35
16 Roger Clemens	6.00	1.80
17 Tim Hudson	3.00	.90
18 Rick Ankiel	1.50	.45
19 Troy Glaus	1.25	.35
20 Chipper Jones	3.00	.90
21 Nomar Garciaparra	5.00	1.50
22 Jeff Bagwell	2.00	.60
23 Shawn Green	1.25	.35
24 Vladimir Guerrero	3.00	.90
25 Mike Piazza	5.00	1.50
26 Jim Edmonds	1.25	.35
27 Rafael Palmeiro	2.00	.60
28 Cal Ripken	10.00	3.00
29 Sammy Sosa	5.00	1.50
30 Frank Thomas	3.00	.90
31 Ken Griffey Jr.	5.00	1.50
32 Gary Sheffield	1.25	.35
33 Barry Bonds	8.00	2.40
34 Alex Rodriguez	5.00	1.50
35 Mark McGwire	8.00	2.40
36 Carlos Delgado	1.25	.35

2000 Pacific Omega MLB Generations

Randomly inserted into packs at one in 145, this 20-card insert features dual-player cards that picture a modern day superstar with a top prospect.

Card	Nm-Mt	Ex-Mt
COMPLETE SET (20)	250.00	75.00
1 Mark McGwire	40.00	12.00
Pat Burrell		
2 Cal Ripken	50.00	15.00
Alex Rodriguez		
3 Randy Johnson	15.00	4.50
Rick Ankiel		
4 Tony Gwynn	20.00	6.00
Darin Erstad		
5 Barry Bonds	40.00	12.00
Magglio Ordonez		
6 Frank Thomas	15.00	4.50
Jason Giambi		
7 Roger Clemens	30.00	9.00
Kerry Wood		
8 Mike Piazza	25.00	7.50
Mitch Meluskey		
9 Ken Griffey Jr.	25.00	7.50
Andruw Jones		
10 Bernie Williams	10.00	3.00
J.D. Drew		
11 Chipper Jones	15.00	4.50
Troy Glaus		
12 Andres Galarraga	10.00	3.00
Todd Helton		
13 Juan Gonzalez	15.00	4.50
Vladimir Guerrero		
14 Craig Biggio	10.00	3.00
Rafael Furcal		
15 Sammy Sosa	25.00	7.50
Jermaine Dye		
16 Larry Walker	10.00	3.00
Richard Hidalgo		
17 Greg Maddux	25.00	7.50
Adam Eaton		
18 Barry Larkin	40.00	12.00
Derek Jeter		
19 Roberto Alomar	10.00	3.00
Jose Vidro		
20 Jeff Kent	6.00	1.80
Edgardo Alfonzo		

2000 Pacific Omega Signatures

Randomly inserted into packs, this nine-card insert features autographed cards from players like Nomar Garciaparra and Frank Thomas.

Card	Nm-Mt	Ex-Mt
1 Darin Erstad	25.00	7.50
2 Nomar Garciaparra	150.00	45.00
4 Magglio Ordonez	25.00	7.50
5 Frank Thomas	60.00	18.00
6 Brady Clark	15.00	4.50
7 Richard Hidalgo	15.00	4.50
8 Gary Sheffield	40.00	12.00
9 Pat Burrell	25.00	7.50
10 Jim Edmonds	40.00	12.00

2000 Pacific Omega Stellar Performers

Randomly inserted into packs at one in 37, this 20-card insert features superstar caliber players.

Card	Nm-Mt	Ex-Mt
COMPLETE SET (20)	120.00	36.00
1 Darin Erstad	2.50	.75
2 Chipper Jones	6.00	1.80
3 Greg Maddux	10.00	3.00
4 Cal Ripken	20.00	6.00
5 Pedro Martinez	6.00	1.80
6 Nomar Garciaparra	10.00	3.00
7 Sammy Sosa	10.00	3.00
8 Frank Thomas	6.00	1.80
9 Ken Griffey Jr.	10.00	3.00
10 Todd Helton	4.00	1.20
11 Jeff Bagwell	4.00	1.20
12 Vladimir Guerrero	6.00	1.80
13 Mike Piazza	10.00	3.00
14 Derek Jeter	15.00	4.50
15 Roger Clemens	12.00	3.60
16 Tony Gwynn	8.00	2.40
17 Barry Bonds	15.00	4.50
18 Alex Rodriguez	10.00	3.00
19 Mark McGwire	15.00	4.50
20 Ivan Rodriguez	6.00	1.80

1999 Pacific Private Stock

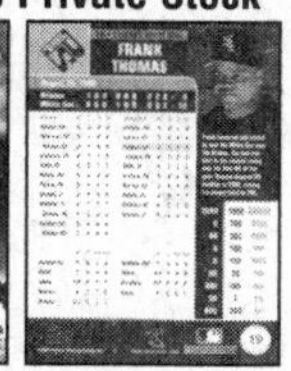

This 150-card set was distributed in six card packs with a suggested retail price of $4.49. The fronts feature color action player photos printed on super-thick 30 pt. card stock in holographic silver foil. The backs display selected box scores from the 1998 season.

Card	Nm-Mt	Ex-Mt
COMPLETE SET (150)	80.00	24.00
1 Jeff Bagwell	.75	.23
2 Roger Clemens	2.50	.75
3 J.D. Drew	.50	.15
4 Nomar Garciaparra	2.00	.60
5 Juan Gonzalez	.75	.23
6 Ken Griffey Jr.	2.00	.60
7 Tony Gwynn	1.50	.45
8 Derek Jeter	3.00	.90
9 Chipper Jones	1.25	.35
10 Travis Lee	.30	.09
11 Greg Maddux	2.00	.60
12 Mark McGwire	3.00	.90
13 Mike Piazza	2.00	.60
14 Manny Ramirez	.75	.23
15 Cal Ripken	4.00	1.20
16 Alex Rodriguez	2.00	.60
17 Ivan Rodriguez	1.25	.35
18 Sammy Sosa	2.00	.60
19 Frank Thomas	1.25	.35
20 Kerry Wood	1.25	.35
21 Roberto Alomar	.75	.23
22 Moises Alou	.50	.15
23 Albert Belle	.50	.15
24 Craig Biggio	.75	.23
25 Wade Boggs	.75	.23
26 Barry Bonds	3.00	.90
27 Jose Canseco	1.25	.35
28 Jim Edmonds	.50	.15
29 Darin Erstad	.50	.15
30 Andres Galarraga	.50	.15
31 Tom Glavine	.75	.23
32 Ben Grieve	.30	.09
33 Vladimir Guerrero	1.25	.35
34 Wilton Guerrero	.30	.09
35 Todd Helton	.75	.23
36 Andruw Jones	.50	.15
37 Ryan Klesko	.50	.15
38 Kenny Lofton	.50	.15
39 Javy Lopez	.50	.15
40 Pedro Martinez	1.25	.35
41 Paul Molitor	.75	.23
42 Raul Mondesi	.50	.15
43 Rafael Palmeiro	.75	.23
44 Tim Salmon	.75	.23
45 Jim Thome	1.25	.35
46 Mo Vaughn	.50	.15
47 Larry Walker	.75	.23
48 David Wells	.50	.15
49 Bernie Williams	.75	.23
50 Jaret Wright	.30	.09
51 Bob Abreu	.50	.15
52 Garret Anderson	.50	.15
53 Rolando Arrojo	.30	.09
54 Tony Batista	.50	.15
55 Rod Beck	.30	.09
56 Derek Bell	.30	.09
57 Marvin Benard	.30	.09
58 Dave Berg	.30	.09
59 Dante Bichette	.50	.15
60 Aaron Boone	.50	.15
61 Bret Boone	.50	.15
62 Scott Brosius	.50	.15
63 Brant Brown	.30	.09
64 Kevin Brown	.75	.23
65 Jeromy Burnitz	.50	.15
66 Ken Caminiti	.50	.15
67 Mike Caruso	.30	.09
68 Sean Casey	.50	.15
69 Vinny Castilla	.50	.15
70 Eric Chavez	.50	.15
71 Ryan Christenson	.30	.09
72 Jeff Cirillo	.30	.09
73 Tony Clark	.30	.09
74 Will Clark	1.25	.35
75 Edgard Clemente	.30	.09
76 David Cone	.50	.15
77 Marty Cordova	.30	.09
78 Jose Cruz Jr.	.30	.09
79 Eric Davis	.50	.15
80 Carlos Delgado	.50	.15
81 David Dellucci	.30	.09
82 Delino DeShields	.30	.09
83 Gary DiSarcina	.30	.09
84 Damion Easley	.30	.09
85 Dennis Eckersley	.50	.15
86 Cliff Floyd	.50	.15
87 Jason Giambi	.50	.15
88 Doug Glanville	.30	.09
89 Alex Gonzalez	.30	.09
90 Mark Grace	.75	.23
91 Rusty Greer	.50	.15
92 Jose Guillen	.50	.15
93 Carlos Guillen	.50	.15
94 Jeffrey Hammonds	.50	.15
95 Rick Helling	.30	.09
96 Bob Henley	.30	.09
97 Livan Hernandez	.30	.09
98 Orlando Hernandez	.30	.09
99 Bob Higginson	.50	.15
100 Trevor Hoffman	.50	.15
101 Randy Johnson	1.25	.35
102 Brian Jordan	.50	.15
103 Wally Joyner	.50	.15
104 Eric Karros	.50	.15
105 Jason Kendall	.50	.15
106 Jeff Kent	.50	.15
107 Jeff King	.30	.09
108 Mark Kotsay	.30	.09
109 Ray Lankford	.30	.09
110 Barry Larkin	.75	.23
111 Mark Loretta	.50	.15
112 Edgar Martinez	.75	.23
113 Tino Martinez	.75	.23
114 Quinton McCracken	.30	.09
115 Fred McGriff	.75	.23
116 Ryan Minor	.30	.09
117 Hal Morris	.30	.09
118 Bill Mueller	.50	.15
119 Mike Mussina	.75	.23
120 Dave Nilsson	.30	.09
121 Otis Nixon	.30	.09
122 Hideo Nomo	1.25	.35
123 Paul O'Neill	.75	.23
124 Jose Offerman	.30	.09
125 John Olerud	.50	.15
126 Rey Ordonez	.30	.09
127 David Ortiz	.75	.23
128 Dean Palmer	.50	.15
129 Chan Ho Park	.50	.15
130 Aramis Ramirez	.50	.15
131 Edgar Renteria	.50	.15
132 Armando Rios	.30	.09
133 Henry Rodriguez	.30	.09
134 Scott Rolen	1.25	.35
135 Curt Schilling	.50	.15
136 David Segui	.30	.09
137 Richie Sexson	.50	.15
138 Gary Sheffield	.50	.15
139 John Smoltz	.75	.23
140 Matt Stairs	.30	.09
141 Justin Thompson	.30	.09
142 Greg Vaughn	.30	.09
143 Omar Vizquel	.75	.23
144 Tim Wakefield	.50	.15
145 Todd Walker	.30	.09
146 Devon White	.50	.15
147 Rondell White	.50	.15
148 Matt Williams	.50	.15
149 Enrique Wilson	.30	.09
150 Kevin Young	.50	.15

1999 Pacific Private Stock Exclusive

Randomly inserted in hobby packs, this 20-card set features action color photos of top players with an alternate photo of the player on the front and back and a special foil logo. The first 20 players in the regular set are featured in this set. Only 299 sets were produced and serially numbered.

Card	Nm-Mt	Ex-Mt
COMPLETE SET (20)	500.00	150.00
*STARS: 3X TO 8X BASIC CARDS		

1999 Pacific Private Stock Platinum

Randomly inserted in packs, this 50-card set features action color photos of the first 50 players in the same design as the base set only with alternate foil color and a special foil logo. Only 199 sets were produced and serially numbered.

Nm-Mt Ex-Mt

*STARS: 5X TO 12X BASIC CARDS

1999 Pacific Private Stock Preferred

Randomly inserted in packs, this 20-card set features action color photos of the first 20 players with alternate team logo and background and a special foil logo. Only 399 sets were produced and serially numbered.

Card	Nm-Mt	Ex-Mt
COMPLETE SET (20)	400.00	120.00
*STARS: 2.5X TO 6X BASIC CARDS		

1999 Pacific Private Stock Vintage

Randomly inserted in packs, this 50-card set features action color photos of the first 50 players in the same design as the base set only with a special foil logo. Only 99 sets were produced and serially numbered.

Nm-Mt Ex-Mt

*STARS: 8X TO 20X BASIC CARDS

1999 Pacific Private Stock PS-206

Inserted one per pack, this 150-card set is a smaller parallel version of the base set. The cards measure approximately 1 1/2" by 2 5/8" and feature blue ink backs.

Nm-Mt Ex-Mt

*SINGLES: .75X TO 2X BASIC PRI. STOCK

1999 Pacific Private Stock PS-206 Red

Randomly inserted one in 25 hobby only packs and one in 33 retail packs, this 150-card set is a smaller parallel version of the base set and features red ink backs. The cards measure approximately 1 1/2" by 2. 5/8".

Nm-Mt Ex-Mt

*PS-206 RED: 5X TO 12X BASIC PRI.STOCK

1999 Pacific Private Stock Home Run History

Randomly inserted in hobby packs at the rate of 2:25 and in retail packs at 1:17, this 22-card set features action color photos commemorating the spectacular feats of Mark McGwire and Sammy Sosa with holographic silver foil highlights.

Card	Nm-Mt	Ex-Mt
COMMON MCGWIRE	6.00	1.80
COMMON SOSA	4.00	1.20
1 Mark McGwire 61	6.00	1.80
3 Mark McGwire 62	10.00	3.00
15 Mark McGwire 70	15.00	4.50
16 Sammy Sosa 66	12.00	3.60
17 Mark McGwire	10.00	3.00
w/J.D. Drew		
18 Sammy Sosa	4.00	1.20
A Season of Celebration		
19 Sammy Sosa	8.00	2.40
Mark McGwire		
Awesome Power		
20 Mark McGwire	8.00	2.40
Sammy Sosa		
Transcending Sports		
21 Mark McGwire	15.00	4.50
Crown Die Cut		
22 Cal Ripken	20.00	6.00
Crown Die Cut		

2000 Pacific Private Stock

This 150 card set was issued in seven card packs with 24 packs in a box. The SRP on these packs are $4.49 and the set includes 25 short printed cards (notated in our checklist with SP) of 2000 Rookies. The set is sequenced in alphabetical order in team order which is also alphabetical.

Card	Nm-Mt	Ex-Mt
COMPLETE SET (150)	100.00	30.00
COMP.SET w/o SP's (125)	40.00	12.00
COMMON CARD (1-150)	.50	.15
COMMON SP PROSPECT	5.00	1.50
1 Darin Erstad	.50	.15
2 Troy Glaus	.50	.15
3 Tim Salmon	.75	.23
4 Mo Vaughn	.50	.15
5 Jay Bell	.50	.15
6 Luis Gonzalez	.50	.15
7 Randy Johnson	1.25	.35
8 Matt Williams	.50	.15
9 Andruw Jones	.50	.15
10 Chipper Jones	1.25	.35
11 Brian Jordan	.50	.15
12 Greg Maddux	2.00	.60
13 Kevin Millwood	.50	.15
14 Albert Belle	.50	.15
15 Mike Mussina	.75	.23
16 Cal Ripken	4.00	1.20
17 B.J. Surhoff	.50	.15
18 Nomar Garciaparra	2.00	.60
19 Butch Huskey	.50	.15
20 Pedro Martinez	1.25	.35
21 Troy O'Leary	.50	.15
22 Mark Grace	.75	.23
23 Bo Porter SP	5.00	1.50
24 Henry Rodriguez	.50	.15
25 Sammy Sosa	2.00	.60
26 Kerry Wood	1.25	.35
27 Jason Dellaero SP	5.00	1.50
28 Ray Durham	.50	.15
29 Paul Konerko	.50	.15
30 Carlos Lee	.50	.15
31 Magglio Ordonez	.50	.15
32 Frank Thomas	1.25	.35
33 Mike Cameron	.50	.15
34 Sean Casey	.50	.15
35 Barry Larkin	.75	.23
36 Greg Vaughn	.50	.15
37 Roberto Alomar	.75	.23
38 Russell Branyan SP	5.00	1.50
39 Kenny Lofton	.50	.15
40 Manny Ramirez	.75	.23
41 Richie Sexson	.50	.15
42 Jim Thome	1.25	.35
43 Omar Vizquel	.75	.23
44 Pedro Astacio	.50	.15
45 Vinny Castilla	.50	.15
46 Todd Helton	.75	.23
47 Ben Petrick SP	5.00	1.50
48 Juan Sosa SP RC	5.00	1.50

49 Larry Walker .75 .23
50 Tony Clark .50 .15
51 Damion Easley .50 .15
52 Juan Encarnacion .50 .15
53 Robert Fick SP 5.00 1.50
54 Dean Palmer .50 .15
55 A.J. Burnett SP 5.00 1.50
56 Luis Castillo .50 .15
57 Alex Gonzalez .50 .15
58 Julio Ramirez SP 5.00 1.50
59 Preston Wilson .50 .15
60 Jeff Bagwell .75 .23
61 Craig Biggio .75 .23
62 Ken Caminiti .50 .15
63 Carl Everett .50 .15
64 Mike Hampton .50 .15
65 Billy Wagner .50 .15
66 Carlos Beltran .75 .23
67 Dermal Brown SP 5.00 1.50
68 Jermaine Dye .50 .15
69 Carlos Febles .50 .15
70 Mark Quinn SP 5.00 1.50
71 Mike Sweeney .50 .15
72 Kevin Brown .75 .23
73 Eric Gagne SP 12.00 3.60
74 Eric Karros .50 .15
75 Raul Mondesi .50 .15
76 Gary Sheffield .50 .15
77 Jeromy Burnitz .50 .15
78 Jeff Cirillo .50 .15
79 Geoff Jenkins .50 .15
80 David Nilsson .50 .15
81 Ron Coomer .50 .15
82 Jacque Jones .50 .15
83 Corey Koskie .50 .15
84 Brad Radke .50 .15
85 Tony Armas Jr. SP 5.00 1.50
86 Peter Bergeron SP 5.00 1.50
87 Vladimir Guerrero 1.25 .35
88 Jose Vidro .50 .15
89 Rondell White .50 .15
90 Edgardo Alfonzo .50 .15
91 Roger Cedeno .50 .15
92 Rickey Henderson 1.25 .35
93 Jay Payton SP 5.00 1.50
94 Mike Piazza 2.00 .60
95 Jorge Toca SP 5.00 1.50
96 Robin Ventura .75 .23
97 Roger Clemens 2.50 .75
98 David Cone .50 .15
99 Derek Jeter 3.00 .90
100 D'Angelo Jimenez SP 5.00 1.50
101 Tino Martinez .75 .23
102 Alfonso Soriano SP 8.00 2.40
103 Bernie Williams .75 .23
104 Jason Giambi .50 .15
105 Ben Grieve .50 .15
106 Tim Hudson .50 .15
107 Matt Stairs .50 .15
108 Bob Abreu .50 .15
109 Doug Glanville .50 .15
110 Scott Rolen 1.25 .35
111 Curt Schilling .50 .15
112 Brian Giles .50 .15
113 Chad Hermansen SP 5.00 1.50
114 Jason Kendall .50 .15
115 Warren Morris .50 .15
116 Rick Ankiel SP 5.00 1.50
117 J.D. Drew .50 .15
118 Adam Kennedy SP 5.00 1.50
119 Ray Lankford .50 .15
120 Mark McGwire 3.00 .90
121 Fernando Tatis .50 .15
122 Mike Darr SP 5.00 1.50
123 Ben Davis .50 .15
124 Tony Gwynn 1.50 .45
125 Trevor Hoffman .50 .15
126 Reggie Sanders .50 .15
127 Barry Bonds 3.00 .90
128 Ellis Burks .50 .15
129 Jeff Kent .50 .15
130 J.T. Snow .50 .15
131 Freddy Garcia .50 .15
132 Ken Griffey Jr. 2.00 .60
133 Carlos Guillen SP 5.00 1.50
134 Edgar Martinez .75 .23
135 Alex Rodriguez 2.00 .60
136 Miguel Cairo .50 .15
137 Jose Canseco 1.25 .35
138 Steve Cox SP 5.00 1.50
139 Roberto Hernandez .50 .15
140 Fred McGriff .75 .23
141 Juan Gonzalez .75 .23
142 Rusty Greer .50 .15
143 Ruben Mateo SP 5.00 1.50
144 Rafael Palmeiro .75 .23
145 Ivan Rodriguez 1.25 .35
146 Carlos Delgado .50 .15
147 Tony Fernandez .50 .15
148 Shawn Green .50 .15
149 Shannon Stewart .50 .15
150 Vernon Wells SP 5.00 1.50

2000 Pacific Private Stock Gold Portraits

Randomly inserted in hobby packs, this parallel set to the regular Pacific Private Stock set is framed in gold foil. These cards are serial numbered to 99.

Nm-Mt Ex-Mt
*STARS: 6X TO 15X BASIC CARDS....
*PROSPECTS: .5X TO 1.2X BASIC CARDS

2000 Pacific Private Stock Premiere Date

Inserted one per hobby box, this parallel set is serial numbered to 34. Each card carries a small Premiere Date foil logo on front with the serial numbering.

Nm-Mt Ex-Mt
*STARS: 10X TO 25X BASIC CARDS..
*PROSPECTS: .75X TO 2X BASIC CARDS

2000 Pacific Private Stock Silver Portraits

Randomly inserted into retail packs, this set parallels the regular Private Stock set. The cards have silver foil framing and are serial numbered to 199.

Nm-Mt Ex-Mt
*STARS: 4X TO 10X BASIC CARDS....
*PROSPECTS: .3X TO .8X BASIC CARDS

2000 Pacific Private Stock Artist's Canvas

Inserted one every 49 packs, these 20 cards featuring leading baseball stars are printed on real artist's canvas.

Nm-Mt Ex-Mt
PROOFS RANDOM INSERTS IN PACKS
PROOFS PRINT RUN 1 SERIAL #'d SET
PROOFS NOT PRICED DUE TO SCARCITY
1 Chipper Jones 10.00 3.00
2 Greg Maddux 15.00 4.50
3 Cal Ripken 30.00 9.00
4 Nomar Garciaparra 15.00 4.50
5 Sammy Sosa 15.00 4.50
6 Frank Thomas 10.00 3.00
7 Manny Ramirez 6.00 1.80
8 Larry Walker 6.00 1.80
9 Jeff Bagwell 6.00 1.80
10 Vladimir Guerrero 10.00 3.00
11 Mike Piazza 15.00 4.50
12 Roger Clemens 20.00 6.00
13 Derek Jeter 25.00 7.50
14 Mark McGwire 25.00 7.50
15 Tony Gwynn 12.00 3.60
16 Barry Bonds 25.00 7.50
17 Ken Griffey Jr. 15.00 4.50
18 Alex Rodriguez 15.00 4.50
19 Juan Gonzalez 6.00 1.80
20 Ivan Rodriguez 10.00 3.00

2000 Pacific Private Stock Extreme Action

Inserted two every 25 packs, this 20 card set features excellent photos of many of baseball top stars.

Nm-Mt Ex-Mt
COMPLETE SET (20) 80.00 24.00
1 Andruw Jones 2.00 .60
2 Chipper Jones 5.00 1.50
3 Cal Ripken 15.00 4.50
4 Nomar Garciaparra 8.00 2.40
5 Sammy Sosa 8.00 2.40
6 Frank Thomas 5.00 1.50
7 Roberto Alomar 3.00 .90
8 Manny Ramirez 3.00 .90
9 Larry Walker 3.00 .90
10 Jeff Bagwell 3.00 .90
11 Vladimir Guerrero 5.00 1.50
12 Mike Piazza 8.00 2.40
13 Derek Jeter 12.00 3.60
14 Bernie Williams 3.00 .90
15 Scott Rolen 5.00 1.50
16 Mark McGwire 12.00 3.60
17 Tony Gwynn 6.00 1.80
18 Ken Griffey Jr. 8.00 2.40
19 Alex Rodriguez 8.00 2.40
20 Ivan Rodriguez 5.00 1.50

2000 Pacific Private Stock Reserve

Issued one every 25 hobby packs, these 20 cards feature players on an unusual paper stock with a special foil seal on the front.

Nm-Mt Ex-Mt
COMPLETE SET (20) 150.00 45.00
1 Chipper Jones 8.00 2.40
2 Greg Maddux 12.00 3.60
3 Cal Ripken 25.00 7.50
4 Nomar Garciaparra 12.00 3.60
5 Sammy Sosa 12.00 3.60
6 Frank Thomas 8.00 2.40
7 Manny Ramirez 5.00 1.50
8 Larry Walker 5.00 1.50
9 Jeff Bagwell 5.00 1.50
10 Vladimir Guerrero 8.00 2.40
11 Mike Piazza 12.00 3.60
12 Roger Clemens 15.00 4.50
13 Derek Jeter 20.00 6.00
14 Mark McGwire 20.00 6.00
15 Tony Gwynn 10.00 3.00
16 Barry Bonds 20.00 6.00
17 Ken Griffey Jr. 12.00 3.60
18 Alex Rodriguez 12.00 3.60
19 Ivan Rodriguez 8.00 2.40
20 Shawn Green 3.00 .90

2000 Pacific Private Stock PS-2000 Action

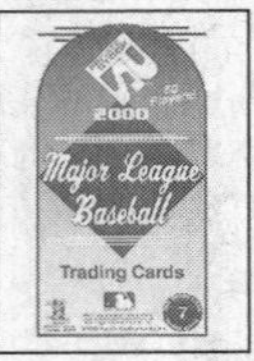

Issued two per pack, these cards features 60 of the best players from the Private Stock set. These cards are printed in a smaller size than the regular cards and features high action photos of these players.

Nm-Mt Ex-Mt
COMPLETE SET (60) 40.00 12.00
1 Mo Vaughn .40 .12
2 Greg Maddux 1.50 .45
3 Andruw Jones .40 .12
4 Chipper Jones 1.00 .30
5 Cal Ripken 3.00 .90
6 Nomar Garciaparra 1.50 .45
7 Pedro Martinez 1.00 .30
8 Sammy Sosa 1.50 .45
9 Jason Dellaero .40 .12
10 Magglio Ordonez .40 .12
11 Frank Thomas 1.00 .30
12 Sean Casey .40 .12
13 Russell Branyan .40 .12
14 Manny Ramirez .60 .18
15 Richie Sexson .40 .12
16 Ben Petrick .40 .12
17 Juan Sosa .40 .12
18 Larry Walker .60 .18
19 Robert Fick .40 .12
20 Craig Biggio .60 .18
21 Jeff Bagwell .60 .18
22 Carlos Beltran .60 .18
23 Dermal Brown 4.00 1.20
24 Mark Quinn 4.00 1.20
25 Eric Gagne 10.00 3.00
26 Jeromy Burnitz .40 .12
27 Tony Armas Jr. 4.00 1.20
28 Peter Bergeron 4.00 1.20
29 Vladimir Guerrero 1.00 .30
30 Edgardo Alfonzo .40 .12
31 Mike Piazza 1.50 .45
32 Jorge Toca 4.00 1.20
33 Roger Clemens 2.00 .60
34 Alfonso Soriano 6.00 1.80
35 Bernie Williams .60 .18
36 Derek Jeter 2.50 .75
37 Tim Hudson .40 .12
38 Bob Abreu .40 .12
39 Scott Rolen 1.00 .30
40 Brian Giles .40 .12
41 Chad Hermansen 4.00 1.20
42 Warren Morris .40 .12
43 Rick Ankiel 4.00 1.20
44 J.D. Drew .40 .12
45 Adam Kennedy 4.00 1.20
46 Mark McGwire 2.50 .75
47 Mike Darr 4.00 1.20
48 Tony Gwynn 1.25 .35
49 Barry Bonds 2.50 .75
50 Ken Griffey Jr. 1.50 .45
51 Carlos Guillen 4.00 1.20
52 Alex Rodriguez 1.50 .45
53 Juan Gonzalez .60 .18
54 Ruben Mateo 4.00 1.20
55 Ivan Rodriguez 1.00 .30
56 Rafael Palmeiro .60 .18
57 Jose Canseco 1.00 .30
58 Steve Cox 4.00 1.20
59 Shawn Green .40 .12
60 Vernon Wells 4.00 1.20

2000 Pacific Private Stock PS-2000 New Wave

Randomly inserted in packs, this set features 20 of baseball's youngest stars and are serial numbered to 199.

Nm-Mt Ex-Mt
COMPLETE SET (20) 120.00 36.00
1 Andruw Jones 5.00 1.50
2 Chipper Jones 12.00 3.60
3 Nomar Garciaparra 20.00 6.00
4 Magglio Ordonez 5.00 1.50
5 Sean Casey 5.00 1.50
6 Manny Ramirez 8.00 2.40
7 Richie Sexson 5.00 1.50
8 Carlos Beltran 8.00 2.40
9 Jeromy Burnitz 5.00 1.50
10 Vladimir Guerrero 12.00 3.60
11 Edgardo Alfonzo 5.00 1.50
12 Derek Jeter 30.00 9.00
13 Tim Hudson 5.00 1.50
14 Bob Abreu 5.00 1.50
15 Scott Rolen 12.00 3.60
16 Brian Giles 5.00 1.50
17 Warren Morris 5.00 1.50
18 J.D. Drew 5.00 1.50
19 Alex Rodriguez 20.00 6.00
20 Shawn Green 5.00 1.50

2000 Pacific Private Stock PS-2000 Rookies

Randomly inserted into packs, these 20 cards feature players assumed to be among the best rookies of 2000 and are serial numbered to 99.

Nm-Mt Ex-Mt
COMPLETE SET (20) 100.00 30.00
1 Jason Dellaero 8.00 2.40
2 Russell Branyan 8.00 2.40
3 Ben Petrick 8.00 2.40
4 Juan Sosa 8.00 2.40
5 Robert Fick 8.00 2.40
6 Dermal Brown 8.00 2.40
7 Mark Quinn 8.00 2.40
8 Eric Gagne 15.00 4.50
9 Tony Armas Jr. 8.00 2.40
10 Peter Bergeron 8.00 2.40
11 Jorge Toca 8.00 2.40
12 Alfonso Soriano 10.00 3.00
13 Chad Hermansen 8.00 2.40
14 Rick Ankiel 8.00 2.40
15 Adam Kennedy 8.00 2.40
16 Mike Darr 8.00 2.40
17 Carlos Guillen 8.00 2.40
18 Steve Cox 8.00 2.40
19 Ruben Mateo 8.00 2.40
20 Vernon Wells 8.00 2.40

2000 Pacific Private Stock PS-2000 Stars

Randomly inserted into Private Stock packs, these cards feature classic portrait photos of 20 superstars. This set is sequentially numbered to 299.

Nm-Mt Ex-Mt
COMPLETE SET (20) 150.00 45.00
1 Mo Vaughn 4.00 1.20
2 Greg Maddux 15.00 4.50
3 Cal Ripken 30.00 9.00
4 Pedro Martinez 10.00 3.00
5 Sammy Sosa 15.00 4.50
6 Frank Thomas 10.00 3.00
7 Larry Walker 6.00 1.80
8 Craig Biggio 6.00 1.80
9 Jeff Bagwell 6.00 1.80
10 Mike Piazza 15.00 4.50
11 Roger Clemens 20.00 6.00
12 Bernie Williams 6.00 1.80
13 Mark McGwire 25.00 7.50
14 Tony Gwynn 12.00 3.60
15 Barry Bonds 25.00 7.50
16 Ken Griffey Jr. 15.00 4.50
17 Juan Gonzalez 6.00 1.80
18 Ivan Rodriguez 10.00 3.00
19 Rafael Palmeiro 6.00 1.80
20 Jose Canseco 10.00 3.00

2001 Pacific Private Stock

The 2001 Private Stock product was released in late December, 2000 and offers a 150-card base set. Cards 1-125 focused on veteran players and were commonly seeded at a rate of about four per pack. Cards 126-150 focused on prospects and were seeded at a rate of 1:4 hobby packs. Each hobby pack contained seven cards, and carried a suggested retail price of $14.99. Please note that each hobby pack included one memorabilia card. Retail packs contained five cards, carried an SRP of $2.99 and did not include a memorabilia card in every pack. This was Pacific's last MLB licensed baseball product issued as they decided to not renew their baseball license as of January 1st, 2001.

Nm-Mt Ex-Mt
COMPLETE SET (150) 150.00 45.00
COMP.SET w/o SP's (125) 50.00 15.00
COMMON CARD (1-125) .50 .15
COMMON (126-150) 5.00 1.50
1 Darin Erstad .50 .15
2 Troy Glaus .50 .15
3 Tim Salmon .75 .23
4 Mo Vaughn .50 .15
5 Steve Finley .50 .15
6 Luis Gonzalez .50 .15
7 Randy Johnson 1.25 .35
8 Matt Williams .50 .15
9 Rafael Furcal .50 .15
10 Andres Galarraga .50 .15
11 Tom Glavine .75 .23
12 Andruw Jones .50 .15
13 Chipper Jones 1.25 .35
14 Greg Maddux 2.00 .60
15 B.J. Surhoff .50 .15
16 Brady Anderson .50 .15
17 Albert Belle .50 .15
18 Mike Mussina .75 .23
19 Cal Ripken 4.00 1.20
20 Carl Everett .50 .15
21 Nomar Garciaparra 2.00 .60
22 Pedro Martinez 1.25 .35
23 Mark Grace .75 .23
24 Sammy Sosa 2.00 .60
25 Kerry Wood 1.25 .35
26 Carlos Lee .50 .15
27 Magglio Ordonez .50 .15
28 Frank Thomas 1.25 .35
29 Sean Casey .50 .15
30 Ken Griffey Jr. 2.00 .60
31 Barry Larkin .75 .23
32 Pokey Reese .50 .15
33 Roberto Alomar .75 .23
34 Kenny Lofton .50 .15
35 Manny Ramirez .75 .23
36 Jim Thome 1.25 .35
37 Omar Vizquel .75 .23
38 Jeff Cirillo .50 .15
39 Jeffrey Hammonds .50 .15
40 Todd Helton .75 .23
41 Larry Walker .75 .23
42 Tony Clark .50 .15
43 Juan Encarnacion .50 .15
44 Juan Gonzalez .75 .23
45 Hideo Nomo 1.25 .35
46 Cliff Floyd .50 .15
47 Derrek Lee .50 .15
48 Henry Rodriguez .50 .15
49 Preston Wilson .50 .15
50 Jeff Bagwell .75 .23
51 Craig Biggio .75 .23
52 Richard Hidalgo .50 .15
53 Moises Alou .50 .15
54 Carlos Beltran .75 .23
55 Johnny Damon .75 .23
56 Jermaine Dye .50 .15
57 Mac Suzuki .50 .15
58 Mike Sweeney .50 .15
59 Adrian Beltre .75 .23
60 Kevin Brown .50 .15
61 Shawn Green .50 .15
62 Eric Karros .50 .15
63 Chan Ho Park .50 .15
64 Gary Sheffield .50 .15
65 Jeromy Burnitz .50 .15
66 Geoff Jenkins .50 .15
67 Richie Sexson .50 .15
68 Jacque Jones .50 .15
69 Matt Lawton .50 .15
70 Eric Milton .50 .15
71 Vladimir Guerrero 1.25 .35
72 Jose Vidro .50 .15
73 Edgardo Alfonzo .50 .15
74 Mike Hampton .50 .15
75 Mike Piazza 2.00 .60
76 Robin Ventura .50 .15
77 Jose Canseco 1.25 .35
78 Roger Clemens 2.50 .75
79 Derek Jeter 3.00 .90
80 David Justice .50 .15
81 Jorge Posada .75 .23
82 Bernie Williams .75 .23
83 Jason Giambi .50 .15
84 Ben Grieve .50 .15
85 Tim Hudson .50 .15
86 Terrence Long .50 .15
87 Miguel Tejada .50 .15
88 Bob Abreu .50 .15
89 Pat Burrell .50 .15
90 Mike Lieberthal .50 .15
91 Scott Rolen 1.25 .35
92 Kris Benson .50 .15
93 Brian Giles .50 .15
94 Jason Kendall .50 .15
95 Aramis Ramirez .50 .15
96 Rick Ankiel .50 .15
97 Will Clark 1.25 .35
98 J.D. Drew .50 .15
99 Jim Edmonds .50 .15
100 Mark McGwire 3.00 .90
101 Fernando Tatis .50 .15
102 Adam Eaton .50 .15
103 Tony Gwynn 1.50 .45
104 Phil Nevin .50 .15
105 Eric Owens .50 .15
106 Barry Bonds 3.00 .90
107 Jeff Kent .50 .15
108 J.T. Snow .50 .15
109 Rickey Henderson 1.25 .35
110 Edgar Martinez .75 .23
111 John Olerud .50 .15
112 Alex Rodriguez 2.00 .60
113 Kazuhiro Sasaki .50 .15
114 Vinny Castilla .50 .15
115 Fred McGriff .75 .23
116 Greg Vaughn .50 .15
117 Gabe Kapler .50 .15
118 Ruben Mateo .50 .15
119 Rafael Palmeiro .75 .23
120 Ivan Rodriguez 1.25 .35
121 Tony Batista .50 .15
122 Jose Cruz Jr. .50 .15
123 Carlos Delgado .50 .15
124 Shannon Stewart .50 .15
125 David Wells .50 .15
126 Shawn Wooten SP 5.00 1.50
127 George Lombard SP 5.00 1.50
128 Morgan Burkhart SP 5.00 1.50
129 Ross Gload SP 5.00 1.50
130 Corey Patterson SP 8.00 2.40
131 Julio Zuleta SP 5.00 1.50
132 Joe Crede SP 5.00 1.50
133 Matt Ginter SP 5.00 1.50

134 Travis Dawkins SP 5.00 1.50
135 Eric Munson SP 5.00 1.50
136 Dee Brown SP 5.00 1.50
137 Luke Prokopec SP 5.00 1.50
138 Timo Perez SP 5.00 1.50
139 Alfonso Soriano SP 8.00 2.40
140 Jake Westbrook SP 5.00 1.50
141 Eric Byrnes SP 5.00 1.50
142 Adam Hyzdu SP 5.00 1.50
143 Jimmy Rollins SP 8.00 2.40
144 Xavier Nady SP 5.00 1.50
145 Ryan Vogelsong SP 5.00 1.50
146 Joel Pineiro SP 10.00 3.00
147 Aubrey Huff SP 8.00 2.40
148 Kenny Kelly SP 5.00 1.50
149 Josh Phelps SP 5.00 1.50
150 Vernon Wells SP 8.00 2.40

2001 Pacific Private Stock Gold Portraits

Randomly inserted into hobby packs, this 150-card insert is a complete parallel of the 2001 Pacific Private Stock base set. These cards are individually serial numbered to 75, and feature a gold border.

Nm-Mt Ex-Mt
*STARS 1-125: 8X TO 20X BASIC CARDS
*PROSPECTS 126-150: .75X TO 2X BASIC

2001 Pacific Private Stock Premiere Date

Randomly inserted into packs at two in 21 hobby, this 150-card insert is a complete parallel of the 2001 Pacific Private Stock base set. These cards are individually serial numbered to 90, and feature a "Premiere Date" stamp on the card fronts.

Nm-Mt Ex-Mt
*STARS 1-125: 8X TO 20X BASIC CARDS
*PROSPECTS 126-150: .75X TO 2X BASIC

2001 Pacific Private Stock Silver

Produced as the basic issue cards in retail packs, this 150-card set is a straight parallel of the regular issue gold foil cards distributed in hobby packs. Two to three Silver cards came seeded in each retail pack.

Nm-Mt Ex-Mt
*STARS 1-125: .75X TO 2X BASIC CARDS
*PROSPECTS: 126-150: .4X TO 1X BASIC

2001 Pacific Private Stock Silver Portraits

Randomly inserted into retail packs at three in 25, this 150-card insert is a complete parallel of the 2001 Pacific Private Stock base set. These cards are individually serial numbered to 290, and feature a silver border.

Nm-Mt Ex-Mt
*STARS 1-125: 3X TO 8X BASIC CARDS
*PROSPECTS 126-150: .5X TO 1.2X BASIC

2001 Pacific Private Stock Artist's Canvas

Randomly inserted into packs at one in 21 hobby and one in 49 retail, this 20-card insert features some of baseball's top stars. These cards were printed on actual canvas paper.

Nm-Mt Ex-Mt
COMPLETE SET (20) 400.00 120.00
PROOFS PRINT RUN 1 SERIAL #'d SET
PROOFS NOT PRICED DUE TO SCARCITY
1 Randy Johnson 12.00 3.60
2 Chipper Jones 12.00 3.60
3 Greg Maddux 20.00 6.00
4 Cal Ripken 40.00 12.00
5 Nomar Garciaparra 20.00 6.00
6 Pedro Martinez 12.00 3.60
7 Sammy Sosa 20.00 6.00
8 Frank Thomas 12.00 3.60
9 Ken Griffey Jr. 20.00 6.00
10 Manny Ramirez 8.00 2.40
11 Vladimir Guerrero 12.00 3.60
12 Mike Piazza 20.00 6.00
13 Roger Clemens 25.00 7.50
14 Derek Jeter 30.00 9.00
15 Jason Giambi 8.00 2.40
16 Rick Ankiel 8.00 2.40
17 Mark McGwire 30.00 9.00
18 Barry Bonds 30.00 9.00
19 Alex Rodriguez 20.00 6.00
20 Ivan Rodriguez 12.00 3.60

2001 Pacific Private Stock Extreme Action

Randomly inserted into packs at two in 21 hobby and 1:25 retail, this 20-card insert features players that are extremely talented.

Nm-Mt Ex-Mt
COMPLETE SET (20) 120.00 36.00
1 Darin Erstad 2.00 .60
2 Troy Glaus 2.00 .60
3 Rafael Furcal 2.00 .60
4 Cal Ripken 15.00 4.50
5 Nomar Garciaparra 8.00 2.40
6 Sammy Sosa 8.00 2.40
7 Frank Thomas 5.00 1.50
8 Ken Griffey Jr. 8.00 2.40
9 Roberto Alomar 3.00 .90
10 Vladimir Guerrero 5.00 1.50
11 Derek Jeter 12.00 3.60
12 Mike Piazza 8.00 2.40
13 Jason Giambi 2.00 .60
14 Miguel Tejada 2.00 .60
15 Jim Edmonds 2.00 .60
16 Mark McGwire 12.00 3.60
17 Barry Bonds 12.00 3.60
18 Jeff Kent 2.00 .60
19 Alex Rodriguez 8.00 2.40
20 Ivan Rodriguez 5.00 1.50

2001 Pacific Private Stock Game Gear

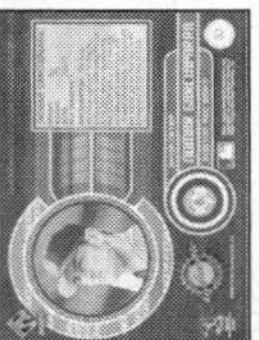

Inserted into packs at one per pack hobby and one in 49 retail, this 178-card insert features game-used memorabilia cards from some of the Major League's top players. Please note that cards 100, 176, and 177 do not exist. Though originally claimed by Pacific not to exist, a few copies of number 37, Sammy Sosa, later surfaced in the secondary market a few months after the products rlelease. Not much is known about this card but we will continue to monitor this card.

Nm-Mt Ex-Mt
1 Garret Anderson Bat 10.00 3.00
2 Darin Erstad Jsy 10.00 3.00
3 Ron Gant Bat 10.00 3.00
4 Troy Glaus Jsy 10.00 3.00
5 Tim Salmon Bat 15.00 4.50
6 Mo Vaughn Jsy 10.00 3.00
Grey Away Uniform
7 Mo Vaughn Jsy 10.00 3.00
White Home Uniform
8 Mo Vaughn Bat 10.00 3.00
9 Jay Bell Jsy 10.00 3.00
10 Jay Bell Bat 10.00 3.00
11 Erubiel Durazo Jsy 10.00 3.00
Black Away Uniform
12 Erubiel Durazo Jsy 10.00 3.00
White Home Uniform
13 Erubiel Durazo Bat 10.00 3.00
14 Steve Finley Bat 10.00 3.00
15 Randy Johnson Jsy 15.00 4.50
16 Byung-Hyun Kim Jsy 10.00 3.00
White Home Uniform
17 Byung-Hyun Kim Jsy 10.00 3.00
Grey Away Uniform
18 Matt Williams Jsy 10.00 3.00
Grey Home Uniform
19 Matt Williams Jsy 10.00 3.00
White Home Uniform
20 Matt Williams Jsy 10.00 3.00
Purple Away Uniform
21 Bobby Bonilla Jsy 10.00 3.00
22 Rafael Furcal Bat 10.00 3.00
23 Andruw Jones Bat 10.00 3.00
24 Chipper Jones Jsy 15.00 4.50
25 Chipper Jones Bat 15.00 4.50
26 Brian Jordan Jsy 10.00 3.00
27 Javier Lopez Bat 10.00 3.00
28 Greg Maddux Jsy 15.00 4.50
29 Greg Maddux Bat 15.00 4.50
30 Brady Anderson Bat 10.00 3.00
31 Albert Belle Bat 10.00 3.00
32 Nomar Garciaparra Bat 20.00 6.00
33 Pedro Martinez Bat 15.00 4.50
34 Jose Offerman Bat 10.00 3.00
35 Damon Buford Jsy 10.00 3.00
36 Jose Nieves Bat 10.00 3.00
37 Sammy Sosa Jsy SP
38 Kerry Wood Bat 15.00 4.50
39 James Baldwin Jsy 10.00 3.00
40 Ray Durham Jsy 10.00 3.00
41 Ray Durham Bat 10.00 3.00
42 Carlos Lee Bat 10.00 3.00
43 Magglio Ordonez Jsy 10.00 3.00
44 Magglio Ordonez Bat 10.00 3.00
45 Chris Singleton Jsy 10.00 3.00
46 Aaron Boone Bat 10.00 3.00
47 Sean Casey Bat 10.00 3.00
48 Barry Larkin Jsy 15.00 4.50
49 Pokey Reese Jsy 10.00 3.00
50 Pokey Reese Bat 10.00 3.00
51 Dmitri Young Bat 10.00 3.00
52 Roberto Alomar Bat 15.00 4.50
53 Einar Diaz Bat 10.00 3.00
54 Kenny Lofton Jsy 10.00 3.00
55 David Segui Bat 10.00 3.00
56 Omar Vizquel Jsy 15.00 4.50
57 Luis Castillo Jsy 10.00 3.00
58 Jeff Cirillo Jsy 10.00 3.00
59 Jeff Frye Bat 10.00 3.00
60 Todd Helton Jsy 15.00 4.50
61 Todd Helton Bat 15.00 4.50
62 Neifi Perez Bat 10.00 3.00
63 Larry Walker Jsy 15.00 4.50
64 Larry Walker Bat 15.00 4.50
65 Masato Yoshii Jsy 10.00 3.00
66 Brad Ausmus Jsy 10.00 3.00
67 Rich Becker Bat 10.00 3.00
68 Tony Clark Bat 10.00 3.00
69 Deivi Cruz Bat 10.00 3.00
70 Juan Gonzalez Bat 15.00 4.50
71 Dean Palmer Bat 10.00 3.00
72 Cliff Floyd Jsy 10.00 3.00
White Home Uniform
73 Cliff Floyd Jsy 10.00 3.00
Teal Away Uniform
74 Cliff Floyd Bat 10.00 3.00
75 Alex Gonzalez Jsy 10.00 3.00
76 Alex Gonzalez 10.00 3.00
Marlins Bat
77 Mark Kotsay Bat 10.00 3.00
78 Derrek Lee Bat 10.00 3.00
79 Pablo Ozuna Jsy 10.00 3.00
80 Craig Biggio Bat 15.00 4.50
81 Ken Caminiti Bat 10.00 3.00
82 Roger Cedeno Bat 10.00 3.00
83 Ricky Bottalico Bat 10.00 3.00
84 Dee Brown Bat 10.00 3.00
85 Jermaine Dye Bat 10.00 3.00
86 David McCarty Bat 10.00 3.00
87 Hector Ortiz Bat 10.00 3.00
88 Joe Randa Bat 10.00 3.00
89 Adrian Beltre Jsy 15.00 4.50
90 Kevin Brown Jsy 10.00 3.00
91 Alex Cora Bat 10.00 3.00
92 Darren Dreifort Bat 10.00 3.00
93 Shawn Green Jsy 10.00 3.00
White Home Uniform
94 Shawn Green Jsy 10.00 3.00
Grey Away Uniform
95 Shawn Green Bat 10.00 3.00
96 Todd Hundley Jsy 10.00 3.00
97 Eric Karros Bat 10.00 3.00
98 Chan Ho Park Jsy 10.00 3.00
99 Chan Ho Park Bat 10.00 3.00
101 Gary Sheffield Bat 10.00 3.00
102 Ismael Valdes Bat 10.00 3.00
103 Jeromy Burnitz Bat 10.00 3.00
104 Marquis Grissom Bat 10.00 3.00
105 Matt Lawton Bat 10.00 3.00
106 Fernando Seguignol 10.00 3.00
Bat
107 Edgardo Alfonzo Jsy 10.00 3.00
White Home Uniform - Full Swing
108 Edgardo Alfonzo Jsy 10.00 3.00
White Home Uniform - Dropping Bat
109 Edgardo Alfonzo Jsy 10.00 3.00
Black Home Uniform
110 Derek Bell Jsy 10.00 3.00
White Home Uniform
111 Derek Bell Jsy 10.00 3.00
Black Away Uniform
112 Armando Benitez Bat 10.00 3.00
113 Al Leiter Bat 10.00 3.00
114 Rey Ordonez Jsy 10.00 3.00
Grey Away Uniform - Fielding
115 Rey Ordonez 10.00 3.00
Jsy White
White Home Uniform
116 Rey Ordonez Jsy 10.00 3.00
Grey Away Uniform - Bunting
117 Rey Ordonez Bat 10.00 3.00
118 Jay Payton Bat 10.00 3.00
119 Mike Piazza Jsy 20.00 6.00
120 Robin Ventura Jsy 10.00 3.00
Black Away Uniform - Hitting
121 Robin Ventura Jsy 10.00 3.00
Black Away Uniform - Fielding
122 Robin Ventura Jsy 10.00 3.00
White Home Uniform
123 Luis Polonia Bat 10.00 3.00
124 Bernie Williams Bat 15.00 4.50
125 Eric Chavez Jsy 10.00 3.00
126 Jason Giambi Jsy 10.00 3.00
127 Jason Giambi Bat 10.00 3.00
128 Ben Grieve Jsy 10.00 3.00
129 Ben Grieve Bat 10.00 3.00
130 Ramon Hernandez Bat 10.00 3.00
131 Tim Hudson Jsy 10.00 3.00
132 Terrence Long Bat 10.00 3.00
133 Mark Mulder Jsy 10.00 3.00
134 Adam Piatt Jsy 10.00 3.00
135 Olmedo Saenz Bat 10.00 3.00
136 Matt Stairs Bat 10.00 3.00
137 Mike Stanley Bat 10.00 3.00
138 Miguel Tejada Bat 10.00 3.00
139 Travis Lee Bat 10.00 3.00
140 Brian Giles Bat 10.00 3.00
141 Jason Kendall Jsy 10.00 3.00
142 Will Clark Bat 15.00 4.50
143 J.D. Drew Bat 10.00 3.00
144 Jim Edmonds Bat 10.00 3.00
145 Mark McGwire Bat 100.00 30.00
146 Edgar Renteria Bat 10.00 3.00
147 Garrett Stephenson 10.00 3.00
Jsy
148 Tony Gwynn Jsy 15.00 4.50
149 Ruben Rivera Bat 10.00 3.00
150 Barry Bonds Jsy 30.00 9.00
151 Barry Bonds Bat 30.00 9.00
152 Ellis Burks Jsy 10.00 3.00
153 J.T. Snow Bat 10.00 3.00
154 Jay Buhner Jsy 10.00 3.00
155 Jay Buhner Bat 10.00 3.00
156 Carlos Guillen Jsy 10.00 3.00
157 Carlos Guillen Bat 10.00 3.00
158 Rickey Henderson Bat 15.00 4.50
159 Edgar Martinez Bat 15.00 4.50
160 Gil Meche Jsy 10.00 3.00
161 John Olerud Bat 10.00 3.00
162 Joe Oliver Bat 10.00 3.00
163 Alex Rodriguez Jsy SP 100.00 30.00
164 Kazuhiro Sasaki Jsy 10.00 3.00
165 Dan Wilson Jsy 10.00 3.00
166 Dan Wilson Bat 10.00 3.00
167 Vinny Castilla Bat 10.00 3.00
168 Jose Guillen Bat 10.00 3.00
169 Fred McGriff Jsy 15.00 4.50
170 Rusty Greer Bat 10.00 3.00
171 Mike Lamb Bat 10.00 3.00
172 Ruben Mateo Jsy 10.00 3.00
173 Ruben Mateo Bat 10.00 3.00
174 Rafael Palmeiro Jsy 15.00 4.50
175 Rafael Palmeiro Bat 15.00 4.50
178 Tony Batista Bat 10.00 3.00
179 Marty Cordova Bat 10.00 3.00
180 Jose Cruz Jr. Bat 10.00 3.00
181 Alex Gonzalez 10.00 3.00
Blue Jays Bat
182 Raul Mondesi Bat 10.00 3.00

2001 Pacific Private Stock Game Jersey Patch

These premium inserts parallel the more common Game Gear jersey cards. Unlike those cards, however, instead of a basic jersey swatch each of these cards features a swatch of fabric that incorporates part of a patch from the featured players jersey. Please note, in addition to the patch itself, that you can distinguish these cards from the jersey cards due to the fact that these cards state "Authentic Game Worn Patch" on the gold rim around the patch swatch on the card front. The set is skip-numbered due to the fact that it's card numbering scheme hails from the Game Gear set which included bats and jerseys.

Nm-Mt Ex-Mt
2 Darin Erstad 25.00 7.50
4 Troy Glaus 25.00 7.50
6 Mo Vaughn Grey 25.00 7.50
7 Mo Vaughn White 25.00 7.50
9 Jay Bell 25.00 7.50
11 Erubiel Durazo Black 15.00 4.50
12 Erubiel Durazo White 15.00 4.50
15 Randy Johnson 60.00 18.00
16 Byung-Hyun Kim White 25.00 7.50
17 Byung-Hyun Kim Grey 25.00 7.50
18 Matt Williams Grey 25.00 7.50
19 Matt Williams White 25.00 7.50
20 Matt Williams Purple 25.00 7.50
21 Bobby Bonilla 25.00 7.50
24 Chipper Jones 60.00 18.00
26 Brian Jordan 25.00 7.50
28 Greg Maddux 120.00 36.00
35 Damon Buford 15.00 4.50
39 James Baldwin 15.00 4.50
40 Ray Durham 25.00 7.50
43 Magglio Ordonez 25.00 7.50
45 Chris Singleton 15.00 4.50
48 Barry Larkin 40.00 12.00
49 Pokey Reese 15.00 4.50
54 Kenny Lofton 25.00 7.50
56 Omar Vizquel 40.00 12.00
57 Luis Castillo 15.00 4.50
58 Jeff Cirillo 15.00 4.50
60 Todd Helton 40.00 12.00
63 Larry Walker 40.00 12.00
65 Masato Yoshii 15.00 4.50
66 Brad Ausmus 15.00 4.50
72 Cliff Floyd White 25.00 7.50
73 Cliff Floyd Teal 25.00 7.50
75 Alex Gonzalez 15.00 4.50
79 Pablo Ozuna 15.00 4.50
89 Adrian Beltre 40.00 12.00
90 Kevin Brown 25.00 7.50
93 Shawn Green White 25.00 7.50
94 Shawn Green Grey 25.00 7.50
96 Todd Hundley 15.00 4.50
98 Chan Ho Park 25.00 7.50
107 Edgardo Alfonzo 15.00 4.50
White Swing
108 Edgardo Alfonzo 15.00 4.50
White Drop
109 Edgardo Alfonzo 15.00 4.50
Black
110 Derek Bell White 15.00 4.50
111 Derek Bell Black 15.00 4.50
114 Rey Ordonez 15.00 4.50
Grey Field
115 Rey Ordonez White 15.00 4.50
116 Rey Ordonez 15.00 4.50
Grey Bunt
119 Mike Piazza 120.00 36.00
120 Robin Ventura 25.00 7.50
Black Hit
121 Robin Ventura 25.00 7.50
Black Field
122 Robin Ventura White 25.00 7.50
125 Eric Chavez 25.00 7.50
126 Jason Giambi 25.00 7.50
128 Ben Grieve 15.00 4.50
131 Tim Hudson 25.00 7.50
133 Mark Mulder 25.00 7.50
134 Adam Piatt 15.00 4.50
141 Jason Kendall 25.00 7.50
147 Garrett Stephenson 15.00 4.50
148 Tony Gwynn 100.00 30.00
150 Barry Bonds 150.00 45.00
152 Ellis Burks 25.00 7.50
154 Jay Buhner 25.00 7.50
156 Carlos Guillen 25.00 7.50
160 Gil Meche 15.00 4.50
163 Alex Rodriguez SP
164 Kazuhiro Sasaki 25.00 7.50
165 Dan Wilson 15.00 4.50
169 Fred McGriff 40.00 12.00
172 Ruben Mateo 15.00 4.50
174 Rafael Palmeiro 40.00 12.00

2001 Pacific Private Stock PS-206 Action

Randomly inserted into packs at two in one, this 60-card insert features a design very similar to the T-206 cards from the past. These cards are much smaller than basic sized cards, and feature top players in action photos.

Nm-Mt Ex-Mt
COMPLETE SET (60) 25.00 7.50
1 Darin Erstad .40 .12
2 Troy Glaus .40 .12
3 Randy Johnson 1.00 .30
4 Rafael Furcal .40 .12

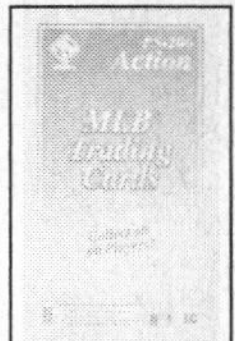

5 Tom Glavine .60 .18
6 Andruw Jones .40 .12
7 Chipper Jones 1.00 .30
8 Greg Maddux 1.50 .45
9 Albert Belle .40 .12
10 Mike Mussina .60 .18
11 Cal Ripken 3.00 .90
12 Nomar Garciaparra 1.50 .45
13 Pedro Martinez 1.00 .30
14 Mark Grace .60 .18
15 Sammy Sosa 1.50 .45
16 Kerry Wood 1.00 .30
17 Magglio Ordonez .40 .12
18 Frank Thomas 1.00 .30
19 Ken Griffey Jr. 1.50 .45
20 Barry Larkin .60 .18
21 Roberto Alomar .60 .18
22 Manny Ramirez .60 .18
23 Jim Thome 1.00 .30
24 Jeff Cirillo .40 .12
25 Todd Helton .60 .18
26 Larry Walker .60 .18
27 Juan Gonzalez .60 .18
28 Hideo Nomo 1.00 .30
29 Preston Wilson .40 .12
30 Jeff Bagwell .60 .18
31 Craig Biggio .60 .18
32 Johnny Damon .60 .18
33 Jermaine Dye .40 .12
34 Shawn Green .40 .12
35 Gary Sheffield .40 .12
36 Vladimir Guerrero 1.00 .30
37 Mike Piazza 1.50 .45
38 Jose Canseco 1.00 .30
39 Roger Clemens 2.00 .60
40 Derek Jeter 2.50 .75
41 Bernie Williams .60 .18
42 Jason Giambi .40 .12
43 Ben Grieve .40 .12
44 Pat Burrell .40 .12
45 Scott Rolen 1.00 .30
46 Rick Ankiel .40 .12
47 J.D. Drew .40 .12
48 Jim Edmonds .40 .12
49 Mark McGwire 2.50 .75
50 Tony Gwynn 1.25 .35
51 Barry Bonds 2.50 .75
52 Jeff Kent .40 .12
53 Edgar Martinez .60 .18
54 Alex Rodriguez 1.50 .45
55 Kazuhiro Sasaki .40 .12
56 Fred McGriff .60 .18
57 Rafael Palmeiro .60 .18
58 Ivan Rodriguez 1.00 .30
59 Tony Batista .40 .12
60 Carlos Delgado .40 .12

2001 Pacific Private Stock PS-206 New Wave

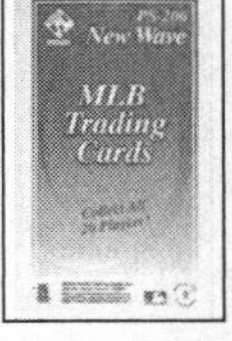

Randomly inserted into packs at one in 60 hobby and one in 480 retail, this 20-card insert features some of today's top young talents on cards that resemble the T-206 design. Each card in this set is individually serial numbered to 199.

Nm-Mt Ex-Mt
COMPLETE SET (20) 120.00 36.00
1 Darin Erstad 5.00 1.50
2 Troy Glaus 5.00 1.50
3 Rafael Furcal 5.00 1.50
4 Andruw Jones 5.00 1.50
5 Magglio Ordonez 5.00 1.50
6 Carlos Lee 5.00 1.50
7 Todd Helton 8.00 2.40
8 Johnny Damon 8.00 2.40
9 Jermaine Dye 5.00 1.50
10 Vladimir Guerrero 12.00 3.60
11 Jason Giambi 5.00 1.50
12 Ben Grieve 5.00 1.50
13 Pat Burrell 5.00 1.50
14 Rick Ankiel 5.00 1.50
15 J.D. Drew 5.00 1.50
16 Adam Eaton 5.00 1.50
17 Kazuhiro Sasaki 5.00 1.50
18 Ruben Mateo 5.00 1.50
19 Tony Batista 5.00 1.50
20 Carlos Delgado 5.00 1.50

2001 Pacific Private Stock PS-206 Rookies

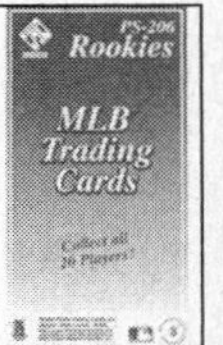

Randomly inserted into packs at one in 120 hobby and one in 480 retail, this 20-card insert features top rookies on cards that resemble the T-206 design. Each card in this set is individually serial numbered to 125.

	Nm-Mt	Ex-Mt
COMPLETE SET (20)	150.00	45.00
1 George Lombard	10.00	3.00
2 Morgan Burkhart	10.00	3.00
3 Corey Patterson	10.00	3.00
4 Julio Zuleta	10.00	3.00
5 Joe Crede	10.00	3.00
6 Matt Ginter	10.00	3.00
7 Aaron Myette	10.00	3.00
8 Travis Dawkins	10.00	3.00
9 Eric Munson	10.00	3.00
10 Dee Brown	10.00	3.00
11 Luke Prokopec	10.00	3.00
12 Jorge Toca	10.00	3.00
13 Alfonso Soriano	15.00	4.50
14 Eric Byrnes	10.00	3.00
15 Adam Hyzdu	10.00	3.00
16 Jimmy Rollins	10.00	3.00
17 Joel Pineiro	20.00	6.00
18 Aubrey Huff	10.00	3.00
19 Kenny Kelly	10.00	3.00
20 Vernon Wells	10.00	3.00

2001 Pacific Private Stock PS-206 Stars

Randomly inserted into packs at one in 40 hobby and one in 240 retail, this 20-card insert features some of today's top superstars on cards that resemble the T-206 design. Each card in this set is individually serial numbered to 315.

	Nm-Mt	Ex-Mt
COMPLETE SET (20)	250.00	75.00
1 Chipper Jones	10.00	3.00
2 Greg Maddux	15.00	4.50
3 Cal Ripken	30.00	9.00
4 Nomar Garciaparra	15.00	4.50
5 Pedro Martinez	10.00	3.00
6 Sammy Sosa	15.00	4.50
7 Frank Thomas	10.00	3.00
8 Ken Griffey Jr.	15.00	4.50
9 Manny Ramirez	8.00	2.40
10 Jeff Bagwell	8.00	2.40
11 Gary Sheffield	8.00	2.40
12 Mike Piazza	15.00	4.50
13 Roger Clemens	20.00	6.00
14 Derek Jeter	25.00	7.50
15 Rick Ankiel	8.00	2.40
16 Mark McGwire	25.00	7.50
17 Tony Gwynn	12.00	3.60
18 Barry Bonds	25.00	7.50
19 Alex Rodriguez	15.00	4.50
20 Ivan Rodriguez	10.00	3.00

2001 Pacific Private Stock Reserve

Randomly inserted into packs at one in 21 hobby, this 20-card insert features some of the Major League's finest athletes on canvas type paper with gold foil lettering.

	Nm-Mt	Ex-Mt
COMPLETE SET (20)	250.00	75.00
1 Randy Johnson	8.00	2.40
2 Chipper Jones	8.00	2.40
3 Greg Maddux	12.00	3.60
4 Cal Ripken	25.00	7.50
5 Nomar Garciaparra	12.00	3.60
6 Pedro Martinez	8.00	2.40
7 Sammy Sosa	12.00	3.60
8 Frank Thomas	8.00	2.40
9 Ken Griffey Jr.	12.00	3.60
10 Todd Helton	5.00	1.50
11 Vladimir Guerrero	8.00	2.40
12 Mike Piazza	12.00	3.60
13 Roger Clemens	15.00	4.50
14 Derek Jeter	20.00	6.00
15 Rick Ankiel	5.00	1.50
16 Mark McGwire	20.00	6.00
17 Tony Gwynn	10.00	3.00
18 Barry Bonds	20.00	6.00
19 Alex Rodriguez	12.00	3.60
20 Ivan Rodriguez	8.00	2.40

2000 Pacific Vanguard

The 2000 Pacific Vanguard product was released in May, 2000 as a 100-card set. The set features a blend of veterans and prospects. Each pack contained four cards and carried a suggested retail price of $3.99.

	Nm-Mt	Ex-Mt
COMPLETE SET (100)	25.00	7.50
1 Troy Glaus	.30	.09
2 Tim Salmon	.30	.09
3 Mo Vaughn	.30	.09
4 Albert Belle	.30	.09
5 Mike Mussina	.50	.15
6 Cal Ripken	2.50	.75
7 Nomar Garciaparra	1.25	.35
8 Pedro Martinez	.75	.23
9 Troy O'Leary	.30	.09
10 Wilton Veras	.30	.09
11 Magglio Ordonez	.30	.09
12 Chris Singleton	.30	.09
13 Frank Thomas	.75	.23
14 Roberto Alomar	.50	.15
15 Russell Branyan	.30	.09
16 Manny Ramirez	.50	.15
17 Jim Thome	.75	.23
18 Omar Vizquel	.50	.15
19 Tony Clark	.30	.09
20 Juan Gonzalez	.50	.15
21 Dean Palmer	.30	.09
22 Carlos Beltran	.50	.15
23 Johnny Damon	.50	.15
24 Jermaine Dye	.30	.09
25 Mark Quinn	.30	.09
26 Jacque Jones	.30	.09
27 Corey Koskie	.30	.09
28 Brad Radke	.30	.09
29 Roger Clemens	1.50	.45
30 Derek Jeter	2.00	.60
31 Alfonso Soriano	.75	.23
32 Bernie Williams	.50	.15
33 Eric Chavez	.30	.09
34 Jason Giambi	.30	.09
35 Ben Grieve	.30	.09
36 Tim Hudson	.30	.09
37 Mike Cameron	.30	.09
38 Freddy Garcia	.30	.09
39 Edgar Martinez	.50	.15
40 Alex Rodriguez	1.25	.35
41 Jose Canseco	.75	.23
42 Vinny Castilla	.30	.09
43 Fred McGriff	.50	.15
44 Rusty Greer	.30	.09
45 Ruben Mateo	.30	.09
46 Rafael Palmeiro	.50	.15
47 Ivan Rodriguez	.75	.23
48 Carlos Delgado	.30	.09
49 Shannon Stewart	.30	.09
50 Vernon Wells	.30	.09
51 Erubiel Durazo	.30	.09
52 Randy Johnson	.75	.23
53 Matt Williams	.30	.09
54 Andruw Jones	.30	.09
55 Chipper Jones	.75	.23
56 Greg Maddux	1.25	.35
57 Mark Grace	.50	.15
58 Sammy Sosa	1.25	.35
59 Kerry Wood	.75	.23
60 Sean Casey	.30	.09
61 Ken Griffey Jr.	1.25	.35
62 Barry Larkin	.50	.15
63 Todd Helton	.50	.15
64 Ben Petrick	.30	.09
65 Larry Walker	.50	.15
66 Luis Castillo	.30	.09
67 Alex Gonzalez	.30	.09
68 Preston Wilson	.30	.09
69 Jeff Bagwell	.50	.15
70 Craig Biggio	.50	.15
71 Billy Wagner	.30	.09
72 Kevin Brown	.50	.15
73 Shawn Green	.30	.09
74 Gary Sheffield	.30	.09
75 Kevin Barker	.30	.09
76 Ron Belliard	.30	.09
77 Jeromy Burnitz	.30	.09
78 Michael Barrett	.30	.09
79 Peter Bergeron	.30	.09
80 Vladimir Guerrero	.75	.23
81 Edgardo Alfonzo	.30	.09
82 Rey Ordonez	.30	.09
83 Mike Piazza	1.25	.35
84 Robin Ventura	.50	.15
85 Bobby Abreu	.30	.09
86 Mike Lieberthal	.30	.09
87 Scott Rolen	.75	.23
88 Brian Giles	.30	.09
89 Chad Hermansen	.30	.09
90 Jason Kendall	.30	.09
91 Rick Ankiel	.30	.09
92 J.D. Drew	.30	.09
93 Mark McGwire	2.00	.60
94 Fernando Tatis	.30	.09
95 Ben Davis	.30	.09
96 Tony Gwynn	1.00	.30
97 Trevor Hoffman	.30	.09
98 Barry Bonds	2.00	.60
99 Ellis Burks	.30	.09
100 Jeff Kent	.30	.09
SAMP Tony Gwynn	1.50	.45

2000 Pacific Vanguard Green

Randomly inserted into packs, this 100-card green-foiled set is a complete parallel of the Vanguard base set. The 50 A.L. players in this set are individually serial numbered to 99, and the 50 N.L. players are individually serial numbered to 199.

Nm-Mt Ex-Mt
*AL STARS 1-50: 4X TO 10X BASIC...
*NL STARS 51-100: 2.5X TO 6X BASIC

2000 Pacific Vanguard Holographic Gold

Randomly inserted into packs, this 100-card gold-foiled set is a complete parallel of the Vanguard base set. The 50 A.L. players in this set are individually serial numbered to 199, and the N.L. players are individually serial numbered to 99.

Nm-Mt Ex-Mt
*AL STARS 1-50: 4X TO 10X BASIC...
*NL STARS 51-100: 6X TO 15X BASIC

2000 Pacific Vanguard Premiere Date

Randomly inserted into hobby packs at one in 25, this 100-card set is a complete parallel of the Vanguard base set. There were only 135 serial numbered sets produced of this insert.

Nm-Mt Ex-Mt
*STARS: 4X TO 10X BASIC CARDS....

2000 Pacific Vanguard Cosmic Force

Randomly inserted into packs at one in 73, this insert features headshots of ten of the major leagues most popular stars.

	Nm-Mt	Ex-Mt
COMPLETE SET (10)	50.00	15.00
1 Chipper Jones	4.00	1.20
2 Cal Ripken	12.00	3.60
3 Nomar Garciaparra	6.00	1.80
4 Sammy Sosa	6.00	1.80
5 Ken Griffey Jr.	6.00	1.80
6 Mike Piazza	6.00	1.80
7 Derek Jeter	10.00	3.00
8 Mark McGwire	10.00	3.00
9 Tony Gwynn	8.00	2.40
10 Alex Rodriguez	6.00	1.80

2000 Pacific Vanguard Diamond Architects

Randomly inserted into packs at one in 25, this insert set features the blueprints of different ballparks, and the superstars that play there.

	Nm-Mt	Ex-Mt
COMPLETE SET (20)	50.00	15.00
1 Chipper Jones	2.50	.75
2 Greg Maddux	4.00	1.20
3 Cal Ripken	8.00	2.40
4 Nomar Garciaparra	4.00	1.20
5 Sammy Sosa	4.00	1.20
6 Ken Griffey Jr.	4.00	1.20
7 Manny Ramirez	1.50	.45
8 Larry Walker	1.50	.45
9 Jeff Bagwell	1.50	.45
10 Vladimir Guerrero	2.50	.75
11 Mike Piazza	4.00	1.20
12 Roger Clemens	5.00	1.50
13 Derek Jeter	6.00	1.80
14 Bernie Williams	1.50	.45
15 Scott Rolen	2.50	.75
16 Mark McGwire	6.00	1.80
17 Tony Gwynn	5.00	1.50
18 Alex Rodriguez	4.00	1.20
19 Rafael Palmeiro	1.50	.45
20 Ivan Rodriguez	2.50	.75

2000 Pacific Vanguard Game-Worn Jerseys

Randomly inserted into packs at one in 120, this five card insert set features swatches from actual game-used jerseys.

	Nm-Mt	Ex-Mt
1 Chipper Jones	15.00	4.50
2 Greg Maddux	25.00	7.50
3 Frank Thomas	15.00	4.50
4 Tony Gwynn	20.00	6.00
5 Alex Rodriguez	25.00	7.50

2000 Pacific Vanguard High Voltage

Inserted into packs at a stated rate of one per pack, this 36-card insert set features some of the most electrifying players in major league baseball. Please note that there are four parallels to this insert (Green, Gold, Holo-Silver, and Red).

	Nm-Mt	Ex-Mt
COMPLETE SET (36)	15.00	4.50

*GOLD: 5X TO 12X BASIC VOLTAGE
GOLD PRINT RUN 199 SERIAL #'d SETS
*GREEN: 8X TO 20X BASIC VOLTAGE
GREEN PRINT RUN 99 SERIAL #'d SETS
HOLO.SILVER PRINT RUN 10 SERIAL #'d SETS
HOLO.SILVER NOT PRICED DUE TO SCARCITY
*RED: 3X TO 8X BASIC VOLTAGE
RED PRINT RUN 299 SERIAL #'d SETS
PARALLELS RANDOM IN HOB/RET PACKS

	Nm-Mt	Ex-Mt
1 Mo Vaughn	.25	.07
2 Erubiel Durazo	.25	.07
3 Randy Johnson	.60	.18
4 Andruw Jones	.25	.07
5 Chipper Jones	.60	.18
6 Greg Maddux	1.00	.30
7 Cal Ripken	2.00	.60
8 Nomar Garciaparra	1.00	.30
9 Pedro Martinez	.60	.18
10 Sammy Sosa	1.00	.30
11 Frank Thomas	.60	.18
12 Sean Casey	.25	.07
13 Ken Griffey Jr.	1.00	.30
14 Barry Larkin	.40	.12
15 Manny Ramirez	.40	.12
16 Jim Thome	.60	.18
17 Larry Walker	.40	.12
18 Jeff Bagwell	.40	.12
19 Craig Biggio	.40	.12
20 Carlos Beltran	.40	.12
21 Shawn Green	.25	.07
22 Vladimir Guerrero	.60	.18
23 Edgardo Alfonzo	.25	.07
24 Mike Piazza	1.00	.30
25 Roger Clemens	1.25	.35
26 Derek Jeter	1.50	.45
27 Bernie Williams	.40	.12
28 Scott Rolen	.60	.18
29 Brian Giles	.25	.07
30 Rick Ankiel	.25	.07
31 Mark McGwire	1.50	.45
32 Tony Gwynn	.75	.23
33 Barry Bonds	1.50	.45
34 Alex Rodriguez	1.00	.30
35 Rafael Palmeiro	.40	.12
36 Ivan Rodriguez	.60	.18

2000 Pacific Vanguard Press

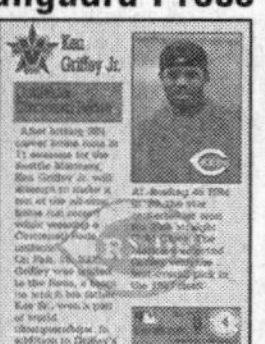

Randomly inserted into packs at two in 25, this 20-card set features 10 A.L. players and 10 N.L. players.

	Nm-Mt	Ex-Mt
COMPLETE A.L. SET (10)	15.00	4.50
COMPLETE N.L. SET (10)	15.00	4.50
A1 Cal Ripken	4.00	1.20
A2 Nomar Garciaparra	2.00	.60
A3 Pedro Martinez	1.25	.35
A4 Manny Ramirez	.75	.23
A5 Carlos Beltran	.75	.23
A6 Roger Clemens	2.50	.75
A7 Derek Jeter	3.00	.90
A8 Alex Rodriguez	2.00	.60
A9 Rafael Palmeiro	.75	.23
A10 Ivan Rodriguez	1.25	.35
N1 Chipper Jones	1.25	.35
N2 Greg Maddux	2.00	.60
N3 Sammy Sosa	2.00	.60
N4 Ken Griffey Jr.	2.00	.60
N5 Larry Walker	.75	.23
N6 Jeff Bagwell	.75	.23
N7 Vladimir Guerrero	1.25	.35
N8 Mike Piazza	2.00	.60
N9 Mark McGwire	3.00	.90
N10 Tony Gwynn	1.50	.45

1992 Pinnacle

The 1992 Pinnacle set (issued by Score) consists of two series each with 310 standard-size cards. Cards were distributed in first and second series 16-card foil packs and 27-card cello packs. An anti-counterfeit device appears in the bottom border of each card back. A special ribbed plastic lenticular detector card was made available that allowed the user to view the anti-counterfeit device and unscramble the coding with the word "Pinnacle" appearing. Special subsets featured include '92 Rookie Prospects (52, 55, 168, 247-261, 263-280), Idols (281-286/584-591), Sidelines (287-294/592-596), Draft Picks (295-304), Shades (305-310/601-605), Grips (606-612), and Technicians (614-620). Rookie Cards in the set include Brian Jordan, Jeff Kent and Manny Ramirez.

	Nm-Mt	Ex-Mt
COMPLETE SET (620)	40.00	12.00
COMP. SERIES 1 (310)	25.00	7.50
COMP. SERIES 2 (310)	15.00	4.50
1 Frank Thomas	.50	.15
2 Benito Santiago	.20	.06
3 Carlos Baerga	.10	.03
4 Cecil Fielder	.20	.06
5 Barry Larkin	.30	.09
6 Ozzie Smith	.75	.23
7 Willie McGee	.20	.06
8 Paul Molitor	.30	.09
9 Andy Van Slyke	.20	.06
10 Ryne Sandberg	.75	.23
11 Kevin Seitzer	.10	.03
12 Len Dykstra	.20	.06
13 Edgar Martinez	.30	.09
14 Ruben Sierra	.10	.03
15 Howard Johnson	.10	.03
16 Dave Henderson	.10	.03
17 Devon White	.20	.06
18 Terry Pendleton	.20	.06
19 Steve Finley	.20	.06
20 Kirby Puckett	.50	.15
21 Orel Hershiser	.20	.06
22 Hal Morris	.10	.03
23 Don Mattingly	1.25	.35
24 Delino DeShields	.10	.03
25 Dennis Eckersley	.20	.06
26 Ellis Burks	.20	.06
27 Jay Buhner	.20	.06
28 Matt Williams	.20	.06
29 Lou Whitaker	.20	.06
30 Alex Fernandez	.10	.03
31 Albert Belle	.20	.06
32 Todd Zeile	.10	.03
33 Tony Pena	.10	.03
34 Jay Bell	.20	.06
35 Rafael Palmeiro	.30	.09
36 Wes Chamberlain	.10	.03
37 George Bell	.10	.03
38 Robin Yount	.75	.23
39 Vince Coleman	.10	.03
40 Bruce Hurst	.10	.03
41 Harold Baines	.20	.06
42 Chuck Finley	.20	.06
43 Ken Caminiti	.20	.06
44 Ben McDonald	.10	.03
45 Roberto Alomar	.30	.09
46 Chili Davis	.20	.06
47 Bill Doran	.10	.03
48 Jerald Clark	.10	.03
49 Jose Lind	.10	.03
50 Nolan Ryan	2.00	.60
51 Phil Plantier	.10	.03
52 Gary DiSarcina	.10	.03
53 Kevin Bass	.10	.03
54 Pat Kelly	.10	.03
55 Mark Wohlers	.10	.03
56 Walt Weiss	.10	.03
57 Lenny Harris	.10	.03
58 Ivan Calderon	.10	.03
59 Harold Reynolds	.20	.06
60 George Brett	1.25	.35
61 Gregg Olson	.10	.03
62 Orlando Merced	.10	.03
63 Steve Decker	.10	.03
64 John Franco	.20	.06
65 Greg Maddux	.75	.23
66 Alex Cole	.10	.03
67 Dave Hollins	.10	.03
68 Kent Hrbek	.20	.06
69 Tom Pagnozzi	.10	.03
70 Jeff Bagwell	.50	.15
71 Jim Gantner	.10	.03
72 Matt Nokes	.10	.03
73 Brian Harper	.10	.03
74 Andy Benes	.10	.03
75 Tom Glavine	.30	.09
76 Terry Steinbach	.10	.03
77 Dennis Martinez	.20	.06
78 John Olerud	.20	.06
79 Ozzie Guillen	.10	.03
80 Darryl Strawberry	.20	.06
81 Gary Gaetti	.20	.06
82 Dave Righetti	.20	.06
83 Chris Hoiles	.10	.03
84 Andujar Cedeno	.10	.03
85 Jack Clark	.20	.06
86 David Howard	.10	.03
87 Bill Gullickson	.10	.03
88 Bernard Gilkey	.10	.03
89 Kevin Elster	.10	.03
90 Kevin Maas	.10	.03
91 Mark Lewis	.10	.03
92 Greg Vaughn	.10	.03
93 Bret Barberie	.10	.03
94 Dave Smith	.10	.03
95 Roger Clemens	1.00	.30
96 Doug Drabek	.10	.03
97 Omar Vizquel	.30	.09
98 Jose Guzman	.10	.03
99 Juan Samuel	.10	.03
100 Dave Justice	.20	.06
101 Tom Browning	.10	.03
102 Mark Gubicza	.10	.03
103 Mickey Morandini	.10	.03
104 Ed Whitson	.10	.03
105 Lance Parrish	.20	.06
106 Scott Erickson	.10	.03
107 Jack McDowell	.10	.03
108 Dave Stieb	.10	.03
109 Mike Moore	.10	.03
110 Travis Fryman	.20	.06
111 Dwight Gooden	.20	.06
112 Fred McGriff	.30	.09
113 Alan Trammell	.20	.06
114 Roberto Kelly	.10	.03
115 Andre Dawson	.20	.06
116 Bill Landrum	.10	.03
117 Brian McRae	.10	.03
118 B.J. Surhoff	.20	.06
119 Chuck Knoblauch	.20	.06
120 Steve Olin	.10	.03
121 Robin Ventura	.20	.06
122 Will Clark	.50	.15
123 Tino Martinez	.30	.09
124 Dale Murphy	.50	.15
125 Pete O'Brien	.10	.03
126 Ray Lankford	.10	.03
127 Juan Gonzalez	.30	.09
128 Ron Gant	.20	.06
129 Marquis Grissom	.20	.06
130 Jose Canseco	.50	.15

131 Mike Greenwell .10 .03
132 Mark Langston .10 .03
133 Brett Butler .20 .06
134 Kelly Gruber .10 .03
135 Chris Sabo .10 .03
136 Mark Grace .30 .09
137 Tony Fernandez .10 .03
138 Glenn Davis .10 .03
139 Pedro Munoz .10 .03
140 Craig Biggio .30 .09
141 Pete Schourek .10 .03
142 Mike Boddicker .10 .03
143 Robby Thompson .10 .03
144 Mel Hall .10 .03
145 Bryan Harvey .10 .03
146 Mike LaValliere .10 .03
147 John Kruk .20 .06
148 Joe Carter .20 .06
149 Greg Olson .10 .03
150 Julio Franco .20 .06
151 Darryl Hamilton .10 .03
152 Felix Fermin .10 .03
153 Jose Offerman .10 .03
154 Paul O'Neill .30 .09
155 Tommy Greene .10 .03
156 Ivan Rodriguez .50 .15
157 Dave Stewart .20 .06
158 Jeff Reardon .20 .06
159 Felix Jose .10 .03
160 Doug Dascenzo .10 .03
161 Tim Wallach .10 .03
162 Dan Plesac .10 .03
163 Luis Gonzalez .20 .06
164 Mike Henneman .10 .03
165 Mike Devereaux .10 .03
166 Luis Polonia .10 .03
167 Mike Sharperson .10 .03
168 Chris Donnels .10 .03
169 Greg W. Harris .10 .03
170 Deion Sanders .30 .09
171 Mike Schooler .10 .03
172 Jose DeJesus .10 .03
173 Jeff Montgomery .10 .03
174 Milt Cuyler .10 .03
175 Wade Boggs .30 .09
176 Kevin Tapani .10 .03
177 Bill Spiers .10 .03
178 Tim Raines .20 .06
179 Randy Milligan .10 .03
180 Rob Dibble .20 .06
181 Kirt Manwaring .10 .03
182 Pascual Perez .10 .03
183 Juan Guzman .10 .03
184 John Smiley .10 .03
185 David Segui .10 .03
186 Omar Olivares .10 .03
187 Joe Slusarski .10 .03
188 Erik Hanson .10 .03
189 Mark Portugal .10 .03
190 Walt Terrell .10 .03
191 John Smoltz .30 .09
192 Wilson Alvarez .10 .03
193 Jimmy Key .20 .06
194 Larry Walker .30 .09
195 Lee Smith .20 .06
196 Pete Harnisch .10 .03
197 Mike Harkey .10 .03
198 Frank Tanana .10 .03
199 Terry Mulholland .10 .03
200 Cal Ripken 1.50 .45
201 Dave Magadan .10 .03
202 Bud Black .10 .03
203 Terry Shumpert .10 .03
204 Mike Mussina .50 .15
205 Mo Vaughn .20 .06
206 Steve Farr .10 .03
207 Darrin Jackson .10 .03
208 Jerry Browne .10 .03
209 Jeff Russell .10 .03
210 Mike Scioscia .10 .03
211 Rick Aguilera .20 .06
212 Jaime Navarro .10 .03
213 Randy Tomlin .10 .03
214 Bobby Thigpen .10 .03
215 Mark Gardner .10 .03
216 Norm Charlton .10 .03
217 Mark McGwire 1.25 .35
218 Skeeter Barnes .10 .03
219 Bob Tewksbury .10 .03
220 Junior Felix .10 .03
221 Sam Horn .10 .03
222 Jody Reed .10 .03
223 Luis Sojo .10 .03
224 Jerome Walton .10 .03
225 Darryl Kile .20 .06
226 Mickey Tettleton .10 .03
227 Dan Pasqua .10 .03
228 Jim Gott .10 .03
229 Bernie Williams .30 .09
230 Shane Mack .10 .03
231 Steve Avery .10 .03
232 Dave Valle .10 .03
233 Mark Leonard .10 .03
234 Spike Owen .10 .03
235 Gary Sheffield .20 .06
236 Steve Chitren .10 .03
237 Zane Smith .10 .03
238 Tom Gordon .10 .03
239 Jose Oquendo .10 .03
240 Todd Stottlemyre .10 .03
241 Darren Daulton .20 .06
242 Tim Naehring .10 .03
243 Tony Phillips .10 .03
244 Shawon Dunston .10 .03
245 Manuel Lee .10 .03
246 Mike Pagliarulo .10 .03
247 Jim Thome .50 .15
248 Luis Mercedes .10 .03
249 Cal Eldred .10 .03
250 Derek Bell .20 .06
251 Arthur Rhodes .10 .03
252 Scott Cooper .10 .03
253 Roberto Hernandez .10 .03
254 Mo Sanford .10 .03
255 Scott Servais .10 .03
256 Eric Karros .20 .06
257 Andy Mota .10 .03
258 Keith Mitchell .10 .03
259 Joel Johnston .10 .03
260 John Wehner .10 .03
261 Gino Minutelli .10 .03
262 Greg Gagne .10 .03
263 Stan Royer .10 .03
264 Carlos Garcia .10 .03
265 Andy Ashby .10 .03
266 Kim Batiste .10 .03
267 Julio Valera .10 .03
268 Royce Clayton .10 .03
269 Gary Scott .10 .03
270 Kirk Dressendorfer .10 .03
271 Sean Berry .10 .03
272 Lance Dickson .10 .03
273 Rob Maurer .10 .03
274 Scott Brosius RC .50 .15
275 Dave Fleming .10 .03
276 Lenny Webster .10 .03
277 Mike Humphreys .10 .03
278 Freddie Benavides .10 .03
279 Harvey Pulliam .10 .03
280 Jeff Carter .10 .03
281 Jim Abbott I .50 .15
Nolan Ryan
282 Wade Boggs I .50 .15
George Brett
283 Ken Griffey Jr. I .50 .15
Rickey Henderson
284 Wally Joyner .30 .09
Dale Murphy
285 Chuck Knoblauch I .30 .09
Ozzie Smith
286 Robin Ventura I .50 .15
Lou Gehrig
287 Robin Yount SIDE .50 .15
288 Bob Tewksbury SIDE .10 .03
289 Kirby Puckett SIDE .30 .09
290 Kenny Lofton SIDE .20 .06
291 Jack McDowell SIDE .10 .03
292 John Burkett SIDE .10 .03
293 Dwight Smith SIDE .10 .03
294 Nolan Ryan SIDE 1.00 .30
295 M.Ramirez DP RC 2.50 .75
296 Cliff Floyd RC DP UER .50 .15
(Throws right, not left as indicated on back)
297 Al Shirley DP RC .15 .04
298 Brian Barber DP RC .15 .04
299 Jon Farrell DP RC .15 .04
300 Scott Ruffcorn DP RC .15 .04
301 Tyrone Hill DP RC .15 .04
302 Benji Gil DP RC .25 .07
303 Tyler Green DP RC .15 .04
304 Allen Watson DP RC .15 .04
305 Jay Buhner SH .10 .03
306 Roberto Alomar SH .20 .06
307 Chuck Knoblauch SH .10 .03
308 Darryl Strawberry SH .10 .03
309 Danny Tartabull SH .10 .03
310 Bobby Bonilla SH .10 .03
311 Mike Felder .10 .03
312 Storm Davis .10 .03
313 Tim Teufel .10 .03
314 Tom Brunansky .10 .03
315 Rex Hudler .10 .03
316 Dave Otto .10 .03
317 Jeff King .10 .03
318 Dan Gladden .10 .03
319 Bill Pecota .10 .03
320 Franklin Stubbs .10 .03
321 Gary Carter .20 .06
322 Melido Perez .10 .03
323 Eric Davis .20 .06
324 Greg Myers .10 .03
325 Pete Incaviglia .10 .03
326 Von Hayes .10 .03
327 Greg Swindell .10 .03
328 Steve Sax .10 .03
329 Chuck McElroy .10 .03
330 Gregg Jefferies .10 .03
331 Joe Oliver .10 .03
332 Paul Faries .10 .03
333 David West .10 .03
334 Craig Grebeck .10 .03
335 Chris Hammond .10 .03
336 Billy Ripken .10 .03
337 Scott Sanderson .10 .03
338 Dick Schofield .10 .03
339 Bob Milacki .10 .03
340 Kevin Reimer .10 .03
341 Jose DeLeon .10 .03
342 Henry Cotto .10 .03
343 Daryl Boston .10 .03
344 Kevin Gross .10 .03
345 Milt Thompson .10 .03
346 Luis Rivera .10 .03
347 Al Osuna .10 .03
348 Rob Deer .10 .03
349 Tim Leary .10 .03
350 Mike Stanton .10 .03
351 Dean Palmer .20 .06
352 Trevor Wilson .10 .03
353 Mark Eichhorn .10 .03
354 Scott Aldred .10 .03
355 Mark Whiten .10 .03
356 Leo Gomez .10 .03
357 Rafael Belliard .10 .03
358 Carlos Quintana .10 .03
359 Mark Davis .10 .03
360 Chris Nabholz .10 .03
361 Carlton Fisk .30 .09
362 Joe Orsulak .10 .03
363 Eric Anthony .10 .03
364 Greg Hibbard .10 .03
365 Scott Leius .10 .03
366 Hensley Meulens .10 .03
367 Chris Bosio .10 .03
368 Brian Downing .10 .03
369 Sammy Sosa .75 .23
370 Stan Belinda .10 .03
371 Joe Grahe .10 .03
372 Luis Salazar .10 .03
373 Lance Johnson .10 .03
374 Kal Daniels .10 .03
375 Dave Winfield .20 .06
376 Brook Jacoby .10 .03
377 Mariano Duncan .10 .03
378 Ron Darling .10 .03
379 Randy Johnson .50 .15
380 Chito Martinez .10 .03
381 Andres Galarraga .20 .06
382 Willie Randolph .20 .06
383 Charles Nagy .10 .03
384 Tim Belcher .10 .03
385 Duane Ward .10 .03
386 Vicente Palacios .10 .03
387 Mike Gallego .10 .03
388 Rich DeLucia .10 .03
389 Scott Radinsky .10 .03
390 Damon Berryhill .10 .03
391 Kirk McCaskill .10 .03
392 Pedro Guerrero .20 .06
393 Kevin Mitchell .10 .03
394 Dickie Thon .10 .03
395 Bobby Bonilla .20 .06
396 Bill Wegman .10 .03
397 Dave Martinez .10 .03
398 Rick Sutcliffe .20 .06
399 Larry Andersen .10 .03
400 Tony Gwynn .60 .18
401 Rickey Henderson .50 .15
402 Greg Cadaret .10 .03
403 Keith Miller .10 .03
404 Bip Roberts .10 .03
405 Kevin Brown .20 .06
406 Mitch Williams .10 .03
407 Frank Viola .20 .06
408 Darren Lewis .10 .03
409 Bob Welch .10 .03
410 Bob Walk .10 .03
411 Todd Frohwirth .10 .03
412 Brian Hunter .10 .03
413 Ron Karkovice .10 .03
414 Mike Morgan .10 .03
415 Joe Hesketh .10 .03
416 Don Slaught .10 .03
417 Tom Henke .10 .03
418 Kurt Stillwell .10 .03
419 Hector Villaneuva .10 .03
420 Glenallen Hill .10 .03
421 Pat Borders .10 .03
422 Charlie Hough .20 .06
423 Charlie Leibrandt .10 .03
424 Eddie Murray .50 .15
425 Jesse Barfield .10 .03
426 Mark Lemke .10 .03
427 Kevin McReynolds .10 .03
428 Gilberto Reyes .10 .03
429 Ramon Martinez .10 .03
430 Steve Buechele .10 .03
431 David Wells .20 .06
432 Kyle Abbott .10 .03
433 John Habyan .10 .03
434 Kevin Appier .20 .06
435 Gene Larkin .10 .03
436 Sandy Alomar Jr. .10 .03
437 Mike Jackson .10 .03
438 Todd Benzinger .10 .03
439 Teddy Higuera .10 .03
440 Reggie Sanders .10 .03
441 Mark Carreon .10 .03
442 Bret Saberhagen .20 .06
443 Gene Nelson .10 .03
444 Jay Howell .10 .03
445 Roger McDowell .10 .03
446 Sid Bream .10 .03
447 Mackey Sasser .10 .03
448 Bill Swift .10 .03
449 Hubie Brooks .10 .03
450 David Cone .20 .06
451 Bobby Witt .10 .03
452 Brady Anderson .20 .06
453 Lee Stevens .10 .03
454 Luis Aquino .10 .03
455 Carney Lansford .20 .06
456 Carlos Hernandez .10 .03
457 Danny Jackson .10 .03
458 Gerald Young .10 .03
459 Tom Candiotti .10 .03
460 Billy Hatcher .10 .03
461 John Wetteland .20 .06
462 Mike Bordick .10 .03
463 Don Robinson .10 .03
464 Jeff Johnson .10 .03
465 Lonnie Smith .10 .03
466 Paul Assenmacher .10 .03
467 Alvin Davis .10 .03
468 Jim Eisenreich .10 .03
469 Brent Mayne .10 .03
470 Jeff Brantley .10 .03
471 Tim Burke .10 .03
472 Pat Mahomes RC .25 .07
473 Ryan Bowen .10 .03
474 Bryn Smith .10 .03
475 Mike Flanagan .10 .03
476 Reggie Jefferson .10 .03
477 Jeff Blauser .10 .03
478 Craig Lefferts .10 .03
479 Todd Worrell .10 .03
480 Scott Scudder .10 .03
481 Kirk Gibson .20 .06
482 Kenny Rogers .20 .06
483 Jack Morris .20 .06
484 Russ Swan .10 .03
485 Mike Huff .10 .03
486 Ken Hill .10 .03
487 Geronimo Pena .10 .03
488 Charlie O'Brien .10 .03
489 Mike Maddux .10 .03
490 Scott Livingstone .10 .03
491 Carl Willis .10 .03
492 Kelly Downs .10 .03
493 Dennis Cook .10 .03
494 Joe Magrane .10 .03
495 Bob Kipper .10 .03
496 Jose Mesa .10 .03
497 Charlie Hayes .10 .03
498 Joe Girardi .10 .03
499 Doug Jones .10 .03
500 Barry Bonds 1.25 .35
501 Bill Krueger .10 .03
502 Glenn Braggs .10 .03
503 Eric King .10 .03
504 Frank Castillo .10 .03
505 Mike Gardiner .10 .03
506 Cory Snyder .10 .03
507 Steve Howe .10 .03
508 Jose Rijo .10 .03
509 Sid Fernandez .10 .03
510 Archi Cianfrocco RC .15 .04
511 Mark Guthrie .10 .03
512 Bob Ojeda .10 .03
513 John Doherty RC .15 .04
514 Dante Bichette .20 .06
515 Juan Berenguer .10 .03
516 Jeff M. Robinson .10 .03
517 Mike Macfarlane .10 .03
518 Matt Young .10 .03
519 Otis Nixon .10 .03
520 Brian Holman .10 .03
521 Chris Haney .10 .03
522 Jeff Kent RC 1.50 .45
523 Chad Curtis RC .25 .07
524 Vince Horsman .10 .03
525 Rod Nichols .10 .03
526 Peter Hoy .10 .03
527 Shawn Boskie .10 .03
528 Alejandro Pena .10 .03
529 Dave Burba .10 .03
530 Ricky Jordan .10 .03
531 Dave Silvestri .10 .03
532 John Patterson UER RC .10 .03
(Listed as being born in 1960; should be 1967)
533 Jeff Branson .10 .03
534 Derrick May .10 .03
535 Esteban Beltre .10 .03
536 Jose Melendez .10 .03
537 Wally Joyner .20 .06
538 Eddie Taubensee RC .25 .07
539 Jim Abbott .30 .09
540 Brian Williams RC .15 .04
541 Donovan Osborne .10 .03
542 Patrick Lennon .10 .03
543 Mike Groppuso RC .15 .04
544 Jarvis Brown .10 .03
545 Shawn Livsey RC .15 .04
546 Jeff Ware .10 .03
547 Danny Tartabull .10 .03
548 Bobby Jones RC .25 .07
549 Ken Griffey Jr. .75 .23
550 Rey Sanchez RC .25 .07
551 Pedro Astacio RC .25 .07
552 Juan Guerrero .10 .03
553 Jacob Brumfield .10 .03
554 Ben Rivera .10 .03
555 Brian Jordan RC .50 .15
556 Denny Neagle .20 .06
557 Cliff Brantley .10 .03
558 Anthony Young .10 .03
559 John Vander Wal .10 .03
560 Monty Fariss .10 .03
561 Russ Springer RC .15 .04
562 Pat Listach RC .25 .07
563 Pat Hentgen .10 .03
564 Andy Stankiewicz .10 .03
565 Mike Perez .10 .03
566 Mike Bielecki .10 .03
567 Butch Henry RC .15 .04
568 Dave Nilsson .10 .03
569 Scott Hatteberg RC .25 .07
570 Ruben Amaro .10 .03
571 Todd Hundley .10 .03
572 Moises Alou .20 .06
573 Hector Fajardo RC .15 .04
574 Todd Van Poppel .10 .03
575 Willie Banks .10 .03
576 Bob Zupcic RC .15 .04
577 J.J. Johnson RC .15 .04
578 John Burkett .10 .03
579 Trever Miller RC .15 .04
580 Scott Bankhead .10 .03
581 Rich Amaral .10 .03
582 Kenny Lofton .30 .09
583 Matt Stairs RC .25 .07
584 Don Mattingly .50 .15
Rod Carew IDOLS
585 Steve Avery .10 .03
Jack Morris IDOLS
586 Roberto Alomar .20 .06
Sandy Alomar SR. IDOLS
587 Scott Sanderson .20 .06
Catfish Hunter IDOLS
588 Dave Justice .20 .06
Willie Stargell IDOLS
589 Rex Hudler .50 .15
Roger Staubach IDOLS
590 David Cone .20 .06
Jackie Gleason IDOLS
591 Tony Gwynn .30 .09
Willie Davis IDOLS
592 Orel Hershiser SIDE .10 .03
593 John Wetteland SIDE .10 .03
594 Tom Glavine SIDE .20 .06
595 Randy Johnson SIDE .30 .09
596 Jim Gott SIDE .10 .03
597 Donald Harris .10 .03
598 Shawn Hare RC .15 .04
599 Chris Gardner .10 .03
600 Rusty Meacham .10 .03
601 Benito Santiago .20 .06
602 Eric Davis SHADE .10 .03
603 Jose Lind SHADE .10 .03
604 Dave Justice SHADE .10 .03
605 Tim Raines SHADE .10 .03
606 Randy Tomlin GRIP .10 .03
607 Jack McDowell GRIP .10 .03
608 Greg Maddux GRIP .50 .15
609 Charles Nagy GRIP .10 .03
610 Tom Candiotti GRIP .10 .03
611 David Cone GRIP .10 .03
612 Steve Avery GRIP .10 .03
613 Rod Beck GRIP RC .25 .07
614 R. Henderson TECH .30 .09
615 Benito Santiago TECH .10 .03
616 Ruben Sierra TECH .10 .03
617 Ryne Sandberg TECH .50 .15
618 Nolan Ryan TECH 1.00 .30
619 Brett Butler TECH .10 .03
620 Dave Justice TECH .10 .03

1992 Pinnacle Rookie Idols

This 18-card insert set is a spin-off on the Idols subset featured in the regular series. The cards were randomly inserted in Series II wax packs. The set features full-bleed color photos of 18 rookies along with their pick of sports figures or other individuals who had the greatest impact on their careers. The fronts carry a close-up photo of the rookie superimposed on an action game shot of his idol.

Nm-Mt Ex-Mt
COMPLETE SET (18) 120.00 36.00
1 Reggie Sanders 3.00 .90
and Eric Davis
2 Hector Fajardo 5.00 1.50
and Jim Abbott
3 Gary Cooper 20.00 6.00
and George Brett
4 Mark Wohlers 15.00 4.50
and Roger Clemens
5 Luis Mercedes 3.00 .90
and Julio Franco
6 Willie Banks 3.00 .90
and Doc Gooden
7 Kenny Lofton 8.00 2.40
and Rickey Henderson
8 Keith Mitchell 1.50 .45
and Dave Henderson
9 Kim Batiste 5.00 1.50
and Barry Larkin
10 Todd Hundley 8.00 2.40
and Thurman Munson
11 Eddie Zosky 25.00 7.50
and Cal Ripken
12 Todd Van Poppel 30.00 9.00
and Nolan Ryan
13 Jim Thome 12.00 3.60
and Ryne Sandberg
14 Dave Fleming 3.00 .90
and Bobby Murcer
15 Royce Clayton 12.00 3.60
and Ozzie Smith
16 Donald Harris 3.00 .90
and Darryl Strawberry
17 Chad Curtis 3.00 .90
and Alan Trammell
18 Derek Bell 3.00 .90
and Dave Winfield

1992 Pinnacle Slugfest

This 15-card set highlights the games top sluggers. The cards were issued exclusively as an one per pack insert in specially marked cello packs.

Nm-Mt Ex-Mt
COMPLETE SET (15) 30.00 9.00
1 Cecil Fielder .75 .23
2 Mark McGwire 5.00 1.50
3 Jose Canseco 2.00 .60
4 Barry Bonds 5.00 1.50
5 David Justice .75 .23
6 Bobby Bonilla .75 .23
7 Ken Griffey Jr. 3.00 .90
8 Ron Gant .75 .23
9 Ryne Sandberg 3.00 .90
10 Ruben Sierra .40 .12
11 Frank Thomas 2.00 .60
12 Will Clark 2.00 .60
13 Kirby Puckett 2.00 .60
14 Cal Ripken 6.00 1.80
15 Jeff Bagwell 2.00 .60

1992 Pinnacle Team 2000

This 80-card standard-size set focuses on young players who were projected to be stars in the year 2000. Cards 1-40 were inserted in Series 1 jumbo packs while cards 41-80 were featured in Series 2 jumbo packs. The insertion rate was three per jumbo pack in either series.

Nm-Mt Ex-Mt
COMPLETE SET (80) 30.00 9.00
COMPLETE SERIES 1 (40) 20.00 6.00
COMPLETE SERIES 2 (40) 10.00 3.00
1 Mike Mussina 1.25 .35
2 Phil Plantier .25 .07
3 Frank Thomas 1.25 .35
4 Travis Fryman .50 .15
5 Kevin Appier .50 .15
6 Chuck Knoblauch .50 .15
7 Pat Kelly .25 .07
8 Ivan Rodriguez 1.25 .35
9 Dave Justice .50 .15
10 Jeff Bagwell 1.25 .35
11 Marquis Grissom .50 .15
12 Andy Benes .25 .07
13 Gregg Olson .25 .07
14 Kevin Morton .25 .07
15 Tim Naehring .25 .07
16 Dave Hollins .25 .07
17 Sandy Alomar Jr. .25 .07
18 Albert Belle .50 .15

19 Charles Nagy .25 .07
20 Brian McRae .25 .07
21 Larry Walker .75 .23
22 Delino DeShields .25 .07
23 Jeff Johnson .25 .07
24 Bernie Williams .75 .23
25 Jose Offerman .25 .07
26 Juan Gonzalez .75 .23
27A Juan Guzman .25 .07
(Pinnacle logo at top)
27B Juan Guzman .25 .07
(Pinnacle logo at bottom)
28 Eric Anthony .25 .07
29 Brian Hunter .25 .07
30 John Smoltz .75 .23
31 Deion Sanders .75 .23
32 Greg Maddux 2.00 .60
33 Andujar Cedeno .25 .07
34 Royce Clayton .25 .07
35 Kenny Lofton .75 .23
36 Cal Eldred .25 .07
37 Jim Thome 1.25 .35
38 Gary DiSarcina .25 .07
39 Brian Jordan 1.25 .35
40 Chad Curtis .60 .18
41 Ben McDonald .25 .07
42 Jim Abbott .75 .23
43 Robin Ventura .50 .15
44 Milt Cuyler .25 .07
45 Gregg Jefferies .25 .07
46 Scott Radinsky .25 .07
47 Ken Griffey Jr. 2.00 .60
48 Roberto Alomar .75 .23
49 Ramon Martinez .25 .07
50 Bret Barberie .25 .07
51 Ray Lankford .25 .07
52 Leo Gomez .25 .07
53 Tommy Greene .25 .07
54 Mo Vaughn .50 .15
55 Sammy Sosa 2.00 .60
56 Carlos Baerga .25 .07
57 Mark Lewis .25 .07
58 Tom Gordon .25 .07
59 Gary Sheffield .50 .15
60 Scott Erickson .25 .07
61 Pedro Munoz .25 .07
62 Tino Martinez .75 .23
63 Darren Lewis .25 .07
64 Dean Palmer .50 .15
65 John Olerud .50 .15
66 Steve Avery .25 .07
67 Pete Harnisch .25 .07
68 Luis Gonzalez .50 .15
69 Kim Batiste .25 .07
70 Reggie Sanders .25 .07
71 Luis Mercedes .25 .07
72 Todd Van Poppel .25 .07
73 Gary Scott .25 .07
74 Monty Fariss .25 .07
75 Kyle Abbott .25 .07
76 Eric Karros .50 .15
77 Mo Sanford .25 .07
78 Todd Hundley .25 .07
79 Reggie Jefferson .25 .07
80 Pat Mahomes .60 .18

1992 Pinnacle Team Pinnacle

This 12-card, double-sided insert set features the National League and American League All-Star team as selected by Pinnacle. The standard-size cards were randomly inserted in Series I wax packs. The cards feature illustrations by sports artist Chris Greco with the National League All-Star on one side and the corresponding American League All-Star by position on the other. The words "Team Pinnacle" are printed vertically down the left side of the card in red for American League on one side and blue for National League on the other.

Nm-Mt Ex-Mt
COMPLETE SET (12) 80.00 24.00
1 Roger Clemens 12.00 3.60
and Ramon Martinez
2 Jim Abbott 4.00 1.20
and Steve Avery
3 Ivan Rodriguez 6.00 1.80
and Benito Santiago
4 Frank Thomas 6.00 1.80
and Will Clark
5 Roberto Alomar 10.00 3.00
and Ryne Sandberg
6 Robin Ventura 2.50 .75
and Matt Williams
7 Cal Ripken 20.00 6.00
and Barry Larkin
8 Danny Tartabull 15.00 4.50
and Barry Bonds
9 Ken Griffey Jr. 10.00 3.00
and Brett Butler
10 Ruben Sierra 2.50 .75
and Dave Justice
11 Dennis Eckersley 2.50 .75
and Rob Dibble
12 Scott Radinsky 2.50 .75
and John Franco

1993 Pinnacle

The 1993 Pinnacle set (by Score) contains 620 standard-size cards issued in two series of 310 cards each. Cards were distributed in hobby and retail foil packs and 27-card jumbo superpacks. The set includes the following topical subsets: Rookies (238-288, 575-620), Now and Then (289-296, 470-476), Idols (297-303, 477-483), Hometown Heroes (304-310, 484-490), and Draft Picks (455-469). Rookie Cards in this set include Derek Jeter, Jason Kendall and Shannon Stewart.

Nm-Mt Ex-Mt
COMPLETE SET (620) 40.00 12.00
COMP. SERIES 1 (310) 15.00 4.50
COMP. SERIES 2 (310) 25.00 7.50
1 Gary Sheffield .30 .09
2 Cal Eldred .15 .04
3 Larry Walker .50 .15
4 Deion Sanders .50 .15
5 Dave Fleming .15 .04
6 Carlos Baerga .15 .04
7 Bernie Williams .50 .15
8 John Kruk .30 .09
9 Jimmy Key .30 .09
10 Jeff Bagwell .50 .15
11 Jim Abbott .50 .15
12 Terry Steinbach .15 .04
13 Bob Tewksbury .15 .04
14 Eric Karros .30 .09
15 Ryne Sandberg 1.25 .35
16 Will Clark .75 .23
17 Edgar Martinez .50 .15
18 Eddie Murray .75 .23
19 Andy Van Slyke .30 .09
20 Cal Ripken Jr. 2.50 .75
21 Ivan Rodriguez .75 .23
22 Barry Larkin .50 .15
23 Don Mattingly 2.00 .60
24 Gregg Jefferies .15 .04
25 Roger Clemens 1.50 .45
26 Cecil Fielder .30 .09
27 Kent Hrbek .30 .09
28 Robin Ventura .30 .09
29 Rickey Henderson .75 .23
30 Roberto Alomar .50 .15
31 Luis Polonia .15 .04
32 Andujar Cedeno .15 .04
33 Pat Listach .15 .04
34 Mark Grace .50 .15
35 Otis Nixon .15 .04
36 Felix Jose .15 .04
37 Mike Sharperson .15 .04
38 Dennis Martinez .30 .09
39 Willie McGee .30 .09
40 Kenny Lofton .30 .09
41 Randy Johnson .75 .23
42 Andy Benes .15 .04
43 Bobby Bonilla .30 .09
44 Mike Mussina .50 .15
45 Len Dykstra .30 .09
46 Ellis Burks .30 .09
47 Chris Sabo .15 .04
48 Jay Bell .30 .09
49 Jose Canseco .75 .23
50 Craig Biggio .50 .15
51 Wally Joyner .30 .09
52 Mickey Tettleton .15 .04
53 Tim Raines .30 .09
54 Brian Harper .15 .04
55 Rene Gonzales .15 .04
56 Mark Langston .15 .04
57 Jack Morris .30 .09
58 Mark McGwire 2.00 .60
59 Ken Caminiti .30 .09
60 Terry Pendleton .30 .09
61 Dave Nilsson .15 .04
62 Tom Pagnozzi .15 .04
63 Mike Morgan .15 .04
64 Darryl Strawberry .30 .09
65 Charles Nagy .15 .04
66 Ken Hill .15 .04
67 Matt Williams .30 .09
68 Jay Buhner .30 .09
69 Vince Coleman .15 .04
70 Brady Anderson .30 .09
71 Fred McGriff .50 .15
72 Ben McDonald .15 .04
73 Terry Mulholland .15 .04
74 Randy Tomlin .15 .04
75 Nolan Ryan 3.00 .90
76 Frank Viola UER .30 .09
(Card incorrectly states he has a surgically repaired elbow)
77 Jose Rijo .15 .04
78 Shane Mack .15 .04
79 Travis Fryman .30 .09
80 Jack McDowell .15 .04
81 Mark Gubicza .15 .04
82 Matt Nokes .15 .04
83 Bert Blyleven .30 .09
84 Eric Anthony .15 .04
85 Mike Bordick .15 .04
86 John Olerud .30 .09
87 B.J. Surhoff .30 .09
88 Bernard Gilkey .15 .04
89 Shawon Dunston .15 .04
90 Tom Glavine .50 .15
91 Brett Butler .30 .09
92 Moises Alou .30 .09
93 Albert Belle .30 .09
94 Darren Lewis .15 .04
95 Omar Vizquel .50 .15
96 Dwight Gooden .30 .09
97 Gregg Olson .15 .04
98 Tony Gwynn 1.00 .30
99 Darren Daulton .30 .09
100 Dennis Eckersley .30 .09
101 Rob Dibble .30 .09
102 Mike Greenwell .15 .04
103 Jose Lind .15 .04
104 Julio Franco .30 .09
105 Tom Gordon .15 .04
106 Scott Livingstone .15 .04
107 Chuck Knoblauch .30 .09
108 Frank Thomas .75 .23
109 Melido Perez .15 .04
110 Ken Griffey Jr. 1.25 .35
111 Harold Baines .30 .09
112 Gary Gaetti .30 .09
113 Pete Harnisch .15 .04
114 David Wells .30 .09
115 Charlie Leibrandt .15 .04
116 Ray Lankford .15 .04
117 Kevin Seitzer .15 .04
118 Robin Yount 1.25 .35
119 Lenny Harris .15 .04
120 Chris James .15 .04
121 Delino DeShields .15 .04
122 Kirt Manwaring .15 .04
123 Glenallen Hill .15 .04
124 Hensley Meulens .15 .04
125 Darrin Jackson .15 .04
126 Todd Hundley .15 .04
127 Dave Hollins .15 .04
128 Sam Horn .15 .04
129 Roberto Hernandez .15 .04
130 Vicente Palacios .15 .04
131 George Brett 2.00 .60
132 Dave Martinez .15 .04
133 Kevin Appier .30 .09
134 Pat Kelly .15 .04
135 Pedro Munoz .15 .04
136 Mark Carreon .15 .04
137 Lance Johnson .15 .04
138 Devon White .30 .09
139 Julio Valera .15 .04
140 Eddie Taubensee .15 .04
141 Willie Wilson .15 .04
142 Stan Belinda .15 .04
143 John Smoltz .50 .15
144 Darryl Hamilton .15 .04
145 Sammy Sosa 1.25 .35
146 Carlos Hernandez .15 .04
147 Tom Candiotti .15 .04
148 Mike Felder .15 .04
149 Rusty Meacham .15 .04
150 Ivan Calderon .15 .04
151 Pete O'Brien .15 .04
152 Erik Hanson .15 .04
153 Billy Ripken .15 .04
154 Kurt Stillwell .15 .04
155 Jeff Kent .75 .23
156 Mickey Morandini .15 .04
157 Randy Milligan .15 .04
158 Reggie Sanders .15 .04
159 Luis Rivera .15 .04
160 Orlando Merced .15 .04
161 Dean Palmer .30 .09
162 Mike Perez .15 .04
163 Scott Erickson .15 .04
164 Kevin McReynolds .15 .04
165 Kevin Maas .15 .04
166 Ozzie Guillen .15 .04
167 Rob Deer .15 .04
168 Danny Tartabull .15 .04
169 Lee Stevens .15 .04
170 Dave Henderson .15 .04
171 Derek Bell .15 .04
172 Steve Finley .30 .09
173 Greg Olson .15 .04
174 Geronimo Pena .15 .04
175 Paul Quantrill .15 .04
176 Steve Buechele .15 .04
177 Kevin Gross .15 .04
178 Tim Wallach .15 .04
179 Dave Valle .15 .04
180 Dave Silvestri .15 .04
181 Bud Black .15 .04
182 Henry Rodriguez .15 .04
183 Tim Teufel .15 .04
184 Mark McLemore .15 .04
185 Bret Saberhagen .30 .09
186 Chris Hoiles .15 .04
187 Ricky Jordan .15 .04
188 Don Slaught .15 .04
189 Mo Vaughn .30 .09
190 Joe Oliver .15 .04
191 Juan Gonzalez .50 .15
192 Scott Leius .15 .04
193 Milt Cuyler .15 .04
194 Chris Haney .15 .04
195 Ron Karkovice .15 .04
196 Steve Farr .15 .04
197 John Orton .15 .04
198 Kelly Gruber .15 .04
199 Ron Darling .15 .04
200 Ruben Sierra .15 .04
201 Chuck Finley .30 .09
202 Mike Moore .15 .04
203 Pat Borders .15 .04
204 Sid Bream .15 .04
205 Todd Zeile .15 .04
206 Rick Wilkins .15 .04
207 Jim Gantner .15 .04
208 Frank Castillo .15 .04
209 Dave Hansen .15 .04
210 Trevor Wilson .15 .04
211 Sandy Alomar Jr. .15 .04
212 Sean Berry .15 .04
213 Tino Martinez .50 .15
214 Chito Martinez .15 .04
215 Dan Walters .15 .04
216 John Franco .30 .09
217 Glenn Davis .15 .04
218 Mariano Duncan .15 .04
219 Mike LaValliere .15 .04
220 Rafael Palmeiro .50 .15
221 Jack Clark .30 .09
222 Hal Morris .15 .04
223 Ed Sprague .15 .04
224 John Valentin .15 .04
225 Sam Militello .15 .04
226 Bob Wickman .15 .04
227 Damion Easley .15 .04
228 John Jaha .15 .04
229 Bob Ayrault .15 .04
230 Mo Sanford .15 .04
231 Walt Weiss .15 .04
232 Dante Bichette .30 .09
233 Steve Decker .15 .04
234 Jerald Clark .15 .04
235 Bryan Harvey .15 .04
236 Joe Girardi .15 .04
237 Dave Magadan .15 .04
238 David Nied .15 .04
239 Eric Wedge RC .40 .12
240 Rico Brogna .15 .04
241 J.T. Bruett .15 .04
242 Jonathan Hurst .15 .04
243 Bret Boone .50 .15
244 Manny Alexander .15 .04
245 Scooter Tucker .15 .04
246 Troy Neel .15 .04
247 Eddie Zosky .15 .04
248 Melvin Nieves .15 .04
249 Ryan Thompson .15 .04
250 Shawn Barton RC .15 .04
251 Ryan Klesko .30 .09
252 Mike Piazza 2.00 .60
253 Steve Hosey .15 .04
254 Shane Reynolds .15 .04
255 Dan Wilson .30 .09
256 Tom Marsh .15 .04
257 Barry Manuel .15 .04
258 Paul Miller .15 .04
259 Pedro Martinez 1.50 .45
260 Steve Cooke .15 .04
261 Johnny Guzman .15 .04
262 Mike Butcher .15 .04
263 Bien Figueroa .15 .04
264 Rich Rowland .15 .04
265 Shawn Jeter .15 .04
266 Gerald Williams .15 .04
267 Derek Parks .15 .04
268 Henry Mercedes .15 .04
269 David Hulse RC .15 .04
270 Tim Pugh RC .15 .04
271 William Suero .15 .04
272 Ozzie Canseco .15 .04
273 Fernando Ramsey RC .15 .04
274 Bernardo Brito .15 .04
275 Dave Mlicki .15 .04
276 Tim Salmon .50 .15
277 Mike Raczka .15 .04
278 Ken Ryan RC .40 .12
279 Rafael Bournigal .15 .04
280 Wil Cordero .15 .04
281 Billy Ashley .15 .04
282 Paul Wagner .15 .04
283 Blas Minor .15 .04
284 Rick Trlicek .15 .04
285 Willie Greene .15 .04
286 Ted Wood .15 .04
287 Phil Clark .15 .04
288 Jesse Levis .15 .04
289 Tony Gwynn NT .50 .15
290 Nolan Ryan NT 1.50 .45
291 Dennis Martinez NT .15 .04
292 Eddie Murray NT .50 .15
293 Robin Yount NT .75 .23
294 George Brett NT 1.00 .30
295 Dave Winfield NT .15 .04
296 Bert Blyleven NT .15 .04
297 Jeff Bagwell .75 .23
Carl Yastrzemski
298 John Smoltz .30 .09
Jack Morris
299 Larry Walker .50 .15
Mike Bossy
300 Gary Sheffield .30 .09
Barry Larkin
301 Ivan Rodriguez .50 .15
Carlton Fisk
302 Delino DeShields .75 .23
Malcolm X
303 Tim Salmon .50 .15
Dwight Evans
304 Bernard Gilkey HH .15 .04
305 Cal Ripken Jr. HH 1.25 .35
306 Barry Larkin HH .30 .09
307 Kent Hrbek HH .15 .04
308 Rickey Henderson HH .50 .15
309 Darryl Strawberry HH .15 .04
310 John Franco HH .15 .04
311 Todd Stottlemyre .15 .04
312 Luis Gonzalez .30 .09
313 Tommy Greene .15 .04
314 Randy Velarde .15 .04
315 Steve Avery .15 .04
316 Jose Oquendo .15 .04
317 Rey Sanchez .15 .04
318 Greg Vaughn .15 .04
319 Orel Hershiser .30 .09
320 Paul Sorrento .15 .04
321 Royce Clayton .15 .04
322 John Vander Wal .15 .04
323 Henry Cotto .15 .04
324 Pete Schourek .15 .04
325 David Segui .15 .04
326 Arthur Rhodes .15 .04
327 Bruce Hurst .15 .04
328 Wes Chamberlain .15 .04
329 Ozzie Smith 1.25 .35
330 Scott Cooper .15 .04
331 Felix Fermin .15 .04
332 Mike Macfarlane .15 .04
333 Dan Gladden .15 .04
334 Kevin Tapani .15 .04
335 Steve Sax .15 .04
336 Jeff Montgomery .15 .04
337 Gary DiSarcina .15 .04
338 Lance Blankenship .15 .04
339 Brian Williams .15 .04
340 Duane Ward .15 .04
341 Chuck McElroy .15 .04
342 Joe Magrane .15 .04
343 Jaime Navarro .15 .04
344 Dave Justice .30 .09
345 Jose Offerman .15 .04
346 Marquis Grissom .30 .09
347 Bill Swift .15 .04
348 Jim Thome .75 .23
349 Archi Cianfrocco .15 .04
350 Anthony Young .15 .04
351 Leo Gomez .15 .04
352 Bill Gullickson .15 .04
353 Alan Trammell .30 .09
354 Dan Pasqua .15 .04
355 Jeff King .15 .04
356 Kevin Brown .30 .09
357 Tim Belcher .15 .04
358 Bip Roberts .15 .04
359 Brent Mayne .15 .04
360 Rheal Cormier .15 .04
361 Mark Guthrie .15 .04
362 Craig Grebeck .15 .04
363 Andy Stankiewicz .15 .04
364 Juan Guzman .15 .04
365 Bobby Witt .15 .04
366 Mark Portugal .15 .04
367 Brian McRae .15 .04
368 Mark Lemke .15 .04
369 Bill Wegman .15 .04
370 Donovan Osborne .15 .04
371 Derrick May .15 .04
372 Carl Willis .15 .04
373 Chris Nabholz .15 .04
374 Mark Lewis .15 .04
375 John Burkett .15 .04
376 Luis Mercedes .15 .04
377 Ramon Martinez .15 .04
378 Kyle Abbott .15 .04
379 Mark Wohlers .15 .04
380 Bob Walk .15 .04
381 Kenny Rogers .30 .09
382 Tim Naehring .15 .04
383 Alex Fernandez .15 .04
384 Keith Miller .15 .04
385 Mike Henneman .15 .04
386 Rick Aguilera .15 .04
387 George Bell .15 .04
388 Mike Gallego .15 .04
389 Howard Johnson .15 .04
390 Kim Batiste .15 .04
391 Jerry Browne .15 .04
392 Damon Berryhill .15 .04
393 Ricky Bones .15 .04
394 Omar Olivares .15 .04
395 Mike Harkey .15 .04
396 Pedro Astacio .15 .04
397 John Wetteland .30 .09
398 Rod Beck .15 .04
399 Thomas Howard .15 .04
400 Mike Devereaux .15 .04
401 Tim Wakefield .75 .23
402 Curt Schilling .30 .09
403 Zane Smith .15 .04
404 Bob Zupcic .15 .04
405 Tom Browning .15 .04
406 Tony Phillips .15 .04
407 John Doherty .15 .04
408 Pat Mahomes .15 .04
409 John Habyan .15 .04
410 Steve Olin .15 .04
411 Chad Curtis .15 .04
412 Joe Grahe .15 .04
413 John Patterson .15 .04
414 Brian Hunter .15 .04
415 Doug Henry .15 .04
416 Lee Smith .30 .09
417 Bob Scanlan .15 .04
418 Kent Mercker .15 .04
419 Mel Rojas .15 .04
420 Mark Whiten .15 .04
421 Carlton Fisk .50 .15
422 Candy Maldonado .15 .04
423 Doug Drabek .15 .04
424 Wade Boggs .50 .15
425 Mark Davis .15 .04
426 Kirby Puckett .75 .23
427 Joe Carter .30 .09
428 Paul Molitor .50 .15
429 Eric Davis .30 .09
430 Darryl Kile .30 .09
431 Jeff Parrett .15 .04
432 Jeff Blauser .15 .04
433 Dan Plesac .15 .04
434 Andres Galarraga .30 .09
435 Jim Gott .15 .04
436 Jose Mesa .15 .04
437 Ben Rivera .15 .04
438 Dave Winfield .30 .09
439 Norm Charlton .15 .04
440 Chris Bosio .15 .04
441 Wilson Alvarez .15 .04
442 Dave Stewart .30 .09
443 Doug Jones .15 .04
444 Jeff Russell .15 .04
445 Ron Gant .30 .09
446 Paul O'Neill .50 .15
447 Charlie Hayes .15 .04
448 Joe Hesketh .15 .04
449 Chris Hammond .15 .04
450 Hipolito Pichardo .15 .04
451 Scott Radinsky .15 .04
452 Bobby Thigpen .15 .04
453 Xavier Hernandez .15 .04
454 Lonnie Smith .15 .04
455 Jamie Arnold DP RC .15 .04
456 B.J. Wallace DP .15 .04
457 Derek Jeter DP RC 10.00 3.00
458 Jason Kendall DP RC 1.00 .30
459 Rick Helling DP .15 .04
460 Derek Wallace DP RC .15 .04
461 Sean Lowe DP RC .15 .04
462 S. Stewart DP RC 1.00 .30
463 Benji Grigsby DP RC .15 .04
464 T. Steverson DP RC .15 .04
465 Dan Serafini DP RC .15 .04
466 Michael Tucker DP .30 .09
467 Chris Roberts DP .15 .04
468 Pete Janicki DP RC .15 .04
469 Jeff Schmidt DP RC .15 .04
470 Don Mattingly NT 1.00 .30
471 Cal Ripken Jr. NT 1.25 .35
472 Jack Morris NT .15 .04
473 Terry Pendleton NT .15 .04
474 Dennis Eckersley NT .30 .09
475 Carlton Fisk NT .30 .09
476 Wade Boggs NT .30 .09
477 Len Dykstra .30 .09
Ken Stabler
478 Danny Tartabull .15 .04
Jose Tartabull
479 Jeff Conine .50 .15
Dale Murphy
480 Gregg Jefferies .15 .04
Ron Cey
481 Paul Molitor .30 .09
Harmon Killebrew
482 John Valentin .15 .04
Dave Concepcion
483 Alex Arias .15 .04
Dave Winfield
484 Barry Bonds HH 1.00 .30

485 Doug Drabek HH .15 .04
486 Dave Winfield HH .15 .04
487 Brett Butler HH .15 .04
488 Harold Baines HH .15 .04
489 David Cone HH .15 .04
490 Willie McGee HH .15 .04
491 Robby Thompson .15 .04
492 Pete Incaviglia .15 .04
493 Manuel Lee .15 .04
494 Rafael Belliard .15 .04
495 Scott Fletcher .15 .04
496 Jeff Frye .15 .04
497 Andre Dawson .30 .09
498 Mike Scioscia .15 .04
499 Spike Owen .15 .04
500 Sid Fernandez .15 .04
501 Joe Orsulak .15 .04
502 Benito Santiago .30 .09
503 Dale Murphy .75 .23
504 Barry Bonds 2.00 .60
505 Jose Guzman .15 .04
506 Tony Pena .15 .04
507 Greg Swindell .15 .04
508 Mike Pagliarulo .15 .04
509 Lou Whitaker .30 .09
510 Greg Gagne .15 .04
511 Butch Henry .15 .04
512 Jeff Brantley .15 .04
513 Jack Armstrong .15 .04
514 Danny Jackson .15 .04
515 Junior Felix .15 .04
516 Milt Thompson .15 .04
517 Greg Maddux 1.25 .35
518 Eric Young .15 .04
519 Jody Reed .15 .04
520 Roberto Kelly .15 .04
521 Darren Holmes .15 .04
522 Craig Lefferts .15 .04
523 Charlie Hough .30 .09
524 Bo Jackson .75 .23
525 Bill Spiers .15 .04
526 Orestes Destrade .15 .04
527 Greg Hibbard .15 .04
528 Roger McDowell .15 .04
529 Cory Snyder .15 .04
530 Harold Reynolds .30 .09
531 Kevin Reimer .15 .04
532 Rick Sutcliffe .30 .09
533 Tony Fernandez .15 .04
534 Tom Brunansky .15 .04
535 Jeff Reardon .30 .09
536 Chili Davis .30 .09
537 Bob Ojeda .15 .04
538 Greg Colbrunn .15 .04
539 Phil Plantier .15 .04
540 Brian Jordan .30 .09
541 Pete Smith .15 .04
542 Frank Tanana .15 .04
543 John Smiley .15 .04
544 David Cone .30 .09
545 Daryl Boston .15 .04
546 Tom Henke .15 .04
547 Bill Krueger .15 .04
548 Freddie Benavides .15 .04
549 Randy Myers .15 .04
550 Reggie Jefferson .15 .04
551 Kevin Mitchell .15 .04
552 Dave Stieb .15 .04
553 Bret Barberie .15 .04
554 Tim Crews .15 .04
555 Doug Dascenzo .15 .04
556 Alex Cole .15 .04
557 Jeff Innis .15 .04
558 Carlos Garcia .15 .04
559 Steve Howe .15 .04
560 Kirk McCaskill .15 .04
561 Frank Seminara .15 .04
562 Cris Carpenter .15 .04
563 Mike Stanley .15 .04
564 Carlos Quintana .15 .04
565 Mitch Williams .15 .04
566 Juan Bell .15 .04
567 Eric Fox .15 .04
568 Al Leiter .30 .09
569 Mike Stanton .15 .04
570 Scott Kamieniecki .15 .04
571 Ryan Bowen .15 .04
572 Andy Ashby .15 .04
573 Bob Welch .15 .04
574 Scott Sanderson .15 .04
575 Joe Kmak .15 .04
576 Scott Pose RC .15 .04
577 Ricky Gutierrez .15 .04
578 Mike Trombley .15 .04
579 Sterling Hitchcock RC .40 .12
580 Rodney Bolton .15 .04
581 Tyler Green .15 .04
582 Tim Costo .15 .04
583 Tim Laker RC .15 .04
584 Steve Reed RC .15 .04
585 Tom Kramer RC .15 .04
586 Robb Nen .30 .09
587 Jim Tatum RC .15 .04
588 Frank Bolick .15 .04
589 Kevin Young .30 .09
590 Matt Whiteside RC .15 .04
591 Cesar Hernandez .15 .04
592 Mike Mohler RC .40 .12
593 Alan Embree .75 .23
594 Terry Jorgensen .15 .04
595 John Cummings RC .15 .04
596 Domingo Martinez RC .15 .04
597 Benji Gil .15 .04
598 Todd Pratt RC .40 .12
599 Rene Arocha RC .40 .12
600 Dennis Moeller .15 .04
601 Jeff Conine .30 .09
602 Trevor Hoffman .30 .09
603 Daniel Smith .15 .04
604 Lee Tinsley .15 .04
605 Dan Peltier .15 .04
606 Billy Brewer .15 .04
607 Matt Walbeck RC .40 .12
608 Richie Lewis RC .15 .04
609 J.T. Snow RC .60 .18
610 Pat Gomez RC .15 .04
611 Phil Hiatt .15 .04
612 Alex Arias .15 .04
613 Kevin Rogers .15 .04
614 Al Martin .15 .04
615 Greg Gohr .15 .04
616 Graeme Lloyd RC .40 .12
617 Kent Bottenfield .15 .04
618 Chuck Carr .15 .04
619 Darrell Sherman RC .15 .04
620 Mike Lansing RC .40 .12

1993 Pinnacle Expansion Opening Day

This nine-card standard-size dual-sided set was issued to commemorate openning day for the two 1993 expansion teams, the Colorado Rockies and the Florida Marlins. The cards were inserted on top of sealed series two hobby boxes. These cards were also available through a mail-in offer. An anti-counterfeit device is printed in the bottom black border. The backs carry the same design as the fronts with a player from the Rockies appearing on one side and a Marlin's player on the flip side. The cards are numbered on both sides.

Nm-Mt Ex-Mt
COMPLETE SET (9) 25.00 7.50
1 Charlie Hough 5.00 1.50
David Nied
2 Benito Santiago 5.00 1.50
Joe Girardi
3 Orestes Destrade 5.00 1.50
Andres Galarraga
4 Bret Barberie 2.50 .75
Eric Young
5 Dave Magadan 2.50 .75
Charlie Hayes
6 Walt Weiss 2.50 .75
Freddie Benavides
7 Jeff Conine 5.00 1.50
Jerald Clark
8 Scott Pose 2.50 .75
Alex Cole
9 Junior Felix 5.00 1.50
Dante Bichette

1993 Pinnacle Rookie Team Pinnacle

Cards from this 10-card standard-size set were randomly inserted into one in every 90 series two foil packs and each features an American League rookie on one side and a National League rookie on the other. Each double-sided card displays paintings by artist Christopher Greco encased by a bold black border. The cards are numbered on the front and back.

Nm-Mt Ex-Mt
COMPLETE SET (10) 100.00 30.00
1 Pedro Martinez 15.00 4.50
Mike Trombley
2 Kevin Rogers 5.00 1.50
Sterling Hitchcock
3 Mike Piazza 25.00 7.50
Jesse Levis
4 Ryan Klesko 8.00 2.40
J.T. Snow
5 John Patterson 10.00 3.00
Bret Boone
6 Kevin Young 5.00 1.50
Domingo Martinez
7 Wil Cordero 5.00 1.50
Manny Alexander
8 Steve Hosey 10.00 3.00
Tim Salmon
9 Ryan Thompson 5.00 1.50
Gerald Williams
10 Melvin Nieves 5.00 1.50
David Hulse

1993 Pinnacle Slugfest

These 30 standard-size cards salute baseball's top hitters and were inserted one per series two jumbo superpacks.

Nm-Mt Ex-Mt
COMPLETE SET (30) 60.00 18.00
1 Juan Gonzalez 2.50 .75
2 Mark McGwire 10.00 3.00
3 Cecil Fielder 1.50 .45
4 Joe Carter 1.50 .45
5 Fred McGriff 2.50 .75
6 Barry Bonds 10.00 3.00
7 Gary Sheffield 1.50 .45
8 Dave Hollins .75 .23
9 Frank Thomas 4.00 1.20
10 Danny Tartabull .75 .23
11 Albert Belle 1.50 .45
12 Ruben Sierra .75 .23
13 Larry Walker 2.50 .75
14 Jeff Bagwell 2.50 .75
15 David Justice 1.50 .45
16 Kirby Puckett 4.00 1.20
17 John Kruk 1.50 .45
18 Howard Johnson .75 .23
19 Darryl Strawberry 1.50 .45
20 Will Clark 4.00 1.20
21 Kevin Mitchell .75 .23
22 Mickey Tettleton .75 .23
23 Don Mattingly 10.00 3.00
24 Jose Canseco 4.00 1.20
25 George Bell .75 .23
26 Andre Dawson 1.50 .45
27 Ryne Sandberg 6.00 1.80
28 Ken Griffey Jr. 6.00 1.80
29 Carlos Baerga .75 .23
30 Travis Fryman 1.50 .45

1993 Pinnacle Team 2001

This 30-card standard-size set salutes players expected to be stars in the year 2001. The cards were inserted one per pack in first series jumbo superpacks and feature color player action shots on their fronts.

Nm-Mt Ex-Mt
COMPLETE SET (30) 40.00 12.00
1 Wil Cordero .75 .23
2 Cal Eldred .75 .23
3 Mike Mussina 2.50 .75
4 Chuck Knoblauch 1.50 .45
5 Melvin Nieves .75 .23
6 Tim Wakefield 4.00 1.20
7 Carlos Baerga .75 .23
8 Bret Boone 2.50 .75
9 Jeff Bagwell 2.50 .75
10 Travis Fryman 1.50 .45
11 Royce Clayton .75 .23
12 Delino DeShields .75 .23
13 Juan Gonzalez 2.50 .75
14 Pedro Martinez 8.00 2.40
15 Bernie Williams 2.50 .75
16 Billy Ashley .75 .23
17 Marquis Grissom 1.50 .45
18 Kenny Lofton 1.50 .45
19 Ray Lankford .75 .23
20 Tim Salmon 2.50 .75
21 Steve Hosey .75 .23
22 Charles Nagy .75 .23
23 Dave Fleming .75 .23
24 Reggie Sanders .75 .23
25 Sam Militello .75 .23
26 Eric Karros 1.50 .45
27 Ryan Klesko 1.50 .45
28 Dean Palmer 1.50 .45
29 Ivan Rodriguez 4.00 1.20
30 Sterling Hitchcock 2.00 .60

1993 Pinnacle Team Pinnacle

Cards from this ten-card dual-sided set, featuring a selection of top stars paired of by position, were randomly inserted into one in every 24 first series foil packs. Each double-sided card displays paintings by artist Christopher Greco. A special bonus Team Pinnacle card (11) was available to collectors only through a mail-in offer for ten 1993 Pinnacle baseball wrappers plus 1.50 for shipping and handling. Moreover, hobby dealers who ordered Pinnacle received two bonus cards and an advertisement display promoting the offer.

Nm-Mt Ex-Mt
COMPLETE SET (10) 80.00 24.00
1 Greg Maddux 15.00 4.50
Mike Mussina
2 Tom Glavine 6.00 1.80
John Smiley
3 Darren Daulton 10.00 3.00
Ivan Rodriguez
4 Fred McGriff 10.00 3.00
Frank Thomas
5 Delino DeShields 2.00 .60
Carlos Baerga
6 Gary Sheffield 4.00 1.20
Edgar Martinez
7 Ozzie Smith 15.00 4.50
Pat Listach
8 Barry Bonds 25.00 7.50
Juan Gonzalez
9 Andy Van Slyke 10.00 3.00
Kirby Puckett
10 Larry Walker 6.00 1.80
Joe Carter
B11 Rob Dibble 2.00 .60
Rick Aguilera

1993 Pinnacle Tribute

Inserted in second-series packs at a rate of one in 24, these ten standard-size cards pay tribute to two recent retirees from baseball: George Brett (1-5), and Nolan Ryan (6-10). Score estimates that the chances of finding a tribute chase card are not less than one in 24 count good packs.

Nm-Mt Ex-Mt
COMPLETE SET (10) 60.00 18.00
COMMON BRETT (1-5) 5.00 1.50
COMMON RYAN (6-10) 10.00 3.00

1993 Pinnacle DiMaggio

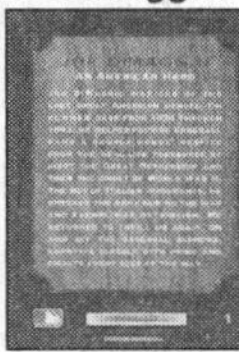

This 30-card standard-size set commemorates the life and career of Joe DiMaggio. Production was limited to 209,000 sets, with each set packaged in a black and gold collector's tin that features a color picture of DiMaggio. A certificate of authenticity card is also included that carries the production number of the set. DiMaggio also signed 9,000 cards for this set. One of 9,000 autographed cards from a special five-card set were randomly inserted into 30-card boxed hobby sets of 1993 Pinnacle Joe DiMaggio.

Nm-Mt Ex-Mt
COMP. FACT SET (30) 20.00 6.00
COMMON CARD (1-30) .75 .23
11 Joe DiMaggio 2.00 .60
Bob Feller
Rapid Robert Feller
vs. Joltin' Joe
21 Joe DiMaggio 1.00 .30
Joe McCarthy MG

1993 Pinnacle DiMaggio Autographs

Joe DiMaggio personally signed a total of 9,000 cards, and one autographed card from this five-card set was randomly inserted in selected 30-card boxed 1993 Pinnacle Joe DiMaggio hobby sets. These five autographed cards are slightly smaller (narrower) than standard size and feature white-bordered black-and-white action shots from DiMaggio's career that place special emphasis on the skills that made him great. DiMaggio's signature appears below the photo within the wide white lower margin.

Nm-Mt Ex-Mt
COMPLETE SET (5) 1000.00 300.00
COMMON CARD (1-5) 200.00 60.00

1994 Pinnacle

The 540-card 1994 Pinnacle standard-size set was issued in two series of 270. Cards were issued in hobby and retail foil-wrapped packs. The card fronts feature full-bleed color action player photos with a small foil logo and players name at the base. Subsets include Rookie Prospects (224-261) and Draft Picks (262-270/430-438). Notable Rookie Cards include Trot Nixon, Chan Ho Park and Billy Wagner. A Carlos Delgado Super Rookie one shot insert was put into packs at a rate of one in 360. It is labeled SR1 and is listed at the end of the set.

Nm-Mt Ex-Mt
COMPLETE SET (540) 20.00 6.00
COMP. SERIES 1 (270) 10.00 3.00
COMP. SERIES 2 (270) 10.00 3.00
1 Frank Thomas .50 .15
2 Carlos Baerga .10 .03
3 Sammy Sosa .75 .23
4 Tony Gwynn .60 .18
5 John Olerud .20 .06
6 Ryne Sandberg .75 .23
7 Moises Alou .20 .06
8 Steve Avery .10 .03
9 Tim Salmon .30 .09
10 Cecil Fielder .20 .06
11 Greg Maddux .75 .23
12 Barry Larkin .30 .09
13 Mike Devereaux .10 .03
14 Charlie Hayes .10 .03
15 Albert Belle .20 .06
16 Andy Van Slyke .20 .06
17 Mo Vaughn .20 .06
18 Brian McRae .10 .03
19 Cal Eldred .10 .03
20 Craig Biggio .30 .09
21 Kirby Puckett .50 .15
22 Derek Bell .10 .03
23 Don Mattingly 1.25 .35
24 John Burkett .10 .03
25 Roger Clemens 1.00 .30
26 Barry Bonds 1.25 .35
27 Paul Molitor .30 .09
28 Mike Piazza 1.00 .30
29 Robin Ventura .20 .06
30 Jeff Conine .20 .06
31 Wade Boggs .30 .09
32 Dennis Eckersley .20 .06
33 Bobby Bonilla .20 .06
34 Lenny Dykstra .20 .06
35 Manny Alexander .10 .03
36 Ray Lankford .10 .03
37 Greg Vaughn .10 .03
38 Chuck Finley .20 .06
39 Todd Benzinger .10 .03
40 Dave Justice .20 .06
41 Rob Dibble .20 .06
42 Tom Henke .10 .03
43 David Nied .10 .03
44 Sandy Alomar Jr. .10 .03
45 Pete Harnisch .10 .03
46 Jeff Russell .10 .03
47 Terry Mulholland .10 .03
48 Kevin Appier .20 .06
49 Randy Tomlin .10 .03
50 Cal Ripken Jr. 1.50 .45
51 Andy Benes .10 .03
52 Jimmy Key .20 .06
53 Kirt Manwaring .10 .03
54 Kevin Tapani .10 .03
55 Jose Guzman .10 .03
56 Todd Stottlemyre .10 .03
57 Jack McDowell .10 .03
58 Orel Hershiser .20 .06
59 Chris Hammond .10 .03
60 Chris Nabholz .10 .03
61 Ruben Sierra .10 .03
62 Dwight Gooden .20 .06
63 John Kruk .20 .06
64 Omar Vizquel .30 .09
65 Tim Naehring .10 .03
66 Dwight Smith .10 .03
67 Mickey Tettleton .10 .03
68 J.T. Snow .20 .06
69 Greg McMichael .10 .03
70 Kevin Mitchell .10 .03
71 Kevin Brown .20 .06
72 Scott Cooper .10 .03
73 Jim Thome .50 .15
74 Joe Girardi .10 .03
75 Eric Anthony .10 .03
76 Orlando Merced .10 .03
77 Felix Jose .10 .03
78 Tommy Greene .10 .03
79 Bernard Gilkey .10 .03
80 Phil Plantier .10 .03
81 Danny Tartabull .10 .03
82 Trevor Wilson .10 .03
83 Chuck Knoblauch .20 .06
84 Rick Wilkins .10 .03
85 Devon White .20 .06
86 Lance Johnson .10 .03
87 Eric Karros .20 .06
88 Gary Sheffield .20 .06
89 Wil Cordero .10 .03
90 Ron Darling .10 .03
91 Darren Daulton .20 .06
92 Joe Orsulak .10 .03
93 Steve Cooke .10 .03
94 Darryl Hamilton .10 .03
95 Aaron Sele .10 .03
96 John Doherty .10 .03
97 Gary DiSarcina .10 .03
98 Jeff Blauser .10 .03
99 John Smiley .10 .03
100 Ken Griffey Jr. .75 .23
101 Dean Palmer .20 .06
102 Felix Fermin .10 .03
103 Jerald Clark .10 .03
104 Doug Drabek .10 .03
105 Curt Schilling .20 .06
106 Jeff Montgomery .10 .03
107 Rene Arocha .10 .03
108 Carlos Garcia .10 .03
109 Wally Whitehurst .10 .03
110 Jim Abbott .30 .09
111 Royce Clayton .10 .03
112 Chris Hoiles .10 .03
113 Mike Morgan .10 .03
114 Joe Magrane .10 .03
115 Tom Candiotti .10 .03
116 Ron Karkovice .10 .03
117 Ryan Bowen .10 .03
118 Rod Beck .10 .03
119 John Wetteland .20 .06
120 Terry Steinbach .10 .03
121 Dave Hollins .10 .03
122 Jeff Kent .20 .06
123 Ricky Bones .10 .03
124 Brian Jordan .20 .06
125 Chad Kreuter .10 .03
126 John Valentin .10 .03
127 Hilly Hathaway .10 .03
128 Wilson Alvarez .10 .03
129 Tino Martinez .30 .09
130 Rodney Bolton .10 .03
131 David Segui .10 .03
132 Wayne Kirby .10 .03
133 Eric Young .10 .03
134 Scott Servais .10 .03
135 Scott Radinsky .10 .03

136 Bret Barberie .10 .03
137 John Roper .10 .03
138 Ricky Gutierrez .10 .03
139 Bernie Williams .30 .09
140 Bud Black .10 .03
141 Jose Vizcaino .10 .03
142 Gerald Williams .10 .03
143 Duane Ward .10 .03
144 Danny Jackson .10 .03
145 Allen Watson .10 .03
146 Scott Fletcher .10 .03
147 Delino DeShields .10 .03
148 Shane Mack .10 .03
149 Jim Eisenreich .10 .03
150 Troy Neel .10 .03
151 Jay Bell .20 .06
152 B.J. Surhoff .20 .06
153 Mark Whiten .10 .03
154 Mike Henneman .10 .03
155 Todd Hundley .10 .03
156 Greg Myers .10 .03
157 Ryan Klesko .20 .06
158 Dave Fleming .10 .03
159 Mickey Morandini .10 .03
160 Blas Minor .10 .03
161 Reggie Jefferson .10 .03
162 David Hulse .10 .03
163 Greg Swindell .10 .03
164 Roberto Hernandez .10 .03
165 Brady Anderson .20 .06
166 Jack Armstrong .10 .03
167 Phil Clark .10 .03
168 Melido Perez .10 .03
169 Darren Lewis .10 .03
170 Sam Horn .10 .03
171 Mike Harkey .10 .03
172 Juan Guzman .10 .03
173 Bob Natal .10 .03
174 Deion Sanders .30 .09
175 Carlos Quintana .10 .03
176 Mel Rojas .10 .03
177 Willie Banks .10 .03
178 Ben Rivera .10 .03
179 Kenny Lofton .20 .06
180 Leo Gomez .10 .03
181 Roberto Mejia .10 .03
182 Mike Perez .10 .03
183 Travis Fryman .20 .06
184 Ben McDonald .10 .03
185 Steve Frey .10 .03
186 Kevin Young .10 .03
187 Dave Magadan .10 .03
188 Bobby Munoz .10 .03
189 Pat Rapp .10 .03
190 Jose Offerman .10 .03
191 Vinny Castilla .20 .06
192 Ivan Calderon .10 .03
193 Ken Caminiti .20 .06
194 Benji Gil .10 .03
195 Chuck Carr .10 .03
196 Derrick May .10 .03
197 Pat Kelly .10 .03
198 Jeff Brantley .10 .03
199 Jose Lind .10 .03
200 Steve Buechele .10 .03
201 Wes Chamberlain .10 .03
202 Eduardo Perez .10 .03
203 Bret Saberhagen .20 .06
204 Gregg Jefferies .10 .03
205 Darrin Fletcher .10 .03
206 Kent Hrbek .20 .06
207 Kim Batiste .10 .03
208 Jeff King .10 .03
209 Donovan Osborne .10 .03
210 Dave Nilsson .10 .03
211 Al Martin .10 .03
212 Mike Moore .10 .03
213 Sterling Hitchcock .10 .03
214 Geronimo Pena .10 .03
215 Kevin Higgins .10 .03
216 Norm Charlton .10 .03
217 Don Slaught .10 .03
218 Mitch Williams .10 .03
219 Derek Lilliquist .10 .03
220 Armando Reynoso .10 .03
221 Kenny Rogers .20 .06
222 Doug Jones .10 .03
223 Luis Aquino .10 .03
224 Mike Oquist .10 .03
225 Darryl Scott .10 .03
226 Kurt Abbott RC .25 .07
227 Andy Tomberlin .10 .03
228 Norberto Martin .10 .03
229 Pedro Castellano .10 .03
230 Curtis Pride RC .25 .07
231 Jeff McNeely .10 .03
232 Scott Lydy .10 .03
233 Darren Oliver RC .25 .07
234 Danny Bautista .10 .03
235 Butch Huskey .10 .03
236 Chipper Jones .50 .15
237 Eddie Zambrano RC .10 .03
238 Domingo Jean .10 .03
239 Javier Lopez .20 .06
240 Nigel Wilson .10 .03
241 Drew Denson .10 .03
242 Raul Mondesi .20 .06
243 Luis Ortiz .10 .03
244 Manny Ramirez .30 .09
245 Greg Blosser .10 .03
246 Rondell White .20 .06
247 Steve Karsay .10 .03
248 Scott Stahoviak .10 .03
249 Jose Valentin .10 .03
250 Marc Newfield .10 .03
251 Keith Kessinger .10 .03
252 Carl Everett .20 .06
253 John O'Donoghue .10 .03
254 Turk Wendell .10 .03
255 Scott Ruffcorn .10 .03
256 Tony Tarasco .10 .03
257 Andy Cook .10 .03
258 Matt Mieske .10 .03
259 Luis Lopez .10 .03
260 Ramon Caraballo .10 .03
261 Salomon Torres .10 .03
262 Brooks Kieschnick RC .25 .07
263 Daron Kirkreit .10 .03
264 Bill Wagner RC .50 .15
265 Matt Drews RC .10 .03
266 Scott Christman RC .10 .03
267 Torii Hunter RC 2.00 .60
268 Jamey Wright RC .10 .03
269 Jeff Granger .10 .03
270 Trot Nixon RC 1.00 .30
271 Randy Myers .10 .03
272 Trevor Hoffman .20 .06
273 Bob Wickman .10 .03
274 Willie McGee .20 .06
275 Hipolito Pichardo .10 .03
276 Bobby Witt .10 .03
277 Gregg Olson .10 .03
278 Randy Johnson .50 .15
279 Robb Nen .20 .06
280 Paul O'Neill .30 .09
281 Lou Whitaker .20 .06
282 Chad Curtis .10 .03
283 Doug Henry .10 .03
284 Tom Glavine .30 .09
285 Mike Greenwell .10 .03
286 Roberto Kelly .10 .03
287 Roberto Alomar .30 .09
288 Charlie Hough .20 .06
289 Alex Fernandez .10 .03
290 Jeff Bagwell .30 .09
291 Wally Joyner .20 .06
292 Andujar Cedeno .10 .03
293 Rick Aguilera .10 .03
294 Darryl Strawberry .20 .06
295 Mike Mussina .30 .09
296 Jeff Gardner .10 .03
297 Chris Gwynn .10 .03
298 Matt Williams .20 .06
299 Brent Gates .10 .03
300 Mark McGwire 1.25 .35
301 Jim Deshaies .10 .03
302 Edgar Martinez .30 .09
303 Danny Darwin .10 .03
304 Pat Meares .10 .03
305 Benito Santiago .20 .06
306 Jose Canseco .50 .15
307 Jim Gott .10 .03
308 Paul Sorrento .10 .03
309 Scott Kamieniecki .10 .03
310 Larry Walker .30 .09
311 Mark Langston .10 .03
312 John Jaha .10 .03
313 Stan Javier .10 .03
314 Hal Morris .10 .03
315 Robby Thompson .10 .03
316 Pat Hentgen .10 .03
317 Tom Gordon .10 .03
318 Joey Cora .10 .03
319 Luis Alicea .10 .03
320 Andre Dawson .20 .06
321 Darryl Kile .20 .06
322 Jose Rijo .10 .03
323 Luis Gonzalez .20 .06
324 Billy Ashley .10 .03
325 David Cone .20 .06
326 Bill Swift .10 .03
327 Phil Hiatt .10 .03
328 Craig Paquette .10 .03
329 Bob Welch .10 .03
330 Tony Phillips .10 .03
331 Archi Cianfrocco .10 .03
332 Dave Winfield .20 .06
333 David McCarty .10 .03
334 Al Leiter .20 .06
335 Tom Browning .10 .03
336 Mark Grace .30 .09
337 Jose Mesa .10 .03
338 Mike Stanley .10 .03
339 Roger McDowell .10 .03
340 Damion Easley .10 .03
341 Angel Miranda .10 .03
342 John Smoltz .30 .09
343 Jay Buhner .20 .06
344 Bryan Harvey .10 .03
345 Joe Carter .20 .06
346 Dante Bichette .20 .06
347 Jason Bere .10 .03
348 Frank Viola .20 .06
349 Ivan Rodriguez .50 .15
350 Juan Gonzalez .30 .09
351 Steve Finley .20 .06
352 Mike Felder .10 .03
353 Ramon Martinez .10 .03
354 Greg Gagne .10 .03
355 Ken Hill .10 .03
356 Pedro Munoz .10 .03
357 Todd Van Poppel .10 .03
358 Marquis Grissom .20 .06
359 Milt Cuyler .10 .03
360 Reggie Sanders .20 .06
361 Scott Erickson .10 .03
362 Billy Hatcher .10 .03
363 Gene Harris .10 .03
364 Rene Gonzales .10 .03
365 Kevin Rogers .10 .03
366 Eric Plunk .10 .03
367 Todd Zeile .10 .03
368 John Franco .20 .06
369 Brett Butler .20 .06
370 Bill Spiers .10 .03
371 Terry Pendleton .20 .06
372 Chris Bosio .10 .03
373 Orestes Destrade .10 .03
374 Dave Stewart .20 .06
375 Darren Holmes .10 .03
376 Doug Strange .10 .03
377 Brian Turang .10 .03
378 Carl Willis .10 .03
379 Mark McLemore .10 .03
380 Bobby Jones .10 .03
381 Scott Sanders .10 .03
382 Kirk Rueter .20 .06
383 Randy Velarde .10 .03
384 Fred McGriff .30 .09
385 Charles Nagy .10 .03
386 Rich Amaral .10 .03
387 Geronimo Berroa .10 .03
388 Eric Davis .20 .06
389 Ozzie Smith .75 .23
390 Alex Arias .10 .03
391 Brad Ausmus .10 .03
392 Cliff Floyd .20 .06
393 Roger Salkeld .10 .03
394 Jim Edmonds .50 .15
395 Jeromy Burnitz .20 .06
396 Dave Staton .10 .03
397 Rob Butler .10 .03
398 Marcos Armas .10 .03
399 Darrell Whitmore .10 .03
400 Ryan Thompson .10 .03
401 Ross Powell RC .10 .03
402 Joe Oliver .10 .03
403 Paul Carey .10 .03
404 Bob Hamelin .10 .03
405 Chris Turner .10 .03
406 Nate Minchey .10 .03
407 Lonnie Maclin RC .10 .03
408 Harold Baines .20 .06
409 Brian Williams .10 .03
410 Johnny Ruffin .10 .03
411 Julian Tavarez RC .10 .03
412 Mark Hutton .10 .03
413 Carlos Delgado .30 .09
414 Chris Gomez .10 .03
415 Mike Hampton .20 .06
416 Alex Diaz RC .10 .03
417 Jeffrey Hammonds .10 .03
418 Jayhawk Owens .10 .03
419 J.R. Phillips .10 .03
420 Cory Bailey RC .10 .03
421 Denny Hocking .10 .03
422 Jon Shave .10 .03
423 Damon Buford .10 .03
424 Troy O'Leary .10 .03
425 Tripp Cromer .10 .03
426 Albie Lopez .10 .03
427 Tony Fernandez .10 .03
428 Ozzie Guillen .10 .03
429 Alan Trammell .20 .06
430 John Wasdin RC .10 .03
431 Marc Valdes .10 .03
432 Brian Anderson RC .25 .07
433 Matt Brunson RC .10 .03
434 Wayne Gomes RC .10 .03
435 Jay Powell RC .10 .03
436 Kirk Presley RC .10 .03
437 Jon Ratliff RC .10 .03
438 Derrek Lee RC .50 .15
439 Tom Pagnozzi .10 .03
440 Kent Mercker .10 .03
441 Phil Leftwich RC .10 .03
442 Jamie Moyer .20 .06
443 John Flaherty .10 .03
444 Mark Wohlers .10 .03
445 Jose Bautista .10 .03
446 Andres Galarraga .20 .06
447 Mark Lemke .10 .03
448 Tim Wakefield .20 .06
449 Pat Listach .10 .03
450 Rickey Henderson .50 .15
451 Mike Gallego .10 .03
452 Bob Tewksbury .10 .03
453 Kirk Gibson .20 .06
454 Pedro Astacio .10 .03
455 Mike Lansing .10 .03
456 Sean Berry .10 .03
457 Bob Walk .10 .03
458 Chili Davis .20 .06
459 Ed Sprague .10 .03
460 Kevin Stocker .10 .03
461 Mike Stanton .10 .03
462 Tim Raines .20 .06
463 Mike Bordick .10 .03
464 David Wells .20 .06
465 Tim Laker .10 .03
466 Cory Snyder .10 .03
467 Alex Cole .10 .03
468 Pete Incaviglia .10 .03
469 Roger Pavlik .10 .03
470 Greg W. Harris .10 .03
471 Xavier Hernandez .10 .03
472 Erik Hanson .10 .03
473 Jesse Orosco .10 .03
474 Greg Colbrunn .10 .03
475 Harold Reynolds .20 .06
476 Greg A. Harris .10 .03
477 Pat Borders .10 .03
478 Melvin Nieves .10 .03
479 Mariano Duncan .10 .03
480 Greg Hibbard .10 .03
481 Tim Pugh .10 .03
482 Bobby Ayala .10 .03
483 Sid Fernandez .10 .03
484 Tim Wallach .10 .03
485 Randy Milligan .10 .03
486 Walt Weiss .10 .03
487 Matt Walbeck .10 .03
488 Mike Macfarlane .10 .03
489 Jerry Browne .10 .03
490 Chris Sabo .10 .03
491 Tim Belcher .10 .03
492 Spike Owen .10 .03
493 Rafael Palmeiro .30 .09
494 Brian Harper .10 .03
495 Eddie Murray .50 .15
496 Ellis Burks .20 .06
497 Karl Rhodes .10 .03
498 Otis Nixon .10 .03
499 Lee Smith .20 .06
500 Bip Roberts .10 .03
501 Pedro Martinez .50 .15
502 Brian Hunter .10 .03
503 Tyler Green .10 .03
504 Bruce Hurst .10 .03
505 Alex Gonzalez .10 .03
506 Mark Portugal .10 .03
507 Bob Ojeda .10 .03
508 Dave Henderson .10 .03
509 Bo Jackson .50 .15
510 Bret Boone .20 .06
511 Mark Eichhorn .10 .03
512 Luis Polonia .10 .03
513 Will Clark .50 .15
514 Dave Valle .10 .03
515 Dan Wilson .10 .03
516 Dennis Martinez .20 .06
517 Jim Leyritz .10 .03
518 Howard Johnson .10 .03
519 Jody Reed .10 .03
520 Julio Franco .20 .06
521 Jeff Reardon .20 .06
522 Willie Greene .10 .03
523 Shawon Dunston .10 .03
524 Keith Mitchell .10 .03
525 Rick Helling .10 .03
526 Mark Kiefer .10 .03
527 Chan Ho Park RC .40 .12
528 Tony Longmire .10 .03
529 Rich Becker .10 .03
530 Tim Hyers RC .10 .03
531 Darrin Jackson .10 .03
532 Jack Morris .20 .06
533 Rick White .10 .03
534 Mike Kelly .10 .03
535 James Mouton .10 .03
536 Steve Trachsel .10 .03
537 Tony Eusebio .10 .03
538 Kelly Stinnett RC .25 .07
539 Paul Spoljaric .10 .03
540 Darren Dreifort .10 .03
SR1 Carlos Delgado 5.00 1.50
Super Rookie

1994 Pinnacle Artist's Proofs

Randomly inserted at a rate of one in 26 hobby and retail packs, cards from this 540-card set parallel that of the basic Pinnacle issue. Each card is embossed with a gold-foil-stamped "Artist's Proof" logo just above the player name. The Pinnacle logo is also done in gold foil. Just 1,000 of each card were printed although none are serial numbered.

Nm-Mt Ex-Mt
*STARS: 10X TO 25X BASIC CARDS..
*ROOKIES: 5X TO 12X BASIC CARDS

1994 Pinnacle Museum Collection

This 540-card set is a parallel dufex to that of the basic Pinnacle issue. They were randomly inserted at a rate of one in four hobby and retail packs. A Museum Collection logo replaces the anti-counterfeit device. Only 6,500 of each card were printed. Five cards (numbers 279, 313, 328, 382 and 387) were available only by mailing in a redemption card randomly seeded into packs. Due to a low response of mailing, these five cards are now by far the toughest cards to find in the set.

Nm-Mt Ex-Mt
*STARS: 2.5X TO 6X BASIC CARDS...
*ROOKIES: 2X TO 5X BASIC CARDS...
279 Robb Nen TRADE 25.00 7.50
313 Stan Javier TRADE 15.00 4.50
328 Craig Paquette TRADE 15.00 4.50
382 Kirk Rueter TRADE 25.00 7.50
387 G.Berroa TRADE 15.00 4.50

1994 Pinnacle Rookie Team Pinnacle

These nine double-front standard-size cards of the "Rookie Team Pinnacle" set feature a top AL and a top NL rookie prospect by position. The insertion rate for these is one per 48 first series packs. These special portrait cards were painted by artists Christopher Greco and Ron DeFelice. The front features the National League player and card number. Both sides contain a gold Rookie Team Pinnacle logo.

Nm-Mt Ex-Mt
COMPLETE SET (9) 60.00 18.00
1 Carlos Delgado 8.00 2.40
Javier Lopez
2 Bob Hamelin 4.00 1.20
J.R. Phillips
3 Jon Shave 4.00 1.20
Keith Kessinger
4 Luis Ortiz 4.00 1.20
Butch Huskey
5 Kurt Abbott 10.00 3.00
Chipper Jones
6 Manny Ramirez 8.00 2.40
Rondell White
7 Jeffrey Hammonds 6.00 1.80
Cliff Floyd
8 Marc Newfield 4.00 1.20
Nigel Wilson
9 Mark Hutton 4.00 1.20
Salomon Torres

1994 Pinnacle Run Creators

Randomly inserted in either series Pinnacle packs at an approximate rate of one in four jumbo packs, this 44-card standard-size set spotlights top run producers.

Nm-Mt Ex-Mt
COMPLETE SET (44) 80.00 24.00
COMPLETE SERIES 1 (22) 50.00 15.00
COMPLETE SERIES 2 (22) 30.00 9.00
RC1 John Olerud 1.00 .30
RC2 Frank Thomas 2.50 .75
RC3 Ken Griffey Jr. 4.00 1.20
RC4 Paul Molitor 1.50 .45
RC5 Rafael Palmeiro 1.50 .45
RC6 Roberto Alomar 1.50 .45
RC7 Juan Gonzalez 1.50 .45
RC8 Albert Belle 1.00 .30
RC9 Travis Fryman 1.00 .30
RC10 Rickey Henderson 2.50 .75
RC11 Tony Phillips .50 .15
RC12 Mo Vaughn 1.00 .30
RC13 Tim Salmon 1.50 .45
RC14 Kenny Lofton 1.00 .30
RC15 Carlos Baerga .50 .15
RC16 Greg Vaughn .50 .15
RC17 Jay Buhner 1.00 .30
RC18 Chris Hoiles .50 .15
RC19 Mickey Tettleton .50 .15
RC20 Kirby Puckett 2.50 .75
RC21 Danny Tartabull .50 .15
RC22 Devon White 1.00 .30
RC23 Barry Bonds 6.00 1.80
RC24 Lenny Dykstra 1.00 .30
RC25 John Kruk 1.00 .30
RC26 Fred McGriff 1.50 .45
RC27 Gregg Jefferies .50 .15
RC28 Mike Piazza 5.00 1.50
RC29 Jeff Blauser .50 .15
RC30 Andres Galarraga 1.00 .30
RC31 Darren Daulton 1.00 .30
RC32 Dave Justice 1.00 .30
RC33 Craig Biggio 1.50 .45
RC34 Mark Grace 1.50 .45
RC35 Tony Gwynn 3.00 .90
RC36 Jeff Bagwell 1.50 .45
RC37 Jay Bell 1.00 .30
RC38 Marquis Grissom 1.00 .30
RC39 Matt Williams 1.00 .30
RC40 Charlie Hayes .50 .15
RC41 Dante Bichette 1.00 .30
RC42 Bernard Gilkey .50 .15
RC43 Brett Butler 1.00 .30
RC44 Rick Wilkins .50 .15

1994 Pinnacle Team Pinnacle

Identical in design to the Rookie Team Pinnacle set, these double-front cards feature top players from each of the nine positions. Randomly inserted in second series hobby and retail packs at a rate of one in 48, these special portrait cards were painted by artists Christopher Greco and Ron DeFelice. The front features the National League player and card number. Both sides contain a gold Team Pinnacle logo.

Nm-Mt Ex-Mt
COMPLETE SET (9) 100.00 30.00
1 Jeff Bagwell 6.00 1.80
Frank Thomas
2 Carlos Baerga 1.25 .35
Robby Thompson
3 Matt Williams 2.50 .75
Dean Palmer
4 Cal Ripken Jr. 20.00 6.00
Jay Bell
5 Ivan Rodriguez 12.00 3.60
Mike Piazza
6 Lenny Dykstra 10.00 3.00
Ken Griffey Jr.
7 Juan Gonzalez 15.00 4.50
Barry Bonds
8 Tim Salmon 2.50 .75
Dave Justice
9 Greg Maddux 10.00 3.00
Jack McDowell

1994 Pinnacle Tribute

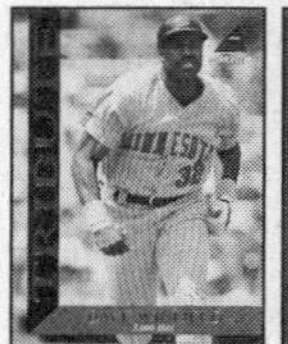

Randomly inserted in hobby packs at a rate of one in 18, this 18-card set was issued in two series of nine. Showcasing some of the top superstar veterans, the fronts have a color player photo with "Tribute" up the left border in a black stripe.

Nm-Mt Ex-Mt
COMPLETE SET (18) 100.00 30.00
COMPLETE SERIES 1 (9) 30.00 9.00
COMPLETE SERIES 2 (9) 70.00 21.00
TR1 Paul Molitor 2.50 .75
TR2 Jim Abbott 2.50 .75
TR3 Dave Winfield 1.50 .45
TR4 Bo Jackson 4.00 1.20
TR5 David Justice 1.50 .45
TR6 Len Dykstra 1.50 .45
TR7 Mike Piazza 8.00 2.40
TR8 Barry Bonds 10.00 3.00
TR9 Randy Johnson 4.00 1.20
TR10 Ozzie Smith 6.00 1.80
TR11 Mark Whiten .75 .23
TR12 Greg Maddux 6.00 1.80
TR13 Cal Ripken Jr. 12.00 3.60
TR14 Frank Thomas 4.00 1.20
TR15 Juan Gonzalez 2.50 .75
TR16 Roberto Alomar 2.50 .75
TR17 Ken Griffey Jr. 6.00 1.80
TR18 Lee Smith 1.50 .45

1995 Pinnacle

This 450-card standard-size set was issued in two series of 225 cards. They were released in 12-card packs, 24 packs to a box and 18 boxes

in a case. The full-bleed fronts feature action photos. The player's last name is printed in black ink against a dramatic gold foil background at the base of the card. There are no notable Rookie Cards in this set.

	Nm-Mt	Ex-Mt
COMPLETE SET (450)	30.00	9.00
COMP. SERIES 1 (225)	15.00	4.50
COMP. SERIES 2 (225)	15.00	4.50
1 Jeff Bagwell	.30	.09
2 Roger Clemens	1.00	.30
3 Mark Whiten	.10	.03
4 Shawon Dunston	.10	.03
5 Bobby Bonilla	.20	.06
6 Kevin Tapani	.10	.03
7 Eric Karros	.20	.06
8 Cliff Floyd	.20	.06
9 Pat Kelly	.10	.03
10 Jeffrey Hammonds	.10	.03
11 Jeff Conine	.20	.06
12 Fred McGriff	.30	.09
13 Chris Bosio	.10	.03
14 Mike Mussina	.30	.09
15 Danny Bautista	.10	.03
16 Mickey Morandini	.10	.03
17 Chuck Finley	.20	.06
18 Jim Thome	.50	.15
19 Luis Ortiz	.10	.03
20 Walt Weiss	.10	.03
21 Don Mattingly	1.25	.35
22 Bob Hamelin	.10	.03
23 Melido Perez	.10	.03
24 Keith Mitchell	.10	.03
25 John Smoltz	.30	.09
26 Hector Carrasco	.10	.03
27 Pat Hentgen	.10	.03
28 Derrick May	.10	.03
29 Mike Kingery	.10	.03
30 Chuck Carr	.10	.03
31 Billy Ashley	.10	.03
32 Todd Hundley	.10	.03
33 Luis Gonzalez	.20	.06
34 Marquis Grissom	.20	.06
35 Jeff King	.10	.03
36 Eddie Williams	.10	.03
37 Tom Pagnozzi	.10	.03
38 Chris Hoiles	.10	.03
39 Sandy Alomar Jr.	.10	.03
40 Mike Greenwell	.10	.03
41 Lance Johnson	.10	.03
42 Junior Felix	.10	.03
43 Felix Jose	.10	.03
44 Scott Leius	.10	.03
45 Ruben Sierra	.10	.03
46 Kevin Seitzer	.10	.03
47 Wade Boggs	.30	.09
48 Reggie Jefferson	.10	.03
49 Jose Canseco	.50	.15
50 David Justice	.20	.06
51 John Smiley	.10	.03
52 Joe Carter	.20	.06
53 Rick Wilkins	.10	.03
54 Ellis Burks	.20	.06
55 Dave Weathers	.10	.03
56 Pedro Astacio	.10	.03
57 Ryan Thompson	.10	.03
58 James Mouton	.10	.03
59 Mel Rojas	.10	.03
60 Orlando Merced	.10	.03
61 Matt Williams	.20	.06
62 Bernard Gilkey	.10	.03
63 J.R. Phillips	.10	.03
64 Lee Smith	.20	.06
65 Jim Edmonds	.30	.09
66 Darrin Jackson	.10	.03
67 Scott Cooper	.10	.03
68 Ron Karkovice	.10	.03
69 Chris Gomez	.10	.03
70 Kevin Appier	.20	.06
71 Bobby Jones	.10	.03
72 Doug Drabek	.10	.03
73 Matt Mieske	.10	.03
74 Sterling Hitchcock	.10	.03
75 John Valentin	.10	.03
76 Reggie Sanders	.10	.03
77 Wally Joyner	.20	.06
78 Turk Wendell	.10	.03
79 Charlie Hayes	.10	.03
80 Bret Barberie	.10	.03
81 Troy Neel	.10	.03
82 Ken Caminiti	.20	.06
83 Milt Thompson	.10	.03
84 Paul Sorrento	.10	.03
85 Trevor Hoffman	.20	.06
86 Jay Bell	.20	.06
87 Mark Portugal	.10	.03
88 Sid Fernandez	.10	.03
89 Charles Nagy	.10	.03
90 Jeff Montgomery	.10	.03
91 Chuck Knoblauch	.20	.06
92 Jeff Frye	.10	.03
93 Tony Gwynn	.60	.18
94 John Olerud	.20	.06
95 David Nied	.10	.03
96 Chris Hammond	.10	.03
97 Edgar Martinez	.30	.09
98 Kevin Stocker	.10	.03
99 Jeff Fassero	.10	.03
100 Curt Schilling	.20	.06
101 Dave Clark	.10	.03
102 Delino DeShields	.10	.03
103 Leo Gomez	.10	.03
104 Dave Hollins	.10	.03
105 Tim Naehring	.10	.03
106 Otis Nixon	.10	.03
107 Ozzie Guillen	.10	.03
108 Jose Lind	.10	.03
109 Stan Javier	.10	.03
110 Greg Vaughn	.10	.03
111 Chipper Jones	.50	.15
112 Ed Sprague	.10	.03
113 Mike Macfarlane	.10	.03
114 Steve Finley	.20	.06
115 Ken Hill	.10	.03
116 Carlos Garcia	.10	.03
117 Lou Whitaker	.20	.06
118 Todd Zeile	.10	.03
119 Gary Sheffield	.20	.06
120 Ben McDonald	.10	.03
121 Pete Harnisch	.10	.03
122 Ivan Rodriguez	.50	.15
123 Wilson Alvarez	.10	.03
124 Travis Fryman	.20	.06
125 Pedro Munoz	.10	.03
126 Mark Lemke	.10	.03
127 Jose Valentin	.10	.03
128 Ken Griffey Jr.	.75	.23
129 Omar Vizquel	.30	.09
130 Milt Cuyler	.10	.03
131 Steve Trachsel	.10	.03
132 Alex Rodriguez	1.25	.35
133 Garret Anderson	.20	.06
134 Armando Benitez	.20	.06
135 Shawn Green	.20	.06
136 Jorge Fabregas	.10	.03
137 Orlando Miller	.10	.03
138 Rikkert Faneyte	.10	.03
139 Ismael Valdes	.10	.03
140 Jose Oliva	.10	.03
141 Aaron Small	.10	.03
142 Tim Davis	.10	.03
143 Ricky Bottalico	.10	.03
144 Mike Matheny	.30	.09
145 Roberto Petagine	.10	.03
146 Fausto Cruz	.10	.03
147 Bryce Florie	.10	.03
148 Jose Lima	.10	.03
149 John Hudek	.10	.03
150 Duane Singleton	.10	.03
151 John Mabry	.10	.03
152 Robert Eenhoorn	.10	.03
153 Jon Lieber	.10	.03
154 Garey Ingram	.10	.03
155 Paul Shuey	.10	.03
156 Mike Lieberthal	.20	.06
157 Steve Dunn	.10	.03
158 Charles Johnson	.20	.06
159 Ernie Young	.10	.03
160 Jose Martinez	.10	.03
161 Kurt Miller	.10	.03
162 Joey Eischen	.10	.03
163 Dave Stevens	.10	.03
164 Brian L.Hunter	.10	.03
165 Jeff Cirillo	.10	.03
166 Mark Smith	.10	.03
167 M. Christensen RC	.10	.03
168 C.J. Nitkowski	.10	.03
169 A. Williamson RC	.10	.03
170 Paul Konerko	.20	.06
171 Scott Elarton RC	.25	.07
172 Jacob Shumate	.10	.03
173 Terrence Long	.20	.06
174 Mark Johnson RC	.25	.07
175 Ben Grieve	.20	.06
176 Jayson Peterson RC	.10	.03
177 Checklist	.10	.03
178 Checklist	.10	.03
179 Checklist	.10	.03
180 Checklist	.10	.03
181 Brian Anderson	.10	.03
182 Steve Buechele	.10	.03
183 Mark Clark	.10	.03
184 Cecil Fielder	.20	.06
185 Steve Avery	.10	.03
186 Devon White	.20	.06
187 Craig Shipley	.10	.03
188 Brady Anderson	.20	.06
189 Kenny Lofton	.20	.06
190 Alex Cole	.10	.03
191 Brent Gates	.10	.03
192 Dean Palmer	.20	.06
193 Alex Gonzalez	.10	.03
194 Steve Cooke	.10	.03
195 Ray Lankford	.10	.03
196 Mark McGwire	1.25	.35
197 Marc Newfield	.10	.03
198 Pat Rapp	.10	.03
199 Darren Lewis	.10	.03
200 Carlos Baerga	.10	.03
201 Rickey Henderson	.50	.15
202 Kurt Abbott	.10	.03
203 Kirt Manwaring	.10	.03
204 Cal Ripken	1.50	.45
205 Darren Daulton	.20	.06
206 Greg Colbrunn	.10	.03
207 Darryl Hamilton	.10	.03
208 Bo Jackson	.50	.15
209 Tony Phillips	.10	.03
210 Geronimo Berroa	.10	.03
211 Rich Becker	.10	.03
212 Tony Tarasco	.10	.03
213 Karl Rhodes	.10	.03
214 Phil Plantier	.10	.03
215 J.T. Snow	.20	.06
216 Mo Vaughn	.20	.06
217 Greg Gagne	.10	.03
218 Ricky Bones	.10	.03
219 Mike Bordick	.10	.03
220 Chad Curtis	.10	.03
221 Royce Clayton	.10	.03
222 Roberto Alomar	.30	.09
223 Jose Rijo	.10	.03
224 Ryan Klesko	.20	.06
225 Mark Langston	.10	.03
226 Frank Thomas	.50	.15
227 Juan Gonzalez	.30	.09
228 Ron Gant	.20	.06
229 Javier Lopez	.20	.06
230 Sammy Sosa	.75	.23
231 Kevin Brown	.20	.06
232 Gary DiSarcina	.10	.03
233 Albert Belle	.20	.06
234 Jay Buhner	.20	.06
235 Pedro Martinez	.50	.15
236 Bob Tewksbury	.10	.03
237 Mike Piazza	.75	.23
238 Darryl Kile	.20	.06
239 Bryan Harvey	.10	.03
240 Andres Galarraga	.20	.06
241 Jeff Blauser	.10	.03
242 Jeff Kent	.20	.06
243 Bobby Munoz	.10	.03
244 Greg Maddux	.75	.23
245 Paul O'Neill	.30	.09
246 Lenny Dykstra	.20	.06
247 Todd Van Poppel	.10	.03
248 Bernie Williams	.30	.09
249 Glenallen Hill	.10	.03
250 Duane Ward	.10	.03
251 Dennis Eckersley	.20	.06
252 Pat Mahomes	.10	.03
253 Rusty Greer	.20	.06
254 Roberto Kelly	.10	.03
255 Randy Myers	.10	.03
256 Scott Ruffcorn	.10	.03
257 Robin Ventura	.20	.06
258 Eduardo Perez	.10	.03
259 Aaron Sele	.10	.03
260 Paul Molitor	.30	.09
261 Juan Guzman	.10	.03
262 Darren Oliver	.10	.03
263 Mike Stanley	.10	.03
264 Tom Glavine	.30	.09
265 Rico Brogna	.10	.03
266 Craig Biggio	.30	.09
267 Darrell Whitmore	.10	.03
268 Jimmy Key	.20	.06
269 Will Clark	.50	.15
270 David Cone	.20	.06
271 Brian Jordan	.20	.06
272 Barry Bonds	1.25	.35
273 Danny Tartabull	.10	.03
274 Ramon J.Martinez	.10	.03
275 Al Martin	.10	.03
276 Fred McGriff SM	.20	.06
277 Carlos Delgado SM	.10	.03
278 Juan Gonzalez SM	.20	.06
279 Shawn Green SM	.10	.03
280 Carlos Baerga SM	.10	.03
281 Cliff Floyd SM	.10	.03
282 Ozzie Smith SM	.50	.15
283 Alex Rodriguez SM	.50	.15
284 Kenny Lofton SM	.10	.03
285 Dave Justice SM	.10	.03
286 Tim Salmon SM	.20	.06
287 Manny Ramirez SM	.20	.06
288 Will Clark SM	.20	.06
289 Garret Anderson SM	.10	.03
290 Billy Ashley SM	.10	.03
291 Tony Gwynn SM	.30	.09
292 Raul Mondesi SM	.10	.03
293 Rafael Palmeiro SM	.20	.06
294 Matt Williams SM	.10	.03
295 Don Mattingly SM	.60	.18
296 Kirby Puckett SM	.30	.09
297 Paul Molitor SM	.20	.06
298 Albert Belle SM	.10	.03
299 Barry Bonds SM	.60	.18
300 Mike Piazza SM	.50	.15
301 Jeff Bagwell SM	.20	.06
302 Frank Thomas SM	.30	.09
303 Chipper Jones SM	.30	.09
304 Ken Griffey Jr. SM	.50	.15
305 Cal Ripken Jr. SM	.75	.23
306 Eric Anthony	.10	.03
307 Todd Benzinger	.10	.03
308 Jacob Brumfield	.10	.03
309 Wes Chamberlain	.10	.03
310 Tino Martinez	.30	.09
311 Roberto Mejia	.10	.03
312 Jose Offerman	.10	.03
313 David Segui	.10	.03
314 Eric Young	.10	.03
315 Rey Sanchez	.10	.03
316 Raul Mondesi	.20	.06
317 Bret Boone	.20	.06
318 Andre Dawson	.20	.06
319 Brian McRae	.10	.03
320 Dave Nilsson	.10	.03
321 Moises Alou	.20	.06
322 Don Slaught	.10	.03
323 Dave McCarty	.10	.03
324 Mike Huff	.10	.03
325 Rick Aguilera	.10	.03
326 Rod Beck	.10	.03
327 Kenny Rogers	.20	.06
328 Andy Benes	.10	.03
329 Allen Watson	.10	.03
330 Randy Johnson	.50	.15
331 Willie Greene	.10	.03
332 Hal Morris	.10	.03
333 Ozzie Smith	.75	.23
334 Jason Bere	.10	.03
335 Scott Erickson	.10	.03
336 Dante Bichette	.20	.06
337 Willie Banks	.10	.03
338 Eric Davis	.20	.06
339 Rondell White	.20	.06
340 Kirby Puckett	.50	.15
341 Deion Sanders	.30	.09
342 Eddie Murray	.50	.15
343 Mike Harkey	.10	.03
344 Joey Hamilton	.10	.03
345 Roger Salkeld	.10	.03
346 Wil Cordero	.10	.03
347 John Wetteland	.20	.06
348 Geronimo Pena	.10	.03
349 Kirk Gibson	.20	.06
350 Manny Ramirez	.30	.09
351 Wm.VanLandingham	.10	.03
352 B.J. Surhoff	.20	.06
353 Ken Ryan	.10	.03
354 Terry Steinbach	.10	.03
355 Bret Saberhagen	.20	.06
356 John Jaha	.10	.03
357 Joe Girardi	.10	.03
358 Steve Karsay	.10	.03
359 Alex Fernandez	.10	.03
360 Salomon Torres	.10	.03
361 John Burkett	.10	.03
362 Derek Bell	.10	.03
363 Tom Henke	.10	.03
364 Gregg Jefferies	.10	.03
365 Jack McDowell	.10	.03
366 Andujar Cedeno	.10	.03
367 Dave Winfield	.20	.06
368 Carl Everett	.20	.06
369 Danny Jackson	.10	.03
370 Jeromy Burnitz	.20	.06
371 Mark Grace	.30	.09
372 Larry Walker	.30	.09
373 Bill Swift	.10	.03
374 Dennis Martinez	.20	.06
375 Mickey Tettleton	.10	.03
376 Mel Nieves	.10	.03
377 Cal Eldred	.10	.03
378 Orel Hershiser	.20	.06
379 David Wells	.20	.06
380 Gary Gaetti	.20	.06
381 Tim Raines	.20	.06
382 Barry Larkin	.30	.09
383 Jason Jacome	.10	.03
384 Tim Wallach	.10	.03
385 Robby Thompson	.10	.03
386 Frank Viola	.20	.06
387 Dave Stewart	.20	.06
388 Bip Roberts	.10	.03
389 Ron Darling	.10	.03
390 Carlos Delgado	.20	.06
391 Tim Salmon	.30	.09
392 Alan Trammell	.20	.06
393 Kevin Foster	.10	.03
394 Jim Abbott	.30	.09
395 John Kruk	.20	.06
396 Andy Van Slyke	.20	.06
397 Dave Magadan	.10	.03
398 Rafael Palmeiro	.30	.09
399 Mike Devereaux	.10	.03
400 Benito Santiago	.20	.06
401 Brett Butler	.20	.06
402 John Franco	.20	.06
403 Matt Walbeck	.10	.03
404 Terry Pendleton	.20	.06
405 Chris Sabo	.10	.03
406 Andrew Lorraine	.10	.03
407 Dan Wilson	.10	.03
408 Mike Lansing	.10	.03
409 Ray McDavid	.10	.03
410 Shane Andrews	.10	.03
411 Tom Gordon	.10	.03
412 Chad Ogea	.10	.03
413 James Baldwin	.10	.03
414 Russ Davis	.10	.03
415 Ray Holbert	.10	.03
416 Ray Durham	.20	.06
417 Matt Nokes	.10	.03
418 Rod Henderson	.10	.03
419 Gabe White	.10	.03
420 Todd Hollandsworth	.10	.03
421 Midre Cummings	.10	.03
422 Harold Baines	.20	.06
423 Troy Percival	.20	.06
424 Joe Vitiello	.10	.03
425 Andy Ashby	.10	.03
426 Michael Tucker	.10	.03
427 Mark Gubicza	.10	.03
428 Jim Bullinger	.10	.03
429 Jose Malave	.10	.03
430 Pete Schourek	.10	.03
431 Bobby Ayala	.10	.03
432 Marvin Freeman	.10	.03
433 Pat Listach	.10	.03
434 Eddie Taubensee	.10	.03
435 Steve Howe	.10	.03
436 Kent Mercker	.10	.03
437 Hector Fajardo	.10	.03
438 Scott Kamieniecki	.10	.03
439 Robb Nen	.20	.06
440 Mike Kelly	.10	.03
441 Tom Candiotti	.10	.03
442 Albie Lopez	.10	.03
443 Jeff Granger	.10	.03
444 Rich Aude	.10	.03
445 Luis Polonia	.10	.03
446 Frank Thomas CL	.30	.09
447 Ken Griffey Jr. CL	.50	.15
448 Mike Piazza CL	.50	.15
449 Jeff Bagwell CL	.20	.06
450 Jeff Bagwell CL Frank Thomas Ken Griffey Jr. Mike Piazza	.50	.15

1995 Pinnacle Artist's Proofs

Inserted one per 36 first series packs and one per 26 second series packs, this is a parallel set to the regular Pinnacle issue. The words "Artist Proof" are clearly labeled in silver on the card front. The name on the bottom is also set against a silver background.

Nm-Mt Ex-Mt
*STARS: 10X TO 25X BASIC CARDS..
*ROOKIES: 6X TO 15X BASIC.........

1995 Pinnacle Museum Collection

Inserted one in four packs for hobby and retail and 1:3 for ANCO, this is a parallel to the regular Pinnacle issue. These cards use the Dufex technology on front and are clearly labeled on the back as Museum Collection cards. Seven series two cards (numbers 410, 413, 416, 420, 423, 426 and 444) were available only with randomly inserted trade cards. These trade cards expired Dec. 31, 1995. Due to a low response of mailing, these seven cards are by far the toughest to find in this set.

	Nm-Mt	Ex-Mt
COMMON CARD (1-450)	1.25	.35
*STARS: 4X TO 10X BASIC CARDS...		
*ROOKIES/PROSPECTS: 2.5X to 6X BASIC CARDS		
410 S. Andrews TRADE	5.00	1.50
413 J. Baldwin TRADE	5.00	1.50
416 Ray Durham TRADE	10.00	3.00
420 T. Hollandsworth TRADE	5.00	1.50
423 Troy Percival TRADE	10.00	3.00
426 M. Tucker TRADE	5.00	1.50
444 Rich Aude TRADE	5.00	1.50

1995 Pinnacle ETA

This six-card standard-sized set was randomly inserted approximately one in every 24 first series hobby packs. This set features players

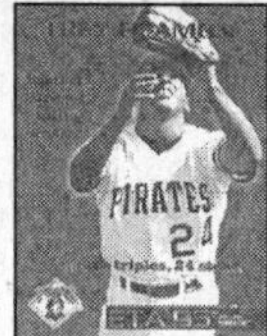

who were among the leading prospects for major league stardom. The fronts feature a player photo as well as a quick information bit. The player's name is located on the top. The busy full-bleed backs feature a player photo and some quick comments.

	Nm-Mt	Ex-Mt
COMPLETE SET (6)	15.00	4.50
ETA1 Ben Grieve	3.00	.90
ETA2 Alex Ochoa	2.00	.60
ETA3 Joe Vitiello	2.00	.60
ETA4 Johnny Damon	3.00	.90
ETA5 Trey Beamon	2.00	.60
ETA6 Brooks Kieschnick	2.00	.60

1995 Pinnacle Gate Attractions

This 18-card standard-size set was inserted approximately one every 12 second series jumbo packs.

	Nm-Mt	Ex-Mt
COMPLETE SET (18)	80.00	24.00
GA1 Ken Griffey Jr.	5.00	1.50
GA2 Frank Thomas	3.00	.90
GA3 Cal Ripken	10.00	3.00
GA4 Jeff Bagwell	2.00	.60
GA5 Mike Piazza	5.00	1.50
GA6 Barry Bonds	8.00	2.40
GA7 Kirby Puckett	3.00	.90
GA8 Albert Belle	1.25	.35
GA9 Tony Gwynn	4.00	1.20
GA10 Raul Mondesi	1.25	.35
GA11 Will Clark	3.00	.90
GA12 Don Mattingly	8.00	2.40
GA13 Roger Clemens	6.00	1.80
GA14 Paul Molitor	2.00	.60
GA15 Matt Williams	1.25	.35
GA16 Greg Maddux	5.00	1.50
GA17 Kenny Lofton	1.25	.35
GA18 Cliff Floyd	1.25	.35

1995 Pinnacle New Blood

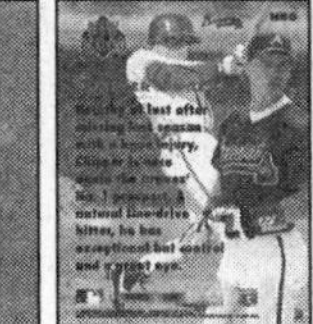

This nine-card standard-size set was inserted approximately one in every 90 second series hobby and retail packs. This set features nine players who were leading prospects entering the 1995 season. The Dufex enhanced fronts feature two player photos.

	Nm-Mt	Ex-Mt
COMPLETE SET (9)	60.00	18.00
NB1 Alex Rodriguez	20.00	6.00
NB2 Shawn Green	4.00	1.20
NB3 Brian Hunter	2.50	.75
NB4 Garret Anderson	4.00	1.20
NB5 Charles Johnson	4.00	1.20
NB6 Chipper Jones	8.00	2.40
NB7 Carlos Delgado	4.00	1.20
NB8 Billy Ashley	2.50	.75
NB9 J.R. Phillips UER Dodgers logo on back Phillips played for the Giants	2.50	.75

1995 Pinnacle Performers

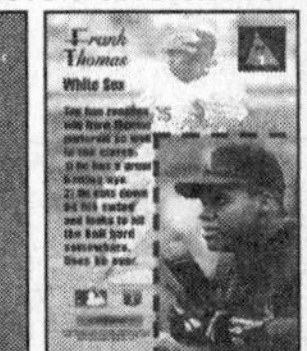

These 18 standard-size cards were randomly inserted approximately one in every 12 first series jumbo packs.

	Nm-Mt	Ex-Mt
COMPLETE SET (18)	100.00	30.00
PP1 Frank Thomas	6.00	1.80
PP2 Albert Belle	2.50	.75
PP3 Barry Bonds	15.00	4.50
PP4 Juan Gonzalez	4.00	1.20
PP5 Andres Galarraga	2.50	.75
PP6 Raul Mondesi	2.50	.75
PP7 Paul Molitor	4.00	1.20
PP8 Tim Salmon	4.00	1.20
PP9 Mike Piazza	10.00	3.00

PP10 Gregg Jefferies 1.25 .35
PP11 Will Clark 6.00 1.80
PP12 Greg Maddux 10.00 3.00
PP13 Manny Ramirez 4.00 1.20
PP14 Kirby Puckett 6.00 1.80
PP15 Shawn Green 2.50 .75
PP16 Rafael Palmeiro 4.00 1.20
PP17 Paul O'Neill 4.00 1.20
PP18 Jason Bere 1.25 .35

1995 Pinnacle Pin Redemption

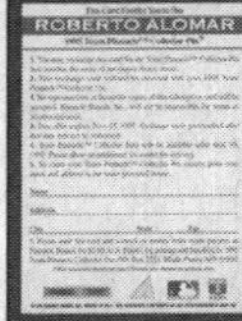

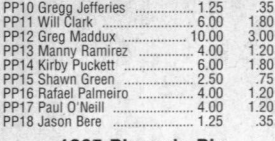

This 18-card standard-size set was randomly inserted in all second series packs. Printed odds indicate that these cards were inserted approximately one every in 48 hobby and retail packs and one in every 36 jumbo packs. The horizontal full-bleed fronts feature an action photo, a team logo and another small player photo. The backs explain the rules for ordering the "Team Pinnacle" Collector Pin. The offer expired on November 15, 1995.

Nm-Mt Ex-Mt
COMPLETE SET (18) 60.00 18.00
*PINS: .75X TO 1.5X BASIC PIN REDEMPTION
ONE PIN VIA MAIL PER REDEMPTION CARD
1 Greg Maddux 4.00 1.20
2 Mike Mussina 1.50 .45
3 Mike Piazza 4.00 1.20
4 Carlos Delgado 1.00 .30
5 Jeff Bagwell 1.50 .45
6 Frank Thomas 2.50 .75
7 Craig Biggio 1.50 .45
8 Roberto Alomar 1.50 .45
9 Ozzie Smith 4.00 1.20
10 Cal Ripken Jr. 8.00 2.40
11 Matt Williams 1.00 .30
12 Travis Fryman 1.00 .30
13 Barry Bonds 6.00 1.80
14 Ken Griffey Jr. 4.00 1.20
15 Dave Justice 1.00 .30
16 Albert Belle 1.00 .30
17 Tony Gwynn 3.00 .90
18 Kirby Puckett 2.50 .75

1995 Pinnacle Red Hot

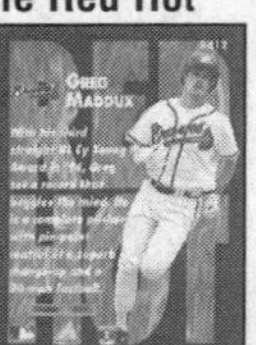

Cards from this 25-card standard-size set were randomly inserted into second series hobby and retail packs. The fronts feature a player photo on the right, with his name, an inset portrait and the words "Red Hot" on the left.

Nm-Mt Ex-Mt
COMPLETE SET (25) 80.00 24.00
*WHITE HOT: 1.5X TO 4X RED HOTS
WHITE HOT SER.2 ODDS 1:36 HOBBY
RH1 Cal Ripken Jr. 8.00 2.40
RH2 Ken Griffey Jr. 4.00 1.20
RH3 Frank Thomas 2.50 .75
RH4 Jeff Bagwell 1.50 .45
RH5 Mike Piazza 4.00 1.20
RH6 Barry Bonds 6.00 1.80
RH7 Albert Belle 1.00 .30
RH8 Tony Gwynn 3.00 .90
RH9 Kirby Puckett 2.50 .75
RH10 Don Mattingly 6.00 1.80
RH11 Matt Williams 1.00 .30
RH12 Greg Maddux 4.00 1.20
RH13 Raul Mondesi 1.00 .30
RH14 Paul Molitor 1.50 .45
RH15 Manny Ramirez 1.50 .45
RH16 Joe Carter 1.00 .30
RH17 Will Clark 2.50 .75
RH18 Roger Clemens 5.00 1.50
RH19 Tim Salmon 1.50 .45
RH20 Dave Justice 1.00 .30
RH21 Kenny Lofton 1.00 .30
RH22 Deion Sanders 1.50 .45
RH23 Roberto Alomar 1.50 .45
RH24 Cliff Floyd 1.00 .30
RH25 Carlos Baerga .50 .15

1995 Pinnacle Team Pinnacle

Randomly inserted in series one hobby and retail packs at a rate of one in 90, this nine-card standard-size set showcases the game's top players in an etched-foil design. Cards are numbered with the prefix "TP". All cards were intentionally issued with two variations, whereby one side of the card or the other had the Dufex effect. Premiums of up to 25 percent may exist for the player with the enhanced side.

Nm-Mt Ex-Mt
COMPLETE SET (9) 150.00 45.00
TP1 Mike Mussina 15.00 4.50
Greg Maddux
TP2 Carlos Delgado 15.00 4.50
Mike Piazza
TP3 Frank Thomas 10.00 3.00
Jeff Bagwell
TP4 Roberto Alomar 6.00 1.80
Craig Biggio
TP5 Cal Ripken 30.00 9.00
Ozzie Smith
TP6 Travis Fryman 4.00 1.20
Matt Williams
TP7 Ken Griffey Jr. 15.00 4.50
Barry Bonds
TP8 Albert Belle 4.00 1.20
David Justice
TP9 Kirby Puckett 10.00 3.00
Tony Gwynn

1995 Pinnacle Upstarts

Top young players are featured in this 30-card standard-size set. The cards were randomly inserted in series one hobby and retail packs at a rate of one in eight. Backs are full-bleed color action photos of the player and are numbered at the top right with the prefix "US".

Nm-Mt Ex-Mt
COMPLETE SET (30) 50.00 15.00
US1 Frank Thomas 3.00 .90
US2 Roberto Alomar 2.00 .60
US3 Mike Piazza 5.00 1.50
US4 Javier Lopez 1.25 .35
US5 Albert Belle 1.25 .35
US6 Carlos Delgado 1.25 .35
US7 Brent Gates .60 .18
US8 Tim Salmon 2.00 .60
US9 Raul Mondesi 1.25 .35
US10 Juan Gonzalez 2.00 .60
US11 Manny Ramirez 2.00 .60
US12 Sammy Sosa 5.00 1.50
US13 Jeff Kent 1.25 .35
US14 Melvin Nieves .60 .18
US15 Rondell White 1.25 .35
US16 Shawn Green 1.25 .35
US17 Bernie Williams 2.00 .60
US18 Aaron Sele .60 .18
US19 Jason Bere .60 .18
US20 Joey Hamilton .60 .18
US21 Mike Kelly .60 .18
US22 Wil Cordero .60 .18
US23 Moises Alou 1.25 .35
US24 Roberto Kelly .60 .18
US25 Deion Sanders 2.00 .60
US26 Steve Karsay .60 .18
US27 Bret Boone 1.25 .35
US28 Willie Greene .60 .18
US29 Billy Ashley .60 .18
US30 Brian Anderson .60 .18

1996 Pinnacle

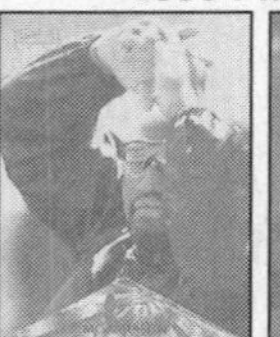

The 1996 Pinnacle set was issued in two separate series of 200 cards each. The 10-card packs retailed for $2.49. On 20-point card stock, the fronts feature full-bleed color action photos, bordered at the bottom by a gold foil triangle. The Series I set features the following topical subsets: The Naturals (134-163), '95 Rookies (164-193) and Checklists (194-200). Series II set features these subsets: Hardball Heroes (30 cards), 300 Series (17 cards), Rookies (25 cards), and Checklists (7 cards). Numbering for the 300 Series subset was based on player's career batting average. At that time, both Paul Molitor and Jeff Bagwell had identical career batting averages of .305, thus Pinnacle numbered both of their 300 Series subset cards as 305. Due to this quirky numbering, the set only runs through card 399, but actually contains 400 cards. A special Cal Ripken Jr. Tribute card was inserted in first series packs at the rate of one in 150.

Nm-Mt Ex-Mt
COMPLETE SET (400) 30.00 9.00
COMP. SERIES 1 (200) 15.00 4.50
COMP. SERIES 2 (200) 15.00 4.50
1 Greg Maddux .75 .23
2 Bill Pulsipher .20 .06
3 Dante Bichette .20 .06
4 Mike Piazza .75 .23
5 Garret Anderson .20 .06
6 Steve Finley .20 .06
7 Andy Benes .20 .06
8 Chuck Knoblauch .20 .06
9 Tom Gordon .20 .06
10 Jeff Bagwell .30 .09
11 Wil Cordero .20 .06
12 John Mabry .20 .06
13 Jeff Frye .20 .06
14 Travis Fryman .20 .06
15 John Wetteland .20 .06
16 Jason Bates .20 .06
17 Danny Tartabull .20 .06
18 Charles Nagy .20 .06
19 Robin Ventura .20 .06
20 Reggie Sanders .20 .06
21 Dave Clark .20 .06
22 Jaime Navarro .20 .06
23 Joey Hamilton .20 .06
24 Al Leiter .20 .06
25 Deion Sanders .30 .09
26 Tim Salmon .30 .09
27 Tino Martinez .30 .09
28 Mike Greenwell .20 .06
29 Phil Plantier .20 .06
30 Bobby Bonilla .20 .06
31 Kenny Rogers .20 .06
32 Chili Davis .20 .06
33 Joe Carter .20 .06
34 Mike Mussina .30 .09
35 Matt Mieske .20 .06
36 Jose Canseco .50 .15
37 Brad Radke .20 .06
38 Juan Gonzalez .30 .09
39 David Segui .20 .06
40 Alex Fernandez .20 .06
41 Jeff Kent .20 .06
42 Todd Zeile .20 .06
43 Darryl Strawberry .20 .06
44 Jose Rijo .20 .06
45 Ramon Martinez .20 .06
46 Manny Ramirez .30 .09
47 Gregg Jefferies .20 .06
48 Bryan Rekar .20 .06
49 Jeff King .20 .06
50 John Olerud .20 .06
51 Marc Newfield .20 .06
52 Charles Johnson .20 .06
53 Robby Thompson .20 .06
54 Brian L. Hunter .20 .06
55 Mike Blowers .20 .06
56 Keith Lockhart .20 .06
57 Ray Lankford .20 .06
58 Tim Wallach .20 .06
59 Ivan Rodriguez .50 .15
60 Ed Sprague .20 .06
61 Paul Molitor .30 .09
62 Eric Karros .20 .06
63 Glenallen Hill .20 .06
64 Jay Bell .20 .06
65 Tom Pagnozzi .20 .06
66 Greg Colbrunn .20 .06
67 Edgar Martinez .30 .09
68 Paul Sorrento .20 .06
69 Kirt Manwaring .20 .06
70 Pete Schourek .20 .06
71 Orlando Merced .20 .06
72 Shawon Dunston .20 .06
73 Ricky Bottalico .20 .06
74 Brady Anderson .20 .06
75 Steve Ontiveros .20 .06
76 Jim Abbott .30 .09
77 Carl Everett .20 .06
78 Mo Vaughn .20 .06
79 Pedro Martinez .50 .15
80 Harold Baines .20 .06
81 Alan Trammell .20 .06
82 Steve Avery .20 .06
83 Jeff Cirillo .20 .06
84 John Valentin .20 .06
85 Bernie Williams .30 .09
86 Andre Dawson .20 .06
87 Dave Winfield .20 .06
88 B.J. Surhoff .20 .06
89 Jeff Blauser .20 .06
90 Barry Larkin .30 .09
91 Cliff Floyd .20 .06
92 Sammy Sosa .75 .23
93 Andres Galarraga .20 .06
94 Dave Nilsson .20 .06
95 James Mouton .20 .06
96 Marquis Grissom .20 .06
97 Matt Williams .20 .06
98 John Jaha .20 .06
99 Don Mattingly 1.25 .35
100 Tim Naehring .20 .06
101 Kevin Appier .20 .06
102 Bobby Higginson .20 .06
103 Andy Pettitte .30 .09
104 Ozzie Smith .75 .23
105 Kenny Lofton .20 .06
106 Ken Caminiti .20 .06
107 Walt Weiss .20 .06
108 Jack McDowell .20 .06
109 Brian McRae .20 .06
110 Gary Gaetti .20 .06
111 Curtis Goodwin .20 .06
112 Dennis Martinez .20 .06
113 Omar Vizquel .30 .09
114 Chipper Jones .50 .15
115 Mark Gubicza .20 .06
116 Ruben Sierra .20 .06
117 Eddie Murray .50 .15
118 Chad Curtis .20 .06
119 Hal Morris .20 .06
120 Ben McDonald .20 .06
121 Marty Cordova .20 .06
122 Ken Griffey Jr. UER .75 .23
Card says Ken homered from both sides
He is only a left hitter
123 Gary Sheffield .20 .06
124 Charlie Hayes .20 .06
125 Shawn Green UER .20 .06
Picture on back is Ed Sprague
126 Jason Giambi .20 .06
127 Mark Langston .20 .06
128 Mark Whiten .20 .06
129 Greg Vaughn .20 .06
130 Mark McGwire 1.25 .35
131 Hideo Nomo .50 .15
132 Eric Karros .50 .15
Mike Piazza
Raul Mondesi
Hideo Nomo
133 Jason Bere .20 .06
134 Ken Griffey Jr. NAT .50 .15
135 Frank Thomas NAT .30 .09
136 Cal Ripken NAT .75 .23
137 Albert Belle NAT .20 .06
138 Mike Piazza NAT .50 .15
139 Dante Bichette NAT .20 .06
140 Sammy Sosa NAT .50 .15
141 Mo Vaughn NAT .20 .06
142 Tim Salmon NAT .20 .06
143 Reggie Sanders NAT .20 .06
144 Cecil Fielder NAT .20 .06
145 Jim Edmonds NAT .20 .06
146 Rafael Palmeiro NAT .20 .06
147 Edgar Martinez NAT .20 .06
148 Barry Bonds NAT .50 .15
149 Manny Ramirez NAT .20 .06
150 Larry Walker NAT .20 .06
151 Jeff Bagwell NAT .20 .06
152 Ron Gant NAT .20 .06
153 Andres Galarraga NAT .20 .06
154 Eddie Murray NAT .30 .09
155 Kirby Puckett NAT .30 .09
156 Will Clark NAT .20 .06
157 Don Mattingly NAT .60 .18
158 Mark McGwire NAT .60 .18
159 Dean Palmer NAT .20 .06
160 Matt Williams NAT .20 .06
161 Fred McGriff NAT .20 .06
162 Joe Carter NAT .20 .06
163 Juan Gonzalez NAT .20 .06
164 Alex Ochoa .20 .06
165 Ruben Rivera .20 .06
166 Tony Clark .20 .06
167 Brian Barber .20 .06
168 Matt Lawton RC .50 .15
169 Terrell Wade .20 .06
170 Johnny Damon .30 .09
171 Derek Jeter 1.25 .35
172 Phil Nevin .20 .06
173 Robert Perez .20 .06
174 C.J. Nitkowski .20 .06
175 Joe Vitiello .20 .06
176 Roger Cedeno .20 .06
177 Ron Coomer .20 .06
178 Chris Widger .20 .06
179 Jimmy Haynes .20 .06
180 Mike Sweeney RC 1.00 .30
181 Howard Battle .20 .06
182 John Wasdin .20 .06
183 Jim Pittsley .20 .06
184 Bob Wolcott .20 .06
185 LaTroy Hawkins .20 .06
186 Nigel Wilson .20 .06
187 Dustin Hermanson .20 .06
188 Chris Snopek .20 .06
189 Mariano Rivera .30 .09
190 Jose Herrera .20 .06
191 Chris Stynes .20 .06
192 Larry Thomas .20 .06
193 David Bell .20 .06
194 Frank Thomas CL .30 .09
195 Ken Griffey Jr. CL .50 .15
196 Cal Ripken CL .75 .23
197 Jeff Bagwell CL .20 .06
198 Mike Piazza CL .50 .15
199 Barry Bonds CL .50 .15
200 Garret Anderson CL .30 .09
Chipper Jones
201 Frank Thomas .50 .15
202 Michael Tucker .20 .06
203 Kirby Puckett .50 .15
204 Alex Gonzalez .20 .06
205 Tony Gwynn .60 .18
206 Moises Alou .20 .06
207 Albert Belle .20 .06
208 Barry Bonds 1.25 .35
209 Fred McGriff .30 .09
210 Dennis Eckersley .20 .06
211 Craig Biggio .30 .09
212 David Cone .20 .06
213 Will Clark .50 .15
214 Cal Ripken 1.50 .45
215 Wade Boggs .30 .09
216 Pete Schourek .20 .06
217 Darren Daulton .20 .06
218 Carlos Baerga .20 .06
219 Larry Walker .30 .09
220 Denny Neagle .20 .06
221 Jim Edmonds .20 .06
222 Lee Smith .20 .06
223 Jason Isringhausen .20 .06
224 Jay Buhner .20 .06
225 John Olerud .20 .06
226 Jeff Conine .20 .06
227 Dean Palmer .20 .06
228 Jim Abbott .30 .09
229 Raul Mondesi .20 .06
230 Tom Glavine .30 .09
231 Kevin Seitzer .20 .06
232 Lenny Dykstra .20 .06
233 Brian Jordan .20 .06
234 Rondell White .20 .06
235 Bret Boone .20 .06
236 Randy Johnson .50 .15
237 Paul O'Neill .30 .09
238 Jim Thome .50 .15
239 Edgardo Alfonzo .20 .06
240 Terry Pendleton .20 .06
241 Harold Baines .20 .06
242 Roberto Alomar .30 .09
243 Mark Grace .30 .09
244 Derek Bell .20 .06
245 Vinny Castilla .20 .06
246 Cecil Fielder .20 .06
247 Roger Clemens 1.00 .30
248 Orel Hershiser .20 .06
249 J.T. Snow .20 .06
250 Rafael Palmeiro .30 .09
251 Bret Saberhagen .20 .06
252 Todd Hollandsworth .20 .06
253 Ryan Klesko .20 .06
254 Greg Maddux HH .50 .15
255 Ken Griffey Jr. HH .50 .15
256 Hideo Nomo HH .30 .09
257 Frank Thomas HH .30 .09
258 Cal Ripken HH .75 .23
259 Jeff Bagwell HH .20 .06
260 Barry Bonds HH .50 .15
261 Mo Vaughn HH .20 .06
262 Albert Belle HH .20 .06
263 Sammy Sosa HH .50 .15
264 Reggie Sanders HH .20 .06
265 Mike Piazza HH .50 .15
266 Chipper Jones HH .30 .09
267 Tony Gwynn HH .30 .09
268 Kirby Puckett HH .30 .09
269 Wade Boggs HH .20 .06
270 Will Clark HH .20 .06
271 Gary Sheffield HH .20 .06
272 Dante Bichette HH .20 .06
273 Randy Johnson HH .30 .09
274 Matt Williams HH .20 .06
275 Alex Rodriguez HH 1.00 .30
276 Tim Salmon HH .20 .06
277 Johnny Damon HH .20 .06
278 Manny Ramirez HH .20 .06
279 Derek Jeter HH .60 .18
280 Eddie Murray HH .30 .09
281 Ozzie Smith HH .50 .15
282 Garret Anderson HH .20 .06
283 Raul Mondesi HH .20 .06
284 Terry Steinbach .20 .06
285 Carlos Garcia .20 .06
286 Dave Justice .20 .06
287 Eric Anthony .20 .06
288 Benji Gil .20 .06
289 Bob Hamelin .20 .06
290 Dwayne Hosey .20 .06
291 Andy Pettitte HH .20 .06
292 Rod Beck .20 .06
293 Shane Andrews .20 .06
294 Julian Tavarez .20 .06
295 Willie Greene .20 .06
296 Ismael Valdes .20 .06
297 Glenallen Hill .20 .06
298 Troy Percival .20 .06
299 Ray Durham .20 .06
300 Jeff Conine 300 .20 .06
301 Ken Griffey Jr. 300 .50 .15
302 Will Clark 300 .20 .06
303 Mike Greenwell 300 .20 .06
304 Carlos Baerga 300 .20 .06
305A Paul Molitor 300 .20 .06
305B Jeff Bagwell 300 .20 .06
306 Mark Grace 300 .20 .06
307 Don Mattingly 300 .60 .18
308 Hal Morris 300 .20 .06
309 Butch Huskey .20 .06
310 Ozzie Guillen .20 .06
311 Erik Hanson .20 .06
312 Kenny Lofton 300 .20 .06
313 Edgar Martinez 300 .20 .06
314 Kurt Abbott .20 .06
315 John Smoltz .30 .09
316 Ariel Prieto .20 .06
317 Mark Carreon .20 .06
318 Kirby Puckett 300 .30 .09
319 Carlos Perez .20 .06
320 Gary DiSarcina .20 .06
321 Trevor Hoffman .20 .06
322 Mike Piazza 300 .50 .15
323 Frank Thomas 300 .30 .09
324 Juan Acevedo .20 .06
325 Bip Roberts .20 .06
326 Javier Lopez .20 .06
327 Benito Santiago .20 .06
328 Mark Lewis .20 .06
329 Royce Clayton .20 .06
330 Tom Gordon .20 .06
331 Ben McDonald .20 .06
332 Dan Wilson .20 .06
333 Ron Gant .20 .06
334 Wade Boggs 300 .20 .06
335 Paul Molitor .30 .09
336 Tony Gwynn 300 .30 .09
337 Sean Berry .20 .06
338 Rickey Henderson .50 .15
339 Wil Cordero .20 .06
340 Kent Mercker .20 .06
341 Kenny Rogers .20 .06
342 Ryne Sandberg .75 .23
343 Charlie Hayes .20 .06
344 Andy Benes .20 .06
345 Sterling Hitchcock .20 .06
346 Bernard Gilkey .20 .06
347 Julio Franco .20 .06
348 Ken Hill .20 .06
349 Russ Davis .20 .06
350 Mike Blowers .20 .06
351 B.J. Surhoff .20 .06
352 Lance Johnson .20 .06
353 Darryl Hamilton .20 .06
354 Shawon Dunston .20 .06
355 Rick Aguilera .20 .06
356 Danny Tartabull .20 .06
357 Todd Stottlemyre .20 .06
358 Mike Bordick .20 .06
359 Jack McDowell .20 .06
360 Todd Zeile .20 .06
361 Tino Martinez .30 .09
362 Greg Gagne .20 .06
363 Mike Kelly .20 .06
364 Tim Raines .20 .06
365 Ernie Young .20 .06
366 Mike Stanley .20 .06
367 Wally Joyner .20 .06
368 Karim Garcia .20 .06
369 Paul Wilson .20 .06
370 Sal Fasano .20 .06
371 Jason Schmidt .30 .09
372 Livan Hernandez RC .50 .15
373 George Arias .20 .06
374 Steve Gibralter .20 .06
375 Jermaine Dye .20 .06
376 Jason Kendall .20 .06
377 Brooks Kieschnick .20 .06
378 Jeff Ware .20 .06
379 Alan Benes .20 .06
380 Rey Ordonez .20 .06
381 Jay Powell .20 .06
382 O. Fernandez RC .25 .07
383 Wilton Guerrero RC .40 .12
384 Eric Owens .20 .06
385 George Williams RC .25 .07
386 Chan Ho Park .20 .06
387 Jeff Suppan .20 .06
388 F.P. Santangelo RC .40 .12
389 Terry Adams .20 .06
390 Bob Abreu .20 .06
391 Quinton McCracken .20 .06
392 Mike Busby RC .25 .07
393 Cal Ripken CL .75 .23
394 Ken Griffey Jr. CL .50 .15
395 Frank Thomas CL .30 .09
396 Chipper Jones CL .30 .09
397 Greg Maddux CL .50 .15
398 Mike Piazza CL .50 .15

399 Ken Griffey Jr CL .50 .15
Cal Ripken Jr.
Chipper Jones
Frank Thomas
Greg Maddux
Mike Piazza
CR1 Cal Ripken Tribute 15.00 4.50

1996 Pinnacle Foil

This 200-card set is a parallel set to the 1996 Pinnacle second series set and was issued in five-card retail super packs which retailed for $2.99. Produced with micro-etched foil fronts, this limited version is similar in design to the regular second series set.

Nm-Mt Ex-Mt
COMPLETE SET (200) 30.00 9.00
*STARS: .75 TO 2X BASIC CARDS....

1996 Pinnacle Starburst

Randomly inserted in first and second series packs at a rate of one in seven hobby/retail packs, one in six jumbo packs and one in 10 magazine packs, this 200-card quasi-parallel insert set features a select group of major league baseball's hottest superstars derived from the 399-card regular set. Unlike the basic cards, Starburst's are printed on all-foil Dufex card stock. The numbering also differs from the regular issue.

Nm-Mt Ex-Mt
*STARS: 3X TO 8X BASIC CARDS......

1996 Pinnacle Starburst Artist's Proofs

Randomly inserted in hobby and retail packs at a rate of one in 47, jumbo packs at a rate of one in 39 and magazine packs at a rate of one in 67; this 200-card set is a parallel issue to the more common Starburst inserts. The cards are identical to their Starburst counterparts except for the foil "Artist's Proofs" wording on their fronts.

Nm-Mt Ex-Mt
*STARS: 1X TO 2.5X BASIC STARBURST

1996 Pinnacle Christie Brinkley Collection

Randomly inserted at the rate of one in 23 packs, this 16-card set features the 1995 World Series participants captured by the lens of supermodel and photographer Christie Brinkley. The fronts feature color player photos in various poses with different backgrounds. The backs carry a color portrait of the player and Ms. Brinkley with an explanation as to why she posed them as she did.

Nm-Mt Ex-Mt
COMPLETE SET (16) 60.00 18.00
1 Greg Maddux 12.00 3.60
2 Ryan Klesko 3.00 .90
3 Dave Justice 3.00 .90
4 Tom Glavine 5.00 1.50
5 Chipper Jones 8.00 2.40
6 Fred McGriff 5.00 1.50
7 Javier Lopez 3.00 .90
8 Marquis Grissom 3.00 .90
9 Jason Schmidt 5.00 1.50
10 Albert Belle 3.00 .90
11 Manny Ramirez 5.00 1.50
12 Carlos Baerga 3.00 .90
13 Sandy Alomar Jr. 3.00 .90
14 Jim Thome 8.00 2.40
15 Julio Franco 3.00 .90
16 Kenny Lofton 3.00 .90
PCB Christie Brinkley 3.00 .90
Promo, On the Beach

1996 Pinnacle Essence of the Game

Randomly inserted in hobby packs only at a rate of one in 23, this 18-card standard-size set takes a unique perspective, photographically capturing the persona of some of the game's most popular icons. Using a micro-etched print technology, the fronts display a color player cutout on an acetate card studded with stars, with "Essence of the Game" appearing on a holographic design across the top.

Nm-Mt Ex-Mt
COMPLETE SET (18) 120.00 36.00
1 Cal Ripken 20.00 6.00
2 Greg Maddux 10.00 3.00
3 Frank Thomas 6.00 1.80
4 Matt Williams 2.50 .75
5 Chipper Jones 6.00 1.80
6 Reggie Sanders 2.50 .75
7 Ken Griffey Jr. 10.00 3.00
8 Kirby Puckett 6.00 1.80
9 Hideo Nomo 6.00 1.80
10 Mike Piazza 10.00 3.00
11 Jeff Bagwell 4.00 1.20
12 Mo Vaughn 2.50 .75
13 Albert Belle 2.50 .75
14 Tim Salmon 4.00 1.20
15 Don Mattingly 15.00 4.50
16 Will Clark 6.00 1.80
17 Eddie Murray 6.00 1.80
18 Barry Bonds 15.00 4.50

1996 Pinnacle First Rate

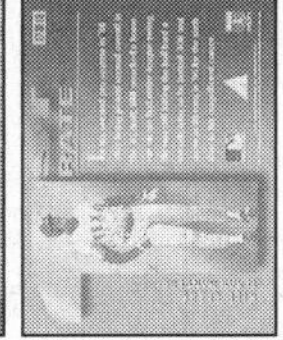

Randomly inserted in retail packs only at a rate of one in 23, this 18-card set features former first-round draft picks who have become major league superstars done in Dufex print.

Nm-Mt Ex-Mt
COMPLETE SET (18) 120.00 36.00
1 Ken Griffey Jr. 12.00 3.60
2 Frank Thomas 8.00 2.40
3 Mo Vaughn 3.00 .90
4 Chipper Jones 8.00 2.40
5 Alex Rodriguez 15.00 4.50
6 Kirby Puckett 8.00 2.40
7 Gary Sheffield 3.00 .90
8 Matt Williams 3.00 .90
9 Barry Bonds 20.00 6.00
10 Craig Biggio 5.00 1.50
11 Robin Ventura 3.00 .90
12 Michael Tucker 3.00 .90
13 Derek Jeter 20.00 6.00
14 Manny Ramirez 5.00 1.50
15 Barry Larkin 5.00 1.50
16 Shawn Green 3.00 .90
17 Will Clark 8.00 2.40
18 Mark McGwire 20.00 6.00

1996 Pinnacle Power

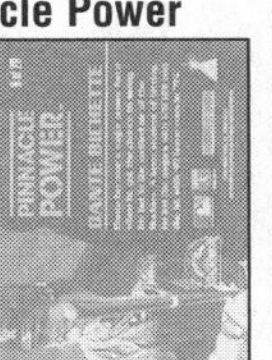

Randomly inserted in packs at a rate of one in 35 retail and hobby packs, or one in 29 jumbo packs, this 20-card set highlights the league's top long-ball hitters in die-cut holographic foil technology.

Nm-Mt Ex-Mt
COMPLETE SET (20) 100.00 30.00
1 Frank Thomas 8.00 2.40
2 Mo Vaughn 3.00 .90
3 Ken Griffey Jr. 12.00 3.60
4 Matt Williams 3.00 .90
5 Barry Bonds 20.00 6.00
6 Reggie Sanders 3.00 .90
7 Mike Piazza 12.00 3.60
8 Jim Edmonds 3.00 .90
9 Dante Bichette 3.00 .90
10 Sammy Sosa 12.00 3.60
11 Jeff Bagwell 5.00 1.50
12 Fred McGriff 5.00 1.50
13 Albert Belle 3.00 .90
14 Tim Salmon 5.00 1.50
15 Joe Carter 3.00 .90
16 Manny Ramirez 5.00 1.50
17 Eddie Murray 8.00 2.40
18 Cecil Fielder 3.00 .90
19 Larry Walker 5.00 1.50
20 Juan Gonzalez 5.00 1.50

1996 Pinnacle Project Stardom

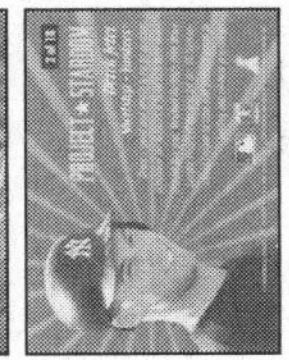

This 18-card set was randomly inserted in hobby packs at the rate of one in 35.

Nm-Mt Ex-Mt
COMPLETE SET (18) 120.00 36.00
1 Paul Wilson 4.00 1.20
2 Derek Jeter 25.00 7.50
3 Karim Garcia 4.00 1.20
4 Johnny Damon 6.00 1.80
5 Alex Rodriguez 20.00 6.00
6 Chipper Jones 10.00 3.00
7 Charles Johnson 4.00 1.20
8 Bob Abreu 4.00 1.20
9 Alan Benes 4.00 1.20
10 Richard Hidalgo 4.00 1.20
11 Brooks Kieschnick 4.00 1.20
12 Garret Anderson 4.00 1.20
13 Livan Hernandez 10.00 3.00
14 Manny Ramirez 6.00 1.80
15 Jermaine Dye 4.00 1.20
16 Todd Hollandsworth 4.00 1.20
17 Raul Mondesi 4.00 1.20
18 Ryan Klesko 4.00 1.20

1996 Pinnacle Skylines

Randomly inserted in magazine packs at the rate of one in 29, this 18-card set features baseball's best players pictured against their city's skyline and printed on clear plastic stock. The backs carry the same player portrait with information about the player and the city printed below.

Nm-Mt Ex-Mt
COMPLETE SET (18) 300.00 90.00
1 Ken Griffey Jr. 50.00 15.00
2 Frank Thomas 30.00 9.00
3 Greg Maddux 50.00 15.00
4 Cal Ripken 100.00 30.00
5 Albert Belle 12.00 3.60
6 Mo Vaughn 12.00 3.60
7 Mike Piazza 50.00 15.00
8 Wade Boggs 20.00 6.00
9 Will Clark 30.00 9.00
10 Barry Bonds 80.00 24.00
11 Gary Sheffield 12.00 3.60
12 Hideo Nomo 30.00 9.00
13 Tony Gwynn 40.00 12.00
14 Kirby Puckett 30.00 9.00
15 Chipper Jones 30.00 9.00
16 Jeff Bagwell 20.00 6.00
17 Manny Ramirez 20.00 6.00
18 Raul Mondesi 12.00 3.60

1996 Pinnacle Slugfest

Randomly inserted exclusively into one in every 35 series two retail packs, cards from this 18 cards set feature a selection of baseball's top slugging stars.

Nm-Mt Ex-Mt
COMPLETE SET (18) 150.00 45.00
1 Frank Thomas 10.00 3.00
2 Ken Griffey Jr. 15.00 4.50
3 Jeff Bagwell 6.00 1.80
4 Barry Bonds 25.00 7.50
5 Mo Vaughn 4.00 1.20
6 Albert Belle 4.00 1.20
7 Mike Piazza 15.00 4.50
8 Matt Williams 4.00 1.20
9 Dante Bichette 4.00 1.20
10 Sammy Sosa 15.00 4.50
11 Gary Sheffield 4.00 1.20
12 Reggie Sanders 4.00 1.20
13 Manny Ramirez 6.00 1.80
14 Eddie Murray 10.00 3.00
15 Juan Gonzalez 6.00 1.80
16 Dean Palmer 4.00 1.20
17 Rafael Palmeiro 6.00 1.80
18 Cecil Fielder 4.00 1.20

1996 Pinnacle Team Pinnacle

Randomly inserted in series one packs at a rate of one in 72, this nine-card set spotlights double-front all-foil Dufex card designs featuring nine top AL and NL players, by position, back-to-back. Only one side of each card is Dufexed.

Nm-Mt Ex-Mt
COMPLETE SET (9) 100.00 30.00
1 Frank Thomas 8.00 2.40
Jeff Bagwell
2 Chuck Knoblauch 5.00 1.50
Craig Biggio
3 Jim Thome 8.00 2.40
Matt Williams
4 Barrry Larkin 25.00 7.50
Cal Ripken
5 Barry Bonds 20.00 6.00
Tim Salmon
6 Ken Griffey Jr. 12.00 3.60
Reggie Sanders
7 Albert Belle 12.00 3.60
Sammy Sosa
8 Ivan Rodriguez 12.00 3.60
Mike Piazza
9 Greg Maddux 12.00 3.60
Randy Johnson

1996 Pinnacle Team Spirit

Randomly inserted in series two packs at the rate of one in 72, this 12-card set features color action player images in holographic foil stamping over a silver foil ball outlined in baseball stitching.

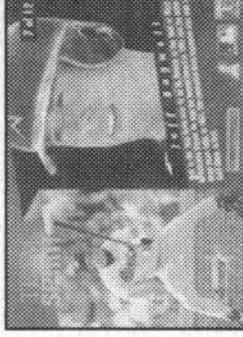

Nm-Mt Ex-Mt
COMPLETE SET (12) 150.00 45.00
1 Greg Maddux 15.00 4.50
2 Ken Griffey Jr. 15.00 4.50
3 Derek Jeter 25.00 7.50
4 Mike Piazza 15.00 4.50
5 Cal Ripken 30.00 9.00
6 Frank Thomas 10.00 3.00
7 Jeff Bagwell 6.00 1.80
8 Mo Vaughn 4.00 1.20
9 Albert Belle 4.00 1.20
10 Chipper Jones 10.00 3.00
11 Johnny Damon 6.00 1.80
12 Barry Bonds 25.00 7.50

1996 Pinnacle Team Tomorrow

Randomly inserted in series one jumbo packs at a rate of one in 19, this 10-card set is a jumbo exclusive and features the next crop of superstars. The fronts are printed in an all-foil Dufex design with two of the same color player action cutouts--one close up and the other full-length.

Nm-Mt Ex-Mt
COMPLETE SET (10) 60.00 18.00
1 Ruben Rivera 4.00 1.20
2 Johnny Damon 6.00 1.80
3 Raul Mondesi 4.00 1.20
4 Manny Ramirez 6.00 1.80
5 Hideo Nomo 10.00 3.00
6 Chipper Jones 10.00 3.00
7 Garret Anderson 4.00 1.20
8 Alex Rodriguez 20.00 6.00
9 Derek Jeter 25.00 7.50
10 Karim Garcia 4.00 1.20

1997 Pinnacle

The 1997 Pinnacle set was issued as one series of 200 cards. Cards were distributed in 10-card hobby and retail packs (SRP $2.49) and seven-card magazine packs. This set was released in February, 1997. The set contains the following subsets: Rookies (156-185), Clout (186-197) and Checklists (198-200).

Nm-Mt Ex-Mt
COMPLETE SET (200) 20.00 6.00
1 Cecil Fielder .30 .09
2 Garret Anderson .30 .09
3 Charles Nagy .30 .09
4 Darryl Hamilton .30 .09
5 Greg Myers .30 .09
6 Eric Davis .30 .09
7 Jeff Frye .30 .09
8 Marquis Grissom .30 .09
9 Curt Schilling .30 .09
10 Jeff Fassero .30 .09
11 Alan Benes .30 .09
12 Orlando Miller .30 .09
13 Alex Fernandez .30 .09
14 Andy Pettitte .50 .15
15 Andre Dawson .30 .09
16 Mark Grudzielanek .30 .09
17 Joe Vitiello .30 .09
18 Juan Gonzalez .50 .15
19 Mark Whiten .30 .09
20 Lance Johnson .30 .09
21 Trevor Hoffman .30 .09
22 Marc Newfield .30 .09
23 Jim Eisenreich .30 .09
24 Joe Carter .30 .09
25 Jose Canseco .75 .23
26 Bill Swift .30 .09
27 Ellis Burks .30 .09
28 Ben McDonald .30 .09
29 Edgar Martinez .50 .15
30 Jamie Moyer .30 .09
31 Chan Ho Park .30 .09
32 Carlos Delgado .30 .09
33 Kevin Mitchell .30 .09
34 Carlos Garcia .30 .09
35 Darryl Strawberry .30 .09
36 Jim Thome .75 .23
37 Jose Offerman .30 .09
38 Ryan Klesko .30 .09
39 Ruben Sierra .30 .09
40 Devon White .30 .09
41 Brian Jordan .30 .09
42 Tony Gwynn 1.00 .30
43 Rafael Palmeiro .50 .15
44 Dante Bichette .30 .09
45 Scott Stahoviak .30 .09
46 Roger Cedeno .30 .09
47 Ivan Rodriguez .75 .23
48 Bob Abreu .30 .09
49 Darryl Kile .30 .09
50 Darren Dreifort .30 .09
51 Shawon Dunston .30 .09
52 Mark McGwire 2.00 .60
53 Tim Salmon .50 .15
54 Gene Schall .30 .09
55 Roger Clemens 1.50 .45
56 Rondell White .30 .09
57 Ed Sprague .30 .09
58 Craig Paquette .30 .09
59 David Segui .30 .09
60 Jaime Navarro .30 .09
61 Tom Glavine .50 .15
62 Jeff Brantley .30 .09
63 Kimera Bartee .30 .09
64 Fernando Vina .30 .09
65 Eddie Murray .75 .23
66 Lenny Dykstra .30 .09
67 Kevin Elster .30 .09
68 Vinny Castilla .30 .09
69 Mike Fetters .30 .09
70 Brett Butler .30 .09
71 Robby Thompson .30 .09
72 Reggie Jefferson .30 .09
73 Todd Hundley .30 .09
74 Jeff King .30 .09
75 Ernie Young .30 .09
76 Jeff Bagwell .50 .15
77 Dan Wilson .30 .09
78 Paul Molitor .50 .15
79 Kevin Seitzer .30 .09
80 Kevin Brown .30 .09
81 Ron Gant .30 .09
82 Dwight Gooden .30 .09
83 Todd Stottlemyre .30 .09
84 Ken Caminiti .30 .09
85 James Baldwin .30 .09
86 Jermaine Dye .30 .09
87 Harold Baines .30 .09
88 Pat Hentgen .30 .09
89 Frank Rodriguez .30 .09
90 Mark Johnson .30 .09
91 Jason Kendall .30 .09
92 Alex Rodriguez 1.25 .35
93 Alan Trammell .30 .09
94 Scott Brosius .30 .09
95 Delino DeShields .30 .09
96 Chipper Jones .75 .23
97 Barry Bonds 2.00 .60
98 Brady Anderson .30 .09
99 Ryne Sandberg 1.25 .35
100 Albert Belle .30 .09
101 Jeff Cirillo .30 .09
102 Frank Thomas .75 .23
103 Mike Piazza 1.25 .35
104 Rickey Henderson .75 .23
105 Rey Ordonez .30 .09
106 Mark Grace .50 .15
107 Terry Steinbach .30 .09
108 Ray Durham .30 .09
109 Barry Larkin .50 .15
110 Tony Clark .30 .09
111 Bernie Williams .50 .15
112 John Smoltz .50 .15
113 Moises Alou .30 .09
114 Alex Gonzalez .30 .09
115 Rico Brogna .30 .09
116 Eric Karros .30 .09
117 Jeff Conine .30 .09
118 Todd Hollandsworth .30 .09
119 Troy Percival .30 .09
120 Paul Wilson .30 .09
121 Orel Hershiser .30 .09
122 Ozzie Smith 1.25 .35
123 Dave Hollins .30 .09
124 Ken Hill .30 .09
125 Rick Wilkins .30 .09
126 Scott Servais .30 .09
127 Fernando Valenzuela .30 .09
128 Mariano Rivera .50 .15
129 Mark Loretta .30 .09
130 Shane Reynolds .30 .09
131 Darren Oliver .30 .09
132 Steve Trachsel .30 .09
133 Darren Bragg .30 .09
134 Jason Dickson .30 .09
135 Darrin Fletcher .30 .09
136 Gary Gaetti .30 .09
137 Joey Cora .30 .09
138 Terry Pendleton .30 .09
139 Derek Jeter 2.00 .60
140 Danny Tartabull .30 .09
141 John Flaherty .30 .09
142 B.J. Surhoff .30 .09
143 Mike Sweeney .30 .09
144 Chad Mottola .30 .09
145 Andujar Cedeno .30 .09
146 Tim Belcher .30 .09
147 Mark Thompson .30 .09
148 Rafael Bournigal .30 .09
149 Marty Cordova .30 .09
150 Osvaldo Fernandez .30 .09
151 Mike Stanley .30 .09
152 Ricky Bottalico .30 .09
153 Donne Wall .30 .09
154 Omar Vizquel .50 .15
155 Mike Mussina .50 .15
156 Brant Brown .30 .09
157 F.P. Santangelo .30 .09
158 Ryan Hancock .30 .09
159 Jeff D'Amico .30 .09
160 Luis Castillo .30 .09
161 Darin Erstad .30 .09
162 Ugueth Urbina .30 .09
163 Andruw Jones .30 .09
164 Steve Gibralter .30 .09
165 Robin Jennings .30 .09
166 Mike Cameron .30 .09
167 George Arias .30 .09
168 Chris Stynes .30 .09
169 Justin Thompson .30 .09
170 Jamey Wright .30 .09
171 Todd Walker .30 .09
172 Nomar Garciaparra 1.25 .35
173 Jose Paniagua .30 .09
174 Marvin Benard .30 .09
175 Rocky Coppinger .30 .09
176 Quinton McCracken .30 .09

177 Amaury Telemaco .30 .09
178 Neifi Perez .30 .09
179 Todd Greene .30 .09
180 Jason Thompson .30 .09
181 Wilton Guerrero .30 .09
182 Edgar Renteria .30 .09
183 Billy Wagner .30 .09
184 Alex Ochoa .30 .09
185 Dmitri Young .30 .09
186 Kenny Lofton CT .30 .09
187 Andres Galarraga CT .30 .09
188 Chuck Knoblauch CT .30 .09
189 Greg Maddux CT 1.25 .35
190 Mo Vaughn CT .30 .09
191 Cal Ripken CT 2.50 .75
192 Hideo Nomo CT .75 .23
193 Ken Griffey Jr. CT 1.25 .35
194 Sammy Sosa CT 1.25 .35
195 Jay Buhner CT .30 .09
196 Manny Ramirez CT .30 .09
197 Matt Williams CT .30 .09
198 Andruw Jones CL .30 .09
199 Darin Erstad CL .30 .09
200 Trey Beamon CL .30 .09

1997 Pinnacle Artist's Proofs

After three years of producing Artist's Proofs cards, Pinnacle decided to add some changes to their line of scarce parallel cards. Instead of the typical one per box parallel with a little foil logo on front the set was completely redesigned in 1997. Following a similar promotion run in the 1996 Finest brand, the 200-card first series set was broken down into three different groups of cards; 125 bronze, 50 silver and 25 gold. One in every 47 first series packs contained either a bronze, silver or gold Artist's Proofs card. The gold cards are scarcest (only 300 of each were produced), and silver cards are scarcer than bronze cards. Print runs for the bronze and silver cards were never announced. Each group of cards is easy to identify by their bold color-specific backgrounds (i.e. gold cards have gold backgrounds). All three groups share the same Artist's Proof logo on front. These cards were inserted at the following ratios; one in every 47 hobby and retail packs and one in every 55 magazine packs.

Nm-Mt Ex-Mt
*BRONZE CARDS: 8X TO 20X BASE CARD HI
*SILVER CARDS: 10X TO 25X BASE CARD HI
*GOLD CARDS: 12.5X TO 30X BASE CARD HI

1997 Pinnacle Museum Collection

Randomly inserted in hobby and retail packs at a rate of one in nine and magazine packs at a rate of one in 13; these cards parallel the regular issue. Etched foil fronts differentiate them from the regular cards.

Nm-Mt Ex-Mt
*STARS: 5X TO 12X BASIC CARDS....

1997 Pinnacle Cardfrontations

Randomly inserted in hobby packs only at a rate of one in 23, this 20-card set displays color player photos on rainbow holographic foil. The card design features a top pitcher on one side with a top home run hitter on the flip side. Both sides are covered with an opaque peel and reveal protective cover.

Nm-Mt Ex-Mt
COMPLETE SET (20) 200.00 60.00
1 Greg Maddux 15.00 4.50
Mike Piazza
2 Tom Glavine 6.00 1.80
Ken Caminiti
3 Randy Johnson 30.00 9.00
Cal Ripken
4 Kevin Appier 25.00 7.50
Mark McGwire
5 Andy Pettitte 6.00 1.80
Juan Gonzalez
6 Pat Hentgen 4.00 1.20
Albert Belle
7 Hideo Nomo 10.00 3.00
Chipper Jones
8 Ismael Valdes 15.00 4.50
Sammy Sosa
9 Mike Mussina 4.00 1.20
Manny Ramirez
10 David Cone 4.00 1.20
Jay Buhner
11 Mark Wohlers 10.00 3.00
Gary Sheffield
12 Andy Benes 25.00 7.50
Barry Bonds
13 Roger Clemens 20.00 6.00
Ivan Rodriguez
14 Mariano Rivera 15.00 4.50
Ken Griffey Jr.
15 Dwight Gooden 10.00 3.00
Frank Thomas
16 John Wetteland 4.00 1.20
Darin Erstad
17 John Smoltz 6.00 1.80
Brian Jordan
18 Kevin Brown 6.00 1.80
Jeff Bagwell
19 Jack McDowell 15.00 4.50
Alex Rodriguez
20 Charles Nagy 6.00 1.80
Bernie Williams

1997 Pinnacle Home/Away

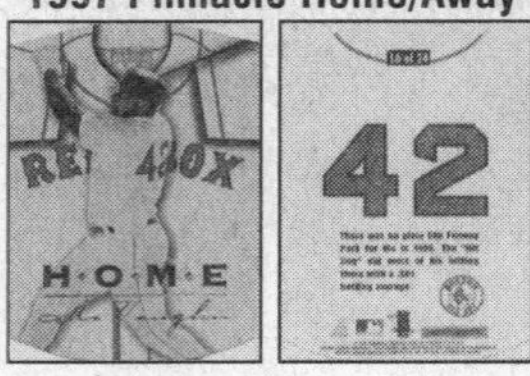

Randomly inserted in only jumbo packs at a rate of one in 33, this 24-card set features color player photos on die-cut cards. The cards were designed and shaped to resemble a player's actual jersey.

Nm-Mt Ex-Mt
1 Chipper Jones AWAY 12.00 3.60
3 Ken Griffey Jr. AWAY 20.00 6.00
5 Mike Piazza AWAY 20.00 6.00
7 Frank Thomas AWAY 12.00 3.60
9 Jeff Bagwell AWAY 8.00 2.40
11 Alex Rodriguez AWAY 20.00 6.00
13 Barry Bonds AWAY 30.00 9.00
15 Mo Vaughn AWAY 5.00 1.50
17 Derek Jeter AWAY 30.00 9.00
19 Mark McGwire AWAY 30.00 9.00
21 Cal Ripken AWAY 40.00 12.00
23 Albert Belle AWAY 5.00 1.50

1997 Pinnacle Passport to the Majors

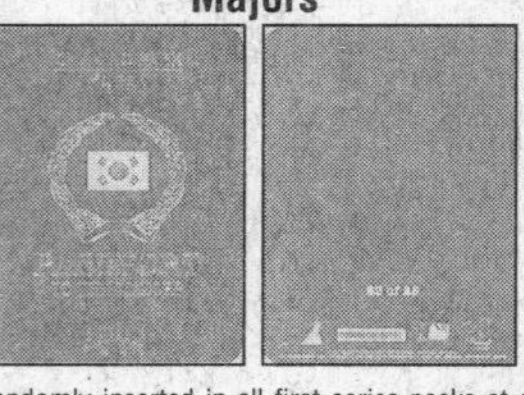

Randomly inserted in all first series packs at a rate of one in 36, this 25-card set features color player photos on a bookfold miniature passport card design and honors the rise to fame of some of the League's most high profile superstars.

Nm-Mt Ex-Mt
COMPLETE SET (25) 120.00 36.00
1 Greg Maddux 10.00 3.00
2 Ken Griffey Jr. 10.00 3.00
3 Frank Thomas 6.00 1.80
4 Cal Ripken 20.00 6.00
5 Mike Piazza 10.00 3.00
6 Alex Rodriguez 10.00 3.00
7 Mo Vaughn 2.50 .75
8 Chipper Jones 6.00 1.80
9 Roberto Alomar 6.00 1.80
10 Edgar Martinez 4.00 1.20
11 Javier Lopez 2.50 .75
12 Ivan Rodriguez 6.00 1.80
13 Juan Gonzalez 4.00 1.20
14 Carlos Baerga 2.50 .75
15 Sammy Sosa 10.00 3.00
16 Manny Ramirez 2.50 .75
17 Raul Mondesi 2.50 .75
18 Henry Rodriguez 2.50 .75
19 Rafael Palmeiro 4.00 1.20
20 Rey Ordonez 2.50 .75
21 Hideo Nomo 6.00 1.80
22 Mac Suzuki 2.50 .75
23 Chan Ho Park 2.50 .75
24 Larry Walker 2.50 .75
25 Ruben Rivera 2.50 .75

1997 Pinnacle Shades

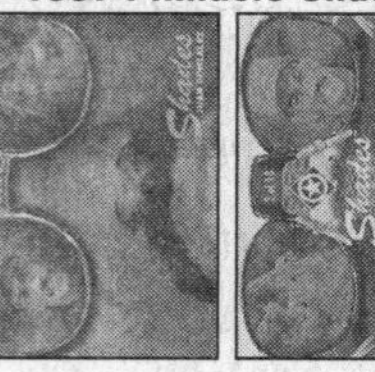

Randomly inserted in magazine packs at a rate of one in 23, this 10-card set features color upclose photos of some of the league's best players wearing their favorite pair of sunglasses. The cards have a die-cut design and mirror mylar finish.

Nm-Mt Ex-Mt
COMPLETE SET (10) 60.00 18.00
1 Ken Griffey Jr. 4.00 1.20
2 Juan Gonzalez 1.50 .45
3 John Smoltz 1.50 .45
4 Gary Sheffield 1.00 .30
5 Cal Ripken 8.00 2.40
6 Mo Vaughn 1.00 .30
7 Brian Jordan 1.00 .30
8 Mike Piazza 4.00 1.20
9 Frank Thomas 2.50 .75
10 Alex Rodriguez 4.00 1.20

1997 Pinnacle Team Pinnacle

Randomly inserted in packs at a rate of one in 90, this 10-card set matches color player photos of the top American and National League players by position on double-fronted, all-foil Dufex cards. The tenth card is a computer design that makes a full Team Pinnacle picture.

Nm-Mt Ex-Mt
COMPLETE SET (10) 120.00 36.00
1 Frank Thomas 12.00 3.60
Jeff Bagwell

2 Chuck Knoblauch 5.00 1.50
Eric Young
3 Ken Caminiti 5.00 1.50
Jim Thome
4 Alex Rodriguez 20.00 6.00
Chipper Jones
5 Mike Piazza 20.00 6.00
Ivan Rodriguez
6 Albert Belle 30.00 9.00
Barry Bonds
7 Ken Griffey Jr. 20.00 6.00
Ellis Burks
8 Juan Gonzalez 8.00 2.40
Gary Sheffield
9 John Smoltz 8.00 2.40
Andy Pettitte
10 Frank Thomas 10.00 3.00
Jeff Bagwell
Chuck Knoblauch
Eric Young
Ken Caminiti
Jim Thome
Alex Rodriguez
Chipper Jones
Mike Piazza
Ivan Rodriguez
Albert Belle
Barry Bonds
Ken Griffey Jr.
Ellis Burks
Juan Gonzalez
Gary Sheffield
John Smoltz
Andy Pettitte

1998 Pinnacle

The 1998 Pinnacle set was issued in one series totalling 200 cards and was distributed in 10-card packs with a suggested retail price of $2.99. The fronts feature borderless color player photos with player information on the backs. The set contains the following subsets: Rookies (158-181), Field of Vision (182-187), Goin' Jake (188-197) and Checklists (198-200). Three variations of each card 1-157 were issued. The cards have home, away or seasonal stats on the back and were all produced in equal quantities. This concept of variations on the statistics was met with utter lack of interest and all three versions trade for equal values. In fact, complete sets typically carry a mix of all three stat variations.

Nm-Mt Ex-Mt
COMPLETE SET (200) 25.00 7.50
1 Tony Gwynn 1.00 .30
2 Pedro Martinez .75 .23
3 Kenny Lofton .30 .09
4 Curt Schilling .30 .09
5 Shawn Estes .30 .09
6 Tom Glavine .50 .15
7 Mike Piazza 1.25 .35
8 Ray Lankford .30 .09
9 Barry Larkin .50 .15
10 Tony Womack .30 .09
11 Jeff Blauser .30 .09
12 Rod Beck .30 .09
13 Larry Walker .50 .15
14 Greg Maddux 1.25 .35
15 Mark Grace .50 .15
16 Ken Caminiti .30 .09
17 Bobby Jones .30 .09
18 Chipper Jones .75 .23
19 Javier Lopez .30 .09
20 Moises Alou .30 .09
21 Royce Clayton .30 .09
22 Darryl Kile .30 .09
23 Barry Bonds 2.00 .60
24 Steve Finley .30 .09
25 Andres Galarraga .30 .09
26 Denny Neagle .30 .09
27 Todd Hundley .30 .09
28 Jeff Bagwell .50 .15
29 Andy Pettitte .50 .15
30 Darin Erstad .30 .09
31 Carlos Delgado .30 .09
32 Matt Williams .30 .09
33 Will Clark .75 .23
34 Vinny Castilla .30 .09
35 Brad Radke .30 .09
36 John Olerud .30 .09
37 Andruw Jones .30 .09
38 Jason Giambi .30 .09
39 Scott Rolen .75 .23
40 Gary Sheffield .30 .09
41 Jimmy Key .30 .09
42 Kevin Appier .30 .09
43 Wade Boggs .50 .15
44 Hideo Nomo .75 .23
45 Manny Ramirez .50 .15
46 Wilton Guerrero .30 .09
47 Travis Fryman .30 .09
48 Chili Davis .30 .09
49 Jeromy Burnitz .30 .09
50 Craig Biggio .50 .15
51 Tim Salmon .50 .15
52 Jose Cruz Jr. .30 .09
53 Sammy Sosa 1.25 .35
54 Hideki Irabu .30 .09
55 Chan Ho Park .30 .09
56 Robin Ventura .30 .09
57 Jose Guillen .30 .09
58 Deion Sanders .50 .15
59 Jose Canseco .75 .23
60 Jay Buhner .30 .09
61 Rafael Palmeiro .50 .15
62 Vladimir Guerrero .75 .23
63 Mark McGwire 2.00 .60
64 Derek Jeter 2.00 .60
65 Bobby Bonilla .30 .09
66 Raul Mondesi .30 .09
67 Paul Molitor .50 .15
68 Joe Carter .30 .09
69 Marquis Grissom .30 .09
70 Juan Gonzalez .50 .15
71 Kevin Orie .30 .09
72 Rusty Greer .30 .09
73 Henry Rodriguez .30 .09
74 Fernando Tatis .30 .09
75 John Valentin .30 .09
76 Matt Morris .30 .09
77 Ray Durham .30 .09
78 Geronimo Berroa .30 .09
79 Scott Brosius .30 .09
80 Willie Greene .30 .09
81 Rondell White .30 .09
82 Doug Drabek .30 .09
83 Derek Bell .30 .09
84 Butch Huskey .30 .09
85 Doug Jones .30 .09
86 Jeff Kent .30 .09
87 Jim Edmonds .30 .09
88 Mark McLemore .30 .09
89 Todd Zeile .30 .09
90 Edgardo Alfonzo .30 .09
91 Carlos Baerga .30 .09
92 Jorge Fabregas .30 .09
93 Alan Benes .30 .09
94 Troy Percival .30 .09
95 Edgar Renteria .30 .09
96 Jeff Fassero .30 .09
97 Reggie Sanders .30 .09
98 Dean Palmer .30 .09
99 J.T. Snow .30 .09
100 Dave Nilsson .30 .09
101 Dan Wilson .30 .09
102 Robb Nen .30 .09
103 Damion Easley .30 .09
104 Kevin Foster .30 .09
105 Jose Offerman .30 .09
106 Steve Cooke .30 .09
107 Matt Stairs .30 .09
108 Darryl Hamilton .30 .09
109 Steve Karsay .30 .09
110 Gary DiSarcina .30 .09
111 Dante Bichette .30 .09
112 Billy Wagner .30 .09
113 David Segui .30 .09
114 Bobby Higginson .30 .09
115 Jeffrey Hammonds .30 .09
116 Kevin Brown .30 .09
117 Paul Sorrento .30 .09
118 Mark Leiter .30 .09
119 Charles Nagy .30 .09
120 Danny Patterson .30 .09
121 Brian McRae .30 .09
122 Jay Bell .30 .09
123 Jamie Moyer .30 .09
124 Carl Everett .30 .09
125 Greg Colbrunn .30 .09
126 Jason Kendall .30 .09
127 Luis Sojo .30 .09
128 Mike Lieberthal .30 .09
129 Reggie Jefferson .30 .09
130 Cal Eldred .30 .09
131 Orel Hershiser .30 .09
132 Doug Glanville .30 .09
133 Willie Blair .30 .09
134 Neifi Perez .30 .09
135 Sean Berry .30 .09
136 Chuck Finley .30 .09
137 Alex Gonzalez .30 .09
138 Dennis Eckersley .30 .09
139 Kenny Rogers .30 .09
140 Troy O'Leary .30 .09
141 Roger Bailey .30 .09
142 Yamil Benitez .30 .09
143 Wally Joyner .30 .09
144 Bobby Witt .30 .09
145 Pete Schourek .30 .09
146 Terry Steinbach .30 .09
147 B.J. Surhoff .30 .09
148 Esteban Loaiza .30 .09
149 Heathcliff Slocumb .30 .09
150 Ed Sprague .30 .09
151 Gregg Jefferies .30 .09
152 Scott Erickson .30 .09
153 Jaime Navarro .30 .09
154 David Wells .30 .09
155 Alex Fernandez .30 .09
156 Tim Belcher .30 .09
157 Mark Grudzielanek .30 .09
158 Scott Hatteberg .30 .09
159 Paul Konerko .30 .09
160 Ben Grieve .30 .09
161 Abraham Nunez .30 .09
162 Shannon Stewart .30 .09
163 Jaret Wright .30 .09
164 Derrek Lee .30 .09
165 Todd Dunwoody .30 .09
166 Steve Woodard .30 .09
167 Ryan McGuire .30 .09
168 Jeremi Gonzalez .30 .09
169 Mark Kotsay .30 .09
170 Brett Tomko .30 .09
171 Bobby Estalella .30 .09
172 Livan Hernandez .30 .09
173 Todd Helton .50 .15
174 Garrett Stephenson .30 .09
175 Pokey Reese .30 .09
176 Tony Saunders .30 .09
177 Antone Williamson .30 .09
178 Bartolo Colon .30 .09
179 Karim Garcia .30 .09
180 Juan Encarnacion .30 .09
181 Jacob Cruz .30 .09
182 Alex Rodriguez FV 1.25 .35
183 Cal Ripken FV 2.00 .60
Roberto Alomar
184 Roger Clemens FV 1.50 .45
185 Derek Jeter FV 2.00 .60
186 Frank Thomas FV .75 .23
187 Ken Griffey Jr. FV 1.25 .35
188 Mark McGwire GJ 2.00 .60
189 Tino Martinez GJ .50 .15
190 Larry Walker GJ .50 .15
191 Brady Anderson GJ .30 .09
192 Jeff Bagwell GJ .50 .15
193 Ken Griffey Jr. GJ 1.25 .35
194 Chipper Jones GJ .50 .15
195 Ray Lankford GJ .30 .09
196 Jim Thome GJ .75 .23
197 Nomar Garciaparra GJ 1.25 .35
198 Brady Anderson .50 .15
Jeff Bagwell
Nomar Garciaparra
Ken Griffey Jr.
Chipper Jones
Ray Lankford
Tino Martinez
Mark McGwire
Jim Thome
Larry Walker
199 Tino Martinez CL .50 .15
200 Jacobs Field CL .30 .09

1998 Pinnacle Artist's Proofs

Only the top 100 cards from the regular issue of the 1998 Pinnacle set were selected for inclusion in this year's Artist's Proofs gold-foil Dufex partial parallel version. The cards were randomly seeded into packs at a rate of 1:39.

Nm-Mt Ex-Mt
*STARS: 1X TO 2.5X MUSEUM COLL

1998 Pinnacle Museum Collection

Only the top 100 cards from the regular issue 1998 Pinnacle set were selected for inclusion in this year's Museum Collection all-foil Dufex partial parallel version. The cards were randomly seeded into packs at a rate of 1:9.

Nm-Mt Ex-Mt
*STARS: 4X TO 10X BASIC CARDS....
MC NUMBERS DON'T MATCH BASIC CARDS

1998 Pinnacle Press Plates

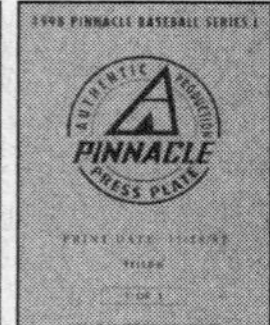

Randomly inserted in packs at the rate of one in 1,250, this 284-card set features the actual press plates used to create the 1998 Pinnacle base set as well as all the insert sets. Each card had eight Press Plates inserts, four of each color for the card front and four for the card back. Unlike the 1997 Press Plates, these were not signed by then CEO Jerry Meyer of Pinnacle. Due to scarcity, no pricing is provided.

Nm-Mt Ex-Mt
COMMON FRONT 50.00 15.00
COMMON BACK 30.00 9.00

1998 Pinnacle Hit It Here

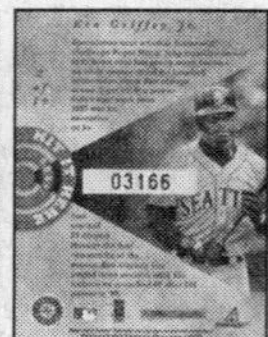

Randomly inserted one in 19 retail and magazine first series packs, and one in 17 first series hobby packs, this 10-card set features color player cut-outs of hot hitters in the league printed on micro-etched silver foil cards with a target in the background. If one of these hitters hit for the cycle on opening day, one lucky collector holding that specific player's card could win $1million. Each card back featured a special serial number that would be entered into a drawing to determine the winner.

Nm-Mt Ex-Mt
COMPLETE SET (10) 30.00 9.00
1 Larry Walker 1.50 .45
2 Ken Griffey Jr. 4.00 1.20
3 Mike Piazza 4.00 1.20
4 Frank Thomas 2.50 .75
5 Barry Bonds 6.00 1.80
6 Albert Belle 1.00 .30
7 Tino Martinez 1.00 .30
8 Mark McGwire 6.00 1.80
9 Juan Gonzalez 1.50 .45
10 Jeff Bagwell 1.50 .45

1998 Pinnacle Spellbound

Randomly inserted in hobby packs only at the rate of one in 17, this 50-card set features game action color photos of nine top players printed on full-foil, micro-etched cards and superimposed over one of the letters of the player's name or nickname. All the cards of the same player needed to be collected in order to spell out the player's name when laid side-by-side.

Nm-Mt Ex-Mt
COMMON M.MCGWIRE 10.00 3.00

COMMON R.CLEMENS 8.00 2.40
COMMON F.THOMAS.................. 4.00 1.20
COMMON S.ROLEN..................... 4.00 1.20
COMMON K.GRIFFEY.................. 6.00 1.80
COMMON L.WALKER................... 2.50 .75
COMMON GARCIAPARRA.......... 6.00 1.80
COMMON C.RIPKEN 12.00 3.60
COMMON T.GWYNN 5.00 1.50

1998 Pinnacle Epix Game Orange

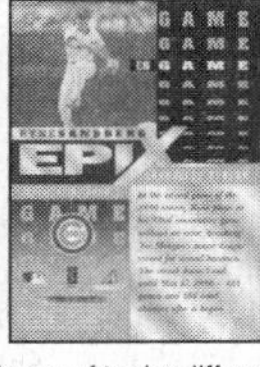

This 18-card partial set is one of twelve different Epix parallel versions. Cards E1-E6 were distributed in basic 1998 Pinnacle packs. Cards E7-E12 were distributed in 1998 Score packs and cards E19-E24 were distributed in 1998 Zenith packs. Missing cards E13-E18 were intended to be seeded within 1998 Pinnacle Certified, but Pinnacle went bankrupt in mid-1998, prior to the intended release of the product. Seeding ratios were only released as a cumulative rate for all versions of Epix cards and they are as follows: Pinnacle 1:21 packs, Score 1:61 packs and Zenith 1:11 packs. Card back text for each GAME card features a highlight of the most memorable game for each player featured. Orange foil fronts and the word "GAME" running down the side furthermore distinguish these cards.

Nm-Mt Ex-Mt
*GAME EMERALD: 1.25X TO 3X ORANGE
*GAME PURPLE: .6X TO 1.5X ORANGE
E1 Ken Griffey Jr. 5.00 1.50
E2 Juan Gonzalez.......................... 2.00 .60
E3 Jeff Bagwell .... 2.00 .60
E4 Ivan Rodriguez.......................... 3.00 .90
E5 Nomar Garciaparra................... 5.00 1.50
E6 Ryne Sandberg .... 3.00 .90
E7 Frank Thomas............................ 3.00 .90
E8 Derek Jeter................................ 8.00 2.40
E9 Tony Gwynn 4.00 1.20
E10 Albert Belle.............................. 2.00 .60
E11 Scott Rolen............................... 3.00 .90
E12 Barry Larkin .... 2.00 .60
E19 Mike Piazza.............................. 5.00 1.50
E20 Andruw Jones........................... 1.25 .35
E21 Greg Maddux 5.00 1.50
E22 Barry Bonds............................. 8.00 2.40
E23 Paul Molitor .... 2.00 .60
E24 Eddie Murray .... 3.00 .90

1998 Pinnacle Epix Moment Orange

This 18-card partial set is one of twelve different Epix parallel versions. Cards E7-E12 were distributed in 1998 Zenith packs. Cards E13-E18 were distributed in basic 1998 Pinnacle packs and cards E19-E24 were distributed in 1998 Score packs. Missing cards E1-E6 were intended to be seeded within 1998 Pinnacle Certified, but Pinnacle went bankrupt in mid-1998, prior to the intended release of the product. Seeding ratios were only released as a cumulative rate for all versions of Epix cards and they are as follows: Pinnacle 1:21 packs, Score 1:61 packs and Zenith 1:11 packs. Card back text for each MOMENT card features a highlight of the most memorable moment for each player featured. Orange foil fronts and the word "MOMENT" running down the side furthermore distinguish these cards.

Nm-Mt Ex-Mt
*MOMENT EMERALD: 1.25X TO 3X ORANGE
MOMENT EMERALD PRINT RUN 30 SETS
*MOMENT PURPLE: .6X TO 1.5X ORANGE
E7 Frank Thomas........................ 4.00 1.20
E8 Derek Jeter........................... 10.00 3.00
E9 Tony Gwynn............................ 5.00 1.50
E10 Albert Belle.......................... 2.50 .75
E11 Scott Rolen........................... 4.00 1.20
E12 Barry Larkin .... 2.50 .75
E13 Alex Rodriguez...................... 6.00 1.80
E14 Cal Ripken........................... 10.00 3.00
E15 Chipper Jones....................... 4.00 1.20
E16 Mo Vaughn .... 1.50 .45
E17 Roger Clemens 8.00 2.40
E18 Mark McGwire 10.00 3.00
E19 Mike Piazza........................... 6.00 1.80
E20 Andruw Jones........................ 1.50 .45
E21 Greg Maddux 6.00 1.80
E22 Barry Bonds......................... 10.00 3.00
E23 Paul Molitor .... 2.50 .75
E24 Eddie Murray 4.00 1.20

1998 Pinnacle Epix Play Orange

This 24-card set is one of twelve different Epix parallel versions. Cards E1-E6 were distributed in 1998 Score packs. Cards E13-E18 were distributed in 1998 Zenith packs and cards E19-E24 were distributed in basic 1998 Pinnacle packs. Missing cards E7-E12 were intended to be seeded within 1998 Pinnacle Certified, but Pinnacle went bankrupt in mid-1998, prior to the intended release of the product. Seeding ratios were only released as a cumulative rate for all versions of Epix cards and they are as follows: Pinnacle 1:21 packs, Score 1:61 packs and Zenith 1:11 packs. Card back text for each PLAY card features a highlight of the most memorable play for each player featured. Orange foil fronts and the word "PLAY" running down the side furthermore distinguish these cards.

Nm-Mt Ex-Mt
*PLAY EMERALD: 1.25X TO 3X ORANGE
*PLAY PURPLE: .6X TO 1.5X ORANGE
E1 Ken Griffey Jr. .... 3.00 .90
E2 Juan Gonzalez........................... 1.25 .35
E3 Jeff Bagwell .... 1.25 .35
E4 Ivan Rodriguez.......................... 2.00 .60
E5 Nomar Garciaparra.................... 3.00 .90
E6 Ryne Sandberg .... 2.00 .60
E13 Alex Rodriguez......................... 3.00 .90
E14 Cal Ripken............................... 5.00 1.50
E15 Chipper Jones........................... 2.00 .60
E16 Mo Vaughn .... .75 .23
E17 Roger Clemens 4.00 1.20
E18 Mark McGwire 5.00 1.50
E19 Mike Piazza............................... 3.00 .90
E20 Andruw Jones............................. .75 .23
E21 Greg Maddux .... 3.00 .90
E22 Barry Bonds.............................. 5.00 1.50
E23 Paul Molitor .... 1.25 .35
E24 Eddie Murray .... 2.00 .60

1998 Pinnacle Epix Season Orange

This 18-card partial set is one of twelve different Epix parallel versions. Cards E1-E6 were distributed in 1998 Zenith packs. Cards E7-E12 were distributed in basic 1998 Pinnacle packs and cards E13-E18 were distributed in 1998 Score packs. Missing cards E19-E24 were intended to be seeded within 1998 Pinnacle Certified, but Pinnacle went bankrupt in mid-1998, prior to the intended release of the product. Seeding ratios were only released as a cumulative rate for all versions of Epix cards and they are as follows: Pinnacle 1:21 packs, Score 1:61 packs and Zenith 1:11 packs. Card back text for each SEASON card features a highlight of the most memorable season for each player featured. Orange foil fronts and the word "SEASON" running down the side furthermore distinguish these cards.

Nm-Mt Ex-Mt
*SEASON EMERALD: 1.25X TO 3X ORANGE
*SEASON PURPLE: .6X TO 1.5X ORANGE
E1 Ken Griffey Jr. 10.00 3.00
E2 Juan Gonzalez.......................... 4.00 1.20
E3 Jeff Bagwell 4.00 1.20
E4 Ivan Rodriguez......................... 6.00 1.80
E5 Nomar Garciaparra................. 10.00 3.00
E6 Ryne Sandberg 6.00 1.80
E7 Frank Thomas........................... 6.00 1.80
E8 Derek Jeter............................. 15.00 4.50
E9 Tony Gwynn 8.00 2.40
E10 Albert Belle............................. 4.00 1.20
E11 Scott Rolen.............................. 6.00 1.80
E12 Barry Larkin 4.00 1.20
E13 Alex Rodriguez...................... 10.00 3.00
E14 Cal Ripken............................. 15.00 4.50
E15 Chipper Jones.......................... 6.00 1.80
E16 Mo Vaughn .... 2.50 .75
E17 Roger Clemens 12.00 3.60
E18 Mark McGwire 15.00 4.50

1997 Pinnacle Totally Certified Platinum Blue

This 150-card set is a parallel version of the more-common 1997 Pinnacle Totally Certified Platinum Red set. Platinum Blue cards were seeded at a rate of one per pack. Only 1,999 sets were produced and each card is sequentially numbered on back.

Nm-Mt Ex-Mt
*STARS: .6X TO 1.5X PLAT.RED........
*ROOKIES: .4X TO 1X PLAT.RED.......

1997 Pinnacle Totally Certified Platinum Gold

This 150-card set is a parallel version of the 1997 Pinnacle Totally Certified Platinum Red set. Platinum Gold cards were randomly seeded into one in every 79 packs. Only 30 sets were produced and each card is sequentially numbered on back.

Nm-Mt Ex-Mt
*STARS: 8X TO 20X PLAT. RED........
*ROOKIES: 2.5X TO 6X PLAT.RED......

1997 Pinnacle Totally Certified Platinum Red

This 150-card set is a quasi-parallel version of the 1997 Pinnacle Certified set. The product was distributed in three-card packs with a suggested retail price of $6.99. The checklist and player content is identical, but the photos are all different and the cards are designed a little differently. The fronts feature color action player images utilizing full micro-etched, holographic mylar print technology, highlighted with red vignette accent and foil stamping. Platinum Red cards were seeded at a rate of two per pack. Only 3,999 Platinum Red sets were produced and each card is sequentially numbered on back.

Nm-Mt Ex-Mt
COMPLETE SET (150)............ 150.00 45.00
1 Barry Bonds.......................... 10.00 3.00
2 Mo Vaughn .... 1.50 .45
3 Matt Williams........................ 1.50 .45
4 Ryne Sandberg 6.00 1.80
5 Jeff Bagwell .... 2.50 .75
6 Alan Benes............................ 1.50 .45
7 John Wetteland .... 1.50 .45
8 Fred McGriff.......................... 2.50 .75
9 Craig Biggio .... 2.50 .75
10 Bernie Williams................... 2.50 .75
11 Brian Hunter........................ 1.50 .45
12 Sandy Alomar Jr. .... 1.50 .45
13 Ray Lankford .... 1.50 .45
14 Ryan Klesko .... 1.50 .45
15 Jermaine Dye....................... 1.50 .45
16 Andy Benes.......................... 1.50 .45
17 Albert Belle.......................... 1.50 .45
18 Tony Clark............................ 1.50 .45
19 Dean Palmer .... 1.50 .45
20 Bernard Gilkey .... 1.50 .45
21 Ken Caminiti......................... 1.50 .45
22 Alex Rodriguez.................... 6.00 1.80
23 Tim Salmon .... 2.50 .75
24 Larry Walker .... 2.50 .75
25 Barry Larkin .... 2.50 .75
26 Mike Piazza 6.00 1.80
27 Brady Anderson .... 1.50 .45
28 Cal Ripken.......................... 12.00 3.60
29 Charles Nagy....................... 1.50 .45
30 Paul Molitor .... 2.50 .75
31 Darin Erstad .... 1.50 .45
32 Rey Ordonez .... 1.50 .45
33 Wally Joyner .... 1.50 .45
34 David Cone.......................... 1.50 .45
35 Sammy Sosa........................ 6.00 1.80
36 Dante Bichette..................... 1.50 .45
37 Eric Karros .... 1.50 .45
38 Omar Vizquel .... 2.50 .75
39 Roger Clemens 8.00 2.40
40 Joe Carter .... 1.50 .45
41 Frank Thomas 4.00 1.20
42 Javy Lopez........................... 1.50 .45
43 Mike Mussina....................... 2.50 .75
44 Gary Sheffield .... 1.50 .45
45 Tony Gwynn 5.00 1.50
46 Jason Kendall....................... 1.50 .45
47 Jim Thome............................ 4.00 1.20
48 Andres Galarraga .... 1.50 .45
49 Mark McGwire 10.00 3.00
50 Troy Percival .... 1.50 .45
51 Derek Jeter......................... 10.00 3.00
52 Todd Hollandsworth............. 1.50 .45
53 Ken Griffey Jr. 6.00 1.80
54 Randy Johnson 4.00 1.20
55 Pat Hentgen .... 1.50 .45
56 Rusty Greer.......................... 1.50 .45
57 John Jaha .... 1.50 .45
58 Kenny Lofton .... 1.50 .45
59 Chipper Jones 4.00 1.20
60 Robb Nen............................. 1.50 .45
61 Rafael Palmeiro.................... 2.50 .75
62 Mariano Rivera..................... 2.50 .75
63 Hideo Nomo......................... 4.00 1.20
64 Greg Vaughn .... 1.50 .45
65 Ron Gant.............................. 1.50 .45
66 Eddie Murray 4.00 1.20
67 John Smoltz.......................... 2.50 .75
68 Manny Ramirez .... 2.50 .75
69 Juan Gonzalez .... 2.50 .75
70 F.P. Santangelo..................... 1.50 .45
71 Moises Alou .... 1.50 .45
72 Alex Ochoa........................... 1.50 .45
73 Chuck Knoblauch .... 1.50 .45
74 Raul Mondesi .... 1.50 .45
75 J.T. Snow .... 1.50 .45
76 Rickey Henderson................. 4.00 1.20
77 Bobby Bonilla....................... 1.50 .45
78 Wade Boggs......................... 2.50 .75
79 Ivan Rodriguez..................... 4.00 1.20
80 Brian Jordan .... 1.50 .45
81 Al Leiter .... 1.50 .45
82 Jay Buhner........................... 1.50 .45
83 Greg Maddux 6.00 1.80
84 Edgar Martinez..................... 2.50 .75
85 Kevin Brown......................... 1.50 .45
86 Eric Young .... 1.50 .45
87 Todd Hundley .... 1.50 .45
88 Ellis Burks............................ 1.50 .45
89 Marquis Grissom .... 1.50 .45
90 Jose Canseco....................... 4.00 1.20
91 Henry Rodriguez .... 1.50 .45
92 Andy Pettitte .... 2.50 .75
93 Mark Grudzielanek .... 1.50 .45
94 Dwight Gooden .... 1.50 .45
95 Roberto Alomar .... 2.50 .75
96 Paul Wilson.......................... 1.50 .45
97 Will Clark 4.00 1.20
98 Rondell White .... 1.50 .45
99 Charles Johnson .... 1.50 .45
100 Jim Edmonds...................... 1.50 .45
101 Jason Giambi .... 1.50 .45
102 Billy Wagner....................... 1.50 .45
103 Edgar Renteria .... 1.50 .45
104 Johnny Damon.................... 2.50 .75
105 Jason Isringhausen............. 1.50 .45
106 Andruw Jones..................... 1.50 .45
107 Jose Guillen .... 1.50 .45
108 Kevin Orie .... 1.50 .45
109 Brian Giles RC.................. 12.00 3.60
110 Danny Patterson .... 1.50 .45
111 Vladimir Guerrero 4.00 1.20
112 Scott Rolen 4.00 1.20
113 Damon Mashore .... 1.50 .45
114 Nomar Garciaparra............. 6.00 1.80
115 Todd Walker....................... 1.50 .45
116 Wilton Guerrero .... 1.50 .45
117 Bob Abreu .... 1.50 .45
118 Brooks Kieschnick .... 1.50 .45
119 Pokey Reese .... 1.50 .45
120 Todd Greene....................... 1.50 .45
121 Dmitri Young....................... 1.50 .45
122 Raul Casanova .... 1.50 .45
123 Glendon Rusch .... 1.50 .45
124 Jason Dickson .... 1.50 .45
125 Jorge Posada .... 2.50 .75
126 Rod Myers .... 1.50 .45
127 Bubba Trammell RC .... 1.50 .45
128 Scott Spiezio....................... 1.50 .45
129 Hideki Irabu RC.................. 1.50 .45
130 Wendell Magee .... 1.50 .45
131 Bartolo Colon...................... 1.50 .45
132 Chris Holt............................ 1.50 .45
133 Calvin Maduro..................... 1.50 .45
134 Ray Montgomery .... 1.50 .45
135 Shannon Stewart .... 1.50 .45
136 Ken Griffey Jr. CERT 4.00 1.20
137 Vl.Guerrero CERT .... 2.50 .75
138 Roger Clemens CERT.......... 4.00 1.20
139 Mark McGwire CERT 5.00 1.50
140 Albert Belle CERT................ 1.50 .45
141 Derek Jeter CERT................ 5.00 1.50
142 Juan Gonzalez CERT .... 1.50 .45
143 Greg Maddux CERT............. 4.00 1.20
144 Alex Rodriguez CERT........... 4.00 1.20
145 Jeff Bagwell CERT............... 1.50 .45
146 Cal Ripken CERT................. 6.00 1.80
147 Tony Gwynn CERT .... 2.50 .75
148 Frank Thomas CERT .... 2.50 .75
149 Hideo Nomo CERT............... 1.50 .45
150 Andruw Jones CERT .... 1.50 .45

1939 Play Ball

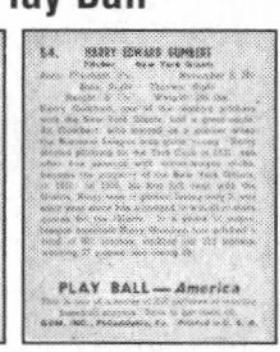

The cards in this 161-card set measure approximately 2 1/2" by 3 1/8". Gum Incorporated introduced a brief (war-shortened) but innovative era of baseball card production with its set of 1939. The combination of actual player photos (black and white), large card size, and extensive biography proved extremely popular. Player names are found either entirely capitalized or with initial caps only, and a "sample card" overprint is not uncommon. The "sample card" overprint variations are valued at double the prices below. Card number 126 was never issued, and cards 116-162 were produced in lesser quantities than cards 1-115. A card of Ted Williams in his rookie season as well as an early card of Joe DiMaggio are the key cards in the set.

Ex-Mt VG
COMPLETE SET (161)......... 10000.00 5000.00
COMMON CARD (1-115) 20.00 10.00
COMMON (116-162)................. 75.00 38.00
WRAPPER (1-CENT).............. 200.00 100.00
1 Jake Powell........................... 60.00 18.00
2 Lee Grissom......................... 20.00 10.00
3 Red Ruffing.......................... 75.00 38.00
4 Eldon Auker 20.00 10.00
5 Luke Sewell.......................... 25.00 12.50
6 Leo Durocher 100.00 50.00
7 Bobby Doerr......................... 75.00 38.00
8 Henry Pippen 20.00 10.00
9 James Tobin......................... 20.00 10.00
10 James DeShong.................. 20.00 10.00
11 Johnny Rizzo 20.00 10.00
12 Hershel Martin 20.00 10.00
13 Luke Hamlin........................ 20.00 10.00
14 Jim Tabor 20.00 10.00
15 Paul Derringer..................... 30.00 15.00
16 John Peacock...................... 20.00 10.00
17 Emerson Dickman............... 20.00 10.00
18 Harry Danning..................... 20.00 10.00
19 Paul Dean............................ 40.00 20.00
20 Joe Heving 20.00 10.00
21 Dutch Leonard 30.00 15.00
22 Bucky Walters..................... 30.00 15.00
23 Burgess Whitehead 20.00 10.00
24 Richard Coffman 20.00 10.00
25 George Selkirk 40.00 20.00
26 Joe DiMaggio................... 1400.00 700.00
27 Fred Ostermueller 20.00 10.00
28 Sylvester Johnson 20.00 10.00
29 John(Jack) Wilson 20.00 10.00
30 Bill Dickey 125.00 60.00
31 Sam West 20.00 10.00
32 Bob Seeds........................... 20.00 10.00
33 Del Young 20.00 10.00
34 Frank Demaree.................... 20.00 10.00
35 Bill Jurges 20.00 10.00
36 Frank McCormick................ 20.00 10.00
37 Virgil Davis.......................... 20.00 10.00
38 Billy Myers........................... 20.00 10.00
39 Rick Ferrell 75.00 38.00
40 James Bagby Jr.................. 20.00 10.00
41 Lon Warneke....................... 25.00 12.50
42 Arndt Jorgens 20.00 10.00
43 Melo Almada 25.00 12.50
44 Don Heffner 20.00 10.00
45 Merrill May.......................... 20.00 10.00
46 Morris Arnovich 20.00 10.00
47 Buddy Lewis 20.00 10.00
48 Lefty Gomez..................... 125.00 60.00
49 Eddie Miller......................... 20.00 10.00
50 Charley Gehringer 125.00 60.00
51 Mel Ott 125.00 60.00
52 Tommy Henrich................... 40.00 20.00
53 Carl Hubbell 125.00 60.00
54 Harry Gumpert 20.00 10.00
55 Arky Vaughan..................... 75.00 38.00
56 Hank Greenberg.............. 200.00 75.00
57 Buddy Hassett..................... 20.00 10.00
58 Lou Chiozza 20.00 10.00
59 Ken Chase........................... 20.00 10.00
60 Schoolboy Rowe................. 40.00 20.00
61 Tony Cuccinello.................. 25.00 12.50
62 Tom Carey........................... 20.00 10.00
63 Emmett Mueller 20.00 10.00
64 Wally Moses 25.00 12.50
65 Harry Craft 25.00 12.50
66 Jimmy Ripple....................... 20.00 10.00
67 Ed Joost.............................. 25.00 12.50
68 Fred Sington 20.00 10.00
69 Elbie Fletcher 20.00 10.00
70 Fred Frankhouse 20.00 10.00
71 Monte Pearson.................... 30.00 15.00
72 Debs Garms........................ 20.00 10.00
73 Hal Schumacher.................. 25.00 12.50
74 Cookie Lavagetto 25.00 12.50
75 Stan Bordagaray 20.00 10.00
76 Goody Rosen 20.00 10.00
77 Lew Riggs........................... 20.00 10.00
78 Julius Solters....................... 20.00 10.00
79 Jo Jo Moore......................... 20.00 10.00
80 Pete Fox.............................. 20.00 10.00
81 Babe Dahlgren 30.00 15.00
82 Chuck Klein...................... 100.00 50.00
83 Gus Suhr............................. 20.00 10.00
84 Skeeter Newsom 20.00 10.00
85 Johnny Cooney 20.00 10.00
86 Dolph Camilli 25.00 12.50
87 Milburn Shoffner.................. 20.00 10.00
88 Charlie Keller....................... 40.00 20.00
89 Lloyd Waner........................ 75.00 38.00
90 Robert Klinger..................... 20.00 10.00
91 John Knott 20.00 10.00
92 Ted Williams 1500.00 750.00
93 Charles Gelbert 20.00 10.00
94 Heinie Manush 75.00 38.00
95 Whit Wyatt.......................... 25.00 12.50
96 Babe Phelps 20.00 10.00
97 Bob Johnson........................ 30.00 15.00
98 Pinky Whitney 20.00 10.00
99 Wally Berger 30.00 15.00
100 Buddy Myer 25.00 12.50
101 Roger Cramer 25.00 12.50
102 Lem Young......................... 20.00 10.00
103 Moe Berg 125.00 60.00
104 Tom Bridges....................... 25.00 12.50
105 Rabbit McNair.................... 20.00 10.00
106 Dolly Stark UMP 30.00 15.00
107 Joe Vosmik 20.00 10.00
108 Frank Hayes 20.00 10.00
109 Myril Hoag 20.00 10.00
110 Fred Fitzsimmons............... 25.00 12.50
111 Van Lingle Mungo.............. 30.00 15.00
112 Paul Waner 100.00 50.00
113 Al Schacht.......................... 30.00 15.00
114 Cecil Travis......................... 25.00 12.50
115 Ralph Kress 20.00 10.00
116 Gene Desautels 75.00 38.00
117 Wayne Ambler.................... 75.00 38.00
118 Lynn Nelson 75.00 38.00
119 Will Hershberger.............. 100.00 50.00
120 Rabbit Warstler 75.00 38.00
121 Bill Posedel 75.00 38.00
122 George McQuinn 75.00 38.00
123 Ray T. Davis 75.00 38.00
124 Walter Brown 75.00 38.00
125 Cliff Melton 75.00 38.00
126 Not issued.........................
127 Gil Brack 75.00 38.00
128 Joe Bowman 75.00 38.00
129 Bill Swift............................. 75.00 38.00
130 Bill Brubaker 75.00 38.00
131 Mort Cooper.................... 100.00 50.00
132 Jim Brown 75.00 38.00
133 Lynn Myers......................... 75.00 38.00
134 Tot Presnell 75.00 38.00
135 Mickey Owen 100.00 50.00
136 Roy Bell 75.00 38.00
137 Pete Appleton..................... 75.00 38.00
138 George Case.................... 100.00 50.00
139 Vito Tamulis 75.00 38.00
140 Ray Hayworth 75.00 38.00
141 Pete Coscarart 75.00 38.00
142 Ira Hutchinson 75.00 38.00
143 Earl Averill...................... 175.00 90.00
144 Zeke Bonura.................... 100.00 50.00
145 Hugh Mulcahy.................... 75.00 38.00
146 Tom Sunkel 75.00 38.00
147 George Coffman................. 75.00 38.00
148 Bill Trotter 75.00 38.00
149 Max West............................ 75.00 38.00
150 James Walkup.................... 75.00 38.00
151 Hugh Casey...................... 100.00 50.00
152 Roy Weatherly.................... 75.00 38.00
153 Dizzy Trout 100.00 50.00
154 Johnny Hudson................... 75.00 38.00
155 Jimmy Outlaw..................... 75.00 38.00
156 Ray Berres 75.00 38.00
157 Don Padgett........................ 75.00 38.00
158 Bud Thomas........................ 75.00 38.00
159 Red Evans........................... 75.00 38.00
160 Gene Moore 75.00 38.00
161 Lonnie Frey 75.00 38.00
162 Whitey Moore 100.00 50.00

1940 Play Ball

The cards in this 240-card series measure approximately 2 1/2" by 3 1/8". Gum Inc. improved upon its 1939 design by enclosing the 1940 black and white player photo with a frame line and printing the player's name in a panel below the picture (often using a nickname). The set included many Hall of Famers and Old Timers. Cards 1-114 are numbered in team groupings. Cards 181-240 are scarcer than cards 1-180. The backs contain an extensive biography and a dated copyright line. The key cards in the set are the cards of Joe DiMaggio, Shoeless Joe Jackson, and Ted Williams.

Ex-Mt VG
COMPLETE SET (240)......... 15000.00 7500.00
COMMON CARD (1-120) 20.00 10.00
COMMON (121-180)................ 20.00 10.00
COMMON (181-240)................ 70.00 35.00
WRAP.(1-CENT, DIFF. COLORS) 800.00 400.00
1 Joe DiMaggio.................... 2500.00 1000.00
2 Art Jorgens 25.00 12.50
3 Babe Dahlgren 25.00 12.50
4 Tommy Henrich..................... 35.00 17.50
5 Monte Pearson....................... 25.00 12.50
6 Lefty Gomez....................... 150.00 75.00

1940 Play Ball

7 Bill Dickey 175.00 90.00
8 George Selkirk 25.00 12.50
9 Charlie Keller 35.00 17.50
10 Red Ruffing 90.00 45.00
11 Jake Powell 25.00 12.50
12 Johnny Schulte 20.00 10.00
13 Jack Knott 20.00 10.00
14 Rabbit McNair 20.00 10.00
15 George Case 25.00 12.50
16 Cecil Travis 25.00 12.50
17 Buddy Myer 25.00 12.50
18 Charlie Gelbert 20.00 10.00
19 Ken Chase 20.00 10.00
20 Buddy Lewis 20.00 10.00
21 Rick Ferrell 80.00 40.00
22 Sammy West 20.00 10.00
23 Dutch Leonard 25.00 12.50
24 Frank Hayes 20.00 10.00
25 Bob Johnson 25.00 12.50
26 Wally Moses 25.00 12.50
27 Ted Williams 1200.00 600.00
28 Gene Desautels 20.00 10.00
29 Doc Cramer 25.00 12.50
30 Moe Berg 150.00 75.00
31 Jack Wilson 20.00 10.00
32 Jim Bagby 20.00 10.00
33 Fritz Ostermueller 20.00 10.00
34 John Peacock 20.00 10.00
35 Joe Heving 20.00 10.00
36 Jim Tabor 20.00 10.00
37 Emerson Dickman 20.00 10.00
38 Bobby Doerr 90.00 45.00
39 Tom Carey 20.00 10.00
40 Hank Greenberg 200.00 100.00
41 Charley Gehringer 150.00 75.00
42 Bud Thomas 20.00 10.00
43 Pete Fox 20.00 10.00
44 Dizzy Trout 25.00 12.50
45 Red Kress 20.00 10.00
46 Earl Averill 90.00 45.00
47 Oscar Vitt 20.00 10.00
48 Luke Sewell 25.00 12.50
49 Stormy Weatherly 20.00 10.00
50 Hal Trosky 25.00 12.50
51 Don Heffner 20.00 10.00
52 Myril Hoag 20.00 10.00
53 George McQuinn 25.00 12.50
54 Bill Trotter 20.00 10.00
55 Slick Coffman 20.00 10.00
56 Eddie Miller 25.00 12.50
57 Max West 20.00 10.00
58 Bill Posedel 20.00 10.00
59 Rabbit Warstler 20.00 10.00
60 John Cooney 20.00 10.00
61 Tony Cuccinello 25.00 12.50
62 Buddy Hassett 20.00 10.00
63 Pete Coscarart 20.00 10.00
64 Van Lingle Mungo 25.00 12.50
65 Fred Fitzsimmons 25.00 12.50
66 Babe Phelps 20.00 10.00
67 Whit Wyatt 25.00 12.50
68 Dolph Camilli 25.00 12.50
69 Cookie Lavagetto 25.00 12.50
70 Luke Hamlin 20.00 10.00
(Hot Potato)
71 Mel Almada 20.00 10.00
72 Chuck Dressen 25.00 12.50
73 Bucky Walters 25.00 12.50
74 Paul(Duke) Derringer 25.00 12.50
75 Frank(Buck)McCormick 25.00 12.50
76 Lonny Frey 20.00 10.00
77 Willard Hershberger 25.00 12.50
78 Lew Riggs 20.00 10.00
79 Harry Craft 25.00 12.50
80 Billy Myers 20.00 10.00
81 Wally Berger 25.00 12.50
82 Hank Gowdy CO 25.00 12.50
83 Cliff Melton 20.00 10.00
84 Jo Jo Moore 20.00 10.00
85 Hal Schumacher 25.00 12.50
86 Harry Gumbert 20.00 10.00
87 Carl Hubbell 125.00 60.00
88 Mel Ott 175.00 90.00
89 Bill Jurges 20.00 10.00
90 Frank Demaree 20.00 10.00
91 Bob Seeds 20.00 10.00
92 Whitey Whitehead 20.00 10.00
93 Harry Danning 20.00 10.00
94 Gus Suhr 20.00 10.00
95 Hugh Mulcahy 20.00 10.00
96 Heinie Mueller 20.00 10.00
97 Morry Arnovich 20.00 10.00
98 Pinky May 20.00 10.00
99 Syl Johnson 20.00 10.00
100 Hersh Martin 20.00 10.00
101 Del Young 20.00 10.00
102 Chuck Klein 100.00 50.00
103 Elbie Fletcher 20.00 10.00
104 Paul Waner 90.00 45.00
105 Lloyd Waner 80.00 40.00
106 Pep Young 20.00 10.00
107 Arky Vaughan 80.00 40.00
108 Johnny Rizzo 20.00 10.00
109 Don Padgett 20.00 10.00
110 Tom Sunkel 20.00 10.00
111 Mickey Owen 25.00 12.50
112 Jimmy Brown 20.00 10.00
113 Mort Cooper 25.00 12.50
114 Lon Warneke 25.00 12.50
115 Mike Gonzalez CO 25.00 12.50
116 Al Schacht 25.00 12.50
117 Dolly Stark UMP 25.00 12.50
118 Waite Hoyt 90.00 45.00
119 Grover C. Alexander 175.00 90.00
120 Walter Johnson 200.00 100.00
121 Atley Donald 25.00 12.50
122 Sandy Sundra 25.00 12.50
123 Hildy Hildebrand 25.00 12.50
124 Earle Combs 100.00 50.00
125 Art Fletcher 25.00 12.50
126 Jake Solters 20.00 10.00
127 Muddy Ruel 20.00 10.00
128 Pete Appleton 20.00 10.00
129 Bucky Harris 80.00 40.00
130 Clyde Milan 25.00 12.50
131 Zeke Bonura 25.00 12.50
132 Connie Mack MG 150.00 75.00
133 Jimmie Foxx 200.00 100.00
134 Joe Cronin 100.00 50.00
135 Line Drive Nelson 20.00 10.00
136 Cotton Pippen 20.00 10.00
137 Bing Miller 20.00 10.00
138 Beau Bell 20.00 10.00
139 Elden Auker 20.00 10.00
140 Dick Coffman 20.00 10.00
141 Casey Stengel MG 175.00 90.00
142 George Kelly 90.00 45.00
143 Gene Moore 20.00 10.00
144 Joe Vosmik 20.00 10.00
145 Vito Tamulis 20.00 10.00
146 Tot Pressnell 20.00 10.00
147 Johnny Hudson 20.00 10.00
148 Hugh Casey 25.00 12.50
149 Pinky Shoffner 20.00 10.00
150 Whitey Moore 20.00 10.00
151 Edwin Joost 25.00 12.50
152 Jimmy Wilson 20.00 10.00
153 Bill McKechnie MG 80.00 40.00
154 Jumbo Brown 20.00 10.00
155 Ray Hayworth 20.00 10.00
156 Daffy Dean 35.00 17.50
157 Lou Chiozza 20.00 10.00
158 Travis Jackson 90.00 45.00
159 Pancho Snyder 20.00 10.00
160 Hans Lobert CO 20.00 10.00
161 Debs Garms 20.00 10.00
162 Joe Bowman 20.00 10.00
163 Spud Davis 20.00 10.00
164 Ray Berres 20.00 10.00
165 Bob Klinger 20.00 10.00
166 Bill Brubaker 20.00 10.00
167 Frankie Frisch MG 90.00 45.00
168 Honus Wagner CO 200.00 100.00
169 Gabby Street 20.00 10.00
170 Tris Speaker 175.00 90.00
171 Harry Heilmann 80.00 40.00
172 Chief Bender 80.00 40.00
173 Napoleon Lajoie 175.00 90.00
174 Johnny Evers 90.00 45.00
175 Christy Mathewson 250.00 125.00
176 Heinie Manush 90.00 45.00
177 Frank Baker 100.00 50.00
178 Max Carey 90.00 45.00
179 George Sisler 125.00 60.00
180 Mickey Cochrane 150.00 75.00
181 Spud Chandler 80.00 40.00
182 Knick Knickerbocker 70.00 35.00
183 Marvin Breuer 70.00 35.00
184 Mule Haas 70.00 35.00
185 Joe Kuhel 70.00 35.00
186 Taft Wright 70.00 35.00
187 Jimmy Dykes MG 80.00 40.00
188 Joe Krakauskas 70.00 35.00
189 Jim Bloodworth 70.00 35.00
190 Charley Berry 70.00 35.00
191 John Babich 70.00 35.00
192 Dick Siebert 70.00 35.00
193 Chubby Dean 70.00 35.00
194 Sam Chapman 70.00 35.00
195 Dee Miles 70.00 35.00
196 Red(Nonny)Nonnenkamp 70.00 35.00
197 Lou Finney 70.00 35.00
198 Denny Galehouse 70.00 35.00
199 Pinky Higgins 70.00 35.00
200 Soup Campbell 70.00 35.00
201 Barney McCosky 70.00 35.00
202 Al Milnar 70.00 35.00
203 Bad News Hale 70.00 35.00
204 Harry Eisenstat 70.00 35.00
205 Rollie Hemsley 70.00 35.00
206 Chet Laabs 70.00 35.00
207 Gus Mancuso 70.00 35.00
208 Lee Gamble 70.00 35.00
209 Hy Vandenberg 70.00 35.00
210 Bill Lohrman 70.00 35.00
211 Pop Joiner 70.00 35.00
212 Babe Young 70.00 35.00
213 John Rucker 70.00 35.00
214 Ken O'Dea 70.00 35.00
215 Johnnie McCarthy 70.00 35.00
216 Joe Marty 70.00 35.00
217 Walter Beck 70.00 35.00
218 Wally Millies 70.00 35.00
219 Russ Bauers 70.00 35.00
220 Mace Brown 70.00 35.00
221 Lee Handley 70.00 35.00
222 Max Butcher 70.00 35.00
223 Hughie Jennings 150.00 75.00
224 Pie Traynor 175.00 90.00
225 Joe Jackson 2500.00 1250.00
226 Harry Hooper 150.00 75.00
227 Jesse Haines 150.00 75.00
228 Charlie Grimm 80.00 40.00
229 Buck Herzog 70.00 35.00
230 Red Faber 175.00 90.00
231 Dolf Luque 100.00 50.00
232 Goose Goslin 150.00 75.00
233 George Earnshaw 80.00 40.00
234 Frank Chance 150.00 75.00
235 John McGraw 175.00 90.00
236 Jim Bottomley 150.00 75.00
237 Willie Keeler 175.00 90.00
238 Tony Lazzeri 175.00 90.00
239 George Uhle 70.00 35.00
240 Bill Atwood 100.00 50.00

1941 Play Ball

The cards in this 72-card set measure approximately 2 1/2" by 3 1/8". Many of the cards in the 1941 Play Ball series are simply color versions of pictures appearing in the 1940 set. This was the only color baseball card set produced by Gum, Inc.. Card numbers 49-72 are slightly more difficult to obtain as they were not issued until 1942. In 1942, numbers 1-48 were also reissued but without the copyright date. The cards were also printed on paper without a cardboard backing; these are generally encountered in sheets or strips. The set features a card of Pee Wee Reese in his rookie year.

Ex-Mt VG
COMPLETE SET (72) 10000.00 5000.00
COMMON CARD (1-48) 40.00 20.00
COMMON CARD (49-72) 60.00 30.00
WRAPPER (1-CENT) 800.00 400.00
1 Eddie Miller 125.00 60.00
2 Max West 40.00 20.00
3 Bucky Walters 45.00 22.00
4 Paul Derringer 50.00 25.00
5 Frank(Buck) McCormick 45.00 22.00
6 Carl Hubbell 175.00 90.00
7 Harry Danning 40.00 20.00
8 Mel Ott 225.00 110.00
9 Pinky May 40.00 20.00
10 Arky Vaughan 100.00 50.00
11 Debs Garms 40.00 20.00
12 Jimmy Brown 40.00 20.00
13 Jimmie Foxx 300.00 150.00
14 Ted Williams 1500.00 900.00
15 Joe Cronin 125.00 60.00
16 Hal Trosky 45.00 22.00
17 Roy Weatherly 40.00 20.00
18 Hank Greenberg 300.00 150.00
19 Charley Gehringer 200.00 100.00
20 Red Ruffing 125.00 60.00
21 Charlie Keller 60.00 30.00
22 Bob Johnson 50.00 25.00
23 George McQuinn 40.00 20.00
24 Dutch Leonard 45.00 22.00
25 Gene Moore 40.00 20.00
26 Harry Gumpert 40.00 20.00
27 Babe Young 40.00 20.00
28 Joe Marty 40.00 20.00
29 Jack Wilson 40.00 20.00
30 Lou Finney 40.00 20.00
31 Joe Kuhel 40.00 20.00
32 Taft Wright 40.00 20.00
33 Al Milnar 40.00 20.00
34 Rollie Hemsley 40.00 20.00
35 Pinky Higgins 45.00 22.00
36 Barney McCosky 40.00 20.00
37 Bruce Campbell 40.00 20.00
38 Atley Donald 50.00 25.00
39 Tommy Henrich 60.00 30.00
40 John Babich 40.00 20.00
41 Frank(Blimp) Hayes 40.00 20.00
42 Wally Moses 45.00 22.00
43 Al Brancato 40.00 20.00
44 Sam Chapman 40.00 20.00
45 Eldon Auker 40.00 20.00
46 Sid Hudson 40.00 20.00
47 Buddy Lewis 40.00 20.00
48 Cecil Travis 45.00 22.00
49 Babe Dahlgren 65.00 32.00
50 Johnny Cooney 60.00 30.00
51 Dolph Camilli 65.00 32.00
52 Kirby Higbe 65.00 32.00
53 Luke Hamlin 60.00 30.00
54 Pee Wee Reese 600.00 300.00
55 Whit Wyatt 65.00 32.00
56 Johnny VanderMeer 100.00 50.00
57 Moe Arnovich 60.00 30.00
58 Frank Demaree 60.00 30.00
59 Bill Jurges 60.00 30.00
60 Chuck Klein 150.00 75.00
61 Vince DiMaggio 225.00 110.00
62 Elbie Fletcher 60.00 30.00
63 Dom DiMaggio 250.00 125.00
64 Bobby Doerr 175.00 90.00
65 Tommy Bridges 65.00 32.00
66 Harland Clift 60.00 30.00
67 Walt Judnich 60.00 30.00
68 John Knott 60.00 30.00
69 George Case 65.00 32.00
70 Bill Dickey 400.00 200.00
71 Joe DiMaggio 2500.00 1250.00
72 Lefty Gomez 475.00 240.00

2004 Playoff Honors

This 250-card set was released in July, 2004. The set was issued in six-card packs with an $6 SRP which came 12 packs to a box and 12 boxes to a case. Cards numbered 1-200 featured veterans while cards numbered 201-250 featured rookies. The rookies who did not sign cards for this set were issued to a stated print run of 1999 serial numbered sets while the rookies who did sign were issued to stated print runs of between 675 and 1000 cards. The specific print run information for each card is located in our checklist.

Nm-Mt Ex-Mt
COMP.SET w/o SP's (200) 50.00 15.00
COMMON ACTIVE (1-200) .40 .12
COMMON RETIRED (1-200) .50 .15
COMMON RC/1999 (201-250) 4.00 1.20
RC/1999 PRINT RUN 1999 SERIAL #'d SETS
COMMON AUTO (201-250) 8.00 2.40
AUTO PRINT RUNS B/WN 675-1000 PER
201-250 RANDOM INSERTS IN PACKS
1 Bartolo Colon .40 .12
2 Garret Anderson .40 .12
3 Tim Salmon .60 .18
4 Troy Glaus .40 .12
5 Vladimir Guerrero 1.00 .30
6 Brandon Webb .40 .12
7 Brian Bruney .40 .12
8 Luis Gonzalez .40 .12
9 Randy Johnson 1.00 .30
10 Richie Sexson .40 .12
11 Robby Hammock .40 .12
12 Roberto Alomar .60 .18
13 Shea Hillenbrand .40 .12
14 Steve Finley .40 .12
15 Adam LaRoche .40 .12
16 Andruw Jones .40 .12
17 Bubba Nelson .40 .12
18 Chipper Jones 1.00 .30
19 Dale Murphy .60 .18
20 J.D. Drew .40 .12
21 John Smoltz .60 .18
22 Marcus Giles .40 .12
23 Rafael Furcal .40 .12
24 Warren Spahn .75 .23
25 Greg Maddux 1.50 .45
26 Adam Loewen .40 .12
27 Cal Ripken 5.00 1.50
28 Javy Lopez .40 .12
29 Jay Gibbons .40 .12
30 Luis Matos .40 .12
31 Miguel Tejada .40 .12
32 Rafael Palmeiro .40 .12
33 Bobby Doerr .50 .15
34 Curt Schilling 1.00 .30
35 Edwin Almonte .40 .12
36 Jason Varitek .60 .18
37 Kevin Youkilis .40 .12
38 Manny Ramirez .60 .18
39 Nomar Garciaparra 1.50 .45
40 Pedro Martinez 1.00 .30
41 Trot Nixon .40 .12
42 Andre Dawson .50 .15
43 Aramis Ramirez .40 .12
44 Brendan Harris .40 .12
45 Derrek Lee .40 .12
46 Ernie Banks 1.25 .35
47 Kerry Wood 1.00 .30
48 Mark Prior 1.00 .30
49 Ryne Sandberg 2.50 .75
50 Sammy Sosa 1.50 .45
51 Carlos Lee .40 .12
52 Frank Thomas 1.00 .30
53 Joe Borchard .40 .12
54 Joe Crede .40 .12
55 Magglio Ordonez .40 .12
56 Adam Dunn .60 .18
57 Austin Kearns .40 .12
58 Barry Larkin .60 .18
59 Brandon Larson .40 .12
60 Ken Griffey Jr. 1.50 .45
61 Ryan Wagner .40 .12
62 Sean Casey .40 .12
63 Bob Feller .50 .15
64 Brian Tallet .40 .12
65 C.C. Sabathia .40 .12
66 Jeremy Guthrie .40 .12
67 Jody Gerut .40 .12
68 Clint Barmes .40 .12
69 Jeff Baker .40 .12
70 Joe Kennedy .40 .12
71 Larry Walker .60 .18
72 Preston Wilson .40 .12
73 Todd Helton .60 .18
74 Alan Trammell .50 .15
75 Dmitri Young .40 .12
76 Ivan Rodriguez 1.00 .30
77 Jeremy Bonderman .40 .12
78 Preston Larrison .40 .12
79 Dontrelle Willis .40 .12
80 Josh Beckett .40 .12
81 Juan Pierre .40 .12
82 Luis Castillo .40 .12
83 Miguel Cabrera .60 .18
84 Mike Lowell .40 .12
85 Andy Pettitte .60 .18
86 Chris Burke .40 .12
87 Craig Biggio .60 .18
88 Jeff Bagwell .60 .18
89 Jeff Kent .40 .12
90 Lance Berkman .40 .12
91 Morgan Ensberg .40 .12
92 Richard Hidalgo .40 .12
93 Roger Clemens 2.00 .60
94 Roy Oswalt .40 .12
95 Angel Berroa .40 .12
96 Byron Gettis .40 .12
97 Carlos Beltran .60 .18
98 George Brett 3.00 .90
99 Juan Gonzalez .60 .18
100 Mike Sweeney .40 .12
101 Duke Snider .75 .23
102 Edwin Jackson .40 .12
103 Eric Gagne 1.00 .30
104 Hideo Nomo 1.00 .30
105 Hong-Chih Kuo .40 .12
106 Kazuhisa Ishii .40 .12
107 Paul Lo Duca .40 .12
108 Robin Ventura .40 .12
109 Shawn Green .40 .12
110 Junior Spivey .40 .12
111 Rickie Weeks .40 .12
112 Scott Podsednik .40 .12
113 J.D. Durbin .40 .12
114 Jacque Jones .40 .12
115 Jason Kubel .40 .12
116 Johan Santana .60 .18
117 Shannon Stewart .40 .12
118 Torii Hunter .40 .12
119 Brad Wilkerson .40 .12
120 Jose Vidro .40 .12
121 Nick Johnson .40 .12
122 Orlando Cabrera .40 .12
123 Gary Carter .50 .15
124 Jae Weong Seo .40 .12
125 Lenny Dykstra .50 .15
126 Mike Piazza 1.50 .45
127 Tom Glavine .60 .18
128 Alex Rodriguez 1.50 .45
129 Bernie Williams .60 .18
130 Chien-Ming Wang .60 .18
131 Derek Jeter 2.00 .60
132 Don Mattingly 3.00 .90
133 Gary Sheffield .40 .12
134 Hideki Matsui 1.50 .45
135 Jason Giambi .40 .12
136 Javier Vazquez .40 .12
137 Jorge Posada .60 .18
138 Jose Contreras .40 .12
139 Kevin Brown .40 .12
140 Mariano Rivera .60 .18
141 Mike Mussina .60 .18
142 Whitey Ford .75 .23
143 Barry Zito .40 .12
144 Eric Chavez .40 .12
145 Mark Mulder .40 .12
146 Rich Harden .40 .12
147 Tim Hudson .40 .12
148 Reggie Jackson .75 .23
149 Rickey Henderson 1.00 .30
150 Brett Myers .40 .12
151 Bobby Abreu .40 .12
152 Jim Thome 1.00 .30
153 Kevin Millwood .40 .12
154 Marlon Byrd .40 .12
155 Mike Schmidt 2.50 .75
156 Ryan Howard .40 .12
157 Jack Wilson .40 .12
158 Jason Kendall .40 .12
159 Brian Giles .40 .12
160 David Wells .40 .12
161 Jay Payton .40 .12
162 Phil Nevin .40 .12
163 Ryan Klesko .40 .12
164 Sean Burroughs .40 .12
165 A.J. Pierzynski .40 .12
166 J.T. Snow .40 .12
167 Jason Schmidt .40 .12
168 Jerome Williams .40 .12
169 Will Clark 1.25 .35
170 Bret Boone .40 .12
171 Chris Snelling .40 .12
172 Edgar Martinez .60 .18
173 Ichiro Suzuki 1.50 .45
174 Randy Winn .40 .12
175 Rich Aurilia .40 .12
176 Shigetoshi Hasegawa .40 .12
177 Albert Pujols 2.00 .60
178 Dan Haren .40 .12
179 Edgar Renteria .40 .12
180 Jim Edmonds .40 .12
181 Matt Morris .40 .12
182 Scott Rolen 1.00 .30
183 Stan Musial 2.00 .60
184 Aubrey Huff .40 .12
185 Chad Gaudin .40 .12
186 Delmon Young .60 .18
187 Fred McGriff .60 .18
188 Rocco Baldelli .40 .12
189 Alfonso Soriano .60 .18
190 Hank Blalock .40 .12
191 Mark Teixeira .40 .12
192 Nolan Ryan 3.00 .90
193 Alexis Rios .40 .12
194 Carlos Delgado .40 .12
195 Dustin McGowan .40 .12
196 Guillermo Quiroz .40 .12
197 Josh Phelps .40 .12
198 Roy Halladay .40 .12
199 Vernon Wells .40 .12
200 Vinnie Chulk .40 .12
201 Jose Capellan/1999 RC 6.00 1.80
202 Kazuo Matsui/1999 RC 8.00 2.40
203 Dave Crouthers/1999 RC 4.00 1.20
204 Akinori Otsuka/1999 RC 4.00 1.20
205 Nick Regilio/1999 RC 4.00 1.20
206 Justin Hampson/1999 RC 4.00 1.20
207 Lincoln Holdzkom/1999 RC 4.00 1.20
208 Jorge Sequea/1999 RC 4.00 1.20
209 Justin Leone/1999 RC 5.00 1.50
210 Renyel Pinto/1999 RC 5.00 1.50
211 Mariano Gomez/1999 RC 4.00 1.20
212 Onil Joseph AU/1000 RC 8.00 2.40
213 J.Labandeira AU/1000 RC 8.00 2.40
214 Cory Sullivan/1999 RC 4.00 1.20
215 Carlos Vasquez AU/675 RC 10.00 3.00
216 Chris Shelton/1999 RC 5.00 1.50
217 Willy Taveras/1999 RC 5.00 1.50
218 John Gall/1999 RC 5.00 1.50
219 Jerry Gil/1999 RC 4.00 1.20
220 Jason Frasor/1999 RC 4.00 1.20
221 Justin Knoedler/1999 RC 4.00 1.20
222 Ronald Belisario/1999 RC 4.00 1.20
223 Mike Rouse/1999 RC 4.00 1.20
224 Dennis Sarfate/1999 RC 4.00 1.20
225 Casey Daigle/1999 RC 4.00 1.20
226 S.Takatsu AU/800 RC 25.00 7.50
227 Jason Bartlett AU/800 RC 10.00 3.00
228 Alfredo Simon AU/1000 RC 8.00 2.40
229 Chris Oxspring/1999 RC 5.00 1.50
230 Fern Nieve AU/1000 RC 8.00 2.40
231 Ruddy Yan AU/800 8.00 2.40
232 Ryan Wing/1999 RC 4.00 1.20
233 Tim Bittner AU/1000 RC 8.00 2.40
234 Ram Ramirez AU/1000 RC 8.00 2.40
235 Sean Henn AU/1000 RC 8.00 2.40
236 Roberto Novoa AU/800 RC 10.00 3.00
237 Jerome Gamble AU/800 RC 8.00 2.40
238 Jamie Brown AU/800 RC 8.00 2.40
239 Ian Snell AU/800 RC 10.00 3.00
240 Freddy Guzman AU/800 RC 8.00 2.40
241 Aarom Baldiris AU/1000 RC 10.00 3.00
242 Greg Dobbs/1999 RC 4.00 1.20
243 Ivan Ochoa/1999 RC 4.00 1.20
244 Angel Chavez AU/800 RC 8.00 2.40
245 Merkin Valdez AU/800 RC 10.00 3.00
246 Mike Gosling AU/800 RC 8.00 2.40
247 Carlos Hines AU/800 RC 8.00 2.40
248 Graham Koonce AU/1000 8.00 2.40
249 Will Bergolla AU/1000 RC 8.00 2.40
250 Hect Gimenez AU/1000 RC 8.00 2.40

2004 Playoff Honors Signature Bronze

Nm-Mt Ex-Mt
RANDOM INSERTS IN PACKS
PRINT RUNS B/WN 1-100 COPIES PER
NO PRICING ON QTY OF 10 OR LESS
NO RC PRICING ON QTY OF 25 OR LESS
2 Garret Anderson/100 15.00 4.50
5 Vladimir Guerrero/50 50.00 15.00
6 Brandon Webb/100 10.00 3.00

7 Brian Bruney/96 10.00 3.00
9 Randy Johnson/5
10 Richie Sexson/5
11 Robby Hammock/100 10.00 3.00
13 Shea Hillenbrand/100 15.00 4.50
14 Steve Finley/50
15 Adam LaRoche/100 10.00 3.00
16 Andruw Jones/25 30.00 9.00
17 Bubba Nelson/100 10.00 3.00
18 Chipper Jones/10
22 Marcus Giles/100 15.00 4.50
23 Rafael Furcal/50 20.00 6.00
24 Warren Spahn/10
26 Adam Loewen/100 10.00 3.00
27 Cal Ripken/25 200.00 60.00
29 Jay Gibbons/100 10.00 3.00
30 Luis Matos/100 10.00 3.00
32 Rafael Palmeiro/10
33 Bobby Doerr/100 15.00 4.50
34 Curt Schilling/10
35 Edwin Almonte/99 10.00 3.00
36 Jason Varitek/50
37 Kevin Youkilis/100 15.00 4.50
38 Manny Ramirez/10
41 Trot Nixon/50 20.00 6.00
42 Andre Dawson/100 15.00 4.50
43 Aramis Ramirez/25 30.00 9.00
44 Brendan Harris/100 10.00 3.00
45 Derrek Lee/100 15.00 4.50
46 Ernie Banks/25 60.00 18.00
47 Kerry Wood/25 60.00 18.00
48 Mark Prior/50 80.00 24.00
50 Sammy Sosa/50 150.00 45.00
51 Carlos Lee/100 15.00 4.50
52 Frank Thomas/25 60.00 18.00
53 Joe Borchard/100 10.00 3.00
54 Joe Crede/50 12.00 3.60
55 Magglio Ordonez/50 20.00 6.00
58 Barry Larkin/25 50.00 15.00
59 Brandon Larson/100 10.00 3.00
61 Ryan Wagner/100 10.00 3.00
63 Bob Feller/100 25.00 7.50
64 Brian Tallet/100 10.00 3.00
66 Jeremy Guthrie/100 10.00 3.00
67 Jody Gerut/100 15.00 4.50
68 Clint Barmes/100 10.00 3.00
69 Jeff Baker/25 20.00 6.00
70 Joe Kennedy/10
72 Preston Wilson/100 15.00 4.50
73 Todd Helton/10
74 Alan Trammell/100 15.00 4.50
78 Preston Larrison/100 10.00 3.00
79 Dontrelle Willis/25 30.00 9.00
80 Josh Beckett/10
82 Luis Castillo/10
83 Miguel Cabrera/100 25.00 7.50
85 Andy Pettitte/25 60.00 18.00
86 Chris Burke/100 10.00 3.00
88 Jeff Bagwell/25 60.00 18.00
90 Lance Berkman/10
91 Morgan Ensberg/100 10.00 3.00
94 Roy Oswalt/10
96 Byron Gettis/100 10.00 3.00
97 Carlos Beltran/100 40.00 12.00
98 George Brett/25 120.00 36.00
99 Juan Gonzalez/10
101 Duke Snider/100 25.00 7.50
102 Edwin Jackson/100 15.00 4.50
104 Hideo Nomo/1
105 Hong-Chih Kuo/100 15.00 4.50
106 Kazuhisa Ishii/25 50.00 15.00
107 Paul Lo Duca/100 15.00 4.50
108 Robin Ventura/50 20.00 6.00
109 Shawn Green/10
110 Junior Spivey/50 12.00 3.60
111 Rickie Weeks/5
112 Scott Podsednik/100 15.00 4.50
113 J.D. Durbin/100 10.00 3.00
114 Jacque Jones/100 15.00 4.50
115 Jason Kubel/50 15.00 4.50
116 Johan Santana/100 40.00 12.00
117 Shannon Stewart/50 12.00 3.60
118 Torii Hunter/10
120 Jose Vidro/10
122 Orlando Cabrera/10
123 Gary Carter/100 15.00 4.50
125 Lenny Dykstra/100 15.00 4.50
126 Mike Piazza/5
127 Tom Glavine/5
129 Bernie Williams/10
130 Chien-Ming Wang/100 25.00 7.50
132 Don Mattingly/25 100.00 30.00
133 Gary Sheffield/50 30.00 9.00
137 Jorge Posada/50 30.00 9.00
138 Jose Contreras/10
142 Whitey Ford/50 30.00 9.00
143 Barry Zito/10
144 Eric Chavez/10
145 Mark Mulder/100 15.00 4.50
146 Rich Harden/100 15.00 4.50
147 Tim Hudson/25 50.00 15.00
148 Reggie Jackson/25 60.00 18.00
149 Rickey Henderson/25 100.00 30.00
150 Brett Myers/100 10.00 3.00
154 Marlon Byrd/100 10.00 3.00
155 Mike Schmidt/50 80.00 24.00
156 Ryan Howard/100 15.00 4.50
161 Jay Payton/100 10.00 3.00
166 J.T. Snow/25
168 Jerome Williams/50 20.00 6.00
169 Will Clark/50 50.00 15.00
171 Chris Snelling/100 10.00 3.00
175 Rich Aurilia/25
176 Shigetoshi Hasegawa/100 60.00 18.00
177 Albert Pujols/5
178 Dan Haren/100 10.00 3.00
180 Jim Edmonds/25 50.00 15.00
182 Scott Rolen/50 50.00 15.00
183 Stan Musial/50 60.00 18.00
184 Aubrey Huff/100 15.00 4.50
185 Chad Gaudin/100 10.00 3.00
186 Delmon Young/50 30.00 9.00
188 Rocco Baldelli/10
191 Mark Teixeira/50 30.00 9.00
192 Nolan Ryan/50 120.00 36.00
193 Alexis Rios/100 15.00 4.50
195 Dustin McGowan/100 10.00 3.00
196 Guillermo Quiroz/50 12.00 3.60
197 Josh Phelps/25 20.00 6.00
198 Roy Halladay/25 20.00 6.00
200 Vinnie Chulk/25 20.00 6.00
201 Jose Capellan/100 30.00 9.00
203 Dave Crouthers/100 10.00 3.00
204 Akinori Otsuka/100 40.00 12.00
205 Nick Regilio/100 10.00 3.00
206 Justin Hampson/100 10.00 3.00
207 Lincoln Holdzkom/100 10.00 3.00
208 Jorge Sequea/100 10.00 3.00
209 Justin Leone/100 15.00 4.50
210 Renyel Pinto/100 15.00 4.50
211 Mariano Gomez/100 10.00 3.00
214 Cory Sullivan/100 10.00 3.00
216 Chris Shelton/100 20.00 6.00
217 Willy Taveras/25
218 John Gall/100 15.00 4.50
219 Jerry Gil/25
220 Jason Frasor/15
222 Ronald Belisario/100 10.00 3.00
223 Mike Rouse/100 10.00 3.00
224 Dennis Sarfate/100 10.00 3.00
225 Casey Daigle/10

2004 Playoff Honors Signature Gold

Nm-Mt Ex-Mt
*GOLD p/r 50: .5X TO 1.2X BRONZE p/r 100
*GOLD p/r 50: .4X TO 1X BRONZE p/r 50
*GOLD p/r 25: .75 TO 2X BRONZE p/r 100
*GOLD p/r 25: .5X TO 1.2X BRONZE p/r 50
RANDOM INSERTS IN PACKS
PRINT RUNS B/WN 1-50 COPIES PER
NO PRICING ON QTY OF 11 OR LESS
NO RC PRICING ON QTY OF 25 OR LESS
2 Garret Anderson/25
5 Vladimir Guerrero/25
6 Brandon Webb/50 12.00 3.60
7 Brian Bruney/50
9 Randy Johnson/5
10 Richie Sexson/5
11 Robby Hammock/5
13 Shea Hillenbrand/50 20.00 6.00
14 Steve Finley/25 25.00 7.50
15 Adam LaRoche/50 12.00 3.60
16 Andruw Jones/5
17 Bubba Nelson/50 12.00 3.60
18 Chipper Jones/5
22 Marcus Giles/50 20.00 6.00
23 Rafael Furcal/25 25.00 7.50
24 Warren Spahn/5
26 Adam Loewen/50 12.00 3.60
27 Cal Ripken/8
29 Jay Gibbons/50 12.00 3.60
30 Luis Matos/50 12.00 3.60
32 Rafael Palmeiro/5
33 Bobby Doerr/50 20.00 6.00
35 Edwin Almonte/50 12.00 3.60
36 Jason Varitek/25 50.00 15.00
37 Kevin Youkilis/50 20.00 6.00
38 Manny Ramirez/5
40 Pedro Martinez/5
41 Trot Nixon/25 25.00 7.50
42 Andre Dawson/50 20.00 6.00
43 Aramis Ramirez/10
44 Brendan Harris/50 12.00 3.60
45 Derrek Lee/5
46 Ernie Banks/5
47 Kerry Wood/5
48 Mark Prior/10
50 Sammy Sosa/25 200.00 60.00
51 Carlos Lee/50 20.00 6.00
52 Frank Thomas/10
53 Joe Borchard/50
54 Joe Crede/10
55 Magglio Ordonez/10
56 Adam Dunn/1
57 Austin Kearns/25 25.00 7.50
58 Barry Larkin/5
59 Brandon Larson/50 12.00 3.60
61 Ryan Wagner/50 12.00 3.60
63 Bob Feller/50 30.00 9.00
64 Brian Tallet/50 12.00 3.60
66 Jeremy Guthrie/25 20.00 6.00
67 Jody Gerut/50 20.00 6.00
68 Clint Barmes/50 12.00 3.60
69 Jeff Baker/5
70 Joe Kennedy/5
72 Preston Wilson/50 20.00 6.00
73 Todd Helton/5
74 Alan Trammell/50 20.00 6.00
78 Preston Larrison/50
79 Dontrelle Willis/10
80 Josh Beckett/5
82 Luis Castillo/5
83 Miguel Cabrera/50 30.00 9.00
84 Mike Lowell/5
85 Andy Pettitte/5
86 Chris Burke/50 12.00 3.60
87 Craig Biggio/5
88 Jeff Bagwell/5
90 Lance Berkman/5
91 Morgan Ensberg/50 12.00 3.60
94 Roy Oswalt/5
96 Byron Gettis/50 12.00 3.60
97 Carlos Beltran/25 80.00 24.00
98 George Brett/5
99 Juan Gonzalez/5
101 Duke Snider/50 30.00 9.00
102 Edwin Jackson/50 20.00 6.00
104 Hideo Nomo/5
105 Hong-Chih Kuo/50 20.00 6.00
106 Kazuhisa Ishii/5
107 Paul Lo Duca/25 30.00 9.00
108 Robin Ventura/25 25.00 7.50
109 Shawn Green/5
110 Junior Spivey/25 15.00 4.50
111 Rickie Weeks/5
112 Scott Podsednik/50 20.00 6.00
113 J.D. Durbin/50 12.00 3.60
114 Jacque Jones/50 20.00 6.00
115 Jason Kubel/50 15.00 4.50
116 Johan Santana/50 50.00 15.00
117 Shannon Stewart/10
118 Torii Hunter/5
120 Jose Vidro/5
121 Nick Johnson/5
122 Orlando Cabrera/5
123 Gary Carter/50 20.00 6.00
124 Jae Weong Seo/25 25.00 7.50
125 Lenny Dykstra/50 20.00 6.00
126 Mike Piazza/5
127 Tom Glavine/5
128 Alex Rodriguez/5
129 Bernie Williams/5
130 Chien-Ming Wang/25
132 Don Mattingly/10
133 Gary Sheffield/25 40.00 12.00
136 Javier Vazquez/5
137 Jorge Posada/5
138 Jose Contreras/5
142 Whitey Ford/10
143 Barry Zito/5
144 Eric Chavez/5
145 Mark Mulder/25 30.00 9.00
146 Rich Harden/50 20.00 6.00
147 Tim Hudson/5
148 Reggie Jackson/10
149 Rickey Henderson/10
150 Brett Myers/50 12.00 3.60
154 Marlon Byrd/50 12.00 3.60
155 Mike Schmidt/10
156 Ryan Howard/50 20.00 6.00
161 Jay Payton/50 12.00 3.60
166 J.T. Snow/10
168 Jerome Williams/25
169 Will Clark/10
171 Chris Snelling/11
172 Edgar Martinez/5
175 Rich Aurilia/10
176 Shigetoshi Hasegawa/50 80.00 24.00
177 Albert Pujols/5
178 Dan Haren/50 12.00 3.60
180 Jim Edmonds/10
182 Scott Rolen/25 60.00 18.00
183 Stan Musial/6
184 Aubrey Huff/50 20.00 6.00
185 Chad Gaudin/50 12.00 3.60
186 Delmon Young/10
187 Fred McGriff/5
188 Rocco Baldelli/5
191 Mark Teixeira/10
192 Nolan Ryan/10
193 Alexis Rios/50 20.00 6.00
195 Dustin McGowan/50
196 Guillermo Quiroz/25 15.00 4.50
197 Josh Phelps/10
198 Roy Halladay/10
200 Vinnie Chulk/10
201 Jose Capellan/25
203 Dave Crouthers/50 12.00 3.60
204 Akinori Otsuka/50 50.00 15.00
205 Nick Regilio/50 12.00 3.60
206 Justin Hampson/50 12.00 3.60
207 Lincoln Holdzkom/50 12.00 3.60
208 Jorge Sequea/50 12.00 3.60
209 Justin Leone/50 20.00 6.00
210 Renyel Pinto/50 20.00 6.00
211 Mariano Gomez/5
214 Cory Sullivan/50 12.00 3.60
216 Chris Shelton/50 25.00 7.50
217 Willy Taveras/5
218 John Gall/50 20.00 6.00
219 Jerry Gil/5
220 Jason Frasor/10
221 Justin Knoedler/25
222 Ronald Belisario/50 12.00 3.60
223 Mike Rouse/50
224 Dennis Sarfate/50 12.00 3.60
225 Casey Daigle/5

2004 Playoff Honors Signature Silver

Nm-Mt Ex-Mt
*SILVER p/r 85-100: .4X TO 1X BRZ p/r 100
*SILVER p/r 95-100: .3X TO .8X BRZ p/r 50
*SILVER p/r 50-59: .5X TO 1.2X BRZ p/r 100
*SILVER p/r 50-59: .4X TO 1X BRZ p/r 50
*SILVER p/r 27-34: .5X TO 1.2X BRZ p/r 50
*SILVER p/r 20-25: .75X TO 2X BRZ p/r 100
*SILVER p/r 20-25: .5X TO 1.2X BRZ p/r 50
*SILVER p/r 20-25: .4X TO 1X BRZ p/r 25
RANDOM INSERTS IN PACKS
PRINT RUNS B/WN 5-100 COPIES PER
NO PRICING ON QTY OF 11 OR LESS
2 Garret Anderson/100 15.00 4.50
5 Vladimir Guerrero/27 60.00 18.00
6 Brandon Webb/100 10.00 3.00
7 Brian Bruney/100 10.00 3.00
9 Randy Johnson/5
10 Richie Sexson/10
11 Robby Hammock/51 12.00 3.60
13 Shea Hillenbrand/100 15.00 4.50
14 Steve Finley/25 25.00 7.50
15 Adam LaRoche/100 10.00 3.00
16 Andruw Jones/10
17 Bubba Nelson/100 10.00 3.00
18 Chipper Jones/10
22 Marcus Giles/100 15.00 4.50
23 Rafael Furcal/50 20.00 6.00
24 Warren Spahn/10
26 Adam Loewen/100 10.00 3.00
27 Cal Ripken/10
29 Jay Gibbons/100 10.00 3.00
30 Luis Matos/100 10.00 3.00
32 Rafael Palmeiro/10
33 Bobby Doerr/100 15.00 4.50
35 Edwin Almonte/100 10.00 3.00
36 Jason Varitek/25 60.00 18.00
37 Kevin Youkilis/100 15.00 4.50
41 Trot Nixon/25 25.00 7.50
42 Andre Dawson/100 15.00 4.50
43 Aramis Ramirez/25 30.00 9.00
44 Brendan Harris/85 10.00 3.00
45 Derrek Lee/25 30.00 9.00
46 Ernie Banks/20 60.00 18.00
47 Kerry Wood/10
48 Mark Prior/25 100.00 30.00
50 Sammy Sosa/25 200.00 60.00
51 Carlos Lee/100 15.00 4.50
52 Frank Thomas/25 60.00 18.00
53 Joe Borchard/100 10.00 3.00
54 Joe Crede/25
55 Magglio Ordonez/25 25.00 7.50
58 Barry Larkin/10
59 Brandon Larson/100 10.00 3.00
61 Ryan Wagner/100 10.00 3.00
63 Bob Feller/100 25.00 7.50
64 Brian Tallet/100 10.00 3.00
66 Jeremy Guthrie/100 10.00 3.00
67 Jody Gerut/100 15.00 4.50
68 Clint Barmes/50 12.00 3.60
69 Jeff Baker/10
72 Preston Wilson/100 15.00 4.50
73 Todd Helton/10
74 Alan Trammell/100 15.00 4.50
78 Preston Larrison/50 12.00 3.60
79 Dontrelle Willis/10
80 Josh Beckett/10
82 Luis Castillo/10
83 Miguel Cabrera/100 25.00 7.50
84 Mike Lowell/5
85 Andy Pettitte/10
86 Chris Burke/100 10.00 3.00
87 Craig Biggio/5
88 Jeff Bagwell/10
90 Lance Berkman/5
94 Roy Oswalt/5
96 Byron Gettis/100 10.00 3.00
97 Carlos Beltran/50 50.00 15.00
98 George Brett/25 120.00 36.00
99 Juan Gonzalez/10
101 Duke Snider/100 25.00 7.50
102 Edwin Jackson/100 15.00 4.50
104 Hideo Nomo/5
105 Hong-Chih Kuo/100 15.00 4.50
106 Kazuhisa Ishii/10
107 Paul Lo Duca/50 20.00 6.00
108 Robin Ventura/25 25.00 7.50
109 Shawn Green/10
110 Junior Spivey/25 15.00 4.50
111 Rickie Weeks/5
112 Scott Podsednik/100 15.00 4.50
113 J.D. Durbin/100 10.00 3.00
114 Jacque Jones/100 15.00 4.50
115 Jason Kubel/100 12.00 3.60
116 Johan Santana/100 40.00 12.00
117 Shannon Stewart/50 12.00 3.60
118 Torii Hunter/10
120 Jose Vidro/10
122 Orlando Cabrera/10
123 Gary Carter/100 15.00 4.50
124 Jae Weong Seo/5
125 Lenny Dykstra/100 15.00 4.50
126 Mike Piazza/5
127 Tom Glavine/5
128 Alex Rodriguez/5
129 Bernie Williams/10
130 Chien-Ming Wang/100 25.00 7.50
132 Don Mattingly/25 100.00 30.00
133 Gary Sheffield/25 40.00 12.00
136 Javier Vazquez/5
137 Jorge Posada/25 40.00 12.00
138 Jose Contreras/5
142 Whitey Ford/25
143 Barry Zito/10
145 Mark Mulder/50 20.00 6.00
146 Rich Harden/100 15.00 4.50
147 Tim Hudson/10
148 Reggie Jackson/10
149 Rickey Henderson/10
150 Brett Myers/25 20.00 6.00
155 Mike Schmidt/20 100.00 30.00
156 Ryan Howard/100 15.00 4.50
161 Jay Payton/100 10.00 3.00
166 J.T. Snow/10
168 Jerome Williams/50 20.00 6.00
169 Will Clark/25 60.00 18.00
171 Chris Snelling/100 10.00 3.00
172 Edgar Martinez/11
175 Rich Aurilia/10
176 Shigetoshi Hasegawa/50 80.00 24.00
177 Albert Pujols/5
178 Dan Haren/100 10.00 3.00
180 Jim Edmonds/25 50.00 15.00
182 Scott Rolen/50 50.00 15.00
183 Stan Musial/25 80.00 24.00
184 Aubrey Huff/100 15.00 4.50
185 Chad Gaudin/100 10.00 3.00
186 Delmon Young/25 40.00 12.00
187 Fred McGriff/5
188 Rocco Baldelli 5
191 Mark Teixeira/25 40.00 12.00
192 Nolan Ryan/34 150.00 45.00
193 Alexis Rios/100 15.00 4.50
195 Dustin McGowan/59 12.00 3.60
196 Guillermo Quiroz/59 12.00 3.60
197 Josh Phelps/25 20.00 6.00
198 Roy Halladay/25 20.00 6.00
200 Vinnie Chulk/25 20.00 6.00
201 Jose Capellan/100 30.00 9.00
203 Dave Crouthers/100 10.00 3.00
204 Akinori Otsuka/100 40.00 12.00
205 Nick Regilio/100 10.00 3.00
206 Justin Hampson/100 10.00 3.00
207 Lincoln Holdzkom/100 10.00 3.00
208 Jorge Sequea/100 10.00 3.00
209 Justin Leone/100 15.00 4.50
210 Renyel Pinto/100 15.00 4.50
214 Cory Sullivan/100 10.00 3.00
216 Chris Shelton/100 20.00 6.00
217 Willy Taveras/10
218 John Gall/100 15.00 4.50
219 Jerry Gil/10
220 Jason Frasor/10
221 Justin Knoedler/52
222 Ronald Belisario/100 10.00 3.00
223 Mike Rouse/100 10.00 3.00
224 Dennis Sarfate/100 10.00 3.00
225 Casey Daigle/5

2004 Playoff Honors Awards

Nm-Mt Ex-Mt
RANDOM INSERTS IN PACKS
PRINT RUNS B/WN 1940-2003 COPIES PER
1 Phil Rizzuto/1950 4.00 1.20
2 Fred Lynn/1975 3.00 .90
3 George Brett/1980 10.00 3.00
4 Cal Ripken/1983 15.00 4.50
5 Don Mattingly/1985 10.00 3.00
6 Rickey Henderson/1990 3.00 .90
7 Stan Musial/1943 6.00 1.80
8 Marty Marion/1944 3.00 .90
9 Ernie Banks/1958 4.00 1.20
10 Sammy Sosa/1998 5.00 1.50
11 Terry Pendleton/1991 3.00 .90
12 Ryne Sandberg/1984 8.00 2.40
13 Andre Dawson/1987 3.00 .90
14 George Foster/1977 3.00 .90
15 Dave Parker/1978 3.00 .90
16 Keith Hernandez/1979 3.00 .90
17 Mike Schmidt/1980 8.00 2.40
18 Dale Murphy/1982 4.00 1.20
19 Whitey Ford/1961 4.00 1.20
20 Roy Halladay/2003 3.00 .90
21 Orel Hershiser/1988 4.00 1.20
22 Bob Feller/1940 3.00 .90
23 Dwight Gooden/1985 3.00 .90
24 Steve Carlton/1972 3.00 .90
25 Randy Johnson/2002 3.00 .90

2004 Playoff Honors Awards Signature

Nm-Mt Ex-Mt
RANDOM INSERTS IN PACKS
PRINT RUNS B/WN 1-100 COPIES PER
NO PRICING ON QTY OF 10 OR LESS
1 Phil Rizzuto/50 30.00 9.00
2 Fred Lynn/100 15.00 4.50
3 George Brett/5
4 Cal Ripken/8
5 Don Mattingly/5
6 Rickey Henderson/5
7 Stan Musial/50
8 Marty Marion/50 12.00 3.60
9 Ernie Banks/1
10 Sammy Sosa/21 150.00 45.00
11 Terry Pendleton/100 10.00 3.00
13 Andre Dawson/100 15.00 4.50
14 George Foster/100 10.00 3.00
15 Dave Parker/88 15.00 4.50
16 Keith Hernandez/100 15.00 4.50
17 Mike Schmidt/10
18 Dale Murphy/1
19 Whitey Ford/50 30.00 9.00
20 Roy Halladay/25 20.00 6.00
21 Orel Hershiser/25 50.00 15.00
22 Bob Feller/100 15.00 4.50
23 Dwight Gooden/100 15.00 4.50
25 Randy Johnson/5

2004 Playoff Honors Champions

Nm-Mt Ex-Mt
RANDOM INSERTS IN PACKS
PRINT RUNS B/WN 1951-2002 COPIES PER
1 Stan Musial/1951 6.00 1.80
2 Warren Spahn/1958 4.00 1.20
3 Bob Gibson/1968 4.00 1.20
4 Mike Schmidt/1980 8.00 2.40
5 Dale Murphy/1982 4.00 1.20
6 Steve Carlton/1983 3.00 .90
7 Will Clark/1988 4.00 1.20
8 Nolan Ryan/1990 10.00 3.00
9 Ryne Sandberg/1990 8.00 2.40
10 Roger Clemens/1990 6.00 1.80
11 George Brett/1990 10.00 3.00
12 Tony Gwynn/1997 5.00 1.50
13 Todd Helton/2000 3.00 .90
14 Troy Glaus/2000 3.00 .90
15 Sammy Sosa/2000 5.00 1.50
16 Pedro Martinez/2000 3.00 .90

17 Mark Mulder/2001 3.00 .90
18 Manny Ramirez/2002 3.00 .90
19 Lance Berkman/2002 3.00 .90
20 Alex Rodriguez Rgr/2002 5.00 1.50

2004 Playoff Honors Champions Jersey

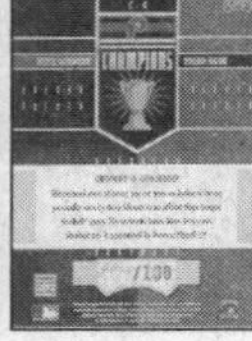

Nm-Mt Ex-Mt
PRINT RUNS B/WN 82-250 COPIES PER
PRIME PRINT RUNS B/WN 1-10 COPIES PER
NO PRIME PRICING DUE TO SCARCITY
RANDOM INSERTS IN PACKS
1 Stan Musial/100 40.00 12.00
2 Warren Spahn/100 15.00 4.50
3 Bob Gibson/100 15.00 4.50
4 Mike Schmidt/100 25.00 7.50
5 Dale Murphy/82
6 Steve Carlton/100 10.00 3.00
7 Will Clark/100 15.00 4.50
8 Nolan Ryan/100 30.00 9.00
9 Ryne Sandberg/100 25.00 7.50
10 Roger Clemens/100 15.00 4.50
11 George Brett/100 25.00 7.50
12 Tony Gwynn/250 15.00 4.50
13 Todd Helton/250 8.00 2.40
14 Troy Glaus/250 5.00 1.50
15 Sammy Sosa/250 10.00 3.00
16 Pedro Martinez/250 8.00 2.40
17 Mark Mulder/250 5.00 1.50
18 Manny Ramirez/250 8.00 2.40
19 Lance Berkman/250 5.00 1.50
20 Alex Rodriguez Rgr/250 10.00 3.00

2004 Playoff Honors Champions Jersey Signature

Nm-Mt Ex-Mt
STATED PRINT RUN 5 SERIAL #'d SETS
PRIME PRINT RUNS B/WN 1-5 COPIES PER
NO PRICING DUE TO SCARCITY
RANDOM INSERTS IN PACKS
1 Stan Musial
2 Warren Spahn
3 Bob Gibson
4 Mike Schmidt
7 Will Clark
8 Nolan Ryan
11 George Brett
12 Tony Gwynn
13 Todd Helton
15 Sammy Sosa
17 Mark Mulder
18 Manny Ramirez
19 Lance Berkman
20 Alex Rodriguez Rgr

2004 Playoff Honors Champions Signature

Nm-Mt Ex-Mt
RANDOM INSERTS IN PACKS
PRINT RUNS B/WN 1-50 COPIES PER
NO PRICING ON QTY OF 10 OR LESS
1 Stan Musial/50 60.00 18.00
2 Warren Spahn/5
3 Bob Gibson/50 30.00 9.00
4 Mike Schmidt/10
7 Will Clark/50 50.00 15.00
8 Nolan Ryan/34 150.00 45.00
11 George Brett/10
12 Tony Gwynn/10
13 Todd Helton/10
15 Sammy Sosa/10
17 Mark Mulder/10
18 Manny Ramirez/1
19 Lance Berkman/10
20 Alex Rodriguez Rgr/5

2004 Playoff Honors Class Reunion

Nm-Mt Ex-Mt
RANDOM INSERTS IN PACKS
PRINT RUNS B/WN 1973-2003 COPIES PER
1 Eddie Murray 4.00 1.20
Gary Carter/2003
2 Carlton Fisk 4.00 1.20
Tony Perez/2000
3 Nolan Ryan 12.00 3.60
George Brett/1999

4 Rod Carew 4.00 1.20
Fergie Jenkins/1991
5 Joe Morgan 3.00 .90
Jim Palmer/1990
6 Carl Yastrzemski 6.00 1.80
Johnny Bench/1989
7 Harmon Killebrew 4.00 1.20
Luis Aparicio/1984
8 Brooks Robinson 4.00 1.20
Juan Marichal/1983
9 Al Kaline 4.00 1.20
Duke Snider/1980
10 Roberto Clemente 10.00 3.00
Warren Spahn/1973
11 Mark Prior 4.00 1.20
Mark Teixeira/2001
12 Josh Beckett 3.00 .90
Barry Zito/1999
13 Mark Mulder 3.00 .90
Adam Dunn/1998
14 Vernon Wells 3.00 .90
Lance Berkman/1997
15 Eric Chavez 3.00 .90
Nick Johnson/1996
16 Kerry Wood 3.00 .90
Roy Halladay/1995
17 Todd Helton 3.00 .90
Carlos Beltran/1995
18 Derek Jeter 6.00 1.80
Jason Giambi/1992
19 Manny Ramirez 3.00 .90
Shawn Green/1991
20 Chipper Jones 3.00 .90
Mike Mussina/1990

2004 Playoff Honors Class Reunion Material

Nm-Mt Ex-Mt
RANDOM INSERTS IN PACKS
PRINT RUNS B/WN 25-250 COPIES PER
1 Eddie Murray Jsy 20.00 6.00
Gary Carter Jsy/100
2 Carlton Fisk Jsy 25.00 7.50
Tony Perez Bat/250
3 Nolan Ryan Jsy 60.00 18.00
George Brett Jsy/100
4 Rod Carew Jsy 15.00 4.50
Fergie Jenkins Pants/250
5 Joe Morgan Jsy 12.00 3.60
Jim Palmer Jsy/100
6 Carl Yastrzemski Jsy 40.00 12.00
Johnny Bench Jsy/250
7 Harmon Killebrew Jsy 15.00 4.50
Luis Aparicio Jsy/250
8 Brooks Robinson Jsy 20.00 6.00
Juan Marichal Jsy/100
9 Al Kaline Jsy 40.00 12.00
Duke Snider Jsy/25
10 Roberto Clemente Jsy 100.00 30.00
Warren Spahn Jsy/100
11 Mark Prior Jsy 15.00 4.50
Mark Teixeira Jsy/250
12 Josh Beckett Jsy 8.00 2.40
Barry Zito Jsy/250
13 Mark Mulder Jsy 10.00 3.00
Adam Dunn Jsy/250
14 Vernon Wells Jsy 8.00 2.40
Lance Berkman Jsy/250
15 Eric Chavez Jsy 8.00 2.40
Nick Johnson Jsy/250
16 Kerry Wood Jsy 10.00 3.00
Roy Halladay Jsy/250
17 Todd Helton Jsy 10.00 3.00
Carlos Beltran Jsy/250
18 Derek Jeter Jsy 25.00 7.50
Jason Giambi Jsy/250
19 Manny Ramirez Jsy 20.00 6.00
Shawn Green Jsy/50
20 Chipper Jones Jsy 10.00 3.00
Mike Mussina Jsy/250

2004 Playoff Honors Fans of the Game

Nm-Mt Ex-Mt
RANDOM INSERTS IN PACKS
251 Charlie Sheen 3.00 .90
252 Corbin Bernsen 2.00 .60
253 Peter Gammons 3.00 .90
254 Jeff Garlin 2.00 .60
255 Larry King 3.00 .90

2004 Playoff Honors Fans of the Game Signature

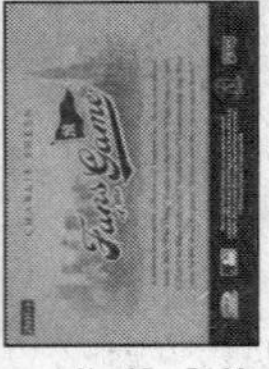

Nm-Mt Ex-Mt
RANDOM INSERTS IN PACKS
251 Charlie Sheen 120.00 36.00
252 Corbin Bernsen 25.00 7.50
253 Peter Gammons 40.00 12.00
254 Jeff Garlin SP 100.00 30.00
255 Larry King 60.00 18.00

2004 Playoff Honors Game Day Souvenir

Nm-Mt Ex-Mt
RANDOM INSERTS IN PACKS
PRINT RUNS B/WN 9-100 COPIES PER
NO PRICING ON QTY OF 9 OR LESS
1 Nolan Ryan Hat/9
2 Bob Gibson Jsy/75 15.00 4.50
3 Frank Robinson Bat/61 12.00 3.60
4 Tony Gwynn Pants/99 25.00 7.50
5 Warren Spahn Jsy/53 20.00 6.00
6 George Brett Bat/77 30.00 9.00
7 Cal Ripken Hat/19 150.00 45.00
8 Frank Thomas Bat/93 10.00 3.00
9 Sammy Sosa Jsy/100 15.00 4.50
10 Harmon Killebrew Bat/75 15.00 4.50

2004 Playoff Honors Game Day Souvenir Signature

Nm-Mt Ex-Mt
RANDOM INSERTS IN PACKS
STATED PRINT RUN 5 SERIAL #'d SETS
NO PRICING DUE TO SCARCITY
1 Nolan Ryan Hat
2 Bob Gibson Jsy
3 Frank Robinson Bat
4 Tony Gwynn Pants
5 Warren Spahn Jsy
6 George Brett Bat
7 Cal Ripken Hat
8 Frank Thomas Bat
9 Sammy Sosa Jsy

2004 Playoff Honors Piece of the Game Jersey

Nm-Mt Ex-Mt
PRINT RUNS B/WN 50-250 COPIES PER
*COMBO p/r 100: 1X TO 2.5X JSY p/r 250
*COMBO p/r 100: .6X TO 1.5X JSY p/r 100
*COMBO p/r 100: .5X TO 1.2X JSY p/r 50
*COMBO p/r 50: 1.25X TO 3X JSY p/r 250
*COMBO p/r 50: .6X TO 1.5X JSY p/r 50
*COMBO p/r 25: 1.25X TO 3X JSY p/r 100
COMBO PRINT RUNS B/WN 25-100 PER
*NBR p/r 250: .4X TO 1X JSY p/r 250
*NBR p/r 100: .5X TO 1.2X JSY p/r 250
*NBR p/r 100: .4X TO 1X JSY p/r 100
*NBR p/r 75: .6X TO 1.5X JSY p/r 250
*NBR p/r 50: .75X TO 2X JSY p/r 250
*NBR p/r 50: .4X TO 1X JSY p/r 50
*NBR p/r 20: .75X TO 2X JSY p/r 100
*NBR p/r 20: .6X TO 1.5X JSY p/r 50
NUMBER PRINTS B/WN 11-250 COPIES PER
NO NBR PRICING ON QTY OF 11 OR LESS
*POS p/r 250: .4X TO 1X JSY p/r 250
*POS p/r 250: .3X TO .8X JSY p/r 100
*POS p/r 100: .5X TO 1.2X JSY p/r 250
*POS p/r 100: .4X TO 1X JSY p/r 100
*POS p/r 50: .4X TO 1X JSY p/r 50
*POS p/r 20: .75X TO 2X JSY p/r 100
*POS p/r 20: .6X TO 1.5X JSY p/r 50
POSITION PRINTS B/WN 20-250 COPIES PER
RANDOM INSERTS IN PACKS
1 Albert Pujols/250 15.00 4.50
2 Angel Berroa/250 5.00 1.50
3 Aubrey Huff/250 5.00 1.50
4 Barry Zito/250 5.00 1.50
5 Bobby Abreu/250 5.00 1.50
6 Carlos Beltran/250 8.00 2.40
7 Chipper Jones/250 8.00 2.40
8 Derek Jeter/50 40.00 12.00
9 Eric Chavez/250 5.00 1.50
10 Eric Hinske/100 8.00 2.40
12 George Brett/250 15.00 4.50
13 Jay Gibbons/250 5.00 1.50
14 Jim Edmonds/250 5.00 1.50
15 Josh Beckett/250 5.00 1.50
16 Manny Ramirez/250 8.00 2.40
17 Mark Mulder/100 8.00 2.40
18 Marlon Byrd/250 5.00 1.50
19 Mike Lowell/250 5.00 1.50
20 Mike Schmidt/50 40.00 12.00
21 Nolan Ryan/100 30.00 9.00
22 Rafael Furcal/250 5.00 1.50
23 Randy Johnson/250 8.00 2.40
24 Rod Carew/100 10.00 3.00
25 Torii Hunter/250 5.00 1.50

2004 Playoff Honors Piece of the Game Jersey Signature

Nm-Mt Ex-Mt
PRINT RUNS B/WN 1-10 COPIES PER
BAT PRINT RUN B/WN 1-10 COPIES PER
COMBO PRINT RUN B/WN 1-10 COPIES PER
NUMBER PRINT RUN B/WN 1-5 COPIES PER
POSITION PRINT B/WN 1-5 COPIES PER
NO PRICING DUE TO SCARCITY
RANDOM INSERTS IN PACKS
1 Albert Pujols/1
2 Angel Berroa/10
3 Aubrey Huff/10
4 Barry Zito/5
6 Carlos Beltran/10
7 Chipper Jones/5
9 Eric Chavez/3
10 Eric Hinske/10
12 George Brett/1
13 Jay Gibbons/10
14 Jim Edmonds/5
15 Josh Beckett/5
16 Manny Ramirez/1
17 Mark Mulder/10
18 Marlon Byrd/10
19 Mike Lowell/5
20 Mike Schmidt/1
21 Nolan Ryan/1
22 Rafael Furcal/10
23 Randy Johnson/1
24 Rod Carew/5
25 Torii Hunter/10

2004 Playoff Honors Prime Signature Insert

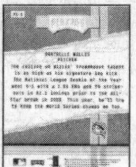

Nm-Mt Ex-Mt
RANDOM INSERTS IN PACKS
STATED PRINT RUN 2500 SERIAL #'d SETS
1 Garret Anderson 3.00 .90
2 Rafael Palmeiro 4.00 1.20
3 Vladimir Guerrero 4.00 1.20
4 Alex Rodriguez 5.00 1.50
5 Dontrelle Willis 3.00 .90
6 Miguel Cabrera 4.00 1.20
7 Shannon Stewart 3.00 .90
8 Mike Piazza 5.00 1.50
9 Gary Sheffield 3.00 .90
10 Ivan Rodriguez 4.00 1.20
11 Randy Johnson 4.00 1.20
12 Tom Glavine 4.00 1.20
13 Brandon Webb 3.00 .90
14 Carlos Lee 3.00 .90
15 Hideo Nomo 4.00 1.20
16 Mike Mussina 4.00 1.20
17 Magglio Ordonez 3.00 .90
18 Austin Kearns 3.00 .90
19 Andruw Jones 3.00 .90
20 Mariano Rivera 4.00 1.20
21 Sammy Sosa 5.00 1.50
22 Juan Gonzalez 4.00 1.20
23 Jeff Bagwell 4.00 1.20
24 Rickey Henderson 4.00 1.20
25 Mike Schmidt 8.00 2.40
26 Jim Rice 3.00 .90
27 Billy Williams 3.00 .90
28 Lou Brock 4.00 1.20
29 Robin Yount 6.00 1.80
30 Nolan Ryan 10.00 3.00
31 Darryl Strawberry 3.00 .90
32 Cal Ripken 15.00 4.50
33 Andre Dawson 3.00 .90
34 Don Mattingly 10.00 3.00
35 Paul Molitor 4.00 1.20
36 Bo Jackson 4.00 1.20
37 Ernie Banks 4.00 1.20
38 Orel Hershiser 4.00 1.20
39 Mark Grace 4.00 1.20
40 Carlton Fisk 4.00 1.20

2004 Playoff Honors Prime Signature Autograph

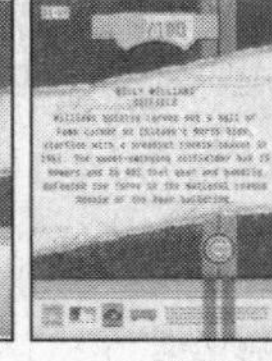

Nm-Mt Ex-Mt
PRINT RUNS B/WN 5-100 COPIES PER
NO PRICING ON QTY OF 10 OR LESS
AU BAT PRINT RUN B/WN 1-10 COPIES PER
NO AU BAT PRICING DUE TO SCARCITY
*AU JSY p/r 20-25: 1X TO 2.5X AU p/r 100
*AU JSY p/r 23-25: .75X TO 2X AU p/r 50
*AU JSY p/r 19: .6X TO 1.5X AU p/r 25
*AU JSY p/r 17: 1X TO 2.5X AU p/r 50
*AU JSY p/r 16: 1.25X TO 3X AU p/r 100
AU JSY PRINT RUN B/WN 1-25 COPIES PER
NO AU JSY PRICING ON QTY OF 14 OR LESS
RANDOM INSERTS IN PACKS
1 Garret Anderson/100 15.00 4.50
2 Rafael Palmeiro/50 50.00 15.00
3 Vladimir Guerrero/50 50.00 15.00
4 Alex Rodriguez/10
5 Dontrelle Willis/50 20.00 6.00
6 Miguel Cabrera/100 25.00 7.50
7 Shannon Stewart/100 10.00 3.00
8 Mike Piazza/10
9 Gary Sheffield/100 25.00 7.50
11 Randy Johnson/10
12 Tom Glavine/25 50.00 15.00
13 Brandon Webb/100 10.00 3.00
14 Carlos Lee/100 15.00 4.50
15 Hideo Nomo/5
17 Magglio Ordonez/100 15.00 4.50
19 Andruw Jones/50 20.00 6.00
21 Sammy Sosa/50 150.00 45.00
22 Juan Gonzalez/50 30.00 9.00
23 Jeff Bagwell/25 60.00 18.00
24 Rickey Henderson/25 100.00 30.00
25 Mike Schmidt/50 80.00 24.00
26 Jim Rice/100 15.00 4.50
27 Billy Williams/100 15.00 4.50
28 Lou Brock/100 25.00 7.50
29 Robin Yount/25 80.00 24.00
30 Nolan Ryan/50 120.00 36.00
31 Darryl Strawberry/100 15.00 4.50
32 Cal Ripken/25 200.00 60.00
33 Andre Dawson/100 15.00 4.50
34 Don Mattingly/50 80.00 24.00
35 Paul Molitor/25 50.00 15.00
36 Bo Jackson/50 100.00 30.00
37 Ernie Banks/50 50.00 15.00
38 Orel Hershiser/100 25.00 7.50
39 Mark Grace/50 50.00 15.00
40 Carlton Fisk/50 30.00 9.00

2004 Playoff Honors Quad Material

Nm-Mt Ex-Mt
PRINT RUNS B/WN 10-100 COPIES PER
NO PRICING ON QTY OF 10 OR LESS
ALL ARE FOUR JSY SWATCH UNLESS NOTED
FERGIE JENKINS SWATCH IS PANTS.
COMBO PRINT RUNS B/WN 1-10 COPIES PER
NO COMBO PRICING DUE TO SCARCITY
ALL COMBO ARE BAT-JSY FOR EACH PLAYER
RANDOM INSERTS IN PACKS
1 Don Mattingly Jsy 60.00 18.00
Mark Grace Jsy
Will Clark Jsy
Keith Hernandez Jsy/100
2 Jason Giambi Jsy 25.00 7.50
Jim Thome Jsy
Carlos Delgado Jsy
Rafael Palmeiro Jsy/100
3 Albert Pujols Jsy 60.00 18.00
Ernie Banks Jsy
Jeff Bagwell Jsy
Frank Thomas Jsy/100
4 Paul Molitor Jsy 60.00 18.00
Joe Morgan Jsy
Ryne Sandberg Jsy
Alfonso Soriano Jsy/50
5 Cal Ripken Jsy 80.00 24.00
Derek Jeter Jsy
Alex Rodriguez Rgr Jsy
Nomar Garciaparra Jsy/100
6 Ozzie Smith Jsy 60.00 18.00
Robin Yount Jsy
Alan Trammell Jsy
Dave Concepcion Jsy/50
7 George Brett Jsy
Mike Schmidt Jsy
Brooks Robinson Jsy
Wade Boggs Jsy/25
8 Johnny Bench Jsy 60.00 18.00
Carlton Fisk Jsy
Gary Carter Jsy
Mike Piazza Jsy/100
9 Todd Helton Jsy 50.00 15.00
Marcus Giles Jsy
Edgar Renteria Jsy
Scott Rolen Jsy/25
10 Carlos Delgado Jsy 25.00 7.50

Alfonso Soriano Jsy
Alex Rodriguez Jsy
Troy Glaus Jsy/100
11 Harmon Killebrew Jsy 80.00 24.00
Reggie Jackson Jsy
Mike Schmidt Jsy
Sammy Sosa Jsy/100
12 Stan Musial Jsy 100.00 30.00
Rickey Henderson Jsy
Tony Gwynn Jsy
Lou Brock Jsy/25
13 Cal Ripken Jsy 80.00 24.00
George Brett Jsy
Paul Molitor Jsy
Rod Carew Jsy/100
14 Sammy Sosa Jsy 40.00 12.00
Vladimir Guerrero Jsy
Manny Ramirez Jsy
Magglio Ordonez Jsy/100
15 Andruw Jones Jsy 25.00 7.50
Jim Edmonds Jsy
Torii Hunter Jsy
Vernon Wells Jsy/100
16 Chipper Jones Jsy 25.00 7.50
Shawn Green Jsy
Garret Anderson Jsy
Lance Berkman Jsy/100
17 Tony Gwynn Jsy.................. 50.00 15.00
Dale Murphy Jsy
Kirby Puckett Jsy
Andre Dawson Jsy/100
18 Stan Musial Jsy............................
Roberto Clemente Jsy
Al Kaline Jsy
Carl Yastrzemski Jsy/10
19 Nolan Ryan Jsy.................... 80.00 24.00
Roger Clemens Jsy
Kerry Wood Jsy
Josh Beckett Jsy/100
20 Bob Gibson Jsy.............................
Fergie Jenkins Pants
Tom Seaver Jsy
Jim Palmer Jsy/10
21 Dennis Eckersley Jsy 60.00 18.00
John Smoltz Jsy
Mariano Rivera Jsy
Lee Smith Jsy/100
22 Mike Mussina Jsy................ 40.00 12.00
Greg Maddux Jsy
Jack Morris Jsy
Bert Blyleven Jsy/100
23 Steve Carlton Jsy................ 25.00 7.50
Tom Glavine Jsy
Barry Zito Jsy
Andy Pettitte Jsy/100
24 Whitey Ford Jsy 80.00 24.00
Warren Spahn Jsy
Bob Feller Jsy
Juan Marichal Jsy/25
25 Nolan Ryan Jsy.................... 80.00 24.00
Roger Clemens Jsy
Steve Carlton Jsy
Randy Johnson Jsy/100

2004 Playoff Honors Rookie Year Jersey Number

Nm-Mt Ex-Mt
RANDOM INSERTS IN PACKS ....
PRINT RUNS B/WN 25-100 COPIES PER
1 Gary Carter/50 .... 12.00 3.60
2 Robin Yount/50....................... 40.00 12.00
3 Roger Clemens/25 .... 50.00 15.00
4 Gary Sheffield/50 .... 10.00 3.00
5 Mike Piazza/25....................... 40.00 12.00
6 Hideo Nomo/25....................... 40.00 12.00
7 Alex Rodriguez/50.................. 25.00 7.50
8 Mark Prior/25......................... 25.00 7.50
9 Dontrelle Willis/100 .... 8.00 2.40
10 Angel Berroa/100................... 8.00 2.40

2004 Playoff Honors Rookie Year Jersey Signature

Nm-Mt Ex-Mt
RANDOM INSERTS IN PACKS ....
PRINT RUNS B/WN 1-10 COPIES PER
NO PRICING DUE TO SCARCITY ....
1 Gary Carter/8 ....
2 Robin Yount/3...................................
4 Gary Sheffield/10 ....
5 Mike Piazza/1....................................
6 Hideo Nomo/1....................................
7 Alex Rodriguez/3...............................
8 Mark Prior/3......................................
9 Dontrelle Willis/10.............................
10 Angel Berroa/10...............................

2004 Playoff Honors Signs of Greatness

Nm-Mt Ex-Mt
RANDOM INSERTS IN PACKS ....
PRINT RUNS B/WN 20-25 COPIES PER
1 Mark Prior/25......................... 80.00 24.00
2 Scott Podsednik/25................. 30.00 9.00
4 Dontrelle Willis/25.................. 30.00 9.00
5 Rocco Baldelli/20.................... 30.00 9.00
6 Brandon Webb/25.................... 20.00 6.00
7 Rich Harden/25....................... 30.00 9.00
8 Miguel Cabrera/25................... 50.00 15.00
9 Josh Beckett/25...................... 50.00 15.00
10 Mark Teixeira/25 .... 50.00 15.00

2004 Playoff Honors Tandem Material

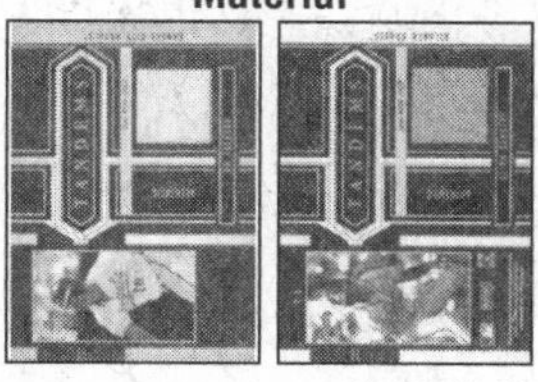

Nm-Mt Ex-Mt
PRINT RUNS B/WN 5-250 COPIES PER
NO PRICING ON QTY OF 5 OR LESS ..
ALL ARE DUAL JSY SWATCH UNLESS NOTED
*COMBO p/r 25: 1.5X TO 4X TANDEM p/r 250
*COMBO p/r 25: .75X TO 2X TANDEM p/r 100
COMBO PRINTS B/WN 1-25 COPIES PER
NO COMBO PRICING ON QTY OF 10 OR LESS
ALL COMBO ARE BAT-JSY FOR EACH PLAYER
RANDOM INSERTS IN PACKS ....
1 Bo Jackson Jsy 40.00 12.00
Deion Sanders Jsy/100
2 Eddie Murray Jsy.................. 15.00 4.50
Rafael Palmeiro Jsy/250
3 Alex Rodriguez Rgr Jsy 15.00 4.50
Dale Murphy Jsy/250
4 Carlton Fisk Jsy 15.00 4.50
Ivan Rodriguez Jsy/250
5 Rickey Henderson Jsy 40.00 12.00
Lou Brock Jsy/50
6 Sammy Sosa Jsy 25.00 7.50
Ernie Banks Jsy/250
7 Warren Spahn Jsy.................. 15.00 4.50
Steve Carlton Jsy/100
8 Carl Yastrzemski Jsy.............. 25.00 7.50
Dwight Evans Jsy/250
9 Keith Hernandez Bat............... 10.00 3.00
Lenny Dykstra Bat/250
10 Pee Wee Reese Jsy.............. 15.00 4.50
Marty Marion Jsy/100
11 Hideo Nomo Jsy 15.00 4.50
Chipper Jones Jsy/250
12 Willie McCovey Jsy............... 25.00 7.50
Reggie Jackson Jsy/100
13 Mark Prior Jsy 15.00 4.50
Barry Zito Jsy/250
14 Cal Ripken Jsy 50.00 15.00
Miguel Tejada Bat/100
15 Roberto Clemente Jsy........... 80.00 24.00
Vladimir Guerrero Bat/100
16 Gary Carter Jsy 15.00 4.50
Mike Piazza Jsy/250
17 Jim Rice Jsy 25.00 7.50
Fred Lynn Jsy/50
18 Willie Stargell Jsy 15.00 4.50
Keith Hernandez Jsy/250
19 Nomar Garciaparra Jsy 25.00 7.50
Mark Teixeira Jsy/100
20 Derek Jeter Jsy 60.00 18.00
Phil Rizzuto Jsy/50
21 Eric Chavez Jsy 10.00 3.00
Hank Blalock Jsy/100
22 Eric Davis Jsy 20.00 6.00
Darryl Strawberry Jsy/100
23 Rickey Henderson Jsy 40.00 12.00
Deion Sanders Jsy/100
24 Dave Parker Jsy 15.00 4.50
Austin Kearns Jsy/250
25 Luis Aparicio Jsy 20.00 6.00
Dave Concepcion Jsy/100
26 Rafael Palmeiro Jsy.............. 25.00 7.50
Will Clark Jsy/100
27 Ryne Sandberg Jsy............... 50.00 15.00
Ozzie Smith Jsy/250
28 Alex Rodriguez M's Jsy 15.00 4.50
Jose Canseco Jsy/250
29 Sammy Sosa Jsy 15.00 4.50
Juan Gonzalez Jsy/250
30 Pedro Martinez Jsy 25.00 7.50
Juan Marichal Jsy/50
31 Stan Musial Jsy.........................
Duke Snider Jsy/5
32 Dwight Gooden Jsy............... 10.00 3.00
Gary Sheffield Jsy/250
33 Lou Boudreau Jsy................. 20.00 6.00
Omar Vizquel Jsy/100
34 Mark Prior Hat 40.00 12.00
Ron Santo Bat/100
35 Albert Pujols Jsy 25.00 7.50
Ken Boyer Jsy/250
36 Tom Seaver Jsy 15.00 4.50
Curt Schilling Jsy/250
37 Joe Morgan Jsy 10.00 3.00
Jeff Kent Jsy/250
38 Steve Garvey Jsy 25.00 7.50
Ozzie Smith Jsy/250
39 Mike Piazza Jsy.................... 15.00 4.50
Ivan Rodriguez Jsy/250
40 Mike Schmidt Jsy 30.00 9.00
Jim Thome Jsy/100

2003 Playoff Prestige

This 210 card set was issued in two separate series. The primary product - containing cards 1-200 from the basic set - was released in May, 2003. The set was issued in six-card packs which were issued 24 packs to a box and 20 boxes to a case. The first 180 cards in the set featured veterans while the final 20 cards featured leading rookies and prospects. Those final 20 cards were inserted at a stated rate of one in three. Cards 201-210 were issued in DLP Rookies and Traded packs of which was distributed in December, 2003.

Nm-Mt Ex-Mt
COMP.LO SET (200)................. 40.00 12.00
COMP.LO SET w/o SP's (180) .. 25.00 7.50
COMP.UPDATE SET (10)............ 8.00 2.40
COMMON CARD (1-180) .... .40 .12
COMMON CARD (181-200) .... 1.50 .45
COMMON CARD (201-210) .... .50 .15
201-210 ISSUED IN DLP R/T PACKS..
1 Darin Erstad .... .40 .12
2 David Eckstein .... .40 .12
3 Garret Anderson...................... .40 .12
4 Jarrod Washburn..................... .40 .12
5 Tim Salmon .... .60 .18
6 Troy Glaus.............................. .40 .12
7 Jay Gibbons............................ .40 .12
8 Marty Cordova .... .40 .12
9 Melvin Mora............................ .40 .12
10 Rodrigo Lopez .... .40 .12
11 Tony Batista .... .40 .12
12 Cliff Floyd.............................. .40 .12
13 Derek Lowe............................ .40 .12
14 Johnny Damon...................... 1.00 .30
15 Manny Ramirez .... .60 .18
16 Nomar Garciaparra .... 1.50 .45
17 Pedro Martinez...................... 1.00 .30
18 Rickey Henderson................. 1.00 .30
19 Shea Hillenbrand.................... .40 .12
20 Carlos Lee.............................. .40 .12
21 Frank Thomas .... 1.00 .30
22 Magglio Ordonez.................... .40 .12
23 Mark Buehrle .... .40 .12
24 Paul Konerko .... .40 .12
25 C.C. Sabathia .... .40 .12
26 Danys Baez .... .40 .12
27 Ellis Burks.............................. .40 .12
28 Travis Hafner......................... .40 .12
29 Omar Vizquel .... .60 .18
30 Bobby Higginson .... .40 .12
31 Carlos Pena........................... .40 .12
32 Mark Redman .... .40 .12
33 Robert Fick............................ .40 .12
34 Steve Sparks .... .40 .12
35 Carlos Beltran........................ .60 .18
36 Joe Randa .... .40 .12
37 Mike Sweeney .... .40 .12
38 Paul Byrd .... .40 .12
39 Raul Ibanez .... .40 .12
40 Runelvys Hernandez .... .40 .12
41 Brad Radke .... .40 .12
42 Corey Koskie.......................... .40 .12
43 Cristian Guzman..................... .40 .12
44 David Ortiz .... .60 .18
45 Doug Mientkiewicz.................. .40 .12
46 Dustin Mohr............................ .40 .12
47 Jacque Jones .... .40 .12
48 Torii Hunter............................ .40 .12
49 Alfonso Soriano .... .60 .18
50 Andy Pettitte .... .60 .18
51 Bernie Williams....................... .60 .18
52 David Wells............................ .40 .12
53 Derek Jeter.......................... 2.50 .75
54 Jason Giambi .... .40 .12
55 Jeff Weaver .... .40 .12
56 Jorge Posada......................... .60 .18
57 Mike Mussina......................... .60 .18
58 Roger Clemens .... 2.00 .60
59 Barry Zito.............................. .40 .12
60 David Justice .... .40 .12
61 Eric Chavez .... .40 .12
62 Jermaine Dye......................... .40 .12
63 Mark Mulder .... .40 .12
64 Miguel Tejada......................... .40 .12
65 Ray Durham........................... .40 .12
66 Tim Hudson .... .40 .12
67 Bret Boone............................. .40 .12
68 Chris Snelling......................... .40 .12
69 Edgar Martinez....................... .60 .18
70 Freddy Garcia........................ .40 .12
71 Ichiro Suzuki....................... 2.00 .60
72 Jamie Moyer .... .40 .12
73 John Olerud .... .40 .12
74 Kazuhiro Sasaki .... .40 .12
75 Aubrey Huff........................... .40 .12
76 Joe Kennedy .... .40 .12
77 Paul Wilson........................... .40 .12
78 Alex Rodriguez.................... 2.00 .60
79 Chan Ho Park......................... .40 .12
80 Hank Blalock .... .60 .18
81 Ivan Rodriguez.................... 1.00 .30
82 Juan Gonzalez .... .60 .18
83 Kevin Mench .... .40 .12
84 Rafael Palmeiro...................... .60 .18
85 Carlos Delgado....................... .40 .12
86 Eric Hinske............................. .40 .12
87 Jose Cruz Jr. .... .40 .12
88 Josh Phelps .... .40 .12
89 Roy Halladay.......................... .40 .12
90 Shannon Stewart .... .40 .12
91 Vernon Wells.......................... .40 .12
92 Curt Schilling .... .40 .12
93 Junior Spivey .... .40 .12
94 Luis Gonzalez......................... .40 .12
95 Mark Grace .... .60 .18
96 Randy Johnson.................... 1.00 .30
97 Andruw Jones......................... .40 .12
98 Chipper Jones..................... 1.00 .30
99 Gary Sheffield .... .40 .12
100 Greg Maddux .... 1.50 .45
101 John Smoltz......................... .60 .18
102 Kevin Millwood .... .40 .12
103 Mike Hampton .... .40 .12
104 Corey Patterson .... .40 .12
105 Fred McGriff......................... .60 .18
106 Kerry Wood....................... 1.00 .30
107 Mark Prior......................... 1.00 .30
108 Moises Alou .... .40 .12
109 Sammy Sosa..................... 1.50 .45
110 Adam Dunn.......................... .60 .18
111 Austin Kearns...................... .40 .12
112 Barry Larkin .... .60 .18
113 Ken Griffey Jr. .... 1.50 .45
114 Sean Casey .... .40 .12
115 Jason Jennings.................... .40 .12
116 Jay Payton .... .40 .12
117 Larry Walker .... .60 .18
118 Todd Helton .... .60 .18
119 A.J. Burnett......................... .40 .12
120 Josh Beckett .... .40 .12
121 Juan Encarnacion................. .40 .12
122 Mike Lowell.......................... .40 .12
123 Craig Biggio .... .60 .18
124 Daryle Ward .... .40 .12
125 Jeff Bagwell .... .60 .18
126 Lance Berkman .... .40 .12
127 Roy Oswalt........................... .40 .12
128 Adrian Beltre .... .60 .18
129 Hideo Nomo....................... 1.00 .30
130 Kazuhisa Ishii....................... .40 .12
131 Kevin Brown......................... .40 .12
132 Odalis Perez......................... .40 .12
133 Paul Lo Duca .... .40 .12
134 Shawn Green .... .40 .12
135 Jeff Kent............................... .40 .12
136 Ben Sheets........................... .40 .12
137 Jeffrey Hammonds................ .40 .12
138 Jose Hernandez .... .40 .12
139 Richie Sexson .... .40 .12
140 Bartolo Colon .... .40 .12
141 Brad Wilkerson .... .40 .12
142 Javier Vazquez .... .40 .12
143 Jose Vidro............................. .40 .12
144 Michael Barrett...................... .40 .12
145 Vladimir Guerrero .... 1.00 .30
146 Al Leiter .... .40 .12
147 Mike Piazza .... 1.50 .45
148 Mo Vaughn .... .40 .12
149 Pedro Astacio........................ .40 .12
150 Roberto Alomar .... .60 .18
151 Roger Cedeno .... .40 .12
152 Tom Glavine.......................... .60 .18
153 Bobby Abreu .... .40 .12
154 Jimmy Rollins........................ .40 .12
155 Mike Lieberthal .... .40 .12
156 Pat Burrell............................. .40 .12
157 Vicente Padilla .... .40 .12
158 Jim Thome........................ 1.00 .30
159 Aramis Ramirez .... .40 .12
160 Brian Giles .... .40 .12
161 Jason Kendall........................ .40 .12
162 Josh Fogg .... .40 .12
163 Kip Wells............................... .40 .12
164 Mark Kotsay.......................... .40 .12
165 Oliver Perez.......................... .40 .12
166 Phil Nevin.............................. .40 .12
167 Ryan Klesko .... .40 .12
168 Sean Burroughs..................... .40 .12
169 Trevor Hoffman...................... .40 .12
170 Barry Bonds .... 2.50 .75
171 Benito Santiago..................... .40 .12
172 Reggie Sanders..................... .40 .12
173 Rich Aurilia .... .40 .12
174 Russ Ortiz .... .40 .12
175 Albert Pujols .... 2.00 .60
176 J.D. Drew .... .40 .12
177 Jim Edmonds......................... .40 .12
178 Matt Morris............................ .40 .12
179 Tino Martinez .... .60 .18
180 Scott Rolen .... 1.00 .30
181 Joe Borchard ROO .... 1.50 .45
182 Freddy Sanchez ROO .... 1.50 .45
183 Jose Contreras ROO RC...... 2.50 .75
184 Jeff Baker ROO .... 1.50 .45
185 Ryan Church ROO.............. 1.50 .45
186 Mario Ramos ROO............. 1.50 .45
187 Corwin Malone ROO .... 1.50 .45
188 Jimmy Gobble ROO .... 1.50 .45
189 Jon Adkins ROO................. 1.50 .45
190 Tim Kalita ROO .... 1.50 .45
191 Nelson Castro ROO............ 1.50 .45
192 Colin Young ROO............... 1.50 .45
193 Luis Martinez ROO............. 1.50 .45
194 Todd Donovan ROO .... 1.50 .45
195 Jeremy Ward ROO .... 1.50 .45
196 Wilson Valdez ROO .... 1.50 .45
197 Hideki Matsui ROO RC......... 5.00 1.50
198 Mitch Wylie ROO .... 1.50 .45
199 Adam Walker ROO .... 1.50 .45
200 Cliff Bartosh ROO.............. 1.50 .45
201 Jeremy Bonderman ROO RC . .50 .15
202 Brandon Webb ROO RC......... .60 .18
203 Adam Loewen ROO RC.......... .60 .18
204 Chien-Ming Wang ROO RC .... .60 .18
205 Hong-Chih Kuo ROO RC .... .50 .15
206 Delmon Young ROO RC .... 2.00 .60
207 Ryan Wagner ROO RC .... .50 .15
208 Dan Haren ROO RC................ .50 .15
209 Rickie Weeks ROO RC .... 1.50 .45
210 Ramon Nivar ROO RC............ .50 .15

2003 Playoff Prestige Autographs

These 10 cards were inserted into the DLP Update Packs. It is interesting to note that although the Rookie Cards were issued in a parallel autograph form for the updates, there were no "parallel" autograph cards issued as part of the regular issue.

MINT NRMT
201 Jeremy Bonderman ROO/100 20.00 9.00
202 Brandon Webb ROO/100.... 25.00 11.00
203 Adam Loewen ROO/100..... 25.00 11.00
204 Chien-Ming Wang ROO/50. 50.00 22.00
205 Hong-Chih Kuo ROO/100... 30.00 13.50
206 Delmon Young ROO/25...................
207 Ryan Wagner ROO/100...... 15.00 6.75
208 Dan Haren ROO/100 .... 20.00 9.00
209 Rickie Weeks ROO/10 ....
210 Ramon Nivar ROO/100 ...... 20.00 9.00

2003 Playoff Prestige Xtra Points Green

Nm-Mt Ex-Mt
*GREEN 1-180: 3X TO 8X BASIC........
1-180 PRINT RUN 150 SERIAL #'d SETS
*GREEN 181-200: 1.25X TO 3X BASIC
*GREEN 201-210: 6X TO 15X BASIC..
181-210 PRINT RUN 50 SERIAL #'d SETS
1-200 RANDOM INSERTS IN RETAIL PACKS
201-210 RANDOM IN DLP R/T PACKS

2003 Playoff Prestige Xtra Points Purple

Nm-Mt Ex-Mt
*PURPLE 1-180: 3X TO 8X BASIC......
1-180 PRINT RUN 150 SERIAL #'d SETS
*PURPLE 181-200: 1.25X TO 3X BASIC
*PURPLE 201-210: 6X TO 15X BASIC
181-200 PRINT RUN 50 SERIAL #'d SETS
RANDOM INSERTS IN RETAIL PACKS

2003 Playoff Prestige Award Winners

Nm-Mt Ex-Mt
RANDOM INSERTS IN PACKS ....
SERIAL NUMBERED TO YEAR OF AWARD
1 Barry Zito CY/2002 .... 3.00 .90
2 Barry Bonds MVP/2001 .... 8.00 2.40
3 Randy Johnson CY/2002......... 3.00 .90
4 Roger Clemens CY/2001 .... 6.00 1.80
5 Ichiro Suzuki MVP/2001 .... 5.00 1.50
6 Chipper Jones MVP/1999 .... 3.00 .90
7 Ken Griffey Jr. MVP/1997 .... 5.00 1.50
8 Miguel Tejada MVP/2002 .... 3.00 .90
9 Greg Maddux CY/1995............ 5.00 1.50
10 Jeff Bagwell MVP/1994........... 3.00 .90
11 Rickey Henderson MVP/1990 3.00 .90
12 Tom Glavine CY/1998 .... 3.00 .90
13 Albert Pujols ROY/2001 .... 6.00 1.80
14 Nomar Garciaparra ROY/1997 5.00 1.50
15 Derek Jeter ROY/1996 .... 8.00 2.40

2003 Playoff Prestige Connections

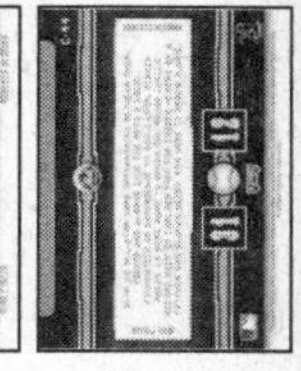

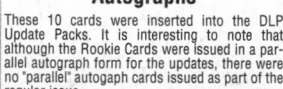

Nm-Mt Ex-Mt
STATED ODDS 1:8 HOBBY/RETAIL .....
*PARALLEL 100: 1.5X TO 4X BASIC ..
PARALLEL 100 RANDOM IN PACKS...
PARALLEL 100 PRINT RUN 100 #'d SETS
1 Troy Glaus............................ 2.00 .60
Garret Anderson
2 Troy Glaus............................ 2.00 .60
Tim Salmon
3 Randy Johnson..................... 2.50 .75
Curt Schilling
4 Matt Williams........................ 2.00 .60
Luis Gonzalez
5 Greg Maddux 4.00 1.20
John Smoltz
6 Andruw Jones....................... 2.50 .75
Chipper Jones
7 Greg Maddux 4.00 1.20
Kevin Millwood
8 Tony Batista .... 2.00 .60
Geronimo Gil
9 Pedro Martinez..................... 4.00 1.20
Nomar Garciaparra
10 Manny Ramirez................... 4.00 1.20
Nomar Garciaparra
11 Nomar Garciaparra.............. 4.00 1.20
Rickey Henderson
12 Trot Nixon .... 2.00 .60
Manny Ramirez
13 Kerry Wood......................... 2.50 .75
Mark Prior

14 Sammy Sosa 4.00 1.20
Fred McGriff
15 Sammy Sosa 4.00 1.20
Corey Patterson
16 Frank Thomas .... 2.50 .75
Magglio Ordonez
17 Joe Borchard .... 2.00 .60
Magglio Ordonez
18 Adam Dunn .... 2.00 .60
Austin Kearns
19 Barry Larkin 4.00 1.20
Ken Griffey Jr.
20 Adam Dunn .... 2.00 .60
Barry Larkin
21 Adam Dunn 4.00 1.20
Ken Griffey Jr.
22 Victor Martinez .... 2.00 .60
Omar Vizquel
23 C.C. Sabathia .... 2.00 .60
Victor Martinez
24 Larry Walker .... 2.00 .60
Todd Helton
25 Carlos Pena .... 2.00 .60
Robert Fick
26 Josh Beckett .... 2.00 .60
Juan Encarnacion
27 Jeff Bagwell .... 2.00 .60
Craig Biggio
28 Lance Berkman .... 2.00 .60
Roy Oswalt
29 Lance Berkman .... 2.00 .60
Jeff Bagwell
30 Mike Sweeney .... 2.00 .60
Carlos Beltran
31 Mike Sweeney .... 2.00 .60
Angel Berroa
32 Kazuhisa Ishii .... 2.00 .60
Shawn Green
33 Adrian Beltre .... 2.00 .60
Shawn Green
34 Kazuhisa Ishii 5.00 1.50
Hideo Nomo
35 Richie Sexson .... 2.00 .60
Ben Sheets
36 Jacque Jones .... 2.00 .60
Torii Hunter
37 Doug Mientkiewicz .... 2.00 .60
David Ortiz
38 Vladimir Guerrero .... 2.50 .75
Jose Vidro
39 Derek Jeter 6.00 1.80
Jason Giambi
40 Derek Jeter 6.00 1.80
Bernie Williams
41 Roger Clemens 5.00 1.50
Mike Mussina
42 Alfonso Soriano .... 2.00 .60
Jorge Posada
43 Derek Jeter 6.00 1.80
Alfonso Soriano
44 Mike Piazza 4.00 1.20
Roberto Alomar
45 Mike Piazza 4.00 1.20
Mo Vaughn
46 Eric Chavez .... 2.00 .60
Miguel Tejada
47 Mark Mulder .... 2.00 .60
Barry Zito
48 Tim Hudson .... 2.00 .60
Barry Zito
49 Pat Burrell .... 2.00 .60
Bobby Abreu
50 Jim Thome .... 2.50 .75
Pat Burrell
51 Jim Thome .... 2.50 .75
Marlon Byrd
52 Brian Giles .... 2.00 .60
Aramis Ramirez
53 Ryan Klesko .... 2.00 .60
Phil Nevin
54 Barry Bonds 6.00 1.80
Benito Santiago
55 Jeff Kent .... 2.00 .60
Rich Aurilia
56 Barry Bonds 6.00 1.80
Jeff Kent
57 Ichiro Suzuki 4.00 1.20
Kazuhiro Sasaki
58 Edgar Martinez .... 2.00 .60
John Olerud
59 Albert Pujols 5.00 1.50
Scott Rolen
60 Jim Edmonds .... 2.00 .60
J.D. Drew
61 Albert Pujols 5.00 1.50
Jim Edmonds
62 Dewon Brazelton .... 2.00 .60
Joe Kennedy
63 Alex Rodriguez 4.00 1.20
Ivan Rodriguez
64 Juan Gonzalez .... 2.00 .60
Rafael Palmeiro
65 Mark Teixeira .... 2.00 .60
Hank Blalock
66 Alex Rodriguez 4.00 1.20
Rafael Palmeiro
67 Alex Rodriguez 4.00 1.20
Juan Gonzalez
68 Shannon Stewart .... 2.00 .60
Carlos Delgado
69 Josh Phelps .... 2.00 .60
Eric Hinske
70 Vernon Wells .... 2.00 .60
Roy Halladay

2003 Playoff Prestige Connections Materials

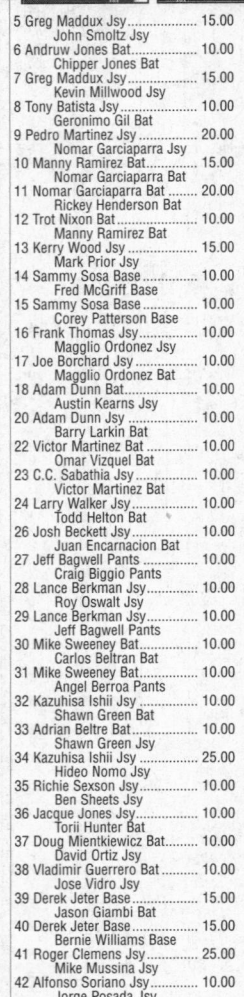

Randomly inserted into packs, this is a parallel to the Connections insert set. These cards feature a game-used memorabilia piece from each player pictured and were issued to a stated print run of 400 serial numbered sets.

Nm-Mt Ex-Mt
1 Troy Glaus Jsy 10.00 3.00
Garret Anderson Bat
2 Troy Glaus Jsy 10.00 3.00
Tim Salmon Bat
4 Matt Williams Jsy 10.00 3.00
Luis Gonzalez Bat

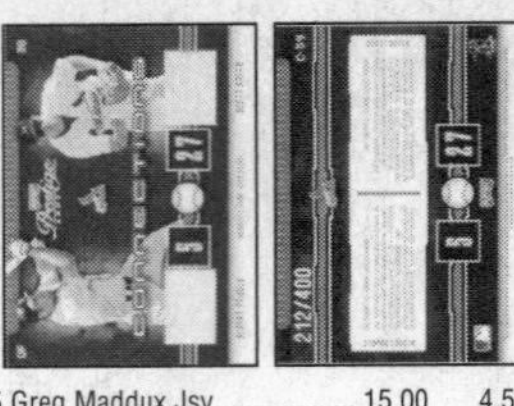

5 Greg Maddux Jsy 15.00 4.50
John Smoltz Jsy
6 Andruw Jones Bat 10.00 3.00
Chipper Jones Bat
7 Greg Maddux Jsy 15.00 4.50
Kevin Millwood Jsy
8 Tony Batista Jsy 10.00 3.00
Geronimo Gil Bat
9 Pedro Martinez Jsy 20.00 6.00
Nomar Garciaparra Jsy
10 Manny Ramirez Bat 15.00 4.50
Nomar Garciaparra Bat
11 Nomar Garciaparra Bat 20.00 6.00
Rickey Henderson Bat
12 Trot Nixon Bat 10.00 3.00
Manny Ramirez Bat
13 Kerry Wood Jsy 15.00 4.50
Mark Prior Jsy
14 Sammy Sosa Base 10.00 3.00
Fred McGriff Base
15 Sammy Sosa Base 10.00 3.00
Corey Patterson Base
16 Frank Thomas Jsy 10.00 3.00
Magglio Ordonez Jsy
17 Joe Borchard Jsy 10.00 3.00
Magglio Ordonez Bat
18 Adam Dunn Bat 10.00 3.00
Austin Kearns Jsy
20 Adam Dunn Jsy 10.00 3.00
Barry Larkin Bat
22 Victor Martinez Bat 10.00 3.00
Omar Vizquel Bat
23 C.C. Sabathia Jsy 10.00 3.00
Victor Martinez Bat
24 Larry Walker Jsy 10.00 3.00
Todd Helton Bat
26 Josh Beckett Jsy 10.00 3.00
Juan Encarnacion Bat
27 Jeff Bagwell Pants 10.00 3.00
Craig Biggio Pants
28 Lance Berkman Jsy 10.00 3.00
Roy Oswalt Jsy
29 Lance Berkman Jsy 10.00 3.00
Jeff Bagwell Pants
30 Mike Sweeney Bat 10.00 3.00
Carlos Beltran Bat
31 Mike Sweeney Bat 10.00 3.00
Angel Berroa Pants
32 Kazuhisa Ishii Jsy 10.00 3.00
Shawn Green Bat
33 Adrian Beltre Bat 10.00 3.00
Shawn Green Jsy
34 Kazuhisa Ishii Jsy 25.00 7.50
Hideo Nomo Jsy
35 Richie Sexson Jsy 10.00 3.00
Ben Sheets Jsy
36 Jacque Jones Jsy 10.00 3.00
Torii Hunter Bat
37 Doug Mientkiewicz Bat 10.00 3.00
David Ortiz Jsy
38 Vladimir Guerrero Bat 10.00 3.00
Jose Vidro Jsy
39 Derek Jeter Base 15.00 4.50
Jason Giambi Bat
40 Derek Jeter Base 15.00 4.50
Bernie Williams Base
41 Roger Clemens Jsy 25.00 7.50
Mike Mussina Jsy
42 Alfonso Soriano Jsy 10.00 3.00
Jorge Posada Jsy
43 Derek Jeter Base 25.00 7.50
Alfonso Soriano Base
44 Mike Piazza Bat 15.00 4.50
Roberto Alomar Jsy
45 Mike Piazza Bat 15.00 4.50
Mo Vaughn Bat
46 Eric Chavez Jsy 10.00 3.00
Miguel Tejada Jsy
47 Mark Mulder Jsy 10.00 3.00
Barry Zito Jsy
48 Tim Hudson Jsy 10.00 3.00
Barry Zito Jsy
49 Pat Burrell Bat 10.00 3.00
Bobby Abreu Bat
50 Jim Thome Bat 10.00 3.00
Pat Burrell Bat
51 Jim Thome Bat 10.00 3.00
Marlon Byrd Jsy
52 Brian Giles Bat 10.00 3.00
Aramis Ramirez Jsy
53 Ryan Klesko Jsy 10.00 3.00
Phil Nevin Jsy
54 Barry Bonds Base 15.00 4.50
Benito Santiago Base
55 Jeff Kent Jsy 10.00 3.00
Rich Aurilia Jsy
56 Barry Bonds Base 15.00 4.50
Jeff Kent Base
57 Ichiro Suzuki Base 25.00 7.50
Kazuhiro Sasaki Base
58 Edgar Martinez Bat 10.00 3.00
John Olerud Jsy
59 Albert Pujols Base 15.00 4.50
Scott Rolen Base
60 Jim Edmonds Bat 10.00 3.00
J.D. Drew Jsy
61 Albert Pujols Base 15.00 4.50
Jim Edmonds Base
62 Dewon Brazelton Jsy 10.00 3.00
Joe Kennedy Jsy
63 Alex Rodriguez Jsy 15.00 4.50
Ivan Rodriguez Bat
64 Juan Gonzalez Pants 10.00 3.00
Rafael Palmeiro Pants
65 Mark Teixeira Bat 10.00 3.00
Hank Blalock Bat
66 Alex Rodriguez Jsy 15.00 4.50
Rafael Palmeiro Pants
67 Alex Rodriguez Bat 15.00 4.50
Juan Gonzalez Pants
68 Shannon Stewart Bat 10.00 3.00
Carlos Delgado Jsy
69 Josh Phelps Bat 10.00 3.00
Eric Hinske Bat
70 Vernon Wells Jsy 10.00 3.00
Roy Halladay Jsy

2003 Playoff Prestige Diamond Heritage

Nm-Mt Ex-Mt
STATED ODDS 1:21 HOBBY, 1:43 RETAIL
*GOLDEN: 1.25X TO 3X BASIC
GOLDEN RANDOM INSERTS IN PACKS
GOLDEN PRINT RUN 50 SERIAL #'d SETS
1 Larry Walker 4.00 1.20
2 Troy Glaus 4.00 1.20
3 Magglio Ordonez 4.00 1.20
4 Roy Oswalt 4.00 1.20
5 Barry Zito 4.00 1.20
6 Nomar Garciaparra 6.00 1.80
7 Kerry Wood 4.00 1.20
8 Roger Clemens 8.00 2.40
9 Pedro Martinez 4.00 1.20
10 Mark Prior 4.00 1.20
11 Sammy Sosa 6.00 1.80
12 Randy Johnson 4.00 1.20
13 Greg Maddux 6.00 1.80
14 Manny Ramirez 4.00 1.20
15 Torii Hunter 4.00 1.20
16 Alex Rodriguez 6.00 1.80
17 Mike Piazza 6.00 1.80
18 Vladimir Guerrero 4.00 1.20
19 Ivan Rodriguez 4.00 1.20
20 Lance Berkman 4.00 1.20
21 Miguel Tejada 4.00 1.20
22 Chipper Jones 4.00 1.20
23 Todd Helton 4.00 1.20
24 Shawn Green 4.00 1.20
25 Scott Rolen 4.00 1.20
26 Adam Dunn 4.00 1.20
27 Jim Thome 4.00 1.20
28 Rafael Palmeiro 4.00 1.20
29 Eric Chavez 4.00 1.20
30 Andruw Jones 4.00 1.20

2003 Playoff Prestige Diamond Heritage Material

Randomly inserted into packs, this is a parallel of the Diamond Heritage insert set. These cards were issued to a stated print run of 200 serial numbered sets for the jersey cards and 100 serial numbered sets for the bat cards.

Nm-Mt Ex-Mt
*MULTI-COLOR PATCH 1-15: 1X TO 1.5X HI
1 Larry Walker Jsy 10.00 3.00
2 Troy Glaus Jsy 8.00 2.40
3 Magglio Ordonez Jsy 8.00 2.40
4 Roy Oswalt Jsy 8.00 2.40
5 Barry Zito Jsy 8.00 2.40
6 Nomar Garciaparra Jsy 15.00 4.50
7 Kerry Wood Jsy 10.00 3.00
8 Roger Clemens Jsy 20.00 6.00
9 Pedro Martinez Jsy 10.00 3.00
10 Mark Prior Jsy 10.00 3.00
11 Sammy Sosa Jsy 15.00 4.50
12 Randy Johnson Jsy 10.00 3.00
13 Greg Maddux Jsy 15.00 4.50
14 Manny Ramirez Jsy 10.00 3.00
15 Torii Hunter Jsy 8.00 2.40
16 Alex Rodriguez Bat 20.00 6.00
17 Mike Piazza Bat 15.00 4.50
18 Vladimir Guerrero Bat 15.00 4.50
19 Ivan Rodriguez Bat 15.00 4.50
20 Lance Berkman Bat 10.00 3.00
21 Miguel Tejada Bat 10.00 3.00
22 Chipper Jones Bat 15.00 4.50
23 Todd Helton Bat 15.00 4.50
24 Shawn Green Bat 10.00 3.00
25 Scott Rolen Bat 15.00 4.50
26 Adam Dunn Bat 15.00 4.50
27 Jim Thome Bat 15.00 4.50
28 Rafael Palmeiro Bat 15.00 4.50
29 Eric Chavez Bat 10.00 3.00
30 Andruw Jones Bat 10.00 3.00

2003 Playoff Prestige Diamond Heritage Material Autographs

Randomly inserted into packs, this is a partial parallel to the Heritage Material insert set. These 10 cards feature not only a memorabilia piece but also an authentic signature from the player. Please note that since no card was issued to a stated print run of more than 25 cards, there is no pricing for this set.

Nm-Mt Ex-Mt
2 Troy Glaus Jsy/15 ....
3 Magglio Ordonez Jsy/25 ....

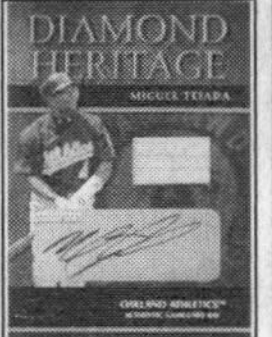

7 Kerry Wood Jsy/15 ....
15 Torii Hunter Jsy/25 ....
20 Lance Berkman Bat/15 ....
21 Miguel Tejada Bat/25 ....
25 Scott Rolen Bat/15 ....
26 Adam Dunn Bat/25 ....
27 Jim Thome Bat/25 ....
29 Eric Chavez Bat/25 ....

2003 Playoff Prestige Draft Class Reunion

Nm-Mt Ex-Mt
STATED ODDS 1:24 HOBBY, 1:42 RETAIL
1 Mike Piazza 5.00 1.50
John Olerud
2 Derek Jeter 8.00 2.40
Shannon Stewart
3 Alex Rodriguez 5.00 1.50
Torii Hunter
4 Nomar Garciaparra 5.00 1.50
Paul Konerko
5 Kerry Wood .... 3.00 .90
Todd Helton
6 Eric Chavez .... 3.00 .90
Billy Koch
7 Lance Berkman .... 3.00 .90
Troy Glaus
8 Pat Burrell .... 3.00 .90
Mark Mulder
9 Barry Zito .... 3.00 .90
Jason Jennings
10 Mark Prior .... 3.00 .90
Mark Teixeira

2003 Playoff Prestige Infield/Outfield Tandems Materials

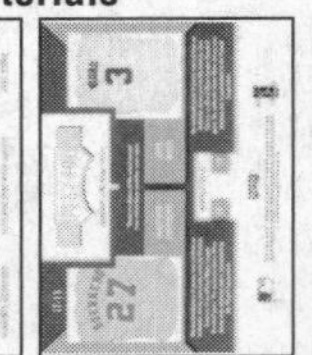

Randomly inserted into packs, these cards feature an outfielder and infielder from the same team along with a game-used memorabilia piece from each player. These cards were issued to a stated print run of 100 serial numbered sets.

Nm-Mt Ex-Mt
1 Troy Glaus Jsy 10.00 3.00
Garret Anderson Bat
2 Mark Grace Bat 15.00 4.50
Luis Gonzalez Jsy
3 Nomar Garciaparra Jsy 25.00 7.50
Manny Ramirez Jsy
4 Alfonso Soriano Jsy 15.00 4.50
Bernie Williams Jsy
5 Jeff Bagwell Jsy 15.00 4.50
Lance Berkman Jsy
6 Alex Rodriguez Jsy 25.00 7.50
Juan Gonzalez Jsy
7 Barry Larkin Jsy 15.00 4.50
Adam Dunn Jsy
8 Scott Rolen Bat 25.00 7.50
Jim Edmonds Jsy
9 Todd Helton Jsy 15.00 4.50
Larry Walker Jsy
10 Adrian Beltre Jsy 15.00 4.50
Shawn Green Jsy
11 Jose Vidro Jsy 15.00 4.50
Vladimir Guerrero Jsy
12 Mike Sweeney Jsy 15.00 4.50
Carlos Beltran Jsy
13 Josh Phelps Jsy 10.00 3.00
Vernon Wells Jsy
14 Paul Konerko Jsy 10.00 3.00
Magglio Ordonez Jsy
15 Phil Nevin Jsy 10.00 3.00
Ryan Klesko Jsy

2003 Playoff Prestige Inside the Numbers

Nm-Mt Ex-Mt
STATED PRINT RUN 2002 SERIAL #'d SETS
*DIE CUT p/r 45-75: 2X TO 5X BASIC
*DIE CUT p/r 27-38: 2.5X TO 6X BASIC
DIE CUT PRINT RUN BASED ON UNIFORM
NO DIE CUT PRICING ON QTY OF 25 OR LESS
RANDOM INSERTS IN PACKS ....
1 Roger Clemens 6.00 1.80
2 Greg Maddux 5.00 1.50
3 Miguel Tejada .... 3.00 .90
4 Alex Rodriguez 5.00 1.50
5 Ichiro Suzuki 5.00 1.50
6 Sammy Sosa 5.00 1.50
7 Jim Thome .... 3.00 .90
8 Derek Jeter 8.00 2.40
9 Randy Johnson .... 3.00 .90
10 Barry Zito .... 3.00 .90
11 Jason Giambi .... 3.00 .90
12 Shawn Green .... 3.00 .90
13 Curt Schilling .... 3.00 .90
14 Albert Pujols 6.00 1.80
15 Vladimir Guerrero .... 3.00 .90
16 Pedro Martinez .... 3.00 .90
17 Alfonso Soriano .... 3.00 .90
18 Barry Bonds 8.00 2.40
19 Magglio Ordonez .... 3.00 .90
20 Chipper Jones .... 3.00 .90
21 Pat Burrell .... 3.00 .90
22 Luis Gonzalez .... 3.00 .90
23 Jeff Bagwell .... 3.00 .90
24 Garret Anderson .... 3.00 .90
25 Larry Walker .... 3.00 .90

2003 Playoff Prestige League Leaders

Nm-Mt Ex-Mt
RANDOM INSERTS IN PACKS ....
STATED PRINT RUN 2002 SERIAL #'d SETS
1 Manny Ramirez AVG .... 3.00 .90
2 Sammy Sosa HR 5.00 1.50
3 Alex Rodriguez RBI 5.00 1.50
4 Alfonso Soriano Runs .... 3.00 .90
5 Vladimir Guerrero Hits .... 3.00 .90
6 Nomar Garciaparra 2B 5.00 1.50
7 Johnny Damon 3B .... 3.00 .90
8 Alfonso Soriano SB .... 3.00 .90
9 Barry Bonds Walks 8.00 2.40
10 Barry Zito Wins .... 3.00 .90
11 Pedro Martinez ERA .... 3.00 .90
12 John Smoltz SV .... 3.00 .90
13 Randy Johnson CG .... 3.00 .90
14 Lance Berkman RBI .... 3.00 .90
15 Randy Johnson SO .... 3.00 .90

2003 Playoff Prestige League Leaders Materials

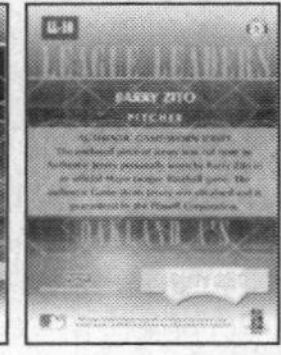

Nm-Mt Ex-Mt
RANDOM INSERTS IN PACKS ....
STATED PRINT RUN 250 SERIAL #'d SETS
1 Manny Ramirez AVG Jsy 10.00 3.00
2 Sammy Sosa HR Base 10.00 3.00
3 Alex Rodriguez RBI Jsy 15.00 4.50
4 Alfonso Soriano Runs Jsy 10.00 3.00
5 Vladimir Guerrero Hits Jsy 10.00 3.00
6 Nomar Garciaparra 2B Jsy 20.00 6.00
7 Johnny Damon 3B Bat 10.00 3.00
8 Alfonso Soriano SB Jsy 10.00 3.00
9 Barry Bonds Walks Base 15.00 4.50
10 Barry Zito Wins Jsy 8.00 2.40
11 Pedro Martinez ERA Jsy 10.00 3.00
12 John Smoltz SV Jsy 10.00 3.00
13 Randy Johnson CG Jsy 10.00 3.00
14 Lance Berkman RBI Jsy 8.00 2.40
15 Randy Johnson SO Jsy 10.00 3.00

2003 Playoff Prestige Patches of MLB

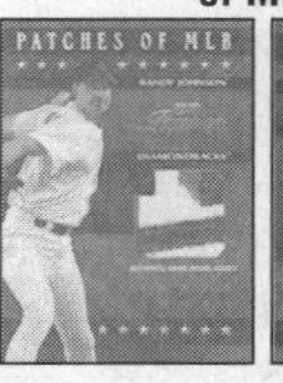

Randomly inserted into packs, these 20 cards feature patch pieces from the game-used jerseys used in this product. These cards were issued to a stated print run of 25 serial numbered sets and no pricing is available due to market scarcity.

Nm-Mt Ex-Mt
1 Roger Clemens ....
2 Randy Johnson ....
3 Sammy Sosa ....
4 Vladimir Guerrero ....

5 Lance Berkman
6 Alfonso Soriano
7 Alex Rodriguez
8 Roberto Alomar
9 Miguel Tejada
10 Pedro Martinez
11 Greg Maddux
12 Barry Zito
13 Magglio Ordonez
14 Chipper Jones
15 Manny Ramirez
16 Troy Glaus
17 Pat Burrell
18 Roy Oswalt
19 Mike Piazza
20 Nomar Garciaparra

2003 Playoff Prestige Patches of MLB Autographs

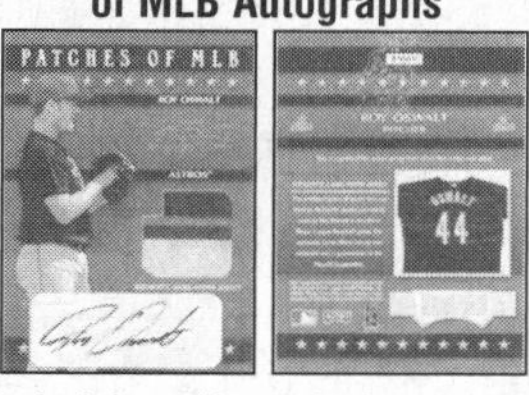

Randomly inserted into packs, these cards feature not only a game-used patch piece but also an authentic autograph from the featured player. Please note that since no card was issued to a stated print run of more than 10 copies, there is no pricing due to market scarcity.

Card	Nm-Mt	Ex-Mt
1 Roger Clemens/5		
4 Vladimir Guerrero/5		
5 Lance Berkman/10		
6 Alfonso Soriano/5		
7 Alex Rodriguez/5		
9 Miguel Tejada/10		
10 Pedro Martinez/5		
11 Greg Maddux/5		
12 Barry Zito/10		
13 Magglio Ordonez/10		
14 Chipper Jones/5		
16 Troy Glaus/5		
17 Pat Burrell/5		
18 Roy Oswalt/10		

2003 Playoff Prestige Player Collection

Randomly inserted into packs, these 100 cards feature leading players as well as various memorabilia pieces. Each of these cards was issued to a stated print run of 325 serial numbered sets. It is believed that this design on card style was used on more than one product issued by Playoff/Donruss during 2003 but each card was easily identifiable from what product it was pulled from.

Card	Nm-Mt	Ex-Mt
*MULTI-COLOR PATCH: 1.25X TO 3X HI		
1 Roberto Alomar Bat	10.00	3.00
2 Jeff Bagwell Bat	10.00	3.00
3 Jeff Bagwell Jsy	10.00	3.00
4 Jeff Bagwell Pants	10.00	3.00
5 Jay Bell Jsy	8.00	2.40
6 Adrian Beltre Jsy	10.00	3.00
7 Lance Berkman Jsy	8.00	2.40
8 Craig Biggio Bat	10.00	3.00
9 Craig Biggio Jsy	10.00	3.00
10 Bret Boone Jsy	8.00	2.40
11 Joe Borchard Jsy	8.00	2.40
12 Kevin Brown Jsy	8.00	2.40
13 Jeromy Burnitz Jsy	8.00	2.40
14 Pat Burrell Bat	8.00	2.40
15 Marlon Byrd Bat	8.00	2.40
16 Marlon Byrd Jsy	8.00	2.40
17 Roger Clemens Stand Jsy	15.00	4.50
18 Roger Clemens Throw Jsy	15.00	4.50
19 Doug Davis Jsy	8.00	2.40
20 Carlos Delgado Jsy	8.00	2.40
21 J.D. Drew Jsy	8.00	2.40
22 Adam Dunn Jsy	10.00	3.00
23 Jim Edmonds Jsy	8.00	2.40
24 Steve Finley Jsy	8.00	2.40
25 Freddy Garcia Jsy	8.00	2.40
26 Nomar Garciaparra Jsy	15.00	4.50
27 Jason Giambi Bat	8.00	2.40
28 Jason Giambi Jsy	8.00	2.40
29 Troy Glaus Jsy	8.00	2.40
30 Juan Gonzalez Bat	10.00	3.00
31 Juan Gonzalez Jsy	10.00	3.00
32 Luis Gonzalez Bat	8.00	2.40
33 Shawn Green Jsy	8.00	2.40
34 Ben Grieve Jsy	8.00	2.40
35 Vladimir Guerrero Jsy	10.00	3.00
36 Tony Gwynn Jsy	10.00	3.00
37 Toby Hall Jsy	8.00	2.40
38 Wes Helms Jsy	8.00	2.40
39 Todd Helton Bat	10.00	3.00
40 Todd Helton Jsy	10.00	3.00
41 Rickey Henderson Bat	10.00	3.00
42 Rickey Henderson Jsy	10.00	3.00
43 Rickey Henderson Pants	10.00	3.00
44 Tim Hudson Jsy	8.00	2.40
45 Jason Jennings Jsy	8.00	2.40
46 Andruw Jones Bat	8.00	2.40
47 Andruw Jones Jsy	8.00	2.40
48 Chipper Jones Jsy	10.00	3.00
49 Ryan Klesko Jsy	8.00	2.40
50 Paul Konerko Jsy	8.00	2.40
51 Barry Larkin Bat	10.00	3.00
52 Barry Larkin Jsy	10.00	3.00
53 Travis Lee Jsy	8.00	2.40
54 Paul Lo Duca Jsy	8.00	2.40
55 Terrence Long Jsy	8.00	2.40
56 Pedro Martinez Jsy	10.00	3.00
57 Joe Mays Jsy	8.00	2.40
58 Mark Mulder Jsy	8.00	2.40
59 John Olerud Jsy	8.00	2.40
60 Magglio Ordonez Bat	8.00	2.40
61 Magglio Ordonez Jsy	8.00	2.40
62 Roy Oswalt Jsy	8.00	2.40
63 Rafael Palmeiro Pants	10.00	3.00
64 Chan Ho Park Jsy	8.00	2.40
65 Jay Payton Jsy	8.00	2.40
66 Robert Person Jsy	8.00	2.40
67 Andy Pettitte Jsy	10.00	3.00
68 Mike Piazza Bat	10.00	3.00
69 Mike Piazza Jsy	10.00	3.00
70 Mark Prior Bat	10.00	3.00
71 Mark Prior Jsy	10.00	3.00
72 Manny Ramirez Bat	10.00	3.00
73 Manny Ramirez Jsy	10.00	3.00
74 Cal Ripken Jsy	40.00	12.00
75 Alex Rodriguez Bat	10.00	3.00
76 Alex Rodriguez M's Jsy	10.00	3.00
77 Alex Rodriguez Rgr Jsy	10.00	3.00
78 Ivan Rodriguez Bat	10.00	3.00
79 Ivan Rodriguez Jsy	10.00	3.00
80 C.C. Sabathia Jsy	8.00	2.40
81 Reggie Sanders Jsy	8.00	2.40
82 Kazuhiro Sasaki Jsy	8.00	2.40
83 Curt Schilling Jsy	8.00	2.40
84 Richie Sexson Jsy	8.00	2.40
85 Tsuyoshi Shinjo Jsy	8.00	2.40
86 Alfonso Soriano Bat	10.00	3.00
87 Alfonso Soriano Jsy	10.00	3.00
88 Sammy Sosa Jsy	15.00	4.50
89 Miguel Tejada Jsy	8.00	2.40
90 Frank Thomas Jsy	10.00	3.00
91 Jim Thome Jsy	10.00	3.00
92 Larry Walker Bat	10.00	3.00
93 Larry Walker Jsy	10.00	3.00
94 David Wells Jsy	8.00	2.40
95 Vernon Wells Jsy	8.00	2.40
96 Bernie Williams Jsy	10.00	3.00
97 Matt Williams Jsy	8.00	2.40
98 Preston Wilson Jsy	8.00	2.40
99 Kerry Wood Jsy	10.00	3.00
100 Barry Zito Jsy	8.00	2.40

2003 Playoff Prestige Signature Impressions

Randomly inserted into packs, these 50 cards feature authentic autographs from the player pictured on the card. These cards were printed to varying quantities and we have notated that information next to the player's name in our checklist.

Card	Nm-Mt	Ex-Mt
1 A.J. Pierzynski/50	25.00	7.50
2 Adam Dunn/25		
3 Barry Zito/25		
4 Bobby Abreu/20		
5 Brandon Phillips/25		
6 Chipper Jones/5		
7 Don Mattingly/15		
8 Edgar Martinez/25		
9 Eric Hinske/25		
10 Greg Maddux/5		
11 Joe Borchard/25		
12 John Candelaria/50		
13 Jose Canseco/10		
14 Kerry Wood/5		
15 Kevin Mench/25		
16 Lance Berkman/25		
17 Magglio Ordonez/5		
18 Miguel Tejada/25		
19 Nolan Ryan/5		
20 Rafael Palmeiro/5		
21 Roberto Alomar/5		
22 Roy Oswalt/25		
23 Bobby Doerr/25		
24 Scott Rolen/5		
25 Tim Hudson/15		
26 Will Clark/10		
27 Yogi Berra/15		
28 Joe Kennedy/50	15.00	4.50
29 Johnny Bench/10		
30 Lenny Dykstra/50	25.00	7.50
31 Mark Mulder/5		
32 Mark Prior/25		
33 Mike Schmidt/5		
34 Ozzie Smith/5		
35 Paul Lo Duca/25		
36 Reggie Jackson/5		
37 Roger Clemens/5		
38 Steve Garvey/25		
39 Toby Hall/50	15.00	4.50
40 Victor Martinez/25		
41 Vladimir Guerrero/5		
42 Adrian Beltre/15		
43 Al Kaline/15		
44 Albert Pujols/15		
45 Barry Larkin/15		
46 Brian Giles/15		
47 C.C. Sabathia/15		
48 Dale Murphy/15		
49 George Brett/5		
50 Jeremy Bonderman/100	20.00	6.00

2003 Playoff Prestige Stars of MLB Jersey

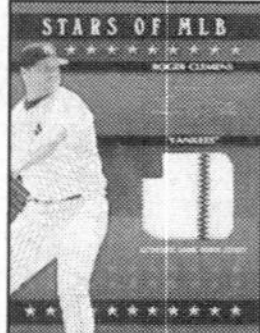

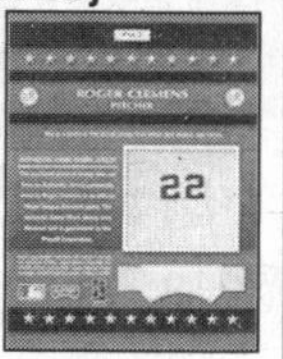

Randomly inserted into packs, these 20 cards feature game-used jersey swatches of the featured players. Each of these cards were issued to a stated print run of 150 serial numbered sets.

Card	Nm-Mt	Ex-Mt
1 Roger Clemens	20.00	6.00
2 Randy Johnson	10.00	3.00
3 Sammy Sosa	20.00	6.00
4 Vladimir Guerrero	10.00	3.00
5 Lance Berkman	8.00	2.40
6 Alfonso Soriano	10.00	3.00
7 Alex Rodriguez	15.00	4.50
8 Roberto Alomar	10.00	3.00
9 Miguel Tejada	8.00	2.40
10 Pedro Martinez	10.00	3.00
11 Greg Maddux	15.00	4.50
12 Barry Zito	8.00	2.40
13 Magglio Ordonez	8.00	2.40
14 Chipper Jones	10.00	3.00
15 Manny Ramirez	10.00	3.00
16 Troy Glaus	8.00	2.40
17 Pat Burrell	8.00	2.40
18 Roy Oswalt	8.00	2.40
19 Mike Piazza	15.00	4.50
20 Nomar Garciaparra	20.00	6.00

2003 Playoff Prestige Stars of MLB Jersey Autographs

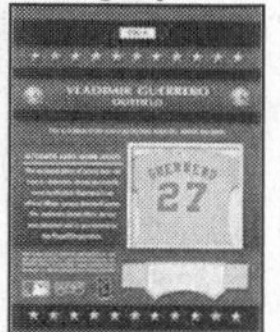

Randomly inserted into packs, these eight cards feature not only game-used jersey swatches but authentic autographs from the player. Each of these cards were issued to a stated print run of 25 serial numbered sets and no pricing is available due to market scarcity.

Card	Nm-Mt	Ex-Mt
4 Vladimir Guerrero		
5 Lance Berkman		
9 Miguel Tejada		
12 Barry Zito		
13 Magglio Ordonez		
14 Chipper Jones		
16 Troy Glaus		
18 Roy Oswalt		

2004 Playoff Prestige

This 200 card set was released in March, 2004. The set was issued in six card packs with an $3 SRP which came 24 packs to a box and 12 boxes to a case. Interspersed into this set are various prospect cards which were printed to the same quantity as the other cards.

Card	Nm-Mt	Ex-Mt
COMPLETE SET (200)	40.00	12.00
1 Bengie Molina	.40	.12
2 Garret Anderson	.40	.12
3 Jarrod Washburn	.40	.12
4 Scott Spiezio	.40	.12
5 Tim Salmon	.60	.18
6 Troy Glaus	.40	.12
7 Alex Cintron	.40	.12
8 Brandon Webb	.40	.12
9 Curt Schilling	.40	.12
10 Edgar Gonzalez PROS	.50	.15
11 Luis Gonzalez	.40	.12
12 Randy Johnson	1.00	.30
13 Steve Finley	.40	.12
14 Andruw Jones	.40	.12
15 Bubba Nelson PROS	.50	.15
16 Chipper Jones	1.00	.30
17 Gary Sheffield	.40	.12
18 Greg Maddux	1.50	.45
19 Javy Lopez	.40	.12
20 John Smoltz	.60	.18
21 Marcus Giles	.40	.12
22 Rafael Furcal	.40	.12
23 Brian Roberts	.40	.12
24 Jason Johnson	.40	.12
25 Jay Gibbons	.40	.12
26 Luis Matos	.40	.12
27 Melvin Mora	.40	.12
28 Tony Batista	.40	.12
29 Bill Mueller	.40	.12
30 David Ortiz	1.00	.30
31 Johnny Damon	1.00	.30
32 Kevin Youkilis PROS	.50	.15
33 Manny Ramirez	.60	.18
34 Nomar Garciaparra	1.50	.45
35 Pedro Martinez	1.00	.30
36 Trot Nixon	.40	.12
37 Aramis Ramirez	.40	.12
38 Brendan Harris PROS	.50	.15
39 Carlos Zambrano	.40	.12
40 Corey Patterson	.40	.12
41 Kenny Lofton	.40	.12
42 Kerry Wood	1.00	.30
43 Mark Prior	1.00	.30
44 Sammy Sosa	1.50	.45
45 Bartolo Colon	.40	.12
46 Carlos Lee	.40	.12
47 Esteban Loaiza	.40	.12
48 Frank Thomas	1.00	.30
49 Joe Crede	.40	.12
50 Magglio Ordonez	.40	.12
51 Roberto Alomar	.60	.18
52 Adam Dunn	.60	.18
53 Austin Kearns	.40	.12
54 Josh Hall	.40	.12
55 Ken Griffey Jr.	1.50	.45
56 Sean Casey	.40	.12
57 Mike Nakamura	.40	.12
58 C.C. Sabathia	.40	.12
59 Casey Blake	.40	.12
60 Jody Gerut	.40	.12
61 Matt Lawton	.40	.12
62 Milton Bradley	.40	.12
63 Omar Vizquel	.60	.18
64 Jason Jennings	.40	.12
65 Jay Payton	.40	.12
66 Larry Walker	.60	.18
67 Preston Wilson	.40	.12
68 Todd Helton	.60	.18
69 Bobby Higginson	.40	.12
70 Carlos Pena	.40	.12
71 Dmitri Young	.40	.12
72 Jeremy Bonderman	.40	.12
73 Preston Larrison PROS	.50	.15
74 Derrek Lee	.40	.12
75 Dontrelle Willis	.40	.12
76 Ivan Rodriguez	1.00	.30
77 Josh Beckett	.40	.12
78 Juan Pierre	.40	.12
79 Miguel Cabrera	.60	.18
80 Mike Lowell	.40	.12
81 Chris Burke PROS	.50	.15
82 Craig Biggio	.60	.18
83 Jeff Bagwell	.60	.18
84 Jeff Kent	.40	.12
85 Lance Berkman	.40	.12
86 Richard Hidalgo	.40	.12
87 Roy Oswalt	.40	.12
88 Aaron Guiel	.40	.12
89 Angel Berroa	.40	.12
90 Carlos Beltran	.60	.18
91 Jeremy Affeldt	.40	.12
92 Mike Sweeney	.40	.12
93 Runelvys Hernandez	.40	.12
94 Dave Roberts	.40	.12
95 Eric Gagne	1.00	.30
96 Hideo Nomo	1.00	.30
97 Kevin Brown	.40	.12
98 Paul Lo Duca	.40	.12
99 Shawn Green	.40	.12
100 Ben Sheets	.40	.12
101 Geoff Jenkins	.40	.12
102 Richie Sexson	.40	.12
103 Rickie Weeks PROS	.50	.15
104 Scott Podsednik	.40	.12
105 J.D. Durbin PROS	.50	.15
106 Jacque Jones	.40	.12
107 Jason Kubel PROS	.50	.15
108 Shannon Stewart	.40	.12
109 Torii Hunter	.40	.12
110 Chad Cordero PROS	.50	.15
111 Javier Vazquez	.40	.12
112 Jose Vidro	.40	.12
113 Livan Hernandez	.40	.12
114 Orlando Cabrera	.40	.12
115 Tony Armas Jr.	.40	.12
116 Vladimir Guerrero	1.00	.30
117 Al Leiter	.40	.12
118 Cliff Floyd	.40	.12
119 Jae Weong Seo	.40	.12
120 Jose Reyes	.40	.12
121 Mike Piazza	1.50	.45
122 Tom Glavine	.60	.18
123 Aaron Boone	.40	.12
124 Alfonso Soriano	.60	.18
125 Andy Pettitte	.60	.18
126 Derek Jeter	2.00	.60
127 Hideki Matsui	1.50	.45
128 Jason Giambi	.40	.12
129 Jorge Posada	.60	.18
130 Jose Contreras	.40	.12
131 Mike Mussina	.60	.18
132 Barry Zito	.40	.12
133 Eric Byrnes	.40	.12
134 Eric Chavez	.40	.12
135 Jose Guillen	.40	.12
136 Mark Mulder	.40	.12
137 Miguel Tejada	.40	.12
138 Ramon Hernandez	.40	.12
139 Rich Harden	.40	.12
140 Tim Hudson	.40	.12
141 Bobby Abreu	.40	.12
142 Brett Myers	.40	.12
143 Jim Thome	1.00	.30
144 Kevin Millwood	.40	.12
145 Mike Lieberthal	.40	.12
146 Ryan Howard PROS	.50	.15
147 Craig Wilson	.40	.12
148 Jack Wilson	.40	.12
149 Jason Kendall	.40	.12
150 Kip Wells	.40	.12
151 Reggie Sanders	.40	.12
152 Albert Pujols	2.00	.60
153 Edgar Renteria	.40	.12
154 Jim Edmonds	.40	.12
155 Matt Morris	.40	.12
156 Scott Rolen	1.00	.30
157 Tino Martinez	.60	.18
158 Woody Williams	.40	.12
159 Brian Giles	.40	.12
160 Freddy Guzman PROS RC	.50	.15
161 Jake Peavy	.40	.12
162 Khalil Greene PROS	.75	.23
163 Phil Nevin	.40	.12
164 Ryan Klesko	.40	.12
165 Ray Durham	.40	.12
166 Jason Schmidt	.40	.12
167 Jerome Williams PROS	.50	.15
168 Jesse Foppert	.40	.12
169 Jose Cruz Jr.	.40	.12
170 Marquis Grissom	.40	.12
171 Merkin Valdez PROS RC	1.00	.30
172 Rich Aurilia	.40	.12
173 Bret Boone	.40	.12
174 Freddy Garcia	.40	.12
175 Ichiro Suzuki	1.50	.45
176 Jamie Moyer	.40	.12
177 John Olerud	.40	.12
178 Mike Cameron	.40	.12
179 Randy Winn	.40	.12
180 Aubrey Huff	.40	.12
181 Carl Crawford	.40	.12
182 Chad Gaudin PROS	.50	.15
183 Rocco Baldelli	.40	.12
184 Toby Hall	.40	.12
185 Travis Lee	.40	.12
186 Alex Rodriguez	1.50	.45
187 Hank Blalock	.40	.12
188 John Thomson	.40	.12
189 Juan Gonzalez	.60	.18
190 Mark Teixeira	.40	.12
191 Michael Young	.40	.12
192 Rafael Palmeiro	.60	.18
193 Ramon Nivar PROS	.50	.15
194 Carlos Delgado	.40	.12
195 Dustin McGowan PROS	.50	.15
196 Frank Catalanotto	.40	.12
197 Vinny Chulk	.40	.12
198 Orlando Hudson	.40	.12
199 Roy Halladay	.40	.12
200 Vernon Wells	.40	.12

2004 Playoff Prestige Autographs

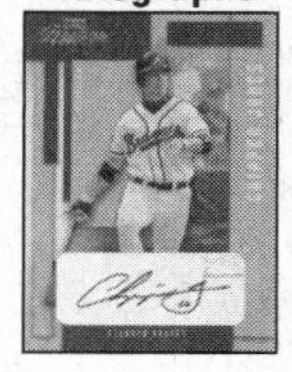

Card	Nm-Mt	Ex-Mt
RANDOM INSERTS IN PACKS		
PRINT RUNS B/WN 4-500 COPIES PER		
PRINT RUNS PROVIDED BY DONRUSS		
CARDS ARE NOT SERIAL-NUMBERED		
SEE BECKETT.COM OPG FOR PRINT RUNS		
NO PRICING ON QTY OF 25 OR LESS		
8 Brandon Webb/100	10.00	3.00
10 Edgar Gonzalez PROS/150	10.00	3.00
15 Bubba Nelson PROS/250	10.00	3.00
25 Jay Gibbons/50	12.00	3.60
32 Kevin Youkilis PROS/100	15.00	4.50
38 Brendan Harris PROS/400	10.00	3.00
57 Mike Nakamura/250	10.00	3.00
60 Jody Gerut/50	20.00	6.00
73 Preston Larrison PROS/250	10.00	3.00
79 Miguel Cabrera/100	25.00	7.50
81 Chris Burke PROS/250	10.00	3.00
93 Runelvys Hernandez/50	12.00	3.60
105 J.D. Durbin PROS/500	10.00	3.00
106 Jacque Jones/50	12.00	3.60
107 Jason Kubel PROS/400	15.00	4.50
108 Shannon Stewart/50	12.00	3.60
133 Eric Byrnes/50	20.00	6.00
139 Rich Harden/50	20.00	6.00
146 Ryan Howard PROS/400	15.00	4.50
193 Ramon Nivar PROS/100	10.00	3.00
195 Dustin McGowan PROS/100	10.00	3.00
197 Vinny Chulk/112	10.00	3.00
198 Orlando Hudson/100	10.00	3.00

2004 Playoff Prestige Xtra Bases Black Autographs

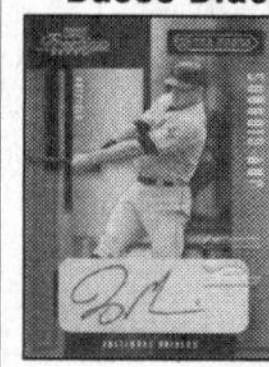

	Nm-Mt	Ex-Mt
RANDOM INSERTS IN HOBBY PACKS		
STATED PRINT RUN 25 SERIAL #'d SETS		
NO PRICING DUE TO SCARCITY		

2004 Playoff Prestige Xtra Bases Green Autographs

Card	Nm-Mt	Ex-Mt
RANDOM INSERTS IN RETAIL PACKS		
STATED PRINT RUN 100 SERIAL #'d SETS		
10 Edgar Gonzalez PROS	10.00	3.00
15 Bubba Nelson PROS	10.00	3.00
38 Brendan Harris PROS	10.00	3.00
57 Mike Nakamura	10.00	3.00
81 Chris Burke PROS	10.00	3.00
105 J.D. Durbin PROS	15.00	4.50
107 Jason Kubel PROS	15.00	4.50
146 Ryan Howard PROS	15.00	4.50
195 Dustin McGowan PROS	10.00	3.00

2004 Playoff Prestige Xtra Bases Purple Autographs

Card	Nm-Mt	Ex-Mt
RANDOM INSERTS IN HOBBY PACKS		
STATED PRINT RUN 100 SERIAL #'d SETS		
10 Edgar Gonzalez PROS	10.00	3.00
15 Bubba Nelson PROS	10.00	3.00
32 Kevin Youkilis PROS	15.00	4.50
38 Brendan Harris PROS	10.00	3.00

57 Mike Nakamura 10.00 3.00
73 Preston Larrison PROS 10.00 3.00
79 Miguel Cabrera 25.00 7.50
81 Chris Burke PROS 10.00 3.00
105 J.D. Durbin PROS 15.00 4.50
107 Jason Kubel PROS 15.00 4.50
146 Ryan Howard PROS 15.00 4.50
193 Ramon Nivar PROS 10.00 3.00
195 Dustin McGowan PROS 10.00 3.00
198 Orlando Hudson 10.00 3.00

2004 Playoff Prestige Xtra Bases Red Autographs

Nm-Mt Ex-Mt
RANDOM INSERTS IN RETAIL PACKS
STATED PRINT RUN 25 SERIAL #'d SETS
NO PRICING DUE TO SCARCITY ....

2004 Playoff Prestige Achievements

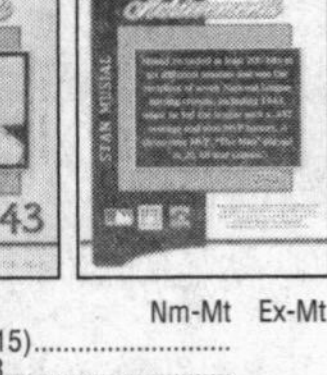

Nm-Mt Ex-Mt
COMPLETE SET (15) ....
STATED ODDS 1:8 ....
1 Hideo Nomo 95 ROY .... 3.00 .90
2 Don Mattingly 85 MVP 10.00 3.00
3 Roger Clemens 86 CY/MVP 6.00 1.80
4 Greg Maddux 95 CY 5.00 1.50
5 Stan Musial 43 MVP 6.00 1.80
6 Roberto Clemente 66 MVP 10.00 3.00
7 Derek Jeter 96 ROY 6.00 1.80
8 Albert Pujols 01 ROY 6.00 1.80
9 Cal Ripken 91 MVP 12.00 3.60
10 George Brett 80 MVP 10.00 3.00
11 Carl Yastrzemski 67 MVP 6.00 1.80
12 Rickey Henderson 90 MVP ..... 3.00 .90
13 Sammy Sosa 98 MVP 5.00 1.50
14 Randy Johnson 02 CY .... 3.00 .90
15 Bob Gibson 68 CY/MVP 4.00 1.20

2004 Playoff Prestige Changing Stripes

Nm-Mt Ex-Mt
STATED ODDS 1:11 ....
*FOIL: .75X TO 2X BASIC ....
FOIL PRINT RUN 150 SERIAL #'d SETS
*HOLO-FOIL: 1.5X TO 4X BASIC ....
HOLO-FOIL PRINT RUN 50 SERIAL #'d SETS
FOIL/HOLO-FOIL RANDOM IN PACKS
1 Rickey Henderson A's-Yanks ... 4.00 1.20
2 Mike Mussina O's-Yanks 4.00 1.20
3 Jim Thome Indians-Phils 4.00 1.20
4 Hideo Nomo Sox-Dodgers 4.00 1.20
5 Scott Rolen Phils-Cards 4.00 1.20
6 Jason Giambi A's-Yanks 4.00 1.20
7 R.Johnson Astros-D'backs 4.00 1.20
8 Shawn Green Jays-Dodgers 4.00 1.20
9 Curt Schilling Phils-D'backs 4.00 1.20
10 Alex Rodriguez M's-Rangers . 6.00 1.80
11 Greg Maddux Cubs-Braves 6.00 1.80
12 Randy Johnson M's-Astros ... 4.00 1.20
13 Hideo Nomo Dodgers-Mets ... 4.00 1.20
14 Ivan Rodriguez Rgr-Marlins ... 4.00 1.20
15 Juan Gonzalez Indians-Rangers 4.00 1.20
16 Manny Ramirez Indians-Sox .. 4.00 1.20
17 Mike Piazza Dodgers-Mets 6.00 1.80
18 Nolan Ryan Angels-Astros 10.00 3.00
19 Nolan Ryan Astros-Rangers. 10.00 3.00
20 Pedro Martinez Expos-Sox 4.00 1.20
21 Reg Jackson Yanks-Angels 4.00 1.20
22 Roberto Alomar Mets-Sox 4.00 1.20
23 Rod Carew Twins-Angels 4.00 1.20
24 Roger Clemens Sox-Yanks 8.00 2.40
25 Sammy Sosa Sox-Cubs 6.00 1.80

2004 Playoff Prestige Changing Stripes Dual Jersey

Nm-Mt Ex-Mt
STATED PRINT RUN 150 SERIAL #'d SETS
PRIME PRINT RUN 25 SERIAL #'d SETS
NO PRIME PRICING DUE TO SCARCITY
RANDOM INSERTS IN PACKS ....
1 Rickey Henderson A's-Yanks . 15.00 4.50
2 Mike Mussina O's-Yanks 15.00 4.50
3 Jim Thome Indians-Phils 15.00 4.50
4 Hideo Nomo Sox-Dodgers 25.00 7.50
5 Scott Rolen Phils-Cards 15.00 4.50
6 Jason Giambi A's-Yanks 10.00 3.00

7 R.Johnson Astros-D'backs 15.00 4.50
8 Shawn Green Jays-Dodgers ... 10.00 3.00
9 Curt Schilling Phils-D'backs .. 10.00 3.00
10 Alex Rodriguez M's-Rangers 15.00 4.50
12 Randy Johnson M's-Astros . 15.00 4.50
13 Hideo Nomo Dodgers-Mets . 25.00 7.50
14 Ivan Rodriguez Rgr-Marlins. 15.00 4.50
15 Juan Gonzalez Indians-Rangers 15.00 4.50
16 Manny Ramirez Indians-Sox 15.00 4.50
17 Mike Piazza Dodgers-Mets ... 15.00 4.50
18 Nolan Ryan Angels-Astros ... 50.00 15.00
19 Nolan Ryan Astros-Rangers. 50.00 15.00
20 Pedro Martinez Expos-Sox ... 15.00 4.50
22 Roberto Alomar Mets-Sox 15.00 4.50
23 Rod Carew Twins-Angels 15.00 4.50
24 Roger Clemens Sox-Yanks ... 20.00 6.00
25 Sammy Sosa Sox-Cubs 20.00 6.00

2004 Playoff Prestige Connections

Nm-Mt Ex-Mt
STATED ODDS 1:9 ....
*FOIL: 1.5X TO 4X BASIC ....
FOIL PRINT RUN 100 SERIAL #'d SETS
HOLO-FOIL PRINT RUN 21 SERIAL #'d SETS
NO HOLO-FOIL PRICING DUE TO SCARCITY
FOIL/HOLO-FOIL RANDOM IN PACKS
1 Derek Jeter .... 2.00 .60
Alfonso Soriano
2 Greg Maddux 4.00 1.20
Chipper Jones
3 Albert Pujols 5.00 1.50
Scott Rolen
4 Randy Johnson .... 2.50 .75
Curt Schilling
5 Nomar Garciaparra 4.00 1.20
Manny Ramirez
6 Alex Rodriguez 4.00 1.20
Mark Teixeira
7 Barry Zito .... 2.00 .60
Tim Hudson
8 Sammy Sosa 4.00 1.20
Mark Prior
9 Derek Jeter 5.00 1.50
Jason Giambi
10 Roger Clemens 5.00 1.50
Mike Mussina
11 Mark Prior .... 2.50 .75
Kerry Wood
12 Alex Rodriguez 4.00 1.20
Hank Blalock
13 Frank Thomas .... 2.50 .75
Magglio Ordonez
14 Nomar Garciaparra 4.00 1.20
Pedro Martinez
15 Carlos Delgado .... 2.00 .60
Vernon Wells
16 Miguel Tejada .... 2.00 .60
Eric Chavez
17 Jeff Bagwell .... 2.00 .60
Lance Berkman
18 Jim Thome .... 2.50 .75
Bobby Abreu
19 Todd Helton .... 2.00 .60
Preston Wilson
20 Vladimir Guerrero .... 2.50 .75
Javier Vazquez

2004 Playoff Prestige Connections Material

Nm-Mt Ex-Mt
RANDOM INSERTS IN PACKS ....
STATED PRINT RUN 250 SERIAL #'d SETS
1 Derek Jeter Bat 25.00 7.50
Alfonso Soriano Bat
2 Greg Maddux Bat 15.00 4.50
Chipper Jones Jsy
3 Albert Pujols Bat 20.00 6.00
Scott Rolen Bat
4 Randy Johnson Bat 15.00 4.50
Curt Schilling Bat
5 Nomar Garciaparra Bat 15.00 4.50
Manny Ramirez Bat
6 Alex Rodriguez Bat 15.00 4.50
Mark Texeira Bat
7 Barry Zito Bat 10.00 3.00
Tim Hudson Bat
8 Sammy Sosa Bat 25.00 7.50
Mark Prior Bat
9 Derek Jeter Bat 25.00 7.50
Jason Giambi Bat
10 Roger Clemens Jsy 20.00 6.00
Mike Mussina Bat
11 Mark Prior Bat 15.00 4.50
Kerry Wood Bat
12 Alex Rodriguez Bat 15.00 4.50
Hank Blalock Bat
13 Frank Thomas Bat 15.00 4.50
Magglio Ordonez Bat
14 Nomar Garciaparra Bat 25.00 7.50
Pedro Martinez Bat
15 Carlos Delgado Bat 10.00 3.00
Vernon Wells Bat
16 Miguel Tejada Bat 10.00 3.00
Eric Chavez Bat
17 Jeff Bagwell Bat 15.00 4.50
Lance Berkman Bat
18 Jim Thome Jsy 15.00 4.50
Bobby Abreu Bat
19 Todd Helton Bat 15.00 4.50
Preston Wilson Bat
20 Vladimir Guerrero Bat 15.00 4.50
Javier Vazquez Jsy

2004 Playoff Prestige Diamond Heritage

Nm-Mt Ex-Mt
STATED ODDS 1:13 ....
1 Mike Piazza 5.00 1.50
2 Greg Maddux 5.00 1.50
3 Nomar Garciaparra 5.00 1.50
4 Chipper Jones .... 3.00 .90
5 Albert Pujols 6.00 1.80
6 Derek Jeter 6.00 1.80
7 Shawn Green .... 3.00 .90
8 Alex Rodriguez 5.00 1.50
9 Jim Thome .... 3.00 .90
10 Jason Giambi .... 3.00 .90
11 Sammy Sosa 5.00 1.50
12 Hank Blalock .... 3.00 .90
13 Garret Anderson .... 3.00 .90
14 Manny Ramirez .... 3.00 .90
15 Scott Rolen .... 3.00 .90
16 Jeff Bagwell .... 3.00 .90
17 Randy Johnson .... 3.00 .90
18 Ichiro Suzuki 5.00 1.50
19 Ivan Rodriguez .... 3.00 .90
20 Alfonso Soriano .... 3.00 .90

2004 Playoff Prestige Diamond Heritage Material

Nm-Mt Ex-Mt
STATED ODDS 1:92 ....
1 Mike Piazza Bat 15.00 4.50
2 Greg Maddux Bat 15.00 4.50
3 Nomar Garciaparra Bat 15.00 4.50
4 Chipper Jones Jsy 10.00 3.00
5 Albert Pujols Bat 20.00 6.00
6 Derek Jeter Jsy 25.00 7.50
7 Shawn Green Bat 8.00 2.40
8 Alex Rodriguez Bat 15.00 4.50
9 Jim Thome Jsy 10.00 3.00
10 Jason Giambi Bat 8.00 2.40
11 Sammy Sosa Bat 15.00 4.50
12 Hank Blalock Bat 8.00 2.40
13 Garret Anderson Bat 8.00 2.40
14 Manny Ramirez Bat 10.00 3.00
15 Scott Rolen Bat 10.00 3.00
16 Jeff Bagwell Bat 10.00 3.00
17 Randy Johnson Bat 10.00 3.00
19 Ivan Rodriguez Bat 10.00 3.00
20 Alfonso Soriano Bat 10.00 3.00

2004 Playoff Prestige League Leaders Single

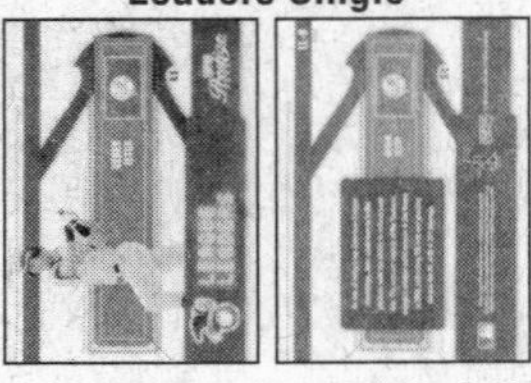

Nm-Mt Ex-Mt
STATED ODDS 1:18 ....
*FOIL: 1.5X TO 4X BASIC ....
FOIL PRINT RUN 100 SERIAL #'d SETS
HOLO-FOIL PRINT RUN 25 SERIAL #'d SETS
NO HOLO-FOIL PRICING DUE TO SCARCITY
FOIL/HOLO-FOIL RANDOM IN PACKS
1 Alex Rodriguez AL HR 4.00 1.20
2 Albert Pujols NL Hit 5.00 1.50
3 Albert Pujols NL Avg 5.00 1.50
4 Nomar Garciaparra AL Hit 4.00 1.20
5 Mark Prior NL ERA .... 2.50 .75
6 Pedro Martinez AL ERA .... 2.50 .75
7 Kerry Wood NL SO .... 2.50 .75
8 Derek Jeter AL Avg 5.00 1.50
9 Jason Giambi AL BB .... 2.00 .60
10 Roger Clemens AL SO 5.00 1.50

2004 Playoff Prestige League Leaders Single Material

Nm-Mt Ex-Mt
RANDOM INSERTS IN PACKS
STATED PRINT RUN 250 SERIAL #'d SETS
1 Alex Rodriguez AL HR Bat 10.00 3.00
2 Albert Pujols NL Hit Bat 15.00 4.50
3 Albert Pujols NL Avg Bat 15.00 4.50
4 Nomar Garciaparra AL Hit Bat 10.00 3.00
5 Mark Prior NL ERA Jsy 10.00 3.00
6 Pedro Martinez AL ERA Jsy ... 10.00 3.00
7 Kerry Wood NL SO Jsy 10.00 3.00
8 Derek Jeter AL Avg Jsy 20.00 6.00
9 Jason Giambi AL BB Jsy 8.00 2.40
10 Roger Clemens AL SO Jsy ....

2004 Playoff Prestige League Leaders Double

Nm-Mt Ex-Mt
STATED PRINT RUN 500 SERIAL #'d SETS
*FOIL: .75X TO 2X BASIC ....
FOIL PRINT RUN 75 SERIAL #'d SETS
HOLO-FOIL PRINT RUN 10 SERIAL #'d SETS
NO HOLO-FOIL PRICING DUE TO SCARCITY
RANDOM INSERTS IN PACKS ....
1 Alex Rodriguez 10.00 3.00
Jim Thome HR
2 Mark Prior 10.00 3.00
Pedro Martinez ERA
3 Roger Clemens 12.00 3.60
Kerry Wood SO
4 Nomar Garciaparra 12.00 3.60
Albert Pujols Hit
5 Derek Jeter 15.00 4.50
Albert Pujols Avg

2004 Playoff Prestige League Leaders Double Material

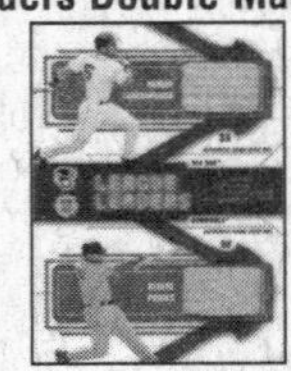

Nm-Mt Ex-Mt
RANDOM INSERTS IN PACKS ....
STATED PRINT RUN 100 SERIAL #'d SETS
1 Alex Rodriguez Bat 25.00 7.50
Jim Thome Bat HR
2 Mark Prior Jsy 25.00 7.50
Pedro Martinez Jsy ERA
3 Roger Clemens Jsy 30.00 9.00
Kerry Wood Jsy SO
4 Nomar Garciaparra Bat 30.00 9.00
Albert Pujols Bat Hits
5 Derek Jeter Jsy 40.00 12.00
Albert Pujols Bat Avg

2004 Playoff Prestige League Leaders Quad

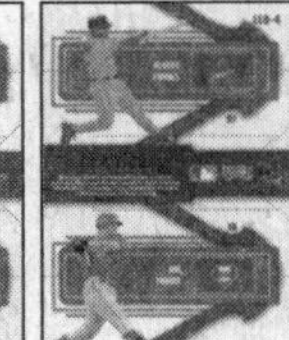

Nm-Mt Ex-Mt
STATED PRINT RUN 250 SERIAL #'d SETS
*FOIL: .75X TO 2X BASIC ....
FOIL PRINT RUN 50 SERIAL #'d SETS
HOLO-FOIL PRINT RUN 5 SERIAL #'d SETS
NO HOLO-FOIL PRICING DUE TO SCARCITY
RANDOM INSERTS IN PACKS ....
1 Albert Pujols 15.00 4.50
Todd Helton
Edgar Renteria
Gary Sheffield NL Avg
2 Derek Jeter 20.00 6.00
Manny Ramirez
Nomar Garciaparra
Ichiro Suzuki AL Avg
3 Mark PriorCurt Schilling 12.00 3.60
Hideo Nomo
Kevin Brown NL ERA
4 Richie Sexson 12.00 3.60
Sammy Sosa
Albert Pujols
Jim Thome NL HR
5 Alex Rodriguez 12.00 3.60
Frank Thomas
Jason Giambi
Carlos Delgado AL HR

2004 Playoff Prestige League Leaders Quad Material

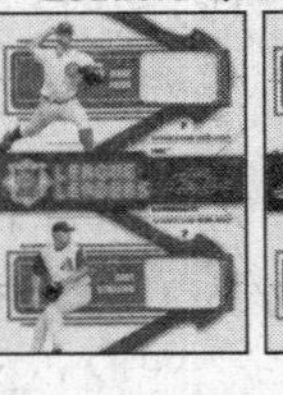
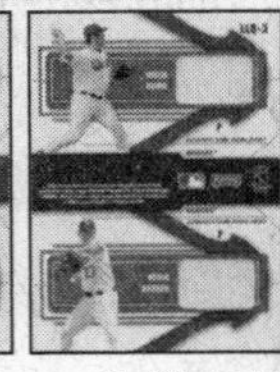

Nm-Mt Ex-Mt
RANDOM INSERTS IN PACKS ....
STATED PRINT RUN 50 SERIAL #'d SETS
1 Albert Pujols Bat 40.00 12.00
Todd Helton Bat
Edgar Renteria Jsy
Gary Sheffield Jsy NL Avg
3 Mark Prior Jsy 40.00 12.00
Curt Schilling Jsy
Hideo Nomo Jsy
Kevin Brown Jsy NL ERA
4 Richie Sexson Jsy 50.00 15.00
Sammy Sosa Bat
Albert Pujols Bat
Jim Thome Bat NL HR
5 Alex Rodriguez Jsy 40.00 12.00
Frank Thomas Jsy
Jason Giambi Jsy
Carlos Delgado Jsy AL HR

2004 Playoff Prestige Players Collection Jersey

Nm-Mt Ex-Mt
STATED ODDS 1:79 ....
*PLATINUM: .75X TO 2X BASIC ....
PLATINUM RANDOM INSERTS IN PACKS
PLATINUM PRINT RUN 50 SERIAL #'d SETS
1 Adam Dunn AS 8.00 2.40
2 Adam Dunn Gray 8.00 2.40
3 Adam Dunn White 8.00 2.40
4 Alex Rodriguez M's 10.00 3.00
5 Alex Rodriguez Rgr AS 10.00 3.00
6 Alex Rodriguez Rgr Blue 10.00 3.00
7 Alex Rodriguez Rgr White 10.00 3.00
8 Andruw Jones Home 5.00 1.50
9 Andruw Jones Road 5.00 1.50
10 Austin Kearns 5.00 1.50
11 Brandon Webb 5.00 1.50
12 C.C. Sabathia 5.00 1.50
13 Cal Ripken 40.00 12.00
14 Carlos Beltran 8.00 2.40
15 Carlos Delgado 5.00 1.50
16 Carlos Lee 5.00 1.50
17 Chipper Jones Home 8.00 2.40
18 Chipper Jones Road 8.00 2.40
19 Craig Biggio 8.00 2.40
20 Curt Schilling 5.00 1.50
21 David Wells 5.00 1.50
22 Don Mattingly 20.00 6.00
23 Dontrelle Willis 5.00 1.50
24 Frank Thomas Black 8.00 2.40
25 Frank Thomas White 8.00 2.40
26 Fred McGriff 8.00 2.40
27 Garret Anderson AS 5.00 1.50
28 Gary Sheffield Braves 5.00 1.50
29 Gary Sheffield Dodgers 5.00 1.50
30 Greg Maddux Gray 10.00 3.00
31 Hank Blalock Home 5.00 1.50
32 Hank Blalock Road 5.00 1.50
33 Hee Seop Choi 5.00 1.50
34 Hideo Nomo Mets 8.00 2.40
35 Hideo Nomo Dodgers Gray 8.00 2.40
36 Hideo Nomo Dodgers White .. 8.00 2.40
37 Ivan Rodriguez Marlins 8.00 2.40
38 Ivan Rodriguez Rgr 8.00 2.40
39 Jason Giambi Home 5.00 1.50
40 Jim Edmonds 5.00 1.50
41 Jim Thome 8.00 2.40
42 John Olerud 5.00 1.50
43 John Smoltz 8.00 2.40
44 Josh Beckett 5.00 1.50
45 Josh Phelps 5.00 1.50
46 Juan Gonzalez Rgr 8.00 2.40
47 Juan Gonzalez Indians 8.00 2.40
48 Kazuhisa Ishii 5.00 1.50
49 Lance Berkman White 5.00 1.50
50 Larry Walker Home 8.00 2.40
51 Larry Walker Road 8.00 2.40
52 Luis Gonzalez AS 5.00 1.50
53 Magglio Ordonez Home 5.00 1.50
54 Magglio Ordonez Road 5.00 1.50
55 Manny Ramirez 8.00 2.40
56 Manny Ramirez AS 8.00 2.40
57 Mark Prior Home 8.00 2.40
58 Mark Prior Road 8.00 2.40

59 Mark Teixeira.......... 5.00 1.50
60 Mike Mussina.......... 8.00 2.40
61 Mike Piazza AS.......... 10.00 3.00
62 Mike Piazza Black.......... 10.00 3.00
63 Mike Piazza White.......... 10.00 3.00
64 Nomar Garciaparra Gray.......... 10.00 3.00
65 Nomar Garciaparra White.......... 10.00 3.00
66 Pat Burrell.......... 5.00 1.50
67 Paul Konerko.......... 5.00 1.50
68 Paul Lo Duca.......... 5.00 1.50
69 Pedro Martinez.......... 8.00 2.40
70 Rafael Furcal.......... 5.00 1.50
71 Rafael Palmeiro Blue.......... 8.00 2.40
72 Rafael Palmeiro Gray.......... 8.00 2.40
73 Ramon Hernandez.......... 5.00 1.50
74 Rickey Henderson.......... 8.00 2.40
75 Rickey Henderson Black.......... 8.00 2.40
76 Rickey Henderson White.......... 8.00 2.40
77 Roberto Alomar Indians.......... 8.00 2.40
78 Roberto Alomar Mets.......... 8.00 2.40
79 Robin Ventura AS.......... 5.00 1.50
80 Roger Clemens Away.......... 15.00 4.50
81 Roger Clemens Home.......... 15.00 4.50
82 Roy Halladay.......... 5.00 1.50
83 Sammy Sosa AS.......... 10.00 3.00
84 Sammy Sosa Gray.......... 10.00 3.00
85 Sammy Sosa White.......... 10.00 3.00
86 Scott Rolen.......... 8.00 2.40
87 Shannon Stewart.......... 5.00 1.50
88 Shawn Green Blue.......... 5.00 1.50
89 Shawn Green Gray.......... 5.00 1.50
90 Shawn Green White.......... 5.00 1.50
91 Terrence Long.......... 5.00 1.50
92 Tim Hudson.......... 5.00 1.50
93 Todd Helton Away.......... 8.00 2.40
94 Todd Helton Home.......... 8.00 2.40
95 Tom Glavine Braves.......... 8.00 2.40
96 Tom Glavine Mets.......... 8.00 2.40
97 Torii Hunter.......... 5.00 1.50
98 Vernon Wells.......... 5.00 1.50
99 Vladimir Guerrero.......... 8.00 2.40
100 Vladimir Guerrero AS.......... 8.00 2.40

2004 Playoff Prestige Prestigious Pros

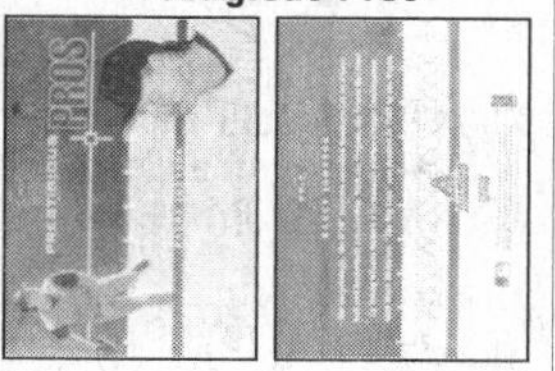

Nm-Mt Ex-Mt
STATED ODDS 1:23..........
1 Mark Prior.......... 4.00 1.20
2 Derek Jeter.......... 8.00 2.40
3 Mike Mussina.......... 4.00 1.20
4 Nomar Garciaparra.......... 6.00 1.80
5 Roger Clemens.......... 8.00 2.40
6 Jason Giambi.......... 4.00 1.20
7 Randy Johnson.......... 4.00 1.20
8 Rafael Palmeiro.......... 4.00 1.20
9 Barry Zito.......... 4.00 1.20
10 Pat Burrell.......... 4.00 1.20

2004 Playoff Prestige Stars of MLB

Nm-Mt Ex-Mt
STATED ODDS 1:36..........
*FOIL: .75X TO 2X BASIC..........
FOIL PRINT RUN 100 SERIAL #'d SETS
HOLO-FOIL PRINT RUN 25 SERIAL #'d SETS
NO HOLO-FOIL PRICING DUE TO SCARCITY
FOIL/HOLO-FOIL RANDOM IN PACKS
1 Albert Pujols.......... 10.00 3.00
2 Derek Jeter.......... 10.00 3.00
3 Mike Piazza.......... 8.00 2.40
4 Greg Maddux.......... 8.00 2.40
5 Ichiro Suzuki.......... 8.00 2.40
6 Nomar Garciaparra.......... 8.00 2.40
7 Ivan Rodriguez.......... 5.00 1.50
8 Randy Johnson.......... 5.00 1.50
9 Alex Rodriguez.......... 8.00 2.40
10 Sammy Sosa.......... 8.00 2.40
11 Alfonso Soriano.......... 5.00 1.50
12 Vladimir Guerrero.......... 5.00 1.50
13 Jason Giambi.......... 5.00 1.50
14 Mark Prior.......... 5.00 1.50
15 Chipper Jones.......... 5.00 1.50

2004 Playoff Prestige Stars of MLB Jersey

Nm-Mt Ex-Mt
STATED PRINT RUN 250 SERIAL #'d SETS
*PRIME: 1X TO 2.5X BASIC..........
PRIME PRINT RUN 50 SERIAL #'d SETS
RANDOM INSERTS IN PACKS..........
1 Albert Pujols.......... 15.00 4.50
2 Derek Jeter.......... 20.00 6.00
3 Mike Piazza.......... 10.00 3.00
4 Greg Maddux.......... 10.00 3.00
6 Nomar Garciaparra.......... 10.00 3.00
7 Ivan Rodriguez.......... 10.00 3.00
8 Randy Johnson.......... 10.00 3.00
9 Alex Rodriguez.......... 10.00 3.00
10 Sammy Sosa.......... 15.00 4.50
11 Alfonso Soriano.......... 10.00 3.00
12 Vladimir Guerrero.......... 10.00 3.00
13 Jason Giambi.......... 8.00 2.40
14 Mark Prior.......... 10.00 3.00
15 Chipper Jones.......... 10.00 3.00

2004 Playoff Prestige Stars of MLB Jersey Autographs

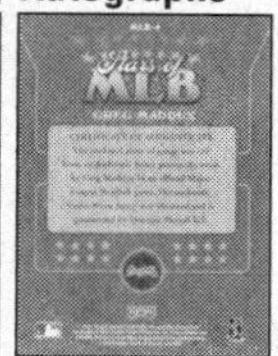

Nm-Mt Ex-Mt
RANDOM INSERTS IN PACKS..........
PRINT RUNS B/WN 1-50 COPIES PER
NO PRICING ON QTY OF 25 OR LESS
14 Mark Prior/50.......... 100.00 30.00

2004 Prime Cuts

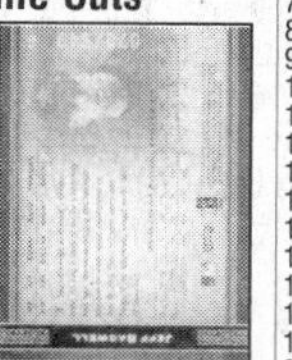

This 50-card set was released in November, 2003. Each four-card pack retailed for $150 and contained four cards per pack along with an encased (but not Graded) BGS card. Each case continued fifteen of these one-pack boxes. Please note a Babe Ruth "Santa" card was randomly inserted into packs and is not considered part of the basic set.

MINT NRMT
COMPLETE SET (50).......... 225.00 100.00
STATED PRINT RUN 949 SERIAL #'d SETS
B.RUTH SANTA STATED ODDS 1:15....
1 Roger Clemens Yanks.......... 10.00 4.50
2 Nomar Garciaparra.......... 8.00 3.60
3 Albert Pujols.......... 10.00 4.50
4 Sammy Sosa.......... 8.00 3.60
5 Greg Maddux Braves.......... 8.00 3.60
6 Jason Giambi.......... 4.00 1.80
7 Hideo Nomo Dodgers.......... 5.00 2.20
8 Mike Piazza Mets.......... 8.00 3.60
9 Ichiro Suzuki.......... 8.00 3.60
10 Jeff Bagwell.......... 5.00 2.20
11 Derek Jeter.......... 10.00 4.50
12 Manny Ramirez.......... 5.00 2.20
13 R.Henderson Dodgers.......... 5.00 2.20
14 Alex Rodriguez Rgr.......... 8.00 3.60
15 Troy Glaus.......... 4.00 1.80
16 Mike Mussina.......... 5.00 2.20
17 Kerry Wood.......... 5.00 2.20
18 Kazuhisa Ishii.......... 4.00 1.80
19 Hideki Matsui.......... 8.00 3.60
20 Frank Thomas.......... 5.00 2.20
21 Barry Bonds Giants.......... 12.00 5.50
22 Adam Dunn.......... 5.00 2.20
23 Randy Johnson D'backs.......... 5.00 2.20
24 Alfonso Soriano.......... 5.00 2.20
25 Pedro Martinez Sox.......... 5.00 2.20
26 Andruw Jones.......... 4.00 1.80
27 Mark Prior.......... 5.00 2.20
28 Vladimir Guerrero.......... 5.00 2.20
29 Chipper Jones.......... 5.00 2.20
30 Todd Helton.......... 5.00 2.20
31 Rafael Palmeiro.......... 5.00 2.20
32 Mark Grace.......... 5.00 2.20
33 Pedro Martinez Dodgers.......... 5.00 2.20
34 Randy Johnson M's.......... 5.00 2.20
35 Randy Johnson Astros.......... 5.00 2.20
36 Roger Clemens Sox.......... 10.00 4.50
37 Roger Clemens Jays.......... 10.00 4.50
38 Alex Rodriguez M's.......... 8.00 3.60
39 Greg Maddux Cubs.......... 8.00 3.60
40 Mike Piazza Dodgers.......... 8.00 3.60
41 Mike Piazza Marlins.......... 8.00 3.60
42 Hideo Nomo Mets.......... 5.00 2.20
43 R.Henderson Yanks.......... 5.00 2.20
44 Rickey Henderson A's.......... 5.00 2.20
45 Barry Bonds Pirates.......... 12.00 5.50
46 Ivan Rodriguez.......... 5.00 2.20
47 George Brett.......... 10.00 4.50
48 Cal Ripken.......... 20.00 9.00
49 Nolan Ryan.......... 12.00 5.50
50 Don Mattingly.......... 10.00 4.50
BRS1 Babe Ruth Santa.......... 15.00 6.75

2004 Prime Cuts Century

MINT NRMT
*CENTURY 1-45: .75X TO 2X BASIC..
*CENTURY MATSUI: 1X TO 2.5X BASIC
*CENTURY 47-50: 1.25X TO 3X BASIC
RANDOM INSERTS IN PACKS..........
STATED PRINT RUN 100 SERIAL #'d SETS

2004 Prime Cuts Century Gold

MINT NRMT
RANDOM INSERTS IN PACKS..........
STATED PRINT RUN 10 SERIAL #'d SETS
NO PRICING DUE TO SCARCITY..........

2004 Prime Cuts Century Proofs

MINT NRMT
RANDOM INSERTS IN PACKS..........
STATED PRINT RUN 1 SERIAL #'d SET
NO PRICING DUE TO SCARCITY..........

2004 Prime Cuts Material

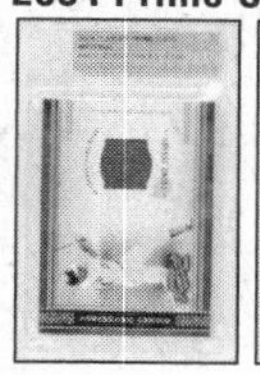

MINT NRMT
RANDOM INSERTS IN PACKS..........
PRINT RUNS B/WN 10-50 COPIES PER
NO PRICING ON QTY OF 10 OR LESS
ALL CARDS FEATURE PRIME SWATCHES
1 Roger Clemens Yanks Jsy/50 40.00 18.00
2 Nomar Garciaparra Jsy/50.......... 40.00 18.00
3 Albert Pujols Jsy/50.......... 50.00 22.00
4 Sammy Sosa Jsy/50.......... 40.00 18.00
5 Greg Maddux Jsy/50.......... 40.00 18.00
6 Jason Giambi Jsy/25.......... 25.00 11.00
7 H.Nomo Dodgers Jsy/50.......... 40.00 18.00
8 Mike Piazza Mets Jsy/50.......... 40.00 18.00
9 Ichiro Suzuki Base/25.......... 80.00 36.00
10 Jeff Bagwell Jsy/25.......... 40.00 18.00
11 Derek Jeter Base/25.......... 80.00 36.00
12 Manny Ramirez Jsy/25.......... 40.00 18.00
13 R.Henderson Dodgers Jsy/50 25.00 11.00
14 Alex Rodriguez Rgr Jsy/25.. 50.00 22.00
15 Troy Glaus Jsy/25.......... 25.00 11.00
16 Mike Mussina Jsy/10..........
17 Kerry Wood Jsy/25.......... 40.00 18.00
18 Kazuhisa Ishii Jsy/25.......... 25.00 11.00
19 Hideki Matsui Base/25.......... 80.00 36.00
20 Frank Thomas Jsy/25.......... 40.00 18.00
21 Barry Bonds Base/25.......... 80.00 36.00
22 Adam Dunn Jsy/25.......... 40.00 18.00
23 R.Johnson D'backs Jsy/25.. 40.00 18.00
24 Alfonso Soriano Jsy/35.......... 25.00 11.00
25 Pedro Martinez Sox Jsy/25.. 40.00 18.00
26 Andruw Jones Jsy/25.......... 25.00 11.00
27 Mark Prior Jsy/50.......... 25.00 11.00
28 Vladimir Guerrero Jsy/25.......... 40.00 18.00
29 Chipper Jones Jsy/25.......... 40.00 18.00
30 Todd Helton Jsy/25.......... 40.00 18.00
31 Rafael Palmeiro Jsy/25.......... 40.00 18.00
32 Mark Grace Jsy/25.......... 40.00 18.00
33 P.Martinez Dodgers Jsy/25.. 40.00 18.00
34 Randy Johnson M's Jsy/25. 40.00 18.00
35 R.Johnson Astros Jsy/25.......... 40.00 18.00
36 Roger Clemens Sox Jsy/25.......... 40.00 18.00
38 Alex Rodriguez M's Jsy/25.. 60.00 27.00
40 Mike Piazza Dodgers Jsy/50 40.00 18.00
42 Hideo Nomo Mets Jsy/50.......... 40.00 18.00
43 R.Henderson Yanks Jsy/50.. 25.00 11.00
44 R.Henderson A's Jsy/50.......... 25.00 11.00
46 Ivan Rodriguez Jsy/25.......... 40.00 18.00
47 George Brett Jsy/50.......... 50.00 22.00
48 Cal Ripken Jsy/50.......... 60.00 27.00
49 Nolan Ryan Jsy/50.......... 50.00 22.00
50 Don Mattingly Jsy/50.......... 50.00 22.00

2004 Prime Cuts Material Combos

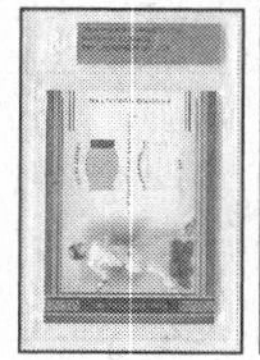

MINT NRMT
RANDOM INSERTS IN PACKS..........
STATED PRINT RUN 25 SERIAL #'d SETS
ALL CARDS FEATURE PRIME SWATCHES
1 R.Clemens Yanks Bat-Jsy.......... 60.00 27.00
2 Nomar Garciaparra Bat-Jsy.... 60.00 27.00
3 Albert Pujols Bat-Jsy.......... 100.00 45.00
4 Sammy Sosa Bat-Jsy.......... 60.00 27.00
5 Greg Maddux Bat-Jsy.......... 60.00 27.00
6 Jason Giambi Bat-Jsy.......... 40.00 18.00
7 H.Nomo Dodgers Bat-Jsy.......... 60.00 27.00
8 Mike Piazza Mets Bat-Jsy.......... 60.00 27.00
9 Ichiro Suzuki Ball-Base.......... 80.00 36.00
10 Jeff Bagwell Bat-Jsy.......... 50.00 22.00
11 Derek Jeter Ball-Base.......... 80.00 36.00
12 Manny Ramirez Bat-Jsy.......... 50.00 22.00
13 R.Henderson Dodgers Bat-Jsy 50.00 22.00
14 Alex Rodriguez Rgr Bat-Jsy. 60.00 27.00
15 Troy Glaus Bat-Jsy.......... 40.00 18.00
16 Mike Mussina Bat-Jsy.......... 50.00 22.00
17 Kerry Wood Bat-Jsy.......... 50.00 22.00
18 Kazuhisa Ishii Bat-Jsy.......... 40.00 18.00
19 Hideki Matsui Ball-Base.......... 100.00 45.00
20 Frank Thomas Bat-Jsy.......... 50.00 22.00
21 Barry Bonds Ball-Base.......... 100.00 45.00
22 Adam Dunn Bat-Jsy.......... 50.00 22.00
23 R.Johnson D'backs Bat-Jsy. 50.00 22.00
24 Alfonso Soriano Bat-Jsy.......... 50.00 22.00
25 Pedro Martinez Sox Bat-Jsy. 50.00 22.00
26 Andruw Jones Bat-Jsy.......... 40.00 18.00
27 Mark Prior Bat-Jsy.......... 50.00 22.00
28 Vladimir Guerrero Bat-Jsy.... 50.00 22.00
29 Chipper Jones Bat-Jsy.......... 50.00 22.00
30 Todd Helton Bat-Jsy.......... 50.00 22.00
31 Rafael Palmeiro Bat-Jsy.......... 50.00 22.00
32 Mark Grace Bat-Jsy.......... 50.00 22.00
33 P.Martinez Dodgers Bat-Jsy. 50.00 22.00
34 Randy Johnson M's Bat-Jsy 50.00 22.00
35 R.Johnson Astros Bat-Jsy.... 50.00 22.00
36 Roger Clemens Sox Bat-Jsy 60.00 27.00
38 Alex Rodriguez M's Bat-Jsy. 60.00 27.00
40 M.Piazza Dodgers Bat-Jsy.... 60.00 27.00
42 Hideo Nomo Mets Bat-Jsy.... 60.00 27.00
43 R.Henderson Yanks Bat-Jsy. 50.00 22.00
44 R.Henderson A's Bat-Jsy.......... 50.00 22.00
46 Ivan Rodriguez Bat-Jsy.......... 50.00 22.00
47 George Brett Bat-Jsy.......... 100.00 45.00
48 Cal Ripken Bat-Jsy.......... 120.00 55.00
49 Nolan Ryan Bat-Jsy.......... 100.00 45.00
50 Don Mattingly Bat-Jsy.......... 100.00 45.00

2004 Prime Cuts Material Signature

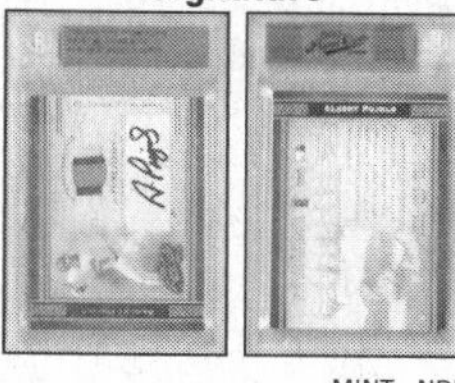

MINT NRMT
RANDOM INSERTS IN PACKS..........
PRINT RUNS B/WN 5-50 COPIES PER
NO PRICING ON QTY OF 10 OR LESS
ALL CARDS FEATURE PRIME SWATCHES
1 R.Clemens Yanks Jsy/25.......... 250.00 110.00
3 Albert Pujols Jsy/25.......... 250.00 110.00
5 Greg Maddux Jsy/25.......... 150.00 70.00
7 H.Nomo Dodgers Jsy/10..........
8 Mike Piazza Mets Jsy/10..........
10 Jeff Bagwell Jsy/25.......... 100.00 45.00
12 Manny Ramirez Jsy/25.......... 100.00 45.00
13 R.Hend Dodgers Jsy/25.......... 100.00 45.00
14 Alex Rodriguez Rgr Jsy/25 250.00 110.00
15 Troy Glaus Jsy/50.......... 40.00 18.00
16 Mike Mussina Jsy/25.......... 80.00 36.00
17 Kerry Wood Jsy/25.......... 100.00 45.00
18 Kazuhisa Ishii Jsy/50.......... 40.00 18.00
20 Frank Thomas Jsy/25.......... 100.00 45.00
22 Adam Dunn Jsy/50.......... 60.00 27.00
23 R.Johnson D'backs Jsy/10..........
24 Alfonso Soriano Jsy/25.......... 80.00 36.00
25 Pedro Martinez Sox Jsy/10..........
26 Andruw Jones Jsy/25.......... 50.00 22.00
27 Mark Prior Jsy/50.......... 120.00 55.00
28 Vladimir Guerrero Jsy/50.......... 80.00 36.00
29 Chipper Jones Jsy/50.......... 80.00 36.00
30 Todd Helton Jsy/50.......... 60.00 27.00
31 Rafael Palmeiro Jsy/25.......... 100.00 45.00
32 Mark Grace Jsy/50.......... 80.00 36.00
33 P.Martinez Dodgers Jsy/10..........
34 Randy Johnson M's Jsy/10..........
35 R.Johnson Astros Jsy/10..........
36 Roger Clemens Sox Jsy/25 250.00 110.00
38 Alex Rodriguez M's Jsy/25 250.00 110.00
40 Mike Piazza Dodgers Jsy/10..........
42 Hideo Nomo Mets Jsy/5..........
43 R.Henderson Yanks Jsy/5..........
44 R.Henderson A's Jsy/25.......... 100.00 45.00
46 Ivan Rodriguez Jsy/25.......... 100.00 45.00
47 George Brett Jsy/50.......... 150.00 70.00
48 Cal Ripken Jsy/50.......... 250.00 110.00
49 Nolan Ryan Jsy/50.......... 200.00 90.00
50 Don Mattingly Jsy/50.......... 150.00 70.00

2004 Prime Cuts MLB Icons Material

MINT NRMT
RANDOM INSERTS IN PACKS..........
PRINT RUNS B/WN 9-50 COPIES PER
NO PRICING ON QTY OF 9 OR LESS..
1 Ty Cobb Pants/9..........
2 Babe Ruth Pants/9..........
3 Lou Gehrig Pants/9..........
4 Johnny Bench Jsy/50.......... 50.00 22.00
5 Lefty Grove A's Hat/25.......... 150.00 70.00
6 Carlton Fisk Jsy/50.......... 40.00 18.00
7 Mel Ott Jsy/25.......... 100.00 45.00
8 Bob Feller Jsy/25.......... 40.00 18.00
9 Jackie Robinson Jsy/25.......... 120.00 55.00
10 Ted Williams Jsy/50.......... 120.00 55.00
11 Roy Campanella Pants/50.... 60.00 27.00
12 Stan Musial Jsy/50.......... 60.00 27.00
13 Yogi Berra Jsy/50.......... 50.00 22.00
14 Babe Ruth Jsy/25.......... 1500.00 700.00
15 Roberto Clemente Jsy/50.... 150.00 70.00
16 Warren Spahn Jsy/50.......... 50.00 22.00
17 Ernie Banks Jsy/50.......... 50.00 22.00
18 Eddie Mathews Jsy/50.......... 50.00 22.00
19 Ryne Sandberg Jsy/50.......... 60.00 27.00
20 Rod Carew Angels Jsy/50.... 40.00 18.00
21 Duke Snider Jsy/50.......... 40.00 18.00
22 Jim Palmer Jsy/50.......... 25.00 11.00
24 Frank Robinson Jsy/50.......... 25.00 11.00
25 Brooks Robinson Jsy/50.......... 40.00 18.00
26 Harmon Killebrew Jsy/50.......... 50.00 22.00
27 Carl Yastrzemski Jsy/50.......... 60.00 27.00
28 Reggie Jackson A's Jsy/50.. 40.00 18.00
29 Mike Schmidt Jsy/50.......... 50.00 22.00
30 Robin Yount Jsy/50.......... 50.00 22.00
31 George Brett Jsy/50.......... 60.00 27.00
32 Nolan Ryan Rgr Jsy/50.......... 60.00 27.00
33 Kirby Puckett Jsy/50.......... 50.00 22.00
34 Cal Ripken Jsy/50.......... 80.00 36.00
35 Don Mattingly Jsy/50.......... 60.00 27.00
36 Tony Gwynn Jsy/19.......... 80.00 36.00
37 Deion Sanders Jsy/19.......... 50.00 22.00
38 Dave Winfield Yanks Jsy/19. 40.00 18.00
39 Eddie Murray Jsy/19.......... 60.00 27.00
40 Tom Seaver Jsy/19.......... 50.00 22.00
41 Willie Stargell Jsy/19.......... 50.00 22.00
42 Wade Boggs Yanks Jsy/19... 50.00 22.00
43 Ozzie Smith Jsy/19.......... 60.00 27.00
44 Willie McCovey Jsy/19.......... 40.00 18.00
45 R.Jackson Angels Jsy/19.......... 50.00 22.00
46 Whitey Ford Jsy/19.......... 50.00 22.00
47 Lou Brock Jsy/19.......... 50.00 22.00
48 Lou Boudreau Jsy/19.......... 40.00 18.00
49 Steve Carlton Jsy/19.......... 40.00 18.00
50 Rod Carew Twins Jsy/19.......... 50.00 22.00
51 Bob Gibson Jsy/19.......... 50.00 22.00
52 Thurman Munson Jsy/19.......... 60.00 27.00
53 Roger Maris Jsy/19.......... 120.00 55.00
54 Nolan Ryan Astros Jsy/50.......... 60.00 27.00
55 Nolan Ryan Angels Jsy/50.......... 60.00 27.00
56 Bo Jackson Jsy/19.......... 60.00 27.00
57 Joe Morgan Jsy/19.......... 40.00 18.00
58 Phil Rizzuto Jsy/19.......... 50.00 22.00
59 Gary Carter Jsy/19.......... 40.00 18.00
60 Paul Molitor Jsy/19.......... 50.00 22.00
61 Don Drysdale Jsy/19.......... 60.00 27.00
62 Catfish Hunter Jsy/19.......... 50.00 22.00
63 Fergie Jenkins Pants/19.......... 40.00 18.00
64 Pee Wee Reese Jsy/19.......... 50.00 22.00
65 Dave Winfield Padres Jsy/19 40.00 18.00
66 Wade Boggs Sox Jsy/19.......... 50.00 22.00
67 Lefty Grove Sox Hat/19.......... 150.00 70.00
68 Rickey Henderson Jsy/19.......... 60.00 27.00
69 Roger Clemens Sox Jsy/19.. 60.00 27.00
70 R.Clemens Yanks Jsy/19.......... 60.00 27.00

2004 Prime Cuts MLB Icons Material Combos Prime

MINT NRMT
RANDOM INSERTS IN PACKS..........
PRINT RUNS B/WN 1-25 COPIES PER
NO PRICING ON QTY OF 15 OR LESS
1 Ty Cobb Bat-Pants/9..........
2 Babe Ruth Bat-Pants/9..........
3 Lou Gehrig Bat-Pants/9..........
4 Johnny Bench Bat-Jsy/5..........
6 Carlton Fisk Bat-Jsy/25.......... 80.00 36.00
7 Mel Ott Bat-Jsy/25..........
10 Ted Williams Bat-Jsy/9..........
11 R.Campanella Bat-Pants/25 100.00 45.00
12 Stan Musial Bat-Jsy/1..........
13 Yogi Berra Bat-Jsy/1..........
15 R.Clemente Bat-Jsy/25..........
17 Ernie Banks Bat-Jsy/25.......... 100.00 45.00
18 Eddie Mathews Bat-Jsy/25. 100.00 45.00
19 Ryne Sandberg Bat-Jsy/25 120.00 55.00
20 R.Carew Angels Bat-Jsy/25.. 80.00 36.00
21 Duke Snider Bat-Jsy/15..........
24 Frank Robinson Bat-Jsy/25.. 60.00 27.00
25 Brooks Robinson Bat-Jsy/25 80.00 36.00
26 Harmon Killebrew Bat-Jsy/5..........
27 Carl Yastrzemski Bat-Jsy/25 150.00 70.00
28 R.Jackson A's Bat-Jsy/25.... 80.00 36.00
29 Mike Schmidt Bat-Jsy/25.... 100.00 45.00
30 Robin Yount Bat-Jsy/25.... 100.00 45.00
31 George Brett Bat-Jsy/25.... 120.00 55.00
32 Nolan Ryan Rgr Bat-Jsy/25 120.00 55.00
33 Kirby Puckett Bat-Jsy/25... 100.00 45.00
34 Cal Ripken Bat-Jsy/25.......... 150.00 70.00
35 Don Mattingly Bat-Jsy/25... 120.00 55.00
36 Tony Gwynn Bat-Jsy/19.... 120.00 55.00
37 Deion Sanders Bat-Jsy/19... 80.00 36.00
38 D.Winfield Yanks Bat-Jsy/19 60.00 27.00
39 Eddie Murray Bat-Jsy/19.... 120.00 55.00
41 Willie Stargell Bat-Jsy/19.... 80.00 36.00
42 W.Boggs Yanks Bat-Jsy/19.. 80.00 36.00
43 Ozzie Smith Bat-Jsy/19.......... 150.00 70.00
44 Willie McCovey Bat-Jsy/19.. 60.00 27.00
45 R.Jackson Angels Bat-Jsy/19 80.00 36.00
46 Whitey Ford Jsy-Pants/19.... 80.00 36.00
47 Lou Brock Bat-Jsy/19.......... 100.00 45.00
48 Lou Boudreau Jsy-Jsy/19.... 60.00 27.00
49 Steve Carlton Bat-Jsy/19.... 60.00 27.00
50 Rod Carew Twins Bat-Jsy/19 80.00 36.00
52 T.Munson Bat-Jsy/19.......... 120.00 55.00
53 Roger Maris Bat-Jsy/19.......... 200.00 90.00
54 N.Ryan Astros Bat-Jsy/19.. 150.00 70.00
55 N.Ryan Angels Bat-Jsy/19. 150.00 70.00
56 Bo Jackson Bat-Jsy/19.......... 100.00 45.00
57 Joe Morgan Bat-Jsy/19.......... 60.00 27.00
58 Phil Rizzuto Bat-Pants/19.... 80.00 36.00
59 Gary Carter Bat-Jsy/19.......... 60.00 27.00
60 Paul Molitor Bat-Jsy/19.......... 80.00 36.00
63 F.Jenkins Fld Glv-Pants/19... 60.00 27.00
64 P.Reese Bat-Jsy/19.......... 100.00 45.00
65 D.Winfield Padres Bat-Jsy/19 60.00 27.00
66 W.Boggs Sox Bat-Jsy/19.... 80.00 36.00
68 R.Henderson Bat-Jsy/19.... 100.00 45.00
69 R.Clemens Sox Bat-Jsy/19 100.00 45.00
70 R.Clemens Yanks Bat-Jsy/19 100.00 45.00

2004 Prime Cuts MLB Icons Material Prime

MINT NRMT
RANDOM INSERTS IN PACKS..........
PRINT RUNS B/WN 1-25 COPIES PER
NO PRICING ON QTY OF 9 OR LESS..
1 Ty Cobb Pants/9..........
2 Babe Ruth Pants/9..........
3 Lou Gehrig Pants/9..........

4 Johnny Bench Jsy/1
5 Lefty Grove A's Hat/9
6 Carlton Fisk Jsy/25 ... 60.00 27.00
7 Mel Ott Jsy/25 ... 200.00 90.00
8 Bob Feller Jsy/5
9 Jackie Robinson Jsy/9
10 Ted Williams Jsy/9
11 Roy Campanella Pants/25 ... 80.00 36.00
12 Stan Musial Jsy/1
13 Yogi Berra Jsy/1
15 Roberto Clemente Jsy/25
16 Warren Spahn Jsy/25 ... 120.00 55.00
17 Ernie Banks Jsy/25 ... 80.00 36.00
18 Eddie Mathews Jsy/25 ... 80.00 36.00
19 Ryne Sandberg Jsy/25 ... 100.00 45.00
20 Rod Carew Angels Jsy/25 ... 60.00 27.00
21 Duke Snider Jsy/9
22 Jim Palmer Jsy/25 ... 50.00 22.00
24 Frank Robinson Jsy/25 ... 50.00 22.00
25 Brooks Robinson Jsy/25 ... 60.00 27.00
26 Harmon Killebrew Jsy/8
27 Carl Yastrzemski Jsy/25 ... 100.00 45.00
28 Reggie Jackson A's Jsy/25 ... 60.00 27.00
29 Mike Schmidt Jsy/25 ... 100.00 45.00
30 Robin Yount Jsy/25 ... 80.00 36.00
31 George Brett Jsy/25 ... 100.00 45.00
32 Nolan Ryan Rgr Jsy/25 ... 100.00 45.00
33 Kirby Puckett Jsy/25 ... 80.00 36.00
34 Cal Ripken Jsy/25 ... 120.00 55.00
35 Don Mattingly Jsy/25 ... 80.00 36.00
36 Tony Gwynn Jsy/19 ... 100.00 45.00
37 Deion Sanders Jsy/19 ... 60.00 27.00
38 Dave Winfield Yanks Jsy/19 ... 50.00 22.00
39 Eddie Murray Jsy/19 ... 100.00 45.00
40 Tom Seaver Jsy/19 ... 60.00 27.00
41 Willie Stargell Jsy/19 ... 60.00 27.00
42 Wade Boggs Yanks Jsy/19 ... 60.00 27.00
43 Ozzie Smith Jsy/19 ... 80.00 36.00
44 Willie McCovey Jsy/19 ... 50.00 22.00
45 R.Jackson Angels Jsy/19 ... 60.00 27.00
46 Whitey Ford Jsy/19 ... 60.00 27.00
47 Lou Brock Jsy/19 ... 80.00 36.00
48 Lou Boudreau Jsy/19 ... 50.00 22.00
49 Steve Carlton Jsy/19 ... 50.00 22.00
50 Rod Carew Twins Jsy/19 ... 60.00 27.00
51 Bob Gibson Jsy/19 ... 80.00 36.00
52 Thurman Munson Jsy/19 ... 100.00 45.00
53 Roger Maris Jsy/19 ... 150.00 70.00
54 Nolan Ryan Astros Jsy/19 ... 100.00 45.00
55 Nolan Ryan Angels Jsy/19 ... 100.00 45.00
56 Bo Jackson Jsy/19 ... 80.00 36.00
57 Joe Morgan Jsy/19 ... 50.00 22.00
58 Phil Rizzuto Jsy/5
59 Gary Carter Jsy/19 ... 50.00 22.00
60 Paul Molitor Jsy/19 ... 60.00 27.00
61 Don Drysdale Jsy/19 ... 100.00 45.00
62 Catfish Hunter Jsy/19 ... 60.00 27.00
63 Fergie Jenkins Pants/19 ... 50.00 22.00
64 Pee Wee Reese Jsy/19 ... 60.00 27.00
65 Dave Winfield Padres Jsy/19 ... 50.00 22.00
66 Wade Boggs Sox Jsy/19 ... 60.00 27.00
67 Lefty Grove Sox Hat/19 ... 180.00 80.00
68 Rickey Henderson Jsy/19 ... 80.00 36.00
69 Roger Clemens Sox Jsy/19 ... 80.00 36.00
70 R.Clemens Yanks Jsy/19 ... 80.00 36.00

2004 Prime Cuts MLB Icons Material Signature

MINT NRMT
RANDOM INSERTS IN PACKS
PRINT RUNS B/WN 16-45 COPIES PER
4 Johnny Bench Jsy/18 ... 150.00 70.00
8 Bob Feller Jsy/45 ... 80.00 36.00
12 Stan Musial Jsy/30 ... 150.00 70.00
13 Yogi Berra Jsy/42 ... 120.00 55.00
21 Duke Snider Jsy/35 ... 100.00 45.00
26 Harmon Killebrew Jsy/30 ... 120.00 55.00
33 Kirby Puckett Jsy/16 ... 150.00 70.00
69 Roger Clemens Sox Jsy/25 200.00 90.00

2004 Prime Cuts MLB Icons Material Signature Prime

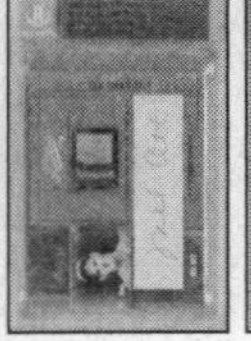
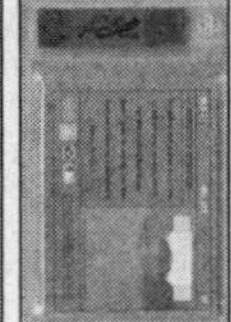

MINT NRMT
RANDOM INSERTS IN PACKS
PRINT RUNS B/WN 1-50 COPIES PER
NO PRICING ON QTY OF 15 OR LESS
1 Ty Cobb Pants/1
2 Babe Ruth Pants/1
3 Lou Gehrig Pants/1
4 Johnny Bench Jsy/5
5 Lefty Grove A's Hat/1
6 Carlton Fisk Jsy/50 ... 80.00 36.00
7 Mel Ott Jsy/1
8 Bob Feller Jsy/5
9 Jackie Robinson Jsy/1
10 Ted Williams Jsy/1
11 Roy Campanella Pants/1
12 Stan Musial Jsy/20 ... 200.00 90.00
13 Yogi Berra Jsy/8
16 Warren Spahn Jsy/25 ... 200.00 90.00
17 Ernie Banks Jsy/50 ... 120.00 55.00
18 Eddie Mathews Jsy/1
19 Ryne Sandberg Jsy/50 ... 150.00 70.00
20 Rod Carew Angels Jsy/50 ... 80.00 36.00
21 Duke Snider Jsy/15
22 Jim Palmer Jsy/50 ... 60.00 27.00
24 Frank Robinson Jsy/50 ... 60.00 27.00
25 Brooks Robinson Jsy/50 ... 80.00 36.00
26 Harmon Killebrew Jsy/20 ... 150.00 70.00
27 Carl Yastrzemski Jsy/50 ... 150.00 70.00
28 Reggie Jackson A's Jsy/50 100.00 45.00
29 Mike Schmidt Jsy/20 ... 200.00 90.00
30 Robin Yount Jsy/50 ... 120.00 55.00
31 George Brett Jsy/50 ... 150.00 70.00
32 Nolan Ryan Rgr Jsy/50 ... 200.00 90.00
33 Kirby Puckett Jsy/34 ... 100.00 45.00
34 Cal Ripken Jsy/50 ... 250.00 110.00
35 Don Mattingly Jsy/50 ... 150.00 70.00
36 Tony Gwynn Jsy/50 ... 100.00 45.00
37 Deion Sanders Jsy/50 ... 120.00 55.00
38 Dave Winfield Yanks Jsy/50. 80.00 36.00
39 Eddie Murray Jsy/50 ... 120.00 55.00
40 Tom Seaver Jsy/10
41 Willie Stargell Jsy/1
42 Wade Boggs Yanks Jsy/50. 100.00 45.00
43 Ozzie Smith Jsy/50 ... 150.00 70.00
44 Willie McCovey Jsy/50 ... 80.00 36.00
45 R.Jackson Angels Jsy/50 ... 100.00 45.00
46 Whitey Ford Jsy/50 ... 100.00 45.00
47 Lou Brock Jsy/25 ... 100.00 45.00
48 Lou Boudreau Jsy/50 ... 150.00 70.00
49 Steve Carlton Jsy/50 ... 80.00 36.00
50 Rod Carew Twins Jsy/50 ... 80.00 36.00
51 Bob Gibson Jsy/50 ... 120.00 55.00
52 Thurman Munson Jsy/1
53 Roger Maris Jsy/1
54 Nolan Ryan Astros Jsy/50 . 200.00 90.00
55 Nolan Ryan Angels Jsy/50 . 200.00 90.00
56 Bo Jackson Jsy/50 ... 120.00 55.00
57 Joe Morgan Jsy/50 ... 60.00 27.00
58 Phil Rizzuto Pants/50 ... 80.00 36.00
59 Gary Carter Jsy/50 ... 60.00 27.00
60 Paul Molitor Jsy/50 ... 80.00 36.00
61 Don Drysdale Jsy/1
62 Catfish Hunter Jsy/1
63 Fergie Jenkins Pants/50 ... 60.00 27.00
64 Pee Wee Reese Jsy/1
65 D.Winfield Padres Jsy/50 ... 80.00 36.00
66 Wade Boggs Sox Jsy/50 ... 100.00 45.00
67 Lefty Grove Sox Hat/1
68 Rickey Henderson Jsy/50 .. 150.00 70.00
69 Roger Clemens Sox Jsy/25 250.00 110.00
70 R.Clemens Yanks Jsy/50 ... 200.00 90.00

2004 Prime Cuts MLB Icons Signature

MINT NRMT
RANDOM INSERTS IN PACKS
PRINT RUNS B/WN 1-50 COPIES PER
NO PRICING ON QTY OF 12 OR LESS
4 Johnny Bench/50 ... 80.00 36.00
6 Carlton Fisk/50 ... 60.00 27.00
8 Bob Feller/50 ... 50.00 22.00
12 Stan Musial/50 ... 100.00 45.00
13 Yogi Berra/50 ... 80.00 36.00
16 Warren Spahn/25 ... 150.00 70.00
17 Ernie Banks/50 ... 100.00 45.00
18 Eddie Mathews/12
19 Ryne Sandberg/50 ... 120.00 55.00
20 Rod Carew Angels/5
21 Duke Snider/25 ... 80.00 36.00
22 Jim Palmer/25 ... 60.00 27.00
24 Frank Robinson/50 ... 50.00 22.00
25 Brooks Robinson/50 ... 60.00 27.00
26 Harmon Killebrew/25 ... 120.00 55.00
27 Carl Yastrzemski/50 ... 100.00 45.00
28 Reggie Jackson A's/50 ... 80.00 36.00
29 Mike Schmidt/20 ... 120.00 55.00
30 Robin Yount/25 ... 120.00 55.00
31 George Brett/25 ... 150.00 70.00
32 Nolan Ryan Rgr/50 ... 150.00 70.00
33 Kirby Puckett/25 ... 100.00 45.00
34 Cal Ripken/25 ... 250.00 110.00
35 Don Mattingly/50 ... 120.00 55.00
36 Tony Gwynn/25 ... 100.00 45.00
37 Deion Sanders/25
38 Dave Winfield Yanks/25 ... 80.00 36.00
39 Eddie Murray/25 ... 120.00 55.00
40 Tom Seaver/25
42 Wade Boggs Yanks/25 ... 100.00 45.00
43 Ozzie Smith/25 ... 150.00 70.00
44 Willie McCovey/25 ... 80.00 36.00
45 Reggie Jackson Angels/25. 100.00 45.00
46 Whitey Ford/10
47 Lou Brock/25 ... 80.00 36.00
48 Lou Boudreau/25 ... 150.00 70.00
49 Steve Carlton/10
50 Rod Carew Twins/5
51 Bob Gibson/25 ... 80.00 36.00
53 Roger Maris/1
54 Nolan Ryan Astros/10
55 Nolan Ryan Angels/10
56 Bo Jackson/25 ... 120.00 55.00
57 Joe Morgan/25 ... 60.00 27.00
58 Phil Rizzuto/10
59 Gary Carter/25 ... 60.00 27.00
60 Paul Molitor/25 ... 80.00 36.00
61 Don Drysdale/1
62 Catfish Hunter/1
63 Fergie Jenkins/10
64 Pee Wee Reese/1
65 Dave Winfield Padres/25 ... 80.00 36.00
66 Wade Boggs Sox/25 ... 100.00 45.00
67 Lefty Grove/1
68 Rickey Henderson A's/10
69 Roger Clemens Sox/10
70 Roger Clemens Yanks/10

2004 Prime Cuts Signature

MINT NRMT
RANDOM INSERTS IN PACKS
PRINT RUNS B/WN 5-25 COPIES PER
NO PRICING ON QTY OF 14 OR LESS
1 Roger Clemens Yanks/25 ... 150.00 70.00
3 Albert Pujols/25 ... 200.00 90.00
5 Greg Maddux Braves/10
7 Hideo Nomo Dodgers/10
8 Mike Piazza Mets/10
10 Jeff Bagwell/25 ... 80.00 36.00
12 Manny Ramirez/14
13 R.Henderson Dodgers/25 ... 80.00 36.00
14 Alex Rodriguez Rgr/25 ... 150.00 70.00
15 Troy Glaus/25 ... 40.00 18.00
16 Mike Mussina/25 ... 60.00 27.00
17 Kerry Wood/25 ... 80.00 36.00
18 Kazuhisa Ishii/25 ... 40.00 18.00
20 Frank Thomas/25 ... 80.00 36.00
22 Adam Dunn/25 ... 60.00 27.00
23 Randy Johnson D'backs/10
24 Alfonso Soriano/25 ... 60.00 27.00
25 Pedro Martinez Sox/10
26 Andruw Jones/25 ... 40.00 18.00
27 Mark Prior/25 ... 120.00 55.00
28 Vladimir Guerrero/25 ... 80.00 36.00
29 Chipper Jones/25 ... 80.00 36.00
30 Todd Helton/17 ... 60.00 27.00
31 Rafael Palmeiro/25 ... 80.00 36.00
32 Mark Grace/25 ... 80.00 36.00
33 Pedro Martinez Dodgers/10
34 Randy Johnson M's/10
35 Randy Johnson Astros/10
36 Roger Clemens Sox/25 ... 150.00 70.00
37 Roger Clemens Jays/25 ... 150.00 70.00
38 Alex Rodriguez M's/25 ... 150.00 70.00
39 Greg Maddux Cubs/10
40 Mike Piazza Dodgers/10
41 Mike Piazza Marlins/5
42 Hideo Nomo Mets/5
43 Rickey Henderson Yanks/25 80.00 36.00
44 Rickey Henderson A's/25 ... 80.00 36.00
46 Ivan Rodriguez/25 ... 80.00 36.00
47 George Brett/25 ... 150.00 70.00
48 Cal Ripken/25 ... 200.00 90.00
49 Nolan Ryan/25 ... 150.00 70.00
50 Don Mattingly/25 ... 120.00 55.00

2004 Prime Cuts Timeline Dual Achievements Material

MINT NRMT
RANDOM INSERTS IN PACKS
PRINT RUNS B/WN 9-19 COPIES PER
NO PRICING ON QTY OF 9 OR LESS
1 Roy Campanella Pants
Yogi Berra Jsy/9
2 Jackie Robinson Jsy
Ted Williams Jsy/9
3 Stan Musial Jsy ... 200.00 90.00
Ted Williams Jsy/19
4 Mike Schmidt Jsy ... 120.00 55.00
George Brett Jsy/19
5 Dale Murphy Jsy ... 120.00 55.00
Cal Ripken Jsy/19
6 Roger Clemens Jsy ... 100.00 45.00
Mike Schmidt Jsy/19
7 Ty Cobb Pants
Babe Ruth Pants/9
8 Roy Campanella Pants
Stan Musial Jsy/9
10 George Brett Jsy ... 120.00 55.00
Nolan Ryan Jsy/19
11 Jackie Robinson Jsy
Roy Campanella Pants/9
12 Al Kaline Pants ... 80.00 36.00
Duke Snider Jsy/19

2004 Prime Cuts Timeline Dual Achievements Material Combos

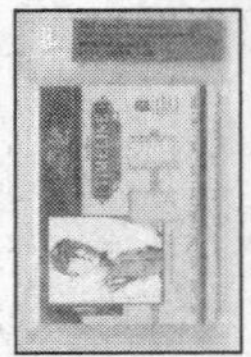

MINT NRMT
RANDOM INSERTS IN PACKS
PRINT RUNS B/WN 1-19 COPIES PER
NO PRICING ON QTY OF 15 OR LESS
1 Roy Campanella Bat-Pants
Yogi Berra Bat-Jsy/1
3 Stan Musial Bat-Jsy
Ted Williams Bat-Jsy/1
4 Mike Schmidt Bat-Jsy ... 250.00 110.00
George Brett Bat-Jsy/19
5 Dale Murphy Bat-Jsy ... 200.00 90.00
Cal Ripken Bat-Jsy/19
6 Roger Clemens Bat-Jsy ... 150.00 70.00
Mike Schmidt Bat-Jsy/19
7 Ty Cobb Bat-Pants
Babe Ruth Bat-Pants/9
8 Roy Campanella Bat-Pants
Stan Musial Bat-Jsy/2
10 George Brett Bat-Jsy ... 250.00 110.00
Nolan Ryan Bat-Jsy/19
12 Al Kaline Bat-Pants
Duke Snider Bat-Jsy/15

2004 Prime Cuts Timeline Dual Achievements Material Prime

MINT NRMT
RANDOM INSERTS IN PACKS
PRINT RUNS B/WN 1-19 COPIES PER
NO PRICING ON QTY OF 15 OR LESS
1 Roy Campanella Pants
Yogi Berra Jsy/1
2 Jackie Robinson Jsy
Ted Williams Jsy/9
3 Stan Musial Jsy
Ted Williams Jsy/2
4 Mike Schmidt Jsy ... 200.00 90.00
George Brett Jsy/19
5 Dale Murphy Jsy ... 200.00 90.00
Cal Ripken Jsy/19
6 Roger Clemens Jsy ... 150.00 70.00
Mike Schmidt Jsy/19
7 Ty Cobb Pants
Babe Ruth Pants/9
8 Roy Campanella Pants
Stan Musial Jsy/2
10 George Brett Jsy ... 200.00 90.00
Nolan Ryan Jsy/19
11 Jackie Robinson Jsy
Roy Campanella Pants/9
12 Al Kaline Pants
Duke Snider Jsy/15

2004 Prime Cuts Timeline Dual Achievements Material Signature

MINT NRMT
RANDOM INSERTS IN PACKS
PRINT RUNS B/WN 1-25 COPIES PER
NO PRICING ON QTY OF 15 OR LESS
2 Jackie Robinson Jsy
Ted Williams Jsy/1
3 Stan Musial Jsy
Ted Williams Jsy/1
4 Mike Schmidt Jsy ... 300.00 135.00
George Brett Jsy/24
5 Dale Murphy Jsy ... 300.00 135.00
Cal Ripken Jsy/25
6 Roger Clemens Jsy ... 300.00 135.00
Mike Schmidt Jsy/24
7 Ty Cobb Pants
Babe Ruth Pants/1
10 George Brett Jsy ... 350.00 160.00
Nolan Ryan Jsy/25
12 Al Kaline Pants
Duke Snider Jsy/15

2004 Prime Cuts Timeline Dual Achievements Signature

MINT NRMT
RANDOM INSERTS IN PACKS
PRINT RUNS B/WN 24-25 COPIES PER
4 Mike Schmidt ... 250.00 110.00
George Brett/24
5 Dale Murphy ... 250.00 110.00
Cal Ripken/25
6 Roger Clemens ... 250.00 110.00
Mike Schmidt/24
10 George Brett ... 300.00 135.00
Nolan Ryan/25
12 Al Kaline ... 150.00 70.00
Duke Snider/25

2004 Prime Cuts Timeline Dual League Leaders Material

MINT NRMT
RANDOM INSERTS IN PACKS
PRINT RUNS B/WN 9-19 COPIES PER
NO PRICING ON QTY OF 9 OR LESS
1 Mel Ott Jsy
Lou Gehrig Pants/9
2 Mel Ott Jsy
Ted Williams Jsy/9
4 Steve Carlton Jsy ... 60.00 27.00
Jim Palmer Jsy/19

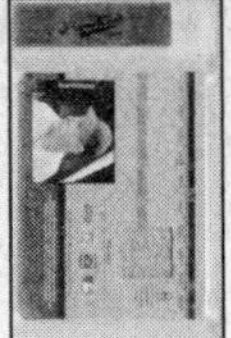

6 Roberto Clemente Jsy
Carl Yastrzemski Jsy/9
7 Steve Carlton Jsy ... 100.00 45.00
Nolan Ryan Jsy/19
8 Don Mattingly Jsy ... 120.00 55.00
Tony Gwynn Jsy/19
9 Roger Clemens Jsy ... 120.00 55.00
Nolan Ryan Jsy/19
10 Babe Ruth Pants
Lou Gehrig Pants/9

2004 Prime Cuts Timeline Dual League Leaders Material Combos

MINT NRMT
RANDOM INSERTS IN PACKS
PRINT RUNS B/WN 9-19 COPIES PER
NO PRICING ON QTY OF 9 OR LESS
1 Mel Ott Bat-Jsy
Lou Gehrig Bat-Pants/9
2 Mel Ott Bat-Jsy
Ted Williams Bat-Jsy/9
6 Roberto Clemente Bat-Jsy
Carl Yastrzemski Bat-Jsy/9
7 Steve Carlton Bat-Jsy ... 150.00 70.00
Nolan Ryan Bat-Jsy/19
8 Don Mattingly Bat-Jsy ... 200.00 90.00
Tony Gwynn Bat-Jsy/19
9 Roger Clemens Bat-Jsy ... 200.00 90.00
Nolan Ryan Bat-Jsy/19
10 Babe Ruth Bat-Pants
Lou Gehrig Bat-Pants/9

2004 Prime Cuts Timeline Dual League Leaders Material Prime

MINT NRMT
RANDOM INSERTS IN PACKS
PRINT RUNS B/WN 9-19 COPIES PER
NO PRICING DUE TO SCARCITY
1 Mel Ott Jsy
Lou Gehrig Pants/9
2 Mel Ott Jsy
Ted Williams Jsy/9
4 Steve Carlton Jsy ... 100.00 45.00
Jim Palmer Jsy/19
6 Roberto Clemente Jsy
Carl Yastrzemski Jsy/9
7 Steve Carlton Jsy ... 150.00 70.00
Nolan Ryan Jsy/19
8 Don Mattingly Jsy ... 200.00 90.00
Tony Gwynn Jsy/19
9 Roger Clemens Jsy ... 200.00 90.00
Nolan Ryan Jsy/19
10 Babe Ruth Pants
Lou Gehrig Pants/9

2004 Prime Cuts Timeline Dual League Leaders Material Signature

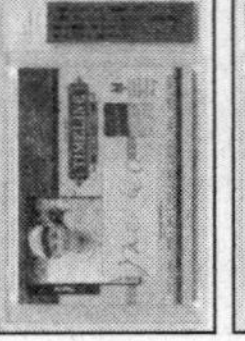

MINT NRMT
RANDOM INSERTS IN PACKS
PRINT RUNS B/WN 1-50 COPIES PER
NO PRICING ON QTY OF 1
1 Mel Ott Jsy
Lou Gehrig Pants/1
2 Mel Ott Jsy
Ted Williams Jsy/1
4 Steve Carlton Jsy ... 120.00 55.00
Jim Palmer Jsy/50
6 Roberto Clemente Jsy
Carl Yastrzemski Jsy/1
7 Steve Carlton Jsy ... 300.00 135.00
Nolan Ryan Jsy/25
8 Don Mattingly Jsy ... 300.00 135.00
Tony Gwynn Jsy/25
9 Roger Clemens Jsy ... 500.00 220.00
Nolan Ryan Jsy/25
10 Babe Ruth Pants
Lou Gehrig Pants/1

2004 Prime Cuts Timeline Dual League Leaders Signature

MINT NRMT
RANDOM INSERTS IN PACKS
PRINT RUNS B/WN 25-50 COPIES PER
4 Steve Carlton ... 100.00 45.00
Jim Palmer/50
7 Steve Carlton ... 250.00 110.00
Nolan Ryan/25
8 Don Mattingly ... 250.00 110.00
Tony Gwynn/25

9 Roger Clemens 400.00 180.00
Nolan Ryan/25

2004 Prime Cuts Timeline Material

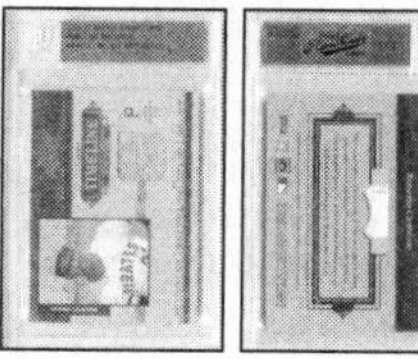
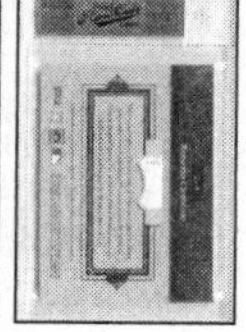

MINT NRMT
RANDOM INSERTS IN PACKS
NO PRICING ON QTY OF 9 OR LESS
1 Ty Cobb Pants/9
2 Babe Ruth Pants/9
3 Lou Gehrig Pants/9
4 Ted Williams TC Jsy/50 120.00 55.00
5 Roy Campanella Pants/50 60.00 27.00
6 Stan Musial MVP Jsy/50 60.00 27.00
7 Yogi Berra 51M Jsy/50 50.00 22.00
9 R.Clemente MVP Jsy/50 150.00 70.00
10 Will Clark Jsy/25 60.00 27.00
12 Carl Yastrzemski Jsy/50 60.00 27.00
13 Mike Schmidt Jsy/50 50.00 22.00
14 George Brett MVP Jsy/50 60.00 27.00
15 Nolan Ryan WIN Jsy/50 60.00 27.00
16 Stan Musial BA Jsy/50 60.00 27.00
17 Ted Williams BA Jsy/50 120.00 55.00
18 R.Clemente BTG Jsy/50 150.00 70.00
19 Greg Maddux Jsy/50 50.00 22.00
21 Robin Yount Jsy/50 50.00 22.00
22 Nolan Ryan HOF Jsy/50 60.00 27.00
23 Ted Williams RET Jsy/50 120.00 55.00
24 George Brett RET Jsy/50 60.00 27.00
25 Yogi Berra 55M Jsy/50 50.00 22.00
26 Rod Carew Jsy/50 40.00 18.00
27 Dale Murphy Jsy/25 60.00 27.00

2004 Prime Cuts Timeline Material Combos

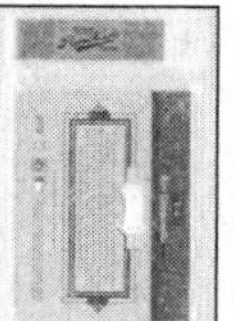

MINT NRMT
RANDOM INSERTS IN PACKS
PRINT RUNS B/WN 1-19 COPIES PER
NO PRICING ON QTY OF 9 OR LESS
1 Ty Cobb Bat-Pants/9
2 Babe Ruth Bat-Pants/9
3 Lou Gehrig Bat-Pants/9
4 Ted Williams TC Bat-Jsy/9
5 Roy Campanella Bat-Pants/9
6 Stan Musial MVP Bat-Jsy/1
7 Yogi Berra 51M Bat-Jsy/2
9 R.Clemente MVP Bat-Jsy/9
10 Will Clark Bat-Jsy/19 150.00 70.00
12 Carl Yastrzemski Bat-Jsy/19 150.00 70.00
13 Mike Schmidt Bat-Jsy/19 120.00 55.00
14 G.Brett MVP Bat-Jsy/19 150.00 70.00
15 N.Ryan WIN Bat-Jsy/19 150.00 70.00
16 Stan Musial BA Bat-Jsy/1
17 Ted Williams BA Bat-Jsy/9
18 R.Clemente BTG Bat-Jsy/9
19 Greg Maddux Bat-Jsy/19 100.00 45.00
21 Robin Yount Bat-Jsy/19 120.00 55.00
22 N.Ryan HOF Bat-Jsy/19 150.00 70.00
23 Ted Williams RET Bat-Jsy/9
24 G.Brett RET Bat-Jsy/19 150.00 70.00
25 Yogi Berra 55M Bat-Jsy/2
26 Rod Carew Bat-Jsy/19 80.00 36.00
27 Dale Murphy Bat-Jsy/19 100.00 45.00

2004 Prime Cuts Timeline Material Prime

MINT NRMT
RANDOM INSERTS IN PACKS
PRINT RUNS B/WN 1-25 COPIES PER
NO PRICING ON QTY OF 9 OR LESS
1 Ty Cobb Pants/9
2 Babe Ruth Pants/9
3 Lou Gehrig Pants/9
4 Ted Williams TC Jsy/9
5 Roy Campanella Pants/25 80.00 36.00
6 Stan Musial MVP Jsy/2
7 Yogi Berra 51M Jsy/1
9 R.Clemente MVP Jsy/25
10 Will Clark Jsy/25 80.00 36.00
12 Carl Yastrzemski Jsy/25 120.00 55.00
13 Mike Schmidt Jsy/25 100.00 45.00
14 George Brett MVP Jsy/25 100.00 45.00
15 Nolan Ryan WIN Jsy/25 100.00 45.00
16 Stan Musial BA Jsy/2
17 Ted Williams BA Jsy/9
18 R.Clemente BTG Jsy/25 150.00 70.00
19 Greg Maddux Jsy/25 80.00 36.00
21 Robin Yount Jsy/25 80.00 36.00
22 Nolan Ryan HOF Jsy/25 100.00 45.00
23 Ted Williams RET Jsy/9
24 George Brett RET Jsy/25 100.00 45.00
25 Yogi Berra 55M Jsy/1
26 Rod Carew Jsy/25 80.00 36.00
27 Dale Murphy Jsy/25 80.00 36.00

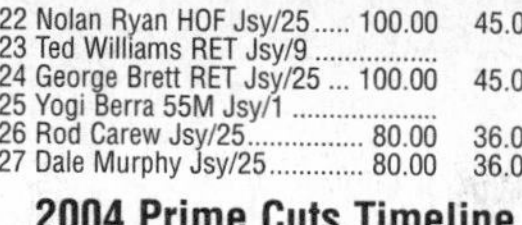

2004 Prime Cuts Timeline Material Signature

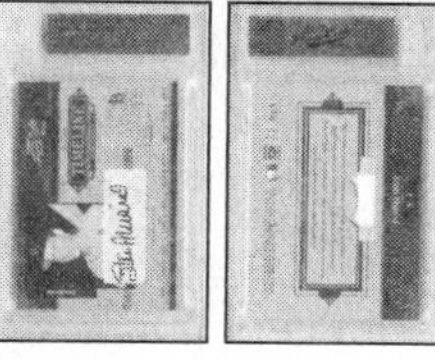

MINT NRMT
RANDOM INSERTS IN PACKS
PRINT RUNS B/WN 33-42 COPIES PER
6 Stan Musial MVP Jsy/33 150.00 70.00
7 Yogi Berra 51M Jsy/42 120.00 55.00
16 Stan Musial BA Jsy/38 150.00 70.00
25 Yogi Berra 55M Jsy/42 120.00 55.00

2004 Prime Cuts Timeline Material Signature Prime

MINT NRMT
RANDOM INSERTS IN PACKS
PRINT RUNS B/WN 1-50 COPIES PER
NO PRICING ON QTY OF 10 OR LESS
1 Ty Cobb Pants/1
2 Babe Ruth Pants/1
3 Lou Gehrig Pants/1
6 Stan Musial MVP Jsy/10
7 Yogi Berra 51M Jsy/8
9 Roberto Clemente Jsy/1
10 Will Clark Jsy/50 120.00 55.00
12 Carl Yastrzemski Jsy/50 150.00 70.00
13 Mike Schmidt Jsy/20 200.00 90.00
14 George Brett MVP Jsy/25 200.00 90.00
15 Nolan Ryan WIN Jsy/50 200.00 90.00
16 Stan Musial BA Jsy/10
19 Greg Maddux Jsy/50 200.00 90.00
21 Robin Yount Jsy/50 120.00 55.00
22 Nolan Ryan HOF Jsy/50 200.00 90.00
24 George Brett RET Jsy/25 200.00 90.00
25 Yogi Berra 55M Jsy/8
26 Rod Carew Jsy/50 80.00 36.00
27 Dale Murphy Jsy/50 100.00 45.00

2004 Prime Cuts Timeline Signature

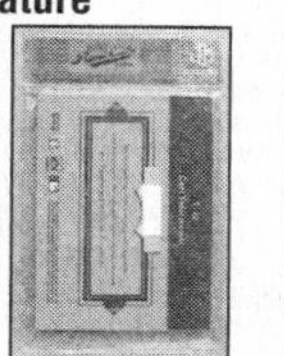

MINT NRMT
RANDOM INSERTS IN PACKS
PRINT RUNS B/WN 10-50 COPIES PER
NO PRICING ON QTY OF 20 OR LESS
6 Stan Musial MVP/50 100.00 45.00
7 Yogi Berra 51M/50 80.00 36.00
10 Will Clark/25 150.00 70.00
12 Carl Yastrzemski/50 100.00 45.00
13 Mike Schmidt/20 120.00 55.00
14 George Brett MVP/25 150.00 70.00
15 Nolan Ryan WIN/50 150.00 70.00
16 Stan Musial BA/50 100.00 45.00
19 Greg Maddux/31 150.00 70.00
21 Robin Yount/25 120.00 55.00
22 Nolan Ryan HOF/50 150.00 70.00
24 George Brett RET/25 150.00 70.00
25 Yogi Berra 55M/50 80.00 36.00
26 Rod Carew/10
27 Dale Murphy/25 100.00 45.00

2004 Prime Cuts II

Nm-Mt Ex-Mt
COMPLETE SET (100)
COMMON CARD (1-91) 4.00 1.20
COMMON CARD (92-100) 4.00 1.20
1 Mark Prior 5.00 1.50
2 Derek Jeter 10.00 3.00
3 Eric Chavez 4.00 1.20
4 Carlos Delgado 4.00 1.20
5 Albert Pujols 10.00 3.00
6 Miguel Cabrera 5.00 1.50
7 Ivan Rodriguez 5.00 1.50
8 Javy Lopez 4.00 1.20
9 Hank Blalock 4.00 1.20
10 Chipper Jones 5.00 1.50
11 Gary Sheffield 4.00 1.20
12 Alfonso Soriano 5.00 1.50
13 Alex Rodriguez Yanks 8.00 2.40
14 Edgar Renteria 4.00 1.20
15 Jim Edmonds 4.00 1.20
16 Garret Anderson 4.00 1.20
17 Lance Berkman 4.00 1.20
18 Brandon Webb 4.00 1.20
19 Mike Lowell 4.00 1.20
20 Mark Mulder 4.00 1.20
21 Sammy Sosa 8.00 2.40
22 Roger Clemens Astros 8.00 2.40
23 Mark Teixeira 4.00 1.20
24 Manny Ramirez 5.00 1.50
25 Rafael Palmeiro 5.00 1.50
26 Ichiro Suzuki 8.00 2.40
27 Vladimir Guerrero 5.00 1.50
28 Austin Kearns 4.00 1.20
29 Troy Glaus 4.00 1.20
30 Ken Griffey Jr. 8.00 2.40
31 Greg Maddux 8.00 2.40
32 Roy Halladay 4.00 1.20
33 Roy Oswalt 4.00 1.20
34 Kerry Wood 5.00 1.50
35 Mike Mussina Yanks 5.00 1.50
36 Michael Young 4.00 1.20
37 Juan Gonzalez 5.00 1.50
38 Curt Schilling 5.00 1.50
39 Shannon Stewart 4.00 1.20
40 Todd Helton 5.00 1.50
41 Larry Walker 5.00 1.50
42 Mariano Rivera 5.00 1.50
43 Nomar Garciaparra 8.00 2.40
44 Adam Dunn 5.00 1.50
45 Pedro Martinez Sox 5.00 1.50
46 Bernie Williams 5.00 1.50
47 Tom Glavine 5.00 1.50
48 Torii Hunter 4.00 1.20
49 David Ortiz 5.00 1.50
50 Frank Thomas 5.00 1.50
51 Randy Johnson D'backs 5.00 1.50
52 Jason Giambi 4.00 1.20
53 Carlos Lee 4.00 1.20
54 Mike Sweeney 4.00 1.20
55 Hideki Matsui 8.00 2.40
56 Dontrelle Willis 4.00 1.20
57 Tim Hudson 4.00 1.20
58 Jose Vidro 4.00 1.20
59 Jeff Bagwell 5.00 1.50
60 Rocco Baldelli 4.00 1.20
61 Craig Biggio 5.00 1.50
62 Mike Piazza Mets 8.00 2.40
63 Magglio Ordonez 4.00 1.20
64 Hideo Nomo 5.00 1.50
65 Miguel Tejada 4.00 1.20
66 Vernon Wells 4.00 1.20
67 Barry Larkin 5.00 1.50
68 Jacque Jones 4.00 1.20
69 Scott Rolen 5.00 1.50
70 Jeff Kent 4.00 1.20
71 Steve Finley 4.00 1.20
72 Kazuo Matsui RC 8.00 2.40
73 Carlos Beltran 5.00 1.50
74 Shawn Green 4.00 1.20
75 Barry Zito 4.00 1.20
76 Aramis Ramirez 4.00 1.20
77 Paul Lo Duca 4.00 1.20
78 Kazuhisa Ishii 4.00 1.20
79 Aubrey Huff 4.00 1.20
80 Jim Thome 5.00 1.50
81 Andy Pettitte Astros 5.00 1.50
82 Andruw Jones 4.00 1.20
83 Josh Beckett 4.00 1.20
84 Sean Casey 4.00 1.20
85 Alex Rodriguez M's 8.00 2.40
86 Roger Clemens Yanks 8.00 2.40
87 Mike Mussina O's 5.00 1.50
88 Pedro Martinez Dgr 5.00 1.50
89 Randy Johnson Astros 5.00 1.50
90 Mike Piazza Dgr 8.00 2.40
91 Andy Pettitte Yanks 5.00 1.50
92 Cal Ripken 20.00 6.00
93 Dale Murphy 5.00 1.50
94 Don Mattingly 10.00 3.00
95 Gary Carter 4.00 1.20
96 George Brett 10.00 3.00
97 Nolan Ryan 12.00 3.60
98 Ozzie Smith 8.00 2.40
99 Steve Carlton 4.00 1.20
100 Tony Gwynn 8.00 2.40

2004 Prime Cuts II Century Gold

Nm-Mt Ex-Mt
*GOLD 1-91: 1.25X TO 3X BASIC
*GOLD 92-100: 1.25X TO 3X BASIC
RANDOM INSERTS IN PACKS
STATED PRINT RUN 25 SERIAL #'d SETS
NO RC YR PRICING DUE TO SCARCITY

2004 Prime Cuts II Century Platinum

Nm-Mt Ex-Mt
RANDOM INSERTS IN PACKS
STATED PRINT RUN 1 SERIAL #'d SET
NO PRICING DUE TO SCARCITY

2004 Prime Cuts II Century Silver

Nm-Mt Ex-Mt
*SILVER 1-91: .75X TO 2X BASIC
*SILVER 92-100: .75X TO 2X BASIC
RANDOM INSERTS IN PACKS
STATED PRINT RUN 50 SERIAL #'d SETS

2004 Prime Cuts II Material Number

Nm-Mt Ex-Mt
*1-91 p/r 25: .3X TO .8X COMBO p/r 22
*92-100 p/r 25: .3X TO .8X COMBO p/r 25
OVERALL AU-GU ODDS 1:1
PRINT RUNS B/WN 1-25 COPIES PER
NO PRICING ON QTY OF 10 OR LESS

2004 Prime Cuts II Material Prime

Nm-Mt Ex-Mt
OVERALL AU-GU ODDS 1:1
PRINT RUNS B/WN 1-10 COPIES PER
NO PRICING DUE TO SCARCITY

2004 Prime Cuts II Material Combo

Nm-Mt Ex-Mt
OVERALL AU-GU ODDS 1:1
PRINT RUNS B/WN 1-35 COPIES PER
NO PRICING ON QTY OF 10 OR LESS
1 Mark Prior Hat-Jsy/22 30.00 9.00
3 Eric Chavez Bat-Jsy/3
4 Carlos Delgado Bat-Jsy/1
5 Albert Pujols Bat-Jsy/5
6 Miguel Cabrera Bat-Jsy/5
7 Ivan Rodriguez Bat-Jsy/7
8 Javy Lopez Bat-Jsy/5
9 Hank Blalock Bat-Jsy/1
10 Chipper Jones Bat-Jsy/10
12 Alfonso Soriano Bat-Jsy/25 25.00 7.50
14 Edgar Renteria Bat-Jsy/1
15 Jim Edmonds Bat-Jsy/15 20.00 6.00
16 Garret Anderson Bat-Jsy/16 20.00 6.00
17 Lance Berkman Hat-Jsy/17 20.00 6.00
19 Mike Lowell Bat-Jsy/1
20 Mark Mulder Bat-Jsy/1
21 Sammy Sosa Bat-Jsy/21 50.00 15.00
22 R.Clem Astros Bat-Jsy/22 50.00 15.00
23 Mark Teixeira Fld Glv-Jsy/1
24 Manny Ramirez Bat-Jsy/24 25.00 7.50
25 Rafael Palmeiro Bat-Jsy/25 25.00 7.50
27 Vlad Guerrero Bat-Jsy/27 30.00 9.00
29 Troy Glaus Bat-Jsy/1
31 Greg Maddux Bat-Jsy/31 50.00 15.00
32 Roy Halladay Jsy-Jsy/1
33 Roy Oswalt Fld Glv-Jsy/1
34 Kerry Wood Jsy-Pants/10
35 M.Muss Yanks Bat-Jsy/35 25.00 7.50
36 Michael Young Bat-Jsy/1
37 Juan Gonzalez Bat-Jsy/1
38 Curt Schilling Bat-Jsy/1
40 Todd Helton Bat-Jsy/17 30.00 9.00
44 Adam Dunn Bat-Jsy/1
45 P.Martinez Sox Jsy-Pants/1
46 Bernie Williams Jsy-Jsy/1
47 Tom Glavine Bat-Jsy/1
48 Torii Hunter Bat-Jsy/1
49 David Ortiz Bat-Jsy/1
50 Frank Thomas Jsy-Pants/1
51 R.John D'backs Bat-Jsy/10
52 Jason Giambi Bat-Jsy/1
55 Hideki Matsui Bat-Jsy/5
56 Dontrelle Willis Jsy-Jsy/1
57 Tim Hudson Hat-Jsy/1
59 Jeff Bagwell Bat-Jsy/5
60 Rocco Baldelli Bat-Jsy/1
61 Craig Biggio Bat-Jsy/1
62 Mike Piazza Mets Jsy-Jsy/10
63 Magglio Ordonez Bat-Jsy/10
64 Hideo Nomo Jsy-Pants/10
65 Miguel Tejada Bat-Jsy/1
66 Vernon Wells Bat-Jsy/1
67 Barry Larkin Bat-Jsy/1
69 Scott Rolen Bat-Jsy/5
72 Kazuo Matsui Bat-Jsy/5
73 Carlos Beltran Bat-Jsy/1
74 Shawn Green Bat-Jsy/1
75 Barry Zito Bat-Jsy/1
78 Kazuhisa Ishii Bat-Jsy/1
80 Jim Thome Bat-Jsy/1
81 A.Pettitte Astros Bat-Jsy/1
82 Andruw Jones Bat-Jsy/1
83 Josh Beckett Bat-Jsy/1
84 Sean Casey Bat-Jsy/1
86 R.Clem Ynk Fld Glv-Jsy/22 50.00 15.00
87 M.Muss O's Jsy-Pants/1
88 P.Martinez Dgr Bat-Jsy/1
89 R.John Astros Bat-Jsy/10
90 Mike Piazza Dgr Bat-Jsy/10
91 A.Pettitte Yanks Jsy-Jsy/1
92 Cal Ripken Bat-Jsy/25 100.00 30.00
93 Dale Murphy Bat-Jsy/25 30.00 9.00
94 Don Mattingly Bat-Jsy/25 60.00 18.00
95 Gary Carter Jkt-Jsy/10
96 George Brett Bat-Jsy/25 60.00 18.00
97 Nolan Ryan Bat-Jkt/25 60.00 18.00
98 Ozzie Smith Bat-Jsy/25 50.00 15.00
99 Steve Carlton Bat-Jsy/10
100 Tony Gwynn Bat-Jsy/10

2004 Prime Cuts II Material Combo Prime

Nm-Mt Ex-Mt
OVERALL AU-GU ODDS 1:1
PRINT RUNS B/WN 1-9 COPIES PER
NO PRICING DUE TO SCARCITY

2004 Prime Cuts II Signature Century Gold

Nm-Mt Ex-Mt
*1-91 p/r 15-19: .5X TO 1.2X SILV p/r 25
*92-100 p/r 15-19: .5X TO 1.2X SILV p/r 25
OVERALL AU-GU ODDS 1:1
PRINT RUNS B/WN 1-19 COPIES PER
NO PRICING ON QTY OF 11 OR LESS

2004 Prime Cuts II Signature Century Platinum

Nm-Mt Ex-Mt
OVERALL AU-GU ODDS 1:1
STATED PRINT RUN 1 SERIAL #'d SET
NO PRICING DUE TO SCARCITY

2004 Prime Cuts II Signature Century Silver

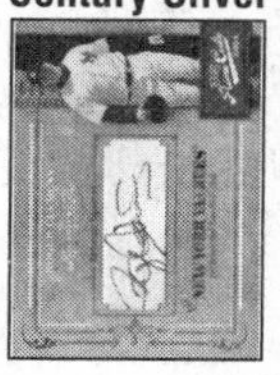

Nm-Mt Ex-Mt
OVERALL AU-GU ODDS 1:1
PRINT RUNS B/WN 1- COPIES PER
NO PRICING ON QTY OF OR LESS
1 Mark Prior/22 50.00 15.00
3 Eric Chavez/10
5 Albert Pujols/10
6 Miguel Cabrera/24 40.00 12.00
9 Hank Blalock/25 40.00 12.00
10 Chipper Jones/1
11 Gary Sheffield/25 40.00 12.00
14 Edgar Renteria/10
15 Jim Edmonds/25 40.00 12.00
16 Garret Anderson/25 25.00 7.50
17 Lance Berkman/25 40.00 12.00
19 Mike Lowell/19 30.00 9.00
20 Mark Mulder/20 25.00 7.50
21 Sammy Sosa/21 120.00 36.00
22 Roger Clemens Astros/10
23 Mark Teixeira/23 40.00 12.00
24 Manny Ramirez/24 80.00 24.00
25 Rafael Palmeiro/25 60.00 18.00
27 Vladimir Guerrero/5
31 Greg Maddux/31 120.00 36.00
34 Kerry Wood/34 50.00 15.00
35 Mike Mussina Yanks/35 40.00 12.00
37 Juan Gonzalez/22 40.00 12.00
38 Curt Schilling/10
40 Todd Helton/17 50.00 15.00
44 Adam Dunn/44 30.00 9.00
45 Pedro Martinez Sox/10
46 Bernie Williams/10
48 Torii Hunter/10
49 David Ortiz/34 50.00 15.00
50 Frank Thomas/35 50.00 15.00
51 Randy Johnson D'backs/10
56 Dontrelle Willis/10
57 Tim Hudson/15 30.00 9.00
59 Jeff Bagwell/10
61 Craig Biggio/25 40.00 12.00
62 Mike Piazza Mets/10
63 Magglio Ordonez/30 25.00 7.50
64 Hideo Nomo/1
66 Vernon Wells/25 25.00 7.50
67 Barry Larkin/11
69 Scott Rolen/27 50.00 15.00
73 Carlos Beltran/15 60.00 18.00
74 Shawn Green/15 30.00 9.00
75 Barry Zito/10
78 Kazuhisa Ishii/17 50.00 15.00
81 Andy Pettitte Astros/10
82 Andruw Jones/25 40.00 12.00
83 Josh Beckett/21 25.00 7.50
84 Sean Casey/10
86 Roger Clemens Yanks/10
87 Mike Mussina O's/35 40.00 12.00
88 Pedro Martinez Dgr/10
89 Randy Johnson Astros/10
90 Mike Piazza Dgr/10
91 Andy Pettitte Yanks/10
92 Cal Ripken/25 200.00 60.00
93 Dale Murphy/25 40.00 12.00
94 Don Mattingly/23 80.00 24.00
95 Gary Carter/25 25.00 7.50
96 George Brett/10
97 Nolan Ryan/34 120.00 36.00
98 Ozzie Smith/10
99 Steve Carlton/32 40.00 12.00
100 Tony Gwynn/25 60.00 18.00

2004 Prime Cuts II Signature Material Number

Nm-Mt Ex-Mt
*1-91 p/r 20-35: .5X TO 1.2X SILV p/r 20-35
*1-91 p/r 15-19: .6X TO 1.5X SILV p/r 20-25
*1-91 p/r 15-19: .5X TO 1.2X SILV p/r 15-19
*92-100 p/r 20-35: .5X TO 1.2X SILV p/r 20-35
*92-100 p/r 15-19: .6X TO 1.5X SILV p/r 20-25
OVERALL AU-GU ODDS 1:1
PRINT RUNS B/WN 1- COPIES PER
NO PRICING ON QTY OF OR LESS

2004 Prime Cuts II Signature Material Prime

Nm-Mt Ex-Mt
OVERALL AU-GU ODDS 1:1
PRINT RUNS B/WN 1-9 COPIES PER
NO PRICING DUE TO SCARCITY

2004 Prime Cuts II Signature Material Combo

Nm-Mt Ex-Mt
*1-91 p/r 20-35: .6X TO 1.5X SILV p/r 20-35
*1-91 p/r 15-19: .75X TO 2X SILV p/r 20-35
*1-91 p/r 15-19: .6X TO 1.5X SILV p/r 15-19
*92-100 p/r 20-35: .6X TO 1.5X SILV p/r 20-35
OVERALL AU-GU ODDS 1:1
PRINT RUNS B/WN 1-25 COPIES PER
NO PRICING ON QTY OF 10 OR LESS

2004 Prime Cuts II Signature Material Combo Prime

Nm-Mt Ex-Mt
OVERALL AU-GU ODDS 1:1
PRINT RUNS B/WN 1-9 COPIES PER
NO PRICING DUE TO SCARCITY

2004 Prime Cuts II MLB Icons

Nm-Mt Ex-Mt
RANDOM INSERTS IN PACKS
STATED PRINT RUN 50 SERIAL #'d SETS
1 Dale Murphy 8.00 2.40
2 Eddie Mathews 10.00 3.00
3 Brooks Robinson 8.00 2.40
4 Cal Ripken Right 40.00 12.00
5 Cal Ripken Left 40.00 12.00
6 Eddie Murray 10.00 3.00
7 Frank Robinson 5.00 1.50
8 Jim Palmer 5.00 1.50
9 Bobby Doerr 5.00 1.50
10 Carl Yastrzemski 15.00 4.50
11 Carlton Fisk R.Sox 8.00 2.40
12 Dennis Eckersley 8.00 2.40
13 Luis Aparicio 5.00 1.50
14 Luis Tiant 5.00 1.50
15 Ted Williams 15.00 4.50
16 Wade Boggs Sox 8.00 2.40
17 Duke Snider Dgr 8.00 2.40
18 Jackie Robinson 8.00 2.40
19 Pee Wee Reese 8.00 2.40
20 Burleigh Grimes 5.00 1.50
21 Nolan Ryan Angels 25.00 7.50
22 Reggie Jackson Angels 8.00 2.40
23 Rod Carew White 8.00 2.40
24 Rod Carew Navy 8.00 2.40
25 Billy Williams 5.00 1.50
26 Ernie Banks 10.00 3.00
27 Mark Grace 8.00 2.40
28 Ron Santo 8.00 2.40
29 Paul Molitor Brew 8.00 2.40
30 Bo Jackson Sox 10.00 3.00
31 Carlton Fisk W.Sox 8.00 2.40
32 Johnny Bench 10.00 3.00
33 Tom Seaver Reds 8.00 2.40
34 Tony Perez 5.00 1.50
35 Bob Feller 5.00 1.50
36 Lou Boudreau 5.00 1.50
37 Al Kaline 10.00 3.00
38 Alan Trammell 5.00 1.50
39 Ty Cobb 10.00 3.00
40 Don Sutton 5.00 1.50
41 Nolan Ryan Astros 25.00 7.50
42 Roger Maris A's 10.00 3.00
43 Bo Jackson Royals 10.00 3.00
44 George Brett Gray 20.00 6.00
45 George Brett White 20.00 6.00
46 Maury Wills 5.00 1.50
47 Warren Spahn 8.00 2.40
48 Robin Yount 15.00 4.50
49 Harmon Killebrew Twins 10.00 3.00
50 Kirby Puckett 15.00 4.50
51 Paul Molitor Twins 8.00 2.40
52 Andre Dawson 5.00 1.50
53 Mel Ott Pinstripe 8.00 2.40
54 Mel Ott White 8.00 2.40
55 Duke Snider Mets 8.00 2.40
56 Rickey Henderson Mets 10.00 3.00
57 Tom Seaver Mets 8.00 2.40
58 Babe Ruth w/Bats 15.00 4.50
59 Babe Ruth Gray 15.00 4.50
60 Catfish Hunter 8.00 2.40
61 Dave Righetti 5.00 1.50
62 Dave Winfield Yanks 5.00 1.50
63 Don Mattingly White 20.00 6.00
64 Don Mattingly Navy 20.00 6.00
65 Lou Gehrig w/o Cap 10.00 3.00
66 Lou Gehrig w/Cap 10.00 3.00
67 Phil Niekro 5.00 1.50
68 Phil Rizzuto 8.00 2.40
69 Reggie Jackson Yanks 8.00 2.40
70 Rickey Henderson Yanks 10.00 3.00
71 Roger Maris Yanks 10.00 3.00
72 Thurman Munson w/Bat 10.00 3.00
73 Thurman Munson w/o Bat 10.00 3.00
74 Wade Boggs Yanks 8.00 2.40
75 Whitey Ford 8.00 2.40
76 Yogi Berra 10.00 3.00
77 Lefty Grove 5.00 1.50
78 Mike Schmidt w/Bat 15.00 4.50
79 Mike Schmidt w/o Bat 15.00 4.50
80 Steve Carlton Phils 5.00 1.50
81 Ralph Kiner 5.00 1.50
82 Roberto Clemente w/Bat 25.00 7.50
83 Roberto Clemente w/o Bat 25.00 7.50
84 Dave Winfield Padres 5.00 1.50
85 Rickey Henderson Padres 10.00 3.00
86 Steve Garvey 5.00 1.50
87 Tony Gwynn Gray 15.00 4.50
88 Tony Gwynn White 15.00 4.50
89 Gaylord Perry 5.00 1.50
90 Joe Morgan 5.00 1.50
91 Juan Marichal 5.00 1.50
92 Steve Carlton Giants 5.00 1.50
93 Will Clark 10.00 3.00
94 Willie McCovey 8.00 2.40
95 Bob Gibson 8.00 2.40
96 Lou Brock 8.00 2.40
97 Stan Musial 15.00 4.50
98 Fergie Jenkins 5.00 1.50
99 Nolan Ryan Rgr 25.00 7.50
100 Harmon Killebrew Senators 10.00 3.00

2004 Prime Cuts II MLB Icons Century Gold

Nm-Mt Ex-Mt
RANDOM INSERTS IN PACKS
STATED PRINT RUN 10 SERIAL #'d SETS
NO PRICING DUE TO SCARCITY

2004 Prime Cuts II MLB Icons Century Platinum

Nm-Mt Ex-Mt
RANDOM INSERTS IN PACKS
STATED PRINT RUN 1 SERIAL #'d SET
NO PRICING DUE TO SCARCITY

2004 Prime Cuts II MLB Icons Century Silver

Nm-Mt Ex-Mt
*SILVER: .6X TO 1.5X BASIC
RANDOM INSERTS IN PACKS
STATED PRINT RUN 25 SERIAL #'d SETS

2004 Prime Cuts II MLB Icons Material Number

Nm-Mt Ex-Mt
*RUTH SWATCH W/P'STRIPE: ADD 25%
OVERALL AU-GU ODDS 1:1
PRINT RUNS B/WN 1- COPIES PER
NO PRICING ON QTY OF OR LESS
1 Dale Murphy Jsy/25 25.00 7.50
2 Eddie Mathews Jsy/5
3 Brooks Robinson Jsy/25 25.00 7.50
4 Cal Ripken Jsy/25 80.00 24.00
5 Cal Ripken Jkt/25 80.00 24.00
6 Eddie Murray Jsy/25 40.00 12.00
7 Frank Robinson Jsy/25 15.00 4.50
8 Jim Palmer Jsy/25 15.00 4.50
9 Bobby Doerr Jsy/25 15.00 4.50
10 Carl Yastrzemski Jsy/25 50.00 15.00
11 Carlton Fisk R.Sox Jsy/25 25.00 7.50
12 Dennis Eckersley Jsy/10
13 Luis Aparicio Jsy/10
14 Luis Tiant Jsy/1
15 Ted Williams Jsy/50 100.00 30.00
16 Wade Boggs Sox Jsy/10
17 Duke Snider Dgr Jsy/25 25.00 7.50
18 Jackie Robinson Jkt/50 80.00 24.00
19 Pee Wee Reese Jsy/25 25.00 7.50
20 Burleigh Grimes Pants/25 60.00 18.00
21 Nolan Ryan Angels Jsy/25 50.00 15.00
22 R.Jackson Angels Jsy/25 25.00 7.50
23 Rod Carew Jsy/25 25.00 7.50
24 Rod Carew Jkt/25 25.00 7.50
25 Billy Williams Jsy/25 15.00 4.50
26 Ernie Banks Jsy/25 30.00 9.00
27 Mark Grace Jsy/1
28 Ron Santo Bat/10
29 Paul Molitor Brew Pants/25 25.00 7.50
30 Bo Jackson Sox Jsy/1
31 Carlton Fisk W.Sox Jsy/25 25.00 7.50
32 Johnny Bench Jsy/25 30.00 9.00
33 Tom Seaver Reds Jsy/25 25.00 7.50
35 Bob Feller Jsy/25 15.00 4.50
36 Lou Boudreau Jsy/25 30.00 9.00
37 Al Kaline Pants/6
38 Alan Trammell Jsy/3
39 Ty Cobb Pants/50 120.00 36.00
40 Don Sutton Jsy/5
41 Nolan Ryan Astros Jsy/25 50.00 15.00
42 Roger Maris A's Jsy/25 60.00 18.00
43 Bo Jackson Royals Jsy/10
44 George Brett Jsy/25 50.00 15.00
45 George Brett Jsy/25 50.00 15.00
46 Maury Wills Jsy/1
47 Warren Spahn Jsy/25 30.00 9.00
48 Robin Yount Jsy/25 40.00 12.00
49 H.Killebrew Twins Jsy/25 40.00 12.00
50 Kirby Puckett Jsy/25 30.00 9.00
51 Paul Molitor Twins Jsy/25 25.00 7.50
52 Andre Dawson Jsy/1
53 Mel Ott Jsy/25 50.00 15.00
54 Mel Ott Pants/25 50.00 15.00
55 Duke Snider Mets Jsy/25 25.00 7.50
56 R.Henderson Mets Jsy/1
57 Tom Seaver Mets Jsy/5
58 Babe Ruth Jsy/25 400.00 120.00
59 Babe Ruth Pants/50 225.00 70.00
60 Catfish Hunter Jsy/25 25.00 7.50
61 Dave Righetti Jsy/1
62 D.Winfield Yanks Pants/10
63 Don Mattingly Jsy/25 50.00 15.00
64 Don Mattingly Jkt/25 50.00 15.00
65 Lou Gehrig Jsy/25 200.00 60.00
66 Lou Gehrig Pants/50 150.00 45.00
67 Phil Niekro Jsy/5
68 Phil Rizzuto Pants/25 25.00 7.50
69 R.Jackson Yanks Jsy/25 25.00 7.50
70 R.Henderson Yanks Jsy/1
71 R.Maris Yanks Pants/25 50.00 15.00
72 Thurman Munson Jsy/50 40.00 12.00
73 Thurman Munson Pants/50 40.00 12.00
74 Wade Boggs Yanks Jsy/10
75 Whitey Ford Pants/16 40.00 12.00
76 Yogi Berra Jsy/8
77 Lefty Grove Hat/25 150.00 45.00
78 Mike Schmidt Jsy/20 50.00 15.00
79 Mike Schmidt Jkt/20 50.00 15.00
80 S.Carlton Phils Pants/10
81 Ralph Kiner Bat/10
82 Roberto Clemente Jsy/21 150.00 45.00
83 Roberto Clemente Hat/21 150.00 45.00
84 Dave Winfield Padres Jsy/10
85 R.Henderson Padres Jsy/1
86 Steve Garvey Jsy/6
87 Tony Gwynn White Jsy/10
88 Tony Gwynn Navy Jsy/10
89 Gaylord Perry Jsy/10
90 Joe Morgan Jsy/8
91 Juan Marichal Jsy/25 15.00 4.50
92 Steve Carlton Giants Jsy/10
93 Will Clark Jsy/22 30.00 9.00
94 Willie McCovey Jsy/25 25.00 7.50
95 Bob Gibson Jsy/25 25.00 7.50
96 Lou Brock Jkt/20 25.00 7.50
97 Stan Musial Jsy/6
98 Fergie Jenkins Hat/10
99 Nolan Ryan Rgr Pants/25 50.00 15.00
100 H.Killebrew Senators Jsy/25 40.00 12.00

2004 Prime Cuts II MLB Icons Material Prime

Nm-Mt Ex-Mt
OVERALL AU-GU ODDS 1:1
PRINT RUNS B/WN 1-10 COPIES PER
NO PRICING DUE TO SCARCITY

2004 Prime Cuts II MLB Icons Material Combo

Nm-Mt Ex-Mt
*p/r 20-25: .6X TO 1.5X NBR p/r 50
*p/r 20-25: .5X TO 1.2X NBR p/r 25
*p/r 16-19: .6X TO 1.5X NBR p/r 25
*p/r 16-19: .5X TO 1.2X NBR p/r 16
OVERALL AU-GU ODDS 1:1
PRINT RUNS B/WN 1-25 COPIES PER
NO PRICING ON QTY OF 14 OR LESS
39 Ty Cobb Bat-Pants/25 200.00 60.00
58 Babe Ruth Bat-Jsy/25 400.00 120.00
59 Babe Ruth Bat-Pants/25 350.00 105.00
65 Lou Gehrig Bat-Jsy/25 300.00 90.00
66 Lou Gehrig Bat-Pants/25 250.00 75.00

2004 Prime Cuts II MLB Icons Material Combo Prime

Nm-Mt Ex-Mt
OVERALL AU-GU ODDS 1:1
PRINT RUNS B/WN 1-10 COPIES PER
NO PRICING DUE TO SCARCITY

2004 Prime Cuts II MLB Icons Signature Century Gold

Nm-Mt Ex-Mt
*p/r 20-25: .5X TO 1.2X SILV p/r 36-50
*p/r 20-25: .4X TO 1X SILV p/r 20-35
*p/r 16-19: .6X TO 1.5X SILV p/r 36-50
*p/r 16-19: .5X TO 1.2X SILV p/r 20-35
OVERALL AU-GU ODDS 1:1
PRINT RUNS B/WN 1-25 COPIES PER
NO PRICING ON QTY OF 11 OR LESS

2004 Prime Cuts II MLB Icons Signature Century Platinum

Nm-Mt Ex-Mt
OVERALL AU-GU ODDS 1:1
STATED PRINT RUN 1 SERIAL #'d SET
NO PRICING DUE TO SCARCITY

2004 Prime Cuts II MLB Icons Signature Century Silver

Nm-Mt Ex-Mt
OVERALL AU-GU ODDS 1:1
PRINT RUNS B/WN 1-50 COPIES PER
NO PRICING ON QTY OF 12 OR LESS
1 Dale Murphy/25 40.00 12.00
3 Brooks Robinson/50 30.00 9.00

4 Cal Ripken Right/25 200.00 60.00
5 Cal Ripken Left/25 200.00 60.00
6 Eddie Murray/25 60.00 18.00
7 Frank Robinson/50 30.00 9.00
8 Jim Palmer/50 30.00 9.00
9 Bobby Doerr/25 25.00 7.50
10 Carl Yastrzemski/25 80.00 24.00
11 Carlton Fisk R.Sox/27 40.00 12.00
12 Dennis Eckersley/43 30.00 9.00
13 Luis Aparicio/25 25.00 7.50
14 Luis Tiant/1
16 Wade Boggs Sox/26 40.00 12.00
17 Duke Snider Dgr/50 30.00 9.00
21 Nolan Ryan Angels/30 120.00 36.00
22 Reggie Jackson Angels/25 60.00 18.00
23 Rod Carew White/29 40.00 12.00
24 Rod Carew Navy/29 40.00 12.00
25 Billy Williams/26 25.00 7.50
27 Mark Grace/1
28 Ron Santo/1
29 Paul Molitor Brew/25 40.00 12.00
30 Bo Jackson Sox/25 60.00 18.00
31 Carlton Fisk W.Sox/25 40.00 12.00
32 Johnny Bench/50 50.00 15.00
33 Tom Seaver Reds/25 40.00 12.00
34 Tony Perez/25 40.00 12.00
35 Bob Feller/25 25.00 7.50
37 Al Kaline/50 50.00 15.00
38 Alan Trammell/1
40 Don Sutton/20 25.00 7.50
41 Nolan Ryan Astros/34 120.00 36.00
43 Bo Jackson Royals/25 60.00 18.00
44 George Brett Gray/25 100.00 30.00
45 George Brett White/25 100.00 30.00
46 Maury Wills/1
47 Warren Spahn/1
48 Robin Yount/19 80.00 24.00
49 H.Killebrew Twins/50 50.00 15.00
50 Kirby Puckett/10
51 Paul Molitor Twins/50 30.00 9.00
52 Andre Dawson/1
55 Duke Snider Mets/50 30.00 9.00
56 Rickey Henderson Mets/24 60.00 18.00
57 Tom Seaver Mets/25 40.00 12.00
62 Dave Winfield Yanks/31 40.00 12.00
63 Don Mattingly White/50 60.00 18.00
64 Don Mattingly Navy/50 60.00 18.00
67 Phil Niekro/35 25.00 7.50
68 Phil Rizzuto/25 40.00 12.00
69 Reggie Jackson Yanks/25 60.00 18.00
70 Rickey Henderson Yanks/24 60.00 18.00
74 Wade Boggs Yanks/12
75 Whitey Ford/25 60.00 18.00
76 Yogi Berra/25 60.00 18.00
78 Mike Schmidt w/Bat/20 80.00 24.00
79 Mike Schmidt w/o Bat/20 80.00 24.00
80 Steve Carlton Phils/32 40.00 12.00
81 Ralph Kiner/25 40.00 12.00
84 Dave Winfield Padres/31 40.00 12.00
85 R.Henderson Padres/24 60.00 18.00
86 Steve Garvey/1
87 Tony Gwynn Gray/50 50.00 15.00
88 Tony Gwynn White/50 50.00 15.00
89 Gaylord Perry/36 20.00 6.00
90 Joe Morgan/24 25.00 7.50
91 Juan Marichal/27 25.00 7.50
92 Steve Carlton Giants/32 40.00 12.00
93 Will Clark/22 60.00 18.00
94 Willie McCovey/25 40.00 12.00
95 Bob Gibson/45 30.00 9.00
96 Lou Brock/50 30.00 9.00
97 Stan Musial/50 80.00 24.00
98 Fergie Jenkins/31 25.00 7.50
99 Nolan Ryan Rgr/34 120.00 36.00
100 H.Killebrew Senators/50 50.00 15.00

2004 Prime Cuts II MLB Icons Signature Material Number

Nm-Mt Ex-Mt
*p/r 36-50: .5X TO 1.2X SILV p/r 36-50
*p/r 36-50: .4X TO 1X SILV p/r 20-35
*p/r 20-35: .6X TO 1.5X SILV p/r 36-50
*p/r 20-35: .5X TO 1.2X SILV p/r 20-35
*p/r 20-35: .4X TO 1X SILV p/r 15-19
*p/r 15-19: .75X TO 2X SILV p/r 36-50
*p/r 15-19: .6X TO 1.5X SILV p/r 20-35
OVERALL AU-GU ODDS 1:1
PRINT RUNS B/WN 1-45 COPIES PER
NO PRICING ON QTY OF 12 OR LESS
27 Mark Grace Jsy/17 60.00 18.00

2004 Prime Cuts II MLB Icons Signature Material Prime

Nm-Mt Ex-Mt
OVERALL AU-GU ODDS 1:1
PRINT RUNS B/WN 1-10 COPIES PER
NO PRICING DUE TO SCARCITY

2004 Prime Cuts II MLB Icons Signature Material Combo

Nm-Mt Ex-Mt
*p/r 20-35: .75X TO 2X SILV p/r 36-50
*p/r 20-35: .6X TO 1.5X SILV p/r 20-35
*p/r 15-19: 1X TO 2.5X SILV p/r 36-50
*p/r 15-19: .75X TO 2X SILV p/r 20-35
*p/r 15-19: .6X TO 1.5X SILV p/r 15-19
OVERALL AU-GU ODDS 1:1
PRINT RUNS B/WN 1-32 COPIES PER
NO PRICING ON QTY OF 11 OR LESS

2004 Prime Cuts II MLB Icons Signature Material Combo Prime

Nm-Mt Ex-Mt
OVERALL AU-GU ODDS 1:1
PRINT RUNS B/WN 1-10 COPIES PER
NO PRICING DUE TO SCARCITY

2004 Prime Cuts II Timeline

Nm-Mt Ex-Mt
RANDOM INSERTS IN PACKS
STATED PRINT RUN 50 SERIAL #'d SETS
1 Al Kaline 10.00 3.00
2 Alex Rodriguez 15.00 4.50
3 Andre Dawson 5.00 1.50
4 Babe Ruth 15.00 4.50
5 Barry Zito 5.00 1.50
6 Bob Feller 5.00 1.50
7 Bob Gibson 8.00 2.40
8 Bobby Doerr 5.00 1.50
9 Brooks Robinson 8.00 2.40
10 Cal Ripken 40.00 12.00
11 Carl Hubbell 5.00 1.50
12 Carl Yastrzemski 15.00 4.50
13 Carlton Fisk 8.00 2.40
14 Catfish Hunter 8.00 2.40
15 Chipper Jones 10.00 3.00
16 Cy Young 8.00 2.40
17 Dale Murphy 8.00 2.40
18 Dave Parker 5.00 1.50
19 Dennis Eckersley 8.00 2.40
20 Don Drysdale 8.00 2.40
21 Don Mattingly 20.00 6.00
22 Duke Snider 8.00 2.40
23 Dwight Gooden 5.00 1.50
24 Early Wynn 5.00 1.50
25 Eddie Mathews 10.00 3.00
26 Eddie Murray 10.00 3.00
27 Enos Slaughter 5.00 1.50
28 Ernie Banks 10.00 3.00
29 Fergie Jenkins 5.00 1.50
30 Frank Robinson 5.00 1.50
31 Frank Thomas 10.00 3.00
32 Frankie Frisch 5.00 1.50
33 Fred Lynn 5.00 1.50
34 Gary Carter 5.00 1.50
35 Gaylord Perry 5.00 1.50
36 George Brett 20.00 6.00
37 Greg Maddux 15.00 4.50
38 Hal Newhouser 5.00 1.50
39 Harmon Killebrew 10.00 3.00
40 Honus Wagner 8.00 2.40
41 Hoyt Wilhelm 5.00 1.50
42 Ivan Rodriguez 10.00 3.00
43 Jackie Robinson 8.00 2.40
44 Jason Giambi 5.00 1.50
45 Jeff Bagwell 8.00 2.40
46 Jim Palmer 5.00 1.50
47 Jimmie Foxx 8.00 2.40
48 Joe Morgan 5.00 1.50
49 Johnny Bench 10.00 3.00
50 Johnny Mize 5.00 1.50
51 Jose Canseco 10.00 3.00
52 Juan Gonzalez 8.00 2.40
53 Juan Marichal 5.00 1.50
54 Keith Hernandez 5.00 1.50
55 Kirby Puckett 15.00 4.50
56 Lefty Grove 5.00 1.50
57 Lou Boudreau 5.00 1.50
58 Lou Brock 8.00 2.40
59 Lou Gehrig 10.00 3.00
60 Luis Aparicio 5.00 1.50
61 Marty Marion 5.00 1.50
62 Mel Ott 8.00 2.40

63 Miguel Tejada 5.00 1.50
64 Mike Schmidt 15.00 4.50
65 Nellie Fox 8.00 2.40
66 Nolan Ryan 25.00 7.50
67 Orel Hershiser 5.00 1.50
68 Orlando Cepeda 5.00 1.50
69 Paul Molitor 8.00 2.40
70 Pedro Martinez 10.00 3.00
71 Pee Wee Reese 8.00 2.40
72 Phil Niekro 5.00 1.50
73 Phil Rizzuto 8.00 2.40
74 Ralph Kiner 5.00 1.50
75 Randy Johnson 10.00 3.00
76 Red Schoendienst 5.00 1.50
77 Reggie Jackson 8.00 2.40
78 Rickey Henderson 10.00 3.00
79 Roberto Clemente 25.00 7.50
80 Robin Yount 15.00 4.50
81 Rod Carew 8.00 2.40
82 Roger Clemens 15.00 4.50
83 Roger Maris 10.00 3.00
84 Rogers Hornsby 8.00 2.40
85 Roy Campanella 10.00 3.00
86 Ozzie Smith 15.00 4.50
87 Sammy Sosa 15.00 4.50
88 Satchel Paige 8.00 2.40
89 Stan Musial 15.00 4.50
90 Steve Carlton 5.00 1.50
91 Ted Williams 15.00 4.50
92 Thurman Munson 10.00 3.00
93 Tom Seaver 8.00 2.40
94 Ty Cobb 10.00 3.00
95 Walter Johnson 8.00 2.40
96 Warren Spahn 8.00 2.40
97 Whitey Ford 8.00 2.40
98 Willie McCovey 8.00 2.40
99 Willie Stargell 8.00 2.40
100 Yogi Berra 10.00 3.00

2004 Prime Cuts II Timeline Century Gold

Nm-Mt Ex-Mt
RANDOM INSERTS IN PACKS
STATED PRINT RUN 10 SERIAL #'d SETS
NO PRICING DUE TO SCARCITY

2004 Prime Cuts II Timeline Century Platinum

Nm-Mt Ex-Mt
RANDOM INSERTS IN PACKS
STATED PRINT RUN 1 SERIAL #'d SET
NO PRICING DUE TO SCARCITY

2004 Prime Cuts II Timeline Century Silver

Nm-Mt Ex-Mt
*SILVER: .6X TO 1.5X BASIC
RANDOM INSERTS IN PACKS
STATED PRINT RUN 25 SERIAL #'d SETS

2004 Prime Cuts II Timeline Material Number

Nm-Mt Ex-Mt
RUTH SWATCH W/P'STRIPE: ADD 25%
OVERALL AU-GU ODDS 1:1
PRINT RUNS B/WN 1-42 COPIES PER
NO PRICING ON QTY OF 11 OR LESS
Al Kaline Pants/6
Babe Ruth Jsy/25 400.00 120.00
Bob Feller Pants/19 20.00 6.00
Bob Gibson Jsy/25 25.00 7.50
Bobby Doerr Jsy/5
Brooks Robinson Jsy/5
0 Cal Ripken Jsy/25 80.00 24.00
2 Carl Yastrzemski Jsy/25 50.00 15.00
3 Carlton Fisk Jsy/27 25.00 7.50
4 Catfish Hunter Jsy/27 25.00 7.50
7 Dale Murphy Jsy/10
0 Don Drysdale Jsy/25 50.00 15.00
1 Don Mattingly Pants/10
2 Duke Snider Pants/25 25.00 7.50
4 Early Wynn Jsy/24 15.00 4.50
5 Eddie Mathews Jsy/25 40.00 12.00
6 Eddie Murray Jsy/25 40.00 12.00
7 Enos Slaughter Jsy/9
8 Ernie Banks Jsy/25 30.00 9.00
9 Fergie Jenkins Pants/1
0 Frank Robinson Jsy/5
2 Frankie Frisch Jkt/25 50.00 15.00
4 Gary Carter Jsy/8
6 George Brett Jsy/25 50.00 15.00
8 Hal Newhouser Jsy/16 40.00 12.00
9 Harmon Killebrew Jsy/25 40.00 12.00
1 Hoyt Wilhelm Jsy/5
3 Jackie Robinson Jkt/42 80.00 24.00
6 Jim Palmer Jsy/22 15.00 4.50
7 Jimmie Foxx Fld Glv/25 100.00 30.00
8 Joe Morgan Jsy/8
9 Johnny Bench Jsy/25 30.00 9.00
0 Johnny Mize Pants/10
3 Juan Marichal Jsy/25 15.00 4.50
5 Kirby Puckett Jsy/25 30.00 9.00
6 Lefty Grove Hat/10
7 Lou Boudreau Jsy/5
8 Lou Brock Jsy/20 25.00 7.50
9 Lou Gehrig Jsy/25 200.00 60.00
Luis Aparicio Jsy/11
Marty Marion Jsy/4
2 Mel Ott Pants/25 50.00 15.00
4 Mike Schmidt Jsy/20 50.00 15.00
5 Nellie Fox Bat/2
66 Nolan Ryan Jsy/25 50.00 15.00
67 Orel Hershiser Jsy/5
68 Orlando Cepeda Pants/25 15.00 4.50
69 Paul Molitor Jsy/4
71 Pee Wee Reese Jsy/25 25.00 7.50
72 Phil Niekro Jsy/5
73 Phil Rizzuto Pants/10
74 Ralph Kiner Bat/25 15.00 4.50
76 Red Schoendienst Jsy/2
77 Reggie Jackson Jsy/25 25.00 7.50
78 Rickey Henderson Jsy/5
79 Roberto Clemente Jsy/5
80 Robin Yount Jsy/19 50.00 15.00
81 Rod Carew Jsy/25 25.00 7.50
82 Roger Clemens Jsy/21 30.00 9.00
83 Roger Maris Jsy/25 60.00 18.00
84 Rogers Hornsby Bat/25 80.00 24.00
85 Roy Campanella Pants/25 30.00 9.00
86 Ozzie Smith Jsy/25 40.00 12.00
87 Sammy Sosa Jsy/21 30.00 9.00
88 Satchel Paige CO Jsy/25 80.00 24.00
89 Stan Musial Jsy/6
90 Steve Carlton Jsy/25 15.00 4.50
91 Ted Williams Jsy/25 120.00 36.00
92 Thurman Munson Jsy/25 50.00 15.00
93 Tom Seaver Pants/25 25.00 7.50
94 Ty Cobb Pants/25 150.00 45.00
96 Warren Spahn Jsy/21 30.00 9.00
97 Whitey Ford Jsy/16 40.00 12.00
98 Willie McCovey Jsy/25 25.00 7.50
99 Willie Stargell Jsy/8
100 Yogi Berra Jsy/8

2004 Prime Cuts II Timeline Material Position

Nm-Mt Ex-Mt
*RET p/r 36-50: .4X TO 1X NBR p/r 36-50
*ACT p/r 20-35: .4X TO 1X NBR p/r 20-35
*RET p/r 20-35: .4X TO 1X NBR p/r 20-35
*RET p/r 15-19: .5X TO 1.2X NBR p/r 20-35
*RET p/r 15-19: .4X TO 1X NBR p/r 15-19
OVERALL AU-GU ODDS 1:1
PRINT RUNS B/WN 1-42 COPIES PER
NO PRICING ON QTY OF 11 OR LESS
4 Babe Ruth Jsy/25 400.00 120.00
59 Lou Gehrig Jsy/25 200.00 60.00

2004 Prime Cuts II Timeline Material Prime

Nm-Mt Ex-Mt
OVERALL AU-GU ODDS 1:1
PRINT RUNS B/WN 1-10 COPIES PER
NO PRICING DUE TO SCARCITY

2004 Prime Cuts II Timeline Material Combo

Nm-Mt Ex-Mt
*RET p/r 36-50: .5X TO 1.2X NBR p/r 36-50
*RET p/r 36-50: .4X TO 1X NBR p/r 20-35
*ACT p/r 20-35: .5X TO 1.2X NBR p/r 20-35
*RET p/r 20-35: .5X TO 1.2X NBR p/r 20-35
*RET p/r 15-19: .6X TO 1.5X NBR p/r 20-35
*RET p/r 15-19: .5X TO 1.2X NBR p/r 15-19
OVERALL AU-GU ODDS 1:1
PRINT RUNS B/WN 1-42 COPIES PER
NO PRICING ON QTY OF 14 OR LESS
4 Babe Ruth Jsy-Jsy/25 500.00 150.00
17 Dale Murphy Bat-Jsy/25 30.00 9.00
21 D.Matt Btg Glv-Pants/25 60.00 18.00
59 Lou Gehrig Jsy-Pants/25 300.00 90.00
79 R.Clemente Hat-Jsy/21 200.00 60.00

2004 Prime Cuts II Timeline Material Combo CY

Nm-Mt Ex-Mt
*ACT p/r 20-35: .5X TO 1.2X NBR p/r 20-35
*RET p/r 20-35: .5X TO 1.2X NBR p/r 20-35
*RET p/r 15-19: .5X TO 1.2X NBR p/r 15-19
OVERALL AU-GU ODDS 1:1
PRINT RUNS B/WN 1-32 COPIES PER
NO PRICING ON QTY OF 10 OR LESS
70 Pedro Martinez Bat-Jsy/25. 120.00 36.00

2004 Prime Cuts II Timeline Material Trio

Nm-Mt Ex-Mt
*ACT p/r 20-35: .6X TO 1.5X NBR p/r 20-35
*RET p/r 20-35: .6X TO 1.5X NBR p/r 20-35
*RET p/r 15-19: .75X TO 2X NBR p/r 20-35
*RET p/r 15-19: .6X TO 1.5X NBR p/r 15-19
OVERALL AU-GU ODDS 1:1
PRINT RUNS B/WN 1-25 COPIES PER
NO PRICING ON QTY OF 10 OR LESS
17 Dale Murphy Bat-Jsy-Jsy/25 40.00 12.00
21 D.Matt Bat-Jkt-Pants/25 80.00 24.00
26 E.Murray Bat-Jsy-Shoe/25. 120.00 36.00

2004 Prime Cuts II Timeline Material Trio HOF

Nm-Mt Ex-Mt
OVERALL AU-GU ODDS 1:1
PRINT RUNS B/WN 1-9 COPIES PER
NO PRICING DUE TO SCARCITY

2004 Prime Cuts II Timeline Material Trio MVP

Nm-Mt Ex-Mt
*RET p/r 15-19: .75X TO 2X NBR p/r 20-35
OVERALL AU-GU ODDS 1:1
PRINT RUNS B/WN 1-15 COPIES PER
NO PRICING ON QTY OF 10 OR LESS

2004 Prime Cuts II Timeline Material Trio Stats

Nm-Mt Ex-Mt
*RET p/r 15-19: .75X TO 2X NBR p/r 20-35
OVERALL AU-GU ODDS 1:1
PRINT RUNS B/WN 1-15 COPIES PER
NO PRICING ON QTY OF 10 OR LESS

2004 Prime Cuts II Timeline Material Quad

Nm-Mt Ex-Mt
OVERALL AU-GU ODDS 1:1
PRINT RUNS B/WN 1-25 COPIES PER
NO PRICING ON QTY OF 10 OR LESS
B ='s Bat, BG ='s Btg Glv, FG ='s Fld Glv
H ='s Hat, J ='s Jsy, JK ='s Jkt, P ='s Pants
4 Babe Ruth B-J-J-P/25 800.00 240.00
91 Ted Williams B-JK-J-J/25 250.00 75.00

2004 Prime Cuts II Timeline Signature Century Gold

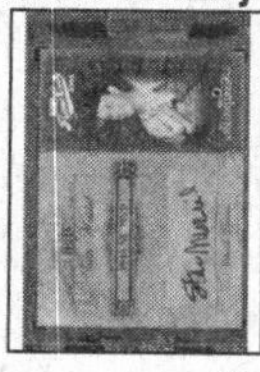

Nm-Mt Ex-Mt
OVERALL AU-GU ODDS 1:1
PRINT RUNS B/WN 1-5 COPIES PER
NO PRICING DUE TO SCARCITY

2004 Prime Cuts II Timeline Signature Century Platinum

Nm-Mt Ex-Mt
OVERALL AU-GU ODDS 1:1
STATED PRINT RUN 1 SERIAL #'d SET
NO PRICING DUE TO SCARCITY

2004 Prime Cuts II Timeline Signature Century Silver

Nm-Mt Ex-Mt
OVERALL AU-GU ODDS 1:1
PRINT RUNS B/WN 1-10 COPIES PER
NO PRICING DUE TO SCARCITY

2004 Prime Cuts II Timeline Signature Material Number

Nm-Mt Ex-Mt
OVERALL AU-GU ODDS 1:1
PRINT RUNS B/WN 1-34 COPIES PER
NO PRICING ON QTY OF 11 OR LESS
1 Al Kaline Pants/6
3 Andre Dawson Jsy/8
4 Babe Ruth Jsy/1
5 Barry Zito Jsy/5
6 Bob Feller Pants/19 40.00 12.00
7 Bob Gibson Jsy/25 50.00 15.00
8 Bobby Doerr Jsy/25 30.00 9.00
9 Brooks Robinson Jsy/5
10 Cal Ripken Jsy/1
12 Carl Yastrzemski Jsy/8
13 Carlton Fisk Jsy/5
15 Chipper Jones Jsy/10
17 Dale Murphy Jsy/3
18 Dave Parker Jsy/1
20 Don Drysdale Jsy/1
21 Don Mattingly Pants/23 100.00 30.00
22 Duke Snider Pants/4
23 Dwight Gooden Jsy/5
26 Eddie Murray Jsy/1
27 Enos Slaughter Jsy/1
29 Fergie Jenkins Pants/1
30 Frank Robinson Jsy/5
31 Frank Thomas Jsy/5
32 Frankie Frisch Jkt/1
33 Fred Lynn Jsy/1
34 Gary Carter Jsy/8
35 Gaylord Perry Jsy/10
36 George Brett Jsy/5
37 Greg Maddux Jsy/5
38 Hal Newhouser Jsy/1
39 Harmon Killebrew Jsy/3
41 Hoyt Wilhelm Jsy/5
45 Jeff Bagwell Jsy/5
46 Jim Palmer Jsy/22 50.00 15.00
47 Jimmie Foxx Fld Glv/1
48 Joe Morgan Jsy/8
49 Johnny Bench Jsy/5
50 Johnny Mize Pants/1
51 Jose Canseco Jsy/5
52 Juan Gonzalez Jsy/5
53 Juan Marichal Jsy/27 30.00 9.00
54 Keith Hernandez Jsy/5
54 Keith Hernandez Jsy/5
55 Kirby Puckett Jsy/1
56 Lefty Grove Hat/1
57 Lou Boudreau Jsy/1
58 Lou Brock Jsy/20 50.00 15.00
60 Luis Aparicio Jsy/11
61 Marty Marion Jsy/1
64 Mike Schmidt Jsy/5
66 Nolan Ryan Jsy/34 150.00 45.00
67 Orel Hershiser Jsy/5
68 Orlando Cepeda Pants/1
69 Paul Molitor Jsy/4
70 Pedro Martinez Jsy/1
71 Pee Wee Reese Jsy/1
72 Phil Niekro Jsy/5
73 Phil Rizzuto Pants/10
74 Ralph Kiner Bat/4
75 Randy Johnson Jsy/1
76 Red Schoendienst Jsy/2
77 Reggie Jackson Jsy/9
78 Rickey Henderson Jsy/1
79 Roberto Clemente Jsy/1
80 Robin Yount Jsy/5
81 Rod Carew Jsy/5
82 Roger Clemens Jsy/1
84 Rogers Hornsby Bat/1
86 Ozzie Smith Jsy/1
87 Sammy Sosa Jsy/1
88 Satchel Paige CO Jsy/1
89 Stan Musial Jsy/6
90 Steve Carlton Jsy/32 50.00 15.00
91 Ted Williams Jsy/1
93 Tom Seaver Pants/5
94 Ty Cobb Pants/1
96 Warren Spahn Jsy/1
97 Whitey Ford Jsy/5
98 Willie McCovey Jsy/4
100 Yogi Berra Jsy/8

2004 Prime Cuts II Timeline Signature Material Position

Nm-Mt Ex-Mt
*RET p/r 20-35: .4X TO 1X NBR p/r 20-35
*RET p/r 15-19: .4X TO 1X NBR p/r 15-19
OVERALL AU-GU ODDS 1:1
PRINT RUNS B/WN 1-34 COPIES PER
NO PRICING ON QTY OF 11 OR LESS

2004 Prime Cuts II Timeline Signature Material Prime

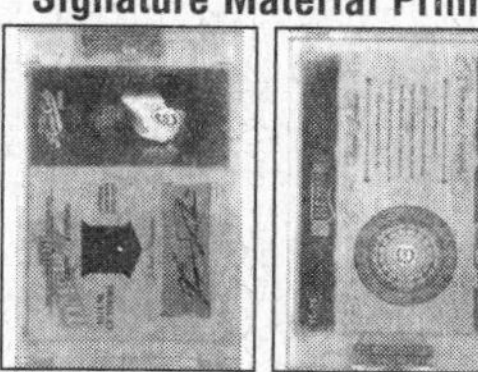

Nm-Mt Ex-Mt
OVERALL AU-GU ODDS 1:1
PRINT RUNS B/WN 1-9 COPIES PER
NO PRICING DUE TO SCARCITY

2004 Prime Cuts II Timeline Signature Material Combo

Nm-Mt Ex-Mt
*RET p/r 20-35: .5X TO 1.2X NBR p/r 20-35
OVERALL AU-GU ODDS 1:1
PRINT RUNS B/WN 1-25 COPIES PER
NO PRICING ON QTY OF 11 OR LESS

2004 Prime Cuts II Timeline Signature Material Combo CY

Nm-Mt Ex-Mt
*RET p/r 20-35: .5X TO 1.2X NBR p/r 20-35
OVERALL AU-GU ODDS 1:1
PRINT RUNS B/WN 1-25 COPIES PER
NO PRICING ON QTY OF 5 OR LESS

2004 Prime Cuts II Timeline Signature Material Trio

Nm-Mt Ex-Mt
OVERALL AU-GU ODDS 1:1
PRINT RUNS B/WN 1-9 COPIES PER
NO PRICING DUE TO SCARCITY

2004 Prime Cuts II Timeline Signature Material Trio HOF

Nm-Mt Ex-Mt
OVERALL AU-GU ODDS 1:1
PRINT RUNS B/WN 1-9 COPIES PER
NO PRICING DUE TO SCARCITY

2004 Prime Cuts II Timeline Signature Material Trio MVP

Nm-Mt Ex-Mt
OVERALL AU-GU ODDS 1:1
PRINT RUNS B/WN 1-8 COPIES PER
NO PRICING DUE TO SCARCITY

2004 Prime Cuts II Timeline Signature Material Trio Stats

Nm-Mt Ex-Mt
OVERALL AU-GU ODDS 1:1
PRINT RUNS B/WN 1-9 COPIES PER
NO PRICING DUE TO SCARCITY

2004 Prime Cuts II Timeline Signature Material Quad

Nm-Mt Ex-Mt
OVERALL AU-GU ODDS 1:1
PRINT RUNS B/WN 1-25 COPIES PER
NO PRICING ON QTY OF 11 OR LESS
B ='s Bat, BG ='s Btg Glv, FG ='s Fld Glv
H ='s Hat, J ='s Jsy, JK ='s Jkt, P ='s Pants
17 Dale Murphy B-J-J-J/25 120.00 36.00

2004 Reflections

This 390-card set was released in May, 2004. The set was issued in four card packs with an $15 SRP which came eight packs to a box and 14 boxes to a case. Cards numbered 1 through 100 feature veterans while cards to 130 feature rookies. Those cards numbered 101 through 130 were inserted at a stated rate of one in eight and were issued to a stated print run of 1250 serial numbered sets. Cards numbered 131 through 298 feature jersey swatches and were inserted at an overall stated rate of one in two packs. Cards numbered 299 through 340 feature autographed cards with a stated print run of 35 serial numbered sets which were inserted at a stated rate of one in 16 packs. Cards numbered 341 through 390 were issued as "random insert sets" in Upper Deck series 2 boxes. An Ichiro Suzuki promo card for this set was released during the Hawaii trade show. That card is printed to a stated serial number print run of 500 sets.

Nm-Mt Ex-Mt
COMP.SET w/o SP's (100) 40.00 12.00
COMP.UPDATE SET (50) 30.00 9.00
COMMON CARD (1-100) .75 .23
COMMON CARD (101-130) 4.00 1.20
COMMON CARD (131-214) 6.00 1.80
SP CL: 132/142/144/146/153/156/159
SP CL: 161-162/164/178/184/186/188
SP CL: 190-191/197-198/201/207/214
SP INFO PROVIDED BY UPPER DECK
COMMON CARD (215-298) 8.00 2.40
COMMON CARD (299-340) 25.00 7.50
COMMON CARD (341-390) .60 .18
1 Adam Dunn 1.25 .35
2 Albert Pujols 4.00 1.20
3 Alex Rodriguez Yanks 3.00 .90
4 Alfonso Soriano 1.25 .35
5 Andruw Jones .75 .23
6 Austin Kearns .75 .23
7 Rafael Furcal .75 .23
8 Barry Zito .75 .23
9 Bartolo Colon .75 .23
10 Ben Sheets .75 .23
11 Bernie Williams 1.25 .35
12 Bobby Abreu .75 .23
13 Brandon Webb .75 .23
14 Bret Boone .75 .23
15 Brian Giles .75 .23
16 Carlos Beltran 1.25 .35
17 Carlos Delgado .75 .23
18 Carlos Lee .75 .23
19 Chipper Jones 2.00 .60
20 Corey Patterson .75 .23
21 Curt Schilling 2.00 .60
22 Delmon Young 1.25 .35
23 Derek Jeter 4.00 1.20
24 Dmitri Young .75 .23
25 Dontrelle Willis .75 .23
26 Edgar Martinez 1.25 .35
27 Edgar Renteria .75 .23
28 Eric Chavez .75 .23
29 Eric Gagne 2.00 .60
30 Frank Thomas 2.00 .60
31 Garrett Anderson .75 .23
32 Gary Sheffield .75 .23
33 Geoff Jenkins .75 .23
34 Greg Maddux 3.00 .90
35 Hank Blalock .75 .23
36 Hideki Matsui 3.00 .90
37 Hideo Nomo 2.00 .60
38 Ichiro Suzuki 3.00 .90
39 Ivan Rodriguez 2.00 .60
40 Jacque Jones .75 .23
41 Jason Giambi .75 .23
42 Jason Schmidt .75 .23
43 Javy Lopez .75 .23
44 Jay Gibbons .75 .23
45 Jeff Bagwell 1.25 .35
46 Jeff Kent .75 .23
47 Jeremy Bonderman .75 .23
48 Jim Edmonds .75 .23
49 Jim Thome 2.00 .60
50 Johnny Damon 2.00 .60
51 Jorge Posada 1.25 .35
52 Jose Contreras .75 .23
53 Jose Reyes .75 .23
54 Jose Vidro .75 .23
55 Josh Beckett .75 .23
56 Juan Gonzalez 1.25 .35
57 Ken Griffey Jr. 3.00 .90
58 Kerry Wood 2.00 .60
59 Kevin Brown .75 .23
60 Kevin Millwood .75 .23
61 Lance Berkman .75 .23
62 Larry Walker 1.25 .35
63 Luis Gonzalez .75 .23
64 Magglio Ordonez .75 .23
65 Manny Ramirez 1.25 .35
66 Mark Mulder .75 .23
67 Mark Prior 2.00 .60
68 Mark Teixeira .75 .23
69 Miguel Cabrera 1.25 .35
70 Miguel Tejada .75 .23
71 Mike Lowell .75 .23
72 Mike Mussina 1.25 .35
73 Mike Piazza 3.00 .90
74 Mike Sweeney .75 .23
75 Milton Bradley .75 .23
76 Nomar Garciaparra 3.00 .90
77 Orlando Cabrera .75 .23
78 Pedro Martinez 2.00 .60
79 Phil Nevin .75 .23
80 Preston Wilson .75 .23
81 Rafael Palmeiro 1.25 .35
82 Randy Johnson 2.00 .60
83 Rich Harden .75 .23
84 Richie Sexson .75 .23
85 Rickie Weeks .75 .23
86 Rocco Baldelli .75 .23
87 Roy Halladay .75 .23
88 Roy Oswalt .75 .23
89 Ryan Klesko .75 .23
90 Sammy Sosa 3.00 .90
91 Scott Rolen 2.00 .60
92 Shannon Stewart .75 .23
93 Shawn Green .75 .23
94 Tim Hudson .75 .23
95 Todd Helton 1.25 .35
96 Torii Hunter .75 .23
97 Trot Nixon .75 .23
98 Troy Glaus .75 .23
99 Vernon Wells .75 .23
100 Vladimir Guerrero 2.00 .60
101 Brandon Medders RC 4.00 1.20
102 Colby Miller RC 4.00 1.20
103 Dave Crouthers RC 4.00 1.20
104 Dennis Sarfate RC 4.00 1.20
105 Donnie Kelly RC 4.00 1.20
106 Alec Zumwalt RC 4.00 1.20
107 Chris Aguila RC 4.00 1.20
108 Greg Dobbs RC 4.00 1.20
109 Ian Snell RC 5.00 1.50
110 Jake Woods RC 4.00 1.20
111 Jamie Brown RC 4.00 1.20
112 Jason Frasor RC 4.00 1.20
113 Jerome Gamble RC 4.00 1.20
114 Jesse Harper RC 4.00 1.20
115 Josh Labandeira RC 4.00 1.20
116 Justin Hampson RC 4.00 1.20
117 Justin Huisman RC 4.00 1.20
118 Justin Leone RC 5.00 1.50
119 Kazuo Matsui RC 8.00 2.40
120 Lincoln Holdzkom RC 4.00 1.20
121 Mike Bumatay RC 4.00 1.20
122 Mike Gosling RC 4.00 1.20
123 Mike Johnston RC 4.00 1.20
124 Mike Rouse RC 4.00 1.20
125 Nick Regilio RC 4.00 1.20
126 Ryan Meaux RC 4.00 1.20
127 Scott Dohmann RC 4.00 1.20
128 Sean Henn RC 4.00 1.20
129 Tim Bausher RC 4.00 1.20
130 Tim Bittner RC 4.00 1.20
131 Adam Dunn Jsy L1 10.00 3.00
132 Andruw Jones Jsy L1 SP 8.00 2.40
133 Austin Kearns Jsy L1 6.00 1.80
134 Bartolo Colon Jsy L1 6.00 1.80
135 Ben Sheets Jsy L1 6.00 1.80
136 Bernie Williams Jsy L1 10.00 3.00
137 Bobby Abreu Jsy L1 6.00 1.80
138 Brian Giles Jsy L1 6.00 1.80
139 Carlos Lee Jsy L1 6.00 1.80
140 Chipper Jones Jsy L1 10.00 3.00
141 Corey Patterson Jsy L1 6.00 1.80
142 Darin Erstad Jsy L1 SP 8.00 2.40
143 Edgar Martinez Jsy L1 10.00 3.00
144 Vladimir Guerrero Jsy L1 SP 12.00 3.60
145 Eric Gagne Jsy L1 10.00 3.00
146 Frank Thomas Jsy L1 SP 12.00 3.60
147 Garret Anderson Jsy L1 6.00 1.80
148 Roger Clemens Jsy L1 15.00 4.50
149 Greg Maddux Jsy L1 10.00 3.00
150 Jacque Jones Jsy L1 6.00 1.80
151 Randy Johnson Jsy L1 10.00 3.00
152 Javy Lopez Jsy L1 6.00 1.80
153 Mike Piazza Jsy L1 SP 15.00 4.50
154 Albert Pujols Jsy L1 15.00 4.50
155 Jim Edmonds Jsy L1 6.00 1.80
156 Eric Milton Jsy L1 SP 8.00 2.40
157 Jorge Posada Jsy L1 10.00 3.00
158 J.D. Drew Jsy L1 6.00 1.80
159 Jose Vidro Jsy L1 SP 8.00 2.40
160 Kevin Millwood Jsy L1 6.00 1.80
161 Larry Walker Jsy L1 SP 12.00 3.60
162 Luis Gonzalez Jsy L1 SP 8.00 2.40
163 Mike Sweeney Jsy L1 6.00 1.80
164 Kerry Wood Jsy L1 SP 12.00 3.60
165 Mike Cameron Jsy L1 6.00 1.80
166 Phil Nevin Jsy L1 6.00 1.80
167 Rocco Baldelli Jsy L1 6.00 1.80
168 Ryan Klesko Jsy L1 6.00 1.80
169 Shannon Stewart Jsy L1 6.00 1.80
170 Torii Hunter Jsy L1 6.00 1.80
171 Trot Nixon Jsy L1 6.00 1.80
172 Vernon Wells Jsy L1 6.00 1.80
173 Alfonso Soriano Jsy L2 10.00 3.00
174 Andruw Jones Jsy L2 6.00 1.80
175 Barry Zito Jsy L2 6.00 1.80
176 Brandon Webb Jsy L2 6.00 1.80
177 Bret Boone Jsy L2 6.00 1.80
178 Scott Rolen Jsy L2 SP 12.00 3.60
179 Carlos Delgado Jsy L2 6.00 1.80
180 Curt Schilling Jsy L2 10.00 3.00
181 Dontrelle Willis Jsy L2 6.00 1.80
182 Eric Chavez Jsy L2 6.00 1.80
183 Frank Thomas Jsy L2 10.00 3.00
184 Gary Sheffield Jsy L2 SP 8.00 2.40
185 Greg Maddux Jsy L2 10.00 3.00
186 Hank Blalock Jsy L2 SP 8.00 2.40
187 Hideki Matsui Jsy L2 25.00 7.50
188 Hideo Nomo Jsy L2 SP 12.00 3.60
189 Ichiro Suzuki Jsy L2 15.00 4.50
190 Ivan Rodriguez Jsy L2 SP 12.00 3.60
191 Jason Giambi Jsy L2 SP 8.00 2.40
192 Rafael Furcal Jsy L2 6.00 1.80
193 Jeff Bagwell Jsy L2 10.00 3.00
194 Jeff Kent Jsy L2 6.00 1.80
195 Jim Thome Jsy L2 10.00 3.00
196 Jose Reyes Jsy L2 6.00 1.80
197 Josh Beckett Jsy L2 SP 8.00 2.40
198 Juan Gonzalez Jsy L2 SP 12.00 3.60
199 Ken Griffey Jr. Jsy L2 15.00 4.50
200 Kevin Brown Jsy L2 6.00 1.80
201 Lance Berkman Jsy L2 SP 8.00 2.40
202 Magglio Ordonez Jsy L2 6.00 1.80
203 Mark Mulder Jsy L2 6.00 1.80
204 Mark Teixeira Jsy L2 6.00 1.80
205 Miguel Tejada Jsy L2 6.00 1.80
206 Mike Mussina Jsy L2 10.00 3.00
207 Preston Wilson Jsy L2 SP 8.00 2.40
208 Rafael Palmeiro Jsy L2 10.00 3.00
209 Alex Rodriguez Jsy L2 15.00 4.50
210 Richie Sexson Jsy L2 6.00 1.80
211 Roy Halladay Jsy L2 6.00 1.80
212 Roy Oswalt Jsy L2 6.00 1.80
213 Tim Hudson Jsy L2 6.00 1.80
214 Troy Glaus Jsy L2 SP 8.00 2.40
215 Adam Dunn Jsy L3 12.00 3.60
216 Austin Kearns Jsy L3 8.00 2.40
217 Bartolo Colon Jsy L3 8.00 2.40
218 Ben Sheets Jsy L3 8.00 2.40
219 Bernie Williams Jsy L3 12.00 3.60
220 Bobby Abreu Jsy L3 8.00 2.40
221 Bret Boone Jsy L3 8.00 2.40
222 Todd Helton Jsy L3 12.00 3.60
223 Chipper Jones Jsy L3 12.00 3.60
224 Corey Patterson Jsy L3 8.00 2.40
225 Darin Erstad Jsy L3 8.00 2.40
226 Dontrelle Willis Jsy L3 8.00 2.40
227 Edgar Martinez Jsy L3 12.00 3.60
228 Eric Gagne Jsy L3 12.00 3.60
229 Garret Anderson Jsy L3 8.00 2.40
230 Roger Clemens Jsy L3 20.00 6.00
231 Hank Blalock Jsy L3 8.00 2.40
232 Jacque Jones Jsy L3 8.00 2.40
233 Jeff Bagwell Jsy L3 12.00 3.60
234 Jeff Kent Jsy L3 8.00 2.40
235 Jeremy Bonderman Jsy L3 8.00 2.40
236 Jim Edmonds Jsy L3 8.00 2.40
237 Jorge Posada Jsy L3 12.00 3.60
238 J.D. Drew Jsy L3 8.00 2.40
239 Jose Reyes Jsy L3 8.00 2.40
240 Jose Vidro Jsy L3 8.00 2.40
241 Kevin Millwood Jsy L3 8.00 2.40
242 Luis Gonzalez Jsy L3 8.00 2.40
243 Mike Sweeney Jsy L3 8.00 2.40
244 Jason Giambi Jsy L3 8.00 2.40
245 Manny Ramirez Jsy L3 12.00 3.60
246 Phil Nevin Jsy L3 8.00 2.40
247 Preston Wilson Jsy L3 8.00 2.40
248 Alex Rodriguez Jsy L3 20.00 6.00
249 Richie Sexson Jsy L3 8.00 2.40
250 Rocco Baldelli Jsy L3 8.00 2.40
251 Ryan Klesko Jsy L3 8.00 2.40
252 Sammy Sosa Jsy L3 15.00 4.50
253 Torii Hunter Jsy L3 8.00 2.40
254 Mike Lowell Jsy L3 8.00 2.40
255 Troy Glaus Jsy L3 8.00 2.40
256 Vernon Wells Jsy L3 8.00 2.40
257 Albert Pujols Jsy L4 25.00 7.50
258 Alex Rodriguez Jsy L4 20.00 6.00
259 Alfonso Soriano Jsy L4 12.00 3.60
260 Roger Clemens Jsy L4 20.00 6.00
261 Barry Zito Jsy L4 8.00 2.40
262 Brandon Webb Jsy L4 8.00 2.40
263 Carlos Delgado Jsy L4 8.00 2.40
264 Curt Schilling Jsy L4 12.00 3.60
265 Derek Jeter Jsy L4 30.00 9.00
266 Eric Chavez Jsy L4 8.00 2.40
267 Gary Sheffield Jsy L4 8.00 2.40
268 Hideki Matsui Jsy L4 30.00 9.00
269 Hideo Nomo Jsy L4 12.00 3.60
270 Ichiro Suzuki Jsy L4 25.00 7.50
271 Ivan Rodriguez Jsy L4 12.00 3.60
272 Jason Giambi Jsy L4 8.00 2.40
273 Jim Thome Jsy L4 12.00 3.60
274 Josh Beckett Jsy L4 8.00 2.40
275 Juan Gonzalez Jsy L4 12.00 3.60
276 Ken Griffey Jr. Jsy L4 20.00 6.00
277 Kerry Wood Jsy L4 12.00 3.60
278 Kevin Brown Jsy L4 8.00 2.40
279 Lance Berkman Jsy L4 8.00 2.40
280 Magglio Ordonez Jsy L4 8.00 2.40
281 Manny Ramirez Jsy L4 12.00 3.60
282 Mark Mulder Jsy L4 8.00 2.40
283 Mark Prior Jsy L4 12.00 3.60
284 Mark Teixeira Jsy L4 8.00 2.40
285 Miguel Tejada Jsy L4 8.00 2.40
286 Mike Mussina Jsy L4 12.00 3.60
287 Mike Piazza Jsy L4 20.00 6.00
288 Pedro Martinez Jsy L4 12.00 3.60
289 Rafael Palmeiro Jsy L4 12.00 3.60
290 Randy Johnson Jsy L4 12.00 3.60
291 Roy Halladay Jsy L4 8.00 2.40
292 Roy Oswalt Jsy L4 8.00 2.40
293 Sammy Sosa Jsy L4 20.00 6.00
294 Scott Rolen Jsy L4 12.00 3.60
295 Shawn Green Jsy L4 8.00 2.40
296 Tim Hudson Jsy L4 8.00 2.40
297 Todd Helton Jsy L4 12.00 3.60
298 Vladimir Guerrero Jsy L4 12.00 3.60
299 Bret Boone AU 40.00 12.00
300 Alex Rodriguez AU 200.00 60.00
301 Dontrelle Willis AU 40.00 12.00
302 Barry Larkin AU 50.00 15.00
303 Barry Zito AU 50.00 15.00
304 Eric Chavez AU 40.00 12.00
305 Bernie Williams AU 120.00 36.00
306 Brandon Webb AU 25.00 7.50
307 Cal Ripken AU 200.00 60.00
308 Carl Yastrzemski AU 80.00 24.00
309 Carlos Delgado AU 40.00 12.00
310 Shawn Green AU 40.00 12.00
311 Eric Gagne AU 60.00 18.00
312 Frank Thomas AU 60.00 18.00
313 Carlos Lee AU 25.00 7.50
314 Garret Anderson AU 40.00 12.00
315 Hideki Matsui AU 350.00 105.00
316 Jim Edmonds AU 50.00 15.00
317 Jeff Bagwell AU 50.00 15.00
318 Luis Gonzalez AU 40.00 12.00
319 Mike Mussina AU 50.00 15.00
320 John Smoltz AU 100.00 30.00
321 Jose Reyes AU 40.00 12.00
322 Josh Beckett AU 50.00 15.00
323 Juan Gonzalez AU 50.00 15.00
324 Ken Griffey Jr. AU 150.00 45.00
325 Rich Harden AU 25.00 7.50
326 Pat Burrell AU 40.00 12.00
327 Mark Teixeira AU 40.00 12.00
328 Roy Oswalt AU 40.00 12.00
329 Miguel Tejada AU 40.00 12.00
330 Mike Hampton AU 40.00 12.00
331 Mike Piazza AU 200.00 60.00
332 Nolan Ryan AU 150.00 45.00
333 Orlando Hernandez AU 40.00 12.00
334 Paul Lo Duca AU 40.00 12.00
335 Roberto Alomar AU 50.00 15.00
336 Rocco Baldelli AU 40.00 12.00
337 Trevor Hoffman AU 50.00 15.00
338 Tom Glavine AU 50.00 15.00
339 Tom Seaver AU 60.00 18.00
340 Mark Prior AU 100.00 30.00
341 Shingo Takatsu RC 3.00 .90
342 Franklyn Gracesqui RC .60 .18
343 Angel Chavez RC 1.00 .30
344 Jorge Sequea RC 1.00 .30
345 David Aardsma RC 1.00 .30
346 Ramon Ramirez RC 1.00 .30
347 Lino Urdaneta RC 1.00 .30
348 Orlando Rodriguez RC 1.00 .30
349 Jason Szuminski RC .60 .18
350 Luis A. Gonzalez RC 1.50 .45
351 John Gall RC 1.50 .45
352 Kevin Cave RC 1.50 .45
353 Chris Oxspring RC 1.50 .45
354 Freddy Guzman RC 1.00 .30
355 Jeff Bennett RC 1.00 .30
356 Jorge Vasquez RC 1.00 .30
357 Merkin Valdez RC 3.00 .90
358 Tim Hamulack RC .60 .18
359 Hector Gimenez RC .60 .18
360 Jerry Gil RC 1.00 .30
361 Ryan Wing RC 1.00 .30
362 Shawn Hill RC 1.00 .30
363 Jason Bartlett RC 1.50 .45
364 Renyel Pinto RC 1.50 .45
365 Carlos Vasquez RC 1.50 .45
366 Mike Vento RC 1.50 .45
367 Casey Daigle RC 1.00 .30
368 Chad Bentz RC 1.00 .30
369 Chris Saenz RC .60 .18
370 Shawn Camp RC .60 .18
371 Carlos Hines RC 1.00 .30
372 Edwin Moreno RC 1.00 .30
373 Michael Wuertz RC 1.50 .45
374 Aarom Baldiris RC 1.50 .45
375 Ronny Cedeno RC 1.00 .30
376 Akinori Otsuka RC 4.00 1.20
377 Jose Capellan RC 5.00 1.50
378 Justin Germano RC 1.00 .30
379 Justin Knoedler RC 1.00 .30
380 Mariano Gomez RC 1.00 .30
381 Fernando Nieve RC 1.00 .30
382 Scott Proctor RC 5.00 1.50
383 Roman Colon RC .60 .18
384 Onil Joseph RC 1.00 .30
385 Eddy Rodriguez RC 1.50 .45
386 Enemencio Pacheco RC 1.00 .30
387 William Bergolla RC 1.00 .30
388 Ivan Ochoa RC 1.00 .30
389 Rusty Tucker RC 1.50 .45
390 Roberto Novoa RC 1.50 .45
S38 Ichiro Suzuki Promo

2004 Reflections Black

Nm-Mt Ex-Mt
1-100 OVERALL PARALLEL ODDS 1:4
101-130/299-340 OVERALL AU ODDS 1:16
173-214/257-298 OVERALL GU ODDS 1:2
1-100/173-340 PRINT RUN 1 SERIAL #'d SET
101-130 PRINT RUN 5 SERIAL #'d SETS
NO PRICING DUE TO SCARCITY

2004 Reflections Gold

Nm-Mt Ex-Mt
*GOLD 1-100: 5X TO 12X BASIC
1-100 PRINT RUN 15 SERIAL #'d SETS
101-130 PRINT RUN 250 SERIAL #'d SETS
*GOLD JSY 131-172: 1.5X TO 4X BASIC
*GOLD JSY 131-172: 1.25X TO 3X BASIC SP
131-172 PRINT RUN 15 SERIAL #'d SETS
257-298 PRINT RUN 5 SERIAL #'d SETS
257-398 NO PRICING DUE TO SCARCITY
*GOLD AU JSY 299-340: .6X TO 1.2X BASIC
299-340 PRINT RUN 15 SERIAL #'d SETS
1-100 OVERALL PARALLEL ODDS 1:4
101-130/299-340 OVERALL AU ODDS 1:16
131-172/257-298 OVERALL GU ODDS 1:2
101 Brandon Medders AU 10.00 3.00
102 Colby Miller AU 10.00 3.00
103 Dave Crouthers AU 10.00 3.00
104 Dennis Sarfate AU 10.00 3.00
105 Donnie Kelly AU 10.00 3.00
106 Alec Zumwalt AU 10.00 3.00
107 Chris Aguila AU 10.00 3.00
108 Greg Dobbs AU 10.00 3.00
109 Ian Snell AU 15.00 4.50
110 Jake Woods AU 10.00 3.00
111 Jamie Brown AU 10.00 3.00
112 Jason Frasor AU 10.00 3.00
113 Jerome Gamble AU 10.00 3.00
114 Jesse Harper AU 10.00 3.00
115 Josh Labandeira AU 10.00 3.00
116 Justin Hampson AU 10.00 3.00
117 Justin Huisman AU 10.00 3.00
118 Justin Leone AU 15.00 4.50
120 Lincoln Holdzkom AU 10.00 3.00
121 Mike Bumatay AU 10.00 3.00
122 Mike Gosling AU 10.00 3.00
123 Mike Johnston AU 10.00 3.00
124 Mike Rouse AU 10.00 3.00
125 Nick Regilio AU 10.00 3.00
126 Ryan Meaux AU 10.00 3.00
127 Scott Dohmann AU 10.00 3.00
128 Sean Henn AU 10.00 3.00
129 Tim Bausher AU 10.00 3.00
130 Tim Bittner AU 10.00 3.00

2004 Reflections Gold Rookie Autograph 125

Nm-Mt Ex-Mt
*GOLD AU 125: .4X TO 1X GOLD AU 250
OVERALL AU ODDS 1:16
STATED PRINT RUN 125 SERIAL #'d SETS

2004 Reflections Red

Nm-Mt Ex-Mt
*RED 1-100: 2X TO 5X BASIC
1-100 OVERALL PARALLEL ODDS 1:4
*RED JSY 131-214: .6X TO 1.5X BASIC
*RED JSY 131-214: .5X TO 1.2X BASIC SP
*RED JSY 215-256: .5X TO 1.2X BASIC
131-256 OVERALL GU ODDS 1:2
STATED PRINT RUN 50 SERIAL #'d SETS

1998 Revolution

The 1998 Revolution set (produced by Pacific) consists of 150 standard size cards. The three card packs retailed for a suggested price of $5.99. The fronts feature a color action photo atop a state-of-the-art silver foil sparkling background. The backs provide collectors with full year-by-year statistics of the featured player. The set release date was September, 1998. Rookie Cards inlcude Magglio Ordonez.

Nm-Mt Ex-Mt
COMPLETE SET (150) 100.00 30.00
1 Garret Anderson 1.00 .30
2 Jim Edmonds 1.00 .30
3 Darin Erstad 1.00 .30
4 Chuck Finley 1.00 .30
5 Tim Salmon 1.50 .45
6 Jay Bell 1.00 .30
7 Travis Lee .60 .18
8 Devon White 1.00 .30
9 Matt Williams 1.00 .30
10 Andres Galarraga 1.00 .30
11 Tom Glavine 1.50 .45
12 Andruw Jones 1.00 .30
13 Chipper Jones 2.50 .75
14 Ryan Klesko 1.00 .30
15 Javy Lopez 1.00 .30
16 Greg Maddux 4.00 1.20
17 Walt Weiss 1.00 .30
18 Roberto Alomar 1.50 .45
19 Joe Carter 1.00 .30
20 Mike Mussina 1.50 .45
21 Rafael Palmeiro 1.50 .45
22 Cal Ripken 8.00 2.40
23 B.J. Surhoff 1.00 .30
24 Nomar Garciaparra 4.00 1.20
25 Reggie Jefferson .60 .18
26 Pedro Martinez 2.50 .75
27 Troy O'Leary .60 .18
28 Mo Vaughn 1.00 .30
29 Mark Grace 1.50 .45
30 Mickey Morandini .60 .18
31 Henry Rodriguez .60 .18
32 Sammy Sosa 4.00 1.20
33 Kerry Wood 2.50 .75
34 Albert Belle 1.00 .30
35 Ray Durham 1.00 .30
36 Magglio Ordonez RC 5.00 1.50
37 Frank Thomas 2.50 .75
38 Robin Ventura 1.00 .30
39 Bret Boone 1.00 .30
40 Barry Larkin 1.50 .45
41 Reggie Sanders .60 .18
42 Brett Tomko .60 .18
43 Sandy Alomar Jr. .60 .18
44 David Justice 1.00 .30
45 Kenny Lofton 1.00 .30
46 Manny Ramirez 1.50 .45
47 Jim Thome 2.50 .75
48 Omar Vizquel 1.50 .45
49 Jaret Wright .60 .18
50 Dante Bichette 1.00 .30
51 Ellis Burks 1.00 .30
52 Vinny Castilla 1.00 .30
53 Todd Helton 1.50 .45
54 Larry Walker 1.50 .45
55 Tony Clark .60 .18
56 Deivi Cruz .60 .18
57 Damion Easley .60 .18
58 Bobby Higginson 1.00 .30
59 Brian Hunter .60 .18
60 Cliff Floyd 1.00 .30
61 Livan Hernandez .60 .18
62 Derrek Lee 1.00 .30
63 Edgar Renteria 1.00 .30
64 Moises Alou 1.00 .30
65 Jeff Bagwell 1.50 .45
66 Derek Bell .60 .18
67 Craig Biggio 1.50 .45
68 Richard Hidalgo .60 .18
69 Johnny Damon 1.50 .45
70 Jeff King .60 .18
71 Hal Morris .60 .18
72 Dean Palmer 1.00 .30
73 Bobby Bonilla 1.00 .30
74 Charles Johnson 1.00 .30
75 Eric Karros 1.00 .30
76 Raul Mondesi 1.00 .30
77 Gary Sheffield 1.00 .30
78 Jeromy Burnitz 1.00 .30
79 Marquis Grissom 1.00 .30
80 Dave Nilsson .60 .18
81 Fernando Vina .60 .18
82 Marty Cordova .60 .18
83 Pat Meares .60 .18
84 Paul Molitor 1.50 .45
85 Brad Radke 1.00 .30
86 Terry Steinbach .60 .18
87 Todd Walker .60 .18
88 Brad Fullmer .60 .18
89 Vladimir Guerrero 2.50 .75
90 Carl Pavano 1.50 .45
91 Rondell White 1.00 .30
92 Bernard Gilkey .60 .18
93 Hideo Nomo 2.50 .75
94 John Olerud 1.00 .30
95 Rey Ordonez .60 .18
96 Mike Piazza 4.00 1.20
97 Masato Yoshii RC 1.50 .45
98 Hideki Irabu .60 .18
99 Derek Jeter 6.00 1.80
100 Chuck Knoblauch 1.00 .30

101 Tino Martinez 1.50 .45
102 Paul O'Neill 1.50 .45
103 Darryl Strawberry 1.00 .30
104 Bernie Williams 1.50 .45
105 Jason Giambi 1.00 .30
106 Ben Grieve .60 .18
107 Rickey Henderson 2.50 .75
108 Matt Stairs .60 .18
109 Doug Glanville .60 .18
110 Desi Relaford .60 .18
111 Scott Rolen 2.50 .75
112 Curt Schilling 1.00 .30
113 Jason Kendall 1.00 .30
114 Al Martin .60 .18
115 Jason Schmidt 1.00 .30
116 Kevin Young 1.00 .30
117 Delino DeShields .60 .18
118 Gary Gaetti 1.00 .30
119 Brian Jordan 1.00 .30
120 Ray Lankford .60 .18
121 Mark McGwire 6.00 1.80
122 Kevin Brown 1.50 .45
123 Steve Finley 1.00 .30
124 Tony Gwynn 3.00 .90
125 Wally Joyner 1.00 .30
126 Greg Vaughn .60 .18
127 Barry Bonds 6.00 1.80
128 Orel Hershiser 1.00 .30
129 Jeff Kent 1.00 .30
130 Bill Mueller 1.00 .30
131 Jay Buhner 1.00 .30
132 Ken Griffey Jr. 4.00 1.20
133 Randy Johnson 2.50 .75
134 Edgar Martinez 1.50 .45
135 Alex Rodriguez 4.00 1.20
136 David Segui .60 .18
137 Rolando Arrojo RC 1.00 .30
138 Wade Boggs 1.50 .45
139 Quinton McCracken .60 .18
140 Fred McGriff 1.50 .45
141 Will Clark 2.50 .75
142 Juan Gonzalez 1.50 .45
143 Tom Goodwin .60 .18
144 Ivan Rodriguez 2.50 .75
145 Aaron Sele .60 .18
146 John Wetteland 1.00 .30
147 Jose Canseco 2.50 .75
148 Roger Clemens 5.00 1.50
149 Jose Cruz Jr. .60 .18
150 Carlos Delgado 1.00 .30

1998 Revolution Shadow Series

The 1998 Revolution Shadow Series consists of 150 cards and is a parallel to the 1998 Revolution base set. The cards are randomly inserted in hobby packs. Only 99 sets were produced and each card is embossed with the words "Shadow Series" and is serial numbered "X of 99" in thin small, black print on back.

Nm-Mt Ex-Mt
*STARS: 4X TO 10X BASIC CARDS....
*ROOKIES: 3X TO 8X BASIC CARDS..

1998 Revolution Foul Pole

The 1998 Revolution Foul Pole Laser Cuts set consists of 20 cards and is an insert to the 1998 Revolution base set. The cards are randomly inserted in packs at a rate of one in 49. The fronts feature color action photography with a unique laser-cut design recreating the look of an actual foul pole.

Nm-Mt Ex-Mt
COMPLETE SET (20) 300.00 90.00
1 Cal Ripken 50.00 15.00
2 Nomar Garciaparra 25.00 7.50
3 Mo Vaughn 6.00 1.80
4 Frank Thomas 15.00 4.50
5 Manny Ramirez 10.00 3.00
6 Bernie Williams 10.00 3.00
7 Ben Grieve 4.00 1.20
8 Ken Griffey Jr. 25.00 7.50
9 Alex Rodriguez 25.00 7.50
10 Juan Gonzalez 10.00 3.00
11 Ivan Rodriguez 15.00 4.50
12 Travis Lee 4.00 1.20
13 Chipper Jones 15.00 4.50
14 Sammy Sosa 25.00 7.50
15 Vinny Castilla 6.00 1.80
16 Moises Alou 6.00 1.80
17 Gary Sheffield 6.00 1.80
18 Mike Piazza 25.00 7.50
19 Mark McGwire 40.00 12.00
20 Barry Bonds 40.00 12.00

1998 Revolution Major League Icons

The 1998 Revolution Major League Icons set consists of 10 cards and is an insert to the 1998 Revolution base set. The cards are randomly inserted in packs at a rate of one 121. The fronts feature color action photos of the MLB's best atop a die-cut "shield of honor" design.

Nm-Mt Ex-Mt
COMPLETE SET (10) 100.00 30.00
1 Cal Ripken 40.00 12.00
2 Nomar Garciaparra 20.00 6.00
3 Frank Thomas 12.00 3.60
4 Ken Griffey Jr. 20.00 6.00
5 Alex Rodriguez 20.00 6.00
6 Chipper Jones 12.00 3.60
7 Kerry Wood 12.00 3.60
8 Mike Piazza 20.00 6.00
9 Mark McGwire 30.00 9.00
10 Tony Gwynn 15.00 4.50

1998 Revolution Prime Time Performers

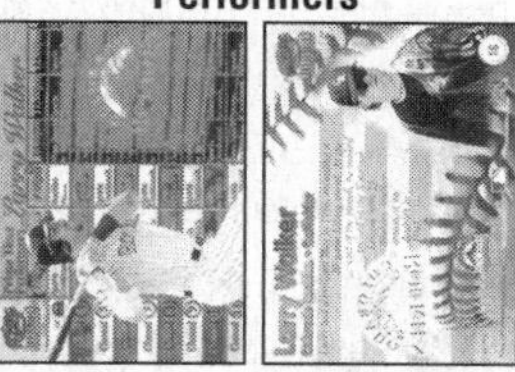

The 1998 Revolution Prime Time Performers Laser-Cuts set consists of 20 card and is an insert to the 1998 Revolution base set. The cards are randomly inserted in packs at a rate of one in 25. The fronts feature color action photography, a laser-cut logo in the upper left corner and an eye-catching "television" and "Prime Time" television schedule design.

Nm-Mt Ex-Mt
COMPLETE SET (20) 150.00 45.00
1 Cal Ripken 25.00 7.50
2 Nomar Garciaparra 12.00 3.60
3 Frank Thomas 8.00 2.40
4 Jim Thome 8.00 2.40
5 Hideki Irabu 2.00 .60
6 Derek Jeter 20.00 6.00
7 Ben Grieve 2.00 .60
8 Ken Griffey Jr. 12.00 3.60
9 Alex Rodriguez 12.00 3.60
10 Juan Gonzalez 5.00 1.50
11 Ivan Rodriguez 8.00 2.40
12 Travis Lee 2.00 .60
13 Chipper Jones 8.00 2.40
14 Greg Maddux 12.00 3.60
15 Kerry Wood 8.00 2.40
16 Larry Walker 5.00 1.50
17 Jeff Bagwell 5.00 1.50
18 Mike Piazza 12.00 3.60
19 Mark McGwire 20.00 6.00
20 Tony Gwynn 10.00 3.00

1998 Revolution Rookies and Hardball Heroes

This 30 card set was inserted one every six hobby packs. This set features 30 of either the leading players in baseball or some of the most promising young stars.

Nm-Mt Ex-Mt
COMPLETE SET (30) 50.00 15.00
*GOLD 1-20: 6X TO 15X BASIC ROOK/HARDBALL
GOLD 1-20 RANDOM INSERTS IN HOBBY PACKS
GOLD 1-20 PRINT RUN 50 SERIAL #'d SETS
1 Justin Baughman 1.00 .30
2 Jarrod Washburn 1.00 .30
3 Travis Lee 1.00 .30
4 Kerry Wood 4.00 1.20
5 Magglio Ordonez 6.00 1.80
6 Todd Helton 2.50 .75
7 Derrek Lee 1.50 .45
8 Richard Hidalgo 1.00 .30
9 Mike Caruso 1.00 .30
10 David Ortiz 1.50 .45
11 Brad Fullmer 1.00 .30
12 Masato Yoshii 2.50 .75
13 Orlando Hernandez 4.00 1.20
14 Ricky Ledee 1.50 .45
15 Ben Grieve 1.00 .30
16 Carlton Loewer 1.00 .30
17 Desi Relaford 1.00 .30
18 Ruben Rivera 1.50 .45
19 Rolando Arrojo 1.00 .30
20 Matt Perisho 1.00 .30
21 Chipper Jones 4.00 1.20
22 Greg Maddux 6.00 1.80
23 Cal Ripken 12.00 3.60
24 Nomar Garciaparra 6.00 1.80
25 Frank Thomas 4.00 1.20
26 Mark McGwire 10.00 3.00
27 Tony Gwynn 5.00 1.50
28 Ken Griffey Jr. 6.00 1.80
29 Alex Rodriguez 6.00 1.80
30 Juan Gonzalez 2.50 .75

1998 Revolution Showstoppers

The 1998 Revolution Showstoppers set consists of 36 cards and is an insert to the 1998 Revolution base set. The cards are randomly inserted in packs at a rate of two in 25. The fronts feature color action photos of 36 of the most exciting stars in the MLB.

Nm-Mt Ex-Mt
COMPLETE SET (36) 200.00 60.00
1 Cal Ripken 20.00 6.00
2 Nomar Garciaparra 10.00 3.00

3 Pedro Martinez 6.00 1.80
4 Mo Vaughn 2.50 .75
5 Frank Thomas 6.00 1.80
6 Manny Ramirez 4.00 1.20
7 Jim Thome 6.00 1.80
8 Jaret Wright 1.50 .45
9 Paul Molitor 4.00 1.20
10 Orlando Hernandez 6.00 1.80
11 Derek Jeter 15.00 4.50
12 Bernie Williams 4.00 1.20
13 Ben Grieve 1.50 .45
14 Ken Griffey Jr. 10.00 3.00
15 Alex Rodriguez 10.00 3.00
16 Wade Boggs 4.00 1.20
17 Juan Gonzalez 4.00 1.20
18 Ivan Rodriguez 6.00 1.80
19 Jose Canseco 6.00 1.80
20 Roger Clemens 12.00 3.60
21 Travis Lee 1.50 .45
22 Andres Galarraga 2.50 .75
23 Chipper Jones 6.00 1.80
24 Greg Maddux 10.00 3.00
25 Sammy Sosa 10.00 3.00
26 Kerry Wood 6.00 1.80
27 Vinny Castilla 2.50 .75
28 Larry Walker 4.00 1.20
29 Moises Alou 2.50 .75
30 Raul Mondesi 2.50 .75
31 Gary Sheffield 2.50 .75
32 Hideki Irabu 1.50 .45
33 Mike Piazza 10.00 3.00
34 Mark McGwire 15.00 4.50
35 Tony Gwynn 8.00 2.40
36 Barry Bonds 15.00 4.50

1999 Revolution

The 1999 Revolution set (produced by Pacific) was issued in one series totalling 150 cards and distributed in three-card packs with a suggested retail price of $3.99. The set features color action player photos on dual-foiled, etched and embossed cards. The set contains a short-printed 25-card rookies subset inserted in packs at the rate of one in four. Rookie Cards include Freddy Garcia.

Nm-Mt Ex-Mt
COMPLETE SET (150) 80.00 24.00
COMMON CARD (1-150) .60 .18
COMMON SP 2.00 .60
1 Jim Edmonds 1.00 .30
2 Darin Erstad 1.00 .30
3 Troy Glaus 1.00 .30
4 Tim Salmon 1.50 .45
5 Mo Vaughn 1.00 .30
6 Steve Finley 1.00 .30
7 Luis Gonzalez 1.00 .30
8 Randy Johnson 2.50 .75
9 Travis Lee .60 .18
10 Matt Williams 1.00 .30
11 Andruw Jones 1.00 .30
12 Chipper Jones 2.50 .75
13 Brian Jordan 1.00 .30
14 Javy Lopez 1.00 .30
15 Greg Maddux 4.00 1.20
16 Kevin McGlinchy SP 2.00 .60
17 John Smoltz 1.50 .45
18 Brady Anderson 1.00 .30
19 Albert Belle 1.00 .30
20 Will Clark 2.50 .75
21 Willis Otanez SP 2.00 .60
22 Calvin Pickering SP 2.00 .60
23 Cal Ripken 8.00 2.40
24 Nomar Garciaparra 4.00 1.20
25 Pedro Martinez 2.50 .75
26 Troy O'Leary .60 .18
27 Jose Offerman .60 .18
28 Mark Grace 1.50 .45
29 Mickey Morandini .60 .18
30 Henry Rodriguez .60 .18
31 Sammy Sosa 4.00 1.20
32 Ray Durham 1.00 .30
33 Carlos Lee SP 2.00 .60
34 Jeff Liefer SP 2.00 .60
35 Magglio Ordonez 1.00 .30
36 Frank Thomas 2.50 .75
37 Mike Cameron 1.00 .30
38 Sean Casey 1.00 .30
39 Barry Larkin 1.50 .45
40 Greg Vaughn .60 .18
41 Roberto Alomar 1.50 .45
42 Sandy Alomar Jr. .60 .18
43 David Justice 1.00 .30
44 Kenny Lofton 1.00 .30
45 Manny Ramirez 1.50 .45
46 Richie Sexson 1.00 .30
47 Jim Thome 2.50 .75
48 Dante Bichette 1.00 .30
49 Vinny Castilla 1.00 .30
50 Darryl Hamilton .60 .18
51 Todd Helton 1.50 .45
52 Larry Walker 1.50 .45
53 Tony Clark .60 .18
54 Damion Easley .60 .18
55 Bob Higginson 1.00 .30
56 Gabe Kapler SP 2.00 .60
57 Alex Gonzalez SP 2.00 .60
58 Mark Kotsay .60 .18
59 Kevin Orie .60 .18
60 Preston Wilson SP 2.00 .60
61 Jeff Bagwell 1.50 .45
62 Derek Bell .60 .18
63 Craig Biggio 1.50 .45
64 Ken Caminiti 1.00 .30
65 Carlos Beltran SP 2.00 .60
66 Johnny Damon 1.50 .45
67 Jermaine Dye 1.00 .30
68 Carlos Febles SP 2.00 .60
69 Kevin Brown 1.50 .45
70 Todd Hundley .60 .18
71 Eric Karros 1.00 .30
72 Raul Mondesi 1.00 .30
73 Gary Sheffield 1.00 .30
74 Jeromy Burnitz 1.00 .30
75 Jeff Cirillo .60 .18
76 Marquis Grissom 1.00 .30
77 Fernando Vina .60 .18
78 Chad Allen SP RC 2.00 .60
79 Corey Koskie SP 2.00 .60
80 D.Mientkiewicz SP RC 3.00 .90
81 Brad Radke 1.00 .30
82 Todd Walker .60 .18
83 Michael Barrett SP 2.00 .60
84 Vladimir Guerrero 2.50 .75
85 Wilton Guerrero .60 .18
86 Guillermo Mota SP RC 2.00 .60
87 Rondell White 1.00 .30
88 Edgardo Alfonzo .60 .18
89 Rickey Henderson 2.50 .75
90 John Olerud 1.00 .30
91 Mike Piazza 4.00 1.20
92 Robin Ventura 1.00 .30
93 Roger Clemens 5.00 1.50
94 Chili Davis 1.00 .30
95 Derek Jeter 6.00 1.80
96 Chuck Knoblauch 1.00 .30
97 Tino Martinez 1.50 .45
98 Paul O'Neill 1.50 .45
99 Bernie Williams 1.50 .45
100 Eric Chavez SP 2.00 .60
101 Jason Giambi 1.00 .30
102 Ben Grieve .60 .18
103 John Jaha .60 .18
104 Olmedo Saenz SP 2.00 .60
105 Bobby Abreu 1.00 .30
106 Doug Glanville .60 .18
107 Desi Relaford .60 .18
108 Scott Rolen 2.50 .75
109 Curt Schilling 1.00 .30
110 Brian Giles 1.00 .30
111 Jason Kendall 1.00 .30
112 Pat Meares .60 .18
113 Kevin Young 1.00 .30
114 J.D. Drew SP 2.00 .60
115 Ray Lankford .60 .18
116 Eli Marrero .60 .18
117 Joe McEwing SP RC 2.00 .60
118 Mark McGwire 6.00 1.80
119 Fernando Tatis .60 .18
120 Tony Gwynn 3.00 .90
121 Trevor Hoffman 1.00 .30
122 Wally Joyner 1.00 .30
123 Reggie Sanders .60 .18
124 Barry Bonds 6.00 1.80
125 Ellis Burks 1.00 .30
126 Jeff Kent 1.00 .30
127 Ramon E.Martinez SP RC 2.00 .60
128 Joe Nathan SP RC 3.00 .90
129 Freddy Garcia SP RC 3.00 .90
130 Ken Griffey Jr. 4.00 1.20
131 Brian Hunter .60 .18
132 Edgar Martinez 1.50 .45
133 Alex Rodriguez 4.00 1.20
134 David Segui .60 .18
135 Wade Boggs 1.50 .45
136 Jose Canseco 2.50 .75
137 Quinton McCracken .60 .18
138 Fred McGriff 1.50 .45
139 K.Dransfeldt SP RC 2.00 .60
140 Juan Gonzalez 1.50 .45
141 Rusty Greer 1.00 .30
142 Rafael Palmeiro 1.50 .45
143 Ivan Rodriguez 2.50 .75
144 Lee Stevens .60 .18
145 Jose Cruz Jr. .60 .18
146 Carlos Delgado 1.00 .30
147 Shawn Green 1.00 .30
148 Roy Halladay SP 2.00 .60
149 Shannon Stewart 1.00 .30
150 Kevin Witt SP 2.00 .60

1999 Revolution Premiere Date

Randomly inserted in hobby packs only at the rate of one in 25, this 150-card set is parallel to the base set. Only 49 serial-numbered sets were produced.

Nm-Mt Ex-Mt
*STARS: 5X TO 12X BASIC CARDS....
*SP'S: 2X TO 5X BASIC SP'S..........
*SP RC'S: 2X TO 5X BASIC SP RC'S .

1999 Revolution Red

Randomly inserted in retail packs only, this 150-card set is a red foil parallel version of the base set. Only 299 serial-numbered sets were produced.

Nm-Mt Ex-Mt
*STARS: 2X TO 5X BASIC CARDS.....
*SP'S: .75X TO 2X BASIC SP'S.........
*SP RC'S: .6X TO 1.5X BASIC SP RC'S

1999 Revolution Shadow Series

Randomly inserted in hobby packs only, this 150-card set is a gold foil parallel version of the base set. Only 99 serial-numbered sets were produced.

Nm-Mt Ex-Mt
*STARS: 4X TO 10X BASIC CARDS....
*SP'S: 1.5X TO 4X BASIC SP'S.........
*SP RC'S: 1.25X TO 3X BASIC SP RC'S

1999 Revolution Diamond Legacy

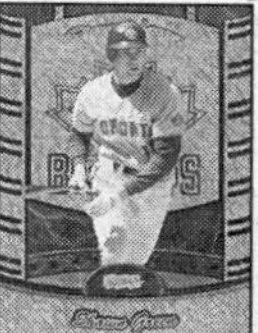

Randomly inserted in packs at the rate of two in 25, this 36-card set features color action photos of some of the league's elite players printed on cards with a new holographic patterned foil design.

Nm-Mt Ex-Mt
COMPLETE SET (36) 150.00 45.00
1 Troy Glaus 2.50 .75
2 Mo Vaughn 2.50 .75
3 Matt Williams 2.50 .75
4 Chipper Jones 6.00 1.80
5 Andruw Jones 2.50 .75
6 Greg Maddux 10.00 3.00
7 Albert Belle 2.50 .75
8 Cal Ripken 20.00 6.00
9 Nomar Garciaparra 10.00 3.00
10 Sammy Sosa 10.00 3.00
11 Frank Thomas 6.00 1.80
12 Manny Ramirez 4.00 1.20
13 Todd Helton 4.00 1.20
14 Larry Walker 4.00 1.20
15 Gabe Kapler 2.00 .60
16 Jeff Bagwell 4.00 1.20
17 Craig Biggio 4.00 1.20
18 Raul Mondesi 2.50 .75
19 Vladimir Guerrero 6.00 1.80
20 Mike Piazza 10.00 3.00
21 Roger Clemens 12.00 3.60
22 Derek Jeter 15.00 4.50
23 Bernie Williams 4.00 1.20
24 Ben Grieve 1.50 .45
25 Scott Rolen 6.00 1.80
26 J.D. Drew 2.00 .60
27 Mark McGwire 15.00 4.50
28 Fernando Tatis 1.50 .45
29 Tony Gwynn 8.00 2.40
30 Barry Bonds 15.00 4.50
31 Ken Griffey Jr. 10.00 3.00
32 Alex Rodriguez 10.00 3.00
33 Jose Canseco 6.00 1.80
34 Juan Gonzalez 4.00 1.20
35 Ivan Rodriguez 6.00 1.80
36 Shawn Green 2.50 .75

1999 Revolution Foul Pole

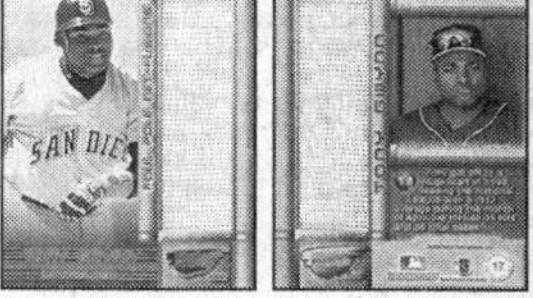

Randomly inserted in packs at the rate of one in 49, this 20-card set features color photos of MLB hitting stars printed on partially foiled cards with an all-new net-fusion technology using actual netting.

Nm-Mt Ex-Mt
COMPLETE SET (20) 250.00 75.00
1 Chipper Jones 15.00 4.50
2 Andruw Jones 6.00 1.80
3 Cal Ripken 50.00 15.00
4 Nomar Garciaparra 25.00 7.50
5 Sammy Sosa 25.00 7.50
6 Frank Thomas 15.00 4.50
7 Manny Ramirez 10.00 3.00
8 Jeff Bagwell 10.00 3.00
9 Raul Mondesi 6.00 1.80
10 Vladimir Guerrero 15.00 4.50
11 Mike Piazza 25.00 7.50
12 Derek Jeter 40.00 12.00
13 Bernie Williams 10.00 3.00
14 Scott Rolen 15.00 4.50
15 J.D. Drew 5.00 1.50
16 Mark McGwire 40.00 12.00
17 Tony Gwynn 20.00 6.00
18 Ken Griffey Jr. 25.00 7.50
19 Alex Rodriguez 25.00 7.50
20 Juan Gonzalez 10.00 3.00

1999 Revolution MLB Icons

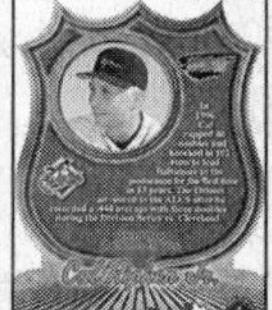

Randomly inserted in packs at the rate of one in 121, this 10-card set features color action photos of some of the hottest players printed on fully silver foiled and etched cards die-cut in the shape of a shield of honor.

Nm-Mt Ex-Mt
1 Cal Ripken 80.00 24.00
2 Nomar Garciaparra 40.00 12.00
3 Sammy Sosa 40.00 12.00
4 Frank Thomas 25.00 7.50
5 Mike Piazza 40.00 12.00

	Nm-Mt	Ex-Mt
6 Derek Jeter	60.00	18.00
7 Mark McGwire	60.00	18.00
8 Tony Gwynn	30.00	9.00
9 Ken Griffey Jr.	40.00	12.00
10 Alex Rodriguez	40.00	12.00

1999 Revolution Thorn in the Side

Randomly inserted in packs at the rate of one in 25, this 20-card set features color action player photos printed on full holographic silver foil die-cut cards.

	Nm-Mt	Ex-Mt
COMPLETE SET (20)	120.00	36.00
1 Mo Vaughn	3.00	.90
2 Chipper Jones	8.00	2.40
3 Greg Maddux	12.00	3.60
4 Cal Ripken	25.00	7.50
5 Nomar Garciaparra	12.00	3.60
6 Sammy Sosa	12.00	3.60
7 Frank Thomas	8.00	2.40
8 Manny Ramirez	5.00	1.50
9 Jeff Bagwell	5.00	1.50
10 Mike Piazza	12.00	3.60
11 Derek Jeter	20.00	6.00
12 Bernie Williams	5.00	1.50
13 J.D. Drew	2.50	.75
14 Mark McGwire	20.00	6.00
15 Tony Gwynn	10.00	3.00
16 Barry Bonds	20.00	6.00
17 Ken Griffey Jr.	12.00	3.60
18 Alex Rodriguez	12.00	3.60
19 Juan Gonzalez	5.00	1.50
20 Ivan Rodriguez	8.00	2.40

1999 Revolution Tripleheader

Randomly inserted in hobby packs only at the rate of four in 25, this 30-card set features color photos of top stars and rookies printed on cards with a gold foil design. A three tier serial-numbered parallel silver foil set was also produced. Only 99 serial-numbered sets of Tier 1 which consists of cards 1-10 was produced; 199 serial-numbered Tier 2 sets were produced which consists of cards 11-20; and 299 serial-numbered Tier 3 sets, which consist of cards 21-30, were also produced.

	Nm-Mt	Ex-Mt
COMPLETE SET (30)	80.00	24.00

*TIER 1 (1-10): 3X TO 8X BASIC TRIPLEHEADER
TIER 1 PRINT RUN 99 SERIAL #'d SETS
*TIER 2 (11-20): 2X TO 5X BASIC TRIPLEHEADER
*TIER 2 DREW: 1X TO 2.5X BASE SP HI
TIER 2 PRINT RUN 199 SERIAL #'d SETS
*TIER 3: 1.25X TO 3X BASIC TRIPLEHEADER
TIER 3 PRINT RUN 299 SERIAL #'d SETS
TIER CARDS RANDOM IN HOBBY PACKS

	Nm-Mt	Ex-Mt
1 Greg Maddux	5.00	1.50
2 Cal Ripken	10.00	3.00
3 Nomar Garciaparra	5.00	1.50
4 Sammy Sosa	5.00	1.50
5 Frank Thomas	3.00	.90
6 Mike Piazza	5.00	1.50
7 Mark McGwire	8.00	2.40
8 Tony Gwynn	4.00	1.20
9 Ken Griffey Jr.	5.00	1.50
10 Alex Rodriguez	5.00	1.50
11 Mo Vaughn	1.25	.35
12 Chipper Jones	3.00	.90
13 Manny Ramirez	2.00	.60
14 Larry Walker	2.00	.60
15 Jeff Bagwell	2.00	.60
16 Vladimir Guerrero	3.00	.90
17 Derek Jeter	8.00	2.40
18 J.D. Drew	1.00	.30
19 Barry Bonds	8.00	2.40
20 Juan Gonzalez	2.00	.60
21 Troy Glaus	1.25	.35
22 Andruw Jones	1.25	.35
23 Matt Williams	1.25	.35
24 Craig Biggio	2.00	.60
25 Raul Mondesi	1.25	.35
26 Roger Clemens	6.00	1.80
27 Bernie Williams	2.00	.60
28 Scott Rolen	3.00	.90
29 Jose Canseco	3.00	.90
30 Ivan Rodriguez	3.00	.90

2000 Revolution

The 2000 Revolution product (produced by Pacific) was released in July, 2000. The product featured a 150-card base set with short-printed prospects (1:4). Each pack contained three cards and carried a suggested retail price of $3.99.

	Nm-Mt	Ex-Mt
COMPLETE SET (150)	100.00	30.00
COMMON CARD (1-150)	1.00	.30
COMMON SP	3.00	.90
1 Darin Erstad	1.00	.30
2 Troy Glaus	1.00	.30
3 Adam Kennedy SP	3.00	.90
4 Mo Vaughn	1.00	.30
5 Erubiel Durazo	1.00	.30
6 Steve Finley	1.00	.30
7 Luis Gonzalez	1.00	.30
8 Randy Johnson	2.50	.75
9 Travis Lee	1.00	.30
10 Vicente Padilla SP RC	3.00	.90
11 Matt Williams	1.00	.30
12 Rafael Furcal SP	3.00	.90
13 Andres Galarraga	1.00	.30
14 Andruw Jones	1.00	.30
15 Chipper Jones	2.50	.75
16 Greg Maddux	4.00	1.20
17 Luis Rivera SP RC	3.00	.90
18 Albert Belle	1.00	.30
19 Mike Bordick	1.00	.30
20 Will Clark	2.50	.75
21 Mike Mussina	1.50	.45
22 Cal Ripken	8.00	2.40
23 B.J. Surhoff	1.00	.30
24 Carl Everett	1.00	.30
25 Nomar Garciaparra	4.00	1.20
26 Pedro Martinez	2.50	.75
27 Jason Varitek	1.50	.45
28 Wilton Veras SP	3.00	.90
29 Shane Andrews	1.00	.30
30 Scott Downs SP RC	3.00	.90
31 Mark Grace	1.50	.45
32 Sammy Sosa	4.00	1.20
33 Kerry Wood	2.50	.75
34 Ray Durham	1.00	.30
35 Paul Konerko	1.00	.30
36 Carlos Lee	1.00	.30
37 Magglio Ordonez	1.00	.30
38 Frank Thomas	2.50	.75
39 Rob Bell SP	3.00	.90
40 Sean Casey	1.00	.30
41 Ken Griffey Jr.	4.00	1.20
42 Barry Larkin	1.50	.45
43 Pokey Reese	1.00	.30
44 Roberto Alomar	1.50	.45
45 David Justice	1.00	.30
46 Kenny Lofton	1.00	.30
47 Manny Ramirez	1.50	.45
48 Richie Sexson	1.00	.30
49 Jim Thome	2.50	.75
50 Jeff Cirillo	1.00	.30
51 Jeffrey Hammonds	1.00	.30
52 Todd Helton	1.50	.45
53 Larry Walker	1.50	.45
54 Tony Clark	1.00	.30
55 Juan Gonzalez	1.50	.45
56 Hideo Nomo	2.50	.75
57 Dean Palmer	1.00	.30
58 Alex Gonzalez	1.00	.30
59 Mike Lowell	1.00	.30
60 Pablo Ozuna SP	3.00	.90
61 Brad Penny SP	3.00	.90
62 Preston Wilson	1.00	.30
63 Moises Alou	1.00	.30
64 Jeff Bagwell	1.50	.45
65 Craig Biggio	1.50	.45
66 Ken Caminiti	1.00	.30
67 Julio Lugo SP	3.00	.90
68 Carlos Beltran	1.50	.45
69 Johnny Damon UER Carlos Beltran pictured on front	1.50	.45
70 Jermaine Dye	1.00	.30
71 Carlos Febles	1.00	.30
72 Mark Quinn SP	3.00	.90
73 Kevin Brown	1.00	.30
74 Shawn Green	1.00	.30
75 Chan Ho Park	1.00	.30
76 Gary Sheffield	1.00	.30
77 Kevin Barker SP	3.00	.90
78 Ron Belliard	1.00	.30
79 Jeromy Burnitz	1.00	.30
80 Geoff Jenkins	1.00	.30
81 Cristian Guzman	1.00	.30
82 Jacque Jones	1.00	.30
83 Corey Koskie	1.00	.30
84 Matt Lawton	1.00	.30
85 Peter Bergeron SP	3.00	.90
86 Vladimir Guerrero	2.50	.75
87 Andy Tracy SP RC	3.00	.90
88 Jose Vidro	1.00	.30
89 Rondell White	1.00	.30
90 Edgardo Alfonzo	1.00	.30
91 Derek Bell	1.00	.30
92 Eric Cammack SP RC	3.00	.90
93 Mike Piazza	4.00	1.20
94 Robin Ventura	1.00	.30
95 Roger Clemens	5.00	1.50
96 Orlando Hernandez	1.00	.30
97 Derek Jeter	6.00	1.80
98 Tino Martinez	1.50	.45
99 Alfonso Soriano SP	5.00	1.50
100 Bernie Williams	1.50	.45
101 Eric Chavez	1.00	.30
102 Jason Giambi	1.00	.30
103 Ben Grieve	1.00	.30
104 Terrence Long SP	3.00	.90
105 Mark Mulder SP	3.00	.90
106 Adam Piatt SP	3.00	.90
107 Bobby Abreu	1.00	.30
108 Pat Burrell SP	3.00	.90
109 Rico Brogna	1.00	.30
110 Doug Glanville	1.00	.30
111 Mike Lieberthal	1.00	.30
112 Scott Rolen	2.50	.75
113 Brian Giles	1.00	.30
114 Jason Kendall	1.00	.30
115 Warren Morris	1.00	.30
116 Rick Ankiel SP	3.00	.90
117 J.D. Drew	1.00	.30
118 Jim Edmonds	1.00	.30
119 Mark McGwire	6.00	1.80
120 Fernando Tatis	1.00	.30
121 Fernando Vina	1.00	.30
122 Tony Gwynn	3.00	.90
123 Trevor Hoffman	1.00	.30
124 Ryan Klesko	1.00	.30
125 Eric Owens	1.00	.30
126 Barry Bonds	6.00	1.80
127 Ellis Burks	1.00	.30
128 Bobby Estalella	1.00	.30
129 Jeff Kent	1.00	.30
130 Scott Linebrink SP RC	3.00	.90
131 Jay Buhner	1.00	.30
132 Stan Javier	1.00	.30
133 Edgar Martinez	1.50	.45
134 John Olerud	1.00	.30
135 Alex Rodriguez	4.00	1.20
136 K.Sasaki SP RC	5.00	1.50
137 Jose Canseco	2.50	.75
138 Vinny Castilla	1.00	.30
139 Fred McGriff	1.50	.45
140 Greg Vaughn	1.00	.30
141 Gabe Kapler	1.00	.30
142 Mike Lamb SP RC	3.00	.90
143 Ruben Mateo SP	3.00	.90
144 Rafael Palmeiro	1.50	.45
145 Ivan Rodriguez	2.50	.75
146 Tony Batista	1.00	.30
147 Jose Cruz Jr.	1.00	.30
148 Carlos Delgado	1.00	.30
149 Brad Fullmer	1.00	.30
150 Raul Mondesi	1.00	.30

2000 Revolution Premiere Date

Randomly inserted in hobby packs at one in 25 packs, this 150-card set is a parallel version of the base set. Only 99 serial-numbered sets were produced.

Nm-Mt Ex-Mt
*STARS: 3X TO 8X BASIC CARDS
*SP's: 1X TO 2.5X BASIC SP's
*RC SP's: 3X TO 8X BASIC RC SP's

2000 Revolution Red

Randomly inserted in retail packs only, this 150-card set is a red foil parallel version of the base set. Only 63 serial-numbered sets were produced.

Nm-Mt Ex-Mt
*STARS: 4X TO 10X BASIC CARDS
*SP's: 1.25X TO 3X BASIC SP's
*SP RC's: 5X TO 12X BASIC RC SP's

2000 Revolution Shadow Series

Randomly inserted in hobby packs at one in 25, this 150-card set is a parallel version of the base set. Only 99 serial-numbered sets were produced.

Nm-Mt Ex-Mt
*STARS: 3X TO 8X BASIC CARDS
*SP's: 1X TO 2.5X BASIC SP's
*RC SP's: 3X TO 8X BASIC RC SP's

2000 Revolution Foul Pole

Inserted one every 49 packs, these 20 cards feature players who hit the longball. These cards feature a swatch of netting.

	Nm-Mt	Ex-Mt
COMPLETE SET (20)	250.00	75.00
1 Chipper Jones	12.00	3.60
2 Cal Ripken	40.00	12.00
3 Nomar Garciaparra	20.00	6.00
4 Pedro Martinez	12.00	3.60
5 Sammy Sosa	20.00	6.00
6 Frank Thomas	12.00	3.60
7 Ken Griffey Jr.	20.00	6.00
8 Manny Ramirez	8.00	2.40
9 Jeff Bagwell	8.00	2.40
10 Shawn Green	5.00	1.50
11 Vladimir Guerrero	12.00	3.60
12 Mike Piazza	20.00	6.00
13 Derek Jeter	30.00	9.00
14 Pat Burrell	15.00	4.50
15 Rick Ankiel	15.00	4.50
16 Mark McGwire	30.00	9.00
17 Tony Gwynn	15.00	4.50
18 Barry Bonds	30.00	9.00
19 Alex Rodriguez	20.00	6.00
20 Ivan Rodriguez	12.00	3.60

2000 Revolution MLB Game Ball Signatures

Randomly inserted into packs, these 25 cards feature MLB player's autographs on actual swatches of baseball. A couple of players are not priced due to lack of market information.

	Nm-Mt	Ex-Mt
1 Randy Johnson	100.00	30.00
2 Greg Maddux	100.00	30.00
3 Rafael Furcal	15.00	4.50
4 Shane Andrews	10.00	3.00
5 Sean Casey	15.00	4.50
6 Travis Dawkins	10.00	3.00
7 Alex Gonzalez	10.00	3.00
8 Shane Reynolds	10.00	3.00
9 Eric Gagne	60.00	18.00
10 Kevin Barker	10.00	3.00
11 Eric Milton	10.00	3.00
12 Mark Quinn	10.00	3.00
13 Alfonso Soriano	50.00	15.00
14 Brian Giles	15.00	4.50
15 Mark Mulder	15.00	4.50
16 Adam Piatt	10.00	3.00
17 Warren Morris	10.00	3.00
18 Rick Ankiel	15.00	4.50
19 Adam Kennedy	15.00	4.50
20 Fernando Tatis	10.00	3.00
21 Barry Bonds	250.00	75.00
22 Alex Rodriguez	100.00	30.00
23 Ruben Mateo	10.00	3.00
24 Billy Koch	15.00	4.50
25 Brad Penny	15.00	4.50

2000 Revolution MLB Icons

Inserted one every 121 packs, these 20 cards feature players that are looked upon as icons of their community.

	Nm-Mt	Ex-Mt
1 Randy Johnson	15.00	4.50
2 Chipper Jones	15.00	4.50
3 Greg Maddux	25.00	7.50
4 Cal Ripken	50.00	15.00
5 Nomar Garciaparra	25.00	7.50
6 Pedro Martinez	15.00	4.50
7 Sammy Sosa	25.00	7.50
8 Frank Thomas	15.00	4.50
9 Ken Griffey Jr.	25.00	7.50
10 Juan Gonzalez	10.00	3.00
11 Jeff Bagwell	10.00	3.00
12 Vladimir Guerrero	15.00	4.50
13 Mike Piazza	25.00	7.50
14 Roger Clemens	30.00	9.00
15 Derek Jeter	40.00	12.00
16 Mark McGwire	40.00	12.00
17 Tony Gwynn	20.00	6.00
18 Barry Bonds	40.00	12.00
19 Alex Rodriguez	25.00	7.50
20 Ivan Rodriguez	15.00	4.50

2000 Revolution On Deck

Inserted one in every 25 packs, these 20 cards feature players who strike fear into the hearts of pitchers that see them on deck.

	Nm-Mt	Ex-Mt
COMPLETE SET (20)	120.00	36.00
1 Chipper Jones	8.00	2.40
2 Cal Ripken	25.00	7.50
3 Nomar Garciaparra	12.00	3.60
4 Sammy Sosa	12.00	3.60
5 Frank Thomas	8.00	2.40
6 Ken Griffey Jr.	12.00	3.60
7 Manny Ramirez	5.00	1.50
8 Larry Walker	5.00	1.50
9 Juan Gonzalez	5.00	1.50
10 Jeff Bagwell	5.00	1.50
11 Shawn Green	3.00	.90
12 Vladimir Guerrero	8.00	2.40
13 Mike Piazza	12.00	3.60
14 Derek Jeter	20.00	6.00
15 Scott Rolen	8.00	2.40
16 Mark McGwire	20.00	6.00
17 Tony Gwynn	10.00	3.00
18 Alex Rodriguez	12.00	3.60
19 Jose Canseco	8.00	2.40
20 Ivan Rodriguez	8.00	2.40

2000 Revolution Season Opener

Inserted two in every 25 packs, these 36 cards feature players who will be starting come opening day.

	Nm-Mt	Ex-Mt
COMPLETE SET (36)	150.00	45.00
1 Erubiel Durazo	2.50	.75
2 Randy Johnson	6.00	1.80
3 Andruw Jones	2.50	.75
4 Chipper Jones	6.00	1.80
5 Greg Maddux	10.00	3.00
6 Cal Ripken	20.00	6.00
7 Nomar Garciaparra	10.00	3.00
8 Pedro Martinez	6.00	1.80
9 Sammy Sosa	10.00	3.00
10 Frank Thomas	6.00	1.80
11 Magglio Ordonez	2.50	.75
12 Ken Griffey Jr.	10.00	3.00
13 Barry Larkin	4.00	1.20
14 Kenny Lofton	2.50	.75
15 Manny Ramirez	4.00	1.20
16 Jim Thome	6.00	1.80
17 Larry Walker	4.00	1.20
18 Juan Gonzalez	4.00	1.20
19 Jeff Bagwell	4.00	1.20
20 Craig Biggio	4.00	1.20
21 Carlos Beltran	4.00	1.20
22 Shawn Green	2.50	.75
23 Vladimir Guerrero	6.00	1.80
24 Mike Piazza	10.00	3.00
25 Orlando Hernandez	2.50	.75
26 Derek Jeter	15.00	4.50
27 Bernie Williams	4.00	1.20
28 Eric Chavez	2.50	.75
29 Scott Rolen	6.00	1.80
30 Jim Edmonds	2.50	.75
31 Tony Gwynn	8.00	2.40
32 Barry Bonds	15.00	4.50
33 Alex Rodriguez	10.00	3.00
34 Jose Canseco	6.00	1.80
35 Ivan Rodriguez	6.00	1.80
36 Rafael Palmeiro	4.00	1.20

2000 Revolution Triple Header

Inserted four in every 25 packs, these 30 cards feature players that lead the league in just about every statistical category.

	Nm-Mt	Ex-Mt
COMPLETE SET (30)	60.00	18.00
1 Chipper Jones	2.50	.75
2 Cal Ripken	8.00	2.40
3 Nomar Garciaparra	4.00	1.20
4 Frank Thomas	2.50	.75
5 Larry Walker	1.50	.45
6 Vladimir Guerrero	2.50	.75
7 Mike Piazza	4.00	1.20
8 Derek Jeter	6.00	1.80
9 Tony Gwynn	3.00	.90
10 Ivan Rodriguez	2.50	.75
11 Sammy Sosa	4.00	1.20
12 Ken Griffey Jr.	4.00	1.20
13 Manny Ramirez	1.50	.45
14 Jeff Bagwell	1.50	.45
15 Shawn Green	1.00	.30
16 Mark McGwire	6.00	1.80
17 Barry Bonds	6.00	1.80
18 Alex Rodriguez	4.00	1.20
19 Jose Canseco	2.50	.75
20 Rafael Palmeiro	1.50	.45
21 Randy Johnson	2.50	.75
22 Tom Glavine	2.00	.60
23 Greg Maddux	4.00	1.20
24 Mike Mussina	1.50	.45
25 Pedro Martinez	2.50	.75
26 Kerry Wood	2.50	.75
27 Chuck Finley	1.00	.30
28 Kevin Brown	1.00	.30
29 Roger Clemens	5.00	1.50
30 Rick Ankiel	3.00	.90

1988 Score

This set consists of 660 standard-size cards. The set was distributed by Major League Marketing and features six distinctive border colors on the front. Subsets include Reggie Jackson Tribute (500-504), Highlights (652-660) and Rookie Prospects (623-647). Card number 501, showing Reggie as a member of the Baltimore Orioles, is one of the few opportunities collectors have to visually remember Reggie's one-year stay with the Orioles. The set is distinguished by the fact that each card back shows a full-color picture of the player. Rookie Cards in this set include Ellis Burks, Ken Caminiti, Tom Glavine and Matt Williams.

	Nm-Mt	Ex-Mt
COMPLETE SET (660)	10.00	4.00
COMP.FACT.SET (660)	12.00	4.80
1 Don Mattingly	.60	.24
2 Wade Boggs	.15	.06
3 Tim Raines	.10	.04
4 Andre Dawson	.10	.04
5 Mark McGwire	1.50	.60
6 Kevin Seitzer	.05	.02
7 Wally Joyner	.10	.04
8 Jesse Barfield	.10	.04
9 Pedro Guerrero	.10	.04
10 Eric Davis	.10	.04
11 George Brett	.50	.20
12 Ozzie Smith	.30	.12
13 Rickey Henderson	.20	.08
14 Jim Rice	.10	.04
15 Matt Nokes RC*	.25	.10
16 Mike Schmidt	.50	.20
17 Dave Parker	.10	.04

18 Eddie Murray .20 .08
19 Andres Galarraga .10 .04
20 Tony Fernandez .05 .02
21 Kevin McReynolds .05 .02
22 B.J. Surhoff .10 .04
23 Pat Tabler .05 .02
24 Kirby Puckett .20 .08
25 Benny Santiago .10 .04
26 Ryne Sandberg .40 .16
27 Kelly Downs .05 .02
(Will Clark in back-ground, out of focus)
28 Jose Cruz .10 .04
29 Pete O'Brien .05 .02
30 Mark Langston .05 .02
31 Lee Smith .10 .04
32 Juan Samuel .05 .02
33 Kevin Bass .05 .02
34 R.J. Reynolds .05 .02
35 Steve Sax .05 .02
36 John Kruk .10 .04
37 Alan Trammell .10 .04
38 Chris Bosio .05 .02
39 Brook Jacoby .05 .02
40 Willie McGee UER .10 .04
(Excited misspelled as excitd)
41 Dave Magadan .05 .02
42 Fred Lynn .10 .04
43 Kent Hrbek .10 .04
44 Brian Downing .10 .04
45 Jose Canseco .20 .08
46 Jim Presley .05 .02
47 Mike Stanley .05 .02
48 Tony Pena .05 .02
49 David Cone .10 .04
50 Rick Sutcliffe .10 .04
51 Doug Drabek .05 .02
52 Bill Doran .05 .02
53 Mike Scioscia .10 .04
54 Candy Maldonado .05 .02
55 Dave Winfield .10 .04
56 Lou Whitaker .10 .04
57 Tom Henke .05 .02
58 Ken Gerhart .05 .02
59 Glenn Braggs .05 .02
60 Julio Franco .10 .04
61 Charlie Leibrandt .05 .02
62 Gary Gaetti .10 .04
63 Bob Boone .10 .04
64 Luis Polonia RC* .25 .10
65 Dwight Evans .10 .04
66 Phil Bradley .05 .02
67 Mike Boddicker .05 .02
68 Vince Coleman .05 .02
69 Howard Johnson .10 .04
70 Tim Wallach .05 .02
71 Keith Moreland .05 .02
72 Barry Larkin .15 .06
73 Alan Ashby .05 .02
74 Rick Rhoden .05 .02
75 Darrell Evans .10 .04
76 Dave Stieb .10 .04
77 Dan Plesac .05 .02
78 Will Clark UER .20 .08
(Born 3/17/64, should be 3/13/64)
79 Frank White .10 .04
80 Joe Carter .10 .04
81 Mike Witt .05 .02
82 Terry Steinbach .10 .04
83 Alvin Davis .05 .02
84 Tommy Herr .10 .04
(Will Clark shown sliding into second)
85 Vance Law .05 .02
86 Kal Daniels .05 .02
87 Rick Honeycutt UER .05 .02
(Wrong years for stats on back)
88 Alfredo Griffin .05 .02
89 Bret Saberhagen .10 .04
90 Bert Blyleven .10 .04
91 Jeff Reardon .10 .04
92 Cory Snyder .05 .02
93A Greg Walker ERR 2.00 .80
(93 of 66)
93B Greg Walker COR .05 .02
(93 of 660)
94 Joe Magrane RC* .25 .10
95 Rob Deer .05 .02
96 Ray Knight .10 .04
97 Casey Candaele .05 .02
98 John Cerutti .05 .02
99 Buddy Bell .10 .04
100 Jack Clark .10 .04
101 Eric Bell .05 .02
102 Willie Wilson .10 .04
103 Dave Schmidt .05 .02
104 Dennis Eckersley UER .15 .06
(Complete games stats are wrong)
105 Don Sutton .10 .04
106 Danny Tartabull .05 .02
107 Fred McGriff .20 .08
108 Les Straker .05 .02
109 Lloyd Moseby .05 .02
110 Roger Clemens .50 .20
111 Glenn Hubbard .05 .02
112 Ken Williams RC .05 .02
113 Ruben Sierra .10 .04
114 Stan Jefferson .05 .02
115 Milt Thompson .05 .02
116 Bobby Bonilla .10 .04
117 Wayne Tolleson .05 .02
118 Matt Williams RC .75 .30
119 Chet Lemon .10 .04
120 Dale Sveum .05 .02
121 Dennis Boyd .05 .02
122 Brett Butler .10 .04
123 Terry Kennedy .05 .02
124 Jack Howell .05 .02
125 Curt Young .05 .02
126A Dave Valle ERR .10 .04
(Misspelled Dale on card front)
126B Dave Valle COR .05 .02
127 Curt Wilkerson .05 .02
128 Tim Teufel .05 .02
129 Ozzie Virgil .05 .02
130 Brian Fisher .05 .02
131 Lance Parrish .10 .04
132 Tom Browning .05 .02
133A Larry Andersen ERR .10 .04
(Misspelled Anderson on card front)
133B Larry Andersen COR .05 .02
134A Bob Brenly ERR .10 .04
(Misspelled Brenley on card front)
134B Bob Brenly COR .05 .02
135 Mike Marshall .05 .02
136 Gerald Perry .05 .02
137 Bobby Meacham .05 .02
138 Larry Herndon .05 .02
139 Fred Manrique .05 .02
140 Charlie Hough .10 .04
141 Ron Darling .10 .04
142 Herm Winningham .05 .02
143 Mike Diaz .05 .02
144 Mike Jackson RC* .25 .10
145 Denny Walling .05 .02
146 Robby Thompson .05 .02
147 Franklin Stubbs .05 .02
148 Albert Hall .05 .02
149 Bobby Witt .05 .02
150 Lance McCullers .05 .02
151 Scott Bradley .05 .02
152 Mark McLemore .05 .02
153 Tim Laudner .05 .02
154 Greg Swindell .05 .02
155 Marty Barrett .05 .02
156 Mike Heath .05 .02
157 Gary Ward .05 .02
158A Lee Mazzilli ERR .10 .04
(Misspelled Mazilli on card front)
158B Lee Mazzilli COR .10 .04
159 Tom Foley .05 .02
160 Robin Yount .30 .12
161 Steve Bedrosian .05 .02
162 Bob Walk .05 .02
163 Nick Esasky .05 .02
164 Ken Caminiti RC .75 .30
165 Jose Uribe .05 .02
166 Dave Anderson .05 .02
167 Ed Whitson .05 .02
168 Ernie Whitt .05 .02
169 Cecil Cooper .10 .04
170 Mike Pagliarulo .05 .02
171 Pat Sheridan .05 .02
172 Chris Bando .05 .02
173 Lee Lacy .05 .02
174 Steve Lombardozzi .05 .02
175 Mike Greenwell .05 .02
176 Greg Minton .05 .02
177 Moose Haas .05 .02
178 Mike Kingery .05 .02
179 Greg A. Harris .05 .02
180 Bo Jackson .20 .08
181 Carmelo Martinez .05 .02
182 Alex Trevino .05 .02
183 Ron Oester .05 .02
184 Danny Darwin .05 .02
185 Mike Krukow .05 .02
186 Rafael Palmeiro .40 .16
187 Tim Burke .05 .02
188 Roger McDowell .05 .02
189 Garry Templeton .10 .04
190 Terry Pendleton .10 .04
191 Larry Parrish .05 .02
192 Rey Quinones .05 .02
193 Joaquin Andujar .10 .04
194 Tom Brunansky .05 .02
195 Donnie Moore .05 .02
196 Dan Pasqua .05 .02
197 Jim Gantner .05 .02
198 Mark Eichhorn .05 .02
199 John Grubb .05 .02
200 Bill Ripken RC* .25 .10
201 Sam Horn RC .10 .04
202 Todd Worrell .05 .02
203 Terry Leach .05 .02
204 Garth Iorg .05 .02
205 Brian Dayett .05 .02
206 Bo Diaz .05 .02
207 Craig Reynolds .05 .02
208 Brian Holton .05 .02
209 Marvell Wynne UER .05 .02
(Misspelled Marvelle on card front)
210 Dave Concepcion .10 .04
211 Mike Davis .05 .02
212 Devon White .10 .04
213 Mickey Brantley .05 .02
214 Greg Gagne .05 .02
215 Oddibe McDowell .05 .02
216 Jimmy Key .10 .04
217 Dave Bergman .05 .02
218 Calvin Schiraldi .05 .02
219 Larry Sheets .05 .02
220 Mike Easler .05 .02
221 Kurt Stillwell .05 .02
222 Chuck Jackson .05 .02
223 Dave Martinez .05 .02
224 Tim Leary .05 .02
225 Steve Garvey .10 .04
226 Greg Mathews .05 .02
227 Doug Sisk .05 .02
228 Dave Henderson .05 .02
(Wearing Red Sox uniform; Red Sox logo on back)
229 Jimmy Dwyer .05 .02
230 Larry Owen .05 .02
231 Andre Thornton .05 .02
232 Mark Salas .05 .02
233 Tom Brookens .05 .02
234 Greg Brock .05 .02
235 Rance Mulliniks .05 .02
236 Bob Brower .05 .02
237 Joe Niekro .05 .02
238 Scott Bankhead .05 .02
239 Doug DeCinces .05 .02
240 Tommy John .10 .04
241 Rich Gedman .05 .02
242 Ted Power .05 .02
243 Dave Meads .05 .02
244 Jim Sundberg .10 .04
245 Ken Oberkfell .05 .02
246 Jimmy Jones .05 .02
247 Ken Landreaux .05 .02
248 Jose Oquendo .05 .02
249 John Mitchell RC .10 .04
250 Don Baylor .10 .04
251 Scott Fletcher .05 .02
252 Al Newman .05 .02
253 Carney Lansford .10 .04
254 Johnny Ray .05 .02
255 Gary Pettis .05 .02
256 Ken Phelps .05 .02
257 Rick Leach .05 .02
258 Tim Stoddard .05 .02
259 Ed Romero .05 .02
260 Sid Bream .05 .02
261A T.Niedenfuer ERR .10 .04
Misspelled Neidenfuer on card front
261B T.Niedenfuer COR .05 .02
262 Rick Dempsey .05 .02
263 Lonnie Smith .05 .02
264 Bob Forsch .05 .02
265 Barry Bonds 2.00 .80
266 Willie Randolph .10 .04
267 Mike Ramsey .05 .02
268 Don Slaught .05 .02
269 Mickey Tettleton .05 .02
270 Jerry Reuss .05 .02
271 Marc Sullivan .05 .02
272 Jim Morrison .05 .02
273 Steve Balboni .05 .02
274 Dick Schofield .05 .02
275 John Tudor .10 .04
276 Gene Larkin RC* .25 .10
277 Harold Reynolds .10 .04
278 Jerry Browne .05 .02
279 Willie Upshaw .05 .02
280 Ted Higuera .05 .02
281 Terry McGriff .05 .02
282 Terry Puhl .05 .02
283 Mark Wasinger .05 .02
284 Luis Salazar .05 .02
285 Ted Simmons .10 .04
286 John Shelby .05 .02
287 John Smiley RC* .25 .10
288 Curt Ford .05 .02
289 Steve Crawford .05 .02
290 Dan Quisenberry .05 .02
291 Alan Wiggins .05 .02
292 Randy Bush .05 .02
293 John Candelaria .05 .02
294 Tony Phillips .05 .02
295 Mike Morgan .05 .02
296 Bill Wegman .05 .02
297A Terry Francona ERR .10 .04
(Misspelled Franconia on card front)
297B Terry Francona COR .10 .04
298 Mickey Hatcher .05 .02
299 Andres Thomas .05 .02
300 Bob Stanley .05 .02
301 Al Pedrique .05 .02
302 Jim Lindeman .05 .02
303 Wally Backman .05 .02
304 Paul O'Neill .15 .06
305 Hubie Brooks .05 .02
306 Steve Buechele .05 .02
307 Bobby Thigpen .05 .02
308 George Hendrick .10 .04
309 John Moses .05 .02
310 Ron Guidry .10 .04
311 Bill Schroeder .05 .02
312 Jose Nunez .05 .02
313 Bud Black .05 .02
314 Joe Sambito .05 .02
315 Scott McGregor .05 .02
316 Rafael Santana .05 .02
317 Frank Williams .05 .02
318 Mike Fitzgerald .05 .02
319 Rick Mahler .05 .02
320 Jim Gott .05 .02
321 Mariano Duncan .05 .02
322 Jose Guzman .05 .02
323 Lee Guetterman .05 .02
324 Dan Gladden .05 .02
325 Gary Carter .10 .04
326 Tracy Jones .05 .02
327 Floyd Youmans .05 .02
328 Bill Dawley .05 .02
329 Paul Noce .05 .02
330 Angel Salazar .05 .02
331 Goose Gossage .10 .04
332 George Frazier .05 .02
333 Ruppert Jones .05 .02
334 Billy Joe Robidoux .05 .02
335 Mike Scott .10 .04
336 Randy Myers .10 .04
337 Bob Sebra .05 .02
338 Eric Show .05 .02
339 Mitch Williams .05 .02
340 Paul Molitor .15 .06
341 Gus Polidor .05 .02
342 Steve Trout .05 .02
343 Jerry Don Gleaton .05 .02
344 Bob Knepper .05 .02
345 Mitch Webster .05 .02
346 John Morris .05 .02
347 Andy Hawkins .05 .02
348 Dave Leiper .05 .02
349 Ernest Riles .05 .02
350 Dwight Gooden .10 .04
351 Dave Righetti .10 .04
352 Pat Dodson .05 .02
353 John Habyan .05 .02
354 Jim Deshaies .05 .02
355 Butch Wynegar .05 .02
356 Bryn Smith .05 .02
357 Matt Young .05 .02
358 Tom Pagnozzi RC .10 .04
359 Floyd Rayford .05 .02
360 Darryl Strawberry .10 .04
361 Sal Butera .05 .02
362 Domingo Ramos .05 .02
363 Chris Brown .05 .02
364 Jose Gonzalez .05 .02
365 Dave Smith .05 .02
366 Andy McGaffigan .05 .02
367 Stan Javier .05 .02
368 Henry Cotto .05 .02
369 Mike Birkbeck .05 .02
370 Len Dykstra .10 .04
371 Dave Collins .05 .02
372 Spike Owen .05 .02
373 Geno Petralli .05 .02
374 Ron Karkovice .05 .02
375 Shane Rawley .05 .02
376 DeWayne Buice .05 .02
377 Bill Pecota RC* .10 .04
378 Leon Durham .05 .02
379 Ed Olwine .05 .02
380 Bruce Hurst .05 .02
381 Bob McClure .05 .02
382 Mark Thurmond .05 .02
383 Buddy Biancalana .05 .02
384 Tim Conroy .05 .02
385 Tony Gwynn .30 .12
386 Greg Gross .05 .02
387 Barry Lyons .05 .02
388 Mike Felder .05 .02
389 Pat Clements .05 .02
390 Ken Griffey .10 .04
391 Mark Davis .05 .02
392 Jose Rijo .10 .04
393 Mike Young .05 .02
394 Willie Fraser .05 .02
395 Dion James .05 .02
396 Steve Shields .05 .02
397 Randy St.Claire .05 .02
398 Danny Jackson .05 .02
399 Cecil Fielder .10 .04
400 Keith Hernandez .10 .04
401 Don Carman .05 .02
402 Chuck Crim .05 .02
403 Rob Woodward .05 .02
404 Junior Ortiz .05 .02
405 Glenn Wilson .05 .02
406 Ken Howell .05 .02
407 Jeff Kunkel .05 .02
408 Jeff Reed .05 .02
409 Chris James .05 .02
410 Zane Smith .05 .02
411 Ken Dixon .05 .02
412 Ricky Horton .05 .02
413 Frank DiPino .05 .02
414 Shane Mack .05 .02
415 Danny Cox .05 .02
416 Andy Van Slyke .10 .04
417 Danny Heep .05 .02
418 John Cangelosi .05 .02
419A J.Christensen ERR .10 .04
Christiansen on card front
419B J.Christensen COR .05 .02
420 Joey Cora RC .25 .10
421 Mike LaValliere .05 .02
422 Kelly Gruber .05 .02
423 Bruce Benedict .05 .02
424 Len Matuszek .05 .02
425 Kent Tekulve .05 .02
426 Rafael Ramirez .05 .02
427 Mike Flanagan .05 .02
428 Mike Gallego .05 .02
429 Juan Castillo .05 .02
430 Neal Heaton .05 .02
431 Phil Garner .10 .04
432 Mike Dunne .05 .02
433 Wallace Johnson .05 .02
434 Jack O'Connor .05 .02
435 Steve Jeltz .05 .02
436 Donell Nixon .05 .02
437 Jack Lazorko .05 .02
438 Keith Comstock .05 .02
439 Jeff D. Robinson .05 .02
440 Graig Nettles .10 .04
441 Mel Hall .05 .02
442 Gerald Young .05 .02
443 Gary Redus .05 .02
444 Charlie Moore .05 .02
445 Bill Madlock .10 .04
446 Mark Clear .05 .02
447 Greg Booker .05 .02
448 Rick Schu .05 .02
449 Ron Kittle .05 .02
450 Dale Murphy .15 .06
451 Bob Dernier .05 .02
452 Dale Mohorcic .05 .02
453 Rafael Belliard .05 .02
454 Charlie Puleo .05 .02
455 Dwayne Murphy .05 .02
456 Jim Eisenreich .05 .02
457 David Palmer .05 .02
458 Dave Stewart .10 .04
459 Pascual Perez .05 .02
460 Glenn Davis .05 .02
461 Dan Petry .05 .02
462 Jim Winn .05 .02
463 Darrell Miller .05 .02
464 Mike Moore .05 .02
465 Mike LaCoss .05 .02
466 Steve Farr .05 .02
467 Jerry Mumphrey .05 .02
468 Kevin Gross .05 .02
469 Bruce Bochy .05 .02
470 Orel Hershiser .10 .04
471 Eric King .05 .02
472 Ellis Burks RC .40 .16
473 Darren Daulton .10 .04
474 Mookie Wilson .10 .04
475 Frank Viola .10 .04
476 Ron Robinson .05 .02
477 Bob Melvin .05 .02
478 Jeff Musselman .05 .02
479 Charlie Kerfeld .05 .02
480 Richard Dotson .05 .02
481 Kevin Mitchell .10 .04
482 Gary Roenicke .05 .02
483 Tim Flannery .05 .02
484 Rich Yett .05 .02
485 Pete Incaviglia .05 .02
486 Rick Cerone .05 .02
487 Tony Armas .10 .04
488 Jerry Reed .05 .02
489 Dave Lopes .10 .04
490 Frank Tanana .10 .04
491 Mike Loynd .05 .02
492 Bruce Ruffin .05 .02
493 Chris Speier .05 .02
494 Tom Hume .05 .02
495 Jesse Orosco .05 .02
496 Robbie Wine UER .05 .02
(Misspelled Robby on card front)
497 Jeff Montgomery RC .25 .10
498 Jeff Dedmon .05 .02
499 Luis Aguayo .05 .02
500 Reggie Jackson A's .15 .06
501 Reggie Jackson O's .15 .06
502 Reggie Jackson Yanks .15 .06
503 Reggie Jackson Angels .15 .06
504 Reggie Jackson A's .15 .06
505 Billy Hatcher .05 .02
506 Ed Lynch .05 .02
507 Willie Hernandez .05 .02
508 Jose DeLeon .05 .02
509 Joel Youngblood .05 .02
510 Bob Welch .10 .04
511 Steve Ontiveros .05 .02
512 Randy Ready .05 .02
513 Juan Nieves .05 .02
514 Jeff Russell .05 .02
515 Von Hayes .05 .02
516 Mark Gubicza .05 .02
517 Ken Dayley .05 .02
518 Don Aase .05 .02
519 Rick Reuschel .10 .04
520 Mike Henneman RC* .25 .10
521 Rick Aguilera .05 .02
522 Jay Howell .05 .02
523 Ed Correa .05 .02
524 Manny Trillo .05 .02
525 Kirk Gibson .20 .08
526 Wally Ritchie .05 .02
527 Al Nipper .05 .02
528 Atlee Hammaker .05 .02
529 Shawon Dunston .05 .02
530 Jim Clancy .05 .02
531 Tom Paciorek .05 .02
532 Joel Skinner .05 .02
533 Scott Garrelts .05 .02
534 Tom O'Malley .05 .02
535 John Franco .10 .04
536 Paul Kilgus .05 .02
537 Darrell Porter .05 .02
538 Walt Terrell .05 .02
539 Bill Long .05 .02
540 George Bell .10 .04
541 Jeff Sellers .05 .02
542 Joe Boever .05 .02
543 Steve Howe .05 .02
544 Scott Sanderson .05 .02
545 Jack Morris .10 .04
546 Todd Benzinger RC* .25 .10
547 Steve Henderson .05 .02
548 Eddie Milner .05 .02
549 Jeff M. Robinson .05 .02
550 Cal Ripken .75 .30
551 Jody Davis .05 .02
552 Kirk McCaskill .05 .02
553 Craig Lefferts .05 .02
554 Darnell Coles .05 .02
555 Phil Niekro .10 .04
556 Mike Aldrete .05 .02
557 Pat Perry .05 .02
558 Juan Agosto .05 .02
559 Rob Murphy .05 .02
560 Dennis Rasmussen .05 .02
561 Manny Lee .05 .02
562 Jeff Blauser RC .25 .10
563 Bob Ojeda .05 .02
564 Dave Dravecky .05 .02
565 Gene Garber .05 .02
566 Ron Roenicke .05 .02
567 Tommy Hinzo .05 .02
568 Eric Nolte .05 .02
569 Ed Hearn .05 .02
570 Mark Davidson .05 .02
571 Jim Walewander .05 .02
572 Donnie Hill UER .05 .02
(84 Stolen Base total listed as 7)
573 Jamie Moyer .10 .04
574 Ken Schrom .05 .02
575 Nolan Ryan 1.00 .40
576 Jim Acker .05 .02
577 Jamie Quirk .05 .02
578 Jay Aldrich .05 .02
579 Claudell Washington .05 .02
580 Jeff Leonard .05 .02
581 Carmen Castillo .05 .02
582 Daryl Boston .05 .02
583 Jeff DeWillis .05 .02
584 John Marzano .05 .02
585 Bill Gullickson .05 .02
586 Andy Allanson .05 .02
587 Lee Tunnell UER .05 .02
(1987 stat line reads .4.84 ERA)
588 Gene Nelson .05 .02
589 Dave LaPoint .05 .02
590 Harold Baines .10 .04
591 Bill Buckner .10 .04
592 Carlton Fisk .15 .06
593 Rick Manning .05 .02
594 Doug Jones RC .25 .10
595 Tom Candiotti .05 .02
596 Steve Lake .05 .02
597 Jose Lind RC .25 .10
598 Ross Jones .05 .02
599 Gary Matthews .10 .04
600 Fernando Valenzuela .10 .04
601 Dennis Martinez .10 .04
602 Les Lancaster .05 .02
603 Ozzie Guillen .05 .02
604 Tony Bernazard .05 .02
605 Chili Davis .10 .04
606 Roy Smalley .05 .02
607 Ivan Calderon .05 .02
608 Jay Tibbs .05 .02
609 Guy Hoffman .05 .02
610 Doyle Alexander .05 .02
611 Mike Bielecki .05 .02
612 Shawn Hillegas .05 .02
613 Keith Atherton .05 .02
614 Eric Plunk .05 .02
615 Sid Fernandez .05 .02
616 Dennis Lamp .05 .02
617 Dave Engle .05 .02
618 Harry Spilman .05 .02
619 Don Robinson .05 .02
620 John Farrell RC .10 .04
621 Nelson Liriano .05 .02

622 Floyd Bannister .05 .02
623 Randy Milligan RC .10 .04
624 Kevin Elster .05 .02
625 Jody Reed RC .25 .10
626 Shawn Abner .05 .02
627 Kirt Manwaring RC .25 .10
628 Pete Stanicek .05 .02
629 Rob Ducey .05 .02
630 Steve Kiefer .05 .02
631 Gary Thurman .05 .02
632 Darrel Akerfelds .05 .02
633 Dave Clark .05 .02
634 Roberto Kelly RC .25 .10
635 Keith Hughes .05 .02
636 John Davis .05 .02
637 Mike Devereaux RC .25 .10
638 Tom Glavine RC 1.50 .60
639 Keith A. Miller RC .25 .10
640 Chris Gwynn UER RC .25 .10
(Wrong batting and throwing on back)
641 Tim Crews RC .25 .10
642 Mackey Sasser RC .25 .10
643 Vicente Palacios .05 .02
644 Kevin Romine .05 .02
645 Gregg Jefferies RC .25 .10
646 Jeff Treadway RC .25 .10
647 Ron Gant RC .40 .16
648 Mark McGwire .75 .30
Matt Nokes
649 Eric Davis .10 .04
Tim Raines
650 Don Mattingly .30 .12
Jack Clark
651 Tony Fernandez .25 .10
Alan Trammell
Cal Ripken
652 Vince Coleman HL .05 .02
653 Kirby Puckett HL .15 .06
654 Benito Santiago HL .05 .02
655 Juan Nieves HL .05 .02
656 Steve Bedrosian HL .05 .02
657 Mike Schmidt HL .20 .08
658 Don Mattingly HL .30 .12
659 Mark McGwire HL .75 .30
660 Paul Molitor HL .10 .04

1988 Score Glossy

This 660 card set is a parallel to the regular 1988 Score set. According to the manufacturer, 5,000 of these sets were produced. These sets are considered glossy as "UV Coating" was added to the fronts of the card. These sets were issued in factory set versions only and released solely through Major League Marketing's hobby accounts.

Nm-Mt Ex-Mt
COMP.FACT.SET (660) 120.00 47.50
*STARS: 6X TO 15X BASIC CARDS
*ROOKIES: 6X TO 15X BASIC CARDS

1988 Score Box Cards

There are six different wax box bottom panels each featuring three players and a trivia (related to a particular stadium for a given year) question. The players and trivia question cards are individually numbered. The trivia are numbered below with the prefix T in order to avoid confusion. The trivia cards are very unpopular with collectors since they do not picture any players. When panels of four are cut into individuals, the cards are standard size. The card backs of the players feature the respective League logos most prominently.

Nm-Mt Ex-Mt
COMPLETE SET (24) 10.00 4.00
1 Terry Kennedy .10 .04
2 Don Mattingly 1.50 .60
3 Willie Randolph .20 .08
4 Wade Boggs 1.00 .40
5 Cal Ripken 3.00 1.20
6 George Bell .10 .04
7 Rickey Henderson 1.25 .50
8 Dave Winfield .75 .30
9 Bret Saberhagen .20 .08
10 Gary Carter .75 .30
11 Jack Clark .20 .08
12 Ryne Sandberg 1.50 .60
13 Mike Schmidt .75 .30
14 Ozzie Smith 1.50 .60
15 Eric Davis .20 .08
16 Andre Dawson .50 .20
17 Darryl Strawberry .20 .08
18 Mike Scott .10 .04
T1 Ted Williams 2.00 .80
Fenway Park '60
T2 Fred Lynn .20 .08
Comiskey Park '83
T3 Mark McGwire 2.00 .80
Anaheim Stadium '87
T4 Gabby Hartnett .20 .08
Wrigley Field '38
T5 Red Schoendienst .20 .08
Comiskey Park '50
T6 John Farrell .50 .20
Paul Molitor
County Stadium '87

1988 Score Rookie/Traded

This 110-card standard-size set issued exclusively in a boxes factory-set form features traded players (1-65) and rookies (66-110) for the 1988 season. The cards are distinguishable from the regular Score set by the orange borders and by the fact that the numbering on the back has a

T suffix. Apparently Score's first attempt at a Rookie/Traded set was produced very conservatively, resulting in a set which is now recognized as being much tougher to find than the other Rookie/Traded sets from the other major companies of that year. Extended Rookie Cards in this set include Roberto Alomar, Brady Anderson, Craig Biggio, Jay Buhner and Mark Grace.

Nm-Mt Ex-Mt
COMP.FACT.SET (110) 40.00 16.00
1T Jack Clark .75 .30
2T Danny Jackson .25 .10
3T Brett Butler .75 .30
4T Kurt Stillwell .25 .10
5T Tom Brunansky .25 .10
6T Dennis Lamp .25 .10
7T Jose DeLeon .25 .10
8T Tom Herr .25 .10
9T Keith Moreland .25 .10
10T Kirk Gibson 2.00 .80
11T Bud Black .25 .10
12T Rafael Ramirez .25 .10
13T Luis Salazar .25 .10
14T Goose Gossage .75 .30
15T Bob Welch .75 .30
16T Vance Law .25 .10
17T Ray Knight .75 .30
18T Dan Quisenberry .75 .30
19T Don Slaught .25 .10
20T Lee Smith .75 .30
21T Rick Cerone .25 .10
22T Pat Tabler .25 .10
23T Larry McWilliams .25 .10
24T Ricky Horton .25 .10
25T Graig Nettles .75 .30
26T Dan Petry .25 .10
27T Jose Rijo .75 .30
28T Chili Davis .75 .30
29T Dickie Thon .25 .10
30T Mackey Sasser .25 .10
31T Mickey Tettleton .25 .10
32T Rick Dempsey .25 .10
33T Ron Hassey .25 .10
34T Phil Bradley .25 .10
35T Jay Howell .25 .10
36T Bill Buckner .75 .30
37T Alfredo Griffin .25 .10
38T Gary Pettis .25 .10
39T Calvin Schiraldi .25 .10
40T John Candelaria .25 .10
41T Joe Orsulak .25 .10
42T Willie Upshaw .25 .10
43T Herm Winningham .25 .10
44T Ron Kittle .25 .10
45T Bob Dernier .25 .10
46T Steve Balboni .25 .10
47T Steve Shields .25 .10
48T Henry Cotto .25 .10
49T Dave Henderson .25 .10
50T Dave Parker .75 .30
51T Mike Young .25 .10
52T Mark Salas .25 .10
53T Mike Davis .25 .10
54T Rafael Santana .25 .10
55T Don Baylor .75 .30
56T Dan Pasqua .25 .10
57T Ernest Riles .25 .10
58T Glenn Hubbard .25 .10
59T Mike Smithson .25 .10
60T Richard Dotson .25 .10
61T Jerry Reuss .25 .10
62T Mike Jackson .75 .30
63T Floyd Bannister .25 .10
64T Jesse Orosco .25 .10
65T Larry Parrish .25 .10
66T Jeff Bittiger .25 .10
67T Ray Hayward .25 .10
68T Ricky Jordan XRC .75 .30
69T Tommy Gregg .25 .10
70T Brady Anderson XRC 1.25 .50
71T Jeff Montgomery .75 .30
72T Darryl Hamilton XRC .75 .30
73T Cecil Espy .25 .10
74T Greg Briley XRC .25 .10
75T Joey Meyer .25 .10
76T Mike Macfarlane XRC .75 .30
77T Oswald Peraza .25 .10
78T Jack Armstrong XRC .25 .10
79T Don Heinkel .25 .10
80T Mark Grace XRC 8.00 3.20
81T Steve Curry .25 .10
82T Damon Berryhill XRC .75 .30
83T Steve Ellsworth .25 .10
84T Pete Smith XRC* .25 .10
85T Jack McDowell XRC 1.25 .50
86T Rob Dibble XRC 2.00 .80
87T Bryan Harvey UER .75 .30
(Games Pitched 47, Innings 5) XRC
88T John Dopson .25 .10
89T Dave Gallagher .25 .10
90T Todd Stottlemyre XRC .75 .30
91T Mike Schooler .25 .10
92T Don Gordon .25 .10
93T Sil Campusano .25 .10
94T Jeff Pico .25 .10
95T Jay Buhner XRC 2.00 .80
96T Nelson Santovenia .25 .10
97T Al Leiter XRC* 3.00 1.20
98T Luis Alicea XRC .75 .30
99T Pat Borders XRC .75 .30
100T Chris Sabo XRC 1.25 .50
101T Tim Belcher .25 .10
102T Walt Weiss XRC* 1.25 .50
103T Craig Biggio XRC 8.00 3.20
104T Don August .25 .10
105T Roberto Alomar XRC 20.00 8.00
106T Todd Burns .25 .10
107T John Costello .25 .10
108T Melido Perez XRC* .75 .30
109T Darrin Jackson XRC .25 .10
110T O.Destrade XRC .25 .10

1988 Score Rookie/Traded Glossy

This 110-card standard-size set was issued as a parallel vesion to the regular Score Rookie/Traded set. This set was issued only in boxed factory-set form. According to published reports, only 3,000 of these sets were created. The sets were sold solely through Score's dealer's accounts of the time.

Nm-Mt Ex-Mt
COMP.FACT.SET (110) 150.00 60.00
*STARS: 1.25X TO 3X BASIC CARDS
*ROOKIES: 1X TO 2.5X BASIC CARDS

1988 Score Young Superstars I

This attractive high-gloss 40-card standard-size set of "Young Superstars" was distributed in a small blue box which had the checklist of the set on a side panel of the box. The cards were also distributed as an insert, one per rack pack. These attractive cards are in full color on the front and also have a full-color small portrait on the card back. The cards in this series are distinguishable from the cards in Series II by the fact that this series has a blue and green border on the card front instead of the (Series II) blue and pink border.

Nm-Mt Ex-Mt
COMPLETE SET (40) 8.00 3.20
1 Mark McGwire 4.00 1.60
2 Benito Santiago .10 .04
3 Sam Horn .05 .02
4 Chris Bosio .05 .02
5 Matt Nokes .05 .02
6 Ken Williams .10 .04
7 Dion James .05 .02
8 B.J. Surhoff .15 .06
9 Joe Magrane .05 .02
10 Kevin Seitzer .05 .02
11 Stanley Jefferson .05 .02
12 Devon White .10 .04
13 Nelson Liriano .05 .02
14 Chris James .05 .02
15 Mike Henneman .10 .04
16 Terry Steinbach .05 .02
17 John Kruk .10 .04
18 Matt Williams 1.00 .40
19 Kelly Downs .05 .02
20 Bill Ripken .05 .02
21 Ozzie Guillen .10 .04
22 Luis Polonia .05 .02
23 Dave Magadan .05 .02
24 Mike Greenwell .05 .02
25 Will Clark 1.00 .40
26 Mike Dunne .05 .02
27 Wally Joyner .10 .04
28 Robby Thompson .05 .02
29 Ken Caminiti .50 .20
30 Jose Canseco 1.00 .40
31 Todd Benzinger .05 .02
32 Pete Incaviglia .05 .02
33 John Farrell .05 .02
34 Casey Candaele .05 .02
35 Mike Aldrete .05 .02
36 Ruben Sierra .10 .04
37 Ellis Burks .20 .08
38 Tracy Jones .05 .02
39 Kal Daniels .05 .02
40 Cory Snyder .05 .02

1988 Score Young Superstars II

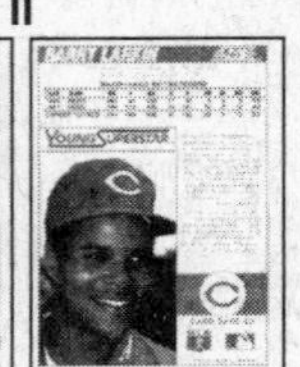

This attractive high-gloss 40-card standard-size set of "Young Superstars" was distributed in a small purple box which had the checklist of the set on a side panel of the box. The cards were not distributed as an insert with rak paks as the first series was, but were only available as a complete set from hobby dealers or through a mail-in offer direct from the company. These attractive cards are in full color on the front and also have a full-color small portrait on the card back. The cards in this series are distinguishable from the cards in Series I by the fact that this series has a blue and pink border on the card front instead of the (Series I) blue and green border.

Nm-Mt Ex-Mt
COMP.FACT SET (40) 5.00 2.00
1 Don Mattingly 1.00 .40
2 Glenn Braggs .05 .02
3 Dwight Gooden .15 .06
4 Jose Lind .05 .02
5 Danny Tartabull .05 .02
6 Tony Fernandez .15 .06
7 Julio Franco .15 .06
8 Andres Galarraga .20 .08
9 Bobby Bonilla .05 .02
10 Eric Davis .15 .06
11 Gerald Young .05 .02
12 Barry Bonds 1.00 .40
13 Jerry Browne .05 .02
14 Jeff Blauser .15 .06
15 Mickey Brantley .05 .02
16 Floyd Youmans .05 .02
17 Bret Saberhagen .15 .06
18 Shawon Dunston .05 .02
19 Len Dykstra .15 .06
20 Darryl Strawberry .15 .06
21 Rick Aguilera .15 .06
22 Ivan Calderon .05 .02
23 Roger Clemens 1.00 .40
24 Vince Coleman .05 .02
25 Gary Thurman .05 .02
26 Jeff Treadway .05 .02
27 Oddibe McDowell .05 .02
28 Fred McGriff .20 .08
29 Mark McLemore .15 .06
30 Jeff Musselman .05 .02
31 Mitch Williams .05 .02
32 Dan Plesac .05 .02
33 Juan Nieves .05 .02
34 Barry Larkin .20 .08
35 Greg Mathews .05 .02
36 Shane Mack .05 .02
37 Scott Bankhead .05 .02
38 Eric Bell .05 .02
39 Greg Swindell .05 .02
40 Kevin Elster .05 .02

1989 Score

This 660-card standard-size set was distributed by Major League Marketing. Cards were issued primarily in fin-wrapped plastic packs and factory sets. Cards feature six distinctive inner border (inside a white outer border) colors on the front. Subsets include Highlights (652-660) and Rookie Prospects (621-651). Rookie Cards in this set include Brady Anderson, Craig Biggio, Randy Johnson, Gary Sheffield, and John Smoltz.

Nm-Mt Ex-Mt
COMPLETE SET (660) 15.00 6.00
COMP.FACT.SET (660) 15.00 6.00
1 Jose Canseco .25 .10
2 Andre Dawson .10 .04
3 Mark McGwire UER 1.00 .40
4 Benito Santiago .10 .04
5 Rick Reuschel .10 .04
6 Fred McGriff .15 .06
7 Kal Daniels .05 .02
8 Gary Gaetti .10 .04
9 Ellis Burks .10 .04
10 Darryl Strawberry .10 .04
11 Julio Franco .10 .04
12 Lloyd Moseby .05 .02
13 Jeff Pico .05 .02
14 Johnny Ray .05 .02
15 Cal Ripken .75 .30
16 Dick Schofield .05 .02
17 Mel Hall .05 .02
18 Bill Ripken .05 .02
19 Brook Jacoby .05 .02
20 Kirby Puckett .25 .10
21 Bill Doran .05 .02
22 Pete O'Brien .05 .02
23 Matt Nokes .05 .02
24 Brian Fisher .05 .02
25 Jack Clark .10 .04
26 Gary Pettis .05 .02
27 Dave Valle .05 .02
28 Willie Wilson .10 .04
29 Curt Young .05 .02
30 Dale Murphy .15 .06
31 Barry Larkin .15 .06
32 Dave Stewart .10 .04
33 Mike LaValliere .05 .02
34 Glenn Hubbard .05 .02
35 Ryne Sandberg .40 .16
36 Tony Pena .05 .02
37 Greg Walker .05 .02
38 Von Hayes .05 .02
39 Kevin Mitchell .10 .04
40 Tim Raines .10 .04
41 Keith Hernandez .10 .04
42 Keith Moreland .05 .02
43 Ruben Sierra .05 .02
44 Chet Lemon .05 .02
45 Willie Randolph .10 .04
46 Andy Allanson .05 .02
47 Candy Maldonado .05 .02
48 Sid Bream .05 .02
49 Denny Walling .05 .02
50 Dave Winfield .10 .04
51 Alvin Davis .05 .02
52 Cory Snyder .05 .02
53 Hubie Brooks .05 .02
54 Chili Davis .10 .04
55 Kevin Seitzer .05 .02
56 Jose Uribe .05 .02
57 Tony Fernandez .05 .02
58 Tim Teufel .05 .02
59 Oddibe McDowell .05 .02
60 Les Lancaster .05 .02
61 Billy Hatcher .05 .02
62 Dan Gladden .05 .02
63 Marty Barrett .05 .02
64 Nick Esasky .05 .02
65 Wally Joyner .10 .04
66 Mike Greenwell .05 .02
67 Ken Williams .05 .02
68 Bob Horner .10 .04
69 Steve Sax .05 .02
70 Rickey Henderson .25 .10
71 Mitch Webster .05 .02
72 Rob Deer .05 .02
73 Jim Presley .05 .02
74 Albert Hall .05 .02
75 George Brett COR .60 .24
(At age 35)
75A George Brett ERR 1.00 .40
(At age 33)
76 Brian Downing .10 .04
77 Dave Martinez .05 .02
78 Scott Fletcher .05 .02
79 Phil Bradley .05 .02
80 Ozzie Smith .40 .16
81 Larry Sheets .05 .02
82 Mike Aldrete .05 .02
83 Darnell Coles .05 .02
84 Len Dykstra .10 .04
85 Jim Rice .10 .04
86 Jeff Treadway .05 .02
87 Jose Lind .05 .02
88 Willie McGee .10 .04
89 Mickey Brantley .05 .02
90 Tony Gwynn .30 .12
91 R.J. Reynolds .05 .02
92 Milt Thompson .05 .02
93 Kevin McReynolds .05 .02
94 Eddie Murray UER .25 .10
('86 batting .205, should be .305)
95 Lance Parrish .10 .04
96 Ron Kittle .05 .02
97 Gerald Young .05 .02
98 Ernie Whitt .05 .02
99 Jeff Reed .05 .02
100 Don Mattingly .60 .24
101 Gerald Perry .05 .02
102 Vance Law .05 .02
103 John Shelby .05 .02
104 Chris Sabo RC * .40 .16
105 Danny Tartabull .05 .02
106 Glenn Wilson .05 .02
107 Mark Davidson .05 .02
108 Dave Parker .10 .04
109 Eric Davis .10 .04
110 Alan Trammell .10 .04
111 Ozzie Virgil .05 .02
112 Frank Tanana .10 .04
113 Rafael Ramirez .05 .02
114 Dennis Martinez .10 .04
115 Jose DeLeon .05 .02
116 Bob Ojeda .05 .02
117 Doug Drabek .05 .02
118 Andy Hawkins .05 .02
119 Greg Maddux .50 .20
120 Cecil Fielder UER .10 .04
Reversed Photo on back
121 Mike Scioscia .10 .04
122 Dan Petry .05 .02
123 Terry Kennedy .05 .02
124 Kelly Downs .05 .02
125 Greg Gross UER .05 .02
(Gregg on back)
126 Fred Lynn .10 .04
127 Barry Bonds 1.25 .50
128 Harold Baines .10 .04
129 Doyle Alexander .05 .02
130 Kevin Elster .05 .02
131 Mike Heath .05 .02
132 Teddy Higuera .05 .02
133 Charlie Leibrandt .05 .02
134 Tim Laudner .05 .02
135A Ray Knight ERR .10 .04
(Reverse negative)
135B Ray Knight COR .10 .04
136 Howard Johnson .10 .04
137 Terry Pendleton .10 .04
138 Andy McGaffigan .05 .02
139 Ken Oberkfell .05 .02
140 Butch Wynegar .05 .02
141 Rob Murphy .05 .02
142 Rich Renteria .05 .02
143 Jose Guzman .05 .02
144 Andres Galarraga .10 .04
145 Ricky Horton .05 .02
146 Frank DiPino .05 .02
147 Glenn Braggs .05 .02
148 John Kruk .10 .04
149 Mike Schmidt .50 .20
150 Lee Smith .10 .04
151 Robin Yount .40 .16
152 Mark Eichhorn .05 .02
153 DeWayne Buice .05 .02
154 B.J. Surhoff .10 .04
155 Vince Coleman .05 .02
156 Tony Phillips .05 .02
157 Willie Fraser .05 .02
158 Lance McCullers .05 .02
159 Greg Gagne .05 .02
160 Jesse Barfield .10 .04
161 Mark Langston .05 .02
162 Kurt Stillwell .05 .02
163 Dion James .05 .02
164 Glenn Davis .05 .02
165 Walt Weiss .05 .02
166 Dave Concepcion .10 .04
167 Alfredo Griffin .05 .02
168 Don Heinkel .05 .02
169 Luis Rivera .05 .02
170 Shane Rawley .05 .02
171 Darrell Evans .10 .04
172 Robby Thompson .05 .02
173 Jody Davis .05 .02
174 Andy Van Slyke .10 .04
175 Wade Boggs UER .15 .06
(Bio says .364, should be .356)
176 Garry Templeton .10 .04
('85 stats off-centered)
177 Gary Redus .05 .02
178 Craig Lefferts .05 .02
179 Carney Lansford .10 .04
180 Ron Darling .10 .04
181 Kirk McCaskill .05 .02
182 Tony Armas .10 .04
183 Steve Farr .05 .02
184 Tom Brunansky .05 .02

185 B.Harvey RC UER .25 .10
'87 games 47,
should be 3
186 Mike Marshall .05 .02
187 Bo Diaz .05 .02
188 Willie Upshaw .05 .02
189 Mike Pagliarulo .05 .02
190 Mike Krukow .05 .02
191 Tommy Herr .05 .02
192 Jim Pankovits .05 .02
193 Dwight Evans .10 .04
194 Kelly Gruber .05 .02
195 Bobby Bonilla .10 .04
196 Wallace Johnson .05 .02
197 Dave Stieb .10 .04
198 Pat Borders RC * .25 .10
199 Rafael Palmeiro .25 .10
200 Dwight Gooden .10 .04
201 Pete Incaviglia .05 .02
202 Chris James .05 .02
203 Marvell Wynne .05 .02
204 Pat Sheridan .05 .02
205 Don Baylor .10 .04
206 Paul O'Neill .15 .06
207 Pete Smith .05 .02
208 Mark McLemore .05 .02
209 Henry Cotto .05 .02
210 Kirk Gibson .10 .04
211 Claudell Washington .05 .02
212 Randy Bush .05 .02
213 Joe Carter .10 .04
214 Bill Buckner .10 .04
215 Bert Blyleven UER .10 .04
(Wrong birth year)
216 Brett Butler .10 .04
217 Lee Mazzilli .10 .04
218 Spike Owen .05 .02
219 Bill Swift .05 .02
220 Tim Wallach .05 .02
221 David Cone .10 .04
222 Don Carman .05 .02
223 Rich Gossage .10 .04
224 Bob Walk .05 .02
225 Dave Righetti .10 .04
226 Kevin Bass .05 .02
227 Kevin Gross .05 .02
228 Tim Burke .05 .02
229 Rick Mahler .05 .02
230 Lou Whitaker UER .10 .04
(252 games in '85,
should be 152)
231 Luis Alicea RC * .25 .10
232 Roberto Alomar .25 .10
233 Bob Boone .10 .04
234 Dickie Thon .05 .02
235 Shawon Dunston .05 .02
236 Pete Stanicek .05 .02
237 Craig Biggio RC .75 .30
(Inconsistent design,
portrait on front)
238 Dennis Boyd .05 .02
239 Tom Candiotti .05 .02
240 Gary Carter .10 .04
241 Mike Stanley .05 .02
242 Ken Phelps .05 .02
243 Chris Bosio .05 .02
244 Les Straker .05 .02
245 Dave Smith .05 .02
246 John Candelaria .05 .02
247 Joe Orsulak .05 .02
248 Storm Davis .05 .02
249 Floyd Bannister UER .05 .02
(ML Batting Record)
250 Jack Morris .10 .04
251 Bret Saberhagen .10 .04
252 Tom Niedenfuer .05 .02
253 Neal Heaton .05 .02
254 Eric Show .05 .02
255 Juan Samuel .05 .02
256 Dale Sveum .05 .02
257 Jim Gott .05 .02
258 Scott Garrelts .05 .02
259 Larry McWilliams .05 .02
260 Steve Bedrosian .05 .02
261 Jack Howell .05 .02
262 Jay Tibbs .05 .02
263 Jamie Moyer .10 .04
264 Doug Sisk .05 .02
265 Todd Worrell .05 .02
266 John Farrell .05 .02
267 Dave Collins .05 .02
268 Sid Fernandez .05 .02
269 Tom Brookens .05 .02
270 Shane Mack .05 .02
271 Paul Kilgus .05 .02
272 Chuck Crim .05 .02
273 Bob Knepper .05 .02
274 Mike Moore .05 .02
275 Guillermo Hernandez .05 .02
276 Dennis Eckersley .15 .06
277 Graig Nettles .10 .04
278 Rich Dotson .05 .02
279 Larry Herndon .05 .02
280 Gene Larkin .05 .02
281 Roger McDowell .05 .02
282 Greg Swindell .05 .02
283 Juan Agosto .05 .02
284 Jeff M. Robinson .05 .02
285 Mike Dunne .05 .02
286 Greg Mathews .05 .02
287 Kent Tekulve .05 .02
288 Jerry Mumphrey .05 .02
289 Jack McDowell .10 .04
290 Frank Viola .10 .04
291 Mark Gubicza .05 .02
292 Dave Schmidt .05 .02
293 Mike Henneman .05 .02
294 Jimmy Jones .05 .02
295 Charlie Hough .10 .04
296 Rafael Santana .05 .02
297 Chris Speier .05 .02
298 Mike Witt .05 .02
299 Pascual Perez .05 .02
300 Nolan Ryan 1.00 .40
301 Mitch Williams .05 .02
302 Mookie Wilson .10 .04
303 Mackey Sasser .05 .02
304 John Cerutti .05 .02
305 Jeff Reardon .10 .04
306 Randy Myers UER .10 .04
(6 hits in '87,
should be 61)
307 Greg Brock .05 .02
308 Bob Welch .10 .04
309 Jeff D. Robinson .05 .02
310 Harold Reynolds .10 .04
311 Jim Walewander .05 .02
312 Dave Magadan .05 .02
313 Jim Gantner .05 .02
314 Walt Terrell .05 .02
315 Wally Backman .05 .02
316 Luis Salazar .05 .02
317 Rick Rhoden .05 .02
318 Tom Henke .05 .02
319 Mike Macfarlane RC * .25 .10
320 Dan Plesac .05 .02
321 Calvin Schiraldi .05 .02
322 Stan Javier .05 .02
323 Devon White .10 .04
324 Scott Bradley .05 .02
325 Bruce Hurst .05 .02
326 Manny Lee .05 .02
327 Rick Aguilera .05 .02
328 Bruce Ruffin .05 .02
329 Ed Whitson .05 .02
330 Bo Jackson .25 .10
331 Ivan Calderon .05 .02
332 Mickey Hatcher .05 .02
333 Barry Jones .05 .02
334 Ron Hassey .05 .02
335 Bill Wegman .05 .02
336 Damon Berryhill .05 .02
337 Steve Ontiveros .05 .02
338 Dan Pasqua .05 .02
339 Bill Pecota .05 .02
340 Greg Cadaret .05 .02
341 Scott Bankhead .05 .02
342 Ron Guidry .10 .04
343 Danny Heep .05 .02
344 Bob Brower .05 .02
345 Rich Gedman .05 .02
346 Nelson Santovenia .05 .02
347 George Bell .10 .04
348 Ted Power .05 .02
349 Mark Grant .05 .02
350 Roger Clemens COR .50 .20
(78 career wins)
350A Roger Clemens ERR 1.25 .50
(778 career wins)
351 Bill Long .05 .02
352 Jay Bell .10 .04
353 Steve Balboni .05 .02
354 Bob Kipper .05 .02
355 Steve Jeltz .05 .02
356 Jesse Orosco .05 .02
357 Bob Dernier .05 .02
358 Mickey Tettleton .05 .02
359 Duane Ward .05 .02
360 Darrin Jackson .10 .04
361 Rey Quinones .05 .02
362 Mark Grace .25 .10
363 Steve Lake .05 .02
364 Pat Perry .05 .02
365 Terry Steinbach .10 .04
366 Alan Ashby .05 .02
367 Jeff Montgomery .05 .02
368 Steve Buechele .05 .02
369 Chris Brown .05 .02
370 Orel Hershiser .10 .04
371 Todd Benzinger .05 .02
372 Ron Gant .10 .04
373 Paul Assenmacher .05 .02
374 Joey Meyer .05 .02
375 Neil Allen .05 .02
376 Mike Davis .05 .02
377 Jeff Parrett .05 .02
378 Jay Howell .05 .02
379 Rafael Belliard .05 .02
380 Luis Polonia UER .05 .02
(2 triples in '87,
should be 10)
381 Keith Atherton .05 .02
382 Kent Hrbek .10 .04
383 Bob Stanley .05 .02
384 Dave LaPoint .05 .02
385 Rance Mulliniks .05 .02
386 Melido Perez .05 .02
387 Doug Jones .05 .02
388 Steve Lyons .05 .02
389 Alejandro Pena .05 .02
390 Frank White .10 .04
391 Pat Tabler .05 .02
392 Eric Plunk .05 .02
393 Mike Maddux .05 .02
394 Allan Anderson .05 .02
395 Bob Brenly .05 .02
396 Rick Cerone .05 .02
397 Scott Terry .05 .02
398 Mike Jackson .05 .02
399 Bobby Thigpen UER .05 .02
Bio says 37 saves in
'88, should be 34
400 Don Sutton .10 .04
401 Cecil Espy .05 .02
402 Junior Ortiz .05 .02
403 Mike Smithson .05 .02
404 Bud Black .05 .02
405 Tom Foley .05 .02
406 Andres Thomas .05 .02
407 Rick Sutcliffe .10 .04
408 Brian Harper .05 .02
409 John Smiley .05 .02
410 Juan Nieves .05 .02
411 Shawn Abner .05 .02
412 Wes Gardner .05 .02
413 Darren Daulton .10 .04
414 Juan Berenguer .05 .02
415 Charles Hudson .05 .02
416 Rick Honeycutt .05 .02
417 Greg Booker .05 .02
418 Tim Belcher .05 .02
419 Don August .05 .02
420 Dale Mohorcic .05 .02
421 Steve Lombardozzi .05 .02
422 Atlee Hammaker .05 .02
423 Jerry Don Gleaton .05 .02
424 Scott Bailes .05 .02
425 Bruce Sutter .10 .04
426 Randy Ready .05 .02
427 Jerry Reed .05 .02
428 Bryn Smith .05 .02
429 Tim Leary .05 .02
430 Mark Clear .05 .02
431 Terry Leach .05 .02
432 John Moses .05 .02
433 Ozzie Guillen .05 .02
434 Gene Nelson .05 .02
435 Gary Ward .05 .02
436 Luis Aguayo .05 .02
437 Fernando Valenzuela .10 .04
438 Jeff Russell UER .05 .02
(Saves total does
not add up correctly)
439 Cecilio Guante .05 .02
440 Don Robinson .05 .02
441 Rick Anderson .05 .02
442 Tom Glavine .25 .10
443 Daryl Boston .05 .02
444 Joe Price .05 .02
445 Stu Cliburn .05 .02
446 Manny Trillo .05 .02
447 Joel Skinner .05 .02
448 Charlie Puleo .05 .02
449 Carlton Fisk .15 .06
450 Will Clark .25 .10
451 Otis Nixon .05 .02
452 Rick Schu .05 .02
453 Todd Stottlemyre UER .05 .02
(ML Batting Record)
454 Tim Birtsas .05 .02
455 Dave Gallagher .05 .02
456 Barry Lyons .05 .02
457 Fred Manrique .05 .02
458 Ernest Riles .05 .02
459 Doug Jennings .05 .02
460 Joe Magrane .05 .02
461 Jamie Quirk .05 .02
462 Jack Armstrong RC * .25 .10
463 Bobby Witt .05 .02
464 Keith A. Miller .05 .02
465 Todd Burns .05 .02
466 John Dopson .05 .02
467 Rich Yett .05 .02
468 Craig Reynolds .05 .02
469 Dave Bergman .05 .02
470 Rex Hudler .05 .02
471 Eric King .05 .02
472 Joaquin Andujar .10 .04
473 Sil Campusano .05 .02
474 Terry Mulholland .05 .02
475 Mike Flanagan .05 .02
476 Greg A. Harris .05 .02
477 Tommy John .10 .04
478 Dave Anderson .05 .02
479 Fred Toliver .05 .02
480 Jimmy Key .10 .04
481 Donell Nixon .05 .02
482 Mark Portugal .05 .02
483 Tom Pagnozzi .05 .02
484 Jeff Kunkel .05 .02
485 Frank Williams .05 .02
486 Jody Reed .05 .02
487 Roberto Kelly .05 .02
488 Shawn Hillegas UER .05 .02
(165 innings in '87,
should be 165.2)
489 Jerry Reuss .05 .02
490 Mark Davis .05 .02
491 Jeff Sellers .05 .02
492 Zane Smith .05 .02
493 Al Newman .05 .02
494 Mike Young .05 .02
495 Larry Parrish .05 .02
496 Herm Winningham .05 .02
497 Carmen Castillo .05 .02
498 Joe Hesketh .05 .02
499 Darrell Miller .05 .02
500 Mike LaCoss .05 .02
501 Charlie Lea .05 .02
502 Bruce Benedict .05 .02
503 Chuck Finley .10 .04
504 Brad Wellman .05 .02
505 Tim Crews .05 .02
506 Ken Gerhart .05 .02
507A Brian Holton ERR .05 .02
(Born 1/25/65 Denver,
should be 11/29/59
in McKeesport)
507B Brian Holton COR 2.00 .80
508 Dennis Lamp .05 .02
509 Bobby Meacham UER .05 .02
('84 games 099)
510 Tracy Jones .05 .02
511 Mike R. Fitzgerald .05 .02
512 Jeff Bittiger .05 .02
513 Tim Flannery .05 .02
514 Ray Hayward .05 .02
515 Dave Leiper .05 .02
516 Rod Scurry .05 .02
517 Carmelo Martinez .05 .02
518 Curtis Wilkerson .05 .02
519 Stan Jefferson .05 .02
520 Dan Quisenberry .05 .02
521 Lloyd McClendon .05 .02
522 Steve Trout .05 .02
523 Larry Andersen .05 .02
524 Don Aase .05 .02
525 Bob Forsch .05 .02
526 Geno Petralli .05 .02
527 Angel Salazar .05 .02
528 Mike Schooler .05 .02
529 Jose Oquendo .05 .02
530 Jay Buhner UER .10 .04
(Wearing 43 on front,
listed as 34 on back)
531 Tom Bolton .05 .02
532 Al Nipper .05 .02
533 Dave Henderson .05 .02
534 John Costello .05 .02
535 Donnie Moore .05 .02
536 Mike Laga .05 .02
537 Mike Gallego .05 .02
538 Jim Clancy .05 .02
539 Joel Youngblood .05 .02
540 Rick Leach .05 .02
541 Kevin Romine .05 .02
542 Mark Salas .05 .02
543 Greg Minton .05 .02
544 Dave Palmer .05 .02
545 Dwayne Murphy UER .05 .02
(Game-sinning)
546 Jim Deshaies .05 .02
547 Don Gordon .05 .02
548 Ricky Jordan RC * .25 .10
549 Mike Boddicker .05 .02
550 Mike Scott .10 .04
551 Jeff Ballard .05 .02
552A Jose Rijo ERR .10 .04
(Uniform listed as
27 on back)
552B Jose Rijo COR .10 .04
(Uniform listed as
24 on back)
553 Danny Darwin .05 .02
554 Tom Browning .05 .02
555 Danny Jackson .05 .02
556 Rick Dempsey .05 .02
557 Jeffrey Leonard .05 .02
558 Jeff Musselman .05 .02
559 Ron Robinson .05 .02
560 John Tudor .10 .04
561 Don Slaught UER .05 .02
(237 games in 1987)
562 Dennis Rasmussen .05 .02
563 Brady Anderson RC .40 .16
564 Pedro Guerrero .10 .04
565 Paul Molitor .15 .06
566 Terry Clark .05 .02
567 Terry Puhl .05 .02
568 Mike Campbell .05 .02
569 Paul Mirabella .05 .02
570 Jeff Hamilton .05 .02
571 Oswald Peraza .05 .02
572 Bob McClure .05 .02
573 Jose Bautista RC .10 .04
574 Alex Trevino .05 .02
575 John Franco .10 .04
576 Mark Parent .05 .02
577 Nelson Liriano .05 .02
578 Steve Shields .05 .02
579 Odell Jones .05 .02
580 Al Leiter .25 .10
581 Dave Stapleton .05 .02
582 Orel Hershiser .10 .04
Jose Canseco
Kirk Gibson
Dave Stewart WS
583 Donnie Hill .05 .02
584 Chuck Jackson .05 .02
585 Rene Gonzales .05 .02
586 Tracy Woodson .05 .02
587 Jim Adduci .05 .02
588 Mario Soto .10 .04
589 Jeff Blauser .05 .02
590 Jim Traber .05 .02
591 Jon Perlman .05 .02
592 Mark Williamson .05 .02
593 Dave Meads .05 .02
594 Jim Eisenreich .05 .02
595A Paul Gibson P1 1.00 .40
595B Paul Gibson P2 .05 .02
(Airbrushed leg on
player in background)
596 Mike Birkbeck .05 .02
597 Terry Francona .10 .04
598 Paul Zuvella .05 .02
599 Franklin Stubbs .05 .02
600 Gregg Jefferies .15 .06
601 John Cangelosi .05 .02
602 Mike Sharperson .05 .02
603 Mike Diaz .05 .02
604 Gary Varsho .05 .02
605 Terry Blocker .05 .02
606 Charlie O'Brien .05 .02
607 Jim Eppard .05 .02
608 John Davis .05 .02
609 Ken Griffey Sr. .10 .04
610 Buddy Bell .10 .04
611 Ted Simmons UER .10 .04
('78 stats Cardinal)
612 Matt Williams .25 .10
613 Danny Cox .05 .02
614 Al Pedrique .05 .02
615 Ron Oester .05 .02
616 John Smoltz RC 1.00 .40
617 Bob Melvin .05 .02
618 Rob Dibble RC * .50 .20
619 Kirt Manwaring .05 .02
620 Felix Fermin .05 .02
621 Doug Dascenzo .05 .02
622 Bill Brennan .05 .02
623 Carlos Quintana RC .10 .04
624 Mike Harkey RC UER .10 .04
(13 and 31 walks in '88,
should be 35 and 33
625 Gary Sheffield RC 1.50 .60
626 Tom Prince .05 .02
627 Steve Searcy .05 .02
628 Charlie Hayes RC .25 .10
(Listed as outfielder)
629 Felix Jose RC UER .10 .04
(Modesto misspelled
as Modesta)
630 Sandy Alomar Jr. RC .40 .16
(Inconsistent design,
portrait on front)
631 Derek Lilliquist RC .10 .04
632 Geronimo Berroa .05 .02
633 Luis Medina .05 .02
634 Tom Gordon RC UER .40 .16
Height 6'0"
635 Ramon Martinez RC .25 .10
636 Craig Worthington .05 .02
637 Edgar Martinez .25 .10
638 Chad Kreuter RC .25 .10
639 Ron Jones .10 .04
640 Van Snider RC .10 .04
641 Lance Blankenship RC .10 .04
642 Dwight Smith RC UER .25 .10
10 HR's in '87, should be 18
643 Cameron Drew .05 .02
644 Jerald Clark RC .10 .04
645 Randy Johnson RC 4.00 1.20
646 Norm Charlton RC .25 .10
647 Todd Frohwirth UER .05 .02
(Southpaw on back)
648 Luis De Los Santos .05 .02
649 Tim Jones .05 .02
650 Dave West RC UER .10 .04
ML hits 3
should be 6
651 Bob Milacki .05 .02
652 Wrigley Field HL .10 .04
653 Orel Hershiser HL .05 .02
654A W.Boggs HL ERR .15 .06
("seaason" on back
654B W.Boggs HL COR .10 .04
655 Jose Canseco HL .15 .06
656 Doug Jones HL .05 .02
657 Rickey Henderson HL .15 .06
658 Tom Browning HL .05 .02
659 Mike Greenwell HL .05 .02
660 Boston Red Sox HL .05 .02

1989 Score Rookie/Traded

The 1989 Score Rookie and Traded set contains 110 standard-size cards. The set was issued exclusively in factory set form through hobby dealers. The set was distributed in a blue box with 10 Magic Motion trivia cards. The fronts have coral green borders with pink diamonds at the bottom. Cards 1-80 feature traded players; cards 81-110 feature 1989 rookies. Rookie Cards in this set include Jim Abbott, Joey (Albert) Belle, Ken Griffey Jr. and John Wetteland.

Nm-Mt Ex-Mt
COMP.FACT.SET (110) 15.00 6.00
1T Rafael Palmeiro .25 .10
2T Nolan Ryan 1.50 .60
3T Jack Clark .10 .04
4T Dave LaPoint .05 .02
5T Mike Moore .05 .02
6T Pete O'Brien .05 .02
7T Jeffrey Leonard .05 .02
8T Rob Murphy .05 .02
9T Tom Herr .05 .02
10T Claudell Washington .05 .02
11T Mike Pagliarulo .05 .02
12T Steve Lake .05 .02
13T Spike Owen .05 .02
14T Andy Hawkins .05 .02
15T Todd Benzinger .05 .02
16T Mookie Wilson .10 .04
17T Bert Blyleven .10 .04
18T Jeff Treadway .05 .02
19T Bruce Hurst .05 .02
20T Steve Sax .05 .02
21T Juan Samuel .05 .02
22T Jesse Barfield .10 .04
23T Carmen Castillo .05 .02
24T Terry Leach .05 .02
25T Mark Langston .05 .02
26T Eric King .05 .02
27T Steve Balboni .05 .02
28T Len Dykstra .10 .04
29T Keith Moreland .05 .02
30T Terry Kennedy .05 .02
31T Eddie Murray .25 .10
32T Mitch Williams .05 .02
33T Jeff Parrett .05 .02
34T Wally Backman .05 .02
35T Julio Franco .10 .04
36T Lance Parrish .10 .04
37T Nick Esasky .05 .02
38T Luis Polonia .05 .02
39T Kevin Gross .05 .02
40T John Dopson .05 .02
41T Willie Randolph .10 .04
42T Jim Clancy .05 .02
43T Tracy Jones .05 .02
44T Phil Bradley .05 .02
45T Milt Thompson .05 .02
46T Chris James .05 .02
47T Scott Fletcher .05 .02
48T Kal Daniels .05 .02
49T Steve Bedrosian .05 .02
50T Rickey Henderson .25 .10
51T Dion James .05 .02
52T Tim Leary .05 .02
53T Roger McDowell .05 .02
54T Mel Hall .05 .02
55T Dickie Thon .05 .02
56T Zane Smith .05 .02
57T Danny Heep .05 .02
58T Bob McClure .05 .02
59T Brian Holton .05 .02
60T Randy Ready .05 .02
61T Bob Melvin .05 .02
62T Harold Baines .10 .04
63T Lance McCullers .05 .02
64T Jody Davis .05 .02
65T Darrell Evans .10 .04
66T Joel Youngblood .05 .02
67T Frank Viola .10 .04
68T Mike Aldrete .05 .02
69T Greg Cadaret .05 .02
70T John Kruk .10 .04
71T Pat Sheridan .05 .02
72T Oddibe McDowell .05 .02
73T Tom Brookens .05 .02
74T Bob Boone .10 .04
75T Walt Terrell .05 .02
76T Joel Skinner .05 .02
77T Randy Johnson 2.50 .80
78T Felix Fermin .05 .02
79T Rick Mahler .05 .02
80T Richard Dotson .05 .02
81T Cris Carpenter RC * .10 .04
82T Bill Spiers RC .25 .10
83T Junior Felix RC .10 .04
84T Joe Girardi RC .40 .16
85T Jerome Walton RC .25 .10
86T Greg Litton .05 .02
87T Greg W.Harris RC .10 .04
88T Jim Abbott RC* .50 .20
89T Kevin Brown .25 .10

90T John Wetteland RC	.40	.16
91T Gary Wayne	.05	.02
92T Rich Monteleone	.05	.02
93T Bob Geren RC	.05	.02
94T Clay Parker	.05	.02
95T Steve Finley RC	.50	.20
96T Gregg Olson RC	.25	.10
97T Ken Patterson	.05	.02
98T Ken Hill RC	.25	.10
99T Scott Scudder RC	.10	.04
100T Ken Griffey Jr. RC	8.00	3.20
101T Jeff Brantley RC	.25	.10
102T Donn Pall	.05	.02
103T Carlos Martinez RC	.10	.04
104T Joe Oliver RC	.25	.10
105T Omar Vizquel RC	.75	.30
106T Joey Belle RC	1.00	.40
107T Kenny Rogers RC	.75	.30
108T Mark Carreon	.05	.02
109T Rolando Roomes	.05	.02
110T Pete Harnisch RC	.25	.10

1989 Scoremasters

The 1989 Scoremasters set contains 42 standard-size cards. The fronts are "pure" with attractively drawn action portraits. The backs feature write-ups of the players' careers. The set was issued in factory set form only. A first year card of Ken Griffey Jr. highlights the set.

	Nm-Mt	Ex-Mt
COMP.FACT.SET (42)	10.00	4.00
1 Bo Jackson	.25	.10
2 Jerome Walton	.10	.04
3 Cal Ripken	.75	.30
4 Mike Scott	.05	.02
5 Nolan Ryan	1.00	.40
6 Don Mattingly	.60	.24
7 Tom Gordon	.25	.10
8 Jack Morris	.10	.04
9 Carlton Fisk	.20	.08
10 Will Clark	.25	.10
11 George Brett	.60	.24
12 Kevin Mitchell	.10	.04
13 Mark Langston	.05	.02
14 Dave Stewart	.10	.04
15 Dale Murphy	.25	.10
16 Gary Gaetti	.10	.04
17 Wade Boggs	.15	.06
18 Eric Davis	.10	.04
19 Kirby Puckett	.25	.10
20 Roger Clemens	.50	.20
21 Orel Hershiser	.10	.04
22 Mark Grace	.25	.10
23 Ryne Sandberg	.40	.16
24 Barry Larkin	.15	.06
25 Ellis Burks	.15	.06
26 Dwight Gooden	.10	.04
27 Ozzie Smith	.40	.16
28 Andre Dawson	.10	.04
29 Julio Franco	.10	.04
30 Ken Griffey Jr.	8.00	3.20
31 Ruben Sierra	.05	.02
32 Mark McGwire	.75	.30
33 Andres Galarraga	.10	.04
34 Joe Carter	.15	.06
35 Vince Coleman	.05	.02
36 Mike Greenwell	.05	.02
37 Tony Gwynn	.30	.12
38 Andy Van Slyke	.10	.04
39 Gregg Jefferies	.10	.04
40 Jose Canseco	.25	.10
41 Dave Winfield	.10	.04
42 Darryl Strawberry	.10	.04
NNO Don Mattingly Promo	5.00	2.00
Issued for National Convention		

1989 Score Young Superstars I

The 1989 Score Young Superstars I set contains 42 standard-size cards. The fronts are pink, white and blue. The vertically oriented backs have color facial shots, 1988 and career stats, and biographical information. One card was included in each 1989 Score rack pack, and the cards were also distributed as a boxed set with five Magic Motion trivia cards.

	Nm-Mt	Ex-Mt
COMPLETE SET (42)	8.00	3.20
1 Gregg Jefferies	.40	.16
2 Jody Reed	.25	.10
3 Mark Grace	1.00	.40
4 Dave Gallagher	.25	.10
5 Bo Jackson	1.00	.40
6 Jay Buhner	.40	.16
7 Melido Perez	.25	.10
8 Bobby Witt	.25	.10
9 David Cone	.40	.16
10 Chris Sabo	.25	.10
11 Pat Borders	.25	.10
12 Mark Grant	.25	.10
13 Mike Macfarlane	.25	.10
14 Mike Jackson	.25	.10
15 Ricky Jordan	.25	.10
16 Ron Gant	.40	.16
17 Al Leiter	1.00	.40
18 Jeff Parrett	.25	.10
19 Pete Smith	.25	.10
20 Walt Weiss	.40	.16
21 Doug Drabek	.25	.10
22 Kirt Manwaring	.25	.10
23 Keith Miller	.25	.10
24 Damon Berryhill	.25	.10
25 Gary Sheffield	4.00	1.60
26 Brady Anderson	.60	.24
27 Mitch Williams	.25	.10
28 Roberto Alomar	1.00	.40
29 Bobby Thigpen	.25	.10
30 Bryan Harvey UER	.25	.10
(47 games in '87)		
31 Jose Rijo	.25	.10
32 Dave West	.25	.10
33 Joey Meyer	.25	.10
34 Allan Anderson	.25	.10
35 Rafael Palmeiro	1.00	.40
36 Tim Belcher	.25	.10
37 John Smiley	.25	.10
38 Mackey Sasser	.25	.10
39 Greg Maddux	2.00	.80
40 Ramon Martinez	.40	.16
41 Randy Myers	.40	.16
42 Scott Bankhead	.25	.10

1989 Score Young Superstars II

The 1989 Score Young Superstars II set contains 42 standard-size cards. The fronts are orange, white and purple. The vertically oriented backs have color facial shots, 1988 and career stats, and biographical information. The cards were distributed as a boxed set with five Magic Motion trivia cards. A first year card of Ken Griffey Jr. highlights the set.

	Nm-Mt	Ex-Mt
COMP.FACT.SET (42)	25.00	10.00
1 Sandy Alomar Jr.	.60	.24
2 Tom Gordon	1.00	.40
3 Ron Jones	.25	.10
4 Todd Burns	.25	.10
5 Paul O'Neill	.60	.24
6 Gene Larkin	.25	.10
7 Eric King	.25	.10
8 Jeff M. Robinson	.25	.10
9 Bill Wegman	.25	.10
10 Cecil Espy	.25	.10
11 Jose Guzman	.25	.10
12 Kelly Gruber	.25	.10
13 Duane Ward	.25	.10
14 Mark Gubicza	.25	.10
15 Norm Charlton	.40	.16
16 Jose Oquendo	.25	.10
17 Geronimo Berroa	.25	.10
18 Ken Griffey Jr.	15.00	6.00
19 Lance McCullers	.25	.10
20 Todd Stottlemyre	.60	.24
21 Craig Worthington	.25	.10
22 Mike Devereaux	.25	.10
23 Tom Glavine	1.00	.40
24 Dale Sveum	.25	.10
25 Roberto Kelly	.40	.16
26 Luis Medina	.25	.10
27 Steve Searcy	.25	.10
28 Don August	.25	.10
29 Shawn Hillegas	.25	.10
30 Mike Campbell	.25	.10
31 Mike Harkey	.25	.10
32 Randy Johnson	8.00	3.20
33 Craig Biggio	3.00	1.20
34 Mike Schooler	.25	.10
35 Andres Thomas	.25	.10
36 Jerome Walton	.40	.16
37 Cris Carpenter	.25	.10
38 Kevin Mitchell	.40	.16
39 Eddie Williams	.25	.10
40 Chad Kreuter	.25	.10
41 Danny Jackson	.25	.10
42 Kurt Stillwell	.25	.10

1990 Score

The 1990 Score set contains 704 standard-size cards. Cards were distributed in plastic-wrap packs and factory sets. The front borders are red, blue, green or white. The vertically oriented backs are white with borders that match the fronts, and feature color mugshots. Subsets include Draft Picks (661-682) and Dream Team (683-695). A special black and white horizontal-designed card of Bo Jackson in football pads holding a bat above his shoulders was a big hit in 1990. That card traded for as much as $10 but has since cooled off. Nevertheless, it remains one of the most noteworthy cards issued in the early 1990's. Rookie Cards of note include Juan Gonzalez, Dave Justice, Chuck Knoblauch, Dean Palmer, Sammy Sosa, Frank Thomas, Mo Vaughn, Larry Walker and Bernie Williams. A ten-card set of Dream Team Rookies was inserted into each hobby factory set, but was not included in retail factory sets.

	Nm-Mt	Ex-Mt
COMPLETE SET (704)	15.00	4.50
COMP.RETAIL SET (704)	15.00	4.50
COMP.HOBBY SET (714)	15.00	4.50
1 Don Mattingly	.60	.18
2 Cal Ripken	.75	.23
3 Dwight Evans	.10	.03
4 Barry Bonds	.60	.18
5 Kevin McReynolds	.05	.02
6 Ozzie Guillen	.05	.02
7 Terry Kennedy	.05	.02
8 Bryan Harvey	.05	.02
9 Alan Trammell	.10	.03
10 Cory Snyder	.05	.02
11 Jody Reed	.05	.02
12 Roberto Alomar	.15	.04
13 Pedro Guerrero	.05	.02
14 Gary Redus	.05	.02
15 Marty Barrett	.05	.02
16 Ricky Jordan	.05	.02
17 Joe Magrane	.05	.02
18 Sid Fernandez	.05	.02
19 Richard Dotson	.05	.02
20 Jack Clark	.10	.03
21 Bob Walk	.05	.02
22 Ron Karkovice	.05	.02
23 Lenny Harris	.05	.02
24 Phil Bradley	.05	.02
25 Andres Galarraga	.10	.03
26 Brian Downing	.05	.02
27 Dave Martinez	.05	.02
28 Eric King	.05	.02
29 Barry Lyons	.05	.02
30 Dave Schmidt	.05	.02
31 Mike Boddicker	.05	.02
32 Tom Foley	.05	.02
33 Brady Anderson	.10	.03
34 Jim Presley	.05	.02
35 Lance Parrish	.05	.02
36 Von Hayes	.05	.02
37 Lee Smith	.10	.03
38 Herm Winningham	.05	.02
39 Alejandro Pena	.05	.02
40 Mike Scott	.05	.02
41 Joe Orsulak	.05	.02
42 Rafael Ramirez	.05	.02
43 Gerald Young	.05	.02
44 Dick Schofield	.05	.02
45 Dave Smith	.05	.02
46 Dave Magadan	.05	.02
47 Dennis Martinez	.10	.03
48 Greg Minton	.05	.02
49 Milt Thompson	.05	.02
50 Orel Hershiser	.10	.03
51 Bip Roberts	.05	.02
52 Jerry Browne	.05	.02
53 Bob Ojeda	.05	.02
54 Fernando Valenzuela	.10	.03
55 Matt Nokes	.05	.02
56 Brook Jacoby	.05	.02
57 Frank Tanana	.05	.02
58 Scott Fletcher	.05	.02
59 Ron Oester	.05	.02
60 Bob Boone	.10	.03
61 Dan Gladden	.05	.02
62 Darnell Coles	.05	.02
63 Gregg Olson	.10	.03
64 Todd Burns	.05	.02
65 Todd Benzinger	.05	.02
66 Dale Murphy	.25	.07
67 Mike Flanagan	.05	.02
68 Jose Oquendo	.05	.02
69 Cecil Espy	.05	.02
70 Chris Sabo	.05	.02
71 Shane Rawley	.05	.02
72 Tom Brunansky	.05	.02
73 Vance Law	.05	.02
74 B.J. Surhoff	.10	.03
75 Lou Whitaker	.10	.03
76 Ken Caminiti UER	.10	.03
Euclid and Ohio should be Hanford and California		
77 Nelson Liriano	.05	.02
78 Tommy Gregg	.05	.02
79 Don Slaught	.05	.02
80 Eddie Murray	.25	.07
81 Joe Boever	.05	.02
82 Charlie Leibrandt	.05	.02
83 Jose Lind	.05	.02
84 Tony Phillips	.05	.02
85 Mitch Webster	.05	.02
86 Dan Plesac	.05	.02
87 Rick Mahler	.05	.02
88 Steve Lyons	.05	.02
89 Tony Fernandez	.05	.02
90 Ryne Sandberg	.40	.12
91 Nick Esasky	.05	.02
92 Luis Salazar	.05	.02
93 Pete Incaviglia	.05	.02
94 Ivan Calderon	.05	.02
95 Jeff Treadway	.05	.02
96 Kurt Stillwell	.05	.02
97 Gary Sheffield	.25	.07
98 Jeffrey Leonard	.05	.02
99 Andres Thomas	.05	.02
100 Roberto Kelly	.05	.02
101 Alvaro Espinoza	.05	.02
102 Greg Gagne	.05	.02
103 John Farrell	.05	.02
104 Willie Wilson	.05	.02
105 Glenn Braggs	.05	.02
106 Chet Lemon	.05	.02
107A Jamie Moyer ERR	.10	.03
(Scintilating)		
107B Jamie Moyer COR	.50	.15
(Scintillating)		
108 Chuck Crim	.05	.02
109 Dave Valle	.05	.02
110 Walt Weiss	.05	.02
111 Larry Sheets	.05	.02
112 Don Robinson	.05	.02
113 Danny Heep	.05	.02
114 Carmelo Martinez	.05	.02
115 Dave Gallagher	.05	.02
116 Mike LaValliere	.05	.02
117 Bob McClure	.05	.02
118 Rene Gonzales	.05	.02
119 Mark Parent	.05	.02
120 Wally Joyner	.10	.03
121 Mark Gubicza	.05	.02
122 Tony Pena	.05	.02
123 Carmelo Castillo	.05	.02
124 Howard Johnson	.05	.02
125 Steve Sax	.05	.02
126 Tim Belcher	.05	.02
127 Tim Burke	.05	.02
128 Al Newman	.05	.02
129 Dennis Rasmussen	.05	.02
130 Doug Jones	.05	.02
131 Fred Lynn	.05	.02
132 Jeff Hamilton	.05	.02
133 German Gonzalez	.05	.02
134 John Morris	.05	.02
135 Dave Parker	.10	.03
136 Gary Pettis	.05	.02
137 Dennis Boyd	.05	.02
138 Candy Maldonado	.05	.02
139 Rick Cerone	.05	.02
140 George Brett	.60	.18
141 Dave Clark	.05	.02
142 Dickie Thon	.05	.02
143 Junior Ortiz	.05	.02
144 Don August	.05	.02
145 Gary Gaetti	.10	.03
146 Kirt Manwaring	.05	.02
147 Jeff Reed	.05	.02
148 Jose Alvarez	.05	.02
149 Mike Schooler	.05	.02
150 Mark Grace	.15	.04
151 Geronimo Berroa	.05	.02
152 Barry Jones	.05	.02
153 Geno Petralli	.05	.02
154 Jim Deshaies	.05	.02
155 Barry Larkin	.15	.04
156 Alfredo Griffin	.05	.02
157 Tom Henke	.05	.02
158 Mike Jeffcoat	.05	.02
159 Bob Welch	.05	.02
160 Julio Franco	.10	.03
161 Henry Cotto	.05	.02
162 Terry Steinbach	.05	.02
163 Damon Berryhill	.05	.02
164 Tim Crews	.05	.02
165 Tom Browning	.05	.02
166 Fred Manrique	.05	.02
167 Harold Reynolds	.10	.03
168A Ron Hassey ERR	.05	.02
(27 on back)		
168B Ron Hassey COR	.50	.15
(24 on back)		
169 Shawon Dunston	.05	.02
170 Bobby Bonilla	.10	.03
171 Tommy Herr	.05	.02
172 Mike Heath	.05	.02
173 Rich Gedman	.05	.02
174 Bill Ripken	.05	.02
175 Pete O'Brien	.05	.02
176A L.McClendon ERR	.05	.02
Uniform number on back listed as 1		
176B L.McClendon COR	.50	.15
Uniform number on back listed as 10		
177 Brian Holton	.05	.02
178 Jeff Blauser	.05	.02
179 Jim Eisenreich	.05	.02
180 Bert Blyleven	.10	.03
181 Rob Murphy	.05	.02
182 Bill Doran	.05	.02
183 Curt Ford	.05	.02
184 Mike Henneman	.05	.02
185 Eric Davis	.10	.03
186 Lance McCullers	.05	.02
187 Steve Davis	.05	.02
188 Bill Wegman	.05	.02
189 Brian Harper	.05	.02
190 Mike Moore	.05	.02
191 Dale Mohorcic	.05	.02
192 Tim Wallach	.05	.02
193 Keith Hernandez	.10	.03
194 Dave Righetti	.05	.02
195A B.Saberhagen ERR	.10	.03
Joke		
195B B.Saberhagen COR	.50	.15
Joker		
196 Paul Kilgus	.05	.02
197 Bud Black	.05	.02
198 Juan Samuel	.05	.02
199 Kevin Seitzer	.05	.02
200 Darryl Strawberry	.10	.03
201 Dave Stieb	.10	.03
202 Charlie Hough	.10	.03
203 Jack Morris	.10	.03
204 Rance Mulliniks	.05	.02
205 Alvin Davis	.05	.02
206 Jack Howell	.05	.02
207 Ken Patterson	.05	.02
208 Terry Pendleton	.10	.03
209 Craig Lefferts	.05	.02
210 Kevin Brown UER	.10	.03
(First mention of '89 Rangers should be '88)		
211 Dan Petry	.05	.02
212 Dave Leiper	.05	.02
213 Daryl Boston	.05	.02
214 Kevin Hickey	.05	.02
215 Mike Krukow	.05	.02
216 Terry Francona	.10	.03
217 Kirk McCaskill	.05	.02
218 Scott Bailes	.05	.02
219 Bob Forsch	.05	.02
220A Mike Aldrete ERR	.05	.02
(25 on back)		
220B Mike Aldrete COR	.50	.15
(24 on back)		
221 Steve Buechele	.05	.02
222 Jesse Barfield	.05	.02
223 Juan Berenguer	.05	.02
224 Andy McGaffigan	.05	.02
225 Pete Smith	.05	.02
226 Mike Witt	.05	.02
227 Jay Howell	.05	.02
228 Scott Bradley	.05	.02
229 Jerome Walton	.05	.02
230 Greg Swindell	.05	.02
231 Atlee Hammaker	.05	.02
232A Mike Devereaux ERR	.05	.02
(RF on front)		
232B M.Devereaux COR	.50	.15
CF on front		
233 Ken Hill	.10	.03
234 Craig Worthington	.05	.02
235 Scott Terry	.05	.02
236 Brett Butler	.10	.03
237 Doyle Alexander	.05	.02
238 Dave Anderson	.05	.02
239 Bob Milacki	.05	.02
240 Dwight Smith	.05	.02
241 Otis Nixon	.05	.02
242 Pat Tabler	.05	.02
243 Derek Lilliquist	.05	.02
244 Danny Tartabull	.05	.02
245 Wade Boggs	.15	.04
246 Scott Garrelts	.05	.02
(Should say Relief Pitcher on front)		
247 Spike Owen	.05	.02
248 Norm Charlton	.05	.02
249 Gerald Perry	.05	.02
250 Nolan Ryan	1.00	.30
251 Kevin Gross	.05	.02
252 Randy Milligan	.05	.02
253 Mike LaCoss	.05	.02
254 Dave Bergman	.05	.02
255 Tony Gwynn	.30	.09
256 Felix Fermin	.05	.02
257 Greg W. Harris	.05	.02
258 Junior Felix	.05	.02
259 Mark Davis	.05	.02
260 Vince Coleman	.05	.02
261 Paul Gibson	.05	.02
262 Mitch Williams	.05	.02
263 Jeff Russell	.05	.02
264 Omar Vizquel	.25	.07
265 Andre Dawson	.10	.03
266 Storm Davis	.05	.02
267 Guillermo Hernandez	.05	.02
268 Mike Felder	.05	.02
269 Tom Candiotti	.05	.02
270 Bruce Hurst	.05	.02
271 Fred McGriff	.25	.07
272 Glenn Davis	.05	.02
273 John Franco	.10	.03
274 Rich Yett	.05	.02
275 Craig Biggio	.15	.04
276 Gene Larkin	.05	.02
277 Rob Dibble	.10	.03
278 Randy Bush	.05	.02
279 Kevin Bass	.05	.02
280A Bo Jackson ERR	.25	.07
(Watham)		
280B Bo Jackson COR	.75	.23
(Wathan)		
281 Wally Backman	.05	.02
282 Larry Andersen	.05	.02
283 Chris Bosio	.05	.02
284 Juan Agosto	.05	.02
285 Ozzie Smith	.40	.12
286 George Bell	.05	.02
287 Rex Hudler	.05	.02
288 Pat Borders	.05	.02
289 Danny Jackson	.05	.02
290 Carlton Fisk	.15	.04
291 Tracy Jones	.05	.02
292 Allan Anderson	.05	.02
293 Johnny Ray	.05	.02
294 Lee Guetterman	.05	.02
295 Paul O'Neill	.15	.04
296 Carney Lansford	.05	.02
297 Tom Brookens	.05	.02
298 Claudell Washington	.05	.02
299 Hubie Brooks	.05	.02
300 Will Clark	.25	.07
301 Kenny Rogers	.10	.03
302 Darrell Evans	.10	.03
303 Greg Briley	.05	.02
304 Donn Pall	.05	.02
305 Teddy Higuera	.05	.02
306 Dan Pasqua	.05	.02
307 Dave Winfield	.10	.03
308 Dennis Powell	.05	.02
309 Jose DeLeon	.05	.02
310 Roger Clemens UER	.50	.15
(Dominate, should say dominant)		
311 Melido Perez	.05	.02
312 Devon White	.10	.03
313 Dwight Gooden	.10	.03
314 Carlos Martinez	.05	.02
315 Dennis Eckersley	.10	.03
316 Clay Parker UER	.05	.02
(Height 6'11")		
317 Rick Honeycutt	.05	.02
318 Tim Laudner	.05	.02
319 Joe Carter	.10	.03
320 Robin Yount	.40	.12
321 Felix Jose	.05	.02
322 Mickey Tettleton	.05	.02
323 Mike Gallego	.05	.02
324 Edgar Martinez	.15	.04
325 Dave Henderson	.05	.02
326 Chili Davis	.10	.03
327 Steve Balboni	.05	.02
328 Jody Davis	.05	.02
329 Shawn Hillegas	.05	.02
330 Jim Abbott	.15	.04
331 John Dopson	.05	.02
332 Mark Williamson	.05	.02
333 Jeff D. Robinson	.05	.02
334 John Smiley	.05	.02
335 Bobby Thigpen	.05	.02
336 Garry Templeton	.05	.02
337 Marvell Wynne	.05	.02
338A Ken Griffey Sr. ERR	.10	.03
(Uniform number on back listed as 25)		
338B Ken Griffey Sr. COR	.50	.15
(Uniform number on back listed as 30)		
339 Steve Finley	.10	.03
340 Ellis Burks	.15	.04
341 Frank Williams	.05	.02
342 Mike Morgan	.05	.02
343 Kevin Mitchell	.05	.02
344 Joel Youngblood	.05	.02
345 Mike Greenwell	.05	.02
346 Glenn Wilson	.05	.02
347 John Costello	.05	.02

348 Wes Gardner .05 .02
349 Jeff Ballard .05 .02
350 Mark Thurmond UER .05 .02
(ERA is 192,
should be 1.92)
351 Randy Myers .10 .03
352 Shawn Abner .05 .02
353 Jesse Orosco .05 .02
354 Greg Walker .05 .02
355 Pete Harnisch .05 .02
356 Steve Farr .05 .02
357 Dave LaPoint .05 .02
358 Willie Fraser .05 .02
359 Mickey Hatcher .05 .02
360 Rickey Henderson .25 .07
361 Mike Fitzgerald .05 .02
362 Bill Schroeder .05 .02
363 Mark Carreon .05 .02
364 Ron Jones .05 .02
365 Jeff Montgomery .10 .03
366 Bill Krueger .05 .02
367 John Cangelosi .05 .02
368 Jose Gonzalez .05 .02
369 Greg Hibbard RC .10 .03
370 John Smoltz .25 .07
371 Jeff Brantley .05 .02
372 Frank White .10 .03
373 Ed Whitson .05 .02
374 Willie McGee .10 .03
375 Jose Canseco .25 .07
376 Randy Ready .05 .02
377 Don Aase .05 .02
378 Tony Armas .05 .02
379 Steve Bedrosian .05 .02
380 Chuck Finley .10 .03
381 Kent Hrbek .10 .03
382 Jim Gantner .05 .02
383 Mel Hall .05 .02
384 Mike Marshall .05 .02
385 Mark McGwire .60 .18
386 Wayne Tolleson .05 .02
387 Brian Holman .05 .02
388 John Wetteland .25 .07
389 Darren Daulton .10 .03
390 Rob Deer .05 .02
391 John Moses .05 .02
392 Todd Worrell .05 .02
393 Chuck Cary .05 .02
394 Stan Javier .05 .02
395 Willie Randolph .10 .03
396 Bill Buckner .05 .02
397 Robby Thompson .05 .02
398 Mike Scioscia .05 .02
399 Lonnie Smith .05 .02
400 Kirby Puckett .25 .07
401 Mark Langston .05 .02
402 Danny Darwin .05 .02
403 Greg Maddux .40 .12
404 Lloyd Moseby .05 .02
405 Rafael Palmeiro .15 .04
406 Chad Kreuter .05 .02
407 Jimmy Key .10 .03
408 Tim Birtsas .05 .02
409 Tim Raines .10 .03
410 Dave Stewart .10 .03
411 Eric Yelding .05 .02
412 Kent Anderson .05 .02
413 Les Lancaster .05 .02
414 Rick Dempsey .05 .02
415 Randy Johnson .50 .12
416 Gary Carter .10 .03
417 Rolando Roomes .05 .02
418 Dan Schatzeder .05 .02
419 Bryn Smith .05 .02
420 Ruben Sierra .05 .02
421 Steve Jeltz .05 .02
422 Ken Oberkfell .05 .02
423 Sid Bream .05 .02
424 Jim Clancy .05 .02
425 Kelly Gruber .05 .02
426 Rick Leach .05 .02
427 Len Dykstra .10 .03
428 Jeff Pico .05 .02
429 John Cerutti .05 .02
430 David Cone .10 .03
431 Jeff Kunkel .05 .02
432 Luis Aquino .05 .02
433 Ernie Whitt .05 .02
434 Bo Diaz .05 .02
435 Steve Lake .05 .02
436 Pat Perry .05 .02
437 Mike Davis .05 .02
438 Cecilio Guante .05 .02
439 Duane Ward .05 .02
440 Andy Van Slyke .10 .03
441 Gene Nelson .05 .02
442 Luis Polonia .05 .02
443 Kevin Elster .05 .02
444 Keith Moreland .05 .02
445 Roger McDowell .05 .02
446 Ron Darling .05 .02
447 Ernest Riles .05 .02
448 Mookie Wilson .10 .03
449A Billy Spiers ERR .05 .02
(No birth year)
449B Billy Spiers COR .50 .15
(Born in 1966)
450 Rick Sutcliffe .10 .03
451 Nelson Santovenia .05 .02
452 Andy Allanson .05 .02
453 Bob Melvin .05 .02
454 Benito Santiago .10 .03
455 Jose Uribe .05 .02
456 Bill Landrum .05 .02
457 Bobby Witt .05 .02
458 Kevin Romine .05 .02
459 Lee Mazzilli .05 .02
460 Paul Molitor .15 .04
461 Ramon Martinez .05 .02
462 Frank DiPino .05 .02
463 Walt Terrell .05 .02
464 Bob Geren .05 .02
465 Rick Reuschel .05 .02
466 Mark Grant .05 .02
467 John Kruk .10 .03
468 Gregg Jefferies .10 .03
469 R.J. Reynolds .05 .02
470 Harold Baines .10 .03
471 Dennis Lamp .05 .02
472 Tom Gordon .10 .03
473 Terry Puhl .05 .02
474 Curt Wilkerson .05 .02
475 Dan Quisenberry .05 .02
476 Oddibe McDowell .05 .02
477A Zane Smith ERR .05 .02
(Career ERA .393)
477B Zane Smith COR .50 .15
(career ERA 3.93)
478 Franklin Stubbs .05 .02
479 Wallace Johnson .05 .02
480 Jay Tibbs .05 .02
481 Tom Glavine .15 .04
482 Manny Lee .05 .02
483 Joe Hesketh UER .05 .02
Says Rookiess on back,
should say Rookies
484 Mike Bielecki .05 .02
485 Greg Brock .05 .02
486 Pascual Perez .05 .02
487 Kirk Gibson .10 .03
488 Scott Sanderson .05 .02
489 Domingo Ramos .05 .02
490 Kal Daniels .05 .02
491A David Wells ERR .10 .03
(Reverse negative
photo on card back)
491B David Wells COR .50 .15
492 Jerry Reed .05 .02
493 Eric Show .05 .02
494 Mike Pagliarulo .05 .02
495 Ron Robinson .05 .02
496 Brad Komminsk .05 .02
497 Greg Litton .05 .02
498 Chris James .05 .02
499 Luis Quinones .05 .02
500 Frank Viola .05 .02
501 Tim Teufel UER .05 .02
(Twins '85, the s is
lower case, should
be upper case)
502 Terry Leach .05 .02
503 Matt Williams UER .10 .03
(Wearing 10 on front,
listed as 9 on back)
504 Tim Leary .05 .02
505 Doug Drabek .05 .02
506 Mariano Duncan .05 .02
507 Charlie Hayes .05 .02
508 Joey Belle .15 .04
509 Pat Sheridan .05 .02
510 Mackey Sasser .05 .02
511 Jose Rijo .05 .02
512 Mike Smithson .05 .02
513 Gary Ward .05 .02
514 Dion James .05 .02
515 Jim Gott .05 .02
516 Drew Hall .05 .02
517 Doug Bair .05 .02
518 Scott Scudder .05 .02
519 Rick Aguilera .10 .03
520 Rafael Belliard .05 .02
521 Jay Buhner .10 .03
522 Jeff Reardon .10 .03
523 Steve Rosenberg .05 .02
524 Randy Velarde .05 .02
525 Jeff Musselman .05 .02
526 Bill Long .05 .02
527 Gary Wayne .05 .02
528 Dave Johnson (P) .05 .02
529 Ron Kittle .05 .02
530 Erik Hanson UER .05 .02
(5th line on back
says seson, should
say season)
531 Steve Wilson .05 .02
532 Joey Meyer .05 .02
533 Curt Young .05 .02
534 Kelly Downs .05 .02
535 Joe Girardi .15 .04
536 Lance Blankenship .05 .02
537 Greg Mathews .05 .02
538 Donell Nixon .05 .02
539 Mark Knudson .05 .02
540 Jeff Wetherby .05 .02
541 Darrin Jackson .05 .02
542 Terry Mulholland .05 .02
543 Eric Hetzel .05 .02
544 Rick Reed RC .25 .07
545 Dennis Cook .05 .02
546 Mike Jackson .05 .02
547 Brian Fisher .05 .02
548 Gene Harris .05 .02
549 Jeff King .05 .02
550 Dave Dravecky .25 .07
551 Randy Kutcher .05 .02
552 Mark Portugal .05 .02
553 Jim Corsi .05 .02
554 Todd Stottlemyre .10 .03
555 Scott Bankhead .05 .02
556 Ken Dayley .05 .02
557 Rick Wrona .05 .02
558 Sammy Sosa RC 5.00 1.50
559 Keith Miller .05 .02
560 Ken Griffey Jr. .75 .23
561A R.Sandberg HL ERR 8.00 2.40
Position on front
listed as 3B
561B R.Sandberg HL COR .25 .07
562 Billy Hatcher .05 .02
563 Jay Bell .10 .03
564 Jack Daugherty .05 .02
565 Rich Monteleone .05 .02
566 Bo Jackson AS-MVP .10 .03
567 Tony Fossas .05 .02
568 Roy Smith .05 .02
569 Jaime Navarro .05 .02
570 Lance Johnson .05 .02
571 Mike Dyer RC .05 .02
572 Kevin Ritz .05 .02
573 Dave West .05 .02
574 Gary Mielke .05 .02
575 Scott Lusader .05 .02
576 Joe Oliver .05 .02
577 Sandy Alomar Jr. .10 .03
578 Andy Benes UER .10 .03
(Extra comma between
day and year)
579 Tim Jones .05 .02
580 Randy McCament .05 .02
581 Curt Schilling 1.00 .30
582 John Orton RC .10 .03
583A Milt Cuyler ERR RC .10 .03
(998 games)
583B Milt Cuyler RC COR .50 .15
(98 games; the extra 9
was ghosted out and
may still be visible)
584 Eric Anthony RC .10 .03
585 Greg Vaughn .05 .02
586 Deion Sanders .25 .07
587 Jose DeJesus .05 .02
588 Chip Hale .05 .02
589 John Olerud RC .50 .15
590 Steve Olin RC .25 .07
591 Marquis Grissom RC .40 .12
592 Moises Alou RC .75 .23
593 Mark Lemke .05 .02
594 Dean Palmer RC .25 .07
595 Robin Ventura .25 .07
596 Tino Martinez .25 .07
597 Mike Huff .05 .02
598 Scott Hemond RC .10 .03
599 Wally Whitehurst .05 .02
600 Todd Zeile .10 .03
601 Glenallen Hill .05 .02
602 Hal Morris .05 .02
603 Juan Bell .05 .02
604 Bobby Rose .05 .02
605 Matt Merullo .05 .02
606 Kevin Maas RC .25 .07
607 Randy Nosek .05 .02
608A Billy Bates .05 .02
(Text mentions 12
triples in tenth line)
608B Billy Bates .05 .02
(Text has no mention
of triples)
609 Mike Stanton RC .25 .07
610 Mauro Gozzo .05 .02
611 Charles Nagy .05 .02
612 Scott Coolbaugh .05 .02
613 Jose Vizcaino RC .25 .07
614 Greg Smith .05 .02
615 Jeff Huson RC .10 .03
616 Mickey Weston .05 .02
617 John Pawlowski .05 .02
618A Joe Skalski ERR .05 .02
(27 on back)
618B Joe Skalski COR .50 .15
(67 on back)
619 Bernie Williams RC 1.00 .30
620 Shawn Holman .05 .02
621 Gary Eave .05 .02
622 Darrin Fletcher UER .10 .03
Elmherst, should be Elmhurst
623 Pat Combs .05 .02
624 Mike Blowers RC .10 .03
625 Kevin Appier .10 .03
626 Pat Austin .05 .02
627 Kelly Mann .05 .02
628 Matt Kinzer .05 .02
629 Chris Hammond RC .10 .03
630 Dean Wilkins .05 .02
631 Larry Walker RC UER 1.00 .30
Uniform number 55 on front
and 33 on back;
Home is Maple Ridge,
not Maple River
632 Blaine Beatty .05 .02
633A Tommy Barrett ERR .05 .02
(29 on back)
633B Tommy Barrett COR .50 .15
(14 on back)
634 Stan Belinda RC .10 .03
635 Mike (Tex) Smith .05 .02
636 Hensley Meulens .05 .02
637 J.Gonzalez RC UER 1.50 .45
Sarasots on back,
should be Sarasota
638 Lenny Webster RC .10 .03
639 Mark Gardner RC .10 .03
640 Tommy Greene RC .10 .03
641 Mike Hartley .05 .02
642 Phil Stephenson .05 .02
643 Kevin Mmahat .05 .02
644 Ed Whited .05 .02
645 Delino DeShields RC .25 .07
646 Kevin Blankenship .05 .02
647 Paul Sorrento RC .25 .07
648 Mike Roesler .05 .02
649 Jason Grimsley RC .10 .03
650 Dave Justice RC .50 .15
651 Scott Cooper RC .10 .03
652 Dave Eiland .05 .02
653 Mike Munoz .05 .02
654 Jeff Fischer .05 .02
655 Terry Jorgensen .05 .02
656 George Canale .05 .02
657 Brian DuBois UER .05 .02
(Misspelled Dubois
on card)
658 Carlos Quintana .05 .02
659 Luis de los Santos .05 .02
660 Jerald Clark .05 .02
661 Donald Harris DC .05 .02
662 Paul Coleman DC RC .10 .03
663 Frank Thomas DC RC 2.00 .60
664 Brent Mayne DC RC .25 .07
665 Eddie Zosky DC RC .10 .03
666 Steve Hosey DC RC .10 .03
667 Scott Bryant DC .10 .03
668 Tom Goodwin DC RC .25 .07
669 Cal Eldred DC RC .25 .07
670 E.Cunningham DC RC .10 .03
671 Alan Zinter DC RC .10 .03
672 C.Knoblauch DC RC .40 .12
673 Kyle Abbott DC .05 .02
674 Roger Salkeld DC RC .05 .02
675 M.Vaughn DC RC .50 .15
676 Keith (Kiki) Jones DC .05 .02
677 Tyler Houston DC RC .25 .07
678 Jeff Jackson DC RC .05 .02
679 Greg Gohr DC RC .10 .03
680 Ben McDonald DC RC .25 .07
681 Greg Blosser DC RC .10 .03
682 W.Greene RC DC UER .25 .07
Name spelled as Green
683A W.Boggs DT ERR .10 .03
Text says 215 hits in
'89, should be 205
683B W.Boggs DT COR .50 .15
Text says 205 hits in '89
684 Will Clark DT .10 .03
685 Tony Gwynn DT UER .15 .04
(Text reads battling
instead of batting)
686 Rickey Henderson DT .15 .04
687 Bo Jackson DT .10 .03
688 Mark Langston DT .05 .02
689 Barry Larkin DT .10 .03
690 Kirby Puckett DT .15 .04
691 Ryne Sandberg DT .25 .07
692 Mike Scott DT .05 .02
693A Terry Steinbach DT .05 .02
ERR (cathers)
693B Terry Steinbach DT .05 .02
COR (catchers)
694 Bobby Thigpen DT .05 .02
695 Mitch Williams DT .05 .02
696 Nolan Ryan HL .40 .12
697 Bo Jackson FB/BB .50 .15
698 Rickey Henderson .15 .04
ALCS-MVP
699 Will Clark .10 .03
NLCS-MVP
700 Dave Stewart .10 .03
Mike Moore WS
701 Lights Out .25 .07
702 Carney Lansford .15 .04
Rickey Henderson
Jose Canseco
Dave Henderson WS
703 WS Game 4/Wrap-up .05 .02
704 Wade Boggs HL .10 .03

1990 Score Rookie Dream Team

A ten-card set of Dream Team Rookies was inserted only into hobby factory sets.These standard size cards carry a B prefix on the card number and include a player at each position plus a commemorative card honoring the late Baseball Commissioner A. Bartlett Giamatti.

	Nm-Mt	Ex-Mt
COMPLETE SET (10)	4.00	1.20
B1 A.Bartlett Giamatti COMM MEM	1.00	.30
B2 Pat Combs	.20	.06
B3 Todd Zeile	.40	.12
B4 Luis de los Santos	.20	.06
B5 Mark Lemke	.20	.06
B6 Robin Ventura	1.00	.30
B7 Jeff Huson	.40	.12
B8 Greg Vaughn	.20	.06
B9 Marquis Grissom	1.50	.45
B10 Eric Anthony	.40	.12

1990 Score Rookie/Traded

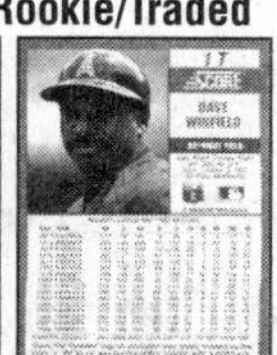

The standard-size 110-card 1990 Score Rookie and Traded set marked the third consecutive year Score had issued an end of the year set to note trades and give rookies early cards. The set was issued through hobby accounts and only in factory set form. The first 66 cards are traded players while the last 44 cards are rookie cards. Hockey star Eric Lindros is included in this set. Rookie Cards in the set include Derek Bell, Todd Hundley and Ray Lankford.

	Nm-Mt	Ex-Mt
COMP.FACT.SET (110)	3.00	.90
1T Dave Winfield	.10	.03
2T Kevin Bass	.05	.02
3T Nick Esasky	.05	.02
4T Mitch Webster	.05	.02
5T Pascual Perez	.05	.02
6T Gary Pettis	.05	.02
7T Tony Pena	.05	.02
8T Candy Maldonado	.05	.02
9T Cecil Fielder	.10	.03
10T Carmelo Martinez	.05	.02
11T Mark Langston	.10	.03
12T Dave Parker	.10	.03
13T Don Slaught	.05	.02
14T Tony Phillips	.05	.02
15T John Franco	.10	.03
16T Randy Myers	.10	.03
17T Jeff Reardon	.10	.03
18T Sandy Alomar Jr.	.10	.03
19T Joe Carter	.10	.03
20T Fred Lynn	.05	.02
21T Storm Davis	.05	.02
22T Craig Lefferts	.05	.02
23T Pete O'Brien	.05	.02
24T Dennis Boyd	.05	.02
25T Lloyd Moseby	.05	.02
26T Mark Davis	.05	.02
27T Tim Leary	.05	.02
28T Gerald Perry	.05	.02
29T Don Aase	.05	.02
30T Ernie Whitt	.05	.02
31T Dale Murphy	.25	.07
32T Alejandro Pena	.05	.02
33T Juan Samuel	.05	.02
34T Hubie Brooks	.05	.02
35T Gary Carter	.10	.03
36T Jim Presley	.05	.02
37T Wally Backman	.05	.02
38T Matt Nokes	.05	.02
39T Dan Petry	.05	.02
40T Franklin Stubbs	.05	.02
41T Jeff Huson	.05	.02
42T Billy Hatcher	.05	.02
43T Terry Leach	.05	.02
44T Phil Bradley	.05	.02
45T Claudell Washington	.05	.02
46T Luis Polonia	.05	.02
47T Daryl Boston	.05	.02
48T Lee Smith	.10	.03
49T Tom Brunansky	.05	.02
50T Mike Witt	.05	.02
51T Willie Randolph	.10	.03
52T Stan Javier	.05	.02
53T Brad Komminsk	.05	.02
54T John Candelaria	.05	.02
55T Bryn Smith	.05	.02
56T Glenn Braggs	.05	.02
57T Keith Hernandez	.10	.03
58T Ken Oberkfell	.05	.02
59T Steve Jeltz	.05	.02
60T Chris James	.05	.02
61T Scott Sanderson	.05	.02
62T Bill Long	.05	.02
63T Rick Cerone	.05	.02
64T Scott Bailes	.05	.02
65T Larry Sheets	.05	.02
66T Junior Ortiz	.05	.02
67T Francisco Cabrera	.05	.02
68T Gary DiSarcina RC	.25	.07
69T Greg Olson	.05	.02
70T Beau Allred RC	.05	.02
71T Oscar Azocar	.05	.02
72T Kent Mercker RC	.25	.07
73T John Burkett	.05	.02
74T Carlos Baerga RC	.25	.07
75T Dave Hollins RC	.25	.07
76T Todd Hundley RC	.25	.07
77T Rick Parker	.05	.02
78T Steve Cummings RC	.05	.02
79T Bill Sampen	.05	.02
80T Jerry Kutzler	.05	.02
81T Derek Bell RC	.25	.07
82T Kevin Tapani RC	.25	.07
83T Jim Leyritz RC	.25	.07
84T Ray Lankford RC	.25	.07
85T Wayne Edwards	.05	.02
86T Frank Thomas	2.00	.60
87T Tim Naehring RC	.10	.03
88T Willie Blair RC	.10	.03
89T Alan Mills RC	.10	.03
90T Scott Radinsky RC	.10	.03
91T Howard Farmer	.05	.02
92T Julio Machado	.05	.02
93T Rafael Valdez	.05	.02
94T Shawn Boskie RC	.10	.03
95T David Segui RC	.25	.07
96T Chris Hoiles RC	.25	.07
97T D.J. Dozier RC	.10	.03
98T Hector Villanueva	.05	.02
99T Eric Gunderson	.05	.02
100T Eric Lindros	1.00	.30
101T Dave Otto	.05	.02
102T Dana Kiecker	.05	.02
103T Tim Drummond	.05	.02
104T Mickey Pina	.05	.02
105T Craig Grebeck RC	.10	.03
106T Bernard Gilkey RC	.25	.07
107T Tim Layana	.05	.02
108T Scott Chiamparino	.05	.02
109T Steve Avery	.05	.02
110T Terry Shumpert	.05	.02

1990 Score Rising Stars

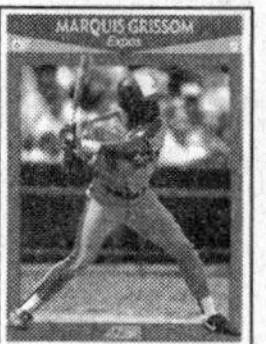

The 1990 Score Rising Stars set contains 100 standard size cards. The fronts are green, blue and white. The vertically oriented backs feature a large color facial shot and career highlights. The cards were distributed as a set in a blister pack, which also included a full color booklet with more information about each player.

	Nm-Mt	Ex-Mt
COMP.FACT.SET (100)	15.00	4.50
1 Tom Gordon	.25	.07
2 Jerome Walton	.10	.03
3 Ken Griffey Jr.	2.00	.60
4 Dwight Smith	.10	.03
5 Jim Abbott	.40	.12
6 Todd Zeile	.25	.07
7 Donn Pall	.10	.03
8 Rick Reed	.60	.18
9 Joey Belle	.60	.18
10 Gregg Jefferies	.25	.07
11 Kevin Ritz	.10	.03
12 Charlie Hayes	.10	.03
13 Kevin Appier	.25	.07
14 Jeff Huson	.10	.03
15 Gary Wayne	.10	.03
16 Eric Yelding	.10	.03
17 Clay Parker	.10	.03
18 Junior Felix	.10	.03
19 Derek Lilliquist	.10	.03
20 Gary Sheffield	.60	.18
21 Craig Worthington	.10	.03
22 Jeff Brantley	.10	.03
23 Eric Hetzel	.10	.03
24 Greg W.Harris	.10	.03
25 John Wetteland	.60	.18
26 Joe Oliver	.10	.03
27 Kevin Maas	.25	.07
28 Kevin Brown	.25	.07
29 Mike Stanton	.10	.03

30 Greg Vaughn .10 .03
31 Ron Jones .10 .03
32 Gregg Olson .25 .07
33 Joe Girardi .40 .12
34 Ken Hill .25 .07
35 Sammy Sosa 8.00 2.40
36 Geronimo Berroa .10 .03
37 Omar Vizquel .60 .18
38 Dean Palmer .60 .18
39 John Olerud 1.00 .30
40 Deion Sanders .60 .18
41 Randy Kramer .10 .03
42 Scott Lusader .10 .03
43 Dave Johnson (P) .10 .03
44 Jeff Wetherby .10 .03
45 Eric Anthony .10 .03
46 Kenny Rogers .25 .07
47 Matt Winters .10 .03
48 Mauro Gozzo .10 .03
49 Carlos Quintana .10 .03
50 Bob Geren .10 .03
51 Chad Kreuter .10 .03
52 Randy Johnson 1.25 .30
53 Hensley Meulens .10 .03
54 Gene Harris .10 .03
55 Bill Spiers .10 .03
56 Kelly Mann .10 .03
57 Tom McCarthy .10 .03
58 Steve Finley .25 .07
59 Ramon Martinez .10 .03
60 Greg Briley .10 .03
61 Jack Daugherty .10 .03
62 Tim Jones .10 .03
63 Doug Strange .10 .03
64 John Orton .10 .03
65 Scott Scudder .10 .03
66 Mark Gardner .10 .03
67 Mark Carreon .10 .03
68 Bob Milacki .10 .03
69 Andy Benes .25 .07
70 Carlos Martinez .10 .03
71 Jeff King .10 .03
72 Brad Arnsberg .10 .03
73 Rick Wrona .10 .03
74 Cris Carpenter .10 .03
75 Dennis Cook .10 .03
76 Pete Harnisch .10 .03
77 Greg Hibbard .10 .03
78 Ed Whited .10 .03
79 Scott Coolbaugh .10 .03
80 Billy Bates .10 .03
81 German Gonzalez .10 .03
82 Lance Blankenship .10 .03
83 Lenny Harris .10 .03
84 Milt Cuyler .10 .03
85 Erik Hanson .10 .03
86 Kent Anderson .10 .03
87 Hal Morris .10 .03
88 Mike Brumley .10 .03
89 Ken Patterson .10 .03
90 Mike Devereaux .10 .03
91 Greg Litton .10 .03
92 Rolando Roomes .10 .03
93 Ben McDonald .10 .03
94 Curt Schilling 2.00 .60
95 Jose DeJesus .10 .03
96 Robin Ventura .60 .18
97 Steve Searcy .10 .03
98 Chip Hale .10 .03
99 Marquis Grissom .60 .18
100 Luis de los Santos .10 .03

1990 Score Young Superstars I

1990 Score Young Superstars I are glossy full color cards featuring 42 standard-size cards of popular young players. The first series was issued with 1990 Score baseball rack packs while the second series was available only via a mailaway from the company.

Nm-Mt Ex-Mt
COMPLETE SET (42) 10.00 3.00
1 Bo Jackson 1.25 .35
2 Dwight Smith .25 .07
3 Albert Belle 1.25 .35
4 Gregg Olson .50 .15
5 Jim Abbott .75 .23
6 Felix Fermin .25 .07
7 Brian Holman .25 .07
8 Clay Parker .25 .07
9 Junior Felix .25 .07
10 Joe Oliver .25 .07
11 Steve Finley .50 .15
12 Greg Briley .25 .07
13 Greg Vaughn .25 .07
14 Bill Spiers .25 .07
15 Eric Yelding .25 .07
16 Jose Gonzalez .25 .07
17 Mark Carreon .25 .07
18 Greg W. Harris .25 .07
19 Felix Jose .25 .07
20 Bob Milacki .25 .07
21 Kenny Rogers .50 .15
22 Rolando Roomes .25 .07
23 Bip Roberts .25 .07
24 Jeff Brantley .25 .07
25 Jeff Ballard .25 .07
26 John Dopson .25 .07
27 Ken Patterson .25 .07
28 Omar Vizquel 1.25 .35
29 Kevin Brown .50 .15
30 Derek Lilliquist .25 .07
31 David Wells .50 .15
32 Ken Hill .50 .15
33 Greg Litton .25 .07
34 Rob Ducey .25 .07
35 Carlos Martinez .25 .07
36 John Smoltz 1.25 .35
37 Lenny Harris .25 .07
38 Charlie Hayes .25 .07
39 Tommy Gregg .25 .07
40 John Wetteland 1.25 .35
41 Jeff Huson .25 .07
42 Eric Anthony .25 .07

1990 Score Young Superstars II

1990 Score Young Superstars II are glossy full color cards featuring 42 standard-size cards of popular young players. Whereas the first series was issued with 1990 Score baseball rack packs, this second series was available only via a mailaway from the company.

Nm-Mt Ex-Mt
COMP.FACT.SET (42) 25.00 7.50
1 Todd Zeile .50 .15
2 Ben McDonald .25 .07
3 Delino DeShields 1.50 .45
4 Pat Combs .25 .07
5 John Olerud 3.00 .90
6 Marquis Grissom 1.50 .45
7 Mike Stanton .25 .07
8 Robin Ventura 1.50 .45
9 Larry Walker 4.00 1.20
10 Dante Bichette .50 .15
11 Jack Armstrong .25 .07
12 Jay Bell .50 .15
13 Andy Benes .50 .15
14 Joey Cora .50 .15
15 Rob Dibble .50 .15
16 Jeff King .25 .07
17 Jeff Hamilton .25 .07
18 Erik Hanson .25 .07
19 Pete Harnisch .25 .07
20 Greg Hibbard .25 .07
21 Stan Javier .25 .07
22 Mark Lemke .25 .07
23 Steve Olin .50 .15
24 Tommy Greene .25 .07
25 Sammy Sosa 15.00 4.50
26 Gary Wayne .25 .07
27 Deion Sanders 1.50 .45
28 Steve Wilson .25 .07
29 Joe Girardi .50 .15
30 John Orton .25 .07
31 Kevin Tapani 1.50 .45
32 Carlos Baerga .50 .15
33 Glenallen Hill .25 .07
34 Mike Blowers .50 .15
35 Dave Hollins .50 .15
36 Lance Blankenship .25 .07
37 Hal Morris .25 .07
38 Lance Johnson .25 .07
39 Chris Gwynn .25 .07
40 Doug Dascenzo .25 .07
41 Jerald Clark .25 .07
42 Carlos Quintana .25 .07

1991 Score

The 1991 Score set contains 893 standard-size cards issued in two separate series of 441 and 452 cards each. This set marks the fourth consecutive year that Score issued a major set but the first time Score issued the set in two series. Cards were distributed in plastic-wrap packs, blister packs and factory sets. The card fronts feature one of four different solid color borders (black, blue, teal and white) framing the full-color photo of the cards. Subsets include Rookie Prospects (331-379), First Draft Picks (380-391, 671-682), AL All-Stars (392-401), Master Blasters (402-406, 689-693), K-Men (407-411, 684-688), Rifleman (412-416, 694-698), NL All-Stars (661-670), No-Hitters (699-707), Franchise (849-874), Award Winners (875-881) and Dream Team (882-893). An American Flag card (737) was issued to honor the American soldiers involved in Desert Storm. Rookie Cards in the set include Carl Everett, Jeff Conine, Chipper Jones, Mike Mussina and Rondell White. There are a number of pitchers whose card backs show Innings Pitched totals which do not equal the added year-by-year total; the following card numbers were affected, 4, 24, 29, 30, 51, 81, 109, 111, 118, 141, 150, 156, 177, 204, 218, 232, 235, 255, 287, 289, 311, and 328.

Nm-Mt Ex-Mt
COMPLETE SET (893) 20.00 6.00
COMP.FACT.SET (900) 25.00 7.50
1 Jose Canseco .25 .07
2 Ken Griffey Jr. .50 .15
3 Ryne Sandberg .40 .12
4 Nolan Ryan 1.00 .30
5 Bo Jackson .25 .07
6 Bret Saberhagen UER .05 .02
(In bio, missed misspelled as mised)
7 Will Clark .25 .07
8 Ellis Burks .10 .03
9 Joe Carter .10 .03
10 Rickey Henderson .25 .07
11 Ozzie Guillen .05 .02
12 Wade Boggs .15 .04
13 Jerome Walton .05 .02
14 John Franco .10 .03
15 Ricky Jordan UER .05 .02
(League misspelled as legue)
16 Wally Backman .05 .02
17 Rob Dibble .10 .03
18 Glenn Braggs .05 .02
19 Cory Snyder .05 .02
20 Kal Daniels .05 .02
21 Mark Langston .05 .02
22 Kevin Gross .05 .02
23 Don Mattingly UER .60 .18
First line, ' is missing from Yankee
24 Dave Righetti .10 .03
25 Roberto Alomar .15 .04
26 Robby Thompson .05 .02
27 Jack McDowell .05 .02
28 Bip Roberts UER .05 .02
(Bio reads playd)
29 Jay Howell .05 .02
30 Dave Stieb UER .05 .02
(17 wins in bio, 18 in stats)
31 Johnny Ray .05 .02
32 Steve Sax .05 .02
33 Terry Mulholland .05 .02
34 Lee Guetterman .05 .02
35 Tim Raines .10 .03
36 Scott Fletcher .05 .02
37 Lance Parrish .10 .03
38 Tony Phillips UER .05 .02
(Born 4/15 should be 4/25)
39 Todd Stottlemyre .05 .02
40 Alan Trammell .10 .03
41 Todd Burns .05 .02
42 Mookie Wilson .10 .03
43 Chris Bosio .05 .02
44 Jeffrey Leonard .05 .02
45 Doug Jones .05 .02
46 Mike Scott UER .05 .02
(In first line, dominate should read dominating)
47 Andy Hawkins .05 .02
48 Harold Reynolds .10 .03
49 Paul Molitor .15 .04
50 John Farrell .05 .02
51 Danny Darwin .05 .02
52 Jeff Blauser .05 .02
53 John Tudor UER .05 .02
(41 wins in '81)
54 Milt Thompson .05 .02
55 Dave Justice .10 .03
56 Greg Olson .05 .02
57 Willie Blair .05 .02
58 Rick Parker .05 .02
59 Shawn Boskie .05 .02
60 Kevin Tapani .05 .02
61 Dave Hollins .05 .02
62 Scott Radinsky .05 .02
63 Francisco Cabrera .05 .02
64 Tim Layana .05 .02
65 Jim Leyritz .05 .02
66 Wayne Edwards .05 .02
67 Lee Stevens .05 .02
68 Bill Sampen UER .05 .02
Fourth line, long is spelled along
69 Craig Grebeck UER .05 .02
Born in Cerritos, not Johnstown
70 John Burkett .05 .02
71 Hector Villanueva .05 .02
72 Oscar Azocar .05 .02
73 Alan Mills .05 .02
74 Carlos Baerga .05 .02
75 Charles Nagy .05 .02
76 Tim Drummond .05 .02
77 Dana Kiecker .05 .02
78 Tom Edens .05 .02
79 Kent Mercker .05 .02
80 Steve Avery .05 .02
81 Lee Smith .10 .03
82 Dave Martinez .05 .02
83 Dave Winfield .10 .03
84 Bill Spiers .05 .02
85 Dan Pasqua .05 .02
86 Randy Milligan .05 .02
87 Tracy Jones .05 .02
88 Greg Myers .05 .02
89 Keith Hernandez .10 .03
90 Todd Benzinger .05 .02
91 Mike Jackson .05 .02
92 Mike Stanley .05 .02
93 Candy Maldonado .05 .02
94 John Kruk UER .10 .03
(No decimal point before 1990 BA)
95 Cal Ripken UER .75 .23
(Genius spelled genuis)
96 Willie Fraser .05 .02
97 Mike Felder .05 .02
98 Bill Landrum .05 .02
99 Chuck Crim .05 .02
100 Chuck Finley .10 .03
101 Kirt Manwaring .05 .02
102 Jaime Navarro .05 .02
103 Dickie Thon .05 .02
104 Brian Downing .05 .02
105 Jim Abbott .15 .04
106 Tom Brookens .05 .02
107 Darryl Hamilton UER .05 .02
(Bio info is for Jeff Hamilton)
108 Bryan Harvey .05 .02
109 Greg A. Harris UER .05 .02
Shown pitching lefty, bio says righty
110 Greg Swindell .05 .02
111 Juan Berenguer .05 .02
112 Mike Heath .05 .02
113 Scott Bradley .05 .02
114 Jack Morris .10 .03
115 Barry Jones .05 .02
116 Kevin Romine .05 .02
117 Garry Templeton .05 .02
118 Scott Sanderson .05 .02
119 Roberto Kelly .05 .02
120 George Brett .60 .18
121 Oddibe McDowell .05 .02
122 Jim Acker .05 .02
123 Bill Swift UER .05 .02
(Born 12/27/61, should be 10/27)
124 Eric King .05 .02
125 Jay Buhner .10 .03
126 Matt Young .05 .02
127 Alvaro Espinoza .05 .02
128 Greg Hibbard .05 .02
129 Jeff M. Robinson .05 .02
130 Mike Greenwell .05 .02
131 Dion James .05 .02
132 Donn Pall UER .05 .02
(1988 ERA in stats 0.00)
133 Lloyd Moseby .05 .02
134 Randy Velarde .05 .02
135 Allan Anderson .05 .02
136 Mark Davis .05 .02
137 Eric Davis .10 .03
138 Phil Stephenson .05 .02
139 Felix Fermin .05 .02
140 Pedro Guerrero .10 .03
141 Charlie Hough .10 .03
142 Mike Henneman .05 .02
143 Jeff Montgomery .05 .02
144 Lenny Harris .05 .02
145 Bruce Hurst .05 .02
146 Eric Anthony .05 .02
147 Paul Assenmacher .05 .02
148 Jesse Barfield .05 .02
149 Carlos Quintana .05 .02
150 Dave Stewart .10 .03
151 Roy Smith .05 .02
152 Paul Gibson .05 .02
153 Mickey Hatcher .05 .02
154 Jim Eisenreich .05 .02
155 Kenny Rogers .10 .03
156 Dave Schmidt .05 .02
157 Lance Johnson .05 .02
158 Dave West .05 .02
159 Steve Balboni .05 .02
160 Jeff Brantley .05 .02
161 Craig Biggio .15 .04
162 Brook Jacoby .05 .02
163 Dan Gladden .05 .02
164 Jeff Reardon UER .10 .03
(Total IP shown as 943.2, should be 943.1)
165 Mark Carreon .05 .02
166 Mel Hall .05 .02
167 Gary Mielke .05 .02
168 Cecil Fielder .10 .03
169 Darrin Jackson .05 .02
170 Rick Aguilera .10 .03
171 Walt Weiss .05 .02
172 Steve Farr .05 .02
173 Jody Reed .05 .02
174 Mike Jeffcoat .05 .02
175 Mark Grace .15 .04
176 Larry Sheets .05 .02
177 Bill Gullickson .05 .02
178 Chris Gwynn .05 .02
179 Melido Perez .05 .02
180 Sid Fernandez UER .05 .02
(779 runs in 1990)
181 Tim Burke .05 .02
182 Gary Pettis .05 .02
183 Rob Murphy .05 .02
184 Craig Lefferts .05 .02
185 Howard Johnson .05 .02
186 Ken Caminiti .10 .03
187 Tim Belcher .05 .02
188 Greg Cadaret .05 .02
189 Matt Williams .10 .03
190 Dave Magadan .05 .02
191 Geno Petralli .05 .02
192 Jeff D. Robinson .05 .02
193 Jim Deshaies .05 .02
194 Willie Randolph .10 .03
195 George Bell .05 .02
196 Hubie Brooks .05 .02
197 Tom Gordon .05 .02
198 Mike Fitzgerald .05 .02
199 Mike Pagliarulo .05 .02
200 Kirby Puckett .25 .07
201 Shawon Dunston .05 .02
202 Dennis Boyd .05 .02
203 Junior Felix UER .05 .02
(Text has him in NL)
204 Alejandro Pena .05 .02
205 Pete Smith .05 .02
206 Tom Glavine UER .15 .04
(Lefty spelled leftie)
207 Luis Salazar .05 .02
208 John Smoltz .15 .04
209 Doug Dascenzo .05 .02
210 Tim Wallach .05 .02
211 Greg Gagne .05 .02
212 Mark Gubicza .05 .02
213 Mark Parent .05 .02
214 Ken Oberkfell .05 .02
215 Gary Carter .10 .03
216 Rafael Palmeiro .15 .04
217 Tom Niedenfuer .05 .02
218 Dave LaPoint .05 .02
219 Jeff Treadway .05 .02
220 Mitch Williams UER .05 .02
('89 ERA shown as 2.76, should be 2.64)
221 Jose DeLeon .05 .02
222 Mike LaValliere .05 .02
223 Darrel Akerfelds .05 .02
224A Kent Anderson ERR .10 .03
(First line& flachy should read flashy)
224B Kent Anderson COR .10 .03
(Corrected in factory sets)
225 Dwight Evans .10 .03
226 Gary Redus .05 .02
227 Paul O'Neill .15 .04
228 Marty Barrett .05 .02
229 Tom Browning .05 .02
230 Terry Pendleton .10 .03
231 Jack Armstrong .05 .02
232 Mike Boddicker .05 .02
233 Neal Heaton .05 .02
234 Marquis Grissom .10 .03
235 Bert Blyleven .10 .03
236 Curt Young .05 .02
237 Don Carman .05 .02
238 Charlie Hayes .05 .02
239 Mark Knudson .05 .02
240 Todd Zeile .05 .02
241 Larry Walker UER .25 .07
(Maple River, should be Maple Ridge)
242 Jerald Clark .05 .02
243 Jeff Ballard .05 .02
244 Jeff King .05 .02
245 Tom Brunansky .05 .02
246 Darren Daulton .10 .03
247 Scott Terry .05 .02
248 Rob Deer .05 .02
249 Brady Anderson UER .10 .03
(1990 Hagerstown 1 hit, should say 13 hits)
250 Len Dykstra .10 .03
251 Greg W. Harris .05 .02
252 Mike Hartley .05 .02
253 Joey Cora .05 .02
254 Ivan Calderon .05 .02
255 Ted Power .05 .02
256 Sammy Sosa .50 .15
257 Steve Buechele .05 .02
258 Mike Devereaux UER .05 .02
(No comma between city and state)
259 Brad Komminsk UER .05 .02
(Last text line, Ba should be BA)
260 Ted Higuera .05 .02
261 Shawn Abner .05 .02
262 Dave Valle .05 .02
263 Jeff Huson .05 .02
264 Edgar Martinez .15 .04
265 Carlton Fisk .15 .04
266 Steve Finley .10 .03
267 John Wetteland .10 .03
268 Kevin Appier .10 .03
269 Steve Lyons .05 .02
270 Mickey Tettleton .05 .02
271 Luis Rivera .05 .02
272 Steve Jeltz .05 .02
273 R.J. Reynolds .05 .02
274 Carlos Martinez .05 .02
275 Dan Plesac .05 .02
276 Mike Morgan UER .05 .02
Total IP shown as 1149.1, should be 1149
277 Jeff Russell .05 .02
278 Pete Incaviglia .05 .02
279 Kevin Seitzer UER .05 .02
Bio has 200 hits twice and .300 four times, should be once and three times
280 Bobby Thigpen .05 .02
281 Stan Javier UER .05 .02
(Born 1/9, should say 9/1)
282 Henry Cotto .05 .02
283 Gary Wayne .05 .02
284 Shane Mack .05 .02
285 Brian Holman .05 .02
286 Gerald Perry .05 .02
287 Steve Crawford .05 .02
288 Nelson Liriano .05 .02
289 Don Aase .05 .02
290 Randy Johnson .30 .09
291 Harold Baines .10 .03
292 Kent Hrbek .10 .03
293A Les Lancaster ERR .05 .02
(No comma between Dallas and Texas)
293B Les Lancaster COR .05 .02
(Corrected in factory sets)
294 Jeff Musselman .05 .02
295 Kurt Stillwell .05 .02
296 Stan Belinda .05 .02
297 Lou Whitaker .10 .03
298 Glenn Wilson .05 .02
299 Omar Vizquel UER .15 .04
Born 5/15, should be 4/24, there is a decimal before GP total for '90
300 Ramon Martinez .05 .02
301 Dwight Smith .05 .02
302 Tim Crews .05 .02
303 Lance Blankenship .05 .02
304 Sid Bream .05 .02
305 Rafael Ramirez .05 .02
306 Steve Wilson .05 .02
307 Mackey Sasser .05 .02
308 Franklin Stubbs .05 .02
309 Jack Daugherty UER .05 .02
(Born 6/3/60, should say July)
310 Eddie Murray .25 .07
311 Bob Welch .05 .02
312 Brian Harper .05 .02
313 Lance McCullers .05 .02
314 Dave Smith .05 .02
315 Bobby Bonilla .10 .03
316 Jerry Don Gleaton .05 .02
317 Greg Maddux .40 .12
318 Keith Miller .05 .02
319 Mark Portugal .05 .02
320 Robin Ventura .10 .03
321 Bob Ojeda .05 .02
322 Mike Harkey .05 .02
323 Jay Bell .10 .03
324 Mark McGwire .60 .18
325 Gary Gaetti .10 .03
326 Jeff Pico .05 .02
327 Kevin McReynolds .05 .02
328 Frank Tanana .05 .02
329 Eric Yelding UER .05 .02
(Listed as 6'3" should be 5'11")
330 Barry Bonds .60 .18
331 Brian McRae RC UER .25 .07
(No comma between city and state)
332 Pedro Munoz RC .10 .03

333 Daryl Irvine .05 .02
334 Chris Hoiles .05 .02
335 Thomas Howard .05 .02
336 Jeff Schulz .05 .02
337 Jeff Manto .05 .02
338 Beau Allred .05 .02
339 Mike Bordick RC .40 .12
340 Todd Hundley .05 .02
341 Jim Vatcher UER .05 .02
(Height 6'9",
should be 5'9")
342 Luis Sojo .05 .02
343 Jose Offerman UER .05 .02
(Born 1969, should
say 1968)
344 Pete Coachman .05 .02
345 Mike Benjamin .05 .02
346 Ozzie Canseco .05 .02
347 Tim McIntosh .05 .02
348 Phil Plantier RC .10 .03
349 Terry Shumpert .05 .02
350 Darren Lewis .05 .02
351 David Walsh RC .05 .02
352A Scott Chiamparino .10 .03
ERR
Bats left, should be right
352B Scott Chiamparino .10 .03
COR
corrected in factory sets
353 Julio Valera .05 .02
UER (Progressed mis-
spelled as progessed)
354 Anthony Telford .05 .02
355 Kevin Wickander .05 .02
356 Tim Naehring .05 .02
357 Jim Poole .05 .02
358 Mark Whiten UER .05 .02
Shown hitting lefty, bio says righty
359 Terry Wells .05 .02
360 Rafael Valdez .05 .02
361 Mel Stottlemyre Jr. .05 .02
362 David Segui .05 .02
363 Paul Abbott RC .10 .03
364 Steve Howard .05 .02
365 Karl Rhodes .05 .02
366 Rafael Novoa .05 .02
367 Joe Grahe RC .05 .02
368 Darren Reed .05 .02
369 Jeff McKnight .05 .02
370 Scott Leius .05 .02
371 Mark Dewey .05 .02
372 Mark Lee UER RC .10 .03
(Shown hitting left,
bio says righty,
born in Dakota,
should say North Dakota
373 Rosario Rodriguez UER .05 .02
Shown hitting lefty, bio says righty
374 Chuck McElroy .05 .02
375 Mike Bell .05 .02
376 Mickey Morandini .05 .02
377 Bill Haselman .05 .02
378 Dave Pavlas .05 .02
379 Derrick May .05 .02
380 J.Burnitz FDP RC .50 .15
381 Donald Peters FDP .05 .02
382 Alex Fernandez FDP .05 .02
383 Mike Mussina FDP RC 1.25 .35
384 Dan Smith FDP RC .10 .03
385 L.Dickson FDP RC .10 .03
386 Carl Everett FDP RC .40 .12
387 Tom Nevers FDP RC .10 .03
388 Adam Hyzdu FDP RC .25 .07
389 T.Van Poppel FDP RC .25 .07
390 R.White FDP RC .40 .12
391 M.Newfield FDP RC .10 .03
392 Julio Franco AS .05 .02
393 Wade Boggs AS .10 .03
394 Ozzie Guillen AS .05 .02
395 Cecil Fielder AS .05 .02
396 Ken Griffey Jr. AS .25 .07
397 Rickey Henderson AS .15 .04
398 Jose Canseco AS .10 .03
399 Roger Clemens AS .25 .07
400 Sandy Alomar Jr. AS .05 .02
401 Bobby Thigpen AS .05 .02
402 Bobby Bonilla MB .05 .02
403 Eric Davis MB .05 .02
404 Fred McGriff MB .10 .03
405 Glenn Davis MB .05 .02
406 Kevin Mitchell MB .05 .02
407 Rob Dibble KM .05 .02
408 Ramon Martinez KM .05 .02
409 David Cone KM .05 .02
410 Bobby Witt KM .05 .02
411 Mark Langston KM .05 .02
412 Bo Jackson RIF .10 .03
413 Shawon Dunston RIF .05 .02
UER
In the baseball, should say in baseball
414 Jesse Barfield RIF .05 .02
415 Ken Caminiti RIF .05 .02
416 Benito Santiago RIF .05 .02
417 Nolan Ryan HL .50 .15
418 B.Thigpen HL UER .05 .02
Back refers to Hal
McRae Jr., should
say Brian McRae
419 Ramon Martinez HL .05 .02
420 Bo Jackson HL .10 .03
421 Carlton Fisk HL .10 .03
422 Jimmy Key .10 .03
423 Junior Noboa .05 .02
424 Al Newman .05 .02
425 Pat Borders .05 .02
426 Von Hayes .05 .02
427 Tim Teufel .05 .02
428 Eric Plunk UER .05 .02
Text says Eric's had, no apostrophe
needed
429 John Moses .05 .02
430 Mike Witt .05 .02
431 Otis Nixon .05 .02
432 Tony Fernandez .05 .02
433 Rance Mulliniks .05 .02
434 Dan Petry .05 .02
435 Bob Geren .05 .02
436 Steve Frey .05 .02
437 Jamie Moyer .10 .03
438 Junior Ortiz .05 .02
439 Tom O'Malley .05 .02
440 Pat Combs .05 .02
441 Jose Canseco DT .25 .07
442 Alfredo Griffin .05 .02
443 Andres Galarraga .10 .03
444 Bryn Smith .05 .02
445 Andre Dawson .10 .03
446 Juan Samuel .05 .02
447 Mike Aldrete .05 .02
448 Ron Gant .10 .03
449 Fernando Valenzuela .10 .03
450 Vince Coleman UER .05 .02
Should say topped
majors in steals four
times, not three times
451 Kevin Mitchell .05 .02
452 Spike Owen .05 .02
453 Mike Bielecki .05 .02
454 Dennis Martinez .10 .03
455 Brett Butler .10 .03
456 Ron Darling .05 .02
457 Dennis Rasmussen .05 .02
458 Ken Howell .05 .02
459 Steve Bedrosian .05 .02
460 Frank Viola .10 .03
461 Jose Lind .05 .02
462 Chris Sabo .05 .02
463 Dante Bichette .10 .03
464 Rick Mahler .05 .02
465 John Smiley .05 .02
466 Devon White .10 .03
467 John Orton .05 .02
468 Mike Stanton .05 .02
469 Billy Hatcher .05 .02
470 Wally Joyner .10 .03
471 Gene Larkin .05 .02
472 Doug Drabek .05 .02
473 Gary Sheffield .10 .03
474 David Wells .05 .02
475 Andy Van Slyke .10 .03
476 Mike Gallego .05 .02
477 B.J. Surhoff .10 .03
478 Gene Nelson .05 .02
479 Mariano Duncan .05 .02
480 Fred McGriff .15 .04
481 Jerry Browne .05 .02
482 Alvin Davis .05 .02
483 Bill Wegman .05 .02
484 Dave Parker .10 .03
485 Dennis Eckersley .10 .03
486 Erik Hanson UER .05 .02
(Basketball misspelled
as baseketball)
487 Bill Ripken .05 .02
488 Tom Candiotti .05 .02
489 Mike Schooler .05 .02
490 Gregg Olson .05 .02
491 Chris James .05 .02
492 Pete Harnisch .05 .02
493 Julio Franco .10 .03
494 Greg Briley .05 .02
495 Ruben Sierra .05 .02
496 Steve Olin .05 .02
497 Mike Fetters .05 .02
498 Mark Williamson .05 .02
499 Bob Tewksbury .05 .02
500 Tony Gwynn .30 .09
501 Randy Myers .05 .02
502 Keith Comstock .05 .02
503 C.Worthington UER .05 .02
DeCinces misspelled
DiCinces on back
504 Mark Eichhorn UER .05 .02
Stats incomplete,
doesn't have '89 Braves stint
505 Barry Larkin .15 .04
506 Dave Johnson .05 .02
507 Bobby Witt .05 .02
508 Joe Orsulak .05 .02
509 Pete O'Brien .05 .02
510 Brad Arnsberg .05 .02
511 Storm Davis .05 .02
512 Bob Milacki .05 .02
513 Bill Pecota .05 .02
514 Glenallen Hill .05 .02
515 Danny Tartabull .05 .02
516 Mike Moore .05 .02
517 Ron Robinson UER .05 .02
(577 K's in 1990)
518 Mark Gardner .05 .02
519 Rick Wrona .05 .02
520 Mike Scioscia .05 .02
521 Frank Wills .05 .02
522 Greg Brock .05 .02
523 Jack Clark .10 .03
524 Bruce Ruffin .05 .02
525 Robin Yount .40 .12
526 Tom Foley .05 .02
527 Pat Perry .05 .02
528 Greg Vaughn .05 .02
529 Wally Whitehurst .05 .02
530 Norm Charlton .05 .02
531 Marvell Wynne .05 .02
532 Jim Gantner .05 .02
533 Greg Litton .05 .02
534 Manny Lee .05 .02
535 Scott Bailes .05 .02
536 Charlie Leibrandt .05 .02
537 Roger McDowell .05 .02
538 Andy Benes .05 .02
539 Rick Honeycutt .05 .02
540 Dwight Gooden .10 .03
541 Scott Garrelts .05 .02
542 Dave Clark .05 .02
543 Lonnie Smith .05 .02
544 Rick Reuschel .05 .02
545 Delino DeShields UER .10 .03
(Rockford misspelled
as Rock Ford in '88)
546 Mike Sharperson .05 .02
547 Mike Kingery .05 .02
548 Terry Kennedy .05 .02
549 David Cone .10 .03
550 Orel Hershiser .10 .03
551 Matt Nokes .05 .02
552 Eddie Williams .05 .02
553 Frank DiPino .05 .02
554 Fred Lynn .05 .02
555 Alex Cole .05 .02
556 Terry Leach .05 .02
557 Chet Lemon .05 .02
558 Paul Mirabella .05 .02
559 Bill Long .05 .02
560 Phil Bradley .05 .02
561 Duane Ward .05 .02
562 Dave Bergman .05 .02
563 Eric Show .05 .02
564 Xavier Hernandez .05 .02
565 Jeff Parrett .05 .02
566 Chuck Cary .05 .02
567 Ken Hill .05 .02
568 Bob Welch Hand .05 .02
(Complement should be
compliment) UER
569 John Mitchell .05 .02
570 Travis Fryman .10 .03
571 Derek Lilliquist .05 .02
572 Steve Lake .05 .02
573 John Barfield .05 .02
574 Randy Bush .05 .02
575 Joe Magrane .05 .02
576 Eddie Diaz .05 .02
577 Casey Candaele .05 .02
578 Jesse Orosco .05 .02
579 Tom Henke .05 .02
580 Rick Cerone UER .05 .02
(Actually his third
go-round with Yankees)
581 Drew Hall .05 .02
582 Tony Castillo .05 .02
583 Jimmy Jones .05 .02
584 Rick Reed .05 .02
585 Joe Girardi .05 .02
586 Jeff Gray .05 .02
587 Luis Polonia .05 .02
588 Joe Klink .05 .02
589 Rex Hudler .05 .02
590 Kirk McCaskill .05 .02
591 Juan Agosto .05 .02
592 Wes Gardner .05 .02
593 Rich Rodriguez .05 .02
594 Mitch Webster .05 .02
595 Kelly Gruber .05 .02
596 Dale Mohorcic .05 .02
597 Willie McGee .10 .03
598 Bill Krueger .05 .02
599 Bob Walk UER .05 .02
Cards says he's 33,
but actually he's 34
600 Kevin Maas .05 .02
601 Danny Jackson .05 .02
602 Craig McMurtry UER .05 .02
(Anonymously misspelled
anonimously)
603 Curtis Wilkerson .05 .02
604 Adam Peterson .05 .02
605 Sam Horn .05 .02
606 Tommy Gregg .05 .02
607 Ken Dayley .05 .02
608 Carmelo Castillo .05 .02
609 John Shelby .05 .02
610 Don Slaught .05 .02
611 Calvin Schiraldi .05 .02
612 Dennis Lamp .05 .02
613 Andres Thomas .05 .02
614 Jose Gonzalez .05 .02
615 Randy Ready .05 .02
616 Kevin Bass .05 .02
617 Mike Marshall .05 .02
618 Daryl Boston .05 .02
619 Andy McGaffigan .05 .02
620 Joe Oliver .05 .02
621 Jim Gott .05 .02
622 Jose Oquendo .05 .02
623 Jose DeJesus .05 .02
624 Mike Brumley .05 .02
625 John Olerud .10 .03
626 Ernest Riles .05 .02
627 Gene Harris .05 .02
628 Jose Uribe .05 .02
629 Darnell Coles .05 .02
630 Carney Lansford .10 .03
631 Tim Leary .05 .02
632 Tim Hulett .05 .02
633 Kevin Elster .05 .02
634 Tony Fossas .05 .02
635 Francisco Oliveras .05 .02
636 Bob Patterson .05 .02
637 Gary Ward .05 .02
638 Rene Gonzales .05 .02
639 Don Robinson .05 .02
640 Darryl Strawberry .10 .03
641 Dave Anderson .05 .02
642 Scott Scudder .05 .02
643 Reggie Harris UER .05 .02
(Hepatitis misspelled
as hepititis)
644 Dave Henderson .05 .02
645 Ben McDonald .05 .02
646 Bob Kipper .05 .02
647 Hal Morris UER .05 .02
(It's should be its)
648 Tim Birtsas .05 .02
649 Steve Searcy .05 .02
650 Dale Murphy .25 .07
651 Ron Oester .05 .02
652 Mike LaCoss .05 .02
653 Ron Jones .05 .02
654 Kelly Downs .05 .02
655 Roger Clemens .50 .15
656 Herm Winningham .05 .02
657 Trevor Wilson .05 .02
658 Jose Rijo .05 .02
659 Dann Bilardello UER .05 .02
Bio has 13 games, 1 hit,
and 32 AB, stats show 19, 2, and 37
660 Gregg Jefferies .05 .02
661 Doug Drabek AS UER .05 .02
(Through is mis-
spelled though)
662 Randy Myers AS .05 .02
663 Benny Santiago AS .05 .02
664 Will Clark AS .10 .03
665 Ryne Sandberg AS .25 .07
666 Barry Larkin AS UER .10 .03
Line 13, coolly misspelled cooly
667 Matt Williams AS .05 .02
668 Barry Bonds AS .30 .09
669 Eric Davis AS .05 .02
670 Bobby Bonilla AS .05 .02
671 C.Jones FDP RC 4.00 1.20
672 E.Christopherson RC .10 .03
FDP
673 R.Beckett FDP RC .10 .03
674 S.Andrews FDP RC .25 .07
675 Steve Karsay FDP RC .25 .07
676 Aaron Holbert FDP RC .10 .03
677 D.Osborne FDP RC .10 .03
678 Todd Ritchie FDP RC .25 .07
679 Ron Walden FDP RC .10 .03
680 Tim Costo FDP RC .10 .03
681 Dan Wilson FDP RC .25 .07
682 Kurt Miller FDP RC .10 .03
683 M.Lieberthal FDP RC .40 .12
684 Roger Clemens KM .25 .07
685 Dwight Gooden KM .05 .02
686 Nolan Ryan KM .50 .15
687 Frank Viola KM .05 .02
688 Erik Hanson KM .05 .02
689 Matt Williams MB .05 .02
690 J.Canseco MB UER .10 .03
Mammoth misspelled
as monmouth
691 Darryl Strawberry MB .05 .02
692 Bo Jackson MB .10 .03
693 Cecil Fielder MB .05 .02
694 Sandy Alomar Jr. RF .05 .02
695 Cory Snyder RF .05 .02
696 Eric Davis RF .05 .02
697 Ken Griffey Jr. RF .25 .07
698 A.Van Slyke RF UER .05 .02
Line 2, outfielders
does not need
699 Mark Langston NH .05 .02
Mike Witt
700 Randy Johnson NH .15 .04
701 Nolan Ryan NH .50 .15
702 Dave Stewart NH .05 .02
703 F.Valenzuela NH .05 .02
704 Andy Hawkins NH .05 .02
705 Melido Perez NH .05 .02
706 Terry Mulholland NH .05 .02
707 Dave Stieb NH .05 .02
708 Brian Barnes RC .05 .02
709 Bernard Gilkey .05 .02
710 Steve Decker .05 .02
711 Paul Faries .05 .02
712 Paul Marak .05 .02
713 Wes Chamberlain RC .10 .03
714 Kevin Belcher .05 .02
715 Dan Boone UER .05 .02
(IP adds up to 101,
but card has 101.2)
716 Steve Adkins .05 .02
717 Geronimo Pena .05 .02
718 Howard Farmer .05 .02
719 Mark Leonard .05 .02
720 Tom Lampkin .05 .02
721 Mike Gardiner .05 .02
722 Jeff Conine RC .40 .12
723 Efrain Valdez .05 .02
724 Chuck Malone .05 .02
725 Leo Gomez .05 .02
726 Paul McClellan .05 .02
727 Mark Leiter RC .10 .03
728 Rich DeLucia UER .05 .02
(Line 2, all told
is written alltold)
729 Mel Rojas .05 .02
730 Hector Wagner .05 .02
731 Ray Lankford .05 .02
732 Turner Ward RC .10 .03
733 Gerald Alexander .05 .02
734 Scott Anderson .05 .02
735 Tony Perezchica .05 .02
736 Jimmy Kremers .05 .02
737 American Flag .25 .07
(Pray for Peace)
738 Mike York .05 .02
739 Mike Rochford .05 .02
740 Scott Aldred .05 .02
741 Rico Brogna .05 .02
742 Dave Burba RC .25 .07
743 Ray Stephens .05 .02
744 Eric Gunderson .05 .02
745 Troy Afenir .05 .02
746 Jeff Shaw .05 .02
747 Orlando Merced RC .10 .03
748 O.Olivares UER RC .10 .03
Line 9, league is
misspelled legaue
749 Jerry Kutzler .05 .02
750 Mo Vaughn UER .10 .03
(44 SB's in 1990)
751 Matt Stark .05 .02
752 Randy Hennis .05 .02
753 Andujar Cedeno .05 .02
754 Kelvin Torve .05 .02
755 Joe Kraemer .05 .02
756 Phil Clark RC .10 .03
757 Ed Vosberg .05 .02
758 Mike Perez RC .10 .03
759 Scott Lewis .05 .02
760 Steve Chitren .05 .02
761 Ray Young .05 .02
762 Andres Santana .05 .02
763 Rodney McCray .05 .02
764 Sean Berry UER RC .10 .03
(Name misspelled
Barry on card front)
765 Brent Mayne .05 .02
766 Mike Simms .05 .02
767 Glenn Sutko .05 .02
768 Gary DiSarcina .05 .02
769 George Brett HL .25 .07
770 Cecil Fielder HL .05 .02
771 Jim Presley .05 .02
772 John Dopson .05 .02
773 Bo Jackson Breaker .10 .03
774 Brent Knackert UER .05 .02
Born in 1954,
shown throwing righty,
but bio says lefty
775 Bill Doran UER .05 .02
(Reds in NL East)
776 Dick Schofield .05 .02
777 Nelson Santovenia .05 .02
778 Mark Guthrie .05 .02
779 Mark Lemke .05 .02
780 Terry Steinbach .05 .02
781 Tom Bolton .05 .02
782 Randy Tomlin RC .10 .03
783 Jeff Kunkel .05 .02
784 Felix Jose .05 .02
785 Rick Sutcliffe .10 .03
786 John Cerutti .05 .02
787 Jose Vizcaino UER .05 .02
(Offerman, not Opperman)
788 Curt Schilling .25 .07
789 Ed Whitson .05 .02
790 Tony Pena .05 .02
791 John Candelaria .05 .02
792 Carmelo Martinez .05 .02
793 Sandy Alomar Jr. UER .05 .02
(Indian's should
say Indians')
794 Jim Neidlinger .05 .02
795 Barry Larkin WS .10 .03
and Chris Sabo
796 Paul Sorrento .05 .02
797 Tom Pagnozzi .05 .02
798 Tino Martinez .15 .04
799 Scott Ruskin UER .05 .02
(Text says first three
seasons but lists
averages for four)
800 Kirk Gibson .10 .03
801 Walt Terrell .05 .02
802 John Russell .05 .02
803 Chili Davis .10 .03
804 Chris Nabholz .05 .02
805 Juan Gonzalez .15 .04
806 Ron Hassey .05 .02
807 Todd Worrell .05 .02
808 Tommy Greene .05 .02
809 Joel Skinner UER .05 .02
Joel, not Bob, was drafted in 1979
810 Benito Santiago .10 .03
811 Pat Tabler UER .05 .02
Line 3, always misspelled always
812 Scott Erickson UER .05 .02
(Record spelled rcord)
813 Moises Alou .10 .03
814 Dale Sveum .05 .02
815 R.Sandberg MANYR .25 .07
816 Rick Dempsey .05 .02
817 Scott Bankhead .05 .02
818 Jason Grimsley .05 .02
819 Doug Jennings .05 .02
820 Tom Herr .05 .02
821 Rob Ducey .05 .02
822 Luis Quinones .05 .02
823 Greg Minton .05 .02
824 Mark Grant .05 .02
825 Ozzie Smith UER .40 .12
(Shortstop misspelled
shortsop)
826 Dave Eiland .05 .02
827 Danny Heep .05 .02
828 Hensley Meulens .05 .02
829 Charlie O'Brien .05 .02
830 Glenn Davis .05 .02
831 John Marzano UER .05 .02
(International mis-
spelled Internaional)
832 Steve Ontiveros .05 .02
833 Ron Karkovice .05 .02
834 Jerry Goff .05 .02
835 Ken Griffey Sr. .10 .03
836 Kevin Reimer .05 .02
837 Randy Kutcher UER .05 .02
(Infectious mis-
spelled infectous)
838 Mike Blowers .05 .02
839 Mike Macfarlane .05 .02
840 Frank Thomas UER .25 .07
1989 Sarasota stats,
15 games but 188 AB
841 Ken Griffey Jr. .40 .12
Ken Griffey Sr.
842 Jack Howell .05 .02
843 Goose Gozzo .05 .02
844 Gerald Young .05 .02
845 Zane Smith .05 .02
846 Kevin Brown .10 .03
847 Sil Campusano .05 .02
848 Larry Andersen .05 .02
849 Cal Ripken FRAN .40 .12
850 Roger Clemens FRAN .25 .07
851 S.Alomar Jr. FRAN .05 .02
852 Alan Trammell FRAN .10 .03
853 George Brett FRAN .25 .07
854 Robin Yount FRAN .25 .07
855 Kirby Puckett FRAN .15 .04
856 Don Mattingly FRAN .30 .09
857 R.Henderson FRAN .15 .04
858 Ken Griffey Jr. FRAN .25 .07
859 Ruben Sierra FRAN .05 .02
860 John Olerud FRAN .05 .02
861 Dave Justice FRAN .05 .02
862 Ryne Sandberg FRAN .25 .07
863 Eric Davis FRAN .05 .02
864 D.Strawberry FRAN .05 .02
865 Tim Wallach FRAN .05 .02
866 Dwight Gooden FRAN .05 .02
867 Len Dykstra FRAN .05 .02
868 Barry Bonds FRAN .30 .09
869 Todd Zeile FRAN UER .05 .02
(Powerful misspelled
as poweful)
870 Benito Santiago FRAN .05 .02
871 Will Clark FRAN .10 .03
872 Craig Biggio FRAN .10 .03
873 Wally Joyner FRAN .05 .02
874 Frank Thomas FRAN .15 .04
875 R.Henderson MVP .15 .04
876 Barry Bonds MVP .30 .09
877 Bob Welch CY .05 .02
878 Doug Drabek CY .05 .02
879 S.Alomar Jr. ROY .05 .02
880 Dave Justice ROY .05 .02
881 Damon Berryhill .05 .02
882 Frank Viola DT .05 .02
883 Dave Stewart DT .05 .02
884 Doug Jones DT .05 .02
885 Randy Myers DT .05 .02
886 Will Clark DT .10 .03
887 Roberto Alomar DT .10 .03
888 Barry Larkin DT .10 .03
889 Wade Boggs DT .15 .04

Card	Nm-Mt	Ex-Mt
890 Rickey Henderson DT	.25	.07
891 Kirby Puckett DT	.15	.04
892 Ken Griffey Jr DT	.50	.15
893 Benny Santiago DT	.10	.03

1991 Score Cooperstown

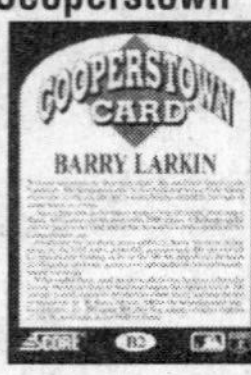

This seven-card standard-size set was available only in complete set form as an insert with 1991 Score factory sets. The card design is not like the regular 1991 Score cards. The card front features a portrait of the player in an oval on a white background. The words "Cooperstown Card" are prominently displayed on the front. The cards are numbered on the back with a B prefix.

	Nm-Mt	Ex-Mt
COMPLETE SET (7)	6.00	1.80
B1 Wade Boggs	.60	.18
B2 Barry Larkin	.60	.18
B3 Ken Griffey Jr.	2.00	.60
B4 Rickey Henderson	1.00	.30
B5 George Brett	2.50	.75
B6 Will Clark	1.00	.30
B7 Nolan Ryan	4.00	1.20

1991 Score Hot Rookies

This ten-card standard-size set was inserted in the one per 1991 Score 100-card blister pack. The front features a color action player photo, with white borders and the words "Hot Rookie" in yellow above the picture. The card background shades from orange to yellow to orange as one moves down the card face. In a horizontal format, the left half of the back has a color head shot, while the right half has career summary.

	Nm-Mt	Ex-Mt
COMPLETE SET (10)	8.00	2.40
1 Dave Justice	1.00	.30
2 Kevin Maas	.50	.15
3 Hal Morris	.50	.15
4 Frank Thomas	2.00	.60
5 Jeff Conine	1.00	.30
6 Sandy Alomar Jr.	.50	.15
7 Ray Lankford	.50	.15
8 Steve Decker	.50	.15
9 Juan Gonzalez	1.00	.30
10 Jose Offerman	.50	.15

1991 Score Mantle

This seven-card standard-size set features Mickey Mantle at various points in his career. The fronts are full-color glossy shots of Mantle while the backs are in a horizontal format with a full-color photo and some narrative information. The cards were randomly inserted in second series packs. 2,500 serial numbered cards were actually signed by Mantle and stamped with certification press. A similar version of this set was also released to dealers and media members on Score's mailing list and was individually to 5,000 numbered on the back. The cards were sent in seven-card packs. The card number and the set serial number appear on the back.

	Nm-Mt	Ex-Mt
COMPLETE SET (7)	100.00	30.00
COMMON MANTLE (1-7)	15.00	4.50
AU Mickey Mantle AU (Autographed with certified signature)	500.00	150.00

1991 Score Rookie/Traded

The 1991 Score Rookie and Traded contains 110 standard-size player cards and was issued exclusively in factory set form along with 10 "World Series II" magic motion trivia cards through hobby dealers. The front design is identical to the regular issue 1991 Score set except for the distinctive mauve borders and T-suffixed numbering. Cards 1T-80T feature traded players, while cards 81T-110T focus on rookies. Rookie Cards in the set include Jeff Bagwell and Ivan Rodriguez.

	Nm-Mt	Ex-Mt
COMP.FACT.SET (110)	5.00	1.50
1T Bo Jackson	.50	.15
2T Mike Flanagan	.10	.03
3T Pete Incaviglia	.10	.03
4T Jack Clark	.25	.07
5T Hubie Brooks	.10	.03
6T Ivan Calderon	.10	.03
7T Glenn Davis	.10	.03
8T Wally Backman	.10	.03
9T Dave Smith	.10	.03
10T Tim Raines	.25	.07
11T Joe Carter	.25	.07
12T Sid Bream	.10	.03
13T George Bell	.10	.03
14T Steve Bedrosian	.10	.03
15T Willie Wilson	.10	.03
16T Darryl Strawberry	.25	.07
17T Danny Jackson	.10	.03
18T Kirk Gibson	.25	.07
19T Willie McGee	.25	.07
20T Junior Felix	.10	.03
21T Steve Farr	.10	.03
22T Pat Tabler	.10	.03
23T Brett Butler	.25	.07
24T Danny Darwin	.10	.03
25T Mickey Tettleton	.10	.03
26T Gary Carter	.25	.07
27T Mitch Williams	.10	.03
28T Candy Maldonado	.10	.03
29T Otis Nixon	.10	.03
30T Brian Downing	.10	.03
31T Tom Candiotti	.10	.03
32T John Candelaria	.10	.03
33T Rob Murphy	.10	.03
34T Deion Sanders	.40	.12
35T Willie Randolph	.25	.07
36T Pete Harnisch	.10	.03
37T Dante Bichette	.25	.07
38T Garry Templeton	.10	.03
39T Gary Gaetti	.25	.07
40T John Cerutti	.10	.03
41T Rick Cerone	.10	.03
42T Mike Pagliarulo	.10	.03
43T Ron Hassey	.10	.03
44T Roberto Alomar	.40	.12
45T Mike Boddicker	.10	.03
46T Bud Black	.10	.03
47T Rob Deer	.10	.03
48T Devon White	.25	.07
49T Luis Sojo	.10	.03
50T Terry Pendleton	.25	.07
51T Kevin Gross	.10	.03
52T Mike Huff	.10	.03
53T Dave Righetti	.25	.07
54T Matt Young	.10	.03
55T Earnest Riles	.10	.03
56T Bill Gullickson	.10	.03
57T Vince Coleman	.10	.03
58T Fred McGriff	.40	.12
59T Franklin Stubbs	.10	.03
60T Eric King	.10	.03
61T Cory Snyder	.10	.03
62T Dwight Evans	.25	.07
63T Gerald Perry	.10	.03
64T Eric Show	.10	.03
65T Shawn Hillegas	.10	.03
66T Tony Fernandez	.10	.03
67T Tim Teufel	.10	.03
68T Mitch Webster	.10	.03
69T Mike Heath	.10	.03
70T Chili Davis	.25	.07
71T Larry Andersen	.10	.03
72T Gary Varsho	.10	.03
73T Juan Berenguer	.10	.03
74T Jack Morris	.25	.07
75T Barry Jones	.10	.03
76T Rafael Belliard	.10	.03
77T Steve Buechele	.10	.03
78T Scott Sanderson	.10	.03
79T Bob Ojeda	.10	.03
80T Curt Schilling	.50	.15
81T Brian Drahman	.10	.03
82T Ivan Rodriguez RC	2.00	.60
83T David Howard	.10	.03
84T H.Slocumb RC	.25	.07
85T Mike Timlin RC	.40	.12
86T Darryl Kile	.25	.07
87T Pete Schourek RC	.10	.03
88T Bruce Walton	.10	.03
89T Al Osuna RC	.10	.03
90T Gary Scott RC	.10	.03
91T Doug Simons	.10	.03
92T Chris Jones RC	.10	.03
93T Chuck Knoblauch	.25	.07
94T Dana Allison RC	.10	.03
95T Erik Pappas	.10	.03
96T Jeff Bagwell RC	1.50	.45
97T K.Dressendorfer RC	.10	.03
98T Freddie Benavides	.10	.03
99T Luis Gonzalez RC	.50	.15
100T Wade Taylor	.10	.03
101T Ed Sprague	.10	.03
102T Bob Scanlan	.10	.03
103T Rick Wilkins RC	.10	.03
104T Chris Donnels	.10	.03
105T Joe Slusarski	.10	.03
106T Mark Lewis	.10	.03
107T Pat Kelly RC	.10	.03
108T John Briscoe	.10	.03
109T Luis Lopez RC	.10	.03
110T Jeff Johnson	.10	.03

1992 Score

The 1992 Score set marked the second year that Score released their set in two different series. The first series contains 442 cards while the second series contains 451 cards. Cards were distributed in plastic wrapped packs, blister packs, jumbo packs and factory sets. Each pack included a special "World Series II" trivia card. Topical subsets include Rookie Prospects (395-424/736-772/814-877), No-Hit Club (425-428/784-787), Highlights (429-430), AL All-Stars (431-440; with color montages displaying

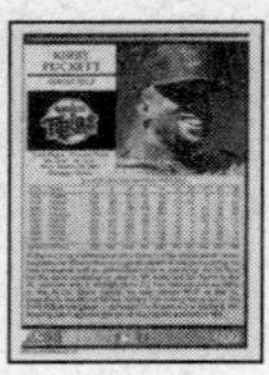

Chris Greco's player caricatures), Dream Team (441-442/883-893), NL All-Stars (773-782), Highlights (783, 795-797), Draft Picks (799-810), and Memorabilia (878-882). All of the Rookie Prospects (736-772) can be found with or without the Rookie Prospect stripe. Rookie Cards in the set include Vinny Castilla and Manny Ramirez. Chuck Knoblauch, 1991 American League Rookie of the Year, autographed 3,000 of his own 1990 Score Draft Pick cards (card number 672) in gold ink, 2,989 were randomly inserted in Series two poly packs, while the other 11 were given away in a sweepstakes. The backs of these Knoblauch autograph cards have special holograms to differentiate them.

	Nm-Mt	Ex-Mt
COMPLETE SET (893)	15.00	4.50
COMP.FACT.SET (910)	20.00	6.00
COMP. SERIES 1 (442)	8.00	2.40
COMP. SERIES 2 (451)	8.00	2.40
1 Ken Griffey Jr.	.40	.12
2 Nolan Ryan	1.00	.30
3 Will Clark	.25	.07
4 Dave Justice	.10	.03
5 Dave Henderson	.05	.02
6 Bret Saberhagen	.10	.03
7 Fred McGriff	.15	.04
8 Erik Hanson	.05	.02
9 Darryl Strawberry	.10	.03
10 Dwight Gooden	.10	.03
11 Juan Gonzalez	.15	.04
12 Mark Langston	.05	.02
13 Lonnie Smith	.05	.02
14 Jeff Montgomery	.05	.02
15 Roberto Alomar	.15	.04
16 Delino DeShields	.05	.02
17 Steve Bedrosian	.05	.02
18 Terry Pendleton	.10	.03
19 Mark Carreon	.05	.02
20 Mark McGwire	.60	.18
21 Roger Clemens	.50	.15
22 Chuck Crim	.05	.02
23 Don Mattingly	.60	.18
24 Dickie Thon	.05	.02
25 Ron Gant	.10	.03
26 Milt Cuyler	.05	.02
27 Mike Macfarlane	.05	.02
28 Dan Gladden	.05	.02
29 Melido Perez	.05	.02
30 Willie Randolph	.10	.03
31 Albert Belle	.10	.03
32 Dave Winfield	.10	.03
33 Jimmy Jones	.05	.02
34 Kevin Gross	.05	.02
35 Andres Galarraga	.10	.03
36 Mike Devereaux	.05	.02
37 Chris Bosio	.05	.02
38 Mike LaValliere	.05	.02
39 Gary Gaetti	.10	.03
40 Felix Jose	.05	.02
41 Alvaro Espinoza	.05	.02
42 Rick Aguilera	.10	.03
43 Mike Gallego	.05	.02
44 Eric Davis	.10	.03
45 George Bell	.05	.02
46 Tom Brunansky	.05	.02
47 Steve Farr	.05	.02
48 Duane Ward	.05	.02
49 David Wells	.10	.03
50 Cecil Fielder	.10	.03
51 Walt Weiss	.05	.02
52 Todd Zeile	.05	.02
53 Doug Jones	.05	.02
54 Bob Walk	.05	.02
55 Rafael Palmeiro	.15	.04
56 Rob Deer	.05	.02
57 Paul O'Neill	.15	.04
58 Jeff Reardon	.10	.03
59 Randy Ready	.05	.02
60 Scott Erickson	.05	.02
61 Paul Molitor	.15	.04
62 Jack McDowell	.05	.02
63 Jim Acker	.05	.02
64 Jay Buhner	.10	.03
65 Travis Fryman	.10	.03
66 Marquis Grissom	.10	.03
67 Mike Harkey	.05	.02
68 Luis Polonia	.05	.02
69 Ken Caminiti	.10	.03
70 Chris Sabo	.05	.02
71 Gregg Olson	.05	.02
72 Carlton Fisk	.15	.04
73 Juan Samuel	.05	.02
74 Todd Stottlemyre	.05	.02
75 Andre Dawson	.10	.03
76 Alvin Davis	.05	.02
77 Bill Doran	.05	.02
78 B.J. Surhoff	.10	.03
79 Kirk McCaskill	.05	.02
80 Dale Murphy	.25	.07
81 Jose DeLeon	.05	.02
82 Alex Fernandez	.05	.02
83 Ivan Calderon	.05	.02
84 Brent Mayne	.05	.02
85 Jody Reed	.05	.02
86 Randy Tomlin	.05	.02
87 Randy Milligan	.05	.02
88 Pascual Perez	.05	.02
89 Hensley Meulens	.05	.02
90 Joe Carter	.10	.03
91 Mike Moore	.05	.02
92 Ozzie Guillen	.05	.02
93 Shawn Hillegas	.05	.02
94 Chili Davis	.10	.03
95 Vince Coleman	.05	.02
96 Jimmy Key	.10	.03
97 Billy Ripken	.05	.02
98 Dave Smith	.05	.02
99 Tom Bolton	.05	.02
100 Barry Larkin	.15	.04
101 Kenny Rogers	.10	.03
102 Mike Boddicker	.05	.02
103 Kevin Elster	.05	.02
104 Ken Hill	.05	.02
105 Charlie Leibrandt	.05	.02
106 Pat Combs	.05	.02
107 Hubie Brooks	.05	.02
108 Julio Franco	.10	.03
109 Vicente Palacios	.05	.02
110 Kal Daniels	.05	.02
111 Bruce Hurst	.05	.02
112 Willie McGee	.10	.03
113 Ted Power	.05	.02
114 Milt Thompson	.05	.02
115 Doug Drabek	.05	.02
116 Rafael Belliard	.05	.02
117 Scott Garrelts	.05	.02
118 Terry Mulholland	.05	.02
119 Jay Howell	.05	.02
120 Danny Jackson	.05	.02
121 Scott Ruskin	.05	.02
122 Robin Ventura	.10	.03
123 Bip Roberts	.05	.02
124 Jeff Russell	.05	.02
125 Hal Morris	.05	.02
126 Teddy Higuera	.05	.02
127 Luis Sojo	.05	.02
128 Carlos Baerga	.05	.02
129 Jeff Ballard	.05	.02
130 Tom Gordon	.05	.02
131 Sid Bream	.05	.02
132 Rance Mulliniks	.05	.02
133 Andy Benes	.05	.02
134 Mickey Tettleton	.05	.02
135 Rich DeLucia	.05	.02
136 Tom Pagnozzi	.05	.02
137 Harold Baines	.10	.03
138 Danny Darwin	.05	.02
139 Kevin Bass	.05	.02
140 Chris Nabholz	.05	.02
141 Pete O'Brien	.05	.02
142 Jeff Treadway	.05	.02
143 Mickey Morandini	.05	.02
144 Eric King	.05	.02
145 Danny Tartabull	.05	.02
146 Lance Johnson	.05	.02
147 Casey Candaele	.05	.02
148 Felix Fermin	.05	.02
149 Rich Rodriguez	.05	.02
150 Dwight Evans	.10	.03
151 Joe Klink	.05	.02
152 Kevin Reimer	.05	.02
153 Orlando Merced	.05	.02
154 Mel Hall	.05	.02
155 Randy Myers	.05	.02
156 Greg A. Harris	.05	.02
157 Jeff Brantley	.05	.02
158 Jim Eisenreich	.05	.02
159 Luis Rivera	.05	.02
160 Cris Carpenter	.05	.02
161 Bruce Ruffin	.05	.02
162 Omar Vizquel	.15	.04
163 Gerald Alexander	.05	.02
164 Mark Guthrie	.05	.02
165 Scott Lewis	.05	.02
166 Bill Sampen	.05	.02
167 Dave Anderson	.05	.02
168 Kevin McReynolds	.05	.02
169 Jose Vizcaino	.05	.02
170 Bob Geren	.05	.02
171 Mike Morgan	.05	.02
172 Jim Gott	.05	.02
173 Mike Pagliarulo	.05	.02
174 Mike Jeffcoat	.05	.02
175 Craig Lefferts	.05	.02
176 Steve Finley	.10	.03
177 Wally Backman	.05	.02
178 Kent Mercker	.05	.02
179 John Cerutti	.05	.02
180 Jay Bell	.10	.03
181 Dale Sveum	.05	.02
182 Greg Gagne	.05	.02
183 Donnie Hill	.05	.02
184 Rex Hudler	.05	.02
185 Pat Kelly	.05	.02
186 Jeff D. Robinson	.05	.02
187 Jeff Gray	.05	.02
188 Jerry Willard	.05	.02
189 Carlos Quintana	.05	.02
190 Dennis Eckersley	.10	.03
191 Kelly Downs	.05	.02
192 Gregg Jefferies	.05	.02
193 Darrin Fletcher	.05	.02
194 Mike Jackson	.05	.02
195 Eddie Murray	.25	.07
196 Bill Landrum	.05	.02
197 Eric Yelding	.05	.02
198 Devon White	.10	.03
199 Larry Walker	.15	.04
200 Ryne Sandberg	.40	.12
201 Dave Magadan	.05	.02
202 Steve Chitren	.05	.02
203 Scott Fletcher	.05	.02
204 Dwayne Henry	.05	.02
205 Scott Coolbaugh	.05	.02
206 Tracy Jones	.05	.02
207 Von Hayes	.05	.02
208 Bob Melvin	.05	.02
209 Scott Scudder	.05	.02
210 Luis Gonzalez	.10	.03
211 Scott Sanderson	.05	.02
212 Chris Donnels	.05	.02
213 Heathcliff Slocumb	.05	.02
214 Mike Timlin	.05	.02
215 Brian Harper	.05	.02
216 Juan Berenguer UER (Decimal point missing in IP total)	.05	.02
217 Mike Henneman	.05	.02
218 Bill Spiers	.05	.02
219 Scott Terry	.05	.02
220 Frank Viola	.10	.03
221 Mark Eichhorn	.05	.02
222 Ernest Riles	.05	.02
223 Ray Lankford	.05	.02
224 Pete Harnisch	.05	.02
225 Bobby Bonilla	.10	.03
226 Mike Scioscia	.05	.02
227 Joel Skinner	.05	.02
228 Brian Holman	.05	.02
229 Gilberto Reyes	.05	.02
230 Matt Williams	.10	.03
231 Jaime Navarro	.05	.02
232 Jose Rijo	.05	.02
233 Atlee Hammaker	.05	.02
234 Tim Teufel	.05	.02
235 John Kruk	.10	.03
236 Kurt Stillwell	.05	.02
237 Dan Pasqua	.05	.02
238 Tim Crews	.05	.02
239 Dave Gallagher	.05	.02
240 Leo Gomez	.05	.02
241 Steve Avery	.05	.02
242 Bill Gullickson	.05	.02
243 Mark Portugal	.05	.02
244 Lee Guetterman	.05	.02
245 Benito Santiago	.10	.03
246 Jim Gantner	.05	.02
247 Robby Thompson	.05	.02
248 Terry Shumpert	.05	.02
249 Mike Bell	.05	.02
250 Harold Reynolds	.10	.03
251 Mike Felder	.05	.02
252 Bill Pecota	.05	.02
253 Bill Krueger	.05	.02
254 Alfredo Griffin	.05	.02
255 Lou Whitaker	.10	.03
256 Roy Smith	.05	.02
257 Jerald Clark	.05	.02
258 Sammy Sosa	.40	.12
259 Tim Naehring	.05	.02
260 Dave Righetti	.10	.03
261 Paul Gibson	.05	.02
262 Chris James	.05	.02
263 Larry Andersen	.05	.02
264 Storm Davis	.05	.02
265 Jose Lind	.05	.02
266 Greg Hibbard	.05	.02
267 Norm Charlton	.05	.02
268 Paul Kilgus	.05	.02
269 Greg Maddux	.40	.12
270 Ellis Burks	.10	.03
271 Frank Tanana	.05	.02
272 Gene Larkin	.05	.02
273 Ron Hassey	.05	.02
274 Jeff M. Robinson	.05	.02
275 Steve Howe	.05	.02
276 Daryl Boston	.05	.02
277 Mark Lee	.05	.02
278 Jose Segura	.05	.02
279 Lance Blankenship	.05	.02
280 Don Slaught	.05	.02
281 Russ Swan	.05	.02
282 Bob Tewksbury	.05	.02
283 Geno Petralli	.05	.02
284 Shane Mack	.05	.02
285 Bob Scanlan	.05	.02
286 Tim Leary	.05	.02
287 John Smoltz	.15	.04
288 Pat Borders	.05	.02
289 Mark Davidson	.05	.02
290 Sam Horn	.05	.02
291 Lenny Harris	.05	.02
292 Franklin Stubbs	.05	.02
293 Thomas Howard	.05	.02
294 Steve Lyons	.05	.02
295 Francisco Oliveras	.05	.02
296 Terry Leach	.05	.02
297 Barry Jones	.05	.02
298 Lance Parrish	.10	.03
299 Wally Whitehurst	.05	.02
300 Bob Welch	.05	.02
301 Charlie Hayes	.05	.02
302 Charlie Hough	.10	.03
303 Gary Redus	.05	.02
304 Scott Bradley	.05	.02
305 Jose Oquendo	.05	.02
306 Pete Incaviglia	.05	.02
307 Marvin Freeman	.05	.02
308 Gary Pettis	.05	.02
309 Joe Slusarski	.05	.02
310 Kevin Seitzer	.05	.02
311 Jeff Reed	.05	.02
312 Pat Tabler	.05	.02
313 Mike Maddux	.05	.02
314 Bob Milacki	.05	.02
315 Eric Anthony	.05	.02
316 Dante Bichette	.10	.03
317 Steve Decker	.05	.02
318 Jack Clark	.10	.03
319 Doug Dascenzo	.05	.02
320 Scott Leius	.05	.02
321 Jim Lindeman	.05	.02
322 Bryan Harvey	.05	.02
323 Spike Owen	.05	.02
324 Roberto Kelly	.05	.02
325 Stan Belinda	.05	.02
326 Joey Cora	.05	.02
327 Jeff Innis	.05	.02
328 Willie Wilson	.05	.02
329 Juan Agosto	.05	.02
330 Charles Nagy	.05	.02
331 Scott Bailes	.05	.02
332 Pete Schourek	.05	.02
333 Mike Flanagan	.05	.02
334 Omar Olivares	.05	.02
335 Dennis Lamp	.05	.02
336 Tommy Greene	.05	.02
337 Randy Velarde	.05	.02
338 Tom Lampkin	.05	.02
339 John Russell	.05	.02
340 Bob Kipper	.05	.02
341 Todd Burns	.05	.02
342 Ron Jones	.05	.02
343 Dave Valle	.05	.02
344 Mike Heath	.05	.02
345 John Olerud	.10	.03
346 Gerald Young	.05	.02
347 Ken Patterson	.05	.02
348 Les Lancaster	.05	.02
349 Steve Crawford	.05	.02
350 John Candelaria	.05	.02
351 Mike Aldrete	.05	.02
352 Mariano Duncan	.05	.02
353 Julio Machado	.05	.02
354 Ken Williams	.05	.02

355 Walt Terrell .05 .02
356 Mitch Williams .05 .02
357 Al Newman .05 .02
358 Bud Black .05 .02
359 Joe Hesketh .05 .02
360 Paul Assenmacher .05 .02
361 Bo Jackson .25 .07
362 Jeff Blauser .05 .02
363 Mike Brumley .05 .02
364 Jim Deshaies .05 .02
365 Brady Anderson .10 .03
366 Chuck McElroy .05 .02
367 Matt Merullo .05 .02
368 Tim Belcher .05 .02
369 Luis Aquino .05 .02
370 Joe Oliver .05 .02
371 Greg Swindell .05 .02
372 Lee Stevens .05 .02
373 Mark Knudson .05 .02
374 Bill Wegman .05 .02
375 Jerry Don Gleaton .05 .02
376 Pedro Guerrero .10 .03
377 Randy Bush .05 .02
378 Greg W. Harris .05 .02
379 Eric Plunk .05 .02
380 Jose DeJesus .05 .02
381 Bobby Witt .05 .02
382 Curtis Wilkerson .05 .02
383 Gene Nelson .05 .02
384 Wes Chamberlain .05 .02
385 Tom Henke .05 .02
386 Mark Lemke .05 .02
387 Greg Briley .05 .02
388 Rafael Ramirez .05 .02
389 Tony Fossas .05 .02
390 Henry Cotto .05 .02
391 Tim Hulett .05 .02
392 Dean Palmer .10 .03
393 Glenn Braggs .05 .02
394 Mark Salas .05 .02
395 Rusty Meacham .05 .02
396 Andy Ashby .05 .02
397 Jose Melendez .05 .02
398 Warren Newson .05 .02
399 Frank Castillo .05 .02
400 Chito Martinez .05 .02
401 Bernie Williams .15 .04
402 Derek Bell .10 .03
403 Javier Ortiz .05 .02
404 Tim Sherrill .05 .02
405 Rob MacDonald .05 .02
406 Phil Plantier .05 .02
407 Troy Afenir .05 .02
408 Gino Minutelli .05 .02
409 Reggie Jefferson .05 .02
410 Mike Remlinger .05 .02
411 Carlos Rodriguez .05 .02
412 Joe Redfield .05 .02
413 Alonzo Powell .05 .02
414 S.Livingstone UER .05 .02
(Travis Fryman, not Woodie, should be referenced on back)
415 Scott Kamieniecki .05 .02
416 Tim Spehr .05 .02
417 Brian Hunter .05 .02
418 Ced Landrum .05 .02
419 Bret Barberie .05 .02
420 Kevin Morton .05 .02
421 Doug Henry RC .10 .03
422 Doug Piatt .05 .02
423 Pat Rice .05 .02
424 Juan Guzman .05 .02
425 Nolan Ryan NH .50 .15
426 Tommy Greene NH .05 .02
427 Bob Milacki and .05 .02
Mike Flanagan NH (Mark Williamson and Gregg Olson)
428 Wilson Alvarez NH .05 .02
429 Otis Nixon HL .05 .02
430 Rickey Henderson HL .15 .04
431 Cecil Fielder AS .05 .02
432 Julio Franco AS .05 .02
433 Cal Ripken AS .40 .12
434 Wade Boggs AS .10 .03
435 Joe Carter AS .05 .02
436 Ken Griffey Jr. AS .25 .07
437 Ruben Sierra AS .05 .02
438 Scott Erickson AS .05 .02
439 Tom Henke AS .05 .02
440 Terry Steinbach AS .05 .02
441 Rickey Henderson DT .25 .07
442 Ryne Sandberg DT .40 .12
443 Otis Nixon .05 .02
444 Scott Radinsky .05 .02
445 Mark Grace .15 .04
446 Tony Pena .05 .02
447 Billy Hatcher .05 .02
448 Glenallen Hill .05 .02
449 Chris Gwynn .05 .02
450 Tom Glavine .15 .04
451 John Habyan .05 .02
452 Al Osuna .05 .02
453 Tony Phillips .05 .02
454 Greg Cadaret .05 .02
455 Rob Dibble .10 .03
456 Rick Honeycutt .05 .02
457 Jerome Walton .05 .02
458 Mookie Wilson .10 .03
459 Mark Gubicza .05 .02
460 Craig Biggio .15 .04
461 Dave Cochrane .05 .02
462 Keith Miller .05 .02
463 Alex Cole .05 .02
464 Pete Smith .05 .02
465 Brett Butler .10 .03
466 Jeff Huson .05 .02
467 Steve Lake .05 .02
468 Lloyd Moseby .05 .02
469 Tim McIntosh .05 .02
470 Dennis Martinez .10 .03
471 Greg Myers .05 .02
472 Mackey Sasser .05 .02
473 Junior Ortiz .05 .02
474 Greg Olson .05 .02
475 Steve Sax .05 .02
476 Ricky Jordan .05 .02
477 Max Venable .05 .02
478 Brian McRae .05 .02
479 Doug Simons .05 .02
480 Rickey Henderson .25 .07
481 Gary Varsho .05 .02
482 Carl Willis .05 .02
483 Rick Wilkins .05 .02
484 Donn Pall .05 .02
485 Edgar Martinez .15 .04
486 Tom Foley .05 .02
487 Mark Williamson .05 .02
488 Jack Armstrong .05 .02
489 Gary Carter .10 .03
490 Ruben Sierra .05 .02
491 Gerald Perry .05 .02
492 Rob Murphy .05 .02
493 Zane Smith .05 .02
494 Darryl Kile .10 .03
495 Kelly Gruber .05 .02
496 Jerry Browne .05 .02
497 Darryl Hamilton .05 .02
498 Mike Stanton .05 .02
499 Mark Leonard .05 .02
500 Jose Canseco .25 .07
501 Dave Martinez .05 .02
502 Jose Guzman .05 .02
503 Terry Kennedy .05 .02
504 Ed Sprague .05 .02
505 Frank Thomas UER .25 .07
(His Gulf Coast League stats are wrong)
506 Darren Daulton .10 .03
507 Kevin Tapani .05 .02
508 Luis Salazar .05 .02
509 Paul Faries .05 .02
510 Sandy Alomar Jr. .05 .02
511 Jeff King .05 .02
512 Gary Thurman .05 .02
513 Chris Hammond .05 .02
514 Pedro Munoz .05 .02
515 Alan Trammell .10 .03
516 Geronimo Pena .05 .02
517 Rodney McCray UER .05 .02
Stole 6 bases in 1990, not 5; career totals are correct at 7
518 Manny Lee .05 .02
519 Junior Felix .05 .02
520 Kirk Gibson .10 .03
521 Darrin Jackson .05 .02
522 John Burkett .05 .02
523 Jeff Johnson .05 .02
524 Jim Corsi .05 .02
525 Robin Yount .40 .12
526 Jamie Quirk .05 .02
527 Bob Ojeda .05 .02
528 Mark Lewis .05 .02
529 Bryn Smith .05 .02
530 Kent Hrbek .10 .03
531 Dennis Boyd .05 .02
532 Ron Karkovice .05 .02
533 Don August .05 .02
534 Todd Frohwirth .05 .02
535 Wally Joyner .10 .03
536 Dennis Rasmussen .05 .02
537 Andy Allanson .05 .02
538 Rich Gossage .10 .03
539 John Marzano .05 .02
540 Cal Ripken .75 .23
541 Bill Swift UER .05 .02
(Brewers logo on front)
542 Kevin Appier .10 .03
543 Dave Bergman .05 .02
544 Bernard Gilkey .05 .02
545 Mike Greenwell .05 .02
546 Jose Uribe .05 .02
547 Jesse Orosco .05 .02
548 Bob Patterson .05 .02
549 Mike Stanley .05 .02
550 Howard Johnson .05 .02
551 Joe Orsulak .05 .02
552 Dick Schofield .05 .02
553 Dave Hollins .05 .02
554 David Segui .05 .02
555 Barry Bonds .60 .18
556 Mo Vaughn .10 .03
557 Craig Wilson .05 .02
558 Bobby Rose .05 .02
559 Rod Nichols .05 .02
560 Len Dykstra .10 .03
561 Craig Grebeck .05 .02
562 Darren Lewis .05 .02
563 Todd Benzinger .05 .02
564 Ed Whitson .05 .02
565 Jesse Barfield .05 .02
566 Lloyd McClendon .05 .02
567 Dan Plesac .05 .02
568 Danny Cox .05 .02
569 Skeeter Barnes .05 .02
570 Bobby Thigpen .05 .02
571 Deion Sanders .15 .04
572 Chuck Knoblauch .10 .03
573 Matt Nokes .05 .02
574 Herm Winningham .05 .02
575 Tom Candiotti .05 .02
576 Jeff Bagwell .25 .07
577 Brook Jacoby .05 .02
578 Chico Walker .05 .02
579 Brian Downing .05 .02
580 Dave Stewart .10 .03
581 Francisco Cabrera .05 .02
582 Rene Gonzales .05 .02
583 Stan Javier .05 .02
584 Randy Johnson .25 .07
585 Chuck Finley .10 .03
586 Mark Gardner .05 .02
587 Mark Whiten .05 .02
588 Garry Templeton .05 .02
589 Gary Sheffield .10 .03
590 Ozzie Smith .40 .12
591 Candy Maldonado .05 .02
592 Mike Sharperson .05 .02
593 Carlos Martinez .05 .02
594 Scott Bankhead .05 .02
595 Tim Wallach .05 .02
596 Tino Martinez .15 .04
597 Roger McDowell .05 .02
598 Cory Snyder .05 .02
599 Andujar Cedeno .05 .02
600 Kirby Puckett .25 .07
601 Rick Parker .05 .02
602 Todd Hundley .05 .02
603 Greg Litton .05 .02
604 Dave Johnson .05 .02
605 John Franco .10 .03
606 Mike Fetters .05 .02
607 Luis Alicea .05 .02
608 Trevor Wilson .05 .02
609 Rob Ducey .05 .02
610 Ramon Martinez .05 .02
611 Dave Burba .05 .02
612 Dwight Smith .05 .02
613 Kevin Maas .05 .02
614 John Costello .05 .02
615 Glenn Davis .05 .02
616 Shawn Abner .05 .02
617 Scott Hemond .05 .02
618 Tom Prince .05 .02
619 Wally Ritchie .05 .02
620 Jim Abbott .15 .04
621 Charlie O'Brien .05 .02
622 Jack Daugherty .05 .02
623 Tommy Gregg .05 .02
624 Jeff Shaw .05 .02
625 Tony Gwynn .30 .09
626 Mark Leiter .05 .02
627 Jim Clancy .05 .02
628 Tim Layana .05 .02
629 Jeff Schaefer .05 .02
630 Lee Smith .10 .03
631 Wade Taylor .05 .02
632 Mike Simms .05 .02
633 Terry Steinbach .05 .02
634 Shawon Dunston .05 .02
635 Tim Raines .10 .03
636 Kirt Manwaring .05 .02
637 Warren Cromartie .05 .02
638 Luis Quinones .05 .02
639 Greg Vaughn .05 .02
640 Kevin Mitchell .05 .02
641 Chris Hoiles .05 .02
642 Tom Browning .05 .02
643 Mitch Webster .05 .02
644 Steve Olin .05 .02
645 Tony Fernandez .05 .02
646 Juan Bell .05 .02
647 Joe Boever .05 .02
648 Carney Lansford .10 .03
649 Mike Benjamin .05 .02
650 George Brett .60 .18
651 Tim Burke .05 .02
652 Jack Morris .10 .03
653 Orel Hershiser .10 .03
654 Mike Schooler .05 .02
655 Andy Van Slyke .10 .03
656 Dave Stieb .05 .02
657 Dave Clark .05 .02
658 Ben McDonald .05 .02
659 John Smiley .05 .02
660 Wade Boggs .15 .04
661 Eric Bullock .05 .02
662 Eric Show .05 .02
663 Lenny Webster .05 .02
664 Mike Huff .05 .02
665 Rick Sutcliffe .10 .03
666 Jeff Manto .05 .02
667 Mike Fitzgerald .05 .02
668 Matt Young .05 .02
669 Dave West .05 .02
670 Mike Hartley .05 .02
671 Curt Schilling .15 .04
672 Brian Bohanon .05 .02
673 Cecil Espy .05 .02
674 Joe Grahe .05 .02
675 Sid Fernandez .05 .02
676 Edwin Nunez .05 .02
677 Hector Villanueva .05 .02
678 Sean Berry .05 .02
679 Dave Eiland .05 .02
680 David Cone .10 .03
681 Mike Bordick .05 .02
682 Tony Castillo .05 .02
683 John Barfield .05 .02
684 Jeff Hamilton .05 .02
685 Ken Dayley .05 .02
686 Carmelo Martinez .05 .02
687 Mike Capel .05 .02
688 Scott Chiamparino .05 .02
689 Rich Gedman .05 .02
690 Rich Monteleone .05 .02
691 Alejandro Pena .05 .02
692 Oscar Azocar .05 .02
693 Jim Poole .05 .02
694 Mike Gardiner .05 .02
695 Steve Buechele .05 .02
696 Rudy Seanez .05 .02
697 Paul Abbott .05 .02
698 Steve Searcy .05 .02
699 Jose Offerman .05 .02
700 Ivan Rodriguez .25 .07
701 Joe Girardi .05 .02
702 Tony Perezchica .05 .02
703 Paul McClellan .05 .02
704 David Howard .05 .02
705 Dan Petry .05 .02
706 Jack Howell .05 .02
707 Jose Mesa .05 .02
708 Randy St. Claire .05 .02
709 Kevin Brown .10 .03
710 Ron Darling .05 .02
711 Jason Grimsley .05 .02
712 John Orton .05 .02
713 Shawn Boskie .05 .02
714 Pat Clements .05 .02
715 Brian Barnes .05 .02
716 Luis Lopez .05 .02
717 Bob McClure .05 .02
718 Mark Davis .05 .02
719 Dann Bilardello .05 .02
720 Tom Edens .05 .02
721 Willie Fraser .05 .02
722 Curt Young .05 .02
723 Neal Heaton .05 .02
724 Craig Worthington .05 .02
725 Mel Rojas .05 .02
726 Daryl Irvine .05 .02
727 Roger Mason .05 .02
728 Kirk Dressendorfer .05 .02
729 Scott Aldred .05 .02
730 Willie Blair .05 .02
731 Allan Anderson .05 .02
732 Dana Kiecker .05 .02
733 Jose Gonzalez .05 .02
734 Brian Drahman .05 .02
735 Brad Komminsk .05 .02
736 Arthur Rhodes .05 .02
737 Terry Mathews .05 .02
738 Jeff Fassero .05 .02
739 Mike Magnante RC .10 .03
740 Kip Gross .05 .02
741 Jim Hunter .05 .02
742 Jose Mota .05 .02
743 Joe Bitker .05 .02
744 Tim Mauser .05 .02
745 Ramon Garcia .05 .02
746 Rod Beck RC .25 .07
747 Jim Austin RC .05 .02
748 Keith Mitchell .05 .02
749 Wayne Rosenthal .05 .02
750 Bryan Hickerson RC .10 .03
751 Bruce Egloff .05 .02
752 John Wehner .05 .02
753 Darren Holmes .05 .02
754 Dave Hansen .05 .02
755 Mike Mussina .25 .07
756 Anthony Young .05 .02
757 Ron Tingley .05 .02
758 Ricky Bones .05 .02
759 Mark Wohlers .05 .02
760 Wilson Alvarez .05 .02
761 Harvey Pulliam .05 .02
762 Ryan Bowen .05 .02
763 Terry Bross .05 .02
764 Joel Johnston .05 .02
765 Terry McDaniel .05 .02
766 Esteban Beltre .05 .02
767 Rob Maurer .05 .02
768 Ted Wood .05 .02
769 Mo Sanford .05 .02
770 Jeff Carter .05 .02
771 Gil Heredia RC .25 .07
772 Monty Fariss .05 .02
773 Will Clark AS .10 .03
774 Ryne Sandberg AS .25 .07
775 Barry Larkin AS .10 .03
776 Howard Johnson AS .05 .02
777 Barry Bonds AS .30 .09
778 Brett Butler AS .05 .02
779 Tony Gwynn AS .15 .04
780 Ramon Martinez AS .05 .02
781 Lee Smith AS .05 .02
782 Mike Scioscia AS .05 .02
783 D.Martinez HL UER .05 .02
Card has both 13th and 15th perfect game in Major League history
784 Dennis Martinez NH .05 .02
785 Mark Gardner NH .05 .02
786 Bret Saberhagen NH .05 .02
787 Kent Mercker NH .05 .02
Mark Wohlers
Alejandro Pena
788 Cal Ripken MVP .40 .12
789 Terry Pendleton MVP .05 .02
790 Roger Clemens CY .25 .07
791 Tom Glavine CY .10 .03
792 C.Knoblauch ROY .05 .02
793 Jeff Bagwell ROY .15 .04
794 Cal Ripken MANYR .40 .12
795 David Cone HL .05 .02
796 Kirby Puckett HL .15 .04
797 Steve Avery HL .05 .02
798 Jack Morris HL .05 .02
799 Allen Watson DC RC .10 .03
800 M.Ramirez DC RC 2.50 .75
801 Cliff Floyd DC RC .40 .12
802 Al Shirley DC RC .10 .03
803 Brian Barber DC RC .10 .03
804 Jon Farrell DC RC .10 .03
805 Brent Gates DC RC .10 .03
806 Scott Ruffcorn DC RC .10 .03
807 Tyrone Hill DC RC .10 .03
808 Benji Gil DC RC .25 .07
809 Aaron Sele DC RC .40 .12
810 Tyler Green DC RC .10 .03
811 Chris Jones .05 .02
812 Steve Wilson .05 .02
813 Freddie Benavides .05 .02
814 Don Wakamatsu .05 .02
815 Mike Humphreys .05 .02
816 Scott Servais .05 .02
817 Rico Rossy .05 .02
818 John Ramos .05 .02
819 Rob Mallicoat .05 .02
820 Milt Hill .05 .02
821 Carlos Garcia .05 .02
822 Stan Royer .05 .02
823 Jeff Plympton .05 .02
824 Braulio Castillo .05 .02
825 David Haas .05 .02
826 Luis Mercedes .05 .02
827 Eric Karros .10 .03
828 Shawn Hare RC .10 .03
829 Reggie Sanders .05 .02
830 Tom Goodwin .05 .02
831 Dan Gakeler .05 .02
832 Stacy Jones .05 .02
833 Kim Batiste .05 .02
834 Cal Eldred .05 .02
835 Chris George .05 .02
836 Wayne Housie .05 .02
837 Mike Ignasiak .05 .02
838 Josias Manzanillo RC .10 .03
839 Jim Olander .05 .02
840 Gary Cooper .05 .02
841 Royce Clayton .05 .02
842 Hector Fajardo RC .10 .03
843 Blaine Beatty .05 .02
844 Jorge Pedre .05 .02
845 Kenny Lofton .15 .04
846 Scott Brosius RC .40 .12
847 Chris Cron .05 .02
848 Denis Boucher .05 .02
849 Kyle Abbott .05 .02
850 Bob Zupcic RC .10 .03
851 Rheal Cormier .05 .02
852 Jimmy Lewis RC .05 .02
853 Anthony Telford .05 .02
854 Cliff Brantley .05 .02
855 Kevin Campbell .05 .02
856 Craig Shipley .05 .02
857 Chuck Carr .05 .02
858 Tony Eusebio .10 .03
859 Jim Thome .25 .07
860 Vinny Castilla RC .75 .23
861 Dann Howitt .05 .02
862 Kevin Ward .05 .02
863 Steve Wapnick .05 .02
864 Rod Brewer RC .10 .03
865 Todd Van Poppel .05 .02
866 Jose Hernandez RC .40 .12
867 Amalio Carreno .05 .02
868 Calvin Jones .05 .02
869 Jeff Gardner .05 .02
870 Jarvis Brown .05 .02
871 Eddie Taubensee RC .25 .07
872 Andy Mota .05 .02
873 Chris Haney .05 .02
874 Roberto Hernandez .05 .02
875 Laddie Renfroe .05 .02
876 Scott Cooper .05 .02
877 Armando Reynoso RC .25 .07
878 Ty Cobb MEMO .25 .07
879 Babe Ruth MEMO .50 .15
880 Honus Wagner MEMO .25 .07
881 Lou Gehrig MEMO .40 .12
882 Satchel Paige MEMO .25 .07
883 Will Clark DT .10 .03
884 Cal Ripken DT 2.00 .60
885 Wade Boggs DT .10 .03
886 Kirby Puckett DT .15 .04
887 Tony Gwynn DT .15 .04
888 Craig Biggio DT .10 .03
889 Scott Erickson DT .05 .02
890 Tom Glavine DT .10 .03
891 Rob Dibble DT .10 .03
892 Mitch Williams DT .05 .02
893 Frank Thomas DT .15 .04
X672 Chuck Knoblauch AU 25.00 7.50
1990 Score card,
3000 copies signed

1992 Score DiMaggio

This five-card standard-size insert set was issued in honor of one of baseball's all-time greats, Joe DiMaggio. These cards were randomly inserted in first series packs. According to sources at Score, 30,000 of each card were produced. On a white card face, the fronts have vintage photos that have been colorized and accented by red, white, and blue border stripes. DiMaggio autographed 2,500 cards for this promotion. 2,495 of these cards were inserted in packs while the other five were used as prizes in a mail-in sweepstakes. The autographed cards are individually numbered out of 2,500.

	Nm-Mt	Ex-Mt
COMPLETE SET (5)	80.00	24.00
COMMON CARD (1-5)	15.00	4.50
AU Joe DiMaggio AU	400.00	120.00

(Autographed with certified signature)

1992 Score Factory Inserts

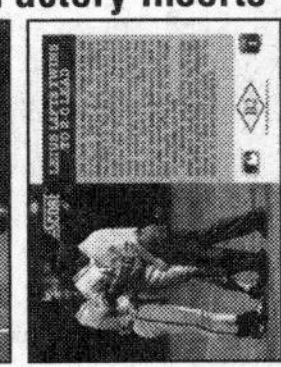

This 17-card insert standard-size set was distributed only in 1992 Score factory sets and consists of four topical subsets. Cards B1-B7 capture a moment from each game of the 1991 World Series. Cards B8-B11 are Cooperstown cards, honoring future Hall of Famers. Cards B12-B14 form a "Joe D" subset paying tribute to Joe DiMaggio. Cards B15-B17, subtitled "Yaz", conclude the set by commemorating Carl Yastrzemski's heroic feats twenty-five years ago in winning the Triple Crown and lifting the Red Sox to their first American League pennant in 21 years. Each subset displayed a different front design. The World Series cards carry full-bleed color action photos except for a blue stripe at the bottom, while the Cooperstown cards have a color portrait on a white card face. Both the DiMaggio and Yastrzemski subsets have action photos with silver borders; they differ in that the DiMaggio photos are black and white, the Yastrzemski photos color. The DiMaggio and Yastrzemski subsets are numbered on the back within each subset (e.g., "1 of 3") and as a part of the 17-card insert set (e.g., "B1"). In the DiMaggio and Yastrzemski subsets, Score varied the insert set slightly in retail versus hobby factory sets. In the hobby set, the DiMaggio cards display different black-and-white photos that are bordered beneath by a dark blue stripe (the stripe is green in the retail factory insert). On the backs, these hobby inserts have a red stripe at the bottom; the same stripe is dark blue on the retail inserts. The Yastrzemski cards in the hobby set have different color photos on their fronts than the retail inserts.

	Nm-Mt	Ex-Mt
COMPLETE SET (17)	6.00	1.80
B1 Greg Gagne WS	.40	.12
B2 Scott Leius WS	.40	.12
B3 Mark Lemke WS David Justice	.40	.12
B4 Lonnie Smith WS Brian Harper	.40	.12

B5 David Justice WS .75 .23
B6 Kirby Puckett WS 2.00 .60
B7 Gene Larkin WS .40 .12
B8 Carlton Fisk 1.25 .35
B9 Ozzie Smith 3.00 .90
B10 Dave Winfield .75 .23
B11 Robin Yount 3.00 .90
B12 Joe DiMaggio 1.00 .30
The Hard Hitter
B13 Joe DiMaggio 1.00 .30
The Stylish Fielder
B14 Joe DiMaggio 1.00 .30
The Championship Player
B15 Carl Yastrzemski .50 .15
The Impossible Dream
B16 Carl Yastrzemski .50 .15
The Triple Crown
B17 Carl Yastrzemski .50 .15
The World Series

1992 Score Franchise

This four-card standard-size set features three all-time greats, Stan Musial, Mickey Mantle, and Carl Yastrzemski. Each former player autographed 2,000 of his 1992 Score cards, and 500 of the combo cards were signed by all three. In addition to these signed cards, Score produced 150,000 of each Franchise card, and both signed and unsigned cards were randomly inserted in 1992 Score Series II poly packs, blister packs, and cello packs.

Nm-Mt Ex-Mt
COMPLETE SET (4) 30.00 9.00
1 Stan Musial 5.00 1.50
2 Mickey Mantle 12.00 3.60
3 Carl Yastrzemski 5.00 1.50
4 The Franchise Players 10.00 3.00
Stan Musial
Mickey Mantle
Carl Yastrzemski
AU1 Stan Musial 80.00 24.00
(Autographed with certified signature)
AU2 Mickey Mantle 500.00 150.00
(Autographed with certified signature)
AU3 Carl Yastrzemski 80.00 24.00
(Autographed with certified signature)
AU4 Franchise Players 1000.00 300.00
Stan Musial
Mickey Mantle
Carl Yastrzemski
(Autographed with certified signatures of all three)

1992 Score Hot Rookies

This ten-card standard-size set features color action player photos on a white face. These cards were inserted one per blister pack.

Nm-Mt Ex-Mt
COMPLETE SET (10) 8.00 2.40
1 Cal Eldred .50 .15
2 Royce Clayton .50 .15
3 Kenny Lofton 2.00 .60
4 Todd Van Poppel .50 .15
5 Scott Cooper .50 .15
6 Todd Hundley .50 .15
7 Tino Martinez 2.00 .60
8 Anthony Telford .50 .15
9 Derek Bell .50 .15
10 Reggie Jefferson .50 .15

1992 Score Impact Players

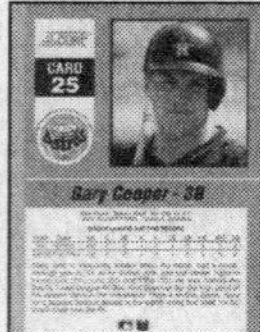

The 1992 Score Impact Players insert set was issued in two series each with 45 standard-size cards with the respective series of the 1992 regular issue Score cards. Five of these cards were inserted in each 1992 Score jumbo pack.

Nm-Mt Ex-Mt
COMPLETE SERIES 1 (45) 12.00 3.60
COMPLETE SERIES 2 (45) 6.00 1.80
1 Chuck Knoblauch .30 .09
2 Jeff Bagwell .75 .23
3 Juan Guzman .15 .04
4 Milt Cuyler .15 .04
5 Ivan Rodriguez .75 .23
6 Rich DeLucia .15 .04
7 Orlando Merced .15 .04
8 Ray Lankford .15 .04
9 Brian Hunter .15 .04
10 Roberto Alomar .50 .15
11 Wes Chamberlain .15 .04
12 Steve Avery .15 .04
13 Scott Erickson .15 .04
14 Jim Abbott .50 .15
15 Mark Whiten .15 .04
16 Leo Gomez .15 .04
17 Doug Henry .30 .09
18 Brent Mayne .15 .04
19 Charles Nagy .15 .04
20 Phil Plantier .15 .04
21 Mo Vaughn .30 .09
22 Craig Biggio .50 .15
23 Derek Bell .30 .09
24 Royce Clayton .15 .04
25 Gary Cooper .15 .04
26 Scott Cooper .15 .04
27 Juan Gonzalez .50 .15
28 Ken Griffey Jr. 1.25 .35
29 Larry Walker .50 .15
30 John Smoltz .50 .15
31 Todd Hundley .15 .04
32 Kenny Lofton .50 .15
33 Andy Mota .15 .04
34 Todd Zeile .15 .04
35 Arthur Rhodes .15 .04
36 Jim Thome .75 .23
37 Todd Van Poppel .15 .04
38 Mark Wohlers .15 .04
39 Anthony Young .15 .04
40 Sandy Alomar Jr. .15 .04
41 John Olerud .30 .09
42 Robin Ventura .30 .09
43 Frank Thomas .75 .23
44 Dave Justice .30 .09
45 Hal Morris .15 .04
46 Ruben Sierra .15 .04
47 Travis Fryman .30 .09
48 Mike Mussina .75 .23
49 Tom Glavine .50 .15
50 Barry Larkin .50 .15
51 Will Clark UER .75 .23
Career Totals spelled To als
52 Jose Canseco .75 .23
53 Bo Jackson .75 .23
54 Dwight Gooden .30 .09
55 Barry Bonds 2.00 .60
56 Fred McGriff .50 .15
57 Roger Clemens 1.50 .45
58 Benito Santiago .30 .09
59 Darryl Strawberry .30 .09
60 Cecil Fielder .30 .09
61 John Franco .30 .09
62 Matt Williams .30 .09
63 Marquis Grissom .30 .09
64 Danny Tartabull .15 .04
65 Ron Gant .30 .09
66 Paul O'Neill .50 .15
67 Devon White .30 .09
68 Rafael Palmeiro .50 .15
69 Tom Gordon .15 .04
70 Shawon Dunston .15 .04
71 Rob Dibble .30 .09
72 Eddie Zosky .15 .04
73 Jack McDowell .15 .04
74 Len Dykstra .30 .09
75 Ramon Martinez .15 .04
76 Reggie Sanders .15 .04
77 Greg Maddux 1.25 .35
78 Ellis Burks .30 .09
79 John Smiley .15 .04
80 Roberto Kelly .15 .04
81 Ben McDonald .15 .04
82 Mark Lewis .15 .04
83 Jose Rijo .15 .04
84 Ozzie Guillen .15 .04
85 Lance Dickson .15 .04
86 Kim Batiste .15 .04
87 Gregg Olson .15 .04
88 Andy Benes .15 .04
89 Cal Eldred .15 .04
90 David Cone .30 .09

1992 Score Rookie/Traded

The 1992 Score Rookie and Traded set contains 110 standard-size cards featuring traded veterans and rookies. This set was issued in complete set form and was released through hobby dealers. The set is arranged numerically such that cards 1T-79T are traded players and cards 80T-110T feature rookies. Notable Rookie Cards in this set include Brian Jordan and Jeff Kent.

Nm-Mt Ex-Mt
COMP.FACT.SET (110) 8.00 2.40
1T Gary Sheffield .30 .09
2T Kevin Seitzer .20 .06
3T Danny Tartabull .20 .06
4T Steve Sax .20 .06
5T Bobby Bonilla .30 .09
6T Frank Viola .30 .09
7T Dave Winfield .30 .09
8T Rick Sutcliffe .30 .09
9T Jose Canseco .75 .23
10T Greg Swindell .20 .06
11T Eddie Murray .75 .23
12T Randy Myers .20 .06
13T Wally Joyner .30 .09
14T Kenny Lofton .50 .15
15T Jack Morris .30 .09
16T Charlie Hayes .20 .06
17T Pete Incaviglia .20 .06
18T Kevin Mitchell .20 .06
19T Kurt Stillwell .20 .06
20T Bret Saberhagen .30 .09
21T Steve Buechele .20 .06
22T John Smiley .20 .06
23T Sammy Sosa 1.25 .35
24T George Bell .20 .06
25T Curt Schilling .50 .15
26T Dick Schofield .20 .06
27T David Cone .30 .09
28T Dan Gladden .20 .06
29T Kirk McCaskill .20 .06
30T Mike Gallego .20 .06
31T Kevin McReynolds .20 .06
32T Bill Swift .20 .06
33T Dave Martinez .20 .06
34T Storm Davis .20 .06
35T Willie Randolph .30 .09
36T Melido Perez .20 .06
37T Mark Carreon .20 .06
38T Doug Jones .20 .06
39T Gregg Jefferies .20 .06
40T Mike Jackson .20 .06
41T Dickie Thon .20 .06
42T Eric King .20 .06
43T Herm Winningham .20 .06
44T Derek Lilliquist .20 .06
45T Dave Anderson .20 .06
46T Jeff Reardon .30 .09
47T Scott Bankhead .20 .06
48T Cory Snyder .20 .06
49T Al Newman .20 .06
50T Keith Miller .20 .06
51T Dave Burba .20 .06
52T Bill Pecota .20 .06
53T Chuck Crim .20 .06
54T Mariano Duncan .20 .06
55T Dave Gallagher .20 .06
56T Chris Gwynn .20 .06
57T Scott Ruskin .20 .06
58T Jack Armstrong .20 .06
59T Gary Carter .30 .09
60T Andres Galarraga .30 .09
61T Ken Hill .20 .06
62T Eric Davis .30 .09
63T Ruben Sierra .20 .06
64T Darrin Fletcher .20 .06
65T Tim Belcher .20 .06
66T Mike Morgan .20 .06
67T Scott Scudder .20 .06
68T Tom Candiotti .20 .06
69T Hubie Brooks .20 .06
70T Kal Daniels .20 .06
71T Bruce Ruffin .20 .06
72T Billy Hatcher .20 .06
73T Bob Melvin .20 .06
74T Lee Guetterman .20 .06
75T Rene Gonzales .20 .06
76T Kevin Bass .20 .06
77T Tom Bolton .20 .06
78T John Wetteland .30 .09
79T Bip Roberts .20 .06
80T Pat Listach RC .40 .12
81T John Doherty RC .20 .06
82T Sam Militello .20 .06
83T Brian Jordan RC .60 .18
84T Jeff Kent RC 2.00 .60
85T Dave Fleming .20 .06
86T Jeff Tackett .20 .06
87T Chad Curtis RC .40 .12
88T Eric Fox RC .20 .06
89T Denny Neagle .30 .09
90T Donovan Osborne .20 .06
91T Carlos Hernandez .20 .06
92T Tim Wakefield RC 4.00 1.20
93T Tim Salmon .75 .23
94T Dave Nilsson .20 .06
95T Mike Perez .20 .06
96T Pat Hentgen .20 .06
97T Frank Seminara RC .20 .06
98T Ruben Amaro .20 .06
99T Archi Cianfrocco RC .20 .06
100T Andy Stankiewicz .20 .06
101T Jim Bullinger .20 .06
102T Pat Mahomes RC .40 .12
103T Hipolito Pichardo RC .20 .06
104T Bret Boone .75 .23
105T John Vander Wal .20 .06
106T Vince Horsman .20 .06
107T Jim Austin .20 .06
108T Brian Williams RC .20 .06
109T Dan Walters .20 .06
110T Wil Cordero .20 .06

1993 Score

The 1993 Score baseball set consists of 660 standard-size cards issued in one single series. The cards were distributed in 16-card poly packs and 35-card jumbo superpacks. Topical subsets featured are Award Winners (481-486), Draft Picks (487-501), All-Star Caricature (502-512 [AL], 522-531 [NL]), Highlights (513-519), World Series Highlights (520-521), Dream Team (532-542) and Rookies (sprinkled throughout the set). Rookie Cards in this set include Derek Jeter, Jason Kendall and Shannon Stewart.

Nm-Mt Ex-Mt
COMPLETE SET (660) 40.00 12.00
1 Ken Griffey Jr. .75 .23
2 Gary Sheffield .20 .06
3 Frank Thomas .50 .15
4 Ryne Sandberg .75 .23
5 Larry Walker .30 .09
6 Cal Ripken Jr. 1.50 .45
7 Roger Clemens 1.00 .30
8 Bobby Bonilla .20 .06
9 Carlos Baerga .10 .03
10 Darren Daulton .20 .06
11 Travis Fryman .20 .06
12 Andy Van Slyke .20 .06
13 Jose Canseco .50 .15
14 Roberto Alomar .30 .09
15 Tom Glavine .30 .09
16 Barry Larkin .30 .09
17 Gregg Jefferies .10 .03
18 Craig Biggio .30 .09
19 Shane Mack .10 .03
20 Brett Butler .20 .06
21 Dennis Eckersley .20 .06
22 Will Clark .50 .15
23 Don Mattingly 1.25 .35
24 Tony Gwynn .60 .18
25 Ivan Rodriguez .50 .15
26 Shawon Dunston .10 .03
27 Mike Mussina .30 .09
28 Marquis Grissom .20 .06
29 Charles Nagy .10 .03
30 Len Dykstra .20 .06
31 Cecil Fielder .20 .06
32 Jay Bell .20 .06
33 B.J. Surhoff .20 .06
34 Bob Tewksbury .10 .03
35 Danny Tartabull .10 .03
36 Terry Pendleton .20 .06
37 Jack Morris .20 .06
38 Hal Morris .10 .03
39 Luis Polonia .10 .03
40 Ken Caminiti .20 .06
41 Robin Ventura .20 .06
42 Darryl Strawberry .20 .06
43 Wally Joyner .20 .06
44 Fred McGriff .30 .09
45 Kevin Tapani .10 .03
46 Matt Williams .20 .06
47 Robin Yount .75 .23
48 Ken Hill .10 .03
49 Edgar Martinez .30 .09
50 Mark Grace .30 .09
51 Juan Gonzalez .30 .09
52 Curt Schilling .20 .06
53 Dwight Gooden .20 .06
54 Chris Hoiles .10 .03
55 Frank Viola .20 .06
56 Ray Lankford .10 .03
57 George Brett 1.25 .35
58 Kenny Lofton .20 .06
59 Nolan Ryan 2.00 .60
60 Mickey Tettleton .10 .03
61 John Smoltz .30 .09
62 Howard Johnson .10 .03
63 Eric Karros .20 .06
64 Rick Aguilera .10 .03
65 Steve Finley .20 .06
66 Mark Langston .10 .03
67 Bill Swift .10 .03
68 John Olerud .20 .06
69 Kevin McReynolds .10 .03
70 Jack McDowell .10 .03
71 Rickey Henderson .50 .15
72 Brian Harper .10 .03
73 Mike Morgan .10 .03
74 Rafael Palmeiro .30 .09
75 Dennis Martinez .20 .06
76 Tino Martinez .30 .09
77 Eddie Murray .50 .15
78 Ellis Burks .20 .06
79 John Kruk .20 .06
80 Gregg Olson .10 .03
81 Bernard Gilkey .10 .03
82 Milt Cuyler .10 .03
83 Mike LaValliere .10 .03
84 Albert Belle .20 .06
85 Bip Roberts .10 .03
86 Melido Perez .10 .03
87 Otis Nixon .10 .03
88 Bill Spiers .10 .03
89 Jeff Bagwell .30 .09
90 Orel Hershiser .20 .06
91 Andy Benes .10 .03
92 Devon White .20 .06
93 Willie McGee .20 .06
94 Ozzie Guillen .10 .03
95 Ivan Calderon .10 .03
96 Keith Miller .10 .03
97 Steve Buechele .10 .03
98 Kent Hrbek .20 .06
99 Dave Hollins .10 .03
100 Mike Bordick .10 .03
101 Randy Tomlin .10 .03
102 Omar Vizquel .30 .09
103 Lee Smith .20 .06
104 Leo Gomez .10 .03
105 Jose Rijo .10 .03
106 Mark Whiten .10 .03
107 Dave Justice .20 .06
108 Eddie Taubensee .10 .03
109 Lance Johnson .10 .03
110 Felix Jose .10 .03
111 Mike Harkey .10 .03
112 Randy Milligan .10 .03
113 Anthony Young .10 .03
114 Rico Brogna .10 .03
115 Bret Saberhagen .20 .06
116 Sandy Alomar Jr. .10 .03
117 Terry Mulholland .10 .03
118 Darryl Hamilton .10 .03
119 Todd Zeile .10 .03
120 Bernie Williams .30 .09
121 Zane Smith .10 .03
122 Derek Bell .10 .03
123 Deion Sanders .30 .09
124 Luis Sojo .10 .03
125 Joe Oliver .10 .03
126 Craig Grebeck .10 .03
127 Andujar Cedeno .10 .03
128 Brian McRae .10 .03
129 Jose Offerman .10 .03
130 Pedro Munoz .10 .03
131 Bud Black .10 .03
132 Mo Vaughn .20 .06
133 Bruce Hurst .10 .03
134 Dave Henderson .10 .03
135 Tom Pagnozzi .10 .03
136 Erik Hanson .10 .03
137 Orlando Merced .10 .03
138 Dean Palmer .20 .06
139 John Franco .20 .06
140 Brady Anderson .20 .06
141 Ricky Jordan .10 .03
142 Jeff Blauser .10 .03
143 Sammy Sosa .75 .23
144 Bob Walk .10 .03
145 Delino DeShields .10 .03
146 Kevin Brown .20 .06
147 Mark Lemke .10 .03
148 Chuck Knoblauch .20 .06
149 Chris Sabo .10 .03
150 Bobby Witt .10 .03
151 Luis Gonzalez .20 .06
152 Ron Karkovice .10 .03
153 Jeff Brantley .10 .03
154 Kevin Appier .20 .06
155 Darrin Jackson .10 .03
156 Kelly Gruber .10 .03
157 Royce Clayton .10 .03
158 Chuck Finley .20 .06
159 Jeff King .10 .03
160 Greg Vaughn .10 .03
161 Geronimo Pena .10 .03
162 Steve Farr .10 .03
163 Jose Oquendo .10 .03
164 Mark Lewis .10 .03
165 John Wetteland .20 .06
166 Mike Henneman .10 .03
167 Todd Hundley .10 .03
168 Wes Chamberlain .10 .03
169 Steve Avery .10 .03
170 Mike Devereaux .10 .03
171 Reggie Sanders .20 .06
172 Jay Buhner .20 .06
173 Eric Anthony .10 .03
174 John Burkett .10 .03
175 Tom Candiotti .10 .03
176 Phil Plantier .10 .03
177 Doug Henry .10 .03
178 Scott Leius .10 .03
179 Kirt Manwaring .10 .03
180 Jeff Parrett .10 .03
181 Don Slaught .10 .03
182 Scott Radinsky .10 .03
183 Luis Alicea .10 .03
184 Tom Gordon .10 .03
185 Rick Wilkins .10 .03
186 Todd Stottlemyre .10 .03
187 Moises Alou .20 .06
188 Joe Grahe .10 .03
189 Jeff Kent .50 .15
190 Bill Wegman .10 .03
191 Kim Batiste .10 .03
192 Matt Nokes .10 .03
193 Mark Wohlers .10 .03
194 Paul Sorrento .10 .03
195 Chris Hammond .10 .03
196 Scott Livingstone .10 .03
197 Doug Jones .10 .03
198 Scott Cooper .10 .03
199 Ramon Martinez .10 .03
200 Dave Valle .10 .03
201 Mariano Duncan .10 .03
202 Ben McDonald .10 .03
203 Darren Lewis .10 .03
204 Kenny Rogers .20 .06
205 Manuel Lee .10 .03
206 Scott Erickson .10 .03
207 Dan Gladden .10 .03
208 Bob Welch .10 .03
209 Greg Olson .10 .03
210 Dan Pasqua .10 .03
211 Tim Wallach .10 .03
212 Jeff Montgomery .10 .03
213 Derrick May .10 .03
214 Ed Sprague .10 .03
215 David Haas .10 .03
216 Darrin Fletcher .10 .03
217 Brian Jordan .20 .06
218 Jaime Navarro .10 .03
219 Randy Velarde .10 .03
220 Ron Gant .20 .06
221 Paul Quantrill .10 .03
222 Damion Easley .10 .03
223 Charlie Hough .20 .06
224 Brad Brink .10 .03
225 Barry Manuel .10 .03
226 Kevin Koslofski .10 .03
227 Ryan Thompson .10 .03
228 Mike Munoz .10 .03
229 Dan Wilson .20 .06
230 Peter Hoy .10 .03
231 Pedro Astacio .10 .03
232 Matt Stairs .10 .03
233 Jeff Reboulet .10 .03
234 Manny Alexander .10 .03
235 Willie Banks .10 .03
236 John Jaha .10 .03
237 Scooter Tucker .10 .03
238 Russ Springer .10 .03
239 Paul Miller .10 .03
240 Dan Peltier .10 .03
241 Ozzie Canseco .10 .03
242 Ben Rivera .10 .03
243 John Valentin .10 .03
244 Henry Rodriguez .10 .03
245 Derek Parks .10 .03
246 Carlos Garcia .10 .03
247 Tim Pugh RC .10 .03
248 Melvin Nieves .10 .03
249 Rich Amaral .10 .03
250 Willie Greene .10 .03
251 Tim Scott .10 .03
252 Dave Silvestri .10 .03
253 Rob Mallicoat .10 .03
254 Donald Harris .10 .03
255 Craig Colbert .10 .03
256 Jose Guzman .10 .03
257 Domingo Martinez RC .10 .03
258 William Suero .10 .03
259 Juan Guerrero .10 .03
260 J.T. Snow RC .50 .15
261 Tony Pena .10 .03
262 Tim Fortugno .10 .03
263 Tom Marsh .10 .03
264 Kurt Knudsen .10 .03
265 Tim Costo .10 .03
266 Steve Shifflett .10 .03
267 Billy Ashley .10 .03
268 Jerry Nielsen .10 .03
269 Pete Young .10 .03
270 Johnny Guzman .10 .03
271 Greg Colbrunn .10 .03
272 Jeff Nelson .10 .03
273 Kevin Young .20 .06

74 Jeff Frye .10 .03
75 J.T. Bruett .10 .03
76 Todd Pratt RC .25 .07
77 Mike Butcher .10 .03
78 John Flaherty .10 .03
79 John Patterson .10 .03
80 Eric Hillman .10 .03
81 Bien Figueroa .10 .03
82 Shane Reynolds .10 .03
83 Rich Rowland .10 .03
84 Steve Foster .10 .03
85 Dave Mlicki .10 .03
86 Mike Piazza 1.50 .45
87 Mike Trombley .10 .03
88 Jim Pena .10 .03
89 Bob Ayrault .10 .03
90 Henry Mercedes .10 .03
91 Bob Wickman .10 .03
92 Jacob Brumfield .10 .03
93 David Hulse RC .10 .03
94 Ryan Klesko .20 .06
95 Doug Linton .10 .03
96 Steve Cooke .10 .03
97 Eddie Zosky .10 .03
98 Gerald Williams .10 .03
99 Jonathan Hurst .10 .03
00 Larry Carter RC .10 .03
01 William Pennyfeather .10 .03
02 Cesar Hernandez .10 .03
03 Steve Hosey .10 .03
04 Blas Minor .10 .03
05 Jeff Grotewald .10 .03
06 Bernardo Brito .10 .03
07 Rafael Bournigal .10 .03
08 Jeff Branson .10 .03
09 Tom Quinlan RC .30 .09
10 Pat Gomez RC .10 .03
11 Sterling Hitchcock RC .25 .07
12 Kent Bottenfield .10 .03
13 Alan Trammell .20 .06
14 Cris Colon .10 .03
15 Paul Wagner .10 .03
16 Matt Maysey .10 .03
17 Mike Stanton .10 .03
18 Rick Trlicek .10 .03
19 Kevin Rogers .10 .03
20 Mark Clark .10 .03
21 Pedro Martinez 1.00 .30
22 Al Martin .10 .03
23 Mike Macfarlane .10 .03
24 Rey Sanchez .10 .03
25 Roger Pavlik .10 .03
26 Troy Neel .10 .03
27 Kerry Woodson .10 .03
28 Wayne Kirby .10 .03
29 Ken Ryan RC .25 .07
30 Jesse Levis .10 .03
31 Jim Austin .10 .03
32 Dan Walters .10 .03
33 Brian Williams .10 .03
34 Wil Cordero .10 .03
35 Bret Boone .30 .09
36 Hipolito Pichardo .10 .03
37 Pat Mahomes .10 .03
38 Andy Stankiewicz .10 .03
39 Jim Bullinger .10 .03
40 Archi Cianfrocco .10 .03
41 Ruben Amaro .10 .03
42 Frank Seminara .10 .03
43 Pat Hentgen .10 .03
44 Dave Nilsson .10 .03
45 Mike Perez .10 .03
46 Tim Salmon .30 .09
47 Tim Wakefield .50 .15
48 Carlos Hernandez .10 .03
49 Donovan Osborne .10 .03
50 Denny Neagle .20 .06
51 Sam Militello .10 .03
52 Eric Fox .10 .03
53 John Doherty .10 .03
54 Chad Curtis .10 .03
55 Jeff Tackett .10 .03
56 Dave Fleming .10 .03
57 Pat Listach .10 .03
58 Kevin Wickander .10 .03
59 John Vander Wal .10 .03
60 Arthur Rhodes .10 .03
61 Bob Scanlan .10 .03
62 Bob Zupcic .10 .03
63 Mel Rojas .10 .03
64 Jim Thome .50 .15
65 Bill Pecota .10 .03
66 Mark Carreon .10 .03
67 Mitch Williams .10 .03
68 Cal Eldred .10 .03
69 Stan Belinda .10 .03
70 Pat Kelly .10 .03
71 Rheal Cormier .10 .03
72 Juan Guzman .10 .03
73 Damon Berryhill .10 .03
74 Gary DiSarcina .10 .03
75 Norm Charlton .10 .03
76 Roberto Hernandez .10 .03
77 Scott Kamieniecki .10 .03
78 Rusty Meacham .10 .03
79 Kurt Stillwell .10 .03
80 Lloyd McClendon .10 .03
81 Mark Leonard .10 .03
82 Jerry Browne .10 .03
83 Glenn Davis .10 .03
84 Randy Johnson .50 .15
85 Mike Greenwell .10 .03
86 Scott Chiamparino .10 .03
87 George Bell .10 .03
88 Steve Olin .10 .03
89 Chuck McElroy .10 .03
90 Mark Gardner .10 .03
91 Rod Beck .10 .03
92 Dennis Rasmussen .10 .03
93 Charlie Leibrandt .10 .03
94 Julio Franco .20 .06
95 Pete Harnisch .10 .03
96 Sid Bream .10 .03
97 Milt Thompson .10 .03
98 Glenallen Hill .10 .03
99 Chico Walker .10 .03
00 Alex Cole .10 .03
01 Trevor Wilson .10 .03
02 Jeff Conine .20 .06
03 Kyle Abbott .10 .03
404 Tom Browning .10 .03
405 Jerald Clark .10 .03
406 Vince Horsman .10 .03
407 Kevin Mitchell .10 .03
408 Pete Smith .10 .03
409 Jeff Innis .10 .03
410 Mike Timlin .10 .03
411 Charlie Hayes .10 .03
412 Alex Fernandez .10 .03
413 Jeff Russell .10 .03
414 Jody Reed .10 .03
415 Mickey Morandini .10 .03
416 Darnell Coles .10 .03
417 Xavier Hernandez .10 .03
418 Steve Sax .10 .03
419 Joe Girardi .10 .03
420 Mike Fetters .10 .03
421 Danny Jackson .10 .03
422 Jim Gott .10 .03
423 Tim Belcher .10 .03
424 Jose Mesa .10 .03
425 Junior Felix .10 .03
426 Thomas Howard .10 .03
427 Julio Valera .10 .03
428 Dante Bichette .20 .06
429 Mike Sharperson .10 .03
430 Darryl Kile .20 .06
431 Lonnie Smith .10 .03
432 Monty Fariss .10 .03
433 Reggie Jefferson .10 .03
434 Bob McClure .10 .03
435 Craig Lefferts .10 .03
436 Duane Ward .10 .03
437 Shawn Abner .10 .03
438 Roberto Kelly .10 .03
439 Paul O'Neill .30 .09
440 Alan Mills .10 .03
441 Roger Mason .10 .03
442 Gary Pettis .10 .03
443 Steve Lake .10 .03
444 Gene Larkin .10 .03
445 Larry Andersen .10 .03
446 Doug Dascenzo .10 .03
447 Daryl Boston .10 .03
448 John Candelaria .10 .03
449 Storm Davis .10 .03
450 Tom Edens .10 .03
451 Mike Maddux .10 .03
452 Tim Naehring .10 .03
453 John Orton .10 .03
454 Joey Cora .10 .03
455 Chuck Crim .10 .03
456 Dan Plesac .10 .03
457 Mike Bielecki .10 .03
458 Terry Jorgensen .10 .03
459 John Habyan .10 .03
460 Pete O'Brien .10 .03
461 Jeff Treadway .10 .03
462 Frank Castillo .10 .03
463 Jimmy Jones .10 .03
464 Tommy Greene .10 .03
465 Tracy Woodson .10 .03
466 Rich Rodriguez .10 .03
467 Joe Hesketh .10 .03
468 Greg Myers .10 .03
469 Kirk McCaskill .10 .03
470 Ricky Bones .10 .03
471 Lenny Webster .10 .03
472 Francisco Cabrera .10 .03
473 Turner Ward .10 .03
474 Dwayne Henry .10 .03
475 Al Osuna .10 .03
476 Craig Wilson .10 .03
477 Chris Nabholz .10 .03
478 Rafael Belliard .10 .03
479 Terry Leach .10 .03
480 Tim Teufel .10 .03
481 Dennis Eckersley AW .20 .06
482 Barry Bonds AW .60 .18
483 Dennis Eckersley AW .20 .06
484 Greg Maddux AW .50 .15
485 Pat Listach AW .10 .03
486 Eric Karros AW .10 .03
487 Jamie Arnold DP RC .10 .03
488 B.J. Wallace DP .10 .03
489 Derek Jeter DP RC 10.00 3.00
490 Jason Kendall DP RC .75 .23
491 Rick Helling DP .10 .03
492 Derek Wallace DP RC .10 .03
493 Sean Lowe DP RC .10 .03
494 S.Stewart DP RC .75 .23
495 Benji Grigsby DP RC .10 .03
496 T.Steverson DP RC .10 .03
497 Dan Serafini DP RC .10 .03
498 Michael Tucker DP .20 .06
499 Chris Roberts DP .10 .03
500 Pete Janicki DP RC .10 .03
501 Jeff Schmidt DP RC .10 .03
502 Edgar Martinez AS .20 .06
503 Omar Vizquel AS .20 .06
504 Ken Griffey Jr. AS .50 .15
505 Kirby Puckett AS .30 .09
506 Joe Carter AS .10 .03
507 Ivan Rodriguez AS .30 .09
508 Jack Morris AS .10 .03
509 Dennis Eckersley AS .20 .06
510 Frank Thomas AS .30 .09
511 Roberto Alomar AS .20 .06
512 Mickey Morandini AS .10 .03
513 Dennis Eckersley HL .20 .06
514 Jeff Reardon HL .10 .03
515 Danny Tartabull HL .10 .03
516 Bip Roberts HL .10 .03
517 George Brett HL .60 .18
518 Robin Yount HL .50 .15
519 Kevin Gross HL .10 .03
520 Ed Sprague WS .10 .03
521 Dave Winfield WS .10 .03
522 Ozzie Smith AS .50 .15
523 Barry Bonds AS .60 .18
524 Andy Van Slyke AS .10 .03
525 Tony Gwynn AS .30 .09
526 Darren Daulton AS .10 .03
527 Greg Maddux AS .50 .15
528 Fred McGriff AS .30 .09
529 Lee Smith AS .10 .03
530 Ryne Sandberg AS .50 .15
531 Gary Sheffield AS .10 .03
532 Ozzie Smith DT .50 .15
533 Kirby Puckett DT .30 .09
534 Gary Sheffield DT .10 .03
535 Andy Van Slyke DT .10 .03
536 Ken Griffey Jr. DT .50 .15
537 Ivan Rodriguez DT .30 .09
538 Charles Nagy DT .10 .03
539 Tom Glavine DT .20 .06
540 Dennis Eckersley DT .20 .06
541 Frank Thomas DT .30 .09
542 Roberto Alomar DT .20 .06
543 Sean Berry .10 .03
544 Mike Schooler .10 .03
545 Chuck Carr .10 .03
546 Lenny Harris .10 .03
547 Gary Scott .10 .03
548 Derek Lilliquist .10 .03
549 Brian Hunter .10 .03
550 Kirby Puckett MOY .30 .09
551 Jim Eisenreich .10 .03
552 Andre Dawson .20 .06
553 David Nied .10 .03
554 Spike Owen .10 .03
555 Greg Gagne .10 .03
556 Sid Fernandez .10 .03
557 Mark McGwire 1.25 .35
558 Bryan Harvey .10 .03
559 Harold Reynolds .20 .06
560 Barry Bonds 1.25 .35
561 Eric Wedge RC .25 .07
562 Ozzie Smith .75 .23
563 Rick Sutcliffe .20 .06
564 Jeff Reardon .20 .06
565 Alex Arias .10 .03
566 Greg Swindell .10 .03
567 Brook Jacoby .10 .03
568 Pete Incaviglia .10 .03
569 Butch Henry .10 .03
570 Eric Davis .20 .06
571 Kevin Seitzer .10 .03
572 Tony Fernandez .10 .03
573 Steve Reed RC .10 .03
574 Cory Snyder .10 .03
575 Joe Carter .20 .06
576 Greg Maddux .75 .23
577 Bert Blyleven UER .20 .06
(Should say 3701
career strikeouts)
578 Kevin Bass .10 .03
579 Carlton Fisk .30 .09
580 Doug Drabek .10 .03
581 Mark Gubicza .10 .03
582 Bobby Thigpen .10 .03
583 Chili Davis .20 .06
584 Scott Bankhead .10 .03
585 Harold Baines .20 .06
586 Eric Young .10 .03
587 Lance Parrish .20 .06
588 Juan Bell .10 .03
589 Bob Ojeda .10 .03
590 Joe Orsulak .10 .03
591 Benito Santiago .20 .06
592 Wade Boggs .30 .09
593 Robby Thompson .10 .03
594 Eric Plunk .10 .03
595 Hensley Meulens .10 .03
596 Lou Whitaker .20 .06
597 Dale Murphy .50 .15
598 Paul Molitor .30 .09
599 Greg W. Harris .10 .03
600 Darren Holmes .10 .03
601 Dave Martinez .10 .03
602 Tom Henke .10 .03
603 Mike Benjamin .10 .03
604 Rene Gonzales .10 .03
605 Roger McDowell .10 .03
606 Kirby Puckett .50 .15
607 Randy Myers .10 .03
608 Ruben Sierra .10 .03
609 Wilson Alvarez .10 .03
610 David Segui .10 .03
611 Juan Samuel .10 .03
612 Tom Brunansky .10 .03
613 Willie Randolph .20 .06
614 Tony Phillips .10 .03
615 Candy Maldonado .10 .03
616 Chris Bosio .10 .03
617 Bret Barberie .10 .03
618 Scott Sanderson .10 .03
619 Ron Darling .10 .03
620 Dave Winfield .20 .06
621 Mike Felder .10 .03
622 Greg Hibbard .10 .03
623 Mike Scioscia .10 .03
624 John Smiley .10 .03
625 Alejandro Pena .10 .03
626 Terry Steinbach .10 .03
627 Freddie Benavides .10 .03
628 Kevin Reimer .10 .03
629 Braulio Castillo .10 .03
630 Dave Stieb .10 .03
631 Dave Magadan .10 .03
632 Scott Fletcher .10 .03
633 Cris Carpenter .10 .03
634 Kevin Maas .10 .03
635 Todd Worrell .10 .03
636 Rob Deer .10 .03
637 Dwight Smith .10 .03
638 Chito Martinez .10 .03
639 Jimmy Key .20 .06
640 Greg A. Harris .10 .03
641 Mike Moore .10 .03
642 Pat Borders .10 .03
643 Bill Gullickson .10 .03
644 Gary Gaetti .20 .06
645 David Howard .10 .03
646 Jim Abbott .30 .09
647 Willie Wilson .10 .03
648 David Wells .20 .06
649 Andres Galarraga .20 .06
650 Vince Coleman .10 .03
651 Rob Dibble .20 .06
652 Frank Tanana .10 .03
653 Steve Decker .10 .03
654 David Cone .20 .06
655 Jack Armstrong .10 .03
656 Dave Stewart .20 .06
657 Billy Hatcher .10 .03
658 Tim Raines .20 .06
659 Walt Weiss .10 .03
660 Jose Lind .10 .03

1993 Score Boys of Summer

Randomly inserted exclusively into one in every four 1993 Score 35-card super packs, cards from this standard-size set feature 30 rookies expected to be the best in their class. Early cards of Pedro Martinez and Mike Piazza highlight this set.

	Nm-Mt	Ex-Mt
COMPLETE SET (30)	50.00	15.00
1 Billy Ashley	1.50	.45
2 Tim Salmon	3.00	.90
3 Pedro Martinez	10.00	3.00
4 Luis Mercedes	1.50	.45
5 Mike Piazza	10.00	3.00
6 Troy Neel	1.50	.45
7 Melvin Nieves	1.50	.45
8 Ryan Klesko	2.00	.60
9 Ryan Thompson	1.50	.45
10 Kevin Young	2.00	.60
11 Gerald Williams	1.50	.45
12 Willie Greene	1.50	.45
13 John Patterson	1.50	.45
14 Carlos Garcia	1.50	.45
15 Ed Zosky	1.50	.45
16 Sean Berry	1.50	.45
17 Rico Brogna	1.50	.45
18 Larry Carter	1.50	.45
19 Bobby Ayala	1.50	.45
20 Alan Embree	3.00	.90
21 Donald Harris	1.50	.45
22 Sterling Hitchcock	2.00	.60
23 David Nied	1.50	.45
24 Henry Mercedes	1.50	.45
25 Ozzie Canseco	1.50	.45
26 David Hulse	1.50	.45
27 Al Martin	1.50	.45
28 Dan Wilson	1.50	.45
29 Paul Miller	1.50	.45
30 Rich Rowland	1.50	.45

1993 Score Franchise

This 28-card set honors the top player on each of the major league teams. These cards were randomly inserted into one in every 24 16-card packs.

	Nm-Mt	Ex-Mt
COMPLETE SET (28)	120.00	36.00
1 Cal Ripken	25.00	7.50
2 Roger Clemens	15.00	4.50
3 Mark Langston	1.50	.45
4 Frank Thomas	8.00	2.40
5 Carlos Baerga	1.50	.45
6 Cecil Fielder	3.00	.90
7 Gregg Jefferies	1.50	.45
8 Robin Yount	12.00	3.60
9 Kirby Puckett	8.00	2.40
10 Don Mattingly	20.00	6.00
11 Dennis Eckersley	3.00	.90
12 Ken Griffey Jr.	12.00	3.60
13 Juan Gonzalez	5.00	1.50
14 Roberto Alomar	5.00	1.50
15 Terry Pendleton	3.00	.90
16 Ryne Sandberg	12.00	3.60
17 Barry Larkin	5.00	1.50
18 Jeff Bagwell	5.00	1.50
19 Brett Butler	3.00	.90
20 Larry Walker	5.00	1.50
21 Bobby Bonilla	3.00	.90
22 Darren Daulton	3.00	.90
23 Andy Van Slyke	3.00	.90
24 Ray Lankford	1.50	.45
25 Gary Sheffield	3.00	.90
26 Will Clark	8.00	2.40
27 Bryan Harvey	1.50	.45
28 David Nied	1.50	.45

1993 Score Gold Dream Team

Cards from this 12-card standard-size set feature Score's selection of the best players in baseball at each position. The cards were available only through a mail-in offer. Each card front features sepia tone photos of the players out of uniform, with the exception of Griffey's card (of whom is pictured in his Mariners togs). The photo edges are rounded with an airbrush effect.

	Nm-Mt	Ex-Mt
COMPLETE SET (12)	5.00	1.50
1 Ozzie Smith	.75	.23
2 Kirby Puckett	.50	.15
3 Gary Sheffield	.20	.06
4 Andy Van Slyke	.20	.06
5 Ken Griffey Jr.	.75	.23
6 Ivan Rodriguez	.50	.15
7 Charles Nagy	.10	.03
8 Tom Glavine	.30	.09
9 Dennis Eckersley	.20	.06
10 Frank Thomas	.50	.15
11 Roberto Alomar	.30	.09
NNO Header Card	.10	.03

1994 Score

The 1994 Score set of 660 standard-size cards was issued in two series of 330. Cards were distributed in 14-card hobby and retail packs. Each pack contained 13 basic cards plus one Gold Rush parallel card. Cards were also distributed in retail Jumbo packs. 4,875 cases of 1994 Score baseball were printed for the hobby. This figure does not take into account additional product printed for retail outlets. Among the subsets are American League stadiums (317-330) and National League stadiums (647-660). Rookie Cards include Trot Nixon and Billy Wagner.

	Nm-Mt	Ex-Mt
COMPLETE SET (660)	24.00	7.25
COMP.SERIES 1 (330)	12.00	3.60
COMP.SERIES 2 (330)	12.00	3.60
1 Barry Bonds	1.25	.35
2 John Olerud	.20	.06
3 Ken Griffey Jr.	.75	.23
4 Jeff Bagwell	.30	.09
5 John Burkett	.10	.03
6 Jack McDowell	.10	.03
7 Albert Belle	.20	.06
8 Andres Galarraga	.20	.06
9 Mike Mussina	.30	.09
10 Will Clark	.50	.15
11 Travis Fryman	.20	.06
12 Tony Gwynn	.60	.18
13 Robin Yount	.75	.23
14 Dave Magadan	.10	.03
15 Paul O'Neill	.30	.09
16 Ray Lankford	.10	.03
17 Damion Easley	.10	.03
18 Andy Van Slyke	.20	.06
19 Brian McRae	.10	.03
20 Ryne Sandberg	.75	.23
21 Kirby Puckett	.50	.15
22 Dwight Gooden	.20	.06
23 Don Mattingly	1.25	.35
24 Kevin Mitchell	.10	.03
25 Roger Clemens	1.00	.30
26 Eric Karros	.20	.06
27 Juan Gonzalez	.30	.09
28 John Kruk	.20	.06
29 Gregg Jefferies	.10	.03
30 Tom Glavine	.30	.09
31 Ivan Rodriguez	.50	.15
32 Jay Bell	.20	.06
33 Randy Johnson	.50	.15
34 Darren Daulton	.20	.06
35 Rickey Henderson	.50	.15
36 Eddie Murray	.50	.15
37 Brian Harper	.10	.03
38 Delino DeShields	.10	.03
39 Jose Lind	.10	.03
40 Benito Santiago	.20	.06
41 Frank Thomas	.50	.15
42 Mark Grace	.30	.09
43 Roberto Alomar	.30	.09
44 Andy Benes	.10	.03
45 Luis Polonia	.10	.03
46 Brett Butler	.20	.06
47 Terry Steinbach	.10	.03
48 Craig Biggio	.30	.09
49 Greg Vaughn	.10	.03
50 Charlie Hayes	.10	.03
51 Mickey Tettleton	.10	.03
52 Jose Rijo	.10	.03
53 Carlos Baerga	.10	.03
54 Jeff Blauser	.10	.03
55 Leo Gomez	.10	.03
56 Bob Tewksbury	.10	.03
57 Mo Vaughn	.20	.06
58 Orlando Merced	.10	.03
59 Tino Martinez	.30	.09
60 Lenny Dykstra	.20	.06
61 Jose Canseco	.50	.15
62 Tony Fernandez	.10	.03
63 Donovan Osborne	.10	.03
64 Ken Hill	.10	.03
65 Kent Hrbek	.20	.06
66 Bryan Harvey	.10	.03
67 Wally Joyner	.20	.06
68 Derrick May	.10	.03
69 Lance Johnson	.10	.03
70 Willie McGee	.20	.06
71 Mark Langston	.10	.03
72 Terry Pendleton	.20	.06
73 Joe Carter	.20	.06
74 Barry Larkin	.30	.09
75 Jimmy Key	.20	.06
76 Joe Girardi	.10	.03
77 B.J. Surhoff	.20	.06
78 Pete Harnisch	.10	.03
79 Lou Whitaker UER (Milt Cuyler pictured on front)	.20	.06
80 Cory Snyder	.10	.03
81 Kenny Lofton	.20	.06
82 Fred McGriff	.30	.09
83 Mike Greenwell	.10	.03
84 Mike Perez	.10	.03
85 Cal Ripken	1.50	.45
86 Don Slaught	.10	.03
87 Omar Vizquel	.30	.09

88 Curt Schilling .20 .06
89 Chuck Knoblauch .20 .06
90 Moises Alou .20 .06
91 Greg Gagne .10 .03
92 Bret Saberhagen .20 .06
93 Ozzie Guillen .10 .03
94 Matt Williams .20 .06
95 Chad Curtis .10 .03
96 Mike Harkey .10 .03
97 Devon White .20 .06
98 Walt Weiss .10 .03
99 Kevin Brown .20 .06
100 Gary Sheffield .20 .06
101 Wade Boggs .30 .09
102 Orel Hershiser .20 .06
103 Tony Phillips .10 .03
104 Andujar Cedeno .10 .03
105 Bill Spiers .10 .03
106 Otis Nixon .10 .03
107 Felix Fermin .10 .03
108 Bip Roberts .10 .03
109 Dennis Eckersley .20 .06
110 Dante Bichette .20 .06
111 Ben McDonald .10 .03
112 Jim Poole .10 .03
113 John Dopson .10 .03
114 Rob Dibble .20 .06
115 Jeff Treadway .10 .03
116 Ricky Jordan .10 .03
117 Mike Henneman .10 .03
118 Willie Blair .10 .03
119 Doug Henry .10 .03
120 Gerald Perry .10 .03
121 Greg Myers .10 .03
122 John Franco .20 .06
123 Roger Mason .10 .03
124 Chris Hammond .10 .03
125 Hubie Brooks .10 .03
126 Kent Mercker .10 .03
127 Jim Abbott .30 .09
128 Kevin Bass .10 .03
129 Rick Aguilera .10 .03
130 Mitch Webster .10 .03
131 Eric Plunk .10 .03
132 Mark Carreon .10 .03
133 Dave Stewart .20 .06
134 Willie Wilson .10 .03
135 Dave Fleming .10 .03
136 Jeff Tackett .10 .03
137 Geno Petralli .10 .03
138 Gene Harris .10 .03
139 Scott Bankhead .10 .03
140 Trevor Wilson .10 .03
141 Alvaro Espinoza .10 .03
142 Ryan Bowen .10 .03
143 Mike Moore .10 .03
144 Bill Pecota .10 .03
145 Jaime Navarro .10 .03
146 Jack Daugherty .10 .03
147 Bob Wickman .10 .03
148 Chris Jones .10 .03
149 Todd Stottlemyre .10 .03
150 Brian Williams .10 .03
151 Chuck Finley .20 .06
152 Lenny Harris .10 .03
153 Alex Fernandez .10 .03
154 Candy Maldonado .10 .03
155 Jeff Montgomery .10 .03
156 David West .10 .03
157 Mark Williamson .10 .03
158 Milt Thompson .10 .03
159 Ron Darling .10 .03
160 Stan Belinda .10 .03
161 Henry Cotto .10 .03
162 Mel Rojas .10 .03
163 Doug Strange .10 .03
164 Rene Arocha .10 .03
165 Tim Hulett .10 .03
166 Steve Avery .10 .03
167 Jim Thome .50 .15
168 Tom Browning .10 .03
169 Mario Diaz .10 .03
170 Steve Reed .10 .03
171 Scott Livingstone .10 .03
172 Chris Donnels .10 .03
173 John Jaha .10 .03
174 Carlos Hernandez .10 .03
175 Dion James .10 .03
176 Bud Black .10 .03
177 Tony Castillo .10 .03
178 Jose Guzman .10 .03
179 Torey Lovullo .10 .03
180 John Vander Wal .10 .03
181 Mike LaValliere .10 .03
182 Sid Fernandez .10 .03
183 Brent Mayne .10 .03
184 Terry Mulholland .10 .03
185 Willie Banks .10 .03
186 Steve Cooke .10 .03
187 Brent Gates .10 .03
188 Erik Pappas .10 .03
189 Bill Haselman .10 .03
190 Fernando Valenzuela .20 .06
191 Gary Redus .10 .03
192 Danny Darwin .10 .03
193 Mark Portugal .10 .03
194 Derek Lilliquist .10 .03
195 Charlie O'Brien .10 .03
196 Matt Nokes .10 .03
197 Danny Sheaffer .10 .03
198 Bill Gullickson .10 .03
199 Alex Arias .10 .03
200 Mike Fetters .10 .03
201 Brian Jordan .20 .06
202 Joe Grahe .10 .03
203 Tom Candiotti .10 .03
204 Jeremy Hernandez .10 .03
205 Mike Stanton .10 .03
206 David Howard .10 .03
207 Darren Holmes .10 .03
208 Rick Honeycutt .10 .03
209 Danny Jackson .10 .03
210 Rich Amaral .10 .03
211 Blas Minor .10 .03
212 Kenny Rogers .20 .06
213 Jim Leyritz .10 .03
214 Mike Morgan .10 .03
215 Dan Gladden .10 .03
216 Randy Velarde .10 .03
217 Mitch Williams .10 .03
218 Hipolito Pichardo .10 .03
219 Dave Burba .10 .03
220 Wilson Alvarez .10 .03
221 Bob Zupcic .10 .03
222 Francisco Cabrera .10 .03
223 Julio Valera .10 .03
224 Paul Assenmacher .10 .03
225 Jeff Branson .10 .03
226 Todd Frohwirth .10 .03
227 Armando Reynoso .10 .03
228 Rich Rowland .10 .03
229 Freddie Benavides .10 .03
230 Wayne Kirby .10 .03
231 Darryl Kile .20 .06
232 Skeeter Barnes .10 .03
233 Ramon Martinez .10 .03
234 Tom Gordon .10 .03
235 Dave Gallagher .10 .03
236 Ricky Bones .10 .03
237 Larry Andersen .10 .03
238 Pat Meares .10 .03
239 Zane Smith .10 .03
240 Tim Leary .10 .03
241 Phil Clark .10 .03
242 Danny Cox .10 .03
243 Mike Jackson .10 .03
244 Mike Gallego .10 .03
245 Lee Smith .20 .06
246 Todd Jones .10 .03
247 Steve Bedrosian .10 .03
248 Troy Neel .10 .03
249 Jose Bautista .10 .03
250 Steve Frey .10 .03
251 Jeff Reardon .20 .06
252 Stan Javier .10 .03
253 Mo Sanford .10 .03
254 Steve Sax .10 .03
255 Luis Aquino .10 .03
256 Domingo Jean .10 .03
257 Scott Servais .10 .03
258 Brad Pennington .10 .03
259 Dave Hansen .10 .03
260 Rich Gossage .20 .06
261 Jeff Fassero .10 .03
262 Junior Ortiz .10 .03
263 Anthony Young .10 .03
264 Chris Bosio .10 .03
265 Ruben Amaro .10 .03
266 Mark Eichhorn .10 .03
267 Dave Clark .10 .03
268 Gary Thurman .10 .03
269 Les Lancaster .10 .03
270 Jamie Moyer .20 .06
271 Ricky Gutierrez .10 .03
272 Greg A. Harris .10 .03
273 Mike Benjamin .10 .03
274 Gene Nelson .10 .03
275 Damon Berryhill .10 .03
276 Scott Radinsky .10 .03
277 Mike Aldrete .10 .03
278 Jerry DiPoto .10 .03
279 Chris Haney .10 .03
280 Richie Lewis .10 .03
281 Jarvis Brown .10 .03
282 Juan Bell .10 .03
283 Joe Klink .10 .03
284 Graeme Lloyd .10 .03
285 Casey Candaele .10 .03
286 Bob MacDonald .10 .03
287 Mike Sharperson .10 .03
288 Gene Larkin .10 .03
289 Brian Barnes .10 .03
290 David McCarty .10 .03
291 Jeff Innis .10 .03
292 Bob Patterson .10 .03
293 Ben Rivera .10 .03
294 John Habyan .10 .03
295 Rich Rodriguez .10 .03
296 Edwin Nunez .10 .03
297 Rod Brewer .10 .03
298 Mike Timlin .10 .03
299 Jesse Orosco .10 .03
300 Gary Gaetti .20 .06
301 Todd Benzinger .10 .03
302 Jeff Nelson .10 .03
303 Rafael Belliard .10 .03
304 Matt Whiteside .10 .03
305 Vinny Castilla .20 .06
306 Matt Turner .10 .03
307 Eduardo Perez .10 .03
308 Joel Johnston .10 .03
309 Chris Gomez .10 .03
310 Pat Rapp .10 .03
311 Jim Tatum .10 .03
312 Kirk Rueter .20 .06
313 John Flaherty .10 .03
314 Tom Kramer .10 .03
315 Mark Whiten .10 .03
316 Chris Bosio .10 .03
317 Baltimore Orioles CL .10 .03
318 Bos.Red Sox CL UER .10 .03
Viola listed as 316; should be 331
319 California Angels CL .10 .03
320 Chicago White Sox CL .10 .03
321 Cleveland Indians CL .10 .03
322 Detroit Tigers CL .10 .03
323 KC Royals CL .10 .03
324 Milw. Brewers CL .10 .03
325 Minnesota Twins CL .10 .03
326 New York Yankees CL .10 .03
327 Oakland Athletics CL .10 .03
328 Seattle Mariners CL .10 .03
329 Texas Rangers CL .10 .03
330 Toronto Blue Jays CL .10 .03
331 Frank Viola .20 .06
332 Ron Gant .20 .06
333 Charles Nagy .10 .03
334 Roberto Kelly .10 .03
335 Brady Anderson .20 .06
336 Alex Cole .10 .03
337 Alan Trammell .20 .06
338 Derek Bell .10 .03
339 Bernie Williams .30 .09
340 Jose Offerman .10 .03
341 Bill Wegman .10 .03
342 Ken Caminiti .20 .06
343 Pat Borders .10 .03
344 Kirt Manwaring .10 .03
345 Chili Davis .20 .06
346 Steve Buechele .10 .03
347 Robin Ventura .20 .06
348 Teddy Higuera .10 .03
349 Jerry Browne .10 .03
350 Scott Kamieniecki .10 .03
351 Kevin Tapani .10 .03
352 Marquis Grissom .20 .06
353 Jay Buhner .20 .06
354 Dave Hollins .10 .03
355 Dan Wilson .10 .03
356 Bob Walk .10 .03
357 Chris Hoiles .10 .03
358 Todd Zeile .10 .03
359 Kevin Appier .20 .06
360 Chris Sabo .10 .03
361 David Segui .10 .03
362 Jerald Clark .10 .03
363 Tony Pena .10 .03
364 Steve Finley .20 .06
365 Roger Pavlik .10 .03
366 John Smoltz .30 .09
367 Scott Fletcher .10 .03
368 Jody Reed .10 .03
369 David Wells .20 .06
370 Jose Vizcaino .10 .03
371 Pat Listach .10 .03
372 Orestes Destrade .10 .03
373 Danny Tartabull .10 .03
374 Greg W. Harris .10 .03
375 Juan Guzman .10 .03
376 Larry Walker .30 .09
377 Gary DiSarcina .10 .03
378 Bobby Bonilla .20 .06
379 Tim Raines .20 .06
380 Tommy Greene .10 .03
381 Chris Gwynn .10 .03
382 Jeff King .10 .03
383 Shane Mack .10 .03
384 Ozzie Smith .75 .23
385 Eddie Zambrano RC .10 .03
386 Mike Devereaux .10 .03
387 Erik Hanson .10 .03
388 Scott Cooper .10 .03
389 Dean Palmer .20 .06
390 John Wetteland .20 .06
391 Reggie Jefferson .10 .03
392 Mark Lemke .10 .03
393 Cecil Fielder .20 .06
394 Reggie Sanders .10 .03
395 Darryl Hamilton .10 .03
396 Daryl Boston .10 .03
397 Pat Kelly .10 .03
398 Joe Orsulak .10 .03
399 Ed Sprague .10 .03
400 Eric Anthony .10 .03
401 Scott Sanderson .10 .03
402 Jim Gott .10 .03
403 Ron Karkovice .10 .03
404 Phil Plantier .10 .03
405 David Cone .20 .06
406 Robby Thompson .10 .03
407 Dave Winfield .20 .06
408 Dwight Smith .10 .03
409 Ruben Sierra .10 .03
410 Jack Armstrong .10 .03
411 Mike Felder .10 .03
412 Wil Cordero .10 .03
413 Julio Franco .20 .06
414 Howard Johnson .10 .03
415 Mark McLemore .10 .03
416 Pete Incaviglia .10 .03
417 John Valentin .10 .03
418 Tim Wakefield .20 .06
419 Jose Mesa .10 .03
420 Bernard Gilkey .10 .03
421 Kirk Gibson .20 .06
422 Dave Justice .20 .06
423 Tom Brunansky .10 .03
424 John Smiley .10 .03
425 Kevin Maas .10 .03
426 Doug Drabek .10 .03
427 Paul Molitor .30 .09
428 Darryl Strawberry .20 .06
429 Tim Naehring .10 .03
430 Bill Swift .10 .03
431 Ellis Burks .20 .06
432 Greg Hibbard .10 .03
433 Felix Jose .10 .03
434 Bret Barberie .10 .03
435 Pedro Munoz .10 .03
436 Darrin Fletcher .10 .03
437 Bobby Witt .10 .03
438 Wes Chamberlain .10 .03
439 Mackey Sasser .10 .03
440 Mark Whiten .10 .03
441 Harold Reynolds .20 .06
442 Greg Olson .10 .03
443 Billy Hatcher .10 .03
444 Joe Oliver .10 .03
445 Sandy Alomar Jr. .10 .03
446 Tim Wallach .10 .03
447 Karl Rhodes .10 .03
448 Royce Clayton .10 .03
449 Cal Eldred .10 .03
450 Rick Wilkins .10 .03
451 Mike Stanley .10 .03
452 Charlie Hough .20 .06
453 Jack Morris .20 .06
454 Jon Ratliff RC .10 .03
455 Rene Gonzales .10 .03
456 Eddie Taubensee .10 .03
457 Roberto Hernandez .10 .03
458 Todd Hundley .10 .03
459 Mike Macfarlane .10 .03
460 Mickey Morandini .10 .03
461 Scott Erickson .10 .03
462 Lonnie Smith .10 .03
463 Dave Henderson .10 .03
464 Ryan Klesko .20 .06
465 Edgar Martinez .30 .09
466 Tom Pagnozzi .10 .03
467 Charlie Leibrandt .10 .03
468 Brian Anderson RC .25 .07
469 Harold Baines .20 .06
470 Tim Belcher .10 .03
471 Andre Dawson .20 .06
472 Eric Young .10 .03
473 Paul Sorrento .10 .03
474 Luis Gonzalez .20 .06
475 Rob Deer .10 .03
476 Mike Piazza 1.00 .30
477 Kevin Reimer .10 .03
478 Jeff Gardner .10 .03
479 Melido Perez .10 .03
480 Darren Lewis .10 .03
481 Duane Ward .10 .03
482 Rey Sanchez .10 .03
483 Mark Lewis .10 .03
484 Jeff Conine .20 .06
485 Joey Cora .10 .03
486 Trot Nixon RC 1.00 .30
487 Kevin McReynolds .10 .03
488 Mike Lansing .10 .03
489 Mike Pagliarulo .10 .03
490 Mariano Duncan .10 .03
491 Mike Bordick .10 .03
492 Kevin Young .10 .03
493 Dave Valle .10 .03
494 Wayne Gomes RC .10 .03
495 Rafael Palmeiro .30 .09
496 Deion Sanders .30 .09
497 Rick Sutcliffe .20 .06
498 Randy Milligan .10 .03
499 Carlos Quintana .10 .03
500 Chris Turner .10 .03
501 Thomas Howard .10 .03
502 Greg Swindell .10 .03
503 Chad Kreuter .10 .03
504 Eric Davis .20 .06
505 Dickie Thon .10 .03
506 Matt Drews RC .10 .03
507 Spike Owen .10 .03
508 Rod Beck .10 .03
509 Pat Hentgen .10 .03
510 Sammy Sosa .75 .23
511 J.T. Snow .20 .06
512 Chuck Carr .10 .03
513 Bo Jackson .50 .15
514 Dennis Martinez .20 .06
515 Phil Hiatt .10 .03
516 Jeff Kent .20 .06
517 Brooks Kieschnick RC .25 .07
518 Kirk Presley RC .10 .03
519 Kevin Seitzer .10 .03
520 Carlos Garcia .10 .03
521 Mike Blowers .10 .03
522 Luis Alicea .10 .03
523 David Hulse .10 .03
524 Greg Maddux UER .75 .23
(career strikeout totals listed as 113; should be 1134)
525 Gregg Olson .10 .03
526 Hal Morris .10 .03
527 Daron Kirkreit .10 .03
528 David Nied .10 .03
529 Jeff Russell .10 .03
530 Kevin Gross .10 .03
531 John Doherty .10 .03
532 Matt Brunson RC .10 .03
533 Dave Nilsson .10 .03
534 Randy Myers .10 .03
535 Steve Farr .10 .03
536 Billy Wagner RC .50 .15
537 Darnell Coles .10 .03
538 Frank Tanana .10 .03
539 Tim Salmon .30 .09
540 Kim Batiste .10 .03
541 George Bell .10 .03
542 Tom Henke .10 .03
543 Sam Horn .10 .03
544 Doug Jones .10 .03
545 Scott Leius .10 .03
546 Al Martin .10 .03
547 Bob Welch .10 .03
548 Scott Christman RC .10 .03
549 Norm Charlton .10 .03
550 Mark McGwire 1.25 .35
551 Greg McMichael .10 .03
552 Tim Costo .10 .03
553 Rodney Bolton .10 .03
554 Pedro Martinez .50 .15
555 Marc Valdes .10 .03
556 Darrell Whitmore .10 .03
557 Tim Bogar .10 .03
558 Steve Karsay .10 .03
559 Danny Bautista .10 .03
560 Jeffrey Hammonds .10 .03
561 Aaron Sele .10 .03
562 Russ Springer .10 .03
563 Jason Bere .10 .03
564 Billy Brewer .10 .03
565 Sterling Hitchcock .10 .03
566 Bobby Munoz .10 .03
567 Craig Paquette .10 .03
568 Bret Boone .20 .06
569 Dan Peltier .10 .03
570 Jeromy Burnitz .20 .06
571 John Wasdin RC .10 .03
572 Chipper Jones .50 .15
573 Jamey Wright RC .10 .03
574 Jeff Granger .10 .03
575 Jay Powell RC .10 .03
576 Ryan Thompson .10 .03
577 Lou Frazier .10 .03
578 Paul Wagner .10 .03
579 Brad Ausmus .10 .03
580 Jack Voigt .10 .03
581 Kevin Rogers .10 .03
582 Damon Buford .10 .03
583 Paul Quantrill .10 .03
584 Marc Newfield .10 .03
585 Derrek Lee RC .50 .15
586 Shane Reynolds .10 .03
587 Cliff Floyd .20 .06
588 Jeff Schwarz .10 .03
589 Ross Powell RC .10 .03
590 Gerald Williams .10 .03
591 Mike Trombley .10 .03
592 Ken Ryan .10 .03
593 John O'Donoghue .10 .03
594 Rod Correia .10 .03
595 Darrell Sherman .10 .03
596 Steve Scarsone .10 .03
597 Sherman Obando .10 .03
598 Kurt Abbott RC .25 .07
599 Dave Telgheder .10 .03
600 Rick Trlicek .10 .03
601 Carl Everett .20 .06
602 Luis Ortiz .10 .03
603 Larry Luebbers .10 .03
604 Kevin Roberson .10 .03
605 Butch Huskey .10 .03
606 Benji Gil .10 .03
607 Todd Van Poppel .10 .03
608 Mark Hutton .10 .03
609 Chip Hale .10 .03
610 Matt Maysey .10 .03
611 Scott Ruffcorn .10 .03
612 Hilly Hathaway .10 .03
613 Allen Watson .10 .03
614 Carlos Delgado .30 .09
615 Roberto Mejia .10 .03
616 Turk Wendell .10 .03
617 Tony Tarasco .10 .03
618 Raul Mondesi .20 .06
619 Kevin Stocker .10 .03
620 Javier Lopez .20 .06
621 Keith Kessinger .10 .03
622 Bob Hamelin .10 .03
623 John Roper .10 .03
624 Lenny Dykstra WS .10 .03
625 Joe Carter WS .10 .03
626 Jim Abbott HL .20 .06
627 Lee Smith HL .10 .03
628 Ken Griffey Jr. HL .50 .15
629 Dave Winfield HL .10 .03
630 Darryl Kile HL .10 .03
631 F.Thomas AL MVP .30 .09
632 Barry Bonds NL MVP .60 .18
633 Jack McDowell AL CY .10 .03
634 Greg Maddux NL CY .50 .15
635 Tim Salmon AL ROY .20 .06
636 Mike Piazza NL ROY .50 .15
637 Brian Turang RC .10 .03
638 Rondell White .20 .06
639 Nigel Wilson .10 .03
640 Torii Hunter RC 2.00 .60
641 Salomon Torres .10 .03
642 Kevin Higgins .10 .03
643 Eric Wedge .10 .03
644 Roger Salkeld .10 .03
645 Manny Ramirez .30 .09
646 Jeff McNeely .10 .03
647 Atlanta Braves CL .10 .03
648 Chicago Cubs CL .10 .03
649 Cincinnati Reds CL .10 .03
650 Colorado Rockies CL .10 .03
651 Florida Marlins CL .10 .03
652 Houston Astros CL .10 .03
653 L.A. Dodgers CL .10 .03
654 Montreal Expos CL .10 .03
655 New York Mets CL .10 .03
656 Phi. Phillies CL .10 .03
657 Pittsburgh Pirates CL .10 .03
658 St. Louis Cardinals CL .10 .03
659 San Diego Padres CL .10 .03
660 S.F. Giants CL .10 .03

1994 Score Gold Rush

This 660-card standard-size set is parallel to the basic Score issue. This set features metallicized and gold-bordered fronts. Gold Rush cards came one per 14-card pack or super pack. They were also issued two per jumbo. These cards were inserted into both hobby and retail packs.

	Nm-Mt	Ex-Mt
COMPLETE SET (660)	120.00	36.00
COMP. SERIES 1 (330)	60.00	18.00
COMP. SERIES 2 (330)	60.00	18.00

*STARS: 1.5X to 4X BASIC CARDS
*ROOKIES: 1.25X TO 3X BASIC

1994 Score Boys of Summer

Randomly inserted in super packs at a rate of one in four, this 60-card set features top young stars and hopefuls. The set was issued in two series of 30 cards.

	Nm-Mt	Ex-Mt
COMPLETE SET (60)	60.00	18.00
COMPLETE SERIES 1 (30)	25.00	7.50
COMPLETE SERIES 2 (30)	35.00	10.50
1 Jeff Conine	2.00	.60
2 Aaron Sele	1.00	.30
3 Kevin Stocker	1.00	.30
4 Pat Meares	1.00	.30
5 Jeromy Burnitz	2.00	.60
6 Mike Piazza	8.00	2.40
7 Allen Watson	1.00	.30
8 Jeffrey Hammonds	1.00	.30
9 Kevin Roberson	1.00	.30
10 Hilly Hathaway	1.00	.30
11 Kirk Rueter	2.00	.60
12 Eduardo Perez	1.00	.30
13 Ricky Gutierrez	1.00	.30
14 Domingo Jean	1.00	.30
15 David Nied	1.00	.30
16 Wayne Kirby	1.00	.30
17 Mike Lansing	1.00	.30
18 Jason Bere	1.00	.30
19 Brent Gates	1.00	.30
20 Javier Lopez	2.00	.60
21 Greg McMichael	1.00	.30
22 David Hulse	1.00	.30
23 Roberto Mejia	1.00	.30
24 Tim Salmon	3.00	.90
25 Rene Arocha	1.00	.30
26 Bret Boone	2.00	.60
27 David McCarty	1.00	.30
28 Todd Van Poppel	1.00	.30
29 Lance Painter	1.00	.30
30 Erik Pappas	1.00	.30
31 Chuck Carr	1.00	.30
32 Mark Hutton	1.00	.30
33 Jeff McNeely	1.00	.30
34 Willie Greene	1.00	.30
35 Nigel Wilson	1.00	.30

6 Rondell White 2.00 .60
7 Brian Turang 1.00 .30
8 Manny Ramirez 3.00 .90
9 Salomon Torres 1.00 .30
0 Melvin Nieves 1.00 .30
1 Ryan Klesko 2.00 .60
2 Keith Kessinger 1.00 .30
3 Brad Ausmus 1.00 .30
4 Bob Hamelin 1.00 .30
5 Carlos Delgado 3.00 .90
6 Marc Newfield 1.00 .30
7 Raul Mondesi 2.00 .60
8 Tim Costo 1.00 .30
9 Pedro Martinez 5.00 1.50
0 Steve Karsay 1.00 .30
1 Danny Bautista 1.00 .30
2 Butch Huskey 1.00 .30
3 Kurt Abbott 2.00 .60
4 Darrell Sherman 1.00 .30
5 Damon Buford 1.00 .30
6 Ross Powell 1.00 .30
7 Darrell Whitmore 1.00 .30
8 Chipper Jones 5.00 1.50
9 Jeff Granger 1.00 .30
0 Cliff Floyd 2.00 .60

1994 Score Cycle

his 20-card set was randomly inserted in sec-nd series foil at a rate of one in 72 and jumbo acks at a rate of one in 36. The set is arranged ccording to players with the most singles (1-5), oubles (6-10), triples (11-15) and home runs 16-20). The cards are number with a "TC" pre-x.

Nm-Mt Ex-Mt
OMPLETE SET (20) 150.00 45.00
C1 Brett Butler 5.00 1.50
C2 Kenny Lofton 5.00 1.50
C3 Paul Molitor 8.00 2.40
C4 Carlos Baerga 2.50 .75
C5 Gregg Jefferies 2.50 .75
Tony Phillips
C6 John Olerud 5.00 1.50
C7 Charlie Hayes 2.50 .75
C8 Lenny Dykstra 5.00 1.50
C9 Dante Bichette 5.00 1.50
C10 Devon White 5.00 1.50
C11 Lance Johnson 2.50 .75
C12 Joey Cora 5.00 1.50
Steve Finley
C13 Tony Fernandez 2.50 .75
C14 David Hulse 5.00 1.50
Brett Butler
C15 Jay Bell 5.00 1.50
Brian McRae
Mickey Morandini
C16 Juan Gonzalez 30.00 9.00
Barry Bonds
C17 Ken Griffey Jr. 20.00 6.00
C18 Frank Thomas 12.00 3.60
C19 Dave Justice 5.00 1.50
C20 Matt Williams 5.00 1.50
Albert Belle

1994 Score Dream Team

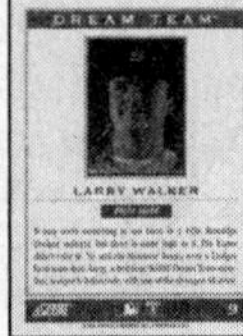

andomly inserted in first series foil and jumbo acks at a rate of one in 72, this ten-card set fea-ure's baseball's Dream Team as selected by innacle Brands. Banded by forest green stripes bove and below, the player photos on the fronts eature ten of baseball's best players sporting istorical team uniforms from the 1930's. A arry Larkin promo card was distributed to deal-rs and hobby media to preview the set.

Nm-Mt Ex-Mt
OMPLETE SET (10) 60.00 18.00
Mike Mussina 8.00 2.40
Tom Glavine 8.00 2.40
Don Mattingly 30.00 9.00
Carlos Baerga 2.50 .75
Barry Larkin 8.00 2.40
Matt Williams 5.00 1.50
Juan Gonzalez 8.00 2.40
Andy Van Slyke 5.00 1.50
Larry Walker 8.00 2.40
0 Mike Stanley 2.50 .75
5 Barry Larkin Sample 1.00 .30

1994 Score Gold Stars

Randomly inserted at a rate of one in every 18 hobby packs, this 60-card set features National and American stars. Split into two series of 30 cards, the first series (1-30) comprises of National League players and the second series (31-60) American Leaguers.

Nm-Mt Ex-Mt
COMPLETE SET (60) 250.00 75.00
COMPLETE NL (30) 100.00 30.00
COMPLETE AL (30) 150.00 45.00
1 Barry Bonds 20.00 6.00
2 Orlando Merced 1.50 .45
3 Mark Grace 5.00 1.50
4 Darren Daulton 3.00 .90
5 Jeff Blauser 1.50 .45
6 Deion Sanders 5.00 1.50
7 John Kruk 3.00 .90
8 Jeff Bagwell 5.00 1.50
9 Gregg Jefferies 1.50 .45
10 Matt Williams 3.00 .90
11 Andres Galarraga 3.00 .90
12 Jay Bell 3.00 .90
13 Mike Piazza 15.00 4.50
14 Ron Gant 3.00 .90
15 Barry Larkin 5.00 1.50
16 Tom Glavine 5.00 1.50
17 Lenny Dykstra 3.00 .90
18 Fred McGriff 5.00 1.50
19 Andy Van Slyke 3.00 .90
20 Gary Sheffield 3.00 .90
21 John Burkett 1.50 .45
22 Dante Bichette 3.00 .90
23 Tony Gwynn 10.00 3.00
24 Dave Justice 3.00 .90
25 Marquis Grissom 3.00 .90
26 Bobby Bonilla 3.00 .90
27 Larry Walker 5.00 1.50
28 Brett Butler 3.00 .90
29 Robby Thompson 1.50 .45
30 Jeff Conine 3.00 .90
31 Joe Carter 3.00 .90
32 Ken Griffey Jr. 12.00 3.60
33 Juan Gonzalez 5.00 1.50
34 Rickey Henderson 8.00 2.40
35 Bo Jackson 8.00 2.40
36 Cal Ripken 25.00 7.50
37 John Olerud 3.00 .90
38 Carlos Baerga 1.50 .45
39 Jack McDowell 1.50 .45
40 Cecil Fielder 3.00 .90
41 Kenny Lofton 3.00 .90
42 Roberto Alomar 5.00 1.50
43 Randy Johnson 8.00 2.40
44 Tim Salmon 5.00 1.50
45 Frank Thomas 8.00 2.40
46 Albert Belle 3.00 .90
47 Greg Vaughn 1.50 .45
48 Travis Fryman 3.00 .90
49 Don Mattingly 20.00 6.00
50 Wade Boggs 5.00 1.50
51 Mo Vaughn 3.00 .90
52 Kirby Puckett 8.00 2.40
53 Devon White 3.00 .90
54 Tony Phillips 1.50 .45
55 Brian Harper 1.50 .45
56 Chad Curtis 1.50 .45
57 Paul Molitor 5.00 1.50
58 Ivan Rodriguez 8.00 2.40
59 Rafael Palmeiro 5.00 1.50
60 Brian McRae 1.50 .45

1994 Score Rookie/Traded

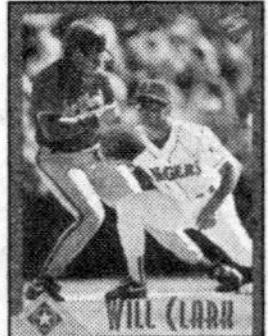

The 1994 Score Rookie and Traded set consists of 165 standard-size cards featuring rookie standouts, traded players, and new young prospects. The set is delineated by traded players (RT1-RT70) and rookies/young prospects (RT71-RT163). The set closes with checklists (RT164-RT165). Each foil pack contained one Gold Rush card. The cards are numbered on the back with an "RT" prefix. Several leading dealers are under the belief that Jose Lima's card (number RT158) was short-printed. Conversely, extra cards of John Mabry are typically found in place of the short Lima's. A special unnumbered September Call-Up Redemption card could be exchanged for an Alex Rodriguez card. The expiration date was January 31, 1995. Odds of finding a redemption card were approximately one in 240 retail and hobby packs. Rookie Cards include Jose Lima and Chan Ho Park.

Nm-Mt Ex-Mt
COMPLETE SET (165) 15.00 4.50
RT1 Will Clark .75 .23
RT2 Lee Smith .30 .09
RT3 Bo Jackson .75 .23
RT4 Ellis Burks .30 .09
RT5 Eddie Murray .75 .23
RT6 Delino DeShields .15 .04
RT7 Erik Hanson .15 .04
RT8 Rafael Palmeiro .50 .15
RT9 Luis Polonia .15 .04
RT10 Omar Vizquel .50 .15
RT11 Kurt Abbott .30 .09
RT12 Vince Coleman .15 .04
RT13 Rickey Henderson .75 .23
RT14 Terry Mulholland .15 .04
RT15 Greg Hibbard .15 .04
RT16 Walt Weiss .15 .04
RT17 Chris Sabo .15 .04
RT18 Dave Henderson .15 .04
RT19 Rick Sutcliffe .30 .09
RT20 Harold Reynolds .30 .09
RT21 Jack Morris .30 .09
RT22 Dan Wilson .15 .04
RT23 Dave Magadan .15 .04
RT24 Dennis Martinez .30 .09
RT25 Wes Chamberlain .15 .04
RT26 Otis Nixon .15 .04
RT27 Eric Anthony .15 .04
RT28 Randy Milligan .15 .04
RT29 Julio Franco .30 .09
RT30 Kevin McReynolds .15 .04
RT31 Anthony Young .15 .04
RT32 Brian Harper .15 .04
RT33 Gene Harris .15 .04
RT34 Eddie Taubensee .15 .04
RT35 David Segui .15 .04
RT36 Stan Javier .15 .04
RT37 Felix Fermin .15 .04
RT38 Darrin Jackson .15 .04
RT39 Tony Fernandez .15 .04
RT40 Jose Vizcaino .15 .04
RT41 Willie Banks .15 .04
RT42 Brian Hunter .15 .04
RT43 Reggie Jefferson .15 .04
RT44 Junior Felix .15 .04
RT45 Jack Armstrong .15 .04
RT46 Bip Roberts .15 .04
RT47 Jerry Browne .15 .04
RT48 Marvin Freeman .15 .04
RT49 Jody Reed .15 .04
RT50 Alex Cole .15 .04
RT51 Sid Fernandez .15 .04
RT52 Pete Smith .15 .04
RT53 Xavier Hernandez .15 .04
RT54 Scott Sanderson .15 .04
RT55 Turner Ward .15 .04
RT56 Rex Hudler .15 .04
RT57 Deion Sanders .50 .15
RT58 Sid Bream .15 .04
RT59 Tony Pena .15 .04
RT60 Bret Boone .30 .09
RT61 Bobby Ayala .15 .04
RT62 Pedro Martinez .75 .23
RT63 Howard Johnson .15 .04
RT64 Mark Portugal .15 .04
RT65 Roberto Kelly .15 .04
RT66 Spike Owen .15 .04
RT67 Jeff Treadway .15 .04
RT68 Mike Harkey .15 .04
RT69 Doug Jones .15 .04
RT70 Steve Farr .15 .04
RT71 Billy Taylor RC .15 .04
RT72 Manny Ramirez .50 .15
RT73 Bob Hamelin .15 .04
RT74 Steve Karsay .15 .04
RT75 Ryan Klesko .30 .09
RT76 Cliff Floyd .30 .09
RT77 Jeffrey Hammonds .15 .04
RT78 Javier Lopez .30 .09
RT79 Roger Salkeld .15 .04
RT80 Hector Carrasco .15 .04
RT81 Gerald Williams .15 .04
RT82 Raul Mondesi .30 .09
RT83 Sterling Hitchcock .15 .04
RT84 Danny Bautista .15 .04
RT85 Chris Turner .15 .04
RT86 Shane Reynolds .15 .04
RT87 Rondell White .30 .09
RT88 Salomon Torres .15 .04
RT89 Turk Wendell .15 .04
RT90 Tony Tarasco .15 .04
RT91 Shawn Green .75 .23
RT92 Greg Colbrunn .15 .04
RT93 Eddie Zambrano .15 .04
RT94 Rich Becker .15 .04
RT95 Chris Gomez .15 .04
RT96 John Patterson .15 .04
RT97 Derek Parks .15 .04
RT98 Rich Rowland .15 .04
RT99 James Mouton .15 .04
RT100 Tim Hyers RC .15 .04
RT101 Jose Valentin .15 .04
RT102 Carlos Delgado .50 .15
RT103 Robert Eenhoorn .15 .04
RT104 John Hudek RC .15 .04
RT105 Domingo Cedeno .15 .04
RT106 Denny Hocking .15 .04
RT107 Greg Pirkl .15 .04
RT108 Mark Smith .15 .04
RT109 Paul Shuey .15 .04
RT110 Jorge Fabregas .15 .04
RT111 Rikkert Faneyte RC .15 .04
RT112 Rob Butler .15 .04
RT113 Darren Oliver RC .30 .09
RT114 Troy O'Leary .15 .04
RT115 Scott Brow .15 .04
RT116 Tony Eusebio .15 .04
RT117 Carlos Reyes .15 .04
RT118 J.R. Phillips .15 .04
RT119 Alex Diaz .15 .04
RT120 Charles Johnson .30 .09
RT121 Nate Minchey .15 .04
RT122 Scott Sanders .15 .04
RT123 Daryl Boston .15 .04
RT124 Joey Hamilton .15 .04
RT125 Brian Anderson .30 .09
RT126 Dan Miceli .15 .04
RT127 Tom Brunansky .15 .04
RT128 Dave Staton .15 .04
RT129 Mike Oquist .15 .04
RT130 John Mabry RC .30 .09
RT131 Norberto Martin .15 .04
RT132 Hector Fajardo .15 .04
RT133 Mark Hutton .15 .04
RT134 Fernando Vina .15 .04
RT135 Lee Tinsley .15 .04
RT136 Chan Ho Park RC .50 .15
RT137 Paul Spoljaric .15 .04
RT138 Matias Carrillo .15 .04
RT139 Mark Kiefer .15 .04
RT140 Stan Royer .15 .04
RT141 Bryan Eversgerd .15 .04
RT142 Brian L. Hunter .15 .04
RT143 Joe Hall .15 .04
RT144 Johnny Ruffin .15 .04
RT145 Alex Gonzalez .15 .04
RT146 Keith Lockhart RC .30 .09
RT147 Tom Marsh .15 .04
RT148 Tony Longmire .15 .04
RT149 Keith Mitchell .15 .04
RT150 Melvin Nieves .15 .04
RT151 Kelly Stinnett RC .15 .04
RT152 Miguel Jimenez .15 .04
RT153 Jeff Juden .15 .04
RT154 Matt Walbeck .15 .04
RT155 Marc Newfield .15 .04
RT156 Matt Mieske .15 .04
RT157 Marcus Moore .15 .04
RT158 Jose Lima RC SP 5.00 1.50
RT159 Mike Kelly .15 .04
RT160 Jim Edmonds .75 .23
RT161 Steve Trachsel .15 .04
RT162 Greg Blosser .15 .04
RT163 Marc Acre RC .15 .04
RT164 AL Checklist .15 .04
RT165 NL Checklist .15 .04
HC1 Alex Rodriguez 400.00 120.00
Call-Up Redemption
NNO Sept. Call-Up Trade EXP 2.00 .60

1994 Score Rookie/Traded Gold Rush

Issued one per pack, these cards are a gold foil version of the 165-card Rookie/Traded set. The differences between the basic card and Gold Rush version are the gold foil borders that surround a metallicized player photo. The only difference on the back is a Gold Rush logo.

Nm-Mt Ex-Mt
COMPLETE SET (165) 50.00 15.00
*STARS: 1X TO 2.5X BASIC CARDS...
*ROOKIES: 1X TO 2.5X BASIC CARDS

1994 Score Rookie/Traded Changing Places

Randomly inserted in both retail and hobby packs at a rate of one in 36 Rookie/Traded packs, this 10-card standard-size set focuses on ten veteran superstar players who were traded prior to or during the 1994 season. Cards fronts feature a color photo with a slanted design. The backs have a short write-up and a distorted photo.

Nm-Mt Ex-Mt
COMPLETE SET (10) 30.00 9.00
CP1 Will Clark 10.00 3.00
CP2 Rafael Palmeiro 6.00 1.80
CP3 Roberto Kelly 2.00 .60
CP4 Bo Jackson 10.00 3.00
CP5 Otis Nixon 2.00 .60
CP6 Rickey Henderson 10.00 3.00
CP7 Ellis Burks 4.00 1.20
CP8 Lee Smith 4.00 1.20
CP9 Delino DeShields 2.00 .60
CP10 Deion Sanders 6.00 1.80

1994 Score Rookie/Traded Super Rookies

Randomly inserted in hobby packs at a rate of one in 36, this 18-card standard-size set focuses on top rookies of 1994. Odds of finding one of these cards is approximately one in 36 hobby packs. Designed much like the Gold Rush, the cards have an all-foil design. The fronts have a player photo and the backs have a photo that serves as background to the Super Rookies logo and text.

Nm-Mt Ex-Mt
COMPLETE SET (18) 60.00 18.00
SU1 Carlos Delgado 8.00 2.40
SU2 Manny Ramirez 8.00 2.40
SU3 Ryan Klesko 5.00 1.50
SU4 Raul Mondesi 5.00 1.50
SU5 Bob Hamelin 2.50 .75
SU6 Steve Karsay 2.50 .75
SU7 Jeffrey Hammonds 2.50 .75
SU8 Cliff Floyd 5.00 1.50
SU9 Kurt Abbott 5.00 1.50
SU10 Marc Newfield 2.50 .75
SU11 Javier Lopez 5.00 1.50
SU12 Rich Becker 2.50 .75
SU13 Greg Pirkl 2.50 .75
SU14 Rondell White 5.00 1.50
SU15 James Mouton 2.50 .75
SU16 Tony Tarasco 2.50 .75
SU17 Brian Anderson 5.00 1.50
SU18 Jim Edmonds 10.00 3.00

1995 Score

The 1995 Score set consists of 605 standard-size cards issued in hobby, retail and jumbo packs. Hobby packs featured a special signed Ryan Klesko (RG1)card. Retail packs also had a Klesko card (SG1) but these were not signed.

Nm-Mt Ex-Mt
COMPLETE SET (605) 24.00 7.25
COMP. SERIES 1 (330) 12.00 3.60
COMP. SERIES 2 (275) 12.00 3.60
1 Frank Thomas .50 .15
2 Roberto Alomar .30 .09
3 Cal Ripken 1.50 .45
4 Jose Canseco .50 .15
5 Matt Williams .20 .06
6 Esteban Beltre .10 .03
7 Domingo Cedeno .10 .03
8 John Valentin .10 .03
9 Glenallen Hill .10 .03
10 Rafael Belliard .10 .03
11 Randy Myers .10 .03
12 Mo Vaughn .20 .06
13 Hector Carrasco .10 .03
14 Chili Davis .20 .06
15 Dante Bichette .20 .06
16 Darrin Jackson .10 .03
17 Mike Piazza .75 .23
18 Junior Felix .10 .03
19 Moises Alou .20 .06
20 Mark Gubicza .10 .03
21 Bret Saberhagen .20 .06
22 Lenny Dykstra .20 .06
23 Steve Howe .10 .03
24 Mark Dewey .10 .03
25 Brian Harper .10 .03
26 Ozzie Smith .75 .23
27 Scott Erickson .10 .03
28 Tony Gwynn .60 .18
29 Bob Welch .10 .03
30 Barry Bonds 1.25 .35
31 Leo Gomez .10 .03
32 Greg Maddux .75 .23
33 Mike Greenwell .10 .03
34 Sammy Sosa .75 .23
35 Darnell Coles .10 .03
36 Tommy Greene .10 .03
37 Will Clark .50 .15
38 Steve Ontiveros .10 .03
39 Stan Javier .10 .03
40 Bip Roberts .10 .03
41 Paul O'Neill .30 .09
42 Bill Haselman .10 .03
43 Shane Mack .10 .03
44 Orlando Merced .10 .03
45 Kevin Seitzer .10 .03
46 Trevor Hoffman .20 .06
47 Greg Gagne .10 .03
48 Jeff Kent .20 .06
49 Tony Phillips .10 .03
50 Ken Hill .10 .03
51 Carlos Baerga .10 .03
52 Henry Rodriguez .10 .03
53 Scott Sanderson .10 .03
54 Jeff Conine .20 .06
55 Chris Turner .10 .03
56 Ken Caminiti .20 .06
57 Harold Baines .20 .06
58 Charlie Hayes .10 .03
59 Roberto Kelly .10 .03
60 John Olerud .20 .06
61 Tim Davis .10 .03
62 Rich Rowland .10 .03
63 Rey Sanchez .10 .03
64 Junior Ortiz .10 .03
65 Ricky Gutierrez .10 .03
66 Rex Hudler .10 .03
67 Johnny Ruffin .10 .03
68 Jay Buhner .20 .06
69 Tom Pagnozzi .10 .03
70 Julio Franco .20 .06
71 Eric Young .10 .03
72 Mike Bordick .10 .03
73 Don Slaught .10 .03
74 Goose Gossage .20 .06
75 Lonnie Smith .10 .03
76 Jimmy Key .20 .06
77 Dave Hollins .10 .03
78 Mickey Tettleton .10 .03
79 Luis Gonzalez .20 .06
80 Dave Winfield .20 .06
81 Ryan Thompson .10 .03
82 Felix Jose .10 .03
83 Rusty Meacham .10 .03
84 Darryl Hamilton .10 .03
85 John Wetteland .20 .06
86 Tom Brunansky .10 .03
87 Mark Lemke .10 .03
88 Spike Owen .10 .03
89 Shawon Dunston .10 .03
90 Wilson Alvarez .10 .03
91 Lee Smith .20 .06
92 Scott Kamieniecki .10 .03
93 Jacob Brumfield .10 .03
94 Kirk Gibson .20 .06
95 Joe Girardi .10 .03
96 Mike Macfarlane .10 .03
97 Greg Colbrunn .10 .03
98 Ricky Bones .10 .03
99 Delino DeShields .10 .03
100 Pat Meares .10 .03
101 Jeff Fassero .10 .03
102 Jim Leyritz .10 .03
103 Gary Redus .10 .03
104 Terry Steinbach .10 .03
105 Kevin McReynolds .10 .03
106 Felix Fermin .10 .03
107 Danny Jackson .10 .03
108 Chris James .10 .03
109 Jeff King .10 .03
110 Pat Hentgen .10 .03
111 Gerald Perry .10 .03
112 Tim Raines .20 .06
113 Eddie Williams .10 .03
114 Jamie Moyer .20 .06
115 Bud Black .10 .03
116 Chris Gomez .10 .03
117 Luis Lopez .10 .03
118 Roger Clemens 1.00 .30
119 Javier Lopez .20 .06
120 Dave Nilsson .10 .03
121 Karl Rhodes .10 .03
122 Rick Aguilera .10 .03
123 Tony Fernandez .10 .03
124 Bernie Williams .30 .09
125 James Mouton .10 .03

126 Mark Langston .10 .03
127 Mike Lansing .10 .03
128 Tino Martinez .30 .09
129 Joe Orsulak .10 .03
130 David Hulse .10 .03
131 Pete Incaviglia .10 .03
132 Mark Clark .10 .03
133 Tony Eusebio .10 .03
134 Chuck Finley .20 .06
135 Lou Frazier .10 .03
136 Craig Grebeck .10 .03
137 Kelly Stinnett .10 .03
138 Paul Shuey .10 .03
139 David Nied .10 .03
140 Billy Brewer .10 .03
141 Dave Weathers .10 .03
142 Scott Leius .10 .03
143 Brian Jordan .20 .06
144 Melido Perez .10 .03
145 Tony Tarasco .10 .03
146 Dan Wilson .10 .03
147 Rondell White .20 .06
148 Mike Henneman .10 .03
149 Brian Johnson .10 .03
150 Tom Henke .10 .03
151 John Patterson .10 .03
152 Bobby Witt .10 .03
153 Eddie Taubensee .10 .03
154 Pat Borders .10 .03
155 Ramon Martinez .10 .03
156 Mike Kingery .10 .03
157 Zane Smith .10 .03
158 Benito Santiago .20 .06
159 Matias Carrillo .10 .03
160 Scott Brosius .20 .06
161 Dave Clark .10 .03
162 Mark McLemore .10 .03
163 Curt Schilling .20 .06
164 J.T. Snow .20 .06
165 Rod Beck .10 .03
166 Scott Fletcher .10 .03
167 Bob Tewksbury .10 .03
168 Mike LaValliere .10 .03
169 Dave Hansen .10 .03
170 Pedro Martinez .50 .15
171 Kirk Rueter .10 .03
172 Jose Lind .10 .03
173 Luis Alicea .10 .03
174 Mike Moore .10 .03
175 Andy Ashby .10 .03
176 Jody Reed .10 .03
177 Darryl Kile .20 .06
178 Carl Willis .10 .03
179 Jeromy Burnitz .20 .06
180 Mike Gallego .10 .03
181 Bill VanLandingham .10 .03
182 Sid Fernandez .10 .03
183 Kim Batiste .10 .03
184 Greg Myers .10 .03
185 Steve Avery .10 .03
186 Steve Farr .10 .03
187 Robb Nen .20 .06
188 Dan Pasqua .10 .03
189 Bruce Ruffin .10 .03
190 Jose Valentin .10 .03
191 Willie Banks .10 .03
192 Mike Aldrete .10 .03
193 Randy Milligan .10 .03
194 Steve Karsay .10 .03
195 Mike Stanley .10 .03
196 Jose Mesa .10 .03
197 Tom Browning .10 .03
198 John Vander Wal .10 .03
199 Kevin Brown .20 .06
200 Mike Oquist .10 .03
201 Greg Swindell .10 .03
202 Eddie Zambrano .10 .03
203 Joe Boever .10 .03
204 Gary Varsho .10 .03
205 Chris Gwynn .10 .03
206 David Howard .10 .03
207 Jerome Walton .10 .03
208 Danny Darwin .10 .03
209 Darryl Strawberry .20 .06
210 Todd Van Poppel .10 .03
211 Scott Livingstone .10 .03
212 Dave Fleming .10 .03
213 Todd Worrell .10 .03
214 Carlos Delgado .20 .06
215 Bill Pecota .10 .03
216 Jim Lindeman .10 .03
217 Rick White .10 .03
218 Jose Oquendo .10 .03
219 Tony Castillo .10 .03
220 Fernando Vina .10 .03
221 Jeff Bagwell .30 .09
222 Randy Johnson .50 .15
223 Albert Belle .10 .03
224 Chuck Carr .10 .03
225 Mark Leiter .10 .03
226 Hal Morris .10 .03
227 Robin Ventura .20 .06
228 Mike Munoz .10 .03
229 Jim Thome .50 .15
230 Mario Diaz .10 .03
231 John Doherty .10 .03
232 Bobby Jones .10 .03
233 Raul Mondesi .20 .06
234 Ricky Jordan .10 .03
235 John Jaha .10 .03
236 Carlos Garcia .10 .03
237 Kirby Puckett .50 .15
238 Orel Hershiser .20 .06
239 Don Mattingly 1.25 .35
240 Sid Bream .10 .03
241 Brent Gates .10 .03
242 Tony Longmire .10 .03
243 Robby Thompson .10 .03
244 Rick Sutcliffe .20 .06
245 Dean Palmer .20 .06
246 Marquis Grissom .20 .06
247 Paul Molitor .30 .09
248 Mark Carreon .10 .03
249 Jack Voigt .10 .03
250 Greg McMichael UER .10 .03
(photo on front is Mike Stanton)
251 Damon Berryhill .10 .03
252 Brian Dorsett .10 .03
253 Jim Edmonds .30 .09
254 Barry Larkin .30 .09
255 Jack McDowell .10 .03
256 Wally Joyner .20 .06
257 Eddie Murray .50 .15
258 Lenny Webster .10 .03
259 Milt Cuyler .10 .03
260 Todd Benzinger .10 .03
261 Vince Coleman .10 .03
262 Todd Stottlemyre .10 .03
263 Turner Ward .10 .03
264 Ray Lankford .10 .03
265 Matt Walbeck .10 .03
266 Deion Sanders .30 .09
267 Gerald Williams .10 .03
268 Jim Gott .10 .03
269 Jeff Frye .10 .03
270 Jose Rijo .10 .03
271 Dave Justice .20 .06
272 Ismael Valdes .10 .03
273 Ben McDonald .10 .03
274 Darren Lewis .10 .03
275 Graeme Lloyd .10 .03
276 Luis Ortiz .10 .03
277 Julian Tavarez .10 .03
278 Mark Dalesandro .10 .03
279 Brett Merriman .10 .03
280 Ricky Bottalico .10 .03
281 Robert Eenhoorn .10 .03
282 Rikkert Faneyte .10 .03
283 Mike Kelly .10 .03
284 Mark Smith .10 .03
285 Turk Wendell .10 .03
286 Greg Blosser .10 .03
287 Garey Ingram .10 .03
288 Jorge Fabregas .10 .03
289 Blaise Ilsley .10 .03
290 Joe Hall .10 .03
291 Orlando Miller .10 .03
292 Jose Lima .10 .03
293 Greg O'Halloran RC .10 .03
294 Mark Kiefer .10 .03
295 Jose Oliva .10 .03
296 Rich Becker .10 .03
297 Brian L. Hunter .10 .03
298 Dave Silvestri .10 .03
299 Armando Benitez .20 .06
300 Darren Dreifort .10 .03
301 John Mabry .10 .03
302 Greg Pirkl .10 .03
303 J.R. Phillips .10 .03
304 Shawn Green .20 .06
305 Roberto Petagine .10 .03
306 Keith Lockhart .10 .03
307 Jonathan Hurst .10 .03
308 Paul Spoljaric .10 .03
309 Mike Lieberthal .20 .06
310 Garret Anderson .20 .06
311 John Johnstone .10 .03
312 Alex Rodriguez 1.25 .35
313 Kent Mercker HL .10 .03
314 John Valentin HL .10 .03
315 Kenny Rogers HL .20 .06
316 Fred McGriff HL .20 .06
317 Team Checklists .10 .03
318 Team Checklists .10 .03
319 Team Checklists .10 .03
320 Team Checklists .10 .03
321 Team Checklists .10 .03
322 Team Checklists .10 .03
323 Team Checklists .10 .03
324 Team Checklists .10 .03
325 Team Checklists .10 .03
326 Team Checklists .10 .03
327 Team Checklists .10 .03
328 Team Checklists .10 .03
329 Team Checklists .10 .03
330 Team Checklists .10 .03
331 Pedro Munoz .10 .03
332 Ryan Klesko .20 .06
333 Andre Dawson .20 .06
334 Derrick May .10 .03
335 Aaron Sele .10 .03
336 Kevin Mitchell .10 .03
337 Steve Trachsel .10 .03
338 Andres Galarraga .20 .06
339 Terry Pendleton .20 .06
340 Gary Sheffield .20 .06
341 Travis Fryman .20 .06
342 Bo Jackson .50 .15
343 Gary Gaetti .20 .06
344 Brett Butler .20 .06
345 B.J. Surhoff .20 .06
346 Larry Walker .30 .09
347 Kevin Tapani .10 .03
348 Rick Wilkins .10 .03
349 Wade Boggs .30 .09
350 Mariano Duncan .10 .03
351 Ruben Sierra .10 .03
352 Andy Van Slyke .20 .06
353 Reggie Jefferson .10 .03
354 Gregg Jefferies .10 .03
355 Tim Naehring .10 .03
356 John Roper .10 .03
357 Joe Carter .20 .06
358 Kurt Abbott .10 .03
359 Lenny Harris .10 .03
360 Lance Johnson .10 .03
361 Brian Anderson .10 .03
362 Jim Eisenreich .10 .03
363 Jerry Browne .10 .03
364 Mark Grace .30 .09
365 Devon White .20 .06
366 Reggie Sanders .10 .03
367 Ivan Rodriguez .50 .15
368 Kirt Manwaring .10 .03
369 Pat Kelly .10 .03
370 Ellis Burks .20 .06
371 Charles Nagy .10 .03
372 Kevin Bass .10 .03
373 Lou Whitaker .20 .06
374 Rene Arocha .10 .03
375 Derek Parks .10 .03
376 Mark Whiten .10 .03
377 Mark McGwire 1.25 .35
378 Doug Drabek .10 .03
379 Greg Vaughn .10 .03
380 Al Martin .10 .03
381 Ron Darling .10 .03
382 Tim Wallach .10 .03
383 Alan Trammell .20 .06
384 Randy Velarde .10 .03
385 Chris Sabo .10 .03
386 Wil Cordero .10 .03
387 Darrin Fletcher .10 .03
388 David Segui .10 .03
389 Steve Buechele .10 .03
390 Dave Gallagher .10 .03
391 Thomas Howard .10 .03
392 Chad Curtis .10 .03
393 Cal Eldred .10 .03
394 Jason Bere .10 .03
395 Bret Barberie .10 .03
396 Paul Sorrento .10 .03
397 Steve Finley .20 .06
398 Cecil Fielder .20 .06
399 Eric Karros .20 .06
400 Jeff Montgomery .10 .03
401 Cliff Floyd .20 .06
402 Matt Mieske .10 .03
403 Brian Hunter .10 .03
404 Alex Cole .10 .03
405 Kevin Stocker .10 .03
406 Eric Davis .20 .06
407 Marvin Freeman .10 .03
408 Dennis Eckersley .20 .06
409 Todd Zeile .10 .03
410 Keith Mitchell .10 .03
411 Andy Benes .10 .03
412 Juan Bell .10 .03
413 Royce Clayton .10 .03
414 Ed Sprague .10 .03
415 Mike Mussina .30 .09
416 Todd Hundley .10 .03
417 Pat Listach .10 .03
418 Joe Oliver .10 .03
419 Rafael Palmeiro .30 .09
420 Tim Salmon .30 .09
421 Brady Anderson .20 .06
422 Kenny Lofton .20 .06
423 Craig Biggio .30 .09
424 Bobby Bonilla .20 .06
425 Kenny Rogers .20 .06
426 Derek Bell .10 .03
427 Scott Cooper .10 .03
428 Ozzie Guillen .10 .03
429 Omar Vizquel .30 .09
430 Phil Plantier .10 .03
431 Chuck Knoblauch .20 .06
432 Darren Daulton .20 .06
433 Bob Hamelin .10 .03
434 Tom Glavine .30 .09
435 Walt Weiss .10 .03
436 Jose Vizcaino .10 .03
437 Ken Griffey Jr. .75 .23
438 Jay Bell .20 .06
439 Juan Gonzalez .30 .09
440 Jeff Blauser .10 .03
441 Rickey Henderson .50 .15
442 Bobby Ayala .10 .03
443 David Cone .20 .06
444 Pedro Martinez .50 .15
445 Manny Ramirez .30 .09
446 Mark Portugal .10 .03
447 Damion Easley .10 .03
448 Gary DiSarcina .10 .03
449 Roberto Hernandez .10 .03
450 Jeffrey Hammonds .10 .03
451 Jeff Treadway .10 .03
452 Jim Abbott .30 .09
453 Carlos Rodriguez .10 .03
454 Joey Cora .10 .03
455 Bret Boone .20 .06
456 Danny Tartabull .10 .03
457 John Franco .20 .06
458 Roger Salkeld .10 .03
459 Fred McGriff .30 .09
460 Pedro Astacio .10 .03
461 Jon Lieber .10 .03
462 Luis Polonia .10 .03
463 Geronimo Pena .10 .03
464 Tom Gordon .10 .03
465 Brad Ausmus .10 .03
466 Willie McGee .20 .06
467 Doug Jones .10 .03
468 John Smoltz .30 .09
469 Troy Neel .10 .03
470 Luis Sojo .10 .03
471 John Smiley .10 .03
472 Rafael Bournigal .10 .03
473 Bill Taylor .10 .03
474 Juan Guzman .10 .03
475 Dave Magadan .10 .03
476 Mike Devereaux .10 .03
477 Andujar Cedeno .10 .03
478 Edgar Martinez .30 .09
479 Milt Thompson .10 .03
480 Allen Watson .10 .03
481 Ron Karkovice .10 .03
482 Joey Hamilton .10 .03
483 Vinny Castilla .20 .06
484 Tim Belcher .10 .03
485 Bernard Gilkey .10 .03
486 Scott Servais .10 .03
487 Cory Snyder .10 .03
488 Mel Rojas .10 .03
489 Carlos Reyes .10 .03
490 Chip Hale .10 .03
491 Bill Swift .10 .03
492 Pat Rapp .10 .03
493 Brian McRae .10 .03
494 Mickey Morandini .10 .03
495 Tony Pena .10 .03
496 Danny Bautista .10 .03
497 Armando Reynoso .10 .03
498 Ken Ryan .10 .03
499 Billy Ripken .10 .03
500 Pat Mahomes .10 .03
501 Mark Acre .10 .03
502 Geronimo Berroa .10 .03
503 Norberto Martin .10 .03
504 Chad Kreuter .10 .03
505 Howard Johnson .10 .03
506 Eric Anthony .10 .03
507 Mark Wohlers .10 .03
508 Scott Sanders .10 .03
509 Pete Harnisch .10 .03
510 Wes Chamberlain .10 .03
511 Tom Candiotti .10 .03
512 Albie Lopez .10 .03
513 Denny Neagle .20 .06
514 Sean Berry .10 .03
515 Billy Hatcher .10 .03
516 Todd Jones .10 .03
517 Wayne Kirby .10 .03
518 Butch Henry .10 .03
519 Sandy Alomar Jr. .10 .03
520 Kevin Appier .20 .06
521 Roberto Mejia .10 .03
522 Steve Cooke .10 .03
523 Terry Shumpert .10 .03
524 Mike Jackson .10 .03
525 Kent Mercker .10 .03
526 David Wells .20 .06
527 Juan Samuel .10 .03
528 Salomon Torres .10 .03
529 Duane Ward .10 .03
530 Rob Dibble .20 .06
531 Mike Blowers .10 .03
532 Mark Eichhorn .10 .03
533 Alex Diaz .10 .03
534 Dan Miceli .10 .03
535 Jeff Branson .10 .03
536 Dave Stevens .10 .03
537 Charlie O'Brien .10 .03
538 Shane Reynolds .10 .03
539 Rich Amaral .10 .03
540 Rusty Greer .20 .06
541 Alex Arias .10 .03
542 Eric Plunk .10 .03
543 John Hudek .10 .03
544 Kirk McCaskill .10 .03
545 Jeff Reboulet .10 .03
546 Sterling Hitchcock .10 .03
547 Warren Newson .10 .03
548 Bryan Harvey .10 .03
549 Mike Huff .10 .03
550 Lance Parrish .20 .06
551 Ken Griffey Jr. HIT .50 .15
552 Matt Williams HIT .10 .03
553 R.Alomar HIT UER .20 .06
Card says he's a NL All-Star
He plays in the AL
554 Jeff Bagwell HIT .20 .06
555 Dave Justice HIT .10 .03
556 Cal Ripken Jr. HIT .75 .23
557 Albert Belle HIT .10 .03
558 Mike Piazza HIT .40 .12
559 Kirby Puckett HIT .30 .09
560 Wade Boggs HIT .20 .06
561 Tony Gwynn HIT UER .30 .09
card has him winning AL batting titles
he's played whole career in the NL
562 Barry Bonds HIT .60 .18
563 Mo Vaughn HIT .10 .03
564 Don Mattingly HIT .60 .18
565 Carlos Baerga HIT .10 .03
566 Paul Molitor HIT .20 .06
567 Raul Mondesi HIT .10 .03
568 Manny Ramirez HIT .20 .06
569 Alex Rodriguez HIT .50 .15
570 Will Clark HIT .20 .06
571 Frank Thomas HIT .30 .09
572 Moises Alou HIT .10 .03
573 Jeff Conine HIT .10 .03
574 Joe Ausanio .10 .03
575 Charles Johnson .20 .06
576 Ernie Young .10 .03
577 Jeff Granger .10 .03
578 Robert Perez .10 .03
579 Melvin Nieves .10 .03
580 Gar Finnvold .10 .03
581 Duane Singleton .10 .03
582 Chan Ho Park .20 .06
583 Fausto Cruz .10 .03
584 Dave Staton .10 .03
585 Denny Hocking .10 .03
586 Nate Minchey .10 .03
587 Marc Newfield .10 .03
588 Jayhawk Owens UER .10 .03
Front Photo is Jim Tatum
589 Darren Bragg .10 .03
590 Kevin King .10 .03
591 Kurt Miller .10 .03
592 Aaron Small .10 .03
593 Troy O'Leary .10 .03
594 Phil Stidham .10 .03
595 Steve Dunn .10 .03
596 Cory Bailey .10 .03
597 Alex Gonzalez .10 .03
598 Jim Bowie RC .10 .03
599 Jeff Cirillo .10 .03
600 Mark Hutton .10 .03
601 Russ Davis .10 .03
602 Checklist .10 .03
603 Checklist .10 .03
604 Checklist .10 .03
605 Checklist .10 .03
RG1 R.Klesko Rook.Great. 1.00 .30
SG1 Ryan Klesko AU/6100 10.00 3.00

1995 Score Gold Rush

Parallel to the basic Score issue, these cards were inserted one per foil pack and two per jumbo pack. The fronts were printed in gold foil and the backs contain the Gold Rush logo. As part of the Gold Rush program, one Platinum Team Redemption card was randomly inserted in Score packs at a rate of one in 36. This redemption card and up to four Gold Rush team sets (and $2) could be redeemed for platinum versions of the team set(s). The Gold Rush sets that were sent in would be returned with a stamp indicating they were already used for redemption purposes. The Platinum Upgrade offer was good through 7/13/95 for series 1, 10/1/95 for series 2.

	Nm-Mt	Ex-Mt
COMPLETE SET (605)	100.00	30.00
COMP. SERIES 1 (330)	50.00	15.00
COMP. SERIES 2 (275)	50.00	15.00

*STARS: 2X TO 5X BASIC CARDS

1995 Score Platinum Team Sets

After completing a Score Gold Rush team set in either series, a collector could mail in those cards along with a platinum redemption card. In return, the collector would receive a complete Platinum Team Set. The cards are similar to the gold cards except they have sparkling platinum-foil fronts and come in a small card case. The top card is the certificate for the team set. Only 4,950 of each platinum team set was produced.

Nm-Mt Ex-Mt

*STARS: 5X TO 12X BASIC CARDS

1995 Score You Trade Em

This skip-numbered 11-card set was available only by redeeming the randomly inserted Score You Trade Em redemption card. The set features a selection of veteran players that were traded to new teams at the beginning of the 1995 season. The numbering and card design parallel the corresponding cards within the regular issue 1995 Score set, but these Trade cards feature the players in their new uniforms.

	Nm-Mt	Ex-Mt
COMPLETE SET (11)	1.50	.45
333T Andre Dawson UER position listed as DH	.40	.12
339T Terry Pendleton	.40	.12
344T Brett Butler	.40	.12
346T Larry Walker	.60	.18
352T Andy Van Slyke	.40	.12
392T Chad Curtis	.20	.06
427T Scott Cooper	.20	.06
443T David Cone	.40	.12
452T Jim Abbott	.60	.18
493T Brian McRae	.20	.06
530T Rob Dibble	.40	.12
NNO Expired Trade Card	.50	.15

1995 Score Airmail

This 18-card set was randomly inserted in series two jumbo packs at a rate of one in 24.

	Nm-Mt	Ex-Mt
COMPLETE SET (18)	50.00	15.00
AM1 Bob Hamelin	1.50	.45
AM2 John Mabry	1.50	.45
AM3 Marc Newfield	1.50	.45
AM4 Jose Oliva	1.50	.45
AM5 Charles Johnson	2.50	.75
AM6 Russ Davis	1.50	.45
AM7 Ernie Young	1.50	.45
AM8 Billy Ashley	1.50	.45
AM9 Ryan Klesko	2.50	.75
AM10 J.R. Phillips	1.50	.45
AM11 Cliff Floyd	2.50	.75
AM12 Carlos Delgado	2.50	.75
AM13 Melvin Nieves	1.50	.45
AM14 Raul Mondesi	2.50	.75
AM15 Manny Ramirez	4.00	1.20
AM16 Mike Kelly	1.50	.45
AM17 Alex Rodriguez	15.00	4.50
AM18 Rusty Greer	2.50	.75

1995 Score Double Gold Champs

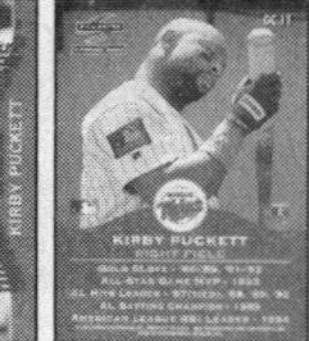

This 12-card set was randomly inserted in second series hobby packs at a rate of one in 36.

	Nm-Mt	Ex-Mt
COMPLETE SET (12)	80.00	24.00
GC1 Frank Thomas	5.00	1.50
GC2 Ken Griffey Jr.	8.00	2.40
GC3 Barry Bonds	12.00	3.60
GC4 Tony Gwynn	6.00	1.80
GC5 Don Mattingly	12.00	3.60
GC6 Greg Maddux	8.00	2.40
GC7 Roger Clemens	10.00	3.00
GC8 Kenny Lofton	2.00	.60
GC9 Jeff Bagwell	3.00	.90
GC10 Matt Williams	2.00	.60
GC11 Kirby Puckett	5.00	1.50
GC12 Cal Ripken	15.00	4.50

1995 Score Draft Picks

Randomly inserted in first series hobby packs at a rate of one in 36, this 18-card set takes a look at top picks selected in June of 1994. The cards are numbered with a "DP" prefix.

Nm-Mt Ex-Mt
COMPLETE SET (18) 25.00 7.50
DP1 McKay Christensen 1.00 .30
DP2 Bret Wagner 1.00 .30
DP3 Paul Wilson 1.00 .30
DP4 C.J. Nitkowski 1.00 .30
DP5 Josh Booty 1.50 .45
DP6 Antone Williamson 1.00 .30
DP7 Paul Konerko 1.50 .45
DP8 Scott Elarton 1.50 .45
DP9 Jacob Shumate 1.00 .30
DP10 Terrence Long 1.50 .45
DP11 Mark Johnson 1.50 .45
DP12 Ben Grieve 1.50 .45
DP13 Doug Million 1.00 .30
DP14 Jayson Peterson 1.00 .30
DP15 Dustin Hermanson 1.00 .30
DP16 Matt Smith 1.00 .30
DP17 Kevin Witt 1.00 .30
DP18 Brian Buchanan 1.50 .45

1995 Score Dream Team

Randomly inserted in first series hobby and retail packs at a rate of one in 72 packs, this 12-card hologram set showcases top performers from the 1994 season. The cards are numbered with a "DG" prefix.

Nm-Mt Ex-Mt
COMPLETE SET (12) 100.00 30.00
DG1 Frank Thomas 8.00 2.40
DG2 Roberto Alomar 5.00 1.50
DG3 Cal Ripken 25.00 7.50
DG4 Matt Williams 3.00 .90
DG5 Mike Piazza 12.00 3.60
DG6 Albert Belle 3.00 .90
DG7 Ken Griffey Jr. 12.00 3.60
DG8 Tony Gwynn 10.00 3.00
DG9 Paul Molitor 5.00 1.50
DG10 Jimmy Key 3.00 .90
DG11 Greg Maddux 12.00 3.60
DG12 Lee Smith 3.00 .90

1995 Score Hall of Gold

Randomly inserted in packs at a rate one in six, this 110-card multi-series set is a collection of top stars and young hopefuls. Cards numbered one through 55 were seeded in first series packs and cards 56-100 were seeded in second series packs.

Nm-Mt Ex-Mt
COMP. SERIES 1 (55) 50.00 15.00
COMP.SERIES 2 (55) 30.00 9.00
*YTE CARDS: .4X TO 1X BASIC HALL 3.00 .90
ONE YTE SET VIA MAIL PER YTE TRADE CARD
HG1 Ken Griffey Jr. 5.00 1.50
HG2 Matt Williams 1.25 .35
HG3 Roberto Alomar 2.00 .60
HG4 Jeff Bagwell 2.00 .60
HG5 Dave Justice 1.25 .35
HG6 Cal Ripken 10.00 3.00
HG7 Randy Johnson 3.00 .90
HG8 Barry Larkin 2.00 .60
HG9 Albert Belle 1.25 .35
HG10 Mike Piazza 5.00 1.50
HG11 Kirby Puckett 3.00 .90
HG12 Moises Alou 1.25 .35
HG13 Jose Canseco 3.00 .90
HG14 Tony Gwynn 4.00 1.20
HG15 Roger Clemens 6.00 1.80
HG16 Barry Bonds 8.00 2.40
HG17 Mo Vaughn 1.25 .35
HG18 Greg Maddux 5.00 1.50
HG19 Dante Bichette 1.25 .35
HG20 Will Clark 3.00 .90
HG21 Lenny Dykstra 1.25 .35
HG22 Don Mattingly 8.00 2.40
HG23 Carlos Baerga .60 .18
HG24 Ozzie Smith 5.00 1.50
HG25 Paul Molitor 2.00 .60
HG26 Paul O'Neill 2.00 .60
HG27 Deion Sanders 2.00 .60
HG28 Jeff Conine 1.25 .35
HG29 John Olerud 1.25 .35
HG30 Jose Rijo .60 .18
HG31 Sammy Sosa 5.00 1.50
HG32 Robin Ventura 1.25 .35
HG33 Raul Mondesi 1.25 .35
HG34 Eddie Murray 3.00 .90
HG35 Marquis Grissom 1.25 .35
HG36 Darryl Strawberry 1.25 .35
HG37 Dave Nilsson .60 .18
HG38 Manny Ramirez 2.00 .60
HG39 Delino DeShields .60 .18
HG40 Lee Smith 1.25 .35
HG41 Alex Rodriguez 8.00 2.40
HG42 Julio Franco 1.25 .35
HG43 Bret Saberhagen 1.25 .35
HG44 Ken Hill .60 .18
HG45 Roberto Kelly .60 .18
HG46 Hal Morris .60 .18
HG47 Jimmy Key 1.25 .35
HG48 Terry Steinbach .60 .18
HG49 Mickey Tettleton .60 .18
HG50 Tony Phillips .60 .18
HG51 Carlos Garcia .60 .18
HG52 Jim Edmonds 2.00 .60
HG53 Rod Beck .60 .18
HG54 Shane Mack .60 .18
HG55 Ken Caminiti 1.25 .35
HG56 Frank Thomas 3.00 .90
HG57 Kenny Lofton 1.25 .35
HG58 Juan Gonzalez 2.00 .60
HG59 Jason Bere .60 .18
HG60 Joe Carter 1.25 .35
HG61 Gary Sheffield 1.25 .35
HG62 Andres Galarraga 1.25 .35
HG63 Ellis Burks 1.25 .35
HG64 Bobby Bonilla 1.25 .35
HG65 Tom Glavine 2.00 .60
HG66 John Smoltz 2.00 .60
HG67 Fred McGriff 2.00 .60
HG68 Craig Biggio 2.00 .60
HG69 Reggie Sanders .60 .18
HG70 Kevin Mitchell .60 .18
HG71 Larry Walker 2.00 .60
HG72 Carlos Delgado 1.25 .35
HG73 Alex Gonzalez .60 .18
HG74 Ivan Rodriguez 3.00 .90
HG75 Ryan Klesko 1.25 .35
HG76 John Kruk .60 .18
HG77 Brian McRae .60 .18
HG78 Tim Salmon 2.00 .60
HG79 Travis Fryman 1.25 .35
HG80 Chuck Knoblauch 1.25 .35
HG81 Jay Bell 1.25 .35
HG82 Cecil Fielder 1.25 .35
HG83 Cliff Floyd 1.25 .35
HG84 Ruben Sierra .60 .18
HG85 Mike Mussina 2.00 .60
HG86 Mark Grace 2.00 .60
HG87 Dennis Eckersley 1.25 .35
HG88 Dennis Martinez .60 .18
HG89 Rafael Palmeiro 2.00 .60
HG90 Ben McDonald .60 .18
HG91 Dave Hollins .60 .18
HG92 Steve Avery .60 .18
HG93 David Cone 1.25 .35
HG94 Darren Daulton 1.25 .35
HG95 Bret Boone 1.25 .35
HG96 Wade Boggs 2.00 .60
HG97 Doug Drabek .60 .18
HG98 Andy Benes .60 .18
HG99 Jim Thome 3.00 .90
HG100 Chili Davis 1.25 .35
HG101 J.Hammonds .60 .18
HG102 R.Henderson 3.00 .90
HG103 Brett Butler 1.25 .35
HG104 Tim Wallach .60 .18
HG105 Wil Cordero .60 .18
HG106 Mark Whiten .60 .18
HG107 Bob Hamelin .60 .18
HG108 Rondell White 1.25 .35
HG109 Devon White 1.25 .35
HG110 Tony Tarasco .60 .18

1995 Score Hall of Gold You Trade Em

This skip-numbered five-card set was available only by redeeming the randomly inserted Hall of Gold Trade card inserted in second series packs of 1995 Score. The set features a selection of veterans that joined new teams prior to the 1995 season. The design and numbering of the cards parallel the regular Hall of Gold inserts.

Nm-Mt Ex-Mt
HG71T Larry Walker 2.00 .60
HG76T John Kruk .60 .18
HG77T Brian McRae .60 .18
HG93T David Cone 1.25 .35
HG110T Tony Tarasco .60 .18
NNO Exp. Hall of Gold Trade Card .50 .15

1995 Score Rookie Dream Team

This 12-card set was randomly inserted in second series retail and hobby packs at a rate of one in 12. The cards are numbered with a "RDT" prefix.

Nm-Mt Ex-Mt
COMPLETE SET (12) 60.00 18.00
RDT1 J.R. Phillips 2.50 .75
RDT2 Alex Gonzalez 2.50 .75
RDT3 Alex Rodriguez 20.00 6.00
RDT4 Jose Oliva 2.50 .75
RDT5 Charles Johnson 5.00 1.50
RDT6 Shawn Green 5.00 1.50
RDT7 Brian Hunter 2.50 .75
RDT8 Garret Anderson 5.00 1.50
RDT9 Julian Tavarez 2.50 .75
RDT10 Jose Lima 2.50 .75
RDT11 Armando Benitez 5.00 1.50
RDT12 Ricky Bottalico 2.50 .75

1995 Score Rules

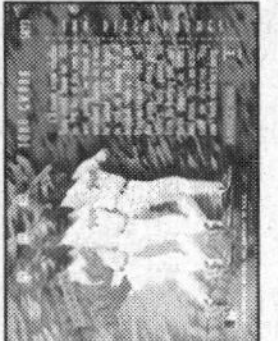

Randomly inserted in first series jumbo packs, this 30-card standard-size set features top big league players. The cards are numbered with an "SR" prefix.

Nm-Mt Ex-Mt
COMPLETE SET (30) 120.00 36.00
*JUMBO'S: .5X TO 1.2X 5.00 1.50
JUMBOS ISSUED ONE PER COLLECTOR KIT
SR1 Ken Griffey Jr. 8.00 2.40
SR2 Frank Thomas 5.00 1.50
SR3 Mike Piazza 8.00 2.40
SR4 Jeff Bagwell 3.00 .90
SR5 Alex Rodriguez 12.00 3.60
SR6 Albert Belle 2.00 .60
SR7 Matt Williams 2.00 .60
SR8 Roberto Alomar 3.00 .90
SR9 Barry Bonds 12.00 3.60
SR10 Raul Mondesi 2.00 .60
SR11 Jose Canseco 5.00 1.50
SR12 Kirby Puckett 5.00 1.50
SR13 Fred McGriff 3.00 .90
SR14 Kenny Lofton 2.00 .60
SR15 Greg Maddux 8.00 2.40
SR16 Juan Gonzalez 3.00 .90
SR17 Cliff Floyd 2.00 .60
SR18 Cal Ripken Jr. 15.00 4.50
SR19 Will Clark 5.00 1.50
SR20 Tim Salmon 3.00 .90
SR21 Paul O'Neill 3.00 .90
SR22 Jason Bere 1.00 .30
SR23 Tony Gwynn 6.00 1.80
SR24 Manny Ramirez 3.00 .90
SR25 Don Mattingly 12.00 3.60
SR26 Dave Justice 2.00 .60
SR27 Javier Lopez 2.00 .60
SR28 Ryan Klesko 2.00 .60
SR29 Carlos Delgado 2.00 .60
SR30 Mike Mussina 3.00 .90

1996 Score

This set consists of 517 standard-size cards. These cards were issued in packs of 10 that retailed for 99 cents per pack. The fronts feature an action photo surrounded by white borders. The "Score 96" logo is in the upper left, while the player is identified on the bottom. The backs have season and career stats as well as a player photo and some text. A Cal Ripken tribute card was issued at a rate of 1 every 300 packs.

Nm-Mt Ex-Mt
COMPLETE SET (517) 24.00 7.25
COMP. SERIES 1 (275) 12.00 3.60
COMP. SERIES 2 (242) 12.00 3.60
1 Will Clark .50 .15
2 Rich Becker .20 .06
3 Ryan Klesko .20 .06
4 Jim Edmonds .20 .06
5 Barry Larkin .30 .09
6 Jim Thome .50 .15
7 Raul Mondesi .20 .06
8 Don Mattingly 1.25 .35
9 Jeff Conine .20 .06
10 Rickey Henderson .50 .15
11 Chad Curtis .20 .06
12 Darren Daulton .20 .06
13 Larry Walker .30 .09
14 Carlos Garcia .20 .06
15 Carlos Baerga .20 .06
16 Tony Gwynn .60 .18
17 Jon Nunnally .20 .06
18 Deion Sanders .30 .09
19 Mark Grace .30 .09
20 Alex Rodriguez 1.00 .30
21 Frank Thomas .50 .15
22 Brian Jordan .20 .06
23 J.T. Snow .20 .06
24 Shawn Green .20 .06
25 Tim Wakefield .20 .06
26 Curtis Goodwin .20 .06
27 John Smoltz .30 .09
28 Devon White .20 .06
29 Brian L. Hunter .20 .06
30 Tim Salmon .30 .09
31 Rafael Palmeiro .30 .09
32 Bernard Gilkey .20 .06
33 John Valentin .20 .06
34 Randy Johnson .50 .15
35 Garret Anderson .20 .06
36 Rikkert Faneyte .20 .06
37 Ray Durham .20 .06
38 Bip Roberts .20 .06
39 Jaime Navarro .20 .06
40 Mark Johnson .20 .06
41 Darren Lewis .20 .06
42 Tyler Green .20 .06
43 Bill Pulsipher .20 .06
44 Jason Giambi .20 .06
45 Kevin Ritz .20 .06
46 Jack McDowell .20 .06
47 Felipe Lira .20 .06
48 Rico Brogna .20 .06
49 Terry Pendleton .20 .06
50 Rondell White .20 .06
51 Andre Dawson .20 .06
52 Kirby Puckett .50 .15
53 Wally Joyner .20 .06
54 B.J. Surhoff .20 .06
55 Randy Velarde .20 .06
56 Greg Vaughn .20 .06
57 Roberto Alomar .30 .09
58 David Justice .20 .06
59 Kevin Seitzer .20 .06
60 Cal Ripken 1.50 .45
61 Ozzie Smith .75 .23
62 Mo Vaughn .20 .06
63 Ricky Bones .20 .06
64 Gary DiSarcina .20 .06
65 Matt Williams .20 .06
66 Wilson Alvarez .20 .06
67 Lenny Dykstra .20 .06
68 Brian McRae .20 .06
69 Todd Stottlemyre .20 .06
70 Bret Boone .20 .06
71 Sterling Hitchcock .20 .06
72 Albert Belle .20 .06
73 Todd Hundley .20 .06
74 Vinny Castilla .20 .06
75 Moises Alou .20 .06
76 Cecil Fielder .20 .06
77 Brad Radke .20 .06
78 Quilvio Veras .20 .06
79 Eddie Murray .50 .15
80 James Mouton .20 .06
81 Pat Listach .20 .06
82 Mark Gubicza .20 .06
83 Dave Winfield .20 .06
84 Fred McGriff .30 .09
85 Darryl Hamilton .20 .06
86 Jeffrey Hammonds .20 .06
87 Pedro Munoz .20 .06
88 Craig Biggio .30 .09
89 Cliff Floyd .20 .06
90 Tim Naehring .20 .06
91 Brett Butler .20 .06
92 Kevin Foster .20 .06
93 Pat Kelly .20 .06
94 John Smiley .20 .06
95 Terry Steinbach .20 .06
96 Orel Hershiser .20 .06
97 Darrin Fletcher .20 .06
98 Walt Weiss .20 .06
99 John Wetteland .20 .06
100 Alan Trammell .20 .06
101 Steve Avery .20 .06
102 Tony Eusebio .20 .06
103 Sandy Alomar Jr. .20 .06
104 Joe Girardi .20 .06
105 Rick Aguilera .20 .06
106 Tony Tarasco .20 .06
107 Chris Hammond .20 .06
108 Mike Macfarlane .20 .06
109 Doug Drabek .20 .06
110 Derek Bell .20 .06
111 Ed Sprague .20 .06
112 Todd Hollandsworth .20 .06
113 Otis Nixon .20 .06
114 Keith Lockhart .20 .06
115 Donovan Osborne .20 .06
116 Dave Magadan .20 .06
117 Edgar Martinez .30 .09
118 Chuck Carr .20 .06
119 J.R. Phillips .20 .06
120 Sean Bergman .20 .06
121 Andujar Cedeno .20 .06
122 Eric Young .20 .06
123 Al Martin .20 .06
124 Mark Lemke .20 .06
125 Jim Eisenreich .20 .06
126 Benito Santiago .20 .06
127 Ariel Prieto .20 .06
128 Jim Bullinger .20 .06
129 Russ Davis .20 .06
130 Jim Abbott .30 .09
131 Jason Isringhausen .20 .06
132 Carlos Perez .20 .06
133 David Segui .20 .06
134 Troy O'Leary .20 .06
135 Pat Meares .20 .06
136 Chris Hoiles .20 .06
137 Ismael Valdes .20 .06
138 Jose Oliva .20 .06
139 Carlos Delgado .20 .06
140 Tom Goodwin .20 .06
141 Bob Tewksbury .20 .06
142 Chris Gomez .20 .06
143 Jose Oquendo .20 .06
144 Mark Lewis .20 .06
145 Salomon Torres .20 .06
146 Luis Gonzalez .20 .06
147 Mark Carreon .20 .06
148 Lance Johnson .20 .06
149 Melvin Nieves .20 .06
150 Lee Smith .20 .06
151 Jacob Brumfield .20 .06
152 Armando Benitez .20 .06
153 Curt Schilling .20 .06
154 Javier Lopez .20 .06
155 Frank Rodriguez .20 .06
156 Alex Gonzalez .20 .06
157 Todd Worrell .20 .06
158 Benji Gil .20 .06
159 Greg Gagne .20 .06
160 Tom Henke .20 .06
161 Randy Myers .20 .06
162 Joey Cora .20 .06
163 Scott Ruffcorn .20 .06
164 W. VanLandingham .20 .06
165 Tony Phillips .20 .06
166 Eddie Williams .20 .06
167 Bobby Bonilla .20 .06
168 Denny Neagle .20 .06
169 Troy Percival .20 .06
170 Billy Ashley .20 .06
171 Andy Van Slyke .20 .06
172 Jose Offerman .20 .06
173 Mark Parent .20 .06
174 Edgardo Alfonzo .20 .06
175 Trevor Hoffman .20 .06
176 David Cone .20 .06
177 Dan Wilson .20 .06
178 Steve Ontiveros .20 .06
179 Dean Palmer .20 .06
180 Mike Kelly .20 .06
181 Jim Leyritz .20 .06
182 Ron Karkovice .20 .06
183 Kevin Brown .20 .06
184 Jose Valentin .20 .06
185 Jorge Fabregas .20 .06
186 Jose Mesa .20 .06
187 Brent Mayne .20 .06
188 Carl Everett .20 .06
189 Paul Sorrento .20 .06
190 Pete Schourek .20 .06
191 Scott Kamieniecki .20 .06
192 Roberto Hernandez .20 .06
193 Randy Johnson RR .30 .09
194 Greg Maddux RR .50 .15
195 Hideo Nomo RR .30 .09
196 David Cone RR .20 .06
197 Mike Mussina RR .20 .06
198 Andy Benes RR .20 .06
199 Kevin Appier RR .20 .06
200 John Smoltz RR .20 .06
201 John Wetteland RR .20 .06
202 Mark Wohlers RR .20 .06
203 Stan Belinda .20 .06
204 Brian Anderson .20 .06
205 Mike Devereaux .20 .06
206 Mark Wohlers .20 .06
207 Omar Vizquel .30 .09
208 Jose Rijo .20 .06
209 Willie Blair .20 .06
210 Jamie Moyer .20 .06
211 Craig Shipley .20 .06
212 Shane Reynolds .20 .06
213 Chad Fonville .20 .06
214 Jose Vizcaino .20 .06
215 Sid Fernandez .20 .06
216 Andy Ashby .20 .06
217 Frank Castillo .20 .06
218 Kevin Tapani .20 .06
219 Kent Mercker .20 .06
220 Karim Garcia .20 .06
221 Antonio Osuna .20 .06
222 Tim Unroe .20 .06
223 Johnny Damon .30 .09
224 LaTroy Hawkins .20 .06
225 Mariano Rivera .30 .09
226 Jose Alberro .20 .06
227 Angel Martinez .20 .06
228 Jason Schmidt .30 .09
229 Tony Clark .20 .06
230 Kevin Jordan UER .20 .06
Ricky Jordan pictured on both sides
231 Mark Thompson .20 .06
232 Jim Dougherty .20 .06
233 Roger Cedeno .20 .06
234 Ugueth Urbina .20 .06
235 Ricky Otero .20 .06
236 Mark Smith .20 .06
237 Brian Barber .20 .06
238 Kevin Flora .20 .06
239 Joe Rosselli .20 .06
240 Derek Jeter 1.25 .35
241 Michael Tucker .20 .06
242 Ben Blomdahl .20 .06
243 Joe Vitiello .20 .06
244 Todd Steverson .20 .06
245 James Baldwin .20 .06
246 Alan Embree .20 .06
247 Shannon Penn .20 .06
248 Chris Stynes .20 .06
249 Oscar Munoz .20 .06
250 Jose Herrera .20 .06
251 Scott Sullivan .20 .06
252 Reggie Williams .20 .06
253 Mark Grudzielanek .20 .06
254 Steve Rodriguez .20 .06
255 Terry Bradshaw .20 .06
256 F.P. Santangelo .20 .06
257 Lyle Mouton .20 .06
258 George Williams .20 .06
259 Larry Thomas .20 .06
260 Rudy Pemberton .20 .06
261 Jim Pittsley .20 .06
262 Les Norman .20 .06
263 Ruben Rivera .20 .06
264 Cesar Devarez .20 .06
265 Greg Zaun .20 .06
266 Dustin Hermanson .20 .06
267 John Frascatore .20 .06
268 Joe Randa .20 .06
269 Jeff Bagwell CL .20 .06
270 Mike Piazza CL .50 .15
271 Dante Bichette CL .20 .06
272 Frank Thomas CL .30 .09
273 Ken Griffey Jr. CL .50 .15
274 Cal Ripken CL .75 .23
275 Greg Maddux CL .20 .06
Albert Belle
276 Greg Maddux .75 .23
277 Pedro Martinez .50 .15
278 Bobby Higginson .20 .06
279 Ray Lankford .20 .06
280 Shawon Dunston .20 .06
281 Gary Sheffield .20 .06
282 Ken Griffey Jr. .75 .23
283 Paul Molitor .30 .09
284 Kevin Appier .20 .06
285 Chuck Knoblauch .20 .06
286 Alex Fernandez .20 .06
287 Steve Finley .20 .06
288 Jeff Blauser .20 .06
289 Charles Johnson .20 .06
290 John Franco .20 .06
291 Mark Langston .20 .06
292 Bret Saberhagen .20 .06
293 John Mabry .20 .06
294 Ramon Martinez .20 .06
295 Mike Blowers .20 .06
296 Paul O'Neill .30 .09
297 Dave Nilsson .20 .06
298 Dante Bichette .20 .06
299 Marty Cordova .20 .06
300 Jay Bell .20 .06
301 Mike Mussina .30 .09
302 Ivan Rodriguez .50 .15
303 Jose Canseco .50 .15
304 Jeff Bagwell .30 .09

305 Manny Ramirez .30 .09
306 Dennis Martinez .20 .06
307 Charlie Hayes .20 .06
308 Joe Carter .20 .06
309 Travis Fryman .20 .06
310 Mark McGwire 1.25 .35
311 Reggie Sanders UER .20 .06
Photo on front is John Roper
312 Julian Tavarez .20 .06
313 Jeff Montgomery .20 .06
314 Andy Benes .20 .06
315 John Jaha .20 .06
316 Jeff Kent .20 .06
317 Mike Piazza .75 .23
318 Erik Hanson .20 .06
319 Kenny Rogers .20 .06
320 Hideo Nomo .50 .15
321 Gregg Jefferies .20 .06
322 Chipper Jones .50 .15
323 Jay Buhner .20 .06
324 Dennis Eckersley .20 .06
325 Kenny Lofton .20 .06
326 Robin Ventura .20 .06
327 Tom Glavine .30 .09
328 Tim Salmon .30 .09
329 Andres Galarraga .20 .06
330 Hal Morris .20 .06
331 Brady Anderson .20 .06
332 Chili Davis .20 .06
333 Roger Clemens 1.00 .30
334 Marquis Grissom .20 .06
335 Mike Greenwell UER .20 .06
Name spelled Jeff on Front
336 Sammy Sosa .75 .23
337 Ron Gant .20 .06
338 Ken Caminiti .20 .06
339 Danny Tartabull .20 .06
340 Barry Bonds 1.25 .35
341 Ben McDonald .20 .06
342 Ruben Sierra .20 .06
343 Bernie Williams .30 .09
344 Wil Cordero .20 .06
345 Wade Boggs .30 .09
346 Gary Gaetti .20 .06
347 Greg Colbrunn .20 .06
348 Juan Gonzalez .30 .09
349 Marc Newfield .20 .06
350 Charles Nagy .20 .06
351 Robby Thompson .20 .06
352 Roberto Petagine .20 .06
353 Darryl Strawberry .20 .06
354 Tino Martinez .30 .09
355 Eric Karros .20 .06
356 Cal Ripken SS .75 .23
357 Cecil Fielder SS .20 .06
358 Kirby Puckett SS .30 .09
359 Jim Edmonds SS .20 .06
360 Matt Williams SS .20 .06
361 Alex Rodriguez SS .50 .15
362 Barry Larkin SS .20 .06
363 Rafael Palmeiro SS .20 .06
364 David Cone SS .20 .06
365 Roberto Alomar SS .20 .06
366 Eddie Murray SS .30 .09
367 Randy Johnson SS .30 .09
368 Ryan Klesko SS .20 .06
369 Raul Mondesi SS .20 .06
370 Mo Vaughn SS .20 .06
371 Will Clark SS .20 .06
372 Carlos Baerga SS .20 .06
373 Frank Thomas SS .30 .09
374 Larry Walker SS .20 .06
375 Garret Anderson SS .20 .06
376 Edgar Martinez SS .20 .06
377 Don Mattingly SS .60 .18
378 Tony Gwynn SS .30 .09
379 Albert Belle SS .20 .06
380 J.Isringhausen SS .20 .06
381 Ruben Rivera SS .20 .06
382 Johnny Damon SS .20 .06
383 Karim Garcia SS .20 .06
384 Derek Jeter SS .60 .18
385 David Justice SS .20 .06
386 Royce Clayton .20 .06
387 Mark Whiten .20 .06
388 Mickey Tettleton .20 .06
389 Steve Trachsel .20 .06
390 Danny Bautista .20 .06
391 Midre Cummings .20 .06
392 Scott Leius .20 .06
393 Manny Alexander .20 .06
394 Brent Gates .20 .06
395 Rey Sanchez .20 .06
396 Andy Pettitte .30 .09
397 Jeff Cirillo .20 .06
398 Kurt Abbott .20 .06
399 Lee Tinsley .20 .06
400 Paul Assenmacher .20 .06
401 Scott Erickson .20 .06
402 Todd Zeile .20 .06
403 Tom Pagnozzi .20 .06
404 Ozzie Guillen .20 .06
405 Jeff Frye .20 .06
406 Kirt Manwaring .20 .06
407 Chad Ogea .20 .06
408 Harold Baines .20 .06
409 Jason Bere .20 .06
410 Chuck Finley .20 .06
411 Jeff Fassero .20 .06
412 Joey Hamilton .20 .06
413 John Olerud .20 .06
414 Kevin Stocker .20 .06
415 Eric Anthony .20 .06
416 Aaron Sele .20 .06
417 Chris Bosio .20 .06
418 Michael Mimbs .20 .06
419 Orlando Miller .20 .06
420 Stan Javier .20 .06
421 Matt Mieske .20 .06
422 Jason Bates .20 .06
423 Orlando Merced .20 .06
424 John Flaherty .20 .06
425 Reggie Jefferson .20 .06
426 Scott Stahoviak .20 .06
427 John Burkett .20 .06
428 Rod Beck .20 .06
429 Bill Swift .20 .06
430 Scott Cooper .20 .06
431 Mel Rojas .20 .06
432 Todd Van Poppel .20 .06
433 Bobby Jones .20 .06
434 Mike Harkey .20 .06
435 Sean Berry .20 .06
436 Glenallen Hill .20 .06
437 Ryan Thompson .20 .06
438 Luis Alicea .20 .06
439 Esteban Loaiza .20 .06
440 Jeff Reboulet .20 .06
441 Vince Coleman .20 .06
442 Ellis Burks .20 .06
443 Allen Battle .20 .06
444 Jimmy Key .20 .06
445 Ricky Bottalico .20 .06
446 Delino DeShields .20 .06
447 Albie Lopez .20 .06
448 Mark Petkovsek .20 .06
449 Tim Raines .20 .06
450 Bryan Harvey .20 .06
451 Pat Hentgen .20 .06
452 Tim Laker .20 .06
453 Tom Gordon .20 .06
454 Phil Plantier .20 .06
455 Ernie Young .20 .06
456 Pete Harnisch .20 .06
457 Roberto Kelly .20 .06
458 Mark Portugal .20 .06
459 Mark Leiter .20 .06
460 Tony Pena .20 .06
461 Roger Pavlik .20 .06
462 Jeff King .20 .06
463 Bryan Rekar .20 .06
464 Al Leiter .20 .06
465 Phil Nevin .20 .06
466 Jose Lima .20 .06
467 Mike Stanley .20 .06
468 David McCarty .20 .06
469 Herb Perry .20 .06
470 Geronimo Berroa .20 .06
471 David Wells .20 .06
472 Vaughn Eshelman .20 .06
473 Greg Swindell .20 .06
474 Steve Sparks .20 .06
475 Luis Sojo .20 .06
476 Derrick May .20 .06
477 Joe Oliver .20 .06
478 Alex Arias .20 .06
479 Brad Ausmus .20 .06
480 Gabe White .20 .06
481 Pat Rapp .20 .06
482 Damon Buford .20 .06
483 Turk Wendell .20 .06
484 Jeff Brantley .20 .06
485 Curtis Leskanic .20 .06
486 Robb Nen .20 .06
487 Lou Whitaker .20 .06
488 Melido Perez .20 .06
489 Luis Polonia .20 .06
490 Scott Brosius .20 .06
491 Robert Perez .20 .06
492 Mike Sweeney RC 1.00 .30
493 Mark Loretta .20 .06
494 Alex Ochoa .20 .06
495 Matt Lawton RC .30 .09
496 Shawn Estes .20 .06
497 John Wasdin .20 .06
498 Marc Kroon .20 .06
499 Chris Snopek .20 .06
500 Jeff Suppan .20 .06
501 Terrell Wade .20 .06
502 Marvin Benard RC .20 .06
503 Chris Widger .20 .06
504 Quinton McCracken .20 .06
505 Bob Wolcott .20 .06
506 C.J. Nitkowski .20 .06
507 Aaron Ledesma .20 .06
508 Scott Hatteberg .20 .06
509 Jimmy Haynes .20 .06
510 Howard Battle .20 .06
511 Marty Cordova CL .20 .06
512 Randy Johnson CL .30 .09
513 Mo Vaughn CL .20 .06
514 Hideo Nomo CL .20 .06
515 Greg Maddux CL .50 .15
516 Barry Larkin CL .20 .06
517 Tom Glavine CL .20 .06
NNO Cal Ripken 2131 20.00 6.00

1996 Score All-Stars

Randomly inserted in second series jumbo packs at a rate of one in nine, this 20-card set was printed in rainbow holographic prismatic foil.

	Nm-Mt	Ex-Mt
COMPLETE SET (20)	60.00	18.00
1 Frank Thomas	3.00	.90
2 Albert Belle	1.25	.35
3 Ken Griffey Jr.	5.00	1.50
4 Cal Ripken	10.00	3.00
5 Mo Vaughn	1.25	.35
6 Matt Williams	1.25	.35
7 Barry Bonds	8.00	2.40
8 Dante Bichette	1.25	.35
9 Tony Gwynn	4.00	1.20
10 Greg Maddux	5.00	1.50
11 Randy Johnson	3.00	.90
12 Hideo Nomo	3.00	.90
13 Tim Salmon	2.00	.60
14 Jeff Bagwell	2.00	.60
15 Edgar Martinez	2.00	.60
16 Reggie Sanders	1.25	.35
17 Larry Walker	2.00	.60
18 Chipper Jones	3.00	.90
19 Manny Ramirez	2.00	.60
20 Eddie Murray	3.00	.90

1996 Score Big Bats

This 20-card set was randomly inserted in retail packs at a rate of approximately one in 31. The cards are numbered "X" of 20 in the upper left corner.

	Nm-Mt	Ex-Mt
COMPLETE SET (20)	100.00	30.00
1 Cal Ripken	15.00	4.50
2 Ken Griffey Jr.	8.00	2.40
3 Frank Thomas	5.00	1.50
4 Jeff Bagwell	3.00	.90
5 Mike Piazza	8.00	2.40
6 Barry Bonds	12.00	3.60
7 Matt Williams	2.00	.60
8 Raul Mondesi	2.00	.60
9 Tony Gwynn	6.00	1.80
10 Albert Belle	2.00	.60
11 Manny Ramirez	3.00	.90
12 Carlos Baerga	2.00	.60
13 Mo Vaughn	2.00	.60
14 Derek Bell	2.00	.60
15 Larry Walker	3.00	.90
16 Kenny Lofton	2.00	.60
17 Edgar Martinez	3.00	.90
18 Reggie Sanders	2.00	.60
19 Eddie Murray	5.00	1.50
20 Chipper Jones	5.00	1.50

1996 Score Diamond Aces

This 30-card set features some of baseball's best players. The cards were inserted approximately one every eight jumbo packs.

	Nm-Mt	Ex-Mt
COMPLETE SET (30)	120.00	36.00
1 Hideo Nomo	5.00	1.50
2 Brian L.Hunter	2.00	.60
3 Ray Durham	2.00	.60
4 Frank Thomas	5.00	1.50
5 Cal Ripken	15.00	4.50
6 Barry Bonds	12.00	3.60
7 Greg Maddux	8.00	2.40
8 Chipper Jones	5.00	1.50
9 Raul Mondesi	2.00	.60
10 Mike Piazza	8.00	2.40
11 Derek Jeter	12.00	3.60
12 Bill Pulsipher	2.00	.60
13 Larry Walker	3.00	.90
14 Ken Griffey Jr.	8.00	2.40
15 Alex Rodriguez	10.00	3.00
16 Manny Ramirez	3.00	.90
17 Mo Vaughn	2.00	.60
18 Reggie Sanders	2.00	.60
19 Derek Bell	2.00	.60
20 Jim Edmonds	2.00	.60
21 Albert Belle	2.00	.60
22 Eddie Murray	5.00	1.50
23 Tony Gwynn	6.00	1.80
24 Jeff Bagwell	3.00	.90
25 Carlos Baerga	2.00	.60
26 Matt Williams	2.00	.60
27 Garret Anderson	2.00	.60
28 Todd Hollandsworth	2.00	.60
29 Johnny Damon	2.00	.60
30 Tim Salmon	3.00	.90

1996 Score Dream Team

This nine-card set was randomly inserted in approximately one in 72 packs. This set features a leading player at each position. The cards are numbered in the upper right as "X" of nine.

	Nm-Mt	Ex-Mt
COMPLETE SET (9)	60.00	18.00
1 Cal Ripken	15.00	4.50
2 Frank Thomas	5.00	1.50
3 Carlos Baerga	2.00	.60
4 Matt Williams	2.00	.60
5 Mike Piazza	8.00	2.40
6 Barry Bonds	12.00	3.60
7 Ken Griffey Jr.	8.00	2.40
8 Manny Ramirez	3.00	.90
9 Greg Maddux	8.00	2.40

1996 Score Dugout Collection

This set is a mini-parallel to the regular issue. Only 110 cards of each Series 1 and Series 2 were selected. Randomly inserted approximately one in every three packs, these cards have all gold foil printing that gives them a shiny copper cast. The words "Dugout Collection" are printed on the back.

	Nm-Mt	Ex-Mt
COMP. SERIES 1 (110)	50.00	15.00
COMP. SERIES 2 (110)	50.00	15.00

*DUGOUT: 1.5X TO 4X BASIC
STATED ODDS 1:3 HOB/RET
*AP DUGOUT: 10X TO 25X BASIC
AP STATED ODDS 1:36 HOB/RET

1996 Score Future Franchise

Randomly inserted in retail packs at a rate of one in 72, this 16-card set honors young stars of the game.

	Nm-Mt	Ex-Mt
COMPLETE SET (16)	100.00	30.00
1 Jason Isringhausen	4.00	1.20
2 Chipper Jones	10.00	3.00
3 Derek Jeter	25.00	7.50
4 Alex Rodriguez	20.00	6.00
5 Alex Ochoa	4.00	1.20
6 Manny Ramirez	6.00	1.80
7 Johnny Damon	4.00	1.20
8 Ruben Rivera	4.00	1.20
9 Karim Garcia	4.00	1.20
10 Garret Anderson	4.00	1.20
11 Marty Cordova	4.00	1.20
12 Bill Pulsipher	4.00	1.20
13 Hideo Nomo	10.00	3.00
14 Marc Newfield	4.00	1.20
15 Charles Johnson	4.00	1.20
16 Raul Mondesi	4.00	1.20

1996 Score Gold Stars

Randomly inserted in packs at a rate of one in 15, this 30-card set features borderless color action player photos with a special sepia player cutout inserted behind a gold foil stamp designating the star player.

	Nm-Mt	Ex-Mt
COMPLETE SET (30)	50.00	15.00
1 Ken Griffey Jr.	4.00	1.20
2 Frank Thomas	2.50	.75
3 Reggie Sanders	1.00	.30
4 Tim Salmon	1.50	.45
5 Mike Piazza	4.00	1.20
6 Tony Gwynn	3.00	.90
7 Gary Sheffield	1.00	.30
8 Matt Williams	1.00	.30
9 Bernie Williams	1.50	.45
10 Jason Isringhausen	1.00	.30
11 Albert Belle	1.00	.30
12 Chipper Jones	2.50	.75
13 Edgar Martinez	1.50	.45
14 Barry Larkin	1.50	.45
15 Barry Bonds	6.00	1.80
16 Jeff Bagwell	1.50	.45
17 Greg Maddux	4.00	1.20
18 Mo Vaughn	1.00	.30
19 Ryan Klesko	1.00	.30
20 Sammy Sosa	4.00	1.20
21 Darren Daulton	1.00	.30
22 Ivan Rodriguez	2.50	.75
23 Dante Bichette	1.00	.30
24 Hideo Nomo	2.50	.75
25 Cal Ripken	8.00	2.40
26 Rafael Palmeiro	1.50	.45
27 Larry Walker	1.50	.45
28 Carlos Baerga	1.00	.30
29 Randy Johnson	2.50	.75
30 Manny Ramirez	1.50	.45

1996 Score Numbers Game

This 30-card set was inserted approximately one in every 15 packs. The cards are numbered as "X" of 30 in the upper left corner.

	Nm-Mt	Ex-Mt
COMPLETE SET (30)	60.00	18.00
1 Cal Ripken	8.00	2.40
2 Frank Thomas	2.50	.75
3 Ken Griffey Jr.	4.00	1.20
4 Mike Piazza	4.00	1.20
5 Barry Bonds	6.00	1.80
6 Greg Maddux	4.00	1.20
7 Jeff Bagwell	1.50	.45
8 Derek Bell	1.00	.30
9 Tony Gwynn	3.00	.90
10 Hideo Nomo	2.50	.75
11 Raul Mondesi	1.00	.30
12 Manny Ramirez	1.50	.45
13 Albert Belle	1.00	.30
14 Matt Williams	1.00	.30
15 Jim Edmonds	1.00	.30
16 Edgar Martinez	1.50	.45
17 Mo Vaughn	1.00	.30
18 Reggie Sanders	1.00	.30
19 Chipper Jones	2.50	.75
20 Larry Walker	1.50	.45
21 Juan Gonzalez	1.50	.45
22 Kenny Lofton	1.00	.30
23 Don Mattingly	6.00	1.80
24 Ivan Rodriguez	2.50	.75
25 Randy Johnson	2.50	.75
26 Derek Jeter	6.00	1.80
27 J.T. Snow	1.00	.30
28 Will Clark	2.50	.75
29 Rafael Palmeiro	1.50	.45
30 Alex Rodriguez	5.00	1.50

1996 Score Power Pace

Randomly inserted in retail packs at a rate of one in 31, this 18-card set features homerun hitters.

	Nm-Mt	Ex-Mt
COMPLETE SET (18)	60.00	18.00
1 Mark McGwire	10.00	3.00
2 Albert Belle	1.50	.45
3 Jay Buhner	1.50	.45
4 Frank Thomas	4.00	1.20
5 Matt Williams	1.50	.45
6 Gary Sheffield	1.50	.45
7 Mike Piazza	6.00	1.80
8 Larry Walker	2.50	.75
9 Mo Vaughn	1.50	.45
10 Rafael Palmeiro	2.50	.75
11 Dante Bichette	1.50	.45
12 Ken Griffey Jr.	6.00	1.80
13 Barry Bonds	10.00	3.00
14 Manny Ramirez	2.50	.75
15 Sammy Sosa	6.00	1.80
16 Tim Salmon	2.50	.75
17 Dave Justice	1.50	.45
18 Eric Karros	1.50	.45

1996 Score Reflextions

This 20-card set was randomly inserted approximately one in every 31 hobby packs. Two players per card are featured, a veteran player and a younger star playing the same position.

	Nm-Mt	Ex-Mt
COMPLETE SET (20)	100.00	30.00
1 Cal Ripken Chipper Jones	15.00	4.50
2 Ken Griffey Jr. Alex Rodriguez	8.00	2.40
3 Frank Thomas Mo Vaughn	5.00	1.50
4 Kenny Lofton Brian L.Hunter	2.00	.60
5 Don Mattingly J.T.Snow	12.00	3.60
6 Manny Ramirez Raul Mondesi	3.00	.90
7 Tony Gwynn Garret Anderson	6.00	1.80
8 Roberto Alomar Carlos Baerga	3.00	.90
9 Andre Dawson Larry Walker	2.00	.60
10 Barry Larkin Derek Jeter	12.00	3.60
11 Barry Bonds Reggie Sanders	12.00	3.60
12 Mike Piazza Albert Belle	8.00	2.40
13 Wade Boggs Edgar Martinez	3.00	.90
14 David Cone John Smoltz	2.00	.60
15 Will Clark Jeff Bagwell	3.00	.90
16 Mark McGwire Cecil Fielder	12.00	3.60
17 Greg Maddux Mike Mussina	8.00	2.40
18 Randy Johnson Hideo Nomo	5.00	1.50
19 Jim Thome Dean Palmer	5.00	1.50
20 Chuck Knoblauch Craig Biggio	3.00	.90

1996 Score Titanic Taters

Randomly inserted in hobby packs at a rate of one in 31, this 18-card set features long home run hitters.

	Nm-Mt	Ex-Mt
COMPLETE SET (18)	80.00	24.00
1 Albert Belle	2.00	.60
2 Frank Thomas	5.00	1.50
3 Mo Vaughn	2.00	.60
4 Ken Griffey Jr.	8.00	2.40
5 Matt Williams	2.00	.60
6 Mark McGwire	12.00	3.60
7 Dante Bichette	2.00	.60
8 Tim Salmon	3.00	.90
9 Jeff Bagwell	3.00	.90
10 Rafael Palmeiro	3.00	.90
11 Mike Piazza	8.00	2.40
12 Cecil Fielder	2.00	.60
13 Larry Walker	3.00	.90
14 Sammy Sosa	8.00	2.40
15 Manny Ramirez	3.00	.90
16 Gary Sheffield	2.00	.60
17 Barry Bonds	12.00	3.60
18 Jay Buhner	2.00	.60

1997 Score

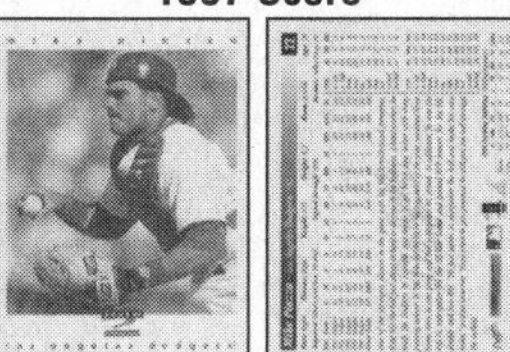

The 1997 Score set has a total of 550 cards. With cards 1-330 distributed in series one packs and cards 331-550 in series two packs. The 10-card Series one packs and the 12-card Series two packs carried a suggested retail price of $.99 each and were distributed exclusively to retail outlets. The fronts feature color player action photos in a white border. The backs carry player information and career statistics. The Hideki Irabu card (551A and B) is shortprinted (about twice as tough to pull as a basic card). One final note on the Irabu card, in the retail packs and factory sets, the card text is in English. In the Hobby Reserve packs, text is in Japanese. Notable Rookie Cards include Brian Giles.

	Nm-Mt	Ex-Mt
COMPLETE SET (551)	40.00	12.00
COMP.FACT.SET (551)	40.00	12.00
COMP.SERIES 1 (330)	15.00	4.50
COMP.SERIES 2 (221)	25.00	7.50
1 Jeff Bagwell	.30	.09
2 Mickey Tettleton	.20	.06
3 Johnny Damon	.30	.09
4 Jeff Conine	.20	.06
5 Bernie Williams	.30	.09
6 Will Clark	.50	.15
7 Ryan Klesko	.20	.06
8 Cecil Fielder	.20	.06
9 Paul Wilson	.20	.06
10 Gregg Jefferies	.20	.06
11 Chili Davis	.20	.06
12 Albert Belle	.20	.06
13 Ken Hill	.20	.06
14 Cliff Floyd	.20	.06
15 Jaime Navarro	.20	.06
16 Ismael Valdes	.20	.06
17 Jeff King	.20	.06
18 Chris Bosio	.20	.06
19 Reggie Sanders	.20	.06
20 Darren Daulton	.20	.06
21 Ken Caminiti	.20	.06
22 Mike Piazza	.75	.23
23 Chad Mottola	.20	.06
24 Darin Erstad	.20	.06
25 Dante Bichette	.20	.06
26 Frank Thomas	.50	.15
27 Ben McDonald	.20	.06
28 Raul Casanova	.20	.06
29 Kevin Ritz	.20	.06
30 Garret Anderson	.20	.06
31 Jason Kendall	.20	.06
32 Billy Wagner	.20	.06
33 Dave Justice	.20	.06
34 Marty Cordova	.20	.06
35 Derek Jeter	1.25	.35
36 Trevor Hoffman	.20	.06
37 Geronimo Berroa	.20	.06
38 Walt Weiss	.20	.06
39 Kirt Manwaring	.20	.06
40 Alex Gonzalez	.20	.06
41 Sean Berry	.20	.06
42 Kevin Appier	.20	.06
43 Rusty Greer	.20	.06
44 Pete Incaviglia	.20	.06
45 Rafael Palmeiro	.30	.09
46 Eddie Murray	.50	.15
47 Moises Alou	.20	.06
48 Mark Lewis	.20	.06
49 Hal Morris	.20	.06
50 Edgar Renteria	.20	.06
51 Rickey Henderson	.50	.15
52 Pat Listach	.20	.06
53 John Wasdin	.20	.06
54 James Baldwin	.20	.06
55 Brian Jordan	.20	.06
56 Edgar Martinez	.30	.09
57 Wil Cordero	.20	.06
58 Danny Tartabull	.20	.06
59 Keith Lockhart	.20	.06
60 Rico Brogna	.20	.06
61 Ricky Bottalico	.20	.06
62 Terry Pendleton	.20	.06
63 Bret Boone	.20	.06
64 Charlie Hayes	.20	.06
65 Marc Newfield	.20	.06
66 Sterling Hitchcock	.20	.06
67 Roberto Alomar	.30	.09
68 John Jaha	.20	.06
69 Greg Colbrunn	.20	.06
70 Sal Fasano	.20	.06
71 Brooks Kieschnick	.20	.06
72 Pedro Martinez	.50	.15
73 Kevin Elster	.20	.06
74 Ellis Burks	.20	.06
75 Chuck Finley	.20	.06
76 John Olerud	.20	.06
77 Jay Bell	.20	.06
78 Allen Watson	.20	.06
79 Darryl Strawberry	.20	.06
80 Orlando Miller	.20	.06
81 Jose Herrera	.20	.06
82 Andy Pettitte	.30	.09
83 Juan Guzman	.20	.06
84 Alan Benes	.20	.06
85 Jack McDowell	.20	.06
86 Ugueth Urbina	.20	.06
87 Rocky Coppinger	.20	.06
88 Jeff Cirillo	.20	.06
89 Tom Glavine	.30	.09
90 Robby Thompson	.20	.06
91 Barry Bonds	1.25	.35
92 Carlos Delgado	.20	.06
93 Mo Vaughn	.20	.06
94 Ryne Sandberg	.75	.23
95 Alex Rodriguez	.75	.23
96 Brady Anderson	.20	.06
97 Scott Brosius	.20	.06
98 Dennis Eckersley	.20	.06
99 Brian McRae	.20	.06
100 Rey Ordonez	.20	.06
101 John Valentin	.20	.06
102 Brett Butler	.20	.06
103 Eric Karros	.20	.06
104 Harold Baines	.20	.06
105 Javier Lopez	.20	.06
106 Alan Trammell	.20	.06
107 Jim Thome	.50	.15
108 Frank Rodriguez	.20	.06
109 Bernard Gilkey	.20	.06
110 Reggie Jefferson	.20	.06
111 Scott Stahoviak	.20	.06
112 Steve Gibralter	.20	.06
113 Todd Hollandsworth	.20	.06
114 Ruben Rivera	.20	.06
115 Dennis Martinez	.20	.06
116 Mariano Rivera	.30	.09
117 John Smoltz	.30	.09
118 John Mabry	.20	.06
119 Tom Gordon	.20	.06
120 Alex Ochoa	.20	.06
121 Jamey Wright	.20	.06
122 Dave Nilsson	.20	.06
123 Bobby Bonilla	.20	.06
124 Al Leiter	.20	.06
125 Rick Aguilera	.20	.06
126 Jeff Brantley	.20	.06
127 Kevin Brown	.20	.06
128 George Arias	.20	.06
129 Darren Oliver	.20	.06
130 Bill Pulsipher	.20	.06
131 Roberto Hernandez	.20	.06
132 Delino DeShields	.20	.06
133 Mark Grudzielanek	.20	.06
134 John Wetteland	.20	.06
135 Carlos Baerga	.20	.06
136 Paul Sorrento	.20	.06
137 Leo Gomez	.20	.06
138 Andy Ashby	.20	.06
139 Julio Franco	.20	.06
140 Brian Hunter	.20	.06
141 Jermaine Dye	.20	.06
142 Tony Clark	.20	.06
143 Ruben Sierra	.20	.06
144 Donovan Osborne	.20	.06
145 Mark McLemore	.20	.06
146 Terry Steinbach	.20	.06
147 Bob Wells	.20	.06
148 Chan Ho Park	.20	.06
149 Tim Salmon	.30	.09
150 Paul O'Neill	.30	.09
151 Cal Ripken	1.50	.45
152 Wally Joyner	.20	.06
153 Omar Vizquel	.30	.09
154 Mike Mussina	.30	.09
155 Andres Galarraga	.20	.06
156 Ken Griffey Jr.	.75	.23
157 Kenny Lofton	.20	.06
158 Ray Durham	.20	.06
159 Hideo Nomo	.50	.15
160 Ozzie Guillen	.20	.06
161 Roger Pavlik	.20	.06
162 Manny Ramirez	.30	.09
163 Mark Lemke	.20	.06
164 Mike Stanley	.20	.06
165 Chuck Knoblauch	.20	.06
166 Kimera Bartee	.20	.06
167 Wade Boggs	.30	.09
168 Jay Buhner	.20	.06
169 Eric Young	.20	.06
170 Jose Canseco	.50	.15
171 Dwight Gooden	.20	.06
172 Fred McGriff	.30	.09
173 Sandy Alomar Jr.	.20	.06
174 Andy Benes	.20	.06
175 Dean Palmer	.20	.06
176 Larry Walker	.30	.09
177 Charles Nagy	.20	.06
178 David Cone	.20	.06
179 Mark Grace	.30	.09
180 Robin Ventura	.20	.06
181 Roger Clemens	1.00	.30
182 Bobby Witt	.20	.06
183 Vinny Castilla	.20	.06
184 Gary Sheffield	.20	.06
185 Dan Wilson	.20	.06
186 Roger Cedeno	.20	.06
187 Mark McGwire	1.25	.35
188 Darren Bragg	.20	.06
189 Quinton McCracken	.20	.06
190 Randy Myers	.20	.06
191 Jeromy Burnitz	.20	.06
192 Randy Johnson	.50	.15
193 Chipper Jones	.50	.15
194 Greg Vaughn	.20	.06
195 Travis Fryman	.20	.06
196 Tim Naehring	.20	.06
197 B.J. Surhoff	.20	.06
198 Juan Gonzalez	.30	.09
199 Terrell Wade	.20	.06
200 Jeff Frye	.20	.06
201 Joey Cora	.20	.06
202 Raul Mondesi	.20	.06
203 Ivan Rodriguez	.50	.15
204 Armando Reynoso	.20	.06
205 Jeffrey Hammonds	.20	.06
206 Darren Dreifort	.20	.06
207 Kevin Seitzer	.20	.06
208 Tino Martinez	.30	.09
209 Jim Bruske	.20	.06
210 Jeff Suppan	.20	.06
211 Mark Carreon	.20	.06
212 Wilson Alvarez	.20	.06
213 John Burkett	.20	.06
214 Tony Phillips	.20	.06
215 Greg Maddux	.75	.23
216 Mark Whiten	.20	.06
217 Curtis Pride	.20	.06
218 Lyle Mouton	.20	.06
219 Todd Hundley	.20	.06
220 Greg Gagne	.20	.06
221 Rich Amaral	.20	.06
222 Tom Goodwin	.20	.06
223 Chris Hoiles	.20	.06
224 Jayhawk Owens	.20	.06
225 Kenny Rogers	.20	.06
226 Mike Greenwell	.20	.06
227 Mark Wohlers	.20	.06
228 Henry Rodriguez	.20	.06
229 Robert Perez	.20	.06
230 Jeff Kent	.20	.06
231 Darryl Hamilton	.20	.06
232 Alex Fernandez	.20	.06
233 Ron Karkovice	.20	.06
234 Jimmy Haynes	.20	.06
235 Craig Biggio	.30	.09
236 Ray Lankford	.20	.06
237 Lance Johnson	.20	.06
238 Matt Williams	.20	.06
239 Chad Curtis	.20	.06
240 Mark Thompson	.20	.06
241 Jason Giambi	.20	.06
242 Barry Larkin	.30	.09
243 Paul Molitor	.30	.09
244 Sammy Sosa	.75	.23
245 Kevin Tapani	.20	.06
246 Marquis Grissom	.20	.06
247 Joe Carter	.20	.06
248 Ramon Martinez	.20	.06
249 Tony Gwynn	.60	.18
250 Andy Fox	.20	.06
251 Troy O'Leary	.20	.06
252 Warren Newson	.20	.06
253 Troy Percival	.20	.06
254 Jamie Moyer	.20	.06
255 Danny Graves	.20	.06
256 David Wells	.20	.06
257 Todd Zeile	.20	.06
258 Raul Ibanez	.20	.06
259 Tyler Houston	.20	.06
260 LaTroy Hawkins	.20	.06
261 Joey Hamilton	.20	.06
262 Mike Sweeney	.20	.06
263 Brant Brown	.20	.06
264 Pat Hentgen	.20	.06
265 Mark Johnson	.20	.06
266 Robb Nen	.20	.06
267 Justin Thompson	.20	.06
268 Ron Gant	.20	.06
269 Jeff D'Amico	.20	.06
270 Shawn Estes	.20	.06
271 Derek Bell	.20	.06
272 Fernando Valenzuela	.20	.06
273 Tom Pagnozzi	.20	.06
274 John Burke	.20	.06
275 Ed Sprague	.20	.06
276 F.P. Santangelo	.20	.06
277 Todd Greene	.20	.06
278 Butch Huskey	.20	.06
279 Steve Finley	.20	.06
280 Eric Davis	.20	.06
281 Shawn Green	.20	.06
282 Al Martin	.20	.06
283 Michael Tucker	.20	.06
284 Shane Reynolds	.20	.06
285 Matt Mieske	.20	.06
286 Jose Rosado	.20	.06
287 Mark Langston	.20	.06
288 Ralph Milliard	.20	.06
289 Mike Lansing	.20	.06
290 Scott Servais	.20	.06
291 Royce Clayton	.20	.06
292 Mike Grace	.20	.06
293 James Mouton	.20	.06
294 Charles Johnson	.20	.06
295 Gary Gaetti	.20	.06
296 Kevin Mitchell	.20	.06
297 Carlos Garcia	.20	.06
298 Desi Relaford	.20	.06
299 Jason Thompson	.20	.06
300 Osvaldo Fernandez	.20	.06
301 Fernando Vina	.20	.06
302 Jose Offerman	.20	.06
303 Yamil Benitez	.20	.06
304 J.T. Snow	.20	.06
305 Rafael Bournigal	.20	.06
306 Jason Isringhausen	.20	.06
307 Bobby Higginson	.20	.06
308 Nerio Rodriguez RC	.20	.06
309 Brian Giles RC	1.00	.30
310 Andruw Jones	.20	.06
311 Tony Graffanino	.20	.06
312 Arquimedez Pozo	.20	.06
313 Jermaine Allensworth	.20	.06
314 Jeff Darwin	.20	.06
315 George Williams	.20	.06
316 Karim Garcia	.20	.06
317 Trey Beamon	.20	.06
318 Mac Suzuki	.20	.06
319 Robin Jennings	.20	.06
320 Danny Patterson	.20	.06
321 Damon Mashore	.20	.06
322 Wendell Magee	.20	.06
323 Dax Jones	.20	.06
324 Kevin Brown	.20	.06
325 Marvin Benard	.20	.06
326 Mike Cameron	.20	.06
327 Marcus Jensen	.20	.06
328 Eddie Murray CL	.30	.09
329 Paul Molitor CL	.20	.06
330 Todd Hundley CL	.20	.06
331 Norm Charlton	.20	.06
332 Bruce Ruffin	.20	.06
333 John Wetteland	.20	.06
334 Marquis Grissom	.20	.06
335 Sterling Hitchcock	.20	.06
336 John Olerud	.20	.06
337 David Wells	.20	.06
338 Chili Davis	.20	.06
339 Mark Lewis	.20	.06
340 Kenny Lofton	.20	.06
341 Alex Fernandez	.20	.06
342 Ruben Sierra	.20	.06
343 Delino DeShields	.20	.06
344 John Wasdin	.20	.06
345 Dennis Martinez	.20	.06
346 Kevin Elster	.20	.06
347 Bobby Bonilla	.20	.06
348 Jaime Navarro	.20	.06
349 Chad Curtis	.20	.06
350 Terry Steinbach	.20	.06
351 Ariel Prieto	.20	.06
352 Jeff Kent	.20	.06
353 Carlos Garcia	.20	.06
354 Mark Whiten	.20	.06
355 Todd Zeile	.20	.06
356 Eric Davis	.20	.06
357 Greg Colbrunn	.20	.06
358 Moises Alou	.20	.06
359 Allen Watson	.20	.06
360 Jose Canseco	.50	.15
361 Matt Williams	.20	.06
362 Jeff King	.20	.06
363 Darryl Hamilton	.20	.06
364 Mark Clark	.20	.06
365 J.T. Snow	.20	.06
366 Kevin Mitchell	.20	.06
367 Orlando Miller	.20	.06
368 Rico Brogna	.20	.06
369 Mike James	.20	.06
370 Brad Ausmus	.20	.06
371 Darryl Kile	.20	.06
372 Edgardo Alfonzo	.20	.06
373 Julian Tavarez	.20	.06
374 Darren Lewis	.20	.06
375 Steve Karsay	.20	.06
376 Lee Stevens	.20	.06
377 Albie Lopez	.20	.06
378 Orel Hershiser	.20	.06
379 Lee Smith	.20	.06
380 Rick Helling	.20	.06
381 Carlos Perez	.20	.06
382 Tony Tarasco	.20	.06
383 Melvin Nieves	.20	.06
384 Benji Gil	.20	.06
385 Devon White	.20	.06
386 Armando Benitez	.20	.06
387 Bill Swift	.20	.06
388 John Smiley	.20	.06
389 Midre Cummings	.20	.06
390 Tim Belcher	.20	.06
391 Tim Raines	.20	.06
392 Todd Worrell	.20	.06
393 Quilvio Veras	.20	.06
394 Matt Lawton	.20	.06
395 Aaron Sele	.20	.06
396 Bip Roberts	.20	.06
397 Denny Neagle	.20	.06
398 Tyler Green	.20	.06
399 Hipolito Pichardo	.20	.06
400 Scott Erickson	.20	.06
401 Bobby Jones	.20	.06
402 Jim Edmonds	.20	.06
403 Chad Ogea	.20	.06
404 Cal Eldred	.20	.06
405 Pat Listach	.20	.06
406 Todd Stottlemyre	.20	.06
407 Phil Nevin	.20	.06
408 Otis Nixon	.20	.06
409 Billy Ashley	.20	.06
410 Jimmy Key	.20	.06
411 Mike Timlin	.20	.06
412 Joe Vitiello	.20	.06
413 Rondell White	.20	.06
414 Jeff Fassero	.20	.06
415 Rex Hudler	.20	.06
416 Curt Schilling	.20	.06
417 Rich Becker	.20	.06
418 W.Van Landingham	.20	.06
419 Chris Snopek	.20	.06
420 David Segui	.20	.06
421 Eddie Murray	.50	.15
422 Shane Andrews	.20	.06
423 Gary DiSarcina	.20	.06
424 Brian Hunter	.20	.06
425 Willie Greene	.20	.06
426 Felipe Crespo	.20	.06
427 Jason Bates	.20	.06
428 Albert Belle	.20	.06
429 Rey Sanchez	.20	.06
430 Roger Clemens	1.00	.30
431 Deion Sanders	.30	.09
432 Ernie Young	.20	.06
433 Jay Bell	.20	.06
434 Jeff Blauser	.20	.06
435 Lenny Dykstra	.20	.06
436 Chuck Carr	.20	.06
437 Russ Davis	.20	.06
438 Carl Everett	.20	.06
439 Damion Easley	.20	.06
440 Pat Kelly	.20	.06
441 Pat Rapp	.20	.06
442 Dave Justice	.20	.06
443 Graeme Lloyd	.20	.06
444 Damon Buford	.20	.06
445 Jose Valentin	.20	.06
446 Jason Schmidt	.20	.06
447 Dave Martinez	.20	.06
448 Danny Tartabull	.20	.06
449 Jose Vizcaino	.20	.06
450 Steve Avery	.20	.06
451 Mike Devereaux	.20	.06
452 Jim Eisenreich	.20	.06
453 Mark Leiter	.20	.06
454 Roberto Kelly	.20	.06
455 Benito Santiago	.20	.06
456 Steve Trachsel	.20	.06
457 Gerald Williams	.20	.06
458 Pete Schourek	.20	.06
459 Esteban Loaiza	.20	.06
460 Mel Rojas	.20	.06
461 Tim Wakefield	.20	.06
462 Tony Fernandez	.20	.06
463 Doug Drabek	.20	.06
464 Joe Girardi	.20	.06
465 Mike Bordick	.20	.06
466 Jim Leyritz	.20	.06
467 Erik Hanson	.20	.06
468 Michael Tucker	.20	.06
469 Tony Womack RC	.30	.09
470 Doug Glanville	.20	.06
471 Rudy Pemberton	.20	.06
472 Keith Lockhart	.20	.06
473 Nomar Garciaparra	.75	.23
474 Scott Rolen	.50	.15
475 Jason Dickson	.20	.06
476 Glendon Rusch	.20	.06
477 Todd Walker	.20	.06
478 Dmitri Young	.20	.06
479 Rod Myers	.20	.06
480 Wilton Guerrero	.20	.06
481 Jorge Posada	.30	.09
482 Brant Brown	.20	.06
483 Bubba Trammell RC	.20	.06
484 Jose Guillen	.20	.06
485 Scott Spiezio	.20	.06
486 Bob Abreu	.20	.06
487 Chris Holt	.20	.06
488 Deivi Cruz RC	.20	.06
489 Vladimir Guerrero	.50	.15
490 Julio Santana	.20	.06
491 Ray Montgomery RC	.20	.06
492 Kevin Orie	.20	.06
493 Todd Hundley GY	.20	.06
494 Tim Salmon GY	.20	.06
495 Albert Belle GY	.20	.06
496 Manny Ramirez GY	.20	.06
497 Rafael Palmeiro GY	.20	.06
498 Juan Gonzalez GY	.20	.06
499 Ken Griffey Jr. GY	.50	.15
500 Andruw Jones GY	.20	.06
501 Mike Piazza GY	.50	.15
502 Jeff Bagwell GY	.20	.06
503 Bernie Williams GY	.20	.06
504 Barry Bonds GY	.50	.15
505 Ken Caminiti GY	.20	.06
506 Darin Erstad GY	.20	.06
507 Alex Rodriguez GY	.50	.15
508 Frank Thomas GY	.30	.09
509 Chipper Jones GY	.30	.09
510 Mo Vaughn GY	.20	.06
511 Mark McGwire GY	.60	.18
512 Fred McGriff GY	.20	.06
513 Jay Buhner GY	.20	.06
514 Gary Sheffield GY	.20	.06
515 Jim Thome GY	.30	.09
516 Dean Palmer GY	.20	.06
517 Henry Rodriguez GY	.20	.06
518 Andy Pettitte RF	.20	.06
519 Mike Mussina RF	.20	.06
520 Greg Maddux RF	.50	.15
521 John Smoltz RF	.20	.06
522 Hideo Nomo RF	.20	.06
523 Troy Percival RF	.20	.06
524 John Wetteland RF	.20	.06
525 Roger Clemens RF	.50	.15
526 Charles Nagy RF	.20	.06
527 Mariano Rivera RF	.20	.06
528 Tom Glavine RF	.20	.06
529 Randy Johnson RF	.30	.09
530 J.Isringhausen RF	.20	.06
531 Alex Fernandez RF	.20	.06
532 Kevin Brown RF	.20	.06
533 Chuck Knoblauch TG	.20	.06
534 Rusty Greer TG	.20	.06
535 Tony Gwynn TG	.30	.09
536 Ryan Klesko TG	.20	.06
537 Ryne Sandberg TG	.50	.15
538 Barry Larkin TG	.20	.06
539 Will Clark TG	.20	.06
540 Kenny Lofton TG	.20	.06
541 Paul Molitor TG	.20	.06
542 Roberto Alomar TG	.20	.06
543 Rey Ordonez TG	.20	.06
544 Jason Giambi TG	.20	.06
545 Derek Jeter TG	.60	.18
546 Cal Ripken TG	.75	.23
547 Ivan Rodriguez TG	.30	.09
548 Ken Griffey Jr. CL	.50	.15
549 Frank Thomas CL	.30	.09
550 Mike Piazza CL	.50	.15
551A Hideki Irabu SP	2.50	.75
551B Hideki Irabu Japanese SP	2.50	.75

1997 Score Artist's Proofs White Border

Artist's Proofs White Border cards were randomly inserted exclusively into Score Series 1 retail packs. The cards share the similar "Artist's Proof" logo as seen on the more commonly traded Showcase Series Artist's Proofs. Unlike the silver-foiled Showcase Series Artist's Proofs, however, the White Border cards have plain white stock card fronts - making them easy to misidentify with a basic issue Score card. Please note that Series 2 Artist Proofs do not exist.

Nm-Mt Ex-Mt

*STARS: 12.5X TO 30X BASIC CARDS
*ROOKIES: 4X TO 10X BASIC CARDS

1997 Score Premium Stock

A special Premium Stock version of the base series one set was produced exclusively for hobby outlets. The cards parallel the regular issue set except for a grey border, thicker card stock and a prominent gold foil "Premium Stock" logo on front. The cards were distributed in Premium Stock hobby packs. Second series Premium Stock cards were called "Hobby Reserve."

	Nm-Mt	Ex-Mt
COMPLETE SET (551)	80.00	24.00
COMP.SERIES 1 (330)	40.00	12.00
COMP.SERIES 2 (221)	40.00	12.00

*STARS: .75X TO 2X BASIC CARDS
*ROOKIES: .6X TO 1.5X BASIC CARDS
*IRABU: .4X TO 1X BASIC IRABU

1997 Score Reserve Collection

Randomly inserted in second series hobby reserve packs only at a rate of one in 11, this set is parallel to the regular second series set. The cards are printed on thick 20 pt. foil card stock with screen printing for a raised ink effect. A large grey "Reserve Collection" logo is printed on each card back.

	Nm-Mt	Ex-Mt
*STARS: 5X TO 12X BASIC CARDS		
*ROOKIES: 2.5X TO 6X BASIC CARDS		
*IRABU: 1.5X TO 3X BASIC IRABU		

1997 Score Showcase Series

Randomly inserted in first series packs at a rate of one in seven hobby packs, one in two jumbo packs, one in four magazine and one in seven retail packs, and second series packs at a rate of one in five hobby packs and one in seven retail packs, cards from this set are silver-coated parallel versions of the regular Score set.

	Nm-Mt	Ex-Mt
*STARS: 3X TO 8X BASIC CARDS		
*ROOKIES: 1.5X TO 4X BASIC CARDS		
*IRABU: .5X TO 1.2X BASIC IRABU		

1997 Score Showcase Series Artist's Proofs

Randomly inserted in first series hobby and retail packs at a rate of one in 35, and second series hobby 1:23 and second series retail 1:35, cards from this 551-card set are parallel to the more common Showcase Series set. The cards are printed on holographic laminated card stock with a prismatic foil background and stamped with an Artist's Proof logo on front.

	Nm-Mt	Ex-Mt
*STARS: 10X TO 25X BASIC CARDS		
*ROOKIES: 4X TO 10X BASIC CARDS		
*IRABU: 2X TO 5X BASIC IRABU		

1997 Score Blast Masters

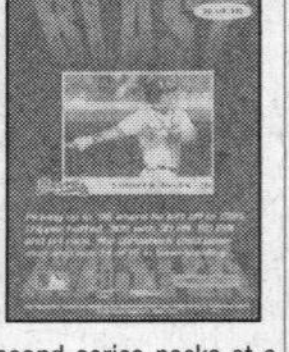

Randomly inserted in second series packs at a rate of 1:35 (retail) and 1:23 (hobby reserve), this 18-card set features color player photos on a gold prismatic foil card.

	Nm-Mt	Ex-Mt
COMPLETE SET (18)	100.00	30.00
1 Mo Vaughn	2.00	.60
2 Mark McGwire	12.00	3.60
3 Juan Gonzalez	3.00	.90
4 Albert Belle	2.00	.60
5 Barry Bonds	12.00	3.60
6 Ken Griffey Jr.	8.00	2.40
7 Andruw Jones	2.00	.60
8 Chipper Jones	5.00	1.50
9 Mike Piazza	8.00	2.40
10 Jeff Bagwell	3.00	.90
11 Dante Bichette	2.00	.60
12 Alex Rodriguez	8.00	2.40
13 Gary Sheffield	2.00	.60
14 Ken Caminiti	2.00	.60
15 Sammy Sosa	8.00	2.40
16 Vladimir Guerrero	5.00	1.50
17 Brian Jordan	2.00	.60
18 Tim Salmon	3.00	.90

1997 Score Franchise

Randomly inserted in series one hobby packs only at a rate of one in 72, this nine-card set honors superstar players for their irreplaceable contribution to their team. The fronts display sepia player portraits on a white baseball replica background. The backs carry an action player photo with a sentence about the player which explains why he was selected for this set.

	Nm-Mt	Ex-Mt
COMPLETE SET (9)	20.00	6.00
*GLOWING: 1.25X TO 3X BASIC FRANCHISE		
GLOW.SER.1 ODDS 1:240H/R, 1:79J, 1:120M		
1 Ken Griffey Jr.	2.00	.60
2 John Smoltz	.75	.23
3 Cal Ripken	4.00	1.20
4 Chipper Jones	1.25	.35
5 Mike Piazza	2.00	.60
6 Albert Belle	.50	.15
7 Frank Thomas	1.25	.35
8 Sammy Sosa	2.00	.60
9 Roberto Alomar	.75	.23

1997 Score Heart of the Order

Randomly inserted in packs at a rate of 1:23 (retail) and 1:15 (hobby reserve), this 36-card set features color photos of players on six teams with a panorama of the stadium in the background. Each team's three cards form one collectible unit. Eighteen of these cards are found in

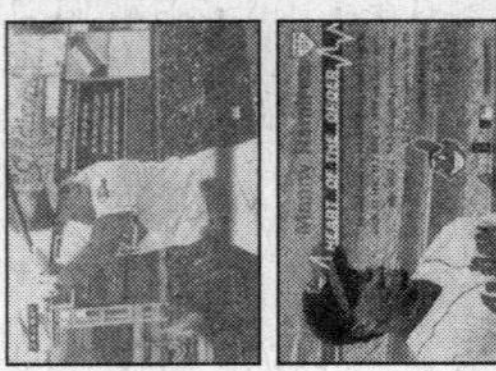

retail packs, and eighteen in Hobby Reserve packs.

	Nm-Mt	Ex-Mt
COMPLETE SET (36)	100.00	30.00
1 Will Clark	4.00	1.20
2 Ivan Rodriguez	4.00	1.20
3 Juan Gonzalez	2.50	.75
4 Frank Thomas	4.00	1.20
5 Albert Belle	1.50	.45
6 Robin Ventura	1.50	.45
7 Alex Rodriguez	6.00	1.80
8 Jay Buhner	1.50	.45
9 Ken Griffey Jr.	6.00	1.80
10 Rafael Palmeiro	2.50	.75
11 Roberto Alomar	2.50	.75
12 Cal Ripken	12.00	3.60
13 Manny Ramirez	2.50	.75
14 Matt Williams	1.50	.45
15 Jim Thome	4.00	1.20
16 Derek Jeter	10.00	3.00
17 Wade Boggs	2.50	.75
18 Bernie Williams	2.50	.75
19 Chipper Jones	4.00	1.20
20 Andruw Jones	1.50	.45
21 Ryan Klesko	1.50	.45
22 Mike Piazza	6.00	1.80
23 Wilton Guerrero	1.50	.45
24 Raul Mondesi	1.50	.45
25 Tony Gwynn	5.00	1.50
26 Greg Vaughn	1.50	.45
27 Ken Caminiti	1.50	.45
28 Brian Jordan	1.50	.45
29 Ron Gant	1.50	.45
30 Dmitri Young	1.50	.45
31 Darin Erstad	1.50	.45
32 Tim Salmon	2.50	.75
33 Jim Edmonds	1.50	.45
34 Chuck Knoblauch	1.50	.45
35 Paul Molitor	2.50	.75
36 Todd Walker	1.50	.45

1997 Score Highlight Zone

Randomly inserted in series one hobby packs only at a rate of one in 35, this 18-card set honors those mega-stars who have the incredible ability to consistently make the highlight films. The set is printed on thicker card stock with special foil stamping and a dot matrix holographic background.

	Nm-Mt	Ex-Mt
COMPLETE SET (18)	150.00	45.00
1 Frank Thomas	6.00	1.80
2 Ken Griffey Jr.	10.00	3.00
3 Mo Vaughn	2.50	.75
4 Albert Belle	2.50	.75
5 Mike Piazza	10.00	3.00
6 Barry Bonds	15.00	4.50
7 Greg Maddux	10.00	3.00
8 Sammy Sosa	10.00	3.00
9 Jeff Bagwell	4.00	1.20
10 Alex Rodriguez	10.00	3.00
11 Chipper Jones	6.00	1.80
12 Brady Anderson	2.50	.75
13 Ozzie Smith	2.50	.75
14 Edgar Martinez	4.00	1.20
15 Cal Ripken	20.00	6.00
16 Ryan Klesko	2.50	.75
17 Randy Johnson	6.00	1.80
18 Eddie Murray	6.00	1.80

1997 Score Pitcher Perfect

Randomly inserted in series one packs at a rate of one in 23, this 15-card set features players photographed by Randy Johnson in unique poses and foil stamping. The backs carry player information.

	Nm-Mt	Ex-Mt
COMPLETE SET (15)	5.00	1.50
1 Cal Ripken	1.50	.45
2 Alex Rodriguez	.75	.23
3 Alex Rodriguez Cal Ripken	3.00	.90
4 Edgar Martinez	.30	.09
5 Ivan Rodriguez	.50	.15
6 Mark McGwire	1.25	.35
7 Tim Salmon	.30	.09
8 Chili Davis	.20	.06
9 Joe Carter	.20	.06
10 Frank Thomas	.50	.15
11 Will Clark	.50	.15
12 Mo Vaughn	.20	.06
13 Wade Boggs	.30	.09
14 Ken Griffey Jr.	.75	.23
15 Randy Johnson	.50	.15

1997 Score Stand and Deliver

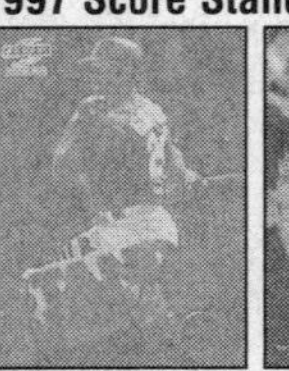

Randomly inserted in series two packs at a rate of 1:71 (retail) and 1:47 (hobby reserve), this 24-card set features color player photos printed on silver foil card stock. The set is broken into six separate 4-card groupings. Groups contain players from the following teams: 1-4 (Braves), 5-8 (Mariners), 9-12 (Yankees), 13-16 (Dodgers), 17-20 (Indians) and 21-24 (Wild Card). The four players featured within the Wild Card group are from "lesser" teams not given a shot at winning the World Series. Each of these cards, unlike cards 1-20, has a "Wild Card" logo stamped on front. Collectors were then supposed to gather up the particular group that won the 1997 World Series, in this case - the Florida Marlins. Since none of the featured teams won, the 4-card Wild Card group was designated as the winner. The winning cards could then be mailed into Pinnacle for a special gold upgrade version of the set, framed in glass.

	Nm-Mt	Ex-Mt
COMPLETE SET (24)	250.00	75.00
1 Andruw Jones	4.00	1.20
2 Greg Maddux	15.00	4.50
3 Chipper Jones	10.00	3.00
4 John Smoltz	6.00	1.80
5 Ken Griffey Jr.	15.00	4.50
6 Alex Rodriguez	15.00	4.50
7 Jay Buhner	4.00	1.20
8 Randy Johnson	10.00	3.00
9 Derek Jeter	25.00	7.50
10 Andy Pettitte	6.00	1.80
11 Bernie Williams	6.00	1.80
12 Mariano Rivera	6.00	1.80
13 Mike Piazza	15.00	4.50
14 Hideo Nomo	10.00	3.00
15 Raul Mondesi	4.00	1.20
16 Todd Hollandsworth	4.00	1.20
17 Manny Ramirez	6.00	1.80
18 Jim Thome	10.00	3.00
19 Dave Justice	4.00	1.20
20 Matt Williams	4.00	1.20
21 Juan Gonzalez W	6.00	1.80
22 Jeff Bagwell W	6.00	1.80
23 Cal Ripken W	30.00	9.00
24 Frank Thomas W	10.00	3.00

1997 Score Stellar Season

Randomly inserted in series one pre-priced magazine packs only at a rate of one in 35, this 18-card set features players who had a star season. The cards are printed using dot matrix holographic printing.

	Nm-Mt	Ex-Mt
COMPLETE SET (18)	60.00	18.00
1 Juan Gonzalez	2.50	.75
2 Chuck Knoblauch	1.50	.45
3 Jeff Bagwell	2.50	.75
4 John Smoltz	2.50	.75
5 Mark McGwire	10.00	3.00
6 Ken Griffey Jr.	6.00	1.80
7 Frank Thomas	4.00	1.20
8 Alex Rodriguez	6.00	1.80
9 Mike Piazza	6.00	1.80
10 Albert Belle	1.50	.45
11 Roberto Alomar	2.50	.75
12 Sammy Sosa	6.00	1.80
13 Mo Vaughn	1.50	.45
14 Brady Anderson	1.50	.45
15 Henry Rodriguez	1.50	.45
16 Eric Young	1.50	.45
17 Gary Sheffield	1.50	.45
18 Ryan Klesko	1.50	.45

1997 Score Titanic Taters

Randomly inserted in series one retail packs only at a rate of one in 35, this 18-card set honors the long-ball ability of some of the league's top sluggers and uses dot matrix holographic printing.

	Nm-Mt	Ex-Mt
COMPLETE SET (18)	120.00	36.00
1 Mark McGwire	15.00	4.50
2 Mike Piazza	10.00	3.00
3 Ken Griffey Jr.	10.00	3.00
4 Juan Gonzalez	4.00	1.20
5 Frank Thomas	6.00	1.80
6 Albert Belle	2.50	.75
7 Sammy Sosa	10.00	3.00
8 Jeff Bagwell	4.00	1.20
9 Todd Hundley	2.50	.75
10 Ryan Klesko	2.50	.75
11 Brady Anderson	2.50	.75
12 Mo Vaughn	2.50	.75
13 Jay Buhner	2.50	.75
14 Chipper Jones	6.00	1.80
15 Barry Bonds	15.00	4.50
16 Gary Sheffield	2.50	.75
17 Alex Rodriguez	10.00	3.00
18 Cecil Fielder	2.50	.75

1998 Score

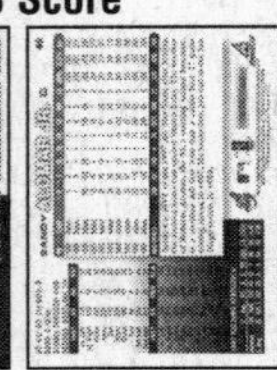

This 270-card set was distributed in 10-card packs exclusively to retail outlets with a suggested retail price of $.99. The fronts feature color player photos in a thin white border. The backs carry player information and statistics. In addition, two unnumbered checklist cards were created. The first card was available only in regular issue packs and provided listings for the standard 270-card set. A blank-backed checklist card was randomly seeded exclusively into All-Star Edition packs (released about three months after the regular packs went live). This checklist card provided listings only for the three insert sets exclusively distributed in All-Star Edition packs (First Pitch, Loaded Lineup and New Season).

	Nm-Mt	Ex-Mt
COMPLETE SET (270)	40.00	12.00
1 Andruw Jones	.20	.06
2 Dan Wilson	.20	.06
3 Hideo Nomo	.50	.15
4 Chuck Carr	.20	.06
5 Barry Bonds	1.25	.35
6 Jack McDowell	.20	.06
7 Albert Belle	.20	.06
8 Francisco Cordova	.20	.06
9 Greg Maddux	.75	.23
10 Alex Rodriguez	.75	.23
11 Steve Avery	.20	.06
12 Chuck McElroy	.20	.06
13 Larry Walker	.30	.09
14 Hideki Irabu	.20	.06
15 Roberto Alomar	.30	.09
16 Neifi Perez	.20	.06
17 Jim Thome	.50	.15
18 Rickey Henderson	.50	.15
19 Andres Galarraga	.20	.06
20 Jeff Fassero	.20	.06
21 Kevin Young	.20	.06
22 Derek Jeter	1.25	.35
23 Andy Benes	.20	.06
24 Mike Piazza	.75	.23
25 Todd Stottlemyre	.20	.06
26 Michael Tucker	.20	.06
27 Denny Neagle	.20	.06
28 Javier Lopez	.20	.06
29 Aaron Sele	.20	.06
30 Ryan Klesko	.20	.06
31 Dennis Eckersley	.20	.06
32 Quinton McCracken	.20	.06
33 Brian Anderson	.20	.06
34 Ken Griffey Jr.	.75	.23
35 Shawn Estes	.20	.06
36 Tim Wakefield	.20	.06
37 Jimmy Key	.20	.06
38 Jeff Bagwell	.30	.09
39 Edgardo Alfonzo	.20	.06
40 Mike Cameron	.20	.06
41 Mark McGwire	1.25	.35
42 Tino Martinez	.30	.09
43 Cal Ripken	1.50	.45
44 Curtis Goodwin	.20	.06
45 Bobby Ayala	.20	.06
46 Sandy Alomar Jr.	.20	.06
47 Bobby Jones	.20	.06
48 Omar Vizquel	.20	.06
49 Roger Clemens	1.00	.30
50 Tony Gwynn	.60	.18
51 Chipper Jones	.50	.15
52 Ron Coomer	.20	.06
53 Dmitri Young	.20	.06
54 Brian Giles	.20	.06
55 Steve Finley	.20	.06
56 David Cone	.20	.06
57 Andy Pettitte	.30	.09
58 Wilton Guerrero	.20	.06
59 Deion Sanders	.30	.09
60 Carlos Delgado	.20	.06
61 Jason Giambi	.20	.06
62 Ozzie Guillen	.20	.06
63 Jay Bell	.20	.06
64 Barry Larkin	.30	.09
65 Sammy Sosa	.75	.23
66 Bernie Williams	.30	.09
67 Terry Steinbach	.20	.06
68 Scott Rolen	.50	.15
69 Melvin Nieves	.20	.06
70 Craig Biggio	.30	.09
71 Todd Greene	.20	.06
72 Greg Gagne	.20	.06
73 Shigetoshi Hasegawa	.20	.06
74 Mark McLemore	.20	.06
75 Darren Bragg	.20	.06
76 Brett Butler	.20	.06
77 Ron Gant	.20	.06
78 Mike Difelice RC	.20	.06
79 Charles Nagy	.20	.06
80 Scott Hatteberg	.20	.06
81 Brady Anderson	.20	.06
82 Jay Buhner	.20	.06
83 Todd Hollandsworth	.20	.06
84 Geronimo Berroa	.20	.06
85 Jeff Suppan	.20	.06
86 Pedro Martinez	.50	.15
87 Roger Cedeno	.20	.06
88 Ivan Rodriguez	.50	.15
89 Jaime Navarro	.20	.06
90 Chris Hoiles	.20	.06
91 Nomar Garciaparra	.75	.23
92 Rafael Palmeiro	.30	.09
93 Darin Erstad	.20	.06
94 Kenny Lofton	.20	.06
95 Mike Timlin	.20	.06
96 Chris Clemons	.20	.06
97 Vinny Castilla	.20	.06
98 Charlie Hayes	.20	.06
99 Lyle Mouton	.20	.06
100 Jason Dickson	.20	.06
101 Justin Thompson	.20	.06
102 Pat Kelly	.20	.06
103 Chan Ho Park	.20	.06
104 Ray Lankford	.20	.06
105 Frank Thomas	.50	.15
106 Jermaine Allensworth	.20	.06
107 Doug Drabek	.20	.06
108 Todd Hundley	.20	.06
109 Carl Everett	.20	.06
110 Edgar Martinez	.30	.09
111 Robin Ventura	.20	.06
112 John Wetteland	.20	.06
113 Mariano Rivera	.30	.09
114 Jose Rosado	.20	.06
115 Ken Caminiti	.20	.06
116 Paul O'Neill	.30	.09
117 Tim Salmon	.30	.09
118 Eduardo Perez	.20	.06
119 Mike Jackson	.20	.06
120 John Smoltz	.30	.09
121 Brant Brown	.20	.06
122 John Mabry	.20	.06
123 Chuck Knoblauch	.20	.06
124 Reggie Sanders	.20	.06
125 Ken Hill	.20	.06
126 Mike Mussina	.30	.09
127 Chad Curtis	.20	.06
128 Todd Worrell	.20	.06
129 Chris Widger	.20	.06
130 Damon Mashore	.20	.06
131 Kevin Brown	.30	.09
132 Bip Roberts	.20	.06
133 Tim Naehring	.20	.06
134 Dave Martinez	.20	.06
135 Jeff Blauser	.20	.06
136 David Justice	.20	.06
137 Dave Hollins	.20	.06
138 Pat Hentgen	.20	.06
139 Darren Daulton	.20	.06
140 Ramon Martinez	.20	.06
141 Raul Casanova	.20	.06
142 Tom Glavine	.30	.09
143 J.T. Snow	.20	.06
144 Tony Graffanino	.20	.06
145 Randy Johnson	.50	.15
146 Orlando Merced	.20	.06
147 Jeff Juden	.20	.06
148 Darryl Kile	.20	.06
149 Ray Durham	.20	.06
150 Alex Fernandez	.20	.06
151 Joey Cora	.20	.06
152 Royce Clayton	.20	.06
153 Randy Myers	.20	.06
154 Charles Johnson	.20	.06
155 Alan Benes	.20	.06
156 Mike Bordick	.20	.06
157 Heathcliff Slocumb	.20	.06
158 Roger Bailey	.20	.06
159 Reggie Jefferson	.20	.06
160 Ricky Bottalico	.20	.06
161 Scott Erickson	.20	.06
162 Matt Williams	.20	.06
163 Robb Nen	.20	.06
164 Matt Stairs	.20	.06
165 Ismael Valdes	.20	.06
166 Lee Stevens	.20	.06
167 Gary DiSarcina	.20	.06
168 Brad Radke	.20	.06
169 Mike Lansing	.20	.06
170 Armando Benitez	.20	.06
171 Mike James	.20	.06
172 Russ Davis	.20	.06
173 Lance Johnson	.20	.06
174 Joey Hamilton	.20	.06
175 John Valentin	.20	.06
176 David Segui	.20	.06
177 David Wells	.20	.06
178 Delino DeShields	.20	.06
179 Eric Karros	.20	.06
180 Jim Leyritz	.20	.06
181 Raul Mondesi	.20	.06
182 Travis Fryman	.20	.06
183 Todd Zeile	.20	.06
184 Brian Jordan	.20	.06
185 Rey Ordonez	.20	.06
186 Jim Edmonds	.20	.06
187 Terrell Wade	.20	.06
188 Marquis Grissom	.20	.06
189 Chris Snopek	.20	.06
190 Shane Reynolds	.20	.06
191 Jeff Frye	.20	.06
192 Paul Sorrento	.20	.06
193 James Baldwin	.20	.06
194 Brian McRae	.20	.06
195 Fred McGriff	.30	.09
196 Troy Percival	.20	.06
197 Rich Amaral	.20	.06
198 Juan Guzman	.20	.06
199 Cecil Fielder	.20	.06
200 Willie Blair	.20	.06
201 Chili Davis	.20	.06
202 Gary Gaetti	.20	.06
203 B.J. Surhoff	.20	.06
204 Steve Cooke	.20	.06
205 Chuck Finley	.20	.06
206 Jeff Kent	.20	.06
207 Ben McDonald	.20	.06
208 Jeffrey Hammonds	.20	.06
209 Tom Goodwin	.20	.06
210 Billy Ashley	.20	.06
211 Wil Cordero	.20	.06
212 Shawon Dunston	.20	.06

213 Tony Phillips .20 .06
214 Jamie Moyer .20 .06
215 John Jaha .20 .06
216 Troy O'Leary .20 .06
217 Brad Ausmus .20 .06
218 Garret Anderson .20 .06
219 Wilson Alvarez .20 .06
220 Kent Mercker .20 .06
221 Wade Boggs .30 .09
222 Mark Wohlers .20 .06
223 Kevin Appier .20 .06
224 Tony Fernandez .20 .06
225 Ugueth Urbina .20 .06
226 Gregg Jefferies .20 .06
227 Mo Vaughn .20 .06
228 Arthur Rhodes .20 .06
229 Jorge Fabregas .20 .06
230 Mark Gardner .20 .06
231 Shane Mack .20 .06
232 Jorge Posada .30 .09
233 Jose Cruz Jr. .20 .06
234 Paul Konerko .20 .06
235 Derrek Lee .20 .06
236 Steve Woodard .20 .06
237 Todd Dunwoody .20 .06
238 Fernando Tatis .20 .06
239 Jacob Cruz .20 .06
240 Pokey Reese .20 .06
241 Mark Kotsay .20 .06
242 Matt Morris .20 .06
243 Antone Williamson .20 .06
244 Ben Grieve .20 .06
245 Ryan McGuire .20 .06
246 Lou Collier .20 .06
247 Shannon Stewart .20 .06
248 Brett Tomko .20 .06
249 Bobby Estalella .20 .06
250 Livan Hernandez .20 .06
251 Todd Helton .30 .09
252 Jaret Wright .20 .06
253 Darryl Hamilton IM .20 .06
254 Stan Javier IM .20 .06
255 Glenallen Hill IM .20 .06
256 Mark Gardner IM .20 .06
257 Cal Ripken IM .75 .23
258 Mike Mussina IM .20 .06
259 Mike Piazza IM .50 .15
260 Sammy Sosa IM .50 .15
261 Todd Hundley IM .20 .06
262 Eric Karros IM .20 .06
263 Denny Neagle IM .20 .06
264 Jeromy Burnitz IM .20 .06
265 Greg Maddux IM .50 .15
266 Tony Clark IM .20 .06
267 Vladimir Guerrero IM .30 .09
268 Cal Ripken CL UER .75 .23
269 Ken Griffey Jr. CL .50 .15
270 Mark McGwire CL .60 .18
NNO CL Regular Issue .20 .06
NNO CL All-Star Edition .30 .09

1998 Score Showcase Series

Randomly inserted in packs at the rate of one in seven, this 160-card set is an all silver-foil partial parallel rendition of the base set.

Nm-Mt Ex-Mt
*SHOWCASE: 2X TO 5X BASIC CARDS
STATED ODDS 1:7

1998 Score Showcase Series Artist's Proofs

Randomly inserted in packs at the rate of one in 35, this 160-card set is a partial parallel to the base set and features color player photos printed on full prismatic foil with the "Artist Proof" stamp on the fronts.

Nm-Mt Ex-Mt
*STARS: 1.5X TO 4X BASIC SHOWCASE
STATED ODDS 1:35

1998 Score All Score Team

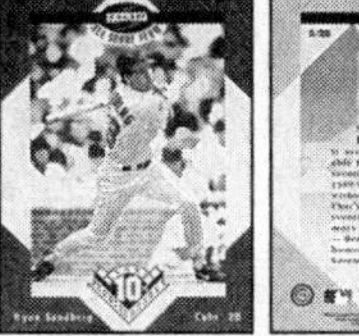

Randomly inserted in packs at the rate of one in 35, this 20-card set features color player images on a metallic foil background. The backs carry a small player head photo with information stating why the player was selected to this appear in this set.

Nm-Mt Ex-Mt
COMPLETE SET (20) 100.00 30.00
1 Mike Piazza 8.00 2.40
2 Ivan Rodriguez 5.00 1.50
3 Frank Thomas 5.00 1.50
4 Mark McGwire 12.00 3.60
5 Ryne Sandberg 5.00 1.50
6 Roberto Alomar 3.00 .90
7 Cal Ripken 15.00 4.50
8 Barry Larkin 3.00 .90
9 Paul Molitor 5.00 1.50
10 Travis Fryman 2.00 .60
11 Kirby Puckett 10.00 3.00
12 Tony Gwynn 6.00 1.80
13 Ken Griffey Jr. 8.00 2.40
14 Juan Gonzalez 5.00 1.50
15 Barry Bonds 12.00 3.60
16 Andruw Jones 2.00 .60
17 Roger Clemens 10.00 3.00
18 Randy Johnson 5.00 1.50
19 Greg Maddux 8.00 2.40
20 Dennis Eckersley 2.00 .60

1998 Score Complete Players

Randomly inserted in packs at the rate of one in 23, this 30-card set features three photos of each of the ten listed players with full holo

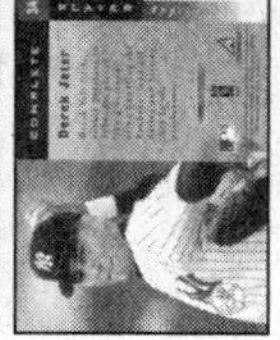

graphic foil stamping.

Nm-Mt Ex-Mt
COMPLETE SET (30) 150.00 45.00
*GOLD: .4X TO 1X BASIC COMP.PLAY.
GOLD: RANDOM IN SCORE TEAM SETS
1A Ken Griffey Jr. 6.00 1.80
2A Mark McGwire 10.00 3.00
3A Derek Jeter 10.00 3.00
4A Cal Ripken 12.00 3.60
5A Mike Piazza 6.00 1.80
6A Darin Erstad 1.50 .45
7A Frank Thomas 4.00 1.20
8A Andruw Jones 1.50 .45
9A Nomar Garciaparra 6.00 1.80
10A Manny Ramirez 4.00 1.20

1998 Score First Pitch

This 20 card insert set features star players anxiously awaiting opening day. The player's name is at top with the "First Pitch" words on the bottom of the card. These cards were inserted one every 11 All-Star Edition packs.

Nm-Mt Ex-Mt
COMPLETE SET (20) 60.00 18.00
1 Ken Griffey Jr. 4.00 1.20
2 Frank Thomas 2.50 .75
3 Alex Rodriguez 4.00 1.20
4 Cal Ripken 8.00 2.40
5 Chipper Jones 2.50 .75
6 Juan Gonzalez 2.50 .75
7 Derek Jeter 6.00 1.80
8 Mike Piazza 4.00 1.20
9 Andruw Jones 1.00 .30
10 Nomar Garciaparra 4.00 1.20
11 Barry Bonds 6.00 1.80
12 Jeff Bagwell 1.50 .45
13 Scott Rolen 2.50 .75
14 Hideo Nomo 2.50 .75
15 Roger Clemens 5.00 1.50
16 Mark McGwire 6.00 1.80
17 Greg Maddux 4.00 1.20
18 Albert Belle 1.00 .30
19 Ivan Rodriguez 2.50 .75
20 Mo Vaughn 1.00 .30

1998 Score Loaded Lineup

This 10-card set was inserted one every 45 Score All-Star Edition packs. The cards feature a player for each position and the cards are printed on all-foil micro etched cards.

Nm-Mt Ex-Mt
COMPLETE SET (10) 60.00 18.00
LL1 Chuck Knoblauch 2.00 .60
LL2 Tony Gwynn 6.00 1.80
LL3 Frank Thomas 5.00 1.50
LL4 Ken Griffey Jr. 8.00 2.40
LL5 Mike Piazza 8.00 2.40
LL6 Barry Bonds 12.00 3.60
LL7 Cal Ripken 15.00 4.50
LL8 Paul Molitor 5.00 1.50
LL9 Nomar Garciaparra 8.00 2.40
LL10 Greg Maddux 8.00 2.40

1998 Score New Season

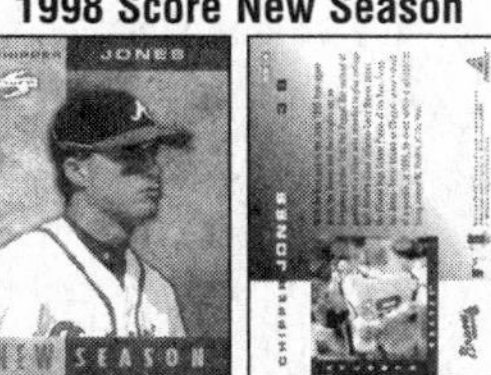

This 15 card insert set features a mix of young and veteran players waiting for the new season to begin. The players photo take up most of the borderless cards with his name on top and the words "New Season" on the bottom.

Nm-Mt Ex-Mt
COMPLETE SET (15) 50.00 15.00
NS1 Kenny Lofton 2.00 .60
NS2 Nomar Garciaparra 6.00 1.80
NS3 Todd Helton 2.50 .75
NS4 Miguel Tejada 2.00 .60
NS5 Jaret Wright 1.50 .45
NS6 Alex Rodriguez 6.00 1.80
NS7 Vladimir Guerrero 3.00 .90
NS8 Ken Griffey Jr. 8.00 2.40
NS9 Ben Grieve 1.50 .45
NS10 Travis Lee 1.50 .45
NS11 Jose Cruz Jr. 1.50 .45
NS12 Paul Konerko 2.00 .60
NS13 Frank Thomas 3.00 .90
NS14 Chipper Jones 3.00 .90
NS15 Cal Ripken 12.00 3.60

1998 Score Rookie Traded

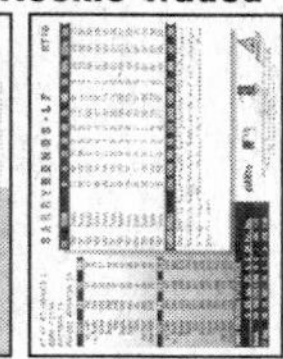

The 1998 Score Rookie and Traded set was issued in one series totalling 270 cards. The 10-card packs retail for $.99 each. The set contains the subset: Spring Training (253-267). Cards numbered one through 50 were inserted one per pack making them short prints compared to the other cards in the set. Paul Konerko signed 500 cards which were also randomly seeded into packs. Notable Rookie Cards include Magglio Ordonez.

Nm-Mt Ex-Mt
COMPLETE SET (270) 40.00 12.00
COMMON SP (1-50) .30 .09
COMMON CARD (51-270) .20 .06
1 Tony Clark .30 .09
2 Juan Gonzalez .50 .15
3 Frank Thomas .75 .23
4 Greg Maddux 1.25 .35
5 Barry Larkin .50 .15
6 Derek Jeter 2.00 .60
7 Randy Johnson .75 .23
8 Roger Clemens 1.50 .45
9 Tony Gwynn 1.00 .30
10 Barry Bonds 2.00 .60
11 Jim Edmonds .30 .09
12 Bernie Williams .50 .15
13 Ken Griffey Jr. 1.25 .35
14 Tim Salmon .50 .15
15 Mo Vaughn .30 .09
16 David Justice .30 .09
17 Jose Cruz Jr. .30 .09
18 Andruw Jones .30 .09
19 Sammy Sosa 1.25 .35
20 Jeff Bagwell .50 .15
21 Scott Rolen .75 .23
22 Darin Erstad .30 .09
23 Andy Pettitte .50 .15
24 Mike Mussina .50 .15
25 Mark McGwire 2.00 .60
26 Hideo Nomo .75 .23
27 Chipper Jones .75 .23
28 Cal Ripken 2.50 .75
29 Chuck Knoblauch .30 .09
30 Alex Rodriguez 1.25 .35
31 Jim Thome .75 .23
32 Mike Piazza 1.25 .35
33 Ivan Rodriguez .75 .23
34 Roberto Alomar .50 .15
35 Nomar Garciaparra 1.25 .35
36 Albert Belle .30 .09
37 Vladimir Guerrero .75 .23
38 Raul Mondesi .30 .09
39 Larry Walker .50 .15
40 Manny Ramirez .50 .15
41 Tino Martinez .50 .15
42 Craig Biggio .50 .15
43 Jay Buhner .30 .09
44 Kenny Lofton .30 .09
45 Pedro Martinez .75 .23
46 Edgar Martinez .50 .15
47 Gary Sheffield .30 .09
48 Jose Guillen .30 .09
49 Ken Caminiti .30 .09
50 Bobby Higginson .30 .09
51 Alan Benes .20 .06
52 Shawn Green .20 .06
53 Ron Coomer .20 .06
54 Charles Nagy .20 .06
55 Steve Karsay .20 .06
56 Matt Morris .20 .06
57 Bobby Jones .20 .06
58 Jason Kendall .20 .06
59 Jeff Conine .20 .06
60 Joe Girardi .20 .06
61 Mark Kotsay .20 .06
62 Eric Karros .20 .06
63 Bartolo Colon .20 .06
64 Mariano Rivera .30 .09
65 Alex Gonzalez .20 .06
66 Scott Spiezio .20 .06
67 Luis Castillo .20 .06
68 Joey Cora .20 .06
69 Mark McLemore .20 .06
70 Reggie Jefferson .20 .06
71 Lance Johnson .20 .06
72 Damian Jackson .20 .06
73 Jeff D'Amico .20 .06
74 David Ortiz .50 .15
75 J.T. Snow .20 .06
76 Todd Hundley .20 .06
77 Billy Wagner .20 .06
78 Vinny Castilla .20 .06
79 Ismael Valdes .20 .06
80 Neifi Perez .20 .06
81 Derek Bell .20 .06
82 Ryan Klesko .20 .06
83 Rey Ordonez .20 .06
84 Carlos Garcia .20 .06
85 Curt Schilling .30 .09
86 Robin Ventura .20 .06
87 Pat Hentgen .20 .06
88 Glendon Rusch .20 .06
89 Hideki Irabu .20 .06
90 Antone Williamson .20 .06
91 Denny Neagle .20 .06
92 Kevin Orie .20 .06
93 Reggie Sanders .20 .06
94 Brady Anderson .20 .06
95 Andy Benes .20 .06
96 John Valentin .20 .06
97 Bobby Bonilla .20 .06
98 Walt Weiss .20 .06
99 Robin Jennings .20 .06
100 Marty Cordova .20 .06
101 Brad Ausmus .20 .06
102 Brian Rose .20 .06
103 Calvin Maduro .20 .06
104 Raul Casanova .20 .06
105 Jeff King .20 .06
106 Sandy Alomar Jr. .20 .06
107 Tim Naehring .20 .06
108 Mike Cameron .20 .06
109 Omar Vizquel .30 .09
110 Brad Radke .20 .06
111 Jeff Fassero .20 .06
112 Deivi Cruz .20 .06
113 Dave Hollins .20 .06
114 Dean Palmer .20 .06
115 Esteban Loaiza .20 .06
116 Brian Giles .20 .06
117 Steve Finley .20 .06
118 Jose Canseco .50 .15
119 Al Martin .20 .06
120 Eric Young .20 .06
121 Curtis Goodwin .20 .06
122 Ellis Burks .20 .06
123 Mike Hampton .20 .06
124 Lou Collier .20 .06
125 John Olerud .20 .06
126 Ramon Martinez .20 .06
127 Todd Dunwoody .20 .06
128 Jermaine Allensworth .20 .06
129 Eduardo Perez .20 .06
130 Dante Bichette .20 .06
131 Edgar Renteria .20 .06
132 Bob Abreu .20 .06
133 Rondell White .20 .06
134 Michael Coleman .20 .06
135 Jason Giambi .20 .06
136 Brant Brown .20 .06
137 Michael Tucker .20 .06
138 Dave Nilsson .20 .06
139 Benito Santiago .20 .06
140 Ray Durham .20 .06
141 Jeff Kent .20 .06
142 Matt Stairs .20 .06
143 Kevin Young .20 .06
144 Eric Davis .20 .06
145 John Wetteland .20 .06
146 Esteban Yan RC .20 .06
147 Wilton Guerrero .20 .06
148 Moises Alou .20 .06
149 Edgardo Alfonzo .20 .06
150 Andy Ashby .20 .06
151 Todd Walker .20 .06
152 Jermaine Dye .20 .06
153 Brian Hunter .20 .06
154 Shawn Estes .20 .06
155 Bernard Gilkey .20 .06
156 Tony Womack .20 .06
157 John Smoltz .30 .09
158 Delino DeShields .20 .06
159 Jacob Cruz .20 .06
160 Javier Valentin .20 .06
161 Chris Hoiles .20 .06
162 Garret Anderson .20 .06
163 Dan Wilson .20 .06
164 Paul O'Neill .30 .09
165 Matt Williams .20 .06
166 Travis Fryman .20 .06
167 Javier Lopez .20 .06
168 Ray Lankford .20 .06
169 Bobby Estalella .20 .06
170 Henry Rodriguez .20 .06
171 Quinton McCracken .20 .06
172 Jaret Wright .20 .06
173 Darryl Kile .20 .06
174 Wade Boggs .50 .15
175 Orel Hershiser .20 .06
176 B.J. Surhoff .20 .06
177 Fernando Tatis .20 .06
178 Carlos Delgado .20 .06
179 Jorge Fabregas .20 .06
180 Tony Saunders .20 .06
181 Devon White .20 .06
182 Dmitri Young .20 .06
183 Ryan McGuire .20 .06
184 Mark Bellhorn .20 .06
185 Joe Carter .20 .06
186 Kevin Stocker .20 .06
187 Mike Lansing .20 .06
188 Jason Dickson .20 .06
189 Charles Johnson .20 .06
190 Will Clark .50 .15
191 Shannon Stewart .20 .06
192 Johnny Damon .30 .09
193 Todd Greene .20 .06
194 Carlos Baerga .20 .06
195 David Cone .20 .06
196 Pokey Reese .20 .06
197 Livan Hernandez .20 .06
198 Tom Glavine .30 .09
199 Geronimo Berroa .20 .06
200 Darryl Hamilton .20 .06
201 Terry Steinbach .20 .06
202 Robb Nen .20 .06
203 Ron Gant .20 .06
204 Rafael Palmeiro .30 .09
205 Rickey Henderson .50 .15
206 Justin Thompson .20 .06
207 Jeff Suppan .20 .06
208 Kevin Brown .30 .09
209 Jimmy Key .20 .06
210 Brian Jordan .20 .06
211 Aaron Sele .20 .06
212 Fred McGriff .30 .09
213 Jay Bell .20 .06
214 Andres Galarraga .20 .06
215 Mark Grace .30 .09
216 Brett Tomko .20 .06
217 Francisco Cordova .20 .06
218 Rusty Greer .20 .06
219 Bubba Trammell .20 .06
220 Derrek Lee .20 .06
221 Brian Anderson .20 .06
222 Mark Grudzielanek .20 .06
223 Marquis Grissom .20 .06
224 Gary DiSarcina .20 .06
225 Jim Leyritz .20 .06
226 Jeffrey Hammonds .20 .06
227 Karim Garcia .20 .06
228 Chan Ho Park .20 .06
229 Brooks Kieschnick .20 .06
230 Trey Beamon .20 .06
231 Kevin Appier .20 .06
232 Wally Joyner .20 .06
233 Richie Sexson .20 .06
234 Frank Catalanotto RC .30 .09
235 Rafael Medina .20 .06
236 Travis Lee .20 .06
237 Eli Marrero .20 .06
238 Carl Pavano .30 .06
239 Enrique Wilson .20 .06
240 Richard Hidalgo .20 .06
241 Todd Helton .30 .09
242 Ben Grieve .20 .06
243 Mario Valdez .20 .06
244 Magglio Ordonez RC 1.00 .30
245 Juan Encarnacion .20 .06
246 Russell Branyan .20 .06
247 Sean Casey .20 .06
248 Abraham Nunez .20 .06
249 Brad Fullmer .20 .06
250 Paul Konerko .20 .06
251 Miguel Tejada .20 .06
252 Mike Lowell RC 1.00 .30
253 Ken Griffey Jr. ST .50 .15
254 Frank Thomas ST .30 .09
255 Alex Rodriguez ST .50 .15
256 Jose Cruz Jr. ST .20 .06
257 Jeff Bagwell ST .50 .15
258 Chipper Jones ST .30 .09
259 Mo Vaughn ST .20 .06
260 Nomar Garciaparra ST .50 .15
261 Jim Thome ST .30 .09
262 Derek Jeter ST .60 .18
263 Mike Piazza ST .50 .15
264 Tony Gwynn ST .30 .09
265 Scott Rolen ST .30 .09
266 Andruw Jones ST .20 .06
267 Cal Ripken ST .75 .23
268 Checklist 1 .20 .06
269 Checklist 2 .20 .06
270 Checklist 3 .20 .06
S250 Paul Konerko AU/500 10.00 3.00

1998 Score Rookie Traded Showcase Series

Randomly inserted in packs at a rate of one in seven, this 160-card set is a parallel to the Score Rookie Traded base set.

Nm-Mt Ex-Mt
*STARS 1-50: 1.25X TO 3X BASIC CARDS
*SHOWCASE 51-270: 2X TO 5X BASIC
*SHOWCASE RC'S 51-270: 1.5X TO 4X BASIC
STATED ODDS 1:7

1998 Score Rookie Traded Showcase Series Artist's Proofs

Randomly inserted in packs at a rate of one in 35, this 160-card set is a parallel to the Score Rookie Traded base set.

Nm-Mt Ex-Mt
*SHOWCASE AP 1-50: 5X TO 12X BASIC
*SHOWCASE AP 51-270: 8X TO 20X BASIC
*SHOWCASE AP RC'S 51-270: 3X TO 8X BASIC
STATED ODDS 1:35

1998 Score Rookie Traded Showcase Series Artist's Proofs 1 of 1's

These extremely scarce parallel Artist's Proofs cards were randomly seeded into Rookie Traded hobby packs. Only one of each card was produced. They're easy to spot due to the gold foil circular logo directly on the middle of the card front that says "SCORE ONE OF ONE . . . 001/001". Due to scarcity no pricing is provided.

Nm-Mt Ex-Mt
RANDOM INSERTS IN HOBBY PACKS
STATED PRINT RUN 1 SET
NO PRICING DUE TO SCARCITY

1998 Score Rookie Traded All-Star Epix

Randomly inserted in packs at a rate of one in 61, these cards are an insert to the Score Rookie Traded brand. The fronts feature 12 top players in color action photos printed on high-tech dot matrix orange, purple, and emerald variations. The cards were actually seeded in both Score Rookie Traded and Pinnacle Plus in a cross-brand promotion. Please see 1998 Pinnacle Plus All-Star Epix for pricing.

Nm-Mt Ex-Mt
PLEASE SEE 1998 PINNACLE PLUS AS EPIX

1998 Score Rookie Traded Complete Players

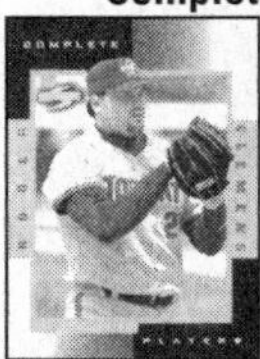

Randomly inserted in packs at a rate of one in 11, this 30-card set is an insert to the Score Rookie Traded base set. The card fronts feature special holographic foil stamping. Each player has three different cards highlighting his own power, speed and approach to the game. Put them together and form the Complete Player.

Nm-Mt Ex-Mt
COMPLETE SET (30) 50.00 15.00
1A Ken Griffey Jr. 3.00 .90
2A Larry Walker 1.25 .35
3A Alex Rodriguez 3.00 .90
4A Jose Cruz Jr. .75 .23
5A Jeff Bagwell 1.25 .35
6A Greg Maddux 3.00 .90
7A Ivan Rodriguez 2.00 .60
8A Roger Clemens 4.00 1.20
9A Chipper Jones 2.00 .60
10A Hideo Nomo 2.00 .60

1998 Score Rookie Traded Star Gazing

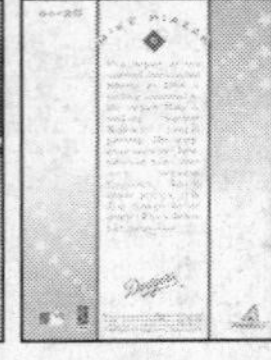

Randomly inserted in packs at a rate of one in 35, this 20-card set is an insert to the Score Rookie Traded base set. The fronts feature color action photos printed on a diamond-shaped star-gazing background. The player's name sits atop the player photo with the Score logo in the upper right corner.

Nm-Mt Ex-Mt
COMPLETE SET (20) 25.00 7.50
1 Ken Griffey Jr. 2.50 .75
2 Frank Thomas 1.50 .45
3 Chipper Jones 1.50 .45
4 Mark McGwire 4.00 1.20
5 Cal Ripken 5.00 1.50
6 Mike Piazza 2.50 .75
7 Nomar Garciaparra 2.50 .75
8 Derek Jeter 4.00 1.20
9 Juan Gonzalez 1.00 .30
10 Vladimir Guerrero 1.50 .45
11 Alex Rodriguez 2.50 .75
12 Tony Gwynn 2.00 .60
13 Andruw Jones .60 .18
14 Scott Rolen 1.50 .45
15 Jose Cruz Jr. .60 .18
16 Mo Vaughn .60 .18
17 Bernie Williams 1.00 .30
18 Greg Maddux 2.50 .75
19 Tony Clark .60 .18
20 Ben Grieve .40 .12

1993 Select

Seeking a niche in the premium, mid-price market, Score produced a new 405-card standard-size set entitled Select in 1993. The set includes regular players, rookies, and draft picks, and was sold in 15-card hobby and retail packs and 28-card super packs. Subset cards include Draft Picks and Rookies, both sprinkled throughout the latter part of the set. Rookie Cards in this set include Derek Jeter, Jason Kendall and Shannon Stewart.

Nm-Mt Ex-Mt
COMPLETE SET (405) 25.00 7.50
1 Barry Bonds 1.25 .35
2 Ken Griffey Jr. .75 .23
3 Will Clark .50 .15
4 Kirby Puckett .50 .15
5 Tony Gwynn .60 .18
6 Frank Thomas .50 .15
7 Tom Glavine .30 .09
8 Roberto Alomar .30 .09
9 Andre Dawson .20 .06
10 Ron Darling .15 .04
11 Bobby Bonilla .20 .06
12 Danny Tartabull .15 .04
13 Darren Daulton .20 .06
14 Roger Clemens 1.00 .30
15 Ozzie Smith .75 .23
16 Mark McGwire 1.25 .35
17 Terry Pendleton .20 .06
18 Cal Ripken 1.50 .45
19 Fred McGriff .30 .09
20 Cecil Fielder .20 .06
21 Darryl Strawberry .20 .06
22 Robin Yount .75 .23
23 Barry Larkin .30 .09
24 Don Mattingly 1.25 .35
25 Craig Biggio .30 .09
26 Sandy Alomar Jr. .15 .04
27 Larry Walker .30 .09
28 Junior Felix .15 .04
29 Eddie Murray .50 .15
30 Robin Ventura .20 .06
31 Greg Maddux .75 .23
32 Dave Winfield .20 .06
33 John Kruk .20 .06
34 Wally Joyner .20 .06
35 Andy Van Slyke .20 .06
36 Chuck Knoblauch .20 .06
37 Tom Pagnozzi .15 .04
38 Dennis Eckersley .20 .06
39 Dave Justice .20 .06
40 Juan Gonzalez .30 .09
41 Gary Sheffield .20 .06
42 Paul Molitor .30 .09
43 Delino DeShields .15 .04
44 Travis Fryman .20 .06
45 Hal Morris .15 .04
46 Greg Olson .15 .04
47 Ken Caminiti .20 .06
48 Wade Boggs .30 .09
49 Orel Hershiser .20 .06
50 Albert Belle .20 .06
51 Bill Swift .15 .04
52 Mark Langston .15 .04
53 Joe Girardi .15 .04
54 Keith Miller .15 .04
55 Gary Carter .20 .06
56 Brady Anderson .20 .06
57 Dwight Gooden .20 .06
58 Julio Franco .20 .06
59 Lenny Dykstra .20 .06
60 Mickey Tettleton .15 .04
61 Randy Tomlin .15 .04
62 B.J. Surhoff .20 .06
63 Todd Zeile .15 .04
64 Roberto Kelly .15 .04
65 Rob Dibble .20 .06
66 Leo Gomez .15 .04
67 Doug Jones .15 .04
68 Ellis Burks .20 .06
69 Mike Scioscia .15 .04
70 Charles Nagy .15 .04
71 Cory Snyder .15 .04
72 Devon White .20 .06
73 Mark Grace .30 .09
74 Luis Polonia .15 .04
75 John Smiley 2X .15 .04
76 Carlton Fisk .30 .09
77 Luis Sojo .15 .04
78 George Brett 1.25 .35
79 Mitch Williams .15 .04
80 Kent Hrbek .20 .06
81 Jay Bell .20 .06
82 Edgar Martinez .30 .09
83 Lee Smith .20 .06
84 Deion Sanders .30 .09
85 Bill Gullickson .15 .04
86 Paul O'Neill .30 .09
87 Kevin Seitzer .15 .04
88 Steve Finley .20 .06
89 Mel Hall .15 .04
90 Nolan Ryan 2.00 .60
91 Eric Davis .20 .06
92 Mike Mussina .30 .09
93 Tony Fernandez .15 .04
94 Frank Viola .20 .06
95 Matt Williams .20 .06
96 Joe Carter .20 .06
97 Ryne Sandberg .75 .23
98 Jim Abbott .30 .09
99 Marquis Grissom .20 .06
100 George Bell .15 .04
101 Howard Johnson .15 .04
102 Kevin Appier .20 .06
103 Dale Murphy .50 .15
104 Shane Mack .15 .04
105 Jose Lind .15 .04
106 Rickey Henderson .50 .15
107 Bob Tewksbury .15 .04
108 Kevin Mitchell .15 .04
109 Steve Avery .15 .04
110 Candy Maldonado .15 .04
111 Bip Roberts .15 .04
112 Lou Whitaker .20 .06
113 Jeff Bagwell .30 .09
114 Dante Bichette .20 .06
115 Brett Butler .20 .06
116 Melido Perez .15 .04
117 Andy Benes .15 .04
118 Randy Johnson .50 .15
119 Willie McGee .20 .06
120 Jody Reed .15 .04
121 Shawon Dunston .15 .04
122 Carlos Baerga .15 .04
123 Bret Saberhagen .20 .06
124 John Olerud .20 .06
125 Ivan Calderon .15 .04
126 Bryan Harvey .15 .04
127 Terry Mulholland .15 .04
128 Ozzie Guillen .15 .04
129 Steve Buechele .15 .04
130 Kevin Tapani .15 .04
131 Felix Jose .15 .04
132 Terry Steinbach .15 .04
133 Ron Gant .20 .06
134 Harold Reynolds .20 .06
135 Chris Sabo .15 .04
136 Ivan Rodriguez .50 .15
137 Eric Anthony .15 .04
138 Mike Henneman .15 .04
139 Robby Thompson .15 .04
140 Scott Fletcher .15 .04
141 Bruce Hurst .15 .04
142 Kevin Maas .15 .04
143 Tom Candiotti .15 .04
144 Chris Hoiles .15 .04
145 Mike Morgan .15 .04
146 Mark Whiten .15 .04
147 Dennis Martinez .20 .06
148 Tony Pena .15 .04
149 Dave Magadan .15 .04
150 Mark Lewis .15 .04
151 Mariano Duncan .15 .04
152 Gregg Jefferies .15 .04
153 Doug Drabek .15 .04
154 Brian Harper .15 .04
155 Ray Lankford .15 .04
156 Carney Lansford .20 .06
157 Mike Sharperson .15 .04
158 Jack Morris .20 .06
159 Otis Nixon .15 .04
160 Steve Sax .15 .04
161 Mark Lemke .15 .04
162 Rafael Palmeiro .30 .09
163 Jose Rijo .15 .04
164 Omar Vizquel .30 .09
165 Sammy Sosa .75 .23
166 Milt Cuyler .15 .04
167 John Franco .20 .06
168 Darryl Hamilton .15 .04
169 Ken Hill .15 .04
170 Mike Devereaux .15 .04
171 Don Slaught .15 .04
172 Steve Farr .15 .04
173 Bernard Gilkey .15 .04
174 Mike Fetters .15 .04
175 Vince Coleman .15 .04
176 Kevin McReynolds .15 .04
177 John Smoltz .30 .09
178 Greg Gagne .15 .04
179 Greg Swindell .15 .04
180 Juan Guzman .15 .04
181 Kal Daniels .15 .04
182 Rick Sutcliffe .20 .06
183 Orlando Merced .15 .04
184 Bill Wegman .15 .04
185 Mark Gardner .15 .04
186 Rob Deer .15 .04
187 Dave Hollins .15 .04
188 Jack Clark .20 .06
189 Brian Hunter .15 .04
190 Tim Wallach .15 .04
191 Tim Belcher .15 .04
192 Walt Weiss .15 .04
193 Kurt Stillwell .15 .04
194 Charlie Hayes .15 .04
195 Willie Randolph .20 .06
196 Jack McDowell .15 .04
197 Jose Offerman .15 .04
198 Chuck Finley .20 .06
199 Darrin Jackson .15 .04
200 Kelly Gruber .15 .04
201 John Wetteland .20 .06
202 Jay Buhner .20 .06
203 Mike LaValliere .15 .04
204 Kevin Brown .20 .06
205 Luis Gonzalez .20 .06
206 Rick Aguilera .15 .04
207 Norm Charlton .15 .04
208 Mike Bordick .15 .04
209 Charlie Leibrandt .15 .04
210 Tom Brunansky .15 .04
211 Tom Henke .15 .04
212 Randy Milligan .15 .04
213 Ramon Martinez .15 .04
214 Mo Vaughn .20 .06
215 Randy Myers .15 .04
216 Greg Hibbard .15 .04
217 Wes Chamberlain .15 .04
218 Tony Phillips .15 .04
219 Pete Harnisch .15 .04
220 Mike Gallego .15 .04
221 Bud Black .15 .04
222 Greg Vaughn .15 .04
223 Milt Thompson .15 .04
224 Ben McDonald .15 .04
225 Billy Hatcher .15 .04
226 Paul Sorrento .15 .04
227 Mark Gubicza .15 .04
228 Mike Greenwell .15 .04
229 Curt Schilling .20 .06
230 Alan Trammell .20 .06
231 Zane Smith .15 .04
232 Bobby Thigpen .15 .04
233 Greg Olson .15 .04
234 Joe Orsulak .15 .04
235 Joe Oliver .15 .04
236 Tim Raines .20 .06
237 Juan Samuel .15 .04
238 Chili Davis .20 .06
239 Spike Owen .15 .04
240 Dave Stewart .20 .06
241 Jim Eisenreich .15 .04
242 Phil Plantier .15 .04
243 Sid Fernandez .15 .04
244 Dan Gladden .15 .04
245 Mickey Morandini .15 .04
246 Tino Martinez .30 .09
247 Kirt Manwaring .15 .04
248 Dean Palmer .20 .06
249 Tom Browning .15 .04
250 Brian McRae .15 .04
251 Scott Leius .15 .04
252 Bert Blyleven .20 .06
253 Scott Erickson .15 .04
254 Bob Welch .15 .04
255 Pat Kelly .15 .04
256 Felix Fermin .15 .04
257 Harold Baines .20 .06
258 Duane Ward .15 .04
259 Bill Spiers .15 .04
260 Jaime Navarro .15 .04
261 Scott Sanderson .15 .04
262 Gary Gaetti .20 .06
263 Bob Ojeda .15 .04
264 Jeff Montgomery .15 .04
265 Scott Bankhead .15 .04
266 Lance Johnson .15 .04
267 Rafael Belliard .15 .04
268 Kevin Reimer .15 .04
269 Benito Santiago .20 .06
270 Mike Moore .15 .04
271 Dave Fleming .15 .04
272 Moises Alou .20 .06
273 Pat Listach .15 .04
274 Reggie Sanders .15 .04
275 Kenny Lofton .20 .06
276 Donovan Osborne .15 .04
277 Rusty Meacham .15 .04
278 Eric Karros .20 .06
279 Andy Stankiewicz .15 .04
280 Brian Jordan .20 .06
281 Gary DiSarcina .15 .04
282 Mark Wohlers .15 .04
283 Dave Nilsson .15 .04
284 Anthony Young .15 .04
285 Jim Bullinger .15 .04
286 Derek Bell .15 .04
287 Brian Williams .15 .04
288 Julio Valera .15 .04
289 Dan Walters .15 .04
290 Chad Curtis .15 .04
291 Michael Tucker DP .20 .06
292 Bob Zupcic .15 .04
293 Todd Hundley .15 .04
294 Jeff Tackett .15 .04
295 Greg Colbrunn .15 .04
296 Cal Eldred .15 .04
297 Chris Roberts DP .15 .04
298 John Doherty .15 .04
299 Denny Neagle .20 .06
300 Arthur Rhodes .15 .04
301 Mark Clark .15 .04
302 Scott Cooper .15 .04
303 Jamie Arnold DP RC .15 .04
304 Jim Thome .50 .15
305 Frank Seminara .15 .04
306 Kurt Knudsen .15 .04
307 Tim Wakefield .50 .15
308 John Jaha .15 .04
309 Pat Hentgen .15 .04
310 B.J. Wallace DP .15 .04
311 Roberto Hernandez .15 .04
312 Hipolito Pichardo .15 .04
313 Eric Fox .15 .04
314 Willie Banks .15 .04
315 Sam Militello .15 .04
316 Vince Horsman .15 .04
317 Carlos Hernandez .15 .04
318 Jeff Kent .50 .15
319 Mike Perez .15 .04
320 Scott Livingstone .15 .04
321 Jeff Conine .20 .06
322 Jim Austin .15 .04
323 John Vander Wal .15 .04
324 Pat Mahomes .15 .04
325 Pedro Astacio .15 .04
326 Bret Boone UER .30 .09
(Misspelled Brett)
327 Matt Stairs .15 .04
328 Damion Easley .15 .04
329 Ben Rivera .15 .04
330 Reggie Jefferson .15 .04
331 Luis Mercedes .15 .04
332 Kyle Abbott .15 .04
333 Eddie Taubensee .15 .04
334 Tim McIntosh .15 .04
335 Phil Clark .15 .04
336 Wil Cordero .15 .04
337 Russ Springer .15 .04
338 Craig Colbert .15 .04
339 Tim Salmon .30 .09
340 Braulio Castillo .15 .04
341 Donald Harris .15 .04
342 Eric Young .15 .04
343 Bob Wickman .15 .04
344 John Valentin .15 .04
345 Dan Wilson .20 .06
346 Steve Hosey .15 .04
347 Mike Piazza 1.50 .45
348 Willie Greene .15 .04
349 Tom Goodwin .15 .04
350 Eric Hillman .15 .04
351 Steve Reed RC .15 .04
352 Dan Serafini DP RC .15 .04
353 T.Steverson DP RC .15 .04
354 Benji Grigsby DP RC .15 .04
355 S.Stewart DP RC .75 .23
356 Sean Lowe DP RC .15 .04
357 Derek Wallace DP RC .15 .04
358 Rick Helling DP .15 .04
359 Jason Kendall DP RC .75 .23
360 Derek Jeter DP RC 10.00 3.00
361 David Cone .20 .06
362 Jeff Reardon .20 .06
363 Bobby Witt .15 .04
364 Jose Canseco .50 .15
365 Jeff Russell .15 .04
366 Ruben Sierra .15 .04
367 Alan Mills .15 .04
368 Matt Nokes .15 .04
369 Pat Borders .15 .04
370 Pedro Munoz .15 .04
371 Danny Jackson .15 .04
372 Geronimo Pena .15 .04
373 Craig Lefferts .15 .04
374 Joe Grahe .15 .04
375 Roger McDowell .15 .04
376 Jimmy Key .20 .06
377 Steve Olin .15 .04
378 Glenn Davis .15 .04
379 Rene Gonzales .15 .04
380 Manuel Lee .15 .04
381 Ron Karkovice .15 .04
382 Sid Bream .15 .04
383 Gerald Williams .15 .04
384 Lenny Harris .15 .04
385 J.T. Snow RC .50 .15
386 Dave Stieb .15 .04
387 Kirk McCaskill .15 .04
388 Lance Parrish .20 .06
389 Craig Grebeck .15 .04
390 Rick Wilkins .15 .04
391 Manny Alexander .15 .04
392 Mike Schooler .15 .04
393 Bernie Williams .30 .09
394 Kevin Koslofski .15 .04
395 Willie Wilson .15 .04
396 Jeff Parrett .15 .04
397 Mike Harkey .15 .04
398 Frank Tanana .15 .04
399 Doug Henry .15 .04
400 Royce Clayton .15 .04
401 Eric Wedge RC .25 .07
402 Derrick May .15 .04
403 Carlos Garcia .15 .04
404 Henry Rodriguez .15 .04
405 Ryan Klesko .20 .06

1993 Select Aces

This 24-card standard-size set features some of the top starting pitchers in both leagues. The cards were randomly inserted into one in every eight 28-card super packs.

Nm-Mt Ex-Mt
COMPLETE SET (24) 50.00 15.00
1 Roger Clemens 15.00 4.50
2 Tom Glavine 5.00 1.50
3 Jack McDowell 2.50 .75
4 Greg Maddux 12.00 3.60
5 Jack Morris 3.00 .90
6 Dennis Martinez 3.00 .90
7 Kevin Brown 3.00 .90
8 Dwight Gooden 3.00 .90
9 Kevin Appier 3.00 .90
10 Mike Morgan 2.50 .75
11 Juan Guzman 2.50 .75
12 Charles Nagy 2.50 .75
13 John Smiley 2.50 .75
14 Ken Hill 2.50 .75
15 Bob Tewksbury 2.50 .75
16 Doug Drabek 2.50 .75
17 John Smoltz 5.00 1.50
18 Greg Swindell 2.50 .75
19 Bruce Hurst 2.50 .75
20 Mike Mussina 5.00 1.50
21 Cal Eldred 2.50 .75
22 Melido Perez 2.50 .75
23 Dave Fleming 2.50 .75
24 Kevin Tapani 2.50 .75

1993 Select Chase Rookies

This 21-card standard-size set showcases 1992's best rookies. The cards were randomly inserted into one in every eighteen 15-card hobby packs.

Nm-Mt Ex-Mt
COMPLETE SET (21) 50.00 15.00
1 Pat Listach 2.50 .75
2 Moises Alou 5.00 1.50
3 Reggie Sanders 2.50 .75
4 Kenny Lofton 5.00 1.50
5 Eric Karros 5.00 1.50
6 Brian Williams 2.50 .75
7 Donovan Osborne 2.50 .75
8 Sam Militello 2.50 .75
9 Chad Curtis 2.50 .75
10 Bob Zupcic 2.50 .75
11 Tim Salmon 8.00 2.40
12 Jeff Conine 5.00 1.50
13 Pedro Astacio 2.50 .75
14 Arthur Rhodes 2.50 .75
15 Cal Eldred 2.50 .75
16 Tim Wakefield 10.00 3.00
17 Andy Stankiewicz 2.50 .75
18 Wil Cordero 2.50 .75
19 Todd Hundley 2.50 .75
20 Dave Fleming 2.50 .75
21 Bret Boone 8.00 2.40

1993 Select Chase Stars

This 24-card standard-size set showcases the top players in Major League Baseball. The cards were randomly inserted into one in every eighteen retail 15-card packs. The fronts exhibit Score's "dufex" printing process, in which a color photo is printed on a metallic base creating an unusual, three-dimensional look.

Nm-Mt Ex-Mt
COMPLETE SET (24) 100.00 30.00
1 Fred McGriff 4.00 1.20
2 Ryne Sandberg 10.00 3.00
3 Ozzie Smith 10.00 3.00
4 Gary Sheffield 2.50 .75
5 Darren Daulton 2.50 .75
6 Andy Van Slyke 2.50 .75
7 Barry Bonds 15.00 4.50
8 Tony Gwynn 8.00 2.40
9 Greg Maddux 10.00 3.00
10 Tom Glavine 4.00 1.20
11 John Franco 2.50 .75
12 Lee Smith 2.50 .75
13 Cecil Fielder 2.50 .75
14 Roberto Alomar 4.00 1.20
15 Cal Ripken 20.00 6.00
16 Edgar Martinez 4.00 1.20
17 Ivan Rodriguez 6.00 1.80
18 Kirby Puckett 6.00 1.80
19 Ken Griffey Jr. 10.00 3.00
20 Joe Carter 2.50 .75
21 Roger Clemens 12.00 3.60
22 Dave Fleming 2.00 .60
23 Paul Molitor 4.00 1.20
24 Dennis Eckersley 2.50 .75

1993 Select Stat Leaders

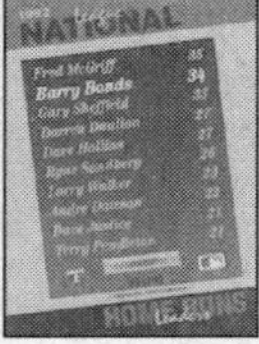

Featuring 45 cards from each league, these 90 Stat Leaders were inserted one per 1993 Score pack in every regular pack and super pack.

Nm-Mt Ex-Mt
COMPLETE SET (90) 8.00 2.40
1 Edgar Martinez .20 .06
2 Kirby Puckett .30 .09

3 Frank Thomas .30 .09
4 Gary Sheffield .10 .03
5 Andy Van Slyke .10 .03
6 John Kruk .10 .03
7 Kirby Puckett .30 .09
8 Carlos Baerga .10 .03
9 Paul Molitor .20 .06
10 Terry Pendleton .10 .03
Andy Van Slyke
11 Ryne Sandberg .50 .15
12 Mark Grace .20 .06
13 Frank Thomas .30 .09
Edgar Martinez
14 Don Mattingly .75 .23
Robin Yount
15 Ken Griffey .50 .15
16 Andy Van Slyke .10 .03
17 Mariano Duncan .10 .03
Will Clark
Ray Lankford
18 Marquis Grissom .10 .03
Terry Pendleton
19 Lance Johnson .10 .03
20 Mike Devereaux .10 .03
21 Brady Anderson .10 .03
22 Deion Sanders .20 .06
23 Steve Finley .10 .03
24 Andy Van Slyke .10 .03
25 Juan Gonzalez .20 .06
26 Mark McGwire .75 .23
27 Cecil Fielder .10 .03
28 Fred McGriff .20 .06
29 Barry Bonds .75 .23
30 Gary Sheffield .10 .03
31 Cecil Fielder .10 .03
32 Joe Carter .10 .03
33 Frank Thomas .30 .09
34 Darren Daulton .10 .03
35 Terry Pendleton .10 .03
36 Fred McGriff .20 .06
37 Tony Phillips .10 .03
38 Frank Thomas .30 .09
39 Roberto Alomar .20 .06
40 Barry Bonds .75 .23
41 Dave Hollins .10 .03
42 Andy Van Slyke .10 .03
43 Mark McGwire .75 .23
44 Edgar Martinez .20 .06
45 Frank Thomas .30 .09
46 Barry Bonds .75 .23
47 Gary Sheffield .10 .03
48 Fred McGriff .20 .06
49 Frank Thomas .30 .09
50 Danny Tartabull .10 .03
51 Roberto Alomar .20 .06
52 Barry Bonds .75 .23
53 John Kruk .10 .03
54 Brett Butler .10 .03
55 Kenny Lofton .10 .03
56 Pat Listach .10 .03
57 Brady Anderson .10 .03
58 Marquis Grissom .10 .03
59 Delino DeShields .10 .03
60 Bip Roberts .10 .03
Steve Finley
61 Jack McDowell .10 .03
62 Kevin Brown .60 .18
Roger Clemens
63 Charles Nagy .10 .03
Melido Perez
64 Terry Mulholland .10 .03
65 Curt Schilling .10 .03
Doug Drabek
66 Greg Maddux .50 .15
John Smoltz
67 Dennis Eckersley .10 .03
68 Rick Aguilera .10 .03
69 Jeff Montgomery .10 .03
70 Lee Smith .10 .03
71 Randy Myers .10 .03
72 John Wetteland .10 .03
73 Randy Johnson .30 .09
74 Melido Perez .10 .03
75 Roger Clemens .60 .18
76 John Smoltz .20 .06
77 David Cone .10 .03
78 Greg Maddux .50 .15
79 Roger Clemens .60 .18
80 Kevin Appier .10 .03
81 Mike Mussina .20 .06
82 Bill Swift .10 .03
83 Bob Tewksbury .10 .03
84 Greg Maddux .50 .15
85 Jack Morris .10 .03
Kevin Brown
86 Jack McDowell .10 .03
87 Roger Clemens .60 .18
Mike Mussina
88 Tom Glavine .50 .15
Greg Maddux
89 Ken Hill .10 .03
Bob Tewksbury
90 Mike Morgan .10 .03
Dennis Martinez

1993 Select Triple Crown

Honoring the three most recent Triple Crown winners since 1993, cards from this three-card standard-size set were randomly inserted in 15-card hobby packs.

	Nm-Mt	Ex-Mt
COMPLETE SET (3)	50.00	15.00
1 Mickey Mantle	40.00	12.00
2 Frank Robinson	10.00	3.00
3 Carl Yastrzemski	10.00	3.00

1993 Select Rookie/Traded

These 150 standard-size cards feature rookies and traded veteran players. The production run comprised 1,950 individually numbered cases. Cards were distributed in foil packs. Card design is similar to the regular 1993 Select cards excpt for the dramatic royal blue borders (instead of emerald green for the regular cards) and T-suffixed numbering. There are no key Rookie Cards in this set. Two Rookie of the Year insert cards and a Nolan Ryan Tribute card were randomly inserted in the foil packs. The chances of finding a Nolan Ryan card was listed at not less than one per 288 packs. The two ROY cards, featuring American League Rookie of the Year, Tim Salmon and National League Rookie of the Year, Mike Piazza were randomly inserted into one in every 576 packs.

	Nm-Mt	Ex-Mt
COMPLETE SET (150)	15.00	4.50
COMMON CARD (1T-150T)	.40	.12
COMMON RC	.40	.12
1T Rickey Henderson	1.50	.45
2T Rob Deer	.40	.12
3T Tim Belcher	.40	.12
4T Gary Sheffield	.60	.18
5T Fred McGriff	1.00	.30
6T Mark Whiten	.40	.12
7T Jeff Russell	.40	.12
8T Harold Baines	.60	.18
9T Dave Winfield	.60	.18
10T Ellis Burks	.60	.18
11T Andre Dawson	.60	.18
12T Gregg Jefferies	.40	.12
13T Jimmy Key	.60	.18
14T Harold Reynolds	.60	.18
15T Tom Henke	.40	.12
16T Paul Molitor	1.00	.30
17T Wade Boggs	1.00	.30
18T David Cone	.60	.18
19T Tony Fernandez	.40	.12
20T Roberto Kelly	.40	.12
21T Paul O'Neill	1.00	.30
22T Jose Lind	.40	.12
23T Barry Bonds	4.00	1.20
24T Dave Stewart	.60	.18
25T Randy Myers	.40	.12
26T Benito Santiago	.60	.18
27T Tim Wallach	.40	.12
28T Greg Gagne	.40	.12
29T Kevin Mitchell	.40	.12
30T Jim Abbott	1.00	.30
31T Lee Smith	.60	.18
32T Bobby Munoz	.40	.12
33T Mo Sanford	.40	.12
34T John Roper	.40	.12
35T David Hulse RC	.40	.12
36T Pedro Martinez	3.00	.90
37T Chuck Carr	.40	.12
38T Armando Reynoso	.40	.12
39T Ryan Thompson	.40	.12
40T Carlos Garcia	.40	.12
41T Matt Whiteside RC	.40	.12
42T Benji Gil	.40	.12
43T Rodney Bolton	.40	.12
44T J.T. Snow	1.00	.30
45T David McCarty	.40	.12
46T Paul Quantrill	.40	.12
47T Al Martin	.40	.12
48T Lance Painter RC	.40	.12
49T Lou Frazier RC	.40	.12
50T Eduardo Perez	.40	.12
51T Kevin Young	.60	.18
52T Mike Trombley	.40	.12
53T Sterling Hitchcock RC	.60	.18
54T Tim Bogar RC	.40	.12
55T Hilly Hathaway RC	.40	.12
56T Wayne Kirby	.40	.12
57T Craig Paquette	.40	.12
58T Bret Boone	1.00	.30
59T Greg McMichael RC	.40	.12
60T Mike Lansing RC	.60	.18
61T Brent Gates	.40	.12
62T Rene Arocha RC	.60	.18
63T Ricky Gutierrez	.40	.12
64T Kevin Rogers	.40	.12
65T Ken Ryan RC	.40	.12
66T Phil Hiatt	.40	.12
67T Pat Meares RC	.60	.18
68T Troy Neel	.40	.12
69T Steve Cooke	.40	.12
70T Sherman Obando RC	.40	.12
71T Blas Minor	.40	.12
72T Angel Miranda	.40	.12
73T Tom Kramer RC	.40	.12
74T Chip Hale	.40	.12
75T Brad Pennington	.40	.12
76T Graeme Lloyd RC	.60	.18
77T Darrell Whitmore RC	.40	.12
78T David Nied	.40	.12
79T Todd Van Poppel	.40	.12
80T Chris Gomez RC	.60	.18
81T Jason Bere	.40	.12
82T Jeffrey Hammonds	.40	.12
83T Brad Ausmus	.40	.12
84T Kevin Stocker	.40	.12
85T Jeromy Burnitz	.60	.18
86T Aaron Sele	.40	.12
87T Roberto Mejia RC	.40	.12
88T Kirk Rueter RC	1.00	.30
89T Kevin Roberson RC	.40	.12
90T Allen Watson	.40	.12
91T Charlie Leibrandt	.40	.12
92T Eric Davis	.60	.18
93T Jody Reed	.40	.12
94T Danny Jackson	.40	.12
95T Gary Gaetti	.60	.18
96T Norm Charlton	.40	.12
97T Doug Drabek	.40	.12
98T Scott Fletcher	.40	.12
99T Greg Swindell	.40	.12
100T John Smiley	.40	.12
101T Kevin Reimer	.40	.12
102T Andres Galarraga	.60	.18
103T Greg Hibbard	.40	.12
104T Chris Hammond	.40	.12
105T Darnell Coles	.40	.12
106T Mike Felder	.40	.12
107T Jose Guzman	.40	.12
108T Chris Bosio	.40	.12
109T Spike Owen	.40	.12
110T Felix Jose	.40	.12
111T Cory Snyder	.40	.12
112T Craig Lefferts	.40	.12
113T David Wells	.60	.18
114T Pete Incaviglia	.40	.12
115T Mike Pagliarulo	.40	.12
116T Dave Magadan	.40	.12
117T Charlie Hough	.60	.18
118T Ivan Calderon	.40	.12
119T Manuel Lee	.40	.12
120T Bob Patterson	.40	.12
121T Bob Ojeda	.40	.12
122T Scott Bankhead	.40	.12
123T Greg Maddux	2.50	.75
124T Chili Davis	.60	.18
125T Milt Thompson	.40	.12
126T Dave Martinez	.40	.12
127T Frank Tanana	.40	.12
128T Phil Plantier	.40	.12
129T Juan Samuel	.40	.12
130T Eric Young	.40	.12
131T Joe Orsulak	.40	.12
132T Derek Bell	.40	.12
133T Darrin Jackson	.40	.12
134T Tom Brunansky	.40	.12
135T Jeff Reardon	.60	.18
136T Kevin Higgins	.40	.12
137T Joel Johnston	.40	.12
138T Rick Trlicek	.40	.12
139T Richie Lewis RC	.40	.12
140T Jeff Gardner	.40	.12
141T Jack Voigt RC	.40	.12
142T Rod Correia RC	.40	.12
143T Billy Brewer	.40	.12
144T Terry Jorgensen	.40	.12
145T Rich Amaral	.40	.12
146T Sean Berry	.40	.12
147T Dan Peltier	.40	.12
148T Paul Wagner	.40	.12
149T Damon Buford	.40	.12
150T Wil Cordero	.40	.12
NR1 Nolan Ryan Tribute	40.00	12.00
ROY1 T.Salmon AL ROY	5.00	1.50
ROY2 Mike Piazza NL ROY	25.00	7.50

1993 Select Rookie/Traded All-Star Rookies

This ten-card standard-size set was randomly inserted in foil packs of 1993 Select Rookie and Traded. The insertion rate was reportedly not less than one in 36 packs.

	Nm-Mt	Ex-Mt
COMPLETE SET (10)	100.00	30.00
1 Jeff Conine	10.00	3.00
2 Brent Gates	5.00	1.50
3 Mike Lansing	10.00	3.00
4 Kevin Stocker	5.00	1.50
5 Mike Piazza	40.00	12.00
6 Jeffrey Hammonds	5.00	1.50
7 David Hulse	5.00	1.50
8 Tim Salmon	10.00	3.00
9 Rene Arocha	10.00	3.00
10 Greg McMichael	5.00	1.50

1994 Select

Measuring the standard size, the 1994 Select set consists of 420 cards that were issued in two series of 210. The horizontal fronts feature a color player action photo and a duo-tone player shot. The backs are vertical and contain a photo, 1993 and career statistics and highlights. Special Dave Winfield and Cal Ripken cards were inserted in first series packs. A Paul Molitor MVP card and a Carlos Delgado Rookie of the Year card were inserted in second series packs. The insertion rate for each card was one in 360 packs. Rookie Cards include Chan Ho Park.

	Nm-Mt	Ex-Mt
COMPLETE SET (420)	25.00	7.50
COMP. SERIES 1 (210)	15.00	4.50
COMP. SERIES 2 (210)	10.00	3.00
1 Ken Griffey Jr.	1.25	.35
2 Greg Maddux	1.25	.35
3 Paul Molitor	.50	.15
4 Mike Piazza	1.50	.45
5 Jay Bell	.30	.09
6 Frank Thomas	.75	.23
7 Barry Larkin	.50	.15
8 Paul O'Neill	.50	.15
9 Darren Daulton	.30	.09
10 Mike Greenwell	.15	.04
11 Chuck Carr	.15	.04
12 Joe Carter	.30	.09
13 Lance Johnson	.15	.04
14 Jeff Blauser	.15	.04
15 Chris Hoiles	.15	.04
16 Rick Wilkins	.15	.04
17 Kirby Puckett	.75	.23
18 Larry Walker	.50	.15
19 Randy Johnson	.75	.23
20 Bernard Gilkey	.15	.04
21 Devon White	.30	.09
22 Randy Myers	.15	.04
23 Don Mattingly	2.00	.60
24 John Kruk	.30	.09
25 Ozzie Guillen	.15	.04
26 Jeff Conine	.30	.09
27 Mike Macfarlane	.15	.04
28 Dave Hollins	.15	.04
29 Chuck Knoblauch	.30	.09
30 Ozzie Smith	1.25	.35
31 Harold Baines	.30	.09
32 Ryne Sandberg	1.25	.35
33 Ron Karkovice	.15	.04
34 Terry Pendleton	.30	.09
35 Wally Joyner	.30	.09
36 Mike Mussina	.50	.15
37 Felix Jose	.15	.04
38 Derrick May	.15	.04
39 Scott Cooper	.15	.04
40 Jose Rijo	.15	.04
41 Robin Ventura	.30	.09
42 Charlie Hayes	.15	.04
43 Jimmy Key	.30	.09
44 Eric Karros	.30	.09
45 Ruben Sierra	.15	.04
46 Ryan Thompson	.15	.04
47 Brian McRae	.15	.04
48 Pat Hentgen	.15	.04
49 John Valentin	.15	.04
50 Al Martin	.15	.04
51 Jose Lind	.15	.04
52 Kevin Stocker	.15	.04
53 Mike Gallego	.15	.04
54 Dwight Gooden	.30	.09
55 Brady Anderson	.30	.09
56 Jeff King	.15	.04
57 Mark McGwire	2.00	.60
58 Sammy Sosa	1.25	.35
59 Ryan Bowen	.15	.04
60 Mark Lemke	.15	.04
61 Roger Clemens	1.50	.45
62 Brian Jordan	.30	.09
63 Andres Galarraga	.30	.09
64 Kevin Appier	.30	.09
65 Don Slaught	.15	.04
66 Mike Blowers	.15	.04
67 Wes Chamberlain	.15	.04
68 Troy Neel	.15	.04
69 John Wetteland	.30	.09
70 Joe Girardi	.15	.04
71 Reggie Sanders	.15	.04
72 Edgar Martinez	.50	.15
73 Todd Hundley	.15	.04
74 Pat Borders	.15	.04
75 Roberto Mejia	.15	.04
76 David Cone	.30	.09
77 Tony Gwynn	1.00	.30
78 Jim Abbott	.50	.15
79 Jay Buhner	.30	.09
80 Mark McLemore	.15	.04
81 Wil Cordero	.15	.04
82 Pedro Astacio	.15	.04
83 Bob Tewksbury	.15	.04
84 Dave Winfield	.30	.09
85 Jeff Kent	.30	.09
86 Todd Van Poppel	.15	.04
87 Steve Avery	.15	.04
88 Mike Lansing	.15	.04
89 Lenny Dykstra	.30	.09
90 Jose Guzman	.15	.04
91 Brian R. Hunter	.15	.04
92 Tim Raines	.30	.09
93 Andre Dawson	.30	.09
94 Joe Orsulak	.15	.04
95 Ricky Jordan	.15	.04
96 Billy Hatcher	.15	.04
97 Jack McDowell	.15	.04
98 Tom Pagnozzi	.15	.04
99 Darryl Strawberry	.30	.09
100 Mike Stanley	.15	.04
101 Bret Saberhagen	.30	.09
102 Willie Greene	.15	.04
103 Bryan Harvey	.15	.04
104 Tim Bogar	.15	.04
105 Jack Voigt	.15	.04
106 Brad Ausmus	.15	.04
107 Ramon Martinez	.15	.04
108 Mike Perez	.15	.04
109 Jeff Montgomery	.15	.04
110 Danny Darwin	.15	.04
111 Wilson Alvarez	.15	.04
112 Kevin Mitchell	.15	.04
113 David Nied	.15	.04
114 Rich Amaral	.15	.04
115 Stan Javier	.15	.04
116 Mo Vaughn	.30	.09
117 Ben McDonald	.15	.04
118 Tom Gordon	.15	.04
119 Carlos Garcia	.15	.04
120 Phil Plantier	.15	.04
121 Mike Morgan	.15	.04
122 Pat Meares	.15	.04
123 Kevin Young	.15	.04
124 Jeff Fassero	.15	.04
125 Gene Harris	.15	.04
126 Bob Welch	.15	.04
127 Walt Weiss	.15	.04
128 Bobby Witt	.15	.04
129 Andy Van Slyke	.30	.09
130 Steve Cooke	.15	.04
131 Mike Devereaux	.15	.04
132 Joey Cora	.15	.04
133 Bret Barberie	.15	.04
134 Orel Hershiser	.30	.09
135 Ed Sprague	.15	.04
136 Shawon Dunston	.15	.04
137 Alex Arias	.15	.04
138 Archi Cianfrocco	.15	.04
139 Tim Wallach	.15	.04
140 Bernie Williams	.50	.15
141 Karl Rhodes	.15	.04
142 Pat Kelly	.15	.04
143 Dave Magadan	.15	.04
144 Kevin Tapani	.15	.04
145 Eric Young	.15	.04
146 Derek Bell	.15	.04
147 Dante Bichette	.30	.09
148 Geronimo Pena	.15	.04
149 Joe Oliver	.15	.04
150 Orestes Destrade	.15	.04
151 Tim Naehring	.15	.04
152 Ray Lankford	.15	.04
153 Phil Clark	.15	.04
154 David McCarty	.15	.04
155 Tommy Greene	.15	.04
156 Wade Boggs	.50	.15
157 Kevin Gross	.15	.04
158 Hal Morris	.15	.04
159 Moises Alou	.30	.09
160 Rick Aguilera	.15	.04
161 Curt Schilling	.30	.09
162 Chip Hale	.15	.04
163 Tino Martinez	.50	.15
164 Mark Whiten	.15	.04
165 Dave Stewart	.30	.09
166 Steve Buechele	.15	.04
167 Bobby Jones	.15	.04
168 Darrin Fletcher	.15	.04
169 John Smiley	.15	.04
170 Cory Snyder	.15	.04
171 Scott Erickson	.15	.04
172 Kirk Rueter	.30	.09
173 Dave Fleming	.15	.04
174 John Smoltz	.50	.15
175 Ricky Gutierrez	.15	.04
176 Mike Bordick	.15	.04
177 Chan Ho Park RC	.50	.15
178 Alex Gonzalez	.15	.04
179 Steve Karsay	.15	.04
180 Jeffrey Hammonds	.15	.04
181 Manny Ramirez	.50	.15
182 Salomon Torres	.15	.04
183 Raul Mondesi	.30	.09
184 James Mouton	.15	.04
185 Cliff Floyd	.30	.09
186 Danny Bautista	.15	.04
187 Kurt Abbott RC	.30	.09
188 Javier Lopez	.30	.09
189 John Patterson	.15	.04
190 Greg Blosser	.15	.04
191 Bob Hamelin	.15	.04
192 Tony Eusebio	.15	.04
193 Carlos Delgado	.50	.15
194 Chris Gomez	.15	.04
195 Kelly Stinnett RC	.30	.09
196 Shane Reynolds	.15	.04
197 Ryan Klesko	.30	.09
198 Jim Edmonds UER	.75	.23
Mark Dalesandro pictured on front		
199 James Hurst RC	.15	.04
200 Dave Staton	.15	.04
201 Rondell White	.30	.09
202 Keith Mitchell	.15	.04
203 Darren Oliver RC	.30	.09
204 Mike Matheny RC	2.00	.60
205 Chris Turner	.15	.04
206 Matt Mieske	.15	.04
207 NL Team Checklist	.15	.04
208 NL Team Checklist	.15	.04
209 AL Team Checklist	.15	.04
210 AL Team Checklist	.15	.04
211 Barry Bonds	2.00	.60
212 Juan Gonzalez	.50	.15
213 Jim Eisenreich	.15	.04
214 Ivan Rodriguez	.75	.23
215 Tony Phillips	.15	.04
216 John Jaha	.15	.04
217 Lee Smith	.30	.09
218 Bip Roberts	.15	.04
219 Dave Hansen	.15	.04
220 Pat Listach	.15	.04
221 Willie McGee	.30	.09
222 Damion Easley	.15	.04
223 Dean Palmer	.30	.09
224 Mike Moore	.15	.04
225 Brian Harper	.15	.04
226 Gary DiSarcina	.15	.04
227 Delino DeShields	.15	.04
228 Otis Nixon	.15	.04
229 Roberto Alomar	.50	.15
230 Mark Grace	.50	.15
231 Kenny Lofton	.30	.09
232 Gregg Jefferies	.15	.04
233 Cecil Fielder	.30	.09
234 Jeff Bagwell	.50	.15
235 Albert Belle	.30	.09
236 Dave Justice	.30	.09
237 Tom Henke	.15	.04
238 Bobby Bonilla	.30	.09
239 John Olerud	.30	.09
240 Robby Thompson	.15	.04
241 Dave Valle	.15	.04
242 Marquis Grissom	.30	.09
243 Greg Swindell	.15	.04
244 Todd Zeile	.15	.04
245 Dennis Eckersley	.30	.09
246 Jose Offerman	.15	.04
247 Greg McMichael	.15	.04
248 Tim Belcher	.15	.04
249 Cal Ripken Jr.	2.50	.75
250 Tom Glavine	.50	.15
251 Luis Polonia	.15	.04
252 Bill Swift	.15	.04
253 Juan Guzman	.15	.04
254 Rickey Henderson	.75	.23
255 Terry Mulholland	.15	.04
256 Gary Sheffield	.30	.09
257 Terry Steinbach	.15	.04
258 Brett Butler	.30	.09
259 Jason Bere	.15	.04
260 Doug Strange	.15	.04
261 Kent Hrbek	.30	.09
262 Graeme Lloyd	.15	.04
263 Lou Frazier	.15	.04
264 Charles Nagy	.15	.04
265 Bret Boone	.30	.09
266 Kirk Gibson	.30	.09

267 Kevin Brown .30 .09
268 Fred McGriff .50 .15
269 Matt Williams .30 .09
270 Greg Gagne .15 .04
271 Mariano Duncan .15 .04
272 Jeff Russell .15 .04
273 Eric Davis .30 .09
274 Shane Mack .15 .04
275 Jose Vizcaino .15 .04
276 Jose Canseco .75 .23
277 Roberto Hernandez .15 .04
278 Royce Clayton .15 .04
279 Carlos Baerga .15 .04
280 Pete Incaviglia .15 .04
281 Brent Gates .15 .04
282 Jeromy Burnitz .30 .09
283 Chili Davis .30 .09
284 Pete Harnisch .15 .04
285 Alan Trammell .30 .09
286 Eric Anthony .15 .04
287 Ellis Burks .30 .09
288 Julio Franco .30 .09
289 Jack Morris .30 .09
290 Erik Hanson .15 .04
291 Chuck Finley .30 .09
292 Reggie Jefferson .15 .04
293 Kevin McReynolds .15 .04
294 Greg Hibbard .15 .04
295 Travis Fryman .30 .09
296 Craig Biggio .50 .15
297 Kenny Rogers .30 .09
298 Dave Henderson .15 .04
299 Jim Thome .75 .23
300 Rene Arocha .15 .04
301 Pedro Munoz .15 .04
302 David Hulse .15 .04
303 Greg Vaughn .15 .04
304 Darren Lewis .15 .04
305 Deion Sanders .50 .15
306 Danny Tartabull .15 .04
307 Darryl Hamilton .15 .04
308 Andujar Cedeno .15 .04
309 Tim Salmon .50 .15
310 Tony Fernandez .15 .04
311 Alex Fernandez .15 .04
312 Roberto Kelly .15 .04
313 Harold Reynolds .30 .09
314 Chris Sabo .15 .04
315 Howard Johnson .15 .04
316 Mark Portugal .15 .04
317 Rafael Palmeiro .50 .15
318 Pete Smith .15 .04
319 Will Clark .75 .23
320 Henry Rodriguez .15 .04
321 Omar Vizquel .50 .15
322 David Segui .15 .04
323 Lou Whitaker .30 .09
324 Felix Fermin .15 .04
325 Spike Owen .15 .04
326 Darryl Kile .30 .09
327 Chad Kreuter .15 .04
328 Rod Beck .15 .04
329 Eddie Murray .75 .23
330 B.J. Surhoff .30 .09
331 Mickey Tettleton .15 .04
332 Pedro Martinez .75 .23
333 Roger Pavlik .15 .04
334 Eddie Taubensee .15 .04
335 John Doherty .15 .04
336 Jody Reed .15 .04
337 Aaron Sele .15 .04
338 Leo Gomez .15 .04
339 Dave Nilsson .15 .04
340 Rob Dibble .30 .09
341 John Burkett .15 .04
342 Wayne Kirby .15 .04
343 Dan Wilson .15 .04
344 Armando Reynoso .15 .04
345 Chad Curtis .15 .04
346 Dennis Martinez .30 .09
347 Cal Eldred .15 .04
348 Luis Gonzalez .30 .09
349 Doug Drabek .15 .04
350 Jim Leyritz .15 .04
351 Mark Langston .15 .04
352 Darrin Jackson .15 .04
353 Sid Fernandez .15 .04
354 Benito Santiago .30 .09
355 Kevin Seitzer .15 .04
356 Bo Jackson .75 .23
357 David Wells .30 .09
358 Paul Sorrento .15 .04
359 Ken Caminiti .30 .09
360 Eduardo Perez .15 .04
361 Orlando Merced .15 .04
362 Steve Finley .30 .09
363 Andy Benes .15 .04
364 Manuel Lee .15 .04
365 Todd Benzinger .15 .04
366 Sandy Alomar Jr. .15 .04
367 Rex Hudler .15 .04
368 Mike Henneman .15 .04
369 Vince Coleman .15 .04
370 Kirt Manwaring .15 .04
371 Ken Hill .15 .04
372 Glenallen Hill .15 .04
373 Sean Berry .15 .04
374 Geronimo Berroa .15 .04
375 Duane Ward .15 .04
376 Allen Watson .15 .04
377 Marc Newfield .15 .04
378 Dan Miceli .15 .04
379 Denny Hocking .15 .04
380 Mark Kiefer .15 .04
381 Tony Tarasco .15 .04
382 Tony Longmire .15 .04
383 Brian Anderson RC .30 .09
384 Fernando Vina .15 .04
385 Hector Carrasco .15 .04
386 Mike Kelly .15 .04
387 Greg Colbrunn .15 .04
388 Roger Salkeld .15 .04
389 Steve Trachsel .15 .04
390 Rich Becker .15 .04
391 Billy Taylor RC .30 .09
392 Rich Rowland .15 .04
393 Carl Everett .30 .09
394 Johnny Ruffin .15 .04
395 Keith Lockhart RC .30 .09
396 J.R. Phillips .15 .04
397 Sterling Hitchcock .15 .04
398 Jorge Fabregas .15 .04
399 Jeff Granger .15 .04
400 Eddie Zambrano RC .15 .04
401 Rikkert Faneyte RC .15 .04
402 Gerald Williams .15 .04
403 Joey Hamilton .15 .04
404 Joe Hall RC .15 .04
405 John Hudek RC .15 .04
406 Roberto Petagine .15 .04
407 Charles Johnson .30 .09
408 Mark Smith .15 .04
409 Jeff Juden .15 .04
410 Carlos Pulido RC .15 .04
411 Paul Shuey .15 .04
412 Rob Butler .15 .04
413 Mark Acre RC .15 .04
414 Greg Pirkl .15 .04
415 Melvin Nieves .15 .04
416 Tim Hyers RC .15 .04
417 NL Checklist .15 .04
418 NL Checklist .15 .04
419 AL Checklist .15 .04
420 AL Checklist .15 .04
RY1 Carlos Delgado 5.00 1.50
SS1 Cal Ripken Jr. 20.00 6.00
Salute
SS2 Dave Winfield 4.00 1.20
Salute
MVP1 Paul Molitor 5.00 1.50

1994 Select Crown Contenders

This ten-card set showcases top contenders for various awards such as batting champion, Cy Young Award winner and Most Valuable Player. The cards were inserted in first series packs at a rate of one in 24 and measure the standard size.

Nm-Mt Ex-Mt
COMPLETE SET (10) 60.00 18.00
CC1 Lenny Dykstra 2.00 .60
CC2 Greg Maddux 8.00 2.40
CC3 Roger Clemens 10.00 3.00
CC4 Randy Johnson 5.00 1.50
CC5 Frank Thomas 5.00 1.50
CC6 Barry Bonds 12.00 3.60
CC7 Juan Gonzalez 3.00 .90
CC8 John Olerud 2.00 .60
CC9 Mike Piazza 10.00 3.00
CC10 Ken Griffey Jr. 8.00 2.40

1994 Select Rookie Surge

This 18-card standard-size set showcased potential top rookies for 1994. The set was divided into two series of nine cards. The cards were randomly inserted in packs at a rate of one in 48. The fronts exhibit Score's "dufex" printing process, in which a color photo is printed on a metallic base creating an unusual, three-dimensional look.

Nm-Mt Ex-Mt
COMPLETE SET (18) 80.00 24.00
COMPLETE SERIES 1 (9) 30.00 9.00
COMPLETE SERIES 2 (9) 50.00 15.00
RS1 Cliff Floyd 6.00 1.80
RS2 Bob Hamelin 4.00 1.20
RS3 Ryan Klesko 6.00 1.80
RS4 Carlos Delgado 10.00 3.00
RS5 Jeffrey Hammonds 4.00 1.20
RS6 Rondell White 6.00 1.80
RS7 Salomon Torres 4.00 1.20
RS8 Steve Karsay 4.00 1.20
RS9 Javier Lopez 6.00 1.80
RS10 Manny Ramirez 10.00 3.00
RS11 Tony Tarasco 4.00 1.20
RS12 Kurt Abbott 6.00 1.80
RS13 Chan Ho Park 10.00 3.00
RS14 Rich Becker 4.00 1.20
RS15 James Mouton 4.00 1.20
RS16 Alex Gonzalez 4.00 1.20
RS17 Raul Mondesi 6.00 1.80
RS18 Steve Trachsel 4.00 1.20

1994 Select Skills

This 10-card standard-size set takes an up close look at the leagues top statistical leaders. The cards were randomly inserted in second series packs at a rate of approximately one in 24.

Nm-Mt Ex-Mt
COMPLETE SET (10) 50.00 15.00
SK1 Randy Johnson 12.00 3.60
SK2 Barry Larkin 8.00 2.40
SK3 Lenny Dykstra 5.00 1.50
SK4 Kenny Lofton 5.00 1.50
SK5 Juan Gonzalez 8.00 2.40
SK6 Barry Bonds 30.00 9.00
SK7 Marquis Grissom 5.00 1.50
SK8 Ivan Rodriguez 12.00 3.60
SK9 Larry Walker 8.00 2.40
SK10 Travis Fryman 5.00 1.50

1995 Select

This 250-card set was issued in 12-card packs with 24 packs per box and 24 boxes per case. There was an announced production run of 4,950 cases. A special card of Hideo Nomo (number 251) was issued to hobby dealers who had bought cases of the Select product.

Nm-Mt Ex-Mt
COMPLETE SET (250) 15.00 4.50
1 Cal Ripken Jr. 1.50 .45
2 Robin Ventura .20 .06
3 Al Martin .10 .03
4 Jeff Frye .10 .03
5 Darryl Strawberry .20 .06
6 Chan Ho Park .20 .06
7 Steve Avery .10 .03
8 Bret Boone .20 .06
9 Danny Tartabull .10 .03
10 Dante Bichette .20 .06
11 Rondell White .20 .06
12 Dave McCarty .10 .03
13 Bernard Gilkey .10 .03
14 Mark McGwire 1.25 .35
15 Ruben Sierra .10 .03
16 Wade Boggs .30 .09
17 Mike Piazza .75 .23
18 Jeffrey Hammonds .10 .03
19 Mike Mussina .30 .09
20 Darryl Kile .20 .06
21 Greg Maddux .75 .23
22 Frank Thomas .50 .15
23 Kevin Appier .20 .06
24 Jay Bell .20 .06
25 Kirk Gibson .20 .06
26 Pat Hentgen .10 .03
27 Joey Hamilton .10 .03
28 Bernie Williams .30 .09
29 Aaron Sele .10 .03
30 Delino DeShields .10 .03
31 Danny Bautista .10 .03
32 Jim Thome .50 .15
33 Rikkert Faneyte .10 .03
34 Roberto Alomar .30 .09
35 Paul Molitor .30 .09
36 Allen Watson .10 .03
37 Jeff Bagwell .30 .09
38 Jay Buhner .20 .06
39 Marquis Grissom .20 .06
40 Jim Edmonds .30 .09
41 Ryan Klesko .20 .06
42 Fred McGriff .30 .09
43 Tony Tarasco .10 .03
44 Darren Daulton .20 .06
45 Marc Newfield .10 .03
46 Barry Bonds 1.25 .35
47 Bobby Bonilla .20 .06
48 Greg Pirkl .10 .03
49 Steve Karsay .10 .03
50 Bob Hamelin .10 .03
51 Javier Lopez .20 .06
52 Barry Larkin .30 .09
53 Kevin Young .10 .03
54 Sterling Hitchcock .10 .03
55 Tom Glavine .30 .09
56 Carlos Delgado .20 .06
57 Darren Oliver .10 .03
58 Cliff Floyd .20 .06
59 Tim Salmon .30 .09
60 Albert Belle .20 .06
61 Salomon Torres .10 .03
62 Gary Sheffield .20 .06
63 Ivan Rodriguez .50 .15
64 Charles Nagy .10 .03
65 Eduardo Perez .10 .03
66 Terry Steinbach .10 .03
67 Dave Justice .20 .06
68 Jason Bere .10 .03
69 Dave Nilsson .10 .03
70 Brian Anderson .10 .03
71 Billy Ashley .10 .03
72 Roger Clemens 1.00 .30
73 Jimmy Key .20 .06
74 Wally Joyner .20 .06
75 Andy Benes .10 .03
76 Ray Lankford .10 .03
77 Jeff Kent .20 .06
78 Moises Alou .20 .06
79 Kirby Puckett .50 .15
80 Joe Carter .20 .06
81 Manny Ramirez .30 .09
82 J.R. Phillips .10 .03
83 Matt Mieske .10 .03
84 John Olerud .20 .06
85 Andres Galarraga .20 .06
86 Juan Gonzalez .30 .09
87 Pedro Martinez .50 .15
88 Dean Palmer .20 .06
89 Ken Griffey Jr. .75 .23
90 Brian Jordan .20 .06
91 Hal Morris .10 .03
92 Lenny Dykstra .20 .06
93 Wil Cordero .10 .03
94 Tony Gwynn .60 .18
95 Alex Gonzalez .10 .03
96 Cecil Fielder .20 .06
97 Mo Vaughn .20 .06
98 John Valentin .10 .03
99 Will Clark .50 .15
100 Geronimo Pena .10 .03
101 Don Mattingly 1.25 .35
102 Charles Johnson .20 .06
103 Raul Mondesi .20 .06
104 Reggie Sanders .10 .03
105 Royce Clayton .10 .03
106 Reggie Jefferson .10 .03
107 Craig Biggio .30 .09
108 Jack McDowell .10 .03
109 James Mouton .10 .03
110 Mike Greenwell .10 .03
111 David Cone .20 .06
112 Matt Williams .20 .06
113 Garret Anderson .20 .06
114 Carlos Garcia .10 .03
115 Alex Fernandez .10 .03
116 Deion Sanders .30 .09
117 Chili Davis .20 .06
118 Mike Kelly .10 .03
119 Jeff Conine .20 .06
120 Kenny Lofton .20 .06
121 Rafael Palmeiro .30 .09
122 Chuck Knoblauch .20 .06
123 Ozzie Smith .75 .23
124 Carlos Baerga .10 .03
125 Brett Butler .20 .06
126 Sammy Sosa .75 .23
127 Ellis Burks .20 .06
128 Bret Saberhagen .20 .06
129 Doug Drabek .10 .03
130 Dennis Martinez .20 .06
131 Paul O'Neill .30 .09
132 Travis Fryman .20 .06
133 Brent Gates .10 .03
134 Rickey Henderson .50 .15
135 Randy Johnson .50 .15
136 Mark Langston .10 .03
137 Greg Colbrunn .10 .03
138 Jose Rijo .10 .03
139 Bryan Harvey .10 .03
140 Dennis Eckersley .20 .06
141 Ron Gant .20 .06
142 Carl Everett .20 .06
143 Jeff Granger .10 .03
144 Ben McDonald .10 .03
145 Kurt Abbott UER .10 .03
(Mariners logo on front
146 Jim Abbott .30 .09
147 Jason Jacome .10 .03
148 Rico Brogna .10 .03
149 Cal Eldred .10 .03
150 Rich Becker .10 .03
151 Pete Harnisch .10 .03
152 Roberto Petagine .10 .03
153 Jacob Brumfield .10 .03
154 Todd Hundley .10 .03
155 Roger Cedeno .10 .03
156 Harold Baines .20 .06
157 Steve Dunn .10 .03
158 Tim Belk .10 .03
159 Marty Cordova .10 .03
160 Russ Davis .10 .03
161 Jose Malave .10 .03
162 Brian Hunter .10 .03
163 Andy Pettitte .30 .09
164 Brooks Kieschnick .10 .03
165 Midre Cummings .10 .03
166 Frank Rodriguez .10 .03
167 Chad Mottola .10 .03
168 Brian Barber .10 .03
169 Tim Unroe RC .10 .03
170 Shane Andrews .10 .03
171 Kevin Flora .10 .03
172 Ray Durham .20 .06
173 Chipper Jones .50 .15
174 Butch Huskey .10 .03
175 Ray McDavid .10 .03
176 Jeff Cirillo .10 .03
177 Terry Pendleton .20 .06
178 Scott Ruffcorn .10 .03
179 Ray Holbert .10 .03
180 Joe Randa .10 .03
181 Jose Oliva .10 .03
182 Andy Van Slyke .20 .06
183 Albie Lopez .10 .03
184 Chad Curtis .10 .03
185 Ozzie Guillen .10 .03
186 Chad Ogea .10 .03
187 Dan Wilson .10 .03
188 Tony Fernandez .10 .03
189 John Smoltz .30 .09
190 Willie Greene .10 .03
191 Darren Lewis .10 .03
192 Orlando Miller .10 .03
193 Kurt Miller .10 .03
194 Andrew Lorraine .10 .03
195 Ernie Young .10 .03
196 Jimmy Haynes .10 .03
197 Raul Casanova RC .25 .07
198 Joe Vitiello .10 .03
199 Brad Woodall RC .10 .03
200 Juan Acevedo RC .10 .03
201 Michael Tucker .10 .03
202 Shawn Green .20 .06
203 Alex Rodriguez 1.25 .35
204 Julian Tavarez .10 .03
205 Jose Lima .10 .03
206 Wilson Alvarez .10 .03
207 Rich Aude .10 .03
208 Armando Benitez .20 .06
209 Dwayne Hosey .10 .03
210 Gabe White .10 .03
211 Joey Eischen .10 .03
212 Bill Pulsipher .10 .03
213 Robby Thompson .10 .03
214 Toby Borland .10 .03
215 Rusty Greer .20 .06
216 Fausto Cruz .10 .03
217 Luis Ortiz .10 .03
218 Duane Singleton .10 .03
219 Troy Percival .20 .06
220 Gregg Jefferies .10 .03
221 Mark Grace .30 .09
222 Mickey Tettleton .10 .03
223 Phil Plantier .10 .03
224 Larry Walker .30 .09
225 Ken Caminiti .20 .06
226 Dave Winfield .20 .06
227 Brady Anderson .20 .06
228 Kevin Brown .20 .06
229 Andujar Cedeno .10 .03
230 Roberto Kelly .10 .03
231 Jose Canseco .50 .15
232 Scott Ruffcorn ST .10 .03
233 Billy Ashley ST .10 .03
234 J.R. Phillips ST .10 .03
235 Chipper Jones ST .30 .09
236 Charles Johnson ST .10 .03
237 Midre Cummings ST .10 .03
238 Brian L.Hunter ST .10 .03
239 Garret Anderson ST .10 .03
240 Shawn Green ST .10 .03
241 Alex Rodriguez ST .50 .15
242 Frank Thomas CL .30 .09
243 Ken Griffey Jr. CL .50 .15
244 Albert Belle CL .10 .03
245 Cal Ripken Jr. CL .75 .23
246 Barry Bonds CL .60 .18
247 Raul Mondesi CL .10 .03
248 Mike Piazza CL .50 .15
249 Jeff Bagwell CL .20 .06
250 Jeff Bagwell .50 .15
Ken Griffey Jr.
Frank Thomas
Mike Piazza CL
251S Hideo Nomo 1.50 .45

1995 Select Artist's Proofs

This 250-card set is parallel to the regular Select set. These cards were inserted at a rate of one per 24 packs. The only difference between these cards and the regular issue cards are the words "Artist's Proof" printed in the lower left corner. Based upon the announced print run of 4,950 cases, approximately 238 complete sets of Artist's Proofs were produced. Please note, however, that these cards are not serial numbered and that number has never been verified by the manufacturer. The Hideo Nomo card was randomly distributed directly to hobby dealers and never inserted in packs.

Nm-Mt Ex-Mt
*STARS: 12.5X TO 30X BASIC CARDS

1995 Select Big Sticks

Randomly inserted in packs, these 12 cards feature leading hitters. The cards are numbered in the upper right corner with a "BS" prefix.

Nm-Mt Ex-Mt
COMPLETE SET (12) 120.00 36.00
BS1 Frank Thomas 8.00 2.40
BS2 Ken Griffey Jr. 12.00 3.60
BS3 Cal Ripken Jr. 25.00 7.50
BS4 Mike Piazza 12.00 3.60
BS5 Don Mattingly 20.00 6.00
BS6 Will Clark 8.00 2.40
BS7 Tony Gwynn 10.00 3.00
BS8 Jeff Bagwell 5.00 1.50
BS9 Barry Bonds 20.00 6.00
BS10 Paul Molitor 5.00 1.50
BS11 Matt Williams 3.00 .90
BS12 Albert Belle 3.00 .90

1995 Select Can't Miss

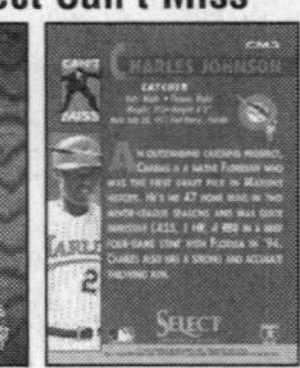

These 12 cards featuring promising young players were inserted one per 24 packs. The cards are numbered with a "CM" prefix in the upper right corner.

Nm-Mt Ex-Mt
COMPLETE SET (12) 50.00 15.00
CM1 Cliff Floyd 2.50 .75
CM2 Ryan Klesko 2.50 .75
CM3 Charles Johnson 2.50 .75
CM4 Raul Mondesi 2.50 .75
CM5 Manny Ramirez 3.00 .90
CM6 Billy Ashley 1.50 .45
CM7 Alex Gonzalez 1.50 .45
CM8 Carlos Delgado 2.50 .75
CM9 Garret Anderson 2.50 .75
CM10 Alex Rodriguez 12.00 3.60
CM11 Chipper Jones 5.00 1.50
CM12 Shawn Green 2.50 .75

1995 Select Sure Shots

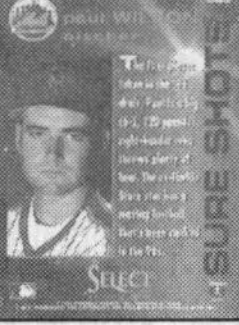

These ten cards were randomly inserted into packs at a rate of one in 90. This set features some of the top 1994 draft picks. The cards are numbered with an "SS" prefix in the upper right corner.

	Nm-Mt	Ex-Mt
COMPLETE SET (10)	30.00	9.00
SS1 Ben Grieve	3.00	.90
SS2 Kevin Witt	3.00	.90
SS3 Mark Farris	3.00	.90
SS4 Paul Konerko	3.00	.90
SS5 Dustin Hermanson	3.00	.90
SS6 Ramon Castro	3.00	.90
SS7 McKay Christensen	3.00	.90
SS8 Brian Buchanan	3.00	.90
SS9 Paul Wilson	3.00	.90
SS10 Terrence Long	3.00	.90

1996 Select

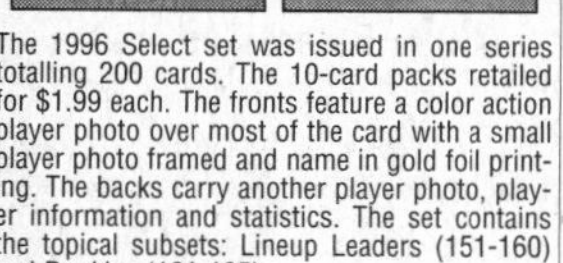

The 1996 Select set was issued in one series totalling 200 cards. The 10-card packs retailed for $1.99 each. The fronts feature a color action player photo over most of the card with a small player photo framed and name in gold foil printing. The backs carry another player photo, player information and statistics. The set contains the topical subsets: Lineup Leaders (151-160) and Rookies (161-195).

	Nm-Mt	Ex-Mt
COMPLETE SET (200)	15.00	4.50
1 Wade Boggs	.30	.09
2 Shawn Green	.20	.06
3 Andres Galarraga	.20	.06
4 Bill Pulsipher	.20	.06
5 Chuck Knoblauch	.20	.06
6 Ken Griffey Jr.	.75	.23
7 Greg Maddux	.75	.23
8 Manny Ramirez	.30	.09
9 Ivan Rodriguez	.50	.15
10 Tim Salmon	.30	.09
11 Frank Thomas	.50	.15
12 Jeff Bagwell	.30	.09
13 Travis Fryman	.20	.06
14 Kenny Lofton	.20	.06
15 Matt Williams	.20	.06
16 Jay Bell	.20	.06
17 Ken Caminiti	.20	.06
18 Ray Lankford	.20	.06
19 Cal Ripken	1.50	.45
20 Roger Clemens	1.00	.30
21 Carlos Baerga	.20	.06
22 Mike Piazza	.75	.23
23 Gregg Jefferies	.20	.06
24 Reggie Sanders	.20	.06
25 Rondell White	.20	.06
26 Sammy Sosa	.75	.23
27 Kevin Appier	.20	.06
28 Kevin Seitzer	.20	.06
29 Gary Sheffield	.20	.06
30 Mike Mussina	.30	.09
31 Mark McGwire	1.25	.35
32 Barry Larkin	.30	.09
33 Marc Newfield	.20	.06
34 Ismael Valdes	.20	.06
35 Marty Cordova	.20	.06
36 Albert Belle	.20	.06
37 Johnny Damon	.30	.09
38 Garret Anderson	.20	.06
39 Cecil Fielder	.20	.06
40 John Mabry	.20	.06
41 Chipper Jones	.50	.15
42 Omar Vizquel	.30	.09
43 Jose Rijo	.20	.06
44 Charles Johnson	.20	.06
45 Alex Rodriguez	1.00	.30
46 Rico Brogna	.20	.06
47 Joe Carter	.20	.06
48 Mo Vaughn	.20	.06
49 Moises Alou	.20	.06
50 Raul Mondesi	.20	.06
51 Robin Ventura	.20	.06
52 Jim Thome	.50	.15
53 David Justice	.20	.06
54 Jeff King	.20	.06
55 Brian L.Hunter	.20	.06
56 Juan Gonzalez	.30	.09
57 John Olerud	.20	.06
58 Rafael Palmeiro	.30	.09
59 Tony Gwynn	.60	.18
60 Eddie Murray	.50	.15
61 Jason Isringhausen	.20	.06
62 Dante Bichette	.20	.06
63 Randy Johnson	.50	.15
64 Kirby Puckett	.50	.15
65 Jim Edmonds	.20	.06
66 David Cone	.20	.06
67 Ozzie Smith	.75	.23
68 Fred McGriff	.30	.09
69 Darren Daulton	.20	.06
70 Edgar Martinez	.30	.09
71 J.T. Snow	.20	.06
72 Butch Huskey	.20	.06
73 Hideo Nomo	.50	.15
74 Pedro Martinez	.50	.15
75 Bobby Bonilla	.20	.06
76 Jeff Conine	.20	.06
77 Ryan Klesko	.20	.06
78 Bernie Williams	.30	.09
79 Andre Dawson	.20	.06
80 Trevor Hoffman	.20	.06
81 Mark Grace	.30	.09
82 Benji Gil	.20	.06
83 Eric Karros	.20	.06
84 Pete Schourek	.20	.06
85 Edgardo Alfonzo	.20	.06
86 Jay Buhner	.20	.06
87 Vinny Castilla	.20	.06
88 Bret Boone	.20	.06
89 Ray Durham	.20	.06
90 Brian Jordan	.20	.06
91 Jose Canseco	.50	.15
92 Paul O'Neill	.30	.09
93 Chili Davis	.20	.06
94 Tom Glavine	.30	.09
95 Julian Tavarez	.20	.06
96 Derek Bell	.20	.06
97 Will Clark	.50	.15
98 Larry Walker	.30	.09
99 Denny Neagle	.20	.06
100 Alex Fernandez	.20	.06
101 Barry Bonds	1.25	.35
102 Ben McDonald	.20	.06
103 Andy Pettitte	.30	.09
104 Tino Martinez	.30	.09
105 Sterling Hitchcock	.20	.06
106 Royce Clayton	.20	.06
107 Jim Abbott	.30	.09
108 Rickey Henderson	.50	.15
109 Ramon Martinez	.20	.06
110 Paul Molitor	.30	.09
111 Dennis Eckersley	.20	.06
112 Alex Gonzalez	.20	.06
113 Marquis Grissom	.20	.06
114 Greg Vaughn	.20	.06
115 Lance Johnson	.20	.06
116 Todd Stottleymyre	.20	.06
117 Jack McDowell	.20	.06
118 Ruben Sierra	.20	.06
119 Brady Anderson	.20	.06
120 Julio Franco	.20	.06
121 Brooks Kieschnick	.20	.06
122 Roberto Alomar	.30	.09
123 Greg Gagne	.20	.06
124 Wally Joyner	.20	.06
125 John Smoltz	.30	.09
126 John Valentin	.20	.06
127 Russ Davis	.20	.06
128 Joe Vitiello	.20	.06
129 Shawon Dunston	.20	.06
130 Frank Rodriguez	.20	.06
131 Charlie Hayes	.20	.06
132 Andy Benes	.20	.06
133 B.J. Surhoff	.20	.06
134 Dave Nilsson	.20	.06
135 Carlos Delgado	.20	.06
136 Walt Weiss	.20	.06
137 Mike Stanley	.20	.06
138 Greg Colbrunn	.20	.06
139 Mike Kelly	.20	.06
140 Ryne Sandberg	.75	.23
141 Lee Smith	.20	.06
142 Dennis Martinez	.20	.06
143 Bernard Gilkey	.20	.06
144 Lenny Dykstra	.20	.06
145 Danny Tartabull	.20	.06
146 Dean Palmer	.20	.06
147 Craig Biggio	.30	.09
148 Juan Acevedo	.20	.06
149 Michael Tucker	.20	.06
150 Bobby Higginson	.20	.06
151 Ken Griffey Jr. LUL	.50	.15
152 Frank Thomas LUL	.30	.09
153 Cal Ripken LUL	.75	.23
154 Albert Belle LUL	.20	.06
155 Mike Piazza LUL	.50	.15
156 Barry Bonds LUL	.50	.15
157 Sammy Sosa LUL	.50	.15
158 Mo Vaughn LUL	.20	.06
159 Greg Maddux LUL	.50	.15
160 Jeff Bagwell LUL	.20	.06
161 Derek Jeter	1.25	.35
162 Paul Wilson	.20	.06
163 Chris Snopek	.20	.06
164 Jason Schmidt	.30	.09
165 Jimmy Haynes	.20	.06
166 George Arias	.20	.06
167 Steve Gibralter	.20	.06
168 Bob Wolcott	.20	.06
169 Jason Kendall	.20	.06
170 Greg Zaun	.20	.06
171 Quinton McCracken	.20	.06
172 Alan Benes	.20	.06
173 Rey Ordonez	.20	.06
174 Livan Hernandez RC	.50	.15
175 Osvaldo Fernandez	.20	.06
176 Marc Barcelo	.20	.06
177 Sal Fasano	.20	.06
178 Mike Grace	.20	.06
179 Chan Ho Park	.20	.06
180 Robert Perez	.20	.06
181 Todd Hollandsworth	.20	.06
182 Wilton Guerrero RC	.20	.06
183 John Wasdin	.20	.06
184 Jim Pittsley	.20	.06
185 LaTroy Hawkins	.20	.06
186 Jay Powell	.20	.06
187 Felipe Crespo	.20	.06
188 Jermaine Dye	.20	.06
189 Bob Abreu	.20	.06
190 Matt Luke	.20	.06
191 Richard Hidalgo	.20	.06
192 Karim Garcia	.20	.06
193 Marvin Benard RC	.20	.06
194 Andy Fox	.20	.06
195 Terrell Wade	.20	.06
196 Frank Thomas CL	.30	.09
197 Ken Griffey Jr. CL	.50	.15
198 Greg Maddux CL	.50	.15
199 Mike Piazza CL	.50	.15
200 Cal Ripken CL	.75	.23

1996 Select Artist's Proofs

Randomly inserted one in 35 packs, this 200-card set is parallel and similar in design to the regular set. The difference is the holographic foil-stamped Artist's Proof logo on the card front.

Nm-Mt Ex-Mt

*STARS: 12.5X TO 30X BASIC CARDS
*ROOKIES: 8X TO 20X BASIC CARDS

1996 Select Claim To Fame

Randomly inserted in packs at a rate of one in 72, this 20-card set features potential Hall of Famers. The fronts display a color player portrait on a diecut plaque similar to the ones that enshrine Hall of Famers. The backs carry information about the player's claim to fame. Only 2100 of these sets were produced. A Sammy

Sosa Sample card was distributed to dealers and hobby media to preview the set.

	Nm-Mt	Ex-Mt
COMPLETE SET (20)	250.00	75.00
1 Cal Ripken	30.00	9.00
2 Greg Maddux	15.00	4.50
3 Ken Griffey Jr.	15.00	4.50
4 Frank Thomas	10.00	3.00
5 Mo Vaughn	4.00	1.20
6 Albert Belle	4.00	1.20
7 Jeff Bagwell	6.00	1.80
8 Sammy Sosa	15.00	4.50
9 Reggie Sanders	4.00	1.20
10 Hideo Nomo	10.00	3.00
11 Chipper Jones	10.00	3.00
12 Mike Piazza	15.00	4.50
13 Matt Williams	4.00	1.20
14 Tony Gwynn	12.00	3.60
15 Johnny Damon	6.00	1.80
16 Dante Bichette	4.00	1.20
17 Kirby Puckett	10.00	3.00
18 Barry Bonds	25.00	7.50
19 Randy Johnson	10.00	3.00
20 Eddie Murray	10.00	3.00
S8 Sammy Sosa Sample	2.00	.60

1996 Select En Fuego

Randomly inserted in packs at a rate of one in 48, this 25-card set is printed with all-foil Dufex technology, etched highlights and transparent inks that make each card shine. Spanish for "on fire," En Fuego is an expression popularized by ESPN sportscaster Dan Patrick, who provides the commentary for each player on the card back. The fronts feature color action player photos while the backs display more player photos and the commentary.

	Nm-Mt	Ex-Mt
COMPLETE SET (25)	200.00	60.00
1 Ken Griffey Jr.	12.00	3.60
2 Frank Thomas	8.00	2.40
3 Cal Ripken	25.00	7.50
4 Greg Maddux	12.00	3.60
5 Jeff Bagwell	5.00	1.50
6 Barry Bonds	20.00	6.00
7 Mo Vaughn	3.00	.90
8 Albert Belle	3.00	.90
9 Sammy Sosa	12.00	3.60
10 Reggie Sanders	3.00	.90
11 Mike Piazza	12.00	3.60
12 Chipper Jones	8.00	2.40
13 Tony Gwynn	10.00	3.00
14 Kirby Puckett	8.00	2.40
15 Wade Boggs	5.00	1.50
16 Dan Patrick ANN	3.00	.90
17 Gary Sheffield	3.00	.90
18 Dante Bichette	3.00	.90
19 Randy Johnson	8.00	2.40
20 Matt Williams	3.00	.90
21 Alex Rodriguez	15.00	4.50
22 Tim Salmon	5.00	1.50
23 Johnny Damon	5.00	1.50
24 Manny Ramirez	5.00	1.50
25 Hideo Nomo	8.00	2.40

1996 Select Team Nucleus

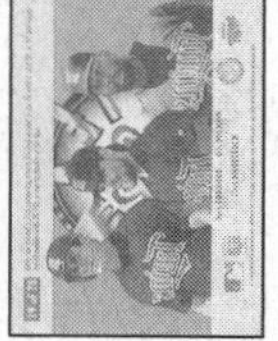

Randomly inserted in packs at a rate of one in 18, this 28-card set is printed on clear plastic with holographic and micro-etched highlights and gold foil stamping.

	Nm-Mt	Ex-Mt
COMPLETE SET (28)	100.00	30.00
1 Albert Belle	2.50	.75
Manny Ramirez		
Carlos Baerga		
2 Ray Lankford	6.00	1.80
Brian Jordan		
Ozzie Smith		
3 Jay Bell	1.50	.45
Jeff King		
Denny Neagle		
4 Dante Bichette	1.50	.45
Andres Galarraga		
Larry Walker		
5 Mark McGwire	10.00	3.00
Mike Bordick		
Terry Steinbach		
6 Bernie Williams	2.50	.75
Wade Boggs		
David Cone		
7 Joe Carter	1.50	.45
Alex Gonzalez		
Shawn Green		
8 Roger Clemens	8.00	2.40
Mo Vaughn		
Jose Canseco		
9 Ken Griffey Jr.	6.00	1.80
Edgar Martinez		
Randy Johnson		
10 Gregg Jefferies	1.50	.45
Darren Daulton		
Len Dykstra		
11 Mike Piazza	6.00	1.80
Raul Mondesi		
Hideo Nomo		
12 Greg Maddux	6.00	1.80
Chipper Jones		
Ryan Klesko		
13 Cecil Fielder	1.50	.45
Travis Fryman		
Phil Nevin		
14 Ivan Rodriguez	4.00	1.20
Will Clark		
Juan Gonzalez		
15 Ryne Sandberg	6.00	1.80
Sammy Sosa		
Mark Grace		
16 Gary Sheffield	1.50	.45
Charles Johnson		
Andre Dawson		
17 Johnny Damon	2.50	.75
Michael Tucker		
Kevin Appier		
18 Barry Bonds	10.00	3.00
Matt Williams		
Rod Beck		
19 Kirby Puckett	4.00	1.20
Chuck Knoblauch		
Marty Cordova		
20 Cal Ripken	12.00	3.60
Barry Bonilla		
Mike Mussina		
21 Jason Isringhausen	1.50	.45
Bill Pulsipher		
Rico Brogna		
22 Tony Gwynn	5.00	1.50
Ken Caminiti		
Mark Newfield		
23 Tim Salmon	1.50	.45
Garret Anderson		
Jim Edmonds		
24 Moises Alou	1.50	.45
Rondell White		
Cliff Floyd		
25 Barry Larkin	2.50	.75
Reggie Sanders		
Bret Boone		
26 Jeff Bagwell	2.50	.75
Craig Biggio		
Derek Bell		
27 Frank Thomas	4.00	1.20
Robin Ventura		
Alex Fernandez		
28 John Jaha	1.50	.45
Greg Vaughn		
Kevin Seitzer		

1997 Select

The 1997 Select set was issued in two series totalling 200 cards and was distributed in hobby only six-card packs with a suggested retail price of $2.99. The 150-card first series set contains 100 common "Red" cards and 50 short-printed Blue cards. Each card featues a distinctive silver-foil treatment with either a red or blue foil accent. The red cards are twice as easy to find than the blue cards. The fronts display a color action player photo over most of the card with a small player photo at the bottom. The backs carry another player photo, player information and statistics.

	Nm-Mt	Ex-Mt
COMPLETE SET (200)	65.00	19.50
COMP. SERIES 1 (150)	40.00	12.00
COMP. HI SERIES (50)	25.00	7.50
COMMON RED (1-150)	.30	.09
COMMON BLUE (1-150)	.60	.18
COMMON (151-200)	.60	.18
1 Juan Gonzalez B	1.00	.30
2 Mo Vaughn B	.60	.18
3 Tony Gwynn R	1.00	.30
4 Manny Ramirez B	1.00	.30
5 Jose Canseco R	.75	.23
6 David Cone R	.30	.09
7 Chan Ho Park R	.30	.09
8 Frank Thomas B	1.50	.45
9 Todd Hollandsworth R	.30	.09
10 Marty Cordova R	.30	.09
11 Gary Sheffield B	.60	.18
12 John Smoltz B	1.00	.30
13 Mark Grudzielanek R	.30	.09
14 Sammy Sosa B	2.50	.75
15 Paul Molitor R	.50	.15
16 Kevin Brown R	.30	.09
17 Albert Belle B	.60	.18
18 Eric Young R	.30	.09
19 John Wetteland R	.30	.09
20 Ryan Klesko B	.60	.18
21 Joe Carter R	.30	.09
22 Alex Ochoa R	.30	.09
23 Greg Maddux B	2.50	.75
24 Roger Clemens B	3.00	.90
25 Ivan Rodriguez B	1.50	.45
26 Barry Bonds B	4.00	1.20
27 Kenny Lofton B	.60	.18
28 Javy Lopez R	.30	.09
29 Hideo Nomo B	1.50	.45
30 Rusty Greer R	.30	.09
31 Rafael Palmeiro R	.50	.15
32 Mike Piazza B	2.50	.75
33 Ryne Sandberg R	1.25	.35
34 Wade Boggs R	.50	.15
35 Jim Thome B	1.50	.45
36 Ken Caminiti B	.60	.18
37 Mark Grace R	.50	.15
38 Brian Jordan B	.60	.18
39 Craig Biggio R	.50	.15
40 Henry Rodriguez R	.30	.09
41 Dean Palmer R	.30	.09
42 Jason Kendall R	.30	.09
43 Bill Pulsipher R	.30	.09
44 Tim Salmon B	1.00	.30
45 Marc Newfield R	.30	.09
46 Pat Hentgen R	.30	.09
47 Ken Griffey Jr. B	2.50	.75
48 Paul Wilson R	.30	.09
49 Jay Buhner B	.60	.18
50 Rickey Henderson R	.75	.23
51 Jeff Bagwell B	1.00	.30
52 Cecil Fielder R	.30	.09
53 Alex Rodriguez B	2.00	.60
54 John Jaha R	.30	.09
55 Brady Anderson B	.60	.18
56 Andres Galarraga R	.30	.09
57 Raul Mondesi R	.30	.09
58 Andy Pettitte R	.50	.15
59 Roberto Alomar B	1.00	.30
60 Derek Jeter B	4.00	1.20
61 Charles Johnson R	.30	.09
62 Travis Fryman R	.30	.09
63 Chipper Jones B	1.50	.45
64 Edgar Martinez R	.50	.15
65 Bobby Bonilla R	.30	.09
66 Greg Vaughn R	.30	.09
67 Bobby Higginson R	.30	.09
68 Garret Anderson R	.30	.09
69 Chuck Knoblauch B	.60	.18
70 Jermaine Dye R	.30	.09
71 Cal Ripken B	5.00	1.50
72 Jason Giambi R	.30	.09
73 Trey Beamon R	.30	.09
74 Shawn Green R	.30	.09
75 Mark McGwire B	4.00	1.20
76 Carlos Delgado R	.30	.09
77 Jason Isringhausen R	.30	.09
78 Randy Johnson B	1.50	.45
79 Troy Percival B	.60	.18
80 Ron Gant R	.30	.09
81 Ellis Burks R	.30	.09
82 Mike Mussina B	1.00	.30
83 Todd Hundley R	.30	.09
84 Jim Edmonds R	.30	.09
85 Charles Nagy R	.30	.09
86 Dante Bichette B	.60	.18
87 Mariano Rivera R	.50	.15
88 Matt Williams B	.60	.18
89 Rondell White R	.30	.09
90 Steve Finley R	.30	.09
91 Alex Fernandez R	.30	.09
92 Barry Larkin R	.50	.15
93 Tom Goodwin R	.30	.09
94 Will Clark R	.75	.23
95 Michael Tucker R	.30	.09
96 Derek Bell R	.30	.09
97 Larry Walker R	.50	.15
98 Alan Benes R	.30	.09
99 Tom Glavine R	.50	.15
100 Darin Erstad B	.60	.18
101 Andruw Jones B	.60	.18
102 Scott Rolen R	.50	.15
103 Todd Walker B	.60	.18
104 Dmitri Young R	.30	.09
105 Vladimir Guerrero B	1.50	.45
106 Nomar Garciaparra R	1.25	.35
107 Danny Patterson R	.30	.09
108 Karim Garcia R	.30	.09
109 Todd Greene R	.30	.09
110 Ruben Rivera R	.30	.09
111 Raul Casanova R	.30	.09
112 Mike Cameron R	.30	.09
113 Bartolo Colon R	.30	.09
114 Rod Myers R	.30	.09
115 Todd Dunn R	.30	.09
116 Torii Hunter R	.30	.09
117 Jason Dickson R	.30	.09
118 Eugene Kingsale R	.30	.09
119 Rafael Medina R	.30	.09
120 Raul Ibanez R	.30	.09
121 Bobby Henley R RC	.30	.09
122 Scott Spiezio R	.30	.09
123 Bobby Smith R	.30	.09
124 J.J. Johnson R	.30	.09
125 Bubba Trammell R RC	.50	.15
126 Jeff Abbott R	.30	.09
127 Neifi Perez R	.30	.09
128 Derrek Lee R	.30	.09
129 Kevin Brown C R	.30	.09
130 Mendy Lopez R	.30	.09
131 Kevin Orie R	.30	.09
132 Ryan Jones R	.30	.09
133 Juan Encarnacion R	.30	.09
134 Jose Guillen B	.30	.09
135 Greg Norton R	.30	.09
136 Richie Sexson R	.30	.09
137 Jay Payton R	.30	.09
138 Bob Abreu R	.30	.09
139 Ron Belliard R RC	.75	.23
140 Wilton Guerrero B	.60	.18
141 Alex Rodriguez SS B	1.25	.35
142 Juan Gonzalez SS B	1.00	.30
143 Ken Caminiti SS B	.60	.18
144 Frank Thomas SS B	1.50	.45
145 Ken Griffey Jr. SS B	1.50	.45
146 John Smoltz SS B	1.00	.30
147 Mike Piazza SS B	.75	.23
148 Derek Jeter SS B	2.00	.60
149 Frank Thomas CL R	.50	.15
150 Ken Griffey Jr. CL R	.75	.23
151 Jose Cruz Jr. RC	1.50	.45
152 Moises Alou	.60	.18
153 Hideki Irabu RC	1.00	.30
154 Glendon Rusch	.60	.18
155 Ron Coomer	.60	.18
156 Jeremi Gonzalez RC	.60	.18
157 Fernando Tatis RC	2.00	.60
158 John Olerud	.60	.18
159 Rickey Henderson	.75	.23
160 Shannon Stewart	.60	.18

161 Kevin Polcovich RC .60 .18
162 Jose Rosado .60 .18
163 Ray Lankford .60 .18
164 David Justice .60 .18
165 Mark Kotsay RC 2.50 .75
166 Deivi Cruz RC 1.00 .30
167 Billy Wagner .60 .18
168 Jacob Cruz .60 .18
169 Matt Morris .30 .09
170 Brian Banks .60 .18
171 Brett Tomko .60 .18
172 Todd Helton 1.50 .45
173 Eric Young .60 .18
174 Bernie Williams 1.00 .30
175 Jeff Fassero .60 .18
176 Ryan McGuire .60 .18
177 Darryl Kile .60 .18
178 Kelvim Escobar RC 1.50 .45
179 Dave Nilsson .60 .18
180 Geronimo Berroa .60 .18
181 Livan Hernandez .60 .18
182 Tony Womack RC 1.50 .45
183 Deion Sanders 1.00 .30
184 Jeff Kent .60 .18
185 Brian Hunter .60 .18
186 Jose Malave .60 .18
187 Steve Woodard RC .60 .18
188 Brad Radke .60 .18
189 Todd Dunwoody .60 .18
190 Joey Hamilton .60 .18
191 Denny Neagle .60 .18
192 Bobby Jones .60 .18
193 Tony Clark .60 .18
194 Jaret Wright RC 2.50 .75
195 Matt Stairs .60 .18
196 Francisco Cordova .60 .18
197 Justin Thompson .60 .18
198 Pokey Reese .60 .18
199 Garrett Stephenson .60 .18
200 Carl Everett .60 .18

1997 Select Artist's Proofs

Randomly inserted in packs at the rate of one in 71 for red cards and one in 355 for blue cards, this 150-card parallel set is a holographic foil rendition of the Series 1 base set with either red or blue foil treatment and the unique Artist's Proof logo.

Nm-Mt Ex-Mt
*STARS: 5X TO 12X BASIC CARDS....

1997 Select Company

Randomly inserted one in every Select Hi Series pack, this 200-card set is a fractured parallel version of the Select base set. The difference is found in the full foil card stock with puffed ink accented highlights. The first level features 100 players from the base set with a red bordered design. The second level features the 50 players found only in the Select High Series. The final level features 50 parallel cards of top superstars utilizing a blue puffed ink border.

Nm-Mt Ex-Mt
*BLUE 1-150: .4X TO 1X BASIC
*RED 1-150: .75X TO 2X BASIC
*HI SERIES 151-200: .4X TO 1X BASIC
P121 B.Henley PROMO .50 .15

1997 Select Registered Gold

Randomly inserted in packs at the rate of one in 11 for red cards and one in 47 for blue cards, this 150-card set is parallel to the regular Select Series 1 set. The difference is found in the fractured gold foil treatment which replaces the silver foil treatment of the regular set.

Nm-Mt Ex-Mt
*STARS: 1.25X TO 3X BASIC CARDS.

1997 Select Rookie Autographs

This four-card set features color player photos of potential Rookie of the Year candidates with their autographs. Each player signed 3000 cards except for Andruw Jones who only signed 2500.

Nm-Mt Ex-Mt
1 Jose Guillen/3000 15.00 4.50
2 Wilton Guerrero/3000 8.00 2.40
3 Andruw Jones/2500 25.00 7.50
4 Todd Walker/3000 15.00 4.50

1997 Select Rookie Revolution

Randomly inserted in packs at a rate of one in 56, this 20-card set features color photos of top rookies on a micro-etched, full mylar card.

Nm-Mt Ex-Mt
COMPLETE SET (20) 100.00 30.00
1 Andruw Jones 3.00 .90
2 Derek Jeter 15.00 4.50
3 Todd Hollandsworth 2.00 .60
4 Edgar Renteria 3.00 .90
5 Jason Kendall 3.00 .90
6 Rey Ordonez 2.00 .60
7 F.P. Santangelo 2.00 .60
8 Jermaine Dye 3.00 .90
9 Alex Ochoa 2.00 .60
10 Vladimir Guerrero 6.00 1.80
11 Dmitri Young 3.00 .90
12 Todd Walker 2.00 .60
13 Scott Rolen 6.00 1.80
14 Nomar Garciaparra 10.00 3.00
15 Ruben Rivera 2.00 .60
16 Darin Erstad 3.00 .90
17 Todd Greene 2.00 .60
18 Mariano Rivera 5.00 1.50
19 Trey Beamon 2.00 .60
20 Karim Garcia 2.00 .60

1997 Select Tools of the Trade

Randomly inserted in packs at a rate of one in nine, this 25-card set matches color photos of 25 young players with 25 veteran superstars printed back-to-back on a double-fronted full silver foil card stock with gold foil stamping.

Nm-Mt Ex-Mt
COMPLETE SET (25) 120.00 36.00
*MIRROR BLUE: 2X TO 5X BASIC MIRROR
MIRROR BLUE STATED ODDS 1:240..
1 Ken Griffey Jr. 6.00 1.80
Andruw Jones
2 Greg Maddux 6.00 1.80
Andy Pettitte
3 Cal Ripken 8.00 2.40
Chipper Jones
4 Mike Piazza 6.00 1.80
Jason Kendall
5 Albert Belle 1.25 .35
Karim Garcia
6 Mo Vaughn 1.25 .35
Dmitri Young
7 Juan Gonzalez 3.00 .90
Vladimir Guerrero
8 Tony Gwynn 5.00 1.50
Jermaine Dye
9 Barry Bonds 10.00 3.00
Alex Ochoa
10 Jeff Bagwell 2.00 .60
Jason Giambi
11 Kenny Lofton 1.25 .35
Darin Erstad
12 Gary Sheffield 2.00 .60
Manny Ramirez
13 Tim Salmon 2.00 .60
Todd Hollandsworth
14 Sammy Sosa 6.00 1.80
Ruben Rivera
15 Paul Molitor 2.00 .60
George Arias
16 Jim Thome 3.00 .90
Todd Walker
17 Wade Boggs 3.00 .90
Scott Rolen
18 Ryne Sandberg 6.00 1.80
Chuck Knoblauch
19 Mark McGwire 8.00 2.40
Frank Thomas
20 Ivan Rodriguez 3.00 .90
Charles Johnson
21 Brian Jordan 1.25 .35
Rusty Greer
22 Roger Clemens 8.00 2.40
Troy Percival
23 John Smoltz 2.00 .60
Mike Mussina
24 Alex Rodriguez 6.00 1.80
Rey Ordonez
25 Derek Jeter 8.00 2.40
Nomar Garciaparra

1995 Select Certified

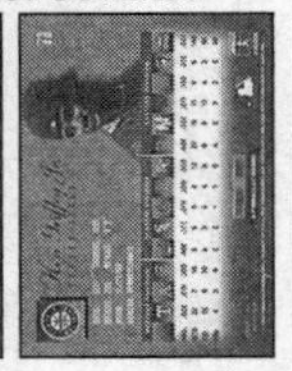

This 135-card standard-size set was issued through hobby outlets only. This product was issued in six-card packs. The cards are made with 24-point stock and are all metallic and double laminated. Rookie Cards in this set include Bobby Higginson and Hideo Nomo. Card number 18 was never printed; Cal Ripken is featured on a special card numbered 2131, which is included in the complete set of 135.

Nm-Mt Ex-Mt
COMPLETE SET (135) 40.00 12.00
1 Barry Bonds 3.00 .90
2 Reggie Sanders .25 .07
3 Terry Steinbach .25 .07
4 Eduardo Perez .25 .07
5 Frank Thomas 1.25 .35
6 Wil Cordero .25 .07
7 John Olerud .50 .15
8 Deion Sanders .75 .23
9 Mike Mussina .75 .23
10 Mo Vaughn .50 .15
11 Will Clark 1.25 .35
12 Chili Davis .50 .15
13 Jimmy Key .50 .15
14 Eddie Murray 1.25 .35
15 Bernard Gilkey .25 .07
16 David Cone .50 .15
17 Tim Salmon .75 .23
19 Steve Ontiveros .25 .07
20 Andres Galarraga .50 .15
21 Don Mattingly 3.00 .90
22 Kevin Appier .50 .15
23 Paul Molitor .75 .23
24 Edgar Martinez .75 .23
25 Andy Benes .25 .07
26 Rafael Palmeiro .75 .23
27 Barry Larkin .75 .23
28 Gary Sheffield .50 .15
29 Wally Joyner .50 .15
30 Wade Boggs .75 .23
31 Rico Brogna .25 .07
32 Eddie Murray .75 .23
3000th Hit
33 Kirby Puckett 1.25 .35
34 Bobby Bonilla .50 .15
35 Hal Morris .25 .07
36 Moises Alou .50 .15
37 Javier Lopez .50 .15
38 Chuck Knoblauch .50 .15
39 Mike Piazza 2.00 .60
40 Travis Fryman .50 .15
41 Rickey Henderson 1.25 .35
42 Jim Thome 1.25 .35
43 Carlos Baerga .25 .07
44 Dean Palmer .50 .15
45 Kirk Gibson .50 .15
46 Bret Saberhagen .50 .15
47 Cecil Fielder .50 .15
48 Manny Ramirez .75 .23
49 Derek Bell .25 .07
50 Mark McGwire 3.00 .90
51 Jim Edmonds .75 .23
52 Robin Ventura .50 .15
53 Ryan Klesko .50 .15
54 Jeff Bagwell .75 .23
55 Ozzie Smith 2.00 .60
56 Albert Belle .50 .15
57 Darren Daulton .50 .15
58 Jeff Conine .50 .15
59 Greg Maddux 2.00 .60
60 Lenny Dykstra .50 .15
61 Randy Johnson 1.25 .35
62 Fred McGriff .75 .23
63 Ray Lankford .25 .07
64 David Justice .50 .15
65 Paul O'Neill .75 .23
66 Tony Gwynn 1.50 .45
67 Matt Williams .50 .15
68 Dante Bichette .50 .15
69 Craig Biggio .75 .23
70 Ken Griffey Jr. 2.00 .60
71 J.T. Snow .50 .15
72 Cal Ripken 4.00 1.20
73 Jay Bell .50 .15
74 Joe Carter .50 .15
75 Roberto Alomar .75 .23
76 Benji Gil .25 .07
77 Ivan Rodriguez 1.25 .35
78 Raul Mondesi .50 .15
79 Cliff Floyd .50 .15
80 Eric Karros 1.25 .35
Mike Piazza
Raul Mondesi
81 Royce Clayton .25 .07
82 Billy Ashley .25 .07
83 Joey Hamilton .25 .07
84 Sammy Sosa 2.00 .60
85 Jason Bere .25 .07
86 Dennis Martinez .50 .15
87 Greg Vaughn .25 .07
88 Roger Clemens 2.50 .75
89 Larry Walker .75 .23
90 Mark Grace .75 .23
91 Kenny Lofton .50 .15
92 Carlos Perez RC .50 .15
93 Roger Cedeno .25 .07
94 Scott Ruffcorn .25 .07
95 Jim Pittsley .25 .07
96 Andy Pettitte .75 .23
97 James Baldwin .25 .07
98 Hideo Nomo RC 3.00 .90
99 Ismael Valdes .25 .07
100 Armando Benitez .50 .15
101 Jose Malave .25 .07
102 Bob Higginson RC 1.00 .30
103 LaTroy Hawkins .25 .07
104 Russ Davis .25 .07
105 Shawn Green .50 .15
106 Joe Vitiello .25 .07
107 Chipper Jones 1.25 .35
108 Shane Andrews .25 .07
109 Jose Oliva .25 .07
110 Ray Durham .50 .15
111 Jon Nunnally .25 .07
112 Alex Gonzalez .25 .07
113 Vaughn Eshelman .25 .07
114 Marty Cordova .25 .07
115 Mark Grudzielanek RC .50 .15
116 Brian L.Hunter .25 .07
117 Charles Johnson .50 .15
118 Alex Rodriguez 3.00 .90
119 David Bell .25 .07
120 Todd Hollandsworth .25 .07
121 Joe Randa .25 .07
122 Derek Jeter 3.00 .90
123 Frank Rodriguez .25 .07
124 Curtis Goodwin .25 .07
125 Bill Pulsipher .25 .07
126 John Mabry .25 .07
127 Julian Tavarez .25 .07
128 Edgardo Alfonzo .50 .15
129 Orlando Miller .25 .07
130 Juan Acevedo RC .25 .07
131 Jeff Cirillo .25 .07
132 Roberto Petagine .25 .07
133 Antonio Osuna .25 .07
134 Michael Tucker .25 .07
135 Garret Anderson .50 .15
2131 Cal Ripken TRIB 4.00 1.20

1995 Select Certified Mirror Gold

This 135-card set is a parallel to the regular issue. Pinnacle used their all-holographic foil technology on the fronts. The backs are identical to the regular issue but the words "Mirror Gold" are in the middle. These cards were inserted approximately one every five packs.

Nm-Mt Ex-Mt
*STARS: 4X TO 10X BASIC CARDS....
*ROOKIES: 5X TO 12X BASIC.........

1995 Select Certified Checklists

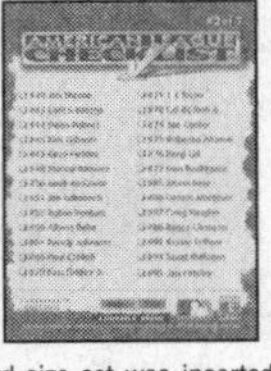

This seven-card standard-size set was inserted one per Select Certified pack. These cards were not made of the same card stock as the regular Certified cards.

Nm-Mt Ex-Mt
COMPLETE SET (7) 3.00 .90
1 Ken Griffey Jr. .50 .15
2 Frank Thomas .30 .09
3 Cal Ripken 1.00 .30
4 Jeff Bagwell .20 .06
5 Mike Piazza .50 .15
6 Barry Bonds .75 .23
7 Manny Ramirez .20 .06
Raul Mondesi

1995 Select Certified Future

This ten-card set was inserted approximately one in every 19 packs. Ten leading 1995 rookie players are included in this set. These cards were produced using Pinnacle's Dufex technology.

Nm-Mt Ex-Mt
COMPLETE SET (10) 40.00 12.00
1 Chipper Jones 5.00 1.50
2 Curtis Goodwin 1.00 .30
3 Hideo Nomo 6.00 1.80
4 Shawn Green 2.00 .60
5 Ray Durham 2.00 .60
6 Todd Hollandsworth 1.00 .30
7 Brian L.Hunter 1.00 .30
8 Carlos Delgado 2.00 .60
9 Michael Tucker UER 1.00 .30
(Front photo is Jon Nunnally)
10 Alex Rodriguez 12.00 3.60

1995 Select Certified Gold Team

This 12-card was inserted approximately one in every 41 packs. This set features some of the leading players in baseball. These cards feature double-sided all-gold-foil Dufex technology.

Nm-Mt Ex-Mt
COMPLETE SET (12) 200.00 60.00
1 Ken Griffey Jr. 20.00 6.00
2 Frank Thomas 12.00 3.60
3 Cal Ripken 40.00 12.00
4 Jeff Bagwell 8.00 2.40
5 Mike Piazza 20.00 6.00
6 Barry Bonds 30.00 9.00
7 Matt Williams 5.00 1.50
8 Don Mattingly 30.00 9.00
9 Will Clark 12.00 3.60
10 Tony Gwynn 15.00 4.50
11 Kirby Puckett 12.00 3.60
12 Jose Canseco 12.00 3.60

1995 Select Certified Potential Unlimited 1975

Cards from this 20-card set were randomly inserted into one in every 29 packs. The cards feature Pinnacle's all-foil Dufex printing technology. Only 1,975 sets were made and each card is numbered 1 of 1,975 at the bottom right.

Nm-Mt Ex-Mt
COMPLETE SET (20) 120.00 36.00
*903 CARDS: .6X TO 1.5X 1975 CARDS
ONE 903 CARD PER SEALED BOX......
STATED PRINT RUN 903 SETS..........
1 Cliff Floyd 4.00 1.20
2 Manny Ramirez 6.00 1.80
3 Raul Mondesi 4.00 1.20
4 Scott Ruffcorn 4.00 1.20
5 Billy Ashley 4.00 1.20
6 Alex Gonzalez 4.00 1.20
7 Midre Cummings 4.00 1.20
8 Charles Johnson 4.00 1.20
9 Garret Anderson 4.00 1.20
10 Hideo Nomo 15.00 4.50
11 Chipper Jones 10.00 3.00
12 Curtis Goodwin 4.00 1.20
13 Frank Rodriguez 4.00 1.20
14 Shawn Green 4.00 1.20
15 Ray Durham 4.00 1.20
16 Todd Hollandsworth 4.00 1.20
17 Brian L.Hunter 4.00 1.20
18 Carlos Delgado 4.00 1.20
19 Michael Tucker 4.00 1.20
20 Alex Rodriguez 30.00 9.00

1996 Select Certified

The 1996 Select Certified hobby only set was issued in one series totalling 144 cards. Each six-card pack carried a suggested retail price of $4.99. Printed on special 24-point silver mirror mylar card stock, the fronts feature a color player photo on a gray and black background. The backs carry another color player photo with information about his playing abilities.

Nm-Mt Ex-Mt
COMPLETE SET (144) 40.00 12.00
1 Frank Thomas 1.00 .30
2 Tino Martinez .60 .18
3 Gary Sheffield .40 .12
4 Kenny Lofton .40 .12
5 Joe Carter .40 .12
6 Alex Rodriguez 2.00 .60
7 Chipper Jones 1.00 .30
8 Roger Clemens 2.00 .60
9 Jay Bell .40 .12
10 Eddie Murray 1.00 .30
11 Will Clark 1.00 .30
12 Mike Mussina .60 .18
13 Hideo Nomo 1.00 .30
14 Andres Galarraga .40 .12
15 Marc Newfield .25 .07
16 Jason Isringhausen .40 .12
17 Randy Johnson 1.00 .30
18 Chuck Knoblauch .40 .12
19 J.T. Snow .40 .12
20 Mark McGwire 2.50 .75
21 Tony Gwynn 1.25 .35
22 Albert Belle .40 .12
23 Gregg Jefferies .25 .07
24 Reggie Sanders .25 .07
25 Bernie Williams .60 .18
26 Ray Lankford .25 .07
27 Johnny Damon .60 .18
28 Ryne Sandberg 1.50 .45
29 Rondell White .40 .12
30 Mike Piazza 1.50 .45
31 Barry Bonds 2.50 .75
32 Greg Maddux 1.50 .45
33 Craig Biggio .60 .18
34 John Valentin .25 .07
35 Ivan Rodriguez 1.00 .30
36 Rico Brogna .25 .07
37 Tim Salmon .60 .18
38 Sterling Hitchcock .25 .07
39 Charles Johnson .40 .12
40 Travis Fryman .40 .12
41 Barry Larkin .60 .18
42 Tom Glavine .60 .18
43 Marty Cordova .25 .07
44 Shawn Green .40 .12
45 Ben McDonald .25 .07
46 Robin Ventura .40 .12
47 Ken Griffey Jr. 1.50 .45
48 Orlando Merced .25 .07
49 Paul O'Neill .60 .18
50 Ozzie Smith 1.50 .45
51 Manny Ramirez .60 .18
52 Ismael Valdes .25 .07
53 Cal Ripken 3.00 .90
54 Jeff Bagwell .60 .18
55 Greg Vaughn .25 .07
56 Juan Gonzalez .60 .18
57 Raul Mondesi .40 .12
58 Carlos Baerga .25 .07
59 Sammy Sosa 1.50 .45
60 Mike Kelly .25 .07
61 Edgar Martinez .60 .18
62 Kirby Puckett 1.00 .30
63 Cecil Fielder .40 .12
64 David Cone .40 .12
65 Moises Alou .40 .12
66 Fred McGriff .60 .18
67 Mo Vaughn .40 .12
68 Edgardo Alfonzo .25 .07
69 Jim Thome 1.00 .30
70 Rickey Henderson 1.00 .30
71 Dante Bichette .40 .12
72 Lenny Dykstra .40 .12
73 Benji Gil .25 .07
74 Wade Boggs .60 .18
75 Jim Edmonds .40 .12
76 Michael Tucker .25 .07
77 Carlos Delgado .40 .12

78 Butch Huskey .25 .07
79 Billy Ashley .25 .07
80 Dean Palmer .40 .12
81 Paul Molitor .60 .18
82 Ryan Klesko .40 .12
83 Brian L.Hunter .25 .07
84 Jay Buhner .40 .12
85 Larry Walker .60 .18
86 Mike Bordick .25 .07
87 Matt Williams .40 .12
88 Jack McDowell .25 .07
89 Hal Morris .25 .07
90 Brian Jordan .40 .12
91 Andy Pettitte .60 .18
92 Melvin Nieves .25 .07
93 Pedro Martinez 1.00 .30
94 Mark Grace .60 .18
95 Garret Anderson .40 .12
96 Andre Dawson .40 .12
97 Ray Durham .40 .12
98 Jose Canseco 1.00 .30
99 Roberto Alomar .60 .18
100 Derek Jeter 2.50 .75
101 Alan Benes .25 .07
102 Karim Garcia .25 .07
103 Robin Jennings .25 .07
104 Bob Abreu .40 .12
105 Sal Fasano UER .25 .07
(name on front is Livan Hernandez)
105A Sal Fasano
Correct Name on Front of Card
106 Steve Gibralter .25 .07
107 Jermaine Dye .40 .12
108 Jason Kendall .40 .12
109 Mike Grace RC .25 .07
110 Jason Schmidt .60 .18
111 Paul Wilson .25 .07
112 Rey Ordonez .25 .07
113 Wilton Guerrero RC .40 .12
114 Brooks Kieschnick .25 .07
115 George Arias .25 .07
116 O.Fernandez RC .25 .07
117 Todd Hollandsworth .25 .07
118 John Wasdin .25 .07
119 Eric Owens .25 .07
120 Chan Ho Park .40 .12
121 Mark Loretta .40 .12
122 Richard Hidalgo .25 .07
123 Jeff Suppan .25 .07
124 Jim Pittsley .25 .07
125 LaTroy Hawkins .25 .07
126 Chris Snopek .25 .07
127 Justin Thompson .25 .07
128 Jay Powell .25 .07
129 Alex Ochoa .25 .07
130 Felipe Crespo .25 .07
131 Matt Lawton RC .60 .18
132 Jimmy Haynes .25 .07
133 Terrell Wade .25 .07
134 Ruben Rivera .25 .07
135 Frank Thomas PP .60 .18
136 Ken Griffey Jr. PP 1.00 .30
137 Greg Maddux PP 1.00 .30
138 Mike Piazza PP 1.00 .30
139 Cal Ripken PP 1.50 .45
140 Albert Belle PP .40 .12
141 Mo Vaughn PP .25 .07
142 Chipper Jones PP .60 .18
143 Hideo Nomo PP .60 .18
144 Ryan Klesko PP .25 .07

1996 Select Certified Artist's Proofs

Randomly inserted in packs at a rate of one in 18, this 144-card set is parallel to the base set with only 500 sets being produced. The design is similar to the regular set with the exception of a holographic gold foil Artist's proof stamp on the front.

Nm-Mt Ex-Mt
*STARS: 2.5X TO 6X BASIC CARDS...

1996 Select Certified Certified Blue

Randomly inserted in packs at a rate of one in 50, this 144-card set is parallel to the base set with only 180 sets being produced. This set is a blue all-foil rendition of the base set.

Nm-Mt Ex-Mt
*STARS: 5X TO 12X BASIC CARDS....
*ROOKIES: 2.5X TO 6X BASIC CARDS

1996 Select Certified Certified Red

Randomly inserted in packs at a rate of one in five, this 144-card set is parallel to the base set with only 1,800 sets being produced. This set is a red all-foil rendition of the base set.

Nm-Mt Ex-Mt
*STARS: 1X TO 2.5X BASIC CARDS...

1996 Select Certified Mirror Blue

Randomly inserted in packs at a rate of one in 200, this 144-card set is parallel to the base set with only 45 sets being produced. This set is a blue holographic foil rendition of the base set. No set price has been provided due to scarcity.

Nm-Mt Ex-Mt
*STARS: 25X TO 60X BASIC CARDS..
*PP STARS 135-144: 20X TO 50X BASIC
*ROOKIES: 12.5X TO 30X BASIC........

1996 Select Certified Mirror Gold

Randomly inserted in packs at a rate of one in 300, this 144-card set is parallel to the base set with only 30 sets being produced. This set is a gold holographic foil rendition of the base set. No set price has been provided due to scarcity.

Nm-Mt Ex-Mt
*STARS: 125X TO 250X BASIC CARDS
*PP STARS 135-144: 125X TO 250X BASIC
*ROOKIES: 60X TO 120X BASIC CARDS

1996 Select Certified Mirror Red

Randomly inserted in packs at a rate of one in 100, this 144-card set is parallel to the base set with only 90 sets being produced. This set is a red holographic foil rendition of the base set. No set price has been provided due to scarcity.

Nm-Mt Ex-Mt
*STARS: 15X TO 40X BASIC CARDS..
*ROOKIES: 8X TO 20X BASIC CARDS

1996 Select Certified Interleague Preview

Randomly inserted in packs at a rate of one in 42, this 25-card set gets ready for the start of interleague play in the 1997 season. Printed on Silver Prime Frost foil stock with gold lettering, the fronts feature color player cutouts of two opposing players. The backs carry another color cutout of the two players with information as to why they are a great matchup.

Nm-Mt Ex-Mt
COMPLETE SET (25) 200.00 60.00
1 Ken Griffey Jr. 8.00 2.40
Hideo Nomo
2 Greg Maddux 8.00 2.40
Mo Vaughn
3 Frank Thomas 8.00 2.40
Sammy Sosa
4 Mike Piazza 8.00 2.40
Jim Edmonds
5 Ryan Klesko 10.00 3.00
Roger Clemens
6 Derek Jeter 12.00 3.60
Rey Ordonez
7 Johnny Damon 3.00 .90
Ray Lankford
8 Manny Ramirez 3.00 .90
Reggie Sanders
9 Barry Bonds 12.00 3.60
Jay Buhner
10 Jason Isringhausen 3.00 .90
Wade Boggs
11 David Cone 5.00 1.50
Chipper Jones
12 Jeff Bagwell 3.00 .90
Will Clark
13 Tony Gwynn 6.00 1.80
Randy Johnson
14 Cal Ripken 15.00 4.50
Tom Glavine
15 Kirby Puckett 5.00 1.50
Andy Benes
16 Gary Sheffield 3.00 .90
Mike Mussina
17 Raul Mondesi 3.00 .90
Tim Salmon
18 Rondell White 2.00 .60
Carlos Delgado
19 Cecil Fielder 8.00 2.40
Ryne Sandberg
20 Kenny Lofton 2.00 .60
Brian L.Hunter
21 Paul Wilson 3.00 .90
Paul O'Neill
22 Ismael Valdes 3.00 .90
Edgar Martinez
23 Matt Williams 12.00 3.60
Mark McGwire
24 Albert Belle 3.00 .90
Barry Larkin
25 Brady Anderson 2.00 .60
Marquis Grissom
S7 Johnny Damon
Ray Lankford SAMPLE

1996 Select Certified Select Few

Randomly inserted in packs at a rate of one in 60, this 18-card set honors superstar athletes with unmatched playing field talents. Utilizing the all-new Dot Matrix hologram technology, the fronts feature color action player cutouts. Several of the cards were erroneously printed without player's name on the front. These uncorrected errors are worth the same as the corrected cards.

Nm-Mt Ex-Mt
COMPLETE SET (18) 100.00 30.00
1 Sammy Sosa 8.00 2.40
2 Derek Jeter 12.00 3.60
3 Ken Griffey Jr. 8.00 2.40
4 Albert Belle 2.00 .60
5 Cal Ripken 15.00 4.50
6 Greg Maddux 8.00 2.40
7 Frank Thomas 5.00 1.50
8 Mo Vaughn 2.00 .60
9 Chipper Jones 5.00 1.50
10 Mike Piazza 8.00 2.40
11 Ryan Klesko 2.00 .60
12 Hideo Nomo 5.00 1.50
13 Alan Benes 1.25 .35
14 Manny Ramirez 3.00 .90
15 Gary Sheffield 2.00 .60
16 Barry Bonds 12.00 3.60
17 Matt Williams 2.00 .60
18 Johnny Damon 3.00 .90

2000 SkyBox

The 2000 SkyBox product was released in late May, 2000 as a 250-card set that featured 200-player cards, and 50-short printed prospect cards. The set also includes a horizontal parallel version of each of the 50 prospect cards (1:8). The last ten cards in the set feature dual player cards of some of the hottest prospects in baseball. The horizontal parallel version of these ten cards were inserted at one in 12 packs. Each pack contained 10-cards and carried a suggested retail price of 2.99.

Nm-Mt Ex-Mt
COMP.MASTER SET (300) 120.00 36.00
COMP.SET w/o SP's (250) 40.00 12.00
COMMON CARD (1-200) .30 .09
COMMON (201S-240S) 2.00 .60
COMMON (241S-250S) .75 .23
1 Cal Ripken 2.50 .75
2 Ivan Rodriguez .75 .23
3 Chipper Jones .75 .23
4 Dean Palmer .30 .09
5 Devon White .30 .09
6 Ugueth Urbina .30 .09
7 Doug Glanville .30 .09
8 Damian Jackson .30 .09
9 Jose Canseco .75 .23
10 Billy Koch .30 .09
11 Brady Anderson .30 .09
12 Vladimir Guerrero .75 .23
13 Dan Wilson .30 .09
14 Kevin Brown .50 .15
15 Eddie Taubensee .30 .09
16 Jose Lima .30 .09
17 Greg Maddux 1.25 .35
18 Manny Ramirez .50 .15
19 Brad Fullmer .30 .09
20 Ron Gant .30 .09
21 Edgar Martinez .50 .15
22 Pokey Reese .30 .09
23 Jason Varitek .50 .15
24 Neifi Perez .30 .09
25 Shane Reynolds .30 .09
26 Robin Ventura .50 .15
27 Scott Rolen .75 .23
28 Trevor Hoffman .30 .09
29 John Valentin .30 .09
30 Shannon Stewart .30 .09
31 Troy Glaus .30 .09
32 Kerry Wood .75 .23
33 Jim Thome .75 .23
34 Rafael Roque .30 .09
35 Tino Martinez .50 .15
36 Jeffrey Hammonds .30 .09
37 Orlando Hernandez .30 .09
38 Kris Benson .30 .09
39 Fred McGriff .50 .15
40 Brian Jordan .30 .09
41 Trot Nixon .30 .09
42 Matt Clement .30 .09
43 Ray Durham .30 .09
44 Johnny Damon .50 .15
45 Todd Hollandsworth .30 .09
46 Edgardo Alfonzo .30 .09
47 Tim Hudson .30 .09
48 Tony Gwynn 1.00 .30
49 Barry Bonds 2.00 .60
50 Andruw Jones .30 .09
51 Pedro Martinez .75 .23
52 Mike Hampton .30 .09
53 Miguel Tejada .30 .09
54 Kevin Young .30 .09
55 J.T. Snow .30 .09
56 Carlos Delgado .30 .09
57 Bobby Howry .30 .09
58 Andres Galarraga .30 .09
59 Paul Konerko .30 .09
60 Mike Cameron .30 .09
61 Jeremy Giambi .30 .09
62 Todd Hundley .30 .09
63 Al Leiter .30 .09
64 Matt Stairs .30 .09
65 Edgar Renteria .30 .09
66 Jeff Kent .30 .09
67 John Wetteland .30 .09
68 Nomar Garciaparra 1.25 .35
69 Jeff Weaver .30 .09
70 Matt Williams .30 .09
71 Kyle Farnsworth .30 .09
72 Brad Radke .30 .09
73 Eric Chavez .30 .09
74 J.D. Drew .30 .09
75 Steve Finley .30 .09
76 Pete Harnisch .30 .09
77 Chad Kreuter .30 .09
78 Todd Pratt .30 .09
79 John Jaha .30 .09
80 Armando Rios .30 .09
81 Luis Gonzalez .30 .09
82 Ryan Minor .30 .09
83 Juan Gonzalez .50 .15
84 Rickey Henderson .75 .23
85 Jason Giambi .30 .09
86 Shawn Estes .30 .09
87 Chad Curtis .30 .09
88 Jeff Cirillo .30 .09
89 Juan Encarnacion .30 .09
90 Tony Womack .30 .09
91 Mike Mussina .50 .15
92 Jeff Bagwell .50 .15
93 Rey Ordonez .30 .09
94 Joe McEwing .30 .09
95 Robb Nen .30 .09
96 Will Clark .75 .23
97 Chris Singleton .30 .09
98 Jason Kendall .30 .09
99 Ken Griffey Jr. 1.25 .35
100 Rusty Greer .30 .09
101 Charles Johnson .30 .09
102 Carlos Lee .30 .09
103 Brad Ausmus .30 .09
104 Preston Wilson .30 .09
105 Ronnie Belliard .30 .09
106 Mike Lieberthal .30 .09
107 Alex Rodriguez 1.25 .35
108 Jay Bell .30 .09
109 Frank Thomas .75 .23
110 Adrian Beltre .50 .15
111 Ron Coomer .30 .09
112 Ben Grieve .30 .09
113 Darryl Kile .30 .09
114 Erubiel Durazo .30 .09
115 Magglio Ordonez .30 .09
116 Gary Sheffield .30 .09
117 Joe Mays .30 .09
118 Fernando Tatis .30 .09
119 David Wells .30 .09
120 Tim Salmon .50 .15
121 Troy O'Leary .30 .09
122 Roberto Alomar .50 .15
123 Damion Easley .30 .09
124 Brant Brown .30 .09
125 Carlos Beltran .50 .15
126 Eric Karros .30 .09
127 Geoff Jenkins .30 .09
128 Roger Clemens 1.50 .45
129 Warren Morris .30 .09
130 Eric Owens .30 .09
131 Jose Cruz Jr. .30 .09
132 Mo Vaughn .30 .09
133 Eric Young .30 .09
134 Kenny Lofton .30 .09
135 Marquis Grissom .30 .09
136 A.J. Burnett .30 .09
137 Bernie Williams .50 .15
138 Javy Lopez .30 .09
139 Jose Offerman .30 .09
140 Sean Casey .30 .09
141 Alex Gonzalez .30 .09
142 Carlos Febles .30 .09
143 Mike Piazza 1.25 .35
144 Curt Schilling .30 .09
145 Ben Davis .30 .09
146 Rafael Palmeiro .50 .15
147 Scott Williamson .30 .09
148 Darin Erstad .30 .09
149 Joe Girardi .30 .09
150 Gerald Williams .30 .09
151 Richie Sexson .30 .09
152 Corey Koskie .30 .09
153 Paul O'Neill .50 .15
154 Chad Hermansen .30 .09
155 Randy Johnson .75 .23
156 Henry Rodriguez .30 .09
157 Bartolo Colon .30 .09
158 Tony Clark .30 .09
159 Mike Lowell .30 .09
160 Moises Alou .30 .09
161 Todd Walker .30 .09
162 Mariano Rivera .50 .15
163 Mark McGwire 2.00 .60
164 Roberto Hernandez .30 .09
165 Larry Walker .50 .15
166 Albert Belle .30 .09
167 Barry Larkin .50 .15
168 Rolando Arrojo .30 .09
169 Mark Kotsay .30 .09
170 Ken Caminiti .30 .09
171 Dermal Brown .30 .09
172 Michael Barrett .30 .09
173 Jay Buhner .30 .09
174 Ruben Mateo .30 .09
175 Jim Edmonds .30 .09
176 Sammy Sosa 1.25 .35
177 Omar Vizquel .50 .15
178 Todd Helton .50 .15
179 Kevin Barker .30 .09
180 Derek Jeter 2.00 .60
181 Brian Giles .30 .09
182 Greg Vaughn .30 .09
183 Roy Halladay .30 .09
184 Tom Glavine .50 .15
185 Craig Biggio .50 .15
186 Jose Vidro .30 .09
187 Andy Ashby .30 .09
188 Freddy Garcia .30 .09
189 Garret Anderson .30 .09
190 Mark Grace .50 .15
191 Travis Fryman .30 .09
192 Jeromy Burnitz .30 .09
193 Jacque Jones .30 .09
194 David Cone .30 .09
195 Ryan Rupe .30 .09
196 John Smoltz .50 .15
197 Daryle Ward .30 .09
198 Rondell White .30 .09
199 Bobby Abreu .30 .09
200 Justin Thompson .30 .09
201 Norm Hutchins .30 .09
201S Norm Hutchins SP 2.00 .60
202 Ramon Ortiz .30 .09
202S Ramon Ortiz SP 2.00 .60
203 Dan Wheeler .30 .09
203S Dan Wheeler SP 2.00 .60
204 Matt Riley .30 .09
204S Matt Riley SP 2.00 .60
205 Steve Lomasney .30 .09
205S Steve Lomasney SP 2.00 .60
206 Chad Meyers .30 .09
206S Chad Meyers SP 2.00 .60
207 Gary Glover RC .50 .15
207S Gary Glover SP 2.00 .60
208 Joe Crede .30 .09
208S Joe Crede SP 2.00 .60
209 Kip Wells .30 .09
209S Kip Wells SP 2.00 .60
210 Travis Dawkins .30 .09
210S Travis Dawkins SP 2.00 .60
211 Denny Stark RC .50 .15
211S Denny Stark SP 2.00 .60
212 Ben Petrick .30 .09
212S Ben Petrick SP 2.00 .60
213 Eric Munson .30 .09
213S Eric Munson SP 2.00 .60
214 Josh Beckett .50 .15
214S Josh Beckett SP 2.50 .75
215 Pablo Ozuna .30 .09
215S Pablo Ozuna SP 2.00 .60
216 Brad Penny .30 .09
216S Brad Penny SP 2.00 .60
217 Julio Ramirez .30 .09
217S Julio Ramirez SP 2.00 .60
218 Danny Peoples .30 .09
218S Danny Peoples SP 2.00 .60
219 W.Rodriguez RC .50 .15
219S W.Rodriguez SP 2.00 .60
220 Julio Lugo .30 .09
220S Julio Lugo SP 2.00 .60
221 Mark Quinn .30 .09
221S Mark Quinn SP 2.00 .60
222 Eric Gagne 1.25 .35
222S Eric Gagne SP 6.00 1.80
223 Chad Green .30 .09
223S Chad Green SP 2.00 .60
224 Tony Armas Jr. .30 .09
224S Tony Armas Jr. SP 2.00 .60
225 Milton Bradley .30 .09
225S Milton Bradley SP 2.00 .60
226 Rob Bell .30 .09
226S Rob Bell SP 2.00 .60
227 Alfonso Soriano .75 .23
227S Alfonso Soriano SP 4.00 1.20
228 Wily Pena .30 .09
228S Wily Pena SP 2.00 .60
229 Nick Johnson .30 .09
229S Nick Johnson SP 2.00 .60
230 Ed Yarnall .30 .09
230S Ed Yarnall SP 2.00 .60
231 Ryan Bradley .30 .09
231S Ryan Bradley SP 2.00 .60
232 Adam Piatt .30 .09
232S Adam Piatt SP 2.00 .60
233 Chad Harville .30 .09
233S Chad Harville SP 2.00 .60
234 Alex Sanchez .30 .09
234S Alex Sanchez SP 2.00 .60
235 Michael Coleman .30 .09
235S Michael Coleman SP 2.00 .60
236 Pat Burrell .30 .09
236S Pat Burrell SP 2.00 .60
237 Wascar Serrano RC .50 .15
237S Wascar Serrano SP 2.00 .60
238 Rick Ankiel .30 .09
238S Rick Ankiel SP 2.00 .60
239 Mike Lamb RC .50 .15
239S Mike Lamb SP 2.00 .60
240 Vernon Wells .30 .09
240S Vernon Wells SP 2.00 .60
241 Jorge Toca .30 .09
Geofrey Tomlinson
241S Jorge Toca .75 .23
Geofrey Tomlinson SP
242 Josh Phelps RC .75 .23
Shea Hillenbrand
242S Josh Phelps 2.00 .60
Shea Hillenbrand SP
243 Aaron Myette .30 .09
Doug Davis
243S Aaron Myette .75 .23
Doug Davis SP
244 Brett Laxton .30 .09
Rob Ramsay
244S Brett Laxton .75 .23
Rob Ramsay SP
245 B.J. Ryan .30 .09
Corey Lee
245S B.J.Ryan .75 .23
Corey Lee SP
246 Chris Haas .30 .09
Wilton Veras
246S Chris Haas .75 .23
Wilton Veras SP
247 Jimmy Anderson .30 .09
Kyle Peterson
247S Jimmy Anderson .75 .23
Kyle Peterson SP
248 Jason Dewey .30 .09
Giuseppe Chiaramonte
248S Jason Dewey .75 .23
Giuseppe Chiaramonte SP
249 Guillermo Mota .30 .09
Orber Moreno
249S Guillermo Mota .75 .23
Orber Moreno SP
250 Julio Zuleta RC .50 .15
Steve Cox
250S Julio Zuleta .75 .23
Steve Cox SP

2000 SkyBox Star Rubies

Randomly inserted into packs at one in 12, this set parallels the 250-card base issued Skybox set. Card fronts feature red foil. Card backs carry a "SR" prefix.

Nm-Mt Ex-Mt
*STARS: 4X TO 10X BASIC CARDS....
*ROOKIES: 2X TO 5X BASIC VERTICAL

2000 SkyBox Star Rubies Extreme

Randomly inserted into packs, this set parallels the 250-card base issued Skybox set. There were 50 serial numbered sets produced. Card fronts feature red foil. Card backs carry a "SRE" prefix.

Nm-Mt Ex-Mt
*STARS: 15X TO 40X BASIC CARDS..
*ROOKIES: 6X TO 15X BASIC CARDS

2000 SkyBox Autographics

Randomly inserted in numerous Fleer/SkyBox brands insert set features autographed cards of a wide array of major league veterans and youngsters. Stated odds per brand are as follows: Dominion 1:144, E-X 1:24, Impact 1:216, Metal 1:96 and SkyBox 1:72.

Nm-Mt Ex-Mt
*PURPLE FOIL: 1X TO 2.5X BASIC.....
PURPLE RANDOM IN SKYBOX PRODUCTS
PURPLE STATED PRINT RUN 50 #'d SETS
1 Bobby Abreu EX-IM-MT......... 15.00 4.50
2 Chad Allen MT................. 10.00 3.00
3 Moises Alou EX................ 15.00 4.50
4 Marlon Anderson IM-MT 10.00 3.00
5 Rick Ankiel.................... 15.00 4.50
DM-EX-IM-MT-SB
6 Glen Barker MT................ 10.00 3.00
7 Michael Barrett EX-SB 10.00 3.00
8 Josh Beckett EX-SB 25.00 7.50
9 Rob Bell EX-IM-MT-SB 10.00 3.00
10 Mark Bellhorn MT............ 50.00 15.00
11 Carlos Beltran EX-IM 40.00 12.00
12 Adrian Beltre EX-SB 25.00 7.50
13 Peter Bergeron................ 10.00 3.00
DM-MT-SB
14 Lance Berkman MT-SB 25.00 7.50
15 Wade Boggs.................. 40.00 12.00
DM-EX-IM-MT
16 Barry Bonds.................. 250.00 75.00
DM-EX-IM-MT
17 Kent Bottenfield EX-MT........ 10.00 3.00
18 Milton Bradley EX-IM.......... 15.00 4.50
19 Rico Brogna SB 10.00 3.00
20 Pat Burrell.................... 15.00 4.50
DM-EX-IM-MT-SB
21 Orlando Cabrera IM-SB........ 15.00 4.50
22 Miguel Cairo DM-MT 10.00 3.00
23 Mike Cameron................ 15.00 4.50
DM-MT-SB
24 Chris Carpenter................ 10.00 3.00
EX-IM-MT
25 Sean Casey EX-IM 15.00 4.50
26 Roger Cedeno MT-SB 10.00 3.00
27 Eric Chavez EX-SB 15.00 4.50
28 Bruce Chen SB................. 10.00 3.00
29 Will Clark EX.................. 40.00 12.00
30 Johnny Damon EX-SB 25.00 7.50
31 Mike Darr EX-MT 10.00 3.00
32 Ben Davis EX-DM-SB........... 10.00 3.00
33 Russ Davis EX-DM.............. 10.00 3.00
34 Carlos Delgado EX-IM......... 25.00 7.50
35 Jason Dewey EX-SB............ 10.00 3.00
36 Einar Diaz DM-MT.............. 10.00 3.00
37 Octavio Dotel EX-SB 10.00 3.00
38 J.D. Drew..................... 25.00 7.50
EX-IM-MT-SB
39 Erubiel Durazo MT-SB......... 15.00 4.50
40 Ray Durham EX-IM-MT 15.00 4.50
41 Damion Easley EX-MT 10.00 3.00
42 Scott Elarton DM-MT 10.00 3.00
43 Kelvim Escobar EX-IM 10.00 3.00
44 Carlos Febles EX............... 10.00 3.00
45 Freddy Garcia EX............. 15.00 4.50
46 Jason Giambi SB.............. 25.00 7.50
47 Jeremy Giambi................ 10.00 3.00
DM-EX-MT
48 Doug Glanville MT-SB......... 10.00 3.00
49 Troy Glaus SB................ 15.00 4.50
50 Alex Gonzalez SB............. 10.00 3.00
51 Shawn Green MT-SB........... 15.00 4.50
52 Todd Greene DM-EX 10.00 3.00
53 Jason Grilli EX-SB............ 10.00 3.00
54 Vladimir Guerrero 40.00 12.00
DM-EX-IM
55 Tony Gwynn.................. 50.00 15.00
DM-EX-IM-SB
56 Jerry Hairston Jr. 10.00 3.00
EX-IM-MT
57 Mike Hampton EX-SB 15.00 4.50
58 Todd Helton EX-IM............ 25.00 7.50
59 Trevor Hoffman EX............ 25.00 7.50
60 Bobby Howry DM-MT........... 10.00 3.00
61 Tim Hudson DM-EX-SB 25.00 7.50
62 Norm Hutchins MT-SB.......... 10.00 3.00
63 John Jaha EX-SB.............. 10.00 3.00
64 Derek Jeter EX-SB 120.00 36.00
65 D'Angelo Jimenez 10.00 3.00
EX-SB
66 Nick Johnson IM.............. 15.00 4.50
67 Russ Johnson................ 80.00 24.00
DM-EX-MT-SB
68 Andruw Jones DM-SB 15.00 4.50
69 Jacque Jones DM-MT.......... 15.00 4.50
70 Gabe Kapler MT-SB............ 10.00 3.00
71 Jason Kendall................ 15.00 4.50
EX-IM-SB
72 Adam Kennedy EX-SB.......... 10.00 3.00
73 Cesar King EX-MT-SB.......... 10.00 3.00
74 Paul Konerko EX-SB 15.00 4.50
75 Mark Kotsay................... 15.00 4.50
EX-IM-MT-SB
76 Ray Lankford EX............... 10.00 3.00
77 Jason LaRue DM-EX........... 10.00 3.00
78 Matt Lawton DM-EX............ 10.00 3.00
79 Carlos Lee EX-SB.............. 15.00 4.50
80 Mike Lieberthal EX-SB 15.00 4.50
81 Cole Liniak EX-IM-MT.......... 10.00 3.00
82 Steve Lomasney EX-SB 10.00 3.00
83 Jose Macias EX-IM 10.00 3.00
84 Greg Maddux.................. 80.00 24.00
DM-EX-MT-SB-IM
85 Edgar Martinez EX-SB......... 40.00 12.00
86 Pedro Martinez............. 100.00 30.00
DM-EX-MT
87 Ruben Mateo 10.00 3.00
EX-IM-MT
88 Gary Matthews Jr. EX 10.00 3.00
89 Aaron McNeal EX-SB 10.00 3.00
90 Kevin Millwood SB............ 15.00 4.50
91 Raul Mondesi EX-SB.......... 15.00 4.50
92 Orber Moreno EX-IM 10.00 3.00
93 Warren Morris EX-MT.......... 10.00 3.00
94 Eric Munson EX-IM............ 10.00 3.00
95 Heath Murray EX-MT 10.00 3.00
96 Mike Mussina EX............... 25.00 7.50
97 Joe Nathan..................... 15.00 4.50
EX-IM-MT-SB
98 Magglio Ordonez SB 15.00 4.50
99 Eric Owens SB.................. 10.00 3.00
100 Rafael Palmeiro.............. 40.00 12.00
EX-SB
101 Jim Parque EX-MT............. 10.00 3.00
102 Angel Pena.................... 10.00 3.00
EX-IM-MT-SB
103 Adam Piatt IM.................. 10.00 3.00
104 Wily Pena EX-SB.............. 25.00 7.50
105 Pokey Reese DM-EX 15.00 4.50
106 Matt Riley EX-IM.............. 15.00 4.50
107 Cal Ripken................... 120.00 36.00
EX-IM-MT-SB
108 Alex Rodriguez............... 100.00 30.00
DM-EX-IM-MT-SB
109 Scott Rolen EX-IM-SB 40.00 12.00
110 Jimmy Rollins.................. 15.00 4.50
EX-IM-SB
111 Ryan Rupe DM-MT............ 10.00 3.00
112 B.J. Ryan EX-IM-SB........... 10.00 3.00
113 Tim Salmon SB................ 25.00 7.50
114 Randall Simon EX-MT......... 10.00 3.00
115 Chris Singleton 10.00 3.00
EX-MT-SB
116 J.T. Snow DM-SB.............. 15.00 4.50
117 Alfonso Soriano 40.00 12.00
EX-IM
118 Shannon Stewart EX 15.00 4.50
119 Mike Sweeney.................. 15.00 4.50
EX-MT-SB
120 Miguel Tejada EX.............. 15.00 4.50
121 Frank Thomas EX-IM 40.00 12.00
122 Wilton Veras 10.00 3.00
EX-IM-MT
123 Jose Vidro DM-SB 10.00 3.00
124 Billy Wagner EX-IM........... 25.00 7.50
125 Jeff Weaver EX-IM............ 15.00 4.50
126 Rondell White EX-SB 15.00 4.50
127 Scott Williamson.............. 10.00 3.00
EX-IM-MT
128 Randy Wolf EX-MT 15.00 4.50
129 Tony Womack 10.00 3.00
DM-MT
130 Jaret Wright EX-SB........... 10.00 3.00
131 Ed Yarnall DM-EX.............. 10.00 3.00
132 Kevin Young DM-EX............ 10.00 3.00

2000 SkyBox E-Ticket

Randomly inserted into packs at one in four, this 15-card insert features players that are Hall of Fame bound. Card backs carry an "ET" prefix.

Nm-Mt Ex-Mt
COMPLETE SET (15).............. 20.00 6.00
*STAR RUBY: 8X TO 20X BASIC E-TICKET
STAR RUBIES: RANDOM IN HOBBY PACKS
STAR RUBIES PR.RUN 100 SERIAL #'d SETS
ET1 Alex Rodriguez.............. 1.50 .45
ET2 Derek Jeter................. 2.50 .75
ET3 Nomar Garciaparra.......... 1.50 .45
ET4 Cal Ripken.................. 3.00 .90
ET5 Sean Casey .... .40 .12
ET6 Mark McGwire .... 2.50 .75
ET7 Sammy Sosa................. 1.50 .45
ET8 Ken Griffey Jr.............. 1.50 .45
ET9 Tony Gwynn................. 1.25 .35
ET10 Pedro Martinez............ 1.00 .30
ET11 Chipper Jones............. 1.00 .30
ET12 Vladimir Guerrero .... 1.00 .30
ET13 Roger Clemens .... 2.00 .60
ET14 Mike Piazza .... 1.50 .45
ET15 Randy Johnson............. 1.00 .30

2000 SkyBox Genuine Coverage

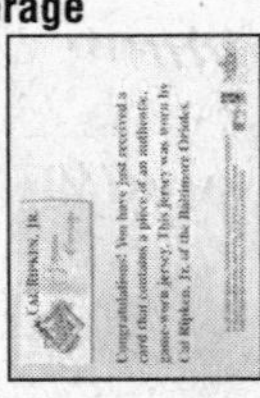

This insert features game-used jersey cards of 10 of the major league's top athletes. All cards are unnumbered and checklisted below alphabetically by player name. The set was split into two five card groups for hobby and retail distribution. The five "common" cards - tagged with an "HR" in the checklist below - were distributed in both hobby and retail packs at a rate of 1:399. The five "hobby-only" cards - tagged with an "H" in the checklist below - were seeded hobby packs at a rate of 1:144. In addition, Cal Ripken and Alex Rodriguez each signed 20 serial numbered copies of their jersey cards. These rare cards were seeded exclusively into hobby packs and are listed at the end of the checklist.

Nm-Mt Ex-Mt
AUTOS RANDOM INSERTS IN HOBBY
AU PRINT RUN 20 SERIAL #'d SETS .
NO AU PRICING DUE TO SCARCITY...
1 Jose Canseco H 15.00 4.50
2 J.D. Drew H 10.00 3.00
3 Troy Glaus HR.................. 10.00 3.00
4 Manny Ramirez H 15.00 4.50
5 Cal Ripken HR.................. 40.00 12.00
6 Alex Rodriguez HR............. 25.00 7.50
7 Ivan Rodriguez H 15.00 4.50
8 Frank Thomas H................ 15.00 4.50
9 Robin Ventura HR 10.00 3.00
10 Matt Williams HR.............. 10.00 3.00
AU1 Cal Ripken AU/20 ....
AU2 Alex Rodriguez AU 20 ....

2000 SkyBox Higher Level

Randomly inserted into packs at one in 24, this insert features 10 players that take their game to the next level. Card backs carry a "HL" prefix.

Nm-Mt Ex-Mt
COMPLETE SET (10)............... 50.00 15.00
*STAR RUBIES: 5X TO 12X BASIC HIGH.LEVEL
STAR RUBIES: RANDOM IN HOBBY PACKS
STAR RUBIES PRINT RUN 50 SERIAL #'d SETS
HL1 Cal Ripken 10.00 3.00
HL2 Derek Jeter 8.00 2.40
HL3 Nomar Garciaparra............ 5.00 1.50
HL4 Chipper Jones .... 3.00 .90
HL5 Mike Piazza 5.00 1.50
HL6 Ivan Rodriguez .... 3.00 .90
HL7 Ken Griffey Jr. 5.00 1.50
HL8 Sammy Sosa.................. 5.00 1.50
HL9 Alex Rodriguez 5.00 1.50
HL10 Mark McGwire 8.00 2.40

2000 SkyBox Preeminence

Randomly inserted into packs at one in 24, this insert set features 10 of major league baseball's top athletes. Card backs carry a "P" prefix.

Nm-Mt Ex-Mt
COMPLETE SET (10)................ 40.00 12.00
*STAR RUBIES: 5X TO 12X BASIC PRE-EM
STAR RUBIES: RANDOM IN HOBBY PACKS
STAR RUBIES PRINT RUN 50 SERIAL #'d SETS
P1 Pedro Martinez .... 3.00 .90
P2 Derek Jeter 8.00 2.40
P3 Nomar Garciaparra 5.00 1.50
P4 Alex Rodriguez 5.00 1.50
P5 Mark McGwire................... 8.00 2.40
P6 Sammy Sosa 5.00 1.50
P7 Sean Casey...................... 1.25 .35
P8 Mike Piazza.................... 5.00 1.50
P9 Chipper Jones.................. 3.00 .90
P10 Ivan Rodriguez .... 3.00 .90

2000 SkyBox Skylines

Randomly inserted into packs at one in 11, this insert set features ten MLB stars against the backdrop of the city they play in. Card backs carry a "SL" prefix.

Nm-Mt Ex-Mt
COMPLETE SET (10)............... 25.00 7.50
*STAR RUBIES: 10X TO 25X BASIC SKYLINES
STAR RUBIES: RANDOM IN HOBBY PACKS
STAR RUBIES PRINT RUN 50 SERIAL #'d SETS
SL1 Cal Ripken 5.00 1.50
SL2 Mark McGwire 4.00 1.20
SL3 Alex Rodriguez............... 2.50 .75
SL4 Sammy Sosa .... 2.50 .75
SL5 Derek Jeter 4.00 1.20
SL6 Mike Piazza................... 2.50 .75
SL7 Nomar Garciaparra .... 2.50 .75
SL8 Chipper Jones................. 1.50 .45
SL9 Ken Griffey Jr. .... 2.50 .75
SL10 Manny Ramirez .... 1.00 .30

2000 SkyBox Speed Merchants

Randomly inserted into packs at one in 8, this set features 10 players who exhibit speed including baserunning, bat speed, pitching and fielding. Card backs carry a "SM" prefix.

Nm-Mt Ex-Mt
COMPLETE SET (10)............... 20.00 6.00
*STAR RUBIES: 6X TO 15X BASIC MERCHANT
STAR RUBIES: RANDOM IN HOBBY PACKS
STAR RUBIES PRINT RUN 100 SERIAL #'d SETS
SM1 Derek Jeter .... 3.00 .90
SM2 Sammy Sosa .... 2.00 .60
SM3 Nomar Garciaparra .... 2.00 .60
SM4 Alex Rodriguez .... 2.00 .60
SM5 Randy Johnson............... 1.25 .35
SM6 Ken Griffey Jr. .... 2.00 .60
SM7 Pedro Martinez .... 1.25 .35
SM8 Pat Burrell..................... .50 .15
SM9 Barry Bonds.................. 3.00 .90
SM10 Mark McGwire .... 3.00 .90

2000 SkyBox Technique

Randomly inserted into packs at one in 11, this insert set features 15 players that get the job done with their exceptional fundamentals and technique. Card backs carry a "T" prefix.

Nm-Mt Ex-Mt
COMPLETE SET (15)............... 40.00 12.00
*STAR RUBIES: 8X TO 20X BASIC TECHNIQUE
STAR RUBIES: RANDOM IN HOBBY PACKS
STAR RUBIES PRINT RUN 50 SERIAL #'d SETS
T1 Alex Rodriguez................. 3.00 .90
T2 Tony Gwynn.................... 2.50 .75
T3 Sean Casey .... .75 .23
T4 Mark McGwire.................. 5.00 1.50
T5 Sammy Sosa.................... 3.00 .90
T6 Ken Griffey Jr. .... 3.00 .90
T7 Mike Piazza .... 3.00 .90
T8 Nomar Garciaparra............. 3.00 .90
T9 Derek Jeter..................... 5.00 1.50
T10 Vladimir Guerrero .... 2.00 .60
T11 Cal Ripken.................... 6.00 1.80
T12 Chipper Jones .... 2.00 .60
T13 Frank Thomas .... 2.00 .60
T14 Manny Ramirez .... 1.25 .35
T15 Jeff Bagwell .... 1.25 .35

2004 Skybox Autographics

This 100 card set was released in April, 2004. The set was issued in five-card hobby packs with an $34.99 SRP which came four packs to a hobby box and four boxes to a case. Cards numbered 1 through 65 feature veterans while cards numbered 66 through 100 feature leading rookies and prosepcts. Those prospect cards were issued at a stated rate of one per hobby pack and one per 72 retail packs and were issued to a stated print run of 1500 serial numbered sets.

Nm-Mt Ex-Mt
COMMON CARD (1-65) .... 1.50 .45
COMMON CARD (66-100) .... 3.00 .90
1 Albert Pujols 8.00 2.40
2 Richie Sexson .... 1.50 .45
3 Scott Rolen 4.00 1.20
4 Rafael Palmeiro................ 2.50 .75
5 Ichiro Suzuki................... 6.00 1.80
6 Craig Biggio .... 2.50 .75
7 Todd Helton .... 2.50 .75
8 Miguel Cabrera................. 2.50 .75
9 Ken Griffey Jr. 6.00 1.80
10 Pat Burrell..................... 1.50 .45
11 Jose Reyes.................... 1.50 .45
12 Hideki Matsui 6.00 1.80
13 Geoff Jenkins .... 1.50 .45
14 Mark Prior...................... 4.00 1.20
15 Gary Sheffield .... 1.50 .45
16 Nomar Garciaparra............ 6.00 1.80
17 Luis Gonzalez.................. 1.50 .45
18 Troy Glaus..................... 1.50 .45
19 Rocco Baldelli .... 1.50 .45
20 Hank Blalock .... 1.50 .45
21 Bret Boone..................... 1.50 .45
22 Mike Sweeney.................. 1.50 .45
23 Dmitri Young................... 1.50 .45
24 Dontrelle Willis................. 1.50 .45
25 Austin Kearns................... 1.50 .45
26 Jason Kendall.................. 1.50 .45
27 Derek Jeter..................... 8.00 2.40
28 Miguel Tejada .... 1.50 .45
29 Torii Hunter .... 1.50 .45
30 Sammy Sosa................... 6.00 1.80
31 Chipper Jones.................. 4.00 1.20
32 Pedro Martinez................. 4.00 1.20
33 Curt Schilling 4.00 1.20
34 Roy Halladay................... 1.50 .45
35 Jim Edmonds .... 1.50 .45
36 Alex Rodriguez Yanks 6.00 1.80
37 Jason Schmidt.................. 1.50 .45
38 Jeff Bagwell .... 2.50 .75
39 Omar Vizquel .... 2.50 .75
40 Ivan Rodriguez.................. 4.00 1.20
41 Magglio Ordonez .... 1.50 .45
42 Jim Thome....................... 4.00 1.20
43 Mike Piazza 6.00 1.80
44 Alfonso Soriano .... 2.50 .75
45 Hideo Nomo..................... 4.00 1.20
46 Kerry Wood...................... 4.00 1.20
47 Greg Maddux 6.00 1.80
48 Tony Batista .... 1.50 .45
49 Randy Johnson.................. 4.00 1.20
50 Garret Anderson................. 1.50 .45
51 Mark Teixeira................... 1.50 .45
52 Carlos Delgado.................. 1.50 .45
53 Darin Erstad .... 1.50 .45
54 Shawn Green .... 1.50 .45
55 Josh Beckett .... 1.50 .45
56 Lance Berkman .... 1.50 .45
57 Adam Dunn....................... 2.50 .75
58 Brian Giles .... 1.50 .45
59 Jason Giambi .... 1.50 .45
60 Barry Zito .... 1.50 .45
61 Vladimir Guerrero 4.00 1.20
62 Frank Thomas 4.00 1.20
63 Jay Gibbons...................... 1.50 .45
64 Manny Ramirez.................. 2.50 .75
65 Andruw Jones.................... 1.50 .45
66 Rickie Weeks PR................ 3.00 .90
67 Chad Bentz PR RC .... 3.00 .90
68 Bobby Crosby PR................ 5.00 1.50
69 Greg Dobbs PR RC .... 3.00 .90
70 John Gall PR RC 5.00 1.50
71 Kaz Matsui PR RC 8.00 2.40
72 Dallas McPherson PR 5.00 1.50
73 Brandon Watson PR .... 3.00 .90
74 Jerry Gil PR RC.................. 3.00 .90
75 Garrett Atkins PR .... 3.00 .90
76 Cory Sullivan PR RC .... 3.00 .90
77 Khalil Greene PR 5.00 1.50
78 Shawn Hill PR RC .... 3.00 .90
79 Graham Koonce PR .... 3.00 .90
80 Chien-Ming Wang PR .... 3.00 .90
81 John Labandeira PR RC......... 3.00 .90
82 Jonny Gomes PR .... 3.00 .90
83 Edwin Jackson PR .... 3.00 .90
84 Alfredo Simon PR RC .... 3.00 .90
85 Delmon Young PR 5.00 1.50
86 Jason Bartlett PR RC 5.00 1.50
87 Angel Chavez PR RC .... 3.00 .90
88 Angel Guzman PR................ 3.00 .90
89 Ryan Howard PR .... 3.00 .90
90 Scott Hairston PR .... 3.00 .90
91 Ronny Cedeno PR RC............ 3.00 .90
92 Don Kelly PR RC .... 3.00 .90
93 Ivan Ochoa PR RC............... 3.00 .90
94 Edwin Encarnarcion PR.......... 3.00 .90
95 Byron Gettis PR .... 3.00 .90
96 Kevin Youkilis PR................ 3.00 .90
97 Grady Sizemore PR.............. 3.00 .90
98 Mariano Gomez PR RC .... 3.00 .90
99 Hector Gimenez PR RC.......... 3.00 .90
100 Ruddy Yan PR................... 3.00 .90

2004 Skybox Autographics Insignia

Nm-Mt Ex-Mt
*INSIGNIA 1-65: .6X TO 1.5X BASIC..
*INSIGNIA 66-100: .6X TO 1.5X BASIC
OVERALL PARALLEL ODDS 1:4 H, 1:192 R
STATED PRINT RUN 150 SERIAL #'d SETS
INSIGNIA IS SILVER BACKGROUND...
71 Kaz Matsui PR 12.00 3.60

2004 Skybox Autographics Royal Insignia

Nm-Mt Ex-Mt
*ROYAL INS. 1-65: 2X TO 5X BASIC..
*ROYAL INS. 66-100: 1.5X TO 4X BASIC
OVERALL PARALLEL ODDS 1:4 H, 1:192 R
STATED PRINT RUN 25 SERIAL #'d SETS
ROYAL INSIGNIA IS PURPLE BACKGROUND

2004 Skybox Autographics Autoclassics

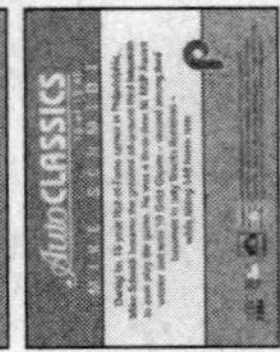

Nm-Mt Ex-Mt
STATED ODDS 1:12 HOBBY/RETAIL ...
1 Johnny Bench 6.00 1.80
2 Steve Carlton 5.00 1.50
3 Carlton Fisk.................... 6.00 1.80
4 Bill Mazeroski.................. 6.00 1.80
5 Jim Palmer...................... 5.00 1.50
6 Warren Spahn 6.00 1.80
7 Duke Snider 6.00 1.80
8 Wade Boggs.................... 6.00 1.80
9 Nolan Ryan 15.00 4.50
10 Mike Schmidt................. 12.00 3.60
11 Albert Chandler 5.00 1.50
12 Ty Cobb........................ 8.00 2.40
13 Sal Maglie 5.00 1.50
14 George Kelly................... 5.00 1.50
15 Joe Sewell..................... 5.00 1.50

2004 Skybox Autographics Autoclassics Memorabilia

Nm-Mt Ex-Mt
OVERALL AU-GU ODDS 1:1 HOB, 1:24 RET
STATED PRINT RUN 350 SERIAL #'d SETS
BM Bill Mazeroski Bat 15.00 4.50
CF Carlton Fisk Jsy 15.00 4.50
DS Duke Snider Jsy 15.00 4.50
JB Johnny Bench Jsy 15.00 4.50
JP Jim Palmer Jsy 10.00 3.00

Card	Nm-Mt	Ex-Mt
MS Mike Schmidt Bat	15.00	4.50
NR Nolan Ryan Jsy	25.00	7.50
SC Steve Carlton Jsy	10.00	3.00
WB Wade Boggs Jsy	15.00	4.50
WS Warren Spahn Jsy	15.00	4.50

2004 Skybox Autographics Autoclassics Signature

	Nm-Mt	Ex-Mt
OVERALL AU-GU ODDS 1:1 HOB, 1:24 RET		
PRINT RUNS B/WN 3-50 COPIES PER		
NO PRICING ON QTY OF 3 OR LESS		
AC Albert Chandler/25	150.00	45.00
BM Bill Mazeroski/50	40.00	12.00
CF Carlton Fisk/50	40.00	12.00
DS Duke Snider/50	40.00	12.00
GK George Kelly/25	175.00	52.50
JB Johnny Bench/50	50.00	15.00
JP Jim Palmer/50	25.00	7.50
JS Joe Sewell/25	150.00	45.00
NR Nolan Ryan/38	150.00	45.00
SC Steve Carlton/50	40.00	12.00
SM Mike Schmidt/25	120.00	36.00
SM Sal Maglie/25	175.00	52.50
TC Ty Cobb/3		
WB Wade Boggs/50	40.00	12.00
WS Warren Spahn/50	40.00	12.00

2004 Skybox Autographics Jerseygraphics Blue

	Nm-Mt	Ex-Mt
STATED PRINT RUN 250 SERIAL #'d SETS		
*GOLD: 1X TO 2.5X BLUE		
GOLD PRINT RUN 25 SERIAL #'d SETS		
PURPLE PRINT RUN 1 SERIAL #'d SET		
NO PURPLE PRICING DUE TO SCARCITY		
*SILVER: .5X TO 1.2X BLUE		
SILVER PRINT RUN 100 SERIAL #'d SETS		
OVERALL AU-GU ODDS 1:1 HOB, 1:24 RET		
AD Adam Dunn	10.00	3.00
AJ Andruw Jones	8.00	2.40
AK Austin Kearns	8.00	2.40
AP Albert Pujols	15.00	4.50
AR Alex Rodriguez	12.00	3.60
AS Alfonso Soriano	10.00	3.00
BA Bobby Abreu	8.00	2.40
BZ Barry Zito	8.00	2.40
CB Craig Biggio	10.00	3.00
CD Carlos Delgado	8.00	2.40
CJ Chipper Jones	10.00	3.00
CS Curt Schilling	8.00	2.40
DE Darin Erstad	8.00	2.40
DJ Derek Jeter	20.00	6.00
DO David Ortiz	10.00	3.00
DW Dontrelle Willis	8.00	2.40
FT Frank Thomas	10.00	3.00
GM Greg Maddux	12.00	3.60
HB Hank Blalock	8.00	2.40
HN Hideo Nomo	10.00	3.00
IR Ivan Rodriguez	10.00	3.00
JB Josh Beckett	8.00	2.40
JE Jim Edmonds	8.00	2.40
JG1 Jason Giambi	8.00	2.40
JG2 Jay Gibbons	8.00	2.40
JR Jose Reyes	8.00	2.40
JT Jim Thome	10.00	3.00
KM Kevin Millwood	8.00	2.40
KW Kerry Wood	10.00	3.00
LB Lance Berkman	8.00	2.40
MC Miguel Cabrera	10.00	3.00
MO Magglio Ordonez	8.00	2.40
MP1 Mike Piazza	12.00	3.60
MP2 Mark Prior	10.00	3.00
MR Manny Ramirez	10.00	3.00
MT1 Mark Teixeira	8.00	2.40
MT2 Miguel Tejada	8.00	2.40
NG Nomar Garciaparra	12.00	3.60
PB Pat Burrell	8.00	2.40
PM Pedro Martinez	10.00	3.00
RB Rocco Baldelli	8.00	2.40
RH Roy Halladay	8.00	2.40
RP Rafael Palmeiro	10.00	3.00
SG Shawn Green	8.00	2.40
SR Scott Rolen	10.00	3.00
SS Sammy Sosa	12.00	3.60
TG Troy Glaus	8.00	2.40
TH1 Todd Helton	10.00	3.00
TH2 Torii Hunter	8.00	2.40
VG Vladimir Guerrero	10.00	3.00

2004 Skybox Autographics Jeter Legacy Collection

	Nm-Mt	Ex-Mt
OVERALL AU-GU ODDS 1:1 HOB, 1:24 RET		
STATED PRINT RUN 25 SERIAL #'d CARDS		
DJ Derek Jeter AU/25		

2004 Skybox Autographics Prospects Endorsed

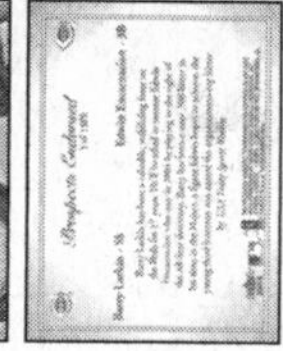

	Nm-Mt	Ex-Mt
STATED ODDS 1:4 HOBBY, 1:8 RETAIL		
1 Albert Pujols	8.00	2.40
Delmon Young		
2 Eric Gagne	4.00	1.20
Bobby Jenks		
3 Barry Larkin	4.00	1.20
Kaz Matsui		
4 Andruw Jones	3.00	.90
Jonny Gomes		
5 Hideo Nomo	4.00	1.20
Chien-Ming Wang		
6 Gary Sheffield	3.00	.90
Cory Sullivan		
7 Billy Wagner	3.00	.90
Ryan Howard		
8 Jorge Posada	4.00	1.20
Koyie Hill		
9 Curt Schilling	4.00	1.20
Ryan Wagner		
10 Jose Reyes	3.00	.90
Rickie Weeks		
11 Alfonso Soriano	4.00	1.20
Matt Kata		
12 Barry Zito	3.00	.90
Rich Harden		
13 Randy Johnson	4.00	1.20
Brandon Webb		
14 Alex Rodriguez	6.00	1.80
Angel Berroa		
15 Dontrelle Willis	3.00	.90
Edwin Jackson		

2004 Skybox Autographics Prospects Endorsed Dual Autograph

	Nm-Mt	Ex-Mt
OVERALL AU-GU ODDS 1:1 HOB, 1:24 RET		
STATED PRINT RUN 50 SERIAL #'d SETS		
AJJG Andruw Jones		
Jonny Gomes		
APDY Albert Pujols	200.00	60.00
Delmon Young		
BWRH Billy Wagner	25.00	7.50
Ryan Howard		
EGBJ Eric Gagne	60.00	18.00
Bobby Jenks		
GSCS Gary Sheffield	40.00	12.00
Cory Sullivan		
JRRW Jose Reyes	40.00	12.00
Rickie Weeks		

2004 Skybox Autographics Prospects Endorsed Dual Jersey

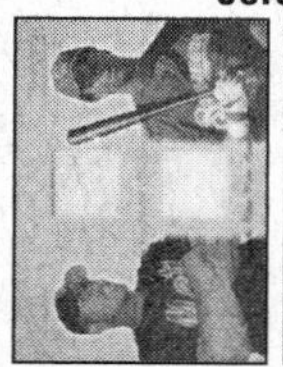

	Nm-Mt	Ex-Mt
STATED PRINT RUN 500 SERIAL #'d SETS		
*PATCH: 1.25X TO 3X BASIC		
PATCH PRINT RUN 50 SERIAL #'d SETS		
OVERALL AU-GU ODDS 1:1 HOB, 1:24 RET		
APDY Albert Pujols	15.00	4.50
Delmon Young		
ARAB Alex Rodriguez	12.00	3.60
Angel Berroa		
ASMK Alfonso Soriano	10.00	3.00
Matt Kata		
BLKM Barry Larkin	15.00	4.50
Kaz Matsui Bat		
BZRH Barry Zito	8.00	2.40
Rich Harden		
CSRW Curt Schilling	10.00	3.00
Ryan Wagner		
DWEJ Dontrelle Willis	8.00	2.40
Edwin Jackson		
HNCW Hideo Nomo	10.00	3.00
Chein-Ming Wang		
JRRW Jose Reyes	8.00	2.40
Rickie Weeks		
RJBW Randy Johnson	10.00	3.00
Brandon Webb		

2004 Skybox Autographics Signatures Blue

	Nm-Mt	Ex-Mt
PRINT RUNS B/WN 100-485 COPIES PER		
*GOLD: 1X TO 2X BLUE p/r 200-485		
*GOLD: 1X TO 2X BLUE p/r 100-197		
GOLD PRINT RUN 25 SERIAL #'d SETS		
*ON LOCATION: .4X TO 1X BLUE p/r 200-485		
*ON LOCATION: .4X TO 1X BLUE p/r 100-197		
ON LOCATION PRINT 99 SERIAL #'d SETS		
PURPLE PRINT RUN 1 SERIAL #'d SET		
NO PURPLE PRICING DUE TO SCARCITY		
*SILVER: .4X TO 1X BLUE p/r 200-485		
*SILVER: .4X TO 1X BLUE p/r 100-197		
SILVER PRINT RUN 100 SERIAL #'d SETS		
OVERALL AU-GU ODDS 1:1 HOB, 1:24 RET		
AB1 Angel Berroa/182	10.00	3.00
AB2 A.J. Burnett/485	10.00	3.00
AH Aubrey Huff/296	15.00	4.50
AK Austin Kearns/275	15.00	4.50
AM Aaron Miles/140	15.00	4.50
AP Albert Pujols/103	120.00	36.00
BJ Bobby Jenks/307	10.00	3.00
BL Barry Larkin/195	25.00	7.50
BW1 Billy Wagner/180	25.00	7.50
BW2 Brandon Webb/310	10.00	3.00
CP Corey Patterson/220	15.00	4.50
CS1 Chris Snelling/200	10.00	3.00
CS2 Cory Sullivan/170	10.00	3.00
CW Chien-Ming Wang/195	25.00	7.50
DH Dan Haren/176	10.00	3.00
DM Dallas McPherson/179	25.00	7.50
DW Dontrelle Willis/225	15.00	4.50
DY Delmon Young/205	25.00	7.50
EE Edwin Encarnarcion/188	10.00	3.00
EG Eric Gagne/225	40.00	12.00
EJ Edwin Jackson/224	15.00	4.50
GA Garrett Atkins/175	10.00	3.00
GK Graham Koonce/190	10.00	3.00
GS Gary Sheffield/210	25.00	7.50
HB Hank Blalock/205	15.00	4.50
JB Josh Beckett/100	25.00	7.50
JG Jonny Gomes/265	10.00	3.00
JP Juan Pierre/220	15.00	4.50
JR1 Jose Reyes/195	15.00	4.50
JR2 Juan Richardson/345	10.00	3.00
JV Javier Vazquez/210	15.00	4.50
KG Khalil Greene/190	40.00	12.00
KH Koyie Hill/240	10.00	3.00
KW Kerry Wood/191	40.00	12.00
LN Laynce Nix/185	15.00	4.50
MB Marlon Byrd/240	10.00	3.00
MK Matt Kata/197	10.00	3.00
MM Mark Mulder/186	15.00	4.50
RB Rocco Baldelli/255	15.00	4.50
RH1 Rich Harden/185	15.00	4.50
RH2 Ryan Howard/170	15.00	4.50
RW Rickie Weeks/187	15.00	4.50
SH Shea Hillenbrand/213	15.00	4.50
SP Scott Podsednik/210	15.00	4.50
SS Shannon Stewart/340	15.00	4.50
TH1 Tim Hudson/169	25.00	7.50
TH2 Torii Hunter/215	15.00	4.50
TN Trot Nixon/210	15.00	4.50

2004 Skybox Autographics Signatures Game Jersey

	Nm-Mt	Ex-Mt
STATED PRINT RUN 125 SERIAL #'d SETS		
*PATCH: 1X TO 2X BASIC		
PATCH PRINT RUN 25 SERIAL #'d SETS		
OVERALL AU-GU ODDS 1:1 HOB, 1:24 RET		
AP Albert Pujols	150.00	45.00
BW1 Billy Wagner	40.00	12.00
BW2 Brandon Webb	15.00	4.50
CP Corey Patterson	25.00	7.50
DW Dontrelle Willis	25.00	7.50
HB Hank Blalock	25.00	7.50
JB Josh Beckett	40.00	12.00
RB Rocco Baldelli	25.00	7.50
TH2 Torii Hunter	25.00	7.50

2000 SkyBox Dominion

This 300 card set was issued in 10 cards packs with a SRP of $1.49. The following subsets are included in this set: League Leaders (1-8), Highlights (9-23), Prospects (251-270), Future Stars (271-300). The Future Star cards feature two players from each team. The regular cards have color photos against a black and white background. An Alex Rodriguez Promo card was distributed to dealers and hobby media several weeks prior to the product's release. The promo is easy to distinguish by the text "PROMOTIONAL SAMPLE" running diagonally across the card front.

	Nm-Mt	Ex-Mt
COMPLETE SET (300)	40.00	12.00
COMMON CARD (1-250)	.20	.06
COMMON (251-300)	.40	.12
1 Mark McGwire LL	.50	.15
Ken Griffey Jr.		
2 Mark McGwire LL	.50	.15
Manny Ramirez		
3 Larry Walker LL	.50	.15
Nomar Garciaparra		
4 Tony Womack LL	.20	.06
Brian Hunter		
5 Mike Hampton LL	.30	.09
Pedro Martinez		
6 Randy Johnson LL	.30	.09
Pedro Martinez		
7 Randy Johnson LL	.30	.09
Pedro Martinez		
8 Ugueth Urbina LL	.20	.06
Mariano Rivera		
9 Vinny Castilla HL	.20	.06
10 Orioles/Cuban Nat'l HL	.20	.06
11 Jose Canseco HL	.30	.09
12 Fernando Tatis HL	.20	.06
13 Robin Ventura HL	.20	.06
14 Roger Clemens HL	.50	.15
15 Jose Jimenez HL	.20	.06
16 David Cone HL	.20	.06
17 Mark McGwire HL	.60	.18
18 Cal Ripken HL	.75	.23
19 Tony Gwynn HL	.30	.09
20 Wade Boggs HL	.20	.06
21 Ivan Rodriguez HL	.30	.09
22 Chuck Finley HL UER	.20	.06
23 Eric Milton HL	.20	.06
24 Adrian Beltre	.30	.09
25 Brad Radke	.20	.06
26 Derek Bell	.20	.06
27 Garret Anderson	.20	.06
28 Ivan Rodriguez	.50	.15
29 Jeff Kent	.20	.06
30 Jeremy Giambi	.20	.06
31 John Franco	.20	.06
32 Jose Hernandez	.20	.06
33 Jose Offerman	.20	.06
34 Jose Rosado	.20	.06
35 Kevin Appier	.20	.06
36 Kris Benson	.20	.06
37 Mark McGwire	1.25	.35
38 Matt Williams	.20	.06
39 Paul O'Neill	.30	.09
40 Rickey Henderson	.50	.15
41 Todd Greene	.20	.06
42 Russ Ortiz	.20	.06
43 Sean Casey	.20	.06
44 Tony Womack	.20	.06
45 Troy O'Leary	.20	.06
46 Ugueth Urbina	.20	.06
47 Tom Glavine	.30	.09
48 Mike Mussina	.30	.09
49 Carlos Febles	.20	.06
50 Jon Lieber	.20	.06
51 Juan Gonzalez	.30	.09
52 Matt Clement	.20	.06
53 Moises Alou	.20	.06
54 Ray Durham	.20	.06
55 Robb Nen	.20	.06
56 Tino Martinez	.30	.09
57 Troy Glaus	.20	.06
58 Curt Schilling	.20	.06
59 Mike Sweeney	.20	.06
60 Steve Finley	.20	.06
61 Roger Cedeno	.20	.06
62 Bobby Jones	.20	.06
63 John Smoltz	.30	.09
64 Darin Erstad	.20	.06
65 Carlos Delgado	.20	.06
66 Ray Lankford	.20	.06
67 Todd Stottlemyre	.20	.06
68 Andy Ashby	.20	.06
69 Bob Abreu	.20	.06
70 Chuck Finley	.20	.06
71 Damion Easley	.20	.06
72 Dustin Hermanson	.20	.06
73 Frank Thomas	.50	.15
74 Kevin Brown	.30	.09
75 Kevin Millwood	.20	.06
76 Mark Grace	.30	.09
77 Matt Stairs	.20	.06
78 Mike Hampton	.20	.06
79 Omar Vizquel	.30	.09
80 Preston Wilson	.20	.06
81 Robin Ventura	.30	.09
82 Todd Helton	.30	.09
83 Tony Clark	.20	.06
84 Al Leiter	.20	.06
85 Alex Fernandez	.20	.06
86 Bernie Williams	.30	.09
87 Edgar Martinez	.30	.09
88 Edgar Renteria	.20	.06
89 Fred McGriff	.30	.09
90 Jermaine Dye	.20	.06
91 Joe McEwing	.20	.06
92 John Halama	.20	.06
93 Lee Stevens	.20	.06
94 Matt Lawton	.20	.06
95 Mike Piazza	.75	.23
96 Pete Harnisch	.20	.06
97 Scott Karl	.20	.06
98 Tony Fernandez	.20	.06
99 Sammy Sosa	.75	.23
100 Bobby Higginson	.20	.06
101 Tony Gwynn	.60	.18
102 J.D. Drew	.20	.06
103 Roberto Hernandez	.20	.06
104 Rondell White	.20	.06
105 David Nilsson	.20	.06
106 Shane Reynolds	.20	.06
107 Jaret Wright	.20	.06
108 Jeff Bagwell	.30	.09
109 Jay Bell	.20	.06
110 Kevin Tapani	.20	.06
111 Michael Barrett	.20	.06
112 Neifi Perez	.20	.06
113 Pat Hengen	.20	.06
114 Roger Clemens	1.00	.30
115 Travis Fryman	.20	.06
116 Aaron Sele	.20	.06
117 Eric Davis	.20	.06
118 Trevor Hoffman	.20	.06
119 Chris Singleton	.20	.06
120 Ryan Klesko	.20	.06
121 Scott Rolen	.50	.15
122 Jorge Posada	.30	.09
123 Abraham Nunez	.20	.06
124 Alex Gonzalez	.20	.06
125 B.J. Surhoff	.20	.06
126 Barry Bonds	1.25	.35
127 Billy Koch	.20	.06
128 Billy Wagner	.20	.06
129 Brad Ausmus	.20	.06
130 Bret Boone	.20	.06
131 Cal Ripken	1.50	.45
132 Chad Allen	.20	.06
133 Chris Carpenter	.20	.06
134 Craig Biggio	.30	.09
135 Dante Bichette	.20	.06
136 Dean Palmer	.20	.06
137 Derek Jeter	1.25	.35
138 Ellis Burks	.20	.06
139 Freddy Garcia	.20	.06
140 Gabe Kapler	.20	.06
141 Greg Maddux	.75	.23
142 Greg Vaughn	.20	.06
143 Jason Kendall	.20	.06
144 Jim Parque	.20	.06
145 John Valentin	.20	.06
146 Jose Vidro	.20	.06
147 Ken Griffey Jr.	.75	.23
148 Kenny Lofton	.20	.06
149 Kenny Rogers	.20	.06
150 Kent Bottenfield	.20	.06
151 Chuck Knoblauch	.20	.06
152 Larry Walker	.30	.09
153 Manny Ramirez	.30	.09
154 Mickey Morandini	.20	.06
155 Mike Cameron	.20	.06
156 Mike Lieberthal	.20	.06
157 Mo Vaughn	.20	.06
158 Randy Johnson	.50	.15
159 Rey Ordonez	.20	.06
160 Roberto Alomar	.30	.09
161 Scott Williamson	.20	.06
162 Shawn Estes	.20	.06
163 Tim Wakefield	.20	.06
164 Tony Batista	.20	.06
165 Will Clark	.50	.15
166 Wade Boggs	.30	.09
167 David Cone	.20	.06
168 Doug Glanville	.20	.06
169 Jeff Cirillo	.20	.06
170 John Jaha	.20	.06
171 Mariano Rivera	.30	.09
172 Tom Gordon	.20	.06
173 Wally Joyner	.20	.06
174 Alex Gonzalez	.20	.06
175 Andruw Jones	.20	.06
176 Barry Larkin	.30	.09
177 Bartolo Colon	.20	.06
178 Brian Giles	.20	.06
179 Carlos Lee	.20	.06
180 Darren Dreifort	.20	.06
181 Eric Chavez	.20	.06
182 Henry Rodriguez	.20	.06
183 Ismael Valdes	.20	.06
184 Jason Giambi	.20	.06
185 John Wetteland	.20	.06
186 Juan Encarnacion	.20	.06
187 Luis Gonzalez	.20	.06
188 Reggie Sanders	.20	.06
189 Richard Hidalgo	.20	.06
190 Ryan Rupe	.20	.06
191 Sean Berry	.20	.06
192 Rick Helling	.20	.06
193 Randy Wolf	.20	.06
194 Cliff Floyd	.20	.06
195 Jose Lima	.20	.06
196 Chipper Jones	.50	.15
197 Charles Johnson	.20	.06
198 Nomar Garciaparra	.75	.23
199 Magglio Ordonez	.20	.06
200 Shawn Green	.20	.06
201 Travis Lee	.20	.06
202 Jose Canseco	.50	.15
203 Fernando Tatis	.20	.06
204 Bruce Aven	.20	.06
205 Johnny Damon	.30	.09
206 Gary Sheffield	.20	.06
207 Ken Caminiti	.20	.06
208 Ben Grieve	.20	.06
209 Sidney Ponson	.20	.06
210 Vinny Castilla	.20	.06
211 Alex Rodriguez	.75	.23
212 Chris Widger	.20	.06
213 Carl Pavano	.20	.06
214 J.T. Snow	.20	.06
215 Jim Thome	.50	.15
216 Kevin Young	.20	.06
217 Mike Sirotka	.20	.06
218 Rafael Palmeiro	.30	.09
219 Rico Brogna	.20	.06
220 Todd Walker	.20	.06
221 Todd Zeile	.20	.06
222 Brian Rose	.20	.06
223 Chris Fussell	.20	.06
224 Corey Koskie	.20	.06
225 Rich Aurilia	.20	.06
226 Geoff Jenkins	.20	.06
227 Pedro Martinez	.50	.15
228 Todd Hundley	.20	.06
229 Brian Jordan	.20	.06
230 Cristian Guzman	.20	.06
231 Raul Mondesi	.20	.06
232 Tim Hudson	.20	.06
233 Albert Belle	.20	.06
234 Andy Pettitte	.30	.09
235 Brady Anderson	.20	.06
236 Brian Bohanon	.20	.06
237 Carlos Beltran	.30	.09
238 Doug Mientkiewicz	.20	.06
239 Jason Schmidt	.20	.06
240 Jeff Zimmerman	.20	.06
241 John Olerud	.20	.06
242 Paul Byrd	.20	.06
243 Vladimir Guerrero	.50	.15
244 Warren Morris	.20	.06
245 Eric Karros	.20	.06
246 Jeff Weaver	.20	.06
247 Jeromy Burnitz	.20	.06
248 David Bell	.20	.06
249 Rusty Greer	.20	.06
250 Kevin Stocker	.20	.06
251 S.Hillenbrand PROS	.40	.12
252 A.Soriano PROS	.75	.23
253 Micah Bowie PROS	.40	.12

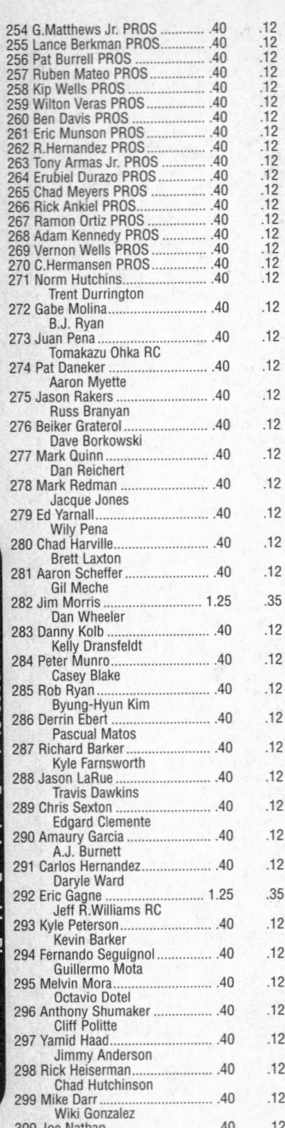

254 G.Matthews Jr. PROS .40 .12
255 Lance Berkman PROS .40 .12
256 Pat Burrell PROS .40 .12
257 Ruben Mateo PROS .40 .12
258 Kip Wells PROS .40 .12
259 Wilton Veras PROS .40 .12
260 Ben Davis PROS .40 .12
261 Eric Munson PROS .40 .12
262 R.Hernandez PROS .40 .12
263 Tony Armas Jr. PROS .40 .12
264 Erubiel Durazo PROS .40 .12
265 Chad Meyers PROS .40 .12
266 Rick Ankiel PROS .40 .12
267 Ramon Ortiz PROS .40 .12
268 Adam Kennedy PROS .40 .12
269 Vernon Wells PROS .40 .12
270 C.Hermansen PROS .40 .12
271 Norm Hutchins .40 .12
Trent Durrington
272 Gabe Molina .40 .12
B.J. Ryan
273 Juan Pena .40 .12
Tomakazu Ohka RC
274 Pat Daneker .40 .12
Aaron Myette
275 Jason Rakers .40 .12
Russ Branyan
276 Beiker Graterol .40 .12
Dave Borkowski
277 Mark Quinn .40 .12
Dan Reichert
278 Mark Redman .40 .12
Jacque Jones
279 Ed Yarnall .40 .12
Wily Pena
280 Chad Harville .40 .12
Brett Laxton
281 Aaron Scheffer .40 .12
Gil Meche
282 Jim Morris 1.25 .35
Dan Wheeler
283 Danny Kolb .40 .12
Kelly Dransfeldt
284 Peter Munro .40 .12
Casey Blake
285 Rob Ryan .40 .12
Byung-Hyun Kim
286 Derrin Ebert .40 .12
Pascual Matos
287 Richard Barker .40 .12
Kyle Farnsworth
288 Jason LaRue .40 .12
Travis Dawkins
289 Chris Sexton .40 .12
Edgard Clemente
290 Amaury Garcia .40 .12
A.J. Burnett
291 Carlos Hernandez .40 .12
Daryle Ward
292 Eric Gagne 1.25 .35
Jeff R.Williams RC
293 Kyle Peterson .40 .12
Kevin Barker
294 Fernando Seguignol .40 .12
Guillermo Mota
295 Melvin Mora .40 .12
Octavio Dotel
296 Anthony Shumaker .40 .12
Cliff Politte
297 Yamid Haad .40 .12
Jimmy Anderson
298 Rick Heiserman .40 .12
Chad Hutchinson
299 Mike Darr .40 .12
Wiki Gonzalez
300 Joe Nathan .40 .12
Calvin Murray
P211 A.Rodriguez Promo 2.00 .60

2000 Skybox Dominion Double Play

Inserted one every nine packs, this 10 card set highlights two stars on each card. The cards are double-sided with one of the players featured on each side.

Nm-Mt Ex-Mt
COMPLETE SET (10) 25.00 7.50
*PLUS: 1.5X TO 4X BASIC DOUBLE PLAY
PLUS STATED ODDS 1:90
*WARP TEK: 8X TO 20X BASIC DOUBLE PLAY
WARP TEK STATED ODDS 1:900
DP1 Nomar Garciaparra 2.50 .75
Alex Rodriguez
DP2 Pedro Martinez 1.50 .45
Randy Johnson
DP3 Chipper Jones 1.50 .45
Scott Rolen
DP4 Mark McGwire 4.00 1.20
Ken Griffey Jr.
DP5 Cal Ripken 4.00 1.20
Derek Jeter
DP6 Roger Clemens 2.50 .75
Greg Maddux
DP7 Juan Gonzalez 1.00 .30
Manny Ramirez
DP8 Tony Gwynn 2.00 .60
Shawn Green
DP9 Sammy Sosa 1.50 .45
Frank Thomas
DP10 Mike Piazza 2.50 .75
Ivan Rodriguez

2000 Skybox Dominion Eye on October

Inserted one every 24 packs, these 15 cards feature players who are striving to appear in the post season. Card backs carry an "EO" prefix.

Nm-Mt Ex-Mt
COMPLETE SET (15) 80.00 24.00
*PLUS: 2X TO 5X BASIC OCTOBER
PLUS STATED ODDS 1:240
EO1 Ken Griffey Jr. 5.00 1.50
EO2 Mark McGwire 8.00 2.40
EO3 Derek Jeter 8.00 2.40
EO4 Juan Gonzalez 2.00 .60
EO5 Chipper Jones 3.00 .90
EO6 Sammy Sosa 5.00 1.50
EO7 Greg Maddux 5.00 1.50
EO8 Frank Thomas 3.00 .90
EO9 Nomar Garciaparra 5.00 1.50
EO10 Shawn Green 1.25 .35
EO11 Cal Ripken 10.00 3.00
EO12 Manny Ramirez 2.00 .60
EO13 Scott Rolen 3.00 .90
EO14 Mike Piazza 5.00 1.50
EO15 Alex Rodriguez 5.00 1.50

2000 Skybox Dominion Eye on October Warp Tek

Randomly inserted into packs, these cards parallel the Eye on October insert set. These cards, are printed on lenticular, three dimensional stock and are serial numbered to the players uniform number. Due to the scarcity of these cards, no pricing is provided.

Nm-Mt Ex-Mt
EO1 Ken Griffey Jr./24
EO2 Mark McGwire/25
EO3 Derek Jeter/2
EO4 Juan Gonzalez/19
EO5 Chipper Jones/10
EO6 Sammy Sosa/21
EO7 Greg Maddux/31
EO8 Frank Thomas/35
EO9 Nomar Garciaparra/5
EO10 Shawn Green/15
EO11 Cal Ripken/8
EO12 Manny Ramirez/24
EO13 Scott Rolen/17
EO14 Mike Piazza/31
EO15 Alex Rodriguez/3

2000 Skybox Dominion Hats Off

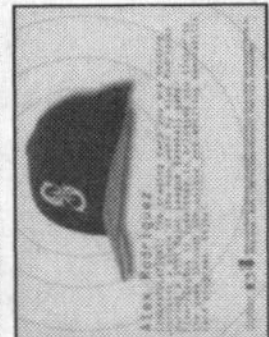

Inserted into hobby packs at a rate of one in 467, these 15 cards feature a piece of a a game worn hat along with a picture of that player.

Nm-Mt Ex-Mt
1 Wade Boggs 25.00 7.50
2 Barry Bonds 60.00 18.00
3 J.D. Drew 15.00 4.50
4 Shawn Green 15.00 4.50
5 Vladimir Guerrero 25.00 7.50
6 Randy Johnson 25.00 7.50
7 Andruw Jones 15.00 4.50
8 Greg Maddux 50.00 15.00
9 Pedro Martinez 25.00 7.50
10 Mike Mussina 25.00 7.50
11 Rafael Palmeiro 25.00 7.50
12 Alex Rodriguez 50.00 15.00
13 Scott Rolen 25.00 7.50
14 Tim Salmon 25.00 7.50
15 Robin Ventura 15.00 4.50

2000 Skybox Dominion Milestones

Issued one every 1999 packs, these six cards feature players who reached important career milestones during the 1999 season. The horizontal cards have the players photo against a background in which the milestone is identified.

Nm-Mt Ex-Mt
COMPLETE SET (6) 300.00 90.00
M1 Mark McGwire 80.00 24.00
M2 Roger Clemens 60.00 18.00
M3 Tony Gwynn 40.00 12.00
M4 Wade Boggs 20.00 6.00
M5 Cal Ripken 100.00 30.00
M6 Jose Canseco 30.00 9.00

2000 SkyBox Dominion New Era

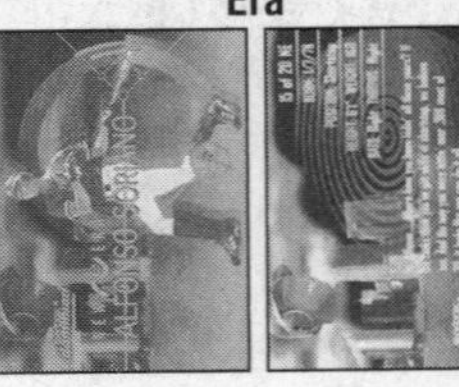

Issued one every three packs these 20 cards feature some of the leading young players who are expected to be stars in the 21st century. These cards are printed on silver foil board.

Nm-Mt Ex-Mt
COMPLETE SET (20) 10.00 3.00
*PLUS: 1.5X TO 4X BASIC NEW ERA
PLUS STATED ODDS 1:30
*WARP TEK: 5X TO 12X BASIC NEW ERA
WARP TEK STATED ODDS 1:300
N1 Pat Burrell 1.00 .30
N2 Ruben Mateo 1.00 .30
N3 Wilton Veras 1.00 .30
N4 Eric Munson 1.00 .30
N5 Jeff Weaver 1.00 .30
N6 Tim Hudson 1.00 .30
N7 Carlos Beltran 1.00 .30
N8 Chris Singleton 1.00 .30
N9 Lance Berkman 1.00 .30
N10 Freddy Garcia 1.00 .30
N11 Erubiel Durazo 1.00 .30
N12 Randy Wolf 1.00 .30
N13 Shea Hillenbrand 1.00 .30
N14 Kip Wells 1.00 .30
N15 Alfonso Soriano 1.50 .45
N16 Rick Ankiel 1.00 .30
N17 Ramon Ortiz 1.00 .30
N18 Adam Kennedy 1.00 .30
N19 Vernon Wells 1.00 .30
N20 Chad Hermansen 1.00 .30

2004 Skybox LE

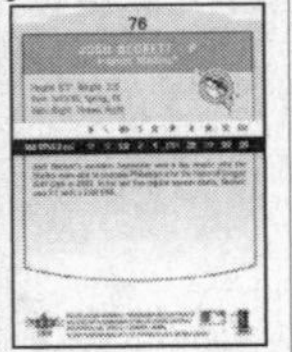

This 160 card set was released in March, 2004. This set was issued in three-card packs which came in both hobby and retail versions. The hobby packs were issued with an $3 SRP and came 18 packs to a box and 16 boxes to a case. Retail packs had a $2 SRP and were not as insert laden as the hobby packs. The first 110 cards of this set featured veterans while cards number 111 through 160 feature leading prospects. Please note that these cards were all issued to a print run of 99 or 299.

Nm-Mt Ex-Mt
COMP.SET w/o SP'S (110) 40.00 12.00
COMMON CARD (1-110) .75 .23
1-110 HOBBY CARDS ARE ALL DIE-CUT
COMMON CARD p/r 299 5.00 1.50
COMMON CARD p/r 99 10.00 3.00
111-160 ODDS 1:18 HOBBY, 1:144 RETAIL
111-160 PRINTS B/WN 99-299 COPIES PER
1 Juan Pierre .75 .23
2 Derek Jeter 4.00 1.20
3 Brandon Webb .75 .23
4 Jeff Bagwell 1.25 .35
5 Jason Schmidt .75 .23
6 Marlon Byrd .75 .23
7 Garret Anderson .75 .23
8 Miguel Cabrera 1.25 .35
9 Jose Reyes .75 .23
10 Rocco Baldelli .75 .23
11 Tony Batista .75 .23
12 Carlos Beltran 1.25 .35
13 Nomar Garciaparra 3.00 .90
14 Shawn Green .75 .23
15 Albert Pujols 4.00 1.20
16 Magglio Ordonez .75 .23
17 Kip Wells .75 .23
18 Andruw Jones .75 .23
19 Ryan Wagner .75 .23
20 Alex Rodriguez 2.50 .75
21 Vernon Wells .75 .23
22 Todd Helton 1.25 .35
23 David Ortiz 2.00 .60
24 Troy Glaus .75 .23
25 Jim Thome 2.00 .60
26 Greg Maddux 3.00 .90
27 Roberto Alomar 1.25 .35
28 Edgardo Alfonzo .75 .23
29 Hee Seop Choi .75 .23
30 Ken Griffey Jr. 3.00 .90
31 Tim Hudson .75 .23
32 Shannon Stewart .75 .23
33 Ichiro Suzuki 3.00 .90
34 Luis Gonzalez .75 .23
35 Darin Erstad .75 .23
36 Dmitri Young .75 .23
37 Ivan Rodriguez 2.00 .60
38 Scott Podsednik .75 .23
39 Jose Vidro .75 .23
40 Mark Prior 2.00 .60
41 Mike Mussina 1.25 .35
42 Gary Sheffield .75 .23
43 Manny Ramirez 1.25 .35
44 C.C. Sabathia .75 .23
45 Curt Schilling .75 .23
46 Scott Rolen 2.00 .60
47 Hideo Nomo 2.00 .60
48 Torii Hunter .75 .23
49 Aubrey Huff .75 .23
50 Javy Lopez .75 .23
51 Austin Kearns .75 .23
52 Mike Piazza 3.00 .90
53 Sean Burroughs .75 .23
54 Kerry Wood 2.00 .60
55 Marquis Grissom .75 .23
56 Preston Wilson .75 .23
57 Angel Berroa .75 .23
58 Jason Kendall .75 .23
59 Rafael Palmeiro 1.25 .35
60 Mike Lowell .75 .23
61 Eric Chavez .75 .23
62 Bartolo Colon .75 .23
63 Adam Dunn 1.25 .35
64 Pedro Martinez 2.00 .60
65 Lance Berkman .75 .23
66 Bret Boone .75 .23
67 Eric Gagne 2.00 .60
68 Vladimir Guerrero 2.00 .60
69 Jay Gibbons .75 .23
70 Larry Walker 1.25 .35
71 Orlando Cabrera .75 .23
72 Jorge Posada 1.25 .35
73 Jamie Moyer .75 .23
74 Carl Crawford .75 .23
75 Hank Blalock .75 .23
76 Josh Beckett .75 .23
77 Jody Gerut .75 .23
78 Kevin Brown .75 .23
79 Sammy Sosa 3.00 .90
80 Chipper Jones 2.00 .60
81 Tom Glavine 1.25 .35
82 Barry Zito .75 .23
83 Edgar Renteria .75 .23
84 Esteban Loaiza .75 .23
85 Jason Giambi .75 .23
86 Miguel Tejada .75 .23
87 Randy Johnson 2.00 .60
88 A.J. Burnett .75 .23
89 Richie Sexson .75 .23
90 Reggie Sanders .75 .23
91 Carlos Delgado .75 .23
92 Pat Burrell .75 .23
93 Jacque Jones .75 .23
94 Roy Oswalt .75 .23
95 Frank Thomas 2.00 .60
96 Melvin Mora .75 .23
97 Jeremy Bonderman .75 .23
98 Mike Sweeney .75 .23
99 Brian Giles .75 .23
100 Edgar Martinez 1.25 .35
101 Mark Teixeira .75 .23
102 Sean Casey .75 .23
103 Javier Vazquez .75 .23
104 Hideki Matsui 3.00 .90
105 Jim Edmonds .75 .23
106 Roy Halladay .75 .23
107 Craig Biggio 1.25 .35
108 Geoff Jenkins .75 .23
109 Alfonso Soriano 1.25 .35
110 Barry Larkin 1.25 .35
111 Chris Bootcheck PR/299 5.00 1.50
112 Dallas McPherson PR/99 15.00 4.50
113 Matt Kata PR/99 10.00 3.00
114 Scott Hairston PR/299 5.00 1.50
115 Bobby Crosby PR/299 8.00 2.40
116 Adam Wainright PR/99 10.00 3.00
117 Daniel Cabrera PR/299 5.00 1.50
118 Kevin Youkilis PR/299 5.00 1.50
119 Ronny Cedeno PR/299 RC 5.00 1.50
120 Ruddy Yan PR/299 5.00 1.50
121 Ryan Wing PR/299 RC 5.00 1.50
122 William Bergolla PR/299 RC 5.00 1.50
123 Edwin Encarnacion PR/299 5.00 1.50
124 Jonny Gomes PR/299 5.00 1.50
125 Garrett Atkins PR/299 5.00 1.50
126 Clint Barmes PR/299 5.00 1.50
127 Wilfredo Ledezma PR/299 5.00 1.50
128 Cody Ross PR/299 5.00 1.50
129 Josh Willingham PR/99 10.00 3.00
130 Chin-Hui Tsao PR/299 5.00 1.50
131 Hector Gimenez PR/299 RC 5.00 1.50
132 David DeJesus PR/299 5.00 1.50
133 Jimmy Gobble PR/299 5.00 1.50
134 Edwin Jackson PR/99 10.00 3.00
135 Koyie Hill PR/299 5.00 1.50
136 Rickie Weeks PR/99 10.00 3.00
137 Graham Koonce PR/299 5.00 1.50
138 Rob Bowen PR/299 5.00 1.50
139 Shawn Hill PR/299 RC 5.00 1.50
140 Craig Brazell PR/299 5.00 1.50
141 Mike Hessman PR/299 5.00 1.50
142 Jorge De Paula PR/299 5.00 1.50
143 Chien-Ming Wang PR/99 10.00 3.00
144 Rich Harden PR/299 5.00 1.50
145 Ryan Howard PR/99 10.00 3.00
146 Alfredo Simon PR/299 RC 5.00 1.50
147 Ian Snell PR RC/299 RC 8.00 2.40
148 Ryan Doumit PR/299 5.00 1.50
149 Khalil Greene PR/99 15.00 4.50
150 Angel Chavez PR/299 RC 5.00 1.50
151 Dan Haren PR/299 5.00 1.50
152 Chris Snelling PR/299 5.00 1.50
153 Aaron Miles PR/299 5.00 1.50
154 John Gall PR/299 RC 8.00 2.40
155 Chris Narveson PR/299 5.00 1.50
156 Delmon Young PR/99 15.00 4.50
157 Chad Gaudin PR/299 5.00 1.50
158 Gerald Laird PR/299 5.00 1.50
159 Alexis Rios PR/299 5.00 1.50
160 Jason Arnold PR/299 5.00 1.50

2004 Skybox LE Artist Proof

Nm-Mt Ex-Mt
*AP 1-110: 2.5X TO 6X BASIC
*AP 111-160: .75X TO 2X BASIC p/r 299
*AP 111-160: .4X TO 1X BASIC p/r 99
OVERALL PARALLEL ODDS 1:6 H, 1:48 R
STATED PRINT RUN 50 SERIAL #'d SETS

2004 Skybox LE Executive Proof

Nm-Mt Ex-Mt
OVERALL PARALLEL ODDS 1:6 H, 1:48 R
STATED PRINT RUN 1 SERIAL #'d SET
NO PRICING DUE TO SCARCITY

2004 Skybox LE Gold Proof

Nm-Mt Ex-Mt
*GOLD 1-110: 1.25X TO 3X BASIC
*GOLD 111-160: .4X TO 1X BASIC p/r 299
*GOLD 111-160: .2X TO .5X BASIC p/r 99
OVERALL PARALLEL ODDS 1:6 H, 1:48 R
STATED PRINT RUN 150 SERIAL #'d SETS

2004 Skybox LE Photographer Proof

Nm-Mt Ex-Mt
*PHOTO 1-110: 4X TO 10X BASIC
*PHOTO 111-160: 1X TO 2.5X BASIC p/r 299
*PHOTO 111-160: .5X TO 1.2X BASIC p/r 99
OVERALL PARALLEL ODDS 1:6 H, 1:48 R
STATED PRINT RUN 25 SERIAL #'d SETS

2004 SkyBox LE Retail

Nm-Mt Ex-Mt
*RETAIL 1-110: .15X TO .4X BASIC
ISSUED ONLY IN RETAIL PACKS
RETAIL CARDS ARE NOT DIE CUT

2004 Skybox LE Jersey Proof

Nm-Mt Ex-Mt
STATED PRINT RUN 299 SERIAL #'d SETS
GOLD PRINT RUN 10 SERIAL #'d SETS
NO GOLD PRICING DUE TO SCARCITY
*SILVER: .6X TO 1.5X BASIC
SILVER PRINT RUN 50 SERIAL #'d SETS
OVERALL GU ODDS 1:9 H, 1:48 R
1 Troy Glaus 8.00 2.40
2 Curt Schilling 8.00 2.40
3 Randy Johnson 10.00 3.00
4 Brandon Webb 8.00 2.40
5 Gary Sheffield 8.00 2.40
6 Greg Maddux 15.00 4.50
7 Chipper Jones 10.00 3.00
8 David Ortiz 10.00 3.00
9 Nomar Garciaparra 15.00 4.50
10 Pedro Martinez 10.00 3.00
11 Manny Ramirez 10.00 3.00
12 Kerry Wood 10.00 3.00
13 Mark Prior 10.00 3.00
14 Sammy Sosa 15.00 4.50
15 Frank Thomas 10.00 3.00
16 Austin Kearns
17 Todd Helton 10.00 3.00
18 Preston Wilson 8.00 2.40
19 Juan Pierre 8.00 2.40
20 Josh Beckett 8.00 2.40
21 Ivan Rodriguez 10.00 3.00
22 Miguel Cabrera 10.00 3.00
23 Mike Lowell 8.00 2.40
24 Lance Berkman 8.00 2.40
25 Jeff Bagwell 10.00 3.00
26 Angel Berroa 8.00 2.40
27 Hideo Nomo 15.00 4.50
28 Eric Gagne 10.00 3.00
29 Scott Podsednik 8.00 2.40
30 Richie Sexson 8.00 2.40
31 Torii Hunter 8.00 2.40
32 Mike Piazza 15.00 4.50
33 Jose Reyes 8.00 2.40
34 Tom Glavine 10.00 3.00
35 Derek Jeter 30.00 9.00
36 Jorge Posada 10.00 3.00
37 Jason Giambi 8.00 2.40
38 Alfonso Soriano 10.00 3.00
39 Eric Chavez 8.00 2.40
40 Miguel Tejada 8.00 2.40
41 Jim Thome 10.00 3.00
42 Albert Pujols 20.00 6.00
43 Scott Rolen 10.00 3.00
44 Rocco Baldelli 8.00 2.40
45 Alex Rodriguez 12.00 3.60
46 Hank Blalock 8.00 2.40
47 Mark Teixeira 8.00 2.40
48 Rafael Palmeiro 10.00 3.00
49 Carlos Delgado 8.00 2.40
50 Roy Halladay 8.00 2.40

2004 Skybox LE History Draft 90's Autograph Black

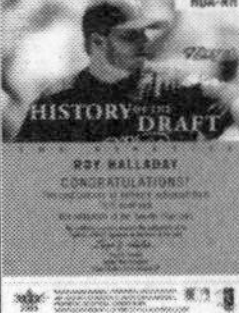

Nm-Mt Ex-Mt
STATED PRINT RUN 199 SERIAL #'d SETS
*COPPER: .4X TO 1X BASIC
COPPER PRINTS B/WN 93-99 COPIES PER
GOLD PRINT RUN 10 SERIAL #'d SETS
NO GOLD PRICING DUE TO SCARCITY
*SILVER: .5X TO 1.2X BASIC
SILVER PRINT RUN 50 SERIAL #'d SETS
OVERALL AUTO ODDS 1:18 HOBBY
AH Aubrey Huff 15.00 4.50
AK Austin Kearns 15.00 4.50
AP Albert Pujols 120.00 36.00
CP Corey Patterson 15.00 4.50
HB Hank Blalock 15.00 4.50
JP Juan Pierre 15.00 4.50
MB Marlon Byrd 10.00 3.00

ML Mike Lowell 15.00 4.50
RH Roy Halladay 10.00 3.00
SP Scott Podsednik 15.00 4.50
SR Scott Rolen 40.00 12.00
TH Torii Hunter 15.00 4.50
VW Vernon Wells 15.00 4.50

2004 Skybox LE History Draft 90's Jersey

Nm-Mt Ex-Mt
PRINT RUNS B/WN 90-99 COPIES PER
GOLD PRINT RUN 10 SERIAL #'d SETS
NO GOLD PRICING DUE TO SCARCITY
*SILVER: .5X TO 1.2X BASIC
SILVER PRINT RUN 50 SERIAL #'d SETS
OVERALL GU ODDS 1:9 H, 1:48 R
AB A.J. Burnett/95 10.00 3.00
AD Adam Dunn/98 12.00 3.60
AH Aubrey Huff/98 10.00 3.00
AK Austin Kearns/98 10.00 3.00
AP Albert Pujols/99 25.00 7.50
AR Alex Rodriguez/93 15.00 4.50
BB Bret Boone/90 10.00 3.00
BZ Barry Zito/99 10.00 3.00
CB Carlos Beltran/95 12.00 3.60
CJ Chipper Jones/90 12.00 3.60
CP Corey Patterson/98 10.00 3.00
DE Darin Erstad/95 10.00 3.00
DJ Derek Jeter/92 40.00 12.00
EC Eric Chavez/96 10.00 3.00
GA Garret Anderson/90 10.00 3.00
HB Hank Blalock/99 10.00 3.00
JB Josh Beckett/99 10.00 3.00
JG Jason Giambi/92 10.00 3.00
JPI Juan Pierre/98 10.00 3.00
JPO Jorge Posada/90 12.00 3.60
JS Jason Schmidt/91 10.00 3.00
JV Javier Vazquez/94 10.00 3.00
KW Kerry Wood/95 12.00 3.60
LB Lance Berkman/97 10.00 3.00
MB Marlon Byrd/99 10.00 3.00
ML Mike Lowell/95 10.00 3.00
MM Mike Mussina/90 12.00 3.60
MR Manny Ramirez/91 12.00 3.60
NG Nomar Garciaparra/94 20.00 6.00
PB Pat Burrell/98 10.00 3.00
RH Roy Halladay/95 10.00 3.00
RS Richie Sexson/93 10.00 3.00
SG Shawn Green/91 10.00 3.00
SP Scott Podsednik/94 10.00 3.00
SR Scott Rolen/93 12.00 3.60
SS Shannon Stewart/92 10.00 3.00
THE Todd Helton/95 12.00 3.60
THN Torii Hunter/93 10.00 3.00
THU Tim Hudson/97 10.00 3.00
VW Vernon Wells/97 10.00 3.00

2004 Skybox LE League Leaders

Nm-Mt Ex-Mt
STATED ODDS 1:18 HOBBY, 1:12 RETAIL
EXECUTIVE RANDOM INSERTS IN PACKS
EXECUTIVE PRINT RUN 1 SERIAL #'d SET
NO EXECUTIVE PRICING DUE TO SCARCITY
1 Alex Rodriguez 6.00 1.80
2 Jim Thome 4.00 1.20
3 Albert Pujols 8.00 2.40
4 Pedro Martinez 4.00 1.20
5 Roy Halladay 3.00 .90
6 Jason Schmidt 3.00 .90
7 Kerry Wood 4.00 1.20
8 Juan Pierre 3.00 .90
9 Preston Wilson 3.00 .90
10 Carlos Delgado 3.00 .90

2004 Skybox LE League Leaders Jersey

Nm-Mt Ex-Mt
STATED PRINT RUN 75 SERIAL #'d SETS
GOLD PRINT RUN 10 SERIAL #'d SETS
NO GOLD PRICING DUE TO SCARCITY
*SILVER: .5X TO 1.2X BASIC
SILVER PRINT RUN 50 SERIAL #'d SETS
OVERALL GU ODDS 1:9 H, 1:48 R
AP Albert Pujols 25.00 7.50
AR Alex Rodriguez 15.00 4.50
CD Carlos Delgado 10.00 3.00
JP Juan Pierre 10.00 3.00
JS Jason Schmidt 10.00 3.00
JT Jim Thome 12.00 3.60
KW Kerry Wood 12.00 3.60
PM Pedro Martinez 12.00 3.60
PW Preston Wilson 10.00 3.00
RH Roy Halladay 10.00 3.00

2004 Skybox LE Rare Form

Nm-Mt Ex-Mt
STATED ODDS 1:288 HOBBY, 1:576 RETAIL
NO MORE THAN 130 SETS PRODUCED
PRINT RUN INFO PROVIDED BY FLEER
EXECUTIVE RANDOM INSERTS IN PACKS
EXECUTIVE PRINT RUN 1 SERIAL #'d SET
NO EXECUTIVE PRICING DUE TO SCARCITY
1 Albert Pujols 30.00 9.00
2 Miguel Cabrera 15.00 4.50
3 Jim Thome 15.00 4.50
4 Derek Jeter 30.00 9.00
5 Nomar Garciaparra 25.00 7.50
6 Mike Piazza 25.00 7.50
7 Alex Rodriguez 25.00 7.50
8 Delmon Young 15.00 4.50
9 Chipper Jones 15.00 4.50
10 Rickie Weeks 15.00 4.50

2004 Skybox LE Rare Form Autograph Black

Nm-Mt Ex-Mt
STATED PRINT RUN 299 SERIAL #'d SETS
*COPPER: .5X TO 1.2X BASIC
COPPER PRINT RUN 99 SERIAL #'d SETS
GOLD PRINT RUN 10 SERIAL #'d SETS
NO GOLD PRICING DUE TO SCARCITY
*SILVER: .6X TO 1.5X BASIC
SILVER PRINT RUN 50 SERIAL #'d SETS
OVERALL AUTO ODDS 1:18 HOBBY
1 Dallas McPherson 25.00 7.50
2 Delmon Young 25.00 7.50
3 Rickie Weeks 15.00 4.50
4 Brandon Webb 10.00 3.00
5 Matt Kata 10.00 3.00
6 Edwin Jackson 15.00 4.50
7 Rocco Baldelli 15.00 4.50
8 Angel Berroa 10.00 3.00
9 Rich Harden 15.00 4.50

2004 Skybox LE Rare Form Game Used Silver

Nm-Mt Ex-Mt
STATED PRINT RUN 50 SERIAL #'d SETS
GOLD PRINT RUN 10 SERIAL #'d SETS
NO GOLD PRICING DUE TO SCARCITY
*NUMBER p/r 31: .5X TO 1.2X BASIC
*NUMBER p/r 20-25: .6X TO 1.5X BASIC
NUMBER PRINTS B/WN 2-31 COPIES PER
NO NUMBER PRICING ON 25 OR LESS
OVERALL GU ODDS 1:9 H, 1:48 R
AP Albert Pujols Jsy 30.00 9.00
AR Alex Rodriguez Jsy 20.00 6.00
CJ Chipper Jones Jsy 15.00 4.50
DJ Derek Jeter Jsy 50.00 15.00
JT Jim Thome Jsy 15.00 4.50
MC Miguel Cabrera Jsy 15.00 4.50
MP Mike Piazza Jsy 25.00 7.50
NG Nomar Garciaparra Jsy 25.00 7.50
RB Rocco Baldelli Jsy 12.00 3.60
RW Rickie Weeks Bat 12.00 3.60

2004 Skybox LE Sky's the Limit

Nm-Mt Ex-Mt
STATED ODDS 1:6 HOBBY, 1:8 RETAIL
EXECUTIVE RANDOM INSERTS IN PACKS
EXECUTIVE PRINT RUN 1 SERIAL #'d SET
NO EXECUTIVE PRICING DUE TO SCARCITY
1 Dontrelle Willis 2.00 .60
2 Rocco Baldelli 2.00 .60
3 Miguel Cabrera 3.00 .90
4 Mark Prior 3.00 .90
5 Hideki Matsui 5.00 1.50
6 Kerry Wood 3.00 .90
7 Alfonso Soriano 3.00 .90
8 Ichiro Suzuki 5.00 1.50
9 Brandon Webb 2.00 .60
10 Alex Rodriguez 5.00 1.50
11 Barry Zito 2.00 .60
12 Hank Blalock 2.00 .60
13 Jose Reyes 2.00 .60
14 Torii Hunter 2.00 .60
15 Josh Beckett 2.00 .60
16 Manny Ramirez 3.00 .90
17 Andruw Jones 2.00 .60
18 Vladimir Guerrero 3.00 .90
19 Miguel Tejada 2.00 .60
20 Carlos Delgado 2.00 .60

2004 Skybox LE Sky's the Limit Jersey

Nm-Mt Ex-Mt
STATED PRINT RUN 99 SERIAL #'d SETS
GOLD PRINT RUN 10 SERIAL #'d SETS
NO GOLD PRICING DUE TO SCARCITY
*SILVER: .5X TO 1.2X BASIC
SILVER PRINT RUN 50 SERIAL #'d SETS
OVERALL GU ODDS 1:9 H, 1:48 R
AJ Andruw Jones 10.00 3.00
AR Alex Rodriguez 15.00 4.50
AS Alfonso Soriano 12.00 3.60
BW Brandon Webb 10.00 3.00
BZ Barry Zito 10.00 3.00
CD Carlos Delgado 10.00 3.00
DW Dontrelle Willis 10.00 3.00
HB Hank Blalock 10.00 3.00
JB Josh Beckett 10.00 3.00
JR Jose Reyes 10.00 3.00
KW Kerry Wood 12.00 3.60
MC Miguel Cabrera 12.00 3.60
MP Mark Prior 12.00 3.60
MR Manny Ramirez 12.00 3.60
MT Miguel Tejada 10.00 3.00
RB Rocco Baldelli 10.00 3.00
TH Torii Hunter 10.00 3.00
VG Vladimir Guerrero 12.00 3.60

1999 SkyBox Premium

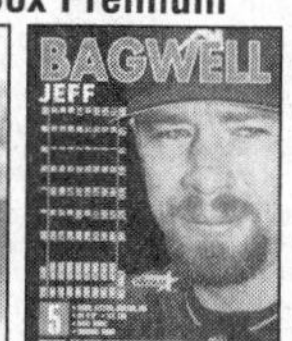

The 1999 SkyBox Premium set was issued in one series for a total of 350 cards and distributed in eight-card packs with a suggested retail price of $2.69. The set features color action player photos with a team colored action-trail and gold-foil stamping. The set contains the following subsets: Spring Fling (273-297) and two versions of the 50 Rookies. In an effoty to satisfy fans of both complete sets and short-printed Rookie Cards, dual version rookie and prospect cards were created. The commonly available versions feature close-up shots of the players and these are considered the true Rookie Card. The short-printed versions feature full-body action shots and are seeded at a rate of one in eight packs. Both versions of these cards are numbered but we've added an "S" suffix on the short-prints for checklisting purposes. Notable Rookie Cards include Pat Burrell and Freddy Garcia.

Nm-Mt Ex-Mt
COMP.MASTER SET (350) 200.00 60.00
COMP.SET w/o SP's (300) 25.00 7.50
COMMON (1-222/273-300) .20 .06
COMMON (223-272) .30 .09
COMMON SP (223-272) 2.00 .60
1 Alex Rodriguez 1.25 .35
2 Sidney Ponson .20 .06
3 Shawn Green .30 .09
4 Dan Wilson .20 .06
5 Rolando Arrojo .20 .06
6 Roberto Alomar .50 .15
7 Matt Anderson .20 .06
8 David Segui .20 .06
9 Alex Gonzalez .20 .06
10 Edgar Renteria .30 .09
11 Benito Santiago .30 .09
12 Todd Stottlemyre .20 .06
13 Rico Brogna .20 .06
14 Troy Glaus .30 .09
15 Al Leiter .30 .09
16 Pedro Martinez .75 .23
17 Paul O'Neill .50 .15
18 Manny Ramirez .50 .15
19 Scott Rolen .75 .23
20 Curt Schilling .30 .09
21 Bob Abreu .30 .09
22 Robb Nen .30 .09
23 Andy Pettitte .50 .15
24 John Wetteland .30 .09
25 Bobby Bonilla .30 .09
26 Darin Erstad .30 .09
27 Shawn Estes .20 .06
28 John Franco .30 .09
29 Nomar Garciaparra 1.25 .35
30 Rick Helling .20 .06
31 David Justice .30 .09
32 Chuck Knoblauch .30 .09
33 Quinton McCracken .20 .06
34 Kenny Rogers .30 .09
35 Brian Giles .30 .09
36 Armando Benitez .20 .06
37 Trevor Hoffman .30 .09
38 Charles Johnson .30 .09
39 Travis Lee .20 .06
40 Tom Glavine .50 .15
41 Rondell White .30 .09
42 Orlando Hernandez .20 .06
43 Mickey Morandini .20 .06
44 Darryl Kile .30 .09
45 Greg Vaughn .20 .06
46 Gregg Jefferies .20 .06
47 Mark McGwire 2.00 .60
48 Kerry Wood .75 .23
49 Jeromy Burnitz .30 .09
50 Ron Gant .30 .09
51 Vinny Castilla .30 .09
52 Doug Glanville .20 .06
53 Juan Guzman .20 .06
54 Dustin Hermanson .20 .06
55 Jose Hernandez .20 .06
56 Bobby Higginson .30 .09
57 A.J. Hinch .20 .06
58 Randy Johnson .75 .23
59 Eli Marrero .20 .06
60 Rafael Palmeiro .50 .15
61 Carl Pavano .30 .09
62 Brett Tomko .20 .06
63 Jose Guillen .30 .09
64 Mike Lieberthal .30 .09
65 Jim Abbott .50 .15
66 Dante Bichette .30 .09
67 Jeff Cirillo .20 .06
68 Eric Davis .30 .09
69 Delino DeShields .20 .06
70 Steve Finley .30 .09
71 Mark Grace .50 .15
72 Jason Kendall .30 .09
73 Jeff Kent .30 .09
74 Desi Relaford .20 .06
75 Ivan Rodriguez .75 .23
76 Shannon Stewart .30 .09
77 Geoff Jenkins .30 .09
78 Ben Grieve .20 .06
79 Cliff Floyd .30 .09
80 Jason Giambi .30 .09
81 Rod Beck .20 .06
82 Derek Bell .20 .06
83 Will Clark .75 .23
84 David Dellucci .20 .06
85 Joey Hamilton .20 .06
86 Livan Hernandez .20 .06
87 Barry Larkin .50 .15
88 Matt Mantei .20 .06
89 Dean Palmer .30 .09
90 Chan Ho Park .30 .09
91 Jim Thome .75 .23
92 Miguel Tejada .30 .09
93 Justin Thompson .20 .06
94 David Wells .30 .09
95 Bernie Williams .50 .15
96 Jeff Bagwell .50 .15
97 Derrek Lee .30 .09
98 Devon White .30 .09
99 Jeff Shaw .20 .06
100 Brad Radke .30 .09
101 Mark Grudzielanek .20 .06
102 Javy Lopez .30 .09
103 Mike Sirotka .20 .06
104 Robin Ventura .30 .09
105 Andy Ashby .20 .06
106 Juan Gonzalez .50 .15
107 Albert Belle .30 .09
108 Andy Benes .20 .06
109 Jay Buhner .30 .09
110 Ken Caminiti .30 .09
111 Roger Clemens 1.50 .45
112 Mike Hampton .30 .09
113 Pete Harnisch .20 .06
114 Mike Piazza 1.25 .35
115 J.T. Snow .30 .09
116 John Olerud .30 .09
117 Tony Womack .20 .06
118 Todd Zeile .30 .09
119 Tony Gwynn 1.00 .30
120 Brady Anderson .30 .09
121 Sean Casey .30 .09
122 Jose Cruz Jr. .20 .06
123 Carlos Delgado .30 .09
124 Edgar Martinez .50 .15
125 Jose Mesa .20 .06
126 Shane Reynolds .20 .06
127 John Valentin .20 .06
128 Mo Vaughn .30 .09
129 Kevin Young .30 .09
130 Jay Bell .30 .09
131 Aaron Boone .30 .09
132 John Smoltz .50 .15
133 Mike Stanley .20 .06
134 Bret Saberhagen .30 .09
135 Tim Salmon .50 .15
136 Mariano Rivera .50 .15
137 Ken Griffey Jr. 1.25 .35
138 Jose Offerman .20 .06
139 Troy Percival .30 .09
140 Greg Maddux 1.25 .35
141 Frank Thomas .75 .23
142 Steve Avery .20 .06
143 Kevin Millwood .30 .09
144 Sammy Sosa 1.25 .35
145 Larry Walker .50 .15
146 Matt Williams .30 .09
147 Mike Caruso .20 .06
148 Todd Helton .50 .15
149 Andruw Jones .30 .09
150 Ray Lankford .20 .06
151 Craig Biggio .50 .15
152 Ugueth Urbina .20 .06
153 Wade Boggs .50 .15
154 Derek Jeter 2.00 .60
155 Wally Joyner .30 .09
156 Mike Mussina .50 .15
157 Gregg Olson .20 .06
158 Henry Rodriguez .20 .06
159 Reggie Sanders .20 .06
160 Fernando Tatis .20 .06
161 Dmitri Young .30 .09
162 Rick Aguilera .20 .06
163 Marty Cordova .20 .06
164 Johnny Damon .50 .15
165 Ray Durham .30 .09
166 Brad Fullmer .20 .06
167 Chipper Jones .75 .23
168 Bobby Smith .20 .06
169 Omar Vizquel .50 .15
170 Todd Hundley .20 .06
171 David Cone .30 .09
172 Royce Clayton .20 .06
173 Ryan Klesko .30 .09
174 Jeff Montgomery .20 .06
175 Magglio Ordonez .30 .09
176 Billy Wagner .30 .09
177 Masato Yoshii .20 .06
178 Jason Christiansen .20 .06
179 Chuck Finley .30 .09
180 Tom Gordon .20 .06
181 Wilton Guerrero .20 .06
182 Rickey Henderson .75 .23
183 Sterling Hitchcock .20 .06
184 Kenny Lofton .30 .09
185 Tino Martinez .50 .15
186 Fred McGriff .50 .15
187 Matt Stairs .20 .06
188 Neifi Perez .20 .06
189 Bob Wickman .20 .06
190 Barry Bonds 2.00 .60
191 Jose Canseco .75 .23
192 Damion Easley .20 .06
193 Jim Edmonds .30 .09
194 Juan Encarnacion .20 .06
195 Travis Fryman .30 .09
196 Tom Goodwin .20 .06
197 Rusty Greer .30 .09
198 Roberto Hernandez .20 .06
199 B.J. Surhoff .30 .09
200 Scott Brosius .30 .09
201 Brian Jordan .30 .09
202 Paul Konerko .30 .09
203 Ismael Valdes .20 .06
204 Eric Milton .20 .06
205 Adrian Beltre .50 .15
206 Tony Clark .20 .06
207 Bartolo Colon .30 .09
208 Cal Ripken 2.50 .75
209 Moises Alou .30 .09
210 Wilson Alvarez .20 .06
211 Kevin Brown .50 .15
212 Orlando Cabrera .20 .06
213 Vladimir Guerrero .75 .23
214 Jose Rosado .20 .06
215 Raul Mondesi .30 .09
216 David Nilsson .20 .06
217 Carlos Perez .20 .06
218 Jason Schmidt .30 .09
219 Richie Sexson .30 .09
220 Gary Sheffield .30 .09
221 Fernando Vina .20 .06
222 Todd Walker .20 .06
223 Scott Sauerbeck RC .30 .09
223S Scott Sauerbeck SP 2.00 .60
224 Pascual Matos RC .30 .09
224S Pascual Matos SP 2.00 .60
225 Kyle Farnsworth RC .30 .09
225S Kyle Farnsworth SP 2.00 .60
226 Freddy Garcia RC .75 .23
226S Freddy Garcia SP 3.00 .90
227 David Lundquist RC .30 .09
227S David Lundquist SP 2.00 .60
228 Jolbert Cabrera RC .30 .09
228S Jolbert Cabrera SP 2.00 .60
229 Dan Perkins RC .30 .09
229S Dan Perkins SP 2.00 .60
230 Warren Morris .30 .09
230S Warren Morris SP 2.00 .60
231 Carlos Febles .30 .09
231S Carlos Febles SP 2.00 .60
232 Brett Hinchliffe RC .30 .09
232S Brett Hinchliffe SP 2.00 .60
233 Jason Phillips RC .30 .09
233S Jason Phillips SP 2.00 .60
234 Glen Barker RC .30 .09
234S Glen Barker SP 2.00 .60
235 Jose Macias RC .30 .09
235S Jose Macias SP 2.00 .60
236 Joe Mays RC .30 .09
236S Joe Mays SP 2.00 .60
237 Chad Allen RC .30 .09
237S Chad Allen SP 2.00 .60
238 Miguel Del Toro RC .30 .09
238S Miguel Del Toro SP 2.00 .60
239 Chris Singleton .30 .09
239S Chris Singleton SP 2.00 .60
240 Jesse Garcia RC .30 .09
240S Jesse Garcia SP 2.00 .60
241 Kris Benson .30 .09
241S Kris Benson SP 2.00 .60
242 Clay Bellinger RC .30 .09
242S Clay Bellinger SP 2.00 .60
243 Scott Williamson .30 .09
243S Scott Williamson SP 2.00 .60
244 Masao Kida RC .30 .09
244S Masao Kida SP 2.00 .60
245 Guillermo Garcia RC .30 .09
245S Guillermo Garcia SP 2.00 .60
246 A.J. Burnett RC .75 .23
246S A.J. Burnett SP 3.00 .90
247 Bo Porter RC .30 .09
247S Bo Porter SP 2.00 .60
248 Pat Burrell RC 1.00 .30
248S Pat Burrell SP 5.00 1.50
249 Carlos Lee .30 .09
249S Carlos Lee SP 2.00 .60
250 Jeff Weaver RC .50 .15
250S Jeff Weaver SP 2.00 .60
251 Ruben Mateo .30 .09
251S Ruben Mateo SP 2.00 .60
252 J.D. Drew .30 .09
252S J.D. Drew SP 2.00 .60
253 Jeremy Giambi .30 .09
253S Jeremy Giambi SP 2.00 .60
254 Gary Bennett RC .30 .09
254S Gary Bennett SP 2.00 .60
255 Edwards Guzman RC .30 .09
255S Edwards Guzman SP 2.00 .60

256 Ramon E.Martinez RC .30 .09
256S RamonE.Martinez SP 2.00 .60
257 Giomar Guevara RC .30 .09
257S Giomar Guevara SP 2.00 .60
258 Joe McEwing RC .30 .09
258S Joe McEwing SP 2.00 .60
259 Tom Davey RC .30 .09
259S Tom Davey SP 2.00 .60
260 Gabe Kapler .30 .09
260S Gabe Kapler SP 2.00 .60
261 Ryan Rupe RC .30 .09
261S Ryan Rupe SP 2.00 .60
262 Kelly Dransfeldt RC .30 .09
262S Kelly Dransfeldt SP 2.00 .60
263 Michael Barrett .30 .09
263S Michael Barrett SP 2.00 .60
264 Eric Chavez .30 .09
264S Eric Chavez SP 2.00 .60
265 Orber Moreno RC .30 .09
265S Orber Moreno SP 2.00 .60
266 Marlon Anderson .30 .09
266S Marlon Anderson SP 2.00 .60
267 Carlos Beltran .50 .15
267S Carlos Beltran SP 2.00 .60
268 D.Mientkiewicz RC .75 .23
268S D.Mientkiewicz SP 3.00 .90
269 Roy Halladay .30 .09
269S Roy Halladay SP 2.00 .60
270 Torii Hunter .30 .09
270S Torii Hunter SP 2.00 .60
271 Stan Spencer .30 .09
271S Stan Spencer SP 2.00 .60
272 Alex Gonzalez .30 .09
272S Alex Gonzalez SP 2.00 .60
273 Mark McGwire SF 1.00 .30
274 Scott Rolen SF .50 .15
275 Jeff Bagwell SF .30 .09
276 Derek Jeter SF 1.00 .30
277 Tony Gwynn SF .50 .15
278 Frank Thomas SF .50 .15
279 Sammy Sosa SF .75 .23
280 Nomar Garciaparra SF .75 .23
281 Cal Ripken SF 1.25 .35
282 Albert Belle SF .20 .06
283 Kerry Wood SF .50 .15
284 Greg Maddux SF .75 .23
285 Barry Bonds SF .75 .23
286 Juan Gonzalez SF .30 .09
287 Ken Griffey Jr. SF .75 .23
288 Alex Rodriguez SF .75 .23
289 Ben Grieve SF .20 .06
290 Travis Lee SF .20 .06
291 Mo Vaughn SF .20 .06
292 Mike Piazza SF .75 .23
293 Roger Clemens SF .75 .23
294 J.D. Drew SF .20 .06
295 Randy Johnson SF .50 .15
296 Chipper Jones SF .50 .15
297 Vladimir Guerrero SF .50 .15
298 Nomar Garciaparra CL .75 .23
299 Ken Griffey Jr. CL .75 .23
300 Mark McGwire CL 1.00 .30
S83 Ben Grieve Sample 1.00 .30

1999 SkyBox Premium Star Rubies

Randomly inserted into packs, this 300-card set is parallel to the base set. Only 50 serial-numbered sets were produced with the short-printed full-body action shot rookie and prospect cards sequentially numbered to just 15. Like the rest of the cards in this set, the close-up rookie and prospect cards are serial numbered to 50.

Nm-Mt Ex-Mt
COMMON CARD (1-300) 8.00 2.40
*STARS 1-300: 12.5X TO 30X BASIC CARDS
*PROSPECTS 223-272: 12.5X TO 30X BASIC
*ROOKIES 223-272: 8X TO 20X BASIC RC'S

1999 SkyBox Premium Autographics

Randomly inserted in packs at the rate of one in 68, this 52-card set features autographed color photos of top players. The cards are unnumbered and checklisted in alphabetical order.

Nm-Mt Ex-Mt
1 Roberto Alomar 25.00 7.50
2 Paul Bako 10.00 3.00
3 Michael Barrett 10.00 3.00
4 Kris Benson 10.00 3.00
5 Micah Bowie 10.00 3.00
6 Roosevelt Brown 10.00 3.00
7 A.J. Burnett 15.00 4.50
8 Pat Burrell 20.00 6.00
9 Ken Caminiti 25.00 7.50
10 Royce Clayton 10.00 3.00
11 Edgard Clemente 10.00 3.00
12 Bartolo Colon 15.00 4.50
13 J.D. Drew 25.00 7.50
14 Damion Easley 10.00 3.00
15 Derrin Ebert 10.00 3.00
16 Mario Encarnacion 10.00 3.00
17 Juan Encarnacion 10.00 3.00
18 Troy Glaus 15.00 4.50
19 Tom Glavine 40.00 12.00
20 Juan Gonzalez SP 150.00 45.00
21 Shawn Green 15.00 4.50
22 Wilton Guerrero 10.00 3.00
23 Jose Guillen 15.00 4.50
24 Tony Gwynn 50.00 15.00
25 Mark Harriger 10.00 3.00
26 Todd Hollandsworth 10.00 3.00
27 Scott Hunter 10.00 3.00
28 Gabe Kapler 10.00 3.00
29 Scott Karl 10.00 3.00
30 Mike Kinkade 10.00 3.00
31 Ray Lankford 10.00 3.00
32 Barry Larkin 25.00 7.50
33 Matt Lawton 10.00 3.00
34 Ricky Ledee 10.00 3.00
35 Travis Lee 10.00 3.00
36 Eli Marrero 10.00 3.00
37 Ruben Mateo 10.00 3.00
38 Joe McEwing 15.00 4.50
39 Doug Mientkiewicz 15.00 4.50
40 Russ Ortiz 15.00 4.50
41 Jim Parque 10.00 3.00
42 Robert Person 10.00 3.00
43 Alex Rodriguez 100.00 30.00
44 Scott Rolen 40.00 12.00
45 Benj Sampson 10.00 3.00
46 Luis Saturria 10.00 3.00
47 Curt Schilling 40.00 12.00
48 David Segui 10.00 3.00
49 Fernando Tatis 10.00 3.00
50 Peter Tucci 10.00 3.00
51 Javier Vazquez 15.00 4.50
52 Robin Ventura 15.00 4.50

1999 SkyBox Premium Autographics Blue Ink

Randomly inserted in packs, this 52-card set is a blue ink parallel version of the regular insert set. Only 50 serial-numbered sets were produced.

Nm-Mt Ex-Mt
*BLUE INK STARS: 1X TO 2.5X BASIC AU'S
*BLUE INK RC'S: .75X TO 2X BASIC AU'S

1999 SkyBox Premium Diamond Debuts

Randomly inserted in packs at the rate of one in 49, this 15-card set features color photos of the best rookies of 1999 printed on silver rainbow holo-foil and etched cards.

Nm-Mt Ex-Mt
COMPLETE SET (15) 80.00 24.00
1 Eric Chavez 8.00 2.40
2 Kyle Farnsworth 8.00 2.40
3 Ryan Rupe 8.00 2.40
4 Jeremy Giambi 8.00 2.40
5 Marlon Anderson 8.00 2.40
6 J.D. Drew 8.00 2.40
7 Carlos Febles 8.00 2.40
8 Joe McEwing 8.00 2.40
9 Jeff Weaver 12.00 3.60
10 Alex Gonzalez 5.00 1.50
11 Chad Allen 8.00 2.40
12 Michael Barrett 8.00 2.40
13 Gabe Kapler 8.00 2.40
14 Carlos Lee 8.00 2.40
15 Edwards Guzman 8.00 2.40

1999 SkyBox Premium Intimidation Nation

Randomly inserted in packs, this 15-card set features color photos of top players stamped on gold rainbow holo-foil cards. Only 99 serial-numbered sets were produced.

Nm-Mt Ex-Mt
1 Cal Ripken 100.00 30.00
2 Tony Gwynn 40.00 12.00
3 Nomar Garciaparra 50.00 15.00
4 Frank Thomas 30.00 9.00
5 Mike Piazza 50.00 15.00
6 Mark McGwire 80.00 24.00
7 Scott Rolen 30.00 9.00
8 Chipper Jones 30.00 9.00
9 Greg Maddux 50.00 15.00
10 Ken Griffey Jr. 50.00 15.00
11 Juan Gonzalez 20.00 6.00
12 Derek Jeter 80.00 24.00
13 J.D. Drew 20.00 6.00
14 Roger Clemens 60.00 18.00
15 Alex Rodriguez 50.00 15.00

1999 SkyBox Premium Live Bats

Randomly inserted in packs at the rate of one in seven, this 15-card set features color photos of some of baseball's best hitters on foil stamped cards.

Nm-Mt Ex-Mt
COMPLETE SET (15) 25.00 7.50
1 Juan Gonzalez .75 .23
2 Mark McGwire 3.00 .90
3 Jeff Bagwell .75 .23
4 Frank Thomas 1.25 .35
5 Mike Piazza 2.00 .60
6 Nomar Garciaparra 2.00 .60
7 Alex Rodriguez 2.00 .60
8 Scott Rolen 1.25 .35
9 Travis Lee .30 .09
10 Tony Gwynn 1.50 .45
11 Derek Jeter 3.00 .90
12 Ben Grieve .30 .09
13 Chipper Jones 1.25 .35
14 Ken Griffey Jr. 2.00 .60
15 Cal Ripken 4.00 1.20

1999 SkyBox Premium Show Business

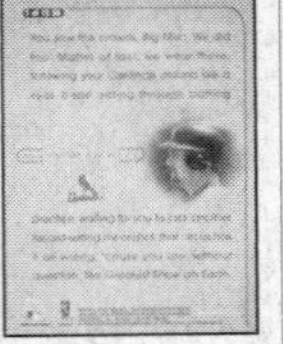

Randomly inserted in packs at the rate of one in 70, this 15-card set features top players printed on double foil-stamped cards.

Nm-Mt Ex-Mt
COMPLETE SET (15) 200.00 60.00
1 Mark McGwire 20.00 6.00
2 Tony Gwynn 10.00 3.00
3 Nomar Garciaparra 12.00 3.60
4 Juan Gonzalez 5.00 1.50
5 Roger Clemens 15.00 4.50
6 Chipper Jones 8.00 2.40
7 Cal Ripken 25.00 7.50
8 Alex Rodriguez 12.00 3.60
9 Orlando Hernandez 2.00 .60
10 Greg Maddux 12.00 3.60
11 Mike Piazza 12.00 3.60
12 Frank Thomas 8.00 2.40
13 Ken Griffey Jr. 12.00 3.60
14 Scott Rolen 8.00 2.40
15 Derek Jeter 20.00 6.00

1999 SkyBox Premium Soul of the Game

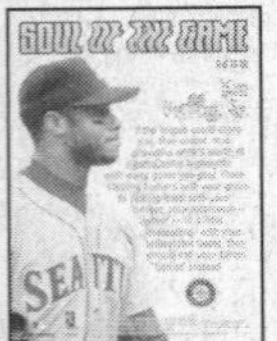

Randomly inserted into packs at the rate of one in 14, this 15-card set features players who are fan favorites printed on rainbow foil stamped cards.

Nm-Mt Ex-Mt
COMPLETE SET (15) 60.00 18.00
1 Alex Rodriguez 4.00 1.20
2 Vladimir Guerrero 2.50 .75
3 Chipper Jones 2.50 .75
4 Derek Jeter 6.00 1.80
5 Tony Gwynn 3.00 .90
6 Scott Rolen 2.50 .75
7 Juan Gonzalez 1.50 .45
8 Mark McGwire 6.00 1.80
9 Ken Griffey Jr. 4.00 1.20
10 Jeff Bagwell 1.50 .45
11 Cal Ripken 8.00 2.40
12 Frank Thomas 2.50 .75
13 Mike Piazza 4.00 1.20
14 Nomar Garciaparra 4.00 1.20
15 Sammy Sosa 4.00 1.20

1993 SP

This 290-card standard-size set, produced by Upper Deck, features fronts with action color player photos. Special subsets include All Star players (1-18) and Foil Prospects (271-290). Cards 19-270 are in alphabetical order by team nickname. Notable Rookie Cards include Johnny Damon and Derek Jeter.

Nm-Mt Ex-Mt
COMPLETE SET (290) 80.00 24.00
COMMON CARD (1-270) .50 .15
COMMON FOIL (271-290) 1.00 .30
1 Roberto Alomar AS 1.25 .35
2 Wade Boggs AS 1.25 .35
3 Joe Carter AS .50 .15
4 Ken Griffey Jr. AS 3.00 .90
5 Mark Langston AS .50 .15
6 John Olerud AS .75 .23
7 Kirby Puckett AS 2.00 .60
8 Cal Ripken Jr. AS 6.00 1.80
9 Ivan Rodriguez AS 2.00 .60
10 Barry Bonds AS 5.00 1.50
11 Darren Daulton AS .75 .23
12 Marquis Grissom AS .75 .23
13 David Justice AS .75 .23
14 John Kruk AS .75 .23
15 Barry Larkin AS 1.25 .35
16 Terry Mulholland AS .50 .15
17 Ryne Sandberg AS 3.00 .90
18 Gary Sheffield AS .75 .23
19 Chad Curtis .50 .15
20 Chili Davis .75 .23
21 Gary DiSarcina .50 .15
22 Damion Easley .75 .23
23 Chuck Finley .75 .23
24 Luis Polonia .50 .15
25 Tim Salmon 1.25 .35
26 J.T. Snow RC 1.25 .35
27 Russ Springer .50 .15
28 Jeff Bagwell 1.25 .35
29 Craig Biggio 1.25 .35
30 Ken Caminiti .75 .23
31 Andujar Cedeno .50 .15
32 Doug Drabek .50 .15
33 Steve Finley .75 .23
34 Luis Gonzalez .75 .23
35 Pete Harnisch .50 .15
36 Darryl Kile .75 .23
37 Mike Bordick .50 .15
38 Dennis Eckersley .75 .23
39 Brent Gates .50 .15
40 Rickey Henderson 2.00 .60
41 Mark McGwire 5.00 1.50
42 Craig Paquette .50 .15
43 Ruben Sierra .50 .15
44 Terry Steinbach .50 .15
45 Todd Van Poppel .50 .15
46 Pat Borders .50 .15
47 Tony Fernandez .50 .15
48 Juan Guzman .50 .15
49 Pat Hentgen .50 .15
50 Paul Molitor 1.25 .35
51 Jack Morris .75 .23
52 Ed Sprague .50 .15
53 Duane Ward .50 .15
54 Devon White .75 .23
55 Steve Avery .50 .15
56 Jeff Blauser .50 .15
57 Ron Gant .75 .23
58 Tom Glavine 1.25 .35
59 Greg Maddux 3.00 .90
60 Fred McGriff 1.25 .35
61 Terry Pendleton .75 .23
62 Deion Sanders 1.25 .35
63 John Smoltz 1.25 .35
64 Cal Eldred .50 .15
65 Darryl Hamilton .50 .15
66 John Jaha .50 .15
67 Pat Listach .50 .15
68 Jaime Navarro .50 .15
69 Kevin Reimer .50 .15
70 B.J. Surhoff .75 .23
71 Greg Vaughn .50 .15
72 Robin Yount 3.00 .90
73 Rene Arocha RC .75 .23
74 Bernard Gilkey .50 .15
75 Gregg Jefferies .50 .15
76 Ray Lankford .50 .15
77 Tom Pagnozzi .50 .15
78 Lee Smith .75 .23
79 Ozzie Smith 3.00 .90
80 Bob Tewksbury .50 .15
81 Mark Whiten .50 .15
82 Steve Buechele .50 .15
83 Mark Grace 1.25 .35
84 Jose Guzman .50 .15
85 Derrick May .50 .15
86 Mike Morgan .50 .15
87 Randy Myers .50 .15
88 Kevin Roberson RC .50 .15
89 Sammy Sosa 3.00 .90
90 Rick Wilkins .50 .15
91 Brett Butler .75 .23
92 Eric Davis .75 .23
93 Orel Hershiser .75 .23
94 Eric Karros .75 .23
95 Ramon Martinez .50 .15
96 Raul Mondesi .75 .23
97 Jose Offerman .50 .15
98 Mike Piazza 5.00 1.50
99 Darryl Strawberry .75 .23
100 Moises Alou .75 .23
101 Wil Cordero .50 .15
102 Delino DeShields .50 .15
103 Darrin Fletcher .50 .15
104 Ken Hill .50 .15
105 Mike Lansing RC .75 .23
106 Dennis Martinez .75 .23
107 Larry Walker 1.25 .35
108 John Wetteland .75 .23
109 Rod Beck .50 .15
110 John Burkett .50 .15
111 Will Clark 2.00 .60
112 Royce Clayton .50 .15
113 Darren Lewis .50 .15
114 Willie McGee .75 .23
115 Bill Swift .50 .15
116 Robby Thompson .50 .15
117 Matt Williams .75 .23
118 Sandy Alomar Jr. .50 .15
119 Carlos Baerga .50 .15
120 Albert Belle .75 .23
121 Reggie Jefferson .50 .15
122 Wayne Kirby .50 .15
123 Kenny Lofton .75 .23
124 Carlos Martinez .50 .15
125 Charles Nagy .50 .15
126 Paul Sorrento .50 .15
127 Rich Amaral .50 .15
128 Jay Buhner .75 .23
129 Norm Charlton .50 .15
130 Dave Fleming .50 .15
131 Erik Hanson .50 .15
132 Randy Johnson 2.00 .60
133 Edgar Martinez 1.25 .35
134 Tino Martinez 1.25 .35
135 Omar Vizquel 1.25 .35
136 Bret Barberie .50 .15
137 Chuck Carr .50 .15
138 Jeff Conine .75 .23
139 Orestes Destrade .50 .15
140 Chris Hammond .50 .15
141 Bryan Harvey .50 .15
142 Benito Santiago .75 .23
143 Walt Weiss .50 .15
144 Darrell Whitmore RC .50 .15
145 Tim Bogar RC .50 .15
146 Bobby Bonilla .75 .23
147 Jeromy Burnitz .75 .23
148 Vince Coleman .50 .15
149 Dwight Gooden .75 .23
150 Todd Hundley .50 .15
151 Howard Johnson .50 .15
152 Eddie Murray 2.00 .60
153 Bret Saberhagen .75 .23
154 Brady Anderson .75 .23
155 Mike Devereaux .50 .15
166 Jeffrey Hammonds .50 .15
157 Chris Hoiles .50 .15
158 Ben McDonald .50 .15
159 Mark McLemore .50 .15
160 Mike Mussina 1.25 .35
161 Gregg Olson .50 .15
162 David Segui .50 .15
163 Derek Bell .50 .15
164 Andy Benes .50 .15
165 Archi Cianfrocco .50 .15
166 Ricky Gutierrez .50 .15
167 Tony Gwynn 2.50 .75
168 Gene Harris .50 .15
169 Trevor Hoffman .75 .23
170 Ray McDavid RC .50 .15
171 Phil Plantier .50 .15
172 Mariano Duncan .50 .15
173 Len Dykstra .75 .23
174 Tommy Greene .50 .15
175 Dave Hollins .50 .15
176 Pete Incaviglia .50 .15
177 Mickey Morandini .50 .15
178 Curt Schilling .75 .23
179 Kevin Stocker .50 .15
180 Mitch Williams .50 .15
181 Stan Belinda .50 .15
182 Jay Bell .75 .23
183 Steve Cooke .50 .15
184 Carlos Garcia .50 .15
185 Jeff King .50 .15
186 Orlando Merced .50 .15
187 Don Slaught .50 .15
188 Andy Van Slyke .75 .23
189 Kevin Young .75 .23
190 Kevin Brown .75 .23
191 Jose Canseco 2.00 .60
192 Julio Franco .75 .23
193 Benji Gil .50 .15
194 Juan Gonzalez 1.25 .35
195 Tom Henke .50 .15
196 Rafael Palmeiro 1.25 .35
197 Dean Palmer .75 .23
198 Nolan Ryan 8.00 2.40
199 Roger Clemens 4.00 1.20
200 Scott Cooper .50 .15
201 Andre Dawson .75 .23
202 Mike Greenwell .50 .15
203 Carlos Quintana .50 .15
204 Jeff Russell .50 .15
205 Aaron Sele .75 .23
206 Mo Vaughn .75 .23
207 Frank Viola .75 .23
208 Rob Dibble .75 .23
209 Roberto Kelly .50 .15
210 Kevin Mitchell .50 .15
211 Hal Morris .50 .15
212 Joe Oliver .50 .15
213 Jose Rijo .50 .15
214 Bip Roberts .50 .15
215 Chris Sabo .50 .15
216 Reggie Sanders .50 .15
217 Dante Bichette .75 .23
218 Jerald Clark .50 .15
219 Alex Cole .50 .15
220 Andres Galarraga .75 .23
221 Joe Girardi .50 .15
222 Charlie Hayes .50 .15
223 Roberto Mejia RC .50 .15
224 Armando Reynoso .50 .15
225 Eric Young .50 .15
226 Kevin Appier .75 .23
227 George Brett 5.00 1.50
228 David Cone .75 .23
229 Phil Hiatt .50 .15
230 Felix Jose .50 .15
231 Wally Joyner .75 .23
232 Mike Macfarlane .50 .15
233 Brian McRae .50 .15
234 Jeff Montgomery .50 .15
235 Rob Deer .50 .15
236 Cecil Fielder .75 .23
237 Travis Fryman .75 .23
238 Mike Henneman .50 .15
239 Tony Phillips .50 .15
240 Mickey Tettleton .50 .15
241 Alan Trammell .75 .23
242 David Wells .75 .23
243 Lou Whitaker .75 .23
244 Rick Aguilera .50 .15
245 Scott Erickson .50 .15
246 Brian Harper .50 .15
247 Kent Hrbek .75 .23
248 Chuck Knoblauch .75 .23
249 Shane Mack .50 .15
250 David McCarty .50 .15
251 Pedro Munoz .50 .15
252 Dave Winfield .75 .23
253 Alex Fernandez .50 .15
254 Ozzie Guillen .50 .15
255 Bo Jackson 2.00 .60
256 Lance Johnson .50 .15
257 Ron Karkovice .50 .15
258 Jack McDowell .50 .15
259 Tim Raines .75 .23
260 Frank Thomas 2.00 .60
261 Robin Ventura .75 .23
262 Jim Abbott 1.25 .35
263 Steve Farr .50 .15
264 Jimmy Key .75 .23
265 Don Mattingly 5.00 1.50
266 Paul O'Neill 1.25 .35
267 Mike Stanley .50 .15
268 Danny Tartabull .50 .15
269 Bob Wickman .50 .15
270 Bernie Williams 1.25 .35
271 Jason Bere FOIL 1.00 .30
272 R.Cedeno FOIL RC 1.50 .45

273 J.Damon FOIL RC 10.00 3.00
274 Russ Davis FOIL RC 1.50 .45
275 Carlos Delgado FOIL 4.00 1.20
276 Carl Everett FOIL 1.50 .45
277 Cliff Floyd FOIL .75 .23
278 Alex Gonzalez FOIL 1.00 .30
279 Derek Jeter FOIL RC 60.00 18.00
280 Chipper Jones FOIL 4.00 1.20
281 Javier Lopez FOIL 1.25 .35
282 Chad Mottola FOIL RC 1.00 .30
283 Marc Newfield FOIL 1.00 .30
284 Eduardo Perez FOIL 1.00 .30
285 Manny Ramirez FOIL 4.00 1.20
286 T.Steverson FOIL RC 1.00 .30
287 Michael Tucker FOIL 1.50 .45
288 Allen Watson FOIL 1.00 .30
289 Rondell White FOIL 1.50 .45
290 Dmitri Young FOIL 1.50 .45

1993 SP Platinum Power

Cards from this 20-card standard-size were inserted one every nine packs and feature power hitters from the American and National Leagues.

Nm-Mt Ex-Mt
COMPLETE SET (20) 80.00 24.00
PP1 Albert Belle 2.00 .60
PP2 Barry Bonds 12.00 3.60
PP3 Joe Carter 1.25 .35
PP4 Will Clark 5.00 1.50
PP5 Darren Daulton 2.00 .60
PP6 Cecil Fielder 2.00 .60
PP7 Ron Gant 2.00 .60
PP8 Juan Gonzalez 3.00 .90
PP9 Ken Griffey Jr. 8.00 2.40
PP10 Dave Hollins 1.25 .35
PP11 David Justice 2.00 .60
PP12 Fred McGriff 3.00 .90
PP13 Mark McGwire 12.00 3.60
PP14 Dean Palmer 2.00 .60
PP15 Mike Piazza 12.00 3.60
PP16 Tim Salmon 3.00 .90
PP17 Ryne Sandberg 8.00 2.40
PP18 Gary Sheffield 2.00 .60
PP19 Frank Thomas 5.00 1.50
PP20 Matt Williams 2.00 .60

1994 SP Previews

These 15 cards were distributed regionally as inserts in second series Upper Deck hobby packs. They were inserted at a rate of one in 35. The manner of distribution was five cards per Central, East and West region. The cards are nearly identical to the basic SP issue. Card fronts differ in that the region is at bottom right where the team name is located on the SP cards.

Nm-Mt Ex-Mt
COMPLETE SET (15) 160.00 47.50
COMPLETE CENTRAL (5) 60.00 18.00
COMPLETE EAST (5) 40.00 12.00
COMPLETE WEST (5) 60.00 18.00
CR1 Jeff Bagwell 5.00 1.50
CR2 Michael Jordan 25.00 7.50
CR3 Kirby Puckett 8.00 2.40
CR4 Manny Ramirez 5.00 1.50
CR5 Frank Thomas 8.00 2.40
ER1 Roberto Alomar 5.00 1.50
ER2 Cliff Floyd 3.00 .90
ER3 Javier Lopez 3.00 .90
ER4 Don Mattingly 20.00 6.00
ER5 Cal Ripken 25.00 7.50
WR1 Barry Bonds 20.00 6.00
WR2 Juan Gonzalez 5.00 1.50
WR3 Ken Griffey Jr. 12.00 3.60
WR4 Mike Piazza 15.00 4.50
WR5 Tim Salmon 5.00 1.50

1994 SP

This 200-card standard-size set distributed in foil packs contains the game's top players and prospects. The first 20 cards in the set are Foil Prospects which are brighter and more metallic than the rest of the set. These cards therefore are highly condition sensitive. Cards 21-200 are in alphabetical order by team nickname. Rookie Cards include Brad Fullmer, Derrek Lee, Chan Ho Park and Alex Rodriguez.

Nm-Mt Ex-Mt
COMPLETE SET (200) 100.00 30.00
COMMON CARD (21-200) .20 .06
COMMON FOIL (1-20) .50 .15
1 Mike Bell FOIL RC .50 .15
2 D.J. Boston FOIL RC .50 .15
3 Johnny Damon FOIL 2.00 .60
4 Brad Fullmer FOIL RC 1.25 .35
5 Joey Hamilton FOIL .50 .15
6 T.Hollandsworth FOIL .50 .15
7 Brian L. Hunter FOIL .50 .15
8 L.Hawkins FOIL RC 1.25 .35
9 B.Kieschnick FOIL RC .75 .23
10 Derrek Lee FOIL RC 2.00 .60
11 Trot Nixon FOIL RC 2.50 .75
12 Alex Ochoa FOIL .50 .15
13 Chan Ho Park FOIL RC 1.25 .35
14 Kirk Presley FOIL RC .50 .15
15 A.Rodriguez FOIL RC 80.00 24.00
16 Jose Silva FOIL RC .50 .15
17 Terrell Wade FOIL RC .50 .15
18 Billy Wagner FOIL RC 2.00 .60
19 G.Williams FOIL RC .50 .15
20 Preston Wilson FOIL .75 .23
21 Brian Anderson RC .40 .12
22 Chad Curtis .20 .06
23 Chili Davis .40 .12
24 Bo Jackson 1.00 .30
25 Mark Langston .20 .06
26 Tim Salmon .60 .18
27 Jeff Bagwell .60 .18
28 Craig Biggio .60 .18
29 Ken Caminiti .40 .12
30 Doug Drabek .20 .06
31 John Hudek RC .20 .06
32 Greg Swindell .20 .06
33 Brent Gates .20 .06
34 Rickey Henderson 1.00 .30
35 Steve Karsay .20 .06
36 Mark McGwire 2.50 .75
37 Ruben Sierra .20 .06
38 Terry Steinbach .20 .06
39 Roberto Alomar .60 .18
40 Joe Carter .40 .12
41 Carlos Delgado .60 .18
42 Alex Gonzalez .20 .06
43 Juan Guzman .20 .06
44 Paul Molitor .60 .18
45 John Olerud .40 .12
46 Devon White .40 .12
47 Steve Avery .20 .06
48 Jeff Blauser .20 .06
49 Tom Glavine .60 .18
50 David Justice .40 .12
51 Roberto Kelly .20 .06
52 Ryan Klesko .40 .12
53 Javier Lopez .40 .12
54 Greg Maddux 1.50 .45
55 Fred McGriff .60 .18
56 Ricky Bones .20 .06
57 Cal Eldred .20 .06
58 Brian Harper .20 .06
59 Pat Listach .20 .06
60 B.J. Surhoff .40 .12
61 Greg Vaughn .20 .06
62 Bernard Gilkey .20 .06
63 Gregg Jefferies .20 .06
64 Ray Lankford .20 .06
65 Ozzie Smith 1.50 .45
66 Bob Tewksbury .20 .06
67 Mark Whiten .20 .06
68 Todd Zeile .20 .06
69 Mark Grace .60 .18
70 Randy Myers .20 .06
71 Ryne Sandberg 1.50 .45
72 Sammy Sosa 1.50 .45
73 Steve Trachsel .20 .06
74 Rick Wilkins .20 .06
75 Brett Butler .40 .12
76 Delino DeShields .20 .06
77 Orel Hershiser .40 .12
78 Eric Karros .40 .12
79 Raul Mondesi .40 .12
80 Mike Piazza 2.00 .60
81 Tim Wallach .20 .06
82 Moises Alou .40 .12
83 Cliff Floyd .40 .12
84 Marquis Grissom .40 .12
85 Pedro Martinez 1.00 .30
86 Larry Walker .60 .18
87 John Wetteland .40 .12
88 Rondell White .40 .12
89 Rod Beck .20 .06
90 Barry Bonds 2.50 .75
91 John Burkett .20 .06
92 Royce Clayton .20 .06
93 Billy Swift .20 .06
94 Robby Thompson .20 .06
95 Matt Williams .40 .12
96 Carlos Baerga .20 .06
97 Albert Belle .40 .12
98 Kenny Lofton .40 .12
99 Dennis Martinez .40 .12
100 Eddie Murray 1.00 .30
101 Manny Ramirez .60 .18
102 Eric Anthony .20 .06
103 Chris Bosio .20 .06
104 Jay Buhner .40 .12
105 Ken Griffey Jr. 1.50 .45
106 Randy Johnson 1.00 .30
107 Edgar Martinez .60 .18
108 Chuck Carr .20 .06
109 Jeff Conine .40 .12
110 Carl Everett .40 .12
111 Chris Hammond .20 .06
112 Bryan Harvey .20 .06
113 Charles Johnson .40 .12
114 Gary Sheffield .40 .12
115 Bobby Bonilla .40 .12
116 Dwight Gooden .40 .12
117 Todd Hundley .20 .06
118 Bobby Jones .20 .06
119 Jeff Kent .40 .12
120 Bret Saberhagen .40 .12
121 Jeffrey Hammonds .20 .06
122 Chris Hoiles .20 .06
123 Ben McDonald .20 .06
124 Mike Mussina .60 .18
125 Rafael Palmeiro .60 .18
126 Cal Ripken Jr. 3.00 .90
127 Lee Smith .40 .12
128 Derek Bell .20 .06
129 Andy Benes .20 .06
130 Tony Gwynn 1.25 .35
131 Trevor Hoffman .40 .12
132 Phil Plantier .20 .06
133 Bip Roberts .20 .06
134 Darren Daulton .40 .12
135 Lenny Dykstra .40 .12
136 Dave Hollins .20 .06
137 Danny Jackson .20 .06
138 John Kruk .40 .12
139 Kevin Stocker .20 .06
140 Jay Bell .40 .12
141 Carlos Garcia .20 .06
142 Jeff King .20 .06
143 Orlando Merced .20 .06
144 Andy Van Slyke .40 .12
145 Rick White .20 .06
146 Jose Canseco 1.00 .30
147 Will Clark 1.00 .30
148 Juan Gonzalez .60 .18
149 Rick Helling .20 .06
150 Dean Palmer .40 .12
151 Ivan Rodriguez 1.00 .30
152 Roger Clemens 2.00 .60
153 Scott Cooper .20 .06
154 Andre Dawson .40 .12
155 Mike Greenwell .20 .06
156 Aaron Sele .20 .06
157 Mo Vaughn .40 .12
158 Bret Boone .40 .12
159 Barry Larkin .60 .18
160 Kevin Mitchell .20 .06
161 Jose Rijo .20 .06
162 Deion Sanders .60 .18
163 Reggie Sanders .20 .06
164 Dante Bichette .40 .12
165 Ellis Burks .40 .12
166 Andres Galarraga .40 .12
167 Charlie Hayes .20 .06
168 David Nied .20 .06
169 Walt Weiss .20 .06
170 Kevin Appier .40 .12
171 David Cone .40 .12
172 Jeff Granger .20 .06
173 Felix Jose .20 .06
174 Wally Joyner .40 .12
175 Brian McRae .20 .06
176 Cecil Fielder .40 .12
177 Travis Fryman .40 .12
178 Mike Henneman .20 .06
179 Tony Phillips .20 .06
180 Mickey Tettleton .20 .06
181 Alan Trammell .40 .12
182 Rick Aguilera .20 .06
183 Rich Becker .20 .06
184 Scott Erickson .20 .06
185 Chuck Knoblauch .40 .12
186 Kirby Puckett 1.00 .30
187 Dave Winfield .40 .12
188 Wilson Alvarez .20 .06
189 Jason Bere .20 .06
190 Alex Fernandez .20 .06
191 Julio Franco .40 .12
192 Jack McDowell .20 .06
193 Frank Thomas 1.00 .30
194 Robin Ventura .40 .12
195 Jim Abbott .60 .18
196 Wade Boggs .60 .18
197 Jimmy Key .40 .12
198 Don Mattingly 2.50 .75
199 Paul O'Neill .60 .18
200 Danny Tartabull .20 .06
P24 Ken Griffey Jr. Promo 2.00 .60

1994 SP Die Cuts

This 200-card die-cut set is parallel to that of the basic SP issue. The cards were inserted one per SP pack. The difference, of course, is the unique die-cut shape. The backs have a silver Upper Deck hologram as opposed to gold on the basic issue.

Nm-Mt Ex-Mt
COMPLETE SET (200) 150.00 45.00
*STARS: .75X TO 2X BASIC CARDS...
*ROOKIES: .5X TO 1.2X BASIC CARDS
15 Alex Rodriguez FOIL 100.00 30.00

1994 SP Holoviews

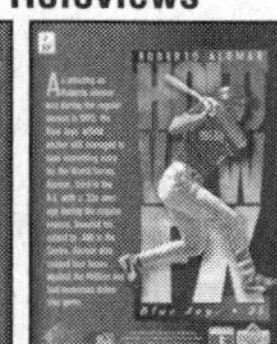

Randomly inserted in SP foil packs at a rate of one in five, this 38-card set contains top stars and prospects.

Nm-Mt Ex-Mt
1 Roberto Alomar 3.00 .90
2 Kevin Appier 2.00 .60
3 Jeff Bagwell 3.00 .90
4 Jose Canseco 5.00 1.50
5 Roger Clemens 10.00 3.00
6 Carlos Delgado 2.00 .60
7 Cecil Fielder 2.00 .60
8 Cliff Floyd 2.00 .60
9 Travis Fryman 2.00 .60
10 Andres Galarraga 2.00 .60
11 Juan Gonzalez 3.00 .90
12 Ken Griffey Jr. 8.00 2.40
13 Tony Gwynn 6.00 1.80
14 Jeffrey Hammonds 1.50 .45
15 Bo Jackson 5.00 1.50
16 Michael Jordan 25.00 7.50
17 David Justice 2.00 .60
18 Steve Karsay 1.50 .45
19 Jeff Kent 2.00 .60
20 Brooks Kieschnick 2.00 .60
21 Ryan Klesko 2.00 .60
22 John Kruk 2.00 .60
23 Barry Larkin 3.00 .90
24 Pat Listach 1.50 .45
25 Don Mattingly 12.00 3.60
26 Mark McGwire 12.00 3.60
27 Raul Mondesi 2.00 .60
28 Trot Nixon 5.00 1.50
29 Mike Piazza 8.00 2.40
30 Kirby Puckett 5.00 1.50
31 Manny Ramirez 3.00 .90
32 Cal Ripken 15.00 4.50
33 Alex Rodriguez 50.00 15.00
34 Tim Salmon 3.00 .90
35 Gary Sheffield 2.00 .60
36 Ozzie Smith 8.00 2.40
37 Sammy Sosa 8.00 2.40
38 Andy Van Slyke 2.00 .60

1994 SP Holoviews Die Cuts

Parallel to the blue Holoview set, this 38-card red-bordered issue was also randomly inserted in SP packs. They are much more difficult to pull than the blue version with an insertion rate of one in 75.

Nm-Mt Ex-Mt
*DIE CUTS: 4X TO 10X BASIC HOLO .
*DIE CUTS: 2.5X TO 6X BASIC HOLO RC YR
16 Michael Jordan 150.00 45.00
28 Trot Nixon 30.00 9.00
33 Alex Rodriguez 500.00 150.00

1995 SP

This set consists of 207 cards being sold in eight-card, hobby-only packs with a suggested retail price of $3.99. Subsets featured are Salute (1-4) and Premier Prospects (5-24). The only notable Rookie Card in this set is Hideo Nomo. Dealers who ordered a certain quantity of Upper Deck baseball cases received as a bonus, a certified autographed SP card of Ken Griffey Jr.

Nm-Mt Ex-Mt
COMPLETE SET (207) 40.00 12.00
COMMON CARD (1-207) .20 .06
COMMON FOIL (5-24) .50 .15
GRIFFEY AU SENT TO DEALERS AS BONUS
1 Cal Ripken Salute 3.00 .90
2 Nolan Ryan Salute 4.00 1.20
3 George Brett Salute 2.50 .75
4 Mike Schmidt Salute 1.50 .45
5 Dustin Hermanson FOIL .50 .15
6 Antonio Osuna FOIL .50 .15
7 M.Grudzielanek FOIL RC .75 .23
8 Ray Durham FOIL .75 .23
9 Ugueth Urbina FOIL .50 .15
10 Ruben Rivera FOIL .50 .15
11 Curtis Goodwin FOIL .50 .15
12 Jimmy Hurst FOIL .50 .15
13 Jose Malave FOIL .50 .15
14 Hideo Nomo FOIL RC 3.00 .90
15 Juan Acevedo RC FOIL .50 .15
16 Tony Clark FOIL .50 .15
17 Jim Pittsley FOIL .50 .15
18 Freddy A. Garcia RC FOIL .50 .15
19 Carlos Perez RC FOIL .75 .23
20 R.Casanova FOIL RC .50 .15
21 Quilvio Veras FOIL .50 .15
22 Edgardo Alfonzo FOIL .50 .15
23 Marty Cordova FOIL .50 .15
24 C.J. Nitkowski FOIL .50 .15
25 Wade Boggs CL .40 .12
26 Dave Winfield CL .20 .06
27 Eddie Murray CL .60 .18
28 David Justice .40 .12
29 Marquis Grissom .40 .12
30 Fred McGriff .60 .18
31 Greg Maddux 1.50 .45
32 Tom Glavine .60 .18
33 Steve Avery .20 .06
34 Chipper Jones 1.00 .30
35 Sammy Sosa 1.50 .45
36 Jaime Navarro .20 .06
37 Randy Myers .20 .06
38 Mark Grace .60 .18
39 Todd Zeile .20 .06
40 Brian McRae .20 .06
41 Reggie Sanders .20 .06
42 Ron Gant .40 .12
43 Deion Sanders .60 .18
44 Bret Boone .40 .12
45 Barry Larkin .60 .18
46 Jose Rijo .20 .06
47 Jason Bates .20 .06
48 Andres Galarraga .40 .12
49 Bill Swift .20 .06
50 Larry Walker .60 .18
51 Vinny Castilla .40 .12
52 Dante Bichette .40 .12
53 Jeff Conine .40 .12
54 John Burkett .20 .06
55 Gary Sheffield .40 .12
56 Andre Dawson .40 .12
57 Terry Pendleton .40 .12
58 Charles Johnson .40 .12
59 Brian L. Hunter .20 .06
60 Jeff Bagwell .60 .18
61 Craig Biggio .60 .18
62 Phil Nevin .40 .12
63 Doug Drabek .20 .06
64 Derek Bell .20 .06
65 Raul Mondesi .40 .12
66 Eric Karros .40 .12
67 Roger Cedeno .20 .06
68 Delino DeShields .20 .06
69 Ramon Martinez .20 .06
70 Mike Piazza 1.50 .45
71 Billy Ashley .20 .06
72 Jeff Fassero .20 .06
73 Shane Andrews .20 .06
74 Wil Cordero .20 .06
75 Tony Tarasco .20 .06
76 Rondell White .40 .12
77 Pedro Martinez 1.00 .30
78 Moises Alou .40 .12
79 Rico Brogna .20 .06
80 Bobby Bonilla .40 .12
81 Jeff Kent .40 .12
82 Brett Butler .40 .12
83 Bobby Jones .20 .06
84 Bill Pulsipher .20 .06
85 Bret Saberhagen .40 .12
86 Gregg Jefferies .20 .06
87 Lenny Dykstra .40 .12
88 Dave Hollins .20 .06
89 Charlie Hayes .20 .06
90 Darren Daulton .40 .12
91 Curt Schilling .40 .12
92 Heathcliff Slocumb .20 .06
93 Carlos Garcia .20 .06
94 Denny Neagle .40 .12
95 Jay Bell .40 .12
96 Orlando Merced .20 .06
97 Dave Clark .20 .06
98 Bernard Gilkey .20 .06
99 Scott Cooper .20 .06
100 Ozzie Smith 1.50 .45
101 Tom Henke .20 .06
102 Ken Hill .20 .06
103 Brian Jordan .40 .12
104 Ray Lankford .20 .06
105 Tony Gwynn 1.25 .35
106 Andy Benes .20 .06
107 Ken Caminiti .40 .12
108 Steve Finley .40 .12
109 Joey Hamilton .20 .06
110 Bip Roberts .20 .06
111 Eddie Williams .20 .06
112 Rod Beck .20 .06
113 Matt Williams .40 .12
114 Glenallen Hill .20 .06
115 Barry Bonds 2.50 .75
116 Robby Thompson .20 .06
117 Mark Portugal .20 .06
118 Brady Anderson .40 .12
119 Mike Mussina .60 .18
120 Rafael Palmeiro .60 .18
121 Chris Hoiles .20 .06
122 Harold Baines .40 .12
123 Jeffrey Hammonds .20 .06
124 Tim Naehring .20 .06
125 Mo Vaughn .40 .12
126 Mike Macfarlane .20 .06
127 Roger Clemens 2.00 .60
128 John Valentin .20 .06
129 Aaron Sele .20 .06
130 Jose Canseco 1.00 .30
131 J.T. Snow .40 .12
132 Mark Langston .20 .06
133 Chili Davis .40 .12
134 Chuck Finley .40 .12
135 Tim Salmon .60 .18
136 Tony Phillips .20 .06
137 Jason Bere .20 .06
138 Robin Ventura .40 .12
139 Tim Raines .40 .12
140 Frank Thomas COR 1.00 .30
140A Frank Thomas ERR 1.00 .30
141 Alex Fernandez .20 .06
142 Jim Abbott .60 .18
143 Wilson Alvarez .20 .06
144 Carlos Baerga .20 .06
145 Albert Belle .40 .12
146 Jim Thome 1.00 .30
147 Dennis Martinez .40 .12
148 Eddie Murray 1.00 .30
149 Dave Winfield .40 .12
150 Kenny Lofton .40 .12
151 Manny Ramirez .60 .18
152 Chad Curtis .20 .06
153 Lou Whitaker .40 .12
154 Alan Trammell .40 .12
155 Cecil Fielder .40 .12
156 Kirk Gibson .40 .12
157 Michael Tucker .20 .06
158 Jon Nunnally .20 .06
159 Wally Joyner .40 .12
160 Kevin Appier .40 .12
161 Jeff Montgomery .20 .06
162 Greg Gagne .20 .06
163 Ricky Bones .20 .06
164 Cal Eldred .20 .06
165 Greg Vaughn .20 .06
166 Kevin Seitzer .20 .06
167 Jose Valentin .20 .06
168 Joe Oliver .20 .06
169 Rick Aguilera .20 .06
170 Kirby Puckett 1.00 .30
171 Scott Stahoviak .20 .06
172 Kevin Tapani .20 .06
173 Chuck Knoblauch .40 .12
174 Rich Becker .20 .06
175 Don Mattingly 2.50 .75
176 Jack McDowell .20 .06
177 Jimmy Key .40 .12
178 Paul O'Neill .60 .18
179 John Wetteland .40 .12
180 Wade Boggs .60 .18
181 Derek Jeter 2.50 .75
182 Rickey Henderson 1.00 .30
183 Terry Steinbach .20 .06
184 Ruben Sierra .20 .06
185 Mark McGwire 2.50 .75
186 Todd Stottlemyre .20 .06
187 Dennis Eckersley .40 .12
188 Alex Rodriguez 2.50 .75
189 Randy Johnson 1.00 .30
190 Ken Griffey Jr. 1.50 .45
191 Tino Martinez UER .60 .18
Mike Blowers pictured on back
192 Jay Buhner .40 .12
193 Edgar Martinez .60 .18
194 Mickey Tettleton .20 .06
195 Juan Gonzalez .60 .18
196 Benji Gil .20 .06
197 Dean Palmer .40 .12
198 Ivan Rodriguez 1.00 .30
199 Kenny Rogers .40 .12
200 Will Clark 1.00 .30
201 Roberto Alomar .60 .18
202 David Cone .40 .12
203 Paul Molitor .60 .18
204 Shawn Green .40 .12
205 Joe Carter .40 .12
206 Alex Gonzalez .20 .06
207 Pat Hentgen .20 .06
P100 K.Griffey Jr. Promo 2.00 .60
AU190 Ken Griffey Jr. AU 150.00 45.00

1995 SP Silver

This 207-card set parallels that of the regular SP set and was inserted one per pack. The only difference between the regular 180 cards in the two sets is that the chevron of the parallel version on the left side of the front uses rainbow-colored foil instead of blue or red. The subset cards have a die-cut design to differentiate them from the regular edition cards. The only other difference is the silver (rather than gold) hologram on the back.

Nm-Mt Ex-Mt
COMPLETE SET (207) 100.00 30.00
*STARS: 1X to 2.5X BASIC CARDS
*ROOKIES: .6X to 1.5X BASIC CARDS

1995 SP Platinum Power

This 20-card set was randomly inserted in packs at a rate of one in five. This die-cut set is comprised of the top home run hitters in baseball.

Nm-Mt Ex-Mt
COMPLETE SET (20) 20.00 6.00
PP1 Jeff Bagwell .75 .23
PP2 Barry Bonds 3.00 .90
PP3 Ron Gant .50 .15
PP4 Fred McGriff .75 .23
PP5 Raul Mondesi .50 .15
PP6 Mike Piazza 2.00 .60
PP7 Larry Walker .75 .23
PP8 Matt Williams .50 .15
PP9 Albert Belle .50 .15
PP10 Cecil Fielder .50 .15
PP11 Juan Gonzalez .75 .23
PP12 Ken Griffey Jr. 2.00 .60
PP13 Mark McGwire 3.00 .90
PP14 Eddie Murray 1.25 .35
PP15 Manny Ramirez .75 .23
PP16 Cal Ripken 4.00 1.20
PP17 Tim Salmon .75 .23
PP18 Frank Thomas 1.25 .35
PP19 Jim Thome 1.25 .35
PP20 Mo Vaughn .50 .15

1995 SP Special FX

This 48-card set was randomly inserted in packs at a rate of one in 75. The set is comprised of the top names in baseball. The cards are numbered on the back "X/48."

Nm-Mt Ex-Mt
COMPLETE SET (48) 300.00 90.00
1 Jose Canseco 15.00 4.50
2 Roger Clemens 30.00 9.00
3 Mo Vaughn 6.00 1.80
4 Tim Salmon 10.00 3.00
5 Chuck Finley 6.00 1.80
6 Robin Ventura 6.00 1.80
7 Jason Bere 3.00 .90
8 Carlos Baerga 3.00 .90
9 Albert Belle 6.00 1.80
10 Kenny Lofton 6.00 1.80
11 Manny Ramirez 10.00 3.00
12 Jeff Montgomery 3.00 .90
13 Kirby Puckett 15.00 4.50
14 Wade Boggs 10.00 3.00
15 Don Mattingly 40.00 12.00
16 Cal Ripken 50.00 15.00
17 Ruben Sierra 3.00 .90
18 Ken Griffey Jr. 25.00 7.50
19 Randy Johnson 15.00 4.50
20 Alex Rodriguez 40.00 12.00
21 Will Clark 15.00 4.50
22 Juan Gonzalez 10.00 3.00
23 Roberto Alomar 10.00 3.00
24 Joe Carter 6.00 1.80
25 Alex Gonzalez 3.00 .90
26 Paul Molitor 10.00 3.00
27 Ryan Klesko 6.00 1.80
28 Fred McGriff 10.00 3.00
29 Greg Maddux 25.00 7.50
30 Sammy Sosa 25.00 7.50
31 Bret Boone 6.00 1.80
32 Barry Larkin 10.00 3.00
33 Reggie Sanders 3.00 .90
34 Dante Bichette 6.00 1.80
35 Andres Galarraga 6.00 1.80
36 Charles Johnson 6.00 1.80
37 Gary Sheffield 6.00 1.80
38 Jeff Bagwell 10.00 3.00
39 Craig Biggio 10.00 3.00
40 Eric Karros 6.00 1.80
41 Billy Ashley 3.00 .90
42 Raul Mondesi 6.00 1.80
43 Mike Piazza 25.00 7.50
44 Rondell White 6.00 1.80
45 Bret Saberhagen 6.00 1.80
46 Tony Gwynn 20.00 6.00
47 Melvin Nieves 3.00 .90
48 Matt Williams 6.00 1.80

1996 SP

The 1996 SP set was issued in one series totalling 188 cards. The eight-card packs retailed for $4.19 each. Cards number 1-20 feature color action player photos with "Premier Prospects" printed in silver foil across the top and the player's name and team at the bottom in the border. The backs carry player information and statistics. Cards number 21-185 display unique player photos with an outer wood-grain border and

inner thin platinum foil border as well as a small inset player shot. The only notable Rookie Card in this set is Darin Erstad.

Nm-Mt Ex-Mt
COMPLETE SET (188) 40.00 12.00
1 Rey Ordonez FOIL .40 .12
2 George Arias FOIL .40 .12
3 Osvaldo Fernandez FOIL .40 .12
4 Darin Erstad FOIL RC 4.00 1.20
5 Paul Wilson FOIL .40 .12
6 Richard Hidalgo FOIL .40 .12
7 Justin Thompson FOIL .40 .12
8 Jimmy Haynes FOIL .40 .12
9 Edgar Renteria FOIL .40 .12
10 Ruben Rivera FOIL .40 .12
11 Chris Snopek FOIL .40 .12
12 Billy Wagner FOIL .40 .12
13 Mike Grace FOIL RC .40 .12
14 Todd Greene FOIL .40 .12
15 Karim Garcia FOIL .40 .12
16 John Wasdin FOIL .40 .12
17 Jason Kendall FOIL .40 .12
18 Bob Abreu FOIL .40 .12
19 Jermaine Dye FOIL .40 .12
20 Jason Schmidt FOIL .60 .18
21 Javy Lopez .40 .12
22 Ryan Klesko .40 .12
23 Tom Glavine .60 .18
24 John Smoltz .60 .18
25 Greg Maddux 1.50 .45
26 Chipper Jones 1.00 .30
27 Fred McGriff .60 .18
28 David Justice .40 .12
29 Roberto Alomar .60 .18
30 Cal Ripken 3.00 .90
31 B.J. Surhoff .40 .12
32 Bobby Bonilla .40 .12
33 Mike Mussina .60 .18
34 Randy Myers .40 .12
35 Rafael Palmeiro .60 .18
36 Brady Anderson .40 .12
37 Tim Naehring .40 .12
38 Jose Canseco 1.00 .30
39 Roger Clemens 2.00 .60
40 Mo Vaughn .40 .12
41 John Valentin .40 .12
42 Kevin Mitchell .40 .12
43 Chili Davis .40 .12
44 Garret Anderson .40 .12
45 Tim Salmon .60 .18
46 Chuck Finley .40 .12
47 Troy Percival .40 .12
48 Jim Abbott .60 .18
49 J.T. Snow .40 .12
50 Jim Edmonds .40 .12
51 Sammy Sosa 1.50 .45
52 Brian McRae .40 .12
53 Ryne Sandberg 1.50 .45
54 Jaime Navarro .40 .12
55 Mark Grace .60 .18
56 Harold Baines .60 .18
57 Robin Ventura .40 .12
58 Tony Phillips .40 .12
59 Alex Fernandez .40 .12
60 Frank Thomas 1.00 .30
61 Ray Durham .40 .12
62 Bret Boone .40 .12
63 Reggie Sanders .40 .12
64 Pete Schourek .40 .12
65 Barry Larkin .60 .18
66 John Smiley .40 .12
67 Carlos Baerga .40 .12
68 Jim Thome 1.00 .30
69 Eddie Murray 1.00 .30
70 Albert Belle .40 .12
71 Dennis Martinez .40 .12
72 Jack McDowell .40 .12
73 Kenny Lofton .40 .12
74 Manny Ramirez .60 .18
75 Dante Bichette .40 .12
76 Vinny Castilla .40 .12
77 Andres Galarraga .40 .12
78 Walt Weiss .40 .12
79 Ellis Burks .40 .12
80 Larry Walker .60 .18
81 Cecil Fielder .40 .12
82 Melvin Nieves .40 .12
83 Travis Fryman .40 .12
84 Chad Curtis .40 .12
85 Alan Trammell .60 .18
86 Gary Sheffield .40 .12
87 Charles Johnson .40 .12
88 Andre Dawson .40 .12
89 Jeff Conine .40 .12
90 Greg Colbrunn .40 .12
91 Derek Bell .40 .12
92 Brian L.Hunter .40 .12
93 Doug Drabek .40 .12
94 Craig Biggio .60 .18
95 Jeff Bagwell .60 .18
96 Kevin Appier .40 .12
97 Jeff Montgomery .40 .12
98 Michael Tucker .40 .12
99 Bip Roberts .40 .12
100 Johnny Damon .60 .18
101 Eric Karros .40 .12
102 Raul Mondesi .40 .12
103 Ramon Martinez .40 .12
104 Ismael Valdes .40 .12
105 Mike Piazza 1.50 .45
106 Hideo Nomo 1.00 .30
107 Chan Ho Park .40 .12
108 Ben McDonald .40 .12
109 Kevin Seitzer .40 .12
110 Greg Vaughn .40 .12
111 Jose Valentin .40 .12
112 Rick Aguilera .40 .12
113 Marty Cordova .40 .12
114 Brad Radke .40 .12
115 Kirby Puckett 1.00 .30
116 Chuck Knoblauch .40 .12
117 Paul Molitor .60 .18
118 Pedro Martinez 1.00 .30
119 Mike Lansing .40 .12
120 Rondell White .40 .12
121 Moises Alou .40 .12
122 Mark Grudzielanek .40 .12
123 Jeff Fassero .40 .12
124 Rico Brogna .40 .12
125 Jason Isringhausen .40 .12
126 Jeff Kent .40 .12
127 Bernard Gilkey .40 .12
128 Todd Hundley .40 .12
129 David Cone .40 .12
130 Andy Pettitte .60 .18
131 Wade Boggs .60 .18
132 Paul O'Neill .60 .18
133 Ruben Sierra .40 .12
134 John Wetteland .40 .12
135 Derek Jeter 2.50 .75
136 Geronimo Berroa .40 .12
137 Terry Steinbach .40 .12
138 Ariel Prieto .40 .12
139 Scott Brosius .40 .12
140 Mark McGwire 2.50 .75
141 Lenny Dykstra .40 .12
142 Todd Zeile .40 .12
143 Benito Santiago .40 .12
144 Mickey Morandini .40 .12
145 Gregg Jefferies .40 .12
146 Denny Neagle .40 .12
147 Orlando Merced .40 .12
148 Charlie Hayes .40 .12
149 Carlos Garcia .40 .12
150 Jay Bell .40 .12
151 Ray Lankford .40 .12
152 Alan Benes .40 .12
Andy Benes
153 Dennis Eckersley .40 .12
154 Gary Gaetti .40 .12
155 Ozzie Smith 1.50 .45
156 Ron Gant .40 .12
157 Brian Jordan .40 .12
158 Ken Caminiti .40 .12
159 Rickey Henderson 1.00 .30
160 Tony Gwynn 1.25 .35
161 Wally Joyner .40 .12
162 Andy Ashby .40 .12
163 Steve Finley .40 .12
164 Glenallen Hill .40 .12
165 Matt Williams .40 .12
166 Barry Bonds 2.50 .75
167 W. VanLandingham .40 .12
168 Rod Beck .40 .12
169 Randy Johnson 1.00 .30
170 Ken Griffey Jr. 1.50 .45
171 Alex Rodriguez 2.00 .60
172 Edgar Martinez .60 .18
173 Jay Buhner .40 .12
174 Russ Davis .40 .12
175 Juan Gonzalez .60 .18
176 Mickey Tettleton .40 .12
177 Will Clark 1.00 .30
178 Ken Hill .40 .12
179 Dean Palmer .40 .12
180 Ivan Rodriguez 1.00 .30
181 Carlos Delgado .40 .12
182 Alex Gonzalez .40 .12
183 Shawn Green .40 .12
184 Juan Guzman .40 .12
185 Joe Carter .40 .12
186 Hideo Nomo CL UER .60 .18
Checklist lists Livan Hernandez as #4
187 Cal Ripken CL 1.50 .45
188 Ken Griffey Jr. CL 1.00 .30

1996 SP Baseball Heroes

This 10-card set was randomly inserted at the rate of one in 96 packs. It continues the insert set that was started in 1990 featuring ten of the top players in baseball. Please note these cards are condition sensitive and trade for premiums in Mint.

Nm-Mt Ex-Mt
COMPLETE SET (10) 150.00 45.00
82 Frank Thomas 12.00 3.60
83 Albert Belle 5.00 1.50
84 Barry Bonds 30.00 9.00
85 Chipper Jones 12.00 3.60
86 Hideo Nomo 12.00 3.60
87 Mike Piazza 20.00 6.00
88 Manny Ramirez 8.00 2.40
89 Greg Maddux 20.00 6.00
90 Ken Griffey Jr. 20.00 6.00
NNO Ken Griffey Jr. HDR 20.00 6.00

1996 SP Marquee Matchups

Randomly inserted at the rate of one in five packs, this 20-card set highlights two superstars' cards with a common matching stadium background photograph in a blue border.

Nm-Mt Ex-Mt
COMPLETE SET (20) 40.00 12.00
*DIE CUTS: 2X TO 5X BASIC MARQUEE
DC STATED ODDS 1:61
MM1 Ken Griffey Jr. 3.00 .90
MM2 Hideo Nomo 2.00 .60
MM3 Derek Jeter 5.00 1.50
MM4 Rey Ordonez .75 .23
MM5 Tim Salmon 1.25 .35
MM6 Mike Piazza 3.00 .90
MM7 Mark McGwire 5.00 1.50
MM8 Barry Bonds 5.00 1.50
MM9 Cal Ripken 6.00 1.80
MM10 Greg Maddux 3.00 .90
MM11 Albert Belle .75 .23
MM12 Barry Larkin 1.25 .35
MM13 Jeff Bagwell 1.25 .35
MM14 Juan Gonzalez 1.25 .35
MM15 Frank Thomas 2.00 .60
MM16 Sammy Sosa 3.00 .90
MM17 Mike Mussina 1.25 .35
MM18 Chipper Jones 2.00 .60
MM19 Roger Clemens 4.00 1.20
MM20 Fred McGriff 1.25 .35

1996 SP Special FX

Randomly inserted at the rate of one in five packs, this 48-card set features a color action player cutout on a gold foil background with a holoview diamond shaped insert containing a black-and-white player portrait.

Nm-Mt Ex-Mt
COMPLETE SET (48) 150.00 45.00
*DIE CUTS: 2X TO 5X BASIC SPECIAL FX
DIE CUTS STATED ODDS 1:75
1 Greg Maddux 8.00 2.40
2 Eric Karros 2.00 .60
3 Mike Piazza 8.00 2.40
4 Raul Mondesi 2.00 .60
5 Hideo Nomo 5.00 1.50
6 Jim Edmonds 2.00 .60
7 Jason Isringhausen 2.00 .60
8 Jay Buhner 2.00 .60
9 Barry Larkin 3.00 .90
10 Ken Griffey Jr. 8.00 2.40
11 Gary Sheffield 2.00 .60
12 Craig Biggio 3.00 .90
13 Paul Wilson 2.00 .60
14 Rondell White 2.00 .60
15 Chipper Jones 5.00 1.50
16 Kirby Puckett 5.00 1.50
17 Ron Gant 2.00 .60
18 Wade Boggs 3.00 .90
19 Fred McGriff 3.00 .90
20 Cal Ripken 15.00 4.50
21 Jason Kendall 2.00 .60
22 Johnny Damon 3.00 .90
23 Kenny Lofton 2.00 .60
24 Roberto Alomar 3.00 .90
25 Barry Bonds 12.00 3.60
26 Dante Bichette 2.00 .60
27 Mark McGwire 12.00 3.60
28 Rafael Palmeiro 3.00 .90
29 Juan Gonzalez 3.00 .90
30 Albert Belle 2.00 .60
31 Randy Johnson 5.00 1.50
32 Jose Canseco 5.00 1.50
33 Sammy Sosa 8.00 2.40
34 Eddie Murray 5.00 1.50
35 Frank Thomas 5.00 1.50
36 Tom Glavine 3.00 .90
37 Matt Williams 2.00 .60
38 Roger Clemens 10.00 3.00
39 Paul Molitor 3.00 .90
40 Tony Gwynn 6.00 1.80
41 Mo Vaughn 2.00 .60
42 Tim Salmon 3.00 .90
43 Manny Ramirez 3.00 .90
44 Jeff Bagwell 3.00 .90
45 Edgar Martinez 3.00 .90
46 Rey Ordonez 2.00 .60
47 Osvaldo Fernandez 2.00 .60
48 Derek Jeter 12.00 3.60

1997 SP

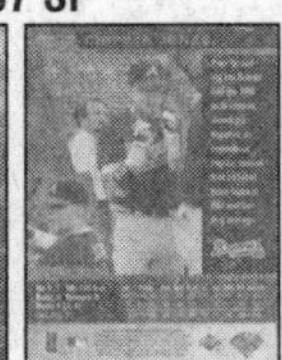

The 1997 SP set was issued in one series totalling 183 cards and was distributed in eight-card packs with a suggested retail of $4.39. Although unconfirmed by the manufacturer, it is perceived in some circles that cards numbered between 160 and 180 are in slightly shorter supply. Notable Rookie Cards include Jose Cruz Jr. and Hideki Irabu.

Nm-Mt Ex-Mt
COMPLETE SET (184) 40.00 12.00
1 Andruw Jones FOIL .75 .23
2 Kevin Orie FOIL .50 .15
3 Nomar Garciaparra FOIL 2.50 .75
4 Jose Guillen FOIL .75 .23
5 Todd Walker FOIL .50 .15
6 Derrick Gibson FOIL .50 .15
7 Aaron Boone FOIL .75 .23
8 Bartolo Colon FOIL .75 .23
9 Derrek Lee FOIL .75 .23
10 Vladimir Guerrero FOIL 1.50 .45
11 Wilton Guerrero FOIL .50 .15
12 Luis Castillo FOIL .50 .15
13 Jason Dickson FOIL .50 .15
14 B.Trammell FOIL RC .75 .23
15 Jose Cruz Jr. FOIL RC 1.00 .30
16 Eddie Murray 1.00 .30
17 Darin Erstad .40 .12
18 Garret Anderson .40 .12
19 Jim Edmonds .40 .12
20 Tim Salmon .60 .18
21 Chuck Finley .40 .12
22 John Smoltz .60 .18
23 Greg Maddux 1.50 .45
24 Kenny Lofton .40 .12
25 Chipper Jones 1.00 .30
26 Ryan Klesko .40 .12
27 Javy Lopez .40 .12
28 Fred McGriff .60 .18
29 Roberto Alomar .60 .18
30 Rafael Palmeiro .60 .18
31 Mike Mussina .60 .18
32 Brady Anderson .40 .12
33 Rocky Coppinger .40 .12
34 Cal Ripken 3.00 .90
35 Mo Vaughn .40 .12
36 Steve Avery .40 .12
37 Tom Gordon .40 .12
38 Tim Naehring .40 .12
39 Troy O'Leary .40 .12
40 Sammy Sosa 1.50 .45
41 Brian McRae .40 .12
42 Mel Rojas .40 .12
43 Ryne Sandberg 1.50 .45
44 Mark Grace .60 .18
45 Albert Belle .40 .12
46 Robin Ventura .40 .12
47 Roberto Hernandez .40 .12
48 Ray Durham .40 .12
49 Harold Baines .40 .12
50 Frank Thomas 1.00 .30
51 Bret Boone .40 .12
52 Reggie Sanders .40 .12
53 Deion Sanders .60 .18
54 Hal Morris .40 .12
55 Barry Larkin .60 .18
56 Jim Thome 1.00 .30
57 Marquis Grissom .40 .12
58 David Justice .40 .12
59 Charles Nagy .40 .12
60 Manny Ramirez .60 .18
61 Matt Williams .40 .12
62 Jack McDowell .40 .12
63 Vinny Castilla .40 .12
64 Dante Bichette .40 .12
65 Andres Galarraga .40 .12
66 Ellis Burks .40 .12
67 Larry Walker .60 .18
68 Eric Young .40 .12
69 Brian L. Hunter .40 .12
70 Travis Fryman .40 .12
71 Tony Clark .40 .12
72 Bobby Higginson .40 .12
73 Melvin Nieves .40 .12
74 Jeff Conine .40 .12
75 Gary Sheffield .40 .12
76 Moises Alou .40 .12
77 Edgar Renteria .40 .12
78 Alex Fernandez .40 .12
79 Charles Johnson .40 .12
80 Bobby Bonilla .40 .12
81 Darryl Kile .40 .12
82 Derek Bell .40 .12
83 Shane Reynolds .40 .12
84 Craig Biggio .60 .18
85 Jeff Bagwell .60 .18
86 Billy Wagner .40 .12
87 Chili Davis .40 .12
88 Kevin Appier .40 .12
89 Jay Bell .40 .12
90 Johnny Damon .60 .18
91 Jeff King .40 .12
92 Hideo Nomo 1.00 .30
93 Todd Hollandsworth .40 .12
94 Eric Karros .40 .12
95 Mike Piazza 1.50 .45
96 Ramon Martinez .40 .12
97 Todd Worrell .40 .12
98 Raul Mondesi .40 .12
99 Dave Nilsson .40 .12
100 John Jaha .40 .12
101 Jose Valentin .40 .12
102 Jeff Cirillo .40 .12
103 Jeff D'Amico .40 .12
104 Ben McDonald .40 .12
105 Paul Molitor .60 .18
106 Rich Becker .40 .12
107 Frank Rodriguez .40 .12
108 Marty Cordova .40 .12
109 Terry Steinbach .40 .12
110 Chuck Knoblauch .40 .12
111 Mark Grudzielanek .40 .12
112 Mike Lansing .40 .12
113 Pedro Martinez 1.00 .30
114 Henry Rodriguez .40 .12
115 Rondell White .40 .12
116 Rey Ordonez .40 .12
117 Carlos Baerga .40 .12
118 Lance Johnson .40 .12
119 Bernard Gilkey .40 .12
120 Todd Hundley .40 .12
121 John Franco .40 .12
122 Bernie Williams .60 .18
123 David Cone .40 .12
124 Cecil Fielder .40 .12
125 Derek Jeter 2.50 .75
126 Tino Martinez .60 .18
127 Mariano Rivera .60 .18
128 Andy Pettitte .60 .18
129 Wade Boggs .60 .18
130 Mark McGwire 2.50 .75
131 Jose Canseco 1.00 .30
132 Geronimo Berroa .40 .12
133 Jason Giambi .40 .12
134 Ernie Young .40 .12
135 Scott Rolen 1.00 .30
136 Ricky Bottalico .40 .12
137 Curt Schilling .40 .12

138 Gregg Jefferies .40 .12
139 Mickey Morandini .40 .12
140 Jason Kendall .40 .12
141 Kevin Elster .40 .12
142 Al Martin .40 .12
143 Joe Randa .40 .12
144 Jason Schmidt .40 .12
145 Ray Lankford .40 .12
146 Brian Jordan .40 .12
147 Andy Benes .40 .12
148 Alan Benes .40 .12
149 Gary Gaetti .40 .12
150 Ron Gant .40 .12
151 Dennis Eckersley .40 .12
152 Rickey Henderson 1.00 .30
153 Joey Hamilton .40 .12
154 Ken Caminiti .40 .12
155 Tony Gwynn 1.25 .35
156 Steve Finley .40 .12
157 Trevor Hoffman .40 .12
158 Greg Vaughn .40 .12
159 J.T.Snow .40 .12
160 Barry Bonds 2.50 .75
161 Glenallen Hill .40 .12
162 Bill Van Landingham .40 .12
163 Jeff Kent .40 .12
164 Jay Buhner .40 .12
165 Ken Griffey Jr. 1.50 .45
166 Alex Rodriguez 1.50 .45
167 Randy Johnson 1.00 .30
168 Edgar Martinez .60 .18
169 Dan Wilson .40 .12
170 Ivan Rodriguez 1.00 .30
171 Roger Pavlik .40 .12
172 Will Clark 1.00 .30
173 Dean Palmer .40 .12
174 Rusty Greer .40 .12
175 Juan Gonzalez .60 .18
176 John Wetteland .40 .12
177 Joe Carter .40 .12
178 Ed Sprague .40 .12
179 Carlos Delgado .40 .12
180 Roger Clemens 2.00 .60
181 Juan Guzman .40 .12
182 Pat Hentgen .40 .12
183 Ken Griffey Jr. CL 1.00 .30
184 Hideki Irabu RC .40 .12

1997 SP Game Film

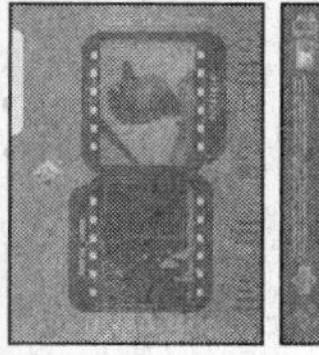

Randomly inserted in packs, this 10-card set features actual game film that highlights the accomplishments of some of the League's greatest players. Only 500 of each card in this crash numbered, limited edition set were produced.

Nm-Mt Ex-Mt
COMPLETE SET (10) 200.00 60.00
GF1 Alex Rodriguez 25.00 7.50
GF2 Frank Thomas 15.00 4.50
GF3 Andruw Jones 12.00 3.60
GF4 Cal Ripken 50.00 15.00
GF5 Mike Piazza 25.00 7.50
GF6 Derek Jeter 40.00 12.00
GF7 Mark McGwire 40.00 12.00
GF8 Chipper Jones 15.00 4.50
GF9 Barry Bonds 40.00 12.00
GF10 Ken Griffey Jr. 25.00 7.50

1997 SP Griffey Heroes

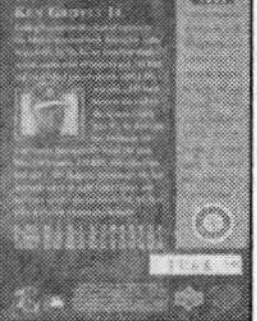

This 10-card continuation insert set pays special tribute to one of the game's most talented players and features color photos of Ken Griffey Jr. Only 2,000 of each card in this crash numbered, limited edition set were produced.

Nm-Mt Ex-Mt
COMPLETE SET (10) 50.00 15.00
COMMON CARD (91-100) 8.00 2.40

1997 SP Inside Info

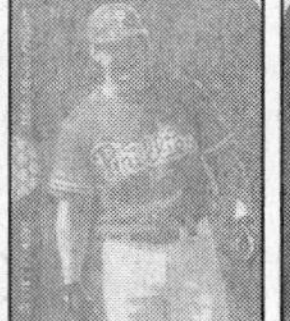

Inserted one in every 30-pack box, this 25-card set features color player photos on original cards with an exclusive pull-out panel that details the accomplishments of the League's brightest stars. Please note these cards are condition sensitive and trade for premium values in Mint condition.

Nm-Mt Ex-Mt
COMPLETE SET (25) 150.00 45.00
1 Ken Griffey Jr. 10.00 3.00
2 Mark McGwire 15.00 4.50
3 Kenny Lofton 2.50 .75
4 Paul Molitor 4.00 1.20
5 Frank Thomas 6.00 1.80
6 Greg Maddux 10.00 3.00
7 Mo Vaughn 2.50 .75
8 Cal Ripken 20.00 6.00
9 Jeff Bagwell 4.00 1.20
10 Alex Rodriguez 10.00 3.00
11 John Smoltz 4.00 1.20
12 Manny Ramirez 4.00 1.20
13 Sammy Sosa 10.00 3.00
14 Vladimir Guerrero 10.00 3.00
15 Albert Belle 2.50 .75
16 Mike Piazza 10.00 3.00
17 Derek Jeter 15.00 4.50
18 Scott Rolen 6.00 1.80
19 Tony Gwynn 8.00 2.40
20 Barry Bonds 15.00 4.50
21 Ken Caminiti 2.50 .75
22 Chipper Jones 6.00 1.80
23 Juan Gonzalez 4.00 1.20
24 Roger Clemens 12.00 3.60
25 Andruw Jones 5.00 1.50

1997 SP Marquee Matchups

Randomly inserted in packs at a rate of one in five, this 20-card set features color player images on die-cut cards that match-up the best pitchers and hitters from around the League.

Nm-Mt Ex-Mt
COMPLETE SET (20) 50.00 15.00
MM1 Ken Griffey Jr. 3.00 .90
MM2 Andres Galarraga .75 .23
MM3 Barry Bonds 5.00 1.50
MM4 Mark McGwire 5.00 1.50
MM5 Mike Piazza 3.00 .90
MM6 Tim Salmon 1.25 .35
MM7 Tony Gwynn 2.50 .75
MM8 Alex Rodriguez 3.00 .90
MM9 Chipper Jones 2.00 .60
MM10 Derek Jeter 5.00 1.50
MM11 Manny Ramirez 1.25 .35
MM12 Jeff Bagwell 1.25 .35
MM13 Greg Maddux 3.00 .90
MM14 Cal Ripken 6.00 1.80
MM15 Mo Vaughn .75 .23
MM16 Gary Sheffield .75 .23
MM17 Jim Thome 2.00 .60
MM18 Barry Larkin 1.25 .35
MM19 Frank Thomas 2.00 .60
MM20 Sammy Sosa 3.00 .90

1997 SP Special FX

Randomly inserted in packs at a rate of one in nine, this 48-card set features color player photos on Holoview cards with the Special F/X die-cut design. Cards numbers 1-47 are from 1997 with card number 49 featuring a design from 1996. There is no card number 48.

Nm-Mt Ex-Mt
COMPLETE SET (48) 200.00 60.00
1 Ken Griffey Jr. 8.00 2.40
2 Frank Thomas 5.00 1.50
3 Barry Bonds 12.00 3.60
4 Albert Belle 2.00 .60
5 Mike Piazza 8.00 2.40
6 Greg Maddux 8.00 2.40
7 Chipper Jones 5.00 1.50
8 Cal Ripken 15.00 4.50
9 Jeff Bagwell 3.00 .90
10 Alex Rodriguez 8.00 2.40
11 Mark McGwire 12.00 3.60
12 Kenny Lofton 2.00 .60
13 Juan Gonzalez 3.00 .90
14 Mo Vaughn 2.00 .60
15 John Smoltz 3.00 .90
16 Derek Jeter 12.00 3.60
17 Tony Gwynn 6.00 1.80
18 Ivan Rodriguez 5.00 1.50
19 Barry Larkin 3.00 .90
20 Sammy Sosa 8.00 2.40
21 Mike Mussina 3.00 .90
22 Gary Sheffield 2.00 .60
23 Brady Anderson 2.00 .60
24 Roger Clemens 10.00 3.00
25 Ken Caminiti 2.00 .60
26 Roberto Alomar 3.00 .90
27 Hideo Nomo 5.00 1.50
28 Bernie Williams 3.00 .90
29 Todd Hundley 2.00 .60
30 Manny Ramirez 3.00 .90
31 Eric Karros 2.00 .60
32 Tim Salmon 3.00 .90
33 Jay Buhner 2.00 .60
34 Andy Pettitte 3.00 .90
35 Jim Thome 5.00 1.50
36 Ryne Sandberg 8.00 2.40
37 Matt Williams 2.00 .60
38 Ryan Klesko 2.00 .60
39 Jose Canseco 5.00 1.50
40 Paul Molitor 3.00 .90
41 Eddie Murray 5.00 1.50
42 Darin Erstad 2.00 .60
43 Todd Walker 2.50 .75
44 Wade Boggs 3.00 .90
45 Andruw Jones 4.00 1.20
46 Scott Rolen 5.00 1.50
47 Vladimir Guerrero 8.00 2.40
49 Alex Rodriguez '96 10.00 3.00

1997 SP SPx Force

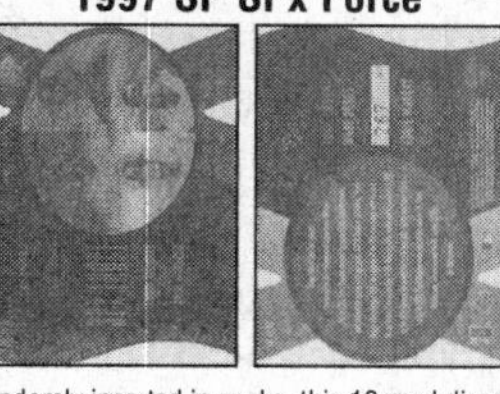

Randomly inserted in packs, this 10-card die-cut set features head photos of four of the very best players on each card with an "X" in the background and players' and teams' names on one side. Only 500 of each card in this crash numbered, limited edition set were produced.

Nm-Mt Ex-Mt
COMPLETE SET (10) 200.00 60.00
1 Ken Griffey Jr. 25.00 7.50
Jay Buhner
Andres Galarraga
Dante Bichette
2 Albert Belle 40.00 12.00
Brady Anderson
Mark McGwire
Cecil Fielder
3 Mo Vaughn 15.00 4.50
Ken Caminiti
Frank Thomas
Jeff Bagwell
4 Gary Sheffield 25.00 7.50
Sammy Sosa
Barry Bonds
Jose Canseco
5 Greg Maddux 25.00 7.50
Roger Clemens
John Smoltz
Randy Johnson
6 Alex Rodriguez 40.00 12.00
Derek Jeter
Chipper Jones
Rey Ordonez
7 Todd Hollandsworth 25.00 7.50
Mike Piazza
Raul Mondesi
Hideo Nomo
8 Juan Gonzalez 15.00 4.50
Manny Ramirez
Roberto Alomar
Ivan Rodriguez
9 Tony Gwynn 20.00 6.00
Wade Boggs
Eddie Murray
Paul Molitor
10 Andruw Jones 25.00 7.50
Vladimir Guerrero
Todd Walker
Scott Rolen

1997 SP SPx Force Autographs

Randomly inserted in packs, this 10-card set is an autographed parallel version of the regular SPx Force set. Only 100 of each card in this crash numbered, limited edition set were produced. Mo Vaughn packed out as an exchange card.

Nm-Mt Ex-Mt
1 Ken Griffey Jr. 150.00 45.00
2 Albert Belle 50.00 15.00
3 Mo Vaughn 50.00 15.00
4 Gary Sheffield 80.00 24.00
5 Greg Maddux 150.00 45.00
6 Alex Rodriguez 200.00 60.00
7 Todd Hollandsworth 30.00 9.00
8 Roberto Alomar 80.00 24.00
9 Tony Gwynn 100.00 30.00
10 Andruw Jones 80.00 24.00

1997 SP Vintage Autographs

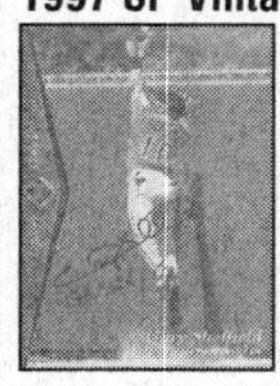

Randomly inserted in packs, this set features authenticated original 1993-1996 SP cards that have been autographed by the pictured player. The print runs are listed after year following the player's name in our checklist. Some of the very short printed autographs are listed but not priced. Each card came in the pack along with a standard size certificate of authenticity. These certificates are usually included when these autographed cards are traded. The 1997 Mo Vaughn card was available only as a mail-in exchange. Upper Deck seeded 250 '97 SP Vaughn cards into packs each carrying a large circular sticker on front. UD sent Mo 300 cards to sign, hoping that he'd sign at least 250 cards and actually received 293 cards back. The additional 43 cards were sent to UD's Quality Assurance area. An additional Mo Vaughn card, hailing from 1995, surfaced in early 2001. This set now stands as one of the most important issues of the 1990's in that it was the first to feature the popular "buy-back" concept widely used in the 2000's.

Nm-Mt Ex-Mt
1 Jeff Bagwell 93/7
2 Jeff Bagwell 95/173 50.00 15.00
3 Jeff Bagwell 96/292 50.00 15.00
4 Jeff Bagwell 96 MM/23
5 Jay Buhner 95/57 40.00 12.00
6 Jay Buhner 96/79 40.00 12.00
7 Jay Buhner 96 FX/27 50.00 15.00
8 Ken Griffey Jr. 93/16
9 Ken Griffey Jr. 93 PP/5
10 Ken Griffey Jr. 94/103 100.00 30.00
11 Ken Griffey Jr. 95/38 150.00 45.00
12 Ken Griffey Jr. 96/312 100.00 30.00
13 Tony Gwynn 93/17
14 Tony Gwynn 94/367 40.00 12.00
15 Tony Gwynn 94 HV/31 120.00 36.00
16 Tony Gwynn 95/64 60.00 18.00
17 Tony Gwynn 96/20
18 Todd Hollandsworth 94/167 15.00 4.50
19 Chipper Jones 93/34 100.00 30.00
20 Chipper Jones 95/60 80.00 24.00
21 Chipper Jones 96/102 60.00 18.00
22 Rey Ordonez 96/111 15.00 4.50
23 R.Ordonez '96 MM/40 25.00 7.50
24 Alex Rodriguez 94/94 1500.00 450.00
25 Alex Rodriguez 95/63 150.00 45.00
26 Alex Rodriguez 96/73 150.00 45.00
27 Gary Sheffield 94/130 40.00 12.00
28 Gary Sheffield 94 HVDC/4
29 Gary Sheffield 95/221 25.00 7.50
30 Gary Sheffield 96/58 60.00 18.00
31 Mo Vaughn 95/75 40.00 12.00
32 Mo Vaughn 97/293 15.00 4.50

1998 SP Authentic

The 1998 SP Authentic set was issued in one series totalling 198 cards. The five-card packs retailed for $4.99 each. The set contains the topical subset: Future Watch (1-30). Rookie Cards include Magglio Ordonez. A sample card featuring Ken Griffey Jr. was issued prior to the product's release and distributed along with dealer order forms. The card is identical to the basic issue Griffey Jr. card (number 123) except for the term "SAMPLE" in red print running diagonally against the card back.

Nm-Mt Ex-Mt
COMPLETE SET (198) 40.00 12.00
1 Travis Lee FOIL .40 .12
2 Mike Caruso FOIL .40 .12
3 Kerry Wood FOIL 2.00 .60
4 Mark Kotsay FOIL .40 .12
5 M.Ordonez FOIL RC 10.00 3.00
6 Scott Elarton FOIL .40 .12
7 Carl Pavano FOIL .60 .12
8 A.J. Hinch FOIL .40 .12
9 Rolando Arrojo FOIL RC .40 .12
10 Ben Grieve FOIL .40 .12
11 Gabe Alvarez FOIL .40 .12
12 Mike Kinkade FOIL RC .40 .12
13 Bruce Chen FOIL .40 .12
14 Juan Encarnacion FOIL .40 .12
15 Todd Helton FOIL .60 .18
16 Aaron Boone FOIL .40 .12
17 Sean Casey FOIL .40 .12
18 R.Hernandez FOIL .40 .12
19 Daryle Ward FOIL .40 .12
20 Paul Konerko FOIL .40 .12
21 David Ortiz FOIL 1.00 .30
22 Derrek Lee FOIL .40 .12
23 Brad Fullmer FOIL .40 .12
24 Javier Vazquez FOIL .40 .12
25 Miguel Tejada FOIL .40 .12
26 Dave Dellucci FOIL RC .60 .18
27 Alex Gonzalez FOIL .40 .12
28 Matt Clement FOIL .40 .12
29 Masato Yoshii FOIL RC .60 .18
30 Russell Branyan FOIL .40 .12
31 Chuck Finley .40 .12
32 Jim Edmonds .40 .12
33 Darin Erstad .40 .12
34 Jason Dickson .40 .12
35 Tim Salmon .60 .18
36 Cecil Fielder .40 .12
37 Todd Greene .40 .12
38 Andy Benes .40 .12
39 Jay Bell .40 .12
40 Matt Williams .40 .12
41 Brian Anderson .40 .12
42 Karim Garcia .40 .12
43 Javy Lopez .40 .12
44 Tom Glavine .60 .18
45 Greg Maddux 1.50 .45
46 Andruw Jones .40 .12
47 Chipper Jones 1.00 .30
48 Ryan Klesko .40 .12
49 John Smoltz .60 .18
50 Andres Galarraga .40 .12
51 Rafael Palmeiro .60 .18
52 Mike Mussina .60 .18
53 Roberto Alomar .60 .18
54 Joe Carter .40 .12
55 Cal Ripken 3.00 .90
56 Brady Anderson .40 .12
57 Mo Vaughn .40 .12
58 John Valentin .40 .12
59 Dennis Eckersley .40 .12
60 Nomar Garciaparra 1.50 .45
61 Pedro Martinez 1.00 .30
62 Jeff Blauser .40 .12
63 Kevin Orie .40 .12
64 Henry Rodriguez .40 .12
65 Mark Grace .60 .18
66 Albert Belle .40 .12
67 Mike Cameron .40 .12
68 Robin Ventura .40 .12
69 Frank Thomas 1.00 .30
70 Barry Larkin .60 .18
71 Brett Tomko UER .40 .12
1 Yr Total is Wrong
72 Willie Greene .40 .12
73 Reggie Sanders .40 .12
74 Sandy Alomar Jr. .40 .12
75 Kenny Lofton .40 .12
76 Jaret Wright .40 .12
77 David Justice .40 .12
78 Omar Vizquel .60 .18
79 Manny Ramirez .60 .18
80 Jim Thome 1.00 .30
81 Travis Fryman .40 .12
82 Neifi Perez .40 .12
83 Mike Lansing .40 .12
84 Vinny Castilla .40 .12
85 Larry Walker .60 .18
86 Dante Bichette .40 .12
87 Darryl Kile .40 .12
88 Justin Thompson .40 .12
89 Damion Easley .40 .12
90 Tony Clark .40 .12
91 Bobby Higginson .40 .12
92 Brian Hunter .40 .12
93 Edgar Renteria .40 .12
94 Craig Counsell .40 .12
95 Mike Piazza 1.50 .45
96 Livan Hernandez .40 .12
97 Todd Zeile .40 .12
98 Richard Hidalgo .40 .12
99 Moises Alou .40 .12
100 Jeff Bagwell .60 .18
101 Mike Hampton .40 .12
102 Craig Biggio .60 .18
103 Dean Palmer .40 .12
104 Tim Belcher .40 .12
105 Jeff King .40 .12
106 Jeff Conine .40 .12
107 Johnny Damon .60 .18
108 Hideo Nomo 1.00 .30
109 Raul Mondesi .40 .12
110 Gary Sheffield .40 .12
111 Ramon Martinez .40 .12
112 Chan Ho Park .40 .12
113 Eric Young .40 .12
114 Charles Johnson .40 .12
115 Eric Karros .40 .12
116 Bobby Bonilla .40 .12
117 Jeromy Burnitz .40 .12
118 Cal Eldred .40 .12
119 Jeff D'Amico .40 .12
120 Marquis Grissom .40 .12
121 Dave Nilsson .40 .12
122 Brad Radke .40 .12
123 Marty Cordova .40 .12
124 Ron Coomer .40 .12
125 Paul Molitor .60 .18
126 Todd Walker .40 .12
127 Rondell White .40 .12
128 Mark Grudzielanek .40 .12
129 Carlos Perez .40 .12
130 Vladimir Guerrero 1.00 .30
131 Dustin Hermanson .40 .12
132 Butch Huskey .40 .12
133 John Franco .40 .12
134 Rey Ordonez .40 .12
135 Todd Hundley .40 .12
136 Edgardo Alfonzo .40 .12
137 Bobby Jones .40 .12
138 John Olerud .40 .12
139 Chili Davis .40 .12
140 Tino Martinez .60 .18
141 Andy Pettitte .60 .18
142 Chuck Knoblauch .40 .12
143 Bernie Williams .60 .18
144 David Cone .40 .12
145 Derek Jeter 2.50 .75
146 Paul O'Neill .60 .18
147 Rickey Henderson 1.00 .30
148 Jason Giambi .40 .12
149 Kenny Rogers .40 .12
150 Scott Rolen 1.00 .30
151 Curt Schilling .40 .12
152 Ricky Bottalico .40 .12
153 Mike Lieberthal .40 .12
154 Francisco Cordova .40 .12
155 Jose Guillen .40 .12
156 Jason Schmidt .40 .12
157 Jason Kendall .40 .12
158 Kevin Young .40 .12
159 Delino DeShields .40 .12
160 Mark McGwire 2.50 .75
161 Ray Lankford .40 .12
162 Brian Jordan .40 .12
163 Ron Gant .40 .12
164 Todd Stottlemyre .40 .12
165 Ken Caminiti .40 .12
166 Kevin Brown .60 .18
167 Trevor Hoffman .40 .12
168 Steve Finley .40 .12
169 Wally Joyner .40 .12
170 Tony Gwynn 1.25 .35
171 Shawn Estes .40 .12
172 J.T. Snow .40 .12
173 Jeff Kent .40 .12
174 Robb Nen .40 .12
175 Barry Bonds 2.50 .75
176 Randy Johnson 1.00 .30
177 Edgar Martinez .60 .18
178 Jay Buhner .40 .12
179 Alex Rodriguez 1.50 .45
180 Ken Griffey Jr. 1.50 .45
181 Ken Cloude .40 .12
182 Wade Boggs .60 .18
183 Tony Saunders .40 .12
184 Wilson Alvarez .40 .12
185 Fred McGriff .60 .18
186 Roberto Hernandez .40 .12
187 Kevin Stocker .40 .12
188 Fernando Tatis .40 .12
189 Will Clark 1.00 .30
190 Juan Gonzalez .60 .18
191 Rusty Greer .40 .12
192 Ivan Rodriguez 1.00 .30
193 Jose Canseco 1.00 .30
194 Carlos Delgado .40 .12
195 Roger Clemens 2.00 .60
196 Pat Hentgen .40 .12
197 Randy Myers .40 .12
198 Ken Griffey Jr. CL 1.00 .30
S123 Ken Griffey Jr. Sample 2.00 .60

1998 SP Authentic Chirography

Randomly inserted in packs at a rate of one in 25, this 31-card set is autographed by the league's top players. The Ken Griffey Jr. card was actually not available in packs. Instead, an exchange card was printed and seeded into packs. Collectors had until July 27th, 1999 to redeem these Griffey exchange cards. A selection of players were short-printed to 400 or 800 copies. These cards, however, are not serial numbered.

	Nm-Mt	Ex-Mt
AJ Andruw Jones	15.00	4.50
AR Alex Rodriguez SP/800	100.00	30.00
BG Ben Grieve	15.00	4.50
CJ Charles Johnson	15.00	4.50
CP Chipper Jones SP/800	40.00	12.00
DE Darin Erstad	15.00	4.50
GS Gary Sheffield	25.00	7.50
IR Ivan Rodriguez	40.00	12.00
JC Jose Cruz Jr.	15.00	4.50
JW Jaret Wright	15.00	4.50
KG Ken Griffey Jr. SP/400	100.00	30.00
KG-EX K.Griffey Jr. EXCH	15.00	4.50
LH Livan Hernandez	15.00	4.50
MK Mark Kotsay	15.00	4.50
MM Mike Mussina	25.00	7.50
MT Miguel Tejada	15.00	4.50
MV Mo Vaughn SP800	15.00	4.50
NG N. Garciaparra SP400	150.00	45.00
PK Paul Konerko	15.00	4.50
PM Paul Molitor SP/800	25.00	7.50
RA R. Alomar SP/800	25.00	7.50
RB Russell Branyan	15.00	4.50
RC R. Clemens SP/400	120.00	36.00
RL Ray Lankford	15.00	4.50
SC Sean Casey	15.00	4.50
SR Scott Rolen	40.00	12.00
TC Tony Clark	15.00	4.50
TG Tony Gwynn SP/850	40.00	12.00
TH Todd Helton	25.00	7.50
TL Travis Lee	15.00	4.50
VG Vladimir Guerrero	40.00	12.00

1998 SP Authentic Game Jersey 5 x 7

These attractive 5" by 7" memorabilia cards are the items one received when redeeming the SP Authentic Trade Cards (of which were randomly seeded into 1998 SP Authentic packs at a rate of 1:291). The 5 x 7 cards feature a larger swatch of the jersey on them as compared to a standard size Game Jersey card. The exchange deadline expired back on August 1st, 1999.

	Nm-Mt	Ex-Mt
1 Ken Griffey Jr./125	60.00	18.00
2 Gary Sheffield/125	25.00	7.50
3 Greg Maddux/125	60.00	18.00
4 Alex Rodriguez/125	60.00	18.00
5 Tony Gwynn/415	50.00	15.00
6 Jay Buhner/125	25.00	7.50

1998 SP Authentic Sheer Dominance

Randomly inserted in packs at a rate of one in three, this 42-card set has a mix of stars and young players and were issued in three different versions.

	Nm-Mt	Ex-Mt
COMPLETE SET (42)	100.00	30.00
*GOLD: 1.25X TO 3X BASIC DOMINANCE		
GOLD: RANDOM INSERTS IN PACKS		
GOLD PRINT RUN 2000 SERIAL #'d SETS		
*TITANIUM: 3X TO 8X BASIC DOMINANCE		
TITANIUM: RANDOM INSERTS IN PACKS		
TITANIUM PRINT RUN 100 SERIAL #'d SETS		
SD1 Ken Griffey Jr.	4.00	1.20
SD2 Rickey Henderson	2.50	.75
SD3 Jaret Wright	1.00	.30
SD4 Craig Biggio	1.50	.45
SD5 Travis Lee	1.00	.30
SD6 Kenny Lofton	1.00	.30
SD7 Raul Mondesi	1.00	.30
SD8 Cal Ripken	8.00	2.40
SD9 Matt Williams	1.00	.30
SD10 Mark McGwire	6.00	1.80
SD11 Alex Rodriguez	4.00	1.20
SD12 Fred McGriff	1.50	.45
SD13 Scott Rolen	2.50	.75
SD14 Paul Molitor	1.50	.45
SD15 Nomar Garciaparra	4.00	1.20
SD16 Vladimir Guerrero	2.50	.75
SD17 Andruw Jones	1.00	.30
SD18 Manny Ramirez	1.50	.45
SD19 Tony Gwynn	3.00	.90
SD20 Barry Bonds	6.00	1.80
SD21 Ben Grieve	1.00	.30
SD22 Ivan Rodriguez	2.50	.75
SD23 Jose Cruz Jr.	2.50	.75
SD24 Pedro Martinez	2.50	.75
SD25 Chipper Jones	2.50	.75
SD26 Albert Belle	1.00	.30
SD27 Todd Helton	1.50	.45
SD28 Paul Konerko	1.00	.30
SD29 Sammy Sosa	2.50	.75
SD30 Frank Thomas	2.50	.75
SD31 Greg Maddux	4.00	1.20
SD32 Randy Johnson	2.50	.75
SD33 Larry Walker	1.50	.45
SD34 Roberto Alomar	1.50	.45
SD35 Roger Clemens	5.00	1.50
SD36 Mo Vaughn	1.00	.30
SD37 Jim Thome	2.50	.75
SD38 Jeff Bagwell	1.50	.45
SD39 Tino Martinez	1.50	.45
SD40 Mike Piazza	4.00	1.20
SD41 Derek Jeter	6.00	1.80
SD42 Juan Gonzalez	1.50	.45

1998 SP Authentic Trade Cards

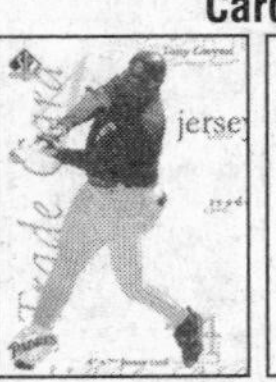

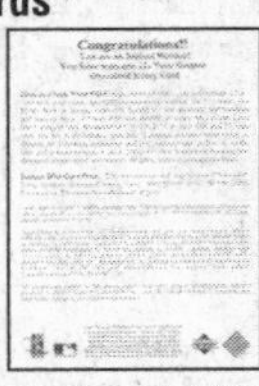

Randomly seeded into packs at a rate of 1:291, these fifteen different trade cards could be redeemed for an assortion of UDA material. Specific quantities for each item are detailed below after each player name. The deadline to redeem these cards was August 1st, 1999. It is important to note that the redemption items came from UDA back stock and in many cases the card is far mor valuable than the redemption prize.

	Nm-Mt	Ex-Mt
COMMON CARD (B1-B5)	15.00	4.50
COMMON CARD (J1-J6)	15.00	4.50
COMMON CARD (KG1-KG4)	15.00	4.50
B1 Roberto Alomar	25.00	7.50
Ball 100		
B2 Albert Belle	15.00	4.50
Ball 100		
B3 Brian Jordan	15.00	4.50
Ball 50		
B4 Raul Mondesi	15.00	4.50
Ball 100		
B5 Robin Ventura	25.00	7.50
Ball 50		
J1 Jay Buhner	15.00	4.50
Jersey Card 125		
J2 Ken Griffey Jr.	60.00	18.00
Jersey Card 125		
J3 Tony Gwynn	25.00	7.50
Jersey Card 415		
J4 Greg Maddux	60.00	18.00
Jersey Card 125		
J5 Alex Rodriguez	50.00	15.00
Jersey Card 125		
J6 Gary Sheffield	15.00	4.50
Jersey Card 125		
KG1 Ken Griffey Jr.	15.00	4.50
300 Card 1000 made		
KG2 Ken Griffey Jr.		
Auto Glove 30		
KG3 Ken Griffey Jr.		
Auto Jersey 30		
KG4 Ken Griffey Jr.	25.00	7.50
Standee 200		

1999 SP Authentic

The 1999 SP Authentic set was issued in one series totalling 135 cards and distributed in five-card packs with a suggested retail price of $4.99. The fronts feature color action player photos with player information printed on the backs. The set features the following limited edition subsets: Future Watch (91-120) serially numbered to 2700 and Season to Remember (121-135) numbered to 2700 also. 350 Ernie Banks A Piece of History 500 Club bat cards were randomly seeded into packs. Also, Banks signed and numbered twenty additional copies. Pricing for these bat cards can be referenced under 1999 Upper Deck A Piece of History 500 Club.

	Nm-Mt	Ex-Mt
COMP.SET w/o SP's (90)	25.00	7.50
COMMON CARD (1-90)	.40	.12
COMMON FW (91-120)	10.00	3.00
COMMON STR (121-135)	3.00	.90
1 Mo Vaughn	.40	.12
2 Jim Edmonds	.40	.12
3 Darin Erstad	.40	.12
4 Travis Lee	.40	.12
5 Matt Williams	.40	.12
6 Randy Johnson	1.00	.30
7 Chipper Jones	1.00	.30
8 Greg Maddux	1.50	.45
9 Andruw Jones	.40	.12
10 Andres Galarraga	.40	.12
11 Tom Glavine	.60	.18
12 Cal Ripken	3.00	.90
13 Brady Anderson	.40	.12
14 Albert Belle	.40	.12
15 Nomar Garciaparra	1.50	.45
16 Donnie Sadler	.40	.12
17 Pedro Martinez	1.00	.30
18 Sammy Sosa	1.50	.45
19 Kerry Wood	1.00	.30
20 Mark Grace	.60	.18
21 Mike Caruso	.40	.12
22 Frank Thomas	1.00	.30
23 Paul Konerko	.40	.12
24 Sean Casey	.40	.12
25 Barry Larkin	.60	.18
26 Kenny Lofton	.40	.12
27 Manny Ramirez	.60	.18
28 Jim Thome	1.00	.30
29 Bartolo Colon	.40	.12
30 Jaret Wright	.40	.12
31 Larry Walker	.60	.18
32 Todd Helton	.60	.18
33 Tony Clark	.40	.12
34 Dean Palmer	.40	.12
35 Mark Kotsay	.40	.12
36 Cliff Floyd	.40	.12
37 Ken Caminiti	.40	.12
38 Craig Biggio	.60	.18
39 Jeff Bagwell	.60	.18
40 Moises Alou	.40	.12
41 Johnny Damon	.60	.18
42 Larry Sutton	.40	.12
43 Kevin Brown	.60	.18
44 Gary Sheffield	.40	.12
45 Raul Mondesi	.40	.12
46 Jeromy Burnitz	.40	.12
47 Jeff Cirillo	.40	.12
48 Todd Walker	.40	.12
49 David Ortiz	.60	.18
50 Brad Radke	.40	.12
51 Vladimir Guerrero	1.00	.30
52 Rondell White	.40	.12
53 Brad Fullmer	.40	.12
54 Mike Piazza	1.50	.45
55 Robin Ventura	.40	.12
56 John Olerud	.40	.12
57 Derek Jeter	2.50	.75
58 Tino Martinez	.60	.18
59 Bernie Williams	.60	.18
60 Roger Clemens	2.00	.60
61 Ben Grieve	.40	.12
62 Miguel Tejada	.40	.12
63 A.J. Hinch	.40	.12
64 Scott Rolen	1.00	.30
65 Curt Schilling	.40	.12
66 Doug Glanville	.40	.12
67 Aramis Ramirez	.40	.12
68 Tony Womack	.40	.12
69 Jason Kendall	.40	.12
70 Tony Gwynn	1.25	.35
71 Wally Joyner	.40	.12
72 Greg Vaughn	.40	.12
73 Barry Bonds	2.50	.75
74 Ellis Burks	.40	.12
75 Jeff Kent	.40	.12
76 Ken Griffey Jr.	1.50	.45
77 Alex Rodriguez	1.50	.45
78 Edgar Martinez	.60	.18
79 Mark McGwire	2.50	.75
80 Eli Marrero	.40	.12
81 Matt Morris	.40	.12
82 Rolando Arrojo	.40	.12
83 Quinton McCracken	.40	.12
84 Jose Canseco	1.00	.30
85 Ivan Rodriguez	1.00	.30
86 Juan Gonzalez	.60	.18
87 Royce Clayton	.40	.12
88 Shawn Green	.40	.12
89 Jose Cruz Jr.	.40	.12
90 Carlos Delgado	.40	.12
91 Troy Glaus FW	10.00	3.00
92 George Lombard FW	10.00	3.00
93 Ryan Minor FW	10.00	3.00
94 Calvin Pickering FW	10.00	3.00
95 Jin Ho Cho FW	10.00	3.00
96 Russ Branyan FW	10.00	3.00
97 Derrick Gibson FW	10.00	3.00
98 Gabe Kapler FW	10.00	3.00
99 Matt Anderson FW	10.00	3.00
100 Preston Wilson FW	10.00	3.00
101 Alex Gonzalez FW	10.00	3.00
102 Carlos Beltran FW	12.00	3.60
103 Dee Brown FW	10.00	3.00
104 Jeremy Giambi FW	10.00	3.00
105 Angel Pena FW	10.00	3.00
106 Geoff Jenkins FW	10.00	3.00
107 Corey Koskie FW	10.00	3.00
108 A.J. Pierzynski FW	10.00	3.00
109 Michael Barrett FW	10.00	3.00
110 F.Seguignol FW	10.00	3.00
111 Mike Kinkade FW	10.00	3.00
112 Ricky Ledee FW	10.00	3.00
113 Mike Lowell FW	10.00	3.00
114 Eric Chavez FW	10.00	3.00
115 Matt Clement FW	10.00	3.00
116 Shane Monahan FW	10.00	3.00
117 J.D. Drew FW	10.00	3.00
118 Bubba Trammell FW	10.00	3.00
119 Kevin Witt FW	10.00	3.00
120 Roy Halladay FW	10.00	3.00
121 Mark McGwire STR	12.00	3.60
122 Mark McGwire STR	10.00	3.00
Sammy Sosa		
123 Sammy Sosa STR	8.00	2.40
124 Ken Griffey Jr. STR	8.00	2.40
125 Cal Ripken STR	15.00	4.50
126 Juan Gonzalez STR	3.00	.90
127 Kerry Wood STR	5.00	1.50
128 Trevor Hoffman STR	3.00	.90
129 Barry Bonds STR	12.00	3.60
130 Alex Rodriguez STR	8.00	2.40
131 Ben Grieve STR	3.00	.90
132 Tom Glavine STR	3.00	.90
133 David Wells STR	3.00	.90
134 Mike Piazza STR	8.00	2.40
135 Scott Brosius STR	3.00	.90

1999 SP Authentic Chirography

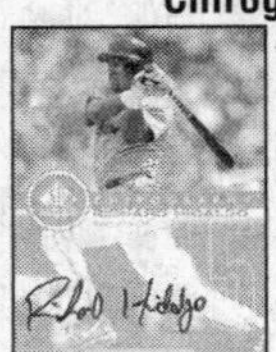

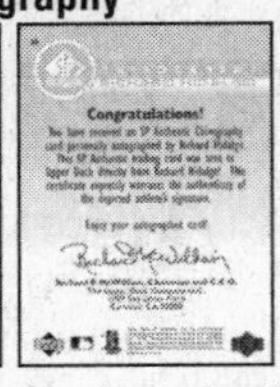

Randomly inserted in packs at the rate of one in 24, this 39-card set features color player photos with the pictured player's autograph at the bottom of the photo. Exchange cards for Ken Griffey Jr., Cal Ripken, Ruben Rivera and Scott Rolen were seeded into packs. The expiration date for the exchange cards was February 24th, 2000. Prices in our checklist refer to the actual autograph cards.

	Nm-Mt	Ex-Mt
AG Alex Gonzalez	10.00	3.00
BC Bruce Chen	10.00	3.00
BF Brad Fullmer	10.00	3.00
BG Ben Grieve	10.00	3.00
CB Carlos Beltran	40.00	12.00
CJ Chipper Jones	40.00	12.00
CK Corey Koskie	15.00	4.50
CP Calvin Pickering	10.00	3.00
CR Cal Ripken	120.00	36.00
EC Eric Chavez	15.00	4.50
GK Gabe Kapler	10.00	3.00
GL George Lombard	10.00	3.00
GM Greg Maddux	100.00	30.00
GMJ Gary Matthews Jr.	10.00	3.00
GV Greg Vaughn	10.00	3.00
IR Ivan Rodriguez	40.00	12.00
JD J.D. Drew	25.00	7.50
JG Jeremy Giambi	10.00	3.00
JR Ken Griffey Jr.	100.00	30.00
JT Jim Thome	40.00	12.00
KW Kevin Witt	10.00	3.00
KW Kerry Wood	40.00	12.00
MA Matt Anderson	10.00	3.00
MK Mike Kinkade	10.00	3.00
ML Mike Lowell	15.00	4.50
NG Nomar Garciaparra	120.00	36.00
RB Russell Branyan	10.00	3.00
RH Richard Hidalgo	10.00	3.00
RL Ricky Ledee	10.00	3.00
RM Ryan Minor	10.00	3.00
RR Ruben Rivera	10.00	3.00
SM Shane Monahan	10.00	3.00
SR Scott Rolen	40.00	12.00
TG Tony Gwynn	40.00	12.00
TGL Troy Glaus	15.00	4.50
TH Todd Helton	25.00	7.50
TL Travis Lee	10.00	3.00
TW Todd Walker	15.00	4.50
VG Vladimir Guerrero	40.00	12.00
CR-X Cal Ripken EXCH	15.00	4.50
JR-X Ken Griffey Jr. EXCH	12.00	3.60
RR-X Ruben Rivera EXCH	1.00	.30
SR-X Scott Rolen EXCH	2.50	.75

1999 SP Authentic Chirography Gold

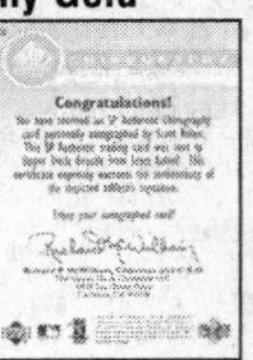

These scarce parallel versions of the Chirography cards were all serial numbered to the featured player's jersey number. The serial numbering was done by hand and is on the front of the card. In addition, gold ink was used on the card fronts (a flat grey front was used on the more common basic Chirography cards). While we only have pricing on some of the cards in this set, we are printing the checklist so collectors can know how many cards are available of each player. The same four players featured on exchange cards in the basic chirography (Griffey, Ripken, Rivera and Rolen) also had exchange cards in this set. The deadline for redeeming these cards was February 24th, 2000. Our listed price refers to the actual autograph cards.

	Nm-Mt	Ex-Mt
AG Alex Gonzalez/22		
BC Bruce Chen/48	25.00	7.50
BF Brad Fullmer/20		
BG Ben Grieve/14		
CB Carlos Beltran/36	100.00	30.00
CJ Chipper Jones/10		
CK Corey Koskie/47	40.00	12.00
CP Calvin Pickering/6		
CR Cal Ripken/8		
EC Eric Chavez/30	40.00	12.00
GK Gabe Kapler/51	25.00	7.50
GL George Lombard/26	25.00	7.50
GM Greg Maddux/31	250.00	75.00
GMJ G.Matthews Jr./68	25.00	7.50
GV Greg Vaughn/23		
IR Ivan Rodriguez/7		
JD J.D. Drew/8		
JG Jeremy Giambi/15		
JR Ken Griffey Jr./24		
JT Jim Thome/25		
KW Kevin Witt/6		
KW Kerry Wood/34	120.00	36.00
MA Matt Anderson/14		
MK Mike Kinkade/33	25.00	7.50
ML Mike Lowell/60	40.00	12.00
NG Nomar Garciaparra/5		
RB Russ Branyan/66	25.00	7.50
RH Richard Hidalgo/15		
RL Ricky Ledee/38	25.00	7.50
RM Ryan Minor/10		
RR Ruben Rivera/28	25.00	7.50
SM Shane Monahan/12		
SR Scott Rolen/17		
TG Tony Gwynn/19		
TGL Troy Glaus/14		
TH Todd Helton/17		
TL Travis Lee/16		
TW Todd Walker/12		
VG Vladimir Guerrero/27	120.00	36.00
CR-X Cal Ripken EXCH		
JR-X Ken Griffey Jr. EXCH		
RR-X Ruben Rivera EXCH		
SR-X Scott Rolen EXCH		

1999 SP Authentic Epic Figures

Randomly inserted in packs at the rate of one in seven, this 30-card set features action color photos of some of the game's most impressive players.

	Nm-Mt	Ex-Mt
COMPLETE SET (30)	100.00	30.00
E1 Mo Vaughn	1.50	.45
E2 Travis Lee	1.50	.45
E3 Andres Galarraga	1.50	.45
E4 Andruw Jones	1.50	.45
E5 Chipper Jones	4.00	1.20
E6 Greg Maddux	6.00	1.80
E7 Cal Ripken	12.00	3.60
E8 Nomar Garciaparra	6.00	1.80
E9 Sammy Sosa	6.00	1.80
E10 Frank Thomas	4.00	1.20
E11 Kerry Wood	4.00	1.20
E12 Kenny Lofton	1.50	.45
E13 Manny Ramirez	2.50	.75
E14 Larry Walker	2.50	.75
E15 Jeff Bagwell	2.50	.75
E16 Paul Molitor	4.00	1.20
E17 Vladimir Guerrero	4.00	1.20
E18 Derek Jeter	10.00	3.00
E19 Tino Martinez	2.50	.75
E20 Mike Piazza	6.00	1.80
E21 Ben Grieve	1.50	.45
E22 Scott Rolen	4.00	1.20
E23 Mark McGwire	10.00	3.00
E24 Tony Gwynn	5.00	1.50
E25 Barry Bonds	10.00	3.00
E26 Ken Griffey Jr.	6.00	1.80
E27 Alex Rodriguez	6.00	1.80
E28 J.D. Drew	1.50	.45
E29 Juan Gonzalez	2.50	.75
E30 Kevin Brown	2.50	.75

1999 SP Authentic Home Run Chronicles

Inserted one per pack, this 70-card set features action color photos of players who were the leading sluggers of the 1998 season.

	Nm-Mt	Ex-Mt
COMPLETE SET (70)	120.00	36.00
*DIE CUTS: 8X TO 20X BASIC HR CHRON.		
DIE CUTS RANDOM INSERTS IN PACKS		
DIE CUT PRINT RUN 70 SERIAL #'d SETS		
HR1 Mark McGwire	4.00	1.20
HR2 Sammy Sosa	1.50	.45
HR3 Ken Griffey Jr.	1.50	.45
HR4 Mark McGwire	2.50	.75
HR5 Mark McGwire	2.50	.75
HR6 Albert Belle	.40	.12
HR7 Jose Canseco	1.00	.30
HR8 Juan Gonzalez	.60	.18
HR9 Manny Ramirez	.60	.18
HR10 Rafael Palmeiro	1.00	.30
HR11 Mo Vaughn	.40	.12
HR12 Carlos Delgado	.40	.12
HR13 Nomar Garciaparra	1.50	.45
HR14 Barry Bonds	2.50	.75
HR15 Alex Rodriguez	1.50	.45
HR16 Tony Clark	.40	.12
HR17 Jim Thome	1.00	.30
HR18 Edgar Martinez	.60	.18
HR19 Frank Thomas	1.00	.30
HR20 Greg Vaughn	.40	.12
HR21 Vinny Castilla	.40	.12
HR22 Andres Galarraga	.40	.12
HR23 Moises Alou	.40	.12
HR24 Jeromy Burnitz	.40	.12
HR25 Vladimir Guerrero	1.00	.30
HR26 Jeff Bagwell	.60	.18
HR27 Chipper Jones	1.00	.30
HR28 Javier Lopez	.40	.12
HR29 Mike Piazza	1.50	.45
HR30 Andruw Jones	.40	.12
HR31 Henry Rodriguez	.40	.12
HR32 Jeff Kent	.40	.12
HR33 Ray Lankford	.40	.12

HR34 Scott Rolen 1.00 .30
HR35 Raul Mondesi .40 .12
HR36 Ken Caminiti .40 .12
HR37 J.D. Drew .40 .12
HR38 Troy Glaus .40 .12
HR39 Gabe Kapler .40 .12
HR40 Alex Rodriguez 1.50 .45
HR41 Ken Griffey Jr. 1.50 .45
HR42 Sammy Sosa 1.50 .45
HR43 Mark McGwire 2.50 .75
HR44 Sammy Sosa 1.50 .45
HR45 Mark McGwire 2.50 .75
HR46 Vinny Castilla .40 .12
HR47 Sammy Sosa 1.50 .45
HR48 Mark McGwire 2.50 .75
HR49 Sammy Sosa 1.50 .45
HR50 Greg Vaughn .40 .12
HR51 Sammy Sosa 1.50 .45
HR52 Mark McGwire 2.50 .75
HR53 Sammy Sosa 1.50 .45
HR54 Mark McGwire 2.50 .75
HR55 Sammy Sosa 1.50 .45
HR56 Ken Griffey Jr. 1.50 .45
HR57 Sammy Sosa 1.50 .45
HR58 Mark McGwire 2.50 .75
HR59 Sammy Sosa 1.50 .45
HR60 Mark McGwire 2.50 .75
HR61 Mark McGwire 4.00 .20
HR62 Mark McGwire 5.00 1.50
HR63 Mark McGwire 2.50 .75
HR64 Mark McGwire 2.50 .75
HR65 Mark McGwire 2.50 .75
HR66 Sammy Sosa 8.00 2.40
HR67 Mark McGwire 2.50 .75
HR68 Mark McGwire 2.50 .75
HR69 Mark McGwire 2.50 .75
HR70 Mark McGwire 10.00 3.00

1999 SP Authentic Redemption Cards

Randomly inserted in packs at the rate of one in 864, this 10-card set features hand-numbered cards that could be redeemed for various items autographed by the player named on the card. The expiration date for these cards was March 1st, 2000.

Nm-Mt Ex-Mt
1 K.Griffey Jr. AU Jersey/25
2 K.Griffey Jr. AU Baseball/75
3 K.Griffey Jr. AU SI Cover/75
4 K.Griffey Jr. AU Mini Helmet/75
5 M.McGwire AU 62 Ticket/1
6 M.McGwire AU 70 Ticket/3
7 Ken Griffey Jr. 12.00 3.60
Standee/300
8 Ken Griffey Jr. 40.00 12.00
Glove Card/200
9 Ken Griffey Jr. 25.00 7.50
HE Cel Card/346
10 Ken Griffey Jr. 20.00 6.00
SI Cover/200

1999 SP Authentic Reflections

Randomly inserted in packs at the rate of one in 23, this 30-card set features color action photos of some of the game's best players and printed using Dot Matrix technology.

Nm-Mt Ex-Mt
COMPLETE SET (30) 300.00 90.00
R1 Mo Vaughn 3.00 .90
R2 Travis Lee 3.00 .90
R3 Andres Galarraga 3.00 .90
R4 Andruw Jones 3.00 .90
R5 Chipper Jones 8.00 2.40
R6 Greg Maddux 12.00 3.60
R7 Cal Ripken 25.00 7.50
R8 Nomar Garciaparra 12.00 3.60
R9 Sammy Sosa 12.00 3.60
R10 Frank Thomas 8.00 2.40
R11 Kerry Wood 8.00 2.40
R12 Kenny Lofton 3.00 .90
R13 Manny Ramirez 5.00 1.50
R14 Larry Walker 5.00 1.50
R15 Jeff Bagwell 5.00 1.50
R16 Paul Molitor 8.00 2.40
R17 Vladimir Guerrero 8.00 2.40
R18 Derek Jeter 20.00 6.00
R19 Tino Martinez 5.00 1.50
R20 Mike Piazza 12.00 3.60
R21 Ben Grieve 3.00 .90
R22 Scott Rolen 8.00 2.40
R23 Mark McGwire 20.00 6.00
R24 Tony Gwynn 10.00 3.00
R25 Barry Bonds 20.00 6.00
R26 Ken Griffey Jr 12.00 3.60
R27 Alex Rodriguez 12.00 3.60
R28 J.D. Drew 3.00 .90
R29 Juan Gonzalez 5.00 1.50
R30 Roger Clemens 15.00 4.50

2000 SP Authentic

The 2000 SP Authentic product was initially released in late July, 2000 as a 135-card set. Each pack contained five cards and carried a suggested retail price of $4.99. The basic set features 90 veteran players, a 15-card SP Superstars subset serial numbered to 2500, and a 30-card Future Watch subset also serial numbered to 2500. In late December, Upper Deck released their UD Rookie Update brand, which contained a selection of cards to append the 2000 SP Authentic, SPx and UD Pros and Prospects brands. For SP Authentic, sixty new cards were intended, but card number 165 was never created due to problems at the manufacturer. Cards 136-164 are devoted to an extension of the Future Watch prospect subset established in the basic set. Similar to the basic set's FW cards, these Update cards are serial numbered, but only 1,700 copies of each card were produced (as compared to the 2,500 print run for the "first series" cards). Cards 166-195 feature a selection of established veterans either initially not included in the basic set or traded to new teams. Notable Rookie Cards include Xavier Nady, Kazuhiro Sasaki and Barry Zito. Also, a selection of A Piece of History 3000 Club Tris Speaker and Paul Waner memorabilia cards were randomly seeded into packs. 350 bat cards and five hand-numbered, combination bat chip and autograph cut cards for each player were produced. Pricing for these memorabilia cards can be referenced under 2000 Upper Deck A Piece of History 3000 Club. Finally, a Ken Griffey Jr. sample card was distributed to dealers and hobby media in June, 2000 (several weeks prior to the basic product's national release). The card can be readily distinguished by the large "SAMPLE" text running diagonally across the back.

Nm-Mt Ex-Mt
COMP.BASIC w/o SP's (90) 25.00 7.50
COMP.UPDATE w/o SP'S (30) 10.00 3.00
COMMON CARD (1-90) .40 .12
COMMON SUP (91-105) 3.00 .90
COMMON FW (106-135) 5.00 1.50
COMMON FW (136-164) 5.00 1.50
COMMON (166-195) .60 .18
1 Mo Vaughn .40 .12
2 Troy Glaus .40 .12
3 Jason Giambi .40 .12
4 Tim Hudson .40 .12
5 Eric Chavez .40 .12
6 Shannon Stewart .40 .12
7 Raul Mondesi .40 .12
8 Carlos Delgado .40 .12
9 Jose Canseco 1.00 .30
10 Vinny Castilla .40 .12
11 Greg Vaughn .40 .12
12 Manny Ramirez .60 .18
13 Roberto Alomar .60 .18
14 Jim Thome 1.00 .30
15 Richie Sexson .40 .12
16 Alex Rodriguez 1.50 .45
17 Freddy Garcia .40 .12
18 John Olerud .40 .12
19 Albert Belle .40 .12
20 Cal Ripken 3.00 .90
21 Mike Mussina .60 .18
22 Ivan Rodriguez 1.00 .30
23 Gabe Kapler .40 .12
24 Rafael Palmeiro .60 .18
25 Nomar Garciaparra 1.50 .45
26 Pedro Martinez 1.00 .30
27 Carl Everett .40 .12
28 Carlos Beltran .60 .18
29 Jermaine Dye .40 .12
30 Juan Gonzalez .60 .18
31 Dean Palmer .40 .12
32 Corey Koskie .40 .12
33 Jacque Jones .40 .12
34 Frank Thomas 1.00 .30
35 Paul Konerko .40 .12
36 Magglio Ordonez .40 .12
37 Bernie Williams .60 .18
38 Derek Jeter 2.50 .75
39 Roger Clemens 2.00 .60
40 Mariano Rivera .60 .18
41 Jeff Bagwell .60 .18
42 Craig Biggio .60 .18
43 Jose Lima .40 .12
44 Moises Alou .40 .12
45 Chipper Jones 1.00 .30
46 Greg Maddux 1.50 .45
47 Andruw Jones .40 .12
48 Andres Galarraga .40 .12
49 Jeromy Burnitz .40 .12
50 Geoff Jenkins .40 .12
51 Mark McGwire 2.50 .75
52 Fernando Tatis .40 .12
53 J.D. Drew .40 .12
54 Sammy Sosa 1.50 .45
55 Kerry Wood 1.00 .30
56 Mark Grace .60 .18
57 Matt Williams .40 .12
58 Randy Johnson 1.00 .30
59 Erubiel Durazo .40 .12
60 Gary Sheffield .40 .12
61 Kevin Brown .60 .18
62 Shawn Green .40 .12
63 Vladimir Guerrero 1.00 .30
64 Michael Barrett .40 .12
65 Barry Bonds 2.50 .75
66 Jeff Kent .40 .12
67 Russ Ortiz .40 .12
68 Preston Wilson .40 .12
69 Mike Lowell .40 .12
70 Mike Piazza 1.50 .45
71 Mike Hampton .40 .12
72 Robin Ventura .40 .12
73 Edgardo Alfonzo .40 .12
74 Tony Gwynn 1.25 .35
75 Ryan Klesko .40 .12
76 Trevor Hoffman .40 .12
77 Scott Rolen 1.00 .30
78 Bob Abreu .40 .12
79 Mike Lieberthal .40 .12
80 Curt Schilling .40 .12
81 Jason Kendall .40 .12
82 Brian Giles .40 .12
83 Kris Benson .40 .12
84 Ken Griffey Jr. 1.50 .45
85 Sean Casey .40 .12
86 Pokey Reese .40 .12
87 Barry Larkin .60 .18
88 Larry Walker .60 .18
89 Todd Helton .60 .18
90 Jeff Cirillo .40 .12
91 Ken Griffey Jr. SUP 8.00 2.40
92 Mark McGwire SUP 12.00 3.60
93 Chipper Jones SUP 5.00 1.50
94 Derek Jeter SUP 12.00 3.60
95 Shawn Green SUP 3.00 .90
96 Pedro Martinez SUP 5.00 1.50
97 Mike Piazza SUP 8.00 2.40
98 Alex Rodriguez SUP 8.00 2.40
99 Jeff Bagwell SUP 3.00 .90
100 Cal Ripken SUP 15.00 4.50
101 Sammy Sosa SUP 8.00 2.40
102 Barry Bonds SUP 12.00 3.60
103 Jose Canseco SUP 5.00 1.50
104 N.Garciaparra SUP 8.00 2.40
105 Ivan Rodriguez SUP 5.00 1.50
106 Rick Ankiel FW 5.00 1.50
107 Pat Burrell FW 3.00 .90
108 Vernon Wells FW 5.00 1.50
109 Nick Johnson FW 5.00 1.50
110 Kip Wells FW 5.00 1.50
111 Matt Riley FW 5.00 1.50
112 Alfonso Soriano FW 8.00 2.40
113 Josh Beckett FW 8.00 2.40
114 Danys Baez FW RC 5.00 1.50
115 Travis Dawkins FW 5.00 1.50
116 Eric Gagne FW 15.00 4.50
117 Mike Lamb FW RC 5.00 1.50
118 Eric Munson FW 5.00 1.50
119 W.Rodriguez FW RC 5.00 1.50
120 K.Sasaki FW RC 8.00 2.40
121 Chad Hutchinson FW 5.00 1.50
122 Peter Bergeron FW 5.00 1.50
123 W.Serrano FW RC 5.00 1.50
124 Tony Armas Jr. FW 5.00 1.50
125 Ramon Ortiz FW 5.00 1.50
126 Adam Kennedy FW 5.00 1.50
127 Joe Crede FW 5.00 1.50
128 Roosevelt Brown FW 5.00 1.50
129 Mark Mulder FW 5.00 1.50
130 Brad Penny FW 5.00 1.50
131 Terrence Long FW 5.00 1.50
132 Ruben Mateo FW 5.00 1.50
133 Wily Mo Pena FW 5.00 1.50
134 Rafael Furcal FW 5.00 1.50
135 M.Encarnacion FW 5.00 1.50
136 Barry Zito FW RC 15.00 4.50
137 Aaron McNeal FW RC 5.00 1.50
138 Timo Perez FW RC 5.00 1.50
139 Sun Woo Kim FW RC 5.00 1.50
140 Xavier Nady FW RC 8.00 2.40
141 M.Wheatland FW RC 5.00 1.50
142 B.Abernathy FW RC 5.00 1.50
143 Cory Vance FW RC 5.00 1.50
144 Scott Heard FW RC 5.00 1.50
145 Mike Meyers FW RC 5.00 1.50
146 Ben Diggins FW RC 5.00 1.50
147 Luis Matos FW RC 5.00 1.50
148 Ben Sheets FW RC 15.00 4.50
149 K.Ainsworth FW RC 5.00 1.50
150 Dave Krynzel FW RC 5.00 1.50
151 Alex Cabrera FW RC 5.00 1.50
152 Mike Tonis FW RC 5.00 1.50
153 Dane Sardinha FW RC 5.00 1.50
154 Keith Ginter FW RC 5.00 1.50
155 D.Espinosa FW RC 5.00 1.50
156 Joe Torres FW RC 5.00 1.50
157 Daylan Holt FW RC 5.00 1.50
158 Koyie Hill FW RC 5.00 1.50
159 B.Wilkerson FW RC 8.00 2.40
160 Juan Pierre FW RC 8.00 2.40
161 Matt Ginter FW RC 5.00 1.50
162 Dane Artman FW RC 5.00 1.50
163 Jon Rauch FW RC 5.00 1.50
164 Sean Burnett FW RC 8.00 2.40
165 Does Not Exist
166 Darin Erstad .60 .18
167 Ben Grieve .60 .18
168 David Wells .60 .18
169 Fred McGriff 1.00 .30
170 Bob Wickman .60 .18
171 Al Martin .60 .18
172 Melvin Mora .60 .18
173 Ricky Ledee .60 .18
174 Dante Bichette .60 .18
175 Mike Sweeney .60 .18
176 Bobby Higginson .60 .18
177 Matt Lawton .60 .18
178 Charles Johnson .60 .18
179 David Justice .60 .18
180 Richard Hidalgo .60 .18
181 B.J. Surhoff .60 .18
182 Richie Sexson .60 .18
183 Jim Edmonds .60 .18
184 Rondell White .60 .18
185 Curt Schilling .60 .18
186 Tom Goodwin .60 .18
187 Jose Vidro .60 .18
188 Ellis Burks .60 .18
189 Henry Rodriguez .60 .18
190 Mike Bordick .60 .18
191 Eric Owens .60 .18
192 Travis Lee .60 .18
193 Kevin Young .60 .18
194 Aaron Boone .60 .18
195 Todd Hollandsworth .60 .18
SPA K.Griffey Jr. Sample 2.00 .60

2000 SP Authentic Limited

Randomly inserted into packs, this 135-card set is a complete parallel of the 2000 SP Authentic base set. These cards are individually serial numbered to 100.

Nm-Mt Ex-Mt
*STARS 1-90: 8X TO 20X BASIC CARDS
*SUP 91-105: 1.25X TO 3X BASIC SUP
*FW 106-135: 1X TO 2.5X BASIC FW.
*FW 106-135 RC: 1X TO 2.5X BASIC FW RC

2000 SP Authentic Buybacks

Representatives at Upper Deck purchased back a selection of vintage SP brand trading cards from 1993-1999, featuring 29 different players. The "vintage" cards were all purchased in 2000 through hobby dealers. Each card was then hand-numbered in blue ink sharpie on front (please see listings for print runs), affixed with a serial numbered UDA hologram on back and packaged with a 2 1/2" by 3 1/2" UDA Certificate of Authenticity (of which had a hologram with a matching serial number of the signed card). The Certificate of Authenticity and the signed card were placed together in a soft plastic "penny" sleeve and then randomly seeded into 2000 SP Authentic packs at a rate of 1:95. Jeff Bagwell, Ken Griffey, Andruw Jones, Chipper Jones, Manny Ramirez and Alex Rodriguez did not manage to sign their cards in time for packout, thus exchange cards were created and seeded into packs for these players. The exchange cards did NOT specify the actual vintage card that the bearer would receive back in the mail. The deadline to redeem the exchange cards was March 30th, 2001. Pricing for cards with production of 25 or fewer cards is not provided due to scarcity.

Nm-Mt Ex-Mt
1 Jeff Bagwell 93/58 50.00 15.00
2 Jeff Bagwell 94/46 50.00 15.00
3 Jeff Bagwell 95/60 50.00 15.00
4 Jeff Bagwell 96/74 50.00 15.00
5 Jeff Bagwell 97/53 50.00 15.00
6 Jeff Bagwell 98/38 50.00 15.00
7 Jeff Bagwell 99/539 50.00 15.00
8 Jeff Bagwell EXCH 3.00 .90
9 Craig Biggio 93/59 40.00 12.00
10 Craig Biggio 94/69 40.00 12.00
11 Craig Biggio 95/171 25.00 7.50
12 Craig Biggio 96/71 40.00 12.00
13 Craig Biggio 97/46 40.00 12.00
14 Craig Biggio 98/40 40.00 12.00
15 Craig Biggio 99/125 25.00 7.50
16 Barry Bonds 93/12
17 Barry Bonds 94/12
18 Barry Bonds 95/21
19 Barry Bonds 96/9
20 Barry Bonds 97/5
21 Barry Bonds 98/22
22 Barry Bonds 99/520 250.00 75.00
23 Jose Canseco 93/29 60.00 18.00
24 Jose Canseco 94/20
25 Jose Canseco 95/6
26 Jose Canseco 96/23
27 Jose Canseco 97/23
28 Jose Canseco 98/24
29 Jose Canseco 99/502 40.00 12.00
30 Sean Casey 98/5
31 Sean Casey 99/139 15.00 4.50
32 Roger Clemens 93/68 120.00 36.00
33 Roger Clemens 94/60 120.00 36.00
34 Roger Clemens 95/68 120.00 36.00
35 Roger Clemens 96/68 120.00 36.00
36 Roger Clemens 97/7
37 Roger Clemens 98/25
38 Roger Clemens 99/134 100.00 30.00
39 Jason Giambi 97/34 50.00 15.00
40 Jason Giambi 98/25
41 Tom Glavine 93/99 40.00 12.00
42 Tom Glavine 94/107 40.00 12.00
43 Tom Glavine 95/97 40.00 12.00
44 Tom Glavine 96/42 50.00 15.00
45 Tom Glavine 98/40 50.00 15.00
46 Tom Glavine 99/138 40.00 12.00
47 Shawn Green 96/55 25.00 7.50
48 Shawn Green 99/530 15.00 4.50
49 Ken Griffey Jr. 93/19
50 Ken Griffey Jr. 94/8
51 Ken Griffey Jr. 95/9
52 Ken Griffey Jr. 96/12
53 Ken Griffey Jr. 97/10
54 Ken Griffey Jr. 98/22
55 Ken Griffey Jr. 99/403 80.00 24.00
56 Ken Griffey Jr. EXCH 10.00 3.00
57 Tony Gwynn 93/17
58 Tony Gwynn 94/7
59 Tony Gwynn 95/11
60 Tony Gwynn 96/11
61 Tony Gwynn 97/24
62 Tony Gwynn 98/21
63 Tony Gwynn 99/129 40.00 12.00
64 Tony Gwynn 99/369 40.00 12.00
65 Derek Jeter 93/5
66 Derek Jeter 95/17
67 Derek Jeter 96/10
68 Derek Jeter 97/12
69 Derek Jeter 98/11
70 Derek Jeter 99/119 200.00 60.00
71 Randy Johnson 93/60 80.00 24.00
72 Randy Johnson 94/45 80.00 24.00
73 Randy Johnson 95/70 80.00 24.00
74 Randy Johnson 96/60 80.00 24.00
75 Randy Johnson 97/10
76 Randy Johnson 98/21
77 Randy Johnson 99/113 80.00 24.00
78 Andruw Jones 97/70 15.00 4.50
79 Andruw Jones 98/56 25.00 7.50
80 Andruw Jones 99/531 15.00 4.50
81 Andruw Jones EXCH 3.00 .90
82 Chipper Jones 93/3
83 Chipper Jones 95/9
84 Chipper Jones 96/17
85 Chipper Jones 97/63 60.00 18.00
86 Chipper Jones 98/23
87 Chipper Jones 99/541 40.00 12.00
88 Chipper Jones EXCH 5.00 1.50
89 Kenny Lofton 94/100 25.00 7.50
90 Kenny Lofton 95/84 25.00 7.50
91 Kenny Lofton 96/34 50.00 15.00
92 Kenny Lofton 97/82 25.00 7.50
93 Kenny Lofton 98/21
94 Kenny Lofton 99/99 25.00 7.50
95 Javy Lopez 93/106 15.00 4.50
96 Javy Lopez 94/160 15.00 4.50
97 Javy Lopez 96/99 15.00 4.50
98 Javy Lopez 97/61 25.00 7.50
99 Javy Lopez 98/26 30.00 9.00
100 Greg Maddux 93/22
101 Greg Maddux 94/19
102 Greg Maddux 95/14
103 Greg Maddux 96/13
104 Greg Maddux 97/8
105 Greg Maddux 98/11
106 Greg Maddux 99/504 80.00 24.00
107 Paul O'Neill 93/110 25.00 7.50
108 Paul O'Neill 94/97 25.00 7.50
109 Paul O'Neill 95/142 25.00 7.50
110 Paul O'Neill 96/70 25.00 7.50
111 Paul O'Neill 98/23
112 Manny Ramirez 93/6
113 Manny Ramirez 94/7
114 Manny Ramirez 95/22
115 Manny Ramirez 96/13
116 Manny Ramirez 97/42 50.00 15.00
117 Manny Ramirez 98/36 50.00 15.00
118 M. Ramirez 99/532 50.00 15.00
119 Manny Ramirez EXCH 4.00 1.20
120 Cal Ripken 93/7
121 Cal Ripken 94/22
122 Cal Ripken 95/10
123 Cal Ripken 96/12
124 Cal Ripken 97/12
125 Cal Ripken 98/13
126 Cal Ripken 99/510 120.00 36.00
127 Alex Rodriguez 94/5
128 Alex Rodriguez 95/57 150.00 45.00
129 Alex Rodriguez 96/37 150.00 45.00
130 Alex Rodriguez 97/10
131 Alex Rodriguez 98/22
132 A.Rodriguez 99/408 100.00 30.00
133 Alex Rodriguez EXCH 8.00 2.40
134 Ivan Rodriguez 93/29 60.00 18.00
135 Ivan Rodriguez 94/16
136 Ivan Rodriguez 95/18
137 Ivan Rodriguez 96/22
138 Ivan Rodriguez 97/14
139 Ivan Rodriguez 98/27 60.00 18.00
140 Ivan Rodriguez 99/2
141 Scott Rolen 97/23
142 Scott Rolen 98/31 60.00 18.00
143 Frank Thomas 93/1
144 Frank Thomas 94/20
145 Frank Thomas 95/5
146 Frank Thomas 96/10
147 Frank Thomas 97/20
148 Frank Thomas 98/29 60.00 18.00
149 F.Thomas 99/100 40.00 12.00
150 Greg Vaughn 93/79 10.00 3.00
151 Greg Vaughn 94/75 10.00 3.00
152 Greg Vaughn 95/155 10.00 3.00
153 Greg Vaughn 96/113 10.00 3.00
154 Greg Vaughn 97/29 20.00 6.00
155 Greg Vaughn 99/527 10.00 3.00
156 Mo Vaughn 93/119 15.00 4.50
157 Mo Vaughn 94/96 15.00 4.50
158 Mo Vaughn 95/121 15.00 4.50
159 Mo Vaughn 96/114 15.00 4.50
160 Mo Vaughn 97/61 25.00 7.50
161 Mo Vaughn 98/29 30.00 9.00
162 Mo Vaughn 99/537 15.00 4.50
163 Robin Ventura 93/59 25.00 7.50
164 Robin Ventura 94/49 25.00 7.50
165 R.Ventura 95/125 15.00 4.50
166 Robin Ventura 96/55 25.00 7.50
167 Robin Ventura 97/44 25.00 7.50
168 Robin Ventura 98/28 30.00 9.00
169 R.Ventura 99/370 15.00 4.50
170 Matt Williams 93/55 25.00 7.50
171 Matt Williams 94/50 25.00 7.50
172 Matt Williams 95/137 15.00 4.50
173 Matt Williams 96/77 15.00 4.50
174 Matt Williams 97/54 25.00 7.50
175 Matt Williams 98/29 30.00 9.00
176 Matt Williams 99/529 15.00 4.50
177 P.Wilson 94/249 15.00 4.50
178 P.Wilson 99/195 15.00 4.50
179 Authentication Card .50 .15

2000 SP Authentic Chirography

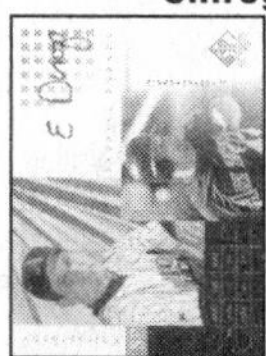
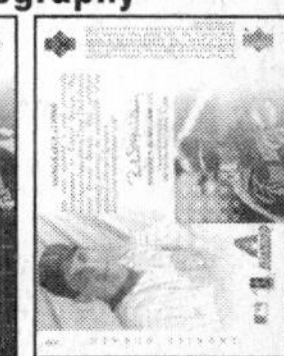

Randomly inserted into packs at one in 23, this 42-card insert features autographed cards of modern superstar players. Please note that there were also autographs of Sandy Koufax inserted into this set. There were a number of cards in this set that packed out as exchange cards, the exchange cards must be sent to Upper Deck by 03/30/01.

Nm-Mt Ex-Mt
AJ Andruw Jones 15.00 4.50
AR Alex Rodriguez 100.00 30.00

AS Alfonso Soriano 40.00 12.00
BB Barry Bonds 250.00 75.00
BP Ben Petrick 10.00 3.00
CBE Carlos Beltran 40.00 12.00
CJ Chipper Jones 40.00 12.00
CR Cal Ripken 120.00 36.00
DJ Derek Jeter 150.00 45.00
EC Eric Chavez 15.00 4.50
ED Erubiel Durazo 15.00 4.50
EM Eric Munson 10.00 3.00
EY Ed Yarnall 10.00 3.00
IR Ivan Rodriguez 40.00 12.00
JB Jeff Bagwell 50.00 15.00
JC Jose Canseco 40.00 12.00
JD J.D. Drew 25.00 7.50
JG Jason Giambi 25.00 7.50
JK Josh Kalinowski 10.00 3.00
JL Jose Lima 15.00 4.50
JMA Joe Mays 10.00 3.00
JMO Jim Morris 25.00 7.50
JOB John Bale 10.00 3.00
KL Kenny Lofton 25.00 7.50
MQ Mark Quinn 10.00 3.00
MR Manny Ramirez 50.00 15.00
MRI Matt Riley 15.00 4.50
MV Mo Vaughn 15.00 4.50
NJ Nick Johnson 15.00 4.50
PB Pat Burrell 15.00 4.50
RA Rick Ankiel 15.00 4.50
RC Roger Clemens 120.00 36.00
RF Rafael Furcal 15.00 4.50
RP Robert Person 10.00 3.00
SC Sean Casey 15.00 4.50
SK Sandy Koufax 250.00 75.00
SR Scott Rolen 40.00 12.00
TG Tony Gwynn 50.00 15.00
TGL Troy Glaus 15.00 4.50
VG Vladimir Guerrero 40.00 12.00
VW Vernon Wells 15.00 4.50
WG Wilton Guerrero 10.00 3.00

2000 SP Authentic Chirography Gold

Randomly inserted into packs, this 42-card insert is a complete parallel of the SP Authentic Chirography set. All Gold cards have a G suffix on the card number (for example Rick Ankiel's card is number G-RA). For the handful of exchange cards that were seeded into packs, this was the key manner to differentiate them from basic Chirography cards. Please note exchange cards (with a redemption deadline of 03/30/01) were seeded into packs for Andruw Jones, Alex Rodriguez, Chipper Jones, Jeff Bagwell, Manny Ramirez, Pat Burrell, Rick Ankiel and Scott Rolen. In addition, about 50% of Jose Lima's cards went into packs as real autographs and the remainder packed out as exchange cards.

Nm-Mt Ex-Mt
G-AJ Andruw Jones/25
G-AR Alex Rodriguez/3
G-AS Alfonso Soriano/53 50.00 15.00
G-BB Barry Bonds/25
G-BP Ben Petrick/15
G-CJ Cal Ripken/8
G-CR Chipper Jones/10
G-DJ Derek Jeter/2
G-EC Eric Chavez/3
G-ED Erubiel Durazo/44 25.00 7.50
G-EM Eric Munson/17
G-EY Ed Yarnall/41 15.00 4.50
G-IR Ivan Rodriguez/7
G-JB Jeff Bagwell/5
G-JC Jose Canseco/33 120.00 36.00
G-JD J.D. Drew/7
G-JG Jason Giambi/16
G-JK Josh Kalinowski/62 15.00 4.50
G-JL Jose Lima/42 25.00 7.50
G-JMA Joe Mays/53 15.00 4.50
G-JMO Jim Morris/63 40.00 12.00
G-JOB John Bale/49 15.00 4.50
G-KL Kenny Lofton/7
G-MQ Mark Quinn/14
G-MR Manny Ramirez/24
G-MRI Matt Riley/25
G-MV Mo Vaughn/42 25.00 7.50
G-NJ Nick Johnson/63 25.00 7.50
G-PB Pat Burrell/33 25.00 7.50
G-RA Rick Ankiel/66 25.00 7.50
G-RC Roger Clemens/22
G-RF Rafael Furcal/1
G-RP Robert Person/31 25.00 7.50
G-SC Sean Casey/21
G-SK Sandy Koufax/32
G-SR Scott Rolen/17
G-TG Tony Gwynn/19
G-TGL Troy Glaus/14
G-VG V.Guerrero/27 120.00 36.00
G-VW Vernon Wells/10
G-WG Wilton Guerrero/4
GCBE Carlos Beltran/15

2000 SP Authentic Cornerstones

Randomly inserted into packs at one in 23, this seven-card insert features players that are the cornerstones of their teams. Card backs carry a "C" prefix.

Nm-Mt Ex-Mt
COMPLETE SET (7) 60.00 18.00
C1 Ken Griffey Jr. 6.00 1.80
C2 Cal Ripken 12.00 3.60
C3 Mike Piazza 6.00 1.80
C4 Derek Jeter 10.00 3.00
C5 Mark McGwire 10.00 3.00

C6 Nomar Garciaparra 6.00 1.80
C7 Sammy Sosa 6.00 1.80

2000 SP Authentic DiMaggio Memorabilia

Randomly inserted into packs, this three-card insert features game-used memorabilia cards of Joe DiMaggio. This set features a Game-Used Jersey card (numbered to 500), a Game-Used Jersey card Gold (numbered to 56), and a Game-Used Jersey/Cut Autograph card (numbered to 5).

Nm-Mt Ex-Mt
1 Joe DiMaggio 120.00 36.00
Jsy/500
2 Joe DiMaggio 250.00 75.00
Jsy Gold/56
3 Joe DiMaggio
Jsy-Cut AU/5

2000 SP Authentic Midsummer Classics

Randomly inserted into packs at one in 12, this 10-card insert features perennial All-Stars. Card backs carry a "MC" prefix.

Nm-Mt Ex-Mt
COMPLETE SET (10) 30.00 9.00
MC1 Cal Ripken 8.00 2.40
MC2 Roger Clemens 5.00 1.50
MC3 Jeff Bagwell 1.50 .45
MC4 Barry Bonds 6.00 1.80
MC5 Jose Canseco 2.50 .75
MC6 Frank Thomas 2.50 .75
MC7 Mike Piazza 4.00 1.20
MC8 Tony Gwynn 3.00 .90
MC9 Juan Gonzalez 1.50 .45
MC10 Greg Maddux 4.00 1.20

2000 SP Authentic Premier Performers

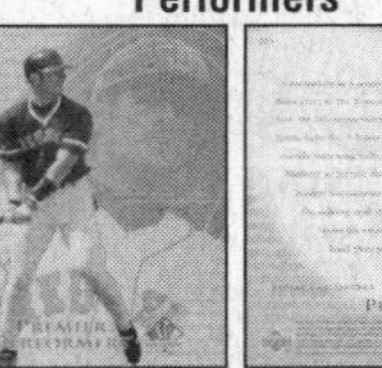

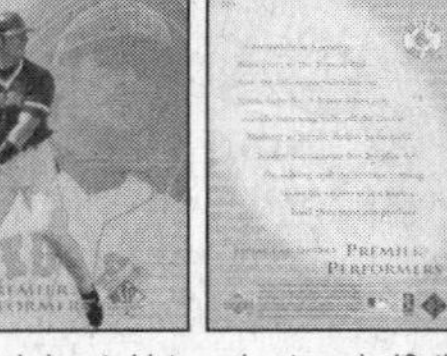

Randomly inserted into packs at one in 12, this 10-card insert features prime-time players that leave it all on the field and hold nothing back. Card backs carry a "PP" prefix.

Nm-Mt Ex-Mt
COMPLETE SET (10) 50.00 15.00
PP1 Mark McGwire 6.00 1.80
PP2 Alex Rodriguez 4.00 1.20
PP3 Cal Ripken 8.00 2.40
PP4 Nomar Garciaparra 4.00 1.20
PP5 Ken Griffey Jr. 4.00 1.20
PP6 Chipper Jones 2.50 .75
PP7 Derek Jeter 6.00 1.80
PP8 Ivan Rodriguez 2.50 .75
PP9 Vladimir Guerrero 2.50 .75
PP10 Sammy Sosa 4.00 1.20

2000 SP Authentic Supremacy

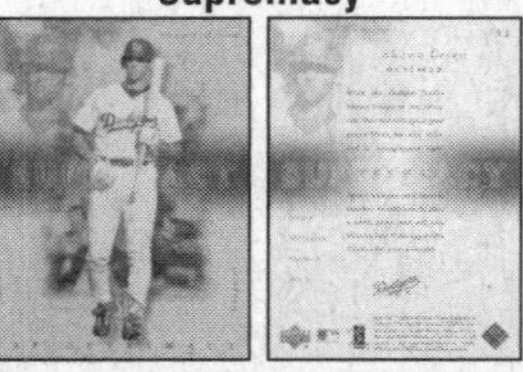

Randomly inserted into packs at one in 23, this seven-card insert features players that any team would like to have. Card backs carry a "S" prefix.

Nm-Mt Ex-Mt
COMPLETE SET (7) 30.00 9.00
S1 Alex Rodriguez 6.00 1.80
S2 Shawn Green 1.50 .45
S3 Pedro Martinez 4.00 1.20
S4 Chipper Jones 4.00 1.20
S5 Tony Gwynn 5.00 1.50
S6 Ivan Rodriguez 4.00 1.20
S7 Jeff Bagwell 2.50 .75

2000 SP Authentic United Nations

Randomly inserted into packs at one in four, this 10-card insert features players that have come from other countries to play in the Major Leagues. Card backs carry a "UN" prefix.

Nm-Mt Ex-Mt
COMPLETE SET (10) 10.00 3.00
UN1 Sammy Sosa 2.00 .60
UN2 Ken Griffey Jr. 2.00 .60
UN3 Orlando Hernandez .50 .15
UN4 Andres Galarraga .50 .15
UN5 Kazuhiro Sasaki 1.25 .35
UN6 Larry Walker .75 .23
UN7 Vinny Castilla .50 .15
UN8 Andruw Jones .50 .15
UN9 Ivan Rodriguez 1.25 .35
UN10 Chan Ho Park .50 .15

2001 SP Authentic

SP Authentic was initially released as a 180-card set in September, 2001. An additional 60-card Update set was distributed within Upper Deck Rookie Update packs in late December, 2001. Each basic sealed box contained 24 packs plus two three-card bonus packs (one entitled Stars of Japan and another entitled Mantle Pinstripe Exclusives). Each basic pack of SP Authentic contained five cards and carried a suggested retail price of $4.99. Upper Deck Rookie Update packs contained four cards and carried an SRP of $4.99. The basic set is broken into the following components: basic veterans (1-90), Future Watch (91-135) and Superstars (136-180). Each Future Watch and Superstar subset card from the first series is serial numbered of 1250 copies. Though odds were not released by the manufacturer, information supplied by dealers breaking several cases indicate on average one in every 18 basic packs contains one of these serial-numbered cards. The Update set is broken down as follows: basic veterans (181-210) and Future Watch (211-240). Each Update Future Watch is serial numbered to 1500 copies. Notable Rookie Cards in the basic set include Albert Pujols, Tsuyoshi Shinjo and Ichiro Suzuki. Notable Rookie Cards in the Update set include Mark Prior and Mark Teixeira.

Nm-Mt Ex-Mt
COMP.BASIC w/o SP's (90) 25.00 7.50
COMP.UPDATE w/o SP's (30) 10.00 3.00
COMMON CARD (1-90) .40 .12
COMMON FW (91-135) 8.00 2.40
COMMON SS (136-180) 5.00 1.50
COMMON (181-210) .60 .18
COMMON (211-240) 6.00 1.80
1 Troy Glaus .40 .12
2 Darin Erstad .40 .12
3 Jason Giambi .40 .12
4 Tim Hudson .40 .12
5 Eric Chavez .40 .12
6 Miguel Tejada .40 .12
7 Jose Ortiz .40 .12
8 Carlos Delgado .40 .12
9 Tony Batista .40 .12
10 Raul Mondesi .40 .12
11 Aubrey Huff .40 .12
12 Greg Vaughn .40 .12
13 Roberto Alomar .60 .18
14 Juan Gonzalez .60 .18
15 Jim Thome 1.00 .30
16 Omar Vizquel .60 .18
17 Edgar Martinez .60 .18
18 Freddy Garcia .40 .12
19 Cal Ripken 3.00 .90
20 Ivan Rodriguez 1.00 .30
21 Rafael Palmeiro .60 .18
22 Alex Rodriguez 1.50 .45
23 Manny Ramirez .60 .18
24 Pedro Martinez 1.00 .30
25 Nomar Garciaparra 1.50 .45
26 Mike Sweeney .40 .12
27 Jermaine Dye .40 .12
28 Bobby Higginson .40 .12
29 Dean Palmer .40 .12
30 Matt Lawton .40 .12
31 Eric Milton .40 .12
32 Frank Thomas 1.00 .30
33 Magglio Ordonez .40 .12
34 David Wells .40 .12
35 Paul Konerko .40 .12
36 Derek Jeter 2.50 .75
37 Bernie Williams .60 .18
38 Roger Clemens 2.00 .60
39 Mike Mussina .60 .18
40 Jorge Posada .60 .18
41 Jeff Bagwell .60 .18
42 Richard Hidalgo .40 .12
43 Craig Biggio .60 .18
44 Greg Maddux 1.50 .45
45 Chipper Jones 1.00 .30
46 Andruw Jones .40 .12
47 Rafael Furcal .40 .12
48 Tom Glavine .60 .18
49 Jeromy Burnitz .40 .12
50 Jeffrey Hammonds .40 .12
51 Mark McGwire 2.50 .75
52 Jim Edmonds .40 .12
53 Rick Ankiel .40 .12
54 J.D. Drew .40 .12
55 Sammy Sosa 1.50 .45
56 Corey Patterson .40 .12
57 Kerry Wood 1.00 .30
58 Randy Johnson 1.00 .30
59 Luis Gonzalez .40 .12
60 Curt Schilling .40 .12
61 Gary Sheffield .40 .12
62 Shawn Green .40 .12
63 Kevin Brown .40 .12
64 Vladimir Guerrero 1.00 .30
65 Jose Vidro .40 .12
66 Barry Bonds 2.50 .75
67 Jeff Kent .40 .12
68 Livan Hernandez .40 .12
69 Preston Wilson .40 .12
70 Charles Johnson .40 .12
71 Ryan Dempster .40 .12
72 Mike Piazza 1.50 .45
73 Al Leiter .40 .12
74 Edgardo Alfonzo .40 .12
75 Robin Ventura .40 .12
76 Tony Gwynn 1.25 .35
77 Phil Nevin .40 .12
78 Trevor Hoffman .40 .12
79 Scott Rolen 1.00 .30
80 Pat Burrell .40 .12
81 Bob Abreu .40 .12
82 Jason Kendall .40 .12
83 Brian Giles .40 .12
84 Kris Benson .40 .12
85 Ken Griffey Jr. 1.50 .45
86 Barry Larkin .60 .18
87 Sean Casey .40 .12
88 Todd Helton .60 .18
89 Mike Hampton .40 .12
90 Larry Walker .60 .18
91 Ichiro Suzuki FW RC 120.00 36.00
92 Wilson Betemit FW RC 8.00 2.40
93 A. Hernandez FW RC 8.00 2.40
94 Juan Uribe FW RC 10.00 3.00
95 Travis Hafner FW RC 20.00 6.00
96 M. Ensberg FW RC 12.00 3.60
97 Sean Douglass FW RC 8.00 2.40
98 Juan Diaz FW RC 8.00 2.40
99 Erick Almonte FW RC 8.00 2.40
100 Ryan Freel FW RC 8.00 2.40
101 E. Guzman FW RC 8.00 2.40
102 C. Parker FW RC 8.00 2.40
103 Josh Fogg FW RC 8.00 2.40
104 Bert Snow FW RC 8.00 2.40
105 H. Ramirez FW RC 10.00 3.00
106 R. Rodriguez FW RC 8.00 2.40
107 Tyler Walker FW RC 8.00 2.40
108 Jose Mieses FW RC 8.00 2.40
109 Billy Sylvester FW RC 8.00 2.40
110 Martin Vargas FW RC 8.00 2.40
111 Andres Torres FW RC 8.00 2.40
112 Greg Miller FW RC 8.00 2.40
113 Alexis Gomez FW RC 8.00 2.40
114 Grant Balfour FW RC 8.00 2.40
115 Henry Mateo FW RC 8.00 2.40
116 Esix Snead FW RC 8.00 2.40
117 J. Melian FW RC 8.00 2.40
118 Nate Teut FW RC 8.00 2.40
119 T. Shinjo FW RC 10.00 3.00
120 C. Valderrama FW RC 8.00 2.40
121 J. Estrada FW RC 20.00 6.00
122 J. Michaels FW RC 8.00 2.40
123 William Ortega FW RC 8.00 2.40
124 Jason Smith FW RC 8.00 2.40
125 B. Lawrence FW RC 8.00 2.40
126 Albert Pujols FW RC 250.00 75.00
127 Wilkin Ruan FW RC 8.00 2.40
128 Josh Towers FW RC 8.00 2.40
129 Kris Keller FW RC 8.00 2.40
130 Nick Maness FW RC 8.00 2.40
131 Jack Wilson FW RC 15.00 4.50
132 B. Duckworth FW RC 8.00 2.40
133 Mike Penney FW RC 8.00 2.40
134 Jay Gibbons FW RC 12.00 3.60
135 Cesar Crespo FW RC 8.00 2.40
136 Ken Griffey Jr. SS 10.00 3.00
137 Mark McGwire SS 15.00 4.50
138 Derek Jeter SS 15.00 4.50
139 Alex Rodriguez SS 10.00 3.00
140 Sammy Sosa SS 10.00 3.00
141 Carlos Delgado SS 5.00 1.50
142 Cal Ripken SS 20.00 6.00
143 Pedro Martinez SS 6.00 1.80
144 Frank Thomas SS 6.00 1.80
145 Juan Gonzalez SS 6.00 1.80
146 Troy Glaus SS 5.00 1.50
147 Jason Giambi SS 5.00 1.50
148 Ivan Rodriguez SS 6.00 1.80
149 Chipper Jones SS 6.00 1.80
150 Vladimir Guerrero SS 6.00 1.80
151 Mike Piazza SS 10.00 3.00
152 Jeff Bagwell SS 5.00 1.50
153 Randy Johnson SS 6.00 1.80
154 Todd Helton SS 5.00 1.50
155 Gary Sheffield SS 5.00 1.50
156 Tony Gwynn SS 8.00 2.40
157 Barry Bonds SS 15.00 4.50
158 N. Garciaparra SS 10.00 3.00
159 Bernie Williams SS 5.00 1.50
160 Greg Vaughn SS 5.00 1.50
161 David Wells SS 5.00 1.50
162 Roberto Alomar SS 5.00 1.50
163 Jermaine Dye SS 5.00 1.50
164 Rafael Palmeiro SS 5.00 1.50
165 Andruw Jones SS 5.00 1.50
166 Preston Wilson SS 5.00 1.50
167 Edgardo Alfonzo SS 5.00 1.50
168 Pat Burrell SS 5.00 1.50
169 Jim Edmonds SS 5.00 1.50
170 Mike Hampton SS 5.00 1.50
171 Jeff Kent SS 5.00 1.50
172 Kevin Brown SS 5.00 1.50
173 Manny Ramirez SS 5.00 1.50
174 Magglio Ordonez SS 5.00 1.50
175 Roger Clemens SS 12.00 3.60
176 Jim Thome SS 6.00 1.80
177 Barry Zito SS 5.00 1.50
178 Brian Giles SS 5.00 1.50
179 Rick Ankiel SS 5.00 1.50
180 Corey Patterson SS 5.00 1.50
181 Garret Anderson .60 .18
182 Jermaine Dye .60 .18
183 Shannon Stewart .60 .18
184 Ben Grieve .60 .18
185 Ellis Burks .60 .18
186 John Olerud .60 .18
187 Tony Batista .60 .18
188 Ruben Sierra .60 .18
189 Carl Everett .60 .18
190 Neifi Perez .60 .18
191 Tony Clark .60 .18
192 Doug Mientkiewicz .60 .18
193 Carlos Lee .60 .18
194 Jorge Posada 1.00 .30
195 Lance Berkman 5.00 1.50
196 Ken Caminiti .60 .18
197 Ben Sheets 1.00 .30
198 Matt Morris .60 .18
199 Fred McGriff 1.00 .30
200 Mark Grace 1.00 .30
201 Paul LoDuca .60 .18
202 Tony Armas Jr. .60 .18
203 Andres Galarraga .60 .18
204 Cliff Floyd .60 .18
205 Matt Lawton .60 .18
206 Ryan Klesko .60 .18
207 Jimmy Rollins .60 .18
208 Aramis Ramirez .60 .18
209 Aaron Boone .60 .18
210 Jose Ortiz .60 .18
211 Mark Prior FW RC 150.00 45.00
212 Mark Teixeira FW RC 60.00 18.00
213 Bud Smith FW RC 6.00 1.80
214 W.Caceres FW RC 6.00 1.80
215 Dave Williams FW RC 6.00 1.80
216 Delvin James FW RC 6.00 1.80
217 Endy Chavez FW RC 6.00 1.80
218 Doug Nickle FW RC 6.00 1.80
219 Bret Prinz FW RC 6.00 1.80
220 Troy Mattes FW RC 6.00 1.80
221 D.Sanchez FW RC 6.00 1.80
222 D.Brazelton FW RC 8.00 2.40
223 Brian Bowles FW RC 6.00 1.80
224 D.Mendez FW RC 6.00 1.80
225 Jorge Julio FW RC 6.00 1.80
226 Matt White FW RC 6.00 1.80
227 Casey Fossum FW RC 6.00 1.80
228 Mike Rivera FW RC 6.00 1.80
229 Joe Kennedy FW RC 8.00 2.40
230 Kyle Lohse FW RC 8.00 2.40
231 Juan Cruz FW RC 6.00 1.80
232 Jeremy Affeldt FW RC 8.00 2.40
233 Brandon Lyon FW RC 6.00 1.80
234 Brian Roberts FW RC 6.00 1.80
235 Willie Harris FW RC 6.00 1.80
236 Pedro Santana FW RC 6.00 1.80
237 Rafael Soriano FW RC 8.00 2.40
238 Steve Green FW RC 6.00 1.80
239 Junior Spivey FW RC 8.00 2.40
240 R.Mackowiak FW RC 8.00 2.40
NNO K.Griffey Jr. Promo 2.00 .60

2001 SP Authentic Limited

This 180-card set is a straight parallel of the basic set. Only fifty sets were produced and each card features serial-numbering in thin gold foil on front and a gold foil brand logo (basic cards feature silver foil brand logos).

Nm-Mt Ex-Mt
*STARS 1-90: 10X TO 25X BASIC 1-90
*FW 91-135: .75X TO 2X BASIC 91-135
*SS 136-180: 1.5X TO 4X BASIC 136-180
91 Ichiro Suzuki FW 300.00 90.00
126 Albert Pujols FW 600.00 180.00

2001 SP Authentic BuyBacks

For the third time in the history of the brand (including 1997 and 2000), Upper Deck incorporated Buyback cards into SP Authentic packs. Representatives from UD purchased varying quantities of actual previously released SP Authentic cards ranging from 1993 to 2000. The cards were then signed by the featured ballplayer, hand-numbered in blue ink on front and affixed with a serial-numbered hologram sticker on back (note: it's believed all 2001 hologram sticker numbers begin with the letters "AAA"). In addition to the actual signed card, each Buyback was distributed with a 2 1/2" by 3 1/2" Authenticity Guarantee card. Each of these cards featured a hologram with a matching serial-number and a note of congratulations from Upper Deck's CEO Richard McWilliam. Our listings for these cards feature the year of the card followed by the quantity produced. Thus, "Edgardo Alfonzo 95/77" indicates a 1995 SP Authentic Edgardo Alfonzo card of which 77 copies were made. Please note that several Buyback cards are too scarce for us to provide accurate pricing. Please see our magazine or website for pricing information on these cards as it's made available. The following players were seeded into packs as exchange cards: Roger

Clemens, Cal Ripken and Frank Thomas. Collectors did not know which card of these players they would receive until it was mailed to them. Exchange deadline was 8/30/04.

	Nm-Mt	Ex-Mt
1 Edgardo Alfonzo 95/77	15.00	4.50
2 Edgardo Alfonzo 98/15		
3 Edgardo Alfonzo 00/280	10.00	3.00
4 Barry Bonds 93/75	250.00	75.00
5 Barry Bonds 94/103	250.00	75.00
6 Barry Bonds 95/31	250.00	75.00
7 Barry Bonds 95 Silver/2		
8 Barry Bonds 96/49	250.00	75.00
9 Barry Bonds 97/15		
10 Barry Bonds 98/15		
11 Barry Bonds 00/146	250.00	75.00
12 Roger Clemens 00/145	120.00	36.00
13 R.Clemens 99/150 EXCH	120.00	36.00
15 Carlos Delgado 93/24		
16 Carlos Delgado 94/272	15.00	4.50
17 Carlos Delgado 96/81	25.00	7.50
18 Carlos Delgado 97/8		
19 Carlos Delgado 98/29	50.00	15.00
20 Carlos Delgado 00/169	15.00	4.50
21 Jim Edmonds 96/72	40.00	12.00
22 Jim Edmonds 97/38	60.00	18.00
23 Jim Edmonds 98/23		
24 Jason Giambi 97/14		
25 Jason Giambi 98/6		
26 Jason Giambi 00/290	15.00	4.50
27 Troy Glaus 00/340	15.00	4.50
28 Shawn Green 00/340	15.00	4.50
29 Ken Griffey Jr. 93/34	150.00	45.00
30 Ken Griffey Jr. 94/182	100.00	30.00
31 Ken Griffey Jr. 95/116	100.00	30.00
32 Ken Griffey Jr. 95 Silver/2		
33 Ken Griffey Jr. 96/53	150.00	45.00
34 Ken Griffey Jr. 97/7		
35 Ken Griffey Jr. 98/8		
36 Ken Griffey Jr. 00/333	80.00	24.00
37 Tony Gwynn 93/101	60.00	18.00
38 Tony Gwynn 94/88	60.00	18.00
39 Tony Gwynn 95/179	50.00	15.00
40 Tony Gwynn 96/92	60.00	18.00
41 Tony Gwynn 97/9		
42 Tony Gwynn 98/16		
43 Tony Gwynn 00/95	60.00	18.00
44 Todd Helton 00/194	25.00	7.50
45 Tim Hudson 00/291	25.00	7.50
46 Randy Johnson 93/97	100.00	30.00
47 Randy Johnson 94/146	60.00	18.00
48 Randy Johnson 95/121	60.00	18.00
49 Randy Johnson 95 Silver/6		
50 Randy Johnson 96/78	100.00	30.00
51 Randy Johnson 97/8		
52 Randy Johnson 98/12		
53 Randy Johnson 00/213	60.00	18.00
54 Andruw Jones 97/20		
55 Andruw Jones 98/12		
56 Andruw Jones 00/336	15.00	4.50
57 Chipper Jones 93/13		
58 Chipper Jones 95/118	50.00	15.00
59 Chipper Jones 96/72	60.00	18.00
60 Chipper Jones 97/15		
61 Chipper Jones 98/11		
62 Chipper Jones 00/303	40.00	12.00
63 Cal Ripken 93/22		
64 Cal Ripken 94/99	120.00	36.00
65 Cal Ripken 95/37	200.00	60.00
66 Cal Ripken 96/16		
67 Cal Ripken 96 CL/10		
68 Cal Ripken 97/23		
69 Cal Ripken 98/11		
70 Cal Ripken 00/266	120.00	36.00
72 Alex Rodriguez 95/117	120.00	36.00
73 Alex Rodriguez 95 Silver/2		
74 Alex Rodriguez 96/72	150.00	45.00
75 Alex Rodriguez 97/14		
76 Alex Rodriguez 98/11		
77 Alex Rodriguez 00/332	100.00	30.00
78 Ivan Rodriguez 93/89	50.00	15.00
79 Ivan Rodriguez 95/16		
80 Ivan Rodriguez 95 Silver/2		
81 Ivan Rodriguez 96/64	80.00	24.00
82 Ivan Rodriguez 97/8		
83 Ivan Rodriguez 98/13		
84 Ivan Rodriguez 00/163	40.00	12.00
85 Gary Sheffield 93/82	40.00	12.00
86 Gary Sheffield 94/2		
87 Gary Sheffield 95/70	40.00	12.00
88 Gary Sheffield 96/67	40.00	12.00
89 Gary Sheffield 97/43	60.00	18.00
90 Gary Sheffield 98/27	80.00	24.00
91 Gary Sheffield 00/146	25.00	7.50
92 Sammy Sosa 93/73	200.00	60.00
93 Sammy Sosa 94/19		
94 Sammy Sosa 95/30	250.00	75.00
95 Sammy Sosa 96/9		
96 Sammy Sosa 97/14		
97 Fernando Tatis 00/267	10.00	3.00
98 Frank Thomas 93/79	60.00	18.00
99 Frank Thomas 94/165	40.00	12.00
100 Frank Thomas 95/3		
101 Frank Thomas 97/34	100.00	30.00
102 Frank Thomas 98/10		
103 Frank Thomas 00/302	40.00	12.00
105 Mo Vaughn 93/94	25.00	7.50
106 Mo Vaughn 94/102	25.00	7.50
107 Mo Vaughn 95/129	15.00	4.50
108 Mo Vaughn 95 Silver/3		
109 Mo Vaughn 96/81	25.00	7.50
110 Mo Vaughn 97/36	40.00	12.00
111 Mo Vaughn 98/23		
112 Mo Vaughn 00/309	15.00	4.50
113 Robin Ventura 00/340	15.00	4.50
114 Matt Williams 00/310	15.00	4.50
115 Authentication Card		

2001 SP Authentic Chirography

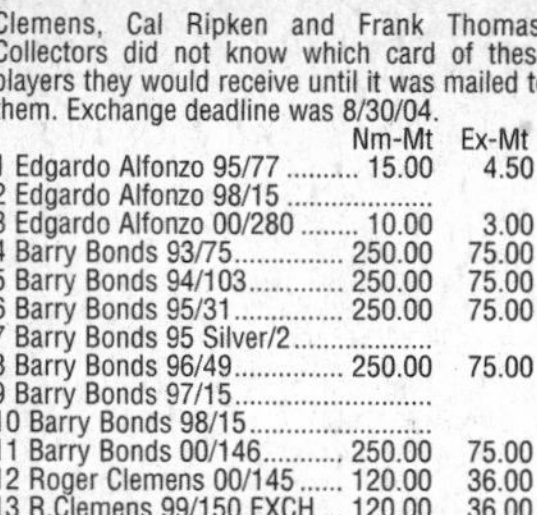

Signed Chirography inserts were brought back for the fourth straight year within SP Authentic. Over 40 players were featured in the 2001 issue, with announced odds of 1:72 packs. Each card features a horizontal design and a small black and white action photo of the player at the side to allow the maximum amount of room for the featured player's autograph (of which is typically found signed in blue ink). Quantities produced for each card varied dramatically and shortly after the product was released, representatives at Upper Deck publicly announced print runs on a selection of the toughest cards to obtain. Those quantities have been added to our checklist following the featured player's name.

	Nm-Mt	Ex-Mt
AB Albert Belle	15.00	4.50
AJ Andruw Jones	15.00	4.50
ALP Albert Pujols	300.00	90.00
AR Alex Rodriguez SP/229	120.00	36.00
BS Ben Sheets	25.00	7.50
CB Carlos Beltran	40.00	12.00
CD Carlos Delgado	15.00	4.50
CF Cliff Floyd	15.00	4.50
CJ Chipper Jones SP/184	40.00	12.00
CR Cal Ripken SP/109	150.00	45.00
DD Darren Dreifort SP/206	10.00	3.00
DER Darin Erstad	15.00	4.50
DES David Espinosa	10.00	3.00
DJ David Justice	15.00	4.50
DS Dane Sardinha	10.00	3.00
DW David Wells	15.00	4.50
EA Edgardo Alfonzo	10.00	3.00
JC Jose Canseco	40.00	12.00
JD J.D. Drew	25.00	7.50
JE Jim Edmonds	25.00	7.50
JG Jason Giambi	15.00	4.50
KG Ken Griffey Jr. SP/126	120.00	36.00
LG Luis Gonzalez SP/271	25.00	7.50
MB Milton Bradley	15.00	4.50
MK Mark Kotsay SP/228	15.00	4.50
MS Mike Sweeney	15.00	4.50
MV Mo Vaughn SP/103	15.00	4.50
MW Matt Williams	15.00	4.50
PB Pat Burrell	15.00	4.50
RF Rafael Furcal SP/222	15.00	4.50
RH Rick Helling SP/211	10.00	3.00
RJ R. Johnson SP/143	60.00	15.00
RV Robin Ventura SP/92		
RW Rondell White	15.00	4.50
SG Shawn Green SP/82	40.00	12.00
SS Sammy Sosa SP/76	200.00	60.00
TIH Tim Hudson	25.00	7.50
TL Travis Lee SP/226	10.00	3.00
TOG Tony Gwynn SP/76	50.00	15.00
TOH Todd Helton SP/152	40.00	12.00
TRG Troy Glaus	15.00	4.50

2001 SP Authentic Chirography Gold

These scarce autograph cards are a straight parallel of the more commonly available Chirography cards. The Gold cards, however, were all produced to quantities mirroring the featured player's uniform number. Furthermore, the cards are individually numbered on front in blue ink and the imagery and design accents are printed in a subdued gold color (rather than the black and white design used on the basic Chirography cards). Many of these cards are too scarce for us to provide accurate pricing on.

	Nm-Mt	Ex-Mt
G-AB Albert Belle/88	50.00	15.00
G-AJ Andruw Jones/25		
G-ALP Albert Pujols/5		
G-AR Alex Rodriguez/3		
G-BS Ben Sheets/15		
G-CB Carlos Beltran/15		
G-CD Carlos Delgado/25		
G-CF Cliff Floyd/30		
G-CJ Chipper Jones/10		
G-CR Cal Ripken/8		
G-DD Darren Dreifort/37	25.00	7.50
G-DER Darin Erstad/17		
G-DES David Espinosa/79	25.00	7.50
G-DJ David Justice/28	50.00	15.00
G-DS Dane Sardinha/50	25.00	7.50
G-DW David Wells/33	50.00	15.00
G-EA Edgardo Alfonzo/13		
G-JD J.D. Drew/7		
G-JE Jim Edmonds/15		
G-JG Jason Giambi/16		
G-KG Ken Griffey Jr./30	200.00	60.00
G-LG Luis Gonzalez/20		
G-MB Milton Bradley/24		
G-MK Mark Kotsay/14		
G-MS Mike Sweeney/29	50.00	15.00
G-MV Mo Vaughn/42	50.00	15.00
G-MW Matt Williams/9		
G-PB Pat Burrell/5		
G-RF Rafael Furcal/1		
G-RH Rick Helling/32	25.00	7.50
G-RJ Randy Johnson/51	120.00	36.00
G-RV Robin Ventura/4		
G-RW Rondell White/22		
G-SG Shawn Green/15		
G-SS Sammy Sosa/21		
G-TIH Tim Hudson/15		
G-TL Travis Lee/16		
G-TOG Tony Gwynn/21		
G-TOH Todd Helton/17		
G-TRG Troy Glaus/25		

2001 SP Authentic Chirography Update

Randomly inserted into Upper Deck Rookie Update packs, thse eight cards feature autographs from leading players in the game. Cal Ripken and Ichiro Suuzki did not return their cards in time for inclusion in these packs and these cards are available as exchange cards. Those cards could be redeemed until September 13th, 2004. These cards are serial numbered to 250.

	Nm-Mt	Ex-Mt
SP-CR Cal Ripken	150.00	45.00
SP-DM Doug Mientkiewicz	15.00	4.50
SP-IS Ichiro Suzuki	400.00	120.00
SP-JP Jorge Posada	40.00	12.00
SP-KG Ken Griffey Jr.	100.00	30.00
SP-LB Lance Berkman	25.00	7.50
SP-MS Mike Sweeney	15.00	4.50
SP-TG Tony Gwynn	40.00	12.00

2001 SP Authentic Chirography Update Silver

Randomly inserted into Upper Deck Rookie Update packs, thse eight cards parallel the Chirography Update insert set and feature autographs from leading players in the game. Cal Ripken Jr. and Ichiro Suuzki did not return their cards in time for inclusion in these packs and these cards are available as exchange cards. These cards are serial numbered to 100.

	Nm-Mt	Ex-Mt
SPCR Cal Ripken		
SPDM Doug Mientkiewicz	25.00	7.50
SPIS Ichiro Suzuki		
SPJP Jorge Posada	40.00	12.00
SPKG Ken Griffey Jr.	120.00	36.00
SPLB Lance Berkman	40.00	12.00
SPMS Mike Sweeney	25.00	7.50
SPTG Tony Gwynn	60.00	18.00

2001 SP Authentic Cooperstown Calling Game Jersey

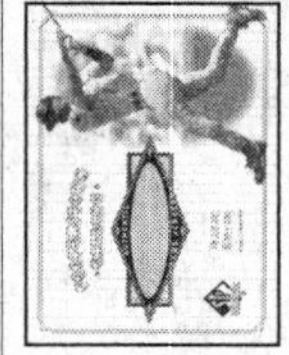

This 22-card set features a selection of players that were voted in (or were soon to be voted in) to the baseball Hall of Fame in Cooperstown, NY. Each card features a swatch of game-used jersey incorporated into an attractive horizontal design. Though specific odds per pack were not released for this set, Upper Deck did release cumulative odds of 1:24 packs for finding a game-used jersey card from either of the Cooperstown Calling, UD Exclusives or UD Exclusives Combos sets within the SP Authentic product.

	Nm-Mt	Ex-Mt
CC-AD Andre Dawson	10.00	3.00
CC-BM Bill Mazeroski	15.00	4.50
CC-CR Cal Ripken	40.00	12.00
CC-DM Don Mattingly	40.00	12.00
CC-DW Dave Winfield	10.00	3.00
CC-EM Eddie Murray	15.00	4.50
CC-GC Gary Carter	10.00	3.00
CC-GG Goose Gossage	10.00	3.00
CC-JB Jeff Bagwell	15.00	4.50
CC-KP Kirby Puckett	15.00	4.50
CC-KS Kazuhiro Sasaki	10.00	3.00
CC-MP Mike Piazza SP	25.00	7.50
CC-MR M. Ramirez SP	15.00	4.50
CC-OS Ozzie Smith	15.00	4.50
CC-PM Pedro Martinez SP	15.00	4.50
CC-PM Paul Molitor	15.00	4.50
CC-RC Roger Clemens	40.00	12.00
CC-RM R. Maris SP/243	80.00	24.00
CC-RS Ryne Sandberg	30.00	9.00
CC-SG Steve Garvey	10.00	3.00
CC-TG Tony Gwynn	20.00	6.00
CC-WB Wade Boggs	15.00	4.50

2001 SP Authentic Stars of Japan

This 30-card dual player set features a selection of Japanese stars active in Major League baseball at the time of issue. The cards were distributed in special Stars of Japan packs of which were available as a bonus pack within each sealed box of 2001 SP Authentic baseball. Each Stars of Japan pack contained three cards and one in every 12 packs contained a memorabilia card.

	Nm-Mt	Ex-Mt
COMPLETE SET (30)	80.00	24.00
RS1 Ichiro Suzuki Tsuyoshi Shinjo	8.00	2.40
RS2 Shigetoshi Hasegawa Hideki Irabu	2.00	.60
RS3 Tomo Ohka Mac Suzuki	2.00	.60
RS4 Tsuyoshi Shinjo Hideki Irabu	2.00	.60
RS5 Ichiro Suzuki Hideo Nomo	10.00	3.00
RS6 Tsuyoshi Shinjo Mac Suzuki	2.00	.60
RS7 Tsuyoshi Shinjo Kazuhiro Sasaki	2.00	.60
RS8 Hideo Nomo Tomo Ohka	2.00	.60
RS9 Ichiro Suzuki Mac Suzuki	8.00	2.40
RS10 Hideo Nomo Shigetoshi Hasegawa	2.00	.60
RS11 Hideo Nomo Masato Yoshii	2.00	.60
RS12 Hideo Nomo Hideki Irabu	2.00	.60
RS13 Shig. Hasegawa Kazuhiro Sasaki	2.00	.60
RS14 Shig. Hasegawa Mac Suzuki	2.00	.60
RS15 Tsuyoshi Shinjo Hideo Nomo	2.00	.60
RS16 Tsuyoshi Shinjo Tomo Ohka	2.00	.60
RS17 Ichiro Suzuki Kazuhiro Sasaki	10.00	3.00
RS18 Masato Yoshii Hideki Irabu	2.00	.60
RS19 Ichiro Suzuki Tomo Ohka	8.00	2.40
RS20 Hideki Irabu Kazuhiro Sasaki	2.00	.60
RS21 Tsuyoshi Shinjo Masato Yoshii	2.00	.60
RS22 Ichiro Suzuki Shigetoshi Hasegawa	8.00	2.40
RS23 Mac Suzuki Kazuhiro Sasaki	2.00	.60
RS24 Ichiro Suzuki Hideki Irabu	8.00	2.40
RS25 Tomo Ohka Kazuhiro Sasaki	2.00	.60
RS26 Tsuyoshi Shinjo Shigetoshi Hasegawa	2.00	.60
RS27 Masato Yoshii Kazuhiro Sasaki	2.00	.60
RS28 Hideo Nomo Kazuhiro Sasaki	2.00	.60
RS29 Ichiro Suzuki Masato Yoshii	8.00	2.40
RS30 Hideo Nomo Mac Suzuki	2.00	.60

2001 SP Authentic Stars of Japan Game Ball

This six-card set features a selection of Japanese stars actively playing in the Major Leagues at the time of issue. Each card features a patch of game-used baseball. The cards were distributed in special Stars of Japan packs. Each sealed box of 2001 SP Authentic contained one three-card Stars of Japan pack inside.Though individual Jersey card odds were not announced, the cumulative odds of finding a memorabilia card (ball, base, bat or jersey) from a Stars of Japan packs was 1:12.

	Nm-Mt	Ex-Mt
GOLD RANDOM INSERTS IN PACKS		
GOLD PRINT RUN 25 SERIAL #'d SETS		
GOLD NO PRICING DUE TO SCARCITY		
BB-HI Hideki Irabu	10.00	3.00
BB-IS Ichiro Suzuki	80.00	24.00
BB-KS Kazuhiro Sasaki	10.00	3.00
BB-MY Masato Yoshii	10.00	3.00
BB-SH Shig. Hasegawa SP/30		
BB-TS T. Shinjo SP/50	15.00	4.50

2001 SP Authentic Stars of Japan Game Ball-Base Combos

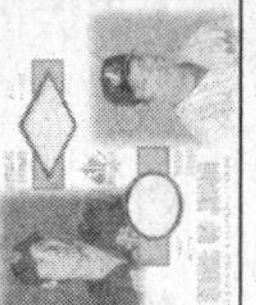

This 14-card dual player set features a selection of Japanese stars actively playing in the Major Leagues at the time of issue. Each card features a piece of a game-used baseball coupled with a piece of game-used base. The cards were distributed in special Stars of Japan packs. Each sealed box of 2001 SP Authentic contained one three-card Stars of Japan pack inside.Though individual Jersey card odds were not announced, the cumulative odds of finding a memorabilia card (ball, base, bat or jersey) from a Stars of Japan packs was 1:12.

	Nm-Mt	Ex-Mt
GOLD RANDOM INSERTS IN PACKS		
GOLD PRINT RUN 25 SERIAL #'d SETS		
GOLD NO PRICING DUE TO SCARCITY		
HI-KS Hideki Irabu Kazuhiro Sasaki SP/30		
HN-KS Hideo Nomo Kazuhiro Sasaki SP/50	80.00	24.00
HN-SH Hideo Nomo Shigetosi Hasegawa	25.00	7.50
IS-KS Ichiro Suzuki Kazuhiro Sasaki SP/30		
IS-MY Ichiro Suzuki Masato Yoshii	80.00	24.00
IS-SH Ichiro Suzuki Shigestosi Hasegawa SP/72	120.00	36.00
IS-TS Ichiro Suzuki Tsuyoshi Shinjo SP/40		
MS-KS Mac Suzuki Kazuhiro Sasaki SP/30		
MY-KS Masato Yoshii Kazuhiro Sasaki SP/30		
SH-KS S. Hasegawa Kazuhiro Sasaki SP/30		
TO-KS Tomokazu Ohka Kazuhiro Sasaki	10.00	3.00
TS-HI Tsuyoshi Shinjo Hideki Irabu SP/30		
TS-KS Tsuyoshi Shinjo Kazuhiro Sasaki SP/30		
TS-SH Tsuyoshi Shinjo Shigetosi Hasegawa SP/30		

2001 SP Authentic Stars of Japan Game Ball-Base Trio

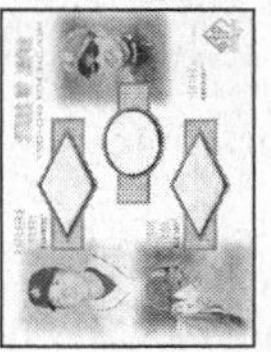

This card features the three greatest Japanese stars actively playing in the Major Leagues at the time of issue. The card features two pieces of game-used bases and one piece of a game-used baseball from the highlighted players. The card was distributed in special Stars of Japan packs. Each sealed box of 2001 SP Authentic contained one three-card Stars of Japan pack inside.Though individual Jersey card odds were not announced, the cumulative odds of finding a memorabilia card (ball, base, bat or jersey) from a Stars of Japan packs was 1:12.

	Nm-Mt	Ex-Mt
GOLD RANDOM INSERTS IN PACKS		
GOLD PRINT RUN 25 SERIAL #'d SETS		
GOLD NO PRICING DUE TO SCARCITY		
RS Kazuhiro Sasaki Ichiro Suzuki Hideo Nomo SP/30		

2001 SP Authentic Stars of Japan Game Base

This eight-card set features a selection of Japanese stars actively playing in the Major Leagues at the time of issue. Each card features a piece of game used base. The cards were distributed in special Stars of Japan packs. Each sealed box of 2001 SP Authentic contained one three-card Stars of Japan pack inside.Though individual Jersey card odds were not announced, the cumulative odds of finding a memorabilia card (ball, base, bat or jersey) from a Stars of Japan packs was 1:12.

	Nm-Mt	Ex-Mt
GOLD RANDOM INSERTS IN PACKS		
GOLD PRINT RUN 25 SERIAL #'d SETS		
GOLD NO PRICING DUE TO SCARCITY		
HI Hideki Irabu SP/33		
IS Ichiro Suzuki SP/23		
KS Kazuhiro Sasaki SP/33		
MS Mac Suzuki SP/23		
MY Masato Yoshii SP/33		
SH S. Hasegawa SP/33		
TO Tomokazu Ohka SP/33		
TS Tsuyoshi Shinjo SP/33		

2001 SP Authentic Stars of Japan Game Bat

This three-card set features a selection of Japanese stars actively playing in the Major

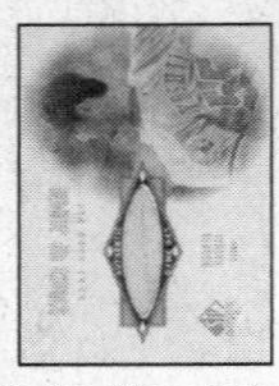

Leagues at the time of issue. Each card features a piece of game-used bat. The cards were distributed in special Stars of Japan packs. Each sealed box of 2001 SP Authentic contained one three-card Stars of Japan pack inside.Though individual Jersey card odds were not announced, the cumulative odds of finding a memorabilia card (ball, base, bat or jersey) from a Stars of Japan packs was 1:12.

Nm-Mt Ex-Mt
GOLD RANDOM INSERTS IN PACKS..
GOLD PRINT RUN 25 SERIAL #'d SETS
GOLD NO PRICING DUE TO SCARCITY
B-HN Hideo Nomo SP/30....................
B-MY Masato Yoshii 10.00 3.00
B-TS T. Shinjo SP/30....................

2001 SP Authentic Stars of Japan Game Bat-Jersey Combos

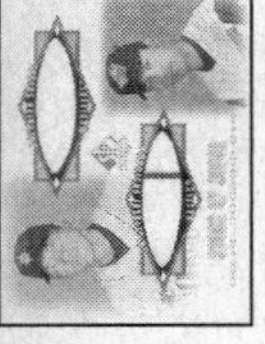

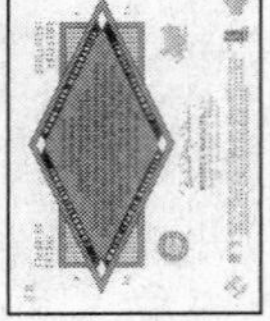

This 4-card dual player set features a selection of Japanese stars actively playing in the Major Leagues at the time of issue. Each card features a combination of a game-used bat chip or game-used jersey swatch from the featured players. The cards were distributed in special Stars of Japan packs. Each sealed box of 2001 SP Authentic contained one 3-card Stars of Japan pack inside.Though individual Jersey card odds were not announced, the cumulative odds of finding a memorabilia card (ball, base, bat or jersey) from a Stars of Japan packs was 1:12.

Nm-Mt Ex-Mt
GOLD RANDOM INSERTS IN PACKS..
GOLD PRINT RUN 25 SERIAL #'d SETS
GOLD NO PRICING DUE TO SCARCITY
BB-HS S. Hasegawa................. 25.00 7.50
Tsuyoshi Shinjo
JB-NN Hideo Nomo.................. 60.00 18.00
Hideo Nomo
JB-SN Kazuhiro Sasaki 25.00 7.50
Hideo Nomo
JJ-SH Kazuhiro Sasaki.............. 15.00 4.50
Shigetosi Hasegawa

2001 SP Authentic Stars of Japan Game Jersey

This six-card set features a selection of Japanese stars actively playing in the Major Leagues at the time of issue. Each card features a swatch of game-used jersey. The cards were distributed in special Stars of Japan packs. Each sealed box of 2001 SP Authentic contained one three-card Stars of Japan pack inside. Though individual Jersey card odds were not announced, the cumulative odds of finding a memorabilia card (ball, base, bat or jersey) from a Stars of Japan packs was 1:12. Ichiro Suzuki's jersey card was not available at time of packout and an exchange card was seeded into packs in it's place. The exchange card had a redemption deadline of August 30th, 2004. Though not serial-numbered, officials at Upper Deck announced that only 260 copies of Ichiro's jersey card were produced.

Nm-Mt Ex-Mt
GOLD RANDOM INSERTS IN PACKS..
GOLD PRINT RUN 25 SERIAL #'d SETS
NO GOLD PRICING DUE TO SCARCITY
J-HN Hideo Nomo.................... 15.00 4.50
J-IS I. Suzuki SP/260 EXCH.... 100.00 30.00
J-KS Kazuhiro Sasaki............. 10.00 3.00
J-MY Masato Yoshii................ 10.00 3.00
J-SH S. Hasegawa 10.00 3.00
J-TS Tsuyoshi Shinjo.............. 15.00 4.50

2001 SP Authentic Stars of Japan Game Jersey Gold

These Gold cards are straight parallels to the standard Stars of Japan Game Jersey inserts. However, only 25 Gold sets were produced and each card carries gold-foil serial-numbering "XX/25" on front. In addition, gold ink design highlights on the card fronts and backs replace the silver ink highlights seen on the standard Stars of Japan memorabilia cards. The cards were randomly inserted into Stars of Japan packs at an unspecified ratio. No Ichiro Suzuki game jersey gold card was issued.

Nm-Mt Ex-Mt
J-HN Hideo Nomo..............................
J-KS Kazuhiro Sasaki..........................
J-MY Masato Yoshii...........................
J-SH S. Hasegawa.............................
J-TS Tsuyoshi Shinjo..........................

2001 SP Authentic Sultan of Swatch Memorabilia

This 21-card set features a selection of significant achievements from legendary slugger Babe Ruth's storied career. Each card features a swatch of game-used uniform (most likely pants) and is hand-numbered in blue ink on front to the year or statisitical figure of the featured event (i.e. card SOS3 highlights Ruth's 94 career wins as a pitcher, thus only 94 hand-numbered copies of that card were produced). Quantities on each card vary from as many as 94 copies to as few as 14 copies. The cards were randomly inserted into packs at an unspecified ratio.

Nm-Mt Ex-Mt
SOS1 B.Ruth Red Sox/14 ....
SOS2 B.Ruth 29.2 Inn/29 .... 400.00 120.00
SOS3 B.Ruth 94 Wins/94....... 400.00 120.00
SOS4 B.Ruth 54 HRs/54........ 400.00 120.00
SOS5 B.Ruth 59 HRs/59........ 400.00 120.00
SOS6 Babe Ruth 400.00 120.00
3 HRs WS/26
SOS7 B.Ruth 60 HRs/27......... 400.00 120.00
SOS8 Babe Ruth 400.00 120.00
Called Shot/32
SOS9 B.Ruth HR Title/20 ....
SOS10 B.Ruth HR Title/21 ....
SOS11 B.Ruth Christens/23..................
SOS12 B.Ruth 46 HRs/24 ....
SOS13 B.Ruth 40 HRs/26....... 400.00 120.00
SOS14 B.Ruth HR Title/27...... 400.00 120.00
SOS15 B.Ruth 50 HRs/28....... 400.00 120.00
SOS16 Babe Ruth 400.00 120.00
Leads Way/29
SOS17 B.Ruth 49 HRs/30....... 400.00 120.00
SOS18 Babe Ruth 400.00 120.00
Last Title/31
SOS19 Babe Ruth 400.00 120.00
1st AS/33
SOS20 B.Ruth 1st HOF/36...... 400.00 120.00
SOS21 B.Ruth House/48........ 400.00 120.00

2001 SP Authentic Sultan of Swatch Memorabilia Signature Cuts

Each of these cards features an actual Babe Ruth autograph taken from an autographed "cut" (an industry term for a signed piece of paper - often old checks or 3 x 5 note cards) incorporated directly into the card through a window of cardboard. Though only one copy of each card was made for this set, three cards are actually identical parallels of each other save for the SOS-prefixed card numbering on back and the variations in the cut signatures used for each. The signature on card SOS2 has been verified as "Babe Ruth" and for card SOS3 as "G.H. Ruth". Due to the extreme scarcity of these cards, we cannot provide an accurate value as they rarely are seen for public sale.

Nm-Mt Ex-Mt
JC1 Babe Ruth Jsy-Cut AU/1 ....
JC2 Babe Ruth Jsy-Cut AU ....
Cut signed as "Babe Ruth"
JC3 Babe Ruth Jsy-Cut AU ....
Cut signed as G.H. Ruth"

2001 SP Authentic UD Exclusives Game Jersey

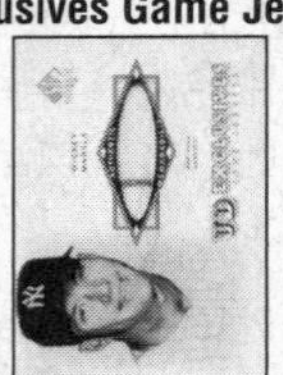

This 6-card set features a selection of superstars signed exclusively to Upper Deck for the rights to produce game-used jersey cards. Each card features a swatch of game-used jersey incorporated into an attractive horizontal design. Though specific odds per pack were not released for this set, Upper Deck did release cumulative odds of 1:24 packs for finding a game-used jersey card from either of the Cooperstown Calling, UD Exclusives or UD Exclusives Combos sets within the SP Authentic product. Shortly after release, representatives at Upper Deck publicly released print run information on several short prints. These quantities have been added to the end of the card description within our checklist.

Nm-Mt Ex-Mt
AR Alex Rodriguez 15.00 4.50
GS Gary Sheffield..................... 10.00 3.00
JD J.DiMaggio SP/243............ 100.00 30.00
KG Ken Griffey Jr. 15.00 4.50
MM M.Mantle SP/243............ 200.00 60.00
SS Sammy Sosa 15.00 4.50

2001 SP Authentic UD Exclusives Game Jersey Combos

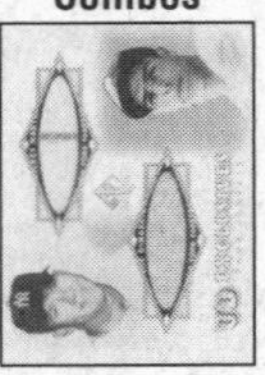

This six-card set features a selection of superstars signed exclusively to Upper Deck for the rights to produce game-used jersey cards. Each card features a swatch of game-used jersey from each featured player incorporated into an attractive horizontal design. Though specific odds per pack were not released for this set, Upper Deck did release cumulative odds of 1:24 packs for finding a game-used jersey card from either of the Cooperstown Calling, UD Exclusives or UD Exclusives Combos sets within the SP Authentic product. Shortly after release, representatives at Upper Deck publicly released print run information on several short prints. These quantities have been added to the end of the card description within our checklist.

Nm-Mt Ex-Mt
GD Ken Griffey Jr. 120.00 36.00
Joe DiMaggio SP/98
MD Mickey Mantle 400.00 120.00
Joe DiMaggio SP/98
MG Mickey Mantle 200.00 60.00
Ken Griffey Jr. SP/98
RS Alex Rodriguez 50.00 15.00
Ozzie Smith
SD Sammy Sosa 40.00 12.00
Andre Dawson
SW Gary Sheffiel...................... 25.00 7.50
Dave Winfield

2002 SP Authentic

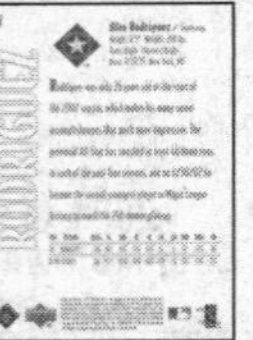

This 230 card set was released in two separate series. The basic SP Authentic product (containing cards 1-170) was issued in September, 2002. Update cards 171-230 were distributed within packs of 2002 Upper Deck Rookie Update in mid-December, 2002. SP Authentic packs were issued in five card packs with a $5 SRP. Boxes contained 24 packs and were packed five to a case. Cards numbered 1 through 90 featured veterans while cards number 91 through 135 were part of the Future Watch subset and were printed to a stated print run of 1999 serial numbered sets. Cards numbered 136 through 170 were signed by the player and most of the cards were printed to a stated print run of 999 serial numbered sets. Cards number 146, 152 and 157 were printed to a stated print run of 249 serial numbered sets. Update cards 201-230 continued the Future Watch subset (focusing on rookies and prospects) and each card was serial numbered to 1999. Though pack odds for these cards was never released, we estimate the cards were seeded at an approximate rate of 1:7 Rookie Update packs. In addition, an exchange card good for a signed Joe DiMaggio poster was randomly inserted into SP Authentic packs.

Nm-Mt Ex-Mt
COMP.LOW w/o SP's (90) 15.00 4.50
COMP.UPDATE w/o SP's (30).... 10.00 3.00
COMMON CARD (1-90) .... .40 .12
COMMON (91-135/201-230) 5.00 1.50
COMMON CARD (136-170) 15.00 4.50
COMMON CARD (171-200) .... .60 .18
1 Troy Glaus.................................. .40 .12
2 Darin Erstad .... .40 .12
3 Barry Zito.................................... .40 .12
4 Eric Chavez .... .40 .12
5 Tim Hudson .... .40 .12
6 Miguel Tejada............................... .40 .12
7 Carlos Delgado............................. .40 .12
8 Shannon Stewart .... .40 .12
9 Ben Grieve .... .40 .12
10 Jim Thome................................ 1.00 .30
11 C.C. Sabathia .... .40 .12
12 Ichiro Suzuki .... 1.50 .45
13 Freddy Garcia.............................. .40 .12
14 Edgar Martinez............................ .60 .18
15 Bret Boone .... .40 .12
16 Jeff Conine................................... .40 .12
17 Alex Rodriguez.......................... 1.50 .45
18 Juan Gonzalez............................. .60 .18
19 Ivan Rodriguez.......................... 1.00 .30
20 Rafael Palmeiro.......................... .60 .18
21 Hank Blalock .... 1.00 .30
22 Pedro Martinez.......................... 1.00 .30
23 Manny Ramirez............................ .60 .18
24 Nomar Garciaparra.................. 1.50 .45
25 Carlos Beltran .... .60 .18
26 Mike Sweeney .... .40 .12
27 Randall Simon .... .40 .12
28 Dmitri Young............................... .40 .12
29 Bobby Higginson .... .40 .12
30 Corey Koskie .... .40 .12
31 Eric Milton .... .40 .12
32 Torii Hunter .... .40 .12
33 Joe Mays .... .40 .12
34 Frank Thomas .... 1.00 .30
35 Mark Buehrle .... .40 .12
36 Magglio Ordonez......................... .40 .12
37 Kenny Lofton .... .40 .12
38 Roger Clemens .... 2.00 .60
39 Derek Jeter............................... 2.50 .75
40 Jason Giambi .... .40 .12
41 Bernie Williams.......................... .60 .18
42 Alfonso Soriano .... .60 .18
43 Lance Berkman .... .40 .12
44 Roy Oswalt.................................. .40 .12
45 Jeff Bagwell .... .60 .18
46 Craig Biggio .... .60 .18
47 Chipper Jones .... 1.00 .30
48 Greg Maddux .... 1.50 .45
49 Gary Sheffield............................. .40 .12
50 Andruw Jones.............................. .40 .12
51 Ben Sheets.................................. .40 .12
52 Richie Sexson .... .40 .12
53 Albert Pujols .... 2.00 .60
54 Matt Morris................................. .40 .12
55 J.D. Drew.................................... .40 .12
56 Sammy Sosa............................. 1.50 .45
57 Kerry Wood.............................. 1.00 .30
58 Corey Patterson .... .40 .12
59 Mark Prior................................ 1.50 .45
60 Randy Johnson .... 1.00 .30
61 Luis Gonzalez.............................. .40 .12
62 Curt Schilling .... .40 .12
63 Shawn Green .... .40 .12
64 Kevin Brown................................ .40 .12
65 Hideo Nomo.............................. 1.00 .30
66 Vladimir Guerrero .... 1.00 .30
67 Jose Vidro................................... .40 .12
68 Barry Bonds .... 2.50 .75
69 Jeff Kent..................................... .40 .12
70 Rich Aurilia .... .40 .12
71 Preston Wilson .... .40 .12
72 Josh Beckett .... .40 .12
73 Mike Lowell................................. .40 .12
74 Roberto Alomar .... .60 .18
75 Mo Vaughn .... .40 .12
76 Jeromy Burnitz............................ .40 .12
77 Mike Piazza .... 1.50 .45
78 Sean Burroughs .... .40 .12
79 Phil Nevin................................... .40 .12
80 Bobby Abreu .... .40 .12
81 Pat Burrell................................... .40 .12
82 Scott Rolen .... 1.00 .30
83 Jason Kendall.............................. .40 .12
84 Brian Giles .... .40 .12
85 Ken Griffey Jr. .... 1.50 .45
86 Adam Dunn................................. .60 .18
87 Sean Casey .... .40 .12
88 Todd Helton .... .60 .18
89 Larry Walker .... .60 .18
90 Mike Hampton .... .40 .12
91 Brandon Puffer FW 5.00 1.50
92 Tom Shearn FW RC.................. 5.00 1.50
93 Chris Baker FW RC 5.00 1.50
94 Gustavo Chacin FW RC............ 8.00 2.40
95 Joe Orloski FW RC 5.00 1.50
96 Mike Smith FW RC................... 5.00 1.50
97 John Ennis FW RC 5.00 1.50
98 John Foster FW RC.................. 5.00 1.50
99 Kevin Gryboski FW RC 5.00 1.50
100 Brian Mallette FW RC 5.00 1.50
101 Takahito Nomura FW RC........ 5.00 1.50
102 So Taguchi FW RC 8.00 2.40
103 Jeremy Lambert FW RC.......... 5.00 1.50
104 J.Simontacchi FW RC 5.00 1.50
105 Jorge Sosa FW RC.................. 5.00 1.50
106 Brandon Backe FW RC 8.00 2.40
107 P.J. Bevis FW RC 5.00 1.50
108 Jeremy Ward FW RC.............. 5.00 1.50
109 Doug Devore FW RC.............. 5.00 1.50
110 Ron Chiavacci FW 5.00 1.50
111 Ron Calloway FW RC 5.00 1.50
112 Nelson Castro FW RC 5.00 1.50
113 Deivis Santos FW.................... 5.00 1.50
114 Earl Snyder FW RC 8.00 2.40
115 Julio Mateo FW RC 5.00 1.50
116 J.J. Putz FW RC 5.00 1.50
117 Allan Simpson FW RC............ 5.00 1.50
118 Satoru Komiyama FW RC 5.00 1.50
119 Adam Walker FW RC.............. 5.00 1.50
120 Oliver Perez FW RC 15.00 4.50
121 Cliff Bartosh FW RC 5.00 1.50
122 Todd Donovan FW RC 5.00 1.50
123 Elio Serrano FW RC 5.00 1.50
124 Pete Zamora FW RC 5.00 1.50
125 Mike Gonzalez FW RC 5.00 1.50
126 Travis Hughes FW RC............ 5.00 1.50
127 J.De La Rosa FW RC.............. 5.00 1.50
128 An.Martinez FW RC................ 5.00 1.50
129 Colin Young FW RC 5.00 1.50
130 Nate Field FW RC 5.00 1.50
131 Tim Kalita FW RC................... 5.00 1.50
132 Julius Matos FW RC 5.00 1.50
133 Terry Pearson FW RC............. 5.00 1.50
134 Kyle Kane FW RC................... 5.00 1.50
135 Mitch Wylie FW RC................ 5.00 1.50
136 Rodrigo Rosario AU RC 15.00 4.50
137 Franklyn German AU RC 15.00 4.50
138 Reed Johnson AU RC 20.00 6.00
139 Luis Martinez AU RC 15.00 4.50
140 Michael Crudale AU RC 15.00 4.50
141 Francis Beltran AU RC 15.00 4.50
142 Steve Kent AU RC 15.00 4.50
143 Felix Escalona AU RC 15.00 4.50
144 Jose Valverde AU RC 20.00 6.00
145 Victor Alvarez AU RC 15.00 4.50
146 Kazuhisa Ishii AU/249 RC .. 50.00 15.00
147 Jorge Nunez AU RC 15.00 4.50
148 Eric Good AU RC 15.00 4.50
149 Luis Ugueto AU RC 15.00 4.50
150 Matt Thornton AU RC 15.00 4.50
151 Wilson Valdez AU RC 15.00 4.50
152 Han Izquierdo AU/249 RC.. 40.00 12.00
153 Jaime Cerda AU RC 15.00 4.50
154 Mark Corey AU RC 15.00 4.50
155 Tyler Yates AU RC 20.00 6.00
156 Steve Bechler AU RC 15.00 4.50
157 Ben Howard AU/249 RC 40.00 12.00
158 And. Machado AU RC 15.00 4.50
159 Jorge Padilla AU RC 15.00 4.50
160 Eric Junge AU RC 15.00 4.50
161 Adrian Burnside AU RC 15.00 4.50
162 Josh Hancock AU RC 15.00 4.50
163 Chris Booker AU RC 15.00 4.50
164 Cam Esslinger AU RC 15.00 4.50
165 Rene Reyes AU RC 15.00 4.50
166 Aaron Cook AU RC 15.00 4.50
167 Juan Brito AU RC 15.00 4.50
168 Miguel Ascencio AU RC 15.00 4.50
169 Kevin Frederick AU RC 15.00 4.50
170 Edwin Almonte AU RC 15.00 4.50
171 Erubiel Durazo .... .60 .18
172 Junior Spivey .... .60 .18
173 Geronimo Gil............................ .60 .18
174 Cliff Floyd .... .60 .18
175 Brandon Larson .... .60 .18
176 Aaron Boone .... .60 .18
177 Shawn Estes .... .60 .18
178 Austin Kearns.......................... .60 .18
179 Joe Borchard............................ .60 .18
180 Russell Branyan .... .60 .18
181 Jay Payton .... .60 .18
182 Andres Torres .... .60 .18
183 Andy Van Hekken..................... .60 .18
184 Alex Sanchez............................ .60 .18
185 Endy Chavez............................ .60 .18
186 Bartolo Colon .... .60 .18
187 Raul Mondesi .... .60 .18
188 Robin Ventura.......................... .60 .18
189 Mike Mussina......................... 1.00 .30
190 Jorge Posada .... 1.00 .30
191 Ted Lilly................................... .60 .18
192 Ray Durham .... .60 .18
193 Brett Myers .... .60 .18
194 Marlon Byrd .... .60 .18
195 Vicente Padilla .... .60 .18
196 Josh Fogg .... .60 .18
197 Kenny Lofton .... .60 .18
198 Scott Rolen .... 1.50 .45
199 Jason Lane............................... .60 .18
200 Josh Phelps .... .60 .18
201 Travis Driskill FW RC 5.00 1.50
202 Howie Clark FW RC.............. 5.00 1.50
203 Mike Mahoney FW 5.00 1.50
204 Brian Tallet FW RC............... 5.00 1.50
205 Kirk Saarloos FW RC 5.00 1.50
206 Barry Wesson FW RC 5.00 1.50
207 Aaron Guiel FW RC 5.00 1.50
208 Shawn Sedlacek FW RC........ 5.00 1.50
209 Jose Diaz FW RC 5.00 1.50
210 Jorge Nunez FW.................... 5.00 1.50
211 Danny Mota FW RC 5.00 1.50
212 David Ross FW RC 5.00 1.50
213 Jayson Durocher FW RC....... 5.00 1.50
214 Shane Nance FW RC 5.00 1.50
215 Wil Nieves FW RC................. 5.00 1.50
216 Freddy Sanchez FW RC......... 5.00 1.50
217 Alex Pelaez FW RC............... 5.00 1.50
218 Jamey Carroll FW RC............ 5.00 1.50
219 J.J. Trujillo FW RC 5.00 1.50
220 Kevin Pickford FW RC........... 5.00 1.50
221 Clay Condrey FW RC............. 5.00 1.50
222 Chris Snelling FW RC............ 5.00 1.50
223 Cliff Lee FW RC..................... 8.00 2.40
224 Jeremy Hill FW RC 5.00 1.50
225 Jose Rodriguez FW RC 5.00 1.50
226 Lance Carter FW RC.............. 5.00 1.50
227 Ken Huckaby FW RC............. 5.00 1.50
228 Scott Wiggins FW RC 5.00 1.50
229 Corey Thurman FW RC.......... 5.00 1.50
230 Kevin Cash FW RC 5.00 1.50
RJ-D J.DiMaggio Poster AU EX 200.00 60.00

2002 SP Authentic Limited

Randomly inserted into packs, this is a parallel to the basic 170-card SP Authentic first series set. These cards have a stated print run of 125 serial numbered sets.

Nm-Mt Ex-Mt
*LTD 1-90: 5X TO 12X BASIC...........
*LTD 91-135: .4X TO 1X BASIC...........
*LTD 136-170: .4X TO 1X BASIC........
*LTD 146/152/157: .3X TO .8X BASIC
104 Jason Simontacchi FW 5.00 1.50
120 Oliver Perez FW 20.00 6.00
146 Kazuhisa Ishii FW AU......... 50.00 15.00

2002 SP Authentic Limited Gold

Randomly inserted into packs, this is a parallel to the basic 170-card SP Authentic first series set. These cards have a stated print run of 50 serial numbered sets.

Nm-Mt Ex-Mt
*GOLD 1-90: 10X TO 25X BASIC......
*GOLD 91-135: .6X TO 1.5X BASIC......
*GOLD 136-170: .6X TO 1.5X BASIC..
*GOLD 146/152/157: .5X TO 1.2X BASIC

2002 SP Authentic Big Mac Missing Link

Randomly inserted into packs, these five cards feature autographs of Mark McGwire. Each card was issued to a stated print run of 25 serial numbered sets and thus no pricing is available due to market scarcity.

	Nm-Mt	Ex-Mt
MMC Mark McGwire 98		
MM Mark McGwire 99		
MAM Mark McGwire 00		
SP-MM Mark McGwire 01		
MAMC Mark McGwire 02		

2002 SP Authentic Chirography

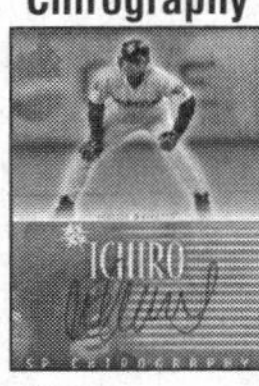

Bret Boone and Tony Gwynn are available only in the basic Chirography set. No Gold parallels were created for them. The following players packed out as redemption cards: Alex Rodriguez, Bret Boone, Sammy Sosa and Tony Gwynn. The deadline for exchange cards to be received by Upper Deck was September 10th, 2005.

	Nm-Mt	Ex-Mt
AD Adam Dunn/348	25.00	7.50
AG Alex Graman/418	10.00	3.00
AR Alex Rodriguez/391 EXCH	120.00	36.00
BB Barry Bonds/112	250.00	75.00
BBo Bret Boone/500 EXCH	15.00	4.50
BZ Barry Zito/419	25.00	7.50
CF Cliff Floyd/313	10.00	3.00
CS C.C. Sabathia/442	15.00	4.50
DE Darin Erstad/80	15.00	4.50
DM Doug Mientkiewicz/478	15.00	4.50
FG Freddy Garcia/456	15.00	4.50
HB Hank Blalock/282	40.00	12.00
IS Ichiro Suzuki/78	400.00	120.00
JB John Buck/427	10.00	3.00
JG Jason Giambi/244	15.00	4.50
JL Jon Lieber/462	10.00	3.00
JM Joe Mays/469	10.00	3.00
KG Ken Griffey Jr./238	100.00	30.00
MBr Milton Bradley/470	15.00	4.50
MBu Mark Buehrle/438	15.00	4.50
MM Mark McGwire/50	400.00	120.00
MS Mike Sweeney/265	15.00	4.50
RS Richie Sexson/483	15.00	4.50
SB Sean Burroughs/275	15.00	4.50
SS Sammy Sosa/247 EXCH	150.00	45.00
TG Tom Glavine/376	40.00	12.00
TGw Tony Gwynn/75 EXCH	50.00	15.00

2002 SP Authentic Chirography Gold

Gold parallel cards were not created for Tony Gwynn and Bret Boone. Sammy Sosa and Alex Rodriguez packed out as exchange cards with a redemption deadline of September 10th, 2005.

	Nm-Mt	Ex-Mt
AD Adam Dunn/44	50.00	15.00
AG Alex Graman/76	25.00	7.50
AR Alex Rodriguez/3 EXCH		
BB Barry Bonds/25		
BZ Barry Zito/75	40.00	12.00
CF Cliff Floyd/30	30.00	9.00
CS C.C. Sabathia/52	30.00	9.00
DE Darin Erstad/17		
DM Doug Mientkiewicz/16		
FG Freddy Garcia/34	50.00	15.00
HB Hank Blalock/12		
IS Ichiro Suzuki/51	400.00	120.00
JB John Buck/67		
JG Jason Giambi/25		
JL Jon Lieber/32	30.00	9.00
JM Joe Mays/25		
KG Ken Griffey Jr./30	200.00	60.00
MBr Milton Bradley/24		
MBu Mark Buehrle/56	30.00	9.00
MM Mark McGwire/25		
MS Mike Sweeney/29	50.00	15.00
RS Richie Sexson/11		
SB Sean Burroughs/21		
SS Sammy Sosa/21 EXCH		
TG Tom Glavine/47	80.00	24.00

2002 SP Authentic Excellence

Randomly inserted into packs, theis card featues signatures of many of Upper Deck's spokespeople. This card was issued to a stated print run of 25 serial numbered sets and no pricing is available due to market scarcity. Please note that this card was issued as an exchange card and was redeemable until September 10, 2005.

	Nm-Mt	Ex-Mt
AE Ken Griffey Jr.		

Sammy Sosa
Cal Ripken
Jason Giambi
Mark McGwire
Ichiro Suzuki

2002 SP Authentic Game Jersey

Inserted into packs at stated odds of one in 24, these 38 cards feature some of the leading players along with a game-used memorabilia swatch. A few cards were issued in shorter supply and we have notated that in our checklist along with a stated print run when available.

	Nm-Mt	Ex-Mt
J-AJ Andruw Jones	10.00	3.00
J-AP Andy Pettitte	15.00	4.50
J-AR Alex Rodriguez	20.00	6.00
J-BW Bernie Williams	15.00	4.50
J-BZ Barry Zito	10.00	3.00
J-CC C.C. Sabathia	10.00	3.00
J-CD Carlos Delgado	10.00	3.00
J-CJ Chipper Jones	15.00	4.50
J-CS Curt Schilling	10.00	3.00
J-DE Darin Erstad	10.00	3.00
J-GM Greg Maddux	15.00	4.50
J-GS Gary Sheffield	10.00	3.00
J-IR Ivan Rodriguez	15.00	4.50
J-IS Ichiro Suzuki SP	60.00	18.00
J-JBA Jeff Bagwell	15.00	4.50
J-JBU Jeromy Burnitz SP	15.00	4.50
J-JE Jim Edmonds	10.00	3.00
J-JGO Juan Gonzalez	15.00	4.50
J-JGR Jason Giambi	10.00	3.00
J-JK Jason Kendall	10.00	3.00
J-JT Jim Thome	15.00	4.50
J-KG Ken Griffey Jr. SP/95	40.00	12.00
J-KI Kazuhisa Ishii	15.00	4.50
J-MM Mark McGwire SP	150.00	45.00
J-MO Magglio Ordonez	10.00	3.00
J-MP Mike Piazza	15.00	4.50
J-MR Manny Ramirez	15.00	4.50
J-OV Omar Vizquel	15.00	4.50
J-PW Preston Wilson	10.00	3.00
J-RA Roberto Alomar	15.00	4.50
J-RC Roger Clemens	20.00	6.00
J-RJ Randy Johnson	15.00	4.50
J-RV Robin Ventura	10.00	3.00
J-SG Shawn Green	10.00	3.00
J-SR Scott Rolen	15.00	4.50
J-SS Sammy Sosa	20.00	6.00
J-TH Todd Helton	15.00	4.50
J-TS Tsuyoshi Shinjo	10.00	3.00

2002 SP Authentic Game Jersey Gold

Randomly inserted into packs, this is a parallel to the Game Jersey insert set. Each of these cards have a stated print run which matches the featured player's uniform number and we have notated that information in our checklist. If a card was issued to a stated print run of 25 or fewer, it is not priced due to market scarcity.

	Nm-Mt	Ex-Mt
J-AJ Andruw Jones/25		
J-AP Andy Pettitte/46	30.00	9.00
J-AR Alex Rodriguez/3		
J-BW Bernie Williams/51	30.00	9.00
J-BZ Barry Zito/75	20.00	6.00
J-CC C.C. Sabathia/52	20.00	6.00
J-CD Carlos Delgado/25		
J-CJ Chipper Jones/10		
J-CS Curt Schilling/38	25.00	7.50
J-DE Darin Erstad/17		
J-GM Greg Maddux/31	80.00	24.00
J-GS Gary Sheffield/11		
J-IR Ivan Rodriguez/7		
J-IS Ichiro Suzuki/51	120.00	36.00
J-JBA Jeff Bagwell/5		
J-JBU Jeromy Burnitz/20		
J-JE Jim Edmonds/15		
J-JGO Juan Gonzalez/19		
J-JGR Jason Giambi/25		
J-JK Jason Kendall/18		
J-JT Jim Thome/25		
J-KG Ken Griffey Jr./30	80.00	24.00
J-KI Kazuhisa Ishii/17		
J-MM Mark McGwire/25		
J-MO Magglio Ordonez/30	25.00	7.50
J-MP Mike Piazza/31	80.00	24.00
J-MR Manny Ramirez/24		
J-OV Omar Vizquel/13		
J-PW Preston Wilson/44	20.00	6.00
J-RA Roberto Alomar/12		
J-RC Roger Clemens/22		
J-RJ Randy Johnson/51	40.00	12.00
J-RV Robin Ventura/19		
J-SG Shawn Green/15		
J-SR Scott Rolen/17		
J-SS Sammy Sosa/21		
J-TH Todd Helton/17		
J-TS Tsuyoshi Shinjo/5		

2002 SP Authentic Prospects Signatures

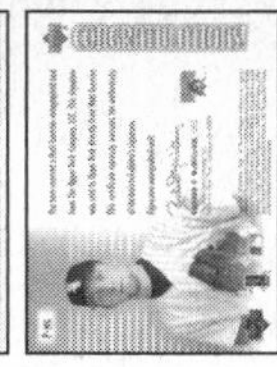

Inserted into packs at a stated rate of one in 36, these 12 cards feature signed cards of some leading baseball prospects.

	Nm-Mt	Ex-Mt
P-AG Alex Graman	8.00	2.40
P-BH Bill Hall	8.00	2.40
P-DM Dustan Mohr	8.00	2.40
P-DW Danny Wright	8.00	2.40
P-JC Jose Cueto	8.00	2.40
P-JDE Jeff Deardorff	8.00	2.40
P-JDI Jose Diaz	10.00	3.00
P-KH Ken Huckaby	8.00	2.40
P-MG Matt Guerrier	8.00	2.40
P-MS Marcos Scutaro	8.00	2.40
P-ST Steve Torrealba	8.00	2.40
P-XN Xavier Nady	8.00	2.40

2002 SP Authentic Signed Big Mac

Randomly inserted into packs, these 10 cards feature authentic autographs of retired superstar Mark McGwire. Each of these cards were signed to a different stated print run and we have notated that information in our checklist. If a card was signed to 25 or fewer copies, there is no pricing provided due to market scarcity.

	Nm-Mt	Ex-Mt
MM1 Mark McGwire/1		
MM2 Mark McGwire/25		
MM3 Mark McGwire/5		
MM4 Mark McGwire/4		
MM5 Mark McGwire/12		
MM6 Mark McGwire/70	300.00	90.00
MM7 Mark McGwire/4		
MM8 Mark McGwire/7		
MM9 Mark McGwire/5		
MM10 Mark McGwire/16		

2002 SP Authentic Signs of Greatness

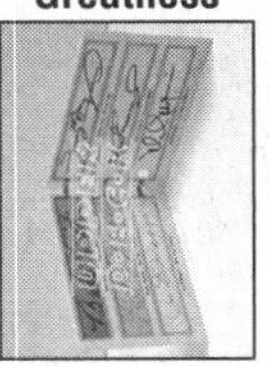

Randomly inserted into packs, this is a one card set featuring five autograph on the same card. Since only one of these cards was produced, there is no pricing due to market scarcity.

	Nm-Mt	Ex-Mt
SOG Babe Ruth		

Joe DiMaggio
Mickey Mantle
Ken Griffey Jr.
Sammy Sosa
Mark McGwire

2002 SP Authentic USA Future Watch

Randomly inserted into packs, these 22 cards feature players from the USA National Team. Each card was issued to a stated print run of 1999 serial numbered sets.

	Nm-Mt	Ex-Mt
USA1 Chad Cordero	8.00	2.40
USA2 Philip Humber	10.00	3.00
USA3 Grant Johnson	8.00	2.40
USA4 Wes Littleton	10.00	3.00
USA5 Kyle Sleeth	12.00	3.60
USA6 Huston Street	12.00	3.60
USA7 Brad Sullivan	10.00	3.00
USA8 Bob Zimmermann	8.00	2.40
USA9 Abe Alvarez	10.00	3.00
USA10 Kyle Bakker	8.00	2.40
USA11 Landon Powell	10.00	3.00
USA12 Clint Sammons	8.00	2.40
USA13 Michael Aubrey	25.00	7.50
USA14 Aaron Hill	12.00	3.60
USA15 Conor Jackson	30.00	9.00
USA16 Eric Patterson	10.00	3.00
USA17 Dustin Pedroia	20.00	6.00
USA18 Rickie Weeks	50.00	15.00
USA19 Shane Costa	10.00	3.00
USA20 Mark Jurich	8.00	2.40
USA21 Sam Fuld	8.00	2.40
USA22 Carlos Quentin	30.00	9.00

2003 SP Authentic

This 239-card set was distributed in two separate series. The primary SP Authentic product was originally issued as a 189-card set released in May, 2003. These cards were issued in five card packs with an $5 SRP which were issued 24 packs to a box and 12 boxes to a case. Update cards 190-239 were issued randomly within packs of 2003 Upper Deck Finite and released in December, 2003. Cards numbered 1-90 featured commonly seeded veterans while cards 91-123 featured what was titled SP Rookie Archives (RA) and those cards were issued to a stated print run of 2500 serial numbered sets. Cards numbered 124 to 150 feature a subset called Back to 93 and those cards were issued to a stated print run of 1993 serial numbered sets. Cards numbered 151 through 189 feature Future Watch prospects (with 181 to 189 being autographed). Please note that cards numbered 151-180 were also issued to a stated print run of 2003 serial numbered sets and cards numbered 181-189 were issued to a stated print run of 500 serial numbered sets. The Jose Contreras signed card was issued either as a live card or an exchange card. The Contreras exchange card could be redeemed until May 21, 2006. Cards 190-239 (released at year's end) continued the Future Watch subset but each card was serial numbered to 699 copies.

	Nm-Mt	Ex-Mt
COMP.LO SET w/o SP's (90)	15.00	4.50
COMMON CARD (1-90)	.40	.12
COMMON CARD (91-123)	3.00	.90
COMMON CARD (124-150)	3.00	.90
COMMON CARD (151-180)	5.00	1.50
COMMON CARD (181-189)	15.00	4.50
91-189 RANDOM INSERTS IN PACKS		
COMMON CARD (190-239)	5.00	1.50
190-239 RANDOM IN 03 UD FINITE PACKS		
190-239 PRINT RUN 699 SERIAL #'d SETS		
1 Darin Erstad	.40	.12
2 Garret Anderson	.40	.12
3 Troy Glaus	.40	.12
4 Eric Chavez	.40	.12
5 Barry Zito	.40	.12
6 Miguel Tejada	.40	.12
7 Eric Hinske	.40	.12
8 Carlos Delgado	.40	.12
9 Josh Phelps	.40	.12
10 Ben Grieve	.40	.12
11 Carl Crawford	.40	.12
12 Omar Vizquel	.60	.18
13 Matt Lawton	.40	.12
14 C.C. Sabathia	.40	.12
15 Ichiro Suzuki	1.50	.45
16 John Olerud	.40	.12
17 Freddy Garcia	.40	.12
18 Jay Gibbons	.40	.12
19 Tony Batista	.40	.12
20 Melvin Mora	.40	.12
21 Alex Rodriguez	1.50	.45
22 Rafael Palmeiro	.60	.18
23 Hank Blalock	.60	.18
24 Nomar Garciaparra	1.50	.45
25 Pedro Martinez	1.00	.30
26 Johnny Damon	1.00	.30
27 Mike Sweeney	.40	.12
28 Carlos Febles	.40	.12
29 Carlos Beltran	.60	.18
30 Carlos Pena	.40	.12
31 Eric Munson	.40	.12
32 Bobby Higginson	.40	.12
33 Torii Hunter	.40	.12
34 Doug Mientkiewicz	.40	.12
35 Jacque Jones	.40	.12
36 Paul Konerko	.40	.12
37 Bartolo Colon	.40	.12
38 Magglio Ordonez	.40	.12
39 Derek Jeter	2.50	.75
40 Bernie Williams	.60	.18
41 Jason Giambi	.40	.12
42 Alfonso Soriano	.60	.18
43 Roger Clemens	2.00	.60
44 Jeff Bagwell	.60	.18
45 Jeff Kent	.40	.12
46 Lance Berkman	.40	.12
47 Chipper Jones	1.00	.30
48 Andruw Jones	.40	.12
49 Gary Sheffield	.40	.12
50 Ben Sheets	.40	.12
51 Richie Sexson	.40	.12
52 Geoff Jenkins	.40	.12
53 Jim Edmonds	.40	.12
54 Albert Pujols	2.00	.60
55 Scott Rolen	1.00	.30
56 Sammy Sosa	1.50	.45
57 Kerry Wood	1.00	.30
58 Eric Karros	.40	.12
59 Luis Gonzalez	.40	.12
60 Randy Johnson	1.00	.30
61 Curt Schilling	.60	.18
62 Fred McGriff	.60	.18
63 Shawn Green	.40	.12
64 Paul Lo Duca	.40	.12
65 Vladimir Guerrero	1.00	.30
66 Jose Vidro	.40	.12
67 Barry Bonds	2.50	.75
68 Rich Aurilia	.40	.12
69 Edgardo Alfonzo	.40	.12
70 Ivan Rodriguez	1.00	.30
71 Mike Lowell	.40	.12
72 Derrek Lee	.40	.12
73 Tom Glavine	.60	.18
74 Mike Piazza	1.50	.45
75 Roberto Alomar	.60	.18
76 Ryan Klesko	.40	.12
77 Phil Nevin	.40	.12
78 Mark Kotsay	.40	.12
79 Jim Thome	1.00	.30
80 Pat Burrell	.40	.12
81 Bobby Abreu	.40	.12
82 Jason Kendall	.40	.12
83 Brian Giles	.40	.12
84 Aramis Ramirez	.40	.12
85 Austin Kearns	.40	.12
86 Ken Griffey Jr.	1.50	.45
87 Adam Dunn	.60	.18
88 Larry Walker	.60	.18
89 Todd Helton	.60	.18
90 Preston Wilson	.40	.12
91 Derek Jeter RA	8.00	2.40
92 Johnny Damon RA	3.00	.90
93 Chipper Jones RA	3.00	.90
94 Manny Ramirez RA	3.00	.90
95 Trot Nixon RA	3.00	.90
96 Alex Rodriguez RA	5.00	1.50
97 Chan Ho Park RA	3.00	.90
98 Brad Fullmer RA	3.00	.90
99 Billy Wagner RA	3.00	.90
100 Hideo Nomo RA	3.00	.90
101 Freddy Garcia RA	3.00	.90
102 Darin Erstad RA	3.00	.90
103 Jose Cruz Jr. RA	3.00	.90
104 Nomar Garciaparra RA	5.00	1.50
105 Magglio Ordonez RA	3.00	.90
106 Kerry Wood RA	3.00	.90
107 Troy Glaus RA	3.00	.90
108 J.D. Drew RA	3.00	.90
109 Alfonso Soriano RA	3.00	.90
110 Danys Baez RA	3.00	.90
111 Kazuhiro Sasaki RA	3.00	.90
112 Barry Zito RA	3.00	.90
113 Brent Abernathy RA	3.00	.90
114 Ben Diggins RA	3.00	.90
115 Ben Sheets RA	3.00	.90
116 Brad Wilkerson RA	3.00	.90
117 Juan Pierre RA	3.00	.90
118 Jon Rauch RA	3.00	.90
119 Ichiro Suzuki RA	5.00	1.50
120 Albert Pujols RA	6.00	1.80
121 Mark Prior RA	3.00	.90
122 Mark Teixeira RA	3.00	.90
123 Kazuhisa Ishii RA	3.00	.90
124 Troy Glaus B93	3.00	.90
125 Randy Johnson B93	3.00	.90
126 Curt Schilling B93	3.00	.90
127 Chipper Jones B93	3.00	.90
128 Greg Maddux B93	5.00	1.50
129 Nomar Garciaparra B93	5.00	1.50
130 Pedro Martinez B93	3.00	.90
131 Sammy Sosa B93	5.00	1.50
132 Mark Prior B93	3.00	.90
133 Ken Griffey Jr. B93	5.00	1.50
134 Adam Dunn B93	3.00	.90
135 Jeff Bagwell B93	3.00	.90
136 Vladimir Guerrero B93	3.00	.90
137 Mike Piazza B93	5.00	1.50
138 Tom Glavine B93	3.00	.90
139 Derek Jeter B93	8.00	2.40
140 Roger Clemens B93	6.00	1.80
141 Jason Giambi B93	3.00	.90
142 Alfonso Soriano B93	3.00	.90
143 Miguel Tejada B93	3.00	.90
144 Barry Zito B93	3.00	.90
145 Jim Thome B93	3.00	.90
146 Barry Bonds B93	8.00	2.40
147 Ichiro Suzuki B93	5.00	1.50
148 Albert Pujols B93	6.00	1.80
149 Alex Rodriguez B93	5.00	1.50
150 Carlos Delgado B93	3.00	.90
151 Rich Fischer FW RC	5.00	1.50
152 Brandon Webb FW RC	10.00	3.00
153 Rob Hammock FW RC	8.00	2.40
154 Matt Kata FW RC	8.00	2.40
155 Tim Olson FW RC	8.00	2.40
156 Oscar Villarreal FW RC	5.00	1.50
157 Michael Hessman FW RC	5.00	1.50
158 Daniel Cabrera FW RC	8.00	2.40
159 Jon Leicester FW RC	5.00	1.50
160 Todd Wellemeyer FW RC	8.00	2.40
161 Felix Sanchez FW RC	5.00	1.50
162 David Sanders FW RC	5.00	1.50
163 Josh Stewart FW RC	5.00	1.50
164 Arnie Munoz FW RC	5.00	1.50
165 Ryan Cameron FW RC	5.00	1.50
166 Clint Barmes FW RC	8.00	2.40
167 Josh Willingham FW RC	8.00	2.40
169 Willie Eyre FW RC	5.00	1.50
170 Brent Hoard FW RC	5.00	1.50
171 Termmel Sledge FW RC	8.00	2.40
172 Phil Seibel FW RC	5.00	1.50
173 Craig Brazell FW RC	8.00	2.40
174 Jeff Duncan FW RC	8.00	2.40
176 Bernie Castro FW RC	5.00	1.50
177 Mike Nicolas FW RC	5.00	1.50
178 Rett Johnson FW RC	8.00	2.40
179 Bobby Madritsch FW RC	15.00	4.50
180 Chris Capuano FW RC	5.00	1.50
181 Hid Matsui FW AU RC	250.00	75.00
182 J.Contreras FW AU RC	40.00	12.00
183 Lew Ford FW AU RC	40.00	12.00
184 Jer. Griffiths FW AU RC	25.00	7.50
185 G. Quiroz FW AU RC	25.00	7.50
186 Alej Machado FW AU RC	15.00	4.50
187 Fran Cruceta FW AU RC	15.00	4.50
188 Pr. Redman FW AU RC	15.00	4.50
189 S.Bazzell FW AU RC	15.00	4.50
190 Aaron Looper FW RC	5.00	1.50
191 Alex Prieto FW RC	5.00	1.50
192 Alfredo Gonzalez FW RC	5.00	1.50
193 Andrew Brown FW RC	8.00	2.40
194 Anthony Ferrari FW RC	5.00	1.50
195 Aquilino Lopez FW RC	5.00	1.50
196 Beau Kemp FW RC	5.00	1.50
197 Bo Hart FW RC	8.00	2.40
198 Chad Gaudin FW RC	5.00	1.50
199 Colin Porter FW RC	5.00	1.50
200 D.J. Carrasco FW RC	5.00	1.50
201 Dan Haren FW RC	8.00	2.40
202 Danny Garcia FW RC	5.00	1.50
203 Jon Switzer FW	5.00	1.50
204 Edwin Jackson FW RC	20.00	6.00
205 Fernando Cabrera FW RC	5.00	1.50
206 Garrett Atkins FW	5.00	1.50
207 Gerald Laird FW	5.00	1.50
208 Greg Jones FW RC	5.00	1.50
209 Ian Ferguson FW RC	5.00	1.50
210 Jason Roach FW RC	5.00	1.50
211 Jason Shiell FW RC	5.00	1.50

Card	Nm-Mt	Ex-Mt
212 Jeremy Bonderman FW RC	8.00	2.40
213 Jeremy Wedel FW RC	5.00	1.50
214 Jhonny Peralta FW	5.00	1.50
215 Delmon Young FW RC	30.00	9.00
216 Jorge DePaula FW	5.00	1.50
217 Josh Hall FW RC	8.00	2.40
218 Julio Manon FW RC	5.00	1.50
219 Kevin Correia FW RC	5.00	1.50
220 Kevin Ohme FW RC	5.00	1.50
221 Kevin Tolar FW RC	5.00	1.50
222 Luis Ayala FW RC	5.00	1.50
223 Luis De Los Santos FW	5.00	1.50
224 Chad Cordero FW RC	5.00	1.50
225 Mark Malaska FW RC	5.00	1.50
226 Khalil Greene FW	15.00	4.50
227 Michael Nakamura FW RC	5.00	1.50
228 Michel Hernandez FW RC	5.00	1.50
229 Miguel Ojeda FW RC	5.00	1.50
230 Mike Neu FW RC	5.00	1.50
231 Nate Bland FW RC	5.00	1.50
232 Pete LaForest FW RC	8.00	2.40
233 Rickie Weeks FW RC	20.00	6.00
234 Rosman Garcia FW RC	5.00	1.50
235 Ryan Wagner FW RC	8.00	2.40
236 Lance Niekro FW	5.00	1.50
237 Tom Gregorio FW RC	5.00	1.50
238 Tommy Phelps FW	5.00	1.50
239 Wilfredo Ledezma FW RC	8.00	2.40

2003 SP Authentic Matsui Future Watch Autograph Parallel

Card	Nm-Mt	Ex-Mt
RANDOM INSERTS IN PACKS		
PRINT RUNS B/WN 10-75 COPIES PER		
NO PRICING ON QTY OF 25 OR LESS		
181A H.Matsui Bronze/75	300.00	90.00
181B H.Matsui Silver/25		
181C H.Matsui Gold/10		

2003 SP Authentic 500 HR Club

Randomly inserted into packs, this card featured members of the 500 homer club along with a game-used memorabilia piece from each player. A gold parallel was also issued for this card and that card was issued to a stated print run of 25 serial numbered sets. The gold version is not priced due to market scarcity.

Card	Nm-Mt	Ex-Mt
500 Sammy Sosa Jsy/Pants / Ted Williams Pants / Mickey Mantle Jsy/Pants / Mark McGwire Jsy/Pants / Barry Bonds Base	400.00	120.00
500G Sammy Sosa Jsy/Pants / Ted Williams Pants / Mickey Mantle Jsy/Pants / Mark McGwire Jsy/Pants / Barry Bonds Base Gold/25		

2003 SP Authentic Chirography

Randomly inserted into packs, these cards feature authentic autographs from the player pictured on the card. These cards marked the debut of Upper Deck using the "Band-Aid" approach to putting autographs on cards. What that means is that the player does not actually sign the card, instead the player signs a sticker which is then attached to the card. Please note that since these cards were issued to varying print runs, we have notated the stated print run next to the player's name in our checklist. Several players did not get their cards signed in time for inclusion in this product and those exchange cards could be redeemed until April 21, 2006. Please note that many cards in the various sets have notations but neither Mark Prior nor Corey Patterson used whatever notations they were supposed to throughout the course of this product.

Card	Nm-Mt	Ex-Mt
AD Adam Dunn/170	30.00	9.00
BA Jeff Bagwell/175	60.00	18.00
CR Cal Ripken/250	100.00	30.00
FC Rafael Furcal/150	20.00	6.00
FG Freddy Garcia/345	15.00	4.50
FL Cliff Floyd/125	15.00	4.50
GA1 Garret Anderson/350	15.00	4.50
GI Jason Giambi/250	15.00	4.50
GJ Ken Griffey Jr./350 EXCH	80.00	24.00
GL Brian Giles/225	15.00	4.50
IC Ichiro Suzuki/85	350.00	105.00
IS Ichiro Suzuki/75	350.00	105.00
JD Johnny Damon/245	40.00	12.00
JE2 Jim Edmonds/350	25.00	7.50
JM Joe Mays/245	10.00	3.00
JR Ken Griffey Jr./350 EXCH	80.00	24.00
JT1 Jim Thome/250 EXCH	40.00	12.00
KE Jason Kendall/145	20.00	6.00
LG1 Luis Gonzalez/195	20.00	6.00
MM Mark McGwire/50	400.00	120.00
RO Scott Rolen/345	40.00	12.00
RS Richie Sexson/245	15.00	4.50
SA Sammy Sosa/335 EXCH	150.00	45.00
SO Sammy Sosa/335 EXCH	150.00	45.00
SW Mike Sweeney/125	20.00	6.00
TO Torii Hunter/245	15.00	4.50
TS Tim Salmon/350	25.00	7.50

2003 SP Authentic Chirography Bronze

Randomly inserted into packs, this is a partial parallel to the Chirography insert set. A few of these cards have special notations and we have noted that information in our checklist. Again, a few cards were issued as exchange cards and those cards could be redeemed until May 21, 2006.

Card	Nm-Mt	Ex-Mt
AD Adam Dunn/50	50.00	15.00
BA Jeff Bagwell/50	100.00	30.00
CR Cal Ripken/75	150.00	45.00
FC Rafael Furcal/50	30.00	9.00
FG Freddy Garcia/100	25.00	7.50
FL Cliff Floyd/50	25.00	7.50
GI Jason Giambi/50	25.00	7.50
GJ Ken Griffey Jr./100 EXCH	100.00	30.00
GL Brian Giles/50	25.00	7.50
IC Ichiro Suzuki ROY/50	500.00	150.00
IS Ichiro Suzuki MVP/50	500.00	150.00
JD Johnny Damon/100	60.00	18.00
JM Joe Mays/100	15.00	4.50
JR Ken Griffey Jr./100 EXCH	100.00	30.00
KE Jason Kendall/50	30.00	9.00
MM Mark McGwire/25		
RO Scott Rolen/100	60.00	18.00
RS Richie Sexson Milwaukee Notation/100	25.00	7.50
SA Sammy Sosa/100 EXCH	150.00	45.00
SO Sammy Sosa/100 EXCH	150.00	45.00
SW Mike Sweeney/75 EXCH	30.00	9.00
TO Torii Hunter/100 Gold Glove Notation	25.00	7.50

2003 SP Authentic Chirography Silver

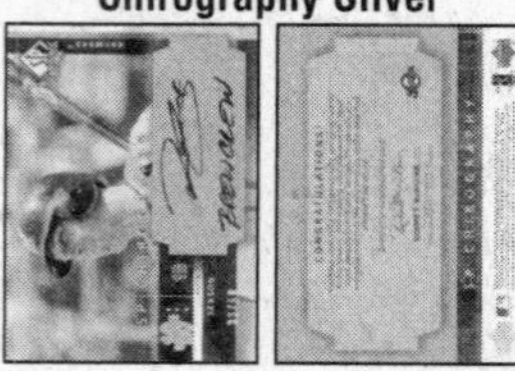

Card	Nm-Mt	Ex-Mt
AD Adam Dunn/25		
BA Jeff Bagwell/25		
CR Cal Ripken/25		
FC Rafael Furcal/25		
FG Freddy Garcia/50	40.00	12.00
FL Cliff Floyd/25		
GI Jason Giambi/25		
GJ Ken Griffey Jr./25 EXCH		
GL Brian Giles/25		
IC Ichiro Suzuki/25		
IS Ichiro Suzuki/25		
JD Johnny Damon/50	100.00	30.00
JM Joe Mays/50	25.00	7.50
JR Ken Griffey Jr./25 EXCH		
KE Jason Kendall/25		
MM Mark McGwire/15		
RO Scott Rolen/50	100.00	30.00
RS Richie Sexson/50	40.00	12.00
SA Sammy Sosa/50 EXCH	150.00	45.00
SO Sammy Sosa/50 EXCH	150.00	45.00
SW Mike Sweeney/25 EXCH		
TO Torii Hunter/50	40.00	12.00

2003 SP Authentic Chirography Dodgers Stars

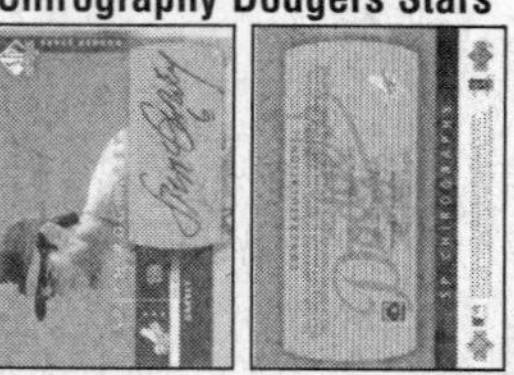

Randomly inserted in packs, these 11 cards feature retired Dodger stars and were issued to varying print runs. We have noted the stated print run in our checklist next to the player's name.

Card	Nm-Mt	Ex-Mt
BB Bill Buckner/245	15.00	4.50
BI Bill Russell/245	15.00	4.50
CE Ron Cey/345	15.00	4.50
DL Davey Lopes/245	15.00	4.50
DN Don Newcombe/345	15.00	4.50
DS Duke Snider/345	40.00	12.00
JN Tommy John/170	15.00	4.50
MW Maury Wills/320	15.00	4.50
SG Steve Garvey/320	25.00	7.50
SU Don Sutton/245	15.00	4.50
SY Steve Yeager/345	15.00	4.50

2003 SP Authentic Chirography Dodgers Stars Bronze

Randomly inserted in packs, this is a partial parallel to the Dodgers Stars insert set. Please note that all of these cards have the word "Dodgers" as an inscription.

	Nm-Mt	Ex-Mt
*BRONZE: .6X TO 1.5X BASIC DODGER		

2003 SP Authentic Chirography Dodgers Stars Silver

Randomly inserted into packs, this is a partial parallel to the Dodgers Stars insert set. Each of these cards were issued to a stated print run of 50 serial numbered sets and most of these cards had a 1981 WS Champs Notation. Please note that the player's who signed cards for this set and were not on the 81 Dodgers used different notations which we have identified in our checklist.

	Nm-Mt	Ex-Mt
*SILVER: .75X TO 2X BASIC DODGER		

2003 SP Authentic Chirography Doubles

Randomly inserted into packs, these 15 cards feature signatures from two different players, who had a reason for commonality. These cards were issued to a stated print run of anywhere from 10 to 150 copies and we have placed that information next to the player's name in our checklist. Please note that cards with a stated print run of 25 or fewer are not priced due to market scarcity. In addition, a few cards were issued as exchange cards and those cards could be redeemed until May 21, 2006.

Card	Nm-Mt	Ex-Mt
FB Whitey Ford / Yogi Berra/75	150.00	45.00
FE Carlton Fisk / Dwight Evans/75	80.00	24.00
FM Carlton Fisk / Bill Mazeroski/75	60.00	18.00
GG Ken Griffey Jr. / Jason Giambi/75 EXCH	120.00	36.00
GR Steve Garvey / Ron Cey/75	60.00	18.00
JI Ken Griffey Jr. / Ichiro Suzuki/125 EXCH	400.00	120.00
KR Tony Kubek / Bobby Richardson/75	100.00	30.00
KT Jerry Koosman / Tom Seaver/75	80.00	24.00
MG Don Mattingly / Jason Giambi/25		
MJ Mark McGwire / Ken Griffey Jr./10		
MS Mark McGwire / Sammy Sosa/15 EXCH		
RT Nolan Ryan / Tom Seaver/25		
SE Tim Salmon / Darin Erstad/25		
SJ Sammy Sosa / Jason Giambi/75 EXCH	200.00	60.00
WB Mookie Wilson / Bill Buckner/150	50.00	15.00

2003 SP Authentic Chirography Flashback

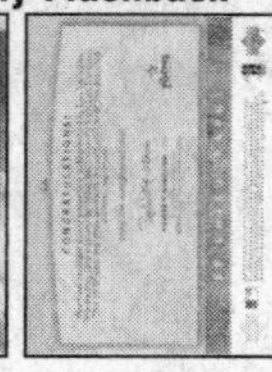

Randomly inserted into packs, these cards feature an important moment from the player's career as well as authentic autograph. Most of these cards were issued to a stated print run of 350 copies but a few were issued to differing amounts so we have noted the print run information next to the player's name in our checklist. In addition, some players did not return their autograph in time and those cards could be exchanged until May 21, 2006.

Card	Nm-Mt	Ex-Mt
BN Brian Giles/245	15.00	4.50
CF1 Cliff Floyd/350	15.00	4.50
GM Ken Griffey Jr./350 EXCH	80.00	24.00
JA Jason Giambi/350	15.00	4.50
JE1 Jim Edmonds/350	25.00	7.50
LA Luis Gonzalez/200	20.00	6.00
MA Mark McGwire/55	400.00	120.00
SR Sammy Sosa/245 EXCH	150.00	45.00

2003 SP Authentic Chirography Flashback Bronze

Randomly inserted in packs, this is a partial parallel to the Flashback insert set. All of the cards live at the time of issue had special notations and we have noted those notations in our checklist. These cards were issued to varying print runs and we have identified the stated print runs in our checklist. Ken Griffey Jr and Sammy Sosa did not return their autographs in time for inclusion and those exchange cards could be redeemed until May 21, 2006.

Card	Nm-Mt	Ex-Mt
BN Brian Giles/50	25.00	7.50
GM Ken Griffey Jr./100 EXCH	100.00	30.00
JA Jason Giambi 2000 MVP/100	25.00	7.50
LA Luis Gonzalez 2001 Champs/75	30.00	9.00
MA Mark McGwire 500 HR Club/25		
SR Sammy Sosa/100 EXCH	150.00	45.00

2003 SP Authentic Chirography Flashback Silver

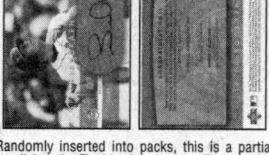

Randomly inserted into packs, this is a partial parallel to the Flashback insert set. These cards were issued to stated print runs of between 15 and 50 copies and for those copies with stated print runs fo 25 or fewer, no pricing is provided due to market scarcity.

Card	Nm-Mt	Ex-Mt
BN Brian Giles/25		
GM Ken Griffey Jr./25 EXCH		
JA0 Jason Giambi A's/50	30.00	9.00
LA Luis Gonzalez 25		
MA Mark McGwire/15		
SR Sammy Sosa/50 EXCH	150.00	45.00

2003 SP Authentic Chirography Hall of Famers

Randomly inserted into packs, these 14 cards feature autographs of Hall of Famers. Since these cards were issued to varying print runs, we have identified the stated print run next to the player's name in our checklist.

Card	Nm-Mt	Ex-Mt
BG Bob Gibson/245	40.00	12.00
CF Carlton Fisk/240	40.00	12.00
DS Duke Snider/250	40.00	12.00
DW2 Dave Winfield/350	25.00	7.50
GC1 Gary Carter/350	25.00	7.50
JB1 Johnny Bench/350	50.00	15.00
NR Nolan Ryan/170	150.00	45.00
OC Orlando Cepeda/245	25.00	7.50
RF Rollie Fingers/170	25.00	7.50
RR Robin Roberts/170	40.00	12.00
RY Robin Yount/350	50.00	15.00
TP Tony Perez/320	25.00	7.50
TS Tom Seaver/170	40.00	12.00
WF Whitey Ford/150	40.00	12.00

2003 SP Authentic Chirography Hall of Famers Bronze

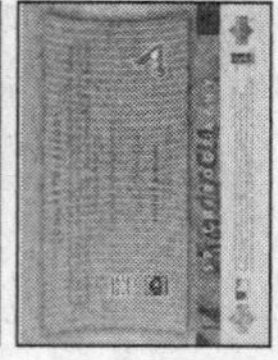

Randomly inserted into packs, this is a partial parallel to the Hall of Famers insert set. These cards all feature an HOF (or some close variation) notation as part of the autograph. These cards were issued to stated print runs between 50 and 100 copies and we have noted the specific information next to the player's name in our checklist.

Card	Nm-Mt	Ex-Mt
BG Bob Gibson/100	60.00	18.00
CF Carlton Fisk/100	60.00	18.00
DS Duke Snider/100	60.00	18.00
NR Nolan Ryan/50	200.00	60.00
OC Orlando Cepeda/100	40.00	12.00
RF Rollie Fingers/50	40.00	12.00
RR Robin Roberts/50	60.00	18.00
TP Tony Perez/100	40.00	12.00
TS Tom Seaver/75	60.00	18.00
WF Whitey Ford/75	60.00	18.00

2003 SP Authentic Chirography Hall of Famers Silver

Randomly inserted into packs, this is a partial parallel to the Hall of Famers insert set. All of these cards have the HOF (and specific year of the player's induction) notation. These cards were issued to a stated print run of either 25 or 50 copies. Please note that for cards with a stated print run of 25 copies there is no pricing due to market scarcity.

Card	Nm-Mt	Ex-Mt
BG Bob Gibson/50	80.00	24.00
CF Carlton Fisk/50	80.00	24.00
DS Duke Snider/50	80.00	24.00
NR Nolan Ryan/25		
OC Orlando Cepeda/50	50.00	15.00
RF Rollie Fingers/25		
RR Robin Roberts/25		
TP Tony Perez/50	50.00	15.00
TS Tom Seaver/50	80.00	24.00
WF Whitey Ford/25		

2003 SP Authentic Chirography Triples

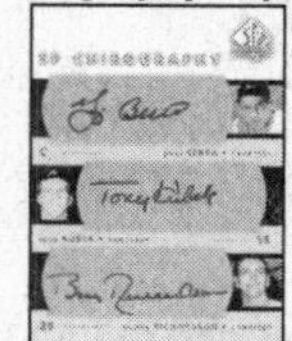

Randomly inserted in packs, these 12 cards feature autographs from three leading players. These cards were issued to stated print runs of anywhere from 10 to 75 copies and we are only providing pricing for cards with a stated print run of more than 10 copies. The following cards were available only as an exchange and those cards could be redeemed until May 21, 2006: Berra/Kubek/Richardson, Fisk/Carter/Gibson, Griffey Jr./Ichiro/Sosa, Griffey Jr./Sosa/Giambi, Giambi/Sosa/Griffey Jr., Ichiro/Sosa/Giambi, McGwire/Sosa/Griffey Jr., McGwire/Sosa/Ichiro and Seaver/Koosman/McGraw.

Card	Nm-Mt	Ex-Mt
BKR Yogi Berra / Tony Kubek / Bobby Richardson/75	200.00	60.00
FCG Carlton Fisk / Gary Carter / Kirk Gibson/75 EXCH	120.00	36.00
GIS Ken Griffey Jr. / Ichiro Suzuki / Sammy Sosa/75 EXCH	500.00	150.00
GLC Steve Garvey / Davy Lopes / Ron Cey/75	100.00	30.00
GRC Steve Garvey / Bill Russell / Ron Cey/75	100.00	30.00

GSG Ken Griffey Jr.	250.00	75.00
Sammy Sosa		
Jason Giambi/75 EXCH		
GSJ Jason Giambi	250.00	75.00
Sammy Sosa		
Ken Griffey Jr./75		
ISG Ichiro Suzuki	500.00	150.00
Sammy Sosa		
Jason Giambi/75		
MSG Mark McGwire		
Sammy Sosa		
Ken Griffey Jr./10		
MSI Mark McGwire		
Sammy Sosa		
Ichiro Suzuki/10		
SEA Tim Salmon	120.00	36.00
Darin Erstad		
Garret Anderson/75		
SKM Tom Seaver	150.00	45.00
Jerry Koosman		
Tug McGraw/75 EXCH		

2003 SP Authentic Chirography World Series Heroes

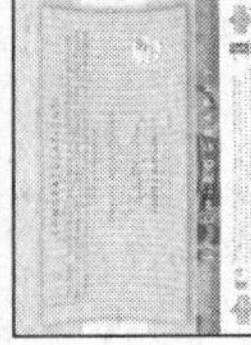

Randomly inserted into packs, these 17 cards feature players who were leading players in at least one World Series. Each of these cards were issued to varying print runs and we have identified the stated print run next to the player's name in our checklist. Andruw Jones did not return his cards in time for inclusion in this product so those exchange cards could be redeemed until May 21, 2006.

	Nm-Mt	Ex-Mt
AJ1 Andruw Jones/350 EXCH	20.00	6.00
BM Bill Mazeroski/245	25.00	7.50
CF Carlton Fisk/200	40.00	12.00
CR Cal Ripken/295	100.00	30.00
CS Curt Schilling/345	40.00	12.00
DE Darin Erstad/245	20.00	6.00
DJ David Justice/170	25.00	7.50
ER Edgar Renteria/220	20.00	6.00
GA Garret Anderson/245	25.00	7.50
GC Gary Carter/345	20.00	6.00
GO Luis Gonzalez/225	20.00	6.00
GS Ken Griffey Sr./295	20.00	6.00
JK Jerry Koosman/170	25.00	7.50
JP Jorge Posada/350	40.00	12.00
KG Kirk Gibson/145	25.00	7.50
TI Tim Salmon/245	25.00	7.50
TM Tug McGraw/170	50.00	15.00

2003 SP Authentic Chirography World Series Heroes Bronze

Randomly inserted into packs, this is a partial parallel to the World Series Heroes insert set. Each of these cards have not only an autograph but a notation identifying a key world series this player's career. Each of these cards were issued to a stated print run of between 50 and 100 copies.

	Nm-Mt	Ex-Mt
BM Bill Mazeroski/100	40.00	12.00
CF Carlton Fisk/75	60.00	18.00
CS Curt Schilling/100	60.00	18.00
DE Darin Erstad/100	30.00	9.00
DJ David Justice/75 EXCH	40.00	12.00
ER Edgar Renteria/75	40.00	12.00
GA Garret Anderson/100	40.00	12.00
GC Gary Carter/100	30.00	9.00
GO Luis Gonzalez/100	30.00	9.00
GS Ken Griffey Sr./100	30.00	9.00
JK Jerry Koosman/75	40.00	12.00
KG Kirk Gibson/50	40.00	12.00
TI Tim Salmon/100	40.00	12.00
TM Tug McGraw/100	80.00	24.00

2003 SP Authentic Chirography World Series Heroes Silver

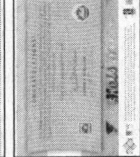

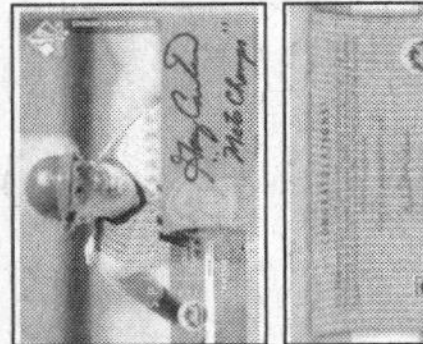
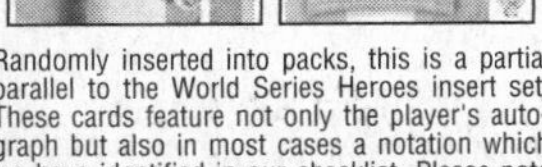

Randomly inserted into packs, this is a partial parallel to the World Series Heroes insert set. These cards feature not only the player's autograph but also in most cases a notation which we have identified in our checklist. Please note that these cards have stated print runs of either 25 or 50 cards. Cards with stated print runs of 25 are not printed due to market scarcity. Of note, Tug McGraw's card, inscribed "Ya Gotta Believe" took on a much deeper meaning after his unfortunate death less than a year after the card was issued.

	Nm-Mt	Ex-Mt
BM Bill Mazeroski	50.00	15.00
Buc's 60/50		
CF Carlton Fisk		
Home Run/25		
CS Curt Schilling/50	80.00	24.00
DE Darin Erstad/50	40.00	12.00
DJ David Justice/50	50.00	15.00
ER Edgar Renteria		
Marlins 97/25		
GA Garret Anderson/50	50.00	15.00
GC Gary Carter	40.00	12.00
Mets Champs/50		
GO Luis Gonzalez	40.00	12.00
D-Backs 01/50		
GS Ken Griffey Sr.	40.00	12.00
Big Red Machine/50		
JK Jerry Koosman/50	50.00	15.00
KG Kirk Gibson		
Home Run/25		
TI Tim Salmon	50.00	15.00
2002 Champs/50		
TM Tug McGraw	100.00	30.00
Ya Gotta Believe/50		

2003 SP Authentic Chirography Yankees Stars

Randomly inserted into packs, these 14 cards feature not only Yankee stars of the past and present but also authentic autographs of the featured players. Since these cards were issued to varying print runs, we have identified the stated print run next to the player's name in our checklist.

	Nm-Mt	Ex-Mt
BR Bobby Richardson/320	25.00	7.50
DM Don Mattingly/295	60.00	18.00
DW1 Dave Winfield/350	25.00	7.50
HK Ralph Houk/245	15.00	4.50
JB Jim Bouton/345	15.00	4.50
JG Jason Giambi/275	15.00	4.50
KS Ken Griffey Sr./350	15.00	4.50
RC Roger Clemens/210	120.00	36.00
SL Sparky Lyle/345	15.00	4.50
ST Mel Stottlemyre/345	15.00	4.50
TH Tommy Henrich/345	15.00	4.50
TJ Tommy John/245	15.00	4.50
TK Tony Kubek/345	25.00	7.50
YB Yogi Berra/320	40.00	12.00

2003 SP Authentic Chirography Yankees Stars Bronze

Randomly inserted into packs, this is a partial parallel to the Yankee Stars insert set. Most of these cards were issued to a stated print run of 100 copies and most have an "Yankees" inscription. Please note that for the few players who did not put an Yankees inscription we put a NO next to the player's name. In addition, since a few cards have a print run of fewer than 100 copies we have noted all print runs in our checklist.

	Nm-Mt	Ex-Mt
BR Bobby Richardson/100	40.00	12.00
DM Don Mattingly NO/100	100.00	30.00
HK Ralph Houk/100	25.00	7.50
JB Jim Bouton/100	25.00	7.50
JG Jason Giambi/60	25.00	7.50
KS Ken Griffey Sr./100	25.00	7.50
RC Roger Clemens NO/75	150.00	45.00
SL Sparky Lyle/100	25.00	7.50
ST Mel Stottlemyre/100	25.00	7.50
TH Tommy Henrich/100	25.00	7.50
TJ Tommy John/100	25.00	7.50
TK Tony Kubek/100	40.00	12.00
YB Yogi Berra NO/100	60.00	18.00

2003 SP Authentic Chirography Yankees Stars Silver

Randomly inserted into packs, this is a partial parallel to the Yankee Stars insert set. Each of these cards was issued to a stated print run of either 25 or 50 copies and we have noted that information in our checklist. Since there is a mix in this set about cards with notations, what the notations are -- we have put the notation information, when it exists, in our checklist.

	Nm-Mt	Ex-Mt
BR Bobby Richardson	50.00	15.00
New York/50		
DM Don Mattingly/50	120.00	36.00
HK Ralph Houk	30.00	9.00
New York/50		
JB Jim Bouton	30.00	9.00
New York/50		
JG Jason Giambi/25		
KS Ken Griffey Sr./25		
RC Roger Clemens/50	150.00	45.00
SL Sparky Lyle/50	30.00	9.00
ST Mel Stottlemyre/50	30.00	9.00
TH Tommy Henrich	30.00	9.00
Yankees/50		
TJ Tommy John/50	30.00	9.00
TK Tony Kubek	50.00	15.00
New York/50		
YB Yogi Berra/75	80.00	24.00

2003 SP Authentic Chirography Young Stars

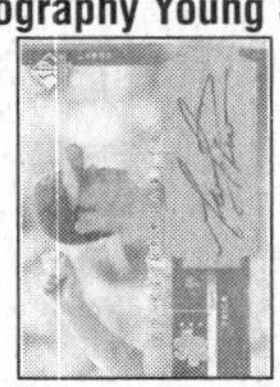

Randomly inserted into packs, these 25 cards feature autographs of some of the leading young stars in baseball. These cards were issued to stated print runs of between 150 and 350 cards and we have notated that information in our checklist. Please note that Hee Seop Choi did not return his autographs in time for pack out and those exchange cards could be redeemed until May 21, 2006.

	Nm-Mt	Ex-Mt
AP A.J. Pierzynski/245	15.00	4.50
BO Joe Borchard/245	10.00	3.00
BP1 Brandon Phillips/350	10.00	3.00
BZ Barry Zito/350	25.00	7.50
CP Corey Patterson/245	15.00	4.50
DH Drew Henson/245	25.00	7.50
DI1 Ben Diggins/350	10.00	3.00
EH Eric Hinske/245	10.00	3.00
FS Freddy Sanchez/350	10.00	3.00
HB Hank Blalock/245	25.00	7.50
HC Hee Seop Choi/245 EXCH	60.00	18.00
JJ Jacque Jones/245	15.00	4.50
JJ1 Jimmy Journell/350	10.00	3.00
JL Jason Lane/245	10.00	3.00
JP Josh Phelps/245	10.00	3.00
JS Jayson Werth/350	10.00	3.00
MB Marlon Byrd/245	10.00	3.00
MI Doug Mientkiewicz/245	15.00	4.50
MP Mark Prior/150	60.00	18.00
MY Brett Myers/245	10.00	3.00
OH Orlando Hudson/245	10.00	3.00
OP Oliver Perez/245	15.00	4.50
PE Carlos Pena/245	10.00	3.00
SB Sean Burroughs/245	15.00	4.50
TX Mark Teixeira/245	25.00	7.50

2003 SP Authentic Chirography Young Stars Bronze

Randomly inserted into packs, this is a partial parallel to the Young Stars insert set. Please note that most of these cards (with the exception of the Mark Prior card) were issued to a stated print run of 100 serial numbered sets and most of these cards had a notation of what city the player was playing in at the time of issue for this set. We have put the city information when applicable in our checklist.

	Nm-Mt	Ex-Mt
*BRONZE: .6X TO 1.5X BASIC YS		

2003 SP Authentic Chirography Young Stars Silver

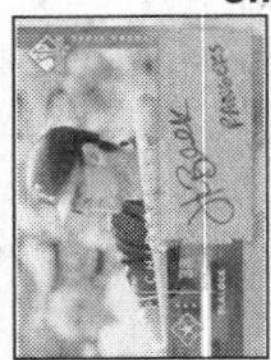

Randomly inserted into packs, this is a partial parallel to the Young Stars insert set. Most of these cards have a team notation and we have put that information next to tha players name in our checklist. Please note that most of these cards, with the exception of Mark Prior was issued to a stated print run of 50 serial numbered sets. The Prior card was issued to a stated print run of 25 serial numbered sets and there is no pricing due to market scarcity on that card.

	Nm-Mt	Ex-Mt
*SILVER: .75X TO 2X BASIC YS		

2003 SP Authentic Simply Splendid

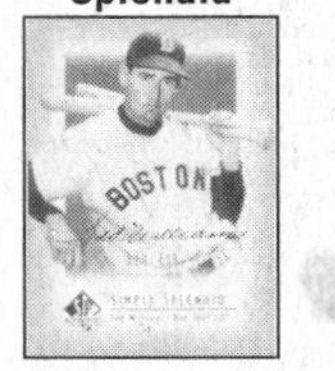

	Nm-Mt	Ex-Mt
COMMON CARD (TW1-TW30)	8.00	2.40
RANDOM INSERTS IN PACKS		
STATED PRINT RUN 406 SERIAL #'d SETS		

2003 SP Authentic Splendid Jerseys

	Nm-Mt	Ex-Mt
RANDOM INSERTS IN PACKS		
STATED PRINT RUN 406 SERIAL #'d SETS		
SJTW Ted Williams	100.00	30.00

2003 SP Authentic Splendid Signatures

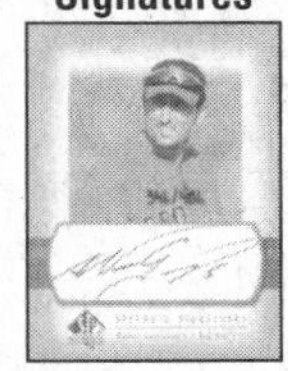

Randomly inserted in packs, these two cards feature autographs of current Red Sox star Nomar Garciaparra and retired Red Sox legend Ted Williams. Please note, that since these cards were issued after Williams passed on, that the Williams autographs are "cuts" while the Nomar autographs were signed for this product. Since the Williams card was issued to a stated print run of five serial numbered copies, no pricing is available for that card.

	Nm-Mt	Ex-Mt
GA Nomar Garciaparra/406	150.00	45.00
TWSIG Ted Williams/5		

2003 SP Authentic Splendid Signatures Pairs

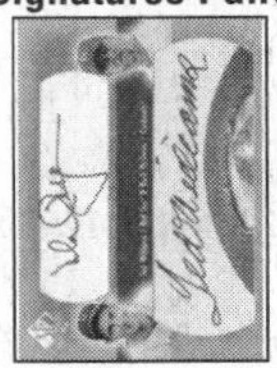

Randomly inserted into packs, these six cards feature a Ted Williams autograph "cut" to go with an autograph of an modern star. Each of these cards were issued to a stated print run of 3 serial numbered copies and no pricing is available due to market scarcity. Of note, all three copies of the Ken Griffey Jr./Ted Williams combo signature actually packed erroneously featuring Ken Griffey Sr. signatures. It's been verified that at least one of the three copies was returned to Upper Deck by a dealer and a Griffey Jr. signature was switched out.

	Nm-Mt	Ex-Mt
IS2 Ted Williams		
Ichiro Suzuki		
JG2 Ted Williams		
Jason Giambi		
KG2 Ted Williams		
Ken Griffey Jr.		
MM2 Ted Williams		
Mark McGwire		
NM3 Ted Williams		
Nomar Garciaparra		
SS2 Ted Williams		
Sammy Sosa		

2003 SP Authentic Splendid Swatches Pairs

Randomly inserted into packs, these nine cards feature a game-worn jersey swatch of retired Red Sox legend Ted Williams along with a game-used jersey swatch of another star. Each of the these cards were issued to a stated print run of

406 serial numbered sets. The two Williams/Nomar cards were not ready for pack-out and those were issued as a exchange cards with a redemption date of May 21, 2006.

	Nm-Mt	Ex-Mt
IS Ted Williams	100.00	30.00
Ichiro Suzuki		
JG Ted Williams	60.00	18.00
Jason Giambi		
KG Ted Williams	80.00	24.00
Ken Griffey Jr.		
MM Ted Williams	120.00	36.00
Mark McGwire		
NM1 Ted Williams	100.00	30.00
Nomar Garciaparra EXCH		
NM2 Ted Williams	100.00	30.00
Nomar Garciaparra EXCH		
SS Ted Williams	100.00	30.00
Sammy Sosa		
TW Ted Williams	200.00	60.00
Mickey Mantle		

2003 SP Authentic Superstar Flashback

	Nm-Mt	Ex-Mt
RANDOM INSERTS IN PACKS		
STATED PRINT RUN 2003 SERIAL #'d SETS		
SF1 Tim Salmon	3.00	.90
SF2 Darin Erstad	3.00	.90
SF3 Troy Glaus	3.00	.90
SF4 Randy Johnson	3.00	.90
SF5 Curt Schilling	3.00	.90
SF6 Steve Finley	3.00	.90
SF7 Greg Maddux	5.00	1.50
SF8 Chipper Jones	3.00	.90
SF9 Andruw Jones	3.00	.90
SF10 Gary Sheffield	3.00	.90
SF11 Manny Ramirez	3.00	.90
SF12 Pedro Martinez	3.00	.90
SF13 Nomar Garciaparra	5.00	1.50
SF14 Sammy Sosa	5.00	1.50
SF15 Frank Thomas	3.00	.90
SF16 Kerry Wood	3.00	.90
SF17 Paul Konerko	3.00	.90
SF18 Corey Patterson	3.00	.90
SF19 Mark Prior	3.00	.90
SF20 Ken Griffey Jr.	5.00	1.50
SF21 Adam Dunn	3.00	.90
SF22 Larry Walker	3.00	.90
SF23 Preston Wilson	3.00	.90
SF24 Todd Helton	3.00	.90
SF25 Ivan Rodriguez	3.00	.90
SF26 Josh Beckett	3.00	.90
SF27 Jeff Bagwell	3.00	.90
SF28 Jeff Kent	3.00	.90
SF29 Lance Berkman	3.00	.90
SF30 Carlos Beltran	3.00	.90
SF31 Shawn Green	3.00	.90
SF32 Richie Sexson	3.00	.90
SF33 Vladimir Guerrero	3.00	.90
SF34 Mike Piazza	5.00	1.50
SF35 Roberto Alomar	3.00	.90
SF36 Roger Clemens	6.00	1.80
SF37 Derek Jeter	8.00	2.40
SF38 Jason Giambi	3.00	.90
SF39 Bernie Williams	3.00	.90
SF40 Nick Johnson	3.00	.90
SF41 Alfonso Soriano	3.00	.90
SF42 Miguel Tejada	3.00	.90
SF43 Eric Chavez	3.00	.90
SF44 Barry Zito	3.00	.90
SF45 Jim Thome	3.00	.90
SF46 Pat Burrell	3.00	.90
SF47 Marlon Byrd	3.00	.90
SF48 Jason Kendall	3.00	.90
SF49 Aramis Ramirez	3.00	.90
SF50 Brian Giles	3.00	.90
SF51 Phil Nevin	3.00	.90
SF52 Barry Bonds	8.00	2.40
SF53 Ichiro Suzuki	5.00	1.50
SF54 Scott Rolen	3.00	.90
SF55 J.D. Drew	3.00	.90
SF56 Albert Pujols	6.00	1.80
SF57 Mark Teixeira	3.00	.90
SF58 Hank Blalock	3.00	.90
SF59 Carlos Delgado	3.00	.90
SF60 Roy Halladay	3.00	.90

2004 SP Authentic

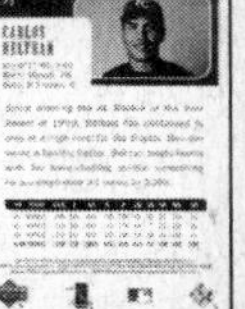

This 191 card set was released in June, 2004. The set was issued in five card packs with an $5 SRP which came 24 packs to a box and 12 boxes to a case. Cards numbered 1 through 90 featured veterans while cards numbered 91 through 132 and 178 through 191 feature rookies.With the exception of card 180, there were parallel versions issued of these cards and those cards all begin their serial numbering with 296. Card number 180 featuring Kazuo Matsui has a straight serial print run of card 1 through 999. Cards numbered 133 through 177 feature a mix of active and retired players with All-Star game memories and those cards were inserted at a stated rate of one in 24 with a stated print run of 999 serial numbered sets.

Nm-Mt Ex-Mt
COMP.SET w/o SP's (90) 15.00 4.50
COMMON CARD (1-90) .... .40 .12
COMMON (91-132/178-191) 5.00 1.50
91-132/178-191 OVERALL FW ODDS 1:24
91-132/178-191 PRINT 704 #'d SETS
91-132/178-179/181-191 #'d FROM 296-999
CARD 180 PRINT RUN 999 #'d COPIES
CARD 180 #'d FROM 1-999
COMMON CARD (133-177) .... 3.00 .90
133-177 STATED ODDS 1:24
133-177 PRINT RUN 999 SERIAL #'d SETS
1 Bret Boone .40 .12
2 Gary Sheffield .40 .12
3 Rafael Palmeiro .60 .18
4 Jorge Posada .60 .18
5 Derek Jeter 2.00 .60
6 Garret Anderson .40 .12
7 Bartolo Colon .40 .12
8 Kevin Brown .40 .12
9 Shea Hillenbrand .40 .12
10 Ryan Klesko .40 .12
11 Bobby Abreu .40 .12
12 Scott Rolen 1.00 .30
13 Alfonso Soriano .60 .18
14 Jason Giambi .40 .12
15 Tom Glavine .60 .18
16 Hideo Nomo 1.00 .30
17 Johan Santana .60 .18
18 Sammy Sosa 1.50 .45
19 Rickie Weeks .40 .12
20 Barry Zito .40 .12
21 Kerry Wood 1.00 .30
22 Austin Kearns .40 .12
23 Shawn Green .40 .12
24 Miguel Cabrera .60 .18
25 Richard Hidalgo .40 .12
26 Andruw Jones .40 .12
27 Randy Wolf .40 .12
28 David Ortiz 1.00 .30
29 Roy Oswalt .40 .12
30 Vernon Wells .40 .12
31 Ben Sheets .40 .12
32 Mike Lowell .40 .12
33 Todd Helton .60 .18
34 Jacque Jones .40 .12
35 Mike Sweeney .40 .12
36 Hank Blalock .40 .12
37 Jason Schmidt .40 .12
38 Jeff Kent .40 .12
39 Josh Beckett .40 .12
40 Manny Ramirez .60 .18
41 Torii Hunter .40 .12
42 Brian Giles .40 .12
43 Javier Vazquez .40 .12
44 Jim Edmonds .40 .12
45 Dmitri Young .40 .12
46 Preston Wilson .40 .12
47 Jeff Bagwell .60 .18
48 Pedro Martinez 1.00 .30
49 Eric Chavez .40 .12
50 Ken Griffey Jr. 1.50 .45
51 Shannon Stewart .40 .12
52 Rafael Furcal .40 .12
53 Brandon Webb .40 .12
54 Juan Pierre .40 .12
55 Roger Clemens 2.00 .60
56 Geoff Jenkins .40 .12
57 Lance Berkman .40 .12
58 Albert Pujols 2.00 .60
59 Frank Thomas 1.00 .30
60 Edgar Martinez .60 .18
61 Tim Hudson .40 .12
62 Eric Gagne 1.00 .30
63 Richie Sexson .40 .12
64 Corey Patterson .40 .12
65 Nomar Garciaparra 1.50 .45
66 Hideki Matsui 1.50 .45
67 Mark Teixeira .40 .12
68 Troy Glaus .40 .12
69 Carlos Lee .40 .12
70 Mike Mussina .60 .18
71 Magglio Ordonez .40 .12
72 Roy Halladay .40 .12
73 Ichiro Suzuki 1.50 .45
74 Randy Johnson 1.00 .30
75 Luis Gonzalez .40 .12
76 Mark Prior 1.00 .30
77 Carlos Beltran .60 .18
78 Ivan Rodriguez 1.00 .30
79 Alex Rodriguez 1.50 .45
80 Dontrelle Willis .40 .12
81 Mike Piazza 1.50 .45
82 Curt Schilling 1.00 .30
83 Vladimir Guerrero 1.00 .30
84 Greg Maddux 1.50 .45
85 Jim Thome 1.00 .30
86 Miguel Tejada .40 .12
87 Carlos Delgado .40 .12
88 Jose Reyes .40 .12
89 Matt Morris .40 .12
90 Mark Mulder .40 .12
91 Angel Chavez FW RC 5.00 1.50
92 Brandon Medders FW RC 5.00 1.50
93 Carlos Vasquez FW RC 8.00 2.40
94 Chris Aguila FW RC 5.00 1.50
95 Colby Miller FW RC 5.00 1.50
96 Dave Crouthers FW RC 5.00 1.50
97 Dennis Sarfate FW RC 5.00 1.50
98 Donnie Kelly FW RC 5.00 1.50
99 Merkin Valdez FW RC 8.00 2.40
100 Eddy Rodriguez FW RC 8.00 2.40
101 Edwin Moreno FW RC 5.00 1.50
102 Enemencio Pacheco FW RC. 5.00 1.50
103 Roberto Novoa FW RC 8.00 2.40
104 Greg Dobbs FW RC 5.00 1.50
105 Hector Gimenez FW RC 5.00 1.50
106 Ian Snell FW RC 8.00 2.40
107 Jake Woods FW RC 5.00 1.50
108 Jamie Brown FW RC 5.00 1.50
109 Jason Frasor FW RC 5.00 1.50
110 Jerome Gamble FW RC 5.00 1.50
111 Jerry Gil FW RC 5.00 1.50
112 Jesse Harper FW RC 5.00 1.50
113 Jorge Vasquez FW RC 5.00 1.50
114 Jose Capellan FW RC 8.00 2.40
115 Josh Labandeira FW RC 5.00 1.50
116 Justin Hampson FW RC 5.00 1.50
117 Justin Huisman FW RC 5.00 1.50
118 Justin Leone FW RC 8.00 2.40
119 Lincoln Holdzkom FW RC 5.00 1.50
120 Lino Urdaneta FW RC 5.00 1.50
121 Mike Gosling FW RC 5.00 1.50
122 Mike Johnston FW RC 5.00 1.50
123 Mike Rouse FW RC 5.00 1.50
124 Scott Proctor FW RC 8.00 2.40
125 Roman Colon FW RC 5.00 1.50
126 Ronny Cedeno FW RC 5.00 1.50
127 Ryan Meaux FW RC 5.00 1.50
128 Scott Dohmann FW RC 5.00 1.50
129 Sean Henn FW RC 5.00 1.50
130 Tim Bausher FW RC 5.00 1.50
131 Tim Bittner FW RC 5.00 1.50
132 William Bergolla FW RC 5.00 1.50
133 Rick Ferrell ASM 3.00 .90
134 Joe DiMaggio ASM 5.00 1.50
135 Bob Feller ASM 3.00 .90
136 Ted Williams ASM 8.00 2.40
137 Stan Musial ASM 5.00 1.50
138 Larry Doby ASM 3.00 .90
139 Red Schoendienst ASM 3.00 .90
140 Enos Slaughter ASM 3.00 .90
141 Stan Musial ASM 5.00 1.50
142 Mickey Mantle ASM 10.00 3.00
143 Ted Williams ASM 8.00 2.40
144 Mickey Mantle ASM 10.00 3.00
145 Stan Musial ASM 5.00 1.50
146 Tom Seaver ASM 4.00 1.20
147 Willie McCovey ASM 4.00 1.20
148 Bob Gibson ASM 4.00 1.20
149 Frank Robinson ASM 3.00 .90
150 Joe Morgan ASM 3.00 .90
151 Billy Williams ASM 3.00 .90
152 Catfish Hunter ASM 4.00 1.20
153 Joe Morgan ASM 3.00 .90
154 Joe Morgan ASM 3.00 .90
155 Mike Schmidt ASM 8.00 2.40
156 Tommy Lasorda ASM 3.00 .90
157 Robin Yount ASM 5.00 1.50
158 Nolan Ryan ASM 10.00 3.00
159 John Franco ASM 3.00 .90
160 Nolan Ryan ASM 10.00 3.00
161 Ken Griffey Jr. ASM 5.00 1.50
162 Cal Ripken ASM 10.00 3.00
163 Ken Griffey Jr. ASM 5.00 1.50
164 Gary Sheffield ASM 3.00 .90
165 Fred McGriff ASM 4.00 1.20
166 Hideo Nomo ASM 4.00 1.20
167 Mike Piazza ASM 5.00 1.50
168 Sandy Alomar Jr. ASM 3.00 .90
169 Roberto Alomar ASM 4.00 1.20
170 Ted Williams ASM 8.00 2.40
171 Pedro Martinez ASM 4.00 1.20
172 Derek Jeter ASM 6.00 1.80
173 Cal Ripken ASM 10.00 3.00
174 Torii Hunter ASM 3.00 .90
175 Alfonso Soriano ASM 4.00 1.20
176 Hank Blalock ASM 3.00 .90
177 Ichiro Suzuki ASM 5.00 1.50
178 Orlando Rodriguez FW RC 5.00 1.50
179 Ramon Ramirez FW RC 5.00 1.50
180 Kazuo Matsui FW RC 10.00 3.00
181 Kevin Cave FW RC 8.00 2.40
182 John Gall FW RC 8.00 2.40
183 Freddy Guzman FW RC 5.00 1.50
184 Chris Oxspring FW RC 8.00 2.40
185 Rusty Tucker FW RC 8.00 2.40
186 Jorge Sequea FW RC 5.00 1.50
187 Carlos Hines FW RC 5.00 1.50
188 Michael Vento FW RC 8.00 2.40
189 Ryan Wing FW RC 5.00 1.50
190 Jeff Bennett FW RC 5.00 1.50
191 Luis A. Gonzalez FW RC 8.00 2.40

2004 SP Authentic 199/99

Nm-Mt Ex-Mt
*199/99 1-90: 3X TO 8X BASIC
*199/99 91-132/178-191: .75X TO 2X BASIC
1-132/178-191 PRINT RUN SER. 99 #'d SETS
*199/99 133-177: .75X TO 2X BASIC
133-177 PRINT RUN 199 SERIAL #'d SETS
OVERALL PARALLEL ODDS 1:8
180 Kazuo Matsui FW 25.00 7.50

2004 SP Authentic 499/249

Nm-Mt Ex-Mt
*499/249 1-90: 1.25X TO 3X BASIC
*499/249 133-177: .6X TO 1.5X BASIC
1-90/133-177 PRINT RUN 499 #'d SETS
*499/249 91-132/178-191: .5X TO 1.2X BASIC
91-132/178-191 PRINT RUN 249 #'d SETS
OVERALL PARALLEL ODDS 1:8
180 Kazuo Matsui FW 15.00 4.50

2004 SP Authentic Future Watch Autograph

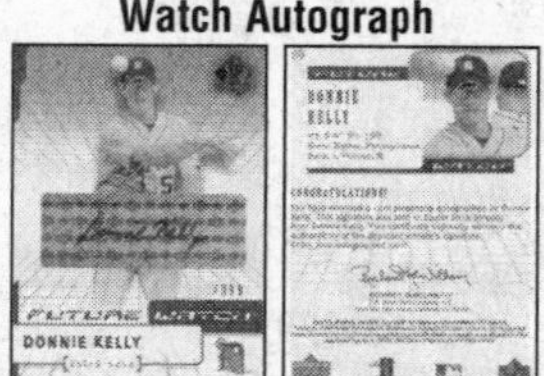

Nm-Mt Ex-Mt
STATED PRINT RUN 295 SERIAL #'d SETS
*AUTO 195: .5X TO 1.2X BASIC
AUTO 195 PRINT RUN 195 SERIAL #'d SETS
OVERALL FUTURE WATCH ODDS 1:24
91 Angel Chavez FW 10.00 3.00
92 Brandon Medders FW 10.00 3.00
93 Carlos Vasquez FW 15.00 4.50
94 Chris Aguila FW 10.00 3.00
95 Colby Miller FW 10.00 3.00
96 Dave Crouthers FW 10.00 3.00
97 Dennis Sarfate FW 10.00 3.00
98 Donnie Kelly FW 10.00 3.00
99 Merkin Valdez FW 25.00 7.50
100 Eddy Rodriguez FW 15.00 4.50
101 Edwin Moreno FW 10.00 3.00
102 Enemencio Pacheco FW 10.00 3.00
103 Roberto Novoa FW 15.00 4.50
104 Greg Dobbs FW 10.00 3.00
105 Hector Gimenez FW 10.00 3.00
106 Ian Snell FW 20.00 6.00
107 Jake Woods FW 10.00 3.00
108 Jamie Brown FW 10.00 3.00
109 Jason Frasor FW 10.00 3.00
110 Jerome Gamble FW 10.00 3.00
111 Jerry Gil FW 10.00 3.00
112 Jesse Harper FW 10.00 3.00
113 Jorge Vasquez FW 10.00 3.00
114 Jose Capellan FW 25.00 7.50
115 Josh Labandeira FW 10.00 3.00
116 Justin Hampson FW 10.00 3.00
117 Justin Huisman FW 10.00 3.00
118 Justin Leone FW 15.00 4.50
119 Lincoln Holdzkom FW 10.00 3.00
120 Lino Urdaneta FW 10.00 3.00
121 Mike Gosling FW 10.00 3.00
122 Mike Johnston FW 10.00 3.00
123 Mike Rouse FW 10.00 3.00
124 Scott Proctor FW 15.00 4.50
125 Roman Colon FW 10.00 3.00
126 Ronny Cedeno FW 10.00 3.00
127 Ryan Meaux FW 10.00 3.00
128 Scott Dohmann FW 10.00 3.00
129 Sean Henn FW 10.00 3.00
130 Tim Bausher FW 10.00 3.00
131 Tim Bittner FW 10.00 3.00
132 William Bergolla FW 10.00 3.00
178 Orlando Rodriguez FW 10.00 3.00
179 Ramon Ramirez FW 10.00 3.00
181 Kevin Cave FW 15.00 4.50
182 John Gall FW 15.00 4.50
183 Freddy Guzman FW 10.00 3.00
184 Chris Oxspring FW 15.00 4.50
185 Rusty Tucker FW 15.00 4.50
186 Jorge Sequea FW 10.00 3.00
187 Carlos Hines FW 10.00 3.00
188 Michael Vento FW 15.00 4.50
189 Ryan Wing FW 10.00 3.00
190 Jeff Bennett FW 10.00 3.00
191 Luis A. Gonzalez FW 15.00 4.50

2004 SP Authentic Game-Dated

Nm-Mt Ex-Mt
OVERALL GAME DATED ODDS 1:288.
STATED PRINT RUN 1 SERIAL #'d SET
MULTIPLE VERSIONS OF EACH CARD EXIST
NO PRICING DUE TO SCARCITY

2004 SP Authentic Game-Dated Autographs

Nm-Mt Ex-Mt
OVERALL GAME DATED ODDS 1:288.
STATED PRINT RUN 1 SERIAL #'d SET
CL: 1/5/6/10/11/19-20/22/24-25/27/29
CL: 31/34/36/43/49-50/59-60/62/67/69
CL: 72/76/78/80/86-88
MULTIPLE VERSIONS OF EACH CARD EXIST
NO PRICING DUE TO SCARCITY

2004 SP Authentic Buybacks

Jorge Posada did not return his cards in time for pack out and those cards could be redeemed until June 4, 2007.

Nm-Mt Ex-Mt
OVERALL AUTO INSERT ODDS 1:12
PRINT RUNS B/WN 1-105 COPIES PER
NO PRICING ON QTY OF 14 OR LESS
AB1 Angel Berroa 04 VIN/70 10.00 3.00
AD1 Andre Dawson 04 SSC/50. 20.00 6.00
AKE1 Austin Kearns 03 40M/5
AKE2 Austin Kearns 03 CP/1
AKE3 Austin Kearns 03 PC/1
AKE4 Austin Kearns 03 SPx/1
AKE5 Austin Kearns 03 SS/5
AKE6 Austin Kearns 03 UDA/1
AKE7 Austin Kearns 04 DAS/1
AKE8 Austin Kearns 04 VIN/5
AK1 Al Kaline 03 SP LC/20 60.00 18.00
AK2 Al Kaline 04 SSC/70 50.00 15.00
AL1 Al Leiter 04 FP/80 15.00 4.50
AL2 Al Leiter 04 UD/60 20.00 6.00
BA1 Bobby Abreu 03 CP/63 15.00 4.50
BA2 Bobby Abreu 03 HR/53
BA3 Bobby Abreu 03 SPx/63 15.00 4.50
BA4 Bobby Abreu 03 SS/64 15.00 4.50
BA5 Bobby Abreu 03 UDA/63 15.00 4.50
BA6 Bobby Abreu 04 DAS/53 20.00 6.00
BA7 Bobby Abreu 04 FP/53 20.00 6.00
BA8 Bobby Abreu 04 UD/65 15.00 4.50
BA9 Bobby Abreu 04 VIN/53 20.00 6.00
BB1 Bret Boone 03 CP/66 40.00 12.00
BB2 Bret Boone 03 PC/15 60.00 18.00
BB3 Bret Boone 03 SPx/29 50.00 15.00
BB4 Bret Boone 03 SS/44 40.00 12.00
BB5 Bret Boone 03 UDA/63 40.00 12.00
BB6 Bret Boone 04 DAS/57 40.00 12.00
BB7 Bret Boone 04 VIN/53 40.00 12.00
BD1 Bobby Doerr 03 SP LCB/50 20.00 6.00
BD2 Bobby Doerr 04 SSC/73 15.00 4.50
BG1 Bob Gibson 04 SSC/23 40.00 12.00
BHI1 Bobby Hill 03 40M/40 12.00 3.60
BHI2 Bobby Hill 03 UDA/17 20.00 6.00
BHI3 Bobby Hill 04 FP/17 20.00 6.00
BHI4 Bobby Hill 04 UD/17 20.00 6.00
BHI5 Bobby Hill 04 VIN/34 15.00 4.50
BH1 Bo Hart 03 SPx/50 12.00 3.60
BH2 Bo Hart 04 VIN/45 12.00 3.60
BL1 Barry Larkin 03 FP/10
BR1 B.Robinson 03 SP LC/50 30.00 9.00
BR2 B.Robinson 04 SSC/70 25.00 7.50
BS1 Ben Sheets 03 40M/25 25.00 7.50
BS2 Ben Sheets 03 CP/15 30.00 9.00
BS3 Ben Sheets 03 PC/15 30.00 9.00
BS4 Ben Sheets 03 SPx/15 30.00 9.00
BS5 Ben Sheets 04 DAS/15 30.00 9.00
BS6 Ben Sheets 04 FP/15
BS7 Ben Sheets 04 UD/25 25.00 7.50
BS8 Ben Sheets 04 VIN/15 30.00 9.00
BW1 Brandon Webb 03 SPx/20 15.00 4.50
BW2 Brandon Webb 03 UD/65 10.00 3.00
BW3 Brandon Webb 03 UDA/10
BW4 Brandon Webb 04 DAS/50 12.00 3.60
BW5 Brandon Webb 04 FP/30 15.00 4.50
BW6 Brandon Webb 04 VIN/85 10.00 3.00
BZ1 Barry Zito 03 40M/30 40.00 12.00
BZ2 Barry Zito 03 CP/41 30.00 9.00
BZ3 Barry Zito 03 HR/60 30.00 9.00
BZ4 Barry Zito 03 PC/15 50.00 15.00
BZ5 Barry Zito 03 SPx/46 30.00 9.00
BZ6 Barry Zito 03 SS/63 25.00 7.50
BZ7 Barry Zito 03 UDA/40 30.00 9.00
BZ8 Barry Zito 04 FP/69 25.00 7.50
BZ9 Barry Zito 04 UD/61 25.00 7.50
BZ10 Barry Zito 04 VIN/50 30.00 9.00
CB1 Carlos Beltran 03 40M/25
CB2 Carlos Beltran 03 CP/15 60.00 18.00
CB3 Carlos Beltran 03 PC/15 60.00 18.00
CB4 Carlos Beltran 03 SPx/15
CB5 Carlos Beltran 03 SS/15 60.00 18.00
CB6 Carlos Beltran 04 DAS/15 60.00 18.00
CB7 Carlos Beltran 04 VIN/15 60.00 18.00
CD1 Carlos Delgado 03 CP/1
CD2 Carlos Delgado 03 HR/1
CD3 Carlos Delgado 03 SPx/1
CD4 Carlos Delgado 03 SS/1
CD5 C.Delgado 03 UDA/43 20.00 6.00
CD6 Carlos Delgado 04 DAS/1
CD7 Carlos Delgado 04 VIN/1
CF1 C.Fisk 03 SP LC/38 50.00 15.00
CF2 C.Fisk 03 SP LCB/55 50.00 15.00
CLL1 Cliff Lee 04 FP/40 12.00 3.60
CLL2 Cliff Lee 04 UD/50 12.00 3.60
CL1 Carlos Lee 04 FP/70 15.00 4.50
CL2 Carlos Lee 04 UD/70 15.00 4.50
CL3 Carlos Lee 04 VIN/70 15.00 4.50
CPO1 Colin Porter 03 CP/60 12.00 3.60
CPO2 Colin Porter 03 SS/10
CPO3 Colin Porter 04 FP/70 10.00 3.00
CP1 C.Patterson 03 40M/20 25.00 7.50
CP2 C.Patterson 03 PC/20 25.00 7.50
CP3 C.Patterson 03 SPx/20 25.00 7.50
CP4 C.Patterson 03 SS/20 25.00 7.50
CP5 C.Patterson 04 FP/20 25.00 7.50
CP6 C.Patterson 04 UD/20 25.00 7.50
CP7 C.Patterson 04 VIN/20 25.00 7.50
CR1 Cal Ripken 03 SSC/45 150.00 45.00
CW1 C.Wang 04 FP/26 40.00 12.00
CY1 C.Yastrzemski 04 SSC/22 80.00 24.00
CZ1 C.Zambrano 04 VIN/70 25.00 7.50
DJ1 Derek Jeter 03 40M/30 180.00 55.00
DJ2 Derek Jeter 03 CP/2
DJ3 Derek Jeter 03 HR/25 200.00 60.00
DJ4 Derek Jeter 03 PC/25 200.00 60.00
DJ5 Derek Jeter 03 SPx/2
DJ6 Derek Jeter 03 SS/30 180.00 55.00
DJ7 Derek Jeter 03 UDA/2
DJ8 Derek Jeter 04 DAS/12
DJ9 Derek Jeter 04 FP/12
DJ10 Derek Jeter 04 UD/25 200.00 60.00
DJ11 Derek Jeter 04 VIN/25 200.00 60.00
DS1 Duke Snider 04 SSC/23 40.00 12.00
DW1 D.Willis 04 DAS/70 15.00 4.50
DW2 D.Willis 04 FP/80 15.00 4.50
DW3 D.Willis 04 UD SR/45 20.00 6.00
DW4 D.Willis 04 VIN/105 15.00 4.50
DY1 Delmon Young 04 DAS/5
DY2 Delmon Young 04 FP/5
DY3 Delmon Young 04 VIN/35 40.00 12.00
EC1 Eric Chavez 03 40M/30 25.00 7.50
EC2 Eric Chavez 03 CP/3
EC3 Eric Chavez 03 HR/3
EC4 Eric Chavez 03 SPx/3
EC5 Eric Chavez 03 SS/25 25.00 7.50
EC6 Eric Chavez 04 FP/3
EC7 Eric Chavez 04 DAS/2
EC8 Eric Chavez 04 UD/3
EC9 Eric Chavez 04 VIN/3
EG1 Eric Gagne 03 40M/38 40.00 12.00
EG2 Eric Gagne 04 FP/26 50.00 15.00
EG3 Eric Gagne 04 UD/38 40.00 12.00
EG4 Eric Gagne 04 VIN/38 40.00 12.00
EM1 E.Martinez 04 DAS/70 40.00 12.00
GA1 G.Anderson 03 40M/30 25.00 7.50
GA2 G.Anderson 03 CP/16
GA3 G.Anderson 03 SPx/16
GA4 G.Anderson 03 SS/20 25.00 7.50
GA5 G.Anderson 04 DAS/16 30.00 9.00
GA6 G.Anderson 04 VIN/16 30.00 9.00
HB1 Hank Blalock 03 40M/20 25.00 7.50
HB2 Hank Blalock 03 CP/9
HB3 Hank Blalock 03 PC/9
HB4 Hank Blalock 03 SPx/9
HB5 Hank Blalock 03 SS/15 30.00 9.00
HB6 Hank Blalock 04 FP/10
HB7 Hank Blalock 04 UD/9
HB8 Hank Blalock 04 VIN/9
HK1 H.Killebrew 03 SP LC/20 60.00 18.00
HK2 Harmon Killebrew 04 SSC/3
HR1 H.Ramirez 03 40M/25 15.00 4.50
HR2 Horacio Ramirez 04 FP/5
HR3 Horacio Ramirez 04 UD/15 20.00 6.00
JB1 Josh Beckett 03 40M/21 40.00 12.00
JB2 Josh Beckett 03 CP/5
JB3 Josh Beckett 03 HR/21 40.00 12.00
JB4 Josh Beckett 03 PC/12
JB5 Josh Beckett 03 SPx/5
JB6 Josh Beckett 03 SS/21 40.00 12.00
JB7 Josh Beckett 04 VIN/5
JE1 Jim Edmonds 03 CP/25 40.00 12.00
JE2 Jim Edmonds 03 HR/15 50.00 15.00
JE3 Jim Edmonds 03 SPx/25 40.00 12.00
JE4 Jim Edmonds 03 SS/45 30.00 9.00
JE5 Jim Edmonds 03 UDA/25 40.00 12.00
JE6 Jim Edmonds 04 DAS/15 50.00 15.00
JE7 Jim Edmonds 04 FP/15 50.00 15.00
JE8 Jim Edmonds 04 UD/25 40.00 12.00
JE9 Jim Edmonds 04 VIN/15 50.00 15.00
JGE1 Jody Gerut 04 DAS/70 15.00 4.50
JGE2 Jody Gerut 04 VIN/70 15.00 4.50
JG1 Juan Gonzalez 03 40M/19 50.00 15.00
JG2 Juan Gonzalez 03 CP/19
JG3 Juan Gonzalez 03 PC/19 50.00 15.00
JG4 Juan Gonzalez 03 SS/19 50.00 15.00
JG5 Juan Gonzalez 04 FP/5
JG6 Juan Gonzalez 04 UD/19 50.00 15.00
JG7 Juan Gonzalez 04 VIN/20 40.00 12.00
JJ1 Jacque Jones 03 40M/40 20.00 6.00
JJ2 Jacque Jones 03 CP/11
JJ3 Jacque Jones 03 SPx/35 25.00 7.50
JJ4 Jacque Jones 03 SS/35 25.00 7.50
JJ5 Jacque Jones 03 UDA/11
JJ6 Jacque Jones 04 DAS/1
JJ7 Jacque Jones 04 VIN/11
JL1 Javy Lopez 03 40M/30 25.00 7.50
JL2 Javy Lopez 04 FP/18 30.00 9.00
JL3 Javy Lopez 04 UD/29 25.00 7.50
JL4 Javy Lopez 04 VIN/18 30.00 9.00
JO1 John Olerud 03 CP/50 30.00 9.00
JO2 John Olerud 03 SS/45 30.00 9.00
JO3 John Olerud 04 VIN/70 25.00 7.50
JP1 Jorge Posada 03 40M/20 EXCH
JP2 Jorge Posada 03 CP/5 EXCH
JP3 Jorge Posada 03 SPx/5 EXCH
JP4 Jorge Posada 03 SS/20 EXCH
JP5 Jorge Posada 04 FP/5 EXCH
JP6 Jorge Posada 04 UD/20 EXCH
JP7 Jorge Posada 04 VIN/20 EXCH
JP8 Jorge Posada EXCH 50.00 15.00
JR1 Jose Reyes 04 DAS/7
JS1 John Smoltz 04 FP/67 60.00 18.00
JS2 John Smoltz 04 UD/67 60.00 18.00
JS3 John Smoltz 04 VIN/70 60.00 18.00
JT1 Joe Torre 04 SSC/70 25.00 7.50
JV1 Javier Vazquez 04 DAS/70. 15.00 4.50
JV2 Javier Vazquez 04 VIN/70. 15.00 4.50
JWS1 Jae Seo 03 SS/10
JWS2 Jae Seo 04 FP/5
JWS3 Jae Seo 04 UD/15 30.00 9.00
JWS4 Jae Seo 04 VIN/15 30.00 9.00
JW1 Jer.Williams 04 UD/70 25.00 7.50
JW2 Jer.Williams 04 VIN/60 30.00 9.00
KG1 K.Grif 02 SUP Silv/45 120.00 36.00
KG2 K.Grif 02 SUP SK 92 AS/6
KG3 K.Grif 02 SUP SK Blue/19 150.00 45.00
KG4 K.Grif 03 40M Blue/20 150.00 45.00
KG5 K.Grif 03 40M Red/10
KG6 K.Grif 03 40M 92 AS/18 150.00 45.00
KG7 K.Grif 03 40M 97 AL/18 150.00 45.00
KG8 K.Grif 03 40MHR94 Blk/31 150.00 45.00
KG9 K.Grif 03 40MHR94 Blu/27 150.00 45.00
KG10 K.Grif 03 40MHR98 Sil/28 150.00 45.00
KG11 K.Grif 03 40M HR98 AS/12
KG12 K.Grif 03 40M HR98 GG/14
KG13 K.Grif 03 40M HR99 Sil/48 120.00 36.00
KG14 K.Grif 03 40M T40 Blu/35 150.00 45.00
KG15 K.Grif 03 40M T40 AL/29 120.00 36.00
KG16 K.Grif 03 GF Black/40 150.00 45.00
KG17 K.Grif 03 GF Blue/23 150.00 45.00
KG18 K.Grif 03 GF Red/10
KG19 K.Grif 03 GF 92AS/19 150.00 45.00
KG20 K.Grif 03 HR 92AS/15 150.00 45.00
KG21 K.Grif 03 HR 97AL/37 150.00 45.00
KG22 K.Grif 03 HR Red/10
KG23 K.Grif 03 MVP Blk/56 120.00 36.00
KG24 K.Grif 03 MVP Red/10
KG25 K.Grif 03 MVP GG/15 150.00 45.00
KG26 K.Grif 03 MVP GG92/1
KG27 K.Grif 03 PC Black/27 150.00 45.00
KG28 K.Grif 03 PC Blue/7
KG29 K.Grif 03 PC 92 AS/8
KG30 K.Grif 03 PB Black/15 150.00 45.00
KG31 K.Grif 03 PB Blue/11
KG32 K.Grif 03 PB 56 HR/15 150.00 45.00
KG33 K.Grif 03 PB 92 AS/9
KG34 K.Grif 03 SPA 56 HR/15 150.00 45.00
KG35 K.Grif 03 SPA 92 AS/20 150.00 45.00
KG36 K.Grif 03 SPA B93/20 150.00 45.00
KG37 K.Grif 03 SPA B93 AS MVP/1
KG38 K.Grif 03 SPA Red/5
KG39 K.Grif 03 SPx 97 AL/26. 150.00 45.00
KG40 K.Grif 03 SS 97 AL/32 150.00 45.00
KG41 K.Grif 03 UDA Red/5
KG42 K.Grif 03 VIC Blk/57 120.00 36.00
KG43 K.Grif 03 VIC 92 AS/18 150.00 45.00
KW1 Kerry Wood 03 40M/34 50.00 15.00
KW2 Kerry Wood 03 40M RWB/13
KW3 Kerry Wood 03 CP/1
KW4 Kerry Wood 03 PC/10
KW5 Kerry Wood 03 SPx/5
KW6 Kerry Wood 03 SS/34 50.00 15.00
KW7 Kerry Wood 03 UDA/5
KW8 Kerry Wood 04 DAS/1
KW9 Kerry Wood 04 VIN/5
LA1 L.Aparicio 03 SP LC/20 25.00 7.50
LA2 Luis Aparicio 04 SSC/3
LG1 L.Gonzalez 03 40M HR/25. 25.00 7.50
LG2 Luis Gonzalez 03 CP/20
LG3 Luis Gonzalez 03 HR/20 25.00 7.50
LG4 Luis Gonzalez 03 SPx/1
LG5 Luis Gonzalez 03 SS/40 20.00 6.00
LG6 Luis Gonzalez 03 UDA/1
LG7 Luis Gonzalez 04 FP/20
LG8 Luis Gonzalez 04 UD/10
LG9 Luis Gonzalez 04 VIN/20 25.00 7.50

MB1 Marlon Byrd 04 VIN/70 ..... 10.00 3.00
MC1 M.Cabrera 03 SPx/25 .... 40.00 12.00
MC2 M.Cabrera 04 DAS/20 .... 40.00 12.00
MC3 M.Cabrera 04 FP/20 .... 40.00 12.00
MC4 M.Cabrera 04 VIN/20 .... 40.00 12.00
ME1 M.Ensberg 04 FP/70 .... 10.00 3.00
ME2 M.Ensberg 04 UD/70 .... 10.00 3.00
ME3 M.Ensberg 04 VIN/70 .... 10.00 3.00
MG1 Marcus Giles 04 VIN/70 .... 15.00 4.50
MH1 Mike Hampton 03 UDA/60 12.00 3.60
MH2 Mike Hampton 04 FP/34 ... 15.00 4.50
MH3 Mike Hampton 04 UD/47 .. 12.00 3.60
MI1 Monte Irvin 03 SP LC/20 .... 25.00 7.50
MI2 Monte Irvin 04 SSC/3 ....
ML1 Mike Lowell 03 40M/19 .... 20.00 6.00
ML2 Mike Lowell 04 DAS/19 .... 20.00 6.00
ML3 Mike Lowell 04 FP/19 ...... 20.00 6.00
ML4 Mike Lowell 04 UD/19 ...... 20.00 6.00
ML5 Mike Lowell 04 VIN/19 ....
MM1 Mike Mussina 03 CP/45 ....
MM2 Mike Mussina 03 HR/20 .. 40.00 12.00
MM3 Mike Mussina 03 HR/25 .. 40.00 12.00
MM4 Mike Mussina 03 SPx/45 ....
MM5 Mike Mussina 03 SS/60 ... 30.00 9.00
MM6 Mike Mussina 03 UDA/45 30.00 9.00
MM7 Mike Mussina 04 FP/58 ... 30.00 9.00
MM8 Mike Mussina 04 UD/45 ... 30.00 9.00
MM9 Mike Mussina 04 VIN/45 . 30.00 9.00
MPI1 Mike Piazza 03 40M/5 ....
MPI2 Mike Piazza 03 CP/1 ....
MPI3 Mike Piazza 03 HR/1 ....
MPI4 Mike Piazza 03 PC/1 ....
MPI5 Mike Piazza 03 SPx/1 ....
MPI6 Mike Piazza 03 SS/1 ....
MPI7 Mike Piazza 03 UDA/1 ....
MPI8 Mike Piazza 04 DAS/1 ....
MPI9 Mike Piazza 04 FP/2 ....
MPI10 Mike Piazza 04 UD/5 ....
MPI11 Mike Piazza 04 VIN/1 ....
MP1 Mark Prior 03 40M/22 ...... 80.00 24.00
MP2 Mark Prior 03 40M RWB/5 ....
MP3 Mark Prior 03 CP/5 ....
MP4 Mark Prior 03 HR/22 .... 80.00 24.00
MP5 Mark Prior 03 PC/22 .... 80.00 24.00
MP6 Mark Prior 03 SPx/22 .... 80.00 24.00
MP7 Mark Prior 03 SS/22 .... 80.00 24.00
MP8 Mark Prior 03 UDA/10 ....
MP9 Mark Prior 04 DAS/4 ....
MP10 Mark Prior 04 FP/22 .... 80.00 24.00
MP11 Mark Prior 04 UD/22 .... 80.00 24.00
MP12 Mark Prior 04 VIN/22 ...... 80.00 24.00
MS1 M.Schmidt 03 SP LC/20. 100.00 30.00
MS2 Mike Schmidt 04 SSC/3 ....
MTE1 Miguel Tejada 03 CP/38 .. 20.00 6.00
MTE2 Miguel Tejada 03 HR/36 .. 20.00 6.00
MTE3 M.Tejada 03 SPx/30 .... 25.00 7.50
MTE4 M.Tejada 03 UDA/58 .... 20.00 6.00
MTE5 Miguel Tejada 04 DAS/37 20.00 6.00
MTE6 Miguel Tejada 04 VIN/70. 15.00 4.50
MT1 M.Teix 03 40M RWB/45 ..... 30.00 9.00
MT2 Mark Teixeira 03 CP/23 ....
MT3 Mark Teixeira 03 PC/3 ....
MT4 Mark Teixeira 03 SPx/40 ... 30.00 9.00
MT5 Mark Teixeira 03 SS/23 ...... 40.00 12.00
MT6 Mark Teixeira 03 SS/25 ...... 40.00 12.00
MT7 Mark Teixeira 03 UDA/21 .. 40.00 12.00
MT8 Mark Teixeira 04 DAS/5 ....
MT9 Mark Teixeira 04 FP/10 ....
MT10 Mark Teixeira 04 UD/23 .. 40.00 12.00
MT11 Mark Teixeira 04 VIN/23 ....
MW1 Maury Wills 04 SSC/70 .... 15.00 4.50
NR1 Nolan Ryan 03 UDA/20 ... 150.00 45.00
NR2 Nolan Ryan 04 SSC/3 ....
OD1 Octavio Dotel 04 FP/70 ..... 10.00 3.00
OD2 Octavio Dotel 04 UD/70 ..... 10.00 3.00
OD3 Octavio Dotel 04 VIN/70 .... 10.00 3.00
PB1 Pat Burrell 03 CP/50 .... 20.00 6.00
PB2 Pat Burrell 03 HR/25 .... 25.00 7.50
PB3 Pat Burrell 03 SS/50 .... 20.00 6.00
PB4 Pat Burrell 03 UDA/50 .... 20.00 6.00
PB5 Pat Burrell 04 VIN/68 .... 15.00 4.50
PL1 P.LoDuca 03 40M RWB/60 20.00 6.00
PL2 Paul Lo Duca 04 VIN/60 ..... 20.00 6.00
PL3 P.Lo Duca 04 VIN BW/20 .... 25.00 7.50
PR1 Phil Rizzuto 03 SP LC/21 .. 40.00 12.00
PR2 Phil Rizzuto 04 SSC/2 ....
RB1 Rocco Baldelli 03 40M/20 ....
RB2 Rocco Baldelli 03 PC/20 ....
RB3 Rocco Baldelli 03 SPx/15 .. 30.00 9.00
RB4 Rocco Baldelli 03 UDA/10 ....
RB5 Rocco Baldelli 04 DAS/5 ....
RB6 Rocco Baldelli 04 FP/10 ....
RB7 R.Baldelli 04 PB Red/25 ..... 25.00 7.50
RB8 R.Baldelli 04 PB Blue/25 .... 25.00 7.50
RB9 Rocco Baldelli 04 UD/5 ....
RB10 Rocco Baldelli 04 VIN/5 ....
RF1 Rollie Fingers 03 SP LC/1 ....
RF2 Rollie Fingers 03 UDA/5 ....
RF3 Rollie Fingers 04 SSC/10 ....
RHL1 Roy Halladay 03 40M/32. 15.00 4.50
RHL2 Roy Halladay 03 HR/10 ....
RHL3 Roy Halladay 04 DAS/10 ....
RHL4 Roy Halladay 04 FP/10 ....
RHL5 Roy Halladay 04 UD/32 .... 15.00 4.50
RHL6 Roy Halladay 04 VIN/1 ....
RHM1 R.Hammock 03 40M/35. 15.00 4.50
RHM2 R.Hammock 03 PC/15 .... 20.00 6.00
RHM3 R.Hammock 04 FP/7 ....
RHM4 R.Hammock 04 UD/30 .... 15.00 4.50
RHM5 R.Hammock 04 VIN/7 ....
RHR1 R.Hernandez 03 40M/55. 12.00 3.60
RHR2 R.Hernandez 03 UDA/40. 12.00 3.60
RI1 Raul Ibanez 04 FP/70 .... 10.00 3.00
RI2 Raul Ibanez 04 UD/65 .... 10.00 3.00
RI3 Raul Ibanez 04 VIN/70 .... 10.00 3.00
RK1 Ralph Kiner 03 SP LC/20 .. 40.00 12.00
RK2 Ralph Kiner 04 SSC/3 ....
RO1 Roy Oswalt 03 40M/44 ...... 20.00 6.00
RO2 Roy Oswalt 03 HR/55 .... 20.00 6.00
RO3 Roy Oswalt 03 SS/20 .... 25.00 7.50
RO4 Roy Oswalt 04 UD/52 .... 20.00 6.00
RR1 R.Roberts 03 SP LC/15 ...... 30.00 9.00
RR2 Robin Roberts 03 UDA/5 ....
RR3 Robin Roberts 04 SSC/3 ....
RW1 Rickie Weeks 03 UD/30 .... 25.00 7.50
RW2 Rickie Weeks 04 FP/15 ..... 30.00 9.00
RW3 Rickie Weeks 04 VIN/50 .... 20.00 6.00
RY1 Robin Yount 03 SP LC/20 100.00 30.00
RY2 Robin Yount 04 SSC/3 ....
SG1 Shawn Green 03 CP/2 ....
SG2 Shawn Green 03 HR/10 ....
SG3 Shawn Green 03 SS/15 ...... 30.00 9.00
SG4 Shawn Green 03 UDA/5 ....
SG5 Shawn Green 04 DAS/5 ....
SG6 Shawn Green 04 FP/15 ...... 30.00 9.00
SG7 Shawn Green 04 UD/1 ....
SG8 Shawn Green 04 VIN/15 ..... 30.00 9.00
SM1 S.Musial 03 SP LC/16 ..... 100.00 30.00
SM2 Stan Musial 03 UDA/6 ....
SM3 Stan Musial 04 SSC/1 ....
THO1 T.Hoffman 04 FP/67 .... 25.00 7.50
THO2 T.Hoffman 04 UD/51 .... 30.00 9.00
TH1 Travis Hafner 03 40M/32 .... 15.00 4.50
TH2 Travis Hafner 03 HR/10 ....
TH3 Travis Hafner 03 SPx/1 ....
TH4 Travis Hafner 03 SS/32 .... 15.00 4.50
TH5 Travis Hafner 03 UDA/5 ....
TH6 Travis Hafner 04 VIN/10 ....
TP1 Tony Perez 03 SP LC/20 ....
TP2 Tony Perez 04 SSC/3 ....
TS1 Tom Seaver 03 SP LC/15 .... 80.00 24.00
TS2 Tom Seaver 03 UDA/6 ....
TS3 Tom Seaver 04 SSC/2 ....
VG1 Vlad Guerrero 03 CP/20 ..... 50.00 15.00
VG2 Vlad Guerrero 03 HR/27 ....
VG3 Vlad Guerrero 03 SPx/34 .. 50.00 15.00
VG4 Vlad Guerrero 03 SS/27 ..... 50.00 15.00
VG5 Vlad Guerrero 03 UDA/54 . 40.00 12.00
VG6 Vlad Guerrero 04 DAS/27.. 50.00 15.00
VG7 Vlad Guerrero 04 FP/28 ...... 50.00 15.00
VG8 Vlad Guerrero 04 UD/27 ....
VG9 Vlad Guerrero 04 VIN/27 .... 50.00 15.00
VW1 Vernon Wells 03 40M/15.. 30.00 9.00
VW2 Vernon Wells 03 CP/10 ....
VW3 Vernon Wells 03 PC/10 ....
VW4 Vernon Wells 03 SPx/10 ....
VW5 Vernon Wells 03 SS/10 ....
VW6 Vernon Wells 04 DAS/10 ....
VW7 Vernon Wells 04 FP/10 ....
VW8 Vernon Wells 04 UD/10 ....
VW9 Vernon Wells 04 VIN/10 ....
WE1 Willie Eyre 03 40M/45 .... 12.00 3.60
WE2 W.Eyre 03 40M RWB/45 .... 12.00 3.60
YB1 Yogi Berra 03 SP LC/23 ..... 60.00 18.00

2004 SP Authentic Chirography

Jorge Posada and Ken Griffey Jr. did not return their cards in time for pack out and those cards could be redeemed until June 4, 2007. It is interesting to note that Griffey did return his buy-backed cards in time for inclusion in this product.

Nm-Mt Ex-Mt
STATED PRINT RUN 75 SERIAL #'d SETS
BASIC CHIRO. HAVE RED BACKGROUNDS
*DT w/NOTE: .5X TO 1.2X BASIC ......
*DT w/o NOTE: .4X TO 1X BASIC ......
DUO TONE PRINT RUN 75 SERIAL #'d SETS
MOST DT FEATURE UNIFORM # NOTATION
*BRONZE: .4X TO 1X BASIC ....
BRONZE PRINT RUN 65 SERIAL #'d SETS
*BRONZE DT w/NOTE: .5X TO 1.2X BASIC
*BRONZE DT w/o NOTE: .4X TO 1X BASIC
BRONZE DUO TONE PRINT RUN 60 #'d SETS
MOST BRONZE DT FEATURE TEAM NAMES
*SILVER: .4X TO 1X BASIC ....
SILVER PRINT RUN 60 SERIAL #'d SETS
*SILVER DT w/NOTE: .6X TO 1.5X BASIC
*SILVER DT w/o NOTE: .5X TO 1.2X BASIC
SILVER DT PRINT RUN 30 SERIAL #'d SETS
MOST SILVER DT HAVE KEY ACHIEVEMENT
OVERALL AUTO INSERT ODDS 1:12 ..
AK Austin Kearns 20.00 6.00
BA Bobby Abreu 20.00 6.00
BB Bret Boone 30.00 9.00
BH Bo Hart 12.00 3.60
BS Ben Sheets 20.00 6.00
BW Brandon Webb 12.00 3.60
BZ Barry Zito 30.00 9.00
CB Carlos Beltran 50.00 15.00
CL Cliff Lee 12.00 3.60
CP Colin Porter 12.00 3.60
CR Cal Ripken 120.00 36.00
CW Chien-Ming Wang 30.00 9.00
DE Dennis Eckersley 30.00 9.00
DJ Derek Jeter 150.00 45.00
DW Dontrelle Willis 20.00 6.00
DY Delmon Young 30.00 9.00
EC Eric Chavez 20.00 6.00
EG Eric Gagne 50.00 15.00
GA Garret Anderson 20.00 6.00
HA Robby Hammock 12.00 3.60
HB Hank Blalock 20.00 6.00
HE Runelvys Hernandez 12.00 3.60
HI Bobby Hill 12.00 3.60
HR Horacio Ramirez 12.00 3.60
HY Roy Halladay 12.00 3.60
JB Josh Beckett 30.00 9.00
JG Juan Gonzalez 30.00 9.00
JJ Jacque Jones 11 .... 20.00 6.00
JL Javy Lopez 30.00 9.00
JP Jorge Posada EXCH 30.00 9.00
JR Jose Reyes 20.00 6.00
JS Jae Weong Seo 20.00 6.00
JV Javier Vazquez 20.00 6.00
JW Jerome Williams 20.00 6.00
KG Ken Griffey Jr. EXCH 120.00 36.00
KW Kerry Wood 50.00 15.00
MC Miguel Cabrera 30.00 9.00
ML Mike Lowell 20.00 6.00
MP Mark Prior 60.00 18.00
MT Mark Teixeira 30.00 9.00
PA Corey Patterson 20.00 6.00
PI Mike Piazza 180.00 55.00
PL Paul Lo Duca 20.00 6.00
RB Rocco Baldelli 20.00 6.00
RO Roy Oswalt 20.00 6.00
RW Rickie Weeks 20.00 6.00
TH Travis Hafner 12.00 3.60
VW Vernon Wells 20.00 6.00
WE Willie Eyre 12.00 3.60

2004 SP Authentic Chirography Gold

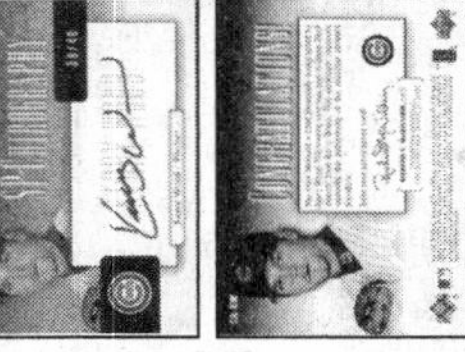

Nm-Mt Ex-Mt
*GOLD p/r 40: .5X TO 1.2X BASIC .....
STATED PRINT RUN 40 SERIAL #'d SETS
EDGAR/LEITER/SMOLTZ 75 #'d COPIES PER
*GLD DT p/r 20 w/NOTE: .6X TO 1.5X p/r 40
*GLD DT p/r20 w/o NOTE:.5X TO 1.2X p/r 40
*GOLD DT p/r 75: .4X TO 1X GOLD p/r 75
GOLD DT PRINT RUN 20 SERIAL #'d SETS
MOST GOLD DT HAVE KEY ACHIEVEMENT
OVERALL AUTO INSERT ODDS 1:12 ..
EXCHANGE DEADLINE 06/04/07
AL Al Leiter/75 .... 20.00 6.00
AR Alex Rodriguez 200.00 60.00
EM Edgar Martinez/75 .... 30.00 9.00
SM John Smoltz/75 .... 50.00 15.00

2004 SP Authentic Chirography Dual

A few cards were not ready in time for pack out and those cards could be exchanged until June 4, 2007.

Nm-Mt Ex-Mt
OVERALL AUTO INSERT ODDS 1:12 ..
STATED PRINT RUN 50 SERIAL #'d SETS
BC Bret Boone 80.00 24.00
Eric Chavez
BL Josh Beckett 80.00 24.00
Mike Lowell
BP Carlos Beltran 80.00 24.00
Corey Patterson
BT Hank Blalock 80.00 24.00
Mark Teixeira
EG Dennis Eckersley 80.00 24.00
Eric Gagne
HW Roy Halladay 60.00 18.00
Vernon Wells
JM Johnny Bench 300.00 90.00
Mike Piazza
KG Austin Kearns 120.00 36.00
Ken Griffey Jr. EXCH
PB Jorge Posada 120.00 36.00
Yogi Berra
RR Alex Rodriguez 500.00 150.00
Cal Ripken
SG Ichiro Suzuki 500.00 150.00
Ken Griffey Jr. EXCH
SM Ozzie Smith 200.00 60.00
Stan Musial
WC Dontrelle Willis 80.00 24.00
Miguel Cabrera
WJ Chien-Ming Wang 250.00 75.00
Derek Jeter
WR Kerry Wood 300.00 90.00
Nolan Ryan
WW Brandon Webb 60.00 18.00
Dontrelle Willis
YW Delmon Young 80.00 24.00
Rickie Weeks EXCH
ZC Barry Zito 80.00 24.00
Eric Chavez

2004 SP Authentic Chirography Hall of Famers

Nm-Mt Ex-Mt
STATED PRINT RUN 40 SERIAL #'d SETS
*DUO TONE: .5X TO 1.2X BASIC ....
DUO TONE PRINT RUN 25 SERIAL #'d SETS
SOME DT FEATURE HOF NOTATION ...
OVERALL AUTO INSERT ODDS 1:12 ..
AK Al Kaline 60.00 18.00
BD Bobby Doerr 25.00 7.50
BG Bob Gibson 40.00 12.00
BR B.Robinson UER B/W 40.00 12.00
CF Carlton Fisk 40.00 12.00
CY Carl Yastrzemski HOF 89 ... 100.00 30.00
DE Dennis Eckersley 40.00 12.00
DS Duke Snider 40.00 12.00
HK Harmon Killebrew 60.00 18.00
JB Johnny Bench 60.00 18.00
KP Kirby Puckett 100.00 30.00
LA Luis Aparicio Hall of Famer . 25.00 7.50
MI Monte Irvin 25.00 7.50
MS Mike Schmidt 120.00 36.00
NR Nolan Ryan 150.00 45.00
OS Ozzie Smith 100.00 30.00
PM Paul Molitor 40.00 12.00
PR Phil Rizzuto Hall of Famer ... 40.00 12.00
RK Ralph Kiner HOF 1975 .... 25.00 7.50
RR Robin Roberts Hall of Famer 40.00 12.00
RY Robin Yount 100.00 30.00
SM Stan Musial 120.00 36.00
TP Tony Perez Hall of Famer 25.00 7.50
TS Tom Seaver 40.00 12.00
YB Yogi Berra 60.00 18.00

2004 SP Authentic Chirography Quad

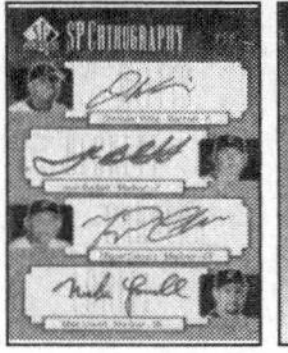
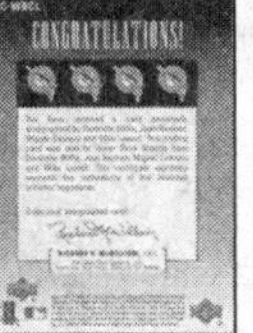

Nm-Mt Ex-Mt
OVERALL AUTO INSERT ODDS 1:12 ..
STATED PRINT RUN 10 SERIAL #'d SETS
NO PRICING DUE TO SCARCITY ....
EXCHANGE DEADLINE 06/04/07 ....
GRRS Bob Gibson ....
Nolan Ryan
Robin Roberts
Tom Seaver
RRRS Alex Rodriguez ....
Cal Ripken
Jose Reyes
Ozzie Smith
RTCW Jose Reyes ....
Mark Teixeira
Miguel Cabrera
Rickie Weeks EXCH
RYYM Cal Ripken ....
Carl Yastrzemski
Robin Yount
Stan Musial
SIRB Duke Snider ....
Monte Irvin
Nolan Ryan
Yogi Berra
WBCL Dontrelle Willis ....
Josh Beckett
Miguel Cabrera
Mike Lowell
WBWP Dontrelle Willis ....
Josh Beckett
Kerry Wood
Mark Prior
WJVP Chien-Ming Wang ....
Derek Jeter
Javier Vazquez
Jorge Posada EXCH
WPRS Kerry Wood ....
Mark Prior
Nolan Ryan
Tom Seaver
WWRW Brandon Webb ....
Dontrelle Willis
Horacio Ramirez
Jerome Williams

2004 SP Authentic Chirography Triple

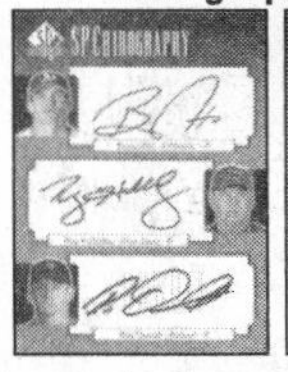
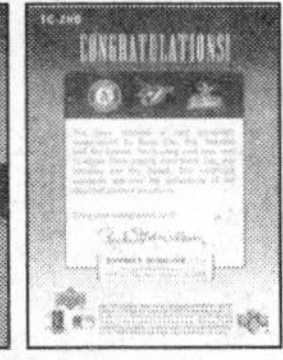

A couple of cards were not totally ready at pack-out time and those cards could be exchanged until June 4, 2007.

Nm-Mt Ex-Mt
OVERALL AUTO INSERT ODDS 1:12 ..
STATED PRINT RUN 25 SERIAL #'d SETS
BWR Josh Beckett 300.00 90.00
Kerry Wood
Nolan Ryan EXCH
FBB Carlton Fisk 400.00 120.00
Johnny Bench
Yogi Berra
GSM Bob Gibson 300.00 90.00
Ozzie Smith
Stan Musial
JVB Derek Jeter 400.00 120.00
Javier Vazquez
Yogi Berra
PRC Colin Porter 150.00 45.00
Jose Reyes
Miguel Cabrera
RBT Alex Rodriguez 300.00 90.00
Hank Blalock
Mark Teixeira
RRR Alex Rodriguez 600.00 180.00
Cal Ripken
Phil Rizzuto EXCH
SJB Ichiro Suzuki 400.00 120.00
Jacque Jones
Rocco Baldelli
WLE Chien-Ming Wang 150.00 45.00
Cliff Lee
Willie Eyre
WPB Brandon Webb 300.00 90.00
Mark Prior
Josh Beckett
YYM Carl Yastrzemski 400.00 120.00
Robin Yount
Stan Musial
ZHO Barry Zito 250.00 75.00
Roy Halladay
Roy Oswalt

2004 SP Authentic USA Signatures 445

Nm-Mt Ex-Mt
STATED PRINT RUN 445 SERIAL #'d SETS
*USA SIG 50: .6X TO 1.5X BASIC ....
USA SIG 50 PRINT RUN 50 #'d SETS
OVERALL AUTO INSERT ODDS 1:12 ..
1 Ernie Young 10.00 3.00
2 Chris Burke 15.00 4.50
3 Jesse Crain 15.00 4.50
4 Justin Duchscherer 15.00 4.50
5 J.D. Durbin 15.00 4.50
6 Gerald Laird 15.00 4.50
7 John Grabow 10.00 3.00
8 Gabe Gross 15.00 4.50
9 J.J. Hardy 15.00 4.50
10 Jeremy Reed 25.00 7.50
11 Graham Koonce 10.00 3.00
12 Mike Lamb 10.00 3.00
13 Justin Leone 15.00 4.50
14 Ryan Madson 10.00 3.00
15 Joe Mauer 40.00 12.00
16 Todd Williams 10.00 3.00
17 Horacio Ramirez 10.00 3.00
18 Mike Rouse 10.00 3.00
19 Jason Stanford 10.00 3.00
20 John Van Benschoten 15.00 4.50
21 Grady Sizemore 15.00 4.50

2001 SP Game Bat Milestone

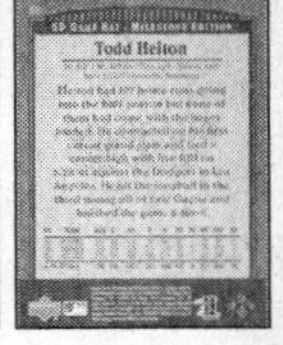

This ninety-six card set was issued in October, 2001. This set was issued in four-card packs with an SRP of $19.99 per pack. Cards numbered 91-96 were short printed and these cards were serial numbered to 500.

Nm-Mt Ex-Mt
COMP.SET w/o SP's (90) 80.00 24.00
COMMON CARD (1-90) .... 1.00 .30
COMMON BAT (91-96) 8.00 2.40
1 Troy Glaus .... 1.00 .30
2 Darin Erstad .... 1.00 .30
3 Jason Giambi .... 1.00 .30
4 Jermaine Dye .... 1.00 .30
5 Eric Chavez .... 1.00 .30
6 Carlos Delgado .... 1.00 .30
7 Raul Mondesi .... 1.00 .30
8 Shannon Stewart .... 1.00 .30
9 Greg Vaughn .... 1.00 .30
10 Aubrey Huff .... 1.00 .30
11 Juan Gonzalez .... 1.50 .45
12 Roberto Alomar .... 1.50 .45
13 Jim Thome .... 2.50 .75
14 Omar Vizquel .... 1.50 .45
15 Mike Cameron .... 1.00 .30
16 Edgar Martinez .... 1.50 .45
17 John Olerud .... 1.00 .30
18 Bret Boone .... 1.00 .30
19 Cal Ripken 8.00 2.40
20 Tony Batista .... 1.00 .30
21 Alex Rodriguez 4.00 1.20
22 Ivan Rodriguez .... 2.50 .75
23 Rafael Palmeiro .... 1.50 .45
24 Manny Ramirez .... 1.50 .45
25 Pedro Martinez .... 2.50 .75
26 Nomar Garciaparra 4.00 1.20
27 Carl Everett .... 1.00 .30
28 Mike Sweeney .... 1.00 .30
29 Neifi Perez .... 1.00 .30
30 Mark Quinn .... 1.00 .30
31 Bobby Higginson .... 1.00 .30
32 Tony Clark .... 1.00 .30
33 Doug Mientkiewicz .... 1.00 .30
34 Cristian Guzman .... 1.00 .30
35 Joe Mays .... 1.00 .30
36 David Ortiz .... 1.50 .45
37 Frank Thomas .... 2.50 .75
38 Magglio Ordonez .... 1.00 .30
39 Carlos Lee .... 1.00 .30
40 Alfonso Soriano .... 1.50 .45
41 Bernie Williams .... 1.50 .45
42 Derek Jeter 6.00 1.80
43 Roger Clemens 5.00 1.50
44 Jeff Bagwell .... 1.50 .45
45 Richard Hidalgo .... 1.00 .30
46 Moises Alou .... 1.00 .30
47 Chipper Jones .... 2.50 .75
48 Greg Maddux 4.00 1.20
49 Rafael Furcal .... 1.00 .30
50 Andruw Jones .... 1.00 .30
51 Jeromy Burnitz .... 1.00 .30
52 Geoff Jenkins .... 1.00 .30
53 Richie Sexson .... 1.00 .30
54 Edgar Renteria .... 1.00 .30
55 Mark McGwire 6.00 1.80
56 Jim Edmonds .... 1.00 .30
57 J.D. Drew .... 1.00 .30
58 Sammy Sosa 4.00 1.20

59 Fred McGriff	1.50	.45
60 Luis Gonzalez	1.00	.30
61 Randy Johnson	2.50	.75
62 Gary Sheffield	1.00	.30
63 Shawn Green	1.00	.30
64 Kevin Brown	1.00	.30
65 Vladimir Guerrero	2.50	.75
66 Jose Vidro	1.00	.30
67 Fernando Tatis	1.00	.30
68 Barry Bonds	6.00	1.80
69 Jeff Kent	1.00	.30
70 Rich Aurilia	1.00	.30
71 Preston Wilson	1.00	.30
72 Charles Johnson	1.00	.30
73 Cliff Floyd	1.00	.30
74 Mike Piazza	4.00	1.20
75 Matt Lawton	1.00	.30
76 Edgardo Alfonzo	1.00	.30
77 Tony Gwynn	3.00	.90
78 Phil Nevin	1.00	.30
79 Scott Rolen	2.50	.75
80 Pat Burrell	1.00	.30
81 Bobby Abreu	1.00	.30
82 Brian Giles	1.00	.30
83 Jason Kendall	1.00	.30
84 Aramis Ramirez	1.00	.30
85 Sean Casey	1.00	.30
86 Ken Griffey Jr.	4.00	1.20
87 Barry Larkin	1.50	.45
88 Todd Helton	1.50	.45
89 Mike Hampton	1.00	.30
90 Larry Walker	1.50	.45
91 Ichiro Suzuki BAT RC	50.00	15.00
92 Albert Pujols BAT RC	60.00	18.00
93 T. Shinjo BAT RC	10.00	3.00
94 Jack Wilson BAT RC	15.00	4.50
95 D. Mendez BAT RC	8.00	2.40
96 Junior Spivey BAT RC	10.00	3.00

2001 SP Game Bat Milestone Art of Hitting

Inserted at a rate of one in five and featured a mix of batting champions and other leading hitters who made hitting an art.

	Nm-Mt	Ex-Mt
COMPLETE SET (12)	50.00	15.00
AH1 Tony Gwynn	4.00	1.20
AH2 Manny Ramirez	2.00	.60
AH3 Todd Helton	2.00	.60
AH4 Nomar Garciaparra	5.00	1.50
AH5 Vladimir Guerrero	3.00	.90
AH6 Ichiro Suzuki	20.00	6.00
AH7 Darin Erstad	2.00	.60
AH8 Alex Rodriguez	5.00	1.50
AH9 Carlos Delgado	2.00	.60
AH10 Edgar Martinez	2.00	.60
AH11 Luis Gonzalez	2.00	.60
AH12 Barry Bonds	8.00	2.40

2001 SP Game Bat Milestone Piece of Action Autographs

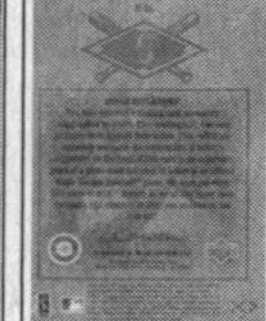

Inserted at a rate of one per 100 packs, these 13 cards feature signed cards of some of the leading players in the game. A few players were printed in lower quantities than the others and we have notated those players with both and SP and officially released print information from Upper Deck. Jose Vidro did not return his cards in time for inclusion in this product, these cards were available via exchange until October 12, 2004.

	Nm-Mt	Ex-Mt
S-AR A. Rodriguez SP/97	150.00	45.00
S-CD C. Delgado SP/97	50.00	15.00
S-GS G. Sheffield SP/194	60.00	18.00
S-IS Ichiro Suzuki SP/53	1200.00	350.00
S-JD J.D. Drew	60.00	18.00
S-JD Jermaine Dye	40.00	12.00
S-JK Jason Kendall	40.00	12.00
S-JK Jeff Kent SP/194	60.00	18.00
S-JV Jose Vidro	25.00	7.50
S-LG Luis Gonzalez	40.00	12.00
S-MT Miguel Tejada	40.00	12.00
S-PW Preston Wilson	40.00	12.00
S-RB Russell Branyan	25.00	7.50

2001 SP Game Bat Milestone Piece of Action Bound for the Hall

Randomly inserted in packs, these 16 cards feature bat clippings of players who look like they are on their way to enshriment in Cooperstown. A few players seemed to be available in larger supply, we have notated those players with an asterisk next to their name.

	Nm-Mt	Ex-Mt
BAR A.Rodriguez Rangers	15.00	4.50
BBB Barry Bonds	25.00	7.50
BCD Carlos Delgado	10.00	3.00
BCR Cal Ripken	40.00	12.00
BEM Edgar Martinez	15.00	4.50

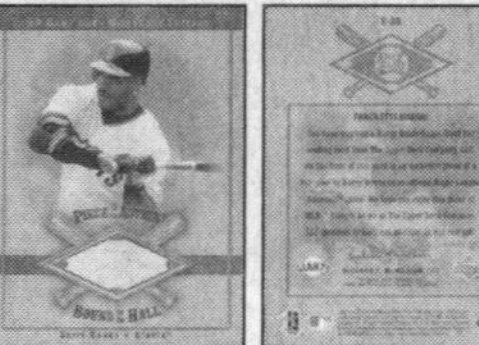

BFM Fred McGriff	15.00	4.50
BGM Greg Maddux	15.00	4.50
BIR Ivan Rodriguez	15.00	4.50
BJG Jason Giambi	10.00	3.00
BMP Mike Piazza	15.00	4.50
BRC R.Clemens SP/203	40.00	12.00
BRP Rafael Palmeiro	15.00	4.50
BSS Sammy Sosa	20.00	6.00
BTG Tony Gwynn	15.00	4.50
BKGM Ken Griffey Jr. M's*	20.00	6.00
BKGR K.Griffey Jr. Reds	20.00	6.00

2001 SP Game Bat Milestone Piece of Action International

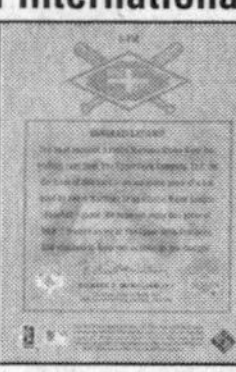

Randomly inserted into packs, these 16 cards feature bat pieces of some of the finest imports playing major league baseball. A couple of players were printed in lesser quantity then the other cards in this set and we have notated those with an SP as well as the print information. Omar Vizquel seems to have been printed in larger quantites and we have notated that with an asterisk.

	Nm-Mt	Ex-Mt
IAB Adrian Beltre	15.00	4.50
IAJ Andruw Jones	10.00	3.00
IAP Albert Pujols	50.00	15.00
ICP Chan Ho Park	10.00	3.00
IHN Hideo Nomo SP/275	15.00	4.50
IIS Ichiro Suzuki SP/203	80.00	24.00
IJG Juan Gonzalez	15.00	4.50
IJP Jorge Posada	15.00	4.50
IMO Magglio Ordonez	10.00	3.00
IMR Manny Ramirez	15.00	4.50
IMT Miguel Tejada	10.00	3.00
IOV Omar Vizquel *	10.00	3.00
IPM Pedro Martinez	15.00	4.50
IRA Roberto Alomar	15.00	4.50
IRF Rafael Furcal	10.00	3.00
ITS Tsuyoshi Shinjo	15.00	4.50

2001 SP Game Bat Milestone Piece of Action International Gold

Randomly inserted in packs, these 16 cards parallel the Piece of History International insert set. These cards are serial numbered to 35.

	Nm-Mt	Ex-Mt
I-AB Adrian Beltre	40.00	12.00
I-AJ Andruw Jones	25.00	7.50
I-AP Albert Pujols	150.00	45.00
I-CP Chan Ho Park	25.00	7.50
I-HN Hideo Nomo	40.00	12.00
I-IS Ichiro Suzuki	120.00	36.00
I-JG Juan Gonzalez	40.00	12.00
I-JP Jorge Posada	40.00	12.00
I-MO Magglio Ordonez	25.00	7.50
I-MR Manny Ramirez	40.00	12.00
I-MT Miguel Tejada	25.00	7.50
I-OV Omar Vizquel	40.00	12.00
I-PM Pedro Martinez	40.00	12.00
I-RA Roberto Alomar	40.00	12.00
I-RF Rafael Furcal	25.00	7.50
I-TS Tsuyoshi Shinjo	40.00	12.00

2001 SP Game Bat Milestone Piece of Action Milestone

Randomly inserted into packs, these 18 cards feature some of the best hitters in baseball. Each card features a bat sliver on it.

	Nm-Mt	Ex-Mt
AR A.Rodriguez Mariners	15.00	4.50
BB Barry Bonds	25.00	7.50
CHJ Chipper Jones	15.00	4.50
CR Cal Ripken	40.00	12.00
DE Darin Erstad	10.00	3.00
FT Frank Thomas *	15.00	4.50
GS Gary Sheffield	10.00	3.00
IS Ichiro Suzuki SP/203	80.00	24.00
JB Jeff Bagwell	15.00	4.50
JBU Jeromy Burnitz	10.00	3.00
JT Jim Thome	10.00	3.00
KG Ken Griffey Jr.	20.00	6.00
LG Luis Gonzalez *	10.00	3.00
MP Mike Piazza	15.00	4.50
RB Russell Branyan	10.00	3.00
RC Roger Clemens	20.00	6.00
SS Sammy Sosa *	15.00	4.50
TH Todd Helton	15.00	4.50

2001 SP Game Bat Milestone Piece of Action Milestone Gold

Randomly inserted in packs, these 16 cards parallel the Piece of History Milestone set. These cards are serial numbered to 35.

	Nm-Mt	Ex-Mt
AR Alex Rodriguez	60.00	18.00
BB Barry Bonds	80.00	24.00
CHJ Chipper Jones	40.00	12.00
CR Cal Ripken	100.00	30.00
DE Darin Erstad	25.00	7.50
FT Frank Thomas	40.00	12.00
GS Gary Sheffield	25.00	7.50
IS Ichiro Suzuki	120.00	36.00
JB Jeff Bagwell	40.00	12.00
JBU Jeromy Burnitz	25.00	7.50
JT Jim Thome	40.00	12.00
KG Ken Griffey Jr.	60.00	18.00
LG Luis Gonzalez	25.00	7.50
MP Mike Piazza	80.00	24.00
RB Russell Branyan	25.00	7.50
RC Roger Clemens	80.00	24.00
SS Sammy Sosa	60.00	18.00
TH Todd Helton	40.00	12.00

2001 SP Game Bat Milestone Piece of Action Quads

Inserted in packs at a rate of one in 50, these 15 cards feature four pieces of game-used bats from four different major league stars.

	Nm-Mt	Ex-Mt
GDBS Ken Griffey Jr. J.D. Drew Jeromy Burnitz Sammy Sosa	50.00	15.00
GGRR Ken Griffey Jr. Ken Griffey Jr. Alex Rodriguez Alex Rodriguez	80.00	24.00
GHSK Luis Gonzalez Todd Helton Gary Sheffield Jeff Kent	40.00	12.00
GRBM Tony Gwynn Cal Ripken Barry Bonds Fred McGriff	150.00	45.00
GRSB Ken Griffey Jr. Alex Rodriguez Sammy Sosa Barry Bonds	150.00	45.00
JJFM Chipper Jones Andruw Jones Rafael Furcal Greg Maddux	40.00	12.00
JVBW Chipper Jones Robin Ventura Pat Burrell Preston Wilson	40.00	12.00
OJCP Paul O'Neill David Justice Roger Clemens Jorge Posada	100.00	30.00
ONRD Paul O'Neill Hideo Nomo Cal Ripken Carlos Delgado	100.00	30.00
PWSG Kirby Puckett Dave Winfield Ozzie Smith Steve Garvey	40.00	12.00
RGGM Alex Rodriguez Troy Glaus Jason Giambi Edgar Martinez	50.00	15.00
RRPM Alex Rodriguez Ivan Rodriguez Rafael Palmeiro Ruben Mateo	50.00	15.00
SGBP Gary Sheffield Shawn Green Adrian Beltre Chan Ho Park	40.00	12.00
TDTA Frank Thomas Jermaine Dye Jim Thome Roberto Alomar	40.00	12.00
TVAL Jim Thome Omar Vizquel Roberto Alomar Kenny Lofton	40.00	12.00

2001 SP Game Bat Milestone Piece of Action Trios

Inserted in packs at a rate of one in 50, these 14 cards feature four pieces of game-used bats from three different major league stars.

	Nm-Mt	Ex-Mt
CMG Roger Clemens Greg Maddux Tom Glavine	50.00	15.00
GBM Ken Griffey Jr. Barry Bonds Fred McGriff	40.00	12.00
GRB Tony Gwynn Cal Ripken Barry Bonds	80.00	24.00
GRS Ken Griffey Jr. Alex Rodriguez Sammy Sosa	40.00	12.00
JJF Chipper Jones Andruw Jones Rafael Furcal	40.00	12.00
KGR Jason Kendall Brian Giles Aramis Ramirez	25.00	7.50
OJC Paul O'Neill David Justice Roger Clemens	50.00	15.00
OTA Rey Ordonez Frank Thomas Sandy Alomar Jr.	40.00	12.00
PWS Kirby Puckett Dave Winfield Ozzie Smith	40.00	12.00
RRP Alex Rodriguez Ivan Rodriguez Rafael Palmeiro	50.00	15.00
SFR Alfonso Soriano Rafael Furcal Aramis Ramirez	40.00	12.00
SGB Gary Sheffield Shawn Green Adrian Beltre	40.00	12.00
TVA Jim Thome Omar Vizquel Roberto Alomar	40.00	12.00
VSA Robin Ventura Tsuyoshi Shinjo Edgardo Alfonzo	40.00	12.00

2001 SP Game Bat Milestone Slugging Sensations

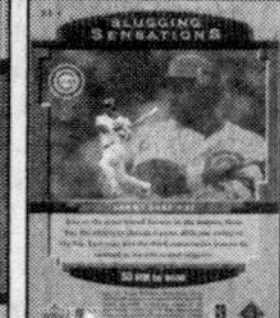

Inserted in packs at a rate of one in five, these 12 cards feature the players who hit a baseball harder and farther than other players.

	Nm-Mt	Ex-Mt
COMPLETE SET (12)	40.00	12.00
SS1 Troy Glaus	1.25	.35
SS2 Mark McGwire	8.00	2.40
SS3 Sammy Sosa	5.00	1.50
SS4 Juan Gonzalez	2.00	.60
SS5 Barry Bonds	8.00	2.40
SS6 Jeff Bagwell	2.00	.60
SS7 Jason Giambi	1.25	.35
SS8 Ivan Rodriguez	3.00	.90
SS9 Mike Piazza	5.00	1.50
SS10 Chipper Jones	3.00	.90
SS11 Ken Griffey Jr.	5.00	1.50
SS12 Gary Sheffield	1.25	.35

2001 SP Game Bat Milestone Trophy Room

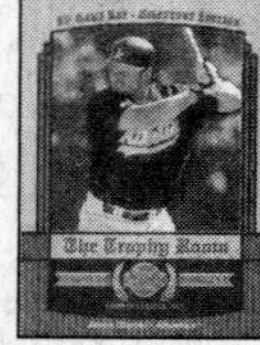
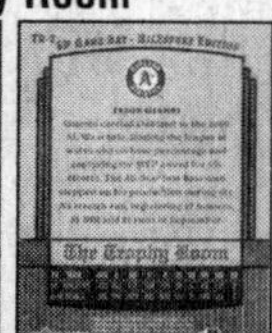

Inserted at a rate of one in ten, these six cards feature players who have won key awards during their career.

	Nm-Mt	Ex-Mt
COMPLETE SET (6)	30.00	9.00
TR1 Sammy Sosa	5.00	1.50
TR2 Jason Giambi	3.00	.90
TR3 Todd Helton	3.00	.90
TR4 Alex Rodriguez	5.00	1.50
TR5 Mark McGwire	8.00	2.40
TR6 Ken Griffey Jr.	5.00	1.50

2001 SP Game Used Edition

This 90-card set was distributed in three-card packs with a suggested retail value of $29.99 and features color action player photos. The set includes the following subset: Super Prospects (61-90).

	Nm-Mt	Ex-Mt
COMP.SET w/o SP's (60)	80.00	24.00
COMMON CARD (1-60)	1.25	.35
COMMON CARD (61-90)	8.00	2.40
1 Garret Anderson	1.25	.35
2 Troy Glaus	1.25	.35
3 Darin Erstad	1.25	.35
4 Jason Giambi	1.25	.35
5 Tim Hudson	1.25	.35
6 Johnny Damon	2.00	.60
7 Carlos Delgado	1.25	.35
8 Greg Vaughn	1.25	.35
9 Juan Gonzalez	2.00	.60
10 Roberto Alomar	2.00	.60
11 Jim Thome	3.00	.90
12 Edgar Martinez	2.00	.60
13 Cal Ripken	10.00	3.00
14 Andres Galarraga	1.25	.35
15 Alex Rodriguez	5.00	1.50
16 Rafael Palmeiro	2.00	.60
17 Ivan Rodriguez	3.00	.90
18 Manny Ramirez	2.00	.60
19 Nomar Garciaparra	5.00	1.50
20 Pedro Martinez	3.00	.90
21 Jermaine Dye	1.25	.35
22 Dean Palmer	1.25	.35
23 Matt Lawton	1.25	.35
24 Frank Thomas	3.00	.90
25 David Wells	1.25	.35
26 Magglio Ordonez	1.25	.35
27 Derek Jeter	8.00	2.40
28 Bernie Williams	2.00	.60
29 Roger Clemens	6.00	1.80
30 Jeff Bagwell	2.00	.60
31 Richard Hidalgo	1.25	.35
32 Chipper Jones	3.00	.90
33 Andruw Jones	1.25	.35
34 Greg Maddux	5.00	1.50
35 Jeffrey Hammonds	1.25	.35
36 Mark McGwire	8.00	2.40
37 Jim Edmonds	1.25	.35
38 Sammy Sosa	5.00	1.50
39 Corey Patterson	1.25	.35
40 Randy Johnson	3.00	.90
41 Luis Gonzalez	1.25	.35
42 Gary Sheffield	1.25	.35
43 Shawn Green	1.25	.35
44 Kevin Brown	1.25	.35
45 Vladimir Guerrero	3.00	.90
46 Barry Bonds	8.00	2.40
47 Jeff Kent	1.25	.35
48 Preston Wilson	1.25	.35
49 Charles Johnson	1.25	.35
50 Mike Piazza	5.00	1.50
51 Edgardo Alfonzo	1.25	.35
52 Tony Gwynn	4.00	1.20
53 Scott Rolen	3.00	.90
54 Pat Burrell	1.25	.35
55 Brian Giles	1.25	.35
56 Jason Kendall	1.25	.35
57 Ken Griffey Jr.	5.00	1.50
58 Mike Hampton	1.25	.35
59 Todd Helton	2.00	.60
60 Larry Walker	2.00	.60
61 Wilson Betemit RC	8.00	2.40
62 Travis Hafner RC	15.00	4.50
63 Ichiro Suzuki RC	60.00	18.00
64 Juan Diaz RC	8.00	2.40
65 Morgan Ensberg RC	10.00	3.00
66 Horacio Ramirez RC	10.00	3.00
67 Ricardo Rodriguez RC	8.00	2.40
68 Sean Douglass RC	8.00	2.40
69 Brandon Duckworth RC	8.00	2.40
70 Jackson Melian RC	8.00	2.40
71 Adrian Hernandez RC	8.00	2.40
72 Kyle Kessel RC	8.00	2.40
73 Jason Michaels RC	8.00	2.40
74 Esix Snead RC	8.00	2.40
75 Jason Smith RC	8.00	2.40
76 Tyler Walker RC	8.00	2.40
77 Juan Uribe RC	10.00	3.00
78 Adam Pettyjohn RC	8.00	2.40
79 Tsuyoshi Shinjo RC	10.00	3.00
80 Mike Penney RC	8.00	2.40
81 Josh Towers RC	8.00	2.40
82 Erick Almonte RC	8.00	2.40
83 Ryan Freel RC	8.00	2.40
84 Juan Pena	8.00	2.40
85 Albert Pujols RC	120.00	36.00
86 Henry Mateo RC	8.00	2.40
87 Greg Miller RC	8.00	2.40
88 Jose Mieses RC	8.00	2.40
89 Jack Wilson RC	12.00	3.60
90 Carlos Valderrama RC	8.00	2.40

2001 SP Game Used Edition Authentic Fabric

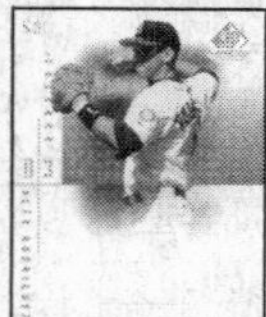

Randomly inserted one in every pack, this 82-card set features color player portraits with a swatch of a game-used jersey embedded in the card.

	Nm-Mt	Ex-Mt
AH Aubrey Huff	10.00	3.00
AJ Andruw Jones	10.00	3.00
AL Al Leiter	10.00	3.00
AP Adam Piatt	10.00	3.00
ARH A.Rodriguez Rangers	15.00	4.50
ARM A.Rodriguez Mariners*	15.00	4.50
BB Barry Bonds	25.00	7.50
BG Brian Giles SP	25.00	7.50
BL Barry Larkin	15.00	4.50
CD Carlos Delgado SP	25.00	7.50
CJ Chipper Jones	15.00	4.50
CJO Charles Johnson	10.00	3.00
CR Cal Ripken	40.00	12.00
DE Darin Erstad	10.00	3.00
DW David Wells SP	25.00	7.50
DY Dmitri Young	10.00	3.00
EA Edgardo Alfonzo	10.00	3.00
EC Eric Chavez	10.00	3.00
EM Edgar Martinez *	15.00	4.50

FM Fred McGriff 15.00 4.50
FTA Fernando Tatis 10.00 3.00
FTH Frank Thomas 15.00 4.50
GM Greg Maddux * 15.00 4.50
GS Gary Sheffield 10.00 3.00
GV Greg Vaughn 10.00 3.00
IR Ivan Rodriguez 15.00 4.50
JB Jeromy Burnitz 10.00 3.00
JCB Jose Canseco BLC
JCH Jose Canseco 15.00 4.50
JCI Jeff Cirillo 10.00 3.00
JDI Joe DiMaggio SP/50
JDR J.D. Drew * 10.00 3.00
JDY Jermaine Dye SP 25.00 7.50
JE Jim Edmonds * 10.00 3.00
JG Jason Giambi 10.00 3.00
JI Jason Isringhausen SP 25.00 7.50
JK Jason Kendall 10.00 3.00
JK Jeff Kent 10.00 3.00
JO John Olerud 10.00 3.00
JT Jim Thome 15.00 4.50
JV Jose Vidro 10.00 3.00
KB Kevin Brown 10.00 3.00
KGH Ken Griffey Jr. Reds 15.00 4.50
KGM K.Griffey Jr. Mariners* 15.00 4.50
KGR Ken Griffey Jr. Road
KL Kenny Lofton 10.00 3.00
KM Kevin Millwood 10.00 3.00
LG Luis Gonzalez 10.00 3.00
MG Mark Grace 15.00 4.50
MH Mike Hampton 10.00 3.00
MM Mickey Mantle SP/50 250.00 75.00
MO Magglio Ordonez 10.00 3.00
MR Mariano Rivera 15.00 4.50
MT Miguel Tejada 10.00 3.00
MW Matt Williams 10.00 3.00
NR Nolan Ryan Rangers SP/50 50.00 15.00
NRA Nolan Ryan Astros SP/50 50.00 15.00
PB Pat Burrell 10.00 3.00
PN Phil Nevin 10.00 3.00
PW Preston Wilson 10.00 3.00
RA Rick Ankiel * 10.00 3.00
RAL Roberto Alomar 15.00 4.50
RC Roger Clemens 15.00 4.50
RJ Randy Johnson 15.00 4.50
RM Roger Maris SP 80.00 24.00
RV Robin Ventura 10.00 3.00
SG Shawn Green 10.00 3.00
SR Scott Rolen 15.00 4.50
SSH Sammy Sosa Home 15.00 4.50
SSR Sammy Sosa Road 15.00 4.50
TB Tony Batista SP 25.00 7.50
TGL Troy Glaus 10.00 3.00
TGW Tony Gwynn * 15.00 4.50
TH Tim Hudson 10.00 3.00
THE Todd Helton 15.00 4.50
TL Terrence Long 10.00 3.00
TM Tino Martinez 15.00 4.50
TOG Tom Glavine 15.00 4.50
TRH Trevor Hoffman 10.00 3.00
TS Tom Seaver Mets SP/50 40.00 12.00
TSR Tom Seaver Reds SP/50 40.00 12.00
TZ Todd Zeile 10.00 3.00

2001 SP Game Used Edition Authentic Fabric Autographs

Randomly inserted in packs, this 21-card set is an autographed, partial parallel version of the regular insert set. Only 50 serially numbered sets were produced. An exchange card was seeded into packs for Alex Rodriguez.

Nm-Mt Ex-Mt
S-AJ Andruw Jones 50.00 15.00
S-AR A.Rodriguez EXCH 200.00 60.00
S-BB Barry Bonds 300.00 90.00
S-CD Carlos Delgado 50.00 15.00
S-CJ Chipper Jones 120.00 36.00
S-CR Cal Ripken 250.00 75.00
S-DW David Wells 50.00 15.00
S-EA Edgardo Alfonzo 50.00 15.00
S-FTH Frank Thomas 120.00 36.00
S-IR Ivan Rodriguez 120.00 36.00
S-JC Jose Canseco 120.00 36.00
S-JDR J.D. Drew 80.00 24.00
S-JG Jason Giambi 50.00 15.00
S-KG Ken Griffey Jr. 150.00 45.00
S-NR Nolan Ryan 250.00 75.00
S-RA Rick Ankiel 50.00 15.00
S-RJ Randy Johnson 120.00 36.00
S-SS Sammy Sosa 300.00 90.00
S-TGL Troy Glaus 50.00 15.00
S-TH Tim Hudson 80.00 24.00
S-TS Tom Seaver Mets

2001 SP Game Used Edition Authentic Fabric Duos

Randomly inserted in packs, this 14-card set features color photos of two players to a card with two game jersey swatches embedded in each card. Only 50 serially numbered sets were produced.

Nm-Mt Ex-Mt
B-C Barry Bonds / Jose Canseco 80.00 24.00
C-W Roger Clemens / Bernie Williams 50.00 15.00
G-R Ken Griffey Jr. / Alex Rodriguez 60.00 18.00
G-S Ken Griffey Jr. / Sammy Sosa 60.00 18.00
H-G Tim Hudson / Jason Giambi 40.00 12.00
J-J Chipper Jones / Andruw Jones 50.00 15.00
J-R Randy Johnson / Nolan Ryan 100.00 30.00
M-D Mickey Mantle / Joe DiMaggio 700.00 210.00
M-M Mickey Mantle / Roger Maris 600.00 180.00
R-R Alex Rodriguez / Ivan Rodriguez 60.00 18.00
R-S Nolan Ryan / Tom Seaver 120.00 36.00
S-G Gary Sheffield / Shawn Green 40.00 12.00
S-R Sammy Sosa / Alex Rodriguez 60.00 18.00
S-T Sammy Sosa / Frank Thomas 50.00 15.00

2001 SP Game Used Edition Authentic Fabric Trios

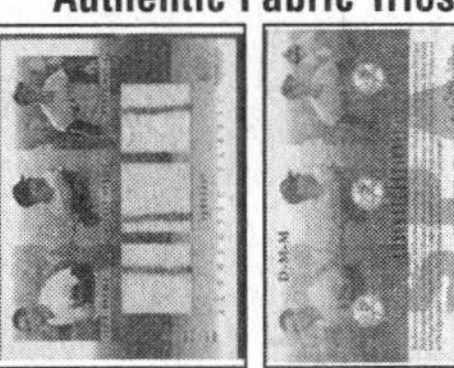

Randomly inserted in packs, this six-card set features color photos of three players to a card with three game jersey swatches embedded in each card. Only 25 serially numbered sets were produced. Due to market scarcity, no pricing is provided for these cards.

Nm-Mt Ex-Mt
D-G-S Joe DiMaggio / Ken Griffey Jr. / Sammy Sosa
D-M-M Joe DiMaggio / Mickey Mantle / Roger Maris
G-R-S Ken Griffey Jr. / Alex Rodriguez / Sammy Sosa
J-B-S Andruw Jones / Barry Bonds / Sammy Sosa
J-S-M Randy Johnson / Tom Seaver / Greg Maddux
M-J-J Greg Maddux / Chipper Jones / Andruw Jones

2004 SP Game Used Patch

The initial 119 card set was released in April, 2004. This set was issued in three-card pack with an $150 SRP which came one pack to box and 12 boxes to a case. Cards numbered 1 through 60 feature active veterans while cards 61 through 90 feature veterans in a significant number subset in which cards were issued to an important number of their career. Cards numbered 91 through 119 feature rookies and those cards were issued to a stated print run of 375 serial numbered sets. Cards 121-170 were issued as a complete sealed factory set randomly seeded into one in every 48 hobby boxes of 2004 Upper Deck Series 2 baseball in June, 2004. Please note, card 120 was never produced, thus the set is complete at 169 cards despite being checklisted from 1-170.

Nm-Mt Ex-Mt
COMP.UPDATE SET (50) 100.00 30.00
COMMON CARD 1-60 4.00 1.20
61-90 PRINT RUN B/WN 86-684 COPIES PER
COMMON CARD (91-119) 8.00 2.40
COMMON CARD (121-135) 2.50 .75
COMMON CARD (136-170) 2.50 .75
ONE UPDATE SET PER 48 UD2 HOB.BOXES
1 Miguel Cabrera 4.00 1.20
2 Alex Rodriguez Yanks 8.00 2.40
3 Edgar Renteria 4.00 1.20
4 Juan Gonzalez 4.00 1.20
5 Mike Lowell 4.00 1.20
6 Andruw Jones 4.00 1.20
7 Eric Chavez 4.00 1.20
8 Jim Edmonds 4.00 1.20
9 Mike Piazza 8.00 2.40
10 Angel Berroa 4.00 1.20
11 Eric Gagne 5.00 1.50
12 Jody Gerut 4.00 1.20
13 Orlando Cabrera 4.00 1.20
14 Austin Kearns 4.00 1.20
15 Frank Thomas 5.00 1.50
16 Johan Santana 4.00 1.20
17 Randy Johnson 5.00 1.50
18 Preston Wilson 4.00 1.20
19 Garret Anderson 4.00 1.20
20 Jorge Posada 4.00 1.20
21 Rich Harden 4.00 1.20
22 Barry Zito 4.00 1.20
23 Gary Sheffield 4.00 1.20
24 Jose Reyes 4.00 1.20
25 Roy Halladay 4.00 1.20
26 Ben Sheets 4.00 1.20
27 Geoff Jenkins 4.00 1.20
28 Josh Beckett 4.00 1.20
29 Roy Oswalt 4.00 1.20
30 Bobby Abreu 4.00 1.20
31 Hank Blalock 4.00 1.20
32 Kerry Wood 5.00 1.50
33 Ryan Klesko 4.00 1.20
34 Rafael Furcal 4.00 1.20
35 Tom Glavine 4.00 1.20
36 Kevin Brown 4.00 1.20
37 Scott Rolen 5.00 1.50
38 Bret Boone 4.00 1.20
39 Ichiro Suzuki 8.00 2.40
40 Lance Berkman 4.00 1.20
41 Tim Hudson 4.00 1.20
42 Carlos Delgado 4.00 1.20
43 Ivan Rodriguez 5.00 1.50
44 Luis Gonzalez 4.00 1.20
45 Torii Hunter 4.00 1.20
46 Carlos Lee 4.00 1.20
47 Jacque Jones 4.00 1.20
48 Manny Ramirez 4.00 1.20
49 Troy Glaus 4.00 1.20
50 Corey Patterson 4.00 1.20
51 Jason Schmidt 4.00 1.20
52 Mark Mulder 4.00 1.20
53 Vernon Wells 4.00 1.20
54 Curt Schilling 5.00 1.50
55 Javy Lopez 4.00 1.20
56 Mark Prior 5.00 1.50
57 Dontrelle Willis 4.00 1.20
58 Derek Jeter 10.00 3.00
59 Jeff Bagwell 4.00 1.20
60 Marlon Byrd 4.00 1.20
61 Rafael Palmeiro SN/500 5.00 1.50
62 Kevin Millwood SN/165 5.00 1.50
63 Greg Maddux SN/273 10.00 3.00
64 Adam Dunn SN/400 5.00 1.50
65 Richie Sexson SN/469 5.00 1.50
66 Magglio Ordonez SN/567 5.00 1.50
67 Hideo Nomo SN/236 6.00 1.80
68 Albert Pujols SN/194 12.00 3.60
69 Rocco Baldelli SN/368 5.00 1.50
70 Mark Teixeira SN/86 6.00 1.80
71 Jason Giambi SN/660 5.00 1.50
72 Alfonso Soriano SN/230 5.00 1.50
73 Roger Clemens SN/300 12.00 3.60
74 Miguel Tejada SN/359 5.00 1.50
75 Jeff Kent SN/684 5.00 1.50
76 Bernie Williams SN/342 5.00 1.50
77 Sammy Sosa SN/470 10.00 3.00
78 Mike Mussina SN/641 5.00 1.50
79 Jim Thome SN/334 6.00 1.80
80 Brian Giles SN/506 5.00 1.50
81 Shawn Green SN/234 5.00 1.50
82 Mike Sweeney SN/340 5.00 1.50
83 John Smoltz SN/262 5.00 1.50
84 Carlos Beltran SN/319 5.00 1.50
85 Todd Helton SN/384 5.00 1.50
86 Nomar Garciaparra SN/372 10.00 3.00
87 Ken Griffey Jr. SN/481 10.00 3.00
88 Chipper Jones SN/633 6.00 1.80
89 Vladimir Guerrero SN/226 6.00 1.80
90 Pedro Martinez SN/313 6.00 1.80
91 Brandon Medders RD RC 8.00 2.40
92 Colby Miller RD RC 8.00 2.40
93 Dave Crouthers RD RC 8.00 2.40
94 Dennis Sarfate RD RC 8.00 2.40
95 Donald Kelly RD RC 8.00 2.40
96 Alec Zumwalt RD RC 8.00 2.40
97 Chris Aguila RD RC 8.00 2.40
98 Greg Dobbs RD RC 8.00 2.40
99 Ian Snell RD RC 10.00 3.00
100 Jake Woods RD RC 8.00 2.40
101 Jamie Brown RD RC 8.00 2.40
102 Jason Frasor RD RC 8.00 2.40
103 Jerome Gamble RD RC 8.00 2.40
104 Jesse Harper RD RC 8.00 2.40
105 Josh Labandeira RD RC 8.00 2.40
106 Justin Hampson RD RC 8.00 2.40
107 Justin Huisman RD RC 8.00 2.40
108 Justin Leone RD RC 10.00 3.00
109 Lincoln Holdzkom RD RC 8.00 2.40
110 Mike Bumatay RD RC 8.00 2.40
111 Mike Gosling RD RC 8.00 2.40
112 Mike Johnston RD RC 8.00 2.40
113 Mike Rouse RD RC 8.00 2.40
114 Nick Regilio RD RC 8.00 2.40
115 Ryan Meaux RD RC 8.00 2.40
116 Scott Dohmann RD RC 8.00 2.40
117 Sean Henn RD RC 8.00 2.40
118 Tim Bausher RD RC 8.00 2.40
119 Tim Bittner RD RC 8.00 2.40
121 Richie Sexson 2.50 .75
122 Javier Vazquez 2.50 .75
123 Alex Rodriguez Yanks 8.00 2.40
124 Javy Lopez 2.50 .75
125 Miguel Tejada 2.50 .75
126 Bartolo Colon 2.50 .75
127 Ivan Rodriguez 5.00 1.50
128 Rafael Palmeiro 4.00 1.20
129 Kevin Brown 2.50 .75
130 Gary Sheffield 2.50 .75
131 Greg Maddux 8.00 2.40
132 Curt Schilling 5.00 1.50
133 Roger Clemens 10.00 3.00
134 Alfonso Soriano 4.00 1.20
135 Vladimir Guerrero 5.00 1.50
136 Carlos Vasquez RC 2.50 .75
137 Roman Colon RC 2.50 .75
138 William Bergolla RC 2.50 .75
139 Jason Bartlett RC 3.00 .90
140 Casey Daigle RC 2.50 .75
141 Ryan Wing RC 2.50 .75
142 Chris Saenz RC 2.50 .75
143 Edwin Moreno RC 2.50 .75
144 Shawn Hill RC 2.50 .75
145 Eddy Rodriguez RC 3.00 .90
146 Justin Knoedler RC 2.50 .75
147 Renyel Pinto RC 3.00 .90
148 Kevin Cave RC 3.00 .90
149 Carlos Hines RC 2.50 .75
150 Merkin Valdez RC 5.00 1.50
151 Tim Hamulack RC 2.50 .75
152 Hector Gimenez RC 2.50 .75
153 Mike Vento RC 3.00 .90
154 Scott Proctor RC 3.00 .90
155 Rusty Tucker RC 3.00 .90
156 Akinori Otsuka RC 2.50 .75
157 Ronny Cedeno RC 2.50 .75
158 Jose Capellan RC 8.00 2.40
159 Justin Germano RC 2.50 .75
160 Shingo Takatsu RC 6.00 1.80
161 Fernando Nieve RC 2.50 .75
162 Michael Wuertz RC 3.00 .90
163 Jerry Gil RC 2.50 .75
164 Jorge Vasquez RC 2.50 .75
165 Chad Bentz RC 2.50 .75
166 Luis A. Gonzalez RC 3.00 .90
167 Ivan Ochoa RC 2.50 .75
168 Onil Joseph RC 2.50 .75
169 Enemencio Pacheco RC 2.50 .75
170 Kazuo Matsui RC 10.00 3.00

2004 SP Game Used Patch 300 Win Club

Nm-Mt Ex-Mt
RANDOM INSERTS IN PACKS
STATED PRINT RUN 10 SERIAL #'d SETS
NO PRICING DUE TO SCARCITY
DS Don Sutton
LG Lefty Grove
NR Nolan Ryan
RC Roger Clemens
SC Steve Carlton
TS Tom Seaver
WS Warren Spahn

2004 SP Game Used Patch 300 Win Club Autograph

Nm-Mt Ex-Mt
RANDOM INSERTS IN PACKS
STATED PRINT RUN 10 SERIAL #'d SETS
NO PRICING DUE TO SCARCITY
DS Don Sutton
GP Gaylord Perry
NR Nolan Ryan Astros
NR1 Nolan Ryan Mets
NR2 Nolan Ryan Angels
NR3 Nolan Ryan Rgr
PN Phil Niekro
SC Steve Carlton
TS Tom Seaver Mets
TS1 Tom Seaver W.Sox

2004 SP Game Used Patch 3000 Hit Club

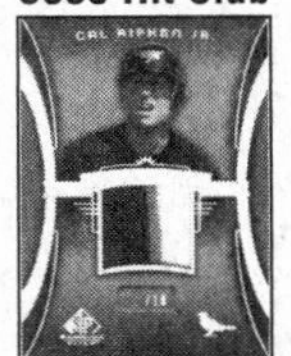

Nm-Mt Ex-Mt
RANDOM INSERTS IN PACKS
STATED PRINT RUN 10 SERIAL #'d SETS
NO PRICING DUE TO SCARCITY
CR Cal Ripken
CY Carl Yastrzemski
SM Stan Musial
TG Tony Gwynn

2004 SP Game Used Patch 3000 Hit Club Autograph

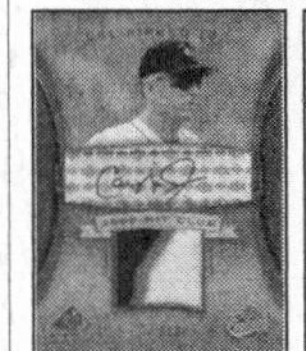

Nm-Mt Ex-Mt
RANDOM INSERTS IN PACKS
STATED PRINT RUN 10 SERIAL #'d SETS
NO PRICING DUE TO SCARCITY
CR Cal Ripken
CY Carl Yastrzemski
LB Lou Brock Cards
LB1 Lou Brock Cubs
PM Paul Molitor Brewers
PM1 Paul Molitor Jays
PM2 Paul Molitor Twins
RY Robin Yount
TG Tony Gwynn
WB Wade Boggs

2004 SP Game Used Patch 500 HR Club

Nm-Mt Ex-Mt
RANDOM INSERTS IN PACKS
STATED PRINT RUN 10 SERIAL #'d SETS
NO PRICING DUE TO SCARCITY
EM Eddie Mathews
FR Frank Robinson
HK Harmon Killebrew
MS Mike Schmidt
RP Rafael Palmeiro
SS Sammy Sosa
TW Ted Williams

2004 SP Game Used Patch 500 HR Club Autograph

Nm-Mt Ex-Mt
RANDOM INSERTS IN PACKS
STATED PRINT RUN 10 SERIAL #'d SETS
NO PRICING DUE TO SCARCITY
FR Frank Robinson Reds
FR1 Frank Robinson O's
HK Harmon Killebrew Twins
HK1 Harmon Killebrew Royals
HK2 Harmon Killebrew Senators
RP Rafael Palmeiro Rgr
RP1 Rafael Palmeiro O's

2004 SP Game Used Patch 500 HR Club Triple

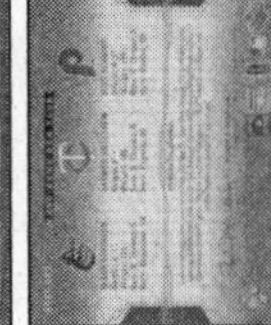

Nm-Mt Ex-Mt
RANDOM INSERTS IN PACKS
STATED PRINT RUN 10 SERIAL #'d SETS
NO PRICING DUE TO SCARCITY
MSW Eddie Mathews / Sammy Sosa / Ted Williams
RKS Frank Robinson / Harmon Killebrew / Mike Schmidt

2004 SP Game Used Patch All-Star

Nm-Mt Ex-Mt
RANDOM INSERTS IN PACKS
STATED PRINT RUN 50 SERIAL #'d SETS
AP Albert Pujols 80.00 24.00
AR Alex Rodriguez 60.00 18.00
AS Alfonso Soriano 40.00 12.00
BZ Barry Zito 25.00 7.50
CD Carlos Delgado 25.00 7.50
CJ Chipper Jones 40.00 12.00
CS Curt Schilling 40.00 12.00
DJ Derek Jeter 100.00 30.00
EC Eric Chavez 25.00 7.50
FT Frank Thomas 40.00 12.00
GS Gary Sheffield 25.00 7.50
HE Todd Helton 40.00 12.00
HN Hideo Nomo 80.00 24.00
IS Ichiro Suzuki 100.00 30.00
JG Juan Gonzalez 40.00 12.00
JT Jim Thome 40.00 12.00
KG Ken Griffey Jr. 60.00 18.00
MP Mark Prior 40.00 12.00
SS Sammy Sosa 50.00 15.00
TH Tim Hudson 25.00 7.50
VW Vernon Wells 25.00 7.50

2004 SP Game Used Patch All-Star Number

	Nm-Mt	Ex-Mt
RANDOM INSERTS IN PACKS		
PRINT RUNS B/WN 3-50 COPIES PER		
NO PRICING ON QTY OF 12 OR LESS		
AJ Andruw Jones/25	40.00	12.00
AP Andy Pettitte/42	40.00	12.00
AR Alex Rodriguez/3		
AS Alfonso Soriano/12		
BZ Barry Zito/50	25.00	7.50
CD Carlos Delgado/25	40.00	12.00
CD1 Carlos Delgado/25	40.00	12.00
CJ Chipper Jones/10		
CS Curt Schilling Sox/38	40.00	12.00
CS1 Curt Schilling D'backs/38	25.00	7.50
CY Carl Yastrzemski/8		
EC Eric Chavez/3		
EC1 Eric Chavez/3		
FT Frank Thomas/35	40.00	12.00
GA Garret Anderson/16	40.00	12.00
GM Greg Maddux Braves/31	60.00	18.00
GM1 Greg Maddux Cubs/31	60.00	18.00
GS Gary Sheffield/11		
HE Todd Helton/17	50.00	15.00
HN Hideo Nomo/10		
IR Ivan Rodriguez/7		
IS Ichiro Suzuki/50	100.00	30.00
JG Juan Gonzalez/19	50.00	15.00
JP Jorge Posada/20	50.00	15.00
JT Jim Thome/25	50.00	15.00
KG Ken Griffey Jr./30	80.00	24.00
MM Mike Mussina/35	40.00	12.00
MO Magglio Ordonez/30	25.00	7.50
MP Mark Prior/5		
MT Miguel Tejada/4		
PM Pedro Martinez/45	40.00	12.00
PU Albert Pujols/7		
RC Roger Clemens/22	80.00	24.00
RH Roy Halladay/32	25.00	7.50
RP Rafael Palmeiro/25	50.00	15.00
SG Shawn Green/15	40.00	12.00
SR Scott Rolen/27	40.00	12.00
SS Sammy Sosa Cubs/21	100.00	30.00
SS1 Sammy Sosa Sox/21	100.00	30.00
TH Tim Hudson/15	40.00	12.00
TH1 Tim Hudson/15	40.00	12.00
VW Vernon Wells/10		

2004 SP Game Used Patch All-Star Autograph

	Nm-Mt	Ex-Mt
RANDOM INSERTS IN PACKS		
STATED PRINT RUN 10 SERIAL #'d SETS		
NO PRICING DUE TO SCARCITY		

2004 SP Game Used Patch Cut Signatures

	Nm-Mt	Ex-Mt
RANDOM INSERTS IN PACKS		
PRINT RUNS B/WN 1-2 COPIES PER		
NO PRICING DUE TO SCARCITY		
AD John Adams/1		
AE Albert Einstein/1		
DE1 Dwight Eisenhower/1		
HH Herbert Hoover/1		
JA James Monroe/1		
JPG Jean Paul Getty/2		
MLK Martin Luther King Jr./1		
OW Orville Wright/1		
REL Robert E. Lee/1		
SH William Sherman/1		
TE Thomas Edison/1		

2004 SP Game Used Patch Famous Nicknames

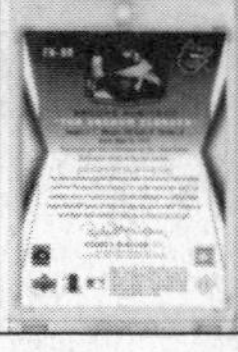

	Nm-Mt	Ex-Mt
RANDOM INSERTS IN PACKS		
PRINT RUNS B/WN 1-27 COPIES PER		
NO PRICING ON QTY OF 14 OR LESS		
AR Alex Rodriguez/10		
BM Bill Mazeroski/1		
BR Brooks Robinson/23	50.00	15.00
CR Cal Ripken Glove Down/21	200.00	60.00
CR1 Cal Ripken Glove Up/21	200.00	60.00
CY Carl Yastrzemski/23	80.00	24.00
DM Don Mattingly/14		
DS Darryl Strawberry/17	40.00	12.00
DW Dontrelle Willis/1		
ES Duke Snider/18	50.00	15.00
FT Frank Thomas/14		
GA Sparky Anderson/27	25.00	7.50
GC Gary Carter/19	40.00	12.00
HK Harmon Killebrew/22	100.00	30.00
HM Hideki Matsui/1		
IR Ivan Rodriguez/13		
JB Jeff Bagwell/13		
JD Joe DiMaggio/13		
JF Nellie Fox/19	200.00	60.00
JG Juan Gonzalez/15	50.00	15.00
JH Catfish Hunter/15	50.00	15.00
KG Ken Griffey Jr./15	120.00	36.00
LB Yogi Berra/19	100.00	30.00
LJ Chipper Jones Hand Up/10		
LJ1 Chipper Jones Arms Out/10		
MU Mike Mussina Yanks/13		
MU1 Mike Mussina O's/13		
NR Nolan Ryan Astros/27	100.00	30.00
NR1 Nolan Ryan Rgr/27	100.00	30.00
OC Orlando Cepeda/17	40.00	12.00
OS Ozzie Smith/19	80.00	24.00
PN Phil Niekro/24	40.00	12.00
RC Roger Clemens/20	80.00	24.00
RI Phil Rizzuto/13		
RJ Randy Johnson/16	50.00	15.00
RR Red Rolfe/10		
RY Robin Yount/20	80.00	24.00
SM Stan Musial/22	150.00	45.00
SS Sammy Sosa Cubs/15	120.00	36.00
SS1 Sammy Sosa Sox/15	120.00	36.00
TS Tom Seaver/20	50.00	15.00
WS Willie Stargell/21	50.00	15.00

2004 SP Game Used Patch Famous Nicknames Autograph

	Nm-Mt	Ex-Mt
RANDOM INSERTS IN PACKS		
STATED PRINT RUN 50 SERIAL #'d SETS		
AD Andre Dawson	60.00	18.00
AR Alex Rodriguez Rgr	200.00	60.00
AR1 Alex Rodriguez M's	200.00	60.00
BM Bill Mazeroski	80.00	24.00
BR Brooks Robinson	80.00	24.00
DM Don Mattingly	150.00	45.00
FT Frank Thomas	100.00	30.00
HK Harmon Killebrew	100.00	30.00
HM Hideki Matsui	400.00	120.00
JB Jeff Bagwell	120.00	36.00
JG Juan Gonzalez	80.00	24.00
KG Ken Griffey Jr.	200.00	60.00
LJ Chipper Jones Hand Up	100.00	30.00
MM Mike Mussina	80.00	24.00
NR Nolan Ryan	200.00	60.00
OS Ozzie Smith	120.00	36.00
PN Phil Niekro	60.00	18.00
RC Roger Clemens	175.00	52.50
RY Robin Yount	120.00	36.00
TS Tom Seaver	80.00	24.00
WI Dontrelle Willis	60.00	18.00

2004 SP Game Used Patch HOF Numbers

	Nm-Mt	Ex-Mt
RANDOM INSERTS IN PACKS		
PRINT RUNS B/WN 1-50 COPIES PER		
NO PRICING ON QTY OF 11 OR LESS		
AJ Andruw Jones/25	40.00	12.00
AP Albert Pujols/5		
AR Alex Rodriguez/3		
BE Johnny Bench/5		
BG Bob Gibson/45	40.00	12.00
BM Bill Mazeroski/1		
BR Brooks Robinson/5		
BW Billy Williams/26	40.00	12.00
CD Carlos Delgado/25	40.00	12.00
CH Catfish Hunter/27	40.00	12.00
CJ Chipper Jones/10		
CL Roger Clemens/22	80.00	24.00
CR Cal Ripken/8		
CS Curt Schilling/38	40.00	12.00
CY Carl Yastrzemski/8		
DD Don Drysdale/50	60.00	18.00
DJ Derek Jeter Cap/2		
DJ1 Derek Jeter No Cap/2		
DS Don Sutton/20	40.00	12.00
EC Eric Chavez/3		
EG Eric Gagne/38	40.00	12.00
EM Eddie Mathews/41	80.00	24.00
FR Frank Robinson/20	40.00	12.00
FT Frank Thomas/35	40.00	12.00
GC Gary Carter/8		
GL Tom Glavine/47	40.00	12.00
GM Greg Maddux/31	60.00	18.00
GO Juan Gonzalez Royals/19	50.00	15.00
GO1 Juan Gonzalez Rgr/19	50.00	15.00
GP Gaylord Perry/36	25.00	7.50
GS Gary Sheffield/11		
HE Todd Helton/17	50.00	15.00
HK Harmon Killebrew/3		
HN Hideo Nomo/10		
IR Ivan Rodriguez/7		
IS Ichiro Suzuki/51	100.00	30.00
JB Jeff Bagwell/5		
JC Jose Canseco/33	40.00	12.00
JD Joe DiMaggio/5		
JG Jason Giambi/25	40.00	12.00
JI Jim Thome/25	50.00	15.00
JM Joe Morgan/8		
JP Jim Palmer/22	40.00	12.00
JT Joe Torre/9		
KG Ken Griffey Jr./30	80.00	24.00
LA Luis Aparicio/11		
LD Leo Durocher/2		
MA Juan Marichal/27	40.00	12.00
MP Mike Piazza/31	60.00	18.00
MR Manny Ramirez/24	50.00	15.00
MS Mike Schmidt/20	80.00	24.00
MZ Pedro Martinez/45	40.00	12.00
NF Nellie Fox/2		
NG Nomar Garciaparra/5		
NR Nolan Ryan/34	80.00	24.00
OC Orlando Cepeda/30	25.00	7.50
OS Ozzie Smith/1		
PI Mark Prior Look Right/22	40.00	12.00
PI1 Mark Prior Look Left/22	40.00	12.00
PM Paul Molitor/4		
PR Phil Rizzuto/10		
RC Roberto Clemente/21	350.00	105.00
RF Rollie Fingers/34	25.00	7.50
RH Rickey Henderson/25	50.00	15.00
RP Rafael Palmeiro O's/25	50.00	15.00
RP1 Rafael Palmeiro Rgr/25	50.00	15.00
RY Robin Yount/19	80.00	24.00
SA Sparky Anderson/2		
SC Steve Carlton/32	25.00	7.50
SG Shawn Green/15	40.00	12.00
SM Stan Musial/6		
SN Duke Snider/4		
SR Scott Rolen/27	40.00	12.00
SS Sammy Sosa Cubs/21	100.00	30.00
SS1 Sammy Sosa Sox/21	100.00	30.00
ST Willie Stargell/8		
TG Tony Gwynn/19		
TH Tim Hudson/15	40.00	12.00
TS Tom Seaver/41	40.00	12.00
WB Wade Boggs/26	40.00	12.00
WS Warren Spahn/21	80.00	24.00
YB Yogi Berra/8		

2004 SP Game Used Patch Legendary Combo Cuts

	Nm-Mt	Ex-Mt
RANDOM INSERTS IN PACKS		
STATED PRINT RUN 1 SERIAL #'d SET		
NO PRICING DUE TO SCARCITY		
AECL Amelia Earhart Charles Lindbergh		
BRMM Babe Ruth Mickey Mantle		
ERFR Eleanor Roosevelt Franklin D.Roosevelt		
GWTJ George Washington Thomas Jefferson		
JKRK John F. Kennedy Robert Kennedy		

2004 SP Game Used Patch Legendary Fabrics

	Nm-Mt	Ex-Mt
RANDOM INSERTS IN PACKS		
PRINT RUNS B/WN 6-50 COPIES PER		
NO PRICING ON QTY OF 10 OR LESS		
BE Johnny Bench w/Mask/50	40.00	12.00
BE1 Johnny Bench Hitting/50	40.00	12.00
BG Bob Gibson/50	40.00	12.00
BR Brooks Robinson/9		
BR1 Brooks Robinson/10		
BW Billy Williams/50	25.00	7.50
CH Catfish Hunter/50	40.00	12.00
CR Cal Ripken Fielding/50	100.00	30.00
CR1 Cal Ripken Running/50	100.00	30.00
CY Carl Yastrzemski/31	60.00	18.00
EM Eddie Mathews/50	80.00	24.00
FR Frank Robinson O's/50	40.00	12.00
FR1 Frank Robinson Reds/50	40.00	12.00
GP Gaylord Perry/50	25.00	7.50
HK Harmon Killebrew Twins/50	80.00	24.00
HK1 H.Killebrew Senators/50	80.00	24.00
JC Jose Canseco/50	40.00	12.00
JM Joe Morgan Reds/50	25.00	7.50
JM1 Joe Morgan Giants/50	25.00	7.50
JP Jim Palmer/6		
JP1 Jim Palmer/7		
JT Joe Torre/50	40.00	12.00
LA Luis Aparicio/50	25.00	7.50
LD Leo Durocher/50	40.00	12.00
MS Mike Schmidt Bat Hand/50	60.00	18.00
MS1 Mike Schmidt Swing/50	60.00	18.00
NR Nolan Ryan Astros/50	60.00	18.00
NR1 Nolan Ryan Rgr/50	60.00	18.00
OC Orlando Cepeda/50	25.00	7.50
OS Ozzie Smith/50	50.00	15.00
PO Paul O'Neill/50	40.00	12.00
RF Rollie Fingers/50	25.00	7.50
RY Robin Yount Bat Up/50	50.00	15.00
RY1 Robin Yount Bat Down/50	50.00	15.00
SC Steve Carlton/50	25.00	7.50
TS Tom Seaver Mets/50	40.00	12.00
TS1 Tom Seaver Reds/50	40.00	12.00
WS W.Spahn Arms Down/50	50.00	15.00
WS1 W.Spahn Arms Up/50	50.00	15.00

2004 SP Game Used Patch Legendary Fabrics Autograph Dual

	Nm-Mt	Ex-Mt
RANDOM INSERTS IN PACKS		
PRINT RUNS B/WN 10-25 COPIES PER		
NO PRICING ON QTY OF 13 OR LESS		
AD Andre Dawson/25	100.00	30.00
BE Johnny Bench/25	150.00	45.00
BM Bill Mazeroski/10		
BR Brooks Robinson/25	120.00	36.00
BW Billy Williams/25	120.00	36.00
CR Cal Ripken/25	350.00	105.00
CY Carl Yastrzemski/17	200.00	60.00
DE Dwight Evans/25	100.00	30.00
DM Don Mattingly/25	250.00	75.00
DS Don Sutton/25	80.00	24.00
FL Fred Lynn/25	80.00	24.00
FR Frank Robinson/25	120.00	36.00
GP Gaylord Perry/25	80.00	24.00
HK Harmon Killebrew/25	150.00	45.00
JC Jose Canseco/25	150.00	45.00
JM Joe Morgan/25	100.00	30.00
JP Jim Palmer/25	100.00	30.00
JT Joe Torre Cards 25	120.00	36.00
JT1 Joe Torre Braves/25	120.00	36.00
KP Kirby Puckett/25	150.00	45.00
KP1 Kirby Puckett/12		
LA Luis Aparicio/25	80.00	24.00
LB Lou Brock/13		
NR Nolan Ryan Astros/25	250.00	75.00
NR1 Nolan Ryan Rgr/25	250.00	75.00
OC Orlando Cepeda/25	100.00	30.00
OS Ozzie Smith/25	175.00	52.50
PM Paul Molitor/25	120.00	36.00
PO Paul O'Neill/25	120.00	36.00
RC Roger Clemens/25	250.00	75.00
RF Rollie Fingers/25	100.00	30.00
RY Robin Yount Look Ahead/25	175.00	52.50
SG Steve Garvey/25	100.00	30.00
ST Darryl Strawberry/25	100.00	30.00
TG Tony Gwynn Look Left/25	150.00	45.00
TG1 Tony Gwynn Look Right/25	150.00	45.00
TS Tom Seaver Mets/25	120.00	36.00
TS1 Tom Seaver Reds/25	120.00	36.00
WB Wade Boggs Yanks/25	120.00	36.00
WB1 Wade Boggs Sox/25	120.00	36.00
WI Maury Wills/25	80.00	24.00
YO Robin Yount Look Right/25	175.00	52.50

2004 SP Game Used Patch Logo Threads

	Nm-Mt	Ex-Mt
RANDOM INSERTS IN PACKS		
STATED PRINT RUN 1 SERIAL #'d SET		
NO PRICING DUE TON SCARCITY		

2004 SP Game Used Patch Logo Threads Autograph

	Nm-Mt	Ex-Mt
RANDOM INSERTS IN PACKS		
STATED PRINT RUN 1 SERIAL #'d SET		
NO PRICING DUE TO SCARCITY		

2004 SP Game Used Patch Logo Threads Autograph Dual

	Nm-Mt	Ex-Mt
RANDOM INSERTS IN PACKS		
STATED PRINT RUN 1 SERIAL #'d SET		
NO PRICING DUE TO SCARCITY		

2004 SP Game Used Patch MLB Masters

	Nm-Mt	Ex-Mt
RANDOM INSERTS IN PACKS		
PRINT RUNS B/WN 3-50 COPIES PER		
NO PRICING ON QTY OF 12 OR LESS		
AJ Andruw Jones/25	40.00	12.00
AP Albert Pujols/5		
AR Alex Rodriguez/3		
AS Alfonso Soriano/12		
BE Josh Beckett/25	40.00	12.00
CD Carlos Delgado/25	40.00	12.00
CJ Chipper Jones/10		
CS Curt Schilling/38	40.00	12.00
EC Eric Chavez/3		
FT Frank Thomas/35	40.00	12.00
GM Greg Maddux Braves/31	60.00	18.00
GM1 Greg Maddux Cubs/31	60.00	18.00
GO Juan Gonzalez/19	50.00	15.00
GS Gary Sheffield/11		
HE Todd Helton/17	50.00	15.00
HN Hideo Nomo Dodgers/10		
HN1 Hideo Nomo Sox/10		
IR Ivan Rodriguez/7		
IS Ichiro Suzuki/50	100.00	30.00
JB Jeff Bagwell/5		
JG Jason Giambi/25	40.00	12.00
JP Jorge Posada/20	50.00	15.00
JT Jim Thome Phils/25	50.00	15.00
JT1 Jim Thome Indians/25	50.00	15.00
KG Ken Griffey Jr./30	80.00	24.00
MO Magglio Ordonez/30	25.00	7.50
MP Mark Prior/22	50.00	15.00
MR Manny Ramirez/24	50.00	15.00
PI Mike Piazza/31	60.00	18.00
PM Pedro Martinez/45	40.00	12.00
RC Roger Clemens/22	80.00	24.00
RH Roy Halladay/32	25.00	7.50
SG Shawn Green/15	40.00	12.00
SR Scott Rolen/27	40.00	12.00
SS Sammy Sosa/21	100.00	30.00
TH Tim Hudson Glove Up/15	40.00	12.00
TH1 Tim Hudson Glove Down/15	40.00	12.00
VW Vernon Wells/10		

2004 SP Game Used Patch MVP

	Nm-Mt	Ex-Mt
RANDOM INSERTS IN PACKS		
STATED PRINT RUN 25 SERIAL #'d SETS		
AR Alex Rodriguez	60.00	18.00
BR Brooks Robinson	50.00	15.00
BW Bernie Williams	50.00	15.00
CJ Chipper Jones	50.00	15.00
CR Cal Ripken	150.00	45.00
CS Curt Schilling	50.00	15.00
DJ Derek Jeter	120.00	36.00
FT Frank Thomas	50.00	15.00
GA Garret Anderson	40.00	12.00
IS Ichiro Suzuki	120.00	36.00
IV Ivan Rodriguez	50.00	15.00
JB Josh Beckett	40.00	12.00
JG Jason Giambi	40.00	12.00
KG Ken Griffey Jr.	80.00	24.00
MP Mike Piazza	60.00	18.00
MT Miguel Tejada	40.00	12.00
PM Pedro Martinez	50.00	15.00
RC Roger Clemens	80.00	24.00
RJ Randy Johnson	50.00	15.00
SS Sammy Sosa	60.00	18.00
TG Troy Glaus	40.00	12.00

2004 SP Game Used Patch Premium

	Nm-Mt	Ex-Mt
RANDOM INSERTS IN PACKS		
STATED PRINT RUN 50 SERIAL #'d SETS		
GARCIAPARRA PRINT RUN 11 #'d CARDS		
MATSUI PRINT RUN 17 #'d CARDS		
SORIANO PRINT RUN 34 #'d CARDS.		

NO PRICING ON QTY OF 11 OR LESS
AD Adam Dunn 40.00 12.00
AP Albert Pujols 80.00 24.00
AR Alex Rodriguez Rgr 60.00 18.00
AR1 A.Rodriguez Yanks Cap 80.00 24.00
AR2 A.Rodriguez Yanks Helmet 80.00 24.00
AS Alfonso Soriano/34 40.00 12.00
BE Josh Beckett 25.00 7.50
BW Bernie Williams 40.00 12.00
BZ Barry Zito 25.00 7.50
CD Carlos Delgado 25.00 7.50
CJ Chipper Jones 40.00 12.00
CS Curt Schilling Glove Up 40.00 12.00
CS1 Curt Schilling Hand in Air 40.00 12.00
DJ Derek Jeter 100.00 30.00
DW Dontrelle Willis 25.00 7.50
EC Eric Chavez 25.00 7.50
FT Frank Thomas 40.00 12.00
GM Greg Maddux Braves 50.00 15.00
GM1 Greg Maddux Cubs 50.00 15.00
GO Juan Gonzalez 40.00 12.00
HM Hideki Matsui/17 200.00 60.00
IR Ivan Rodriguez 40.00 12.00
IS Ichiro Suzuki Profile 100.00 30.00
IS1 Ichiro Suzuki Arm Out 100.00 30.00
JB Jeff Bagwell 40.00 12.00
JG Jason Giambi 25.00 7.50
JP Jorge Posada 40.00 12.00
JT Jim Thome 40.00 12.00
KB Kevin Brown 25.00 7.50
KG Ken Griffey Jr. Arm Out 60.00 18.00
KG1 K.Griffey Jr. Red Helmet 60.00 18.00
MO Magglio Ordonez 25.00 7.50
MP Mark Prior 40.00 12.00
MR Manny Ramirez 40.00 12.00
MT Miguel Tejada 25.00 7.50
NG Nomar Garciaparra/11
NR Nolan Ryan 60.00 18.00
PI Mike Piazza 50.00 15.00
PM Pedro Martinez 40.00 12.00
RC Roger Clemens 50.00 15.00
RH Roy Halladay 25.00 7.50
RI Mariano Rivera 40.00 12.00
RJ Randy Johnson 40.00 12.00
RP Rafael Palmeiro 40.00 12.00
SG Shawn Green 25.00 7.50
SR Scott Rolen 40.00 12.00
SS Sammy Sosa Swing 50.00 15.00
SS1 Sammy Sosa Bat Down 50.00 15.00
TE Mark Teixeira 25.00 7.50
TG Tom Glavine 40.00 12.00
TH Tim Hudson 25.00 7.50

2004 SP Game Used Patch Premium Update

Nm-Mt Ex-Mt
ONE PER SPGU UPDATE FACTORY SET
ONE UPDATE SET PER 48 UD2 HOB.BOXES
STATED PRINT RUN 20 SERIAL #'d SETS
V.WELLS PRINT RUN 21 SERIAL #'d CARDS
AK Austin Kearns 40.00 12.00
BA Bobby Abreu 40.00 12.00
BB Bret Boone 40.00 12.00
BC Bartolo Colon 40.00 12.00
BW Brandon Webb 40.00 12.00
CP Corey Patterson 40.00 12.00
EG Eric Gagne 80.00 24.00
EM Edgar Martinez 60.00 18.00
GA Garret Anderson 40.00 12.00
HB Hank Blalock 40.00 12.00
HN Hideo Nomo 80.00 24.00
JE Jim Edmonds 40.00 12.00
JJ Jacque Jones 40.00 12.00
JK Jeff Kent 40.00 12.00
JR Jose Reyes 40.00 12.00
KM Kevin Millwood 40.00 12.00
KW Kerry Wood 80.00 24.00
LB Lance Berkman 40.00 12.00
MM Mark Mulder 40.00 12.00
MS Mike Sweeney 40.00 12.00
RB Rocco Baldelli 40.00 12.00
RK Ryan Klesko 40.00 12.00
RO Roy Oswalt 40.00 12.00
RS Richie Sexson 40.00 12.00
TG Troy Glaus 40.00 12.00
TH Torii Hunter 40.00 12.00
VG Vladimir Guerrero 80.00 24.00
VW Vernon Wells /21 40.00 12.00

2004 SP Game Used Patch Premium Autograph

Nm-Mt Ex-Mt
RANDOM INSERTS IN PACKS
STATED PRINT RUN 50 SERIAL #'d SETS
GARCIAPARRA PRINT 33 SERIAL #'d CARDS
AK Austin Kearns 60.00 18.00
AR Alex Rodriguez 200.00 60.00
BZ Barry Zito 80.00 24.00
CD Carlos Delgado 60.00 18.00
DW Dontrelle Willis 60.00 18.00
EC Eric Chavez 60.00 18.00
EG Eric Gagne 100.00 30.00

HM Hideki Matsui 400.00 120.00
IR Ivan Rodriguez 100.00 30.00
IS Ichiro Suzuki 400.00 120.00
KB Kevin Brown 60.00 18.00
KG Ken Griffey Jr. Reds 200.00 60.00
KG1 Ken Griffey Jr. M's 200.00 60.00
MP Mark Prior 120.00 36.00
MT Miguel Tejada 60.00 18.00
NG Nomar Garciaparra/33 250.00 75.00
RC Roger Clemens 175.00 52.50
SG Shawn Green 60.00 18.00
TG Troy Glaus 60.00 18.00
TH Tim Hudson 80.00 24.00
VG Vladimir Guerrero 100.00 30.00

2004 SP Game Used Patch Significant Numbers

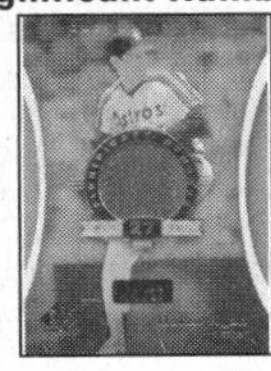

Nm-Mt Ex-Mt
RANDOM INSERTS IN PACKS
PRINT RUNS B/WN 1-27 COPIES PER
NO PRICING ON QTY OF 14 OR LESS
AJ Andruw Jones/8
AP Albert Pujols/3
AR Alex Rodriguez/10
BE Josh Beckett/3
BW Brandon Webb/1
CD Carlos Delgado/11
CJ Chipper Jones/10
CR Cal Ripken/21 200.00 60.00
CS Curt Schilling/16 50.00 15.00
CY Carl Yastrzemski/23 80.00 24.00
DJ Derek Jeter/9
DS Darryl Strawberry/17 40.00 12.00
EC Eric Chavez/6
EG Eric Gagne/5
EM Eddie Mathews/17 120.00 36.00
FT Frank Thomas/14
GM Greg Maddux/18 80.00 24.00
GO Juan Gonzalez/15 50.00 15.00
GS Gary Sheffield/16 40.00 12.00
HM Hideki Matsui/1
IS Ichiro Suzuki/3
JB Jeff Bagwell/13
JG Jason Giambi/9
KG Ken Griffey Jr./15 120.00 36.00
MM Mike Mussina/13
MP Mike Piazza/12
MR Manny Ramirez/11
MT Mark Teixeira/1
NR Nolan Ryan/27 100.00 30.00
PM Pedro Martinez/12
PO Paul O'Neill/17 50.00 15.00
PR Mark Prior/2
RC Roger Clemens/20 80.00 24.00
RF Rollie Fingers/17 40.00 12.00
RH Roy Halladay/6
RJ Randy Johnson/16 50.00 15.00
RP Rafael Palmeiro/18 50.00 15.00
SG Shawn Green/11
SN Duke Snider/18 50.00 15.00
SS Sammy Sosa/15 120.00 36.00
TG Tom Glavine/17 50.00 15.00
TS Tom Seaver/20 50.00 15.00

2004 SP Game Used Patch Significant Numbers Autograph

Nm-Mt Ex-Mt
RANDOM INSERTS IN PACKS
STATED PRINT RUN 50 SERIAL #'d SETS
BROCK PRINT RUN 16 SERIAL #'d CARDS
PUCKETT PRINT RUN 3 SERIAL #'d CARDS
NO PUCKETT PRICING DUE TO SCARCITY
AR Alex Rodriguez Rgr 200.00 60.00
AR1 Alex Rodriguez M's 200.00 60.00
BA Bobby Abreu 60.00 18.00
BG Brian Giles 60.00 18.00
BW Bernie Williams 120.00 36.00
BZ Barry Zito 80.00 24.00
CD Carlos Delgado 60.00 18.00
CJ Chipper Jones 100.00 30.00
EC Eric Chavez 60.00 18.00
EG Eric Gagne 100.00 30.00
GM Greg Maddux 150.00 45.00
HE Todd Helton 80.00 24.00
HM Hideki Matsui 400.00 120.00
JG Juan Gonzalez Royals 80.00 24.00
JG1 Juan Gonzalez Rgr 80.00 24.00
KB Kevin Brown 60.00 18.00
KG Ken Griffey Jr. Reds 200.00 60.00
KG1 Ken Griffey Jr. M's 200.00 60.00
KP Kirby Puckett/3
LB Lou Brock/16 100.00 30.00
LG Luis Gonzalez 60.00 18.00
MM Mike Mussina Yanks 80.00 24.00
MM1 Mike Mussina O's 80.00 24.00
MP Mike Piazza 250.00 75.00
MS Mike Schmidt 120.00 36.00
MT Miguel Tejada O's 60.00 18.00
MT1 Miguel Tejada A's 60.00 18.00
NR Nolan Ryan 200.00 60.00
PB Pat Burrell 60.00 18.00

PO Paul O'Neill 80.00 24.00
PR Mark Prior 120.00 36.00
RA Roberto Alomar 80.00 24.00
RB Rocco Baldelli 60.00 18.00
RF Rollie Fingers 60.00 18.00
RO Roy Oswalt Arm Up 60.00 18.00
RO1 Roy Oswalt Elbow Out 60.00 18.00
RP Rafael Palmeiro 100.00 30.00
RS Ryne Sandberg 120.00 36.00
SG Shawn Green 60.00 18.00
TG Tom Glavine 80.00 24.00
TH Tim Hudson 80.00 24.00
VG Vladimir Guerrero 100.00 30.00

2004 SP Game Used Patch Star Potential

Nm-Mt Ex-Mt
RANDOM INSERTS IN PACKS
PRINT RUNS B/WN 3-50 COPIES PER
NO PRICING ON QTY OF 12 OR LESS
AS Alfonso Soriano/12
BW Brandon Webb/50 25.00 7.50
CP Corey Patterson/20 40.00 12.00
DW0 D.Willis Arm Up/35 25.00 7.50
DW1 D.Willis Arm Down/35 25.00 7.50
EC Eric Chavez/3
HA Roy Halladay/32 25.00 7.50
HB Hank Blalock/9
IS Ichiro Suzuki/50 100.00 30.00
JB Josh Beckett/21 40.00 12.00
JR Jose Reyes/7
LB Lance Berkman/17 40.00 12.00
MM Mark Mulder/20 40.00 12.00
MP0 M.Prior Hand in Glove/22 50.00 15.00
MP1 Mark Prior Throwing/22 50.00 15.00
MT M.Teixeira Hands Back/23 40.00 12.00
MT1 M.Teixeira Hands Fwd/23 40.00 12.00
RB Rocco Baldelli/5
RH Rich Harden/40 25.00 7.50
RO Roy Oswalt/44 25.00 7.50
RS Richie Sexson/11
RW Rickie Weeks/23 40.00 12.00
TE Miguel Tejada/4
TG Troy Glaus/25 40.00 12.00
TH Tim Hudson/15 40.00 12.00
VW Vernon Wells/10

2004 SP Game Used Patch Stellar Combos Dual

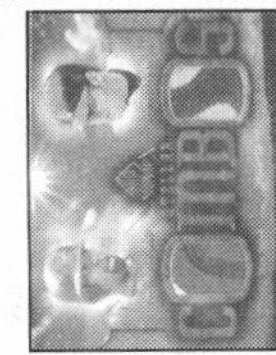

Nm-Mt Ex-Mt
RANDOM INSERTS IN PACKS
PRINT RUNS B/WN 1-25 COPIES PER
NO PRICING ON QTY OF 8 OR LESS
AD Alfonso Soriano 120.00 36.00
Derek Jeter/8
AJ Alex Rodriguez 80.00 24.00
Juan Gonzalez/25
AT Bobby Abreu 60.00 18.00
Jim Thome/25
BK Jeff Bagwell 60.00 18.00
Jeff Kent/25
BT Hank Blalock 50.00 15.00
Mark Teixeira/25
CA Joe Carter 60.00 18.00
Roberto Alomar/25
CO Roger Clemens 80.00 24.00
Roy Oswalt/25
CR Curt Schilling 60.00 18.00
Randy Johnson/25
DG Carlos Delgado 50.00 15.00
Jason Giambi/25
DK Adam Dunn 60.00 18.00
Austin Kearns/25
DL Derek Jeter
Lou Gehrig/25
GH Eric Gagne 60.00 18.00
Trevor Hoffman/25
GT Greg Maddux 100.00 30.00
Tom Glavine/25
JD Derek Jeter
Joe DiMaggio/10
JG Derek Jeter
Nomar Garciaparra/3
JJ Andruw Jones 60.00 18.00
Chipper Jones/25
KR Jerry Koosman 175.00 52.50
Nolan Ryan/25
LP Al Leiter 80.00 24.00
Mike Piazza/25
LS Fred Lynn 120.00 36.00
Ichiro Suzuki/25
MG Don Mattingly 100.00 30.00
Jason Giambi/25
MM Hideki Matsui
Mickey Mantle/1
MN Hideki Matsui
Hideo Nomo/5
MT Edgar Martinez 60.00 18.00
Frank Thomas/25
MY Paul Molitor 100.00 30.00
Robin Yount/25
NB Hideo Nomo 60.00 18.00

Kevin Brown/25
NY Alfonso Soriano 50.00 15.00
Jose Reyes/25
PC Mark Prior 100.00 30.00
Roger Clemens/25
PE Albert Pujols 120.00 36.00
Jim Edmonds/25
PM Andy Pettitte 60.00 18.00
Mike Mussina/25
PP Jorge Posada 80.00 24.00
Mike Piazza/25
PS Rafael Palmeiro 80.00 24.00
Sammy Sosa/25
RB Ivan Rodriguez 60.00 18.00
Josh Beckett/25
RG1 Manny Ramirez
Nomar Garciaparra/3
RG2 Cal Ripken 500.00 150.00
Lou Gehrig/25
RJ1 Alex Rodriguez Rgr 150.00 45.00
Derek Jeter/25
RJ2 Alex Rodriguez Yanks 200.00 60.00
Derek Jeter/25
RR Alex Rodriguez 250.00 75.00
Cal Ripken/25
RS Brooks Robinson 150.00 45.00
Mike Schmidt/25
SC Ichiro Suzuki 250.00 75.00
Ty Cobb/25
SG Duke Snider 60.00 18.00
Shawn Green/25
SJ Gary Sheffield 60.00 18.00
Randy Johnson/25
SM Curt Schilling 60.00 18.00
Pedro Martinez/25
SR Curt Schilling 100.00 30.00
Nolan Ryan/25
TO Frank Thomas 60.00 18.00
Magglio Ordonez/25
WC David Wells 80.00 24.00
Roger Clemens/25
WH Larry Walker 60.00 18.00
Todd Helton/25
WS Billy Williams 80.00 24.00
Sammy Sosa/25
WW Honus Wagner
Ted Williams/1
ZH Barry Zito 50.00 15.00
Tim Hudson/25

2004 SP Game Used Patch Team Threads Triple

Nm-Mt Ex-Mt
RANDOM INSERTS IN PACKS
STATED PRINT RUN 10 SERIAL #'d SETS
MANNY/NOMAR/PEDRO PRINT 3 #'d CARDS
A.ROD/JETER/MATSUI PRINT 5 #'d CARDS
NO PRICING DUE TO SCARCITY
AB Andruw Jones
Chipper Jones
Gary Sheffield
AD Curt Schilling
Luis Gonzalez
Randy Johnson
BR Manny Ramirez
Nomar Garciaparra
Pedro Martinez/3
CC Kerry Wood
Mark Prior
Sammy Sosa
CW Frank Thomas
Magglio Ordonez
Roberto Alomar
HA Craig Biggio
Jeff Bagwell
Lance Berkman
NY Bernie Williams
Hideki Matsui
Jason Giambi
PP Bobby Abreu
Jim Thome
Kevin Millwood
RJG Alex Rodriguez
Derek Jeter
Jason Giambi
RJM Alex Rodriguez
Derek Jeter
Hideki Matsui/5
RSB Alex Rodriguez
Gary Sheffield
Kevin Brown
SC Albert Pujols
Jim Edmonds
Scott Rolen
SM Bret Boone
Edgar Martinez
Ichiro Suzuki
WSM Honus Wagner
Ichiro Suzuki
Mickey Mantle

2004 SP Game Used Patch Triple Authentic

Nm-Mt Ex-Mt
RANDOM INSERTS IN PACKS
STATED PRINT RUN 10 SERIAL #'d SETS
A.ROD/JETER/NOMAR PRINT 3 #'d CARDS
A.ROD/MANNY/NOMAR PRINT 3 #'d CARDS
NO PRICING DUE TO SCARCITY
BTH Jeff Bagwell
Jim Thome
Todd Helton
CBG Eric Chavez
Hank Blalock
Troy Glaus
CRB Eric Chavez
Scott Rolen
Tony Batista
DGP Carlos Delgado
Jason Giambi
Rafael Palmeiro
DHW Carlos Delgado
Roy Halladay
Vernon Wells
DKG Adam Dunn
Austin Kearns
Ken Griffey Jr.
FCB Carlton Fisk
Gary Carter
Johnny Bench
GNG Eric Gagne
Hideo Nomo
Shawn Green
GPS Ken Griffey Jr.
Rafael Palmeiro
Sammy Sosa
JAB Andruw Jones
Bobby Abreu
Pat Burrell
JBJ Jason Jennings
Kevin Brown
Randy Johnson
JJP Randy Johnson
Jacque Jones
Mark Prior
KSB Adam Kennedy
Alfonso Soriano
Bret Boone
LHG Al Leiter
Mike Hampton
Tom Glavine
LTP Javy Lopez
Miguel Tejada
Rafael Palmeiro
MMG Greg Maddux
Kevin Millwood
Tom Glavine
MYW Paul Molitor
Robin Yount
Rickie Weeks
PBS Albert Pujols
Lance Berkman
Sammy Sosa
PDH Albert Pujols
Carlos Delgado
Todd Helton
PMO Mark Prior
Matt Morris
Roy Oswalt
RJG Alex Rodriguez
Derek Jeter
Nomar Garciaparra/3
RPP Ivan Rodriguez
Jorge Posada
Mike Piazza
RRG Alex Rodriguez
Manny Ramirez
Nomar Garciaparra/3
RVS Cal Ripken
Omar Vizquel
Ozzie Smith
SCM Ichiro Suzuki
Roberto Clemente
Stan Musial
SJM Alfonso Soriano
Derek Jeter
Hideki Matsui
SSB Curt Schilling
Gary Sheffield
Kevin Brown
WWP Brandon Webb
Dontrelle Willis
Mark Prior
ZMC Barry Zito
Pedro Martinez
Roger Clemens
ZMH Barry Zito
Mark Mulder
Tim Hudson

2004 SP Game Used Patch World Series

Nm-Mt Ex-Mt
RANDOM INSERTS IN PACKS
PRINT RUNS B/WN 15-50 COPIES PER
AJ Andruw Jones/50 25.00 7.50
AP Andy Pettitte/15 50.00 15.00
AS0 A.Soriano Hands on Bat/15 50.00 15.00
AS1 A.Soriano Hands Apart/15 50.00 15.00
BL Barry Larkin/50 40.00 12.00
BW Bernie Williams/50 40.00 12.00
CA Jose Canseco/50 40.00 12.00
CJ Chipper Jones/50 40.00 12.00
CS Curt Schilling D'backs/50 25.00 7.50
CS1 Curt Schilling Sox/50 40.00 12.00
CY Carl Yastrzemski/31 60.00 18.00
DW Dontrelle Willis/50 25.00 7.50
GA Garret Anderson/50 25.00 7.50
GL Troy Glaus Run/50 25.00 7.50

GL1 Troy Glaus Walk/50 .... 25.00 7.50
GM Greg Maddux Arm Up/50 ... 50.00 15.00
GM1 Greg Maddux Cubs/50 ..... 50.00 15.00
GM2 G.Maddux Glove Out/50 ... 50.00 15.00
HM Hideki Matsui/17 .... 200.00 60.00
IR Ivan Rodriguez/50 .... 40.00 12.00
JB Josh Beckett Leaning/50...... 25.00 7.50
JB1 Josh Beckett Leg Kick/50... 25.00 7.50
JE Derek Jeter Gray/50 .... 100.00 30.00
JE1 Derek Jeter Stripes/50 ..... 100.00 30.00
JM Joe Morgan/50................... 25.00 7.50
JP Jorge Posada/50................ 40.00 12.00
JT Jim Thome Indians/50 .... 40.00 12.00
JT1 Jim Thome Phils/50........... 40.00 12.00
KB Kevin Brown/50.................. 25.00 7.50
MM Mike Mussina Yanks/50...... 40.00 12.00
MM1 Mike Mussina O's/43........ 40.00 12.00
MP Mike Piazza Mets/50.......... 50.00 15.00
MP1 Mike Piazza Dodgers/50 ... 50.00 15.00
MR Mariano Rivera/50 .... 40.00 12.00
MS Mike Schmidt/50 .... 60.00 18.00
PM Paul Molitor/50.................. 40.00 12.00
PO Paul O'Neill/50 .... 40.00 12.00
RC Roger Clemens/50.............. 50.00 15.00
RF Rollie Fingers/50 .... 40.00 12.00
RJ Randy Johnson/50.............. 40.00 12.00
TG Tom Glavine/50.................. 40.00 12.00

2004 SP Game Used Patch World Series Autograph Dual

Nm-Mt Ex-Mt
RANDOM INSERTS IN PACKS
STATED PRINT RUN 1 SERIAL #'d SET
NO PRICING DUE TO SCARCITY ....

2001 SP Legendary Cuts

The SP Lengendary Cuts product was released in October, 2001 and featured a 90-card base set. Each pack contained four cards and carried a suggested retail price of $9.99.

Nm-Mt Ex-Mt
COMPLETE SET (90)................ 25.00 7.50
1 Al Simmons .... .30 .09
2 Jimmie Foxx.............................. .75 .23
3 Mickey Cochrane .... .50 .15
4 Phil Niekro .... .30 .09
5 Eddie Mathews.......................... .75 .23
6 Gary Matthews.......................... .30 .09
7 Hank Aaron .... 1.50 .45
8 Joe Adcock .... .30 .09
9 Warren Spahn .... .50 .15
10 George Sisler .... .30 .09
11 Stan Musial.............................. 1.25 .35
12 Dizzy Dean .... .75 .23
13 Frankie Frisch.......................... .30 .09
14 Harvey Haddix.......................... .30 .09
15 Johnny Mize............................. .50 .15
16 Ken Boyer .... .30 .09
17 Rogers Hornsby........................ .75 .23
18 Cap Anson .... .75 .23
19 Andre Dawson .... .30 .09
20 Billy Williams .... .30 .09
21 Billy Herman .... .30 .09
22 Hack Wilson............................. .50 .15
23 Ron Santo .... .50 .15
24 Ryne Sandberg .... 1.25 .35
25 Ernie Banks .... .75 .23
26 Burleigh Grimes .... .30 .09
27 Don Drysdale .... .75 .23
28 Gil Hodges .... .75 .23
29 Jackie Robinson....................... .75 .23
30 Tommy Lasorda .... .30 .09
31 Pee Wee Reese .... .75 .23
32 Roy Campanella .... .75 .23
33 Tommy Davis .... .30 .09
34 Branch Rickey.......................... .30 .09
35 Leo Durocher .... .50 .15
36 Walt Alston .... .30 .09
37 Bill Terry................................... .30 .09
38 Carl Hubbell .... .50 .15
39 Eddie Stanky .... .30 .09
40 George Kelly............................. .30 .09
41 Mel Ott .... .75 .23
42 Juan Marichal .... .30 .09
43 Rube Marquard......................... .30 .09
44 Travis Jackson .... .30 .09
45 Bob Feller................................. .30 .09
46 Earl Averill................................ .30 .09
47 Elmer Flick .... .30 .09
48 Ken Keltner............................... .30 .09
49 Lou Boudreau .... .50 .15
50 Early Wynn............................... .50 .15
51 Satchel Paige........................... .75 .23
52 Ron Hunt .... .30 .09
53 Tom Seaver.............................. .50 .15
54 Richie Ashburn .... .50 .15
55 Mike Schmidt........................... 1.50 .45
56 Honus Wagner......................... 1.00 .30
57 Lloyd Waner............................. .50 .15
58 Max Carey................................ .30 .09
59 Paul Waner .... .50 .15
60 Roberto Clemente .... 2.00 .60
61 Nolan Ryan .... 2.00 .60
62 Bobby Doerr............................. .50 .15
63 Carlton Fisk.............................. .50 .15
64 Joe Cronin .... .30 .09
65 Joe Wood................................. .50 .15
66 Tony Conigliaro .... .50 .15
67 Edd Roush .... .30 .09
68 Johnny VanderMeer................. .30 .09
69 Walter Johnson........................ .75 .23
70 Charlie Gehringer .... .30 .09
71 Al Kaline.................................. .75 .23
72 Ty Cobb.................................. 1.25 .35
73 Tony Oliva .... .30 .09
74 Luke Appling .... .30 .09
75 Minnie Minoso .... .30 .09
76 Nellie Fox .... .50 .15
77 Joe Jackson .... 1.50 .45
78 Babe Ruth .... 2.50 .75
79 Bill Dickey .... .50 .15
80 Elston Howard .... .50 .15
81 Joe DiMaggio .... 1.50 .45
82 Lefty Gomez .... .75 .23
83 Lou Gehrig .... 1.50 .45
84 Mickey Mantle .... 3.00 .90
85 Reggie Jackson .... .50 .15
86 Roger Maris .... .75 .23
87 Whitey Ford .... .50 .15
88 Waite Hoyt .... .30 .09
89 Yogi Berra .... .75 .23
90 Casey Stengel .... .75 .23

2001 SP Legendary Cuts Autographs

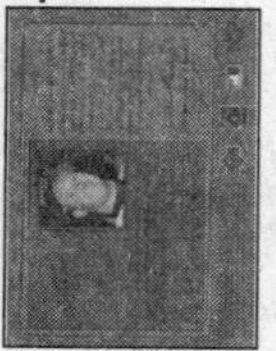

Randomly inserted into packs at a rate of one in 252 (a.k.a. - one per case), this 85-card set features more than 3,300 autographs of deceased legends that were cut off of checks, contracts, letters, etc that Upper Deck purchased on the secondary market. The card backs carry the players initials as numbering. Cards with a print run of less than 25 are not priced due to scarcity. A couple of players: Joe DiMaggio and Ted Lyons were printed to different quantities.

Nm-Mt Ex-Mt
C-BD Bill Dickey/28................ 500.00 150.00
C-BG Burleigh Grimes/18..........
C-BHA Bucky Harris/10.............
C-BHE Billy Herman/88 .... 150.00 45.00
C-BL Bob Lemon/23.................
C-BM Bob Meusel/23...............
C-BRI Branch Rickey/16...........
C-BRU Babe Ruth/7 ....
C-BS Bob Shawkey/39 .... 250.00 75.00
C-BT Bill Terry/184.................. 250.00 75.00
C-BW Bucky Walters/13...........
C-CA Cap Anson/2 ....
C-CH Carl Hubbell/30.............. 600.00 180.00
C-CK Charlie Keller/16.............
C-CS Casey Stengel/10 ....
C-DDE Dizzy Dean/56............. 900.00 275.00
C-DDR Don Drysdale/12 ....
C-EA Earl Averill/189.............. 120.00 36.00
C-EB Ed Barrow/16 ....
C-EF Elmer Flick/22.................
C-EL Eddie Lopat/22 ....
C-ER Edd Roush/83 .... 150.00 45.00
C-FF Ford Frick/21...................
C-FF Frankie Frisch/3 ....
C-FL Freddy Lindstrom/2 ....
C-GA Grover Alexander/1 ....
C-GH Gabby Hartnett/32 .... 400.00 120.00
C-GH Gil Hodges/6...................
C-GK George Kelly/52 .... 200.00 60.00
C-GS George Selkirk/15 ....
C-GS George Sisler/1 ....
C-HH Harvey Haddix/4 ....
C-HH Harry Hooper/14..............
C-HM Heinie Manush/50.......... 350.00 105.00
C-HW Honus Wagner/24...........
C-HW Hack Wilson/4 ....
C-JC Jocko Conlan/26............. 500.00 150.00
C-JC Joe Cronin/12 ....
C-JD1 Joe DiMaggio/25 ....
C-JD2 Joe DiMaggio/50........... 500.00 150.00
C-JD3 Joe DiMaggio/150......... 500.00 150.00
C-JD4 Joe DiMaggio/275......... 400.00 120.00
C-JF Jimmie Foxx/16 ....
C-JJ Judy Johnson/9 ....
C-JM Joe Medwick/18 ....
C-JMC Joe McCarthy/40 .... 500.00 150.00
C-JMI Johnny Mize/84 .... 300.00 90.00
C-JR Jackie Robinson/147.... 1200.00 350.00
C-JS Joe Sewell/55................. 300.00 90.00
C-JW Joe Wood/43................. 600.00 180.00
C-KC Kiki Cuyler/6...................
C-KK Ken Keltner/11 ....
C-KL Kenesaw Landis/4 ....
C-LA Luke Appling/45 .... 300.00 90.00
C-LD Leo Durocher/45 .... 400.00 120.00
C-LG Lefty Grove/34 .... 500.00 150.00
C-LGE Lou Gehrig/7 ....
C-LGO Lefty Gomez/85 .... 300.00 90.00
C-LW Lloyd Waner/217 .... 175.00 52.50
C-MC Max Carey/73 .... 250.00 75.00
C-MK Mark Koenig/30............. 400.00 120.00
C-MM Mickey Mantle/8 ....
C-MO Mel Ott/8 ....
C-NF Nellie Fox/9 ....
C-PW Paul Waner/4 ....
C-RC Roberto Clemente/4..........
C-RF Rick Ferrell/8...................
C-RH Rogers Hornsby/4 ....
C-ROM Roger Maris/73 .... 1500.00 450.00
C-RP R.Peckinpaugh/45......... 250.00 75.00
C-RR Red Ruffing/5 ....
C-RS Rip Sewell/39................ 300.00 90.00
C-RUM Rube Marquard/23 ....
C-SC Stanley Coveleski/42 ...... 250.00 75.00
C-SM Sal Maglie/19 ....
C-SP Satchel Paige/36 .... 2000.00 600.00
C-TC Ty Cobb/24 ....
C-TJ Travis Jackson/35........... 300.00 90.00
C-TL1 Ted Lyons/2 ....
C-TL2 Ted Lyons/59 .... 300.00 90.00
C-VM J. VanderMeer/65.......... 250.00 75.00
C-VR Vic Raschi/26............... 500.00 150.00
C-WA Walt Alston/34 .... 400.00 120.00
C-WG Warren Giles/10..............
C-WH Waite Hoyt/38............... 400.00 120.00
C-WJ Walter Johnson/113 .... 1500.00 450.00

2001 SP Legendary Cuts Debut Game Bat

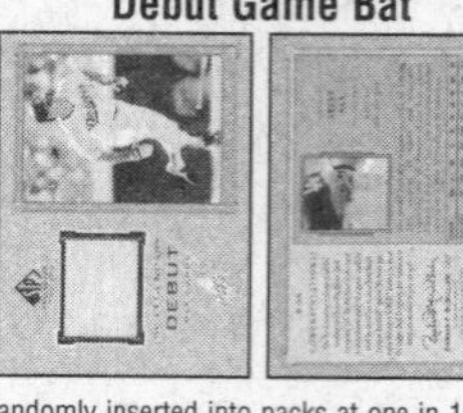

Randomly inserted into packs at one in 18, this 35-card set features the first game-used pieces of bat cards for each player. Card backs carry the player's initials as numbering. Cards with a perceived larger supply carry an asterisk and all short-print cards carry an SP designation.

Nm-Mt Ex-Mt
B-AT Alan Trammell * 10.00 3.00
B-BB Bobby Bonds 10.00 3.00
B-BF Bill Freehan.................... 10.00 3.00
B-GL Greg Luzinski 10.00 3.00
B-LW Lou Whitaker................. 10.00 3.00
B-SS Steve Sax * 10.00 3.00
B-SY Steve Yeager 10.00 3.00
B-WH Willie Horton................. 10.00 3.00
B-WP Wes Parker * 10.00 3.00
D-BB Bill Buckner * 10.00 3.00
D-BD Bobby Doerr SP............. 25.00 7.50
D-BF Bob Feller SP 25.00 7.50
D-BH Billy Herman SP 25.00 7.50
D-BM Bill Mazeroski 15.00 4.50
D-BR B.Richardson SP 25.00 7.50
D-CG Charlie Gehringer........... 25.00 7.50
D-EH Elston Howard SP.......... 25.00 7.50
D-ES Eddie Stanky 10.00 3.00
D-FF Frankie Frisch SP........... 25.00 7.50
D-GM Gary Matthews 10.00 3.00
D-GS George Sisler................ 25.00 7.50
D-HW Hack Wilson SP............ 60.00 18.00
D-JA Joe Adcock SP 25.00 7.50
D-JC Joe Cronin..................... 15.00 4.50
D-JJ Joe Jackson.................. 200.00 60.00
D-KB Ken Boyer SP................ 25.00 7.50
D-LA Luke Appling SP 40.00 12.00
D-LB Lou Boudreau 15.00 4.50
D-MC Mickey Cochrane 40.00 12.00
D-MM Minnie Minoso SP 25.00 7.50
D-PW Paul Waner SP............. 50.00 15.00
D-RA Richie Ashburn SP 40.00 12.00
D-RH Ron Hunt...................... 10.00 3.00
D-TC Tony Conigliaro SP 25.00 7.50
D-TO Tony Oliva 10.00 3.00

2001 SP Legendary Cuts Game Bat

Randomly inserted into packs at one in 18, this 36-card set features game-used pieces of bat cards for each player. Card backs carry the player's initials as numbering. Cards with a perceived larger supply carry an asterisk and all short-print cards carry an SP designation.

Nm-Mt Ex-Mt
B-AD Andre Dawson * 10.00 3.00
B-AS Al Simmons SP............... 40.00 12.00
B-BR Babe Ruth SP 200.00 60.00
B-BT Bill Terry SP 40.00 12.00
B-CF Carlton Fisk 15.00 4.50
B-DD Don Drysdale SP 40.00 12.00
B-DJ Davey Johnson............... 10.00 3.00
B-EM Eddie Mathews 15.00 4.50
B-GB George Brett * 15.00 4.50
B-GH Gil Hodges SP 60.00 18.00
B-HA Hank Aaron SP 60.00 18.00
B-JD Joe DiMaggio SP 120.00 36.00
B-JF Jimmie Foxx 50.00 15.00
B-JR Jackie Robinson SP 100.00 30.00
B-KC Kiki Cuyler..................... 25.00 7.50
B-MM Mickey Mantle SP 150.00 45.00
B-MM Manny Mota 10.00 3.00
B-MO Mel Ott SP 60.00 18.00
B-MW Maury Wills * 10.00 3.00
B-NF Nellie Fox 15.00 4.50
B-NR Nolan Ryan SP 40.00 12.00
B-PM Paul Molitor 15.00 4.50
B-RC Rico Carty...................... 10.00 3.00
B-RCA R.Campanella SP 50.00 15.00
B-RCL Roberto Clemente 80.00 24.00
B-RJ Reggie Jackson * 15.00 4.50
B-RM Roger Maris SP 80.00 24.00
B-RS Ryne Sandberg * 25.00 7.50
B-RY Robin Yount * 15.00 4.50
B-TC Ty Cobb SP 150.00 45.00
B-TD Tommy Davis SP 80.00 24.00
B-THO Tommy Holmes UER 10.00 3.00
Eddie Mathews pictured
B-VP Vada Pinson................... 10.00 3.00
B-WB Wade Boggs * 15.00 4.50
B-WMC Willie McCovey * 10.00 3.00
B-YB Yogi Berra 15.00 4.50

2001 SP Legendary Cuts Game Bat Combo

Randomly inserted into packs, these 24 cards feature dual player game-used bat pieces from some of the games greatest stars. Card backs carry both players' initials as numbering. Please note that there were only 25 serial numbered sets produced. Due to market scarcity, no pricing is provided for these cards.

Nm-Mt Ex-Mt
BMRC Bill Mazeroski ....
Roberto Clemente
BRMM Babe Ruth ....
Mickey Mantle
GSBT George Sisler ....
Bill Terry
HABR Hank Aaron......................
Babe Ruth
HWBH Hack Wilson ....
Billy Herman
JCBD Joe Cronin........................
Bobby Doerr
JDMM Joe DiMaggio ....
Mickey Mantle
JFAS Jimmie Foxx ....
Al Simmons
JFBR Jimmie Foxx ....
Babe Ruth
JRRC Jackie Robinson...............
Roy Campanella
LBBF Lou Boudreau ....
Bob Feller
MMNF Minnie Minoso.................
Nellie Fox
MOBT Mel Ott ....
Bill Terry
MOJD Mel Ott ....
Joe DiMaggio
NRBF Nolan Ryan......................
Bob Feller
RJMM Reggie Jackson ....
Mickey Mantle
RMMM Roger Maris ....
Mickey Mantle
RSAD Ryne Sandberg ....
Andre Dawson
SJPW Joe Jackson......................
Paul Waner
TCBR Ty Cobb...........................
Babe Ruth
TCCG Ty Cobb...........................
Charlie Gehringer
TDDD Tommy Davis...................
Don Drysdale
TORC Tony Oliva.......................
Roberto Clemente
YBEH Yogi Berra ....
Elston Howard

2001 SP Legendary Cuts Game Jersey

Randomly inserted into packs at one in 18, this 35-card set features game-worn jersey or uniform pieces for each player. Card backs carry the player's initials as numbering. Cards with a perceived larger supply carry an asterisk and all short-print cards carry an SP designation.

Nm-Mt Ex-Mt
J-BD Bill Dickey Uni 40.00 12.00
J-BL Bob Lemon Uni............... 15.00 4.50
J-BM B.Mazeroski Uni SP 80.00 24.00
J-BR B.Richardson Uni 10.00 3.00
J-BR Babe Ruth Uni SP ....
J-BRO B.Robinson Uni............. 15.00 4.50
J-BT Bobby Thomson Uni......... 15.00 4.50
J-BW Billy Williams Jsy 10.00 3.00
J-CS Casey Stengel Uni 15.00 4.50
J-GH Gil Hodges Jsy............... 15.00 4.50
J-GP Gaylord Perry Jsy 10.00 3.00
J-HW H.Wagner Uni SP...........
J-JD Joe DiMaggio Uni SP.......
J-JF Jim Fregosi Jsy 10.00 3.00
J-JM Juan Marichal Jsy * 10.00 3.00
J-JN Joe Nuxhall Jsy 15.00 4.50
J-LD Leo Durocher Jsy............ 15.00 4.50
J-MM M. Mantle Uni SP ....
J-MW Maury Wills Jsy............. 10.00 3.00
J-NF Nellie Fox Uni 15.00 4.50
J-NR Nolan Ryan Jsy 40.00 12.00
J-RC R. Clemente Jsy 100.00 30.00
J-RJ Reggie Jackson Jsy 15.00 4.50
J-RM Roger Maris Uni SP 250.00 75.00
J-RY Robin Yount Jsy.............. 15.00 4.50
J-TC Tony Conigliaro Jsy 15.00 4.50
J-TC Ty Cobb Uni SP ....
J-THO T.Holmes Uni* 10.00 3.00
J-TK Ted Kluszewski Jsy 15.00 4.50
J-TS Tom Seaver Jsy SP......... 150.00 45.00
J-VL Vic Lombardi Jsy............. 10.00 3.00
J-WB Wade Boggs Jsy............. 15.00 4.50
J-WF Whitey Ford Uni.............. 15.00 4.50
J-WM Willie McCovey Uni* 10.00 3.00
J-YB Yogi Berra Uni 15.00 4.50

2002 SP Legendary Cuts

This 90 card set was released in October, 2002. The set was issued in four card packs which came 12 packs to a box and 16 boxes to a case. In addition to these basic cards, an exchange card for a Mark McGwire "private signings" card was randomly inserted into packs. That card has a stated print run of 100 copies inserted and a redemption deadline of 09/12/03.

Nm-Mt Ex-Mt
COMPLETE SET (90)................ 25.00 7.50
1 Al Kaline.................................. 1.50 .45
2 Alvin Dark .... .60 .18
3 Andre Dawson .... .60 .18
4 Babe Ruth 5.00 1.50
5 Ernie Banks.............................. 1.50 .45
6 Bob Lemon .... 1.00 .30
7 Bobby Bonds .... .60 .18
8 Carl Erskine............................... .60 .18
9 Carl Hubbell............................. 1.00 .30
10 Casey Stengel .... 1.50 .45
11 Charlie Gehringer .... 1.00 .30
12 Christy Mathewson .... 1.50 .45
13 Dale Murphy .... 1.50 .45
14 Dave Concepcion .... .60 .18
15 Dave Parker .... .60 .18
16 Dazzy Vance............................ .60 .18
17 Dizzy Dean .... 1.00 .30
18 Don Baylor .... .60 .18
19 Don Drysdale........................... 1.50 .45
20 Duke Snider .... 1.00 .30
21 Earl Averill .... .60 .18
22 Early Wynn................................ .60 .18
23 Edd Roush .... .60 .18
24 Elston Howard .... .60 .18
25 Ferguson Jenkins .... .60 .18
26 Frank Crosetti............................ .60 .18
27 Frankie Frisch............................ .60 .18
28 Gaylord Perry .... .60 .18
29 George Foster .... .60 .18
30 George Kell .... .60 .18
31 Gil Hodges .... 1.00 .30
32 Hank Greenberg .... 1.50 .45
33 Phil Niekro .... .60 .18
34 Harvey Haddix........................... .60 .18
35 Harvey Kuenn .... .60 .18
36 Honus Wagner........................ 2.50 .75
37 Jackie Robinson...................... 1.50 .45
38 Orlando Cepeda .... .60 .18
39 Joe Adcock .... .60 .18
40 Joe Cronin .... .60 .18
41 Joe DiMaggio.......................... 3.00 .90
42 Joe Morgan................................ .60 .18
43 Johnny Mize............................... .60 .18
44 Lefty Gomez .... 1.00 .30
45 Lefty Grove .... 1.00 .30
46 Jim Palmer................................. .60 .18
47 Lou Boudreau .... .60 .18
48 Lou Gehrig .... 3.00 .90
49 Luke Appling............................... .60 .18
50 Mark McGwire 5.00 1.50
51 Mel Ott.................................... 1.50 .45
52 Mickey Cochrane .... 1.00 .30
53 Mickey Mantle......................... 6.00 1.80
54 Minnie Minoso............................ .60 .18
55 Brooks Robinson .... 1.00 .30
56 Nellie Fox .... 1.00 .30
57 Nolan Ryan.............................. 4.00 1.20
58 Rollie Fingers............................. .60 .18
59 Pee Wee Reese....................... 1.00 .30
60 Phil Rizzuto............................. 1.00 .30
61 Ralph Kiner .... .60 .18
62 Ray Dandridge .... .60 .18
63 Richie Ashburn .... 1.00 .30
64 Robin Yount .... 2.50 .75
65 Rocky Colavito......................... 1.00 .30
66 Roger Maris .... 1.50 .45
67 Rogers Hornsby....................... 1.50 .45
68 Ron Santo .... .60 .18
69 Ryne Sandberg .... 3.00 .90
70 Stan Musial.............................. 2.50 .75
71 Sam McDowell............................ .60 .18
72 Satchel Paige........................... 1.50 .45
73 Willie McCovey............................ .60 .18
74 Steve Garvey............................... .60 .18
75 Ted Kluszewski.......................... 1.00 .30
76 Catfish Hunter............................ 1.00 .30
77 Terry Moore .... .40 .12
78 Thurman Munson .... 1.50 .45
79 Tom Seaver................................ 1.00 .30
80 Tommy John................................. .60 .18
81 Tony Gwynn .... 2.00 .60
82 Tony Kubek.................................. .60 .18
83 Tony Lazzeri .... .60 .18
84 Ty Cobb...................................... 2.50 .75
85 Wade Boggs............................... 1.00 .30
86 Waite Hoyt .... .60 .18
87 Walter Johnson........................... 1.50 .45
88 Willie Stargell............................. 1.00 .30
89 Yogi Berra .... 1.50 .45
90 Zack Wheat .... .60 .18
MM M.McGwire AU/100 EX ....

2002 SP Legendary Cuts Autographs

Inserted in packs at stated odds of one in 128, these 97 cards feature "cut" autographs of a mix of retired greats and tough to track down early players dating back to the 1910's. Each card has

a different stated serial numbered print run and we have notated that information next to the player's name in our checklist. Edd Roush has two different varieties issued. Also, if a player has a stated print run of 25 or fewer copies, there is no pricing provided due to market scarcity.

	Nm-Mt	Ex-Mt
BDA Babe Dahlgren/51	200.00	60.00
BFA Bibb Falk/44	200.00	60.00
BGO Bill Goodman/53	120.00	36.00
BHA Buddy Hassett/56	200.00	60.00
BIL Bill Lee/40	200.00	60.00
BKA Bob Kahle/53	120.00	36.00
BOL Bob Lemon/91	150.00	45.00
BRU Babe Ruth/3		
BSC Bob Scheffing/19		
BSE Bill Serena/16		
BSH Bill Sherdel/10		
BSH Bob Shawkey/118	150.00	45.00
BSZ Billy Shantz/17		
BVE Bill Veeck/11		
BWA Bucky Walters/31	250.00	75.00
CGE Charlie Gehringer/3		
CHM Chet Morgan/27	250.00	75.00
CHRM Christy Mathewson/2		
CHU Carl Hubbell/17		
CKE Charlie Keller/29	250.00	75.00
CLA Cookie Lavagetto/22		
CST Casey Stengel/8		
DDE Dizzy Dean/4		
DDO Dick Donovan/23		
DDR Don Drysdale/14		
DVA Dazzy Vance/5		
EAV Earl Averill/22		
EJO Earl Johnson/31	250.00	75.00
ELO Ed Lopat/58	150.00	45.00
ERO Edd Roush/101	120.00	36.00
ERO2 Edd Roush/155	120.00	36.00
EWY Early Wynn/4		
FFR Frankie Frisch/35	400.00	120.00
FOF Ford Frick/1		
GBU Guy Bush/38	150.00	45.00
GCA George Case/35	200.00	60.00
GHO Gil Hodges/1		
GPI George Pipgras/34	200.00	60.00
HCH Happy Chandler/96	150.00	45.00
HGR Hank Greenberg/94	400.00	120.00
HHA Harvey Haddix/37	250.00	75.00
HKU Harvey Kuenn/23		
HMA Hank Majeski/21		
HNE Hal Newhouser/81	150.00	45.00
HSC Hal Schumacher/17		
HWA Honus Wagner/6		
JAD Joe Adcock/48	250.00	75.00
JBE Johnny Berardino/12		
JCO Johnny Cooney/64	120.00	36.00
JCR Joe Cronin/185	150.00	45.00
JDI Joe DiMaggio/103	500.00	150.00
JDU Joe Dugan/39	200.00	60.00
JJO Judy Johnson/86	250.00	75.00
JMI Johnny Mize/3		
JMO Johnny Moore/22		
JSE Joe Sewell/136	150.00	45.00
KKE Ken Keltner/11		
LAP Luke Appling/53	150.00	45.00
LBO Lou Boudreau/85	150.00	45.00
LGE Lou Gehrig/3		
LGO Lefty Gomez/3		
LGR Lefty Grove/194	250.00	75.00
LJA Larry Jackson/37	200.00	60.00
LRI Lance Richbourg/3		
LSE Luke Sewell/2		
MCO Mickey Cochrane/2		
MKO Mark Koenig/22		
MMA Mickey Mantle/2		
NFO Nellie Fox/1		
NJA Bucky Jacobs/44	200.00	60.00
ORO Oscar Roettger/9		
PRE Pete Reiser/73	200.00	60.00
PWE Pee Wee Reese/23		
PWI Pete Whisenant/13		
RAS Richie Ashburn/10		
RDA Ray Dandridge/179	120.00	36.00
RFE Rick Ferrell/19		
RHO Rogers Hornsby/1		
RMA Roger Maris/1		
RMC Roy McMillan/18		
RRE Rip Repulski/19		
SCH Spud Chandler/17		
SCO Stan Coveleski/85	150.00	45.00
SHA Stan Hack/36	250.00	75.00
SMA Sal Maglie/29	250.00	75.00
TDO Taylor Douthit/60	150.00	45.00
TKL Ted Kluszewski/23		
TMO Terry Moore/86	120.00	36.00
TYC Ty Cobb/2		
VRA Vic Raschi/98	150.00	45.00
VWE Vic Wertz/17		
WHO Waite Hoyt/61	250.00	75.00
WJO Walter Johnson/20		
WKA Willie Kamm/57	120.00	36.00
WSC Willard Schmidt/10		
WST Willie Stargell/153	120.00	36.00
ZWH Zack Wheat/127	200.00	60.00

2002 SP Legendary Cuts Bat Barrel

Randomly inserted into packs, these 26 cards feature "barrel" pieces of the featured player. Each card has a stated print run of 11 or fewer and there is no pricing provided due to market scarcity.

	Nm-Mt	Ex-Mt
BB-ADA Alvin Dark/4		
BB-AND Andre Dawson/4		

BB-BBO Bobby Bonds/3		
BB-BRU Babe Ruth/3		
BB-DBA Don Baylor/5		
BB-DMU Dale Murphy/3		
BB-DPA Dave Parker/6		
BB-DSN Duke Snider/2		
BB-EWY Early Wynn/1		
BB-GFO George Foster/5		
BB-HGR Hank Greenberg/1		
BB-JAR Jackie Robinson/1		
BB-JMI Johnny Mize/2		
BB-LGR Lefty Grove/1		
BB-MMA Mickey Mantle/7		
BB-MMC Mark McGwire/4		
BB-NRY Nolan Ryan/9		
BB-PWE Pee Wee Reese/4		
BB-RCO Rocky Colavito/2		
BB-RMA Roger Maris/1		
BB-RSA Ryne Sandberg/3		
BB-RYO Robin Yount/8		
BB-TGW Tony Gwynn/11		
BB-TLA Tony Lazzeri/1		
BB-TMU Thurman Munson/4		
BB-WST Willie Stargell/5		

2002 SP Legendary Cuts Buybacks

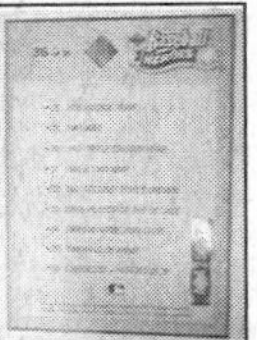

Randomly inserted into packs, this is a one card set featuring "bought-back" signed cards from the 1992 Upper Deck Heroes set featuring Ted Williams autograph. These bought back cards have a stated print run of nine serial numbered sets and there is no pricing due to market scarcity.

	Nm-Mt	Ex-Mt
NNO Ted Williams 92 Heroes AU/9		

2002 SP Legendary Cuts Game Bat

Inserted in packs at a stated rate of one in eight, these 36 cards feature game-used bat chips of some leading retired superstars. A few cards were issued in shorter supply and we have either notated that information with an SP next to the players name or an asterisk.

	Nm-Mt	Ex-Mt
B-ADA Alvin Dark *	10.00	3.00
B-AND Andre Dawson *	8.00	2.40
B-BBO Bobby Bonds *	8.00	2.40
B-BRU Babe Ruth SP	200.00	60.00
B-CRI Cal Ripken	30.00	9.00
B-DBA Don Baylor *	8.00	2.40
B-DMU Dale Murphy *	15.00	4.50
B-DPA Dave Parker *	8.00	2.40
B-DSN Duke Snider	15.00	4.50
B-EHO Elston Howard SP *	15.00	4.50
B-EWY Early Wynn	10.00	3.00
B-GFO George Foster *	8.00	2.40
B-GKE George Kell	10.00	3.00
B-GPE Gaylord Perry	8.00	2.40
B-HGR Hank Greenberg SP	50.00	15.00
B-JAR Jackie Robinson SP *	50.00	15.00
B-JMI Johnny Mize SP *	15.00	4.50
B-LGR Lefty Grove	25.00	7.50
B-MMA Mickey Mantle SP	150.00	45.00
B-MMC Mark McGwire *	60.00	18.00
B-NFO Nellie Fox	15.00	4.50
B-NRY Nolan Ryan	40.00	12.00
B-PWE Pee Wee Reese *	15.00	4.50
B-RCO Rocky Colavito *	15.00	4.50
B-RKI Ralph Kiner	10.00	3.00
B-RMA Roger Maris SP *	60.00	18.00
B-RSA Ryne Sandberg *	15.00	4.50
B-RYO Robin Yount *	15.00	4.50
B-SGA Steve Garvey	8.00	2.40
B-TGW Tony Gwynn SP *	20.00	6.00
B-TKU Tony Kubek UER Name spelled Tonk on the front	15.00	4.50
B-TLA Tony Lazzeri	10.00	3.00
B-TMU Thurman Munson	25.00	7.50
B-TSE Tom Seaver SP	20.00	6.00
B-WST Willie Stargell	10.00	3.00
B-YBE Yogi Berra SP	25.00	7.50

2002 SP Legendary Cuts Game Jersey

Inserted in packs at stated odds of one in 24, these 15 cards feature pieces of game-worn jerseys. A few players cards actually feature pant pieces and we have notated that next to their name in our checklist. In addition, a few cards were issued in shorter supply and we have notated that information in our checklist as well.

	Nm-Mt	Ex-Mt
J-AND Andre Dawson	8.00	2.40
J-BBO Bobby Bonds Pants	8.00	2.40
J-DBA Don Baylor	8.00	2.40
J-DPA Dave Parker Pants *	8.00	2.40
J-FCR Frank Crosetti	10.00	3.00
J-GFO George Foster	8.00	2.40
J-JRO J.Robinson Pants SP *	50.00	15.00
J-MMA M.Mantle Pants SP *	120.00	36.00
J-NRY Nolan Ryan Pants	40.00	12.00
J-PWE Pee Wee Reese	15.00	4.50
J-RMA Roger Maris Pants	50.00	15.00
J-RSA Ryne Sandberg SP *	25.00	7.50
J-SGA Steve Garvey	8.00	2.40
J-TSE Tom Seaver	10.00	3.00
J-YBE Yogi Berra Pants *	25.00	7.50

2002 SP Legendary Cuts Game Swatches

Inserted in packs at stated odds of one in 24, these 15 cards feature game-used memorabilia swatches of the featured players.

	Nm-Mt	Ex-Mt
S-CER Carl Erskine Pants	10.00	3.00
S-CRJ Cal Ripken	25.00	7.50
S-DBA Don Baylor	8.00	2.40
S-DDR Don Drysdale Pants	25.00	7.50
S-DPA Dave Parker	8.00	2.40
S-FCR Frank Crosetti	10.00	3.00
S-FJE Ferguson Jenkins Pants	8.00	2.40
S-JMO Joe Morgan	8.00	2.40
S-MMI Minnie Minoso	10.00	3.00
S-MOT Mel Ott Pants	25.00	7.50
S-RSA Ron Santo	15.00	4.50
S-SMC Sam McDowell	8.00	2.40
S-TGW Tony Gwynn	15.00	4.50
S-TJO Tommy John	8.00	2.40
S-WBO Wade Boggs	10.00	3.00

2003 SP Legendary Cuts

This 130-card set was released in December, 2003. This set was issued in four-card packs with an $10 SRP which came 12 packs to a box and 16 boxes to a case. Thirty cards in this set were short printed and each of those cards were issued to a stated print run of 1299 serial numbered sets and were inserted at a stated rate of one in 12.

	MINT	NRMT
COMP.SET w/o SP's (100)	40.00	18.00
COMMON CARD	.40	.18
COMMON SP	8.00	3.60
1 Luis Aparicio	.60	.25
2 Al Barlick	.40	.18
3 Al Lopez	.60	.25
4 Ernie Banks	1.50	.70
5 Alexander Cartwright	.60	.25
6 Lou Brock	1.00	.45
7 Babe Ruth/1299	15.00	6.75
8 Bill Dickey	1.00	.45
9 Bill Mazeroski	1.00	.45
10 Bob Feller	.60	.25
11 Billy Herman	.60	.25
12 Billy Williams	.60	.25
13 Bob Gibson/1299	10.00	4.50
14 Bob Lemon	.60	.25
15 Bobby Doerr	.60	.25
16 Branch Rickey	.60	.25
17 Gary Carter	.60	.25
18 Burleigh Grimes	.60	.25
19 Cap Anson	1.00	.45
20 Carl Hubbell	1.00	.45
21 Carlton Fisk	1.00	.45
22 Casey Stengel	1.00	.45
23 Charlie Gehringer	.60	.25
24 Chief Bender	.60	.25
25 Christy Mathewson/1299	10.00	4.50
26 Cy Young	1.50	.70
27 Dave Winfield	.60	.25
28 Dazzy Vance	.60	.25
29 Dizzy Dean/1299	10.00	4.50
30 Don Drysdale/1299	10.00	4.50
31 Duke Snider/1299	10.00	4.50
32 Earl Averill	.60	.25
33 Earle Combs	.60	.25
34 Edd Roush	.60	.25
35 Earl Weaver	.60	.25
36 Eddie Collins	.60	.25
37 Eddie Plank	.60	.25
38 Elmer Flick	.60	.25
39 Enos Slaughter	.60	.25
40 Ernie Lombardi	.60	.25
41 Ford Frick	.40	.18
42 Jim Hunter	1.00	.45
43 Frankie Frisch	.60	.25
44 Gabby Hartnett	.60	.25
45 George Kell	.60	.25
46 Early Wynn	.60	.25
47 Ferguson Jenkins	.60	.25
48 Al Kaline	1.50	.70
49 Harmon Killebrew	1.50	.70
50 Hal Newhouser	.60	.25
51 Hank Greenberg/1299	10.00	4.50
52 Harry Caray	1.00	.45
53 Tommy Lasorda	.60	.25
54 Honus Wagner/1299	10.00	4.50
55 Hoyt Wilhelm/1299	8.00	3.60
56 Jackie Robinson/1299	10.00	4.50
57 Jim Bottomley	.60	.25
58 Jim Bunning/1299	10.00	4.50
59 Jimmie Foxx/1299	10.00	4.50
60 Eddie Mathews	1.50	.70
61 Joe Cronin	.60	.25
62 Joe DiMaggio/1299	10.00	4.50
63 Joe McCarthy/1299	8.00	3.60
64 Joe Morgan/1299	8.00	3.60
65 Willie McCovey	.60	.25
66 Joe Tinker	.60	.25
67 Johnny Bench/1299	10.00	4.50
68 Johnny Evers/1299	8.00	3.60
69 Johnny Mize/1299	8.00	3.60
70 Josh Gibson/1299	10.00	4.50
71 Juan Marichal	.60	.25
72 Judy Johnson	.60	.25
73 Stan Musial	2.50	1.10
74 Kiki Cuyler	.60	.25
75 Larry Doby	.60	.25
76 Nap Lajoie	1.00	.45
77 Larry MacPhail	.40	.18
78 Phil Niekro	.60	.25
79 Lefty Gomez/1299	10.00	4.50
80 Lefty Grove/1299	10.00	4.50
81 Leo Durocher/1299	8.00	3.60
82 Leon Day	.60	.25
83 Gaylord Perry/1299	8.00	3.60
84 Lou Boudreau	.60	.25
85 Lou Gehrig	3.00	1.35
86 Luke Appling	.60	.25
87 Max Carey	.60	.25
88 Mel Allen/1299	8.00	3.60
89 Mel Ott/1299	10.00	4.50
90 Mickey Cochrane	.60	.25
91 Mickey Mantle	5.00	2.20
92 Brooks Robinson	1.00	.45
93 Monte Irvin	.60	.25
94 Nellie Fox	1.00	.45
95 Nolan Ryan/1299	12.00	5.50
96 Ozzie Smith/1299	10.00	4.50
97 Mike Schmidt	3.00	1.35
98 Pee Wee Reese/1299	10.00	4.50
99 Phil Rizzuto	1.00	.45
100 Ralph Kiner	.60	.25
101 Ray Dandridge	.60	.25
102 Richie Ashburn	1.00	.45
103 Rick Ferrell	.60	.25
104 Roberto Clemente	4.00	1.80
105 Robin Roberts	.60	.25
106 Robin Yount	2.50	1.10
107 Rogers Hornsby	1.50	.70
108 Rollie Fingers	.60	.25
109 Roy Campanella	1.50	.70
110 Rube Marquard	.60	.25
111 Sam Crawford	.60	.25
112 Steve Carlton	.60	.25
113 Satchel Paige/1299	10.00	4.50
114 Sparky Anderson	.60	.25
115 Stan Coveleski	.60	.25
116 Red Schoendienst	1.00	.45
117 Ted Williams	3.00	1.35
118 Tom Seaver	1.00	.45
119 Tom Yawkey	.40	.18
120 Tony Lazzeri	.60	.25
121 Tony Perez	.60	.25
122 Tris Speaker	1.50	.70
123 Ty Cobb	2.50	1.10
124 Waite Hoyt/1299	8.00	3.60
125 Walter Alston	.60	.25
126 Walter Johnson	1.50	.70
127 Warren Spahn	1.50	.70
128 Whitey Ford	1.00	.45
129 Willie Stargell	1.00	.45
130 Yogi Berra	1.50	.70

2003 SP Legendary Cuts Blue

	MINT	NRMT
*BLUE POST-WAR: 2X TO 5X BASIC		
*BLUE PRE-WAR: 1.5X TO 4X BASIC		
*BLUE POST-WAR: .6X TO 1.5X BASIC SP		
*BLUE PRE-WAR: .5X TO 1.2X BASIC SP		
RANDOM INSERTS IN PACKS		
STATED PRINT RUN 275 SERIAL #'d SETS		

2003 SP Legendary Cuts Green

	MINT	NRMT
RANDOM INSERTS IN PACKS		
STATED PRINT RUN 25 SERIAL #'d SETS		
NO PRICING DUE TO SCARCITY		

2003 SP Legendary Cuts Autographs

All the autograph cards in this insert set feature HOFers. After having a mix in 2002 of HOFers and retired players of varying note, Upper Deck decided that this product was better off with only HOFers involved in the cut signature insert set. Please note that several players: Bob Lemon, Charlie Gehringer, Carl Hubbell, Hal Newhouser, Joe DiMaggio and Ray Dandridge had two different varieties in the main autograph set. In addition, for the first time, Upper Deck made some "color" variations in the autograph cut insert set.

This set includes a "cut" signature of Alexander Cartwright who is believed by most historians to be the true founder of baseball.

	MINT	NRMT
OVERALL CUT SIG ODDS 1:196		
PRINT RUNS B/WN 1-96 COPIES PER		
NO PRICING ON QTY OF 25 OR LESS		
AL Alexander Cartwright/1		
BD Bill Dickey/25		
BG Burleigh Grimes/34	300.00	135.00
BI Billy Herman/30	150.00	70.00
BL Bob Lemon/34	150.00	70.00
BL1 Bob Lemon/41	150.00	70.00
CG Charlie Gehringer/17		
CG1 Charlie Gehringer/20		
CH Carl Hubbell/47	300.00	135.00
CH1 Carl Hubbell/63	300.00	135.00
CS Casey Stengel/3		
CY Cy Young/2		
DD Dizzy Dean/8		
DO Don Drysdale/12		
DV Dazzy Vance/2		
EA Earl Averill/96	120.00	55.00
EC Earle Combs/45	250.00	110.00
EF Elmer Flick/6		
EL Ernie Lombardi/1		
ER Edd Roush/15		
ER1 Edd Roush/14		
ES Enos Slaughter/30	200.00	90.00
FF Ford Frick/10		
FR Frankie Frisch/4		
GH Gabby Hartnett/20		
HC Harry Caray/29	300.00	135.00
HC1 Harry Caray/35	300.00	135.00
HG Hank Greenberg/30	500.00	220.00
HN Hal Newhouser TC/22		
HN1 Hal Newhouser B2B/22		
HW Honus Wagner/1		
JB Jim Bottomley/2		
JC Joe Cronin/15		
JD Joe DiMaggio/50	500.00	220.00
JD1 Joe DiMaggio/28	600.00	275.00
JF Jimmie Foxx/3		
JJ Judy Johnson/23		
JM Johnny Mize/18		
JM1 Johnny Mize/12		
JO Joe McCarthy/22		
JR Jackie Robinson/4		
LA Leon Day/6		
LB Lou Boudreau/82	120.00	55.00
LB1 Lou Boudreau/49	150.00	70.00
LD Leo Durocher/20		
LE Lefty Grove/9		
LG Lefty Gomez/21		
LM Larry MacPhail/2		
LU Luke Appling/52	150.00	70.00
MA Mel Allen/2		
MC Max Carey/18		
MI Mickey Cochrane/3		
MM Mickey Mantle/2		
NF Nellie Fox/5		
NL Nap Lajoie/2		
RA Richie Ashburn/10		
RD Ray Dandridge Hands/20		
RD1 Ray Dandridge MVP/20		
RH Rogers Hornsby/1		
RM Rube Marquard/40	250.00	110.00
RO Roy Campanella/1		
SC Sam Crawford/3		
SP Satchel Paige/1		
ST Stanley Coveleski/19		
ST1 Stan Coveleski/20		
TC Ty Cobb/6		
TJ Travis Jackson/19		
TO Tony Lazzeri/8		
TS Tris Speaker/2		
TW Ted Williams/7		
TY Tom Yawkey/1		
WA Walter Alston/30		
WJ Walter Johnson/1		
WS Willie Stargell/4		
ZW Zack Wheat/19		

2003 SP Legendary Cuts Autographs Blue

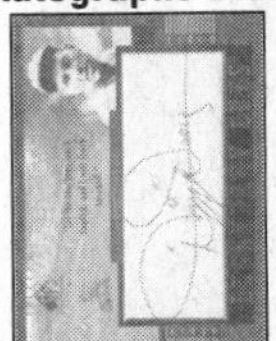

	MINT	NRMT
OVERALL CUT SIG ODDS 1:196		
PRINT RUNS B/WN 1-50 COPIES PER		
NO PRICING ON QTY OF 25 OR LESS		
BD Bill Dickey/12		
BG Burleigh Grimes/22		
BI Billy Herman/15		
BL1 Bob Lemon/25		
BR Branch Rickey/1		
CG1 Charlie Gehringer/4		
CH1 Carl Hubbell/25		
CS Casey Stengel/1		
CY Cy Young/1		
DD Dizzy Dean/4		
DO Don Drysdale/6		
DV Dazzy Vance/1		
EA Earl Averill/50	150.00	70.00
EC Earle Combs/16		

ED Eddie Collins/1
EF Elmer Flick/4
EL Ernie Lombardi/1
ER Edd Roush/15
ES Enos Slaughter/11
FF Ford Frick/7
FR Frankie Frisch/2
GH Gabby Hartnett/5
HC1 Harry Caray/35 .... 300.00 135.00
HG Hank Greenberg/15
HN1 Hal Newhouser B2B/29 ... 150.00 70.00
HW Honus Wagner/1
JB Jim Bottomley/2
JC Joe Cronin/5
JD1 Joe DiMaggio/40 .... 500.00 220.00
JE Johnny Evers/1
JF Jimmie Foxx/2
JJ Judy Johnson/8
JM Johnny Mize/15
JO Joe McCarthy/15
JR Jackie Robinson/2
JT Joe Tinker/1
LA Leon Day/5
LB Lou Boudreau/25
LD Leo Durocher/5
LE Lefty Grove/4
LG Lefty Gomez/14
LM Larry MacPhail/1
LO Lou Gehrig/1
LU Luke Appling/18
MA Mel Allen/1
MC Max Carey/5
MI Mickey Cochrane/2
MM Mickey Mantle/1
MO Mel Ott/1
NF Nellie Fox/1
NL Nap Lajoie/1
RA Richie Asburn/5
RC Roberto Clemente/1
RD1 Ray Dandridge MVP/9
RH Rogers Hornsby/1
RM Rube Marquard/16
RO Roy Campanella/1
SC Sam Crawford/2
SP Satchel Paige/4
ST1 Stan Coveleski/20
TC Ty Cobb/2
TJ Travis Jackson/5
TO Tony Lazzeri/3
TS Tris Speaker/1
TW Ted Williams/1
TY Tom Yawkey/1
WA Walter Alston/10
WJ Walter Johnson/1
WS Willie Stargell/2
ZW Zack Wheat/5

2003 SP Legendary Cuts Autographs Green

MINT NRMT
OVERALL CUT SIG ODDS 1:196
PRINT RUNS B/WN 1-5 COPIES PER
NO PRICING DUE TO SCARCITY

2003 SP Legendary Cuts Combo Cuts

MINT NRMT
OVERALL CUT SIG ODDS 1:196
STATED PRINT RUN 1 SERIAL #'d SET
NO PRICING DUE TO SCARCITY
BJ Branch Rickey
Jackie Robinson
BL Babe Ruth
Lou Gehrig
HM Harry Caray
Mel Allen
HT Honus Wagner
Ty Cobb
JC Jackie Robinson
Roy Campanella
JM Joe DiMaggio
Mickey Mantle
JT Joe DiMaggio
Ted Williams
SJ Satchel Paige
Jackie Robinson

2003 SP Legendary Cuts Etched in Time 400

MINT NRMT
STATED PRINT RUN 400 SERIAL #'d SETS
*ETCHED 300: .4X TO 1X BASIC 400
ETCHED 300 PRINT RUN 300 #'d SETS
*ETCHED 175: .5X TO 1.2X BASIC 400
ETCHED 175 PRINT RUN 175 #'d SETS
OVERALL ETCHED ODDS 1:12
AB Al Barlick 5.00 2.20
AC Alexander Cartwright 5.00 2.20
BR Babe Ruth 15.00 6.75
CG Charlie Gehringer 5.00 2.20
CH Carl Hubbell 8.00 3.60
CM Christy Mathewson 8.00 3.60
CS Casey Stengel 8.00 3.60
CY Cy Young 8.00 3.60
DD Dizzy Dean 8.00 3.60
DO Don Drysdale 8.00 3.60
EC Eddie Collins 5.00 2.20
EL Ernie Lombardi 5.00 2.20
GH Gabby Hartnett 5.00 2.20
HC Harry Caray 8.00 3.60
HG Hank Greenberg 8.00 3.60
HW Honus Wagner 8.00 3.60
JD Joe DiMaggio 10.00 4.50
JF Jimmie Foxx 8.00 3.60
JG Josh Gibson 8.00 3.60
JM Joe McCarthy 5.00 2.20
JO Johnny Mize 5.00 2.20
JR Jackie Robinson 8.00 3.60
LB Lou Boudreau 5.00 2.20
LD Leo Durocher 5.00 2.20
LE Lefty Grove 8.00 3.60
LG Lefty Gomez 8.00 3.60
LO Lou Gehrig 12.00 5.50
ME Mel Allen 5.00 2.20
MM Mickey Mantle 25.00 11.00
MO Mel Ott 8.00 3.60
PR Pee Wee Reese 8.00 3.60
RA Richie Ashburn 8.00 3.60
RC Roberto Clemente 15.00 6.75
RH Rogers Hornsby 8.00 3.60
RO Roy Campanella 8.00 3.60
SP Satchel Paige 8.00 3.60
TC Ty Cobb 10.00 4.50
TL Tony Lazzeri 5.00 2.20
TS Tris Speaker 8.00 3.60
TW Ted Williams 10.00 4.50

2003 SP Legendary Cuts Hall Marks Autographs

MINT NRMT
OVERALL HALL MARKS ODDS 1:196.
BLACK INK PRINTS B/WN 10-99 COPIES PER
BLUE INK PRINTS B/WN 10-15 COPIES PER
RED INK PRINT RUN 5 #'d COPIES PER
NO PRICING ON QTY OF 15 OR LESS
BD1 Bobby Doerr Black/50 .... 40.00 18.00
BD2 Bobby Doerr Blue/15
BD3 Bobby Doerr Red/5
BG1 Bob Gibson Black/30
BG2 Bob Gibson Blue/15
BG3 Bob Gibson Red/5
BM1 Bill Mazeroski Black/50..... 60.00 27.00
BM2 Bill Mazeroski Blue/15
BM3 Bill Mazeroski Red/5
CF1 Carlton Fisk Black/50 .... 60.00 27.00
CF2 Carlton Fisk Blue/15
CF3 Carlton Fisk Red/5
CY1 Carl Yastrzemski Black/45 100.00 45.00
CY2 Carl Yastrzemski Blue/15
CY3 Carl Yastrzemski Red/5
DS1 Duke Snider Black/50 .... 60.00 27.00
DS2 Duke Snider Blue/15
DS3 Duke Snider Red/5
DW1 Dave Winfield Black/10
DW2 Dave Winfield Blue/15
DW3 Dave Winfield Red/5
GC1 Gary Carter Black/50 .... 40.00 18.00
GC2 Gary Carter Blue/15
GC3 Gary Carter Red/5
GK1 George Kell Black/50 .... 25.00 11.00
GK2 George Kell Blue/15
GK3 George Kell Red/5
JB2 Johnny Bench Blue/10
JB3 Johnny Bench Red/5
JM1 Juan Marichal Black/50..... 40.00 18.00
JM2 Juan Marichal Blue/15
JM3 Juan Marichal Red/5
JO1 Joe Morgan Black/75 .... 40.00 18.00
JO2 Joe Morgan Blue/15
JO3 Joe Morgan Red/5
LA1 Luis Aparicio Black/45 .... 40.00 18.00
LA2 Luis Aparicio Blue/15
LA3 Luis Aparicio Red/5
MI1 Monte Irvin Black/85 .... 50.00 22.00
MI2 Monte Irvin Blue/15
MI3 Monte Irvin Red/5
NR3 Nolan Ryan Red/5
OS1 Ozzie Smith Black/45....... 100.00 45.00
OS2 Ozzie Smith Blue/15
OS3 Ozzie Smith Red/5
PR1 Phil Rizzuto Black/50 .... 60.00 27.00
PR2 Phil Rizzuto Blue/15
PR3 Phil Rizzuto Red/5
RF1 Rollie Fingers Black/99 ..... 25.00 11.00
RF2 Rollie Fingers Blue/15
RF3 Rollie Fingers Red/5
RK1 Ralph Kiner Black/50 .... 40.00 18.00
RK2 Ralph Kiner Blue/15
RK3 Ralph Kiner Red/5
RR1 Robin Roberts Black/65 .... 60.00 27.00
RR2 Robin Roberts Blue/15
RR3 Robin Roberts Red/5
RY1 Robin Yount Black/45 ...... 100.00 45.00
RY2 Robin Yount Blue/15
RY3 Robin Yount Red/5
SA1 Sparky Anderson Black/30 40.00 18.00
SA2 Sparky Anderson Blue/15
SA3 Sparky Anderson Red/5
TP1 Tony Perez Black/50 .... 40.00 18.00
TP2 Tony Perez Blue/15
TP3 Tony Perez Red/5
TS2 Tom Seaver Blue/10
TS3 Tom Seaver Red/5
WS1 Warren Spahn Black/35 ... 80.00 36.00
WS2 Warren Spahn Blue/15
WS3 Warren Spahn Red/5
YB1 Yogi Berra Black/50 .... 80.00 36.00
YB2 Yogi Berra Blue/15
YB3 Yogi Berra Red/5

2003 SP Legendary Cuts Hall Marks Autographs Blue

MINT NRMT
OVERALL HALL MARKS ODD 1:196
STATED PRINT RUN 25 SERIAL #'d SETS
NO PRICING DUE TO SCARCITY

2003 SP Legendary Cuts Hall Marks Autographs Green

MINT NRMT
OVERALL HALL MARKS ODDS 1:196.
STATED PRINT RUN 10 SERIAL #'d SETS
NO PRICING DUE TO SCARCITY

2003 SP Legendary Cuts Historic Lumber

MINT NRMT
OVERALL GAME USED ODDS 1:12
PRINT RUNS B/WN 50-350 COPIES PER
BR Babe Ruth Away/150 .... 150.00 70.00
BR1 Babe Ruth Home/150 .... 150.00 70.00
CF Carlton Fisk R.Sox/50 .... 25.00 11.00
CF1 Carlton Fisk W.Sox/50 .... 25.00 11.00
CY C.Yastrzemski w/Bat/300 ..... 30.00 13.50
CY1 C.Yastrzemski w/Cap/350 .. 30.00 13.50
CY2 C.Yaz w/Helmet/350 .... 30.00 13.50
DW Dave Winfield Padres/350 .. 10.00 4.50
DW1 Dave Winfield Yanks/350 . 10.00 4.50
FR Frank Robinson O's/300 ...... 15.00 6.75
FR1 Frank Robinson Reds/350 . 15.00 6.75
FR2 Frank Robinson Angels/350 15.00 6.75
GC Gary Carter Mets/300 .... 10.00 4.50
GC1 G.Carter Helmet Expos/100 10.00 4.50
GC2 G.Carter Cap Expos/100 .... 10.00 4.50
HK Harmon Killebrew/350 .... 15.00 6.75
JB Johnny Bench w/Bat/350 ..... 15.00 6.75
JB1 Johnny Bench Swing/350 .. 15.00 6.75
JM Joe Morgan Reds/350 .... 10.00 4.50
JM1 Joe Morgan Astros/350 .... 10.00 4.50
MM Mickey Mantle/300 .... 120.00 55.00
NR Nolan Ryan Rgr/225 .... 30.00 13.50
OS Ozzie Smith Cards/300 .... 25.00 11.00
OS1 Ozzie Smith Padres/350 .... 25.00 11.00
RS R.Schoen Look Right/165 ... 15.00 6.75
RS1 R.Schoen Look Left/165 .... 15.00 6.75
SC Steve Carlton/350 .... 10.00 4.50
TP Tony Perez Swing/350 .... 10.00 4.50
TP1 Tony Perez Portrait/350 ..... 10.00 4.50
TS Tom Seaver/100 .... 15.00 6.75
TW Ted Williams w/3 Bats/150 . 80.00 36.00
TW1 Ted Williams Portrait/150 . 80.00 36.00
WS W.Stargell Arms Down/150 15.00 6.75
WS1 W.Stargell Arms Up/150 ... 15.00 6.75
YB Yogi Berra Shout/350 .... 15.00 6.75
YB1 Yogi Berra w/Bat/350 .... 15.00 6.75

2003 SP Legendary Cuts Historic Lumber Green

MINT NRMT
OVERALL GAME USED ODDS 1:12
PRINT RUNS BETWEEN 50-125 COPIES PER
BR Babe Ruth Away/75 .... 200.00 90.00
BR1 Babe Ruth Home/75 .... 200.00 90.00
CY C.Yastrzemski w/Bat/125 ..... 40.00 18.00
CY1 C.Yastrzemski w/Cap/125 .. 40.00 18.00
CY2 C.Yaz w/Helmet/125 .... 40.00 18.00
DW Dave Winfield Padres/125 .. 10.00 4.50
DW1 Dave Winfield Yanks/125 . 10.00 4.50
FR Frank Robinson O's/125 ...... 15.00 6.75
FR1 Frank Robinson Reds/125 . 15.00 6.75
FR2 Frank Robinson Angels/125 15.00 6.75
GC Gary Carter Mets/125 .... 10.00 4.50
GC1 G.Carter Helmet Expos/125 10.00 4.50
GC2 G.Carter Cap Expos/125 .... 10.00 4.50
HK Harmon Killebrew/125 .... 15.00 6.75
JB Johnny Bench w/Bat/125 ..... 15.00 6.75
JB1 Johnny Bench Swing/125 .. 15.00 6.75
JM Joe Morgan Reds/125 .... 10.00 4.50
JM1 Joe Morgan Astros/125 .... 10.00 4.50
MM Mickey Mantle/75 .... 150.00 70.00
NR Nolan Ryan Astros/50 .... 60.00 27.00
OS Ozzie Smith Cards/125 .... 30.00 13.50
OS1 Ozzie Smith Padres/125 .... 30.00 13.50
RS R.Schoen Look Right/125 ... 15.00 6.75
RS1 R.Schoen Look Left/125 .... 15.00 6.75
SC Steve Carlton/125 .... 10.00 4.50
TP Tony Perez Swing/125 .... 10.00 4.50
TP1 Tony Perez Portrait/125 ..... 10.00 4.50
TS Tom Seaver/50 .... 25.00 11.00
TW Ted Williams w/3 Bats/75 . 100.00 45.00
TW1 Ted Williams Portrait/75 . 100.00 45.00
WS W.Stargell Arms Down/125 15.00 6.75
WS1 W.Stargell Arms Up/125 ... 15.00 6.75
YB Yogi Berra Shout/125 .... 15.00 6.75
YB1 Yogi Berra w/Bat/125 .... 15.00 6.75

2003 SP Legendary Cuts Historic Swatches

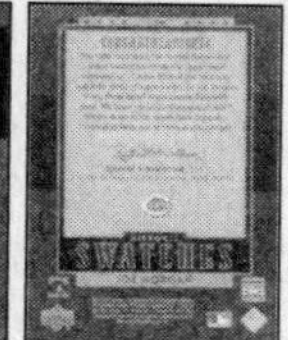

MINT NRMT
OVERALL GAME USED ODDS 1:12
PRINT RUNS B/WN 48-350 COPIES PER
BG Bob Gibson CO Jsy/350 .... 15.00 6.75
BM Bill Mazeroski Pants/50 ..... 25.00 11.00
BW Billy Williams Jsy/190 .... 10.00 4.50
CF Carlton Fisk Pants/350 .... 15.00 6.75
CM C.Mathewson Pants/300 ... 100.00 45.00
CS Casey Stengel Jsy/275 .... 15.00 6.75
CY Carl Yastrzemski Jsy/350 .... 25.00 11.00
CY1 Carl Yastrzemski Pants/350 25.00 11.00
DS Duke Snider Jsy/350 .... 15.00 6.75
DW1 D.Winfield Twins Jsy/300. 10.00 4.50
FR F.Robinson O's Jsy/350 .... 15.00 6.75
FR1 F.Robinson Angels Jsy/350 15.00 6.75
GC G.Carter Mets Jsy/350 .... 10.00 4.50
GC1 G.Carter Expos Jsy/350 .... 10.00 4.50
HW Honus Wagner Pants/275 100.00 45.00
JB Johnny Bench Jsy/150 .... 15.00 6.75
JM Joe Morgan Jsy/350 .... 10.00 4.50
JN Juan Marichal Pants/225 ..... 10.00 4.50
JN1 Juan Marichal Jsy/48 .... 15.00 6.75
LA Luis Aparicio Jsy/230 .... 10.00 4.50
LB Lou Boudreau Jsy/265 .... 10.00 4.50
MM Mickey Mantle Pants/350 120.00 55.00
NR N.Ryan Rgr Pants/350 .... 30.00 13.50
NR1 N.Ryan Astros Pants/350 .. 30.00 13.50
OS Ozzie Smith Jsy/85 .... 40.00 18.00
RF Rollie Fingers Jsy/105 .... 10.00 4.50
RY R.Yount Portrait Jsy/350 ..... 15.00 6.75
RY1 R.Yount Swing Jsy/350 ..... 15.00 6.75
SA Sparky Anderson Jsy/350 .... 10.00 4.50
SC Steve Carlton Jsy/350 .... 10.00 4.50
SM Stan Musial Jsy/350 .... 40.00 18.00
TC Ty Cobb Pants/300 .... 100.00 45.00
TP Tony Perez Jsy/350 .... 10.00 4.50
TS Tom Seaver Jsy/350 .... 15.00 6.75
TS1 Tom Seaver Pants/350 .... 15.00 6.75
TW Ted Williams Jsy/250 .... 80.00 36.00
WA W.Alston Look Left Jsy/350 10.00 4.50
WA1 W.Alston Ahead Jsy/350 ... 10.00 4.50
WI Willie Stargell Jsy/55 .... 25.00 11.00
WS Warren Spahn CO Jsy/350 . 15.00 6.75
YB Yogi Berra Jsy/300 .... 15.00 6.75

2003 SP Legendary Cuts Historic Swatches Blue

MINT NRMT
*BLUE: .6X TO 1.5X BASIC p/r 225-350
*BLUE: .6X TO 1.5X BASIC p/r 150-190
OVERALL GAME USED ODDS 1:12
STATED PRINT RUN 50 SERIAL #'d SETS

2003 SP Legendary Cuts Historic Swatches Green

MINT NRMT
*GREEN: .5X TO 1.2X BASIC SWATCH
OVERALL GAME USED ODDS 1:12
PRINT RUNS B/WN 160-250 COPIES PER
DW D.Winfield Yanks Jsy/160 .. 10.00 4.50

2003 SP Legendary Cuts Historic Swatches Purple

MINT NRMT
*PURPLE p/r 150: .5X TO 1.2X BASIC
*PURPLE p/r 75-100: .6X TO 1.5X BASIC
OVERALL GAME USED ODDS 1:12
PRINT RUNS B/WN 75-150 COPIES PER

2003 SP Legendary Cuts Historical Impressions

MINT NRMT
STATED PRINT RUN 350 SERIAL #'d SETS
*GOLD 200: .6X TO 1.5X BASIC
GOLD 200 PRINT RUN 200 SERIAL #'d SETS
*GOLD 75: 1.25X TO 3X BASIC
GOLD 75 PRINT RUN 75 SERIAL #'d SETS
*SILVER: .75X TO 2X BASIC
SILVER PRINT RUN 250 SERIAL #'d SETS
OVERALL HIST.IMP.ODDS 1:12
AC Alexander Cartwright 8.00 3.60
BR Babe Ruth 20.00 9.00
CG Charlie Gehringer 8.00 3.60
CH Carl Hubbell 10.00 4.50
CM Christy Mathewson 10.00 4.50
CS Casey Stengel 10.00 4.50
CY Cy Young 10.00 4.50
DD Dizzy Dean 10.00 4.50
DO Don Drysdale 10.00 4.50
EC Eddie Collins 8.00 3.60
ES Enos Slaughter 8.00 3.60
GH Gabby Hartnett 8.00 3.60
HC Harry Caray 10.00 4.50
HG Hank Greenberg 10.00 4.50
HO Hoyt Wilhelm 8.00 3.60
HW Honus Wagner 10.00 4.50
JD Joe DiMaggio 12.00 5.50
JF Jimmie Foxx 10.00 4.50
JM Johnny Mize 8.00 3.60
JO Joe McCarthy 8.00 3.60
JR Jackie Robinson 10.00 4.50
LB Lou Boudreau 8.00 3.60
LD Leo Durocher 8.00 3.60
LE Lefty Grove 10.00 4.50
LG Lefty Gomez 10.00 4.50
LO Lou Gehrig 12.00 5.50
MA Mel Allen 8.00 3.60
MC Mickey Cochrane 8.00 3.60
MM Mickey Mantle 30.00 13.50
MO Mel Ott 10.00 4.50
PR Pee Wee Reese 10.00 4.50
RA Richie Ashburn 10.00 4.50
RC Roberto Clemente 20.00 9.00
RH Rogers Hornsby 10.00 4.50
RO Roy Campanella 10.00 4.50
SP Satchel Paige 10.00 4.50
TL Tony Lazzeri 8.00 3.60
TS Tris Speaker 10.00 4.50
TW Ted Williams 12.00 5.50
TY Ty Cobb 12.00 5.50

2003 SP Legendary Cuts Presidential Cut Signatures

Randomly inserted into packs, these cards featured autographs of deceased United States Presidents. It is believed that these cards were originally supposed to be included in the 2003 Upper Deck "American History" set which was never produced. We have put the stated print runs for these cards next to the President's name in our checklist. Please note that due to market scarcity, no pricing is provided for these cards. Many collectors were somewhat dismayed to discover that Upper Deck actually put their serial numbering on the cut itself.

MINT NRMT
AJ Andrew Johnson/2
BH Benjamin Harrison/2
CA Chester Arthur/3
CC Calvin Coolidge/2
DE Dwight Eisenhower/2
FDR Franklin D. Roosevelt/3
GW George Washington /1
HT Harry Truman/2
JK John F. Kennedy /2
LJ Lyndon Johnson/2
RN Richard Nixon/2
UG Ulysses S. Grant/2
WT William Taft/2
WW Woodrow Wilson/2

1999 SP Signature

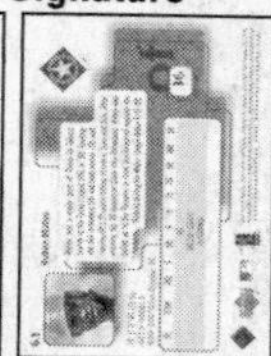

The 1999 SP Signature set was issued in one series totalling 180 cards and distributed in three card packs with a suggested retail price of $19.99. The expensive SRP was due to the fact that there is one autograph card per pack. The set features color action player photos with player information on the cardback. Rookie Cards include A.J. Burnett and Pat Burrell. 350 Mel Ott A Piece of History 500 Club bat cards were randomly seeded into packs. Pricing for these bat cards can be referenced under 1999 Upper Deck A Piece of History 500 Club.

Nm-Mt Ex-Mt
COMPLETE SET (180) 150.00 45.00
1 Nomar Garciaparra 4.00 1.20
2 Ken Griffey Jr. 4.00 1.20
3 J.D. Drew .... 1.00 .30
4 Alex Rodriguez 4.00 1.20
5 Juan Gonzalez .... 1.50 .45
6 Mo Vaughn .... 1.00 .30
7 Greg Maddux 4.00 1.20
8 Chipper Jones .... 2.50 .75
9 Frank Thomas .... 2.50 .75
10 Vladimir Guerrero .... 2.50 .75

11 Mike Piazza 4.00 1.20
12 Eric Chavez 1.00 .30
13 Tony Gwynn 3.00 .90
14 Orlando Hernandez .75 .23
15 Pat Burrell RC 6.00 1.80
16 Darin Erstad 1.00 .30
17 Greg Vaughn .75 .23
18 Russ Branyan .75 .23
19 Gabe Kapler .75 .23
20 Craig Biggio 1.50 .45
21 Troy Glaus 1.00 .30
22 Pedro Martinez 2.50 .75
23 Carlos Beltran 1.50 .45
24 Derrek Lee 1.00 .30
25 Manny Ramirez 1.50 .45
26 Shea Hillenbrand RC 4.00 1.20
27 Carlos Lee 1.00 .30
28 Angel Pena .75 .23
29 Rafael Roque RC 1.00 .30
30 Octavio Dotel .75 .23
31 Jeromy Burnitz 1.00 .30
32 Jeremy Giambi .75 .23
33 Andruw Jones 1.00 .30
34 Todd Helton 1.50 .45
35 Scott Rolen 2.50 .75
36 Jason Kendall 1.00 .30
37 Trevor Hoffman 1.00 .30
38 Barry Bonds 6.00 1.80
39 Ivan Rodriguez 2.50 .75
40 Roy Halladay .75 .23
41 Rickey Henderson 2.50 .75
42 Ryan Minor .75 .23
43 Brian Jordan 1.00 .30
44 Alex Gonzalez .75 .23
45 Raul Mondesi 1.00 .30
46 Corey Koskie 1.00 .30
47 Paul O'Neill 1.50 .45
48 Todd Walker .75 .23
49 Carlos Febles .75 .23
50 Travis Fryman 1.00 .30
51 Albert Belle 1.00 .30
52 Travis Lee .75 .23
53 Bruce Chen .75 .23
54 Reggie Taylor .75 .23
55 Jerry Hairston Jr. 1.00 .30
56 Carlos Guillen 1.00 .30
57 Michael Barrett .75 .23
58 Jason Conti .75 .23
59 Joe Lawrence .75 .23
60 Jeff Cirillo .75 .23
61 Juan Melo .75 .23
62 Chad Hermansen .75 .23
63 Ruben Mateo .75 .23
64 Ben Davis .75 .23
65 Mike Caruso .75 .23
66 Jason Giambi 1.00 .30
67 Jose Canseco 2.50 .75
68 Chad Hutchinson RC 1.50 .45
69 Mitch Meluskey .75 .23
70 Adrian Beltre 1.50 .45
71 Mark Kotsay .75 .23
72 Juan Encarnacion .75 .23
73 Dermal Brown .75 .23
74 Kevin Witt .75 .23
75 Vinny Castilla 1.00 .30
76 Aramis Ramirez 1.00 .30
77 Marlon Anderson .75 .23
78 Mike Kinkade .75 .23
79 Kevin Barker .75 .23
80 Ron Belliard .75 .23
81 Chris Haas .75 .23
82 Bob Henley .75 .23
83 Fernando Seguignol .75 .23
84 Damon Minor .75 .23
85 A.J. Burnett RC 4.00 1.20
86 Calvin Pickering .75 .23
87 Mike Darr .75 .23
88 Cesar King .75 .23
89 Rob Bell .75 .23
90 Derrick Gibson .75 .23
91 Orber Moreno RC 1.00 .30
92 Robert Fick .75 .23
93 Doug Mientkiewicz RC 4.00 1.20
94 A.J. Pierzynski 1.00 .30
95 Orlando Palmeiro .75 .23
96 Sidney Ponson .75 .23
97 Ivanon Coffie RC 1.00 .30
98 Juan Pena RC 1.00 .30
99 Matt Karchner .75 .23
100 Carlos Castillo .75 .23
101 Bryan Ward RC 1.00 .30
102 Mario Valdez .75 .23
103 Billy Wagner 1.00 .30
104 Miguel Tejada 1.00 .30
105 Jose Cruz Jr. .75 .23
106 George Lombard .75 .23
107 Geoff Jenkins 1.00 .30
108 Ray Lankford .75 .23
109 Todd Stottlemyre .75 .23
110 Mike Lowell 1.00 .30
111 Matt Clement .75 .23
112 Scott Brosius 1.00 .30
113 Preston Wilson 1.00 .30
114 Bartolo Colon 1.00 .30
115 Rolando Arrojo .75 .23
116 Jose Guillen 1.00 .30
117 Ron Gant 1.00 .30
118 Ricky Ledee .75 .23
119 Carlos Delgado 1.00 .30
120 Abraham Nunez .75 .23
121 John Olerud 1.00 .30
122 Chan Ho Park 1.00 .30
123 Brad Radke 1.00 .30
124 Al Leiter 1.00 .30
125 Gary Matthews Jr. .75 .23
126 F.P. Santangelo .75 .23
127 Brad Fullmer .75 .23
128 Matt Anderson .75 .23
129 A.J. Hinch .75 .23
130 Sterling Hitchcock .75 .23
131 Edgar Martinez 1.50 .45
132 Fernando Tatis .75 .23
133 Bobby Smith .75 .23
134 Paul Konerko 1.00 .30
135 Sean Casey 1.00 .30
136 Donnie Sadler .75 .23
137 Denny Neagle .75 .23
138 Sandy Alomar Jr. .75 .23
139 Mariano Rivera 1.50 .45
140 Emil Brown .75 .23
141 J.T. Snow 1.00 .30
142 Eli Marrero .75 .23
143 Rusty Greer 1.00 .30
144 Johnny Damon 1.50 .45
145 Damion Easley .75 .23
146 Eric Milton .75 .23
147 Rico Brogna .75 .23
148 Ray Durham 1.00 .30
149 Wally Joyner 1.00 .30
150 Royce Clayton .75 .23
151 David Ortiz 1.50 .45
152 Wade Boggs 1.50 .45
153 Ugueth Urbina .75 .23
154 Richard Hidalgo .75 .23
155 Bob Abreu 1.00 .30
156 Robb Nen 1.00 .30
157 David Segui .75 .23
158 Sean Berry .75 .23
159 Kevin Tapani .75 .23
160 Jason Varitek 1.50 .45
161 Fernando Vina .75 .23
162 Jim Leyritz .75 .23
163 Enrique Wilson .75 .23
164 Jim Parque .75 .23
165 Doug Glanville .75 .23
166 Jesus Sanchez .75 .23
167 Nolan Ryan 6.00 1.80
168 Robin Yount 4.00 1.20
169 Stan Musial 4.00 1.20
170 Tom Seaver 1.50 .45
171 Mike Schmidt 5.00 1.50
172 Willie Stargell 1.50 .45
173 Rollie Fingers 1.00 .30
174 Willie McCovey 1.00 .30
175 Harmon Killebrew 2.50 .75
176 Eddie Mathews 2.50 .75
177 Reggie Jackson 1.50 .45
178 Frank Robinson 1.50 .45
179 Ken Griffey Sr. 1.00 .30
180 Eddie Murray 2.50 .75
S1 Ken Griffey Jr. Sample 2.00 .60

1999 SP Signature Autographs

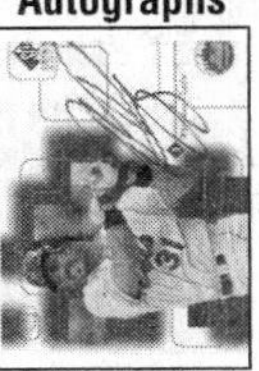

Inserted one per pack, this 150-card set is a partial parallel autographed version of the base set. Though print runs were not released, the amount of cards each player signed varied greatly. Many of the active veteran stars are noticeably tougher to find than the other cards in the set. In addition, several players had exchange cards of which expired on May 12th, 2000. The following players originally packed out as exchange cards: A.J. Burnett, Sean Casey, Vinny Castilla, Bartolo Colon, Pedro Martinez, Ruben Mateo, Jim Parque, Mike Piazza, Scott Rolen, J.T. Snow and Willie Stargell.

Nm-Mt Ex-Mt
AB Albert Belle 25.00 7.50
ABE Adrian Beltre 25.00 7.50
AG Alex Gonzalez 8.00 2.40
AJ Andruw Jones 15.00 4.50
AJB A.J. Burnett 10.00 3.00
AJP A.J. Pierzynski 15.00 4.50
AL Al Leiter 15.00 4.50
AN Abraham Nunez 8.00 2.40
AP Angel Pena 8.00 2.40
AR Alex Rodriguez 150.00 45.00
ARA Aramis Ramirez 15.00 4.50
BA Bob Abreu 15.00 4.50
BB Barry Bonds 300.00 90.00
BC Bruce Chen 8.00 2.40
BCO Bartolo Colon 15.00 4.50
BD Ben Davis 8.00 2.40
BF Brad Fullmer 8.00 2.40
BH Bob Henley 8.00 2.40
BR Brad Radke 15.00 4.50
BS Bobby Smith 8.00 2.40
BW Bryan Ward 8.00 2.40
BWA Billy Wagner 25.00 7.50
CBE Carlos Beltran 40.00 12.00
CC Carlos Castillo 8.00 2.40
CD Carlos Delgado 25.00 7.50
CF Carlos Febles 8.00 2.40
CH Chad Hermansen 8.00 2.40
CHA Chris Haas 8.00 2.40
CHU Chad Hutchinson 8.00 2.40
CJ Chipper Jones 40.00 12.00
CK Corey Koskie 15.00 4.50
CKI Cesar King 8.00 2.40
CL Carlos Lee 15.00 4.50
CP Calvin Pickering 8.00 2.40
DAM Damon Minor 8.00 2.40
DB Dermal Brown 8.00 2.40
DE Darin Erstad 15.00 4.50
DEA Damion Easley 8.00 2.40
DG Derrick Gibson 8.00 2.40
DGL Doug Glanville 8.00 2.40
DL Derrek Lee 15.00 4.50
DO David Ortiz 25.00 7.50
DOM Doug Mientkiewicz 10.00 3.00
DS Donnie Sadler 8.00 2.40
DSE David Segui 8.00 2.40
EB Emil Brown 8.00 2.40
EC Eric Chavez 15.00 4.50
ED Orlando Hernandez SP 80.00 24.00
ELI Eli Marrero 8.00 2.40
EM Edgar Martinez 40.00 12.00
EMA Eddie Mathews 60.00 18.00
EMI Eric Milton 8.00 2.40
EW Enrique Wilson 8.00 2.40
FR Frank Robinson 25.00 7.50
FS Fernando Seguignol 8.00 2.40
FT Frank Thomas 60.00 18.00
FTA Fernando Tatis 8.00 2.40
FV Fernando Vina 8.00 2.40
GJ Geoff Jenkins 15.00 4.50
GK Gabe Kapler 8.00 2.40
GM Greg Maddux 100.00 30.00
GMJ Gary Matthews Jr. 8.00 2.40
GV Greg Vaughn 8.00 2.40
HK Harmon Killebrew 40.00 12.00
IC Ivanon Coffie 8.00 2.40
JAG Jason Giambi 25.00 7.50
JC Jason Conti 8.00 2.40
JCI Jeff Cirillo 8.00 2.40
JD J.D. Drew 25.00 7.50
JDA Johnny Damon 25.00 7.50
JE Juan Encarnacion 8.00 2.40
JEG Jeremy Giambi 8.00 2.40
JG Jose Guillen 15.00 4.50
JHJ Jerry Hairston Jr. 8.00 2.40
JK Jason Kendall 15.00 4.50
JLA Joe Lawrence 8.00 2.40
JLE Jim Leyritz 8.00 2.40
JM Juan Melo 8.00 2.40
JO John Olerud 25.00 7.50
JOC Jose Canseco 40.00 12.00
JP Jim Parque 8.00 2.40
JR Ken Griffey Jr. 120.00 36.00
JS Jesus Sanchez 8.00 2.40
JT J.T. Snow 15.00 4.50
JV Jason Varitek 40.00 12.00
KB Kevin Barker 8.00 2.40
KW Kevin Witt 8.00 2.40
MA Marlon Anderson 8.00 2.40
MB Michael Barrett 8.00 2.40
MC Mike Caruso 8.00 2.40
MCL Matt Clement 15.00 2.40
MK Mark Kotsay 15.00 4.50
MKA Matt Karchner 8.00 2.40
MKI Mike Kinkade 8.00 2.40
MME Mitch Meluskey 8.00 2.40
MO Mo Vaughn 15.00 4.50
MP Mike Piazza 250.00 75.00
MR Manny Ramirez 50.00 15.00
MRI Mariano Rivera 60.00 18.00
MS Mike Schmidt 60.00 18.00
MT Miguel Tejada 15.00 4.50
MV Mario Valdez 8.00 2.40
NG Nomar Garciaparra 150.00 45.00
NR Nolan Ryan 150.00 45.00
OD Octavio Dotel 8.00 2.40
OP Orlando Palmeiro 8.00 2.40
PB Pat Burrell 20.00 6.00
PG Ivan Rodriguez 40.00 12.00
PK Paul Konerko 15.00 4.50
PM Pedro Martinez 120.00 36.00
PO Paul O'Neill 25.00 7.50
POP Willie Stargell 60.00 18.00
RB Russ Branyan 8.00 2.40
RBE Ron Belliard 8.00 2.40
RC Royce Clayton 8.00 2.40
RD Ray Durham 15.00 4.50
RGA Ron Gant SP 50.00 15.00
RGR Rusty Greer 15.00 4.50
RH Roy Halladay 8.00 2.40
RJ Reggie Jackson SP 60.00 18.00
RL Ray Lankford 8.00 2.40
RM Ryan Minor 8.00 2.40
RMA Ruben Mateo 8.00 2.40
RN Robb Nen 15.00 4.50
ROB Rob Bell 8.00 2.40
ROB Robert Fick 8.00 2.40
ROL Rollie Fingers 15.00 4.50
RR Rafael Roque 8.00 2.40
RT Reggie Taylor 8.00 2.40
RY Robin Yount 50.00 15.00
SA Sandy Alomar Jr. 8.00 2.40
SB Scott Brosius SP 60.00 18.00
SC Sean Casey 15.00 4.50
SHH Shea Hillenbrand 10.00 3.00
SM Stan Musial 60.00 18.00
SP Sidney Ponson 8.00 2.40
SR Ken Griffey Sr. 15.00 4.50
SR Scott Rolen 40.00 12.00
STH Sterling Hitchcock 8.00 2.40
TG Tony Gwynn 40.00 12.00
TGL Troy Glaus 15.00 4.50
THE Todd Helton 25.00 7.50
THO Trevor Hoffman 25.00 7.50
TSE Tom Seaver 40.00 12.00
TST Todd Stottlemyre 8.00 2.40
TW Todd Walker 15.00 4.50
VC Vinny Castilla 15.00 4.50
VG Vladimir Guerrero 40.00 12.00
WJ Wally Joyner 15.00 4.50
WMC Willie McCovey 40.00 12.00

1999 SP Signature Autographs Gold

Randomly inserted into packs, this 90-card set is a gold signature style partial parallel version of the base set. The only difference in design is a thin strip of gold foil squares on the card front. According to Upper Deck, 11 players did not sign their cards and are marked "NO AU" in the checklist below. Only 50 serial-numbered sets were produced. In addition, the following players had exchange cards of which expired on May 12th, 2000: Mike Piazza, Pedro Martinez, Scott Rolen and Vinny Castilla. Finally, a mere 20 copies of A.J. Burnett's cards packed out. All twenty made their way into packs as exchange cards with a May 12th, 2000 deadline. The Burnett card is not priced due to scarcity.

Nm-Mt Ex-Mt
AB Albert Belle 60.00 18.00
ABE Adrian Beltre 60.00 18.00
AG Alex Gonzalez 25.00 7.50
AJ Andruw Jones 40.00 12.00
AJB A.J. Burnett SP/20
AP Angel Pena 25.00 7.50
AR Alex Rodriguez 250.00 75.00
ARA Aramis Ramirez 40.00 12.00
BB Barry Bonds 400.00 120.00
BC Bruce Chen 25.00 7.50
BD Ben Davis 25.00 7.50
BH Bob Henley 25.00 7.50
CBE Carlos Beltran 100.00 30.00
CF Carlos Febles 25.00 7.50
CH Chad Hermansen 25.00 7.50
CHA Chris Haas 25.00 7.50
CHU Chad Hutchinson 25.00 7.50
CJ Chipper Jones 100.00 30.00
CK Corey Koskie 40.00 12.00
CKI Cesar King 25.00 7.50
CL Carlos Lee 40.00 12.00
CP Calvin Pickering 25.00 7.50
DAM Damon Minor 25.00 7.50
DB Dermal Brown 25.00 7.50
DE Darin Erstad 40.00 12.00
DG Derrick Gibson 25.00 7.50
DL Derrek Lee 40.00 12.00
EC Eric Chavez 40.00 12.00
ED Orlando Hernandez 25.00 7.50
FS Fernando Seguignol 25.00 7.50
FT Frank Thomas 100.00 30.00
GK Gabe Kapler 25.00 7.50
GM Greg Maddux 200.00 60.00
GV Greg Vaughn 25.00 7.50
JAG Jason Giambi 60.00 18.00
JC Jason Conti 25.00 7.50
JCI Jeff Cirillo 25.00 7.50
JD J.D. Drew 60.00 18.00
JE Juan Encarnacion 25.00 7.50
JHJ Jerry Hairston Jr. 25.00 7.50
JK Jason Kendall 40.00 12.00
JLA Joe Lawrence 25.00 7.50
JM Juan Melo 25.00 7.50
JOC Jose Canseco 100.00 30.00
JR Ken Griffey Jr. 200.00 60.00
KB Kevin Barker 25.00 7.50
KW Kevin Witt 25.00 7.50
MA Marlon Anderson 25.00 7.50
MB Michael Barrett 25.00 7.50
MC Mike Caruso 25.00 7.50
MK Mark Kotsay 40.00 12.00
MKI Mike Kinkade 25.00 7.50
MME Mitch Meluskey 25.00 7.50
MO Mo Vaughn 40.00 12.00
MP Mike Piazza 350.00 105.00
MR Manny Ramirez 100.00 30.00
NG Nomar Garciaparra 250.00 75.00
OD Octavio Dotel 25.00 7.50
PB Pat Burrell 60.00 18.00
PG Ivan Rodriguez 100.00 30.00
PM Pedro Martinez 200.00 60.00
PO Paul O'Neill 60.00 18.00
RB Russ Branyan 25.00 7.50
RBE Ron Belliard 25.00 7.50
RH Roy Halladay 25.00 7.50
RM Ryan Minor 25.00 7.50
RMA Ruben Mateo 25.00 7.50
ROB Rob Bell 25.00 7.50
RR Rafael Roque 25.00 7.50
RT Reggie Taylor 25.00 7.50
SHH Shea Hillenbrand 40.00 12.00
SR Scott Rolen 100.00 30.00
TG Tony Gwynn 100.00 30.00
TGL Troy Glaus 40.00 12.00
THE Todd Helton 60.00 18.00
THO Trevor Hoffman 60.00 18.00
TW Todd Walker 40.00 12.00
VC Vinny Castilla 40.00 12.00
VG Vladimir Guerrero 100.00 30.00

1999 SP Signature Legendary Cuts

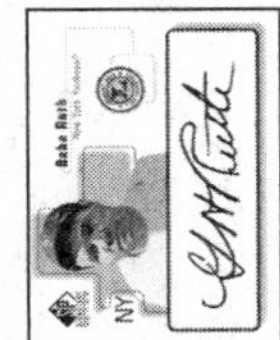

Randomly inserted into packs, this eight-card set features a "cut" signature from one of baseball's legends. Only one of each card was produced. No pricing is available due to scarcity but a checklist is provided.

Nm-Mt Ex-Mt
ROY Roy Campanella
XX Jimmie Foxx
LG Lefty Grove
W Walter Johnson
MEL1 Mel Ott
MEL2 Mel Ott
BR Babe Ruth
CY Cy Young

1997 Sports Illustrated

The 1997 Sports Illustrated set (created by Fleer) was issued in one series totalling 180 cards. Each pack contained six cards and carried a $1.99 SRP. The fronts feature Sports Illustrated action player photos with player stories on the backs. The set contains the topical subsets: Fresh Faces (1-27), Season Highlights (28-36), Inside Baseball (37-54), S.I.BER Vision 55-72) and Classic Covers (169-180). An unnumbered Jose Cruz Jr. foldout checklist was also seeded in approximately 1:4 packs.

Nm-Mt Ex-Mt
COMPLETE SET (180) 40.00 12.00
1 Bob Abreu .30 .09
2 Jaime Bluma .30 .09
3 Emil Brown RC .30 .09
4 Jose Cruz Jr. RC .75 .23
5 Jason Dickson .30 .09
6 Nomar Garciaparra 1.25 .35
7 Todd Greene .30 .09
8 Vladimir Guerrero .75 .23
9 Wilton Guerrero .30 .09
10 Jose Guillen .30 .09
11 Hideki Irabu RC .50 .15
12 Russ Johnson .30 .09
13 Andruw Jones .30 .09
14 Damon Mashore .30 .09
15 Jason McDonald .30 .09
16 Ryan McGuire .30 .09
17 Matt Morris .30 .09
18 Kevin Orie .30 .09
19 Dante Powell .30 .09
20 Pokey Reese .30 .09
21 Joe Roa RC .30 .09
22 Scott Rolen .75 .23
23 Glendon Rusch .30 .09
24 Scott Spiezio .30 .09
25 Bubba Trammell RC .50 .15
26 Todd Walker .30 .09
27 Jamey Wright .30 .09
28 Ken Griffey Jr. SH .75 .23
29 Tino Martinez SH .30 .09
30 Roger Clemens SH .75 .23
31 Hideki Irabu SH .30 .09
32 Kevin Brown SH .30 .09
33 Chipper Jones SH 1.00 .30
Cal Ripken
34 Sandy Alomar Jr. SH .30 .09
35 Ken Caminiti SH .30 .09
36 Randy Johnson SH .50 .15
37 Andy Ashby IB .30 .09
38 Jay Buhner IB .30 .09
39 Joe Carter IB .30 .09
40 Darren Daulton IB .30 .09
41 Jeff Fassero IB .30 .09
42 Andres Galarraga IB .30 .09
43 Rusty Greer IB .30 .09
44 Marquis Grissom IB .30 .09
45 Joey Hamilton IB .30 .09
46 Jimmy Key IB .30 .09
47 Ryan Klesko IB .30 .09
48 Eddie Murray IB .50 .15
49 Charles Nagy IB .30 .09
50 Dave Nilsson IB .30 .09
51 Ricardo Rincon IB RC .30 .09
52 Billy Wagner IB .30 .09
53 Dan Wilson IB .30 .09
54 Dmitri Young IB .30 .09
55 Roberto Alomar SIV .30 .09
56 Sandy Alomar Jr. SIV .30 .09
57 Scott Brosius SIV .30 .09
58 Tony Clark SIV .30 .09
59 Carlos Delgado SIV .30 .09
60 Jermaine Dye SIV .30 .09
61 Darin Erstad SIV .30 .09
62 Derek Jeter SIV 1.00 .30
63 Jason Kendall SIV .30 .09
64 Hideo Nomo SIV .30 .09
65 Rey Ordonez SIV .30 .09
66 Andy Pettitte SIV .30 .09
67 Manny Ramirez SIV .30 .09
68 Edgar Renteria SIV .30 .09
69 Shane Reynolds SIV .30 .09
70 Alex Rodriguez SIV .75 .23
71 Ivan Rodriguez SIV .50 .15
72 Jose Rosado SIV .30 .09
73 John Smoltz .50 .15
74 Tom Glavine .50 .15
75 Greg Maddux 1.25 .35
76 Chipper Jones .75 .23
77 Kenny Lofton .30 .09
78 Fred McGriff .50 .15
79 Kevin Brown .30 .09
80 Alex Fernandez .30 .09
81 Al Leiter .30 .09
82 Bobby Bonilla .30 .09
83 Gary Sheffield .30 .09
84 Moises Alou .30 .09
85 Henry Rodriguez .30 .09
86 Mark Grudzielanek .30 .09
87 Pedro Martinez .75 .23
88 Todd Hundley .30 .09
89 Bernard Gilkey .30 .09
90 Bobby Jones .30 .09
91 Curt Schilling .30 .09
92 Ricky Bottalico .30 .09
93 Mike Lieberthal .30 .09
94 Sammy Sosa 1.25 .35
95 Ryne Sandberg 1.25 .35
96 Mark Grace .50 .15
97 Deion Sanders .50 .15
98 Reggie Sanders .30 .09
99 Barry Larkin .50 .15
100 Craig Biggio .50 .15
101 Jeff Bagwell .50 .15
102 Derek Bell .30 .09
103 Brian Jordan .30 .09
104 Ray Lankford .30 .09
105 Ron Gant .30 .09
106 Al Martin .30 .09
107 Kevin Elster .30 .09
108 Jermaine Allensworth .30 .09
109 Vinny Castilla .30 .09
110 Dante Bichette .30 .09
111 Larry Walker .50 .15
112 Mike Piazza 1.25 .35
113 Eric Karros .30 .09
114 Todd Hollandsworth .30 .09
115 Raul Mondesi .30 .09
116 Hideo Nomo .75 .23
117 Ramon Martinez .30 .09
118 Ken Caminiti .30 .09
119 Tony Gwynn 1.00 .30
120 Steve Finley .30 .09
121 Barry Bonds 2.00 .60
122 J.T. Snow .30 .09
123 Rod Beck .30 .09
124 Cal Ripken 2.50 .75
125 Mike Mussina .50 .15
126 Brady Anderson .30 .09
127 Bernie Williams .50 .15
128 Derek Jeter 2.00 .60
129 Tino Martinez .50 .15
130 Andy Pettitte .50 .15
131 David Cone .30 .09
132 Mariano Rivera .50 .15
133 Roger Clemens 1.50 .45
134 Pat Hentgen .30 .09
135 Juan Guzman .30 .09
136 Bob Higginson .30 .09
137 Tony Clark .30 .09
138 Travis Fryman .30 .09
139 Mo Vaughn .30 .09

140 Tim Naehring .30 .09
141 John Valentin .30 .09
142 Matt Williams .30 .09
143 David Justice .30 .09
144 Jim Thome .75 .23
145 Chuck Knoblauch .30 .09
146 Paul Molitor .50 .15
147 Marty Cordova .30 .09
148 Frank Thomas .75 .23
149 Albert Belle .30 .09
150 Robin Ventura .30 .09
151 John Jaha .30 .09
152 Jeff Cirillo .30 .09
153 Jose Valentin .30 .09
154 Jay Bell .30 .09
155 Jeff King .30 .09
156 Kevin Appier .30 .09
157 Ken Griffey Jr. 1.25 .35
158 Alex Rodriguez 1.25 .35
159 Randy Johnson .75 .23
160 Juan Gonzalez .50 .15
161 Will Clark .75 .23
162 Dean Palmer .30 .09
163 Tim Salmon .50 .15
164 Jim Edmonds .30 .09
165 Jim Leyritz .30 .09
166 Jose Canseco .75 .23
167 Jason Giambi .30 .09
168 Mark McGwire 2.00 .60
169 Barry Bonds CC .75 .23
170 Alex Rodriguez CC .75 .23
171 Roger Clemens CC .75 .23
172 Ken Griffey Jr. CC .75 .23
173 Greg Maddux CC .75 .23
174 Mike Piazza CC .75 .23
175 Will Clark CC .75 .23
Mark McGwire
176 Hideo Nomo CC .30 .09
177 Cal Ripken CC 1.25 .35
178 Ken Griffey Jr. CC .75 .23
Frank Thomas
179 Alex Rodriguez CC 1.25 .35
Derek Jeter
180 John Wetteland CC .30 .09
P158 A.Rodriguez Promo 1.50 .45
NNO Jose Cruz Jr. CL .25 .07

1997 Sports Illustrated Extra Edition

Randomly inserted in packs, this 180-card set if parallel to the base set with etched holofoil accents. Only 500 of each card were produced and are sequentially numbered.

Nm-Mt Ex-Mt
*STARS: 6X TO 15X BASIC CARDS....
*ROOKIES: 3X TO 8X BASIC CARDS..

1997 Sports Illustrated Autographed Mini-Covers

Redemptions for these autographed cards were randomly inserted in packs. This six-card set features color photos of three current and three retired players on miniature SI covers. Only 250 of each card was produced and serially numbered and autographed.

	Nm-Mt	Ex-Mt
1 Alex Rodriguez	120.00	36.00
2 Cal Ripken	150.00	45.00
3 Kirby Puckett	50.00	15.00
4 Willie Mays	150.00	45.00
5 Frank Robinson	25.00	7.50
6 Hank Aaron	150.00	45.00

1997 Sports Illustrated Cooperstown Collection

Randomly inserted in packs at the rate of one in 12, this 12-card set features classic Sports Illustrated baseball covers with a description of the issue on the back.

	Nm-Mt	Ex-Mt
COMPLETE SET (12)	60.00	18.00
1 Hank Aaron	10.00	3.00
2 Yogi Berra	6.00	1.80
3 Lou Brock	5.00	1.50
4 Rod Carew	5.00	1.50
5 Juan Marichal	5.00	1.50
6 Al Kaline	6.00	1.80
7 Joe Morgan	5.00	1.50
8 Brooks Robinson	5.00	1.50
9 Willie Stargell	5.00	1.50
10 Kirby Puckett	5.00	1.50
11 Willie Mays	12.00	3.60
12 Frank Robinson	5.00	1.50

1997 Sports Illustrated Great Shots

Randomly inserted one per pack, this 25-card set showcases some of the greatest photography in Sports Illustrated history and features color player photos that unfold into mini posters. When unfolded the blank backed posters measure 5" by 7".

	Nm-Mt	Ex-Mt
COMPLETE SET (25)	8.00	2.40
1 Chipper Jones	.50	.15
2 Ryan Klesko	.20	.06
3 Kenny Lofton	.20	.06
4 Greg Maddux	.75	.23
5 John Smoltz	.30	.09
6 Roberto Alomar	.20	.06
7 Cal Ripken	1.50	.45
8 Mo Vaughn	.20	.06
9 Albert Belle	.20	.06
10 Frank Thomas	.50	.15
11 Ryne Sandberg	.75	.23
12 Deion Sanders	.30	.09
13 Vinny Castilla	.20	.06
Andres Galarraga		
14 Eric Karros	.20	.06
15 Mike Piazza	.75	.23
16 Derek Jeter	1.25	.35
17 Mark McGwire	1.25	.35
18 Darren Daulton	.20	.06
19 Andy Ashby	.20	.06
20 Barry Bonds	1.25	.35
21 Jay Buhner	.20	.06
22 Randy Johnson	.50	.15
23 Alex Rodriguez	.75	.23
24 Juan Gonzalez	.30	.09
25 Ken Griffey Jr.	.75	.23

1998 Sports Illustrated

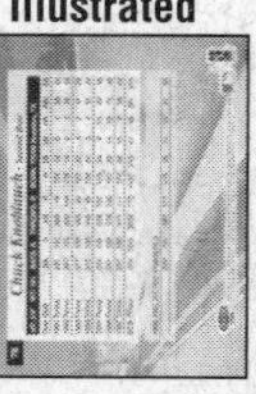

The 1998 Sports Illustrated set (created by Fleer) was issued in one series totalling 200 cards and was distributed in six-card packs with a suggested retail price of $1.99. The cards feature exclusive Sports Illustrated photography and commentary. The set contains the topical subsets: Baseball's Best (129-148), One to Watch (149-176/201), and 97 in Review (177-200). A Travis Lee One to Watch subset card (number 201) was inserted into the product just before going to press. Though official numbers were never released, it appears the card was seeded into approximately one in every four boxes, making it about two times tougher to pull than any of the other regular issue cards. Notable Rookie Cards include Magglio Ordonez. Also, a 3 1/2" by 5" Alex Rodriguez bonus card was randomly inserted one in every six packs displaying an action color player photo with the complete Sports Illustrated checklisted printed on the card. In addition a promotional card featuring Alex Rodriguez was distributed to dealers and hobby media severla weeks prior to the products release. The "Promotional Sample" text running diagonally across the front and back of the card makes it easy to distinguish.

	Nm-Mt	Ex-Mt
COMPLETE SET (200)	25.00	7.50
1 Edgardo Alfonzo	.30	.09
2 Roberto Alomar	.50	.15
3 Sandy Alomar Jr.	.30	.09
4 Moises Alou	.30	.09
5 Brady Anderson	.30	.09
6 Garret Anderson	.30	.09
7 Kevin Appier	.30	.09
8 Jeff Bagwell	.50	.15
9 Jay Bell	.30	.09
10 Albert Belle	.30	.09
11 Dante Bichette	.30	.09
12 Craig Biggio	.50	.15
13 Barry Bonds	2.00	.60
14 Bobby Bonilla	.30	.09
15 Kevin Brown	.50	.15
16 Jay Buhner	.30	.09
17 Ellis Burks	.30	.09
18 Mike Cameron	.30	.09
19 Ken Caminiti	.30	.09
20 Jose Canseco	.75	.23
21 Joe Carter	.30	.09
22 Vinny Castilla	.30	.09
23 Jeff Cirillo	.30	.09
24 Tony Clark	.30	.09
25 Will Clark	.75	.23
26 Roger Clemens	1.50	.45
27 David Cone	.30	.09
28 Jose Cruz Jr.	.30	.09
29 Carlos Delgado	.30	.09
30 Jason Dickson	.30	.09
31 Dennis Eckersley	.30	.09
32 Jim Edmonds	.30	.09
33 Scott Erickson	.30	.09
34 Darin Erstad	.30	.09
35 Shawn Estes	.30	.09
36 Jeff Fassero	.30	.09
37 Alex Fernandez	.30	.09
38 Chuck Finley	.30	.09
39 Steve Finley	.30	.09
40 Travis Fryman	.30	.09
41 Andres Galarraga	.30	.09
42 Ron Gant	.30	.09
43 Nomar Garciaparra	1.25	.35
44 Jason Giambi	.30	.09
45 Tom Glavine	.50	.15
46 Juan Gonzalez	.75	.23
47 Mark Grace	.50	.15
48 Willie Greene	.30	.09
49 Rusty Greer	.30	.09
50 Ben Grieve	.30	.09
51 Ken Griffey Jr.	1.25	.35
52 Mark Grudzielanek	.30	.09
53 Vladimir Guerrero	.75	.23
54 Juan Guzman	.30	.09
55 Tony Gwynn	1.00	.30
56 Joey Hamilton	.30	.09
57 Rickey Henderson	.75	.23
58 Pat Hentgen	.30	.09
59 Livan Hernandez	.30	.09
60 Bobby Higginson	.30	.09
61 Todd Hundley	.30	.09
62 Hideki Irabu	.30	.09
63 John Jaha	.30	.09
64 Derek Jeter	2.00	.60
65 Charles Johnson	.30	.09
66 Randy Johnson	.75	.23
67 Andruw Jones	.30	.09
68 Bobby Jones	.30	.09
69 Chipper Jones	.75	.23
70 Brian Jordan	.30	.09
71 David Justice	.30	.09
72 Eric Karros	.30	.09
73 Jeff Kent	.30	.09
74 Jimmy Key	.30	.09
75 Darryl Kile	.30	.09
76 Jeff King	.30	.09
77 Ryan Klesko	.30	.09
78 Chuck Knoblauch	.30	.09
79 Ray Lankford	.30	.09
80 Barry Larkin	.50	.15
81 Kenny Lofton	.30	.09
82 Greg Maddux	1.25	.35
83 Al Martin	.30	.09
84 Edgar Martinez	.50	.15
85 Pedro Martinez	.75	.23
86 Tino Martinez	.50	.15
87 Mark McGwire	2.00	.60
88 Paul Molitor	.50	.15
89 Raul Mondesi	.30	.09
90 Jamie Moyer	.30	.09
91 Mike Mussina	.50	.15
92 Tim Naehring	.30	.09
93 Charles Nagy	.30	.09
94 Denny Neagle	.30	.09
95 Dave Nilsson	.30	.09
96 Hideo Nomo	.75	.23
97 Rey Ordonez	.30	.09
98 Dean Palmer	.30	.09
99 Rafael Palmeiro	.50	.15
100 Andy Pettitte	.50	.15
101 Mike Piazza	1.25	.35
102 Brad Radke	.30	.09
103 Manny Ramirez	.50	.15
104 Edgar Renteria	.30	.09
105 Cal Ripken	2.50	.75
106 Alex Rodriguez	1.25	.35
107 Henry Rodriguez	.30	.09
108 Ivan Rodriguez	.75	.23
109 Scott Rolen	.75	.23
110 Tim Salmon	.50	.15
111 Curt Schilling	.30	.09
112 Gary Sheffield	.30	.09
113 John Smoltz	.30	.09
114 J.T. Snow	.30	.09
115 Sammy Sosa	1.25	.35
116 Matt Stairs	.30	.09
117 Shannon Stewart	.30	.09
118 Frank Thomas	.75	.23
119 Jim Thome	.75	.23
120 Justin Thompson	.30	.09
121 Mo Vaughn	.30	.09
122 Robin Ventura	.30	.09
123 Larry Walker	.50	.15
124 Rondell White	.30	.09
125 Bernie Williams	.50	.15
126 Matt Williams	.30	.09
127 Tony Womack	.30	.09
128 Jaret Wright	.30	.09
129 Edgar Renteria BB	.30	.09
130 Kenny Lofton BB	.30	.09
131 Tony Gwynn BB	.50	.15
132 Mark McGwire BB	1.00	.30
133 Craig Biggio BB	.30	.09
134 Charles Johnson BB	.30	.09
135 J.T. Snow BB	.30	.09
136 Ken Caminiti BB	.30	.09
137 Vladimir Guerrero BB	.50	.15
138 Jim Edmonds BB	.30	.09
139 Randy Johnson BB	.50	.15
140 Darryl Kile BB	.30	.09
141 John Smoltz BB	.30	.09
142 Greg Maddux BB	.75	.23
143 Andy Pettitte BB	.30	.09
144 Ken Griffey Jr. BB	.75	.23
145 Mike Piazza BB	.75	.23
146 Todd Greene BB	.30	.09
147 Vinny Castilla BB	.30	.09
148 Derek Jeter BB	1.00	.30
149 R.Machado OW RC	.30	.09
150 Mike Gulan OW RC	.30	.09
151 Randall Simon OW	.30	.09
152 Michael Coleman OW	.30	.09
153 Brian Rose OW	.30	.09
154 Scott Eyre OW RC	.30	.09
155 M.Ordonez OW RC	2.00	.60
156 Todd Helton OW	.50	.15
157 Juan Encarnacion OW	.30	.09
158 Mark Kotsay OW	.30	.09
159 Josh Booty OW	.30	.09
160 Melvin Rosario OW	.30	.09
161 Shane Halter OW	.30	.09
162 Paul Konerko OW	.30	.09
163 Henry Blanco OW	.30	.09
164 A.Williamson OW	.30	.09
165 Brad Fullmer OW	.30	.09
166 Ricky Ledee OW	.30	.09
167 Ben Grieve OW	.30	.09
168 F.Catalanotto OW RC	.50	.15
169 Bobby Estalella OW	.30	.09
170 Dennis Reyes OW	.30	.09
171 Kevin Polcovich OW	.30	.09
172 Jacob Cruz OW	.30	.09
173 Ken Cloude OW	.30	.09
174 Eli Marrero OW	.30	.09
175 Fernando Tatis OW	.30	.09
176 Tom Evans OW	.30	.09
177 Rafael Palmeiro	.50	.15
Chipper Jones '97		
178 Eric Davis '97	.30	.09
179 Roger Clemens '97	.75	.23
180 Brett Butler	.50	.15
Eddie Murray '97		
181 Frank Thomas '97	.50	.15
182 Curt Schilling '97	.30	.09
183 Jeff Bagwell '97	.30	.09
184 Mark McGwire	.75	.23
Ken Griffey Jr. '97		
185 Kevin Brown '97	.30	.09
186 Francisco Cordova	.30	.09
Ricardo Rincon '97		
187 Charles Johnson '97	.30	.09
188 Hideki Irabu '97	.30	.09
189 Tony Gwynn '97	.50	.15
190 Sandy Alomar Jr. '97	.30	.09
191 Ken Griffey Jr. '97	.75	.23
192 Larry Walker '97	.30	.09
193 Roger Clemens '97	.75	.23
194 Pedro Martinez '97	.50	.15
195 Nomar Garciaparra '97	.75	.23
196 Scott Rolen '97	.50	.15
197 Brian Anderson '97	.30	.09
198 Tony Saunders '97	.30	.09
199 Florida Marlins '97	.30	.09
200 Livan Hernandez '97	.30	.09
201 Travis Lee OW SP	2.00	.60
P106 Alex Rodriguez PROMO	2.00	.60
NNO Alex Rodriguez CL	.50	.15

1998 Sports Illustrated Extra Edition

Randomly inserted in packs, this 201-card set is a holofoil-stamped parallel version of the base set and is serially numbered to 250.

Nm-Mt Ex-Mt
*STARS: 6X TO 15X BASIC CARDS....
*ROOKIES: 4X TO 10X BASIC CARDS

1998 Sports Illustrated Autographs

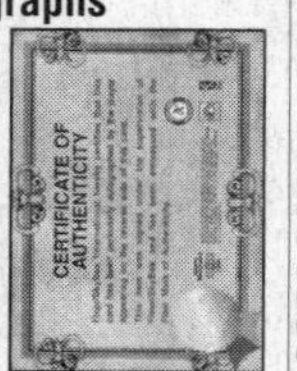

These six cards were randomly seeded into packs. The Grieve and Konerko cards are actually exchange cards with a deadline that expired on November 1st, 1999; but the other four are signed by the player. Only 500 serial numbered sets were made. The cards are unnumbered and listed in alphabetical order below.

	Nm-Mt	Ex-Mt
1 Lou Brock/500	25.00	7.50
2 Jose Cruz Jr./250	15.00	4.50
3 Rollie Fingers/500	15.00	4.50
4 Ben Grieve/250	15.00	4.50
5 Paul Konerko/250	15.00	4.50
6 Brooks Robinson/500	25.00	7.50

1998 Sports Illustrated Covers

Randomly inserted in packs at the rate of one in nine, this 10-card set features trading-card sized versions of actual Sports Illustrated covers displaying photos of the listed active players.

	Nm-Mt	Ex-Mt
COMPLETE SET (10)	25.00	7.50
C1 Ken Griffey	4.00	1.20
Mike Piazza		
C2 Derek Jeter	6.00	1.80
C3 Ken Griffey Jr.	4.00	1.20
C4 Cal Ripken	8.00	2.40
C5 Manny Ramirez	1.50	.45
C6 Jay Buhner	1.00	.30
C7 Matt Williams	1.00	.30
C8 Randy Johnson	2.50	.75
C9 Deion Sanders	1.00	.30
C10 Jose Canseco	2.50	.75

1998 Sports Illustrated Editor's Choice

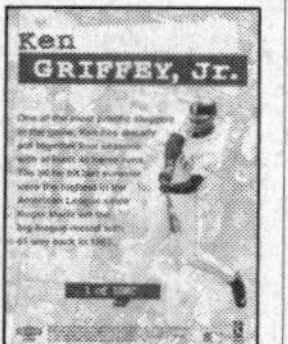

Randomly inserted in packs at the rate of one in 24, this 10-card set features color action photos of top stars for 1998 as profiled by the editors of Sports Illustrated.

	Nm-Mt	Ex-Mt
COMPLETE SET (10)	80.00	24.00
EC1 Ken Griffey Jr.	10.00	3.00
EC2 Alex Rodriguez	10.00	3.00
EC3 Frank Thomas	6.00	1.80
EC4 Mark McGwire	15.00	4.50
EC5 Greg Maddux	10.00	3.00
EC6 Derek Jeter	15.00	4.50
EC7 Cal Ripken	20.00	6.00
EC8 Nomar Garciaparra	10.00	3.00
EC9 Jeff Bagwell	4.00	1.20
EC10 Jose Cruz Jr.	2.50	.75

1998 Sports Illustrated Opening Day Mini Posters

Inserted at a rate of one per pack, this 30-card set features 5" by 7" blank-backed mini-posters with color photos of a top player from each team plus the team's 1998 schedule.

	Nm-Mt	Ex-Mt
COMPLETE SET (30)	10.00	3.00
OD1 Tim Salmon	.30	.09
OD2 Matt Williams	.20	.06
OD3 John Smoltz	.75	.23
Greg Maddux		
OD4 Cal Ripken	1.50	.45
OD5 Nomar Garciaparra	.75	.23
OD6 Sammy Sosa	.75	.23
OD7 Frank Thomas	.50	.15
OD8 Barry Larkin	.30	.09
OD9 David Justice	.20	.06
OD10 Larry Walker	.30	.09
OD11 Tony Clark	.20	.06
OD12 Livan Hernandez	.20	.06
OD13 Jeff Bagwell	.30	.09
OD14 Kevin Appier	.20	.06
OD15 Mike Piazza	.75	.23
OD16 Fernando Vina	.20	.06
OD17 Paul Molitor	.30	.09
OD18 Vladimir Guerrero	.50	.15
OD19 Rey Ordonez	.20	.06
OD20 Bernie Williams	.30	.09
OD21 Matt Stairs	.20	.06
OD22 Curt Schilling	.20	.06
OD23 Tony Womack	.20	.06
OD24 Mark McGwire	1.25	.35
OD25 Tony Gwynn	.60	.18
OD26 Barry Bonds	1.25	.35
OD27 Ken Griffey Jr.	.75	.23
OD28 Fred McGriff	.30	.09
OD29 Juan Gonzalez	.50	.15
Ivan Rodriguez		
OD30 Roger Clemens	1.00	.30

1999 Sports Illustrated

Released in mid-March, 1999, this set was produced by Fleer/SkyBox. Each pack contained six cards and carried an SRP of $1.99. The 180-card basic set features full-bleed action player photos printed on thick 20-pt. stock and contains the following subsets: Post-Season (1-9), Award Winners (10-20), Season Highlights (21-41), Prospects 2000 (42-71) and Checklists (179-180). In addition, a Kerry Wood sample card was distributed to dealers and hobby media a few months prior to the product's release. The card can be easily identified by the bold "SAMPLE" text running diagonally across the back.

	Nm-Mt	Ex-Mt
COMPLETE SET (180)	50.00	15.00
1 Yankees POST	.30	.09
2 Scott Brosius POST	.20	.06
3 David Wells POST	.20	.06
4 Sterling Hitchcock POST	.20	.06
5 David Justice POST	.20	.06
6 David Cone POST	.20	.06
7 Greg Maddux POST	.75	.23
8 Jim Leyritz POST	.20	.06
9 Gary Gaetti POST	.20	.06
10 Mark McGwire	.75	.23
Ken Griffey Jr. AW		
11 Sammy Sosa	.75	.23
Juan Gonzalez AW		
12 Larry Walker	.30	.09
Bernie Williams AW		
13 Tony Womack	.50	.15
Rickey Henderson AW		
14 Tom Glavine	.30	.09
Roger Clemens		
David Cone		
Rick Helling AW		
15 Curt Schilling	.50	.15
Roger Clemens AW		
16 Greg Maddux	.75	.23
Roger Clemens AW		
17 Trevor Hoffman	.30	.09
Tom Gordon AW		
18 Kerry Wood	.50	.15
Ben Grieve AW		
19 Tom Glavine	.50	.15
Roger Clemens AW		
20 Sammy Sosa	.50	.15
Juan Gonzalez AW		
21 Travis Lee SH	.20	.06
22 Roberto Alomar SH	.30	.09
23 Roger Clemens SH	.75	.23
24 Barry Bonds SH	.75	.23
25 Paul Molitor SH	.30	.09
26 Todd Stottlemyre SH	.20	.06
27 Chris Hoiles SH	.20	.06
28 Albert Belle SH	.20	.06
29 Tony Clark SH	.20	.06
30 Kerry Wood SH	.50	.15
31 David Wells SH	.20	.06
32 Dennis Eckersley SH	.30	.09
33 Mark McGwire SH	1.00	.30

34 Cal Ripken SH 1.25 .35
35 Ken Griffey Jr. SH .75 .23
36 Alex Rodriguez SH .75 .23
37 Craig Biggio SH .30 .09
38 Sammy Sosa SH .75 .23
39 Dennis Martinez SH .20 .06
40 Curt Schilling SH .20 .06
41 Orlando Hernandez SH .20 .06
42 Troy Glaus .50 .15
Ben Molina RC
Todd Greene
43 Mitch Meluskey .20 .06
Daryle Ward
Mike Grzanich RC
44 Eric Chavez .30 .09
Blake Stein
Mike Neill
45 Roy Halladay .20 .06
Tom Evans
Kevin Witt
46 George Lombard .20 .06
Adam Butler
Bruce Chen
47 Rafael Roque RC .20 .06
Ron Belliard
Valerio de los Santos
48 J.D.Drew .30 .09
Placido Polanco
Mark Little
49 Jason Maxwell .20 .06
Jose Nieves RC
Jeremi Gonzalez
50 Scott McClain .20 .06
Kerry Robinson
Mike Duvall RC
51 Ben Ford .20 .06
Bryan Corey RC
Danny Klassen
52 Angel Pena .30 .09
Jeff Kubenka
Paul LoDuca
53 Fernando Seguignol .20 .06
Kirk Bullinger
Tim Young
54 Ramon E. Martinez RC .20 .06
Wilson Delgado
Armando Rios
55 Jolbert Cabrera RC .20 .06
Russell Branyan
Jason Rakers
56 Carlos Guillen .30 .09
Dave Holdridge RC
Giomar Guevara
57 Alex Gonzalez .20 .06
Joe Fontenot
Preston Wilson
58 Mike Kinkade .20 .06
Jay Payton
Masato Yoshii
59 Calvin Pickering .20 .06
Ryan Minor
Willis Otanez
60 Ben Davis .20 .06
Matt Clement
Stan Spencer
61 Marlon Anderson .20 .06
Mike Welch
Gary Bennett RC
62 Abraham Nunez .30 .09
Sean Lawrence
Aramis Ramirez
63 Jonathan Johnson .20 .06
Robert Sasser RC
Scott Sheldon
64 Keith Glauber .20 .06
Guillermo Garcia
Eddie Priest
65 Brian Barkley .20 .06
Jin Ho Cho
Donnie Sadler
66 Derrick Gibson .20 .06
Mark Strittmatter
Edgard Clemente
67 Jeremy Giambi .20 .06
Dermal Brown
Chris Hatcher
68 Gabe Kapler .20 .06
Robert Fick
Marino Santana
69 Corey Koskie .30 .09
A.J.Pierzynski
Benji Sampson
70 Brian Simmons .20 .06
Mark Johnson
Craig Wilson
71 Ryan Bradley .30 .09
Mike Lowell
Jay Tessmer
72 Ben Grieve .20 .06
73 Shawn Green .30 .09
74 Rafael Palmeiro .50 .15
75 Juan Gonzalez .50 .15
76 Mike Piazza 1.25 .35
77 Devon White .30 .09
78 Jim Thome .75 .23
79 Barry Larkin .50 .15
80 Scott Rolen .75 .23
81 Raul Mondesi .30 .09
82 Jason Giambi .30 .09
83 Jose Canseco .75 .23
84 Tony Gwynn 1.00 .30
85 Cal Ripken 2.50 .75
86 Andy Pettitte .50 .15
87 Carlos Delgado .30 .09
88 Jeff Cirillo .20 .06
89 Bret Saberhagen .30 .09
90 John Olerud .30 .09
91 Ron Coomer .20 .06
92 Todd Helton .50 .15
93 Ray Lankford .20 .06
94 Tim Salmon .50 .15
95 Fred McGriff .50 .15
96 Matt Stairs .20 .06
97 Ken Griffey Jr. 1.25 .35
98 Chipper Jones .75 .23
99 Mark Grace .50 .15
100 Ivan Rodriguez .75 .23
101 Jeromy Burnitz .30 .09
102 Kenny Rogers .30 .09
103 Kevin Millwood .30 .09
104 Vinny Castilla .30 .09
105 Jim Edmonds .30 .09
106 Craig Biggio .50 .15
107 Andres Galarraga .30 .09
108 Sammy Sosa 1.25 .35
109 Juan Encarnacion .20 .06
110 Larry Walker .50 .15
111 John Smoltz .50 .15
112 Randy Johnson .75 .23
113 Bobby Higginson .30 .09
114 Albert Belle .30 .09
115 Jaret Wright .20 .06
116 Edgar Renteria .30 .09
117 Andruw Jones .30 .09
118 Barry Bonds 2.00 .60
119 Rondell White .30 .09
120 Jamie Moyer .30 .09
121 Darin Erstad .30 .09
122 Al Leiter .30 .09
123 Mark McGwire 2.00 .60
124 Mo Vaughn .30 .09
125 Livan Hernandez .20 .06
126 Jason Kendall .30 .09
127 Frank Thomas .75 .23
128 Denny Neagle .20 .06
129 Johnny Damon .50 .15
130 Derek Bell .20 .06
131 Jeff Kent .30 .09
132 Tony Womack .20 .06
133 Trevor Hoffman .20 .06
134 Gary Sheffield .30 .09
135 Tino Martinez .50 .15
136 Travis Fryman .30 .09
137 Rolando Arrojo .20 .06
138 Dante Bichette .30 .09
139 Nomar Garciaparra 1.25 .35
140 Moises Alou .30 .09
141 Chuck Knoblauch .30 .09
142 Robin Ventura .30 .09
143 Scott Erickson .20 .06
144 David Cone .30 .09
145 Greg Vaughn .20 .06
146 Wade Boggs .50 .15
147 Mike Mussina .50 .15
148 Tony Clark .20 .06
149 Alex Rodriguez 1.25 .35
150 Javy Lopez .30 .09
151 Bartolo Colon .30 .09
152 Derek Jeter 2.00 .60
153 Greg Maddux 1.25 .35
154 Kevin Brown .50 .15
155 Curt Schilling .30 .09
156 Jeff King .20 .06
157 Bernie Williams .50 .15
158 Roberto Alomar .50 .15
159 Travis Lee .20 .06
160 Kerry Wood .75 .23
161 Jeff Bagwell .50 .15
162 Roger Clemens 1.50 .45
163 Matt Williams .30 .09
164 Chan Ho Park .30 .09
165 Damion Easley .20 .06
166 Manny Ramirez .50 .15
167 Quinton McCracken .20 .06
168 Todd Walker .20 .06
169 Eric Karros .30 .09
170 Will Clark .75 .23
171 Edgar Martinez .50 .15
172 Cliff Floyd .30 .09
173 Vladimir Guerrero .75 .23
174 Tom Glavine .50 .15
175 Pedro Martinez .75 .23
176 Chuck Finley .30 .09
177 Dean Palmer .30 .09
178 Omar Vizquel .50 .15
179 Checklist .20 .06
180 Checklist .20 .06
S160 Kerry Wood Sample 1.00 .30

1999 Sports Illustrated Diamond Dominators

Randomly inserted in packs, this 10-card set features color action photos of star pitchers and hitters. The Pitchers (1-5) have an insertion rate of 1:90. The Hitters (6-10) are inserted 1:180.

	Nm-Mt	Ex-Mt
COMPLETE SET (10)	250.00	75.00
1 Kerry Wood	12.00	3.60
2 Roger Clemens	25.00	7.50
3 Randy Johnson	12.00	3.60
4 Greg Maddux	20.00	6.00
5 Pedro Martinez	12.00	3.60
6 Ken Griffey Jr.	30.00	9.00
7 Sammy Sosa	30.00	9.00
8 Nomar Garciaparra	30.00	9.00
9 Mark McGwire	50.00	15.00
10 Alex Rodriguez	30.00	9.00

1999 Sports Illustrated Fabulous 40's

Randomly inserted in packs at the rate of one in 20, this 13-card set features color action photos of players who hit 40 or more home runs during the season and are printed on sculpture embossed foil-stamped cards showing the player's 1998 home run total.

	Nm-Mt	Ex-Mt
COMPLETE SET (13)	60.00	18.00
1 Mark McGwire	12.00	3.60
2 Sammy Sosa	8.00	2.40
3 Ken Griffey Jr.	8.00	2.40
4 Greg Vaughn	1.25	.35
5 Albert Belle	2.00	.60
6 Jose Canseco	5.00	1.50
7 Vinny Castilla	2.00	.60
8 Juan Gonzalez	3.00	.90
9 Manny Ramirez	3.00	.90
10 Andres Galarraga	2.00	.60
11 Rafael Palmeiro	3.00	.90
12 Alex Rodriguez	8.00	2.40
13 Mo Vaughn	2.00	.60

1999 Sports Illustrated Fabulous 40's Extra

Randomly inserted in hobby packs only, this 13-card set is a silver patterned holo-foil stamped parallel version of the Sports Illustrated Fabulous 40's regular insert set. Each card is hand-numbered to the amount of home runs the pictured player hit during the season.

	Nm-Mt	Ex-Mt
1 Mark McGwire/70	60.00	18.00
2 Sammy Sosa/66	40.00	12.00
3 Ken Griffey Jr./56	40.00	12.00
4 Greg Vaughn/50	10.00	3.00
5 Albert Belle/49	10.00	3.00
6 Jose Canseco/46	25.00	7.50
7 Vinny Castilla/46	10.00	3.00
8 Juan Gonzalez/45	15.00	4.50
9 Manny Ramirez/45	15.00	4.50
10 Andres Galarraga/44	10.00	3.00
11 Rafael Palmeiro/43	15.00	4.50
12 Alex Rodriguez/42	40.00	12.00
13 Mo Vaughn/40	10.00	3.00

1999 Sports Illustrated Headliners

Randomly inserted in packs at the rate of one in four, this 25-card set features color action photos of leaders and star players printed on silver-foil stamped, team-color coded cards.

	Nm-Mt	Ex-Mt
COMPLETE SET (25)	40.00	12.00
1 Vladimir Guerrero	1.50	.45
2 Randy Johnson	1.50	.45
3 Mo Vaughn	.60	.18
4 Chipper Jones	1.50	.45
5 Jeff Bagwell	1.00	.30
6 Juan Gonzalez	1.00	.30
7 Mark McGwire	4.00	1.20
8 Cal Ripken	5.00	1.50
9 Frank Thomas	1.50	.45
10 Manny Ramirez	1.00	.30
11 Ken Griffey Jr.	2.50	.75
12 Scott Rolen	1.50	.45
13 Alex Rodriguez	2.50	.75
14 Barry Bonds	4.00	1.20
15 Roger Clemens	3.00	.90
16 Darin Erstad	.60	.18
17 Nomar Garciaparra	2.50	.75
18 Mike Piazza	2.50	.75
19 Greg Maddux	2.50	.75
20 Ivan Rodriguez	1.50	.45
21 Derek Jeter	4.00	1.20
22 Sammy Sosa	2.50	.75
23 Andruw Jones	.60	.18
24 Pedro Martinez	1.50	.45
25 Kerry Wood	1.50	.45

1999 Sports Illustrated One's To Watch

Featuring a selection of the league's top young prospects, these silver board foil cards were seeded into packs at consumer friendly 1:12 rate. In addition, young slugger J.D. Drew signed 250 serial-numbered cards, of which were randomly seeded into packs.

	Nm-Mt	Ex-Mt
COMPLETE SET (15)	20.00	6.00
1 J.D. Drew	1.50	.45
2 Marlon Anderson	1.00	.30
3 Roy Halladay	1.00	.30
4 Ben Grieve	1.00	.30
5 Todd Helton	2.50	.75
6 Gabe Kapler	1.00	.30
7 Troy Glaus	2.50	.75
8 Ben Davis	1.00	.30
9 Eric Chavez	1.50	.45
10 Richie Sexson	1.50	.45
11 Fernando Seguignol	1.00	.30
12 Kerry Wood	4.00	1.20
13 Bobby Smith	1.00	.30
14 Ryan Minor	1.00	.30
15 Jeremy Giambi	1.00	.30
NNO J.D. Drew AU/250	40.00	12.00

1999 Sports Illustrated Greats of the Game

The 1999 Sports Illustrated Greats of the Game (created by Fleer) was issued in one series totalling 90 cards and was distributed in seven-card packs with a suggested retail price of $15. The fronts feature color photos of some of Baseball's greatest players (including reproductions of numerous SI front covers). The backs carry player information.

	Nm-Mt	Ex-Mt
COMPLETE SET (90)	80.00	24.00
1 Jimmie Foxx	1.50	.45
2 Red Schoendienst	1.00	.30
3 Babe Ruth	5.00	1.50
4 Lou Gehrig	3.00	.90
5 Mel Ott	1.50	.45
6 Stan Musial	2.50	.75
7 Mickey Mantle	6.00	1.80
8 Carl Yastrzemski	2.50	.75
9 Enos Slaughter	.60	.18
10 Andre Dawson	.60	.18
11 Luis Aparicio	.60	.18
12 Ferguson Jenkins	.60	.18
13 Christy Mathewson	1.50	.45
14 Ernie Banks	1.50	.45
15 Johnny Podres	.60	.18
16 George Foster	.60	.18
17 Jerry Koosman	.60	.18
18 Curt Simmons	.40	.12
19 Bob Feller	.60	.18
20 Frank Robinson	1.00	.30
21 Gary Carter	.60	.18
22 Frank Thomas	.40	.12
23 Bill Lee	.60	.18
24 Willie Mays	3.00	.90
25 Tommie Agee	.60	.18
26 Boog Powell	.60	.18
27 Jim Wynn	.60	.18
28 Sparky Lyle	.60	.18
29 Bo Belinsky	.40	.12
30 Maury Wills	.60	.18
31 Bill Buckner	.60	.18
32 Steve Carlton	.60	.18
33 Harmon Killebrew	1.50	.45
34 Nolan Ryan	4.00	1.20
35 Randy Jones	.40	.12
36 Robin Roberts	.60	.18
37 Al Oliver	.60	.18
38 Rico Petrocelli	.40	.12
39 Dave Parker	.60	.18
40 Eddie Mathews	1.50	.45
41 Earl Weaver	.60	.18
42 Jackie Robinson	1.50	.45
43 Lou Brock	1.00	.30
44 Reggie Jackson	1.00	.30
45 Bob Gibson	1.00	.30
46 Jeff Burroughs	.40	.12
47 Jim Bouton	.60	.18
48 Bob Forsch	.40	.12
49 Ron Guidry	.60	.18
50 Ty Cobb	2.50	.75
51 Roy White	.60	.18
52 Joe Rudi	.60	.18
53 Moose Skowron	.60	.18
54 Goose Gossage	.60	.18
55 Ed Kranepool	.40	.12
56 Paul Blair	.40	.12
57 Kent Hrbek	.60	.18
58 Orlando Cepeda	.60	.18
59 Buck O'Neill	.60	.18
60 Al Kaline	1.50	.45
61 Vida Blue	.60	.18
62 Sam McDowell	.40	.12
63 Jesse Barfield	.40	.12
64 Dave Kingman	.60	.18
65 Ron Santo	1.00	.30
66 Steve Garvey	.60	.18
67 Gaylord Perry	.60	.18
68 Darrell Evans	.60	.18
69 Rollie Fingers	.60	.18
70 Walter Johnson	1.50	.45
71 Al Hrabosky	.60	.18
72 Mickey Rivers	.40	.12
73 Mike Torrez	.40	.12
74 Hank Bauer	.60	.18
75 Tug McGraw	.60	.18
76 David Clyde	.40	.12
77 Jim Lonborg	.40	.12
78 Clete Boyer	.60	.18
79 Harry Walker	.40	.12
80 Cy Young	1.50	.45
81 Bud Harrelson	.40	.12
82 Paul Splittorff	.40	.12
83 Bert Campaneris	.60	.18
84 Joe Niekro	.60	.18
85 Bob Horner	.60	.18
86 Jerry Royster	.40	.12
87 Tommy John	.60	.18
88 Mark Fidrych	.60	.18
89 Dick Williams	.60	.18
90 Graig Nettles	.60	.18

1999 Sports Illustrated Greats of the Game Autographs

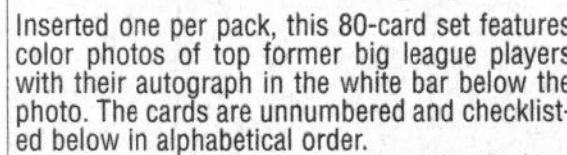

Inserted one per pack, this 80-card set features color photos of top former big league players with their autograph in the white bar below the photo. The cards are unnumbered and checklisted below in alphabetical order.

	Nm-Mt	Ex-Mt
1 Tommie Agee	25.00	7.50
2 Luis Aparicio	15.00	4.50
3 Ernie Banks	40.00	12.00
4 Jesse Barfield	8.00	2.40
5 Hank Bauer	15.00	4.50
6 Bo Belinsky	15.00	4.50
7 Paul Blair	8.00	2.40
8 Vida Blue	15.00	4.50
9 Jim Bouton	15.00	4.50
10 Clete Boyer	15.00	4.50
11 Lou Brock	25.00	7.50
12 Bill Buckner	15.00	4.50
13 Jeff Burroughs	8.00	2.40
14 Bert Campaneris	15.00	4.50
15 Steve Carlton	25.00	7.50
16 Gary Carter	15.00	4.50
17 Orlando Cepeda	15.00	4.50
18 David Clyde	8.00	2.40
19 Andre Dawson	15.00	4.50
20 Darrell Evans	15.00	4.50
21 Bob Feller	15.00	4.50
22 Mark Fidrych	25.00	7.50
23 Rollie Fingers	15.00	4.50
24 Bob Forsch	8.00	2.40
25 George Foster	15.00	4.50
26 Steve Garvey	15.00	4.50
27 Bob Gibson	25.00	7.50
28 Goose Gossage	15.00	4.50
29 Ron Guidry	25.00	7.50
30 Bud Harrelson	15.00	4.50
31 Bob Horner	15.00	4.50
32 Al Hrabosky	15.00	4.50
33 Kent Hrbek	15.00	4.50
34A Reggie Jackson	150.00	45.00
34B Reggie Jackson Mr. October	250.00	75.00
34C Reggie Jackson HOF 93	250.00	75.00
35 Ferguson Jenkins	15.00	4.50
36 Tommy John	15.00	4.50
37 Randy Jones	8.00	2.40
38 Al Kaline	40.00	12.00
39 Harmon Killebrew	40.00	12.00
40 Dave Kingman	15.00	4.50
41 Jerry Koosman	15.00	4.50
42 Ed Kranepool	15.00	4.50
43 Bill Lee	15.00	4.50
44 Jim Lonborg	8.00	2.40
45 Sparky Lyle	15.00	4.50
46 Eddie Mathews	80.00	24.00
47 Willie Mays	200.00	60.00
48 Sam McDowell	15.00	4.50
49 Tug McGraw	40.00	12.00
50 Stan Musial	120.00	36.00
51 Graig Nettles	15.00	4.50
52 Joe Niekro	15.00	4.50
53 Buck O'Neill	25.00	7.50
54 Al Oliver	15.00	4.50
55 Dave Parker	15.00	4.50
56 Gaylord Perry	15.00	4.50
57 Rico Petrocelli	15.00	4.50
58 Johnny Podres	25.00	7.50
59 Boog Powell	25.00	7.50
60 Mickey Rivers	15.00	4.50
61 Robin Roberts	25.00	7.50
62 Frank Robinson	25.00	7.50
63 Jerry Royster	8.00	2.40
64 Joe Rudi	15.00	4.50
65 Nolan Ryan	200.00	60.00
66 Ron Santo	25.00	7.50
67 Red Schoendienst	15.00	4.50
68 Curt Simmons	8.00	2.40
69 Moose Skowron	25.00	7.50
70 Enos Slaughter	25.00	7.50
71 Paul Splittorff	8.00	2.40
72 Frank Thomas	8.00	2.40
73 Mike Torrez	8.00	2.40
74 Harry Walker	8.00	2.40
75 Earl Weaver	15.00	4.50
76 Roy White	15.00	4.50
77 Dick Williams	15.00	4.50
78 Maury Wills	15.00	4.50
79 Jim Wynn	15.00	4.50
80 Carl Yastrzemski	80.00	24.00

1999 Sports Illustrated Greats of the Game Cover Collection

Randomly inserted one per pack, this 50-card set features reproductions of 50 classic Sports Illustrated covers covering over 40 years of baseball history.

	Nm-Mt	Ex-Mt
COMPLETE SET (50)	60.00	18.00
1 Johnny Podres	1.00	.30
2 Mickey Mantle	10.00	3.00
3 Stan Musial	4.00	1.20
4 Eddie Mathews	2.50	.75
5 Frank Thomas	.60	.18
6 Willie Mays	5.00	1.50
7 Red Schoendienst	1.50	.45
8 Luis Aparicio	1.00	.30
9 Mickey Mantle	10.00	3.00
10 Al Kaline	2.50	.75
11 Maury Wills	1.00	.30

12 Sam McDowell .60 .18
13 Harry Walker .60 .18
14 Carl Yastrzemski 4.00 1.20
15 Carl Yastrzemski 4.00 1.20
16 Lou Brock 1.50 .45
17 Ron Santo 1.50 .45
18 Reggie Jackson 1.50 .45
19 Frank Robinson 1.50 .45
20 Jerry Koosman 1.00 .30
21 Bud Harrelson .60 .18
22 Vida Blue 1.00 .30
23 Ferguson Jenkins 1.00 .30
24 Sparky Lyle 1.00 .30
25 Steve Carlton 1.00 .30
26 Bert Campaneris 1.00 .30
27 Jim Wynn 1.00 .30
28 Steve Garvey 1.00 .30
29 Nolan Ryan 6.00 1.80
30 Randy Jones .60 .18
31 Reggie Jackson 1.50 .45
32 Joe Rudi 1.00 .30
33 Reggie Jackson 1.50 .45
34 Dave Parker 1.00 .30
35 Mark Fidrych 1.00 .30
36 Earl Weaver 1.00 .30
37 Nolan Ryan 6.00 1.80
38 Steve Carlton 1.00 .30
39 Reggie Jackson 1.50 .45
40 Rollie Fingers 1.00 .30
41 Gary Carter 1.00 .30
42 Graig Nettles 1.00 .30
43 Gaylord Perry 1.00 .30
44 Kent Hrbek 1.00 .30
45 Gary Carter 1.00 .30
46 Steve Garvey 1.00 .30
47 Steve Carlton 1.00 .30
48 Nolan Ryan 6.00 1.80
49 Nolan Ryan 6.00 1.80
50 Mickey Mantle 10.00 3.00

1999 Sports Illustrated Greats of the Game Record Breakers

Randomly inserted in packs at the rate of one in 12, this 10-card set features action color photos of some of Baseball's record-setters printed on silver-foil stamped cards.

Nm-Mt Ex-Mt
COMPLETE SET (10) 120.00 36.00
*GOLD: 2X TO 5X BASIC RB'S
GOLD STATED ODDS 1:120
1 Mickey Mantle 30.00 9.00
2 Stan Musial 12.00 3.60
3 Babe Ruth 25.00 7.50
4 Christy Mathewson 8.00 2.40
5 Cy Young 8.00 2.40
6 Nolan Ryan 20.00 6.00
7 Jackie Robinson 8.00 2.40
8 Lou Gehrig 15.00 4.50
9 Ty Cobb 12.00 3.60
10 Walter Johnson 8.00 2.40

1998 Sports Illustrated Then and Now

The 1998 Sports Illustrated Then and Now set (created by Fleer) was issued in one series totalling 150 cards and was distributed in six-card packs containing five cards and one mini-poster with a suggested retail price of $1.99. The fronts feature color photos of active and retired players plus 1998 rookies and prospects. The backs carry ratings for each player in key skill areas. The set contains the topical subset: A Place in History (37-53) which displays statistical comparison between current players and retired greats. Notable Rookie Cards include Magglio Ordonez. An Alex Rodriguez checklist mini-poster was randomly seeded into 1:12 packs. In addition, an Alex Rodriguez promo card was distributed to dealers and hobby media several weeks to the product's release.

Nm-Mt Ex-Mt
COMPLETE SET (150) 25.00 7.50
1 Luis Aparicio .30 .09
2 Richie Ashburn .50 .15
3 Ernie Banks .75 .23
4 Yogi Berra .75 .23
5 Lou Boudreau .30 .09
6 Lou Brock .50 .15
7 Jim Bunning .30 .09
8 Rod Carew .50 .15
9 Bob Feller .30 .09
10 Rollie Fingers .30 .09
11 Bob Gibson .50 .15
12 Ferguson Jenkins .30 .09
13 Al Kaline .75 .23
14 George Kell .50 .15
15 Harmon Killebrew .75 .23
16 Ralph Kiner .30 .09
17 Tommy Lasorda .30 .09
18 Juan Marichal .30 .09
19 Eddie Mathews .75 .23
20 Willie Mays 1.50 .45
21 Willie McCovey .30 .09
22 Joe Morgan .30 .09
23 Gaylord Perry .30 .09
24 Kirby Puckett .75 .23
25 Pee Wee Reese .50 .15
26 Phil Rizzuto .50 .15
27 Robin Roberts .30 .09
28 Brooks Robinson .50 .15
29 Frank Robinson .50 .15
30 Red Schoendienst .30 .09
31 Enos Slaughter .30 .09
32 Warren Spahn .50 .15
33 Willie Stargell .50 .15
34 Earl Weaver .30 .09
35 Billy Williams .30 .09
36 Early Wynn .30 .09
37 R. Henderson HIST .50 .15
38 Greg Maddux HIST .75 .23
39 Mike Mussina HIST .30 .09
40 Cal Ripken HIST 1.25 .35
41 Albert Belle HIST .30 .09
42 Frank Thomas HIST .50 .15
43 Jeff Bagwell HIST .30 .09
44 Paul Molitor HIST .30 .09
45 Chuck Knoblauch HIST .30 .09
46 Todd Hundley HIST .30 .09
47 Bernie Williams HIST .30 .09
48 Tony Gwynn HIST .50 .15
49 Barry Bonds HIST .75 .23
50 Ken Griffey Jr. HIST .75 .23
51 Randy Johnson HIST .50 .15
52 Mark McGwire HIST 1.00 .30
53 Roger Clemens HIST .75 .23
54 Jose Cruz Jr. HIST .30 .09
55 Roberto Alomar .50 .15
56 Sandy Alomar Jr. .30 .09
57 Brady Anderson .30 .09
58 Kevin Appier .30 .09
59 Jeff Bagwell .50 .15
60 Albert Belle .30 .09
61 Dante Bichette .30 .09
62 Craig Biggio .50 .15
63 Barry Bonds 2.00 .60
64 Kevin Brown .50 .15
65 Jay Buhner .30 .09
66 Ellis Burks .30 .09
67 Ken Caminiti .30 .09
68 Jose Canseco .75 .23
69 Joe Carter .30 .09
70 Vinny Castilla .30 .09
71 Tony Clark .30 .09
72 Roger Clemens 1.50 .45
73 David Cone .30 .09
74 Jose Cruz Jr. .30 .09
75 Jason Dickson .30 .09
76 Jim Edmonds .30 .09
77 Scott Erickson .30 .09
78 Darin Erstad .30 .09
79 Alex Fernandez .30 .09
80 Steve Finley .30 .09
81 Travis Fryman .30 .09
82 Andres Galarraga .30 .09
83 Nomar Garciaparra 1.25 .35
84 Tom Glavine .50 .15
85 Juan Gonzalez .50 .15
86 Mark Grace .50 .15
87 Willie Greene .30 .09
88 Ken Griffey Jr. 1.25 .35
89 Vladimir Guerrero .75 .23
90 Tony Gwynn 1.00 .30
91 Livan Hernandez .30 .09
92 Bobby Higginson .30 .09
93 Derek Jeter 2.00 .60
94 Charles Johnson .30 .09
95 Randy Johnson .75 .23
96 Andruw Jones .30 .09
97 Chipper Jones .75 .23
98 David Justice .30 .09
99 Eric Karros .30 .09
100 Jason Kendall .30 .09
101 Jimmy Key .30 .09
102 Darryl Kile .30 .09
103 Chuck Knoblauch .30 .09
104 Ray Lankford .30 .09
105 Barry Larkin .50 .15
106 Kenny Lofton .30 .09
107 Greg Maddux 1.25 .35
108 Al Martin .30 .09
109 Edgar Martinez .50 .15
110 Pedro Martinez .75 .23
111 Ramon Martinez .30 .09
112 Tino Martinez .50 .15
113 Mark McGwire 2.00 .60
114 Raul Mondesi .30 .09
115 Matt Morris .30 .09
116 Charles Nagy .30 .09
117 Denny Neagle .30 .09
118 Hideo Nomo .75 .23
119 Dean Palmer .30 .09
120 Andy Pettitte .50 .15
121 Mike Piazza 1.25 .35
122 Manny Ramirez .50 .15
123 Edgar Renteria .30 .09
124 Cal Ripken 2.50 .75
125 Alex Rodriguez 1.25 .35
126 Henry Rodriguez .30 .09
127 Ivan Rodriguez .75 .23
128 Scott Rolen .50 .15
129 Tim Salmon .50 .15
130 Curt Schilling .30 .09
131 Gary Sheffield .30 .09
132 John Smoltz .50 .15
133 Sammy Sosa 1.25 .35
134 Frank Thomas .75 .23
135 Jim Thome .75 .23
136 Mo Vaughn .30 .09
137 Robin Ventura .30 .09
138 Larry Walker .50 .15
139 Bernie Williams .50 .15
140 Matt Williams .30 .09
141 Jaret Wright .30 .09
142 Michael Coleman .30 .09
143 Juan Encarnacion .30 .09
144 Brad Fullmer .30 .09
145 Ben Grieve .30 .09
146 Todd Helton .50 .15
147 Paul Konerko .30 .09
148 Derrek Lee .30 .09
149 Magglio Ordonez RC 2.00 .60
150 Enrique Wilson .30 .09
P125 A. Rodriguez PROMO 2.00 .60
NNO Alex Rodriguez CL .50 .15

1998 Sports Illustrated Then and Now Extra Edition

Randomly inserted in packs, this 150-card set is parallel to the base set and is distinguished by the "Extra Edition" stamp on the front. Only 500 sets were produced and each card is serial numbered on back.

Nm-Mt Ex-Mt
*STARS: 4X TO 10X BASIC CARDS
*ROOKIES: 3X TO 8X BASIC CARDS

1998 Sports Illustrated Then and Now Art of the Game

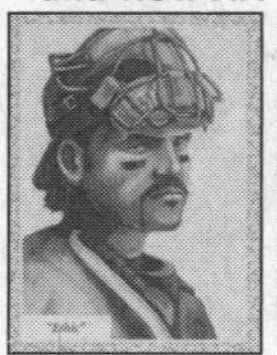

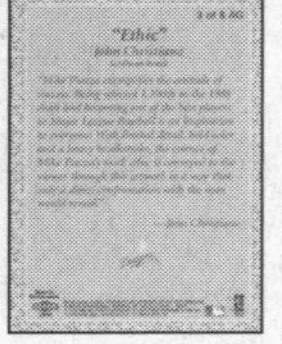

Randomly inserted in packs at the rate of one in nine, this eight-card set features reproductions of original artwork of past and present baseball heroes by eight popular sports artists.

Nm-Mt Ex-Mt
COMPLETE SET (8) 20.00 6.00
AG1 Ken Griffey Jr. 3.00 .90
AG2 Alex Rodriguez 3.00 .90
AG3 Mike Piazza 3.00 .90
AG4 Brooks Robinson 1.25 .35
AG5 David Justice .75 .23
AG6 Cal Ripken 6.00 1.80
AG7 Prospect 'n Prospector .75 .23
AG8 Barry Bonds 5.00 1.50

1998 Sports Illustrated Then and Now Autographs

These six different signed cards were distributed via mail to lucky collectors that sent in an Autograph Redemption card prior to the November 1st, 1999 deadline. Each card is embossed with a Fleer logo for authenticity. Each player signed a total of 250 cards, except for Bob Gibson and Harmon Killebrew who each signed 500 cards.

Nm-Mt Ex-Mt
*EXCHANGE: .1X TO .25X BASIC AUTO
1 Roger Clemens/250 100.00 30.00
2 Bob Gibson/500 40.00 12.00
3 Tony Gwynn/250 60.00 18.00
4 Harmon Killebrew/500 40.00 12.00
5 Willie Mays/250 150.00 45.00
6 Scott Rolen/250 40.00 12.00

1998 Sports Illustrated Then and Now Covers

Randomly inserted in packs at the rate of one in 18, this 12-card set features color photos printed as Sports Illustrated Covers of six active and six retired players.

Nm-Mt Ex-Mt
COMPLETE SET (12) 80.00 24.00
C1 Lou Brock 3.00 .90
C2 Kirby Puckett 5.00 1.50
C3 Harmon Killebrew 5.00 1.50
C4 Eddie Mathews 5.00 1.50
C5 Willie Mays 10.00 3.00
C6 Frank Robinson 3.00 .90
C7 Cal Ripken 15.00 4.50
C8 Roger Clemens 10.00 3.00
C9 Ken Griffey Jr. 8.00 2.40
C10 Mark McGwire 12.00 3.60
C11 Tony Gwynn 6.00 1.80
C12 Ivan Rodriguez 5.00 1.50

1998 Sports Illustrated Then and Now Great Shots

Inserted one in every pack, this 25-card set features Sports Illustrated photos of top players on fold-out blank-backed mini-posters that measure approximately 5" by 7".

Nm-Mt Ex-Mt
COMPLETE SET (25) 10.00 3.00
1 Ken Griffey Jr. .75 .23
2 Frank Thomas .50 .15
3 Alex Rodriguez .75 .23
4 Andruw Jones .20 .06
5 Chipper Jones .50 .15
6 Cal Ripken 1.50 .45
7 Mark McGwire 1.25 .35
8 Derek Jeter 1.25 .35
9 Greg Maddux .75 .23
10 Jeff Bagwell .30 .09
11 Mike Piazza .75 .23
12 Scott Rolen .50 .15
13 Nomar Garciaparra .75 .23
14 Jose Cruz Jr. .20 .06
15 Charles Johnson .20 .06
16 Fergie Jenkins .20 .06
17 Lou Brock .30 .09
18 Bob Gibson .30 .09
19 Harmon Killebrew .50 .15
20 Juan Marichal .20 .06
21 Brooks Robinson Frank Robinson .30 .09
22 Rod Carew .30 .09
23 Yogi Berra .50 .15
24 Willie Mays 1.00 .30
25 Kirby Puckett .50 .15

1998 Sports Illustrated Then and Now Road to Cooperstown

Randomly inserted in packs at the rate of one in 24, this 10-card set features color photos of current players having Hall of Fame caliber careers.

Nm-Mt Ex-Mt
COMPLETE SET (10) 80.00 24.00
RC1 Barry Bonds 15.00 4.50
RC2 Roger Clemens 12.00 3.60
RC3 Ken Griffey Jr. 10.00 3.00
RC4 Tony Gwynn 8.00 2.40
RC5 Rickey Henderson 4.00 1.20
RC6 Greg Maddux 10.00 3.00
RC7 Paul Molitor 2.50 .75
RC8 Mike Piazza 10.00 3.00
RC9 Cal Ripken 20.00 6.00
RC10 Frank Thomas 6.00 1.80

1998 Sports Illustrated World Series Fever

The 1998 Sports Illustrated World Series Fever set (created by Fleer) was issued in one series totalling 150 cards. The set contains the topical subsets: Covers (1-20), and Magnificent Moments (21-30). Notable Rookie Cards include Orlando Hernandez and Magglio Ordonez. A Cal Ripken promo card was distributed to dealers and hobby media to preview the brand a few month's before th product's national release. The promo is similar in design to the basic Ripken except for the text "PROMOTIONAL SAMPLE" running diagonally across the front and back of the card.

Nm-Mt Ex-Mt
COMPLETE SET (150) 25.00 7.50
1 Mickey Mantle COV 3.00 .90
2 W.S. Preview COV .30 .09
3 W.S. Preview COV .30 .09
4 Chicago (AL) COV .30 .09
5 W.S. Preview COV .30 .09
6 Lou Brock COV .30 .09
7 Brooks Robinson COV .30 .09
8 Frank Robinson COV .30 .09
9 L.A. Oakland COV .30 .09
10 Reggie Jackson COV .30 .09
11 Kansas City COV .30 .09
12 Minnesota COV .30 .09
13 Orel Hershiser COV .30 .09
14 Rickey Henderson COV .50 .15
15 Minnesota COV .30 .09
16 Toronto COV .30 .09
17 Joe Carter COV .30 .09
18 Atlanta COV .30 .09
19 N.Y. Yankees COV .30 .09
20 Edgar Renteria COV .30 .09
21 Bill Mazeroski MM .30 .09
22 Joe Carter MM .30 .09
23 Carlton Fisk MM .30 .09
24 Bucky Dent MM .30 .09
25 Mookie Wilson MM .30 .09
26 Enos Slaughter MM .30 .09
27 Mickey Lolich MM .30 .09
28 Bobby Richardson MM .30 .09
29 Kirk Gibson MM .30 .09
30 Edgar Renteria MM .30 .09
31 Albert Belle .30 .09
32 Kevin Brown .50 .15
33 Brian Rose .30 .09
34 Ron Gant .30 .09
35 Jeromy Burnitz .30 .09
36 Andres Galarraga .30 .09
37 Jim Edmonds .30 .09
38 Jose Cruz Jr. .30 .09
39 Mark Grudzielanek .30 .09
40 Shawn Estes .30 .09
41 Mark Grace .50 .15
42 Nomar Garciaparra 1.25 .35
43 Juan Gonzalez .50 .15
44 Tom Glavine .50 .15
45 Brady Anderson .30 .09
46 Tony Clark .30 .09
47 Jeff Cirillo .30 .09
48 Dante Bichette .30 .09
49 Ben Grieve .30 .09
50 Ken Griffey Jr. 1.25 .35
51 Edgardo Alfonzo .30 .09
52 Roger Clemens 1.50 .45
53 Pat Hentgen .30 .09
54 Todd Helton .50 .15
55 Andy Benes .30 .09
56 Tony Gwynn 1.00 .30
57 Andruw Jones .30 .09
58 Bobby Higginson .30 .09
59 Bobby Jones .30 .09
60 Darryl Kile .30 .09
61 Chan Ho Park .30 .09
62 Charles Johnson .30 .09
63 Rusty Greer .30 .09
64 Travis Fryman .30 .09
65 Derek Jeter 2.00 .60
66 Jay Buhner .30 .09
67 Chuck Knoblauch .30 .09
68 David Justice .30 .09
69 Brian Hunter .30 .09
70 Eric Karros .30 .09
71 Edgar Martinez .50 .15
72 Chipper Jones .75 .23
73 Barry Larkin .50 .15
74 Mike Lansing .30 .09
75 Craig Biggio .50 .15
76 Al Martin .30 .09
77 Barry Bonds 2.00 .60
78 Randy Johnson .75 .23
79 Ryan Klesko .30 .09
80 Mark McGwire 2.00 .60
81 Fred McGriff .50 .15
82 Javy Lopez .30 .09
83 Kenny Lofton .30 .09
84 Sandy Alomar Jr. .30 .09
85 Matt Morris .30 .09
86 Paul Konerko .30 .09
87 Ray Lankford .30 .09
88 Kerry Wood .75 .23
89 Roberto Alomar .50 .15
90 Greg Maddux 1.25 .35
91 Travis Lee .30 .09
92 Moises Alou .30 .09
93 Dean Palmer .30 .09
94 Hideo Nomo .75 .23
95 Ken Caminiti .30 .09
96 Pedro Martinez .75 .23
97 Raul Mondesi .30 .09
98 Denny Neagle .30 .09
99 Tino Martinez .50 .15
100 Mike Mussina .50 .15
101 Kevin Appier .30 .09
102 Vinny Castilla .30 .09
103 Jeff Bagwell .50 .15
104 Paul O'Neill .50 .15
105 Rey Ordonez .30 .09
106 Vladimir Guerrero .75 .23
107 Rafael Palmeiro .50 .15
108 Alex Rodriguez 1.25 .35
109 Andy Pettitte .50 .15
110 Carl Pavano .50 .15
111 Henry Rodriguez .30 .09
112 Gary Sheffield .30 .09
113 Curt Schilling .30 .09
114 John Smoltz .50 .15
115 Reggie Sanders .30 .09
116 Scott Rolen .75 .23
117 Mike Piazza 1.25 .35
118 Manny Ramirez .50 .15
119 Cal Ripken 2.50 .75
120 Brad Radke .30 .09
121 Tim Salmon .50 .15
122 Brett Tomko .30 .09
123 Robin Ventura .30 .09
124 Mo Vaughn .30 .09
125 A.J. Hinch .30 .09
126 Derrek Lee .30 .09
127 Orl. Hernandez RC 1.00 .30
128 Aramis Ramirez .30 .09
129 Frank Thomas .75 .23
130 J.T. Snow .30 .09
131 Magglio Ordonez RC 2.00 .60
132 Bobby Bonilla .30 .09
133 Marquis Grissom .30 .09
134 Jim Thome .75 .23
135 Justin Thompson .30 .09
136 Matt Williams .30 .09
137 Matt Stairs .30 .09
138 Wade Boggs .50 .15
139 Chuck Finley .30 .09
140 Jaret Wright .30 .09
141 Ivan Rodriguez .75 .23
142 Brad Fullmer .30 .09
143 Bernie Williams .50 .15
144 Jason Giambi .30 .09
145 Larry Walker .50 .15
146 Tony Womack .30 .09
147 Sammy Sosa 1.25 .35
148 Rondell White .30 .09
149 Todd Stottlemyre .30 .09
150 Shane Reynolds .30 .09
P8 Cal Ripken Promo 2.00 .60

1998 Sports Illustrated World Series Fever Extra Edition

This 150-card set is a parallel to the basic set. The cards are paralleled on gold holofoil and serially numbered to 98.

Nm-Mt Ex-Mt
*STARS: 10X TO 25X BASIC CARDS
*ROOKIES: 8X TO 20X BASIC CARDS

1998 Sports Illustrated World Series Fever Autumn Excellence

Randomly inserted in packs at a rate of 1:24, this set honors the great show Series records have stood the test of time.

	Nm-Mt	Ex-Mt
COMPLETE SET (10)	60.00	18.00
1 Willie Mays	8.00	2.40
2 Kirby Puckett	4.00	1.20
3 Babe Ruth	10.00	3.00
4 Reggie Jackson	2.50	.75
5 Whitey Ford	2.50	.75
6 Lou Brock	2.50	.75
7 Mickey Mantle	15.00	4.50
8 Yogi Berra	4.00	1.20
9 Bob Gibson	2.50	.75
10 Don Larsen	1.50	.45

1998 Sports Illustrated World Series Fever MVP Collection

Randomly inserted in packs at a rate of 1:4, this 10-card set profiles the Most Valuable Players from World Series history and how they achieved that status. The fronts feature color action photos with the player's name, team, and year he played in the World Series.

	Nm-Mt	Ex-Mt
COMPLETE SET (10)	8.00	2.40
1 Frank Robinson	1.25	.35
2 Brooks Robinson	1.25	.35
3 Willie Stargell	1.25	.35
4 Bret Saberhagen	.75	.23
5 Rollie Fingers	.75	.23
6 Orel Hershiser	.75	.23
7 Paul Molitor	1.25	.35
8 Tom Glavine	1.25	.35
9 John Wetteland	.75	.23
10 Livan Hernandez	.75	.23

1998 Sports Illustrated World Series Fever Reggie Jackson's Picks

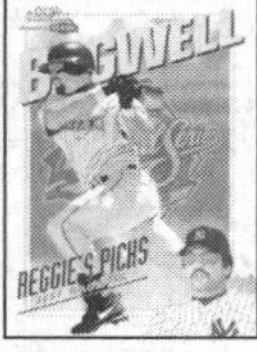

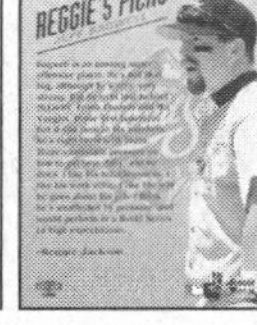

Randomly inserted in packs at a rate of 1:12, this 15-card set spotlights the World Series legend known as "Mr. October" as he gives his insight on current players he thinks can be World Series stars. The fronts feature an embossed player image and graphics.

	Nm-Mt	Ex-Mt
COMPLETE SET (15)	40.00	12.00
1 Paul O'Neill	1.50	.45
2 Barry Bonds	6.00	1.80
3 Ken Griffey Jr.	4.00	1.20
4 Juan Gonzalez	1.50	.45
5 Greg Maddux	4.00	1.20
6 Mike Piazza	4.00	1.20
7 Larry Walker	1.50	.45
8 Mo Vaughn	1.00	.30
9 Roger Clemens	5.00	1.50
10 John Smoltz	1.50	.45
11 Alex Rodriguez	4.00	1.20
12 Frank Thomas	2.50	.75
13 Mark McGwire	6.00	1.80
14 Jeff Bagwell	1.50	.45
15 Randy Johnson	2.50	.75

1996 SPx

This 1996 SPx set (produced by Upper Deck) was issued in one series totalling 60 cards. The one-card packs had a suggested retail price of $3.49. Printed on 32 pt. card stock with Holoview technology and a perimeter diecut design, the set features color player photos with a Holography background on the fronts and decorative foil stamping on the back. Two special cards are included in the set: a Ken Griffey Jr. Commemorative card was inserted one in every 75 packs and a Mike Piazza Tribute card inserted one in every 95 packs. An autographed version of each of these cards was inserted at the rate of one in 2,000.

	Nm-Mt	Ex-Mt
COMPLETE SET (60)	50.00	15.00
1 Greg Maddux	3.00	.90
2 Chipper Jones	2.00	.60
3 Fred McGriff	1.25	.35
4 Tom Glavine	1.25	.35
5 Cal Ripken	6.00	1.80
6 Roberto Alomar	1.25	.35
7 Rafael Palmeiro	1.25	.35
8 Jose Canseco	2.00	.60
9 Roger Clemens	4.00	1.20
10 Mo Vaughn	.75	.23
11 Jim Edmonds	.75	.23
12 Tim Salmon	1.25	.35
13 Sammy Sosa	3.00	.90
14 Ryne Sandberg	3.00	.90
15 Mark Grace	1.25	.35
16 Frank Thomas	2.00	.60
17 Barry Larkin	1.25	.35
18 Kenny Lofton	.75	.23
19 Albert Belle	.75	.23
20 Eddie Murray	2.00	.60
21 Manny Ramirez	1.25	.35
22 Dante Bichette	.75	.23
23 Larry Walker	1.25	.35
24 Vinny Castilla	.75	.23
25 Andres Galarraga	.75	.23
26 Cecil Fielder	.75	.23
27 Gary Sheffield	.75	.23
28 Craig Biggio	1.25	.35
29 Jeff Bagwell	1.25	.35
30 Derek Bell	.75	.23
31 Johnny Damon	1.25	.35
32 Eric Karros	.75	.23
33 Mike Piazza	3.00	.90
34 Raul Mondesi	.75	.23
35 Hideo Nomo	2.00	.60
36 Kirby Puckett	2.00	.60
37 Paul Molitor	1.25	.35
38 Marty Cordova	.75	.23
39 Rondell White	.75	.23
40 Jason Isringhausen	.75	.23
41 Paul Wilson	.75	.23
42 Rey Ordonez	.75	.23
43 Derek Jeter	5.00	1.50
44 Wade Boggs	1.25	.35
45 Mark McGwire	5.00	1.50
46 Jason Kendall	.75	.23
47 Ron Gant	.75	.23
48 Ozzie Smith	3.00	.90
49 Tony Gwynn	2.50	.75
50 Ken Caminiti	.75	.23
51 Barry Bonds	5.00	1.50
52 Matt Williams	.75	.23
53 Osvaldo Fernandez	.75	.23
54 Jay Buhner	.75	.23
55 Ken Griffey Jr.	3.00	.90
56 Randy Johnson	2.00	.60
57 Alex Rodriguez	4.00	1.20
58 Juan Gonzalez	1.25	.35
59 Joe Carter	.75	.23
60 Carlos Delgado	.75	.23
KG1 K.Griffey Jr. Comm.	5.00	1.50
MP1 Mike Piazza Trib.	5.00	1.50
KGA1 Ken Griffey Jr. Auto.	150.00	45.00
MPA1 Mike Piazza Auto.	200.00	60.00

1996 SPx Gold

Parallel to the regular version, this 60-card set was randomly inserted in hobby packs only at a rate of one in seven. The design is similar to the regular set with the exception being the gold foil borders on front.

Nm-Mt Ex-Mt

*STARS: 1.25X TO 3X BASIC CARDS.

1996 SPx Bound for Glory

Randomly inserted in packs at a rate of one in 24, this 10-card set features players with a chance to be long remembered.

	Nm-Mt	Ex-Mt
COMPLETE SET (10)	80.00	24.00
1 Ken Griffey Jr.	8.00	2.40
2 Frank Thomas	5.00	1.50
3 Barry Bonds	12.00	3.60
4 Cal Ripken	15.00	4.50
5 Greg Maddux	8.00	2.40
6 Chipper Jones	5.00	1.50
7 Roberto Alomar	3.00	.90
8 Manny Ramirez	3.00	.90
9 Tony Gwynn	6.00	1.80
10 Mike Piazza	8.00	2.40

1997 SPx

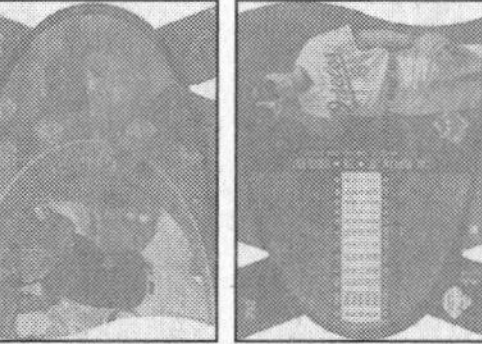

The 1997 SPx set (produced by Upper Deck) was issued in one series totalling 50 cards and was distributed in three-card hobby only packs with a suggested retail price of $5.99. The fronts feature color player images on a Holoview perimeter die cut design. The backs carry a player photo, player information, and career statistics. A sample card featuring Ken Griffey Jr. was distributed to dealers and hobby media several weeks prior to the products release.

	Nm-Mt	Ex-Mt
COMPLETE SET (50)	60.00	18.00
1 Eddie Murray	1.50	.45
2 Darin Erstad	.60	.18
3 Tim Salmon	1.00	.30
4 Andruw Jones	.60	.18
5 Chipper Jones	1.50	.45
6 John Smoltz	1.00	.30
7 Greg Maddux	2.50	.75
8 Kenny Lofton	.60	.18
9 Roberto Alomar	1.00	.30
10 Rafael Palmeiro	1.00	.30
11 Brady Anderson	.60	.18
12 Cal Ripken	5.00	1.50
13 Nomar Garciaparra	2.50	.75
14 Mo Vaughn	.60	.18
15 Ryne Sandberg	2.50	.75
16 Sammy Sosa	2.50	.75
17 Frank Thomas	1.50	.45
18 Albert Belle	.60	.18
19 Barry Larkin	1.00	.30
20 Deion Sanders	1.00	.30
21 Manny Ramirez	1.00	.30
22 Jim Thome	1.50	.45
23 Dante Bichette	.60	.18
24 Andres Galarraga	.60	.18
25 Larry Walker	1.00	.30
26 Gary Sheffield	.60	.18
27 Jeff Bagwell	1.00	.30
28 Raul Mondesi	.60	.18
29 Hideo Nomo	1.50	.45
30 Mike Piazza	2.50	.75
31 Paul Molitor	1.00	.30
32 Todd Walker	.60	.18
33 Vladimir Guerrero	1.50	.45
34 Todd Hundley	.60	.18
35 Andy Pettitte	1.00	.30
36 Derek Jeter	4.00	1.20
37 Jose Canseco	1.50	.45
38 Mark McGwire	4.00	1.20
39 Scott Rolen	1.50	.45
40 Ron Gant	.60	.18
41 Ken Caminiti	.60	.18
42 Tony Gwynn	2.00	.60
43 Barry Bonds	4.00	1.20
44 Jay Buhner	.60	.18
45 Ken Griffey Jr.	2.50	.75
46 Alex Rodriguez	2.50	.75
47 Jose Cruz Jr. RC	1.50	.45
48 Juan Gonzalez	1.00	.30
49 Ivan Rodriguez	1.50	.45
50 Roger Clemens	3.00	.90
S45 Ken Griffey Jr. Sample	2.00	.60

1997 SPx Bronze

Randomly inserted in packs at the approximate rate of one in three, cards from this 50-card set are a parallel version of the base set with bronze etched foil enhancements.

Nm-Mt Ex-Mt

*STARS: 1X TO 2.5X BASIC CARDS...
*ROOKIES: .6X TO 1.5X BASIC CARDS

1997 SPx Gold

Randomly inserted in packs at the rate of one in 17, This 50-card set is parallel to the base set and features etched gold foil enhancements.

Nm-Mt Ex-Mt

*STARS: 2.5X TO 6X BASIC CARDS...
*ROOKIES: 1.5X TO 4X BASIC CARDS

1997 SPx Grand Finale

Randomly inserted in packs, cards from this 50-card set are an extremely limited edition parallel version of the base set and features an all gold holoview image. Only 50 of each card was produced. The set was entitled Grand Finale to signify the fact that this would be the last baseball product Upper Deck would ever use the holoview technology on.

Nm-Mt Ex-Mt

*STARS: 12.5X TO 30X BASIC CARDS
*ROOKIES: 5X TO 12X BASIC CARDS

1997 SPx Silver

Randomly inserted in packs at an approximate rate of one in six, cards from this 50-card set are a parallel version of the base set with etched silver foil enhancements.

Nm-Mt Ex-Mt

*STARS: 1.5X TO 4X BASIC CARDS...
*ROOKIES: 1X TO 2.5X BASIC CARDS

1997 SPx Steel

Randomly inserted one in approximately one in every two packs, cards from this 50-card set are a parallel version of the base set. Many dealers and collectors believe that cards numbered 25-50 were printed in shorter supply. These cards can be distinguished from the similar looking silver cards by the holographic background behind the SPx logo and the player's number. Silvers lack the holographic background behind the SPx logo.

Nm-Mt Ex-Mt

*STARS: .6X TO 1.5X BASIC CARDS..
*ROOKIES: .5X TO 1.2X BASIC CARDS

1997 SPx Bound for Glory

Randomly inserted in packs, this 20-card set features color photos of promising great players on a Holoview die cut card design. Only 1,500 of each card was produced and are sequentially numbered.

	Nm-Mt	Ex-Mt
COMPLETE SET (20)	250.00	75.00
1 Andruw Jones	4.00	1.20
2 Chipper Jones	10.00	3.00
3 Greg Maddux	15.00	4.50
4 Kenny Lofton	4.00	1.20
5 Cal Ripken	30.00	9.00
6 Mo Vaughn	4.00	1.20
7 Frank Thomas	10.00	3.00
8 Albert Belle	4.00	1.20
9 Manny Ramirez	6.00	1.80
10 Gary Sheffield	4.00	1.20
11 Jeff Bagwell	6.00	1.80
12 Mike Piazza	15.00	4.50
13 Derek Jeter	25.00	7.50
14 Mark McGwire	25.00	7.50
15 Tony Gwynn	12.00	3.60
16 Ken Caminiti	4.00	1.20
17 Barry Bonds	25.00	7.50
18 Alex Rodriguez	15.00	4.50
19 Ken Griffey Jr.	15.00	4.50
20 Juan Gonzalez	6.00	1.80

1997 SPx Bound for Glory Supreme Signatures

Randomly inserted in packs, this five-card set features unnumbered autographed Bound for Glory cards. Only 250 of each card was produced and signed and are sequentially numbered. The cards are checklisted below in alphabetical order.

	Nm-Mt	Ex-Mt
1 Jeff Bagwell	80.00	24.00
2 Ken Griffey Jr.	150.00	45.00
3 Andruw Jones	50.00	15.00
4 Alex Rodriguez	200.00	60.00
5 Gary Sheffield	50.00	15.00

1997 SPx Cornerstones of the Game

Randomly inserted in packs, cards from this 10-card set display color photos of 20 top players. Two players are featured on each card using double Holoview technology. Only 500 of each card was produced and each is sequentially numbered on back.

	Nm-Mt	Ex-Mt
COMPLETE SET (10)	250.00	75.00
1 Ken Griffey Jr. Barry Bonds	25.00	7.50
2 Frank Thomas Albert Belle	15.00	4.50
3 Chipper Jones Greg Maddux	25.00	7.50
4 Tony Gwynn Paul Molitor	20.00	6.00
5 Andruw Jones Vladimir Guerrero	15.00	4.50
6 Jeff Bagwell Ryne Sandberg	25.00	7.50
7 Mike Piazza Ivan Rodriguez	25.00	7.50
8 Cal Ripken Eddie Murray	50.00	15.00
9 Mo Vaughn Mark McGwire	40.00	12.00
10 Alex Rodriguez Derek Jeter	40.00	12.00

1998 SPx Finite

The 1998 SPx Finite set contains a total of 180 cards, all serial numbered based upon specific subsets. The three-card packs retailed for $5.99 each and hit the market in June, 1998. The subsets and serial numbering are as follows: Youth Movement (1-30) - 5000 of each card, Power Explosion (31-50) - 4000 of each card, Basic Cards (51-140) - 9000 of each card, Star Focus (141-170) - 7000 of each card, Heroes of the Game (171-180) - 2000 of each card, Youth Movement (181-210) - 5000 of each card, Power Passion (211-240) - 7000 of each card, Basic Cards (241-330) - 9000 of each card, Tradewinds (331-350) - 4000 of each card and Cornerstones of the Game (351-360) -2000 of each card. Notable Rookie Cards include Kevin Millwood and Magglio Ordonez.

	Nm-Mt	Ex-Mt
COMP.YM SER.1 (30)	40.00	12.00
COMMON YM (1-30)	1.50	.45
COMP.PE SER.1 (20)	120.00	36.00
COMMON PE (31-50)	2.50	.75
COMP.BASIC SER.1 (90)	80.00	24.00
COMMON CARD (51-140)	1.00	.30
COMP.SF SER.1 (30)	100.00	30.00
COMMON SF (141-170)	1.25	.35
COMP.HG SER.1 (10)	150.00	45.00
COMMON HG (171-180)	10.00	3.00
COMP.YM SER.2 (30)	60.00	18.00
COMMON YM (181-210)	1.50	.45
COMP.PP SER.2 (30)	80.00	24.00
COMMON PP (211-240)	1.25	.35
COMP.BASIC SER.2 (90)	50.00	15.00
COMMON (241-330)	1.00	.30
COMP.TW SER.2 (20)	30.00	9.00
COMMON TW (331-350)	2.50	.75
COMP.CG SER.2 (10)	150.00	45.00
COMMON CG (351-360)	4.00	1.20
1 Nomar Garciaparra YM	6.00	1.80
2 Miguel Tejada YM	1.50	.45
3 Mike Cameron YM	1.50	.45
4 Ken Cloude YM	1.50	.45
5 Jaret Wright YM	1.50	.45
6 Mark Kotsay YM	1.50	.45
7 Craig Counsell YM	1.50	.45
8 Jose Guillen YM	1.50	.45
9 Neifi Perez YM	1.50	.45
10 Jose Cruz Jr. YM	1.50	.45
11 Brett Tomko YM	1.50	.45
12 Matt Morris YM	1.50	.45
13 Justin Thompson YM	1.50	.45
14 Jeremi Gonzalez YM	1.50	.45
15 Scott Rolen YM	4.00	1.20
16 Vladimir Guerrero YM	4.00	1.20
17 Brad Fullmer YM	1.50	.45
18 Brian Giles YM	1.50	.45
19 Todd Dunwoody YM	1.50	.45
20 Ben Grieve YM	1.50	.45
21 Juan Encarnacion YM	1.50	.45
22 Aaron Boone YM	1.50	.45
23 Richie Sexson YM	1.50	.45
24 Richard Hidalgo YM	1.50	.45
25 Andruw Jones YM	1.50	.45
26 Todd Helton YM	2.50	.75
27 Paul Konerko YM	1.50	.45
28 Dante Powell YM	1.50	.45
29 Eli Marrero YM	1.50	.45
30 Derek Jeter YM	10.00	3.00
31 Mike Piazza PE	10.00	3.00
32 Tony Clark PE	2.50	.75
33 Larry Walker PE	4.00	1.20
34 Jim Thome PE	6.00	1.80
35 Juan Gonzalez PE	5.00	1.50
36 Jeff Bagwell PE	4.00	1.20
37 Jay Buhner PE	2.50	.75
38 Tim Salmon PE	4.00	1.20
39 Albert Belle PE	2.50	.75
40 Mark McGwire PE	15.00	4.50
41 Sammy Sosa PE	10.00	3.00
42 Mo Vaughn PE	2.50	.75
43 Manny Ramirez PE	4.00	1.20
44 Tino Martinez PE	4.00	1.20
45 Frank Thomas PE	6.00	1.80
46 Nomar Garciaparra PE	10.00	3.00
47 Alex Rodriguez PE	10.00	3.00
48 Chipper Jones PE	6.00	1.80
49 Barry Bonds PE	15.00	4.50
50 Ken Griffey Jr. PE	10.00	3.00
51 Jason Dickson	1.00	.30
52 Jim Edmonds	1.00	.30
53 Darin Erstad	1.00	.30
54 Tim Salmon	1.50	.45
55 Chipper Jones	2.50	.75
56 Ryan Klesko	1.00	.30
57 Tom Glavine	1.50	.45
58 Denny Neagle	1.00	.30
59 John Smoltz	1.50	.45
60 Javy Lopez	1.00	.30
61 Roberto Alomar	1.50	.45
62 Rafael Palmeiro	1.50	.45
63 Mike Mussina	1.50	.45
64 Cal Ripken	8.00	2.40
65 Mo Vaughn	1.00	.30
66 Tim Naehring	1.00	.30
67 John Valentin	1.00	.30
68 Mark Grace	1.50	.45
69 Kevin Orie	1.00	.30
70 Sammy Sosa	4.00	1.20
71 Albert Belle	1.00	.30
72 Frank Thomas	2.50	.75
73 Robin Ventura	1.00	.30
74 David Justice	1.00	.30
75 Kenny Lofton	1.00	.30
76 Omar Vizquel	1.50	.45
77 Manny Ramirez	1.50	.45
78 Jim Thome	2.50	.75
79 Dante Bichette	1.00	.30
80 Larry Walker	1.50	.45
81 Vinny Castilla	1.00	.30
82 Ellis Burks	1.00	.30
83 Bobby Higginson	1.00	.30
84 Brian Hunter	1.00	.30
85 Tony Clark	1.00	.30
86 Mike Hampton	1.00	.30
87 Jeff Bagwell	1.50	.45
88 Craig Biggio	1.50	.45
89 Derek Bell	1.00	.30
90 Mike Piazza	4.00	1.20
91 Ramon Martinez	1.00	.30
92 Raul Mondesi	1.00	.30
93 Hideo Nomo	2.50	.75
94 Eric Karros	1.00	.30
95 Paul Molitor	1.50	.45
96 Marty Cordova	1.00	.30
97 Brad Radke	1.00	.30
98 Mark Grudzielanek	1.00	.30
99 Carlos Perez	1.00	.30
100 Rondell White	1.00	.30

101 Todd Hundley 1.00 .30
102 Edgardo Alfonzo 1.00 .30
103 John Franco 1.00 .30
104 John Olerud 1.00 .30
105 Tino Martinez 1.50 .45
106 David Cone 1.00 .30
107 Paul O'Neill 1.50 .45
108 Andy Pettitte 1.50 .45
109 Bernie Williams 1.50 .45
110 Rickey Henderson 4.00 1.20
111 Jason Giambi 1.00 .30
112 Matt Stairs 1.00 .30
113 Gregg Jefferies 1.00 .30
114 Rico Brogna 1.00 .30
115 Curt Schilling 1.00 .30
116 Jason Schmidt 1.00 .30
117 Jose Guillen 1.00 .30
118 Kevin Young 1.00 .30
119 Ray Lankford 1.00 .30
120 Mark McGwire 6.00 1.80
121 Delino DeShields 1.00 .30
122 Ken Caminiti 1.00 .30
123 Tony Gwynn 3.00 .90
124 Trevor Hoffman 1.00 .30
125 Barry Bonds 6.00 1.80
126 Jeff Kent 1.00 .30
127 Shawn Estes 1.00 .30
128 J.T. Snow 1.00 .30
129 Jay Buhner 1.00 .30
130 Ken Griffey Jr. 4.00 1.20
131 Dan Wilson 1.00 .30
132 Edgar Martinez 1.50 .45
133 Alex Rodriguez 4.00 1.20
134 Rusty Greer 1.00 .30
135 Juan Gonzalez 1.50 .45
136 Fernando Tatis 1.00 .30
137 Ivan Rodriguez 2.50 .75
138 Carlos Delgado 1.00 .30
139 Pat Hentgen 1.00 .30
140 Roger Clemens 5.00 1.50
141 Chipper Jones SF 3.00 .90
142 Greg Maddux SF 5.00 1.50
143 Rafael Palmeiro SF 2.00 .60
144 Mike Mussina SF 2.00 .60
145 Cal Ripken SF 10.00 3.00
146 Nomar Garciaparra SF 5.00 1.50
147 Mo Vaughn SF 1.25 .35
148 Sammy Sosa SF 5.00 1.50
149 Albert Belle SF 1.25 .35
150 Frank Thomas SF 3.00 .90
151 Jim Thome SF 3.00 .90
152 Kenny Lofton SF 1.25 .35
153 Manny Ramirez SF 2.00 .60
154 Larry Walker SF 2.00 .60
155 Jeff Bagwell SF 2.00 .60
156 Craig Biggio SF 2.00 .60
157 Mike Piazza SF 5.00 1.50
158 Paul Molitor SF 2.00 .60
159 Derek Jeter SF 8.00 2.40
160 Tino Martinez SF 2.00 .60
161 Curt Schilling SF 1.25 .35
162 Mark McGwire SF 8.00 2.40
163 Tony Gwynn SF 4.00 1.20
164 Barry Bonds SF 8.00 2.40
165 Ken Griffey Jr. SF 5.00 1.50
166 Randy Johnson SF 3.00 .90
167 Alex Rodriguez SF 5.00 1.50
168 Juan Gonzalez SF 2.00 .60
169 Ivan Rodriguez SF 3.00 .90
170 Roger Clemens SF 6.00 1.80
171 Greg Maddux HG 15.00 4.50
172 Cal Ripken HG 30.00 9.00
173 Frank Thomas HG 10.00 3.00
174 Jeff Bagwell HG 10.00 3.00
175 Mike Piazza HG 15.00 4.50
176 Mark McGwire HG 25.00 7.50
177 Barry Bonds HG 25.00 7.50
178 Ken Griffey Jr. HG 15.00 4.50
179 Alex Rodriguez HG 15.00 4.50
180 Roger Clemens HG 20.00 6.00
181 Mike Caruso YM 1.50 .45
182 David Ortiz YM 4.00 1.20
183 Gabe Alvarez YM 1.50 .45
184 G.Matthews Jr. YM RC 1.50 .45
185 Kerry Wood YM 4.00 1.20
186 Carl Pavano YM 2.50 .45
187 Alex Gonzalez YM 1.50 .45
188 Masato Yoshii YM RC 2.50 .75
189 Larry Sutton YM 1.50 .45
190 Russell Branyan YM 1.50 .45
191 Bruce Chen YM 1.50 .45
192 R. Arrojo YM RC 1.50 .45
193 R.Christenson YM RC 1.50 .45
194 Cliff Politte YM 1.50 .45
195 A.J. Hinch YM 1.50 .45
196 Kevin Witt YM 1.50 .45
197 Daryle Ward YM 1.50 .45
198 Corey Koskie YM RC 4.00 1.20
199 Mike Lowell YM RC 8.00 2.40
200 Travis Lee YM 1.50 .45
201 K.Millwood YM RC 4.00 1.20
202 Robert Smith YM 1.50 .45
203 M.Ordonez YM RC 12.00 3.60
204 Eric Milton YM 1.50 .45
205 Geoff Jenkins YM 1.50 .45
206 Rich Butler YM RC 1.50 .45
207 Mike Kinkade YM RC 1.50 .45
208 Braden Looper YM 1.50 .45
209 Matt Clement YM 1.50 .45
210 Derrek Lee YM 1.50 .45
211 Randy Johnson PP 3.00 .90
212 John Smoltz PP 2.00 .60
213 Roger Clemens PP 6.00 1.80
214 Curt Schilling PP 1.25 .35
215 Pedro Martinez PP 3.00 .90
216 Vinny Castilla PP 1.25 .35
217 Jose Cruz Jr. PP 1.25 .35
218 Jim Thome PP 3.00 .90
219 Alex Rodriguez PP 5.00 1.50
220 Frank Thomas PP 3.00 .90
221 Tim Salmon PP 2.00 .60
222 Larry Walker PP 2.00 .60
223 Albert Belle PP 1.25 .35
224 Manny Ramirez PP 2.00 .60
225 Mark McGwire PP 8.00 2.40
226 Mo Vaughn PP 1.25 .35
227 Andres Galarraga PP 1.25 .35
228 Scott Rolen PP 3.00 .90
229 Travis Lee PP 1.25 .35
230 Mike Piazza PP 5.00 1.50
231 N.Garciaparra PP 5.00 1.50
232 Andruw Jones PP 1.25 .35
233 Barry Bonds PP 8.00 2.40
234 Jeff Bagwell PP 2.00 .60
235 Juan Gonzalez PP 2.00 .60
236 Tino Martinez PP 2.00 .60
237 Vladimir Guerrero PP 3.00 .90
238 Rafael Palmeiro PP 2.00 .60
239 Russell Branyan PP 1.25 .35
240 Ken Griffey Jr. PP 5.00 1.50
241 Cecil Fielder 1.00 .30
242 Chuck Finley 1.00 .30
243 Jay Bell 1.00 .30
244 Andy Benes 1.00 .30
245 Matt Williams 1.00 .30
246 Brian Anderson 1.00 .30
247 Dave Dellucci RC 1.50 .45
248 Andres Galarraga 1.00 .30
249 Andruw Jones 1.00 .30
250 Greg Maddux 4.00 1.20
251 Brady Anderson 1.00 .30
252 Joe Carter 1.00 .30
253 Eric Davis 1.00 .30
254 Pedro Martinez 2.50 .75
255 Nomar Garciaparra 4.00 1.20
256 Dennis Eckersley 1.00 .30
257 Henry Rodriguez 1.00 .30
258 Jeff Blauser 1.00 .30
259 Jaime Navarro 1.00 .30
260 Ray Durham 1.00 .30
261 Chris Stynes 1.00 .30
262 Willie Greene 1.00 .30
263 Reggie Sanders 1.00 .30
264 Bret Boone 1.00 .30
265 Barry Larkin 1.50 .45
266 Travis Fryman 1.00 .30
267 Charles Nagy 1.00 .30
268 Sandy Alomar Jr. 1.00 .30
269 Darryl Kile 1.00 .30
270 Mike Lansing 1.00 .30
271 Pedro Astacio 1.00 .30
272 Damion Easley 1.00 .30
273 Joe Randa 1.00 .30
274 Luis Gonzalez 1.00 .30
275 Mike Piazza 4.00 1.20
276 Todd Zeile 1.00 .30
277 Edgar Renteria 1.00 .30
278 Livan Hernandez 1.00 .30
279 Cliff Floyd 1.00 .30
280 Moises Alou 1.00 .30
281 Billy Wagner 1.00 .30
282 Jeff King 1.00 .30
283 Hal Morris 1.00 .30
284 Johnny Damon 1.50 .45
285 Dean Palmer 1.00 .30
286 Tim Belcher 1.00 .30
287 Eric Young 1.00 .30
288 Bobby Bonilla 1.00 .30
289 Gary Sheffield 1.00 .30
290 Chan Ho Park 1.00 .30
291 Charles Johnson 1.00 .30
292 Jeff Cirillo 1.00 .30
293 Jeromy Burnitz 1.00 .30
294 Jose Valentin 1.00 .30
295 Marquis Grissom 1.00 .30
296 Todd Walker 1.00 .30
297 Terry Steinbach 1.00 .30
298 Rick Aguilera 1.00 .30
299 Vladimir Guerrero 2.50 .75
300 Rey Ordonez 1.00 .30
301 Butch Huskey 1.00 .30
302 Bernard Gilkey 1.00 .30
303 Mariano Rivera 1.50 .45
304 Chuck Knoblauch 1.00 .30
305 Derek Jeter 6.00 1.80
306 Ricky Bottalico 1.00 .30
307 Bob Abreu 1.00 .30
308 Scott Rolen 2.50 .75
309 Al Martin 1.00 .30
310 Jason Kendall 1.00 .30
311 Brian Jordan 1.00 .30
312 Ron Gant 1.00 .30
313 Todd Stottlemyre 1.00 .30
314 Greg Vaughn 1.00 .30
315 Kevin Brown 1.50 .45
316 Wally Joyner 1.00 .30
317 Robb Nen 1.00 .30
318 Orel Hershiser 1.00 .30
319 Russ Davis 1.00 .30
320 Randy Johnson 2.50 .75
321 Quinton McCracken 1.00 .30
322 Tony Saunders 1.00 .30
323 Wilson Alvarez 1.00 .30
324 Wade Boggs 1.50 .45
325 Fred McGriff 1.50 .45
326 Lee Stevens 1.00 .30
327 John Wetteland 1.00 .30
328 Jose Canseco 2.50 .75
329 Randy Myers 1.00 .30
330 Jose Cruz Jr. 1.00 .30
331 Matt Williams TW 2.50 .75
332 Andres Galarraga TW 2.50 .75
333 Walt Weiss TW 2.50 .75
334 Joe Carter TW 2.50 .75
335 Pedro Martinez TW 6.00 1.80
336 Henry Rodriguez TW 2.50 .75
337 Travis Fryman TW 2.50 .75
338 Darryl Kile TW 2.50 .75
339 Mike Lansing TW 2.50 .75
340 Mike Piazza TW 10.00 3.00
341 Moises Alou TW 2.50 .75
342 Charles Johnson TW 2.50 .75
343 Chuck Knoblauch TW 2.50 .75
344 Rickey Henderson TW 6.00 1.80
345 Kevin Brown TW 4.00 1.20
346 Orel Hershiser TW 2.50 .75
347 Wade Boggs TW 4.00 1.20
348 Fred McGriff TW 4.00 1.20
349 Jose Canseco TW 6.00 1.80
350 Gary Sheffield TW 2.50 .75
351 Travis Lee CG 4.00 1.20
352 N.Garciaparra CG 15.00 4.50
353 Frank Thomas CG 10.00 3.00
354 Cal Ripken CG 30.00 9.00
355 Mark McGwire CG 25.00 7.50
356 Mike Piazza CG 15.00 4.50
357 Alex Rodriguez CG 15.00 4.50
358 Barry Bonds CG 25.00 7.50
359 Tony Gwynn CG 12.00 3.60
360 Ken Griffey Jr. CG 15.00 4.50

1998 SPx Finite Radiance

Randomly inserted in packs, this 360-card set is a parallel to the SPx Finite base set. Due to problems in the manufacturing process, exchange cards had to be inserted into packs for Power Explosion cards 40, 41 and 45. The deadline to redeem these exchange cards was June 2nd, 1999. Serial numbering of the various subsets is as follows: Youth Movement (1-30) - 2500 of each card, Power Explosion (31-50) - 1000 of each card, Basic Cards (51-140) - 4500 of each card, Star Focus (141-170) - 3500 of each card, Heroes of the Game (171-180) - 100 of each card, Youth Movement (181-210) - 2500 of each card, Power Passion (211-240) - 3500 of each card, Basic Cards (241-330) - 4500 of each card, Tradewinds (331-350) -1000 of each card, Cornerstones of the Game (351-360) -100 of each card.

Nm-Mt Ex-Mt
*YOUTH: .6X TO 1.5X BASIC YOUTH
*PE RADIANCE: 1.25X TO 3X BASIC POW.EXP.
*BASIC RADIANCE: .75X TO 2X BASIC CARDS
*SF RADIANCE: .75X TO 2X BASIC SF
*HG RADIANCE: 1.5X TO 4X BASIC HG
*YM RADIANCE: .6X TO 1.5X BASIC YM
*YM RADIANCE RC's: .3X TO .8X BASIC YM
*PP RADIANCE: .6X TO 1.5X BASIC PP
*BASIC RADIANCE: .75X TO 2X BASIC CARDS
*TW RADIANCE: 1.25X TO 3X BASIC TW
*CG RADIANCE: 1.5X TO 4X BASIC CG

1998 SPx Finite Spectrum

Randomly inserted in packs, this 360-card set is a parallel to the SPx Finite base set. Due to problems in the manufacturing process, exchange cards had to be inserted into packs for Power Explosion cards 40, 41 and 45. The deadline to redeem these exchange cards was June 2nd, 1999. This version is the most difficult to obtain of the three varieties of SPx Finite. Serial numbering for the various subsets is as follows: Youth Movement (1-30) - 1250 of each card, Power Explosion (31-50) - 50 of each card, Basic Cards (51-140) - 2250 of each card, Star Focus (141-170) - 1750 of each card, Heroes of the Game (171-180) - 1 of each card, Youth Movement (181-210) - 1250 of each card, Power Passion (211-240) -1750 of each card, Basic Cards (241-330) - 2250 of each card, Tradewinds (331-350) - 50 of each card and Cornerstones of the Game (351-360) - 1 of each card. Neither the Heroes of the Game nor the Cornerstones of the Game subsets are priced due to scarcity.

Nm-Mt Ex-Mt
*YM SPECTRUM: 1X TO 2.5X BASIC YM
*PE SPECTRUM: 4X TO 10X BASIC PE
*BASIC SPECTRUM: 1.25X TO 3X BASIC
*SF SPECTRUM: 1.25X TO 3X BASIC SF
*YM SPECTRUM: .75X TO 2X BASIC YM
*YM SPECTRUM RC's: .5X TO 1.2X BASIC YM
*PP SPECTRUM: 1.25X TO 3X BASIC PP
*BASIC SPECTRUM: 1.25X TO 3X BASIC
*TW SPECTRUM: 4X TO 10X BASIC TW

1998 SPx Finite Home Run Hysteria

Randomly seeded exclusively into second series packs, these ten different inserts chronicle the epic home run race of the 1998 season. Each card is serial numbered to 62 on back.

Nm-Mt Ex-Mt
HR1 Ken Griffey Jr. 80.00 24.00
HR2 Mark McGwire 120.00 36.00
HR3 Sammy Sosa 80.00 24.00
HR4 Albert Belle 20.00 6.00
HR5 Alex Rodriguez 80.00 24.00
HR6 Greg Vaughn 20.00 6.00
HR7 Andres Galarraga 20.00 6.00
HR8 Vinny Castilla 20.00 6.00
HR9 Juan Gonzalez 30.00 9.00
HR10 Chipper Jones 50.00 15.00

1999 SPx

The 1999 SPx set (produced by Upper Deck) was issued in one series for a total of 120 cards and distributed in thee-card packs with a suggested retail price of $5.99. The set features color photos of 80 MLB verteran players (1-80) with 40 top rookies on subset cards (81-120) numbered to 1,999. J.D. Drew and Gabe Kapler autographed all 1,999 of their respective rookie cards. A Ken Griffey Jr. Sample card was distributed to dealers and hobby media several weeks prior to the product's release. This card is serial numbered "0000/0000" on front, has the word "SAMPLE" pasted across the back in red ink and is oddly numbered "24 East" on back (even though the basic cards have no regional references). Also, 350 Willie Mays A Piece of History 500 Home Run bat cards were randomly seeded into packs. Mays personally signed an additional 24 cards (matching his jersey number) - all of which were then serial numbered by hand and randomly seeded into packs. Pricing for these bat cards can be referenced under 1999 Upper Deck A Piece of History 500 Club.

Nm-Mt Ex-Mt
COMP.SET w/o SP's (80) 25.00 7.50
COMMON (1-10) 1.50 .45
COMMON CARD (11-80) .50 .15
COMMON SP (81-120) 10.00 3.00
1 Mark McGwire 61 3.00 .90
2 Mark McGwire 62 3.00 .90
3 Mark McGwire 63 1.50 .45
4 Mark McGwire 64 1.50 .45
5 Mark McGwire 65 1.50 .45
6 Mark McGwire 66 1.50 .45
7 Mark McGwire 67 1.50 .45
8 Mark McGwire 68 1.50 .45
9 Mark McGwire 69 1.50 .45
10 Mark McGwire 70 4.00 1.20
11 Mo Vaughn .50 .15
12 Darin Erstad .50 .15
13 Travis Lee .50 .15
14 Randy Johnson 1.25 .35
15 Matt Williams .50 .15
16 Chipper Jones 1.25 .35
17 Greg Maddux 2.00 .60
18 Andruw Jones .50 .15
19 Andres Galarraga .50 .15
20 Cal Ripken 4.00 1.20
21 Albert Belle .50 .15
22 Mike Mussina .75 .23
23 Nomar Garciaparra 2.00 .60
24 Pedro Martinez 1.25 .35
25 John Valentin .50 .15
26 Kerry Wood 1.25 .35
27 Sammy Sosa 2.00 .60
28 Mark Grace .75 .23
29 Frank Thomas 1.25 .35
30 Mike Caruso .50 .15
31 Barry Larkin .75 .23
32 Sean Casey .50 .15
33 Jim Thome 1.25 .35
34 Kenny Lofton .50 .15
35 Manny Ramirez .75 .23
36 Larry Walker .75 .23
37 Todd Helton .75 .23
38 Vinny Castilla .50 .15
39 Tony Clark .50 .15
40 Derrek Lee .50 .15
41 Mark Kotsay .50 .15
42 Jeff Bagwell .75 .23
43 Craig Biggio .75 .23
44 Moises Alou .50 .15
45 Larry Sutton .50 .15
46 Johnny Damon .75 .23
47 Gary Sheffield .50 .15
48 Raul Mondesi .50 .15
49 Jeromy Burnitz .50 .15
50 Todd Walker .50 .15
51 David Ortiz .75 .23
52 Vladimir Guerrero 1.25 .35
53 Rondell White .50 .15
54 Mike Piazza 2.00 .60
55 Derek Jeter 3.00 .90
56 Tino Martinez .75 .23
57 Roger Clemens 2.50 .75
58 Ben Grieve .50 .15
59 A.J. Hinch .50 .15
60 Scott Rolen 1.25 .35
61 Doug Glanville .50 .15
62 Aramis Ramirez .50 .15
63 Jose Guillen .50 .15
64 Tony Gwynn 1.50 .45
65 Greg Vaughn .50 .15
66 Ruben Rivera .50 .15
67 Barry Bonds 3.00 .90
68 J.T. Snow .50 .15
69 Alex Rodriguez 2.00 .60
70 Ken Griffey Jr. 2.00 .60
71 Jay Buhner .50 .15
72 Mark McGwire 3.00 .90
73 Fernando Tatis .50 .15
74 Quinton McCracken .50 .15
75 Wade Boggs .75 .23
76 Ivan Rodriguez 1.25 .35
77 Juan Gonzalez .75 .23
78 Rafael Palmeiro .75 .23
79 Jose Cruz Jr. .50 .15
80 Carlos Delgado .50 .15
81 Troy Glaus SP 10.00 3.00
82 Vladimir Nunez SP 10.00 3.00
83 George Lombard SP 10.00 3.00
84 Bruce Chen SP 10.00 3.00
85 Ryan Minor SP 10.00 3.00
86 Calvin Pickering SP 10.00 3.00
87 Jin Ho Cho SP 10.00 3.00
88 Russ Branyan SP 10.00 3.00
89 Derrick Gibson SP 10.00 3.00
90 Gabe Kapler SP AU 15.00 4.50
91 Matt Anderson SP 10.00 3.00
92 Robert Fick SP 10.00 3.00
93 Juan Encarnacion SP 10.00 3.00
94 Preston Wilson SP 10.00 3.00
95 Alex Gonzalez SP 10.00 3.00
96 Carlos Beltran SP 15.00 4.50
97 Jeremy Giambi SP 10.00 3.00
98 Dee Brown SP 10.00 3.00
99 Adrian Beltre SP 15.00 4.50
100 Alex Cora SP 10.00 3.00
101 Angel Pena SP 10.00 3.00
102 Geoff Jenkins SP 10.00 3.00
103 Ronnie Belliard SP 10.00 3.00
104 Corey Koskie SP 10.00 3.00
105 A.J. Pierzynski SP 10.00 3.00
106 Michael Barrett SP 10.00 3.00
107 Fern.Seguignol SP 10.00 3.00
108 Mike Kinkade SP 10.00 3.00
109 Mike Lowell SP 10.00 3.00
110 Ricky Ledee SP 10.00 3.00
111 Eric Chavez SP 10.00 3.00
112 Abraham Nunez SP 10.00 3.00
113 Matt Clement SP 10.00 3.00
114 Ben Davis SP 10.00 3.00
115 Mike Darr SP 10.00 3.00
116 Ramon E.Martinez SP RC 10.00 3.00
117 Carlos Guillen SP 10.00 3.00
118 Shane Monahan SP 10.00 3.00
119 J.D. Drew SP AU 25.00 7.50
120 Kevin Witt SP 10.00 3.00
24EAST K.Griffey Jr. SAMP 2.00 .60

1999 SPx Finite Radiance

Randomly inserted in Finite Radiance Hot Packs only, this 120-card set is parallel to the SPx base set. Only 100 serial-numbered sets were produced.

Nm-Mt Ex-Mt
*RADIANCE 1-10: 5X TO 12X BASIC 1-10
*RADIANCE 11-80: 8X TO 20X BASIC 11-80
*RADIANCE 81-120: .75X TO 2X BASIC 81-120
90 Gabe Kapler AU 25.00 7.50
119 J.D. Drew AU 40.00 12.00

1999 SPx Dominance

Randomly inserted into packs at the rate of one in 17, this 20-card set features color photos of some of the most dominant MLB superstars.

Nm-Mt Ex-Mt
COMPLETE SET (20) 120.00 36.00
FB1 Chipper Jones 6.00 1.80
FB2 Greg Maddux 10.00 3.00
FB3 Cal Ripken 20.00 6.00
FB4 Nomar Garciaparra 10.00 3.00
FB5 Mo Vaughn 2.50 .75
FB6 Sammy Sosa 10.00 3.00
FB7 Albert Belle 2.50 .75
FB8 Frank Thomas 6.00 1.80
FB9 Jim Thome 6.00 1.80
FB10 Jeff Bagwell 4.00 1.20
FB11 Vladimir Guerrero 6.00 1.80
FB12 Mike Piazza 10.00 3.00
FB13 Derek Jeter 15.00 4.50
FB14 Tony Gwynn 8.00 2.40
FB15 Barry Bonds 15.00 4.50
FB16 Ken Griffey Jr. 10.00 3.00
FB17 Alex Rodriguez 10.00 3.00
FB18 Mark McGwire 15.00 4.50
FB19 J.D. Drew 2.50 .75
FB20 Juan Gonzalez 4.00 1.20

1999 SPx Power Explosion

Randomly inserted in packs at the rate of one in three, this 30-card set features color action photos of some of the top power hitters of the game.

Nm-Mt Ex-Mt
COMPLETE SET (30) 40.00 12.00
PE1 Troy Glaus .75 .23
PE2 Mo Vaughn .75 .23
PE3 Travis Lee .75 .23
PE4 Chipper Jones 2.00 .60
PE5 Andres Galarraga .75 .23
PE6 Brady Anderson .75 .23
PE7 Albert Belle .75 .23
PE8 Nomar Garciaparra 3.00 .90
PE9 Sammy Sosa 3.00 .90
PE10 Frank Thomas 2.00 .60
PE11 Jim Thome 2.00 .60
PE12 Manny Ramirez 1.25 .35
PE13 Larry Walker 1.25 .35
PE14 Tony Clark .75 .23
PE15 Jeff Bagwell 1.25 .35
PE16 Moises Alou .75 .23
PE17 Ken Caminiti .75 .23
PE18 Vladimir Guerrero 2.00 .60
PE19 Mike Piazza 3.00 .90
PE20 Tino Martinez 1.25 .35
PE21 Ben Grieve .75 .23
PE22 Scott Rolen 2.00 .60
PE23 Greg Vaughn .75 .23
PE24 Barry Bonds 5.00 1.50
PE25 Ken Griffey Jr. 3.00 .90
PE26 Alex Rodriguez 3.00 .90
PE27 Mark McGwire 5.00 1.50
PE28 J.D. Drew .75 .23
PE29 Juan Gonzalez 1.25 .35
PE30 Ivan Rodriguez 2.00 .60

1999 SPx Premier Stars

Randomly inserted in packs at the rate of one in 17, this 30-card set features color action photos of some of the game's most powerful players captured on cards with a unique rainbow-foil design.

Nm-Mt Ex-Mt
PS1 Mark McGwire 20.00 6.00
PS2 Sammy Sosa 12.00 3.60
PS3 Frank Thomas 8.00 2.40

	Nm-Mt	Ex-Mt
PS4 J.D. Drew	3.00	.90
PS5 Kerry Wood	8.00	2.40
PS6 Moises Alou	3.00	.90
PS7 Kenny Lofton	3.00	.90
PS8 Jeff Bagwell	5.00	1.50
PS9 Tony Clark	3.00	.90
PS10 Roberto Alomar	8.00	2.40
PS11 Cal Ripken	25.00	7.50
PS12 Derek Jeter	20.00	6.00
PS13 Mike Piazza	12.00	3.60
PS14 Jose Cruz Jr.	3.00	.90
PS15 Chipper Jones	8.00	2.40
PS16 Nomar Garciaparra	12.00	3.60
PS17 Greg Maddux	12.00	3.60
PS18 Scott Rolen	8.00	2.40
PS19 Vladimir Guerrero	8.00	2.40
PS20 Albert Belle	3.00	.90
PS21 Ken Griffey Jr.	12.00	3.60
PS22 Alex Rodriguez	12.00	3.60
PS23 Ben Grieve	3.00	.90
PS24 Juan Gonzalez	5.00	1.50
PS25 Barry Bonds	20.00	6.00
PS26 Roger Clemens	15.00	4.50
PS27 Tony Gwynn	10.00	3.00
PS28 Randy Johnson	8.00	2.40
PS29 Travis Lee	3.00	.90
PS30 Mo Vaughn	3.00	.90

1999 SPx Star Focus

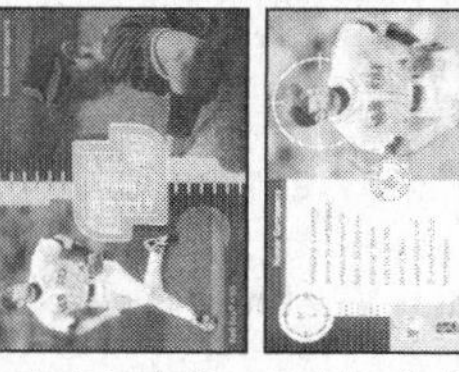
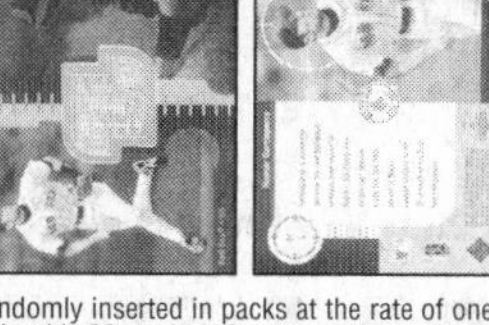

Randomly inserted in packs at the rate of one in eight, this 30-card set features action color photos of some of the brightest stars in the game beside a black-and-white portrait of the player.

	Nm-Mt	Ex-Mt
COMPLETE SET (30)	120.00	36.00
SF1 Chipper Jones	5.00	1.50
SF2 Greg Maddux	8.00	2.40
SF3 Cal Ripken	15.00	4.50
SF4 Nomar Garciaparra	8.00	2.40
SF5 Mo Vaughn	2.00	.60
SF6 Sammy Sosa	8.00	2.40
SF7 Albert Belle	2.00	.60
SF8 Frank Thomas	5.00	1.50
SF9 Jim Thome	5.00	1.50
SF10 Kenny Lofton	2.00	.60
SF11 Manny Ramirez	3.00	.90
SF12 Larry Walker	3.00	.90
SF13 Jeff Bagwell	3.00	.90
SF14 Craig Biggio	3.00	.90
SF15 Randy Johnson	5.00	1.50
SF16 Vladimir Guerrero	5.00	1.50
SF17 Mike Piazza	8.00	2.40
SF18 Derek Jeter	12.00	3.60
SF19 Tino Martinez	3.00	.90
SF20 Bernie Williams	5.00	1.50
SF21 Curt Schilling	2.00	.60
SF22 Tony Gwynn	6.00	1.80
SF23 Barry Bonds	12.00	3.60
SF24 Ken Griffey Jr.	8.00	2.40
SF25 Alex Rodriguez	8.00	2.40
SF26 Mark McGwire	12.00	3.60
SF27 J.D. Drew	2.00	.60
SF28 Juan Gonzalez	3.00	.90
SF29 Ivan Rodriguez	5.00	1.50
SF30 Ben Grieve	2.00	.60

1999 SPx Winning Materials

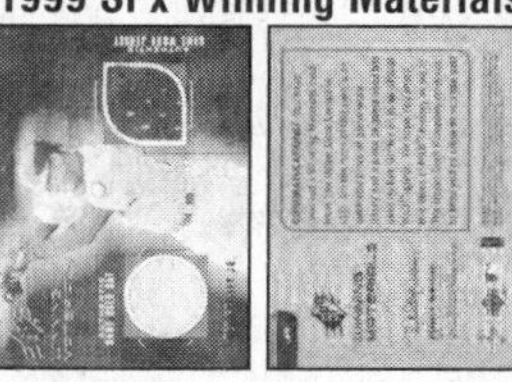

Randomly inserted into packs at the rate of one in 251, this eight-card set features color photos of top players with a piece of the player's game-worn jersey and game-used bat embedded in the card.

	Nm-Mt	Ex-Mt
IR Ivan Rodriguez	25.00	7.50
JD J.D. Drew	15.00	4.50
JR Ken Griffey Jr.	50.00	15.00
TG Tony Gwynn	40.00	12.00
TH Todd Helton	25.00	7.50
TL Travis Lee	10.00	3.00
VC Vinny Castilla	15.00	4.50
VG Vladimir Guerrero	25.00	7.50

2000 SPx

The 2000 SPx (produced by Upper Deck) set was initially released in May, 2000 as a 120-card set. Each pack contained four cards and carried a suggested retail price of $5.99. The set featured 90-player cards, and a 30-card "Young Stars" subset. There are three tiers within the Young Stars subset. Tier one cards are serial numbered to 1000, Tier two cards are serial numbered to 1500 and autographed by the player and Tier three cards are serial numbered to 500 and autographed by the player. Redemption cards were issued for several of the autograph cards and they were to be postmarked by 1/24/01 and received by 2/3/01 to be valid for exchange. In late December, 2000, Upper Deck issued a new product called Rookie Update which contained a selection of new cards for SP Authentic, SPx and UD Pros and Prospects. Rookie Update packs contained four cards and the collector was guaranteed one card from each featured brand, plus a fourth card. For SPx, these "high series" cards were numbered 121-196. The Young Stars subset was extended with cards 121-151 and cards 182-196. Cards 121-135 and 182-196 featured a selection of prospects each serial numbered to 1600. Cards 136-151 featured a selection of prospect cards signed by the player and each serial numbered to 1500. Cards 152-181 contained a selection of veteran players that were either initially not included in the basic 120-card "first series" set or traded to new teams. Notable Rookie Cards include Xavier Nady, Kazuhiro Sasaki, Ben Sheets and Barry Zito. Also, a selection of A Piece of History 3000 Club Ty Cobb memorabilia cards were randomly seeded into packs. 350 bat cards, three hand-numbered autograph cut cards and one hand-numbered, combination bat chip and autograph cut card were produced. Pricing for these memorabilia cards can be referenced under 2000 Upper Deck A Piece of History 3000 Club.

	Nm-Mt	Ex-Mt
COMP.BASIC w/o SP's (90)	25.00	7.50
COMP.UPDATE w/o SP's (30)	10.00	3.00
COMMON CARD (1-90)	.50	.15
COMMON AU/1500 (91-120)	10.00	3.00
COMMON (121-135/182-196)	8.00	2.40
COMMON (136-151)	10.00	3.00
COMMON (152-181)	.75	.23
1 Troy Glaus	.50	.15
2 Mo Vaughn	.50	.15
3 Ramon Ortiz	.50	.15
4 Jeff Bagwell	.75	.23
5 Moises Alou	.50	.15
6 Craig Biggio	.75	.23
7 Jose Lima	.50	.15
8 Jason Giambi	.50	.15
9 John Jaha	.50	.15
10 Matt Stairs	.50	.15
11 Chipper Jones	1.25	.35
12 Greg Maddux	2.00	.60
13 Andres Galarraga	.50	.15
14 Andruw Jones	.50	.15
15 Jeromy Burnitz	.50	.15
16 Ron Belliard	.50	.15
17 Carlos Delgado	.50	.15
18 David Wells	.50	.15
19 Tony Batista	.50	.15
20 Shannon Stewart	.50	.15
21 Sammy Sosa	2.00	.60
22 Mark Grace	.75	.23
23 Henry Rodriguez	.50	.15
24 Mark McGwire	3.00	.90
25 J.D. Drew	.50	.15
26 Luis Gonzalez	.50	.15
27 Randy Johnson	1.25	.35
28 Matt Williams	.50	.15
29 Steve Finley	.50	.15
30 Shawn Green	.50	.15
31 Kevin Brown	.75	.23
32 Gary Sheffield	.50	.15
33 Jose Canseco	1.25	.35
34 Greg Vaughn	.50	.15
35 Vladimir Guerrero	1.25	.35
36 Michael Barrett	.50	.15
37 Russ Ortiz	.50	.15
38 Barry Bonds	3.00	.90
39 Jeff Kent	.50	.15
40 Richie Sexson	.50	.15
41 Manny Ramirez	.50	.15
42 Jim Thome	1.25	.35
43 Roberto Alomar	.75	.23
44 Edgar Martinez	.75	.23
45 Alex Rodriguez	2.00	.60
46 John Olerud	.50	.15
47 Alex Gonzalez	.50	.15
48 Cliff Floyd	.50	.15
49 Mike Piazza	2.00	.60
50 Al Leiter	.50	.15
51 Robin Ventura	.75	.23
52 Edgardo Alfonzo	.50	.15
53 Albert Belle	.50	.15
54 Cal Ripken	4.00	1.20
55 B.J. Surhoff	.50	.15
56 Tony Gwynn	1.50	.45
57 Trevor Hoffman	.50	.15
58 Brian Giles	.50	.15
59 Jason Kendall	.50	.15
60 Kris Benson	.50	.15
61 Bob Abreu	.50	.15
62 Scott Rolen	1.25	.35
63 Curt Schilling	.50	.15
64 Mike Lieberthal	.50	.15
65 Sean Casey	.50	.15
66 Dante Bichette	.50	.15
67 Ken Griffey Jr.	2.00	.60
68 Pokey Reese	.50	.15
69 Mike Sweeney	.50	.15
70 Carlos Febles	.50	.15
71 Ivan Rodriguez	1.25	.35
72 Ruben Mateo	.50	.15
73 Rafael Palmeiro	.75	.23
74 Larry Walker	.75	.23
75 Todd Helton	.75	.23
76 Nomar Garciaparra	2.00	.60
77 Pedro Martinez	1.25	.35
78 Troy O'Leary	.50	.15
79 Jacque Jones	.50	.15
80 Corey Koskie	.50	.15
81 Juan Gonzalez	.75	.23
82 Dean Palmer	.50	.15
83 Juan Encarnacion	.50	.15
84 Frank Thomas	1.25	.35
85 Magglio Ordonez	.50	.15
86 Paul Konerko	.50	.15
87 Bernie Williams	.75	.23
88 Derek Jeter	3.00	.90
89 Roger Clemens	2.50	.75
90 Orlando Hernandez	.50	.15
91 Vernon Wells AU/1500	15.00	4.50
92 Rick Ankiel AU/1500	40.00	12.00
93 Eric Chavez AU/1500	25.00	7.50
94 A.Soriano/1500 AU	60.00	18.00
95 Eric Gagne AU/1500	100.00	30.00
96 Rob Bell AU/1500	10.00	3.00
97 Matt Riley AU/1500	15.00	4.50
98 Josh Beckett AU/1500	60.00	18.00
99 Ben Petrick AU/1500	10.00	3.00
100 Rob Ramsay AU/1500	10.00	3.00
101 Scott Williamson 1500 AU	10.00	3.00
102 Doug Davis AU/1500	10.00	3.00
103 E.Munson/1500 AU*	10.00	3.00
104 Pat Burrell AU/500	50.00	15.00
105 Jim Morris AU/1500	25.00	7.50
106 Gabe Kapler AU/500	25.00	7.50
107 Lance Berkman/1000	8.00	2.40
108 E.Durazo/1500 AU	15.00	4.50
109 Tim Hudson AU/1500	40.00	7.50
110 Ben Davis AU/1500	10.00	3.00
111 N.Johnson/1500 AU	15.00	4.50
112 O.Dotel/1500 AU	10.00	3.00
113 Jerry Hairston/1000	8.00	2.40
114 Ruben Mateo/1000	8.00	2.40
115 Chris Singleton/1000	8.00	2.40
116 Bruce Chen AU/1500	10.00	3.00
117 Derrick Gibson/1000	8.00	2.40
118 Carlos Beltran AU/500	175.00	52.50
119 F.Garcia/1500 AU	15.00	4.50
120 P.Wilson/1500 AU	15.00	4.50
121 B.Wilkerson/1600 RC	10.00	3.00
122 Roy Oswalt/1600 RC	50.00	15.00
123 W.Serrano/1600 RC	8.00	2.40
124 Sean Burnett/1600 RC	10.00	3.00
125 Alex Cabrera/1600 RC	8.00	2.40
126 Timo Perez/1600 RC	8.00	2.40
127 Juan Pierre/1600 RC	10.00	3.00
128 Daylan Holt/1600 RC	8.00	2.40
129 T.Ohka/1600 RC	8.00	2.40
130 K.Sasaki/1600 RC	10.00	3.00
131 K.Ainsworth/1600 RC	8.00	2.40
132 B.Abernathy/1600 RC	8.00	2.40
133 Danys Baez/1600 RC	8.00	2.40
134 Brad Cresse/1600 RC	8.00	2.40
135 R.Franklin/1600 RC	8.00	2.40
136 M.Lamb/1500 AU RC	10.00	3.00
137 David Espinosa 1500 AU RC	10.00	3.00
138 Matt Wheatland 1500 AU RC	10.00	3.00
139 X.Nady/1500 AU RC	15.00	4.50
140 S.Heard/1500 AU RC	10.00	3.00
141 P.Coco/1500 AU RC Card erroneously numbered 54 instead of 141	10.00	3.00
142 J.Miller/1500 AU RC	10.00	3.00
143 Dave Krynzel 1500 AU RC	10.00	3.00
144 Dane Sardinha 1500 AU RC	10.00	3.00
145 B.Sheets/1500 AU RC	60.00	18.00
146 L.Estrella/1500 AU RC	10.00	3.00
147 Ben Diggins 1500 AU RC	10.00	3.00
148 B.Zito/1500 AU RC	70.00	21.00
149 J.Torres/1500 AU RC	10.00	3.00
150 Mike Meyers 1500 AU RC	10.00	3.00
151 K.Wilson/1500 AU RC	10.00	3.00
152 Darin Erstad	.75	.23
153 Richard Hidalgo	.75	.23
154 Eric Chavez	.75	.23
155 B.J. Surhoff	.75	.23
156 Richie Sexson	.75	.23
157 Raul Mondesi	.75	.23
158 Rondell White	.75	.23
159 Jim Edmonds	.75	.23
160 Curt Schilling	.75	.23
161 Tom Goodwin	.75	.23
162 Fred McGriff	1.25	.35
163 Jose Vidro	.75	.23
164 Ellis Burks	.75	.23
165 David Segui	.75	.23
166 Aaron Sele	.75	.23
167 Henry Rodriguez	.75	.23
168 Mike Bordick	.75	.23
169 Mike Mussina	1.25	.35
170 Ryan Klesko	.75	.23
171 Kevin Young	.75	.23
172 Travis Lee	.75	.23
173 Aaron Boone	.75	.23
174 Jermaine Dye	.75	.23
175 Ricky Ledee	.75	.23
176 Jeffrey Hammonds	.75	.23
177 Carl Everett	.75	.23
178 Matt Lawton	.75	.23
179 Bobby Higginson	.75	.23
180 Charles Johnson	.75	.23
181 David Justice	.75	.23
182 Joey Nation/1600 RC	8.00	2.40
183 Rico Washington 1600 RC	8.00	2.40
184 Luis Matos/1600 RC	8.00	2.40
185 C.Wakeland/1600 RC	8.00	2.40
186 SW Kim/1600 RC	8.00	2.40
187 Keith Ginter/1600 RC	8.00	2.40
188 G.Guzman/1600 RC	8.00	2.40
189 J.Spurgeon/1600 RC	8.00	2.40
190 Jace Brewer/1600 RC	8.00	2.40
191 J.Guzman/1600 RC	8.00	2.40
192 Ross Gload/1600 RC	8.00	2.40
193 P.Crawford/1600 RC	8.00	2.40
194 R.Kohlmeier/1600 RC	8.00	2.40
195 Julio Zuleta/1600 RC	8.00	2.40
196 Matt Ginter/1600 RC	8.00	2.40

2000 SPx Radiance

Randomly inserted into packs, this 135-card insert is a parallel of the SPx base set. Each card in the set is individually serial numbered to 100. Please note the cards with asterisks next to their name were not issued in the basic set but were prepared and accidentally issued in the 2000 SPx packs. They are numbered and packed out to 100 just like the other Radiance cards.

	Nm-Mt	Ex-Mt
COMMON CARD (1-90)	4.00	1.20
*STARS 1-90: 6X TO 15X BASIC CARDS		
COMMON CARD (91-120)	8.00	2.40
91 Vernon Wells	8.00	2.40
92 Rick Ankiel	8.00	2.40
93 Eric Chavez	8.00	2.40
94 Alfonso Soriano	15.00	4.50
95 Eric Gagne	25.00	7.50
96 Rob Bell	8.00	2.40
97 Matt Riley	8.00	2.40
98 Josh Beckett	10.00	3.00
98A John Bale *	8.00	2.40
98B Alex Escobar *	8.00	2.40
98C Joe Mays *	8.00	2.40
98D Calvin Pickering *	8.00	2.40
98E Dave Roberts *	8.00	2.40
98F Jared Sandberg *	8.00	2.40
98G Dernell Stenson *	8.00	2.40
98H Reggie Taylor *	8.00	2.40
98I Ed Yarnall *	8.00	2.40
99 Ben Petrick	8.00	2.40
100 Rob Ramsay	8.00	2.40
101 Scott Williamson	8.00	2.40
102 Doug Davis	8.00	2.40
103 Eric Munson	8.00	2.40
103A Tony Armas Jr. *	8.00	2.40
103B Travis Dawkins *	8.00	2.40
103C Mike Lamb *	8.00	2.40
103D Rico Washington *	8.00	2.40
104 Pat Burrell	8.00	2.40
105 Jim Morris	15.00	4.50
106 Gabe Kapler	8.00	2.40
106A Adam Piatt *	8.00	2.40
106B Mark Quinn *	8.00	2.40
107 Lance Berkman	8.00	2.40
108 Erubiel Durazo	8.00	2.40
109 Tim Hudson	8.00	2.40
110 Ben Davis	8.00	2.40
111 Nick Johnson	8.00	2.40
112 Octavio Dotel	8.00	2.40
113 Jerry Hairston	8.00	2.40
114 Ruben Mateo	8.00	2.40
115 Chris Singleton	8.00	2.40
116 Bruce Chen	8.00	2.40
117 Derrick Gibson	8.00	2.40
118 Carlos Beltran	10.00	3.00
119 Freddy Garcia	8.00	2.40
120 Preston Wilson	8.00	2.40

2000 SPx Foundations

Randomly inserted into packs at one 32, this 10-card insert features players that are the cornerstones teams build around. Card backs carry a "F" prefix.

	Nm-Mt	Ex-Mt
COMPLETE SET (10)	100.00	30.00
F1 Ken Griffey Jr.	10.00	3.00
F2 Nomar Garciaparra	10.00	3.00
F3 Cal Ripken	20.00	6.00
F4 Chipper Jones	6.00	1.80
F5 Mike Piazza	10.00	3.00
F6 Derek Jeter	15.00	4.50
F7 Manny Ramirez	4.00	1.20
F8 Jeff Bagwell	4.00	1.20
F9 Tony Gwynn	8.00	2.40
F10 Larry Walker	4.00	1.20

2000 SPx Heart of the Order

Randomly inserted into packs at one in eight, this 20-card insert features players that can lift their teams to victory with one swing of the bat. Card backs carry a "H" prefix.

	Nm-Mt	Ex-Mt
COMPLETE SET (20)	60.00	18.00
H1 Bernie Williams	2.00	.60
H2 Mike Piazza	5.00	1.50
H3 Ivan Rodriguez	3.00	.90
H4 Mark McGwire	8.00	2.40
H5 Manny Ramirez	2.00	.60
H6 Ken Griffey Jr.	5.00	1.50
H7 Matt Williams	1.25	.35
H8 Sammy Sosa	5.00	1.50
H9 Mo Vaughn	1.25	.35
H10 Carlos Delgado	1.25	.35
H11 Brian Giles	1.25	.35
H12 Chipper Jones	3.00	.90
H13 Sean Casey	1.25	.35
H14 Tony Gwynn	4.00	1.20
H15 Barry Bonds	8.00	2.40
H16 Carlos Beltran	2.00	.60
H17 Scott Rolen	3.00	.90
H18 Juan Gonzalez	2.00	.60
H19 Larry Walker	2.00	.60
H20 Vladimir Guerrero	3.00	.90

2000 SPx Highlight Heroes

Randomly inserted into packs at one in 16, this 10-card insert features players that have a flair for heroics. Card backs carry a "HH" prefix.

	Nm-Mt	Ex-Mt
COMPLETE SET (10)	30.00	9.00
HH1 Pedro Martinez	3.00	.90
HH2 Ivan Rodriguez	3.00	.90
HH3 Carlos Beltran	2.00	.60
HH4 Nomar Garciaparra	5.00	1.50
HH5 Ken Griffey Jr.	5.00	1.50
HH6 Randy Johnson	3.00	.90
HH7 Chipper Jones	3.00	.90
HH8 Scott Williamson	1.00	.30
HH9 Larry Walker	2.00	.60
HH10 Mark McGwire	8.00	2.40

2000 SPx Power Brokers

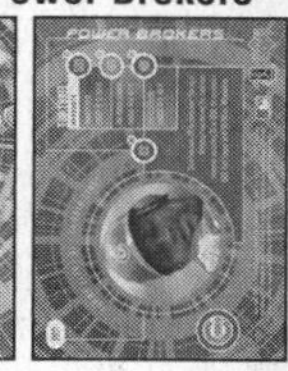

Randomly inserted into packs at one in eight, this 20-card insert features some of the greatest power hitters of all time. Card backs carry a "PB" prefix.

	Nm-Mt	Ex-Mt
COMPLETE SET (20)	60.00	18.00
PB1 Rafael Palmeiro	2.00	.60
PB2 Carlos Delgado	1.25	.35
PB3 Ken Griffey Jr.	5.00	1.50
PB4 Matt Stairs	1.25	.35
PB5 Mike Piazza	5.00	1.50
PB6 Vladimir Guerrero	3.00	.90
PB7 Chipper Jones	3.00	.90
PB8 Mark McGwire	8.00	2.40
PB9 Matt Williams	1.25	.35
PB10 Juan Gonzalez	2.00	.60
PB11 Shawn Green	1.25	.35
PB12 Sammy Sosa	5.00	1.50
PB13 Brian Giles	1.25	.35
PB14 Jeff Bagwell	2.00	.60
PB15 Alex Rodriguez	5.00	1.50
PB16 Frank Thomas	3.00	.90
PB17 Larry Walker	2.00	.60
PB18 Albert Belle	1.25	.35
PB19 Dean Palmer	1.25	.35
PB20 Mo Vaughn	1.25	.35

2000 SPx Signatures

Randomly inserted into packs at one in 179, this 15-card insert features autographed cards of some of the hottest players in major league baseball. The following players went out as stickered exchange cards: Jeff Bagwell (100 percent), Ken Griffey Jr. (100 percent), Tony Gwynn (25 percent), Vladimir Guerrero (50 percent), Manny Ramirez (100 percent) and Ivan Rodriguez (25 percent). The exchange deadline for the stickered cards was February 3rd, 2001. Card backs carry a "X" prefix followed by the players initials.

	Nm-Mt	Ex-Mt
XBB Barry Bonds	250.00	75.00
XCJ Chipper Jones	40.00	12.00
XCR Cal Ripken	150.00	45.00
XDJ Derek Jeter	150.00	45.00
XIR I.Rodriguez EXCH *	40.00	12.00
XJB Jeff Bagwell	50.00	15.00
XJC Jose Canseco	40.00	12.00
XKG Ken Griffey Jr.	100.00	30.00
XMR M.Ramirez EXCH	50.00	15.00
XOH Orlando Hernandez	60.00	18.00
XRC Roger Clemens	120.00	36.00
XSC Sean Casey	15.00	4.50
XSR Scott Rolen	40.00	12.00
XTG Tony Gwynn	50.00	15.00
XVG V.Guerrero EXCH *	40.00	12.00

2000 SPx SPXcitement

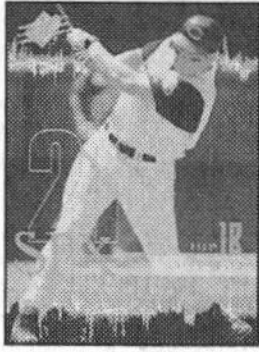

Randomly inserted into packs at one in four, this 20-card insert features some of the most exciting players in the major leagues. Card backs carry a "XC" prefix.

	Nm-Mt	Ex-Mt
COMPLETE SET (20)	30.00	9.00
XC1 Nomar Garciaparra	2.50	.75
XC2 Mark McGwire	4.00	1.20

XC3 Derek Jeter 4.00 1.20
XC4 Cal Ripken 5.00 1.50
XC5 Barry Bonds 4.00 1.20
XC6 Alex Rodriguez 2.50 .75
XC7 Scott Rolen 1.50 .45
XC8 Pedro Martinez 1.50 .45
XC9 Sean Casey .60 .18
XC10 Sammy Sosa 2.50 .75
XC11 Randy Johnson 1.50 .45
XC12 Ivan Rodriguez 1.50 .45
XC13 Frank Thomas 1.50 .45
XC14 Greg Maddux 2.50 .75
XC15 Tony Gwynn 2.00 .60
XC16 Ken Griffey Jr. 2.50 .75
XC17 Carlos Beltran .60 .18
XC18 Mike Piazza 2.50 .75
XC19 Chipper Jones 1.50 .45
XC20 Craig Biggio 1.00 .30

2000 SPx Untouchable Talents

Randomly inserted into packs at one in 96, this 10-card insert features players that have skills that are unmatched. Card backs carry a "UT" prefix.

Nm-Mt Ex-Mt
COMPLETE SET (10) 200.00 60.00
UT1 Mark McGwire 40.00 12.00
UT2 Ken Griffey Jr. 25.00 7.50
UT3 Shawn Green 6.00 1.80
UT4 Ivan Rodriguez 15.00 4.50
UT5 Sammy Sosa 25.00 7.50
UT6 Derek Jeter 40.00 12.00
UT7 Sean Casey 6.00 1.80
UT8 Chipper Jones 15.00 4.50
UT9 Pedro Martinez 15.00 4.50
UT10 Vladimir Guerrero 15.00 4.50

2000 SPx Winning Materials

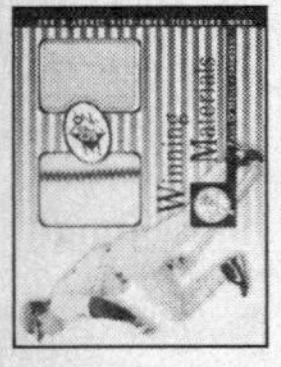

Randomly inserted into first series packs, this 30-card insert features game-used memorabilia cards from some of the top names in baseball. The set includes Bat/Jersey cards, Cap/Jersey cards, Ball/Jersey cards, and autographed Bat/Jersey cards. Card backs carry the players initals. Please note that the Ken Griffey Jr. autographed Bat/Jersey cards, and the Manny Ramirez autographed Bat/Jersey cards were both redemptions with an exchang deadline of 12/31/2000.

Nm-Mt Ex-Mt
AR1 Alex Rodriguez 25.00 7.50
Bat-Jsy
AR2 Alex Rodriguez 50.00 15.00
Cap-Jsy/100
AR3 Alex Rodriguez 60.00 18.00
Ball-Jsy/50
BB1 Barry Bonds 40.00 12.00
Bat-Jsy
BB2 Barry Bonds 60.00 18.00
Cap-Jsy/100
BB3 Barry Bonds
Bat-Jsy AU/25
BW Bernie Williams 15.00 4.50
Bat-Jsy
DJ1 Derek Jeter 50.00 15.00
Bat-Jsy
DJ2 Derek Jeter 100.00 30.00
Ball-Jsy/50
DJ3 Derek Jeter
Bat-Jsy AU/2
EC1 Eric Chavez 10.00 3.00
Bat-Jsy
EC2 Eric Chavez 15.00 4.50
Cap-Jsy/100
GM Greg Maddux 25.00 7.50
Bat-Jsy
IR Ivan Rodriguez 15.00 4.50
Bat-Jsy
JB1 Jeff Bagwell 15.00 4.50
Bat-Jsy
JB2 Jeff Bagwell 40.00 12.00
Ball-Jsy/50
JC Jose Canseco 15.00 4.50
Bat-Jsy
JL1 Javy Lopez 10.00 3.00
Bat-Jsy
JL2 Javy Lopez 15.00 4.50
Cap-Jsy
KG1 Ken Griffey Jr. 25.00 7.50
Bat-Jsy
KG2 Ken Griffey Jr. 60.00 18.00
Ball-Jsy/50
KG3 Ken Griffey Jr.
Bat-Jsy AU/24
MM1 Mark McGwire 50.00 15.00
Ball-Base/250
MM2 Mark McGwire 50.00 15.00
Ball-Base/250
MR1 Manny Ramirez 15.00 4.50
Bat-Jsy
MR2 Manny Ramirez
Bat-Jsy AU/24
MW Matt Williams 10.00 3.00
Bat-Jsy
PM Pedro Martinez 25.00 7.50
Cap-Jsy/100
PO Paul O'Neill 15.00 4.50
Bat-Jsy
VG1 Vladimir Guerrero 15.00 4.50
Bat-Jsy
VG2 Vladimir Guerrero 25.00 7.50
Cap-Jsy/100
VG3 Vladimir Guerrero 40.00 12.00
Ball-Jsy/50
TGL Troy Glaus 10.00 3.00
Bat-Jsy
TGW1 Tony Gwynn 15.00 4.50
Bat-Jsy
TGW2 Tony Gwynn 50.00 15.00
Ball-Jsy/50
TGW3 Tony Gwynn 30.00 9.00
Cap-Jsy/100

2000 SPx Winning Materials Update

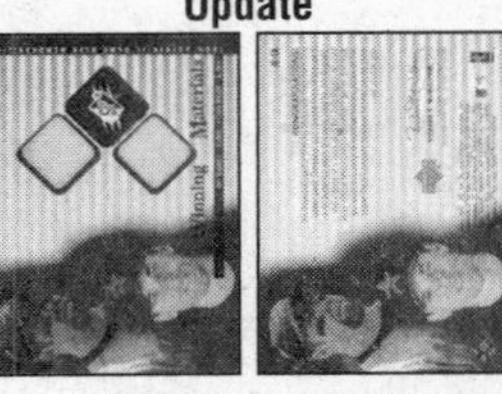

Randomly inserted into packs of 2000 Upper Deck Rookie Update (at an approximate rate of one per box), this 28-card insert features game-used memorabilia cards from some of baseball's top athletes. The set also includes a few members of the 2000 USA Olympic Baseball team. Card backs carry the player's initials as numbering.

Nm-Mt Ex-Mt
MK-GD Travis Dawkins 8.00 2.40
Mike Kinkade Bat-Bat
BA-AE Brent Abernathy 8.00 2.40
Adam Everett Bat-Bat
BW-EY Brad Wilkerson 10.00 3.00
Ernie Young Bat-Bat
CR-TG Cal Ripken 40.00 12.00
Tony Gwynn Base-Base
DJ-AR Derek Jeter 40.00 12.00
Alex Rodriguez Base-Bat
DJ-NG Derek Jeter 50.00 15.00
Nomar Garciaparra Base-Bat
FT-MO Frank Thomas 10.00 3.00
Magglio Ordonez Base-Base
G-S-R Ken Griffey Jr. 50.00 15.00
Sammy Sosa
Alex Rodriguez
Jsy-Jsy-Jsy
GW-BS Ben Sheets 10.00 3.00
Ball-Jsy
GW-DM D.Mientkiewicz 8.00 2.40
Bat-Base
GW-EY Ernie Young 8.00 2.40
Bat-Base
GW-JC John Cotton 8.00 2.40
Bat-Jsy
GW-MN Mike Neill Bat-Jsy 8.00 2.40
GW-SB Sean Burroughs 8.00 2.40
Bat-Jsy
IR-RP Ivan Rodriguez 10.00 3.00
Rafael Palmeiro Ball-Ball
J-G-R Derek Jeter 120.00 36.00
Nomar Garciaparra
Alex Rodriguez
Base-Ball-Bat
JB-CB Jeff Bagwell 10.00 3.00
Craig Biggio Base-Base
JC-BB Jose Canseco 30.00 9.00
Barry Bonds Ball-Ball
KG-SS Ken Griffey Jr. 30.00 9.00
Sammy Sosa Bat-Bat
MM-KG Mark McGwire 50.00 15.00
Ken Griffey Jr. Ball-Bat
MM-RA Mark McGwire 40.00 12.00
Rick Ankiel Base-Base
MM-SS Mark McGwire 50.00 15.00
Sammy Sosa Ball-Ball
MP-RV Mike Piazza 25.00 7.50
Robin Ventura Ball-Ball
NG-PM N.Garciaparra 30.00 9.00
Pedro Martinez Ball-Ball
RC-PM Roger Clemens 40.00 12.00
Pedro Martinez Ball-Ball
SB-BS Sean Burroughs 10.00 3.00
Ben Sheets Bat-Base

2001 SPx

The 2001 SPx product was initially released in early May, 2001, and featured a 150-card base set. 60 additional update cards (151-210) were distributed within Upper Deck Rookie Update packs in late December, 2001. The base set is broken into tiers as follows: Base Veterans (1-90), Young Stars (91-120) serial numbered to 2000, Rookie Jerseys (121-135), and Jersey Autographs (136-150). The Rookie Update SPx cards were broken into tiers as follows: base veterans (151-180) and Young Stars (181-210) serial numbered to 1500. Each basic pack contained four cards and carried a suggested retail price of $6.99. Rookie Update packs contained four cards with an SRP of $4.99.

Nm-Mt Ex-Mt
COMP.BASIC w/o SP's (90) 25.00 7.50
COMP.UPDATE w/o SP's (30) 10.00 3.00
COMMON CARD (1-90) .50 .15
COMMON YS (91-120) 8.00 2.40
COMMON JSY (121-135) 10.00 3.00
COMMON (136-150) 15.00 4.50
COMMON (151-180) .75 .23
COMMON (181-210) 5.00 1.50
1 Darin Erstad .50 .15
2 Troy Glaus .50 .15
3 Mo Vaughn .50 .15
4 Johnny Damon .75 .23
5 Jason Giambi .50 .15
6 Tim Hudson .50 .15
7 Miguel Tejada .50 .15
8 Carlos Delgado .50 .15
9 Raul Mondesi .50 .15
10 Tony Batista .50 .15
11 Ben Grieve .50 .15
12 Greg Vaughn .50 .15
13 Juan Gonzalez .75 .23
14 Jim Thome 1.25 .35
15 Roberto Alomar .75 .23
16 John Olerud .50 .15
17 Edgar Martinez .75 .23
18 Albert Belle .50 .15
19 Cal Ripken 4.00 1.20
20 Ivan Rodriguez 1.25 .35
21 Rafael Palmeiro .75 .23
22 Alex Rodriguez 2.00 .60
23 Nomar Garciaparra 2.00 .60
24 Pedro Martinez 1.25 .35
25 Manny Ramirez .75 .23
26 Jermaine Dye .50 .15
27 Mark Quinn .50 .15
28 Carlos Beltran .75 .23
29 Tony Clark .50 .15
30 Bobby Higginson .50 .15
31 Eric Milton .50 .15
32 Matt Lawton .50 .15
33 Frank Thomas 1.25 .35
34 Magglio Ordonez .50 .15
35 Ray Durham .50 .15
36 David Wells .50 .15
37 Derek Jeter 3.00 .90
38 Bernie Williams .75 .23
39 Roger Clemens UER 2.50 .75
Wrong uniform number on card
40 David Justice .50 .15
41 Jeff Bagwell .75 .23
42 Richard Hidalgo .50 .15
43 Moises Alou .50 .15
44 Chipper Jones 1.25 .35
45 Andruw Jones .50 .15
46 Greg Maddux 2.00 .60
47 Rafael Furcal .50 .15
48 Jeromy Burnitz .50 .15
49 Geoff Jenkins .50 .15
50 Mark McGwire 3.00 .90
51 Jim Edmonds .50 .15
52 Rick Ankiel .50 .15
53 Edgar Renteria .50 .15
54 Sammy Sosa 2.00 .60
55 Kerry Wood 1.25 .35
56 Rondell White .50 .15
57 Randy Johnson 1.25 .35
58 Steve Finley .50 .15
59 Matt Williams .50 .15
60 Luis Gonzalez .50 .15
61 Kevin Brown .50 .15
62 Gary Sheffield .50 .15
63 Shawn Green .50 .15
64 Vladimir Guerrero 1.25 .35
65 Jose Vidro .50 .15
66 Barry Bonds 3.00 .90
67 Jeff Kent .50 .15
68 Livan Hernandez .50 .15
69 Preston Wilson .50 .15
70 Charles Johnson .50 .15
71 Cliff Floyd .50 .15
72 Mike Piazza 2.00 .60
73 Edgardo Alfonzo .50 .15
74 Jay Payton .50 .15
75 Robin Ventura .50 .15
76 Tony Gwynn 1.50 .45
77 Phil Nevin .50 .15
78 Ryan Klesko .50 .15
79 Scott Rolen 1.25 .35
80 Pat Burrell .50 .15
81 Bob Abreu .50 .15
82 Brian Giles .50 .15
83 Kris Benson .50 .15
84 Jason Kendall .50 .15
85 Ken Griffey Jr. 2.00 .60
86 Barry Larkin .75 .23
87 Sean Casey .50 .15
88 Todd Helton .75 .23
89 Larry Walker .75 .23
90 Mike Hampton .50 .15
91 Billy Sylvester YS RC 8.00 2.40
92 Josh Towers YS RC 8.00 2.40
93 Zach Day YS RC 8.00 2.40
94 Martin Vargas YS RC 8.00 2.40
95 Adam Pettyjohn YS RC 8.00 2.40
96 Andres Torres YS RC 8.00 2.40
97 Kris Keller YS RC 8.00 2.40
98 Blaine Neal YS RC 8.00 2.40
99 Kyle Kessel YS RC 8.00 2.40
100 Greg Miller YS RC 8.00 2.40
101 Shawn Sonnier YS 8.00 2.40
102 Alexis Gomez YS RC 8.00 2.40
103 Grant Balfour YS RC 8.00 2.40
104 Henry Mateo YS RC 8.00 2.40
105 Wilken Ruan YS RC 8.00 2.40
106 Nick Maness YS RC 8.00 2.40
107 J. Michaels YS RC 8.00 2.40
108 Esix Snead YS RC 8.00 2.40
109 William Ortega YS RC 8.00 2.40
110 David Elder YS RC 8.00 2.40
111 J. Melian YS RC 8.00 2.40
112 Nate Teut YS RC 8.00 2.40
113 Jason Smith YS RC 8.00 2.40
114 Mike Penney YS RC 8.00 2.40
115 Jose Mieses YS RC 8.00 2.40
116 Juan Pena YS 8.00 2.40
117 B. Lawrence YS RC 8.00 2.40
118 Jeremy Owens YS RC 8.00 2.40
119 C. Valderrama YS RC 8.00 2.40
120 Rafael Soriano YS RC 8.00 2.40
121 H. Ramirez JSY RC 15.00 4.50
122 R. Rodriguez JSY RC 10.00 3.00
123 Juan Diaz JSY RC 10.00 3.00
124 Donnie Bridges JSY 10.00 3.00
125 Tyler Walker JSY RC 10.00 3.00
126 Erick Almonte JSY RC 10.00 3.00
127 Jesus Colome JSY 10.00 3.00
128 Ryan Freel JSY RC 10.00 3.00
129 Elpidio Guzman JSY RC 10.00 3.00
130 Jack Cust JSY 10.00 3.00
131 Eric Hinske JSY RC 15.00 4.50
132 Josh Fogg JSY RC 10.00 3.00
133 Juan Uribe JSY RC 15.00 4.50
134 Bert Snow JSY RC 10.00 3.00
135 Pedro Feliz JSY 10.00 3.00
136 W. Betemit JSY AU RC 15.00 4.50
137 S. Douglass JSY AU RC 15.00 4.50
138 D. Stenson JSY AU 15.00 4.50
139 Brandon Inge JSY AU 15.00 4.50
140 M. Ensberg JSY AU RC 25.00 7.50
141 Brian Cole JSY AU 15.00 4.50
142 A. Hernandez JSY AU RC 15.00 4.50
143 Brandon Duckworth 15.00 4.50
JSY AU RC
144 J. Wilson JSY AU RC 30.00 9.00
145 T. Hafner JSY AU RC 40.00 12.00
146 Carlos Pena JSY AU 15.00 4.50
147 C. Patterson JSY AU 25.00 7.50
148 Xavier Nady JSY AU 15.00 4.50
149 Jason Hart JSY AU 15.00 4.50
150 I.Suzuki JSY AU RC 650.00 200.00
151 Garret Anderson .75 .23
152 Jermaine Dye .75 .23
153 Shannon Stewart .75 .23
154 Toby Hall .75 .23
155 C.C. Sabathia .75 .23
156 Bret Boone .75 .23
157 Tony Batista .75 .23
158 Gabe Kapler .75 .23
159 Carl Everett .75 .23
160 Mike Sweeney .75 .23
161 Dean Palmer .75 .23
162 Doug Mientkiewicz .75 .23
163 Carlos Lee .75 .23
164 Mike Mussina 1.25 .35
165 Lance Berkman .75 .23
166 Ken Caminiti .75 .23
167 Ben Sheets 1.25 .35
168 Matt Morris .75 .23
169 Fred McGriff 1.25 .35
170 Curt Schilling .75 .23
171 Paul LoDuca .75 .23
172 Javier Vazquez .75 .23
173 Rich Aurilia .75 .23
174 A.J. Burnett .75 .23
175 Al Leiter .75 .23
176 Mark Kotsay .75 .23
177 Jimmy Rollins .75 .23
178 Aramis Ramirez .75 .23
179 Aaron Boone .75 .23
180 Jeff Cirillo .75 .23
181 J.Estrada YS RC 15.00 4.50
182 Dave Williams YS RC 5.00 1.50
183 D.Mendez YS RC 5.00 1.50
184 Junior Spivey YS RC 8.00 2.40
185 Jay Gibbons YS RC 8.00 2.40
186 Kyle Lohse YS RC 8.00 2.40
187 Willie Harris YS RC 5.00 1.50
188 Juan Cruz YS RC 5.00 1.50
189 Joe Kennedy YS RC 8.00 2.40
190 D.Sanchez YS RC 5.00 1.50
191 Jorge Julio YS RC 5.00 1.50
192 Cesar Crespo YS RC 5.00 1.50
193 Casey Fossum YS RC 5.00 1.50
194 Brian Roberts YS RC 5.00 1.50
195 Troy Mattes YS RC 5.00 1.50
196 R.Mackowiak YS RC 8.00 2.40
197 T.Shinjo YS RC 8.00 2.40
198 Nick Punto YS RC 5.00 1.50
199 Wilmy Caceres YS RC 5.00 1.50
200 Jeremy Affeldt YS RC 8.00 2.40
201 Bret Prinz YS RC 5.00 1.50
202 Delvin James YS RC 5.00 1.50
203 Luis Pineda YS RC 5.00 1.50
204 Matt White YS RC 5.00 1.50
205 B.Knight YS RC 5.00 1.50
206 Albert Pujols YS AU RC 400.00 120.00
207 M.Teixeira YS AU RC 100.00 30.00
208 Mark Prior YS AU RC 200.00 60.00
209 D.Brazelton YS AU RC 25.00 7.50
210 Bud Smith YS AU RC 15.00 4.50

2001 SPx Spectrum

Randomly inserted into packs, this 120-card insert is a partial parallel of the 2001 SPx base set. Please note that each card is individually serial numbered to 50.

Nm-Mt Ex-Mt
*STARS 1-90: 12.5X TO 30X BASIC CARDS
*YS 91-120: 1X TO 2.5X BASIC CARDS

2001 SPx Foundations

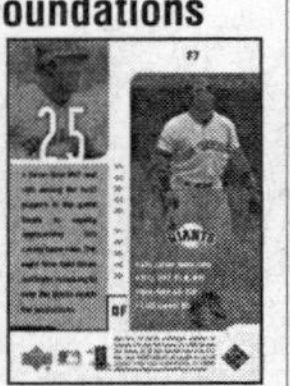

Randomly inserted into packs at one in eight, this 12-card insert features players that are the major foundation that keeps their respective ballclubs together. Card backs carry a "F" prefix.

Nm-Mt Ex-Mt
COMPLETE SET (12) 50.00 15.00
F1 Mark McGwire 8.00 2.40
F2 Jeff Bagwell 2.00 .60
F3 Alex Rodriguez 5.00 1.50
F4 Ken Griffey Jr. 5.00 1.50
F5 Andruw Jones 2.00 .60
F6 Cal Ripken 10.00 3.00
F7 Barry Bonds 8.00 2.40
F8 Derek Jeter 8.00 2.40
F9 Frank Thomas 3.00 .90
F10 Sammy Sosa 5.00 1.50
F11 Tony Gwynn 4.00 1.20
F12 Vladimir Guerrero 3.00 .90

2001 SPx SPXcitement

Randomly inserted into packs at one in eight, this 12-card insert features players that are known for bringing excitement to the game. Card backs carry an "X" prefix.

Nm-Mt Ex-Mt
COMPLETE SET (12) 50.00 15.00
X1 Alex Rodriguez 5.00 1.50
X2 Jason Giambi 2.00 .60
X3 Ken Griffey Jr. 5.00 1.50
X4 Sammy Sosa 5.00 1.50
X5 Frank Thomas 3.00 .90
X6 Todd Helton 2.00 .60
X7 Mark McGwire 8.00 2.40
X8 Mike Piazza 5.00 1.50
X9 Derek Jeter 8.00 2.40
X10 Vladimir Guerrero 3.00 .90
X11 Carlos Delgado 2.00 .60
X12 Chipper Jones 3.00 .90

2001 SPx Untouchable Talents

Randomly inserted into packs at one in 15, this six-card insert features players whose skills are unmatched. Card backs carry a "UT" prefix.

Nm-Mt Ex-Mt
COMPLETE SET (6) 40.00 12.00
UT1 Ken Griffey Jr. 5.00 1.50
UT2 Mike Piazza 5.00 1.50
UT3 Mark McGwire 8.00 2.40
UT4 Alex Rodriguez 5.00 1.50
UT5 Sammy Sosa 5.00 1.50
UT6 Derek Jeter 8.00 2.40

2001 SPx Winning Materials Ball-Base

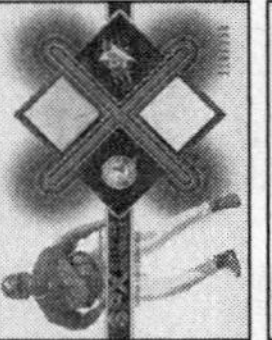
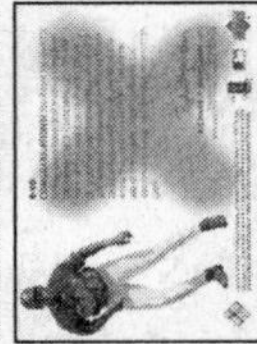

Randomly inserted into packs, this 13-card insert features actual swatches of both game-used baseball and base. Card backs carry a "B" prefix followed by the player's initials. Each card is individually serial numbered to 250.

Nm-Mt Ex-Mt
B-AJ Andruw Jones 15.00 4.50
B-AR Alex Rodriguez 25.00 7.50
B-BB Barry Bonds 50.00 15.00
B-CJ Chipper Jones 25.00 7.50
B-DJ Derek Jeter 50.00 15.00
B-FT Frank Thomas 25.00 7.50
B-KG Ken Griffey Jr. 40.00 12.00
B-MM Mark McGwire 80.00 24.00
B-MP Mike Piazza 25.00 7.50
B-NG Nomar Garciaparra 25.00 7.50
B-PM Pedro Martinez 25.00 7.50
B-SS Sammy Sosa 25.00 7.50
B-VG Vladimir Guerrero 25.00 7.50

2001 SPx Winning Materials Base Duos

Randomly inserted into packs, this 10-card insert features actual swatches of game-used bases. Card backs carry a "B2" prefix followed by the player's initials. Each card is individually serial numbered to 50.

Nm-Mt Ex-Mt
B2-GJ Nomar Garciaparra 100.00 30.00
Derek Jeter
B2-JG Derek Jeter 80.00 24.00
Jason Giambi
B2-JP Derek Jeter 100.00 30.00

Mike Piazza
B2-MG Mark McGwire 100.00 30.00
Ken Griffey Jr.
B2-MR Mark McGwire 100.00 30.00
Alex Rodriguez
B2-MS Mark McGwire 100.00 30.00
Sammy Sosa
B2-PB Mike Piazza 100.00 30.00
Barry Bonds
B2-PM Mike Piazza 100.00 30.00
Mark McGwire
B2-RJ Alex Rodriguez 100.00 30.00
Derek Jeter
B2-TR Frank Thomas 80.00 24.00
Alex Rodriguez

2001 SPx Winning Materials Base Trios

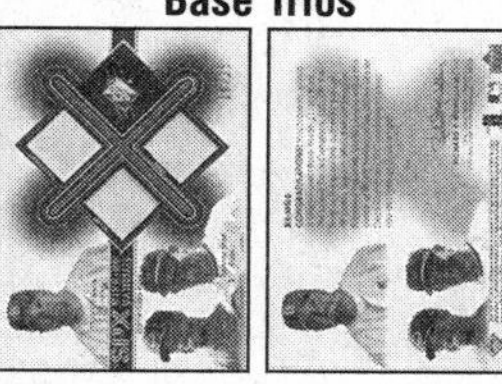

Randomly inserted into packs, this five-card insert set features actual swatches of game-used bases. Card backs carry a "B3" prefix followed by the player's initials. Each card is individually serial numbered to 25. Due to market scarcity, no pricing is provided.

Nm-Mt Ex-Mt
B3-BMS Barry Bonds
Mark McGwire
Sammy Sosa
B3-GJR Ken Griffey Jr.
Derek Jeter
Alex Rodriguez
B3-JRG Derek Jeter
Alex Rodriguez
Nomar Garciaparra
B3-MGS Mark McGwire
Ken Griffey Jr.
Sammy Sosa
B3-PJW Mike Piazza
Derek Jeter
Bernie Williams

2001 SPx Winning Materials Bat-Jersey

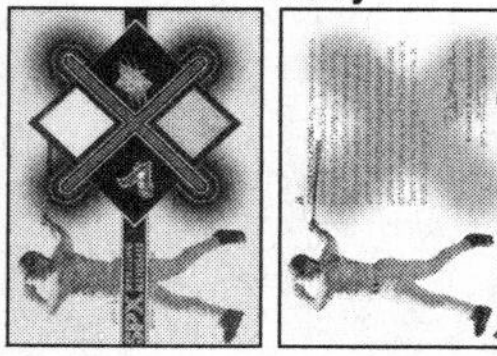

Randomly inserted into packs, this 21-card insert features actual swatches of both game-used bats and jerseys. Card backs carry the player's initials as numbering.

Nm-Mt Ex-Mt
AJ1 Andruw Jones AS 10.00 3.00
AJ2 Andruw Jones 10.00 3.00
AR1 Alex Rodriguez AS 15.00 4.50
AR2 Alex Rodriguez 15.00 4.50
BB1 Barry Bonds AS 25.00 7.50
BB2 Barry Bonds 25.00 7.50
CD Carlos Delgado AS * 10.00 3.00
CJ1 Chipper Jones AS 15.00 4.50
CJ2 Chipper Jones 15.00 4.50
CR Cal Ripken 40.00 12.00
FT Frank Thomas 15.00 4.50
IR1 Ivan Rodriguez AS 15.00 4.50
IR2 Ivan Rodriguez 15.00 4.50
JD Joe DiMaggio 150.00 45.00
JE Jim Edmonds * 10.00 3.00
KG1 Ken Griffey Jr. AS 15.00 4.50
KG2 Ken Griffey Jr. 15.00 4.50
RA Rick Ankiel * 10.00 3.00
RJ1 Randy Johnson AS 15.00 4.50
RJ2 Randy Johnson 15.00 4.50
SS Sammy Sosa 15.00 4.50

2001 SPx Winning Materials Jersey Duos

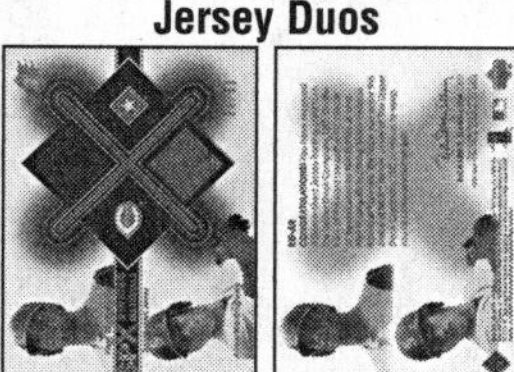
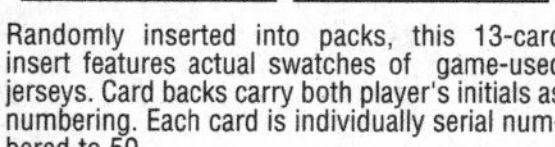

Randomly inserted into packs, this 13-card insert features actual swatches of game-used jerseys. Card backs carry both player's initials as numbering. Each card is individually serial numbered to 50.

Nm-Mt Ex-Mt
AJCJ Andruw Jones 40.00 12.00
Chipper Jones
ARCR Alex Rodriguez 100.00 30.00
Cal Ripken
BBSS Barry Bonds 100.00 30.00
Sammy Sosa
CJDW Chipper Jones 40.00 12.00
David Wells
IRAR Ivan Rodriguez 80.00 24.00
Alex Rodriguez
KGAR Ken Griffey Jr. 80.00 24.00
Alex Rodriguez AS
KGBB Ken Griffey Jr. 100.00 30.00
Barry Bonds AS
KGJD Ken Griffey Jr. 200.00 60.00
Joe DiMaggio
KGKG Ken Griffey Jr. 80.00 24.00
Ken Griffey Jr. AS
KGRJ Ken Griffey Jr. 80.00 24.00
Randy Johnson AS
KGSS Ken Griffey Jr. 80.00 24.00
Sammy Sosa
SSCD Sammy Sosa 50.00 15.00
Carlos Delgado
SSFT Sammy Sosa 50.00 15.00
Frank Thomas

2001 SPx Winning Materials Jersey Trios

Randomly inserted into packs, this seven-card insert set features actual swatches of game-used jerseys. Card backs carry the first letter of each player's last name as numbering. Each card is individually serial numbered to 25. Due to market scarcity, no pricing is provided for these cards.

Nm-Mt Ex-Mt
B-G-J Barry Bonds
Ken Griffey Jr.
Andruw Jones
D-B-S Carlos Delgado
Barry Bonds
Sammy Sosa
D-G-J Joe DiMaggio
Ken Griffey Jr.
Andruw Jones
G-R-B Ken Griffey Jr.
Alex Rodriguez
Barry Bonds
R-J-D Cal Ripken
Chipper Jones
Carlos Delgado
R-R-D Alex Rodriguez
Ivan Rodriguez
Carlos Delgado
S-G-C Sammy Sosa
Ken Griffey Jr.
Chipper Jones

2001 SPx Winning Materials Update Duos

Inserted into 2001 Upper Deck Rookie Update packs at a rate of one in 15, these cards feature two players and a memorabilia piece from each of them.

Nm-Mt Ex-Mt
GOLD RANDOM INSERTS IN PACKS
GOLD PRINT RUN 25 SERIAL #'d SETS
NO GOLD PRICING DUE TO SCARCITY
AP-JE Albert Pujols 40.00 12.00
Jim Edmonds
AS-KS Aaron Sele 10.00 3.00
Kazuhiro Sasaki
BB-LG Barry Bonds 25.00 7.50
Luis Gonzalez
BW-MR Bernie Williams 15.00 4.50
Mariano Rivera
BW-RJ Bernie Williams 15.00 4.50
Reggie Jackson
CP-BK Chan Ho Park 10.00 3.00
Byung-Hyun Kim
CP-FV Chan Ho Park 15.00 4.50
Fernando Valenzuela
CR-EM Cal Ripken 40.00 12.00
Eddie Murray
CR-X2 Cal Ripken 40.00 12.00
Cal Ripken
CS-RJ Curt Schilling 15.00 4.50
Randy Johnson
EM-JM Eric Milton 10.00 3.00
Joe Mays
FT-MO Frank Thomas 15.00 4.50
Magglio Ordonez
GS-SG Gary Sheffield 10.00 3.00
Shawn Green
HN-MY Hideo Nomo 15.00 4.50
Masato Yoshii
IR-AR Ivan Rodriguez 15.00 4.50
Alex Rodriguez
JB-CB Jeff Bagwell 15.00 4.50
Craig Biggio
JB-RY Jeromy Burnitz 15.00 4.50
Robin Yount
JG-BB Jason Giambi 25.00 7.50
Barry Bonds
KG-SC Ken Griffey Jr. 15.00 4.50
Sean Casey
LW-TH Larry Walker 15.00 4.50
Todd Helton
MP-EA Mike Piazza 15.00 4.50
Edgardo Alfonzo
MR-JG Manny Ramirez 15.00 4.50
Juan Gonzalez
PM-GM Pedro Martinez 15.00 4.50
Greg Maddux
PM-RJ Pedro Martinez 15.00 4.50
Randy Johnson
SR-BA Scott Rolen 15.00 4.50
Bobby Abreu
SS-EB Sammy Sosa 25.00 7.50
Ernie Banks
SS-JG Sammy Sosa 15.00 4.50
Jason Giambi
TG-CR Tony Gwynn 40.00 12.00
Cal Ripken
TG-DW Tony Gwynn 15.00 4.50
Dave Winfield
TG-X2 Tony Gwynn 15.00 4.50
Tony Gwynn
TS-HN Tsuyoshi Shinjo 15.00 4.50
Hideo Nomo

2001 SPx Winning Materials Update Trios

Inserted into 2001 Upper Deck Rookie Update Packs at a rate of one in 15, these 22 cards feature three players as well as a piece of memorabilia from each one.

Nm-Mt Ex-Mt
GOLD RANDOM INSERTS IN PACKS
GOLD PRINT RUN 25 SERIAL #'d SETS
NO GOLD PRICING DUE TO SCARCITY
BGG Barry Bonds 40.00 12.00
Luis Gonzalez
Ken Griffey Jr.
BTD Jeff Bagwell 15.00 4.50
Frank Thomas
Carlos Delgado
CHN Roger Clemens 25.00 7.50
Tim Hudson
Hideo Nomo
DEA J.D. Drew 10.00 3.00
Jim Edmonds
Bobby Abreu
DOP Carlos Delgado 50.00 15.00
Magglio Ordonez
Albert Pujols
GWS Luis Gonzalez 10.00 3.00
Matt Williams
Curt Schilling
GZH Jason Giambi 10.00 3.00
Barry Zito
Tim Hudson
HDG Todd Helton 15.00 4.50
Carlos Delgado
Jason Giambi
JAF Chipper Jones 15.00 4.50
Andruw Jones
Rafael Furcal
KBA Jeff Kent 25.00 7.50
Barry Bonds
Rich Aurilia
MGJ Greg Maddux 25.00 7.50
Tom Glavine
Andruw Jones
PPV Jay Payton 20.00 6.00
Mike Piazza
Robin Ventura
PWO Andy Pettitte 15.00 4.50
Bernie Williams
Paul O'Neill
RPK Ivan Rodriguez 20.00 6.00
Mike Piazza
Jason Kendall
RRK Alex Rodriguez 20.00 6.00
Ivan Rodriguez
Gabe Kapler
SJC Curt Schilling 40.00 12.00
Randy Johnson
Roger Clemens
SKB Gary Sheffield 10.00 3.00
Eric Karros
Kevin Brown
SSM Aaron Sele 40.00 12.00
Ichiro Suzuki
Edgar Martinez
SYN Kazuhiro Sasaki 15.00 4.50
Masato Yoshii
Hideo Nomo
TDK Frank Thomas 15.00 4.50
Ray Durham
Paul Konerko
TGA Jim Thome 15.00 4.50
Juan Gonzalez
Roberto Alomar
VRF Omar Vizquel 20.00 6.00
Alex Rodriguez
Rafael Furcal

2002 SPx

This 280-card set was issued in two separate brands. The SPx product itself was released in late April, 2002 and contained cards 1-250. These cards were issued in four card packs of which were distributed at a rate of 18 packs per box and 14 boxes per case. Cards numbered from 91 through 120 feature either a portrait or an action shot of a prospect. Both the portrait and the action shot were issued with separate stated print runs of 1800 serial numbered cards (for a total of 3,600 of each player in the subset). Cards 121-150 were not serial-numbered but instead feature autographs and were seeded into packs at a rate of 1:18. Cards numbered 151 through 190 were issued and featured jersey swatches of leading major league players. These cards had a stated print run of either 700 or 800 serial numbered cards. High series cards 191-250 were distributed in mid-December, 2002 within packs of 2002 Upper Deck Rookie Update. Cards 191-220 feature veterans on new teams and were commonly distributed in all packs. Cards 221-250 feature prospects and were signed by the player. In addition, the card were serial numbered to 825 copies. Though stated pack odds were not released by the manufacturer, we believe these signed cards were seeded at an approximate rate of 1:16 Upper Deck Rookie Update packs.

Nm-Mt Ex-Mt
COMP.LOW w/o SP's (90) 25.00 7.50
COMP.UPDATE w/o SP's (30) 10.00 3.00
COMMON CARD (1-90) .50 .15
COMMON ROOKIE (91A- 8.00 2.40
COMMON CARD (121-150) 15.00 4.50
COMMON CARD (151-190) 8.00 2.40
COMMON CARD (191-220) .75 .23
COMMON CARD (221-250) 10.00 3.00
1 Troy Glaus .50 .15
2 Darin Erstad .50 .15
3 David Justice .50 .15
4 Tim Hudson .50 .15
5 Miguel Tejada .50 .15
6 Barry Zito .50 .15
7 Carlos Delgado .50 .15
8 Shannon Stewart .50 .15
9 Greg Vaughn .50 .15
10 Toby Hall .50 .15
11 Jim Thome 1.25 .35
12 C.C. Sabathia .50 .15
13 Ichiro Suzuki 2.00 .60
14 Edgar Martinez .75 .23
15 Freddy Garcia .50 .15
16 Mike Cameron .50 .15
17 Jeff Conine .50 .15
18 Tony Batista .50 .15
19 Alex Rodriguez 2.00 .60
20 Rafael Palmeiro .75 .23
21 Ivan Rodriguez 1.25 .35
22 Carl Everett .50 .15
23 Pedro Martinez 1.25 .35
24 Manny Ramirez .75 .23
25 Nomar Garciaparra 2.00 .60
26 Johnny Damon Sox 1.25 .35
27 Mike Sweeney .50 .15
28 Carlos Beltran .75 .23
29 Dmitri Young .50 .15
30 Joe Mays .50 .15
31 Doug Mientkiewicz .50 .15
32 Cristian Guzman .50 .15
33 Corey Koskie .50 .15
34 Frank Thomas 1.25 .35
35 Magglio Ordonez .50 .15
36 Mark Buehrle .50 .15
37 Bernie Williams .75 .23
38 Roger Clemens 2.50 .75
39 Derek Jeter 3.00 .90
40 Jason Giambi .50 .15
41 Mike Mussina .75 .23
42 Lance Berkman .50 .15
43 Jeff Bagwell .75 .23
44 Roy Oswalt .50 .15
45 Greg Maddux 2.00 .60
46 Chipper Jones 1.25 .35
47 Andruw Jones .50 .15
48 Gary Sheffield .50 .15
49 Geoff Jenkins .50 .15
50 Richie Sexson .50 .15
51 Ben Sheets .50 .15
52 Albert Pujols 2.50 .75
53 J.D. Drew .50 .15
54 Jim Edmonds .50 .15
55 Sammy Sosa 2.00 .60
56 Moises Alou .50 .15
57 Kerry Wood 1.25 .35
58 Jon Lieber .50 .15
59 Fred McGriff .75 .23
60 Randy Johnson 1.25 .35
61 Luis Gonzalez .50 .15
62 Curt Schilling .50 .15
63 Kevin Brown .50 .15
64 Hideo Nomo 1.25 .35
65 Shawn Green .50 .15
66 Vladimir Guerrero 1.25 .35
67 Jose Vidro .50 .15
68 Barry Bonds 3.00 .90
69 Jeff Kent .50 .15
70 Rich Aurilia .50 .15
71 Cliff Floyd .50 .15
72 Josh Beckett .50 .15
73 Preston Wilson .50 .15
74 Mike Piazza 2.00 .60
75 Mo Vaughn .50 .15
76 Jeromy Burnitz .50 .15
77 Roberto Alomar .75 .23
78 Phil Nevin .50 .15
79 Ryan Klesko .50 .15
80 Scott Rolen 1.25 .35
81 Bobby Abreu .50 .15
82 Jimmy Rollins .50 .15
83 Brian Giles .50 .15
84 Aramis Ramirez .50 .15
85 Ken Griffey Jr. 2.00 .60
86 Sean Casey .50 .15
87 Barry Larkin .75 .23
88 Mike Hampton .50 .15
89 Larry Walker .75 .23
90 Todd Helton .75 .23
91A Ron Calloway YS RC 8.00 2.40
91P Ron Calloway YS RC 8.00 2.40
92A Joe Orloski YS RC 8.00 2.40
92P Joe Orloski YS RC 8.00 2.40
93A An. Machado YS RC 8.00 2.40
93P An. Machado YS RC 8.00 2.40
94A Eric Good YS RC 8.00 2.40
94P Eric Good YS RC 8.00 2.40
95A Reed Johnson YS RC 10.00 3.00
95P Reed Johnson YS RC 10.00 3.00
96A Brendan Donnelly YS RC 8.00 2.40
96P Brendan Donnelly YS RC 8.00 2.40
97A Chris Baker YS RC 8.00 2.40
97P Chris Baker YS RC 8.00 2.40
98A Wilson Valdez YS RC 8.00 2.40
98P Wilson Valdez YS RC 8.00 2.40
99A Scotty Layfield YS RC 8.00 2.40
99P Scotty Layfield YS RC 8.00 2.40
100A P.J. Bevis YS RC 8.00 2.40
100P P.J. Bevis YS RC 8.00 2.40
101A Edwin Almonte YS RC 8.00 2.40
101P Edwin Almonte YS RC 8.00 2.40
102A Francis Beltran YS RC 8.00 2.40
102P Francis Beltran YS RC 8.00 2.40
103A Val Pascucci YS 8.00 2.40
103P Val Pascucci YS 8.00 2.40
104A Nelson Castro YS RC 8.00 2.40
104P Nelson Castro YS RC 8.00 2.40
105A Michael Crudale YS RC 8.00 2.40
105P Michael Crudale YS RC 8.00 2.40
106A Colin Young YS RC 8.00 2.40
106P Colin Young YS RC 8.00 2.40
107A Todd Donovan YS RC 8.00 2.40
107P Todd Donovan YS RC 8.00 2.40
108A Felix Escalona YS RC 8.00 2.40
108P Felix Escalona YS RC 8.00 2.40
109A Brandon Backe YS RC 10.00 3.00
109P Brandon Backe YS RC 10.00 3.00
110A Corey Thurman YS RC 8.00 2.40
110P Corey Thurman YS RC 8.00 2.40
111A Kyle Kane YS RC 8.00 2.40
111P Kyle Kane YS RC 8.00 2.40
112A Allan Simpson YS RC 8.00 2.40
112P Allan Simpson YS RC 8.00 2.40
113A Jose Valverde YS RC 10.00 3.00
113P Jose Valverde YS RC 10.00 3.00
114A Chris Booker YS RC 8.00 2.40
114P Chris Booker YS RC 8.00 2.40
115A Brandon Puffer YS RC 8.00 2.40
115P Brandon Puffer YS RC 8.00 2.40
116A John Foster YS RC 8.00 2.40
116P John Foster YS RC 8.00 2.40
117A Cliff Bartosh YS RC 8.00 2.40
117P Cliff Bartosh YS RC 8.00 2.40
118A Gustavo Chacin YS RC 10.00 3.00
118P Gustavo Chacin YS RC 10.00 3.00
119A Steve Kent YS RC 8.00 2.40
119P Steve Kent YS RC 8.00 2.40
120A Nate Field YS RC 8.00 2.40
120P Nate Field YS RC 8.00 2.40
121 Victor Alvarez AU RC 10.00 3.00
122 Steve Bechler AU RC 10.00 3.00
123 Adrian Burnside AU RC 10.00 3.00
124 Marlon Byrd AU 15.00 4.50
125 Jaime Cerda AU RC 10.00 3.00
126 Brandon Claussen AU 15.00 4.50
127 Mark Corey AU RC 10.00 3.00
128 Doug Devore AU RC 10.00 3.00
129 Kazuhisa Ishii AU SP RC 100.00 30.00
130 John Ennis AU RC 10.00 3.00
131 Kevin Frederick AU RC 10.00 3.00
132 Josh Hancock AU RC 10.00 3.00
133 Ben Howard AU RC 10.00 3.00
134 Orlando Hudson AU 15.00 4.50
135 Hansel Izquierdo AU RC 10.00 3.00
136 Eric Junge AU RC 10.00 3.00
137 Austin Kearns AU 25.00 7.50
138 Victor Martinez AU 40.00 12.00
139 Luis Martinez AU RC 10.00 3.00
140 Danny Mota AU RC 10.00 3.00
141 Jorge Padilla AU RC 10.00 3.00
142 Andy Pratt AU RC 10.00 3.00
143 Rene Reyes AU RC 10.00 3.00
144 Rodrigo Rosario AU RC 10.00 3.00
145 Tom Shearn AU RC 10.00 3.00
146 So Taguchi AU SP RC 40.00 12.00
147 Dennis Tankersley AU 15.00 4.50
148 Matt Thornton AU RC 10.00 3.00
149 Jeremy Ward AU RC 10.00 3.00
150 Mitch Wylie AU RC 10.00 3.00
151 Pedro Martinez JSY/800 10.00 3.00
152 Cal Ripken JSY/800 40.00 12.00
153 Roger Clemens JSY/800 25.00 7.50
154 Bernie Williams JSY/800 10.00 3.00
155 Jason Giambi JSY/700 8.00 2.40
156 Robin Ventura JSY/800 8.00 2.40
157 Carlos Delgado JSY/800 8.00 2.40
158 Frank Thomas JSY/800 10.00 3.00
159 Mag. Ordonez JSY/800 8.00 2.40
160 Jim Thome JSY/800 10.00 3.00
161 Darin Erstad JSY/800 8.00 2.40
162 Tim Salmon JSY/800 10.00 3.00
163 Tim Hudson JSY/800 8.00 2.40
164 Barry Zito JSY/800 8.00 2.40
165 Ichiro Suzuki JSY/800 40.00 12.00
166 Edgar Martinez JSY/800 10.00 3.00
167 Alex Rodriguez JSY/800 20.00 6.00
168 Ivan Rodriguez JSY/800 10.00 3.00
169 Juan Gonzalez JSY/800 10.00 3.00
170 Greg Maddux JSY/800 15.00 4.50
171 Chipper Jones JSY/800 10.00 3.00
172 Andruw Jones JSY/800 8.00 2.40
173 Tom Glavine JSY/800 10.00 3.00
174 Mike Piazza JSY/800 15.00 4.50
175 Roberto Alomar JSY/800 10.00 3.00
176 Scott Rolen JSY/800 10.00 3.00
177 Sammy Sosa JSY/800 20.00 6.00
178 Moises Alou JSY/800 8.00 2.40
179 Ken Griffey Jr. JSY/700 20.00 6.00
180 Jeff Bagwell JSY/800 10.00 3.00
181 Jim Edmonds JSY/800 8.00 2.40
182 J.D. Drew JSY/800 8.00 2.40
183 Brian Giles JSY/800 8.00 2.40
184 Randy Johnson JSY/800 10.00 3.00
185 Curt Schilling JSY/800 8.00 2.40
186 Luis Gonzalez JSY/800 8.00 2.40
187 Todd Helton JSY/800 10.00 3.00
188 Shawn Green JSY/800 8.00 2.40
189 David Wells JSY/800 8.00 2.40
190 Jeff Kent JSY/800 8.00 2.40
191 Tom Glavine 1.25 .35
192 Cliff Floyd .75 .23
193 Mark Prior 3.00 .90
194 Corey Patterson .75 .23
195 Paul Konerko .75 .23
196 Adam Dunn 1.25 .35
197 Joe Borchard .75 .23
198 Carlos Pena .75 .23

199 Juan Encarnacion .75 .23
200 Luis Castillo .75 .23
201 Torii Hunter .75 .23
202 Hee Seop Choi .75 .23
203 Bartolo Colon .75 .23
204 Raul Mondesi .75 .23
205 Jeff Weaver .75 .23
206 Eric Munson .75 .23
207 Alfonso Soriano 1.25 .35
208 Ray Durham .75 .23
209 Eric Chavez .75 .23
210 Brett Myers .75 .23
211 Jeremy Giambi .75 .23
212 Vicente Padilla .75 .23
213 Felipe Lopez .75 .23
214 Sean Burroughs .75 .23
215 Kenny Lofton .75 .23
216 Scott Rolen 2.00 .60
217 Carl Crawford .75 .23
218 Juan Gonzalez 1.25 .35
219 Orlando Hudson .75 .23
220 Eric Hinske .75 .23
221 Adam Walker AU RC 10.00 3.00
222 Aaron Cook AU RC 10.00 3.00
223 Cam Esslinger AU RC 10.00 3.00
224 Kirk Saarloos AU RC 10.00 3.00
225 Jose Diaz AU RC 10.00 3.00
226 David Ross AU RC 10.00 3.00
227 Jayson Durocher AU RC 10.00 3.00
228 Brian Mallette AU RC 10.00 3.00
229 Aaron Guiel AU RC 10.00 3.00
230 Jorge Nunez AU RC 10.00 3.00
231 Satoru Komiyama AU RC 25.00 7.50
232 Tyler Yates AU RC 15.00 4.50
233 Pete Zamora AU RC 10.00 3.00
234 Mike Gonzalez AU RC 10.00 3.00
235 Oliver Perez AU RC 50.00 15.00
236 Julius Matos AU RC 10.00 3.00
237 Andy Shibilo AU RC 10.00 3.00
238 J.Simontacchi AU RC 10.00 3.00
239 Ron Chiavacci AU 10.00 3.00
240 Deivis Santos AU 10.00 3.00
241 Travis Driskill AU RC 10.00 3.00
242 Jorge De La Rosa AU RC 10.00 3.00
243 An. Martinez AU RC 10.00 3.00
244 Earl Snyder AU RC 15.00 4.50
245 Freddy Sanchez AU RC 10.00 3.00
246 Miguel Asencio AU RC 10.00 3.00
247 Juan Brito AU RC 10.00 3.00
248 Franklyn German AU RC 10.00 3.00
249 Chris Snelling AU RC 10.00 3.00
250 Ken Huckaby AU RC 10.00 3.00

2002 SPx SuperStar Swatch Gold

Randomly inserted in packs, these cards parallel the final forty cards of the base set. These cards were printed to a stated print run of 150 serial numbered sets.

Nm-Mt Ex-Mt
*GOLD JSY: .6X TO 1.5X BASIC JSY..

2002 SPx SuperStar Swatch Silver

Randomly inserted in packs, these cards parallel the final forty cards of the base set. These cards were printed to a stated print run of 400 serial numbered sets.

Nm-Mt Ex-Mt
*SILVER JSY: .4X TO 1X BASIC JSY..

2002 SPx Sweet Spot Preview Bat Barrel

Randomly inserted in packs, these cards feature bat "barrel" cards of leading players. Each card was printed to a different amount and we have notated that information next to their name in our checklist. Due to market scarcity, no pricing is provided for these cards.

Nm-Mt Ex-Mt
BB-AJ Andruw Jones/5
BB-AR Alex Rodriguez/5
BB-CB Carlos Beltran/1
BB-CD Carlos Delgado/1
BB-CJ Chipper Jones/5
BB-EC Eric Chavez/1
BB-EM Edgar Martinez/2
BB-FT Frank Thomas/8
BB-GM Greg Maddux/5
BB-GS Gary Sheffield/5
BB-IR Ivan Rodriguez/7
BB-IS Ichiro Suzuki/2
BB-JD J.D. Drew/1
BB-JE Jim Edmonds/1
BB-JG Jason Giambi/1
BB-JT Jim Thome/1
BB-KG Ken Griffey Jr./6
BB-KW Kerry Wood/1
BB-MP Mike Piazza/7
BB-MR Manny Ramirez/4
BB-MW Matt Williams/5
BB-PW Preston Wilson/1
BB-RA Roberto Alomar/3
BB-RC Roger Clemens/1
BB-RP Rafael Palmeiro/1
BB-SG Shawn Green/7
BB-SS Sammy Sosa/5
BB-TG Tom Glavine/5
BB-TH Todd Helton/3

2002 SPx Winning Materials 2-Player Base Combos

Randomly inserted into packs, these cards include bases used by both players featured on the card. These cards were issued to a stated print run of 200 serial numbered sets.

Nm-Mt Ex-Mt
B-BG Barry Bonds 40.00 12.00
Shawn Green
B-GR Troy Glaus 30.00 9.00
Alex Rodriguez
B-GS Ken Griffey Jr. 40.00 12.00
Sammy Sosa
B-IM Ichiro Suzuki 60.00 18.00
Edgar Martinez
B-PE Mike Piazza 25.00 7.50
Jim Edmonds
B-PI Albert Pujols 100.00 30.00
Ichiro Suzuki
B-RJ Alex Rodriguez 60.00 18.00
Derek Jeter
B-SG Sammy Sosa 30.00 9.00
Luis Gonzalez
B-SR Kazuhiro Sasaki 25.00 7.50
Mariano Rivera
B-WJ Bernie Williams 50.00 15.00
Derek Jeter

2002 SPx Winning Materials 2-Player Jersey Combos

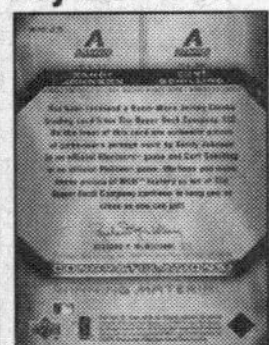

Inserted at stated odds of one in 18, these 29 cards feature not only the players but a jersey swatch from each player. A few players were issued in lesser quantities and we have notated that with an SP in our checklist. Other players were issued in larger quantities and we have notated that with an asterisk next to the player's name.

Nm-Mt Ex-Mt
WM-AR Alex Rodriguez 20.00 6.00
Ivan Rodriguez
WM-BA Jeromy Burnitz 10.00 3.00
Edgardo Alfonzo
WM-BG Jeff Bagwell 15.00 4.50
Juan Gonzalez
WM-BR Jeff Bagwell 15.00 4.50
Alex Rodriguez*
WM-DH Jermaine Dye 10.00 3.00
Tim Hudson
WM-DS Carlos Delgado 10.00 3.00
Shannon Stewart
WM-ED Jim Edmonds 10.00 3.00
J.D. Drew
WM-GC Ken Griffey Jr. 20.00 6.00
Sean Casey SP
WM-GK Shawn Green 10.00 3.00
Eric Karros
WM-GR Juan Gonzalez 15.00 4.50
Ivan Rodriguez
WM-HW Mike Hampton 15.00 4.50
Larry Walker
WM-JJ Chipper Jones 15.00 4.50
Andruw Jones
WM-JS Randy Johnson 15.00 4.50
Curt Schilling
WM-KG Jason Kendall 10.00 3.00
Brian Giles
WM-LH Al Leiter 10.00 3.00
Mike Hampton
WM-MC Edgar Martinez 15.00 4.50
Mike Cameron
WM-MJ Greg Maddux 25.00 7.50
Chipper Jones
WM-NM Hideo Nomo 25.00 7.50
Pedro Martinez SP
WM-PA Mike Piazza 15.00 4.50
Roberto Alomar *
WM-RA Scott Rolen 15.00 4.50
Bob Abreu
WM-RP Ivan Rodriguez 15.00 4.50
Chan Ho Park
WM-SE Aaron Sele 10.00 3.00
Darin Erstad
WM-SH Kazuhiro Sasaki 10.00 3.00
Shigetoshi Hasegawa
WM-SP Sammy Sosa 25.00 7.50
Corey Patterson
WM-TO Frank Thomas 15.00 4.50
Magglio Ordonez
WM-TS Jim Thome 15.00 4.50
C.C. Sabathia*
WM-VR Omar Vizquel 20.00 6.00
Alex Rodriguez
WM-WG Bernie Williams 15.00 4.50
Jason Giambi*
WM-WP David Wells 15.00 4.50
Jorge Posada*

2002 SPx Winning Materials Ball Patch Combos

Randomly inserted into packs, these nine cards feature both a ball piece along with a jersey patch of the featured players. Each of these cards were issued to a stated print run of 25 serial numbered sets and we are not pricing these cards due to market scarcity.

Nm-Mt Ex-Mt
PC-AR Alex Rodriguez
PC-CJ Chipper Jones
PC-IS Ichiro Suzuki
PC-KG Ken Griffey Jr.
PC-MP Mike Piazza
PC-RC Roger Clemens
PC-SG Shawn Green
PC-SS Sammy Sosa
PC-TH Todd Helton

2002 SPx Winning Materials Base Patch Combos

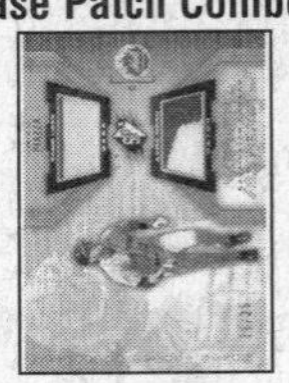

Randomly inserted into packs, these eight cards feature both a base piece along with a jersey patch of the featured players. Each of these cards were issued to a stated print run of 25 serial numbered sets and we are not pricing these cards due to market scarcity.

Nm-Mt Ex-Mt
BP-AR Alex Rodriguez
BP-BW Bernie Williams
BP-IS Ichiro Suzuki
BP-JG Jason Giambi
BP-KG Ken Griffey Jr.
BP-LG Luis Gonzalez
BP-MP Mike Piazza
BP-SS Sammy Sosa

2002 SPx Winning Materials USA Jersey Combos

Randomly inserted into packs, these 23 cards feature two uniform swatches from players who played for the USA National team. These cards had a stated print run of 150 serial numbered sets.

Nm-Mt Ex-Mt
USA-AH Brent Abernathy 15.00 4.50
Orlando Hudson
USA-AW Matt Anderson 15.00 4.50
Jeff Weaver
USA-BT Sean Burroughs 25.00 7.50
MarkTeixeira
USA-GB Jason Giambi 15.00 4.50
Sean Burroughs
USA-GT Jason Giambi 15.00 4.50
Mark Teixeira
USA-HD Orlando Hudson 15.00 4.50
Jeff Deardorff
USA-HP Dustin Hermanson 40.00 12.00
Mark Prior
USA-JC Jacques Jones 15.00 4.50
Michael Cuddyer
USA-KB Austin Kearns 15.00 4.50
Sean Burroughs
USA-KC Aaron Kearns 15.00 4.50
Michael Cuddyer
USA-MG Doug Mientkiewicz 15.00 4.50
Jason Giambi
USA-MO Matt Morris 15.00 4.50
Roy Oswalt
USA-MP Matt Morris 40.00 12.00
Mark Prior
USA-MW Matt Morris 15.00 4.50
Jeff Weaver
USA-PB Mark Prior 40.00 12.00
Dewon Brazelton
USA-RE Brian Roberts 15.00 4.50
Adam Everett
USA-SD Mark Kotsay 15.00 4.50
Sean Burroughs
USA-TB Brent Abernathy 15.00 4.50
Dewon Brazelton
USA-TP Mark Teixeira 50.00 15.00
Mark Prior
USA-WB Jeff Weaver 15.00 4.50
Dewon Brazelton
USA-WH Jeff Weaver 15.00 4.50
Dustin Hermanson
USA-HOU Roy Oswalt 15.00 4.50
Adam Everett
USA-MIN Doug Mientkiewicz 15.00 4.50
Michael Cuddyer

2003 SPx

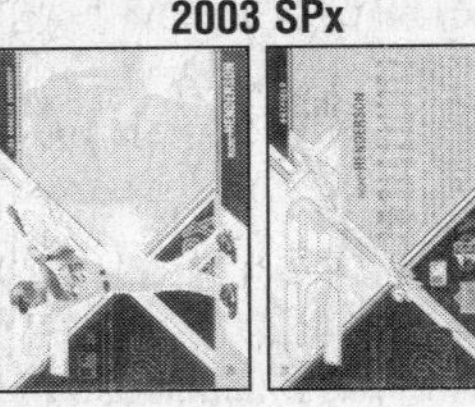

This 199 card set was released in two series. The primary 178-card set was issued in August, 2003 followed up with 21 Update cards randomly seeded within a special rookie pack within sealed boxes of 2003 Upper Deck Finite baseball (of which was released in December, 2003). The primary SPx product was distributed in four card packs carrying an SRP of $7. Each sealed box contained 18 packs and each sealed case contained 14 boxes. Cards numbered 1 to 125 featured veterans with 25 short print cards inserted. Cards numbered 126 through 160 featured rookie cards which were issued to a stated print run of 999 serial numbered sets. Cards 161 and 162 featured New York Yankees rookies Hideki Matsui and Jose Contreras. The Matsui card was issued to a serial numbered print run of 864 copies while the Contreras was issued to a serial numbered print run of 800 copies. Both cards were signed while the Matsui also included a game-used jersey swatch. Cards numbered 163 through 178 featured both autographs and jersey swatches of the featured player and those cards were issued to a stated print run of 1224 cards. The Update cards 179-193 featured a selection of prospects and each card was serial numbered to 150 copies. For reasons unknown to us, the set then skipped to cards 381-387, of which featured additional prospects on cards enriched with both certified autographs and game jersey swatches. These "high number" cards were printed to a serial numbered quantity of 355 copies each.

MINT NRMT
COMP.LO SET w/o SP's (100) 25.00 11.00
COMP.LO SET w/ SP's (125) 100.00 45.00
COMMON CARD (1-125) .50 .23
COMMON SP (1-125) 4.00 1.80
COMMON CARD (126-160) 8.00 3.60
COMMON CARD (163-178) 15.00 6.75
163-178 PRINT RUN 1224 SERIAL #'d SETS
126-178 RANDOM INSERTS IN SPx PACKS
COMMON CARD (179-193) 15.00 6.75
COMMON CARD (381-387) 20.00 9.00
1 Darin Erstad .50 .23
2 Garret Anderson .50 .23
3 Tim Salmon .75 .35
4 Troy Glaus SP 4.00 1.80
5 Luis Gonzalez .50 .23
6 Randy Johnson 1.25 .55
7 Curt Schilling .50 .23
8 Lyle Overbay .50 .23
9 Andruw Jones SP 4.00 1.80
10 Gary Sheffield .50 .23
11 Rafael Furcal .50 .23
12 Greg Maddux 2.00 .90
13 Chipper Jones SP 5.00 2.20
14 Tony Batista .50 .23
15 Rodrigo Lopez .50 .23
16 Jay Gibbons .50 .23
17 Byung-Hyun Kim .50 .23
18 Johnny Damon 1.25 .55
19 Derek Lowe .50 .23
20 Nomar Garciaparra SP 8.00 3.60
21 Pedro Martinez 1.25 .55
22 Manny Ramirez SP 4.00 1.80
23 Mark Prior 1.25 .55
24 Kerry Wood 1.25 .55
25 Corey Patterson .50 .23
26 Sammy Sosa SP 8.00 3.60
27 Moises Alou .50 .23
28 Magglio Ordonez .50 .23
29 Frank Thomas 1.25 .55
30 Paul Konerko .50 .23
31 Bartolo Colon .50 .23
32 Adam Dunn .75 .35
33 Austin Kearns .75 .35
34 Aaron Boone .50 .23
35 Ken Griffey Jr. SP 8.00 3.60
36 Omar Vizquel .75 .35
37 C.C. Sabathia .50 .23
38 Jason Davis .50 .23
39 Travis Hafner .50 .23
40 Brandon Phillips .50 .23
41 Larry Walker .75 .35
42 Preston Wilson .50 .23
43 Jay Payton .50 .23
44 Todd Helton .75 .35
45 Carlos Pena .50 .23
46 Eric Munson .50 .23
47 Ivan Rodriguez 1.25 .55
48 Josh Beckett .50 .23
49 Alex Gonzalez .50 .23
50 Roy Oswalt .50 .23
51 Craig Biggio .75 .35
52 Jeff Bagwell .75 .35
53 Dontrelle Willis SP 4.00 1.80
54 Mike Sweeney .50 .23
55 Carlos Beltran .75 .35
56 Brent Mayne .50 .23
57 Hideo Nomo 1.25 .55
58 Rickey Henderson 1.25 .55
59 Adrian Beltre .75 .35
60 Miguel Cabrera SP 5.00 2.20
61 Kazuhisa Ishii .50 .23
62 Ben Sheets .50 .23
63 Richie Sexson .50 .23
64 Torii Hunter SP 4.00 1.80
65 Jacque Jones .50 .23
66 Joe Mays .50 .23
67 Corey Koskie .50 .23
68 A.J. Pierzynski .50 .23
69 Jose Vidro .50 .23
70 Vladimir Guerrero SP 5.00 2.20
71 Tom Glavine .75 .35
72 Jose Reyes SP 4.00 1.80
73 Aaron Heilman .50 .23
74 Mike Piazza 2.00 .90
75 Jorge Posada .75 .35
76 Mike Mussina .75 .35
77 Robin Ventura .50 .23
78 Mariano Rivera .75 .35
79 Roger Clemens SP 10.00 4.50
80 Jason Giambi .50 .23
81 Bernie Williams .75 .35
82 Alfonso Soriano SP 4.00 1.80
83 Derek Jeter SP 12.00 5.50
84 Miguel Tejada SP 4.00 1.80
85 Eric Chavez .50 .23
86 Tim Hudson .50 .23
87 Barry Zito .50 .23
88 Mark Mulder .50 .23
89 Erubiel Durazo .50 .23
90 Pat Burrell .50 .23
91 Jim Thome SP 5.00 2.20
92 Bobby Abreu .50 .23
93 Brian Giles .50 .23
94 Reggie Sanders SP 4.00 1.80
95 Kenny Lofton .50 .23
96 Ryan Klesko .50 .23
97 Sean Burroughs .50 .23
98 Edgardo Alfonzo .50 .23
99 Rich Aurilia .50 .23
100 Jose Cruz Jr. .50 .23
101 Barry Bonds SP 12.00 5.50
102 Mike Cameron .50 .23
103 Kazuhiro Sasaki .50 .23
104 Bret Boone .50 .23
105 Ichiro Suzuki SP 8.00 3.60
106 J.D. Drew .50 .23
107 Jim Edmonds .50 .23
108 Scott Rolen SP 5.00 2.20
109 Matt Morris .50 .23
110 Tino Martinez .75 .35
111 Albert Pujols SP 10.00 4.50
112 Damian Rolls .50 .23
113 Carl Crawford .50 .23
114 Rocco Baldelli SP 4.00 1.80
115 Hank Blalock .75 .35
116 Alex Rodriguez SP 8.00 3.60
117 Kevin Mench .50 .23
118 Rafael Palmeiro .75 .35
119 Mark Teixeira .50 .23
120 Shannon Stewart .50 .23
121 Vernon Wells .50 .23
122 Josh Phelps .50 .23
123 Eric Hinske .50 .23
124 Orlando Hudson .50 .23
125 Carlos Delgado SP 4.00 1.80
126 Jason Roach ROO RC 8.00 3.60
127 Dan Haren ROO RC 10.00 4.50
128 Luis Ayala ROO RC 8.00 3.60
129 Bo Hart ROO RC 10.00 4.50
130 Wil. Ledezma ROO RC 10.00 4.50
131 Rick Roberts ROO RC 8.00 3.60
132 Miguel Ojeda ROO RC 8.00 3.60
133 Aquilino Lopez ROO RC 8.00 3.60
134 Roger Deago ROO RC 8.00 3.60
135 Arnie Munoz ROO RC 8.00 3.60
136 Brent Hoard ROO RC 8.00 3.60
137 Termel Sledge ROO RC 10.00 4.50
138 Ryan Cameron ROO RC 8.00 3.60
139 Pr. Redman ROO RC 8.00 3.60
140 Clint Barmes ROO RC 10.00 4.50
141 Jeremy Griffiths ROO RC 10.00 4.50
142 Jon Leicester ROO RC 8.00 3.60
143 Brandon Webb ROO RC 10.00 4.50
144 T.Wellemeyer ROO RC 10.00 4.50
145 Felix Sanchez ROO RC 8.00 3.60
146 Anthony Ferrari ROO RC 8.00 3.60
147 Ian Ferguson ROO RC 8.00 3.60
148 Mi. Nakamura ROO RC 8.00 3.60
149 Lew Ford ROO RC 10.00 4.50
150 Nate Bland ROO RC 8.00 3.60
151 David Matranga ROO RC 8.00 3.60
152 Edgar Gonzalez ROO RC 8.00 3.60
153 Carlos Mendez ROO RC 8.00 3.60
154 Jason Gilfillan ROO RC 8.00 3.60
155 Mike Neu ROO RC 8.00 3.60
156 Jason Shiell ROO RC 8.00 3.60
157 Jeff Duncan ROO RC 10.00 4.50
158 Oscar Villarreal ROO RC 8.00 3.60
159 D.Markwell ROO RC 8.00 3.60
160 Joe Valentine ROO RC 8.00 3.60
161 H.Matsui AU JSY RC 300.00 135.00
162 Jose Contreras AU RC 40.00 18.00
163 Willie Eyre AU JSY RC 15.00 6.75
164 Matt Bruback AU JSY RC 15.00 6.75
165 Rett Johnson AU JSY RC 25.00 11.00
166 Jeremy Griffiths AU JSY 25.00 11.00
167 Fran Cruceta AU JSY RC 15.00 6.75
168 Fern Cabrera AU JSY RC 15.00 6.75
169 J.Peralta AU JSY RC 15.00 6.75
170 S.Bazzell AU JSY RC 15.00 6.75
171 B.Madritsch AU JSY RC 50.00 22.00
172 Phil Seibel AU JSY RC 15.00 6.75
173 J.Willingham AU JSY RC 25.00 11.00
174 R.Hammock AU JSY RC 25.00 11.00
175 A.Machado AU JSY RC 15.00 6.75
176 D.Sanders AU JSY RC 15.00 6.75
177 Matt Kata AU JSY RC 25.00 11.00
178 Heath Bell AU JSY RC 15.00 6.75
179 Chad Gaudin ROO RC 15.00 6.75
180 Chris Capuano ROO RC 15.00 6.75
181 Danny Garcia ROO RC 15.00 6.75
182 Delmon Young ROO 50.00 22.00
183 Edwin Jackson ROO RC 40.00 18.00
184 Greg Jones ROO RC 15.00 6.75
185 Jeremy Bonderman ROO RC 20.00 9.00
186 Jorge DePaula ROO 15.00 6.75
187 Khalil Greene ROO 40.00 18.00
188 Chad Cordero ROO RC 15.00 6.75
189 Miguel Cabrera ROO 20.00 9.00
190 Rich Harden ROO 20.00 9.00
191 Rickie Weeks ROO 40.00 18.00
192 Rosman Garcia ROO RC 15.00 6.75
193 Tom Gregorio ROO RC 15.00 6.75
381 Andrew Brown AU JSY RC 25.00 11.00
382 Delm Young AU JSY RC 180.00 80.00
383 Colin Porter AU JSY RC 20.00 9.00
385 Rickie Weeks AU JSY RC 100.00 45.00
386 David Matranga AU JSY RC 20.00 9.00
387 Bo Hart AU JSY 25.00 11.00

2003 SPx Spectrum

MINT NRMT
*SPECTRUM 1-125 p/r 51-75: 5X TO 12X
*SPECTRUM 1-125 p/r 36-50: 6X TO 15X
*SPECTRUM 1-125 p/r 26-35: 8X TO 20X
*SPECTRUM 1-125 p/r 51-75: 1.25X TO 3X SP
*SPECTRUM 1-125 p/r 36-50: 1.5X TO 4X SP
*SPECTRUM 1-125 p/r 26-35: 2X TO 5X SP
1-125 PRINT RUNS B/WN 1-75 COPIES PER
*SPECTRUM 126-160: .6X TO 1.5X BASIC
126-160 PRINT RUN 125 SERIAL #'d SETS
161-178 PRINT RUN 25 SERIAL #'d SETS
161-178 NO PRICING DUE TO SCARCITY
RANDOM INSERTS IN PACKS

2003 SPx Game Used Combos

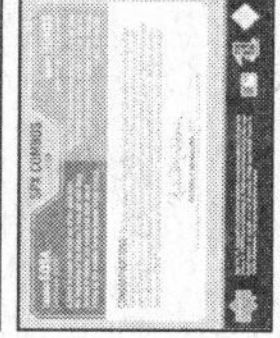

Randomly inserted into packs, these 42 cards feature two players along with game-used memorabilia of each player. Since these cards were issued in varying quantities, we have notated the print run next to the card in our checklist. Please note that if a card was issued to a print run of 25 or fewer copies, no pricing is provided due to market scarcity.

MINT NRMT
BK Jeff Bagwell Patch 40.00 18.00
Jeff Kent Patch/90
BM Barry Bonds Base 120.00 55.00
Roger Maris Jsy/50
BT Barry Bonds Base 250.00 110.00
Ted Williams Patch/50
CA Cal Ripken Patch 200.00 90.00
Alex Rodriguez Patch/50
CC Jose Contreras Base 50.00 22.00
Roger Clemens Patch/50
CL Cal Ripken Patch 400.00 180.00
Lou Gehrig Pants/90
CM Jose Contreras Base 40.00 18.00
Pedro Martinez Patch/90
EG Darin Erstad Patch 25.00 11.00
Troy Glaus Patch/90
FC Carlton Fisk Patch 40.00 18.00
Gary Carter Patch/90
GC Greg Maddux Patch 50.00 22.00
Chipper Jones Patch/90
GD Ken Griffey Jr. Patch 60.00 27.00
Adam Dunn Patch/90
GR Ken Griffey Jr. Patch 60.00 27.00
Sammy Sosa Patch/90
GS Jason Giambi Patch 40.00 18.00
Alfonso Soriano Patch/90
HJ Hideki Matsui Patch 100.00 45.00
Jason Giambi Patch/50
HM Hideki Matsui Patch
Mickey Mantle Bat/10
IA Ichiro Suzuki Patch 250.00 110.00
Albert Pujols Patch/50
JJ Chipper Jones Patch 40.00 18.00
Andruw Jones Patch/90
MB Mickey Mantle Bat 200.00 90.00
Barry Bonds Base/50
MC Hideki Matsui Patch
Jose Contreras Base/10
MD Mickey Mantle Bat 250.00 110.00
Derek Jeter Base/50
MG Pedro Martinez Patch 60.00 27.00
Nomar Garciaparra Base/90
MJ Hideki Matsui Patch 120.00 55.00
Derek Jeter Base/90
MR Mickey Mantle Bat
Roger Maris Jsy/10
MS Hideki Matsui Patch 400.00 180.00
Ichiro Suzuki Patch/50
MW Mickey Mantle Bat 400.00 180.00
Ted Williams Jsy/50
NI Hideo Nomo Patch 80.00 36.00
Kazuhisa Ishii Patch/50
PM Rafael Palmeiro Patch 40.00 18.00
Fred McGriff Patch/90
PS Rafael Palmeiro Patch 60.00 27.00
Sammy Sosa Patch/10
RC Nolan Ryan Patch 150.00 70.00
Roger Clemens Patch/90
RG Alex Rodriguez Patch 60.00 27.00
Nomar Garciaparra Base/90
RM Babe Ruth Bat
Hideki Matsui Patch/10
RR Cal Ripken Patch 100.00 45.00
Scott Rolen Patch/90
RS Nolan Ryan Patch 150.00 70.00
Tom Seaver Patch/90
RT Alex Rodriguez Patch 50.00 22.00
Miguel Tejada Patch/90
RY Nolan Ryan Patch
Pedro Martinez Patch/10
SB Sammy Sosa Patch 60.00 27.00
Barry Bonds Base/90
SJ Curt Schilling Patch 40.00 18.00
Randy Johnson Patch/90
SN Ichiro Suzuki Patch 200.00 90.00
Hideo Nomo Patch/90
SP Sammy Sosa Patch 60.00 27.00
Rafael Palmeiro Patch/90
TB Thurman Munson Patch
Yogi Berra Bat/10
WG Ted Williams Patch
Nomar Garciaparra Base/10
WM Ted Williams Patch
Pedro Martinez Patch/10

2003 SPx Stars Autograph Jersey

Randomly inserted in packs, these cards feature both a game-used jersey swatch as well as an authentic signature. Since these cards were

issued in varying print runs, we have notated the stated print run next to their name in our checklist.

MINT NRMT
SPECTRUM PRINT RUN 1 SERIAL #'d SET
NO SPECTRUM PRICING DUE TO SCARCITY
RANDOM INSERTS IN PACKS
CJO Chipper Jones/195 60.00 27.00
CS Curt Schilling/490 50.00 22.00
JG Jason Giambi/315 40.00 18.00
KG Ken Griffey Jr./690 100.00 45.00
LB Lance Berkman/590 40.00 18.00
LG Luis Gonzalez/790 25.00 11.00
MP Mark Prior/490 80.00 36.00
NM Nomar Garciaparra/195 150.00 70.00
PB Pat Burrell/590 25.00 11.00
TG Troy Glaus/490 25.00 11.00
VG Vladimir Guerrero/390 50.00 22.00

2003 SPx Winning Materials 375

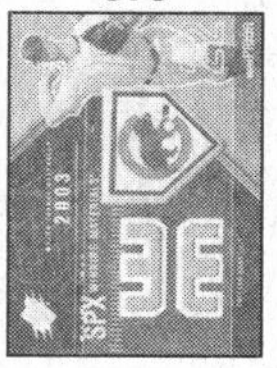

MINT NRMT
LOGO'S CONSECUTIVELY #'d FROM 41-375
NUMBERS CONSECUTIVELY #'d FROM 1-40
CARDS CUMULATIVELY SERIAL #'d TO 375
*WIN.MAT.250: .5X TO 1.2X WIN.MAT.375
NUMBERS CONSECUTIVELY #'d FROM 1-28
LOGOS CONSECUTIVELY #'d FROM 29-250
WM 250 CUMULATIVELY SERIAL #'d TO 250
LOGO/NUMBER PRINTS PROVIDED BY UD
RANDOM INSERTS IN PACKS
AJ1A Andruw Jones Logo 8.00 3.60
AJ1B Andruw Jones Num 15.00 6.75
AP1A Albert Pujols Logo 25.00 11.00
AP1B Albert Pujols Num 50.00 22.00
AR1A Alex Rodriguez Logo 15.00 6.75
AR1B Alex Rodriguez Num 30.00 13.50
AS1A Alfonso Soriano Logo 10.00 4.50
AS1B Alfonso Soriano Num 20.00 9.00
BW1A Bernie Williams Logo 10.00 4.50
BW1B Bernie Williams Num 20.00 9.00
BZ1A Barry Zito Logo 8.00 3.60
BZ1B Barry Zito Num 15.00 6.75
CD1A Carlos Delgado Logo 8.00 3.60
CD1B Carlos Delgado Num 15.00 6.75
CJ1A Chipper Jones Logo 10.00 4.50
CJ1B Chipper Jones Num 20.00 9.00
CS1A Curt Schilling Logo 8.00 3.60
CS1B Curt Schilling Num 15.00 6.75
FT1A Frank Thomas Logo 10.00 4.50
FT1B Frank Thomas Num 20.00 9.00
GM1A Greg Maddux Logo 15.00 6.75
GM1B Greg Maddux Num 30.00 13.50
GS1A Gary Sheffield Logo 8.00 3.60
GS1B Gary Sheffield Num 15.00 6.75
HM1A Hideki Matsui Logo 25.00 11.00
HM1B Hideki Matsui Num 40.00 18.00
HN1A Hideo Nomo Logo 25.00 11.00
HN1B Hideo Nomo Num 50.00 22.00
IR1A Ivan Rodriguez Logo 10.00 4.50
IR1B Ivan Rodriguez Num 20.00 9.00
IS1A Ichiro Suzuki Logo 40.00 18.00
IS1B Ichiro Suzuki Num 80.00 36.00
JB1A Jeff Bagwell Logo 10.00 4.50
JB1B Jeff Bagwell Num 20.00 9.00
JG1A Jason Giambi Logo 8.00 3.60
JG1B Jason Giambi Num 15.00 6.75
JK1A Jeff Kent Logo 8.00 3.60
JK1B Jeff Kent Num 15.00 6.75
JT1A Jim Thome Logo 10.00 4.50
JT1B Jim Thome Num 20.00 9.00
KG1A Ken Griffey Jr. Logo 20.00 9.00
KG1B Ken Griffey Jr. Num 40.00 18.00
LB1A Lance Berkman Logo 8.00 3.60
LB1B Lance Berkman Num 15.00 6.75
LG1A Luis Gonzalez Logo 8.00 3.60
LG1B Luis Gonzalez Num 15.00 6.75
MA1A Mark Prior Logo 10.00 4.50
MA1B Mark Prior Num 20.00 9.00
MP1A Mike Piazza Logo 15.00 6.75
MP1B Mike Piazza Num 30.00 13.50
MR1A Manny Ramirez Logo 10.00 4.50
MR1B Manny Ramirez Num 20.00 9.00
MT1A Miguel Tejada Logo 8.00 3.60
MT1B Miguel Tejada Num 15.00 6.75
PB1A Pat Burrell Logo 8.00 3.60
PB1B Pat Burrell Num 15.00 6.75
PM1A Pedro Martinez Logo 10.00 4.50
PM1B Pedro Martinez Num 20.00 9.00
RA1A Roberto Alomar Logo 10.00 4.50
RA1B Roberto Alomar Num 20.00 9.00
RC1A Roger Clemens Logo 20.00 9.00
RC1B Roger Clemens Num 40.00 18.00
RF1A Rafael Furcal Logo 8.00 3.60
RF1B Rafael Furcal Num 15.00 6.75
RJ1A Randy Johnson Logo 10.00 4.50
RJ1B Randy Johnson Num 20.00 9.00
SG1A Shawn Green Logo 8.00 3.60
SG1B Shawn Green Num 15.00 6.75
SS1A Sammy Sosa Logo 20.00 9.00
SS1B Sammy Sosa Num 40.00 18.00
TG1A Tom Glavine Logo 10.00 4.50
TG1B Tom Glavine Num 20.00 9.00
TH1A Torii Hunter Logo 8.00 3.60
TH1B Torii Hunter Num 15.00 6.75
TO1A Todd Helton Logo 10.00 4.50
TO1B Todd Helton Num 20.00 9.00
TR1A Troy Glaus Logo 8.00 3.60
TR1B Troy Glaus Num 15.00 6.75
VG1A Vladimir Guerrero Logo 10.00 4.50
VG1B Vladimir Guerrero Num 20.00 9.00

2003 SPx Winning Materials 175

MINT NRMT
NUMBERS CONSECUTIVELY #'d FROM 1-20
LOGOS CONSECUTIVELY #'d FROM 21-175
CARDS CUMULATIVELY SERIAL #'d TO 175
*WM LOGO 50: .75X TO 2X WM LOGO 175
WM 50 NUMBERS CONSECUTIVELY #'d 1-10
WM 50 LOGOS CONSECUTIVELY #'d 11-50
WM 50 CUMULATIVELY SERIAL #'d TO 50
NO NUMBER PRICING DUE TO SCARCITY
LOGO/NUMBER PRINTS PROVIDED BY UD
AJ2A Andruw Jones Logo 10.00 4.50
AP2A Albert Pujols Logo 30.00 13.50
AR2A Alex Rodriguez Logo 20.00 9.00
AS2A Alfonso Soriano Logo 12.00 5.50
BW2A Bernie Williams Logo 12.00 5.50
BZ2A Barry Zito Logo 10.00 4.50
CD2A Carlos Delgado Logo 10.00 4.50
CJ2A Chipper Jones Logo 12.00 5.50
CS2A Curt Schilling Logo 10.00 4.50
FT2A Frank Thomas Logo 12.00 5.50
GM2A Greg Maddux Logo 20.00 9.00
GS2A Gary Sheffield Logo 10.00 4.50
HM2A Hideki Matsui Logo 30.00 13.50
HN2A Hideo Nomo Logo 30.00 13.50
IR2A Ivan Rodriguez Logo 12.00 5.50
IS2A Ichiro Suzuki Logo 50.00 22.00
JB2A Jeff Bagwell Logo 12.00 5.50
JG2A Jason Giambi Logo 10.00 4.50
JK2A Jeff Kent Logo 10.00 4.50
JT2A Jim Thome Logo 12.00 5.50
KG2A Ken Griffey Jr. Logo 25.00 11.00
LB2A Lance Berkman Logo 10.00 4.50
LG2A Luis Gonzalez Logo 10.00 4.50
MM2A M.Mantle Pants Logo 150.00 70.00
MP2RA Mark Prior Logo 12.00 5.50
MP2A Mike Piazza Logo 20.00 9.00
MR2A Manny Ramirez Logo 12.00 5.50
MT2A Miguel Tejada Logo 10.00 4.50
PB2A Pat Burrell Logo 10.00 4.50
PM2A Pedro Martinez Logo 12.00 5.50
RA2A Roberto Alomar Logo 12.00 5.50
RC2A Roger Clemens Logo 25.00 11.00
RF2A Rafael Furcal Logo 10.00 4.50
RJ2A Randy Johnson Logo 12.00 5.50
SG2A Shawn Green Logo 10.00 4.50
SS2A Sammy Sosa Logo 25.00 11.00
TGL2A Troy Glaus Logo 10.00 4.50
TG2A Tom Glavine Logo 12.00 5.50
THE2A Todd Helton Logo 12.00 5.50
TH2A Torii Hunter Logo 10.00 4.50
TW2A T.Williams Pants Logo 80.00 36.00
VG2A Vladimir Guerrero Logo 12.00 5.50

2003 SPx Young Stars Autograph Jersey

20 of the 23 cards within this set were randomly inserted in 2003 SPx packs (released in August, 2003). Serial #'d print runs for the 20 low series cards range between 964-1460 copies each. An additional three cards (all of which are much scarcer with serial #'d print runs of only 355 copies per), were randomly seeded in packs of 2003 Upper Deck Finite of which was released in December, 2003. These cards feature game-used jersey swatches and authentic autographs from each player. Since these cards were issued in varying quantities, we have noted the stated print run next to the player's name in our checklist. Rocco Baldelli did not return his autographs prior to packout thus an exchange card with a redemption deadline of August 15th, 2006 was placed into packs.

MINT NRMT
SPECTRUM PRINT RUN 25 SERIAL #'d SETS
NO SPECTRUM PRICING DUE TO SCARCITY
AD Adam Dunn/1295 25.00 11.00
AK Austin Kearns/964 15.00 6.75
BM Brett Myers/1295 10.00 4.50
BP Brandon Phillips/1295 10.00 4.50
CG Chris George/1260 10.00 4.50
DW Dontrelle Willis/355 40.00 18.00
EH Eric Hinske/1295 10.00 4.50
HB Hank Blalock/1295 25.00 11.00
JA Jason Jennings/1295 10.00 4.50
JBA Josh Bard/1295 10.00 4.50
JJ Jacque Jones/1260 15.00 6.75
JP Josh Phelps/1295 10.00 4.50
KA Kurt Ainsworth/1460 10.00 4.50
KG Khalil Greene/355 80.00 36.00
KS Kirk Saarloos/1295 10.00 4.50
MD Michael Cuddyer/1156 10.00 4.50
MK Mike Kinkade/1295 10.00 4.50
MT Mark Teixeira/1295 25.00 11.00
NJ Nick Johnson/1295 10.00 4.50
RB Rocco Baldelli/1295 EXCH 25.00 11.00
RH Rich Harden/355 40.00 18.00
RO Roy Oswalt/1295 15.00 6.75
SB Sean Burroughs/1295 15.00 6.75

1976 SSPC

The cards in this 630-card set measure 2 1/2" by 3 1/2". The 1976 "Pure Card" set issued by TCMA derives its name from the lack of borders, logos,

signatures, etc., which often clutter up the picture areas of some baseball sets. It differs from other sets produced by this company in that it cannot be re-issued due to an agreement entered into by the manufacturer. Thus, while not technically a legitimate issue, it is significant because it cannot be reprinted, unlike other collector issues. The cards are numbered in team groups, i.e., Atlanta (1-21), Cincinnati (22-46), Houston (47-65), Los Angeles (66-91), San Francisco (92-113), San Diego (114-133), Chicago White Sox (134-158), Kansas City (159-185), California (186-204), Minnesota (205-225), Milwaukee (226-251), Texas (252-273), St. Louis (274-300), Chicago Cubs (301-321), Montreal (322-351), Detroit (352-373), Baltimore (374-401), Boston (402-424), New York Yankees (425-455), Philadelphia (456-477), Oakland (478-503), Cleveland (504-532), New York Mets (533-560), and Pittsburgh (561-586). The rest of the numbers are filled in with checklists (589-595), miscellaneous players, and a heavy dose of coaches. There are a few instances in the set where the team identified on the back is different from the team shown on the front due to trades made after the completion of the 1975 season. The set features rookie year cards of Dennis Eckersley and Willie Randolph as well as early cards of George Brett, Gary Carter, and Robin Yount. The card backs were edited by Keith Olbermann, prior to his network broadcasting days. Although some of these cards were copyrighted in 1975, they were not released until spring of 1976 and have always been considered cards from 1976 within the hobby. These cards were originally available directly from SSPC for $10.99 per set.

NM Ex
COMPLETE SET (630) 80.00 32.00
1 Buzz Capra .10 .04
2 Tom House .10 .04
3 Max Leon .10 .04
4 Carl Morton .10 .04
5 Phil Niekro 4.00 1.60
6 Mike Thompson .10 .04
7 Elias Sosa .10 .04
8 Larvell Blanks .10 .04
9 Darrell Evans .20 .08
10 Rod Gilbreath .10 .04
11 Mike Lum .10 .04
12 Craig Robinson .10 .04
13 Earl Williams .10 .04
14 Vic Correll .10 .04
15 Biff Pocoroba .10 .04
16 Dusty Baker .30 .12
17 Ralph Garr .15 .06
18 Cito Gaston .15 .06
19 Dave May .10 .04
20 Rowland Office .10 .04
21 Bob Beall .10 .04
22 Sparky Anderson MG .75 .30
23 Jack Billingham .10 .04
24 Pedro Borbon .10 .04
25 Clay Carroll .10 .04
26 Pat Darcy .10 .04
27 Don Gullett .15 .06
28 Clay Kirby .10 .04
29 Gary Nolan .10 .04
30 Fred Norman .10 .04
31 Johnny Bench 6.00 2.40
32 Bill Plummer .10 .04
33 Darrel Chaney .10 .04
34 Dave Concepcion .30 .12
35 Terry Crowley .10 .04
36 Dan Driessen .15 .06
37 Doug Flynn .10 .04
38 Joe Morgan 3.00 1.20
39 Tony Perez 2.50 1.00
40 Ken Griffey 1.00 .40
41 Pete Rose 8.00 3.20
42 Ed Armbrister .10 .04
43 John Vukovich .10 .04
44 George Foster .50 .20
45 Cesar Geronimo .10 .04
46 Merv Rettenmund .10 .04
47 Jim Crawford .10 .04
48 Ken Forsch .10 .04
49 Doug Konieczny .10 .04
50 Joe Niekro .20 .08
51 Cliff Johnson .10 .04
52 Skip Jutze .10 .04
53 Milt May .10 .04
54 Rob Andrews .10 .04
55 Ken Boswell .10 .04
56 Tommy Helms .10 .04
57 Roger Metzger .10 .04
58 Larry Milbourne .10 .04
59 Doug Rader .15 .06
60 Bob Watson .30 .12
61 Enos Cabell .10 .04
62 Jose Cruz .20 .08
63 Cesar Cedeno .20 .08
64 Greg Gross .10 .04
65 Wilbur Howard .10 .04
66 Al Downing .10 .04
67 Burt Hooton .10 .04
68 Charlie Hough .30 .12
69 Tommy John .75 .30
70 Andy Messersmith .15 .06
71 Doug Rau .10 .04
72 Rick Rhoden .15 .06
73 Don Sutton 2.50 1.00
74 Rick Auerbach .10 .04
75 Ron Cey .30 .12
76 Ivan DeJesus .10 .04
77 Steve Garvey 1.50 .60
78 Lee Lacy .10 .04
79 Dave Lopes .15 .06
80 Ken McMullen .10 .04
81 Joe Ferguson .10 .04
82 Paul Powell .10 .04
83 Steve Yeager .10 .04
84 Willie Crawford .10 .04
85 Henry Cruz .10 .04
86 Charlie Manuel .10 .04
87 Manny Mota .15 .06
88 Tom Paciorek .10 .04
89 Jim Wynn .15 .06
90 Walt Alston MG .75 .30
91 Bill Buckner .30 .12
92 Jim Barr .10 .04
93 Mike Caldwell .10 .04
94 John D'Acquisto .10 .04
95 Dave Heaverlo .10 .04
96 Gary Lavelle .10 .04
97 John Montefusco .15 .06
98 Charlie Williams .10 .04
99 Chris Arnold .10 .04
100 Marc Hill .10 .04
101 Dave Rader .10 .04
102 Bruce Miller .10 .04
103 Willie Montanez .10 .04
104 Steve Ontiveros .10 .04
105 Chris Speier .10 .04
106 Derrel Thomas .10 .04
107 Gary Thomasson .10 .04
108 Glenn Adams .10 .04
109 Von Joshua .10 .04
110 Gary Matthews .15 .06
111 Bobby Murcer .30 .12
112 Horace Speed .10 .04
113 Wes Westrum MG .10 .04
114 Rich Folkers .10 .04
115 Alan Foster .10 .04
116 Dave Freisleben .10 .04
117 Dan Frisella .10 .04
118 Randy Jones .15 .06
119 Dan Spillner .10 .04
120 Larry Hardy .10 .04
121 Randy Hundley .15 .06
122 Fred Kendall .10 .04
123 John McNamara MG .10 .04
124 Tito Fuentes .10 .04
125 Enzo Hernandez .10 .04
126 Steve Huntz .10 .04
127 Mike Ivie .10 .04
128 Hector Torres .10 .04
129 Ted Kubiak .10 .04
130 John Grubb .10 .04
131 John Scott .10 .04
132 Bob Tolan .15 .06
133 Dave Winfield 12.00 4.80
134 Bill Gogolewski .10 .04
135 Dan Osborn .10 .04
136 Jim Kaat .75 .30
137 Claude Osteen .15 .06
138 Cecil Upshaw .10 .04
139 Wilbur Wood .15 .06
140 Lloyd Allen .10 .04
141 Brian Downing .20 .08
142 Jim Essian .10 .04
143 Bucky Dent .15 .06
144 Jorge Orta .10 .04
145 Lee Richard .10 .04
146 Bill Stein .10 .04
147 Ken Henderson .10 .04
148 Carlos May .10 .04
149 Nyls Nyman .10 .04
150 Bob Coluccio .10 .04
151 Chuck Tanner MG .15 .06
152 Pat Kelly .10 .04
153 Jerry Hairston .10 .04
154 Pete Varney .10 .04
155 Bill Melton .10 .04
156 Goose Gossage 1.25 .50
157 Terry Forster .15 .06
158 Rich Hinton .10 .04
159 Nelson Briles .10 .04
160 Al Fitzmorris .10 .04
161 Steve Mingori .10 .04
162 Marty Pattin .10 .04
163 Paul Splittorff .10 .04
164 Dennis Leonard .15 .06
165 Buck Martinez .15 .06
166 Bob Stinson .10 .04
167 George Brett 20.00 8.00
168 Harmon Killebrew 3.00 1.20
169 John Mayberry .15 .06
170 Fred Patek .15 .06
171 Cookie Rojas .15 .06
172 Rodney Scott .10 .04
173 Tony Solaita .10 .04
174 Frank White .30 .12
175 Al Cowens .10 .04
176 Hal McRae .30 .12
177 Amos Otis .20 .08
178 Vada Pinson .30 .12
179 Jim Wohlford .10 .04
180 Doug Bird .10 .04
181 Mark Littell .10 .04
182 Bob McClure .10 .04
183 Steve Busby .15 .06
184 Fran Healy .10 .04
185 Whitey Herzog MG .20 .08
186 Andy Hassler .10 .04
187 Nolan Ryan 25.00 10.00
188 Bill Singer .10 .04
189 Frank Tanana .30 .12
190 Ed Figueroa .10 .04
191 Dave Collins .15 .06
192 Dick Williams MG .15 .06
193 Ellie Rodriguez .10 .04
194 Dave Chalk .10 .04
195 Winston Llenas .10 .04
196 Rudy Meoli .10 .04
197 Orlando Ramirez .10 .04
198 Jerry Remy .10 .04
199 Billy Smith .10 .04
200 Bruce Bochte .10 .04
201 Joe Lahoud .10 .04
202 Morris Nettles .10 .04
203 Mickey Rivers .15 .06
204 Leroy Stanton .10 .04
205 Vic Albury .10 .04
206 Tom Burgmeier .10 .04
207 Bill Butler .10 .04
208 Bill Campbell .10 .04

209 Ray Corbin .10 .04
210 Joe Decker .10 .04
211 Jim Hughes .10 .04
212 Ed Bane UER .10 .04
(Photo actually
Mike Pazik)
213 Glenn Borgmann .10 .04
214 Rod Carew 5.00 2.00
215 Steve Brye .10 .04
216 Dan Ford .10 .04
217 Tony Oliva .75 .30
218 Dave Goltz .10 .04
219 Bert Blyleven .50 .20
220 Larry Hisle .15 .06
221 Steve Braun .10 .04
222 Jerry Terrell .10 .04
223 Eric Soderholm .10 .04
224 Phil Roof .10 .04
225 Danny Thompson .10 .04
226 Jim Colborn .10 .04
227 Tom Murphy .10 .04
228 Ed Rodriguez .10 .04
229 Jim Slaton .10 .04
230 Ed Sprague .10 .04
231 Charlie Moore .10 .04
232 Darrell Porter .15 .06
233 Kurt Bevacqua .15 .06
234 Pedro Garcia .10 .04
235 Mike Hegan .10 .04
236 Don Money .15 .06
237 George Scott .15 .06
238 Robin Yount UER 12.00 4.80
1st mention of career triples should be doubles
239 Hank Aaron 10.00 4.00
240 Rob Ellis .10 .04
241 Sixto Lezcano .15 .06
242 Bob Mitchell .10 .04
243 Gorman Thomas .15 .06
244 Bill Travers .10 .04
245 Pete Broberg .10 .04
246 Bill Sharp .10 .04
247 Bobby Darwin .10 .04
248 Rick Austin UER .10 .04
(Photo actually
Larry Anderson)
249 Larry Anderson UER .10 .04
(Photo actually
Rick Austin)
250 Tom Bianco .10 .04
251 Lafayette Currence .10 .04
252 Steve Foucault .10 .04
253 Bill Hands .10 .04
254 Steve Hargan .10 .04
255 Fergie Jenkins 3.00 1.20
256 Bob Sheldon .10 .04
257 Jim Umbarger .10 .04
258 Clyde Wright .10 .04
259 Bill Fahey .10 .04
260 Jim Sundberg .20 .08
261 Leo Cardenas .10 .04
262 Jim Fregosi .20 .08
263 Mike Hargrove .20 .08
264 Toby Harrah .15 .06
265 Roy Howell .10 .04
266 Lenny Randle .10 .04
267 Roy Smalley .15 .06
268 Jim Spencer .10 .04
269 Jeff Burroughs .15 .06
270 Tom Grieve .15 .06
271 Joe Lovitto .10 .04
272 Frank Lucchesi MG .10 .04
273 Dave Nelson .10 .04
274 Ted Simmons .75 .30
275 Lou Brock 4.00 1.60
276 Ron Fairly .15 .06
277 Bake McBride .10 .04
278 Reggie Smith .20 .08
279 Willie Davis .15 .06
280 Ken Reitz .10 .04
281 Buddy Bradford .10 .04
282 Luis Melendez .10 .04
283 Mike Tyson .10 .04
284 Ted Sizemore .10 .04
285 Mario Guerrero .10 .04
286 Larry Lintz .10 .04
287 Ken Rudolph .10 .04
288 Dick Billings .10 .04
289 Jerry Mumphrey .15 .06
290 Mike Wallace .10 .04
291 Al Hrabosky .15 .06
292 Ken Reynolds .10 .04
293 Mike Garman .10 .04
294 Bob Forsch .15 .06
295 John Denny .15 .06
296 Harry Rasmussen .10 .04
297 Lynn McGlothen .10 .04
298 Mike Barlow .10 .04
299 Greg Terlecky .10 .04
300 Red Schoendienst MG .50 .20
301 Rick Reuschel .20 .08
302 Steve Stone .15 .06
303 Bill Bonham .10 .04
304 Oscar Zamora .10 .04
305 Ken Frailing .10 .04
306 Milt Wilcox .10 .04
307 Darold Knowles .10 .04
308 Jim Marshall MG .10 .04
309 Bill Madlock .50 .20
310 Jose Cardenal .15 .06
311 Rick Monday .15 .06
312 Jerry Morales .10 .04
313 Tim Hosley .10 .04
314 Gene Hiser .10 .04
315 Don Kessinger .15 .06
316 Manny Trillo .15 .06
317 Pete LaCock .15 .06
318 George Mitterwald .10 .04
319 Steve Swisher .10 .04
320 Rob Sperring .10 .04
321 Vic Harris .10 .04
322 Ron Dunn .10 .04
323 Jose Morales .10 .04
324 Pete Mackanin .10 .04
325 Jim Cox .10 .04
326 Larry Parrish .15 .06
327 Mike Jorgensen .10 .04
328 Tim Foli .10 .04
329 Hal Breeden .10 .04
330 Nate Colbert .10 .04
331 Pepe Frias .10 .04
332 Pat Scanlon .10 .04
333 Bob Bailey .10 .04
334 Gary Carter 5.00 2.00
335 Pepe Mangual .10 .04
336 Larry Biittner .10 .04
337 Jim Lyttle .10 .04
338 Gary Roenicke .20 .08
339 Tony Scott .10 .04
340 Jerry White .10 .04
341 Jim Dwyer .10 .04
342 Ellis Valentine .15 .06
343 Fred Scherman .10 .04
344 Dennis Blair .10 .04
345 Woodie Fryman .10 .04
346 Chuck Taylor .10 .04
347 Dan Warthen .10 .04
348 Dan Carrithers .10 .04
349 Steve Rogers .15 .06
350 Dale Murray .10 .04
351 Duke Snider CO 2.00 .80
352 Ralph Houk MG .15 .06
353 John Hiller .10 .04
354 Mickey Lolich .30 .12
355 Dave Lemancyzk .10 .04
356 Lerrin LaGrow .10 .04
357 Fred Arroyo .10 .04
358 Joe Coleman .10 .04
359 Ben Oglivie .15 .06
360 Willie Horton .15 .06
361 John Knox .10 .04
362 Leon Roberts .15 .06
363 Ron LeFlore .15 .06
364 Gary Sutherland .10 .04
365 Dan Meyer .10 .04
366 Aurelio Rodriguez .10 .04
367 Tom Veryzer .10 .04
368 Jack Pierce .10 .04
369 Gene Michael .15 .06
370 Billy Baldwin .10 .04
371 Gates Brown .10 .04
372 Mickey Stanley .15 .06
373 Terry Humphrey .10 .04
374 Doyle Alexander .15 .06
375 Mike Cuellar .20 .08
376 Wayne Garland .10 .04
377 Ross Grimsley .10 .04
378 Grant Jackson .10 .04
379 Dyar Miller .10 .04
380 Jim Palmer 4.00 1.60
381 Mike Torrez .15 .06
382 Mike Willis .10 .04
383 Dave Duncan .15 .06
384 Ellie Hendricks .10 .04
385 Jim Hutto .10 .04
386 Bob Bailor .10 .04
387 Doug DeCinces .20 .08
388 Bob Grich .20 .08
389 Lee May .20 .08
390 Tony Muser .10 .04
391 Tim Nordbrook .10 .04
392 Brooks Robinson 4.00 1.60
393 Royle Stillman .10 .04
394 Don Baylor .75 .30
395 Paul Blair .15 .06
396 Al Bumbry .10 .04
397 Larry Harlow .10 .04
398 Tommy Davis .15 .06
399 Jim Northrup .15 .06
400 Ken Singleton .15 .06
401 Tom Shopay .10 .04
402 Fred Lynn .75 .30
403 Carlton Fisk 5.00 2.00
404 Cecil Cooper .30 .12
405 Jim Rice 2.00 .80
406 Juan Beniquez .10 .04
407 Denny Doyle .10 .04
408 Dwight Evans 1.00 .40
409 Carl Yastrzemski 5.00 2.00
410 Rick Burleson .10 .04
411 Bernie Carbo .10 .04
412 Doug Griffin .10 .04
413 Rico Petrocelli .15 .06
414 Bob Montgomery .10 .04
415 Tim Blackwell .10 .04
416 Rick Miller .10 .04
417 Darrell Johnson MG .10 .04
418 Jim Burton .10 .04
419 Jim Willoughby .10 .04
420 Rogelio Moret .10 .04
421 Bill Lee .15 .06
422 Dick Drago .10 .04
423 Diego Segui .10 .04
424 Luis Tiant .30 .12
425 Jim Hunter 3.00 1.20
426 Rick Sawyer .10 .04
427 Rudy May .10 .04
428 Dick Tidrow .10 .04
429 Sparky Lyle .30 .12
430 Doc Medich .10 .04
431 Pat Dobson .10 .04
432 Dave Pagan .10 .04
433 Thurman Munson 3.00 1.20
434 Chris Chambliss .30 .12
435 Roy White .15 .06
436 Walt Williams .10 .04
437 Graig Nettles .50 .20
438 Rick Dempsey .15 .06
439 Bobby Bonds .75 .30
440 Ed Herrmann .10 .04
441 Sandy Alomar .15 .06
442 Fred Stanley .10 .04
443 Terry Whitfield .10 .04
444 Rich Bladt .10 .04
445 Lou Piniella .50 .20
446 Rich Coggins .10 .04
447 Ed Brinkman .10 .04
448 Jim Mason .10 .04
449 Larry Murray .10 .04
450 Ron Blomberg .10 .04
451 Elliott Maddox .10 .04
452 Kerry Dineen .10 .04
453 Billy Martin MG .75 .30
454 Dave Bergman .10 .04
455 Otto Velez .10 .04
456 Joe Hoerner .10 .04
457 Tug McGraw .30 .12
458 Gene Garber .15 .06
459 Steve Carlton 5.00 2.00
460 Larry Christenson .10 .04
461 Tom Underwood .10 .04
462 Jim Lonborg .15 .06
463 Jay Johnstone .20 .08
464 Larry Bowa .20 .08
465 Dave Cash .10 .04
466 Ollie Brown .10 .04
467 Greg Luzinski .30 .12
468 Johnny Oates .10 .04
469 Mike Anderson .10 .04
470 Mike Schmidt 15.00 6.00
471 Bob Boone .50 .20
472 Tom Hutton .10 .04
473 Rich Allen .75 .30
474 Tony Taylor .15 .06
475 Jerry Martin .10 .04
476 Danny Ozark MG .10 .04
477 Dick Ruthven .10 .04
478 Jim Todd .10 .04
479 Paul Lindblad .10 .04
480 Rollie Fingers 3.00 1.20
481 Vida Blue .20 .08
482 Ken Holtzman .15 .06
483 Dick Bosman .10 .04
484 Sonny Siebert .10 .04
485 Glenn Abbott .10 .04
486 Stan Bahnsen .10 .04
487 Mike Norris .15 .06
488 Alvin Dark MG .15 .06
489 Claudell Washington .15 .06
490 Joe Rudi .15 .06
491 Bill North .10 .04
492 Bert Campaneris .15 .06
493 Gene Tenace .15 .06
494 Reggie Jackson 8.00 3.20
495 Phil Garner .10 .04
496 Billy Williams 3.00 1.20
497 Sal Bando .15 .06
498 Jim Holt .10 .04
499 Ted Martinez .10 .04
500 Ray Fosse .10 .04
501 Matt Alexander .10 .04
502 Larry Haney .10 .04
503 Angel Mangual .10 .04
504 Fred Beene .10 .04
505 Tom Buskey .10 .04
506 Dennis Eckersley 12.00 4.80
507 Roric Harrison .10 .04
508 Don Hood .10 .04
509 Jim Kern .10 .04
510 Dave LaRoche .10 .04
511 Fritz Peterson .10 .04
512 Jim Strickland .10 .04
513 Rick Waits .10 .04
514 Alan Ashby .20 .08
515 John Ellis .10 .04
516 Rick Cerone .20 .08
517 Buddy Bell .20 .08
518 Jack Brohamer .10 .04
519 Rico Carty .15 .06
520 Ed Crosby .10 .04
521 Frank Duffy .10 .04
522 Duane Kuiper UER .10 .04
(Photo actually
Rick Manning)
523 Joe Lis .10 .04
524 Boog Powell 1.00 .40
525 Frank Robinson 4.00 1.60
526 Oscar Gamble .15 .06
527 George Hendrick .15 .06
528 John Lowenstein .10 .04
529 Rick Manning UER .15 .06
(Photo actually
Duane Kuiper)
530 Tommy Smith .10 .04
531 Charlie Spikes .10 .04
532 Steve Kline .10 .04
533 Ed Kranepool .15 .06
534 Mike Vail .10 .04
535 Del Unser .10 .04
536 Felix Millan .10 .04
537 Rusty Staub .30 .12
538 Jesus Alou .10 .04
539 Wayne Garrett .10 .04
540 Mike Phillips .10 .04
541 Joe Torre .50 .20
542 Dave Kingman .50 .20
543 Gene Clines .10 .04
544 Jack Heidemann .10 .04
545 Bud Harrelson .15 .06
546 John Stearns .15 .06
547 John Milner .10 .04
548 Bob Apodaca .10 .04
549 Skip Lockwood .10 .04
550 Ken Sanders .10 .04
551 Tom Seaver 6.00 2.40
552 Rick Baldwin .10 .04
553 Hank Webb .10 .04
554 Jon Matlack .10 .04
555 Randy Tate .10 .04
556 Tom Hall .10 .04
557 George Stone .10 .04
558 Craig Swan .10 .04
559 Jerry Cram .10 .04
560 Roy Staiger .10 .04
561 Kent Tekulve .30 .12
562 Jerry Reuss .15 .06
563 John Candelaria .20 .08
564 Larry Demery .10 .04
565 Dave Giusti .10 .04
566 Jim Rooker .10 .04
567 Ramon Hernandez .10 .04
568 Bruce Kison .10 .04
569 Ken Brett .10 .04
570 Bob Moose .10 .04
571 Manny Sanguillen .15 .06
572 Dave Parker 2.50 1.00
573 Willie Stargell 3.00 1.20
574 Richie Zisk .15 .06
575 Rennie Stennett .10 .04
576 Al Oliver .50 .20
577 Bill Robinson .15 .06
578 Bob Robertson .10 .04
579 Rich Hebner .15 .06
580 Ed Kirkpatrick .10 .04
581 Duffy Dyer .10 .04
582 Craig Reynolds .10 .04
583 Frank Taveras .10 .04
584 Willie Randolph 3.00 1.20
585 Art Howe .30 .12
586 Danny Murtaugh MG .15 .06
587 Rick McKinney .10 .04
588 Ed Goodson .10 .04
589 George Brett 4.00 1.60
Al Cowens CL
590 Keith Hernandez 1.00 .40
Lou Brock CL
591 Jerry Koosman 1.00 .40
Duke Snider CL
592 Maury Wills .15 .06
John Knox CL
593A Jim Hunter 15.00 6.00
Nolan Ryan CL ERR
(Noland on front)
593B Jim Hunter 5.00 2.00
Nolan Ryan CL COR
594 Ralph Branca .20 .08
Carl Erskine
Pee Wee Reese CL
595 Willie Mays 1.50 .60
Herb Score CL
596 Larry Cox .10 .04
597 Gene Mauch MG .15 .06
598 W. Wietelmann CO .10 .04
599 Wayne Simpson .10 .04
600 Mel Thomason .10 .04
601 Ike Hampton .10 .04
602 Ken Crosby .10 .04
603 Ralph Rowe .10 .04
604 Jim Tyrone .10 .04
605 Mick Kelleher .10 .04
606 Mario Mendoza .10 .04
607 Mike Rogodzinski .10 .04
608 Bob Gallagher .10 .04
609 Jerry Koosman .20 .08
610 Joe Frazier MG .10 .04
611 Karl Kuehl MG .10 .04
612 Frank LaCorte .10 .04
613 Ray Bare .10 .04
614 Billy Muffett CO .10 .04
615 Bill Laxton .10 .04
616 Willie Mays CO 8.00 3.20
617 Phil Cavarretta CO .15 .06
618 Ted Kluszewski CO .30 .12
619 Elston Howard CO .20 .08
620 Alex Grammas CO .10 .04
621 Mickey Vernon CO .15 .06
622 Dick Sisler CO .10 .04
623 Harvey Haddix CO .10 .04
624 Bobby Winkles CO .10 .04
625 John Pesky CO .15 .06
626 Jim Davenport CO .10 .04
627 Dave Tomlin .10 .04
628 Roger Craig CO .15 .06
629 Joe Amalfitano CO .10 .04
630 Jim Reese CO .30 .12

1991 Stadium Club

This 600-card standard size set marked Topps first premium quality set. The set was issued in two separate series of 300 cards each. Cards were distributed in plastic wrapped packs. Series II cards were also available at McDonald's restaurants in the Northeast at three cards per pack. The set created a stir in the hobby upon release with dazzling full-color borderless photos and slick, glossy card stock. The back of each card has the basic biographical information as well as making use of the Fastball BARS system and an inset photo of the player's Topps rookie card. Notable Rookie Cards include Jeff Bagwell.

	Nm-Mt	Ex-Mt
COMPLETE SET (600)	60.00	18.00
COMP.SERIES 1 (300)	40.00	12.00
COMP.SERIES 2 (300)	20.00	6.00

1 Dave Stewart TUX .50 .15
2 Wally Joyner .50 .15
3 Shawon Dunston .25 .07
4 Darren Daulton .50 .15
5 Will Clark 1.25 .35
6 Sammy Sosa 2.50 .75
7 Dan Plesac .25 .07
8 Marquis Grissom .50 .15
9 Erik Hanson .25 .07
10 Geno Petralli .25 .07
11 Jose Rijo .25 .07
12 Carlos Quintana .25 .07
13 Junior Ortiz .25 .07
14 Bob Walk .25 .07
15 Mike Macfarlane .25 .07
16 Eric Yelding .25 .07
17 Bryn Smith .25 .07
18 Bip Roberts .25 .07
19 Mike Scioscia .25 .07
20 Mark Williamson .25 .07
21 Don Mattingly 3.00 .90
22 John Franco .50 .15
23 Chet Lemon .25 .07
24 Tom Henke .25 .07
25 Jerry Browne .25 .07
26 Dave Justice .50 .15
27 Mark Langston .25 .07
28 Damon Berryhill .25 .07
29 Kevin Bass .25 .07
30 Scott Fletcher .25 .07
31 Moises Alou .50 .15
32 Dave Valle .25 .07
33 Jody Reed .25 .07
34 Dave West .25 .07
35 Kevin McReynolds .25 .07
36 Pat Combs .25 .07
37 Eric Davis .50 .15
38 Bret Saberhagen .50 .15
39 Stan Javier .25 .07
40 Chuck Cary .25 .07
41 Tony Phillips .25 .07
42 Lee Smith .50 .15
43 Tim Teufel .25 .07
44 Lance Dickson RC .40 .12
45 Greg Litton .25 .07
46 Ted Higuera .25 .07
47 Edgar Martinez .75 .23
48 Steve Avery .25 .07
49 Walt Weiss .25 .07
50 David Segui .25 .07
51 Andy Benes .25 .07
52 Karl Rhodes .25 .07
53 Neal Heaton .25 .07
54 Danny Gladden .25 .07
55 Luis Rivera .25 .07
56 Kevin Brown .50 .15
57 Frank Thomas 1.25 .35
58 Terry Mulholland .25 .07
59 Dick Schofield .25 .07
60 Ron Darling .25 .07
61 Sandy Alomar Jr. .25 .07
62 Dave Stieb .25 .07
63 Alan Trammell .50 .15
64 Matt Nokes .25 .07
65 Lenny Harris .25 .07
66 Milt Thompson .25 .07
67 Storm Davis .25 .07
68 Joe Oliver .25 .07
69 Andres Galarraga .50 .15
70 Ozzie Guillen .25 .07
71 Ken Howell .25 .07
72 Garry Templeton .25 .07
73 Derrick May .25 .07
74 Xavier Hernandez .25 .07
75 Dave Parker .50 .15
76 Rick Aguilera .50 .15
77 Robby Thompson .25 .07
78 Pete Incaviglia .25 .07
79 Bob Welch .25 .07
80 Randy Milligan .25 .07
81 Chuck Finley .50 .15
82 Alvin Davis .25 .07
83 Tim Naehring .25 .07
84 Jay Bell .50 .15
85 Joe Magrane .25 .07
86 Howard Johnson .25 .07
87 Jack McDowell .25 .07
88 Kevin Seitzer .25 .07
89 Bruce Ruffin .25 .07
90 Fernando Valenzuela .50 .15
91 Terry Kennedy .25 .07
92 Barry Larkin .75 .23
93 Larry Walker 1.25 .35
94 Luis Salazar .25 .07
95 Gary Sheffield .50 .15
96 Bobby Witt .25 .07
97 Lonnie Smith .25 .07
98 Bryan Harvey .25 .07
99 Mookie Wilson .50 .15
100 Dwight Gooden .50 .15
101 Lou Whitaker .50 .15
102 Ron Karkovice .25 .07
103 Jesse Barfield .25 .07
104 Jose DeJesus .25 .07
105 Benito Santiago .50 .15
106 Brian Holman .25 .07
107 Rafael Ramirez .25 .07
108 Ellis Burks .50 .15
109 Mike Bielecki .25 .07
110 Kirby Puckett 1.25 .35
111 Terry Shumpert .25 .07
112 Chuck Crim .25 .07
113 Todd Benzinger .25 .07
114 Brian Barnes RC .40 .12
115 Carlos Baerga .25 .07
116 Kal Daniels .25 .07
117 Dave Johnson .25 .07
118 Andy Van Slyke .50 .15
119 John Burkett .25 .07
120 Rickey Henderson 1.25 .35
121 Tim Jones .25 .07
122 Daryl Irvine .25 .07
123 Ruben Sierra .25 .07
124 Jim Abbott .75 .23
125 Daryl Boston .25 .07
126 Greg Maddux 2.00 .60
127 Von Hayes .25 .07
128 Mike Fitzgerald .25 .07
129 Wayne Edwards .25 .07
130 Greg Briley .25 .07
131 Rob Dibble .50 .15
132 Gene Larkin .25 .07
133 David Wells .50 .15
134 Steve Balboni .25 .07
135 Greg Vaughn .25 .07
136 Mark Davis .25 .07
137 Dave Rhode .25 .07
138 Eric Show .25 .07
139 Bobby Bonilla .50 .15
140 Dana Kiecker .25 .07
141 Gary Pettis .25 .07
142 Dennis Boyd .25 .07
143 Mike Benjamin .25 .07
144 Luis Polonia .25 .07
145 Doug Jones .25 .07
146 Al Newman .25 .07
147 Alex Fernandez .25 .07
148 Bill Doran .25 .07
149 Kevin Elster .25 .07
150 Len Dykstra .50 .15
151 Mike Gallego .25 .07
152 Tim Belcher .25 .07
153 Jay Buhner .50 .15
154 Ozzie Smith UER 2.00 .60
(Rookie card is 1979,
but card back says '78)
155 Jose Canseco 1.25 .35
156 Gregg Olson .25 .07
157 Charlie O'Brien .25 .07
158 Frank Tanana .25 .07
159 George Brett 3.00 .90
160 Jeff Huson .25 .07
161 Kevin Tapani .25 .07
162 Jerome Walton .25 .07
163 Charlie Hayes .25 .07
164 Chris Bosio .25 .07
165 Chris Sabo .25 .07
166 Lance Parrish .50 .15
167 Don Robinson .25 .07
168 Manny Lee .25 .07
169 Dennis Rasmussen .25 .07
170 Wade Boggs .75 .23

171 Bob Geren .25 .07
172 Mackey Sasser .25 .07
173 Julio Franco .50 .15
174 Otis Nixon .25 .07
175 Bert Blyleven .50 .15
176 Craig Biggio .75 .23
177 Eddie Murray 1.25 .35
178 Randy Tomlin RC .40 .12
179 Tino Martinez .75 .23
180 Carlton Fisk .75 .23
181 Dwight Smith .25 .07
182 Scott Garrelts .25 .07
183 Jim Gantner .25 .07
184 Dickie Thon .25 .07
185 John Farrell .25 .07
186 Cecil Fielder .50 .15
187 Glenn Braggs .25 .07
188 Allan Anderson .25 .07
189 Kurt Stillwell .25 .07
190 Jose Oquendo .25 .07
191 Joe Orsulak .25 .07
192 Ricky Jordan .25 .07
193 Kelly Downs .25 .07
194 Delino DeShields .25 .07
195 Omar Vizquel .75 .23
196 Mark Carreon .25 .07
197 Mike Harkey .25 .07
198 Jack Howell .25 .07
199 Lance Johnson .25 .07
200 Nolan Ryan TUX 5.00 1.50
201 John Marzano .25 .07
202 Doug Drabek .25 .07
203 Mark Lemke .25 .07
204 Steve Sax .25 .07
205 Greg Harris .25 .07
206 B.J. Surhoff .50 .15
207 Todd Burns .25 .07
208 Jose Gonzalez .25 .07
209 Mike Scott .25 .07
210 Dave Magadan .25 .07
211 Dante Bichette .50 .15
212 Trevor Wilson .25 .07
213 Hector Villanueva .25 .07
214 Dan Pasqua .25 .07
215 Greg Colbrunn RC .60 .18
216 Mike Jeffcoat .25 .07
217 Harold Reynolds .50 .15
218 Paul O'Neill .75 .23
219 Mark Guthrie .25 .07
220 Barry Bonds 3.00 .90
221 Jimmy Key .50 .15
222 Billy Ripken .25 .07
223 Tom Pagnozzi .25 .07
224 Bo Jackson 1.25 .35
225 Sid Fernandez .25 .07
226 Mike Marshall .25 .07
227 John Kruk .50 .15
228 Mike Fetters .25 .07
229 Eric Anthony .25 .07
230 Ryne Sandberg 2.00 .60
231 Carney Lansford .50 .15
232 Melido Perez .25 .07
233 Jose Lind .25 .07
234 Darryl Hamilton .25 .07
235 Tom Browning .25 .07
236 Spike Owen .25 .07
237 Juan Gonzalez .75 .23
238 Felix Fermin .25 .07
239 Keith Miller .25 .07
240 Mark Gubicza .25 .07
241 Kent Anderson .25 .07
242 Alvaro Espinoza .25 .07
243 Dale Murphy 1.25 .35
244 Orel Hershiser .50 .15
245 Paul Molitor .75 .23
246 Eddie Whitson .25 .07
247 Joe Girardi .25 .07
248 Kent Hrbek .50 .15
249 Bill Sampen .25 .07
250 Kevin Mitchell .25 .07
251 Mariano Duncan .25 .07
252 Scott Bradley .25 .07
253 Mike Greenwell .25 .07
254 Tom Gordon .25 .07
255 Todd Zeile .25 .07
256 Bobby Thigpen .25 .07
257 Gregg Jefferies .25 .07
258 Kenny Rogers .50 .15
259 Shane Mack .25 .07
260 Zane Smith .25 .07
261 Mitch Williams .25 .07
262 Jim Deshaies .25 .07
263 Dave Winfield .50 .15
264 Ben McDonald .25 .07
265 Randy Ready .25 .07
266 Pat Borders .25 .07
267 Jose Uribe .25 .07
268 Derek Lilliquist .25 .07
269 Greg Brock .25 .07
270 Ken Griffey Jr. 2.50 .75
271 Jeff Gray .25 .07
272 Danny Tartabull .25 .07
273 Dennis Martinez .50 .15
274 Robin Ventura .50 .15
275 Randy Myers .25 .07
276 Jack Daugherty .25 .07
277 Greg Gagne .25 .07
278 Jay Howell .25 .07
279 Mike LaValliere .25 .07
280 Rex Hudler .25 .07
281 Mike Simms .25 .07
282 Kevin Maas .25 .07
283 Jeff Ballard .25 .07
284 Dave Henderson .25 .07
285 Pete O'Brien .25 .07
286 Brook Jacoby .25 .07
287 Mike Henneman .25 .07
288 Greg Olson .25 .07
289 Greg Myers .25 .07
290 Mark Grace .75 .23
291 Shawn Abner .25 .07
292 Frank Viola .50 .15
293 Lee Stevens .25 .07
294 Jason Grimsley .25 .07
295 Matt Williams .50 .15
296 Ron Robinson .25 .07
297 Tom Brunansky .25 .07
298 Checklist 1-100 .25 .07
299 Checklist 101-200 .25 .07
300 Checklist 201-300 .25 .07
301 Darryl Strawberry .50 .15
302 Bud Black .25 .07
303 Harold Baines .50 .15
304 Roberto Alomar .75 .23
305 Norm Charlton .25 .07
306 Gary Thurman .25 .07
307 Mike Felder .25 .07
308 Tony Gwynn 1.50 .45
309 Roger Clemens 2.50 .75
310 Andre Dawson .50 .15
311 Scott Radinsky .25 .07
312 Bob Melvin .25 .07
313 Kirk McCaskill .25 .07
314 Pedro Guerrero .50 .15
315 Walt Terrell .25 .07
316 Sam Horn .25 .07
317 W.Chamberlain RC UER .60 .18
Card listed as 1989
Debut card, should be 1990
318 Pedro Munoz RC .40 .12
319 Roberto Kelly .25 .07
320 Mark Portugal .25 .07
321 Tim McIntosh .25 .07
322 Jesse Orosco .25 .07
323 Gary Green .25 .07
324 Greg Harris .25 .07
325 Hubie Brooks .25 .07
326 Chris Nabholz .25 .07
327 Terry Pendleton .50 .15
328 Eric King .25 .07
329 Chili Davis .50 .15
330 Anthony Telford .25 .07
331 Kelly Gruber .25 .07
332 Dennis Eckersley .50 .15
333 Mel Hall .25 .07
334 Bob Kipper .25 .07
335 Willie McGee .50 .15
336 Steve Olin .25 .07
337 Steve Buechele .25 .07
338 Scott Leius .25 .07
339 Hal Morris .25 .07
340 Jose Offerman .25 .07
341 Kent Mercker .25 .07
342 Ken Griffey Sr. .50 .15
343 Pete Harnisch .25 .07
344 Kirk Gibson .50 .15
345 Dave Smith .25 .07
346 Dave Martinez .25 .07
347 Atlee Hammaker .25 .07
348 Brian Downing .25 .07
349 Todd Hundley .25 .07
350 Candy Maldonado .25 .07
351 Dwight Evans .50 .15
352 Steve Searcy .25 .07
353 Gary Gaetti .50 .15
354 Jeff Reardon .50 .15
355 Travis Fryman .50 .15
356 Dave Righetti .25 .07
357 Fred McGriff .75 .23
358 Don Slaught .25 .07
359 Gene Nelson .25 .07
360 Billy Spiers .25 .07
361 Lee Guetterman .25 .07
362 Darren Lewis .25 .07
363 Duane Ward .25 .07
364 Lloyd Moseby .25 .07
365 John Smoltz .75 .23
366 Felix Jose .25 .07
367 David Cone .50 .15
368 Wally Backman .25 .07
369 Jeff Montgomery .25 .07
370 Rich Garces RC .40 .12
371 Billy Hatcher .25 .07
372 Bill Swift .25 .07
373 Jim Eisenreich .25 .07
374 Rob Ducey .25 .07
375 Tim Crews .25 .07
376 Steve Finley .50 .15
377 Jeff Blauser .25 .07
378 Willie Wilson .25 .07
379 Gerald Perry .25 .07
380 Jose Mesa .25 .07
381 Pat Kelly RC .60 .18
382 Matt Merullo .25 .07
383 Ivan Calderon .25 .07
384 Scott Chiamparino .25 .07
385 Lloyd McClendon .25 .07
386 Dave Bergman .25 .07
387 Ed Sprague .25 .07
388 Jeff Bagwell RC 3.00 .90
389 Brett Butler .50 .15
390 Larry Andersen .25 .07
391 Glenn Davis .25 .07
392 Alex Cole UER .25 .07
(Front photo actually
Otis Nixon)
393 Mike Heath .25 .07
394 Danny Darwin .25 .07
395 Steve Lake .25 .07
396 Tim Layana .25 .07
397 Terry Leach .25 .07
398 Bill Wegman .25 .07
399 Mark McGwire 3.00 .90
400 Mike Boddicker .25 .07
401 Steve Howe .25 .07
402 Bernard Gilkey .25 .07
403 Thomas Howard .25 .07
404 Rafael Belliard .25 .07
405 Tom Candiotti .25 .07
406 Rene Gonzales .25 .07
407 Chuck McElroy .25 .07
408 Paul Sorrento .25 .07
409 Randy Johnson 1.50 .45
410 Brady Anderson .50 .15
411 Dennis Cook .25 .07
412 Mickey Tettleton .25 .07
413 Mike Stanton .25 .07
414 Ken Oberkfell .25 .07
415 Rick Honeycutt .25 .07
416 Nelson Santovenia .25 .07
417 Bob Tewksbury .25 .07
418 Brent Mayne .25 .07
419 Steve Farr .25 .07
420 Phil Stephenson .25 .07
421 Jeff Russell .25 .07
422 Chris James .25 .07
423 Tim Leary .25 .07
424 Gary Carter .50 .15
425 Glenallen Hill .25 .07
426 Matt Young UER .25 .07
Card mentions 83T/Tr
as RC, but 84T shown
427 Sid Bream .25 .07
428 Greg Swindell .25 .07
429 Scott Aldred .25 .07
430 Cal Ripken 4.00 1.20
431 Bill Landrum .25 .07
432 Earnest Riles .25 .07
433 Danny Jackson .25 .07
434 Casey Candaele .25 .07
435 Ken Hill .25 .07
436 Jaime Navarro .25 .07
437 Lance Blankenship .25 .07
438 Randy Velarde .25 .07
439 Frank DiPino .25 .07
440 Carl Nichols .25 .07
441 Jeff M. Robinson .25 .07
442 Deion Sanders .75 .23
443 Vicente Palacios .25 .07
444 Devon White .50 .15
445 John Cerutti .25 .07
446 Tracy Jones .25 .07
447 Jack Morris .50 .15
448 Mitch Webster .25 .07
449 Bob Ojeda .25 .07
450 Oscar Azocar .25 .07
451 Luis Aquino .25 .07
452 Mark Whiten .25 .07
453 Stan Belinda .25 .07
454 Ron Gant .50 .15
455 Jose DeLeon .25 .07
456 Mark Salas UER .25 .07
Back has 85T photo,
but calls it 86T
457 Junior Felix .25 .07
458 Wally Whitehurst .25 .07
459 Phil Plantier RC .60 .18
460 Juan Berenguer .25 .07
461 Franklin Stubbs .25 .07
462 Joe Boever .25 .07
463 Tim Wallach .25 .07
464 Mike Moore .25 .07
465 Albert Belle .50 .15
466 Mike Witt .25 .07
467 Craig Worthington .25 .07
468 Jerald Clark .25 .07
469 Scott Terry .25 .07
470 Milt Cuyler .25 .07
471 John Smiley .25 .07
472 Charles Nagy .25 .07
473 Alan Mills .25 .07
474 John Russell .25 .07
475 Bruce Hurst .25 .07
476 Andujar Cedeno .25 .07
477 Dave Eiland .25 .07
478 Brian McRae RC .60 .18
479 Mike LaCoss .25 .07
480 Chris Gwynn .25 .07
481 Jamie Moyer .50 .15
482 John Olerud .50 .15
483 Efrain Valdez .25 .07
484 Sil Campusano .25 .07
485 Pascual Perez .25 .07
486 Gary Redus .25 .07
487 Andy Hawkins .25 .07
488 Cory Snyder .25 .07
489 Chris Hoiles .25 .07
490 Ron Hassey .25 .07
491 Gary Wayne .25 .07
492 Mark Lewis .25 .07
493 Scott Coolbaugh .25 .07
494 Gerald Young .25 .07
495 Juan Samuel .25 .07
496 Willie Fraser .25 .07
497 Jeff Treadway .25 .07
498 Vince Coleman .25 .07
499 Cris Carpenter .25 .07
500 Jack Clark .50 .15
501 Kevin Appier .50 .15
502 Rafael Palmeiro .75 .23
503 Hensley Meulens .25 .07
504 George Bell .25 .07
505 Tony Pena .25 .07
506 Roger McDowell .25 .07
507 Luis Sojo .25 .07
508 Mike Schooler .25 .07
509 Robin Yount 2.00 .60
510 Jack Armstrong .25 .07
511 Rick Cerone .25 .07
512 Curt Wilkerson .25 .07
513 Joe Carter .50 .15
514 Tim Burke .25 .07
515 Tony Fernandez .25 .07
516 Ramon Martinez .25 .07
517 Tim Hulett .25 .07
518 Terry Steinbach .25 .07
519 Pete Smith .25 .07
520 Ken Caminiti .50 .15
521 Shawn Boskie .25 .07
522 Mike Pagliarulo .25 .07
523 Tim Raines .50 .15
524 Alfredo Griffin .25 .07
525 Henry Cotto .25 .07
526 Mike Stanley .25 .07
527 Charlie Leibrandt .25 .07
528 Jeff King .25 .07
529 Eric Plunk .25 .07
530 Tom Lampkin .25 .07
531 Steve Bedrosian .25 .07
532 Tom Herr .25 .07
533 Craig Lefferts .25 .07
534 Jeff Reed .25 .07
535 Mickey Morandini .25 .07
536 Greg Cadaret .25 .07
537 Ray Lankford .50 .15
538 John Candelaria .25 .07
539 Rob Deer .25 .07
540 Brad Arnsberg .25 .07
541 Mike Sharperson .25 .07
542 Jeff D. Robinson .25 .07
543 Mo Vaughn .50 .15
544 Jeff Parrett .25 .07
545 Willie Randolph .50 .15
546 Herm Winningham .25 .07
547 Jeff Innis .25 .07
548 Chuck Knoblauch .50 .15
549 Tommy Greene UER .25 .07
(Born in North Carolina,
not South Carolina)
550 Jeff Hamilton .25 .07
551 Barry Jones .25 .07
552 Ken Dayley .25 .07
553 Rick Dempsey .25 .07
554 Greg Smith .25 .07
555 Mike Devereaux .25 .07
556 Keith Comstock .25 .07
557 Paul Faries .25 .07
558 Tom Glavine .75 .23
559 Craig Grebeck .25 .07
560 Scott Erickson .25 .07
561 Joel Skinner .25 .07
562 Mike Morgan .25 .07
563 Dave Gallagher .25 .07
564 Todd Stottlemyre .25 .07
565 Rich Rodriguez .25 .07
566 Craig Wilson .25 .07
567 Jeff Brantley .25 .07
568 Scott Kamieniecki RC .60 .18
569 Steve Decker RC .40 .12
570 Juan Agosto .25 .07
571 Tommy Gregg .25 .07
572 Kevin Wickander .25 .07
573 Jamie Quirk UER .25 .07
(Rookie card is 1976,
but card back is 1990)
574 Jerry Don Gleaton .25 .07
575 Chris Hammond .25 .07
576 Luis Gonzalez RC 1.50 .45
577 Russ Swan .25 .07
578 Jeff Conine RC 1.00 .30
579 Charlie Hough .50 .15
580 Jeff Kunkel .25 .07
581 Darrel Akerfelds .25 .07
582 Jeff Manto .25 .07
583 Alejandro Pena .25 .07
584 Mark Davidson .25 .07
585 Bob MacDonald RC .40 .12
586 Paul Assenmacher .25 .07
587 Dan Wilson RC .60 .18
588 Tom Bolton .25 .07
589 Brian Harper .25 .07
590 John Habyan .25 .07
591 John Orton .25 .07
592 Mark Gardner .25 .07
593 Turner Ward RC .60 .18
594 Bob Patterson .25 .07
595 Ed Nunez .25 .07
596 Gary Scott RC UER .40 .12
(Major League Batting
Record should be
Minor League)
597 Scott Bankhead .25 .07
598 Checklist 301-400 .25 .07
599 Checklist 401-500 .25 .07
600 Checklist 501-600 .25 .07

1992 Stadium Club Dome

The 1992 Stadium Club Dome set (issued by Topps) features 100 top draft picks, 56 1991 All-Star Game cards, 25 1991 Team U.S.A. cards, and 19 1991 Championship and World Series cards, all packaged in a factory set box inside a molded-plastic SkyDome display. Topps actually references this set as a 1991 set and the copyright lines on the card backs say 1991, but the set was released well into 1992. Rookie Cards in this set include Shawn Green and Manny Ramirez.

Nm-Mt Ex-Mt
COMP.FACT.SET (200) 15.00 4.50
1 Terry Adams RC .50 .15
2 Tommy Adams RC .25 .07
3 Rick Aguilera .15 .04
4 Ron Allen RC .25 .07
5 Roberto Alomar .25 .07
6 Sandy Alomar Jr. .10 .03
7 Greg Anthony RC .25 .07
8 James Austin RC .25 .07
9 Steve Avery .10 .03
10 Harold Baines .15 .04
11 Brian Barber RC .25 .07
12 Jon Barnes RC .25 .07
13 George Bell .10 .03
14 Doug Bennett RC .25 .07
15 Sean Bergman RC .50 .15
16 Craig Biggio .25 .07
17 Bill Bliss RC .25 .07
18 Wade Boggs .25 .07
19 Bobby Bonilla .15 .04
20 Russell Brock RC .25 .07
21 Tarrik Brock RC .25 .07
22 Tom Browning .10 .03
23 Brett Butler .15 .04
24 Ivan Calderon .10 .03
25 Joe Carter .15 .04
26 Joe Caruso RC .25 .07
27 Dan Cholowsky RC .25 .07
28 Will Clark .50 .15
29 Roger Clemens 1.00 .30
30 Shawn Curran RC .25 .07
31 Chris Curtis RC .25 .07
32 Chili Davis .15 .04
33 Andre Dawson .15 .04
34 Joe DeBerry RC .25 .07
35 John Dettmer .10 .03
36 Rob Dibble .15 .04
37 John Donati RC .25 .07
38 Dave Doorneweerd RC .25 .07
39 Darren Dreifort .10 .03
40 Mike Durant RC .25 .07
41 Chris Durkin RC .25 .07
42 Dennis Eckersley .15 .04
43 Brian Edmondson RC .25 .07
44 Vaughn Eshelman RC .25 .07
45 Shawn Estes RC .50 .15
46 Jorge Fabregas RC .50 .15
47 Jon Farrell RC .25 .07
48 Cecil Fielder .15 .04
49 Carlton Fisk .25 .07
50 Tim Flannelly RC .25 .07
51 Cliff Floyd RC .75 .23
52 Julio Franco .15 .04
53 Greg Gagne .10 .03
54 Chris Gambs RC .25 .07
55 Ron Gant .15 .04
56 Brent Gates RC .25 .07
57 Dwayne Gerald RC .25 .07
58 Jason Giambi 1.00 .30
59 Benji Gil RC .50 .15
60 Mark Gipner RC .25 .07
61 Danny Gladden .10 .03
62 Tom Glavine .25 .07
63 Jimmy Gonzalez RC .25 .07
64 Jeff Granger .10 .03
65 Dan Grapenthien RC .25 .07
66 Dennis Gray RC .25 .07
67 Shawn Green RC 4.00 1.20
68 Tyler Green RC .25 .07
69 Todd Greene .10 .03
70 Ken Griffey Jr. .75 .23
71 Kelly Gruber .10 .03
72 Ozzie Guillen .10 .03
73 Tony Gwynn .60 .18
74 Shane Halter RC .25 .07
75 Jeffrey Hammonds .15 .04
76 Larry Hanlon RC .25 .07
77 Pete Harnisch .10 .03
78 Mike Harrison RC .25 .07
79 Bryan Harvey .10 .03
80 Scott Hatteberg RC .50 .15
81 Rick Helling .10 .03
82 Dave Henderson .10 .03
83 Rickey Henderson .50 .15
84 Tyrone Hill RC .25 .07
85 T.Hollandsworth RC .50 .15
86 Brian Holliday RC .25 .07
87 Terry Horn RC .25 .07
88 Jeff Hostetler RC .25 .07
89 Kent Hrbek .15 .04
90 Mark Hubbard RC .25 .07
91 Charles Johnson .15 .04
92 Howard Johnson .10 .03
93 Todd Johnson .10 .03
94 Bobby Jones RC .50 .15
95 Dan Jones RC .25 .07
96 Felix Jose .10 .03
97 David Justice .10 .03
98 Jimmy Key .15 .04
99 Marc Kroon RC .25 .07
100 John Kruk .15 .04
101 Mark Langston .10 .03
102 Barry Larkin .25 .07
103 Mike LaValliere .10 .03
104 Scott Leius .10 .03
105 Mark Lemke .10 .03
106 Donnie Leshnock .10 .03
107 Jimmy Lewis RC .25 .07
108 Shane Livesy RC .25 .07
109 Ryan Long RC .25 .07
110 Trevor Mallory RC .25 .07
111 Dennis Martinez .15 .04
112 Justin Mashore RC .25 .07
113 Jason McDonald .10 .03
114 Jack McDowell .10 .03
115 Tom McKinnon RC .25 .07
116 Billy McMillon .10 .03
117 Buck McNabb RC .25 .07
118 Jim Mecir RC .25 .07
119 Dan Melendez .25 .07
120 Shawn Miller RC .25 .07
121 Trever Miller RC .25 .07
122 Paul Molitor .25 .07
123 Vincent Moore RC .25 .07
124 Mike Morgan .10 .03
125 Jack Morris WS .10 .03
126 Jack Morris AS .10 .03
127 Sean Mulligan RC .25 .07
128 Eddie Murray AS .50 .15
129 Mike Neill RC .50 .15
130 Phil Nevin 1.00 .30
131 Mark O'Brien RC .25 .07
132 Alex Ochoa RC .50 .15
133 Chad Ogea RC .25 .07
134 Greg Olson .10 .03
135 Paul O'Neill .25 .07
136 Jared Osentowski RC .25 .07
137 Mike Pagliarulo .10 .03
138 Rafael Palmeiro .25 .07
139 Rodney Pedraza RC .25 .07
140 Tony Phillips (P) .10 .03
141 Scott Pisciotta RC .25 .07
142 C.Pritchett RC .25 .07
143 Jason Pruitt RC .25 .07
144 K.Puckett WS UER .50 .15
Championship series
AB and BA is wrong
145 Kirby Puckett AS .50 .15
146 Manny Ramirez RC 4.00 1.20
147 Eddie Ramos RC .25 .07
148 Mark Ratekin RC .25 .07
149 Jeff Reardon .15 .04
150 Sean Rees RC .25 .07
151 Pokey Reese RC .75 .23
152 Desmond Relaford RC .50 .15
153 Eric Richardson RC .25 .07
154 Cal Ripken 1.50 .45
155 Chris Roberts .10 .03
156 Mike Robertson RC .25 .07
157 Steve Rodriguez .10 .03
158 Mike Rossiter RC .25 .07
159 Scott Ruffcorn RC .25 .07
160 Chris Sabo .10 .03
161 Juan Samuel .10 .03
162 Ryne Sandberg UER .75 .23
(On 5th line, prior
misspelled as prilor)
163 Scott Sanderson .10 .03
164 Benny Santiago .15 .04
165 Gene Schall RC .25 .07
166 Chad Schoenvogel RC .25 .07
167 Chris Seelbach RC .25 .07
168 Aaron Sele RC .75 .23
169 Basil Shabazz RC .25 .07
170 Al Shirley RC .25 .07
171 Paul Shuey .10 .03
172 Ruben Sierra .10 .03
173 John Smiley .10 .03

174 Lee Smith .15 .04
175 Ozzie Smith .75 .23
176 Tim Smith RC .25 .07
177 Zane Smith .10 .03
178 John Smoltz .25 .07
179 Scott Stahoviak RC .25 .07
180 Kennie Steenstra .10 .03
181 Kevin Stocker RC .25 .07
182 Chris Stynes RC .50 .15
183 Danny Tartabull .10 .03
184 Brien Taylor RC .50 .15
185 Todd Taylor .10 .03
186 Larry Thomas RC .25 .07
187 Ozzie Timmons RC .25 .07
(See also 188)
188 David Tuttle UER .10 .03
(Mistakenly numbered as 187 on card)
189 Andy Van Slyke .15 .04
190 Frank Viola .15 .04
191 Michael Walkden RC .25 .07
192 Jeff Ware .10 .03
193 Allen Watson RC .25 .07
194 Steve Whitaker RC .25 .07
195 Jerry Willard .10 .03
196 Craig Wilson .10 .03
197 Chris Wimmer .10 .03
198 S.Wojciechowski RC .25 .07
199 Joel Wolfe RC .25 .07
200 Ivan Zweig .10 .03

1992 Stadium Club

The 1992 Stadium Club baseball card set consists of 900 standard-size cards issued in three series of 300 cards each. Cards were issued in plastic wrapped packs. A card-like application form for membership in Topps Stadium Club was inserted in each pack. Card numbers 591-610 form a "Members Choice" subset.

	Nm-Mt	Ex-Mt
COMPLETE SET (900)	45.00	13.50
COMP.SERIES 1 (300)	15.00	4.50
COMP.SERIES 2 (300)	15.00	4.50
COMP.SERIES 3 (300)	15.00	4.50

1 Cal Ripken UER 1.50 .45
(Misspelled Ripkin on card back)
2 Eric Yelding .10 .03
3 Geno Petralli .10 .03
4 Wally Backman .10 .03
5 Milt Cuyler .10 .03
6 Kevin Bass .10 .03
7 Dante Bichette .15 .04
8 Ray Lankford .15 .04
9 Mel Hall .10 .03
10 Joe Carter .15 .04
11 Juan Samuel .10 .03
12 Jeff Montgomery .10 .03
13 Glenn Braggs .10 .03
14 Henry Cotto .10 .03
15 Deion Sanders .25 .07
16 Dick Schofield .10 .03
17 David Cone .15 .04
18 Chili Davis .15 .04
19 Tom Foley .10 .03
20 Ozzie Guillen .10 .03
21 Luis Salazar .10 .03
22 Terry Steinbach .10 .03
23 Chris James .10 .03
24 Jeff King .10 .03
25 Carlos Quintana .10 .03
26 Mike Maddux .10 .03
27 Tommy Greene .10 .03
28 Jeff Russell .10 .03
29 Steve Finley .15 .04
30 Mike Flanagan .10 .03
31 Darren Lewis .10 .03
32 Mark Lee .10 .03
33 Willie Fraser .10 .03
34 Mike Henneman .10 .03
35 Kevin Maas .10 .03
36 Dave Hansen .10 .03
37 Erik Hanson .10 .03
38 Bill Doran .10 .03
39 Mike Boddicker .10 .03
40 Vince Coleman .10 .03
41 Devon White .15 .04
42 Mark Gardner .10 .03
43 Scott Lewis .10 .03
44 Juan Berenguer .10 .03
45 Carney Lansford .15 .04
46 Curt Wilkerson .10 .03
47 Shane Mack .10 .03
48 Bip Roberts .10 .03
49 Greg A. Harris .10 .03
50 Ryne Sandberg .75 .23
51 Mark Whiten .10 .03
52 Jack McDowell .10 .03
53 Jimmy Jones .10 .03
54 Steve Lake .10 .03
55 Bud Black .10 .03
56 Dave Valle .10 .03
57 Kevin Reimer .10 .03
58 Rich Gedman UER .10 .03
(Wrong BARS chart used)
59 Travis Fryman .15 .04
60 Steve Avery .10 .03
61 Francisco de la Rosa .10 .03
62 Scott Hemond .10 .03
63 Hal Morris .10 .03
64 Hensley Meulens .10 .03
65 Frank Castillo .10 .03
66 Gene Larkin .10 .03
67 Jose DeLeon .10 .03
68 Al Osuna .10 .03
69 Dave Cochrane .10 .03
70 Robin Ventura .15 .04
71 John Cerutti .10 .03
72 Kevin Gross .10 .03
73 Ivan Calderon .10 .03
74 Mike Macfarlane .10 .03
75 Stan Belinda .10 .03
76 Shawn Hillegas .10 .03
77 Pat Borders .10 .03
78 Jim Vatcher .10 .03
79 Bobby Rose .10 .03
80 Roger Clemens 1.00 .30
81 Craig Worthington .10 .03
82 Jeff Treadway .10 .03
83 Jamie Quirk .10 .03
84 Randy Bush .10 .03
85 Anthony Young .10 .03
86 Trevor Wilson .10 .03
87 Jaime Navarro .10 .03
88 Les Lancaster .10 .03
89 Pat Kelly .10 .03
90 Alvin Davis .10 .03
91 Larry Andersen .10 .03
92 Rob Deer .10 .03
93 Mike Sharperson .10 .03
94 Lance Parrish .15 .04
95 Cecil Espy .10 .03
96 Tim Spehr .10 .03
97 Dave Stieb .10 .03
98 Terry Mulholland .10 .03
99 Dennis Boyd .10 .03
100 Barry Larkin .25 .07
101 Ryan Bowen .10 .03
102 Felix Fermin .10 .03
103 Luis Alicea .10 .03
104 Tim Hulett .10 .03
105 Rafael Belliard .10 .03
106 Mike Gallego .10 .03
107 Dave Righetti .15 .04
108 Jeff Schaefer .10 .03
109 Ricky Bones .10 .03
110 Scott Erickson .10 .03
111 Matt Nokes .10 .03
112 Bob Scanlan .10 .03
113 Tom Candiotti .10 .03
114 Sean Berry .10 .03
115 Kevin Morton .10 .03
116 Scott Fletcher .10 .03
117 B.J. Surhoff .15 .04
118 Dave Magadan UER .10 .03
(Born Tampa, not Tamps)
119 Bill Gullickson .10 .03
120 Marquis Grissom .15 .04
121 Lenny Harris .10 .03
122 Wally Joyner .15 .04
123 Kevin Brown .15 .04
124 Braulio Castillo .10 .03
125 Eric King .10 .03
126 Mark Portugal .10 .03
127 Calvin Jones .10 .03
128 Mike Heath .10 .03
129 Todd Van Poppel .10 .03
130 Benny Santiago .15 .04
131 Gary Thurman .10 .03
132 Joe Girardi .10 .03
133 Dave Eiland .10 .03
134 Orlando Merced .10 .03
135 Joe Orsulak .10 .03
136 John Burkett .10 .03
137 Ken Dayley .10 .03
138 Ken Hill .10 .03
139 Walt Terrell .10 .03
140 Mike Scioscia .10 .03
141 Junior Felix .10 .03
142 Ken Caminiti .15 .04
143 Carlos Baerga .10 .03
144 Tony Fossas .10 .03
145 Craig Grebeck .10 .03
146 Scott Bradley .10 .03
147 Kent Mercker .10 .03
148 Derrick May .10 .03
149 Jerald Clark .10 .03
150 George Brett 1.25 .35
151 Luis Quinones .10 .03
152 Mike Pagliarulo .10 .03
153 Jose Guzman .10 .03
154 Charlie O'Brien .10 .03
155 Darren Holmes .10 .03
156 Joe Boever .10 .03
157 Rich Monteleone .10 .03
158 Reggie Harris .10 .03
159 Roberto Alomar .25 .07
160 Robby Thompson .10 .03
161 Chris Hoiles .10 .03
162 Tom Pagnozzi .10 .03
163 Omar Vizquel .25 .07
164 John Candelaria .10 .03
165 Terry Shumpert .10 .03
166 Andy Mota .10 .03
167 Scott Bailes .10 .03
168 Jeff Blauser .10 .03
169 Steve Olin .10 .03
170 Doug Drabek .10 .03
171 Dave Bergman .10 .03
172 Eddie Whitson .10 .03
173 Gilberto Reyes .10 .03
174 Mark Grace .25 .07
175 Paul O'Neill .25 .07
176 Greg Cadaret .10 .03
177 Mark Williamson .10 .03
178 Casey Candaele .10 .03
179 Candy Maldonado .10 .03
180 Lee Smith .15 .04
181 Harold Reynolds .15 .04
182 David Justice .15 .04
183 Lenny Webster .10 .03
184 Donn Pall .10 .03
185 Gerald Alexander .10 .03
186 Jack Clark .15 .04
187 Stan Javier .10 .03
188 Ricky Jordan .10 .03
189 Franklin Stubbs .10 .03
190 Dennis Eckersley .15 .04
191 Danny Tartabull .10 .03
192 Pete O'Brien .10 .03
193 Mark Lewis .10 .03
194 Mike Felder .10 .03
195 Mickey Tettleton .10 .03
196 Dwight Smith .10 .03
197 Shawn Abner .10 .03
198 Jim Leyritz UER .10 .03
(Career totals less than 1991 totals)
199 Mike Devereaux .10 .03
200 Craig Biggio .25 .07
201 Kevin Elster .10 .03
202 Rance Mulliniks .10 .03
203 Tony Fernandez .10 .03
204 Allan Anderson .10 .03
205 Herm Winningham .10 .03
206 Tim Jones .10 .03
207 Ramon Martinez .10 .03
208 Teddy Higuera .10 .03
209 John Kruk .10 .03
210 Jim Abbott .25 .07
211 Dean Palmer .15 .04
212 Mark Davis .10 .03
213 Jay Buhner .15 .04
214 Jesse Barfield .10 .03
215 Kevin Mitchell .10 .03
216 Mike LaValliere .10 .03
217 Mark Wohlers .10 .03
218 Dave Henderson .10 .03
219 Dave Smith .10 .03
220 Albert Belle .15 .04
221 Spike Owen .10 .03
222 Jeff Gray .10 .03
223 Paul Gibson .10 .03
224 Bobby Thigpen .10 .03
225 Mike Mussina .50 .15
226 Darrin Jackson .10 .03
227 Luis Gonzalez .15 .04
228 Greg Briley .10 .03
229 Brent Mayne .10 .03
230 Paul Molitor .25 .07
231 Al Leiter .15 .04
232 Andy Van Slyke .15 .04
233 Ron Tingley .10 .03
234 Bernard Gilkey .10 .03
235 Kent Hrbek .15 .04
236 Eric Karros .15 .04
237 Randy Velarde .10 .03
238 Andy Allanson .10 .03
239 Willie McGee .15 .04
240 Juan Gonzalez .25 .07
241 Karl Rhodes .10 .03
242 Luis Mercedes .10 .03
243 Bill Swift .10 .03
244 Tommy Gregg .10 .03
245 David Howard .10 .03
246 Dave Hollins .10 .03
247 Kip Gross .10 .03
248 Walt Weiss .10 .03
249 Mackey Sasser .10 .03
250 Cecil Fielder .15 .04
251 Jerry Browne .10 .03
252 Doug Dascenzo .10 .03
253 Darryl Hamilton .10 .03
254 Dann Bilardello .10 .03
255 Luis Rivera .10 .03
256 Larry Walker .25 .07
257 Ron Karkovice .10 .03
258 Bob Tewksbury .10 .03
259 Jimmy Key .15 .04
260 Bernie Williams .25 .07
261 Gary Wayne .10 .03
262 Mike Simms UER .10 .03
(Reversed negative)
263 John Orton .10 .03
264 Marvin Freeman .10 .03
265 Mike Jeffcoat .10 .03
266 Roger Mason .10 .03
267 Edgar Martinez .25 .07
268 Henry Rodriguez .10 .03
269 Sam Horn .10 .03
270 Brian McRae .10 .03
271 Kirt Manwaring .10 .03
272 Mike Bordick .10 .03
273 Chris Sabo .10 .03
274 Jim Olander .10 .03
275 Greg W. Harris .10 .03
276 Dan Gakeler .10 .03
277 Bill Sampen .10 .03
278 Joel Skinner .10 .03
279 Curt Schilling .25 .07
280 Dale Murphy .50 .15
281 Lee Stevens .10 .03
282 Lonnie Smith .10 .03
283 Manuel Lee .10 .03
284 Shawn Boskie .10 .03
285 Kevin Seitzer .10 .03
286 Stan Royer .10 .03
287 John Dopson .10 .03
288 Scott Bullett RC .10 .03
289 Ken Patterson .10 .03
290 Todd Hundley .10 .03
291 Tim Leary .10 .03
292 Brett Butler .15 .04
293 Gregg Olson .10 .03
294 Jeff Brantley .10 .03
295 Brian Holman .10 .03
296 Brian Harper .10 .03
297 Brian Bohanon .10 .03
298 Checklist 1-100 .10 .03
299 Checklist 101-200 .10 .03
300 Checklist 201-300 .10 .03
301 Frank Thomas .50 .15
302 Lloyd McClendon .10 .03
303 Brady Anderson .15 .04
304 Julio Valera .10 .03
305 Mike Aldrete .10 .03
306 Joe Oliver .10 .03
307 Todd Stottlemyre .10 .03
308 Rey Sanchez RC .15 .04
309 Gary Sheffield UER .15 .04
(Listed as 5'1", should be 5'11")
310 Andujar Cedeno .10 .03
311 Kenny Rogers .15 .04
312 Bruce Hurst .10 .03
313 Mike Schooler .10 .03
314 Mike Benjamin .10 .03
315 Chuck Finley .15 .04
316 Mark Lemke .10 .03
317 Scott Livingstone .10 .03
318 Chris Nabholz .10 .03
319 Mike Humphreys .10 .03
320 Pedro Guerrero .15 .04
321 Willie Banks .10 .03
322 Tom Goodwin .10 .03
323 Hector Wagner .10 .03
324 Wally Ritchie .10 .03
325 Mo Vaughn .15 .04
326 Joe Klink .10 .03
327 Cal Eldred .10 .03
328 Daryl Boston .10 .03
329 Mike Huff .10 .03
330 Jeff Bagwell .50 .15
331 Bob Milacki .10 .03
332 Tom Prince .10 .03
333 Pat Tabler .10 .03
334 Ced Landrum .10 .03
335 Reggie Jefferson .10 .03
336 Mo Sanford .10 .03
337 Kevin Ritz .10 .03
338 Gerald Perry .10 .03
339 Jeff Hamilton .10 .03
340 Tim Wallach .10 .03
341 Jeff Huson .10 .03
342 Jose Melendez .10 .03
343 Willie Wilson .10 .03
344 Mike Stanton .10 .03
345 Joel Johnston .10 .03
346 Lee Guetterman .10 .03
347 Francisco Oliveras .10 .03
348 Dave Burba .10 .03
349 Tim Crews .10 .03
350 Scott Leius .10 .03
351 Danny Cox .10 .03
352 Wayne Housie .10 .03
353 Chris Donnels .10 .03
354 Chris George .10 .03
355 Gerald Young .10 .03
356 Roberto Hernandez .10 .03
357 Neal Heaton .10 .03
358 Todd Frohwirth .10 .03
359 Jose Vizcaino .10 .03
360 Jim Thome .50 .15
361 Craig Wilson .10 .03
362 Dave Haas .10 .03
363 Billy Hatcher .10 .03
364 John Barfield .10 .03
365 Luis Aquino .10 .03
366 Charlie Leibrandt .10 .03
367 Howard Farmer .10 .03
368 Bryn Smith .10 .03
369 Mickey Morandini .10 .03
370 Jose Canseco .50 .15
(See also 597)
371 Jose Uribe .10 .03
372 Bob MacDonald .10 .03
373 Luis Sojo .10 .03
374 Craig Shipley .10 .03
375 Scott Bankhead .10 .03
376 Greg Gagne .10 .03
377 Scott Cooper .10 .03
378 Jose Offerman .10 .03
379 Bill Spiers .10 .03
380 John Smiley .10 .03
381 Jeff Carter .10 .03
382 Heathcliff Slocumb .10 .03
383 Jeff Tackett .10 .03
384 John Kiely .10 .03
385 John Vander Wal .10 .03
386 Omar Olivares .10 .03
387 Ruben Sierra .10 .03
388 Tom Gordon .10 .03
389 Charles Nagy .10 .03
390 Dave Stewart .15 .04
391 Pete Harnisch .10 .03
392 Tim Burke .10 .03
393 Roberto Kelly .10 .03
394 Freddie Benavides .10 .03
395 Tom Glavine .25 .07
396 Wes Chamberlain .10 .03
397 Eric Gunderson .10 .03
398 Dave West .10 .03
399 Ellis Burks .15 .04
400 Ken Griffey Jr. .75 .23
401 Thomas Howard .10 .03
402 Juan Guzman .10 .03
403 Mitch Webster .10 .03
404 Matt Merullo .10 .03
405 Steve Buechele .10 .03
406 Danny Jackson .10 .03
407 Felix Jose .10 .03
408 Doug Piatt .10 .03
409 Jim Eisenreich .10 .03
410 Bryan Harvey .10 .03
411 Jim Austin .10 .03
412 Jim Poole .10 .03
413 Glenallen Hill .10 .03
414 Gene Nelson .10 .03
415 Ivan Rodriguez .50 .15
416 Frank Tanana .10 .03
417 Steve Decker .10 .03
418 Jason Grimsley .10 .03
419 Tim Layana .10 .03
420 Don Mattingly 1.25 .35
421 Jerome Walton .10 .03
422 Rob Ducey .10 .03
423 Andy Benes .10 .03
424 John Marzano .10 .03
425 Gene Harris .10 .03
426 Tim Raines .15 .04
427 Bret Barberie .10 .03
428 Harvey Pulliam .10 .03
429 Cris Carpenter .10 .03
430 Howard Johnson .10 .03
431 Orel Hershiser .15 .04
432 Brian Hunter .10 .03
433 Kevin Tapani .10 .03
434 Rick Reed .10 .03
435 Ron Witmeyer RC .10 .03
436 Gary Gaetti .15 .04
437 Alex Cole .10 .03
438 Chito Martinez .10 .03
439 Greg Litton .10 .03
440 Julio Franco .15 .04
441 Mike Munoz .10 .03
442 Erik Pappas .10 .03
443 Pat Combs .10 .03
444 Lance Johnson .10 .03
445 Ed Sprague .10 .03
446 Mike Greenwell .10 .03
447 Milt Thompson .10 .03
448 Mike Magnante RC .10 .03
449 Chris Haney .10 .03
450 Robin Yount .75 .23
451 Rafael Ramirez .10 .03
452 Gino Minutelli .10 .03
453 Tom Lampkin .10 .03
454 Tony Perezchica .10 .03
455 Dwight Gooden .15 .04
456 Mark Guthrie .10 .03
457 Jay Howell .10 .03
458 Gary DiSarcina .10 .03
459 John Smoltz .25 .07
460 Will Clark .50 .15
461 Dave Otto .10 .03
462 Rob Maurer .10 .03
463 Dwight Evans .15 .04
464 Tom Brunansky .10 .03
465 Shawn Hare RC .10 .03
466 Geronimo Pena .10 .03
467 Alex Fernandez .10 .03
468 Greg Myers .10 .03
469 Jeff Fassero .10 .03
470 Len Dykstra .15 .04
471 Jeff Johnson .10 .03
472 Russ Swan .10 .03
473 Archie Corbin .10 .03
474 Chuck McElroy .10 .03
475 Mark McGwire 1.25 .35
476 Wally Whitehurst .10 .03
477 Tim McIntosh .10 .03
478 Sid Bream .10 .03
479 Jeff Juden .10 .03
480 Carlton Fisk .25 .07
481 Jeff Plympton .10 .03
482 Carlos Martinez .10 .03
483 Jim Gott .10 .03
484 Bob McClure .10 .03
485 Tim Teufel .10 .03
486 Vicente Palacios .10 .03
487 Jeff Reed .10 .03
488 Tony Phillips .10 .03
489 Mel Rojas .10 .03
490 Ben McDonald .10 .03
491 Andres Santana .10 .03
492 Chris Beasley .10 .03
493 Mike Timlin .10 .03
494 Brian Downing .10 .03
495 Kirk Gibson .15 .04
496 Scott Sanderson .10 .03
497 Nick Esasky .10 .03
498 Johnny Guzman RC .10 .03
499 Mitch Williams .10 .03
500 Kirby Puckett .50 .15
501 Mike Harkey .10 .03
502 Jim Gantner .10 .03
503 Bruce Egloff .10 .03
504 Josias Manzanillo RC .10 .03
505 Delino DeShields .10 .03
506 Rheal Cormier .10 .03
507 Jay Bell .15 .04
508 Rich Rowland RC .10 .03
509 Scott Servais .10 .03
510 Terry Pendleton .15 .04
511 Rich DeLucia .10 .03
512 Warren Newson .10 .03
513 Paul Faries .10 .03
514 Kal Daniels .10 .03
515 Jarvis Brown .10 .03
516 Rafael Palmeiro .25 .07
517 Kelly Downs .10 .03
518 Steve Chitren .10 .03
519 Moises Alou .15 .04
520 Wade Boggs .25 .07
521 Pete Schourek .10 .03
522 Scott Terry .10 .03
523 Kevin Appier .15 .04
524 Gary Redus .10 .03
525 George Bell .10 .03
526 Jeff Kaiser .10 .03
527 Alvaro Espinoza .10 .03
528 Luis Polonia .10 .03
529 Darren Daulton .15 .04
530 Norm Charlton .10 .03
531 John Olerud .15 .04
532 Dan Plesac .10 .03
533 Billy Ripken .10 .03
534 Rod Nichols .10 .03
535 Joey Cora .10 .03
536 Harold Baines .15 .04
537 Bob Ojeda .10 .03
538 Mark Leonard .10 .03
539 Danny Darwin .10 .03
540 Shawon Dunston .10 .03
541 Pedro Munoz .10 .03
542 Mark Gubicza .10 .03
543 Kevin Baez .10 .03
544 Todd Zeile .10 .03
545 Don Slaught .10 .03
546 Tony Eusebio .15 .04
547 Alonzo Powell .10 .03
548 Gary Pettis .10 .03
549 Brian Barnes .10 .03
550 Lou Whitaker .15 .04
551 Keith Mitchell .10 .03
552 Oscar Azocar .10 .03
553 Stu Cole RC .10 .03
554 Steve Wapnick .10 .03
555 Derek Bell .15 .04
556 Luis Lopez .10 .03
557 Anthony Telford .10 .03
558 Tim Mauser .10 .03
559 Glen Sutko .10 .03
560 Darryl Strawberry .15 .04
561 Tom Bolton .10 .03
562 Cliff Young .10 .03
563 Bruce Walton .10 .03
564 Chico Walker .10 .03
565 John Franco .15 .04
566 Paul McClellan .10 .03
567 Paul Abbott .10 .03
568 Gary Varsho .10 .03
569 Carlos Maldonado RC .10 .03
570 Kelly Gruber .10 .03
571 Jose Oquendo .10 .03
572 Steve Frey .10 .03
573 Tino Martinez .25 .07
574 Bill Haselman .10 .03
575 Eric Anthony .10 .03
576 John Habyan .10 .03
577 Jeff McNeely .10 .03
578 Chris Bosio .10 .03
579 Joe Grahe .10 .03
580 Fred McGriff .25 .07
581 Rick Honeycutt .10 .03
582 Matt Williams .15 .04
583 Cliff Brantley .10 .03

584 Rob Dibble .15 .04
585 Skeeter Barnes .10 .03
586 Greg Hibbard .10 .03
587 Randy Milligan .10 .03
588 Checklist 301-400 .10 .03
589 Checklist 401-500 .10 .03
590 Checklist 501-600 .10 .03
591 Frank Thomas MC .25 .07
592 David Justice MC .10 .03
593 Roger Clemens MC .50 .15
594 Steve Avery MC .10 .03
595 Cal Ripken MC .75 .23
596 Barry Larkin MC UER .15 .04
(Ranked in AL, should be NL)
597 J.Canseco MC UER .15 .04
Mistakenly numbered 370 on card back
598 Will Clark MC .15 .04
599 Cecil Fielder MC .10 .03
600 Ryne Sandberg MC .50 .15
601 Chuck Knoblauch MC .10 .03
602 Dwight Gooden MC .10 .03
603 Ken Griffey Jr. MC .50 .15
604 Barry Bonds MC .60 .18
605 Nolan Ryan MC .75 .23
606 Jeff Bagwell MC .25 .07
607 Robin Yount MC .50 .15
608 Bobby Bonilla MC .10 .03
609 George Brett MC .60 .18
610 Howard Johnson MC .10 .03
611 Esteban Beltre .10 .03
612 Mike Christopher .10 .03
613 Troy Afenir .10 .03
614 Mariano Duncan .10 .03
615 Doug Henry RC .10 .03
616 Doug Jones .10 .03
617 Alvin Davis .10 .03
618 Craig Lefferts .10 .03
619 Kevin McReynolds .10 .03
620 Barry Bonds 1.25 .35
621 Turner Ward .10 .03
622 Joe Magrane .10 .03
623 Mark Parent .10 .03
624 Tom Browning .10 .03
625 John Smiley .10 .03
626 Steve Wilson .10 .03
627 Mike Gallego .10 .03
628 Sammy Sosa .75 .23
629 Rico Rossy .10 .03
630 Royce Clayton .10 .03
631 Clay Parker .10 .03
632 Pete Smith .10 .03
633 Jeff McKnight .10 .03
634 Jack Daugherty .10 .03
635 Steve Sax .10 .03
636 Joe Hesketh .10 .03
637 Vince Horsman .10 .03
638 Eric King .10 .03
639 Joe Boever .10 .03
640 Jack Morris .15 .04
641 Arthur Rhodes .10 .03
642 Bob Melvin .10 .03
643 Rick Wilkins .10 .03
644 Scott Scudder .10 .03
645 Bip Roberts .10 .03
646 Julio Valera .10 .03
647 Kevin Campbell .10 .03
648 Steve Searcy .10 .03
649 Scott Kamieniecki .10 .03
650 Kurt Stillwell .10 .03
651 Bob Welch .10 .03
652 Andres Galarraga .15 .04
653 Mike Jackson .10 .03
654 Bo Jackson .50 .15
655 Sid Fernandez .10 .03
656 Mike Bielecki .10 .03
657 Jeff Reardon .15 .04
658 Wayne Rosenthal .10 .03
659 Eric Bullock .10 .03
660 Eric Davis .15 .04
661 Randy Tomlin .10 .03
662 Tom Edens .10 .03
663 Rob Murphy .10 .03
664 Leo Gomez .10 .03
665 Greg Maddux .75 .23
666 Greg Vaughn .10 .03
667 Wade Taylor .10 .03
668 Brad Arnsberg .10 .03
669 Mike Moore .10 .03
670 Mark Langston .10 .03
671 Barry Jones .10 .03
672 Bill Landrum .10 .03
673 Greg Swindell .10 .03
674 Wayne Edwards .10 .03
675 Greg Olson .10 .03
676 Bill Pulsipher RC .10 .03
677 Bobby Witt .10 .03
678 Mark Carreon .10 .03
679 Patrick Lennon .10 .03
680 Ozzie Smith .75 .23
681 John Briscoe .10 .03
682 Matt Young .10 .03
683 Jeff Conine .15 .04
684 Phil Stephenson .10 .03
685 Ron Darling .10 .03
686 Bryan Hickerson RC .10 .03
687 Dale Sveum .10 .03
688 Kirk McCaskill .10 .03
689 Rich Amaral .10 .03
690 Danny Tartabull .10 .03
691 Donald Harris .10 .03
692 Doug Davis .10 .03
693 John Farrell .10 .03
694 Paul Gibson .10 .03
695 Kenny Lofton .25 .07
696 Mike Fetters .10 .03
697 Rosario Rodriguez .10 .03
698 Chris Jones .10 .03
699 Jeff Manto .10 .03
700 Rick Sutcliffe .15 .04
701 Scott Bankhead .10 .03
702 Donnie Hill .10 .03
703 Todd Worrell .10 .03
704 Rene Gonzales .10 .03
705 Rick Cerone .10 .03
706 Tony Pena .10 .03
707 Paul Sorrento .10 .03
708 Gary Scott .10 .03
709 Junior Noboa .10 .03
710 Wally Joyner .15 .04
711 Charlie Hayes .10 .03
712 Rich Rodriguez .10 .03
713 Rudy Seanez .10 .03
714 Jim Bullinger .10 .03
715 Jeff M. Robinson .10 .03
716 Jeff Branson .10 .03
717 Andy Ashby .10 .03
718 Dave Burba .10 .03
719 Rich Gossage .15 .04
720 Randy Johnson .50 .15
721 Dave Wells .15 .04
722 Paul Kilgus .10 .03
723 Dave Martinez .10 .03
724 Denny Neagle .15 .04
725 Andy Stankiewicz .10 .03
726 Rick Aguilera .15 .04
727 Junior Ortiz .10 .03
728 Storm Davis .10 .03
729 Don Robinson .10 .03
730 Ron Gant .15 .04
731 Paul Assenmacher .10 .03
732 Mike Gardiner .10 .03
733 Milt Hill .10 .03
734 Jeremy Hernandez RC .10 .03
735 Ken Hill .10 .03
736 Xavier Hernandez .10 .03
737 Gregg Jefferies .10 .03
738 Dick Schofield .10 .03
739 Ron Robinson .10 .03
740 Sandy Alomar Jr. .15 .04
741 Mike Stanley .10 .03
742 Butch Henry RC .10 .03
743 Floyd Bannister .10 .03
744 Brian Drahman .10 .03
745 Dave Winfield .15 .04
746 Bob Walk .10 .03
747 Chris James .10 .03
748 Don Prybylinski RC .10 .03
749 Dennis Rasmussen .10 .03
750 Rickey Henderson .50 .15
751 Chris Hammond .10 .03
752 Bob Kipper .10 .03
753 Dave Rohde .10 .03
754 Hubie Brooks .10 .03
755 Bret Saberhagen .15 .04
756 Jeff D. Robinson .10 .03
757 Pat Listach RC .15 .04
758 Bill Wegman .10 .03
759 John Wetteland .15 .04
760 Phil Plantier .10 .03
761 Wilson Alvarez .10 .03
762 Scott Aldred .10 .03
763 Armando Reynoso RC .15 .04
764 Todd Benzinger .10 .03
765 Kevin Mitchell .10 .03
766 Gary Sheffield .15 .04
767 Allan Anderson .10 .03
768 Rusty Meacham .10 .03
769 Rick Parker .10 .03
770 Nolan Ryan 2.00 .60
771 Jeff Ballard .10 .03
772 Cory Snyder .10 .03
773 Denis Boucher .10 .03
774 Jose Gonzalez .10 .03
775 Juan Guerrero .10 .03
776 Ed Nunez .10 .03
777 Scott Ruskin .10 .03
778 Terry Leach .10 .03
779 Carl Willis .10 .03
780 Bobby Bonilla .15 .04
781 Duane Ward .10 .03
782 Joe Slusarski .10 .03
783 David Segui .10 .03
784 Kirk Gibson .15 .04
785 Frank Viola .15 .04
786 Keith Miller .10 .03
787 Mike Morgan .10 .03
788 Kim Batiste .10 .03
789 Sergio Valdez .10 .03
790 Eddie Taubensee RC .15 .04
791 Jack Armstrong .10 .03
792 Scott Fletcher .10 .03
793 Steve Farr .10 .03
794 Dan Pasqua .10 .03
795 Eddie Murray .50 .15
796 John Morris .10 .03
797 Francisco Cabrera .10 .03
798 Mike Perez .10 .03
799 Ted Wood .10 .03
800 Jose Rijo .10 .03
801 Danny Gladden .10 .03
802 Archi Cianfrocco RC .10 .03
803 Monty Fariss .10 .03
804 Roger McDowell .10 .03
805 Randy Myers .10 .03
806 Kirk Dressendorfer .10 .03
807 Zane Smith .10 .03
808 Glenn Davis .10 .03
809 Torey Lovullo .10 .03
810 Andre Dawson .15 .04
811 Bill Pecota .10 .03
812 Ted Power .10 .03
813 Willie Blair .10 .03
814 Dave Fleming .10 .03
815 Chris Gwynn .10 .03
816 Jody Reed .10 .03
817 Mark Dewey .10 .03
818 Kyle Abbott .10 .03
819 Tom Henke .10 .03
820 Kevin Seitzer .10 .03
821 Al Newman .10 .03
822 Tim Sherrill .10 .03
823 Chuck Crim .10 .03
824 Darren Reed .10 .03
825 Tony Gwynn .60 .18
826 Steve Foster .10 .03
827 Steve Howe .10 .03
828 Brook Jacoby .10 .03
829 Rodney McCray .10 .03
830 Chuck Knoblauch .15 .04
831 John Wehner .10 .03
832 Scott Garrelts .10 .03
833 Alejandro Pena .10 .03
834 Jeff Parrett UER .10 .03
(Kentucy)
835 Juan Bell .10 .03
836 Lance Dickson .10 .03
837 Darryl Kile .15 .04
838 Efrain Valdez .10 .03
839 Bob Zupcic RC .10 .03
840 George Bell .10 .03
841 Dave Gallagher .10 .03
842 Tim Belcher .10 .03
843 Jeff Shaw .10 .03
844 Mike Fitzgerald .10 .03
845 Gary Carter .15 .04
846 John Russell .10 .03
847 Eric Hillman RC .10 .03
848 Mike Witt .10 .03
849 Curt Wilkerson .10 .03
850 Alan Trammell .15 .04
851 Rex Hudler .10 .03
852 Mike Walkden RC .10 .03
853 Kevin Ward .10 .03
854 Tim Naehring .10 .03
855 Bill Swift .10 .03
856 Damon Berryhill .10 .03
857 Mark Eichhorn .10 .03
858 Hector Villanueva .10 .03
859 Jose Lind .10 .03
860 Dennis Martinez .15 .04
861 Bill Krueger .10 .03
862 Mike Kingery .10 .03
863 Jeff Innis .10 .03
864 Derek Lilliquist .10 .03
865 Reggie Sanders .10 .03
866 Ramon Garcia .10 .03
867 Bruce Ruffin .10 .03
868 Dickie Thon .10 .03
869 Melido Perez .10 .03
870 Ruben Amaro .10 .03
871 Alan Mills .10 .03
872 Matt Sinatro .10 .03
873 Eddie Zosky .10 .03
874 Pete Incaviglia .10 .03
875 Tom Candiotti .10 .03
876 Bob Patterson .10 .03
877 Neal Heaton .10 .03
878 Terrel Hansen RC .10 .03
879 Dave Eiland .10 .03
880 Von Hayes .10 .03
881 Tim Scott .10 .03
882 Otis Nixon .10 .03
883 Herm Winningham .10 .03
884 Dion James .10 .03
885 Dave Wainhouse .10 .03
886 Frank DiPino .10 .03
887 Dennis Cook .10 .03
888 Jose Mesa .10 .03
889 Mark Leiter .10 .03
890 Willie Randolph .15 .04
891 Craig Colbert .10 .03
892 Dwayne Henry .10 .03
893 Jim Lindeman .10 .03
894 Charlie Hough .15 .04
895 Gil Heredia RC .15 .04
896 Scott Chiamparino .10 .03
897 Lance Blankenship .10 .03
898 Checklist 601-700 .10 .03
899 Checklist 701-800 .10 .03
900 Checklist 801-900 .10 .03

1992 Stadium Club First Draft Picks

This three-card standard-size set, featuring Major League Baseball's Number 1 draft pick for 1990, 1991, and 1992, was randomly inserted into 1992 Stadium Club Series III packs at an approximate rate of 1:72. One card also was mailed to each member of Topps Stadium Club.

	Nm-Mt	Ex-Mt
1 Chipper Jones	5.00	1.50
2 Brien Taylor	2.00	.60
3 Phil Nevin	2.00	.60

1992 Stadium Club Master Photos

In the first package of materials sent to 1992 Topps Stadium Club members, along with an 11-card boxed set, members received a randomly chosen "Master Photo" printed on (approximately) 5" by 7" white card stock to demonstrate how the photos are cropped to create a borderless design. Each master photo has the Topps Stadium Club logo and the words "Master Photo" above a gold foil picture frame enclosing the color player photo. The backs are blank. The cards are unnumbered and checklisted below alphabetically. Master photos were also available through a special promotion at Walmart as an insert one-per-box in specially marked wax boxes of regular Topps Stadium Club cards.

	Nm-Mt	Ex-Mt
COMPLETE SET (15)	20.00	6.00
1 Wade Boggs	1.25	.35
2 Barry Bonds	2.50	.75
3 Jose Canseco	1.25	.35
4 Will Clark	1.00	.30
5 Cecil Fielder	.50	.15
6 Dwight Gooden	.50	.15
7 Ken Griffey Jr.	3.00	.90
8 Rickey Henderson	1.50	.45
9 Lance Johnson	.25	.07
10 Cal Ripken	5.00	1.50
11 Nolan Ryan	5.00	1.50
12 Deion Sanders	1.00	.30
13 Darryl Strawberry	.50	.15
14 Danny Tartabull	.25	.07
15 Frank Thomas	1.50	.45

1993 Stadium Club Murphy

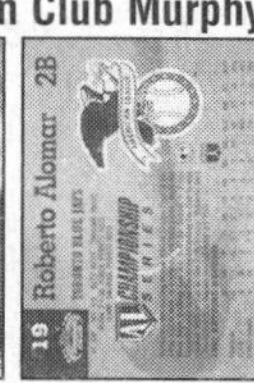

This 200-card boxed set features 1992 All-Star Game cards, 1992 Team USA cards, and 1992 Championship and World Series cards. Topps actually refers to this set as a 1992 issue, but the set was released in 1993. This set is housed in a replica of San Diego's Jack Murphy Stadium, site of the 1992 All-Star Game. Production was limited to 8,000 cases, with 16 boxes per case. The set includes 100 Draft Pick cards, 56 All-Star cards, 25 Team USA cards, and 19 cards commemorating the 1992 National and American League Championship Series and the World Series. Notable Rookie Cards in this set include Derek Jeter, Jason Kendall, Shannon Stewart and Preston Wilson. A second year Team USA Nomar Garciaparra is featured in this set as well.

	Nm-Mt	Ex-Mt
COMP.FACT.SET (212)	40.00	12.00
COMPLETE SET (200)	25.00	7.50
COMMON CARD (1-200)	.15	.04
COMMON RC	.15	.04
1 Dave Winfield	.15	.04
2 Juan Guzman	.15	.04
3 Tony Gwynn	1.00	.30
4 Chris Roberts	.15	.04
5 Benny Santiago	.30	.09
6 Sherard Clinkscales RC	.15	.04
7 Jon Nunnally RC	.50	.15
8 Chuck Knoblauch	.30	.09
9 Bob Wolcott RC	.15	.04
10 Steve Rodriguez	.15	.04
11 Mark Williams RC	.15	.04
12 Danny Clyburn RC	.15	.04
13 Darren Dreifort	.15	.04
14 Andy Van Slyke	.30	.09
15 Wade Boggs	.50	.15
16 Scott Patton RC	.15	.04
17 Gary Sheffield	.30	.09
18 Ron Villone	.15	.04
19 Roberto Alomar	.50	.15
20 Marc Valdes	.15	.04
21 Daron Kirkreit	.15	.04
22 Jeff Granger	.15	.04
23 Levon Largusa RC	.15	.04
24 Jimmy Key	.30	.09
25 Kevin Pearson RC	.15	.04
26 Michael Moore RC	.15	.04
27 Preston Wilson RC	1.50	.45
28 Kirby Puckett	.75	.23
29 Tim Crabtree RC	.15	.04
30 Bip Roberts	.15	.04
31 Kelly Gruber	.15	.04
32 Tony Fernandez	.15	.04
33 Jason Angel RC	.15	.04
34 Calvin Murray	.15	.04
35 Chad McConnell	.15	.04
36 Jason Moler	.15	.04
37 Mark Lemke	.15	.04
38 Tom Knauss RC	.15	.04
39 Larry Mitchell RC	.15	.04
40 Doug Mirabelli RC	.50	.15
41 Everett Stull II RC	.15	.04
42 Chris Wimmer	.15	.04
43 Dan Serafini RC	.15	.04
44 Ryne Sandberg	1.25	.35
45 Steve Lyons RC	.15	.04
46 Ryan Freeburg RC	.15	.04
47 Ruben Sierra	.15	.04
48 David Mysel RC	.15	.04
49 Joe Hamilton RC	.15	.04
50 Steve Rodriguez	.15	.04
51 Tim Wakefield	.75	.23
52 Scott Gentile RC	.15	.04
53 Doug Jones	.15	.04
54 Willie Brown RC	.15	.04
55 Chad Mottola RC	.50	.15
56 Ken Griffey Jr.	1.25	.35
57 Jon Lieber RC	1.00	.30
58 Dennis Martinez	.30	.09
59 Joe Petcka RC	.15	.04
60 Benji Simonton RC	.15	.04
61 Brett Backlund RC	.15	.04
62 Damon Berryhill	.15	.04
63 Juan Guzman	.15	.04
64 Doug Hecker RC	.15	.04
65 Jamie Arnold RC	.15	.04
66 Bob Tewksbury	.15	.04
67 Tim Leger RC	.15	.04
68 Todd Etler RC	.15	.04
69 Lloyd McClendon	.15	.04
70 Kurt Ehmann RC	.15	.04
71 Rick Magdaleno RC	.15	.04
72 Tom Pagnozzi	.15	.04
73 Jeffrey Hammonds	.15	.04
74 Joe Carter	.30	.09
75 Chris Holt RC	.30	.09
76 Charles Johnson	.30	.09
77 Bob Walk	.15	.04
78 Fred McGriff	.50	.15
79 Tom Evans RC	.15	.04
80 Scott Klingenbeck RC	.15	.04
81 Chad McConnell	.15	.04
82 Chris Eddy RC	.15	.04
83 Phil Nevin	.30	.09
84 John Kruk	.30	.09
85 Tony Sheffield RC	.15	.04
86 John Smoltz	.50	.15
87 Trevor Humphry RC	.15	.04
88 Charles Nagy	.15	.04
89 Sean Runyan RC	.15	.04
90 Mike Gulan RC	.15	.04
91 Darren Daulton	.30	.09
92 Otis Nixon	.15	.04
93 Nomar Garciaparra	15.00	4.50
94 Larry Walker	.50	.15
95 Hut Smith RC	.15	.04
96 Rick Helling	.15	.04
97 Roger Clemens	1.50	.45
98 Ron Gant	.30	.09
99 Kenny Felder RC	.15	.04
100 Steve Murphy RC	.15	.04
101 Mike Smith RC	.15	.04
102 Terry Pendleton	.30	.09
103 Tim Davis	.15	.04
104 Jeff Patzke RC	.15	.04
105 Craig Wilson	.15	.04
106 Tom Glavine	.50	.15
107 Mark Langston	.15	.04
108 Mark Thompson RC	.15	.04
109 Eric Owens RC	.50	.15
110 Keith Johnson RC	.15	.04
111 Robin Ventura	.30	.09
112 Ed Sprague	.15	.04
113 Jeff Schmidt RC	.15	.04
114 Don Wengert RC	.15	.04
115 Craig Biggio	.50	.15
116 Kenny Carlyle RC	.15	.04
117 Derek Jeter RC	20.00	6.00
118 Manuel Lee	.15	.04
119 Jeff Haas RC	.15	.04
120 Roger Bailey RC	.15	.04
121 Sean Lowe RC	.15	.04
122 Rick Aguilera	.15	.04
123 Sandy Alomar Jr.	.15	.04
124 Derek Wallace RC	.15	.04
125 B.J. Wallace	.15	.04
126 Greg Maddux	1.25	.35
127 Tim Moore RC	.15	.04
128 Lee Smith	.30	.09
129 Todd Steverson RC	.15	.04
130 Chris Widger RC	.50	.15
131 Paul Molitor	.50	.15
132 Chris Smith RC	.15	.04
133 Chris Gomez RC	.50	.15
134 Jimmy Baron RC	.15	.04
135 John Smoltz	.50	.15
136 Pat Borders	.15	.04
137 Donnie Leshnock	.15	.04
138 Gus Gandarillos RC	.15	.04
139 Will Clark	.75	.23
140 Ryan Luzinski RC	.15	.04
141 Cal Ripken	2.50	.75
142 B.J. Wallace	.15	.04
143 Trey Beamon RC	.50	.15
144 Norm Charlton	.15	.04
145 Mike Mussina	.50	.15
146 Billy Owens RC	.15	.04
147 Ozzie Smith	1.25	.35
148 Jason Kendall RC	1.50	.45
149 Mike Matthews RC	.15	.04
150 David Spykstra RC	.15	.04
151 Benji Grigsby RC	.15	.04
152 Sean Smith RC	.15	.04
153 Mark McGwire	2.00	.60
154 David Cone	.30	.09
155 Shon Walker RC	.15	.04
156 Jason Giambi	1.00	.30
157 Jack McDowell	.15	.04
158 Paxton Briley RC	.15	.04
159 Edgar Martinez	.50	.15
160 Brian Sackinsky RC	.15	.04
161 Barry Bonds	2.00	.60
162 Roberto Kelly	.15	.04
163 Jeff Alkire	.15	.04
164 Mike Sharperson	.15	.04
165 Jamie Taylor RC	.15	.04
166 John Saffer UER RC	.15	.04
167 Jerry Browne	.15	.04
168 Travis Fryman	.30	.09
169 Brady Anderson	.30	.09
170 Chris Roberts	.15	.04
171 Lloyd Peever RC	.15	.04
172 Francisco Cabrera	.15	.04
173 Ramiro Martinez RC	.15	.04
174 Jeff Alkire	.15	.04
175 Ivan Rodriguez	.75	.23
176 Kevin Brown	.30	.09
177 Chad Roper RC	.15	.04
178 Rod Henderson RC	.15	.04
179 Dennis Eckersley	.30	.09
180 Shannon Stewart RC	1.50	.45
181 DeShawn Warren RC	.15	.04
182 Lonnie Smith	.15	.04
183 Willie Adams	.15	.04
184 Jeff Montgomery	.15	.04
185 Damon Hollins RC	.15	.04
186 Byron Mathews RC	.15	.04
187 Harold Baines	.30	.09
188 Rick Greene	.15	.04
189 Carlos Baerga	.15	.04
190 Brandon Cromer RC	.15	.04
191 Roberto Alomar	.50	.15
192 Rich Ireland RC	.15	.04
193 S.Montgomery RC	.15	.04
194 Brant Brown RC	.15	.04
195 Ritchie Moody RC	.15	.04
196 Michael Tucker	.30	.09
197 Jason Varitek	3.00	.90
198 David Manning RC	.15	.04
199 Marquis Riley RC	.15	.04
200 Jason Giambi	1.00	.30

1993 Stadium Club Murphy Master Photos

One Murphy Master Photo was included in each 1993 Stadium Club Murphy Special factory set. Each of these twelve uncropped Murphy Master Photos is inlaid in a 5" by 7" white frame and bordered with a prismatic foil trim. The photo within parallels the corresponding player's regular issue Murphy card. The cards are unnumbered and checklisted below in alphabetical order.

	Nm-Mt	Ex-Mt
COMPLETE SET (12)	5.00	1.50

1 Sandy Alomar Jr. AS .15 .04
2 Tom Glavine AS .50 .15
3 Ken Griffey Jr. AS 1.25 .35
4 Tony Gwynn AS 1.00 .30
5 Chuck Knoblauch AS .30 .09
6 Chad Mottola '92 .50 .15
7 Kirby Puckett AS .75 .23
8 Chris Roberts USA .15 .04
9 Ryne Sandberg AS 1.25 .35
10 Gary Sheffield AS .30 .09
11 Larry Walker AS .50 .15
12 Preston Wilson '92 2.00 .60

1993 Stadium Club

The 1993 Stadium Club baseball set consists of 750 standard-size cards issued in three series of 300, 300, and 150 cards respectively. Each series closes with a Members Choice subset (291-300, 591-600, and 746-750.

	Nm-Mt	Ex-Mt
COMPLETE SET (750)	50.00	15.00
COMP.SERIES 1 (300)	15.00	4.50
COMP.SERIES 2 (300)	20.00	6.00
COMP.SERIES 3 (150)	15.00	4.50

1 Pat Borders .15 .04
2 Greg Maddux 1.25 .35
3 Daryl Boston .15 .04
4 Bob Ayrault .15 .04
5 Tony Phillips IF .15 .04
6 Damion Easley .15 .04
7 Kip Gross .15 .04
8 Jim Thome .75 .23
9 Tim Belcher .15 .04
10 Gary Wayne .15 .04
11 Sam Militello .15 .04
12 Mike Magnante .15 .04
13 Tim Wakefield .75 .23
14 Tim Hulett .15 .04
15 Rheal Cormier .15 .04
16 Juan Guerrero .15 .04
17 Rich Gossage .30 .09
18 Tim Laker RC .15 .04
19 Darrin Jackson .15 .04
20 Jack Clark .30 .09
21 Roberto Hernandez .15 .04
22 Dean Palmer .30 .09
23 Harold Reynolds .30 .09
24 Dan Plesac .15 .04
25 Brent Mayne .15 .04
26 Pat Hentgen .15 .04
27 Luis Sojo .15 .04
28 Ron Gant .30 .09
29 Paul Gibson .15 .04
30 Bip Roberts .15 .04
31 Mickey Tettleton .15 .04
32 Randy Velarde .15 .04
33 Brian McRae .15 .04
34 Wes Chamberlain .15 .04
35 Wayne Kirby .15 .04
36 Rey Sanchez .15 .04
37 Jesse Orosco .15 .04
38 Mike Stanton .15 .04
39 Royce Clayton .15 .04
40 Cal Ripken UER 2.50 .75
(Place of birth Havre de Grave; should be Havre de Grace)
41 John Dopson .15 .04
42 Gene Larkin .15 .04
43 Tim Raines .30 .09
44 Randy Myers .15 .04
45 Clay Parker .15 .04
46 Mike Scioscia .15 .04
47 Pete Incaviglia .15 .04
48 Todd Van Poppel .15 .04
49 Ray Lankford .15 .04
50 Eddie Murray .75 .23
51 Barry Bonds COR 2.00 .60
51A Barry Bonds ERR 2.00 .60
(Missing four stars over name to indicate NL MVP)
52 Gary Thurman .15 .04
53 Bob Wickman .15 .04
54 Joey Cora .15 .04
55 Kenny Rogers .30 .09
56 Mike Devereaux .15 .04
57 Kevin Seitzer .15 .04
58 Rafael Belliard .15 .04
59 David Wells .30 .09
60 Mark Clark .15 .04
61 Carlos Baerga .15 .04
62 Scott Brosius .30 .09
63 Jeff Grotewold .15 .04
64 Rick Wrona .15 .04
65 Kurt Knudsen .15 .04
66 Lloyd McClendon .15 .04
67 Omar Vizquel .50 .15
68 Jose Vizcaino .15 .04
69 Rob Ducey .15 .04
70 Casey Candaele .15 .04
71 Ramon Martinez .15 .04
72 Todd Hundley .15 .04
73 John Marzano .15 .04
74 Derek Parks .15 .04
75 Jack McDowell .15 .04
76 Tim Scott .15 .04
77 Mike Mussina .50 .15
78 Delino DeShields .15 .04
79 Chris Bosio .15 .04
80 Mike Bordick .15 .04
81 Rod Beck .15 .04
82 Ted Power .15 .04
83 John Kruk .30 .09
84 Steve Shifflett .15 .04
85 Danny Tartabull .15 .04
86 Mike Greenwell .15 .04
87 Jose Melendez .15 .04
88 Craig Wilson .15 .04
89 Melvin Nieves .15 .04
90 Ed Sprague .15 .04
91 Willie McGee .30 .09
92 Joe Orsulak .15 .04
93 Jeff King .15 .04
94 Dan Pasqua .15 .04
95 Brian Harper .15 .04
96 Joe Oliver .15 .04
97 Shane Turner .15 .04
98 Lenny Harris .15 .04
99 Jeff Parrett .15 .04
100 Luis Polonia .15 .04
101 Kent Bottenfield .15 .04
102 Albert Belle .30 .09
103 Mike Maddux .15 .04
104 Randy Tomlin .15 .04
105 Andy Stankiewicz .15 .04
106 Rico Rossy .15 .04
107 Joe Hesketh .15 .04
108 Dennis Powell .15 .04
109 Derrick May .15 .04
110 Pete Harnisch .15 .04
111 Kent Mercker .15 .04
112 Scott Fletcher .15 .04
113 Rex Hudler .15 .04
114 Chico Walker .15 .04
115 Rafael Palmeiro .50 .15
116 Mark Leiter .15 .04
117 Pedro Munoz .15 .04
118 Jim Bullinger .15 .04
119 Ivan Calderon .15 .04
120 Mike Timlin .15 .04
121 Rene Gonzales .15 .04
122 Greg Vaughn .15 .04
123 Mike Flanagan .15 .04
124 Mike Hartley .15 .04
125 Jeff Montgomery .15 .04
126 Mike Gallego .15 .04
127 Don Slaught .15 .04
128 Charlie O'Brien .15 .04
129 Jose Offerman .15 .04
(Can be found with home town missing on back)
130 Mark Wohlers .15 .04
131 Eric Fox .15 .04
132 Doug Strange .15 .04
133 Jeff Frye .15 .04
134 Wade Boggs UER .50 .15
(Redundantly lists lefty breakdown)
135 Lou Whitaker .30 .09
136 Craig Grebeck .15 .04
137 Rich Rodriguez .15 .04
138 Jay Bell .30 .09
139 Felix Fermin .15 .04
140 Dennis Martinez .30 .09
141 Eric Anthony .15 .04
142 Roberto Alomar .50 .15
143 Darren Lewis .15 .04
144 Mike Blowers .15 .04
145 Scott Bankhead .15 .04
146 Jeff Reboulet .15 .04
147 Frank Viola .30 .09
148 Bill Pecota .15 .04
149 Carlos Hernandez .15 .04
150 Bobby Witt .15 .04
151 Sid Bream .15 .04
152 Todd Zeile .15 .04
153 Dennis Cook .15 .04
154 Brian Bohanon .15 .04
155 Pat Kelly .15 .04
156 Milt Cuyler .15 .04
157 Juan Bell .15 .04
158 Randy Milligan .15 .04
159 Mark Gardner .15 .04
160 Pat Tabler .15 .04
161 Jeff Reardon .30 .09
162 Ken Patterson .15 .04
163 Bobby Bonilla .30 .09
164 Tony Pena .15 .04
165 Greg Swindell .15 .04
166 Kirk McCaskill .15 .04
167 Doug Drabek .15 .04
168 Franklin Stubbs .15 .04
169 Ron Tingley .15 .04
170 Willie Banks .15 .04
171 Sergio Valdez .15 .04
172 Mark Lemke .15 .04
173 Robin Yount 1.25 .35
174 Storm Davis .15 .04
175 Dan Walters .15 .04
176 Steve Farr .15 .04
177 Curt Wilkerson .15 .04
178 Luis Alicea .15 .04
179 Russ Swan .15 .04
180 Mitch Williams .15 .04
181 Wilson Alvarez .15 .04
182 Carl Willis .15 .04
183 Craig Biggio .50 .15
184 Sean Berry .15 .04
185 Trevor Wilson .15 .04
186 Jeff Tackett .15 .04
187 Ellis Burks .30 .09
188 Jeff Branson .15 .04
189 Matt Nokes .15 .04
190 John Smiley .15 .04
191 Danny Gladden .15 .04
192 Mike Boddicker .15 .04
193 Roger Pavlik .15 .04
194 Paul Sorrento .15 .04
195 Vince Coleman .15 .04
196 Gary DiSarcina .15 .04
197 Rafael Bournigal .15 .04
198 Mike Schooler .15 .04
199 Scott Ruskin .15 .04
200 Frank Thomas .75 .23
201 Kyle Abbott .15 .04
202 Mike Perez .15 .04
203 Andre Dawson .30 .09
204 Bill Swift .15 .04
205 Alejandro Pena .15 .04
206 Dave Winfield .30 .09
207 Andujar Cedeno .15 .04
208 Terry Steinbach .15 .04
209 Chris Hammond .15 .04
210 Todd Burns .15 .04
211 Hipolito Pichardo .15 .04
212 John Kiely .15 .04
213 Tim Teufel .15 .04
214 Lee Guetterman .15 .04
215 Geronimo Pena .15 .04
216 Brett Butler .30 .09
217 Bryan Hickerson .15 .04
218 Rick Trlicek .15 .04
219 Lee Stevens .15 .04
220 Roger Clemens 1.50 .45
221 Carlton Fisk .50 .15
222 Chili Davis .30 .09
223 Walt Terrell .15 .04
224 Jim Eisenreich .15 .04
225 Ricky Bones .15 .04
226 Henry Rodriguez .15 .04
227 Ken Hill .15 .04
228 Rick Wilkins .15 .04
229 Ricky Jordan .15 .04
230 Bernard Gilkey .15 .04
231 Tim Fortugno .15 .04
232 Geno Petralli .15 .04
233 Jose Rijo .15 .04
234 Jim Leyritz .15 .04
235 Kevin Campbell .15 .04
236 Al Osuna .15 .04
237 Pete Smith .15 .04
238 Pete Schourek .15 .04
239 Moises Alou .30 .09
240 Donn Pall .15 .04
241 Denny Neagle .30 .09
242 Dan Peltier .15 .04
243 Scott Scudder .15 .04
244 Juan Guzman .15 .04
245 Dave Burba .15 .04
246 Rick Sutcliffe .30 .09
247 Tony Fossas .15 .04
248 Mike Munoz .15 .04
249 Tim Salmon .50 .15
250 Rob Murphy .15 .04
251 Roger McDowell .15 .04
252 Lance Parrish .30 .09
253 Cliff Brantley .15 .04
254 Scott Leius .15 .04
255 Carlos Martinez .15 .04
256 Vince Horsman .15 .04
257 Oscar Azocar .15 .04
258 Craig Shipley .15 .04
259 Ben McDonald .15 .04
260 Jeff Brantley .15 .04
261 Damon Berryhill .15 .04
262 Joe Grahe .15 .04
263 Dave Hansen .15 .04
264 Rich Amaral .15 .04
265 Tim Pugh RC .15 .04
266 Dion James .15 .04
267 Frank Tanana .15 .04
268 Stan Belinda .15 .04
269 Jeff Kent .75 .23
270 Bruce Ruffin .15 .04
271 Xavier Hernandez .15 .04
272 Darrin Fletcher .15 .04
273 Tino Martinez .50 .15
274 Benny Santiago .30 .09
275 Scott Radinsky .15 .04
276 Mariano Duncan .15 .04
277 Kenny Lofton .30 .09
278 Dwight Smith .15 .04
279 Joe Carter .30 .09
280 Tim Jones .15 .04
281 Jeff Huson .15 .04
282 Phil Plantier .15 .04
283 Kirby Puckett .75 .23
284 Johnny Guzman .15 .04
285 Mike Morgan .15 .04
286 Chris Sabo .15 .04
287 Matt Williams .30 .09
288 Checklist 1-100 .15 .04
289 Checklist 101-200 .15 .04
290 Checklist 201-300 .15 .04
291 Dennis Eckersley MC .30 .09
292 Eric Karros MC .15 .04
293 Pat Listach MC .15 .04
294 Andy Van Slyke MC .15 .04
295 Robin Ventura MC .15 .04
296 Tom Glavine MC .30 .09
297 J.Gonzalez MC UER .30 .09
Misspelled Gonzales
298 Travis Fryman MC .15 .04
299 Larry Walker MC .50 .15
300 Gary Sheffield MC .15 .04
301 Chuck Finley .30 .09
302 Luis Gonzalez .30 .09
303 Darryl Hamilton .15 .04
304 Bien Figueroa .15 .04
305 Ron Darling .15 .04
306 Jonathan Hurst .15 .04
307 Mike Sharperson .15 .04
308 Mike Christopher .15 .04
309 Marvin Freeman .15 .04
310 Jay Buhner .30 .09
311 Butch Henry .15 .04
312 Greg W. Harris .15 .04
313 Darren Daulton .30 .09
314 Chuck Knoblauch .30 .09
315 Greg A. Harris .15 .04
316 John Franco .30 .09
317 John Wehner .15 .04
318 Donald Harris .15 .04
319 Benny Santiago .30 .09
320 Larry Walker .50 .15
321 Randy Knorr .15 .04
322 Ramon Martinez RC .15 .04
323 Mike Stanley .15 .04
324 Bill Wegman .15 .04
325 Tom Candiotti .15 .04
326 Glenn Davis .15 .04
327 Chuck Crim .15 .04
328 Scott Livingstone .15 .04
329 Eddie Taubensee .15 .04
330 George Bell .15 .04
331 Edgar Martinez .50 .15
332 Paul Assenmacher .15 .04
333 Steve Hosey .15 .04
334 Mo Vaughn .30 .09
335 Bret Saberhagen .30 .09
336 Mike Trombley .15 .04
337 Mark Lewis .15 .04
338 Terry Pendleton .30 .09
339 Dave Hollins .15 .04
340 Jeff Conine .30 .09
341 Bob Tewksbury .15 .04
342 Billy Ashley .15 .04
343 Zane Smith .15 .04
344 John Wetteland .30 .09
345 Chris Hoiles .15 .04
346 Frank Castillo .15 .04
347 Bruce Hurst .15 .04
348 Kevin McReynolds .15 .04
349 Dave Henderson .15 .04
350 Ryan Bowen .15 .04
351 Sid Fernandez .15 .04
352 Mark Whiten .15 .04
353 Nolan Ryan 3.00 .90
354 Rick Aguilera .15 .04
355 Mark Langston .15 .04
356 Jack Morris .30 .09
357 Rob Deer .15 .04
358 Dave Fleming .15 .04
359 Lance Johnson .15 .04
360 Joe Millette .15 .04
361 Wil Cordero .15 .04
362 Chito Martinez .15 .04
363 Scott Servais .15 .04
364 Bernie Williams .50 .15
365 Pedro Martinez 1.50 .45
366 Ryne Sandberg 1.25 .35
367 Brad Ausmus .15 .04
368 Scott Cooper .15 .04
369 Rob Dibble .30 .09
370 Walt Weiss .15 .04
371 Mark Davis .15 .04
372 Orlando Merced .15 .04
373 Mike Jackson .15 .04
374 Kevin Appier .30 .09
375 Esteban Beltre .15 .04
376 Joe Slusarski .15 .04
377 William Suero .15 .04
378 Pete O'Brien .15 .04
379 Alan Embree .75 .23
380 Lenny Webster .15 .04
381 Eric Davis .30 .09
382 Duane Ward .15 .04
383 John Habyan .15 .04
384 Jeff Bagwell .50 .15
385 Ruben Amaro .15 .04
386 Julio Valera .15 .04
387 Robin Ventura .30 .09
388 Archi Cianfrocco .15 .04
389 Skeeter Barnes .15 .04
390 Tim Costo .15 .04
391 Luis Mercedes .15 .04
392 Jeremy Hernandez .15 .04
393 Shawon Dunston .15 .04
394 Andy Van Slyke .30 .09
395 Kevin Maas .15 .04
396 Kevin Brown .30 .09
397 J.T. Bruett .15 .04
398 Darryl Strawberry .30 .09
399 Tom Pagnozzi .15 .04
400 Sandy Alomar Jr. .15 .04
401 Keith Miller .15 .04
402 Rich DeLucia .15 .04
403 Shawn Abner .15 .04
404 Howard Johnson .15 .04
405 Mike Benjamin .15 .04
406 Roberto Mejia RC .15 .04
407 Mike Butcher .15 .04
408 Deion Sanders UER .50 .15
(Braves on front and Yankees on back)
409 Todd Stottlemyre .15 .04
410 Scott Kamieniecki .15 .04
411 Doug Jones .15 .04
412 John Burkett .15 .04
413 Lance Blankenship .15 .04
414 Jeff Parrett .15 .04
415 Barry Larkin .50 .15
416 Alan Trammell .30 .09
417 Mark Kiefer .15 .04
418 Gregg Olson .15 .04
419 Mark Grace .50 .15
420 Shane Mack .15 .04
421 Bob Walk .15 .04
422 Curt Schilling .30 .09
423 Erik Hanson .15 .04
424 George Brett 2.00 .60
425 Reggie Jefferson .15 .04
426 Mark Portugal .15 .04
427 Ron Karkovice .15 .04
428 Matt Young .15 .04
429 Troy Neel .15 .04
430 Hector Fajardo .15 .04
431 Dave Righetti .30 .09
432 Pat Listach .15 .04
433 Jeff Innis .15 .04
434 Bob MacDonald .15 .04
435 Brian Jordan .30 .09
436 Jeff Blauser .15 .04
437 Mike Myers RC .15 .04
438 Frank Seminara .15 .04
439 Rusty Meacham .15 .04
440 Greg Briley .15 .04
441 Derek Lilliquist .15 .04
442 John Vander Wal .15 .04
443 Scott Erickson .15 .04
444 Bob Scanlan .15 .04
445 Todd Frohwirth .15 .04
446 Tom Goodwin .15 .04
447 William Pennyfeather .15 .04
448 Travis Fryman .30 .09
449 Mickey Morandini .15 .04
450 Greg Olson .15 .04
451 Trevor Hoffman .30 .09
452 Dave Magadan .15 .04
453 Shawn Jeter .15 .04
454 Andres Galarraga .30 .09
455 Ted Wood .15 .04
456 Freddie Benavides .15 .04
457 Junior Felix .15 .04
458 Alex Cole .15 .04
459 John Orton .15 .04
460 Eddie Zosky .15 .04
461 Dennis Eckersley .30 .09
462 Lee Smith .30 .09
463 John Smoltz .50 .15
464 Ken Caminiti .30 .09
465 Melido Perez .15 .04
466 Tom Marsh .15 .04
467 Jeff Nelson .15 .04
468 Jesse Levis .15 .04
469 Chris Nabholz .15 .04
470 Mike Macfarlane .15 .04
471 Reggie Sanders .15 .04
472 Chuck McElroy .15 .04
473 Kevin Gross .15 .04
474 Matt Whiteside RC .15 .04
475 Cal Eldred .15 .04
476 Dave Gallagher .15 .04
477 Len Dykstra .30 .09
478 Mark McGwire 2.00 .60
479 David Segui .15 .04
480 Mike Henneman .15 .04
481 Bret Barberie .15 .04
482 Steve Sax .15 .04
483 Dave Valle .15 .04
484 Danny Darwin .15 .04
485 Devon White .30 .09
486 Eric Plunk .15 .04
487 Jim Gott .15 .04
488 Scooter Tucker .15 .04
489 Omar Olivares .15 .04
490 Greg Myers .15 .04
491 Brian Hunter .15 .04
492 Kevin Tapani .15 .04
493 Rich Monteleone .15 .04
494 Steve Buechele .15 .04
495 Bo Jackson .75 .23
496 Mike LaValliere .15 .04
497 Mark Leonard .15 .04
498 Daryl Boston .15 .04
499 Jose Canseco .75 .23
500 Brian Barnes .15 .04
501 Randy Johnson .75 .23
502 Tim McIntosh .15 .04
503 Cecil Fielder .30 .09
504 Derek Bell .15 .04
505 Kevin Koslofski .15 .04
506 Darren Holmes .15 .04
507 Brady Anderson .30 .09
508 John Valentin .15 .04
509 Jerry Browne .15 .04
510 Fred McGriff .50 .15
511 Pedro Astacio .15 .04
512 Gary Gaetti .30 .09
513 John Burke RC .15 .04
514 Dwight Gooden .30 .09
515 Thomas Howard .15 .04
516 D.Whitmore RC UER .15 .04
11 games played in 1992; should be 121
517 Ozzie Guillen .15 .04
518 Darryl Kile .30 .09
519 Rich Rowland .15 .04
520 Carlos Delgado .75 .23
521 Doug Henry .15 .04
522 Greg Colbrunn .15 .04
523 Tom Gordon .15 .04
524 Ivan Rodriguez .75 .23
525 Kent Hrbek .30 .09
526 Eric Young .15 .04
527 Rod Brewer .15 .04
528 Eric Karros .30 .09
529 Marquis Grissom .30 .09
530 Rico Brogna .15 .04
531 Sammy Sosa 1.25 .35
532 Bret Boone .50 .15
533 Luis Rivera .15 .04
534 Hal Morris .15 .04
535 Monty Fariss .15 .04
536 Leo Gomez .15 .04
537 Wally Joyner .30 .09
538 Tony Gwynn 1.00 .30
539 Mike Williams .15 .04
540 Juan Gonzalez .50 .15
541 Ryan Klesko .30 .09
542 Ryan Thompson .15 .04
543 Chad Curtis .15 .04
544 Orel Hershiser .30 .09
545 Carlos Garcia .15 .04
546 Bob Welch .15 .04
547 Vinny Castilla .30 .09
548 Ozzie Smith 1.25 .35
549 Luis Salazar .15 .04
550 Mark Guthrie .15 .04
551 Charles Nagy .15 .04
552 Alex Fernandez .15 .04
553 Mel Rojas .15 .04
554 Orestes Destrade .15 .04
555 Mark Gubicza .15 .04
556 Steve Finley .30 .09
557 Don Mattingly 2.00 .60
558 Rickey Henderson .75 .23
559 Tommy Greene .15 .04
560 Arthur Rhodes .15 .04
561 Alfredo Griffin .15 .04
562 Will Clark .75 .23
563 Bob Zupcic .15 .04
564 Chuck Carr .15 .04
565 Henry Cotto .15 .04
566 Billy Spiers .15 .04
567 Jack Armstrong .15 .04
568 Kurt Stillwell .15 .04
569 David McCarty .15 .04
570 Joe Vitiello .15 .04
571 Gerald Williams .15 .04
572 Dale Murphy .75 .23
573 Scott Aldred .15 .04
574 Bill Gullickson .15 .04
575 Bobby Thigpen .15 .04
576 Glenallen Hill .15 .04
577 Dwayne Henry .15 .04
578 Calvin Jones .15 .04
579 Al Martin .15 .04
580 Ruben Sierra .15 .04
581 Andy Benes .15 .04
582 Anthony Young .15 .04
583 Shawn Boskie .15 .04
584 Scott Pose RC .15 .04
585 Mike Piazza 2.00 .60
586 Donovan Osborne .15 .04
587 Jim Austin .15 .04

588 Checklist 301-400 .15 .04
589 Checklist 401-500 .15 .04
590 Checklist 501-600 .15 .04
591 Ken Griffey Jr. MC .75 .23
592 Ivan Rodriguez MC .50 .15
593 Carlos Baerga MC .15 .04
594 Fred McGriff MC .30 .09
595 Mark McGwire MC 1.00 .30
596 Roberto Alomar MC .30 .09
597 Kirby Puckett MC .50 .15
598 Marquis Grissom MC .15 .04
599 John Smoltz MC .30 .09
600 Ryne Sandberg MC .75 .23
601 Wade Boggs .50 .15
602 Jeff Reardon .30 .09
603 Billy Ripken .15 .04
604 Bryan Harvey .15 .04
605 Carlos Quintana .15 .04
606 Greg Hibbard .15 .04
607 Ellis Burks .30 .09
608 Greg Swindell .15 .04
609 Dave Winfield .30 .09
610 Charlie Hough .30 .09
611 Chili Davis .30 .09
612 Jody Reed .15 .04
613 Mark Williamson .15 .04
614 Phil Plantier .15 .04
615 Jim Abbott .50 .15
616 Dante Bichette .30 .09
617 Mark Eichhorn .15 .04
618 Gary Sheffield .30 .09
619 Richie Lewis RC .15 .04
620 Joe Girardi .15 .04
621 Jaime Navarro .15 .04
622 Willie Wilson .15 .04
623 Scott Fletcher .15 .04
624 Bud Black .15 .04
625 Tom Brunansky .15 .04
626 Steve Avery .15 .04
627 Paul Molitor .50 .15
628 Gregg Jefferies .15 .04
629 Dave Stewart .30 .09
630 Javier Lopez .50 .15
631 Greg Gagne .15 .04
632 Roberto Kelly .15 .04
633 Mike Fetters .15 .04
634 Ozzie Canseco .15 .04
635 Jeff Russell .15 .04
636 Pete Incaviglia .15 .04
637 Tom Henke .15 .04
638 Chipper Jones .75 .23
639 Jimmy Key .30 .09
640 Dave Martinez .15 .04
641 Dave Stieb .15 .04
642 Milt Thompson .15 .04
643 Alan Mills .15 .04
644 Tony Fernandez .15 .04
645 Randy Bush .15 .04
646 Joe Magrane .15 .04
647 Ivan Calderon .15 .04
648 Jose Guzman .15 .04
649 John Olerud .30 .09
650 Tom Glavine .50 .15
651 Julio Franco .30 .09
652 Armando Reynoso .15 .04
653 Felix Jose .15 .04
654 Ben Rivera .15 .04
655 Andre Dawson .30 .09
656 Mike Harkey .15 .04
657 Kevin Seitzer .15 .04
658 Lonnie Smith .15 .04
659 Norm Charlton .15 .04
660 David Justice .30 .09
661 Fernando Valenzuela .30 .09
662 Dan Wilson .30 .09
663 Mark Gardner .15 .04
664 Doug Dascenzo .15 .04
665 Greg Maddux 1.25 .35
666 Harold Baines .30 .09
667 Randy Myers .15 .04
668 Harold Reynolds .30 .09
669 Candy Maldonado .15 .04
670 Al Leiter .30 .09
671 Jerald Clark .15 .04
672 Doug Drabek .15 .04
673 Kirk Gibson .30 .09
674 Steve Reed RC .15 .04
675 Mike Felder .15 .04
676 Ricky Gutierrez .15 .04
677 Spike Owen .15 .04
678 Otis Nixon .15 .04
679 Scott Sanderson .15 .04
680 Mark Carreon .15 .04
681 Troy Percival .50 .15
682 Kevin Stocker .15 .04
683 Jim Converse RC .15 .04
684 Barry Bonds 2.00 .60
685 Greg Gohr .15 .04
686 Tim Wallach .15 .04
687 Matt Mieske .15 .04
688 Robby Thompson .15 .04
689 Brien Taylor .15 .04
690 Kirt Manwaring .15 .04
691 Mike Lansing RC .30 .09
692 Steve Decker .15 .04
693 Mike Moore .15 .04
694 Kevin Mitchell .15 .04
695 Phil Hiatt .15 .04
696 Tony Tarasco RC .15 .04
697 Benji Gil .15 .04
698 Jeff Juden .15 .04
699 Kevin Reimer .15 .04
700 Andy Ashby .15 .04
701 John Jaha .15 .04
702 Tim Bogar RC .15 .04
703 David Cone .30 .09
704 Willie Greene .15 .04
705 David Hulse RC .15 .04
706 Cris Carpenter .15 .04
707 Ken Griffey Jr. 1.25 .35
708 Steve Bedrosian .15 .04
709 Dave Nilsson .15 .04
710 Paul Wagner .15 .04
711 B.J. Surhoff .30 .09
712 Rene Arocha RC .30 .09
713 Manuel Lee .15 .04
714 Brian Williams .15 .04
715 Sherman Obando RC .15 .04
716 Terry Mulholland .15 .04
717 Paul O'Neill .50 .15
718 David Nied .15 .04
719 J.T. Snow RC .50 .15
720 Nigel Wilson .15 .04
721 Mike Bielecki .15 .04
722 Kevin Young .30 .09
723 Charlie Leibrandt .15 .04
724 Frank Bolick .15 .04
725 Jon Shave RC .15 .04
726 Steve Cooke .15 .04
727 Domingo Martinez RC .15 .04
728 Todd Worrell .15 .04
729 Jose Lind .15 .04
730 Jim Tatum RC .15 .04
731 Mike Hampton .30 .09
732 Mike Draper .15 .04
733 Henry Mercedes .15 .04
734 John Johnstone RC .15 .04
735 Mitch Webster .15 .04
736 Russ Springer .15 .04
737 Rob Natal .15 .04
738 Steve Howe .15 .04
739 Darrell Sherman RC .15 .04
740 Pat Mahomes .15 .04
741 Alex Arias .15 .04
742 Damon Buford .15 .04
743 Charlie Hayes .15 .04
744 Guillermo Velasquez .15 .04
745 CL 601-750 UER .15 .04
650 Tom Glavine
746 Frank Thomas MC .50 .15
747 Barry Bonds MC 1.00 .30
748 Roger Clemens MC .75 .23
749 Joe Carter MC .15 .04
750 Greg Maddux MC .75 .23

1993 Stadium Club First Day Issue

Two thousand of each 1993 Stadium Club baseball card were produced on the first day and then randomly inserted in packs at a rate of 1:24. These standard-size cards are identical to the regular-issue 1993 Stadium Club cards, except for the embossed prismatic-foil "1st Day Production" logo stamped in an upper corner. Some of the logos have been transferred from "common" 1st day cards to the fronts of better players.

Nm-Mt Ex-Mt
*STARS: 8X TO 20X BASIC CARDS....

1993 Stadium Club Inserts

This 10-card set was randomly inserted in all series of Stadium Club packs, the first four in series 1, the second four in series 2 and the last two in series 3. The themes of the standard-size cards differ from series to series, but the basic design -- borderless color action shots on the fronts -- remains the same throughout. The series 1 and 3 cards are numbered on the back, the series 2 cards are unnumbered. No matter what series, all of these inserts were included one every 15 packs.

Nm-Mt Ex-Mt
COMPLETE SERIES 1 (4) 2.00 .60
COMPLETE SERIES 2 (4) 10.00 3.00
COMPLETE SERIES 3 (2) .50 .15
COMMON SER.1 (A1-A4) .30 .09
COMMON SER.2 (B1-B4) .30 .09
COMMON SER.3 (C1-C2) .30 .09
A1 Robin Yount 2.50 .75
A2 George Brett 4.00 1.20
A3 David Nied FDP .30 .09
A4 Nigel Wilson FDP .30 .09
B1 Will Clark 4.00 1.20
Mark McGwire
B2 Dwight Gooden 4.00 1.20
Don Mattingly
B3 Ryne Sandberg 1.50 .45
Frank Thomas
B4 Darryl Strawberry 2.50 .75
Ken Griffey Jr.
C1 David Nied UER .30 .09
Colorado Rockies Firsts
(Misspelled pitch-
hitter on back)
C2 Charlie Hough .60 .18

1993 Stadium Club Master Photos

Each of the three Stadium Club series features Master Photos, uncropped versions of the regular Stadium Club cards. Each Master Photo is inlaid in a 5" by 7" white frame and bordered with a prismatic foil trim. The Master Photos were made available to the public in two ways. First, one in every 24 packs included a Master Photo winner card redeemable for a group of three Master Photos until Jan. 31, 1994. Second, each hobby box contained one Master Photo. The cards are unnumbered and checklisted below in alphabetical order within series I (1-12), II (13-24), and III (25-30). Two different versions of these master photos were issued, one with and one without the "Members Only" gold foil seal at the upper right corner. The "Members Only" Master Photos were only available with the direct-mail solicited 750-card Stadium Club Members Only set.

Nm-Mt Ex-Mt
COMPLETE SERIES 1 (12) 6.00 1.80
COMPLETE SERIES 2 (12) 8.00 2.40
COMPLETE SERIES 3 (6) 10.00 3.00
1 Carlos Baerga .25 .07
2 Delino DeShields .25 .07
3 Brian McRae .25 .07
4 Sam Militello .25 .07
5 Joe Oliver .25 .07
6 Kirby Puckett 1.25 .35
7 Cal Ripken 4.00 1.20
8 Bip Roberts .25 .07
9 Mike Scioscia .25 .07
10 Rick Sutcliffe .50 .15
11 Danny Tartabull .25 .07
12 Tim Wakefield 1.25 .35
13 George Brett 3.00 .90
14 Jose Canseco 1.25 .35
15 Will Clark 1.25 .35
16 Travis Fryman .50 .15
17 Dwight Gooden .50 .15
18 Mark Grace .75 .23
19 Rickey Henderson 1.25 .35
20 Mark McGwire MC 3.00 .90
21 Nolan Ryan 5.00 1.50
22 Ruben Sierra .25 .07
23 Darryl Strawberry .50 .15
24 Larry Walker .75 .23
25 Barry Bonds 3.00 .90
26 Ken Griffey Jr. 2.00 .60
27 Greg Maddux 2.00 .60
28 David Nied .25 .07
29 J.T. Snow .75 .23
30 Brien Taylor .25 .07

1994 Stadium Club

The 720 standard-size cards comprising this set were issued two series of 270 and a third series of 180. There are a number of subsets including Home Run Club (258-268), Tale of Two Players (525/526), Division Leaders (527-532), Quick Starts (533-538), Career Contributors (541-543), Rookie Rocker (626-630), Rookie Rocket (631-634) and Fantastic Finishes (714-719). Rookie Cards include Jeff Cirillo and Chan Ho Park.

Nm-Mt Ex-Mt
COMPLETE SET (720) 55.00 16.50
COMP.SERIES 1 (270) 20.00 6.00
COMP.SERIES 2 (270) 20.00 6.00
COMP.SERIES 3 (180) 15.00 4.50
1 Robin Yount 1.25 .35
2 Rick Wilkins .15 .04
3 Steve Scarsone .15 .04
4 Gary Sheffield .30 .09
5 George Brett UER 2.00 .60
(birthdate listed as 1963;
should be 1953)
6 Al Martin .15 .04
7 Joe Oliver .15 .04
8 Stan Belinda .15 .04
9 Denny Hocking .15 .04
10 Roberto Alomar .50 .15
11 Luis Polonia .15 .04
12 Scott Hemond .15 .04
13 Jody Reed .15 .04
14 Mel Rojas .15 .04
15 Junior Ortiz .15 .04
16 Harold Baines .30 .09
17 Brad Pennington .15 .04
18 Jay Bell .30 .09
19 Tom Henke .15 .04
20 Jeff Branson .15 .04
21 Roberto Mejia .15 .04
22 Pedro Munoz .15 .04
23 Matt Nokes .15 .04
24 Jack McDowell .15 .04
25 Cecil Fielder .30 .09
26 Tony Fossas .15 .04
27 Jim Eisenreich .15 .04
28 Anthony Young .15 .04
29 Chuck Carr .15 .04
30 Jeff Treadway .15 .04
31 Chris Nabholz .15 .04
32 Tom Candiotti .15 .04
33 Mike Maddux .15 .04
34 Nolan Ryan 3.00 .90
35 Luis Gonzalez .30 .09
36 Tim Salmon .50 .15
37 Mark Whiten .15 .04
38 Roger McDowell .15 .04
39 Royce Clayton .15 .04
40 Troy Neel .15 .04
41 Mike Harkey .15 .04
42 Darrin Fletcher .15 .04
43 Wayne Kirby .15 .04
44 Rich Amaral .15 .04
45 Robb Nen UER .30 .09
(Nenn on back)
46 Tim Teufel .15 .04
47 Steve Cooke .15 .04
48 Jeff McNeely .15 .04
49 Jeff Montgomery .15 .04
50 Skeeter Barnes .15 .04
51 Scott Stahoviak .15 .04
52 Pat Kelly .15 .04
53 Brady Anderson .30 .09
54 Mariano Duncan .15 .04
55 Brian Bohanon .15 .04
56 Jerry Spradlin .15 .04
57 Ron Karkovice .15 .04
58 Jeff Gardner .15 .04
59 Bobby Bonilla .30 .09
60 Tino Martinez .50 .15
61 Todd Benzinger .15 .04
62 Steve Trachsel .15 .04
63 Brian Jordan .30 .09
64 Steve Bedrosian .15 .04
65 Brent Gates .15 .04
66 Shawn Green .75 .23
67 Sean Berry .15 .04
68 Joe Klink .15 .04
69 Fernando Valenzuela .30 .09
70 Andy Tomberlin .15 .04
71 Tony Pena .15 .04
72 Eric Young .15 .04
73 Chris Gomez .15 .04
74 Paul O'Neill .50 .15
75 Ricky Gutierrez .15 .04
76 Brad Holman .15 .04
77 Lance Painter .15 .04
78 Mike Butcher .15 .04
79 Sid Bream .15 .04
80 Sammy Sosa 1.25 .35
81 Felix Fermin .15 .04
82 Todd Hundley .15 .04
83 Kevin Higgins .15 .04
84 Todd Pratt .15 .04
85 Ken Griffey Jr. 1.25 .35
86 John O'Donoghue .15 .04
87 Rick Renteria .15 .04
88 John Burkett .15 .04
89 Jose Vizcaino .15 .04
90 Kevin Seitzer .15 .04
91 Bobby Witt .15 .04
92 Chris Turner .15 .04
93 Omar Vizquel .50 .15
94 David Justice .30 .09
95 David Segui .15 .04
96 Dave Hollins .15 .04
97 Doug Strange .15 .04
98 Jerald Clark .15 .04
99 Mike Moore .15 .04
100 Joey Cora .15 .04
101 Scott Kamieniecki .15 .04
102 Andy Benes .15 .04
103 Chris Bosio .15 .04
104 Rey Sanchez .15 .04
105 John Jaha .15 .04
106 Otis Nixon .15 .04
107 Rickey Henderson .75 .23
108 Jeff Bagwell .50 .15
109 Gregg Jefferies .15 .04
110 Roberto Alomar .30 .09
Paul Molitor
John Olerud
111 Ron Gant .30 .09
David Justice
Fred McGriff
112 Juan Gonzalez .50 .15
Rafael Palmeiro
Dean Palmer
113 Greg Swindell .15 .04
114 Bill Haselman .15 .04
115 Phil Plantier .15 .04
116 Ivan Rodriguez .75 .23
117 Kevin Tapani .15 .04
118 Mike LaValliere .15 .04
119 Tim Costo .15 .04
120 Mickey Morandini .15 .04
121 Brett Butler .30 .09
122 Tom Pagnozzi .15 .04
123 Ron Gant .30 .09
124 Damion Easley .15 .04
125 Dennis Eckersley .30 .09
126 Matt Mieske .15 .04
127 Cliff Floyd .30 .09
128 Julian Tavarez RC .30 .09
129 Arthur Rhodes .15 .04
130 Dave West .15 .04
131 Tim Naehring .15 .04
132 Freddie Benavides .15 .04
133 Paul Assenmacher .15 .04
134 David McCarty .15 .04
135 Jose Lind .15 .04
136 Reggie Sanders .30 .09
137 Don Slaught .15 .04
138 Andujar Cedeno .15 .04
139 Rob Deer .15 .04
140 Mike Piazza UER 1.50 .45
(listed as outfielder)
141 Moises Alou .30 .09
142 Tom Foley .15 .04
143 Benito Santiago .30 .09
144 Sandy Alomar Jr. .15 .04
145 Carlos Hernandez .15 .04
146 Luis Alicea .15 .04
147 Tom Lampkin .15 .04
148 Ryan Klesko .30 .09
149 Juan Guzman .15 .04
150 Scott Servais .15 .04
151 Tony Gwynn 1.00 .30
152 Tim Wakefield .30 .09
153 David Nied .15 .04
154 Chris Haney .15 .04
155 Danny Bautista .15 .04
156 Randy Velarde .15 .04
157 Darrin Jackson .15 .04
158 J.R. Phillips .15 .04
159 Greg Gagne .15 .04
160 Luis Aquino .15 .04
161 John Vander Wal .15 .04
162 Randy Myers .15 .04
163 Ted Power .15 .04
164 Scott Brosius .30 .09
165 Len Dykstra .30 .09
166 Jacob Brumfield .15 .04
167 Bo Jackson .75 .23
168 Eddie Taubensee .15 .04
169 Carlos Baerga .15 .04
170 Tim Bogar .15 .04
171 Jose Canseco .75 .23
172 Greg Blosser UER .15 .04
(Gregg on front)
173 Chili Davis .30 .09
174 Randy Knorr .15 .04
175 Mike Perez .15 .04
176 Henry Rodriguez .15 .04
177 Brian Turang RC .15 .04
178 Roger Pavlik .15 .04
179 Aaron Sele .15 .04
180 Fred McGriff .50 .15
Gary Sheffield
181 J.T. Snow .50 .15
Tim Salmon
182 Roberto Hernandez .15 .04
183 Jeff Reboulet .15 .04
184 John Doherty .15 .04
185 Danny Sheaffer .15 .04
186 Bip Roberts .15 .04
187 Dennis Martinez .30 .09
188 Darryl Hamilton .15 .04
189 Eduardo Perez .15 .04
190 Pete Harnisch .15 .04
191 Rich Gossage .30 .09
192 Mickey Tettleton .15 .04
193 Lenny Webster .15 .04
194 Lance Johnson .15 .04
195 Don Mattingly 2.00 .60
196 Gregg Olson .15 .04
197 Mark Gubicza .15 .04
198 Scott Fletcher .15 .04
199 Jon Shave .15 .04
200 Tim Mauser .15 .04
201 Jeromy Burnitz .30 .09
202 Rob Dibble .30 .09
203 Will Clark .75 .23
204 Steve Buechele .15 .04
205 Brian Williams .15 .04
206 Carlos Garcia .15 .04
207 Mark Clark .15 .04
208 Rafael Palmeiro .50 .15
209 Eric Davis .30 .09
210 Pat Meares .15 .04
211 Chuck Finley .30 .09
212 Jason Bere .15 .04
213 Gary DiSarcina .15 .04
214 Tony Fernandez .15 .04
215 B.J. Surhoff .30 .09
216 Lee Guetterman .15 .04
217 Tim Wallach .15 .04
218 Kirt Manwaring .15 .04
219 Albert Belle .30 .09
220 Dwight Gooden .30 .09
221 Archi Cianfrocco .15 .04
222 Terry Mulholland .15 .04
223 Hipolito Pichardo .15 .04
224 Kent Hrbek .30 .09
225 Craig Grebeck .15 .04
226 Todd Jones .15 .04
227 Mike Bordick .15 .04
228 John Olerud .30 .09
229 Jeff Blauser .15 .04
230 Alex Arias .15 .04
231 Bernard Gilkey .15 .04
232 Denny Neagle .30 .09
233 Pedro Borbon .15 .04
234 Dick Schofield .15 .04
235 Matias Carrillo .15 .04
236 Juan Bell .15 .04
237 Mike Hampton .30 .09
238 Barry Bonds 2.00 .60
239 Cris Carpenter .15 .04
240 Eric Karros .30 .09
241 Greg McMichael .15 .04
242 Pat Hentgen .15 .04
243 Tim Pugh .15 .04
244 Vinny Castilla .30 .09
245 Charlie Hough .30 .09
246 Bobby Munoz .15 .04
247 Kevin Baez .15 .04
248 Todd Frohwirth .15 .04
249 Charlie Hayes .15 .04
250 Mike Macfarlane .15 .04
251 Danny Darwin .15 .04
252 Ben Rivera .15 .04
253 Dave Henderson .15 .04
254 Steve Avery .15 .04
255 Tim Belcher .15 .04
256 Dan Plesac .15 .04
257 Jim Thome .75 .23
258 Albert Belle HR .30 .09
259 Barry Bonds HR 1.00 .30
260 Ron Gant HR .15 .04
261 Juan Gonzalez HR .30 .09
262 Ken Griffey Jr. HR .75 .23
263 David Justice HR .15 .04
264 Fred McGriff HR .30 .09
265 Rafael Palmeiro HR .30 .09
266 Mike Piazza HR .75 .23
267 Frank Thomas HR .50 .15
268 Matt Williams HR .15 .04
269 Checklist 1-135 .15 .04
270 Checklist 136-270 .15 .04
271 Mike Stanley .15 .04
272 Tony Tarasco .15 .04
273 Teddy Higuera .15 .04
274 Ryan Thompson .15 .04
275 Rick Aguilera .15 .04
276 Ramon Martinez .15 .04
277 Orlando Merced .15 .04
278 Guillermo Velasquez .15 .04
279 Mark Hutton .15 .04
280 Larry Walker .50 .15
281 Kevin Gross .15 .04
282 Jose Offerman .15 .04
283 Jim Leyritz .15 .04
284 Jamie Moyer .30 .09
285 Frank Thomas .75 .23
286 Derek Bell .15 .04
287 Derrick May .15 .04
288 Dave Winfield .30 .09
289 Curt Schilling .30 .09
290 Carlos Quintana .15 .04
291 Bob Natal .15 .04
292 David Cone .30 .09
293 Al Osuna .15 .04
294 Bob Hamelin .15 .04
295 Chad Curtis .15 .04
296 Danny Jackson .15 .04
297 Bob Welch .15 .04
298 Felix Jose .15 .04
299 Jay Buhner .30 .09
300 Joe Carter .30 .09
301 Kenny Lofton .30 .09
302 Kirk Rueter .30 .09
303 Kim Batiste .15 .04
304 Mike Morgan .15 .04
305 Pat Borders .15 .04
306 Rene Arocha .15 .04
307 Ruben Sierra .15 .04

308 Steve Finley .30 .09
309 Travis Fryman .30 .09
310 Zane Smith .15 .04
311 Willie Wilson .15 .04
312 Trevor Hoffman .30 .09
313 Terry Pendleton .30 .09
314 Salomon Torres .15 .04
315 Robin Ventura .30 .09
316 Randy Tomlin .15 .04
317 Dave Stewart .30 .09
318 Mike Benjamin .15 .04
319 Matt Turner .15 .04
320 Manny Ramirez .50 .15
321 Kevin Young .15 .04
322 Ken Caminiti .30 .09
323 Joe Girardi .15 .04
324 Jeff McKnight .15 .04
325 Gene Harris .15 .04
326 Devon White .30 .09
327 Darryl Kile .30 .09
328 Craig Paquette .15 .04
329 Cal Eldred .15 .04
330 Bill Swift .15 .04
331 Alan Trammell .30 .09
332 Armando Reynoso .15 .04
333 Brent Mayne .15 .04
334 Chris Donnels .15 .04
335 Darryl Strawberry .30 .09
336 Dean Palmer .30 .09
337 Frank Castillo .15 .04
338 Jeff King .15 .04
339 John Franco .30 .09
340 Kevin Appier .30 .09
341 Lance Blankenship .15 .04
342 Mark McLemore .15 .04
343 Pedro Astacio .15 .04
344 Rich Batchelor .15 .04
345 Ryan Bowen .15 .04
346 Terry Steinbach .15 .04
347 Troy O'Leary .15 .04
348 Willie Blair .15 .04
349 Wade Boggs .50 .15
350 Tim Raines .30 .09
351 Scott Livingstone .15 .04
352 Rod Correia .15 .04
353 Ray Lankford .15 .04
354 Pat Listach .15 .04
355 Milt Thompson .15 .04
356 Miguel Jimenez .15 .04
357 Marc Newfield .15 .04
358 Mark McGwire 2.00 .60
359 Kirby Puckett .75 .23
360 Kent Mercker .15 .04
361 John Kruk .30 .09
362 Jeff Kent .30 .09
363 Hal Morris .15 .04
364 Edgar Martinez .50 .15
365 Dave Magadan .15 .04
366 Dante Bichette .30 .09
367 Chris Hammond .15 .04
368 Bret Saberhagen .30 .09
369 Billy Ripken .15 .04
370 Bill Gullickson .15 .04
371 Andre Dawson .30 .09
372 Roberto Kelly .15 .04
373 Cal Ripken 2.50 .75
374 Craig Biggio .50 .15
375 Dan Pasqua .15 .04
376 Dave Nilsson .15 .04
377 Duane Ward .15 .04
378 Greg Vaughn .15 .04
379 Jeff Fassero .15 .04
380 Jerry DiPoto .15 .04
381 John Patterson .15 .04
382 Kevin Brown .30 .09
383 Kevin Roberson .15 .04
384 Joe Orsulak .15 .04
385 Hilly Hathaway .15 .04
386 Mike Greenwell .15 .04
387 Orestes Destrade .15 .04
388 Mike Gallego .15 .04
389 Ozzie Guillen .15 .04
390 Raul Mondesi .30 .09
391 Scott Lydy .15 .04
392 Tom Urbani .15 .04
393 Wil Cordero .15 .04
394 Tony Longmire .15 .04
395 Todd Zeile .15 .04
396 Scott Cooper .15 .04
397 Ryne Sandberg 1.25 .35
398 Ricky Bones .15 .04
399 Phil Clark .15 .04
400 Orel Hershiser .30 .09
401 Mike Henneman .15 .04
402 Mark Lemke .15 .04
403 Mark Grace .50 .15
404 Ken Ryan .15 .04
405 John Smoltz .50 .15
406 Jeff Conine .30 .09
407 Greg Harris .15 .04
408 Doug Drabek .15 .04
409 Dave Fleming .15 .04
410 Danny Tartabull .15 .04
411 Chad Kreuter .15 .04
412 Brad Ausmus .15 .04
413 Ben McDonald .15 .04
414 Barry Larkin .50 .15
415 Bret Barberie .15 .04
416 Chuck Knoblauch .30 .09
417 Ozzie Smith 1.25 .35
418 Ed Sprague .15 .04
419 Matt Williams .30 .09
420 Jeremy Hernandez .15 .04
421 Jose Bautista .15 .04
422 Kevin Mitchell .15 .04
423 Manuel Lee .15 .04
424 Mike Devereaux .15 .04
425 Omar Olivares .15 .04
426 Rafael Belliard .15 .04
427 Richie Lewis .15 .04
428 Ron Darling .15 .04
429 Shane Mack .15 .04
430 Tim Hulett .15 .04
431 Wally Joyner .30 .09
432 Wes Chamberlain .15 .04
433 Tom Browning .15 .04
434 Scott Radinsky .15 .04
435 Rondell White .30 .09
436 Rod Beck .15 .04
437 Rheal Cormier .15 .04
438 Randy Johnson .75 .23
439 Pete Schourek .15 .04
440 Mo Vaughn .30 .09
441 Mike Timlin .15 .04
442 Mark Langston .15 .04
443 Lou Whitaker .30 .09
444 Kevin Stocker .15 .04
445 Ken Hill .15 .04
446 John Wetteland .30 .09
447 J.T. Snow .30 .09
448 Erik Pappas .15 .04
449 David Hulse .15 .04
450 Darren Daulton .30 .09
451 Chris Hoiles .15 .04
452 Bryan Harvey .15 .04
453 Darren Lewis .15 .04
454 Andres Galarraga .30 .09
455 Joe Hesketh .15 .04
456 Jose Valentin .15 .04
457 Dan Peltier .15 .04
458 Joe Boever .15 .04
459 Kevin Rogers .15 .04
460 Craig Shipley .15 .04
461 Alvaro Espinoza .15 .04
462 Wilson Alvarez .15 .04
463 Cory Snyder .15 .04
464 Candy Maldonado .15 .04
465 Blas Minor .15 .04
466 Rod Bolton .15 .04
467 Kenny Rogers .30 .09
468 Greg Myers .15 .04
469 Jimmy Key .30 .09
470 Tony Castillo .15 .04
471 Mike Stanton .15 .04
472 Deion Sanders .50 .15
473 Tito Navarro .15 .04
474 Mike Gardiner .15 .04
475 Steve Reed .15 .04
476 John Roper .15 .04
477 Mike Trombley .15 .04
478 Charles Nagy .15 .04
479 Larry Casian .15 .04
480 Eric Hillman .15 .04
481 Bill Wertz .15 .04
482 Jeff Schwarz .15 .04
483 John Valentin .15 .04
484 Carl Willis .15 .04
485 Gary Gaetti .30 .09
486 Bill Pecota .15 .04
487 John Smiley .15 .04
488 Mike Mussina .50 .15
489 Mike Ignasiak .15 .04
490 Billy Brewer .15 .04
491 Jack Voigt .15 .04
492 Mike Munoz .15 .04
493 Lee Tinsley .15 .04
494 Bob Wickman .15 .04
495 Roger Salkeld .15 .04
496 Thomas Howard .15 .04
497 Mark Davis .15 .04
498 Dave Clark .15 .04
499 Turk Wendell .15 .04
500 Rafael Bournigal .15 .04
501 Chip Hale .15 .04
502 Matt Whiteside .15 .04
503 Brian Koelling .15 .04
504 Jeff Reed .15 .04
505 Paul Wagner .15 .04
506 Torey Lovullo .15 .04
507 Curt Leskanic .15 .04
508 Derek Lilliquist .15 .04
509 Joe Magrane .15 .04
510 Mackey Sasser .15 .04
511 Lloyd McClendon .15 .04
512 Jayhawk Owens .15 .04
513 Woody Williams .15 .04
514 Gary Redus .15 .04
515 Tim Spehr .15 .04
516 Jim Abbott .50 .15
517 Lou Frazier .15 .04
518 Erik Plantenberg RC .15 .04
519 Tim Worrell .15 .04
520 Brian McRae .15 .04
521 Chan Ho Park RC
522 Mark Wohlers .15 .04
523 Geronimo Pena .15 .04
524 Andy Ashby .15 .04
525 Tim Raines .15 .04
Andre Dawson TALE
526 Paul Molitor TALE .30 .09
527 Joe Carter DL .15 .04
528 F.Thomas DL UER .50 .15
listed as third in RBI in
1993; was actually second
529 Ken Griffey Jr. DL .75 .23
530 David Justice DL .15 .04
531 Gregg Jefferies DL .15 .04
532 Barry Bonds DL 1.00 .30
533 John Kruk QS .15 .04
534 Roger Clemens QS .75 .23
535 Cecil Fielder QS .15 .04
536 Ruben Sierra QS .15 .04
537 Tony Gwynn QS .50 .15
538 Tom Glavine QS .30 .09
539 CL 271-405 UER .15 .04
number on back is 269
540 CL 406-540 UER .15 .04
numbered 270 on back
541 Ozzie Smith ATL .75 .23
542 Eddie Murray ATL .50 .15
543 Lee Smith ATL .15 .04
544 Greg Maddux 1.25 .35
545 Denis Boucher .15 .04
546 Mark Gardner .15 .04
547 Bo Jackson .75 .23
548 Eric Anthony .15 .04
549 Delino DeShields .15 .04
550 Turner Ward .15 .04
551 Scott Sanderson .15 .04
552 Hector Carrasco .15 .04
553 Tony Phillips .15 .04
554 Melido Perez .15 .04
555 Mike Felder .15 .04
556 Jack Morris .30 .09
557 Rafael Palmeiro .50 .15
558 Shane Reynolds .15 .04
559 Pete Incaviglia .15 .04
560 Greg Harris .15 .04
561 Matt Walbeck .15 .04
562 Todd Van Poppel .15 .04
563 Todd Stottlemyre .15 .04
564 Ricky Bones .15 .04
565 Mike Jackson .15 .04
566 Kevin McReynolds .15 .04
567 Melvin Nieves .15 .04
568 Juan Gonzalez .50 .15
569 Frank Viola .30 .09
570 Vince Coleman .15 .04
571 Brian Anderson RC .30 .09
572 Omar Vizquel .50 .15
573 Bernie Williams .50 .15
574 Tom Glavine .50 .15
575 Mitch Williams .15 .04
576 Shawon Dunston .15 .04
577 Mike Lansing .15 .04
578 Greg Pirkl .15 .04
579 Sid Fernandez .15 .04
580 Doug Jones .15 .04
581 Walt Weiss .15 .04
582 Tim Belcher .15 .04
583 Alex Fernandez .15 .04
584 Alex Cole .15 .04
585 Greg Cadaret .15 .04
586 Bob Tewksbury .15 .04
587 Dave Hansen .15 .04
588 Kurt Abbott RC .30 .09
589 Rick White RC .15 .04
590 Kevin Bass .15 .04
591 Geronimo Berroa .15 .04
592 Jaime Navarro .15 .04
593 Steve Farr .15 .04
594 Jack Armstrong .15 .04
595 Steve Howe .15 .04
596 Jose Rijo .15 .04
597 Otis Nixon .15 .04
598 Robby Thompson .15 .04
599 Kelly Stinnett RC .30 .09
600 Carlos Delgado .50 .15
601 Brian Johnson RC .15 .04
602 Gregg Olson .15 .04
603 Jim Edmonds .75 .23
604 Mike Blowers .15 .04
605 Lee Smith .30 .09
606 Pat Rapp .15 .04
607 Mike Magnante .15 .04
608 Karl Rhodes .15 .04
609 Jeff Juden .15 .04
610 Rusty Meacham .15 .04
611 Pedro Martinez .75 .23
612 Todd Worrell .15 .04
613 Stan Javier .15 .04
614 Mike Hampton .30 .09
615 Jose Guzman .15 .04
616 Xavier Hernandez .15 .04
617 David Wells .30 .09
618 John Habyan .15 .04
619 Chris Nabholz .15 .04
620 Bobby Jones .15 .04
621 Chris James .15 .04
622 Ellis Burks .30 .09
623 Erik Hanson .15 .04
624 Pat Meares .15 .04
625 Harold Reynolds .30 .09
626 Bob Hamelin RR .15 .04
627 Manny Ramirez RR .30 .09
628 Ryan Klesko RR .30 .09
629 Carlos Delgado RR .30 .09
630 Javier Lopez RR .30 .09
631 Steve Karsay RR .15 .04
632 Rick Helling RR .15 .04
633 Steve Trachsel RR .15 .04
634 Hector Carrasco RR .15 .04
635 Andy Stankiewicz .15 .04
636 Paul Sorrento .15 .04
637 Scott Erickson .15 .04
638 Chipper Jones .75 .23
639 Luis Polonia .15 .04
640 Howard Johnson .15 .04
641 John Dopson .15 .04
642 Jody Reed .15 .04
643 Lonnie Smith UER .15 .04
Card numbered 543
644 Mark Portugal .15 .04
645 Paul Molitor .50 .15
646 Paul Assenmacher .15 .04
647 Hubie Brooks .15 .04
648 Gary Wayne .15 .04
649 Sean Berry .15 .04
650 Roger Clemens 1.50 .45
651 Brian R. Hunter .15 .04
652 Wally Whitehurst .15 .04
653 Allen Watson .15 .04
654 Rickey Henderson .75 .23
655 Sid Bream .15 .04
656 Dan Wilson .15 .04
657 Ricky Jordan .15 .04
658 Sterling Hitchcock .15 .04
659 Darrin Jackson .15 .04
660 Junior Felix .15 .04
661 Tom Brunansky .15 .04
662 Jose Vizcaino .15 .04
663 Mark Leiter .15 .04
664 Gil Heredia .15 .04
665 Fred McGriff .50 .15
666 Will Clark .75 .23
667 Al Leiter .30 .09
668 James Mouton .15 .04
669 Billy Bean .15 .04
670 Scott Leius .15 .04
671 Bret Boone .30 .09
672 Darren Holmes .15 .04
673 Dave Weathers .15 .04
674 Eddie Murray .75 .23
675 Felix Fermin .15 .04
676 Chris Sabo .15 .04
677 Billy Spiers .15 .04
678 Aaron Sele .15 .04
679 John Samuel .15 .04
680 Julio Franco .30 .09
681 Heathcliff Slocumb .15 .04
682 Dennis Martinez .30 .09
683 Jerry Browne .15 .04
684 Pedro Martinez RC .30 .09
685 Rex Hudler .15 .04
686 Willie McGee .30 .09
687 Andy Van Slyke .30 .09
688 Pat Mahomes .15 .04
689 Dave Henderson .15 .04
690 Tony Eusebio .15 .04
691 Rick Sutcliffe .30 .09
692 Willie Banks .15 .04
693 Alan Mills .15 .04
694 Jeff Treadway .15 .04
695 Alex Gonzalez .15 .04
696 David Segui .15 .04
697 Rick Helling .15 .04
698 Bip Roberts .15 .04
699 Jeff Cirillo RC .50 .15
700 Terry Mulholland .15 .04
701 Marvin Freeman .15 .04
702 Jason Bere .15 .04
703 Javier Lopez .30 .09
704 Greg Hibbard .15 .04
705 Tommy Greene .15 .04
706 Marquis Grissom .30 .09
707 Brian Harper .15 .04
708 Steve Karsay .15 .04
709 Jeff Brantley .15 .04
710 Jeff Russell .15 .04
711 Bryan Hickerson .15 .04
712 Jim Pittsley RC .15 .04
713 Bobby Ayala .15 .04
714 John Smoltz .50 .15
715 Jose Rijo .15 .04
716 Greg Maddux .75 .23
717 Matt Williams .15 .04
718 Frank Thomas .50 .15
719 Ryne Sandberg .75 .23
720 Checklist .15 .04

1994 Stadium Club First Day Issue

Randomly inserted in one of every 24 packs, these First Day Production cards are identical to the regular issues except for a special 1st Day foil stamp engraved on the front of each card. No more than 2,000 of each Stadium Club card was issued as First Day Issue. Some FDI logos have been transferred from "common" players to the front of "star" players.

Nm-Mt Ex-Mt
*STARS: 8X TO 20X BASIC CARDS
*ROOKIES: 6X to 15X BASIC CARDS

1994 Stadium Club Golden Rainbow

Parallel to the basic Stadium Club set, Golden Rainbows differ in that the player's last name on front has gold refracting foil over it. The cards were inserted one per Stadium Club foil pack and two per jumbo.

Nm-Mt Ex-Mt
COMPLETE SET (720) 160.00 47.50
COMP.SERIES 1 (270) 60.00 18.00
COMP.SERIES 2 (270) 60.00 18.00
COMP.SERIES 3 (180) 40.00 12.00
*STARS: 1.25X TO 3X BASIC CARDS
*ROOKIES: 1X TO 2.5X BASIC CARDS

1994 Stadium Club Dugout Dirt

Randomly inserted at a rate of one per six packs, these standard-size cards feature some of baseball's most popular and colorful players by sports cartoonists Daniel Guidera and Steve Benson. The cards resemble basic Stadium Club cards except for a Dugout Dirt logo at the bottom. Backs contain a cartoon. Cards 1-4 were found in first series packs with cards 5-8 and 9-12 were inserted in second series and third series packs respectively.

Nm-Mt Ex-Mt
COMPLETE SERIES 1 (4) 5.00 1.50
COMPLETE SERIES 2 (4) 3.00 .90
COMPLETE SERIES 3 (4) 3.00 .90
DD1 Mike Piazza 1.50 .45
DD2 Dave Winfield .30 .09
DD3 John Kruk .30 .09
DD4 Cal Ripken 2.50 .75
DD5 Jack McDowell .15 .04
DD6 Barry Bonds 2.00 .60
DD7 Ken Griffey Jr. 1.25 .35
DD8 Tim Salmon .50 .15
DD9 Frank Thomas .75 .23
DD10 Jeff Kent .30 .09
DD11 Randy Johnson .75 .23
DD12 Darren Daulton .30 .09

1994 Stadium Club Finest

This set contains 10 standard-size metallic cards of top players. They were randomly inserted one in six third series packs. Jumbo versions measuring approximately five inches by seven inches were issued for retail repacks.

Nm-Mt Ex-Mt
COMPLETE SET (10) 25.00 7.50
*JUMBOS: .6X TO 1.5X BASIC SC FINEST
JUMBOS DISTRIBUTED IN RETAIL PACKS
F1 Jeff Bagwell 1.50 .45
F2 Albert Belle 1.00 .30
F3 Barry Bonds 6.00 1.80
F4 Juan Gonzalez 1.50 .45
F5 Ken Griffey Jr. 4.00 1.20
F6 Marquis Grissom 1.00 .30
F7 David Justice 1.00 .30
F8 Mike Piazza 5.00 1.50
F9 Tim Salmon 1.50 .45
F10 Frank Thomas 2.50 .75

1994 Stadium Club Super Teams

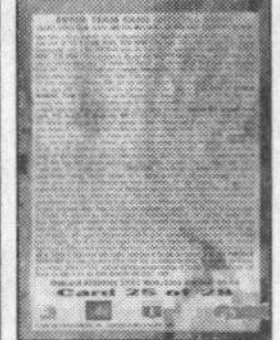

Randomly inserted at a rate of one per 24 first series packs only, this 28-card standard-size features one card for each of the 28 MLB teams. Collectors holding team cards could redeem them for special prizes if those teams won a division title, a league championship, or the World Series. But, since the strike affected the 1994 season, Topps postponed the promotion until the 1995 season. The expiration was pushed back to January 31, 1996.

Nm-Mt Ex-Mt
COMPLETE SET (28) 50.00 15.00
ST1 Jeff Blauser 2.50 .75
Terry Pendleton
ST2 Sammy Sosa 1.00 .30
Derrick May
ST3 Reggie Sanders 1.50 .45
Barry Larkin
ST4 Vinny Castilla 1.00 .30
Eric Young
ST5 Alex Arias 1.00 .30
ST6 Eric Anthony 1.00 .30
Steve Finley
ST7 Mike Piazza 5.00 1.50
ST8 Marquis Grissom 1.00 .30
ST9 Bobby Bonilla 1.00 .30
ST10 Mickey Morandini 1.00 .30
ST11 Andy Van Slyke 1.00 .30
Jay Bell
ST12 Todd Zeile 1.00 .30
Gregg Jefferies
ST13 Ricky Gutierrez 1.00 .30
ST14 Matt Williams 1.00 .30
Kirt Manwaring
ST15 Cal Ripken 8.00 2.40
ST16 Luis Rivera 1.00 .30
John Valentin
ST17 Tim Salmon 1.00 .30
ST18 Joey Cora 1.00 .30
ST19 Kenny Lofton 1.00 .30
Carlos Baerga
Albert Belle
ST20 (Alan Trammell 1.00 .30
Tony Phillips
ST21 Jose Lind 1.00 .30
Curt Wilkerson
ST22 Pat Listach 1.00 .30
John Jaha
Cal Eldred
ST23 Kirby Puckett 2.50 .75
Kent Hrbek
ST24 Don Mattingly 6.00 1.80
Bernie Williams
ST25 Mike Bordick 1.00 .30
Brent Gates
ST26 Jay Buhner 1.00 .30
Mike Blowers
ST27 Ivan Rodriguez 1.50 .45
Dean Palmer
Jose Canseco
Juan Gonzalez
ST28 John Olerud 1.00 .30

1994 Stadium Club Draft Picks

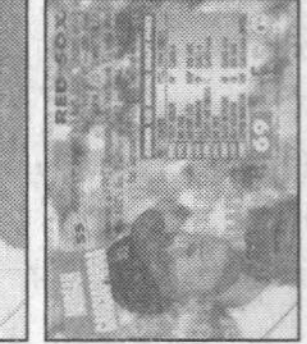

This 90-card standard-size set features players chosen in the June 1994 MLB draft and photographed in their major league uniforms. Each 24-pack box included four First Day Issue Draft Pick cards randomly packed, one in every six packs. Early cards of Nomar Garciaparra, Ben Grieve and Terrence Long are featured in this set.

Nm-Mt Ex-Mt
COMPLETE SET (90) 10.00 3.00
1 Jacob Shumate XRC .25 .07
2 C.J. Nitkowski XRC .25 .07
3 Doug Million XRC .25 .07
4 Matt Smith XRC .25 .07
5 Kevin Lovinger XRC .25 .07
6 Alberto Castillo XRC .25 .07
7 Mike Russell XRC .25 .07
8 Dan Lock XRC .25 .07
9 Tom Szimanski XRC .25 .07
10 Aaron Boone XRC .50 .15
11 Jayson Peterson XRC .25 .07
12 Mark Johnson XRC .25 .07
13 Cade Gaspar XRC .25 .07
14 George Lombard XRC .25 .07
15 Russ Johnson .25 .07
16 Travis Miller XRC .25 .07
17 Jay Payton XRC .50 .15

18 Brian Buchanan XRC .25 .07
19 Jacob Cruz XRC .40 .12
20 Gary Rath XRC .25 .07
21 Ramon Castro XRC .25 .07
22 Tommy Davis XRC .25 .07
23 Tony Terry XRC .25 .07
24 Jerry Whittaker XRC .25 .07
25 Mike Darr XRC .40 .12
26 Doug Webb XRC .25 .07
27 Jason Camilli XRC .25 .07
28 Brad Rigby XRC .25 .07
29 Ryan Nye XRC .25 .07
30 Carl Dale XRC .25 .07
31 Andy Taulbee XRC .25 .07
32 Trey Moore XRC .25 .07
33 John Crowther XRC .25 .07
34 Joe Giuliano XRC .25 .07
35 Brian Rose XRC .25 .07
36 Paul Failla XRC .25 .07
37 Brian Meadows XRC .25 .07
38 Oscar Robles XRC .25 .07
39 Mike Metcalfe XRC .25 .07
40 Larry Barnes XRC .25 .07
41 Paul Ottavinia XRC .25 .07
42 Chris McBride XRC .25 .07
43 Ricky Stone XRC .25 .07
44 Billy Blythe XRC .25 .07
45 Eddie Priest XRC .25 .07
46 Scott Forster XRC .25 .07
47 Eric Pickett XRC .25 .07
48 Matt Beaumont .25 .07
49 Darrell Nicholas XRC .25 .07
50 Mike A. Hampton XRC .25 .07
51 Paul O'Malley XRC .25 .07
52 Steve Shoemaker XRC .25 .07
53 Jason Sikes XRC .25 .07
54 Bryan Farson XRC .25 .07
55 Yates Hall XRC .25 .07
56 Troy Brohawn XRC .25 .07
57 Dan Hower XRC .25 .07
58 Clay Caruthers XRC .25 .07
59 Pepe McNeal XRC .25 .07
60 Ray Ricken XRC .25 .07
61 Scott Shores XRC .25 .07
62 Eddie Brooks XRC .25 .07
63 Dave Kauflin XRC .25 .07
64 David Meyer XRC .25 .07
65 Geoff Blum XRC .40 .12
66 Roy Marsh XRC .25 .07
67 Ryan Beeney XRC .25 .07
68 Derek Dukart XRC .25 .07
69 Nomar Garciaparra 4.00 1.20
70 Jason Kelly XRC .25 .07
71 Jesse Ibarra XRC .25 .07
72 Bucky Buckles XRC .25 .07
73 Mark Little XRC .25 .07
74 Heath Murray XRC .25 .07
75 Greg Morris XRC .25 .07
76 Mike Halperlin XRC .25 .07
77 Wes Helms XRC .50 .15
78 Ray Brown XRC .25 .07
79 Kevin L.Brown XRC .40 .12
80 Paul Konerko XRC 1.50 .45
81 Mike Thurman XRC .25 .07
82 Paul Wilson .40 .12
83 Terrence Long XRC .50 .15
84 Ben Grieve XRC .50 .15
85 Mark Farris XRC .25 .07
86 Bret Wagner .25 .07
87 Dustin Hermanson .40 .12
88 Kevin Witt XRC .40 .12
89 Corey Pointer XRC .25 .07
90 Tim Grieve XRC .25 .07

1994 Stadium Club Draft Picks First Day Issue

Randomly inserted in packs, this 90-card standard-size set is identical in design with the regular Stadium Club Draft Picks cards except for a holographic "1st Day Issue" emblem on the fronts.

Nm-Mt Ex-Mt
*FIRST DAY: 1.5X TO 4X BASIC CARDS

1995 Stadium Club

The 1995 Stadium Club baseball card set was issued in three series of 270, 225 and 135 standard-size cards for a total of 630. The cards were distributed in 14-card packs at a suggested retail price of $2.50 and contained 24 packs per box. Notable Rookie Cards include Mark Grudzielanek, Bobby Higginson and Hideo Nomo.

Nm-Mt Ex-Mt
COMPLETE SET (630) 60.00 18.00
COMP.SERIES 1 (270) 25.00 7.50
COMP.SERIES 2 (225) 20.00 6.00
COMP.SERIES 3 (135) 15.00 4.50
1 Cal Ripken 2.50 .75
2 Bo Jackson .75 .23
3 Bryan Harvey .15 .04
4 Curt Schilling .30 .09
5 Bruce Ruffin .15 .04
6 Travis Fryman .30 .09
7 Jim Abbott .50 .15
8 David McCarty .15 .04
9 Gary Gaetti .30 .09
10 Roger Clemens 1.50 .45
11 Carlos Garcia .15 .04
12 Lee Smith .30 .09
13 Bobby Ayala .15 .04
14 Charles Nagy .15 .04
15 Lou Frazier .15 .04
16 Rene Arocha .15 .04
17 Carlos Delgado .30 .09
18 Steve Finley .30 .09
19 Ryan Klesko .30 .09
20 Cal Eldred .15 .04
21 Rey Sanchez .15 .04
22 Ken Hill .15 .04
23 Benito Santiago .30 .09
24 Julian Tavarez .15 .04
25 Jose Vizcaino .15 .04
26 Andy Benes .15 .04
27 Mariano Duncan .15 .04
28 Checklist A .15 .04
29 Shawon Dunston .15 .04
30 Rafael Palmeiro .50 .15
31 Dean Palmer .30 .09
32 Andres Galarraga .30 .09
33 Joey Cora .15 .04
34 Mickey Tettleton .15 .04
35 Barry Larkin .50 .15
36 Carlos Baerga .15 .04
37 Orel Hershiser .30 .09
38 Jody Reed .15 .04
39 Paul Molitor .50 .15
40 Jim Edmonds .50 .15
41 Bob Tewksbury .15 .04
42 John Patterson .15 .04
43 Ray McDavid .15 .04
44 Zane Smith .15 .04
45 Bret Saberhagen SE .15 .04
46 Greg Maddux SE .75 .23
47 Frank Thomas SE .50 .15
48 Carlos Baerga SE .15 .04
49 Billy Spiers .15 .04
50 Stan Javier .15 .04
51 Rex Hudler .15 .04
52 Denny Hocking .15 .04
53 Todd Worrell .15 .04
54 Mark Clark .15 .04
55 Hipolito Pichardo .15 .04
56 Bob Wickman .15 .04
57 Raul Mondesi .30 .09
58 Steve Cooke .15 .04
59 Rod Beck .15 .04
60 Tim Davis .15 .04
61 Jeff Kent .30 .09
62 John Valentin .15 .04
63 Alex Arias .15 .04
64 Steve Reed .15 .04
65 Ozzie Smith 1.25 .35
66 Terry Pendleton .30 .09
67 Kenny Rogers .30 .09
68 Vince Coleman .15 .04
69 Tom Pagnozzi .15 .04
70 Roberto Alomar .50 .15
71 Darrin Jackson .15 .04
72 Dennis Eckersley .30 .09
73 Jay Buhner .30 .09
74 Darren Lewis .15 .04
75 Dave Weathers .15 .04
76 Matt Walbeck .15 .04
77 Brad Ausmus .15 .04
78 Danny Bautista .15 .04
79 Bob Hamelin .15 .04
80 Steve Trachsel .15 .04
81 Ken Ryan .15 .04
82 Chris Turner .15 .04
83 David Segui .15 .04
84 Ben McDonald .15 .04
85 Wade Boggs .50 .15
86 John Vander Wal .15 .04
87 Sandy Alomar Jr. .15 .04
88 Ron Karkovice .15 .04
89 Doug Jones .15 .04
90 Gary Sheffield .30 .09
91 Ken Caminiti .30 .09
92 Chris Bosio .15 .04
93 Kevin Tapani .15 .04
94 Walt Weiss .15 .04
95 Erik Hanson .15 .04
96 Ruben Sierra .15 .04
97 Nomar Garciaparra 2.00 .60
98 Terrence Long .30 .09
99 Jacob Shumate .15 .04
100 Paul Wilson .15 .04
101 Kevin Witt .15 .04
102 Paul Konerko .30 .09
103 Ben Grieve .30 .09
104 Mark Johnson RC .40 .12
105 Cade Gaspar RC .15 .04
106 Mark Farris RC .15 .04
107 Dustin Hermanson .15 .04
108 Scott Elarton RC .40 .12
109 Doug Million .15 .04
110 Matt Smith RC .15 .04
111 Brian Buchanan RC .40 .12
112 Jayson Peterson RC .15 .04
113 Bret Wagner RC .15 .04
114 C.J. Nitkowski RC .40 .12
115 Ramon Castro RC .40 .12
116 Rafael Bournigal .15 .04
117 Jeff Fassero .15 .04
118 Bobby Bonilla .30 .09
119 Ricky Gutierrez .15 .04
120 Roger Pavlik .15 .04
121 Mike Greenwell .15 .04
122 Deion Sanders .50 .15
123 Charlie Hayes .15 .04
124 Paul O'Neill .30 .09
125 Jay Bell .30 .09
126 Royce Clayton .15 .04
127 Willie Banks .15 .04
128 Mark Wohlers .15 .04
129 Todd Jones .15 .04
130 Todd Stottlemyre .15 .04
131 Will Clark .75 .23
132 Wilson Alvarez .15 .04
133 Chili Davis .30 .09
134 Dave Burba .15 .04
135 Chris Hoiles .15 .04
136 Jeff Blauser .15 .04
137 Jeff Reboulet .15 .04
138 Bret Saberhagen .30 .09
139 Kirk Rueter .15 .04
140 Dave Nilsson .15 .04
141 Pat Borders .15 .04
142 Ron Darling .15 .04
143 Derek Bell .15 .04
144 Dave Hollins .15 .04
145 Juan Gonzalez .50 .15
146 Andre Dawson .30 .09
147 Jim Thome .75 .23
148 Larry Walker .50 .15
149 Mike Piazza 1.25 .35
150 Mike Perez .15 .04
151 Steve Avery .15 .04
152 Dan Wilson .15 .04
153 Andy Van Slyke .30 .09
154 Junior Felix .15 .04
155 Jack McDowell .15 .04
156 Danny Tartabull .15 .04
157 Willie Blair .15 .04
158 Wm.VanLandingham .15 .04
159 Robb Nen .30 .09
160 Lee Tinsley .15 .04
161 Ismael Valdes .15 .04
162 Juan Guzman .15 .04
163 Scott Servais .15 .04
164 Cliff Floyd .30 .09
165 Allen Watson .15 .04
166 Eddie Taubensee .15 .04
167 Scott Hemond .15 .04
168 Jeff Tackett .15 .04
169 Chad Curtis .15 .04
170 Rico Brogna .15 .04
171 Luis Polonia .15 .04
172 Checklist B .15 .04
173 Lance Johnson .15 .04
174 Sammy Sosa 1.25 .35
175 Mike Macfarlane .15 .04
176 Darryl Hamilton .15 .04
177 Rick Aguilera .15 .04
178 Dave West .15 .04
179 Mike Gallego .15 .04
180 Marc Newfield .15 .04
181 Steve Buechele .15 .04
182 David Wells .30 .09
183 Tom Glavine .50 .15
184 Joe Girardi .15 .04
185 Craig Biggio .50 .15
186 Eddie Murray .75 .23
187 Kevin Gross .15 .04
188 Sid Fernandez .15 .04
189 John Franco .30 .09
190 Bernard Gilkey .15 .04
191 Matt Williams .30 .09
192 Darrin Fletcher .15 .04
193 Jeff Conine .30 .09
194 Ed Sprague .15 .04
195 Eduardo Perez .15 .04
196 Scott Livingstone .15 .04
197 Ivan Rodriguez .75 .23
198 Orlando Merced .15 .04
199 Ricky Bones .15 .04
200 Javier Lopez .30 .09
201 Miguel Jimenez .15 .04
202 Terry McGriff .15 .04
203 Mike Lieberthal .30 .09
204 David Cone .30 .09
205 Todd Hundley .15 .04
206 Ozzie Guillen .15 .04
207 Alex Cole .15 .04
208 Tony Phillips .15 .04
209 Jim Eisenreich .15 .04
210 Greg Vaughn BES .15 .04
211 Barry Larkin BES .30 .09
212 Don Mattingly BES 1.00 .30
213 Mark Grace BES .30 .09
214 Jose Canseco BES .30 .09
215 Joe Carter BES .15 .04
216 David Cone BES .15 .04
217 Sandy Alomar Jr. BES .15 .04
218 Al Martin BES .15 .04
219 Roberto Kelly BES .15 .04
220 Paul Sorrento .15 .04
221 Tony Fernandez .15 .04
222 Stan Belinda .15 .04
223 Mike Stanley .15 .04
224 Doug Drabek .15 .04
225 Todd Van Poppel .15 .04
226 Matt Mieske .15 .04
227 Tino Martinez .50 .15
228 Andy Ashby .15 .04
229 Midre Cummings .15 .04
230 Jeff Frye .15 .04
231 Hal Morris .15 .04
232 Jose Lind .15 .04
233 Shawn Green .30 .09
234 Rafael Belliard .15 .04
235 Randy Myers .15 .04
236 Frank Thomas CE .50 .15
237 Darren Daulton CE .15 .04
238 Sammy Sosa CE .75 .23
239 Cal Ripken CE 1.25 .35
240 Jeff Bagwell CE .30 .09
241 Ken Griffey Jr. 1.25 .35
242 Brett Butler .30 .09
243 Derrick May .15 .04
244 Pat Listach .15 .04
245 Mike Bordick .15 .04
246 Mark Langston .15 .04
247 Randy Velarde .15 .04
248 Julio Franco .30 .09
249 Chuck Knoblauch .30 .09
250 Bill Gullickson .15 .04
251 Dave Henderson .15 .04
252 Bret Boone .30 .09
253 Al Martin .15 .04
254 Armando Benitez .30 .09
255 Wil Cordero .15 .04
256 Al Leiter .30 .09
257 Luis Gonzalez .30 .09
258 Charlie O'Brien .15 .04
259 Tim Wallach .15 .04
260 Scott Sanders .15 .04
261 Tom Henke .15 .04
262 Otis Nixon .15 .04
263 Darren Daulton .30 .09
264 Manny Ramirez .50 .15
265 Bret Barberie .15 .04
266 Mel Rojas .15 .04
267 John Burkett .15 .04
268 Brady Anderson .30 .09
269 John Roper .15 .04
270 Shane Reynolds .15 .04
271 Barry Bonds 2.00 .60
272 Alex Fernandez .15 .04
273 Brian McRae .15 .04
274 Todd Zeile .15 .04
275 Greg Swindell .15 .04
276 Johnny Ruffin .15 .04
277 Troy Neel .15 .04
278 Eric Karros .30 .09
279 John Hudek .15 .04
280 Thomas Howard .15 .04
281 Joe Carter .30 .09
282 Mike Devereaux .15 .04
283 Butch Henry .15 .04
284 Reggie Jefferson .15 .04
285 Mark Lemke .15 .04
286 Jeff Montgomery .15 .04
287 Ryan Thompson .15 .04
288 Paul Shuey .15 .04
289 Mark McGwire 2.00 .60
290 Bernie Williams .50 .15
291 Mickey Morandini .15 .04
292 Scott Leius .15 .04
293 David Hulse .15 .04
294 Greg Gagne .15 .04
295 Moises Alou .30 .09
296 Geronimo Berroa .15 .04
297 Eddie Zambrano .15 .04
298 Alan Trammell .30 .09
299 Don Slaught .15 .04
300 Jose Rijo .15 .04
301 Joe Ausanio .15 .04
302 Tim Raines .30 .09
303 Melido Perez .15 .04
304 Kent Mercker .15 .04
305 James Mouton .15 .04
306 Luis Lopez .15 .04
307 Mike Kingery .15 .04
308 Willie Greene .15 .04
309 Cecil Fielder .30 .09
310 Scott Kamieniecki .15 .04
311 Mike Greenwell BES .15 .04
312 Bobby Bonilla BES .15 .04
313 A.Galarraga BES .15 .04
314 Cal Ripken BES 1.25 .35
315 Matt Williams BES .15 .04
316 Tom Pagnozzi BES .15 .04
317 Len Dykstra BES .15 .04
318 Frank Thomas BES .50 .15
319 Kirby Puckett BES .75 .23
320 Mike Piazza BES .75 .23
321 Jason Jacome .15 .04
322 Brian Hunter .15 .04
323 Brent Gates .15 .04
324 Jim Converse .15 .04
325 Damion Easley .15 .04
326 Dante Bichette .30 .09
327 Kurt Abbott .15 .04
328 Scott Cooper .15 .04
329 Mike Henneman .15 .04
330 Orlando Miller .15 .04
331 John Kruk .30 .09
332 Jose Oliva .15 .04
333 Reggie Sanders .30 .09
334 Omar Vizquel .50 .15
335 Devon White .30 .09
336 Mike Morgan .15 .04
337 J.R. Phillips .15 .04
338 Gary DiSarcina .15 .04
339 Joey Hamilton .15 .04
340 Randy Johnson .75 .23
341 Jim Leyritz .15 .04
342 Bobby Jones .15 .04
343 Jaime Navarro .15 .04
344 Bip Roberts .15 .04
345 Steve Karsay .15 .04
346 Kevin Stocker .15 .04
347 Jose Canseco .75 .23
348 Bill Wegman .15 .04
349 Rondell White .30 .09
350 Mo Vaughn .30 .09
351 Joe Orsulak .15 .04
352 Pat Meares .15 .04
353 Albie Lopez .15 .04
354 Edgar Martinez .50 .15
355 Brian Jordan .30 .09
356 Tommy Greene .15 .04
357 Chuck Carr .15 .04
358 Pedro Astacio .15 .04
359 Russ Davis .15 .04
360 Chris Hammond .15 .04
361 Gregg Jefferies .15 .04
362 Shane Mack .15 .04
363 Fred McGriff .50 .15
364 Pat Rapp .15 .04
365 Bill Swift .15 .04
366 Checklist .15 .04
367 Robin Ventura .30 .09
368 Bobby Witt .15 .04
369 Karl Rhodes .15 .04
370 Eddie Williams .15 .04
371 John Jaha .15 .04
372 Steve Howe .15 .04
373 Leo Gomez .15 .04
374 Hector Fajardo .15 .04
375 Jeff Bagwell .50 .15
376 Mark Acre .15 .04
377 Wayne Kirby .15 .04
378 Mark Portugal .15 .04
379 Jesus Tavarez .15 .04
380 Jim Lindeman .15 .04
381 Don Mattingly 2.00 .60
382 Trevor Hoffman .30 .09
383 Chris Gomez .15 .04
384 Garret Anderson .30 .09
385 Bobby Munoz .15 .04
386 Jon Lieber .15 .04
387 Rick Helling .15 .04
388 Marvin Freeman .15 .04
389 Juan Castillo .15 .04
390 Jeff Cirillo .15 .04
391 Sean Berry .15 .04
392 Hector Carrasco .15 .04
393 Mark Grace .50 .15
394 Pat Kelly .15 .04
395 Tim Naehring .15 .04
396 Greg Pirkl .15 .04
397 John Smoltz .50 .15
398 Robby Thompson .15 .04
399 Rick White .15 .04
400 Frank Thomas .75 .23
401 Jeff Conine CS .15 .04
402 Jose Valentin CS .15 .04
403 Carlos Baerga CS .15 .04
404 Rick Aguilera CS .15 .04
405 Wilson Alvarez CS .15 .04
406 Juan Gonzalez CS .30 .09
407 Barry Larkin CS .30 .09
408 Ken Hill CS .15 .04
409 Chuck Carr CS .15 .04
410 Tim Raines CS .15 .04
411 Bryan Eversgerd .15 .04
412 Phil Plantier .15 .04
413 Josias Manzanillo .15 .04
414 Roberto Kelly .15 .04
415 Rickey Henderson .75 .23
416 John Smiley .15 .04
417 Kevin Brown .30 .09
418 Jimmy Key .30 .09
419 Wally Joyner .30 .09
420 Roberto Hernandez .15 .04
421 Felix Fermin .15 .04
422 Checklist .15 .04
423 Greg Vaughn .15 .04
424 Ray Lankford .15 .04
425 Greg Maddux 1.25 .35
426 Mike Mussina .50 .15
427 Geronimo Pena .15 .04
428 David Nied .15 .04
429 Scott Erickson .15 .04
430 Kevin Mitchell .15 .04
431 Mike Lansing .15 .04
432 Brian Anderson .15 .04
433 Jeff King .15 .04
434 Ramon Martinez .15 .04
435 Kevin Seitzer .15 .04
436 Salomon Torres .15 .04
437 Brian L.Hunter .15 .04
438 Melvin Nieves .15 .04
439 Mike Kelly .15 .04
440 Marquis Grissom .30 .09
441 Chuck Finley .30 .09
442 Len Dykstra .30 .09
443 Ellis Burks .30 .09
444 Harold Baines .30 .09
445 Kevin Appier .30 .09
446 David Justice .30 .09
447 Darryl Kile .30 .09
448 John Olerud .30 .09
449 Greg McMichael .15 .04
450 Kirby Puckett .75 .23
451 Jose Valentin .15 .04
452 Rick Wilkins .15 .04
453 Arthur Rhodes .15 .04
454 Pat Hentgen .15 .04
455 Tom Gordon .15 .04
456 Tom Candiotti .15 .04
457 Jason Bere .15 .04
458 Wes Chamberlain .15 .04
459 Greg Colbrunn .15 .04
460 John Doherty .15 .04
461 Kevin Foster .15 .04
462 Mark Whiten .15 .04
463 Terry Steinbach .15 .04
464 Aaron Sele .15 .04
465 Kirt Manwaring .15 .04
466 Darren Hall .15 .04
467 Delino DeShields .15 .04
468 Andujar Cedeno .15 .04
469 Billy Ashley .15 .04
470 Kenny Lofton .30 .09
471 Pedro Munoz .15 .04
472 John Wetteland .30 .09
473 Tim Salmon .50 .15
474 Denny Neagle .30 .09
475 Tony Gwynn 1.00 .30
476 Vinny Castilla .30 .09
477 Steve Dreyer .15 .04
478 Jeff Shaw .15 .04
479 Chad Ogea .15 .04
480 Scott Ruffcorn .15 .04
481 Lou Whitaker .30 .09
482 J.T. Snow .30 .09
483 Rich Rowland .15 .04
484 Denny Martinez .30 .09
485 Pedro Martinez .75 .23
486 Rusty Greer .30 .09
487 Dave Fleming .15 .04
488 John Dettmer .15 .04
489 Albert Belle .30 .09
490 Ravelo Manzanillo .15 .04
491 Henry Rodriguez .15 .04
492 Andrew Lorraine .15 .04
493 Dwayne Hosey .15 .04
494 Mike Blowers .15 .04
495 Turner Ward .15 .04
496 Fred McGriff EC .30 .09
497 Sammy Sosa EC .75 .23
498 Barry Larkin EC .30 .09
499 Andres Galarraga EC .15 .04
500 Gary Sheffield EC .15 .04
501 Jeff Bagwell EC .30 .09
502 Mike Piazza EC .75 .23
503 Moises Alou EC .15 .04
504 Bobby Bonilla EC .15 .04
505 Darren Daulton EC .15 .04
506 Jeff King EC .15 .04
507 Ray Lankford EC .15 .04
508 Tony Gwynn EC .50 .15
509 Barry Bonds EC 1.00 .30
510 Cal Ripken EC 1.25 .35
511 Mo Vaughn EC .15 .04
512 Tim Salmon EC .30 .09
513 Frank Thomas EC .50 .15
514 Albert Belle EC .15 .04
515 Cecil Fielder EC .15 .04
516 Kevin Appier EC .15 .04
517 Greg Vaughn EC .15 .04
518 Kirby Puckett EC .50 .15
519 Paul O'Neill EC .30 .09
520 Ruben Sierra EC .15 .04
521 Ken Griffey Jr. EC .75 .23
522 Will Clark EC .30 .09
523 Joe Carter EC .15 .04
524 Antonio Osuna .15 .04
525 Glenallen Hill .15 .04
526 Alex Gonzalez .15 .04
527 Dave Stewart .30 .09
528 Ron Gant .30 .09
529 Jason Bates .15 .04
530 Mike Macfarlane .15 .04
531 Esteban Loaiza .15 .04
532 Joe Randa .15 .04
533 Dave Winfield .30 .09
534 Danny Darwin .15 .04
535 Pete Harnisch .15 .04
536 Joey Cora .15 .04
537 Jaime Navarro .15 .04

538 Marty Cordova .15 .04
539 Andujar Cedeno .15 .04
540 Mickey Tettleton .15 .04
541 Andy Van Slyke .30 .09
542 Carlos Perez RC .40 .12
543 Chipper Jones .75 .23
544 Tony Fernandez .15 .04
545 Tom Henke .15 .04
546 Pat Borders .15 .04
547 Chad Curtis .15 .04
548 Ray Durham .30 .09
549 Joe Oliver .15 .04
550 Jose Mesa .15 .04
551 Steve Finley .30 .09
552 Otis Nixon .15 .04
553 Jacob Brumfield .15 .04
554 Bill Swift .15 .04
555 Quilvio Veras .15 .04
556 Hideo Nomo RC UER 2.00 .60
Wins and IP totals reversed
557 Joe Vitiello .15 .04
558 Mike Perez .15 .04
559 Charlie Hayes .15 .04
560 Brad Radke RC .75 .23
561 Darren Bragg .15 .04
562 Orel Hershiser .30 .09
563 Edgardo Alfonzo .30 .09
564 Doug Jones .15 .04
565 Andy Pettitte .50 .15
566 Benito Santiago .30 .09
567 John Burkett .15 .04
568 Brad Clontz .15 .04
569 Jim Abbott .50 .15
570 Joe Rosselli .15 .04
571 Mark Grudzielanek RC .40 .12
572 Dustin Hermanson .15 .04
573 Benji Gil .15 .04
574 Mark Whiten .15 .04
575 Mike Ignasiak .15 .04
576 Kevin Ritz .15 .04
577 Paul Quantrill .15 .04
578 Andre Dawson .30 .09
579 Jerald Clark .15 .04
580 Frank Rodriguez .15 .04
581 Mark Kiefer .15 .04
582 Trevor Wilson .15 .04
583 Gary Wilson RC .15 .04
584 Andy Stankiewicz .15 .04
585 Felipe Lira .15 .04
586 Mike Mimbs RC .15 .04
587 Jon Nunnally .15 .04
588 Tomas Perez RC .15 .04
589 Chad Fonville .15 .04
590 Todd Hollandsworth .15 .04
591 Roberto Petagine .15 .04
592 Mariano Rivera .50 .15
593 Mark McLemore .15 .04
594 Bobby Witt .15 .04
595 Jose Offerman .15 .04
596 J.Christiansen RC .15 .04
597 Jeff Manto .15 .04
598 Jim Dougherty RC .15 .04
599 Juan Acevedo RC .15 .04
600 Troy O'Leary .15 .04
601 Ron Villone .15 .04
602 Tripp Cromer .15 .04
603 Steve Scarsone .15 .04
604 Lance Parrish .30 .09
605 Ozzie Timmons .15 .04
606 Ray Holbert .15 .04
607 Tony Phillips .15 .04
608 Phil Plantier .15 .04
609 Shane Andrews .15 .04
610 Heathcliff Slocumb .15 .04
611 Bobby Higginson RC .75 .23
612 Bob Tewksbury .15 .04
613 Terry Pendleton .30 .09
614 Scott Cooper TA .15 .04
615 John Wetteland TA .15 .04
616 Ken Hill TA .15 .04
617 Marquis Grissom TA .15 .04
618 Larry Walker TA .15 .04
619 Derek Bell TA .15 .04
620 David Cone TA .15 .04
621 Ken Caminiti TA .15 .04
622 Jack McDowell TA .15 .04
623 Vaughn Eshelman TA .15 .04
624 Brian McRae TA .15 .04
625 Gregg Jefferies TA .15 .04
626 Kevin Brown TA .15 .04
627 Lee Smith TA .15 .04
628 Tony Tarasco TA .15 .04
629 Brett Butler TA .15 .04
630 Jose Canseco TA .30 .09

1995 Stadium Club First Day Issue

Parallel to the basic first series Stadium Club issue, these cards, were primarily inserted in second series Topps packs. They were also inserted at a rate of ten per Topps factory set. Nine double printed cards were issued in both first and second series Topps packs. Those cards are as follows: 29, 39, 79, 96, 131, 149, 153, 168 and 197. Limited instances of duplicitous parties transferring the FDI foil logos from "common" players to the fronts of "star" players were chronicled shortly after release - thus it's recommended for collectors to take a close look at the logo on front before purchasing these cards.

Nm-Mt Ex-Mt
COMPLETE SET (270) 250.00 75.00
COMMON CARD (1-270) 2.00 .60
*STARS: 5X TO 12X BASIC CARDS
*ROOKIES: 3X TO 8X BASIC CARDS...
*DP STARS: 1.25X TO 3X BASIC CARDS

1995 Stadium Club Super Team Division Winners

Each of these six team sets was available exclusively by mailing in the corresponding winning 1994 Super Team card. Each team set was distributed in a clear plastic sealed wrapper and included ten player cards and a Super Team card (of which was stamped "REDEEMED" on back). The card design and numbering for the player cards parallels regular issue 1995 Stadium Club cards. In fact, the only way to tell these cards apart is by the gold foil "Division Winner" logo on each card front. The cards are listed below alphabetically by team; the prefixes B, D, I, M, R and RS have been added to denote Braves, Dodgers, Indians, Mariners, Reds and Red Sox.

Nm-Mt Ex-Mt
COMP.BRAVES SET (11) 8.00 2.40
COMP.DODGERS (11) 8.00 2.40
COMP.INDIANS SET (11) 6.00 1.80
COMP.MARINERS (11) 8.00 2.40
COMP.REDS SET (11) 3.00 .90
COMP.RED SOX SET (11) 6.00 1.80
COMMON SUPER TEAM 1.00 .30
B1T Braves DW 1.00 .30
Super Team
Jeff Blauser
Terry Pendleton
B19 Ryan Klesko .60 .18
B128 Mark Wohlers .30 .09
B151 Steve Avery .30 .09
B183 Tom Glavine 1.00 .30
B200 Javy Lopez .60 .18
B393 Fred McGriff 1.00 .30
B397 John Smoltz 1.00 .30
B425 Greg Maddux 2.50 .75
B446 Dave Justice .60 .18
B543 Chipper Jones 1.50 .45
D7T Dodgers DW 1.00 .30
Super Team
Mike Piazza
D57 Raul Mondesi .60 .18
D149 Mike Piazza 2.50 .75
D161 Ismael Valdes .30 .09
D242 Brett Butler .60 .18
D259 Tim Wallach .30 .09
D278 Eric Karros .60 .18
D434 Ramon Martinez .30 .09
D456 Tom Candiotti .30 .09
D467 Delino DeShields .30 .09
D556 Hideo Nomo 4.00 1.20
I19T Indians DW 1.00 .30
Super Team
Carlos Baerga
Albert Belle
Kenny Lofton
I36 Carlos Baerga .30 .09
I147 Jim Thome 1.50 .45
I186 Eddie Murray 1.50 .45
I264 Manny Ramirez 1.00 .30
I334 Omar Vizquel 1.00 .30
I470 Kenny Lofton .60 .18
I484 Dennis Martinez .60 .18
I489 Albert Belle .60 .18
I550 Jose Mesa .30 .09
I562 Orel Hershiser .60 .18
M26T Mariners DW 1.00 .16
Super Team
Mike Blowers
Jay Buhner
M73 Jay Buhner .60 .18
M92 Chris Bosio .30 .09
M152 Dan Wilson .30 .09
M227 Tino Martinez 1.00 .30
M241 Ken Griffey Jr. 2.50 .75
M340 Randy Johnson 1.50 .45
M354 Edgar Martinez 1.00 .30
M421 Felix Fermin .30 .09
M494 Mike Blowers .30 .09
M536 Joey Cora .30 .09
RE3T Reds DW
Super Team
Barry Larkin
Reggie Sanders
RE35 Barry Larkin 1.00 .30
RE231 Hal Morris .30 .09
RE252 Bret Boone .60 .18
RE280 Thomas Howard .30 .09
RE300 Jose Rijo .30 .09
RE333 Reggie Sanders .30 .09
RE392 Hector Carrasco .30 .09
RE416 John Smiley .30 .09
RE528 Ron Gant .60 .18
RE566 Benito Santiago .60 .18
RS1T Red Sox DW 1.00 .30
Super Team
Luis Rivera
John Valentin
RS10 Roger Clemens 3.00 .90
RS62 John Valentin .30 .09
RS121 Mike Greenwell .30 .09
RS160 Lee Tinsley .30 .09
RS347 Jose Canseco 1.50 .45
RS350 Mo Vaughn .60 .18
RS395 Tim Naehring .30 .09
RS464 Aaron Sele .30 .09
RS530 Mike Macfarlane .30 .09
RS600 Troy O'Leary .30 .09

1995 Stadium Club Super Team Master Photos

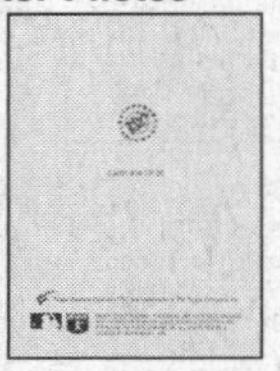

This 20-card set was distributed in two separate 10-card sealed team bags. The cards were available exclusively by mailing in a Braves or Indians 1994 Super Team card. These oversized cards (5" by 7") feature a reproduction of the player's standard 1995 Stadium Club card enframed around a shining blue background. Unlike the standard issue cards they parallel, these are numbered X of 20.

Nm-Mt Ex-Mt
COMP.BRAVES SET (10) 10.00 3.00
COMP.INDIANS SET (10) 8.00 2.40
1 Steve Avery .40 .12
2 Tom Glavine 1.25 .35
3 Chipper Jones 2.00 .60
4 Dave Justice .75 .23
5 Ryan Klesko .75 .23
6 Javy Lopez .75 .23
7 Greg Maddux 3.00 .90
8 Fred McGriff 1.25 .35
9 John Smoltz 1.25 .35
10 Mark Wohlers .40 .12
11 Carlos Baerga .40 .12
12 Albert Belle .75 .23
13 Orel Hershiser .75 .23
14 Kenny Lofton .75 .23
15 Dennis Martinez .75 .23
16 Jose Mesa .40 .12
17 Eddie Murray 2.00 .60
18 Manny Ramirez 1.25 .35
19 Jim Thome 2.00 .60
20 Omar Vizquel 1.25 .35

1995 Stadium Club Super Team World Series

Because of the strike-interrupted season, the 1994 Stadium Club Super Team insert program had to be finished up with the 1995 product. Collectors who redeemed the 1994 Atlanta Braves Super Team card received: 1) a complete 630-card 1995 Stadium Club parallel set stamped with a special gold foil World Series logo (of which was mailed in two separate series of 585 and 45 cards) 2) a Division Winner parallel Braves team set along with the winner card stamped "redeemed" on its back 3) a jumbo-sized (3" by 5") parallel Master Photo Braves team set. Collectors who redeemed the 1994 Cleveland Indians Super Team card got parallel Indians Division Winner and Master Photo team sets. Collectors who redeemed the 1994 Super Team card of a division winner (Dodgers, Mariners, Red Sox and Reds) received a Division Winner parallel team set of the respective team that they sent in. All of these winner cards parallel the 1995 Stadium Club regular series cards.

Nm-Mt Ex-Mt
COMP.WS SET (585) 80.00 24.00
COMP.EC/TA SET (45) 15.00 4.50
*STARS: .6X TO 1.5X BASIC CARDS..
*ROOKIES: .6X TO 1.5X BASIC CARDS

1995 Stadium Club Virtual Reality

This 270-card standard-size set parallels a selection of cards from the regular 1995 Stadium Club set. Differences include the words "Virtual Reality" printed above the player's name and the numbering on the back. These cards were inserted in the first two Stadium Club series on a one per pack, two per rack pack basis.

Nm-Mt Ex-Mt
COMPLETE SET (270) 100.00 30.00
COMP.SERIES 1 (135) 50.00 15.00
COMP.SERIES 2 (135) 50.00 15.00
*STARS: .75X TO 2X BASIC CARDS...

1995 Stadium Club Clear Cut

Randomly inserted at a rate of one in 24 hobby and retail packs, this 28-card set features a full color action photo of the player against a clear acetate background with the player's name printed vertically.

Nm-Mt Ex-Mt
COMPLETE SET (28) 80.00 24.00
COMPLETE SERIES 1 (14) 40.00 12.00
COMP.SERIES 2 (14) 40.00 12.00
CC1 Mike Piazza 10.00 3.00
CC2 Ruben Sierra 1.25 .35
CC3 Tony Gwynn 8.00 2.40
CC4 Frank Thomas 6.00 1.80
CC5 Fred McGriff 4.00 1.20
CC6 Rafael Palmeiro 4.00 1.20
CC7 Bobby Bonilla 2.50 .75
CC8 Chili Davis 2.50 .75
CC9 Hal Morris 1.25 .35
CC10 Jose Canseco 6.00 1.80
CC11 Jay Bell 2.50 .75
CC12 Kirby Puckett 6.00 1.80
CC13 Gary Sheffield 2.50 .75
CC14 Bob Hamelin 1.25 .35
CC15 Jeff Bagwell 4.00 1.20
CC16 Albert Belle 2.50 .75
CC17 Sammy Sosa 10.00 3.00
CC18 Ken Griffey Jr. 10.00 3.00
CC19 Todd Zeile 1.25 .35
CC20 Mo Vaughn 2.50 .75
CC21 Moises Alou 2.50 .75
CC22 Paul O'Neill 4.00 1.20
CC23 Andres Galarraga 2.50 .75
CC24 Greg Vaughn 1.25 .35
CC25 Len Dykstra 2.50 .75
CC26 Joe Carter 2.50 .75
CC27 Barry Bonds 15.00 4.50
CC28 Cecil Fielder 2.50 .75

1995 Stadium Club Crunch Time

This 20-card standard-size set features home run hitters and was randomly inserted in first series rack packs. The cards are numbered as "X" of 20 in the upper right corner.

Nm-Mt Ex-Mt
COMPLETE SET (20) 50.00 15.00
1 Jeff Bagwell 2.00 .60
2 Kirby Puckett 3.00 .90
3 Frank Thomas 3.00 .90

4 Albert Belle 1.25 .35
5 Julio Franco 1.25 .35
6 Jose Canseco 3.00 .90
7 Paul Molitor 2.00 .60
8 Joe Carter 1.25 .35
9 Ken Griffey Jr. 5.00 1.50
10 Larry Walker 2.00 .60
11 Dante Bichette 1.25 .35
12 Carlos Baerga .60 .18
13 Fred McGriff 2.00 .60
14 Ruben Sierra .60 .18
15 Will Clark 3.00 .90
16 Moises Alou 1.25 .35
17 Rafael Palmeiro 2.00 .60
18 Travis Fryman 1.25 .35
19 Barry Bonds 8.00 2.40
20 Cal Ripken 10.00 3.00

1995 Stadium Club Crystal Ball

This 15-card standard-size set was inserted into series three packs at a rate of one in 24. Fifteen leading 1995 rookies and prospects were featured in this set. The player is identified on the top and the cards are numbered with a "CB" prefix in the upper left corner.

Nm-Mt Ex-Mt
COMPLETE SET (15) 80.00 24.00
CB1 Chipper Jones 10.00 3.00
CB2 Dustin Hermanson 2.00 .60
CB3 Ray Durham 4.00 1.20
CB4 Phil Nevin 4.00 1.20
CB5 Billy Ashley 2.00 .60
CB6 Shawn Green 4.00 1.20
CB7 Jason Bates 2.00 .60
CB8 Benji Gil 2.00 .60
CB9 Marty Cordova 2.00 .60
CB10 Quilvio Veras 2.00 .60
CB11 Mark Grudzielanek 4.00 1.20
CB12 Ruben Rivera 2.00 .60
CB13 Bill Pulsipher 2.00 .60
CB14 Derek Jeter 20.00 6.00
CB15 LaTroy Hawkins 2.00 .60

1995 Stadium Club Power Zone

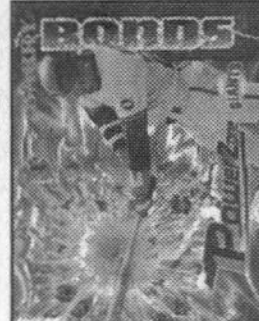

This 12-card standard-size set was inserted into series three packs at a rate of one in 24. The cards are numbered in the upper right corner with a "PZ" prefix.

Nm-Mt Ex-Mt
COMPLETE SET (12) 50.00 15.00
PZ1 Jeff Bagwell 4.00 1.20
PZ2 Albert Belle 2.50 .75
PZ3 Barry Bonds 15.00 4.50
PZ4 Joe Carter 2.50 .75
PZ5 Cecil Fielder 2.50 .75
PZ6 Andres Galarraga 2.50 .75
PZ7 Ken Griffey Jr. 10.00 3.00
PZ8 Paul Molitor 4.00 1.20
PZ9 Fred McGriff 4.00 1.20
PZ10 Rafael Palmeiro 4.00 1.20
PZ11 Frank Thomas 6.00 1.80
PZ12 Matt Williams 2.50 .75

1995 Stadium Club Ring Leaders

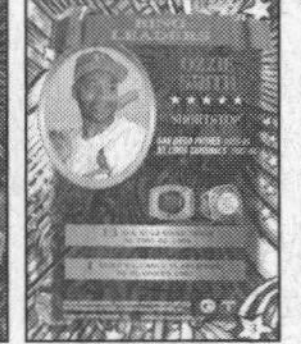

Randomly inserted in packs, this set features players who have won various awards or titles. This set was also redeemable as a prize with winning regular phone cards. This set features Stadium Club's "Power Matrix Technology," which makes the cards shine and glow. The horizontal fronts feature a player photo, rings in both upper corners as well as other designs that make for a very busy front. The backs have information on how the player earned his rings, along with a player photo and some other pertinent information.

Nm-Mt Ex-Mt
COMPLETE SET (40) 100.00 30.00
COMPLETE SERIES 1 (20) 50.00 15.00
COMP.SERIES 2 (20) 50.00 15.00
RL1 Jeff Bagwell 5.00 1.50
RL2 Mark McGwire 20.00 6.00
RL3 Ozzie Smith 12.00 3.60
RL4 Paul Molitor 5.00 1.50
RL5 Darryl Strawberry 1.50 .45
RL6 Eddie Murray 8.00 2.40
RL7 Tony Gwynn 10.00 3.00
RL8 Jose Canseco 8.00 2.40
RL9 Howard Johnson 1.50 .45
RL10 Andre Dawson 3.00 .90
RL11 Matt Williams 3.00 .90
RL12 Tim Raines 3.00 .90
RL13 Fred McGriff 5.00 1.50
RL14 Ken Griffey Jr. 12.00 3.60
RL15 Gary Sheffield 3.00 .90
RL16 Dennis Eckersley 3.00 .90
RL17 Kevin Mitchell 1.50 .45
RL18 Will Clark 8.00 2.40
RL19 Darren Daulton 3.00 .90
RL20 Paul O'Neill 5.00 1.50
RL21 Julio Franco 3.00 .90
RL22 Albert Belle 3.00 .90
RL23 Juan Gonzalez 5.00 1.50
RL24 Kirby Puckett 8.00 2.40
RL25 Joe Carter 3.00 .90
RL26 Frank Thomas 8.00 2.40
RL27 Cal Ripken 25.00 7.50
RL28 John Olerud 3.00 .90
RL29 Ruben Sierra 1.50 .45
RL30 Barry Bonds 20.00 6.00
RL31 Cecil Fielder 3.00 .90
RL32 Roger Clemens 15.00 4.50
RL33 Don Mattingly 20.00 6.00
RL34 Terry Pendleton 3.00 .90
RL35 Rickey Henderson 8.00 2.40
RL36 Dave Winfield 3.00 .90
RL37 Edgar Martinez 5.00 1.50
RL38 Wade Boggs 5.00 1.50
RL39 Willie McGee 3.00 .90
RL40 Andres Galarraga 3.00 .90

1995 Stadium Club Super Skills

This 20-card set was randomly inserted into hobby packs. The cards are numbered in the upper left as "X" of 9.

Nm-Mt Ex-Mt
COMPLETE SERIES 1 (9) 30.00 9.00
COMP.SERIES 2 (11) 40.00 12.00
SS1 Roberto Alomar 4.00 1.20
SS2 Barry Bonds 15.00 4.50
SS3 Jay Buhner 2.50 .75
SS4 Chuck Carr 1.25 .35
SS5 Don Mattingly 15.00 4.50
SS6 Raul Mondesi 2.50 .75
SS7 Tim Salmon 4.00 1.20
SS8 Deion Sanders 4.00 1.20
SS9 Devon White 2.50 .75
SS10 Mark Whiten 1.25 .35
SS11 Ken Griffey Jr. 10.00 3.00
SS12 Marquis Grissom 2.50 .75
SS13 Paul O'Neill 4.00 1.20
SS14 Kenny Lofton 2.50 .75
SS15 Larry Walker 4.00 1.20
SS16 Scott Cooper 1.25 .35
SS17 Barry Larkin 4.00 1.20
SS18 Matt Williams 2.50 .75
SS19 John Wetteland 2.50 .75
SS20 Randy Johnson 6.00 1.80

1995 Stadium Club Virtual Extremists

This 10-card set was inserted randomly into second series rack packs. The fronts feature a player photo against a baseball backdrop. The words "VR Extremist" are spelled vertically down the right side while the player name is in silver foil on the bottom. All of this is surrounded by blue and purple borders. The horizontal backs feature projected full-season 1994 stats. The cards are numbered with a "VRE" prefix in the upper right corner.

Nm-Mt Ex-Mt
COMPLETE SET (10) 80.00 24.00
VRE1 Barry Bonds 25.00 7.50
VRE2 Ken Griffey Jr. 15.00 4.50
VRE3 Jeff Bagwell 6.00 1.80
VRE4 Albert Belle 4.00 1.20
VRE5 Frank Thomas 10.00 3.00
VRE6 Tony Gwynn 12.00 3.60
VRE7 Kenny Lofton 4.00 1.20
VRE8 Deion Sanders 6.00 1.80
VRE9 Ken Hill 2.00 .60
VRE10 Jimmy Key 4.00 1.20

1996 Stadium Club

The 1996 Stadium Club set consists of 450 cards with cards 1-225 in first series packs and 226-450 in second series packs. The product was primarily distributed in first and second series foil-wrapped packs.There was also a factory set, which included the Mantle insert cards, packaged in mini-cereal box type cartons and made available through retail outlets. The set includes a Team TSC subset (181-270). These subset cards were slightly shortprinted in comparison to the other cards in the set. Though not confirmed by the manufacturer, it is believed that card number 22 (Roberto Hernandez) is a short-print.

	Nm-Mt	Ex-Mt
COMPLETE SET (450)	80.00	24.00
COMP.CEREAL SET (454)	80.00	24.00
COMP.SERIES 1 (225)	40.00	12.00
COMP.SERIES 2 (225)	40.00	12.00
COMMON (1-180/271-450)	.30	.09
COMMON SP (181-270)	.50	.15
1 Hideo Nomo	.75	.23
2 Paul Molitor	.50	.15
3 Garret Anderson	.30	.09
4 Jose Mesa	.30	.09
5 Vinny Castilla	.30	.09
6 Mike Mussina	.50	.15
7 Ray Durham	.30	.09
8 Jack McDowell	.30	.09
9 Juan Gonzalez	.50	.15
10 Chipper Jones	.75	.23
11 Deion Sanders	.50	.15
12 Rondell White	.30	.09
13 Tom Henke	.30	.09
14 Derek Bell	.30	.09
15 Randy Myers	.30	.09
16 Randy Johnson	.75	.23
17 Len Dykstra	.30	.09
18 Bill Pulsipher	.30	.09
19 Greg Colbrunn	.30	.09
20 David Wells	.30	.09
21 Chad Curtis	.30	.09
22 Roberto Hernandez SP	5.00	1.50
23 Kirby Puckett	.75	.23
24 Joe Vitiello	.30	.09
25 Roger Clemens	1.50	.45
26 Al Martin	.30	.09
27 Chad Ogea	.30	.09
28 David Segui	.30	.09
29 Joey Hamilton	.30	.09
30 Dan Wilson	.30	.09
31 Chad Fonville	.30	.09
32 Bernard Gilkey	.30	.09
33 Kevin Seitzer	.30	.09
34 Shawn Green	.30	.09
35 Rick Aguilera	.30	.09
36 Gary DiSarcina	.30	.09
37 Jaime Navarro	.30	.09
38 Doug Jones	.30	.09
39 Brent Gates	.30	.09
40 Dean Palmer	.30	.09
41 Pat Rapp	.30	.09
42 Tony Clark	.30	.09
43 Bill Swift	.30	.09
44 Randy Velarde	.30	.09
45 Matt Williams	.30	.09
46 John Mabry	.30	.09
47 Mike Fetters	.30	.09
48 Orlando Miller	.30	.09
49 Tom Glavine	.50	.15
50 Delino DeShields	.30	.09
51 Scott Erickson	.30	.09
52 Andy Van Slyke	.30	.09
53 Jim Bullinger	.30	.09
54 Lyle Mouton	.30	.09
55 Bret Saberhagen	.30	.09
56 Benito Santiago	.30	.09
57 Dan Miceli	.30	.09
58 Carl Everett	.30	.09
59 Rod Beck	.30	.09
60 Phil Nevin	.30	.09
61 Jason Giambi	.30	.09
62 Paul Menhart	.30	.09
63 Eric Karros	.30	.09
64 Allen Watson	.30	.09
65 Jeff Cirillo	.30	.09
66 Lee Smith	.30	.09
67 Sean Berry	.30	.09
68 Luis Sojo	.30	.09
69 Jeff Montgomery	.30	.09
70 Todd Hundley	.30	.09
71 John Burkett	.30	.09
72 Mark Gubicza	.30	.09
73 Don Mattingly	2.00	.60
74 Jeff Brantley	.30	.09
75 Matt Walbeck	.30	.09
76 Steve Parris	.30	.09
77 Ken Caminiti	.30	.09
78 Kirt Manwaring	.30	.09
79 Greg Vaughn	.30	.09
80 Pedro Martinez	.75	.23
81 Benji Gil	.30	.09
82 Heathcliff Slocumb	.30	.09
83 Joe Girardi	.30	.09
84 Sean Bergman	.30	.09
85 Matt Karchner	.30	.09
86 Butch Huskey	.30	.09
87 Mike Morgan	.30	.09
88 Todd Worrell	.30	.09
89 Mike Bordick	.30	.09
90 Bip Roberts	.30	.09
91 Mike Hampton	.30	.09
92 Troy O'Leary	.30	.09
93 Wally Joyner	.30	.09
94 Dave Stevens	.30	.09
95 Cecil Fielder	.30	.09
96 Wade Boggs	.50	.15
97 Hal Morris	.30	.09
98 Mickey Tettleton	.30	.09
99 Jeff Kent	.30	.09
100 Denny Martinez	.30	.09
101 Luis Gonzalez	.30	.09
102 John Jaha	.30	.09
103 Javier Lopez	.30	.09
104 Mark McGwire	2.00	.60
105 Ken Griffey Jr.	1.25	.35
106 Darren Daulton	.30	.09
107 Bryan Rekar	.30	.09
108 Mike Macfarlane	.30	.09
109 Gary Gaetti	.30	.09
110 Shane Reynolds	.30	.09
111 Pat Meares	.30	.09
112 Jason Schmidt	.50	.15
113 Otis Nixon	.30	.09
114 John Franco	.30	.09
115 Marc Newfield	.30	.09
116 Andy Benes	.30	.09
117 Ozzie Guillen	.30	.09
118 Brian Jordan	.30	.09
119 Terry Pendleton	.30	.09
120 Chuck Finley	.30	.09
121 Scott Stahoviak	.30	.09
122 Sid Fernandez	.30	.09
123 Derek Jeter	2.00	.60
124 John Smiley	.30	.09
125 David Bell	.30	.09
126 Brett Butler	.30	.09
127 Doug Drabek	.30	.09
128 J.T. Snow	.30	.09
129 Joe Carter	.30	.09
130 Dennis Eckersley	.30	.09
131 Marty Cordova	.30	.09
132 Greg Maddux	1.25	.35
133 Tom Goodwin	.30	.09
134 Andy Ashby	.30	.09
135 Paul Sorrento	.30	.09
136 Ricky Bones	.30	.09
137 Shawon Dunston	.30	.09
138 Moises Alou	.30	.09
139 Mickey Morandini	.30	.09
140 Ramon Martinez	.30	.09
141 Royce Clayton	.30	.09
142 Brad Ausmus	.30	.09
143 Kenny Rogers	.30	.09
144 Tim Naehring	.30	.09
145 Chris Gomez	.30	.09
146 Bobby Bonilla	.30	.09
147 Wilson Alvarez	.30	.09
148 Johnny Damon	.50	.15
149 Pat Hentgen	.30	.09
150 Andres Galarraga	.30	.09
151 David Cone	.30	.09
152 Lance Johnson	.30	.09
153 Carlos Garcia	.30	.09
154 Doug Johns	.30	.09
155 Midre Cummings	.30	.09
156 Steve Sparks	.30	.09
157 Sandy Martinez	.30	.09
158 Wm. Van Landingham	.30	.09
159 David Justice	.30	.09
160 Mark Grace	.50	.15
161 Robb Nen	.30	.09
162 Mike Greenwell	.30	.09
163 Brad Radke	.30	.09
164 Edgardo Alfonzo	.30	.09
165 Mark Leiter	.30	.09
166 Walt Weiss	.30	.09
167 Mel Rojas	.30	.09
168 Bret Boone	.30	.09
169 Ricky Bottalico	.30	.09
170 Bobby Higginson	.30	.09
171 Trevor Hoffman	.30	.09
172 Jay Bell	.30	.09
173 Gabe White	.30	.09
174 Curtis Goodwin	.30	.09
175 Tyler Green	.30	.09
176 Roberto Alomar	.50	.15
177 Sterling Hitchcock	.30	.09
178 Ryan Klesko	.30	.09
179 Donne Wall	.30	.09
180 Brian McRae	.30	.09
181 Will Clark TSC SP	1.00	.30
182 F.Thomas TSC SP	1.00	.30
183 Jeff Bagwell TSC SP	.50	.15
184 Mo Vaughn TSC SP	.50	.15
185 Tino Martinez TSC SP	.75	.23
186 Craig Biggio TSC SP	.75	.23
187 C. Knoblauch TSC SP	.50	.15
188 Carlos Baerga TSC SP	.50	.15
189 Quilvio Veras TSC SP	.50	.15
190 Luis Alicea TSC SP	.50	.15
191 Jim Thome TSC SP	1.00	.30
192 Mike Blowers TSC SP	.50	.15
193 R.Ventura TSC SP	.50	.15
194 Jeff King TSC SP	.50	.15
195 Tony Phillips TSC SP	.50	.15
196 John Valentin TSC SP	.50	.15
197 Barry Larkin TSC SP	.75	.23
198 Cal Ripken TSC SP	3.00	.90
199 Omar Vizquel TSC SP	.75	.23
200 Kurt Abbott TSC SP	.50	.15
201 Albert Belle TSC SP	.50	.15
202 Barry Bonds TSC SP	2.50	.75
203 Ron Gant TSC SP	.50	.15
204 D.Bichette TSC SP	.50	.15
205 Jeff Conine TSC SP	.50	.15
206 Jim Edmonds TSC SP UER (Greg Myers pictured on front)	.50	.15
207 Stan Javier TSC SP	.50	.15
208 Kenny Lofton TSC SP	.50	.15
209 Ray Lankford TSC SP	.50	.15
210 B.Williams TSC SP	.75	.23
211 Jay Buhner TSC SP	.50	.15
212 Paul O'Neill TSC SP	.75	.23
213 Tim Salmon TSC SP	.75	.23
214 R.Sanders TSC SP	.50	.15
215 M.Ramirez TSC SP	.75	.23
216 Mike Piazza TSC SP	1.50	.45
217 Mike Stanley TSC SP	.50	.15
218 Tony Eusebio TSC SP	.50	.15
219 Chris Hoiles TSC SP	.50	.15
220 R.Karkovice TSC SP	.50	.15
221 E.Martinez TSC SP	.75	.23
222 Chili Davis TSC SP	.50	.15
223 Jose Canseco TSC SP	.75	.23
224 Eddie Murray TSC SP	1.00	.30
225 G.Berroa TSC SP	.50	.15
226 C.Jones TSC SP	1.00	.30
227 G.Anderson TSC SP	.50	.15
228 M.Cordova TSC SP	.50	.15
229 Jon Nunnally TSC SP	.50	.15
230 Brian L.Hunter TSC SP	.50	.15
231 Shawn Green TSC SP	.50	.15
232 Ray Durham TSC SP	.50	.15
233 Alex Gonzalez TSC SP	.50	.15
234 B.Higginson TSC SP	.50	.15
235 R.Johnson TSC SP	1.00	.30
236 Al Leiter TSC SP	.50	.15
237 Tom Glavine TSC SP	.75	.23
238 Kenny Rogers TSC SP	.50	.15
239 M.Hampton TSC SP	.50	.15
240 David Wells TSC SP	.50	.15
241 Jim Abbott TSC SP	.75	.23
242 Denny Neagle TSC SP	.50	.15
243 W.Alvarez TSC SP	.50	.15
244 John Smiley TSC SP	.50	.15
245 Greg Maddux TSC SP	.75	.23
246 Andy Ashby TSC SP	.50	.15
247 Hideo Nomo TSC SP	1.00	.30
248 Pat Rapp TSC SP	.50	.15
249 T.Wakefield TSC SP	.50	.15
250 John Smoltz TSC SP	.75	.23
251 J.Hamilton TSC SP	.50	.15
252 Frank Castillo TSC SP	.50	.15
253 D.Martinez TSC SP	.50	.15
254 J.Navarro TSC SP	.50	.15
255 Karim Garcia TSC SP	.50	.15
256 Bob Abreu TSC SP	.50	.15
257 Butch Huskey TSC SP	.50	.15
258 Ruben Rivera TSC SP	.50	.15
259 J.Damon TSC SP	.75	.23
260 Derek Jeter TSC SP	2.50	.75
261 D. Eckersley TSC SP	.50	.15
262 Jose Mesa TSC SP	.50	.15
263 Tom Henke TSC SP	.50	.15
264 Rick Aguilera TSC SP	.50	.15
265 Randy Myers TSC SP	.50	.15
266 John Franco TSC SP	.50	.15
267 Jeff Brantley TSC SP	.50	.15
268 J.Wetteland TSC SP	.50	.15
269 Mark Wohlers TSC SP	.50	.15
270 Rod Beck TSC SP	.50	.15
271 Barry Larkin	.50	.15
272 Paul O'Neill	.50	.15
273 Bobby Jones	.30	.09
274 Will Clark	.75	.23
275 Steve Avery	.30	.09
276 Jim Edmonds	.30	.09
277 John Olerud	.30	.09
278 Carlos Perez	.30	.09
279 Chris Hoiles	.30	.09
280 Jeff Conine	.30	.09
281 Jim Eisenreich	.30	.09
282 Jason Jacome	.30	.09
283 Ray Lankford	.30	.09
284 John Wasdin	.30	.09
285 Frank Thomas	.75	.23
286 Jason Isringhausen	.30	.09
287 Glenallen Hill	.30	.09
288 Esteban Loaiza	.30	.09
289 Bernie Williams	.50	.15
290 Curtis Leskanic	.30	.09
291 Scott Cooper	.30	.09
292 Curt Schilling	.50	.15
293 Eddie Murray	.75	.23
294 Rick Krivda	.30	.09
295 Domingo Cedeno	.30	.09
296 Jeff Fassero	.30	.09
297 Albert Belle	.30	.09
298 Craig Biggio	.50	.15
299 Fernando Vina	.30	.09
300 Edgar Martinez	.50	.15
301 Tony Gwynn	1.00	.30
302 Felipe Lira	.30	.09
303 Mo Vaughn	.30	.09
304 Alex Fernandez	.30	.09
305 Keith Lockhart	.30	.09
306 Roger Pavlik	.30	.09
307 Lee Tinsley	.30	.09
308 Omar Vizquel	.30	.09
309 Scott Servais	.30	.09
310 Danny Tartabull	.30	.09
311 Chili Davis	.30	.09
312 Cal Eldred	.30	.09
313 Roger Cedeno	.30	.09
314 Chris Hammond	.30	.09
315 Rusty Greer	.30	.09
316 Brady Anderson	.30	.09
317 Ron Villone	.30	.09
318 Mark Carreon	.30	.09
319 Larry Walker	.50	.15
320 Pete Harnisch	.30	.09
321 Robin Ventura	.30	.09
322 Tim Belcher	.30	.09
323 Tony Tarasco	.30	.09
324 Juan Guzman	.30	.09
325 Kenny Lofton	.30	.09
326 Kevin Foster	.30	.09
327 Wil Cordero	.30	.09
328 Troy Percival	.30	.09
329 Turk Wendell	.30	.09
330 Thomas Howard	.30	.09
331 Carlos Baerga	.30	.09
332 B.J. Surhoff	.30	.09
333 Jay Buhner	.30	.09
334 Andujar Cedeno	.30	.09
335 Jeff King	.30	.09
336 Dante Bichette	.30	.09
337 Alan Trammell	.50	.15
338 Scott Leius	.30	.09
339 Chris Snopek	.30	.09
340 Roger Bailey	.30	.09
341 Jacob Brumfield	.30	.09
342 Jose Canseco	.75	.23
343 Rafael Palmeiro	.50	.15
344 Quilvio Veras	.30	.09
345 Darrin Fletcher	.30	.09
346 Carlos Delgado	.30	.09
347 Tony Eusebio	.30	.09
348 Ismael Valdes	.30	.09
349 Terry Steinbach	.30	.09
350 Orel Hershiser	.30	.09
351 Kurt Abbott	.30	.09
352 Jody Reed	.30	.09
353 David Howard	.30	.09
354 Ruben Sierra	.30	.09
355 John Ericks	.30	.09
356 Buck Showalter MG	.30	.09
357 Jim Thome	.75	.23
358 Geronimo Berroa	.30	.09
359 Robby Thompson	.30	.09
360 Jose Vizcaino	.30	.09
361 Jeff Frye	.30	.09
362 Kevin Appier	.30	.09
363 Pat Kelly	.30	.09
364 Ron Gant	.30	.09
365 Luis Alicea	.30	.09
366 Armando Benitez	.30	.09
367 Rico Brogna	.30	.09
368 Manny Ramirez	.50	.15
369 Mike Lansing	.30	.09
370 Sammy Sosa	1.25	.35
371 Don Wengert	.30	.09
372 Dave Nilsson	.30	.09
373 Sandy Alomar Jr.	.30	.09
374 Joey Cora	.30	.09
375 Larry Thomas	.30	.09
376 John Valentin	.30	.09
377 Kevin Ritz	.30	.09
378 Steve Finley	.30	.09
379 Frank Rodriguez	.30	.09
380 Ivan Rodriguez	.75	.23
381 Alex Ochoa	.30	.09
382 Mark Lemke	.30	.09
383 Scott Brosius	.30	.09
384 James Mouton	.30	.09
385 Mark Langston	.30	.09
386 Ed Sprague	.30	.09
387 Joe Oliver	.30	.09
388 Steve Ontiveros	.30	.09
389 Rey Sanchez	.30	.09
390 Mike Henneman	.30	.09
391 Jose Valentin	.30	.09
392 Tom Candiotti	.30	.09
393 Damon Buford	.30	.09
394 Erik Hanson	.30	.09
395 Mark Smith	.30	.09
396 Pete Schourek	.30	.09
397 John Flaherty	.30	.09
398 Dave Martinez	.30	.09
399 Tommy Greene	.30	.09
400 Gary Sheffield	.30	.09
401 Glenn Dishman	.30	.09
402 Barry Bonds	2.00	.60
403 Tom Pagnozzi	.30	.09
404 Todd Stottlemyre	.30	.09
405 Tim Salmon	.50	.15
406 John Hudek	.30	.09
407 Fred McGriff	.50	.15
408 Orlando Merced	.30	.09
409 Brian Barber	.30	.09
410 Ryan Thompson	.30	.09
411 Mariano Rivera	.50	.15
412 Eric Young	.30	.09
413 Chris Bosio	.30	.09
414 Chuck Knoblauch	.30	.09
415 Jamie Moyer	.30	.09
416 Chan Ho Park	.30	.09
417 Mark Portugal	.30	.09
418 Tim Raines	.30	.09
419 Antonio Osuna	.30	.09
420 Todd Zeile	.30	.09
421 Steve Wojciechowski	.30	.09
422 Marquis Grissom	.30	.09
423 Norm Charlton	.30	.09
424 Cal Ripken	2.50	.75
425 Gregg Jefferies	.30	.09
426 Mike Stanton	.30	.09
427 Tony Fernandez	.30	.09
428 Jose Rijo	.30	.09
429 Jeff Bagwell	.50	.15
430 Raul Mondesi	.30	.09
431 Travis Fryman	.30	.09
432 Ron Karkovice	.30	.09
433 Alan Benes	.30	.09
434 Tony Phillips	.30	.09
435 Reggie Sanders	.30	.09
436 Andy Pettitte	.50	.15
437 Matt Lawton RC	.50	.15
438 Jeff Blauser	.30	.09
439 Michael Tucker	.30	.09
440 Mark Loretta	.30	.09
441 Charlie Hayes	.30	.09
442 Mike Piazza	1.25	.35
443 Shane Andrews	.30	.09
444 Jeff Suppan	.30	.09
445 Steve Rodriguez	.30	.09
446 Mike Matheny	.30	.09
447 Trenidad Hubbard	.30	.09
448 Denny Hocking	.30	.09
449 Mark Grudzielanek	.30	.09
450 Joe Randa	.30	.09

1996 Stadium Club Bash and Burn

Randomly inserted in packs at a rate of one in 24 (retail) and one in 48 (hobby), this ten card set features power/speed players.

	Nm-Mt	Ex-Mt
COMPLETE SET (10)	40.00	12.00
BB1 Sammy Sosa	15.00	4.50
BB2 Barry Bonds	25.00	7.50
BB3 Reggie Sanders	4.00	1.20
BB4 Craig Biggio	6.00	1.80
BB5 Raul Mondesi	4.00	1.20
BB6 Ron Gant	4.00	1.20
BB7 Ray Lankford	4.00	1.20
BB8 Glenallen Hill	4.00	1.20
BB9 Chad Curtis	4.00	1.20
BB10 John Valentin	4.00	1.20

1996 Stadium Club Extreme Players Bronze

One hundred and seventy nine different players were featured on Extreme Player game cards randomly issued in 1996 Stadium Club first and second series packs. Each player has three versions: Bronze, Silver and Gold. All of these cards parallel their corresponding regular issue card except for the Bronze foil "Extreme Players" logo on each card front and the "EP" suffix on the card number, thus creating a skip-numbered set. The Bronze cards listed below were seeded at a rate of 1:12 packs. At the conclusion of the 1996 regular season, an Extreme Player from each of ten positions was identified as a winner based on scores calculated from their actual playing statistics. The 10 winning players are noted with a "W" below. Prior to the December 31st, 1996 deadline, each of the ten winning Extreme Players Bronze cards was redeemable for a 10-card set of Extreme Winners Bronze. Unredeemed winners are now in much shorter supply than other cards in this set and carry premium values.

	Nm-Mt	Ex-Mt
COMP.BRONZE SER.1 (90)	120.00	36.00
COMP.BRONZE SER.2 (90)	120.00	36.00
*BRONZE: 2X TO 5X BASE CARD HI		
*SILVER SINGLES: .6X TO 1.5X BRONZE		
*SILVER WIN: .6X TO 1.5X BRONZE WIN		
*GOLD SINGLES: 1.25X TO 3X BRONZE		
*GOLD WIN: 1.25X TO 3X BRONZE WIN		
GOLD STATED ODDS 1:48		
SKIP-NUMBERED 179-CARD SET		
77 Ken Caminiti W	4.00	1.20
88 Todd Worrell W	1.50	.45
105 Ken Griffey Jr. W	12.00	3.60
132 Greg Maddux W	12.00	3.60
150 Andres Galarraga W	4.00	1.20
271 Barry Larkin W	4.00	1.20
400 Gary Sheffield W	5.00	1.50
402 Barry Bonds W	20.00	6.00
414 Chuck Knoblauch W	3.00	.90
442 Mike Piazza W	12.00	3.60

1996 Stadium Club Extreme Winners Bronze

This 10-card skip-numbered set was only available to collectors who redeemed one of the ten winning Bronze Extreme Players cards before the December 31st, 1996 deadline. The cards parallel the Extreme Players cards inserted in Stadium Club packs except for their distinctive diffraction foil fronts.

	Nm-Mt	Ex-Mt
COMPLETE SET (10)	25.00	7.50
*SILVER: 1.25X TO 3X BRONZE WINNERS		
ONE SILV.SET VIA MAIL PER SILV.WINNER		
*GOLD: 5X TO 12X BRONZE WINNERS		
ONE GOLD CARD VIA MAIL PER GOLD WNR.		
EW1 Greg Maddux	4.00	1.20
EW2 Mike Piazza	4.00	1.20
EW3 Andres Galarraga	1.00	.30
EW4 Chuck Knoblauch	1.00	.30
EW5 Ken Caminiti	1.00	.30
EW6 Barry Larkin	1.50	.45
EW7 Barry Bonds	6.00	1.80
EW8 Ken Griffey Jr.	4.00	1.20
EW9 Gary Sheffield	1.00	.30
EW10 Todd Worrell	1.00	.30

1996 Stadium Club Mantle

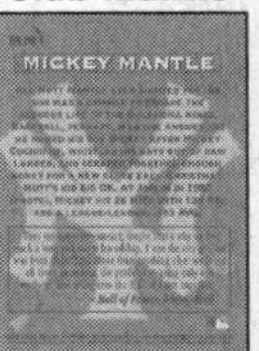

Randomly inserted at a rate of one card in every 24 packs in series one, one in 12 packs in series two, this 19-card retrospective set chronicles Mantle's career with classic photography, celebrity quotes and highlights from each year. The cards are double foil-stamped. The series one cards feature black-and-white photos, series two color photos. Mantle's name is printed across a silver foil facade of Yankee Stadium on each card top. Cereal Box factory sets include these cards with gold foil. They are valued the same as the pack inserts.

	Nm-Mt	Ex-Mt
COMPLETE SET (19)	120.00	36.00
COMMON (MM1-MM9)	10.00	3.00
COMMON (MM10-MM19)	6.00	1.80

1996 Stadium Club Megaheroes

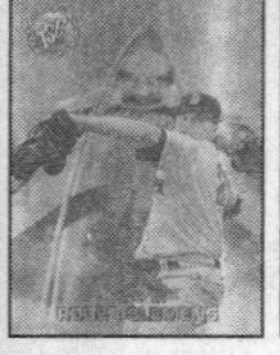

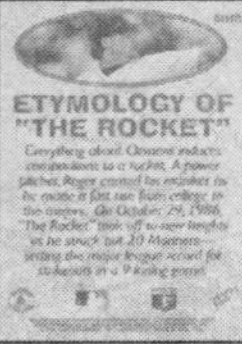

Randomly inserted at a rate of one in every 48 hobby and 24 retail packs, this 10-card set features super-heroic players matched with a comic book-style illustration depicting their nicknames.

	Nm-Mt	Ex-Mt
COMPLETE SET (10)	40.00	12.00
MH1 Frank Thomas	5.00	1.50
MH2 Ken Griffey Jr.	8.00	2.40
MH3 Hideo Nomo	5.00	1.50
MH4 Ozzie Smith	5.00	1.50
MH5 Will Clark	5.00	1.50
MH6 Jack McDowell	2.00	.60
MH7 Andres Galarraga	2.00	.60
MH8 Roger Clemens	10.00	3.00
MH9 Deion Sanders	3.00	.90
MH10 Mo Vaughn	2.00	.60

1996 Stadium Club Metalists

Randomly inserted in packs at a rate of one in 96 (retail) and one in 48 (hobby), this eight-card set features players with two or more MLB awards and is printed on laser-cut foil board.

	Nm-Mt	Ex-Mt
COMPLETE SET (8)	40.00	12.00
M1 Jeff Bagwell	2.50	.75
M2 Barry Bonds	10.00	3.00
M3 Jose Canseco	4.00	1.20
M4 Roger Clemens	8.00	2.40
M5 Dennis Eckersley	1.50	.45
M6 Greg Maddux	6.00	1.80
M7 Cal Ripken	12.00	3.60
M8 Frank Thomas	4.00	1.20

1996 Stadium Club Midsummer Matchups

Randomly inserted at a rate of one in every 48 hobby and 24 retail packs, this 10-card set salutes 1995 National League and American League All-Stars as they are matched back-to-back by position on these two-sided etched foil cards.

	Nm-Mt	Ex-Mt
COMPLETE SET (10)	60.00	18.00
M1 Hideo Nomo / Randy Johnson	5.00	1.50
M2 Mike Piazza / Ivan Rodriguez	8.00	2.40
M3 Fred McGriff / Frank Thomas	5.00	1.50
M4 Craig Biggio / Carlos Baerga	3.00	.90
M5 Vinny Castilla / Wade Boggs	3.00	.90
M6 Barry Larkin / Cal Ripken	15.00	4.50
M7 Barry Bonds / Albert Belle	12.00	3.60
M8 Len Dykstra / Kenny Lofton	2.00	.60
M9 Tony Gwynn / Kirby Puckett	6.00	1.80
M10 Ron Gant / Edgar Martinez	3.00	.90

1996 Stadium Club Power Packed

Randomly inserted in packs at a rate of one in 48, this 15-card set features the biggest, most powerful hitters in the League. Printed on Power Matrix, the cards carry diagrams showing where the players hit the ball over the fence and how far.

	Nm-Mt	Ex-Mt
COMPLETE SET (15)	60.00	18.00
PP1 Albert Belle	2.50	.75
PP2 Mark McGwire	15.00	4.50
PP3 Jose Canseco	6.00	1.80
PP4 Mike Piazza	10.00	3.00
PP5 Ron Gant	2.50	.75
PP6 Ken Griffey Jr.	10.00	3.00
PP7 Mo Vaughn	2.50	.75
PP8 Cecil Fielder	2.50	.75
PP9 Tim Salmon	4.00	1.20
PP10 Frank Thomas	6.00	1.80
PP11 Juan Gonzalez	4.00	1.20
PP12 Andres Galarraga	2.50	.75
PP13 Fred McGriff	4.00	1.20
PP14 Jay Buhner	2.50	.75
PP15 Dante Bichette	2.50	.75

1996 Stadium Club Power Streak

Randomly inserted at a rate of one in every 24 hobby packs and 48 retail packs, this 15-card set spotlights baseball's most awesome power hitters and strikeout artists.

	Nm-Mt	Ex-Mt
COMPLETE SET (15)	60.00	18.00
PS1 Randy Johnson	6.00	1.80
PS2 Hideo Nomo	6.00	1.80
PS3 Albert Belle	2.50	.75
PS4 Dante Bichette	2.50	.75
PS5 Jay Buhner	2.50	.75
PS6 Frank Thomas	6.00	1.80
PS7 Mark McGwire	15.00	4.50
PS8 Rafael Palmeiro	4.00	1.20
PS9 Mo Vaughn	2.50	.75
PS10 Sammy Sosa	10.00	3.00
PS11 Larry Walker	4.00	1.20
PS12 Gary Gaetti	2.50	.75
PS13 Tim Salmon	4.00	1.20
PS14 Barry Bonds	15.00	4.50
PS15 Jim Edmonds	2.50	.75

1996 Stadium Club Prime Cuts

Randomly inserted at a rate of one in every 36 hobby and 72 retail packs, this eight card set this set highlights hitters with the purest swings. The cards are numbered on the back with a "PC" prefix.

	Nm-Mt	Ex-Mt
COMPLETE SET (8)	50.00	15.00
PC1 Albert Belle	2.00	.60
PC2 Barry Bonds	12.00	3.60
PC3 Ken Griffey Jr.	8.00	2.40
PC4 Tony Gwynn	6.00	1.80
PC5 Edgar Martinez	3.00	.90
PC6 Rafael Palmeiro	3.00	.90
PC7 Mike Piazza	8.00	2.40
PC8 Frank Thomas	5.00	1.50

1996 Stadium Club TSC Awards

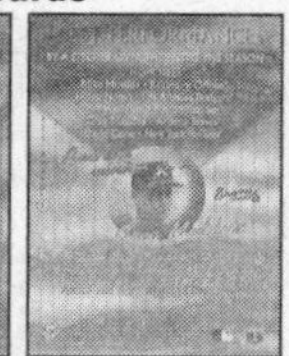

Randomly inserted in packs at a rate of one in 24 (retail) and one in 48 (hobby), this ten-card set features players whom TSC baseball experts voted to win various awards and is printed on diffraction foil.

	Nm-Mt	Ex-Mt
COMPLETE SET (10)	40.00	12.00
1 Cal Ripken	12.00	3.60
2 Albert Belle	1.50	.45
3 Tom Glavine	2.50	.75
4 Jeff Conine	1.50	.45
5 Ken Griffey Jr.	6.00	1.80
6 Hideo Nomo	4.00	1.20
7 Greg Maddux	6.00	1.80
8 Chipper Jones	4.00	1.20
9 Randy Johnson	4.00	1.20
10 Jose Mesa	1.50	.45

1997 Stadium Club

Cards from this 390 card set were distributed in eight-card hobby and retail packs (SRP $3) and 13-card hobby collector packs (SRP $5). Card fronts feature color action player photos printed on 20 pt. card stock with Topps Super Color processing, Hi-gloss laminating, embossing and double foil stamping. The backs carry player

information and statistics. In addition to the standard selection of major leaguers, the set contains a 15-card TSC 2000 subset (181-195) featuring a selection of top young prospects. These subset cards were inserted one in every two eight-card first series packs and one per 13-card first series pack. First series cards were released in February, 1997. The 195-card Series two set was issued in six-card retail packs with a suggested retail price of $2 and in nine-card hobby packs with a suggested retail price of $3. The second series set features a 15-card Stadium Sluggers subset (376-390) with an insertion rate of one in every two hobby and three retail Series 2 packs. Second series cards were released in April, 1997. Please note that cards 361 and 374 do not exist. Due to an error at the manufacturer both Mike Sweeney and Tom Pagnozzi had their cards numbered as 274. In addition, Jermaine Dye and Brant Brown both had their cards numbered as 351. These numbering errors were never corrected and no premiums in value are associated.

	Nm-Mt	Ex-Mt
COMPLETE SET (390)	80.00	24.00
COMP.SERIES 1 (195)	40.00	12.00
COMP.SERIES 2 (195)	40.00	12.00
COMMON (1-180/196-375)	.30	.09
COM.SP (181-195/376-390)	.75	.23
1 Chipper Jones	.75	.23
2 Gary Sheffield	.30	.09
3 Kenny Lofton	.30	.09
4 Brian Jordan	.30	.09
5 Mark McGwire	2.00	.60
6 Charles Nagy	.30	.09
7 Tim Salmon	.50	.15
8 Cal Ripken	2.50	.75
9 Jeff Conine	.30	.09
10 Paul Molitor	.50	.15
11 Mariano Rivera	.50	.15
12 Pedro Martinez	.75	.23
13 Jeff Bagwell	.50	.15
14 Bobby Bonilla	.30	.09
15 Barry Bonds	2.00	.60
16 Ryan Klesko	.30	.09
17 Barry Larkin	.50	.15
18 Jim Thome	.75	.23
19 Jay Buhner	.30	.09
20 Juan Gonzalez	.50	.15
21 Mike Mussina	.50	.15
22 Kevin Appier	.30	.09
23 Eric Karros	.30	.09
24 Steve Finley	.30	.09
25 Ed Sprague	.30	.09
26 Bernard Gilkey	.30	.09
27 Tony Phillips	.30	.09
28 Henry Rodriguez	.30	.09
29 John Smoltz	.50	.15
30 Dante Bichette	.30	.09
31 Mike Piazza	1.25	.35
32 Paul O'Neill	.50	.15
33 Billy Wagner	.30	.09
34 Reggie Sanders	.30	.09
35 John Jaha	.30	.09
36 Eddie Murray	.75	.23
37 Eric Young	.30	.09
38 Roberto Hernandez	.30	.09
39 Pat Hentgen	.30	.09
40 Sammy Sosa	1.25	.35
41 Todd Hundley	.30	.09
42 Mo Vaughn	.30	.09
43 Robin Ventura	.30	.09
44 Mark Grudzielanek	.30	.09
45 Shane Reynolds	.30	.09
46 Andy Pettitte	.50	.15
47 Fred McGriff	.50	.15
48 Rey Ordonez	.30	.09
49 Will Clark	.75	.23
50 Ken Griffey Jr.	1.25	.35
51 Todd Worrell	.30	.09
52 Rusty Greer	.30	.09
53 Mark Grace	.50	.15
54 Tom Glavine	.50	.15
55 Derek Jeter	2.00	.60
56 Rafael Palmeiro	.50	.15
57 Bernie Williams	.50	.15
58 Marty Cordova	.30	.09
59 Andres Galarraga	.30	.09
60 Ken Caminiti	.30	.09
61 Garret Anderson	.30	.09
62 Denny Martinez	.30	.09
63 Mike Greenwell	.30	.09
64 David Segui	.30	.09
65 Julio Franco	.30	.09
66 Rickey Henderson	.75	.23
67 Ozzie Guillen	.30	.09
68 Pete Harnisch	.30	.09
69 Chan Ho Park	.30	.09
70 Harold Baines	.30	.09
71 Mark Clark	.30	.09
72 Steve Avery	.30	.09
73 Brian Hunter	.30	.09
74 Pedro Astacio	.30	.09
75 Jack McDowell	.30	.09
76 Gregg Jefferies	.30	.09
77 Jason Kendall	.30	.09
78 Todd Walker	.30	.09
79 B.J. Surhoff	.30	.09
80 Moises Alou	.30	.09
81 Fernando Vina	.30	.09
82 Darryl Strawberry	.30	.09
83 Jose Rosado	.30	.09
84 Chris Gomez	.30	.09
85 Chili Davis	.30	.09
86 Alan Benes	.30	.09
87 Todd Hollandsworth	.30	.09
88 Jose Vizcaino	.30	.09
89 Edgardo Alfonzo	.30	.09
90 Ruben Rivera	.30	.09
91 Donovan Osborne	.30	.09
92 Doug Glanville	.30	.09
93 Gary DiSarcina	.30	.09
94 Brooks Kieschnick	.30	.09
95 Bobby Jones	.30	.09
96 Raul Casanova	.30	.09
97 Jermaine Allensworth	.30	.09
98 Kenny Rogers	.30	.09
99 Mark McLemore	.30	.09
100 Jeff Fassero	.30	.09
101 Sandy Alomar Jr.	.30	.09
102 Chuck Finley	.30	.09
103 Eric Owens	.30	.09
104 Billy McMillon	.30	.09
105 Dwight Gooden	.30	.09
106 Sterling Hitchcock	.30	.09
107 Doug Drabek	.30	.09
108 Paul Wilson	.30	.09
109 Chris Snopek	.30	.09
110 Al Leiter	.30	.09
111 Bob Tewksbury	.30	.09
112 Todd Greene	.30	.09
113 Jose Valentin	.30	.09
114 Delino DeShields	.30	.09
115 Mike Bordick	.30	.09
116 Pat Meares	.30	.09
117 Mariano Duncan	.30	.09
118 Steve Trachsel	.30	.09
119 Luis Castillo	.30	.09
120 Andy Benes	.30	.09
121 Donne Wall	.30	.09
122 Alex Gonzalez	.30	.09
123 Dan Wilson	.30	.09
124 Omar Vizquel	.50	.15
125 Devon White	.30	.09
126 Darryl Hamilton	.30	.09
127 Orlando Merced	.30	.09
128 Royce Clayton	.30	.09
129 W.VanLandingham	.30	.09
130 Terry Steinbach	.30	.09
131 Jeff Blauser	.30	.09
132 Jeff Cirillo	.30	.09
133 Roger Pavlik	.30	.09
134 Danny Tartabull	.30	.09
135 Jeff Montgomery	.30	.09
136 Bobby Higginson	.30	.09
137 Mike Grace	.30	.09
138 Kevin Elster	.30	.09
139 Brian Giles RC	1.50	.45
140 Rod Beck	.30	.09
141 Ismael Valdes	.30	.09
142 Scott Brosius	.30	.09
143 Mike Fetters	.30	.09
144 Gary Gaetti	.30	.09
145 Mike Lansing	.30	.09
146 Glenallen Hill	.30	.09
147 Shawn Green	.30	.09
148 Mel Rojas	.30	.09
149 Joey Cora	.30	.09
150 John Smiley	.30	.09
151 Marvin Benard	.30	.09
152 Curt Schilling	.30	.09
153 Dave Nilsson	.30	.09
154 Edgar Renteria	.30	.09
155 Joey Hamilton	.30	.09
156 Carlos Garcia	.30	.09
157 Nomar Garciaparra	1.25	.35
158 Kevin Ritz	.30	.09
159 Keith Lockhart	.30	.09
160 Justin Thompson	.30	.09
161 Terry Adams	.30	.09
162 Jamey Wright	.30	.09
163 Otis Nixon	.30	.09
164 Michael Tucker	.30	.09
165 Mike Stanley	.30	.09
166 Ben McDonald	.30	.09
167 John Mabry	.30	.09
168 Troy O'Leary	.30	.09
169 Mel Nieves	.30	.09
170 Bret Boone	.30	.09
171 Mike Timlin	.30	.09
172 Scott Rolen	.75	.23
173 Reggie Jefferson	.30	.09
174 Neifi Perez	.30	.09
175 Brian McRae	.30	.09
176 Tom Goodwin	.30	.09
177 Aaron Sele	.30	.09
178 Benito Santiago	.30	.09
179 Frank Rodriguez	.30	.09
180 Eric Davis	.30	.09
181 A.Jones 2000 SP	.75	.23
182 Todd Walker 2000 SP	.75	.23
183 Wes Helms 2000 SP	.75	.23
184 Nelson Figueroa 2000 SP RC	.75	.23
185 V. Guerrero 2000 SP	1.25	.35
186 B.McMillon 2000 SP	.75	.23
187 Todd Helton 2000 SP	1.25	.35
188 Nomar Garciaparra 2000 SP	2.50	.75
189 K. Maeda 2000 SP	.75	.23
190 R.Branyan 2000 SP	.75	.23
191 G.Rusch 2000 SP	.75	.23
192 B.Colon 2000 SP	.75	.23
193 Scott Rolen 2000 SP	1.25	.35
194 A. Echevarria 2000 SP	.75	.23
195 Bob Abreu 2000 SP	.75	.23
196 Greg Maddux	1.25	.35
197 Joe Carter	.30	.09
198 Alex Ochoa	.30	.09
199 Ellis Burks	.30	.09
200 Ivan Rodriguez	.75	.23
201 Marquis Grissom	.30	.09
202 Trevor Hoffman	.30	.09
203 Matt Williams	.30	.09
204 Carlos Delgado	.30	.09
205 Ramon Martinez	.30	.09
206 Chuck Knoblauch	.30	.09
207 Juan Guzman	.30	.09
208 Derek Bell	.30	.09
209 Roger Clemens	1.50	.45
210 Vladimir Guerrero	.75	.23
211 Cecil Fielder	.30	.09
212 Hideo Nomo	.75	.23
213 Frank Thomas	.75	.23
214 Greg Vaughn	.30	.09
215 Javy Lopez	.30	.09
216 Raul Mondesi	.30	.09
217 Wade Boggs	.50	.15
218 Carlos Baerga	.30	.09
219 Tony Gwynn	1.00	.30
220 Tino Martinez	.50	.15
221 Vinny Castilla	.30	.09
222 Lance Johnson	.30	.09
223 David Justice	.30	.09
224 Rondell White	.30	.09
225 Dean Palmer	.30	.09
226 Jim Edmonds	.30	.09
227 Albert Belle	.30	.09
228 Alex Fernandez	.30	.09
229 Ryne Sandberg	1.25	.35
230 Jose Mesa	.30	.09
231 David Cone	.30	.09
232 Troy Percival	.30	.09
233 Edgar Martinez	.50	.15
234 Jose Canseco	.75	.23
235 Kevin Brown	.30	.09
236 Ray Lankford	.30	.09
237 Karim Garcia	.30	.09
238 J.T. Snow	.30	.09
239 Dennis Eckersley	.30	.09
240 Roberto Alomar	.50	.15
241 John Valentin	.30	.09
242 Ron Gant	.30	.09
243 Geronimo Berroa	.30	.09
244 Manny Ramirez	.50	.15
245 Travis Fryman	.30	.09
246 Denny Neagle	.30	.09
247 Randy Johnson	.75	.23
248 Darin Erstad	.30	.09
249 Mark Wohlers	.30	.09
250 Ken Hill	.30	.09
251 Larry Walker	.50	.15
252 Craig Biggio	.50	.15
253 Brady Anderson	.30	.09
254 John Wetteland	.30	.09
255 Andruw Jones	.30	.09
256 Turk Wendell	.30	.09
257 Jason Isringhausen	.30	.09
258 Jaime Navarro	.30	.09
259 Sean Berry	.30	.09
260 Albie Lopez	.30	.09
261 Jay Bell	.30	.09
262 Bobby Witt	.30	.09
263 Tony Clark	.30	.09
264 Tim Wakefield	.30	.09
265 Brad Radke	.30	.09
266 Tim Belcher	.30	.09
267 Nerio Rodriguez RC	.30	.09
268 Roger Cedeno	.30	.09
269 Tim Naehring	.30	.09
270 Kevin Tapani	.30	.09
271 Joe Randa	.30	.09
272 Randy Myers	.30	.09
273 Dave Burba	.30	.09
274 Mike Sweeney	.30	.09
275 Danny Graves	.30	.09
276 Chad Mottola	.30	.09
277 Ruben Sierra	.30	.09
278 Norm Charlton	.30	.09
279 Scott Servais	.30	.09
280 Jacob Cruz	.30	.09
281 Mike Macfarlane	.30	.09
282 Rich Becker	.30	.09
283 Shannon Stewart	.30	.09
284 Gerald Williams	.30	.09
285 Jody Reed	.30	.09
286 Jeff D'Amico	.30	.09
287 Walt Weiss	.30	.09
288 Jim Leyritz	.30	.09
289 Francisco Cordova	.30	.09
290 F.P. Santangelo	.30	.09
291 Scott Erickson	.30	.09
292 Hal Morris	.30	.09
293 Ray Durham	.30	.09
294 Andy Ashby	.30	.09
295 Darryl Kile	.30	.09
296 Jose Paniagua	.30	.09
297 Mickey Tettleton	.30	.09
298 Joe Girardi	.30	.09
299 Rocky Coppinger	.30	.09
300 Bob Abreu	.30	.09
301 John Olerud	.30	.09
302 Paul Shuey	.30	.09
303 Jeff Brantley	.30	.09
304 Bob Wells	.30	.09
305 Kevin Seitzer	.30	.09
306 Shawon Dunston	.30	.09
307 Jose Herrera	.30	.09
308 Butch Huskey	.30	.09
309 Jose Offerman	.30	.09
310 Rick Aguilera	.30	.09
311 Greg Gagne	.30	.09
312 John Burkett	.30	.09
313 Mark Thompson	.30	.09
314 Alvaro Espinoza	.30	.09
315 Todd Stottlemyre	.30	.09
316 Al Martin	.30	.09
317 James Baldwin	.30	.09
318 Cal Eldred	.30	.09
319 Sid Fernandez	.30	.09
320 Mickey Morandini	.30	.09
321 Robb Nen	.30	.09
322 Mark Lemke	.30	.09
323 Pete Schourek	.30	.09
324 Marcus Jensen	.30	.09
325 Rich Aurilia	.30	.09
326 Jeff King	.30	.09
327 Scott Stahoviak	.30	.09
328 Ricky Otero	.30	.09
329 Antonio Osuna	.30	.09
330 Chris Hoiles	.30	.09
331 Luis Gonzalez	.30	.09
332 Wil Cordero	.30	.09
333 Johnny Damon	.50	.15
334 Mark Langston	.30	.09
335 Orlando Miller	.30	.09
336 Jason Giambi	.30	.09
337 Damian Jackson	.30	.09
338 David Wells	.30	.09
339 Bip Roberts	.30	.09
340 Matt Ruebel	.30	.09
341 Tom Candiotti	.30	.09
342 Wally Joyner	.30	.09
343 Jimmy Key	.30	.09
344 Tony Batista	.30	.09
345 Paul Sorrento	.30	.09
346 Ron Karkovice	.30	.09

47 Wilson Alvarez .30 .09
48 John Flaherty .30 .09
49 Rey Sanchez .30 .09
50 John Vander Wal .30 .09
51 Jermaine Dye .30 .09
52 Mike Hampton .30 .09
53 Greg Colbrunn .30 .09
54 Heathcliff Slocumb .30 .09
55 Ricky Bottalico .30 .09
56 Marty Janzen .30 .09
57 Orel Hershiser .30 .09
58 Rex Hudler .30 .09
59 Amaury Telemaco .30 .09
60 Darrin Fletcher .30 .09
61 Brant Brown UER .30 .09
Card numbered 351
62 Russ Davis .30 .09
63 Allen Watson .30 .09
64 Mike Lieberthal .30 .09
65 Dave Stevens .30 .09
66 Jay Powell .30 .09
67 Tony Fossas .30 .09
68 Bob Wolcott .30 .09
69 Mark Loretta .30 .09
70 Shawn Estes .30 .09
71 Sandy Martinez .30 .09
72 Wendell Magee Jr. .30 .09
73 John Franco .30 .09
74 Tom Pagnozzi UER .30 .09
misnumbered as 274
75 Willie Adams .30 .09
76 Chipper Jones SS SP 1.25 .35
77 Mo Vaughn SS SP .75 .23
78 Frank Thomas SS SP 1.25 .35
79 Albert Belle SS SP .75 .23
80 A.Galarraga SS SP .75 .23
81 Gary Sheffield SS SP .75 .23
82 Jeff Bagwell SS SP .75 .23
83 Mike Piazza SS SP 2.50 .75
84 Mark McGwire SS SP 4.00 1.20
85 Ken Griffey Jr. SS SP 2.50 .75
86 Barry Bonds SS SP 4.00 1.20
87 Juan Gonzalez SS SP .75 .23
88 B.Anderson SS SP .75 .23
89 Ken Caminiti SS SP .75 .23
90 Jay Buhner SS SP .75 .23

1997 Stadium Club Matrix

andomly inserted in first and second series ght-card packs at a rate of one in 12 and in 13-ard packs at a rate of one in six, this 120-card et is parallel to the first 60 cards of both the eries one and series two of the regular set. Each latrix card was reproduced with Power Matrix echnology, giving the card fronts a glittering ffect.

Nm-Mt Ex-Mt
STARS: 4X TO 10X BASIC CARDS....

1997 Stadium Club Co-Signers

andomly inserted in first series eight-card obby packs at a rate of one in 168 and first eries 13-card hobby collector packs at a rate of ne in 96, cards (CO1-CO5) from this dual-ded, dual-player set feature color action player hotos printed on 20pt. card stock with authen-c signatures of two major league stand-outs er card. The last five cards (CO6-CO10) were andomly inserted in second series 10-card obby packs with a rate of one in 168 and insert-d with a rate of one in 96 Hobby Collector acks.

Nm-Mt Ex-Mt
O1 Andy Pettitte 150.00 45.00
Derek Jeter
O2 Paul Wilson 10.00 3.00
Todd Hundley
O3 Jermaine Dye 15.00 4.50
Mark Wohlers
O4 Scott Rolen 40.00 12.00
Gregg Jefferies
O5 Todd Hollandsworth 15.00 4.50
Jason Kendall
O6 Alan Benes 15.00 4.50
Robin Ventura
O7 Eric Karros 15.00 4.50
Raul Mondesi
O8 Rey Ordonez 80.00 24.00
Nomar Garciaparra
O9 Rondell White 15.00 4.50
Marty Cordova
O10 Tony Gwynn 40.00 12.00
Karim Garcia

1997 Stadium Club Firebrand Redemption

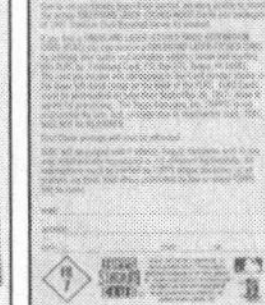

andomly inserted exclusively into first series ight-card retail packs at a rate of one in 36, hese redemption cards feature a selection of the eagues top sluggers. Due to circumstances eyond the manufacturers control, they were not able to insert the actual etched-wood cards into packs and had to resort to these redemption cards.

Nm-Mt Ex-Mt
*WOOD: 5X TO 1.2X BASIC FIREBRAND
ONE WOOD CARD VIA MAIL PER EXCH.CARD
F1 Jeff Bagwell 4.00 1.20
F2 Albert Belle 2.50 .75
F3 Barry Bonds 15.00 4.50
F4 Andres Galarraga 2.50 .75
F5 Ken Griffey Jr. 10.00 3.00
F6 Brady Anderson 2.50 .75
F7 Mark McGwire 15.00 4.50
F8 Chipper Jones 6.00 1.80
F9 Frank Thomas 6.00 1.80
F10 Mike Piazza 10.00 3.00
F11 Mo Vaughn 2.50 .75
F12 Juan Gonzalez 4.00 1.20

1997 Stadium Club Instavision

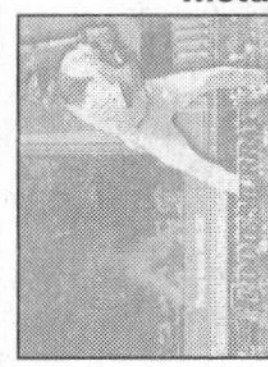

The first ten cards of this 22-card set were randomly inserted in first series eight-card packs at a rate of one in 24 and first series 13-card packs at a rate of 1:12. The last 12 cards were inserted in series two packs at the rate of one in 24 and one in 12 in hobby collector packs. The set highlights some of the 1996 season's most exciting moments through exclusive holographic video action.

Nm-Mt Ex-Mt
COMPLETE SET (22) 50.00 15.00
COMPLETE SERIES 1 (10) 25.00 7.50
COMPLETE SERIES 2 (12) 25.00 7.50
I1 Eddie Murray 4.00 1.20
I2 Paul Molitor 2.50 .75
I3 Todd Hundley 1.50 .45
I4 Roger Clemens 8.00 2.40
I5 Barry Bonds 10.00 3.00
I6 Mark McGwire 10.00 3.00
I7 Brady Anderson 1.50 .45
I8 Barry Larkin 2.50 .75
I9 Ken Caminiti 1.50 .45
I10 Hideo Nomo 4.00 1.20
I11 Bernie Williams 2.50 .75
I12 Juan Gonzalez 2.50 .75
I13 Andy Pettitte 2.50 .75
I14 Albert Belle 1.50 .45
I15 John Smoltz 2.50 .75
I16 Brian Jordan 1.50 .45
I17 Derek Jeter 10.00 3.00
I18 Ken Caminiti 1.50 .45
I19 John Wetteland 1.50 .45
I20 Brady Anderson 1.50 .45
I21 Andruw Jones 1.50 .45
I22 Jim Leyritz 1.50 .45

1997 Stadium Club Millennium

Randomly inserted in first and second series eight-card packs at a rate of one in 24 and 13-card packs at a rate of 1:12, this 40-card set features color player photos of breakthrough stars of Major League Baseball reproduced using state-of-the-art advanced embossed holographic technology.

Nm-Mt Ex-Mt
COMPLETE SET (40) 130.00 39.00
COMPLETE SERIES 1 (20) 50.00 15.00
COMPLETE SERIES 2 (20) 80.00 24.00
M1 Derek Jeter 20.00 6.00
M2 Mark Grudzielanek 1.50 .45
M3 Jacob Cruz 1.50 .45
M4 Ray Durham 2.50 .75
M5 Tony Clark 1.50 .45
M6 Chipper Jones 6.00 1.80
M7 Luis Castillo 1.50 .45
M8 Carlos Delgado 2.50 .75
M9 Brant Brown 1.50 .45
M10 Jason Kendall 2.50 .75
M11 Alan Benes 1.50 .45
M12 Rey Ordonez 1.50 .45
M13 Justin Thompson 1.50 .45
M14 J.Allensworth 1.50 .45
M15 Brian Hunter 1.50 .45
M16 Marty Cordova 1.50 .45
M17 Edgar Renteria 2.50 .75
M18 Karim Garcia 1.50 .45
M19 Todd Greene 1.50 .45
M20 Paul Wilson 1.50 .45

1997 Stadium Club Patent Leather

Randomly inserted in second series retail packs only at a rate of one in 36, this 13-card set features action player images standing in a baseball glove and with an inner die-cut glove background printed on leather card stock.

Nm-Mt Ex-Mt
COMPLETE SET (13) 120.00 36.00
PL1 Ivan Rodriguez 10.00 3.00

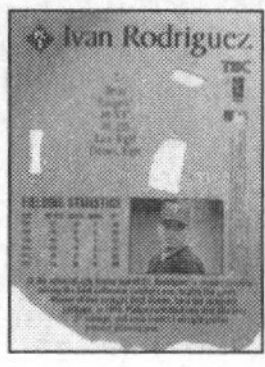

PL2 Ken Caminiti 4.00 1.20
PL3 Barry Bonds 25.00 7.50
PL4 Ken Griffey Jr. 15.00 4.50
PL5 Greg Maddux 15.00 4.50
PL6 Craig Biggio 6.00 1.80
PL7 Andres Galarraga 4.00 1.20
PL8 Kenny Lofton 4.00 1.20
PL9 Barry Larkin 6.00 1.80
PL10 Mark Grace 6.00 1.80
PL11 Rey Ordonez 4.00 1.20
PL12 Roberto Alomar 6.00 1.80
PL13 Derek Jeter 25.00 7.50

1997 Stadium Club Pure Gold

Randomly inserted in first and second series eight-card packs at a rate of one in 72 and 13-card packs at a rate of one in 36, this 20-card set features color action star player photos reproduced on 20 pt. embossed gold mirror foilboard.

Nm-Mt Ex-Mt
COMPLETE SERIES 1 (10) 120.00 36.00
COMPLETE SERIES 2 (10) 200.00 60.00
PG1 Brady Anderson 3.00 .90
PG2 Albert Belle 3.00 .90
PG3 Dante Bichette 3.00 .90
PG4 Barry Bonds 20.00 6.00
PG5 Jay Buhner 3.00 .90
PG6 Tony Gwynn 10.00 3.00
PG7 Chipper Jones 8.00 2.40
PG8 Mark McGwire 20.00 6.00
PG9 Gary Sheffield 3.00 .90
PG10 Frank Thomas 8.00 2.40
PG11 Juan Gonzalez 5.00 1.50
PG12 Ken Caminiti 3.00 .90
PG13 Kenny Lofton 3.00 .90
PG14 Jeff Bagwell 5.00 1.50
PG15 Ken Griffey Jr. 12.00 3.60
PG16 Cal Ripken 25.00 7.50
PG17 Mo Vaughn 3.00 .90
PG18 Mike Piazza 12.00 3.60
PG19 Derek Jeter 20.00 6.00
PG20 Andres Galarraga 3.00 .90

1998 Stadium Club

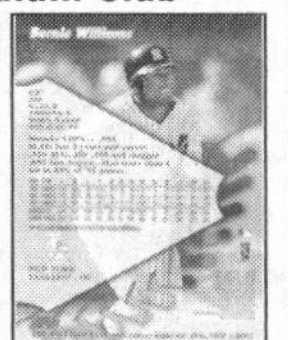

The 1998 Stadium Club set was issued in two separate 200-card series and distributed in six-card retail packs for $2, nine-card hobby packs for $3, and 15-card Home Team Advantage packs for $5. The card fronts feature action color player photos with player information displayed on the backs. The series one set included odd numbered cards only and series two included even numbered cards only. The set contains the topical subsets: Future Stars (odd-numbered 361-379), Draft Picks (odd-numbered 381-399) and Traded (even-numbered 356-400). Two separate Cal Ripken Sound Chip cards were distributed as chiptoppers in Home Team Advantage boxes. The second series features a 23-card Transaction subset (356-400). Second series cards were released in April, 1998. Rookie Cards include Kevin Millwood and Magglio Ordonez.

Nm-Mt Ex-Mt
COMPLETE SET (400) 80.00 24.00
COMP.SERIES 1 (200) 40.00 12.00
COMP.SERIES 2 (200) 40.00 12.00
1 Chipper Jones .75 .23
2 Frank Thomas .75 .23
3 Vladimir Guerrero .75 .23
4 Ellis Burks .30 .09
5 John Franco .30 .09
6 Paul Molitor .50 .15
7 Rusty Greer .30 .09
8 Todd Hundley .30 .09
9 Brett Tomko .30 .09
10 Eric Karros .30 .09
11 Mike Cameron .30 .09
12 Jim Edmonds .30 .09
13 Bernie Williams .50 .15
14 Denny Neagle .30 .09
15 Jason Dickson .30 .09
16 Sammy Sosa 1.25 .35
17 Brian Jordan .30 .09
18 Jose Vidro .30 .09
19 Scott Spiezio .30 .09
20 Jay Buhner .30 .09
21 Jim Thome .75 .23
22 Sandy Alomar Jr. .30 .09
23 Livan Hernandez .30 .09
24 Roberto Alomar .50 .15
25 Chris Gomez .30 .09
26 John Wetteland .30 .09
27 Willie Greene .30 .09
28 Gregg Jefferies .30 .09
29 Johnny Damon .50 .15
30 Barry Larkin .50 .15
31 Chuck Knoblauch .30 .09
32 Mo Vaughn .30 .09
33 Tony Clark .30 .09
34 Marty Cordova .30 .09
35 Vinny Castilla .30 .09
36 Jeff King .30 .09
37 Reggie Jefferson .30 .09
38 Mariano Rivera .50 .15
39 Jermaine Allensworth .30 .09
40 Livan Hernandez .30 .09
41 Heathcliff Slocumb .30 .09
42 Jacob Cruz .30 .09
43 Barry Bonds 2.00 .60
44 Dave Magadan .30 .09
45 Chan Ho Park .30 .09
46 Jeremi Gonzalez .30 .09
47 Jeff Cirillo .30 .09
48 Delino DeShields .30 .09
49 Craig Biggio .50 .15
50 Benito Santiago .30 .09
51 Mark Clark .30 .09
52 Fernando Vina .30 .09
53 F.P. Santangelo .30 .09
54 Pep Harris .30 .09
55 Edgar Renteria .30 .09
56 Jeff Bagwell .50 .15
57 Jimmy Key .30 .09
58 Bartolo Colon .30 .09
59 Curt Schilling .30 .09
60 Steve Finley .30 .09
61 Andy Ashby .30 .09
62 John Burkett .30 .09
63 Orel Hershiser .30 .09
64 Pokey Reese .30 .09
65 Scott Servais .30 .09
66 Todd Jones .30 .09
67 Javy Lopez .30 .09
68 Robin Ventura .30 .09
69 Miguel Tejada .30 .09
70 Raul Casanova .30 .09
71 Reggie Sanders .30 .09
72 Edgardo Alfonzo .30 .09
73 Dean Palmer .30 .09
74 Todd Stottlemyre .30 .09
75 David Wells .30 .09
76 Troy Percival .30 .09
77 Albert Belle .30 .09
78 Pat Hentgen .30 .09
79 Brian Hunter .30 .09
80 Richard Hidalgo .30 .09
81 Darren Oliver .30 .09
82 Mark Wohlers .30 .09
83 Cal Ripken 2.50 .75
84 Hideo Nomo .75 .23
85 Derrek Lee .30 .09
86 Stan Javier .30 .09
87 Rey Ordonez .30 .09
88 Randy Johnson .75 .23
89 Jeff Kent .30 .09
90 Brian McRae .30 .09
91 Manny Ramirez .50 .15
92 Trevor Hoffman .30 .09
93 Doug Glanville .30 .09
94 Todd Walker .30 .09
95 Andy Benes .30 .09
96 Jason Schmidt .30 .09
97 Mike Matheny .30 .09
98 Tim Naehring .30 .09
99 Keith Lockhart .30 .09
100 Jose Rosado .30 .09
101 Roger Clemens 1.50 .45
102 Pedro Astacio .30 .09
103 Mark Bellhorn .30 .09
104 Paul O'Neill .50 .15
105 Darin Erstad .30 .09
106 Mike Lieberthal .30 .09
107 Wilson Alvarez .30 .09
108 Mike Mussina .50 .15
109 George Williams .30 .09
110 Cliff Floyd .30 .09
111 Shawn Estes .30 .09
112 Mark Grudzielanek .30 .09
113 Tony Gwynn 1.00 .30
114 Alan Benes .30 .09
115 Terry Steinbach .30 .09
116 Greg Maddux 1.25 .35
117 Andy Pettitte .50 .15
118 Dave Nilsson .30 .09
119 Deivi Cruz .30 .09
120 Carlos Delgado .30 .09
121 Scott Hatteberg .30 .09
122 John Olerud .30 .09
123 Todd Dunwoody .30 .09
124 Garret Anderson .30 .09
125 Royce Clayton .30 .09
126 Dante Powell .30 .09
127 Tom Glavine .50 .15
128 Gary DiSarcina .30 .09
129 Terry Adams .30 .09
130 Raul Mondesi .30 .09
131 Dan Wilson .30 .09
132 Al Martin .30 .09
133 Mickey Morandini .30 .09
134 Rafael Palmeiro .50 .15
135 Juan Encarnacion .30 .09
136 Jim Pittsley .30 .09
137 Magglio Ordonez RC 2.00 .60
138 Will Clark .75 .23
139 Todd Helton .50 .15
140 Kelvim Escobar .30 .09
141 Esteban Loaiza .30 .09
142 John Jaha .30 .09
143 Jeff Fassero .30 .09
144 Harold Baines .30 .09
145 Butch Huskey .30 .09
146 Pat Meares .30 .09
147 Brian Giles .30 .09
148 Ramiro Mendoza .30 .09
149 John Smoltz .50 .15
150 Felix Martinez .30 .09
151 Jose Valentin .30 .09
152 Brad Rigby .30 .09
153 Ed Sprague .30 .09
154 Mike Hampton .30 .09
155 Carlos Perez .30 .09
156 Ray Lankford .30 .09
157 Bobby Bonilla .30 .09
158 Bill Mueller .30 .09
159 Jeffrey Hammonds .30 .09
160 Charles Nagy .30 .09
161 Rich Loiselle RC .30 .09
162 Al Leiter .30 .09
163 Larry Walker .50 .15
164 Chris Hoiles .30 .09
165 Jeff Montgomery .30 .09
166 Francisco Cordova .30 .09
167 James Baldwin .30 .09
168 Mark McLemore .30 .09
169 Kevin Appier .30 .09
170 Jamey Wright .30 .09
171 Nomar Garciaparra 1.25 .35
172 Matt Franco .30 .09
173 Armando Benitez .30 .09
174 Jeromy Burnitz .30 .09
175 Ismael Valdes .30 .09
176 Lance Johnson .30 .09
177 Paul Sorrento .30 .09
178 Rondell White .30 .09
179 Kevin Elster .30 .09
180 Jason Giambi .30 .09
181 Carlos Baerga .30 .09
182 Russ Davis .30 .09
183 Ryan McGuire .30 .09
184 Eric Young .30 .09
185 Ron Gant .30 .09
186 Manny Alexander .30 .09
187 Scott Karl .30 .09
188 Brady Anderson .30 .09
189 Randall Simon .30 .09
190 Tim Belcher .30 .09
191 Jaret Wright .30 .09
192 Dante Bichette .30 .09
193 John Valentin .30 .09
194 Darren Bragg .30 .09
195 Mike Sweeney .30 .09
196 Craig Counsell .30 .09
197 Jaime Navarro .30 .09
198 Todd Dunn .30 .09
199 Ken Griffey Jr. 1.25 .35
200 Juan Gonzalez .50 .15
201 Billy Wagner .30 .09
202 Tino Martinez .50 .15
203 Mark McGwire 2.00 .60
204 Jeff D'Amico .30 .09
205 Rico Brogna .30 .09
206 Todd Hollandsworth .30 .09
207 Chad Curtis .30 .09
208 Tom Goodwin .30 .09
209 Neifi Perez .30 .09
210 Derek Bell .30 .09
211 Quilvio Veras .30 .09
212 Greg Vaughn .30 .09
213 Kirk Rueter .30 .09
214 Arthur Rhodes .30 .09
215 Cal Eldred .30 .09
216 Bill Taylor .30 .09
217 Todd Greene .30 .09
218 Mario Valdez .30 .09
219 Ricky Bottalico .30 .09
220 Frank Rodriguez .30 .09
221 Rich Becker .30 .09
222 Roberto Duran RC .30 .09
223 Ivan Rodriguez .75 .23
224 Mike Jackson .30 .09
225 Deion Sanders .50 .15
226 Tony Womack .30 .09
227 Mark Kotsay .30 .09
228 Steve Trachsel .30 .09
229 Ryan Klesko .30 .09
230 Ken Cloude .30 .09
231 Luis Gonzalez .30 .09
232 Gary Gaetti .30 .09
233 Michael Tucker .30 .09
234 Shawn Green .30 .09
235 Ariel Prieto .30 .09
236 Kirt Manwaring .30 .09
237 Omar Vizquel .50 .15
238 Matt Beech .30 .09
239 Justin Thompson .30 .09
240 Bret Boone .30 .09
241 Derek Jeter 2.00 .60
242 Ken Caminiti .30 .09
243 Jose Offerman .30 .09
244 Kevin Tapani .30 .09
245 Jason Kendall .30 .09
246 Jose Guillen .30 .09
247 Mike Bordick .30 .09
248 Dustin Hermanson .30 .09
249 Darrin Fletcher .30 .09
250 Dave Hollins .30 .09
251 Ramon Martinez .30 .09
252 Hideki Irabu .30 .09
253 Mark Grace .50 .15
254 Jason Isringhausen .30 .09
255 Jose Cruz Jr. .30 .09
256 Brian Johnson .30 .09
257 Brad Ausmus .30 .09
258 Andruw Jones .30 .09
259 Doug Jones .30 .09
260 Jeff Shaw .30 .09
261 Chuck Finley .30 .09
262 Gary Sheffield .30 .09
263 David Segui .30 .09
264 John Smiley .30 .09
265 Tim Salmon .50 .15
266 J.T. Snow .30 .09
267 Alex Fernandez .30 .09
268 Matt Stairs .30 .09
269 B.J. Surhoff .30 .09
270 Keith Foulke .30 .09
271 Edgar Martinez .50 .15
272 Shannon Stewart .30 .09
273 Eduardo Perez .30 .09
274 Wally Joyner .30 .09
275 Kevin Young .30 .09
276 Eli Marrero .30 .09
277 Brad Radke .30 .09
278 Jamie Moyer .30 .09
279 Joe Girardi .50 .15
280 Troy O'Leary .30 .09
281 Jeff Frye .30 .09
282 Jose Offerman .30 .09
283 Scott Erickson .30 .09
284 Sean Berry .30 .09
285 Shigetoshi Hasegawa .30 .09

286 Felix Heredia	.30	.09
287 Willie McGee	.30	.09
288 Alex Rodriguez	1.25	.35
289 Ugueth Urbina	.30	.09
290 Jon Lieber	.30	.09
291 Fernando Tatis	.30	.09
292 Chris Stynes	.30	.09
293 Bernard Gilkey	.30	.09
294 Joey Hamilton	.30	.09
295 Matt Karchner	.30	.09
296 Paul Wilson	.30	.09
297 Damion Easley	.30	.09
298 Kevin Millwood RC	1.00	.30
299 Ellis Burks	.30	.09
300 Jerry DiPoto	.30	.09
301 Jermaine Dye	.30	.09
302 Travis Lee	.30	.09
303 Ron Coomer	.30	.09
304 Matt Williams	.30	.09
305 Bobby Higginson	.30	.09
306 Jorge Fabregas	.30	.09
307 Jon Nunnally	.30	.09
308 Jay Bell	.30	.09
309 Jason Schmidt	.30	.09
310 Andy Benes	.30	.09
311 Sterling Hitchcock	.30	.09
312 Jeff Suppan	.30	.09
313 Shane Reynolds	.30	.09
314 Willie Blair	.30	.09
315 Scott Rolen	.75	.23
316 Wilson Alvarez	.30	.09
317 David Justice	.30	.09
318 Fred McGriff	.50	.15
319 Bobby Jones	.30	.09
320 Wade Boggs	.50	.15
321 Tim Wakefield	.30	.09
322 Tony Saunders	.30	.09
323 David Cone	.30	.09
324 Roberto Hernandez	.30	.09
325 Jose Canseco	.75	.23
326 Kevin Stocker	.30	.09
327 Gerald Williams	.30	.09
328 Quinton McCracken	.30	.09
329 Mark Gardner	.30	.09
330 Ben Grieve	.30	.09
331 Kevin Brown	.50	.15
332 Mike Lowell RC	1.50	.45
333 Jed Hansen	.30	.09
334 Abraham Nunez	.30	.09
335 John Thomson	.30	.09
336 Masato Yoshii RC	.75	.23
337 Mike Piazza	1.25	.35
338 Brad Fullmer	.30	.09
339 Ray Durham	.30	.09
340 Kerry Wood	.75	.23
341 Kevin Polcovich	.30	.09
342 Russ Johnson	.30	.09
343 Darryl Hamilton	.30	.09
344 David Ortiz	.75	.23
345 Kevin Orie	.30	.09
346 Mike Caruso	.30	.09
347 Juan Guzman	.30	.09
348 Ruben Rivera	.30	.09
349 Rick Aguilera	.30	.09
350 Bobby Estalella	.30	.09
351 Bobby Witt	.30	.09
352 Paul Konerko	.30	.09
353 Matt Morris	.30	.09
354 Carl Pavano	.50	.09
355 Todd Zeile	.30	.09
356 Kevin Brown TR	.50	.15
357 Alex Gonzalez	.30	.09
358 Chuck Knoblauch TR	.30	.09
359 Joey Cora	.30	.09
360 Mike Lansing TR	.30	.09
361 Adrian Beltre	.75	.23
362 Dennis Eckersley TR	.30	.09
363 A.J. Hinch	.30	.09
364 Kenny Lofton TR	.30	.09
365 Alex Gonzalez	.30	.09
366 Henry Rodriguez TR	.30	.09
367 Mike Stoner RC	.30	.09
368 Darryl Kile TR	.30	.09
369 Kevin McGlinchy	.30	.09
370 Walt Weiss TR	.30	.09
371 Kris Benson	.30	.09
372 Cecil Fielder TR	.30	.09
373 Dermal Brown	.30	.09
374 Rod Beck TR	.30	.09
375 Eric Milton	.30	.09
376 Travis Fryman TR	.30	.09
377 Preston Wilson	.30	.09
378 Chili Davis TR	.30	.09
379 Travis Lee	.30	.09
380 Jim Leyritz TR	.30	.09
381 Vernon Wells	.30	.09
382 Joe Carter TR	.30	.09
383 J.J. Davis	.30	.09
384 Marquis Grissom TR	.30	.09
385 Mike Cuddyer RC	.75	.23
386 Rickey Henderson TR	.75	.23
387 Chris Enochs RC	.30	.09
388 Andres Galarraga TR	.30	.09
389 Jason Dellaero	.30	.09
390 Robb Nen TR	.30	.09
391 Mark Mangum	.30	.09
392 Jeff Blauser TR	.30	.09
393 Adam Kennedy	.30	.09
394 Bob Abreu TR	.30	.09
395 Jack Cust RC	.50	.15
396 Jose Vizcaino TR	.30	.09
397 Jon Garland	.30	.09
398 Pedro Martinez TR	.75	.23
399 Aaron Akin	.30	.09
400 Jeff Conine TR	.30	.09
NNO Cal Ripken Sound Chip 1	15.00	4.50
NNO Cal Ripken Sound Chip 2	15.00	4.50

1998 Stadium Club First Day Issue

Randomly inserted in first series retail packs at the rate of one in 42 and second series retail packs at the rate of one in 47, this 400-card set parallels the 1998 Stadium Club base set and features a "First Day Issue" foil stamp on the front. Each card is serial numbered out of 200 on back.

	Nm-Mt	Ex-Mt
*STARS: 6X TO 15X BASIC CARDS....		
*ROOKIES: 6X TO 15X BASIC CARDS		

1998 Stadium Club One Of A Kind

Randomly inserted in first and second series hobby and Home Team Advantage packs this 400-card set parallels the 1998 Stadium Club base set. First series cards were seeded at 1:21 hobby and 1:13 HTA packs. Series 2 cards were seeded at 1:24 hobby and 1:14 HTA packs. Each card front features a special metalized foil treatment coupled with a "One of a Kind" logo. In addition, each card is serial numbered out of 150 on back.

	Nm-Mt	Ex-Mt
*STARS: 8X TO 20X BASIC CARDS....		
*ROOKIES: 8X TO 20X BASIC CARDS		

1998 Stadium Club Co-Signers

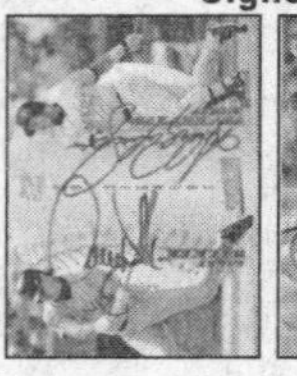

Randomly inserted exclusively in first and second series hobby and Home Team Advantage packs, this 36-card set features color photos of two top players on each card along with their autographs. These cards were released in three different levels of scarcity: A, B and C. Seeding rates are as follows: Series 1 Group A 1:4372 hobby and 1:2623 HTA, Series 1 Group B 1:1457 hobby and 1:874 HTA, Series 1 Group C 1:121 hobby and 1:73 HTA, Series 2 Group A 1:4702 hobby and 1:2821 HTA, Series 2 Group B 1:1567 hobby and 1:940 HTA and Series 2 Group C 1:131 hobby and 1:78 HTA. The scarce group A cards (rumored to be only 25 of each made) are the most difficult to obtain.

	Nm-Mt	Ex-Mt
CS1 Nomar Garciaparra A Scott Rolen	150.00	45.00
CS2 Nomar Garciaparra B Derek Jeter	300.00	90.00
CS3 Nomar Garciaparra C Eric Karros	80.00	24.00
CS4 Scott Rolen C Derek Jeter	120.00	36.00
CS5 Scott Rolen B Eric Karros	60.00	18.00
CS6 Derek Jeter A Eric Karros	150.00	45.00
CS7 Travis Lee B Jose Cruz Jr.	25.00	7.50
CS8 Travis Lee C Mark Kotsay	15.00	4.50
CS9 Travis Lee A Paul Konerko	50.00	15.00
CS10 Jose Cruz Jr. A Mark Kotsay	50.00	15.00
CS11 Jose Cruz Jr. C Paul Konerko	15.00	4.50
CS12 Mark Kotsay B Paul Konerko	40.00	12.00
CS13 Tony Gwynn A Larry Walker	120.00	36.00
CS14 Tony Gwynn C Mark Grudzielanek	40.00	12.00
CS15 Tony Gwynn B Andres Galarraga	80.00	24.00
CS16 Larry Walker B Mark Grudzielanek	60.00	18.00
CS17 Larry Walker C Andres Galarraga	40.00	12.00
CS18 Mark Grudzielanek A Andres Galarraga	50.00	15.00
CS19 Sandy Alomar A Roberto Alomar	80.00	24.00
CS20 Sandy Alomar C Andy Pettitte	25.00	7.50
CS21 Sandy Alomar B Tino Martinez	50.00	15.00
CS22 Roberto Alomar B Andy Pettitte	60.00	18.00
CS23 Roberto Alomar C Tino Martinez	40.00	12.00
CS24 Andy Pettitte A Tino Martinez	100.00	30.00
CS25 Tony Clark A Todd Hundley	50.00	15.00
CS26 Tony Clark B Tim Salmon	50.00	15.00
CS27 Tony Clark C Robin Ventura	15.00	4.50
CS28 Todd Hundley C Tim Salmon	25.00	7.50
CS29 Todd Hundley B Robin Ventura	40.00	12.00
CS30 Tim Salmon A Robin Ventura	80.00	24.00
CS31 Roger Clemens B Randy Johnson	200.00	60.00
CS32 Roger Clemens A Jaret Wright	150.00	45.00
CS33 Roger Clemens C Matt Morris	100.00	30.00
CS34 Randy Johnson C Jaret Wright	60.00	18.00
CS35 Randy Johnson A Matt Morris	120.00	36.00
CS36 Jaret Wright B Matt Morris	40.00	12.00

1998 Stadium Club In The Wings

Randomly inserted in first series hobby and retail packs at the rate of one in 36 and first series Home Team Advantage packs at a rate of

one in 12, this 15-card set features color photos of some of the top young players in the league.

	Nm-Mt	Ex-Mt
COMPLETE SET (15)	40.00	12.00
W1 Juan Encarnacion	4.00	1.20
W2 Brad Fullmer	4.00	1.20
W3 Ben Grieve	4.00	1.20
W4 Todd Helton	6.00	1.80
W5 Richard Hidalgo	4.00	1.20
W6 Russ Johnson	4.00	1.20
W7 Paul Konerko	4.00	1.20
W8 Mark Kotsay	4.00	1.20
W9 Derrek Lee	4.00	1.20
W10 Travis Lee	4.00	1.20
W11 Eli Marrero	4.00	1.20
W12 David Ortiz	10.00	3.00
W13 Randall Simon	4.00	1.20
W14 Shannon Stewart	4.00	1.20
W15 Fernando Tatis	4.00	1.20

1998 Stadium Club Never Compromise

Randomly inserted in first series hobby and retail packs at the rate of one in 12 and first series HTA packs at the rate of one in four, this 20-card set features color photos of top players who never compromise in their game play.

	Nm-Mt	Ex-Mt
COMPLETE SET (20)	80.00	24.00
NC1 Cal Ripken	10.00	3.00
NC2 Ivan Rodriguez	3.00	.90
NC3 Ken Griffey Jr.	5.00	1.50
NC4 Frank Thomas	3.00	.90
NC5 Tony Gwynn	4.00	1.20
NC6 Mike Piazza	5.00	1.50
NC7 Randy Johnson	3.00	.90
NC8 Greg Maddux	5.00	1.50
NC9 Roger Clemens	6.00	1.80
NC10 Derek Jeter	8.00	2.40
NC11 Chipper Jones	3.00	.90
NC12 Barry Bonds	8.00	2.40
NC13 Larry Walker	2.00	.60
NC14 Jeff Bagwell	2.00	.60
NC15 Barry Larkin	2.00	.60
NC16 Ken Caminiti	1.25	.35
NC17 Mark McGwire	8.00	2.40
NC18 Manny Ramirez	2.00	.60
NC19 Tim Salmon	2.00	.60
NC20 Paul Molitor	2.00	.60

1998 Stadium Club Playing With Passion

Randomly seeded into second series hobby and retail packs at a rate of one in 12 and second series Home Team Advantage packs at a rate of one in four, cards from this 10-card set feature a selection of players who've got true fire in their hearts and the burning desire to win.

	Nm-Mt	Ex-Mt
COMPLETE SET (10)	25.00	7.50
P1 Bernie Williams	1.50	.45
P2 Jim Edmonds	1.00	.30
P3 Chipper Jones	2.50	.75
P4 Cal Ripken	8.00	2.40
P5 Craig Biggio	1.50	.45
P6 Juan Gonzalez	1.50	.45
P7 Alex Rodriguez	4.00	1.20
P8 Tino Martinez	1.50	.45
P9 Mike Piazza	4.00	1.20
P10 Ken Griffey Jr.	4.00	1.20

1998 Stadium Club Royal Court

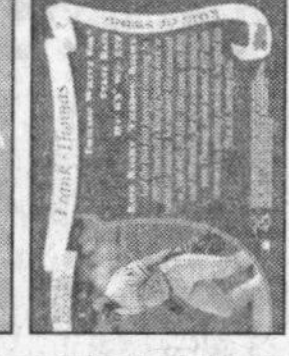

Randomly seeded into second series hobby and retail packs at a rate of one in 36 and second series Home Team Advantage packs at a rate of one in 12, cards from this 15-card set feature a selection of players that have proven their talent and dedication that they've got what it takes to achieve royalty. Players are broken into groups of ten Kings (veterans) and five Princes (rookies). Each card features a special Uniluster technology on front.

	Nm-Mt	Ex-Mt
COMPLETE SET (15)	120.00	36.00
RC1 Ken Griffey Jr.	12.00	3.60
RC2 Frank Thomas	8.00	2.40
RC3 Mike Piazza	12.00	3.60
RC4 Chipper Jones	8.00	2.40
RC5 Mark McGwire	20.00	6.00
RC6 Cal Ripken	25.00	7.50
RC7 Jeff Bagwell	5.00	1.50
RC8 Barry Bonds	20.00	6.00
RC9 Juan Gonzalez	5.00	1.50
RC10 Alex Rodriguez	12.00	3.60
RC11 Travis Lee	3.00	.90
RC12 Paul Konerko	3.00	.90
RC13 Todd Helton	5.00	1.50
RC14 Ben Grieve	3.00	.90
RC15 Mark Kotsay	3.00	.90

1998 Stadium Club Triumvirate Luminous

Randomly inserted in first and second series retail packs at the rate of one in 48, the cards of this 54-card set feature color photos of three teammates that can be fused together to make one big card. These laser cut cards use Luminous technology.

	Nm-Mt	Ex-Mt
*LUMINESCENT: 1.25X TO 3X LUMINOUS		
LUMINESCENT STATED ODDS 1:192 RETAIL		
*ILLUMINATOR: 2X TO 5X LUMINOUS		
ILLUMINATOR STATED ODDS 1:384 RETAIL		
T1A Chipper Jones	6.00	1.80
T1B Andruw Jones	2.50	.75
T1C Kenny Lofton	2.50	.75
T2A Derek Jeter	15.00	4.50
T2B Bernie Williams	4.00	1.20
T2C Tino Martinez	4.00	1.20
T3A Jay Buhner	2.50	.75
T3B Edgar Martinez	4.00	1.20
T3C Ken Griffey Jr.	10.00	3.00
T4A Albert Belle	2.50	.75
T4B Robin Ventura	2.50	.75
T4C Frank Thomas	6.00	1.80
T5A Brady Anderson	2.50	.75
T5B Cal Ripken	20.00	6.00
T5C Rafael Palmeiro	4.00	1.20
T6A Mike Piazza	10.00	3.00
T6B Raul Mondesi	2.50	.75
T6C Eric Karros	2.50	.75
T7A Vinny Castilla	2.50	.75
T7B Andres Galarraga	2.50	.75
T7C Larry Walker	4.00	1.20
T8A Jim Thome	6.00	1.80
T8B Manny Ramirez	4.00	1.20
T8C David Justice	2.50	.75
T9A Mike Mussina	4.00	1.20
T9B Greg Maddux	10.00	3.00
T9C Randy Johnson	6.00	1.80
T10A Mike Piazza	10.00	3.00
T10B Sandy Alomar Jr.	2.50	.75
T10C Ivan Rodriguez	6.00	1.80
T11A Mark McGwire	15.00	4.50
T11B Tino Martinez	4.00	1.20
T11C Frank Thomas	6.00	1.80
T12A Roberto Alomar	4.00	1.20
T12B Chuck Knoblauch	2.50	.75
T12C Craig Biggio	4.00	1.20
T13A Cal Ripken	20.00	6.00
T13B Chipper Jones	6.00	1.80
T13C Ken Caminiti	2.50	.75
T14A Derek Jeter	15.00	4.50
T14B Nomar Garciaparra	10.00	3.00
T14C Alex Rodriguez	10.00	3.00
T15A Barry Bonds	15.00	4.50
T15B David Justice	2.50	.75
T15C Albert Belle	2.50	.75
T16A Bernie Williams	4.00	1.20
T16B Ken Griffey Jr.	10.00	3.00
T16C Ray Lankford	2.50	.75
T17A Tim Salmon	4.00	1.20
T17B Larry Walker	4.00	1.20
T17C Tony Gwynn	8.00	2.40
T18A Paul Molitor	4.00	1.20
T18B Edgar Martinez	4.00	1.20
T18C Juan Gonzalez	4.00	1.20

1999 Stadium Club

This 355-card set of 1999 Stadium Club cards was distributed in two separate series of 170 and 185 cards respectively. Six-card hobby and six-card retail packs each carried a suggested retail price of $2. 15-card Home Team Advantage packs (SRP of $5) were also distributed. All pack types contained a trifold/checklist info card. The card fronts feature color action player photos printed on 20 pt. card stock. The backs carry player information and career statistics. Draft Pick and Future Stars cards 141-160 and 336-355 were shortprinted at the following rates: 1:3 hobby/retail packs, one per HTA pack. Key Rookie Cards include Pat Burrell, Nick Johnson and Austin Kearns.

	Nm-Mt	Ex-Mt
COMPLETE SET (355)	100.00	30.00
COMP.SERIES 1 (170)	50.00	15.00
COMP.SER.1 w/o SP's (150)	25.00	7.50
COMP.SERIES 2 (185)	50.00	15.00
COMP.SER.2 w/o SP's (165)	25.00	7.50
COMMON (1-140/161-170)	.30	.09
COMMON (171-335)	.30	.09
COMMON (141-160/336-355)	1.00	.30
1 Alex Rodriguez	1.25	.35
2 Chipper Jones	.75	.23
3 Rusty Greer	.30	.09
4 Jim Edmonds	.30	.09
5 Ron Gant	.30	.09
6 Kevin Polcovich	.30	.09
7 Darryl Strawberry	.30	.09
8 Bill Mueller	.30	.09
9 Vinny Castilla	.30	.09
10 Wade Boggs	.50	.15
11 Jose Lima	.30	.09
12 Darren Dreifort	.30	.09
13 Jay Bell	.30	.09
14 Ben Grieve	.30	.09
15 Shawn Green	.30	.09
16 Andres Galarraga	.30	.09
17 Bartolo Colon	.30	.09
18 Francisco Cordova	.30	.09
19 Paul O'Neill	.50	.15
20 Trevor Hoffman	.30	.09
21 Darren Oliver	.30	.09
22 John Franco	.30	.09
23 Eli Marrero	.30	.09
24 Roberto Hernandez	.30	.09
25 Craig Biggio	.50	.15
26 Brad Fullmer	.30	.09
27 Scott Erickson	.30	.09
28 Tom Gordon	.30	.09
29 Brian Hunter	.30	.09
30 Raul Mondesi	.30	.09
31 Rick Reed	.30	.09
32 Jose Canseco	.75	.23
33 Robb Nen	.30	.09
34 Turner Ward	.30	.09
35 Orlando Hernandez	.30	.09
36 Jeff Shaw	.30	.09
37 Matt Lawton	.30	.09
38 David Wells	.30	.09
39 Bob Abreu	.30	.09
40 Jeromy Burnitz	.30	.09
41 Deivi Cruz	.30	.09
42 Derek Bell	.30	.09
43 Rico Brogna	.30	.09
44 Dmitri Young	.30	.09
45 Chuck Knoblauch	.30	.09
46 Johnny Damon	.50	.15
47 Brian Meadows	.30	.09
48 Jeremi Gonzalez	.30	.09
49 Gary DiSarcina	.30	.09
50 Frank Thomas	.75	.23
51 F.P. Santangelo	.30	.09
52 Tom Candiotti	.30	.09
53 Shane Reynolds	.30	.09
54 Rod Beck	.30	.09
55 Rey Ordonez	.30	.09
56 Todd Helton	.50	.15
57 Mickey Morandini	.30	.09
58 Jorge Posada	.50	.15
59 Mike Mussina	.50	.15
60 Al Leiter	.30	.09
61 David Segui	.30	.09
62 Brian McRae	.30	.09
63 Fred McGriff	.50	.15
64 Brett Tomko	.30	.09
65 Derek Jeter	2.00	.60
66 Sammy Sosa	1.25	.35
67 Kenny Rogers	.30	.09
68 Dave Nilsson	.30	.09
69 Eric Young	.30	.09
70 Mark McGwire	2.00	.60
71 Kenny Lofton	.30	.09
72 Tom Glavine	.50	.15
73 Joey Hamilton	.30	.09
74 John Valentin	.30	.09
75 Mariano Rivera	.50	.15
76 Ray Durham	.30	.09
77 Tony Clark	.30	.09
78 Livan Hernandez	.30	.09
79 Rickey Henderson	.75	.23
80 Vladimir Guerrero	.75	.23
81 J.T. Snow	.30	.09
82 Juan Guzman	.30	.09
83 Darryl Hamilton	.30	.09
84 Matt Anderson	.30	.09
85 Travis Lee	.30	.09
86 Joe Randa	.30	.09
87 Dave Dellucci	.30	.09
88 Moises Alou	.30	.09
89 Alex Gonzalez	.30	.09
90 Tony Womack	.30	.09
91 Neifi Perez	.30	.09
92 Travis Fryman	.30	.09
93 Masato Yoshii	.30	.09
94 Woody Williams	.30	.09
95 Ray Lankford	.30	.09
96 Roger Clemens	1.50	.45
97 Dustin Hermanson	.30	.09
98 Joe Carter	.30	.09
99 Jason Schmidt	.30	.09
100 Greg Maddux	1.25	.35
101 Kevin Tapani	.30	.09
102 Charles Johnson	.30	.09
103 Derrek Lee	.30	.09
104 Pete Harnisch	.30	.09
105 Dante Bichette	.30	.09
106 Scott Brosius	.30	.09
107 Mike Caruso	.30	.09
108 Eddie Taubensee	.30	.09
109 Jeff Fassero	.30	.09
110 Marquis Grissom	.30	.09
111 Jose Hernandez	.30	.09
112 Chan Ho Park	.30	.09
113 Wally Joyner	.30	.09
114 Bobby Estalella	.30	.09
115 Pedro Martinez	.75	.23

116 Shawn Estes .30 .09
117 Walt Weiss .30 .09
118 John Mabry .30 .09
119 Brian Johnson .30 .09
120 Jim Thome .75 .23
121 Bill Spiers .30 .09
122 John Olerud .30 .09
123 Jeff King .30 .09
124 Tim Belcher .30 .09
125 John Wetteland .30 .09
126 Tony Gwynn 1.00 .30
127 Brady Anderson .30 .09
128 Randy Winn .30 .09
129 Andy Fox .30 .09
130 Eric Karros .30 .09
131 Kevin Millwood .30 .09
132 Andy Benes .30 .09
133 Andy Ashby .30 .09
134 Ron Coomer .30 .09
135 Juan Gonzalez .50 .15
136 Randy Johnson .75 .23
137 Aaron Sele .30 .09
138 Edgardo Alfonzo .30 .09
139 B.J. Surhoff .30 .09
140 Jose Vizcaino .30 .09
141 Chad Moeller SP RC 1.00 .30
142 Mike Zywica SP RC 1.00 .30
143 Angel Pena SP 1.00 .30
144 Nick Johnson SP RC 2.00 .60
145 G. Chiaramonte SP RC 1.00 .30
146 Kit Pellow SP RC 1.00 .30
147 C.Andrews SP RC 1.00 .30
148 Jerry Hairston Jr. SP 1.00 .30
149 Jason Tyner SP RC 1.00 .30
150 Chip Ambres SP RC 1.00 .30
151 Pat Burrell SP RC 2.50 .75
152 Josh McKinley SP RC 1.00 .30
153 Choo Freeman SP RC 1.00 .30
154 Rick Elder SP RC 1.00 .30
155 Eric Valent SP RC 1.00 .30
156 J.Winchester SP RC 1.00 .30
157 Mike Nannini SP RC 1.00 .30
158 Mamon Tucker SP RC 1.00 .30
159 Nate Bump SP RC 1.00 .30
160 Andy Brown SP RC 1.00 .30
161 Troy Glaus .30 .09
162 Adrian Beltre .50 .15
163 Mitch Meluskey .30 .09
164 Alex Gonzalez .30 .09
165 George Lombard .30 .09
166 Eric Chavez .30 .09
167 Ruben Mateo .30 .09
168 Calvin Pickering .30 .09
169 Gabe Kapler .30 .09
170 Bruce Chen .30 .09
171 Darin Erstad .30 .09
172 Sandy Alomar Jr. .30 .09
173 Miguel Cairo .30 .09
174 Jason Kendall .30 .09
175 Cal Ripken 2.50 .75
176 Darryl Kile .30 .09
177 David Cone .30 .09
178 Mike Sweeney .30 .09
179 Royce Clayton .30 .09
180 Curt Schilling .50 .15
181 Barry Larkin .50 .15
182 Eric Milton .30 .09
183 Ellis Burks .30 .09
184 A.J. Hinch .30 .09
185 Garret Anderson .30 .09
186 Sean Bergman .30 .09
187 Shannon Stewart .30 .09
188 Bernard Gilkey .30 .09
189 Jeff Blauser .30 .09
190 Andruw Jones .30 .09
191 Omar Daal .30 .09
192 Jeff Kent .30 .09
193 Mark Kotsay .30 .09
194 Dave Burba .30 .09
195 Bobby Higginson .30 .09
196 Hideki Irabu .30 .09
197 Jamie Moyer .30 .09
198 Doug Glanville .30 .09
199 Quinton McCracken .30 .09
200 Ken Griffey Jr. 1.25 .35
201 Mike Lieberthal .30 .09
202 Carl Everett .30 .09
203 Omar Vizquel .50 .15
204 Mike Lansing .30 .09
205 Manny Ramirez .50 .15
206 Ryan Klesko .30 .09
207 Jeff Montgomery .30 .09
208 Chad Curtis .30 .09
209 Rick Helling .30 .09
210 Justin Thompson .30 .09
211 Tom Goodwin .30 .09
212 Todd Dunwoody .30 .09
213 Kevin Young .30 .09
214 Tony Saunders .30 .09
215 Gary Sheffield .30 .09
216 Jaret Wright .30 .09
217 Quilvio Veras .30 .09
218 Marty Cordova .30 .09
219 Tino Martinez .50 .15
220 Scott Rolen .75 .23
221 Fernando Tatis .30 .95
222 Damion Easley .30 .09
223 Aramis Ramirez .30 .09
224 Brad Radke .30 .09
225 Nomar Garciaparra 1.25 .35
226 Magglio Ordonez .30 .09
227 Andy Pettitte .50 .15
228 David Ortiz .50 .15
229 Todd Jones .30 .09
230 Larry Walker .50 .15
231 Tim Wakefield .30 .09
232 Jose Guillen .30 .09
233 Gregg Olson .30 .09
234 Ricky Gutierrez .30 .09
235 Todd Walker .30 .09
236 Abraham Nunez .30 .09
237 Sean Casey .30 .09
238 Greg Norton .30 .09
239 Bret Saberhagen .30 .09
240 Bernie Williams .50 .15
241 Tim Salmon .50 .15
242 Jason Giambi .30 .09
243 Fernando Vina .30 .09
244 Darrin Fletcher .30 .09
245 Mike Bordick .30 .09
246 Dennis Reyes .30 .09
247 Hideo Nomo .75 .23
248 Kevin Stocker .30 .09
249 Mike Hampton .30 .09
250 Kerry Wood .75 .23
251 Ismael Valdes .30 .09
252 Pat Hentgen .30 .09
253 Scott Spiezio .30 .09
254 Chuck Finley .30 .09
255 Troy Glaus .30 .09
256 Bobby Jones .30 .09
257 Wayne Gomes .30 .09
258 Rondell White .30 .09
259 Todd Zeile .30 .09
260 Matt Williams .30 .09
261 Henry Rodriguez .30 .09
262 Matt Stairs .30 .09
263 Jose Valentin .30 .09
264 David Justice .30 .09
265 Javy Lopez .30 .09
266 Matt Morris .30 .09
267 Steve Trachsel .30 .09
268 Edgar Martinez .50 .15
269 Al Martin .30 .09
270 Ivan Rodriguez .75 .23
271 Carlos Delgado .30 .09
272 Mark Grace .50 .15
273 Ugueth Urbina .30 .09
274 Jay Buhner .30 .09
275 Mike Piazza 1.25 .35
276 Rick Aguilera .30 .09
277 Javier Valentin .30 .09
278 Brian Anderson .30 .09
279 Cliff Floyd .30 .09
280 Barry Bonds 2.00 .60
281 Troy O'Leary .30 .09
282 Seth Greisinger .30 .09
283 Mark Grudzielanek .30 .09
284 Jose Cruz Jr. .30 .09
285 Jeff Bagwell .50 .15
286 John Smoltz .50 .15
287 Jeff Cirillo .30 .09
288 Richie Sexson .30 .09
289 Charles Nagy .30 .09
290 Pedro Martinez .75 .23
291 Juan Encarnacion .30 .09
292 Phil Nevin .30 .09
293 Terry Steinbach .30 .09
294 Miguel Tejada .30 .09
295 Dan Wilson .30 .09
296 Chris Peters .30 .09
297 Brian Moehler .30 .09
298 Jason Christiansen .30 .09
299 Kelly Stinnett .30 .09
300 Dwight Gooden .30 .09
301 Randy Velarde .30 .09
302 Kirt Manwaring .30 .09
303 Jeff Abbott .30 .09
304 Dave Hollins .30 .09
305 Kerry Ligtenberg .30 .09
306 Aaron Boone .30 .09
307 Carlos Hernandez .30 .09
308 Mike Difelice .30 .09
309 Brian Meadows .30 .09
310 Tim Bogar .30 .09
311 Greg Vaughn TR .30 .09
312 Brant Brown TR .30 .09
313 Steve Finley TR .30 .09
314 Bret Boone TR .30 .09
315 Albert Belle TR .30 .09
316 Robin Ventura TR .30 .09
317 Eric Davis TR .30 .09
318 Todd Hundley TR .30 .09
319 Roger Clemens TR 1.50 .45
320 Kevin Brown TR .30 .09
321 Jose Offerman TR .30 .09
322 Brian Jordan TR .30 .09
323 Mike Cameron TR .30 .09
324 Bobby Bonilla TR .30 .09
325 Roberto Alomar TR .50 .15
326 Ken Caminiti TR .30 .09
327 Todd Stottlemyre TR .30 .09
328 Randy Johnson TR .75 .23
329 Luis Gonzalez TR .30 .09
330 Rafael Palmeiro TR .50 .15
331 Devon White TR .30 .09
332 Will Clark TR .75 .23
333 Dean Palmer TR .30 .09
334 Gregg Jefferies TR .30 .09
335 Mo Vaughn TR .30 .09
336 Brad Lidge SP RC 4.00 1.20
337 Chris George SP RC 1.00 .30
338 Austin Kearns SP RC 4.00 1.20
339 Matt Belisle SP RC 1.00 .30
340 Nate Cornejo SP RC 1.00 .30
341 Matt Holliday SP RC 2.00 .60
342 J.M. Gold SP RC 1.00 .30
343 Matt Roney SP RC 1.00 .55
344 Seth Etherton SP RC 1.00 .30
345 Adam Everett SP RC 1.50 .45
346 Marlon Anderson SP 1.00 .30
347 Ron Belliard SP 1.00 .30
348 F.Seguignol SP 1.00 .30
349 Michael Barrett SP 1.00 .30
350 Dernell Stenson SP 1.00 .30
351 Ryan Anderson SP 1.00 .30
352 Ramon Hernandez SP 1.00 .30
353 Jeremy Giambi SP 1.00 .30
354 Ricky Ledee SP 1.00 .30
355 Carlos Lee SP 1.00 .30

1999 Stadium Club First Day Issue

Randomly inserted in retail packs only at the rate of 1:75 series one packs and 1:60 series two packs, this 355-card set is parallel to Stadium Club Series one base set. Only 170 serially numbered series one sets were produced and 200 serial numbered series two sets were produced.

Nm-Mt Ex-Mt
*STARS: 6X TO 15X BASIC CARDS....
*SP 141-160/336-355: 2X TO 5X BASIC SP

1999 Stadium Club One of a Kind

This set is a parallel version of the regular issue printed on mirrorboard and sequentially numbered to 150. The cards were randomly inserted packs at the rate of 1:53 first series hobby packs, 1:21 first series HTA packs, 1:48 second series retail packs and 1:19 second series HTA packs.

Nm-Mt Ex-Mt
*STARS: 6X TO 15X BASIC CARDS....
*SP'S 141-160/336-355: 2X TO 5X BASIC

1999 Stadium Club Autographs

This 10-card set features color player photos with the pictured player's autograph and a gold-foil Topps Certified Autograph Issue stamp on the card front. They were inserted exclusively into retail packs as follows: series 1 1:1107, series 2 1:877.

Nm-Mt Ex-Mt
SCA1 Alex Rodriguez 100.00 30.00
SCA2 Chipper Jones 40.00 12.00
SCA3 Barry Bonds 250.00 75.00
SCA4 Tino Martinez 25.00 7.50
SCA5 Ben Grieve 15.00 4.50
SCA6 Juan Gonzalez 25.00 7.50
SCA7 Vladimir Guerrero 40.00 12.00
SCA8 Albert Belle 15.00 4.50
SCA9 Kerry Wood 40.00 12.00
SCA10 Todd Helton 25.00 7.50

1999 Stadium Club Chrome

Randomly inserted in packs at the rate of one in 24 hobby and retail packs and one in six HTA packs, this 40-card set features color player photos printed using chromium technology which gives the cards the shimmering metallic light of fresh steel.

Nm-Mt Ex-Mt
COMPLETE SERIES 1 (20) 60.00 18.00
COMPLETE SERIES 2 (20) 60.00 18.00
*REFRACTORS: 1X TO 2.5X BASIC CHROME
REFRACTOR ODDS 1:96 HOB/RET, 1:24 HTA
SCC1 Nomar Garciaparra 6.00 1.80
SCC2 Kerry Wood 4.00 1.20
SCC3 Jeff Bagwell 2.50 .75
SCC4 Ivan Rodriguez 4.00 1.20
SCC5 Albert Belle 1.50 .45
SCC6 Gary Sheffield 1.50 .45
SCC7 Andruw Jones 1.50 .45
SCC8 Kevin Brown 1.50 .45
SCC9 David Cone 1.50 .45
SCC10 Darin Erstad 1.50 .45
SCC11 Manny Ramirez 2.50 .75
SCC12 Larry Walker 2.50 .75
SCC13 Mike Piazza 6.00 1.80
SCC14 Cal Ripken 12.00 3.60
SCC15 Pedro Martinez 4.00 1.20
SCC16 Greg Vaughn 1.50 .45
SCC17 Barry Bonds 10.00 3.00
SCC18 Mo Vaughn 1.50 .45
SCC19 Bernie Williams 2.50 .75
SCC20 Ken Griffey Jr. 6.00 1.80
SCC21 Alex Rodriguez 6.00 1.80
SCC22 Chipper Jones 4.00 1.20
SCC23 Ben Grieve 1.50 .45
SCC24 Frank Thomas 4.00 1.20
SCC25 Derek Jeter 10.00 3.00
SCC26 Sammy Sosa 6.00 1.80
SCC27 Mark McGwire 10.00 3.00
SCC28 Vladimir Guerrero 4.00 1.20
SCC29 Greg Maddux 6.00 1.80
SCC30 Juan Gonzalez 2.50 .75
SCC31 Troy Glaus 1.50 .45
SCC32 Adrian Beltre 2.50 .75
SCC33 Mitch Meluskey 1.50 .45
SCC34 Alex Gonzalez 1.50 .45
SCC35 George Lombard 1.50 .45
SCC36 Eric Chavez 1.50 .45
SCC37 Ruben Mateo 1.50 .45
SCC38 Calvin Pickering 1.50 .45
SCC39 Gabe Kapler 1.50 .45
SCC40 Bruce Chen 1.50 .45

1999 Stadium Club Co-Signers

Randomly inserted in hobby packs only, this 42-card set features color player photos with their autographs and Topps "Certified Autograph Issue" stamp. Cards 1-21 were seeded in first series packs and 22-42 in second series. The cards are divided into four groups. Group A was signed by all four players appearing on the cards. Groups B-D are dual player cards featuring two autographs. Series 1 hobby pack insertion rates are as follows: Group A 1:45,213, Group B 1:3617, Group C 1:1006, and Group D 1:102. Series 2 hobby pack insertion rates are as follows: Group A 1:43,369, Group B 1:8984, Group C 1:2975 and Group D 1:251. Series 2 HTA pack insertion rates are as follows: Group A 1:18,171, Group B 1:3533, Group C 1:1189 and Group D 1:100. Pricing is available for all cards where possible.

Nm-Mt Ex-Mt
NO GROUP A PRICING DUE TO SCARCITY
NO SER.2 GROUP B PRICING AVAILABLE
CS1 Ben Grieve 15.00 4.50
Richie Sexson D
CS2 Todd Helton 50.00 15.00
Troy Glaus D
CS3 Alex Rodriguez 150.00 45.00
Scott Rolen D
CS4 Derek Jeter 200.00 60.00
Chipper Jones D
CS5 Cliff Floyd 15.00 4.50
Eli Marrero D
CS6 Jay Buhner 15.00 4.50
Kevin Young D
CS7 Ben Grieve 40.00 12.00
Troy Glaus C
CS8 Todd Helton 50.00 15.00
Richie Sexson C
CS9 Alex Rodriguez 150.00 45.00
Chipper Jones C
CS10 Derek Jeter 150.00 45.00
Scott Rolen C
CS11 Cliff Floyd 15.00 4.50
Kevin Young C
CS12 Jay Buhner 15.00 4.50
Eli Marrero B
CS13 Ben Grieve 60.00 18.00
Todd Helton B
CS14 Richie Sexson 50.00 15.00
Troy Glaus B
CS15 Alex Rodriguez 500.00 150.00
Derek Jeter B
CS16 Chipper Jones 150.00 45.00
Scott Rolen B
CS17 Cliff Floyd 15.00 4.50
Jay Buhner B
CS18 Eli Marrero 25.00 7.50
Kevin Young B
CS19 Ben Grieve
Todd Helton
Richie Sexson
Troy Glaus A
CS20 Alex Rodriguez
Derek Jeter
Chipper Jones
Scott Rolen A
CS21 Cliff Floyd
Jay Buhner
Eli Marrero
Kevin Young A
CS22 Edgardo Alfonzo 15.00 4.50
Jose Guillen D
CS23 Mike Lowell 15.00 4.50
Ricardo Rincon D
CS24 Juan Gonzalez 25.00 7.50
Vinny Castilla D
CS25 Moises Alou 80.00 24.00
Roger Clemens D
CS26 Scott Spiezio 15.00 4.50
Tony Womack D
CS27 Fernando Vina 15.00 4.50
Quilvio Veras D
CS28 Edgardo Alfonzo 15.00 4.50
Ricardo Rincon C
CS29 Jose Guillen 15.00 4.50
Mike Lowell C
CS30 Juan Gonzalez 25.00 7.50
Moises Alou C
CS31 Roger Clemens 120.00 36.00
Vinny Castilla C
CS32 Scott Spiezio 15.00 4.50
Fernando Vina C
CS33 Tony Womack
Quilvio Veras B
CS34 Edgardo Alfonzo
Mike Lowell B
CS35 Jose Guillen
Ricardo Rincon B
CS36 Juan Gonzalez
Roger Clemens B
CS37 Moises Alou
Vinny Castilla B
CS38 Scott Spiezio
Quilvio Veras B
CS39 Tony Womack
Fernando Vina B
CS40 Edgardo Alfonzo
Jose Guillen
Mike Lowell
Ricardo Rincon A
CS41 Juan Gonzalez
Moises Alou
Roger Clemens
Vinny Castilla A
CS42 Scott Spiezio
Tony Womack
Fernando Vina
Quilvio Veras A

1999 Stadium Club Never Compromise

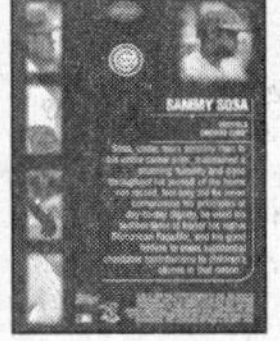

Randomly inserted in packs at the rate of one in 12 hobby and retail packs and one in four HTA packs, this 10-card set features color action photos of top players.

Nm-Mt Ex-Mt
COMPLETE SET (20) 50.00 15.00
COMPLETE SERIES 1 (10) 30.00 9.00
COMPLETE SERIES 2 (10) 20.00 6.00
NC1 Mark McGwire 5.00 1.50
NC2 Sammy Sosa 3.00 .90
NC3 Ken Griffey Jr. 3.00 .90
NC4 Greg Maddux 3.00 .90
NC5 Barry Bonds 5.00 1.50
NC6 Alex Rodriguez 3.00 .90
NC7 Darin Erstad .75 .23
NC8 Roger Clemens 4.00 1.20
NC9 Nomar Garciaparra 3.00 .90
NC10 Derek Jeter 5.00 1.50
NC11 Cal Ripken 6.00 1.80
NC12 Mike Piazza 3.00 .90
NC13 Kerry Wood 2.00 .60
NC14 Andres Galarraga .75 .23
NC15 Vinny Castilla .75 .23
NC16 Jeff Bagwell 1.25 .35
NC17 Chipper Jones 2.00 .60
NC18 Eric Chavez .75 .23
NC19 Orlando Hernandez .75 .23
NC20 Troy Glaus .75 .23

1999 Stadium Club Triumvirate Luminous

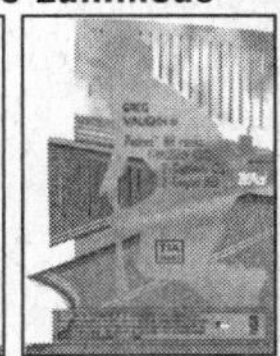

Randomly inserted in hobby packs at the rate of one in 36 and in retail packs at the rate of one in 48, this 24-card set features color player photos printed on cards made to fit together to form eight different long cards.

Nm-Mt Ex-Mt
COMPLETE SERIES 1 (24) 120.00 36.00
COMPLETE SERIES 2 (24) 150.00 45.00
*ILLUMINATOR: 2X TO 5X LUMINOUS
ILLUM.ODDS 1:288 H, 1:384 R, 1:144 HTA
*LUMINESCENT: 1X TO 2.5X LUMINOUS
L'SCENT.ODDS 1:144 H, 1:192 R, 1:72 HTA
T1A Greg Vaughn 2.00 .60
T1B Ken Caminiti 2.00 .60
T1C Tony Gwynn 6.00 1.80
T2A Andruw Jones 2.00 .60
T2B Chipper Jones 5.00 1.50
T2C Andres Galarraga 2.00 .60
T3A Jay Buhner 2.00 .60
T3B Ken Griffey Jr. 8.00 2.40
T3C Alex Rodriguez 8.00 2.40
T4A Derek Jeter 12.00 3.60
T4B Tino Martinez 3.00 .90
T4C Bernie Williams 3.00 .90
T5A Brian Jordan 2.00 .60
T5B Ray Lankford 2.00 .60
T5C Mark McGwire 12.00 3.60
T6A Jeff Bagwell 3.00 .90
T6B Craig Biggio 3.00 .90
T6C Randy Johnson 5.00 1.50
T7A Nomar Garciaparra 8.00 2.40
T7B Pedro Martinez 5.00 1.50
T7C Mo Vaughn 2.00 .60
T8A Sammy Sosa 8.00 2.40
T8B Mark Grace 3.00 .90
T8C Kerry Wood 5.00 1.50
T9A Alex Rodriguez 8.00 2.40
T9B Nomar Garciaparra 8.00 2.40
T9C Derek Jeter 12.00 3.60
T10A Todd Helton 3.00 .90
T10B Travis Lee 2.00 .60
T10C Pat Burrell 2.50 .75
T11A Greg Maddux 8.00 2.40
T11B Kerry Wood 5.00 1.50
T11C Tom Glavine 3.00 .90
T12A Chipper Jones 5.00 1.50
T12B Vinny Castilla 2.00 .60
T12C Scott Rolen 5.00 1.50
T13A Juan Gonzalez 3.00 .90
T13B Ken Griffey Jr. 8.00 2.40
T13C Ben Grieve 2.00 .60
T14A Sammy Sosa 8.00 2.40
T14B Vladimir Guerrero 5.00 1.50
T14C Barry Bonds 12.00 3.60
T15A Frank Thomas 5.00 1.50
T15B Jim Thome 5.00 1.50
T15C Tino Martinez 3.00 .90
T16A Mark McGwire 12.00 3.60
T16B Andres Galarraga 2.00 .60
T16C Jeff Bagwell 3.00 .90

1999 Stadium Club Video Replay

Randomly inserted in Series two hobby and retail packs at the rate of one in 12 and HTA packs at the rate of one in four, this five-card set features live-action video images of top players on lenticular cards.

Nm-Mt Ex-Mt
COMPLETE SET (5) 12.00 3.60
VR1 Mark McGwire 4.00 1.20
VR2 Sammy Sosa 2.50 .75
VR3 Ken Griffey Jr. 2.50 .75

VR4 Kerry Wood 1.50 .45
VR5 Alex Rodriguez 2.50 .75

2000 Stadium Club

This 250-card single series set was released in February, 2000. Six-card hobby and retail packs carried an SRP of $2.00. There was also a HTC (Home Team Collector) fourteen card pack issued with a SRP of $5.00. The last 50 cards were printed in shorter supply the first 200 cards. These cards were inserted one in five packs and one per HTC pack. This was the first time the Stadium Club set was issued in a single series. Notable Rookie Cards include Rick Asadoorian and Bobby Bradley.

Nm-Mt Ex-Mt
COMPLETE SET (250) 120.00 36.00
COMP.SET w/o SP'S (200) 30.00 9.00
COMMON CARD (1-200) .30 .09
COMMON SP (201-250) 3.00 .90
1 Nomar Garciaparra 1.25 .35
2 Brian Jordan .30 .09
3 Mark Grace .50 .15
4 Jeromy Burnitz .30 .09
5 Shane Reynolds .30 .09
6 Alex Gonzalez .30 .09
7 Jose Offerman .30 .09
8 Orlando Hernandez .30 .09
9 Mike Caruso .30 .09
10 Tony Clark .30 .09
11 Sean Casey .30 .09
12 Johnny Damon .50 .15
13 Dante Bichette .30 .09
14 Kevin Young .30 .09
15 Juan Gonzalez .50 .15
16 Chipper Jones .75 .23
17 Quilvio Veras .30 .09
18 Trevor Hoffman .30 .09
19 Roger Cedeno .30 .09
20 Ellis Burks .30 .09
21 Richie Sexson .30 .09
22 Gary Sheffield .30 .09
23 Delino DeShields .30 .09
24 Wade Boggs .50 .15
25 Ray Lankford .30 .09
26 Kevin Appier .30 .09
27 Roy Halladay .30 .09
28 Harold Baines .30 .09
29 Todd Zeile .30 .09
30 Barry Larkin .50 .15
31 Ron Coomer .30 .09
32 Jorge Posada .50 .15
33 Magglio Ordonez .30 .09
34 Brian Giles .30 .09
35 Jeff Kent .30 .09
36 Henry Rodriguez .30 .09
37 Fred McGriff .50 .15
38 Shawn Green .30 .09
39 Derek Bell .30 .09
40 Ben Grieve .30 .09
41 Dave Nilsson .30 .09
42 Mo Vaughn .30 .09
43 Rondell White .30 .09
44 Doug Glanville .30 .09
45 Paul O'Neill .50 .15
46 Carlos Lee .30 .09
47 Vinny Castilla .30 .09
48 Mike Sweeney .30 .09
49 Rico Brogna .30 .09
50 Alex Rodriguez 1.25 .35
51 Luis Castillo .30 .09
52 Kevin Brown .50 .15
53 Jose Vidro .30 .09
54 John Smoltz .50 .15
55 Garret Anderson .30 .09
56 Matt Stairs .30 .09
57 Omar Vizquel .50 .15
58 Tom Goodwin .30 .09
59 Scott Brosius .30 .09
60 Robin Ventura .50 .15
61 B.J. Surhoff .30 .09
62 Andy Ashby .30 .09
63 Chris Widger .30 .09
64 Tim Hudson .30 .09
65 Javy Lopez .30 .09
66 Tim Salmon .50 .15
67 Warren Morris .30 .09
68 John Wetteland .30 .09
69 Gabe Kapler .30 .09
70 Bernie Williams .50 .15
71 Rickey Henderson .75 .23
72 Andruw Jones .30 .09
73 Eric Young .30 .09
74 Bob Abreu .30 .09
75 David Cone .30 .09
76 Rusty Greer .30 .09
77 Ron Belliard .30 .09
78 Troy Glaus .30 .09
79 Mike Hampton .30 .09
80 Miguel Tejada .30 .09
81 Jeff Cirillo .30 .09
82 Todd Hundley .30 .09
83 Roberto Alomar .50 .15
84 Charles Johnson .30 .09
85 Rafael Palmeiro .50 .15
86 Doug Mientkiewicz .30 .09
87 Mariano Rivera .50 .15
88 Neifi Perez .30 .09
89 Jermaine Dye .30 .09
90 Ivan Rodriguez .75 .23
91 Jay Buhner .30 .09
92 Pokey Reese .30 .09
93 John Olerud .30 .09
94 Brady Anderson .30 .09
95 Manny Ramirez .50 .15
96 Keith Osik RC .30 .09
97 Mickey Morandini .30 .09
98 Matt Williams .30 .09
99 Eric Karros .30 .09
100 Ken Griffey Jr. 1.25 .35
101 Bret Boone .30 .09
102 Ryan Klesko .30 .09
103 Craig Biggio .50 .15
104 John Jaha .30 .09
105 Vladimir Guerrero .75 .23
106 Devon White .30 .09
107 Tony Womack .30 .09
108 Marvin Benard .30 .09
109 Kenny Lofton .30 .09
110 Preston Wilson .30 .09
111 Al Leiter .30 .09
112 Reggie Sanders .30 .09
113 Scott Williamson .30 .09
114 Deivi Cruz .30 .09
115 Carlos Beltran .50 .15
116 Ray Durham .30 .09
117 Ricky Ledee .30 .09
118 Torii Hunter .30 .09
119 John Valentin .30 .09
120 Scott Rolen .75 .23
121 Jason Kendall .30 .09
122 Dave Martinez .30 .09
123 Jim Thome .75 .23
124 David Bell .30 .09
125 Jose Canseco .75 .23
126 Jose Lima .30 .09
127 Carl Everett .30 .09
128 Kevin Millwood .30 .09
129 Bill Spiers .30 .09
130 Omar Daal .30 .09
131 Miguel Cairo .30 .09
132 Mark Grudzielanek .30 .09
133 David Justice .30 .09
134 Russ Ortiz .30 .09
135 Mike Piazza 1.25 .35
136 Brian Meadows .30 .09
137 Tony Gwynn 1.00 .30
138 Cal Ripken 2.50 .75
139 Kris Benson .30 .09
140 Larry Walker .50 .15
141 Cristian Guzman .30 .09
142 Tino Martinez .50 .15
143 Chris Singleton .30 .09
144 Lee Stevens .30 .09
145 Rey Ordonez .30 .09
146 Russ Davis .30 .09
147 J.T. Snow .30 .09
148 Luis Gonzalez .30 .09
149 Marquis Grissom .30 .09
150 Greg Maddux 1.25 .35
151 Fernando Tatis .30 .09
152 Jason Giambi .30 .09
153 Carlos Delgado .30 .09
154 Joe McEwing .30 .09
155 Raul Mondesi .30 .09
156 Rich Aurilia .30 .09
157 Alex Fernandez .30 .09
158 Albert Belle .30 .09
159 Pat Meares .30 .09
160 Mike Lieberthal .30 .09
161 Mike Cameron .30 .09
162 Juan Encarnacion .30 .09
163 Chuck Knoblauch .30 .09
164 Pedro Martinez .75 .23
165 Randy Johnson .75 .23
166 Shannon Stewart .30 .09
167 Jeff Bagwell .50 .15
168 Edgar Renteria .30 .09
169 Barry Bonds 2.00 .60
170 Steve Finley .30 .09
171 Brian Hunter .30 .09
172 Tom Glavine .50 .15
173 Mark Kotsay .30 .09
174 Tony Fernandez .30 .09
175 Sammy Sosa 1.25 .35
176 Geoff Jenkins .30 .09
177 Adrian Beltre .50 .15
178 Jay Bell .30 .09
179 Mike Bordick .30 .09
180 Ed Sprague .30 .09
181 Dave Roberts .30 .09
182 Greg Vaughn .30 .09
183 Brian Daubach .30 .09
184 Damion Easley .30 .09
185 Carlos Febles .30 .09
186 Kevin Tapani .30 .09
187 Frank Thomas .75 .23
188 Roger Clemens 1.50 .45
189 Mike Benjamin .30 .09
190 Curt Schilling .30 .09
191 Edgardo Alfonzo .30 .09
192 Mike Mussina .50 .15
193 Todd Helton .50 .15
194 Todd Jones .30 .09
195 Dean Palmer .30 .09
196 John Flaherty .30 .09
197 Derek Jeter 2.00 .60
198 Todd Walker .30 .09
199 Brad Ausmus .30 .09
200 Mark McGwire 2.00 .60
201 Erubiel Durazo SP 3.00 .90
202 Nick Johnson SP 3.00 .90
203 Ruben Mateo SP 3.00 .90
204 Lance Berkman SP 3.00 .90
205 Pat Burrell SP 3.00 .90
206 Pablo Ozuna SP 3.00 .90
207 Roosevelt Brown SP 3.00 .90
208 Alfonso Soriano SP 4.00 1.20
209 A.J. Burnett SP 3.00 .90
210 Rafael Furcal SP 3.00 .90
211 Scott Morgan SP 3.00 .90
212 Adam Piatt SP 3.00 .90
213 Dee Brown SP 3.00 .90
214 Corey Patterson SP 3.00 .90
215 Mickey Lopez SP 3.00 .90
216 Rob Ryan SP 3.00 .90
217 Sean Burroughs SP 3.00 .90
218 Jack Cust SP 3.00 .90
219 John Patterson SP 3.00 .90
220 Kit Pellow SP 3.00 .90
221 Chad Hermansen SP 3.00 .90
222 Daryle Ward SP 3.00 .90
223 Jayson Werth SP 3.00 .90
224 Jason Standridge SP 3.00 .90
225 Mark Mulder SP 3.00 .90
226 Peter Bergeron SP 3.00 .90
227 Willi Mo Pena SP 3.00 .90
228 Aramis Ramirez SP 3.00 .90
229 John Sneed SP RC 3.00 .90
230 Wilton Veras SP 3.00 .90
231 Josh Hamilton SP 3.00 .90
232 Eric Munson SP 3.00 .90
233 Bobby Bradley SP RC 3.00 .90
234 Larry Bigbie SP RC 4.00 1.20
235 B.J. Garbe SP RC 3.00 .90
236 Brett Myers SP RC 4.00 1.20
237 Jason Stumm SP RC 3.00 .90
238 Corey Myers SP RC 3.00 .90
239 R.Christianson SP RC 3.00 .90
240 David Walling SP 3.00 .90
241 Josh Girdley SP 3.00 .90
242 Omar Ortiz SP 3.00 .90
243 Jason Jennings SP 3.00 .90
244 Kyle Snyder SP 3.00 .90
245 Jay Gehrke SP 3.00 .90
246 Mike Paradis SP 3.00 .90
247 Chance Caple SP RC 3.00 .90
248 B.Christensen SP RC 3.00 .90
249 Brad Baker SP RC 3.00 .90
250 R.Asadoorian SP RC 3.00 .90

2000 Stadium Club First Day Issue

This parallel to the Stadium Club set was inserted at a rate of one in 36 retail packs and were serial numbered to 150. These cards can be identified by the first day issue stamp on the front.

Nm-Mt Ex-Mt
*STARS: 10X TO 25X BASIC CARDS
*SP'S 201-250: 1X TO 2.5X BASIC
*SP RC'S 201-250: 1.25X TO 3X BASIC

2000 Stadium Club One of a Kind

This parallel set was issued at a rate of one in 27 hobby and one in 11 HTC packs. The cards are serial numbered to 150 as well. These cards are differentiated from the regular cards by the mirrorboard technology.

Nm-Mt Ex-Mt
*STARS 1-250: 10X TO 25X BASIC CARDS
*SP'S 201-250: 1X TO 2.5X BASIC
*SP RC'S 201-250: 1.25X TO 3X BASIC

2000 Stadium Club Bats of Brilliance

Issued at a rate of one in 12 hobby packs, one in 15 retail packs and one in six HTC packs these 10 cards feature some of the best clutch hitters in the game.

Nm-Mt Ex-Mt
COMPLETE SET (10) 20.00 6.00
*DIE CUTS: 1.25X TO 3X BASIC BATS
DIE CUT ODDS 1:60 HOB, 1:75 RET, 1:30 HTC
BB1 Mark McGwire 4.00 1.20
BB2 Sammy Sosa 2.50 .75
BB3 Jose Canseco 1.50 .45
BB4 Jeff Bagwell 1.00 .30
BB5 Ken Griffey Jr. 2.50 .75
BB6 Nomar Garciaparra 2.50 .75
BB7 Mike Piazza 2.50 .75
BB8 Alex Rodriguez 2.50 .75
BB9 Vladimir Guerrero 1.50 .45
BB10 Chipper Jones 1.50 .45

2000 Stadium Club Capture the Action

Inserted one in 12 hobby and retail packs and one in six HTC packs, these 20 cards feature players who continually hustle when on the field. This set is broken up into three groups: Rookies (CA1 through CA5); Stars (CA6 through CA14) and Legends (CA15 through CA20).

Nm-Mt Ex-Mt
COMPLETE SET (20) 60.00 18.00
*GAME VIEW 1-5: 5X TO 12X BASIC CAPT
*GAME VIEW: 5X TO 12X BASIC CAPTURE
GAME VIEW ODDS 1:508 HOB, 1:203 HTC
GAME VIEW PRINT RUN 100 SERIAL #'d SETS
CA1 Josh Hamilton 1.00 .30
CA2 Pat Burrell 1.00 .30
CA3 Erubiel Durazo 1.00 .30
CA4 Alfonso Soriano 1.25 .35
CA5 A.J. Burnett 1.00 .30
CA6 Alex Rodriguez 4.00 1.20
CA7 Sean Casey 1.00 .30
CA8 Derek Jeter 6.00 1.80
CA9 Vladimir Guerrero 2.50 .75
CA10 Nomar Garciaparra 4.00 1.20
CA11 Mike Piazza 4.00 1.20
CA12 Ken Griffey Jr. 4.00 1.20
CA13 Sammy Sosa 4.00 1.20
CA14 Juan Gonzalez 1.50 .45
CA15 Mark McGwire 6.00 1.80
CA16 Ivan Rodriguez 2.50 .75
CA17 Barry Bonds 6.00 1.80
CA18 Wade Boggs 1.50 .45
CA19 Tony Gwynn 3.00 .90
CA20 Cal Ripken 8.00 2.40

2000 Stadium Club Capture the Action Game View

Inserted at a rate of one in 508 hobby packs, these cards parallel the regular Capture the Action insert set. These cards, issued only through hobby packs, feature a replica of the actual photo slide used to create the card and is viewable from both sides. Each card back has a "Topps3M" sticker to ensure the autenticity.

Nm-Mt Ex-Mt
*GAME VIEW: 5X TO 12X BASIC CAPTURE

2000 Stadium Club Chrome Preview

Inserted at a rate of one in 24 for hobby and retail and one in 12 HTC packs, these 20 cards preview the "Chrome" set. These cards carry a "SCC" prefix.

Nm-Mt Ex-Mt
COMPLETE SET (20) 100.00 30.00
*REFRACTOR: 1.25X TO 3X BASIC CHR.PREV.
REFRACTOR ODDS 1:120 HOB/RET, 1:60 HTC
SCC1 Nomar Garciaparra 6.00 1.80
SCC2 Juan Gonzalez 2.50 .75
SCC3 Chipper Jones 4.00 1.20
SCC4 Alex Rodriguez 6.00 1.80
SCC5 Ivan Rodriguez 4.00 1.20
SCC6 Manny Ramirez 2.50 .75
SCC7 Ken Griffey Jr. 6.00 1.80
SCC8 Vladimir Guerrero 4.00 1.20
SCC9 Mike Piazza 6.00 1.80
SCC10 Pedro Martinez 4.00 1.20
SCC11 Jeff Bagwell 2.50 .75
SCC12 Barry Bonds 10.00 3.00
SCC13 Sammy Sosa 6.00 1.80
SCC14 Derek Jeter 10.00 3.00
SCC15 Mark McGwire 10.00 3.00
SCC16 Erubiel Durazo 1.50 .45
SCC17 Nick Johnson 1.50 .45
SCC18 Pat Burrell 1.50 .45
SCC19 Alfonso Soriano 4.00 1.20
SCC20 Adam Piatt 1.50 .45

2000 Stadium Club Co-Signers

Inserted in hobby packs only at different rates, these 15 cards feature a pair of players who have signed these cards. The odds are broken down like this: Group A was issued one every 10,184 hobby packs and one every 4060 HTC packs. Group B was issued one every 5092 hobby packs and one every 2032 HTC packs. Group C was issued one every 508 hobby packs and one every 203 HTC packs.

Nm-Mt Ex-Mt
CO1 Alex Rodriguez 600.00 180.00
Derek Jeter A
CO2 Derek Jeter 150.00 45.00
Omar Vizquel B
CO3 Alex Rodriguez 150.00 45.00
Rey Ordonez B
CO4 Derek Jeter 150.00 45.00
Rey Ordonez B
CO5 Omar Vizquel 150.00 45.00
Alex Rodriguez B
CO6 Rey Ordonez 40.00 12.00
Omar Vizquel C
CO7 Wade Boggs 40.00 12.00
Robin Ventura C
CO8 Randy Johnson 120.00 36.00
Mike Mussina C
CO9 Pat Burrell 25.00 7.50
Magglio Ordonez C
CO10 Chad Hermansen 25.00 7.50
Pat Burrell C
CO11 Magglio Ordonez 25.00 7.50
Chad Hermansen C
CO12 Josh Hamilton 15.00 4.50
Corey Myers C
CO13 B.J.Garbe 15.00 4.50
Josh Hamilton C
CO14 Corey Myers 15.00 4.50
B.J. Garbe C
CO15 Tino Martinez 50.00 15.00
Fred McGriff C

2000 Stadium Club Lone Star Signatures

Issued at different rates throughout the various packaging, these 16 cards feature signed cards of various stars. The cards were inserted at these rates: Group 1 was inserted at a rate of one in 1981 retail packs, one in 1979 hobby packs and one in 792 HTC packs. Group 2 was inserted at a rate of one in 2421 retail packs, one in 2374 hobby packs and one in 946 HTC packs.

Group 3 was issued at the same rate as Group 1 (1:1979 hobby, 1:1981 retail; 1:792 HTC packs). Group 4 were issued at a rate of one in 424 hobby packs, one in 423 retail packs and one in 169 HTC packs. These cards are authenticated with a "Topps Certified Autograph" stamp as well as a "Topps3M" sticker.

Nm-Mt Ex-Mt
LS1 Derek Jeter G1 120.00 36.00
LS2 Alex Rodriguez G1 120.00 36.00
LS3 Wade Boggs G1 40.00 12.00
LS4 Robin Ventura G1 15.00 4.50
LS5 Randy Johnson G2 80.00 24.00
LS6 Mike Mussina G2 25.00 7.50
LS7 Tino Martinez G3 50.00 15.00
LS8 Fred McGriff G3 50.00 15.00
LS9 Omar Vizquel G4 25.00 7.50
LS10 Rey Ordonez G4 10.00 3.00
LS11 Pat Burrell G4 15.00 4.50
LS12 Chad Hermansen G4 10.00 3.00
LS13 Magglio Ordonez G4 15.00 4.50
LS14 Josh Hamilton G4 10.00 3.00
LS15 Corey Myers G4 10.00 3.00
LS16 B.J. Garbe G4 10.00 3.00

2000 Stadium Club Onyx Extreme

Inserted at a rate of one in 12 hobby, one in 15 retail and one in six HTC packs, these 10 cards feature 10 cards printed using black styrene technology with silver foil stamping.

Nm-Mt Ex-Mt
COMPLETE SET (10) 25.00 7.50
*DIE CUTS: 1.25X TO 3X BASIC ONYX
DIE CUT ODDS 1:60 HOB, 1:75 RET, 1:30 HTC
OE1 Ken Griffey Jr. 2.50 .75
OE2 Derek Jeter 4.00 1.20
OE3 Vladimir Guerrero 1.50 .45
OE4 Nomar Garciaparra 2.50 .75
OE5 Barry Bonds 4.00 1.20
OE6 Alex Rodriguez 2.50 .75
OE7 Sammy Sosa 2.50 .75
OE8 Ivan Rodriguez 1.50 .45
OE9 Larry Walker 1.00 .30
OE10 Andruw Jones .60 .18

2000 Stadium Club Scenes

Inserted as a box-topper in hobby and HTC boxes, these eight cards which measure 2 1/2" by 4 11/16" feature superstar players in a special "widevision" format.

Nm-Mt Ex-Mt
COMPLETE SET (8) 25.00 7.50
SCS1 Mark McGwire 5.00 1.50
SCS2 Alex Rodriguez 3.00 .90
SCS3 Cal Ripken 6.00 1.80
SCS4 Sammy Sosa 3.00 .90
SCS5 Derek Jeter 5.00 1.50
SCS6 Ken Griffey Jr. 3.00 .90
SCS7 Nomar Garciaparra 3.00 .90
SCS8 Chipper Jones 2.00 .60

2000 Stadium Club Souvenir

Inserted exclusively into hobby packs at a rate of one in 339 hobby packs and one in 136 HTC packs, these cards feature die-cut technology which incorporates an actual piece of a game-used uniform.

Nm-Mt Ex-Mt
S1 Wade Boggs 25.00 7.50
S2 Edgardo Alfonzo 10.00 3.00
S3 Robin Ventura 15.00 4.50

2000 Stadium Club 3 X 3 Luminous

Inserted at a rate of one in 18 hobby, one in 24 retail and one in nine HTC packs, these 30 cards can be fused together to form one very oversized card. The luminous variety is the most common of the three forms used (Luminous, Luminescent and Illuminator).

	Nm-Mt	Ex-Mt
COMPLETE SET (30)	120.00	36.00
*ILLUMINATOR: 1.5X TO 4X LUMINOUS		
ILLUM ODDS 1:144 HOB, 1:192 RET, 1:72 HTC		
*L'SCENT: .75X TO 2X LUMINOUS		
L'SCENT ODDS 1:72 HOB, 1:96 RET, 1:36 HTC		
1A Randy Johnson	4.00	1.20
1B Pedro Martinez	4.00	1.20
1C Greg Maddux	6.00	1.80
2A Mike Piazza	6.00	1.80
2B Ivan Rodriguez	4.00	1.20
2C Mike Lieberthal	1.50	.45
3A Mark McGwire	10.00	3.00
3B Jeff Bagwell	2.50	.75
3C Sean Casey	1.50	.45
4A Craig Biggio	2.50	.75
4B Roberto Alomar	2.50	.75
4C Jay Bell	1.50	.45
5A Chipper Jones	4.00	1.20
5B Matt Williams	1.50	.45
5C Robin Ventura	2.50	.75
6A Alex Rodriguez	6.00	1.80
6B Derek Jeter	10.00	3.00
6C Nomar Garciaparra	6.00	1.80
7A Barry Bonds	10.00	3.00
7B Luis Gonzalez	1.50	.45
7C Dante Bichette	1.50	.45
8A Ken Griffey Jr.	6.00	1.80
8B Bernie Williams	2.50	.75
8C Andruw Jones	1.50	.45
9A Manny Ramirez	2.50	.75
9B Sammy Sosa	6.00	1.80
9C Juan Gonzalez	2.50	.75
10A Jose Canseco	4.00	1.20
10B Frank Thomas	4.00	1.20
10C Rafael Palmeiro	2.50	.75

2001 Stadium Club

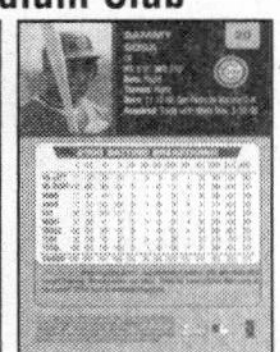

The 2001 Stadium Club product was released in late December, 2000 and features a 200-card base set. The set is broken into tiers as follows: 175 Base Veterans and 25 Prospects (1:6). Each pack contained seven cards and carried a suggested retail price of $1.99.

	Nm-Mt	Ex-Mt
COMPLETE SET (200)	120.00	36.00
COMP.SET w/o SP's (175)	25.00	7.50
COMMON CARD (1-150)	.30	.09
COMMON SP (151-200)	3.00	.90
1 Nomar Garciaparra	1.25	.35
2 Chipper Jones	.75	.23
3 Jeff Bagwell	.50	.15
4 Chad Kreuter	.30	.09
5 Randy Johnson	.75	.23
6 Mike Hampton	.30	.09
7 Barry Larkin	.50	.15
8 Bernie Williams	.50	.15
9 Chris Singleton	.30	.09
10 Larry Walker	.50	.15
11 Brad Ausmus	.30	.09
12 Ron Coomer	.30	.09
13 Edgardo Alfonzo	.30	.09
14 Delino DeShields	.30	.09
15 Tony Gwynn	1.00	.30
16 Andruw Jones	.30	.09
17 Raul Mondesi	.30	.09
18 Troy Glaus	.30	.09
19 Ben Grieve	.30	.09
20 Sammy Sosa	1.25	.35
21 Fernando Vina	.30	.09
22 Jeromy Burnitz	.30	.09
23 Jay Bell	.30	.09
24 Pete Harnisch	.30	.09
25 Barry Bonds	2.00	.60
26 Eric Karros	.30	.09
27 Alex Gonzalez	.30	.09
28 Mike Lieberthal	.30	.09
29 Juan Encarnacion	.30	.09
30 Derek Jeter	2.00	.60
31 Luis Sojo	.30	.09
32 Eric Milton	.30	.09
33 Aaron Boone	.30	.09
34 Roberto Alomar	.50	.15
35 John Olerud	.30	.09
36 Orlando Cabrera	.30	.09
37 Shawn Green	.30	.09
38 Roger Cedeno	.30	.09
39 Garret Anderson	.30	.09
40 Jim Thome	.75	.23
41 Gabe Kapler	.30	.09
42 Mo Vaughn	.30	.09
43 Sean Casey	.30	.09
44 Preston Wilson	.30	.09
45 Javy Lopez	.30	.09
46 Ryan Klesko	.30	.09
47 Ray Durham	.30	.09
48 Dean Palmer	.30	.09
49 Jorge Posada	.50	.15
50 Alex Rodriguez	1.25	.35
51 Tom Glavine	.50	.15
52 Ray Lankford	.30	.09
53 Jose Canseco	.75	.23
54 Tim Salmon	.50	.15
55 Cal Ripken	2.50	.75
56 Bob Abreu	.30	.09
57 Robin Ventura	.30	.09
58 Damion Easley	.30	.09
59 Paul O'Neill	.50	.15
60 Ivan Rodriguez	.75	.23
61 Carl Everett	.30	.09
62 Doug Glanville	.30	.09
63 Jeff Kent	.30	.09
64 Jay Buhner	.30	.09
65 Cliff Floyd	.30	.09
66 Rick Ankiel	.30	.09
67 Mark Grace	.50	.15
68 Brian Jordan	.30	.09
69 Craig Biggio	.50	.15
70 Carlos Delgado	.30	.09
71 Brad Radke	.30	.09
72 Greg Maddux	1.25	.35
73 Al Leiter	.30	.09
74 Pokey Reese	.30	.09
75 Todd Helton	.50	.15
76 Mariano Rivera	.50	.15
77 Shane Spencer	.30	.09
78 Jason Kendall	.30	.09
79 Chuck Knoblauch	.30	.09
80 Scott Rolen	.75	.23
81 Jose Offerman	.30	.09
82 J.T. Snow	.30	.09
83 Pat Meares	.30	.09
84 Quilvio Veras	.30	.09
85 Edgar Renteria	.30	.09
86 Luis Matos	.30	.09
87 Adrian Beltre	.50	.15
88 Luis Gonzalez	.30	.09
89 Rickey Henderson	.75	.23
90 Brian Giles	.30	.09
91 Carlos Febles	.30	.09
92 Tino Martinez	.50	.15
93 Magglio Ordonez	.30	.09
94 Rafael Furcal	.30	.09
95 Mike Mussina	.50	.15
96 Gary Sheffield	.30	.09
97 Kenny Lofton	.30	.09
98 Fred McGriff	.50	.15
99 Ken Caminiti	.30	.09
100 Mark McGwire	2.00	.60
101 Tom Goodwin	.30	.09
102 Mark Grudzielanek	.30	.09
103 Derek Bell	.30	.09
104 Mike Lowell	.30	.09
105 Jeff Cirillo	.30	.09
106 Orlando Hernandez	.30	.09
107 Jose Valentin	.30	.09
108 Warren Morris	.30	.09
109 Mike Williams	.30	.09
110 Greg Zaun	.30	.09
111 Jose Vidro	.30	.09
112 Omar Vizquel	.50	.15
113 Vinny Castilla	.30	.09
114 Gregg Jefferies	.30	.09
115 Kevin Brown	.30	.09
116 Shannon Stewart	.30	.09
117 Marquis Grissom	.30	.09
118 Manny Ramirez	.50	.15
119 Albert Belle	.30	.09
120 Bret Boone	.30	.09
121 Johnny Damon	.50	.15
122 Juan Gonzalez	.50	.15
123 David Justice	.30	.09
124 Jeffrey Hammonds	.30	.09
125 Ken Griffey Jr.	1.25	.35
126 Mike Sweeney	.30	.09
127 Tony Clark	.30	.09
128 Todd Zeile	.30	.09
129 Mark Johnson	.30	.09
130 Matt Williams	.30	.09
131 Geoff Jenkins	.30	.09
132 Jason Giambi	.30	.09
133 Steve Finley	.30	.09
134 Derrek Lee	.30	.09
135 Royce Clayton	.30	.09
136 Joe Randa	.30	.09
137 Rafael Palmeiro	.50	.15
138 Kevin Young	.30	.09
139 Mike Redmond	.30	.09
140 Vladimir Guerrero	.75	.23
141 Greg Vaughn	.30	.09
142 Jermaine Dye	.30	.09
143 Roger Clemens	1.50	.45
144 Denny Hocking	.30	.09
145 Frank Thomas	.75	.23
146 Carlos Beltran	.50	.15
147 Eric Young	.30	.09
148 Pat Burrell	.30	.09
149 Pedro Martinez	.75	.23
150 Mike Piazza	1.25	.35
151 Adrian Gonzalez	.50	.15
152 Adam Johnson	.50	.15
153 Luis Montanez SP RC	3.00	.90
154 Mike Stodolka	.50	.15
155 Phil Dumatrait	.50	.15
156 Sean Burnett SP	3.00	.90
157 Dominic Rich SP RC	3.00	.90
158 Adam Wainwright	.50	.15
159 Scott Thorman	.50	.15
160 Scott Heard SP	3.00	.90
161 Chad Petty SP RC	3.00	.90
162 Matt Wheatland	.50	.15
163 Bryan Digby	.50	.15
164 Rocco Baldelli	.75	.23
165 Grady Sizemore	1.00	.30
166 Brian Sellier SP RC	3.00	.90
167 Rick Brosseau SP RC	3.00	.90
168 Shawn Fagan SP RC	3.00	.90
169 Sean Smith SP	3.00	.90
170 Chris Bass SP RC	3.00	.90
171 Corey Patterson	.50	.15
172 Sean Burroughs	.50	.15
173 Ben Petrick	.50	.15
174 Mike Glendenning	.50	.15
175 Barry Zito	.75	.23
176 Milton Bradley	.50	.15
177 Bobby Bradley	.50	.15
178 Jason Hart	.50	.15
179 Ryan Anderson	.50	.15
180 Ben Sheets	.75	.23
181 Adam Everett	.50	.15
182 Alfonso Soriano	.50	.15
183 Josh Hamilton	.50	.15
184 Eric Munson	.50	.15
185 Chin-Feng Chen	.50	.15
186 Tim Christman SP RC	3.00	.90
187 J.R. House SP	3.00	.90
188 B.Parker SP RC	3.00	.90
189 Sean Fesh SP RC	3.00	.90
190 Joel Pineiro SP	4.00	1.20
191 Oscar Ramirez SP RC	3.00	.90
192 Alex Santos SP RC	3.00	.90
193 Eddy Reyes SP RC	3.00	.90
194 Mike Jacobs SP RC	3.00	.90
195 Erick Almonte SP RC	3.00	.90
196 B.Claussen SP RC	8.00	2.40
197 Kris Keller SP RC	3.00	.90
198 Wilson Betemit SP RC	3.00	.90
199 Andy Phillips SP RC	3.00	.90
200 A.Pettyjohn SP RC	3.00	.90

2001 Stadium Club Beam Team

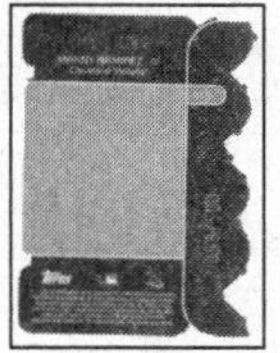

Randomly inserted into packs at one in 175 Hobby, and one in 68 HTA, this 30-card die-cut insert set features players who possess unparalleled style to accompany their world-class talent. Please note that these cards are individually serial numbered to 500, and that the card backs carry a "BT" prefix.

	Nm-Mt	Ex-Mt
BT1 Sammy Sosa	20.00	6.00
BT2 Mark McGwire	30.00	9.00
BT3 Vladimir Guerrero	12.00	3.60
BT4 Chipper Jones	12.00	3.60
BT5 Manny Ramirez	8.00	2.40
BT6 Derek Jeter	30.00	9.00
BT7 Alex Rodriguez	20.00	6.00
BT8 Cal Ripken	40.00	12.00
BT9 Ken Griffey Jr.	20.00	6.00
BT10 Greg Maddux	20.00	6.00
BT11 Barry Bonds	30.00	9.00
BT12 Pedro Martinez	12.00	3.60
BT13 Nomar Garciaparra	20.00	6.00
BT14 Randy Johnson	12.00	3.60
BT15 Frank Thomas	12.00	3.60
BT16 Ivan Rodriguez	12.00	3.60
BT17 Jeff Bagwell	8.00	2.40
BT18 Mike Piazza	20.00	6.00
BT19 Todd Helton	8.00	2.40
BT20 Shawn Green	5.00	1.50
BT21 Juan Gonzalez	8.00	2.40
BT22 Larry Walker	8.00	2.40
BT23 Tony Gwynn	20.00	6.00
BT24 Pat Burrell	5.00	1.50
BT25 Rafael Furcal	5.00	1.50
BT26 Corey Patterson	5.00	1.50
BT27 Chin-Feng Chen	5.00	1.50
BT28 Sean Burroughs	5.00	1.50
BT29 Ryan Anderson	5.00	1.50
BT30 Josh Hamilton	5.00	1.50

2001 Stadium Club Capture the Action

Randomly inserted into packs at one in eight HOB/RET and one in two HTA, this 15-card insert features transformer technology that open up to enlarged action photos of ballplayers at the top of their game. Card backs carry a "CA" prefix.

	Nm-Mt	Ex-Mt
COMPLETE SET (15)	30.00	9.00
*GAME VIEW: 10X TO 25X BASIC CAPTURE		
GAME VIEW ODDS 1:577 HOBBY, 1:224 HTA		
GAME VIEW PRINT RUN 100 SERIAL #'d SETS		
CA1 Cal Ripken	4.00	1.20
CA2 Alex Rodriguez	2.00	.60
CA3 Mike Piazza	2.00	.60
CA4 Mark McGwire	3.00	.90
CA5 Greg Maddux	2.00	.60
CA6 Derek Jeter	3.00	.90
CA7 Chipper Jones	1.25	.35
CA8 Pedro Martinez	1.25	.35
CA9 Ken Griffey Jr.	2.00	.60
CA10 Nomar Garciaparra	2.00	.60
CA11 Randy Johnson	1.25	.35
CA12 Sammy Sosa	2.00	.60
CA13 Vladimir Guerrero	1.25	.35
CA14 Barry Bonds	3.00	.90
CA15 Ivan Rodriguez	1.25	.35

2001 Stadium Club Co-Signers

Randomly inserted into packs at one in 962 Hobby and one in 374 HTA packs, this nine-card insert features authenticated autographs of two players on the same card. Please note that the Chipper Jones/Troy Glaus and the Corey Patterson/Nick Johnson cards packed out as exchange cards, and must be redeemed by 11/30/01.

	Nm-Mt	Ex-Mt
CO1 Nomar Garciaparra / Derek Jeter	500.00	150.00
CO2 Roberto Alomar / Edgardo Alfonzo	50.00	15.00
CO3 Rick Ankiel / Kevin Millwood	25.00	7.50
CO4 Chipper Jones / Troy Glaus	80.00	24.00
CO5 Magglio Ordonez / Bob Abreu	40.00	12.00
CO6 Adam Piatt / Sean Burroughs	40.00	12.00
CO7 Corey Patterson / Nick Johnson	40.00	12.00
CO8 Adrian Gonzalez / Rocco Baldelli	40.00	12.00
CO9 Adam Johnson / Mike Stodolka	25.00	7.50

2001 Stadium Club Diamond Pearls

Randomly inserted into packs at one in eight HOB/RET packs, and one in 3 HTA packs; this 20-card insert features players that are the most sought after treasures in the game today. Card backs carry a "DP" prefix.

	Nm-Mt	Ex-Mt
COMPLETE SET (20)	50.00	15.00
DP1 Ken Griffey Jr.	3.00	.90
DP2 Alex Rodriguez	3.00	.90
DP3 Derek Jeter	5.00	1.50
DP4 Chipper Jones	2.00	.60
DP5 Nomar Garciaparra	3.00	.90
DP6 Vladimir Guerrero	2.00	.60
DP7 Jeff Bagwell	1.50	.45
DP8 Cal Ripken	6.00	1.80
DP9 Sammy Sosa	3.00	.90
DP10 Mark McGwire	5.00	1.50
DP11 Frank Thomas	2.00	.60
DP12 Pedro Martinez	2.00	.60
DP13 Manny Ramirez	1.50	.45
DP14 Randy Johnson	2.00	.60
DP15 Barry Bonds	5.00	1.50
DP16 Ivan Rodriguez	2.00	.60
DP17 Greg Maddux	3.00	.90
DP18 Mike Piazza	3.00	.90
DP19 Todd Helton	1.50	.45
DP20 Shawn Green	1.50	.45

2001 Stadium Club King of the Hill Dirt Relic

Randomly inserted into packs at one in 20 HTA, this five-card insert features game-used dirt cards from the pitchers mound of today's top pitchers. The Topps Company announced that the ten exchange subjects from Stadium Club Play at the Plate, King of the Hill, and Souvenirs contain the wrong card back stating that they were autographed. None of these cards are actually autographed. Also note that these cards were inserted into packs with a white "waxpaper" covering to protect the cards. Card backs carry a "KH" prefix. Please note that Greg Maddux and Rick Ankiel both packed out as exchange cards and must be returned to Topps by 11/30/01.

	Nm-Mt	Ex-Mt
KH1 Pedro Martinez	10.00	3.00
KH2 Randy Johnson	10.00	3.00
KH3 G.Maddux ERR	10.00	3.00
KH4 R.Ankiel ERR	8.00	2.40
KH5 Kevin Brown	8.00	2.40

2001 Stadium Club Lone Star Signatures

Randomly inserted into packs, this 18-card inserrt features authentic autographs from some of the Major Leagues most prolific players. Please note that this insert was broken into four tiers as follows: Group A (1:937 HOB/RET, 1:364 HTA), Group B (1:1010 HOB/RET, 1:392 HTA), Group C (1:1541 HOB/RET, 1:600 HTA), and Group D (1:354 HOB/RET, 1:138 HTA). The overall odds for pulling an autograph was one in 181 HOB/RET and one in 70 HTA.

	Nm-Mt	Ex-Mt
LS1 Nomar Garciaparra A	120.00	36.00
LS2 Derek Jeter A	150.00	45.00
LS3 Edgardo Alfonzo A	40.00	12.00
LS4 Roberto Alomar A	60.00	18.00
LS5 Magglio Ordonez A	25.00	7.50
LS6 Bobby Abreu A	40.00	12.00
LS7 Chipper Jones A	50.00	15.00
LS8 Troy Glaus A	40.00	12.00
LS9 Nick Johnson B	15.00	4.50
LS10 Adam Piatt B	15.00	4.50
LS11 Sean Burroughs B	15.00	4.50
LS12 Corey Patterson B	15.00	4.50
LS13 Rick Ankiel C	10.00	3.00
LS14 Kevin Millwood C	15.00	4.50
LS15 Adrian Gonzalez D	15.00	4.50
LS16 Adam Johnson D	10.00	3.00
LS17 Rocco Baldelli D	25.00	7.50
LS18 Mike Stodolka D	10.00	3.00

2001 Stadium Club Play at the Plate Dirt Relic

Randomly inserted into packs at one in 10 HTA, this nine-card insert features game-used dirt from the batter's box in which these top players played in. The Topps Company announced that the ten exchange subjects from Stadium Club Play at the Plate, King of the Hill, and Souvenirs contain the wrong card back stating that they were autographed. None of these cards are actually autographed. Please note that both Chipper Jones and Jeff Bagwell are number PP6. Also note that these cards were inserted into packs with a white "waxpaper" covering to protect the cards. The exchange deadline for these cards was 11/30/01.

	Nm-Mt	Ex-Mt
PP1 Mark McGwire ERR	40.00	12.00
PP2 S.Sosa ERR	15.00	4.50
PP3 Vladimir Guerrero	10.00	3.00
PP4 Ken Griffey Jr. ERR	15.00	4.50
PP5 Mike Piazza	10.00	3.00
PP6 J.Bagwell ERR	10.00	3.00
PP6 C.Jones ERR	10.00	3.00
PP7 Barry Bonds	25.00	7.50
PP8 Alex Rodriguez	15.00	4.50
PP10 Nomar Garciaparra ERR	15.00	4.50

2001 Stadium Club Prospect Performance

Randomly inserted into packs at one in 262 HOB/RET and one in 102 HTA, this 20-card insert features game-used jersey cards from some of the hottest young players in the Major Leagues. Card backs carry a "PRP" prefix.

	Nm-Mt	Ex-Mt
PRP1 Chin-Feng Chen	80.00	24.00
PRP2 Bobby Bradley	8.00	2.40
PRP3 Tomokazu Ohka	10.00	3.00
PRP4 Kurt Ainsworth	8.00	2.40
PRP5 Craig Anderson	8.00	2.40
PRP6 Josh Hamilton	8.00	2.40
PRP7 Felipe Lopez	8.00	2.40
PRP8 Ryan Anderson	8.00	2.40
PRP9 Alex Escobar	8.00	2.40
PRP10 Ben Sheets	15.00	4.50
PRP11 Ntema Ndungidi	8.00	2.40
PRP12 Eric Munson	8.00	2.40
PRP13 Aaron Myette	8.00	2.40
PRP14 Jack Cust	8.00	2.40
PRP15 Julio Zuleta	8.00	2.40
PRP16 Corey Patterson	10.00	3.00
PRP17 Carlos Pena	8.00	2.40
PRP18 Marcus Giles	10.00	3.00
PRP19 Travis Wilson	8.00	2.40
PRP20 Barry Zito	15.00	4.50

2001 Stadium Club Souvenirs

Randomly inserted into HTA packs, this eight-card insert features game-used bat cards and game-used jersey cards of modern superstars. Card backs carry a "SCS" prefix. Please note that the Topps Company announced that the ten exchange subjects from Stadium Club Play at the Plate, King of the Hill, and Souvenirs contain the wrong card back stating that they were auto

graphed. None of these cards are actually autographed. Also note that cards of Scott Rolen, Matt Lawton, Jose Vidro, and Pat Burrell all packed out as exchange cards. These cards needed to have been returned to Topps by 11/30/01.

Nm-Mt Ex-Mt
SCS1 Scott Rolen 25.00 7.50
Bat A ERR
SCS2 Larry Walker Bat B 15.00 4.50
SCS3 Rafael Furcal Bat A 15.00 4.50
SCS4 Darin Erstad Bat A........... 15.00 4.50
SCS5 Mike Sweeney Jsy........... 10.00 3.00
SCS6 Matt Lawton 10.00 3.00
Jsy ERR
SCS7 Jose Vidro 10.00 3.00
Jsy ERR
SCS8 Pat Burrell 10.00 3.00
Jsy ERR

2002 Stadium Club

This 125 card set was issued in late 2001. The set was issued in either six card regular packs or 15 card HTA packs. Cards numbered 101-125 were short printed and are serial numbered to 2999.

Nm-Mt Ex-Mt
COMP.SET w/o SP's (100)......... 25.00 7.50
COMMON CARD (1-100) .... .30 .09
COMMON (101-125)................ 20.00 6.00
1 Pedro Martinez......................... .75 .23
2 Derek Jeter........................... 2.00 .60
3 Chipper Jones........................... .75 .23
4 Roberto Alomar .... .50 .15
5 Albert Pujols .... 1.50 .45
6 Bret Boone................................ .30 .09
7 Alex Rodriguez........................ 1.25 .35
8 Jose Cruz Jr. .... .30 .09
9 Mike Hampton .... .30 .09
10 Vladimir Guerrero .... .75 .23
11 Jim Edmonds............................ .30 .09
12 Luis Gonzalez........................... .30 .09
13 Jeff Kent.................................. .30 .09
14 Mike Piazza .... 1.25 .35
15 Ben Sheets............................... .30 .09
16 Tsuyoshi Shinjo........................ .30 .09
17 Pat Burrell UER .... .30 .09
Card has a photo of Scott Rolen
18 Jermaine Dye .... .30 .09
19 Rafael Furcal .... .30 .09
20 Randy Johnson......................... .75 .23
21 Carlos Delgado......................... .30 .09
22 Roger Clemens .... 1.50 .45
23 Eric Chavez .... .30 .09
24 Nomar Garciaparra................ 1.25 .35
25 Ivan Rodriguez.......................... .75 .23
26 Juan Gonzalez .... .50 .15
27 Reggie Sanders......................... .30 .09
28 Jeff Bagwell .... .50 .15
29 Kazuhiro Sasaki .... .30 .09
30 Larry Walker .... .50 .15
31 Ben Grieve .... .30 .09
32 David Justice .... .30 .09
33 David Wells............................... .30 .09
34 Kevin Brown.............................. .30 .09
35 Miguel Tejada .... .30 .09
36 Jorge Posada .... .50 .15
37 Javy Lopez .... .30 .09
38 Cliff Floyd.................................. .30 .09
39 Carlos Lee................................. .30 .09
40 Manny Ramirez......................... .30 .09
41 Jim Thome .... .75 .23
42 Pokey Reese .... .30 .09
43 Scott Rolen .... .75 .23
44 Richie Sexson .... .30 .09
45 Dean Palmer .... .30 .09
46 Rafael Palmeiro......................... .50 .15
47 Alfonso Soriano .... .50 .15
48 Craig Biggio .... .50 .15
49 Troy Glaus................................. .30 .09
50 Andruw Jones .... .30 .09
51 Ichiro Suzuki......................... 1.25 .35
52 Kenny Lofton .... .30 .09
53 Hideo Nomo.............................. .75 .23
54 Magglio Ordonez....................... .30 .09
55 Brad Penny .... .30 .09
56 Omar Vizquel .... .50 .15
57 Mike Sweeney........................... .30 .09
58 Gary Sheffield .... .30 .09
59 Ken Griffey Jr. .... 1.25 .35
60 Curt Schilling .... .30 .09
61 Bobby Higginson .... .30 .09
62 Terrence Long........................... .30 .09
63 Moises Alou .... .30 .09
64 Sandy Alomar Jr. .... .30 .09
65 Cristian Guzman........................ .30 .09
66 Sammy Sosa......................... 1.25 .35
67 Jose Vidro................................. .30 .09
68 Edgar Martinez.......................... .50 .15
69 Jason Giambi .... .30 .09
70 Mark McGwire .... 2.00 .60
71 Barry Bonds.......................... 2.00 .60
72 Greg Vaughn .... .30 .09
73 Phil Nevin.................................. .30 .09
74 Jason Kendall............................ .30 .09
75 Greg Maddux .... 1.25 .35
76 Jeromy Burnitz.......................... .30 .09
77 Mike Mussina............................ .50 .15
78 Johnny Damon.......................... .50 .15
79 Shawn Green .... .30 .09
80 Jimmy Rollins............................ .30 .09
81 Edgardo Alfonzo........................ .30 .09
82 Barry Larkin .... .50 .15
83 Raul Mondesi .... .30 .09
84 Preston Wilson .... .30 .09
85 Mike Lieberthal .... .30 .09
86 J.D. Drew .... .30 .09
87 Ryan Klesko.............................. .30 .09
88 David Segui............................... .30 .09
89 Derek Bell.................................. .30 .09
90 Bernie Williams......................... .50 .15
91 Doug Mientkiewicz.................... .30 .09
92 Rich Aurilia .... .30 .09
93 Ellis Burks................................. .30 .09
94 Placido Polanco .... .30 .09
95 Darin Erstad .... .30 .09
96 Brian Giles .... .30 .09
97 Geoff Jenkins............................ .30 .09
98 Kerry Wood............................... .75 .23
99 Mariano Rivera.......................... .50 .15
100 Todd Helton .... .50 .15
101 Adam Dunn FS 20.00 6.00
102 Grant Balfour FS 20.00 6.00
103 Jae Seo FS 20.00 6.00
104 Hank Blalock FS 25.00 7.50
105 Chris George FS.................. 20.00 6.00
106 Jack Cust FS 20.00 6.00
107 Juan Cruz FS....................... 20.00 6.00
108 Adrian Gonzalez FS 20.00 6.00
109 Nick Johnson FS 20.00 6.00
110 Jeff DaVanon FS 20.00 6.00
111 Juan Diaz FS 20.00 6.00
112 B. Duckworth FS 20.00 6.00
113 Jason Lane FS 20.00 6.00
114 Seung Song FS 20.00 6.00
115 Morgan Ensberg FS 20.00 6.00
116 Marlyn Tisdale FY RC 20.00 6.00
117 Jason Botts FY RC 25.00 7.50
118 Henry Pichardo FY RC 20.00 6.00
119 J. Rodriguez FY RC 20.00 6.00
120 Mike Peeples FY RC 20.00 6.00
121 Rob Bowen EFY RC 20.00 6.00
122 Jeremy Affeldt EFY.............. 20.00 6.00
123 Jorge Buret EFY RC 20.00 6.00
124 Manny Ravelo EFY RC 20.00 6.00
125 Eudy Lajara EFY RC 20.00 6.00
NNO B.Bonds AU Ball 300.00 90.00

2002 Stadium Club All-Star Relics

Randomly inserted in packs, these 28 cards feature relics of players who participated in the All-Star game. Depending on which group the player belonged to there could be between 400 and 4800 of each card printed.

Nm-Mt Ex-Mt
GROUP 1 ODDS 1:477 H, 1:548 R, 1:80 HTA
GROUP 1 PRINT RUN 400 SERIAL #'d SETS
GROUP 2 ODDS 1:795 H, 1:915 R, 1:133 HTA
GROUP 2 PRINT RUN 800 SERIAL #'d SETS
GROUP 3 ODDS 1:199 H, 1:247 R, 1:33 HTA
GROUP 3 PRINT RUN 1200 SERIAL #'d SETS
GROUP 4 ODDS 1:199 H, 1:247 R, 1:33 HTA
GROUP 4 PRINT RUN 2400 SERIAL #'d SETS
GROUP 5 ODDS 1:265 H, 1:305 R, 1:44 HTA
GROUP 5 PRINT RUN 3600 SERIAL #'d SETS
GROUP 6 ODDS 1:397 H, 1:457 R, 1:67 HTA
GROUP 6 PRINT RUN 4800 SERIAL #'d SETS
SCAS-AP Albert Pujols............. 40.00 12.00
Bat/800 G2
SCAS-BB Barry Bonds 30.00 9.00
Uni/4800 G6
SCAS-BG Brian Giles.............. 10.00 3.00
Bat/800 G2
SCAS-CF Cliff Floyd................ 10.00 3.00
Bat/400 G1
SCAS-CG C.Guzman............... 10.00 3.00
Bat/400 G1
SCAS-CJ Chipper Jones.......... 15.00 4.50
Jsy/1200 G3
SCAS-EM Edgar Martinez 15.00 4.50
Jsy/1200 G3
SCAS-IR Ivan Rodriguez 15.00 4.50
Uni/2400 G4
SCAS-JG Juan Gonzalez 15.00 4.50
Bat/400 G1
SCAS-JK Jeff Kent 10.00 3.00
Bat/400 G1
SCAS-JO John Olerud 10.00 3.00
Jsy/1200 G3
SCAS-JP Jorge Posada........... 15.00 4.50
Bat/400 G1
SCAS-KS Kaz Sasaki 10.00 3.00
Jsy/1200 G3
SCAS-LW Larry Walker 15.00 4.50
Jsy/2400 G4
SCAS-MA Moises Alou 10.00 3.00
Bat/400 G1
SCAS-MC Mike Cameron 10.00 3.00
Bat/400 G1
SCAS-MO M. Ordonez 10.00 3.00
Bat/400 G1
SCAS-MP Mike Piazza............. 40.00 12.00
Uni/1200 G3
SCAS-MR Manny Ramirez 15.00 4.50
Uni/3600 G5
SCAS-MS Mike Sweeney 10.00 3.00
Bat/400 G1
SCAS-RA Roberto Alomar....... 15.00 4.50
Uni/3600 G5
SCAS-RJ Randy Johnson 15.00 4.50
Jsy/2400 G4
SCAS-RK Ryan Klesko............ 10.00 3.00
Jsy/1200 G3
SCAS-SC Sean Casey............. 10.00 3.00
Bat/400 G1
SCAS-TG Tony Gwynn 20.00 6.00
Jsy/2400 G4
SCAS-TH Todd Helton............. 15.00 4.50
Jsy/1200 G3
SCAS-BRB Bret Boone............ 10.00 3.00
Bat/1200 G3
SCAS-LG3 Luis Gonzalez........ 10.00 3.00
Bat/800 G2

2002 Stadium Club Chasing 500-500

Randomly inserted in packs, these three cards feature memorabilia from Barry Bonds as he chases becoming the first member of the 500 homer, 500 stolen base club.

Nm-Mt Ex-Mt
C55-BB1 Barry Bonds.............. 50.00 15.00
Dual
C55-BB2 Barry Bonds.............. 40.00 12.00
Jsy/600
C55-BB3 Barry Bonds............ 100.00 30.00
Multiple/200

2002 Stadium Club Passport to the Majors

Randomly inserted in packs, these cards feature foreign players as well as a game-used relic. The jersey relics are serial numbered to 1200 while the bats are printed to differing amounts. The specific print information is notated in our checklist.

Nm-Mt Ex-Mt
PTM-AG Andres Galarraga........ 10.00 3.00
Jsy
PTM-AJ Andruw Jones 10.00 3.00
Jsy
PTM-AP Albert Pujols 50.00 15.00
Bat/450
PTM-AS Alfonso Soriano 15.00 4.50
Bat/400
PTM-BA Bob Abreu.................. 10.00 3.00
Bat/450
PTM-BC Bartolo Colon Uni 10.00 3.00
PTM-CL Carlos Lee Jsy............ 10.00 3.00
PTM-CP Chan Ho Park Jsy 10.00 3.00
PTM-EA Edgardo Alfonzo......... 10.00 3.00
Jsy
PTM-IR Ivan Rodriguez............ 15.00 4.50
Uni
PTM-JG Juan Gonzalez............ 15.00 4.50
Jsy
PTM-JL Javier Lopez Jsy.......... 10.00 3.00
PTM-KS Kazuhiro Sasaki 10.00 3.00
Jsy
PTM-LW Larry Walker Jsy 15.00 4.50
PTM-MO Magglio Ordonez 10.00 3.00
Jsy
PTM-MR Manny Ramirez.......... 15.00 4.50
Jsy
PTM-MT Miguel Tejada 10.00 3.00
Bat/375
PTM-PM Pedro Martinez........... 15.00 4.50
Jsy
PTM-RA Roberto Alomar.......... 15.00 4.50
Uni
PTM-RF Rafael Furcal Jsy......... 10.00 3.00
PTM-RM Raul Mondesi............. 10.00 3.00
Jsy
PTM-RP Rafael Palmeiro 15.00 4.50
Jsy
PTM-SH Sh. Hasegawa 10.00 3.00
Jsy
PTM-TS Tsuyoshi Shinjo........... 10.00 3.00
Bat/400
PTM-WB Wilson Betemit 10.00 3.00
Bat/325

2002 Stadium Club Reel Time

Inserted at a rate of one in eight hobby/retail packs and one in four HTA packs this 20 card set features players who constantly make the highlight reel.

Nm-Mt Ex-Mt
COMPLETE SET (20)................ 60.00 18.00
RT1 Luis Gonzalez .... 2.00 .60
RT2 Derek Jeter.......................... 6.00 1.80
RT3 Ken Griffey Jr. 4.00 1.20
RT4 Alex Rodriguez 4.00 1.20
RT5 Barry Bonds......................... 6.00 1.80
RT6 Ichiro Suzuki 4.00 1.20
RT7 Carlos Delgado .... 2.00 .60
RT8 Manny Ramirez.................... 2.00 .60
RT9 Mike Piazza......................... 4.00 1.20
RT10 Mark McGwire................... 6.00 1.80
RT11 Todd Helton .... 2.00 .60
RT12 Vladimir Guerrero.............. 2.50 .75
RT13 Jim Thome......................... 2.50 .75
RT14 Rich Aurilia .... 2.00 .60
RT15 Bret Boone......................... 2.00 .60
RT16 Roberto Alomar.................. 2.00 .60
RT17 Jason Giambi..................... 2.00 .60
RT18 Chipper Jones.................... 2.50 .75
RT19 Albert Pujols 5.00 1.50
RT20 Sammy Sosa 4.00 1.20

2002 Stadium Club Stadium Shots

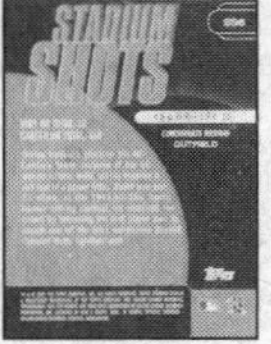

Inserted at a rate of one in 12 hobby/retail packs and one in six HTA packs, these 10 cards feature 10 sluggers known for their long homers.

Nm-Mt Ex-Mt
COMPLETE SET (10)................ 25.00 7.50
SS1 Sammy Sosa 4.00 1.20
SS2 Manny Ramirez .... 2.50 .75
SS3 Jason Giambi...................... 2.50 .75
SS4 Mike Piazza........................ 4.00 1.20
SS5 Barry Bonds........................ 6.00 1.80
SS6 Ken Griffey Jr. 4.00 1.20
SS7 Juan Gonzalez .... 2.50 .75
SS8 Jeff Bagwell .... 2.50 .75
SS9 Jim Thome .... 2.50 .75
SS10 Mark McGwire................... 6.00 1.80

2002 Stadium Club Stadium Slices Barrel Relics

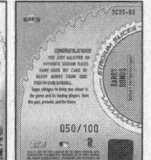

These five cards were inserted in packs and feature bat slices cut from the barrel of the bat. Each card is printed to a different amount and that information is notated in our checklist.

Nm-Mt Ex-Mt
GROUP A ODDS 1:4289 HOBBY, 1:1700 HTA
GROUP B ODDS 1:6768 HOBBY, 1:2680 HTA
GROUP C ODDS 1:6465 HOBBY, 1:2581 HTA
GROUP D ODDS 1:6101 HOBBY, 1:2489 HTA
SCSS-AP A.Pujols/95 B 100.00 30.00
SCSS-BB B.Bonds/100 C 100.00 30.00
SCSS-BW Bernie Williams 30.00 9.00
100 A
SCSS-IR Ivan Rodriguez 50.00 15.00
105 D
SCSS-LG Luis Gonzalez 30.00 9.00
75 A

2002 Stadium Club Stadium Slices Handle Relics

These five cards were inserted in packs and feature bat slices cut from the handle of the bat. Each card is printed to a different amount and that information is notated in our checklist.

Nm-Mt Ex-Mt
GROUP A ODDS 1:3671 HOBBY, 1:1483 HTA
GROUP B ODDS 1:3580 HOBBY, 1:1422 HTA
GROUP C ODDS 1:3384 HOBBY, 1:1366 HTA
GROUP D ODDS 1:3209 HOBBY, 1:1290 HTA
GROUP E ODDS 1:3050 HOBBY, 1:1222 HTA
SCSS-AP A.Pujols/190 C 60.00 18.00
SCSS-BB B.Bonds/175 A 60.00 18.00
SCSS-BW B.Williams/210 E 20.00 6.00
SCSS-IR I.Rodriguez/180 B 30.00 9.00
SCSS-LG L.Gonzalez/200 D 20.00 6.00

2002 Stadium Club Stadium Slices Trademark Relics

These five cards were inserted in packs and feature bat slices cut from the middle of the bat. Each card is printed to a different amount and that information is notated in our checklist.

Nm-Mt Ex-Mt
SCSS-AP A.Pujols/130 C 80.00 24.00

SCSS-BB B.Bonds/105 A 80.00 24.00
SCSS-BW Bernie Williams 25.00 7.50
110 B
SCSS-IR Ivan Rodriguez........... 25.00 7.50
170 E
SCSS-LG Luis Gonzalez............ 25.00 7.50
140 D

2002 Stadium Club World Champion Relics

Inserted at different odds depending on what type of relic, these 69 cards feature game-used relics from World Series ring holders. The Rickey Henderson card was short printed and we have notated this information in our checklist.

Nm-Mt Ex-Mt
BAT ODDS 1:94 H, 1:108 R, 1:16 HTA
JERSEY ODDS 1:106 H, 1:122 R, 1:18 HTA
PANTS ODDS 1:795 H, 1:1022 R, 1:133 HTA
SPIKES 1:38,400 H, 1:51,696 R, 1:6335 HTA
WC-AB Al Bumbry Bat 10.00 3.00
WC-AL Al Leiter Jsy 15.00 4.50
WC-AT Alan Trammell Bat 15.00 4.50
WC-BB Bert Blyleven Jsy 15.00 4.50
WC-BD Bucky Dent Bat.............. 15.00 4.50
WC-BM Bill Madlock Bat............ 15.00 4.50
WC-BW B.Williams Bat 20.00 6.00
WC-BRB Bob Boone Jsy 15.00 4.50
WC-CC C.Chambliss Bat 15.00 4.50
WC-CJ Chipper Jones Bat.......... 25.00 7.50
WC-CK C.Knoblauch Bat 15.00 4.50
WC-DB Don Baylor Bat 15.00 4.50
WC-DC D.Concepcion Bat.......... 15.00 4.50
WC-DJ David Justice Bat........... 15.00 4.50
WC-DL Dave Lopes Bat............. 15.00 4.50
WC-DP Dave Parker Bat............. 15.00 4.50
WC-DW Dave Winfield Bat......... 15.00 4.50
WC-ED Eric Davis Bat 15.00 4.50
WC-ES Ed Sprague Jsy.............. 10.00 3.00
WC-EM1 Eddie Murray Bat 25.00 7.50
WC-EM2 Ed. Murray Jsy............ 25.00 7.50
WC-FM Fred McGriff Bat........... 20.00 6.00
WC-FV F. Valenzuela Bat 15.00 4.50
WC-GB George Brett Bat........... 60.00 18.00
WC-GF George Foster Bat......... 15.00 4.50
WC-GH G. Hendrick Bat 15.00 4.50
WC-GL Greg Luzinski Bat 15.00 4.50
WC-GM Greg Maddux Jsy 40.00 12.00
WC-GC1 Gary Carter Bat........... 15.00 4.50
WC-GC2 Gary Carter Jsy 15.00 4.50
WC-HM Hal McRae Bat............. 15.00 4.50
WC-JB Johnny Bench Bat.......... 25.00 7.50
WC-JC Joe Carter Jsy 15.00 4.50
WC-JL Javy Lopez Bat 15.00 4.50
WC-JO John Olerud Jsy............ 15.00 4.50
WC-JP Jorge Posada Bat........... 20.00 6.00
WC-JS John Smoltz Jsy 20.00 6.00
WC-JV Jose Vizcaino Bat.......... 10.00 3.00
WC-JC1 Jose Canseco.............. 25.00 7.50
Yankees Bat
WC-JC2 Jose Canseco.............. 25.00 7.50
A's Bat
WC-KG Ken Griffey Sr. Bat........ 20.00 6.00
WC-KH K. Hernandez Bat.......... 15.00 4.50
WC-KP Kirby Puckett Bat.......... 25.00 7.50
WC-KG1 Kirk Gibson Bat 20.00 6.00
WC-KG2 Kirk Gibson Jsy 20.00 6.00
WC-LW Lou Whitaker Bat 15.00 4.50
WC-LVP Lou Piniella Bat........... 15.00 4.50
WC-MA Moises Alou Bat........... 15.00 4.50
WC-MS Mike Scioscia Bat 15.00 4.50
WC-MW M. Wilson Bat............. 15.00 4.50
WC-MJS M. Schmidt Bat 60.00 18.00
WC-OH Orel Hershiser Jsy........ 15.00 4.50
WC-OS Ozzie Smith Bat 40.00 12.00
WC-PG Phil Garner Bat............. 10.00 3.00
WC-PM Paul Molitor Bat........... 20.00 6.00
WC-PO Paul O'Neill Pants......... 20.00 6.00
WC-RA R. Alomar Pants 20.00 6.00
WC-RC Ron Cey Bat 15.00 4.50
WC-RH R.Henderson Spikes SP/50 ....
WC-RJ R. Jackson Bat............... 20.00 6.00
WC-SB Scott Brosius Bat.......... 15.00 4.50
WC-TG Tom Glavine Jsy 20.00 6.00
WC-TM T. Munson Bat.............. 60.00 18.00
WC-TP Tony Perez Bat 15.00 4.50
WC-TLM T. Martinez Bat 20.00 6.00
WC-WB Wade Boggs Bat........... 20.00 6.00
WC-WH W. Hernandez Jsy........ 15.00 4.50
WC-WR W. Randolph Bat 15.00 4.50
WC-WS Willie Stargell Bat......... 20.00 6.00

2003 Stadium Club

This 125 card set was released in November, 2002. This set marked the conclusion of the 13 year run of Stadium Club product being released as a baseball brand by Topps. This set was issued in either 10 card packs or 20 card HTA packs. The 10-card packs were issued 10 cards to a pack with 24 packs to a box and 12 boxes to a case with an SRP of $3 per pack. The 20-card HTA packs were issued 10 packs to a box and eight boxes to a case with an SRP of $10 per

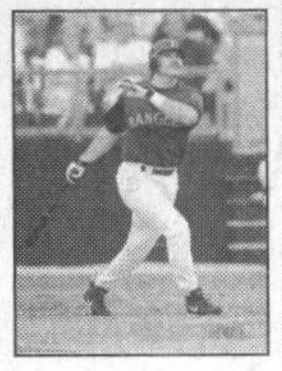
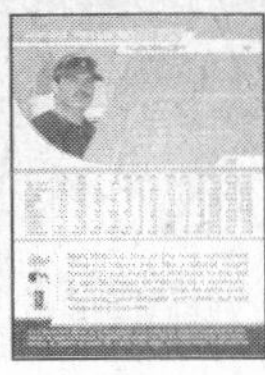

pack. Cards numbered from 101 through 113 featured future stars while cards numbered 114 through 125 feature players in their first year on a Stadium Club card. Cards numbered 101 through 125 were issued with different photos depending on whether or not they came from hobby or retail packs. These cards have two different varieties in all the parallel sets as well. Sets are considered complete at 125 cards - with one copy of either the hobby or retail versions of cards 101-125.

	Nm-Mt	Ex-Mt
COMP.MASTER SET (150)	60.00	18.00
COMPLETE SET (125)	40.00	12.00
COMMON CARD (1-100)	.30	.09
COMMON CARD (101-115)	.50	.15
COMMON CARD (116-125)	1.00	.30
1 Rafael Furcal	.30	.09
2 Randy Winn	.30	.09
3 Eric Chavez	.30	.09
4 Fernando Vina	.30	.09
5 Pat Burrell	.30	.09
6 Derek Jeter	2.00	.60
7 Ivan Rodriguez	.75	.23
8 Eric Hinske	.30	.09
9 Roberto Alomar	.50	.15
10 Tony Batista	.30	.09
11 Jacque Jones	.30	.09
12 Alfonso Soriano	.50	.15
13 Omar Vizquel	.50	.15
14 Paul Konerko	.30	.09
15 Shawn Green	.30	.09
16 Garret Anderson	.30	.09
17 Darin Erstad	.30	.09
18 Johnny Damon	.75	.23
19 Juan Gonzalez	.50	.15
20 Luis Gonzalez	.30	.09
21 Sean Burroughs	.30	.09
22 Mark Prior	.75	.23
23 Javier Vazquez	.30	.09
24 Shannon Stewart	.30	.09
25 Jay Gibbons	.30	.09
26 A.J. Pierzynski	.30	.09
27 Vladimir Guerrero	.75	.23
28 Austin Kearns	.30	.09
29 Shea Hillenbrand	.30	.09
30 Magglio Ordonez	.30	.09
31 Mike Cameron	.30	.09
32 Tim Salmon	.50	.15
33 Brian Jordan	.30	.09
34 Moises Alou	.30	.09
35 Rich Aurilia	.30	.09
36 Nick Johnson	.30	.09
37 Junior Spivey	.30	.09
38 Curt Schilling	.30	.09
39 Jose Vidro	.30	.09
40 Orlando Cabrera	.30	.09
41 Jeff Bagwell	.50	.15
42 Mo Vaughn	.30	.09
43 Luis Castillo	.30	.09
44 Vicente Padilla	.30	.09
45 Pedro Martinez	.75	.23
46 John Olerud	.30	.09
47 Tom Glavine	.50	.15
48 Torii Hunter	.30	.09
49 J.D. Drew	.30	.09
50 Alex Rodriguez	1.25	.35
51 Randy Johnson	.75	.23
52 Richie Sexson	.30	.09
53 Jimmy Rollins	.30	.09
54 Cristian Guzman	.30	.09
55 Tim Hudson	.30	.09
56 Mark Buehrle	.30	.09
57 Paul Lo Duca	.30	.09
58 Aramis Ramirez	.30	.09
59 Todd Helton	.50	.15
60 Lance Berkman	.30	.09
61 Josh Beckett	.30	.09
62 Bret Boone	.30	.09
63 Miguel Tejada	.30	.09
64 Nomar Garciaparra	1.25	.35
65 Albert Pujols	1.50	.45
66 Chipper Jones	.75	.23
67 Scott Rolen	.75	.23
68 Kerry Wood	.75	.23
69 Jorge Posada	.50	.15
70 Ichiro Suzuki	1.25	.35
71 Jeff Kent	.30	.09
72 David Eckstein	.30	.09
73 Phil Nevin	.30	.09
74 Brian Giles	.30	.09
75 Barry Zito	.30	.09
76 Andruw Jones	.30	.09
77 Jim Thome	.75	.23
78 Robert Fick	.30	.09
79 Rafael Palmeiro	.50	.15
80 Barry Bonds	2.00	.60
81 Gary Sheffield	.30	.09
82 Jim Edmonds	.30	.09
83 Kazuhisa Ishii	.30	.09
84 Jose Hernandez	.30	.09
85 Jason Giambi	.30	.09
86 Mark Mulder	.30	.09
87 Roger Clemens	1.50	.45
88 Troy Glaus	.30	.09
89 Carlos Delgado	.30	.09
90 Mike Sweeney	.30	.09
91 Ken Griffey Jr.	1.25	.35
92 Manny Ramirez	.50	.15
93 Ryan Klesko	.30	.09
94 Larry Walker	.50	.15
95 Adam Dunn	.50	.15
96 Raul Ibanez	.30	.09
97 Preston Wilson	.30	.09
98 Roy Oswalt	.30	.09
99 Sammy Sosa	1.25	.35
100 Mike Piazza	1.25	.35

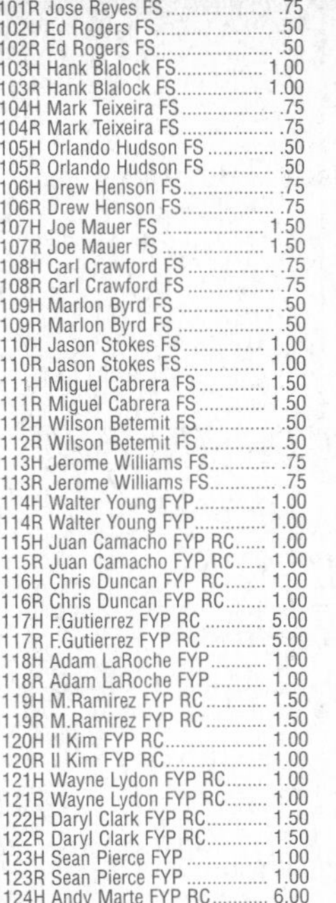

101H Jose Reyes FS	.75	.23
101R Jose Reyes FS	.75	.23
102H Ed Rogers FS	.50	.15
102R Ed Rogers FS	.50	.15
103H Hank Blalock FS	1.00	.30
103R Hank Blalock FS	1.00	.30
104H Mark Teixeira FS	.75	.23
104R Mark Teixeira FS	.75	.23
105H Orlando Hudson FS	.50	.15
105R Orlando Hudson FS	.50	.15
106H Drew Henson FS	.75	.23
106R Drew Henson FS	.75	.23
107H Joe Mauer FS	1.50	.45
107R Joe Mauer FS	1.50	.45
108H Carl Crawford FS	.75	.23
108R Carl Crawford FS	.75	.23
109H Marlon Byrd FS	.50	.15
109R Marlon Byrd FS	.50	.15
110H Jason Stokes FS	1.00	.30
110R Jason Stokes FS	1.00	.30
111H Miguel Cabrera FS	1.50	.45
111R Miguel Cabrera FS	1.50	.45
112H Wilson Betemit FS	.50	.15
112R Wilson Betemit FS	.50	.15
113H Jerome Williams FS	.75	.23
113R Jerome Williams FS	.75	.23
114H Walter Young FYP	1.00	.30
114R Walter Young FYP	1.00	.30
115H Juan Camacho FYP RC	1.00	.30
115R Juan Camacho FYP RC	1.00	.30
116H Chris Duncan FYP RC	1.00	.30
116R Chris Duncan FYP RC	1.00	.30
117H F.Gutierrez FYP RC	5.00	1.50
117R F.Gutierrez FYP RC	5.00	1.50
118H Adam LaRoche FYP	1.00	.30
118R Adam LaRoche FYP	1.00	.30
119H M.Ramirez FYP RC	1.50	.45
119R M.Ramirez FYP RC	1.50	.45
120H Il Kim FYP RC	1.00	.30
120R Il Kim FYP RC	1.00	.30
121H Wayne Lydon FYP RC	1.00	.30
121R Wayne Lydon FYP RC	1.00	.30
122H Daryl Clark FYP RC	1.50	.45
122R Daryl Clark FYP RC	1.50	.45
123H Sean Pierce FYP	1.00	.30
123R Sean Pierce FYP	1.00	.30
124H Andy Marte FYP RC	6.00	1.80
124R Andy Marte FYP RC	6.00	1.80
125H Mat.Peterson FYP RC	1.00	.30
125R Mat.Peterson FYP RC	1.00	.30

2003 Stadium Club Photographer's Proof

Randomly inserted into packs:, this is a parallel to the Stadium Club set. These cards were issued to a stated print run of 299 serial numbered sets.

Nm-Mt Ex-Mt
*PROOF 1-100: 4X TO 10X BASIC......
*PROOF 101-115: 2X TO 5X BASIC......
*PROOF 116-125: 1.5X TO 4X BASIC.
1-100 ODDS 1:39 H, 1:23 HTA, 1:34 R
101-125 ODDS 1:61 H, 1:17 HTA, 1:92 R

2003 Stadium Club Royal Gold

Inserted one per pack, this is a parallel to the Stadium Club set. These cards can be differentiated by their thickness compared to the regular cards. Photo variations were created for cards 101-125 whereby hobby and retail packs each had exclusive distribution on one image per player.

Nm-Mt Ex-Mt
*GOLD 1-100: 1X TO 2.5X BASIC......
*GOLD 101-115: 1X TO 2.5X BASIC......
*GOLD 116-125: .75X TO 2X BASIC......

2003 Stadium Club Beam Team

Inserted into packs at a stated rate of one in 12 hobby, one in 12 retail and one in two HTA, these 20 cards feature some of the hottest talents in baseball.

	Nm-Mt	Ex-Mt
BT1 Lance Berkman	2.00	.60
BT2 Barry Bonds	8.00	2.40
BT3 Carlos Delgado	2.00	.60
BT4 Adam Dunn	3.00	.90
BT5 Nomar Garciaparra	5.00	1.50
BT6 Jason Giambi	2.00	.60
BT7 Brian Giles	2.00	.60
BT8 Shawn Green	2.00	.60
BT9 Vladimir Guerrero	3.00	.90
BT10 Todd Helton	3.00	.90
BT11 Derek Jeter	8.00	2.40
BT12 Chipper Jones	3.00	.90
BT13 Jeff Kent	2.00	.60
BT14 Mike Piazza	5.00	1.50
BT15 Alex Rodriguez	5.00	1.50
BT16 Ivan Rodriguez	3.00	.90
BT17 Sammy Sosa	5.00	1.50
BT18 Ichiro Suzuki	5.00	1.50
BT19 Miguel Tejada	2.00	.60
BT20 Larry Walker	3.00	.90

2003 Stadium Club Born in the USA Relics

Inserted into packs at different odds depending on what type of game-used memorabilia piece was used, these 50 cards feature those memorabilia pieces cut into the shape of the player's home state.

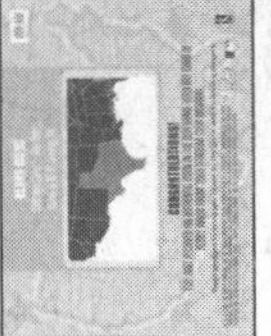

Nm-Mt Ex-Mt
BAT ODDS 1:76 H, 1:23 HTA, 1:89 R..
JERSEY ODDS 1:52 H, 1:15 HTA, 1:61 R
UNIFORM ODDS 1:413 H, 1:126 HTA, 1:484 R

	Nm-Mt	Ex-Mt
AB A.J. Burnett Jsy	10.00	3.00
AD Adam Dunn Bat	15.00	4.50
AR Alex Rodriguez Bat	25.00	7.50
BB Bret Boone Jsy	10.00	3.00
BF Brad Fullmer Bat	10.00	3.00
BL Barry Larkin Jsy	15.00	4.50
CB Craig Biggio Jsy	15.00	4.50
CF Cliff Floyd Bat	10.00	3.00
CJ Chipper Jones Jsy	15.00	4.50
CP Corey Patterson Bat	10.00	3.00
EC Eric Chavez Uni	10.00	3.00
EM Eric Milton Jsy	10.00	3.00
FT Frank Thomas Bat	15.00	4.50
GM Greg Maddux Jsy	15.00	4.50
GS Gary Sheffield Bat	10.00	3.00
JB Jeff Bagwell Jsy	15.00	4.50
JD Johnny Damon Bat	15.00	4.50
JDD J.D. Drew Bat	10.00	3.00
JE Jim Edmonds Jsy	10.00	3.00
JH Josh Hamilton Bat	10.00	3.00
JNB Jeromy Burnitz Bat	10.00	3.00
JO John Olerud Jsy	10.00	3.00
JS John Smoltz Jsy	15.00	4.50
JT Jim Thome Jsy	15.00	4.50
KW Kerry Wood Bat	15.00	4.50
LG Luis Gonzalez Bat	10.00	3.00
MG Mark Grace Jsy	15.00	4.50
MP Mike Piazza Jsy	15.00	4.50
MV Mo Vaughn Bat	10.00	3.00
MW Matt Williams Bat	10.00	3.00
NG Nomar Garciaparra Bat	25.00	7.50
PB Pat Burrell Bat	10.00	3.00
PK Paul Konerko Bat	10.00	3.00
PW Preston Wilson Jsy	10.00	3.00
RA Rich Aurilia Jsy	10.00	3.00
RH Rickey Henderson Bat	15.00	4.50
RJ Randy Johnson Bat	15.00	4.50
RK Ryan Klesko Bat	10.00	3.00
RS Richie Sexson Bat	10.00	3.00
RV Robin Ventura Bat	10.00	3.00
SB Sean Burroughs Bat	10.00	3.00
SG Shawn Green Bat	10.00	3.00
SR Scott Rolen Bat	15.00	4.50
TC Tony Clark Bat	10.00	3.00
TH Todd Helton Bat	15.00	4.50
TJH Toby Hall Bat	10.00	3.00
TL Terrence Long Uni	10.00	3.00
TM Tino Martinez Bat	15.00	4.50
TRL Travis Lee Bat	10.00	3.00
WM Willie Mays Bat	60.00	18.00

2003 Stadium Club Clubhouse Exclusive

Inserted into packs at a different rate depending on how many memorabilia pieces are used, these four cards feature game-worn memorabilia pieces of Cardinals star Albert Pujols.

Nm-Mt Ex-Mt
JSY ODDS 1:488 H, 1:178 HTA......
BAT-JSY ODDS 1:2073 H, 1:758 HTA .
BAT-JSY-SPK ODDS 1:2750 H, 1:1016 HTA
BAT-HAT-JSY-SPK ODDS 1:1016 HTA.

	Nm-Mt	Ex-Mt
CE1 Albert Pujols Jsy	20.00	6.00
CE2 Albert Pujols Bat-Jsy	40.00	12.00
CE3 Albert Pujols Bat-Jsy-Spike	100.00	30.00
CE4 Albert Pujols Bat-Hat-Jsy-Spike...		

2003 Stadium Club Co-Signers

Randomly inserted into packs, these two cards featue a pair of important baseball players who each signed cards for this set. This set features the first Masanori Murakami (the first Japanese player to play in the majors) certified signed cards. Murakami, to honor his heritage, signed an equivalent amount of cards in English and Japanese.

Nm-Mt Ex-Mt
GROUP A STATED ODDS 1: 339 HTA .
GROUP B STATED ODDS 1:1016 HTA.

	Nm-Mt	Ex-Mt
AM Hank Aaron Willie Mays A	500.00	150.00
MI Masanori Murakami Kazuhisa Ishii B	300.00	90.00

2003 Stadium Club License to Drive Bat Relics

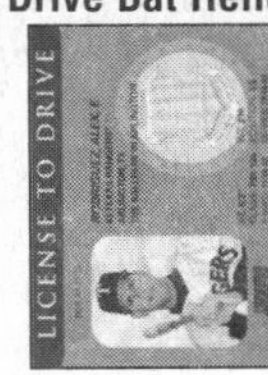

Inserted into packs at a stated rate of one in 98 hobby, one in 114 retail and one in 29 HTA, these 25 cards feature game-used bat relics of players who have driven in 100 runs in a season.

	Nm-Mt	Ex-Mt
AB Adrian Beltre	15.00	4.50
AD Adam Dunn	15.00	4.50
AJ Andruw Jones	10.00	3.00
ANR Aramis Ramirez	10.00	3.00
AP Albert Pujols	20.00	6.00
AR Alex Rodriguez	25.00	7.50
BW Bernie Williams	15.00	4.50
CJ Chipper Jones	15.00	4.50
EC Eric Chavez	10.00	3.00
FT Frank Thomas	15.00	4.50
GS Gary Sheffield	10.00	3.00
IR Ivan Rodriguez	15.00	4.50
JG Juan Gonzalez	15.00	4.50
LB Lance Berkman	10.00	3.00
LG Luis Gonzalez	10.00	3.00
LW Larry Walker	15.00	4.50
MA Moises Alou	10.00	3.00
MP Mike Piazza	25.00	7.50
NG Nomar Garciaparra	25.00	7.50
RA Roberto Alomar	15.00	4.50
RP Rafael Palmeiro	15.00	4.50
SG Shawn Green	10.00	3.00
SR Scott Rolen	15.00	4.50
TH Todd Helton	15.00	4.50
TM Tino Martinez	15.00	4.50

2003 Stadium Club MLB Match-Up Dual Relics

Inserted into hobby packs at a stated rate of one in 485, one in 570 retail and HTA packs at one in 148, these five cards feature both a game-worn jersey swatch as well as a game-used bat relic of the featured players.

	Nm-Mt	Ex-Mt
AJ Andruw Jones	20.00	6.00
AP Albert Pujols	40.00	12.00
BB Bret Boone	20.00	6.00
GM Greg Maddux	30.00	9.00
TH Todd Helton	25.00	7.50

2003 Stadium Club Shots

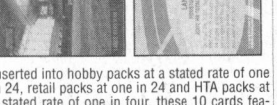

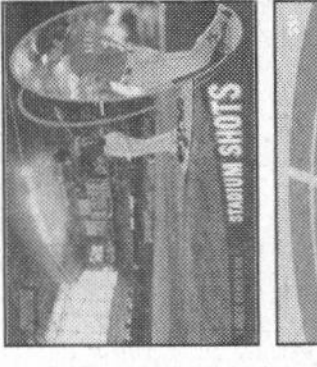

Inserted into hobby packs at a stated rate of one in 24, retail packs at one in 24 and HTA packs at a stated rate of one in four, these 10 cards feature players who are known for their long distance slugging.

	Nm-Mt	Ex-Mt
SS1 Lance Berkman	2.00	.60
SS2 Barry Bonds	8.00	2.40
SS3 Jason Giambi	2.00	.60
SS4 Shawn Green	2.00	.60
SS5 Miguel Tejada	2.00	.60
SS6 Paul Konerko	2.00	.60
SS7 Mike Piazza	5.00	1.50
SS8 Alex Rodriguez	5.00	1.50
SS9 Sammy Sosa	5.00	1.50
SS10 Gary Sheffield	2.00	.60

2003 Stadium Club Stadium Slices Barrel Relics

Inserted into hobby packs at a stated rate of one in 550 and HTA packs at a stated rate of one in 204, these 10 cards feature game-used bat pieces taken from the barrel.

	Nm-Mt	Ex-Mt
AJ Andruw Jones	25.00	7.50
AP Albert Pujols	50.00	15.00
AR Alex Rodriguez	60.00	18.00
CD Carlos Delgado	25.00	7.50
GS Gary Sheffield	25.00	7.50
MP Mike Piazza	60.00	18.00
NG Nomar Garciaparra	80.00	24.00
RA Roberto Alomar	40.00	12.00
RP Rafael Palmeiro	40.00	12.00
TH Todd Helton	40.00	12.00

2003 Stadium Club Stadium Slices Handle Relics

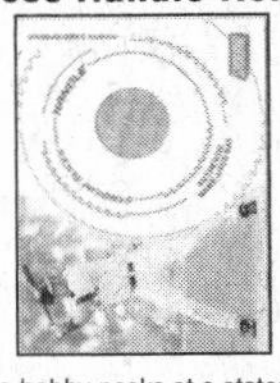

Inserted into hobby packs at a stated rate of one in 237 and HTA packs at a stated rate of one in 86, these 10 cards feature game-used bat pieces taken from the handle.

	Nm-Mt	Ex-Mt
AJ Andruw Jones	12.00	3.60
AP Albert Pujols	25.00	7.50
AR Alex Rodriguez	30.00	9.00
CD Carlos Delgado	12.00	3.60
GS Gary Sheffield	12.00	3.60
MP Mike Piazza	30.00	9.00
NG Nomar Garciaparra	40.00	12.00
RA Roberto Alomar	20.00	6.00
RP Rafael Palmeiro	20.00	6.00
TH Todd Helton	20.00	6.00

2003 Stadium Club Stadium Slices Trademark Relics

Inserted into hobby packs at a stated rate of one in 415 and HTA packs at a stated rate of one in 151, these 10 cards feature game-used bat pieces taken from the middle of the bat.

	Nm-Mt	Ex-Mt
AJ Andruw Jones	15.00	4.50
AP Albert Pujols	30.00	9.00
AR Alex Rodriguez	40.00	12.00
CD Carlos Delgado	15.00	4.50
GS Gary Sheffield	15.00	4.50
MP Mike Piazza	40.00	12.00
NG Nomar Garciaparra	50.00	15.00
RA Roberto Alomar	25.00	7.50
RP Rafael Palmeiro	25.00	7.50
TH Todd Helton	25.00	7.50

2003 Stadium Club World Stage Relics

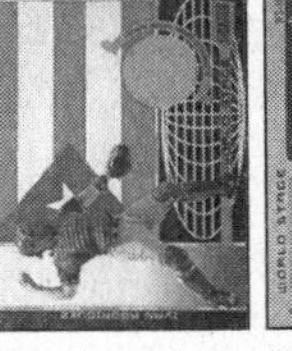
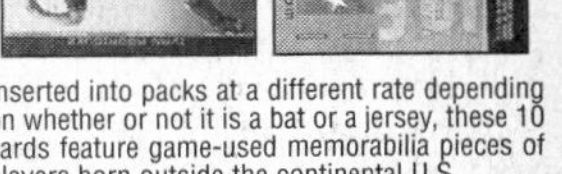

Inserted into packs at a different rate depending on whether or not it is a bat or a jersey, these 10 cards feature game-used memorabilia pieces of players born outside the continental U.S.

Nm-Mt Ex-Mt
BAT ODDS 1:809 H, 1:246 HTA, 1:950 R
JSY ODDS 1:118 H, 1:36 HTA, 1:138 R

	Nm-Mt	Ex-Mt
AB Adrian Beltre Jsy	10.00	3.00
AP Albert Pujols Jsy	20.00	6.00
AS Alfonso Soriano Bat	15.00	4.50
BK Byung-Hyun Kim Jsy	10.00	3.00
HN Hideo Nomo Bat	25.00	7.50
IR Ivan Rodriguez Jsy	10.00	3.00
KI Kazuhisa Ishii Jsy	8.00	2.40
KS Kazuhiro Sasaki Jsy	8.00	2.40
MT Miguel Tejada Jsy	8.00	2.40
TS Tsuyoshi Shinjo Bat	10.00	3.00

2000 Stadium Club Chrome

The 2000 Stadium Club Chrome set was released in May, 2000 as a 250-card set. The set features 200 Player cards, 30 Future Star cards, and 20 Draft Pick cards. Each pack contained five cards and carried a suggested retail price of $4.00. Notable Rookie Cards include Rick Asadoorian and Bobby Bradley.

	Nm-Mt	Ex-Mt
COMPLETE SET (250)	50.00	15.00
COMMON CARD (1-250)	.50	.15

COMMON RC .75 .23
1 Nomar Garciaparra 2.00 .60
2 Brian Jordan .50 .15
3 Mark Grace .75 .23
4 Jeromy Burnitz .50 .15
5 Shane Reynolds .50 .15
6 Alex Gonzalez .50 .15
7 Jose Offerman .50 .15
8 Orlando Hernandez .50 .15
9 Mike Caruso .50 .15
10 Tony Clark .50 .15
11 Sean Casey .50 .15
12 Johnny Damon .75 .23
13 Dante Bichette .50 .15
14 Kevin Young .50 .15
15 Juan Gonzalez .75 .23
16 Chipper Jones 1.25 .35
17 Quilvio Veras .50 .15
18 Trevor Hoffman .50 .15
19 Roger Cedeno .50 .15
20 Ellis Burks .50 .15
21 Richie Sexson .50 .15
22 Gary Sheffield .50 .15
23 Delino DeShields .50 .15
24 Wade Boggs .75 .23
25 Ray Lankford .50 .15
26 Kevin Appier .50 .15
27 Roy Halladay .50 .15
28 Harold Baines .50 .15
29 Todd Zeile .50 .15
30 Barry Larkin .75 .23
31 Ron Coomer .50 .15
32 Jorge Posada .75 .23
33 Magglio Ordonez .50 .15
34 Brian Giles .50 .15
35 Jeff Kent .50 .15
36 Henry Rodriguez .50 .15
37 Fred McGriff .75 .23
38 Shawn Green .50 .15
39 Derek Bell .50 .15
40 Ben Grieve .50 .15
41 Dave Nilsson .50 .15
42 Mo Vaughn .50 .15
43 Rondell White .50 .15
44 Doug Glanville .50 .15
45 Paul O'Neill .75 .23
46 Carlos Lee .50 .15
47 Vinny Castilla .50 .15
48 Mike Sweeney .50 .15
49 Rico Brogna .50 .15
50 Alex Rodriguez 2.00 .60
51 Luis Castillo .50 .15
52 Kevin Brown .75 .23
53 Jose Vidro .50 .15
54 John Smoltz .75 .23
55 Garret Anderson .50 .15
56 Matt Stairs .50 .15
57 Omar Vizquel .75 .23
58 Tom Goodwin .50 .15
59 Scott Brosius .50 .15
60 Robin Ventura .75 .23
61 B.J. Surhoff .50 .15
62 Andy Ashby .50 .15
63 Chris Widger .50 .15
64 Tim Hudson .50 .15
65 Javy Lopez .50 .15
66 Tim Salmon .75 .23
67 Warren Morris .50 .15
68 John Wetteland .50 .15
69 Gabe Kapler .50 .15
70 Bernie Williams .75 .23
71 Rickey Henderson 1.25 .35
72 Andruw Jones .50 .15
73 Eric Young .50 .15
74 Bob Abreu .50 .15
75 David Cone .50 .15
76 Rusty Greer .50 .15
77 Ron Belliard .50 .15
78 Troy Glaus .50 .15
79 Mike Hampton .50 .15
80 Miguel Tejada .50 .15
81 Jeff Cirillo .50 .15
82 Todd Hundley .50 .15
83 Roberto Alomar .75 .23
84 Charles Johnson .50 .15
85 Rafael Palmeiro .75 .23
86 Doug Mientkiewicz .50 .15
87 Mariano Rivera .75 .23
88 Neifi Perez .50 .15
89 Jermaine Dye .50 .15
90 Ivan Rodriguez 1.25 .35
91 Jay Buhner .50 .15
92 Pokey Reese .50 .15
93 John Olerud .50 .15
94 Brady Anderson .50 .15
95 Manny Ramirez .75 .23
96 Keith Osik RC .75 .23
97 Mickey Morandini .50 .15
98 Matt Williams .50 .15
99 Eric Karros .50 .15
100 Ken Griffey Jr. 2.00 .60
101 Bret Boone .50 .15
102 Ryan Klesko .50 .15
103 Craig Biggio .75 .23
104 John Jaha .50 .15
105 Vladimir Guerrero 1.25 .35
106 Devon White .50 .15
107 Tony Womack .50 .15
108 Marvin Benard .50 .15
109 Kenny Lofton .50 .15
110 Preston Wilson .50 .15
111 Al Leiter .50 .15
112 Reggie Sanders .50 .15
113 Scott Williamson .50 .15
114 Deivi Cruz .50 .15
115 Carlos Beltran .75 .23
116 Ray Durham .50 .15
117 Ricky Ledee .50 .15
118 Torii Hunter .50 .15
119 John Valentin .50 .15
120 Scott Rolen 1.25 .35
121 Jason Kendall .50 .15
122 Dave Martinez .50 .15
123 Jim Thome 1.25 .35
124 David Bell .50 .15
125 Jose Canseco 1.25 .35
126 Jose Lima .50 .15
127 Carl Everett .50 .15
128 Kevin Millwood .50 .15
129 Bill Spiers .50 .15
130 Omar Daal .50 .15
131 Miguel Cairo .50 .15
132 Mark Grudzielanek .50 .15
133 David Justice .50 .15
134 Russ Ortiz .50 .15
135 Mike Piazza 2.00 .60
136 Brian Meadows .50 .15
137 Tony Gwynn 1.50 .45
138 Cal Ripken 4.00 1.20
139 Kris Benson .50 .15
140 Larry Walker .75 .23
141 Cristian Guzman .50 .15
142 Tino Martinez .75 .23
143 Chris Singleton .50 .15
144 Lee Stevens .50 .15
145 Rey Ordonez .50 .15
146 Russ Davis .50 .15
147 J.T. Snow .50 .15
148 Luis Gonzalez .50 .15
149 Marquis Grissom .50 .15
150 Greg Maddux 2.00 .60
151 Fernando Tatis .50 .15
152 Jason Giambi .50 .15
153 Carlos Delgado .50 .15
154 Joe McEwing .50 .15
155 Raul Mondesi .50 .15
156 Rich Aurilia .50 .15
157 Alex Fernandez .50 .15
158 Albert Belle .50 .15
159 Pat Meares .50 .15
160 Mike Lieberthal .50 .15
161 Mike Cameron .50 .15
162 Juan Encarnacion .50 .15
163 Chuck Knoblauch .50 .15
164 Pedro Martinez 1.25 .35
165 Randy Johnson 1.25 .35
166 Shannon Stewart .50 .15
167 Jeff Bagwell .75 .23
168 Edgar Renteria .50 .15
169 Barry Bonds 3.00 .90
170 Steve Finley .50 .15
171 Brian Hunter .50 .15
172 Tom Glavine .75 .23
173 Mark Kotsay .50 .15
174 Tony Fernandez .50 .15
175 Sammy Sosa 2.00 .60
176 Geoff Jenkins .50 .15
177 Adrian Beltre .75 .23
178 Jay Bell .50 .15
179 Mike Bordick .50 .15
180 Ed Sprague .50 .15
181 Dave Roberts .50 .15
182 Greg Vaughn .50 .15
183 Brian Daubach .50 .15
184 Damion Easley .50 .15
185 Carlos Febles .50 .15
186 Kevin Tapani .50 .15
187 Frank Thomas 1.25 .35
188 Roger Clemens 2.50 .75
189 Mike Benjamin .50 .15
190 Curt Schilling .50 .15
191 Edgardo Alfonzo .50 .15
192 Mike Mussina .75 .23
193 Todd Helton .75 .23
194 Todd Jones .50 .15
195 Dean Palmer .50 .15
196 John Flaherty .50 .15
197 Derek Jeter 3.00 .90
198 Todd Walker .50 .15
199 Brad Ausmus .50 .15
200 Mark McGwire 3.00 .90
201 Erubiel Durazo .50 .15
202 Nick Johnson .50 .15
203 Ruben Mateo .50 .15
204 Lance Berkman .50 .15
205 Pat Burrell .50 .15
206 Pablo Ozuna .50 .15
207 Roosevelt Brown .50 .15
208 Alfonso Soriano 1.25 .35
209 A.J. Burnett .50 .15
210 Rafael Furcal .50 .15
211 Scott Morgan .50 .15
212 Adam Piatt .50 .15
213 Dee Brown .50 .15
214 Corey Patterson .50 .15
215 Mickey Lopez .50 .15
216 Rob Ryan .50 .15
217 Sean Burroughs .50 .15
218 Jack Cust .50 .15
219 John Patterson .50 .15
220 Kit Pellow .50 .15
221 Chad Hermansen .50 .15
222 Daryle Ward .50 .15
223 Jayson Werth .50 .15
224 Jason Standridge .50 .15
225 Mark Mulder .50 .15
226 Peter Bergeron .50 .15
227 Willi Mo Pena .50 .15
228 Aramis Ramirez .50 .15
229 John Sneed RC .75 .23
230 Wilton Veras .50 .15
231 Josh Hamilton .50 .15
232 Eric Munson .50 .15
233 Bobby Bradley RC .75 .23
234 Larry Bigbie RC 2.00 .60
235 B.J. Garbe RC .75 .23
236 Brett Myers RC 1.25 .35
237 Jason Stumm RC .75 .23
238 Corey Myers RC .75 .23
239 Ryan Christianson RC .75 .23
240 David Walling .50 .15
241 Josh Girdley .50 .15
242 Omar Ortiz .50 .15
243 Jason Jennings .50 .15
244 Kyle Snyder .50 .15
245 Jay Gehrke .50 .15
246 Mike Paradis .50 .15
247 Chance Caple RC .75 .23
248 Ben Christensen RC .75 .23
249 Brad Baker RC .75 .23
250 Rick Asadoorian RC .75 .23

2000 Stadium Club Chrome First Day Issue

Randomly inserted into packs at one in 33, this 250-card insert is a complete parallel of the Stadium Club Chrome base set. Each card is individually serial numbered to 100.

Nm-Mt Ex-Mt
*STARS: 6X TO 15X BASIC CARDS
*ROOKIES: 2.5X TO 6X BASIC CARDS

2000 Stadium Club Chrome First Day Issue Refractors

Randomly inserted into packs at one in 131, this 250-card insert is a complete parallel of the Stadium Club Chrome base set. Each card features Topps' 'refractor' technology. Each card is also individually serial numbered to 25.

Nm-Mt Ex-Mt
*STARS: 15X TO 40X BASIC CARDS

2000 Stadium Club Chrome Refractors

Randomly inserted into packs at one in 12, this 250-card insert is a complete parallel of the Stadium Club Chrome base set. Each card features Topps' 'refractor' technology.

Nm-Mt Ex-Mt
*STARS: 4X TO 10X BASIC CARDS
*ROOKIES: 1.5X TO 4X BASIC CARDS

2000 Stadium Club Chrome Capture the Action

Randomly inserted into packs at one in 18, this 20-card insert features some of the major league's top prospects and veteran players. Card backs carry a "CA" prefix.

Nm-Mt Ex-Mt
COMPLETE SET (20) 150.00 45.00
*REFRACTORS: 1X TO 2.5X BASIC CAPTURE
REFRACTOR STATED ODDS 1:90
CA1 Josh Hamilton 1.25 .35
CA2 Pat Burrell 1.25 .35
CA3 Erubiel Durazo 1.25 .35
CA4 Alfonso Soriano 3.00 .90
CA5 A.J. Burnett 1.25 .35
CA6 Alex Rodriguez 5.00 1.50
CA7 Sean Casey 1.25 .35
CA8 Derek Jeter 8.00 2.40
CA9 Vladimir Guerrero 3.00 .90
CA10 Nomar Garciaparra 5.00 1.50
CA11 Mike Piazza 5.00 1.50
CA12 Ken Griffey Jr. 5.00 1.50
CA13 Sammy Sosa 5.00 1.50
CA14 Juan Gonzalez 2.00 .60
CA15 Mark McGwire 8.00 2.40
CA16 Ivan Rodriguez 3.00 .90
CA17 Barry Bonds 8.00 2.40
CA18 Wade Boggs 2.00 .60
CA19 Tony Gwynn 4.00 1.20
CA20 Cal Ripken 10.00 3.00

2000 Stadium Club Chrome Clear Shots

Randomly inserted into packs at one in 24, this insert features ten of the major leagues most famous stars from both front and back angles at the same time. Card backs carry a "CS" prefix.

Nm-Mt Ex-Mt
COMPLETE SET (10) 30.00 9.00
*REFRACTORS: 1X TO 2.5X BASIC CLEAR
REFRACTOR ODDS 1:120
CS1 Derek Jeter 6.00 1.80
CS2 Bernie Williams 1.50 .45
CS3 Roger Clemens 5.00 1.50
CS4 Chipper Jones 2.50 .75
CS5 Greg Maddux 4.00 1.20
CS6 Andruw Jones 1.00 .30
CS7 Juan Gonzalez 1.50 .45
CS8 Manny Ramirez 1.50 .45
CS9 Ken Griffey Jr. 4.00 1.20
CS10 Josh Hamilton 1.00 .30

2000 Stadium Club Chrome Eyes of the Game

Randomly inserted into packs at one in 16, this 10-card insert features players who have an "eye" for the game. Card backs carry an "EG" prefix.

Nm-Mt Ex-Mt
COMPLETE SET (10) 30.00 9.00
*REFRACTORS: 1X TO 2.5X BASIC EYES
REFRACTOR ODDS 1:80
EG1 Randy Johnson 2.00 .60
EG2 Mike Piazza 3.00 .90
EG3 Nomar Garciaparra 3.00 .90
EG4 Mark McGwire 5.00 1.50
EG5 Alex Rodriguez 3.00 .90
EG6 Derek Jeter 5.00 1.50
EG7 Tony Gwynn 2.50 .75
EG8 Sammy Sosa 3.00 .90
EG9 Larry Walker 1.25 .35
EG10 Ken Griffey Jr. 3.00 .90

2000 Stadium Club Chrome True Colors

Randomly inserted into packs at one in 32, this 10-card insert features players that rise to the occasion when the game's on the line. Card backs carry a "TC" prefix.

Nm-Mt Ex-Mt
COMPLETE SET (10) 50.00 15.00
*REFRACTORS: 1X TO 2.5X BASIC TRUE
REFRACTOR ODDS 1:160
TC1 Sammy Sosa 5.00 1.50
TC2 Nomar Garciaparra 5.00 1.50
TC3 Alex Rodriguez 5.00 1.50
TC4 Derek Jeter 8.00 2.40
TC5 Mark McGwire 8.00 2.40
TC6 Chipper Jones 3.00 .90
TC7 Mike Piazza 5.00 1.50
TC8 Ken Griffey Jr. 5.00 1.50
TC9 Manny Ramirez 2.00 .60
TC10 Vladimir Guerrero 3.00 .90

2000 Stadium Club Chrome Visionaries

Randomly inserted into packs at one in 18, this 20-card insert features some of the major league's most talented prospects. Card backs carry a 'V' prefix.

Nm-Mt Ex-Mt
COMPLETE SET (20) 60.00 18.00
*REF: .75X TO 2X BASIC VISIONARIES
REFRACTOR ODDS 1:90
V1 Alfonso Soriano 3.00 .90
V2 Josh Hamilton 1.25 .35
V3 A.J. Burnett 1.25 .35
V4 Pat Burrell 1.25 .35
V5 Ruben Salazar 1.25 .35
V6 Aaron Rowand 4.00 1.20
V7 Adam Piatt 1.25 .35
V8 Nick Johnson 1.25 .35
V9 Brett Myers 2.00 .60
V10 Jack Cust 1.25 .35
V11 Corey Patterson 1.25 .35
V12 Sean Burroughs 1.25 .35
V13 Pablo Ozuna 1.25 .35
V14 Dee Brown 1.25 .35
V15 John Patterson 1.25 .35
V16 Willi Mo Pena 1.25 .35
V17 Mark Mulder 1.25 .35
V18 Eric Munson 1.25 .35
V19 Alex Escobar 3.00 .90
V20 Rick Asadoorian 1.25 .35

1991 Studio Previews

This 18-card preview set was issued four at a time within 1991 Donruss retail factory sets in order to show dealers and collectors the look of their new Studio cards. The standard-size cards are exactly the same style as those in the Studio series, with black and white player photos bordered in mauve and player information on the backs.

Nm-Mt Ex-Mt
COMPLETE SET (18) 30.00 9.00
1 Juan Bell 1.00 .30
2 Roger Clemens 12.00 3.60
3 Dave Parker 2.00 .60
4 Tim Raines 2.00 .60
5 Kevin Seitzer 1.00 .30
6 Ted Higuera 1.00 .30
7 Bernie Williams 6.00 1.80
8 Harold Baines 2.00 .60
9 Gary Pettis 1.00 .30
10 Dave Justice 2.00 .60
11 Eric Davis 2.00 .60
12 Andujar Cedeno 1.00 .30
13 Tom Foley 1.00 .30
14 Dwight Gooden 2.00 .60
15 Doug Drabek 1.00 .30
16 Steve Decker 1.00 .30
17 Joe Torre MG 2.00 .60
NNO0 Title Card 1.00 .30

1991 Studio

The 1991 Studio set, issued by Donruss/Leaf, contains 264 standard-size cards issued in one series. Cards were distributed in foil packs each of which contained one of 21 different Rod Carew puzzle panels. The Studio card fronts feature posed black and white head-and-shoulders player photos with mauve borders. The team

logo, player's name, and position appear along the bottom of the card face. The cards are ordered alphabetically within and according to teams for each league with American League teams preceding National League. Rookie Cards in the set include Jeff Bagwell, Jeff Conine and Brian McRae.

Nm-Mt Ex-Mt
COMPLETE SET (264) 15.00 4.50
1 Glenn Davis .10 .03
2 Dwight Evans .15 .04
3 Leo Gomez .10 .03
4 Chris Hoiles .10 .03
5 Sam Horn .10 .03
6 Ben McDonald .10 .03
7 Randy Milligan .10 .03
8 Gregg Olson .10 .03
9 Cal Ripken 1.50 .45
10 David Segui .10 .03
11 Wade Boggs .25 .07
12 Ellis Burks .15 .04
13 Jack Clark .15 .04
14 Roger Clemens 1.00 .30
15 Mike Greenwell .10 .03
16 Tim Naehring .10 .03
17 Tony Pena .10 .03
18 Phil Plantier RC .10 .03
19 Jeff Reardon .15 .04
20 Mo Vaughn .15 .04
21 Jimmie Reese CO .15 .04
22 Jim Abbott UER .25 .07
(Born in 1967, not 1969)
23 Bert Blyleven .15 .04
24 Chuck Finley .15 .04
25 Gary Gaetti .15 .04
26 Wally Joyner .15 .04
27 Mark Langston .10 .03
28 Kirk McCaskill .10 .03
29 Lance Parrish .15 .04
30 Dave Winfield .15 .04
31 Alex Fernandez .10 .03
32 Carlton Fisk .25 .07
33 Scott Fletcher .10 .03
34 Greg Hibbard .10 .03
35 Charlie Hough .15 .04
36 Jack McDowell .10 .03
37 Tim Raines .15 .04
38 Sammy Sosa 1.00 .30
39 Bobby Thigpen .10 .03
40 Frank Thomas .50 .15
41 Sandy Alomar Jr. .10 .03
42 John Farrell .10 .03
43 Glenallen Hill .10 .03
44 Brook Jacoby .10 .03
45 Chris James .10 .03
46 Doug Jones .10 .03
47 Eric King .10 .03
48 Mark Lewis .10 .03
49 Greg Swindell UER .10 .03
(Photo actually Turner Ward)
50 Mark Whiten .10 .03
51 Milt Cuyler .10 .03
52 Rob Deer .10 .03
53 Cecil Fielder .15 .04
54 Travis Fryman .15 .04
55 Bill Gullickson .10 .03
56 Lloyd Moseby .10 .03
57 Frank Tanana .10 .03
58 Mickey Tettleton .10 .03
59 Alan Trammell .15 .04
60 Lou Whitaker .15 .04
61 Mike Boddicker .10 .03
62 George Brett 1.25 .35
63 Jeff Conine RC .50 .15
64 Warren Cromartie .10 .03
65 Storm Davis .10 .03
66 Kirk Gibson .15 .04
67 Mark Gubicza .10 .03
68 Brian McRae RC .15 .04
69 Bret Saberhagen .15 .04
70 Kurt Stillwell .10 .03
71 Tim McIntosh .10 .03
72 Candy Maldonado .10 .03
73 Paul Molitor .25 .07
74 Willie Randolph .15 .04
75 Ron Robinson .10 .03
76 Gary Sheffield .15 .04
77 Franklin Stubbs .10 .03
78 B.J. Surhoff .15 .04
79 Greg Vaughn .10 .03
80 Robin Yount .75 .23
81 Rick Aguilera .15 .04
82 Steve Bedrosian .10 .03
83 Scott Erickson .10 .03
84 Greg Gagne .10 .03
85 Dan Gladden .10 .03
86 Brian Harper .10 .03
87 Kent Hrbek .15 .04
88 Shane Mack .10 .03
89 Jack Morris .15 .04
90 Kirby Puckett .50 .15
91 Jesse Barfield .10 .03
92 Steve Farr .10 .03
93 Steve Howe .10 .03
94 Roberto Kelly .10 .03
95 Tim Leary .10 .03
96 Kevin Maas .10 .03
97 Don Mattingly 1.25 .35
98 Hensley Meulens .10 .03
99 Scott Sanderson .10 .03
100 Steve Sax .10 .03
101 Jose Canseco .50 .15
102 Dennis Eckersley .15 .04
103 Dave Henderson .10 .03
104 Rickey Henderson .50 .15
105 Rick Honeycutt .10 .03

106 Mark McGwire 1.25 .35
107 Dave Stewart UER .15 .04
(No-hitter against
Toronto& not Texas)
108 Eric Show .10 .03
109 Todd Van Poppel RC .10 .03
110 Bob Welch .10 .03
111 Alvin Davis .10 .03
112 Ken Griffey Jr. 1.00 .30
113 Ken Griffey Sr. .15 .04
114 Erik Hanson UER .10 .03
(Misspelled Eric)
115 Brian Holman .10 .03
116 Randy Johnson .60 .18
117 Edgar Martinez .25 .07
118 Tino Martinez .25 .07
119 Harold Reynolds .15 .04
120 David Valle .10 .03
121 Kevin Belcher .10 .03
122 Scott Chiamparino .10 .03
123 Julio Franco .15 .04
124 Juan Gonzalez .25 .07
125 Rich Gossage .15 .04
126 Jeff Kunkel .10 .03
127 Rafael Palmeiro .25 .07
128 Nolan Ryan 2.00 .60
129 Ruben Sierra .10 .03
130 Bobby Witt .10 .03
131 Roberto Alomar .25 .07
132 Tom Candiotti .10 .03
133 Joe Carter .15 .04
134 Ken Dayley .10 .03
135 Kelly Gruber .10 .03
136 John Olerud .15 .04
137 Dave Stieb .10 .03
138 Turner Ward RC .15 .04
139 Devon White .15 .04
140 Mookie Wilson .15 .04
141 Steve Avery .10 .03
142 Sid Bream .10 .03
143 Nick Esasky UER .10 .03
(Homers abbreviated RH)
144 Ron Gant .15 .04
145 Tom Glavine .25 .07
146 David Justice .15 .04
147 Kelly Mann .10 .03
148 Terry Pendleton .15 .04
149 John Smoltz .25 .07
150 Jeff Treadway .10 .03
151 George Bell .10 .03
152 Shawn Boskie .10 .03
153 Andre Dawson .15 .04
154 Lance Dickson RC .10 .03
155 Shawon Dunston .10 .03
156 Joe Girardi .10 .03
157 Mark Grace .25 .07
158 Ryne Sandberg .75 .23
159 Gary Scott RC .10 .03
160 Dave Smith .10 .03
161 Tom Browning .10 .03
162 Eric Davis .15 .04
163 Rob Dibble .15 .04
164 Mariano Duncan .10 .03
165 Chris Hammond .10 .03
166 Billy Hatcher .10 .03
167 Barry Larkin .25 .07
168 Hal Morris .10 .03
169 Paul O'Neill .25 .07
170 Chris Sabo .10 .03
171 Eric Anthony .10 .03
172 Jeff Bagwell RC 2.00 .60
173 Craig Biggio .25 .07
174 Ken Caminiti .15 .04
175 Jim Deshaies .10 .03
176 Steve Finley .15 .04
177 Pete Harnisch .10 .03
178 Darryl Kile .15 .04
179 Curt Schilling .50 .15
180 Mike Scott .10 .03
181 Brett Butler .15 .04
182 Gary Carter .15 .04
183 Orel Hershiser .15 .04
184 Ramon Martinez .10 .03
185 Eddie Murray .50 .15
186 Jose Offerman .10 .03
187 Bob Ojeda .10 .03
188 Juan Samuel .10 .03
189 Mike Scioscia .10 .03
190 Darryl Strawberry .15 .04
191 Moises Alou .15 .04
192 Brian Barnes RC .10 .03
193 Oil Can Boyd .10 .03
194 Ivan Calderon .10 .03
195 Delino DeShields .15 .04
196 Mike Fitzgerald .10 .03
197 Andres Galarraga .15 .04
198 Marquis Grissom .15 .04
199 Bill Sampen .10 .03
200 Tim Wallach .10 .03
201 Daryl Boston .10 .03
202 Vince Coleman .10 .03
203 John Franco .15 .04
204 Dwight Gooden .15 .04
205 Tom Herr .10 .03
206 Gregg Jefferies .10 .03
207 Howard Johnson .10 .03
208 Dave Magadan UER .10 .03
(Born 1862&
should be 1962)
209 Kevin McReynolds .10 .03
210 Frank Viola .15 .04
211 Wes Chamberlain RC .10 .03
212 Darren Daulton .15 .04
213 Len Dykstra .15 .04
214 Charlie Hayes .10 .03
215 Ricky Jordan .10 .03
216 Steve Lake .10 .03
(Pictured with parrot
on his shoulder)
217 Roger McDowell .10 .03
218 Mickey Morandini .10 .03
219 Terry Mulholland .10 .03
220 Dale Murphy .50 .15
221 Jay Bell .15 .04
222 Barry Bonds 1.25 .35
223 Bobby Bonilla .15 .04
224 Doug Drabek .10 .03
225 Bill Landrum .10 .03
226 Mike LaValliere .10 .03
227 Jose Lind .10 .03
228 Don Slaught .10 .03
229 John Smiley .10 .03
230 Andy Van Slyke .15 .04
231 Bernard Gilkey .10 .03
232 Pedro Guerrero .15 .04
233 Rex Hudler .10 .03
234 Ray Lankford .10 .03
235 Joe Magrane .10 .03
236 Jose Oquendo .10 .03
237 Lee Smith .15 .04
238 Ozzie Smith .75 .23
239 Milt Thompson .10 .03
240 Todd Zeile .10 .03
241 Larry Andersen .10 .03
242 Andy Benes .10 .03
243 Paul Faries .10 .03
244 Tony Fernandez .10 .03
245 Tony Gwynn .60 .18
246 Atlee Hammaker .10 .03
247 Fred McGriff .25 .07
248 Bip Roberts .10 .03
249 Bentio Santiago .15 .04
250 Ed Whitson .10 .03
251 Dave Anderson .10 .03
252 Mike Benjamin .10 .03
253 John Burkett UER .10 .03
(Front photo actually
Trevor Wilson)
254 Will Clark .50 .15
255 Scott Garrelts .10 .03
256 Willie McGee .15 .04
257 Kevin Mitchell .10 .03
258 Dave Righetti .15 .04
259 Matt Williams .15 .04
260 Bud Black .10 .03
Steve Decker
261 S.Anderson MG CL .15 .04
262 Tom Lasorda MG CL .25 .07
263 Tony LaRussa MG CL .15 .04
NNO Title Card .10 .03

1992 Studio

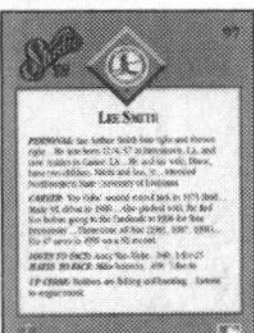

The 1992 Studio set consists of ten players from each of the 26 major league teams, three checklists, and an introduction card for a total of 264 standard-size cards. The key Rookie Cards in this set are Chad Curtis and Brian Jordan.

Nm-Mt Ex-Mt
COMPLETE SET (264) 15.00 4.50
1 Steve Avery .10 .03
2 Sid Bream .10 .03
3 Ron Gant .15 .04
4 Tom Glavine .25 .07
5 David Justice .15 .04
6 Mark Lemke .10 .03
7 Greg Olson .10 .03
8 Terry Pendleton .15 .04
9 Deion Sanders .25 .07
10 John Smoltz .25 .07
11 Doug Dascenzo .10 .03
12 Andre Dawson .15 .04
13 Joe Girardi .10 .03
14 Mark Grace .25 .07
15 Greg Maddux .60 .18
16 Chuck McElroy .10 .03
17 Mike Morgan .10 .03
18 Ryne Sandberg .60 .18
19 Gary Scott .10 .03
20 Sammy Sosa .60 .18
21 Norm Charlton .10 .03
22 Rob Dibble .15 .04
23 Barry Larkin .25 .07
24 Hal Morris .10 .03
25 Paul O'Neill .25 .07
26 Jose Rijo .10 .03
27 Bip Roberts .10 .03
28 Chris Sabo .10 .03
29 Reggie Sanders .10 .03
30 Greg Swindell .10 .03
31 Jeff Bagwell .40 .12
32 Craig Biggio .25 .07
33 Ken Caminiti .15 .04
34 Andujar Cedeno .10 .03
35 Steve Finley .15 .04
36 Pete Harnisch .10 .03
37 Butch Henry RC .15 .04
38 Doug Jones .10 .03
39 Darryl Kile .15 .04
40 Eddie Taubensee RC .25 .07
41 Brett Butler .15 .04
42 Tom Candiotti .10 .03
43 Eric Davis .15 .04
44 Orel Hershiser .15 .04
45 Eric Karros .15 .04
46 Ramon Martinez .10 .03
47 Jose Offerman .10 .03
48 Mike Scioscia .10 .03
49 Mike Sharperson .10 .03
50 Darryl Strawberry .15 .04
51 Bret Barberie .10 .03
52 Ivan Calderon .10 .03
53 Gary Carter .15 .04
54 Delino DeShields .10 .03
55 Marquis Grissom .10 .03
56 Ken Hill .10 .03
57 Dennis Martinez .15 .04
58 Spike Owen .10 .03
59 Larry Walker .25 .07
60 Tim Wallach .10 .03
61 Bobby Bonilla .15 .04
62 Tim Burke .10 .03
63 Vince Coleman .10 .03
64 John Franco .15 .04
65 Dwight Gooden .15 .04
66 Todd Hundley .10 .03
67 Howard Johnson .10 .03
68 Eddie Murray UER .40 .12
(He's not all-time switch
homer leader, but he has
most games with homers
from both sides)
69 Bret Saberhagen .15 .04
70 Anthony Young .10 .03
71 Kim Batiste .10 .03
72 Wes Chamberlain .10 .03
73 Darren Daulton .15 .04
74 Mariano Duncan .10 .03
75 Len Dykstra .15 .04
76 John Kruk .15 .04
77 Mickey Morandini .10 .03
78 Terry Mulholland .10 .03
79 Dale Murphy .40 .12
80 Mitch Williams .10 .03
81 Jay Bell .15 .04
82 Barry Bonds 1.00 .30
83 Steve Buechele .10 .03
84 Doug Drabek .10 .03
85 Mike LaValliere .10 .03
86 Jose Lind .10 .03
87 Denny Neagle .15 .04
88 Randy Tomlin .10 .03
89 Andy Van Slyke .15 .04
90 Gary Varsho .10 .03
91 Pedro Guerrero .15 .04
92 Rex Hudler .10 .03
93 Brian Jordan RC .50 .15
94 Felix Jose .10 .03
95 Donovan Osborne .10 .03
96 Tom Pagnozzi .10 .03
97 Lee Smith .15 .04
98 Ozzie Smith .60 .18
99 Todd Worrell .10 .03
100 Todd Zeile .10 .03
101 Andy Benes .10 .03
102 Jerald Clark .10 .03
103 Tony Fernandez .10 .03
104 Tony Gwynn .50 .15
105 Greg W. Harris .10 .03
106 Fred McGriff .25 .07
107 Benito Santiago .15 .04
108 Gary Sheffield .15 .04
109 Kurt Stillwell .10 .03
110 Tim Teufel .10 .03
111 Kevin Bass .10 .03
112 Jeff Brantley .10 .03
113 John Burkett .10 .03
114 Will Clark .40 .12
115 Royce Clayton .10 .03
116 Mike Jackson .10 .03
117 Darren Lewis .10 .03
118 Bill Swift .10 .03
119 Robby Thompson .10 .03
120 Matt Williams .15 .04
121 Brady Anderson .15 .04
122 Glenn Davis .10 .03
123 Mike Devereaux .10 .03
124 Chris Hoiles .10 .03
125 Sam Horn .10 .03
126 Ben McDonald .10 .03
127 Mike Mussina .40 .12
128 Gregg Olson .10 .03
129 Cal Ripken Jr. 1.25 .35
130 Rick Sutcliffe .15 .04
131 Wade Boggs .25 .07
132 Roger Clemens .75 .23
133 Greg A. Harris .10 .03
134 Tim Naehring .10 .03
135 Tony Pena .10 .03
136 Phil Plantier .10 .03
137 Jeff Reardon .15 .04
138 Jody Reed .10 .03
139 Mo Vaughn .15 .04
140 Frank Viola .15 .04
141 Jim Abbott .25 .07
142 Hubie Brooks .10 .03
143 Chad Curtis RC .25 .07
144 Gary DiSarcina .10 .03
145 Chuck Finley .15 .04
146 Bryan Harvey .10 .03
147 Von Hayes .10 .03
148 Mark Langston .10 .03
149 Lance Parrish .15 .04
150 Lee Stevens .10 .03
151 George Bell .10 .03
152 Alex Fernandez .10 .03
153 Greg Hibbard .10 .03
154 Lance Johnson .10 .03
155 Kirk McCaskill .10 .03
156 Tim Raines .15 .04
157 Steve Sax .10 .03
158 Bobby Thigpen .10 .03
159 Frank Thomas .40 .12
160 Robin Ventura .15 .04
161 Sandy Alomar Jr. .15 .04
162 Jack Armstrong .10 .03
163 Carlos Baerga .10 .03
164 Albert Belle .15 .04
165 Alex Cole .10 .03
166 Glenallen Hill .10 .03
167 Mark Lewis .10 .03
168 Kenny Lofton .25 .07
169 Paul Sorrento .15 .04
170 Mark Whiten .10 .03
171 Milt Cuyler .10 .03
172 Rob Deer .10 .03
173 Cecil Fielder .15 .04
174 Travis Fryman .15 .04
175 Mike Henneman .10 .03
176 Tony Phillips .10 .03
177 Frank Tanana .10 .03
178 Mickey Tettleton .10 .03
179 Alan Trammell .15 .04
180 Lou Whitaker .15 .04
181 George Brett 1.00 .30
182 Tom Gordon .10 .03
183 Mark Gubicza .10 .03
184 Gregg Jefferies .10 .03
185 Wally Joyner .15 .04
186 Brent Mayne .10 .03
187 Brian McRae .10 .03
188 Kevin McReynolds .10 .03
189 Keith Miller .10 .03
190 Jeff Montgomery .10 .03
191 Dante Bichette .15 .04
192 Ricky Bones .10 .03
193 Scott Fletcher .10 .03
194 Paul Molitor .25 .07
195 Jaime Navarro .10 .03
196 Franklin Stubbs .10 .03
197 B.J. Surhoff .15 .04
198 Greg Vaughn .10 .03
199 Bill Wegman .10 .03
200 Robin Yount .60 .18
201 Rick Aguilera .15 .04
202 Scott Erickson .15 .04
203 Greg Gagne .10 .03
204 Brian Harper .10 .03
205 Kent Hrbek .15 .04
206 Scott Leius .10 .03
207 Shane Mack .10 .03
208 Pat Mahomes RC .25 .07
209 Kirby Puckett .40 .12
210 John Smiley .10 .03
211 Mike Gallego .10 .03
212 Charlie Hayes .10 .03
213 Pat Kelly .10 .03
214 Roberto Kelly .10 .03
215 Kevin Maas .10 .03
216 Don Mattingly 1.00 .30
217 Matt Nokes .10 .03
218 Melido Perez .10 .03
219 Scott Sanderson .10 .03
220 Danny Tartabull .10 .03
221 Harold Baines .15 .04
222 Jose Canseco .40 .12
223 Dennis Eckersley .15 .04
224 Dave Henderson .10 .03
225 Carney Lansford .15 .04
226 Mark McGwire 1.00 .30
227 Mike Moore .10 .03
228 Randy Ready .10 .03
229 Terry Steinbach .10 .03
230 Dave Stewart .15 .04
231 Jay Buhner .15 .04
232 Ken Griffey Jr. .60 .18
233 Erik Hanson .10 .03
234 Randy Johnson .40 .12
235 Edgar Martinez .25 .07
236 Tino Martinez .25 .07
237 Kevin Mitchell .10 .03
238 Pete O'Brien .10 .03
239 Harold Reynolds .15 .04
240 David Valle .10 .03
241 Julio Franco .15 .04
242 Juan Gonzalez .25 .07
243 Jose Guzman .10 .03
244 Rafael Palmeiro .25 .07
245 Dean Palmer .15 .04
246 Ivan Rodriguez .40 .12
247 Jeff Russell .10 .03
248 Nolan Ryan 1.50 .45
249 Ruben Sierra .10 .03
250 Dickie Thon .10 .03
251 Roberto Alomar .25 .07
252 Derek Bell .15 .04
253 Pat Borders .10 .03
254 Joe Carter .15 .04
255 Kelly Gruber .10 .03
256 Juan Guzman .10 .03
257 Jack Morris .15 .04
258 John Olerud .15 .04
259 Devon White .15 .04
260 Dave Winfield .15 .04
261 Checklist .10 .03
262 Checklist .10 .03
263 Checklist .10 .03
264 History Card .10 .03

1992 Studio Heritage

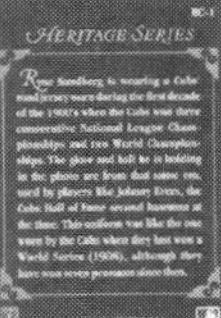

The 1992 Studio Heritage standard-size insert set presents today's star players dressed in vintage uniforms. Cards numbered 1-8 were randomly inserted in 12-card foil packs while cards numbered 9-14 were inserted one per pack in 28-card jumbo packs. The fronts display sepia-toned portraits of the players dressed in vintage uniforms of their current teams. The cards are numbered on the back with a "BC" prefix.

Nm-Mt Ex-Mt
COMPLETE SET (14) 25.00 7.50
COMP.FOIL SET (8) 15.00 4.50
COMP.JUMBO SET (6) 10.00 3.00
BC1 Ryne Sandberg 3.00 .90
BC2 Carlton Fisk 2.00 .60
BC3 Wade Boggs 1.25 .35
BC4 Jose Canseco 2.00 .60
BC5 Don Mattingly 5.00 1.50
BC6 Darryl Strawberry .75 .23
BC7 Cal Ripken 6.00 1.80
BC8 Will Clark 2.00 .60
BC9 Andre Dawson .75 .23
BC10 Andy Van Slyke .75 .23
BC11 Paul Molitor 1.25 .35
BC12 Jeff Bagwell 2.00 .60
BC13 Darren Daulton .75 .23
BC14 Kirby Puckett 2.00 .60

1993 Studio

The 220 standard-size cards comprising this set feature borderless fronts with posed color player photos that are cut out and superposed upon a closeup of an embroidered team logo. The key Rookie Card in this set is J.T. Snow.

Nm-Mt Ex-Mt
COMPLETE SET (220) 20.00 6.00
1 Dennis Eckersley .25 .07
2 Chad Curtis .15 .04
3 Eric Anthony .15 .04
4 Roberto Alomar .40 .12
5 Steve Avery .15 .04
6 Cal Eldred .15 .04
7 Bernard Gilkey .15 .04
8 Steve Buechele .15 .04
9 Brett Butler .25 .07
10 Terry Mulholland .15 .04
11 Moises Alou .25 .07
12 Barry Bonds 1.50 .45
13 Sandy Alomar Jr. .15 .04
14 Chris Bosio .15 .04
15 Scott Sanderson .15 .04
16 Bobby Bonilla .25 .07
17 Brady Anderson .25 .07
18 Derek Bell .15 .04
19 Wes Chamberlain .15 .04
20 Jay Bell .25 .07
21 Kevin Brown .25 .07
22 Roger Clemens 1.25 .35
23 Roberto Kelly .15 .04
24 Dante Bichette .25 .07
25 George Brett 1.50 .45
26 Rob Deer .15 .04
27 Brian Harper .15 .04
28 George Bell .15 .04
29 Jim Abbott .40 .12
30 Dave Henderson .15 .04
31 Wade Boggs .40 .12
32 Chili Davis .25 .07
33 Ellis Burks .25 .07
34 Jeff Bagwell .40 .12
35 Kent Hrbek .25 .07
36 Pat Borders .15 .04
37 Cecil Fielder .25 .07
38 Sid Bream .15 .04
39 Greg Gagne .15 .04
40 Darryl Hamilton .15 .04
41 Jerald Clark .15 .04
42 Mark Grace .40 .12
43 Barry Larkin .40 .12
44 John Burkett .15 .04
45 Scott Cooper .15 .04
46 Mike Lansing RC .25 .07
47 Jose Canseco .60 .18
48 Will Clark .60 .18
49 Carlos Garcia .15 .04
50 Carlos Baerga .15 .04
51 Darren Daulton .25 .07
52 Jay Buhner .25 .07
53 Andy Benes .15 .04
54 Jeff Conine .25 .07
55 Mike Devereaux .15 .04
56 Vince Coleman .15 .04
57 Terry Steinbach .15 .04
58 J.T. Snow RC .40 .12
59 Greg Swindell .15 .04
60 Devon White .25 .07
61 John Smoltz .40 .12
62 Todd Zeile .15 .04
63 Rick Wilkins .15 .04
64 Tim Wallach .15 .04
65 John Wetteland .25 .07
66 Matt Williams .25 .07
67 Paul Sorrento .15 .04
68 David Valle .15 .04
69 Walt Weiss .15 .04
70 John Franco .25 .07
71 Nolan Ryan 2.50 .75
72 Frank Viola .25 .07
73 Chris Sabo .15 .04
74 David Nied .15 .04
75 Kevin McReynolds .15 .04
76 Lou Whitaker .25 .07
77 Dave Winfield .25 .07
78 Robin Ventura .25 .07
79 Spike Owen .15 .04
80 Cal Ripken Jr. 2.00 .60
81 Dan Walters .15 .04
82 Mitch Williams .15 .04
83 Tim Wakefield .60 .18
84 Rickey Henderson .60 .18
85 Gary DiSarcina .15 .04
86 Craig Biggio .40 .12
87 Joe Carter .25 .07
88 Ron Gant .25 .07
89 John Jaha .15 .04
90 Gregg Jefferies .15 .04
91 Jose Guzman .15 .04
92 Eric Karros .25 .07
93 Wil Cordero .15 .04
94 Royce Clayton .15 .04
95 Albert Belle .25 .07
96 Ken Griffey Jr. 1.00 .30
97 Orestes Destrade .15 .04
98 Tony Fernandez .15 .04
99 Leo Gomez .15 .04
100 Tony Gwynn .75 .23
101 Len Dykstra .25 .07
102 Jeff King .15 .04
103 Julio Franco .25 .07
104 Andre Dawson .25 .07
105 Randy Milligan .15 .04
106 Alex Cole .15 .04
107 Phil Hiatt .15 .04
108 Travis Fryman .25 .07
109 Chuck Knoblauch .25 .07
110 Bo Jackson .60 .18
111 Pat Kelly .15 .04
112 Bret Saberhagen .25 .07
113 Ruben Sierra .15 .04
114 Tim Salmon .40 .12
115 Doug Jones .15 .04
116 Ed Sprague .15 .04
117 Terry Pendleton .25 .07
118 Robin Yount 1.00 .30
119 Mark Whiten .15 .04
120 Checklist 1-110 .15 .04
121 Sammy Sosa 1.00 .30
122 Darryl Strawberry .25 .07
123 Larry Walker .40 .12
124 Robby Thompson .15 .04
125 Carlos Martinez .15 .04

126 Edgar Martinez .40 .12
127 Benito Santiago .25 .07
128 Howard Johnson .15 .04
129 Harold Reynolds .25 .07
130 Craig Shipley .15 .04
131 Curt Schilling .25 .07
132 Andy Van Slyke .25 .07
133 Ivan Rodriguez .60 .18
134 Mo Vaughn .25 .07
135 Bip Roberts .15 .04
136 Charlie Hayes .15 .04
137 Brian McRae .15 .04
138 Mickey Tettleton .15 .04
139 Frank Thomas .60 .18
140 Paul O'Neill .40 .12
141 Mark McGwire 1.50 .45
142 Damion Easley .15 .04
143 Ken Caminiti .25 .07
144 Juan Guzman .15 .04
145 Tom Glavine .40 .12
146 Pat Listach .15 .04
147 Lee Smith .25 .07
148 Derrick May .15 .04
149 Ramon Martinez .15 .04
150 Delino DeShields .15 .04
151 Kirt Manwaring .15 .04
152 Reggie Jefferson .15 .04
153 Randy Johnson .60 .18
154 Dave Magadan .15 .04
155 Dwight Gooden .25 .07
156 Chris Hoiles .15 .04
157 Fred McGriff .40 .12
158 Dave Hollins .15 .04
159 Al Martin .15 .04
160 Juan Gonzalez .40 .12
161 Mike Greenwell .15 .04
162 Kevin Mitchell .15 .04
163 Andres Galarraga .25 .07
164 Wally Joyner .25 .07
165 Kirk Gibson .25 .07
166 Pedro Munoz .15 .04
167 Ozzie Guillen .15 .04
168 Jimmy Key .25 .07
169 Kevin Seitzer .15 .04
170 Luis Polonia .15 .04
171 Luis Gonzalez .25 .07
172 Paul Molitor .40 .12
173 David Justice .25 .07
174 B.J. Surhoff .25 .07
175 Ray Lankford .15 .04
176 Ryne Sandberg 1.00 .30
177 Jody Reed .15 .04
178 Marquis Grissom .25 .07
179 Willie McGee .25 .07
180 Kenny Lofton .25 .07
181 Junior Felix .15 .04
182 Jose Offerman .15 .04
183 John Kruk .25 .07
184 Orlando Merced .15 .04
185 Rafael Palmeiro .40 .12
186 Billy Hatcher .15 .04
187 Joe Oliver .15 .04
188 Joe Girardi .15 .04
189 Jose Lind .15 .04
190 Harold Baines .25 .07
191 Mike Pagliarulo .15 .04
192 Lance Johnson .15 .04
193 Don Mattingly 1.50 .45
194 Doug Drabek .15 .04
195 John Olerud .25 .07
196 Greg Maddux 1.00 .30
197 Greg Vaughn .15 .04
198 Tom Pagnozzi .15 .04
199 Willie Wilson .15 .04
200 Jack McDowell .15 .04
201 Mike Piazza 1.50 .45
202 Mike Mussina .40 .12
203 Charles Nagy .15 .04
204 Tino Martinez .40 .12
205 Charlie Hough .25 .07
206 Todd Hundley .15 .04
207 Gary Sheffield .25 .07
208 Mickey Morandini .15 .04
209 Don Slaught .15 .04
210 Dean Palmer .25 .07
211 Jose Rijo .15 .04
212 Vinny Castilla .25 .07
213 Tony Phillips .15 .04
214 Kirby Puckett .60 .18
215 Tim Raines .25 .07
216 Otis Nixon .15 .04
217 Ozzie Smith 1.00 .30
218 Jose Vizcaino .15 .04
219 Randy Tomlin .15 .04
220 Checklist 111-220 .15 .04

1993 Studio Heritage

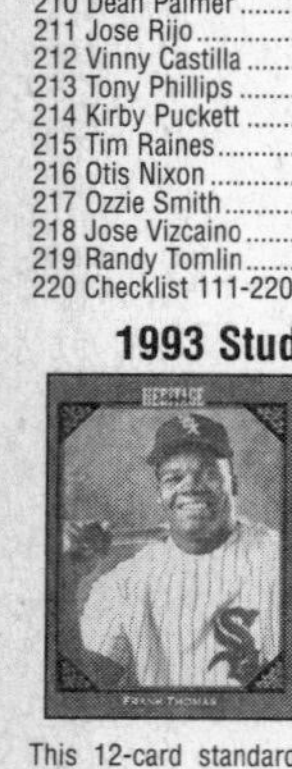

This 12-card standard-size set was randomly inserted in all 1993 Leaf Studio foil packs, and features sepia-toned portraits of current players in vintage team uniforms.

Nm-Mt Ex-Mt
COMPLETE SET (12) 30.00 9.00
1 George Brett 10.00 3.00
2 Juan Gonzalez 2.50 .75
3 Roger Clemens 8.00 2.40
4 Mark McGwire 10.00 3.00
5 Mark Grace 2.50 .75
6 Ozzie Smith 6.00 1.80
7 Barry Larkin 2.50 .75
8 Frank Thomas 4.00 1.20
9 Carlos Baerga 1.00 .30
10 Eric Karros 1.50 .45
11 J.T. Snow 2.50 .75
12 John Kruk 1.50 .45

1993 Studio Silhouettes

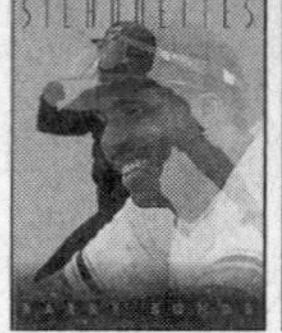

The 1993 Studio Silhouettes 10-card standard-size set was inserted one per 20-card Studio jumbo pack.

Nm-Mt Ex-Mt
COMPLETE SET (10) 25.00 7.50
1 Frank Thomas 2.00 .60
2 Barry Bonds 5.00 1.50
3 Jeff Bagwell 1.25 .35
4 Juan Gonzalez 1.25 .35
5 Travis Fryman .75 .23
6 J.T. Snow 1.25 .35
7 John Kruk .75 .23
8 Jeff Blauser .50 .15
9 Mike Piazza 5.00 1.50
10 Nolan Ryan 8.00 2.40

1993 Studio Superstars on Canvas

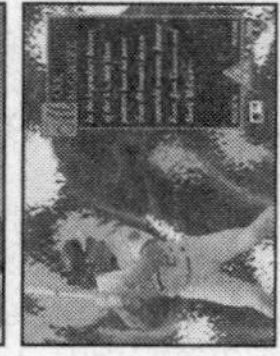

This ten-card standard-size set was randomly inserted in 1993 Studio hobby and retail foil packs.

Nm-Mt Ex-Mt
COMPLETE SET (10) 40.00 12.00
1 Ken Griffey Jr. 6.00 1.80
2 Jose Canseco 4.00 1.20
3 Mark McGwire 10.00 3.00
4 Mike Mussina 2.50 .75
5 Joe Carter 1.50 .45
6 Frank Thomas 4.00 1.20
7 Darren Daulton 1.50 .45
8 Mark Grace 2.50 .75
9 Andres Galarraga 1.50 .45
10 Barry Bonds 10.00 3.00

1993 Studio Thomas

The 1993 Studio Frank Thomas five-card standard-size set was randomly inserted in all 1993 Studio packs. The cards feature borderless posed black-and-white portraits of the Chicago White Sox slugging first baseman.

Nm-Mt Ex-Mt
COMPLETE SET (5) 8.00 2.40
COMMON THOMAS (1-5) 2.00 .60

1994 Studio

The 1994 Studio set consists of 220 full-bleed, standard-size cards. Card fronts offer a player photo with his jersey hanging in a locker room setting in the background. The set is grouped alphabetically within teams.

Nm-Mt Ex-Mt
COMPLETE SET (220) 15.00 4.50
1 Dennis Eckersley .30 .09
2 Brent Gates .15 .04
3 Rickey Henderson .75 .23
4 Mark McGwire 2.00 .60
5 Troy Neel .15 .04
6 Ruben Sierra .15 .04
7 Terry Steinbach .15 .04
8 Chad Curtis .15 .04
9 Chili Davis .30 .09
10 Gary DiSarcina .15 .04
11 Damion Easley .15 .04
12 Bo Jackson .75 .23
13 Mark Langston .15 .04
14 Eduardo Perez .15 .04
15 Tim Salmon .50 .15
16 Jeff Bagwell .50 .15
17 Craig Biggio .50 .15
18 Ken Caminiti .30 .09
19 Andujar Cedeno .15 .04
20 Doug Drabek .15 .04
21 Steve Finley .30 .09
22 Luis Gonzalez .30 .09
23 Darryl Kile .30 .09
24 Roberto Alomar .50 .15
25 Pat Borders .15 .04
26 Joe Carter .30 .09
27 Carlos Delgado .50 .15
28 Pat Hentgen .15 .04
29 Paul Molitor .50 .15
30 John Olerud .30 .09
31 Ed Sprague .15 .04
32 Devon White .30 .09
33 Steve Avery .15 .04
34 Tom Glavine .50 .15
35 David Justice .30 .09
36 Roberto Kelly .15 .04
37 Ryan Klesko .30 .09
38 Javier Lopez .30 .09
39 Greg Maddux 1.25 .35
40 Fred McGriff .50 .15
41 Terry Pendleton .30 .09
42 Ricky Bones .15 .04
43 Darryl Hamilton .15 .04
44 Brian Harper .15 .04
45 John Jaha .15 .04
46 Dave Nilsson .15 .04
47 Kevin Seitzer .15 .04
48 Greg Vaughn .15 .04
49 Turner Ward .15 .04
50 Bernard Gilkey .15 .04
51 Gregg Jefferies .15 .04
52 Ray Lankford .15 .04
53 Tom Pagnozzi .15 .04
54 Ozzie Smith 1.25 .35
55 Bob Tewksbury .15 .04
56 Mark Whiten .15 .04
57 Todd Zeile .15 .04
58 Steve Buechele .15 .04
59 Shawon Dunston .15 .04
60 Mark Grace .50 .15
61 Derrick May .15 .04
62 Karl Rhodes .15 .04
63 Ryne Sandberg 1.25 .35
64 Sammy Sosa 1.25 .35
65 Rick Wilkins .15 .04
66 Brett Butler .30 .09
67 Delino DeShields .15 .04
68 Orel Hershiser .30 .09
69 Eric Karros .30 .09
70 Raul Mondesi .30 .09
71 Jose Offerman .15 .04
72 Mike Piazza 1.50 .45
73 Tim Wallach .15 .04
74 Moises Alou .30 .09
75 Sean Berry .15 .04
76 Wil Cordero .15 .04
77 Cliff Floyd .30 .09
78 Marquis Grissom .30 .09
79 Ken Hill .15 .04
80 Larry Walker .50 .15
81 John Wetteland .30 .09
82 Rod Beck .15 .04
83 Barry Bonds 2.00 .60
84 Royce Clayton .15 .04
85 Darren Lewis .15 .04
86 Willie McGee .30 .09
87 Bill Swift .15 .04
88 Robby Thompson .15 .04
89 Matt Williams .30 .09
90 Sandy Alomar Jr. .15 .04
91 Carlos Baerga .15 .04
92 Albert Belle .30 .09
93 Kenny Lofton .30 .09
94 Eddie Murray .75 .23
95 Manny Ramirez .50 .15
96 Paul Sorrento .15 .04
97 Jim Thome .75 .23
98 Rich Amaral .15 .04
99 Eric Anthony .15 .04
100 Jay Buhner .30 .09
101 Ken Griffey Jr. 1.25 .35
102 Randy Johnson .75 .23
103 Edgar Martinez .50 .15
104 Tino Martinez .50 .15
105 Kurt Abbott RC .30 .09
106 Bret Barberie .15 .04
107 Chuck Carr .15 .04
108 Jeff Conine .30 .09
109 Chris Hammond .15 .04
110 Bryan Harvey .15 .04
111 Benito Santiago .30 .09
112 Gary Sheffield .30 .09
113 Bobby Bonilla .30 .09
114 Dwight Gooden .30 .09
115 Todd Hundley .15 .04
116 Bobby Jones .15 .04
117 Jeff Kent .30 .09
118 Kevin McReynolds .15 .04
119 Bret Saberhagen .15 .04
120 Ryan Thompson .15 .04
121 Harold Baines .30 .09
122 Mike Devereaux .15 .04
123 Jeffrey Hammonds .15 .04
124 Ben McDonald .15 .04
125 Mike Mussina .50 .15
126 Rafael Palmeiro .50 .15
127 Cal Ripken Jr. 2.50 .75
128 Lee Smith .30 .09
129 Brad Ausmus .15 .04
130 Derek Bell .15 .04
131 Andy Benes .15 .04
132 Tony Gwynn 1.00 .30
133 Trevor Hoffman .30 .09
134 Scott Livingstone .15 .04
135 Phil Plantier .15 .04
136 Darren Daulton .30 .09
137 Mariano Duncan .15 .04
138 Lenny Dykstra .30 .09
139 Dave Hollins .15 .04
140 Pete Incaviglia .15 .04
141 Danny Jackson .15 .04
142 John Kruk .30 .09
143 Kevin Stocker .15 .04
144 Jay Bell .30 .09
145 Carlos Garcia .15 .04
146 Jeff King .15 .04
147 Al Martin .15 .04
148 Orlando Merced .15 .04
149 Don Slaught .15 .04
150 Andy Van Slyke .30 .09
151 Kevin Brown .30 .09
152 Jose Canseco .75 .23
153 Will Clark .75 .23
154 Juan Gonzalez .50 .15
155 David Hulse .15 .04
156 Dean Palmer .30 .09
157 Ivan Rodriguez .75 .23
158 Kenny Rogers .30 .09
159 Roger Clemens 1.50 .45
160 Scott Cooper .15 .04
161 Andre Dawson .30 .09
162 Mike Greenwell .15 .04
163 Otis Nixon .15 .04
164 Aaron Sele .15 .04
165 John Valentin .15 .04
166 Mo Vaughn .30 .09
167 Bret Boone .30 .09
168 Barry Larkin .50 .15
169 Kevin Mitchell .15 .04
170 Hal Morris .15 .04
171 Jose Rijo .15 .04
172 Deion Sanders .50 .15
173 Reggie Sanders .15 .04
174 John Smiley .15 .04
175 Dante Bichette .30 .09
176 Ellis Burks .30 .09
177 Andres Galarraga .30 .09
178 Joe Girardi .15 .04
179 Charlie Hayes .15 .04
180 Roberto Mejia .15 .04
181 Walt Weiss .15 .04
182 David Cone .30 .09
183 Gary Gaetti .30 .09
184 Greg Gagne .15 .04
185 Felix Jose .15 .04
186 Wally Joyner .30 .09
187 Mike Macfarlane .15 .04
188 Brian McRae .15 .04
189 Eric Davis .30 .09
190 Cecil Fielder .30 .09
191 Travis Fryman .30 .09
192 Tony Phillips .15 .04
193 Mickey Tettleton .15 .04
194 Alan Trammell .30 .09
195 Lou Whitaker .30 .09
196 Kent Hrbek .30 .09
197 Chuck Knoblauch .30 .09
198 Shane Mack .15 .04
199 Pat Meares .15 .04
200 Kirby Puckett .75 .23
201 Matt Walbeck .15 .04
202 Dave Winfield .30 .09
203 Wilson Alvarez .15 .04
204 Alex Fernandez .15 .04
205 Julio Franco .30 .09
206 Ozzie Guillen .15 .04
207 Jack McDowell .15 .04
208 Tim Raines .30 .09
209 Frank Thomas .75 .23
210 Robin Ventura .30 .09
211 Jim Abbott .50 .15
212 Wade Boggs .50 .15
213 Pat Kelly .15 .04
214 Jimmy Key .30 .09
215 Don Mattingly 2.00 .60
216 Paul O'Neill .50 .15
217 Mike Stanley .15 .04
218 Danny Tartabull .15 .04
219 Checklist .15 .04
220 Checklist .15 .04

1994 Studio Editor's Choice

This eight-card standard-sized set was randomly inserted in foil packs at a rate of one in 36. These cards are acetate and were designed much like a film strip with black borders.

Nm-Mt Ex-Mt
COMPLETE SET (8) 30.00 9.00
1 Barry Bonds 10.00 3.00
2 Frank Thomas 4.00 1.20
3 Ken Griffey Jr. 6.00 1.80
4 Andres Galarraga 1.50 .45
5 Juan Gonzalez 2.50 .75
6 Tim Salmon 2.50 .75
7 Paul O'Neill 2.50 .75
8 Mike Piazza 8.00 2.40

1994 Studio Heritage

Each player in this eight-card insert set (randomly inserted in foil packs at a rate of one in nine) is modelling a vintage uniform of his team. The year of the uniform is noted in gold lettering at the top with a gold Heritage Collection logo at the bottom.

Nm-Mt Ex-Mt
COMPLETE SET (8) 12.00 3.60
1 Barry Bonds 5.00 1.50
2 Frank Thomas 2.00 .60
3 Joe Carter .75 .23
4 Don Mattingly 5.00 1.50
5 Ryne Sandberg 3.00 .90
6 Javier Lopez .75 .23
7 Gregg Jefferies .40 .12
8 Mike Mussina 1.25 .35

1994 Studio Series Stars

This 10-card acetate set showcases top stars and was limited to 10,000 of each card. They were randomly inserted in foil packs at a rate of one in 60. The player cutout is surrounded by a small circle of stars with the player's name at the top. The team name, limited edition notation and the Series Stars logo are at the bottom. The back of the cutout contains a photo. Gold versions of this set were more difficult to obtain in packs (one in 120, 5,000 total).

Nm-Mt Ex-Mt
COMPLETE SET (10) 120.00 36.00
*GOLD: .75X TO 2X BASIC SERIES STARS
GOLD STATED ODDS 1:120
GOLD PRINT RUN 5000 SERIAL #'d SETS
1 Tony Gwynn 10.00 3.00
2 Barry Bonds 20.00 6.00
3 Frank Thomas 8.00 2.40
4 Ken Griffey Jr. 12.00 3.60
5 Joe Carter 3.00 .90
6 Mike Piazza 15.00 4.50
7 Cal Ripken Jr. 25.00 7.50
8 Greg Maddux 12.00 3.60
9 Juan Gonzalez 5.00 1.50
10 Don Mattingly 20.00 6.00

1995 Studio

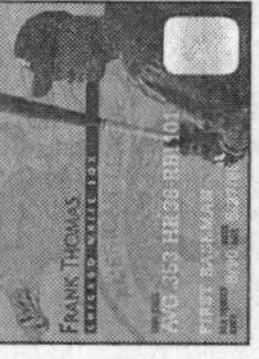

This 200-card horizontal set was issued by Donruss for the fifth consecutive year. Using a different design than past Studio issues, these cards were designed similarly to credit cards. The cards were issued in five-card packs with a suggested retail price of $1.49. There are no Rookie Cards in this set.

Nm-Mt Ex-Mt
COMPLETE SET (200) 50.00 15.00
1 Frank Thomas 1.00 .30
2 Jeff Bagwell .60 .18
3 Don Mattingly 2.50 .75
4 Mike Piazza 1.50 .45
5 Ken Griffey Jr. 1.50 .45
6 Greg Maddux 1.50 .45
7 Barry Bonds 2.50 .75
8 Cal Ripken Jr. 3.00 .90
9 Jose Canseco 1.00 .30
10 Paul Molitor .60 .18
11 Kenny Lofton .40 .12
12 Will Clark 1.00 .30
13 Tim Salmon .60 .18
14 Joe Carter .40 .12
15 Albert Belle .40 .12
16 Roger Clemens 2.00 .60
17 Roberto Alomar .60 .18
18 Alex Rodriguez 2.50 .75
19 Raul Mondesi .40 .12
20 Deion Sanders .60 .18
21 Juan Gonzalez .60 .18
22 Kirby Puckett 1.00 .30
23 Fred McGriff .60 .18
24 Matt Williams .40 .12
25 Tony Gwynn 1.25 .35
26 Cliff Floyd .40 .12
27 Travis Fryman .40 .12
28 Shawn Green .40 .12
29 Mike Mussina .60 .18
30 Bob Hamelin .20 .06
31 David Justice .40 .12
32 Manny Ramirez .60 .18
33 David Cone .40 .12
34 Marquis Grissom .40 .12
35 Moises Alou .40 .12
36 Carlos Baerga .20 .06
37 Barry Larkin .60 .18
38 Robin Ventura .40 .12
39 Mo Vaughn .40 .12
40 Jeffrey Hammonds .20 .06
41 Ozzie Smith 1.50 .45
42 Andres Galarraga .40 .12
43 Carlos Delgado .40 .12
44 Lenny Dykstra .40 .12
45 Cecil Fielder .40 .12
46 Wade Boggs .60 .18
47 Gregg Jefferies .20 .06
48 Randy Johnson 1.00 .30
49 Rafael Palmeiro .60 .18
50 Craig Biggio .60 .18
51 Steve Avery .20 .06
52 Ricky Bottalico .20 .06
53 Chris Gomez .20 .06
54 Carlos Garcia .20 .06
55 Brian Anderson .20 .06
56 Wilson Alvarez .20 .06
57 Roberto Kelly .20 .06
58 Larry Walker .60 .18
59 Dean Palmer .40 .12
60 Rick Aguilera .20 .06
61 Javier Lopez .40 .12
62 Shawon Dunston .20 .06
63 Wm. VanLandingham .20 .06
64 Jeff Kent .40 .12
65 David McCarty .20 .06
66 Armando Benitez .40 .12

67 Brett Butler .40 .12
68 Bernard Gilkey .20 .06
69 Joey Hamilton .20 .06
70 Chad Curtis .20 .06
71 Dante Bichette .40 .12
72 Chuck Carr .20 .06
73 Pedro Martinez 1.00 .30
74 Ramon Martinez .20 .06
75 Rondell White .40 .12
76 Alex Fernandez .20 .06
77 Dennis Martinez .40 .12
78 Sammy Sosa 1.50 .45
79 Bernie Williams .60 .18
80 Lou Whitaker .40 .12
81 Kurt Abbott .20 .06
82 Tino Martinez .60 .18
83 Willie Greene .20 .06
84 Garret Anderson .40 .12
85 Jose Rijo .20 .06
86 Jeff Montgomery .20 .06
87 Mark Langston .20 .06
88 Reggie Sanders .20 .06
89 Rusty Greer .40 .12
90 Delino DeShields .20 .06
91 Jason Bere .20 .06
92 Lee Smith .40 .12
93 Devon White .40 .12
94 John Wetteland .40 .12
95 Luis Gonzalez .40 .12
96 Greg Vaughn .20 .06
97 Lance Johnson .20 .06
98 Alan Trammell .40 .12
99 Bret Saberhagen .40 .12
100 Jack McDowell .20 .06
101 Trevor Hoffman .40 .12
102 Dave Nilsson .20 .06
103 Bryan Harvey .20 .06
104 Chuck Knoblauch .40 .12
105 Bobby Bonilla .40 .12
106 Hal Morris .20 .06
107 Mark Whiten .20 .06
108 Phil Plantier .20 .06
109 Ryan Klesko .40 .12
110 Greg Gagne .20 .06
111 Ruben Sierra .20 .06
112 J.R. Phillips .20 .06
113 Terry Steinbach .20 .06
114 Jay Buhner .40 .12
115 Ken Caminiti .40 .12
116 Gary DiSarcina .20 .06
117 Ivan Rodriguez 1.00 .30
118 Bip Roberts .20 .06
119 Jay Bell .40 .12
120 Ken Hill .20 .06
121 Mike Greenwell .20 .06
122 Rick Wilkins .20 .06
123 Rickey Henderson 1.00 .30
124 Dave Hollins .20 .06
125 Terry Pendleton .40 .12
126 Rich Becker .20 .06
127 Billy Ashley .20 .06
128 Derek Bell .20 .06
129 Dennis Eckersley .40 .12
130 Andujar Cedeno .20 .06
131 John Jaha .20 .06
132 Chuck Finley .40 .12
133 Steve Finley .40 .12
134 Danny Tartabull .20 .06
135 Jeff Conine .40 .12
136 Jon Lieber .20 .06
137 Jim Abbott .60 .18
138 Steve Trachsel .20 .06
139 Bret Boone .40 .12
140 Charles Johnson .40 .12
141 Mark McGwire 2.50 .75
142 Eddie Murray 1.00 .30
143 Doug Drabek .20 .06
144 Steve Cooke .20 .06
145 Kevin Seitzer .20 .06
146 Rod Beck .20 .06
147 Eric Karros .40 .12
148 Tim Raines .40 .12
149 Joe Girardi .20 .06
150 Aaron Sele .20 .06
151 Robby Thompson .20 .06
152 Chan Ho Park .40 .12
153 Ellis Burks .40 .12
154 Brian McRae .20 .06
155 Jimmy Key .40 .12
156 Rico Brogna .20 .06
157 Ozzie Guillen .20 .06
158 Chili Davis .40 .12
159 Darren Daulton .40 .12
160 Chipper Jones 1.00 .30
161 Walt Weiss .20 .06
162 Paul O'Neill .60 .18
163 Al Martin .20 .06
164 John Valentin .20 .06
165 Tim Wallach .20 .06
166 Scott Erickson .20 .06
167 Ryan Thompson .20 .06
168 Todd Zeile .20 .06
169 Scott Cooper .20 .06
170 Matt Mieske .20 .06
171 Allen Watson .20 .06
172 Brian L.Hunter .20 .06
173 Kevin Stocker .20 .06
174 Cal Eldred .20 .06
175 Tony Phillips .20 .06
176 Ben McDonald .20 .06
177 Mark Grace .60 .18
178 Midre Cummings .20 .06
179 Orlando Merced .20 .06
180 Jeff King .20 .06
181 Gary Sheffield .40 .12
182 Tom Glavine .60 .18
183 Edgar Martinez .60 .18
184 Steve Karsay .20 .06
185 Pat Listach .20 .06
186 Wil Cordero .20 .06
187 Brady Anderson .40 .12
188 Bobby Jones .20 .06
189 Andy Benes .20 .06
190 Ray Lankford .20 .06
191 John Doherty .20 .06
192 Wally Joyner .40 .12
193 Jim Thome 1.00 .30
194 Royce Clayton .20 .06
195 John Olerud .40 .12
196 Steve Buechele .20 .06
197 Harold Baines .40 .12
198 Geronimo Berroa .20 .06
199 Checklist .20 .06
200 Checklist .20 .06

1995 Studio Gold Series

This 50-card set was inserted one per packs. This set parallels the first 50 cards of the regular studio set. The only differences between these cards and the regular issue are they were printed with a gold background and are numbered in the right corner as "X" of 50. Also the words "Studio Gold" are printed in the upper front left corner.

Nm-Mt Ex-Mt
COMPLETE SET (50) 30.00 9.00
*GOLD: .5X TO 1.2X BASIC CARDS ...

1995 Studio Platinum Series

This 25-card set was randomly inserted into packs at a rate of one in 10 packs. This set parallels the first 25 cards of the regular issue. These cards are different from the regular issue in that they have a platinum background, the words "Studio Platinum" in the upper left corner and are numbered on the back as "X" of 25.

Nm-Mt Ex-Mt
*PLATINUM: 2.5X TO 6X BASIC CARDS

1996 Studio

The 1996 Studio set was issued in one series totalling 150 cards and was distributed in seven-card packs. The fronts feature color action player photos with a player portrait in the background.

Nm-Mt Ex-Mt
COMPLETE SET (150) 15.00 4.50
1 Cal Ripken 2.00 .60
2 Alex Gonzalez .25 .07
3 Roger Cedeno .25 .07
4 Todd Hollandsworth .25 .07
5 Gregg Jefferies .25 .07
6 Ryne Sandberg 1.00 .30
7 Eric Karros .25 .07
8 Jeff Conine .25 .07
9 Rafael Palmeiro .40 .12
10 Bip Roberts .25 .07
11 Roger Clemens 1.25 .35
12 Tom Glavine .40 .12
13 Jason Giambi .25 .07
14 Rey Ordonez .25 .07
15 Chan Ho Park .25 .07
16 Vinny Castilla .25 .07
17 Butch Huskey .25 .07
18 Greg Maddux 1.00 .30
19 Bernard Gilkey .25 .07
20 Marquis Grissom .25 .07
21 Chuck Knoblauch .25 .07
22 Ozzie Smith 1.00 .30
23 Garret Anderson .25 .07
24 J.T. Snow .25 .07
25 John Valentin .25 .07
26 Barry Larkin .40 .12
27 Bobby Bonilla .25 .07
28 Todd Zeile .25 .07
29 Roberto Alomar .40 .12
30 Ramon Martinez .25 .07
31 Jeff King .25 .07
32 Dennis Eckersley .25 .07
33 Derek Jeter 1.50 .45
34 Edgar Martinez .40 .12
35 Geronimo Berroa .25 .07
36 Hal Morris .25 .07
37 Troy Percival .25 .07
38 Jason Isringhausen .25 .07
39 Greg Vaughn .25 .07
40 Robin Ventura .25 .07
41 Craig Biggio .40 .12
42 Will Clark .60 .18
43 Sammy Sosa 1.00 .30
44 Bernie Williams .40 .12
45 Kenny Lofton .25 .07
46 Wade Boggs .40 .12
47 Javy Lopez .25 .07
48 Reggie Sanders .25 .07
49 Jeff Bagwell .40 .12
50 Fred McGriff .40 .12
51 Charles Johnson .25 .07
52 Darren Daulton .25 .07
53 Jose Canseco .60 .18
54 Cecil Fielder .25 .07
55 Hideo Nomo .60 .18
56 Tim Salmon .40 .12
57 Carlos Delgado .25 .07
58 David Cone .25 .07
59 Tim Raines .25 .07
60 Lyle Mouton .25 .07
61 Wally Joyner .25 .07
62 Bret Boone .25 .07
63 Raul Mondesi .25 .07
64 Gary Sheffield .25 .07
65 Alex Rodriguez 1.25 .35
66 Russ Davis .25 .07
67 Checklist .25 .07
68 Marty Cordova .25 .07
69 Ruben Sierra .25 .07
70 Jose Mesa .25 .07
71 Matt Williams .25 .07
72 Chipper Jones .60 .18
73 Randy Johnson .60 .18
74 Kirby Puckett .60 .18
75 Jim Edmonds .25 .07
76 Barry Bonds 1.50 .45
77 David Segui .25 .07
78 Larry Walker .40 .12
79 Jason Kendall .25 .07
80 Mike Piazza 1.00 .30
81 Brian L.Hunter .25 .07
82 Julio Franco .25 .07
83 Jay Bell .25 .07
84 Kevin Seitzer .25 .07
85 John Smoltz .40 .12
86 Joe Carter .25 .07
87 Ray Durham .25 .07
88 Carlos Baerga .25 .07
89 Ron Gant .25 .07
90 Orlando Merced .25 .07
91 Lee Smith .25 .07
92 Pedro Martinez .60 .18
93 Frank Thomas .60 .18
94 Al Martin .25 .07
95 Chad Curtis .25 .07
96 Eddie Murray .60 .18
97 Rusty Greer .25 .07
98 Jay Buhner .25 .07
99 Rico Brogna .25 .07
100 Todd Hundley .25 .07
101 Moises Alou .25 .07
102 Chili Davis .25 .07
103 Ismael Valdes .25 .07
104 Mo Vaughn .25 .07
105 Juan Gonzalez .40 .12
106 Mark Grudzielanek .25 .07
107 Derek Bell .25 .07
108 Shawn Green .25 .07
109 David Justice .25 .07
110 Paul O'Neill .40 .12
111 Kevin Appier .25 .07
112 Ray Lankford .25 .07
113 Travis Fryman .25 .07
114 Manny Ramirez .40 .12
115 Brooks Kieschnick .25 .07
116 Ken Griffey Jr. 1.00 .30
117 Jeffrey Hammonds .25 .07
118 Mark McGwire 1.50 .45
119 Denny Neagle .25 .07
120 Quilvio Veras .25 .07
121 Alan Benes .25 .07
122 Rondell White .25 .07
123 Osvaldo Fernandez RC .25 .07
124 Andres Galarraga .25 .07
125 Johnny Damon .40 .12
126 Lenny Dykstra .25 .07
127 Jason Schmidt .40 .12
128 Mike Mussina .40 .12
129 Ken Caminiti .25 .07
130 Michael Tucker .25 .07
131 LaTroy Hawkins .25 .07
132 Checklist .25 .07
133 Delino DeShields .25 .07
134 Dave Nilsson .25 .07
135 Jack McDowell .25 .07
136 Joey Hamilton .25 .07
137 Dante Bichette .25 .07
138 Paul Molitor .40 .12
139 Ivan Rodriguez .60 .18
140 Mark Grace .40 .12
141 Paul Wilson .25 .07
142 Orel Hershiser .25 .07
143 Albert Belle .25 .07
144 Tino Martinez .40 .12
145 Tony Gwynn .75 .23
146 George Arias .25 .07
147 Brian Jordan .25 .07
148 Brian McRae .25 .07
149 Rickey Henderson .60 .18
150 Ryan Klesko .25 .07

1996 Studio Bronze Press Proofs

Randomly inserted in packs, this 150-card Bronze set is parallel to the regular set and is similar in design with bronze foil stamping. Only 2,000 sets were produced. Prices below refer to Bronze cards.

Nm-Mt Ex-Mt
*STARS: 5X TO 12X BASIC CARDS....

1996 Studio Gold Press Proofs

Randomly inserted in packs at a rate of 1:24, this 150-card set is parallel to the regular set and is similar in design with gold foil stamping. Only 500 sets were produced.

Nm-Mt Ex-Mt
*STARS: 12.5X TO 30X BASIC CARDS

1996 Studio Silver Press Proofs

Randomly inserted in magazine packs, this 150-card set is parallel to the regular set and is similar in design with silver foil stamping. Only 100 sets were produced.

Nm-Mt Ex-Mt
*STARS: 30X TO 80X BASIC CARDS..

1996 Studio Hit Parade

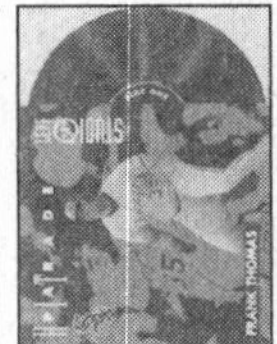

Randomly inserted in packs at a rate of 1:48, cards from this ten-card set feature some of the League's top long-ball hitters. Each card is serial numbered of 5,000 on back.

Nm-Mt Ex-Mt
COMPLETE SET (10) 60.00 18.00
1 Tony Gwynn 8.00 2.40
2 Ken Griffey Jr. 10.00 3.00
3 Frank Thomas 6.00 1.80
4 Jeff Bagwell 4.00 1.20
5 Kirby Puckett 6.00 1.80
6 Mike Piazza 10.00 3.00
7 Barry Bonds 15.00 4.50
8 Albert Belle 2.50 .75
9 Tim Salmon 4.00 1.20
10 Mo Vaughn 2.50 .75

1996 Studio Masterstrokes

Randomly inserted in packs, this eight-card set features some of the League's most popular stars. Each card from this set was also produced in a promo form.

Nm-Mt Ex-Mt
COMPLETE SET (8) 100.00 30.00
1 Tony Gwynn 12.00 3.60
2 Mike Piazza 15.00 4.50
3 Jeff Bagwell 6.00 1.80
4 Manny Ramirez 6.00 1.80
5 Cal Ripken 30.00 9.00
6 Frank Thomas 10.00 3.00
7 Ken Griffey Jr. 15.00 4.50
8 Greg Maddux 15.00 4.50

1996 Studio Stained Glass Stars

Randomly inserted in packs, this 12-card set honors some of the league's hottest superstars. The cards feature color player images on a genuine-look stained glass background and were printed with a clear plastic, die-cut technology.

Nm-Mt Ex-Mt
COMPLETE SET (12) 60.00 18.00
1 Cal Ripken 12.00 3.60
2 Ken Griffey Jr. 6.00 1.80
3 Frank Thomas 4.00 1.20
4 Greg Maddux 6.00 1.80
5 Chipper Jones 4.00 1.20
6 Mike Piazza 6.00 1.80
7 Albert Belle 1.50 .45
8 Jeff Bagwell 2.50 .75
9 Hideo Nomo 4.00 1.20
10 Barry Bonds 10.00 3.00
11 Manny Ramirez 2.50 .75
12 Kenny Lofton 1.50 .45

1997 Studio

The 1997 Studio set was issued in one series totalling 165 cards and was distributed in five-card packs with an 8x10 Studio Portrait for a suggested retail price of $2.49. The fronts feature color player portraits, while the backs carry player information. It is believed that the following cards: 112, 133, 137, 147 and 161 were short printed.

Nm-Mt Ex-Mt
COMPLETE SET (165) 60.00 18.00
SP'S REPORTED BY CASE DEALERS
SP'S NOT CONFIRMED BY MANUFACTURER
SP CL: 112/133/137/147/161
1 Frank Thomas .75 .23
2 Gary Sheffield .30 .09
3 Jason Isringhausen .30 .09
4 Ron Gant .30 .09
5 Andy Pettitte .50 .15
6 Todd Hollandsworth .30 .09
7 Troy Percival .30 .09
8 Mark McGwire 2.00 .60
9 Barry Larkin .50 .15
10 Ken Caminiti .30 .09
11 Paul Molitor .50 .15
12 Travis Fryman .30 .09
13 Kevin Brown .30 .09
14 Robin Ventura .30 .09
15 Andres Galarraga .30 .09
16 Ken Griffey Jr. 1.25 .35
17 Roger Clemens 1.50 .45
18 Alan Benes .30 .09
19 Dave Justice .30 .09
20 Damon Buford .30 .09
21 Mike Piazza 1.25 .35
22 Ray Durham .30 .09
23 Billy Wagner .30 .09
24 Dean Palmer .30 .09
25 David Cone .30 .09
26 Ruben Sierra .30 .09
27 Henry Rodriguez .30 .09
28 Ray Lankford .30 .09
29 Jamey Wright .30 .09
30 Brady Anderson .30 .09
31 Tino Martinez .50 .15
32 Manny Ramirez .50 .15
33 Jeff Conine .30 .09
34 Dante Bichette .30 .09
35 Jose Canseco .75 .23
36 Mo Vaughn .30 .09
37 Sammy Sosa 1.25 .35
38 Mark Grudzielanek .30 .09
39 Mike Mussina .50 .15
40 Bill Pulsipher .30 .09
41 Ryne Sandberg 1.25 .35
42 Rickey Henderson .75 .23
43 Alex Rodriguez 1.25 .35
44 Eddie Murray .75 .23
45 Ernie Young .30 .09
46 Joey Hamilton .30 .09
47 Wade Boggs .50 .15
48 Rusty Greer .30 .09
49 Carlos Delgado .30 .09
50 Ellis Burks .30 .09
51 Cal Ripken 2.50 .75
52 Alex Fernandez .30 .09
53 Wally Joyner .30 .09
54 James Baldwin .30 .09
55 Juan Gonzalez .50 .15
56 John Smoltz .50 .15
57 Omar Vizquel .50 .15
58 Shane Reynolds .30 .09
59 Barry Bonds 2.00 .60
60 Jason Kendall .30 .09
61 Marty Cordova .30 .09
62 Charles Johnson .30 .09
63 John Jaha .30 .09
64 Chan Ho Park .30 .09
65 Jermaine Allensworth .30 .09
66 Mark Grace .50 .15
67 Tim Salmon .50 .15
68 Edgar Martinez .50 .15
69 Marquis Grissom .30 .09
70 Craig Biggio .50 .15
71 Bobby Higginson .30 .09
72 Kevin Seitzer .30 .09
73 Hideo Nomo .75 .23
74 Dennis Eckersley .30 .09
75 Bobby Bonilla .30 .09
76 Dwight Gooden .30 .09
77 Jeff Cirillo .30 .09
78 Brian McRae .30 .09
79 Chipper Jones .75 .23
80 Jeff Fassero .30 .09
81 Fred McGriff .50 .15
82 Garret Anderson .30 .09
83 Eric Karros .30 .09
84 Derek Bell .30 .09
85 Kenny Lofton .30 .09
86 John Mabry .30 .09
87 Pat Hentgen .30 .09
88 Greg Maddux 1.25 .35
89 Jason Giambi .30 .09
90 Al Martin .30 .09
91 Derek Jeter 2.00 .60
92 Rey Ordonez .30 .09
93 Will Clark .75 .23
94 Kevin Appier .30 .09
95 Roberto Alomar .50 .15
96 Joe Carter .30 .09
97 Bernie Williams .50 .15
98 Albert Belle .30 .09
99 Greg Vaughn .30 .09
100 Tony Clark .30 .09
101 Matt Williams .30 .09
102 Jeff Bagwell .50 .15
103 Reggie Sanders .30 .09
104 Mariano Rivera .50 .15
105 Larry Walker .50 .15
106 Shawn Green .30 .09
107 Alex Ochoa .30 .09
108 Ivan Rodriguez .75 .23
109 Eric Young .30 .09
110 Javier Lopez .30 .09
111 Brian Hunter .30 .09
112 Raul Mondesi SP 4.00 1.20
113 Randy Johnson .75 .23
114 Tony Phillips .30 .09
115 Carlos Garcia .30 .09
116 Moises Alou .30 .09
117 Paul O'Neill .50 .15
118 Jim Thome .75 .23
119 Jermaine Dye .30 .09
120 Wilson Alvarez .30 .09
121 Rondell White .30 .09
122 Michael Tucker .30 .09
123 Mike Lansing .30 .09
124 Tony Gwynn 1.00 .30
125 Ryan Klesko .30 .09
126 Jim Edmonds .30 .09
127 Chuck Knoblauch .50 .15
128 Rafael Palmeiro .50 .15
129 Jay Buhner .30 .09
130 Tom Glavine .50 .15
131 Julio Franco .30 .09
132 Cecil Fielder .30 .09
133 Paul Wilson SP 4.00 1.20
134 Deion Sanders .50 .15
135 Alex Gonzalez .30 .09
136 Charles Nagy .30 .09
137 Andy Ashby SP 4.00 1.20
138 Edgar Renteria .30 .09
139 Pedro Martinez .75 .23
140 Brian Jordan .30 .09
141 Todd Hundley .30 .09
142 Marc Newfield .30 .09
143 Darryl Strawberry .30 .09
144 Dan Wilson .30 .09
145 Brian Giles RC 1.50 .45
146 F.P. Santangelo .30 .09
147 Shannon Stewart SP 4.00 1.20
148 Scott Spiezio .30 .09
149 Andruw Jones .30 .09
150 Karim Garcia .30 .09
151 Vladimir Guerrero .75 .23
152 George Arias .30 .09
153 Brooks Kieschnick .30 .09
154 Todd Walker .30 .09
155 Scott Rolen .75 .23
156 Todd Greene .30 .09
157 Dmitri Young .30 .09
158 Ruben Rivera .30 .09
159 Bartolo Colon .30 .09
160 Nomar Garciaparra 1.25 .35
161 Bob Abreu SP 4.00 1.20
162 Darin Erstad .30 .09

163 Ken Griffey Jr. CL .75 .23
164 Frank Thomas CL .50 .15
165 Alex Rodriguez CL .75 .23

1997 Studio Gold Press Proofs

Randomly inserted in packs, this 165-card set is parallel to the regular Studio set. The difference is found in the special micro-etched border with gold holographic foil stamping. Only 500 of each card was produced.

Nm-Mt Ex-Mt
*STARS: 8X TO 20X BASIC CARDS....
*SP'S: .6X TO 1.5X BASIC CARDS.....
*ROOKIES: 2.5X TO 6X BASIC CARDS

1997 Studio Silver Press Proofs

Randomly inserted in packs, this 165-card set is parallel to the regular Studio set. The difference is found in the special micro-etched border with silver holographic foil stamping. Only 1500 of each card was produced.

Nm-Mt Ex-Mt
*STARS: 4X TO 10X BASIC CARDS....
*SP's: .3X TO .8X BASIC CARDS........
*ROOKIES: 1.25X TO 3X BASIC CARDS

1997 Studio Autographs

Randomly inserted in packs at an approximate rate of 1 in every 30 or more boxes, each of these three different cards feature an autographed and serial-numbered parallel version of the 8x10 Studio Portraits insert. Cards are distinguished by a silver "Autographed Signature" stamp on the front. Only a limited number of portraits were signed by each player. The amount each player signed is listed next to his name. Each player signed the first 100 serial #'d cards in blue ink and all the preceding cards in black ink.

Nm-Mt Ex-Mt
PRINT RUNS B/WN 500-1250 PER ....
12 Todd Walker/1250 15.00 4.50
21 Vladimir Guerrero/500 40.00 12.00
24 Scott Rolen/1000 40.00 12.00

1997 Studio Hard Hats

Randomly inserted in packs, this 24-card set features color player images of 24 major league superstars on a unique clear plastic, foil-stamped, die cut batting helmet design. Only 5000 of each card was produced and are sequentially numbered.

Nm-Mt Ex-Mt
COMPLETE SET (24) 150.00 45.00
1 Ivan Rodriguez 6.00 1.80
2 Albert Belle 2.50 .75
3 Ken Griffey Jr. 10.00 3.00
4 Chuck Knoblauch 2.50 .75
5 Frank Thomas 6.00 1.80
6 Cal Ripken 20.00 6.00
7 Todd Walker 2.50 .75
8 Alex Rodriguez 10.00 3.00
9 Jim Thome 6.00 1.80
10 Mike Piazza 10.00 3.00
11 Barry Larkin 4.00 1.20
12 Chipper Jones 6.00 1.80
13 Derek Jeter 15.00 4.50
14 Matt Williams 2.50 .75
15 Jason Giambi 2.50 .75
16 Tim Salmon 4.00 1.20
17 Brady Anderson 2.50 .75
18 Rondell White 2.50 .75
19 Bernie Williams 4.00 1.20
20 Juan Gonzalez 4.00 1.20
21 Karim Garcia 2.50 .75
22 Scott Rolen 6.00 1.80
23 Darin Erstad 2.50 .75
24 Brian Jordan 2.50 .75

1997 Studio Master Strokes

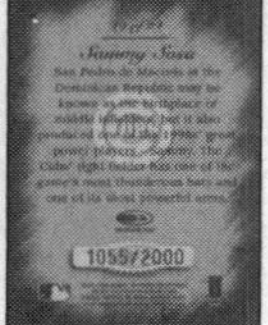

Randomly inserted in packs, this 24-card set features color photos of superstar players on all canvas card stock with gold foil stamping. Only 2,000 of each card was produced and is sequentially numbered.

Nm-Mt Ex-Mt
COMPLETE SET (24) 300.00 90.00
8 X 10: RANDOM INSERTS IN PACKS
8 X 10 PRINT RUN 5000 SERIAL #'d SETS
1 Derek Jeter 30.00 9.00
2 Jeff Bagwell 8.00 2.40
3 Ken Griffey Jr. 20.00 6.00
4 Barry Bonds 30.00 9.00
5 Frank Thomas 12.00 3.60
6 Andy Pettitte 8.00 2.40
7 Mo Vaughn 5.00 1.50
8 Alex Rodriguez 20.00 6.00
9 Andruw Jones 5.00 1.50
10 Kenny Lofton 5.00 1.50
11 Cal Ripken 40.00 12.00
12 Greg Maddux 20.00 6.00
13 Manny Ramirez 8.00 2.40
14 Mike Piazza 20.00 6.00
15 Vladimir Guerrero 12.00 3.60
16 Albert Belle 5.00 1.50
17 Chipper Jones 12.00 3.60
18 Hideo Nomo 12.00 3.60
19 Sammy Sosa 20.00 6.00
20 Tony Gwynn 15.00 4.50
21 Gary Sheffield 5.00 1.50
22 Mark McGwire 30.00 9.00
23 Juan Gonzalez 8.00 2.40
24 Paul Molitor 8.00 2.40

1997 Studio Portraits 8 x 10

Inserted one per pack, this 24-card set is a partial parallel version of the base set and features full-color portraits of star players measuring approximately 8" by 10" with a signable UV coating.

Nm-Mt Ex-Mt
COMPLETE SET (24) 25.00 7.50
1 Ken Griffey Jr. 2.50 .75
2 Frank Thomas 1.50 .45
3 Alex Rodriguez 2.50 .75
4 Andruw Jones .60 .18
5 Cal Ripken 5.00 1.50
6 Greg Maddux 2.50 .75
7 Mike Piazza 2.50 .75
8 Chipper Jones 1.50 .45
9 Albert Belle .60 .18
10 Derek Jeter 4.00 1.20
11 Juan Gonzalez 1.00 .30
12 Todd Walker .60 .18
13 Mark McGwire 4.00 1.20
14 Barry Bonds 4.00 1.20
15 Jeff Bagwell 1.00 .30
16 Manny Ramirez 1.00 .30
17 Kenny Lofton .60 .18
18 Mo Vaughn .60 .18
19 Hideo Nomo 1.50 .45
20 Tony Gwynn 2.00 .60
21 Vladimir Guerrero 1.50 .45
22 Gary Sheffield .60 .18
23 Ryne Sandberg 2.50 .75
24 Scott Rolen 1.50 .45

1998 Studio

The 1998 Studio set consists of 220 cards. The eight-card packs retailed for $2.99 each. Each pack contains 1-8"x10" card and seven standard size cards. The fronts feature candid head/shoulder player photos with game action photography in the background. The player's name lines the bottom border and the Donruss logo sits in the upper left corner. The release date was June, 1998.

Nm-Mt Ex-Mt
COMPLETE SET (220) 50.00 15.00
1 Tony Clark .30 .09
2 Jose Cruz Jr. .30 .09
3 Ivan Rodriguez .75 .23
4 Mo Vaughn .30 .09
5 Kenny Lofton .30 .09
6 Will Clark .75 .23
7 Barry Larkin .50 .15
8 Jay Bell .30 .09
9 Kevin Young .30 .09
10 Francisco Cordova .30 .09
11 Justin Thompson .30 .09
12 Paul Molitor .50 .15
13 Jeff Bagwell .50 .15
14 Jose Canseco .75 .23
15 Scott Rolen .75 .23
16 Wilton Guerrero .30 .09
17 Shannon Stewart .30 .09
18 Hideki Irabu .30 .09
19 Michael Tucker .30 .09
20 Joe Carter .30 .09
21 Gabe Alvarez .30 .09
22 Ricky Ledee .30 .09
23 Karim Garcia .30 .09
24 Eli Marrero .30 .09
25 Scott Elarton .30 .09
26 Mario Valdez .30 .09
27 Ben Grieve .30 .09
28 Paul Konerko .30 .09
29 Esteban Yan RC .30 .09
30 Esteban Loaiza .30 .09
31 Delino DeShields .30 .09
32 Bernie Williams .50 .15
33 Joe Randa .30 .09
34 Randy Johnson .75 .23
35 Brett Tomko .30 .09
36 Todd Erdos RC .30 .09
37 Bobby Higginson .30 .09
38 Jason Kendall .30 .09
39 Ray Lankford .30 .09
40 Mark Grace .50 .15
41 Andy Pettitte .50 .15
42 Alex Rodriguez 1.25 .35
43 Hideo Nomo .75 .23
44 Sammy Sosa 1.25 .35
45 J.T. Snow .30 .09
46 Jason Varitek .75 .23
47 Vinny Castilla .30 .09
48 Neifi Perez .30 .09
49 Todd Walker .30 .09
50 Mike Cameron .30 .09
51 Jeffrey Hammonds .30 .09
52 Deivi Cruz .30 .09
53 Brian Hunter .30 .09
54 Al Martin .30 .09
55 Ron Coomer .30 .09
56 Chan Ho Park .30 .09
57 Pedro Martinez .75 .23
58 Darin Erstad .30 .09
59 Albert Belle .30 .09
60 Nomar Garciaparra 1.25 .35
61 Tony Gwynn 1.00 .30
62 Mike Piazza 1.25 .35
63 Todd Helton .50 .15
64 David Ortiz .75 .23
65 Todd Dunwoody .30 .09
66 Orlando Cabrera .30 .09
67 Ken Cloude .30 .09
68 Andy Benes .30 .09
69 Mariano Rivera .50 .15
70 Cecil Fielder .30 .09
71 Brian Jordan .30 .09
72 Darryl Kile .30 .09
73 Reggie Jefferson .30 .09
74 Shawn Estes .30 .09
75 Bobby Bonilla .30 .09
76 Denny Neagle .30 .09
77 Robin Ventura .30 .09
78 Omar Vizquel .50 .15
79 Craig Biggio .50 .15
80 Moises Alou .30 .09
81 Garret Anderson .30 .09
82 Eric Karros .30 .09
83 Dante Bichette .30 .09
84 Charles Johnson .30 .09
85 Rusty Greer .30 .09
86 Travis Fryman .30 .09
87 Fernando Tatis .30 .09
88 Wilson Alvarez .30 .09
89 Carl Pavano .50 .15
90 Brian Rose .30 .09
91 Geoff Jenkins .30 .09
92 Magglio Ordonez RC 2.00 .60
93 David Segui .30 .09
94 David Cone .30 .09
95 John Smoltz .50 .15
96 Jim Thome .75 .23
97 Gary Sheffield .30 .09
98 Barry Bonds 2.00 .60
99 Andres Galarraga .30 .09
100 Brad Fullmer .30 .09
101 Bobby Estalella .30 .09
102 Enrique Wilson .30 .09
103 Frank Catalanotto RC .50 .15
104 Mike Lowell RC 1.50 .45
105 Kevin Orie .30 .09
106 Matt Morris .30 .09
107 Pokey Reese .30 .09
108 Shawn Green .30 .09
109 Tony Womack .30 .09
110 Ken Caminiti .30 .09
111 Roberto Alomar .50 .15
112 Ken Griffey Jr. 1.25 .35
113 Cal Ripken 2.50 .75
114 Lou Collier .30 .09
115 Larry Walker .50 .15
116 Fred McGriff .50 .15
117 Jim Edmonds .30 .09
118 Edgar Martinez .50 .15
119 Matt Williams .30 .09
120 Ismael Valdes .30 .09
121 Bartolo Colon .30 .09
122 Jeff Cirillo .30 .09
123 Steve Woodard .30 .09
124 Kevin Millwood RC 1.00 .30
125 Derrick Gibson .30 .09
126 Jacob Cruz .30 .09
127 Russell Branyan .30 .09
128 Sean Casey .30 .09
129 Derrek Lee .30 .09
130 Paul O'Neill .50 .15
131 Brad Radke .30 .09
132 Kevin Appier .30 .09
133 John Olerud .30 .09
134 Alan Benes .30 .09
135 Todd Greene .30 .09
136 Carlos Mendoza RC .30 .09
137 Wade Boggs .50 .15
138 Jose Guillen .30 .09
139 Tino Martinez .50 .15
140 Aaron Boone .30 .09
141 Abraham Nunez .30 .09
142 Preston Wilson .30 .09
143 Randall Simon .30 .09
144 Dennis Reyes .30 .09
145 Mark Kotsay .30 .09
146 Richard Hidalgo .30 .09
147 Travis Lee .30 .09
148 Hanley Frias RC .30 .09
149 Ruben Rivera .30 .09
150 Rafael Medina .30 .09
151 Dave Nilsson .30 .09
152 Curt Schilling .30 .09
153 Brady Anderson .30 .09
154 Carlos Delgado .30 .09
155 Jason Giambi .30 .09
156 Pat Hentgen .30 .09
157 Tom Glavine .50 .15
158 Ryan Klesko .30 .09
159 Chipper Jones .75 .23
160 Juan Gonzalez .50 .15
161 Mark McGwire 2.00 .60
162 Vladimir Guerrero .75 .23
163 Derek Jeter 2.00 .60
164 Manny Ramirez .50 .15
165 Mike Mussina .50 .15
166 Rafael Palmeiro .50 .15
167 Henry Rodriguez .30 .09
168 Jeff Suppan .30 .09
169 Eric Milton .30 .09
170 Scott Spiezio .30 .09
171 Wilson Delgado .30 .09
172 Bubba Trammell .30 .09
173 Ellis Burks .30 .09
174 Jason Dickson .30 .09
175 Butch Huskey .30 .09
176 Edgardo Alfonzo .30 .09
177 Eric Young .30 .09
178 Marquis Grissom .30 .09
179 Lance Johnson .30 .09
180 Kevin Brown .50 .15
181 Sandy Alomar Jr. .30 .09
182 Todd Hundley .30 .09
183 Rondell White .30 .09
184 Javier Lopez .30 .09
185 Damian Jackson .30 .09
186 Raul Mondesi .30 .09
187 Rickey Henderson .75 .23
188 David Justice .30 .09
189 Jay Buhner .30 .09
190 Jaret Wright .30 .09
191 Miguel Tejada .30 .09
192 Ron Wright .30 .09
193 Livan Hernandez .30 .09
194 A.J. Hinch .30 .09
195 Richie Sexson .30 .09
196 Bob Abreu .30 .09
197 Luis Castillo .30 .09
198 Michael Coleman .30 .09
199 Greg Maddux 1.25 .35
200 Frank Thomas .75 .23
201 Andruw Jones .30 .09
202 Roger Clemens 1.50 .45
203 Tim Salmon .50 .15
204 Chuck Knoblauch .30 .09
205 Wes Helms .30 .09
206 Juan Encarnacion .30 .09
207 Russ Davis .30 .09
208 John Valentin .30 .09
209 Tony Saunders .30 .09
210 Mike Sweeney .30 .09
211 Steve Finley .30 .09
212 Dave Dellucci RC .50 .15
213 Edgar Renteria .30 .09
214 Jeremi Gonzalez .30 .09
CL1 Jeff Bagwell CL .30 .09
CL2 Mike Piazza CL .75 .23
CL3 Greg Maddux CL .75 .23
CL4 Cal Ripken CL 1.25 .35
CL5 Frank Thomas CL .50 .15
CL6 Ken Griffey Jr. CL .75 .23

1998 Studio Gold Press Proofs

Randomly inserted in packs, this 220-card set is a parallel to the Studio base set. Each card features striking gold foil borders and is sequentially serial numbered to 300 on back.

Nm-Mt Ex-Mt
*STARS: 4X TO 10X BASIC CARDS....
*ROOKIES: 4X TO 10X BASIC CARDS

1998 Studio Silver Press Proofs

Randomly inserted in packs, this 220-card set is a parallel to the Studio base set. Each card features silver foil borders on front. Though they are not serial numbered, each card states "1 of 1,000" on back.

Nm-Mt Ex-Mt
COMMON CARD 2.00 .60
*STARS: 2X TO 5X BASIC CARDS......
*ROOKIES: 2X TO 5X BASIC CARDS..

1998 Studio Autographs 8 x 10

Three of the games youngest and brighest stars signed these 8" by 10" photos . Each player signed a limited amount of autographs and the amount they signed is notated next to their names

Nm-Mt Ex-Mt
1 Travis Lee/500 10.00 3.00
2 Todd Helton/1000 25.00 7.50
3 Ben Grieve/1000 10.00 3.00

1998 Studio Freeze Frame

Randomly inserted in packs, this 30-card set features a selection of top stars in a design mimicking a roll of film. The set is sequentially numbered to 4,000, and the first 500 cards in this set are die cut.

Nm-Mt Ex-Mt
COMPLETE SET (30) 150.00 45.00
DIE CUT PRINT RUN 500 SERIAL #'d SETS
RANDOM INSERTS IN PACKS
1 Ken Griffey Jr. 10.00 3.00
2 Derek Jeter 15.00 4.50
3 Ben Grieve 2.50 .75
4 Cal Ripken 20.00 6.00
5 Alex Rodriguez 10.00 3.00
6 Greg Maddux 10.00 3.00
7 David Justice 2.50 .75
8 Mike Piazza 10.00 3.00
9 Chipper Jones 6.00 1.80
10 Randy Johnson 6.00 1.80
11 Jeff Bagwell 4.00 1.20
12 Nomar Garciaparra 10.00 3.00
13 Andruw Jones 2.50 .75
14 Frank Thomas 6.00 1.80
15 Scott Rolen 6.00 1.80
16 Barry Bonds 15.00 4.50
17 Kenny Lofton 2.50 .75
18 Ivan Rodriguez 6.00 1.80
19 Chuck Knoblauch 2.50 .75
20 Jose Cruz Jr. 2.50 .75
21 Bernie Williams 4.00 1.20
22 Tony Gwynn 8.00 2.40
23 Juan Gonzalez 4.00 1.20
24 Gary Sheffield 2.50 .75
25 Roger Clemens 12.00 3.60
26 Travis Lee 2.50 .75
27 Brad Fullmer 2.50 .75
28 Tim Salmon 4.00 1.20
29 Raul Mondesi 2.50 .75
30 Roberto Alomar 4.00 1.20

1998 Studio Hit Parade

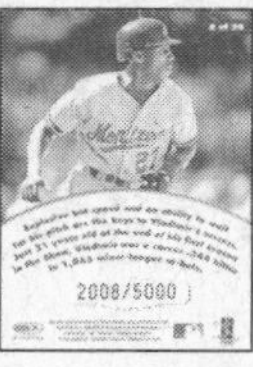

Randomly inserted in packs, this 20-card set is an insert to the Studio base set. The set is sequentially numbered to 5000. The fronts feature 20 of the game's most accomplished batsmen in color action photography. The backgrounds help showcase the players with a sunburst design. The player's name and team logo are found below the photo and the Donruss logo is in the upper left corner.

Nm-Mt Ex-Mt
COMPLETE SET (20) 100.00 30.00
1 Tony Gwynn 8.00 2.40
2 Larry Walker 4.00 1.20
3 Mike Piazza 10.00 3.00
4 Frank Thomas 6.00 1.80
5 Manny Ramirez 4.00 1.20
6 Ken Griffey Jr. 10.00 3.00
7 Todd Helton 4.00 1.20
8 Vladimir Guerrero 6.00 1.80
9 Albert Belle 2.50 .75
10 Jeff Bagwell 4.00 1.20
11 Juan Gonzalez 4.00 1.20
12 Jim Thome 6.00 1.80
13 Scott Rolen 6.00 1.80
14 Tino Martinez 4.00 1.20
15 Mark McGwire 15.00 4.50
16 Barry Bonds 15.00 4.50
17 Tony Clark 2.50 .75
18 Mo Vaughn 2.50 .75
19 Darin Erstad 2.50 .75
20 Paul Konerko 2.50 .75

1998 Studio Masterstrokes

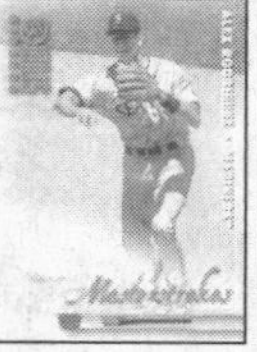

Randomly inserted in packs, this 20-card set is an insert to the Studio base set. The set is sequentially numbered to 1000. Each card resembles an artist's canvas on which a color player photo is featured. An artist's paintbrush sits at the bottom border of the card with the word "Masterstrokes" written in italics above it.

Nm-Mt Ex-Mt
COMPLETE SET (20) 250.00 75.00
1 Travis Lee 5.00 1.50
2 Kenny Lofton 5.00 1.50
3 Mo Vaughn 5.00 1.50
4 Ivan Rodriguez 12.00 3.60
5 Roger Clemens 25.00 7.50
6 Mark McGwire 30.00 9.00
7 Hideo Nomo 12.00 3.60
8 Andruw Jones 5.00 1.50
9 Nomar Garciaparra 20.00 6.00
10 Juan Gonzalez 8.00 2.40
11 Jeff Bagwell 8.00 2.40
12 Derek Jeter 30.00 9.00
13 Tony Gwynn 15.00 4.50
14 Chipper Jones 12.00 3.60
15 Mike Piazza 20.00 6.00
16 Greg Maddux 20.00 6.00
17 Alex Rodriguez 20.00 6.00
18 Cal Ripken 40.00 12.00
19 Frank Thomas 12.00 3.60
20 Ken Griffey Jr. 20.00 6.00

1998 Studio Portraits 8 x 10

Inserted one per Studio pack, this 36-card set is an insert to the Studio base set. Twelve of the Studio Portraits are exclusive to the retail/hobby configuration of the product.

Nm-Mt Ex-Mt
COMPLETE SET (36)................ 40.00 12.00
GOLD: RANDOM INSERTS IN PACKS
GOLD PRINT RUN 300 SERIAL #'d SETS
1 Travis Lee.......................... .50 .15
2 Todd Helton .... .75 .23
3 Ben Grieve .... .50 .15
4 Paul Konerko .... .50 .15
5 Jeff Bagwell .... .75 .23
6 Derek Jeter.......................... 3.00 .90
7 Ivan Rodriguez.......................... 1.25 .35
8 Cal Ripken.......................... 4.00 1.20
9 Mike Piazza.......................... 2.00 .60
10 Chipper Jones.......................... 1.25 .35
11 Frank Thomas.......................... 1.25 .35
12 Tony Gwynn.......................... 1.50 .45
13 Nomar Garciaparra.......................... 2.00 .60
14 Juan Gonzalez.......................... .75 .23
15 Greg Maddux.......................... 2.00 .60
16 Hideo Nomo.......................... 1.25 .35
17 Scott Rolen.......................... 1.25 .35
18 Barry Bonds.......................... 3.00 .90
19 Ken Griffey Jr.......................... 2.00 .60
20 Alex Rodriguez.......................... 2.00 .60
21 Roger Clemens.......................... 2.50 .75
22 Mark McGwire.......................... 3.00 .90
23 Jose Cruz Jr.......................... .50 .15
24 Andruw Jones.......................... .50 .15
25 Tino Martinez.......................... .75 .23
26 Mo Vaughn.......................... .50 .15
27 Vladimir Guerrero.......................... 1.25 .35
28 Tony Clark.......................... .50 .15
29 Andy Pettitte.......................... .75 .23
30 Jaret Wright.......................... .50 .15
31 Paul Molitor.......................... .75 .23
32 Darin Erstad.......................... .50 .15
33 Larry Walker.......................... .75 .23
34 Chuck Knoblauch.......................... .50 .15
35 Barry Larkin.......................... .75 .23
36 Kenny Lofton.......................... .50 .15

1998 Studio MLB 99

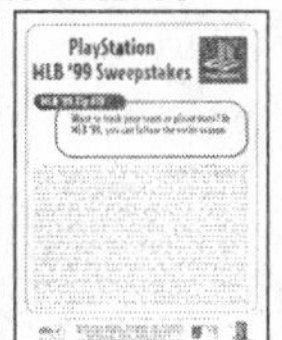

This 20 card set was inserted into both Donruss Update and Studio packs. These cards feature 20 of the leading Baseball players and were widely available because of the insertion into both of the aforementioned brands. Please see 1998 Donruss MLB 99 for pricing.

Nm-Mt Ex-Mt
PLEASE SEE 1998 DONRUSS MLB 99

2001 Studio

This 200 card set was issued in six-card packs with 18 packs per box. Cards numbered 151-200 were shorter printed than cards 1-150. Each of the cards from 151-200 were serial numbered to 700.

Nm-Mt Ex-Mt
COMP.SET w/o SP's (150)........ 40.00 12.00
COMMON CARD (1-150) .... .50 .15
COMMON (151-200).............. 8.00 2.40
1 Alex Rodriguez.......................... 2.00 .60
2 Barry Bonds.......................... 3.00 .90
3 Cal Ripken.......................... 4.00 1.20
4 Chipper Jones.......................... 1.25 .35
5 Derek Jeter.......................... 3.00 .90
6 Troy Glaus.......................... .50 .15
7 Frank Thomas.......................... 1.25 .35
8 Greg Maddux.......................... 2.00 .60
9 Ivan Rodriguez.......................... 1.25 .35
10 Jeff Bagwell.......................... .75 .23
11 Mark Quinn.......................... .50 .15
12 Todd Helton.......................... .75 .23
13 Ken Griffey Jr.......................... 2.00 .60
14 Manny Ramirez.......................... .75 .23
15 Mark McGwire.......................... 3.00 .90
16 Mike Piazza.......................... 2.00 .60
17 Nomar Garciaparra.......................... 2.00 .60
18 Robin Ventura.......................... .50 .15
19 Aramis Ramirez.......................... .50 .15
20 J.T. Snow.......................... .50 .15
21 Pat Burrell.......................... .50 .15
22 Curt Schilling.......................... .50 .15
23 Carlos Delgado.......................... .50 .15
24 J.D. Drew.......................... .50 .15
25 Cliff Floyd.......................... .50 .15
26 Brian Jordan.......................... .50 .15
27 Roberto Alomar.......................... .75 .23
28 Barry Zito.......................... .75 .23
29 Harold Baines.......................... .50 .15
30 Brad Penny.......................... .50 .15
31 Jose Cruz Jr.......................... .50 .15
32 Andy Pettitte.......................... .75 .23
33 Jim Edmonds.......................... .50 .15
34 Darin Erstad.......................... .50 .15
35 Jason Giambi.......................... .50 .15
36 Tom Glavine.......................... .75 .23
37 Juan Gonzalez.......................... .75 .23
38 Mark Grace.......................... .75 .23
39 Shawn Green.......................... .50 .15
40 Tim Hudson.......................... .50 .15
41 Andruw Jones.......................... .50 .15
42 Jeff Kent.......................... .50 .15
43 Barry Larkin.......................... .75 .23
44 Rafael Furcal.......................... .50 .15
45 Mike Mussina.......................... .75 .23
46 Hideo Nomo.......................... 1.25 .35
47 Rafael Palmeiro.......................... .75 .23
48 Scott Rolen.......................... 1.25 .35
49 Gary Sheffield.......................... .50 .15
50 Bernie Williams.......................... .75 .23
51 Bob Abreu.......................... .50 .15
52 Edgardo Alfonzo.......................... .50 .15
53 Edgar Martinez.......................... .75 .23
54 Magglio Ordonez.......................... .50 .15
55 Kerry Wood.......................... 1.25 .35
56 Matt Morris.......................... .50 .15
57 Lance Berkman.......................... .50 .15
58 Kevin Brown.......................... .50 .15
59 Sean Casey.......................... .50 .15
60 Eric Chavez.......................... .50 .15
61 Bartolo Colon.......................... .50 .15
62 Johnny Damon.......................... .75 .23
63 Jermaine Dye.......................... .50 .15
64 Juan Encarnacion.......................... .50 .15
65 Carl Everett.......................... .50 .15
66 Brian Giles.......................... .50 .15
67 Mike Hampton.......................... .50 .15
68 Richard Hidalgo.......................... .50 .15
69 Geoff Jenkins.......................... .50 .15
70 Jacque Jones.......................... .50 .15
71 Jason Kendall.......................... .50 .15
72 Ryan Klesko.......................... .50 .15
73 Chan Ho Park.......................... .50 .15
74 Richie Sexson.......................... .50 .15
75 Mike Sweeney.......................... .50 .15
76 Fernando Tatis.......................... .50 .15
77 Miguel Tejada.......................... .50 .15
78 Jose Vidro.......................... .50 .15
79 Larry Walker.......................... 2.00 .60
80 Preston Wilson.......................... .50 .15
81 Craig Biggio.......................... .75 .23
82 Fred McGriff.......................... .75 .23
83 Jim Thome.......................... 1.25 .35
84 Garret Anderson.......................... .50 .15
85 Mark Mulder.......................... .50 .15
86 Tony Batista.......................... .50 .15
87 Terrence Long.......................... .50 .15
88 Brad Fullmer.......................... .50 .15
89 Rusty Greer.......................... .50 .15
90 Orlando Hernandez.......................... .50 .15
91 Gabe Kapler.......................... .50 .15
92 Paul Konerko.......................... .50 .15
93 Carlos Lee.......................... .50 .15
94 Kenny Lofton.......................... .50 .15
95 Raul Mondesi.......................... .50 .15
96 Jorge Posada.......................... .75 .23
97 Tim Salmon.......................... .75 .23
98 Greg Vaughn.......................... .50 .15
99 Mo Vaughn.......................... .50 .15
100 Omar Vizquel.......................... .75 .23
101 Ben Grieve.......................... .50 .15
102 Luis Gonzalez.......................... .50 .15
103 Ray Durham.......................... .50 .15
104 Ryan Dempster.......................... .50 .15
105 Eric Karros.......................... .50 .15
106 David Justice.......................... .50 .15
107 Pedro Martinez.......................... 1.25 .35
108 Randy Johnson.......................... 1.25 .35
109 Rick Ankiel.......................... .50 .15
110 Rickey Henderson.......................... 1.25 .35
111 Roger Clemens.......................... 2.50 .75
112 Sammy Sosa.......................... 2.00 .60
113 Tony Gwynn.......................... 1.50 .45
114 Vladimir Guerrero.......................... 1.25 .35
115 Kazuhiro Sasaki.......................... .50 .15
116 Phil Nevin.......................... .50 .15
117 Ruben Mateo.......................... .50 .15
118 Shannon Stewart.......................... .50 .15
119 Matt Williams.......................... .50 .15
120 Tino Martinez.......................... .75 .23
121 Ken Caminiti.......................... .50 .15
122 Edgar Renteria.......................... .50 .15
123 Charles Johnson.......................... .50 .15
124 Aaron Sele.......................... .50 .15
125 Javy Lopez.......................... .50 .15
126 Mariano Rivera.......................... .75 .23
127 Shea Hillenbrand.......................... .50 .15
128 Jeff D'Amico.......................... .50 .15
129 Brady Anderson.......................... .50 .15
130 Kevin Millwood.......................... .50 .15
131 Trot Nixon.......................... .50 .15
132 Mike Lieberthal.......................... .50 .15
133 Juan Pierre.......................... .50 .15
134 Russ Ortiz.......................... .50 .15
135 Jose Macias.......................... .50 .15
136 John Smoltz.......................... .75 .23
137 Jason Varitek.......................... .75 .23
138 Dean Palmer.......................... .50 .15
139 Jeff Cirillo.......................... .50 .15
140 Paul O'Neill.......................... .75 .23
141 Andres Galarraga.......................... .50 .15
142 David Wells.......................... .50 .15
143 Brad Radke.......................... .50 .15
144 Wade Miller.......................... .50 .15
145 John Olerud.......................... .50 .15
146 Moises Alou.......................... .50 .15
147 Carlos Beltran.......................... .75 .23
148 Jeromy Burnitz.......................... .50 .15
149 Steve Finley.......................... .50 .15
150 Joe Mays.......................... .50 .15
151 Alex Escobar ROO.......................... 8.00 2.40
152 J. Estrada ROO RC.......................... 10.00 3.00
153 Pedro Feliz ROO.......................... 8.00 2.40
154 Nate Frese ROO RC.......................... 8.00 2.40
155 Dee Brown ROO.......................... 8.00 2.40
156 B. Larson ROO RC.......................... 8.00 2.40
157 A. Gomez ROO RC.......................... 8.00 2.40
158 Jason Hart ROO.......................... 8.00 2.40
159 C.C. Sabathia ROO.......................... 8.00 2.40
160 Josh Towers ROO RC.......................... 8.00 2.40
161 C. Parker ROO RC.......................... 8.00 2.40
162 J. Melian ROO RC.......................... 8.00 2.40
163 Joe Kennedy ROO RC.......................... 10.00 3.00
164 A. Hernandez ROO RC.......................... 8.00 2.40
165 Jimmy Rollins ROO.......................... 8.00 2.40
166 Jose Mieses ROO RC.......................... 8.00 2.40
167 Roy Oswalt ROO.......................... 10.00 3.00
168 Eric Munson ROO.......................... 8.00 2.40
169 Xavier Nady ROO.......................... 8.00 2.40
170 H. Ramirez ROO RC.......................... 10.00 3.00
171 Abraham Nunez ROO.......................... 8.00 2.40
172 Jose Ortiz ROO.......................... 8.00 2.40
173 Jeremy Owens ROO RC UER 8.00 2.40
Eric Owens pictured on front
174 C. Vargas ROO RC.......................... 8.00 2.40
175 Corey Patterson ROO.......................... 8.00 2.40
176 Carlos Pena ROO.......................... 8.00 2.40
177 Bud Smith ROO RC.......................... 8.00 2.40
178 Adam Dunn ROO.......................... 10.00 3.00
179 A. Pettyjohn ROO RC.......................... 8.00 2.40
180 E. Guzman ROO RC.......................... 8.00 2.40
181 Jay Gibbons ROO RC.......................... 10.00 3.00
182 Wilkin Ruan ROO RC.......................... 8.00 2.40
183 T. Shinjo ROO RC.......................... 10.00 3.00
184 Alfonso Soriano ROO.......................... 10.00 3.00
185 Marcus Giles ROO.......................... 8.00 2.40
186 Ichiro Suzuki ROO RC.......................... 80.00 24.00
187 Juan Uribe ROO RC.......................... 10.00 3.00
188 D. Williams ROO RC.......................... 8.00 2.40
189 Carlos Valderrama.......................... 8.00 2.40
ROO RC
190 Matt White ROO RC.......................... 8.00 2.40
191 Albert Pujols ROO RC.......................... 120.00 36.00
192 D. Mendez ROO RC.......................... 8.00 2.40
193 C. Aldridge ROO RC.......................... 8.00 2.40
194 Endy Chavez ROO RC.......................... 8.00 2.40
195 Josh Beckett ROO.......................... 8.00 2.40
196 W. Betemit ROO RC.......................... 8.00 2.40
197 Ben Sheets ROO.......................... 10.00 3.00
198 A. Torres ROO RC.......................... 8.00 2.40
199 Aubrey Huff ROO.......................... 8.00 2.40
200 Jack Wilson ROO RC.......................... 12.00 3.60

2001 Studio Diamond Collection

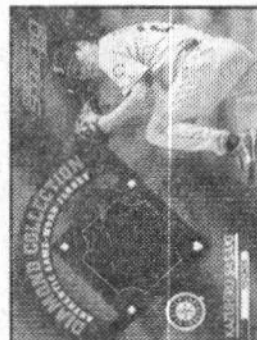

Randomly inserted in packs, these 47 cards feature each of these players along with a game-worn jersey swatch. Cards numbered 24, 35 and 44 were not printed for this set.

Nm-Mt Ex-Mt
DC-1 Vladimir Guerrero.......................... 15.00 4.50
DC-2 Barry Bonds.......................... 25.00 7.50
DC-3 Cal Ripken.......................... 40.00 12.00
DC-4 Nomar Garciaparra.......................... 15.00 4.50
DC-5 Greg Maddux.......................... 15.00 4.50
DC-6 Frank Thomas.......................... 15.00 4.50
DC-7 Roger Clemens.......................... 25.00 7.50
DC-8 Luis Gonzalez SP.......................... 15.00 4.50
DC-9 Tony Gwynn.......................... 15.00 4.50
DC-10 Carlos Lee SP.......................... 15.00 4.50
DC-11 Troy Glaus.......................... 10.00 3.00
DC-12 Randy Johnson.......................... 15.00 4.50
DC-13 Manny Ramirez SP.......................... 25.00 7.50
DC-14 Pedro Martinez.......................... 15.00 4.50
DC-15 Todd Helton.......................... 15.00 4.50
DC-16 Jeff Bagwell.......................... 15.00 4.50
DC-17 Rickey Henderson.......................... 15.00 4.50
DC-18 Kazuhiro Sasaki.......................... 10.00 3.00
DC-19 Albert Pujols SP.......................... 50.00 15.00
DC-20 Ivan Rodriguez.......................... 15.00 4.50
DC-21 Darin Erstad.......................... 10.00 3.00
DC-22 Andruw Jones.......................... 10.00 3.00
DC-23 Roberto Alomar.......................... 15.00 4.50
DC-24 Does Not Exist..........................
DC-25 Juan Gonzalez.......................... 15.00 4.50
DC-26 Shawn Green.......................... 10.00 3.00
DC-27 Lance Berkman.......................... 10.00 3.00
DC-28 Scott Rolen.......................... 15.00 4.50
DC-29 Rafael Palmeiro.......................... 15.00 4.50
DC-30 J.D. Drew.......................... 10.00 3.00
DC-31 Kerry Wood.......................... 15.00 4.50
DC-32 Jim Edmonds.......................... 10.00 3.00
DC-33 Tom Glavine SP.......................... 25.00 7.50
DC-34 Hideo Nomo SP.......................... 25.00 7.50
DC-35 Does Not Exist..........................
DC-36 Tim Hudson.......................... 10.00 3.00
DC-37 Miguel Tejada.......................... 10.00 3.00
DC-38 Chipper Jones.......................... 15.00 4.50
DC-39 Edgar Martinez SP.......................... 25.00 7.50
DC-40 Chan Ho Park.......................... 10.00 3.00
DC-41 Magglio Ordonez.......................... 10.00 3.00
DC-42 Sean Casey.......................... 10.00 3.00
DC-43 Larry Walker.......................... 15.00 4.50
DC-44 Does Not Exist..........................
DC-45 Cliff Floyd.......................... 10.00 3.00
DC-46 Mike Sweeney.......................... 10.00 3.00
DC-47 Kevin Brown.......................... 10.00 3.00
DC-48 Richie Sexson.......................... 10.00 3.00
DC-49 Jermaine Dye.......................... 10.00 3.00
DC-50 Craig Biggio.......................... 15.00 4.50

2001 Studio Diamond Cut Collection

This parallel to the Diamond Cut insert set was randomly inserted in packs. Each card was serial numbered to 75 except for six players for whom only 50 cards were issued. We have notated those cards with an SP/50 in our checklist. Those players signed 25 of these cards for inclusion in this product.

Nm-Mt Ex-Mt
1/8/19/26-28 PRINT RUN 50 #'d OF EACH

2001 Studio Leather and Lumber

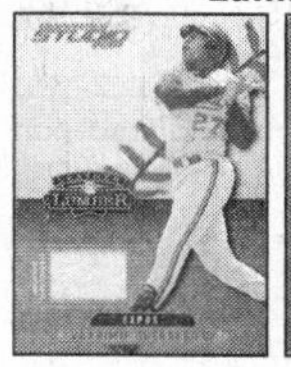

Randomly inserted in packs, these 47 cards feature player cards along with one swatch of a game-used bat. A few players were printed in lesser quantity and we have notated those players with an SP. Also, cards numbered 4,22 and 39 do not exist.

Nm-Mt Ex-Mt
COMBOS PRINT RUN 25 #'d SETS.....
NO COMBO PRICING DUE TO SCARCITY
LL-1 Barry Bonds.......................... 25.00 7.50
LL-2 Cal Ripken.......................... 40.00 12.00
LL-3 Miguel Tejada.......................... 10.00 3.00
LL-4 Does Not Exist..........................
LL-5 Frank Thomas.......................... 15.00 4.50
LL-6 Greg Maddux.......................... 15.00 4.50
LL-7 Ivan Rodriguez.......................... 15.00 4.50
LL-8 Jeff Bagwell SP.......................... 25.00 7.50
LL-9 Sean Casey SP.......................... 15.00 4.50
LL-10 Todd Helton.......................... 15.00 4.50
LL-11 Cliff Floyd.......................... 10.00 3.00
LL-12 Hideo Nomo.......................... 15.00 4.50
LL-13 Chipper Jones.......................... 15.00 4.50
LL-14 Rickey Henderson.......................... 15.00 4.50
LL-15 Richard Hidalgo.......................... 10.00 3.00
LL-16 Mike Piazza.......................... 15.00 4.50
LL-17 Larry Walker.......................... 15.00 4.50
LL-18 Tony Gwynn.......................... 15.00 4.50
LL-19 Vladimir Guerrero.......................... 15.00 4.50
LL-20 Rafael Furcal.......................... 10.00 3.00
LL-21 Roberto Alomar SP.......................... 25.00 7.50
LL-22 Does Not Exist..........................
LL-23 Albert Pujols.......................... 50.00 15.00
LL-24 Raul Mondesi.......................... 10.00 3.00
LL-25 J.D. Drew.......................... 10.00 3.00
LL-26 Jim Edmonds.......................... 10.00 3.00
LL-27 Darin Erstad SP.......................... 15.00 4.50
LL-28 Craig Biggio.......................... 15.00 4.50
LL-29 Kenny Lofton.......................... 10.00 3.00
LL-30 Juan Gonzalez.......................... 15.00 4.50
LL-31 John Olerud.......................... 10.00 3.00
LL-32 Shawn Green.......................... 10.00 3.00
LL-33 Andruw Jones SP.......................... 15.00 4.50
LL-34 Moises Alou.......................... 10.00 3.00
LL-35 Jeff Kent.......................... 10.00 3.00
LL-36 Ryan Klesko.......................... 10.00 3.00
LL-37 Luis Gonzalez.......................... 10.00 3.00
LL-38 Rafael Palmeiro.......................... 15.00 4.50
LL-39 Does Not Exist..........................
LL-40 Scott Rolen.......................... 15.00 4.50
LL-41 Carlos Lee.......................... 10.00 3.00
LL-42 Bob Abreu.......................... 10.00 3.00
LL-43 Edgardo Alfonzo.......................... 10.00 3.00
LL-44 Bernie Williams.......................... 15.00 4.50
LL-45 Brian Giles.......................... 10.00 3.00
LL-46 Jermaine Dye.......................... 10.00 3.00
LL-47 Lance Berkman.......................... 10.00 3.00
LL-48 Edgar Martinez.......................... 15.00 4.50
LL-49 Richie Sexson.......................... 10.00 3.00
LL-50 Magglio Ordonez.......................... 10.00 3.00

2001 Studio Masterstrokes

Randomly inserted in packs, these 30 cards feature the player along with both a swatch of game-used bat and a game-used jersey. These cards are serial numbered to 200 and cards numbered 13 and 15 were not issued.

Nm-Mt Ex-Mt
MS-1 Tony Gwynn.......................... 25.00 7.50
MS-2 Ivan Rodriguez.......................... 25.00 7.50
MS-3 J.D. Drew.......................... 15.00 4.50
MS-4 Cal Ripken.......................... 60.00 18.00
MS-5 Hideo Nomo.......................... 25.00 7.50
MS-6 Darin Erstad.......................... 15.00 4.50
MS-7 Frank Thomas.......................... 25.00 7.50
MS-8 Andruw Jones.......................... 15.00 4.50
MS-9 Roberto Alomar.......................... 25.00 7.50
MS-10 Larry Walker.......................... 25.00 7.50
MS-11 Vladimir Guerrero.......................... 25.00 7.50
MS-12 Barry Bonds.......................... 50.00 15.00
MS-13 Does Not Exist..........................
MS-14 Luis Gonzalez.......................... 15.00 4.50
MS-15 Does Not Exist..........................
MS-16 Juan Gonzalez.......................... 25.00 7.50
MS-17 Todd Helton.......................... 25.00 7.50
MS-18 Jeff Bagwell.......................... 25.00 7.50
MS-19 Albert Pujols.......................... 80.00 24.00
MS-20 Shawn Green.......................... 15.00 4.50
MS-21 Magglio Ordonez.......................... 15.00 4.50
MS-22 Scott Rolen.......................... 25.00 7.50
MS-23 Rafael Palmeiro.......................... 25.00 7.50
MS-24 Sean Casey.......................... 15.00 4.50
MS-25 Jim Edmonds.......................... 15.00 4.50
MS-26 Chipper Jones.......................... 25.00 7.50
MS-27 Cliff Floyd.......................... 15.00 4.50
MS-28 Carlos Lee.......................... 15.00 4.50
MS-29 Edgar Martinez.......................... 25.00 7.50
MS-30 Lance Berkman..........................

2001 Studio Masterstrokes Artist's Proofs

This parallel to the Studio Masterstroke set was issued to a print run of 25 sets. A few of the players signed their cards for inclusion in the set.

Nm-Mt Ex-Mt
2/11/14/19-20/24 ARE AUTO CARDS

2001 Studio Private Signings 5 x 7

Issued one per sealed box, these cards measure 5" by 7" and were signed by the players. A few cards were issued in shorter supply and we have notated them with an SP and print run information supplied by Donruss/Playoff.

Nm-Mt Ex-Mt
1 Bob Abreu.......................... 15.00 4.50
2 Roberto Alomar SP/200.......................... 25.00 7.50
3 Rick Ankiel.......................... 10.00 3.00
4 Josh Beckett.......................... 25.00 7.50
5 Lance Berkman.......................... 25.00 7.50
6 Wilson Betemit.......................... 15.00 4.50
7 Barry Bonds SP/95.......................... 250.00 75.00
8 Sean Casey.......................... 15.00 4.50
9 Roger Clemens SP/200.......................... 100.00 30.00
10 Adam Dunn.......................... 25.00 7.50
11 Darin Erstad SP/25..........................
12 Alex Escobar.......................... 10.00 3.00
13 Cliff Floyd.......................... 15.00 4.50
14 Jason Giambi SP/250.......................... 15.00 4.50
15 Brian Giles.......................... 15.00 4.50
16 Troy Glaus.......................... 15.00 4.50
17 Tom Glavine.......................... 40.00 12.00
18 Luis Gonzalez.......................... 15.00 4.50
19 Shawn Green SP/190.......................... 25.00 7.50
20 Vladimir Guerrero.......................... 40.00 12.00
21 Tony Gwynn SP/190.......................... 80.00 24.00
22 Todd Helton SP/125.......................... 25.00 7.50
23 Andruw Jones SP/250.......................... 15.00 4.50
24 Gabe Kapler.......................... 10.00 3.00
25 Ryan Klesko.......................... 15.00 4.50
26 Carlos Lee.......................... 15.00 4.50
27 Greg Maddux SP/200.......................... 80.00 24.00
28 Edgar Martinez.......................... 40.00 12.00
29 Mike Mussina SP/144.......................... 40.00 12.00
30 Magglio Ordonez.......................... 15.00 4.50
31 R. Palmeiro SP/250.......................... 40.00 12.00
32 Corey Patterson.......................... 15.00 4.50
33 Brad Penny.......................... 10.00 3.00
34 Albert Pujols SP/50..........................
35 Manny Ramirez SP/115.......................... 50.00 15.00
36 Cal Ripken SP/50..........................
37 Alex Rodriguez.......................... 100.00 30.00
38 Ivan Rodriguez SP/150.......................... 40.00 12.00
39 Scott Rolen.......................... 40.00 12.00
40 C.C. Sabathia.......................... 15.00 4.50
41 Curt Schilling.......................... 40.00 12.00
42 Ben Sheets.......................... 25.00 7.50
43 Alfonso Soriano.......................... 40.00 12.00
44 Mike Sweeney.......................... 15.00 4.50
45 Miguel Tejada.......................... 15.00 4.50
46 Frank Thomas.......................... 40.00 12.00
47 Kerry Wood.......................... 40.00 12.00
48 Barry Zito.......................... 25.00 7.50

2001 Studio Warning Track

Randomly inserted in packs, these 35 cards feature the player along with a swatch from an outfield-wall. Card number 26 does not exist in this set.

Nm-Mt Ex-Mt
*OFF THE WALL: RANDOM INSERTS IN PACKS
OFF THE WALL 25 SERIAL #'D SETS
OFF THE WALL: NO PRICING DUE TO SCARCITY
OTW: RANDOM INSERTS IN PACKS...
WT-1 Andruw Jones.......................... 8.00 2.40
WT-2 Rafael Palmeiro.......................... 10.00 3.00
WT-3 Gary Sheffield.......................... 8.00 2.40
WT-4 Larry Walker.......................... 10.00 3.00
WT-5 Shawn Green.......................... 8.00 2.40
WT-6 Mike Piazza.......................... 15.00 4.50
WT-7 Barry Bonds.......................... 25.00 7.50
WT-8 J.D. Drew.......................... 8.00 2.40
WT-9 Magglio Ordonez.......................... 8.00 2.40
WT-10 Todd Helton.......................... 10.00 3.00
WT-11 Juan Gonzalez.......................... 10.00 3.00
WT-12 Pat Burrell.......................... 8.00 2.40
WT-13 Mark McGwire.......................... 30.00 9.00
WT-14 Frank Robinson.......................... 10.00 3.00
WT-15 Manny Ramirez.......................... 10.00 3.00
WT-16 Lance Berkman.......................... 8.00 2.40
WT-17 Kirby Puckett.......................... 10.00 3.00
WT-18 Johnny Bench.......................... 10.00 3.00
WT-19 Chipper Jones.......................... 10.00 3.00
WT-20 Mike Schmidt.......................... 20.00 6.00
WT-21 Vladimir Guerrero.......................... 10.00 3.00
WT-22 Sammy Sosa.......................... 20.00 6.00
WT-23 Cal Ripken.......................... 30.00 9.00
WT-24 Roberto Alomar.......................... 10.00 3.00
WT-25 Willie Stargell.......................... 10.00 3.00
WT-26 Does Not Exist..........................

WT-27 Scott Rolen.................. 10.00 3.00
WT-28 R. Clemente SP 60.00 18.00
WT-29 Tony Gwynn................. 15.00 4.50
WT-30 Ivan Rodriguez 10.00 3.00
WT-31 Sean Casey.................. 8.00 2.40
WT-32 Frank Thomas............... 10.00 3.00
WT-33 Jeff Bagwell................ 10.00 3.00
WT-34 Jeff Kent..................... 8.00 2.40
WT-35 Reggie Jackson 10.00 3.00

2002 Studio

This 275 card set was issued in two separate series. The Studio product, containing cards 1-250, was released in July, 2002. The product was issued in five card packs which came 18 packs to a box and 16 boxes to a case. Cards numbered 1 through 200 feature veterans while cards 201 through 250 feature rookies and prospects and have a stated print run of 1500 serial numbered sets. Cards 251-275 were distributed in 2002 Donruss the Rookies packs in mid-December 2002. Like cards 201-250, these update cards featured a selection of prospects and were each serial-numbered to 1500 copies.

Nm-Mt Ex-Mt
COMP.LOW SET w/o SP's (200) 50.00 15.00
COMMON CARD (1-200) .... .50 .15
COMMON ROOKIE (1-200)........... .50 .15
COMMON CARD (201-275) 4.00 1.20
1 Vladimir Guerrero .... 1.25 .35
2 Chipper Jones....................... 1.25 .35
3 Bob Abreu............................. .50 .15
4 Barry Zito.............................. .50 .15
5 Larry Walker .... .75 .23
6 Miguel Tejada......................... .50 .15
7 Mike Sweeney......................... .50 .15
8 Shannon Stewart .... .50 .15
9 Sammy Sosa......................... 2.00 .60
10 Bud Smith............................ .50 .15
11 Wilson Betemit...................... .50 .15
12 Kevin Brown.......................... .50 .15
13 Ellis Burks............................ .50 .15
14 Pat Burrell............................ .50 .15
15 Cliff Floyd............................. .50 .15
16 Marcus Giles......................... .50 .15
17 Troy Glaus............................ .50 .15
18 Barry Larkin.......................... .75 .23
19 Carlos Lee............................ .50 .15
20 Brian Lawrence...................... .50 .15
21 Paul Lo Duca .... .50 .15
22 Ben Grieve .... .50 .15
23 Shawn Green .... .50 .15
24 Mike Cameron........................ .50 .15
25 Roger Clemens .... 2.50 .75
26 Joe Crede............................. .50 .15
27 Jose Cruz Jr.......................... .50 .15
28 Jeremy Affeldt....................... .50 .15
29 Adrian Beltre......................... .75 .23
30 Josh Beckett .... .50 .15
31 Roberto Alomar .... .75 .23
32 Toby Hall.............................. .50 .15
33 Mike Hampton .... .50 .15
34 Eric Milton .... .50 .15
35 Eric Munson.......................... .50 .15
36 Trot Nixon .... .50 .15
37 Roy Oswalt............................ .50 .15
38 Chan Ho Park........................ .50 .15
39 Charles Johnson .... .50 .15
40 Nick Johnson......................... .50 .15
41 Tim Hudson .... .50 .15
42 Cristian Guzman .... .50 .15
43 Drew Henson .... .50 .15
44 Mark Grace .... .75 .23
45 Luis Gonzalez........................ .50 .15
46 Pedro Martinez.................... 1.25 .35
47 Joe Mays .... .50 .15
48 Jorge Posada .... .75 .23
49 Aramis Ramirez .... .50 .15
50 Kip Wells.............................. .50 .15
51 Moises Alou .... .50 .15
52 Omar Vizquel .... .75 .23
53 Ichiro Suzuki...................... 2.00 .60
54 Jimmy Rollins........................ .50 .15
55 Freddy Garcia........................ .50 .15
56 Steve Green .... .50 .15
57 Brian Jordan .... .50 .15
58 Paul Konerko .... .50 .15
59 Jack Cust.............................. .50 .15
60 Sean Casey........................... .50 .15
61 Bret Boone........................... .50 .15
62 Hideo Nomo....................... 1.25 .35
63 Magglio Ordonez.................... .50 .15
64 Frank Thomas..................... 1.25 .35
65 Josh Towers.......................... .50 .15
66 Javier Vazquez .... .50 .15
67 Robin Ventura .... .50 .15
68 Aubrey Huff........................... .50 .15
69 Richard Hidalgo .... .50 .15
70 Brandon Claussen.................. .50 .15
71 Bartolo Colon........................ .50 .15
72 John Buck............................. .50 .15
73 Dee Brown............................ .50 .15
74 Barry Bonds....................... 3.00 .90
75 Jason Giambi........................ .50 .15
76 Erick Almonte........................ .50 .15
77 Ryan Dempster .... .50 .15
78 Jim Edmonds......................... .50 .15
79 Jay Gibbons.......................... .50 .15
80 Shigetoshi Hasegawa............. .50 .15
81 Todd Helton.......................... .75 .23
82 Erik Bedard........................... .50 .15
83 Carlos Beltran....................... .75 .23
84 Rafael Soriano .... .50 .15
85 Gary Sheffield .... .50 .15
86 Richie Sexson........................ .50 .15
87 Mike Rivera........................... .50 .15
88 Jose Ortiz............................. .50 .15
89 Abraham Nunez .... .50 .15
90 Dave Williams .... .50 .15
91 Preston Wilson .... .50 .15
92 Jason Jennings...................... .50 .15
93 Juan Diaz .... .50 .15
94 Steve Smyth.......................... .50 .15
95 Phil Nevin............................. .50 .15
96 John Olerud .... .50 .15
97 Brad Penny .... .50 .15
98 Andy Pettitte .... .75 .23
99 Juan Pierre........................... .50 .15
100 Manny Ramirez.................... .75 .23
101 Edgardo Alfonzo................... .50 .15
102 Michael Cuddyer................... .50 .15
103 Johnny Damon Sox .... 1.25 .35
104 Carlos Zambrano .... .50 .15
105 Jose Vidro............................ .50 .15
106 Tsuyoshi Shinjo.................... .50 .15
107 Ed Rogers .... .50 .15
108 Scott Rolen .... 1.25 .35
109 Mariano Rivera..................... .75 .23
110 Tim Redding .... .50 .15
111 Josh Phelps .... .50 .15
112 Gabe Kapler .... .50 .15
113 Edgar Martinez...................... .75 .23
114 Fred McGriff.......................... .75 .23
115 Raul Mondesi........................ .50 .15
116 Wade Miller........................... .50 .15
117 Mike Mussina........................ .75 .23
118 Rafael Palmeiro..................... .75 .23
119 Adam Johnson .... .50 .15
120 Rickey Henderson.............. 1.25 .35
121 Bill Hall................................ .50 .15
122 Ken Griffey Jr. .... 2.00 .60
123 Geronimo Gil......................... .50 .15
124 Robert Fick........................... .50 .15
125 Darin Erstad .... .50 .15
126 Brandon Duckworth .... .50 .15
127 Garret Anderson.................... .50 .15
128 Pedro Feliz .... .50 .15
129 Jeff Cirillo............................. .50 .15
130 Brian Giles .... .50 .15
131 Craig Biggio .... .75 .23
132 Willie Harris .... .50 .15
133 Doug Davis .... .50 .15
134 Jeff Kent............................... .50 .15
135 Terrence Long .... .50 .15
136 Carlos Delgado...................... .50 .15
137 Tino Martinez .... .75 .23
138 Donaldo Mendez .... .50 .15
139 Sean Douglass...................... .50 .15
140 Eric Chavez .... .50 .15
141 Rick Ankiel............................ .50 .15
142 Jeremy Giambi .... .50 .15
143 Juan Pena .... .50 .15
144 Bernie Williams..................... .75 .23
145 Craig Wilson .... .50 .15
146 Ricardo Rodriguez .... .50 .15
147 Albert Pujols .... 2.50 .75
148 Antonio Perez........................ .50 .15
149 Russ Ortiz............................. .50 .15
150 Corky Miller .... .50 .15
151 Rich Aurilia .... .50 .15
152 Kerry Wood........................ 1.25 .35
153 Joe Thurston......................... .50 .15
154 Jeff Deardorff........................ .50 .15
155 Jermaine Dye........................ .50 .15
156 Andruw Jones .... .50 .15
157 Victor Martinez.................... 1.25 .35
158 Nick Neugebauer................... .50 .15
159 Matt Morris........................... .50 .15
160 Casey Fossum....................... .50 .15
161 J.D. Drew............................. .50 .15
162 Matt Childers .... .50 .15
163 Mark Buehrle .... .50 .15
164 Jeff Bagwell.......................... .75 .23
165 Kazuhiro Sasaki .... .50 .15
166 Ben Sheets........................... .50 .15
167 Alex Rodriguez.................... 2.00 .60
168 Adam Pettyjohn .... .50 .15
169 Chris Snelling RC.................. .50 .15
170 Robert Person....................... .50 .15
171 Juan Uribe .... .50 .15
172 Mo Vaughn .... .50 .15
173 Alfredo Amezaga................... .50 .15
174 Ryan Drese .... .50 .15
175 Corey Thurman RC .... .50 .15
176 Jim Thome........................ 1.25 .35
177 Orlando Cabrera................... .50 .15
178 Eric Cyr .... .50 .15
179 Greg Maddux .... 2.00 .60
180 Earl Snyder RC...................... .75 .23
181 C.C. Sabathia .... .50 .15
182 Mark Mulder .... .50 .15
183 Jose Mieses .... .50 .15
184 Joe Kennedy .... .50 .15
185 Randy Johnson .... 1.25 .35
186 Tom Glavine .... .75 .23
187 Eric Junge RC .... .50 .15
188 Mike Piazza .... 2.00 .60
189 Corey Patterson .... .50 .15
190 Carlos Pena.......................... .50 .15
191 Curt Schilling .... .50 .15
192 Nomar Garciaparra .... 2.00 .60
193 Lance Berkman .... .50 .15
194 Ryan Klesko .... .50 .15
195 Ivan Rodriguez.................. 1.25 .35
196 Alfonso Soriano .... .75 .23
197 Derek Jeter....................... 3.00 .90
198 David Justice .... .50 .15
199 Juan Gonzalez...................... .75 .23
200 Adam Dunn........................... .75 .23
201 Victor Alvarez ROO RC....... 4.00 1.20
202 Miguel Asencio ROO RC...... 4.00 1.20
203 Brandon Backe ROO RC...... 5.00 1.50
204 Chris Baker ROO RC........... 4.00 1.20
205 Steve Bechler ROO RC........ 4.00 1.20
206 Francis Beltran ROO RC...... 4.00 1.20
207 Angel Berroa ROO............... 4.00 1.20
208 Hank Blalock ROO............... 5.00 1.50
209 Dewon Brazelton ROO 4.00 1.20
210 Sean Burroughs ROO.......... 4.00 1.20
211 Marlon Byrd ROO................ 4.00 1.20
212 Raul Chavez ROO RC.......... 4.00 1.20
213 Juan Cruz ROO 4.00 1.20
214 J.De La Rosa ROO RC........ 4.00 1.20
215 Doug Devore ROO RC......... 4.00 1.20
216 John Ennis ROO RC............ 4.00 1.20
217 Felix Escalona ROO RC....... 4.00 1.20
218 Morgan Ensberg ROO.......... 4.00 1.20
219 Cam Esslinger ROO RC........ 4.00 1.20
220 Kevin Frederick ROO RC...... 4.00 1.20
221 Fr.German ROO RC 4.00 1.20
222 Eric Hinske ROO 4.00 1.20
223 Ben Howard ROO RC.......... 4.00 1.20
224 Orlando Hudson ROO 4.00 1.20
225 Travis Hughes ROO RC....... 4.00 1.20
226 Kazuhisa Ishii ROO RC....... 10.00 3.00
227 Ryan Jamison ROO............. 4.00 1.20
228 Reed Johnson ROO RC........ 5.00 1.50
229 Kyle Kane ROO RC.............. 4.00 1.20
230 Austin Kearns ROO 4.00 1.20
231 Sat.Komiyama ROO RC........ 4.00 1.20
232 Jason Lane ROO 4.00 1.20
233 Jeremy Lambert ROO RC...... 4.00 1.20
234 And. Machado ROO RC........ 4.00 1.20
235 Brian Mallette ROO RC........ 4.00 1.20
236 Tak. Nomura ROO RC.......... 4.00 1.20
237 Jorge Padilla ROO RC......... 4.00 1.20
238 Luis Ugueto ROO RC........... 4.00 1.20
239 Mark Prior ROO 12.00 3.60
240 Rene Reyes ROO RC............ 4.00 1.20
241 Deivis Santos ROO.............. 4.00 1.20
242 Elio Serrano ROO RC........... 4.00 1.20
243 Tom Shearn ROO RC............ 4.00 1.20
244 Allan Simpson ROO RC......... 4.00 1.20
245 So Taguchi ROO RC.............. 5.00 1.50
246 Dennis Tankersley ROO......... 4.00 1.20
247 Mark Teixeira ROO 5.00 1.50
248 Matt Thornton ROO RC......... 4.00 1.20
249 Bobby Hill ROO 4.00 1.20
250 Ramon Vazquez ROO 4.00 1.20
251 Freddy Sanchez ROO RC 4.00 1.20
252 Josh Bard ROO RC............... 4.00 1.20
253 Trey Hodges ROO RC............ 4.00 1.20
254 Jorge Sosa ROO RC.............. 4.00 1.20
255 Ben Kozlowski ROO RC 4.00 1.20
256 Eric Good ROO RC................ 4.00 1.20
257 Brian Tallet ROO RC............. 4.00 1.20
258 P.J. Bevis ROO RC................ 4.00 1.20
259 Rodrigo Rosario ROO RC 4.00 1.20
260 Kirk Saarloos ROO RC........... 4.00 1.20
261 Run. Hernandez ROO RC...... 4.00 1.20
262 Josh Hancock ROO RC.......... 4.00 1.20
263 Tim Kalita ROO RC............... 4.00 1.20
264 J.Simontacchi ROO RC.......... 4.00 1.20
265 Clay Condrey ROO RC.......... 4.00 1.20
266 Cliff Lee ROO RC.................. 5.00 1.50
267 Aaron Guiel ROO RC............. 4.00 1.20
268 Andy Pratt ROO RC............... 4.00 1.20
269 Wilson Valdez ROO RC.......... 4.00 1.20
270 Oliver Perez ROO RC 10.00 3.00
271 Joe Borchard ROO................ 4.00 1.20
272 J.Robertson ROO RC............. 4.00 1.20
273 Aaron Cook ROO RC.............. 4.00 1.20
274 Kevin Cash ROO RC.............. 4.00 1.20
275 Chone Figgins ROO RC 5.00 1.50

2002 Studio Private Signings

Randomly inserted in packs of Studio and Donruss the Rookies, these 210 cards partially parallel the 2002 Studio set. Since these cards are signed to a variable amount of cards, we have listed the print run next to the player's name. Those players who signed 25 or fewer cards are not priced due to market scarcity.

Nm-Mt Ex-Mt
1 Vladimir Guerrero/25
2 Chipper Jones/15
3 Bob Abreu/50.................. 25.00 7.50
4 Barry Zito/25
6 Miguel Tejada/50.............. 25.00 7.50
7 Mike Sweeney/50.............. 25.00 7.50
8 Shannon Stewart/50........... 25.00 7.50
10 Bud Smith/100................. 15.00 4.50
11 Wilson Betemit/250 .... 10.00 3.00
12 Kevin Brown/25
15 Cliff Floyd/50.................. 25.00 7.50
16 Marcus Giles/250.............. 15.00 4.50
17 Troy Glaus/50.................. 25.00 7.50
18 Barry Larkin/25
19 Carlos Lee/25
20 Brian Lawrence/250.......... 10.00 3.00
21 Paul Lo Duca/50.............. 25.00 7.50
25 Roger Clemens/15
26 Joe Crede/250................. 10.00 3.00
28 Jeremy Affeldt/250........... 10.00 3.00
29 Adrian Beltre/25
30 Josh Beckett/25
31 Roberto Alomar/25
32 Toby Hall/250.................. 10.00 3.00
35 Eric Munson/25
37 Roy Oswalt/50................. 25.00 7.50
40 Nick Johnson/250............. 15.00 4.50
41 Tim Hudson/25
43 Drew Henson/150............. 25.00 7.50
45 Luis Gonzalez/15
46 Pedro Martinez/15
47 Joe Mays/100.................. 15.00 4.50
49 Aramis Ramirez/50........... 25.00 7.50
50 Kip Wells/250.................. 10.00 3.00
51 Moises Alou/15
55 Freddy Garcia/50............. 25.00 7.50
56 Steve Green/250.............. 10.00 3.00
59 Jack Cust/250.................. 10.00 3.00
60 Sean Casey/50................. 25.00 7.50
63 Magglio Ordonez/15
64 Frank Thomas/15
65 Josh Towers/250.............. 10.00 3.00
66 Javier Vazquez/100........... 20.00 6.00
68 Aubrey Huff/250............... 15.00 4.50
69 Richard Hidalgo/25
70 Brandon Claussen/250....... 10.00 3.00
72 John Buck/250................. 10.00 3.00
73 Dee Brown/250................. 10.00 3.00
75 Jason Giambi/25
76 Erick Almonte/250 .... 10.00 3.00
79 Jay Gibbons/250.............. 10.00 3.00
81 Todd Helton/15
82 Erik Bedard/250 .... 10.00 3.00
83 Carlos Beltran/15
84 Rafael Soriano/250 .... 10.00 3.00
85 Gary Sheffield/15
86 Richie Sexson/50 .... 25.00 7.50
87 Mike Rivera/250............... 10.00 3.00
88 Jose Ortiz/250................. 10.00 3.00
89 Abraham Nunez/250 .... 10.00 3.00
90 Dave Williams/250............ 10.00 3.00
92 Jason Jennings/250........... 10.00 3.00
93 Juan Diaz/250................. 10.00 3.00
94 Steve Smyth/250.............. 10.00 3.00
97 Brad Penny/80 .... 15.00 4.50
99 Juan Pierre/100 .... 20.00 6.00
100 Manny Ramirez/15
102 Michael Cuddyer/250........ 10.00 3.00
104 Carlos Zambrano/250 .... 25.00 7.50
105 Jose Vidro/100............... 15.00 4.50
107 Ed Rogers/250 .... 10.00 3.00
108 Scott Rolen/15
110 Tim Redding/250 .... 10.00 3.00
111 Josh Phelps/250 .... 10.00 3.00
112 Gabe Kapler/100............. 15.00 4.50
113 Edgar Martinez/50........... 50.00 15.00
116 Wade Miller/250.............. 10.00 3.00
117 Mike Mussina/15
118 Rafael Palmeiro/25
120 Rickey Henderson/15
121 Bill Hall/250.................. 10.00 3.00
123 Geronimo Gil/250............ 10.00 3.00
124 Robert Fick/150 .... 10.00 3.00
125 Darin Erstad/15
126 Brandon Duckworth/250.... 10.00 3.00
128 Pedro Feliz/250 .... 10.00 3.00
130 Brian Giles/15
131 Craig Biggio/15
132 Willie Harris/250 .... 10.00 3.00
133 Doug Davis/250 .... 10.00 3.00
135 Terrence Long/50............ 25.00 7.50
138 Donaldo Mendez/250 .... 10.00 3.00
139 Sean Douglass/250.......... 10.00 3.00
140 Eric Chavez/15
141 Rick Ankiel/250.............. 10.00 3.00
142 Jeremy Giambi/100.......... 15.00 4.50
143 Juan Pena/250 .... 10.00 3.00
144 Bernie Williams/15
145 Craig Wilson/250 .... 15.00 4.50
146 Ricardo Rodriguez/250...... 10.00 3.00
147 Albert Pujols/15
148 Antonio Perez/250 .... 10.00 3.00
150 Corky Miller/250 .... 10.00 3.00
151 Rich Aurilia/25
152 Kerry Wood/25
153 Joe Thurston/250............. 10.00 3.00
154 Jeff Deardorff/250........... 10.00 3.00
155 Jermaine Dye/15
156 Andruw Jones/15
157 Victor Martinez/250 .... 40.00 12.00
158 Nick Neugebauer/150....... 10.00 3.00
160 Casey Fossum/250.......... 10.00 3.00
161 J.D. Drew/25
162 Matt Childers/250 .... 10.00 3.00
163 Mark Buehrle/150 .... 15.00 4.50
164 Jeff Bagwell/15
166 Ben Sheets/100.............. 20.00 6.00
167 Alex Rodriguez/15
168 Adam Pettyjohn/250 .... 10.00 3.00
169 Chris Snelling/250 .... 10.00 3.00
170 Robert Person/250.......... 10.00 3.00
171 Juan Uribe/250 .... 10.00 3.00
173 Alfredo Amezaga/250...... 10.00 3.00
175 Corey Thurman/250 .... 10.00 3.00
176 Jim Thome/15
178 Eric Cyr/250 .... 10.00 3.00
179 Greg Maddux/15
180 Earl Snyder/250 .... 15.00 4.50
181 C.C. Sabathia/50 .... 25.00 7.50
182 Mark Mulder/50 .... 25.00 7.50
183 Jose Mieses/250 .... 10.00 3.00
184 Joe Kennedy/250 .... 10.00 3.00
186 Tom Glavine/15
187 Eric Junge/250.............. 10.00 3.00
189 Corey Patterson/205 ...... 15.00 4.50
190 Carlos Pena/200............ 10.00 3.00
191 Curt Schilling/15
192 Nomar Garciaparra/15
193 Lance Berkman/15
194 Ryan Klesko/15
195 Ivan Rodriguez/15
196 Alfonso Soriano/50 .... 50.00 15.00
198 David Justice/15
199 Juan Gonzalez/15
200 Adam Dunn/25
201 Victor Alvarez ROO/250 ..... 10.00 3.00
203 Brandon Backe ROO/250 ... 25.00 7.50
204 Chris Baker ROO/250 .... 10.00 3.00
205 Steve Bechler ROO/250 .... 10.00 3.00
206 Francis Beltran ROO/250 ... 10.00 3.00
207 Angel Berroa ROO/250...... 10.00 3.00
208 Hank Blalock ROO/100....... 40.00 12.00
209 Dewon Brazelton ROO/200 10.00 3.00
210 Sean Burroughs ROO/50 .... 25.00 7.50
211 Marlon Byrd ROO/200 .... 10.00 3.00
212 Raul Chavez ROO/250 ...... 10.00 3.00
213 Juan Cruz ROO/50 .... 25.00 7.50
214 Jorge De La Rosa ROO/250 10.00 3.00
215 Doug Devore ROO/250 ...... 10.00 3.00
216 John Ennis ROO/250......... 10.00 3.00
217 Felix Escalona ROO/250..... 10.00 3.00
218 Morgan Ensberg ROO/250. 15.00 4.50
219 Cam Esslinger ROO/250 .... 10.00 3.00
220 Kevin Frederick ROO/250.... 10.00 3.00
221 Franklyn German ROO/250 10.00 3.00
222 Eric Hinske ROO/250 .... 10.00 3.00
223 Ben Howard ROO/250........ 10.00 3.00
224 Orlando Hudson ROO/250 . 10.00 3.00
225 Travis Hughes ROO/250..... 10.00 3.00
226 Kazuhisa Ishii ROO/50 ...... 50.00 15.00
227 Ryan Jamison ROO/250...... 10.00 3.00
228 Reed Johnson ROO/250...... 15.00 4.50
229 Kyle Kane ROO/250........... 10.00 3.00
230 Austin Kearns ROO/250..... 15.00 4.50
231 Satoru Komiyama ROO/50. 25.00 7.50
232 Jason Lane ROO/200 .... 10.00 3.00
233 Jeremy Lambert ROO/250 . 10.00 3.00
234 And Machado ROO/200 ..... 10.00 3.00
235 Brian Mallette ROO/250 .... 10.00 3.00
236 Takahito Nomura ROO/100 25.00 7.50
237 Jorge Padilla ROO/200....... 10.00 3.00
238 Luis Ugueto ROO/250 .... 10.00 3.00
239 Mark Prior ROO/100 .... 80.00 24.00
240 Rene Reyes ROO/250 .... 10.00 3.00
241 Deivis Santos ROO/250 ..... 10.00 3.00
242 Elio Serrano ROO/250 .... 10.00 3.00
243 Tom Shearn ROO/250......... 10.00 3.00
244 Allan Simpson ROO/250 ..... 10.00 3.00
245 So Taguchi ROO/100.......... 20.00 6.00
246 Dennis Tankersley ROO/100 15.00 4.50
247 Mark Teixeira ROO/50 .... 40.00 12.00
248 Matt Thornton ROO/250 ..... 10.00 3.00
249 Bobby Hill ROO/100........... 15.00 4.50
250 Ramon Vazquez ROO/250.. 10.00 3.00
252 Josh Bard ROO/100 .... 15.00 4.50
253 Trey Hodges ROO/250 .... 10.00 3.00
255 Ben Kozlowski ROO/200 ..... 10.00 3.00
256 Eric Good ROO/200 .... 10.00 3.00
257 Brian Tallet ROO/100......... 15.00 4.50
258 P.J. Bevis ROO/50 .... 25.00 7.50
259 Rodrigo Rosario ROO/250 . 10.00 3.00
260 Kirk Saarloos ROO/100 ...... 15.00 4.50
263 Tim Kalita ROO/50 .... 15.00 4.50
266 Cliff Lee ROO/100 .... 25.00 7.50
268 Andy Pratt ROO/250 .... 10.00 3.00
269 Wilson Valdez ROO/200..... 10.00 3.00
270 Oliver Perez ROO/25
271 Joe Borchard ROO/100...... 15.00 4.50
274 Kevin Cash ROO/100 .... 15.00 4.50
275 Chone Figgins ROO/100..... 25.00 7.50

2002 Studio Proofs

Randomly issued in Studio and Donruss the Rookies packs, this is a complete parallel of the 2002 Studio set. Cards 1-250 were distributed in Studio packs and 251-275 in Donruss the Rookies. These cards were printed to a stated print run of 100 serial numbered sets.

Nm-Mt Ex-Mt
*PROOFS 1-200: 4X TO 10X BASIC ...
*PROOFS RC'S 1-200: 3X TO 8X BASIC
*PROOFS 201-275: 1X TO 2.5X BASIC
201 Victor Alvarez ROO 10.00 3.00
202 Miguel Asencio ROO........... 10.00 3.00
203 Brandon Backe ROO........... 12.00 3.60
204 Chris Baker ROO............... 10.00 3.00
205 Steve Bechler ROO............ 10.00 3.00
206 Francis Beltran ROO.......... 10.00 3.00
207 Angel Berroa ROO............. 10.00 3.00
208 Hank Blalock ROO............. 12.00 3.60
209 Dewon Brazelton ROO 10.00 3.00
210 Sean Burroughs ROO......... 10.00 3.00
211 Marlon Byrd ROO............... 10.00 3.00
212 Raul Chavez ROO.............. 10.00 3.00
213 Juan Cruz ROO................. 10.00 3.00
214 Jorge De La Rosa ROO...... 10.00 3.00
215 Doug Devore ROO 10.00 3.00
216 John Ennis ROO 10.00 3.00
217 Felix Escalona ROO........... 10.00 3.00
218 Morgan Ensberg ROO......... 10.00 3.00
219 Cam Esslinger ROO 10.00 3.00
220 Kevin Frederick ROO.......... 10.00 3.00
221 Franklyn German ROO 10.00 3.00
222 Eric Hinske ROO 10.00 3.00
223 Ben Howard ROO 10.00 3.00
224 Orlando Hudson ROO 10.00 3.00
225 Travis Hughes ROO 10.00 3.00
226 Kazuhisa Ishii ROO 25.00 7.50
227 Ryan Jamison ROO 10.00 3.00
228 Reed Johnson ROO............ 12.00 3.60
229 Kyle Kane ROO.................. 10.00 3.00
230 Austin Kearns ROO 10.00 3.00
231 Satoru Komiyama ROO 10.00 3.00
232 Jason Lane ROO 10.00 3.00
233 Jeremy Lambert ROO 10.00 3.00
234 Anderson Machado ROO ... 10.00 3.00
235 Brian Mallette ROO 10.00 3.00
236 Takahito Nomura ROO 10.00 3.00
237 Jorge Padilla ROO 10.00 3.00
238 Luis Ugueto ROO 10.00 3.00
239 Mark Prior ROO 30.00 9.00
240 Rene Reyes ROO 10.00 3.00
241 Deivis Santos ROO............. 10.00 3.00
242 Elio Serrano ROO 10.00 3.00
243 Tom Shearn ROO 10.00 3.00
244 Allan Simpson ROO............ 10.00 3.00
245 So Taguchi ROO 12.00 3.60
246 Dennis Tankersley ROO...... 10.00 3.00
247 Mark Teixeira ROO 12.00 3.60
248 Matt Thornton ROO 10.00 3.00
249 Bobby Hill ROO 10.00 3.00
250 Ramon Vazquez ROO 10.00 3.00
251 Freddy Sanchez ROO 10.00 3.00
252 Josh Bard ROO 10.00 3.00
253 Trey Hodges ROO 10.00 3.00
254 Jorge Sosa ROO 10.00 3.00
255 Ben Kozlowski ROO 10.00 3.00
256 Eric Good ROO 10.00 3.00
257 Brian Tallet ROO 10.00 3.00
258 P.J. Bevis ROO 10.00 3.00
259 Rodrigo Rosario ROO 10.00 3.00
260 Kirk Saarloos ROO 10.00 3.00
261 Runelvys Hernandez ROO .. 10.00 3.00
262 Josh Hancock ROO 10.00 3.00
263 Tim Kalita ROO 10.00 3.00
264 Jason Simontacchi ROO 10.00 3.00
265 Clay Condrey ROO 10.00 3.00
266 Cliff Lee ROO 12.00 3.60
267 Aaron Guiel ROO 10.00 3.00
268 Andy Pratt ROO 10.00 3.00
269 Wilson Valdez ROO 10.00 3.00
270 Oliver Perez ROO 25.00 7.50
271 Joe Borchard ROO 10.00 3.00
272 Jeriome Robertson ROO 10.00 3.00
273 Aaron Cook ROO 10.00 3.00
274 Kevin Cash ROO 10.00 3.00
275 Chone Figgins ROO 12.00 3.60

2002 Studio Classic

Randomly inserted in packs, these 25 card feature players elected to the Hall of Fame on the first ballot and have a stated print run of 1,000 serial numbered sets.

Nm-Mt Ex-Mt
COMPLETE SET (25).............. 150.00 45.00
*1ST BALLOT: 2X TO 5X BASIC CLASSIC
1ST BALLOT RANDOM IN PACKS
1ST BALLOT PRINT RUN BASED ON HOF YR
1 Kirby Puckett 8.00 2.40

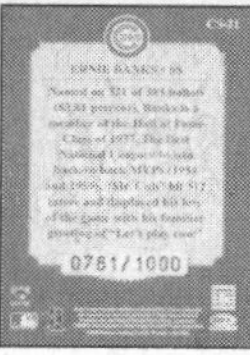

2 George Brett 15.00 4.50
3 Nolan Ryan 15.00 4.50
4 Mike Schmidt 12.00 3.60
5 Steve Carlton 5.00 1.50
6 Reggie Jackson 5.00 1.50
7 Tom Seaver 5.00 1.50
8 Joe Morgan 5.00 1.50
9 Jim Palmer 5.00 1.50
10 Johnny Bench 8.00 2.40
11 Willie McCovey 5.00 1.50
12 Brooks Robinson 5.00 1.50
13 Al Kaline 8.00 2.40
14 Stan Musial 10.00 3.00
15 Ozzie Smith 10.00 3.00
16 Dave Winfield 5.00 1.50
17 Robin Yount 10.00 3.00
18 Rod Carew 5.00 1.50
19 Willie Stargell 5.00 1.50
20 Lou Brock 5.00 1.50
21 Ernie Banks 8.00 2.40
22 Ted Williams 12.00 3.60
23 Jackie Robinson 8.00 2.40
24 Roberto Clemente 15.00 4.50
25 Lou Gehrig 15.00 4.50

2002 Studio Classic Autographs

Randomly inserted in packs, these 19 cards partially parallel the Studio Classic insert set. We have listed the stated print runs next to the player's name and since no player signed more than 20 cards there is no pricing due to market scarcity.

Nm-Mt Ex-Mt
1 Kirby Puckett/15
2 George Brett/15
3 Nolan Ryan/15
4 Mike Schmidt/20
5 Steve Carlton/20
6 Reggie Jackson/15
7 Tom Seaver/15
8 Joe Morgan/20
10 Johnny Bench/20
11 Willie McCovey/15
12 Brooks Robinson/20
13 Al Kaline/20
14 Stan Musial/15
15 Ozzie Smith/15
16 Dave Winfield/15
17 Robin Yount/15
18 Rod Carew/25
20 Lou Brock/20
21 Ernie Banks/20

2002 Studio Diamond Collection

Inserted in packs at stated odds of one in 17, these 25 cards feature some of the most popular players in baseball.

Nm-Mt Ex-Mt
COMPLETE SET (25) 120.00 36.00
1 Todd Helton 4.00 1.20
2 Chipper Jones 4.00 1.20
3 Lance Berkman 4.00 1.20
4 Derek Jeter 10.00 3.00
5 Hideo Nomo 4.00 1.20
6 Kazuhisa Ishii 5.00 1.50
7 Barry Bonds 10.00 3.00
8 Alex Rodriguez 6.00 1.80
9 Ichiro Suzuki 6.00 1.80
10 Mike Piazza 6.00 1.80
11 Jim Thome 4.00 1.20
12 Greg Maddux 6.00 1.80
13 Jeff Bagwell 4.00 1.20
14 Vladimir Guerrero 4.00 1.20
15 Ken Griffey Jr. 6.00 1.80
16 Jason Giambi 4.00 1.20
17 Nomar Garciaparra 6.00 1.80
18 Albert Pujols 8.00 2.40
19 Manny Ramirez 4.00 1.20
20 Pedro Martinez 4.00 1.20
21 Roger Clemens 8.00 2.40
22 Randy Johnson 4.00 1.20
23 Mark Prior 6.00 1.80
24 So Taguchi 4.00 1.20
25 Sammy Sosa 6.00 1.80

2002 Studio Diamond Collection Artist's Proofs

Randomly inserted in packs, these cards partially parallel the Diamond Collection insert set. Each card features a memorabilia piece and we have notated both the information as to what type of piece along with the stated print run next to the player's name in our checklist.

Nm-Mt Ex-Mt
1 Todd Helton Jsy/200 15.00 4.50
2 Chipper Jones Jsy/150 15.00 4.50
3 Lance Berkman Jsy/200 15.00 4.50
4 Derek Jeter Base/200 25.00 7.50
5 Hideo Nomo Jsy/150 80.00 24.00
6 Kazuhisa Ishii Jsy/150 20.00 6.00
7 Barry Bonds Base/200 25.00 7.50
8 Alex Rodriguez Jsy/150 20.00 6.00
9 Ichiro Suzuki Base/200 25.00 7.50
10 Mike Piazza Jsy/150 15.00 4.50
11 Jim Thome Jsy/150 15.00 4.50
12 Greg Maddux Jsy/150 15.00 4.50
13 Jeff Bagwell Jsy/150 15.00 4.50
14 Vladimir Guerrero Jsy/200 15.00 4.50
15 Ken Griffey Jr. Base/200 15.00 4.50
16 Jason Giambi Base/200 15.00 4.50
17 Nomar Garciaparra Jsy/150 20.00 6.00
18 Albert Pujols Base/200 15.00 4.50
19 Manny Ramirez Jsy/150 15.00 4.50
20 Pedro Martinez Jsy/150 15.00 4.50
21 Roger Clemens Jsy/150 25.00 7.50
22 Randy Johnson Jsy/150 15.00 4.50
24 So Taguchi Jsy/200 15.00 4.50
25 Sammy Sosa Base/200 15.00 4.50

2002 Studio Heroes Icons Texans

Randomly inserted in packs, these four cards honor that Texas sports legend, Nolan Ryan. There are four stated print runs with the highlight being an autograph card numbered to a stated print run of 32 serial numbered cards.

Nm-Mt Ex-Mt
HIT-2 Nolan Ryan 10.00 3.00
HIT-2 Nolan Ryan/500 15.00 4.50
HIT-2 Nolan Ryan/100 50.00 15.00
HIT-2 Nolan Ryan AU/32 250.00 75.00

2002 Studio Leather and Lumber

Randomly inserted in packs, these 25 cards feature some of the game's most dominating batsmen. Each card contains one game-used bat piece. And since there are different print runs, we have put that information next to the player's name in our checklist.

Nm-Mt Ex-Mt
1 Nomar Garciaparra/200 25.00 7.50
2 Jeff Bagwell/150 15.00 4.50
3 Alex Rodriguez/200 20.00 6.00
4 Vladimir Guerrero/100 20.00 6.00
5 Luis Gonzalez/200 10.00 3.00
6 Chipper Jones/200 15.00 4.50
7 Shawn Green/200 10.00 3.00
8 Kirby Puckett/100 20.00 6.00
9 Juan Gonzalez/200 15.00 4.50
10 Troy Glaus/200 10.00 3.00
11 Don Mattingly/100 40.00 12.00
12 Todd Helton/200 15.00 4.50
13 Jim Thome/200 15.00 4.50
14 Rickey Henderson/200 15.00 4.50
15 Mike Schmidt/100 60.00 18.00
16 Adam Dunn/100 20.00 6.00
17 Ivan Rodriguez/200 15.00 4.50
18 Manny Ramirez/150 15.00 4.50
19 Tsuyoshi Shinjo/200 10.00 3.00
20 Andruw Jones/150 10.00 3.00
21 Roberto Alomar/200 15.00 4.50
22 Lance Berkman/200 10.00 3.00
23 Derek Jeter Ball/50 80.00 24.00
24 Ichiro Suzuki Ball/50 80.00 24.00
25 Mike Piazza/200 15.00 4.50

2002 Studio Leather and Lumber Artist's Proofs

Randomly inserted in packs, these cards parallel the Leather and Lumber insert set. These cards have a stated print run of 50 serial numbered sets which included not only the bat piece but also either a ball or batting glove piece.

Nm-Mt Ex-Mt
5 Luis Gonzalez SP/25

2002 Studio Masterstrokes

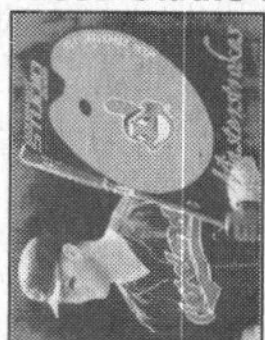

Inserted in packs at stated odds of one in 17, these 25 cards feature baseball's most skilled hitters.

Nm-Mt Ex-Mt
COMPLETE SET (25) 100.00 30.00
1 Vladimir Guerrero 4.00 1.20
2 Frank Thomas 4.00 1.20
3 Alex Rodriguez 6.00 1.80
4 Manny Ramirez 4.00 1.20
5 Jeff Bagwell 4.00 1.20
6 Jim Thome 4.00 1.20
7 Ichiro Suzuki 6.00 1.80
8 Andruw Jones 4.00 1.20
9 Troy Glaus 4.00 1.20
10 Chipper Jones 4.00 1.20
11 Juan Gonzalez 4.00 1.20
12 Lance Berkman 4.00 1.20
13 Mike Piazza 6.00 1.80
14 Darin Erstad 4.00 1.20
15 Albert Pujols 8.00 2.40
16 Kazuhisa Ishii 5.00 1.50
17 Shawn Green 4.00 1.20
18 Rafael Palmeiro 4.00 1.20
19 Todd Helton 4.00 1.20
20 Carlos Delgado 4.00 1.20
21 Ivan Rodriguez 4.00 1.20
22 Luis Gonzalez 4.00 1.20
23 Derek Jeter 10.00 3.00
24 Nomar Garciaparra 6.00 1.80
25 J.D. Drew 4.00 1.20

2002 Studio Masterstrokes Artist's Proofs

Randomly inserted in packs, these 25 cards are a parallel to the Masterstrokes insert set and most of them feature a bat-jersey combo. The Ichiro Suzuki, Derek Jeter and J.D. Drew cards feature a ball-base combo.

Nm-Mt Ex-Mt
1 Vladimir Guerrero/200 20.00 6.00
2 Frank Thomas/200 20.00 6.00
3 Alex Rodriguez/100 40.00 12.00
4 Manny Ramirez/200 20.00 6.00
5 Jeff Bagwell/150 20.00 6.00
6 Jim Thome/200 20.00 6.00
7 Ichiro Suzuki/100 60.00 18.00
8 Andruw Jones/200 15.00 4.50
9 Troy Glaus/200 15.00 4.50
10 Chipper Jones/200 20.00 6.00
11 Juan Gonzalez/200 20.00 6.00
12 Lance Berkman/200 15.00 4.50
13 Mike Piazza/200 40.00 12.00
14 Darin Erstad/200 15.00 4.50
15 Albert Pujols/100 40.00 12.00
16 Kazuhisa Ishii/150 25.00 7.50
17 Shawn Green/200 15.00 4.50
18 Rafael Palmeiro/200 20.00 6.00
19 Todd Helton/200 20.00 6.00
20 Carlos Delgado/200 15.00 4.50
21 Ivan Rodriguez/200 20.00 6.00
22 Luis Gonzalez/200 15.00 4.50
23 Derek Jeter/100 60.00 18.00
24 Nomar Garciaparra/150 40.00 12.00
25 J.D. Drew/150 15.00 4.50

2002 Studio Spirit of the Game

Inserted in packs at a stated odds of one in nine, these 50 cards highlight players who play the game with a real passion.

Nm-Mt Ex-Mt
COMPLETE SET (50) 120.00 36.00
1 Alex Rodriguez 6.00 1.80
2 Curt Schilling 2.50 .75
3 Hideo Nomo 4.00 1.20
4 Derek Jeter 10.00 3.00
5 Mike Sweeney 2.50 .75
6 Mike Piazza 6.00 1.80
7 Roger Clemens 8.00 2.40
8 Shawn Green 2.50 .75
9 Vladimir Guerrero 4.00 1.20
10 Carlos Lee 2.50 .75
11 Edgar Martinez 2.50 .75
12 Albert Pujols 8.00 2.40
13 Mark Prior 6.00 1.80
14 Mark Buehrle 2.50 .75
15 Chipper Jones 4.00 1.20
16 Paul Lo Duca 2.50 .75
17 Frank Thomas 4.00 1.20
18 Randy Johnson 4.00 1.20
19 Cliff Floyd 2.50 .75
20 Todd Helton 2.50 .75
21 Luis Gonzalez 2.50 .75
22 Brandon Duckworth 2.50 .75
23 Jason Giambi 2.50 .75
24 Juan Uribe 2.50 .75
25 Dewon Brazelton 2.50 .75
26 J.D. Drew 2.50 .75
27 Troy Glaus 2.50 .75
28 Wade Miller 2.50 .75
29 Darin Erstad 2.50 .75
30 Brian Giles 2.50 .75
31 Lance Berkman 2.50 .75
32 Shannon Stewart 2.50 .75
33 Kazuhisa Ishii 5.00 1.50
34 Corey Patterson 2.50 .75
35 Rafael Palmeiro 2.50 .75
36 Roy Oswalt 2.50 .75
37 Jason Lane 2.50 .75
38 Andruw Jones 2.50 .75
39 Brad Penny 2.50 .75
40 Bud Smith 2.50 .75
41 Carlos Beltran 2.50 .75
42 Magglio Ordonez 2.50 .75
43 Craig Biggio 2.50 .75
44 Hank Blalock 4.00 1.20
45 Jeff Bagwell 2.50 .75
46 Josh Beckett 2.50 .75
47 Juan Cruz 2.50 .75
48 Kerry Wood 4.00 1.20
49 Brandon Berger 2.50 .75
50 Juan Pierre 2.50 .75

2002 Studio Spirit of the Game Hats Off

Randomly inserted in packs, these 24 cards form a partial parallel to the Spirit of the Game insert set. These cards feature pieces of game-used hats and most are serial numbered to 100. The Kazuishi Ishii card has a stated print run of 50 serial numbered sets.

Nm-Mt Ex-Mt
MLB LOGO PRINT RUN 1 SERIAL #'d SET
NO MLB LOGO PRICING DUE TO SCARCITY
USA FLAG PRINT RUN 1 SERIAL #'d SET
NO USA FLAG PRICING DUE TO SCARCITY
10 Carlos Lee 25.00 7.50
14 Mark Buehrle 25.00 7.50
16 Paul Lo Duca 25.00 7.50
22 Brandon Duckworth 15.00 4.50
26 J.D. Drew 25.00 7.50
28 Wade Miller 15.00 4.50
30 Brian Giles 25.00 7.50
31 Lance Berkman 25.00 7.50
32 Shannon Stewart 25.00 7.50
33 Kazuhisa Ishii SP/50 50.00 15.00
35 Rafael Palmeiro 40.00 12.00
36 Roy Oswalt 25.00 7.50
37 Jason Lane 15.00 4.50
38 Andruw Jones 25.00 7.50
39 Brad Penny 15.00 4.50
40 Bud Smith 15.00 4.50
41 Carlos Beltran 40.00 12.00
42 Magglio Ordonez 25.00 7.50
43 Craig Biggio 40.00 12.00
45 Jeff Bagwell 40.00 12.00
47 Juan Cruz 15.00 4.50
48 Kerry Wood 40.00 12.00
49 Brandon Berger 15.00 4.50
50 Juan Pierre 15.00 7.50

2002 Studio Stars

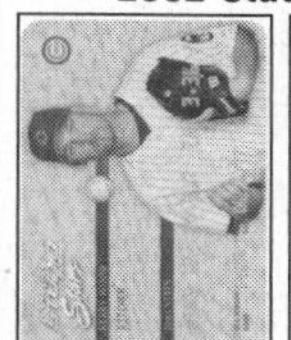
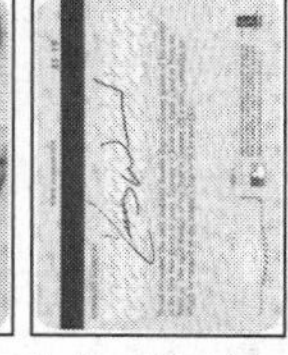

Randomly inserted in packs, these 50 cards feature leading players in a credit charge design. These cards have some key statistics for the players listed across the front of their cards.

Nm-Mt Ex-Mt
COMPLETE SET (50) 100.00 30.00
1 Mike Piazza 4.00 1.20
2 Ivan Rodriguez 2.00 .60
3 Albert Pujols 5.00 1.50
4 Scott Rolen 2.00 .60
5 Alex Rodriguez 4.00 1.20
6 Curt Schilling 2.00 .60
7 Vladimir Guerrero 2.00 .60
8 Jim Thome 2.00 .60
9 Derek Jeter 6.00 1.80
10 C.C. Sabathia 2.00 .60
11 Sammy Sosa 4.00 1.20
12 Adam Dunn 2.00 .60
13 Bernie Williams 2.00 .60
14 Ichiro Suzuki 4.00 1.20
15 Barry Bonds 6.00 1.80
16 Rickey Henderson 2.00 .60
17 Ken Griffey Jr. 4.00 1.20
18 Kazuhisa Ishii 2.50 .75
19 Kerry Wood 2.00 .60
20 Todd Helton 2.00 .60
21 Hideo Nomo 2.00 .60
22 Frank Thomas 2.00 .60
23 Manny Ramirez 2.00 .60
24 Luis Gonzalez 2.00 .60
25 Rafael Palmeiro 2.00 .60
26 Mike Mussina 2.00 .60
27 Roy Oswalt 2.00 .60
28 Darin Erstad 2.00 .60
29 Barry Larkin 2.00 .60
30 Randy Johnson 2.00 .60
31 Tom Glavine 2.00 .60
32 Lance Berkman 2.00 .60
33 Juan Gonzalez 2.00 .60
34 Shawn Green 2.00 .60
35 Nomar Garciaparra 4.00 1.20
36 Troy Glaus 2.00 .60
37 Tim Hudson 2.00 .60
38 Carlos Delgado 2.00 .60
39 Jason Giambi 2.00 .60
40 Andruw Jones 2.00 .60
41 Roberto Alomar 2.00 .60
42 Greg Maddux 4.00 1.20
43 Pedro Martinez 2.00 .60
44 Tony Gwynn 3.00 .90
45 Alfonso Soriano 2.00 .60
46 Chipper Jones 2.00 .60
47 J.D. Drew 2.00 .60
48 Roger Clemens 5.00 1.50
49 Barry Zito 2.00 .60
50 Jeff Bagwell 2.00 .60

2003 Studio

This 210-card set was issued in two separate series. The primary Studio product - containing cards 1-200 from the basic set - was released in June, 2003. The set was issued in six card packs with an $4 SRP which came packed 20 packs to a box and 16 boxes to a case. The first 190 cards feature just one player while the final 10 cards portray two teammates. Cards 201-211 were randomly seeded into packs of DLP Rookies and Traded of which was distributed in December, 2003. Each of these update cards featured a top prospect and was serial numbered to 1500 copies.

Nm-Mt Ex-Mt
COMP.LO SET (200) 50.00 15.00
COMMON CARD (1-190) .50 .15
COMMON RC (1-190) .60 .18
COMMON CARD (191-200) 1.00 .30
COMMON CARD (201-211) 4.00 1.20
1 Darin Erstad .50 .15
2 David Eckstein .50 .15
3 Garret Anderson .50 .15
4 Jarrod Washburn .50 .15
5 Tim Salmon .75 .23
6 Troy Glaus .50 .15
7 Jay Gibbons .50 .15
8 Melvin Mora .50 .15
9 Rodrigo Lopez .50 .15
10 Tony Batista .50 .15
11 Freddy Sanchez .50 .15
12 Derek Lowe .50 .15
13 Johnny Damon 1.25 .35
14 Manny Ramirez .75 .23
15 Nomar Garciaparra 2.00 .60
16 Pedro Martinez 1.25 .35
17 Rickey Henderson 1.25 .35
18 Shea Hillenbrand .50 .15
19 Carlos Lee .50 .15
20 Frank Thomas 1.25 .35
21 Magglio Ordonez .50 .15
22 Bartolo Colon .50 .15
23 Paul Konerko .50 .15
24 Josh Stewart RC .60 .18
25 C.C. Sabathia .50 .15
26 Jeremy Guthrie .50 .15
27 Ellis Burks .50 .15
28 Omar Vizquel .75 .23
29 Victor Martinez .75 .23
30 Cliff Lee .50 .15
31 Jhonny Peralta .50 .15
32 Brian Tallet .50 .15
33 Bobby Higginson .50 .15
34 Carlos Pena .50 .15
35 Nook Logan RC .60 .18
36 Steve Sparks .50 .15
37 Travis Chapman .50 .15
38 Carlos Beltran .75 .23
39 Joe Randa .50 .15
40 Mike Sweeney .50 .15
41 Jimmy Gobble .50 .15
42 Michael Tucker .50 .15
43 Runelvys Hernandez .50 .15
44 Brad Radke .50 .15
45 Corey Koskie .50 .15
46 Cristian Guzman .50 .15
47 J.C. Romero .50 .15
48 Doug Mientkiewicz .50 .15
49 Lew Ford RC 2.00 .60
50 Jacque Jones .50 .15
51 Torii Hunter .50 .15
52 Alfonso Soriano .75 .23
53 Nick Johnson .50 .15
54 Bernie Williams .75 .23
55 Jose Contreras RC 2.00 .60
56 Derek Jeter 3.00 .90
57 Jason Giambi .50 .15
58 Brandon Claussen .50 .15
59 Jorge Posada .75 .23
60 Mike Mussina .75 .23
61 Roger Clemens 2.50 .75
62 Hideki Matsui RC 5.00 1.50
63 Barry Zito .50 .15
64 Adam Morrissey .50 .15
65 Eric Chavez .50 .15
66 Jermaine Dye .50 .15
67 Mark Mulder .50 .15
68 Miguel Tejada .50 .15
69 Joe Valentine RC .60 .18
70 Tim Hudson .50 .15
71 Bret Boone .50 .15
72 Chris Snelling .50 .15
73 Edgar Martinez .75 .23
74 Freddy Garcia .50 .15
75 Ichiro Suzuki 2.00 .60
76 Jamie Moyer .50 .15
77 John Olerud .50 .15

2003 Studio

78 Kazuhiro Sasaki .50 .15
79 Aubrey Huff .50 .15
80 Joe Kennedy .50 .15
81 Dewon Brazelton .50 .15
82 Pete LaForest RC 1.00 .30
83 Alex Rodriguez 2.00 .60
84 Chan Ho Park .50 .15
85 Hank Blalock .75 .23
86 Juan Gonzalez .75 .23
87 Kevin Mench .50 .15
88 Rafael Palmeiro .75 .23
89 Carlos Delgado .50 .15
90 Eric Hinske .50 .15
91 Josh Phelps .50 .15
92 Roy Halladay .50 .15
93 Shannon Stewart .50 .15
94 Vernon Wells .50 .15
95 Vinny Chulk .50 .15
96 Curt Schilling .50 .15
97 Junior Spivey .50 .15
98 Luis Gonzalez .50 .15
99 Mark Grace .75 .23
100 Randy Johnson 1.25 .35
101 Andruw Jones .50 .15
102 Chipper Jones 1.25 .35
103 Gary Sheffield .50 .15
104 Greg Maddux 2.00 .60
105 John Smoltz .75 .23
106 Mike Hampton .50 .15
107 Adam LaRoche .50 .15
108 Michael Hessman RC .60 .18
109 Corey Patterson .50 .15
110 Kerry Wood 1.25 .35
111 Mark Prior 1.25 .35
112 Moises Alou .50 .15
113 Sammy Sosa 2.00 .60
114 Adam Dunn .75 .23
115 Austin Kearns .50 .15
116 Barry Larkin .75 .23
117 Ken Griffey Jr. 2.00 .60
118 Sean Casey .50 .15
119 Jason Jennings .50 .15
120 Jay Payton .50 .15
121 Larry Walker .75 .23
122 Todd Helton .75 .23
123 Jeff Baker .50 .15
124 Clint Barmes RC 1.00 .30
125 Ivan Rodriguez 1.25 .35
126 Josh Beckett .50 .15
127 Juan Encarnacion .50 .15
128 Mike Lowell .50 .15
129 Craig Biggio .75 .23
130 Jason Lane .50 .15
131 Jeff Bagwell .75 .23
132 Lance Berkman .50 .15
133 Roy Oswalt .50 .15
134 Jeff Kent .50 .15
135 Hideo Nomo 1.25 .35
136 Kazuhisa Ishii .50 .15
137 Kevin Brown .50 .15
138 Odalis Perez .50 .15
139 Paul Lo Duca .50 .15
140 Shawn Green .50 .15
141 Adrian Beltre .75 .23
142 Ben Sheets .50 .15
143 Bill Hall .50 .15
144 Jeffrey Hammonds .50 .15
145 Richie Sexson .50 .15
146 Terrmel Sledge RC 1.00 .30
147 Brad Wilkerson .50 .15
148 Javier Vazquez .50 .15
149 Jose Vidro .50 .15
150 Michael Barrett .50 .15
151 Vladimir Guerrero 1.25 .35
152 Al Leiter .50 .15
153 Mike Piazza 2.00 .60
154 Mo Vaughn .50 .15
155 Cliff Floyd .50 .15
156 Roberto Alomar .75 .23
157 Roger Cedeno .50 .15
158 Tom Glavine .75 .23
159 Prentice Redman RC .60 .18
160 Bobby Abreu .50 .15
161 Jimmy Rollins .50 .15
162 Mike Lieberthal .50 .15
163 Pat Burrell .50 .15
164 Vicente Padilla .50 .15
165 Jim Thome 1.25 .35
166 Kevin Millwood .50 .15
167 Aramis Ramirez .50 .15
168 Brian Giles .50 .15
169 Jason Kendall .50 .15
170 Josh Fogg .50 .15
171 Kip Wells .50 .15
172 Jose Castillo .50 .15
173 Mark Kotsay .50 .15
174 Oliver Perez .50 .15
175 Phil Nevin .50 .15
176 Ryan Klesko .50 .15
177 Sean Burroughs .50 .15
178 Brian Lawrence .50 .15
179 Shane Victorino RC .60 .18
180 Barry Bonds 3.00 .90
181 Benito Santiago .50 .15
182 Ray Durham .50 .15
183 Rich Aurilla .50 .15
184 Damian Moss .50 .15
185 Albert Pujols 2.50 .75
186 J.D. Drew .50 .15
187 Jim Edmonds .50 .15
188 Matt Morris .50 .15
189 Tino Martinez .75 .23
190 Scott Rolen 1.25 .35
191 Troy Glaus 1.50 .45
Tim Salmon
192 Sean Casey 1.00 .30
Corky Miller
193 Carlos Lee 1.50 .45
Frank Thomas
194 Lance Berkman 1.00 .30
Jeff Kent
195 Jose Contreras 1.50 .45
Mariano Rivera
196 Alex Rodriguez 1.50 .45
Juan Gonzalez
197 Andy Pettitte 1.50 .45
David Wells
198 Shawn Green 1.00 .30
Dave Roberts
199 Mike Lieberthal 1.00 .30
Jimmy Rollins
200 Mike Mussina 2.00 .60
Hideki Matsui
201 Adam Loewen ROO RC 5.00 1.50
202 Jeremy Bonderman ROO RC 5.00 1.50
203 Brandon Webb ROO RC 5.00 1.50
204 Chien-Ming Wang ROO RC 5.00 1.50
205 Chad Gaudin ROO RC 4.00 1.20
206 Ryan Wagner ROO RC 5.00 1.50
207 Hong-Chih Kuo ROO RC 5.00 1.50
208 Dan Haren ROO RC 5.00 1.50
209 Rickie Weeks ROO RC 8.00 2.40
210 Ramon Nivar ROO RC 5.00 1.50
211 Delmon Young ROO RC 10.00 3.00

2003 Studio Private Signings

Nm-Mt Ex-Mt
1-200 RANDOM INSERTS IN PACKS
201-211 RANDOM IN DLP R/T PACKS
PRINT RUNS B/WN 5-200 COPIES PER
NO PRICING ON QTY OF 35 OR LESS
1 Darin Erstad/5
6 Troy Glaus/15
7 Jay Gibbons/100 15.00 4.50
11 Freddy Sanchez/150 10.00 3.00
16 Pedro Martinez/5
17 Rickey Henderson/10
19 Carlos Lee/25
20 Frank Thomas/5
22 Mark Buehrle/50
24 Josh Stewart/200 10.00 3.00
25 C.C. Sabathia/10
26 Jeremy Guthrie/125 10.00 3.00
29 Victor Martinez/200 25.00 7.50
30 Cliff Lee/150 10.00 3.00
31 Jhonny Peralta/200 15.00 4.50
32 Brian Tallet/35
35 Nook Logan/100 10.00 3.00
37 Travis Chapman/150 10.00 3.00
38 Carlos Beltran/25
40 Mike Sweeney/25
41 Jimmy Gobble/200 10.00 3.00
47 J.C. Romero/200 10.00 3.00
49 Lew Ford/200 20.00 6.00
51 Torii Hunter/50 25.00 7.50
52 Alfonso Soriano/5
53 Nick Johnson/100 15.00 4.50
54 Bernie Williams/5
55 Jose Contreras/100 25.00 7.50
58 Brandon Claussen/200 10.00 3.00
60 Mike Mussina/5
61 Roger Clemens/10
63 Barry Zito/25
64 Adam Morrissey/100
66 Jermaine Dye/25
67 Mark Mulder/15
69 Joe Valentine/200 10.00 3.00
70 Tim Hudson/15
72 Chris Snelling/25
73 Edgar Martinez/15
74 Freddy Garcia/5
79 Aubrey Huff/50 25.00 7.50
80 Joe Kennedy/25
81 Dewon Brazelton/75 15.00 4.50
82 Pete LaForest/200 15.00 4.50
83 Alex Rodriguez/5
85 Hank Blalock/50 40.00 12.00
87 Kevin Mench/200 10.00 3.00
90 Eric Hinske/125 10.00 3.00
95 Vinny Chulk/100 15.00 4.50
97 Junior Spivey/50 15.00 4.50
98 Luis Gonzalez/5
101 Andruw Jones/15
102 Chipper Jones/5
103 Gary Sheffield/10
104 Greg Maddux/10
107 Adam LaRoche/200 10.00 3.00
108 Michael Hessman/200 10.00 3.00
109 Corey Patterson/50
110 Kerry Wood/15
111 Mark Prior/50 80.00 24.00
114 Adam Dunn/25
115 Austin Kearns/25
116 Barry Larkin/15
119 Jason Jennings/50 15.00 4.50
123 Jeff Baker/75 15.00 4.50
124 Clint Barmes/200 15.00 4.50
125 Ivan Rodriguez/5
126 Josh Beckett/10
129 Craig Biggio/10
130 Jason Lane/100 15.00 4.50
132 Lance Berkman/10
133 Roy Oswalt/25
136 Kazuhisa Ishii/10
139 Paul Lo Duca/75 20.00 6.00
140 Shawn Green/5
143 Bill Hall/50 15.00 4.50
145 Richie Sexson/15
146 Terrmel Sledge/125 15.00 4.50
148 Javier Vazquez/25
149 Jose Vidro/50 15.00 4.50
151 Vladimir Guerrero/15
156 Roberto Alomar/15
158 Tom Glavine/15
159 Prentice Redman/200 10.00 3.00
160 Bobby Abreu/50 25.00 7.50
163 Pat Burrell/10
165 Jim Thome/10
167 Aramis Ramirez/15
168 Brian Giles/25
171 Kip Wells/100 15.00 4.50
172 Jose Castillo/175 10.00 3.00
176 Ryan Klesko/20
178 Brian Lawrence/100 15.00 4.50
179 Shane Victorino/200 10.00 3.00
185 Albert Pujols/15
187 Jim Edmonds/5
201 Adam Loewen ROO/100 25.00 7.50
202 Jeremy Bonderman ROO/50 25.00 7.50
203 Brandon Webb ROO/100 25.00 7.50
204 Chien-Ming Wang ROO/50 50.00 15.00
205 Chad Gaudin ROO/25
206 Ryan Wagner ROO/100 15.00 4.50
207 Hong-Chih Kuo ROO/25
208 Dan Haren ROO/100 20.00 6.00
209 Rickie Weeks ROO/10
210 Ramon Nivar ROO/100 20.00 6.00
211 Delmon Young ROO/25

2003 Studio Proofs

Nm-Mt Ex-Mt
*PROOFS 1-190: 4X TO 10X BASIC
*PROOFS RC's 1-190: 2X TO 5X BASIC
*PROOFS 191-200: 1.5X TO 4X BASIC
*PROOFS 201-211: .6X TO 1.5X BASIC
1-200 RANDOM INSERTS IN PACKS
201-211 RANDOM IN DLP R/T PACKS
STATED PRINT RUN 100 SERIAL #'d SETS

2003 Studio Big League Challenge

Nm-Mt Ex-Mt
STATED PRINT RUN 400 SERIAL #'d SETS
*PROOFS: 1.5X TO 4X BASIC BLC
PROOFS PRINT RUN 25 SERIAL #'d SETS
NO PROOFS PRICING DUE TO SCARCITY
1 Jose Canseco 00 WIN 8.00 2.40
2 Magglio Ordonez 03 WIN 5.00 1.50
3 Alex Rodriguez 03 10.00 3.00
4 Lance Berkman 03 5.00 1.50
5 Rafael Palmeiro 03 8.00 2.40
6 Nomar Garciaparra 00 10.00 3.00
7 Nomar Garciaparra 00 10.00 3.00
8 Nomar Garciaparra 00 10.00 3.00
9 Troy Glaus 02 WIN 5.00 1.50
10 Mark McGwire 00 15.00 4.50
11 Mark McGwire 00 15.00 4.50
12 Mark McGwire 00 15.00 4.50
13 Jim Thome 02 8.00 2.40
14 Chipper Jones 00 8.00 2.40
15 Shawn Green 02 5.00 1.50
16 Alex Rodriguez 00 10.00 3.00
17 Alex Rodriguez 00 10.00 3.00
18 Alex Rodriguez 00 10.00 3.00
19 Alex Rodriguez 00 10.00 3.00
20 Jason Giambi 01 5.00 1.50
21 Pat Burrell 03 5.00 1.50
22 Mike Piazza 01 10.00 3.00
23 Mike Piazza 01 10.00 3.00
24 Mike Piazza 01 10.00 3.00
25 Frank Thomas 01 8.00 2.40
26 Rafael Palmeiro 01 WIN 8.00 2.40
27 Todd Helton 01 8.00 2.40
28 Jose Canseco 01 8.00 2.40
29 Albert Pujols 03 10.00 3.00
30 Troy Glaus 01 5.00 1.50
31 Barry Bonds 01 10.00 3.00
32 Barry Bonds 01 10.00 3.00
33 Barry Bonds 01 10.00 3.00
34 Todd Helton 02 8.00 2.40
35 Rafael Palmeiro 02 8.00 2.40
36 Jim Thome 02 8.00 2.40
37 Ozzie Smith 02 15.00 4.50
38 Troy Glaus 02 WIN 5.00 1.50
39 Shawn Green 02 5.00 1.50
40 Barry Bonds 02 10.00 3.00
41 Barry Bonds 02 10.00 3.00
42 Barry Bonds 02 10.00 3.00
43 Magglio Ordonez 03 WIN 5.00 1.50
44 Alex Rodriguez 03 10.00 3.00
45 Alex Rodriguez 03 10.00 3.00
46 Alex Rodriguez 03 10.00 3.00
47 Lance Berkman 03 5.00 1.50
48 Rafael Palmeiro 03 8.00 2.40
49 Pat Burrell 03 5.00 1.50
50 Albert Pujols 03 10.00 3.00

2003 Studio Big League Challenge Materials

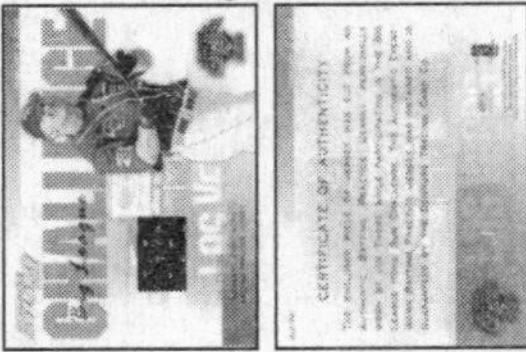

Nm-Mt Ex-Mt
STATED ODDS 1:20
*PRIME 100: 1X TO 2.5X BASIC MATERIAL
*PRIME 50: 1.5X TO 4X BASIC MATERIAL
PRIME RANDOM INSERTS IN PACKS
PRIME PRINT RUN B/WN 50-100 COPIES PER
2 Magglio Ordonez 03 BP Jsy 8.00 2.40
3 Alex Rodriguez 03 BP Jsy 15.00 4.50
4 Lance Berkman 03 Jsy 8.00 2.40
15 Shawn Green 02 BP Jsy 8.00 2.40
29 Albert Pujols 03 Jsy 25.00 7.50
36 Jim Thome 02 BP Jsy 8.00 2.40
39 Shawn Green 02 Pants 8.00 2.40
40 Barry Bonds 02 Base 15.00 4.50
41 Barry Bonds 02 Base 15.00 4.50
42 Barry Bonds 02 Plate 15.00 4.50
43 Magglio Ordonez 03 Jsy 8.00 2.40
45 Alex Rodriguez 03 Jsy 15.00 4.50
46 Alex Rodriguez 03 Pants 15.00 4.50
47 Lance Berkman 03 BP Jsy 8.00 2.40
48 Rafael Palmeiro 03 BP Jsy 8.00 2.40
50 Albert Pujols 03 Pants 15.00 4.50

2003 Studio Enshrinement

Nm-Mt Ex-Mt
STATED PRINT RUN 750 SERIAL #'d SETS
PROOFS PRINT RUN B/WN 20-21 COPIES PER
NO PROOFS PRICING DUE TO SCARCITY
RANDOM INSERTS IN PACKS
1 Gary Carter 5.00 1.50
2 Ozzie Smith 10.00 3.00
3 Kirby Puckett 8.00 2.40
4 Carlton Fisk 8.00 2.40
5 Tony Perez 5.00 1.50
6 Nolan Ryan 15.00 4.50
7 George Brett 15.00 4.50
8 Robin Yount 10.00 3.00
9 Orlando Cepeda 5.00 1.50
10 Phil Niekro 5.00 1.50
11 Mike Schmidt 12.00 3.60
12 Richie Ashburn 8.00 2.40
13 Steve Carlton 5.00 1.50
14 Phil Rizzuto 8.00 2.40
15 Reggie Jackson 8.00 2.40
16 Tom Seaver 8.00 2.40
17 Rollie Fingers 5.00 1.50
18 Rod Carew 8.00 2.40
19 Gaylord Perry 5.00 1.50
20 Fergie Jenkins 5.00 1.50
21 Jim Palmer 5.00 1.50
22 Joe Morgan 5.00 1.50
23 Johnny Bench 8.00 2.40
24 Willie Stargell 8.00 2.40
25 Billy Williams 5.00 1.50
26 Catfish Hunter 8.00 2.40
27 Willie McCovey 5.00 1.50
28 Bobby Doerr 5.00 1.50
29 Lou Brock 8.00 2.40
30 Enos Slaughter 5.00 1.50
31 Hoyt Wilhelm 5.00 1.50
32 Harmon Killebrew 8.00 2.40
33 Pee Wee Reese 8.00 2.40
34 Luis Aparicio 5.00 1.50
35 Brooks Robinson 8.00 2.40
36 Juan Marichal 5.00 1.50
37 Frank Robinson 8.00 2.40
38 Bob Gibson 8.00 2.40
39 Al Kaline 8.00 2.40
40 Duke Snider 8.00 2.40
41 Eddie Mathews 8.00 2.40
42 Robin Roberts 5.00 1.50
43 Ralph Kiner 5.00 1.50
44 Whitey Ford 8.00 2.40
45 Roberto Clemente 12.00 3.60
46 Warren Spahn 8.00 2.40
47 Yogi Berra 8.00 2.40
48 Early Wynn 5.00 1.50
49 Stan Musial 10.00 3.00
50 Bob Feller 5.00 1.50

2003 Studio Enshrinement Autographs

Randomly inserted into packs, this is a partial parallel to the Enshrinement insert set. Each of these cards is signed to bewteen one and 100 copies and we have notated the print run in our checklist. If a card was printed to 25 or fewer copies there is no pricing available due to market scarcity.

Nm-Mt Ex-Mt
1 Gary Carter/50 30.00 9.00
2 Ozzie Smith/5
3 Kirby Puckett/5
4 Carlton Fisk/5
5 Tony Perez/50 50.00 15.00
6 Nolan Ryan/5
7 George Brett/5
8 Robin Yount/5
9 Orlando Cepeda/50 30.00 9.00
10 Phil Niekro/50 30.00 9.00
11 Mike Schmidt/5
13 Steve Carlton/50 50.00 15.00
14 Phil Rizzuto/5
15 Reggie Jackson/5
16 Tom Seaver/5
20 Fergie Jenkins/50 30.00 9.00
21 Jim Palmer/25
22 Joe Morgan/10
23 Johnny Bench/10
27 Willie McCovey/10
28 Bobby Doerr/100 25.00 7.50
29 Lou Brock/25
31 Hoyt Wilhelm/50 30.00 9.00
32 Harmon Killebrew/10
34 Luis Aparicio/100 25.00 7.50
35 Brooks Robinson/25
37 Frank Robinson/25
39 Al Kaline/25
40 Duke Snider/10
43 Ralph Kiner/25
46 Warren Spahn/1
47 Yogi Berra/10
49 Stan Musial/5
50 Bob Feller/100 25.00 7.50

2003 Studio Leather and Lumber

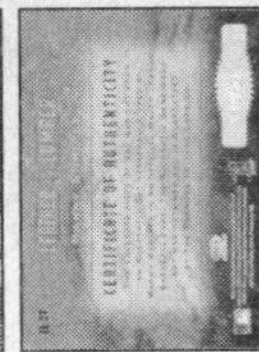

Nm-Mt Ex-Mt
COMMON CARD p/r 300-400 8.00 2.40
RANDOM INSERTS IN PACKS
PRINT RUNS B/WN 100-400 COPIES PER
1 Adam Dunn Bat/400 10.00 3.00
2 Alex Rodriguez Bat/250 20.00 6.00
3 Alfonso Soriano Bat/250 15.00 4.50
4 Andruw Jones Bat/400 8.00 2.40
5 Austin Kearns Bat/400 8.00 2.40
6 Chipper Jones Bat/400 10.00 3.00
7 Derek Jeter Ball/100 40.00 12.00
8 Don Mattingly Bat/100 40.00 12.00
9 Edgar Martinez Bat/400 10.00 3.00
10 Frank Thomas Bat/400 10.00 3.00
11 Fred McGriff Bat/400 10.00 3.00
12 Garret Anderson Bat/400
13 Greg Maddux Bat/150 15.00 4.50
14 Hideki Matsui Ball/100 40.00 12.00
15 Hideo Nomo Bat/150 20.00 6.00
16 Ichiro Suzuki Ball/100 40.00 12.00
17 Ivan Rodriguez Bat/250 15.00 4.50
18 Jason Giambi Bat/400 8.00 2.40
19 Jeff Bagwell Bat/400 10.00 3.00
20 Jim Edmonds Bat/150 10.00 3.00
21 Jim Thome Bat/400 10.00 3.00
22 Juan Gonzalez Bat/400 10.00 3.00
23 Kerry Wood Bat/250 15.00 4.50
24 Kirby Puckett Bat/100 25.00 7.50
25 Lance Berkman Bat/400 8.00 2.40
26 Magglio Ordonez Bat/400 8.00 2.40
27 Manny Ramirez Bat/250 15.00 4.50
28 Mark Prior Bat/400 10.00 3.00
29 Miguel Tejada Bat/200 10.00 3.00
30 Mike Piazza Bat/400 10.00 3.00
31 Mike Schmidt Bat/200 40.00 12.00
32 Nomar Garciaparra Bat/400 15.00 4.50
33 Pat Burrell Bat/400 8.00 2.40
34 Pedro Martinez Bat/150 15.00 4.50
35 Rafael Palmeiro Bat/400
36 Randy Johnson Bat/250 15.00 4.50
37 Rickey Henderson Bat/175 15.00 4.50
38 Sammy Sosa Bat/300 15.00 4.50
39 Shawn Green Bat/400 8.00 2.40
40 Vladimir Guerrero Bat/400 10.00 3.00

2003 Studio Leather and Lumber Combos

Nm-Mt Ex-Mt
RANDOM INSERTS IN PACKS
PRINT RUNS B/WN 25-50 COPIES PER
NO PRICING ON QTY OF 25 OR LESS
1 Adam Dunn Bat-Btg Glv/50 40.00 12.00
2 Alex Rodriguez Bat-Fld Glv/50 50.00 15.00
3 Alfonso Soriano Bat-Ball/25
4 Andruw Jones Bat-Fld Glv/50 25.00 7.50
5 Austin Kearns Bat-Shoe/50 25.00 7.50
6 Chipper Jones Bat-Ball/25
7 Derek Jeter Bat-Ball/25
8 Don Mattingly Bat-Btg Glv/25
9 Edgar Martinez Bat-Ball/25
10 Frank Thomas Bat-Btg Glv/50 40.00 12.00
11 Fred McGriff Bat-Ball/25
12 Garret Anderson Bat-Ball/25
13 Greg Maddux Bat-Shoe/50 40.00 12.00
14 Hideki Matsui Bat-Ball/25
15 Hideo Nomo Bat-Ball/25
16 Ichiro Suzuki Bat-Ball/25
17 Ivan Rodriguez Bat-Btg Glv/50 40.00 12.00
18 Jason Giambi Bat-Ball/25
19 Jeff Bagwell Bat-Ball/25
20 Jim Edmonds Bat-Shoe/50 25.00 7.50
21 Jim Thome Bat-Ball/25
22 Juan Gonzalez Bat-Ball/25
23 Kerry Wood Bat-Fld Glv/50 40.00 12.00
24 Kirby Puckett Bat-Btg Glv/25
25 Lance Berkman Bat-Fld Glv/50 25.00 7.50
26 Magglio Ordonez Bat-Shoe/25
27 Manny Ramirez Bat-Shoe/25
28 Mark Prior Bat-Shoe/25
29 Miguel Tejada Bat-Ball/25
30 Mike Piazza Bat-Shoe/25
31 Mike Schmidt Bat-Btg Glv/25
32 Nomar Garciaparra Bat-Ball/25
33 Pat Burrell Bat-Ball/25
34 Pedro Martinez Bat-Ball/25
35 Rafael Palmeiro Bat-Fld Glv/25
36 Randy Johnson Bat-Ball/25
37 Rickey Henderson Bat-Ball/25
38 Sammy Sosa Bat-Shoe/25
39 Shawn Green Bat-Ball/25
40 Vladimir Guerrero Bat-Ball/25

2003 Studio Masterstrokes

Nm-Mt Ex-Mt
RANDOM INSERTS IN PACKS
STATED PRINT RUN 1000 SERIAL #'d SETS
1 Adam Dunn 5.00 1.50
2 Albert Pujols 10.00 3.00
3 Alex Rodriguez 8.00 2.40

4 Alfonso Soriano 5.00 1.50
5 Andruw Jones 3.00 .90
6 Chipper Jones 5.00 1.50
7 Derek Jeter 12.00 3.60
8 Greg Maddux 8.00 2.40
9 Hideki Matsui 10.00 3.00
10 Hideo Nomo 5.00 1.50
11 Ivan Rodriguez 5.00 1.50
12 Jason Giambi 3.00 .90
13 Jeff Bagwell 5.00 1.50
14 Juan Gonzalez 5.00 1.50
15 Ken Griffey Jr. 8.00 2.40
16 Lance Berkman 3.00 .90
17 Magglio Ordonez 3.00 .90
18 Manny Ramirez 5.00 1.50
19 Mark Prior 5.00 1.50
20 Miguel Tejada 3.00 .90
21 Mike Piazza 8.00 2.40
22 Nomar Garciaparra 8.00 2.40
23 Pat Burrell 3.00 .90
24 Sammy Sosa 8.00 2.40
25 Vladimir Guerrero 5.00 1.50

2003 Studio Masterstrokes Proofs

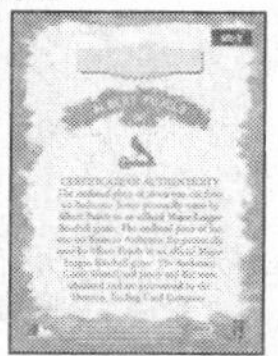

Nm-Mt Ex-Mt
RANDOM INSERTS IN PACKS
STATED PRINT RUN 50 SERIAL #'d SETS
1 Adam Dunn Bat-Jsy 30.00 9.00
2 Albert Pujols Bat-Jsy 60.00 18.00
3 Alex Rodriguez Bat-Jsy 60.00 18.00
4 Alfonso Soriano Bat-Jsy 30.00 9.00
5 Andruw Jones Bat-Jsy 20.00 6.00
6 Chipper Jones Bat-Jsy 30.00 9.00
7 Derek Jeter Base-Ball 80.00 24.00
8 Greg Maddux Bat-Jsy 40.00 12.00
9 Hideki Matsui Base-Ball 80.00 24.00
10 Hideo Nomo Bat-Jsy 120.00 36.00
11 Ivan Rodriguez Bat-Jsy 30.00 9.00
12 Jason Giambi Bat-Jsy 20.00 6.00
13 Jeff Bagwell Bat-Jsy 30.00 9.00
14 Juan Gonzalez Bat-Jsy 30.00 9.00
15 Ken Griffey Jr. Base-Base 50.00 15.00
16 Lance Berkman Bat-Jsy 20.00 6.00
17 Magglio Ordonez Bat-Jsy 20.00 6.00
18 Manny Ramirez Bat-Jsy 30.00 9.00
19 Mark Prior Bat-Jsy 30.00 9.00
20 Miguel Tejada Bat-Jsy 20.00 6.00
21 Mike Piazza Bat-Jsy 40.00 12.00
22 Nomar Garciaparra Bat-Jsy 50.00 15.00
23 Pat Burrell Bat-Jsy 20.00 6.00
24 Sammy Sosa Bat-Jsy 50.00 15.00
25 Vladimir Guerrero Bat-Jsy 30.00 9.00

2003 Studio Player Collection

Nm-Mt Ex-Mt
*PLAY.COLL: .4X TO 1X PRESTIGE PLAY.COLL
RANDOM INSERTS IN PACKS
STATED PRINT RUN 300 SERIAL #'d SETS
SEE 2003 PRESTIGE PLAY.COLL FOR PRICING

2003 Studio Recollection Autographs 5 x 7

Inserted at a stated rate of one per sealed hobby case, these 27 cards feature authentic autographs of the featured players. Please note that these cards are alll 2001 Studio buybacks and we have put the stated print run next to the player's name in our checklist. In addition, if a card has a print run of 25 or fewer copies, there is no pricing due to market scarcity.

Nm-Mt Ex-Mt
1 Josh Beckett/3
2 Lance Berkman/13
3 Sean Casey/125 20.00 6.00
4 Adam Dunn/12
5 Troy Glaus/82 20.00 6.00
6 Tom Glavine/3
7 Shawn Green/3
8 Vladimir Guerrero/125 40.00 12.00
9 Tony Gwynn/13
10 Todd Helton/55 40.00 12.00
11 Andruw Jones/3
12 Ryan Klesko/75 20.00 6.00
13 Greg Maddux/25
14 Edgar Martinez/11
15 Magglio Ordonez/6
16 Cal Ripken/4
17 Alex Rodriguez/3
18 Ivan Rodriguez/50 50.00 15.00
19 C.C. Sabathia/50 25.00 7.50
20 Curt Schilling/75 40.00 12.00
21 Ben Sheets/1
22 Alfonso Soriano/8
23 Mike Sweeney/42 25.00 7.50
24 Miguel Tejada/44 25.00 7.50
25 Frank Thomas/11
26 Kerry Wood/200 25.00 7.50
27 Barry Zito/200 25.00 7.50

2003 Studio Spirit of the Game

Nm-Mt Ex-Mt
RANDOM INSERTS IN PACKS
STATED PRINT RUN 1250 SERIAL #'d SETS
1 Garret Anderson 2.50 .75
2 Nomar Garciaparra 6.00 1.80
3 Pedro Martinez 4.00 1.20
4 Rickey Henderson 4.00 1.20
5 Magglio Ordonez 2.50 .75
6 Torii Hunter 2.50 .75
7 Alfonso Soriano 4.00 1.20
8 Jose Contreras 4.00 1.20
9 Derek Jeter 10.00 3.00
10 Jason Giambi 2.50 .75
11 Roger Clemens 8.00 2.40
12 Hideki Matsui 8.00 2.40
13 Barry Zito 2.50 .75
14 Ichiro Suzuki 6.00 1.80
15 Alex Rodriguez 6.00 1.80
16 Curt Schilling 2.50 .75
17 Randy Johnson 4.00 1.20
18 Andruw Jones 2.50 .75
19 Chipper Jones 4.00 1.20
20 Greg Maddux 6.00 1.80
21 Sammy Sosa 6.00 1.80
22 Adam Dunn 4.00 1.20
23 Ken Griffey Jr. 6.00 1.80
24 Todd Helton 4.00 1.20
25 Ivan Rodriguez 4.00 1.20
26 Lance Berkman 2.50 .75
27 Hideo Nomo 4.00 1.20
28 Shawn Green 2.50 .75
29 Vladimir Guerrero 4.00 1.20
30 Mike Piazza 6.00 1.80
31 Roberto Alomar 2.50 .75
32 Jim Thome 4.00 1.20
33 Barry Bonds 10.00 3.00
34 Albert Pujols 8.00 2.40
35 Scott Rolen 4.00 1.20

2003 Studio Spirit of MLB

Nm-Mt Ex-Mt
RANDOM INSERTS IN PACKS
STATED PRINT RUN 1 SERIAL #'d SET

2003 Studio Stars

Nm-Mt Ex-Mt
STATED ODDS 1:5
*GOLD: 1X TO 2.5X BASIC STARS
GOLD PRINT RUN 100 SERIAL #'d SETS
PLATINUM PRINT RUN 25 SERIAL #'d SETS
NO PLATINUM PRICING DUE TO SCARCITY
GOLD/PLATINUM RANDOM IN PACKS
1 Troy Glaus 2.00 .60
2 Manny Ramirez 2.00 .60
3 Nomar Garciaparra 5.00 1.50
4 Pedro Martinez 3.00 .90
5 Rickey Henderson 3.00 .90
6 Torii Hunter 2.00 .60
7 Frank Thomas 3.00 .90
8 Magglio Ordonez 2.00 .60
9 Alfonso Soriano 2.00 .60
10 Jose Contreras 3.00 .90
11 Derek Jeter 8.00 2.40
12 Jason Giambi 2.00 .60
13 Roger Clemens 6.00 1.80
14 Mike Mussina 2.00 .60
15 Barry Zito 2.00 .60
16 Miguel Tejada 2.00 .60
17 Ichiro Suzuki 5.00 1.50
18 Alex Rodriguez 5.00 1.50
19 Juan Gonzalez 2.00 .60
20 Rafael Palmeiro 2.00 .60
21 Hank Blalock 2.00 .60
22 Curt Schilling 2.00 .60
23 Randy Johnson 3.00 .90
24 Junior Spivey 2.00 .60
25 Andruw Jones 2.00 .60
26 Chipper Jones 3.00 .90
27 Greg Maddux 5.00 1.50
28 Kerry Wood 3.00 .90
29 Mark Prior 3.00 .90
30 Sammy Sosa 5.00 1.50
31 Adam Dunn 2.00 .60
32 Ken Griffey Jr. 5.00 1.50
33 Austin Kearns 2.00 .60
34 Larry Walker 2.00 .60
35 Todd Helton 2.00 .60
36 Ivan Rodriguez 3.00 .90
37 Jeff Bagwell 2.00 .60
38 Lance Berkman 2.00 .60
39 Craig Biggio 2.00 .60
40 Hideo Nomo 3.00 .90
41 Shawn Green 2.00 .60
42 Vladimir Guerrero 3.00 .90
43 Mike Piazza 5.00 1.50
44 Tom Glavine 2.00 .60
45 Roberto Alomar 2.00 .60
46 Pat Burrell 2.00 .60
47 Jim Thome 3.00 .90
48 Barry Bonds 8.00 2.40
49 Albert Pujols 6.00 1.80
50 Scott Rolen 3.00 .90

2004 Studio

Nm-Mt Ex-Mt
COMP.SET w/o SP's (200) 50.00 15.00
COMMON ACTIVE (1-200) .40 .12
COMMON RETIRED (1-200) .50 .15
COMMON RC (1-200) .40 .12
AU'S RANDOM INSERTS IN PACKS
AU PRINT RUNS B/WN 400-800 COPIES PER
COMMON CARD (226-241) 3.00 .90
COMMON CARD (242-275) 3.00 .90
226-275 ODDS 1:23 '05 DONRUSS
CARDS 220/222-225 DO NOT EXIST
1 Bartolo Colon .40 .12
2 Garret Anderson .40 .12
3 Tim Salmon .60 .18
4 Troy Glaus .40 .12
5 Vladimir Guerrero 1.00 .30
6 Brandon Webb .40 .12
7 Brian Bruney .40 .12
8 Casey Fossum .40 .12
9 Luis Gonzalez .40 .12
10 Randy Johnson 1.00 .30
11 Richie Sexson .40 .12
12 Robby Hammock .40 .12
13 Roberto Alomar .60 .18
14 Shea Hillenbrand .40 .12
15 Steve Finley .40 .12
16 Adam LaRoche .40 .12
17 Andruw Jones .40 .12
18 Bubba Nelson .40 .12
19 Chipper Jones 1.00 .30
20 Dale Murphy .60 .18
21 J.D. Drew .40 .12
22 Marcus Giles .40 .12
23 Michael Hessman .40 .12
24 Rafael Furcal .40 .12
25 Warren Spahn .60 .18
26 Adam Loewen .40 .12
27 Cal Ripken 4.00 1.20
28 Javy Lopez .40 .12
29 Jay Gibbons .40 .12
30 Luis Matos .40 .12
31 Miguel Tejada .40 .12
32 Rafael Palmeiro .60 .18
33 Curt Schilling 1.00 .30
34 Jason Varitek .60 .18
35 Kevin Youkilis .40 .12
36 Manny Ramirez .60 .18
37 Nomar Garciaparra 1.50 .45
38 Pedro Martinez 1.00 .30
39 Trot Nixon .40 .12
40 Aramis Ramirez .40 .12
41 Brendan Harris .40 .12
42 Derrek Lee .40 .12
43 Ernie Banks 1.25 .35
44 Greg Maddux 1.50 .45
45 Kerry Wood 1.00 .30
46 Mark Prior 1.00 .30
47 Ryne Sandberg 2.50 .75
48 Sammy Sosa 1.50 .45
49 Todd Wellemeyer .40 .12
50 Carlos Lee .40 .12
51 Edwin Almonte .40 .12
52 Frank Thomas 1.00 .30
53 Joe Borchard .40 .12
54 Joe Crede .40 .12
55 Magglio Ordonez .40 .12
56 Adam Dunn .40 .12
57 Austin Kearns .40 .12
58 Barry Larkin .60 .18
59 Brandon Larson .40 .12
60 Ken Griffey Jr. 1.50 .45
61 Ryan Wagner .40 .12
62 Sean Casey .40 .12
63 Brian Tallet .40 .12
64 C.C. Sabathia .40 .12
65 Jeremy Guthrie .40 .12
66 Jody Gerut .40 .12
67 Travis Hafner .40 .12
68 Clint Barmes .40 .12
69 Jeff Baker .40 .12
70 Joe Kennedy .40 .12
71 Larry Walker .60 .18
72 Preston Wilson .40 .12
73 Todd Helton .60 .18
74 Dmitri Young .40 .12
75 Ivan Rodriguez 1.00 .30
76 Jeremy Bonderman .40 .12
77 Preston Larrison .40 .12
78 Dontrelle Willis .40 .12
79 Josh Beckett .40 .12
80 Juan Pierre .40 .12
81 Luis Castillo .40 .12
82 Miguel Cabrera .60 .18
83 Mike Lowell .40 .12
84 Andy Pettitte .60 .18
85 Chris Burke .40 .12
86 Craig Biggio .60 .18
87 Jeff Bagwell .60 .18
88 Jeff Kent .40 .12
89 Lance Berkman .40 .12
90 Morgan Ensberg .40 .12
91 Richard Hidalgo .40 .12
92 Roger Clemens 2.00 .60
93 Roy Oswalt .40 .12
94 Wade Miller .40 .12
95 Angel Berroa .40 .12
96 Byron Gettis .40 .12
97 Carlos Beltran .60 .18
98 Juan Gonzalez .60 .18
99 Mike Sweeney .40 .12
100 Duke Snider .75 .23
101 Edwin Jackson .40 .12
102 Eric Gagne 1.00 .30
103 Hideo Nomo 1.00 .30
104 Hong-Chih Kuo .40 .12
105 Kazuhisa Ishii .40 .12
106 Paul Lo Duca .40 .12
107 Robin Ventura .40 .12
108 Shawn Green .40 .12
109 Junior Spivey .40 .12
110 Lyle Overbay .40 .12
111 Rickie Weeks .40 .12
112 Scott Podsednik .40 .12
113 J.D. Durbin .40 .12
114 Jacque Jones .40 .12
115 Jason Kubel .40 .12
116 Johan Santana .60 .18
117 Shannon Stewart .40 .12
118 Torii Hunter .40 .12
119 Brad Wilkerson .40 .12
120 Jose Vidro .40 .12
121 Nick Johnson .40 .12
122 Orlando Cabrera .40 .12
123 Zach Day .40 .12
124 Gary Carter .50 .15
125 Jae Weong Seo .40 .12
126 Kazuo Matsui RC 2.50 .75
127 Mike Piazza 1.50 .45
128 Tom Glavine .60 .18
129 Alex Rodriguez Yanks 1.50 .45
130 Bernie Williams .60 .18
131 Chien-Ming Wang .40 .12
132 Derek Jeter 2.00 .60
133 Don Mattingly 2.50 .75
134 Gary Sheffield .40 .12
135 Hideki Matsui 1.50 .45
136 Jason Giambi .40 .12
137 Javier Vazquez .40 .12
138 Jorge Posada .60 .18
139 Jose Contreras .40 .12
140 Kevin Brown .40 .12
141 Mariano Rivera .60 .18
142 Mike Mussina .60 .18
143 Whitey Ford .75 .23
144 Barry Zito .40 .12
145 Eric Chavez .40 .12
146 Mark Mulder .40 .12
147 Rich Harden .40 .12
148 Tim Hudson .40 .12
149 Bobby Abreu .40 .12
150 Jim Thome 1.00 .30
151 Kevin Millwood .40 .12
152 Marlon Byrd .40 .12
153 Mike Schmidt 2.50 .75
154 Ryan Howard .40 .12
155 Jack Wilson .40 .12
156 Jason Kendall .40 .12
157 Akinori Otsuka RC .40 .12
158 Brian Giles .40 .12
159 David Wells .40 .12
160 Jay Payton .40 .12
161 Phil Nevin .40 .12
162 Ryan Klesko .40 .12
163 Sean Burroughs .40 .12
164 A.J. Pierzynski .40 .12
165 J.T. Snow .40 .12
166 Jason Schmidt .40 .12
167 Jerome Williams .40 .12
168 Merkin Valdez RC 1.25 .35
169 Will Clark 1.25 .35
170 Bret Boone .40 .12
171 Chris Snelling .40 .12
172 Edgar Martinez .60 .18
173 Ichiro Suzuki 1.50 .45
174 Jamie Moyer .40 .12
175 Randy Winn .40 .12
176 Rich Aurilia .40 .12
177 Shigetoshi Hasegawa .40 .12
178 Albert Pujols 2.00 .60
179 Dan Haren .40 .12
180 Edgar Renteria .40 .12
181 Jim Edmonds .40 .12
182 Matt Morris .40 .12
183 Scott Rolen 1.00 .30
184 Stan Musial 2.00 .60
185 Aubrey Huff .40 .12
186 Chad Gaudin .40 .12
187 Delmon Young .60 .18
188 Fred McGriff .60 .18
189 Rocco Baldelli .40 .12
190 Alfonso Soriano .60 .18
191 Hank Blalock .40 .12
192 Mark Teixeira .40 .12
193 Nolan Ryan 3.00 .90
194 Alexis Rios .40 .12
195 Carlos Delgado .40 .12
196 Dustin McGowan .40 .12
197 Guillermo Quiroz .40 .12
198 Josh Phelps .40 .12
199 Roy Halladay .40 .12
200 Vernon Wells .40 .12
201 Mike Gosling AU/400 RC 10.00 3.00
202 Ronny Cedeno AU/766 RC 8.00 2.40
203 Ron Belisario AU/400 RC 10.00 3.00
204 Justin Hampson AU/800 RC 8.00 2.40
205 Carlos Vasquez AU/800 RC 8.00 2.40
206 Linc.Holdzkom AU/800 RC 8.00 2.40
207 Casey Daigle AU/550 RC 10.00 3.00
208 Jason Bartlett AU/800 RC 10.00 3.00
209 Mariano Gomez AU/800 RC 8.00 2.40
210 Mike Rouse AU/800 RC 8.00 2.40
211 Chris Shelton AU/800 RC 10.00 3.00
212 Dennis Sarfate AU/800 RC 8.00 2.40
213 Shingo Takatsu AU/400 RC 40.00 12.00
214 Justin Leone AU/800 RC 10.00 3.00
215 Cory Sullivan AU/800 RC 8.00 2.40
216 Michael Wuertz AU/800 RC 10.00 3.00
217 Tim Bausher AU/800 RC 8.00 2.40
218 Jesse Harper AU/800 RC 8.00 2.40
219 Ryan Meaux AU/800 RC 8.00 2.40
220 Does Not Exist
221 Kevin Cave AU/800 RC 10.00 3.00
222 Does Not Exist
223 Does Not Exist
224 Does Not Exist
225 Does Not Exist
226 Abe Alvarez XRC 8.00 2.40
227 Carlos Hines XRC 5.00 1.50
228 Charles Thomas XRC 8.00 2.40
229 Frankie Francisco XRC 5.00 1.50
230 Greg Dobbs XRC 5.00 1.50
231 Hector Gimenez XRC 3.00 .90
232 Jesse Crain XRC 8.00 2.40
233 Joey Gathright XRC 8.00 2.40
234 Justin Knoedler XRC 5.00 1.50
235 Kazuhito Tadano XRC 8.00 2.40
236 Lance Cormier XRC 5.00 1.50
237 Scott Proctor XRC 8.00 2.40
238 Tim Bittner XRC 5.00 1.50
239 Travis Blackley XRC 8.00 2.40
240 Mike Johnston XRC 5.00 1.50
241 Yadier Molina XRC 8.00 2.40
242 B.J. Upton 8.00 2.40
243 Ben Sheets 5.00 1.50
244 Bobby Crosby 8.00 2.40
245 Brad Penny 3.00 .90
246 Carl Crawford 5.00 1.50
247 Carlos Beltran 8.00 2.40
248 Carlos Guillen 5.00 1.50
249 Carlos Zambrano 5.00 1.50
250 Casey Kotchman 8.00 2.40
251 Chase Utley 5.00 1.50
252 Craig Wilson 5.00 1.50
253 Danny Graves 3.00 .90
254 Danny Kolb 3.00 .90
255 David Wright 20.00 6.00
256 Eric Milton 3.00 .90
257 Esteban Loaiza 3.00 .90
258 Francisco Cordero 3.00 .90
259 Francisco Rodriguez 5.00 1.50
260 Jake Peavy 5.00 1.50
261 Jason Bay 5.00 1.50
262 Jermaine Dye 5.00 1.50
263 Joe Nathan 5.00 1.50
264 John Lackey 3.00 .90
265 Ken Harvey 3.00 .90
266 Khalil Greene 8.00 2.40
267 Lew Ford 5.00 1.50
268 Livan Hernandez 3.00 .90
269 Milton Bradley 5.00 1.50
270 Nomar Garciaparra 10.00 3.00
271 Orlando Cabrera Sox 8.00 2.40
272 Paul Lo Duca 5.00 1.50
273 Richard Hidalgo 3.00 .90
274 Steve Finley 5.00 1.50
275 Victor Martinez 5.00 1.50

2004 Studio Proofs Gold

Nm-Mt Ex-Mt
*GOLD 1-200: 5X TO 12X BASIC ACTIVE
*GOLD 1-200: 5X TO 12X BASIC RETIRED
*GOLD 1-200: 2.5X TO 6X BASIC RC'S
*GOLD 201-225: .25X TO .6X AU p/r 766-800
*GOLD 201-225: .2X TO .5X AU p/r 400-550
1-225 RANDOM INSERTS IN PACKS
220/222-225 EXIST ONLY IN PARALLEL SET
*GOLD 226-241: .75X TO 2X BASIC
*GOLD 242-275: .75X TO 2X BASIC
226-275 RANDOM IN '05 DONRUSS
STATED PRINT RUN 50 SERIAL #'d SETS
220 David Aardsma 5.00 1.50
222 Mike Johnston 5.00 1.50
223 Jason Szuminski 5.00 1.50
224 Shawn Camp 5.00 1.50
225 Colby Miller 5.00 1.50

2004 Studio Proofs Platinum

Nm-Mt Ex-Mt
1-225 RANDOM INSERTS IN PACKS
226-275 RANDOM IN '05 DONRUSS
STATED PRINT RUN 10 SERIAL #'d SETS
NO PRICING DUE TO SCARCITY

2004 Studio Proofs Silver

Nm-Mt Ex-Mt
*SILVER 1-200: 3X TO 8X BASIC ACTIVE
*SILVER 1-200: 3X TO 8X BASIC RETIRED
*SILVER 1-200: 1.5X TO 4X BASIC RC'S
*SILVER 201-225: .15X TO .4X AU p/r 766-800
*SILVER 201-225: .12X TO .3X AU p/r 400-550
1-225 RANDOM INSERTS IN PACKS
*SILVER 226-241: .5X TO 1.2X BASIC
*SILVER 242-275: .5X TO 1.2X BASIC
226-275 RANDOM IN '05 DONRUSS
STATED PRINT RUN 100 SERIAL #'d SETS
220/222-225 EXIST ONLY IN PARALLEL SET
220 David Aardsma 3.00 .90
222 Mike Johnston 3.00 .90
223 Jason Szuminski 3.00 .90
224 Shawn Camp 3.00 .90
225 Colby Miller 3.00 .90

2004 Studio Private Signings Gold

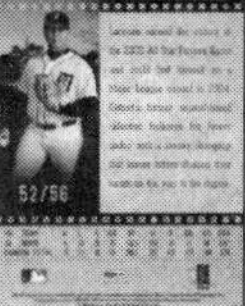

RANDOM INSERTS IN PACKS

PRINT RUNS B/WN 1-100 COPIES PER

NO PRICING ON QTY OF 12 OR LESS

NO RC YR PRICING ON QTY OF 25 OR LESS

	Nm-Mt	Ex-Mt
2 Garret Anderson/16	40.00	12.00
5 Vladimir Guerrero/10		
6 Brandon Webb/55	12.00	3.60
7 Brian Bruney/100	10.00	3.00
8 Casey Fossum/5		
10 Randy Johnson/5		
11 Richie Sexson/5		
12 Robby Hammock/7		
14 Shea Hillenbrand/28	25.00	7.50
15 Steve Finley/12		
16 Adam LaRoche/25	20.00	6.00
17 Andruw Jones/5		
18 Bubba Nelson/100	10.00	3.00
19 Chipper Jones/10		
20 Dale Murphy/5		
21 J.D. Drew/7		
22 Marcus Giles/25	30.00	9.00
23 Michael Hessman/25	20.00	6.00
24 Rafael Furcal/1		
25 Warren Spahn/5		
26 Adam Loewen/1		
27 Cal Ripken/10		
29 Jay Gibbons/25	20.00	6.00
30 Luis Matos/100	10.00	3.00
32 Rafael Palmeiro/5		
33 Curt Schilling/5		
34 Jason Varitek/33	60.00	18.00
35 Kevin Youkilis/100	15.00	4.50
36 Manny Ramirez/1		
39 Trot Nixon/7		
40 Aramis Ramirez/16	40.00	12.00
41 Brendan Harris/75	10.00	3.00
43 Ernie Banks/5		
45 Kerry Wood/5		
46 Mark Prior/22	100.00	30.00
47 Ryne Sandberg/1		
48 Sammy Sosa/10		
49 Todd Wellemeyer/50	12.00	3.60
50 Carlos Lee/45	20.00	6.00
51 Edwin Almonte/56	12.00	3.60
52 Frank Thomas/5		
53 Joe Borchard/25	20.00	6.00
54 Joe Crede/24	20.00	6.00
55 Magglio Ordonez/10		
57 Austin Kearns/28	25.00	7.50
58 Barry Larkin/11		
59 Brandon Larson/16	25.00	7.50
61 Ryan Wagner/38	12.00	3.60
63 Brian Tallet/50	12.00	3.60
65 Jeremy Guthrie/67	10.00	3.00
66 Jody Gerut/25	30.00	9.00
67 Travis Hafner/34	25.00	7.50
68 Clint Barmes/36	12.00	3.60
69 Jeff Baker/62	10.00	3.00
70 Joe Kennedy/37	12.00	3.60
72 Preston Wilson/10		
73 Todd Helton/17	60.00	18.00
77 Preston Larrison/56	12.00	3.60
78 Dontrelle Willis/35	25.00	7.50
79 Josh Beckett/1		
81 Luis Castillo/1		
82 Miguel Cabrera/24	50.00	15.00
84 Andy Pettitte/5		
85 Chris Burke/46	12.00	3.60
86 Craig Biggio/7		
87 Jeff Bagwell/5		
89 Lance Berkman/17	60.00	18.00
90 Morgan Ensberg/25	20.00	6.00
93 Roy Oswalt/5		
94 Wade Miller/10		
95 Angel Berroa/4		
96 Byron Gettis/100	10.00	3.00
97 Carlos Beltran/25	60.00	18.00
98 Juan Gonzalez/22	50.00	15.00
100 Duke Snider/25	50.00	15.00
101 Edwin Jackson/50	20.00	6.00
103 Hideo Nomo/1		
104 Hong-Chih Kuo/100	15.00	4.50
105 Kazuhisa Ishii/17	60.00	18.00
106 Paul Lo Duca/16	40.00	12.00
107 Robin Ventura/25	50.00	15.00
108 Shawn Green/15	40.00	12.00
109 Junior Spivey/37	12.00	3.60
110 Lyle Overbay/10		
111 Rickie Weeks/1		
112 Scott Podsednik/20	30.00	9.00
113 J.D. Durbin/31	15.00	4.50
114 Jacque Jones/25	30.00	9.00
116 Johan Santana/57	50.00	15.00
117 Shannon Stewart/23	20.00	6.00
118 Torii Hunter/10		
120 Jose Vidro/3		
121 Nick Johnson/21	20.00	6.00
122 Orlando Cabrera/18	40.00	12.00
123 Zach Day/1		
124 Gary Carter/25	30.00	9.00
125 Jae Weong Seo/25	30.00	9.00
127 Mike Piazza/1		
128 Tom Glavine/1		
129 Alex Rodriguez Yanks/3		
130 Bernie Williams/1		
131 Chien-Ming Wang/100	25.00	7.50
133 Don Mattingly/5		
134 Gary Sheffield/11		
137 Javier Vazquez/5		
138 Jorge Posada/10		
139 Jose Contreras/5		
142 Mike Mussina/1		
143 Whitey Ford/5		
144 Barry Zito/1		
146 Mark Mulder/10		
147 Rich Harden/53	20.00	6.00
148 Tim Hudson/5		
149 Bobby Abreu/5		
152 Marlon Byrd/29	15.00	4.50
153 Mike Schmidt/5		
154 Ryan Howard/100	15.00	4.50
157 Akinori Otsuka/16		
160 Jay Payton/17	25.00	7.50
165 J.T. Snow/10		
167 Jerome Williams/50	30.00	9.00
168 Merkin Valdez/100	20.00	6.00
169 Will Clark/10		
171 Chris Snelling/32	15.00	4.50
172 Edgar Martinez/11		
174 Jamie Moyer/1		
176 Rich Aurilia/10		
177 Shigetoshi Hasegawa/17	120.00	36.00
178 Albert Pujols/5		
179 Dan Haren/100	10.00	3.00
181 Jim Edmonds/10		
183 Scott Rolen/10		
184 Stan Musial/25	80.00	24.00
185 Aubrey Huff/19	40.00	12.00
186 Chad Gaudin/100	10.00	3.00
187 Delmon Young/73	25.00	7.50
188 Fred McGriff/5		
189 Rocco Baldelli/5		
191 Hank Blalock/5		
192 Mark Teixeira/25	50.00	15.00
193 Nolan Ryan/10		
194 Alexis Rios/50	20.00	6.00
196 Dustin McGowan/50	12.00	3.60
197 Guillermo Quiroz/12		
198 Josh Phelps/17	25.00	7.50
199 Roy Halladay/5		
226 Abe Alvarez/50	15.00	4.50
227 Carlos Hines/50	10.00	3.00
228 Charles Thomas/50	20.00	6.00
229 Frankie Francisco/50	10.00	3.00
231 Hector Gimenez/50	10.00	3.00
232 Jesse Crain/50	20.00	6.00
233 Joey Gathright/50	20.00	6.00
234 Justin Knoedler/50	10.00	3.00
236 Lance Cormier/50	10.00	3.00
237 Scott Proctor/50	15.00	4.50
238 Tim Bittner/50	10.00	3.00
239 Travis Blackley/50	15.00	4.50
240 Mike Johnston/50	10.00	3.00
241 Yadier Molina/50	20.00	6.00
244 Bobby Crosby/5		
245 Brad Penny/5		
246 Carl Crawford/5		
247 Carlos Beltran/5		
252 Craig Wilson/5		
255 David Wright/5		
257 Esteban Loaiza/5		
260 Jake Peavy/5		
261 Jason Bay/5		
262 Jermaine Dye/5		
263 Joe Nathan/5		
264 John Lackey/5		
265 Ken Harvey/5		
267 Lew Ford/5		
269 Milton Bradley/5		
271 Orlando Cabrera/5		
272 Paul Lo Duca/5		
275 Victor Martinez/5		

2004 Studio Private Signings Silver

RANDOM INSERTS IN PACKS

PRINT RUNS B/WN 1-250 COPIES PER

NO PRICING ON QTY OF 10 OR LESS

NO RC YR PRICING ON QTY OF 25 OR LESS

	Nm-Mt	Ex-Mt
2 Garret Anderson/25	30.00	9.00
5 Vladimir Guerrero/5		
6 Brandon Webb/25	20.00	6.00
7 Brian Bruney/200	10.00	3.00
8 Casey Fossum/63	10.00	3.00
10 Randy Johnson/5		
11 Richie Sexson/5		
13 Roberto Alomar/5		
14 Shea Hillenbrand/25	30.00	9.00
15 Steve Finley/10		
16 Adam LaRoche/26	15.00	4.50
17 Andruw Jones/10		
18 Bubba Nelson/250	10.00	3.00
19 Chipper Jones/1		
21 J.D. Drew/1		
22 Marcus Giles/25	30.00	9.00
23 Michael Hessman/95	10.00	3.00
24 Rafael Furcal/25	30.00	9.00
25 Warren Spahn/10		
26 Adam Loewen/25	20.00	6.00
27 Cal Ripken/10		
29 Jay Gibbons/50	12.00	3.60
30 Luis Matos/250	10.00	3.00
32 Rafael Palmeiro/5		
33 Curt Schilling/5		
34 Jason Varitek/10		
35 Kevin Youkilis/250	15.00	4.50
36 Manny Ramirez/1		
39 Trot Nixon/25	30.00	9.00
40 Aramis Ramirez/25	30.00	9.00
41 Brendan Harris/100	10.00	3.00
43 Ernie Banks/25	80.00	24.00
45 Kerry Wood/5		
46 Mark Prior/10		
48 Sammy Sosa/21	150.00	45.00
49 Todd Wellemeyer/92	10.00	3.00
50 Carlos Lee/25	30.00	9.00
51 Edwin Almonte/227	10.00	3.00
52 Frank Thomas/5		
53 Joe Borchard/100	10.00	3.00
54 Joe Crede/10		
55 Magglio Ordonez/10		
57 Austin Kearns/10		
58 Barry Larkin/10		
59 Brandon Larson/100	10.00	3.00
61 Ryan Wagner/50	12.00	3.60
63 Brian Tallet/250	10.00	3.00
65 Jeremy Guthrie/89	10.00	3.00
66 Jody Gerut/100	15.00	4.50
67 Travis Hafner/100	15.00	4.50
68 Clint Barmes/100	10.00	3.00
69 Jeff Baker/50	12.00	3.60
70 Joe Kennedy/100	10.00	3.00
72 Preston Wilson/25	30.00	9.00
73 Todd Helton/5		
77 Preston Larrison/100	10.00	3.00
78 Dontrelle Willis/10		
79 Josh Beckett/1		
81 Luis Castillo/25	20.00	6.00
82 Miguel Cabrera/25	50.00	15.00
84 Andy Pettitte/5		
85 Chris Burke/100	10.00	3.00
86 Craig Biggio/5		
87 Jeff Bagwell/5		
89 Lance Berkman/10		
90 Morgan Ensberg/50	12.00	3.60
93 Roy Oswalt/10		
94 Wade Miller/10		
95 Angel Berroa/10		
96 Byron Gettis/250	10.00	3.00
97 Carlos Beltran/50	50.00	15.00
98 Juan Gonzalez/10		
100 Duke Snider/50	30.00	9.00
101 Edwin Jackson/100	15.00	4.50
103 Hideo Nomo/1		
104 Hong-Chih Kuo/250	15.00	4.50
105 Kazuhisa Ishii/5		
106 Paul Lo Duca/25	30.00	9.00
107 Robin Ventura/25	50.00	15.00
108 Shawn Green/1		
109 Junior Spivey/50	12.00	3.60
111 Rickie Weeks/1		
112 Scott Podsednik/100	15.00	4.50
113 J.D. Durbin/250	10.00	3.00
114 Jacque Jones/50	20.00	6.00
115 Jason Kubel/100	15.00	4.50
116 Johan Santana/25	60.00	18.00
117 Shannon Stewart/25	20.00	6.00
118 Torii Hunter/10		
120 Jose Vidro/15	25.00	7.50
121 Nick Johnson/5		
122 Orlando Cabrera/15	40.00	12.00
123 Zach Day/6		
124 Gary Carter/50	20.00	6.00
127 Mike Piazza/1		
128 Tom Glavine/1		
129 Alex Rodriguez Yanks/3		
130 Bernie Williams/1		
131 Chien-Ming Wang/243	25.00	7.50
133 Don Mattingly/25	100.00	30.00
134 Gary Sheffield/25	50.00	15.00
137 Javier Vazquez/5		
138 Jorge Posada/5		
139 Jose Contreras/5		
143 Whitey Ford/5		
144 Barry Zito/5		
146 Mark Mulder/5		
147 Rich Harden/200	15.00	4.50
148 Tim Hudson/5		
149 Bobby Abreu/5		
152 Marlon Byrd/10		
153 Mike Schmidt/10		
154 Ryan Howard/250	15.00	4.50
157 Akinori Otsuka/25		
160 Jay Payton/50	12.00	3.60
165 J.T. Snow/10		
167 Jerome Williams/57	30.00	9.00
168 Merkin Valdez/250	15.00	4.50
169 Will Clark/25	120.00	36.00
171 Chris Snelling/200	10.00	3.00
172 Edgar Martinez/7		
176 Rich Aurilia/8		
177 Shigetoshi Hasegawa/25	120.00	36.00
178 Albert Pujols/5		
179 Dan Haren/250	10.00	3.00
181 Jim Edmonds/5		
183 Scott Rolen/10		
184 Stan Musial/25	80.00	24.00
185 Aubrey Huff/250	15.00	4.50
186 Chad Gaudin/100	10.00	3.00
187 Delmon Young/25	50.00	15.00
188 Fred McGriff/5		
189 Rocco Baldelli/10		
191 Hank Blalock/5		
192 Mark Teixeira/23	50.00	15.00
193 Nolan Ryan/34	120.00	36.00
194 Alexis Rios/250	15.00	4.50
196 Dustin McGowan/115	10.00	3.00
197 Guillermo Quiroz/120	10.00	3.00
198 Josh Phelps/10		
199 Roy Halladay/5		
226 Abe Alvarez/100	12.00	3.60
227 Carlos Hines/100	8.00	2.40
228 Charles Thomas/100	15.00	4.50
229 Frankie Francisco/100	8.00	2.40
230 Greg Dobbs/40	8.00	2.40
231 Hector Gimenez/100	8.00	2.40
232 Jesse Crain/100	15.00	4.50
233 Joey Gathright/100	15.00	4.50
234 Justin Knoedler/100	8.00	2.40
236 Lance Cormier/100	8.00	2.40
237 Scott Proctor/100	12.00	3.60
238 Tim Bittner/100	8.00	2.40
239 Travis Blackley/100	12.00	3.60
240 Mike Johnston/100	8.00	2.40
241 Yadier Molina/100	15.00	4.50
244 Bobby Crosby/10		
245 Brad Penny/10		
246 Carl Crawford/10		
247 Carlos Beltran/10		
252 Craig Wilson/10		
255 David Wright/10		
257 Esteban Loaiza/10		
260 Jake Peavy/10		
261 Jason Bay/10		
262 Jermaine Dye/10		
263 Joe Nathan/10		
264 John Lackey/10		
265 Ken Harvey/10		
267 Lew Ford/10		
269 Milton Bradley/10		
271 Orlando Cabrera/10		
272 Paul Lo Duca/10		
275 Victor Martinez/10		

2004 Studio Big League Challenge

STATED PRINT RUN 999 SERIAL #'d SETS

*DIE CUT: .6X TO 1.5X BASIC

DIE CUT PRINT RUN 500 SERIAL #'d SETS

RANDOM INSERTS IN PACKS

	Nm-Mt	Ex-Mt
1 Albert Pujols Left	6.00	1.80
2 Albert Pujols Right	6.00	1.80
3 Alex Rodriguez Rgr Left	5.00	1.50
4 Alex Rodriguez Rgr Right	5.00	1.50
5 Magglio Ordonez	3.00	.90
6 Rafael Palmeiro	4.00	1.20
7 Troy Glaus Follow	3.00	.90
8 Troy Glaus Start	3.00	.90
9 Albert Pujols Bat Up	6.00	1.80
10 Alex Rodriguez Rgr Bat Up	5.00	1.50

2004 Studio Big League Challenge Material

STATED PRINT RUN 100 SERIAL #'d SETS

*COMBO: .75X TO 2X BASIC

COMBO PRINT RUN 50 SERIAL #'d SETS

RANDOM INSERTS IN PACKS

	Nm-Mt	Ex-Mt
1 Albert Pujols Jsy	15.00	4.50
2 Albert Pujols Pants	15.00	4.50
3 Alex Rodriguez Rgr Jsy	10.00	3.00
4 Alex Rodriguez Rgr Pants	10.00	3.00
5 Magglio Ordonez Jsy	8.00	2.40
6 Rafael Palmeiro Jsy	10.00	3.00
7 Troy Glaus Jsy	8.00	2.40
8 Troy Glaus Pants	8.00	2.40
9 Albert Pujols Hat	20.00	6.00
10 Alex Rodriguez Rgr Hat	15.00	4.50

2004 Studio Diamond Cuts Material Bat

RANDOM INSERTS IN PACKS

PRINT RUNS B/WN 100-200 COPIES PER

	Nm-Mt	Ex-Mt
1 Derek Jeter/100	25.00	7.50
2 Greg Maddux/100	12.00	3.60
3 Nomar Garciaparra/200	10.00	3.00
4 Miguel Cabrera/200	8.00	2.40
5 Mark Mulder/200	5.00	1.50
6 Rafael Furcal/200	5.00	1.50
7 Mark Prior/200	8.00	2.40
8 Roy Oswalt/200	5.00	1.50
9 Dontrelle Willis/100	8.00	2.40
10 Jay Gibbons/200	5.00	1.50
11 Josh Beckett/200	5.00	1.50
12 Angel Berroa/200	5.00	1.50
13 Adam Dunn/200	8.00	2.40
14 Hank Blalock/200	5.00	1.50
15 Carlos Beltran/200	8.00	2.40
16 Shannon Stewart/200	5.00	1.50
17 Aubrey Huff/200	5.00	1.50
18 Jeff Bagwell/200	8.00	2.40
19 Trot Nixon/200	5.00	1.50
21 Tony Gwynn/200	12.00	3.60
22 Andre Dawson/200	8.00	2.40
23 Don Mattingly/200	15.00	4.50
24 Dale Murphy/200	10.00	3.00
25 Gary Carter/200	8.00	2.40

2004 Studio Diamond Cuts Material Jersey

PRINT RUNS B/WN 200-250 COPIES PER

PRIME PRINT RUN B/WN 5-10 COPIES PER

NO PRIME PRICING DUE TO SCARCITY

RANDOM INSERTS IN PACKS

	Nm-Mt	Ex-Mt
1 Derek Jeter/250	20.00	6.00
2 Greg Maddux/250	10.00	3.00
3 Nomar Garciaparra/200	10.00	3.00
4 Miguel Cabrera/250	8.00	2.40
5 Mark Mulder/250	5.00	1.50
6 Rafael Furcal/250	5.00	1.50
7 Mark Prior/250	8.00	2.40
8 Roy Oswalt/250	5.00	1.50
9 Dontrelle Willis/250	5.00	1.50
10 Jay Gibbons/250	5.00	1.50
11 Josh Beckett/250	5.00	1.50
12 Angel Berroa/250	5.00	1.50
13 Adam Dunn/250	8.00	2.40
14 Hank Blalock/250	5.00	1.50
15 Carlos Beltran/250	8.00	2.40
16 Shannon Stewart/250	5.00	1.50
17 Aubrey Huff/250	5.00	1.50
18 Jeff Bagwell/250	8.00	2.40
19 Trot Nixon/250	5.00	1.50
20 Nolan Ryan Jacket/250	25.00	7.50
21 Tony Gwynn/250	15.00	4.50
22 Andre Dawson/250	8.00	2.40
23 Don Mattingly Jacket/250	15.00	4.50
24 Dale Murphy/250	10.00	3.00
25 Gary Carter/250	8.00	2.40

2004 Studio Diamond Cuts Combo Material

PRINT RUNS B/WN 25-50 COPIES PER

PRIME PRINT RUN 5 SERIAL #'d SETS

NO PRIME PRICING DUE TO SCARCITY

RANDOM INSERTS IN PACKS

	Nm-Mt	Ex-Mt
1 Derek Jeter Bat-Jsy/50	50.00	15.00
2 Greg Maddux Bat-Jsy/50	30.00	9.00
3 N.Garciaparra Bat-Jsy/25		
4 Miguel Cabrera Bat-Jsy/50	20.00	6.00
5 Mark Mulder Bat-Jsy/50	12.00	3.60
6 Rafael Furcal Bat-Jsy/50	12.00	3.60
7 Mark Prior Bat-Jsy/50	20.00	6.00
8 Roy Oswalt Bat-Jsy/50	12.00	3.60
9 Dontrelle Willis Bat-Jsy/25		
10 Jay Gibbons Bat-Jsy/50	12.00	3.60
11 Josh Beckett Bat-Jsy/50	12.00	3.60
12 Angel Berroa Bat-Jsy/50	12.00	3.60
13 Adam Dunn Bat-Jsy/50	20.00	6.00
14 Hank Blalock Bat-Jsy/50	12.00	3.60
15 Carlos Beltran Bat-Jsy/50	20.00	6.00
16 Shannon Stewart Bat-Jsy/50	12.00	3.60
17 Aubrey Huff Bat-Jsy/50	12.00	3.60
18 Jeff Bagwell Bat-Jsy/50	20.00	6.00
19 Trot Nixon Bat-Jsy/50	12.00	3.60
20 Nolan Ryan Bat-Jacket/50	40.00	12.00
21 Tony Gwynn Bat-Jsy/50	40.00	12.00
22 Andre Dawson Bat-Jsy/50	15.00	4.50
23 D.Mattingly Bat-Jacket/50	50.00	15.00
24 Dale Murphy Bat-Jsy/50	25.00	7.50
25 Gary Carter Bat-Jsy/50	15.00	4.50

2004 Studio Diamond Cuts Combo Material Signature

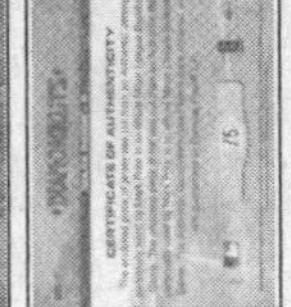

Nm-Mt Ex-Mt

PRINT RUNS B/WN 1-5 COPIES PER

PRIME PRINT RUNS B/WN 1-5 COPIES PER

RANDOM INSERTS IN PACKS

NO PRICING DUE TO SCARCITY

2004 Studio Fans of the Game

RANDOM INSERTS IN PACKS

	Nm-Mt	Ex-Mt
216 Regis Philbin	4.00	1.20
217 Denis Leary	3.00	.90
218 Bode Miller	2.00	.60
219 Steve Schirripa	2.00	.60
220 Adam Mesh	2.00	.60

2004 Studio Fans of the Game Autographs

RANDOM INSERTS IN PACKS

	Nm-Mt	Ex-Mt
216 Regis Philbin	50.00	15.00
217 Denis Leary	40.00	12.00
218 Bode Miller	25.00	7.50
219 Steve Schirripa	30.00	9.00
220 Adam Mesh	25.00	7.50

2004 Studio Game Day Souvenirs Number

Nm-Mt Ex-Mt
PRINT RUNS B/WN 25-300 COPIES PER
*POSITION: .4X TO 1X BASIC
POSITION PRINT B/WN 25-300 COPIES PER
RANDOM INSERTS IN PACKS
1 Garret Anderson Jsy/300 5.00 1.50
2 Troy Glaus Jsy/300 5.00 1.50
3 Vladimir Guerrero Jsy/300 8.00 2.40
4 Steve Finley Jsy/250 5.00 1.50
5 Luis Gonzalez Jsy/25 15.00 4.50
6 Richie Sexson Jsy/250 5.00 1.50
7 Andruw Jones Jsy/300 5.00 1.50
8 Chipper Jones Jsy/250 8.00 2.40
9 Rafael Furcal Jsy/250 5.00 1.50
13 Curt Schilling Jsy/300 8.00 2.40
14 Pedro Martinez Jsy/300 8.00 2.40
15 David Ortiz Jsy/300 8.00 2.40
16 Sammy Sosa Jsy/300 10.00 3.00
17 Corey Patterson Jsy/250 5.00 1.50
18 Moises Alou Jsy/300 5.00 1.50
19 Magglio Ordonez Jsy/250 5.00 1.50
20 Paul Konerko Jsy/300 5.00 1.50
21 Frank Thomas Jsy/300 8.00 2.40
22 Austin Kearns Jsy/50 10.00 3.00
23 Sean Casey Jsy/200 5.00 1.50
24 Adam Dunn Jsy/200 8.00 2.40
25 Omar Vizquel Jsy/250 8.00 2.40
26 C.C. Sabathia Jsy/300 5.00 1.50
27 Jody Gerut Jsy/250 5.00 1.50
28 Todd Helton Jsy/300 8.00 2.40
29 Vinny Castilla Jsy/300 5.00 1.50
30 Jeromy Burnitz Jsy/300 5.00 1.50
31 Fernando Vina Jsy/150 5.00 1.50
32 Ivan Rodriguez Jsy/300 8.00 2.40
33 Jeremy Bonderman Jsy/300 5.00 1.50
34 Mike Lowell Jsy/225 5.00 1.50
35 Luis Castillo Jsy/250 5.00 1.50
36 Miguel Cabrera Jsy/250 8.00 2.40
37 Roger Clemens Jsy/300 10.00 3.00
38 Andy Pettitte Jsy/300 8.00 2.40
39 Jeff Bagwell Jsy/300 8.00 2.40
40 Mike Sweeney Jsy/150 5.00 1.50
41 Carlos Beltran Jsy/200 8.00 2.40
42 Angel Berroa Jsy/100 8.00 2.40
43 Paul Lo Duca Jsy/75 8.00 2.40
44 Shawn Green Jsy/300 5.00 1.50
45 Adrian Beltre Jsy/150 8.00 2.40
46 Ben Sheets Jsy/300 5.00 1.50
47 Geoff Jenkins Jsy/250 5.00 1.50
48 Junior Spivey Jsy/300 5.00 1.50
49 Doug Mientkiewicz Jsy/100 8.00 2.40
50 Shannon Stewart Jsy/100 8.00 2.40
51 Torii Hunter Jsy/300 5.00 1.50
52 Livan Hernandez Jsy/300 5.00 1.50
53 Jose Vidro Jsy/200 5.00 1.50
54 Orlando Cabrera Jsy/300 5.00 1.50
55 Mike Piazza Jsy/250 10.00 3.00
56 Mike Cameron Jsy/250 5.00 1.50
57 Kazuo Matsui Jsy/200 25.00 7.50
58 Derek Jeter Jsy/50 40.00 12.00
59 Jason Giambi Jsy/50 10.00 3.00
61 Barry Zito Jsy/200 5.00 1.50
62 Eric Chavez Jsy/150 5.00 1.50
63 Eric Byrnes Jsy/150 5.00 1.50
65 Jim Thome Jsy/300 8.00 2.40
66 Jimmy Rollins Jsy/250 5.00 1.50
67 Jason Kendall Jsy/250 5.00 1.50
68 Craig Wilson Jsy/250 5.00 1.50
69 Jack Wilson Jsy/250 5.00 1.50
70 Ryan Klesko Jsy/300 5.00 1.50
71 Brian Giles Jsy/300 5.00 1.50
72 Sean Burroughs Jsy/300 5.00 1.50
73 A.J. Pierzynski Jsy/300 5.00 1.50
74 J.T. Snow Jsy/300 5.00 1.50
75 Michael Tucker Jsy/300 5.00 1.50
77 Edgar Martinez Jsy/50 15.00 4.50
79 Scott Rolen Jsy/300 8.00 2.40
80 Albert Pujols Jsy/300 15.00 4.50
81 Jim Edmonds Jsy/300 5.00 1.50
82 Aubrey Huff Jsy/100 8.00 2.40
83 Tino Martinez Jsy/100 10.00 3.00
84 Rocco Baldelli Jsy/100 8.00 2.40
85 Alfonso Soriano Jsy/200 8.00 2.40
86 Michael Young Jsy/250 5.00 1.50
87 Hank Blalock Jsy/200 5.00 1.50
88 Eric Hinske Jsy/200 5.00 1.50
89 Carlos Delgado Jsy/300 5.00 1.50
90 Vernon Wells Jsy/250 5.00 1.50

2004 Studio Game Day Souvenirs Signature Number

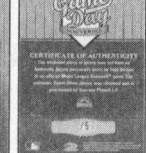

Nm-Mt Ex-Mt
STATED PRINT RUN 5 SERIAL #'d SETS
POSITION PRINT RUN 5 SERIAL #'d SETS
RANDOM INSERTS IN PACKS
NO PRICING DUE TO SCARCITY

2004 Studio Heritage

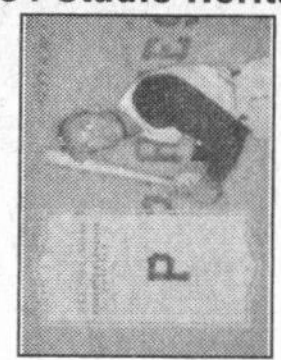

Nm-Mt Ex-Mt
STATED PRINT RUN 999 SERIAL #'d SETS
*DIE CUT: 1.25X TO 3X BASIC
DIE CUT PRINT RUN 100 SERIAL #'d SETS
RANDOM INSERTS IN PACKS
1 George Brett 8.00 2.40
2 Nolan Ryan 8.00 2.40
3 Cal Ripken 10.00 3.00
4 Mike Schmidt 6.00 1.80
5 Roberto Clemente 8.00 2.40
6 Don Mattingly 6.00 1.80
7 Dale Murphy 4.00 1.20
8 Ryne Sandberg 6.00 1.80
9 Harmon Killebrew 4.00 1.20
10 Stan Musial 5.00 1.50

2004 Studio Heritage Material Bat

Nm-Mt Ex-Mt
RANDOM INSERTS IN PACKS
STATED PRINT RUN 50 SERIAL #'d SETS
1 George Brett 40.00 12.00
3 Cal Ripken 60.00 18.00
4 Mike Schmidt 25.00 7.50
5 Roberto Clemente 100.00 30.00
6 Don Mattingly 40.00 12.00
7 Dale Murphy 20.00 6.00
8 Ryne Sandberg 40.00 12.00
9 Harmon Killebrew 20.00 6.00
10 Stan Musial 40.00 12.00

2004 Studio Heritage Material Jersey

Nm-Mt Ex-Mt
PRINT RUNS B/WN 50-200 COPIES PER
PRIME PRINT RUN B/WN 3-10 COPIES PER
NO PRIME PRICING DUE TO SCARCITY
RANDOM INSERTS IN PACKS
1 George Brett/200 15.00 4.50
2 Nolan Ryan Jacket/200 25.00 7.50
3 Cal Ripken/200 40.00 12.00
4 Mike Schmidt Pants/200 15.00 4.50
5 Roberto Clemente/50 100.00 30.00
6 Don Mattingly Jacket/200 15.00 4.50
7 Dale Murphy/200 10.00 3.00
8 Ryne Sandberg/200 25.00 7.50
9 Harmon Killebrew Pants/200 15.00 4.50
10 Stan Musial/100 25.00 7.50

2004 Studio Heritage Material Signature Jersey

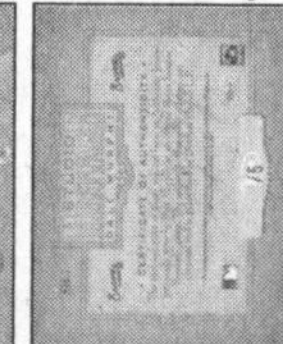

Nm-Mt Ex-Mt
RANDOM INSERTS IN PACKS
STATED PRINT RUN 5 SERIAL #'d SETS
NO PRICING DUE TO SCARCITY

2004 Studio Heroes of the Hall

Nm-Mt Ex-Mt
STATED PRINT RUN 999 SERIAL #'d SETS
*DIE CUT: .6X TO 1.5X BASIC
DIE CUT PRINT RUN 500 SERIAL #'d SETS
RANDOM INSERTS IN PACKS
1 Fergie Jenkins 3.00 .90
2 Gary Carter 3.00 .90
3 Gaylord Perry 3.00 .90
4 George Brett 8.00 2.40
5 Jim Palmer 3.00 .90
6 Nolan Ryan 8.00 2.40
7 Paul Molitor 4.00 1.20
8 Rod Carew 4.00 1.20
9 Steve Carlton 3.00 .90
10 Robin Yount 5.00 1.50

2004 Studio Heroes of the Hall Material Bat

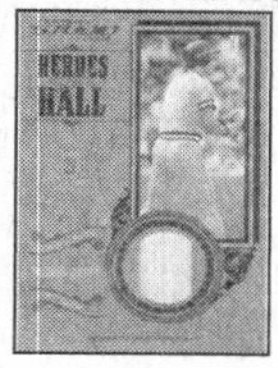

Nm-Mt Ex-Mt
RANDOM INSERTS IN PACKS
STATED PRINT RUN 100 SERIAL #'d SETS
2 Gary Carter 8.00 2.40
4 George Brett 25.00 7.50
7 Paul Molitor 10.00 3.00
8 Rod Carew 10.00 3.00
9 Steve Carlton 8.00 2.40
10 Robin Yount 20.00 6.00

2004 Studio Heroes of the Hall Material Jersey

Nm-Mt Ex-Mt
STATED PRINT RUN 200 SERIAL #'d SETS
PRIME PRINT RUN 10 SERIAL #'d SETS
NO PRIME PRICING DUE TO SCARCITY
RANDOM INSERTS IN PACKS
1 Fergie Jenkins Pants/200 8.00 2.40
2 Gary Carter/200 8.00 2.40
3 Gaylord Perry/100 8.00 2.40
4 George Brett/200 15.00 4.50
5 Jim Palmer/200 8.00 2.40
6 Nolan Ryan/200 25.00 7.50
7 Paul Molitor/200 10.00 3.00
8 Rod Carew/200 10.00 3.00
9 Steve Carlton/200 8.00 2.40
10 Robin Yount/200 15.00 4.50

2004 Studio Heroes of the Hall Material Signature Jersey

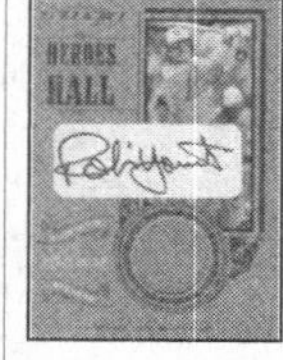

Nm-Mt Ex-Mt
RANDOM INSERTS IN PACKS
PRINT RUNS B/WN 1-10 COPIES PER
NO PRICING DUE TO SCARCITY

2004 Studio Masterstrokes Material Bat

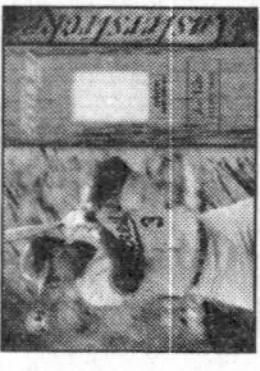

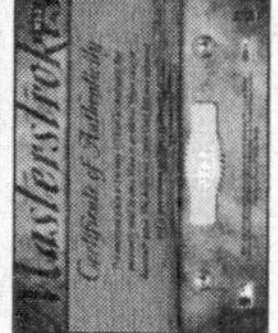

Nm-Mt Ex-Mt
RANDOM INSERTS IN PACKS
STATED PRINT RUN 200 SERIAL #'d SETS
1 Todd Helton 8.00 2.40
2 Jose Vidro 2.00 .60
3 Edgar Renteria 5.00 1.50
4 Mike Lowell 5.00 1.50
5 Gary Sheffield 5.00 1.50
6 Albert Pujols 15.00 4.50
7 Javy Lopez 5.00 1.50
8 Carlos Delgado 5.00 1.50
9 Bret Boone 5.00 1.50
10 Alex Rodriguez Rgr 10.00 3.00
11 Vernon Wells 5.00 1.50
12 Manny Ramirez 8.00 2.40
13 Jorge Posada 8.00 2.40
14 Edgar Martinez 8.00 2.40
15 Bernie Williams 8.00 2.40
16 Magglio Ordonez 5.00 1.50
17 Garret Anderson 5.00 1.50
18 Eric Chavez 5.00 1.50
19 Alfonso Soriano 8.00 2.40
20 Jason Giambi 5.00 1.50
21 Jeff Kent 5.00 1.50
22 Scott Rolen 8.00 2.40
23 Vladimir Guerrero 8.00 2.40
24 Sammy Sosa 10.00 3.00
25 Mike Piazza 10.00 3.00

2004 Studio Masterstrokes Material Jersey

Nm-Mt Ex-Mt
PRINT RUNS B/WN 150-250 COPIES PER
PRIME PRINT RUN 5 SERIAL #'d SETS
NO PRIME PRICING DUE TO SCARCITY
RANDOM INSERTS IN PACKS
1 Todd Helton/250 8.00 2.40
2 Jose Vidro/250 5.00 1.50
3 Edgar Renteria/250 5.00 1.50
4 Mike Lowell/250 5.00 1.50
5 Gary Sheffield/250 5.00 1.50
6 Albert Pujols/250 15.00 4.50
7 Javy Lopez/250 5.00 1.50
8 Carlos Delgado/250 5.00 1.50
9 Bret Boone/250 5.00 1.50
10 Alex Rodriguez Rgr/250 10.00 3.00
11 Vernon Wells/250 5.00 1.50
12 Manny Ramirez/250 8.00 2.40
13 Jorge Posada/250 8.00 2.40
14 Edgar Martinez/250 8.00 2.40
15 Bernie Williams/250 8.00 2.40
16 Magglio Ordonez/250 5.00 1.50
17 Garret Anderson/250 5.00 1.50
18 Eric Chavez/250 5.00 1.50
19 Alfonso Soriano/150 8.00 2.40
20 Jason Giambi/250 5.00 1.50
21 Jeff Kent/250 5.00 1.50
22 Scott Rolen/250 8.00 2.40
23 Vladimir Guerrero/250 8.00 2.40
24 Sammy Sosa/250 10.00 3.00
25 Mike Piazza/250 10.00 3.00

2004 Studio Masterstrokes Combo Material

Nm-Mt Ex-Mt
STATED PRINT RUN 50 SERIAL #'d SETS
PRIME PRINT RUN 5 SERIAL #'d SETS
NO PRIME PRICING DUE TO SCARCITY
RANDOM INSERTS IN PACKS
1 Todd Helton Bat-Jsy/50 20.00 6.00
2 Jose Vidro Bat-Jsy/50 12.00 3.60
3 Edgar Renteria Bat-Jsy/50 12.00 3.60
4 Mike Lowell Bat-Jsy/50 12.00 3.60
5 Gary Sheffield Bat-Jsy/50 12.00 3.60
6 Albert Pujols Bat-Jsy/50 40.00 12.00
7 Javy Lopez Bat-Jsy/50 12.00 3.60
8 Carlos Delgado Bat-Jsy/50 12.00 3.60
9 Bret Boone Bat-Jsy/50 12.00 3.60
10 A.Rodriguez Rgr Bat-Jsy/50 25.00 7.50
11 Vernon Wells Bat-Jsy/50 12.00 3.60
12 Manny Ramirez Bat-Jsy/50 20.00 6.00
13 Jorge Posada Bat-Jsy/50 20.00 6.00
14 Edgar Martinez Bat-Jsy/50 20.00 6.00
15 Bernie Williams Bat-Jsy/50 20.00 6.00
16 Magglio Ordonez Bat-Jsy/50 12.00 3.60
17 Garret Anderson Bat-Jsy/50 12.00 3.60
18 Eric Chavez Bat-Jsy/50 12.00 3.60
19 Alfonso Soriano Bat-Jsy/50 20.00 6.00
20 Jason Giambi Bat-Jsy/50 12.00 3.60
21 Jeff Kent Bat-Jsy/50
22 Scott Rolen Bat-Jsy/50 20.00 6.00
23 Vladimir Guerrero Bat-Jsy/50 20.00 6.00
24 Sammy Sosa Bat-Jsy/50 30.00 9.00
25 Mike Piazza Bat-Jsy/50 30.00 9.00

2004 Studio Masterstrokes Combo Material Signature

Nm-Mt Ex-Mt
PRINT RUNS B/WN 1-10 COPIES PER
PRIME PRINT RUNS B/WN 1-5 COPIES PER
RANDOM INSERTS IN PACKS
NO PRICING DUE TO SCARCITY

2004 Studio Rally Caps

Nm-Mt Ex-Mt
STATED PRINT RUN 999 SERIAL #'d SETS
*DIE CUT: .6X TO 1.5X BASIC
DIE CUT PRINT RUN 500 SERIAL #'d SETS

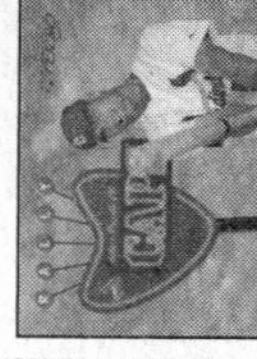

RANDOM INSERTS IN PACKS
1 Adam Dunn 4.00 1.20
2 Adrian Beltre 4.00 1.20
3 Albert Pujols 6.00 1.80
4 Alex Rodriguez 6.00 1.80
5 Andruw Jones 3.00 .90
6 Angel Berroa 3.00 .90
7 Aubrey Huff 3.00 .90
8 Austin Kearns 3.00 .90
9 Ben Sheets 3.00 .90
10 Brad Penny 3.00 .90
11 Carlos Beltran 4.00 1.20
12 Carlos Lee 3.00 .90
13 Casey Fossum 3.00 .90
14 Eric Hinske 3.00 .90
15 Geoff Jenkins 3.00 .90
16 Jack Wilson 3.00 .90
17 Jason Jennings 3.00 .90
18 Joe Kennedy 3.00 .90
19 Lance Berkman 3.00 .90
20 Magglio Ordonez 3.00 .90
21 Kerry Wood 4.00 1.20
22 Mark Buehrle 3.00 .90
23 Mark Prior 4.00 1.20
24 Mark Teixeira 3.00 .90
25 Michael Cuddyer 3.00 .90
26 Jeff Conine 3.00 .90
27 Mike Mussina 4.00 1.20
28 Mike Piazza 5.00 1.50
29 Jose Reyes 3.00 .90
30 Paul Lo Duca 3.00 .90
31 Pedro Martinez 4.00 1.20
32 Roy Oswalt 3.00 .90
33 Ryan Klesko 3.00 .90
34 Sammy Sosa 5.00 1.50
35 Tim Hudson 3.00 .90
36 Todd Helton 4.00 1.20
37 Torii Hunter 3.00 .90
38 Vernon Wells 3.00 .90
39 Craig Wilson 3.00 .90
40 Edgar Renteria 3.00 .90

2004 Studio Spirit of the Game

Nm-Mt Ex-Mt
STATED PRINT RUN 999 SERIAL #'d SETS
*DIE CUT: .6X TO 1.5X BASIC
DIE CUT PRINT RUN 500 SERIAL #'d SETS
RANDOM INSERTS IN PACKS
1 Sammy Sosa 5.00 1.50
2 Alex Rodriguez Rgr 5.00 1.50
3 Nomar Garciaparra 5.00 1.50
4 Derek Jeter 6.00 1.80
5 Albert Pujols 6.00 1.80
6 Roger Clemens 6.00 1.80
7 Mark Prior 4.00 1.20
8 Randy Johnson 4.00 1.20
9 Pedro Martinez 4.00 1.20
10 Vladimir Guerrero 4.00 1.20
11 Todd Helton 4.00 1.20
12 Jeff Bagwell 4.00 1.20
13 Mike Mussina 4.00 1.20
14 Josh Beckett 3.00 .90
15 Hideo Nomo 4.00 1.20
16 Mike Piazza 5.00 1.50
17 Don Mattingly 6.00 1.80
18 George Brett 8.00 2.40
19 Nolan Ryan 8.00 2.40
20 Cal Ripken 10.00 3.00

2004 Studio Spirit of the Game Material Bat

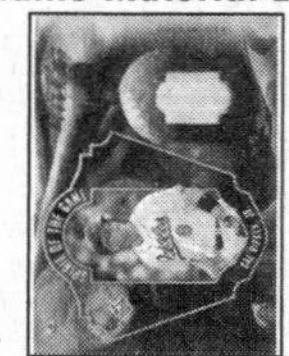

Nm-Mt Ex-Mt
RANDOM INSERTS IN PACKS
PRINT RUNS B/WN 10-100 COPIES PER
NO PRICING ON QTY OF 10 OR LESS
1 Sammy Sosa/100 12.00 3.60
2 Alex Rodriguez Rgr/100 12.00 3.60
3 Nomar Garciaparra/100 12.00 3.60
4 Derek Jeter/100 25.00 7.50
5 Albert Pujols/100 20.00 6.00
6 Roger Clemens/50 25.00 7.50
7 Mark Prior/100 10.00 3.00
8 Randy Johnson/100 10.00 3.00
9 Pedro Martinez/100
10 Vladimir Guerrero/100 10.00 3.00
11 Todd Helton/100 10.00 3.00
12 Jeff Bagwell/100 10.00 3.00
13 Mike Mussina/50 10.00 3.00

14 Josh Beckett/100 .... 8.00 2.40
15 Hideo Nomo/100 .... 10.00 3.00
16 Mike Piazza/100 .... 12.00 3.60
17 Don Mattingly/100 .... 25.00 7.50
18 George Brett/100 .... 25.00 7.50
19 Nolan Ryan/10
20 Cal Ripken/50 .... 60.00 18.00

2004 Studio Spirit of the Game Material Jersey

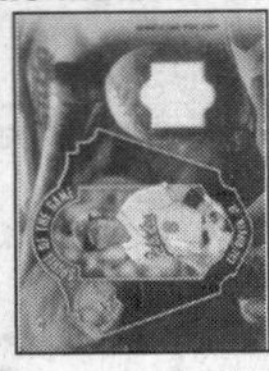

Nm-Mt Ex-Mt

PRINT RUNS B/WN 100-200 COPIES PER
PRIME PRINT RUNS B/WN 1-5 COPIES PER
NO PRIME PRICING DUE TO SCARCITY
RANDOM INSERTS IN PACKS

1 Sammy Sosa/200 .... 10.00 3.00
2 Alex Rodriguez Rgr/200 .... 10.00 3.00
3 Nomar Garciaparra/100 .... 12.00 3.60
4 Derek Jeter/200 .... 20.00 6.00
5 Albert Pujols/100 .... 20.00 6.00
7 Mark Prior/200 .... 8.00 2.40
8 Randy Johnson/100 .... 10.00 3.00
9 Pedro Martinez/200 .... 8.00 2.40
11 Todd Helton/100 .... 10.00 3.00
12 Jeff Bagwell/200 .... 8.00 2.40
13 Mike Mussina/200 .... 8.00 2.40
14 Josh Beckett/200 .... 5.00 1.50
15 Hideo Nomo/200 .... 8.00 2.40
16 Mike Piazza/200 .... 10.00 3.00
17 Don Mattingly Jacket/200 .... 15.00 4.50
18 George Brett/200 .... 15.00 4.50
19 Nolan Ryan/100 .... 40.00 12.00
20 Cal Ripken/100 .... 50.00 15.00

2004 Studio Spirit of the Game Material Signature Jersey

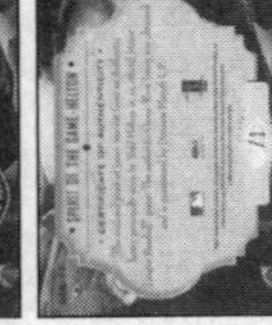

Nm-Mt Ex-Mt

RANDOM INSERTS IN PACKS
PRINT RUNS B/WN 1-5 COPIES PER
NO PRICING DUE TO SCARCITY

2004 Studio Stars

Nm-Mt Ex-Mt

STATED ODDS 1:5
*GOLD: 1.25X TO 3X BASIC
*GOLD K.MATSUI: 1.25X TO 3X BASIC
GOLD PRINT RUN 100 SERIAL #'d SETS
*PLAT: 2.5X TO 6X BASIC
*PLAT K.MATSUI: 4X TO 10X BASIC
PLATINUM PRINT RUN 25 SERIAL #'d SETS
GOLD/PLATINUM RANDOM IN PACKS

1 Albert Pujols 5.00 1.50
2 Alex Rodriguez Yanks 4.00 1.20
3 Alfonso Soriano .... 2.50 .75
4 Andy Pettitte .... 2.50 .75
5 Angel Berroa .... 1.50 .45
6 Aubrey Huff .... 1.50 .45
7 Austin Kearns .... 1.50 .45
8 Barry Zito .... 1.50 .45
9 Brian Giles .... 1.50 .45
10 Carlos Delgado .... 1.50 .45
11 Chipper Jones .... 2.50 .75
12 Craig Biggio .... 2.50 .75
13 Curt Schilling .... 2.50 .75
14 Derek Jeter 5.00 1.50
15 Edgar Martinez .... 2.50 .75
16 Eric Gagne .... 2.50 .75
17 Frank Thomas .... 2.50 .75
18 Hank Blalock .... 1.50 .45
19 Hideki Matsui 4.00 1.20
20 Hideo Nomo .... 2.50 .75
21 Ichiro Suzuki 4.00 1.20
22 Ivan Rodriguez .... 2.50 .75
23 Jason Kendall .... 1.50 .45
24 Jason Schmidt .... 1.50 .45
25 Jeff Bagwell .... 2.50 .75
26 Jim Edmonds .... 1.50 .45
27 Jim Thome .... 2.50 .75
28 Josh Beckett .... 1.50 .45
29 Kazuo Matsui 5.00 1.50
30 Ken Griffey Jr. 4.00 1.20
31 Larry Walker .... 2.50 .75
32 Magglio Ordonez .... 1.50 .45
33 Manny Ramirez .... 2.50 .75
34 Mark Mulder .... 1.50 .45
35 Mark Prior .... 2.50 .75
36 Mark Teixeira .... 1.50 .45
37 Miguel Tejada .... 1.50 .45
38 Mike Mussina .... 2.50 .75
39 Mike Piazza 4.00 1.20
40 Pedro Martinez .... 2.50 .75
41 Randy Johnson .... 2.50 .75
42 Roger Clemens 5.00 1.50
43 Roy Halladay .... 1.50 .45
44 Russ Ortiz .... 1.50 .45
45 Sammy Sosa 4.00 1.20
46 Scott Podsednik .... 1.50 .45
47 Tim Hudson .... 1.50 .45
48 Todd Helton .... 2.50 .75
49 Vernon Wells .... 1.50 .45
50 Vladimir Guerrero .... 2.50 .75

2001 Sweet Spot

The 2001 Upper Deck Sweet Spot product was initially released in February, 2001 and offered a 90-card base set. An additional 60-card Update set was distributed within Upper Deck Rookie Update packs in late December, 2001. The basic 90-card set is broken into tiers as follows: 60 basic veterans (1-60), and 30 Sweet Beginning subset cards (each individually serial numbered to 1000). The Update set was composed of 30 basic veterans (91-120) and 30 Sweet Beginnings subset cards (121-150) each serial numbered to 1500. Basic packs contained four cards and carried a suggested retail price of $2.99. Rookie Update packs contained four cards and carried a suggested retail price of $4.99.

Nm-Mt Ex-Mt

COMP.BASIC w/o SP's (60) 25.00 7.50
COMP.UPDATE w/o SP's (30) 10.00 3.00
COMMON CARD (1-60) .... .40 .12
COMMON CARD (61-90) 10.00 3.00
COMMON CARD (91-120) .... .60 .18
COMMON (121-150) 5.00 1.50

1 Troy Glaus .... .40 .12
2 Darin Erstad .... .40 .12
3 Jason Giambi .... .40 .12
4 Tim Hudson .... .40 .12
5 Ben Grieve .... .40 .12
6 Carlos Delgado .... .40 .12
7 David Wells .... .40 .12
8 Greg Vaughn .... .40 .12
9 Roberto Alomar .... .60 .18
10 Jim Thome .... 1.00 .30
11 John Olerud .... .40 .12
12 Edgar Martinez .... .60 .18
13 Cal Ripken .... 3.00 .90
14 Albert Belle .... .40 .12
15 Ivan Rodriguez .... 1.00 .30
16 Alex Rodriguez Rangers .... 3.00 .90
17 Pedro Martinez .... 1.00 .30
18 Nomar Garciaparra .... 1.50 .45
19 Manny Ramirez .... .60 .18
20 Jermaine Dye .... .40 .12
21 Juan Gonzalez .... .60 .18
22 Dean Palmer .... .40 .12
23 Matt Lawton .... .40 .12
24 Eric Milton .... .40 .12
25 Frank Thomas .... 1.00 .30
26 Magglio Ordonez .... .40 .12
27 Derek Jeter .... 2.50 .75
28 Bernie Williams .... .60 .18
29 Roger Clemens .... 2.00 .60
30 Jeff Bagwell .... .60 .18
31 Richard Hidalgo .... .40 .12
32 Chipper Jones .... 1.00 .30
33 Greg Maddux .... 1.50 .45
34 Richie Sexson .... .40 .12
35 Jeromy Burnitz .... .40 .12
36 Mark McGwire .... 2.50 .75
37 Jim Edmonds .... .40 .12
38 Sammy Sosa .... 1.50 .45
39 Randy Johnson .... 1.00 .30
40 Steve Finley .... .40 .12
41 Gary Sheffield .... .40 .12
42 Shawn Green .... .40 .12
43 Vladimir Guerrero .... 1.00 .30
44 Jose Vidro .... .40 .12
45 Barry Bonds .... 2.50 .75
46 Jeff Kent .... .40 .12
47 Preston Wilson .... .40 .12
48 Luis Castillo .... .40 .12
49 Mike Piazza .... 1.50 .45
50 Edgardo Alfonzo .... .40 .12
51 Tony Gwynn .... 1.25 .35
52 Ryan Klesko .... .40 .12
53 Scott Rolen .... 1.00 .30
54 Bob Abreu .... .40 .12
55 Jason Kendall .... .40 .12
56 Brian Giles .... .40 .12
57 Ken Griffey Jr. .... 1.50 .45
58 Barry Larkin .... .60 .18
59 Todd Helton .... .60 .18
60 Mike Hampton .... .40 .12
Card back has batting header lines UER
61 Corey Patterson SB 10.00 3.00
62 Ichiro Suzuki SB RC 175.00 52.50
63 Jason Grilli SB 10.00 3.00
64 Brian Cole SB 10.00 3.00
65 Juan Pierre SB 10.00 3.00
66 Matt Ginter SB 10.00 3.00
67 Jimmy Rollins SB 10.00 3.00
68 Jason Smith SB RC 10.00 3.00
69 Israel Alcantara SB 10.00 3.00
70 Adam Pettyjohn SB RC 10.00 3.00
71 Luke Prokopec SB 10.00 3.00
72 Barry Zito SB 12.00 3.60
73 Keith Ginter SB 10.00 3.00
74 Sun Woo Kim SB 10.00 3.00
75 Ross Gload SB 10.00 3.00
76 Matt Wise SB 10.00 3.00
77 Aubrey Huff SB 10.00 3.00
78 Ryan Franklin SB 10.00 3.00
79 Brandon Inge SB 10.00 3.00
80 Wes Helms SB 10.00 3.00
81 Junior Spivey SB RC 12.00 3.60
82 Ryan Vogelsong SB 10.00 3.00
83 John Parrish SB 10.00 3.00
84 Joe Crede SB 10.00 3.00
85 Damian Rolls SB 10.00 3.00
86 Esix Snead SB RC 10.00 3.00
87 Rocky Biddle SB 10.00 3.00
88 Brady Clark SB 10.00 3.00
89 Timo Perez SB 10.00 3.00
90 Jay Spurgeon SB 10.00 3.00
91 Garret Anderson .... .60 .18
92 Jermaine Dye .... .60 .18
93 Shannon Stewart .... .60 .18
94 Ben Grieve .... .60 .18
95 Juan Gonzalez .... 1.00 .30
96 Brett Boone .... .60 .18
97 Tony Batista .... .60 .18
98 Rafael Palmeiro .... 1.00 .30
99 Carl Everett .... .60 .18
100 Mike Sweeney .... .60 .18
101 Tony Clark .... .60 .18
102 Doug Mientkiewicz .... .60 .18
103 Jose Canseco .... 1.50 .45
104 Mike Mussina .... 1.00 .30
105 Lance Berkman .... .60 .18
106 Andruw Jones .... .60 .18
107 Geoff Jenkins .... .60 .18
108 Matt Morris .... .60 .18
109 Fred McGriff .... 1.00 .30
110 Luis Gonzalez .... .60 .18
111 Kevin Brown .... .60 .18
112 Tony Armas Jr. .... .60 .18
113 John Vander Wal .... .60 .18
114 Cliff Floyd .... .60 .18
115 Matt Lawton .... .60 .18
116 Phil Nevin .... .60 .18
117 Pat Burrell .... .60 .18
118 Aramis Ramirez .... .60 .18
119 Sean Casey .... .60 .18
120 Larry Walker .... 1.00 .30
121 Albert Pujols SB RC 120.00 36.00
122 J.Estrada SB RC 8.00 2.40
123 Wilson Betemit SB RC 5.00 1.50
124 A.Hernandez SB RC 5.00 1.50
125 M.Ensberg SB RC 8.00 2.40
126 H.Ramirez SB RC 5.00 1.50
127 Josh Towers SB RC 5.00 1.50
128 Juan Uribe SB RC 5.00 1.50
129 Wilken Ruan SB RC 5.00 1.50
130 Andres Torres SB RC 5.00 1.50
131 B.Lawrence SB RC 5.00 1.50
132 Ryan Freel SB RC 5.00 1.50
133 B.Duckworth SB RC 5.00 1.50
134 Juan Diaz SB RC 5.00 1.50
135 Rafael Soriano SB RC 5.00 1.50
136 R.Rodriguez SB RC 5.00 1.50
137 Bud Smith SB RC 5.00 1.50
138 Mark Teixeira SB RC 40.00 12.00
139 Mark Prior SB RC 80.00 24.00
140 J.Melian SB RC 5.00 1.50
141 D.Brazelton SB RC 5.00 1.50
142 Greg Miller SB RC 5.00 1.50
143 Billy Sylvester SB RC 5.00 1.50
144 E.Guzman SB RC 5.00 1.50
145 Jack Wilson SB RC 10.00 3.00
146 Jose Mieses SB RC 5.00 1.50
147 Brandon Lyon SB RC 5.00 1.50
148 T.Shinjo SB RC 5.00 1.50
149 Juan Cruz SB RC 5.00 1.50
150 Jay Gibbons SB RC 8.00 2.40

2001 Sweet Spot Big League Challenge

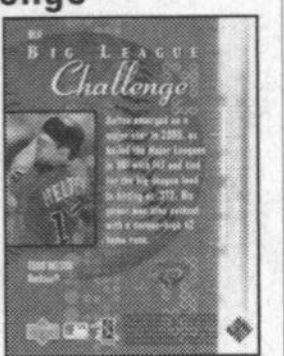

Randomly inserted into packs at one in six, this 20-card insert features the top power-hitting players in the league. Card backs carry a "BL" prefix.

Nm-Mt Ex-Mt

COMPLETE SET (20) 60.00 18.00
BL1 Mark McGwire 8.00 2.40
BL2 Richard Hidalgo .... 2.00 .60
BL3 Alex Rodriguez 5.00 1.50
BL4 Shawn Green .... 2.00 .60
BL5 Frank Thomas .... 3.00 .90
BL6 Chipper Jones .... 3.00 .90
BL7 Rafael Palmeiro .... 2.00 .60
BL8 Troy Glaus .... 2.00 .60
BL9 Mike Piazza 5.00 1.50
BL10 Andruw Jones .... 2.00 .60
BL11 Todd Helton .... 2.00 .60
BL12 Jason Giambi .... 2.00 .60
BL13 Sammy Sosa 5.00 1.50
BL14 Carlos Delgado .... 2.00 .60
BL15 Barry Bonds 8.00 2.40
BL16 Jose Canseco .... 3.00 .90
BL17 Jim Edmonds .... 2.00 .60
BL18 Manny Ramirez .... 2.00 .60
BL19 Gary Sheffield .... 2.00 .60
BL20 Nomar Garciaparra 5.00 1.50

2001 Sweet Spot Game Base Duos

Randomly inserted into packs at one in 18, this 16-card insert set features dual-player cards with a swatch of an actual game-used base. Card backs carry a "B1" prefix followed by the player's initials.

Nm-Mt Ex-Mt

B1-BD Jeff Bagwell 15.00 4.50
Jermaine Dye
B1-BH Barry Bonds 30.00 9.00
Todd Helton
B1-CP Roger Clemens 25.00 7.50

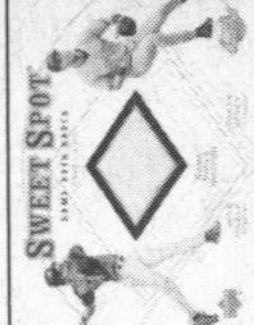

Mike Piazza
B1-GD Vladimir Guerrero 15.00 4.50
Carlos Delgado
B1-HG Jeffrey Hammonds 10.00 3.00
Troy Glaus
B1-JG Chipper Jones 25.00 7.50
Nomar Garciaparra
B1-JP Mike Piazza 40.00 12.00
Derek Jeter
B1-MG Mark McGwire 80.00 24.00
Ken Griffey Jr.
B1-MP Mark McGwire 50.00 15.00
Timo Perez
B1-RJ Alex Rodriguez 50.00 15.00
Derek Jeter
B1-RR Scott Rolen 30.00 9.00
Cal Ripken
B1-SR Gary Sheffield 15.00 4.50
Alex Rodriguez
B1-ST Sammy Sosa 25.00 7.50
Frank Thomas
B1-GRA Ken Griffey Jr. 25.00 7.50
Manny Ramirez
B1-GRO Tony Gwynn 15.00 4.50
Ivan Rodriguez
B1-JGI Randy Johnson 15.00 4.50
Jason Giambi

2001 Sweet Spot Game Base Trios

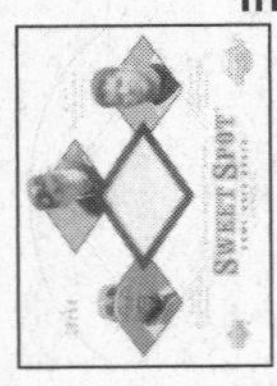

Randomly inserted into packs, this 13-card insert set features three players on one card with a swatch of an actual game-used base. Card backs carry a "B2" prefix followed by the player's initials. Please note that there were only 50 serial numbered sets produced.

Nm-Mt Ex-Mt

BDH Jef Bagwell 40.00 12.00
Jermaine Dye
Richard Hidalgo
BHK Barry Bonds 100.00 30.00
Todd Helton
Jeff Kent
GDM V. Guerrero 40.00 12.00
Carlos Delgado
Raul Mondesi
GRP Tony Gwynn 50.00 15.00
Ivan Rodriguez
Rafael Palmeiro
GRT Ken Griffey Jr. 50.00 15.00
Manny Ramirez
Jim Thome
HGH Jeffrey Hammonds 40.00 12.00
Troy Glaus
Todd Helton
JGC Randy Johnson 40.00 12.00
Jason Giambi
Eric Chavez
JGJ Chipper Jones 60.00 18.00
Nomar Garciaparra
Andruw Jones
MGE Mark McGwire 120.00 36.00
Ken Griffey Jr.
Jim Edmonds
PJW Mike Piazza 100.00 30.00
Derek Jeter
Bernie Williams
RRB Scott Rolen 100.00 30.00
Cal Ripken
Albert Belle
SRM Gary Sheffield 50.00 15.00
Alex Rodriguez
Edgar Martinez
STO Sammy Sosa 60.00 18.00
Frank Thomas
Magglio Ordonez

2001 Sweet Spot Game Bat

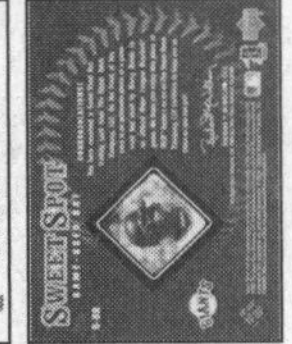

Randomly inserted into packs at one in 18, this 19-card insert set features a swatch of actual game-used bat. Card backs carry a "B" prefix followed by the player's initials.

Nm-Mt Ex-Mt

B-AJ Andruw Jones 10.00 3.00
B-AR Alex Rodriguez 15.00 4.50
B-BB Barry Bonds 25.00 7.50
B-CR Cal Ripken 40.00 12.00
B-FT Frank Thomas 15.00 4.50
B-GS Gary Sheffield 10.00 3.00
B-HA Hank Aaron 60.00 18.00
B-IR Ivan Rodriguez 15.00 4.50
B-JC Jose Canseco 15.00 4.50
B-JD Joe DiMaggio 100.00 30.00
B-KG Ken Griffey Jr. 15.00 4.50
B-MM Mickey Mantle 150.00 45.00
B-NR Nolan Ryan 40.00 12.00
B-RA Rick Ankiel 10.00 3.00
B-RJ Reggie Jackson 15.00 4.50
B-SM Stan Musial 50.00 15.00
B-SS Sammy Sosa 15.00 4.50
B-TC Ty Cobb 150.00 45.00
B-WM Willie Mays 60.00 18.00

2001 Sweet Spot Game Jersey

Randomly inserted into packs at one in 18, this 20-card insert set features a swatch from an actual game-used jersey. Card backs carry a "J" prefix followed by the player's initials. The Ichiro jersey actually was not major league regular-season game worn, but was worn in an spring training game in 1999.

Nm-Mt Ex-Mt

J-AJ Andruw Jones 10.00 3.00
J-AR Alex Rodriguez 15.00 4.50
J-BB Barry Bonds 25.00 7.50
J-CJ Chipper Jones 15.00 4.50
J-CR Cal Ripken 40.00 12.00
J-DS Duke Snider 15.00 4.50
J-FT Frank Thomas 15.00 4.50
J-IR Ivan Rodriguez 15.00 4.50
J-IS Ichiro Suzuki 80.00 24.00
J-JC Jose Canseco 15.00 4.50
J-JD Joe DiMaggio 100.00 30.00
J-KG Ken Griffey Jr. 15.00 4.50
J-MM Mickey Mantle 150.00 45.00
J-NR Nolan Ryan 40.00 12.00
J-RC Roberto Clemente 100.00 30.00
J-RC Roger Clemens 15.00 4.50
J-RJ Randy Johnson 15.00 4.50
J-SM Stan Musial 50.00 15.00
J-SS Sammy Sosa 15.00 4.50
J-WM Willie Mays 80.00 24.00

2001 Sweet Spot Players Party

Inserted at a rate of one in 12 packs, these 10 cards feature some of Baseball's leading players. These cards have a "PP" prefix.

Nm-Mt Ex-Mt

COMPLETE SET (10) 50.00 15.00
PP1 Derek Jeter 8.00 2.40
PP2 Randy Johnson .... 3.00 .90
PP3 Frank Thomas .... 3.00 .90
PP4 Nomar Garciaparra 5.00 1.50
PP5 Ken Griffey Jr. 5.00 1.50
PP6 Carlos Delgado .... 2.00 .60
PP7 Mike Piazza 5.00 1.50
PP8 Barry Bonds 8.00 2.40
PP9 Sammy Sosa 5.00 1.50
PP10 Pedro Martinez .... 3.00 .90

2001 Sweet Spot Signatures

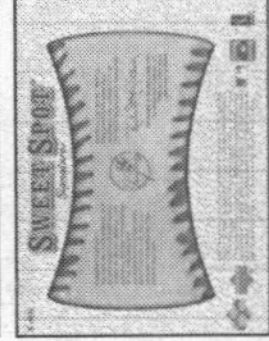

This 52-card insert set features authentic autographs from some of the Major League's top active and retired players. These cards incorporate the leather sweet spots from actual baseballs, whereby the featured athlete signed the leather swatch. The stunning design of these cards made them one of the most popular autograph inserts of the modern era. One in every eighteen packs of Sweet Spot contained either a Game Base insert or one of these Signatures inserts. Please note the following players packed out as exchange cards with a redemption deadline of November 8th, 2001: Roger Clemens and Willie Mays. In addition, the following players packed out as 50% exchange cards and 50% actual signed cards: Albert Belle, Pat Burrell and Rafael Furcal. Though the cards lack actual serial-numbering, representatives at Upper Deck publicly announced specific print runs on several short-printed cards within this set. That information is listed within our checklist. Forty of the 150 serial numbered DiMaggio cards were actually inscribed by DiMaggio as "Joe DiMaggio - Yankee Clipper".Card backs carry a "S" prefix followed by the player's initials.

NO PRICING ON QTY OF 10 OR LESS

	Nm-Mt	Ex-Mt
S-AB Albert Belle	40.00	12.00
S-AH Art Howe	25.00	7.50
S-AJ Andruw Jones	40.00	12.00
S-AR A. Rodriguez SP/154	250.00	75.00
S-AT Alan Trammell	40.00	12.00
S-BB Buddy Bell	40.00	12.00
S-BM Bill Madlock	40.00	12.00
S-BR Babe Ruth SP/1		
S-BV Bobby Valentine	40.00	12.00
S-CB Chris Chambliss	40.00	12.00
S-CD Carlos Delgado	40.00	12.00
S-CJ Chipper Jones	100.00	30.00
S-DB Dusty Baker	50.00	15.00
S-DB Don Baylor	40.00	12.00
S-DE Darin Erstad	40.00	12.00
S-DJ Davey Johnson	40.00	12.00
S-DL Davey Lopes	40.00	12.00
S-FT Frank Thomas	80.00	24.00
S-GS Gary Sheffield	50.00	15.00
S-HM Hal McRae	40.00	12.00
S-IR I. Rodriguez SP/150	120.00	36.00
S-JB Jeff Bagwell SP/214	150.00	45.00
S-JC Jose Canseco	100.00	30.00
S-JD J.DiMaggio SP/110	600.00	180.00
S-JDa DiMag Clipper SP/40	1000.00	300.00
S-JG Joe Garagiola	80.00	24.00
S-JG Jason Giambi	40.00	12.00
S-JR Jim Rice	40.00	12.00
S-KG Ken Griffey Jr. SP/100	400.00	120.00
S-LP Lou Piniella	40.00	12.00
S-MB Milton Bradley	40.00	12.00
S-ML Mike Lamb	25.00	7.50
S-MM Mickey Mantle SP/10		
S-MW Matt Williams	40.00	12.00
S-NR Nolan Ryan	250.00	75.00
S-PB Pat Burrell	40.00	12.00
S-PO Paul O'Neill	50.00	15.00
S-RAI Roberto Alomar	50.00	15.00
S-RAN Rick Ankiel	40.00	12.00
S-RC R. Clemens EXCH	175.00	52.50
S-RF Rafael Furcal	40.00	12.00
S-RJ Randy Johnson	120.00	36.00
S-RV Robin Ventura	40.00	12.00
S-SG Shawn Green	40.00	12.00
S-SM Stan Musial	150.00	45.00
S-SS S. Sosa SP/148	250.00	75.00
S-TC Ty Cobb SP/1		
S-TGL Troy Glaus	40.00	12.00
S-TGW Tony Gwynn	120.00	36.00
S-TH Tim Hudson	50.00	15.00
S-TL Tony LaRussa	40.00	12.00
S-WM Willie Mays	250.00	75.00

2002 Sweet Spot

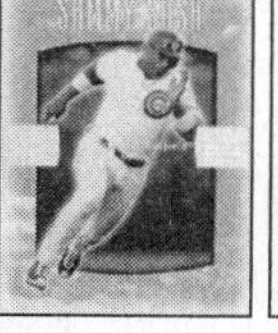

This 175 card set was released in October, 2002. The four card packs were issued 12 packs to a box and 16 boxes to a case with an $10 SRP per pack. Cards numbered 1 through 90 feature veterans while cards numbered 91 through 145 feature rookies and cards numbered 146-175 feature veterans as part of the "Game Face" subset. Cards numbered 91 through 130 were issued to a stated print run of 1300 serial numbered sets while cards 131 through 145 were issued to either a stated print run of 750 or 100 serial numbered sets. Cards numbered 146 through 175 were issued at stated odds of one in 24. Also randomly inserted in packs were redemptions for Mark McGwire autographs which had an exchange deadline of September 12, 2003.

	Nm-Mt	Ex-Mt
COMP.SET w/o SP's (90)	25.00	7.50
COMMON CARD (1-90)	.40	.12
COMMON CARD (91-130)	4.00	1.20
COMMON TIER 1 AU (131-145)	15.00	4.50
COMMON TIER 2 AU (131-145)	25.00	7.50
COMMON CARD (146-175)	10.00	3.00
1 Troy Glaus	.40	.12
2 Darin Erstad	.40	.12
3 Tim Hudson	.40	.12
4 Eric Chavez	.40	.12
5 Barry Zito	.40	.12
6 Miguel Tejada	.40	.12
7 Carlos Delgado	.40	.12
8 Eric Hinske	.40	.12
9 Ben Grieve	.40	.12
10 Jim Thome	1.00	.30
11 C.C. Sabathia	.40	.12
12 Omar Vizquel	.60	.18
13 Ichiro Suzuki	1.50	.45
14 Edgar Martinez	.60	.18
15 Bret Boone	.40	.12
16 Freddy Garcia	.40	.12
17 Tony Batista	.40	.12
18 Geronimo Gil	.40	.12
19 Alex Rodriguez	1.50	.45
20 Rafael Palmeiro	.60	.18
21 Ivan Rodriguez	1.00	.30
22 Hank Blalock	1.00	.30
23 Juan Gonzalez	.60	.18
24 Nomar Garciaparra	1.50	.45
25 Pedro Martinez	1.00	.30
26 Manny Ramirez	.60	.18
27 Mike Sweeney	.40	.12
28 Carlos Beltran	.60	.18
29 Dmitri Young	.40	.12
30 Torii Hunter	.40	.12
31 Eric Milton	.40	.12
32 Corey Koskie	.40	.12
33 Frank Thomas	1.00	.30
34 Mark Buehrle	.40	.12
35 Magglio Ordonez	.40	.12
36 Roger Clemens	2.00	.60
37 Derek Jeter	2.50	.75
38 Jason Giambi	.40	.12
39 Alfonso Soriano	.60	.18
40 Bernie Williams	.60	.18
41 Jeff Bagwell	.60	.18
42 Roy Oswalt	.40	.12
43 Lance Berkman	.40	.12
44 Greg Maddux	1.50	.45
45 Chipper Jones	1.00	.30
46 Gary Sheffield	.40	.12
47 Andruw Jones	.40	.12
48 Richie Sexson	.40	.12
49 Ben Sheets	.40	.12
50 Albert Pujols	2.00	.60
51 Matt Morris	.40	.12
52 J.D. Drew	.40	.12
53 Sammy Sosa	1.50	.45
54 Kerry Wood	1.00	.30
55 Mark Prior	1.50	.45
56 Moises Alou	.40	.12
57 Corey Patterson	.40	.12
58 Randy Johnson	1.00	.30
59 Luis Gonzalez	.40	.12
60 Curt Schilling	.40	.12
61 Shawn Green	.40	.12
62 Kevin Brown	.40	.12
63 Paul Lo Duca	.40	.12
64 Adrian Beltre	.60	.18
65 Vladimir Guerrero	1.00	.30
66 Jose Vidro	.40	.12
67 Javier Vazquez	.40	.12
68 Barry Bonds	2.50	.75
69 Jeff Kent	.40	.12
70 Rich Aurilia	.40	.12
71 Mike Lowell	.40	.12
72 Josh Beckett	.40	.12
73 Brad Penny	.40	.12
74 Roberto Alomar	.60	.18
75 Mike Piazza	1.50	.45
76 Jeromy Burnitz	.40	.12
77 Mo Vaughn	.40	.12
78 Phil Nevin	.40	.12
79 Sean Burroughs	.40	.12
80 Jeremy Giambi	.40	.12
81 Bobby Abreu	.40	.12
82 Jimmy Rollins	.40	.12
83 Pat Burrell	.40	.12
84 Brian Giles	.40	.12
85 Aramis Ramirez	.40	.12
86 Ken Griffey Jr.	1.50	.45
87 Adam Dunn	.60	.18
88 Austin Kearns	.40	.12
89 Todd Helton	.60	.18
90 Larry Walker	.60	.18
91 Earl Snyder SB RC	5.00	1.50
92 Jorge Padilla SB RC	4.00	1.20
93 Felix Escalona SB RC	4.00	1.20
94 John Foster SB RC	4.00	1.20
95 Brandon Puffer SB RC	4.00	1.20
96 Steve Bechler SB RC	4.00	1.20
97 Hansel Izquierdo SB RC	4.00	1.20
98 Chris Baker SB RC	4.00	1.20
99 Jeremy Ward SB RC	4.00	1.20
100 Kevin Frederick SB RC	4.00	1.20
101 Josh Hancock SB RC	4.00	1.20
102 Allan Simpson SB RC	4.00	1.20
103 Mitch Wylie SB RC	4.00	1.20
104 Mark Corey SB RC	4.00	1.20
105 Victor Alvarez SB RC	4.00	1.20
106 Todd Donovan SB RC	4.00	1.20
107 Nelson Castro SB RC	4.00	1.20
108 Chris Booker SB RC	4.00	1.20
109 Corey Thurman SB RC	4.00	1.20
110 Kirk Saarloos SB RC	4.00	1.20
111 Michael Crudale SB RC	4.00	1.20
112 J.Simontacchi SB RC	4.00	1.20
113 Ron Calloway SB RC	4.00	1.20
114 Brandon Backe SB RC	5.00	1.50
115 Tom Shearn SB RC	4.00	1.20
116 Oliver Perez SB RC	10.00	3.00
117 Kyle Kane SB RC	4.00	1.20
118 Francis Beltran SB RC	4.00	1.20
119 So Taguchi SB RC	5.00	1.50
120 Doug Devore SB RC	4.00	1.20
121 Juan Brito SB RC	4.00	1.20
122 Cliff Bartosh SB RC	4.00	1.20
123 Eric Junge SB RC	4.00	1.20
124 Joe Orloski SB RC	4.00	1.20
125 Scotty Layfield SB RC	4.00	1.20
126 Jorge Sosa SB RC	4.00	1.20
127 Satoru Komiyama SB RC	4.00	1.20
128 Edwin Almonte SB RC	4.00	1.20
129 Takahito Nomura SB RC	4.00	1.20
130 John Ennis SB RC	4.00	1.20
131 Kazuhisa Ishii T2 AU RC	120.00	36.00
132 Ben Howard T2 AU RC	25.00	7.50
133 Aaron Cook T1 AU RC	15.00	4.50
134 Andy Machado T1 AU RC	15.00	4.50
135 Luis Ugueto T1 AU RC	15.00	4.50
136 Tyler Yates T1 AU RC	25.00	7.50
137 Rod. Rosario T1 AU RC	15.00	4.50
138 Jaime Cerda T1 AU RC	15.00	4.50
139 Luis Martinez T1 AU RC	15.00	4.50
140 Rene Reyes T1 AU RC	15.00	4.50
141 Eric Good T1 AU RC	15.00	4.50
142 Matt Thornton T2 AU RC	25.00	7.50
143 Steve Kent T1 AU RC	15.00	4.50
144 Jose Valverde T1 AU RC	25.00	7.50
145 A.Burnside T1 AU RC	15.00	4.50
146 Barry Bonds GF	25.00	7.50
147 Ken Griffey Jr. GF	15.00	4.50
148 Alex Rodriguez GF	15.00	4.50
149 Jason Giambi GF	4.00	1.20
150 Chipper Jones GF	10.00	3.00
151 Nomar Garciaparra GF	15.00	4.50
152 Mike Piazza GF	15.00	4.50
153 Sammy Sosa GF	15.00	4.50
154 Derek Jeter GF	25.00	7.50
155 Jeff Bagwell GF	10.00	3.00
156 Albert Pujols GF	20.00	6.00
157 Ichiro Suzuki GF	15.00	4.50
158 Randy Johnson GF	10.00	3.00
159 Frank Thomas GF	10.00	3.00
160 Greg Maddux GF	15.00	4.50
161 Jim Thome GF	10.00	3.00
162 Scott Rolen GF	10.00	3.00
163 Shawn Green GF	10.00	3.00
164 Vladimir Guerrero GF	10.00	3.00
165 Troy Glaus GF	10.00	3.00
166 Carlos Delgado GF	10.00	3.00
167 Luis Gonzalez GF	10.00	3.00
168 Roger Clemens GF	20.00	6.00
169 Todd Helton GF	10.00	3.00
170 Eric Chavez GF	10.00	3.00
171 Rafael Palmeiro GF	10.00	3.00
172 Pedro Martinez GF	10.00	3.00
173 Lance Berkman GF	10.00	3.00
174 Josh Beckett GF	10.00	3.00
175 Sean Burroughs GF	10.00	3.00
MM Mark McGwire AU EXCH/100		

2002 Sweet Spot Game Face Blue Portraits

Randomly inserted in packs, this is a parallel to the Game Face subset. These cards can be differentiated from the regular card by their "blue" tint and were issued to a stated print run of 100 serial numbered sets.

Nm-Mt Ex-Mt

*GAME FACE: .6X TO 1.5X BASIC CARDS

2002 Sweet Spot Bat Barrels

Randomly inserted in packs, these cards feature game-used "barrel" pieces of the featured players. We have included the stated print run information next to the player's name and since each card has a print run of 25 or fewer copies, there is no pricing available due to market scarcity.

	Nm-Mt	Ex-Mt
AJ Andruw Jones/7		
AR Alex Rodriguez/6		
BG Brian Giles/4		
BW Bernie Williams/6		
CJ Chipper Jones/5		
FT Frank Thomas/6		
GM Greg Maddux/3		
GS Gary Sheffield/6		
IR Ivan Rodriguez/7		
IS Ichiro Suzuki/2		
JD J.D. Drew/2		
JGo Juan Gonzalez/1		
JT Jim Thome/3		
KG Ken Griffey Jr./7		
LG Luis Gonzalez/3		
LW Larry Walker/2		
MA Moises Alou/2		
MC Mark McGwire/1		
MO Magglio Ordonez/2		
PW Preston Wilson/1		
RA Roberto Alomar/4		
RAn Rick Ankiel/2		
RC Roger Clemens/1		
RP Rafael Palmeiro/1		
SG Shawn Green/4		
SS Sammy Sosa/5		
TG Tom Glavine/4		
TH Todd Helton/3		

2002 Sweet Spot Legendary Signatures

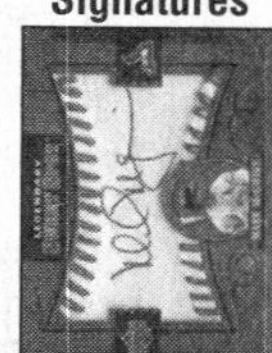

Inserted at stated odds of one in 72, these 16 cards feature signatures of retired greats. Since each player signed a different amount of cards we have notated that stated print run information next to their name in our checklist.

	Nm-Mt	Ex-Mt
AK Al Kaline/835	50.00	15.00
AT Alan Trammell/843	25.00	7.50
BP Boog Powell/944	30.00	9.00
BR Brooks Robinson/TBD	30.00	9.00
CR Cal Ripken/194	200.00	60.00
FJ Ferguson Jenkins/857	25.00	7.50
FL Fred Lynn/853	25.00	7.50
GP Gaylord Perry/921	25.00	7.50
JD Joe DiMaggio/50	800.00	240.00
KH Keith Hernandez/906	25.00	7.50
LA Luis Aparicio/485	25.00	7.50
MM Mark McGwire/90	600.00	180.00
PM Paul Molitor/852	30.00	9.00
RF Rollie Fingers/866	25.00	7.50
SG Steve Garvey/871	25.00	7.50
SK Sandy Koufax/485	300.00	90.00

2002 Sweet Spot Signatures

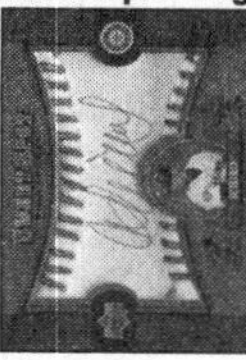

Inserted at stated odds of one in 72, these 25 cards feature signatures of some of today's leading players. Since each player signed a different amount of cards we have notated that stated print run information next to their name in our checklist. The Barry Bonds cards were not returned in time for inclusion in packs and those cards could be redeemed until October 23, 2005.

	Nm-Mt	Ex-Mt
AD Adam Dunn/291	40.00	12.00
AJ Andruw Jones/291	25.00	7.50
AR Alex Rodriguez/291	200.00	60.00
BB Barry Bonds/380 EXCH	400.00	120.00
BG Brian Giles/291	25.00	7.50
BZ Barry Zito/291	40.00	12.00
CD Carlos Delgado/291	25.00	7.50
FG Freddy Garcia/145	25.00	7.50
FT Frank Thomas/291	80.00	24.00
HB Hank Blalock/291	50.00	15.00
IS Ichiro Suzuki/145	400.00	120.00
JB Jeromy Burnitz/291	25.00	7.50
JG Jason Giambi/291	25.00	7.50
JT Jim Thome/291	50.00	15.00
KG Ken Griffey Jr./291	150.00	45.00
LB Lance Berkman/291	40.00	12.00
LG Luis Gonzalez/291	25.00	7.50
MPr Mark Prior/291	150.00	45.00
MS Mike Sweeney/291	25.00	7.50
RC Roger Clemens/194	200.00	60.00
RO Roy Oswalt/291	25.00	7.50
SB Sean Burroughs/291	25.00	7.50
SR Scott Rolen/291	50.00	15.00
SS Sammy Sosa/145	200.00	60.00
TG Tom Glavine/291	50.00	15.00

2002 Sweet Spot Swatches

Inserted at stated odds of one in 12, these 25 cards feature game-used swatches of the featured players.

	Nm-Mt	Ex-Mt
AR Alex Rodriguez	15.00	4.50
BG Brian Giles	10.00	3.00
BW Bernie Williams	10.00	3.00
CJ Chipper Jones	10.00	3.00
DE Darin Erstad	10.00	3.00
EC Eric Chavez	10.00	3.00
FT Frank Thomas	10.00	3.00
GM Greg Maddux	15.00	4.50
IR Ivan Rodriguez	10.00	3.00
IS Ichiro Suzuki	50.00	15.00
JBa Jeff Bagwell	10.00	3.00
JBe Josh Beckett	10.00	3.00
JE Jim Edmonds	10.00	3.00
JGI Jason Giambi	10.00	3.00
JGo Juan Gonzalez	10.00	3.00
KG Ken Griffey Jr.	15.00	4.50
KI Kazuhisa Ishii	15.00	4.50
LG Luis Gonzalez	10.00	3.00
MP Mike Piazza	15.00	4.50
OV Omar Vizquel	10.00	3.00
PM Pedro Martinez	10.00	3.00
SB Sean Burroughs	10.00	3.00
SG Shawn Green	10.00	3.00
SR Scott Rolen	10.00	3.00
SS Sammy Sosa	15.00	4.50

2002 Sweet Spot USA Jerseys

Issued at a stated rate of one in 12, these 17 cards feature jersey swatches from players who represented the USA team in International competition.

	Nm-Mt	Ex-Mt
AE Adam Everett	8.00	2.40
AK Adam Kennedy	8.00	2.40
BA Brent Abernathy	8.00	2.40
DB Dewon Brazelton	8.00	2.40
DG Danny Graves	8.00	2.40
DM Doug Mientkiewicz	8.00	2.40
EM Eric Munson	8.00	2.40
JG Jake Gautreau	8.00	2.40
JK Josh Karp	8.00	2.40
JM Joe Mauer	15.00	4.50
JR Jon Rauch	8.00	2.40
JW Justin Wayne	8.00	2.40
MP Mark Prior	20.00	6.00
MT Mark Teixeira	10.00	3.00
RO Roy Oswalt	8.00	2.40
TB Tagg Bozied	10.00	3.00
XN Xavier Nady	8.00	2.40

2003 Sweet Spot

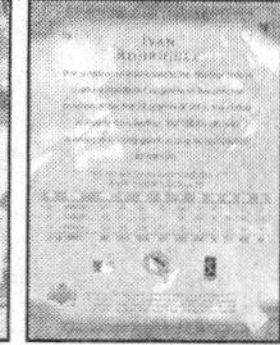

This 231 card set was released in September, 2003. The set was issued in four card packs with an $10 SRP which were issued in 12 pack boxes which came 16 boxes to a case. Thirty of the first 130 cards were issued at a stated rate of one in four packs and we have notated those cards with an SP in our checklist. Cards number 131 through 190 are part of the Sweet Beginning subset and those cards were issued at a stated rate of one in three. Cards numbered 191 through 232 were issued at an overall stated rate of one in nine and those cards were issued in three different tiers. Card number 217 was not issued.

	MINT	NRMT
COMP.SET w/o SP's (100)	25.00	11.00
COMP.SET w/SP's (130)	120.00	55.00
COMMON CARD (1-130)	.50	.23
COMMON SP (1-130)	3.00	1.35
COMMON CARD (131-190)	3.00	1.35
131-190 PRINT RUN 2003 SERIAL #'d SETS		
COMMON P1 (191-232)	4.00	1.80
P1 191-232 PRINT RUN 500 SERIAL #'d SETS		
COMMON P2-P3 (191-232)	3.00	1.35
P2 191-232 PRINT RUN 1200 SERIAL #'d SETS		
P3 191-232 PRINT RUN 1430 SERIAL #'d SETS		
1 Darin Erstad	.50	.23
2 Garret Anderson	.50	.23
3 Tim Salmon	.75	.35
4 Troy Glaus	.50	.23
5 Luis Gonzalez	.50	.23
6 Randy Johnson	1.25	.55
7 Curt Schilling	.50	.23
8 Lyle Overbay	.50	.23
9 Andruw Jones SP	3.00	1.35
10 Gary Sheffield SP	3.00	1.35
11 Rafael Furcal SP	3.00	1.35
12 Greg Maddux SP	6.00	2.70
13 Chipper Jones SP	4.00	1.80
14 Tony Batista	.50	.23
15 Rodrigo Lopez	.50	.23
16 Jay Gibbons	.50	.23
17 Jason Johnson	.50	.23
18 Byung-Hyun Kim SP	3.00	1.35
19 Johnny Damon SP	4.00	1.80
20 Derek Lowe SP	3.00	1.35
21 Nomar Garciaparra SP	6.00	2.70
22 Pedro Martinez SP	4.00	1.80
23 Manny Ramirez SP	4.00	1.80
24 Mark Prior	1.25	.55
25 Kerry Wood	1.25	.55
26 Corey Patterson	.50	.23
27 Sammy Sosa	2.00	.90
28 Moises Alou	.50	.23
29 Magglio Ordonez	.50	.23
30 Frank Thomas	1.25	.55
31 Paul Konerko	.50	.23
32 Roberto Alomar	.75	.35
33 Adam Dunn	.75	.35
34 Austin Kearns	.75	.35
35 Ryan Wagner RC	.75	.35
36 Ken Griffey Jr.	2.00	.90
37 Sean Casey	.50	.23
38 Omar Vizquel	.75	.35
39 C.C. Sabathia	.50	.23
40 Jason Davis	.50	.23
41 Travis Hafner	.50	.23
42 Brandon Phillips	.50	.23
43 Larry Walker	.75	.35
44 Preston Wilson	.50	.23
45 Jay Payton	.50	.23
46 Todd Helton	.75	.35
47 Carlos Pena	.50	.23
48 Eric Munson	.50	.23
49 Ivan Rodriguez	1.25	.55
50 Josh Beckett	.50	.23
51 Alex Gonzalez	.50	.23
52 Roy Oswalt	.50	.23
53 Craig Biggio	.75	.35
54 Jeff Bagwell	.75	.35
55 Lance Berkman	.50	.23
56 Mike Sweeney	.50	.23
57 Carlos Beltran	.75	.35
58 Brent Mayne	.50	.23
59 Mike MacDougal	.50	.23
60 Hideo Nomo	1.25	.55
61 Dave Roberts	.50	.23
62 Adrian Beltre	.75	.35
63 Shawn Green	.50	.23
64 Kazuhisa Ishii	.50	.23
65 Rickey Henderson	1.25	.55
66 Richie Sexson	.50	.23
67 Torii Hunter	.50	.23
68 Jacque Jones	.50	.23
69 Joe Mays	.50	.23
70 Corey Koskie	.50	.23
71 A.J. Pierzynski	.50	.23
72 Jose Vidro	.50	.23
73 Vladimir Guerrero	1.25	.55
74 Tom Glavine	.75	.35
75 Mike Piazza	2.00	.90
76 Jose Reyes	.50	.23
77 Jae Weong Seo	.50	.23
78 Jorge Posada SP	4.00	1.80
79 Mike Mussina SP	4.00	1.80
80 Robin Ventura SP	3.00	1.35
81 Mariano Rivera SP	4.00	1.80
82 Roger Clemens SP	8.00	3.60
83 Jason Giambi SP	3.00	1.35
84 Bernie Williams SP	4.00	1.80
85 Alfonso Soriano SP	4.00	1.80
86 Derek Jeter	3.00	1.35
87 Miguel Tejada	.50	.23
88 Eric Chavez	.50	.23
89 Tim Hudson	.50	.23
90 Barry Zito	.50	.23
91 Mark Mulder	.50	.23
92 Erubiel Durazo	.50	.23
93 Pat Burrell	.50	.23
94 Jim Thome	1.25	.55
95 Bobby Abreu	.50	.23
96 Brian Giles	.50	.23
97 Reggie Sanders	.50	.23
98 Jose Hernandez	.50	.23
99 Ryan Klesko	.50	.23
100 Sean Burroughs	.50	.23
101 Edgardo Alfonzo SP	3.00	1.35
102 Rich Aurilia SP	3.00	1.35
103 Jose Cruz Jr. SP	3.00	1.35
104 Barry Bonds SP	10.00	4.50
105 Andres Galarraga SP	3.00	1.35
106 Mike Cameron	.50	.23
107 Kazuhiro Sasaki	.50	.23

108 Bret Boone .50 .23
109 Ichiro Suzuki 2.00 .90
110 John Olerud .50 .23
111 J.D. Drew SP 3.00 1.35
112 Jim Edmonds SP 3.00 1.35
113 Scott Rolen SP 4.00 1.80
114 Matt Morris SP 3.00 1.35
115 Tino Martinez SP 4.00 1.80
116 Albert Pujols SP 8.00 3.60
117 Jared Sandberg .50 .23
118 Carl Crawford .50 .23
119 Rafael Palmeiro .75 .35
120 Hank Blalock .75 .35
121 Alex Rodriguez SP 6.00 2.70
122 Kevin Mench .50 .23
123 Juan Gonzalez .75 .35
124 Mark Teixeira .50 .23
125 Shannon Stewart .50 .23
126 Vernon Wells .50 .23
127 Josh Phelps .50 .23
128 Eric Hinske .50 .23
129 Orlando Hudson .50 .23
130 Carlos Delgado .50 .23
131 Jason Shiell SB RC 3.00 1.35
132 Kevin Tolar SB RC 3.00 1.35
133 Nathan Bland SB RC 3.00 1.35
134 Brent Hoard SB RC 3.00 1.35
135 Jon Pridie SB RC 3.00 1.35
136 Mike Ryan SB RC 4.00 1.80
137 Francisco Rosario SB RC 3.00 1.35
138 Runelvys Hernandez SB 3.00 1.35
139 Guillermo Quiroz SB RC 4.00 1.80
140 Chin-Hui Tsao SB 3.00 1.35
141 Rett Johnson SB RC 4.00 1.80
142 Colin Porter SB RC 3.00 1.35
143 Jose Castillo SB 3.00 1.35
144 Chris Waters SB RC 3.00 1.35
145 Jeremy Guthrie SB 3.00 1.35
146 Pedro Liriano SB 3.00 1.35
147 Joe Borowski SB 3.00 1.35
148 Felix Sanchez SB RC 3.00 1.35
149 Todd Wellemeyer SB RC 4.00 1.80
150 Gerald Laird SB 3.00 1.35
151 Brandon Webb SB RC 5.00 2.20
152 Tommy Whiteman SB 3.00 1.35
153 Carlos Rivera SB 3.00 1.35
154 Rick Roberts SB RC 3.00 1.35
155 Terrmel Sledge SB RC 4.00 1.80
156 Jeff Duncan SB RC 4.00 1.80
157 Craig Brazell SB RC 4.00 1.80
158 Bernie Castro SB RC 3.00 1.35
159 Cory Stewart SB RC 3.00 1.35
160 Brandon Villafuerte SB 3.00 1.35
161 Tommy Phelps SB 3.00 1.35
162 Josh Hall SB RC 4.00 1.80
163 Ryan Cameron SB RC 3.00 1.35
164 Garret Atkins SB 3.00 1.35
165 Brian Stokes SB RC 3.00 1.35
166 Rafael Betancourt SB RC 4.00 1.80
167 Jaime Cerda SB 3.00 1.35
168 D.J. Carrasco SB RC 3.00 1.35
169 Ian Ferguson SB RC 3.00 1.35
170 Jorge Cordova SB RC 3.00 1.35
171 Eric Munson SB 3.00 1.35
172 Nook Logan SB RC 3.00 1.35
173 Jeremy Bonderman SB RC 4.00 1.80
174 Kyle Snyder SB 3.00 1.35
175 Rich Harden SB 4.00 1.80
176 Kevin Ohme SB RC 3.00 1.35
177 Roger Deago SB RC 3.00 1.35
178 Marlon Byrd SB 3.00 1.35
179 Dontrelle Willis SB 4.00 1.80
180 Bobby Hill SB 3.00 1.35
181 Jesse Foppert SB 3.00 1.35
182 Andrew Good SB 3.00 1.35
183 Chase Utley SB 3.00 1.35
184 Bo Hart SB RC 4.00 1.80
185 Dan Haren SB RC 4.00 1.80
186 Tim Olson SB RC 4.00 1.80
187 Joe Thurston SB 3.00 1.35
188 Jason Anderson SB 3.00 1.35
189 Jason Gilfillan SB RC 3.00 1.35
190 Rickie Weeks SB RC 10.00 4.50
191 Hideki Matsui SB P1 RC 25.00 11.00
192 J.Contreras SB P3 RC 8.00 3.60
193 Willie Eyre SB P3 RC 3.00 1.35
194 Matt Bruback SB P3 RC 3.00 1.35
195 Heath Bell SB P3 RC 3.00 1.35
196 Lew Ford SB P3 RC 8.00 3.60
197 J.Griffiths SB P3 RC 4.00 1.80
198 O.Villarreal SB P1 RC 4.00 1.80
199 Fr. Cruceta SB P3 RC 4.00 1.80
200 Fernn Cabrera SB P3 RC 3.00 1.35
201 Jhonny Peralta SB P3 3.00 1.35
202 Shane Bazzell SB P3 RC 3.00 1.35
203 B.Madritsch SB P1 RC 25.00 11.00
204 Phil Seibel SB P3 RC 3.00 1.35
205 J.Willingham SB P3 RC 4.00 1.80
206 Rob Hammock SB P1 RC 5.00 2.20
207 Al. Machado SB P3 RC 3.00 1.35
208 David Sanders SB P3 RC 3.00 1.35
209 Mike Neu SB P1 RC 4.00 1.80
210 Andrew Brown SB P3 RC 4.00 1.80
211 N. Robertson SB P3 RC 10.00 4.50
212 Miguel Ojeda SB P3 RC 3.00 1.35
213 Beau Kemp SB P3 RC 3.00 1.35
214 Aaron Looper SB P3 RC 3.00 1.35
215 Alf.Gonzalez SB P3 RC 3.00 1.35
216 Rich Fischer SB P1 RC 4.00 1.80
217 Jeremy Wedel SB P3 RC 3.00 1.35
218 Pr.Redman SB P3 RC 3.00 1.35
219 Mi.Hernandez SB P3 RC 3.00 1.35
220 Rocco Baldelli SB P1 4.00 1.80
221 Luis Ayala SB P3 RC 3.00 1.35
222 Arnaldo Munoz SB P3 RC 3.00 1.35
223 Wil.Ledezma SB P3 RC 3.00 1.35
224 Chris Capuano SB P3 RC 3.00 1.35
225 Aquilino Lopez SB P3 RC 3.00 1.35
226 Joe Valentine SB P1 RC 4.00 1.80
227 Matt Kata SB P2 RC 4.00 1.80
228 D.Markwell SB P2 RC 3.00 1.35
229 Clint Barmes SB P2 RC 4.00 1.80
230 Mike Nicolas SB P1 RC 4.00 1.80
231 Jon Leicester SB P2 RC 3.00 1.35

2003 Sweet Spot Sweet Beginnings 75

MINT NRMT
*SB 75: .6X TO 1.5X BASIC P1
*SB 75 MATSUI: .75X TO 1.5X BASIC MATSUI
*SB 75: .75X TO 2X BASIC P2-P3
RANDOM INSERTS IN PACKS
STATED PRINT RUN 75 SERIAL #'d SETS
CARDS ARE NOT GAME-USED MATERIAL

2003 Sweet Spot Sweet Beginnings Game Used 25

RANDOM INSERTS IN PACKS
STATED PRINT RUN 25 SERIAL #'d SETS
NO PRICING DUE TO SCARCITY
191 Hideki Matsui
193 Willie Eyre
194 Matt Bruback
195 Heath Bell
197 Jeremy Griffiths

MINT NRMT

2003 Sweet Spot Sweet Beginnings Game Used 10

MINT NRMT
RANDOM INSERTS IN PACKS
STATED PRINT RUN 10 SERIAL #'d SETS
NO PRICING DUE TO SCARCITY
191 Hideki Matsui
202 Shane Bazzell
203 Bobby Madritsch
204 Phil Seibel
206 Robby Hammock
207 Alejandro Machado

2003 Sweet Spot Bat Barrels

MINT NRMT
STATED ODDS 1:6000
NO PRICING DUE TO SCARCITY
AJ Andruw Jones/7
AR Alex Rodriguez/4
AS Alfonso Soriano/1
BA Bobby Abreu/4
BW Bernie Williams/4
CJ Chipper Jones/1
CS Curt Schilling/1
DE Darin Erstad/4
GM Greg Maddux/2
GS Gary Sheffield/6
HN Hideo Nomo/3
IS Ichiro Suzuki/1
JD Jermaine Dye/3
JE Jeff Kent/4
JT Jim Thome/3
KG Ken Griffey Jr./6
KW Kerry Wood/2
LB Lance Berkman/2
LW Larry Walker/6
MP Mike Piazza/3
MR Manny Ramirez/1
MT Miguel Tejada/2
MW Matt Williams/5
OV Omar Vizquel/5
RA Roberto Alomar/7
RJ Randy Johnson/2
RP Rafael Palmeiro/2
SG Shawn Green/2
SS Sammy Sosa/7
TG Troy Glaus/1

2003 Sweet Spot Instant Win Redemptions

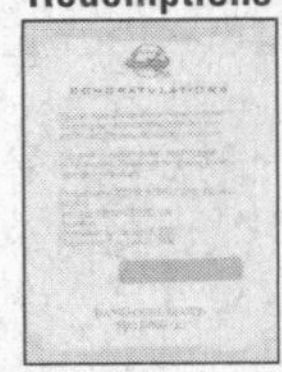

Randomly inserted into packs, these cards enabled a lucky collector to receive a prize from the Upper Deck Company.

MINT NRMT
ONE OR MORE CARDS PER CASE
PRINT RUNS B/WN 1-350 COPIES PER
NO PRICING ON QTY OF 28 OR LESS
EXCHANGE DEADLINE 09/16/06

2003 Sweet Spot Patches

MINT NRMT
*PATCH 75: 1X TO 2.5X BASIC
PATCH 75 PRINT RUN 75 SERIAL #'d SETS
CUMULATIVE PATCHES ODDS 1:8
CARDS ARE NOT GAME-USED MATERIAL
AD1 Adam Dunn 10.00 4.50
AJ1 Andruw Jones 8.00 3.60
AP1 Albert Pujols 15.00 6.75
AR1 Alex Rodriguez 15.00 6.75

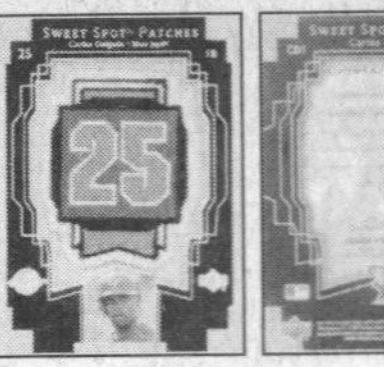

AS1 Alfonso Soriano 10.00 4.50
BB1 Barry Bonds 20.00 9.00
BW1 Bernie Williams 10.00 4.50
BZ1 Barry Zito 8.00 3.60
CD1 Carlos Delgado 8.00 3.60
CJ1 Chipper Jones 10.00 4.50
CP1 Corey Patterson 8.00 3.60
CS1 Curt Schilling 8.00 3.60
DE1 Darin Erstad 8.00 3.60
DJ1 Derek Jeter 20.00 9.00
GM1 Greg Maddux 15.00 6.75
GS1 Gary Sheffield 8.00 3.60
HN1 Hideo Nomo 10.00 4.50
IS1 Ichiro Suzuki 15.00 6.75
JB1 Jeff Bagwell 10.00 4.50
JE1 Jim Edmonds 8.00 3.60
JG1 Jason Giambi 8.00 3.60
JK1 Jeff Kent 8.00 3.60
JT1 Jim Thome 10.00 4.50
KG1 Ken Griffey Jr. 15.00 6.75
KI1 Kazuhisa Ishii 8.00 3.60
LB1 Lance Berkman 8.00 3.60
LG1 Luis Gonzalez 8.00 3.60
MA1 Mark Prior 10.00 4.50
MO1 Magglio Ordonez 8.00 3.60
MP1 Mike Piazza 15.00 6.75
MT1 Miguel Tejada 8.00 3.60
NG1 Nomar Garciaparra 15.00 6.75
PB1 Pat Burrell 8.00 3.60
PM1 Pedro Martinez 10.00 4.50
RC1 Roger Clemens 15.00 6.75
RJ1 Randy Johnson 10.00 4.50
SG1 Shawn Green 8.00 3.60
SS1 Sammy Sosa 15.00 6.75
TG1 Troy Glaus 8.00 3.60
TH1 Torii Hunter 8.00 3.60
TO1 Tom Glavine 10.00 4.50
VG1 Vladimir Guerrero 10.00 4.50

2003 Sweet Spot Patches Game Used 25

MINT NRMT
RANDOM INSERTS IN PACKS
STATED PRINT RUN 25 SERIAL #'d SETS
NO PRICING DUE TO SCARCITY
AS3 Alfonso Soriano
KG3 Ken Griffey Jr.
MP3 Mike Piazza
NG3 Nomar Garciaparra
SS3 Sammy Sosa
TG3 Troy Glaus

2003 Sweet Spot Patches Game Used 10

MINT NRMT
RANDOM INSERTS IN PACKS
STATED PRINT RUN 10 SERIAL #'d SETS
NO PRICING DUE TO SCARCITY
AP3 Albert Pujols
AR3 Alex Rodriguez
IS3 Ichiro Suzuki
JG3 Jason Giambi
JT3 Jim Thome
RC3 Roger Clemens

2003 Sweet Spot Signatures Black Ink

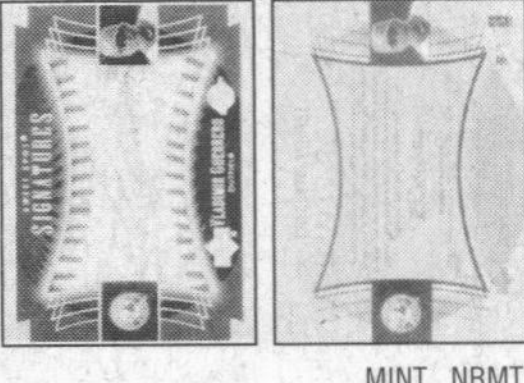

MINT NRMT
CUMULATIVE AUTO ODDS 1:24
SP PRINT RUNS PROVIDED BY UPPER DECK
SP'S ARE NOT SERIAL-NUMBERED
AD Adam Dunn 40.00 18.00
AK Austin Kearns 25.00 11.00
BH Bo Hart 25.00 11.00
BP Brandon Phillips 15.00 6.75
BW Brandon Webb 40.00 18.00
CR Cal Ripken SP/122 200.00 90.00
CS Curt Schilling 50.00 22.00
DH Drew Henson 40.00 18.00
DW Dontrelle Willis 40.00 18.00
GL Tom Glavine 50.00 22.00
GS Gary Sheffield 40.00 18.00
HA Travis Hafner 25.00 11.00
HB Hank Blalock 40.00 18.00
HM Hideki Matsui SP/147 300.00 135.00
JC Jose Contreras 40.00 18.00
JG Jason Giambi SP 50.00 22.00
JR Jose Reyes 25.00 11.00
JT Jim Thome 50.00 22.00
JW Jerome Williams 25.00 11.00
KGJ Ken Griffey Jr. 100.00 45.00
KGS Ken Griffey Sr. 25.00 11.00
KI Kazuhisa Ishii SP 50.00 22.00
LO Lyle Overbay 25.00 11.00
MP Mark Prior 120.00 55.00
MT Mark Teixeira 40.00 18.00
NG Nomar Garciaparra 120.00 55.00
NR Nolan Ryan SP 150.00 70.00
PB Pat Burrell 25.00 11.00
RC Roger Clemens SP/73 150.00 70.00
RO Roy Oswalt 25.00 11.00
TH Todd Helton SP/45 80.00 36.00
TR Troy Glaus 25.00 11.00
TS Tim Salmon 40.00 18.00
VG Vladimir Guerrero 50.00 22.00

2003 Sweet Spot Signatures Black Ink Holo-Foil

MINT NRMT
CUMULATIVE AUTO ODDS 1:24
STATED PRINT RUN 25 SERIAL #'d SETS
SOSA PRINT RUN 7 SERIAL #'d CARDS
NO PRICING DUE TO SCARCITY

2003 Sweet Spot Signatures Blue Ink

Rickie Weeks did not return his cards in time for inclusion in this product. Those cards were issued as exchange cards and were redeemable until September 16, 2006.

MINT NRMT
CUMULATIVE AUTO ODDS 1:24
STATED PRINT RUN 40 SERIAL #'d SETS
T.GWYNN CARD NOT SERIAL-NUMBERED
T.GWYNN AU IN FAR GREATER SUPPLY
AD Adam Dunn 60.00 27.00
AK Austin Kearns 40.00 18.00
BH Bo Hart 40.00 18.00
BP Brandon Phillips 25.00 11.00
BW Brandon Webb 50.00 22.00
CR Cal Ripken 250.00 110.00
CS Curt Schilling 80.00 36.00
DH Drew Henson 60.00 27.00
DW Dontrelle Willis 60.00 27.00
GL Tom Glavine 80.00 36.00
GS Gary Sheffield 60.00 27.00
HA Travis Hafner 40.00 18.00
HB Hank Blalock 60.00 27.00
HM Hideki Matsui 300.00 135.00
IS Ichiro Suzuki 500.00 220.00
JC Jose Contreras 60.00 27.00
JG Jason Giambi 40.00 18.00
JR Jose Reyes 40.00 18.00
JT Jim Thome 80.00 36.00
JW Jerome Williams 40.00 18.00
KGJ Ken Griffey Jr. 150.00 70.00
KGS Ken Griffey Sr. 40.00 18.00
KI Kazuhisa Ishii 60.00 27.00
LO Lyle Overbay 40.00 18.00
MM Mickey Mantle/7
MP Mark Prior 150.00 70.00
MT Mark Teixeira 60.00 27.00
NG Nomar Garciaparra 200.00 90.00
NR Nolan Ryan 200.00 90.00
PB Pat Burrell 40.00 18.00
RC Roger Clemens 200.00 90.00
RO Roy Oswalt 40.00 18.00
RW Rickie Weeks/100 EXCH 80.00 36.00
SS Sammy Sosa 200.00 90.00
TG Tony Gwynn NNO 50.00 22.00
TH Todd Helton 80.00 36.00
TR Troy Glaus 40.00 18.00
TS Tim Salmon 40.00 18.00
TW Ted Williams/9
VG Vladimir Guerrero 80.00 36.00

2003 Sweet Spot Signatures Red Ink

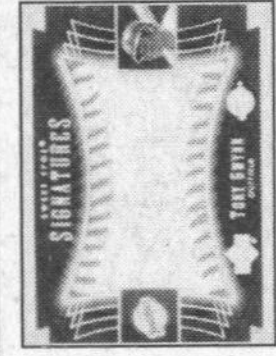

MINT NRMT
CUMULATIVE AUTO ODDS 1:24
PRINT RUNS B/WN 9-35 COPIES PER
GWYNN CARD NOT SERIAL-NUMBERED
NO PRICING ON QTY OF 10 OR LESS

2003 Sweet Spot Signatures Barrel

MINT NRMT
CUMULATIVE AUTO ODDS 1:24
PRINT RUNS B/WN 49-445 COPIES PER
CARDS ARE NOT GAME-USED MATERIAL
AD Adam Dunn/345 50.00 22.00
CR Cal Ripken/149 200.00 90.00
HB Hank Blalock/420 50.00 22.00
HM Hideki Matsui/124 300.00 135.00
JT Jim Thome/345 100.00 45.00
KG Ken Griffey Jr./295 120.00 55.00
NR Nolan Ryan/445 150.00 70.00
PB Pat Burrell/345 40.00 18.00
RC Roger Clemens/49 250.00 110.00
TG Tom Glavine/345 50.00 22.00
TR Troy Glaus/345 40.00 18.00

2003 Sweet Spot Swatches

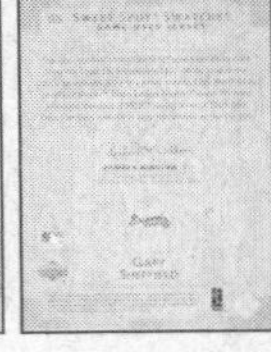

MINT NRMT
SP INFO PROVIDED BY UPPER DECK
SP'S ARE NOT SERIAL-NUMBERED
*SWATCH 75: .6X TO 1.5X BASIC
*SWATCH 75: .5X TO 1.2X BASIC SP
*SWATCH 75: .4X TO 1X BASIC SP p/r 75-100
*SWATCH 75 MATSUI: .5X TO 1.2X BASIC
SWATCH 75 PRINT RUN 75 #'d SETS
CUMULATIVE SWATCHES ODDS 1:20
AJ Andruw Jones 5.00 2.20
AK Austin Kearns 5.00 2.20
AP Albert Pujols 20.00 9.00
AR Alex Rodriguez 10.00 4.50
AS Alfonso Soriano SP/81 15.00 6.75
BW Bernie Williams SP 15.00 6.75
BZ Barry Zito SP 10.00 4.50
CJ Chipper Jones 8.00 3.60
CS Curt Schilling 5.00 2.20
FT Frank Thomas 8.00 3.60
GM Greg Maddux 10.00 4.50
GS Gary Sheffield SP 10.00 4.50
HM Hideki Matsui SP/150 40.00 18.00
IS Ichiro Suzuki 25.00 11.00
JG Jason Giambi 5.00 2.20
JT Jim Thome 8.00 3.60
KG Ken Griffey Jr. 15.00 6.75
LG Luis Gonzalez 5.00 2.20
MM M.Mantle Pants UER SP/100 150.00 70.00
Card erroneously states Game Used Jersey
MP Mike Piazza 10.00 4.50
MP Mark Prior SP 15.00 6.75
MT Miguel Tejada 5.00 2.20
NG Nomar Garciaparra SP/75
PB Pat Burrell 5.00 2.20
RA Roberto Alomar SP 15.00 6.75
RC Roger Clemens 10.00 4.50
RJ Randy Johnson SP 15.00 6.75
RO Roy Oswalt 5.00 2.20
SS Sammy Sosa 10.00 4.50
TG Troy Glaus 5.00 2.20
TG Tom Glavine SP 15.00 6.75
TH Torii Hunter 5.00 2.20
TW Ted Williams Pants SP/100 100.00 45.00
VG Vladimir Guerrero 8.00 3.60

2004 Sweet Spot

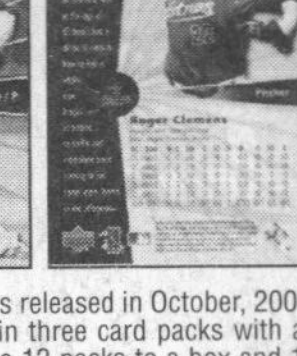

This 262 card set was released in October, 2004. The set was issued in three card packs with an $10 SRP which came 12 packs to a box and 10 boxes to a case. The first 90 cards in this set feature veterans while cards 91 through 170 and 261-262 feature Rookie Cards. Those cards were issued at a stated rate of one in two. Cards numbered 171 through 205 comprise a swinging for the fences subset and cards numbered 206 through 230 are season leader subset cards. Those cards were issued to a stated print run of 399 serial numbered sets. Cards numbered 231 through 250 is a pennant drive subset and those cards were issued to a stated print run of 299 serial numbered sets. Cards numbered 251 through 260 comprise a diamond duo subset and those cards were issued to a stated print run of 199 serial numbered sets.

Nm-Mt Ex-Mt
COMP.SET w/o SP's (90) 25.00 7.50
COMMON CARD (1-90) .50 .15
COMMON (91-170/261-262) 4.00 1.20
91-170/261-262 STATED ODDS 1:12
COMMON CARD (171-230) 4.00 1.20
171-230 PRINT RUN 399 SERIAL #'d SETS
COMMON CARD (231-250) 4.00 1.20
231-250 PRINT RUN 299 SERIAL #'d SETS
COMMON CARD (251-260) 6.00 1.80
251-260 PRINT RUN 199 SERIAL #'d SETS
171-260/Ltd 10/W99 OVERALL ODDS 1:12
OVERALL PLATES ODDS 1:360 HOBBY
PLATES PRINT RUN 1 SET PER COLOR
BLACK-CYAN-MAGENTA-YELLOW ISSUED
NO PLATES PRICING DUE TO SACRCITY
1 Albert Pujols 2.50 .75
2 Alex Rodriguez 2.00 .60
3 Alfonso Soriano .75 .23
4 Andruw Jones .50 .15
5 Andy Pettitte .75 .23

6 Aubrey Huff .50 .15
7 Austin Kearns .50 .15
8 Barry Zito .50 .15
9 Bobby Abreu .50 .15
10 Brandon Webb .50 .15
11 Bret Boone .50 .15
12 Brian Giles .50 .15
13 C.C. Sabathia .50 .15
14 Carlos Beltran .75 .23
15 Carlos Delgado .50 .15
16 Chipper Jones 1.25 .35
17 Cliff Floyd .50 .15
18 Curt Schilling 1.25 .35
19 Delmon Young .75 .23
20 Derek Jeter 2.50 .75
21 Dontrelle Willis .50 .15
22 Edgar Martinez .75 .23
23 Edgar Renteria .50 .15
24 Eric Chavez .50 .15
25 Eric Gagne 1.25 .35
26 Frank Thomas 1.25 .35
27 Garret Anderson .50 .15
28 Gary Sheffield .50 .15
29 Geoff Jenkins .50 .15
30 Greg Maddux 2.00 .60
31 Hank Blalock .50 .15
32 Hideo Nomo 1.25 .35
33 Ichiro Suzuki 2.00 .60
34 Ivan Rodriguez 1.25 .35
35 Jacque Jones .50 .15
36 Jason Giambi .50 .15
37 Jason Schmidt .50 .15
38 Javier Vazquez .50 .15
39 Javy Lopez .50 .15
40 Jeff Bagwell .75 .23
41 Jim Edmonds .50 .15
42 Jim Thome 1.25 .35
43 Joe Mauer .75 .23
44 John Smoltz .50 .15
45 Jose Cruz Jr. .50 .15
46 Jose Reyes .50 .15
47 Jose Vidro .50 .15
48 Josh Beckett .50 .15
49 Ken Griffey Jr. 2.00 .60
50 Kerry Wood 1.25 .35
51 Kevin Brown .50 .15
52 Larry Walker .75 .23
53 Magglio Ordonez .50 .15
54 Manny Ramirez .75 .23
55 Mark Mulder .50 .15
56 Mark Prior 1.25 .35
57 Mark Teixeira .50 .15
58 Miguel Cabrera .75 .23
59 Miguel Tejada .50 .15
60 Mike Lowell .50 .15
61 Mike Mussina .75 .23
62 Mike Piazza 2.00 .60
63 Nomar Garciaparra 2.00 .60
64 Orlando Cabrera .50 .15
65 Pat Burrell .50 .15
66 Pedro Martinez 1.25 .35
67 Phil Nevin .50 .15
68 Preston Wilson .50 .15
69 Rafael Furcal .50 .15
70 Rafael Palmeiro .75 .23
71 Randy Johnson 1.25 .35
72 Craig Wilson .50 .15
73 Rich Harden .50 .15
74 Richie Sexson .50 .15
75 Rickie Weeks .50 .15
76 Rocco Baldelli .50 .15
77 Roger Clemens 2.50 .75
78 Roy Halladay .50 .15
79 Roy Oswalt .50 .15
80 Ryan Klesko .50 .15
81 Sammy Sosa 2.00 .60
82 Scott Podsednik .50 .15
83 Scott Rolen 1.25 .35
84 Shawn Green .50 .15
85 Tim Hudson .50 .15
86 Todd Helton .75 .23
87 Torii Hunter .50 .15
88 Troy Glaus .50 .15
89 Vernon Wells .50 .15
90 Vladimir Guerrero 1.25 .35
91 Aarom Baldiris SB RC 5.00 1.50
92 Akinori Otsuka SB RC 4.00 1.20
93 Andres Blanco SB RC 4.00 1.20
94 Angel Chavez SB RC 4.00 1.20
95 Brian Dallimore SB RC 4.00 1.20
96 Carlos Hines SB RC 4.00 1.20
97 Carlos Vasquez SB RC 5.00 1.50
98 Casey Daigle SB RC 4.00 1.20
99 Chad Bentz SB RC 4.00 1.20
100 Chris Aguila SB RC 4.00 1.20
101 Chris Oxspring SB RC 5.00 1.50
102 Chris Saenz SB RC 4.00 1.20
103 Chris Shelton SB RC 5.00 1.50
104 Colby Miller SB RC 4.00 1.20
105 Dave Crouthers SB RC 4.00 1.20
106 David Aardsma SB RC 4.00 1.20
107 Dennis Sarfate SB RC 4.00 1.20
108 Donnie Kelly SB RC 4.00 1.20
109 Eddy Rodriguez SB RC 5.00 1.50
110 Eduardo Villacis SB RC 4.00 1.20
111 Edwin Moreno SB RC 5.00 1.50
112 Enemencio Pacheco SB RC 4.00 1.20
113 Fernando Nieve SB RC 4.00 1.20
114 Franklyn Gracesqui SB RC 4.00 1.20
115 Freddy Guzman SB RC 4.00 1.20
116 Greg Dobbs SB RC 4.00 1.20
117 Hector Gimenez SB RC 4.00 1.20
118 Ian Snell SB RC 5.00 1.50
119 Ivan Ochoa SB RC 4.00 1.20
120 Jake Woods SB RC 4.00 1.20
121 Jamie Brown SB RC 4.00 1.20
122 Jason Bartlett SB RC 5.00 1.50
123 Jason Frasor SB RC 4.00 1.20
124 Jeff Bennett SB RC 4.00 1.20
125 Jerome Gamble SB RC 4.00 1.20
126 Jerry Gil SB RC 4.00 1.20
127 Brandon Medders SB RC 4.00 1.20
128 Ryan Meaux SB RC 4.00 1.20
129 John Gall SB RC 5.00 1.50
130 Jorge Sequea SB RC 4.00 1.20
131 Jorge Vasquez SB RC 4.00 1.20
132 Jose Capellan SB RC 8.00 2.40
133 Josh Labandeira SB RC 4.00 1.20
134 Justin Germano SB RC 4.00 1.20
135 Justin Hampson SB RC 4.00 1.20
136 Justin Huisman SB RC 4.00 1.20
137 Justin Knoedler SB RC 4.00 1.20
138 Justin Leone SB RC 5.00 1.50
139 Kazuhito Tadano SB RC 5.00 1.50
140 Kazuo Matsui SB RC 8.00 2.40
141 Kevin Cave SB RC 4.00 1.20
142 Lincoln Holdzkom SB RC 4.00 1.20
143 Lino Urdaneta SB RC 4.00 1.20
144 Luis A. Gonzalez SB RC 4.00 1.20
145 Mariano Gomez SB RC 4.00 1.20
146 Merkin Valdez SB RC 5.00 1.50
147 Michael Vento SB RC 5.00 1.50
148 Michael Wuertz SB RC 5.00 1.50
149 Mike Gosling SB RC 4.00 1.20
150 Mike Johnston SB RC 4.00 1.20
151 Mike Rouse SB RC 4.00 1.20
152 Nick Regilio SB RC 4.00 1.20
153 Onil Joseph SB RC 4.00 1.20
154 Orlando Rodriguez SB RC 4.00 1.20
155 Ramon Ramirez SB RC 4.00 1.20
156 Renyel Pinto SB RC 5.00 1.50
157 Roberto Novoa SB RC 5.00 1.50
158 Roman Colon SB RC 4.00 1.20
159 Ronald Belisario SB RC 4.00 1.20
160 Ronny Cedeno SB RC 4.00 1.20
161 Rusty Tucker SB RC 5.00 1.50
162 Ryan Wing SB RC 4.00 1.20
163 Scott Dohmann SB RC 4.00 1.20
164 Scott Proctor SB RC 5.00 1.50
165 Sean Henn SB RC 4.00 1.20
166 Shawn Camp SB RC 4.00 1.20
167 Shawn Hill SB RC 4.00 1.20
168 Shingo Takatsu SB RC 5.00 1.50
169 Tim Hamulack SB RC 4.00 1.20
170 William Bergolla SB RC 4.00 1.20
171 Adam Dunn SF 5.00 1.50
172 Albert Pujols SF 10.00 3.00
173 Alex Rodriguez SF 8.00 2.40
174 Alfonso Soriano SF 5.00 1.50
175 Andruw Jones SF 4.00 1.20
176 Bret Boone SF 4.00 1.20
177 Brian Giles SF 4.00 1.20
178 Carlos Delgado SF 4.00 1.20
179 Derrek Lee SF 4.00 1.20
180 Eric Chavez SF 4.00 1.20
181 Frank Thomas SF 5.00 1.50
182 Garret Anderson SF 4.00 1.20
183 Gary Sheffield SF 4.00 1.20
184 Hank Blalock SF 4.00 1.20
185 Jason Giambi SF 4.00 1.20
186 Javy Lopez SF 4.00 1.20
187 Jeff Bagwell SF 5.00 1.50
188 Jim Edmonds SF 4.00 1.20
189 Jim Thome SF 5.00 1.50
190 Ken Griffey Jr. SF 8.00 2.40
191 Lance Berkman SF 4.00 1.20
192 Magglio Ordonez SF 4.00 1.20
193 Manny Ramirez SF 5.00 1.50
194 Mike Lowell SF 4.00 1.20
195 Mike Piazza SF 8.00 2.40
196 Preston Wilson SF 4.00 1.20
197 Rafael Palmeiro SF 5.00 1.50
198 Richie Sexson SF 4.00 1.20
199 Sammy Sosa SF 8.00 2.40
200 Scott Rolen SF 5.00 1.50
201 Shawn Green SF 4.00 1.20
202 Todd Helton SF 5.00 1.50
203 Troy Glaus SF 4.00 1.20
204 Vernon Wells SF 4.00 1.20
205 Vladimir Guerrero SF 5.00 1.50
206 Garret Anderson 5.00 1.50
Vladimir Guerrero SL
207 Luis Gonzalez 4.00 1.20
Richie Sexson SL
208 Andruw Jones 5.00 1.50
Chipper Jones SL
209 Javy Lopez 4.00 1.20
Miguel Tejada SL
210 Manny Ramirez 5.00 1.50
David Ortiz SL
211 Derrek Lee 8.00 2.40
Sammy Sosa SL
212 Frank Thomas 5.00 1.50
Magglio Ordonez SL
213 Austin Kearns 8.00 2.40
Ken Griffey Jr. SL
214 Preston Wilson 5.00 1.50
Todd Helton SL
215 Dmitri Young 5.00 1.50
Ivan Rodriguez SL
216 Miguel Cabrera 5.00 1.50
Mike Lowell SL
217 Jeff Bagwell 5.00 1.50
Lance Berkman SL
218 Lyle Overbay 4.00 1.20
Geoff Jenkins SL
219 Adrian Beltre 5.00 1.50
Shawn Green SL
220 Jacque Jones 4.00 1.20
Torii Hunter SL
221 Jose Vidro 4.00 1.20
Nick Johnson SL
222 Kazuo Matsui 8.00 2.40
Mike Piazza SL
223 Alex Rodriguez 8.00 2.40
Jason Giambi SL
224 Eric Chavez 4.00 1.20
Jermaine Dye SL
225 Jim Thome 5.00 1.50
Pat Burrell SL
226 Brian Giles 4.00 1.20
Phil Nevin SL
227 Bret Boone 8.00 2.40
Ichiro Suzuki SL
228 Albert Pujols 10.00 3.00
Scott Rolen SL
229 Hank Blalock 4.00 1.20
Mark Teixeira SL
230 Carlos Delgado 4.00 1.20
Vernon Wells SL
231 Albert Pujols PD 10.00 3.00
232 Alex Rodriguez PD 8.00 2.40
233 Chipper Jones PD 5.00 1.50
234 Craig Biggio PD 5.00 1.50
235 Curt Schilling PD 5.00 1.50
236 Derek Jeter PD 10.00 3.00
237 Ivan Rodriguez PD 5.00 1.50
238 Jeff Bagwell PD 5.00 1.50
239 Jim Edmonds PD 4.00 1.20
240 Jim Thome PD 5.00 1.50
241 Josh Beckett PD 4.00 1.20
242 Kerry Wood PD 5.00 1.50
243 Kevin Brown PD 4.00 1.20
244 Mark Prior PD 5.00 1.50
245 Miguel Tejada PD 4.00 1.20
246 Mike Mussina PD 5.00 1.50
247 Nomar Garciaparra PD 8.00 2.40
248 Pedro Martinez PD 5.00 1.50
249 Randy Johnson PD 5.00 1.50
250 Roger Clemens PD 10.00 3.00
251 Alex Rodriguez 15.00 4.50
Derek Jeter DD
252 Alfonso Soriano 8.00 2.40
Hank Blalock DD
253 Bobby Abreu 6.00 1.80
Pat Burrell DD
254 Edgar Renteria 8.00 2.40
Scott Rolen DD
255 Garret Anderson 8.00 2.40
Vladimir Guerrero DD
256 Jeff Bagwell 8.00 2.40
Jeff Kent DD
257 Jose Reyes 10.00 3.00
Kazuo Matsui DD
258 Khalil Greene 8.00 2.40
Sean Burroughs DD
259 Marcus Giles 6.00 1.80
Rafael Furcal DD
260 Manny Ramirez 8.00 2.40
Johnny Damon DD
261 Tim Bausher SB RC 4.00 1.20
262 Tim Bittner SB RC 4.00 1.20

2004 Sweet Spot Limited

Nm-Mt Ex-Mt
Basic 171-260/Ltd 10/Wood 99 ODDS 1:12
STATED PRINT RUN 10 SERIAL #'d SETS
NO PRICING DUE TO SCARCITY

2004 Sweet Spot Wood

Nm-Mt Ex-Mt
*WOOD 1-90: 2.5X TO 6X BASIC
*WOOD 91-170/261-262: .6X TO 1.5X BASIC
*WOOD 171-230: .6X TO 1.5X BASIC
*WOOD 231-250: .6X TO 1.5X BASIC
*WOOD 251-260: .5X TO 1.2X BASIC
Wood 99/Basic 171-260/Ltd 10 ODDS 1:12
STATED PRINT RUN 99 SERIAL #'d SETS
OVERALL PLATES ODDS 1:360 HOBBY
PLATES PRINT RUN 1 SET PER COLOR
BLACK-CYAN-MAGENTA-YELLOW ISSUED
NO PLATES PRICING DUE TO SCARCITY

2004 Sweet Spot Diamond Champs Jersey

Nm-Mt Ex-Mt
STATED PRINT RUN 150 SERIAL #'d SETS
PATCH PRINT RUN 10 SERIAL #'d SETS
A-ROD PATCH PRINT RUN 1 #'d CARD
NO PATCH PRICING DUE TO SCARCITY
OVERALL GAME-USED ODDS 1:6
AP Albert Pujols 20.00 6.00
AR Alex Rodriguez Yanks 15.00 4.50
BZ Barry Zito 8.00 2.40
CJ Chipper Jones 10.00 3.00
CS Curt Schilling 15.00 4.50
DJ Derek Jeter 25.00 7.50
EG Eric Gagne 10.00 3.00
GA Garret Anderson 8.00 2.40
GM Greg Maddux 15.00 4.50
IR Ivan Rodriguez 10.00 3.00
IS Ichiro Suzuki 30.00 9.00
JB Josh Beckett 8.00 2.40
KG Ken Griffey Jr. 15.00 4.50
MP Mike Piazza 15.00 4.50
MT Miguel Tejada 8.00 2.40
PE Andy Pettitte 10.00 3.00
PM Pedro Martinez 10.00 3.00
RC Roger Clemens 15.00 4.50
RH Roy Halladay 8.00 2.40
RJ Randy Johnson 10.00 3.00

2004 Sweet Spot Home Run Heroes Jersey

Nm-Mt Ex-Mt
STATED PRINT RUN 199 SERIAL #'d SETS
*1-2 COLOR PATCH: .75X TO 2X BASIC
*3-4 COLOR PATCH: 1.25X TO 3X BASIC
PATCH PRINT RUN 55 SERIAL #'d SETS
A-ROD PATCH PRINT RUN 10 #'d CARDS
NO A-ROD PATCH PRICING AVAILABLE
OVERALL GAME-USED ODDS 1:6
AB Adrian Beltre 10.00 3.00
AD Adam Dunn 10.00 3.00
AJ Andruw Jones 8.00 2.40
AP Albert Pujols 20.00 6.00
AR A.Rod Yanks Bat Up 15.00 4.50
AR1 A.Rod Yanks Swing 15.00 4.50
AS Alfonso Soriano 10.00 3.00
BB Bret Boone 8.00 2.40
BG Brian Giles 8.00 2.40
BW Bernie Williams 10.00 3.00
CB Carlos Beltran 10.00 3.00
CD Carlos Delgado 8.00 2.40
CJ Chipper Jones 10.00 3.00
DJ Derek Jeter 25.00 7.50
DL Derrek Lee 8.00 2.40
DO David Ortiz 10.00 3.00
EC Eric Chavez 8.00 2.40
FM Fred McGriff 10.00 3.00
FT Frank Thomas 10.00 3.00
GA Garret Anderson 8.00 2.40
GS Gary Sheffield 8.00 2.40
HA Travis Hafner 8.00 2.40
HB Hank Blalock 8.00 2.40
HM Hideki Matsui 30.00 9.00
IR Ivan Rodriguez 10.00 3.00
JB Jeff Bagwell 10.00 3.00
JD J.D. Drew 8.00 2.40
JE Jim Edmonds 8.00 2.40
JG Jason Giambi 8.00 2.40
JK Jeff Kent 8.00 2.40
JM Joe Mauer 10.00 3.00
JP Jorge Posada 10.00 3.00
JT Jim Thome 10.00 3.00
KG Ken Griffey Jr. 15.00 4.50
KG1 Ken Griffey Jr. 15.00 4.50
LB Lance Berkman 8.00 2.40
LG Luis Gonzalez 8.00 2.40
MC Miguel Cabrera 10.00 3.00
ML Mike Lowell 8.00 2.40
MO Magglio Ordonez 8.00 2.40
MP Mike Piazza 15.00 4.50
MR Manny Ramirez 10.00 3.00
MT Mark Teixeira 8.00 2.40
PB Pat Burrell 8.00 2.40
PW Preston Wilson 8.00 2.40
RP Rafael Palmeiro 10.00 3.00
RS Richie Sexson 8.00 2.40
SG Shawn Green 8.00 2.40
SR Scott Rolen 10.00 3.00
SS Sammy Sosa 15.00 4.50
TE Miguel Tejada 8.00 2.40
TG Troy Glaus 8.00 2.40
TH Todd Helton 10.00 3.00
VG Vladimir Guerrero 10.00 3.00
VW Vernon Wells 8.00 2.40

2004 Sweet Spot Marquee Attractions Jersey

Nm-Mt Ex-Mt
STATED PRINT RUN 199 SERIAL #'d SETS
*1-2 COLOR PATCH: 1X TO 2.5X BASIC
*3-4 COLOR PATCH: 1.5X TO 4X BASIC
*5+ COLOR PATCH: 2X TO 5X BASIC
PATCH PRINT RUN 35 SERIAL #'d SETS
A-ROD PATCH PRINT RUN 5 #'d CARDS
NO A-ROD PATCH PRICING AVAILABLE
OVERALL GAME-USED ODDS 1:6
AJ Andruw Jones 8.00 2.40
AP Albert Pujols 20.00 6.00
AR Alex Rodriguez Yanks 15.00 4.50
BG Brian Giles 8.00 2.40
BS Ben Sheets 8.00 2.40
CD Carlos Delgado 8.00 2.40
CS Curt Schilling 10.00 3.00
DJ Derek Jeter 25.00 7.50
EC Eric Chavez 8.00 2.40
EG Eric Gagne 10.00 3.00
FT Frank Thomas 10.00 3.00
HB Hank Blalock 8.00 2.40
HU Torii Hunter 8.00 2.40
IR Ivan Rodriguez 10.00 3.00
IS Ichiro Suzuki 30.00 9.00
JS Jason Schmidt 8.00 2.40
JT Jim Thome 10.00 3.00
KG Ken Griffey Jr. 15.00 4.50
MC Miguel Cabrera 10.00 3.00
MP Mark Prior 10.00 3.00
MS Mike Sweeney 8.00 2.40
MT Miguel Tejada 8.00 2.40
PI Mike Piazza 15.00 4.50
RC Roger Clemens 15.00 4.50
RJ Randy Johnson 10.00 3.00
TH Todd Helton 10.00 3.00
VG Vladimir Guerrero 10.00 3.00

2004 Sweet Spot Signatures

Nm-Mt Ex-Mt
TIER 4 PRINT RUNS 201 COPIES AND UP
TIER 3 PRINT RUNS B/WN 101-200 PER
TIER 2 PRINT RUNS B/WN 51-100 PER
TIER 1 PRINT RUNS B/WN 27-34 PER
TIER 1 PRINT RUNS PROVIDED BY UD
OVERALL AU ODDS 1:12
TIER INFO PROVIDED BY UPPER DECK
CARDS ARE NOT SERIAL-NUMBERED
BASIC SIGNATURES FEATURE RED STITCH
EXCHANGE DEADLINE 11/22/07
AB Angel Berroa T4 15.00 4.50
AD Adam Dunn T4 25.00 7.50
AK Austin Kearns T4 15.00 4.50
AP Albert Pujols T3 200.00 60.00
AR Alex Rodriguez T1/27 *
BB Bret Boone T4 25.00 7.50
BE Josh Beckett T3 25.00 7.50
BG Brian Giles T4 15.00 4.50
BS Ben Sheets T4 15.00 4.50
BW Brandon Webb T4 15.00 4.50
CB Carlos Beltran T3 60.00 18.00
CL Carlos Lee T4 15.00 4.50
CP Corey Patterson T2 EXCH 30.00 9.00
CR Cal Ripken T2 EXCH * 200.00 60.00
CZ Carlos Zambrano T3 40.00 12.00
DJ Derek Jeter T2 200.00 60.00
DL Derrek Lee T4 15.00 4.50
DM Don Mattingly T4 60.00 18.00
DW Dontrelle Willis T4 15.00 4.50
DY Delmon Young T4 15.00 4.50
EC Eric Chavez T4 15.00 4.50
EJ Edwin Jackson T2 EXCH
EL Esteban Loaiza T4 15.00 4.50
EM Edgar Martinez T3 60.00 18.00
FT Frank Thomas T3 60.00 18.00
GA Garret Anderson T4 15.00 4.50
GJ Geoff Jenkins T4 15.00 4.50
GL Tom Glavine T2 50.00 15.00
GS Gary Sheffield T4 40.00 12.00
HA Roy Halladay T3 25.00 7.50
HB Hank Blalock T4 15.00 4.50
HI Richard Hidalgo T4 15.00 4.50
HO Trevor Hoffman T4 15.00 4.50
HU Torii Hunter T4 15.00 4.50
IR Ivan Rodriguez T2 EXCH 80.00 24.00
IS Ichiro Suzuki T4 300.00 90.00
JD J.D. Drew T3 40.00 12.00
JG Juan Gonzalez T2 50.00 15.00
JJ Jacque Jones T4 15.00 4.50
JM Joe Mauer T4 25.00 7.50
JR Jose Reyes T4 15.00 4.50
JS Jason Schmidt T4 25.00 7.50
JV Javier Vazquez T4 15.00 4.50
KG Ken Griffey Jr. T4 80.00 24.00
KW Kerry Wood T4 40.00 12.00
LG Luis Gonzalez T2 30.00 9.00
LO Mike Lowell T3 25.00 7.50
MA Mike Marshall T1/34 *
MC Miguel Cabrera T4 25.00 7.50
MG Marcus Giles T4 15.00 4.50
ML Mike Lieberthal T4 15.00 4.50
MM Mike Mussina T3 40.00 12.00
MP Mark Prior T3 60.00 18.00
MR Manny Ramirez T2 80.00 24.00
MT Mark Teixeira T4 25.00 7.50
MU Mark Mulder T4 15.00 4.50
NG Nomar Garciaparra T4 80.00 24.00
NR Nolan Ryan T2 EXCH * 200.00 60.00
OP Odalis Perez T4 15.00 4.50
PB Pat Burrell T2 30.00 9.00
PI Mike Piazza T2 200.00 60.00
RB Rocco Baldelli T2 50.00 15.00
RC Roger Clemens T2 150.00 45.00
RH Rich Harden T4 15.00 4.50
RK Ryan Klesko T4 15.00 4.50
RO Roy Oswalt T4 15.00 4.50
RS Ryne Sandberg T2 80.00 24.00
RW Randy Wolf T4 15.00 4.50
SA Johan Santana T4 40.00 12.00
SB Sean Burroughs T4 15.00 4.50
SM John Smoltz T3 60.00 18.00
SP Scott Podsednik T4 15.00 4.50
SR Scott Rolen T4 50.00 15.00
TE Miguel Tejada T3 40.00 12.00
TG Tony Gwynn T3 60.00 18.00
TH Todd Helton T2 50.00 15.00
TI Tim Hudson T2 30.00 9.00
TS Tom Seaver T3 60.00 18.00
VG Vladimir Guerrero T2 60.00 18.00
VW Vernon Wells T1/30 *
WA Billy Wagner T4 15.00 4.50
WC Will Clark T4 40.00 12.00
WE Rickie Weeks T4 15.00 4.50

2004 Sweet Spot Signatures Black Stitch

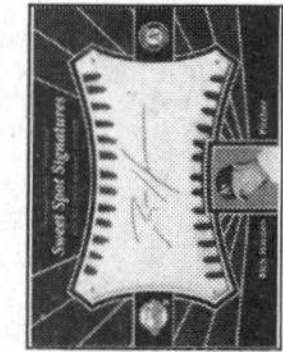

Nm-Mt Ex-Mt
BLK/RED-BLUE/DUAL/HIST AU ODDS 1:180
STATED PRINT RUN 1 SERIAL #'d SET
NO PRICING DUE TO SCARCITY
EXCHANGE DEADLINE 11/22/07

2004 Sweet Spot Signatures Red-Blue Stitch

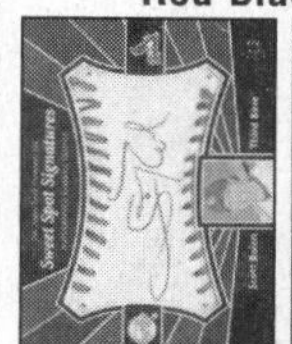

Nm-Mt Ex-Mt
*R/B p/r 40-55: .6X TO 1.5X TIER 4
*R/B p/r 40-55: .5X TO 1.2X TIER 3
*R/B p/r 40-55: .6X TO 1.5X TIER 2
*R/B p/r 20-35: .6X TO 1.5X TIER 3
*R/B p/r 20-35: .5X TO 1.2X TIER 2
*R/B p/r 15: .75X TO 2X TIER 4
BLK/RED-BLUE/DUAL/HIST AU ODDS 1:180
PRINT RUNS B/WN 10-55 COPIES PER
NO PRICING ON QTY OF 10 OR LESS
EXCHANGE DEADLINE 11/22/07
AP Albert Pujols/45 300.00 90.00
CR Cal Ripken/35 EXCH * 300.00 90.00

DJ Derek Jeter/35 .... 400.00 120.00
IS Ichiro Suzuki/25 .... 500.00 150.00
NR Nolan Ryan/40 EXCH 200.00 60.00
PI Mike Piazza/20.................. 250.00 75.00
RC Roger Clemens/30 EXCH * 200.00 60.00

2004 Sweet Spot Signatures Barrel

Nm-Mt Ex-Mt
OVERALL AU ODDS 1:12
PRINT RUNS B/WN 13-74 COPIES PER
CARDS ARE NOT SERIAL-NUMBERED
PRINT RUNS PROVIDED BY UPPER DECK
NO PRICING ON QTY OF 14 OR LESS
EXCHANGE DEADLINE 11/22/07
AB Angel Berroa/64 * 30.00 9.00
AD Adam Dunn/74 * 50.00 15.00
AK Austin Kearns/64 * 40.00 12.00
AP Albert Pujols/64 * 250.00 75.00
AR Alex Rodriguez/28 * 350.00 105.00
BB Bret Boone/64 * 50.00 15.00
BE Josh Beckett/65 * 40.00 12.00
BG Brian Giles/64 * 40.00 12.00
BS Ben Sheets/64 * 40.00 12.00
BW Brandon Webb/64 * 30.00 9.00
CB Carlos Beltran/55 * 100.00 30.00
CL Carlos Lee/64 * 40.00 12.00
CP Corey Patterson/74 EXCH * . 40.00 12.00
CR Cal Ripken/38 * 250.00 75.00
CZ Carlos Zambrano/38 * 60.00 18.00
DJ Derek Jeter/53 * 300.00 90.00
DL Derrek Lee/64 * 40.00 12.00
DM Don Mattingly/38 * 150.00 45.00
DW Dontrelle Willis/64 * 40.00 12.00
DY Delmon Young/74 * 40.00 12.00
EC Eric Chavez/74 * 40.00 12.00
EJ Edwin Jackson/64 EXCH * 30.00 9.00
EL Esteban Loaiza/64 * 30.00 9.00
EM Edgar Martinez/64 * 80.00 24.00
FT Frank Thomas/13 *
GA Garret Anderson/74 * 40.00 12.00
GJ Geoff Jenkins/64 * 40.00 12.00
GL Tom Glavine/64 * 50.00 15.00
GS Gary Sheffield/38 * 80.00 24.00
HA Roy Halladay/64 * 40.00 12.00
HB Hank Blalock/74 * 40.00 12.00
HI Richard Hidalgo/64 * 30.00 9.00
HO Trevor Hoffman/68 * 40.00 12.00
HU Torii Hunter/64 * 40.00 12.00
IR Ivan Rodriguez/64 * 80.00 24.00
IS Ichiro Suzuki/64 * 600.00 180.00
JD J.D. Drew/13 *
JG Juan Gonzalez/13 *
JJ Jacque Jones/64 * 40.00 12.00
JM Joe Mauer/72 * 50.00 15.00
JR Jose Reyes/49 * 40.00 12.00
JS Jason Schmidt/64 * 50.00 15.00
JV Javier Vazquez/64 * 40.00 12.00
KG Ken Griffey Jr./64 * 150.00 45.00
KW Kerry Wood/64 * 60.00 18.00
LG Luis Gonzalez/13 *
LO Mike Lowell/64 * 40.00 12.00
MA Mike Marshall/13 *
MC Miguel Cabrera/64 * 50.00 15.00
MG Marcus Giles/64 * 40.00 12.00
ML Mike Lieberthal/64 * 40.00 12.00
MM Mike Mussina/64 * 60.00 18.00
MP Mark Prior/64 * 80.00 24.00
MR Manny Ramirez/63 * 120.00 36.00
MT Mark Teixeira/64 * 50.00 15.00
MU Mark Mulder/64 * 40.00 12.00
NG Nomar Garciaparra/38 * 120.00 36.00
NR Nolan Ryan/38 * 200.00 60.00
OP Odalis Perez/64 * 30.00 9.00
PB Pat Burrell/13 *
PI Mike Piazza/38 * 175.00 52.50
RB Rocco Baldelli/19 * 80.00 24.00
RH Rich Harden/64 * 40.00 12.00
RK Ryan Klesko/64 * 40.00 12.00
RO Roy Oswalt/64 * 40.00 12.00
RS Ryne Sandberg/14 *
RW Randy Wolf/64 * 30.00 9.00
SA Johan Santana/64 * 60.00 18.00
SB Sean Burroughs/64 * 40.00 12.00
SM John Smoltz/13 *
SP Scott Podsednik/64 * 40.00 12.00
TE Miguel Tejada/64 * 50.00 15.00
TG Tony Gwynn/15 *
TH Todd Helton/38 * 60.00 18.00
TI Tim Hudson/64 * 40.00 12.00
TS Tom Seaver/38 * 80.00 24.00
VG Vladimir Guerrero/38 * 80.00 24.00
VW Vernon Wells/33 * 50.00 15.00
WA Billy Wagner/64 * 40.00 12.00
WC Will Clark/13 *
WE Rickie Weeks/64 * 40.00 12.00

2004 Sweet Spot Signatures Glove

Nm-Mt Ex-Mt
OVERALL AU ODDS 1:12
PRINT RUNS B/WN 5-25 #'d COPIES PER
NO PRICING ON QTY OF 5 OR LESS
EXCHANGE DEADLINE 11/22/07
AB Angel Berroa/25 .... 50.00 15.00
AD Adam Dunn/25 .... 80.00 24.00
AK Austin Kearns/25 .... 60.00 18.00
AP Albert Pujols/25 .... 400.00 120.00
AR Alex Rodriguez/5
BB Bret Boone/25 .... 80.00 24.00
BE Josh Beckett/25 .... 60.00 18.00
BG Brian Giles/25 .... 60.00 18.00
BS Ben Sheets/25 .... 60.00 18.00
BW Brandon Webb/25 .... 50.00 15.00
CB Carlos Beltran/25 .... 120.00 36.00
CL Carlos Lee/25 .... 60.00 18.00
CP Corey Patterson/25 EXCH.... 60.00 18.00
CR Cal Ripken/25 .... 350.00 105.00
CZ Carlos Zambrano/15 .... 100.00 30.00
DJ Derek Jeter/5
DL Derrek Lee/25 .... 60.00 18.00
DM Don Mattingly/25 .... 200.00 60.00
DW Dontrelle Willis/25 .... 60.00 18.00
DY Delmon Young/25 .... 60.00 18.00
EC Eric Chavez/25 .... 60.00 18.00
EJ Edwin Jackson/25 EXCH 50.00 15.00
EL Esteban Loaiza/25 .... 50.00 15.00
EM Edgar Martinez/25 .... 120.00 36.00
FT Frank Thomas/15 .... 150.00 45.00
GA Garret Anderson/25 .... 60.00 18.00
GJ Geoff Jenkins/25 .... 60.00 18.00
GL Tom Glavine/25 .... 80.00 24.00
GS Gary Sheffield/20 .... 100.00 30.00
HA Roy Halladay/24 .... 60.00 18.00
HB Hank Blalock/25 .... 60.00 18.00
HI Richard Hidalgo/15 .... 60.00 18.00
HO Trevor Hoffman/15 .... 80.00 24.00
HU Torii Hunter/25 .... 60.00 18.00
IR Ivan Rodriguez/25 EXCH * . 120.00 36.00
IS Ichiro Suzuki/15
JD J.D. Drew/5
JG Juan Gonzalez/25 .... 80.00 24.00
JJ Jacque Jones/25 .... 60.00 18.00
JM Joe Mauer/25 .... 80.00 24.00
JR Jose Reyes/25 .... 60.00 18.00
JS Jason Schmidt/25 .... 80.00 24.00
JV Javier Vazquez/25 .... 60.00 18.00
KG Ken Griffey Jr./25 .... 250.00 75.00
KW Kerry Wood/25 .... 100.00 30.00
LG Luis Gonzalez/25 .... 60.00 18.00
LO Mike Lowell/5
MA Mike Marshall/25 .... 80.00 24.00
MC Miguel Cabrera/25 .... 80.00 24.00
MG Marcus Giles/25 .... 60.00 18.00
ML Mike Lieberthal/25 .... 60.00 18.00
MM Mike Mussina/25 .... 100.00 30.00
MP Mark Prior/25 .... 150.00 45.00
MR Manny Ramirez/25 .... 150.00 45.00
MT Mark Teixeira/25 .... 80.00 24.00
MU Mark Mulder/25 .... 60.00 18.00
NG Nomar Garciaparra/25 .... 200.00 60.00
NR Nolan Ryan/25 .... 300.00 90.00
OP Odalis Perez/25 .... 50.00 15.00
PB Pat Burrell/25 .... 80.00 24.00
PI Mike Piazza/5
RB Rocco Baldelli/25 .... 80.00 24.00
RH Rich Harden/25 .... 60.00 18.00
RK Ryan Klesko/15 .... 80.00 24.00
RO Roy Oswalt/25 .... 60.00 18.00
RS Ryne Sandberg/20 .... 150.00 45.00
RW Randy Wolf/15 .... 60.00 18.00
SA Johan Santana/25 .... 120.00 36.00
SB Sean Burroughs/25 .... 60.00 18.00
SM John Smoltz/5
SP Scott Podsednik/25 .... 60.00 18.00
TE Miguel Tejada/25 .... 80.00 24.00
TG Tony Gwynn/25 .... 120.00 36.00
TH Todd Helton/25 .... 80.00 24.00
TI Tim Hudson/25 .... 60.00 18.00
TS Tom Seaver/15 .... 120.00 36.00
VG Vladimir Guerrero/25 .... 120.00 36.00
VW Vernon Wells/5
WA Billy Wagner/25 .... 60.00 18.00
WC Will Clark/25 .... 150.00 45.00
WE Rickie Weeks/25 .... 60.00 18.00

2004 Sweet Spot Signatures Dual

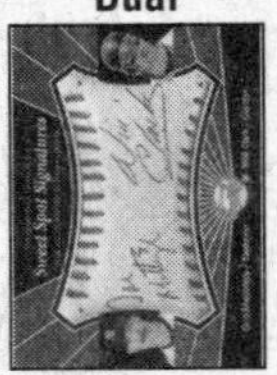

Nm-Mt Ex-Mt
BLK/RED-BLUE/DUAL/HIST AU ODDS 1:180
STATED PRINT RUN 10 SERIAL #'d SETS
NO PRICING DUE TO SCARCITY
EXCHANGE DEADLINE 11/22/07
BC Josh Beckett
Miguel Cabera
CN Nolan Ryan
Cal Ripken
GJ Nomar Garciaparra
Derek Jeter
JS Ichiro Suzuki
Derek Jeter
MC Don Mattingly
Will Clark
MH Mark Mulder
Tim Hudson EXCH
MP Joe Mauer
Mark Prior
OT Akinori Otsuka
Shingo Takatsu
PG Mike Piazza
Tom Glavine
PS Ichiro Suzuki
Albert Pujols
RG Alex Rodriguez
Nomar Garciaparra
RJ Alex Rodriguez
Derek Jeter
RR Alex Rodriguez
Cal Ripken
RS Nolan Ryan
Tom Seaver
TB Mark Teixeira
Hank Blalock EXCH
TC Mark Teixeira
Miguel Cabrera
WP Kerry Wood
Mark Prior EXCH
YW Delmon Young
Rickie Weeks

2004 Sweet Spot Signatures Historical Ball

Nm-Mt Ex-Mt
BLK/RED-BLUE/DUAL/HIST AU ODDS 1:180
STATED PRINT RUN 1 SERIAL #'d SET
NO PRICING DUE TO SCARCITY
BG A. Bartlett Giamatti
DM Joe DiMaggio
Mickey Mantle
GF Gerald Ford
JB Jack Buck
JC Jimmy Carter
JD Joe DiMaggio
MA Mel Allen
RN Richard Nixon
WI Ted Williams

2004 Sweet Spot Sweet Sticks

Nm-Mt Ex-Mt
OVERALL GAME-USED ODDS 1:6
STATED PRINT RUN 199 SERIAL #'d SETS
AB Adrian Beltre 10.00 3.00
AD Adam Dunn 10.00 3.00
AJ Andruw Jones 8.00 2.40
AP Albert Pujols 20.00 6.00
AR Alex Rodriguez 15.00 4.50
AS Alfonso Soriano 10.00 3.00
BA Bobby Abreu 8.00 2.40
BB Bret Boone 8.00 2.40
BE Carlos Beltran 10.00 3.00
BG Brian Giles 8.00 2.40
CB Craig Biggio 10.00 3.00
CD Carlos Delgado 8.00 2.40
CJ Chipper Jones 10.00 3.00
CR Cal Ripken 30.00 9.00
CS Curt Schilling 10.00 3.00
DJ Derek Jeter 25.00 7.50
DL Derrek Lee 8.00 2.40
EC Eric Chavez 8.00 2.40
ER Edgar Renteria 8.00 2.40
FT Frank Thomas 10.00 3.00
GA Garret Anderson 8.00 2.40
GL Tom Glavine 10.00 3.00
GM Greg Maddux 15.00 4.50
GS Gary Sheffield 8.00 2.40
HB Hank Blalock 8.00 2.40
HM Hideki Matsui 30.00 9.00
IR Ivan Rodriguez 10.00 3.00
IS Ichiro Suzuki 30.00 9.00
JB Jeff Bagwell 10.00 3.00
JD J.D. Drew 8.00 2.40
JE Jim Edmonds 8.00 2.40
JG Jason Giambi 8.00 2.40
JK Jeff Kent 8.00 2.40
JR Jose Reyes 8.00 2.40
JT Jim Thome 10.00 3.00
KG Ken Griffey Jr. 15.00 4.50
KM Kazuo Matsui 15.00 4.50
LB Lance Berkman 10.00 3.00
LG Luis Gonzalez 8.00 2.40
LW Larry Walker 10.00 3.00
MA Moises Alou 8.00 2.40
MC Miguel Cabrera 10.00 3.00
MG Marcus Giles 8.00 2.40
ML Mike Lowell 8.00 2.40
MO Magglio Ordonez 8.00 2.40
MP Mike Piazza 15.00 4.50
MR Manny Ramirez 10.00 3.00
MT Mark Teixeira 8.00 2.40
NG Nomar Garciaparra 15.00 4.50
PB Pat Burrell 8.00 2.40
PR Mark Prior 10.00 3.00
PW Preston Wilson 8.00 2.40
RC Roger Clemens 15.00 4.50
RF Rafael Furcal 8.00 2.40
RJ Randy Johnson 10.00 3.00
RP Rafael Palmeiro 10.00 3.00
RS Richie Sexson 8.00 2.40
SG Shawn Green 8.00 2.40
SR Scott Rolen 10.00 3.00
SS Sammy Sosa 15.00 4.50
TE Miguel Tejada 8.00 2.40
TG Troy Glaus 8.00 2.40
TH Todd Helton 10.00 3.00
TW Ted Williams 50.00 15.00
VG Vladimir Guerrero 10.00 3.00

2004 Sweet Spot Sweet Sticks Dual

Nm-Mt Ex-Mt
OVERALL GAME-USED ODDS 1:6
STATED PRINT RUN 100 SERIAL #'d SETS
BT Hank Blalock 15.00 4.50
Mark Teixeira
CL Miguel Cabera 15.00 4.50
Mike Lowell
JC Randy Johnson 30.00 9.00
Roger Clemens
JG Derek Jeter 40.00 12.00
Nomar Garciaparra
JM Jose Reyes 25.00 7.50
Kazuo Matsui
MM Hideki Matsui 60.00 18.00
Kazuo Matsui
PR Albert Pujols 40.00 12.00
Scott Rolen
RG Manny Ramirez 15.00 4.50
Nomar Garciaparra
RJ Alex Rodriguez 60.00 18.00
Derek Jeter
RP Ivan Rodriguez 15.00 4.50
Mike Piazza
TB Jim Thome 15.00 4.50
Pat Burrell
WP Kerry Wood 25.00 7.50
Mark Prior

2004 Sweet Spot Sweet Sticks Triple

Nm-Mt Ex-Mt
OVERALL GAME-USED ODDS 1:6
STATED PRINT RUN 50 SERIAL #'d SETS
GPS Ken Griffey Jr. 50.00 15.00
Rafael Palmeiro
Sammy Sosa
JJD Andruw Jones 30.00 9.00
Chipper Jones
J.D. Drew
JSG Derek Jeter 150.00 45.00
Ichiro Suzuki
Ken Griffey Jr.
MWP Greg Maddux 50.00 15.00
Kerry Wood
Mark Prior
RJG Alex Rodriguez 80.00 24.00
Derek Jeter
Jason Giambi

2004 Sweet Spot Sweet Sticks Quad

Nm-Mt Ex-Mt
OVERALL GAME-USED ODDS 1:6
STATED PRINT RUN 25 SERIAL #'d SETS
PRSG Albert Pujols 150.00 45.00
Alex Rodriguez
Ichiro Suzuki
Ken Griffey Jr.
RGDM Babe Ruth
Lou Gehrig
Joe DiMaggio
Mickey Mantle

2004 Sweet Spot Sweet Threads

Nm-Mt Ex-Mt
*1-2 COLOR PATCH: .75X TO 2X BASIC
*3-4 COLOR PATCH: 1.25X TO 3X BASIC
*1-2 COLOR PATCH: .6X TO 1.5X BASIC SP
*3-4 COLOR PATCH: 1X TO 2.5X BASIC SP
PATCH PRINT RUN 85 SERIAL #'d SETS
MAUER PATCH PRINT RUN 70 #'d CARDS
OVERALL GAME-USED ODDS 1:6
PLATES PRINT RUN 4 SERIAL #'d SETS
BLACK-CYAN-MAGENTA-YELLOW EXIST
NO PLATES PRICING DUE TO SCARCITY
AS Alfonso Soriano 8.00 2.40
BB Bret Boone 5.00 1.50
BC Bartolo Colon 5.00 1.50
BG Brian Giles 5.00 1.50
CB Carlos Beltran 8.00 2.40
CD Carlos Delgado 5.00 1.50
DW Dontrelle Willis 5.00 1.50
DY Delmon Young 8.00 2.40
EC Eric Chavez 5.00 1.50
EM Edgar Martinez 8.00 2.40
FT Frank Thomas 8.00 2.40
GS Gary Sheffield 5.00 1.50
HB Hank Blalock 5.00 1.50
HE Todd Helton 8.00 2.40
HN Hideo Nomo 8.00 2.40
JB Jeff Bagwell 8.00 2.40
JG Jason Giambi 5.00 1.50
JM Joe Mauer 8.00 2.40
JR Jose Reyes 5.00 1.50
JS Jason Schmidt 5.00 1.50
JT Jim Thome 8.00 2.40
KM Kazuo Matsui SP 15.00 4.50
KW Kerry Wood 8.00 2.40
LB Lance Berkman 5.00 1.50
MC Miguel Cabrera 8.00 2.40
ML Mike Lowell 5.00 1.50
MM Mark Mulder 5.00 1.50
MO Magglio Ordonez 5.00 1.50
MP Mark Prior 8.00 2.40
MR Manny Ramirez 8.00 2.40
MT Mark Teixeira 5.00 1.50
PW Preston Wilson 5.00 1.50
RH Rich Harden 5.00 1.50
RO Roy Oswalt 5.00 1.50
RS Richie Sexson 5.00 1.50
RW Rickie Weeks 5.00 1.50
SG Shawn Green 5.00 1.50
SS Sammy Sosa 10.00 3.00
TG Troy Glaus 5.00 1.50
TH Tim Hudson 5.00 1.50
VG Vladimir Guerrero 8.00 2.40
VW Vernon Wells 5.00 1.50

2004 Sweet Spot Sweet Threads Dual

Nm-Mt Ex-Mt
OVERALL GAME-USED ODDS 1:6
STATED PRINT RUN 150 SERIAL #'d SETS
BP Angel Berroa 10.00 3.00
Scott Podsednik
BT Hank Blalock 10.00 3.00
Mark Teixeira
CK Curt Schilling 15.00 4.50
Kevin Brown
CS Roger Clemens 20.00 6.00
Sammy Sosa
DT Carlos Delgado 15.00 4.50
Jim Thome
GH Eric Gagne 15.00 4.50
Roy Halladay
HG Tim Hudson 10.00 3.00
Vladimir Guerrero
JC Randy Johnson 25.00 7.50
Roger Clemens
JH Andruw Jones 10.00 3.00
Torii Hunter
JJ Andruw Jones 15.00 4.50
Chipper Jones
MM Hideki Matsui 50.00 15.00
Kazuo Matsui
MP Joe Mauer 20.00 6.00
Mark Prior
PC Andy Pettitte 20.00 6.00
Roger Clemens
PP Jorge Posada 15.00 4.50
Mike Piazza
PS Albert Pujols 50.00 15.00
Ichiro Suzuki
PW Albert Pujols 20.00 6.00
Kerry Wood
RJ Alex Rodriguez 50.00 15.00
Derek Jeter
RM Jose Reyes 20.00 6.00
Kazuo Matsui
SB Alfonso Soriano 10.00 3.00
Bret Boone
SM Gary Sheffield 15.00 4.50
Pedro Martinez
WP Kerry Wood 25.00 7.50
Mark Prior
YW Delmon Young 15.00 4.50
Rickie Weeks

2004 Sweet Spot Sweet Threads Dual Patch

Nm-Mt Ex-Mt
*PATCHES: 1X TO 2.5X BASIC
OVERALL GAME-USED ODDS 1:6
STATED PRINT RUN 60 SERIAL #'d SETS

A.ROD-JETER PRINT RUN 10 #'d CARDS
NO A.ROD-JETER PRICING AVAILABLE
MM Hideki Matsui.................. 150.00 45.00
Kazuo Matsui
PS Albert Pujols...................... 175.00 52.50
Ichiro Suzuki

2004 Sweet Spot Sweet Threads Triple

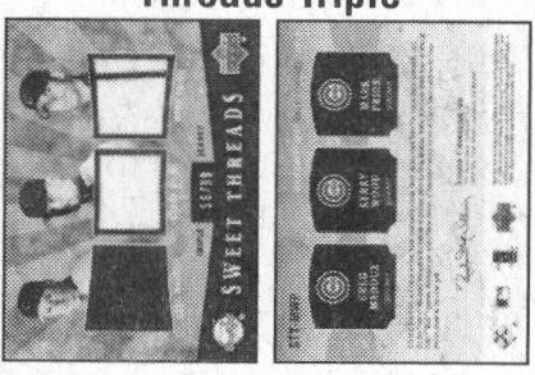

Nm-Mt Ex-Mt
OVERALL GAME-USED ODDS 1:6......
STATED PRINT RUN 99 SERIAL #'d SETS
AGG Garret Anderson 25.00 7.50
Troy Glaus
Vladimir Guerrero
BKE Jeff Bagwell...................... 15.00 4.50
Jeff Kent
Morgan Ensberg
BLR Adrian Beltre 15.00 4.50
Mike Lowell
Scott Rolen
BMS Bret Boone 60.00 18.00
Edgar Martinez
Ichiro Suzuki
BWC Josh Beckett..................... 30.00 9.00
Kerry Wood
Roger Clemens
CMM Bobby Crosby................. 30.00 9.00
Joe Mauer
Kazuo Matsui
DHW Carlos Delgado 15.00 4.50
Roy Halladay
Vernon Wells
DKG Adam Dunn....................... 25.00 7.50
Austin Kearns
Ken Griffey Jr.
DMJ Joe DiMaggio 300.00 90.00
Mickey Mantle
Derek Jeter
DMW Joe DiMaggio............... 300.00 90.00
Mickey Mantle
Ted Williams
DRN Johnny Damon 50.00 15.00
Manny Ramirez
Trot Nixon
FRP Keith Foulke...................... 25.00 7.50
Mariano Rivera
Troy Percival
GPS Ken Griffey Jr. 40.00 12.00
Rafael Palmeiro
Sammy Sosa
JJD Andruw Jones..................... 25.00 7.50
Chipper Jones
J.D. Drew
JTG Derek Jeter 40.00 12.00
Miguel Tejada
Nomar Garciaparra
JWH Edwin Jackson 15.00 4.50
Jerome Williams
Rich Harden
KVG Jeff Kent........................... 15.00 4.50
Jose Vidro
Marcus Giles
LTO Carlos Lee......................... 15.00 4.50
Frank Thomas
Magglio Ordonez
LTP Javy Lopez 15.00 4.50
Miguel Tejada
Rafael Palmeiro
MCF Kazuo Matsui 25.00 7.50
Orlando Cabrera
Rafael Furcal
MMH Mike Mussina.................. 25.00 7.50
Pedro Martinez
Tim Hudson
MSH Joe Mauer 40.00 12.00
Johan Santana
Torii Hunter
MWP Greg Maddux.................. 40.00 12.00
Kerry Wood
Mark Prior
PAS Corey Patterson............... 25.00 7.50
Moises Alou
Sammy Sosa
PCO Andy Pettitte 30.00 9.00
Roger Clemens
Roy Oswalt
PRR Albert Pujols.................... 40.00 12.00
Edgar Renteria
Scott Rolen
PTH Albert Pujols.................... 30.00 9.00
Jim Thome
Todd Helton
RCB Alex Rodriguez................ 25.00 7.50
Eric Chavez
Hank Blalock
RGJ Alex Rodriguez................ 40.00 12.00
Ken Griffey Jr.
Randy Johnson
RGW Jose Reyes 25.00 7.50
Khalil Greene
Rickie Weeks
RJG Alex Rodriguez................ 60.00 18.00
Derek Jeter
Jason Giambi
RMP Jose Reyes...................... 40.00 12.00
Kazuo Matsui
Mike Piazza
SBK Alfonso Soriano.............. 15.00 4.50
Bret Boone
Adam Kennedy
SBP Jason Schmidt 15.00 4.50
Josh Beckett
Mark Prior
SBT Alfonso Soriano.............. 15.00 4.50
Hank Blalock
Mark Teixeira
SLM Curt Schilling.................. 50.00 15.00
Derek Lowe
Pedro Martinez
VBM Javier Vazquez................ 15.00 4.50
Kevin Brown
Mike Mussina
WBP Brandon Webb 15.00 4.50
Josh Beckett
Mark Prior
WGS Billy Wagner................... 25.00 7.50
Eric Gagne
John Smoltz
WRC Kerry Wood.................... 80.00 24.00
Nolan Ryan
Roger Clemens
YCW Delmon Young 25.00 7.50
Miguel Cabrera
Rickie Weeks
ZMH Barry Zito 15.00 4.50
Mark Mulder
Tim Hudson

2004 Sweet Spot Sweet Threads Triple Patch

Nm-Mt Ex-Mt
*PATCH p/r 20-25: 1.5X TO 3X BASIC
OVERALL GAME-USED ODDS 1:6......
PRINT RUNS B/WN 5-25 COPIES PER
NO PRICING ON QTY OF 5 OR LESS..
FRP Keith Foulke..................... 60.00 18.00
Mariano Rivera
Troy Percival/25
GPS Ken Griffey Jr. 80.00 24.00
Rafael Palmeiro
Sammy Sosa/25
JTG Derek Jeter 80.00 24.00
Miguel Tejada
Nomar Garciaparra/25
MSH Joe Mauer 100.00 30.00
Johan Santana
Torii Hunter/20
WRC Kerry Wood.................. 200.00 60.00
Nolan Ryan
Roger Clemens/25

2004 Sweet Spot Sweet Threads Quad

Nm-Mt Ex-Mt
OVERALL GAME-USED ODDS 1:6......
STATED PRINT RUN 99 SERIAL #'d SETS
BADH Carlos Beltran................ 40.00 12.00
Garret Anderson
Johnny Damon
Torii Hunter
BBGS Angel Berroa 25.00 7.50
Carlos Beltran
Juan Gonzalez
Mike Sweeney
BPJC Josh Beckett................... 50.00 15.00
Mark Prior
Randy Johnson
Roger Clemens
BWRC Josh Beckett................. 80.00 24.00
Kerry Wood
Nolan Ryan
Roger Clemens
CAGG Bartolo Colon................. 40.00 12.00
Garret Anderson
Troy Glaus
Vladimir Guerrero
DHHW Carlos Delgado............. 25.00 7.50
Eric Hinske
Roy Halladay
Vernon Wells
DOGP Carlos Delgado.............. 40.00 12.00
David Ortiz
Jason Giambi
Rafael Palmeiro
GNKB Brian Giles 25.00 7.50
Phil Nevin
Ryan Klesko
Sean Burroughs
GNLG Eric Gagne 40.00 12.00
Hideo Nomo
Paul LoDuca
Shawn Green
JBGB Chipper Jones 25.00 7.50
Lance Berkman
Luis Gonzalez
Pat Burrell
JEGW Andruw Jones................ 40.00 12.00
Jim Edmonds
Ken Griffey Jr.
Preston Wilson
JJDF Andruw Jones.................. 40.00 12.00
Chipper Jones
J.D. Drew
Rafael Furcal
JMSH Jacque Jones 40.00 12.00
Joe Mauer
Shannon Stewart
Torii Hunter
JRMT Derek Jeter 50.00 15.00
Edgar Renteria
Kazuo Matsui
Miguel Tejada
KGCS Austin Kearns 25.00 7.50
Brian Giles
Miguel Cabrera
Sammy Sosa
LMRS Carlos Lee 60.00 18.00
Hideki Matsui
Manny Ramirez
Shannon Stewart
LTOK Carlos Lee...................... 25.00 7.50
Frank Thomas
Magglio Ordonez
Paul Konerko
LTPP Javy Lopez 40.00 12.00
Miguel Tejada
Rafael Palmeiro
Sidney Ponson
MMMH Mark Mulder................. 25.00 7.50
Mike Mussina
Pedro Martinez
Roy Halladay
MTTS Edgar Martinez 25.00 7.50
Frank Thomas
Mark Teixeira
Mike Sweeney
NSGH Phil Nevin 25.00 7.50
Richie Sexson
Shawn Green
Todd Helton
PBBC Andy Pettitte 50.00 15.00
Craig Biggio
Jeff Bagwell
Roger Clemens
PLBT Albert Pujols................... 40.00 12.00
Derrek Lee
Jeff Bagwell
Jim Thome
PRER Albert Pujols 80.00 24.00
Edgar Renteria
Jim Edmonds
Scott Rolen
PWPS Corey Patterson 60.00 18.00
Kerry Wood
Mark Prior
Sammy Sosa
RCBG Alex Rodriguez 40.00 12.00
Eric Chavez
Hank Blalock
Troy Glaus
RDRW Alex Rodriguez 200.00 60.00
Joe DiMaggio
Manny Ramirez
Ted Williams
RJDM Alex Rodriguez............ 400.00 120.00
Derek Jeter
Joe DiMaggio
Mickey Mantle
RJGP Alex Rodriguez............. 100.00 30.00
Derek Jeter
Jason Giambi
Jorge Posada
RLPM Ivan Rodriguez.............. 40.00 12.00
Javy Lopez
Jorge Posada
Joe Mauer
RMPG Jose Reyes 50.00 15.00
Kazuo Matsui
Mike Piazza
Tom Glavine
SBKV Alfonso Soriano 25.00 7.50
Bret Boone
Jeff Kent
Jose Vidro
SBMM Curt Schilling................ 40.00 12.00
Kevin Brown
Mike Mussina
Pedro Martinez
SDRM Curt Schilling.............. 100.00 30.00
Johnny Damon
Manny Ramirez
Pedro Martinez
SSOG Gary Sheffield................ 50.00 15.00
Ichiro Suzuki
Magglio Ordonez
Vladimir Guerrero
VCBM Javier Vazquez.............. 25.00 7.50
Jose Contreras
Kevin Brown
Mike Mussina
WATM Billy Wagner 40.00 12.00
Bobby Abreu
Jim Thome
Kevin Millwood
WBCL Dontrelle Willis.............. 25.00 7.50
Josh Beckett
Miguel Cabrera
Mike Lowell
WGJS Brandon Webb 25.00 7.50
Luis Gonzalez
Randy Johnson
Richie Sexson
ZMHH Barry Zito...................... 40.00 12.00
Mark Mulder
Rich Harden
Tim Hudson

2004 Sweet Spot Sweet Threads Quad Patch

Nm-Mt Ex-Mt
*PATCH: 1.5X TO 3X BASIC...............
OVERALL GAME-USED ODDS 1:6 ......
PRINT RUNS B/WN 1-15 #'d COPIES PER
NO PRICING ON QTY OF 10 OR LESS
BWRC Josh Beckett................ 400.00 120.00
Kerry Wood
Nolan Ryan
Roger Clemens/15
LMRS Carlos Lee 150.00 45.00
Hideki Matsui
Manny Ramirez
Shannon Stewart/15
PRER Albert Pujols 200.00 60.00
Edgar Renteria
Jim Edmonds
Scott Rolen/15
PWPS Corey Patterson.......... 150.00 45.00
Kerry Wood
Mark Prior
Sammy Sosa/15
SBMM Curt Schilling................ 80.00 24.00
Kevin Brown
Mike Mussina
Pedro Martinez/15
SDRM Curt Schilling.............. 300.00 90.00
Johnny Damon
Manny Ramirez
Pedro Martinez/15

2002 Sweet Spot Classics

This 90 card set was issued in February, 2002. These cards were issued in four card packs which came 12 packs to a box and eight boxes to a case.

	Nm-Mt	Ex-Mt
COMPLETE SET (90)	40.00	12.00
1 Mickey Mantle	6.00	1.80
2 Joe DiMaggio	3.00	.90
3 Babe Ruth	5.00	1.50
4 Ty Cobb	2.50	.75
5 Nolan Ryan	4.00	1.20
6 Sandy Koufax	3.00	.90
7 Cy Young	1.50	.45
8 Roberto Clemente	4.00	1.20
9 Lefty Grove	1.00	.30
10 Lou Gehrig	3.00	.90
11 Walter Johnson	1.50	.45
12 Honus Wagner	2.00	.60
13 Christy Mathewson	1.50	.45
14 Jackie Robinson	1.50	.45
15 Joe Morgan	1.00	.30
16 Reggie Jackson	1.00	.30
17 Eddie Collins	1.00	.30
18 Cal Ripken	5.00	1.50
19 Hank Greenberg	1.50	.45
20 Harmon Killebrew	1.50	.45
21 Johnny Bench	1.50	.45
22 Ernie Banks	1.50	.45
23 Willie McCovey	1.00	.30
24 Mel Ott	1.50	.45
25 Tom Seaver	1.00	.30
26 Tony Gwynn	2.00	.60
27 Dave Winfield	1.00	.30
28 Willie Stargell	1.00	.30
29 Mark McGwire	4.00	1.20
30 Al Kaline	1.50	.45
31 Jimmie Foxx	1.50	.45
32 Satchel Paige	1.50	.45
33 Eddie Murray	1.50	.45
34 Lou Boudreau	1.00	.30
35 Joe Jackson	3.00	.90
36 Luke Appling	1.00	.30
37 Ralph Kiner	1.00	.30
38 Robin Yount	2.50	.75
39 Paul Molitor	1.00	.30
40 Juan Marichal	1.00	.30
41 Brooks Robinson	1.00	.30
42 Wade Boggs	1.00	.30
43 Kirby Puckett	1.50	.45
44 Yogi Berra	1.50	.45
45 George Sisler	1.00	.30
46 Buck Leonard	1.00	.30
47 Billy Williams	1.00	.30
48 Duke Snider	1.00	.30
49 Don Drysdale	1.50	.45
50 Bill Mazeroski	1.00	.30
51 Tony Oliva	1.00	.30
52 Luis Aparicio	1.00	.30
53 Carlton Fisk	1.00	.30
54 Kirk Gibson	1.00	.30
55 Catfish Hunter	1.00	.30
56 Joe Carter	1.00	.30
57 Gaylord Perry	1.00	.30
58 Don Mattingly	4.00	1.20
59 Eddie Mathews	1.50	.45
60 Fergie Jenkins	1.00	.30
61 Roy Campanella	1.50	.45
62 Orlando Cepeda	1.00	.30
63 Tony Perez	1.00	.30
64 Dave Parker	1.00	.30
65 Richie Ashburn	1.00	.30
66 Andre Dawson	1.00	.30
67 Dwight Evans	1.00	.30
68 Rollie Fingers	1.00	.30
69 Dale Murphy	1.50	.45
70 Ron Santo	1.00	.30
71 Steve Garvey	1.00	.30
72 Monte Irvin	1.00	.30
73 Alan Trammell	1.00	.30
74 Ryne Sandberg	2.50	.75
75 Gary Carter	1.00	.30
76 Fred Lynn	1.00	.30
77 Maury Wills	1.00	.30
78 Ozzie Smith	2.50	.75
79 Bobby Bonds	1.00	.30
80 Mickey Cochrane	1.00	.30
81 Dizzy Dean	1.50	.45
82 Graig Nettles	1.00	.30
83 Keith Hernandez	1.00	.30
84 Boog Powell	1.00	.30
85 Jack Clark	1.00	.30
86 Dave Stewart	1.00	.30
87 Tommy Lasorda	1.00	.30
88 Dennis Eckersley	1.00	.30
89 Ken Griffey Sr.	1.00	.30
90 Bucky Dent	1.00	.30

2002 Sweet Spot Classics Bat Barrels

Randomly inserted in packs, these cards feature pieces of bat barrels from bats that Upper Deck has already cut up for inclusion in this or other products. These bat slivers include the nameplate and player facsimile signature. Each card has a very small print run which we have notated in our checklist. Please note that due to scarcity, no pricing is provided.

Nm-Mt Ex-Mt
BB-AK Al Kaline/4...............................
BB-BM Bill Madlock/1...........................
BB-BR Brooks Robinson/2...................
BB-BW Billy Williams/2........................
BB-BAR Babe Ruth/1............................
BB-BBO Bob Boone/2..........................
BB-CR Cal Ripken/5............................
BB-DE Dwight Evans/1........................
BB-DM Don Mattingly/1........................
BB-DP Dave Parker/4..........................
BB-DW Dave Winfield/1.......................
BB-FJ Ferguson Jenkins/1..................
BB-FL Fred Lynn/2...............................
BB-GC Gary Carter/1...........................
BB-GN Graig Nettles/2........................
BB-HG Hank Greenberg/1....................
BB-JB Johnny Bench/5........................
BB-JD Joe DiMaggio/5.........................
BB-KG Ken Griffey Sr./3......................
BB-KP Kirby Puckett/4.........................
BB-NR Nolan Ryan/4...........................
BB-PM Paul Molitor/4...........................
BB-RC Roberto Clemente/1.................
BB-RJ Reggie Jackson/13...................
BB-SG Steve Garvey/1........................
BB-TG Tony Gwynn/12.........................
BB-TM Thurman Munson/1...................
BB-WB Wade Boggs/2.........................
BB-YB Yogi Berra/3............................

2002 Sweet Spot Classics Game Bat

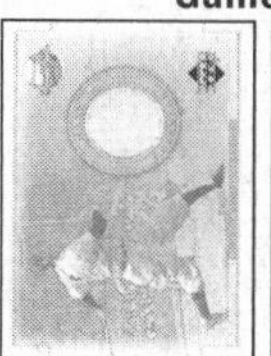

Inserted at stated odds of one in eight, these cards feature the most notable tools of the trade. Please note that if the player has an asterisk next to their name than that card is perceived to be in larger supply. Also note that some player have shorter print runs and that information is notated in our checklist along with a stated print run from the company.

	Nm-Mt	Ex-Mt
GOLD RANDOM INSERTS IN PACKS..		
GOLD PRINT RUN 25 SERIAL #'d SETS		
GOLD NO PRICING DUE TO SCARCITY		
B-AK Al Kaline	15.00	4.50
B-BBO Bob Boone	10.00	3.00
B-BBU Bill Buckner	10.00	3.00
B-BD Bucky Dent	10.00	3.00
B-BM Bill Madlock	10.00	3.00
B-BR Brooks Robinson	15.00	4.50
B-BW Billy Williams	10.00	3.00
B-CR Cal Ripken *	25.00	7.50
B-DE Dwight Evans	10.00	3.00
B-DM Don Mattingly	25.00	7.50
B-DP Dave Parker	10.00	3.00
B-DW Dave Winfield *	10.00	3.00
B-FJ Fergie Jenkins	10.00	3.00
B-FL Fred Lynn	10.00	3.00
B-GC Gary Carter	10.00	3.00
B-GN Graig Nettles	10.00	3.00
B-HG Hank Greenberg SP	60.00	18.00
B-JB Johnny Bench	15.00	4.50
B-JD Joe DiMaggio SP/40		
B-KG Ken Griffey Sr. *	10.00	3.00
B-KP Kirby Puckett *	15.00	4.50
B-NR Nolan Ryan	40.00	12.00
B-PM Paul Molitor	15.00	4.50
B-RC Roberto Clemente	60.00	18.00
B-RJ Reggie Jackson	15.00	4.50
B-SG Steve Garvey	10.00	3.00
B-TG Tony Gwynn *	15.00	4.50
B-TM Thurman Munson	40.00	12.00
B-WB Wade Boggs *	15.00	4.50
B-YB Yogi Berra	15.00	4.50

2002 Sweet Spot Classics Game Jersey

Inserted at stated odds of one in eight, these cards feature memorabilia from the featured player. Please note that if the player has an asterisk next to their name than that card is perceived to be in larger supply. Also note that some player have shorter print runs and that information is

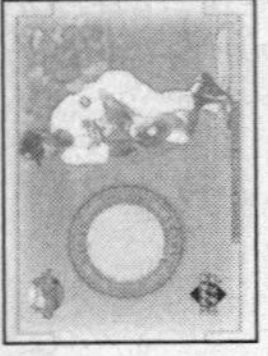

notated in our checklist along with a stated print run from the company.

Nm-Mt Ex-Mt
GOLD RANDOM INSERTS IN PACKS..
GOLD PRINT RUN 25 SERIAL #'d SETS
GOLD NO PRICING DUE TO SCARCITY
J-BM Bill Madlock 10.00 3.00
J-BW Billy Williams 10.00 3.00
J-CR Cal Ripken * 25.00 7.50
J-DM Don Mattingly * 25.00 7.50
J-DP Dave Parker 10.00 3.00
J-DSN Duke Snider SP/53 100.00 30.00
J-DST Dave Stewart 10.00 3.00
J-EM Eddie Murray 15.00 4.50
J-GC Gary Carter 10.00 3.00
J-GN Graig Nettles 10.00 3.00
J-JC Joe Carter 10.00 3.00
J-JD Joe DiMaggio SP/53 200.00 60.00
J-JMA Juan Marichal 10.00 3.00
J-MM Mickey Mantle SP/53 300.00 90.00
J-NR Nolan Ryan * 40.00 12.00
J-OS Ozzie Smith 15.00 4.50
J-PM Paul Molitor * 15.00 4.50
J-RF Rollie Fingers 10.00 3.00
J-RJ Reggie Jackson 15.00 4.50
J-RS Ryne Sandberg 15.00 4.50
J-RY Robin Yount * 15.00 4.50
J-SG Steve Garvey 10.00 3.00
J-SK Sandy Koufax SP 150.00 45.00
J-TG Tony Gwynn * 15.00 4.50
J-TS Tom Seaver 15.00 4.50
J-WB Wade Boggs 15.00 4.50
J-WS Willie Stargell 15.00 4.50

2002 Sweet Spot Classics Signatures

Inserted at stated odds of one in 24, these cards feature the top stars of yesterday with their signature on a "sweet spot". Please note that if the player has an asterisk next to their name than that card is perceived to be in larger supply. Also note that some player have shorter print runs and that information is noted in our checklist along with a stated print run from the company.

Nm-Mt Ex-Mt
GOLD RANDOM INSERTS IN PACKS..
GOLD PRINT RUN 25 SERIAL #'d SETS
GOLD NO PRICING DUE TO SCARCITY
S-AD Andre Dawson SP/100 120.00 36.00
S-AK Al Kaline 50.00 15.00
S-AT Alan Trammell 30.00 9.00
S-BD Bucky Dent 30.00 9.00
S-BM Bill Mazeroski 50.00 15.00
S-BP Boog Powell 30.00 9.00
S-BR Brooks Robinson 40.00 12.00
S-CF Carlton Fisk SP/100 150.00 45.00
S-CR Cal Ripken 175.00 52.50
S-DAM Dale Murphy 50.00 15.00
S-DAS Dave Stewart 30.00 9.00
S-DEE Dennis Eckersley 40.00 12.00
S-DOM Don Mattingly * 100.00 30.00
S-DW Dave Winfield SP/70 150.00 45.00
S-EB Ernie Banks 80.00 24.00
S-FJ Fergie Jenkins 30.00 9.00
S-FL Fred Lynn 30.00 9.00
S-GP Gaylord Perry 30.00 9.00
S-JB Johnny Bench 80.00 24.00
S-JM Joe Morgan 30.00 9.00
S-KG Kirk Gibson/SP 60.00 18.00
S-KH Keith Hernandez 30.00 9.00
S-KP Kirby Puckett SP/74 200.00 60.00
S-NR Nolan Ryan SP/74 350.00 105.00
S-OS Ozzie Smith SP/137 200.00 60.00
S-PM Paul Molitor 40.00 12.00
S-RF Rollie Fingers 30.00 9.00
S-RJ Reggie Jackson SP 120.00 36.00
S-SG Steve Garvey 30.00 9.00
S-SK Sandy Koufax SP 300.00 90.00
S-TL Tommy Lasorda 40.00 12.00
S-TS Tom Seaver 60.00 18.00
S-WM Willie McCovey SP 100.00 30.00
S-YB Yogi Berra SP/100 200.00 60.00

2003 Sweet Spot Classics

This 150 card set was issued in March, 2003. It was issued in five-card packs with an $10 SRP. The packs were issued in 12 pack boxes which came 16 boxes to a case. The following subsets are included: Ted Williams Ball Game (91-120) and Yankee Heritage (121-150). The Williams's cards were printed to a stated print run of 1941 and the Yankee Heritage cards were printed to a stated print run of 1500 serial numbered sets. While this set features mainly retired players, a special Hideki Matsui card (75) was issued. That card was issued to a stated print run of 1999 serial numbered sets. Originally that card was supposed to be Rod Carew and a few Carew cards made it through the production process. However, at this time no pricing information is available on the Carew card which was supposed to be card number 75 originally.

Nm-Mt Ex-Mt
COMP.SET w/o SP's (89) 40.00 12.00
COMMON (1-74/76-90) .75 .23
COMMON CARD (91-120) 8.00 2.40
COMMON CARD (121-150) 5.00 1.50
1 Al Hrabosky .75 .23
2 Al Lopez .75 .23
3 Andre Dawson .75 .23
4 Bill Buckner .75 .23
5 Billy Williams .75 .23
6 Bob Feller .75 .23
7 Bob Lemon .75 .23
8 Bobby Doerr .75 .23
9 Cecil Cooper .75 .23
10 Cal Ripken 6.00 1.80
11 Carlton Fisk 1.25 .35
12 Catfish Hunter 1.25 .35
13 Chris Chambliss .75 .23
14 Dale Murphy 2.00 .60
15 Gaylord Perry .75 .23
16 Dave Kingman .75 .23
17 Dave Parker .75 .23
18 Dave Stewart .75 .23
19 David Cone .75 .23
20 Dennis Eckersley .75 .23
21 Don Baylor .75 .23
22 Don Sutton .75 .23
23 Duke Snider 1.25 .35
24 Dwight Evans .75 .23
25 Dwight Gooden .75 .23
26 Earl Weaver MG .75 .23
27 Early Wynn .75 .23
28 Eddie Mathews 2.00 .60
29 Enos Slaughter .75 .23
30 Ernie Banks 2.00 .60
31 Fred Lynn .75 .23
32 Fred Stanley .75 .23
33 Gary Carter .75 .23
34 George Foster .75 .23
35 Hal Newhouser .75 .23
36 George Kell .75 .23
37 Harmon Killebrew 2.00 .60
38 Hoyt Wilhelm .75 .23
39 Jack Morris .75 .23
40 Jim Bunning .75 .23
41 Jim Gilliam .75 .23
42 Jim Leyritz .75 .23
43 Jimmy Key .75 .23
44 Joe Carter .75 .23
45 Joe Morgan .75 .23
46 John Montefusco .75 .23
47 Johnny Bench 2.00 .60
48 Johnny Podres .75 .23
49 Jose Canseco 2.00 .60
50 Juan Marichal .75 .23
51 Keith Hernandez .75 .23
52 Ken Griffey Sr. .75 .23
53 Kirby Puckett 2.00 .60
54 Kirk Gibson .75 .23
55 Larry Doby .75 .23
56 Lee May .75 .23
57 Lee Mazzilli .75 .23
58 Lou Boudreau .75 .23
59 Mark McGwire 5.00 1.50
60 Maury Wills .75 .23
61 Mike Pagliarulo .75 .23
62 Monte Irvin .75 .23
63 Nolan Ryan 5.00 1.50
64 Orlando Cepeda .75 .23
65 Ozzie Smith 3.00 .90
66 Paul O'Neill 1.25 .35
67 Pee Wee Reese 1.25 .35
68 Phil Niekro .75 .23
69 Ralph Kiner .75 .23
70 Red Schoendienst .75 .23
71 Richie Ashburn 1.25 .35
72 Rick Ferrell .75 .23
73 Robin Roberts .75 .23
74 Robin Yount 3.00 .90
75 Hideki Matsui/1999 XRC 10.00 3.00
75B Rod Carew ERR
Not Intended for Public Release
76 Rollie Fingers .75 .23
77 Ron Cey .75 .23
78 Tom Seaver 1.25 .35
79 Sparky Anderson MG .75 .23
80 Stan Musial 3.00 .90
81 Steve Garvey .75 .23
82 Ted Williams 4.00 1.20
83 Tommy Lasorda .75 .23
84 Tony Gwynn 2.50 .75
85 Tony Perez .75 .23
86 Vida Blue .75 .23
87 Warren Spahn 1.25 .35
88 Bob Gibson 1.25 .35
89 Willie McCovey .75 .23
90 Willie Stargell 1.25 .35
91 Ted Williams TB 8.00 2.40
92 Ted Williams TB 8.00 2.40
93 Ted Williams TB 8.00 2.40
94 Ted Williams TB 8.00 2.40
95 Ted Williams TB 8.00 2.40
96 Ted Williams TB 8.00 2.40
97 Ted Williams TB 8.00 2.40
98 Ted Williams TB 8.00 2.40
99 Ted Williams TB 8.00 2.40
100 Ted Williams TB 8.00 2.40
101 Ted Williams TB 8.00 2.40
102 Ted Williams TB 8.00 2.40
103 Ted Williams TB 8.00 2.40
104 Ted Williams TB 8.00 2.40
105 Ted Williams TB 8.00 2.40
106 Ted Williams TB 8.00 2.40
107 Ted Williams TB 8.00 2.40
108 Ted Williams TB 8.00 2.40
109 Ted Williams TB 8.00 2.40
110 Ted Williams TB 8.00 2.40
111 Ted Williams TB 8.00 2.40
112 Ted Williams TB 8.00 2.40
113 Ted Williams TB 8.00 2.40
114 Ted Williams TB 8.00 2.40
115 Ted Williams TB 8.00 2.40
116 Ted Williams TB 8.00 2.40
117 Ted Williams TB 8.00 2.40
118 Ted Williams TB 8.00 2.40
119 Ted Williams TB 8.00 2.40
120 Ted Williams TB 8.00 2.40
121 Babe Ruth YH 15.00 4.50
122 Bucky Dent YH 5.00 1.50
123 Casey Stengel YH 5.00 1.50
124 Dave Righetti YH 5.00 1.50
125 Dave Winfield YH 5.00 1.50
126 Dick Tidrow YH 5.00 1.50
127 Dock Ellis YH 5.00 1.50
128 Don Mattingly YH 15.00 4.50
129 Hank Bauer YH 5.00 1.50
130 Jim Bouton YH 5.00 1.50
131 Jim Kaat YH 5.00 1.50
132 Joe DiMaggio YH 10.00 3.00
133 Joe Torre YH 8.00 2.40
134 Lou Piniella YH 5.00 1.50
135 Mel Stottlemyre YH 5.00 1.50
136 Mickey Mantle YH 20.00 6.00
137 Mickey Rivers YH 5.00 1.50
138 Phil Rizzuto YH 5.00 1.50
139 Ralph Branca YH 5.00 1.50
140 Ralph Houk YH 5.00 1.50
141 Roger Maris YH 8.00 2.40
142 Ron Guidry YH 5.00 1.50
143 Ruben Amaro Sr. YH 5.00 1.50
144 Sparky Lyle YH 5.00 1.50
145 Thurman Munson YH 8.00 2.40
146 Tommy Henrich YH 5.00 1.50
147 Tommy John YH 5.00 1.50
148 Tony Kubek YH 5.00 1.50
149 Whitey Ford YH 5.00 1.50
150 Yogi Berra YH 8.00 2.40

2003 Sweet Spot Classics Matsui Parallel

Randomly inserted into packs, these cards parallel the Hideki Matsui base card. There are three different versions of this card and they were all issued to different stated print runs. Please note the silver version (75C) was issued to a stated print run of 25 serial numbered sets and there is no pricing due to market scarcity.

Nm-Mt Ex-Mt
75A Hideki Matsui Red/500 15.00 4.50
75B Hideki Matsui Blue/250 20.00 6.00
75C Hideki Matsui Silver/25

2003 Sweet Spot Classics Autographs Black Ink

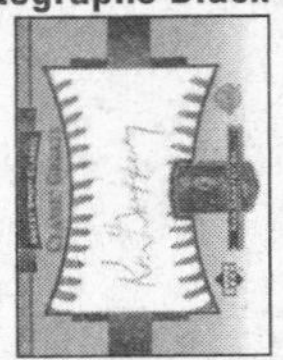

Randomly inserted into packs, these cards feature the players signing in black ink. These autograph cards were in packs at overall rate of one in 24. Each card was printed to a different amount and we have noted that information next to the player's name in our checklist. All the Mark McGwire autos are inscribed "Maris '61"

Nm-Mt Ex-Mt
AD Andre Dawson/75 50.00 15.00
AH Al Hrabosky/100 40.00 12.00
AT Alan Trammell/173 40.00 12.00
BB Bill Buckner/85 40.00 12.00
BW Billy Williams/173 40.00 12.00
CR Cal Ripken/38
DB Don Baylor/50 50.00 15.00
DE Dwight Evans/100 50.00 15.00
DP Dave Parker/113 40.00 12.00
DS Don Sutton/123 40.00 12.00
EB Ernie Banks/73 120.00 36.00
GC Gary Carter/173 40.00 12.00
GF George Foster/173 40.00 12.00
GI Kirk Gibson/173 40.00 12.00
HK Harmon Killebrew/73 120.00 36.00
JB Johnny Bench/73 150.00 45.00
JC Joe Carter/123 40.00 12.00
JM Joe Morgan/169 40.00 12.00
JM Jack Morris/123 40.00 12.00
JP Johnny Podres/173 40.00 12.00
KG Ken Griffey Sr./100 50.00 15.00
KH Keith Hernandez/173 40.00 12.00
KP Kirby Puckett/174 60.00 18.00
MM Mark McGwire/73 700.00 210.00
MW Maury Wills/173 40.00 12.00
OC Orlando Cepeda/34
PN Phil Niekro/173 40.00 12.00
RF Rollie Fingers/73 50.00 15.00
RR Robin Roberts/173 50.00 15.00
RY Robin Yount/73 150.00 45.00
SG Steve Garvey/173 40.00 12.00
SN Duke Snider/100 80.00 24.00
TG Tony Gwynn/101 80.00 24.00
TP Tony Perez/51 80.00 24.00
TS Tom Seaver/74 80.00 24.00

2003 Sweet Spot Classics Autographs Blue Ink

Randomly inserted in packs, these cards feature the players signing their cards in black ink. A few players were issued in shorter quantity and we have notated that information with an SP next to their name in our checklist. In addition, Upper Deck purchased nine Ted Williams cuts and issued nine of these cards to match his uniform number.

Nm-Mt Ex-Mt
AD Andre Dawson 25.00 7.50
AH Al Hrabosky SP 25.00 7.50
BB Bill Buckner SP 25.00 7.50
CF Carlton Fisk 60.00 18.00
CR Cal Ripken 200.00 60.00
DB Don Baylor SP 25.00 7.50
DE Dennis Eckersley 25.00 7.50
DE Dwight Evans * 25.00 7.50
DM Dale Murphy 40.00 12.00
DS Dave Stewart 25.00 7.50
KG Ken Griffey Sr. 25.00 7.50
KP Kirby Puckett 40.00 12.00
OC Orlando Cepeda * 25.00 7.50
SN Duke Snider 50.00 15.00
TG Tony Gwynn 50.00 15.00
TW Ted Williams/9

2003 Sweet Spot Classics Autographs Yankee Greats Black Ink

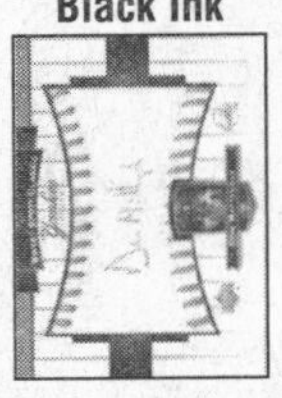

Randomly inserted in packs, these cards feature former New York Yankees who signed their card in black ink. We have notated the stated print run information next to the player's name in our checklist. Please note that the Hideki Matsui card was issued as an exchange card and has an exchange deadline of March 13, 2006.

Nm-Mt Ex-Mt
CC Chris Chambliss/101 60.00 18.00
DC David Cone/74 80.00 24.00
DE Dock Ellis/174 40.00 12.00
DG Dwight Gooden/74 60.00 18.00
DK Dave Kingman/100 60.00 18.00
DM Don Mattingly/74 150.00 45.00
DR Dave Righetti/173 60.00 18.00
DT Dick Tidrow/101 40.00 12.00
DW Dave Winfield/25
FS Fred Stanley/101 40.00 12.00
GU Ron Guidry/100 80.00 24.00
HB Hank Bauer/75 60.00 18.00
HM Hideki Matsui/25 EXCH
JB Jim Bouton/100 40.00 12.00
JC Jose Canseco/73 100.00 30.00
JD Joe DiMaggio/5
JK Jim Kaat/100 40.00 12.00
JK Jimmy Key/100 40.00 12.00
JL Jim Leyritz/100 40.00 12.00
JM John Montefusco/100 40.00 12.00
JT Joe Torre/73 100.00 30.00
LM Lee Mazzilli/100 40.00 12.00
LP Lou Piniella/100 40.00 12.00
MP Mike Pagliarulo/99 40.00 12.00
MR Mickey Rivers/73 60.00 18.00
MS Mel Stottlemyre/73 60.00 18.00
PO Paul O'Neill/100 80.00 24.00
PR Phil Rizzuto/173 80.00 24.00
RA Ruben Amaro Sr./100 40.00 12.00
RB Ralph Branca/100 40.00 12.00
RH Ralph Houk/100 40.00 12.00
SL Sparky Lyle/100 40.00 12.00
TH Tommy Henrich/100 40.00 12.00
TJ Tommy John/100 40.00 12.00
TK Tony Kubek/123 60.00 18.00
YB Yogi Berra/73 120.00 36.00

2003 Sweet Spot Classics Autographs Yankee Greats Blue Ink

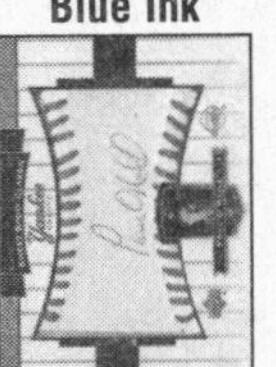

Randomly inserted in packs, these cards feature former New York Yankees who signed their card in blue ink. A few cards were issued in lesser quantity and we have notated those cards with an SP in our checklist. In addition, the Bucky Dent card seems to be in larger supply and we have notated that with an asterisk in our checklist. Also, Upper Deck purchased seven Mickey Mantle autographs and used those as scarce cuts in this product.

Nm-Mt Ex-Mt
BD Bucky Dent * 25.00 7.50
CC Chris Chambliss SP 40.00 12.00
DK Dave Kingman 40.00 12.00
DT Dick Tidrow 25.00 7.50
FS Fred Stanley 25.00 7.50
GU Ron Guidry 50.00 15.00
HB Hank Bauer SP 40.00 12.00
JB Jim Bouton 25.00 7.50
JK Jim Kaat 25.00 7.50
JK Jimmy Key 40.00 12.00
JL Jim Leyritz 25.00 7.50
JM John Montefusco 25.00 7.50
LM Lee Mazzilli 25.00 7.50
LP Lou Piniella SP 40.00 12.00
MM Mickey Mantle/7
MP Mike Pagliarulo 25.00 7.50
PO Paul O'Neill 50.00 15.00
RA Ruben Amaro Sr. 25.00 7.50
RB Ralph Branca 25.00 7.50
RH Ralph Houk 25.00 7.50
SL Sparky Lyle SP 40.00 12.00
TH Tommy Henrich SP 40.00 12.00
TJ Tommy John 25.00 7.50

2003 Sweet Spot Classics Autographs Yankee Greats Matsui Exchange

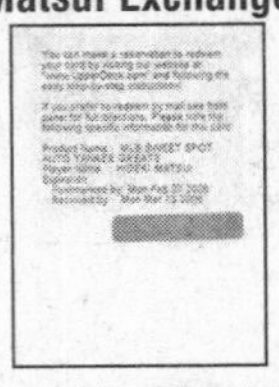

Randomly inserted in packs, this was a card issued as an exchange card for a collector to obtain an Hideki Matsui signed card. This card was issued to a stated print run of 50 sets of which Matsui signed 25 cards in black and 25 cards in red. This card could be exchanged until March 13, 2006.

Nm-Mt Ex-Mt
HM Hideki Matsui EXCH

2003 Sweet Spot Classics Game Jersey

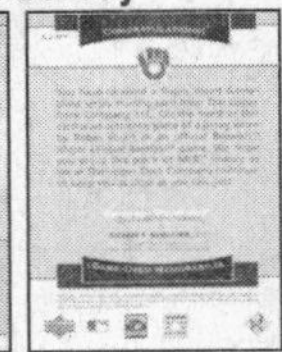

Issued at a stated rate of one in 16, these 30 cards feature game-worn jersey swatches on the card. A few cards were issued in smaller quantities and we have notated those cards with an SP in our checklist.

Nm-Mt Ex-Mt
AD Andre Dawson SP 10.00 3.00
CC Cecil Cooper 10.00 3.00
CF Carlton Fisk 15.00 4.50
CR Cal Ripken 25.00 7.50
DM Dale Murphy 15.00 4.50
DPO Dave Parker Pants 10.00 3.00
DS Duke Snider SP 15.00 4.50
EB Ernie Banks SP 15.00 4.50
FL Fred Lynn 10.00 3.00
GC Gary Carter SP 10.00 3.00
GF George Foster 10.00 3.00
HK Harmon Killebrew 15.00 4.50
JB Johnny Bench 15.00 4.50
JC Jose Canseco 15.00 4.50
JG Jim Gilliam 10.00 3.00
JMO Joe Morgan Pants 10.00 3.00
JP Johnny Podres 10.00 3.00
KP Kirby Puckett 15.00 4.50
LM Lee May 10.00 3.00
MM Mark McGwire 40.00 12.00
NR Nolan Ryan 40.00 12.00
OS Ozzie Smith 15.00 4.50
RC Ron Cey 10.00 3.00
RF Rollie Fingers 10.00 3.00
RY Robin Yount 15.00 4.50
SG Steve Garvey 10.00 3.00
SM Stan Musial SP 40.00 12.00
TG Tony Gwynn 15.00 4.50
TW Ted Williams SP 100.00 30.00
WS Willie Stargell SP 15.00 4.50

2003 Sweet Spot Classics Patch Cards

Inserted at a stated rate of one in six, these 83 cards feature special patch-type pieces. These cards honor different highlights in many player's career and we have notated that information next to their name in our checklist.

Nm-Mt Ex-Mt
BR1 Babe Ruth Red Sox/350 40.00 12.00
BR2 Babe Ruth Yankees 30.00 9.00
BR3 Babe Ruth 27 WS/150 50.00 15.00
BW1 Billy Williams 10.00 3.00
CF1 Carlton Fisk Red Sox 15.00 4.50
CF2 Carlton Fisk White Sox/150 25.00 7.50
CH1 Catfish Hunter A's/350 15.00 4.50
CH2 Catfish Hunter Yankees 15.00 4.50
CH3 Catfish Hunter A's GU/39 60.00 18.00
CH4 Catfish Hunter 72 WS/50 40.00 12.00
CR1 Cal Ripken 25.00 7.50
CR2 Cal Ripken GU/75 150.00 45.00
CR3 Cal Ripken 83 WS/150 60.00 18.00
DS1 Duke Snider 15.00 4.50
DS2 Duke Snider LA/150 25.00 7.50
DS3 Duke Snider Mets/350 15.00 4.50
DS4 Duke Snider Dodgers GU/25

Card	Nm-Mt	Ex-Mt
DS5 Duke Snider Brooklyn/150	25.00	7.50
DS6 Duke Snider 59 WS/150	25.00	7.50
EB1 Ernie Banks	15.00	4.50
FL1 Fred Lynn Red Sox	10.00	3.00
FL2 Fred Lynn Angels/350	10.00	3.00
FL3 Fred Lynn O's/150	15.00	4.50
FL4 Fred Lynn Tigers/50	25.00	7.50
GF1 George Foster Mets/350	10.00	3.00
GF2 George Foster Reds	10.00	3.00
HM1 Hideki Matsui	25.00	7.50
JB1 Johnny Bench	15.00	4.50
JB2 Johnny Bench GU/150	60.00	18.00
JB3 Johnny Bench 76 WS/150	40.00	12.00
JD1 Joe DiMaggio	15.00	4.50
JD2 Joe DiMaggio 47 WS/50	100.00	30.00
JD3 Joe DiMaggio 37 WS/350	30.00	9.00
JD4 Joe DiMaggio 39 WS/150	40.00	12.00
JM1 Joe Morgan Reds	10.00	3.00
JM2 Joe Morgan Astros/350	10.00	3.00
JM3 Joe Morgan Giants/150	15.00	4.50
JM4 Joe Morgan Reds GU/150	40.00	12.00
JM5 Joe Morgan 76 WS/100	15.00	4.50
KG1 Kirk Gibson Dodgers	10.00	3.00
KG2 Kirk Gibson Tigers/350	10.00	3.00
KP1 Kirby Puckett	15.00	4.50
KP2 Kirby Puckett GU/40	100.00	30.00
MC1 Mark McGwire A's	25.00	7.50
MC2 Mark McGwire Cards/350	50.00	15.00
MC3 Mark McGwire Cards GU/9		
MM1 Mickey Mantle	40.00	12.00
MM2 M.Mantle 52 WS/150	120.00	36.00
MM3 M.Mantle 56 WS/150	120.00	36.00
MM4 M.Mantle 60 WS/150	120.00	36.00
MM5 Mickey Mantle Logo/7		
NR1 Nolan Ryan Astros	25.00	7.50
NR2 Nolan Ryan Rangers/350	50.00	15.00
NR3 Nolan Ryan Angels/150	60.00	18.00
NR4 N.Ryan Astros GU/105	120.00	36.00
OS1 Ozzie Smith Cards	15.00	4.50
OS2 Ozzie Smith Padres/350	25.00	7.50
OS3 Ozzie Smith Cards GU/150	60.00	18.00
OS4 Ozzie Smith 82 WS/100	40.00	12.00
OS5 Ozzie Smith 85 WS/100	40.00	12.00
RM1 Roger Maris Yankees	15.00	4.50
RM2 Roger Maris Cards/350	25.00	7.50
RM3 Roger Maris 62 WS/150	40.00	12.00
RM4 Roger Maris 67 WS/50	50.00	15.00
RY1 Robin Yount	15.00	4.50
RY2 Robin Yount GU/150	60.00	18.00
RY3 Robin Yount 82 WS/350	25.00	7.50
SG1 Steve Garvey Dodgers	10.00	3.00
SG2 Steve Garvey Padres/350	10.00	3.00
SG3 S.Garvey Dodgers GU/150	40.00	12.00
SG4 Steve Garvey 77 WS/50	25.00	7.50
SG5 Steve Garvey 81 WS/50	25.00	7.50
TG1 Tony Gwynn	15.00	4.50
TG2 Tony Gwynn GU/150	80.00	24.00
TG3 Tony Gwynn 84 WS/350	25.00	7.50
TW1 Ted Williams	20.00	6.00
TW2 Ted Williams 46 WS/350	40.00	12.00
WS1 Willie Stargell	15.00	4.50
WS2 Willie Stargell GU/137	50.00	15.00
WS3 Willie Stargell 71 WS/150	25.00	7.50
WS4 Willie Stargell 79 WS/50	40.00	12.00
YB1 Yogi Berra	15.00	4.50
YB2 Yogi Berra 53 WS/350	25.00	7.50
YB3 Yogi Berra 56 WS/150	40.00	12.00

2003 Sweet Spot Classics Pinstripes

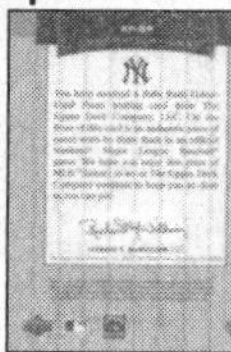

nserted at a stated rate of one in 40, these 12 ards feature authentic game-used pieces of lew York Yankee uniforms. Please note that a ew cards were issued in shorter supply and we ave notated that information with an SP notaon in our checklist.

Card	Nm-Mt	Ex-Mt
RO Babe Ruth Pants SP	350.00	105.00
S Casey Stengel	15.00	4.50
E Bucky Dent	10.00	3.00
G0 Dwight Gooden Pants	10.00	3.00
MO Don Mattingly Pants	40.00	12.00
R Dave Righetti	10.00	3.00
B Jim Bouton	10.00	3.00
D Joe DiMaggio SP	120.00	36.00
M Mickey Mantle SP	180.00	55.00
R Phil Rizzuto	15.00	4.50
M Thurman Munson SP	40.00	12.00
B Yogi Berra	20.00	6.00

2004 Sweet Spot Classic

his 159 card standard-size set was released in ebruary, 2004. The set was issued in four card acks which came 12 packs to a box and 8 oxes to a case. Cards numbered 1-90 were ssued in higher quantity than cards 91-161. The ards 91 through 161 feature "famous firsts" in ayers careers. Each of these cards are numered to that year in issue. Cards numbered 143 nd 148 which were supposed to feature Roger emens were removed from the set when emens came out of a very short retirement to gn with the Houston Astros.

Card	Nm-Mt	Ex-Mt
COMP.SET w/o SP'S (90)	40.00	12.00
COMMON CARD (1-90)	.75	.23
COMMON CARD (91-161)	5.00	1.50
91-161 STATED ODDS 1:3		
1 Al Kaline	2.00	.60
2 Andre Dawson	.75	.23
3 Bert Blyleven	.75	.23
4 Bill Dickey	1.25	.35
5 Bill Mazeroski	1.25	.35
6 Billy Martin	1.25	.35
7 Bob Feller	.75	.23
8 Bob Gibson	1.25	.35
9 Bob Lemon	.75	.23
10 George Kell	.75	.23
11 Bobby Doerr	.75	.23
12 Brooks Robinson	1.25	.35
13 Cal Ripken	6.00	1.80
14 Carl Hubbell	1.25	.35
15 Carl Yastrzemski	3.00	.90
16 Charlie Keller	.75	.23
17 Chuck Dressen	.75	.23
18 Cy Young	2.00	.60
19 Dave Winfield	.75	.23
20 Dizzy Dean	1.25	.35
21 Don Drysdale	2.00	.60
22 Don Larsen	.75	.23
23 Don Mattingly	5.00	1.50
24 Don Newcombe	.75	.23
25 Duke Snider	1.25	.35
26 Early Wynn	.75	.23
27 Eddie Mathews	2.00	.60
28 Elston Howard	.75	.23
29 Frank Robinson	.75	.23
30 Gary Carter	.75	.23
31 Gil Hodges	1.25	.35
32 Gil McDougald	1.25	.35
33 Hank Greenberg	2.00	.60
34 Harmon Killebrew	2.00	.60
35 Harry Caray	.75	.23
36 Honus Wagner	2.00	.60
37 Hoyt Wilhelm	.75	.23
38 Jackie Robinson	2.00	.60
39 Jim Bunning	.75	.23
40 Jim Palmer	.75	.23
41 Jimmie Foxx	2.00	.60
42 Jimmy Wynn	.75	.23
43 Joe DiMaggio	4.00	1.20
44 Joe Torre	1.25	.35
45 Johnny Mize	.75	.23
46 Juan Marichal	.75	.23
47 Larry Doby	.75	.23
48 Lefty Gomez	1.25	.35
49 Lefty Grove	1.25	.35
50 Leo Durocher	.75	.23
51 Lou Boudreau	.75	.23
52 Lou Brock	1.25	.35
53 Lou Gehrig	4.00	1.20
54 Luis Aparicio	.75	.23
55 Maury Wills	.75	.23
56 Mel Allen	.75	.23
57 Mel Ott	2.00	.60
58 Mickey Cochrane	.75	.23
59 Mickey Mantle	8.00	2.40
60 Mike Schmidt	4.00	1.20
61 Monte Irvin	.75	.23
62 Nolan Ryan	5.00	1.50
63 Pee Wee Reese	1.25	.35
64 Phil Rizzuto	1.25	.35
65 Ralph Kiner	.75	.23
66 Richie Ashburn	1.25	.35
67 Rick Ferrell	.75	.23
68 Roberto Clemente	5.00	1.50
69 Robin Roberts	.75	.23
70 Robin Yount	3.00	.90
71 Rogers Hornsby	2.00	.60
72 Rollie Fingers	.75	.23
73 Roy Campanella	2.00	.60
74 Ryne Sandberg	4.00	1.20
75 Tony Gwynn	2.50	.75
76 Satchel Paige	2.00	.60
77 Shoeless Joe Jackson	3.00	.90
78 Stan Musial	3.00	.90
79 Ted Williams	4.00	1.20
80 Thurman Munson	2.00	.60
81 Tom Seaver	1.25	.35
82 Tommy Henrich	.75	.23
83 Tony Perez	.75	.23
84 Tris Speaker	1.25	.35
85 Vida Blue	.75	.23
86 Wade Boggs	1.25	.35
87 Walter Johnson	2.00	.60
88 Warren Spahn	1.25	.35
89 Whitey Ford	1.25	.35
90 Willie McCovey	.75	.23
91 Andre Dawson FF/1987	5.00	1.50
92 Andre Dawson FF/1990	5.00	1.50
93 Ernie Banks FF/1958	8.00	2.40
94 Bob Lemon FF/1948	5.00	1.50
95 Cal Ripken FF/1982	15.00	4.50
96 Cal Ripken FF/1995	15.00	4.50
97 Carl Yastrzemski FF/1979	8.00	2.40
98 Carlton Fisk FF/1972	8.00	2.40
99 Cy Young FF/1910	8.00	2.40
100 Don Larsen FF/1956	5.00	1.50
101 Don Newcombe FF/1949	5.00	1.50
102 Don Newcombe FF/1956	5.00	1.50
103 Dwight Evans FF/1986	8.00	2.40
104 Elston Howard FF/1955	5.00	1.50
105 Frank Robinson FF/1956	5.00	1.50
106 Frank Robinson FF/1966	5.00	1.50
107 Frank Robinson FF/1973	5.00	1.50
108 Gil McDougald FF/1951	8.00	2.40
109 Hank Greenberg FF/1941	8.00	2.40
110 Harmon Killebrew FF/1964	8.00	2.40
111 Hoyt Wilhelm FF/1952	5.00	1.50
112 Hoyt Wilhelm FF/1958	5.00	1.50
113 Jackie Robinson FF/1946	8.00	2.40
114 J.Robinson FF Black/1947	8.00	2.40
115 J.Robinson FF ROY/1947	8.00	2.40
116 Jackie Robinson FF/1997	8.00	2.40
117 Jim Bunning FF/1964	5.00	1.50
118 J.DiMaggio FF Bench/1950	10.00	3.00
119 Joe Morgan FF/1976	5.00	1.50
120 Johnny Mize FF/1939	5.00	1.50
121 Johnny Mize FF/1947	5.00	1.50
122 Juan Marichal FF/1968	5.00	1.50
123 Ken Griffey Sr. FF/1990	5.00	1.50
124 Larry Doby FF/1947	5.00	1.50
125 Lefty Gomez FF/1933	8.00	2.40
126 Lou Boudreau FF/1946	5.00	1.50
127 Lou Gehrig FF Lineup/1939	10.00	3.00
128 Lou Gehrig FF Number/1939	10.00	3.00
129 Mark McGwire FF/1989	12.00	3.60
130 Mark McGwire FF/1998	12.00	3.60
131 Maury Wills FF/1962	5.00	1.50
132 Mel Ott FF/1946	8.00	2.40
133 Mike Schmidt FF/1980	10.00	3.00
134 Nolan Ryan FF/1973	12.00	3.60
135 Nolan Ryan FF/1989	12.00	3.60
136 Pee Wee Reese FF/1955	8.00	2.40
137 Nolan Ryan FF/1979	12.00	3.60
138 Richie Ashburn FF/1962	8.00	2.40
139 Roberto Clemente FF/1971	12.00	3.60
140 Roberto Clemente FF/1973	12.00	3.60
141 Robin Roberts FF/1956	5.00	1.50
142 Robin Yount FF/1982	8.00	2.40
143 Does Not Exist		
144 Rollie Fingers FF/1975	5.00	1.50
145 Rollie Fingers FF/1981	5.00	1.50
146 Roy Campanella FF/1953	8.00	2.40
147 Ryne Sandberg FF/1990	10.00	3.00
148 Does Not Exist		
149 Satchel Paige FF/1948	8.00	2.40
150 Stan Musial FF/1952	8.00	2.40
151 Stan Musial FF/1954	8.00	2.40
152 Stan Musial FF/1963	8.00	2.40
153 Ted Williams FF/1947	10.00	3.00
154 Ted Williams FF/1957	10.00	3.00
155 Tom Seaver FF/1970	8.00	2.40
156 Tom Seaver FF/1975	8.00	2.40
157 Wade Boggs FF/1999	8.00	2.40
158 Warren Spahn FF/1957	8.00	2.40
159 Warren Spahn FF/1958	8.00	2.40
160 Joe DiMaggio FF AS/1950	10.00	3.00
161 Yogi Berra FF/1947	8.00	2.40

2004 Sweet Spot Classic Barrel Signatures

Lou Brock did not return his cards in time for inclusion in this product. Those cards could be redeemed until January 27, 2004. A few cards have been seen on the secondary market with Duke Snider's photo used on Wade Boggs' card.

Card	Nm-Mt	Ex-Mt
OVERALL AUTO ODDS 1:24		
PRINT RUNS B/WN 24-203 COPIES PER		
NO PRICING ON QTY OF 25 OR LESS		
BM Bill Mazeroski/24		
BW Billy Williams/200	50.00	15.00
CR Cal Ripken/25		
HB Harold Baines/200	50.00	15.00
JB Johnny Bench/50		
LB Lou Brock/50 EXCH		
NR Nolan Ryan/25		
RS Ron Santo/203	50.00	15.00
SM Stan Musial/25		
TS Tom Seaver/25		
WB Wade Boggs/200	80.00	24.00

2004 Sweet Spot Classic Game Used Memorabilia

Card	Nm-Mt	Ex-Mt
OVERALL GU MEMORABILIA ODDS 1:24		
STATED PRINT RUN 275 SERIAL #'d SETS		
AD Andre Dawson Expos Jsy	10.00	3.00
AD1 Andre Dawson Cubs Jsy	10.00	3.00
BB Bert Blyleven Jsy	10.00	3.00
BM Billy Martin Pants	15.00	4.50
CD Chuck Dressen Pants	10.00	3.00
CK Charlie Keller Jsy	10.00	3.00
CR Cal Ripken Jsy	40.00	12.00
CY Carl Yastrzemski Jsy	25.00	7.50
DM Don Mattingly Jsy	25.00	7.50
EH Elston Howard Jsy	15.00	4.50
EM Eddie Mathews Jsy	15.00	4.50
FR Frank Robinson Jsy	10.00	3.00
GC Gary Carter Pants	10.00	3.00
GM Gil McDougald Jsy	15.00	4.50
JB Jim Bunning Pants	15.00	4.50
JD Joe DiMaggio Pants	80.00	24.00
JM Juan Marichal Pants	10.00	3.00
JO Johnny Mize Pants	15.00	4.50
JP Jim Palmer Jsy	10.00	3.00
JR Jackie Robinson Pants	40.00	12.00
JT Joe Torre Jsy	15.00	4.50
KG Ken Griffey Sr. Jsy	10.00	3.00
ML Mickey Lolich Jsy	10.00	3.00
MM Mickey Mantle Pants	120.00	36.00
MW Maury Wills Pants	10.00	3.00
NR Nolan Ryan Jsy	40.00	12.00
OS Ozzie Smith Jsy	15.00	4.50
PR Phil Rizzuto Pants	15.00	4.50
RB Ron Blomberg Jsy	10.00	3.00
RC Roberto Clemente Pants	80.00	24.00
RM Roger Maris Pants	60.00	18.00
RY Robin Yount Jsy	15.00	4.50
SA Sparky Anderson Jsy	10.00	3.00
SB Sal Bando Jsy	10.00	3.00
SM Stan Musial Pants	40.00	12.00
TG Tony Gwynn Pants	15.00	4.50
TM Thurman Munson Jsy	30.00	9.00
TS Tom Seaver Pants	15.00	4.50
TW Ted Williams Pants	60.00	18.00
WB Wade Boggs Sox Pants	15.00	4.50
WB1 Wade Boggs Yanks Pants	15.00	4.50

2004 Sweet Spot Classic Game Used Memorabilia Silver Rainbow

Card	Nm-Mt	Ex-Mt
*SILVER RBW: .75X TO 2X BASIC SWATCH		
OVERALL GU MEMORABILIA ODDS 1:24		
STATED PRINT RUN 50 SERIAL #'d SETS		
JD Joe DiMaggio Pants	100.00	30.00
MM Mickey Mantle Pants	200.00	60.00
RC Roberto Clemente Pants	100.00	30.00
TW Ted Williams Pants	80.00	24.00

2004 Sweet Spot Classic Game Used Patch

Card	Nm-Mt	Ex-Mt
PRINT RUNS B/WN 17-176 COPIES PER		
NO PRICING ON QTY OF 23 OR LESS		
SILVER RAINBOW PRINT RUN 10 #'d SETS		
NO SILV.RAIN.PRICING DUE TO SCARCITY		
RANDOM INSERTS IN PACKS		
AD Andre Dawson/100	25.00	7.50
BB Bert Blyleven/113	25.00	7.50
CK Charlie Keller/55	40.00	12.00
CR Cal Ripken/17		
CY Carl Yastrzemski/20		
DM Don Mattingly/176	60.00	18.00
EH Elston Howard/23		
FR Frank Robinson/50	40.00	12.00
GM Gil McDougald/31	50.00	15.00
ML Mickey Lolich/115	25.00	7.50
MW Maury Wills/78	25.00	7.50
NR Nolan Ryan/96	100.00	30.00
RY Robin Yount/100	60.00	18.00
TG Tony Gwynn/100	60.00	18.00
TM Thurman Munson/100	60.00	18.00
TS Tom Seaver/94	40.00	12.00
WB Wade Boggs/90	40.00	12.00

2004 Sweet Spot Classic Patch 300

Card	Nm-Mt	Ex-Mt
STATED PRINT RUN 300 SERIAL #'d SETS		
*PATCH 230: .4X TO 1X BASIC		
PATCH 230 PRINT RUN 230 SERIAL #'d SETS		
*PATCH 200: .4X TO 1X BASIC		
PATCH 200 PRINT RUN 200 SERIAL #'d SETS		
*PATCH 150: .5X TO 1.2X BASIC		
PATCH 150 PRINT RUN 150 SERIAL #'d SETS		
*PATCH 125: .5X TO 1.2X BASIC		
PATCH 125 PRINT RUN 125 SERIAL #'d SETS		
*PATCH 75: .6X TO 1.5X BASIC		
PATCH 75 PRINT RUN 75 SERIAL #'d SETS		
*PATCH 50: .75X TO 2X BASIC		
PATCH 50 PRINT RUN 50 SERIAL #'d SETS		
PATCH 25 PRINT RUN 25 SERIAL #'d SETS		
NO PATCH 25 PRICING DUE TO SCARCITY		
PATCH 10 PRINT RUN 10 SERIAL #'d SETS		
NO PATCH 10 PRICING DUE TO SCARCITY		
OVERALL PATCH ODDS 1:3		
AD Andre Dawson Cubs	10.00	3.00
AK Al Kaline Tigers	20.00	6.00
AL Mel Allen Yanks	10.00	3.00
BD Bill Dickey Yanks	15.00	4.50
BF Bob Feller Indians	10.00	3.00
BG Bob Gibson Cards	15.00	4.50
BL Bob Lemon Indians	10.00	3.00
BM Billy Martin Yanks	15.00	4.50
BR Lou Brock Cards	15.00	4.50
CA Roy Campanella Dodgers	15.00	4.50
CG Charlie Gehringer Tigers	10.00	3.00
CH Carl Hubbell Giants	15.00	4.50
CM Christy Mathewson Giants	15.00	4.50
CO Mickey Cochrane Tigers	10.00	3.00
CR Cal Ripken AS	40.00	12.00
CY Cy Young Indians	15.00	4.50
DD Dizzy Dean Cards	15.00	4.50
DL Don Larsen Yanks	10.00	3.00
DM Don Mattingly Yanks	30.00	9.00
DN Don Newcombe Dodgers	10.00	3.00
DO Bobby Doerr Red Sox	10.00	3.00
DR Don Drysdale Dodgers	15.00	4.50
DS Duke Snider AS	15.00	4.50
DU Leo Durocher Dodgers	10.00	3.00
DW Dave Winfield Yanks	10.00	3.00
EM Eddie Mathews Braves	15.00	4.50
ES Enos Slaughter Cards	10.00	3.00
EW Early Wynn Indians	10.00	3.00
FF Frankie Frisch Cards	10.00	3.00
FI Rollie Fingers A's	10.00	3.00
FJ Ferguson Jenkins Cubs	10.00	3.00
FR Frank Robinson Reds	10.00	3.00
GC Gary Carter Mets	10.00	3.00
GE Lou Gehrig Yanks	20.00	6.00
GH Gil Hodges Dodgers	15.00	4.50
GP Gaylord Perry Giants	10.00	3.00
GR Lefty Grove A's	15.00	4.50
HC Harry Caray Cubs	10.00	3.00
HG Hank Greenberg Tigers	15.00	4.50
HK Harmon Killebrew Twins	20.00	6.00
HW Honus Wagner Pirates	15.00	4.50
IR Monte Irvin Giants	10.00	3.00
JB Jim Bunning Phils	15.00	4.50
JD Joe DiMaggio Yanks	20.00	6.00
JF Jimmie Foxx A's	15.00	4.50
JJ Shoeless Joe Jackson Sox	20.00	6.00
JM Johnny Mize Cards	10.00	3.00
JP Jim Palmer O's	10.00	3.00
JR Jackie Robinson Dodgers	15.00	4.50
JT Joe Torre Braves	15.00	4.50
LA Luis Aparicio White Sox	10.00	3.00
LB Lou Boudreau Indians	10.00	3.00
LD Larry Doby Indians	10.00	3.00
LG Lefty Gomez Yanks	15.00	4.50
MA Juan Marichal Giants	10.00	3.00
MI Mickey Mantle AS	50.00	15.00
ML Mickey Lolich Tigers	10.00	3.00
MO Mel Ott Giants	15.00	4.50
MS Mike Schmidt Phils	25.00	7.50
MW Maury Wills Dodgers	10.00	3.00
NR Nolan Ryan Mets	30.00	9.00
PR Pee Wee Reese Dodgers	15.00	4.50
RA Richie Ashburn Phils	15.00	4.50
RC Roberto Clemente Pirates	30.00	9.00
RF Rick Ferrell Red Sox	10.00	3.00
RH Rogers Hornsby Cards	15.00	4.50
RI Phil Rizzuto Yanks	15.00	4.50
RK Ralph Kiner Pirates	10.00	3.00
RO Brooks Robinson O's	15.00	4.50
RR Robin Roberts Phils	10.00	3.00
RS Ryne Sandberg Cubs	25.00	7.50
RU Babe Ruth AS	30.00	9.00
SK Bill Skowron Yanks	10.00	3.00
SM Stan Musial Cards	20.00	6.00
SP Satchel Paige Indians	15.00	4.50
TC Ty Cobb Tigers	20.00	6.00
TH Tommy Henrich Yanks	10.00	3.00
TL Tommy Lasorda Dodgers	10.00	3.00
TM Thurman Munson Yanks	15.00	4.50
TP Tony Perez Reds	10.00	3.00
TR Tris Speaker Red Sox	15.00	4.50
TS Tom Seaver Mets	15.00	4.50
TW Ted Williams AS	25.00	7.50
WB Wade Boggs Red Sox	15.00	4.50
WF Whitey Ford Yanks	15.00	4.50
WI Hoyt Wilhelm White Sox	10.00	3.00
WJ Walter Johnson Senators	15.00	4.50
WM Willie McCovey Giants	10.00	3.00
WS Warren Spahn Braves	15.00	4.50
YA Carl Yastrzemski Red Sox	25.00	7.50

2004 Sweet Spot Classic Signatures Black

Randomly inserted in packs, these cards feature signatures from the noted personages in black ink. Several people including long-time Phillies announcer Harry Kalas and one time NL consecutive-games played leader Gus Suhr have their 1st certified autograph card in this set. Please note that several people did not return their cards in time for inclusion in pack out and those cards could be redeemed until January 27, 2004. Please note that for players with 25 or fewer signatures that no pricing is provided due to market scarcity.

Card	Nm-Mt	Ex-Mt
OVERALL AUTO ODDS 1:24		
PRINT RUNS B/WN 25-275 COPIES PER		
2 Preacher Roe/225	40.00	12.00
4 Bob Feller/65	50.00	15.00
5 Bob Gibson/50	80.00	24.00
6 Harry Kalas/100	60.00	18.00
7 Bobby Doerr/100	40.00	12.00
8 Cal Ripken/50	175.00	52.50
9 Carl Yastrzemski/35		
10 Carlton Fisk/100	60.00	18.00
11 Chuck Tanner/150	25.00	7.50
12 Cito Gaston/150	25.00	7.50
13 Danny Ozark/150	25.00	7.50
14 Dave Winfield/80	80.00	24.00
15 Davey Johnson/175	40.00	12.00
16 Ernie Harwell/100 EXCH	60.00	18.00
17 Dick Williams/150	25.00	7.50
18 Don Mattingly/40		
19 Don Newcombe/40	50.00	15.00
20 Duke Snider/35	80.00	24.00
21 Steve Carlton/150	60.00	18.00
22 Felipe Alou/175	25.00	7.50
23 Frank Robinson/65	80.00	24.00
24 Gary Carter/100	40.00	12.00
25 Gene Mauch/225	25.00	7.50
26 George Bamberger/225	25.00	7.50
28 Gus Suhr/100	40.00	12.00
30 Harmon Killebrew/50	100.00	30.00
31 Jack McKeon/225	40.00	12.00
32 Jim Bunning/100	80.00	24.00
33 Jimmy Piersall/212	40.00	12.00
35 Johnny Bench/50	100.00	30.00
36 Juan Marichal/50	50.00	15.00
37 Lou Brock/50 EXCH	80.00	24.00
38 George Kell/40	50.00	15.00
39 Maury Wills/40	50.00	15.00
41 Mike Schmidt/40 EXCH		
42 Nolan Ryan/50		
43 Ozzie Smith/65	100.00	30.00
44 Eddie Mayo/140	25.00	7.50
45 Phil Rizzuto/50	80.00	24.00
46 Ralph Kiner/40 EXCH	50.00	15.00
47 Lonny Frey/114	25.00	7.50
48 Bill Mazeroski/50	80.00	24.00
49 Robin Roberts/40	80.00	24.00
50 Robin Yount/40	100.00	30.00
52 Roger Craig/175	40.00	12.00

55 Tony Perez/40 ... 50.00 15.00
56 Sparky Anderson/175 ... 40.00 12.00
57 Stan Musial/40 ...
58 Ted Radcliffe/225 ... 40.00 12.00
60 Tom Seaver/25 ...
61 Tony Gwynn/65 ...
62 Tony LaRussa/275 ... 25.00 7.50
63 Tony Oliva/150 ... 40.00 12.00
64 Tony Pena/150 ... 25.00 7.50
66 Whitey Ford/45 ... 80.00 24.00
67 Yogi Berra/65 ... 100.00 30.00

2004 Sweet Spot Classic Signatures Black Holo-Foil

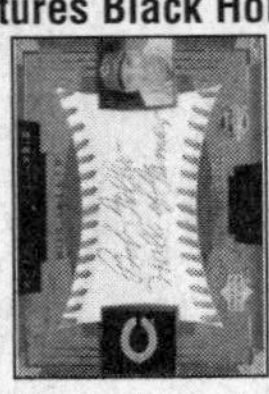

For those people who did not return their cards in time for inclusion in this product, those exchange cards could be returned until January 27, 2007.

Nm-Mt Ex-Mt
OVERALL AUTO ODDS 1:24 ...
PRINT RUNS B/WN 10-100 COPIES PER
NO PRICING ON QTY OF 25 OR LESS
MOST CARDS FEATURE INSCRIPTIONS
11 Chuck Tanner/100 ... 25.00 7.50
12 Cito Gaston/100 ... 25.00 7.50
13 Danny Ozark/100 ... 25.00 7.50
15 Davey Johnson/50 ... 50.00 15.00
17 Dick Williams/100 ... 25.00 7.50
22 Felipe Alou/50 ... 30.00 9.00
24 Gary Carter/50 ... 50.00 15.00
52 Roger Craig/50 ... 50.00 15.00
56 Sparky Anderson/50 ... 50.00 15.00
62 Tony LaRussa/50 ... 30.00 9.00
63 Tony Oliva/100 ... 40.00 12.00
64 Tony Pena/100 ... 25.00 7.50

2004 Sweet Spot Classic Signatures Blue

A few people did not return their cards in time for inclusion in packs, those signed cards could be redeemed until January 27, 2004.

Nm-Mt Ex-Mt
OVERALL AUTO ODDS 1:24 ...
PRINT RUNS B/WN 15-150 COPIES PER
NO PRICING ON QTY OF 25 OR LESS
2 Preacher Roe/150 ... 40.00 12.00
4 Bob Feller/50 ... 50.00 15.00
5 Bob Gibson/25 ...
6 Harry Kalas/50 ... 80.00 24.00
7 Bobby Doerr/50 ... 50.00 15.00
8 Cal Ripken/25 ...
9 Carl Yastrzemski/15 ...
10 Carlton Fisk/50 ... 80.00 24.00
11 Chuck Tanner/125 ... 25.00 7.50
12 Cito Gaston/125 ... 25.00 7.50
13 Danny Ozark/125 ... 25.00 7.50
14 Dave Winfield/35 ... 80.00 24.00
15 Davey Johnson/150 ... 40.00 12.00
16 Ernie Harwell/50 EXCH ... 80.00 24.00
17 Dick Williams/125 ... 25.00 7.50
18 Don Mattingly/25 ...
19 Don Newcombe/25 ...
20 Duke Snider/25 ...
21 Steve Carlton/100 ... 60.00 18.00
22 Felipe Alou/150 ... 25.00 7.50
23 Frank Robinson/50 ... 80.00 24.00
24 Gary Carter/75 ... 50.00 15.00
25 Gene Mauch/150 ... 25.00 7.50
26 George Bamberger/150 ... 25.00 7.50
28 Gus Suhr/85 ... 50.00 15.00
30 Harmon Killebrew/25 ...
31 Jack McKeon/150 ... 40.00 12.00
32 Jim Bunning/65 ... 100.00 30.00
33 Jimmy Piersall/150 ... 40.00 12.00
35 Johnny Bench/20 ...
36 Juan Marichal/25 ...
37 Lou Brock/20 EXCH ...
38 George Kell/25 ...
39 Maury Wills/25 ...
41 Mike Schmidt/25 EXCH ...
42 Nolan Ryan/25 ...
43 Ozzie Smith/50 ... 100.00 30.00
44 Eddie Mayo/50 ... 30.00 9.00
45 Phil Rizzuto/25 ...
46 Ralph Kiner/25 EXCH ...
47 Lonny Frey/75 ... 30.00 9.00
48 Bill Mazeroski/25 ...
49 Robin Roberts/25 ...
50 Robin Yount/25 ...
52 Roger Craig/150 ... 40.00 12.00
55 Tony Perez/25 ...
56 Sparky Anderson/150 ... 40.00 12.00
57 Stan Musial/25 ...
58 Ted Radcliffe/150 ... 40.00 12.00
60 Tom Seaver/15 ...
61 Tony Gwynn/25 ...
62 Tony LaRussa/145 ... 25.00 7.50
63 Tony Oliva/125 ... 40.00 12.00
64 Tony Pena/115 ... 25.00 7.50
66 Whitey Ford/20 ...
67 Yogi Berra/50 ... 100.00 30.00

2004 Sweet Spot Classic Signatures Red

Ernie Harwell, Lou Brock, Mike Schmidt and Ralph Kiner did not return their cards in time for inclusion in packs. Redemption cards with an expiration date of January 27th, 2007 were seeded into packs for these aforementioned athletes. The Joe DiMaggio and Ted Williams cards from this set feature blue ink signed leather baseball patches (as averse to the red ink featured on the other cards). Representatives at Upper Deck have confirmed that they estimate approximately 25% of the Joe DiMaggio cards actually feature the added notation "Yankee Clipper".

Nm-Mt Ex-Mt
OVERALL AUTO ODDS 1:24
PRINT RUNS B/WN 2-86 COPIES PER
NO PRICING ON QTY OF 25 OR LESS
34 Joe DiMaggio/86 ... 700.00 210.00

1911 T205

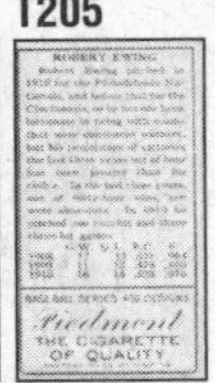

The cards in this 218-card set measure approximately 1 1/2" by 2 5/8". The T205 set (catalog designation), also known as the "Gold Border" set, was issued in 1911 in packages of the following cigarette brands: American Beauty, Broadleaf, Cycle, Drum, Hassan, Honest Long Cut, Piedmont, Polar Bear, Sovereign and Sweet Caporal. All the above were products of the American Tobacco Company, and the ads for the various brands appear below the biographical section on the back of each card. There are pose variations noted in the checklist (which is alphabetized and numbered for reference) and there are 12 minor league cards of a more ornate design which are somewhat scarce. The numbers below correspond to alphabetical order within category, i.e., major leaguers and minor leaguers are alphabetized separately. The gold borders of T205 cards chip easily and they are hard to find in "Mint" or even "Near Mint" condition, due to this there is a high premium on these high condition cards.

Ex-Mt VG COM-
PLETE SET (218) 35000.00 17500.00
COMMON (1-186) ... 100.00 50.00
COMMON (187-198) ... 200.00 100.00
1 Ed Abbaticchio ... 100.00 50.00
2 Red Ames ... 100.00 50.00
3 Jimmy Archer ... 100.00 50.00
4 Jimmy Austin ... 100.00 50.00
5 Bill Bailey ... 100.00 50.00
6 Frank "Homerun" Baker ... 400.00 200.00
7 Neal Ball ... 100.00 50.00
8A Cy Barger ... 100.00 50.00
(Full B)
8B Cy Barger ... 300.00 150.00
Part B
9 Jack Barry ... 100.00 50.00
10 Johnny Bates ... 100.00 50.00
11 Fred Beck ... 100.00 50.00
12 Beals Becker ... 100.00 50.00
13 George Bell ... 100.00 50.00
14 Chief Bender ... 250.00 125.00
15 Bill Bergen ... 100.00 50.00
16 Bob Bescher ... 100.00 50.00
17 Joe Birmingham ... 100.00 50.00
18 Russ Blackburne ... 100.00 50.00
19 Kitty Bransfield ... 100.00 50.00
20A Roger Bresnahan ... 250.00 125.00
(Mouth closed)
20B Roger Bresnahan ... 400.00 200.00
(Mouth open)
21 Al Bridwell ... 100.00 50.00
22 Mordecai Brown ... 400.00 200.00
23 Bobby Byrne ... 100.00 50.00
24 Howie Camnitz ... 100.00 50.00
25 Bill Carrigan ... 100.00 50.00
26 Frank Chance ... 300.00 150.00
27A Hal Chase ... 300.00 150.00
(Chase only)
27B Hal Chase ... 150.00 75.00
(Hal Chase)
28 Eddie Cicotte ... 200.00 100.00
29 Fred Clarke ... 400.00 200.00
30 Ty Cobb ... 5000.00 2500.00
31A Edward T. Collins ... 300.00 150.00
(Mouth closed)
31B Edward T. Collins ... 500.00 250.00
(Mouth open)
32 Frank Corridon ... 100.00 50.00
33A Otis Crandall ... 100.00 50.00
T Crossed in name
33B Otis Crandall ... 100.00 50.00
T Not Crossed in Name
34 Lou Criger ... 100.00 50.00
35 Bill Dahlen ... 150.00 75.00
36 Jake Daubert ... 100.00 50.00
37 Jim Delahanty ... 100.00 50.00
38 Art Devlin ... 100.00 50.00
39 Josh Devore ... 100.00 50.00
40 Walt Dickson ... 100.00 50.00
41 Jiggs Donahue UER ... 150.00 75.00
(Misspelled Donohue on card)
42 Red Dooin ... 100.00 50.00
43 Mickey Doolan ... 100.00 50.00
44A Patsy Dougherty ... 150.00 75.00
(White stocking)
44B Patsy Dougherty ... 100.00 50.00
(Red stocking)
45 Tom Downey ... 100.00 50.00
46 Larry Doyle ... 100.00 50.00
47 Hugh Duffy ... 300.00 150.00
48 Jimmy Dygert ... 100.00 50.00
49 Dick Egan ... 100.00 50.00
50 Kid Elberfeld ... 100.00 50.00
51 Clyde Engle ... 100.00 50.00
52 Steve Evans ... 100.00 50.00
53 Johnny Evers ... 250.00 125.00
54 Bob Ewing ... 100.00 50.00
55 George Ferguson ... 100.00 50.00
56 Ray Fisher ... 150.00 75.00
57 Art Fletcher ... 100.00 50.00
58 John Flynn ... 100.00 50.00
59A Russell Ford ... 100.00 50.00
(Dark cap)
59B Russell Ford ... 150.00 75.00
(Light cap)
60 Bill Foxen ... 100.00 50.00
61 Art Fromme ... 100.00 50.00
62 Earl Gardner ... 100.00 50.00
63 Harry Gaspar ... 100.00 50.00
64 George Gibson ... 100.00 50.00
65 Wilbur Good ... 100.00 50.00
66A George F. Graham ... 100.00 50.00
(Boston Rustlers)
66B George F. Graham ... 400.00 200.00
(Chicago Cubs)
67 Eddie Grant ... 150.00 75.00
68A Dolly Gray ... 100.00 50.00
No stats on back
68B Dolly Gray ... 400.00 200.00
Stats on Back
69 Clark Griffith ... 300.00 150.00
70 Bob Groom ... 100.00 50.00
71A Robert Harmon ... 100.00 50.00
(Both ears)
71B Robert Harmon ... 300.00 150.00
(Left ear only)
72 Topsy Hartsel ... 100.00 50.00
73 Arnold Hauser ... 100.00 50.00
74 Charlie Hemphill ... 100.00 50.00
75 Buck Herzog ... 100.00 50.00
76A Dick Hoblitzell ... 10000.00 5000.00
No Stats
76B Dick Hoblitzell ... 100.00 50.00
No CIN after second 1908
76C Dick Hoblitzell ... 150.00 75.00
CIN after second 1908
76D Dick Hoblitzell ... 100.00 50.00
sic.Hoblitzel
77 Danny Hoffman ... 100.00 50.00
78 Miller Huggins ... 400.00 200.00
79 John Hummell ... 100.00 50.00
80 Fred Jacklitsch ... 100.00 50.00
81 Hughie Jennings ... 300.00 150.00
82 Walter Johnson ... 2000.00 1000.00
83 Davy Jones ... 100.00 50.00
84 Tom Jones ... 100.00 50.00
85 Addie Joss ... 700.00 350.00
86 Ed Karger ... 150.00 75.00
87 Ed Killian ... 100.00 50.00
88 Red Kleinow ... 150.00 75.00
89 John Kling ... 100.00 50.00
90 John Knight ... 100.00 50.00
91 Ed Konetchy ... 100.00 50.00
92 Harry Krause ... 100.00 50.00
93 Rube Kroh ... 100.00 50.00
94 Frank Lang ... 100.00 50.00
95 Frank LaPorte ... 100.00 50.00
96A Arlie Latham ... 100.00 50.00
Back says W.A. Latham
96B Arlie Latham ... 100.00 50.00
A. Latham on back
97 Tommy Leach ... 100.00 50.00
98 Sam Leever ... 100.00 50.00
99A Lefty Leifield ... 100.00 50.00
A.Leifield on front
99B Lefty Leifield ... 100.00 50.00
A.P.Leifield on front
100 Ed Lennox ... 100.00 50.00
101 Paddy Livingston ... 100.00 50.00
102 Hans Lobert ... 100.00 50.00
103 Bris Lord ... 100.00 50.00
104 Harry Lord ... 100.00 50.00
105 John Lush ... 100.00 50.00
106 Nick Maddox ... 100.00 50.00
107 Sherry Magee ... 100.00 50.00
108 Rube Marquard ... 400.00 200.00
109 Christy Mathewson ... 2000.00 1000.00
110 Al Mattern ... 100.00 50.00
111 George McBride ... 100.00 50.00
112 Amby McConnell ... 100.00 50.00
113 Pryor McElveen ... 100.00 50.00
114 John McGraw MG ... 400.00 200.00
115 Harry McIntire ... 100.00 50.00
116 Matty McIntyre ... 100.00 50.00
117 Larry McLean ... 100.00 50.00
118 Fred Merkle ... 100.00 50.00
119 Chief Meyers ... 100.00 50.00
120 Clyde Milan ... 100.00 50.00
121 Dots Miller ... 100.00 50.00
122 Mike Mitchell ... 100.00 50.00
123A Pat Moran ... 300.00 150.00
Extra Stat Line on Card
123B Pat Moran ... 100.00 50.00
124 George Moriarity ... 100.00 50.00
125 George Mullin ... 100.00 50.00
126 Danny Murphy ... 100.00 50.00
127 Red Murray ... 100.00 50.00
128 Tom Needham ... 100.00 50.00
129 Rebel Oakes ... 100.00 50.00
130 Rube Oldring ... 100.00 50.00
131 Charley O'Leary ... 100.00 50.00
132 Fred Olmstead ... 100.00 50.00
133 Orval Overall ... 100.00 50.00
134 Freddy Parent ... 100.00 50.00
135 Dode Paskert ... 100.00 50.00
136 Fred Payne ... 100.00 50.00
137 Barney Pelty ... 100.00 50.00
138 Jack Pfiester ... 100.00 50.00
139 Ed Phelps ... 100.00 50.00
140 Decon Phillippe ... 100.00 50.00
141 Jack Quinn ... 100.00 50.00
142 Bugs Raymond ... 150.00 75.00
143 Ed Reulbach ... 100.00 50.00
144 Lewis Richie ... 100.00 50.00
145 Jack Rowan ... 150.00 75.00
146 Nap Rucker ... 100.00 50.00
147 Doc Scanlan ... 150.00 75.00
148 Germany Schaefer ... 100.00 50.00
149 Admiral Schlei ... 100.00 50.00
150 Boss Schmidt ... 100.00 50.00
151 Wildfire Schulte ... 100.00 50.00
152 Jim Scott ... 100.00 50.00
153 Bayard Sharpe ... 100.00 50.00
154A David Shean ... 100.00 50.00
(Boston Rustlers)
154B David Shean ... 400.00 200.00
(Chicago Cubs)
155 Jimmy Sheckard ... 100.00 50.00
156 Hack Simmons ... 100.00 50.00
157 Tony Smith ... 100.00 50.00
158 Fred Snodgrass ... 100.00 50.00
159 Tris Speaker ... 1000.00 500.00
160 Jake Stahl ... 100.00 50.00
161 Oscar Stanage ... 100.00 50.00
162 Harry Steinfeldt ... 100.00 50.00
163 George Stone ... 100.00 50.00
164 George Stovall ... 100.00 50.00
165 Gabby Street ... 100.00 50.00
166 George Suggs ... 150.00 75.00
167 Ed Summers ... 100.00 50.00
168 Jeff Sweeney ... 150.00 75.00
169 Lee Tannehill ... 100.00 50.00
170 Ira Thomas ... 100.00 50.00
171 Joe Tinker ... 600.00 300.00
172 John Titus ... 100.00 50.00
173 Terry Turner ... 300.00 150.00
174 Hippo Vaughn ... 150.00 75.00
175 Heinie Wagner ... 150.00 75.00
176A Bobby Wallace ... 250.00 125.00
(With cap)
176B Bobby Wallace ... 500.00 250.00
(Without cap)
176C Bobby Wallace ... 300.00 150.00
no cap 2/1910
177 Ed Walsh ... 500.00 250.00
178 Zach Wheat ... 300.00 150.00
179 Doc White ... 100.00 50.00
180 Kirby White ... 150.00 75.00
181 Kaiser Wilhelm ... 150.00 75.00
182 Ed Willett ... 100.00 50.00
183A Hooks Wiltse ... 100.00 50.00
(Both ears)
183B Hooks Wiltse ... 300.00 150.00
(Right ear only)
184 Owen Wilson ... 100.00 50.00
185 Harry Wolter ... 100.00 50.00
186 Cy Young ... 2000.00 1000.00
187 Dr.Merle T. Adkins: ... 200.00 100.00
Baltimore
188 Jack Dunn ... 250.00 125.00
189 George Merritt ... 200.00 100.00
190 Charles Hanford ... 200.00 100.00
191 Hick Cady ... 200.00 100.00
192 James Frick ... 200.00 100.00
193 Wyatt Lee ... 200.00 100.00
194 Lewis McAllister ... 200.00 100.00
195 John Nee ... 200.00 100.00
196 Jimmy Collins ... 500.00 250.00
197 James Phelan ... 200.00 100.00
198 Emil Batch ... 200.00 100.00

1909 T206

The T206 set was and is the most popular of all the tobacco issues. The set was issued from 1909 to 1911 with sixteen different brands of cigarettes: American Beauty, Broadleaf, Cycle, Carolina Brights, Drum, El Principe de Gales, Hindu, Lenox, Old Mill, Piedmont, Polar Bear, Sovereign, Sweet Caporal, Tolstoi, and Uzit. There was also a Ty Cobb back version that was a promotional issue and is very scarce. Only Cobb appears on cards with Ty Cobb backs. The minor league cards are supposedly slightly more difficult to obtain than the cards of the major leaguers, with the Southern League player cards being the most difficult. Minor League players were obtained from the American Association and the Eastern league. Southern League players were obtained from a variety of leagues including the following: South Atlantic League, Southern League, Texas League, and Virginia League. Series 150 was issued between February 1909 thru the end of May, 1909. Series 350 was issued from the end of May, 1909 thru April, 1910. The last series 350-to-406 was issued in late December 1910 through early 1911. The set price below does not include ultra-expensive Wagner, Plank, Magie error, or Doyle variation. The Wagner card is one of the most sought after cards in the hobby. This card (number 366 in the checklist below) was pulled from circulation almost immediately after being issued. While estimates of how many Wagners are in existence vary, the card is considered by many collectors the ultimate card to own. Perhaps the best conditioned example of this card was sold in a public auction in 1991 for $451,000 to hockey great Wayne Gretzky and Bruce McNall. That same card was later used in a major giveaway sponsored by most of the card companies, Treat products and Wal-Mart. That card sold for more than $640,500 in 1996. The next recorded sale of that Wagner card was for more than $1 million dollars. The backs are scarce in the following order: Exceedingly Rare: Ty Cobb; Rare: Drum, Uzit, Lenox, Broadleaf 460 and Hindu; Scarce: Broadleaf 350, Carolina Brights, Hindu (Red); Less Common: American Beauty, Cycle and Tolstoi; Readily Available: El Principe De Gates, Old Mill, Polar Bear and Soverign and Common: Piedmont and Sweet Caporal.

Ex-Mt VG
COMPLETE SET (520) ... 55000.00 27500.00
COMMON (1-389) ... 60.00 30.00
COMMON (390-475) ... 50.00 25.00
COMMON (476-523) ... 125.00 60.00
1 Ed Abbaticchio: ... 60.00 30.00
Pitt
Batting follow thru
2 Ed Abbaticchio: ... 75.00 38.00
Pitt.
Batting waiting pitch
3 Bill Abstein ... 60.00 30.00
4 Whitey Alperman ... 75.00 38.00
5 Red Ames: N.Y. NL ... 75.00 38.00
Portrait
6 Red Ames: N.Y. NL ... 60.00 30.00
Hands over head
7 Red Ames: N.Y. NL ... 75.00 38.00
Hands in front of chest
8 Frank Arellanes ... 60.00 30.00
9 Jake Atz ... 60.00 30.00
10 Frank Baker ... 400.00 150.00
11 Neal Ball: N.Y. AL ... 75.00 38.00
12 Neal Ball: Cleveland ... 60.00 30.00
13 Jap Barbeau ... 60.00 30.00
14 Jack Barry ... 60.00 30.00
15 Johnny Bates ... 75.00 38.00
16 Ginger Beaumont ... 75.00 38.00
17 Fred Beck ... 60.00 30.00
18 Beals Becker ... 60.00 30.00
19 George Bell: ... 60.00 30.00
Brooklyn
pitching follow thru
20 George Bell: ... 75.00 38.00
Brooklyn
Hands
over head
21 Chief Bender ... 500.00 200.00
Phila. AL
Portrait
22 Chief Bender ... 500.00 250.00
Phila. AL
pitching, trees
23 Chief Bender ... 400.00 200.00
Phila AL
pitching, no trees
24 Bill Bergen: ... 60.00 30.00
Brooklyn
Catching
25 Bill Bergen: ... 75.00 38.00
Brooklyn
Batting
26 Heinie Berger ... 60.00 30.00
27 Bob Bescher: Cinc. ... 60.00 30.00
Catching fly ball
28 Bob Bescher: Cinc. ... 60.00 30.00
Portrait
29 Joe Birmingham ... 75.00 38.00
30 Jack Bliss ... 60.00 30.00
31 Frank Bowerman ... 75.00 38.00
32 Bill Bradley: ... 75.00 38.00
Cleveland
Portrait
33 Bill Bradley: ... 60.00 30.00
Cleveland
Batting
34 Kitty Bransfield ... 75.00 38.00
35 Roger Bresnahan: ... 300.00 125.00
St.L. NL
Portrait
36 Roger Bresnahan: ... 300.00 100.00
St.L. NL
Batting
37 Al Bridwell ... 75.00 38.00
N.Y. NL
Portrait
38 Al Bridwell ... 60.00 30.00
N.Y. NL
Wearing sweater
39 George Brown: ... 125.00 60.00
Chicago NL
Sic, Browne
40 George Brown: ... 400.00 200.00
Washington
Sic, Browne
41 Mordecai Brown: ... 500.00 250.00
Chicago NL
Portrait
42 Mordecai Brown: ... 500.00 250.00
Chicago NL
Chicago down front of shirt
43 Mordecai Brown: ... 500.00 250.00
Chicago NL
Cubs Shirt
44 Al Burch: Brooklyn ... 60.00 30.00
Fielding
45 Al Burch: Brooklyn ... 125.00 60.00
Batting
46 Bill Burns ... 60.00 30.00
47 Donie Bush ... 75.00 38.00
48 Bobby Byrne ... 60.00 30.00
49 Howie Camnitz: ... 75.00 38.00
Pitt
Arms folded over chest

50 Howie Camnitz: 60.00 30.00
Pitt
Hands over head
51 Howie Camnitz: 60.00 30.00
Pitt.
Throwing
52 Billy Campbell 60.00 30.00
53 Bill Carrigan 60.00 30.00
54 Frank Chance: 500.00 200.00
Chicago NL
Cubs across chest
55 Frank Chance: 500.00 200.00
Chicago NL
Chicago down front of shirt
56 Frank Chance: 400.00 150.00
Chicago NL
Batting
57 Chappy Charles 60.00 30.00
58 Hal Chase 125.00 60.00
N.Y. AL
Port. blue bkgd.
59 Hal Chase 200.00 100.00
N.Y. AL
Port., pink bkgd.
60 Hal Chase 125.00 60.00
N.Y. AL
Holding cup
61 Hal Chase 125.00 60.00
N.Y. AL
Throwing, dark cap
62 Hal Chase 150.00 75.00
N.Y. AL
Throwing, white cap
63 Jack Chesbro 250.00 125.00
64 Eddie Cicotte 200.00 100.00
65 Fred Clarke: Pitt. 200.00 100.00
Portrait
66 Fred Clarke: Pitt. 200.00 100.00
67 Nig Clarke 75.00 38.00
68 Ty Cobb: Detroit 2500.00 1250.00
Port., red bkgd.
69 Ty Cobb: Detroit 3500.00 1800.00
Port., green background
70 Ty Cobb: Detroit 2500.00 1250.00
Bat on shoulder
71 Ty Cobb: Detroit 2500.00 1250.00
Bat away from shoulder
72 Eddie Collins: 400.00 150.00
Phila. AL
73 Wid Conroy: 75.00 38.00
Washington
Fielding
74 Wid Conroy 60.00 30.00
Washington
Bat on shoulder
75 Harry Covaleski: 75.00 38.00
Phila. NL
76 Doc Crandall 60.00 30.00
N.Y. NL,
without cap
77 Doc Crandall 60.00 30.00
N.Y. NL
sweater and cap
78 Sam Crawford: 500.00 200.00
Detroit, Batting
79 Sam Crawford: 500.00 200.00
Detroit, Throwing
80 Birdie Cree 60.00 30.00
81 Lou Criger 75.00 38.00
82 Dode Criss 75.00 38.00
83 Bill Dahlen: 125.00 60.00
Boston NL
84 Bill Dahlen: 200.00 100.00
Brooklyn
85 George Davis 200.00 100.00
86 Harry Davis 60.00 30.00
Phila. AL
Davis on card
87 Harry Davis 75.00 38.00
Phila. AL
H.Davis on card
88 Jim Delehanty 75.00 38.00
Sic, Delahanty
89 Ray Demmitt 5000.00 2200.00
St.L. AL
90 Ray Demmitt 75.00 38.00
N.Y. AL
91 Art Devlin 75.00 38.00
92 Josh Devore 60.00 30.00
93 Bill Dineen 60.00 30.00
94 Mike Donlin 125.00 60.00
N.Y. NL
Fielding
95 Mike Donlin 125.00 60.00
N.Y. NL
Sitting
96 Mike Donlin 75.00 38.00
N.Y. NL
Batting
97 Jiggs Donohue 75.00 38.00
98 Bill Donovan: 75.00 38.00
Detroit
Portrait
99 Bill Donovan: 60.00 30.00
Detroit
Throwing
100 Red Dooin 75.00 38.00
101 Mickey Doolan: 60.00 30.00
Phila. NL
Fielding
102 Mickey Doolan: 60.00 30.00
Phila. NL
Batting
103 Mickey Doolin (Sic, 75.00 38.00
Doolan): Phila. NL
104 Patsy Dougherty: 75.00 38.00
Chicago AL
Portrait
105 Patsy Dougherty: 60.00 30.00
Chicago AL
Fielding
106 Tom Downey: Cinc. 60.00 30.00
Batting
107 Tom Downey: Cinc. 60.00 30.00
Fielding
108A Joe Doyle: N.Y. 125.00 60.00
Hands over head
108B Joe Doyle: N.Y. 60000.00 30000.00
NAT'L
hands
over head)
109 Larry Doyle: N.Y. 75.00 38.00
NL
Sweater
110 Larry Doyle: N.Y. 125.00 60.00
NL
Throwing
111 Larry Doyle: N.Y. 75.00 38.00
NL
Bat on shoulder
112 Jean Dubuc 60.00 30.00
113 Hugh Duffy 400.00 150.00
114 Joe Dunn 60.00 30.00
115 Bull Durham 75.00 38.00
116 Jimmy Dygert 60.00 30.00
117 Ted Easterly 60.00 30.00
118 Dick Egan 60.00 30.00
119 Kid Elberfeld 60.00 30.00
Wash.
Fielding
120 Kid Elberfeld 1000.00 500.00
Wash.
Portrait
121 Kid Elberfeld 75.00 38.00
N.Y. AL
Portrait
122 Clyde Engle 60.00 30.00
123 Steve Evans 60.00 30.00
124 Johnny Evers: 600.00 250.00
Chicago NL
Portrait
125 Johnny Evers: 500.00 150.00
Chicago NL
Cubs across chest
126 Johnny Evers: 500.00 150.00
Chicago NL
Chicago down front of shirt
127 Bob Ewing 75.00 38.00
128 George Ferguson 60.00 30.00
129 Hobe Ferris 75.00 38.00
130 Lou Fiene 60.00 30.00
Chicago AL
Portrait
131 Lou Fiene 60.00 30.00
Chicago AL
Throwing
132 Art Fletcher 60.00 30.00
133 Elmer Flick 300.00 150.00
134 Russ Ford 60.00 30.00
135 John Frill 60.00 30.00
136 Art Fromme 60.00 30.00
137 Chick Gandil 250.00 125.00
138 Bob Ganley 75.00 38.00
139 Harry Gasper 60.00 30.00
140 Rube Geyer 60.00 30.00
141 George Gibson 75.00 38.00
142 Billy Gilbert 75.00 38.00
143 Wilbur Goode 75.00 38.00
Sic, Good
144 Bill Graham 60.00 30.00
145 Peaches Graham 60.00 30.00
146 Dolly Gray 75.00 38.00
147 Clark Griffith: 250.00 125.00
Cinc.
Portrait
148 Clark Griffith: 250.00 125.00
Cinc.
Batting
149 Bob Groom 60.00 30.00
150 Ed Hahn 75.00 38.00
151 Topsy Hartsel 60.00 30.00
152 Charlie Hemphill 75.00 38.00
153 Buck Herzog 75.00 38.00
N.Y. NL
154 Buck Herzog 60.00 30.00
Boston NL
155 Bill Hinchman 75.00 38.00
156 Doc Hoblitzell 60.00 30.00
157 Danny Hoffman 60.00 30.00
158 Solly Hofman 60.00 30.00
159 Del Howard 60.00 30.00
160 Harry Howell 60.00 30.00
St.L. AL
Portrait
161 Harry Howell 60.00 30.00
St.L. AL
Left hand on hip
162 Miller Huggins: 400.00 200.00
Cinc.
Portrait
163 Miller Huggins: 400.00 200.00
Cinc.
Hands to Mouth
164 Rudy Hulswitt 60.00 30.00
165 John Hummel 60.00 30.00
166 George Hunter 60.00 30.00
167 Frank Isbell 75.00 38.00
168 Fred Jacklitsch 75.00 38.00
169 Hughie Jennings MG: 400.00 200.00
Detroit
Portrait
170 Hughie Jennings MG: 400.00 200.00
Detroit
One
171 Hughie Jennings MG: 400.00 200.00
Detroit
Both
172 Walter Johnson: 1500.00 750.00
Washington
Portrait
173 Walter Johnson: 1200.00 600.00
Washington
Hands at Chest
174 Davy Jones 60.00 30.00
175 Fielder Jones: 75.00 38.00
Chic. AL
Portrait
176 Fielder Jones 75.00 38.00
Chic AL
Hands on hips
177 Tom Jones 75.00 38.00
178 Tim Jordan: 75.00 38.00
Brooklyn
Portrait
179 Tim Jordan: 60.00 30.00
Brooklyn
Batting
180 Addie Joss: 600.00 250.00
Cleveland
Portrait
181 Addie Joss: 500.00 200.00
Cleveland
Ready to pitch
182 Ed Karger 75.00 38.00
183 Willie Keeler 600.00 250.00
N.Y. AL
Portrait
184 Willie Keeler 500.00 200.00
N.Y. AL
Batting
185 Ed Killian: Detroit 75.00 38.00
Portrait
186 Ed Killian: Detroit 60.00 30.00
Pitching
187 Red Kleinow 75.00 38.00
N.Y. AL
Batting
188 Red Kleinow 60.00 30.00
N.Y. AL
Catching
189 Red Kleinow 1000.00 400.00
Boston AL
Catching
190 Johnny Kling: 75.00 38.00
Chicago NL
191 Otto Knabe 60.00 30.00
192 John Knight 60.00 30.00
N.Y. AL
Portrait
193 John Knight 60.00 30.00
N.Y. AL
Batting
194 Ed Konetchy 60.00 30.00
St.L. NL
Awaiting low ball
195 Ed Konetchy 75.00 38.00
St.L. NL
Glove above head
196 Harry Krause 60.00 30.00
Phila. AL
Portrait
197 Harry Krause 60.00 30.00
Phila. AL
Pitching
198 Rube Kroh 60.00 30.00
199 Nap Lajoie: 800.00 400.00
Cleveland
Portrait
200 Nap Lajoie: 600.00 300.00
Cleveland
Batting
201 Nap Lajoie: 600.00 300.00
Cleveland
Throwing
202 Joe Lake 75.00 38.00
N.Y. AL
203 Joe Lake 60.00 30.00
St.L. AL
Hands over head
204 Joe Lake 60.00 30.00
St.L. AL
Throwing
205 Frank LaPorte 60.00 30.00
206 Arlie Latham 75.00 38.00
207 Tommy Leach: Pitt. 75.00 38.00
Portrait
208 Tommy Leach: Pitt. 60.00 30.00
In fielding position
209 Lefty Leifield: 60.00 30.00
Pitt.
Batting
210 Lefty Leifield: 75.00 38.00
Pitt.
Hands behind head
211 Ed Lennox 60.00 30.00
212 Glenn Liebhardt 75.00 38.00
213 Vive Lindaman 125.00 60.00
214 Paddy Livingstone 60.00 30.00
215 Hans Lobert 75.00 38.00
216 Harry Lord 60.00 30.00
217 Harry Lumley 75.00 38.00
218 Carl Lundgren 300.00 150.00
219 Nick Maddox 60.00 30.00
220 Sherry Magee 125.00 60.00
Phila. NL
Portrait
221 Sherry Magee 60.00 30.00
Phila. NL
Batting
222 Sherry Magie 15000.00 7500.00
Phila. NL
Sic, Magee
Portrait,
name misspelled
223 Rube Manning 75.00 38.00
N.Y. AL
Batting
224 Rube Manning 60.00 30.00
N.Y. AL
Hands over head
225 Rube Marquard 500.00 200.00
N.Y. NL
Portrait
226 Rube Marquard 400.00 150.00
N.Y. NL
Pitching
227 Rube Marquard 400.00 150.00
N.Y. NL
Standing
228 Doc Marshall 60.00 30.00
229 Christy Mathewson: 2000.00 750.00
N.Y. NL
Portrait
230 Christy Mathewson: 1500.00 600.00
N.Y. NL
Pitching, white cap
231 Christy Mathewson: 1500.00 600.00
N.Y. NL
Pitching, dark cap
232 Al Mattern 60.00 30.00
233 Jack McAleese 60.00 30.00
234 George McBride 60.00 30.00
235 Moose McCormick 60.00 30.00
236 Pryor McElveen 60.00 30.00
237 John McGraw 500.00 200.00
N.Y. NL
Portrait, no cap
238 John McGraw 500.00 200.00
N.Y. NL
w/Cap
239 John McGraw 500.00 200.00
N.Y. NL
Finger
240 John McGraw 500.00 200.00
N.Y. NL
Glove on hip
241 Matty McIntyre: 75.00 38.00
Brooklyn
242 Matty McIntyre: 60.00 30.00
Brooklyn and
Chicago NL
243 Mike McIntyre: 60.00 30.00
Detroit
244 Larry McLean 60.00 30.00
245 George McQuillan: 75.00 38.00
Phila. NL
Throwing
246 George McQuillan: 60.00 30.00
Phila. NL
Batting
247 Fred Merkle 125.00 60.00
N.Y. NL
Portrait
248 Fred Merkle 125.00 60.00
N.Y. NL
Throwing
249 Chief Meyers 60.00 30.00
250 Chief Meyers 60.00 30.00
Sic, Myers)
N.Y. NL
Fielding
251 Chief Meyers 75.00 38.00
Sic, Myers)
N.Y. NL
Batting
252 Clyde Milan 60.00 30.00
253 Dots Miller 60.00 30.00
254 Mike Mitchell 60.00 30.00
255 Pat Moran 60.00 30.00
256 George Moriarty 60.00 30.00
257 Mike Mowrey 60.00 30.00
258 George Mullin: 60.00 30.00
Detroit
Sic, Mullen
259 George Mullin: 75.00 38.00
Detroit
Throwing
260 George Mullin: 60.00 30.00
Detroit
Batting
261 Danny Murphy 75.00 38.00
Phila. AL
Throwing
262 Danny Murphy 60.00 30.00
Phila. AL
Bat on shoulder
263 Red Murray 60.00 30.00
N.Y. NL
Sweater
264 Red Murray 60.00 30.00
N.Y. NL
Bat on shoulder
265 Tom Needham 60.00 30.00
266 Simon Nicholls 75.00 38.00
Phila AL
267 Simon Nicholls 60.00 30.00
Sic, Nichols:
Phila. AL
268 Harry Niles 75.00 38.00
269 Rebel Oakes 60.00 30.00
270 Bill O'Hara: N.Y. NL 60.00 30.00
271 Bill O'Hara: 5000.00 2500.00
St. Louis NL
272 Rube Oldring 75.00 38.00
Phila. AL
Fielding
273 Rube Oldring 75.00 38.00
Phila. AL
Bat on shoulder
274 Charley O'Leary: 75.00 38.00
Detroit
Portrait
275 Charley O'Leary: 60.00 30.00
Detroit
Hands on knees
276 Orval Overall: 75.00 38.00
Chicago NL
Portrait
277 Orval Overall: 60.00 30.00
Chicago NL
Pitching follow thru
278 Orval Overall: 60.00 30.00
Chicago NL,
Pitching hiding
ball in glove
279 Frank Owen 75.00 38.00
Chicago AL
Sic, Owens)
280 Freddy Parent 75.00 38.00
281 Dode Paskert 60.00 30.00
282 Jim Pastorius 75.00 38.00
283 Harry Pattee 150.00 75.00
284 Fred Payne 60.00 30.00
285 Barney Pelty 125.00 60.00
St.L. AL
HOR
286 Barney Pelty 60.00 30.00
St.L. AL
VERT
287 George Perring 60.00 30.00
288 Jeff Pfeffer 60.00 30.00
289 Jack Pfeister 60.00 30.00
Chic. NL
Sitting
290 Jack Pfeister 60.00 30.00
Chic. NL
Pitching
291 Ed Phelps 60.00 30.00
292 Deacon Phillippe. 125.00 60.00
293 Eddie Plank 30000.00 15000.00
294 Jack Powell 75.00 38.00
295 Mike Powers 125.00 60.00
296 Billy Purtell 60.00 30.00
297 Jack Quinn 60.00 30.00
298 Bugs Raymond 75.00 38.00
299 Ed Reulbach 125.00 60.00
Chicago NL
Pitching
300 Ed Reulbach 125.00 60.00
Chicago NL
Hands at side
301 Bob Rhoades 60.00 30.00
sic,Rhoads
Cleveland
Hand in air
302 Bob Rhoades 60.00 30.00
sic, Rhoads
Cleveland
Ready to pitch
303 Charlie Rhodes 60.00 30.00
304 Claude Ritchey 75.00 38.00
305 Claude Rossman 60.00 30.00
306 Nap Rucker: 125.00 60.00
Brooklyn
Portrait
307 Nap Rucker: 75.00 38.00
Brooklyn
Pitching
308 Germany Schaefer: 75.00 38.00
Washington
309 Germany Schaefer: 75.00 38.00
Detroit
310 Admiral Schlei 60.00 30.00
N.Y. NL
Sweater
311 Admiral Schlei 60.00 30.00
N.Y. NL
Batting
312 Admiral Schlei 75.00 38.00
N.Y. NL
Fielding
313 Boss Schmidt: 60.00 30.00
Detroit
Portrait
314 Boss Schmidt: 75.00 38.00
Detroit
Throwing
315 Frank Schulte: 60.00 30.00
Chicago NL
Batting, back turned
316 Frank Schulte: 75.00 38.00
Chicago NL
Batting, front pose
317 Jim Scott 60.00 30.00
318 Cy Seymour 60.00 30.00
N.Y. NL
Portrait
319 Cy Seymour 60.00 30.00
N.Y. NL
Throwing
320 Cy Seymour 75.00 38.00
N.Y. NL
Batting
321 Al Shaw 75.00 38.00
322 Jimmy Sheckard: 60.00 30.00
Chicago NL
Throwing
323 Jimmy Sheckard: 75.00 38.00
Chicago NL
Side view
324 Bill Shipke 75.00 38.00
325 Frank Smith 60.00 30.00
Chicago AL
Listed as Smith
326 Frank Smith 400.00 200.00
Chicago and Boston AL
327 Frank Smith 75.00 38.00
Chicago AL
Listed as F.Smith
328 Happy Smith 60.00 30.00
329 Fred Snodgrass 75.00 38.00
N.Y. NL
Batting
329A Fred Snodgrass 3000.00 1500.00
N.Y., Battting
Card spelled Nodgrass
Due to a printing glitch
330 Fred Snodgrass 75.00 38.00
N.Y. NL
Catching
331 Bob Spade 75.00 38.00
332 Tris Speaker 1000.00 400.00
333 Tubby Spencer 75.00 38.00
334 Jake Stahl: 75.00 38.00
Boston AL
Catching fly ball
335 Jake Stahl: 75.00 38.00
Boston AL
Standing, arms down
336 Oscar Stanage 60.00 30.00
337 Charlie Starr 60.00 30.00
338 Harry Steinfeldt: 125.00 60.00
Chicago NL
Portrait
339 Harry Steinfeldt: 75.00 38.00
Chicago NL
Batting
340 Jim Stephens 60.00 30.00
341 George Stone 75.00 38.00
342 George Stovall: 75.00 38.00
Cleveland
Portrait
343 George Stovall: 60.00 30.00
Cleveland
Batting
344 Gabby Street: 75.00 38.00
Washington
Portrait
345 Gabby Street: 60.00 30.00
Washington
Catching
346 Billy Sullivan 75.00 38.00
347 Ed Summers 60.00 30.00
348 Jeff Sweeney 60.00 30.00
349 Bill Sweeney 60.00 30.00
350 Jesse Tannehill 60.00 30.00
351 Lee Tannehill: 75.00 38.00
Chicago AL
Listed as L.Tannehill
352 Lee Tannehill: 60.00 30.00
Chicago AL
Listed as Tannehill
353 Fred Tenney 75.00 38.00
354 Ira Thomas 60.00 30.00
355 Joe Tinker 600.00 300.00
Chicago NL
Bat Off Shoulder
356 Joe Tinker 600.00 300.00
Chicago NL
Bat on Shoulder

357 Joe Tinker 800.00 300.00
Chicago NL
Portrait
358 Joe Tinker 600.00 300.00
Chicago NL
Hands on knees
359 John Titus 60.00 30.00
360 Terry Turner 75.00 38.00
361 Bob Unglaub 60.00 30.00
362 Rube Waddell 600.00 250.00
St.L. AL
Portrait
363 Rube Waddell 500.00 200.00
St.L. AL
Pitching
364 Heinie Wagner: 125.00 60.00
Boston AL
Bat on left shoulder
365 Heinie Wagner: 75.00 38.00
Boston AL
Bat on right shoulder
366 Honus Wagner 400000.00 200000.00
367 Bobby Wallace 400.00 150.00
368 Ed Walsh 600.00 250.00
369 Jack Warhop: N.Y. AL 60.00 30.00
370 Jake Weimer: N.Y. NL 75.00 38.00
371 Zach Wheat 300.00 150.00
372 Doc White 75.00 38.00
Chicago AL
Portrait
373 Doc White 60.00 30.00
Chicago AL
Pitching
374 Kaiser Wilhelm: 60.00 30.00
Brooklyn
Batting
375 Kaiser Wilhelm: 75.00 38.00
Brooklyn
Hands to chest
376 Ed Willett: Detroit 60.00 30.00
Batting
377 Ed Willett 60.00 30.00
Sic, Willetts
Detroit
Pitching
378 Jimmy Williams 75.00 38.00
379 Vic Willis: Pitt. 250.00 125.00
380 Vic Willis 200.00 100.00
St.L. NL
Pitching
381 Vic Willis 200.00 100.00
St.L. NL
Batting
382 Chief Wilson 60.00 30.00
383 Hooks Wiltse 75.00 38.00
N.Y. NL
Portrait
384 Hooks Wiltse 60.00 30.00
N.Y.NL
Sweater
385 Hooks Wiltse 60.00 30.00
N.Y. NL
Pitching
386 Cy Young 2000.00 600.00
Cleveland
Portrait
387 Cy Young 1500.00 500.00
Cleveland
Pitch, front view
388 Cy Young 1500.00 500.00
Cleveland
Pitch, side view
389 Heinie Zimmerman: 60.00 30.00
390 Fred Abbott 50.00 25.00
391 Merle(Doc) Adkins 50.00 25.00
392 John Anderson 50.00 25.00
393 Herman Armbruster 50.00 25.00
394 Harry Arndt 50.00 25.00
395 Cy Barger 60.00 30.00
396 John Barry 50.00 25.00
397 Emil H. Batch 50.00 25.00
398 Jake Beckley 250.00 125.00
399 Lena Blackburne 75.00 38.00
400 David Brain 50.00 25.00
401 Roy Brashear 50.00 25.00
402 Fred Burchell 50.00 25.00
403 Jimmy Burke 50.00 25.00
404 John Butler 50.00 25.00
405 Charles Carr 50.00 25.00
406 Doc Casey 50.00 25.00
407 Peter Cassidy 50.00 25.00
408 Wm. Chappelle 60.00 30.00
409 Wm. Clancy 50.00 25.00
410 Joshua Clarke 50.00 25.00
Sic, Clark
411 William Clymer 50.00 25.00
412 Jimmy Collins 400.00 200.00
413 Bunk Congalton 50.00 25.00
414 Gavvy Cravath 125.00 60.00
415 Monte Cross 60.00 30.00
416 Paul Davidson 50.00 25.00
417 Frank Delehanty 75.00 38.00
Sic, Delahanty
418 Rube Dessau 50.00 25.00
419 Gus Dorner 50.00 25.00
420 Jerome Downs 50.00 25.00
421 Jack Dunn 75.00 38.00
422 James Flanagan 50.00 25.00
423 James Freeman 50.00 25.00
424 John Ganzel 50.00 25.00
425 Myron Grimshaw 50.00 25.00
426 Robert Hall 50.00 25.00
427 William Hallman 60.00 30.00
428 John Hannifan 50.00 25.00
429 Jack Hayden 50.00 25.00
430 Harry Hinchman 50.00 25.00
431 Harry C. Hoffman 50.00 25.00
432 James B. Jackson 60.00 30.00
433 Joe Kelley 250.00 125.00
434 Rube Kissinger 60.00 30.00
Sic, Kisinger
435 Otto Krueger 50.00 25.00
Sic, Kruger
436 Wm. Lattimore 50.00 25.00
437 James Lavender 50.00 25.00
438 Carl Lundgren 50.00 25.00
439 Wm. Malarkey 60.00 30.00
440 Wm. Maloney 50.00 25.00
441 Dennis McGann 50.00 25.00
442 James McGinley 50.00 25.00
443 Joe McGinnity 250.00 125.00
444 Ulysses McGlynn 50.00 25.00
445 George Merritt 50.00 25.00
446 Wm. Milligan 50.00 25.00
447 Fred Mitchell 50.00 25.00
448 Dan Moeller 50.00 25.00
449 Joseph H. Moran 50.00 25.00
450 Wm. Nattress 50.00 25.00
451 Frank Oberlin 50.00 25.00
452 Peter O'Brien 50.00 25.00
453 Wm. O'Neil 50.00 25.00
454 James Phelan 50.00 25.00
455 Oliver Pickering 50.00 25.00
456 Philip Poland 50.00 25.00
457 Ambrose Puttman 50.00 25.00
458 Lee Quillen 50.00 25.00
459 Newton Randall 50.00 25.00
460 Louis Ritter 50.00 25.00
461 Dick Rudolph 50.00 25.00
462 George Schirm 50.00 25.00
463 Larry Schlafly 50.00 25.00
464 Ossie Schreckengost 60.00 30.00
Sic Schreck
465 William Shannon 50.00 25.00
466 Bayard Sharpe 50.00 25.00
466A Bayard Sharpe 500.00 250.00
Name is spelled Shappe on front
467 Royal Shaw 50.00 25.00
468 James Slagle 50.00 25.00
469 George Henry Smith 50.00 25.00
470 Samuel Strang 50.00 25.00
471 Dummy Taylor 125.00 60.00
472 John Thielman 50.00 25.00
473 John F. White 50.00 25.00
474 William Wright 50.00 25.00
475 Irving M. Young 60.00 30.00
476 Jack Bastian 125.00 60.00
477 Harry Bay 125.00 60.00
478 Wm. Bernhard 125.00 60.00
479 Ted Breitenstein 125.00 60.00
480 Scoops Carey 125.00 60.00
481 Cad Coles 125.00 60.00
482 Wm. Cranston 125.00 60.00
483 Roy Ellam 125.00 60.00
484 Edward Foster 125.00 60.00
485 Charles Fritz 125.00 60.00
486 Ed Greminger 125.00 60.00
487 Guiheen 125.00 60.00
488 William F. Hart 125.00 60.00
489 James Henry Hart 125.00 60.00
490 J.R. Helm 125.00 60.00
491 Gordon Hickman 125.00 60.00
492 Buck Hooker 125.00 60.00
493 Ernie Howard 125.00 60.00
494 A.O. Jordan 125.00 60.00
495 J.F. Kiernan 125.00 60.00
496 Frank King 125.00 60.00
497 James LaFitte 125.00 60.00
498 Harry Sentz 125.00 60.00
Sic, Lentz
499 Perry Lipe 125.00 60.00
500 George Manion 125.00 60.00
501 McCauley 125.00 60.00
502 Charles B. Miller 125.00 60.00
503 Carlton Molesworth 125.00 60.00
504 Dominic Mullaney 125.00 60.00
505 Albert Orth 125.00 60.00
506 William Otey 125.00 60.00
507 George Paige 125.00 60.00
508 Hub Perdue 150.00 75.00
509 Archie Persons 125.00 60.00
510 Edward Reagan 125.00 60.00
511 R.H. Revelle 125.00 60.00
512 Isaac Rockenfeld 125.00 60.00
513 Ray Ryan 125.00 60.00
514 Charles Seitz 125.00 60.00
515 Frank "Shag" Shaughnessy 150.00 75.00
516 Carlos Smith 125.00 60.00
517 Sid Smith 125.00 60.00
518 Dolly Stark 150.00 75.00
519 Tony Thebo 125.00 60.00
520 Woodie Thornton 125.00 60.00
521 Juan Viola 125.00 60.00
Sic, Violat
522 James Westlake 125.00 60.00
523 Foley White 125.00 60.00

2004 Throwback Threads

This 250-card set was released in August, 2004. The set was issued in five-card packs with an $4 SRP which came 24 packs to a box and 20 boxes to a case. Cards numbered 1-200 feature active veterans while cards numbered 201 through 224 feature retired players and cards 225 through 250 feature a mix of Rookie Cards and leading prospects. All cards numbered 201 through 250 were random inserts in packs and were issued to a stated print run of 1000 serial numbered sets.

Nm-Mt Ex-Mt
COMP.SET w/o SP's (200) 40.00 12.00
COMMON CARD (1-200) .... .30 .09
COMMON RETIRED (201-224) .... 2.00 .60
COMMON ROOKIE (225-250) .... 3.00 .90
1 Bartolo Colon .... .30 .09
2 Darin Erstad .... .30 .09
3 David Eckstein .... .30 .09
4 Garret Anderson .... .30 .09
5 Tim Salmon .... .50 .15
6 Troy Glaus .... .30 .09
7 Vladimir Guerrero .... .75 .23
8 Brandon Webb .... .30 .09
9 Luis Gonzalez .... .30 .09
10 Randy Johnson .... .75 .23
11 Richie Sexson .... .30 .09
12 Roberto Alomar .... .50 .15
13 Shea Hillenbrand .... .30 .09
14 Steve Finley .... .30 .09
15 Adam LaRoche .... .30 .09
16 Andruw Jones .... .30 .09
17 Chipper Jones .... .75 .23
18 J.D. Drew .... .30 .09
19 John Smoltz .... .50 .15
20 Rafael Furcal .... .30 .09
21 Russ Ortiz .... .30 .09
22 Javy Lopez .... .30 .09
23 Jay Gibbons .... .30 .09
24 Larry Bigbie .... .30 .09
25 Luis Matos .... .30 .09
26 Melvin Mora .... .30 .09
27 Miguel Tejada .... .30 .09
28 Rafael Palmeiro .... .50 .15
29 Curt Schilling .... .75 .23
30 David Ortiz .... .75 .23
31 Derek Lowe .... .30 .09
32 Jason Varitek .... .50 .15
33 Johnny Damon .... .75 .23
34 Manny Ramirez .... .50 .15
35 Nomar Garciaparra .... 1.25 .35
36 Pedro Martinez .... .75 .23
37 Trot Nixon .... .30 .09
38 Aramis Ramirez .... .30 .09
39 Corey Patterson .... .30 .09
40 Derrek Lee .... .30 .09
41 Greg Maddux .... 1.25 .35
42 Kerry Wood .... .75 .23
43 Mark Prior .... .75 .23
44 Sammy Sosa .... 1.25 .35
45 Carlos Lee .... .30 .09
46 Esteban Loaiza .... .30 .09
47 Frank Thomas .... .75 .23
48 Joe Borchard .... .30 .09
49 Magglio Ordonez .... .30 .09
50 Mark Buehrle .... .30 .09
51 Paul Konerko .... .30 .09
52 Adam Dunn .... .50 .15
53 Austin Kearns .... .30 .09
54 Barry Larkin .... .50 .15
55 Brandon Larson .... .30 .09
56 Ken Griffey Jr. .... 1.25 .35
57 Ryan Wagner .... .30 .09
58 Sean Casey .... .30 .09
59 C.C. Sabathia .... .30 .09
60 Jody Gerut .... .30 .09
61 Omar Vizquel .... .50 .15
62 Travis Hafner .... .30 .09
63 Victor Martinez .... .30 .09
64 Charles Johnson .... .30 .09
65 Garrett Atkins .... .30 .09
66 Jason Jennings .... .30 .09
67 Joe Kennedy .... .30 .09
68 Larry Walker .... .50 .15
69 Preston Wilson .... .30 .09
70 Todd Helton .... .50 .15
71 Ivan Rodriguez .... .75 .23
72 Jeremy Bonderman .... .30 .09
73 A.J. Burnett .... .30 .09
74 Brad Penny .... .30 .09
75 Dontrelle Willis .... .30 .09
76 Josh Beckett .... .30 .09
77 Juan Pierre .... .30 .09
78 Luis Castillo .... .30 .09
79 Miguel Cabrera .... .50 .15
80 Mike Lowell .... .30 .09
81 Andy Pettitte .... .50 .15
82 Craig Biggio .... .50 .15
83 Jeff Bagwell .... .50 .15
84 Jeff Kent .... .30 .09
85 Lance Berkman .... .30 .09
86 Morgan Ensberg .... .30 .09
87 Richard Hidalgo .... .30 .09
88 Roger Clemens .... 1.50 .45
89 Roy Oswalt .... .30 .09
90 Wade Miller .... .30 .09
91 Angel Berroa .... .30 .09
92 Carlos Beltran .... .50 .15
93 Juan Gonzalez .... .50 .15
94 Ken Harvey .... .30 .09
95 Mike Sweeney .... .30 .09
96 Runelvys Hernandez .... .30 .09
97 Adrian Beltre .... .50 .15
98 Edwin Jackson .... .30 .09
99 Eric Gagne .... .75 .23
100 Hideo Nomo .... .75 .23
101 Hong-Chih Kuo .... .30 .09
102 Kazuhisa Ishii .... .30 .09
103 Paul Lo Duca .... .30 .09
104 Shawn Green .... .30 .09
105 Ben Sheets .... .30 .09
106 Geoff Jenkins .... .30 .09
107 Junior Spivey .... .30 .09
108 Rickie Weeks .... .30 .09
109 Scott Podsednik .... .30 .09
110 Corey Koskie .... .30 .09
111 Doug Mientkiewicz .... .30 .09
112 Jacque Jones .... .30 .09
113 Joe Mays .... .30 .09
114 Johan Santana .... .50 .15
115 Shannon Stewart .... .30 .09
116 Torii Hunter .... .30 .09
117 Brad Wilkerson .... .30 .09
118 Carl Everett .... .30 .09
119 Chad Cordero .... .30 .09
120 Jose Vidro .... .30 .09
121 Nick Johnson .... .30 .09
122 Orlando Cabrera .... .30 .09
123 Al Leiter .... .30 .09
124 Cliff Floyd .... .30 .09
125 Jae Weong Seo .... .30 .09
126 Jose Reyes .... .30 .09
127 Mike Cameron .... .30 .09
128 Mike Piazza .... 1.25 .35
129 Tom Glavine .... .50 .15
130 Alex Rodriguez .... 1.25 .35
131 Bernie Williams .... .50 .15
132 Chien-Ming Wang .... .30 .09
133 Derek Jeter .... 1.50 .45
134 Gary Sheffield .... .30 .09
135 Hideki Matsui .... 1.25 .35
136 Jason Giambi .... .30 .09
137 Javier Vazquez .... .30 .09
138 Jorge Posada .... .50 .15
139 Jose Contreras .... .30 .09
140 Kevin Brown .... .30 .09
141 Mariano Rivera .... .50 .15
142 Mike Mussina .... .50 .15
143 Barry Zito .... .30 .09
144 Bobby Crosby .... .50 .15
145 Eric Chavez .... .30 .09
146 Erubiel Durazo .... .30 .09
147 Jermaine Dye .... .30 .09
148 Mark Kotsay .... .30 .09
149 Mark Mulder .... .30 .09
150 Rich Harden .... .30 .09
151 Tim Hudson .... .30 .09
152 Billy Wagner .... .30 .09
153 Bobby Abreu .... .30 .09
154 Brett Myers .... .30 .09
155 Jim Thome .... .75 .23
156 Jimmy Rollins .... .30 .09
157 Kevin Millwood .... .30 .09
158 Marlon Byrd .... .30 .09
159 Pat Burrell .... .30 .09
160 Jason Bay .... .30 .09
161 Jason Kendall .... .30 .09
162 Brian Giles .... .30 .09
163 Jay Payton .... .30 .09
164 Ryan Klesko .... .30 .09
165 Edgardo Alfonzo .... .30 .09
166 Jason Schmidt .... .30 .09
167 Jerome Williams .... .30 .09
168 Todd Linden .... .30 .09
169 Bret Boone .... .30 .09
170 Edgar Martinez .... .50 .15
171 Freddy Garcia .... .30 .09
172 Ichiro Suzuki .... 1.25 .35
173 Jamie Moyer .... .30 .09
174 John Olerud .... .30 .09
175 Shigetoshi Hasegawa .... .30 .09
176 Albert Pujols .... 1.50 .45
177 Dan Haren .... .30 .09
178 Edgar Renteria .... .30 .09
179 Jim Edmonds .... .30 .09
180 Matt Morris .... .30 .09
181 Scott Rolen .... .75 .23
182 Aubrey Huff .... .30 .09
183 Carl Crawford .... .30 .09
184 Chad Gaudin .... .30 .09
185 Delmon Young .... .50 .15
186 Dewon Brazelton .... .30 .09
187 Fred McGriff .... .50 .15
188 Rocco Baldelli .... .30 .09
189 Alfonso Soriano .... .50 .15
190 Hank Blalock .... .30 .09
191 Laynce Nix .... .30 .09
192 Mark Teixeira .... .30 .09
193 Michael Young .... .30 .09
194 Carlos Delgado .... .30 .09
195 Eric Hinske .... .30 .09
196 Frank Catalanotto .... .30 .09
197 Josh Phelps .... .30 .09
198 Orlando Hudson .... .30 .09
199 Roy Halladay .... .30 .09
200 Vernon Wells .... .30 .09
201 Dale Murphy RET .... 3.00 .90
202 Cal Ripken RET 12.00 3.60
203 Fred Lynn RET .... 2.00 .60
204 Wade Boggs RET .... 3.00 .90
205 Nolan Ryan RET 8.00 2.40
206 Rod Carew RET .... 3.00 .90
207 Andre Dawson RET .... 2.00 .60
208 Ernie Banks RET .... 3.00 .90
209 Ryne Sandberg RET 6.00 1.80
210 Bo Jackson RET .... 3.00 .90
211 Carlton Fisk RET .... 3.00 .90
212 Dave Concepcion RET .... 2.00 .60
213 Alan Trammell RET .... 2.00 .60
214 George Brett RET 6.00 1.80
215 Robin Yount RET 5.00 1.50
216 Gary Carter RET .... 2.00 .60
217 Darryl Strawberry RET .... 2.00 .60
218 Dwight Gooden RET .... 2.00 .60
219 Babe Ruth RET 6.00 1.80
220 Don Mattingly RET 6.00 1.80
221 Reggie Jackson RET .... 3.00 .90
222 Mike Schmidt RET 6.00 1.80
223 Tony Gwynn RET 5.00 1.50
224 Keith Hernandez RET .... 2.00 .60
225 Hector Gimenez ROO RC .... 3.00 .90
226 Graham Koonce ROO .... 3.00 .90
227 John Gall ROO RC 5.00 1.50
228 Jerry Gil ROO RC .... 3.00 .90
229 Jason Frasor ROO RC .... 3.00 .90
230 Justin Knoedler ROO RC .... 3.00 .90
231 Ivan Ochoa ROO RC .... 3.00 .90
232 Greg Dobbs ROO RC .... 3.00 .90
233 Ronald Belisario ROO RC .... 3.00 .90
234 Jerome Gamble ROO RC .... 3.00 .90
235 Roberto Novoa ROO RC .... 3.00 .90
236 Sean Henn ROO RC .... 3.00 .90
237 Willy Taveras ROO RC 5.00 1.50
238 Ramon Ramirez ROO RC .... 3.00 .90
239 Kazuo Matsui ROO RC 8.00 2.40
240 Akinori Otsuka ROO RC .... 3.00 .90
241 Jason Bartlett ROO RC 5.00 1.50
242 Fernando Nieve ROO RC .... 3.00 .90
243 Freddy Guzman ROO RC .... 3.00 .90
244 Aarom Baldiris ROO RC 5.00 1.50
245 Merkin Valdez ROO RC 5.00 1.50
246 Mike Gosling ROO RC .... 3.00 .90
247 Shingo Takatsu ROO RC 5.00 1.50
248 William Bergolla ROO RC .... 3.00 .90
249 Shawn Hill ROO RC .... 3.00 .90
250 Justin Germano ROO RC .... 3.00 .90

2004 Throwback Threads Gold Proof

Nm-Mt Ex-Mt
*GOLD 1-200: 4X TO 10X BASIC........
*GOLD 201-224: 1.25X TO 3X BASIC.
*GOLD 225-250: .6X TO 1.5X BASIC..
RANDOM INSERTS IN PACKS ....
STATED PRINT RUN 100 SERIAL #'d SETS

2004 Throwback Threads Green Proof

Nm-Mt Ex-Mt
*GREEN 1-200: 8X TO 20X BASIC......
*GREEN 201-224: 2.5X TO 6X BASIC.
RANDOM INSERTS IN RETAIL PACKS
STATED PRINT RUN 25 SERIAL #'d SETS
NO PRICING ON 225-250 DUE TO SCARCITY

2004 Throwback Threads Platinum Proof

Nm-Mt Ex-Mt
RANDOM INSERTS IN PACKS ....
STATED PRINT RUN 10 SERIAL #'d SETS
NO PRICING DUE TO SCARCITY ....

2004 Throwback Threads Silver Proof

Nm-Mt Ex-Mt
*SILVER 1-200: 4X TO 10X BASIC .....
*SILVER 201-224: 1.25X TO 3X BASIC
*SILVER 225-250: .6X TO 1.5X BASIC
RANDOM INSERTS IN RETAIL PACKS
STATED PRINT RUN 100 SERIAL #'d SETS

2004 Throwback Threads Material

Nm-Mt Ex-Mt
OVERALL AU-GU ODDS 1:8........
PRINT RUNS B/WN 25-100 COPIES PER
2 Darin Erstad Jsy/100 .... 5.00 1.50
4 Garret Anderson Jsy/100 .... 5.00 1.50
5 Tim Salmon Jsy/100 .... 8.00 2.40
6 Troy Glaus Jsy/100 .... 5.00 1.50
7 Vladimir Guerrero Bat/100 .... 10.00 3.00
8 Brandon Webb Pants/100 .... 5.00 1.50
9 Luis Gonzalez Jsy/100 .... 5.00 1.50
10 Randy Johnson Jsy/100 .... 10.00 3.00
11 Richie Sexson Bat/50 .... 8.00 2.40
12 Roberto Alomar Bat/100 .... 8.00 2.40
14 Steve Finley Jsy/100 .... 5.00 1.50
15 Adam LaRoche Bat/100 .... 5.00 1.50
16 Andruw Jones Jsy/100 .... 5.00 1.50
17 Chipper Jones Jsy/100 .... 10.00 3.00
18 J.D. Drew Bat/100 .... 5.00 1.50
19 John Smoltz Jsy/100 .... 8.00 2.40
20 Rafael Furcal Jsy/100 .... 5.00 1.50
22 Javy Lopez Bat/100 .... 5.00 1.50
23 Jay Gibbons Jsy/100 .... 5.00 1.50
24 Larry Bigbie Jsy/100 .... 5.00 1.50
25 Luis Matos Jsy/100 .... 5.00 1.50
26 Melvin Mora Jsy/100 .... 5.00 1.50
27 Miguel Tejada Bat/100 .... 5.00 1.50
28 Rafael Palmeiro Jsy/100 .... 8.00 2.40
29 Curt Schilling Bat/100 .... 10.00 3.00
30 David Ortiz Bat/100 .... 10.00 3.00
32 Jason Varitek Jsy/100 .... 8.00 2.40
33 Johnny Damon Bat/100 .... 10.00 3.00
34 Manny Ramirez Jsy/100 .... 8.00 2.40
35 Nomar Garciaparra Jsy/100 . 12.00 3.60
36 Pedro Martinez Jsy/100 .... 10.00 3.00
37 Trot Nixon Bat/100 .... 5.00 1.50
38 Aramis Ramirez Jsy/100 .... 5.00 1.50
39 Corey Patterson Pants/100 .... 5.00 1.50
41 Greg Maddux Bat/100 .... 12.00 3.60
42 Kerry Wood Pants/100 .... 10.00 3.00
43 Mark Prior Jsy/100 .... 10.00 3.00
44 Sammy Sosa Jsy/100 .... 12.00 3.60
45 Carlos Lee Jsy/100 .... 5.00 1.50
47 Frank Thomas Pants/100 .... 10.00 3.00
48 Joe Borchard Jsy/100 .... 5.00 1.50
49 Magglio Ordonez Jsy/100 .... 5.00 1.50
50 Mark Buehrle Jsy/100 .... 5.00 1.50
51 Paul Konerko Jsy/100 .... 5.00 1.50
52 Adam Dunn Jsy/100 .... 8.00 2.40
53 Austin Kearns Jsy/100 .... 5.00 1.50
54 Barry Larkin Jsy/100 .... 8.00 2.40
55 Brandon Larson Fld Glv/100 .... 5.00 1.50
58 Sean Casey Jsy/100 .... 5.00 1.50
59 C.C. Sabathia Jsy/100 .... 5.00 1.50
60 Jody Gerut Jsy/100 .... 5.00 1.50
61 Omar Vizquel Jsy/100 .... 8.00 2.40
62 Travis Hafner Jsy/100 .... 5.00 1.50
63 Victor Martinez Bat/100 .... 5.00 1.50
64 Charles Johnson Bat/100 .... 5.00 1.50
65 Garrett Atkins Jsy/100 .... 5.00 1.50
66 Jason Jennings Jsy/100 .... 5.00 1.50
67 Joe Kennedy Bat/100 .... 5.00 1.50
68 Larry Walker Jsy/100 .... 8.00 2.40
69 Preston Wilson Jsy/100 .... 5.00 1.50
70 Todd Helton Jsy/100 .... 8.00 2.40
71 Ivan Rodriguez Bat/100 .... 10.00 3.00
72 Jeremy Bonderman Jsy/100 .... 5.00 1.50
73 A.J. Burnett Jsy/100 .... 5.00 1.50
74 Brad Penny Jsy/100 .... 5.00 1.50
75 Dontrelle Willis Jsy/100 .... 5.00 1.50
76 Josh Beckett Jsy/100 .... 5.00 1.50
77 Juan Pierre Bat/100 .... 5.00 1.50
78 Luis Castillo Jsy/100 .... 5.00 1.50
79 Miguel Cabrera Jsy/100 .... 8.00 2.40
80 Mike Lowell Jsy/50 .... 8.00 2.40
81 Andy Pettitte Bat/100 .... 8.00 2.40
82 Craig Biggio Jsy/100 .... 8.00 2.40
83 Jeff Bagwell Jsy/100 .... 8.00 2.40
84 Jeff Kent Jsy/100 .... 5.00 1.50
85 Lance Berkman Jsy/100 .... 5.00 1.50
86 Morgan Ensberg Jsy/100 .... 5.00 1.50
87 Richard Hidalgo Pants/100 .... 5.00 1.50
88 Roger Clemens Bat/50 .... 20.00 6.00
89 Roy Oswalt Jsy/100 .... 5.00 1.50
90 Wade Miller Jsy/100 .... 5.00 1.50
91 Angel Berroa Pants/100 .... 5.00 1.50
92 Carlos Beltran Jsy/100 .... 8.00 2.40
93 Juan Gonzalez Bat/100 .... 8.00 2.40
94 Ken Harvey Bat/100 .... 5.00 1.50
95 Mike Sweeney Jsy/100 .... 5.00 1.50
96 Runelvys Hernandez Jsy/100 .... 5.00 1.50
97 Adrian Beltre Jsy/100 .... 8.00 2.40
98 Edwin Jackson Jsy/100 .... 5.00 1.50
100 Hideo Nomo Jsy/100 .... 10.00 3.00
101 Hong-Chih Kuo Bat/100 .... 5.00 1.50
102 Kazuhisa Ishii Jsy/100 .... 5.00 1.50

103 Paul Lo Duca Jsy/100 5.00 1.50
104 Shawn Green Jsy/100 5.00 1.50
105 Ben Sheets Jsy/100 5.00 1.50
106 Geoff Jenkins Jsy/100 5.00 1.50
107 Junior Spivey Bat/50 8.00 2.40
108 Rickie Weeks Bat/50 8.00 2.40
111 Doug Mientkiewicz Bat/100 5.00 1.50
112 Jacque Jones Jsy/100 5.00 1.50
113 Joe Mays Jsy/100 5.00 1.50
114 Johan Santana Jsy/100 8.00 2.40
115 Shannon Stewart Jsy/100 5.00 1.50
116 Torii Hunter Jsy/100 5.00 1.50
117 Brad Wilkerson Bat/100 5.00 1.50
118 Carl Everett Bat/100 5.00 1.50
120 Jose Vidro Jsy/100 5.00 1.50
121 Nick Johnson Bat/100 5.00 1.50
122 Orlando Cabrera Jsy/100 5.00 1.50
123 Al Leiter Jsy/100 5.00 1.50
124 Cliff Floyd Bat/100 5.00 1.50
125 Jae Weong Seo Jsy/100 5.00 1.50
126 Jose Reyes Jsy/100 5.00 1.50
128 Mike Piazza Jsy/100 12.00 3.60
129 Tom Glavine Jsy/100 8.00 2.40
130 Alex Rodriguez Bat/100 12.00 3.60
131 Bernie Williams Jsy/100 8.00 2.40
133 Derek Jeter Jsy/100 25.00 7.50
134 Gary Sheffield Bat/100 5.00 1.50
135 Hideki Matsui Jsy/100 30.00 9.00
136 Jason Giambi Jsy/100 5.00 1.50
138 Jorge Posada Jsy/100 8.00 2.40
141 Mariano Rivera Jsy/50 12.00 3.60
142 Mike Mussina Jsy/100 8.00 2.40
143 Barry Zito Jsy/100 5.00 1.50
145 Eric Chavez Jsy/100 5.00 1.50
146 Erubial Durazo Bat/100 5.00 1.50
147 Jermaine Dye Bat/100 5.00 1.50
149 Mark Mulder Jsy/100 5.00 1.50
150 Rich Harden Jsy/100 5.00 1.50
151 Tim Hudson Jsy/100 5.00 1.50
153 Bobby Abreu Jsy/100 5.00 1.50
154 Brett Myers Jsy/100 5.00 1.50
155 Jim Thome Jsy/100 10.00 3.00
157 Kevin Millwood Jsy/100 5.00 1.50
158 Marlon Byrd Jsy/100 5.00 1.50
159 Pat Burrell Jsy/100 5.00 1.50
161 Jason Kendall Jsy/100 5.00 1.50
162 Brian Giles Bat/100 5.00 1.50
164 Ryan Klesko Jsy/100 5.00 1.50
165 Edgardo Alfonzo Bat/100 5.00 1.50
167 Jerome Williams Jsy/100 5.00 1.50
169 Bret Boone Jsy/29
170 Edgar Martinez Jsy/100 8.00 2.40
171 Freddy Garcia Jsy/100 5.00 1.50
173 Jamie Moyer Jsy/100 5.00 1.50
174 John Olerud Jsy/100 5.00 1.50
176 Albert Pujols Jsy/100 20.00 6.00
177 Dan Haren Jsy/100 5.00 1.50
178 Edgar Renteria Jsy/100 5.00 1.50
179 Jim Edmonds Jsy/100 5.00 1.50
180 Matt Morris Jsy/100 5.00 1.50
181 Scott Rolen Jsy/100 10.00 3.00
182 Aubrey Huff Jsy/100 5.00 1.50
183 Carl Crawford Jsy/100 5.00 1.50
184 Chad Gaudin Jsy/100 5.00 1.50
185 Delmon Young Bat/100 8.00 2.40
186 Dewon Brazelton Jsy/100 5.00 1.50
187 Fred McGriff Jsy/100 8.00 2.40
188 Rocco Baldelli Jsy/100 5.00 1.50
189 Alfonso Soriano Bat/100 8.00 2.40
190 Hank Blalock Jsy/100 5.00 1.50
191 Laynce Nix Bat/100 5.00 1.50
192 Mark Teixeira Jsy/23 12.00 3.60
193 Michael Young Bat/100 5.00 1.50
194 Carlos Delgado Jsy/100 5.00 1.50
195 Eric Hinske Jsy/100 5.00 1.50
196 Frank Catalanotto Jsy/100 5.00 1.50
197 Josh Phelps Jsy/100 5.00 1.50
198 Orlando Hudson Jsy/100 5.00 1.50
199 Roy Halladay Jsy/100 5.00 1.50
200 Vernon Wells Jsy/100 5.00 1.50
201 Dale Murphy RET Jsy/100 12.00 3.60
202 Cal Ripken RET Jsy/100 40.00 12.00
203 Fred Lynn RET Bat/100 8.00 2.40
204 Wade Boggs RET Jsy/100 12.00 3.60
205 Nolan Ryan RET Jkt/100 25.00 7.50
206 Rod Carew RET Jkt/100 12.00 3.60
207 A.Dawson RET Pants/100 8.00 2.40
208 Ernie Banks RET Pants/50 20.00 6.00
209 Ryne Sandberg RET Jsy/50 30.00 9.00
210 Bo Jackson RET Jsy/100 15.00 4.50
211 Carlton Fisk RET Jkt/100 12.00 3.60
212 D.Concepcion RET Jsy/100 8.00 2.40
213 Alan Trammell RET Bat/100 8.00 2.40
214 George Brett RET Jsy/100 20.00 6.00
215 Robin Yount RET Jsy/100 15.00 4.50
216 Gary Carter RET Jsy/100 8.00 2.40
217 D.Straw RET Pants/100 8.00 2.40
218 Dwight Gooden RET Jsy/50 10.00 3.00
219 Babe Ruth RET Jsy/25 600.00 180.00
220 Don Mattingly RET Jkt/100 15.00 4.50
221 R.Jackson RET Jkt/100 12.00 3.60
222 Mike Schmidt RET Jkt/100 20.00 6.00
223 Tony Gwynn RET Jsy/100 15.00 4.50
224 K.Hernandez RET Jsy/100 8.00 2.40

2004 Throwback Threads Material Prime

Nm-Mt Ex-Mt
*PRIME p/r 25: 1.25X TO 3X BASIC p/r 100
*PRIME p/r 25: .75X TO 2X BASIC p/r 50
OVERALL AU-GU ODDS 1:8
PRINT RUNS B/WN 5-25 COPIES PER
NO PRICING ON QTY OF 10 OR LESS
156 Jimmy Rollins Jsy/25

2004 Throwback Threads Material Combo

Nm-Mt Ex-Mt
*COMBO p/r 50: .75X TO 2X BASIC p/r 100
*COMBO p/r 50: .6X TO 1.5X BASIC p/r 50
*COMBO p/r 50: .4X TO 1X BASIC p/r 23-29
*COMBO p/r 25: 1X TO 2.5X BASIC p/r 100
*COMBO p/r 25: .75X TO 2X BASIC p/r 50
OVERALL AU-GU ODDS 1:8
PRINT RUNS B/WN 10-50 COPIES PER
NO PRICING ON QTY OF 10 OR LESS
MOST COMBOS FEATURE BAT-JSY

2004 Throwback Threads Material Combo Prime

Nm-Mt Ex-Mt
*COMBO PR p/r 24-25: 1.5X TO 4X p/r 100
*COMBO PR p/r 24-25: 1X TO 2.5X p/r 23
*COMBO PR p/r 15-17: 2X TO 5X p/r 100
OVERALL AU-GU ODDS 1:8
PRINT RUNS B/WN 5-25 COPIES PER
NO PRICING ON QTY OF 12 OR LESS

2004 Throwback Threads Signature Marks

Nm-Mt Ex-Mt
OVERALL AU-GU ODDS 1:8
PRINT RUNS B/WN 5-200 COPIES PER
1-224 NO PRICING ON QTY OF 10 OR LESS
225-250 NO PRICING ON QTY OF 25 OR LESS
4 Garret Anderson/25 25.00 7.50
7 Vladimir Guerrero/5
8 Brandon Webb/50 12.00 3.60
10 Randy Johnson/5
12 Roberto Alomar/5
13 Shea Hillenbrand/50 20.00 6.00
14 Steve Finley/5
15 Adam LaRoche/50 12.00 3.60
16 Andruw Jones/5
17 Chipper Jones/5
20 Rafael Furcal/25 25.00 7.50
23 Jay Gibbons/50 12.00 3.60
24 Larry Bigbie/50 20.00 6.00
25 Luis Matos/50 12.00 3.60
26 Melvin Mora/50 20.00 6.00
29 Curt Schilling/5
30 David Ortiz/25 60.00 18.00
32 Jason Varitek/5
34 Manny Ramirez/5
37 Trot Nixon/25
38 Aramis Ramirez/5
40 Derrek Lee/25 25.00 7.50
42 Kerry Wood/5
43 Mark Prior/25 80.00 24.00
44 Sammy Sosa/5
45 Carlos Lee/50 12.00 3.60
46 Esteban Loaiza/50 12.00 3.60
47 Frank Thomas/5
48 Joe Borchard/25 15.00 4.50
49 Magglio Ordonez/5
50 Mark Buehrle/25 25.00 7.50
52 Adam Dunn/5
53 Austin Kearns/25 25.00 7.50
54 Barry Larkin/5
55 Brandon Larson/25 15.00 4.50
57 Ryan Wagner/5
60 Jody Gerut/50 20.00 6.00
62 Travis Hafner/50 20.00 6.00
63 Victor Martinez/50 20.00 6.00
67 Joe Kennedy/5
69 Preston Wilson/50 20.00 6.00
70 Todd Helton/5
74 Brad Penny/50 12.00 3.60
75 Dontrelle Willis/5
76 Josh Beckett/5
78 Luis Castillo/5
79 Miguel Cabrera/25 40.00 12.00
80 Mike Lowell/25 25.00 7.50
81 Andy Pettitte/5
82 Craig Biggio/5
83 Jeff Bagwell/5
85 Lance Berkman/5
86 Morgan Ensberg/50 12.00 3.60
89 Roy Oswalt/25
91 Angel Berroa/25 15.00 4.50
92 Carlos Beltran/25 50.00 15.00
93 Juan Gonzalez/5
98 Edwin Jackson/50 20.00 6.00
100 Hideo Nomo/5
101 Hong-Chih Kuo/50 20.00 6.00
102 Kazuhisa Ishii/5
103 Paul Lo Duca/10
104 Shawn Green/5
107 Junior Spivey/10
109 Scott Podsednik/50 20.00 6.00
112 Jacque Jones/50 20.00 6.00
114 Johan Santana/25 50.00 15.00
115 Shannon Stewart/25 25.00 7.50
116 Torii Hunter/25 25.00 7.50
119 Chad Cordero/50 12.00 3.60
120 Jose Vidro/25 15.00 4.50
121 Nick Johnson/5
122 Orlando Cabrera/50 20.00 6.00
125 Jae Weong Seo/5
126 Jose Reyes/10
128 Mike Piazza/5
130 Alex Rodriguez/5
131 Bernie Williams/5
132 Chien-Ming Wang/25 40.00 12.00
134 Gary Sheffield/5
137 Javier Vazquez/5
138 Jorge Posada/5
139 Jose Contreras/5
143 Barry Zito/5
145 Eric Chavez/5
147 Jermaine Dye/50 20.00 6.00
149 Mark Mulder/10
150 Rich Harden/5
151 Tim Hudson/5
154 Brett Myers/5
160 Jason Bay/50 20.00 6.00
163 Jay Payton/50 12.00 3.60
167 Jerome Williams/5
168 Todd Linden/50 12.00 3.60
170 Edgar Martinez/5
175 Shigetoshi Hasegawa/25 80.00 24.00
176 Albert Pujols/5
177 Dan Haren/50
179 Jim Edmonds/5
181 Scott Rolen/25 50.00 15.00
182 Aubrey Huff/50 20.00 6.00
184 Chad Gaudin/50 12.00 3.60
185 Delmon Young/5
186 Dewon Brazelton/50 12.00 3.60
187 Fred McGriff/25 60.00 18.00
188 Rocco Baldelli/5
189 Alfonso Soriano/25 50.00 15.00
190 Hank Blalock/25
192 Mark Teixeira/5
193 Michael Young/50 20.00 6.00
197 Josh Phelps/5
198 Orlando Hudson/5
199 Roy Halladay/5
200 Vernon Wells/10
202 Cal Ripken RET/5
203 Fred Lynn RET/50 12.00 3.60
204 Wade Boggs RET/5
205 Nolan Ryan RET/5
206 Rod Carew RET/5
207 Andre Dawson RET/50 20.00 6.00
208 Ernie Banks RET/5
209 Ryne Sandberg RET/5
210 Bo Jackson RET/5
211 Carlton Fisk RET/5
212 Dave Concepcion RET/10
213 Alan Trammell RET/25
214 George Brett RET/5
215 Robin Yount RET/5
216 Gary Carter RET/25 25.00 7.50
217 Darryl Strawberry RET/50 20.00 6.00
218 Dwight Gooden RET/50 20.00 6.00
220 Don Mattingly RET/5
221 Reggie Jackson RET/5
222 Mike Schmidt RET/5
223 Tony Gwynn RET/5
224 Keith Hernandez RET/50 20.00 6.00
225 Hector Gimenez ROO/100 8.00 2.40
226 Graham Koonce ROO/100 8.00 2.40
227 John Gall ROO/25
228 Jerry Gil ROO/100 10.00 3.00
229 Jason Frasor ROO/100 10.00 3.00
230 Justin Knoedler ROO/50 15.00 4.50
231 Ivan Ochoa ROO/25
232 Greg Dobbs ROO/25
233 Ronald Belisario ROO/200 10.00 3.00
234 Jerome Gamble ROO/200 8.00 2.40
235 Roberto Novoa ROO/200 10.00 3.00
236 Sean Henn ROO/200 10.00 3.00
237 Willy Taveras ROO/100 15.00 4.50
238 Ramon Ramirez ROO/200 10.00 3.00
241 Jason Bartlett ROO/25
242 Fernando Nieve ROO/25
243 Freddy Guzman ROO/25
244 Aarom Baldiris ROO/25
245 Merkin Valdez ROO/25
246 Mike Gosling ROO/25
247 Shingo Takatsu ROO/25
248 William Bergolla ROO/100 10.00 3.00
249 Shawn Hill ROO/100 10.00 3.00
250 Justin Germano ROO/100 10.00 3.00

2004 Throwback Threads Blast From the Past

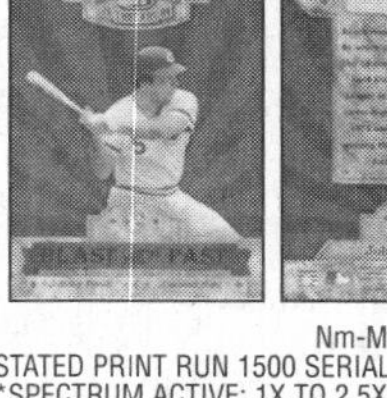

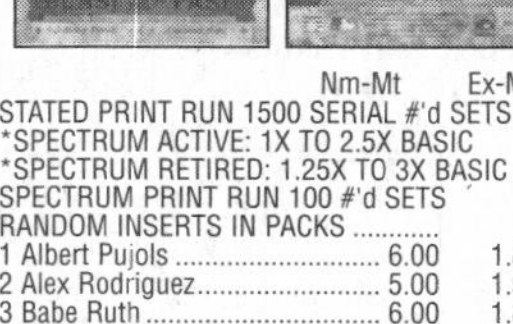

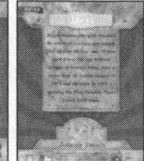

Nm-Mt Ex-Mt
STATED PRINT RUN 1500 SERIAL #'d SETS
*SPECTRUM ACTIVE: 1X TO 2.5X BASIC
*SPECTRUM RETIRED: 1.25X TO 3X BASIC
SPECTRUM PRINT RUN 100 #'d SETS
RANDOM INSERTS IN PACKS
1 Albert Pujols 6.00 1.80
2 Alex Rodriguez 5.00 1.50
3 Babe Ruth 6.00 1.80
4 Cal Ripken 10.00 3.00
5 Carlton Fisk 3.00 .90
6 Eddie Mathews 3.00 .90
7 Eddie Murray 3.00 .90
8 Ernie Banks 3.00 .90
9 Frank Robinson 2.00 .60
10 George Foster 2.00 .60
11 Harmon Killebrew 3.00 .90
12 Jim Rice 2.00 .60
13 Jim Thome 3.00 .90
14 Johnny Bench 3.00 .90
15 Jose Canseco 3.00 .90
16 Juan Gonzalez 3.00 .90
17 Ken Griffey Jr. 5.00 1.50
18 Mike Piazza 5.00 1.50
19 Mike Schmidt 6.00 1.80
20 Reggie Jackson 3.00 .90
21 Roger Maris 3.00 .90
22 Sammy Sosa 5.00 1.50
23 Stan Musial 5.00 1.50
24 Willie McCovey 3.00 .90
25 Willie Stargell 3.00 .90

2004 Throwback Threads Blast From the Past Material Bat

Nm-Mt Ex-Mt
OVERALL AU-GU ODDS 1:8
PRINT RUNS B/WN 50-250 COPIES PER
1 Albert Pujols/250 15.00 4.50
2 Alex Rodriguez/250 10.00 3.00
3 Babe Ruth/50 200.00 60.00
4 Cal Ripken/250 30.00 9.00
5 Carlton Fisk/250 10.00 3.00
6 Eddie Mathews/250 10.00 3.00
7 Eddie Murray/250 10.00 3.00
8 Ernie Banks/250 10.00 3.00
9 Frank Robinson/250 8.00 2.40
10 George Foster/250 8.00 2.40
11 Harmon Killebrew/250 10.00 3.00
12 Jim Rice/250 8.00 2.40
13 Jim Thome/250 10.00 3.00
14 Johnny Bench/250 10.00 3.00
15 Jose Canseco/100 15.00 4.50
16 Juan Gonzalez/250 8.00 2.40
18 Mike Piazza/250 10.00 3.00
19 Mike Schmidt/250 15.00 4.50
20 Reggie Jackson/250 10.00 3.00
21 Roger Maris/250 25.00 7.50
22 Sammy Sosa/250 10.00 3.00
23 Stan Musial/250 20.00 6.00
24 Willie McCovey/250 10.00 3.00
25 Willie Stargell/250 10.00 3.00

2004 Throwback Threads Century Collection Material

Nm-Mt Ex-Mt
PRINT RUNS B/WN 25-250 COPIES PER
*COMBO p/r 50: .75X TO 2X p/r 150-250
*COMBO p/r 50: .75X TO 2X p/r 100
*COMBO p/r 50: .6X TO 1.5X p/r 50
*COMBO p/r 50: .4X TO 1X p/r 25
*COMBO p/r 20-25: 1X TO 2.5X p/r 250
*COMBO p/r 20-25: .5X TO 1.2X p/r 25
*COMBO p/r 15: 1.25X TO 3X p/r 250
COMBO PRINT RUNS B/WN 5-50 PER
NO COMBO PRICING ON QTY OF 5 OR LESS
OVERALL AU-GU ODDS 1:8
1 Alan Trammell Jsy/250 8.00 2.40
2 Alex Rodriguez Jsy/250 10.00 3.00
3 Alfonso Soriano Jsy/250 8.00 2.40
4 Andre Dawson Jsy/250 8.00 2.40
5 Andy Pettitte Jsy/250 8.00 2.40
6 Bert Blyleven Jsy/250 8.00 2.40
7 Bo Jackson Jsy/250 15.00 4.50
8 Bobby Doerr Jsy/250 8.00 2.40
9 Brooks Robinson Jsy/25 25.00 7.50
10 Carl Yastrzemski Jsy/250 20.00 6.00
11 Carlos Delgado Jsy/250 5.00 1.50
12 Carlton Fisk Jkt/250 10.00 3.00
13 Curt Schilling Jsy/250 5.00 1.50
14 Darryl Strawberry Jsy/250 8.00 2.40
15 Dave Concepcion Jsy/250 8.00 2.40
16 Dave Parker Jsy/100 8.00 2.40
17 Dennis Eckersley Jsy/250 10.00 3.00
18 Don Sutton Jsy/250 8.00 2.40
19 Duke Snider Jsy/250 10.00 3.00
20 Dwight Gooden Jsy/250 8.00 2.40
21 Eddie Mathews Jsy/25 40.00 12.00
22 Enos Slaughter Jsy/100 8.00 2.40
23 Ernie Banks Pants/250 10.00 3.00
24 Frankie Frisch Jkt/250 15.00 4.50
25 Frank Robinson Jsy/50 10.00 3.00
26 Frank Thomas Jsy/250 10.00 3.00
27 Garret Anderson Jsy/250 5.00 1.50
28 Gary Carter Jsy/250 8.00 2.40
29 Gary Sheffield Jsy/250 5.00 1.50
30 Harmon Killebrew Jsy/50 20.00 6.00
31 Harold Baines Jsy/250 8.00 2.40
32 Hideo Nomo Jsy/250 10.00 3.00
33 Jack Morris Jsy/250 8.00 2.40
34 Jason Giambi Jsy/250 5.00 1.50
35 Jeff Kent Jsy/250 5.00 1.50
36 Catfish Hunter Jsy/250 10.00 3.00
37 Jim Palmer Jsy/250 10.00 3.00
38 Jim Rice Jsy/250 8.00 2.40
39 Jim Thome Jsy/250 10.00 3.00
40 John Smoltz Jsy/250 8.00 2.40
41 Johnny Mize Pants/250 10.00 3.00
42 Jose Canseco Jsy/250 10.00 3.00
43 Juan Gonzalez Jsy/250 8.00 2.40
44 Juan Marichal Jsy/250 8.00 2.40
45 Keith Hernandez Jsy/250 8.00 2.40
46 Kerry Wood Jsy/250 10.00 3.00
47 Kevin Brown Jsy/250 5.00 1.50
48 Lance Berkman Jsy/250 5.00 1.50
49 Larry Walker Jsy/250 8.00 2.40
50 Lee Smith Jsy/250 8.00 2.40
51 Lenny Dykstra Bat/250 8.00 2.40
52 Luis Tiant Jsy/250 8.00 2.40
53 Magglio Ordonez Jsy/250 5.00 1.50
54 Manny Ramirez Jsy/250 8.00 2.40
55 Mariano Rivera Jsy/100 8.00 2.40
56 Mark Grace Jsy/250 10.00 3.00
57 Mark Mulder Jsy/250 5.00 1.50
58 Mark Teixeira Jsy/150 5.00 1.50
59 Marty Marion Jsy/25 15.00 4.50
60 Mike Mussina Pants/250 8.00 2.40
61 Mike Piazza Jsy/250 10.00 3.00
62 Nellie Fox Bat/250 20.00 6.00
63 Nolan Ryan Jkt/250 25.00 7.50
65 Ozzie Smith Jsy/250 12.00 3.60
66 Pedro Martinez Jsy/250 10.00 3.00
67 Pee Wee Reese Bat/250 10.00 3.00
68 Phil Niekro Jsy/250 8.00 2.40
69 Phil Rizzuto Pants/250 10.00 3.00
70 Rafael Palmeiro Jsy/250 8.00 2.40
71 Ralph Kiner Bat/250 10.00 3.00
72 Randy Johnson Jsy/250 10.00 3.00
73 Reggie Jackson Jkt/250 10.00 3.00
74 Rickey Henderson Jsy/250 10.00 3.00
75 Roberto Alomar Jsy/250 8.00 2.40
76 Robin Ventura Jsy/250 5.00 1.50
77 Rod Carew Jsy/250 10.00 3.00
78 Roger Clemens Jsy/250 10.00 3.00
79 Ron Santo Bat/250 10.00 3.00
80 Scott Rolen Jsy/250 10.00 3.00
81 Shawn Green Jsy/250 5.00 1.50
82 Steve Garvey Jsy/250 8.00 2.40
83 Tim Hudson Jsy/250 5.00 1.50
84 Tom Glavine Jsy/250 8.00 2.40
85 Tom Seaver Jsy/25 25.00 7.50
86 Adam Dunn Jsy/250 8.00 2.40
87 Tommy John Jsy/250 8.00 2.40
88 Tommy Lasorda Jsy/250 8.00 2.40
89 Tony Oliva Jsy/250 8.00 2.40
90 Tony Perez Bat/250 8.00 2.40
91 Torii Hunter Jsy/250 5.00 1.50
92 Troy Glaus Jsy/250 5.00 1.50
93 Vernon Wells Jsy/250 5.00 1.50
94 Vladimir Guerrero Jsy/250 10.00 3.00
95 Wade Boggs Jsy/250 10.00 3.00
96 Warren Spahn Jsy/100 15.00 4.50
97 Will Clark Bat/250 10.00 3.00
98 Willie McCovey Jsy/250 10.00 3.00
99 Willie Stargell Jsy/250 10.00 3.00
100 George Foster Jsy/250 8.00 2.40

2004 Throwback Threads Century Collection Signature Material

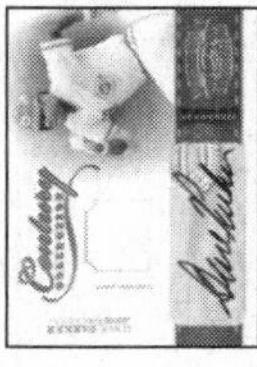

Nm-Mt Ex-Mt
PRINT RUNS B/WN 10-50 COPIES PER
NO PRICING ON QTY OF 10 OR LESS
PRIME PRINT RUNS B/WN 5-10 COPIES PER
NO PRIME PRICING DUE TO SCARCITY
*COMBO p/r 25: .5X TO 1.2X BASIC p/r 50
*COMBO p/r 25: .5X TO 1.2X BASIC p/r 25
COMBO PRINT RUN B/WN 5-25 COPIES PER
NO COMBO PRICE ON QTY OF 10 OR LESS
COMBO PRIME PRINT RUN B/WN 4-10 PER
NO COMBO PR PRICING DUE TO SCARCITY
OVERALL AU-GU ODDS 1:8
1 Alan Trammell Jsy/50 25.00 7.50
3 Alfonso Soriano Jsy/50 50.00 15.00
4 Andre Dawson Jsy/50 25.00 7.50
6 Bert Blyleven Jsy/50 15.00 4.50
7 Bo Jackson Jsy/10
8 Bobby Doerr Jsy/50 25.00 7.50
12 Carlton Fisk Jkt/10
14 Darryl Strawberry Jsy/50 25.00 7.50
15 Dave Concepcion Jsy/50 25.00 7.50
16 Dave Parker Jsy/50 25.00 7.50
17 Dennis Eckersley Jsy/50 40.00 12.00
18 Don Sutton Jsy/50 25.00 7.50
19 Duke Snider Jsy/25 50.00 15.00
20 Dwight Gooden Jsy/50 25.00 7.50
23 Ernie Banks Pants/10
25 Frank Robinson Jsy/10
26 Frank Thomas Jsy/10
27 Garret Anderson Jsy/50 25.00 7.50
28 Gary Carter Jsy/50 25.00 7.50
29 Gary Sheffield Jsy/25 50.00 15.00
31 Harold Baines Jsy/50 25.00 7.50
34 Jack Morris Jsy/50 15.00 4.50
37 Jim Palmer Jsy/25 30.00 9.00
38 Jim Rice Jsy/50 25.00 7.50
42 Jose Canseco Jsy/25 60.00 18.00
44 Juan Marichal Jsy/50 25.00 7.50
45 Keith Hernandez Jsy/50 25.00 7.50
50 Lee Smith Jsy/50 15.00 4.50
51 Lenny Dykstra Bat/50 25.00 7.50
52 Luis Tiant Jsy/50 15.00 4.50
53 Magglio Ordonez Jsy/50 25.00 7.50
56 Mark Grace Jsy/50 40.00 12.00
57 Mark Mulder Jsy/25 30.00 9.00
58 Mark Teixeira Jsy/25 50.00 15.00
59 Marty Marion Jsy/50 15.00 4.50
63 Nolan Ryan Jkt/10
68 Phil Niekro Jsy/50 25.00 7.50
71 Ralph Kiner Bat/50 40.00 12.00
75 Roberto Alomar Jsy/25 50.00 15.00
76 Robin Ventura Jsy/50 25.00 7.50
82 Steve Garvey Jsy/50 40.00 12.00
86 Adam Dunn Jsy/10
87 Tommy John Jsy/50 15.00 4.50
90 Tony Perez Bat/25 60.00 18.00
91 Torii Hunter Jsy/25 30.00 9.00
93 Vernon Wells Jsy/25 30.00 9.00
94 Vladimir Guerrero Jsy/50 50.00 15.00
100 George Foster Jsy/50 15.00 4.50

2004 Throwback Threads Century Stars

Nm-Mt Ex-Mt
STATED PRINT RUN 1500 SERIAL #'d SETS
*SPECTRUM ACTIVE: 1X TO 2.5X BASIC
*SPECTRUM RETIRED: 1.25X TO 3X BASIC
SPECTRUM PRINT RUN 100 #'d SETS
RANDOM INSERTS IN PACKS
1 Al Kaline 3.00 .90
2 Albert Pujols 6.00 1.80
3 Alex Rodriguez 5.00 1.50
4 Barry Larkin 3.00 .90
5 Barry Zito 2.00 .60
6 Billy Williams 2.00 .60
7 Bob Feller 2.00 .60
8 Bob Gibson 3.00 .90
9 Cal Ripken 10.00 3.00
10 Chipper Jones 3.00 .90
11 Curt Schilling 2.00 .60
12 Dale Murphy 3.00 .90
13 Dave Parker 2.00 .60
14 Derek Jeter 6.00 1.80
15 Don Drysdale 3.00 .90
16 Don Mattingly 6.00 1.80
17 Eddie Murray 3.00 .90
18 Fergie Jenkins 2.00 .60
19 Gary Carter 2.00 .60

20 George Brett 6.00 1.80
21 Greg Maddux 5.00 1.50
22 Ivan Rodriguez 3.00 .90
23 Jeff Bagwell 3.00 .90
24 Joe Morgan 2.00 .60
25 Johnny Bench 3.00 .90
26 Kirby Puckett 3.00 .90
27 Lou Boudreau 2.00 .60
28 Lou Brock 3.00 .90
29 Luis Aparicio 2.00 .60
30 Manny Ramirez 3.00 .90
31 Mark Prior 3.00 .90
32 Miguel Tejada 2.00 .60
33 Mike Mussina 3.00 .90
34 Mike Piazza 5.00 1.50
35 Mike Schmidt 6.00 1.80
36 Nolan Ryan 8.00 2.40
37 Nomar Garciaparra 5.00 1.50
38 Ozzie Smith 5.00 1.50
39 Paul Molitor 3.00 .90
40 Pedro Martinez 3.00 .90
41 Rafael Palmeiro 3.00 .90
42 Randy Johnson 3.00 .90
43 Red Schoendienst 2.00 .60
44 Reggie Jackson 3.00 .90
45 Rickey Henderson 3.00 .90
46 Roberto Alomar 3.00 .90
47 Roberto Clemente 8.00 2.40
48 Robin Yount 5.00 1.50
49 Rod Carew 3.00 .90
50 Roger Clemens 6.00 1.80
51 Ryne Sandberg 6.00 1.80
52 Sammy Sosa 5.00 1.50
53 Stan Musial 5.00 1.50
54 Steve Carlton 2.00 .60
55 Todd Helton 3.00 .90
56 Tom Glavine 3.00 .90
57 Tom Seaver 3.00 .90
58 Tony Gwynn 5.00 1.50
59 Wade Boggs 3.00 .90
60 Whitey Ford 3.00 .90

2004 Throwback Threads Century Stars Material

Nm-Mt Ex-Mt
PRINT RUNS B/WN 10-50 COPIES PER
NO PRICING ON QTY OF 10 OR LESS
PRIME PRINT RUN 5 SERIAL #'d SETS
NO PRIME PRICING DUE TO SCARCITY
OVERALL AU-GU ODDS 1:8
1 Al Kaline Pants/25 40.00 12.00
2 Albert Pujols Jsy/50 30.00 9.00
4 Barry Larkin Jsy/50 12.00 3.60
5 Barry Zito Jsy/50 8.00 2.40
6 Billy Williams Jsy/50 10.00 3.00
7 Bob Feller Jsy/10
8 Bob Gibson Jsy/25 25.00 7.50
9 Cal Ripken Jsy/50 60.00 18.00
10 Chipper Jones Jsy/50 15.00 4.50
11 Curt Schilling Jsy/50 8.00 2.40
12 Dale Murphy Jsy/50 15.00 4.50
13 Dave Parker Jsy/50 10.00 3.00
14 Derek Jeter Jsy/50 40.00 12.00
15 Don Drysdale Jsy/50 15.00 4.50
16 Don Mattingly Jkt/50 30.00 9.00
17 Eddie Murray Jsy/50 20.00 6.00
18 Fergie Jenkins Pants/25 15.00 4.50
19 Gary Carter Jsy/50 10.00 3.00
20 George Brett Jsy/50 30.00 9.00
21 Greg Maddux Jsy/50 20.00 6.00
22 Ivan Rodriguez Jsy/50 15.00 4.50
23 Jeff Bagwell Jsy/50 12.00 3.60
24 Joe Morgan Jsy/25 15.00 4.50
25 Johnny Bench Jsy/50 20.00 6.00
26 Kirby Puckett Jsy/50 20.00 6.00
27 Lou Boudreau Jsy/50 10.00 3.00
28 Lou Brock Jsy/25 25.00 7.50
29 Luis Aparicio Pants/50 10.00 3.00
30 Manny Ramirez Jsy/50 12.00 3.60
31 Mark Prior Jsy/50 15.00 4.50
32 Miguel Tejada Jsy/50 8.00 2.40
33 Mike Mussina Jsy/50 12.00 3.60
34 Mike Piazza Jsy/50 20.00 6.00
35 Mike Schmidt Jsy/50 30.00 9.00
36 Nolan Ryan Jsy/50 40.00 12.00
37 Nomar Garciaparra Jsy/50 20.00 6.00
38 Ozzie Smith Jsy/50 25.00 7.50
40 Pedro Martinez Jsy/50 15.00 4.50
41 Rafael Palmeiro Jsy/25 20.00 6.00
42 Randy Johnson Jsy/50 15.00 4.50
43 Red Schoendienst Jsy/50 10.00 3.00
44 Reggie Jackson Pants/50 15.00 4.50
45 Rickey Henderson Jsy/50 20.00 6.00
46 Roberto Alomar Jsy/50 12.00 3.60
47 Roberto Clemente Jsy/10
48 Robin Yount Jsy/50 25.00 7.50
49 Rod Carew Jkt/50 15.00 4.50
50 Roger Clemens Jsy/50 20.00 6.00
51 Ryne Sandberg Jsy/50 30.00 9.00
52 Sammy Sosa Jsy/50 20.00 6.00
53 Stan Musial Jsy/10
54 Steve Carlton Jsy/25 15.00 4.50
55 Todd Helton Jsy/50 12.00 3.60
56 Tom Glavine Jsy/50 12.00 3.60
57 Tom Seaver Jsy/50 15.00 4.50
58 Tony Gwynn Jsy/50 20.00 6.00
59 Wade Boggs Jsy/50 15.00 4.50
60 Whitey Ford Pants/10

2004 Throwback Threads Century Stars Signature

Nm-Mt Ex-Mt
PRINT RUNS B/WN 5-25 COPIES PER
NO PRICING ON QTY OF 10 OR LESS
SIG.MATERIAL PRINT RUN 5 #'d SETS

NO SIG.MTL.PRICING DUE TO SCARCITY
SIG.MATERIAL PRIME PRINT RUN 5 #'d SETS
NO SIG.MTL.PR.PRICING DUE TO SCARCITY
OVERALL AU-GU ODDS 1:8
1 Al Kaline/25 60.00 18.00
2 Albert Pujols/5
3 Alex Rodriguez/5
4 Barry Larkin/10
5 Barry Zito/5
6 Billy Williams/25 40.00 12.00
7 Bob Feller/25 40.00 12.00
8 Bob Gibson/25 40.00 12.00
9 Cal Ripken/5
10 Chipper Jones/5
12 Dale Murphy/25 40.00 12.00
13 Dave Parker/25 25.00 7.50
16 Don Mattingly/10
17 Eddie Murray/5
18 Fergie Jenkins/25 25.00 7.50
19 Gary Carter/25 25.00 7.50
20 George Brett/5
23 Jeff Bagwell/5
24 Joe Morgan/25 25.00 7.50
25 Johnny Bench/5
26 Kirby Puckett/5
28 Lou Brock/25 40.00 12.00
29 Luis Aparicio/25 25.00 7.50
30 Manny Ramirez/5
31 Mark Prior/25 80.00 24.00
33 Mike Mussina/5
35 Mike Schmidt/25 100.00 30.00
36 Nolan Ryan/10
38 Ozzie Smith/25 80.00 24.00
39 Paul Molitor/10
41 Rafael Palmeiro/10
44 Reggie Jackson/10
45 Rickey Henderson/10
46 Roberto Alomar/10
48 Robin Yount/10
49 Rod Carew/10
51 Ryne Sandberg/10
52 Sammy Sosa/5
53 Stan Musial/25 80.00 24.00
54 Steve Carlton/10
55 Todd Helton/5
57 Tom Seaver/5
58 Tony Gwynn/10
59 Wade Boggs/10
60 Whitey Ford/5

2004 Throwback Threads Dynasty

Nm-Mt Ex-Mt
STATED PRINT RUN 1500 SERIAL #'d SETS
*SPECTRUM: 1.25X TO 3X BASIC
SPECTRUM PRINT RUN 100 #'d SETS
RANDOM INSERTS IN PACKS
1 Phil Rizzuto 3.00 .90
Whitey Ford
2 Pee Wee Reese 3.00 .90
Duke Snider
Tommy Lasorda
3 Catfish Hunter 3.00 .90
Reggie Jackson
4 Roger Maris 3.00 .90
Whitey Ford
5 Enos Slaughter 5.00 1.50
Marty Marion
Stan Musial
6 Dwight Gooden 2.00 .60
Gary Carter
Darryl Strawberry
Keith Hernandez
7 Johnny Bench 3.00 .90
Tony Perez
Joe Morgan
George Foster
8 Derek Jeter 6.00 1.80
Jorge Posada
Bernie Williams
Andy Pettitte
9 Frank Robinson 3.00 .90
Brooks Robinson
Jim Palmer
10 Willie Stargell 3.00 .90
Dave Parker
Bill Madlock
11 Bob Gibson 3.00 .90
Lou Brock
Ken Boyer
12 Rickey Henderson 3.00 .90
Paul Molitor
Joe Carter
Roberto Alomar

2004 Throwback Threads Dynasty Material

Nm-Mt Ex-Mt
PRINT RUNS B/WN 5-50 COPIES PER
NO PRICING ON QTY OF 10 OR LESS
ALL ARE JSY SWATCHES UNLESS NOTED
PRIME PRINT RUN 5 SERIAL #'d SETS

NO PRIME PRICING DUE TO SCARCITY
OVERALL AU-GU ODDS 1:8
1 Phil Rizzuto Pants
Whitey Ford Jsy/10
2 Pee Wee Reese Jsy
Duke Snider Jsy
Tommy Lasorda Jsy/5
3 Catfish Hunter Jsy 25.00 7.50
Reggie Jackson Jsy/25
4 Roger Maris Jsy
Whitey Ford Pants/10
5 Enos Slaughter Jsy
Marty Marion Jsy
Stan Musial Jsy/10
6 Dwight Gooden Jsy 25.00 7.50
Gary Carter Jsy
Darryl Strawberry Pants
Keith Hernandez Bat/50
7 Johnny Bench Jsy 120.00 36.00
Tony Perez Bat
Joe Morgan Jsy
George Foster Jsy/25
8 Derek Jeter Jsy 60.00 18.00
Jorge Posada Jsy
Bernie Williams Jsy
Andy Pettitte Jsy/50
9 Frank Robinson Jsy
Brooks Robinson Jsy
Jim Palmer Jsy/10
10 Willie Stargell Jsy 40.00 12.00
Dave Parker Jsy
Bill Madlock Bat/25
11 Bob Gibson Jsy 40.00 12.00
Lou Brock Jsy
Ken Boyer Jsy/25
12 Rickey Henderson Jsy 80.00 24.00
Paul Molitor Bat
Joe Carter Jsy
Roberto Alomar Bat/25

2004 Throwback Threads Fans of the Game

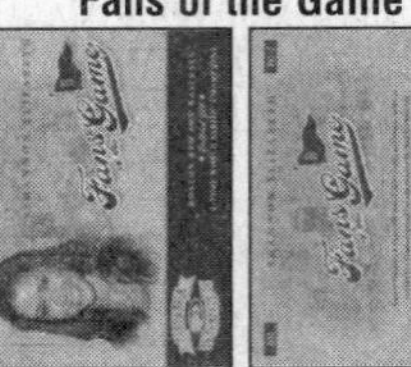

Nm-Mt Ex-Mt
STATED ODDS 1:24
1 Emilio Estevez 3.00 .90
2 Shannon Elizabeth 3.00 .90
3 Joe Mantegna UER 2.00 .60
Incorrectly spelled Montegna
4 Jamie-Lynn DiScala 3.00 .90
5 Jonathan Silverman 2.00 .60

2004 Throwback Threads Fans of the Game Signatures

Nm-Mt Ex-Mt
RANDOM INSERTS IN PACKS
1 Emilio Estevez 50.00 15.00
2 Shannon Elizabeth 80.00 24.00
3 Joe Mantegna UER 40.00 12.00
Incorrectly spelled Montegna
4 Jamie-Lynn DiScala 60.00 18.00
5 Jonathan Silverman 25.00 7.50

2004 Throwback Threads Generations

Nm-Mt Ex-Mt
STATED PRINT RUN 1500 SERIAL #'d SETS
*SPECTRUM: 1.25X TO 3X BASIC
SPECTRUM PRINT RUN 100 #'d SETS
RANDOM INSERTS IN PACKS
1 George Brett 6.00 1.80
Albert Pujols
2 Wade Boggs 3.00 .90
Aubrey Huff
3 Catfish Hunter 3.00 .90
Tim Hudson
4 Steve Garvey 2.00 .60
Shawn Green
5 Tony Gwynn 5.00 1.50
Garret Anderson
6 Fergie Jenkins 3.00 .90
Mark Prior
7 Robin Yount 5.00 1.50
Rickie Weeks
8 Warren Spahn 5.00 1.50
Greg Maddux
9 Brooks Robinson 10.00 3.00
Cal Ripken
Miguel Tejada
10 Bobby Doerr 5.00 1.50
Carl Yastrzemski
Manny Ramirez
11 Al Kaline 3.00 .90
Alan Trammell
Ivan Rodriguez
12 Tom Seaver 3.00 .90
Dwight Gooden
Tom Glavine
13 Stan Musial 5.00 1.50
Lou Brock
Jim Edmonds
14 George Foster 2.00 .60
Dave Parker
Austin Kearns
15 Eddie Mathews 3.00 .90
Dale Murphy
Chipper Jones
16 Don Sutton 8.00 2.40
Nolan Ryan
Roger Clemens
17 Billy Williams 5.00 1.50
Andre Dawson
Sammy Sosa
18 Whitey Ford 3.00 .90
Tommy John
Andy Pettitte
19 Carlton Fisk 6.00 1.80
Roger Clemens
Nomar Garciaparra
20 Marty Marion 5.00 1.50
Ozzie Smith
Edgar Renteria
21 Reggie Jackson 3.00 .90
Rickey Henderson
Eric Chavez
22 Babe Ruth 6.00 1.80
Don Mattingly
Derek Jeter
23 Roberto Clemente 8.00 2.40
Reggie Jackson
Sammy Sosa
24 Bob Feller 6.00 1.80
Tom Seaver
Roger Clemens
25 Ernie Banks 10.00 3.00
Cal Ripken
Alex Rodriguez
26 Pee Wee Reese 6.00 1.80
Ozzie Smith
Derek Jeter
27 Harmon Killebrew 6.00 1.80
Mike Schmidt
Alex Rodriguez
28 Bob Gibson 3.00 .90
Dwight Gooden
Josh Beckett

2004 Throwback Threads Generations Material

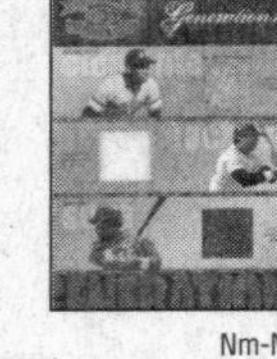

Nm-Mt Ex-Mt
PRINT RUNS B/WN 5-50 COPIES PER
NO PRICING ON QTY OF 10 OR LESS
ALL ARE JSY SWATCHES UNLESS NOTED
PRIME PRINT RUN 5 SERIAL #'d SETS
NO PRIME PRICING DUE TO SCARCITY
OVERALL AU-GU ODDS 1:8
1 George Brett Jsy 40.00 12.00
Albert Pujols Jsy/50
2 Wade Boggs Jsy 15.00 4.50
Aubrey Huff Jsy/50
3 Catfish Hunter Jsy 20.00 6.00
Tim Hudson Jsy/25
4 Steve Garvey Jsy
Shawn Green Jsy/5
5 Tony Gwynn Jsy 25.00 7.50
Garret Anderson Jsy/50
6 Fergie Jenkins Pants 25.00 7.50
Mark Prior Jsy/25
7 Robin Yount Jsy 25.00 7.50
Rickie Weeks Bat/50
8 Warren Spahn Pants 40.00 12.00
Greg Maddux Jsy/25
9 Brooks Robinson Jsy
Cal Ripken Jsy
Miguel Tejada Bat/10
10 Bobby Doerr Bat
Carl Yastrzemski Jsy
Manny Ramirez Jsy/10
11 Al Kaline Pants 50.00 15.00
Alan Trammell Jsy
Ivan Rodriguez Bat/25
12 Tom Seaver Jsy
Dwight Gooden Jsy
Tom Glavine Jsy/5
13 Stan Musial Jsy
Lou Brock Jsy
Jim Edmonds Jsy/10
14 George Foster Jsy 25.00 7.50
Dave Parker Jsy
Austin Kearns Jsy/25
15 Eddie Mathews Jsy
Dale Murphy Jsy
Chipper Jones Jsy/10
16 Don Sutton Jsy 50.00 15.00
Nolan Ryan Jkt
Roger Clemens Bat/50
17 Billy Williams Jsy 25.00 7.50
Andre Dawson Jsy
Sammy Sosa Jsy/50
18 Whitey Ford Jsy 40.00 12.00
Tommy John Jsy
Andy Pettitte Jsy/25
19 Carlton Fisk Jsy 40.00 12.00
Roger Clemens Jsy
Nomar Garciaparra Jsy/50
20 Marty Marion Jsy 60.00 18.00
Ozzie Smith Jsy
Edgar Renteria Jsy/25
21 Reggie Jackson Jkt 40.00 12.00
Rickey Henderson Jsy
Eric Chavez Jsy/50
22 Babe Ruth Jsy
Don Mattingly Jsy
Derek Jeter Jsy/10
23 Roberto Clemente Jsy
Reggie Jackson Jsy
Sammy Sosa Jsy/10
24 Bob Feller Jsy 40.00 12.00
Tom Seaver Jsy
Roger Clemens Jsy/25
25 Ernie Banks Pants 80.00 24.00
Cal Ripken Jsy
Alex Rodriguez Jsy/50
26 Pee Wee Reese Jsy 60.00 18.00
Ozzie Smith Jsy
Derek Jeter Jsy/25
27 Harmon Killebrew Jsy 60.00 18.00
Mike Schmidt Jsy
Alex Rodriguez Bat/25
28 Bob Gibson Jsy 40.00 12.00
Dwight Gooden Jsy
Josh Beckett Jsy/25

2004 Throwback Threads Player Threads

Nm-Mt Ex-Mt
STATED PRINT RUN 250 SERIAL #'d SETS
CARD 57 PRINT RUN 25 SERIAL #'d COPIES
ALL ARE JSY SWATCHES UNLESS NOTED
*PRIME p/r 25: 1.25X TO 3X BASIC
PRIME PRINT RUNS B/WN 10-25 PER
NO PRIME PRICING ON QTY OF 10 OR LESS
OVERALL AU-GU ODDS 1:8
1 Aaron Boone 5.00 1.50
2 Alex Rodriguez M's-Rgr 15.00 4.50
3 A.Gala Braves-Giants-Rgr 15.00 4.50
4 Aramis Ramirez 5.00 1.50
5 Bartolo Colon 5.00 1.50
6 Ben Grieve A's-D'Rays 8.00 2.40
7 Brad Fullmer 5.00 1.50
8 Bret Boone Braves-M's 8.00 2.40
9 Brian Giles 5.00 1.50
10 Brian Jordan 5.00 1.50
11 Byung-Hyun Kim 5.00 1.50
12 Casey Fossum 5.00 1.50
13 Cesar Izturis Pants 5.00 1.50
14 Chan Ho Park 5.00 1.50
15 Charles Johnson 5.00 1.50
16 Cliff Floyd 5.00 1.50
17 D.Straw Dgr-Met-Ynk Pant 10.00 3.00
18 David Ortiz 10.00 3.00
19 David Wells Jays-Yanks 8.00 2.40
20 Derrek Lee 5.00 1.50
21 Dmitri Young 5.00 1.50
22 Edgardo Alfonzo 5.00 1.50
23 Ellis Burks 5.00 1.50
24 G.Shef Braves-Brew-Dgr 10.00 3.00
25 Hee Seop Choi 5.00 1.50
26 I.Rodriguez Marlins-Rgr 12.00 3.60
27 J.D. Drew 5.00 1.50
28 Javier Vazquez 5.00 1.50
29 Jay Payton 5.00 1.50
30 Jeff Kent Astros-Giants-Jays 10.00 3.00
31 Jeromy Burnitz 5.00 1.50
32 Jim Thome Indians-Phils 12.00 3.60
33 Joe Kennedy 5.00 1.50
34 Joe Torre 10.00 3.00
35 Jose Cruz Jr. 5.00 1.50
36 Juan Encarnacion 5.00 1.50
37 Juan Gonzalez Indians-Rgr 10.00 3.00
38 Juan Pierre 5.00 1.50
39 Junior Spivey 5.00 1.50
40 K.Loft Brave Glv-Tribe Hat 8.00 2.40
41 Kevin Millwood Braves-Phils 8.00 2.40
42 Manny Ramirez Indians-Sox 10.00 3.00
43 Mark Grace Cubs-D'backs 10.00 3.00
44 Mike Hampton 5.00 1.50
45 M.Piazza Dgr-Marlins-Mets 20.00 6.00
46 Milton Bradley 5.00 1.50
47 Moises Alou 5.00 1.50
48 Nick Johnson 5.00 1.50
49 N.Ryan Ang Jkt-Ast Jkt-Rgr 50.00 15.00
50 P.Wilson Marlins-Rockies 8.00 2.40
51 Rafael Palmeiro O's-Rgr 10.00 3.00
52 Ray Durham 5.00 1.50
53 R.Jack A's Jkt-Ang-Yank 15.00 4.50
54 Reggie Sanders 5.00 1.50
55 Rich Aurilia 5.00 1.50
56 Richie Sexson 5.00 1.50
57 R.Hend A's-M's-Yanks/25 50.00 15.00
58 R.Hend Dgr-Mets-Padres 15.00 4.50
59 Robert Fick 5.00 1.50
60 Roberto Alomar Mets-Sox 10.00 3.00
61 Roberto Alomar Indians-O's 10.00 3.00
62 R.Ventura Mets-Sox-Yanks 10.00 3.00
63 Rondell White Cubs-Expos 8.00 2.40
64 Ryan Klesko Braves-Padres 8.00 2.40
65 Sean Casey 5.00 1.50
66 S.Stewart Jays-Twins 8.00 2.40

7 Shawn Green Jays-Dgr 8.00 2.40
8 Shea Hillenbrand 5.00 1.50
9 Steve Carlton Giants-Sox 8.00 2.40
0 Terrence Long 5.00 1.50
1 Tony Batista 5.00 1.50
2 Travis Hafner Indians-Rgr 8.00 2.40
3 Travis Lee 5.00 1.50
4 Vladimir Guerrero 10.00 3.00
5 Wes Helms 5.00 1.50

2004 Throwback Threads Player Threads Signature

Nm-Mt Ex-Mt
OVERALL AU-GU ODDS 1:8
PRINT RUNS B/WN 3-25 COPIES PER
NO PRICING ON QTY OF 11 OR LESS
ALL ARE JSY SWATCHES UNLESS NOTED
2 Alex Rodriguez M's-Rgr/5
Aramis Ramirez/25 30.00 9.00
7 D.Straw Dgr-Met-Ynk Pnt/25 50.00 15.00
4 G.Shef Brave-Brw-Dgr/25 50.00 15.00
8 Javier Vazquez/25 30.00 9.00
9 Jay Payton/25 20.00 6.00
3 Joe Kennedy/11
7 J.Gonzalez Indians-Rgr/25 60.00 18.00
9 Junior Spivey/25 20.00 6.00
2 M.Ramirez Indians-Sox/10
3 M.Grace Cubs-D'backs/5
5 M.Piazza Dgr-Marlins-Mets/5
9 N.Ryan Ang Jkt-Ast Jkt-Rgr/5
0 P.Wilson Marlins-Rockies/25 40.00 12.00
1 Rafael Palmeiro O's-Rgr/5
3 R.Jack A's Jkt-Ang-Yank/5
5 Rich Aurilia/25 20.00 6.00
7 R.Hend A's-M's-Yanks/5
8 R.Hend Dgr-Mets-Padres/5
0 Roberto Alomar Mets-Sox/5
1 Roberto Alomar Indians-O's/5
2 R.Vent Mets-Sox-Yanks/25 50.00 15.00
6 S.Stewart Jays-Twins/10
7 Shawn Green Jays-Dgr/5
8 Shea Hillenbrand/25
9 Steve Carlton Giants-Sox/5
2 Travis Hafner Indians-Rgr/3
4 Vladimir Guerrero/25 60.00 18.00

2003 Timeless Treasures

This 100 card standard-size set was released in July, 2003. These cards were issued in four card tins with an $100 SRP which came one group of cards to a tin and 15 tins to a case. Please note that these cards are sequenced in alphabetical order by the player's first name.

Nm-Mt Ex-Mt
STATED PRINT RUN 900 SERIAL #'d SETS
PRODUCED BY DONRUSS/PLAYOFF
1 Adam Dunn 4.00 1.20
2 Al Kaline 5.00 1.50
3 Alan Trammell 4.00 1.20
4 Albert Pujols 8.00 2.40
5 Alex Rodriguez 6.00 1.80
6 Alfonso Soriano 4.00 1.20
7 Andre Dawson 4.00 1.20
8 Andruw Jones 4.00 1.20
9 Austin Kearns 4.00 1.20
10 Babe Ruth 10.00 3.00
11 Barry Bonds 10.00 3.00
12 Barry Larkin 4.00 1.20
13 Barry Zito 4.00 1.20
14 Bernie Williams 4.00 1.20
15 Bo Jackson 5.00 1.50
16 Brooks Robinson 4.00 1.20
17 Cal Ripken 12.00 3.60
18 Carlton Fisk 4.00 1.20
19 Chipper Jones 5.00 1.50
20 Curt Schilling 4.00 1.20
21 Dale Murphy 5.00 1.50
22 Derek Jeter 10.00 3.00
23 Don Mattingly 10.00 3.00
24 Duke Snider 4.00 1.20
25 Eddie Mathews 5.00 1.50
26 Frank Robinson 4.00 1.20
27 Frank Thomas 5.00 1.50
28 Garret Anderson 4.00 1.20
29 Gary Carter 4.00 1.20
30 George Brett 10.00 3.00
31 Greg Maddux 6.00 1.80
32 Harmon Killebrew 5.00 1.50
33 Hideki Matsui RC 10.00 3.00
34 Hideo Nomo 5.00 1.50
35 Ichiro Suzuki 6.00 1.80
36 Ivan Rodriguez 5.00 1.50
37 Jackie Robinson 5.00 1.50
38 Jason Giambi 4.00 1.20
39 Jeff Bagwell 4.00 1.20
40 Jim Edmonds 4.00 1.20
41 Jim Palmer 4.00 1.20
42 Jim Thome 5.00 1.50
43 Joe Morgan 4.00 1.20
44 Jorge Posada 4.00 1.20
45 Jose Contreras RC 5.00 1.50
46 Juan Gonzalez 4.00 1.20
47 Kazuhisa Ishii 4.00 1.20

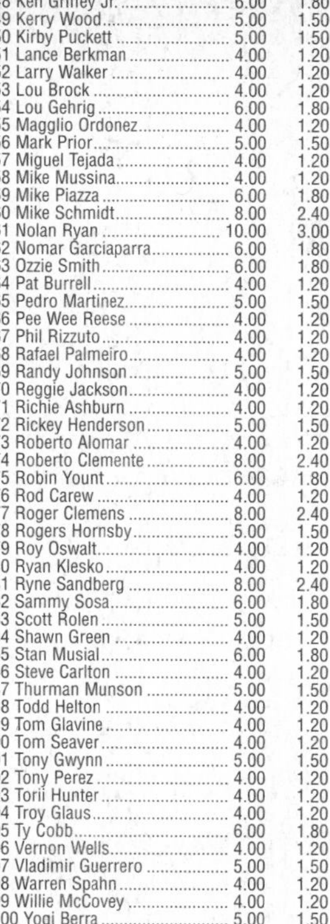

48 Ken Griffey Jr. 6.00 1.80
49 Kerry Wood 5.00 1.50
50 Kirby Puckett 5.00 1.50
51 Lance Berkman 4.00 1.20
52 Larry Walker 4.00 1.20
53 Lou Brock 4.00 1.20
54 Lou Gehrig 6.00 1.80
55 Magglio Ordonez 4.00 1.20
56 Mark Prior 5.00 1.50
57 Miguel Tejada 4.00 1.20
58 Mike Mussina 4.00 1.20
59 Mike Piazza 6.00 1.80
60 Mike Schmidt 8.00 2.40
61 Nolan Ryan 10.00 3.00
62 Nomar Garciaparra 6.00 1.80
63 Ozzie Smith 6.00 1.80
64 Pat Burrell 4.00 1.20
65 Pedro Martinez 5.00 1.50
66 Pee Wee Reese 4.00 1.20
67 Phil Rizzuto 4.00 1.20
68 Rafael Palmeiro 4.00 1.20
69 Randy Johnson 5.00 1.50
70 Reggie Jackson 4.00 1.20
71 Richie Ashburn 4.00 1.20
72 Rickey Henderson 5.00 1.50
73 Roberto Alomar 4.00 1.20
74 Roberto Clemente 8.00 2.40
75 Robin Yount 6.00 1.80
76 Rod Carew 4.00 1.20
77 Roger Clemens 8.00 2.40
78 Rogers Hornsby 5.00 1.50
79 Roy Oswalt 4.00 1.20
80 Ryan Klesko 4.00 1.20
81 Ryne Sandberg 8.00 2.40
82 Sammy Sosa 6.00 1.80
83 Scott Rolen 5.00 1.50
84 Shawn Green 4.00 1.20
85 Stan Musial 6.00 1.80
86 Steve Carlton 4.00 1.20
87 Thurman Munson 5.00 1.50
88 Todd Helton 4.00 1.20
89 Tom Glavine 4.00 1.20
90 Tom Seaver 4.00 1.20
91 Tony Gwynn 5.00 1.50
92 Tony Perez 4.00 1.20
93 Torii Hunter 4.00 1.20
94 Troy Glaus 4.00 1.20
95 Ty Cobb 6.00 1.80
96 Vernon Wells 4.00 1.20
97 Vladimir Guerrero 5.00 1.50
98 Warren Spahn 4.00 1.20
99 Willie McCovey 4.00 1.20
100 Yogi Berra 5.00 1.50

2003 Timeless Treasures Gold

Nm-Mt Ex-Mt
RANDOM INSERTS IN PACKS
STATED PRINT RUN 10 SERIAL #'d SETS
NO PRICING DUE TO SCARCITY

2003 Timeless Treasures Platinum

Nm-Mt Ex-Mt
RANDOM INSERTS IN PACKS
STATED PRINT RUN 1 SERIAL #'d SETS
NO PRICING DUE TO SCARCITY

2003 Timeless Treasures Silver

Nm-Mt Ex-Mt
*ACTIVE STARS: 1.25X TO 3X BASIC.
*RETIRED POST-WAR STARS: 1.5X TO 4X
*RETIRED PRE-WAR STARS: 1X TO 2.5X
*ROOKIES: 1X TO 2.5X BASIC
RANDOM INSERTS IN PACKS
STATED PRINT RUN 50 SERIAL #'d SETS
33 Hideki Matsui 25.00 7.50

2003 Timeless Treasures Award

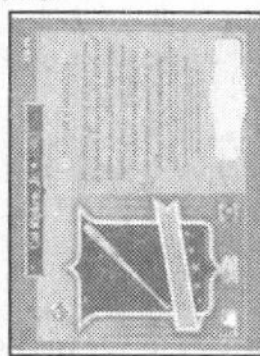

Nm-Mt Ex-Mt
RANDOM INSERTS IN PACKS
PRINT RUNS B/WN 50-100 COPIES PER CARD
1 Ivan Rodriguez Bat/100 20.00 6.00
2 Mike Schmidt Bat-Jsy/50 150.00 45.00
3 Roberto Clemente Bat/50 120.00 36.00
4 Roger Clemens Jsy/50 60.00 18.00
5 Randy Johnson Jsy/100 20.00 6.00
6 Pedro Martinez Jsy/100 20.00 6.00
7 Ivan Rodriguez Chest/100 20.00 6.00
8 Jeff Bagwell Pants/100 20.00 6.00
9 Frank Thomas Jsy/100 20.00 6.00
10 Cal Ripken Bat/75 100.00 30.00
11 Tom Seaver Jsy/50 40.00 12.00

2003 Timeless Treasures Award Autographs

Nm-Mt Ex-Mt
RANDOM INSERTS IN PACKS
PRINT RUNS B/WN 5-15 COPIES PER CARD
NO PRICING DUE TO SCARCITY
2 Mike Schmidt Bat-Jsy/15
4 Roger Clemens Jsy/5
5 Randy Johnson Jsy/5
6 Pedro Martinez Jsy/5
8 Jeff Bagwell Pants/5
9 Frank Thomas Jsy/5
10 Cal Ripken Bat/15
11 Tom Seaver Jsy/10

2003 Timeless Treasures Award MLB Logos

Nm-Mt Ex-Mt
RANDOM INSERTS IN PACKS
STATED PRINT RUN 1 SERIAL #'d SET
NO PRICING DUE TO SCARCITY
5 Randy Johnson
6 Pedro Martinez

2003 Timeless Treasures Award Prime

Nm-Mt Ex-Mt
RANDOM INSERTS IN PACKS
PRINT RUNS B/WN 15-50 COPIES PER CARD
NO PRICING ON QTY OF 30 OR LESS
2 Mike Schmidt Bat-Jsy/25
4 Roger Clemens Jsy/30
5 Randy Johnson Jsy/30
6 Pedro Martinez Jsy/50 60.00 18.00
9 Frank Thomas Jsy/50 60.00 18.00
11 Tom Seaver Jsy/15

2003 Timeless Treasures Award Prime Autographs

Nm-Mt Ex-Mt
RANDOM INSERTS IN PACKS
STATED PRINT RUN 1 SERIAL #'d SET
NO PRICING DUE TO SCARCITY
2 Mike Schmidt Bat-Jsy
4 Roger Clemens Jsy
5 Randy Johnson Jsy
6 Pedro Martinez Jsy
9 Frank Thomas Jsy
11 Tom Seaver Jsy

2003 Timeless Treasures Classic Combos

Nm-Mt Ex-Mt
RANDOM INSERTS IN PACKS
STATED PRINT RUN 100 SERIAL #'d SETS
1 Jason Giambi Hat-Jsy 20.00 6.00
2 Adrian Beltre Hat-Shoes 25.00 7.50
3 Alex Rodriguez Bat-Jsy 40.00 12.00
4 Alfonso Soriano Bat-Jsy 25.00 7.50
5 Andruw Jones Fld Glv-Jsy 20.00 6.00
6 Andre Dawson ST Bat-Jsy 20.00 6.00
7 Barry Larkin Bat-Jsy 25.00 7.50
8 Barry Zito Fld Glv-Jsy 20.00 6.00
9 Cal Ripken Bat-Jsy 100.00 30.00
10 Chipper Jones Bat-Jsy 25.00 7.50
11 Don Mattingly Bat-Jsy 80.00 24.00
12 Eric Chavez Bat-Jsy 20.00 6.00
13 Frank Thomas Bat-Jsy 25.00 7.50
14 Greg Maddux Bat-Jsy 40.00 12.00
15 Ivan Rodriguez Fld Glv-Jsy 25.00 7.50
16 Jeff Bagwell Bat-Jsy 25.00 7.50
17 Jim Thome Bat-Jsy 25.00 7.50
18 Juan Gonzalez Bat-Jsy 25.00 7.50
19 Kazuhisa Ishii Bat-Jsy 20.00 6.00
20 Kerry Wood Jsy-Shoes 25.00 7.50
21 Lance Berkman Fld Glv-Jsy 20.00 6.00
22 Magglio Ordonez Bat-Jsy 20.00 6.00
23 Manny Ramirez Bat-Jsy 25.00 7.50
24 Miguel Tejada Hat-Jsy 20.00 6.00
25 Mike Piazza Bat-Jsy 40.00 12.00
26 Nomar Garciaparra Bat-Jsy 50.00 15.00
27 Pedro Martinez Bat-Jsy 25.00 7.50
28 Randy Johnson Bat-Jsy 25.00 7.50
29 Rickey Henderson Bat-Jsy 25.00 7.50
30 Ryne Sandberg Bat-Jsy 80.00 24.00
31 Sammy Sosa Bat-Jsy
32 Shawn Green Bat-Jsy 20.00 6.00
33 Todd Helton Bat-Jsy 25.00 7.50
34 Tony Gwynn Bat-Jsy 50.00 15.00
35 Vladimir Guerrero Bat-Jsy 25.00 7.50

2003 Timeless Treasures Classic Combos Autographs

Nm-Mt Ex-Mt
RANDOM INSERTS IN PACKS
PRINT RUNS B/WN 5-50 COPIES PER CARD
NO PRICING ON QTY OF 25 OR LESS
3 Alex Rodriguez Bat-Jsy/15
4 Alfonso Soriano Bat-Jsy/5
5 Andruw Jones Fld Glv-Jsy/10
6 Andre Dawson Bat-ST Jsy/50 60.00 18.00

7 Barry Larkin Bat-Jsy/25
8 Barry Zito Fld Glv-Jsy/25
9 Cal Ripken Bat-Jsy/25
10 Chipper Jones Bat-Jsy/5
11 Don Mattingly Bat-Jsy/25
12 Eric Chavez Bat-Jsy/15
13 Frank Thomas Bat-Jsy/5
14 Greg Maddux Bat-Jsy/25
17 Jim Thome Bat-Jsy/10
19 Kazuhisa Ishii Bat-Jsy/25
20 Kerry Wood Jsy-Shoes/15
21 Lance Berkman Fld Glv-Jsy/15
22 Magglio Ordonez Bat-Jsy/25
24 Miguel Tejada Hat-Jsy/15
27 Pedro Martinez Bat-Jsy/10
28 Randy Johnson Bat-Jsy/10
29 Rickey Henderson Bat-Jsy/10
30 Ryne Sandberg Bat-Jsy/50 200.00 60.00
32 Shawn Green Bat-Jsy/25
33 Todd Helton Bat-Jsy/15
34 Tony Gwynn Bat-Jsy/25
35 Vladimir Guerrero Bat-Jsy/50 100.00 30.00

2003 Timeless Treasures Classic Prime Combos

Nm-Mt Ex-Mt
RANDOM INSERTS IN PACKS
STATED PRINT RUN 25 SERIAL #'d SETS
NO PRICING DUE TO SCARCITY

2003 Timeless Treasures Classic Prime Combos Autographs

Nm-Mt Ex-Mt
RANDOM INSERTS IN PACKS
STATED PRINT RUN 1 SERIAL #'d SET
NO PRICING DUE TO SCARCITY
3 Alex Rodriguez Bat-Jsy
4 Alfonso Soriano Bat-Jsy
5 Andruw Jones Fld Glv-Jsy
6 Andre Dawson Bat-ST Jsy
7 Barry Larkin Bat-Jsy
8 Barry Zito Hat-Jsy
9 Cal Ripken Bat-Jsy
10 Chipper Jones Bat-Jsy
11 Don Mattingly Bat-Jsy
12 Eric Chavez Bat-Jsy
13 Frank Thomas Bat-Jsy
14 Greg Maddux Bat-Jsy
17 Jim Thome Bat-Jsy
19 Kazuhisa Ishii Bat-Jsy
20 Kerry Wood Jsy-Shoes
21 Lance Berkman Fld Glv-Jsy
22 Magglio Ordonez Bat-Jsy
24 Miguel Tejada Hat-Jsy
27 Pedro Martinez Bat-Jsy
28 Randy Johnson Bat-Jsy
29 Rickey Henderson Bat-Jsy
30 Ryne Sandberg Bat-Jsy
32 Shawn Green Bat-Jsy
33 Todd Helton Bat-Jsy
34 Tony Gwynn Bat-Jsy
35 Vladimir Guerrero Bat-Jsy

2003 Timeless Treasures Game Day

Nm-Mt Ex-Mt
RANDOM INSERTS IN PACKS
BAT-HAT-JSY PRINT RUN 100 #'d SETS
BALL PRINT RUN 20 SERIAL #'d SETS
NO BALL PRICING DUE TO SCARCITY
1 Tony Gwynn Bat 40.00 12.00
2 Magglio Ordonez Hat 15.00 4.50
3 George Brett Bat 60.00 18.00
4 Rickey Henderson Jsy 20.00 6.00
5 Billy Williams Bat 15.00 4.50
6 Frank Thomas Bat 20.00 6.00
7 Tony Gwynn Jsy 40.00 12.00
8 Billy Williams Ball/20
9 Frank Robinson Ball/20
10 Ryne Sandberg Bat 60.00 18.00
11 Miguel Tejada Jsy 15.00 4.50

2003 Timeless Treasures Game Day Autographs

Nm-Mt Ex-Mt
RANDOM INSERTS IN PACKS

PRINT RUNS B/WN 1-25 COPIES PER CARD
NO PRICING DUE TO SCARCITY
1 Tony Gwynn Bat/10
2 Magglio Ordonez Hat/10
3 George Brett Bat/15
4 Rickey Henderson Jsy/5
5 Billy Williams Bat/25
6 Frank Thomas Bat/1
7 Tony Gwynn Jsy/10
8 Billy Williams Ball/5
9 Frank Robinson Ball/5
10 Ryne Sandberg Bat/25
11 Miguel Tejada Jsy/25

2003 Timeless Treasures Game Day Prime

Nm-Mt Ex-Mt
RANDOM INSERTS IN PACKS
PRINT RUNS B/WN 5-75 COPIES PER CARD
NO PRICING ON QTY OF 25 OR LESS
2 Magglio Ordonez Hat/5
4 Rickey Henderson Jsy/75 50.00 15.00
7 Tony Gwynn Jsy/75 80.00 24.00
11 Miguel Tejada Jsy/75 30.00 9.00

2003 Timeless Treasures Game Day Prime Autographs

Nm-Mt Ex-Mt
RANDOM INSERTS IN PACKS
STATED PRINT RUN 1 SERIAL #'d SET
NO PRICING DUE TO SCARCITY
2 Magglio Ordonez Hat
4 Rickey Henderson Jsy
7 Tony Gwynn Jsy
11 Miguel Tejada Jsy

2003 Timeless Treasures HOF Combos

Nm-Mt Ex-Mt
RANDOM INSERTS IN PACKS
PRINT RUNS B/WN 25-100 COPIES PER CARD
NO PRICING ON QTY 25 OR LESS
1 Al Kaline Bat-Jsy/50 80.00 24.00
2 Babe Ruth Bat-Jsy/25
3 Eddie Mathews Bat-Jsy/50 60.00 18.00
4 Kirby Puckett Bat-Hat/75 50.00 15.00
5 Lou Gehrig Bat-Jsy/25
6 Mike Schmidt Bat-Jsy/100 80.00 24.00
7 Nolan Ryan Fld Glv-Jsy/50 150.00 45.00
8 Phil Rizzuto Bat-Jsy/50 60.00 18.00
9 Reggie Jackson Hat-Jsy/25
10 Roberto Clemente Hat-Jsy/25
11 Rod Carew Bat-Jsy/100 50.00 15.00
12 Stan Musial Bat-Jsy/25
13 Ty Cobb Bat-Pants/25
14 George Brett Bat-Hat/50 150.00 45.00
15 Carlton Fisk Bat-Jsy/100 50.00 15.00

2003 Timeless Treasures HOF Combos Autographs

Nm-Mt Ex-Mt
RANDOM INSERTS IN PACKS
PRINT RUNS B/WN 1-25 COPIES PER CARD
NO PRICING DUE TO SCARCITY
1 Al Kaline Bat-Jsy/25
4 Kirby Puckett Bat-Hat/25
6 Mike Schmidt Bat-Jsy/15
7 Nolan Ryan Fld Glv-Jsy/25
8 Phil Rizzuto Bat-Jsy/25
9 Reggie Jackson Hat-Jsy/1
11 Rod Carew Bat-Jsy/10
12 Stan Musial Bat-Jsy/25
14 George Brett Bat-Hat/15
15 Carlton Fisk Bat-Jsy/25

2003 Timeless Treasures HOF Cuts

Nm-Mt Ex-Mt
RANDOM INSERTS IN PACKS
STATED PRINT RUN 1 SERIAL #'d SET
NO PRICING DUE TO SCARCITY
1 Ty Cobb
2 Babe Ruth
3 Jackie Robinson
4 Pee Wee Reese

2003 Timeless Treasures HOF Induction Year Combos

Nm-Mt Ex-Mt
RANDOM INSERTS IN PACKS
STATED PRINT RUN 25 SERIAL #'d SETS
NO PRICING DUE TO SCARCITY
1 Ty Cobb Bat
Babe Ruth Bat
2 Mel Ott Bat
Jimmie Foxx Bat
3 Yogi Berra Jsy
Early Wynn Jsy
4 Roberto Clemente Jsy
Warren Spahn Jsy
5 Al Kaline Jsy
Duke Snider Jsy
6 Lou Brock Jsy
Enos Slaughter Jsy
7 Jim Palmer Jsy
Joe Morgan Jsy
8 Steve Carlton Jsy
Phil Rizzuto Jsy
9 Mike Schmidt Bat
Richie Ashburn Bat
10 George Brett Jsy
Robin Yount Jsy

2003 Timeless Treasures HOF Induction Year Combos Autographs

Nm-Mt Ex-Mt
RANDOM INSERTS IN PACKS
STATED PRINT RUN 5 SERIAL #'d SETS
NO PRICING DUE TO SCARCITY
5 Al Kaline Jsy
Duke Snider Jsy
7 Jim Palmer Jsy
Joe Morgan Jsy
8 Steve Carlton Jsy
Phil Rizzuto Jsy
10 George Brett Jsy
Robin Yount Jsy

2003 Timeless Treasures HOF Letters

Nm-Mt Ex-Mt
RANDOM INSERTS IN PACKS
PRINT RUNS B/WN 5-25 COPIES PER CARD
NO PRICING DUE TO SCARCITY
28 Brooks Robinson/5
32 Joe Morgan/5
33 Lou Brock/10
35 Mike Schmidt/25
36 Nolan Ryan Angels/15
37 Nolan Ryan Astros/15
38 Nolan Ryan Rangers/15
41 Reggie Jackson/15
44 Rod Carew/20
46 Tom Seaver/25
47 Steve Carlton/15

2003 Timeless Treasures HOF Letters Autographs

Nm-Mt Ex-Mt
RANDOM INSERTS IN PACKS
STATED PRINT RUN 1 SERIAL #'d SET
NO PRICING DUE TO SCARCITY
28 Brooks Robinson
32 Joe Morgan
33 Lou Brock
35 Mike Schmidt
36 Nolan Ryan Angels
37 Nolan Ryan Astros
38 Nolan Ryan Rangers
41 Reggie Jackson
44 Rod Carew
46 Tom Seaver
47 Steve Carlton

2003 Timeless Treasures HOF Logos

Nm-Mt Ex-Mt
RANDOM INSERTS IN PACKS
PRINT RUNS B/WN 1-35 COPIES PER CARD
NO PRICING ON QTY OF 25 OR LESS

25 Al Kaline/5
27 Bobby Doerr/15
28 Brooks Robinson/10
29 Eddie Mathews/35 80.00 24.00
32 Joe Morgan/5
33 Lou Brock/10
35 Mike Schmidt/25
36 Nolan Ryan Angels/35 150.00 45.00
37 Nolan Ryan Astros/35 150.00 45.00
38 Nolan Ryan Rangers/25
39 Phil Rizzuto/5
41 Reggie Jackson/15
42 Roberto Clemente/15
43 Robin Yount/35 100.00 30.00
44 Rod Carew/35 60.00 18.00
45 Stan Musial/1
49 Pee Wee Reese/15
50 Jackie Robinson/5

2003 Timeless Treasures HOF Logos Autographs

Nm-Mt Ex-Mt
RANDOM INSERTS IN PACKS
STATED PRINT RUN 1 SERIAL #'d SET
NO PRICING DUE TO SCARCITY
25 Al Kaline
27 Bobby Doerr
28 Brooks Robinson
32 Joe Morgan
33 Lou Brock
35 Mike Schmidt
36 Nolan Ryan Angels
37 Nolan Ryan Astros
38 Nolan Ryan Rangers
39 Phil Rizzuto
40 Reggie Jackson Yanks
41 Reggie Jackson A's
43 Robin Yount
44 Rod Carew
45 Stan Musial

2003 Timeless Treasures HOF Materials

Nm-Mt Ex-Mt
RANDOM INSERTS IN PACKS
PRINT RUNS B/WN 25-100 COPIES PER CARD
NO PRICING ON QTY OF 25 OR LESS
1 Al Kaline Bat/100 40.00 12.00
2 Babe Ruth Bat/75 250.00 75.00
3 Carlton Fisk Bat/100 25.00 7.50
4 Eddie Mathews Bat/100 40.00 12.00
5 Gary Carter Bat/100 20.00 6.00
6 George Brett Bat/100 60.00 18.00
7 Harmon Killebrew Bat/100 40.00 12.00
8 Joe Morgan Bat/100 20.00 6.00
9 Kirby Puckett Bat/100 25.00 7.50
10 Lou Gehrig Bat/100 150.00 45.00
11 Luis Aparicio Bat/100 20.00 6.00
12 Mike Schmidt Bat/100 50.00 15.00
13 Ozzie Smith Bat/100 40.00 12.00
14 Phil Rizzuto Bat/100 25.00 7.50
15 Reggie Jackson Bat/100 25.00 7.50
16 Richie Ashburn Bat/100 25.00 7.50
17 Roberto Clemente Bat/100 100.00 30.00
18 Robin Yount Bat/100 40.00 12.00
19 Rod Carew Bat/100 25.00 7.50
20 Rogers Hornsby Bat/100 60.00 18.00
21 Stan Musial Bat/100 50.00 15.00
22 Ty Cobb Bat/100 150.00 45.00
23 Willie McCovey Bat/100 20.00 6.00
24 Yogi Berra Bat/100 25.00 7.50
25 Al Kaline Jsy/100 40.00 12.00
26 Babe Ruth Jsy/50 450.00 135.00
27 Bobby Doerr Jsy/100 20.00 6.00
28 Brooks Robinson Jsy/100 25.00 7.50
29 Eddie Mathews Jsy/100 40.00 12.00
30 Harmon Killebrew Jsy/100 40.00 12.00
31 Ty Cobb Pants/100 150.00 45.00
32 Joe Morgan Jsy/100 20.00 6.00
33 Lou Brock Jsy/100 25.00 7.50
34 Lou Gehrig Jsy/50 300.00 90.00
35 Mike Schmidt Jsy/100 50.00 15.00
36 Nolan Ryan Angels Jsy/100 80.00 24.00
37 Nolan Ryan Astros Jsy/100 60.00 18.00
38 Nolan Ryan Rangers Jsy/100 80.00 24.00
39 Phil Rizzuto Jsy/100 25.00 7.50
40 Reggie Jackson Yanks Jsy/25
41 Reggie Jackson A's Jsy/100 25.00 7.50
42 Roberto Clemente Jsy/50 150.00 45.00
43 Robin Yount Jsy/100 40.00 12.00
44 Rod Carew Jsy/100 25.00 7.50
45 Stan Musial Jsy/100 60.00 18.00
46 Tom Seaver Jsy/100 25.00 7.50
47 Steve Carlton Jsy/100 20.00 6.00
48 Carlton Fisk Jsy/100 25.00 7.50
49 Pee Wee Reese Jsy/100 25.00 7.50
50 Jackie Robinson Jsy/50 100.00 30.00

2003 Timeless Treasures HOF Materials Autographs

Nm-Mt Ex-Mt
RANDOM INSERTS IN PACKS
PRINT RUNS B/WN 5-50 COPIES PER CARD
NO PRICING ON QTY OF 25 OR LESS
1 Al Kaline Bat/15
3 Carlton Fisk Bat/15
5 Gary Carter Bat/25
6 George Brett Bat/25
7 Harmon Killebrew Bat/25
8 Joe Morgan Bat/15
9 Kirby Puckett Bat/25
11 Luis Aparicio Bat/25
12 Mike Schmidt Bat/15
13 Ozzie Smith Bat/10
14 Phil Rizzuto Bat/15
15 Reggie Jackson Bat/10
18 Robin Yount Bat/15
19 Rod Carew Bat/10
21 Stan Musial Bat/25
23 Willie McCovey Bat/25
24 Yogi Berra Bat/15
25 Al Kaline Jsy/25
27 Bobby Doerr Jsy/25
28 Brooks Robinson Jsy/25
30 Harmon Killebrew Jsy/50 100.00 30.00
32 Joe Morgan Jsy/25
33 Lou Brock Jsy/50 80.00 24.00
35 Mike Schmidt Jsy/25
36 Nolan Ryan Angels Jsy/25
37 Nolan Ryan Astros Jsy/25
38 Nolan Ryan Rangers Jsy/25
39 Phil Rizzuto Jsy/25
40 Reggie Jackson Yanks Jsy/5
41 Reggie Jackson A's Jsy/15
43 Robin Yount Jsy/25
44 Rod Carew Jsy/15
45 Stan Musial Jsy/50 120.00 36.00
46 Tom Seaver Jsy/25
47 Steve Carlton Jsy/25
48 Carlton Fisk Jsy/25

2003 Timeless Treasures HOF Numbers

Nm-Mt Ex-Mt
RANDOM INSERTS IN PACKS
PRINT RUNS B/WN 5-50 COPIES PER CARD
NO PRICING ON QTY OF 30 OR LESS
26 Babe Ruth/5
28 Brooks Robinson/5
29 Eddie Mathews/35 80.00 24.00
33 Lou Brock/25
34 Lou Gehrig/5
35 Mike Schmidt/50 100.00 30.00
36 Nolan Ryan Angels/35 200.00 60.00
37 Nolan Ryan Astros/25
38 Nolan Ryan Rangers/5
39 Phil Rizzuto/10
41 Reggie Jackson/25
42 Roberto Clemente/15
43 Robin Yount/35 100.00 30.00
44 Rod Carew/25
45 Stan Musial/10
46 Tom Seaver/35 60.00 18.00
47 Steve Carlton/40 50.00 15.00
48 Carlton Fisk/35 60.00 18.00
49 Pee Wee Reese/10
50 Jackie Robinson/5

2003 Timeless Treasures HOF Numbers Autographs

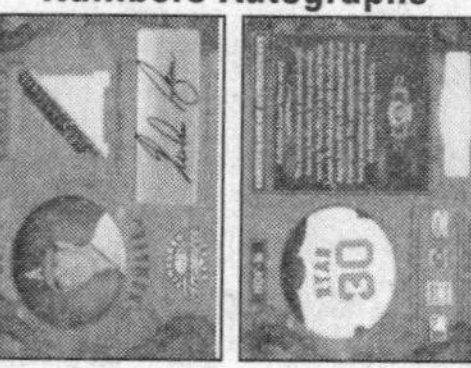

Nm-Mt Ex-Mt
RANDOM INSERTS IN PACKS
STATED PRINT RUN 1 SERIAL #'d SET
NO PRICING DUE TO SCARCITY
25 Al Kaline
28 Brooks Robinson
32 Joe Morgan
33 Lou Brock
35 Mike Schmidt
36 Nolan Ryan Angels
37 Nolan Ryan Astros
38 Nolan Ryan Rangers
39 Phil Rizzuto
41 Reggie Jackson
43 Robin Yount
44 Rod Carew
45 Stan Musial
46 Tom Seaver
47 Steve Carlton
48 Carlton Fisk

2003 Timeless Treasures HOF Prime Combos

Nm-Mt Ex-Mt
RANDOM INSERTS IN PACKS
PRINT RUNS B/WN 5-25 COPIES PER CARD
NO PRICING DUE TO SCARCITY
1 Al Kaline Bat-Jsy/5
2 Babe Ruth Bat-Jsy/5
3 Eddie Mathews Bat-Jsy/25
4 Kirby Puckett Bat-Hat/15
6 Mike Schmidt Bat-Jsy/25
7 Nolan Ryan Fld Glv-Jsy/15
8 Phil Rizzuto Bat-Jsy/5
10 Roberto Clemente Hat-Jsy/5
11 Rod Carew Bat-Jsy/5
14 George Brett Bat-Hat/10
15 Carlton Fisk Bat-Jsy/5

2003 Timeless Treasures HOF Prime Combos Autographs

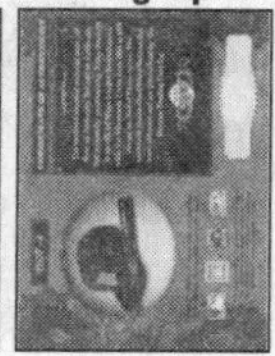

Nm-Mt Ex-Mt
RANDOM INSERTS IN PACKS
STATED PRINT RUN 1 SERIAL #'d SET
NO PRICING DUE TO SCARCITY
1 Al Kaline Bat-Jsy
4 Kirby Puckett Bat-Hat
6 Mike Schmidt Bat-Jsy
7 Nolan Ryan Fld Glv-Jsy
8 Phil Rizzuto Bat-Jsy
9 Reggie Jackson Hat-Jsy
11 Rod Carew Bat-Jsy
14 George Brett Bat-Hat
15 Carlton Fisk Bat-Jsy

2003 Timeless Treasures Home Run

Nm-Mt Ex-Mt
RANDOM INSERTS IN PACKS
BAT-JSY PRINT RUN 100 SERIAL #'d SETS
BALL PRINT RUN 20 SERIAL #'d SETS
NO BALL PRICING DUE TO SCARCITY
1 Harmon Killebrew HR 570 Bat 40.00 12.00
2 Harmon Killebrew HR 565 Bat 40.00 12.00
3 Jose Canseco HR 311 Bat 40.00 12.00
4 Magglio Ordonez 00 HR 17 Bat 15.00 4.50
5 Rafael Palmeiro HR 425 Bat 20.00 6.00
6 Rafael Palmeiro HR 440 Bat 20.00 6.00
7 Rafael Palmeiro HR 448 Jsy 20.00 6.00
8 Alex Rodriguez 00 HR 36 Bat 25.00 7.50
9 Alex Rodriguez 00 HR 37 Bat 25.00 7.50
10 Alex Rodriguez 00 HR 33 Bat 25.00 7.50
11 Alex Rodriguez 98 HR 23 Ball/20
12 Adam Dunn 00 HR 9 Jsy 20.00 6.00

2003 Timeless Treasures Home Run Autographs

Nm-Mt Ex-Mt
RANDOM INSERTS IN PACKS
PRINT RUNS B/WN 1-25 COPIES PER CARD
NO PRICING DUE TO SCARCITY
1 Harmon Killebrew HR 570 Bat/25
2 Harmon Killebrew HR 565 Bat/25
3 Jose Canseco HR 311 Bat/25
4 Magglio Ordonez 00 HR 17 Bat/15
5 Rafael Palmeiro HR 425 Bat/1
6 Rafael Palmeiro HR 440 Bat/1
7 Rafael Palmeiro HR 448 Jsy/1
8 Alex Rodriguez 00 HR 36 Bat/15
9 Alex Rodriguez 00 HR 37 Bat/15
10 Alex Rodriguez 00 HR 33 Bat/15
11 Alex Rodriguez 98 HR 23 Ball/5
12 Adam Dunn 00 HR 9 Jsy/25

2003 Timeless Treasures Home Run MLB Logos

Nm-Mt Ex-Mt
RANDOM INSERTS IN PACKS
STATED PRINT RUN 1 SERIAL #'d SET
NO PRICING DUE TO SCARCITY
7 Rafael Palmeiro HR 448
12 Adam Dunn 00 HR 9

2003 Timeless Treasures Material Ink

Nm-Mt Ex-Mt
COMMON CARD p/r 75-100 40.00 12.00
COMMON CARD p/r 50 60.00 18.00
RANDOM INSERTS IN PACKS
PRINT RUNS B/WN 25-100 COPIES PER CARD
NO PRICING ON QTY OF 25 OR LESS
1 Adam Dunn/50 80.00 24.00
2 Alan Trammell/100 40.00 12.00
3 Alex Rodriguez White Jsy/25
4 Alex Rodriguez Blue Jsy/25
5 Andre Dawson/100 40.00 12.00
6 Barry Zito/50 80.00 24.00
7 Bo Jackson/100 100.00 30.00
8 Bob Feller/25
9 Bobby Doerr/50 60.00 18.00
10 Brooks Robinson/50
11 Cal Ripken No Sleeve/50 300.00 90.00
12 Cal Ripken Black Sleeve/50 300.00 90.00
13 Cal Ripken Throwing/25
14 Dale Murphy/50 80.00 24.00
15 Dave Parker/75 40.00 12.00
16 David Cone/100 40.00 12.00
17 Don Mattingly/100 150.00 45.00
18 Duke Snider/25
19 Edgar Martinez/50 80.00 24.00
20 Gary Carter/100 40.00 12.00
21 Harmon Killebrew/75 100.00 30.00
22 Jim Edmonds/25
23 Jim Thome/50 80.00 24.00
24 Joe Carter/100 40.00 12.00
25 Jose Canseco/50 80.00 24.00
26 Jose Vidro/100 40.00 12.00
27 Kazuhisa Ishii/100 40.00 12.00
28 Kerry Wood/50 80.00 24.00
29 Lance Berkman/50 80.00 24.00
30 Mark Mulder/25
31 Mark Prior/50
32 Mike Schmidt/50 150.00 45.00
33 Nick Johnson/100 40.00 12.00
34 Nolan Ryan Astros/25
35 Nolan Ryan Rangers/25
36 Nolan Ryan Angels/25
37 Paul LoDuca/100 40.00 12.00
38 Paul Molitor/50 80.00 24.00
39 Randy Johnson/25
40 Reggie Jackson/25
41 Roberto Alomar Mets/50 80.00 24.00
42 Roberto Alomar Indians/100 60.00 18.00
43 Robin Yount/50 150.00 45.00
44 Rod Carew/25
45 Roger Clemens Yanks/25
46 Roger Clemens Sox/25
47 Ryan Klesko/75 40.00 12.00
48 Ryne Sandberg/25
50 Shawn Green/25
51 Stan Musial/25
52 Steve Carlton Giants/100 60.00 18.00
53 Steve Carlton Sox/100 60.00 18.00
54 Todd Helton/50 80.00 24.00
55 Tom Seaver/50 80.00 24.00
56 Tony Gwynn/25
57 Torii Hunter/100 40.00 12.00
58 Vladimir Guerrero/100 60.00 18.00
59 Will Clark/50 120.00 36.00

2003 Timeless Treasures Milestone

Nm-Mt Ex-Mt
RANDOM INSERTS IN PACKS
JSY PRINT RUN 100 SERIAL #'d SETS
BALL PRINT RUN 24 SERIAL #'d SETS
NO BALL PRICING DUE TO SCARCITY
1 Cal Ripken Ball/24
2 Willie McCovey Ball/24
3 R.Henderson Padres Jsy/100 25.00 7.50
4 Gaylord Perry Jsy/100 20.00 6.00
5 R.Henderson A's Jsy/100 25.00 7.50

2003 Timeless Treasures Milestone Autographs

Nm-Mt Ex-Mt
RANDOM INSERTS IN PACKS
STATED PRINT RUN 1 SERIAL #'d SET
NO PRICING DUE TO SCARCITY
1 Cal Ripken Ball
2 Willie McCovey Ball
3 Rickey Henderson Padres Jsy
5 Rickey Henderson A's Jsy

2003 Timeless Treasures MLB Logo Ink

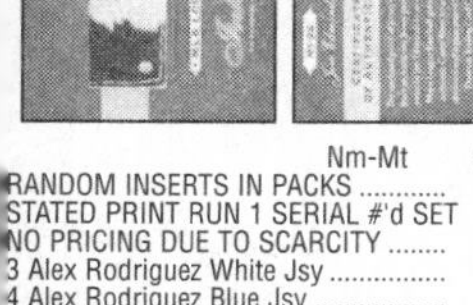

Nm-Mt Ex-Mt
RANDOM INSERTS IN PACKS
STATED PRINT RUN 1 SERIAL #'d SET
NO PRICING DUE TO SCARCITY
3 Alex Rodriguez White Jsy
4 Alex Rodriguez Blue Jsy
6 Barry Zito
13 Cal Ripken Throwing
19 Edgar Martinez
22 Jim Edmonds
23 Jim Thome
26 Jose Vidro
27 Kazuhisa Ishii
28 Kerry Wood
29 Lance Berkman
30 Mark Mulder
31 Mark Prior
33 Nick Johnson
37 Paul LoDuca
39 Randy Johnson
42 Roberto Alomar Indians
45 Roger Clemens Yanks
47 Ryan Klesko
50 Shawn Green
54 Todd Helton
57 Torii Hunter

2003 Timeless Treasures Past and Present

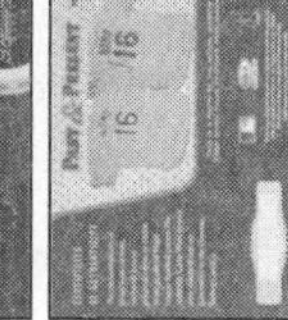

Nm-Mt Ex-Mt
RANDOM INSERTS IN PACKS
STATED PRINT RUN 100 SERIAL #'d SETS
1 Alex Rodriguez 40.00 12.00
2 Hideo Nomo 25.00 7.50
3 Jason Giambi 20.00 6.00
4 Juan Gonzalez 25.00 7.50
5 Mike Piazza 40.00 12.00
6 Pedro Martinez 25.00 7.50
7 Randy Johnson 25.00 7.50
8 Rickey Henderson 25.00 7.50
9 Roberto Alomar 25.00 7.50
10 Roger Clemens 40.00 12.00
11 Sammy Sosa 40.00 12.00

2003 Timeless Treasures Past and Present Autographs

Nm-Mt Ex-Mt
RANDOM INSERTS IN PACKS
PRINT RUNS B/WN 5-25 COPIES PER CARD
NO PRICING DUE TO SCARCITY
1 Alex Rodriguez/25
5 Pedro Martinez/5
7 Randy Johnson/5
8 Rickey Henderson/10
9 Roberto Alomar/25
10 Roger Clemens/15

2003 Timeless Treasures Past and Present Letters

Nm-Mt Ex-Mt
RANDOM INSERTS IN PACKS
PRINT RUNS B/WN 25-75 COPIES PER CARD
NO PRICING ON QTY OF 25 OR LESS
1 Alex Rodriguez/75 80.00 24.00
2 Hideo Nomo/25
4 Juan Gonzalez/75 50.00 15.00
6 Pedro Martinez/75 50.00 15.00
7 Randy Johnson/75 50.00 15.00
9 Roberto Alomar/25

2003 Timeless Treasures Past and Present Letters Autographs

Nm-Mt Ex-Mt
RANDOM INSERTS IN PACKS
STATED PRINT RUN 1 SERIAL #'d SET
NO PRICING DUE TO SCARCITY
1 Alex Rodriguez
7 Randy Johnson
9 Roberto Alomar

2003 Timeless Treasures Past and Present Logos

Nm-Mt Ex-Mt
RANDOM INSERTS IN PACKS
PRINT RUNS B/WN 5-75 COPIES PER CARD
NO PRICING ON QTY OF 25 OR LESS
1 Alex Rodriguez/60 80.00 24.00
2 Hideo Nomo/25
3 Jason Giambi/75 30.00 9.00
4 Juan Gonzalez/25
5 Mike Piazza/50 80.00 24.00
7 Randy Johnson/5
8 Rickey Henderson/25
10 Roger Clemens/35 100.00 30.00
11 Sammy Sosa/25

2003 Timeless Treasures Past and Present Logos Autographs

Nm-Mt Ex-Mt
RANDOM INSERTS IN PACKS
STATED PRINT RUN 1 SERIAL #'d SET
NO PRICING DUE TO SCARCITY
1 Alex Rodriguez
7 Randy Johnson
8 Rickey Henderson
10 Roger Clemens

2003 Timeless Treasures Past and Present Numbers

Nm-Mt Ex-Mt
RANDOM INSERTS IN PACKS
PRINT RUNS B/WN 5-75 COPIES PER CARD
NO PRICING ON QTY OF 25 OR LESS
1 Alex Rodriguez/35 100.00 30.00
2 Hideo Nomo/25
3 Jason Giambi/75 30.00 9.00
4 Juan Gonzalez/25
5 Mike Piazza/5
6 Pedro Martinez/50 60.00 18.00
7 Randy Johnson/50 60.00 18.00
8 Rickey Henderson /25
11 Sammy Sosa/25

2003 Timeless Treasures Past and Present Numbers Autographs

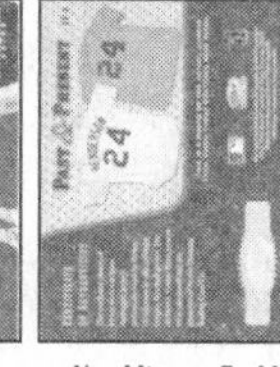

Nm-Mt Ex-Mt
RANDOM INSERTS IN PACKS
STATED PRINT RUN 1 SERIAL #'d SET
NO PRICING DUE TO SCARCITY
1 Alex Rodriguez
6 Pedro Martinez
7 Randy Johnson
8 Rickey Henderson

2003 Timeless Treasures Past and Present Patches

Nm-Mt Ex-Mt
RANDOM INSERTS IN PACKS
PRINT RUNS B/WN 5-20 COPIES PER CARD
NO PRICING DUE TO SCARCITY
1 Alex Rodriguez/10
5 Mike Piazza/15
6 Pedro Martinez/5
8 Rickey Henderson/5
9 Roberto Alomar/20

2003 Timeless Treasures Past and Present Patches Autographs

Nm-Mt Ex-Mt
RANDOM INSERTS IN PACKS
STATED PRINT RUN 1 SERIAL #'d SET
NO PRICING DUE TO SCARCITY
1 Alex Rodriguez
6 Pedro Martinez
8 Rickey Henderson
9 Roberto Alomar

2003 Timeless Treasures Post Season

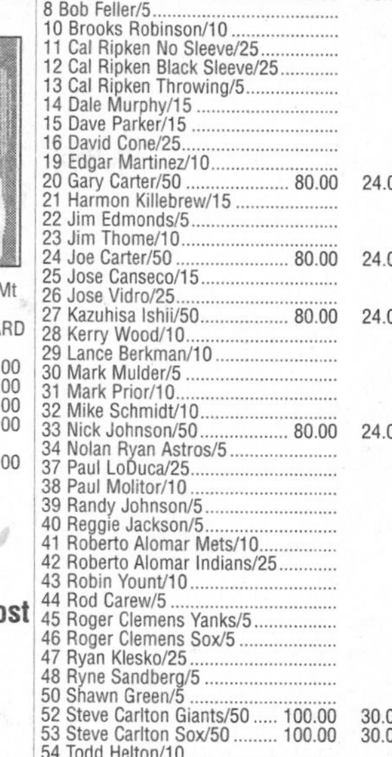

Nm-Mt Ex-Mt
RANDOM INSERTS IN PACKS
PRINT RUNS B/WN 25-100 COPIES PER CARD
NO PRICING ON QTY OF 25 OR LESS
1 Ozzie Smith Jsy/100 40.00 12.00
2 Tom Glavine Jsy/50 40.00 12.00
3 Bernie Williams Bat/100 20.00 6.00
4 Roger Clemens Jsy/100 40.00 12.00
5 Babe Ruth Ball/25
6 Christy Mathewson Seat/100 50.00 15.00
7 Derek Jeter Ball/25
8 Alfonso Soriano Ball/25
9 Randy Johnson NLCS Ball/25
10 Ichiro Suzuki Ball/25
11 Curt Schilling Ball/25
12 Randy Johnson WS Ball/25

2003 Timeless Treasures Post Season Autographs

Nm-Mt Ex-Mt
RANDOM INSERTS IN PACKS
PRINT RUNS B/WN 5-15 COPIES PER CARD
NO PRICING DUE TO SCARCITY
1 Ozzie Smith Jsy/15
3 Bernie Williams Bat/5
4 Roger Clemens Jsy/15
8 Alfonso Soriano Ball/5
9 Randy Johnson NLCS Ball/5
12 Randy Johnson WS Ball/5

2003 Timeless Treasures Post Season Prime

Nm-Mt Ex-Mt
RANDOM INSERTS IN PACKS
PRINT RUNS B/WN 5-75 COPIES PER CARD
NO PRICING ON QTY OF 25 OR LESS
1 Ozzie Smith Jsy/75 60.00 18.00
2 Tom Glavine Jsy/25
4 Roger Clemens Jsy/15
7 Derek Jeter Ball/5
8 Alfonso Soriano Ball/5
9 Randy Johnson NLCS Ball/5
10 Ichiro Suzuki Ball/5
11 Curt Schilling Ball/5
12 Randy Johnson WS Ball/5

2003 Timeless Treasures Post Season Prime Autographs

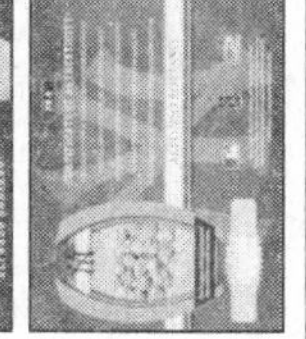

Nm-Mt Ex-Mt
RANDOM INSERTS IN PACKS
STATED PRINT RUN 1 SERIAL #'d SET
NO PRICING DUE TO SCARCITY
1 Ozzie Smith Jsy
2 Tom Glavine Jsy
4 Roger Clemens Jsy
8 Alfonso Soriano Ball
9 Randy Johnson NLCS Ball
12 Randy Johnson WS Ball

2003 Timeless Treasures Prime Ink

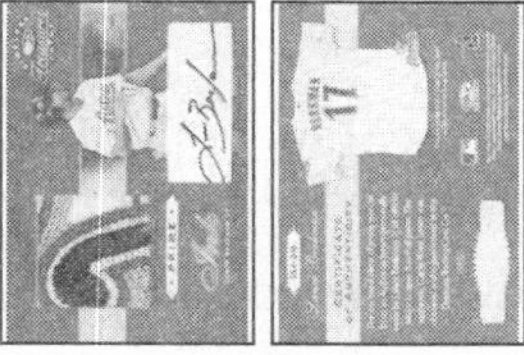
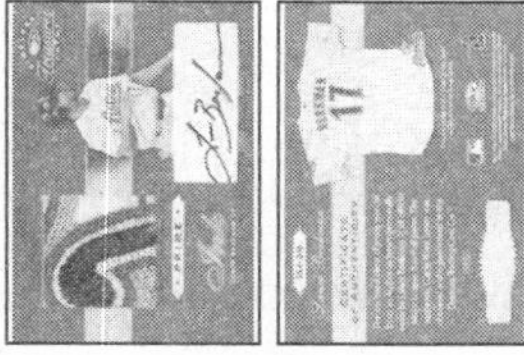
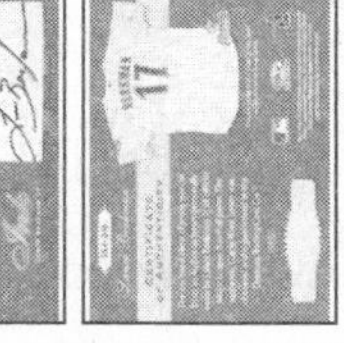

Nm-Mt Ex-Mt
RANDOM INSERTS IN PACKS
PRINT RUNS B/WN 5-50 COPIES PER CARD
NO PRICING ON QTY OF 25 OR LESS
1 Adam Dunn/10
2 Alan Trammell/50 80.00 24.00
3 Alex Rodriguez White Jsy/10
4 Alex Rodriguez Blue Jsy/5
5 Andre Dawson/25
6 Barry Zito/10
7 Bo Jackson/50 200.00 60.00
8 Bob Feller/5
10 Brooks Robinson/10
11 Cal Ripken No Sleeve/25
12 Cal Ripken Black Sleeve/25
13 Cal Ripken Throwing/5
14 Dale Murphy/15
15 Dave Parker/15
16 David Cone/25
19 Edgar Martinez/10
20 Gary Carter/50 80.00 24.00
21 Harmon Killebrew/15
22 Jim Edmonds/5
23 Jim Thome/10
24 Joe Carter/50 80.00 24.00
25 Jose Canseco/15
26 Jose Vidro/25
27 Kazuhisa Ishii/50 80.00 24.00
28 Kerry Wood/10
29 Lance Berkman/10
30 Mark Mulder/5
31 Mark Prior/10
32 Mike Schmidt/10
33 Nick Johnson/50 80.00 24.00
34 Nolan Ryan Astros/5
37 Paul LoDuca/25
38 Paul Molitor/10
39 Randy Johnson/5
40 Reggie Jackson/5
41 Roberto Alomar Mets/10
42 Roberto Alomar Indians/25
43 Robin Yount/10
44 Rod Carew/5
45 Roger Clemens Yanks/5
46 Roger Clemens Sox/5
47 Ryan Klesko/25
48 Ryne Sandberg/5
50 Shawn Green/5
52 Steve Carlton Giants/50 100.00 30.00
53 Steve Carlton Sox/50 100.00 30.00
54 Todd Helton/10
56 Tony Gwynn/10
57 Torii Hunter/50 80.00 24.00
58 Vladimir Guerrero/50 120.00 36.00
59 Will Clark/25

2003 Timeless Treasures Rookie Year

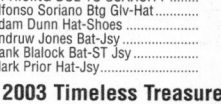

MINT NRMT
COMMON ACTIVE p/r 100 10.00 4.50
COMMON RETIRED p/r 100 15.00 6.75
PRINT RUNS B/WN 50-100 COPIES PER CARD
*PARALLEL p/r 75-100: .4X TO 1X BASIC RY
*PARALLEL p/r 61-68: .5X TO 1.2X BASIC RY
*PARALLEL p/r 42-47: .6X TO 1.5X BASIC RY
PARALLEL PRINT B/WN 42-100 COPIES PER
RANDOM INSERTS IN PACKS
1 Cal Ripken Bat/100 80.00 36.00
2 Mike Schmidt Bat/50 60.00 27.00
3 Rafael Palmeiro Bat/100 15.00 6.75
4 Nomar Garciaparra Jsy/100 40.00 18.00
5 Sean Casey Jsy/100 10.00 4.50
6 Stan Musial Jsy/100 50.00 22.00
7 Yogi Berra Jsy/100 40.00 18.00
8 Bernie Williams Bat/100 15.00 6.75
9 Ivan Rodriguez Jsy/100 15.00 6.75
10 J.D. Drew Jsy/100 10.00 4.50
11 Scott Rolen Jsy/100 15.00 6.75
12 Vladimir Guerrero Jsy/100 15.00 6.75
13 Johnny Bench Bat/100 25.00 11.00
14 Ivan Rodriguez Bat/100 15.00 6.75
15 Andruw Jones Jsy/100 10.00 4.50
16 Andruw Jones Bat/100 10.00 4.50
17 Fred Lynn Jsy/100 15.00 6.75
18 Jeff Kent Jsy/100 10.00 4.50
19 Gary Sheffield Jsy/100 10.00 4.50
20 Ron Santo Bat/100 25.00 11.00
21 Juan Gonzalez Jsy/100 15.00 6.75
22 Alfonso Soriano Jsy/100 15.00 6.75
23 Ryan Klesko Jsy/100 10.00 4.50
24 Adam Dunn Btg Glv/100 15.00 6.75
25 Hideo Nomo Jsy/100 15.00 6.75
26 Mark Prior Jsy/100 15.00 6.75
27 Pat Burrell Bat/50 25.00 11.00
28 Magglio Ordonez Bat/100 10.00 4.50
29 Kirby Puckett Bat/100 40.00 18.00
30 Albert Pujols Jsy/100 40.00 18.00
31 Albert Pujols Bat/100 40.00 18.00

2003 Timeless Treasures Rookie Year Autographs

MINT NRMT
RANDOM INSERTS IN PACKS
PRINT RUNS B/WN 10-25 COPIES PER CARD
NO PRICING DUE TO SCARCITY
1 Cal Ripken Bat/25
2 Mike Schmidt Bat/25
6 Stan Musial Jsy/25
7 Yogi Berra Jsy/15
8 Bernie Williams Bat/25
12 Vladimir Guerrero Jsy/25
13 Johnny Bench Bat/25
15 Andruw Jones Jsy/10
16 Andruw Jones Bat/10
17 Fred Lynn Jsy/25
19 Gary Sheffield Jsy/10
20 Ron Santo Bat/25
22 Alfonso Soriano Jsy/10
23 Ryan Klesko Jsy/25
24 Adam Dunn Btg Glv/10
26 Mark Prior Jsy/25
27 Pat Burrell Bat/10
28 Magglio Ordonez Bat/25
29 Kirby Puckett Bat/15

2003 Timeless Treasures Rookie Year Combos

Nm-Mt Ex-Mt
RANDOM INSERTS IN PACKS
PRINT RUNS B/WN 25-50 COPIES PER CARD
NO PRICJNG ON QTY OF 25 OR LESS
1 Alfonso Soriano Btg Glv-Hat/25
2 Adam Dunn Hat-Shoes/25
3 Andruw Jones Bat-Jsy/50 25.00 7.50
4 Ivan Rodriguez Bat-Jsy/50 40.00 12.00
5 Hank Blalock Bat-ST Jsy/25
6 Mark Prior Hat-Jsy/50 40.00 12.00
7 Albert Pujols Bat-Jsy/50 100.00 30.00

2003 Timeless Treasures Rookie Year Combos Autographs

Nm-Mt Ex-Mt
RANDOM INSERTS IN PACKS
STATED PRINT RUN 1 SERIAL #'d SET
NO PRICING DUE TO SCARCITY
1 Alfonso Soriano Btg Glv-Hat
2 Adam Dunn Hat-Shoes
3 Andruw Jones Bat-Jsy
5 Hank Blalock Bat-ST Jsy
6 Mark Prior Hat-Jsy

2003 Timeless Treasures Rookie Year Letters

Nm-Mt Ex-Mt
RANDOM INSERTS IN PACKS
PRINT RUNS B/WN 15-35 COPIES PER CARD
NO PRICING ON QTY OF 25 OR LESS
4 Nomar Garciaparra/35 60.00 18.00
5 Sean Casey/25
9 Ivan Rodriguez/35 50.00 15.00
10 J.D. Drew/15
11 Scott Rolen/15
12 Vladimir Guerrero/35 50.00 15.00
15 Andruw Jones/25
18 Jeff Kent/15
23 Ryan Klesko/15
25 Hideo Nomo/25
30 Albert Pujols/25

2003 Timeless Treasures Rookie Year Letters Autographs

Nm-Mt Ex-Mt
RANDOM INSERTS IN PACKS
STATED PRINT RUN 1 SERIAL #'d SET
NO PRICING DUE TO SCARCITY
11 Scott Rolen
12 Vladimir Guerrero
15 Andruw Jones
19 Gary Sheffield
23 Ryan Klesko
26 Mark Prior

2003 Timeless Treasures Rookie Year Logos

Nm-Mt Ex-Mt
RANDOM INSERTS IN PACKS
PRINT RUNS B/WN 10-50 COPIES PER CARD
NO PRICING ON QTY OF 25 OR LESS
4 Nomar Garciaparra/15
5 Sean Casey/50 40.00 12.00
6 Stan Musial/15
7 Yogi Berra/10
9 Ivan Rodriguez/10
10 J.D. Drew/50 40.00 12.00
11 Scott Rolen/50 50.00 15.00
12 Vladimir Guerrero/50 50.00 15.00
15 Andruw Jones/50 40.00 12.00
17 Fred Lynn/25
18 Jeff Kent/50 40.00 12.00
19 Gary Sheffield/50 40.00 12.00
21 Juan Gonzalez/25
22 Alfonso Soriano/20
23 Ryan Klesko/50 40.00 12.00
25 Hideo Nomo/25
26 Mark Prior/25
30 Albert Pujols/50 100.00 30.00

2003 Timeless Treasures Rookie Year Logos Autographs

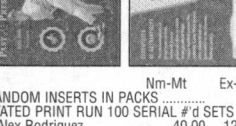

Nm-Mt Ex-Mt
RANDOM INSERTS IN PACKS
STATED PRINT RUN 1 SERIAL #'d SET

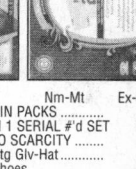

NO PRICING DUE TO SCARCITY
6 Stan Musial
7 Yogi Berra
11 Scott Rolen
12 Vladimir Guerrero
15 Andruw Jones
17 Fred Lynn
19 Gary Sheffield
22 Alfonso Soriano
23 Ryan Klesko
26 Mark Prior

2003 Timeless Treasures Rookie Year Numbers

	MINT	NRMT
RANDOM INSERTS IN PACKS		
PRINT RUNS B/WN 15-50 COPIES PER CARD		
NO PRICING ON QTY OF 30 OR LESS		
5 Sean Casey/30		
6 Stan Musial/15		
7 Yogi Berra/15		
9 Ivan Rodriguez/15		
10 J.D. Drew/25		
11 Scott Rolen/30		
12 Vladimir Guerrero/50	40.00	18.00
15 Andruw Jones/50	25.00	11.00
17 Fred Lynn/30		
18 Jeff Kent/25		
19 Gary Sheffield/25		
21 Juan Gonzalez/30		
22 Alfonso Soriano/35	40.00	18.00
23 Ryan Klesko/35	25.00	11.00
25 Hideo Nomo/25		
26 Mark Prior/35	40.00	18.00
30 Albert Pujols/25		

2003 Timeless Treasures Rookie Year Numbers Autographs

	MINT	NRMT
RANDOM INSERTS IN PACKS		
STATED PRINT RUN 1 SERIAL #'d SET		
NO PRICING DUE TO SCARCITY		
6 Stan Musial		
7 Yogi Berra		
12 Vladimir Guerrero		
15 Andruw Jones		
17 Fred Lynn		
19 Gary Sheffield		
22 Alfonso Soriano		
23 Ryan Klesko		
26 Mark Prior		

2003 Timeless Treasures Rookie Year Patches

	MINT	NRMT
RANDOM INSERTS IN PACKS		
PRINT RUNS B/WN 10-15 COPIES PER CARD		
NO PRICING DUE TO SCARCITY		
5 Sean Casey/15		
11 Scott Rolen/10		
12 Vladimir Guerrero/15		
22 Alfonso Soriano/10		
26 Mark Prior/10		

2003 Timeless Treasures Rookie Year Patches Autographs

	MINT	NRMT
RANDOM INSERTS IN PACKS		
STATED PRINT RUN 1 SERIAL #'d SET		
NO PRICING DUE TO SCARCITY		
12 Vladimir Guerrero		
22 Alfonso Soriano		
23 Ryan Klesko		
26 Mark Prior		

2004 Timeless Treasures

This 100 card set was released in May, 2004. This set was issed in four card packs with an $100 SRP and which came one pack to a box and 15 boxes to a case.

	Nm-Mt	Ex-Mt
COMPLETE SET (100)	250.00	75.00
STATED PRINT RUN 999 SERIAL #'d SETS		
1 Albert Pujols	6.00	1.80
2 Garret Anderson	4.00	1.20
3 Randy Johnson	4.00	1.20
4 Alex Rodriguez Yanks	6.00	1.80
5 Manny Ramirez	4.00	1.20
6 Mark Prior	4.00	1.20
7 Roberto Alomar	4.00	1.20
8 Barry Larkin	4.00	1.20
9 Todd Helton	4.00	1.20
10 Ivan Rodriguez	4.00	1.20
11 Jacque Jones	4.00	1.20
12 Jeff Kent	4.00	1.20
13 Mike Sweeney	4.00	1.20
14 Shawn Green	4.00	1.20
15 Richie Sexson	4.00	1.20
16 Mike Piazza	5.00	1.50
17 Vladimir Guerrero	4.00	1.20
18 Mike Mussina	4.00	1.20
19 Barry Zito	4.00	1.20
20 Don Mattingly	8.00	2.40
21 Ichiro Suzuki	5.00	1.50
22 Rocco Baldelli	4.00	1.20
23 Rafael Palmeiro	4.00	1.20
24 Carlos Delgado	4.00	1.20
25 Roger Clemens	6.00	1.80
26 Luis Gonzalez	4.00	1.20
27 Gary Sheffield	4.00	1.20
28 Jay Gibbons	4.00	1.20
29 Nomar Garciaparra	5.00	1.50
30 Aramis Ramirez	4.00	1.20
31 Frank Thomas	4.00	1.20
32 Ryan Wagner	4.00	1.20
33 Preston Wilson	4.00	1.20
34 Hideki Matsui	5.00	1.50
35 Roy Oswalt	4.00	1.20
36 Angel Berroa	4.00	1.20
37 Kazuhisa Ishii	4.00	1.20
38 Scott Podsednik	4.00	1.20
39 Torii Hunter	4.00	1.20
40 Tom Glavine	4.00	1.20
41 Jason Giambi	4.00	1.20
42 Eric Chavez	4.00	1.20
43 Jim Thome	4.00	1.20
44 Tony Gwynn	4.00	1.20
45 Edgar Martinez	4.00	1.20
46 Jim Edmonds	4.00	1.20
47 Delmon Young	4.00	1.20
48 Hank Blalock	4.00	1.20
49 Vernon Wells	4.00	1.20
50 Curt Schilling	4.00	1.20
51 Chipper Jones	4.00	1.20
52 Cal Ripken	10.00	3.00
53 Jason Varitek	4.00	1.20
54 Kerry Wood	4.00	1.20
55 Magglio Ordonez	4.00	1.20
56 Adam Dunn	4.00	1.20
57 Jay Payton	4.00	1.20
58 Josh Beckett	4.00	1.20
59 Jeff Bagwell	4.00	1.20
60 Carlos Beltran	4.00	1.20
61 Hideo Nomo	4.00	1.20
62 Rickie Weeks	4.00	1.20
63 Alfonso Soriano	4.00	1.20
64 Miguel Tejada	4.00	1.20
65 Bret Boone	4.00	1.20
66 Scott Rolen	4.00	1.20
67 Aubrey Huff	4.00	1.20
68 Juan Gonzalez	4.00	1.20
69 Roy Halladay	4.00	1.20
70 Brandon Webb	4.00	1.20
71 Andruw Jones	4.00	1.20
72 Pedro Martinez	4.00	1.20
73 Carlos Lee	4.00	1.20
74 Lance Berkman	4.00	1.20
75 Paul LoDuca	4.00	1.20
76 Jorge Posada	4.00	1.20
77 Tim Hudson	4.00	1.20
78 Stan Musial	5.00	1.50
79 Mark Teixeira	4.00	1.20
80 Trot Nixon	4.00	1.20
81 Fred McGriff	4.00	1.20
82 Nick Johnson	4.00	1.20
83 Nolan Ryan	8.00	2.40
84 Ken Griffey Jr.	5.00	1.50
85 Mariano Rivera	4.00	1.20
86 Mark Mulder	4.00	1.20
87 Bob Gibson	4.00	1.20
88 Dale Murphy UER	4.00	1.20
89 Bernie Williams	4.00	1.20
90 Carl Yastrzemski	5.00	1.50
91 Sammy Sosa	5.00	1.50
92 Miguel Cabrera	4.00	1.20
93 Craig Biggio	4.00	1.20
94 George Brett	8.00	2.40
95 Rickey Henderson	4.00	1.20
96 Derek Jeter	6.00	1.80
97 Greg Maddux	5.00	1.50
98 Bob Abreu	4.00	1.20
99 Troy Glaus	4.00	1.20
100 Dontrelle Willis	4.00	1.20

2004 Timeless Treasures Bronze

	Nm-Mt	Ex-Mt
*BRONZE ACTIVE: .75X TO 2X BASIC		
*BRONZE RETIRED: 1X TO 2.5X BASIC		
RANDOM INSERTS IN PACKS		
STATED PRINT RUN 100 SERIAL #'d SETS		

2004 Timeless Treasures Gold

	Nm-Mt	Ex-Mt
RANDOM INSERTS IN PACKS		
STATED PRINT RUN 10 SERIAL #'d SETS		
NO PRICING DUE TO SCARCITY		

2004 Timeless Treasures Platinum

	Nm-Mt	Ex-Mt
RANDOM INSERTS IN PACKS		
STATED PRINT RUN 1 SERIAL #'d SET		
NO PRICING DUE TO SCARCITY		

2004 Timeless Treasures Silver

	Nm-Mt	Ex-Mt
*SILVER ACTIVE: 2X TO 5X BASIC		
*SILVER RETIRED: 2X TO 5X BASIC		
RANDOM INSERTS IN PACKS		
STATED PRINT RUN 25 SERIAL #'d SETS		

2004 Timeless Treasures Signature Bronze

	Nm-Mt	Ex-Mt
RANDOM INSERTS IN PACKS		
PRINT RUNS B/WN 1-73 COPIES PER		
NO PRICING ON QTY OF 11 OR LESS		
1 Albert Pujols/25	150.00	45.00
2 Garret Anderson/16	40.00	12.00
3 Randy Johnson/1		
4 Alex Rodriguez/25	200.00	60.00
5 Manny Ramirez/24	60.00	18.00
6 Mark Prior/50	60.00	18.00
7 Roberto Alomar/10		
8 Barry Larkin/25	50.00	15.00
9 Todd Helton/17	60.00	18.00
10 Ivan Rodriguez/10		
11 Jacque Jones/1		
13 Mike Sweeney/5		
14 Shawn Green/15	40.00	12.00
15 Richie Sexson/11		
16 Mike Piazza/10		
17 Vladimir Guerrero/50	50.00	15.00
18 Mike Mussina/1		
19 Barry Zito/10		
20 Don Mattingly/50	80.00	24.00
22 Rocco Baldelli/10		
23 Rafael Palmeiro/25	60.00	18.00
25 Roger Clemens/1		
27 Gary Sheffield/50	30.00	9.00
28 Jay Gibbons/10		
30 Aramis Ramirez/10		
31 Frank Thomas/1		
32 Ryan Wagner/1		
35 Roy Oswalt/5		
36 Angel Berroa/10		
37 Kazuhisa Ishii/17	60.00	18.00
38 Scott Podsednik/1		
39 Torii Hunter/5		
40 Tom Glavine/25	50.00	15.00
42 Eric Chavez/25	30.00	9.00
44 Tony Gwynn/50	60.00	18.00
45 Edgar Martinez/10		
46 Jim Edmonds/15	60.00	18.00
47 Delmon Young/73	25.00	7.50
48 Hank Blalock/10		
49 Vernon Wells/25	30.00	9.00
50 Curt Schilling/38	50.00	15.00
51 Chipper Jones/10		
52 Cal Ripken/8		
53 Jason Varitek/33	60.00	18.00
55 Magglio Ordonez/5		
56 Adam Dunn/25	50.00	15.00
57 Jay Payton/1		
58 Josh Beckett/21	50.00	15.00
59 Jeff Bagwell/25	60.00	18.00
60 Carlos Beltran/15	80.00	24.00
61 Hideo Nomo/10		
62 Rickie Weeks/10		
67 Aubrey Huff/10		
68 Juan Gonzalez/25	50.00	15.00
70 Brandon Webb/10		
71 Andruw Jones/25	30.00	9.00
72 Pedro Martinez/1		
73 Carlos Lee/10		
74 Lance Berkman/5		
75 Paul LoDuca/10		
76 Jorge Posada/25	50.00	15.00
77 Tim Hudson/15	30.00	9.00
78 Stan Musial/50	60.00	18.00
79 Mark Teixeira/23	50.00	15.00
80 Trot Nixon/10		
81 Fred McGriff/10		
82 Nick Johnson/10		
83 Nolan Ryan/50	120.00	36.00
85 Mariano Rivera/10		
86 Mark Mulder/5		
87 Bob Gibson/25	50.00	15.00
88 Dale Murphy UER/50	50.00	15.00
90 Carl Yastrzemski/25	80.00	24.00
91 Sammy Sosa/50	150.00	45.00
92 Miguel Cabrera/24	50.00	15.00
93 Craig Biggio/10		
94 George Brett/25	150.00	45.00
95 Rickey Henderson/25	120.00	36.00
97 Greg Maddux/31	120.00	36.00
98 Bob Abreu/10		
99 Troy Glaus/10		
100 Dontrelle Willis/35	25.00	7.50

2004 Timeless Treasures Signature Silver

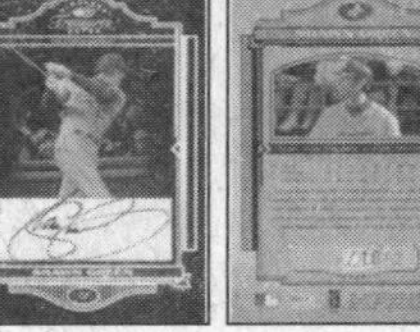

	Nm-Mt	Ex-Mt
RANDOM INSERTS IN PACKS		
PRINT RUNS B/WN 1-34 COPIES PER		
NO PRICING ON QTY OF 13 OR LESS		
6 Mark Prior/22	80.00	24.00
17 Vladimir Guerrero/27	60.00	18.00
20 Don Mattingly/23	120.00	36.00
27 Gary Sheffield/25	50.00	15.00
44 Tony Gwynn/19	100.00	30.00
47 Delmon Young/25	50.00	15.00
68 Juan Gonzalez/22		
76 Jorge Posada/20	50.00	15.00
78 Stan Musial/25	80.00	24.00
83 Nolan Ryan/34	150.00	45.00
88 Dale Murphy UER/25	60.00	18.00
91 Sammy Sosa/21	150.00	45.00

2004 Timeless Treasures Award Materials

	Nm-Mt	Ex-Mt
PRINT RUNS B/WN 9-99 COPIES PER		
NO PRICING ON QTY OF 9 OR LESS		
*NBR p/r 45-51: .5X TO 1.2X BASIC p/r 97		
*NBR p/r 45-51: .4X TO 1X BASIC p/r 68		
*NBR p/r 45-51: .3X TO .8X BASIC p/r 25		
*NBR p/r 33-35: .6X TO 1.5X BASIC p/r 88-94		
*NBR p/r 20-22: .75X TO 2X BASIC p/r 80-81		
*NBR p/r 20-22: .6X TO 1.5X BASIC p/r 50		
*NBR p/r 19: .75X TO 2X BASIC p/r 75		
*NBR p/r 19: .4X TO 1X BASIC p/r 19		
NUMBER PRINT RUNS B/WN 3-51 PER		
NO NUMBER PRICING ON QTY 14 OR LESS		
*PRIME p/r 25: 1X TO 2.5X BASIC p/r 78-97		
*PRIME p/r 25: 1X TO 2.5X BASIC p/r 50-68		
*PRIME p/r 25: .75X TO 2X BASIC p/r 25		
PRIME PRINT RUNS B/WN 1-25 COPIES PER		
NO PRIME PRICING ON QTY OF 10 OR LESS		
RANDOM INSERTS IN PACKS		
1 Jimmie Foxx Bat/9		
2 Stan Musial Jsy/43	40.00	12.00
3 Lou Boudreau Jsy/19	20.00	6.00
4 Roger Maris Pants/61	50.00	15.00
5 Roger Maris Bat/61	50.00	15.00
6 Roberto Clemente Bat/66	60.00	18.00
7 Bob Gibson 68 CY Jsy/68	15.00	4.50
8 Bob Gibson 68 MVP Jsy/68	15.00	4.50
9 Tom Seaver Jsy/19	25.00	7.50
10 Fred Lynn Jsy/75	10.00	3.00
11 Jim Rice Jsy/78	10.00	3.00
12 M.Schmidt 80 MVP Jsy/80	20.00	6.00
13 M.Schmidt 80 MVP Pants/80	20.00	6.00
14 M.Schmidt 80 MVP Stir/80	20.00	6.00
15 M.Schmidt 81 MVP Jsy/81	20.00	6.00
16 M.Schmidt 81 MVP Bat/81	20.00	6.00
17 Dale Murphy Jsy/82	15.00	4.50
18 M.Schmidt 86 MVP Hat/19	50.00	15.00
19 M.Schmidt 86 MVP Shoe/19	50.00	15.00
20 M.Schmidt 86 MVP Bat/86	20.00	6.00
21 M.Schmidt 86 MVP Stir/19	50.00	15.00
22 Jose Canseco Jsy/88	15.00	4.50
23 F.Thomas 93 MVP Bat/93	15.00	4.50
24 F.Thomas 93 MVP Jsy/93	15.00	4.50
25 Jeff Bagwell Pants/94	15.00	4.50
26 F.Thomas 94 MVP Jsy/94	15.00	4.50
27 F.Thomas 94 MVP Pants/94	15.00	4.50
28 Jeff Bagwell Bat/94	15.00	4.50
29 Pedro Martinez 97 CY Jsy/97	15.00	4.50
30 Ivan Rodriguez Bat/99	15.00	4.50
31 R.Johnson 00 CY Jsy/25	20.00	6.00
32 P.Martinez 00 CY Jsy/25	20.00	6.00
33 Roger Clemens Jsy/50	25.00	7.50
34 R.Johnson 02 CY Jsy/25	20.00	6.00
35 Miguel Tejada Jsy/25	15.00	4.50

2004 Timeless Treasures Award Materials Signature

	Nm-Mt	Ex-Mt
PRINT RUNS B/WN 1-78 COPIES PER		
NO PRICING ON QTY OF 9 OR LESS		
*NBR p/r 19: .75X TO 2X BASIC p/r 75		
NUMBER PRINT RUNS B/WN 1-19 PER		
NO NUMBER PRICES ON QTY OF 14 OR LESS		
PRIME PRINT RUNS B/WN 1-14 COPIES PER		
NO PRIME PRICING DUE TO SCARCITY		
RANDOM INSERTS IN PACKS		
2 Stan Musial Jsy/9		
7 Bob Gibson 68 CY Jsy/19	60.00	18.00
8 Bob Gibson 68 MVP Jsy/19	60.00	18.00
9 Tom Seaver Jsy/9		
10 Fred Lynn Jsy/75	20.00	6.00
11 Jim Rice Jsy/78	25.00	7.50
17 Dale Murphy Jsy/9		
22 Jose Canseco Jsy/9		
23 F.Thomas 93 MVP Bat/9		
24 F.Thomas 93 MVP Jsy/9		
25 Jeff Bagwell Pants/9		
26 F.Thomas 94 MVP Jsy/9		
27 F.Thomas 94 MVP Pants/9		
28 Jeff Bagwell Bat/9		
29 Pedro Martinez 97 CY Jsy/1		
30 Ivan Rodriguez Bat/9		
31 Randy Johnson 00 CY Jsy/9		
32 Pedro Martinez 00 CY Jsy/1		
33 Roger Clemens Jsy/9		
34 Randy Johnson 02 CY Jsy/9		

2004 Timeless Treasures Award Materials Combos

	Nm-Mt	Ex-Mt
PRINT RUNS B/WN 25-50 COPIES PER		
*PRIME: .6X TO 1.5X BASIC p/r 25		
PRIME PRINT RUN 19 SERIAL #'d SETS		
RANDOM INSERTS IN PACKS		
4 Roger Maris Bat-Pants/25	80.00	24.00
12 M.Schmidt 80M Jsy-Pant/25	50.00	15.00
13 M.Schmidt 80M Pant-Stir/50	40.00	12.00
14 M.Schmidt 80M Jsy-Stir/50	40.00	12.00
15 M.Schmidt 81M Bat-Jsy/25	50.00	15.00
16 M.Schmidt 81M Bat-Stir/50	40.00	12.00
18 M.Schmidt 86M Hat-Shoe/50	40.00	12.00
19 M.Schmidt 86M Hat-Bat/50	40.00	12.00
20 M.Schmidt 86M Hat-Stir/50	40.00	12.00
21 M.Schmidt 86M Bat-Shoe/50	40.00	12.00
23 F.Thomas 93M Bat-Jsy/25	30.00	9.00
25 Jeff Bagwell Bat-Jsy/25	30.00	9.00
26 F.Thomas 94M Bat-Jsy/25	30.00	9.00
35 Miguel Tejada Bat-Jsy/25	20.00	6.00

2004 Timeless Treasures Award Materials Combos Signature

	Nm-Mt	Ex-Mt
STATED PRINT RUN 5 SERIAL #'d SETS		
PRIME PRINT RUN 5 SERIAL #'d SETS		
RANDOM INSERTS IN PACKS		
NO PRICING DUE TO SCARCITY		
23 F.Thomas 93 MVP Bat-Jsy		
25 Jeff Bagwell Bat-Jsy		
26 F.Thomas 94 MVP Bat-Jsy		

2004 Timeless Treasures Game Day Materials

	Nm-Mt	Ex-Mt
RANDOM INSERTS IN PACKS		
PRINT RUNS B/WN 8-99 COPIES PER		
NO PRICING ON QTY OF 9 OR LESS		
1 Nellie Fox Bat/58	60.00	18.00
2 Frank Robinson Bat/61	15.00	4.50
3 George Brett Bat/77	25.00	7.50
4 George Brett Hat/82	40.00	12.00
5 Nolan Ryan Hat/19	120.00	36.00
6 Cal Ripken Hat/85	60.00	18.00
7 Rod Carew Hat/19	30.00	9.00
8 Ryne Sandberg Bat/91	25.00	7.50
9 Kirby Puckett Bat/92	15.00	4.50
10 Frank Thomas Bat/93	15.00	4.50
11 George Brett Ball/9		
12 Tony Gwynn Pants/99	15.00	4.50
13 Vladimir Guerrero Bat/99	15.00	4.50
14 Tony Gwynn Hat/99	30.00	9.00
15 Magglio Ordonez Hat/15	25.00	7.50
16 Rickey Henderson Bat/50	15.00	4.50
17 Cal Ripken Ball/8		

2004 Timeless Treasures Game Day Materials Signature

	Nm-Mt	Ex-Mt
RANDOM INSERTS IN PACKS		
PRINT RUNS B/WN 8-25 COPIES PER		
NO PRICING ON QTY OF 10 OR LESS		
2 Frank Robinson Bat/25	60.00	18.00
3 George Brett Bat/10		
4 George Brett Hat/10		
5 Nolan Ryan Hat/10		
6 Cal Ripken Hat/8		
7 Rod Carew Hat/10		
8 Ryne Sandberg Bat/10		
9 Kirby Puckett Bat/10		

10 Frank Thomas Bat/10
11 George Brett Ball/5
12 Tony Gwynn Pants/10
13 Vladimir Guerrero Bat/10
14 Tony Gwynn Hat/10
15 Maggio Ordonez Hat/25 50.00 15.00
16 Rickey Henderson Bat/10
17 Cal Ripken Ball/8

2004 Timeless Treasures HOF Materials Signature

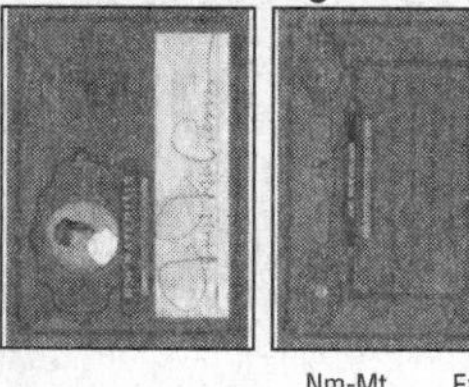
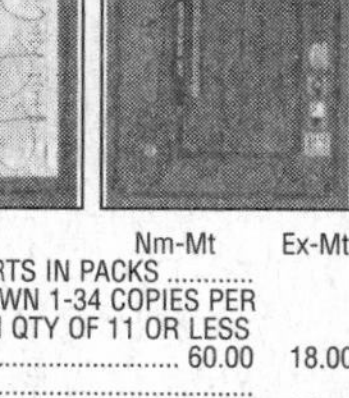

Nm-Mt Ex-Mt
RANDOM INSERTS IN PACKS
PRINT RUNS B/WN 1-34 COPIES PER
NO PRICING ON QTY OF 11 OR LESS
1 Al Kaline/25 60.00 18.00
2 Babe Ruth/1
3 Bob Feller/25 40.00 12.00
4 Bobby Doerr/1
5 Brooks Robinson/25 50.00 15.00
6 Carl Yastrzemski/8
7 Carlton Fisk/27 50.00 15.00
8 Dave Winfield/5
9 Duke Snider/25 50.00 15.00
10 Eddie Murray/5
11 Ernie Banks/25 60.00 18.00
12 Fergie Jenkins/31 40.00 12.00
13 Frank Robinson/20 50.00 15.00
14 Hal Newhouser/5
15 Hoyt Wilhelm/25 40.00 12.00
17 Jim Palmer/22 40.00 12.00
18 Joe Morgan/8
19 Johnny Bench/5
20 Juan Marichal/27 40.00 12.00
21 Kirby Puckett/34 60.00 18.00
22 Lou Brock/20 50.00 15.00
23 Lou Gehrig/1
24 Luis Aparicio/11
26 Orlando Cepeda/30 40.00 12.00
27 Pee Wee Reese/5
28 Phil Rizzuto/25 50.00 15.00
29 Red Schoendienst/25 40.00 12.00
32 Paul Molitor/25 50.00 15.00
34 Warren Spahn/21 60.00 18.00
35 Willie McCovey/25 50.00 15.00

2004 Timeless Treasures HOF Materials Barrel

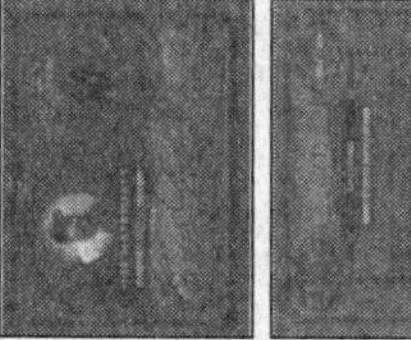

Nm-Mt Ex-Mt
RANDOM INSERTS IN PACKS
STATED PRINT RUN 1 SERIAL #'d SET
NO PRICING DUE TO SCARCITY
1 Al Kaline
2 Babe Ruth
4 Bobby Doerr
5 Brooks Robinson
6 Carl Yastrzemski
7 Carlton Fisk
8 Dave Winfield
9 Duke Snider
10 Eddie Murray
11 Ernie Banks
13 Frank Robinson
18 Joe Morgan
19 Johnny Bench
21 Kirby Puckett
22 Lou Brock
23 Lou Gehrig
24 Luis Aparicio
25 Mel Ott
26 Orlando Cepeda
27 Pee Wee Reese
28 Phil Rizzuto
29 Red Schoendienst
30 Roberto Clemente
31 Roy Campanella
32 Paul Molitor
33 Ty Cobb
36 Willie Stargell

2004 Timeless Treasures HOF Materials Bat

Nm-Mt Ex-Mt
RANDOM INSERTS IN PACKS
PRINT RUNS B/WN 5-50 COPIES PER
NO PRICING ON QTY OF 5 OR LESS
1 Al Kaline/25 40.00 12.00
2 Babe Ruth/50 200.00 60.00
4 Bobby Doerr/25 15.00 4.50
5 Brooks Robinson/25 25.00 7.50
6 Carl Yastrzemski/25 40.00 12.00
7 Carlton Fisk/25 25.00 7.50
8 Dave Winfield/25 20.00 6.00
9 Duke Snider/5
10 Eddie Murray/25 40.00 12.00
11 Ernie Banks/25 40.00 12.00
13 Frank Robinson/25 25.00 7.50
18 Joe Morgan/25 20.00 6.00
19 Johnny Bench/25 40.00 12.00
21 Kirby Puckett/25 40.00 12.00
22 Lou Brock/25 25.00 7.50
23 Lou Gehrig/50 150.00 45.00
24 Luis Aparicio/25 15.00 4.50
25 Mel Ott/25 50.00 15.00
26 Orlando Cepeda/25 20.00 6.00
27 Pee Wee Reese/25 25.00 7.50
28 Phil Rizzuto/25 25.00 7.50
29 Red Schoendienst/25 20.00 6.00
30 Roberto Clemente/25 80.00 24.00
31 Roy Campanella/25 40.00 12.00
32 Paul Molitor/25 25.00 7.50
33 Ty Cobb/25 120.00 36.00
35 Willie McCovey/25 20.00 6.00
36 Willie Stargell/25 25.00 7.50

2004 Timeless Treasures HOF Materials Bat Signature

Nm-Mt Ex-Mt
RANDOM INSERTS IN PACKS
PRINT RUNS B/WN 10-50 COPIES PER
NO PRICING ON QTY OF 10 OR LESS
1 Al Kaline/50 50.00 15.00
4 Bobby Doerr/50 25.00 7.50
5 Brooks Robinson/50 40.00 12.00
6 Carl Yastrzemski/10
7 Carlton Fisk/10
8 Dave Winfield/10
9 Duke Snider/10
10 Eddie Murray/10
11 Ernie Banks/25 80.00 24.00
13 Frank Robinson/50 40.00 12.00
18 Joe Morgan/25 40.00 12.00
19 Johnny Bench/25 80.00 24.00
21 Kirby Puckett/10
22 Lou Brock/50 40.00 12.00
24 Luis Aparicio/50 25.00 7.50
26 Orlando Cepeda/50 30.00 9.00
28 Phil Rizzuto/50 40.00 12.00
29 Red Schoendienst/50 30.00 9.00
32 Paul Molitor/25 50.00 15.00
35 Willie McCovey/10

2004 Timeless Treasures HOF Materials Jersey

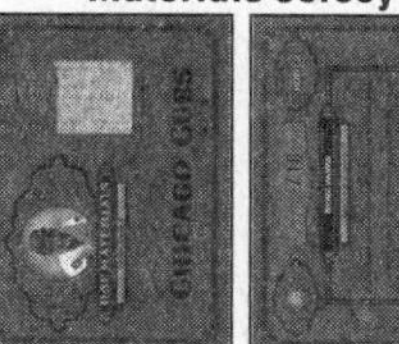
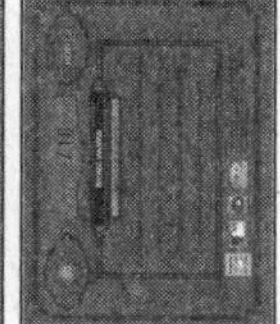

Nm-Mt Ex-Mt
PRINT RUNS B/WN 5-50 COPIES PER
NO PRICING ON QTY OF 10 OR LESS
PRIME PRINT RUNS B/WN 1-10 COPIES PER
NO PRIME PRICING DUE TO SCARCITY
RANDOM INSERTS IN PACKS
1 Al Kaline/6
2 Babe Ruth/25 600.00 180.00
3 Bob Feller/50 15.00 4.50
4 Bobby Doerr/25 15.00 4.50
5 Brooks Robinson/50 20.00 6.00
6 Carl Yastrzemski/50 30.00 9.00
7 Carlton Fisk/50 20.00 6.00
8 Dave Winfield/50 15.00 4.50
9 Duke Snider/10
10 Eddie Murray/25 40.00 12.00
11 Ernie Banks/10
13 Frank Robinson/25 25.00 7.50
14 Hal Newhouser/50 15.00 4.50
15 Hoyt Wilhelm/50 15.00 4.50
16 Jackie Robinson/10
17 Jim Palmer/50 15.00 4.50
18 Joe Morgan/50 15.00 4.50
20 Juan Marichal/50 15.00 4.50
21 Kirby Puckett/50 25.00 7.50
22 Lou Brock/25 25.00 7.50
23 Lou Gehrig/25 200.00 60.00
24 Luis Aparicio/25 15.00 4.50
25 Mel Ott/25 50.00 15.00
26 Orlando Cepeda/5
27 Pee Wee Reese/50 20.00 6.00
28 Phil Rizzuto/50 20.00 6.00
29 Red Schoendienst/25
30 Roberto Clemente/50 80.00 24.00
32 Paul Molitor/50 20.00 6.00
34 Warren Spahn/50 20.00 6.00
35 Willie McCovey/50 15.00 4.50
36 Willie Stargell/50 20.00 6.00

2004 Timeless Treasures HOF Materials Jersey Number

Nm-Mt Ex-Mt
*NUMBER p/r 44: .4X TO 1X BASIC p/r 50
*NUMBER p/r 27-34: .5X TO 1.2X BASIC p/r 50
*NUMBER p/r 27-34: .4X TO 1X BASIC p/r 25
*NUMBER p/r 20-22: .6X TO 1.5X BASIC p/r 50

*NUMBER p/r 20-22: .4X TO 1X BASIC p/r 25
*NUMBER p/r 16-19: .6X TO 1.5X BASIC p/r 50
RANDOM INSERTS IN PACKS
PRINT RUNS B/WN 1-44 COPIES PER
NO PRICING ON QTY OF 14 OR LESS
3 Bob Feller/19 25.00 7.50
16 Jackie Robinson/42 60.00 18.00

2004 Timeless Treasures HOF Materials Jersey Signature

Nm-Mt Ex-Mt
PRINT RUNS B/WN 5-50 COPIES PER
NO PRICING ON QTY OF 10 OR LESS
PRIME PRINT RUNS B/WN 1-10 COPIES PER
NO PRIME PRICING DUE TO SCARCITY
RANDOM INSERTS IN PACKS
1 Al Kaline/25 60.00 18.00
3 Bob Feller/10
4 Bobby Doerr/50 25.00 7.50
5 Brooks Robinson/25 50.00 15.00
6 Carl Yastrzemski/10
7 Carlton Fisk/10
8 Dave Winfield/10
10 Eddie Murray/10
11 Ernie Banks/10
13 Frank Robinson/50 40.00 12.00
15 Hoyt Wilhelm/25 40.00 12.00
17 Jim Palmer/50 30.00 9.00
18 Joe Morgan/25 40.00 12.00
19 Johnny Bench/5
20 Juan Marichal/50 30.00 9.00
21 Kirby Puckett/10
22 Lou Brock/50 40.00 12.00
24 Luis Aparicio/50 25.00 7.50
26 Orlando Cepeda/25 40.00 12.00
28 Phil Rizzuto/50 40.00 12.00
29 Red Schoendienst/50 30.00 9.00
32 Paul Molitor/50 40.00 12.00
34 Warren Spahn/25 80.00 24.00
35 Willie McCovey/10

2004 Timeless Treasures HOF Materials Jersey Signature Number

Nm-Mt Ex-Mt
*NUMBER p/r 25: .5X TO 1.2X BASIC p/r 50
*NUMBER p/r 25: .4X TO 1X BASIC p/r 25
RANDOM INSERTS IN PACKS
PRINT RUNS B/WN 10-25 COPIES PER
NO PRICING ON QTY OF 10 OR LESS
12 Fergie Jenkins Pants/25 40.00 12.00

2004 Timeless Treasures HOF Materials Pants

Nm-Mt Ex-Mt
RANDOM INSERTS IN PACKS
PRINT RUNS B/WN 25-50 COPIES PER
1 Al Kaline/25 40.00 12.00
2 Babe Ruth/50 200.00 60.00
12 Fergie Jenkins/25 20.00 6.00
23 Lou Gehrig/50 150.00 45.00
24 Luis Aparicio/25 15.00 4.50
25 Mel Ott/25 50.00 15.00
31 Roy Campanella/25 40.00 12.00
33 Ty Cobb/25 120.00 36.00

2004 Timeless Treasures HOF Materials Pants Signature

Nm-Mt Ex-Mt
RANDOM INSERTS IN PACKS
STATED PRINT RUN 25 SERIAL #'d SETS
1 Al Kaline 60.00 18.00
12 Fergie Jenkins 40.00 12.00

24 Luis Aparicio 30.00 9.00
28 Phil Rizzuto 50.00 15.00

2004 Timeless Treasures HOF Materials Combos Bat-Jersey

Nm-Mt Ex-Mt
PRINT RUNS B/WN 1-50 COPIES PER
PRIME PRINT RUNS B/WN 1-5 COPIES PER
NO PRIME PRICING DUE TO SCARCITY
RANDOM INSERTS IN PACKS
1 Al Kaline/25 50.00 15.00
2 Babe Ruth/25 600.00 180.00
4 Bobby Doerr/25 20.00 6.00
5 Brooks Robinson/50 25.00 7.50
6 Carl Yastrzemski/50 40.00 12.00
7 Carlton Fisk/50 25.00 7.50
8 Dave Winfield/50 20.00 6.00
10 Eddie Murray/50 40.00 12.00
11 Ernie Banks/10
13 Frank Robinson/50 25.00 7.50
18 Joe Morgan/50 20.00 6.00
19 Johnny Bench/1
21 Kirby Puckett/50 40.00 12.00
22 Lou Brock/50 25.00 7.50
23 Lou Gehrig/25 300.00 90.00
24 Luis Aparicio/25 20.00 6.00
25 Mel Ott/25 80.00 24.00
26 Orlando Cepeda/5
27 Pee Wee Reese/50 25.00 7.50
28 Phil Rizzuto/50 25.00 7.50
29 Red Schoendienst/25 25.00 7.50
30 Roberto Clemente/50 150.00 45.00
32 Paul Molitor/50 25.00 7.50
35 Willie McCovey/50 20.00 6.00
36 Willie Stargell/50 25.00 7.50

2004 Timeless Treasures HOF Materials Combos Bat-Jersey Signature

Nm-Mt Ex-Mt
PRINT RUNS B/WN 1-25 COPIES PER
NO PRICING ON QTY OF 10 OR LESS
PRIME PRINT RUNS B/WN 1-5 COPIES PER
NO PRIME PRICING DUE TO SCARCITY
RANDOM INSERTS IN PACKS
1 Al Kaline/5
4 Bobby Doerr/25 40.00 12.00
5 Brooks Robinson/25 60.00 18.00
6 Carl Yastrzemski/10
7 Carlton Fisk/10
8 Dave Winfield/10
10 Eddie Murray/10
11 Ernie Banks/25 120.00 36.00
13 Frank Robinson/25 60.00 18.00
18 Joe Morgan/25 50.00 15.00
19 Johnny Bench/1
21 Kirby Puckett/10
22 Lou Brock/25 60.00 18.00
24 Luis Aparicio/25 40.00 12.00
26 Orlando Cepeda/10
28 Phil Rizzuto/10
29 Red Schoendienst/25 50.00 15.00
32 Paul Molitor/25 60.00 18.00
35 Willie McCovey/10

2004 Timeless Treasures HOF Materials Combos Bat-Pants

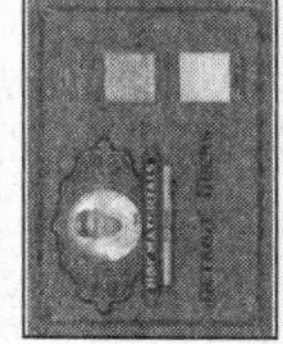

Nm-Mt Ex-Mt
RANDOM INSERTS IN PACKS
STATED PRINT RUN 25 SERIAL #'d SETS
1 Al Kaline/25 50.00 15.00
2 Babe Ruth/25 400.00 120.00
12 F.Jenkins Fld Glv-Pants/25 25.00 7.50
23 Lou Gehrig/25 250.00 75.00
24 Luis Aparicio/25 20.00 6.00
25 Mel Ott/25 80.00 24.00
31 Roy Campanella/25 60.00 18.00
33 Ty Cobb/25 250.00 75.00

2004 Timeless Treasures HOF Materials Combos Bat-Pants Signature

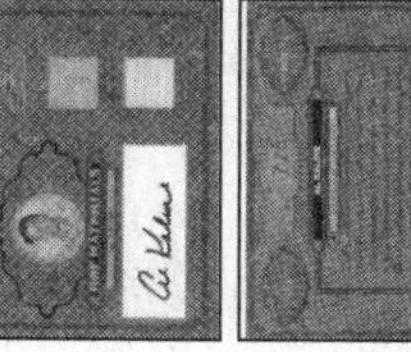

Nm-Mt Ex-Mt
RANDOM INSERTS IN PACKS
STATED PRINT RUN 25 SERIAL #'d SETS
1 Al Kaline/25 100.00 30.00
12 F.Jenkins Fld Glv-Pants/25 50.00 15.00
24 Luis Aparicio/25 40.00 12.00

2004 Timeless Treasures HOF Materials Combos Jersey-Pants

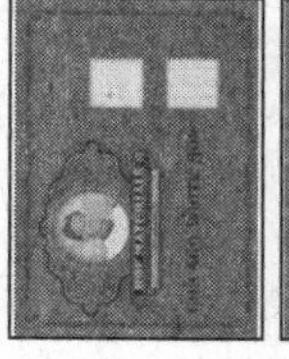

Nm-Mt Ex-Mt
PRINT RUNS B/WN 10-25 COPIES PER
NO PRICING ON QTY OF 10 OR LESS
PRIME PRINT RUNS B/WN 1-5 COPIES PER
NO PRIME PRICING DUE TO SCARCITY
RANDOM INSERTS IN PACKS
1 Al Kaline/10
2 Babe Ruth/25 600.00 180.00
16 J.Robinson Jacket-Jsy/10
23 Lou Gehrig/25 300.00 90.00
24 Luis Aparicio/25 20.00 6.00
25 Mel Ott/10

2004 Timeless Treasures HOF Materials Combos Jersey-Pants Signature

Nm-Mt Ex-Mt
PRINT RUNS B/WN 5-25 COPIES PER
PRIME PRINT RUNS B/WN 1-5 COPIES PER
NO PRIME PRICING DUE TO SCARCITY
RANDOM INSERTS IN PACKS
1 Al Kaline/5
24 Luis Aparicio/25 40.00 12.00

2004 Timeless Treasures Home Away Gamers

Nm-Mt Ex-Mt
PRINT RUNS B/WN 5-100 COPIES PER
NO PRICING ON QTY OF 10 OR LESS
PRIME PRINT RUNS B/WN 3-5 COPIES PER
NO PRIME PRICING DUE TO SCARCITY
1 Babe Ruth Jsy-Jsy/25 800.00 240.00
2 Yogi Berra Jsy-Jsy/8
3 Wade Boggs Jsy-Jsy/50 25.00 7.50
4 Tony Gwynn Jsy-Jsy/50 40.00 12.00
5 Steve Carlton Jsy-Jsy/50 20.00 6.00
6 Stan Musial Jsy-Jsy/10
7 Ryne Sandberg Jsy-Jsy/50 50.00 15.00
8 Rod Carew Jsy-Jsy/50 25.00 7.50
9 R.Henderson Jsy-Jsy/50 40.00 12.00
10 Brooks Robinson Jsy-Jsy/5
11 Ted Williams Jsy-Jsy/100 120.00 36.00
12 Ozzie Smith Jsy-Jsy/50 40.00 12.00
13 Mike Schmidt Jsy-Jsy/50 40.00 12.00
14 Harmon Killebrew Jsy-Jsy/50 40.00 12.00
15 George Brett Jsy-Jsy/100 40.00 12.00
16 Don Mattingly Jsy-Jsy/50 50.00 15.00
17 Dale Murphy Jsy-Jsy/50 25.00 7.50
18 Cal Ripken Jsy-Jsy/100 60.00 18.00
19 Lou Gehrig Jsy-Jsy/50 300.00 90.00
20 Nolan Ryan Jsy-Jsy/100 50.00 15.00

2004 Timeless Treasures Home Away Gamers Signature

Nm-Mt Ex-Mt
RANDOM INSERTS IN PACKS
PRINT RUNS B/WN 1-25 COPIES PER
NO PRICING ON QTY OF 10 OR LESS
1 Babe Ruth Jsy-Jsy/1
2 Yogi Berra Jsy-Jsy/5
3 Wade Boggs Jsy-Jsy/10
4 Tony Gwynn Jsy-Jsy/10
5 Steve Carlton Jsy-Jsy/25 .... 60.00 18.00
6 Stan Musial Jsy-Jsy/10
7 Ryne Sandberg Jsy-Jsy/10
8 Rod Carew Jsy-Jsy/10
9 R.Henderson Jsy-Jsy/10
10 Brooks Robinson Jsy-Jsy/5
11 Ted Williams Jsy-Jsy/1
12 Ozzie Smith Jsy-Jsy/10
13 Mike Schmidt Jsy-Jsy/20... 150.00 45.00
14 H.Killebrew Jsy-Jsy/25 .... 100.00 30.00
15 George Brett Jsy-Jsy/10
16 Don Mattingly Jsy-Jsy/25 .. 200.00 60.00
17 Dale Murphy Jsy-Jsy/25..... 100.00 30.00
18 Cal Ripken Jsy-Jsy/10
19 Lou Gehrig Jsy-Jsy/1
20 Nolan Ryan Jsy-Jsy/10

2004 Timeless Treasures Home Away Gamers Combos

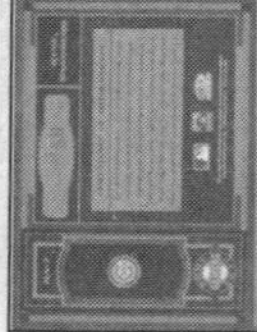

Nm-Mt Ex-Mt
PRINT RUNS B/WN 5-100 COPIES PER
NO PRICING ON QTY OF 8 OR LESS..
PRIME PRINT RUNS B/WN 3-10 COPIES PER
NO PRIME PRICING DUE TO SCARCITY
1 Babe Ruth/25 .... 1000.00 300.00
2 Yogi Berra/8
3 Wade Boggs/50 .... 40.00 12.00
4 Tony Gwynn/50 .... 60.00 18.00
5 Steve Carlton/50 .... 40.00 12.00
6 Stan Musial/25 .... 120.00 36.00
7 Ryne Sandberg/50 .... 60.00 18.00
8 Rod Carew/50 .... 40.00 12.00
9 Rickey Henderson/50 .... 50.00 15.00
10 Brooks Robinson/5
11 Ted Williams/100 .... 150.00 45.00
12 Ozzie Smith/50 .... 50.00 15.00
13 Mike Schmidt/50 .... 60.00 18.00
14 Harmon Killebrew/25 .... 60.00 18.00
15 George Brett/100 .... 60.00 18.00
16 Don Mattingly/50 .... 80.00 24.00
17 Dale Murphy/50 .... 40.00 12.00
18 Cal Ripken/100 .... 80.00 24.00
19 Lou Gehrig/25 .... 600.00 180.00
20 Nolan Ryan/100 .... 80.00 24.00

2004 Timeless Treasures Home Away Gamers Combos Signature

Nm-Mt Ex-Mt
PRINT RUNS B/WN 1-5 COPIES PER.
PRIME PRINT RUN 1 SERIAL #'d SET
RANDOM INSERTS IN PACKS
NO PRICING DUE TO SCARCITY
1 Babe Ruth/1
2 Yogi Berra/5
3 Wade Boggs/5
4 Tony Gwynn/5
5 Steve Carlton/5
6 Stan Musial/5
7 Ryne Sandberg/5
8 Rod Carew/5
9 Rickey Henderson/5
10 Brooks Robinson/5
11 Ted Williams/5
12 Ozzie Smith/5
13 Mike Schmidt/5
14 Harmon Killebrew/5
15 George Brett/5
16 Don Mattingly/5
17 Dale Murphy/5
18 Cal Ripken/5
19 Lou Gehrig/1
20 Nolan Ryan/5

2004 Timeless Treasures Home Run Materials

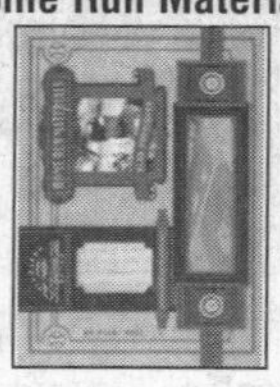

Nm-Mt Ex-Mt
RANDOM INSERTS IN PACKS
PRINT RUNS B/WN 12-100 COPIES PER
NO PRICING ON QTY OF 12 OR LESS
1 Roger Maris Bat/61 .... 50.00 15.00
2 Ron Santo Ball/12
3 H.Killebrew HR 570 Bat/75 .... 25.00 7.50
4 H.Killebrew HR 565 Bat/75 .... 25.00 7.50
5 Jose Canseco Bat/96 .... 15.00 4.50
6 Alex Rodriguez Bat/100 .... 15.00 4.50
7 Sammy Sosa Jsy/100 .... 15.00 4.50
8 Rafael Palmeiro Jsy/25 .... 20.00 6.00
9 Ivan Rodriguez Jsy/25 .... 20.00 6.00

2004 Timeless Treasures Home Run Materials Signature

Nm-Mt Ex-Mt
RANDOM INSERTS IN PACKS
PRINT RUNS B/WN 9-19 COPIES PER
NO PRICING ON QTY OF 12 OR LESS
2 Ron Santo Ball/12
3 H.Killebrew HR 570 Bat/19 .... 80.00 24.00
4 H.Killebrew HR 565 Bat/19 .... 80.00 24.00
5 Jose Canseco Bat/9
6 Alex Rodriguez Bat/9
7 Sammy Sosa Jsy/9
8 Rafael Palmeiro Jsy/9
9 Ivan Rodriguez Jsy/9

2004 Timeless Treasures Material Ink Bat

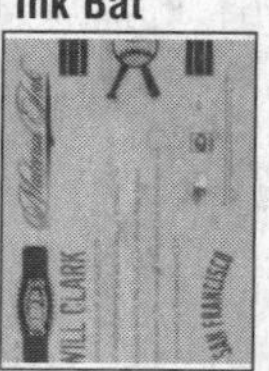

Nm-Mt Ex-Mt
RANDOM INSERTS IN PACKS
PRINT RUNS B/WN 1-50 COPIES PER
NO PRICING ON QTY OF 10 OR LESS
1 Adam Dunn/25 .... 50.00 15.00
2 Alan Trammell/25 .... 40.00 12.00
3 Alex Rodriguez/10
4 Andre Dawson/25 .... 40.00 12.00
5 Bo Jackson/25 .... 100.00 30.00
6 Cal Ripken/8
7 Dale Murphy/25 .... 60.00 18.00
8 Darryl Strawberry/10
9 Dave Parker/10
10 Deion Sanders/5
12 Don Mattingly/50 .... 100.00 30.00
13 Dontrelle Willis/10
14 Hideo Nomo/1
15 Ivan Rodriguez/7
16 Joe Carter/10
17 Jose Canseco/10
19 Mark Grace/10
20 Mark Prior/25 .... 100.00 30.00
21 Mark Teixeira/10
23 Mike Piazza/1
24 Paul Molitor/10
25 Paul O'Neill/25 .... 60.00 18.00
26 Rocco Baldelli/10
29 Ron Santo/50 .... 50.00 15.00
30 Ryne Sandberg/25 .... 120.00 36.00
31 Ernie Banks/10
32 Tony Gwynn/25 .... 100.00 30.00
33 Vladimir Guerrero/10
34 Will Clark/25 .... 60.00 18.00

2004 Timeless Treasures Material Ink Jersey

Nm-Mt Ex-Mt
PRINT RUNS B/WN 10-100 COPIES PER
NO PRICING ON QTY OF 10 OR LESS
*PRIME p/r 25: .75X TO 2X BASIC p/r 100
*PRIME p/r 25: .6X TO 1.5X BASIC p/r 50
PRIME PRINT RUNS B/WN 1-25 COPIES PER
NO PRIME PRICING ON QTY OF 10 OR LESS
RANDOM INSERTS IN PACKS
1 Adam Dunn/25 .... 50.00 15.00
2 Alan Trammell/100 .... 25.00 7.50
3 Alex Rodriguez/10
4 Andre Dawson/100 .... 25.00 7.50
5 Bo Jackson/25 .... 100.00 30.00
6 Cal Ripken/10
7 Dale Murphy/50 .... 50.00 15.00
8 Darryl Strawberry/100 .... 25.00 7.50
9 Dave Parker/25 .... 40.00 12.00
10 Deion Sanders/10
11 Doc Gooden/100 .... 25.00 7.50
12 Don Mattingly/50 .... 100.00 30.00
13 Dontrelle Willis/25 .... 40.00 12.00
14 Hideo Nomo/1
15 Ivan Rodriguez/25 .... 80.00 24.00
16 Joe Carter/25 .... 40.00 12.00
17 Jose Canseco/25 .... 60.00 18.00
18 Kerry Wood/15 .... 120.00 36.00
19 Mark Grace/10
20 Mark Prior/50 .... 80.00 24.00
21 Mark Teixeira/25 .... 50.00 15.00
22 Marty Marion/25 .... 30.00 9.00
23 Mike Piazza/1
24 Paul Molitor/10
26 Rocco Baldelli/25 .... 40.00 12.00
27 Roger Clemens Yanks/5
28 Roger Clemens Sox/5
30 Ryne Sandberg/50 .... 80.00 24.00
31 Ernie Banks/50 .... 60.00 18.00
32 Tony Gwynn/10
33 Vladimir Guerrero/25 .... 80.00 24.00
34 Will Clark/50 .... 50.00 15.00

2004 Timeless Treasures Material Ink Jersey Number

Nm-Mt Ex-Mt
*NUMBER p/r 100: .4X TO 1X BASIC p/r 100
*NUMBER p/r 50: .4X TO 1X BASIC p/r 50
*NUMBER p/r 25: .5X TO 1.2X BASIC p/r 50
*NUMBER p/r 25: .4X TO 1X BASIC p/r 25
RANDOM INSERTS IN PACKS
PRINT RUNS B/WN 1-100 COPIES PER
NO PRICING ON QTY OF 10 OR LESS
10 Deion Sanders/24 .... 80.00 24.00
19 Mark Grace/25 .... 50.00 15.00
32 Tony Gwynn/25

2004 Timeless Treasures Material Ink Combos

Nm-Mt Ex-Mt
PRINT RUNS B/WN 1-50 COPIES PER
NO PRICING ON QTY OF 10 OR LESS
PRIME PRINT RUNS B/WN 1-10 COPIES PER
NO PRIME PRICING DUE TO SCARCITY
RANDOM INSERTS IN PACKS
1 Adam Dunn Bat-Jsy/25 .... 60.00 18.00
2 Alan Trammell Bat-Jsy/25 ...... 50.00 15.00
3 Alex Rodriguez Bat-Jsy/3
4 Andre Dawson Bat-Jsy/25 ...... 50.00 15.00
5 Bo Jackson Bat-Jsy/25 .... 120.00 36.00
6 Cal Ripken Bat-Jsy/8
7 Dale Murphy Bat-Jsy/25 .... 80.00 24.00
8 Darryl Strawberry Bat-Jsy/10
9 Dave Parker Bat-Jsy/10
10 Deion Sanders Bat-Jsy/10
12 Don Mattingly Bat-Jsy/25 .. 200.00 60.00
13 Dontrelle Willis Bat-Jsy/10
14 Hideo Nomo Bat-Jsy/1
15 Ivan Rodriguez Bat-Jsy/7
16 Joe Carter Bat-Jsy/10
17 Jose Canseco Bat-Jsy/25... 100.00 30.00
19 Mark Grace Bat-Jsy/10
20 Mark Prior Bat-Jsy/10
21 Mark Teixeira Bat-Jsy/10
23 Mike Piazza Bat-Jsy/1
24 Paul Molitor Bat-Jsy/5
26 Rocco Baldelli Bat-Jsy/10
30 Ryne Sandberg Bat-Jsy/25 150.00 45.00
31 Ernie Banks Bat-Jsy/5
32 Tony Gwynn Bat-Jsy/25 ...... 120.00 36.00
33 Vladimir Guerrero Bat-Jsy/10
34 Will Clark Bat-Jsy/50 .... 60.00 18.00

2004 Timeless Treasures Milestone Materials

Nm-Mt Ex-Mt
PRINT RUNS B/WN 16-100 COPIES PER
*NBR p/r 35-36: .5X TO 1.2X BASIC p/r 80-82
*NBR p/r 24: .6X TO 1.5X BASIC p/r 100
NUMBER PRINT RUNS B/WN 9-36 PER
NO NUMBER PRICING ON QTY 9 OR LESS
*PRIME p/r 25: 1X TO 2.5X BASIC p/r 80-100
PRIME PRINT RUN 25 SERIAL #'d SETS
RANDOM INSERTS IN PACKS
2 Roger Maris Pants/61 .... 50.00 15.00
3 R.Henderson A's Jsy/80 .... 15.00 4.50
4 Gaylord Perry Jsy/82 .... 10.00 3.00
5 Cal Ripken Ball/16
6 R.Henderson Padres Jsy/100 15.00 4.50

2004 Timeless Treasures Milestone Materials Signature

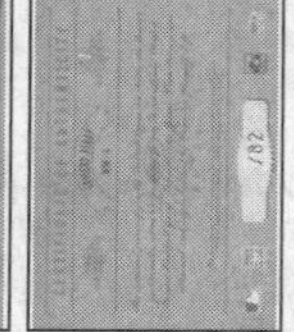

Nm-Mt Ex-Mt
PRINT RUNS B/WN 5-82 COPIES PER
NO PRICING ON QTY OF 8 OR LESS..
*NBR p/r 82: .4X TO 1X BASIC p/r 82
NUMBER PRINT RUNS B/WN 5-82 PER
NO NUMBER PRICING ON QTY 5 OR LESS
*PRIME p/r 19: .75X TO 2X BASIC p/r 82
PRIME PRINT RUNS B/WN 5-19 COPIES PER
NO PRIME PRICING ON QTY OF 5 OR LESS
RANDOM INSERTS IN PACKS
3 R.Henderson A's Jsy/5
4 Gaylord Perry Jsy/82 .... 25.00 7.50
5 Cal Ripken Ball/8
6 R.Henderson Padres Jsy/5

2004 Timeless Treasures No-Hitters Quad Signature

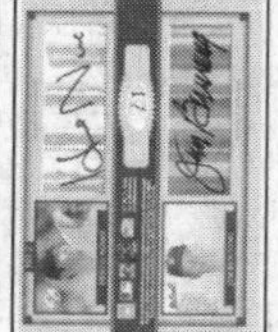

Nm-Mt Ex-Mt
RANDOM INSERTS IN PACKS
STATED PRINT RUN 1 SERIAL #'d SET
NO PRICING DUE TO SCARCITY
1 Cy Young Sox
Nolan Ryan Angels
Hideo Nomo Sox
Jim Bunning Tigers
2 Cy Young Sox
Nolan Ryan Rgr
Hideo Nomo Sox
Jim Bunning Tigers
3 Cy Young Spiders
Nolan Ryan Astros
Hideo Nomo Dodgers
Jim Bunning Phils

2004 Timeless Treasures Rookie Year Materials

Nm-Mt Ex-Mt
PRINT RUNS B/WN 5-100 COPIES PER
NO PRICING ON QTY OF 5 OR LESS..
PRIME PRINT RUNS B/WN 5-10 COPIES PER
NO PRIME PRICING DUE TO SCARCITY
RANDOM INSERTS IN PACKS
1 Stan Musial Jsy/19 .... 50.00 15.00
2 Yogi Berra Stripe Jsy/19 .... 50.00 15.00
3 Yogi Berra Grey Jsy/47 .... 25.00 7.50
4 Whitey Ford Jsy/50 .... 25.00 7.50
5 Catfish Hunter Jsy/65 .... 15.00 4.50
6 Johnny Bench Bat/68 .... 15.00 4.50
7 Mike Schmidt Bat/72 .... 20.00 6.00
8 Gary Carter Jsy/74 .... 10.00 3.00
9 Robin Yount Jsy/74 .... 25.00 7.50
11 Cal Ripken Bat/81 .... 50.00 15.00
12 Kirby Puckett Bat/84 .... 15.00 4.50
13 Roger Clemens Jsy/84 .... 20.00 6.00
15 Gary Sheffield Jsy/89 .... 10.00 3.00
16 Juan Gonzalez Jsy/89 .... 15.00 4.50
17 Randy Johnson Jsy/89 .... 15.00 4.50
18 Ivan Rodriguez Jsy/91 .... 15.00 4.50
20 Pedro Martinez Jsy/92 .... 15.00 4.50
21 Mike Piazza Jsy/93 .... 15.00 4.50
22 Hideo Nomo Jsy/95 .... 15.00 4.50
23 Hideo Nomo Pants/95 .... 15.00 4.50
24 Alex Rodriguez Jsy/95 .... 15.00 4.50
26 Scott Rolen Jsy/96 .... 15.00 4.50
27 Andruw Jones Jsy/96 .... 10.00 3.00
28 Nomar Garciaparra Jsy/97 .... 15.00 4.50
29 Vladimir Guerrero Jsy/97 .... 15.00 4.50
31 Alfonso Soriano Jsy/100 .... 15.00 4.50
32 Albert Pujols White Jsy/100. 20.00 6.00
33 Albert Pujols Grey Jsy/100 .. 20.00 6.00
34 Albert Pujols Bat/100 .... 20.00 6.00
35 Albert Pujols Hat/5
36 Mark Prior Blue Jsy/100 ...... 15.00 4.50
37 Mark Prior Grey Jsy/100 ...... 15.00 4.50
38 Dontrelle Willis Jsy/35 .... 15.00 4.50
39 Rocco Baldelli Jsy/5

2004 Timeless Treasures Rookie Year Materials Signature

Nm-Mt Ex-Mt
PRINT RUNS B/WN 1-97 COPIES PER
NO PRICING ON QTY OF 11 OR LESS
*PRIME p/r 35: .5X TO 1.2X BASIC p/r 35
*PRIME p/r 25: .75X TO 2X BASIC p/r 95-97
*PRIME p/r 22: .5X TO 1.2X BASIC p/r 22
*PRIME p/r 16: .5X TO 1.2X BASIC p/r 19
PRIME PRINT RUNS B/WN 1-35 COPIES PER
NO PRIME PRICING ON QTY OF 11 OR LESS
RANDOM INSERTS IN PACKS
1 Stan Musial Jsy/9
2 Yogi Berra Stripe Jsy/9
3 Yogi Berra Grey Jsy/19 .... 100.00 30.00
4 Whitey Ford Jsy/19 .... 100.00 30.00
6 Johnny Bench Bat/9
7 Mike Schmidt Bat/9
8 Gary Carter Jsy/19 .... 50.00 15.00
9 Robin Yount Jsy/9
10 Fred Lynn Jsy/75 .... 20.00 6.00
11 Cal Ripken Bat/9
12 Kirby Puckett Bat/9
13 Roger Clemens Jsy/9
14 Lenny Dykstra Fld Glv/85 ...... 25.00 7.50
15 Gary Sheffield Jsy/11
16 Juan Gonzalez Jsy/19 .... 60.00 18.00
17 Randy Johnson Jsy/9
18 Ivan Rodriguez Jsy/9
20 Pedro Martinez Jsy/1
21 Mike Piazza Jsy/1
22 Hideo Nomo Jsy/1
23 Hideo Nomo Pants/1
24 Alex Rodriguez Jsy/9
25 Garret Anderson Jsy/95 ...... 25.00 7.50
26 Scott Rolen Jsy/1
27 Andruw Jones Jsy/9
29 Vladimir Guerrero Jsy/9
30 Shannon Stewart Jsy/97 ...... 20.00 6.00
32 Albert Pujols White Jsy/5
33 Albert Pujols Grey Jsy/5
34 Albert Pujols Bat/5
35 Albert Pujols Hat/5
36 Mark Prior Blue Jsy/22 ...... 100.00 30.00
37 Mark Prior Grey Jsy/22 ...... 100.00 30.00
38 Dontrelle Willis Jsy/35 .... 40.00 12.00
39 Rocco Baldelli Jsy/19 .... 50.00 15.00

2004 Timeless Treasures Rookie Year Materials Signature Number

Nm-Mt Ex-Mt
*NBR p/r 35: .4X TO 1X BASIC p/r 35
*NBR p/r 22: .4X TO 1X BASIC p/r 22
*NBR p/r 16-19: .75X TO 2X BASIC p/r 75-95
*NBR p/r 16-19: .4X TO 1X BASIC p/r 19
RANDOM INSERTS IN PACKS
PRINT RUNS B/WN 1-35 COPIES PER
NO PRICING ON QTY OF 11 OR LESS
26 Scott Rolen Jsy/17 .... 80.00 24.00

2004 Timeless Treasures Rookie Year Materials Combos

Nm-Mt Ex-Mt
PRINT RUNS B/WN 5-35 COPIES PER
NO PRICING ON QTY OF 8 OR LESS..
*PRIME: .5X TO 1.2X BASIC
PRIME PRINT RUNS B/WN 1-35 COPIES PER
NO PRIME PRICING ON QTY OF 5 OR LESS
RANDOM INSERTS IN PACKS
2 Yogi Berra Jsy-Jsy/8
22 Hideo Nomo Jsy-Pants/16 ... 40.00 12.00
32 Albert Pujols Jsy-Jsy/5
33 Albert Pujols Bat-Jsy/5
34 Albert Pujols Bat-Jsy/5
35 Albert Pujols Bat-Hat/5
36 Mark Prior Jsy-Jsy/22 .... 30.00 9.00
38 Dontrelle Willis Jsy-Jsy/35 .. 20.00 6.00
39 Rocco Baldelli Jsy-Jsy/5

2004 Timeless Treasures Rookie Year Materials Combos Signature

Nm-Mt Ex-Mt
PRINT RUNS B/WN 1-35 COPIES PER
NO PRICING ON QTY OF 8 OR LESS ..
*PRIME: .5X TO 1.2X BASIC
PRIME PRINT RUNS B/WN 1-35 COPIES PER
NO PRIME PRICING ON QTY OF 5 OR LESS
RANDOM INSERTS IN PACKS
2 Yogi Berra Jsy-Jsy/8
22 Hideo Nomo Jsy-Pants/1
32 Albert Pujols Jsy-Jsy/5
33 Albert Pujols Bat-Jsy/5
34 Albert Pujols Bat-Jsy/5
35 Albert Pujols Bat-Hat/5
36 Mark Prior Jsy-Jsy/22 120.00 36.00
38 Dontrelle Willis Jsy-Jsy/35 40.00 12.00
39 Rocco Baldelli Jsy-Jsy/5

2004 Timeless Treasures Rookie Year Materials Dual

Nm-Mt Ex-Mt
STATED PRINT RUN 25 SERIAL #'d SETS
PRIME PRINT RUN 10 SERIAL #'d SETS
NO PRIME PRICING DUE TO SCARCITY
RANDOM INSERTS IN PACKS
40 Roger Clemens Jsy 60.00 18.00
Nomar Garciaparra Jsy
41 Pedro Martinez Jsy 50.00 15.00
Mike Piazza Jsy
42 Mike Piazza Jsy 50.00 15.00
Hideo Nomo Jsy
43 Pedro Martinez Jsy 30.00 9.00
Hideo Nomo Jsy
44 Yogi Berra Jsy 80.00 24.00
Whitey Ford Jsy
45 Mike Schmidt Bat 60.00 18.00
Scott Rolen Jsy
47 Juan Gonzalez Jsy 30.00 9.00
Ivan Rodriguez Jsy

2004 Timeless Treasures Rookie Year Materials Dual Signature

Nm-Mt Ex-Mt
RANDOM INSERTS IN PACKS
STATED PRINT RUN 5 SERIAL #'d SETS
NO PRICING DUE TO SCARCITY
41 Pedro Martinez Jsy
Mike Piazza Jsy
42 Mike Piazza Jsy
Hideo Nomo Jsy
43 Pedro Martinez Jsy
Hideo Nomo Jsy
44 Yogi Berra Jsy
Whitey Ford Jsy
46 Stan Musial Jsy
Albert Pujols Jsy
47 Juan Gonzalez Jsy
Ivan Rodriguez Jsy

2004 Timeless Treasures Statistical Champions

Nm-Mt Ex-Mt
PRINT RUNS B/WN 3-100 COPIES PER
NO PRICING ON QTY OF 9 OR LESS ..
*NBR p/r 38-51: .4X TO 1X BASIC p/r 68
*NBR p/r 38-51: .3X TO .8X BASIC p/r 19-25
*NBR p/r 26-34: .6X TO 1.5X BASIC p/r 86-100
*NBR p/r 20-25: .75X TO 2X BASIC p/r 88-100
*NBR p/r 20-25: .4X TO 1X BASIC p/r 25
*NBR p/r 21: .3X TO .8X BASIC p/r 19
*NBR p/r 17-19: .5X TO 1.2X BASIC p/r 25
NUMBER PRINT RUNS B/WN 1-51 PER
NO NUMBER PRICES ON QTY 9 OR LESS
PRIME PRINT RUNS B/WN 5-10 COPIES PER
NO PRIME PRICING DUE TO SCARCITY
RANDOM INSERTS IN PACKS
1 Jimmie Foxx Bat/9
2 Stan Musial 43 BA Jsy/19 50.00 15.00
3 Ralph Kiner Bat/49 15.00 4.50
4 Stan Musial 57 BA Jsy/57 40.00 12.00
5 Ted Williams Jsy/25 120.00 36.00
6 Warren Spahn Jsy/25 40.00 12.00
7 Eddie Mathews Jsy/19 50.00 15.00
8 Roger Maris 61 HR Bat/61 50.00 15.00
9 Roger Maris 61 HR Pants/61 50.00 15.00
10 Roger Maris 61 RBI Bat/61 50.00 15.00
11 R.Maris 61 RBI Pants/61 50.00 15.00
12 Roberto Clemente Jsy/19 120.00 36.00
13 Frank Robinson Bat/66 15.00 4.50
14 Bob Gibson 68 ERA Jsy/68 15.00 4.50
15 Bob Gibson 68 K Jsy/68 15.00 4.50
16 Tom Seaver Jsy/19 30.00 9.00
17 Harmon Killebrew Jsy/3
18 Harmon Killebrew Pants/71 25.00 7.50
19 Mike Schmidt Jsy/74 20.00 6.00
20 Reggie Jackson Jsy/19 30.00 9.00
21 Phil Niekro Jsy/5
22 Rod Carew Hat/78 15.00 4.50
23 Jim Rice 78 HR Jsy/78 10.00 3.00
24 Jim Rice 78 RBI Jsy/78 10.00 3.00
25 Reggie Jackson Hat/80 15.00 4.50
26 Dale Murphy 82 RBI Jsy/82 15.00 4.50
27 Steve Carlton Jsy/83 10.00 3.00
28 Dale Murphy 85 HR Jsy/85 15.00 4.50
29 Wade Boggs 86 BA Jsy/86 15.00 4.50
30 Wade Boggs 87 BA Jsy/87 15.00 4.50
31 Will Clark Jsy/88 15.00 4.50
32 Nolan Ryan 89 K Jsy/89 25.00 7.50
33 Nolan Ryan 90 K Jsy/90 25.00 7.50
34 Nolan Ryan 90 K Pants/90 25.00 7.50
35 Ryne Sandberg Jsy/90 25.00 7.50
36 Roger Clemens 90 K Jsy/90 20.00 6.00
37 George Brett Jsy/90 25.00 7.50
38 R.Clemens 92 ERA Jsy/100 20.00 6.00
39 R.Clemens 96 K Jsy/100 20.00 6.00
40 Tony Gwynn Jsy/25 50.00 15.00
41 P.Martinez Expos Jsy/25 20.00 6.00
42 Greg Maddux Jsy/100 15.00 4.50
43 Juan Gonzalez Pants/25 20.00 6.00
44 Manny Ramirez Bat/25 20.00 6.00
45 N.G'parra 99 BA Jsy/100 15.00 4.50
46 N.Garciaparra 99 BA Bat/5
47 N.G'parra 00 BA Jsy/100 15.00 4.50
48 Todd Helton 00 BA Jsy/25 20.00 6.00
49 Todd Helton 00 RBI Jsy/25 20.00 6.00
50 Troy Glaus Jsy/25 15.00 4.50
51 Randy Johnson 00 K Jsy/25 20.00 6.00
52 Tom Glavine Jsy/25 20.00 6.00
53 Sammy Sosa 00 HR Jsy/100 15.00 4.50
54 A.Rodriguez 01 HR Bat/100 15.00 4.50
55 Curt Schilling Jsy/25 15.00 4.50
56 Pedro Martinez 99 K Jsy/25 20.00 6.00
57 A.Rodriguez 01 HR Jsy/100 15.00 4.50
58 Mark Mulder Jsy/25 15.00 4.50
59 S.Sosa 01 RBI Jsy/100 15.00 4.50
60 Manny Ramirez Jsy/25 20.00 6.00
61 Lance Berkman Jsy/25 15.00 4.50
62 Randy Johnson 02 W Jsy/25 20.00 6.00
63 A.Rodriguez 02 HR Jsy/100 15.00 4.50
64 A.Rodriguez 02 RBI Jsy/100 15.00 4.50
65 A.Rodriguez 02 HR Bat/100 15.00 4.50
66 A.Rodriguez 02 RBI Bat/100 15.00 4.50
67 Pedro Martinez 02 K Jsy/25 20.00 6.00
68 P.Martinez 02 ERA Jsy/25 20.00 6.00
69 Sammy Sosa 02 HR Jsy/100 15.00 4.50
70 Jim Thome Jsy/25 20.00 6.00
71 A.Rodriguez 03 HR Bat/100 15.00 4.50
72 Albert Pujols Bat/100 20.00 6.00
73 A.Rodriguez 03 HR Jsy/100 15.00 4.50
74 Albert Pujols Jsy/100 20.00 6.00

2004 Timeless Treasures Statistical Champions Signature

Nm-Mt Ex-Mt
PRINT RUNS B/WN 1-88 COPIES PER
NO PRICING ON QTY OF 10 OR LESS
*NBR p/r 47: .3X TO .8X BASIC p/r 20
*NBR p/r 32-34: .4X TO 1X BASIC p/r 19-25
*NBR p/r 22: 1.25X TO 3X BASIC p/r 88
*NBR p/r 20-25: .4X TO 1X BASIC p/r 20-25
*NBR p/r 19: .4X TO 1X BASIC p/r 19
*NBR p/r 17-19: .5X TO 1.2X BASIC p/r 20-25
NUMBER PRINT RUNS B/WN 1-47 PER
NO NUMBER PRICING ON QTY 14 OR LESS
PRIME PRINT RUNS B/WN 1-10 COPIES PER
NO PRIME PRICING DUE TO SCARCITY
RANDOM INSERTS IN PACKS
2 Stan Musial 43 BA Jsy/10
3 Ralph Kiner Bat/49 50.00 15.00
4 Stan Musial 57 BA Jsy/10
6 Warren Spahn Jsy/25 80.00 24.00
13 Frank Robinson Bat/66 40.00 12.00
14 Bob Gibson 68 ERA Jsy/25 50.00 15.00
15 Bob Gibson 68 K Jsy/25 50.00 15.00
16 Tom Seaver Jsy/10
17 Harmon Killebrew Jsy/71 50.00 15.00
18 Harmon Killebrew Pants/71 50.00 15.00
19 Mike Schmidt Jsy/25 120.00 36.00
20 Reggie Jackson Jsy/25 80.00 24.00
21 Phil Niekro Jsy/50 40.00 12.00
22 Rod Carew Hat/25 50.00 15.00
23 Jim Rice 78 HR Jsy/78 25.00 7.50
24 Jim Rice 78 RBI Jsy/78 25.00 7.50
25 Reggie Jackson Hat/25 80.00 24.00
26 Dale Murphy 82 RBI Jsy/25 60.00 18.00
27 Steve Carlton Jsy/25 50.00 15.00
28 Dale Murphy 85 HR Jsy/25 60.00 18.00
29 Wade Boggs 86 BA Jsy/25 50.00 15.00
30 Wade Boggs 87 BA Jsy/25 50.00 15.00
31 Will Clark Jsy/88 40.00 12.00
32 Nolan Ryan 89 K Jsy/25 150.00 45.00
33 Nolan Ryan 90 K Jsy/25 150.00 45.00
34 Nolan Ryan 90 K Pants/25 150.00 45.00
35 Ryne Sandberg Jsy/25 120.00 36.00
36 Roger Clemens 90 K Jsy/5
37 George Brett Jsy/10
38 R.Clemens 92 ERA Jsy/5
39 Roger Clemens 96 K Jsy/5
40 Tony Gwynn Jsy/25 100.00 30.00
41 Pedro Martinez Expos Jsy/1
42 Greg Maddux Jsy/10
43 Juan Gonzalez Pants/19 60.00 18.00
44 Manny Ramirez Bat/10
48 Todd Helton 00 BA Jsy/10
49 Todd Helton 00 RBI Jsy/10
50 Troy Glaus Jsy/25 40.00 12.00
51 Randy Johnson 00 K Jsy/10
52 Tom Glavine Jsy/20 50.00 15.00
53 Sammy Sosa 00 HR Jsy/25 200.00 60.00
54 A.Rodriguez 01 HR Bat/10
55 Curt Schilling Jsy/25 60.00 18.00
56 Pedro Martinez 99 K Jsy/1
57 A.Rodriguez 01 HR Jsy/10
58 Mark Mulder Jsy/25 40.00 12.00
59 S.Sosa 01 RBI Jsy/25 200.00 60.00
60 Manny Ramirez Jsy/10
61 Lance Berkman Jsy/20 50.00 15.00
62 Randy Johnson 02 W Jsy/9
63 A.Rodriguez 02 HR Jsy/10
64 A.Rodriguez 02 RBI Jsy/10
65 A.Rodriguez 02 HR Bat/10
66 A.Rodriguez 02 RBI Bat/10
67 Pedro Martinez 02 K Jsy/1
68 Pedro Martinez 02 ERA Jsy/1
69 S.Sosa 02 HR Jsy/25 200.00 60.00
71 A.Rodriguez 03 HR Bat/10
72 Albert Pujols Bat/10
73 A.Rodriguez 03 HR Jsy/10
74 Albert Pujols Jsy/10

2004 Timeless Treasures World Series Materials

Nm-Mt Ex-Mt
PRINT RUNS B/WN 2-100 COPIES PER
NO PRICING ON QTY OF 8 OR LESS ..
*PRIME p/r 19-20: 1.25X TO 3X p/r 87-100
PRIME PRINT RUNS B/WN 1-20 COPIES PER
NO PRIME PRICING ON QTY OF 1
RANDOM INSERTS IN PACKS
1 Frank Robinson Bat/61 15.00 4.50
2 Ozzie Smith Jsy/87 20.00 6.00
3 Rickey Henderson Bat/93 15.00 4.50
4 Tom Glavine Jsy/96 15.00 4.50
5 Roger Clemens Jsy/100 20.00 6.00
6 Bob Gibson G1 Ball/6
7 Bob Gibson G4 Ball/3
8 Bob Gibson G7 Ball/7
9 Lou Brock Ball/2
10 Roger Maris Ball/2
11 Carl Yastrzemki Ball/2
12 Bob Gibson
Lou Brock
Roger Maris Ball/2
13 Bob Gibson
Lou Brock
Roger Maris
Carl Yastrzemki Ball/8
14 Bob Gibson G1 Ball/5

2004 Timeless Treasures World Series Materials Signature

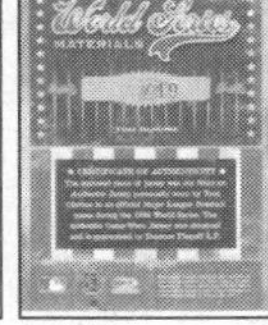

Nm-Mt Ex-Mt
1-11 PRINT RUNS B/WN 2-19 COPIES PER
CARD 14 PRINT RUN 5 SERIAL #'d COPIES
NO CARD 14 PRICING DUE TO SCARCITY
PRIME PRINT RUNS B/WN 9-10 COPIES PER
NO PRIME PRICING DUE TO SCARCITY
RANDOM INSERTS IN PACKS
1 Frank Robinson Bat/19 60.00 18.00
2 Ozzie Smith Jsy/9
3 Rickey Henderson Bat/9
4 Tom Glavine Jsy/19 60.00 18.00
5 Roger Clemens Jsy/9
6 Bob Gibson G1 Ball/5
7 Bob Gibson G4 Ball/2
8 Bob Gibson G7 Ball/7
9 Lou Brock Ball/2
11 Carl Yastrzemski Ball/2
14 Bob Gibson G1 Ball/5

1951 Topps Blue Backs

The cards in this 52-card set measure approximately 2" by 2 5/8". The 1951 Topps series of blue-backed baseball cards could be used to play a baseball game by shuffling the cards and drawing them from a pile. These cards (packaged two adjoined in a penny pack) were marketed with a piece of caramel candy, which often melted or was squashed in such a way as to damage the card and wrapper (despite the fact that a paper shield was inserted between candy and card). Blue Backs are more difficult to obtain than the similarly styled Red Backs. The set is denoted on the cards as "Set B" and the Red Back set is correspondingly Set A. The only notable Rookie Card in the set is Billy Pierce.

NM Ex
COMPLETE SET (52) 1700.00 850.00
WRAPPER (1-CENT) 200.00 100.00
1 Eddie Yost 60.00 18.00
2 Hank Majeski 30.00 15.00
3 Richie Ashburn 200.00 100.00
4 Del Ennis 30.00 15.00
5 Johnny Pesky 30.00 15.00
6 Red Schoendienst 100.00 50.00
7 Gerry Staley 30.00 15.00
8 Dick Sisler 30.00 15.00
9 Johnny Sain 50.00 25.00
10 Joe Page 50.00 25.00
11 Johnny Groth 30.00 15.00
12 Sam Jethroe 40.00 20.00
13 Mickey Vernon 30.00 15.00
14 George Munger 30.00 15.00
15 Eddie Joost 30.00 15.00
16 Murry Dickson 30.00 15.00
17 Roy Smalley 30.00 15.00
18 Ned Garver 30.00 15.00
19 Phil Masi 30.00 15.00
20 Ralph Branca 50.00 25.00
21 Billy Johnson 30.00 15.00
22 Bob Kuzava 30.00 15.00
23 Dizzy Trout 40.00 20.00
24 Sherman Lollar 30.00 15.00
25 Sam Mele 30.00 15.00
26 Chico Carrasquel RC 40.00 20.00
27 Andy Pafko 30.00 15.00
28 Harry Brecheen 30.00 15.00
29 Granville Hamner 30.00 15.00
30 Enos Slaughter 100.00 50.00
31 Lou Brissie 30.00 15.00
32 Bob Elliott 40.00 20.00
33 Don Lenhardt 30.00 15.00
34 Earl Torgeson 30.00 15.00
35 Tommy Byrne 30.00 15.00
36 Cliff Fannin 30.00 15.00
37 Bobby Doerr 100.00 50.00
38 Irv Noren 30.00 15.00
39 Ed Lopat 50.00 25.00
40 Vic Wertz 30.00 15.00
41 Johnny Schmitz 30.00 15.00
42 Bruce Edwards 30.00 15.00
43 Willie Jones 30.00 15.00
44 Johnny Wyrostek 30.00 15.00
45 Billy Pierce RC 50.00 25.00
46 Gerry Priddy 30.00 15.00
47 Herman Wehmeier 30.00 15.00
48 Billy Cox 40.00 20.00
49 Hank Sauer 40.00 20.00
50 Johnny Mize 100.00 50.00
51 Eddie Waitkus 40.00 20.00
52 Sam Chapman 50.00 17.00

1951 Topps Red Backs

The cards in this 52-card set measure approximately 2" by 2 5/8". The 1951 Topps Red Back set is identical in style to the Blue Back set of the same year. The cards have rounded corners and were designed to be used as a baseball game. Zernial, number 36, is listed with either the White Sox or Athletics, and Holmes, number 52, with either the Braves or Hartford. The set is denoted on the cards as "Set A" and the Blue Back set is correspondingly Set B. The cards were packaged as two connected cards along with a piece of caramel in a penny pack. There were 120 penny packs in a box. The most notable Rookie Card in the set is Monte Irvin.

NM Ex
COMPLETE SET (54) 800.00 425.00
WRAPPER (1-CENT) 5.00 2.50
1 Yogi Berra 125.00 45.00
2 Sid Gordon 10.00 5.00
3 Ferris Fain 12.00 6.00
4 Vern Stephens 12.00 6.00
5 Phil Rizzuto 60.00 30.00
6 Allie Reynolds 20.00 10.00
7 Howie Pollet 10.00 5.00
8 Early Wynn 25.00 12.50
9 Roy Sievers 15.00 7.50
10 Mel Parnell 12.00 6.00
11 Gene Hermanski 12.00 6.00
12 Jim Hegan 12.00 6.00
13 Dale Mitchell 12.00 6.00
14 Wayne Terwilliger 10.00 5.00
15 Ralph Kiner 25.00 12.50
16 Preacher Roe 15.00 7.50
17 Gus Bell RC 15.00 7.50
18 Jerry Coleman 15.00 7.50
19 Dick Kokos 10.00 5.00
20 Dom DiMaggio 20.00 10.00
21 Larry Jansen 12.00 6.00
22 Bob Feller 60.00 30.00
23 Ray Boone RC 15.00 7.50
24 Hank Bauer 20.00 10.00
25 Cliff Chambers 10.00 5.00
26 Luke Easter RC 15.00 7.50
27 Wally Westlake 12.00 6.00
28 Elmer Valo 10.00 5.00
29 Bob Kennedy 12.00 6.00
30 Warren Spahn 60.00 30.00
31 Gil Hodges 50.00 25.00
32 Henry Thompson 12.00 6.00
33 William Werle 10.00 5.00
34 Grady Hatton 10.00 5.00
35 Al Rosen 15.00 7.50
36A Gus Zernial 40.00 20.00
(Chicago)
36B Gus Zernial 20.00 10.00
(Philadelphia)
37 Wes Westrum 12.00 6.00
38 Duke Snider 60.00 30.00
39 Ted Kluszewski 25.00 12.50
40 Mike Garcia 15.00 7.50
41 Whitey Lockman 12.00 6.00
42 Ray Scarborough 10.00 5.00
43 Maurice McDermott 10.00 5.00
44 Sid Hudson 10.00 5.00
45 Andy Seminick 12.00 6.00
46 Billy Goodman 12.00 6.00
47 Tommy Glaviano 10.00 5.00
48 Eddie Stanky 12.00 6.00
49 Al Zarilla 10.00 5.00
50 Monte Irvin RC 40.00 20.00
51 Eddie Robinson 10.00 5.00
52A Tommy Holmes 40.00 10.00
(Boston)
52B Tommy Holmes 25.00 6.25
(Hartford)

1952 Topps

The cards in this 407-card set measure approximately 2 5/8" by 3 3/4". The 1952 Topps set is Topps' first truly major set. Card numbers 1 to 80 were issued with red or black backs, both of which are less plentiful than card numbers 81 to 250. In fact, the first series is considered the most difficult with respect to finding perfect condition cards. Card number 48 (Joe Page) and number 49 (Johnny Sain) can be found with each other's write-up on their back. However, many dealers today believe that all cards numbered 1-250 are valued the same. Card numbers 251 to 310 are somewhat scarce and numbers 311 to 407 are quite scarce. Cards 281-300 were single printed compared to the other cards in the next to last series. Cards 311-313 were double printed on the last high number printing sheet. The key card in the set is obviously Mickey Mantle, number 311, Mickey's first of many Topps cards. A really obscure variation on cards from 311 through 313 is that they exist with the stitching on the number circle in the back either clockwise or counter clockwise. There is no price differential for either variation. Card number 307, Frank Campos has been discovered to have a black star next to the words "Topps Baseball" on the back. This card is very scarce but since it is rarely traded in the secondary market -- no value can be established at this time. Many collectors are not aware of this variation. In the early 1980's, Topps issued a standard-size reprint set of the 52 Topps set. These cards were issued only as a factory set and have a current market value of between two and three hundred dollars. Five people portrayed in the regular set: Billy Loes (number 20), Dom DiMaggio (number 22), Saul Rogovin (number 159), Solly Hemus (number 196) and Tommy Holmes (number 289) are not in the reprint set. Although rarely seen, there exist salesman sample panels of three cards containing the fronts of regular cards with ad information on the back. Panels which have been seen are Bob Mahoney/Robin Roberts/Sid Hudson, Bob Wellman/Lou Kretlow/Ray Scarborough, Wally Westlake/Dizzy Trout/Irv Noren and Eddie Joost/Willie Jones/Gordon Goldsberry. The cards were issued in one-card penny packs and six-card nickle packs. The five cent packs were issued 24 packs to a box. The key Rookie Cards in this set are Billy Martin, Eddie Mathews (the last card in the set), and Hoyt Wilhelm. Some cards issued in Canada, (131-190) have also been reported, these cards have a "muted" tone on the front and use a grey stock reverse.

NM Ex
COMP.MASTER SET (487) 80000.00 40000.00
COMPLETE SET (407) 65000.00 32500.00
COMMON CARD (1-80) 60.00 30.00
COMMON CARD (81-250) 40.00 20.00
COMMON (251-310) 50.00 25.00
COMMON (311-407) 250.00 125.00
WRAPPER (1-cent) 250.00 125.00
WRAPPER (5-cent) 100.00 50.00
1 Andy Pafko 5000.00 500.00
1A Andy Pafko Black 3000.00 300.00
2 Pete Runnels RC 250.00 125.00
2A Pete Runnells RC Black 250.00 125.00
3 Hank Thompson 70.00 35.00
3A Hank Thompson Black 70.00 35.00
4 Don Lenhardt 60.00 30.00
4A Don Lenhardt Black 60.00 30.00
5 Larry Jansen 70.00 35.00
5A Larry Jansen Black 70.00 35.00
6 Grady Hatton 60.00 30.00
6A Grady Hatton Black 60.00 30.00

1953 Topps

7 Wayne Terwilliger 60.00 30.00
7A W. Terwilliger Black 60.00 30.00
8 Fred Marsh 60.00 30.00
8A Fred Marsh Black 60.00 30.00
9 Robert Hogue 60.00 30.00
9A Robert Hogue Black 60.00 30.00
10 Al Rosen 70.00 35.00
10A Al Rosen Black 70.00 35.00
11 Phil Rizzuto 400.00 200.00
11A Phil Rizzuto Black 350.00 180.00
12 Monty Basgall 60.00 30.00
12A Monty Basgall Black 60.00 30.00
13 Johnny Wyrostek 60.00 30.00
13A J. Wyrostek Black 60.00 30.00
14 Bob Elliott 70.00 35.00
14A Bob Elliott Black 70.00 35.00
15 Johnny Pesky 70.00 35.00
15A Johnny Pesky Black 70.00 35.00
16 Gene Hermanski 60.00 30.00
16A G. Hermanski Black 60.00 30.00
17 Jim Hegan 70.00 35.00
17A Jim Hegan Black 70.00 35.00
18 Merrill Combs 60.00 30.00
18A Merrill Combs Black 60.00 30.00
19 Johnny Bucha 60.00 30.00
19A Johnny Bucha Black 60.00 30.00
20 Billy Loes RC 125.00 60.00
20A Billy Loes RC Black 125.00 60.00
21 Ferris Fain 70.00 35.00
21A Ferris Fain Black 70.00 35.00
22 Dom DiMaggio 100.00 50.00
22A Dom DiMaggio Black 100.00 50.00
23 Billy Goodman 70.00 35.00
23A Billy Goodman Black 70.00 35.00
24 Luke Easter 80.00 40.00
24A Luke Easter Black 80.00 40.00
25 Johnny Groth 60.00 30.00
25A Johnny Groth Black 60.00 30.00
26 Monte Irvin 150.00 75.00
26A Monte Irvin Black 125.00 60.00
27 Sam Jethroe 70.00 35.00
27A Sam Jethroe Black 70.00 35.00
28 Jerry Priddy 60.00 30.00
28A Jerry Priddy Black 60.00 30.00
29 Ted Kluszewski 125.00 60.00
29A Ted Kluszewski Black 125.00 60.00
30 Mel Parnell 70.00 35.00
30A Mel Parnell Black 70.00 35.00
31 Gus Zernial 80.00 40.00
Posed with seven baseballs
31A Gus Zernial Black 80.00 40.00
Posed with seven baseballs
32 Eddie Robinson 60.00 30.00
32A Eddie Robinson Black 60.00 30.00
33 Warren Spahn 300.00 150.00
33A Warren Spahn Black 250.00 125.00
34 Elmer Valo 60.00 30.00
34A Elmer Valo Black 60.00 30.00
35 Hank Sauer 70.00 35.00
35A Hank Sauer Black 70.00 35.00
36 Gil Hodges 300.00 150.00
36A Gil Hodges Black 250.00 125.00
37 Duke Snider 500.00 250.00
37A Duke Snider Black 400.00 200.00
38 Wally Westlake 60.00 30.00
38A Wally Westlake Black 60.00 30.00
39 Dizzy Trout 70.00 35.00
39A Dizzy Trout Black 70.00 35.00
40 Irv Noren 70.00 35.00
40A Irv Noren Black 70.00 35.00
41 Bob Wellman 60.00 30.00
41A Bob Wellman Black 60.00 30.00
42 Lou Kretlow 60.00 30.00
42A Lou Kretlow Black 60.00 30.00
43 Ray Scarborough 60.00 30.00
43A R. Scarborough Black 60.00 30.00
44 Con Dempsey 60.00 30.00
44A Con Dempsey Black 60.00 30.00
45 Eddie Joost 60.00 30.00
45A Eddie Joost Black 60.00 30.00
46 Gordon Goldsberry 60.00 30.00
46A G. Goldsberry Black 60.00 30.00
47 Willie Jones 70.00 35.00
47A Willie Jones Black 70.00 35.00
48A Joe Page ERR 400.00 200.00
Bio for Sain
Black Back
48B Joe Page COR 125.00 60.00
Black Back
48C Joe Page COR 125.00 60.00
Red Back
49A John Sain ERR 400.00 200.00
Bio for Page
Black Back
49B John Sain COR 125.00 60.00
Black Back
49C John Sain COR 125.00 60.00
Red Back
50 Marv Rickert 60.00 30.00
50A Marv Richert Black 60.00 30.00
51 Jim Russell 60.00 30.00
51A Jim Russell Black 60.00 30.00
52 Don Mueller 70.00 35.00
52A Don Mueller Black 70.00 35.00
53 Chris Van Cuyk 60.00 30.00
53A Chris Van Cuyk Black 60.00 30.00
54 Leo Kiely 60.00 30.00
54A Leo Kiely Black 60.00 30.00
55 Ray Boone 80.00 40.00
55A Ray Boone Black 80.00 40.00
56 Tommy Glaviano 60.00 30.00
56A T. Glaviano Black 60.00 30.00
57 Ed Lopat 100.00 50.00
57A Ed Lopat Black 100.00 50.00
58 Bob Mahoney 60.00 30.00
58A Bob Mahoney Black 60.00 30.00
59 Robin Roberts 175.00 90.00
59A Robin Roberts Black 175.00 90.00
60 Sid Hudson 60.00 30.00
60A Sid Hudson Black 60.00 30.00
61 Tookie Gilbert 60.00 30.00
61A Tookie Gilbert Black 60.00 30.00
62 Chuck Stobbs 60.00 30.00
62A Chuck Stobbs Black 60.00 30.00
63 Howie Pollet 60.00 30.00
63A Howie Pollet Black 60.00 30.00
64 Roy Sievers 70.00 35.00
64A Roy Sievers Black 70.00 35.00
65 Enos Slaughter 175.00 90.00
65A Enos Slaughter Black 175.00 90.00
66 Preacher Roe 100.00 50.00
66A Preacher Roe Black 100.00 50.00
67 Allie Reynolds 125.00 60.00
67A Allie Reynolds Black 100.00 50.00
68 Cliff Chambers 60.00 30.00
68A Cliff Chambers Black 60.00 30.00
69 Virgil Stallcup 60.00 30.00
69A Virgil Stallcup Black 60.00 30.00
70 Al Zarilla 60.00 30.00
70A Al Zarilla Black 60.00 30.00
71 Tom Upton 60.00 30.00
71A Tom Upton Black 60.00 30.00
72 Karl Olson 60.00 30.00
72A Karl Olson Black 60.00 30.00
73 Bill Werle 60.00 30.00
73A Bill Werle Black 60.00 30.00
74 Andy Hansen 60.00 30.00
74A Andy Hansen Black 60.00 30.00
75 Wes Westrum 70.00 35.00
75A Wes Westrum Black 70.00 35.00
76 Eddie Stanky 70.00 35.00
76A Eddie Stanky Black 70.00 35.00
77 Bob Kennedy 70.00 35.00
77A Bob Kennedy Black 70.00 35.00
78 Ellis Kinder 60.00 30.00
78A Ellis Kinder Black 60.00 30.00
79 Gerry Staley 60.00 30.00
79A Gerry Staley Black 60.00 30.00
80 Herman Wehmeier 80.00 40.00
80A H. Wehmeier Black 80.00 40.00
81 Vernon Law 80.00 40.00
82 Duane Pillette 40.00 20.00
83 Billy Johnson 40.00 20.00
84 Vern Stephens 50.00 25.00
85 Bob Kuzava 50.00 25.00
86 Ted Gray 40.00 20.00
87 Dale Coogan 40.00 20.00
88 Bob Feller 250.00 125.00
89 Johnny Lipon 40.00 20.00
90 Mickey Grasso 40.00 20.00
91 Red Schoendienst 100.00 50.00
92 Dale Mitchell 50.00 25.00
93 Al Sima 40.00 20.00
94 Sam Mele 40.00 20.00
95 Ken Holcombe 40.00 20.00
96 Willard Marshall 40.00 20.00
97 Earl Torgeson 40.00 20.00
98 Billy Pierce 50.00 25.00
99 Gene Woodling 60.00 30.00
100 Del Rice 40.00 20.00
101 Max Lanier 40.00 20.00
102 Bill Kennedy 40.00 20.00
103 Cliff Mapes 40.00 20.00
104 Don Kolloway 40.00 20.00
105 Johnny Pramesa 40.00 20.00
106 Mickey Vernon 60.00 30.00
107 Connie Ryan 40.00 20.00
108 Jim Konstanty 60.00 30.00
109 Ted Wilks 40.00 20.00
110 Dutch Leonard 40.00 20.00
111 Peanuts Lowrey 40.00 20.00
112 Hank Majeski 40.00 20.00
113 Dick Sisler 50.00 25.00
114 Willard Ramsdell 40.00 20.00
115 George Munger 40.00 20.00
116 Carl Scheib 40.00 20.00
117 Sherm Lollar 50.00 25.00
118 Ken Raffensberger 40.00 20.00
119 Mickey McDermott 40.00 20.00
120 Bob Chakales 40.00 20.00
121 Gus Niarhos 40.00 20.00
122 Jackie Jensen 80.00 40.00
123 Eddie Yost 50.00 25.00
124 Monte Kennedy 40.00 20.00
125 Bill Rigney 40.00 20.00
126 Fred Hutchinson 50.00 25.00
127 Paul Minner 40.00 20.00
128 Don Bollweg 40.00 20.00
129 Johnny Mize 150.00 75.00
130 Sheldon Jones 40.00 20.00
131 Morrie Martin 40.00 20.00
132 Clyde Kluttz 40.00 20.00
133 Al Widmar 40.00 20.00
134 Joe Tipton 40.00 20.00
135 Dixie Howell 40.00 20.00
136 Johnny Schmitz 40.00 20.00
137 Roy McMillan RC 50.00 25.00
138 Bill MacDonald 40.00 20.00
139 Ken Wood 40.00 20.00
140 Johnny Antonelli 60.00 30.00
141 Clint Hartung 40.00 20.00
142 Harry Perkowski 40.00 20.00
143 Les Moss 40.00 20.00
144 Ed Blake 40.00 20.00
145 Joe Haynes 40.00 20.00
146 Frank House 40.00 20.00
147 Bob Young 40.00 20.00
148 Johnny Klippstein 40.00 20.00
149 Dick Kryhoski 40.00 20.00
150 Ted Beard 40.00 20.00
151 Wally Post RC 50.00 25.00
152 Al Evans 40.00 20.00
153 Bob Rush 40.00 20.00
154 Joe Muir 40.00 20.00
155 Frank Overmire 40.00 20.00
156 Frank Hiller 40.00 20.00
157 Bob Usher 40.00 20.00
158 Eddie Waitkus 40.00 20.00
159 Saul Rogovin 40.00 20.00
160 Owen Friend 40.00 20.00
161 Bud Byerly 40.00 20.00
162 Del Crandall 50.00 25.00
163 Stan Rojek 40.00 20.00
164 Walt Dubiel 40.00 20.00
165 Eddie Kazak 40.00 20.00
166 Paul LaPalme 40.00 20.00
167 Bill Howerton 40.00 20.00
168 Charlie Silvera RC 60.00 30.00
169 Howie Judson 40.00 20.00
170 Gus Bell 50.00 25.00
171 Ed Erautt 40.00 20.00
172 Eddie Miksis 40.00 20.00
173 Roy Smalley 40.00 20.00
174 Clarence Marshall 60.00 30.00
175 Billy Martin RC 500.00 250.00
176 Hank Edwards 40.00 20.00
177 Bill Wight 40.00 20.00
178 Cass Michaels 40.00 20.00
179 Frank Smith 40.00 20.00
180 Charlie Maxwell RC 50.00 25.00
181 Bob Swift 40.00 20.00
182 Billy Hitchcock 40.00 20.00
183 Erv Dusak 40.00 20.00
184 Bob Ramazzotti 40.00 20.00
185 Bill Nicholson 50.00 25.00
186 Walt Masterson 40.00 20.00
187 Bob Miller 40.00 20.00
188 Clarence Podbielan 40.00 20.00
189 Pete Reiser 60.00 30.00
190 Don Johnson 40.00 20.00
191 Yogi Berra 800.00 400.00
192 Myron Ginsberg 40.00 20.00
193 Harry Simpson 50.00 25.00
194 Joe Hatton 40.00 20.00
195 Minnie Minoso RC 150.00 75.00
196 Solly Hemus RC 60.00 30.00
197 George Strickland 40.00 20.00
198 Phil Haugstad 40.00 20.00
199 George Zuverink 40.00 20.00
200 Ralph Houk RC 80.00 40.00
201 Alex Kellner 40.00 20.00
202 Joe Collins RC 60.00 30.00
203 Curt Simmons 60.00 30.00
204 Ron Northey 40.00 20.00
205 Clyde King 60.00 30.00
206 Joe Ostrowski 40.00 20.00
207 Mickey Harris 40.00 20.00
208 Marlin Stuart 40.00 20.00
209 Howie Fox 40.00 20.00
210 Dick Fowler 40.00 20.00
211 Ray Coleman 40.00 20.00
212 Ned Garver 40.00 20.00
213 Nippy Jones 40.00 20.00
214 Johnny Hopp 50.00 25.00
215 Hank Bauer 100.00 50.00
216 Richie Ashburn 250.00 125.00
217 Snuffy Stirnweiss 50.00 25.00
218 Clyde McCullough 40.00 20.00
219 Bobby Shantz 60.00 30.00
220 Joe Presko 40.00 20.00
221 Granny Hamner 40.00 20.00
222 Hoot Evers 40.00 20.00
223 Del Ennis 50.00 25.00
224 Bruce Edwards 40.00 20.00
225 Frank Baumholtz 40.00 20.00
226 Dave Philley 40.00 20.00
227 Joe Garagiola 80.00 40.00
228 Al Brazle 40.00 20.00
229 Gene Bearden UER 40.00 20.00
(Misspelled Beardon)
230 Matt Batts 40.00 20.00
231 Sam Zoldak 40.00 20.00
232 Billy Cox 50.00 25.00
233 Bob Friend RC 80.00 40.00
234 Steve Souchock 40.00 20.00
235 Walt Dropo 40.00 20.00
236 Ed Fitzgerald 40.00 20.00
237 Jerry Coleman 60.00 30.00
238 Art Houtteman 40.00 20.00
239 Rocky Bridges 50.00 25.00
240 Jack Phillips 40.00 20.00
241 Tommy Byrne 40.00 20.00
242 Tom Poholsky 40.00 20.00
243 Larry Doby 80.00 40.00
244 Vic Wertz 40.00 20.00
245 Sherry Robertson 40.00 20.00
246 George Kell 80.00 40.00
247 Randy Gumpert 40.00 20.00
248 Frank Shea 40.00 20.00
249 Bobby Adams 40.00 20.00
250 Carl Erskine 100.00 50.00
251 Chico Carrasquel 50.00 25.00
252 Vern Bickford 50.00 25.00
253 Johnny Berardino 100.00 50.00
254 Joe Dobson 50.00 25.00
255 Clyde Vollmer 50.00 25.00
256 Pete Suder 50.00 25.00
257 Bobby Avila 60.00 30.00
258 Steve Gromek 60.00 30.00
259 Bob Addis 50.00 25.00
260 Pete Castiglione 50.00 25.00
261 Willie Mays 3000.00 1500.00
262 Virgil Trucks 60.00 30.00
263 Harry Brecheen 60.00 30.00
264 Roy Hartsfield 50.00 25.00
265 Chuck Diering 50.00 25.00
266 Murry Dickson 50.00 25.00
267 Sid Gordon 50.00 25.00
268 Bob Lemon 150.00 75.00
269 Willard Nixon 50.00 25.00
270 Lou Brissie 50.00 25.00
271 Jim Delsing 60.00 30.00
272 Mike Garcia 80.00 40.00
273 Erv Palica 50.00 25.00
274 Ralph Branca 125.00 60.00
275 Pat Mullin 50.00 25.00
276 Jim Wilson RC 50.00 25.00
277 Early Wynn 175.00 90.00
278 Allie Clark 50.00 25.00
279 Eddie Stewart 50.00 25.00
280 Cloyd Boyer 80.00 40.00
281 Tommy Brown SP 80.00 40.00
282 Birdie Tebbetts SP 80.00 40.00
283 Phil Masi SP 60.00 30.00
284 Hank Arft SP 60.00 30.00
285 Cliff Fannin SP 60.00 30.00
286 Joe DeMaestri SP 60.00 30.00
287 Steve Bilko SP 60.00 30.00
288 Chet Nichols SP 60.00 30.00
289 Tommy Holmes SP 100.00 50.00
290 Joe Astroth SP 60.00 30.00
291 Gil Coan SP 60.00 30.00
292 Floyd Baker SP 60.00 30.00
293 Sibby Sisti SP 60.00 30.00
294 Walker Cooper SP 60.00 30.00
295 Phil Cavarretta SP 80.00 40.00
296 Red Rolfe MG SP 80.00 40.00
297 Andy Seminick SP 60.00 30.00
298 Bob Ross SP 60.00 30.00
299 Ray Murray SP 60.00 30.00
300 Barney McCosky SP 80.00 40.00
301 Bob Porterfield 50.00 25.00
302 Max Surkont 50.00 25.00
303 Harry Dorish 50.00 25.00
304 Sam Dente 50.00 25.00
305 Paul Richards MG 60.00 30.00
306 Lou Sleater 50.00 25.00
307 Frank Campos 50.00 25.00
307A Frank Campos
Black Star on Back
308 Luis Aloma 50.00 25.00
309 Jim Busby 60.00 30.00
310 George Metkovich 100.00 50.00
311 Mickey Mantle DP 18000.00 9000.00
312 Jackie Robinson DP 2000.00 1000.00
313 Bobby Thomson DP 350.00 180.00
314 Roy Campanella 2500.00 1250.00
315 Leo Durocher MG 600.00 300.00
316 Dave Williams RC 300.00 150.00
317 Conrado Marrero 300.00 150.00
318 Harold Gregg 300.00 150.00
319 Rube Walker 250.00 125.00
320 John Rutherford RC 300.00 150.00
321 Joe Black RC 350.00 180.00
322 Randy Jackson 300.00 150.00
323 Bubba Church 250.00 125.00
324 Warren Hacker 250.00 125.00
325 Bill Serena 300.00 150.00
326 George Shuba RC 400.00 200.00
327 Al Wilson 250.00 125.00
328 Bob Borkowski 300.00 150.00
329 Ike Delock 300.00 150.00
330 Turk Lown 300.00 150.00
331 Tom Morgan 300.00 150.00
332 Anthony Bartirome 300.00 150.00
333 Pee Wee Reese 1800.00 900.00
334 Wilmer Mizell RC 300.00 150.00
335 Ted Lepcio 250.00 125.00
336 Dave Koslo 250.00 125.00
337 Jim Hearn 250.00 125.00
338 Sal Yvars 300.00 150.00
339 Russ Meyer 300.00 150.00
340 Bob Hooper 300.00 150.00
341 Hal Jeffcoat 300.00 150.00
342 Clem Labine RC 400.00 200.00
343 Dick Gernert 250.00 125.00
344 Ewell Blackwell 300.00 150.00
345 Sammy White 250.00 125.00
346 George Spencer 250.00 125.00
347 Joe Adcock 400.00 200.00
348 Robert Kelly 250.00 125.00
349 Bob Cain 300.00 150.00
350 Cal Abrams 300.00 150.00
351 Alvin Dark 300.00 150.00
352 Karl Drews 300.00 150.00
353 Bobby Del Greco 300.00 150.00
354 Fred Hatfield 300.00 150.00
355 Bobby Morgan 300.00 150.00
356 Toby Atwell 300.00 150.00
357 Smoky Burgess 300.00 150.00
358 John Kucab 300.00 150.00
359 Dee Fondy 250.00 125.00
360 George Crowe RC 300.00 150.00
361 William Posedel CO 250.00 125.00
362 Ken Heintzelman 300.00 150.00
363 Dick Rozek 300.00 150.00
364 Clyde Sukeforth CO 300.00 150.00
365 Cookie Lavagetto CO 400.00 200.00
366 Dave Madison 250.00 125.00
367 Ben Thorpe 300.00 150.00
368 Ed Wright 300.00 150.00
369 Dick Groat RC 400.00 200.00
370 Billy Hoeft RC 300.00 150.00
371 Bobby Hofman 250.00 125.00
372 Gil McDougald RC 500.00 250.00
373 Jim Turner CO RC 400.00 200.00
374 John Benton 250.00 125.00
375 John Merson 250.00 125.00
376 Faye Throneberry 250.00 125.00
377 Chuck Dressen MG 400.00 200.00
378 Leroy Fusselman 300.00 150.00
379 Joe Rossi 250.00 125.00
380 Clem Koshorek 250.00 125.00
381 Milton Stock CO 300.00 150.00
382 Sam Jones RC 350.00 180.00
383 Del Wilber 250.00 125.00
384 Frank Crosetti CO 500.00 250.00
385 H.Franks CO RC 250.00 125.00
386 John Yuhas 300.00 150.00
387 Billy Meyer MG 250.00 125.00
388 Bob Chipman 250.00 125.00
389 Ben Wade 300.00 150.00
390 Rocky Nelson 300.00 150.00
391 B.Chapman UER CO 250.00 125.00
Photo actually
Sam Chapman
392 Hoyt Wilhelm RC 800.00 400.00
393 Ebba St.Claire 300.00 150.00
394 Billy Herman CO 600.00 300.00
395 Jake Pitler CO 250.00 125.00
396 Dick Williams RC 400.00 200.00
397 Forrest Main 250.00 125.00
398 Hal Rice 250.00 125.00
399 Jim Fridley 250.00 125.00
400 Bill Dickey CO 1000.00 500.00
401 Bob Schultz 300.00 150.00
402 Earl Harrist 300.00 150.00
403 Bill Miller 300.00 150.00
404 Dick Brodowski 300.00 150.00
405 Eddie Pellagrini 300.00 150.00
406 Joe Nuxhall RC 400.00 200.00
407 Eddie Mathews RC 12000.00 2500.00

1953 Topps

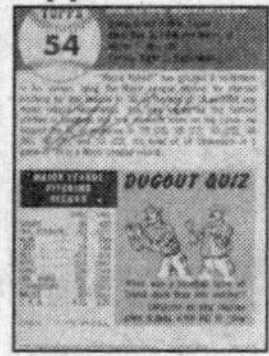

The cards in this 274-card set measure 2 5/8" by 3 3/4". Card number 69, Dick Brodowksi, features the first known drawing of a player during a night game. Although the last card is numbered 280, there are only 274 cards in the set since numbers 253, 261, 267, 268, 271, and 275 were never issued. The 1953 Topps series contains line drawings of players in full color. The name and team panel at the card base is easily damaged, making it very difficult to complete a mint set. The high number series, 221 to 280, was produced in shorter supply late in the year and hence is more difficult to complete than the lower numbers. The key cards in the set are Mickey Mantle (82) and Willie Mays (244). The key Rookie Cards in this set are Roy Face, Jim Gilliam, and Johnny Podres, all from the last series. There are a number of double-printed cards (actually not double but 50 percent more of each of these numbers were printed compared to the other cards in the series) indicated by DP in the checklist below. There were five players (10 Smoky Burgess, 44 Ellis Kinder, 61 Early Wynn, 72 Fred Hutchinson, and 81 Joe Black) that were held out of the first run of 1-85 (but printed in with numbers 86-165), who are each marked by SP in the checklist below. In addition, there are five numbers which were printed with the more plentiful series 166-220; these cards (94, 107, 131, 145, and 156) are also indicated by DP in the checklist below. All these aforementioned cards from 86 through 165 and the five short prints come with the biographical information on the back in either white or black lettering. These seem to be printed in equal quantities and no price differential is given for either variety. The cards were issued in one-card penny packs or six-card nickel packs. The nickel packs were issued 24 to a box. There were some three-card advertising panels produced by Topps; the players include Johnny Mize/Clem Koshorek/Toby Atwell; Jim Hearn/Johnny Groth/Sherman Lollar and Mickey Mantle/Johnny Wyrostek/Sal Yvars. When cut apart, these advertising cards are distinguished by the non-standard card back, i.e., part of an advertisement for the 1953 Topps set instead of the typical statistics and biographical information about the player pictured.

NM Ex
COMPLETE SET (274) 15000.00 7500.00
COMMON CARD (1-165) 30.00 15.00
COMMON (166-220) 25.00 12.50
COMMON DP (1-220) 15.00 7.50
COMMON (221-280) 100.00 50.00
NOT ISSUED (253/261/267)
NOT ISSUED (268/271/275)
WRAP.(1-CENT, DATED) 200.00 100.00
WRAP.(1-CENT, UNDATED) 300.00 150.00
WRAP.(5-CENT, DATED) 400.00 200.00
WRAP.(5-CENT, UNDATED) 350.00 180.00
1 Jackie Robinson DP 800.00 220.00
2 Luke Easter DP 20.00 10.00
3 George Crowe 40.00 20.00
4 Ben Wade 30.00 15.00
5 Joe Dobson 30.00 15.00
6 Sam Jones 40.00 20.00
7 Bob Borkowski DP 15.00 7.50
8 Clem Koshorek DP 15.00 7.50
9 Joe Collins 60.00 30.00
10 Smoky Burgess SP 80.00 40.00
11 Sal Yvars 30.00 15.00
12 Howie Judson DP 15.00 7.50
13 Conrado Marrero DP 15.00 7.50
14 Clem Labine DP 20.00 10.00
15 Bobo Newsom DP 20.00 10.00
16 Peanuts Lowrey DP 15.00 7.50
17 Billy Hitchcock 30.00 15.00
18 Ted Lepcio DP 15.00 7.50
19 Mel Parnell DP 20.00 10.00
20 Hank Thompson 40.00 20.00
21 Billy Johnson 30.00 15.00
22 Howie Fox 30.00 15.00
23 Toby Atwell DP 15.00 7.50
24 Ferris Fain 40.00 20.00
25 Ray Boone 40.00 20.00
26 Dale Mitchell DP 20.00 10.00
27 Roy Campanella DP 300.00 150.00
28 Eddie Pellagrini 30.00 15.00
29 Hal Jeffcoat 30.00 15.00
30 Willard Nixon 30.00 15.00
31 Ewell Blackwell 60.00 30.00
32 Clyde Vollmer 30.00 15.00
33 Bob Kennedy DP 15.00 7.50
34 George Shuba 40.00 20.00
35 Irv Noren DP 15.00 7.50
36 Johnny Groth DP 15.00 7.50
37 Eddie Mathews DP 250.00 125.00
38 Jim Hearn DP 15.00 7.50
39 Eddie Miksis 30.00 15.00
40 John Lipon 30.00 15.00
41 Enos Slaughter 80.00 40.00
42 Gus Zernial DP 20.00 10.00
43 Gil McDougald 60.00 30.00
44 Ellis Kinder SP 50.00 25.00
45 Grady Hatton DP 15.00 7.50
46 Johnny Klippstein DP 15.00 7.50
47 Bubba Church DP 15.00 7.50
48 Bob Del Greco DP 15.00 7.50
49 Faye Throneberry DP 15.00 7.50
50 Chuck Dressen MG DP 20.00 10.00
51 Frank Campos DP 15.00 7.50
52 Ted Gray DP 15.00 7.50
53 Sherm Lollar DP 20.00 10.00
54 Bob Feller DP 150.00 75.00
55 Maurice McDermott DP 15.00 7.50
56 Gerry Staley DP 15.00 7.50
57 Carl Scheib 30.00 15.00
58 George Metkovich 30.00 15.00
59 Karl Drews DP 15.00 7.50
60 Cloyd Boyer DP 15.00 7.50
61 Early Wynn SP 125.00 60.00
62 Monte Irvin DP 50.00 25.00
63 Gus Niarhos DP 15.00 7.50
64 Dave Philley 30.00 15.00
65 Earl Harrist 30.00 15.00
66 Minnie Minoso 60.00 30.00
67 Roy Sievers DP 20.00 10.00
68 Del Rice 30.00 15.00
69 Dick Brodowski 30.00 15.00
70 Ed Yuhas 30.00 15.00
71 Tony Bartirome 30.00 15.00
72 F.Hutchinson MG SP 50.00 25.00
73 Eddie Robinson 30.00 15.00
74 Joe Rossi 30.00 15.00
75 Mike Garcia 40.00 20.00
76 Pee Wee Reese 175.00 90.00
77 Johnny Mize DP 80.00 40.00
78 Red Schoendienst 80.00 40.00
79 Johnny Wyrostek 30.00 15.00
80 Jim Hegan 40.00 20.00
81 Joe Black SP 80.00 40.00
82 Mickey Mantle 3000.00 1800.00

83 Howie Pollet 30.00 15.00
84 Bob Hooper DP 15.00 7.50
85 Bobby Morgan DP 15.00 7.50
86 Billy Martin 125.00 60.00
87 Ed Lopat 60.00 30.00
88 Willie Jones DP 15.00 7.50
89 Chuck Stobbs DP 15.00 7.50
90 Hank Edwards DP 15.00 7.50
91 Ebba St.Claire DP 15.00 7.50
92 Paul Minner DP 15.00 7.50
93 Hal Rice DP 15.00 7.50
94 Bill Kennedy DP 15.00 7.50
95 Willard Marshall DP 15.00 7.50
96 Virgil Trucks 40.00 20.00
97 Don Kolloway DP 15.00 7.50
98 Cal Abrams DP 15.00 7.50
99 Dave Madison 30.00 15.00
100 Bill Miller 30.00 15.00
101 Ted Wilks 30.00 15.00
102 Connie Ryan DP 15.00 7.50
103 Joe Astroth DP 15.00 7.50
104 Yogi Berra 300.00 150.00
105 Joe Nuxhall DP 20.00 10.00
106 Johnny Antonelli 40.00 20.00
107 Danny O'Connell DP 15.00 7.50
108 Bob Porterfield DP 15.00 7.50
109 Alvin Dark 60.00 30.00
110 Herman Wehmeier DP 15.00 7.50
111 Hank Sauer DP 15.00 7.50
112 Ned Garver DP 15.00 7.50
113 Jerry Priddy 30.00 15.00
114 Phil Rizzuto 250.00 125.00
115 George Spencer 30.00 15.00
116 Frank Smith DP 15.00 7.50
117 Sid Gordon DP 15.00 7.50
118 Gus Bell DP 20.00 10.00
119 Johnny Sain SP 60.00 30.00
120 Davey Williams 40.00 20.00
121 Walt Dropo 40.00 20.00
122 Elmer Valo 30.00 15.00
123 Tommy Byrne DP 15.00 7.50
124 Sibby Sisti DP 15.00 7.50
125 Dick Williams DP 20.00 10.00
126 Bill Connelly DP 15.00 7.50
127 Clint Courtney DP 15.00 7.50
128 Wilmer Mizell DP 20.00 10.00
(Inconsistent design, logo on front with black birds)
129 Keith Thomas 30.00 15.00
130 Turk Lown DP 15.00 7.50
131 Harry Byrd DP 15.00 7.50
132 Tom Morgan 30.00 15.00
133 Gil Coan 30.00 15.00
134 Rube Walker 40.00 20.00
135 Al Rosen DP 20.00 10.00
136 Ken Heintzelman DP 15.00 7.50
137 John Rutherford DP 15.00 7.50
138 George Kell 80.00 40.00
139 Sammy White 30.00 15.00
140 Tommy Glaviano 30.00 15.00
141 Allie Reynolds DP 50.00 25.00
142 Vic Wertz 40.00 20.00
143 Billy Pierce 60.00 30.00
144 Bob Schultz DP 15.00 7.50
145 Harry Dorish DP 15.00 7.50
146 Granny Hamner 30.00 15.00
147 Warren Spahn 175.00 90.00
148 Mickey Grasso 30.00 15.00
149 Dom DiMaggio DP 50.00 25.00
150 Harry Simpson DP 15.00 7.50
151 Hoyt Wilhelm 100.00 50.00
152 Bob Adams DP 15.00 7.50
153 Andy Seminick DP 15.00 7.50
154 Dick Groat 40.00 20.00
155 Dutch Leonard 30.00 15.00
156 Jim Rivera DP 20.00 10.00
157 Bob Addis DP 15.00 7.50
158 Johnny Logan RC 40.00 20.00
159 Wayne Terwilliger DP 15.00 7.50
160 Bob Young 30.00 15.00
161 Vern Bickford DP 15.00 7.50
162 Ted Kluszewski 60.00 30.00
163 Fred Hatfield DP 15.00 7.50
164 Frank Shea DP 15.00 7.50
165 Billy Hoeft 30.00 15.00
166 Billy Hunter 25.00 12.50
167 Art Schult 25.00 12.50
168 Willard Schmidt 25.00 12.50
169 Dizzy Trout 30.00 15.00
170 Bill Werle 25.00 12.50
171 Bill Glynn 25.00 12.50
172 Rip Repulski 25.00 12.50
173 Preston Ward 25.00 12.50
174 Billy Loes 30.00 15.00
175 Ron Kline 25.00 12.50
176 Don Hoak RC 40.00 20.00
177 Jim Dyck 25.00 12.50
178 Jim Waugh 25.00 12.50
179 Gene Hermanski 25.00 12.50
180 Virgil Stallcup 25.00 12.50
181 Al Zarilla 25.00 12.50
182 Bobby Hofman 25.00 12.50
183 Stu Miller RC 40.00 20.00
184 Hal Brown 25.00 12.50
185 Jim Pendleton 25.00 12.50
186 Charlie Bishop 25.00 12.50
187 Jim Fridley 25.00 12.50
188 Andy Carey RC 40.00 20.00
189 Ray Jablonski 25.00 12.50
190 Dixie Walker CO 30.00 15.00
191 Ralph Kiner 80.00 40.00
192 Wally Westlake 25.00 12.50
193 Mike Clark 25.00 12.50
194 Eddie Kazak 25.00 12.50
195 Ed McGhee 25.00 12.50
196 Bob Keegan 25.00 12.50
197 Del Crandall 40.00 20.00
198 Forrest Main 25.00 12.50
199 Marion Fricano 25.00 12.50
200 Gordon Goldsberry 25.00 12.50
201 Paul LaPalme 25.00 12.50
202 Carl Sawatski 25.00 12.50
203 Cliff Fannin 25.00 12.50
204 Dick Bokelman 25.00 12.50
205 Vern Benson 25.00 12.50
206 Ed Bailey RC 30.00 15.00
207 Whitey Ford 200.00 100.00
208 Jim Wilson 25.00 12.50
209 Jim Greengrass 25.00 12.50
210 Bob Cerv RC 40.00 20.00
211 J.W. Porter 25.00 12.50
212 Jack Dittmer 25.00 12.50
213 Ray Scarborough 25.00 12.50
214 Bill Bruton RC 40.00 20.00
215 Gene Conley RC 30.00 15.00
216 Jim Hughes 25.00 12.50
217 Murray Wall 25.00 12.50
218 Les Fusselman 25.00 12.50
219 Pete Runnels UER 30.00 15.00
(Photo actually Don Johnson)
220 Satchel Paige UER 600.00 300.00
(Misspelled Satchell on card front)
221 Bob Milliken 100.00 50.00
222 Vic Janowicz DP RC 60.00 30.00
223 Johnny O'Brien DP 50.00 25.00
224 Lou Sleater DP 50.00 25.00
225 Bobby Shantz 125.00 60.00
226 Ed Erautt 100.00 50.00
227 Morrie Martin 100.00 50.00
228 Hal Newhouser 150.00 75.00
229 Rocky Krsnich 100.00 50.00
230 Johnny Lindell DP 50.00 25.00
231 Solly Hemus DP 50.00 25.00
232 Dick Kokos 100.00 50.00
233 Al Aber 100.00 50.00
234 Ray Murray DP 50.00 25.00
235 John Hetki DP 50.00 25.00
236 Harry Perkowski DP 50.00 25.00
237 Bud Podbielan DP 50.00 25.00
238 Cal Hogue DP 50.00 25.00
239 Jim Delsing 100.00 50.00
240 Fred Marsh 100.00 50.00
241 Al Sima DP 50.00 25.00
242 Charlie Silvera 125.00 60.00
243 Carlos Bernier DP 50.00 25.00
244 Willie Mays 2500.00 1250.00
245 Bill Norman CO 100.00 50.00
246 Roy Face DP RC 80.00 40.00
247 Mike Sandlock DP 50.00 25.00
248 Gene Stephens DP 50.00 25.00
249 Eddie O'Brien 100.00 50.00
250 Bob Wilson 100.00 50.00
251 Sid Hudson 100.00 50.00
252 Hank Foiles 100.00 50.00
253 Does not exist
254 Preacher Roe DP 80.00 40.00
255 Dixie Howell 100.00 50.00
256 Les Peden 100.00 50.00
257 Bob Boyd 100.00 50.00
258 Jim Gilliam RC 400.00 200.00
259 Roy McMillan DP 50.00 25.00
260 Sam Calderone 100.00 50.00
261 Does not exist
262 Bob Oldis 100.00 50.00
263 Johnny Podres RC 300.00 150.00
264 Gene Woodling DP 60.00 30.00
265 Jackie Jensen 125.00 60.00
266 Bob Cain 100.00 50.00
267 Does not exist
268 Does not exist
269 Duane Pillette 100.00 50.00
270 Vern Stephens 125.00 60.00
271 Does not exist
272 Bill Antonello 100.00 50.00
273 Harvey Haddix RC 150.00 75.00
274 John Riddle CO 100.00 50.00
275 Does not exist
276 Ken Raffensberger 100.00 50.00
277 Don Lund 100.00 50.00
278 Willie Miranda 100.00 50.00
279 Joe Coleman DP 50.00 25.00
280 Milt Bolling RC 350.00 57.50

1954 Topps

The cards in this 250-card set measure approximately 2 5/8" by 3 3/4". Each of the cards in the 1954 Topps set contains a large "head" shot of the player in color plus a smaller full-length photo in black and white set against a color background. The cards were issued in one-card penny packs or five-card nickel packs. Fifteen-card cello packs have also been seen. The penny packs came 120 to a box while the nickel packs came 24 to a box. This set contains the Rookie Cards of Hank Aaron, Ernie Banks, and Al Kaline and two separate cards of Ted Williams (number 1 and number 250). Conspicuous by his absence is Mickey Mantle who apparently was the exclusive property of Bowman during 1954 (and 1955). The first two issues of Sports Illustrated magazine contained "card" inserts on regular paper stock. The first issue showed actual cards in the set in color, while the second issue showed some created cards of New York Yankees players in black and white, including Mickey Mantle. There was also a Canadian printing of the first 50 cards. These cards can be easily discerned as they have "grey" backs rather than the white backs of the American printed cards. To celebrate this set as the first Topps set to feature Ted Williams, his visage is also featured on the five cent box.

	NM	Ex
COMPLETE SET (250)	8000.00	4000.00
COMMON (1-50/76-250)	15.00	7.50
COMMON CARD (51-75)	25.00	12.50
WRAP.(1-CENT, DATED)	200.00	100.00
WRAP.(1-CENT, UNDATED)	150.00	75.00
WRAP.(5-CENT, DATED)	300.00	150.00
WRAP.(5-CENT, UNDATED)	250.00	125.00

1 Ted Williams 800.00 275.00
2 Gus Zernial 25.00 12.50
3 Monte Irvin 50.00 25.00
4 Hank Sauer 25.00 12.50
5 Ed Lopat 25.00 12.50
6 Pete Runnels 25.00 12.50
7 Ted Kluszewski 50.00 25.00
8 Bob Young 15.00 7.50
9 Harvey Haddix 25.00 12.50
10 Jackie Robinson 400.00 200.00
11 Paul Leslie Smith 15.00 7.50
12 Del Crandall 25.00 12.50
13 Billy Martin 100.00 50.00
14 Preacher Roe UER 25.00 12.50
February is misspelled
15 Al Rosen 25.00 12.50
16 Vic Janowicz 25.00 12.50
17 Phil Rizzuto 125.00 60.00
18 Walt Dropo 25.00 12.50
19 Johnny Lipon 15.00 7.50
Orioles Team Name on Front
White Sox team on Back
Wearing a Red Sox cap
20 Warren Spahn 125.00 60.00
21 Bobby Shantz 25.00 12.50
22 Jim Greengrass 15.00 7.50
23 Luke Easter 25.00 12.50
24 Granny Hamner 15.00 7.50
25 Harvey Kuenn RC 40.00 20.00
26 Ray Jablonski 15.00 7.50
27 Ferris Fain 25.00 12.50
28 Paul Minner 15.00 7.50
29 Jim Hegan 25.00 12.50
30 Eddie Mathews 100.00 50.00
31 Johnny Klippstein 15.00 7.50
32 Duke Snider 200.00 100.00
33 Johnny Schmitz 15.00 7.50
34 Jim Rivera 15.00 7.50
35 Jim Gilliam 50.00 25.00
36 Hoyt Wilhelm 50.00 25.00
37 Whitey Ford 200.00 100.00
38 Eddie Stanky MG 25.00 12.50
39 Sherm Lollar 25.00 12.50
40 Mel Parnell 25.00 12.50
41 Willie Jones 15.00 7.50
42 Don Mueller 25.00 12.50
43 Dick Groat 25.00 12.50
44 Ned Garver 15.00 7.50
45 Richie Ashburn 80.00 40.00
46 Ken Raffensberger 15.00 7.50
47 Ellis Kinder 25.00 12.50
48 Billy Hunter 25.00 12.50
49 Ray Murray 15.00 7.50
50 Yogi Berra 250.00 125.00
51 Johnny Lindell 25.00 12.50
52 Vic Power RC 30.00 15.00
53 Jack Dittmer 25.00 12.50
54 Vern Stephens 30.00 15.00
55 Phil Cavarretta MG 30.00 15.00
56 Willie Miranda 25.00 12.50
57 Luis Aloma 25.00 12.50
58 Bob Wilson 25.00 12.50
59 Gene Conley 30.00 15.00
60 Frank Baumholtz 25.00 12.50
61 Bob Cain 25.00 12.50
62 Eddie Robinson 25.00 12.50
63 Johnny Pesky 30.00 15.00
64 Hank Thompson 25.00 12.50
65 Bob Swift CO 25.00 12.50
66 Ted Lepcio 25.00 12.50
67 Jim Willis 25.00 12.50
68 Sam Calderone 25.00 12.50
69 Bud Podbielan 25.00 12.50
70 Larry Doby 60.00 30.00
71 Frank Smith 25.00 12.50
72 Preston Ward 25.00 12.50
73 Wayne Terwilliger 25.00 12.50
74 Bill Taylor 25.00 12.50
75 Fred Haney MG 25.00 12.50
76 Bob Scheffing CO 15.00 7.50
77 Ray Boone 25.00 12.50
78 Ted Kazanski 15.00 7.50
79 Andy Pafko 25.00 12.50
80 Jackie Jensen 25.00 12.50
81 Dave Hoskins 15.00 7.50
82 Milt Bolling 15.00 7.50
83 Joe Collins 25.00 12.50
84 Dick Cole 15.00 7.50
85 Bob Turley RC 40.00 20.00
86 Billy Herman CO 25.00 12.50
87 Roy Face 25.00 12.50
88 Matt Batts 15.00 7.50
89 Howie Pollet 15.00 7.50
90 Willie Mays 800.00 400.00
91 Bob Oldis 15.00 7.50
92 Wally Westlake 15.00 7.50
93 Sid Hudson 15.00 7.50
94 Ernie Banks RC 1200.00 500.00
95 Hal Rice 15.00 7.50
96 Charlie Silvera 25.00 12.50
97 Jerald Hal Lane 15.00 7.50
98 Joe Black 40.00 20.00
99 Bobby Hofman 15.00 7.50
100 Bob Keegan 15.00 7.50
101 Gene Woodling 25.00 12.50
102 Gil Hodges 80.00 40.00
103 Jim Lemon RC 15.00 7.50
104 Mike Sandlock 15.00 7.50
105 Andy Carey 25.00 12.50
106 Dick Kokos 15.00 7.50
107 Duane Pillette 15.00 7.50
108 Thornton Kipper 15.00 7.50
109 Bill Bruton 25.00 12.50
110 Harry Dorish 15.00 7.50
111 Jim Delsing 15.00 7.50
112 Bill Renna 15.00 7.50
113 Bob Boyd 15.00 7.50
114 Dean Stone 15.00 7.50
115 Rip Repulski 15.00 7.50
116 Steve Bilko 15.00 7.50
117 Solly Hemus 15.00 7.50
118 Carl Scheib 15.00 7.50
119 Johnny Antonelli 25.00 12.50
120 Roy McMillan 25.00 12.50
121 Clem Labine 25.00 12.50
122 Johnny Logan 25.00 12.50
123 Bobby Adams 15.00 7.50
124 Marion Fricano 15.00 7.50
125 Harry Perkowski 15.00 7.50
126 Ben Wade 15.00 7.50
127 Steve O'Neill MG 15.00 7.50
128 Hank Aaron RC 1800.00 750.00
129 Forrest Jacobs 15.00 7.50
130 Hank Bauer 25.00 12.50
131 Reno Bertoia 25.00 12.50
132 Tommy Lasorda RC 250.00 125.00
133 Del Baker CO 15.00 7.50
134 Cal Hogue 15.00 7.50
135 Joe Presko 15.00 7.50
136 Connie Ryan 15.00 7.50
137 Wally Moon RC 40.00 20.00
138 Bob Borkowski 15.00 7.50
139 The O'Briens 50.00 25.00
Johnny O'Brien
Eddie O'Brien
140 Tom Wright 15.00 7.50
141 Joey Jay RC 25.00 12.50
142 Tom Poholsky 15.00 7.50
143 Rollie Hemsley CO 15.00 7.50
144 Bill Werle 15.00 7.50
145 Elmer Valo 15.00 7.50
146 Don Johnson 15.00 7.50
147 Johnny Riddle CO 15.00 7.50
148 Bob Trice 15.00 7.50
149 Al Robertson 15.00 7.50
150 Dick Kryhoski 15.00 7.50
151 Alex Grammas 15.00 7.50
152 Michael Blyzka 15.00 7.50
153 Al Walker 25.00 12.50
154 Mike Fornieles 15.00 7.50
155 Bob Kennedy 25.00 12.50
156 Joe Coleman 25.00 12.50
157 Don Lenhardt 25.00 12.50
158 Peanuts Lowrey 15.00 7.50
159 Dave Philley 15.00 7.50
160 Ralph Kress CO 15.00 7.50
161 John Hetki 15.00 7.50
162 Herman Wehmeier 15.00 7.50
163 Frank House 15.00 7.50
164 Stu Miller 25.00 12.50
165 Jim Pendleton 15.00 7.50
166 Johnny Podres 40.00 20.00
167 Don Lund 15.00 7.50
168 Morrie Martin 25.00 12.50
169 Jim Hughes 40.00 20.00
170 Dusty Rhodes RC 25.00 12.50
171 Leo Kiely 15.00 7.50
172 Harold Brown 15.00 7.50
173 Jack Harshman 15.00 7.50
174 Tom Qualters 15.00 7.50
175 Frank Leja RC 25.00 12.50
176 Robert Keely CO 15.00 7.50
177 Bob Milliken 15.00 7.50
178 Bill Glynn UER 15.00 7.50
Spelled Gylnn on the front
179 Gair Allie 15.00 7.50
180 Wes Westrum 25.00 12.50
181 Mel Roach 15.00 7.50
182 Chuck Harmon 15.00 7.50
183 Earle Combs CO 25.00 12.50
184 Ed Bailey 15.00 7.50
185 Chuck Stobbs 15.00 7.50
186 Karl Olson 15.00 7.50
187 Heinie Manush CO 25.00 12.50
188 Dave Jolly 15.00 7.50
189 Bob Ross 15.00 7.50
190 Ray Herbert 15.00 7.50
191 John(Dick) Schofield RC 25.00 12.50
192 Ellis Deal CO 15.00 7.50
193 Johnny Hopp CO 25.00 12.50
194 Bill Sarni 15.00 7.50
195 Billy Consolo RC 15.00 7.50
196 Stan Jok 15.00 7.50
197 Lynwood Rowe CO 25.00 12.50
("Schoolboy")
198 Carl Sawatski 15.00 7.50
199 Glenn(Rocky) Nelson 15.00 7.50
200 Larry Jansen 25.00 12.50
201 Al Kaline RC 700.00 350.00
202 Bob Purkey RC 25.00 12.50
203 Harry Brecheen CO 25.00 12.50
204 Angel Scull 15.00 7.50
205 Johnny Sain 40.00 20.00
206 Ray Crone 15.00 7.50
207 Tom Oliver CO 15.00 7.50
208 Grady Hatton 15.00 7.50
209 Chuck Thompson 15.00 7.50
210 Bob Buhl RC 25.00 12.50
211 Don Hoak 25.00 12.50
212 Bob Micelotta 15.00 7.50
213 Johnny Fitzpatrick CO 15.00 7.50
214 Arnie Portocarrero 15.00 7.50
215 Ed McGhee 25.00 12.50
216 Al Sima 15.00 7.50
217 Paul Schreiber CO 15.00 7.50
218 Fred Marsh 15.00 7.50
219 Chuck Kress 15.00 7.50
220 Ruben Gomez 25.00 12.50
221 Dick Brodowski 15.00 7.50
222 Bill Wilson 15.00 7.50
223 Joe Haynes CO 15.00 7.50
224 Dick Weik 15.00 7.50
225 Don Liddle 15.00 7.50
226 Jehosie Heard 25.00 12.50
227 Buster Mills CO 15.00 7.50
228 Gene Hermanski 15.00 7.50
229 Bob Talbot 15.00 7.50
230 Bob Kuzava 25.00 12.50
231 Roy Smalley 15.00 7.50
232 Lou Limmer 15.00 7.50
233 Augie Galan CO 15.00 7.50
234 Jerry Lynch RC 15.00 7.50
235 Vern Law 25.00 12.50
236 Paul Penson 15.00 7.50
237 Mike Ryba CO 15.00 7.50
238 Al Aber 15.00 7.50
239 Bill Skowron RC 100.00 50.00
240 Sam Mele 25.00 12.50
241 Robert Miller 15.00 7.50
242 Curt Roberts 15.00 7.50
243 Ray Blades CO 15.00 7.50
244 Leroy Wheat 15.00 7.50
245 Roy Sievers 25.00 12.50
246 Howie Fox 15.00 7.50
247 Ed Mayo CO 15.00 7.50
248 Al Smith RC 25.00 12.50
249 Wilmer Mizell 25.00 12.50
250 Ted Williams 800.00 325.00

1955 Topps

The cards in this 206-card set measure approximately 2 5/8" by 3 3/4". Both the large "head" shot and the smaller full-length photos used on each card of the 1955 Topps set are in color. The card fronts were designed horizontally for the first time in Topps' history. The first card features Dusty Rhodes, hitting star and MVP in the New York Giants' 1954 World Series sweep over the Cleveland Indians. A "high" series, 161 to 210, is more difficult to find than cards 1 to 160. Numbers 175, 186, 203, and 209 were never issued. To fill in for the four cards not issued in the high number series, Topps double printed four players, those appearing on cards 170, 172, 184, and 188. Cards were issued in one-card penny packs or six-card nickel packs (which came 36 packs to a box) and 15-card cello packs (rarely seen). Although rarely seen, there exist salesman sample panels of three cards containing the fronts of regular cards with ad information for the 1955 Topps regular and the 1955 Topps Doubleheaders on the back. One panel depicts (from top to bottom) Danny Schell, Jake Thies, and Howie Pollet. Another Panel consists of Jackie Robinson, Bill Taylor and Curt Roberts. The key Rookie Cards in this set are Ken Boyer, Roberto Clemente, Harmon Killebrew, and Sandy Koufax. The Frank Sullivan card has a very noticable print dot which appears on some of the cards but not all of the cards. We are not listing that card as a variation at this point, but we will continue to monitor information about that card.

	NM	Ex
COMPLETE SET (206)	8000.00	4000.00
COMMON CARD (1-150)	12.00	6.00
COMMON (151-160)	20.00	10.00
COMMON (161-210)	30.00	15.00
NOT ISSUED (175/186/203/209)		
WRAP.(1-CENT, DATED)	150.00	75.00
WRAP.(1-CENT, UNDATED)	50.00	25.00
WRAP.(5-CENT, DATED)	150.00	75.00
WRAP.(5-CENT, UNDATED)	100.00	50.00

1 Dusty Rhodes 125.00 25.00
2 Ted Williams 600.00 300.00
3 Art Fowler 15.00 7.50
4 Al Kaline 150.00 75.00
5 Jim Gilliam 40.00 20.00
6 Stan Hack MG 25.00 12.50
7 Jim Hegan 15.00 7.50
8 Harold Smith 12.00 6.00
9 Robert Miller 12.00 6.00
10 Bob Keegan 12.00 6.00
11 Ferris Fain 15.00 7.50
12 Vernon(Jake) Thies 12.00 6.00
13 Fred Marsh 12.00 6.00
14 Jim Finigan 12.00 6.00
15 Jim Pendleton 12.00 6.00
16 Roy Sievers 15.00 7.50
17 Bobby Hofman 12.00 6.00
18 Russ Kemmerer 12.00 6.00
19 Billy Herman CO 15.00 7.50
20 Andy Carey 15.00 7.50
21 Alex Grammas 12.00 6.00
22 Bill Skowron 40.00 20.00
23 Jack Parks 12.00 6.00
24 Hal Newhouser 40.00 20.00
25 Johnny Podres 25.00 12.50
26 Dick Groat 15.00 7.50
27 Billy Gardner RC 15.00 7.50
28 Ernie Banks 200.00 100.00
29 Herman Wehmeier 12.00 6.00
30 Vic Power 15.00 7.50
31 Warren Spahn 100.00 50.00
32 Warren McGhee 12.00 6.00
33 Tom Qualters 12.00 6.00
34 Wayne Terwilliger 12.00 6.00
35 Dave Jolly 12.00 6.00
36 Leo Kiely 12.00 6.00
37 Joe Cunningham RC 15.00 7.50
38 Bob Turley 15.00 7.50
39 Bill Glynn 12.00 6.00
40 Don Hoak 15.00 7.50
41 Chuck Stobbs 12.00 6.00
42 John(Windy) McCall 12.00 6.00
43 Harvey Haddix 15.00 7.50
44 Harold Valentine 12.00 6.00
45 Hank Sauer 15.00 7.50
46 Ted Kazanski 12.00 6.00
47 Hank Aaron UER 400.00 200.00
(Birth incorrectly listed as 2/10)
48 Bob Kennedy 15.00 7.50
49 J.W. Porter 12.00 6.00
50 Jackie Robinson 500.00 250.00
51 Jim Hughes 15.00 7.50
52 Bill Tremel 12.00 6.00
53 Bill Taylor 12.00 6.00
54 Lou Limmer 12.00 6.00
55 Rip Repulski 12.00 6.00
56 Ray Jablonski 12.00 6.00
57 Billy O'Dell 12.00 6.00
58 Jim Rivera 12.00 6.00
59 Gair Allie 12.00 6.00
60 Dean Stone 12.00 6.00
61 Forrest Jacobs 12.00 6.00
62 Thornton Kipper 12.00 6.00
63 Joe Collins 15.00 7.50
64 Gus Triandos RC 15.00 7.50
65 Ray Boone 15.00 7.50
66 Ron Jackson RC 15.00 7.50
67 Wally Moon 15.00 7.50
68 Jim Davis 12.00 6.00
69 Ed Bailey 15.00 7.50
70 Al Rosen 15.00 7.50
71 Ruben Gomez 12.00 6.00
72 Karl Olson 12.00 6.00
73 Jack Shepard 12.00 6.00
74 Bob Borkowski 12.00 6.00
75 Sandy Amoros RC 40.00 20.00

76 Howie Pollet	12.00	6.00
77 Arnie Portocarrero	12.00	6.00
78 Gordon Jones	12.00	6.00
79 Clyde(Danny) Schell	12.00	6.00
80 Bob Grim RC	15.00	7.50
81 Gene Conley	15.00	7.50
82 Chuck Harmon	12.00	6.00
83 Tom Brewer	12.00	6.00
84 Camilo Pascual RC	15.00	7.50
85 Don Mossi RC	25.00	12.50
86 Bill Wilson	12.00	6.00
87 Frank House	12.00	6.00
88 Bob Skinner RC	15.00	7.50
89 Joe Frazier	15.00	7.50
90 Karl Spooner RC	15.00	7.50
91 Milt Bolling	12.00	6.00
92 Don Zimmer RC	25.00	12.50
93 Steve Bilko	12.00	6.00
94 Reno Bertoia	12.00	6.00
95 Preston Ward	12.00	6.00
96 Chuck Bishop	12.00	6.00
97 Carlos Paula	12.00	6.00
98 John Riddle CO	12.00	6.00
99 Frank Leja	12.00	6.00
100 Monte Irvin	40.00	20.00
101 Johnny Gray	12.00	6.00
102 Wally Westlake	12.00	6.00
103 Chuck White	12.00	6.00
104 Jack Harshman	12.00	6.00
105 Chuck Diering	12.00	6.00
106 Frank Sullivan	12.00	6.00
107 Curt Roberts	12.00	6.00
108 Rube Walker	15.00	7.50
109 Ed Lopat	15.00	7.50
110 Gus Zernial	15.00	7.50
111 Bob Milliken	15.00	7.50
112 Nelson King	12.00	6.00
113 Harry Brecheen CO	15.00	7.50
114 Louis Ortiz	12.00	6.00
115 Ellis Kinder	12.00	6.00
116 Tom Hurd	12.00	6.00
117 Mel Roach	12.00	6.00
118 Bob Purkey	12.00	6.00
119 Bob Lennon	12.00	6.00
120 Ted Kluszewski	80.00	40.00
121 Bill Renna	12.00	6.00
122 Carl Sawatski	12.00	6.00
123 Sandy Koufax RC	800.00	400.00
124 Harmon Killebrew RC	250.00	125.00
125 Ken Boyer RC	80.00	40.00
126 Dick Hall	12.00	6.00
127 Dale Long RC	15.00	7.50
128 Ted Lepcio	12.00	6.00
129 Elvin Tappe	15.00	7.50
130 Mayo Smith MG	12.00	6.00
131 Grady Hatton	12.00	6.00
132 Bob Trice	12.00	6.00
133 Dave Hoskins	12.00	6.00
134 Joey Jay	15.00	7.50
135 Johnny O'Brien	15.00	7.50
136 Veston(Bunky)Stewart	12.00	6.00
137 Harry Elliott	12.00	6.00
138 Ray Herbert	12.00	6.00
139 Steve Kraly	12.00	6.00
140 Mel Parnell	15.00	7.50
141 Tom Wright	12.00	6.00
142 Jerry Lynch	15.00	7.50
143 John(Dick) Schofield	15.00	7.50
144 John(Joe) Amalfitano RC	12.00	6.00
145 Elmer Valo	12.00	6.00
146 Dick Donovan RC	12.00	6.00
147 Hugh Pepper	12.00	6.00
148 Hector Brown	12.00	6.00
149 Ray Crone	12.00	6.00
150 Mike Higgins MG	12.00	6.00
151 Ralph Kress CO	20.00	10.00
152 Harry Agganis RC	100.00	50.00
153 Bud Podbielan	25.00	12.50
154 Willie Miranda	20.00	10.00
155 Eddie Mathews	200.00	60.00
156 Joe Black	50.00	25.00
157 Robert Miller	20.00	10.00
158 Tommy Carroll	25.00	12.50
159 Johnny Schmitz	20.00	10.00
160 Ray Narleski RC	20.00	10.00
161 Chuck Tanner RC	40.00	20.00
162 Joe Coleman	30.00	15.00
163 Faye Throneberry	30.00	15.00
164 Roberto Clemente RC	2000.00	1000.00
165 Don Johnson	30.00	15.00
166 Hank Bauer	80.00	40.00
167 Tom Casagrande	30.00	15.00
168 Duane Pillette	30.00	15.00
169 Bob Oldis	40.00	20.00
170 Jim Pearce DP	15.00	7.50
171 Dick Brodowski	30.00	15.00
172 Frank Baumholtz DP	15.00	7.50
173 Bob Kline	30.00	15.00
174 Rudy Minarcin	30.00	15.00
175 Does not exist		
176 Norm Zauchin	30.00	15.00
177 Al Robertson	30.00	15.00
178 Bobby Adams	30.00	15.00
179 Jim Bolger	30.00	15.00
180 Clem Labine	60.00	30.00
181 Roy McMillan	40.00	20.00
182 Humberto Robinson	30.00	15.00
183 Anthony Jacobs	30.00	15.00
184 Harry Perkowski DP	15.00	7.50
185 Don Ferrarese	30.00	15.00
186 Does not exist		
187 Gil Hodges	175.00	90.00
188 Charlie Silvera DP	15.00	7.50
189 Phil Rizzuto	175.00	90.00
190 Gene Woodling	40.00	20.00
191 Eddie Stanky MG	40.00	20.00
192 Jim Delsing	40.00	20.00
193 Johnny Sain	60.00	30.00
194 Willie Mays	600.00	300.00
195 Ed Roebuck RC	60.00	30.00
196 Gale Wade	30.00	15.00
197 Al Smith	60.00	30.00
198 Yogi Berra	300.00	150.00
199 Bert Hamric	40.00	20.00
200 Jackie Jensen	60.00	30.00
201 Sherman Lollar	40.00	20.00
202 Jim Owens	30.00	15.00
203 Does not exist		
204 Frank Smith	30.00	15.00
205 Gene Freese RC	40.00	20.00
206 Pete Daley	30.00	15.00
207 Billy Consolo	30.00	15.00
208 Ray Moore	40.00	20.00
209 Does not exist		
210 Duke Snider	600.00	180.00

1955 Topps Double Header

The cards in this 66-card set measure approximately 2 1/16" by 4 7/8". Borrowing a design from the T201 Mecca series, Topps issued a 132-player "Double Header" set in a separate wrapper in 1955. Each player is numbered in the biographical section on the reverse. When open, with perforated flap up, one player is revealed; when the flap is lowered, or closed, the player design on top incorporates a portion of the inside player artwork. When the cards are placed side by side, a continuous ballpark background is formed. Some cards have been found without perforations, and all players pictured appear in the low series of the 1955 regular issue. The cards were issued in one-card penny packs which came 120 packs to a box with a piece of bubble gum.

	NM	Ex
COMPLETE SET (66)	4000.00	2000.00
WRAPPER (1-CENT)	200.00	100.00
1 Al Rosen and 2 Chuck Diering	50.00	25.00
3 Monte Irvin and 4 Russ Kemmerer	60.00	30.00
5 Ted Kazanski and 6 Gordon Jones	40.00	20.00
7 Bill Taylor and 8 Billy O'Dell	40.00	20.00
9 J.W. Porter and 10 Thornton Kipper	40.00	20.00
11 Curt Roberts and 12 Arnie Portocarrero	40.00	20.00
13 Wally Westlake and 14 Frank House	50.00	25.00
15 Rube Walker and 16 Lou Limmer	50.00	25.00
17 Dean Stone and 18 Charlie White	40.00	20.00
19 Karl Spooner and 20 Jim Hughes	50.00	25.00
21 Bill Skowron and 22 Frank Sullivan	60.00	30.00
23 Jack Shepard and 24 Stan Hack MG	40.00	20.00
25 Jackie Robinson and 26 Don Hoak	250.00	150.00
27 Dusty Rhodes and 28 Jim Davis	50.00	25.00
29 Vic Power and 30 Ed Bailey	40.00	20.00
31 Howie Pollet and 32 Ernie Banks	200.00	100.00
33 Jim Pendleton and 34 Gene Conley	40.00	20.00
35 Karl Olson and 36 Andy Carey	40.00	20.00
37 Wally Moon and 38 Joe Cunningham	50.00	25.00
39 Freddie Marsh and 40 Vernon Thies	40.00	20.00
41 Eddie Lopat and 42 Harvey Haddix	60.00	30.00
43 Leo Kiely and 44 Chuck Stobbs	40.00	20.00
45 Al Kaline and 46 Harold Valentine	200.00	100.00
47 Forrest Jacobs and 48 Johnny Gray	40.00	20.00
49 Ron Jackson and 50 Jim Finigan	40.00	20.00
51 Ray Jablonski and 52 Bob Keegan	40.00	20.00
53 Billy Herman CO and 54 Sandy Amoros	80.00	40.00
55 Chuck Harmon and 56 Bob Skinner	40.00	20.00
57 Dick Hall and 58 Bob Grim	40.00	20.00
59 Billy Glynn and 60 Bob Miller	50.00	25.00
61 Billy Gardner and 62 John Hetki	40.00	20.00
63 Bob Borkowski and 64 Bob Turley	40.00	20.00
65 Joe Collins and 66 Jack Harshman	40.00	20.00
67 Jim Hegan and 68 Jack Parks	40.00	20.00
69 Ted Williams and 70 Mayo Smith MG	400.00	200.00
71 Gair Allie and 72 Grady Hatton	40.00	20.00
73 Jerry Lynch and 74 Harry Brecheen CO	40.00	20.00
75 Tom Wright and 76 Vernon Stewart	40.00	20.00
77 Dave Hoskins and 78 Warren McGhee	40.00	20.00
79 Roy Sievers and 80 Art Fowler	50.00	25.00
81 Danny Schell and 82 Gus Triandos	40.00	20.00
83 Joe Frazier and 84 Don Mossi	40.00	20.00
85 Elmer Valo and 86 Hector Brown	40.00	20.00
87 Bob Kennedy and 88 Windy McCall	50.00	25.00
89 Ruben Gomez and 90 Jim Rivera	40.00	20.00
91 Louis Ortiz and 92 Milt Bolling	40.00	20.00
93 Carl Sawatski and 94 El Tappe	40.00	20.00
95 Dave Jolly and 96 Bobby Hofman	40.00	20.00
97 Preston Ward and 98 Don Zimmer	60.00	30.00
99 Bill Renna and 100 Dick Groat	50.00	25.00
101 Bill Wilson and 102 Bill Tremel	40.00	20.00
103 Hank Sauer and 104 Camilo Pascual	50.00	25.00
105 Hank Aaron and 106 Ray Herbert	500.00	250.00
107 Alex Grammas and 108 Tom Qualters	40.00	20.00
109 Hal Newhouser and 110 Chuck Bishop	60.00	30.00
111 Harmon Killebrew and 112 John Podres	200.00	100.00
113 Ray Boone and 114 Bob Purkey	40.00	20.00
115 Dale Long and 116 Ferris Fain	50.00	25.00
117 Steve Bilko and 118 Bob Milliken	40.00	20.00
119 Mel Parnell and 120 Tom Hurd	50.00	25.00
121 Ted Kluszewski and 122 Jim Owens	80.00	40.00
123 Gus Zernial and 124 Bob Trice	40.00	20.00
125 Rip Repulski and 126 Ted Lepcio	40.00	20.00
127 Warren Spahn and 128 Tom Brewer	150.00	100.00
129 Jim Gilliam and 130 Ellis Kinder	80.00	40.00
131 Herm Wehmeier and 132 Wayne Terwilliger	40.00	20.00

1956 Topps

The cards in this 340-card set measure approximately 2 5/8" by 3 3/4". Following up with another horizontally oriented card in 1956, Topps improved the format by layering the color "head" shot onto an actual action sequence involving the player. Cards 1 to 180 come with either white or gray backs: in the 1 to 100 sequence, gray backs are less common (worth about 10 percent more) and in the 101 to 180 sequence, white backs are less common (worth 30 percent more). The team cards, used for the first time in a regular set by Topps, are found dated 1955, or undated, with the team name appearing on either side. The dated team cards in the first series were not printed on the gray stock. The two unnumbered checklist cards are highly prized (must be unmarked to qualify as excellent or mint). The complete set price below does not include the unnumbered checklist cards or any of the variations. The set was issued in one-card penny packs or six-card nickel packs. The six card nickel packs came 24 to a box with 24 boxes in a case while the once cent packs came 120 to a box. Both types of packs included a piece of bubble gum. Promotional three card strips were issued for this set. Among those strips were one featuring Johnny O'Brien/Harvey Haddix and Frank House. The key Rookie Cards in this set are Walt Alston, Luis Aparicio, and Roger Craig. There are ten double-printed cards in the first series as evidenced by the discovery of an uncut sheet of 110 cards (10 by 11); these DP's are listed below.

	NM	Ex
COMPLETE SET (340)	8000.00	4000.00
COMMON CARD (1-100)	10.00	5.00
COMMON (101-180)	12.00	6.00
COMMON (261-340)	12.00	6.00
COMMON (181-260)	15.00	7.50
WRAPPER (1-CENT)	250.00	125.00
WRAP.(1-CENT, REPEAT)	100.00	50.00
WRAPPER (5-CENT)	200.00	100.00
1 Will Harridge PRES	125.00	35.00
2 W. Giles PRES RC DP	50.00	25.00
3 Elmer Valo	15.00	7.50
4 Carlos Paula	15.00	7.50
5 Ted Williams	500.00	250.00
6 Ray Boone	25.00	12.50
7 Ron Negray	10.00	5.00
8 Walter Alston MG RC	40.00	20.00
9 Ruben Gomez DP	10.00	5.00
10 Warren Spahn	100.00	50.00
11A Chicago Cubs (Centered)	30.00	15.00
11B Cubs Team (Dated 1955)	80.00	40.00
11C Cubs Team (Name at far left)	30.00	15.00
12 Andy Carey	15.00	7.50
13 Roy Face	15.00	7.50
14 Ken Boyer DP	15.00	7.50
15 Ernie Banks DP	100.00	50.00
16 Hector Lopez RC	15.00	7.50
17 Gene Conley	15.00	7.50
18 Dick Donovan	10.00	5.00
19 Chuck Diering DP	10.00	5.00
20 Al Kaline	125.00	60.00
21 Joe Collins DP	15.00	7.50
22 Jim Finigan	10.00	5.00
23 Fred Marsh	10.00	5.00
24 Dick Groat	15.00	7.50
25 Ted Kluszewski	80.00	40.00
26 Grady Hatton	10.00	5.00
27 Nelson Burbrink DP	10.00	5.00
28 Bobby Hofman	10.00	5.00
29 Jack Harshman	10.00	5.00
30 Jackie Robinson DP	250.00	125.00
31 Hank Aaron UER DP (Small photo actually Willie Mays)	350.00	180.00
32 Frank House	10.00	5.00
33 Roberto Clemente	400.00	200.00
34 Tom Brewer DP	10.00	5.00
35 Al Rosen	15.00	7.50
36 Rudy Minarcin	15.00	7.50
37 Alex Grammas	10.00	5.00
38 Bob Kennedy	15.00	7.50
39 Don Mossi	15.00	7.50
40 Bob Turley	15.00	7.50
41 Hank Sauer	15.00	7.50
42 Sandy Amoros	25.00	12.50
43 Ray Moore	10.00	5.00
44 Windy McCall	10.00	5.00
45 Gus Zernial	15.00	7.50
46 Gene Freese DP	10.00	5.00
47 Art Fowler	10.00	5.00
48 Jim Hegan	15.00	7.50
49 Pedro Ramos	10.00	5.00
50 Dusty Rhodes DP	15.00	7.50
51 Ernie Oravetz	10.00	5.00
52 Bob Grim DP	15.00	7.50
53 Arnie Portocarrero	10.00	5.00
54 Bob Keegan	10.00	5.00
55 Wally Moon	15.00	7.50
56 Dale Long	15.00	7.50
57 Duke Maas	10.00	5.00
58 Ed Roebuck	25.00	12.50
59 Jose Santiago	10.00	5.00
60 Mayo Smith MG DP	10.00	5.00
61 Bill Skowron	25.00	12.50
62 Hal Smith	15.00	7.50
63 Roger Craig RC	40.00	20.00
64 Luis Arroyo RC	10.00	5.00
65 Johnny O'Brien	15.00	7.50
66 Bob Speake DP	10.00	5.00
67 Vic Power	15.00	7.50
68 Chuck Stobbs	10.00	5.00
69 Chuck Tanner	15.00	7.50
70 Jim Rivera	10.00	5.00
71 Frank Sullivan	10.00	5.00
72A Phillies Team (Centered)	30.00	15.00
72B Phillies Team (Dated 1955)	80.00	40.00
72C Phillies Team DP (Name at far left)	30.00	15.00
73 Wayne Terwilliger	10.00	5.00
74 Jim King	10.00	5.00
75 Roy Sievers DP	15.00	7.50
76 Ray Crone	10.00	5.00
77 Harvey Haddix	15.00	7.50
78 Herman Wehmeier	10.00	5.00
79 Sandy Koufax	300.00	180.00
80 Gus Triandos DP	10.00	5.00
81 Wally Westlake	10.00	5.00
82 Bill Renna DP	10.00	5.00
83 Karl Spooner	15.00	7.50
84 Babe Birrer	10.00	5.00
85A Cleveland Indians (Centered)	30.00	15.00
85B Indians Team (Dated 1955)	80.00	40.00
85C Indians Team (Name at far left)	30.00	15.00
86 Ray Jablonski DP	10.00	5.00
87 Dean Stone	10.00	5.00
88 Johnny Kucks RC	15.00	7.50
89 Norm Zauchin	10.00	5.00
90A Cincinnati Redlegs Team (Centered)	30.00	15.00
90B Reds Team (Dated 1955)	80.00	40.00
90C Reds Team (Name at far left)	30.00	15.00
91 Gail Harris	10.00	5.00
92 Bob(Red) Wilson	10.00	5.00
93 George Susce	10.00	5.00
94 Ron Kline	10.00	5.00
95A Milwaukee Braves Team (Centered)	40.00	20.00
95B Braves Team (Dated 1955)	80.00	40.00
95C Braves Team (Name at far left)	40.00	20.00
96 Bill Tremel	10.00	5.00
97 Jerry Lynch	15.00	7.50
98 Camilo Pascual	15.00	7.50
99 Don Zimmer	25.00	12.50
100A Baltimore Orioles Team (centered)	40.00	20.00
100B Orioles Team (Dated 1955)	80.00	40.00
100C Orioles Team (Name at far left)	40.00	20.00
101 Roy Campanella	150.00	75.00
102 Jim Davis	12.00	6.00
103 Willie Miranda	12.00	6.00
104 Bob Lennon	12.00	6.00
105 Al Smith	12.00	6.00
106 Joe Astroth	12.00	6.00
107 Eddie Mathews	100.00	50.00
108 Laurin Pepper	12.00	6.00
109 Enos Slaughter	40.00	20.00
110 Yogi Berra	175.00	90.00
111 Boston Red Sox Team Card	40.00	20.00
112 Dee Fondy	12.00	6.00
113 Phil Rizzuto	150.00	75.00
114 Jim Owens	15.00	7.50
115 Jackie Jensen	15.00	7.50
116 Eddie O'Brien	12.00	6.00
117 Virgil Trucks	15.00	7.50
118 Nellie Fox	80.00	40.00
119 Larry Jackson RC	15.00	7.50
120 Richie Ashburn	60.00	30.00
121 Pittsburgh Pirates Team Card	40.00	20.00
122 Willard Nixon	12.00	6.00
123 Roy McMillan	15.00	7.50
124 Don Kaiser	12.00	6.00
125 Minnie Minoso	40.00	20.00
126 Jim Brady	12.00	6.00
127 Willie Jones	15.00	7.50
128 Eddie Yost	15.00	7.50
129 Jake Martin	12.00	6.00
130 Willie Mays	300.00	150.00
131 Bob Roselli	12.00	6.00
132 Bobby Avila	12.00	6.00
133 Ray Narleski	12.00	6.00
134 St. Louis Cardinals Team Card	40.00	20.00
135 Mickey Mantle	1500.00	750.00
136 Johnny Logan	15.00	7.50
137 Al Silvera	12.00	6.00
138 Johnny Antonelli	15.00	7.50
139 Tommy Carroll	15.00	7.50
140 Herb Score RC	60.00	30.00
141 Joe Frazier	12.00	6.00
142 Gene Baker	12.00	6.00
143 Jim Piersall	15.00	7.50
144 Leroy Powell	12.00	6.00
145 Gil Hodges	60.00	30.00
146 Washington Nationals Team Card	40.00	20.00
147 Earl Torgeson	12.00	6.00
148 Alvin Dark	15.00	7.50
149 Dixie Howell	12.00	6.00
150 Duke Snider	125.00	60.00
151 Spook Jacobs	15.00	7.50
152 Billy Hoeft	15.00	7.50
153 Frank Thomas	15.00	7.50
154 Dave Pope	12.00	6.00
155 Harvey Kuenn	15.00	7.50
156 Wes Westrum	15.00	7.50
157 Dick Brodowski	12.00	6.00
158 Wally Post	15.00	7.50
159 Clint Courtney	12.00	6.00
160 Billy Pierce	15.00	7.50
161 Joe DeMaestri	12.00	6.00
162 Dave(Gus) Bell	15.00	7.50
163 Gene Woodling	15.00	7.50
164 Harmon Killebrew	100.00	50.00
165 Red Schoendienst	40.00	20.00
166 Brooklyn Dodgers Team Card	200.00	100.00
167 Harry Dorish	12.00	6.00
168 Sammy White	12.00	6.00
169 Bob Nelson	12.00	6.00
170 Bill Virdon	15.00	7.50
171 Jim Wilson	12.00	6.00
172 Frank Torre RC	15.00	7.50
173 Johnny Podres	25.00	12.50
174 Glen Gorbous	12.00	6.00
175 Del Crandall	15.00	7.50
176 Alex Kellner	12.00	6.00
177 Hank Bauer	25.00	12.50
178 Joe Black	15.00	7.50
179 Harry Chiti	12.00	6.00
180 Robin Roberts	50.00	25.00
181 Billy Martin	125.00	50.00
182 Paul Minner	15.00	7.50
183 Stan Lopata	20.00	10.00
184 Don Bessent	20.00	10.00
185 Bill Bruton	20.00	10.00
186 Ron Jackson	20.00	10.00
187 Early Wynn	50.00	25.00
188 Chicago White Sox Team Card	50.00	25.00
189 Ned Garver	15.00	7.50
190 Carl Furillo	30.00	15.00
191 Frank Lary	20.00	10.00
192 Smoky Burgess	20.00	10.00
193 Wilmer Mizell	20.00	10.00
194 Monte Irvin	30.00	15.00
195 George Kell	30.00	15.00
196 Tom Poholsky	15.00	7.50
197 Granny Hamner	15.00	7.50
198 Ed Fitzgerald	15.00	7.50
199 Hank Thompson	20.00	10.00
200 Bob Feller	125.00	60.00
201 Rip Repulski	15.00	7.50
202 Jim Hearn	15.00	7.50
203 Bill Tuttle	15.00	7.50
204 Art Swanson	15.00	7.50
205 Whitey Lockman	20.00	10.00
206 Erv Palica	15.00	7.50
207 Jim Small	15.00	7.50
208 Elston Howard	60.00	30.00
209 Max Surkont	15.00	7.50
210 Mike Garcia	20.00	10.00
211 Murry Dickson	15.00	7.50
212 Johnny Temple	15.00	7.50
213 Detroit Tigers Team Card	60.00	30.00
214 Bob Rush	15.00	7.50
215 Tommy Byrne	20.00	10.00
216 Jerry Schoonmaker	15.00	7.50
217 Billy Klaus	15.00	7.50
218 Joe Nuxhall UER (Misspelled Nuxall)	20.00	10.00
219 Lew Burdette	20.00	10.00
220 Del Ennis	20.00	10.00
221 Bob Friend	20.00	10.00
222 Dave Philley	15.00	7.50
223 Randy Jackson	15.00	7.50
224 Bud Podbielan	15.00	7.50
225 Gil McDougald	50.00	25.00
226 New York Giants Team Card	80.00	40.00
227 Russ Meyer	15.00	7.50
228 Mickey Vernon	20.00	10.00
229 Harry Brecheen CO	20.00	10.00
230 Chico Carrasquel	15.00	7.50
231 Bob Hale	15.00	7.50
232 Toby Atwell	15.00	7.50
233 Carl Erskine	30.00	15.00
234 Pete Runnels	15.00	7.50
235 Don Newcombe	50.00	25.00
236 Kansas City Athletics Team Card	40.00	20.00
237 Jose Valdivielso	15.00	7.50
238 Walt Dropo	20.00	10.00
239 Harry Simpson	15.00	7.50
240 Whitey Ford	125.00	60.00
241 Don Mueller UER 6" tall	20.00	10.00
242 Hershell Freeman	15.00	7.50
243 Sherm Lollar	20.00	10.00
244 Bob Buhl	20.00	10.00
245 Billy Goodman	20.00	10.00
246 Tom Gorman	15.00	7.50
247 Bill Sarni	15.00	7.50
248 Bob Porterfield	15.00	7.50

249 Johnny Klippstein 15.00 7.50
250 Larry Doby 30.00 15.00
251 New York Yankees 250.00 125.00
Team Card UER
(Don Larsen misspelled
as Larson on front)
252 Vern Law 20.00 10.00
253 Irv Noren 30.00 15.00
254 George Crowe 15.00 7.50
255 Bob Lemon 50.00 25.00
256 Tom Hurd 15.00 7.50
257 Bobby Thomson 30.00 15.00
258 Art Ditmar 15.00 7.50
259 Sam Jones 20.00 10.00
260 Pee Wee Reese 150.00 75.00
261 Bobby Shantz 15.00 7.50
262 Howie Pollet 12.00 6.00
263 Bob Miller 12.00 6.00
264 Ray Monzant 12.00 6.00
265 Sandy Consuegra 12.00 6.00
266 Don Ferrarese 12.00 6.00
267 Bob Nieman 12.00 6.00
268 Dale Mitchell 15.00 7.50
269 Jack Meyer 12.00 6.00
270 Billy Loes 15.00 7.50
271 Foster Castleman 12.00 6.00
272 Danny O'Connell 12.00 6.00
273 Walker Cooper 12.00 6.00
274 Frank Baumholtz 12.00 6.00
275 Jim Greengrass 12.00 6.00
276 George Zuverink 12.00 6.00
277 Daryl Spencer 12.00 6.00
278 Chet Nichols 12.00 6.00
279 Johnny Groth 12.00 6.00
280 Jim Gilliam 40.00 20.00
281 Art Houtteman 12.00 6.00
282 Warren Hacker 12.00 6.00
283 Hal Smith RC 15.00 7.50
284 Ike Delock 12.00 6.00
285 Eddie Miksis 12.00 6.00
286 Bill Wight 12.00 6.00
287 Bobby Adams 12.00 6.00
288 Bob Cerv 40.00 20.00
289 Hal Jeffcoat 12.00 6.00
290 Curt Simmons 15.00 7.50
291 Frank Kellert 12.00 6.00
292 Luis Aparicio RC 150.00 75.00
293 Stu Miller 25.00 12.50
294 Ernie Johnson 15.00 7.50
295 Clem Labine 15.00 7.50
296 Andy Seminick 12.00 6.00
297 Bob Skinner 15.00 7.50
298 Johnny Schmitz 12.00 6.00
299 Charlie Neal 40.00 20.00
300 Vic Wertz 15.00 7.50
301 Marv Grissom 12.00 6.00
302 Eddie Robinson 12.00 6.00
303 Jim Dyck 12.00 6.00
304 Frank Malzone 15.00 7.50
305 Brooks Lawrence 12.00 6.00
306 Curt Roberts 12.00 6.00
307 Hoyt Wilhelm 40.00 20.00
308 Chuck Harmon 12.00 6.00
309 Don Blasingame RC 15.00 7.50
310 Steve Gromek 12.00 6.00
311 Hal Naragon 12.00 6.00
312 Andy Pafko 15.00 7.50
313 Gene Stephens 12.00 6.00
314 Hobie Landrith 12.00 6.00
315 Milt Bolling 12.00 6.00
316 Jerry Coleman 15.00 7.50
317 Al Aber 12.00 6.00
318 Fred Hatfield 12.00 6.00
319 Jack Crimian 12.00 6.00
320 Joe Adcock 15.00 7.50
321 Jim Konstanty 15.00 7.50
322 Karl Olson 12.00 6.00
323 Willard Schmidt 12.00 6.00
324 Rocky Bridges 15.00 7.50
325 Don Liddle 12.00 6.00
326 Connie Johnson 12.00 6.00
327 Bob Wiesler 12.00 6.00
328 Preston Ward 12.00 6.00
329 Lou Berberet 12.00 6.00
330 Jim Busby 15.00 7.50
331 Dick Hall 12.00 6.00
332 Don Larsen 60.00 30.00
333 Rube Walker 12.00 6.00
334 Bob Miller 15.00 7.50
335 Don Hoak 15.00 7.50
336 Ellis Kinder 12.00 6.00
337 Bobby Morgan 12.00 6.00
338 Jim Delsing 12.00 6.00
339 Rance Pless 12.00 6.00
340 Mickey McDermott 60.00 12.00
NNO Checklist 1/3 300.00 95.00
NNO Checklist 2/4 300.00 95.00

1957 Topps

The cards in this 407-card set measure 2 1/2" by 3 1/2". In 1957, Topps returned to the vertical obverse, adopted what we now call the standard card size, and used a large, uncluttered color photo for the first time since 1952. Cards in the series 265 to 352 and the unnumbered checklist cards are scarcer than other cards in the set. However within this scarce series (265-352) there are 22 cards which were printed in double the quantity of the other cards in the series; these 22 double prints are indicated by DP in the checklist below. The first star combination cards, cards 400 and 407, are quite popular with collectors. They feature the big stars of the previous season's World Series teams, the Dodgers (Furillo, Hodges, Campanella, and Snider) and Yankees (Berra and Mantle). The complete set price below does not include the unnumbered checklist cards. Confirmed packaging includes one-cent penny packs and six-card nickel packs. Cello packs are definately known to exist and some collectors remember buying rack packs of 57's as well. The key Rookie Cards in this set are Jim Bunning, Rocky Colavito, Don Drysdale, Whitey Herzog, Tony Kubek, Bill Mazeroski, Bobby Richardson, Brooks Robinson, and Frank Robinson.

	NM	Ex
COMPLETE SET (407)	10000.00	5000.00
COMMON CARD (1-88)	10.00	5.00
COMMON CARD (89-176)	8.00	4.00
COMMON (177-264)	8.00	4.00
COMMON (265-352)	20.00	10.00
COMMON (353-407)	8.00	4.00
COMMON DP (265-352)	12.00	6.00
WRAPPER (1-CENT)	300.00	150.00
WRAPPER (5-CENT)	200.00	100.00

1 Ted Williams 600.00 150.00
2 Yogi Berra 200.00 100.00
3 Dale Long 20.00 10.00
4 Johnny Logan 20.00 10.00
5 Sal Maglie 20.00 10.00
6 Hector Lopez 15.00 7.50
7 Luis Aparicio 30.00 15.00
8 Don Mossi 15.00 7.50
9 Johnny Temple 15.00 7.50
10 Willie Mays 300.00 125.00
11 George Zuverink 10.00 5.00
12 Dick Groat 20.00 10.00
13 Wally Burnette 10.00 5.00
14 Bob Nieman 10.00 5.00
15 Robin Roberts 30.00 15.00
16 Walt Moryn 10.00 5.00
17 Billy Gardner 10.00 5.00
18 Don Drysdale RC 250.00 125.00
19 Bob Wilson 10.00 5.00
20 Hank Aaron UER 300.00 150.00
(Reverse negative
photo on front)
21 Frank Sullivan 10.00 5.00
22 Jerry Snyder UER 10.00 5.00
Photo actually Ed Fitzgerald
23 Sherm Lollar 15.00 7.50
24 Bill Mazeroski RC 80.00 40.00
25 Whitey Ford 150.00 75.00
26 Bob Boyd 10.00 5.00
27 Ted Kazanski 10.00 5.00
28 Gene Conley 15.00 7.50
29 Whitey Herzog RC 30.00 15.00
30 Pee Wee Reese 80.00 40.00
31 Ron Northey 10.00 5.00
32 Hershell Freeman 10.00 5.00
33 Jim Small 10.00 5.00
34 Tom Sturdivant 15.00 7.50
35 Frank Robinson RC 300.00 125.00
36 Bob Grim 10.00 5.00
37 Frank Torre 15.00 7.50
38 Nellie Fox 50.00 25.00
39 Al Worthington 10.00 5.00
40 Early Wynn 30.00 15.00
41 Hal W. Smith 10.00 5.00
42 Dee Fondy 10.00 5.00
43 Connie Johnson 10.00 5.00
44 Joe DeMaestri 10.00 5.00
45 Carl Furillo 30.00 15.00
46 Robert J. Miller 10.00 5.00
47 Don Blasingame 10.00 5.00
48 Bill Bruton 15.00 7.50
49 Daryl Spencer 10.00 5.00
50 Herb Score 30.00 15.00
51 Clint Courtney 10.00 5.00
52 Lee Walls 10.00 5.00
53 Clem Labine 20.00 10.00
54 Elmer Valo 10.00 5.00
55 Ernie Banks 125.00 60.00
56 Dave Sisler 10.00 5.00
57 Jim Lemon 15.00 7.50
58 Ruben Gomez 10.00 5.00
59 Dick Williams 15.00 7.50
60 Billy Hoeft 15.00 7.50
61 Dusty Rhodes 15.00 7.50
62 Billy Martin 60.00 30.00
63 Ike Delock 10.00 5.00
64 Pete Runnels 15.00 7.50
65 Wally Moon 15.00 7.50
66 Brooks Lawrence 10.00 5.00
67 Chico Carrasquel 10.00 5.00
68 Ray Crone 10.00 5.00
69 Roy McMillan 15.00 7.50
70 Richie Ashburn 50.00 25.00
71 Murry Dickson 10.00 5.00
72 Bill Tuttle 10.00 5.00
73 George Crowe 10.00 5.00
74 Vito Valentinetti 10.00 5.00
75 Jimmy Piersall 15.00 7.50
76 Roberto Clemente 300.00 150.00
77 Paul Foytack 10.00 5.00
78 Vic Wertz 15.00 7.50
79 Lindy McDaniel RC 15.00 7.50
80 Gil Hodges 50.00 25.00
81 Herman Wehmeier 10.00 5.00
82 Elston Howard 30.00 15.00
83 Lou Skizas 10.00 5.00
84 Moe Drabowsky 15.00 7.50
85 Larry Doby 30.00 15.00
86 Bill Sarni 10.00 5.00
87 Tom Gorman 10.00 5.00
88 Harvey Kuenn 15.00 7.50
89 Roy Sievers 15.00 7.50
90 Warren Spahn 80.00 40.00
91 Mack Burk 8.00 4.00
92 Mickey Vernon 15.00 7.50
93 Hal Jeffcoat 8.00 4.00
94 Bobby Del Greco 8.00 4.00
95 Mickey Mantle 1000.00 600.00
96 Hank Aguirre 8.00 4.00
97 New York Yankees 100.00 50.00
Team Card
98 Alvin Dark 15.00 7.50
99 Bob Keegan 8.00 4.00
100 Warren Giles PRES 15.00 7.50
Will Harridge PRES
101 Chuck Stobbs 8.00 4.00
102 Ray Boone 15.00 7.50
103 Joe Nuxhall 15.00 7.50
104 Hank Foiles 8.00 4.00
105 Johnny Antonelli 15.00 7.50
106 Ray Moore 8.00 4.00
107 Jim Rivera 8.00 4.00
108 Tommy Byrne 15.00 7.50
109 Hank Thompson 8.00 4.00
110 Bill Virdon 15.00 7.50
111 Hal R. Smith 8.00 4.00
112 Tom Brewer 8.00 4.00
113 Wilmer Mizell 15.00 7.50
114 Milwaukee Braves 20.00 10.00
Team Card
115 Jim Gilliam 15.00 7.50
116 Mike Fornieles 8.00 4.00
117 Joe Adcock 20.00 10.00
118 Bob Porterfield 8.00 4.00
119 Stan Lopata 8.00 4.00
120 Bob Lemon 30.00 15.00
121 Clete Boyer RC 30.00 15.00
122 Ken Boyer 20.00 10.00
123 Steve Ridzik 8.00 4.00
124 Dave Philley 8.00 4.00
125 Al Kaline 100.00 50.00
126 Bob Wiesler 8.00 4.00
127 Bob Buhl 15.00 7.50
128 Ed Bailey 15.00 7.50
129 Saul Rogovin 8.00 4.00
130 Don Newcombe 20.00 10.00
131 Milt Bolling 8.00 4.00
132 Art Ditmar 15.00 7.50
133 Del Crandall 15.00 7.50
134 Don Kaiser 8.00 4.00
135 Bill Skowron 20.00 10.00
136 Jim Hegan 15.00 7.50
137 Bob Rush 8.00 4.00
138 Minnie Minoso 20.00 10.00
139 Lou Kretlow 8.00 4.00
140 Frank Thomas 15.00 7.50
141 Al Aber 8.00 4.00
142 Charley Thompson 8.00 4.00
143 Andy Pafko 15.00 7.50
144 Ray Narleski 8.00 4.00
145 Al Smith 8.00 4.00
146 Don Ferrarese 8.00 4.00
147 Al Walker 8.00 4.00
148 Don Mueller 15.00 7.50
149 Bob Kennedy 15.00 7.50
150 Bob Friend 15.00 7.50
151 Willie Miranda 8.00 4.00
152 Jack Harshman 8.00 4.00
153 Karl Olson 8.00 4.00
154 Red Schoendienst 30.00 15.00
155 Jim Brosnan 15.00 7.50
156 Gus Triandos 15.00 7.50
157 Wally Post 15.00 7.50
158 Curt Simmons 15.00 7.50
159 Solly Drake 8.00 4.00
160 Billy Pierce 15.00 7.50
161 Pittsburgh Pirates 15.00 7.50
Team Card
162 Jack Meyer 8.00 4.00
163 Sammy White 8.00 4.00
164 Tommy Carroll 8.00 4.00
165 Ted Kluszewski 100.00 50.00
166 Roy Face 15.00 7.50
167 Vic Power 15.00 7.50
168 Frank Lary 15.00 7.50
169 Herb Plews 8.00 4.00
170 Duke Snider 125.00 60.00
171 Boston Red Sox 15.00 7.50
Team Card
172 Gene Woodling 15.00 7.50
173 Roger Craig 15.00 7.50
174 Willie Jones 8.00 4.00
175 Don Larsen 30.00 15.00
176A Gene Baker ERR 350.00 180.00
(Misspelled Bakep
on card back)
176B Gene Baker COR 15.00 7.50
177 Eddie Yost 15.00 7.50
178 Don Bessent 8.00 4.00
179 Ernie Oravetz 8.00 4.00
180 Gus Bell 15.00 7.50
181 Dick Donovan 8.00 4.00
182 Hobie Landrith 8.00 4.00
183 Chicago Cubs 15.00 7.50
Team Card
184 Tito Francona RC 8.00 4.00
185 Johnny Kucks 15.00 7.50
186 Jim King 15.00 7.50
187 Virgil Trucks 15.00 7.50
188 Felix Mantilla RC 15.00 7.50
189 Willard Nixon 8.00 4.00
190 Randy Jackson 8.00 4.00
191 Joe Margoneri 8.00 4.00
192 Jerry Coleman 15.00 7.50
193 Del Rice 8.00 4.00
194 Hal Brown 8.00 4.00
195 Bobby Avila 8.00 4.00
196 Larry Jackson 15.00 7.50
197 Hank Sauer 15.00 7.50
198 Detroit Tigers 15.00 7.50
Team Card
199 Vern Law 15.00 7.50
200 Gil McDougald 15.00 7.50
201 Sandy Amoros 15.00 7.50
202 Dick Gernert 8.00 4.00
203 Hoyt Wilhelm 30.00 15.00
204 Kansas City Athletics 15.00 7.50
Team Card
205 Charlie Maxwell 15.00 7.50
206 Willard Schmidt 8.00 4.00
207 Gordon(Billy) Hunter 8.00 4.00
208 Lou Burdette 15.00 7.50
209 Bob Skinner 15.00 7.50
210 Roy Campanella 150.00 75.00
211 Camilo Pascual 15.00 7.50
212 Rocky Colavito RC 125.00 60.00
213 Les Moss 8.00 4.00
214 Philadelphia Phillies 15.00 7.50
Team Card
215 Enos Slaughter 30.00 15.00
216 Marv Grissom 8.00 4.00
217 Gene Stephens 8.00 4.00
218 Ray Jablonski 8.00 4.00
219 Tom Acker 8.00 4.00
220 Jackie Jensen 20.00 10.00
221 Dixie Howell 8.00 4.00
222 Alex Grammas 8.00 4.00
223 Frank House 8.00 4.00
224 Marv Blaylock 8.00 4.00
225 Harry Simpson 8.00 4.00
226 Preston Ward 8.00 4.00
227 Gerry Staley 8.00 4.00
228 Smoky Burgess UER 15.00 7.50
(Misspelled Smokey
on card back)
229 George Susce 8.00 4.00
230 George Kell 30.00 15.00
231 Solly Hemus 8.00 4.00
232 Whitey Lockman 15.00 7.50
233 Art Fowler 8.00 4.00
234 Dick Cole 8.00 4.00
235 Tom Poholsky 8.00 4.00
236 Joe Ginsberg 8.00 4.00
237 Foster Castleman 8.00 4.00
238 Eddie Robinson 8.00 4.00
239 Tom Morgan 8.00 4.00
240 Hank Bauer 15.00 7.50
241 Joe Lonnett 8.00 4.00
242 Charlie Neal 15.00 7.50
243 St. Louis Cardinals 15.00 7.50
Team Card
244 Billy Loes 15.00 7.50
245 Rip Repulski 8.00 4.00
246 Jose Valdivielso 8.00 4.00
247 Turk Lown 8.00 4.00
248 Jim Finigan 8.00 4.00
249 Dave Pope 8.00 4.00
250 Eddie Mathews 50.00 25.00
251 Baltimore Orioles 15.00 7.50
Team Card
252 Carl Erskine 15.00 7.50
253 Gus Zernial 15.00 7.50
254 Ron Negray 8.00 4.00
255 Charlie Silvera 15.00 7.50
256 Ron Kline 8.00 4.00
257 Walt Dropo 8.00 4.00
258 Steve Gromek 8.00 4.00
259 Eddie O'Brien 8.00 4.00
260 Del Ennis 15.00 7.50
261 Bob Chakales 8.00 4.00
262 Bobby Thomson 15.00 7.50
263 George Strickland 8.00 4.00
264 Bob Turley 15.00 7.50
265 Harvey Haddix DP 12.00 6.00
266 Ken Kuhn DP 12.00 6.00
267 Danny Kravitz 20.00 10.00
268 Jack Collum 20.00 10.00
269 Bob Cerv 30.00 15.00
270 Washington Senators 60.00 30.00
Team Card
271 Danny O'Connell DP 12.00 6.00
272 Bobby Shantz 30.00 15.00
273 Jim Davis 20.00 10.00
274 Don Hoak 15.00 7.50
275 Cleveland Indians 60.00 30.00
Team Card UER
(Text on back credits Tribe
with winning AL title in '28.
The Yankees won that year.)
276 Jim Pyburn 20.00 10.00
277 Johnny Podres DP 40.00 20.00
278 Fred Hatfield DP 12.00 6.00
279 Bob Thurman 20.00 10.00
280 Alex Kellner 20.00 10.00
281 Gail Harris 20.00 10.00
282 Jack Dittmer DP 12.00 6.00
283 Wes Covington DP 12.00 6.00
284 Don Zimmer 40.00 20.00
285 Ned Garver 20.00 10.00
286 Bobby Richardson RC 125.00 60.00
287 Sam Jones 20.00 10.00
288 Ted Lepcio 20.00 10.00
289 Jim Bolger DP 12.00 6.00
290 Andy Carey DP 40.00 20.00
291 Windy McCall 20.00 10.00
292 Billy Klaus 20.00 10.00
293 Ted Abernathy 20.00 10.00
294 Rocky Bridges DP 12.00 6.00
295 Joe Collins DP 40.00 20.00
296 Johnny Klippstein 20.00 10.00
297 Jack Crimian 20.00 10.00
298 Irv Noren DP 12.00 6.00
299 Chuck Harmon 20.00 10.00
300 Mike Garcia 30.00 15.00
301 Sammy Esposito DP 20.00 10.00
302 Sandy Koufax DP 350.00 150.00
303 Billy Goodman 30.00 15.00
304 Joe Cunningham 30.00 15.00
305 Chico Fernandez 20.00 10.00
306 Darrell Johnson DP 12.00 6.00
307 Jack D. Phillips DP 12.00 6.00
308 Dick Hall 20.00 10.00
309 Jim Busby DP 12.00 6.00
310 Max Surkont DP 12.00 6.00
311 Al Pilarcik DP 12.00 6.00
312 Tony Kubek DP RC 100.00 50.00
313 Mel Parnell 15.00 7.50
314 Ed Bouchee DP 12.00 6.00
315 Lou Berberet DP 12.00 6.00
316 Billy O'Dell 20.00 10.00
317 New York Giants 80.00 40.00
Team Card
318 Mickey McDermott 20.00 10.00
319 Gino Cimoli RC 20.00 10.00
320 Neil Chrisley 20.00 10.00
321 John(Red) Murff 20.00 10.00
322 Cincinnati Reds 80.00 40.00
Team Card
323 Wes Westrum 30.00 15.00
324 Brooklyn Dodgers 150.00 75.00
Team Card
325 Frank Bolling 20.00 10.00
326 Pedro Ramos 20.00 10.00
327 Jim Pendleton 20.00 10.00
328 Brooks Robinson RC 400.00 200.00
329 Chicago White Sox 60.00 30.00
Team Card
330 Jim Wilson 20.00 10.00
331 Ray Katt 20.00 10.00
332 Bob Bowman 20.00 10.00
333 Ernie Johnson 20.00 10.00
334 Jerry Schoonmaker 20.00 10.00
335 Granny Hamner 20.00 10.00
336 Haywood Sullivan RC 40.00 20.00
337 Rene Valdes 20.00 10.00
338 Jim Bunning RC 150.00 75.00
339 Bob Speake 20.00 10.00
340 Bill Wight 20.00 10.00
341 Don Gross 20.00 10.00
342 Gene Mauch 30.00 15.00
343 Taylor Phillips 15.00 7.50
344 Paul LaPalme 20.00 10.00
345 Paul Smith 20.00 10.00
346 Dick Littlefield 20.00 10.00
347 Hal Naragon 20.00 10.00
348 Jim Hearn 20.00 10.00
349 Nellie King 20.00 10.00
350 Eddie Miksis 20.00 10.00
351 Dave Hillman 20.00 10.00
352 Ellis Kinder 20.00 10.00
353 Cal Neeman 8.00 4.00
354 Rip Coleman 8.00 4.00
355 Frank Malzone 15.00 7.50
356 Faye Throneberry 8.00 4.00
357 Earl Torgeson 8.00 4.00
358 Jerry Lynch 15.00 7.50
359 Tom Cheney 8.00 4.00
360 Johnny Groth 8.00 4.00
361 Curt Barclay 8.00 4.00
362 Roman Mejias 15.00 7.50
363 Eddie Kasko 8.00 4.00
364 Cal McLish 15.00 7.50
365 Ozzie Virgil 8.00 4.00
366 Ken Lehman 8.00 4.00
367 Ed Fitzgerald 8.00 4.00
368 Bob Purkey 8.00 4.00
369 Milt Graff 8.00 4.00
370 Warren Hacker 8.00 4.00
371 Bob Lennon 8.00 4.00
372 Norm Zauchin 8.00 4.00
373 Pete Whisenant 8.00 4.00
374 Don Cardwell 8.00 4.00
375 Jim Landis 15.00 7.50
376 Don Elston 8.00 4.00
377 Andre Rodgers 8.00 4.00
378 Elmer Singleton 8.00 4.00
379 Don Lee 8.00 4.00
380 Walker Cooper 8.00 4.00
381 Dean Stone 8.00 4.00
382 Jim Bridewеser 8.00 4.00
383 Juan Pizarro 8.00 4.00
384 Bobby G. Smith 8.00 4.00
385 Art Houtteman 8.00 4.00
386 Lyle Luttrell 8.00 4.00
387 Jack Sanford RC 15.00 7.50
388 Pete Daley 8.00 4.00
389 Dave Jolly 8.00 4.00
390 Reno Bertoia 8.00 4.00
391 Ralph Terry RC 15.00 7.50
392 Chuck Tanner 15.00 7.50
393 Raul Sanchez 8.00 4.00
394 Luis Arroyo 15.00 7.50
395 Bubba Phillips 8.00 4.00
396 Casey Wise 8.00 4.00
397 Roy Smalley 8.00 4.00
398 Al Cicotte 15.00 7.50
399 Billy Consolo 8.00 4.00
400 Carl Furillo 250.00 125.00
Gil Hodges
Roy Campanella
Duke Snider
401 Earl Battey RC 15.00 7.50
402 Jim Pisoni 8.00 4.00
403 Dick Hyde 8.00 4.00
404 Harry Anderson 8.00 4.00
405 Duke Maas 8.00 4.00
406 Bob Hale 8.00 4.00
407 Mickey Mantle 500.00 150.00
Yogi Berra
CC1 Contest Card 100.00 25.00
Saturday, May 4th
Boston Red Sox
vs. Cleveland Indians
Cincinnati Redlegs
vs. New York Giants
CC2 Contest Card 100.00 25.00
Saturday, May 25th
Detroit Tigers
vs. Kansas City Athletics
Pittsburgh Pirates
vs. Philadelphia Phillies
CC3 Contest Card 125.00 31.00
Saturday, June 22nd
Brooklyn Dodgers
vs. St. Louis Cardinals
Chicago White Sox
vs. New York Yankees
CC4 Contest Card 125.00 31.00
Saturday, July 19th
Milwaukee Braves
vs. New York Giants
Baltimore Orioles
vs. Kansas City Athletics
NNO Checklist 1/2 250.00 75.00
Bazooka Back
NNO Checklist 1/2 250.00 125.00
Blony Back
NNO Checklist 2/3 400.00 100.00
Bazooka Back
NNO Checklist 2/3 400.00 200.00
Blony Back
NNO Checklist 3/4 800.00 190.00
Bazooka Back
NNO Checklist 3/4 600.00 300.00
Blony Back
NNO Checklist 4/5 1000.00 220.00
Bazooka Back
NNO Checklist 4/5 800.00 400.00
Blony Back
NNO Lucky Penny Charm 100.00 50.00
and Key Chain
offer card

1958 Topps

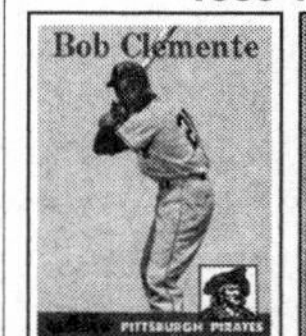

This is a 494-card standard-size set. Card number 145, which was supposedly to be Ed Bouchee, was not issued. The 1958 Topps set contains the first Sport Magazine All-Star

1959 Topps

Selection series (475-495) and expanded use of combination cards. For the first time team cards carried series checklists on back (Milwaukee, Detroit, Baltimore, and Cincinnati are also found with players listed alphabetically). In the first series some cards were issued with yellow name (YL) or team (YT) lettering, as opposed to the common white lettering. They are explicity noted below. Cards were issued in one-card penny packs or six-card nickel packs. In the last series, All-Star cards of Stan Musial and Mickey Mantle were triple printed; the cards they replaced (443, 446, 450, and 462) on the printing sheet were hence printed in shorter supply than other cards in the last series and are marked with an SP in the list below. The All-Star card of Musial marked his first appearence on a Topps card. Technically the New York Giants team card (19) is an error as the Giants had already moved to San Francisco. The key Rookie Cards in this set are Orlando Cepeda, Curt Flood, Roger Maris, and Vada Pinson. These cards were issued in varying formats, including one cent packs which were issued 120 to a box.

NM Ex
COMP. MASTER (534) 12000.00 6000.00
COMPLETE SET (494) 6000.00 3000.00
COMMON CARD (1-110) 12.00 6.00
COMMON (111-495) 8.00 4.00
WRAPPER (1-CENT) 100.00 50.00
WRAPPER (5-CENT) 125.00 60.00
1 Ted Williams 600.00 210.00
2A Bob Lemon 30.00 15.00
2B Bob Lemon YT 60.00 30.00
3 Alex Kellner 12.00 6.00
4 Hank Foiles 12.00 6.00
5 Willie Mays 300.00 150.00
6 George Zuverink 12.00 6.00
7 Dale Long 15.00 7.50
8A Eddie Kasko 12.00 6.00
8B Eddie Kasko YN 40.00 20.00
9 Hank Bauer 20.00 10.00
10 Lou Burdette 20.00 10.00
11A Jim Rivera 12.00 6.00
11B Jim Rivera YT 40.00 20.00
12 George Crowe 12.00 6.00
13A Billy Hoeft 12.00 6.00
13B Billy Hoeft YN 40.00 20.00
14 Rip Repulski 12.00 6.00
15 Jim Lemon 15.00 7.50
16 Charlie Neal 15.00 7.50
17 Felix Mantilla 12.00 6.00
18 Frank Sullivan 12.00 6.00
19 Giants Team Card CL 40.00 8.00
20A Gil McDougald 20.00 10.00
20B Gil McDougald YN 60.00 30.00
21 Curt Barclay 12.00 6.00
22 Hal Naragon 12.00 6.00
23A Bill Tuttle 12.00 6.00
23B Bill Tuttle YN 40.00 20.00
24A Hobie Landrith 12.00 6.00
24B Hobie Landrith YN 40.00 20.00
25 Don Drysdale 100.00 50.00
26 Ron Jackson 12.00 6.00
27 Bud Freeman 12.00 6.00
28 Jim Busby 12.00 6.00
29 Ted Lepcio 12.00 6.00
30A Hank Aaron 200.00 100.00
30B Hank Aaron YN 500.00 250.00
31 Tex Clevenger 12.00 6.00
32A J.W. Porter 12.00 6.00
32B J.W. Porter YN 40.00 20.00
33A Cal Neeman 12.00 6.00
33B Cal Neeman YT 40.00 20.00
34 Bob Thurman 12.00 6.00
35A Don Mossi 15.00 7.50
35B Don Mossi YT 40.00 20.00
36 Ted Kazanski 12.00 6.00
37 Mike McCormick RC 15.00 7.50
UER Photo actually
Ray Monzant
38 Dick Gernert 12.00 6.00
39 Bob Martyn 12.00 6.00
40 George Kell 30.00 15.00
41 Dave Hillman 12.00 6.00
42 John Roseboro RC 30.00 15.00
43 Sal Maglie 15.00 7.50
44 Washington Senators 20.00 4.00
Team Card CL
45 Dick Groat 15.00 7.50
46A Lou Sleater 12.00 6.00
46B Lou Sleater YN 40.00 20.00
47 Roger Maris RC 500.00 250.00
48 Chuck Harmon 12.00 6.00
49 Smoky Burgess 15.00 7.50
50A Billy Pierce 15.00 7.50
50B Billy Pierce YT 40.00 20.00
51 Del Rice 12.00 6.00
52A Roberto Clemente 300.00 150.00
52B Roberto Clemente YT 500.00 250.00
53A Morrie Martin 12.00 6.00
53B Morrie Martin YN 40.00 20.00
54 Norm Siebern RC 20.00 10.00
55 Chico Carrasquel 12.00 6.00
56 Bill Fischer 12.00 6.00
57A Tim Thompson 12.00 6.00
57B Tim Thompson YN 40.00 20.00
58A Art Schult 12.00 6.00
58B Art Schult YT 40.00 20.00
59 Dave Sisler 12.00 6.00
60A Del Ennis 15.00 7.50
60B Del Ennis YN 40.00 20.00
61A Darrell Johnson 12.00 6.00
61B Darrell Johnson YN 40.00 20.00
62 Joe DeMaestri 12.00 6.00
63 Joe Nuxhall 15.00 7.50
64 Joe Lonnett 12.00 6.00
65A Von McDaniel RC 12.00 6.00
65B Von McDaniel YL RC 40.00 20.00
66 Lee Walls 12.00 6.00
67 Joe Ginsberg 12.00 6.00
68 Daryl Spencer 12.00 6.00
69 Wally Burnette 12.00 6.00
70A Al Kaline 100.00 50.00
70B Al Kaline YN 250.00 125.00
71 Dodgers Team CL 60.00 12.00
72 Bud Byerly 12.00 6.00
73 Pete Daley 12.00 6.00
74 Roy Face 15.00 7.50
75 Gus Bell 15.00 7.50
76A Dick Farrell 12.00 6.00
76B Dick Farrell YT 40.00 20.00
77A Don Zimmer 15.00 7.50
77B Don Zimmer YT 40.00 20.00
78A Ernie Johnson 15.00 7.50
78B Ernie Johnson YN 40.00 20.00
79A Dick Williams 15.00 7.50
79B Dick Williams YT 40.00 20.00
80 Dick Drott 12.00 6.00
81A Steve Boros RC 12.00 6.00
81B Steve Boros YT RC 40.00 20.00
82 Ron Kline 12.00 6.00
83 Bob Hazle RC 12.00 6.00
84 Billy O'Dell 12.00 6.00
85A Luis Aparicio 30.00 15.00
85B Luis Aparicio YT 80.00 40.00
86 Valmy Thomas 12.00 6.00
87 Johnny Kucks 12.00 6.00
88 Duke Snider 80.00 40.00
89 Billy Klaus 12.00 6.00
90 Robin Roberts 30.00 15.00
91 Chuck Tanner 15.00 7.50
92A Clint Courtney 12.00 6.00
92B Clint Courtney YN 40.00 20.00
93 Sandy Amoros 15.00 7.50
94 Bob Skinner 15.00 7.50
95 Frank Bolling 12.00 6.00
96 Joe Durham 12.00 6.00
97A Larry Jackson 12.00 6.00
97B Larry Jackson YN 40.00 20.00
98A Billy Hunter 12.00 6.00
98B Billy Hunter YN 40.00 20.00
99 Bobby Adams 12.00 6.00
100A Early Wynn 30.00 15.00
100B Early Wynn YT 80.00 40.00
101A Bobby Richardson 30.00 15.00
101B B.Richardson YN 60.00 30.00
102 George Strickland 12.00 6.00
103 Jerry Lynch 15.00 7.50
104 Jim Pendleton 12.00 6.00
105 Billy Gardner 12.00 6.00
106 Dick Schofield 15.00 7.50
107 Ossie Virgil 12.00 6.00
108A Jim Landis 12.00 6.00
108B Jim Landis YT 40.00 20.00
109 Herb Plews 12.00 6.00
110 Johnny Logan 15.00 7.50
111 Stu Miller 10.00 5.00
112 Gus Zernial 10.00 5.00
113 Jerry Walker RC 8.00 4.00
114 Irv Noren 10.00 5.00
115 Jim Bunning 30.00 15.00
116 Dave Philley 8.00 4.00
117 Frank Torre 10.00 5.00
118 Harvey Haddix 10.00 5.00
119 Harry Chiti 8.00 4.00
120 Johnny Podres 10.00 5.00
121 Eddie Miksis 8.00 4.00
122 Walt Moryn 8.00 4.00
123 Dick Tomanek 8.00 4.00
124 Bobby Usher 8.00 4.00
125 Alvin Dark 10.00 5.00
126 Stan Palys 8.00 4.00
127 Tom Sturdivant 10.00 5.00
128 Willie Kirkland 8.00 4.00
129 Jim Derrington 8.00 4.00
130 Jackie Jensen 10.00 5.00
131 Bob Henrich 8.00 4.00
132 Vern Law 10.00 5.00
133 Russ Nixon RC 8.00 4.00
134 Philadelphia Phillies 15.00 3.00
Team Card CL
135 Mike(Moe)Drabowsky 10.00 5.00
136 Jim Finigan 8.00 4.00
137 Russ Kemmerer 8.00 4.00
138 Earl Torgeson 8.00 4.00
139 George Brunet 8.00 4.00
140 Wes Covington 10.00 5.00
141 Ken Lehman 8.00 4.00
142 Enos Slaughter 25.00 12.50
143 Billy Muffett RC 8.00 4.00
144 Bobby Morgan 8.00 4.00
145 Never issued
146 Dick Gray 8.00 4.00
147 Don McMahon RC 8.00 4.00
148 Billy Consolo 8.00 4.00
149 Tom Acker 8.00 4.00
150 Mickey Mantle 800.00 400.00
151 Buddy Pritchard 8.00 4.00
152 Johnny Antonelli 10.00 5.00
153 Les Moss 8.00 4.00
154 Harry Byrd 8.00 4.00
155 Hector Lopez 10.00 5.00
156 Dick Hyde 8.00 4.00
157 Dee Fondy 8.00 4.00
158 Cleveland Indians 15.00 3.00
Team Card CL
159 Taylor Phillips 8.00 4.00
160 Don Hoak 10.00 5.00
161 Don Larsen 15.00 7.50
162 Gil Hodges 40.00 20.00
163 Jim Wilson 8.00 4.00
164 Bob Taylor 8.00 4.00
165 Bob Nieman 8.00 4.00
166 Danny O'Connell 8.00 4.00
167 Frank Baumann 8.00 4.00
168 Joe Cunningham 8.00 4.00
169 Ralph Terry 10.00 5.00
170 Vic Wertz 10.00 5.00
171 Harry Anderson 8.00 4.00
172 Don Gross 8.00 4.00
173 Eddie Yost 8.00 4.00
174 K.C. Athletics Team CL 15.00 3.00
175 Marv Throneberry RC 15.00 7.50
176 Bob Buhl 8.00 4.00
177 Al Smith 8.00 4.00
178 Ted Kluszewski 25.00 12.50
179 Willie Miranda 8.00 4.00
180 Lindy McDaniel 10.00 5.00
181 Willie Jones 8.00 4.00
182 Joe Caffie 8.00 4.00
183 Dave Jolly 8.00 4.00
184 Elvin Tappe 8.00 4.00
185 Ray Boone 10.00 5.00
186 Jack Meyer 8.00 4.00
187 Sandy Koufax 200.00 100.00
188 Milt Bolling UER 8.00 4.00
(Photo actually
Lou Berberet)
189 George Susce 8.00 4.00
190 Red Schoendienst 25.00 12.50
191 Art Ceccarelli 8.00 4.00
192 Milt Graff 8.00 4.00
193 Jerry Lumpe RC 8.00 4.00
194 Roger Craig 10.00 5.00
195 Whitey Lockman 10.00 5.00
196 Mike Garcia 10.00 5.00
197 Haywood Sullivan 10.00 5.00
198 Bill Virdon 10.00 5.00
199 Don Blasingame 8.00 4.00
200 Bob Keegan 8.00 4.00
201 Jim Bolger 8.00 4.00
202 Woody Held RC 8.00 4.00
203 Al Walker 8.00 4.00
204 Leo Kiely 8.00 4.00
205 Johnny Temple 10.00 5.00
206 Bob Shaw RC 8.00 4.00
207 Solly Hemus 8.00 4.00
208 Cal McLish 8.00 4.00
209 Bob Anderson 8.00 4.00
210 Wally Moon 10.00 5.00
211 Pete Burnside 8.00 4.00
212 Bubba Phillips 8.00 4.00
213 Red Wilson 8.00 4.00
214 Willard Schmidt 8.00 4.00
215 Jim Gilliam 15.00 7.50
216 St. Louis Cardinals 15.00 3.00
Team Card CL
217 Jack Harshman 8.00 4.00
218 Dick Rand 8.00 4.00
219 Camilo Pascual 10.00 5.00
220 Tom Brewer 8.00 4.00
221 Jerry Kindall RC 8.00 4.00
222 Bud Daley 8.00 4.00
223 Andy Pafko 10.00 5.00
224 Bob Grim 10.00 5.00
225 Billy Goodman 10.00 5.00
226 Bob Smith 8.00 4.00
227 Gene Stephens 8.00 4.00
228 Duke Maas 8.00 4.00
229 Frank Zupo 8.00 4.00
230 Richie Ashburn 40.00 20.00
231 Lloyd Merritt 8.00 4.00
232 Reno Bertoia 8.00 4.00
233 Mickey Vernon 10.00 5.00
234 Carl Sawatski 8.00 4.00
235 Tom Gorman 8.00 4.00
236 Ed Fitzgerald 8.00 4.00
237 Bill Wight 8.00 4.00
238 Bill Mazeroski 30.00 15.00
239 Chuck Stobbs 8.00 4.00
240 Bill Skowron 25.00 12.50
241 Dick Littlefield 8.00 4.00
242 Johnny Klippstein 8.00 4.00
243 Larry Raines 8.00 4.00
244 Don Demeter 8.00 4.00
245 Frank Lary 10.00 5.00
246 New York Yankees 100.00 20.00
Team Card CL
247 Casey Wise 8.00 4.00
248 Herman Wehmeier 8.00 4.00
249 Ray Moore 8.00 4.00
250 Roy Sievers 10.00 5.00
251 Warren Hacker 8.00 4.00
252 Bob Trowbridge 8.00 4.00
253 Don Mueller 10.00 5.00
254 Alex Grammas 8.00 4.00
255 Bob Turley 10.00 5.00
256 Chicago White Sox 15.00 3.00
Team Card CL
257 Hal Smith 8.00 4.00
258 Carl Erskine 15.00 7.50
259 Al Pilarcik 8.00 4.00
260 Frank Malzone 10.00 5.00
261 Turk Lown 8.00 4.00
262 Johnny Groth 8.00 4.00
263 Eddie Bressoud 10.00 5.00
264 Jack Sanford 10.00 5.00
265 Pete Runnels 10.00 5.00
266 Connie Johnson 8.00 4.00
267 Sherm Lollar 10.00 5.00
268 Granny Hamner 8.00 4.00
269 Paul Smith 8.00 4.00
270 Warren Spahn 60.00 30.00
271 Billy Martin 40.00 20.00
272 Ray Crone 8.00 4.00
273 Hal Smith 8.00 4.00
274 Rocky Bridges 8.00 4.00
275 Elston Howard 15.00 7.50
276 Bobby Avila 8.00 4.00
277 Virgil Trucks 10.00 5.00
278 Mack Burk 8.00 4.00
279 Bob Boyd 8.00 4.00
280 Jim Piersall 10.00 5.00
281 Sammy Taylor 8.00 4.00
282 Paul Foytack 8.00 4.00
283 Ray Shearer 8.00 4.00
284 Ray Katt 8.00 4.00
285 Frank Robinson 100.00 50.00
286 Gino Cimoli 8.00 4.00
287 Sam Jones 10.00 5.00
288 Harmon Killebrew 100.00 50.00
289 Lou Burdette 10.00 5.00
Bobby Shantz
290 Dick Donovan 8.00 4.00
291 Don Landrum 8.00 4.00
292 Ned Garver 8.00 4.00
293 Gene Freese 8.00 4.00
294 Hal Jeffcoat 8.00 4.00
295 Minnie Minoso 25.00 12.50
296 Ryne Duren RC 15.00 7.50
297 Don Buddin 8.00 4.00
298 Jim Hearn 8.00 4.00
299 Harry Simpson 8.00 4.00
300 Will Harridge PRES 15.00 7.50
Warren Giles
301 Randy Jackson 8.00 4.00
302 Mike Baxes 8.00 4.00
303 Neil Chrisley 8.00 4.00
304 Harvey Kuenn 25.00 12.50
Al Kaline
305 Clem Labine 10.00 5.00
306 Whammy Douglas 8.00 4.00
307 Brooks Robinson 100.00 50.00
308 Paul Giel 10.00 5.00
309 Gail Harris 8.00 4.00
310 Ernie Banks 100.00 50.00
311 Bob Purkey 8.00 4.00
312 Boston Red Sox 15.00 3.00
Team Card CL
313 Bob Rush 8.00 4.00
314 Duke Snider 50.00 25.00
Walt Alston MG
315 Bob Friend 10.00 5.00
316 Tito Francona 10.00 5.00
317 Albie Pearson 10.00 5.00
318 Frank House 8.00 4.00
319 Lou Skizas 8.00 4.00
320 Whitey Ford 60.00 30.00
321 Ted Kluszewski 100.00 50.00
Ted Williams
322 Harding Peterson 10.00 5.00
323 Elmer Valo 8.00 4.00
324 Hoyt Wilhelm 25.00 12.50
325 Joe Adcock 10.00 5.00
326 Bob Miller 8.00 4.00
327 Chicago Cubs 15.00 3.00
Team Card CL
328 Ike Delock 8.00 4.00
329 Bob Cerv 10.00 5.00
330 Ed Bailey 10.00 5.00
331 Pedro Ramos 8.00 4.00
332 Jim King 8.00 4.00
333 Andy Carey 10.00 5.00
334 Bob Friend 10.00 5.00
Billy Pierce
335 Ruben Gomez 8.00 4.00
336 Bert Hamric 8.00 4.00
337 Hank Aguirre 8.00 4.00
338 Walt Dropo 10.00 5.00
339 Fred Hatfield 8.00 4.00
340 Don Newcombe 15.00 7.50
341 Pittsburgh Pirates 15.00 3.00
Team Card CL
342 Jim Brosnan 10.00 5.00
343 Orlando Cepeda RC 100.00 50.00
344 Bob Porterfield 8.00 4.00
345 Jim Hegan 10.00 5.00
346 Steve Bilko 8.00 4.00
347 Don Rudolph 8.00 4.00
348 Chico Fernandez 8.00 4.00
349 Murry Dickson 8.00 4.00
350 Ken Boyer 25.00 12.50
351 Del Crandall 40.00 20.00
Eddie Mathews
Hank Aaron
Joe Adcock
352 Herb Score 15.00 7.50
353 Stan Lopata 8.00 4.00
354 Art Ditmar 10.00 5.00
355 Bill Bruton 10.00 5.00
356 Bob Malkmus 8.00 4.00
357 Danny McDevitt 8.00 4.00
358 Gene Baker 8.00 4.00
359 Billy Loes 10.00 5.00
360 Roy McMillan 10.00 5.00
361 Mike Fornieles 8.00 4.00
362 Ray Jablonski 8.00 4.00
363 Don Elston 8.00 4.00
364 Earl Battey 8.00 4.00
365 Tom Morgan 8.00 4.00
366 Gene Green 8.00 4.00
367 Jack Urban 8.00 4.00
368 Rocky Colavito 50.00 25.00
369 Ralph Lumenti 8.00 4.00
370 Yogi Berra 100.00 50.00
371 Marty Keough 8.00 4.00
372 Don Cardwell 8.00 4.00
373 Joe Pignatano 8.00 4.00
374 Brooks Lawrence 8.00 4.00
375 Pee Wee Reese 80.00 40.00
376 Charley Rabe 8.00 4.00
377A Milwaukee Braves 15.00 7.50
Team Card
(Alphabetical)
377B Milwaukee Team 100.00 20.00
numerical checklist
378 Hank Sauer 10.00 5.00
379 Ray Herbert 8.00 4.00
380 Charlie Maxwell 10.00 5.00
381 Hal Brown 8.00 4.00
382 Al Cicotte 8.00 4.00
383 Lou Berberet 8.00 4.00
384 John Goryl 8.00 4.00
385 Wilmer Mizell 10.00 5.00
386 Ed Bailey 15.00 7.50
Birdie Tebbetts MG
Frank Robinson
387 Wally Post 10.00 5.00
388 Billy Moran 8.00 4.00
389 Bill Taylor 8.00 4.00
390 Del Crandall 10.00 5.00
391 Dave Melton 8.00 4.00
392 Bennie Daniels 8.00 4.00
393 Tony Kubek 30.00 15.00
394 Jim Grant RC 8.00 4.00
395 Willard Nixon 8.00 4.00
396 Dutch Dotterer 8.00 4.00
397A Detroit Tigers 15.00 7.50
Team Card
(Alphabetical)
397B Detroit Team 100.00 20.00
numerical checklist
398 Gene Woodling 10.00 5.00
399 Marv Grissom 8.00 4.00
400 Nellie Fox 40.00 20.00
401 Don Bessent 8.00 4.00
402 Bobby Gene Smith 8.00 4.00
403 Steve Korcheck 8.00 4.00
404 Curt Simmons 10.00 5.00
405 Ken Aspromonte 8.00 4.00
406 Vic Power 10.00 5.00
407 Carlton Willey 10.00 5.00
408A Baltimore Orioles 15.00 7.50
Team Card
(Alphabetical)
408B Baltimore Team 100.00 20.00
numerical checklist
409 Frank Thomas 10.00 5.00
410 Murray Wall 8.00 4.00
411 Tony Taylor RC 10.00 5.00
412 Gerry Staley 8.00 4.00
413 Jim Davenport RC 8.00 4.00
414 Sammy White 8.00 4.00
415 Bob Bowman 8.00 4.00
416 Foster Castleman 8.00 4.00
417 Carl Furillo 15.00 7.50
418 Mickey Mantle 400.00 200.00
Hank Aaron
419 Bobby Shantz 10.00 5.00
420 Vada Pinson RC 40.00 20.00
421 Dixie Howell 8.00 4.00
422 Norm Zauchin 8.00 4.00
423 Phil Clark 8.00 4.00
424 Larry Doby 25.00 12.50
425 Sammy Esposito 8.00 4.00
426 Johnny O'Brien 10.00 5.00
427 Al Worthington 8.00 4.00
428A Cincinnati Reds 15.00 7.50
Team Card
(Alphabetical)
428B Cincinnati Team 100.00 20.00
numerical checklist
429 Gus Triandos 10.00 5.00
430 Bobby Thomson 10.00 5.00
431 Gene Conley 10.00 5.00
432 John Powers 8.00 4.00
433A Pancho Herrer ERR 600.00 300.00
433B Pancho Herrera COR 10.00 5.00
434 Harvey Kuenn 10.00 5.00
435 Ed Roebuck 10.00 5.00
436 Willie Mays 100.00 50.00
Duke Snider
437 Bob Speake 8.00 4.00
438 Whitey Herzog 10.00 5.00
439 Ray Narleski 8.00 4.00
440 Eddie Mathews 80.00 40.00
441 Jim Marshall 10.00 5.00
442 Phil Paine 8.00 4.00
443 Billy Harrell SP 20.00 10.00
444 Danny Kravitz 8.00 4.00
445 Bob Smith 8.00 4.00
446 Carroll Hardy SP 20.00 10.00
447 Ray Monzant 8.00 4.00
448 Charlie Lau RC 10.00 5.00
449 Gene Fodge 8.00 4.00
450 Preston Ward SP 20.00 10.00
451 Joe Taylor 8.00 4.00
452 Roman Mejias 8.00 4.00
453 Tom Qualters 8.00 4.00
454 Harry Hanebrink 8.00 4.00
455 Hal Griggs 8.00 4.00
456 Dick Brown 8.00 4.00
457 Milt Pappas RC 10.00 5.00
458 Julio Becquer 8.00 4.00
459 Ron Blackburn 8.00 4.00
460 Chuck Essegian 8.00 4.00
461 Ed Mayer 8.00 4.00
462 Gary Geiger SP 20.00 10.00
463 Vito Valentinetti 8.00 4.00
464 Curt Flood RC 30.00 15.00
465 Arnie Portocarrero 8.00 4.00
466 Pete Whisenant 8.00 4.00
467 Glen Hobbie 8.00 4.00
468 Bob Schmidt 8.00 4.00
469 Don Ferrarese 8.00 4.00
470 R.C. Stevens 8.00 4.00
471 Lenny Green 8.00 4.00
472 Joey Jay 10.00 5.00
473 Bill Renna 8.00 4.00
474 Roman Semproch 8.00 4.00
475 Fred Haney AS MG 25.00 7.50
Casey Stengel AS MG CL
476 Stan Musial AS TP 50.00 25.00
477 Bill Skowron AS 10.00 5.00
478 J.Temple AS UER 8.00 4.00
Card says record vs American League
Temple was NL AS
479 Nellie Fox AS 15.00 7.50
480 Eddie Mathews AS 30.00 15.00
481 Frank Malzone AS 8.00 4.00
482 Ernie Banks AS 40.00 20.00
483 Luis Aparicio AS 15.00 7.50
484 Frank Robinson AS 40.00 20.00
485 Ted Williams AS 150.00 75.00
486 Willie Mays AS 60.00 30.00
487 Mickey Mantle AS TP 200.00 90.00
488 Hank Aaron AS 60.00 30.00
489 Jackie Jensen AS 10.00 5.00
490 Ed Bailey AS 8.00 4.00
491 Sherm Lollar AS 8.00 4.00
492 Bob Friend AS 8.00 4.00
493 Bob Turley AS 10.00 5.00
494 Warren Spahn AS 25.00 12.50
495 Herb Score AS 15.00 3.00
NNO Contest Cards 40.00 20.00

1959 Topps

The cards in this 572-card set measure 2 1/2" by 3 1/2". The 1959 Topps set contains bust pictures of the players in a colored circle. Card numbers 551 to 572 are Sporting News All-Star Selections. High numbers 507 to 572 have the card number in a black background on the reverse rather than a green background as in the lower numbers. The high numbers are more difficult to obtain. Several cards in the 300s exist with or without an extra traded or option line on the back of the card. Cards 199 to 286 exist with either white or gray backs. There is no price differential for either colored back. Cards 461 to 470 contain "Highlights" while cards 116 to 146 give an alphabetically ordered listing of "Rookie Prospects." These Rookie Prospects (RP) were Topps' first organized inclusion of untested "Rookie" cards. Card 440 features Lew Burdette erroneously posing as a left-handed pitcher. Cards were issued in one-card penny packs or six-card nickel packs. There were some three-card advertising panels produced by Topps; the players included were from the first series. Panels which had Ted Kluszewski's card back on the back included Don McMahon/Red Wilson/Bob Boyd; Joe Pignatano/Sam Jones/Jack Urban also with Kluszewski's card back on back. Strips with Nellie Fox on the back included Billy Hunter/Chuck Stobbs/Carl Sawatski; Vito

Valentinetti/Ken Lehman/Ed Bouchee; Mel Roach/Brooks Lawrence/Warren Spahn. Other panels include Harvey Kuenn/Alex Grammas/ Bob Cerv; and Bob Cerv/Jim Bolger/Mickey Mantle. When separated, these advertising cards are distinguished by the non-standard card back, i.e., part of an advertisement for the 1959 Topps set instead of the typical statistics and biographical information about the player pictured. The key Rookie Cards in this set are Felipe Alou, Sparky Anderson (called George on the card), Norm Cash, Bob Gibson, and Bill White.

	NM	Ex
COMPLETE SET (572)	5000.00	2500.00
COMMON CARD (1-110)	6.00	3.00
COMMON (111-506)	4.00	2.00
COMMON (507-572)	15.00	7.50
WRAPPER (1-CENT)	125.00	60.00
WRAPPER (5-CENT)	100.00	50.00
1 Ford Frick COMM	60.00	16.50
2 Eddie Yost	8.00	4.00
3 Don McMahon	8.00	4.00
4 Albie Pearson	8.00	4.00
5 Dick Donovan	8.00	4.00
6 Alex Grammas	6.00	3.00
7 Al Pilarcik	6.00	3.00
8 Phillies Team CL	80.00	16.00
9 Paul Giel	8.00	4.00
10 Mickey Mantle	800.00	350.00
11 Billy Hunter	8.00	4.00
12 Vern Law	8.00	4.00
13 Dick Gernert	6.00	3.00
14 Pete Whisenant	6.00	3.00
15 Dick Drott	6.00	3.00
16 Joe Pignatano	6.00	3.00
17 Frank Thomas Danny Murtaugh MG Ted Kluszewski	8.00	4.00
18 Jack Urban	6.00	3.00
19 Eddie Bressoud	6.00	3.00
20 Duke Snider	60.00	30.00
21 Connie Johnson	6.00	3.00
22 Al Smith	8.00	4.00
23 Murry Dickson	8.00	4.00
24 Red Wilson	6.00	3.00
25 Don Hoak	8.00	4.00
26 Chuck Stobbs	6.00	3.00
27 Andy Pafko	8.00	4.00
28 Al Worthington	6.00	3.00
29 Jim Bolger	6.00	3.00
30 Nellie Fox	30.00	15.00
31 Ken Lehman	6.00	3.00
32 Don Buddin	6.00	3.00
33 Ed Fitzgerald	6.00	3.00
34 Al Kaline Charley Maxwell	20.00	10.00
35 Ted Kluszewski	12.00	6.00
36 Hank Aguirre	6.00	3.00
37 Gene Green	6.00	3.00
38 Morrie Martin	6.00	3.00
39 Ed Bouchee	6.00	3.00
40A Warren Spahn ERR (Born 1931)	80.00	40.00
40B Warren Spahn ERR (Born 1931, but three is partially obscured)	100.00	50.00
40C Warren Spahn COR (Born 1921)	60.00	30.00
41 Bob Martyn	6.00	3.00
42 Murray Wall	6.00	3.00
43 Steve Bilko	6.00	3.00
44 Vito Valentinetti	6.00	3.00
45 Andy Carey	8.00	4.00
46 Bill R. Henry	6.00	3.00
47 Jim Finigan	6.00	3.00
48 Orioles Team CL	25.00	5.00
49 Bill Hall	6.00	3.00
50 Willie Mays	150.00	75.00
51 Rip Coleman	6.00	3.00
52 Coot Veal	6.00	3.00
53 Stan Williams RC	8.00	4.00
54 Mel Roach	6.00	3.00
55 Tom Brewer	6.00	3.00
56 Carl Sawatski	6.00	3.00
57 Al Cicotte	6.00	3.00
58 Eddie Miksis	6.00	3.00
59 Irv Noren	8.00	4.00
60 Bob Turley	8.00	4.00
61 Dick Brown	6.00	3.00
62 Tony Taylor	8.00	4.00
63 Jim Hearn	6.00	3.00
64 Joe DeMaestri	6.00	3.00
65 Frank Torre	8.00	4.00
66 Joe Ginsberg	6.00	3.00
67 Brooks Lawrence	6.00	3.00
68 Dick Schofield	8.00	4.00
69 Giants Team CL	25.00	5.00
70 Harvey Kuenn	8.00	4.00
71 Don Bessent	6.00	3.00
72 Bill Renna	6.00	3.00
73 Ron Jackson	8.00	4.00
74 Jim Lemon Cookie Lavagetto MG Roy Sievers	8.00	4.00
75 Sam Jones	8.00	4.00
76 Bobby Richardson	20.00	10.00
77 John Goryl	6.00	3.00
78 Pedro Ramos	6.00	3.00
79 Harry Chiti	6.00	3.00
80 Minnie Minoso	12.00	6.00
81 Hal Jeffcoat	6.00	3.00
82 Bob Boyd	6.00	3.00
83 Bob Smith	6.00	3.00
84 Reno Bertoia	6.00	3.00
85 Harry Anderson	6.00	3.00
86 Bob Keegan	8.00	4.00
87 Danny O'Connell	6.00	3.00
88 Herb Score	12.00	6.00
89 Billy Gardner	6.00	3.00
90 Bill Skowron	12.00	6.00
91 Herb Moford	6.00	3.00
92 Dave Philley	6.00	3.00
93 Julio Becquer	6.00	3.00
94 White Sox Team CL	40.00	8.00
95 Carl Willey	6.00	3.00
96 Lou Berberet	6.00	3.00
97 Jerry Lynch	8.00	4.00
98 Arnie Portocarrero	6.00	3.00
99 Ted Kazanski	6.00	3.00
100 Bob Cerv	8.00	4.00
101 Alex Kellner	6.00	3.00
102 Felipe Alou RC	30.00	15.00
103 Billy Goodman	8.00	4.00
104 Del Rice	8.00	4.00
105 Lee Walls	6.00	3.00
106 Hal Woodeshick	6.00	3.00
107 Norm Larker	8.00	4.00
108 Zack Monroe	8.00	4.00
109 Bob Schmidt	6.00	3.00
110 George Witt	8.00	4.00
111 Redlegs Team CL	15.00	3.00
112 Billy Consolo	4.00	2.00
113 Taylor Phillips	4.00	2.00
114 Earl Battey	8.00	4.00
115 Mickey Vernon	8.00	4.00
116 Bob Allison RP RC	12.00	6.00
117 J.Blanchard RP RC	12.00	6.00
118 John Buzhardt RP	5.00	2.50
119 John Callison RP RC	12.00	6.00
120 Chuck Coles RP	5.00	2.50
121 Bob Conley RP	5.00	2.50
122 Bennie Daniels RP	5.00	2.50
123 Don Dillard RP	5.00	2.50
124 Dan Dobbek RP	5.00	2.50
125 Ron Fairly RP RC	12.00	6.00
126 Eddie Haas RP	5.00	2.50
127 Kent Hadley RP	5.00	2.50
128 Bob Hartman RP	5.00	2.50
129 Frank Herrera RP	5.00	2.50
130 Lou Jackson RP	5.00	2.50
131 Deron Johnson RP RC	12.00	6.00
132 Don Lee RP	5.00	2.50
133 Bob Lillis RP RC	5.00	2.50
134 Jim McDaniel RP	5.00	2.50
135 Gene Oliver RP	5.00	2.50
136 Jim O'Toole RP RC	5.00	2.50
137 Dick Ricketts RP	5.00	2.50
138 John Romano RP RC	5.00	2.50
139 Ed Sadowski RP	5.00	2.50
140 Charlie Secrest RP	5.00	2.50
141 Joe Shipley RP	5.00	2.50
142 Dick Stigman RP	5.00	2.50
143 Willie Tasby RP RC	5.00	2.50
144 Jerry Walker RP	5.00	2.50
145 Dom Zanni RP	5.00	2.50
146 Jerry Zimmerman RP	5.00	2.50
147 Dale Long Ernie Banks Walt Moryn	30.00	15.00
148 Mike McCormick	8.00	4.00
149 Jim Bunning	20.00	10.00
150 Stan Musial	125.00	60.00
151 Bob Malkmus	4.00	2.00
152 Johnny Klippstein	4.00	2.00
153 Jim Marshall	4.00	2.00
154 Ray Herbert	4.00	2.00
155 Enos Slaughter	20.00	10.00
156 Billy Pierce Robin Roberts	12.00	6.00
157 Felix Mantilla	4.00	2.00
158 Walt Dropo	4.00	2.00
159 Bob Shaw	8.00	4.00
160 Dick Groat	8.00	4.00
161 Frank Baumann	4.00	2.00
162 Bobby G. Smith	4.00	2.00
163 Sandy Koufax	150.00	75.00
164 Johnny Groth	4.00	2.00
165 Bill Bruton	4.00	2.00
166 Minnie Minoso Rocky Colavito (Misspelled Colovito on card back) Larry Doby	30.00	15.00
167 Duke Maas	4.00	2.00
168 Carroll Hardy	4.00	2.00
169 Ted Abernathy	4.00	2.00
170 Gene Woodling	8.00	4.00
171 Willard Schmidt	4.00	2.00
172 Athletics Team CL	15.00	3.00
173 Bill Monbouquette	8.00	4.00
174 Jim Pendleton	4.00	2.00
175 Dick Farrell	8.00	4.00
176 Preston Ward	4.00	2.00
177 John Briggs	4.00	2.00
178 Ruben Amaro RC	12.00	6.00
179 Don Rudolph	4.00	2.00
180 Yogi Berra	80.00	40.00
181 Bob Porterfield	4.00	2.00
182 Milt Graff	4.00	2.00
183 Stu Miller	8.00	4.00
184 Harvey Haddix	8.00	4.00
185 Jim Busby	4.00	2.00
186 Mudcat Grant	8.00	4.00
187 Bubba Phillips	4.00	2.00
188 Juan Pizarro	4.00	2.00
189 Neil Chrisley	4.00	2.00
190 Bill Virdon	8.00	4.00
191 Russ Kemmerer	4.00	2.00
192 Charlie Beamon	4.00	2.00
193 Sammy Taylor	4.00	2.00
194 Jim Brosnan	8.00	4.00
195 Rip Repulski	4.00	2.00
196 Billy Moran	4.00	2.00
197 Ray Semproch	4.00	2.00
198 Jim Davenport	8.00	4.00
199 Leo Kiely	4.00	2.00
200 W.Giles NL PRES	8.00	4.00
201 Tom Acker	4.00	2.00
202 Roger Maris	125.00	60.00
203 Ossie Virgil	4.00	2.00
204 Casey Wise	4.00	2.00
205 Don Larsen	8.00	4.00
206 Carl Furillo	12.00	6.00
207 George Strickland	4.00	2.00
208 Willie Jones	4.00	2.00
209 Lenny Green	4.00	2.00
210 Ed Bailey	4.00	2.00
211 Bob Blaylock	4.00	2.00
212 Hank Aaron Eddie Mathews	80.00	40.00
213 Jim Rivera	8.00	4.00
214 Marcelino Solis	4.00	2.00
215 Jim Lemon	8.00	4.00
216 Andre Rodgers	4.00	2.00
217 Carl Erskine	12.00	6.00
218 Roman Mejias	4.00	2.00
219 George Zuverink	4.00	2.00
220 Frank Malzone	8.00	4.00
221 Bob Bowman	4.00	2.00
222 Bobby Shantz	8.00	4.00
223 Cardinals Team CL	15.00	3.00
224 Claude Osteen RC	8.00	4.00
225 Johnny Logan	8.00	4.00
226 Art Ceccarelli	4.00	2.00
227 Hal W. Smith	4.00	2.00
228 Don Gross	4.00	2.00
229 Vic Power	8.00	4.00
230 Bill Fischer	4.00	2.00
231 Ellis Burton	4.00	2.00
232 Eddie Kasko	4.00	2.00
233 Paul Foytack	4.00	2.00
234 Chuck Tanner	8.00	4.00
235 Valmy Thomas	4.00	2.00
236 Ted Bowsfield	4.00	2.00
237 Gil McDougald Bob Turley Bobby Richardson	12.00	6.00
238 Gene Baker	4.00	2.00
239 Bob Trowbridge	4.00	2.00
240 Hank Bauer	12.00	6.00
241 Billy Muffett	4.00	2.00
242 Ron Samford	4.00	2.00
243 Marv Grissom	4.00	2.00
244 Ted Gray	4.00	2.00
245 Ned Garver	4.00	2.00
246 J.W. Porter	4.00	2.00
247 Don Ferrarese	4.00	2.00
248 Red Sox Team CL	15.00	3.00
249 Bobby Adams	4.00	2.00
250 Billy O'Dell	4.00	2.00
251 Clete Boyer	12.00	6.00
252 Ray Boone	8.00	4.00
253 Seth Morehead	4.00	2.00
254 Zeke Bella	4.00	2.00
255 Del Ennis	8.00	4.00
256 Jerry Davie	4.00	2.00
257 Leon Wagner RC	8.00	4.00
258 Fred Kipp	4.00	2.00
259 Jim Pisoni	4.00	2.00
260 Early Wynn UER 1957 Cleevland	20.00	10.00
261 Gene Stephens	4.00	2.00
262 Johnny Podres Clem Labine Don Drysdale	12.00	6.00
263 Bud Daley	4.00	2.00
264 Chico Carrasquel	4.00	2.00
265 Ron Kline	4.00	2.00
266 Woody Held	4.00	2.00
267 John Romonosky	4.00	2.00
268 Tito Francona	8.00	4.00
269 Jack Meyer	4.00	2.00
270 Gil Hodges	30.00	15.00
271 Orlando Pena	4.00	2.00
272 Jerry Lumpe	4.00	2.00
273 Joey Jay	8.00	4.00
274 Jerry Kindall	8.00	4.00
275 Jack Sanford	8.00	4.00
276 Pete Daley	4.00	2.00
277 Turk Lown	8.00	4.00
278 Chuck Essegian	4.00	2.00
279 Ernie Johnson	4.00	2.00
280 Frank Bolling	4.00	2.00
281 Walt Craddock	4.00	2.00
282 R.C. Stevens	4.00	2.00
283 Russ Heman	4.00	2.00
284 Steve Korcheck	4.00	2.00
285 Joe Cunningham	4.00	2.00
286 Dean Stone	4.00	2.00
287 Don Zimmer	12.00	6.00
288 Dutch Dotterer	4.00	2.00
289 Johnny Kucks	8.00	4.00
290 Wes Covington	8.00	4.00
291 Pedro Ramos Camilo Pascual	4.00	2.00
292 Dick Williams	8.00	4.00
293 Ray Moore	4.00	2.00
294 Hank Foiles	4.00	2.00
295 Billy Martin	30.00	15.00
296 Ernie Broglio RC	8.00	4.00
297 Jackie Brandt	4.00	2.00
298 Tex Clevenger	4.00	2.00
299 Billy Klaus	4.00	2.00
300 Richie Ashburn	30.00	15.00
301 Earl Averill	4.00	2.00
302 Don Mossi	8.00	4.00
303 Marty Keough	4.00	2.00
304 Cubs Team CL	15.00	3.00
305 Curt Raydon	4.00	2.00
306 Jim Gilliam	8.00	4.00
307 Curt Barclay	4.00	2.00
308 Norm Siebern	4.00	2.00
309 Sal Maglie	8.00	4.00
310 Luis Aparicio	20.00	10.00
311 Norm Zauchin	4.00	2.00
312 Don Newcombe	8.00	4.00
313 Frank House	4.00	2.00
314 Don Cardwell	4.00	2.00
315 Joe Adcock	8.00	4.00
316A Ralph Lumenti UER (Option) (Photo actually Camilo Pascual)	4.00	2.00
316B Ralph Lumenti UER (No option) (Photo actually Camilo Pascual)	80.00	40.00
317 Willie Mays Richie Ashburn	80.00	40.00
318 Rocky Bridges	4.00	2.00
319 Dave Hillman	4.00	2.00
320 Bob Skinner	8.00	4.00
321A Bob Giallombardo (Option)	8.00	4.00
321B Bob Giallombardo (No option)	80.00	40.00
322A Harry Hanebrink (Traded)	8.00	4.00
322B Harry Hanebrink (No trade)	80.00	40.00
323 Frank Sullivan	4.00	2.00
324 Don Demeter	4.00	2.00
325 Ken Boyer	12.00	6.00
326 Marv Throneberry	8.00	4.00
327 Gary Bell	4.00	2.00
328 Lou Skizas	4.00	2.00
329 Tigers Team CL	15.00	3.00
330 Gus Triandos	8.00	4.00
331 Steve Boros	4.00	2.00
332 Ray Monzant	4.00	2.00
333 Harry Simpson	4.00	2.00
334 Glen Hobbie	4.00	2.00
335 Johnny Temple	8.00	4.00
336A Billy Loes (With traded line)	8.00	4.00
336B Billy Loes (No trade)	80.00	40.00
337 George Crowe	4.00	2.00
338 Sparky Anderson RC	60.00	30.00
339 Roy Face	8.00	4.00
340 Roy Sievers	8.00	4.00
341 Tom Qualters	4.00	2.00
342 Ray Jablonski	4.00	2.00
343 Billy Hoeft	4.00	2.00
344 Russ Nixon	4.00	2.00
345 Gil McDougald	12.00	6.00
346 Dave Sisler Tom Brewer	4.00	2.00
347 Bob Buhl	4.00	2.00
348 Ted Lepcio	4.00	2.00
349 Hoyt Wilhelm	20.00	10.00
350 Ernie Banks	80.00	40.00
351 Earl Torgeson	4.00	2.00
352 Robin Roberts	20.00	10.00
353 Curt Flood	8.00	4.00
354 Pete Burnside	4.00	2.00
355 Jimmy Piersall	8.00	4.00
356 Bob Mabe	4.00	2.00
357 Dick Stuart RC	8.00	4.00
358 Ralph Terry	8.00	4.00
359 Bill White RC	20.00	10.00
360 Al Kaline	60.00	30.00
361 Willard Nixon	4.00	2.00
362A Dolan Nichols (With option line)	4.00	2.00
362B Dolan Nichols (No option)	80.00	40.00
363 Bobby Avila	4.00	2.00
364 Danny McDevitt	4.00	2.00
365 Gus Bell	8.00	4.00
366 Humberto Robinson	4.00	2.00
367 Cal Neeman	4.00	2.00
368 Don Mueller	8.00	4.00
369 Dick Tomanek	4.00	2.00
370 Pete Runnels	8.00	4.00
371 Dick Brodowski	4.00	2.00
372 Jim Hegan	8.00	4.00
373 Herb Plews	4.00	2.00
374 Art Ditmar	8.00	4.00
375 Bob Nieman	4.00	2.00
376 Hal Naragon	4.00	2.00
377 John Antonelli	8.00	4.00
378 Gail Harris	8.00	4.00
379 Bob Miller	4.00	2.00
380 Hank Aaron	150.00	60.00
381 Mike Baxes	4.00	2.00
382 Curt Simmons	8.00	4.00
383 Don Larsen Casey Stengel MG	12.00	6.00
384 Dave Sisler	4.00	2.00
385 Sherm Lollar	8.00	4.00
386 Jim Delsing	4.00	2.00
387 Don Drysdale	50.00	25.00
388 Bob Will	4.00	2.00
389 Joe Nuxhall	8.00	4.00
390 Orlando Cepeda	20.00	10.00
391 Milt Pappas	8.00	4.00
392 Whitey Herzog	8.00	4.00
393 Frank Lary	8.00	4.00
394 Randy Jackson	4.00	2.00
395 Elston Howard	12.00	6.00
396 Bob Rush	4.00	2.00
397 Senators Team CL	15.00	3.00
398 Wally Post	8.00	4.00
399 Larry Jackson	4.00	2.00
400 Jackie Jensen	8.00	4.00
401 Ron Blackburn	4.00	2.00
402 Hector Lopez	8.00	4.00
403 Clem Labine	8.00	4.00
404 Hank Sauer	8.00	4.00
405 Roy McMillan	8.00	4.00
406 Solly Drake	4.00	2.00
407 Moe Drabowsky	8.00	4.00
408 Nellie Fox Luis Aparicio	40.00	20.00
409 Gus Zernial	8.00	4.00
410 Billy Pierce	8.00	4.00
411 Whitey Lockman	8.00	4.00
412 Stan Lopata	4.00	2.00
413 Camilo Pascual UER (Listed as Camillo on front and Pasqual on back)	8.00	4.00
414 Dale Long	8.00	4.00
415 Bill Mazeroski	12.00	6.00
416 Haywood Sullivan	8.00	4.00
417 Virgil Trucks	8.00	4.00
418 Gino Cimoli	4.00	2.00
419 Braves Team CL	15.00	3.00
420 Rocky Colavito	30.00	15.00
421 Herman Wehmeier	4.00	2.00
422 Hobie Landrith	4.00	2.00
423 Bob Grim	8.00	4.00
424 Ken Aspromonte	4.00	2.00
425 Del Crandall	8.00	4.00
426 Gerry Staley	8.00	4.00
427 Charlie Neal	8.00	4.00
428 Ron Kline Bob Friend Vernon Law Roy Face	4.00	2.00
429 Bobby Thomson	8.00	4.00
430 Whitey Ford	60.00	30.00
431 Whammy Douglas	4.00	2.00
432 Smoky Burgess	8.00	4.00
433 Billy Harrell	4.00	2.00
434 Hal Griggs	4.00	2.00
435 Frank Robinson	50.00	25.00
436 Granny Hamner	4.00	2.00
437 Ike Delock	4.00	2.00
438 Sammy Esposito	4.00	2.00
439 Brooks Robinson	50.00	25.00
440 Lou Burdette (Posing as if lefthanded)	8.00	4.00
441 John Roseboro	8.00	4.00
442 Ray Narleski	4.00	2.00
443 Daryl Spencer	4.00	2.00
444 Ron Hansen RC	8.00	4.00
445 Cal McLish	4.00	2.00
446 Rocky Nelson	4.00	2.00
447 Bob Anderson	4.00	2.00
448 Vada Pinson UER (Born: 8/8/38 should be 8/11/38)	12.00	6.00
449 Tom Gorman	4.00	2.00
450 Eddie Mathews	40.00	20.00
451 Jimmy Constable	4.00	2.00
452 Chico Fernandez	4.00	2.00
453 Les Moss	4.00	2.00
454 Phil Clark	4.00	2.00
455 Larry Doby	12.00	6.00
456 Jerry Casale	4.00	2.00
457 Dodgers Team CL	30.00	6.00
458 Gordon Jones	4.00	2.00
459 Bill Tuttle	4.00	2.00
460 Bob Friend	8.00	4.00
461 Mickey Mantle HL	125.00	60.00
462 Rocky Colavito HL	12.00	6.00
463 Al Kaline HL	30.00	15.00
464 Willie Mays HL 54 World Series Catch	40.00	20.00
465 Roy Sievers HL	8.00	4.00
466 Billy Pierce HL	8.00	4.00
467 Hank Aaron HL	40.00	20.00
468 Duke Snider HL	20.00	10.00
469 Ernie Banks HL	20.00	10.00
470 Stan Musial HL 3,000 Hits	30.00	15.00
471 Tom Sturdivant	4.00	2.00
472 Gene Freese	4.00	2.00
473 Mike Fornieles	4.00	2.00
474 Moe Thacker	4.00	2.00
475 Jack Harshman	4.00	2.00
476 Indians Team CL	15.00	3.00
477 Barry Latman	4.00	2.00
478 Roberto Clemente	175.00	90.00
479 Lindy McDaniel	8.00	4.00
480 Red Schoendienst	12.00	6.00
481 Charlie Maxwell	8.00	4.00
482 Russ Meyer	4.00	2.00
483 Clint Courtney	4.00	2.00
484 Willie Kirkland	4.00	2.00
485 Ryne Duren	8.00	4.00
486 Sammy White	4.00	2.00
487 Hal Brown	4.00	2.00
488 Walt Moryn	4.00	2.00
489 John Powers	4.00	2.00
490 Frank Thomas	8.00	4.00
491 Don Blasingame	4.00	2.00
492 Gene Conley	8.00	4.00
493 Jim Landis	8.00	4.00
494 Don Pavletich	4.00	2.00
495 Johnny Podres	12.00	6.00
496 W.Terwilliger UER Athlftics on front	4.00	2.00
497 Hal R. Smith	4.00	2.00
498 Dick Hyde	4.00	2.00
499 Johnny O'Brien	8.00	4.00
500 Vic Wertz	8.00	4.00
501 Bob Tiefenauer	4.00	2.00
502 Alvin Dark	8.00	4.00
503 Jim Owens	4.00	2.00
504 Ossie Alvarez	4.00	2.00
505 Tony Kubek	12.00	6.00
506 Bob Purkey	4.00	2.00
507 Bob Hale	15.00	7.50
508 Art Fowler	15.00	7.50
509 Norm Cash RC	80.00	40.00
510 Yankees Team CL	125.00	25.00
511 George Susce	15.00	7.50
512 George Altman	15.00	7.50
513 Tommy Carroll	15.00	7.50
514 Bob Gibson RC	250.00	125.00
515 Harmon Killebrew	125.00	60.00
516 Mike Garcia	20.00	10.00
517 Joe Koppe	15.00	7.50
518 Mike Cueller UER RC Sic, Cuellar	30.00	15.00
519 Pete Runnels Dick Gernert Frank Malzone	20.00	10.00
520 Don Elston	15.00	7.50
521 Gary Geiger	15.00	7.50
522 Gene Snyder	15.00	7.50
523 Harry Bright	15.00	7.50
524 Larry Osborne	15.00	7.50
525 Jim Coates	20.00	10.00
526 Bob Speake	15.00	7.50
527 Solly Hemus	15.00	7.50
528 Pirates Team CL	80.00	16.00
529 G.Bamberger RC	20.00	10.00
530 Wally Moon	20.00	10.00
531 Ray Webster	15.00	7.50
532 Mark Freeman	15.00	7.50
533 Darrell Johnson	20.00	10.00
534 Faye Throneberry	15.00	7.50
535 Ruben Gomez	15.00	7.50
536 Danny Kravitz	15.00	7.50
537 Rudolph Arias	15.00	7.50
538 Chick King	15.00	7.50
539 Gary Blaylock	15.00	7.50
540 Willie Miranda	15.00	7.50
541 Bob Thurman	15.00	7.50
542 Jim Perry RC	30.00	15.00
543 Bob Skinner Bill Virdon Roberto Clemente	125.00	60.00
544 Lee Tate	15.00	7.50
545 Tom Morgan	15.00	7.50
546 Al Schroll	15.00	7.50
547 Jim Baxes	15.00	7.50
548 Elmer Singleton	15.00	7.50
549 Howie Nunn	15.00	7.50
550 Roy Campanella (Symbol of Courage)	150.00	75.00
551 Fred Haney AS MG	15.00	7.50
552 Casey Stengel AS MG	30.00	15.00
553 Orlando Cepeda AS	30.00	15.00
554 Bill Skowron AS	20.00	10.00
555 Bill Mazeroski AS	30.00	15.00
556 Nellie Fox AS	40.00	20.00
557 Ken Boyer AS	30.00	15.00
558 Frank Malzone AS	15.00	7.50
559 Ernie Banks AS	60.00	30.00
560 Luis Aparicio AS	40.00	20.00
561 Hank Aaron AS	125.00	60.00
562 Al Kaline AS	60.00	30.00
563 Willie Mays AS	125.00	60.00
564 Mickey Mantle AS	300.00	150.00

565 Wes Covington AS 20.00 10.00
566 Roy Sievers AS 15.00 7.50
567 Del Crandall AS 15.00 7.50
568 Gus Triandos AS 15.00 7.50
569 Bob Friend AS 15.00 7.50
570 Bob Turley AS 15.00 7.50
571 Warren Spahn AS 50.00 25.00
572 Billy Pierce AS................. 40.00 13.00

1960 Topps

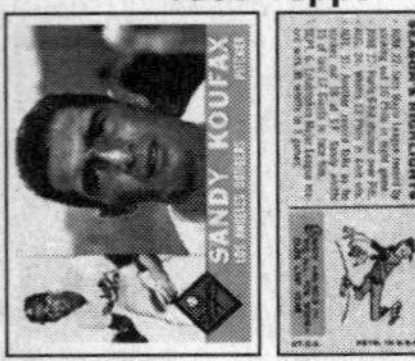

The cards in this 572-card set measure 2 1/2" by 3 1/2". The 1960 Topps set is the only Topps standard size issue to use a horizontally oriented front. World Series cards appeared for the first time (385 to 391), and there is a Rookie Prospect (RP) series (117-148), the most famous of which is Carl Yastrzemski, and a Sport Magazine All-Star Selection (AS) series (553-572). There are 16 manager cards listed alphabetically from 212 through 227. The 1959 Topps All-Rookie team is featured on cards 316-325. The coaching staff of each team was also afforded their own card in a 16-card subset (455-470). There is no price differential for either color back. The high series (507-572) were printed on a more limited basis than the rest of the set. The team cards have series checklists on the reverse. Cards were issued in one-card penny packs, six-card nickel packs (which came 24 to a box), 10 cent cello packs (which came 36 packs to a box) and 36-card rack packs which cost 29 cents . Three card ad-sheets have been seen. One such sheet features Wayne Terwilliger, Kent Hadley and Faye Throneberry on the front with Gene Woodling and an Ad on the back. Another sheet featured Hank Foiles/Hobie Landrith and Hal Smith on the front. The key Rookie Cards in this set are Jim Kaat, Willie McCovey and Carl Yastrzemski. Recently, a Kent Hadley was discovered with a Kansas City A's logo on the front, while this card was rumoured to exist for years, this is the first known spotting of the card. Each series of this set had different card backs. Cards numbered 1-110 had cream colored white back, cards numbered 111-198 had grey backs, cards numbered 119-286 had cream colored white backs, cards numbered 287-374 had grey backs. Cards 375 to 440 come with either gray, white or cream-colored white backs. It is believed that the pure white backs are the most difficult of the three colors in this card range. Cards numbered 441-572 conclude this set and they all have grey backs.

NM Ex
COMPLETE SET (572).......... 5000.00 2000.00
COMMON CARD (1-440) 4.00 1.60
COMMON (441-506) 8.00 3.20
COMMON (507-572) 15.00 6.00
WRAPPER (1-CENT) 900.00 350.00
WRAP. (1-CENT REPEAT) 500.00 200.00
WRAPPER (5-CENT) 40.00 16.00
1 Early Wynn.......................... 40.00 10.00
2 Roman Mejias 4.00 1.60
3 Joe Adcock 6.00 2.40
4 Bob Purkey 4.00 1.60
5 Wally Moon.......................... 6.00 2.40
6 Lou Berberet 4.00 1.60
7 Willie Mays 25.00 10.00
Bill Rigney MG
8 Bud Daley............................. 4.00 1.60
9 Faye Throneberry 4.00 1.60
10 Ernie Banks 50.00 20.00
11 Norm Siebern....................... 4.00 1.60
12 Milt Pappas......................... 6.00 2.40
13 Wally Post........................... 6.00 2.40
14 Jim Grant............................ 6.00 2.40
15 Pete Runnels........................ 6.00 2.40
16 Ernie Broglio 6.00 2.40
17 Johnny Callison 6.00 2.40
18 Dodgers Team CL 50.00 10.00
19 Felix Mantilla 4.00 1.60
20 Roy Face 6.00 2.40
21 Dutch Dotterer 4.00 1.60
22 Rocky Bridges....................... 4.00 1.60
23 Eddie Fisher 4.00 1.60
24 Dick Gray 4.00 1.60
25 Roy Sievers......................... 6.00 2.40
26 Wayne Terwilliger.................. 4.00 1.60
27 Dick Drott........................... 4.00 1.60
28 Brooks Robinson 50.00 20.00
29 Clem Labine 6.00 2.40
30 Tito Francona 4.00 1.60
31 Sammy Esposito 4.00 1.60
32 Jim O'Toole 4.00 1.60
Vada Pinson
33 Tom Morgan 4.00 1.60
34 Sparky Anderson 15.00 6.00
35 Whitey Ford 50.00 20.00
36 Russ Nixon 4.00 1.60
37 Bill Bruton........................... 4.00 1.60
38 Jerry Casale 4.00 1.60
39 Earl Averill 4.00 1.60
40 Joe Cunningham.................... 4.00 1.60
41 Barry Latman 4.00 1.60
42 Hobie Landrith...................... 4.00 1.60
43 Senators Team CL............... 10.00 2.00
44 Bobby Locke 4.00 1.60
45 Roy McMillan........................ 6.00 2.40
46 Jerry Fisher.......................... 4.00 1.60
47 Don Zimmer 6.00 2.40
48 Hal W. Smith 4.00 1.60
49 Curt Raydon 4.00 1.60
50 Al Kaline........................... 50.00 20.00
51 Jim Coates 6.00 2.40
52 Dave Philley 4.00 1.60
53 Jackie Brandt 4.00 1.60
54 Mike Fornieles 4.00 1.60
55 Bill Mazeroski...................... 15.00 6.00
56 Steve Korcheck 4.00 1.60
57 Turk Lown 4.00 1.60
Gerry Staley
58 Gino Cimoli 4.00 1.60
58A Gino Cimoli ....
Cardinals Team Logo
59 Juan Pizarro 4.00 1.60
60 Gus Triandos 6.00 2.40
61 Eddie Kasko 4.00 1.60
62 Roger Craig............................ 6.00 2.40
63 George Strickland 4.00 1.60
64 Jack Meyer............................. 4.00 1.60
65 Elston Howard 6.00 2.40
66 Bob Trowbridge 4.00 1.60
67 Jose Pagan 4.00 1.60
68 Dave Hillman.......................... 4.00 1.60
69 Billy Goodman 6.00 2.40
70 Lew Burdette.......................... 6.00 2.40
Card spelled as Lou on front and back
71 Marty Keough 4.00 1.60
72 Tigers Team CL 25.00 5.00
73 Bob Gibson 50.00 20.00
74 Walt Moryn 4.00 1.60
75 Vic Power.............................. 6.00 2.40
76 Bill Fischer 4.00 1.60
77 Hank Foiles 4.00 1.60
78 Bob Grim 4.00 1.60
79 Walt Dropo............................ 4.00 1.60
80 Johnny Antonelli 6.00 2.40
81 Russ Snyder 4.00 1.60
82 Ruben Gomez 4.00 1.60
83 Tony Kubek 15.00 6.00
84 Hal R. Smith 4.00 1.60
85 Frank Lary............................. 6.00 2.40
86 Dick Gernert.......................... 4.00 1.60
87 John Romonosky.................... 4.00 1.60
88 John Roseboro 6.00 2.40
89 Hal Brown 4.00 1.60
90 Bobby Avila 4.00 1.60
91 Bennie Daniels 4.00 1.60
92 Whitey Herzog 6.00 2.40
93 Art Schult.............................. 4.00 1.60
94 Leo Kiely 4.00 1.60
95 Frank Thomas 6.00 2.40
96 Ralph Terry 6.00 2.40
97 Ted Lepcio............................. 4.00 1.60
98 Gordon Jones 4.00 1.60
99 Lenny Green.......................... 4.00 1.60
100 Nellie Fox 20.00 8.00
101 Bob Miller 4.00 1.60
102 Kent Hadley......................... 4.00 1.60
102A Kent Hadley...............................
Athletics Team Logo
103 Dick Farrell.......................... 6.00 2.40
104 Dick Schofield...................... 6.00 2.40
105 Larry Sherry RC 6.00 2.40
106 Billy Gardner 4.00 1.60
107 Carlton Willey...................... 4.00 1.60
108 Pete Daley........................... 4.00 1.60
109 Clete Boyer 15.00 6.00
110 Cal McLish.......................... 4.00 1.60
111 Vic Wertz 6.00 2.40
112 Jack Harshman 4.00 1.60
113 Bob Skinner 4.00 1.60
114 Ken Aspromonte 4.00 1.60
115 Roy Face 6.00 2.40
Hoyt Wilhelm
116 Jim Rivera............................ 4.00 1.60
117 Tom Borland RP 4.00 1.60
118 Bob Bruce RP 4.00 1.60
119 Chico Cardenas RP 6.00 2.40
120 Duke Carmel RP 4.00 1.60
121 Camilo Carreon RP 4.00 1.60
122 Don Dillard RP 4.00 1.60
123 Dan Dobbek RP 4.00 1.60
124 Jim Donohue RP................... 4.00 1.60
125 Dick Ellsworth RP RC 6.00 2.40
126 Chuck Estrada RP RC 6.00 2.40
127 Ron Hansen RP 6.00 2.40
128 Bill Harris RP 4.00 1.60
129 Bob Hartman RP 4.00 1.60
130 Frank Herrera RP 4.00 1.60
131 Ed Hobaugh RP 4.00 1.60
132 Frank Howard RP RC 25.00 10.00
133 Manuel Javier RC RP 6.00 2.40
(Sic, Julian)
134 Deron Johnson RP.............. 6.00 2.40
135 Ken Johnson RP.................. 4.00 1.60
136 Jim Kaat RP RC 40.00 16.00
137 Lou Klimchock RP 4.00 1.60
138 Art Mahaffey RP RC.............. 6.00 2.40
139 Carl Mathias RP 4.00 1.60
140 Julio Navarro RP RC 4.00 1.60
141 Jim Proctor RP 4.00 1.60
142 Bill Short RP 4.00 1.60
143 Al Spangler RP..................... 4.00 1.60
144 Al Stieglitz RP...................... 4.00 1.60
145 Jim Umbricht RP 4.00 1.60
146 Ted Wieand RP..................... 4.00 1.60
147 Bob Will RP 4.00 1.60
148 C.Yastrzemski RP RC....... 175.00 70.00
149 Bob Nieman 4.00 1.60
150 Billy Pierce 6.00 2.40
151 Giants Team CL................. 10.00 2.00
152 Gail Harris............................. 4.00 1.60
153 Bobby Thomson...................... 6.00 2.40
154 Jim Davenport 6.00 2.40
155 Charlie Neal........................... 6.00 2.40
156 Art Ceccarelli......................... 4.00 1.60
157 Rocky Nelson......................... 6.00 2.40
158 Wes Covington....................... 6.00 2.40
159 Jim Piersall 6.00 2.40
160 Mickey Mantle................. 125.00 50.00
Ken Boyer
161 Ray Narleski 4.00 1.60
162 Sammy Taylor........................ 4.00 1.60
163 Hector Lopez.......................... 6.00 2.40
164 Reds Team CL..................... 10.00 2.00
165 Jack Sanford.......................... 6.00 2.40
166 Chuck Essegian...................... 4.00 1.60
167 Valmy Thomas 4.00 1.60
168 Alex Grammas 4.00 1.60
169 Jake Striker 4.00 1.60
170 Del Crandall 6.00 2.40
171 Johnny Groth 4.00 1.60
172 Willie Kirkland 4.00 1.60
173 Billy Martin......................... 20.00 8.00
174 Indians Team CL 10.00 2.00
175 Pedro Ramos 4.00 1.60
176 Vada Pinson 6.00 2.40
177 Johnny Kucks 4.00 1.60
178 Woody Held 4.00 1.60
179 Rip Coleman 4.00 1.60
180 Harry Simpson......................... 4.00 1.60
181 Billy Loes 6.00 2.40
182 Glen Hobbie 4.00 1.60
183 Eli Grba 4.00 1.60
184 Gary Geiger............................ 4.00 1.60
185 Jim Owens 4.00 1.60
186 Dave Sisler............................. 4.00 1.60
187 Jay Hook 4.00 1.60
188 Dick Williams 6.00 2.40
189 Don McMahon 4.00 1.60
190 Gene Woodling 6.00 2.40
191 Johnny Klippstein 4.00 1.60
192 Danny O'Connell 4.00 1.60
193 Dick Hyde............................... 4.00 1.60
194 Bobby Gene Smith 4.00 1.60
195 Lindy McDaniel 6.00 2.40
196 Andy Carey............................. 6.00 2.40
197 Ron Kline 4.00 1.60
198 Jerry Lynch 6.00 2.40
199 Dick Donovan.......................... 6.00 2.40
200 Willie Mays 125.00 50.00
201 Larry Osborne 4.00 1.60
202 Fred Kipp 4.00 1.60
203 Sammy White 4.00 1.60
204 Ryne Duren 6.00 2.40
205 Johnny Logan 6.00 2.40
206 Claude Osteen 6.00 2.40
207 Bob Boyd 4.00 1.60
208 White Sox Team CL............. 10.00 2.00
209 Ron Blackburn 4.00 1.60
210 Harmon Killebrew 40.00 16.00
211 Taylor Phillips 4.00 1.60
212 Walter Alston MG................. 10.00 4.00
213 Chuck Dressen MG 6.00 2.40
214 Jimmy Dykes MG.................... 6.00 2.40
215 Bob Elliott MG......................... 6.00 2.40
216 Joe Gordon MG 6.00 2.40
217 Charlie Grimm MG 6.00 2.40
218 Solly Hemus MG..................... 4.00 1.60
219 Fred Hutchinson MG................ 6.00 2.40
220 Billy Jurges MG 4.00 1.60
221 Cookie Lavagetto MG.............. 4.00 1.60
222 Al Lopez MG 10.00 4.00
223 Danny Murtaugh MG 6.00 2.40
224 Paul Richards MG 6.00 2.40
225 Bill Rigney MG 4.00 1.60
226 Eddie Sawyer MG.................... 4.00 1.60
227 Casey Stengel MG................ 15.00 6.00
228 Ernie Johnson.......................... 6.00 2.40
229 Joe M. Morgan 4.00 1.60
230 Lou Burdette 10.00 4.00
Warren Spahn
Bob Buhl
231 Hal Naragon 4.00 1.60
232 Jim Busby 4.00 1.60
233 Don Elston 4.00 1.60
234 Don Demeter........................... 4.00 1.60
235 Gus Bell 6.00 2.40
236 Dick Ricketts 4.00 1.60
237 Elmer Valo 4.00 1.60
238 Danny Kravitz.......................... 4.00 1.60
239 Joe Shipley 4.00 1.60
240 Luis Aparicio 15.00 6.00
241 Albie Pearson.......................... 6.00 2.40
242 Cardinals Team CL................ 10.00 2.00
243 Bubba Phillips 4.00 1.60
244 Hal Griggs............................... 4.00 1.60
245 Eddie Yost.............................. 6.00 2.40
246 Lee Maye 6.00 2.40
247 Gil McDougald 10.00 4.00
248 Del Rice 4.00 1.60
249 Earl Wilson RC 6.00 2.40
250 Stan Musial 100.00 40.00
251 Bob Malkmus........................... 4.00 1.60
252 Ray Herbert............................. 4.00 1.60
253 Eddie Bressoud 4.00 1.60
254 Arnie Portocarrero 4.00 1.60
255 Jim Gilliam.............................. 6.00 2.40
256 Dick Brown 4.00 1.60
257 Gordy Coleman RC 6.00 2.40
258 Dick Groat 6.00 2.40
259 George Altman 4.00 1.60
260 Rocky Colavito 15.00 6.00
Tito Francona
261 Pete Burnside.......................... 4.00 1.60
262 Hank Bauer 6.00 2.40
263 Darrell Johnson 4.00 1.60
264 Robin Roberts 15.00 6.00
265 Rip Repulski............................ 4.00 1.60
266 Joey Jay................................. 6.00 2.40
267 Jim Marshall 4.00 1.60
268 Al Worthington 4.00 1.60
269 Gene Green 4.00 1.60
270 Bob Turley 6.00 2.40
271 Julio Becquer 4.00 1.60
272 Fred Green 6.00 2.40
273 Neil Chrisley............................ 4.00 1.60
274 Tom Acker............................... 4.00 1.60
275 Curt Flood 6.00 2.40
276 Ken McBride 4.00 1.60
277 Harry Bright 4.00 1.60
278 Stan Williams.......................... 6.00 2.40
279 Chuck Tanner 6.00 2.40
280 Frank Sullivan 4.00 1.60
281 Ray Boone 6.00 2.40
282 Joe Nuxhall 4.00 1.60
283 John Blanchard........................ 6.00 2.40
284 Don Gross............................... 4.00 1.60
285 Harry Anderson........................ 4.00 1.60
286 Ray Semproch 4.00 1.60
287 Felipe Alou 6.00 2.40
288 Bob Mabe................................ 4.00 1.60
289 Willie Jones 4.00 1.60
290 Jerry Lumpe 4.00 1.60
291 Bob Keegan............................. 4.00 1.60
292 Joe Pignatano 6.00 2.40
John Roseboro
293 Gene Conley............................ 6.00 2.40
294 Tony Taylor 6.00 2.40
295 Gil Hodges 25.00 10.00
296 Nelson Chittum 4.00 1.60
297 Reno Bertoia 4.00 1.60
298 George Witt............................. 4.00 1.60
299 Earl Torgeson 4.00 1.60
300 Hank Aaron 125.00 50.00
301 Jerry Davie.............................. 4.00 1.60
302 Phillies Team CL 10.00 2.00
303 Billy O'Dell 4.00 1.60
304 Joe Ginsberg........................... 4.00 1.60
305 Richie Ashburn 20.00 8.00
306 Frank Baumann 4.00 1.60
307 Gene Oliver 4.00 1.60
308 Dick Hall................................. 4.00 1.60
309 Bob Hale 4.00 1.60
310 Frank Malzone......................... 6.00 2.40
311 Raul Sanchez 4.00 1.60
312 Charley Lau............................ 6.00 2.40
313 Turk Lown 4.00 1.60
314 Chico Fernandez...................... 4.00 1.60
315 Bobby Shantz 10.00 4.00
316 Willie McCovey RC........... 125.00 50.00
317 Pumpsie Green 6.00 2.40
318 Jim Baxes 6.00 2.40
319 Joe Koppe............................... 6.00 2.40
320 Bob Allison.............................. 6.00 2.40
321 Ron Fairly................................ 6.00 2.40
322 Willie Tasby............................ 6.00 2.40
323 John Romano 6.00 2.40
324 Jim Perry 6.00 2.40
325 Jim O'Toole 6.00 2.40
326 Roberto Clemente 175.00 70.00
327 Ray Sadecki RC 4.00 1.60
328 Earl Battey.............................. 4.00 1.60
329 Zack Monroe............................ 4.00 1.60
330 Harvey Kuenn 6.00 2.40
331 Henry Mason 4.00 1.60
332 Yankees Team CL 80.00 16.00
333 Danny McDevitt 4.00 1.60
334 Ted Abernathy......................... 4.00 1.60
335 Red Schoendienst.................. 15.00 6.00
336 Ike Delock 4.00 1.60
337 Cal Neeman............................. 4.00 1.60
338 Ray Monzant 4.00 1.60
339 Harry Chiti.............................. 4.00 1.60
340 Harvey Haddix......................... 6.00 2.40
341 Carroll Hardy........................... 4.00 1.60
342 Casey Wise 4.00 1.60
343 Sandy Koufax 125.00 50.00
344 Clint Courtney 4.00 1.60
345 Don Newcombe 6.00 2.40
346 J.C. Martin UER 6.00 2.40
(Face actually
Gary Peters)
347 Ed Bouchee 4.00 1.60
348 Barry Shetrone........................ 4.00 1.60
349 Moe Drabowsky 6.00 2.40
350 Mickey Mantle 500.00 200.00
351 Don Nottebart 4.00 1.60
352 Gus Bell 10.00 4.00
Frank Robinson
Jerry Lynch
353 Don Larsen 6.00 2.40
354 Bob Lillis................................. 4.00 1.60
355 Bill White 6.00 2.40
356 Joe Amalfitano 4.00 1.60
357 Al Schroll 4.00 1.60
358 Joe DeMaestri.......................... 4.00 1.60
359 Buddy Gilbert 4.00 1.60
360 Herb Score.............................. 6.00 2.40
361 Bob Oldis 6.00 2.40
362 Russ Kemmerer 4.00 1.60
363 Gene Stephens........................ 4.00 1.60
364 Paul Foytack........................... 4.00 1.60
365 Minnie Minoso 10.00 4.00
366 Dallas Green RC.................... 10.00 4.00
367 Bill Tuttle................................ 4.00 1.60
368 Daryl Spencer 4.00 1.60
369 Billy Hoeft 4.00 1.60
370 Bill Skowron......................... 10.00 4.00
371 Bud Byerly 4.00 1.60
372 Frank House........................... 4.00 1.60
373 Don Hoak 6.00 2.40
374 Bob Buhl 6.00 2.40
375 Dale Long............................ 10.00 4.00
376 John Briggs 4.00 1.60
377 Roger Maris....................... 100.00 40.00
378 Stu Miller 6.00 2.40
379 Red Wilson 4.00 1.60
380 Bob Shaw................................ 4.00 1.60
381 Braves Team CL................... 10.00 2.00
382 Ted Bowsfield.......................... 4.00 1.60
383 Leon Wagner........................... 4.00 1.60
384 Don Cardwell 4.00 1.60
385 Charlie Neal WS 8.00 3.20
386 Charlie Neal WS 8.00 3.20
387 Carl Furillo WS 8.00 3.20
388 Gil Hodges WS...................... 10.00 4.00
389 Luis Aparicio WS 12.00 4.80
Maury Wills
390 World Series Game 6.......... 8.00 3.20
391 WS Summary 8.00 3.20
The Champs Celebrate
392 Tex Clevenger......................... 4.00 1.60
393 Smoky Burgess....................... 6.00 2.40
394 Norm Larker............................ 6.00 2.40
395 Hoyt Wilhelm 15.00 6.00
396 Steve Bilko 4.00 1.60
397 Don Blasingame...................... 4.00 1.60
398 Mike Cuellar........................... 6.00 2.40
399 Milt Pappas 6.00 2.40
Jack Fisher
Jerry Walker
400 Rocky Colavito 20.00 8.00
401 Bob Duliba 4.00 1.60
402 Dick Stuart 15.00 6.00
403 Ed Sadowski 4.00 1.60
404 Bob Rush 4.00 1.60
405 Bobby Richardson 15.00 6.00
406 Billy Klaus 4.00 1.60
407 Gary Peters RC UER 6.00 2.40
(Face actually
J.C. Martin)
408 Carl Furillo 10.00 4.00
409 Ron Samford 4.00 1.60
410 Sam Jones 6.00 2.40
411 Ed Bailey 4.00 1.60
412 Bob Anderson 4.00 1.60
413 Athletics Team CL 10.00 2.00
414 Don Williams 4.00 1.60
415 Bob Cerv................................ 4.00 1.60
416 Humberto Robinson................. 4.00 1.60
417 Chuck Cottier RC 4.00 1.60
418 Don Mossi 6.00 2.40
419 George Crowe 4.00 1.60
420 Eddie Mathews 40.00 16.00
421 Duke Maas.............................. 4.00 1.60
422 John Powers 4.00 1.60
423 Ed Fitzgerald 4.00 1.60
424 Pete Whisenant 4.00 1.60
425 Johnny Podres 6.00 2.40
426 Ron Jackson 4.00 1.60
427 Al Grunwald 4.00 1.60
428 Al Smith.................................. 4.00 1.60
429 Nellie Fox 10.00 4.00
Harvey Kuenn
430 Art Ditmar 4.00 1.60
431 Andre Rodgers 4.00 1.60
432 Chuck Stobbs 4.00 1.60
433 Irv Noren 4.00 1.60
434 Brooks Lawrence 6.00 2.40
435 Gene Freese 4.00 1.60
436 Marv Throneberry 6.00 2.40
437 Bob Friend 6.00 2.40
438 Jim Coker............................... 4.00 1.60
439 Tom Brewer 4.00 1.60
440 Jim Lemon 6.00 2.40
441 Gary Bell 10.00 4.00
442 Joe Pignatano 8.00 3.20
443 Charlie Maxwell....................... 8.00 3.20
444 Jerry Kindall........................... 8.00 3.20
445 Warren Spahn 50.00 20.00
446 Ellis Burton 8.00 3.20
447 Ray Moore 8.00 3.20
448 Jim Gentile RC 15.00 6.00
449 Jim Brosnan............................ 8.00 3.20
450 Orlando Cepeda 25.00 10.00
451 Curt Simmons 8.00 3.20
452 Ray Webster 8.00 3.20
453 Vern Law 25.00 10.00
454 Hal Woodeshick 8.00 3.20
455 Eddie Robinson CO 8.00 3.20
Harry Brecheen CO
Luman Harris CO
456 Rudy York CO 10.00 4.00
Billy Herman CO
Sal Maglie CO
Del Baker CO
457 Charlie Root CO 8.00 3.20
Lou Klein CO
Elvin Tappe CO
458 Johnny Cooney CO 8.00 3.20
Don Gutteridge CO
Tony Cuccinello CO
Ray Berres CO
459 Reggie Otero CO 8.00 3.20
Cot Deal CO
Wally Moses CO
460 Mel Harder CO 15.00 6.00
Jo-Jo White CO
Bob Lemon CO
Ralph(Red) Kress CO
461 Tom Ferrick CO 10.00 4.00
Luke Appling CO
Billy Hitchcock CO
462 Fred Fitzsimmons CO............ 8.00 3.20
Don Heffner CO
Walker Cooper CO
463 Bobby Bragan CO 8.00 3.20
Pete Reiser CO
Joe Becker CO
Greg Mulleavy CO
464 Bob Scheffing CO.................... 8.00 3.20
Whitlow Wyatt CO
Andy Pafko CO
George Myatt CO
465 Bill Dickey CO 25.00 10.00
Ralph Houk CO
Frank Crosetti CO
Ed Lopat CO
466 Ken Silvestri CO 8.00 3.20
Dick Carter CO
Andy Cohen CO
467 Mickey Vernon CO 8.00 3.20
Frank Oceak CO
Sam Narron CO
Bill Burwell CO
468 Johnny Keane CO.................... 8.00 3.20
Howie Pollet CO
Ray Katt CO
Harry Walker CO
469 Wes Westrum CO 8.00 3.20
Salty Parker CO
Bill Posedel CO
470 Bob Swift CO 8.00 3.20
Ellis Clary CO
Sam Mele CO
471 Ned Garver.............................. 8.00 3.20
472 Alvin Dark 8.00 3.20
473 Al Cicotte 8.00 3.20
474 Haywood Sullivan 8.00 3.20
475 Don Drysdale 40.00 16.00
476 Lou Johnson 8.00 3.20
477 Don Ferrarese 8.00 3.20
478 Frank Torre............................. 8.00 3.20
479 Georges Maranda.................... 8.00 3.20
480 Yogi Berra 80.00 32.00
481 Wes Stock 8.00 3.20
482 Frank Bolling 8.00 3.20
483 Camilo Pascual 8.00 3.20
484 Pirates Team CL 40.00 8.00
485 Ken Boyer 15.00 6.00
486 Bobby Del Greco 8.00 3.20
487 Tom Sturdivant 8.00 3.20
488 Norm Cash 25.00 10.00
Shown with Indians Cap but listed as a Tiger
489 Steve Ridzik 8.00 3.20
490 Frank Robinson 50.00 20.00
491 Mel Roach............................... 8.00 3.20
492 Larry Jackson 8.00 3.20
493 Duke Snider 50.00 20.00
494 Orioles Team CL................... 25.00 5.00
495 Sherm Lollar 8.00 3.20
496 Bill Virdon 10.00 4.00
497 John Tsitouris 8.00 3.20
498 Al Pilarcik 8.00 3.20
499 Johnny James 10.00 4.00
500 Johnny Temple........................ 8.00 3.20
501 Bob Schmidt 8.00 3.20
502 Jim Bunning 25.00 10.00
503 Don Lee 8.00 3.20
504 Seth Morehead 8.00 3.20
505 Ted Kluszewski 25.00 10.00
506 Lee Walls 8.00 3.20
507 Dick Stigman 15.00 6.00
508 Billy Consolo 15.00 6.00

509 Tommy Davis RC 25.00 10.00
510 Gerry Staley 15.00 6.00
511 Ken Walters 15.00 6.00
512 Joe Gibbon 15.00 6.00
513 Chicago Cubs 30.00 6.00
Team Card CL
514 Steve Barber RC 15.00 6.00
515 Stan Lopata 15.00 6.00
516 Marty Kutyna 15.00 6.00
517 Charlie James 25.00 10.00
518 Tony Gonzalez 15.00 6.00
519 Ed Roebuck 15.00 6.00
520 Don Buddin 15.00 6.00
521 Mike Lee 15.00 6.00
522 Ken Hunt 30.00 12.00
523 Clay Dalrymple 15.00 6.00
524 Bill Henry 15.00 6.00
525 Marv Breeding 15.00 6.00
526 Paul Giel 25.00 10.00
527 Jose Valdivielso 25.00 10.00
528 Ben Johnson 15.00 6.00
529 Norm Sherry RC 20.00 8.00
530 Mike McCormick 15.00 6.00
531 Sandy Amoros 20.00 8.00
532 Mike Garcia 20.00 8.00
533 Lu Clinton 15.00 6.00
534 Ken MacKenzie 15.00 6.00
535 Whitey Lockman 15.00 6.00
536 Wynn Hawkins 15.00 6.00
537 Boston Red Sox 30.00 6.00
Team Card CL
538 Frank Barnes 15.00 6.00
539 Gene Baker 15.00 6.00
540 Jerry Walker 15.00 6.00
541 Tony Curry 15.00 6.00
542 Ken Hamlin 15.00 6.00
543 Elio Chacon 15.00 6.00
544 Bill Monbouquette 20.00 8.00
545 Carl Sawatski 15.00 6.00
546 Hank Aguirre 15.00 6.00
547 Bob Aspromonte 20.00 8.00
548 Don Mincher 15.00 6.00
549 John Buzhardt 15.00 6.00
550 Jim Landis 15.00 6.00
551 Ed Rakow 15.00 6.00
552 Walt Bond 15.00 6.00
553 Bill Skowron AS 20.00 8.00
554 Willie McCovey AS 40.00 16.00
555 Nellie Fox AS 30.00 12.00
556 Charlie Neal AS 15.00 6.00
557 Frank Malzone AS 15.00 6.00
558 Eddie Mathews AS 40.00 16.00
559 Luis Aparicio AS 30.00 12.00
560 Ernie Banks AS 60.00 24.00
561 Al Kaline AS 60.00 24.00
562 Joe Cunningham AS 15.00 6.00
563 Mickey Mantle AS 250.00 100.00
564 Willie Mays AS 100.00 40.00
565 Roger Maris AS 100.00 40.00
566 Hank Aaron AS 100.00 40.00
567 Sherm Lollar AS 15.00 6.00
568 Del Crandall AS 15.00 6.00
569 Camilo Pascual AS 15.00 6.00
570 Don Drysdale AS 40.00 16.00
571 Billy Pierce AS 15.00 6.00
572 Johnny Antonelli AS 30.00 9.00
NNO Iron-on team transfer 5.00 2.00

1961 Topps

The cards in this 587-card set measure 2 1/2" by 3 1/2". In 1961, Topps returned to the vertical obverse format. Introduced for the first time were "League Leaders" (41-50) and separate, numbered checklist cards. Two number 463s exist: the Braves team card carrying that number was meant to be number 426. There are three versions of the second series checklist card number 98; the variations are distinguished by the color of the "CHECKLIST" headline on the front of the card, the color of the printing of the card number on the bottom of the reverse, and the presence of the copyright notice running vertically on the card back. There are two groups of managers (131-139/219-226) as well as separate subsets of World Series cards (306-313), Baseball Thrills (401-410), MVP's of the 1950's (AL 471-478/NL 479-486) and Sporting News All-Stars (566-589). The usual last series scarcity (523-589) exists. Some collectors believe that 61 high numbers are the toughest of all the Topps hi numbers. The set actually totals 587 cards since numbers 587 and 588 were never issued. These card advertising promos have been seen: Dan Dobbek/Russ Nixon/60 NL Pitching Leaders on the front along with an ad and Roger Maris on the back.Other strips feature Jack Kralick/Dick Stigman/Joe Christopher; Ed Roebuck/Bob Schmidt/Zoilo Versalles; Lindy (McDaniel) Shows Larry (Jackson)/John Blanchard/Johnny Kucks. Cards were issued in one-card penny packs, five-card nickel packs, 10 cent cello packs (which came 36 to a box) and 36-card rack packs which cost 29 cents. The one card packs came 120 to a box. The key Rookie Cards in this set are Juan Marichal, Ron Santo and Billy Williams.

	NM	Ex
COMPLETE SET (587)	7000.00	2800.00
COMMON CARD (1-370)	3.00	1.20
COMMON (371-446)	4.00	1.60
COMMON (447-522)	8.00	3.20
COMMON (523-589)	30.00	12.00
NOT ISSUED (587/588)		
WRAPPER (1-CENT)	200.00	80.00
WRAP.(1-CENT, REPEAT)	100.00	40.00
WRAPPER (5-CENT)	40.00	16.00

1 Dick Groat 30.00 6.00
2 Roger Maris 200.00 80.00
3 John Buzhardt 3.00 1.20
4 Lenny Green 3.00 1.20
5 John Romano 3.00 1.20
6 Ed Roebuck 3.00 1.20
7 White Sox Team 8.00 3.20
8 Dick Williams 6.00 2.40
9 Bob Purkey 3.00 1.20
10 Brooks Robinson 50.00 20.00
11 Curt Simmons 6.00 2.40
12 Moe Thacker 3.00 1.20
13 Chuck Cottier 3.00 1.20
14 Don Mossi 6.00 2.40
15 Willie Kirkland 3.00 1.20
16 Billy Muffett 3.00 1.20
17 Checklist 1 10.00 2.00
18 Jim Grant 6.00 2.40
19 Clete Boyer 8.00 3.20
20 Robin Roberts 15.00 6.00
21 Zorro Versalles 8.00 3.20
UER RC
First name should
be Zoilo
22 Clem Labine 6.00 2.40
23 Don Demeter 3.00 1.20
24 Ken Johnson 6.00 2.40
25 Vada Pinson 8.00 3.20
Gus Bell
Frank Robinson
26 Wes Stock 3.00 1.20
27 Jerry Kindall 3.00 1.20
28 Hector Lopez 6.00 2.40
29 Don Nottebart 3.00 1.20
30 Nellie Fox 15.00 6.00
31 Bob Schmidt 3.00 1.20
32 Ray Sadecki 3.00 1.20
33 Gary Geiger 3.00 1.20
34 Wynn Hawkins 3.00 1.20
35 Ron Santo RC 40.00 16.00
36 Jack Kralick 3.00 1.20
37 Charley Maxwell 6.00 2.40
38 Bob Lillis 3.00 1.20
39 Leo Posada 3.00 1.20
40 Bob Turley 6.00 2.40
41 Dick Groat 40.00 16.00
Norm Larker
Willie Mays
Roberto Clemente LL
42 Pete Runnels 8.00 3.20
Al Smith
Minnie Minoso
Bill Skowron LL
43 Ernie Banks 30.00 12.00
Hank Aaron
Ed Mathews
Ken Boyer LL
44 Mickey Mantle 80.00 32.00
Roger Maris
Jim Lemon
Rocky Colavito LL
45 Mike McCormick 8.00 3.20
Ernie Broglio
Don Drysdale
Bob Friend
Stan Williams LL
46 Frank Baumann 8.00 3.20
Jim Bunning
Art Ditmar
Hal Brown LL
47 Ernie Broglio 8.00 3.20
Warren Spahn
Vern Law
Lou Burdette LL
48 Chuck Estrada 8.00 3.20
Jim Perry UER
(Listed as an Oriole)
Bud Daley
Art Ditmar
Frank Lary
Milt Pappas LL
49 Don Drysdale 20.00 8.00
Sandy Koufax
Sam Jones
Ernie Broglio LL
50 Jim Bunning 8.00 3.20
Pedro Ramos
Early Wynn
Frank Lary LL
51 Detroit Tigers 8.00 3.20
Team Card
52 George Crowe 3.00 1.20
53 Russ Nixon 3.00 1.20
54 Earl Francis 3.00 1.20
55 Jim Davenport 6.00 2.40
56 Russ Kemmerer 3.00 1.20
57 Marv Throneberry 6.00 2.40
58 Joe Schaffernoth 3.00 1.20
59 Jim Woods 3.00 1.20
60 Woody Held 3.00 1.20
61 Ron Piche 3.00 1.20
62 Al Pilarcik 3.00 1.20
63 Jim Kaat 8.00 3.20
64 Alex Grammas 3.00 1.20
65 Ted Kluszewski 8.00 3.20
66 Bill Henry 3.00 1.20
67 Ossie Virgil 3.00 1.20
68 Deron Johnson 6.00 2.40
69 Earl Wilson 6.00 2.40
70 Bill Virdon 6.00 2.40
71 Jerry Adair 3.00 1.20
72 Stu Miller 6.00 2.40
73 Al Spangler 3.00 1.20
74 Joe Pignatano 3.00 1.20
75 Lindy McDaniel 6.00 2.40
Larry Jackson
76 Harry Anderson 3.00 1.20
77 Dick Stigman 3.00 1.20
78 Lee Walls 6.00 2.40
79 Joe Ginsberg 3.00 1.20
80 Harmon Killebrew 20.00 8.00
81 Tracy Stallard 3.00 1.20
82 Joe Christopher 3.00 1.20
83 Bob Bruce 3.00 1.20
84 Lee Maye 3.00 1.20
85 Jerry Walker 3.00 1.20
86 Los Angeles Dodgers 8.00 3.20
Team Card
87 Joe Amalfitano 3.00 1.20
88 Richie Ashburn 15.00 6.00
89 Billy Martin 15.00 6.00
90 Gerry Staley 3.00 1.20
91 Walt Moryn 3.00 1.20
92 Hal Naragon 3.00 1.20
93 Tony Gonzalez 3.00 1.20
94 Johnny Kucks 3.00 1.20
95 Norm Cash 8.00 3.20
96 Billy O'Dell 3.00 1.20
97 Jerry Lynch 6.00 2.40
98A Checklist 2 10.00 2.00
(Red "Checklist"
98 black on white)
98B Checklist 2 10.00 2.00
(Yellow "Checklist"
98 black on white)
98C Checklist 2 10.00 2.00
(Yellow "Checklist"
98 white on black
no copyright)
99 Don Buddin UER 3.00 1.20
(66 HR's)
100 Harvey Haddix 6.00 2.40
101 Bubba Phillips 3.00 1.20
102 Gene Stephens 3.00 1.20
103 Ruben Amaro 3.00 1.20
104 John Blanchard 8.00 3.20
105 Carl Willey 3.00 1.20
106 Whitey Herzog 3.00 1.20
107 Seth Morehead 3.00 1.20
108 Dan Dobbek 3.00 1.20
109 Johnny Podres 8.00 3.20
110 Vada Pinson 8.00 3.20
111 Jack Meyer 3.00 1.20
112 Chico Fernandez 3.00 1.20
113 Mike Fornieles 3.00 1.20
114 Hobie Landrith 3.00 1.20
115 Johnny Antonelli 6.00 2.40
116 Joe DeMaestri 3.00 1.20
117 Dale Long 6.00 2.40
118 Chris Cannizzaro 3.00 1.20
119 Norm Siebern 6.00 2.40
Hank Bauer
Jerry Lumpe
120 Eddie Mathews 30.00 12.00
121 Eli Grba 6.00 2.40
122 Chicago Cubs 8.00 3.20
Team Card
123 Billy Gardner 3.00 1.20
124 J.C. Martin 3.00 1.20
125 Steve Barber 3.00 1.20
126 Dick Stuart 6.00 2.40
127 Ron Kline 3.00 1.20
128 Rip Repulski 3.00 1.20
129 Ed Hobaugh 3.00 1.20
130 Norm Larker 3.00 1.20
131 Paul Richards MG 6.00 2.40
132 Al Lopez MG 8.00 3.20
133 Ralph Houk MG 6.00 2.40
134 Mickey Vernon MG 6.00 2.40
135 Fred Hutchinson MG 6.00 2.40
136 Walter Alston MG 8.00 3.20
137 Chuck Dressen MG 6.00 2.40
138 Danny Murtaugh MG 6.00 2.40
139 Solly Hemus MG 6.00 2.40
140 Gus Triandos 6.00 2.40
141 Billy Williams RC 60.00 24.00
142 Luis Arroyo 6.00 2.40
143 Russ Snyder 3.00 1.20
144 Jim Coker 3.00 1.20
145 Bob Buhl 6.00 2.40
146 Marty Keough 3.00 1.20
147 Ed Rakow 3.00 1.20
148 Julian Javier 6.00 2.40
149 Bob Oldis 3.00 1.20
150 Willie Mays 100.00 40.00
151 Jim Donohue 3.00 1.20
152 Earl Torgeson 3.00 1.20
153 Don Lee 3.00 1.20
154 Bobby Del Greco 3.00 1.20
155 Johnny Temple 6.00 2.40
156 Ken Hunt 6.00 2.40
157 Cal McLish 3.00 1.20
158 Pete Daley 3.00 1.20
159 Orioles Team 8.00 3.20
160 Whitey Ford UER 50.00 20.00
Incorrectly listed
as 5'0" tall
161 Sherman Jones UER 3.00 1.20
(Photo actually
Eddie Fisher)
162 Jay Hook 3.00 1.20
163 Ed Sadowski 3.00 1.20
164 Felix Mantilla 3.00 1.20
165 Gino Cimoli 3.00 1.20
166 Danny Kravitz 3.00 1.20
167 San Francisco Giants 8.00 3.20
Team Card
168 Tommy Davis 8.00 3.20
169 Don Elston 3.00 1.20
170 Al Smith 3.00 1.20
171 Paul Foytack 3.00 1.20
172 Don Dillard 3.00 1.20
173 Frank Malzone 6.00 2.40
Vic Wertz
Jackie Jensen
174 Ray Semproch 3.00 1.20
175 Gene Freese 3.00 1.20
176 Ken Aspromonte 3.00 1.20
177 Don Larsen 6.00 2.40
178 Bob Nieman 3.00 1.20
179 Joe Koppe 3.00 1.20
180 Bobby Richardson 12.00 4.80
181 Fred Green 3.00 1.20
182 Dave Nicholson 3.00 1.20
183 Andre Rodgers 3.00 1.20
184 Steve Bilko 6.00 2.40
185 Herb Score 6.00 2.40
186 Elmer Valo 6.00 2.40
187 Billy Klaus 3.00 1.20
188 Jim Marshall 3.00 1.20
189A Checklist 3 10.00 2.00
(Copyright symbol
almost adjacent to
263 Ken Hamlin)
189B Checklist 3 10.00 2.00
(Copyright symbol
adjacent to
264 Glen Hobbie)
190 Stan Williams 6.00 2.40
191 Mike de la Hoz 3.00 1.20
192 Dick Brown 3.00 1.20
193 Gene Conley 6.00 2.40
194 Gordy Coleman 6.00 2.40
195 Jerry Casale 3.00 1.20
196 Ed Bouchee 3.00 1.20
197 Dick Hall 3.00 1.20
198 Carl Sawatski 3.00 1.20
199 Bob Boyd 3.00 1.20
200 Warren Spahn 40.00 16.00
201 Pete Whisenant 3.00 1.20
202 Al Neiger 3.00 1.20
203 Eddie Bressoud 3.00 1.20
204 Bob Skinner 6.00 2.40
205 Billy Pierce 6.00 2.40
206 Gene Green 3.00 1.20
207 Sandy Koufax 30.00 12.00
Johnny Podres
208 Larry Osborne 3.00 1.20
209 Ken McBride 3.00 1.20
210 Pete Runnels 6.00 2.40
211 Bob Gibson 40.00 16.00
212 Haywood Sullivan 6.00 2.40
213 Bill Stafford 3.00 1.20
214 Danny Murphy 6.00 2.40
215 Gus Bell 6.00 2.40
216 Ted Bowsfield 3.00 1.20
217 Mel Roach 3.00 1.20
218 Hal Brown 3.00 1.20
219 Gene Mauch MG 6.00 2.40
220 Alvin Dark MG 6.00 2.40
221 Mike Higgins MG 3.00 1.20
222 Jimmy Dykes MG 6.00 2.40
223 Bob Scheffing MG 3.00 1.20
224 Joe Gordon MG 6.00 2.40
225 Bill Rigney MG 6.00 2.40
226 Cookie Lavagetto MG 6.00 2.40
227 Juan Pizarro 3.00 1.20
228 New York Yankees 60.00 24.00
Team Card
229 Rudy Hernandez 3.00 1.20
230 Don Hoak 6.00 2.40
231 Dick Drott 3.00 1.20
232 Bill White 6.00 2.40
233 Joey Jay 6.00 2.40
234 Ted Lepcio 3.00 1.20
235 Camilo Pascual 6.00 2.40
236 Don Gile 3.00 1.20
237 Billy Loes 6.00 2.40
238 Jim Gilliam 6.00 2.40
239 Dave Sisler 3.00 1.20
240 Ron Hansen 3.00 1.20
241 Al Cicotte 3.00 1.20
242 Hal Smith 3.00 1.20
243 Frank Lary 6.00 2.40
244 Chico Cardenas 6.00 2.40
245 Joe Adcock 6.00 2.40
246 Bob Davis 3.00 1.20
247 Billy Goodman 6.00 2.40
248 Ed Keegan 3.00 1.20
249 Cincinnati Reds 8.00 3.20
Team Card
250 Vern Law 6.00 2.40
Roy Face
251 Bill Bruton 3.00 1.20
252 Bill Short 3.00 1.20
253 Sammy Taylor 3.00 1.20
254 Ted Sadowski 6.00 2.40
255 Vic Power 6.00 2.40
256 Billy Hoeft 3.00 1.20
257 Carroll Hardy 3.00 1.20
258 Jack Sanford 6.00 2.40
259 John Schaive 3.00 1.20
260 Don Drysdale 30.00 12.00
261 Charlie Lau 6.00 2.40
262 Tony Curry 3.00 1.20
263 Ken Hamlin 3.00 1.20
264 Glen Hobbie 3.00 1.20
265 Tony Kubek 12.00 4.80
266 Lindy McDaniel 6.00 2.40
267 Norm Siebern 3.00 1.20
268 Ike Delock 3.00 1.20
269 Harry Chiti 3.00 1.20
270 Bob Friend 6.00 2.40
271 Jim Landis 3.00 1.20
272 Tom Morgan 3.00 1.20
273A Checklist 4 15.00 3.00
(Copyright symbol
adjacent to
336 Don Mincher)
273B Checklist 4 10.00 2.00
(Copyright symbol
adjacent to
339 Gene Baker)
274 Gary Bell 3.00 1.20
275 Gene Woodling 6.00 2.40
276 Ray Rippelmeyer 3.00 1.20
277 Hank Foiles 3.00 1.20
278 Don McMahon 3.00 1.20
279 Jose Pagan 3.00 1.20
280 Frank Howard 8.00 3.20
281 Frank Sullivan 3.00 1.20
282 Faye Throneberry 3.00 1.20
283 Bob Anderson 3.00 1.20
284 Dick Gernert 3.00 1.20
285 Sherm Lollar 6.00 2.40
286 George Witt 3.00 1.20
287 Carl Yastrzemski 50.00 20.00
288 Albie Pearson 6.00 2.40
289 Ray Moore 3.00 1.20
290 Stan Musial 100.00 40.00
291 Tex Clevenger 3.00 1.20
292 Jim Baumer 3.00 1.20
293 Tom Sturdivant 3.00 1.20
294 Don Blasingame 3.00 1.20
295 Milt Pappas 6.00 2.40
296 Wes Covington 6.00 2.40
297 Athletics Team 8.00 3.20
298 Jim Golden 3.00 1.20
299 Clay Dalrymple 3.00 1.20
300 Mickey Mantle 500.00 160.00
301 Chet Nichols 3.00 1.20
302 Al Heist 3.00 1.20
303 Gary Peters 6.00 2.40
304 Rocky Nelson 3.00 1.20
305 Mike McCormick 6.00 2.40
306 Bill Virdon WS 10.00 4.00
307 Mickey Mantle WS 80.00 32.00
308 B.Richardson WS 12.00 4.80
309 Gino Cimoli WS 10.00 4.00
310 Roy Face WS 10.00 4.00
311 Whitey Ford WS 15.00 6.00
312 Bill Mazeroski WS 20.00 8.00
Mazeroski Homer Wins it
313 WS Summary 15.00 6.00
Pirates Celebrate
314 Bob Miller 3.00 1.20
315 Earl Battey 6.00 2.40
316 Bobby Gene Smith 3.00 1.20
317 Jim Brewer 3.00 1.20
318 Danny O'Connell 3.00 1.20
319 Valmy Thomas 3.00 1.20
320 Lou Burdette 6.00 2.40
321 Marv Breeding 3.00 1.20
322 Bill Kunkel 6.00 2.40
323 Sammy Esposito 3.00 1.20
324 Hank Aguirre 3.00 1.20
325 Wally Moon 6.00 2.40
326 Dave Hillman 3.00 1.20
327 Matty Alou RC 12.00 4.80
328 Jim O'Toole 6.00 2.40
329 Julio Becquer 3.00 1.20
330 Rocky Colavito 20.00 8.00
331 Ned Garver 3.00 1.20
332 Dutch Dotterer UER 3.00 1.20
(Photo actually
Tommy Dotterer
Dutch's brother)
333 Fritz Brickell 3.00 1.20
334 Walt Bond 3.00 1.20
335 Frank Bolling 3.00 1.20
336 Don Mincher 6.00 2.40
337 Early Wynn 8.00 3.20
Al Lopez
Herb Score
338 Don Landrum 3.00 1.20
339 Gene Baker 3.00 1.20
340 Vic Wertz 6.00 2.40
341 Jim Owens 3.00 1.20
342 Clint Courtney 3.00 1.20
343 Earl Robinson 3.00 1.20
344 Sandy Koufax 100.00 40.00
345 Jimmy Piersall 8.00 3.20
346 Howie Nunn 3.00 1.20
347 St. Louis Cardinals 8.00 3.20
Team Card
348 Steve Boros 3.00 1.20
349 Danny McDevitt 3.00 1.20
350 Ernie Banks 40.00 16.00
351 Jim King 3.00 1.20
352 Bob Shaw 3.00 1.20
353 Howie Bedell 3.00 1.20
354 Billy Harrell 6.00 2.40
355 Bob Allison 8.00 3.20
356 Ryne Duren 3.00 1.20
357 Daryl Spencer 3.00 1.20
358 Earl Averill 6.00 2.40
359 Dallas Green 3.00 1.20
360 Frank Robinson 40.00 16.00
361A Checklist 5 15.00 3.00
(No ad on back)
361B Checklist 5 15.00 3.00
(Special Feature
ad on back)
362 Frank Funk 3.00 1.20
363 John Roseboro 6.00 2.40
364 Moe Drabowsky 6.00 2.40
365 Jerry Lumpe 3.00 1.20
366 Eddie Fisher 3.00 1.20
367 Jim Rivera 3.00 1.20
368 Bennie Daniels 3.00 1.20
369 Dave Philley 3.00 1.20
370 Roy Face 6.00 2.40
371 Bill Skowron SP 50.00 20.00
372 Bob Hendley 4.00 1.60
373 Boston Red Sox 8.00 3.20
Team Card
374 Paul Giel 4.00 1.60
375 Ken Boyer 12.00 4.80
376 Mike Roarke RC 6.00 2.40
377 Ruben Gomez 4.00 1.60
378 Wally Post 6.00 2.40
379 Bobby Shantz 4.00 1.60
380 Minnie Minoso 8.00 3.20
381 Dave Wickersham 4.00 1.60
382 Frank Thomas 6.00 2.40
383 Mike McCormick 6.00 2.40
Jack Sanford
Billy O'Dell
384 Chuck Essegian 4.00 1.60
385 Jim Perry 6.00 2.40
386 Joe Hicks 4.00 1.60
387 Duke Maas 4.00 1.60
388 Roberto Clemente 125.00 50.00
389 Ralph Terry 6.00 2.40
390 Del Crandall 8.00 3.20
391 Winston Brown 4.00 1.60
392 Reno Bertoia 4.00 1.60
393 Don Cardwell 4.00 1.60
Glen Hobbie
394 Ken Walters 4.00 1.60
395 Chuck Estrada 6.00 2.40
396 Bob Aspromonte 4.00 1.60
397 Hal Woodeshick 4.00 1.60
398 Hank Bauer 6.00 2.40
399 Cliff Cook 4.00 1.60
400 Vern Law 6.00 2.40
401 Babe Ruth HL 60.00 24.00
60th HR
402 Don Larsen HL SP 25.00 10.00
WS Perfect Game
403 Joe Oeschger HL 8.00 3.20
Leon Cadore
26 Inning Tie
404 Rogers Hornsby HL 12.00 4.80
.424 Season BA
405 Lou Gehrig HL 80.00 32.00
Consecutive Game Streak
406 Mickey Mantle HL 100.00 40.00
565 foot HR
407 Jack Chesbro HL 8.00 3.20
41 victories
408 C. Mathewson HL SP 20.00 8.00
267 Strikeouts
409 Walter Johnson SL 12.00 4.80
3 Shutouts in 4 days
410 Harvey Haddix HL 8.00 3.20
12 Perfect Innings
411 Tony Taylor 6.00 2.40
412 Larry Sherry 6.00 2.40
413 Eddie Yost 6.00 2.40
414 Dick Donovan 6.00 2.40

415 Hank Aaron 125.00 50.00
416 Dick Howser RC 8.00 3.20
417 Juan Marichal SP RC 100.00 40.00
418 Ed Bailey 6.00 2.40
419 Tom Borland 4.00 1.60
420 Ernie Broglio 6.00 2.40
421 Ty Cline SP 20.00 8.00
422 Bud Daley 4.00 1.60
423 Charlie Neal SP 20.00 8.00
424 Turk Lown 4.00 1.60
425 Yogi Berra 80.00 32.00
426 Milwaukee Braves 12.00 4.80
Team Card
(Back numbered 463)
427 Dick Ellsworth 6.00 2.40
428 Ray Barker SP 20.00 8.00
429 Al Kaline 50.00 20.00
430 Bill Mazeroski SP 50.00 20.00
431 Chuck Stobbs 4.00 1.60
432 Coot Veal 6.00 2.40
433 Art Mahaffey 4.00 1.60
434 Tom Brewer 4.00 1.60
435 Orlando Cepeda UER 12.00 4.80
(San Francis on card front)
436 Jim Maloney SP RC 20.00 8.00
437A Checklist 6 15.00 3.00
440 Louis Aparicio
437B Checklist 6 15.00 3.00
440 Luis Aparicio
438 Curt Flood 8.00 3.20
439 Phil Regan RC 6.00 2.40
440 Luis Aparicio 12.00 4.80
441 Dick Bertell 4.00 1.60
442 Gordon Jones 4.00 1.60
443 Duke Snider 50.00 20.00
444 Joe Nuxhall 6.00 2.40
445 Frank Malzone 6.00 2.40
446 Bob Taylor 4.00 1.60
447 Harry Bright 8.00 3.20
448 Del Rice 15.00 6.00
449 Bob Bolin 8.00 3.20
450 Jim Lemon 8.00 3.20
451 Daryl Spencer 8.00 3.20
Bill White
Ernie Broglio
452 Bob Allen 8.00 3.20
453 Dick Schofield 8.00 3.20
454 Pumpsie Green 8.00 3.20
455 Early Wynn 15.00 6.00
456 Hal Bevan 8.00 3.20
457 Johnny James 8.00 3.20
(Listed as Angel, but wearing Yankee uniform and cap)
458 Willie Tasby 8.00 3.20
459 Terry Fox RC 10.00 4.00
460 Gil Hodges 25.00 10.00
461 Smoky Burgess 15.00 6.00
462 Lou Klimchock 8.00 3.20
463 Jack Fisher 8.00 3.20
(See also 426)
464 Lee Thomas RC 10.00 4.00
(Pictured with Yankee cap but listed as Los Angeles Angel)
465 Roy McMillan 15.00 6.00
466 Ron Moeller 8.00 3.20
467 Cleveland Indians 12.00 4.80
Team Card
468 John Callison 10.00 4.00
469 Ralph Lumenti 8.00 3.20
470 Roy Sievers 10.00 4.00
471 Phil Rizzuto MVP 25.00 10.00
472 Yogi Berra MVP 50.00 20.00
473 Bob Shantz MVP 8.00 3.20
474 Al Rosen MVP 8.00 3.20
475 Mickey Mantle MVP 200.00 80.00
476 Jackie Jensen MVP 10.00 4.00
477 Nellie Fox MVP 15.00 6.00
478 Roger Maris MVP 60.00 24.00
479 Jim Konstanty MVP 8.00 3.20
480 Roy Campanella MVP 40.00 16.00
481 Hank Sauer MVP 8.00 3.20
482 Willie Mays MVP 50.00 20.00
483 Don Newcombe MVP 10.00 4.00
484 Hank Aaron MVP 50.00 20.00
485 Ernie Banks MVP 40.00 16.00
486 Dick Groat MVP 10.00 4.00
487 Gene Oliver 8.00 3.20
488 Joe McClain 10.00 4.00
489 Walt Dropo 8.00 3.20
490 Jim Bunning 25.00 10.00
491 Philadelphia Phillies 12.00 4.80
Team Card
492 Ron Fairly 10.00 4.00
493 Don Zimmer UER 10.00 4.00
(Brooklyn A.L.)
494 Tom Cheney 15.00 6.00
495 Elston Howard 10.00 4.00
496 Ken MacKenzie 8.00 3.20
497 Willie Jones 8.00 3.20
498 Ray Herbert 8.00 3.20
499 Chuck Schilling RC 8.00 3.20
500 Harvey Kuenn 10.00 4.00
501 John DeMerit 8.00 3.20
502 Clarence Coleman RC 10.00 4.00
503 Tito Francona 8.00 3.20
504 Billy Consolo 8.00 3.20
505 Red Schoendienst 15.00 6.00
506 Willie Davis RC 15.00 6.00
507 Pete Burnside 8.00 3.20
508 Rocky Bridges 8.00 3.20
509 Camilo Carreon 8.00 3.20
510 Art Ditmar 8.00 3.20
511 Joe M. Morgan 8.00 3.20
512 Bob Will 8.00 3.20
513 Jim Brosnan 8.00 3.20
514 Jake Wood 8.00 3.20
515 Jackie Brandt 8.00 3.20
516 Checklist 7 15.00 3.00
517 Willie McCovey 40.00 16.00
518 Andy Carey 8.00 3.20
519 Jim Pagliaroni 8.00 3.20
520 Joe Cunningham 8.00 3.20
521 Norm Sherry 8.00 3.20
Larry Sherry
522 Dick Farrell UER 15.00 6.00
(Phillies cap but listed on Dodgers)
523 Joe Gibbon 30.00 12.00
524 Johnny Logan 30.00 12.00
525 Ron Perranoski RC 60.00 24.00
526 R.C. Stevens 30.00 12.00
527 Gene Leek 30.00 12.00
528 Pedro Ramos 30.00 12.00
529 Bob Roselli 30.00 12.00
530 Bob Malkmus 30.00 12.00
531 Jim Coates 50.00 20.00
532 Bob Hale 30.00 12.00
533 Jack Curtis 30.00 12.00
534 Eddie Kasko 40.00 16.00
535 Larry Jackson 30.00 12.00
536 Bill Tuttle 30.00 12.00
537 Bobby Locke 30.00 12.00
538 Chuck Hiller 30.00 12.00
539 Johnny Klippstein 30.00 12.00
540 Jackie Jensen 40.00 16.00
541 Roland Sheldon RC 50.00 20.00
542 Minnesota Twins 60.00 24.00
Team Card
543 Roger Craig 40.00 16.00
544 George Thomas 50.00 20.00
545 Hoyt Wilhelm 60.00 24.00
546 Marty Kutyna 30.00 12.00
547 Leon Wagner 30.00 12.00
548 Ted Wills 30.00 12.00
549 Hal R. Smith 30.00 12.00
550 Frank Baumann 30.00 12.00
551 George Altman 40.00 16.00
552 Jim Archer 30.00 12.00
553 Bill Fischer 30.00 12.00
554 Pittsburgh Pirates 80.00 32.00
Team Card
555 Sam Jones 30.00 12.00
556 Ken R. Hunt 30.00 12.00
557 Jose Valdivielso 30.00 12.00
558 Don Ferrarese 30.00 12.00
559 Jim Gentile 60.00 24.00
560 Barry Latman 40.00 16.00
561 Charley James 30.00 12.00
562 Bill Monbouquette 30.00 12.00
563 Bob Cerv 60.00 24.00
564 Don Cardwell 30.00 12.00
565 Felipe Alou 50.00 20.00
566 Paul Richards AS MG 30.00 12.00
567 D.Murtaugh AS MG 30.00 12.00
568 Bill Skowron AS 50.00 20.00
569 Frank Herrera AS 40.00 16.00
570 Nellie Fox AS 60.00 24.00
571 Bill Mazeroski AS 60.00 24.00
572 Brooks Robinson AS 80.00 32.00
573 Ken Boyer AS 50.00 20.00
574 Luis Aparicio AS 60.00 24.00
575 Ernie Banks AS 80.00 32.00
576 Roger Maris AS 175.00 70.00
577 Hank Aaron AS 150.00 60.00
578 Mickey Mantle AS 400.00 160.00
579 Willie Mays AS 150.00 60.00
580 Al Kaline AS 80.00 32.00
581 Frank Robinson AS 80.00 32.00
582 Earl Battey AS 30.00 12.00
583 Del Crandall AS 30.00 12.00
584 Jim Perry AS 30.00 12.00
585 Bob Friend AS 30.00 12.00
586 Whitey Ford AS 100.00 40.00
589 Warren Spahn AS 100.00 30.00

1961 Topps Magic Rub-Offs

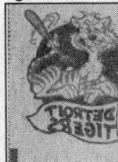

There are 36 "Magic Rub-Offs" in this set of inserts also marketed in packages of 1961 Topps baseball cards. Each rub off measures 2 1/16" by 3 1/16". Of this number, 18 are team designs (numbered 1-18 below), while the remaining 18 depict players (numbered 19-36 below). The latter, one from each team, were apparently selected for their unusual nicknames. Note: The Duke Maas insert is misspelled "Mass".

NM Ex
COMPLETE SET (36) 140.00 55.00
COMMON RUB-OFF (1-18) 2.00 .80
COMMON CARD (19-36) 5.00 2.00
1 Detroit Tigers 3.00 1.20
2 New York Yankees 4.00 1.60
3 Minnesota Twins 2.00 .80
4 Washington Senators 2.00 .80
5 Boston Red Sox 3.00 1.20
6 Los Angeles Angels 2.00 .80
7 Kansas City A's 2.00 .80
8 Baltimore Orioles 2.00 .80
9 Chicago White Sox 2.00 .80
10 Cleveland Indians 2.00 .80
11 Pittsburgh Pirates 2.00 .80
12 San Francisco Giants 2.00 .80
13 Los Angeles Dodgers 4.00 1.60
14 Philadelphia Phillies 2.00 .80
15 Cincinnati Redlegs 2.00 .80
16 St. Louis Cardinals 2.00 .80
17 Chicago Cubs 2.00 .80
18 Milwaukee Braves 2.00 .80
19 John Romano 5.00 2.00
20 Ray Moore 5.00 2.00
21 Ernie Banks 25.00 10.00
22 Charlie Maxwell 5.00 2.00
23 Yogi Berra 25.00 10.00
24 Henry "Dutch" Dotterer 5.00 2.00
25 Jim Brosnan 5.00 2.00
26 Billy Martin 10.00 4.00
27 Jackie Brandt 5.00 2.00
28 Duke Maas 6.00 2.40
sic, Mass
29 Pete Runnels 6.00 2.40
30 Joe Gordon MG 6.00 2.40
31 Sam Jones 5.00 2.00
32 Walt Moryn 5.00 2.00
33 Harvey Haddix 6.00 2.40
34 Frank Howard 8.00 3.20
35 Turk Lown 5.00 2.00
36 Frank Herrera 5.00 2.00

1961 Topps Stamps Inserts

There are 207 different baseball players depicted in this stamp series, which was issued as an insert in packages of the regular Topps cards of 1961. The set is actually comprised of 208 stamps: 104 players are pictured on brown stamps and 104 players appear on green stamps, with Kaline found in both colors. The stamps were issued in attached pairs and an album was sold separately (10 cents) at retail outlets. Each stamp measures 1 3/8" by 1 3/16". Stamps are unnumbered but are presented here in alphabetical order by team, Chicago Cubs (1-12), Cincinnati Reds (13-24), Los Angeles Dodgers (25-36), Milwaukee Braves (37-48), Philadelphia Phillies (49-60), Pittsburgh Pirates (61-72), San Francisco Giants (73-84), St. Louis Cardinals (85-96), Baltimore Orioles AL (97-107), Boston Red Sox (108-119), Chicago White Sox (120-131), Cleveland Indians (132-143), Detroit Tigers (144-155), Kansas City A's (156-168), Los Angeles Angels (169-175), Minnesota Twins (176-187), New York Yankees (188-200) and Washington Senators (201-207).

NM Ex
COMPLETE SET (207) 350.00 140.00
1 George Altman 2.00 .80
2 Bob Anderson 2.00 .80
brown
3 Richie Ashburn 5.00 2.00
4 Ernie Banks 8.00 3.20
5 Ed Bouchee 2.00 .80
6 Jim Brewer 2.00 .80
7 Dick Ellsworth 2.00 .80
8 Don Elston 2.00 .80
9 Ron Santo 5.00 2.00
10 Sammy Taylor 2.00 .80
11 Bob Will 2.00 .80
12 Billy Williams 5.00 2.00
13 Ed Bailey 2.00 .80
14 Gus Bell 2.00 .80
15 Jim Brosnan 2.00 .80
brown
16 Chico Cardenas 2.00 .80
17 Gene Freese 2.00 .80
18 Eddie Kasko 2.00 .80
19 Jerry Lynch 2.00 .80
20 Billy Martin 5.00 2.00
21 Jim O'Toole 2.00 .80
22 Vada Pinson 3.00 1.20
23 Wally Post 2.00 .80
brown
24 Frank Robinson 8.00 3.20
25 Tommy Davis 3.00 1.20
26 Don Drysdale 5.00 2.00
27 Frank Howard 3.00 1.20
brown
28 Norm Larker 2.00 .80
29 Wally Moon 2.00 .80
brown
30 Charlie Neal 2.00 .80
31 Johnny Podres 3.00 1.20
32 Ed Roebuck 2.00 .80
33 Johnny Roseboro 2.00 .80
34 Larry Sherry 2.00 .80
35 Duke Snider 8.00 3.20
36 Stan Williams 2.00 .80
37 Hank Aaron 25.00 10.00
38 Joe Adcock 2.00 .80
39 Bill Bruton 2.00 .80
40 Bob Buhl 2.00 .80
41 Wes Covington 2.00 .80
brown
42 Del Crandall 2.00 .80
43 Joey Jay 2.00 .80
44 Felix Mantilla 2.00 .80
45 Eddie Mathews 8.00 3.20
46 Roy McMillan 2.00 .80
47 Warren Spahn 8.00 3.20
48 Carlton Willey 2.00 .80
brown
49 John Buzhardt 2.00 .80
50 Johnny Callison 2.00 .80
51 Tony Curry 2.00 .80
52 Clay Dalrymple 2.00 .80
brown
53 Bobby Del Greco 2.00 .80
brown
54 Dick Farrell 2.00 .80
brown
55 Tony Gonzalez 2.00 .80
56 Pancho Herrera 2.00 .80
57 Art Mahaffey 2.00 .80
58 Robin Roberts 3.00 1.20
brown
59 Tony Taylor 2.00 .80
60 Lee Walls 2.00 .80
61 Smoky Burgess 2.00 .80
62 Roy Face (brown) 2.00 .80
63 Bob Friend 2.00 .80
64 Dick Groat 3.00 1.20
65 Don Hoak 2.00 .80
66 Vern Law 2.00 .80
67 Bill Mazeroski 3.00 1.20
68 Rocky Nelson 2.00 .80
69 Bob Skinner 2.00 .80
70 Hal Smith 2.00 .80
71 Dick Stuart 2.00 .80
72 Bill Virdon 2.00 .80
73 Don Blasingame 2.00 .80
74 Eddie Bressoud 2.00 .80
brown
75 Orlando Cepeda 3.00 1.20
76 Jim Davenport 2.00 .80
77 Harvey Kuenn 3.00 1.20
brown
78 Hobie Landrith 2.00 .80
79 Juan Marichal 5.00 2.00
80 Willie Mays 25.00 10.00
81 Mike McCormick 2.00 .80
82 Willie McCovey 8.00 3.20
83 Billy O'Dell 2.00 .80
84 Jack Sanford 2.00 .80
85 Ken Boyer 3.00 1.20
86 Curt Flood 3.00 1.20
87 Alex Grammas 2.00 .80
brown
88 Larry Jackson 2.00 .80
89 Julian Javier 2.00 .80
90 Ron Kline 2.00 .80
brown
91 Lindy McDaniel 2.00 .80
92 Stan Musial 15.00 6.00
93 Curt Simmons 2.00 .80
brown
94 Hal Smith 2.00 .80
95 Daryl Spencer 2.00 .80
96 Bill White 2.00 .80
brown
97 Steve Barber 2.00 .80
98 Jackie Brandt 2.00 .80
brown
99 Marv Breeding 2.00 .80
100 Chuck Estrada 2.00 .80
101 Jim Gentile 2.00 .80
102 Ron Hansen 2.00 .80
103 Milt Pappas 2.00 .80
104 Brooks Robinson 8.00 3.20
105 Gene Stephens 2.00 .80
106 Gus Triandos 2.00 .80
107 Hoyt Wilhelm 3.00 1.20
108 Tom Brewer 2.00 .80
109 Gene Conley 2.00 .80
brown
110 Ike Delock 2.00 .80
brown
111 Gary Geiger 2.00 .80
112 Jackie Jensen 3.00 1.20
113 Frank Malzone 2.00 .80
114 Bill Monbouquette 2.00 .80
115 Russ Nixon 2.00 .80
116 Pete Runnels 2.00 .80
117 Willie Tasby 2.00 .80
118 Vic Wertz 2.00 .80
brown
119 Carl Yastrzemski 15.00 6.00
120 Luis Aparicio 3.00 1.20
121 Russ Kemmerer 2.00 .80
brown
122 Jim Landis 2.00 .80
123 Sherman Lollar 2.00 .80
124 J.C. Martin 2.00 .80
125 Minnie Minoso 3.00 1.20
126 Billy Pierce 2.00 .80
127 Bob Shaw 2.00 .80
128 Roy Sievers 2.00 .80
129 Al Smith 2.00 .80
130 Gerry Staley 2.00 .80
brown
131 Early Wynn 3.00 1.20
132 Johnny Antonelli 2.00 .80
brown
133 Ken Aspromonte 2.00 .80
134 Tito Francona 2.00 .80
135 Jim Grant 2.00 .80
136 Woody Held 2.00 .80
137 Barry Latman 2.00 .80
138 Jim Perry 2.00 .80
139 Jimmy Piersall 3.00 1.20
140 Bubba Phillips 2.00 .80
141 Vic Power 2.00 .80
142 John Romano 2.00 .80
143 Johnny Temple 2.00 .80
144 Hank Aguirre 2.00 .80
brown
145 Frank Bolling 2.00 .80
146 Steve Boros 2.00 .80
brown
147 Jim Bunning 3.00 1.20
brown
148 Norm Cash 3.00 1.20
149 Harry Chiti 2.00 .80
150 Chico Fernandez 2.00 .80
151 Dick Gernert 2.00 .80
152A Al Kaline (green) 8.00 3.20
152B Al Kaline (brown) 8.00 3.20
153 Frank Lary 2.00 .80
154 Charlie Maxwell 2.00 .80
155 Dave Sisler 2.00 .80
156 Hank Bauer 2.00 .80
157 Bob Boyd (brown) 2.00 .80
158 Andy Carey 2.00 .80
159 Bud Daley 2.00 .80
160 Dick Hall 2.00 .80
161 J.C. Hartman 2.00 .80
162 Ray Herbert 2.00 .80
163 Whitey Herzog 3.00 1.20
164 Jerry Lumpe 2.00 .80
brown
165 Norm Siebern 2.00 .80
166 Marv Throneberry 2.00 .80
167 Bill Tuttle 2.00 .80
168 Dick Williams 2.00 .80
169 Jerry Casale 2.00 .80
brown
170 Bob Cerv 2.00 .80
171 Ned Garver 2.00 .80
172 Ron Hunt 2.00 .80
173 Ted Kluszewski 5.00 2.00
174 Ed Sadowski 2.00 .80
brown
175 Eddie Yost 2.00 .80
176 Bob Allison 2.00 .80
177 Earl Battey 2.00 .80
brown
178 Reno Bertoia 2.00 .80
179 Billy Gardner 2.00 .80
180 Jim Kaat 3.00 1.20
181 Harmon Killebrew 8.00 3.20
182 Jim Lemon 2.00 .80
183 Camilo Pascual 2.00 .80
184 Pedro Ramos 2.00 .80
185 Chuck Stobbs 2.00 .80
186 Zoilo Versalles 2.00 .80
187 Pete Whisenant 2.00 .80
188 Luis Arroyo 2.00 .80
brown
189 Yogi Berra 12.00 4.80
190 John Blanchard 2.00 .80
191 Clete Boyer 2.00 .80
192 Art Ditmar 2.00 .80
193 Whitey Ford 12.00 4.80
194 Elston Howard 5.00 2.00
195 Tony Kubek 5.00 2.00
196 Mickey Mantle 100.00 40.00
197 Roger Maris 25.00 10.00
198 Bobby Shantz 2.00 .80
199 Bill Stafford 2.00 .80
200 Bob Turley 2.00 .80
201 Bud Daley 2.00 .80
brown
202 Dick Donovan 2.00 .80
203 Bobby Klaus 2.00 .80
204 Johnny Klippstein 2.00 .80
205 Dale Long 2.00 .80
206 Ray Semproch 2.00 .80
207 Gene Woodling 2.00 .80
XX Stamp Album 20.00 8.00

1962 Topps

The cards in this 598-card set measure 2 1/2" by 3 1/2". The 1962 Topps set contains a mini-series spotlighting Babe Ruth (135-144). Other subsets in the set include League Leaders (51-60), World Series cards (232-237), In Action cards (311-319), NL All Stars (390-399), AL All Stars (466-475), and Rookie Prospects (591-598). The All-Star selections were again provided by Sport Magazine, as in 1958 and 1960. The second series had two distinct printings which are distinguishable by numerous color and pose variations. Those cards with a distinctive "green tint" are valued at a slight premuim as they are basically the result of a flawed printing process occurring early in the second series run. Card number 139 exists as A: Babe Ruth Special card, B: Hal Reniff with arms over head, or C: Hal Reniff in the same pose as card number 159. In addition, two poses exist for these cards: 129, 132, 134, 147, 174, 176, and 190. The high number series, 523 to 598, is somewhat more difficult to obtain than other cards in the set. Within the last series (523-598) there are 43 cards which were printed in lesser quantities; these are marked SP in the checklist below. In particular, the Rookie Parade subset (591-598) of this last series is even more difficult. This was the first year Topps produced multi-player Rookie Cards. The set price listed does not include the pose variations (see checklist below for individual values). A three card ad sheet has been seen. The players on the front include AL HR leaders, Barney Schultz and Carl Sawatski, while the back features an ad and a Roger Maris card. Cards were issued in one-card penny packs as well as five-card nickel packs. The five card packs came 24 to a box. The key Rookie Cards in this set are Lou Brock, Tim McCarver, Gaylord Perry, and Bob Uecker.

NM Ex
COMP. MASTER (688) 7000.00 2800.00
COMPLETE SET (598) 6000.00 2400.00
COMMON CARD (1-370) 5.00 2.00
COMMON (371-446) 6.00 2.40
COMMON (447-522) 12.00 4.80
COMMON (523-598) 20.00 8.00
WRAPPER (1-CENT) 100.00 40.00
WRAPPER (5-CENT) 30.00 12.00
1 Roger Maris 300.00 75.00
2 Jim Brosnan 5.00 2.00
3 Pete Runnels 5.00 2.00
4 John DeMerit 8.00 3.20
5 Sandy Koufax UER 150.00 60.00
Struck ou 18
6 Marv Breeding 5.00 2.00
7 Frank Thomas 10.00 4.00
8 Ray Herbert 5.00 2.00
9 Jim Davenport 8.00 3.20
10 Roberto Clemente 175.00 70.00
11 Tom Morgan 5.00 2.00
12 Harry Craft MG 5.00 2.00
13 Dick Howser 8.00 3.20
14 Bill White 8.00 3.20
15 Dick Donovan 5.00 2.00
16 Darrell Johnson 5.00 2.00
17 Johnny Callison 8.00 3.20
18 Mickey Mantle 175.00 70.00
Willie Mays
19 Ray Washburn 5.00 2.00
20 Rocky Colavito 15.00 6.00
21 Jim Kaat 8.00 3.20
22A Checklist 1 ERR 12.00 2.40
(121-176 on back)
22B Checklist 1 COR 12.00 2.40
23 Norm Larker 5.00 2.00
24 Tigers Team 10.00 4.00
25 Ernie Banks 50.00 20.00
26 Chris Cannizzaro 8.00 3.20
27 Chuck Cottier 5.00 2.00
28 Minnie Minoso 10.00 4.00
29 Casey Stengel MG 20.00 8.00
30 Eddie Mathews 40.00 16.00
31 Tom Tresh RC 15.00 6.00
32 John Roseboro 8.00 3.20
33 Don Larsen 8.00 3.20
34 Johnny Temple 8.00 3.20
35 Don Schwall 10.00 4.00
36 Don Leppert 5.00 2.00
37 Barry Latman 5.00 2.00
Dick Stigman
Jim Perry

38 Gene Stephens 5.00 2.00
39 Joe Koppe 5.00 2.00
40 Orlando Cepeda 15.00 6.00
41 Cliff Cook 5.00 2.00
42 Jim King 5.00 2.00
43 Los Angeles Dodgers 10.00 4.00
Team Card
44 Don Taussig 5.00 2.00
45 Brooks Robinson 50.00 20.00
46 Jack Baldschun 5.00 2.00
47 Bob Will 5.00 2.00
48 Ralph Terry 8.00 3.20
49 Hal Jones 5.00 2.00
50 Stan Musial 100.00 40.00
51 Norm Cash 8.00 3.20
Jim Piersall
Al Kaline
Elston Howard LL
52 Roberto Clemente 20.00 8.00
Vada Pinson
Ken Boyer
Wally Moon LL
53 Roger Maris 100.00 40.00
Mickey Mantle
Jim Gentile
Harmon Killebrew LL
54 Orlando Cepeda 20.00 8.00
Willie Mays
Frank Robinson LL
55 Dick Donovan 8.00 3.20
Bill Stafford
Don Mossi
Milt Pappas LL
56 Warren Spahn 8.00 3.20
Jim O'Toole
Curt Simmons
Mike McCormick LL
57 Whitey Ford 8.00 3.20
Frank Lary
Steve Barber
Jim Bunning LL
58 Warren Spahn 8.00 3.20
Joe Jay
Jim O'Toole LL
59 Camilo Pascual 8.00 3.20
Whitey Ford
Jim Bunning
Juan Pizzaro LL
60 Sandy Koufax 20.00 8.00
Stan Williams
Don Drysdale
Jim O'Toole LL
61 Cardinals Team 10.00 4.00
62 Steve Boros 5.00 2.00
63 Tony Cloninger RC 8.00 3.20
64 Russ Snyder 5.00 2.00
65 Bobby Richardson 10.00 4.00
66 Cuno Barragan 5.00 2.00
67 Harvey Haddix 8.00 3.20
68 Ken Hunt 5.00 2.00
69 Phil Ortega 5.00 2.00
70 Harmon Killebrew 25.00 10.00
71 Dick LeMay 5.00 2.00
72 Steve Boros 5.00 2.00
Bob Scheffing MG
Jake Wood
73 Nellie Fox 20.00 8.00
74 Bob Lillis 8.00 3.20
75 Milt Pappas 8.00 3.20
76 Howie Bedell 5.00 2.00
77 Tony Taylor 8.00 3.20
78 Gene Green 5.00 2.00
79 Ed Hobaugh 5.00 2.00
80 Vada Pinson 8.00 3.20
81 Jim Pagliaroni 5.00 2.00
82 Deron Johnson 8.00 3.20
83 Larry Jackson 5.00 2.00
84 Lenny Green 5.00 2.00
85 Gil Hodges 20.00 8.00
86 Donn Clendenon RC 8.00 3.20
87 Mike Roarke 5.00 2.00
88 Ralph Houk MG 8.00 3.20
(Berra in background)
89 Barney Schultz 5.00 2.00
90 Jimmy Piersall 8.00 3.20
91 J.C. Martin 5.00 2.00
92 Sam Jones 5.00 2.00
93 John Blanchard 8.00 3.20
94 Jay Hook 8.00 3.20
95 Don Hoak 8.00 3.20
96 Eli Grba 5.00 2.00
97 Tito Francona 5.00 2.00
98 Checklist 2 12.00 2.40
99 John (Boog) Powell RC 30.00 12.00
100 Warren Spahn 40.00 16.00
101 Carroll Hardy 5.00 2.00
102 Al Schroll 5.00 2.00
103 Don Blasingame 5.00 2.00
104 Ted Savage 5.00 2.00
105 Don Mossi 8.00 3.20
106 Carl Sawatski 5.00 2.00
107 Mike McCormick 8.00 3.20
108 Willie Davis 8.00 3.20
109 Bob Shaw 5.00 2.00
110 Bill Skowron 8.00 3.20
110A Bill Skowron 8.00 3.20
Green Tint
111 Dallas Green 8.00 3.20
111A Dallas Green 8.00 3.20
Green Tint
112 Hank Foiles 5.00 2.00
112A Hank Foiles 5.00 2.00
Green Tint
113 Chicago White Sox 10.00 4.00
Team Card
113A Chicago White Sox 10.00 4.00
Team Card
Green Tint
114 Howie Koplitz 5.00 2.00
114A Howie Koplitz 5.00 2.00
Green Tint
115 Bob Skinner 8.00 3.20
115A Bob Skinner 8.00 3.20
Green Tint
116 Herb Score 8.00 3.20
116A Herb Score 8.00 3.20
Green Tint
117 Gary Geiger 8.00 3.20
117A Gary Geiger 8.00 3.20
Green Tint
118 Julian Javier 8.00 3.20
118A Julian Javier 8.00 3.20
Green Tint
119 Danny Murphy 5.00 2.00
119A Danny Murphy 5.00 2.00
Green Tint
120 Bob Purkey 5.00 2.00
120A Bob Purkey 5.00 2.00
Green Tint
121 Billy Hitchcock MG 5.00 2.00
121A Billy Hitchcock 5.00 2.00
Green Tint
122 Norm Bass 5.00 2.00
122A Norm Bass 5.00 2.00
Green Tint
123 Mike de la Hoz 5.00 2.00
123A Mike de la Hoz 5.00 2.00
Green Tint
124 Bill Pleis 5.00 2.00
124A Bill Pleis 5.00 2.00
Green Tint
125 Gene Woodling 8.00 3.20
125A Gene Woodling 8.00 3.20
Green Tint
126 Al Cicotte 5.00 2.00
126A Al Cicotte 5.00 2.00
Green Tint
127 Norm Siebern 5.00 2.00
Hank Bauer MG
Jerry Lumpe
127A Norm Siebern 5.00 2.00
Hank Bauer MG
Jerry Lumpe
Green Tint
128 Art Fowler 5.00 2.00
128A Art Fowler 5.00 2.00
Green Tint
129A Lee Walls 5.00 2.00
(Facing right)
129B Lee Walls 30.00 12.00
(Facing left)
130 Frank Bolling 5.00 2.00
130A Frank Bolling 5.00 2.00
Green Tint
131 Pete Richert 5.00 2.00
131A Pete Richert 5.00 2.00
Green Tint
132A Angels Team 10.00 4.00
(Without photo)
132B Angels Team 30.00 12.00
(With photo)
133 Felipe Alou 8.00 3.20
133A Felipe Alou 8.00 3.20
Green Tint
134A Billy Hoeft 5.00 2.00
134B Billy Hoeft 30.00 12.00
Green Tint
135 Babe Ruth Special 1 20.00 8.00
Babe as a Boy
135A Babe Ruth Special 20.00 8.00
Base as a Boy
136 Babe Ruth Special 2 20.00 8.00
Jacob Ruppert OWN
Babe Joins Yanks
136A Babe Ruth Special 20.00 8.00
Jacob Ruppert OWN
Babe Joins Yanks
Green Tint
137 Babe Ruth Special 3 20.00 8.00
With Miller Huggins
137A Babe Ruth Special 20.00 8.00
With Miller Huggins
Green Tint
138 Babe Ruth Special 4 20.00 8.00
Famous Slugger
138A Babe Ruth Special 20.00 8.00
Famous Slugger
Green Tint
139A Babe Ruth Special 5 30.00 12.00
Babe Hits 60
139B Hal Reniff PORT RC 15.00 6.00
139C Hal Reniff RC 60.00 24.00
Pitching
140 Babe Ruth Special 6 60.00 24.00
With Lou Gehrig
140A Babe Ruth Special 60.00 24.00
Lou Gehrig
Green Tint
141 Babe Ruth Special 7 20.00 8.00
Twilight Years
141A Babe Ruth Special 20.00 8.00
Twilight Years
Green Tint
142 Babe Ruth Special 8 20.00 8.00
Coaching Dodgers
142A Babe Ruth Special 20.00 8.00
Coaching Dodgers
Green Tint
143 Babe Ruth Special 9 20.00 8.00
Greatest Sports Hero
143A Babe Ruth Special 20.00 8.00
Greatest Sports Hero
Green Tint
144 Babe Ruth Special 10 20.00 8.00
Farewell Speech
144A Babe Ruth Special 20.00 8.00
Babe Ruth Special
Farewell Speech
145 Barry Latman 5.00 2.00
145A Barry Latman 5.00 2.00
Green Tint
146 Don Demeter 5.00 2.00
146A Don Demeter 5.00 2.00
Green Tint
147A Bill Kunkel PORT 5.00 2.00
147B Bill Kunkel 30.00 12.00
(Pitching pose)
148 Wally Post 5.00 2.00
148A Wally Post 5.00 2.00
Green Tint
149 Bob Duliba 5.00 2.00
149A Bob Duliba 5.00 2.00
Green Tint
150 Al Kaline 50.00 20.00
150A Al Kaline 50.00 20.00
Green Tint
151 Johnny Klippstein 5.00 2.00
151A Johnny Klippstein 5.00 2.00
Green Tint
152 Mickey Vernon MG 8.00 3.20
152A Mickey Vernon MG 8.00 3.20
Green Tint
153 Pumpsie Green 6.00 2.40
153A Pumpsie Green 6.00 2.40
Green Tint
154 Lee Thomas 6.00 2.40
154A Lee Thomas 6.00 2.40
Green Tint
155 Stu Miller 6.00 2.40
155A Stu Miller 6.00 2.40
Green Tint
156 Merritt Ranew 5.00 2.00
156A Merritt Ranew 5.00 2.00
Green Tint
157 Wes Covington 8.00 3.20
157A Wes Covington 8.00 3.20
Green Tint
158 Braves Team 10.00 4.00
158A Braves Team 15.00 6.00
Green Tint
159 Hal Reniff RC 8.00 3.20
160 Dick Stuart 8.00 3.20
160A Dick Stuart 8.00 3.20
Green Tint
161 Frank Baumann 5.00 2.00
161A Frank Baumann 5.00 2.00
Green Tint
162 Sammy Drake 5.00 2.00
162A Sammy Drake 5.00 2.00
Green Tint
163 Billy Gardner 8.00 3.20
Cletis Boyer
163A Billy Gardner 8.00 3.20
Clete Boyer
Green Tint
164 Hal Naragon 5.00 2.00
164A Hal Naragon 5.00 2.00
Green Tint
165 Jackie Brandt 5.00 2.00
165A Jackie Brandt 5.00 2.00
Green Tint
166 Don Lee 5.00 2.00
166A Don Lee 5.00 2.00
Green Tint
167 Tim McCarver RC 30.00 12.00
167A Tim McCarver RC 30.00 12.00
Green Tint
168 Leo Posada 5.00 2.00
168A Leo Posada 5.00 2.00
Green Tint
169 Bob Cerv 10.00 4.00
169A Bob Cerv 10.00 4.00
Green Tint
170 Ron Santo 15.00 6.00
170A Ron Santo 15.00 6.00
Green Tint
171 Dave Sisler 5.00 2.00
171A Dave Sisler 5.00 2.00
Green Tint
172 Fred Hutchinson MG 8.00 3.20
172A Fred Hutchinson MG 8.00 3.20
Green Tint
173 Chico Fernandez 5.00 2.00
173A Chico Fernandez 5.00 2.00
Green Tint
174A Carl Willey 5.00 2.00
(Capless)
174B Carl Willey 30.00 12.00
(With cap)
175 Frank Howard 10.00 4.00
175A Frank Howard 10.00 4.00
Green Tint
176A Eddie Yost PORT 5.00 2.00
176B Eddie Yost BATTING 30.00 12.00
177 Bobby Shantz 8.00 3.20
177A Bobby Shantz 8.00 3.20
Green Tint
178 Camilo Carreon 5.00 2.00
178A Camilo Carreon 5.00 2.00
Green Tint
179 Tom Sturdivant 5.00 2.00
179A Tom Sturdivant 5.00 2.00
Green Tint
180 Bob Allison 10.00 4.00
180A Bob Allison 10.00 4.00
Green Tint
181 Paul Brown 5.00 2.00
181A Paul Brown 5.00 2.00
Green Tint
182 Bob Nieman 5.00 2.00
182A Bob Nieman 5.00 2.00
Green Tint
183 Roger Craig 8.00 3.20
183A Roger Craig 8.00 3.20
Green Tint
184 Haywood Sullivan 8.00 3.20
184A Haywood Sullivan 8.00 3.20
Green Tint
185 Roland Sheldon 10.00 4.00
185A Roland Sheldon 10.00 4.00
Green Tint
186 Mack Jones 5.00 2.00
186A Mack Jones 5.00 2.00
Green Tint
187 Gene Conley 5.00 2.00
187A Gene Conley 5.00 2.00
Green Tint
188 Chuck Hiller 5.00 2.00
188A Chuck Hiller 5.00 2.00
Green Tint
189 Dick Hall 5.00 2.00
189A Dick Hall 5.00 2.00
Green Tint
190A Wally Moon PORT 8.00 3.20
190B W.Moon BATTING 30.00 12.00
191 Jim Brewer 5.00 2.00
191A Jim Brewer 5.00 2.00
Green Tint
192A Checklist 3 12.00 2.40
(Without comma)
192B Checklist 3 15.00 3.00
(Comma after
Checklist)
193 Eddie Kasko 5.00 2.00
193A Eddie Kasko 5.00 2.00
Green Tint
194 Dean Chance RC 8.00 3.20
194A Dean Chance RC 8.00 3.20
Green Tint
195 Joe Cunningham 5.00 2.00
195A Joe Cunningham 5.00 2.00
Green Tint
196 Terry Fox 5.00 2.00
196A Terry Fox 5.00 2.00
Green Tint
197 Daryl Spencer 5.00 2.00
198 Johnny Keane MG 5.00 2.00
199 Gaylord Perry RC 80.00 32.00
200 Mickey Mantle 600.00 200.00
201 Ike Delock 5.00 2.00
202 Carl Warwick 5.00 2.00
203 Jack Fisher 5.00 2.00
204 Johnny Weekly 5.00 2.00
205 Gene Freese 5.00 2.00
206 Senators Team 10.00 4.00
207 Pete Burnside 5.00 2.00
208 Billy Martin 20.00 8.00
209 Jim Fregosi RC 15.00 6.00
210 Roy Face 8.00 3.20
211 Frank Bolling 5.00 2.00
Roy McMillan
212 Jim Owens 5.00 2.00
213 Richie Ashburn 20.00 8.00
214 Dom Zanni 5.00 2.00
215 Woody Held 5.00 2.00
216 Ron Kline 5.00 2.00
217 Walter Alston MG 10.00 4.00
218 Joe Torre RC 40.00 16.00
219 Al Downing RC 8.00 3.20
220 Roy Sievers 8.00 3.20
221 Bill Short 5.00 2.00
222 Jerry Zimmerman 5.00 2.00
223 Alex Grammas 5.00 2.00
224 Don Rudolph 5.00 2.00
225 Frank Malzone 8.00 3.20
226 San Francisco Giants 10.00 4.00
Team Card
227 Bob Tiefenauer 5.00 2.00
228 Dale Long 10.00 4.00
229 Jesus McFarlane 5.00 2.00
230 Camilo Pascual 8.00 3.20
231 Ernie Bowman 5.00 2.00
232 World Series Game 1 10.00 4.00
Yanks win opener
233 Joey Jay WS 10.00 4.00
234 Roger Maris WS 25.00 10.00
235 Whitey Ford WS 15.00 6.00
sets new mark
236 World Series Game 5 10.00 4.00
Yanks crush Reds
237 WS Summary 10.00 4.00
Yanks celebrate
238 Norm Sherry 5.00 2.00
239 Cecil Butler 5.00 2.00
240 George Altman 5.00 2.00
241 Johnny Kucks 5.00 2.00
242 Mel McGaha MG 5.00 2.00
243 Robin Roberts 15.00 6.00
244 Don Gile 5.00 2.00
245 Ron Hansen 5.00 2.00
246 Art Ditmar 5.00 2.00
247 Joe Pignatano 5.00 2.00
248 Bob Aspromonte 8.00 3.20
249 Ed Keegan 5.00 2.00
250 Norm Cash 10.00 4.00
251 New York Yankees 50.00 20.00
Team Card
252 Earl Francis 5.00 2.00
253 Harry Chiti CO 5.00 2.00
254 Gordon Windhorn 5.00 2.00
255 Juan Pizarro 5.00 2.00
256 Elio Chacon 8.00 3.20
257 Jack Spring 5.00 2.00
258 Marty Keough 5.00 2.00
259 Lou Klimchock 5.00 2.00
260 Billy Pierce 8.00 3.20
261 George Alusik 5.00 2.00
262 Bob Schmidt 5.00 2.00
263 Bob Purkey 5.00 2.00
Jim Turner CO
Joe Jay
264 Dick Ellsworth 8.00 3.20
265 Joe Adcock 8.00 3.20
266 John Anderson 5.00 2.00
267 Dan Dobbek 5.00 2.00
268 Ken McBride 5.00 2.00
269 Bob Oldis 5.00 2.00
270 Dick Groat 8.00 3.20
271 Ray Rippelmeyer 5.00 2.00
272 Earl Robinson 5.00 2.00
273 Gary Bell 5.00 2.00
274 Sammy Taylor 5.00 2.00
275 Norm Siebern 5.00 2.00
276 Hal Kolstad 5.00 2.00
277 Checklist 4 15.00 3.00
278 Ken Johnson 8.00 3.20
279 Hobie Landrith UER 8.00 3.20
(Wrong birthdate)
280 Johnny Podres 8.00 3.20
281 Jake Gibbs 10.00 4.00
282 Dave Hillman 5.00 2.00
283 Charlie Smith 5.00 2.00
284 Ruben Amaro 5.00 2.00
285 Curt Simmons 8.00 3.20
286 Al Lopez MG 10.00 4.00
287 George Witt 5.00 2.00
288 Billy Williams 30.00 12.00
289 Mike Krsnich 5.00 2.00
290 Jim Gentile 8.00 3.20
291 Hal Stowe 5.00 2.00
292 Jerry Kindall 5.00 2.00
293 Bob Miller 8.00 3.20
294 Phillies Team 10.00 4.00
295 Vern Law 8.00 3.20
296 Ken Hamlin 5.00 2.00
297 Ron Perranoski 8.00 3.20
298 Bill Tuttle 5.00 2.00
299 Don Wert 5.00 2.00
300 Willie Mays 250.00 80.00
301 Galen Cisco RC 5.00 2.00
302 Johnny Edwards 5.00 2.00
303 Frank Torre 8.00 3.20
304 Dick Farrell 8.00 3.20
305 Jerry Lumpe 5.00 2.00
306 Lindy McDaniel 5.00 2.00
Larry Jackson
307 Jim Grant 8.00 3.20
308 Neil Chrisley 8.00 3.20
309 Moe Morhardt 5.00 2.00
310 Whitey Ford 50.00 20.00
311 Tony Kubek IA 8.00 3.20
312 Warren Spahn IA 15.00 6.00
313 Roger Maris IA 80.00 32.00
Blasts 61th
314 Rocky Colavito IA 8.00 3.20
315 Whitey Ford IA 15.00 6.00
316 Harmon Killebrew IA 15.00 6.00
317 Stan Musial IA 20.00 8.00
318 Mickey Mantle IA 150.00 60.00
319 Mike McCormick IA 5.00 2.00
320 Hank Aaron 150.00 60.00
321 Lee Stange 5.00 2.00
322 Alvin Dark MG 8.00 3.20
323 Don Landrum 5.00 2.00
324 Joe McClain 5.00 2.00
325 Luis Aparicio 15.00 6.00
326 Tom Parsons 5.00 2.00
327 Ozzie Virgil 5.00 2.00
328 Ken Walters 5.00 2.00
329 Bob Bolin 5.00 2.00
330 John Romano 5.00 2.00
331 Moe Drabowsky 8.00 3.20
332 Don Buddin 5.00 2.00
333 Frank Cipriani 5.00 2.00
334 Boston Red Sox 10.00 4.00
Team Card
335 Bill Bruton 5.00 2.00
336 Billy Muffett 5.00 2.00
337 Jim Marshall 8.00 3.20
338 Billy Gardner 5.00 2.00
339 Jose Valdivielso 5.00 2.00
340 Don Drysdale 50.00 20.00
341 Mike Hershberger 5.00 2.00
342 Ed Rakow 5.00 2.00
343 Albie Pearson 8.00 3.20
344 Ed Bauta 5.00 2.00
345 Chuck Schilling 5.00 2.00
346 Jack Kralick 5.00 2.00
347 Chuck Hinton 5.00 2.00
348 Larry Burright 8.00 3.20
349 Paul Foytack 5.00 2.00
350 Frank Robinson 50.00 20.00
351 Joe Torre 8.00 3.20
Del Crandall
352 Frank Sullivan 5.00 2.00
353 Bill Mazeroski 15.00 6.00
354 Roman Mejias 8.00 3.20
355 Steve Barber 5.00 2.00
356 Tom Haller RC 5.00 2.00
357 Jerry Walker 5.00 2.00
358 Tommy Davis 8.00 3.20
359 Bobby Locke 5.00 2.00
360 Yogi Berra 80.00 32.00
361 Bob Hendley 5.00 2.00
362 Ty Cline 5.00 2.00
363 Bob Roselli 5.00 2.00
364 Ken Hunt 5.00 2.00
365 Charlie Neal 5.00 2.00
366 Phil Regan 8.00 3.20
367 Checklist 5 15.00 3.00
368 Bob Tillman 5.00 2.00
369 Ted Bowsfield 5.00 2.00
370 Ken Boyer 10.00 4.00
371 Earl Battey 6.00 2.40
372 Jack Curtis 6.00 2.40
373 Al Heist 6.00 2.40
374 Gene Mauch MG 10.00 4.00
375 Ron Fairly 10.00 4.00
376 Bud Daley 8.00 3.20
377 John Orsino 6.00 2.40
378 Bennie Daniels 6.00 2.40
379 Chuck Essegian 6.00 2.40
380 Lou Burdette 10.00 4.00
381 Chico Cardenas 10.00 4.00
382 Dick Williams 8.00 3.20
383 Ray Sadecki 6.00 2.40
384 K.C. Athletics 10.00 4.00
Team Card
385 Early Wynn 15.00 6.00
386 Don Mincher 8.00 3.20
387 Lou Brock RC 125.00 50.00
388 Ryne Duren 8.00 3.20
389 Smoky Burgess 10.00 4.00
390 Orlando Cepeda AS 10.00 4.00
391 Bill Mazeroski AS 10.00 4.00
392 Ken Boyer AS UER 8.00 3.20
Batting Average mistakenly listed as .392
393 Roy McMillan AS 6.00 2.40
394 Hank Aaron AS 50.00 20.00
395 Willie Mays AS 50.00 20.00
396 Frank Robinson AS 15.00 6.00
397 John Roseboro AS 6.00 2.40
398 Don Drysdale AS 15.00 6.00
399 Warren Spahn AS 15.00 6.00
400 Elston Howard 10.00 4.00
401 Roger Maris 60.00 24.00
Orlando Cepeda
402 Gino Cimoli 6.00 2.40
403 Chet Nichols 6.00 2.40
404 Tim Harkness 8.00 3.20
405 Jim Perry 8.00 3.20
406 Bob Taylor 6.00 2.40
407 Hank Aguirre 6.00 2.40
408 Gus Bell 8.00 3.20
409 Pittsburgh Pirates 10.00 4.00
Team Card
410 Al Smith 6.00 2.40
411 Danny O'Connell 6.00 2.40
412 Charlie James 6.00 2.40
413 Matty Alou 10.00 4.00
414 Joe Gaines 6.00 2.40
415 Bill Virdon 10.00 4.00
416 Bob Scheffing MG 6.00 2.40
417 Joe Azcue 6.00 2.40
418 Andy Carey 6.00 2.40
419 Bob Bruce 8.00 3.20
420 Gus Triandos 8.00 3.20
421 Ken MacKenzie 8.00 3.20
422 Steve Bilko 6.00 2.40
423 Roy Face 10.00 4.00
Hoyt Wilhelm
424 Al McBean RC 6.00 2.40
425 Carl Yastrzemski 125.00 50.00
426 Bob Farley 6.00 2.40
427 Jake Wood 6.00 2.40
428 Joe Hicks 6.00 2.40
429 Billy O'Dell 6.00 2.40
430 Tony Kubek 15.00 6.00
431 Bob Rodgers RC 8.00 3.20
432 Jim Pendleton 6.00 2.40

433 Jim Archer 6.00 2.40
434 Clay Dalrymple 6.00 2.40
435 Larry Sherry 8.00 3.20
436 Felix Mantilla 8.00 3.20
437 Ray Moore 6.00 2.40
438 Dick Brown 6.00 2.40
439 Jerry Buchek 6.00 2.40
440 Joey Jay 6.00 2.40
441 Checklist 6 15.00 6.00
442 Wes Stock 6.00 2.40
443 Del Crandall 8.00 3.20
444 Ted Wills 6.00 2.40
445 Vic Power 8.00 3.20
446 Don Elston 6.00 2.40
447 Willie Kirkland 12.00 4.80
448 Joe Gibbon 12.00 4.80
449 Jerry Adair 12.00 4.80
450 Jim O'Toole 15.00 6.00
451 Jose Tartabull RC 15.00 6.00
452 Earl Averill Jr. 12.00 4.80
453 Cal McLish 12.00 4.80
454 Floyd Robinson 12.00 4.80
455 Luis Arroyo 15.00 6.00
456 Joe Amalfitano 15.00 6.00
457 Lou Clinton 12.00 4.80
458A Bob Buhl 15.00 6.00
(Braves emblem on cap)
458B Bob Buhl 50.00 20.00
(No emblem on cap)
459 Ed Bailey 12.00 4.80
460 Jim Bunning 20.00 8.00
461 Ken Hubbs RC 30.00 12.00
462A Willie Tasby 12.00 4.80
(Senators emblem on cap)
462B Willie Tasby 50.00 20.00
(No emblem on cap)
463 Hank Bauer MG 15.00 6.00
464 Al Jackson RC 12.00 4.80
465 Reds Team 20.00 8.00
466 Norm Cash AS 15.00 6.00
467 Chuck Schilling AS 12.00 4.80
468 Brooks Robinson AS 25.00 10.00
469 Luis Aparicio AS 15.00 6.00
470 Al Kaline AS 25.00 10.00
471 Mickey Mantle AS 200.00 80.00
472 Rocky Colavito AS 15.00 6.00
473 Elston Howard AS 15.00 6.00
474 Frank Lary AS 12.00 4.80
475 Whitey Ford AS 20.00 8.00
476 Orioles Team 20.00 8.00
477 Andre Rodgers 12.00 4.80
478 Don Zimmer 20.00 8.00
Shown with Mets cap, but listed with Cincinnati
479 Joel Horlen RC 12.00 4.80
480 Harvey Kuenn 15.00 6.00
481 Vic Wertz 15.00 6.00
482 Sam Mele MG 12.00 4.80
483 Don McMahon 12.00 4.80
484 Dick Schofield 12.00 4.80
485 Pedro Ramos 12.00 4.80
486 Jim Gilliam 15.00 6.00
487 Jerry Lynch 12.00 4.80
488 Hal Brown 12.00 4.80
489 Julio Gotay 12.00 4.80
490 Clete Boyer UER 15.00 6.00
Reversed Negative
491 Leon Wagner 12.00 4.80
492 Hal W. Smith 15.00 6.00
493 Danny McDevitt 12.00 4.80
494 Sammy White 12.00 4.80
495 Don Cardwell 12.00 4.80
496 Wayne Causey 12.00 4.80
497 Ed Bouchee 15.00 6.00
498 Jim Donohue 12.00 4.80
499 Zoilo Versalles 15.00 6.00
500 Duke Snider 60.00 24.00
501 Claude Osteen 15.00 6.00
502 Hector Lopez 15.00 6.00
503 Danny Murtaugh MG 15.00 6.00
504 Eddie Bressoud 12.00 4.80
505 Juan Marichal 40.00 16.00
506 Charlie Maxwell 15.00 6.00
507 Ernie Broglio 15.00 6.00
508 Gordy Coleman 15.00 6.00
509 Dave Giusti RC 15.00 6.00
510 Jim Lemon 12.00 4.80
511 Bubba Phillips 12.00 4.80
512 Mike Fornieles 12.00 4.80
513 Whitey Herzog 15.00 6.00
514 Sherm Lollar 15.00 6.00
515 Stan Williams 15.00 6.00
516A Checklist 7 15.00 3.00
White Boxes
516B Checklist 7 15.00 6.00
Yellow Boxes
517 Dave Wickersham 12.00 4.80
518 Lee Maye 12.00 4.80
519 Bob Johnson 12.00 4.80
520 Bob Friend 15.00 6.00
521 Jacke Davis UER 12.00 4.80
(Listed as OF on front and P on back)
522 Lindy McDaniel 15.00 6.00
523 Russ Nixon SP 30.00 12.00
524 Howie Nunn SP 30.00 12.00
525 George Thomas 20.00 8.00
526 Hal Woodeshick SP 30.00 12.00
527 Dick McAuliffe RC 30.00 12.00
528 Turk Lown 20.00 8.00
529 John Schaive SP 30.00 12.00
530 Bob Gibson SP 125.00 50.00
531 Bobby G. Smith 20.00 8.00
532 Dick Stigman 20.00 8.00
533 Charley Lau SP 30.00 12.00
534 Tony Gonzalez SP 30.00 12.00
535 Ed Roebuck 20.00 8.00
536 Dick Gernert 20.00 8.00
537 Cleveland Indians 50.00 20.00
Team Card
538 Jack Sanford 20.00 8.00
539 Billy Moran 20.00 8.00
540 Jim Landis SP 30.00 12.00
541 Don Nottebart SP 30.00 12.00
542 Dave Philley 20.00 8.00
543 Bob Allen SP 30.00 12.00
544 Willie McCovey SP 125.00 50.00
545 Hoyt Wilhelm SP 50.00 20.00
546 Moe Thacker SP 30.00 12.00
547 Don Ferrarese 20.00 8.00
548 Bobby Del Greco 20.00 8.00
549 Bill Rigney MG SP 30.00 12.00
550 Art Mahaffey SP 30.00 12.00
551 Harry Bright 20.00 8.00
552 Chicago Cubs SP 50.00 20.00
Team Card
553 Jim Coates 30.00 12.00
554 Bubba Morton SP 30.00 12.00
555 John Buzhardt SP 30.00 12.00
556 Al Spangler 20.00 8.00
557 Bob Anderson SP 30.00 12.00
558 John Goryl 20.00 8.00
559 Mike Higgins MG 20.00 8.00
560 Chuck Estrada SP 30.00 12.00
561 Gene Oliver SP 30.00 12.00
562 Bill Henry 20.00 8.00
563 Ken Aspromonte 20.00 8.00
564 Bob Grim 20.00 8.00
565 Jose Pagan 20.00 8.00
566 Marty Kutyna SP 30.00 12.00
567 Tracy Stallard SP 30.00 12.00
568 Jim Golden 20.00 8.00
569 Ed Sadowski SP 30.00 12.00
570 Bill Stafford SP 30.00 12.00
571 Billy Klaus SP 30.00 12.00
572 Bob G. Miller SP 30.00 12.00
573 Johnny Logan 20.00 8.00
574 Dean Stone 20.00 8.00
575 Red Schoendienst SP 50.00 20.00
576 Russ Kemmerer SP 30.00 12.00
577 Dave Nicholson SP 30.00 12.00
578 Jim Duffalo 20.00 8.00
579 Jim Schaffer SP 30.00 12.00
580 Bill Monbouquette 20.00 8.00
581 Mel Roach 20.00 8.00
582 Ron Piche 20.00 8.00
583 Larry Osborne 20.00 8.00
584 Minnesota Twins SP 60.00 24.00
Team Card
585 Glen Hobbie SP 30.00 12.00
586 Sammy Esposito SP 30.00 12.00
587 Frank Funk SP 30.00 12.00
588 Birdie Tebbetts MG 20.00 8.00
589 Bob Turley 30.00 12.00
590 Curt Flood 30.00 12.00
591 Sam McDowell RC 80.00 32.00
Ron Taylor
Ron Nischwitz
Art Quirk
Dick Radatz SP
592 Dan Pfister 80.00 32.00
Bo Belinsky
Dave Stenhouse
Jim Bouton RC
Joe Bonikowski SP
593 Jack Lamabe 50.00 20.00
Craig Anderson
Jack Hamilton
Bob Moorhead
Bob Veale SP
594 Doc Edwards 80.00 32.00
Ken Retzer
Bob Uecker RC
Doug Camilli
Don Pavletich SP
595 Bob Sadowski 50.00 20.00
Felix Torres
Marlan Coughtry
Ed Charles SP
596 Bernie Allen 80.00 32.00
Joe Pepitone RC
Phil Linz
Rich Rollins SP
597 Jim McKnight 50.00 20.00
Rod Kanehl
Amado Samuel
Denis Menke RC SP
598 Al Luplow 80.00 23.00
Manny Jimenez
Howie Goss
Jim Hickman
Ed Olivares SP

1962 Topps Bucks

There are 96 "Baseball Bucks" in this unusual set released in its own one-cent package in 1962. Each "buck" measures 1 3/4" by 4 1/8". Each depicts a player with accompanying biography and facsimile autograph to the left. To the right is found a drawing of the player's home stadium. His team and position are listed under the ribbon design containing his name. The team affiliation and league are also indicated within circles on the reverse.

NM Ex
COMPLETE SET (96) 1250.00 500.00
WRAPPER (1-CENT) 50.00 20.00
1 Hank Aaron 60.00 24.00
2 Joe Adcock 6.00 2.40
3 George Altman 5.00 2.00
4 Jim Archer 5.00 2.00
5 Richie Ashburn 25.00 10.00
6 Ernie Banks 35.00 14.00
7 Earl Battey 5.00 2.00
8 Gus Bell 5.00 2.00
9 Yogi Berra 40.00 16.00
10 Ken Boyer 8.00 3.20
11 Jackie Brandt 5.00 2.00
12 Jim Bunning 25.00 10.00
13 Lew Burdette 6.00 2.40
14 Don Cardwell 5.00 2.00
15 Norm Cash 8.00 3.20
16 Orlando Cepeda 20.00 8.00
17 Roberto Clemente 100.00 40.00
18 Rocky Colavito 15.00 6.00
19 Chuck Cottier 5.00 2.00
20 Roger Craig 6.00 2.40
21 Bennie Daniels 5.00 2.00
22 Don Demeter 5.00 2.00
23 Don Drysdale 30.00 12.00
24 Chuck Estrada 5.00 2.00
25 Dick Farrell 5.00 2.00
26 Whitey Ford 40.00 16.00
27 Nellie Fox 25.00 10.00
28 Tito Francona 5.00 2.00
29 Bob Friend 5.00 2.00
30 Jim Gentile 6.00 2.40
31 Dick Gernert 5.00 2.00
32 Lenny Green 5.00 2.00
33 Dick Groat 6.00 2.40
34 Woodie Held 5.00 2.00
35 Don Hoak 5.00 2.00
36 Gil Hodges 25.00 10.00
37 Elston Howard 15.00 6.00
38 Frank Howard 8.00 3.20
39 Dick Howser 6.00 2.40
40 Ken Hunt 5.00 2.00
41 Larry Jackson 5.00 2.00
42 Joey Jay 5.00 2.00
43 Al Kaline 35.00 14.00
44 Harmon Killebrew 25.00 10.00
45 Sandy Koufax 60.00 24.00
46 Harvey Kuenn 6.00 2.40
47 Jim Landis 5.00 2.00
48 Norm Larker 5.00 2.00
49 Frank Lary 5.00 2.00
50 Jerry Lumpe 5.00 2.00
51 Art Mahaffey 5.00 2.00
52 Frank Malzone 5.00 2.00
53 Felix Mantilla 5.00 2.00
54 Mickey Mantle 200.00 80.00
55 Roger Maris 50.00 20.00
56 Eddie Mathews 25.00 10.00
57 Willie Mays 65.00 26.00
58 Ken McBride 5.00 2.00
59 Mike McCormick 5.00 2.00
60 Stu Miller 5.00 2.00
61 Minnie Minoso 8.00 3.20
62 Wally Moon 6.00 2.40
63 Stan Musial 60.00 24.00
64 Danny O'Connell 5.00 2.00
65 Jim O'Toole 5.00 2.00
66 Camilo Pascual 5.00 2.00
67 Jim Perry 6.00 2.40
68 Jimmy Piersall 6.00 2.40
69 Vada Pinson 8.00 3.20
70 Juan Pizarro 5.00 2.00
71 Johnny Podres 6.00 2.40
72 Vic Power 5.00 2.00
73 Bob Purkey 5.00 2.00
74 Pedro Ramos 5.00 2.00
75 Brooks Robinson 35.00 14.00
76 Floyd Robinson 5.00 2.00
77 Frank Robinson 35.00 14.00
78 John Romano 5.00 2.00
79 Pete Runnels 5.00 2.00
80 Don Schwall 5.00 2.00
81 Bobby Shantz 5.00 2.00
82 Norm Siebern 5.00 2.00
83 Roy Sievers 5.00 2.00
84 Hal Smith 5.00 2.00
85 Warren Spahn 25.00 10.00
86 Dick Stuart 6.00 2.40
87 Tony Taylor 5.00 2.00
88 Lee Thomas 6.00 2.40
89 Gus Triandos 5.00 2.00
90 Leon Wagner 5.00 2.00
91 Jerry Walker 5.00 2.00
92 Bill White 8.00 3.20
93 Billy Williams 25.00 10.00
94 Gene Woodling 6.00 2.40
95 Early Wynn 25.00 10.00
96 Carl Yastrzemski 35.00 14.00

1962 Topps Stamps Inserts

The 201 baseball player stamps inserted into the Topps regular issue of 1962 are color photos set upon red or yellow backgrounds (100 players for each color). They came in two-stamp panels with a small additional strip which contained advertising for an album. Roy Sievers appears with Kansas City or Philadelphia; the set price includes both versions. Each stamp measures 1 3/8" by 1 7/8". Stamps are unnumbered but are presented here in alphabetical order by team, Baltimore Orioles AL (1-10), Boston Red Sox (11-20), Chicago White Sox (21-30), Cleveland Indians (31-40), Detroit Tigers (41-50), Kansas City A's (51-61), Los Angeles Angels (62-71), Minnesota Twins (72-81), New York Yankees (82-91), Washington Senators (92-101), Chicago Cubs NL (102-111), Cincinnati Reds (112-121), Houston Colt .45's (122-131), Los Angeles Dodgers (132-141), Milwaukee Braves (142-151), New York Mets (152-161), Philadelphia Phillies (162-171), Pittsburgh Pirates (172-181), St. Louis Cardinals (182-191) and San Francisco Giants (192-201).

NM Ex
COMPLETE SET (201) 400.00 160.00
1 Baltimore Emblem 1.00 .40
2 Jerry Adair 1.00 .40
3 Jackie Brandt 1.00 .40
4 Chuck Estrada 1.00 .40
5 Jim Gentile 1.50 .60
6 Ron Hansen 1.00 .40
7 Milt Pappas 1.50 .60
8 Brooks Robinson 8.00 3.20
9 Gus Triandos 1.50 .60
10 Hoyt Wilhelm 2.50 1.00
11 Boston Emblem 1.00 .40
12 Mike Fornieles 1.00 .40
13 Gary Geiger 1.00 .40
14 Frank Malzone 1.50 .60
15 Bill Monbouquette 1.00 .40
16 Russ Nixon 1.00 .40
17 Pete Runnels 1.50 .60
18 Chuck Schilling 1.00 .40
19 Don Schwall 1.00 .40
20 Carl Yastrzemski 12.00 4.80
21 Chicago Emblem 1.00 .40
22 Luis Aparicio 2.50 1.00
23 Camilo Carreon 1.00 .40
24 Nellie Fox 4.00 1.60
25 Ray Herbert 1.00 .40
26 Jim Landis 1.00 .40
27 J.C. Martin 1.00 .40
28 Juan Pizzaro 1.00 .40
29 Floyd Robinson 1.00 .40
30 Early Wynn 2.50 1.00
31 Cleveland Emblem 1.00 .40
32 Ty Cline 1.00 .40
33 Dick Donovan 1.00 .40
34 Tito Francona 1.00 .40
35 Woody Held 1.00 .40
36 Barry Latman 1.00 .40
37 Jim Perry 1.50 .60
38 Bubba Phillips 1.00 .40
39 Vic Power 1.00 .40
40 Johnny Romano 1.00 .40
41 Detroit Emblem 1.00 .40
42 Steve Boros 1.00 .40
43 Bill Bruton 1.00 .40
44 Jim Bunning 2.50 1.00
45 Norm Cash 2.50 1.00
46 Rocky Colavito 2.50 1.00
47 Al Kaline 8.00 3.20
48 Frank Lary 1.50 .60
49 Don Mossi 1.50 .60
50 Jake Wood 1.00 .40
51 Kansas City Emblem 1.00 .40
52 Jim Archer 1.00 .40
53 Dick Howser 2.50 1.00
54 Jerry Lumpe 1.00 .40
55 Leo Posada 1.00 .40
56 Bob Shaw 1.00 .40
57 Norm Siebern 1.00 .40
58 Roy Sievers 2.50 1.00
(A's, see also 169
59 Gene Stephens 1.00 .40
60 Haywood Sullivan 1.00 .40
61 Jerry Walker 1.00 .40
62 Los Angeles Emblem 1.00 .40
63 Steve Bilko 1.00 .40
64 Ted Bowsfield 1.00 .40
65 Ken Hunt 1.00 .40
66 Ken McBride 1.00 .40
67 Albie Pearson 1.00 .40
68 Bob Rodgers 1.50 .60
69 George Thomas 1.00 .40
70 Lee Thomas 1.50 .60
71 Leon Wagner 1.00 .40
72 Minnesota Emblem 1.00 .40
73 Bob Allison 1.50 .60
74 Earl Battey 1.00 .40
75 Lenny Green 1.00 .40
76 Harmon Killebrew 6.00 2.40
77 Jack Kralick 1.00 .40
78 Camilo Pascual 1.50 .60
79 Pedro Ramos 1.00 .40
80 Bill Tuttle 1.00 .40
81 Zoilo Versailles 1.00 .40
82 New York Emblem 1.50 .60
83 Yogi Berra 12.00 4.80
84 Clete Boyer 2.50 1.00
85 Whitey Ford 10.00 4.00
86 Elston Howard 4.00 1.60
87 Tony Kubek 2.50 1.00
88 Mickey Mantle 60.00 24.00
89 Roger Maris 20.00 8.00
90 Bobby Richardson 2.50 1.00
91 Bill Skowron 2.50 1.00
92 Washington Emblem 1.00 .40
93 Chuck Cottier 1.00 .40
94 Pete Daley 1.00 .40
95 Bennie Daniels 1.00 .40
96 Chuck Hinton 1.00 .40
97 Bob Johnson 1.00 .40
98 Joe McClain 1.00 .40
99 Danny O'Connell 1.00 .40
100 Jimmy Piersall 2.50 1.00
101 Gene Woodling 1.50 .60
102 Chicago Emblem 1.00 .40
103 George Altman 1.00 .40
104 Ernie Banks 8.00 3.20
105 Dick Bertell 1.00 .40
106 Don Cardwell 1.00 .40
107 Dick Ellsworth 1.00 .40
108 Glen Hobbie 1.00 .40
109 Ron Santo 2.50 1.00
110 Barney Schultz 1.00 .40
111 Billy Williams 2.50 1.00
112 Cincinnati Emblem 1.00 .40
113 Gordon Coleman 1.00 .40
114 Johnny Edwards 1.00 .40
115 Gene Freese 1.00 .40
116 Joey Jay 1.00 .40
117 Eddie Kasko 1.00 .40
118 Jim O'Toole 1.00 .40
119 Vada Pinson 2.50 1.00
120 Bob Purkey 1.00 .40
121 Frank Robinson 8.00 3.20
122 Houston Emblem 1.00 .40
123 Joe Amalfitano 1.00 .40
124 Bob Aspromonte 1.00 .40
125 Dick Farrell 1.00 .40
126 Al Heist 1.00 .40
127 Sam Jones 1.00 .40
128 Bobby Shantz 1.50 .60
129 Hal W. Smith 1.00 .40
130 Al Spangler 1.00 .40
131 Bob Tiefenauer 1.00 .40
132 Los Angeles Emblem 1.00 .40
133 Don Drysdale 6.00 2.40
134 Ron Fairly 1.50 .60
135 Frank Howard 2.50 1.00
136 Sandy Koufax 15.00 6.00
137 Wally Moon 1.50 .60
138 Johnny Podres 2.50 1.00
139 John Roseboro 1.00 .40
140 Duke Snider 10.00 4.00
141 Daryl Spencer 1.00 .40
142 Milwaukee Emblem 1.00 .40
143 Hank Aaron 15.00 6.00
144 Joe Adcock 1.50 .60
145 Frank Bolling 1.00 .40
146 Lou Burdette 2.50 1.00
147 Del Crandall 1.00 .40
148 Eddie Mathews 6.00 2.40
149 Roy McMillan 1.00 .40
150 Warren Spahn 8.00 3.20
151 Joe Torre 5.00 2.00
152 New York Emblem 1.50 .60
153 Gus Bell 1.50 .60
154 Roger Craig 2.50 1.00
155 Gil Hodges 6.00 2.40
156 Jay Hook 1.50 .60
157 Hobie Landrith 1.50 .60
158 Felix Mantilla 1.50 .60
159 Bob L. Miller 1.50 .60
160 Lee Walls 1.50 .60
161 Don Zimmer 2.50 1.00
162 Philadelphia Emblem 1.00 .40
163 Ruben Amaro 1.00 .40
164 Jack Baldschun 1.00 .40
165 Johnny Callison UER 1.50 .60
Name spelled Callizon
166 Clay Dalrymple 1.00 .40
167 Don Demeter 1.00 .40
168 Tony Gonzalez 1.00 .40
169 Roy Sievers 2.50 1.00
Phils, see also 58
170 Tony Taylor 1.50 .60
171 Art Mahaffey 1.00 .40
172 Pittsburgh Emblem 1.00 .40
173 Smoky Burgess 1.50 .60
174 Roberto Clemente 40.00 16.00
175 Roy Face 2.50 1.00
176 Bob Friend 1.50 .60
177 Dick Groat 2.50 1.00
178 Don Hoak 1.00 .40
179 Bill Mazeroski 4.00 1.60
180 Dick Stuart 1.50 .60
181 Bill Virdon 2.50 1.00
182 St. Louis Emblem 1.00 .40
183 Ken Boyer 2.50 1.00
184 Larry Jackson 1.00 .40
185 Julian Javier 1.00 .40
186 Tim McCarver 4.00 1.60
187 Lindy McDaniel 1.00 .40
188 Minnie Minoso 2.50 1.00
189 Stan Musial 15.00 6.00
190 Ray Sadecki 1.00 .40
191 Bill White 1.00 .40
192 S.F. Emblem 1.00 .40
193 Felipe Alou 2.50 1.00
194 Ed Bailey 1.00 .40
195 Orlando Cepeda 2.50 1.00
196 Jim Davenport 1.00 .40
197 Harvey Kuenn 2.50 1.00
198 Juan Marichal 4.00 1.60
199 Willie Mays 20.00 8.00
200 Mike McCormick 1.50 .60
201 Stu Miller 1.00 .40
NNO Stamp Album 20.00 8.00

1963 Topps

The cards in this 576-card set measure 2 1/2" by 3 1/2". The sharp color photographs of the 1963 set are a vivid contrast to the drab pictures of 1962. In addition to the "League Leaders" series (1-10) and World Series cards (142-148), the seventh and last series of cards (523-576) contains seven rookie cards (each depicting four players). Cards were issued, among other ways, in one-card penny packs and five-card nickel packs. There were some three-card advertising panels produced by Topps; the players included are from the first series; one panel shows Hoyt Wilhelm, Don Lock, and Bob Duliba on the front with a Stan Musial ad/endorsement on one of the backs. Key Rookie Cards in this set are Bill Freehan, Tony Oliva, Pete Rose, Willie Stargell and Rusty Staub.

NM Ex
COMPLETE SET (576) 5000.00 2000.00
COMMON CARD (1-196) 4.00 1.60
COMMON (197-283) 5.00 2.00
COMMON (284-370) 5.00 2.00
COMMON (371-446) 5.00 2.00
COMMON (447-522) 25.00 10.00
COMMON (523-576) 15.00 6.00
WRAPPER (1-CENT) 40.00 16.00
WRAPPER (5-CENT) 30.00 12.00
1 Tommy Davis 40.00 8.00
Frank Robinson
Stan Musial
Hank Aaron
Bill White LL
2 Pete Runnels 50.00 20.00
Mickey Mantle
Floyd Robinson
Norm Siebern
Chuck Hinton LL
3 Willie Mays 40.00 16.00
Hank Aaron
Frank Robinson
Orlando Cepeda
Ernie Banks LL
4 Harmon Killebrew 20.00 8.00
Norm Cash
Rocky Colavito
Roger Maris
Jim Gentile
Leon Wagner LL
5 Sandy Koufax 25.00 10.00
Bob Shaw
Bob Purkey
Bob Gibson

Don Drysdale LL
6 Hank Aguirre 10.00 4.00
Robin Roberts
Whitey Ford
Eddie Fisher
Dean Chance LL
7 Don Drysdale 10.00 4.00
Jack Sanford
Bob Purkey
Billy O'Dell
Art Mahaffey
Joe Jay LL
8 Ralph Terry 8.00 3.20
Dick Donovan
Ray Herbert
Jim Bunning
Camilo Pascual LL
9 Don Drysdale 30.00 12.00
Sandy Koufax
Bob Gibson
Billy O'Dell
Dick Farrell LL
10 Camilo Pascual 8.00 3.20
Jim Bunning
Ralph Terry
Juan Pizarro
Jim Kaat LL
11 Lee Walls 4.00 1.60
12 Steve Barber 4.00 1.60
13 Philadelphia Phillies 8.00 3.20
Team Card
14 Pedro Ramos 4.00 1.60
15 Ken Hubbs UER 10.00 4.00
(No position listed
on front of card)
16 Al Smith 4.00 1.60
17 Ryne Duren 8.00 3.20
18 Smoky Burgess 80.00 32.00
Dick Stuart
Bob Clemente
Bob Skinner
19 Pete Burnside 4.00 1.60
20 Tony Kubek 10.00 4.00
21 Marty Keough 4.00 1.60
22 Curt Simmons 8.00 3.20
23 Ed Lopat MG 8.00 3.20
24 Bob Bruce 4.00 1.60
25 Al Kaline 50.00 20.00
26 Ray Moore 4.00 1.60
27 Choo Choo Coleman 8.00 3.20
28 Mike Fornieles 4.00 1.60
29A 1962 Rookie Stars 10.00 4.00
Sammy Ellis
Ray Culp
John Boozer
Jesse Gonder
29B 1963 Rookie Stars 4.00 1.60
Sammy Ellis
Ray Culp
John Boozer
Jesse Gonder
30 Harvey Kuenn 8.00 3.20
31 Cal Koonce 4.00 1.60
32 Tony Gonzalez 4.00 1.60
33 Bo Belinsky 8.00 3.20
34 Dick Schofield 4.00 1.60
35 John Buzhardt 4.00 1.60
36 Jerry Kindall 4.00 1.60
37 Jerry Lynch 4.00 1.60
38 Bud Daley 8.00 3.20
39 Angels Team 8.00 3.20
40 Vic Power 8.00 3.20
41 Charley Lau 8.00 3.20
42 Stan Williams 8.00 3.20
(Listed as Yankee on
card but LA cap)
43 Casey Stengel MG 8.00 3.20
Gene Woodling
44 Terry Fox 4.00 1.60
45 Bob Aspromonte 4.00 1.60
46 Tommie Aaron RC 8.00 3.20
47 Don Lock 4.00 1.60
48 Birdie Tebbetts MG 8.00 3.20
49 Dal Maxvill RC 8.00 3.20
50 Billy Pierce 8.00 3.20
51 George Alusik 4.00 1.60
52 Chuck Schilling 4.00 1.60
53 Joe Moeller 8.00 3.20
54A 1962 Rookie Stars 15.00 6.00
Nelson Mathews
Harry Fanok
Jack Cullen
Dave DeBusschere RC
54B 1963 Rookie Stars 8.00 3.20
Nelson Mathews
Harry Fanok
Jack Cullen
Dave DeBusschere RC
55 Bill Virdon 8.00 3.20
56 Dennis Bennett 4.00 1.60
57 Billy Moran 4.00 1.60
58 Bob Will 4.00 1.60
59 Craig Anderson 4.00 1.60
60 Elston Howard 8.00 3.20
61 Ernie Bowman 4.00 1.60
62 Bob Hendley 4.00 1.60
63 Reds Team 8.00 3.20
64 Dick McAuliffe 8.00 3.20
65 Jackie Brandt 4.00 1.60
66 Mike Joyce 4.00 1.60
67 Ed Charles 4.00 1.60
68 Duke Snider 25.00 10.00
Gil Hodges
69 Bud Zipfel 4.00 1.60
70 Jim O'Toole 8.00 3.20
71 Bobby Wine 8.00 3.20
72 Johnny Romano 4.00 1.60
73 Bobby Bragan MG RC 8.00 3.20
74 Denny Lemaster 4.00 1.60
75 Bob Allison 8.00 3.20
76 Earl Wilson 8.00 3.20
77 Al Spangler 4.00 1.60
78 Marv Throneberry 8.00 3.20
79 Checklist 1 12.00 2.40
80 Jim Gilliam 8.00 3.20
81 Jim Schaffer 4.00 1.60
82 Ed Rakow 4.00 1.60
83 Charley James 4.00 1.60
84 Ron Kline 4.00 1.60
85 Tom Haller 8.00 3.20
86 Charley Maxwell 8.00 3.20
87 Bob Veale 8.00 3.20
88 Ron Hansen 4.00 1.60
89 Dick Stigman 4.00 1.60
90 Gordy Coleman 8.00 3.20
91 Dallas Green 8.00 3.20
92 Hector Lopez 8.00 3.20
93 Galen Cisco 4.00 1.60
94 Bob Schmidt 4.00 1.60
95 Larry Jackson 4.00 1.60
96 Lou Clinton 4.00 1.60
97 Bob Duliba 4.00 1.60
98 George Thomas 4.00 1.60
99 Jim Umbricht 4.00 1.60
100 Joe Cunningham 4.00 1.60
101 Joe Gibbon 4.00 1.60
102A Checklist 2 12.00 2.40
(Red on yellow)
102B Checklist 2 12.00 2.40
(White on red)
103 Chuck Essegian 4.00 1.60
104 Lew Krausse 4.00 1.60
105 Ron Fairly 8.00 3.20
106 Bobby Bolin 4.00 1.60
107 Jim Hickman 8.00 3.20
108 Hoyt Wilhelm 10.00 4.00
109 Lee Maye 4.00 1.60
110 Rich Rollins 8.00 3.20
111 Al Jackson 4.00 1.60
112 Dick Brown 4.00 1.60
113 Don Landrum UER 4.00 1.60
(Photo actually
Ron Santo)
114 Dan Osinski 4.00 1.60
115 Carl Yastrzemski 40.00 16.00
116 Jim Brosnan 8.00 3.20
117 Jacke Davis 4.00 1.60
118 Sherm Lollar 4.00 1.60
119 Bob Lillis 4.00 1.60
120 Roger Maris 80.00 32.00
121 Jim Hannan 4.00 1.60
122 Julio Gotay 4.00 1.60
123 Frank Howard 8.00 3.20
124 Dick Howser 8.00 3.20
125 Robin Roberts 15.00 6.00
126 Bob Uecker 15.00 6.00
127 Bill Tuttle 4.00 1.60
128 Matty Alou 8.00 3.20
129 Gary Bell 4.00 1.60
130 Dick Groat 8.00 3.20
131 Washington Senators 8.00 3.20
Team Card
132 Jack Hamilton 4.00 1.60
133 Gene Freese 4.00 1.60
134 Bob Scheffing MG 4.00 1.60
135 Richie Ashburn 20.00 8.00
136 Ike Delock 4.00 1.60
137 Mack Jones 4.00 1.60
138 Willie Mays 80.00 32.00
Stan Musial
139 Earl Averill 4.00 1.60
140 Frank Lary 8.00 3.20
141 Manny Mota RC 8.00 3.20
142 Whitey Ford WS 10.00 4.00
143 Jack Sanford WS 8.00 3.20
144 Roger Maris WS 15.00 6.00
145 Chuck Hiller WS 8.00 3.20
146 Tom Tresh WS 8.00 3.20
147 Billy Pierce WS 8.00 3.20
148 Ralph Terry WS 8.00 3.20
149 Marv Breeding 4.00 1.60
150 Johnny Podres 8.00 3.20
151 Pirates Team 8.00 3.20
152 Ron Nischwitz 4.00 1.60
153 Hal Smith 4.00 1.60
154 Walter Alston MG 8.00 3.20
155 Bill Stafford 8.00 3.20
156 Roy McMillan 8.00 3.20
157 Diego Segui RC 8.00 3.20
158 Rogelio Alvares 8.00 3.20
Dave Roberts
Tommy Harper RC
Bob Saverine
159 Jim Pagliaroni 4.00 1.60
160 Juan Pizarro 4.00 1.60
161 Frank Torre 8.00 3.20
162 Twins Team 8.00 3.20
163 Don Larsen 8.00 3.20
164 Bubba Morton 4.00 1.60
165 Jim Kaat 8.00 3.20
166 Johnny Keane MG 4.00 1.60
167 Jim Fregosi 8.00 3.20
168 Russ Nixon 4.00 1.60
169 Dick Egan 25.00 10.00
Julio Navarro
Tommie Sisk
Gaylord Perry
170 Joe Adcock 8.00 3.20
171 Steve Hamilton 4.00 1.60
172 Gene Oliver 4.00 1.60
173 Tom Tresh 150.00 60.00
Mickey Mantle
Bobby Richardson
174 Larry Burright 4.00 1.60
175 Bob Buhl 8.00 3.20
176 Jim King 4.00 1.60
177 Bubba Phillips 4.00 1.60
178 Johnny Edwards 4.00 1.60
179 Ron Piche 4.00 1.60
180 Bill Skowron 8.00 3.20
181 Sammy Esposito 4.00 1.60
182 Albie Pearson 8.00 3.20
183 Joe Pepitone 8.00 3.20
184 Vern Law 8.00 3.20
185 Chuck Hiller 4.00 1.60
186 Jerry Zimmerman 4.00 1.60
187 Willie Kirkland 4.00 1.60
188 Eddie Bressoud 4.00 1.60
189 Dave Giusti 8.00 3.20
190 Minnie Minoso 8.00 3.20
191 Checklist 3 12.00 2.40
192 Clay Dalrymple 4.00 1.60
193 Andre Rodgers 4.00 1.60
194 Joe Nuxhall 8.00 3.20
195 Manny Jimenez 4.00 1.60
196 Doug Camilli 4.00 1.60
197 Roger Craig 8.00 3.20
198 Lenny Green 5.00 2.00
199 Joe Amalfitano 5.00 2.00
200 Mickey Mantle 500.00 200.00
201 Cecil Butler 5.00 2.00
202 Boston Red Sox 8.00 3.20
Team Card
203 Chico Cardenas 8.00 3.20
204 Don Nottebart 5.00 2.00
205 Luis Aparicio 15.00 6.00
206 Ray Washburn 5.00 2.00
207 Ken Hunt 5.00 2.00
208 Ron Herbel 5.00 2.00
John Miller
Wally Wolf
Ron Taylor
209 Hobie Landrith 5.00 2.00
210 Sandy Koufax 150.00 60.00
211 Fred Whitfield 5.00 2.00
212 Glen Hobbie 5.00 2.00
213 Billy Hitchcock MG 5.00 2.00
214 Orlando Pena 5.00 2.00
215 Bob Skinner 8.00 3.20
216 Gene Conley 8.00 3.20
217 Joe Christopher 5.00 2.00
218 Frank Lary 8.00 3.20
Don Mossi
Jim Bunning
219 Chuck Cottier 5.00 2.00
220 Camilo Pascual 8.00 3.20
221 Cookie Rojas RC 8.00 3.20
222 Cubs Team 8.00 3.20
223 Eddie Fisher 5.00 2.00
224 Mike Roarke 5.00 2.00
225 Joey Jay 5.00 2.00
226 Julian Javier 8.00 3.20
227 Jim Grant 8.00 3.20
228 Max Alvis 50.00 20.00
Bob Bailey
Tony Oliva
(Listed as Pedro)
Ed Kranepool RC
229 Willie Davis 8.00 3.20
230 Pete Runnels 8.00 3.20
231 Eli Grba UER 5.00 2.00
(Large photo is
Ryne Duren)
232 Frank Malzone 8.00 3.20
233 Casey Stengel MG 20.00 8.00
234 Dave Nicholson 5.00 2.00
235 Billy O'Dell 5.00 2.00
236 Bill Bryan 5.00 2.00
237 Jim Coates 8.00 3.20
238 Lou Johnson 5.00 2.00
239 Harvey Haddix 8.00 3.20
240 Rocky Colavito 15.00 6.00
241 Bob Smith 5.00 2.00
242 Ernie Banks 60.00 24.00
Hank Aaron
243 Don Leppert 5.00 2.00
244 John Tsitouris 5.00 2.00
245 Gil Hodges 20.00 8.00
246 Lee Stange 5.00 2.00
247 Yankees Team 50.00 20.00
248 Tito Francona 5.00 2.00
249 Leo Burke 5.00 2.00
250 Stan Musial 100.00 40.00
251 Jack Lamabe 5.00 2.00
252 Ron Santo 10.00 4.00
253 Len Gabrielson 5.00 2.00
Pete Jernigan
John Wojcik
Deacon Jones
254 Mike Hershberger 5.00 2.00
255 Bob Shaw 5.00 2.00
256 Jerry Lumpe 5.00 2.00
257 Hank Aguirre 5.00 2.00
258 Alvin Dark MG 8.00 3.20
259 Johnny Logan 8.00 3.20
260 Jim Gentile 8.00 3.20
261 Bob Miller 5.00 2.00
262 Ellis Burton 5.00 2.00
263 Dave Stenhouse 5.00 2.00
264 Phil Linz 5.00 2.00
265 Vada Pinson 8.00 3.20
266 Bob Allen 5.00 2.00
267 Carl Sawatski 5.00 2.00
268 Don Demeter 5.00 2.00
269 Don Mincher 5.00 2.00
270 Felipe Alou 8.00 3.20
271 Dean Stone 5.00 2.00
272 Danny Murphy 5.00 2.00
273 Sammy Taylor 5.00 2.00
274 Checklist 4 12.00 2.40
275 Eddie Mathews 30.00 12.00
276 Barry Shetrone 5.00 2.00
277 Dick Farrell 5.00 2.00
278 Chico Fernandez 5.00 2.00
279 Wally Moon 8.00 3.20
280 Bob Rodgers 5.00 2.00
281 Tom Sturdivant 5.00 2.00
282 Bobby Del Greco 5.00 2.00
283 Roy Sievers 8.00 3.20
284 Dave Sisler 5.00 2.00
285 Dick Stuart 8.00 3.20
286 Stu Miller 8.00 3.20
287 Dick Bertell 5.00 2.00
288 Chicago White Sox 10.00 4.00
Team Card
289 Hal Brown 5.00 2.00
290 Bill White 8.00 3.20
291 Don Rudolph 5.00 2.00
292 Pumpsie Green 8.00 3.20
293 Bill Pleis 5.00 2.00
294 Bill Rigney MG 5.00 2.00
295 Ed Roebuck 5.00 2.00
296 Doc Edwards 5.00 2.00
297 Jim Golden 5.00 2.00
298 Don Dillard 5.00 2.00
299 Dave Morehead 8.00 3.20
Bob Dustal
Tom Butters
Dan Schneider
300 Willie Mays 150.00 60.00
301 Bill Fischer 5.00 2.00
302 Whitey Herzog 8.00 3.20
303 Earl Francis 5.00 2.00
304 Harry Bright 5.00 2.00
305 Don Hoak 5.00 2.00
306 Earl Battey 10.00 4.00
Elston Howard
307 Chet Nichols 5.00 2.00
308 Camilo Carreon 5.00 2.00
309 Jim Brewer 5.00 2.00
310 Tommy Davis 8.00 3.20
311 Joe McClain 5.00 2.00
312 Houston Colts 25.00 10.00
Team Card
313 Ernie Broglio 5.00 2.00
314 John Goryl 5.00 2.00
315 Ralph Terry 8.00 3.20
316 Norm Sherry 8.00 3.20
317 Sam McDowell 8.00 3.20
318 Gene Mauch MG 8.00 3.20
319 Joe Gaines 5.00 2.00
320 Warren Spahn 60.00 24.00
321 Gino Cimoli 5.00 2.00
322 Bob Turley 8.00 3.20
323 Bill Mazeroski 15.00 6.00
324 George Williams 8.00 3.20
Pete Ward
Phil Roof
Vic Davalillo
325 Jack Sanford 5.00 2.00
326 Hank Foiles 5.00 2.00
327 Paul Foytack 5.00 2.00
328 Dick Williams 8.00 3.20
329 Lindy McDaniel 8.00 3.20
330 Chuck Hinton 5.00 2.00
331 Bill Stafford 8.00 3.20
Bill Pierce
332 Joel Horlen 8.00 3.20
333 Carl Warwick 5.00 2.00
334 Wynn Hawkins 5.00 2.00
335 Leon Wagner 5.00 2.00
336 Ed Bauta 5.00 2.00
337 Dodgers Team 25.00 10.00
338 Russ Kemmerer 5.00 2.00
339 Ted Bowsfield 5.00 2.00
340 Yogi Berra P/CO 100.00 40.00
341 Jack Baldschun 5.00 2.00
342 Gene Woodling 8.00 3.20
343 Johnny Pesky MG 8.00 3.20
344 Don Schwall 5.00 2.00
345 Brooks Robinson 60.00 24.00
346 Billy Hoeft 5.00 2.00
347 Joe Torre 15.00 6.00
348 Vic Wertz 8.00 3.20
349 Zoilo Versalles 8.00 3.20
350 Bob Purkey 5.00 2.00
351 Al Luplow 5.00 2.00
352 Ken Johnson 5.00 2.00
353 Billy Williams 30.00 12.00
354 Dom Zanni 5.00 2.00
355 Dean Chance 8.00 3.20
356 John Schaive 5.00 2.00
357 George Altman 5.00 2.00
358 Milt Pappas 8.00 3.20
359 Haywood Sullivan 8.00 3.20
360 Don Drysdale 60.00 24.00
361 Clete Boyer 10.00 4.00
362 Checklist 5 12.00 2.40
363 Dick Radatz 8.00 3.20
364 Howie Goss 5.00 2.00
365 Jim Bunning 20.00 8.00
366 Tony Taylor 8.00 3.20
367 Tony Cloninger 5.00 2.00
368 Ed Bailey 5.00 2.00
369 Jim Lemon 5.00 2.00
370 Dick Donovan 5.00 2.00
371 Rod Kanehl 8.00 3.20
372 Don Lee 5.00 2.00
373 Jim Campbell 5.00 2.00
374 Claude Osteen 8.00 3.20
375 Ken Boyer 15.00 6.00
376 John Wyatt 5.00 2.00
377 Baltimore Orioles 10.00 4.00
Team Card
378 Bill Henry 5.00 2.00
379 Bob Anderson 5.00 2.00
380 Ernie Banks UER 100.00 40.00
(Back has career Major
and Minor, but he
never played in Minors)
381 Frank Baumann 5.00 2.00
382 Ralph Houk MG 10.00 4.00
383 Pete Richert 5.00 2.00
384 Bob Tillman 5.00 2.00
385 Art Mahaffey 5.00 2.00
386 Ed Kirkpatrick 5.00 2.00
John Bateman RC
Larry Bearnarth
Garry Roggenburk
387 Al McBean 5.00 2.00
388 Jim Davenport 8.00 3.20
389 Frank Sullivan 5.00 2.00
390 Hank Aaron 150.00 60.00
391 Bill Dailey 5.00 2.00
392 Johnny Romano 5.00 2.00
Tito Francona
393 Ken MacKenzie 8.00 3.20
394 Tim McCarver 15.00 6.00
395 Don McMahon 5.00 2.00
396 Joe Koppe 5.00 2.00
397 Kansas City Athletics 10.00 4.00
Team Card
398 Boog Powell 25.00 10.00
399 Dick Ellsworth 5.00 2.00
400 Frank Robinson 60.00 24.00
401 Jim Bouton 15.00 6.00
402 Mickey Vernon MG 8.00 3.20
403 Ron Perranoski 8.00 3.20
404 Bob Oldis 5.00 2.00
405 Floyd Robinson 5.00 2.00
406 Howie Koplitz 5.00 2.00
407 Frank Kostro 8.00 3.20
Chico Ruiz
Larry Elliot
Dick Simpson
408 Billy Gardner 5.00 2.00
409 Roy Face 8.00 3.20
410 Earl Battey 5.00 2.00
411 Jim Constable 5.00 2.00
412 Johnny Podres 50.00 20.00
Don Drysdale
Sandy Koufax
413 Jerry Walker 5.00 2.00
414 Ty Cline 5.00 2.00
415 Bob Gibson 60.00 24.00
416 Alex Grammas 5.00 2.00
417 Giants Team 10.00 4.00
418 John Orsino 5.00 2.00
419 Tracy Stallard 5.00 2.00
420 Bobby Richardson 15.00 6.00
421 Tom Morgan 5.00 2.00
422 Fred Hutchinson MG 8.00 3.20
423 Ed Hobaugh 5.00 2.00
424 Charlie Smith 5.00 2.00
425 Smoky Burgess 8.00 3.20
426 Barry Latman 5.00 2.00
427 Bernie Allen 5.00 2.00
428 Carl Boles 5.00 2.00
429 Lou Burdette 8.00 3.20
430 Norm Siebern 5.00 2.00
431A Checklist 6 12.00 2.40
(White on red)
431B Checklist 6 30.00 6.00
(Black on orange)
432 Roman Mejias 5.00 2.00
433 Denis Menke 5.00 2.00
434 John Callison 8.00 3.20
435 Woody Held 5.00 2.00
436 Tim Harkness 8.00 3.20
437 Bill Bruton 5.00 2.00
438 Wes Stock 5.00 2.00
439 Don Zimmer 8.00 3.20
440 Juan Marichal 30.00 12.00
441 Lee Thomas 8.00 3.20
442 J.C. Hartman 5.00 2.00
443 Jimmy Piersall 8.00 3.20
444 Jim Maloney 8.00 3.20
445 Norm Cash 10.00 4.00
446 Whitey Ford 60.00 24.00
447 Felix Mantilla 25.00 10.00
448 Jack Kralick 25.00 10.00
449 Jose Tartabull 25.00 10.00
450 Bob Friend 30.00 12.00
451 Indians Team 40.00 16.00
452 Barney Schultz 25.00 10.00
453 Jake Wood 25.00 10.00
454A Art Fowler 25.00 10.00
(Card number on
white background)
454B Art Fowler 30.00 12.00
(Card number on
orange background)
455 Ruben Amaro 25.00 10.00
456 Jim Coker 25.00 10.00
457 Tex Clevenger 25.00 10.00
458 Al Lopez MG 30.00 12.00
459 Dick LeMay 25.00 10.00
460 Del Crandall 30.00 12.00
461 Norm Bass 25.00 10.00
462 Wally Post 25.00 10.00
463 Joe Schaffernoth 25.00 10.00
464 Ken Aspromonte 25.00 10.00
465 Chuck Estrada 25.00 10.00
466 Nate Oliver 60.00 24.00
Tony Martinez
Bill Freehan RC
Jerry Robinson SP
467 Phil Ortega 25.00 10.00
468 Carroll Hardy 30.00 12.00
469 Jay Hook 30.00 12.00
470 Tom Tresh SP 60.00 24.00
471 Ken Retzer 25.00 10.00
472 Lou Brock 80.00 32.00
473 New York Mets 100.00 40.00
Team Card
474 Jack Fisher 25.00 10.00
475 Gus Triandos 30.00 12.00
476 Frank Funk 25.00 10.00
477 Donn Clendenon 30.00 12.00
478 Paul Brown 25.00 10.00
479 Ed Brinkman 25.00 10.00
480 Bill Monbouquette 25.00 10.00
481 Bob Taylor 25.00 10.00
482 Felix Torres 25.00 10.00
483 Jim Owens UER 25.00 10.00
(Stat column for Wins
has an R instead)
484 Dale Long SP 30.00 12.00
485 Jim Landis 25.00 10.00
486 Ray Sadecki 25.00 10.00
487 John Roseboro 30.00 12.00
488 Jerry Adair 25.00 10.00
489 Paul Toth 25.00 10.00
490 Willie McCovey 100.00 40.00
491 Harry Craft MG 25.00 10.00
492 Dave Wickersham 25.00 10.00
493 Walt Bond 25.00 10.00
494 Phil Regan 25.00 10.00
495 Frank Thomas SP 30.00 12.00
496 Steve Dalkowski RC 30.00 12.00
Fred Newman
Jack Smith
Carl Bouldin
497 Bennie Daniels 25.00 10.00
498 Eddie Kasko 25.00 10.00
499 J.C. Martin 25.00 10.00
500 Harmon Killebrew SP 150.00 60.00
501 Joe Azcue 25.00 10.00
502 Daryl Spencer 25.00 10.00
503 Braves Team 40.00 16.00
504 Bob Johnson 25.00 10.00
505 Curt Flood 40.00 16.00
506 Gene Green 25.00 10.00
507 Roland Sheldon 30.00 12.00
508 Ted Savage 25.00 10.00
509A Checklist 7 30.00 6.00
(Copyright centered)
509B Checklist 7 30.00 6.00
(Copyright to right)
510 Ken McBride 25.00 10.00
511 Charlie Neal 30.00 12.00
512 Cal McLish 25.00 10.00
513 Gary Geiger 25.00 10.00
514 Larry Osborne 25.00 10.00
515 Don Elston 25.00 10.00
516 Purnell Goldy 25.00 10.00
517 Hal Woodeshick 25.00 10.00
518 Don Blasingame 25.00 10.00
519 Claude Raymond RC 25.00 10.00
520 Orlando Cepeda 40.00 16.00
521 Dan Pfister 25.00 10.00
522 Mel Nelson 30.00 12.00
Gary Peters
Jim Roland
Art Quirk
523 Bill Kunkel 15.00 6.00
524 Cardinals Team 30.00 12.00
525 Nellie Fox 50.00 20.00
526 Dick Hall 15.00 6.00
527 Ed Sadowski 15.00 6.00

528 Carl Willey 15.00 6.00
529 Wes Covington 15.00 6.00
530 Don Mossi 20.00 8.00
531 Sam Mele MG 15.00 6.00
532 Steve Boros 15.00 6.00
533 Bobby Shantz 20.00 8.00
534 Ken Walters 15.00 6.00
535 Jim Perry 20.00 8.00
536 Norm Larker 15.00 6.00
537 Pedro Gonzalez 800.00 325.00
Ken McMullen
Al Weis
Pete Rose RC
538 George Brunet 15.00 6.00
539 Wayne Causey 15.00 6.00
540 Roberto Clemente 250.00 100.00
541 Ron Moeller 15.00 6.00
542 Lou Klimchock 15.00 6.00
543 Russ Snyder 15.00 6.00
544 Duke Carmel 50.00 20.00
Bill Haas
Rusty Staub RC
Dick Phillips
545 Jose Pagan 15.00 6.00
546 Hal Reniff 20.00 8.00
547 Gus Bell 15.00 6.00
548 Tom Satriano 15.00 6.00
549 Marcelino Lopez 15.00 6.00
Pete Lovrich
Paul Ratliff
Elmo Plaskett
550 Duke Snider 80.00 32.00
551 Billy Klaus 15.00 6.00
552 Detroit Tigers 50.00 20.00
Team Card
553 Brock Davis 125.00 50.00
Jim Gosger
Willie Stargell RC
John Herrnstein
554 Hank Fischer 15.00 6.00
555 John Blanchard 20.00 8.00
556 Al Worthington 15.00 6.00
557 Cuno Barragan 15.00 6.00
558 Bill Faul 20.00 8.00
Ron Hunt RC
Al Moran
Bob Lipski
559 Danny Murtaugh MG 15.00 6.00
560 Ray Herbert 15.00 6.00
561 Mike De La Hoz 15.00 6.00
562 Randy Cardinal 30.00 12.00
Dave McNally RC
Ken Rowe
Don Rowe
563 Mike McCormick 15.00 6.00
564 George Banks 15.00 6.00
565 Larry Sherry 15.00 6.00
566 Cliff Cook 15.00 6.00
567 Jim Duffalo 15.00 6.00
568 Bob Sadowski 15.00 6.00
569 Luis Arroyo 20.00 8.00
570 Frank Bolling 15.00 6.00
571 Johnny Klippstein 15.00 6.00
572 Jack Spring 15.00 6.00
573 Coot Veal 15.00 6.00
574 Hal Kolstad 15.00 6.00
575 Don Cardwell 15.00 6.00
576 Johnny Temple 30.00 11.00

1963 Topps Stick-Ons Inserts

Stick-on inserts were found in several series of the 1963 Topps cards. Each sticker measures 1 1/4" by 2 3/4". They are found either with blank backs or with instructions on the reverse. Stick-ons with the instruction backs are a little tougher to find. The player photo is in color inside an oval with name, team and postion below. Since these inserts were unnumbered, they are ordered below alphabetically.

NM Ex
COMPLETE SET (46) 300.00 120.00
1 Hank Aaron 30.00 12.00
2 Luis Aparicio 10.00 4.00
3 Richie Ashburn 12.00 4.80
4 Bob Aspromonte 3.00 1.20
5 Ernie Banks 15.00 6.00
6 Ken Boyer 6.00 2.40
7 Jim Bunning 10.00 4.00
8 Johnny Callison 3.00 1.20
9 Roberto Clemente 50.00 20.00
10 Orlando Cepeda 10.00 4.00
11 Rocky Colavito 8.00 3.20
12 Tommy Davis 4.00 1.60
13 Dick Donovan 3.00 1.20
14 Don Drysdale 12.00 4.80
15 Dick Farrell 3.00 1.20
16 Jim Gentile 4.00 1.60
17 Ray Herbert 3.00 1.20
18 Chuck Hinton 3.00 1.20
19 Ken Hubbs 6.00 2.40
20 Al Jackson 3.00 1.20
21 Al Kaline 15.00 6.00
22 Harmon Killebrew 10.00 4.00
23 Sandy Koufax 25.00 10.00
24 Jerry Lumpe 3.00 1.20
25 Art Mahaffey 3.00 1.20
26 Mickey Mantle 80.00 32.00
27 Willie Mays 40.00 16.00
28 Bill Mazeroski 8.00 3.20
29 Bill Monbouquette 3.00 1.20
30 Stan Musial 25.00 10.00
31 Camilo Pascual 3.00 1.20
32 Bob Purkey 3.00 1.20
33 Bobby Richardson 6.00 2.40
34 Brooks Robinson 15.00 6.00
35 Floyd Robinson 3.00 1.20
36 Frank Robinson 15.00 6.00
37 Bob Rodgers 3.00 1.20
38 Johnny Romano 3.00 1.20
39 Jack Sanford 3.00 1.20
40 Norm Siebern 3.00 1.20
41 Warren Spahn 10.00 4.00
42 Dave Stenhouse 3.00 1.20
43 Ralph Terry 3.00 1.20
44 Lee Thomas 4.00 1.60
45 Bill White 4.00 1.60
46 Carl Yastrzemski 20.00 8.00

1964 Topps

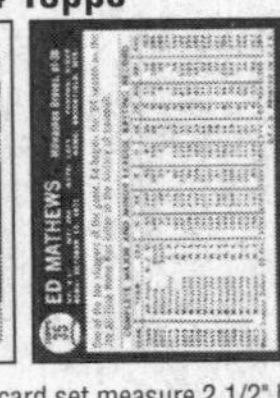

The cards in this 587-card set measure 2 1/2" by 3 1/2". Players in the 1964 Topps baseball series were easy to sort by team due to the giant block lettering found at the top of each card. The name and position of the player are found underneath the picture, and the card is numbered in a ball design on the orange-colored back. The usual last series scarcity holds for this set (523 to 587). Subsets within this set include League Leaders (1-12) and World Series cards (136-140). Among other vehicles, cards were issued in one-card penny packs as well as five-card nickel packs. There were some three-card advertising panels produced by Topps; the players included are from the first series; Panels with Mickey Mantle card backs include Walt Alston/Bill Henry/Vada Pinson; Carl Willey/White Sox Rookies/Bob Friend; and Jimmie Hall/Ernie Broglio/A.L. ERA Leaders on the front with a Mickey Mantle card back on one of the backs. The key Rookie Cards in this set are Richie Allen, Tony Conigliaro, Tommy John, Tony LaRussa, Phil Niekro and Lou Piniella.

NM Ex
COMPLETE SET (587) 3500.00 1800.00
COMMON CARD (1-196) 3.00 1.20
COMMON (197-370) 4.00 1.60
COMMON (371-522) 8.00 3.20
COMMON (523-587) 15.00 6.00
WRAPPER (1-CENT) 100.00 40.00
WRAP. (1-CENT, REPEAT) 125.00 50.00
WRAPPER (5-CENT) 30.00 12.00
WRAP.(5-CENT, COIN) 40.00 16.00
1 Sandy Koufax 30.00 9.00
Dick Ellsworth
Bob Friend LL
2 Gary Peters 8.00 3.20
Juan Pizarro
Camilo Pascual LL
3 Sandy Koufax 20.00 8.00
Juan Marichal
Warren Spahn
Jim Maloney LL
4 Whitey Ford 8.00 3.20
Camilo Pascual
Jim Bouton LL
5 Sandy Koufax 15.00 6.00
Jim Maloney
Don Drysdale LL
6 Camilo Pascual 8.00 3.20
Jim Bunning
Dick Stigman LL
7 Tommy Davis 20.00 8.00
Roberto Clemente
Dick Groat
Hank Aaron LL
8 Carl Yastrzemski 15.00 6.00
Al Kaline
Rich Rollins LL
9 Hank Aaron 30.00 12.00
Willie McCovey
Willie Mays
Orlando Cepeda LL
10 Harmon Killebrew 8.00 3.20
Dick Stuart
Bob Allison LL
11 Hank Aaron 15.00 6.00
Ken Boyer
Bill White LL
12 Dick Stuart 8.00 3.20
Al Kaline
Harmon Killebrew LL
13 Hoyt Wilhelm 12.00 4.80
14 Dick Nen RC 3.00 1.20
Nick Willhite
15 Zoilo Versalles 6.00 2.40
16 John Boozer 3.00 1.20
17 Willie Kirkland 3.00 1.20
18 Billy O'Dell 3.00 1.20
19 Don Wert 3.00 1.20
20 Bob Friend 6.00 2.40
21 Yogi Berra MG 40.00 16.00
22 Jerry Adair 3.00 1.20
23 Chris Zachary 3.00 1.20
24 Carl Sawatski 3.00 1.20
25 Bill Monbouquette 3.00 1.20
26 Gino Cimoli 3.00 1.20
27 New York Mets 8.00 3.20
Team Card
28 Claude Osteen 6.00 2.40
29 Lou Brock 40.00 16.00
30 Ron Perranoski 6.00 2.40
31 Dave Nicholson 3.00 1.20
32 Dean Chance 6.00 2.40
33 Sammy Ellis 6.00 2.40
Mel Queen
34 Jim Perry 6.00 2.40
35 Eddie Mathews 20.00 8.00
36 Hal Reniff 6.00 2.40
37 Smoky Burgess 6.00 2.40
38 Jim Wynn RC 8.00 3.20
39 Hank Aguirre 3.00 1.20
40 Dick Groat 6.00 2.40
41 Willie McCovey 8.00 3.20
Leon Wagner
42 Moe Drabowsky 6.00 2.40
43 Roy Sievers 6.00 2.40
44 Duke Carmel 3.00 1.20
45 Milt Pappas 6.00 2.40
46 Ed Brinkman 3.00 1.20
47 Jesus Alou RC 6.00 2.40
Ron Herbel
48 Bob Perry 3.00 1.20
49 Bill Henry 3.00 1.20
50 Mickey Mantle 350.00 120.00
51 Pete Richert 3.00 1.20
52 Chuck Hinton 3.00 1.20
53 Denis Menke 3.00 1.20
54 Sam Mele MG 3.00 1.20
55 Ernie Banks 40.00 16.00
56 Hal Brown 3.00 1.20
57 Tim Harkness 6.00 2.40
58 Don Demeter 6.00 2.40
59 Ernie Broglio 3.00 1.20
60 Frank Malzone 6.00 2.40
61 Bob Rodgers 6.00 2.40
Ed Sadowski
62 Ted Savage 3.00 1.20
63 John Orsino 3.00 1.20
64 Ted Abernathy 3.00 1.20
65 Felipe Alou 6.00 2.40
66 Eddie Fisher 3.00 1.20
67 Tigers Team 6.00 2.40
68 Willie Davis 6.00 2.40
69 Clete Boyer 6.00 2.40
70 Joe Torre 8.00 3.20
71 Jack Spring 3.00 1.20
72 Chico Cardenas 6.00 2.40
73 Jimmie Hall 8.00 3.20
74 Bob Priddy 3.00 1.20
Tom Butters
75 Wayne Causey 3.00 1.20
76 Checklist 1 10.00 2.00
77 Jerry Walker 3.00 1.20
78 Merritt Ranew 3.00 1.20
79 Bob Heffner 3.00 1.20
80 Vada Pinson 8.00 3.20
81 Nellie Fox 12.00 4.80
Harmon Killebrew
82 Jim Davenport 6.00 2.40
83 Gus Triandos 6.00 2.40
84 Carl Willey 3.00 1.20
85 Pete Ward 3.00 1.20
86 Al Downing 6.00 2.40
87 St. Louis Cardinals 6.00 2.40
Team Card
88 John Roseboro 6.00 2.40
89 Boog Powell 6.00 2.40
90 Earl Battey 3.00 1.20
91 Bob Bailey 6.00 2.40
92 Steve Ridzik 3.00 1.20
93 Gary Geiger 3.00 1.20
94 Jim Britton 3.00 1.20
Larry Maxie
95 George Altman 3.00 1.20
96 Bob Buhl 6.00 2.40
97 Jim Fregosi 6.00 2.40
98 Bill Bruton 3.00 1.20
99 Al Stanek 3.00 1.20
100 Elston Howard 6.00 2.40
101 Walt Alston MG 8.00 3.20
102 Checklist 2 10.00 2.00
103 Curt Flood 6.00 2.40
104 Art Mahaffey 6.00 2.40
105 Woody Held 3.00 1.20
106 Joe Nuxhall 6.00 2.40
107 Bruce Howard 3.00 1.20
Frank Kreutzer
108 John Wyatt 3.00 1.20
109 Rusty Staub 6.00 2.40
110 Albie Pearson 6.00 2.40
111 Don Elston 3.00 1.20
112 Bob Tillman 3.00 1.20
113 Grover Powell 6.00 2.40
114 Don Lock 3.00 1.20
115 Frank Bolling 3.00 1.20
116 Jay Ward 12.00 4.80
Tony Oliva
117 Earl Francis 3.00 1.20
118 John Blanchard 6.00 2.40
119 Gary Kolb 3.00 1.20
120 Don Drysdale 20.00 8.00
121 Pete Runnels 6.00 2.40
122 Don McMahon 3.00 1.20
123 Jose Pagan 3.00 1.20
124 Orlando Pena 3.00 1.20
125 Pete Rose UER 250.00 100.00
Born in 1942
126 Russ Snyder 3.00 1.20
127 Aubrey Gatewood 3.00 1.20
Dick Simpson
128 Mickey Lolich RC 20.00 8.00
129 Amado Samuel 3.00 1.20
130 Gary Peters 6.00 2.40
131 Steve Boros 3.00 1.20
132 Braves Team 6.00 2.40
133 Jim Grant 6.00 2.40
134 Don Zimmer 6.00 2.40
135 Johnny Callison 6.00 2.40
136 Sandy Koufax WS 20.00 8.00
strikes out 15
137 Willie Davis WS 8.00 3.20
138 Ron Fairly WS 8.00 3.20
139 Frank Howard WS 8.00 3.20
140 WS Summary 8.00 3.20
Dodgers celebrate
141 Danny Murtaugh MG 6.00 2.40
142 John Bateman 3.00 1.20
143 Bubba Phillips 3.00 1.20
144 Al Worthington 3.00 1.20
145 Norm Siebern 3.00 1.20
146 Tommy John RC 30.00 12.00
Bob Chance
147 Ray Sadecki 3.00 1.20
148 J.C. Martin 3.00 1.20
149 Paul Foytack 3.00 1.20
150 Willie Mays 125.00 50.00
151 Athletics Team 6.00 2.40
152 Denny Lemaster 3.00 1.20
153 Dick Williams 6.00 2.40
154 Dick Tracewski RC 6.00 2.40
155 Duke Snider 30.00 12.00
156 Bill Dailey 3.00 1.20
157 Gene Mauch MG 6.00 2.40
158 Ken Johnson 3.00 1.20
159 Charlie Dees 3.00 1.20
160 Ken Boyer 6.00 2.40
161 Dave McNally 6.00 2.40
162 Dick Sisler CO 6.00 2.40
Vada Pinson
163 Donn Clendenon 6.00 2.40
164 Bud Daley 3.00 1.20
165 Jerry Lumpe 3.00 1.20
166 Marty Keough 3.00 1.20
167 Mike Brumley 30.00 12.00
Lou Piniella RC
168 Al Weis 3.00 1.20
169 Del Crandall 6.00 2.40
170 Dick Radatz 6.00 2.40
171 Ty Cline 3.00 1.20
172 Indians Team 6.00 2.40
173 Ryne Duren 6.00 2.40
174 Doc Edwards 3.00 1.20
175 Billy Williams 12.00 4.80
176 Tracy Stallard 3.00 1.20
177 Harmon Killebrew 20.00 8.00
178 Hank Bauer MG 6.00 2.40
179 Carl Warwick 3.00 1.20
180 Tommy Davis 6.00 2.40
181 Dave Wickersham 3.00 1.20
182 Carl Yastrzemski 15.00 6.00
Chuck Schilling
183 Ron Taylor 3.00 1.20
184 Al Luplow 3.00 1.20
185 Jim O'Toole 6.00 2.40
186 Roman Mejias 3.00 1.20
187 Ed Roebuck 3.00 1.20
188 Checklist 3 10.00 2.00
189 Bob Hendley 3.00 1.20
190 Bobby Richardson 8.00 3.20
191 Clay Dalrymple 6.00 2.40
192 John Boccabella 3.00 1.20
Billy Cowan
193 Jerry Lynch 3.00 1.20
194 John Goryl 3.00 1.20
195 Floyd Robinson 3.00 1.20
196 Jim Gentile 3.00 1.20
197 Frank Lary 6.00 2.40
198 Len Gabrielson 4.00 1.60
199 Joe Azcue 4.00 1.60
200 Sandy Koufax 100.00 40.00
201 Sam Bowens 6.00 2.40
Wally Bunker
202 Galen Cisco 6.00 2.40
203 John Kennedy 6.00 2.40
204 Matty Alou 6.00 2.40
205 Nellie Fox 12.00 4.80
206 Steve Hamilton 6.00 2.40
207 Fred Hutchinson MG 6.00 2.40
208 Wes Covington 6.00 2.40
209 Bob Allen 4.00 1.60
210 Carl Yastrzemski 40.00 16.00
211 Jim Coker 4.00 1.60
212 Pete Lovrich 4.00 1.60
213 Angels Team 6.00 2.40
214 Ken McMullen 6.00 2.40
215 Ray Herbert 4.00 1.60
216 Mike de la Hoz 4.00 1.60
217 Jim King 4.00 1.60
218 Hank Fischer 4.00 1.60
219 Al Downing 6.00 2.40
Jim Bouton
220 Dick Ellsworth 6.00 2.40
221 Bob Saverine 4.00 1.60
222 Billy Pierce 6.00 2.40
223 George Banks 4.00 1.60
224 Tommie Sisk 4.00 1.60
225 Roger Maris 60.00 24.00
226 Jerry Grote RC 6.00 2.40
Larry Yellen
227 Barry Latman 4.00 1.60
228 Felix Mantilla 4.00 1.60
229 Charley Lau 6.00 2.40
230 Brooks Robinson 40.00 16.00
231 Dick Calmus 4.00 1.60
232 Al Lopez MG 8.00 3.20
233 Hal Smith 4.00 1.60
234 Gary Bell 4.00 1.60
235 Ron Hunt 4.00 1.60
236 Bill Faul 4.00 1.60
237 Cubs Team 6.00 2.40
238 Roy McMillan 6.00 2.40
239 Herm Starrette 4.00 1.60
240 Bill White 6.00 2.40
241 Jim Owens 4.00 1.60
242 Harvey Kuenn 6.00 2.40
243 Richie Allen RC 30.00 12.00
John Herrnstein
244 Tony LaRussa RC 30.00 12.00
245 Dick Stigman 4.00 1.60
246 Manny Mota 6.00 2.40
247 Dave DeBusschere 6.00 2.40
248 Johnny Pesky MG 6.00 2.40
249 Doug Camilli 4.00 1.60
250 Al Kaline 40.00 16.00
251 Choo Choo Coleman 6.00 2.40
252 Ken Aspromonte 4.00 1.60
253 Wally Post 6.00 2.40
254 Don Hoak 6.00 2.40
255 Lee Thomas 6.00 2.40
256 Johnny Weekly 4.00 1.60
257 San Francisco Giants 6.00 2.40
Team Card
258 Garry Roggenburk 4.00 1.60
259 Harry Bright 4.00 1.60
260 Frank Robinson 40.00 16.00
261 Jim Hannan 4.00 1.60
262 Mike Shannon RC 8.00 3.20
Harry Fanok
263 Chuck Estrada 4.00 1.60
264 Jim Landis 4.00 1.60
265 Jim Bunning 12.00 4.80
266 Gene Freese 4.00 1.60
267 Wilbur Wood RC 6.00 2.40
268 Danny Murtaugh MG 6.00 2.40
Bill Virdon
269 Ellis Burton 4.00 1.60
270 Rich Rollins 6.00 2.40
271 Bob Sadowski 4.00 1.60
272 Jake Wood 4.00 1.60
273 Mel Nelson 4.00 1.60
274 Checklist 4 10.00 2.00
275 John Tsitouris 4.00 1.60
276 Jose Tartabull 6.00 2.40
277 Ken Retzer 4.00 1.60
278 Bobby Shantz 6.00 2.40
279 Joe Koppe UER 4.00 1.60
(Glove on wrong hand)
280 Juan Marichal 15.00 6.00
281 Jake Gibbs 6.00 2.40
Tom Metcalf
282 Bob Bruce 4.00 1.60
283 Tom McCraw RC 4.00 1.60
284 Dick Schofield 4.00 1.60
285 Robin Roberts 15.00 6.00
286 Don Landrum 4.00 1.60
287 Tony Conigliaro RC 50.00 20.00
Bill Spanswick
288 Al Moran 4.00 1.60
289 Frank Funk 4.00 1.60
290 Bob Allison 6.00 2.40
291 Phil Ortega 4.00 1.60
292 Mike Roarke 4.00 1.60
293 Phillies Team 6.00 2.40
294 Ken L. Hunt 4.00 1.60
295 Roger Craig 6.00 2.40
296 Ed Kirkpatrick 4.00 1.60
297 Ken MacKenzie 4.00 1.60
298 Harry Craft MG 4.00 1.60
299 Bill Stafford 4.00 1.60
300 Hank Aaron 100.00 40.00
301 Larry Brown 4.00 1.60
302 Dan Pfister 4.00 1.60
303 Jim Campbell 4.00 1.60
304 Bob Johnson 4.00 1.60
305 Jack Lamabe 4.00 1.60
306 Willie Mays 40.00 16.00
Orlando Cepeda
307 Joe Gibbon 4.00 1.60
308 Gene Stephens 4.00 1.60
309 Paul Toth 4.00 1.60
310 Jim Gilliam 6.00 2.40
311 Tom Brown RC 6.00 2.40
312 Fritz Fisher 4.00 1.60
Fred Gladding
313 Chuck Hiller 4.00 1.60
314 Jerry Buchek 4.00 1.60
315 Bo Belinsky 6.00 2.40
316 Gene Oliver 4.00 1.60
317 Al Smith 4.00 1.60
318 Minnesota Twins 6.00 2.40
Team Card
319 Paul Brown 4.00 1.60
320 Rocky Colavito 12.00 4.80
321 Bob Lillis 4.00 1.60
322 George Brunet 4.00 1.60
323 John Buzhardt 4.00 1.60
324 Casey Stengel MG 15.00 6.00
325 Hector Lopez 6.00 2.40
326 Ron Brand 4.00 1.60
327 Don Blasingame 4.00 1.60
328 Bob Shaw 4.00 1.60
329 Russ Nixon 4.00 1.60
330 Tommy Harper 6.00 2.40
331 Roger Maris 150.00 60.00
Norm Cash
Mickey Mantle
Al Kaline
332 Ray Washburn 4.00 1.60
333 Billy Moran 4.00 1.60
334 Lew Krausse 4.00 1.60
335 Don Mossi 6.00 2.40
336 Andre Rodgers 4.00 1.60
337 Al Ferrara 6.00 2.40
Jeff Torborg RC
338 Jack Kralick 4.00 1.60
339 Walt Bond 4.00 1.60
340 Joe Cunningham 4.00 1.60
341 Jim Roland 4.00 1.60
342 Willie Stargell 30.00 12.00
343 Senators Team 6.00 2.40
344 Phil Linz 6.00 2.40
345 Frank Thomas 8.00 3.20
346 Joey Jay 4.00 1.60
347 Bobby Wine 6.00 2.40
348 Ed Lopat MG 6.00 2.40
349 Art Fowler 4.00 1.60
350 Willie McCovey 25.00 10.00
351 Dan Schneider 4.00 1.60
352 Eddie Bressoud 4.00 1.60
353 Wally Moon 6.00 2.40
354 Dave Giusti 6.00 2.40
355 Vic Power 6.00 2.40
356 Bill McCool 6.00 2.40
Chico Ruiz
357 Charley James 4.00 1.60
358 Ron Kline 4.00 1.60
359 Jim Schaffer 4.00 1.60
360 Joe Pepitone 12.00 4.80
361 Jay Hook 4.00 1.60
362 Checklist 5 10.00 2.00
363 Dick McAuliffe 6.00 2.40
364 Joe Gaines 4.00 1.60
365 Cal McLish 6.00 2.40
366 Nelson Mathews 4.00 1.60
367 Fred Whitfield 4.00 1.60
368 Fritz Ackley 6.00 2.40
Don Buford RC
369 Jerry Zimmerman 4.00 1.60
370 Hal Woodeshick 4.00 1.60
371 Frank Howard 8.00 3.20
372 Howie Koplitz 8.00 3.20
373 Pirates Team 12.00 4.80
374 Bobby Bolin 8.00 3.20
375 Ron Santo 10.00 4.00
376 Dave Morehead 8.00 3.20
377 Bob Skinner 8.00 3.20
378 Woody Woodward RC 10.00 4.00
Jack Smith
379 Tony Gonzalez 8.00 3.20
380 Whitey Ford 40.00 16.00
381 Bob Taylor 8.00 3.20
382 Wes Stock 8.00 3.20
383 Bill Rigney MG 8.00 3.20
384 Ron Hansen 8.00 3.20
385 Curt Simmons 10.00 4.00
386 Lenny Green 8.00 3.20
387 Terry Fox 8.00 3.20
388 John O'Donoghue RC 10.00 4.00
George Williams
389 Jim Umbricht 10.00 4.00
(Card back mentions
his death)
390 Orlando Cepeda 25.00 10.00
391 Sam McDowell 10.00 4.00

392 Jim Pagliaroni 8.00 3.20
393 Casey Stengel MG 15.00 6.00
Ed Kranepool
394 Bob Miller 8.00 3.20
395 Tom Tresh 10.00 4.00
396 Dennis Bennett 8.00 3.20
397 Chuck Cottier 8.00 3.20
398 Bill Haas 10.00 4.00
Dick Smith
399 Jackie Brandt 8.00 3.20
400 Warren Spahn 40.00 16.00
401 Charlie Maxwell 8.00 3.20
402 Tom Sturdivant 8.00 3.20
403 Reds Team 12.00 4.80
404 Tony Martinez 8.00 3.20
405 Ken McBride 8.00 3.20
406 Al Spangler 8.00 3.20
407 Bill Freehan 10.00 4.00
408 Jim Stewart 8.00 3.20
Fred Burdette
409 Bill Fischer 8.00 3.20
410 Dick Stuart 10.00 4.00
411 Lee Walls 8.00 3.20
412 Ray Culp 10.00 4.00
413 Johnny Keane MG 8.00 3.20
414 Jack Sanford 8.00 3.20
415 Tony Kubek 15.00 6.00
416 Lee Maye 8.00 3.20
417 Don Cardwell 8.00 3.20
418 Darold Knowles 10.00 4.00
Buster Narum
419 Ken Harrelson RC 15.00 6.00
420 Jim Maloney 10.00 4.00
421 Camilo Carreon 8.00 3.20
422 Jack Fisher 8.00 3.20
423 Hank Aaron 125.00 50.00
Willie Mays
424 Dick Bertell 8.00 3.20
425 Norm Cash 10.00 4.00
426 Bob Rodgers 8.00 3.20
427 Don Rudolph 8.00 3.20
428 Archie Skeen 8.00 3.20
Pete Smith
(Back states Archie
has retired)
429 Tim McCarver 10.00 4.00
430 Juan Pizarro 8.00 3.20
431 George Alusik 8.00 3.20
432 Ruben Amaro 10.00 4.00
433 Yankees Team 40.00 16.00
434 Don Nottebart 8.00 3.20
435 Vic Davalillo 8.00 3.20
436 Charlie Neal 10.00 4.00
437 Ed Bailey 8.00 3.20
438 Checklist 6 15.00 3.00
439 Harvey Haddix 10.00 4.00
440 R.Clemente UER 250.00 100.00
1960 Pittsburfh
441 Bob Duliba 8.00 3.20
442 Pumpsie Green 10.00 4.00
443 Chuck Dressen MG 10.00 4.00
444 Larry Jackson 8.00 3.20
445 Bill Skowron 10.00 4.00
446 Julian Javier 15.00 6.00
447 Ted Bowsfield 8.00 3.20
448 Cookie Rojas 10.00 4.00
449 Deron Johnson 10.00 4.00
450 Steve Barber 8.00 3.20
451 Joe Amalfitano 8.00 3.20
452 Gil Garrido 10.00 4.00
Jim Ray Hart RC
453 Frank Baumann 8.00 3.20
454 Tommie Aaron 10.00 4.00
455 Bernie Allen 8.00 3.20
456 Wes Parker RC 10.00 4.00
John Werhas
457 Jesse Gonder 8.00 3.20
458 Ralph Terry 10.00 4.00
459 Pete Charton 8.00 3.20
Dalton Jones
460 Bob Gibson 40.00 16.00
461 George Thomas 8.00 3.20
462 Birdie Tebbetts MG 8.00 3.20
463 Don Leppert 8.00 3.20
464 Dallas Green 15.00 6.00
465 Mike Hershberger 8.00 3.20
466 Dick Green 10.00 4.00
Aurelio Monteagudo
467 Bob Aspromonte 8.00 3.20
468 Gaylord Perry 40.00 16.00
469 Fred Norman 10.00 4.00
Sterling Slaughter
470 Jim Bouton 10.00 4.00
471 Gates Brown RC 10.00 4.00
472 Vern Law 10.00 4.00
473 Baltimore Orioles 12.00 4.80
Team Card
474 Larry Sherry 10.00 4.00
475 Ed Charles 8.00 3.20
476 Rico Carty RC 15.00 6.00
Dick Kelley
477 Mike Joyce 8.00 3.20
478 Dick Howser 10.00 4.00
479 Dave Bakenhaster 8.00 3.20
Johnny Lewis
480 Bob Purkey 8.00 3.20
481 Chuck Schilling 8.00 3.20
482 John Briggs 10.00 4.00
Danny Cater
483 Fred Valentine 8.00 3.20
484 Bill Pleis 8.00 3.20
485 Tom Haller 8.00 3.20
486 Bob Kennedy MG 8.00 3.20
487 Mike McCormick 10.00 4.00
488 Pete Mikkelsen 15.00 6.00
Bob Meyer
489 Julio Navarro 8.00 3.20
490 Ron Fairly 10.00 4.00
491 Ed Rakow 8.00 3.20
492 Jim Beauchamp RC 8.00 3.20
Mike White
493 Don Lee 8.00 3.20
494 Al Jackson 8.00 3.20
495 Bill Virdon 10.00 4.00
496 White Sox Team 12.00 4.80
497 Jeoff Long 8.00 3.20
498 Dave Stenhouse 8.00 3.20
499 Chico Salmon 8.00 3.20
Gordon Seyfried
500 Camilo Pascual 10.00 4.00
501 Bob Veale 10.00 4.00
502 Bobby Knoop RC 8.00 3.20
Bob Lee
503 Earl Wilson 8.00 3.20
504 Claude Raymond 8.00 3.20
505 Stan Williams 8.00 3.20
506 Bobby Bragan MG 8.00 3.20
507 Johnny Edwards 8.00 3.20
508 Diego Segui 8.00 3.20
509 Gene Alley RC 10.00 4.00
Orlando McFarlane
510 Lindy McDaniel 10.00 4.00
511 Lou Jackson 10.00 4.00
512 Willie Horton RC 15.00 6.00
Joe Sparma
513 Don Larsen 10.00 4.00
514 Jim Hickman 10.00 4.00
515 Johnny Romano 8.00 3.20
516 Jerry Arrigo 8.00 3.20
Dwight Siebler
517A Checklist 7 ERR 25.00 5.00
(Incorrect numbering
sequence on back)
517B Checklist 7 COR 15.00 3.00
(Correct numbering
on back)
518 Carl Bouldin 8.00 3.20
519 Charlie Smith 8.00 3.20
520 Jack Baldschun 10.00 4.00
521 Tom Satriano 8.00 3.20
522 Bob Tiefenauer 8.00 3.20
523 Lou Burdette UER 20.00 8.00
(Pitching lefty)
524 Jim Dickson 15.00 6.00
Bobby Klaus
525 Al McBean 15.00 6.00
526 Lou Clinton 15.00 6.00
527 Larry Bearnarth 15.00 6.00
528 Dave Duncan RC 20.00 8.00
Tommie Reynolds
529 Alvin Dark MG 20.00 8.00
530 Leon Wagner 15.00 6.00
531 Los Angeles Dodgers 25.00 10.00
Team Card
532 Bud Bloomfield 15.00 6.00
(Bloomfield photo
actually Jay Ward)
Joe Nossek RC
533 Johnny Klippstein 15.00 6.00
534 Gus Bell 15.00 6.00
535 Phil Regan 15.00 6.00
536 Larry Elliot 15.00 6.00
John Stephenson
537 Dan Osinski 15.00 6.00
538 Minnie Minoso 20.00 8.00
539 Roy Face 20.00 8.00
540 Luis Aparicio 40.00 16.00
541 Phil Roof 80.00 32.00
Phil Niekro RC
542 Don Mincher 15.00 6.00
543 Bob Uecker 40.00 16.00
544 Steve Hertz 15.00 6.00
Joe Hoerner
545 Max Alvis 15.00 6.00
546 Joe Christopher 15.00 6.00
547 Gil Hodges MG 30.00 12.00
548 Wayne Schurr 20.00 8.00
Paul Speckenbach
549 Joe Moeller 15.00 6.00
550 Ken Hubbs MEM 40.00 16.00
551 Billy Hoeft 15.00 6.00
552 Tom Kelley 15.00 6.00
Sonny Siebert
553 Jim Brewer 15.00 6.00
554 Hank Foiles 15.00 6.00
555 Lee Stange 15.00 6.00
556 Steve Dillon 15.00 6.00
Ron Locke
557 Leo Burke 15.00 6.00
558 Don Schwall 15.00 6.00
559 Dick Phillips 15.00 6.00
560 Dick Farrell 15.00 6.00
561 Dave Bennett UER 20.00 8.00
(19 ... is 18)
Rick Wise RC
562 Pedro Ramos 15.00 6.00
563 Dal Maxvill 20.00 8.00
564 Joe McCabe 20.00 8.00
Jerry McNertney
565 Stu Miller 15.00 6.00
566 Ed Kranepool 20.00 8.00
567 Jim Kaat 20.00 8.00
568 Phil Gagliano 15.00 6.00
Cap Peterson
569 Fred Newman 15.00 6.00
570 Bill Mazeroski 40.00 16.00
571 Gene Conley 15.00 6.00
572 Dave Gray 15.00 6.00
Dick Egan
573 Jim Duffalo 15.00 6.00
574 Manny Jimenez 15.00 6.00
575 Tony Cloninger 15.00 6.00
576 Jerry Hinsley 15.00 6.00
Bill Wakefield
577 Gordy Coleman 15.00 6.00
578 Glen Hobbie 15.00 6.00
579 Red Sox Team 25.00 10.00
580 Johnny Podres 20.00 8.00
581 Pedro Gonzalez 20.00 8.00
Archie Moore
582 Rod Kanehl 20.00 8.00
583 Tito Francona 15.00 6.00
584 Joel Horlen 15.00 6.00
585 Tony Taylor 20.00 8.00
586 Jimmy Piersall 20.00 8.00
587 Bennie Daniels 20.00 8.00

1964 Topps Coins Inserts

This set of 164 unnumbered coins issued in 1964 is sometimes divided into two sets -- the regular series (1-120) and the all-star series (121-164). Each metal coin is approximately 1 1/2" in diameter. The regular series features gold and silver coins with a full color photo of the player, including the background of the photo. The player's name, team and position are delineated on the coin front. The back includes the line "Collect the entire set of 120 all-stars". The all-star series (denoted AS in the checklist

below) contains a full color cutout photo of the player on a solid background. The fronts feature the line "1964 All-stars" along with the name only of the player. The backs contain the line "Collect all 44 special stars". Mantle, Causey and Hinton appear in two variations each. The complete set price below includes all variations. Some dealers believe the following coins are short printed: Callison, Tresh, Rollins, Santo, Pappas, Freehan, Hendley, Staub, Bateman and O'Dell.

NM Ex
COMPLETE SET (167) 600.00 240.00
1 Don Zimmer 3.00 1.20
2 Jim Wynn 2.00 .80
3 Johnny Orsino 1.00 .40
4 Jim Bouton 2.00 .80
5 Dick Groat 2.00 .80
6 Leon Wagner 1.00 .40
7 Frank Malzone 1.00 .40
8 Steve Barber 1.00 .40
9 Johnny Romano 1.00 .40
10 Tom Tresh 3.00 1.20
11 Felipe Alou 2.00 .80
12 Dick Stuart 2.00 .80
13 Claude Osteen 1.00 .40
14 Juan Pizarro 1.00 .40
15 Donn Clendenon 1.00 .40
16 Jimmie Hall 1.00 .40
17 Al Jackson 1.00 .40
18 Brooks Robinson 15.00 6.00
19 Bob Allison 2.00 .80
20 Ed Roebuck 1.00 .40
21 Pete Ward 1.00 .40
22 Willie McCovey 5.00 2.00
23 Elston Howard 5.00 2.00
24 Diego Segui 1.00 .40
25 Ken Boyer 3.00 1.20
26 Carl Yastrzemski 20.00 8.00
27 Bill Mazeroski 5.00 2.00
28 Jerry Lumpe 1.00 .40
29 Woody Held 1.00 .40
30 Dick Radatz 1.00 .40
31 Luis Aparicio 3.00 1.20
32 Dave Nicholson 1.00 .40
33 Eddie Mathews 15.00 6.00
34 Don Drysdale 10.00 4.00
35 Ray Culp 1.00 .40
36 Juan Marichal 5.00 2.00
37 Frank Robinson 20.00 8.00
38 Chuck Hinton 1.00 .40
39 Floyd Robinson 1.00 .40
40 Tommy Harper 2.00 .80
41 Ron Hansen 1.00 .40
42 Ernie Banks 15.00 6.00
43 Jesse Gonder 1.00 .40
44 Billy Williams 3.00 1.20
45 Vada Pinson 2.00 .80
46 Rocky Colavito 5.00 2.00
47 Bill Monbouquette 1.00 .40
48 Max Alvis 1.00 .40
49 Norm Siebern 1.00 .40
50 Johnny Callison 2.00 .80
51 Rich Rollins 1.00 .40
52 Ken McBride 1.00 .40
53 Don Lock 1.00 .40
54 Ron Fairly 2.00 .80
55 Roberto Clemente 40.00 16.00
56 Dick Ellsworth 1.00 .40
57 Tommy Davis 2.00 .80
58 Tony Gonzalez 1.00 .40
59 Bob Gibson 10.00 4.00
60 Jim Maloney 2.00 .80
61 Frank Howard 2.00 .80
62 Jim Pagliaroni 1.00 .40
63 Orlando Cepeda 3.00 1.20
64 Ron Perranoski 1.00 .40
65 Curt Flood 3.00 1.20
66 Alvin McBean 1.00 .40
67 Dean Chance 1.00 .40
68 Ron Santo 3.00 1.20
69 Jack Baldschun 1.00 .40
70 Milt Pappas 2.00 .80
71 Gary Peters 1.00 .40
72 Bobby Richardson 3.00 1.20
73 Frank Thomas 1.00 .40
74 Hank Aguirre 1.00 .40
75 Carlton Willey 1.00 .40
76 Camilo Pascual 2.00 .80
77 Bob Friend 2.00 .80
78 Bill White 2.00 .80
79 Norm Cash 3.00 1.20
80 Willie Mays 40.00 16.00
81 Leon Carmel 1.00 .40
82 Pete Rose 40.00 16.00
83 Hank Aaron 30.00 12.00
84 Bob Aspromonte 1.00 .40
85 Jim O'Toole 1.00 .40
86 Vic Davalillo 2.00 .80
87 Bill Freehan 2.00 .80
88 Warren Spahn 5.00 2.00
89 Ken Hunt 1.00 .40
90 Denis Menke 1.00 .40
91 Dick Farrell 1.00 .40
92 Jim Hickman 1.00 .40
93 Jim Bunning 3.00 1.20
94 Bob Hendley 1.00 .40
95 Ernie Broglio 1.00 .40
96 Rusty Staub 2.00 .80
97 Lou Brock 5.00 2.00
98 Jim Fregosi 2.00 .80
99 Jim Grant 1.00 .40
100 Al Kaline 10.00 4.00
101 Earl Battey 2.00 .80
102 Wayne Causey 1.00 .40
103 Chuck Schilling 1.00 .40
104 Boog Powell 3.00 1.20
105 Dave Wickersham 1.00 .40
106 Sandy Koufax 20.00 8.00
107 John Bateman 2.00 .80
108 Ed Brinkman 1.00 .40
109 Al Downing 1.00 .40
110 Joe Azcue 1.00 .40
111 Albie Pearson 1.00 .40
112 Harmon Killebrew 10.00 4.00
113 Tony Taylor 2.00 .80
114 Larry Jackson 1.00 .40
115 Billy O'Dell 2.00 .80
116 Don Demeter 2.00 .80
117 Ed Charles 1.00 .40
118 Joe Torre 5.00 2.00
119 Don Nottebart 1.00 .40
120 Mickey Mantle 60.00 24.00
121 Joe Pepitone AS 2.00 .80
122 Dick Stuart AS 2.00 .80
123 Bobby Richardson AS 3.00 1.20
124 Jerry Lumpe AS 1.00 .40
125 Brooks Robinson AS 10.00 4.00
126 Frank Malzone AS 1.00 .40
127 Luis Aparicio AS 3.00 1.20
128 Jim Fregosi AS 2.00 .80
129 Al Kaline AS 8.00 3.20
130 Leon Wagner AS 1.00 .40
131A Mickey Mantle AS 50.00 20.00
(right handed)
131B Mickey Mantle AS 50.00 20.00
(left handed)
132 Albie Pearson AS 1.00 .40
133 Harmon Killebrew AS 8.00 3.20
134 Carl Yastrzemski AS 15.00 6.00
135 Elston Howard AS 3.00 1.20
136 Earl Battey AS 1.00 .40
137 Camilo Pascual AS 1.00 .40
138 Jim Bouton AS 2.00 .80
139 Whitey Ford AS 10.00 4.00
140 Gary Peters AS 1.00 .40
141 Bill White AS 2.00 .80
142 Orlando Cepeda AS 3.00 1.20
143 Bill Mazeroski AS 5.00 2.00
144 Tony Taylor AS 1.00 .40
145 Ken Boyer AS 3.00 1.20
146 Ron Santo AS 3.00 1.20
147 Dick Groat AS 2.00 .80
148 Roy McMillan AS 1.00 .40
149 Hank Aaron AS 25.00 10.00
150 Roberto Clemente AS 30.00 12.00
151 Willie Mays AS 30.00 12.00
152 Vada Pinson AS 2.00 .80
153 Tommy Davis AS 2.00 .80
154 Frank Robinson AS 10.00 4.00
155 Joe Torre AS 5.00 2.00
156 Tim McCarver AS 2.00 .80
157 Juan Marichal AS 5.00 2.00
158 Jim Maloney AS 2.00 .80
159 Sandy Koufax AS 15.00 6.00
160 Warren Spahn AS 5.00 2.00
161A Wayne Causey AS 8.00 3.20
National League
161B Wayne Causey AS 2.00 .80
American League
162A Chuck Hinton AS 10.00 4.00
National League
162B Chuck Hinton AS 2.00 .80
American League
163 Bob Aspromonte AS 1.00 .40
164 Ron Hunt AS 1.00 .40

1964 Topps Giants

The cards in this 60-card set measure approximately 3 1/8" by 5 1/4". The 1964 Topps Giants are postcard size cards containing color player photographs. They are numbered on the backs, which also contain biographical information presented in a newspaper format. These "giant size" cards were distributed in both cellophane and waxed gum packs apart from the Topps regular issue of 1964. The gum packs contain three cards. The Cards 3, 28, 42, 45, 47, 51 and 60 are more difficult to find and are indicated by SP in the checklist below.

NM Ex
COMPLETE SET (60) 250.00 100.00
COMMON CARD (1-60) 1.00 .40
COMMON SP'S 10.00 4.00
WRAPPER (5-CENT) 35.00 14.00
1 Gary Peters 1.50 .60
2 Ken Johnson 1.00 .40
3 Sandy Koufax SP 40.00 16.00
4 Bob Bailey 1.00 .40
5 Milt Pappas 1.50 .60
6 Ron Hunt 1.00 .40
7 Whitey Ford 4.00 1.60
8 Roy McMillan 1.00 .40
9 Rocky Colavito 4.00 1.60
10 Jim Bunning 2.50 1.00
11 Roberto Clemente 30.00 12.00
12 Al Kaline 5.00 2.00
13 Nellie Fox 4.00 1.60
14 Tony Gonzalez 1.00 .40
15 Jim Gentile 1.50 .60
16 Dean Chance 1.50 .60
17 Dick Ellsworth 1.50 .60
18 Jim Fregosi 1.50 .60
19 Dick Groat 1.50 .60
20 Chuck Hinton 1.00 .40
21 Elston Howard 1.50 .60
22 Dick Farrell 1.00 .40
23 Albie Pearson 1.00 .40
24 Frank Howard 1.50 .60
25 Mickey Mantle 50.00 20.00
26 Joe Torre 4.00 1.60
27 Eddie Brinkman 1.00 .40
28 Bob Friend SP 10.00 4.00
29 Frank Robinson 4.00 1.60
30 Bill Freehan 1.00 .40
31 Warren Spahn 4.00 1.60
32 Camilo Pascual 1.50 .60
33 Pete Ward 1.00 .40
34 Jim Maloney 1.50 .60
35 Dave Wickersham 1.00 .40
36 Johnny Callison 1.50 .60
37 Juan Marichal 2.50 1.00
38 Harmon Killebrew 5.00 1.60
39 Luis Aparicio 2.50 1.00
40 Dick Radatz 1.00 .40
41 Bob Gibson 4.00 1.60
42 Dick Stuart SP 10.00 4.00
43 Tommy Davis 1.50 .60
44 Tony Oliva 2.50 1.00
45 Wayne Causey SP 10.00 4.00
46 Max Alvis 1.00 .40
47 Galen Cisco SP 10.00 4.00
48 Carl Yastrzemski 5.00 2.00
49 Hank Aaron 10.00 4.00
50 Brooks Robinson 5.00 2.00
51 Willie Mays SP 50.00 20.00
52 Billy Williams 2.50 1.00
53 Juan Pizarro 1.00 .40
54 Leon Wagner 1.00 .40
55 Orlando Cepeda 2.50 1.00
56 Vada Pinson 1.50 .60
57 Ken Boyer 2.50 1.00
58 Ron Santo 2.50 1.00
59 John Romano 1.00 .40
60 Bill Skowron SP 15.00 6.00

1964 Topps Stand Ups

In 1964 Topps produced a die-cut "Stand-Up" card design for the first time since their Connie Mack and Current All Stars of 1951. These cards were issued in both one cent and five cent packs. The cards have full-length, color player photos set against a green and yellow background. Of the 77 cards in the set, 22 were single printed and these are marked in the checklist below with an SP. These unnumbered cards are standard-size (2 1/2" by 3 1/2"), blank backed, and have been numbered here for reference in alphabetical order of players. Interestingly there were four different wrapper designs used for this set. All the design variations are valued at the same price.

NM Ex
COMPLETE SET (77) 3500.00 1400.00
COMMON CARD (1-77) 10.00 4.00
COMMON CARD SP 40.00 16.00
WRAPPER (1-CENT) 150.00 60.00
WRAPPER (5-CENT) 325.00 130.00
1 Hank Aaron 150.00 60.00
2 Hank Aguirre 10.00 4.00
3 George Altman 15.00 6.00
4 Max Alvis 10.00 4.00
5 Bob Aspromonte 10.00 4.00
6 Jack Baldschun SP 40.00 16.00
7 Ernie Banks 80.00 32.00
8 Steve Barber 10.00 4.00
9 Earl Battey 10.00 4.00
10 Ken Boyer 20.00 8.00
11 Ernie Broglio 10.00 4.00
12 John Callison 15.00 6.00
13 Norm Cash SP 60.00 24.00
14 Wayne Causey 10.00 4.00
15 Orlando Cepeda 20.00 8.00
16 Ed Charles 15.00 6.00
17 Roberto Clemente 225.00 90.00
18 Donn Clendenon SP 40.00 16.00
19 Rocky Colavito 30.00 12.00
20 Ray Culp SP 50.00 20.00
21 Tommy Davis 15.00 6.00
22 Don Drysdale SP 125.00 50.00
23 Dick Ellsworth 10.00 4.00
24 Dick Farrell 10.00 4.00
25 Jim Fregosi 15.00 6.00
26 Bob Friend 10.00 4.00
27 Jim Gentile 15.00 6.00
28 Jesse Gonder SP 40.00 16.00
29 Tony Gonzalez SP 40.00 16.00
30 Dick Groat 20.00 8.00
31 Woody Held 10.00 4.00
32 Chuck Hinton 10.00 4.00
33 Elston Howard 20.00 8.00
34 Frank Howard SP 60.00 24.00
35 Ron Hunt 15.00 6.00
36 Al Jackson 10.00 4.00
37 Ken Johnson 10.00 4.00
38 Al Kaline 80.00 32.00
39 Harmon Killebrew 80.00 32.00
40 Sandy Koufax 150.00 60.00
41 Don Lock SP 40.00 16.00
42 Jerry Lumpe SP 40.00 16.00
43 Jim Maloney 15.00 6.00
44 Frank Malzone 10.00 4.00
45 Mickey Mantle 500.00 200.00
46 Juan Marichal SP 100.00 40.00
47 Eddie Mathews SP 125.00 50.00
48 Willie Mays 250.00 100.00
49 Bill Mazeroski 30.00 12.00
50 Ken McBride 10.00 4.00
51 Willie McCovey SP 100.00 40.00
52 Claude Osteen 15.00 6.00
53 Jim O'Toole 10.00 4.00
54 Camilo Pascual 15.00 6.00
55 Albie Pearson SP 50.00 20.00
56 Gary Peters 10.00 4.00
57 Vada Pinson 15.00 6.00
58 Juan Pizarro 10.00 4.00
59 Boog Powell 20.00 8.00
60 Bobby Richardson 20.00 8.00
61 Brooks Robinson 80.00 32.00
62 Floyd Robinson 10.00 4.00
63 Frank Robinson 80.00 32.00
64 Ed Roebuck SP 40.00 16.00
65 Rich Rollins 10.00 4.00
66 John Romano 10.00 4.00
67 Ron Santo SP 60.00 24.00

68 Norm Siebern 10.00 4.00
69 Warren Spahn SP 125.00 50.00
70 Dick Stuart SP 50.00 20.00
71 Lee Thomas 10.00 4.00
72 Joe Torre 20.00 8.00
73 Pete Ward 10.00 4.00
74 Bill White SP 50.00 20.00
75 Billy Williams SP 100.00 40.00
76 Hal Woodeshick SP 40.00 16.00
77 Carl Yastrzemski SP 400.00 160.00

1964 Topps Tattoos Inserts

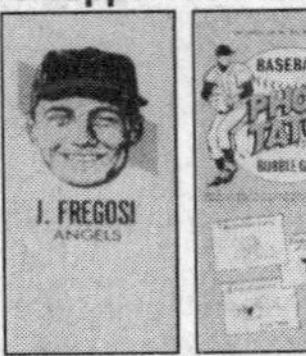

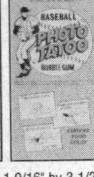

These tattoos measure 1 9/16" by 3 1/2" and are printed in color on very thin paper. One side gives instructions for applying the tattoo. The picture side gives either the team logo and name (on tattoos numbered 1-20 below) or the player's face, name and team (21-75 below). The tattoos are unnumbered and are presented below in alphabetical order within type for convenience. This set was issued in one cent packs which came 120 to a box. The boxes had photos of Whitey Ford on them.

NM Ex
COMPLETE SET (75) 1350.00 550.00
COMMON TATOO (1-20) 4.00 1.60
COMMON TATTOO (21-75) 8.00 3.20
8 Detroit Tigers 5.00 2.00
11 Los Angeles Dodgers 12.00 4.80
14 New York Mets 5.00 2.00
15 New York Yankees 12.00 4.80
21 Hank Aaron 110.00 45.00
22 Max Alvis 8.00 3.20
23 Hank Aguirre 8.00 3.20
24 Ernie Banks 60.00 24.00
25 Steve Barber 8.00 3.20
26 Ken Boyer 12.00 4.80
27 John Callison 8.00 3.20
28 Norm Cash 10.00 4.00
29 Wayne Causey 8.00 3.20
30 Orlando Cepeda 20.00 8.00
31 Rocky Colavito 20.00 8.00
32 Ray Culp 8.00 3.20
33 Vic Davalillo 8.00 3.20
34 Moe Drabowsky 8.00 3.20
35 Dick Ellsworth 8.00 3.20
36 Curt Flood 12.00 4.80
37 Bill Freehan 10.00 4.00
38 Jim Fregosi 10.00 4.00
39 Bob Friend 8.00 3.20
40 Dick Groat 12.00 4.80
41 Woody Held 8.00 3.20
42 Frank Howard 12.00 4.80
43 Al Jackson 8.00 3.20
44 Larry Jackson 8.00 3.20
45 Ken Johnson 8.00 3.20
46 Al Kaline 60.00 24.00
47 Harmon Killebrew 40.00 16.00
48 Sandy Koufax 110.00 45.00
49 Don Lock 8.00 3.20
50 Frank Malzone 10.00 4.00
51 Mickey Mantle 300.00 120.00
52 Eddie Mathews 50.00 20.00
53 Willie Mays 125.00 50.00
54 Bill Mazeroski 15.00 6.00
55 Ken McBride 8.00 3.20
56 Bill Monbouquette 8.00 3.20
57 Dave Nicholson 8.00 3.20
58 Claude Osteen 8.00 3.20
59 Milt Pappas 10.00 4.00
60 Camilo Pascual 8.00 3.20
61 Albie Pearson 8.00 3.20
62 Ron Perranoski 8.00 3.20
63 Gary Peters 8.00 3.20
64 Boog Powell 12.00 4.80
65 Frank Robinson 50.00 20.00
66 Johnny Romano 8.00 3.20
67 Norm Siebern 8.00 3.20
68 Warren Spahn 50.00 20.00
69 Dick Stuart 10.00 4.00
70 Lee Thomas 8.00 3.20
71 Joe Torre 15.00 6.00
72 Pete Ward 8.00 3.20
73 Carlton Willey 8.00 3.20
74 Billy Williams 40.00 16.00
75 Carl Yastrzemski 60.00 24.00

1965 Topps

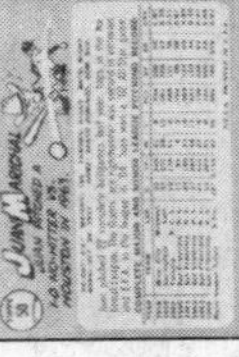

The cards in this 598-card set measure 2 1/2" by 3 1/2". The cards comprising the 1965 Topps set have team names located within a distinctive pennant design below the picture. The cards have blue borders on the reverse and were issued by series. Within this last series (523-598) there are 44 cards that were printed in lesser quantities than the other cards in that series; these shorter-printed cards are marked by SP in the checklist below. Featured subsets within this set include League Leaders (1-12) and World Series cards (132-139). This was the last year Topps issued one-card penny packs. Card were also issued in five-card nickel packs. The key Rookie Cards in this set are Steve Carlton, Jim "Catfish" Hunter, Joe Morgan, Mansori Murakami and Tony Perez.

NM Ex
COMPLETE SET (598) 4000.00 1800.00
COMMON CARD (1-196) 2.00 .80
COMMON (197-283) 2.50 1.00
COMMON (284-370) 4.00 1.60
COMMON (371-598) 8.00 3.20
WRAPPER (1-CENT) 125.00 50.00
WRAPPER (5-CENT) 100.00 40.00
1 Tony Oliva 20.00 6.00
Elston Howard
Brooks Robinson LL
2 Roberto Clemente 25.00 10.00
Hank Aaron
Rico Carty LL
3 Harmon Killebrew 50.00 20.00
Mickey Mantle
Boog Powell LL
4 Willie Mays 15.00 6.00
Billy Williams
Jim Ray Hart
Orlando Cepeda
Johnny Callison LL
5 Brooks Robinson 40.00 16.00
Harmon Killebrew
Mickey Mantle
Dick Stuart LL
6 Ken Boyer 12.00 4.80
Willie Mays
Ron Santo LL
7 Dean Chance 5.00 2.00
Joel Horlen LL
8 Sandy Koufax 20.00 8.00
Don Drysdale LL
9 Dean Chance 5.00 2.00
Gary Peters
Dave Wickersham
Juan Pizarro
Wally Bunker LL
10 Larry Jackson 5.00 2.00
Ray Sadecki
Juan Marichal LL
11 Al Downing 5.00 2.00
Dean Chance
Camilo Pascual LL
12 Bob Veale 10.00 4.00
Don Drysdale
Bob Gibson LL
13 Pedro Ramos 4.00 1.60
14 Len Gabrielson 2.00 .80
15 Robin Roberts 10.00 4.00
16 Joe Morgan RC 60.00 24.00
Sonny Jackson DP
17 Johnny Romano 2.00 .80
18 Bill McCool 2.00 .80
19 Gates Brown 4.00 1.60
20 Jim Bunning 10.00 4.00
21 Don Blasingame 2.00 .80
22 Charlie Smith 2.00 .80
23 Bob Tiefenauer 2.00 .80
24 Minnesota Twins 6.00 2.40
Team Card
25 Al McBean 2.00 .80
26 Bobby Knoop 2.00 .80
27 Dick Bertell 2.00 .80
28 Barney Schultz 2.00 .80
29 Felix Mantilla 2.00 .80
30 Jim Bouton 6.00 2.40
31 Mike White 2.00 .80
32 Herman Franks MG 2.00 .80
33 Jackie Brandt 2.00 .80
34 Cal Koonce 2.00 .80
35 Ed Charles 2.00 .80
36 Bobby Wine 2.00 .80
37 Fred Gladding 2.00 .80
38 Jim King 2.00 .80
39 Gerry Arrigo 2.00 .80
40 Frank Howard 6.00 2.40
41 Bruce Howard 2.00 .80
Marv Staehle
42 Earl Wilson 4.00 1.60
43 Mike Shannon 4.00 1.60
(Name in red, other
Cardinals in yellow)
44 Wade Blasingame 2.00 .80
45 Roy McMillan 4.00 1.60
46 Bob Lee 2.00 .80
47 Tommy Harper 4.00 1.60
48 Claude Raymond 4.00 1.60
49 Curt Blefary RC 4.00 1.60
John Miller
50 Juan Marichal 10.00 4.00
51 Bill Bryan 2.00 .80
52 Ed Roebuck 2.00 .80
53 Dick McAuliffe 4.00 1.60
54 Joe Gibbon 2.00 .80
55 Tony Conigliaro 15.00 6.00
56 Ron Kline 2.00 .80
57 Cardinals Team 6.00 2.40
58 Fred Talbot 2.00 .80
59 Nate Oliver 2.00 .80
60 Jim O'Toole 4.00 1.60
61 Chris Cannizzaro 2.00 .80
62 Jim Kaat UER DP 6.00 2.40
(Misspelled Katt)
63 Ty Cline 2.00 .80
64 Lou Burdette 4.00 1.60
65 Tony Kubek 10.00 4.00
66 Bill Rigney MG 2.00 .80
67 Harvey Haddix 4.00 1.60
68 Del Crandall 4.00 1.60
69 Bill Virdon 4.00 1.60
70 Bill Skowron 6.00 2.40
71 John O'Donoghue 2.00 .80
72 Tony Gonzalez 2.00 .80
73 Dennis Ribant 2.00 .80
74 Rico Petrocelli RC 10.00 4.00
Jerry Stephenson
75 Deron Johnson 4.00 1.60
76 Sam McDowell 6.00 2.40
77 Doug Camilli 2.00 .80
78 Dal Maxvill 2.00 .80
79A Checklist 1 10.00 2.00
(61 Cannizzaro)
79B Checklist 1 10.00 2.00
(61 C.Cannizzaro)
80 Turk Farrell 2.00 .80
81 Don Buford 4.00 1.60
82 Santos Alomar RC 6.00 2.40
John Braun
83 George Thomas 2.00 .80
84 Ron Herbel 2.00 .80
85 Willie Smith 2.00 .80
86 Buster Narum 2.00 .80
87 Nelson Mathews 2.00 .80
88 Jack Lamabe 2.00 .80
89 Mike Hershberger 2.00 .80
90 Rich Rollins 4.00 1.60
91 Cubs Team 6.00 2.40
92 Dick Howser 4.00 1.60
93 Jack Fisher 2.00 .80
94 Charlie Lau 4.00 1.60
95 Bill Mazeroski DP 6.00 2.40
96 Sonny Siebert 4.00 1.60
97 Pedro Gonzalez 2.00 .80
98 Bob Miller 2.00 .80
99 Gil Hodges MG 6.00 2.40
100 Ken Boyer 10.00 4.00
101 Fred Newman 2.00 .80
102 Steve Boros 2.00 .80
103 Harvey Kuenn 4.00 1.60
104 Checklist 2 10.00 2.00
105 Chico Salmon 2.00 .80
106 Gene Oliver 2.00 .80
107 Pat Corrales RC 4.00 1.60
Costen Shockley
108 Don Mincher 2.00 .80
109 Walt Bond 2.00 .80
110 Ron Santo 6.00 2.40
111 Lee Thomas 4.00 1.60
112 Derrell Griffith 2.00 .80
113 Steve Barber 2.00 .80
114 Jim Hickman 4.00 1.60
115 Bobby Richardson 10.00 4.00
116 Dave Dowling 4.00 1.60
Bob Tolan RC
117 Wes Stock 2.00 .80
118 Hal Lanier 4.00 1.60
119 John Kennedy 2.00 .80
120 Frank Robinson 40.00 16.00
121 Gene Alley 4.00 1.60
122 Bill Pleis 2.00 .80
123 Frank Thomas 4.00 1.60
124 Tom Satriano 2.00 .80
125 Juan Pizarro 2.00 .80
126 Dodgers Team 6.00 2.40
127 Frank Lary 2.00 .80
128 Vic Davalillo 2.00 .80
129 Bennie Daniels 2.00 .80
130 Al Kaline 40.00 16.00
131 Johnny Keane MG 2.00 .80
132 Mike Shannon WS 10.00 4.00
133 Mel Stottlemyre WS 6.00 2.40
134 Mickey Mantle WS 80.00 32.00
Mantle's Clutch HR UER
Mantle is shown wearing a road uniform
That game was played in New York
135 Ken Boyer WS 10.00 4.00
136 Tim McCarver WS 6.00 2.40
137 Jim Bouton WS 6.00 2.40
138 Bob Gibson WS 12.00 4.80
139 WS Summary 6.00 2.40
Cards celebrate
140 Dean Chance 4.00 1.60
141 Charlie James 2.00 .80
142 Bill Monbouquette 2.00 .80
143 John Gelnar 2.00 .80
Jerry May
144 Ed Kranepool 4.00 1.60
145 Luis Tiant RC 10.00 4.00
146 Ron Hansen 2.00 .80
147 Dennis Bennett 2.00 .80
148 Willie Kirkland 2.00 .80
149 Wayne Schurr 2.00 .80
150 Brooks Robinson 40.00 16.00
151 Athletics Team 6.00 2.40
152 Phil Ortega 2.00 .80
153 Norm Cash 6.00 2.40
154 Bob Humphreys 2.00 .80
155 Roger Maris 60.00 24.00
156 Bob Sadowski 2.00 .80
157 Zoilo Versalles 4.00 1.60
158 Dick Sisler 2.00 .80
159 Jim Duffalo 2.00 .80
160 R.Clemente UER 175.00 70.00
1960 Pittsburfh
161 Frank Baumann 2.00 .80
162 Russ Nixon 2.00 .80
163 Johnny Briggs 2.00 .80
164 Al Spangler 2.00 .80
165 Dick Ellsworth 2.00 .80
166 George Culver 4.00 1.60
Tommie Agee RC
167 Bill Wakefield 2.00 .80
168 Dick Green 2.00 .80
169 Dave Vineyard 2.00 .80
170 Hank Aaron 125.00 50.00
171 Jim Roland 2.00 .80
172 Jimmy Piersall 6.00 2.40
173 Detroit Tigers 6.00 2.40
Team Card
174 Joey Jay 2.00 .80
175 Bob Aspromonte 2.00 .80
176 Willie McCovey 20.00 8.00
177 Pete Mikkelsen 2.00 .80
178 Dalton Jones 2.00 .80
179 Hal Woodeshick 2.00 .80
180 Bob Allison 4.00 1.60
181 Don Loun 2.00 .80
Joe McCabe
182 Mike de la Hoz 2.00 .80
183 Dave Nicholson 2.00 .80
184 John Boozer 2.00 .80
185 Max Alvis 2.00 .80
186 Billy Cowan 2.00 .80
187 Casey Stengel MG 15.00 6.00
188 Sam Bowens 2.00 .80
189 Checklist 3 10.00 2.00
190 Bill White 6.00 2.40
191 Phil Regan 4.00 1.60
192 Jim Coker 2.00 .80
193 Gaylord Perry 15.00 6.00
194 Bill Kelso 2.00 .80
Rick Reichardt
195 Bob Veale 4.00 1.60
196 Ron Fairly 4.00 1.60
197 Diego Segui 2.50 1.00
198 Smoky Burgess 4.00 1.60
199 Bob Heffner 2.50 1.00
200 Joe Torre 6.00 2.40
201 Sandy Valdespino 4.00 1.60
Cesar Tovar RC
202 Leo Burke 2.50 1.00
203 Dallas Green 4.00 1.60
204 Russ Snyder 2.50 1.00
205 Warren Spahn 30.00 12.00
206 Willie Horton 4.00 1.60
207 Pete Rose 175.00 70.00
208 Tommy John 6.00 2.40
209 Pirates Team 6.00 2.40
210 Jim Fregosi 4.00 1.60
211 Steve Ridzik 2.50 1.00
212 Ron Brand 2.50 1.00
213 Jim Davenport 2.50 1.00
214 Bob Purkey 2.50 1.00
215 Pete Ward 2.50 1.00
216 Al Worthington 2.50 1.00
217 Walter Alston MG 6.00 2.40
218 Dick Schofield 2.50 1.00
219 Bob Meyer 2.50 1.00
220 Billy Williams 10.00 4.00
221 John Tsitouris 2.50 1.00
222 Bob Tillman 2.50 1.00
223 Dan Osinski 2.50 1.00
224 Bob Chance 2.50 1.00
225 Bo Belinsky 4.00 1.60
226 Elvio Jimenez 6.00 2.40
Jake Gibbs
227 Bobby Klaus 2.50 1.00
228 Jack Sanford 2.50 1.00
229 Lou Clinton 2.50 1.00
230 Ray Sadecki 2.50 1.00
231 Jerry Adair 2.50 1.00
232 Steve Blass RC 4.00 1.60
233 Don Zimmer 4.00 1.60
234 White Sox Team 6.00 2.40
235 Chuck Hinton 2.50 1.00
236 Denny McLain RC 25.00 10.00
237 Bernie Allen 2.50 1.00
238 Joe Moeller 2.50 1.00
239 Doc Edwards 2.50 1.00
240 Bob Bruce 2.50 1.00
241 Mack Jones 2.50 1.00
242 George Brunet 2.50 1.00
243 Ted Davidson 4.00 1.60
Tommy Helms RC
244 Lindy McDaniel 4.00 1.60
245 Joe Pepitone 6.00 2.40
246 Tom Butters 4.00 1.60
247 Wally Moon 4.00 1.60
248 Gus Triandos 4.00 1.60
249 Dave McNally 4.00 1.60
250 Willie Mays 150.00 60.00
251 Billy Herman MG 4.00 1.60
252 Pete Richert 2.50 1.00
253 Danny Cater 2.50 1.00
254 Roland Sheldon 2.50 1.00
255 Camilo Pascual 4.00 1.60
256 Tito Francona 2.50 1.00
257 Jim Wynn 4.00 1.60
258 Larry Bearnarth 2.50 1.00
259 Jim Northrup RC 6.00 2.40
Ray Oyler
260 Don Drysdale 20.00 8.00
261 Duke Carmel 2.50 1.00
262 Bud Daley 2.50 1.00
263 Marty Keough 2.50 1.00
264 Bob Buhl 4.00 1.60
265 Jim Pagliaroni 2.50 1.00
266 Bert Campaneris RC 10.00 4.00
267 Senators Team 6.00 2.40
268 Ken McBride 2.50 1.00
269 Frank Bolling 2.50 1.00
270 Milt Pappas 4.00 1.60
271 Don Wert 4.00 1.60
272 Chuck Schilling 2.50 1.00
273 Checklist 4 10.00 2.00
274 Lum Harris MG 2.50 1.00
275 Dick Groat 6.00 2.40
276 Hoyt Wilhelm 10.00 4.00
277 Johnny Lewis 2.50 1.00
278 Ken Retzer 2.50 1.00
279 Dick Tracewski 2.50 1.00
280 Dick Stuart 4.00 1.60
281 Bill Stafford 2.50 1.00
282 Dick Estelle 40.00 16.00
Masanori Murakami RC
283 Fred Whitfield 2.50 1.00
284 Nick Willhite 4.00 1.60
285 Ron Hunt 4.00 1.60
286 Jim Dickson 4.00 1.60
Aurelio Monteagudo
287 Gary Kolb 4.00 1.60
288 Jack Hamilton 4.00 1.60
289 Gordy Coleman 6.00 2.40
290 Wally Bunker 6.00 2.40
291 Jerry Lynch 4.00 1.60
292 Larry Yellen 4.00 1.60
293 Angels Team 6.00 2.40
294 Tim McCarver 10.00 4.00
295 Dick Radatz 6.00 2.40
296 Tony Taylor 6.00 2.40
297 Dave DeBusschere 10.00 4.00
298 Jim Stewart 4.00 1.60
299 Jerry Zimmerman 4.00 1.60
300 Sandy Koufax 100.00 40.00
301 Birdie Tebbetts MG 6.00 2.40
302 Al Stanek 4.00 1.60
303 John Orsino 4.00 1.60
304 Dave Stenhouse 4.00 1.60
305 Rico Carty 6.00 2.40
306 Bubba Phillips 4.00 1.60
307 Barry Latman 4.00 1.60
308 Cleon Jones RC 6.00 2.40
Tom Parsons
309 Steve Hamilton 6.00 2.40
310 Johnny Callison 6.00 2.40
311 Orlando Pena 4.00 1.60
312 Joe Nuxhall 4.00 1.60
313 Jim Schaffer 4.00 1.60
314 Sterling Slaughter 4.00 1.60
315 Frank Malzone 6.00 2.40
316 Reds Team 6.00 2.40
317 Don McMahon 4.00 1.60
318 Matty Alou 6.00 2.40
319 Ken McMullen 4.00 1.60
320 Bob Gibson 50.00 20.00
321 Rusty Staub 10.00 4.00
322 Rick Wise 6.00 2.40
323 Hank Bauer MG 6.00 2.40
324 Bobby Locke 4.00 1.60
325 Donn Clendenon 6.00 2.40
326 Dwight Siebler 4.00 1.60
327 Denis Menke 4.00 1.60
328 Eddie Fisher 4.00 1.60
329 Hawk Taylor 4.00 1.60
330 Whitey Ford 40.00 16.00
331 Al Ferrara 6.00 2.40
John Purdin
332 Ted Abernathy 4.00 1.60
333 Tom Reynolds 4.00 1.60
334 Vic Roznovsky 4.00 1.60
335 Mickey Lolich 6.00 2.40
336 Woody Held 4.00 1.60
337 Mike Cuellar 6.00 2.40
338 Philadelphia Phillies 6.00 2.40
Team Card
339 Ryne Duren 6.00 2.40
340 Tony Oliva 20.00 8.00
341 Bob Bolin 4.00 1.60
342 Bob Rodgers 6.00 2.40
343 Mike McCormick 6.00 2.40
344 Wes Parker 6.00 2.40
345 Floyd Robinson 4.00 1.60
346 Bobby Bragan MG 4.00 1.60
347 Roy Face 6.00 2.40
348 George Banks 4.00 1.60
349 Larry Miller 4.00 1.60
350 Mickey Mantle 500.00 200.00
351 Jim Perry 6.00 2.40
352 Alex Johnson RC 6.00 2.40
353 Jerry Lumpe 4.00 1.60
354 Billy Ott 4.00 1.60
Jack Warner
355 Vada Pinson 10.00 4.00
356 Bill Spanswick 4.00 1.60
357 Carl Warwick 4.00 1.60
358 Albie Pearson 6.00 2.40
359 Ken Johnson 4.00 1.60
360 Orlando Cepeda 15.00 6.00
361 Checklist 5 12.00 2.40
362 Don Schwall 4.00 1.60
363 Bob Johnson 4.00 1.60
364 Galen Cisco 4.00 1.60
365 Jim Gentile 6.00 2.40
366 Dan Schneider 4.00 1.60
367 Leon Wagner 4.00 1.60
368 Ken Berry 6.00 2.40
Joel Gibson
369 Phil Linz 6.00 2.40
370 Tommy Davis 6.00 2.40
371 Frank Kreutzer 8.00 3.20
372 Clay Dalrymple 8.00 3.20
373 Curt Simmons 8.00 3.20
374 Jose Cardenal RC 8.00 3.20
Dick Simpson
375 Dave Wickersham 8.00 3.20
376 Jim Landis 8.00 3.20
377 Willie Stargell 25.00 10.00
378 Chuck Estrada 8.00 3.20
379 Giants Team 8.00 3.20
380 Rocky Colavito 25.00 10.00
381 Al Jackson 8.00 3.20
382 J.C. Martin 8.00 3.20
383 Felipe Alou 15.00 6.00
384 Johnny Klippstein 8.00 3.20
385 Carl Yastrzemski 60.00 24.00
386 Paul Jaeckel 8.00 3.20
Fred Norman
387 Johnny Podres 15.00 6.00
388 John Blanchard 15.00 6.00
389 Don Larsen 15.00 6.00
390 Bill Freehan 15.00 6.00
391 Mel McGaha MG 8.00 3.20
392 Bob Friend 15.00 6.00
393 Ed Kirkpatrick 8.00 3.20
394 Jim Hannan 8.00 3.20
395 Jim Ray Hart 8.00 3.20
396 Frank Bertaina 8.00 3.20
397 Jerry Buchek 8.00 3.20
398 Dan Neville 15.00 6.00
Art Shamsky
399 Ray Herbert 8.00 3.20
400 Harmon Killebrew 50.00 20.00
401 Carl Willey 8.00 3.20
402 Joe Amalfitano 8.00 3.20
403 Boston Red Sox 8.00 3.20
Team Card
404 Stan Williams 8.00 3.20
(Listed as Indian
but Yankee cap)
405 John Roseboro 20.00 8.00
406 Ralph Terry 15.00 6.00
407 Lee Maye 8.00 3.20
408 Larry Sherry 8.00 3.20
409 Jim Beauchamp 15.00 6.00
Larry Dierker RC
410 Luis Aparicio 25.00 10.00
411 Roger Craig 15.00 6.00
412 Bob Bailey 8.00 3.20
413 Hal Reniff 8.00 3.20
414 Al Lopez MG 15.00 6.00
415 Curt Flood 15.00 6.00
416 Jim Brewer 8.00 3.20
417 Ed Brinkman 8.00 3.20
418 Johnny Edwards 8.00 3.20
419 Ruben Amaro 8.00 3.20
420 Larry Jackson 8.00 3.20
421 Gary Dotter 8.00 3.20
Jay Ward
422 Aubrey Gatewood 8.00 3.20
423 Jesse Gonder 8.00 3.20
424 Gary Bell 8.00 3.20
425 Wayne Causey 8.00 3.20
426 Braves Team 8.00 3.20
427 Bob Saverine 8.00 3.20
428 Bob Shaw 8.00 3.20
429 Don Demeter 8.00 3.20
430 Gary Peters 8.00 3.20
431 Nelson Briles RC 15.00 6.00
Wayne Spiezio
432 Jim Grant 15.00 6.00
433 John Bateman 8.00 3.20
434 Dave Morehead 8.00 3.20
435 Willie Davis 15.00 6.00
436 Don Elston 8.00 3.20
437 Chico Cardenas 15.00 6.00
438 Harry Walker MG 8.00 3.20
439 Moe Drabowsky 15.00 6.00

440 Tom Tresh 15.00 6.00
441 Denny Lemaster 8.00 3.20
442 Vic Power 8.00 3.20
443 Checklist 6 12.00 2.40
444 Bob Hendley 8.00 3.20
445 Don Lock 8.00 3.20
446 Art Mahaffey 8.00 3.20
447 Julian Javier 15.00 6.00
448 Lee Stange 8.00 3.20
449 Jerry Hinsley 15.00 6.00
Gary Kroll
450 Elston Howard 15.00 6.00
451 Jim Owens 8.00 3.20
452 Gary Geiger 8.00 3.20
453 Willie Crawford 15.00 6.00
John Werhas
454 Ed Rakow 8.00 3.20
455 Norm Siebern 8.00 3.20
456 Bill Henry 8.00 3.20
457 Bob Kennedy MG 15.00 6.00
458 John Buzhardt 8.00 3.20
459 Frank Kostro 8.00 3.20
460 Richie Allen 40.00 16.00
461 Clay Carroll RC 50.00 20.00
Phil Niekro
462 Lew Krausse UER 8.00 3.20
(Photo actually
Pete Lovrich)
463 Manny Mota 15.00 6.00
464 Ron Piche 8.00 3.20
465 Tom Haller 15.00 6.00
466 Pete Craig 8.00 3.20
Dick Nen
467 Ray Washburn 8.00 3.20
468 Larry Brown 8.00 3.20
469 Don Nottebart 8.00 3.20
470 Yogi Berra P/CO 50.00 20.00
471 Billy Hoeft 8.00 3.20
472 Don Pavletich UER 8.00 3.20
Listed as a pitcher
473 Paul Blair 15.00 6.00
Davey Johnson RC
474 Cookie Rojas 15.00 6.00
475 Clete Boyer 15.00 6.00
476 Billy O'Dell 8.00 3.20
477 Fritz Ackley 150.00 60.00
Steve Carlton RC
478 Wilbur Wood 15.00 6.00
479 Ken Harrelson 15.00 6.00
480 Joel Horlen 8.00 3.20
481 Cleveland Indians 10.00 4.00
Team Card
482 Bob Priddy 8.00 3.20
483 George Smith 8.00 3.20
484 Ron Perranoski 20.00 8.00
485 Nellie Fox P/CO 25.00 10.00
486 Tom Egan 8.00 3.20
Pat Rogan
487 Woody Woodward 15.00 6.00
488 Ted Wills 8.00 3.20
489 Gene Mauch MG 15.00 6.00
490 Earl Battey 8.00 3.20
491 Tracy Stallard 8.00 3.20
492 Gene Freese 8.00 3.20
493 Bill Roman 8.00 3.20
Bruce Brubaker
494 Jay Ritchie 8.00 3.20
495 Joe Christopher 8.00 3.20
496 Joe Cunningham 8.00 3.20
497 Ken Henderson 15.00 6.00
Jack Hiatt
498 Gene Stephens 8.00 3.20
499 Stu Miller 15.00 6.00
500 Eddie Mathews 40.00 16.00
501 Ralph Gagliano 8.00 3.20
Jim Rittwage
502 Don Cardwell 8.00 3.20
503 Phil Gagliano 8.00 3.20
504 Jerry Grote 15.00 6.00
505 Ray Culp 8.00 3.20
506 Sam Mele MG 8.00 3.20
507 Sammy Ellis 8.00 3.20
508 Checklist 7 12.00 2.40
509 Bob Guindon 8.00 3.20
Gerry Vezendy
510 Ernie Banks 80.00 32.00
511 Ron Locke 8.00 3.20
512 Cap Peterson 8.00 3.20
513 New York Yankees 40.00 16.00
Team Card
514 Joe Azcue 8.00 3.20
515 Vern Law 15.00 6.00
516 Al Weis 8.00 3.20
517 Paul Schaal 15.00 6.00
Jack Warner
518 Ken Rowe 8.00 3.20
519 Bob Uecker UER 30.00 12.00
(Posing as a left-
handed batter)
520 Tony Cloninger 8.00 3.20
521 Dave Bennett 8.00 3.20
Morrie Stevens
522 Hank Aguirre 8.00 3.20
523 Mike Brumley SP 12.00 4.80
524 Dave Giusti SP 12.00 4.80
525 Eddie Bressoud 8.00 3.20
526 Rene Lachemann 80.00 32.00
Johnny Odom
Jim Hunter RC UER
(Tim on back)
Skip Lockwood SP
527 Jeff Torborg SP 12.00 4.80
528 George Altman 8.00 3.20
529 Jerry Fosnow SP 12.00 4.80
530 Jim Maloney 15.00 6.00
531 Chuck Hiller 8.00 3.20
532 Hector Lopez 15.00 6.00
533 Dan Napoleon 25.00 10.00
Ron Swoboda RC
Tug McGraw RC
Jim Bethke SP
534 John Herrnstein 8.00 3.20
535 Jack Kralick SP 12.00 4.80
536 Andre Rodgers SP 12.00 4.80
537 Marcelino Lopez 8.00 3.20
Phil Roof
Rudy May RC
538 C.Dressen SP MG 12.00 4.80
539 Herm Starrette 8.00 3.20
540 Lou Brock SP 50.00 20.00
541 Greg Bollo 8.00 3.20
Bob Locker
542 Lou Klimchock 8.00 3.20
543 Ed Connolly SP 12.00 4.80
544 Howie Reed 8.00 3.20
545 Jesus Alou SP 15.00 6.00
546 Bill Davis 8.00 3.20
Mike Hedlund
Ray Barker
Floyd Weaver
547 Jake Wood SP 12.00 4.80
548 Dick Stigman 8.00 3.20
549 Roberto Pena 20.00 8.00
Glenn Beckert RC
550 Mel Stottlemyre SP RC 30.00 12.00
551 New York Mets SP 30.00 12.00
Team Card
552 Julio Gotay 8.00 3.20
553 Dan Coombs 8.00 3.20
Gene Ratliff
Jack McClure
554 Chico Ruiz SP 12.00 4.80
555 Jack Baldschun SP 12.00 4.80
556 Red Schoendienst 25.00 10.00
SP MG
557 Jose Santiago 8.00 3.20
558 Tommie Sisk 8.00 3.20
559 Ed Bailey SP 12.00 4.80
560 Boog Powell SP 25.00 10.00
561 Dennis Daboll 15.00 6.00
Mike Kekich
Hector Valle
Jim Lefebvre RC
562 Billy Moran 8.00 3.20
563 Julio Navarro 8.00 3.20
564 Mel Nelson 8.00 3.20
565 Ernie Broglio SP 12.00 4.80
566 Gil Blanco 12.00 4.80
Ross Moschitto
Art Lopez SP
567 Tommie Aaron 8.00 3.20
568 Ron Taylor SP 12.00 4.80
569 Gino Cimoli SP 12.00 4.80
570 Claude Osteen SP 15.00 6.00
571 Ossie Virgil SP 12.00 4.80
572 Baltimore Orioles SP 25.00 10.00
Team Card
573 Jim Lonborg RC 25.00 10.00
Gerry Moses
Bill Schlesinger
Mike Ryan SP
574 Roy Sievers 15.00 6.00
575 Jose Pagan 8.00 3.20
576 Terry Fox SP 12.00 4.80
577 Darold Knowles 12.00 4.80
Don Buschhorn
Richie Scheinblum SP
578 Camilo Carreon SP 12.00 4.80
579 Dick Smith SP 12.00 4.80
580 Jimmie Hall SP 12.00 4.80
581 Tony Perez RC 80.00 32.00
Dave Ricketts
Kevin Collins SP
582 Bob Schmidt SP 12.00 4.80
583 Wes Covington SP 12.00 4.80
584 Harry Bright 15.00 6.00
585 Hank Fischer 8.00 3.20
586 Tom McCraw SP 12.00 4.80
587 Joe Sparma 8.00 3.20
588 Lenny Green 8.00 3.20
589 Frank Linzy 12.00 4.80
Bob Schroder SP
590 John Wyatt 8.00 3.20
591 Bob Skinner SP 12.00 4.80
592 Frank Bork SP 12.00 4.80
593 Jackie Moore RC 12.00 4.80
John Sullivan SP
594 Joe Gaines 8.00 3.20
595 Don Lee 8.00 3.20
596 Don Landrum SP 12.00 4.80
597 Joe Nossek 8.00 3.20
John Sevcik
Dick Reese
598 Al Downing SP 25.00 7.50

1965 Topps Embossed Inserts

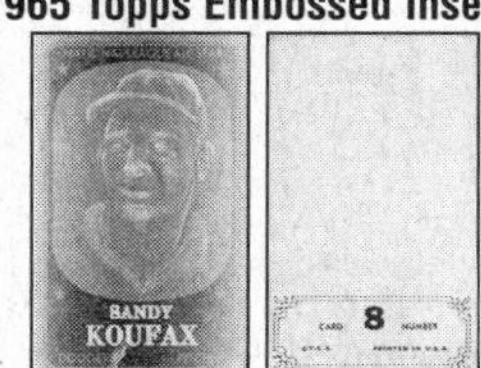

The cards in this 72-card set measure approximately 2 1/8" by 3 1/2". The 1965 Topps Embossed set contains gold foil cameo player portraits. Each league had 36 representatives set on blue backgrounds for the AL and red backgrounds for the NL. The Topps embossed set was distributed as inserts in packages of the regular 1965 baseball series.

NM Ex
COMPLETE SET (72) 200.00 80.00
1 Carl Yastrzemski 8.00 3.20
2 Ron Fairly 1.50 .60
3 Max Alvis 1.50 .60
4 Jim Ray Hart 1.50 .60
5 Bill Skowron 2.50 1.00
6 Ed Kranepool 1.50 .60
7 Tim McCarver 2.50 1.00
8 Sandy Koufax 15.00 6.00
9 Donn Clendenon 1.50 .60
10 John Romano 1.50 .60
11 Mickey Mantle 80.00 32.00
12 Joe Torre 4.00 1.60
13 Al Kaline 8.00 3.20
14 Al McBean 1.50 .60
15 Don Drysdale 4.00 1.60
16 Brooks Robinson 8.00 3.20
17 Jim Bunning 2.50 1.00
18 Gary Peters 1.50 .60
19 Roberto Clemente 40.00 16.00
20 Milt Pappas 1.50 .60
21 Wayne Causey 1.50 .60
22 Frank Robinson 4.00 1.60
23 Bill Mazeroski 4.00 1.60
24 Diego Segui 1.50 .60
25 Jim Bouton 2.50 1.00
26 Eddie Mathews 5.00 2.00
27 Willie Mays 20.00 8.00
28 Ron Santo 2.50 1.00
29 Boog Powell 2.50 1.00
30 Ken McBride 1.50 .60
31 Leon Wagner 1.50 .60
32 Johnny Callison 1.50 .60
33 Zoilo Versalles 1.50 .60
34 Jack Baldschun 1.50 .60
35 Ron Hunt 1.50 .60
36 Richie Allen 4.00 1.60
37 Frank Malzone 1.50 .60
38 Bob Allison 1.50 .60
39 Jim Fregosi 2.50 1.00
40 Billy Williams 2.50 1.00
41 Bill Freehan 2.50 1.00
42 Vada Pinson 2.50 1.00
43 Bill White 2.50 1.00
44 Roy McMillan 1.50 .60
45 Orlando Cepeda 2.50 1.00
46 Rocky Colavito 4.00 1.60
47 Ken Boyer 2.50 1.00
48 Dick Radatz 1.50 .60
49 Tommy Davis 2.50 1.00
50 Walt Bond 1.50 .60
51 John Orsino 1.50 .60
52 Joe Christopher 1.50 .60
53 Al Spangler 1.50 .60
54 Jim King 1.50 .60
55 Mickey Lolich 2.50 1.00
56 Harmon Killebrew 5.00 2.00
57 Bob Shaw 1.50 .60
58 Ernie Banks 8.00 3.20
59 Hank Aaron 20.00 8.00
60 Chuck Hinton 1.50 .60
61 Bob Aspromonte 1.50 .60
62 Lee Maye 1.50 .60
63 Joe Cunningham 1.50 .60
64 Pete Ward 1.50 .60
65 Bobby Richardson 2.50 1.00
66 Dean Chance 1.50 .60
67 Dick Ellsworth 1.50 .60
68 Jim Maloney 1.50 .60
69 Bob Gibson 4.00 1.60
70 Earl Battey 1.50 .60
71 Tony Kubek 2.50 1.00
72 Jack Kralick 1.50 .60

1965 Topps Transfers Inserts

The 1965 Topps transfers (2" by 3") were issued in series of 24 each as inserts in three of the regular 1965 Topps cards series. Thirty-six of the transfers feature blue bands at the top and bottom while 36 feature red bands at the top and bottom. The team name and position are listed in the top band while the player's name is listed in the bottom band. Transfers 1-36 have blue panels whereas 37-72 have red panels. These unnumbered transfers are ordered below alphabetically by player's name within each color group. Transfers of Bob Veale and Carl Yastrzemski are supposedly tougher to find than the others in the set; they are marked below by SP.

NM Ex
COMPLETE SET (72) 400.00 160.00
1 Bob Allison 2.00 .80
2 Max Alvis 2.00 .80
3 Luis Aparicio 5.00 2.00
4 Walt Bond 2.00 .80
5 Jim Bouton 3.00 1.20
6 Jim Bunning 5.00 2.00
7 Rico Carty 3.00 1.20
8 Wayne Causey 2.00 .80
9 Orlando Cepeda 5.00 2.00
10 Dean Chance 3.00 1.20
11 Tony Conigliaro 3.00 1.20
12 Bill Freehan 3.00 1.20
13 Jim Fregosi 3.00 1.20
14 Bob Gibson 8.00 3.20
15 Dick Groat 3.00 1.20
16 Tom Haller 2.00 .80
17 Al Jackson 2.00 .80
18 Bobby Knoop 2.00 .80
19 Jim Maloney 3.00 1.20
20 Juan Marichal 5.00 2.00
21 Lee Maye 2.00 .80
22 Jim O'Toole 2.00 .80
23 Camilo Pascual 2.00 .80
24 Vada Pinson 3.00 1.20
25 Juan Pizarro 2.00 .80
26 Bobby Richardson 5.00 2.00
27 Bob Rodgers 2.00 .80
28 John Roseboro 2.00 .80
29 Dick Stuart 3.00 1.20
30 Luis Tiant 3.00 1.20
31 Joe Torre 5.00 2.00
32 Bob Veale SP 10.00 4.00
33 Leon Wagner 2.00 .80
34 Dave Wickersham 2.00 .80
35 Billy Williams 5.00 2.00
36 Carl Yastrzemski SP 40.00 16.00
37 Hank Aaron 30.00 12.00
38 Richie Allen 8.00 3.20
39 Ken Aspromonte 2.00 .80
40 Ken Boyer 5.00 2.00
41 Johnny Callison 3.00 1.20
42 Dean Chance 2.00 .80
43 Joe Christopher 2.00 .80
44 Roberto Clemente 50.00 20.00
45 Rocky Colavito 8.00 3.20
46 Tommy Davis 3.00 1.20
47 Don Drysdale 8.00 3.20
48 Chuck Hinton 2.00 .80
49 Frank Howard 3.00 1.20
50 Ron Hunt 2.00 .80
51 Al Kaline 15.00 6.00
52 Harmon Killebrew 10.00 4.00
53 Jim King 2.00 .80
54 Ron Kline 2.00 .80
55 Sandy Koufax 30.00 12.00
56 Ed Kranepool 2.00 .80
57 Mickey Mantle 100.00 40.00
58 Willie Mays 30.00 12.00
59 Bill Mazeroski 8.00 3.20
60 Tony Oliva 5.00 2.00
61 Milt Pappas 2.00 .80
62 Gary Peters 2.00 .80
63 Boog Powell 5.00 2.00
64 Dick Radatz 2.00 .80
65 Brooks Robinson 15.00 6.00
66 Frank Robinson 8.00 3.20
67 Ron Santo 5.00 2.00
68 Diego Segui 2.00 .80
69 Bill Skowron 3.00 1.20
70 Al Spangler 2.00 .80
71 Pete Ward 2.00 .80
72 Bill White 3.00 1.20

1966 Topps

The cards in this 598-card set measure 2 1/2" by 3 1/2". There are the same number of cards as in the 1965 set. Once again, the seventh series cards (523 to 598) are considered more difficult to obtain than the cards of any other series in the set. Within this last series there are 43 cards that were printed in lesser quantities than the other cards in that series; these shorter-printed cards are marked by SP in the checklist below. Among other ways, cards were issued in five-card nickel wax packs and in 12-card dime cello packs which came 36 packs to a box. The only featured subset within this set is League Leaders (215-226). Noteworthy Rookie Cards in the set include Jim Palmer (126), Ferguson Jenkins (254), and Don Sutton (288). Jim Palmer is described in the bio (on his card back) as a left-hander.

NM Ex
COMPLETE SET (598) 4000.00 1600.00
COMMON CARD (1-109) 1.50 .60
COMMON (110-283) 2.00 .80
COMMON (284-370) 3.00 1.20
COMMON (371-446) 5.00 2.00
COMMON (447-522) 10.00 4.00
COMMON (523-598) 15.00 6.00
COMMON SP (523-598) 30.00 12.00
WRAPPER (5-CENT) 25.00 10.00
1 Willie Mays 250.00 95.00
2 Ted Abernathy 1.50 .60
3 Sam Mele MG 1.50 .60
4 Ray Culp 1.50 .60
5 Jim Fregosi 2.00 .80
6 Chuck Schilling 1.50 .60
7 Tracy Stallard 1.50 .60
8 Floyd Robinson 1.50 .60
9 Clete Boyer 2.00 .80
10 Tony Cloninger 1.50 .60
11 Brant Alyea 1.50 .60
Pete Craig
12 John Tsitouris 1.50 .60
13 Lou Johnson 2.00 .80
14 Norm Siebern 1.50 .60
15 Vern Law 2.00 .80
16 Larry Brown 1.50 .60
17 John Stephenson 1.50 .60
18 Roland Sheldon 1.50 .60
19 San Francisco Giants 5.00 2.00
Team Card
20 Willie Horton 2.00 .80
21 Don Nottebart 1.50 .60
22 Joe Nossek 1.50 .60
23 Jack Sanford 1.50 .60
24 Don Kessinger RC 4.00 1.60
25 Pete Ward 1.50 .60
26 Ray Sadecki 1.50 .60
27 Darold Knowles 1.50 .60
Andy Etchebarren
28 Phil Niekro 20.00 8.00
29 Mike Brumley 1.50 .60
30 Pete Rose DP UER 100.00 40.00
1963 Hit total is wrong
31 Jack Cullen 2.00 .80
32 Adolfo Phillips 1.50 .60
33 Jim Pagliaroni 1.50 .60
34 Checklist 1 8.00 1.60
35 Ron Swoboda 4.00 1.60
36 Jim Hunter UER 20.00 8.00
Stats say 1963 and 1964
should be 1964 and 1965
37 Billy Herman MG 2.00 .80
38 Ron Nischwitz 1.50 .60
39 Ken Henderson 1.50 .60
40 Jim Grant 1.50 .60
41 Don LeJohn 1.50 .60
42 Aubrey Gatewood 1.50 .60
43A Don Landrum 2.00 .80
(Dark button on pants
showing)
43B Don Landrum 20.00 8.00
(Button on pants
partially airbrushed)
43C Don Landrum 2.00 .80
(Button on pants
not showing)
44 Bill Davis 1.50 .60
Tom Kelley
45 Jim Gentile 2.00 .80
46 Howie Koplitz 1.50 .60
47 J.C. Martin 1.50 .60
48 Paul Blair 2.00 .80
49 Woody Woodward 2.00 .80
50 Mickey Mantle DP 300.00 100.00
51 Gordon Richardson 1.50 .60
52 Wes Covington 4.00 1.60
Johnny Callison
53 Bob Duliba 1.50 .60
54 Jose Pagan 1.50 .60
55 Ken Harrelson 2.00 .80
56 Sandy Valdespino 1.50 .60
57 Jim Lefebvre 2.00 .80
58 Dave Wickersham 1.50 .60
59 Reds Team 5.00 2.00
60 Curt Flood 4.00 1.60
61 Bob Bolin 1.50 .60
62A Merritt Ranew 2.00 .80
(With sold line)
62B Merritt Ranew 30.00 12.00
(Without sold line)
63 Jim Stewart 1.50 .60
64 Bob Bruce 1.50 .60
65 Leon Wagner 1.50 .60
66 Al Weis 1.50 .60
67 Cleon Jones 4.00 1.60
Dick Selma
68 Hal Reniff 1.50 .60
69 Ken Hamlin 1.50 .60
70 Carl Yastrzemski 30.00 12.00
71 Frank Carpin 1.50 .60
72 Tony Perez 25.00 10.00
73 Jerry Zimmerman 1.50 .60
74 Don Mossi 2.00 .80
75 Tommy Davis 2.00 .80
76 Red Schoendienst MG 4.00 1.60
77 John Orsino 1.50 .60
78 Frank Linzy 1.50 .60
79 Joe Pepitone 4.00 1.60
80 Richie Allen 6.00 2.40
81 Ray Oyler 1.50 .60
82 Bob Hendley 1.50 .60
83 Albie Pearson 2.00 .80
84 Jim Beauchamp 1.50 .60
Dick Kelley
85 Eddie Fisher 1.50 .60
86 John Bateman 1.50 .60
87 Dan Napoleon 1.50 .60
88 Fred Whitfield 1.50 .60
89 Ted Davidson 1.50 .60
90 Luis Aparicio 8.00 3.20
91A Bob Uecker TR 10.00 4.00
91B Bob Uecker NTR 40.00 16.00
92 Yankees Team 15.00 6.00
93 Jim Lonborg 2.00 .80
94 Matty Alou 2.00 .80
95 Pete Richert 1.50 .60
96 Felipe Alou 4.00 1.60
97 Jim Merritt 1.50 .60
98 Don Demeter 1.50 .60
99 Willie Stargell 6.00 2.40
Donn Clendenon
100 Sandy Koufax 100.00 32.00
101A Checklist 2 15.00 3.00
(115 W. Spahn) ERR
101B Checklist 2 10.00 2.00
(115 Bill Henry) COR
102 Ed Kirkpatrick 1.50 .60
103A Dick Groat TR 1.50 .60
103B Dick Groat NTR 40.00 16.00
104A Alex Johnson TR 2.00 .80
104B Alex Johnson NTR 30.00 12.00
105 Milt Pappas 2.00 .80
106 Rusty Staub 4.00 1.60
107 Larry Stahl 1.50 .60
Ron Tompkins
108 Bobby Klaus 1.50 .60
109 Ralph Terry 2.00 .80
110 Ernie Banks 30.00 12.00
111 Gary Peters 2.00 .80
112 Manny Mota 4.00 1.60
113 Hank Aguirre 2.00 .80
114 Jim Gosger 2.00 .80
115 Bill Henry 2.00 .80
116 Walter Alston MG 6.00 2.40
117 Jake Gibbs 2.00 .80
118 Mike McCormick 2.00 .80
119 Art Shamsky 2.00 .80
120 Harmon Killebrew 15.00 6.00
121 Ray Herbert 2.00 .80
122 Joe Gaines 2.00 .80
123 Frank Bork 2.00 .80
Jerry May
124 Tug McGraw 4.00 1.60
125 Lou Brock 20.00 8.00
126 Jim Palmer RC UER 100.00 40.00
Described as a
lefthander on
card back
127 Ken Berry 2.00 .80
128 Jim Landis 2.00 .80
129 Jack Kralick 2.00 .80
130 Joe Torre 6.00 2.40
131 Angels Team 5.00 2.00
132 Orlando Cepeda 8.00 3.20
133 Don McMahon 2.00 .80
134 Wes Parker 4.00 1.60
135 Dave Morehead 2.00 .80
136 Woody Held 2.00 .80
137 Pat Corrales 2.00 .80
138 Roger Repoz 2.00 .80
139 Byron Browne 2.00 .80
Don Young
140 Jim Maloney 4.00 1.60
141 Tom McCraw 2.00 .80
142 Don Dennis 2.00 .80
143 Jose Tartabull 4.00 1.60
144 Don Schwall 2.00 .80
145 Bill Freehan 4.00 1.60
146 George Altman 2.00 .80
147 Lum Harris MG 2.00 .80
148 Bob Johnson 2.00 .80
149 Dick Nen 2.00 .80
150 Rocky Colavito 8.00 3.20
151 Gary Wagner 2.00 .80
152 Frank Malzone 4.00 1.60
153 Rico Carty 4.00 1.60
154 Chuck Hiller 2.00 .80
155 Marcelino Lopez 2.00 .80
156 Dick Schofield 2.00 .80
Hal Lanier
157 Rene Lachemann 2.00 .80

158 Jim Brewer 2.00 .80
159 Chico Ruiz 2.00 .80
160 Whitey Ford 30.00 12.00
161 Jerry Lumpe 2.00 .80
162 Lee Maye 2.00 .80
163 Tito Francona 2.00 .80
164 Tommie Agee 4.00 1.60
Marv Staehle
165 Don Lock 2.00 .80
166 Chris Krug 2.00 .80
167 Boog Powell 6.00 2.40
168 Dan Osinski 2.00 .80
169 Duke Sims 2.00 .80
170 Cookie Rojas 4.00 1.60
171 Nick Willhite 2.00 .80
172 Mets Team 5.00 2.00
173 Al Spangler 2.00 .80
174 Ron Taylor 2.00 .80
175 Bert Campaneris 4.00 1.60
176 Jim Davenport 2.00 .80
177 Hector Lopez 2.00 .80
178 Bob Tillman 2.00 .80
179 Dennis Aust 4.00 1.60
Bob Tolan
180 Vada Pinson 4.00 1.60
181 Al Worthington 2.00 .80
182 Jerry Lynch 2.00 .80
183A Checklist 3 8.00 1.60
(Large print
on front)
183B Checklist 3 8.00 1.60
(Small print
on front)
184 Denis Menke 2.00 .80
185 Bob Buhl 4.00 1.60
186 Ruben Amaro 2.00 .80
187 Chuck Dressen MG 4.00 1.60
188 Al Luplow 2.00 .80
189 John Roseboro 4.00 1.60
190 Jimmie Hall 2.00 .80
191 Darrell Sutherland 2.00 .80
192 Vic Power 4.00 1.60
193 Dave McNally 4.00 1.60
194 Senators Team 5.00 2.00
195 Joe Morgan 15.00 6.00
196 Don Pavletich 2.00 .80
197 Sonny Siebert 2.00 .80
198 Mickey Stanley RC 6.00 2.40
199 Bill Skowron 4.00 1.60
Johnny Romano
Floyd Robinson
200 Eddie Mathews 15.00 6.00
201 Jim Dickson 2.00 .80
202 Clay Dalrymple 2.00 .80
203 Jose Santiago 2.00 .80
204 Cubs Team 5.00 2.00
205 Tom Tresh 4.00 1.60
206 Al Jackson 2.00 .80
207 Frank Quilici 2.00 .80
208 Bob Miller 2.00 .80
209 Fritz Fisher 4.00 1.60
John Hiller RC
210 Bill Mazeroski 8.00 3.20
211 Frank Kreutzer 2.00 .80
212 Ed Kranepool 4.00 1.60
213 Fred Newman 2.00 .80
214 Tommy Harper 4.00 1.60
215 Bob Clemente 50.00 20.00
Hank Aaron
Willie Mays LL
216 Tony Oliva 5.00 2.00
Carl Yastrzemski
Vic Davalillo LL
217 Willie Mays 20.00 8.00
Willie McCovey
Billy Williams LL
218 Tony Conigliaro 5.00 2.00
Norm Cash
Willie Horton LL
219 Deron Johnson 12.00 4.80
Frank Robinson
Willie Mays LL
220 Rocky Colavito 5.00 2.00
Willie Horton
Tony Oliva LL
221 Sandy Koufax 12.00 4.80
Juan Marichal
Vern Law LL
222 Sam McDowell 5.00 2.00
Eddie Fisher
Sonny Siebert LL
223 Sandy Koufax 12.00 4.80
Tony Cloninger
Don Drysdale LL
224 Jim Grant 5.00 2.00
Mel Stottlemyre
Jim Kaat LL
225 Sandy Koufax 12.00 4.80
Bob Veale
Bob Gibson LL
226 Sam McDowell 5.00 2.00
Mickey Lolich
Dennis McLain
Sonny Siebert LL
227 Russ Nixon 2.00 .80
228 Larry Dierker 4.00 1.60
229 Hank Bauer MG 4.00 1.60
230 Johnny Callison 4.00 1.60
231 Floyd Weaver 2.00 .80
232 Glenn Beckert 4.00 1.60
233 Dom Zanni 2.00 .80
234 Rich Beck 8.00 3.20
Roy White RC
235 Don Cardwell 2.00 .80
236 Mike Hershberger 2.00 .80
237 Billy O'Dell 2.00 .80
238 Dodgers Team 5.00 2.00
239 Orlando Pena 2.00 .80
240 Earl Battey 2.00 .80
241 Dennis Ribant 2.00 .80
242 Jesus Alou 2.00 .80
243 Nelson Briles 4.00 1.60
244 Chuck Harrison 2.00 .80
Sonny Jackson
245 John Buzhardt 2.00 .80
246 Ed Bailey 2.00 .80
247 Carl Warwick 2.00 .80
248 Pete Mikkelsen 2.00 .80
249 Bill Rigney MG 2.00 .80
250 Sammy Ellis 2.00 .80
251 Ed Brinkman 2.00 .80
252 Denny Lemaster 2.00 .80
253 Don Wert 2.00 .80
254 Fergie Jenkins RC 60.00 24.00
Bill Sorrell
255 Willie Stargell 20.00 8.00
256 Lew Krausse 2.00 .80
257 Jeff Torborg 4.00 1.60
258 Dave Giusti 2.00 .80
259 Boston Red Sox 5.00 2.00
Team Card
260 Bob Shaw 2.00 .80
261 Ron Hansen 2.00 .80
262 Jack Hamilton 2.00 .80
263 Tom Egan 2.00 .80
264 Andy Kosco 2.00 .80
Ted Uhlaender
265 Stu Miller 4.00 1.60
266 Pedro Gonzalez UER 2.00 .80
(Misspelled Gonzales
on card back)
267 Joe Sparma 2.00 .80
268 John Blanchard 2.00 .80
269 Don Heffner MG 2.00 .80
270 Claude Osteen 4.00 1.60
271 Hal Lanier 2.00 .80
272 Jack Baldschun 2.00 .80
273 Bob Aspromonte 4.00 1.60
Rusty Staub
274 Buster Narum 2.00 .80
275 Tim McCarver 4.00 1.60
276 Jim Bouton 4.00 1.60
277 George Thomas 2.00 .80
278 Cal Koonce 2.00 .80
279A Checklist 4 8.00 1.60
(Player's cap black)
279B Checklist 4 8.00 1.60
(Player's cap red)
280 Bobby Knoop 2.00 .80
281 Bruce Howard 2.00 .80
282 Johnny Lewis 2.00 .80
283 Jim Perry 4.00 1.60
284 Bobby Wine 3.00 1.20
285 Luis Tiant 5.00 2.00
286 Gary Geiger 3.00 1.20
287 Jack Aker 3.00 1.20
288 Bill Singer 60.00 20.00
Don Sutton RC
289 Larry Sherry 3.00 1.20
290 Ron Santo 5.00 2.00
291 Moe Drabowsky 5.00 2.00
292 Jim Coker 3.00 1.20
293 Mike Shannon 5.00 2.00
294 Steve Ridzik 3.00 1.20
295 Jim Ray Hart 5.00 2.00
296 Johnny Keane MG 5.00 2.00
297 Jim Owens 3.00 1.20
298 Rico Petrocelli 5.00 2.00
299 Lou Burdette 5.00 2.00
300 Bob Clemente 150.00 60.00
301 Greg Bollo 3.00 1.20
302 Ernie Bowman 3.00 1.20
303 Cleveland Indians 5.00 2.00
Team Card
304 John Herrnstein 3.00 1.20
305 Camilo Pascual 5.00 2.00
306 Ty Cline 3.00 1.20
307 Clay Carroll 5.00 2.00
308 Tom Haller 5.00 2.00
309 Diego Segui 3.00 1.20
310 Frank Robinson 40.00 16.00
311 Tommy Helms 5.00 2.00
Dick Simpson
312 Bob Saverine 3.00 1.20
313 Chris Zachary 3.00 1.20
314 Hector Valle 3.00 1.20
315 Norm Cash 5.00 2.00
316 Jack Fisher 3.00 1.20
317 Dalton Jones 3.00 1.20
318 Harry Walker MG 3.00 1.20
319 Gene Freese 3.00 1.20
320 Bob Gibson 25.00 10.00
321 Rick Reichardt 3.00 1.20
322 Bill Faul 3.00 1.20
323 Ray Barker 3.00 1.20
324 John Boozer 3.00 1.20
325 Vic Davalillo 3.00 1.20
326 Braves Team 5.00 2.00
327 Bernie Allen 3.00 1.20
328 Jerry Grote 5.00 2.00
329 Pete Charton 3.00 1.20
330 Ron Fairly 5.00 2.00
331 Ron Herbel 3.00 1.20
332 Bill Bryan 3.00 1.20
333 Joe Coleman RC 3.00 1.20
Jim French
334 Marty Keough 3.00 1.20
335 Juan Pizarro 3.00 1.20
336 Gene Alley 5.00 2.00
337 Fred Gladding 3.00 1.20
338 Dal Maxvill 3.00 1.20
339 Del Crandall 5.00 2.00
340 Dean Chance 5.00 2.00
341 Wes Westrum MG 5.00 2.00
342 Bob Humphreys 3.00 1.20
343 Joe Christopher 3.00 1.20
344 Steve Blass 5.00 2.00
345 Bob Allison 5.00 2.00
346 Mike de la Hoz 3.00 1.20
347 Phil Regan 5.00 2.00
348 Orioles Team 8.00 3.20
349 Cap Peterson 3.00 1.20
350 Mel Stottlemyre 8.00 3.20
351 Fred Valentine 3.00 1.20
352 Bob Aspromonte 3.00 1.20
353 Al McBean 3.00 1.20
354 Smoky Burgess 5.00 2.00
355 Wade Blasingame 3.00 1.20
356 Owen Johnson 3.00 1.20
Ken Sanders
357 Gerry Arrigo 3.00 1.20
358 Charlie Smith 3.00 1.20
359 Johnny Briggs 3.00 1.20
360 Ron Hunt 3.00 1.20
361 Tom Satriano 3.00 1.20
362 Gates Brown 5.00 2.00
363 Checklist 5 10.00 2.00
364 Nate Oliver 3.00 1.20
365 Roger Maris UER 50.00 20.00
Wrong birth year listed on card
366 Wayne Causey 3.00 1.20
367 Mel Nelson 3.00 1.20
368 Charlie Lau 5.00 2.00
369 Jim King 3.00 1.20
370 Chico Cardenas 3.00 1.20
371 Lee Stange 5.00 2.00
372 Harvey Kuenn 8.00 3.20
373 Jack Hiatt 8.00 3.20
Dick Estelle
374 Bob Locker 5.00 2.00
375 Donn Clendenon 8.00 3.20
376 Paul Schaal 5.00 2.00
377 Turk Farrell 5.00 2.00
378 Dick Tracewski 5.00 2.00
379 Cardinal Team 10.00 4.00
380 Tony Conigliaro 10.00 4.00
381 Hank Fischer 5.00 2.00
382 Phil Roof 5.00 2.00
383 Jackie Brandt 5.00 2.00
384 Al Downing 8.00 3.20
385 Ken Boyer 10.00 4.00
386 Gil Hodges MG 8.00 3.20
387 Howie Reed 5.00 2.00
388 Don Mincher 5.00 2.00
389 Jim O'Toole 8.00 3.20
390 Brooks Robinson 50.00 20.00
391 Chuck Hinton 5.00 2.00
392 Bill Hands 8.00 3.20
Randy Hundley RC
393 George Brunet 5.00 2.00
394 Ron Brand 5.00 2.00
395 Len Gabrielson 5.00 2.00
396 Jerry Stephenson 5.00 2.00
397 Bill White 8.00 3.20
398 Danny Cater 5.00 2.00
399 Ray Washburn 5.00 2.00
400 Zoilo Versalles 8.00 3.20
401 Ken McMullen 5.00 2.00
402 Jim Hickman 5.00 2.00
403 Fred Talbot 5.00 2.00
404 Pittsburgh Pirates 10.00 4.00
Team Card
405 Elston Howard 8.00 3.20
406 Joey Jay 5.00 2.00
407 John Kennedy 5.00 2.00
408 Lee Thomas 8.00 3.20
409 Billy Hoeft 5.00 2.00
410 Al Kaline 40.00 16.00
411 Gene Mauch MG 5.00 2.00
412 Sam Bowens 5.00 2.00
413 Johnny Romano 5.00 2.00
414 Dan Coombs 5.00 2.00
415 Max Alvis 5.00 2.00
416 Phil Ortega 5.00 2.00
417 Jim McGlothlin 5.00 2.00
Ed Sukla
418 Phil Gagliano 5.00 2.00
419 Mike Ryan 5.00 2.00
420 Juan Marichal 15.00 6.00
421 Roy McMillan 8.00 3.20
422 Ed Charles 5.00 2.00
423 Ernie Broglio 5.00 2.00
424 Lee May RC 10.00 4.00
Darrell Osteen
425 Bob Veale 8.00 3.20
426 White Sox Team 10.00 4.00
427 John Miller 5.00 2.00
428 Sandy Alomar 5.00 2.00
429 Bill Monbouquette 5.00 2.00
430 Don Drysdale 20.00 8.00
431 Walt Bond 5.00 2.00
432 Bob Heffner 5.00 2.00
433 Alvin Dark MG 8.00 3.20
434 Willie Kirkland 5.00 2.00
435 Jim Bunning 15.00 6.00
436 Julian Javier 8.00 3.20
437 Al Stanek 5.00 2.00
438 Willie Smith 5.00 2.00
439 Pedro Ramos 5.00 2.00
440 Deron Johnson 8.00 3.20
441 Tommie Sisk 5.00 2.00
442 Ed Barnowski 5.00 2.00
Eddie Watt
443 Bill Wakefield 3.00 1.20
444 Checklist 6 10.00 2.00
445 Jim Kaat 10.00 4.00
446 Mack Jones 5.00 2.00
447 Dick Ellsworth UER 15.00 6.00
(Photo actually
Ken Hubbs)
448 Eddie Stanky MG 10.00 4.00
449 Joe Moeller 10.00 4.00
450 Tony Oliva 15.00 6.00
451 Barry Latman 10.00 4.00
452 Joe Azcue 10.00 4.00
453 Ron Kline 10.00 4.00
454 Jerry Buchek 10.00 4.00
455 Mickey Lolich 15.00 6.00
456 Darrell Brandon 10.00 4.00
Joe Foy
457 Joe Gibbon 10.00 4.00
458 Manny Jiminez 10.00 4.00
459 Bill McCool 10.00 4.00
460 Curt Blefary 10.00 4.00
461 Roy Face 15.00 6.00
462 Bob Rodgers 10.00 4.00
463 Philadelphia Phillies 15.00 6.00
Team Card
464 Larry Bearnarth 10.00 4.00
465 Don Buford 10.00 4.00
466 Ken Johnson 10.00 4.00
467 Vic Roznovsky 10.00 4.00
468 Johnny Podres 15.00 6.00
469 Bobby Murcer RC 30.00 12.00
Dooley Womack
470 Sam McDowell 15.00 6.00
471 Bob Skinner 10.00 4.00
472 Terry Fox 10.00 4.00
473 Rich Rollins 10.00 4.00
474 Dick Schofield 10.00 4.00
475 Dick Radatz 10.00 4.00
476 Bobby Bragan MG 10.00 4.00
477 Steve Barber 10.00 4.00
478 Tony Gonzalez 10.00 4.00
479 Jim Hannan 10.00 4.00
480 Dick Stuart 10.00 4.00
481 Bob Lee 10.00 4.00
482 John Boccabella 10.00 4.00
Dave Dowling
483 Joe Nuxhall 10.00 4.00
484 Wes Covington 10.00 4.00
485 Bob Bailey 10.00 4.00
486 Tommy John 15.00 6.00
487 Al Ferrara 10.00 4.00
488 George Banks 10.00 4.00
489 Curt Simmons 10.00 4.00
490 Bobby Richardson 25.00 10.00
491 Dennis Bennett 10.00 4.00
492 Athletics Team 15.00 6.00
493 Johnny Klippstein 10.00 4.00
494 Gordy Coleman 10.00 4.00
495 Dick McAuliffe 15.00 6.00
496 Lindy McDaniel 10.00 4.00
497 Chris Cannizzaro 10.00 4.00
498 Luke Walker 10.00 4.00
Woody Fryman
499 Wally Bunker 10.00 4.00
500 Hank Aaron 125.00 50.00
501 John O'Donoghue 10.00 4.00
502 Lenny Green UER 10.00 4.00
Born: aJn. 6, 1933
503 Steve Hamilton 15.00 6.00
504 Grady Hatton MG 10.00 4.00
505 Jose Cardenal 10.00 4.00
506 Bo Belinsky 15.00 6.00
507 Johnny Edwards 10.00 4.00
508 Steve Hargan RC 15.00 6.00
509 Jake Wood 10.00 4.00
510 Hoyt Wilhelm 25.00 10.00
511 Bob Barton 10.00 4.00
Tito Fuentes RC
512 Dick Stigman 10.00 4.00
513 Camilo Carreon 10.00 4.00
514 Hal Woodeshick 10.00 4.00
515 Frank Howard 15.00 6.00
516 Eddie Bressoud 10.00 4.00
517A Checklist 7 15.00 3.00
529 White Sox Rookies
544 Cardinals Rookies
517B Checklist 7 15.00 3.00
529 W. Sox Rookies
544 Cards Rookies
518 Herb Hippauf 10.00 4.00
Arnie Umbach
519 Bob Friend 15.00 6.00
520 Jim Wynn 15.00 6.00
521 John Wyatt 10.00 4.00
522 Phil Linz 10.00 4.00
523 Bob Sadowski 10.00 4.00
524 Ollie Brown 30.00 12.00
Don Mason SP
525 Gary Bell SP 30.00 12.00
526 Twins Team SP 100.00 40.00
527 Julio Navarro 15.00 6.00
528 Jesse Gonder SP 30.00 12.00
529 Lee Elia 15.00 6.00
Dennis Higgins
Bill Voss
530 Robin Roberts 50.00 20.00
531 Joe Cunningham 15.00 6.00
532 A.Monteagudo SP 30.00 12.00
533 Jerry Adair SP 30.00 12.00
534 Dave Eilers 15.00 6.00
Rob Gardner
535 Willie Davis SP 40.00 16.00
536 Dick Egan 15.00 6.00
537 Herman Franks MG 15.00 6.00
538 Bob Allen SP 30.00 12.00
539 Bill Heath 25.00 10.00
Carroll Sembera
540 Denny McLain SP 60.00 24.00
541 Gene Oliver SP 30.00 12.00
542 George Smith 15.00 6.00
543 Roger Craig SP 30.00 12.00
544 Joe Hoerner 30.00 12.00
George Kernek
Jimy Williams RC UER SP
(Misspelled Jimmy
on card)
545 Dick Green SP 30.00 12.00
546 Dwight Siebler 25.00 10.00
547 Horace Clarke RC SP 40.00 16.00
548 Gary Kroll SP 30.00 12.00
549 Al Closter 15.00 6.00
Casey Cox
550 Willie McCovey SP 100.00 40.00
551 Bob Purkey SP 30.00 12.00
552 Birdie Tebbetts 30.00 12.00
MG SP
553 Pat Garrett 15.00 6.00
Jackie Warner
554 Jim Northrup SP 30.00 12.00
555 Ron Perranoski SP 30.00 12.00
556 Mel Queen SP 30.00 12.00
557 Felix Mantilla SP 30.00 12.00
558 Guido Grilli 20.00 8.00
Pete Magrini
George Scott RC
559 Roberto Pena SP 30.00 12.00
560 Joel Horlen 15.00 6.00
561 Choo Choo Coleman SP 30.00 12.00
562 Russ Snyder 25.00 10.00
563 Pete Cimino 15.00 6.00
Cesar Tovar
564 Bob Chance SP 30.00 12.00
565 Jimmy Piersall SP 40.00 16.00
566 Mike Cuellar SP 30.00 12.00
567 Dick Howser SP 40.00 16.00
568 Paul Lindblad 15.00 6.00
Ron Stone
569 Orlando McFarlane SP 30.00 12.00
570 Art Mahaffey SP 30.00 12.00
571 Dave Roberts SP 30.00 12.00
572 Bob Priddy 15.00 6.00
573 Derrell Griffith 15.00 6.00
574 Bill Hepler 15.00 6.00
Bill Murphy
575 Earl Wilson 15.00 6.00
576 Dave Nicholson SP 30.00 12.00
577 Jack Lamabe SP 30.00 12.00
578 Chi Chi Olivo SP 30.00 12.00
579 Frank Bertaina 20.00 8.00
Gene Brabender
Dave Johnson
580 Billy Williams SP 60.00 24.00
581 Tony Martinez 15.00 6.00
582 Garry Roggenburk 15.00 6.00
583 Tigers Team SP UER 125.00 50.00
Text on back states Tigers
finished third in 1965 instead
of fourth
584 Frank Fernandez 15.00 6.00
Fritz Peterson
585 Tony Taylor 25.00 10.00
586 Claude Raymond SP 30.00 12.00
587 Dick Bertell 15.00 6.00
588 Chuck Dobson 15.00 6.00
Ken Suarez
589 Lou Klimchock SP 30.00 12.00
590 Bill Skowron SP 40.00 16.00
591 Bart Shirley 40.00 16.00
Grant Jackson RC SP
592 Andre Rodgers 15.00 6.00
593 Doug Camilli SP 30.00 12.00
594 Chico Salmon 15.00 6.00
595 Larry Jackson 15.00 6.00
596 Nate Colbert RC 30.00 12.00
Greg Sims SP
597 John Sullivan 15.00 6.00
598 Gaylord Perry SP 175.00 50.00

1966 Topps Rub-Offs Inserts

There are 120 "rub-offs" in the Topps insert set of 1966, of which 100 depict players and the remaining 20 show team pennants. Each rub off measures 2 1/16" by 3". The color player photos are vertical while the team pennants are horizontal; both types of transfer have a large black printer's mark. These rub-offs were originally printed in rolls of 20 and are frequently still found this way. Since these rub-offs are unnumbered, they are ordered below alphabetically within type, players (1-100) and team pennants (101-120).

NM Ex
COMPLETE SET (120) 375.00 150.00
COMMON (1-100) 1.50 .60
COMMON (101-120) 1.00 .40
1 Hank Aaron 25.00 12.00
2 Jerry Adair 1.50 .60
3 Richie Allen 2.00 .80
4 Jesus Alou 2.00 .80
5 Max Alvis 1.50 .60
6 Bob Aspromonte 1.50 .60
7 Ernie Banks 10.00 4.00
8 Earl Battey 1.50 .60
9 Curt Blefary 1.50 .60
10 Ken Boyer 3.00 1.20
11 Bob Bruce 1.50 .60
12 Jim Bunning 3.00 1.20
13 Johnny Callison 2.00 .80
14 Bert Campaneris 2.00 .80
15 Jose Cardenal 1.50 .60
16 Dean Chance 2.00 .80
17 Ed Charles 1.50 .60
18 Roberto Clemente 30.00 20.00
19 Tony Cloninger 1.50 .60
20 Rocky Colavito 5.00 2.00
21 Tony Conigliaro 2.00 .80
22 Vic Davalillo 1.50 .60
23 Willie Davis 2.00 .80
24 Don Drysdale 5.00 2.00
25 Sammy Ellis 1.50 .60
26 Dick Ellsworth 1.50 .60
27 Ron Fairly 2.00 .80
28 Dick Farrell 1.50 .60
29 Eddie Fisher 1.50 .60
30 Jack Fisher 1.50 .60
31 Curt Flood 2.00 .80
32 Whitey Ford 5.00 2.00
33 Bill Freehan 2.00 .80
34 Jim Fregosi 2.00 .80
35 Bob Gibson 5.00 2.00
36 Jim Grant 1.50 .60
37 Jimmie Hall 1.50 .60
38 Ken Harrelson 2.00 .80
39 Jim Ray Hart 1.50 .60
40 Joel Horlen 1.50 .60
41 Willie Horton 2.00 .80
42 Frank Howard 2.00 .80
43 Deron Johnson 1.50 .60
44 Al Kaline 10.00 4.00
45 Harmon Killebrew 8.00 3.20
46 Bobby Knoop 1.50 .60
47 Sandy Koufax 20.00 6.00
48 Ed Kranepool 1.50 .60
49 Gary Kroll 1.50 .60
50 Don Landrum 1.50 .60
51 Vern Law 2.00 .80
52 Johnny Lewis 1.50 .60
53 Don Lock 1.50 .60
54 Mickey Lolich 2.00 .80
55 Jim Maloney 2.00 .80
56 Felix Mantilla 1.50 .60
57 Mickey Mantle 60.00 40.00
58 Juan Marichal 5.00 2.00
59 Eddie Mathews 8.00 3.20
60 Willie Mays 25.00 12.00
61 Bill Mazeroski 5.00 2.00
62 Dick McAuliffe 2.00 .80
63 Tim McCarver 2.00 .80
64 Willie McCovey 5.00 2.00
65 Sam McDowell 2.00 .80
66 Ken McMullen 1.50 .60
67 Denis Menke 1.50 .60
68 Bill Monbouquette 1.50 .60
69 Joe Morgan 5.00 2.00
70 Fred Newman 1.50 .60
71 John O'Donoghue 1.50 .60
72 Tony Oliva 3.00 1.20
73 Johnny Orsino 1.50 .60
74 Phil Ortega 1.50 .60
75 Milt Pappas 2.00 .80
76 Dick Radatz 2.00 .80
77 Bobby Richardson 3.00 1.20
78 Pete Richert 1.50 .60
79 Brooks Robinson 10.00 4.00

80 Floyd Robinson 1.50 .60
81 Frank Robinson 5.00 2.00
82 Cookie Rojas 1.50 .60
83 Pete Rose 30.00 12.00
84 John Roseboro 2.00 .80
85 Ron Santo 3.00 1.20
86 Bill Skowron 2.00 .80
87 Willie Stargell 5.00 2.00
88 Mel Stottlemyre 2.00 .80
89 Dick Stuart 1.50 .60
90 Ron Swoboda 2.00 .80
91 Fred Talbot 1.50 .60
92 Ralph Terry 2.00 .80
93 Joe Torre 5.00 2.00
94 Tom Tresh 3.00 1.20
95 Bob Veale 1.50 .60
96 Pete Ward 1.50 .60
97 Bill White 2.00 .80
98 Billy Williams 3.00 1.20
99 Jim Wynn 2.00 .80
100 Carl Yastrzemski 12.00 4.80
101 Baltimore Orioles 2.50 1.00
102 Boston Red Sox 2.50 1.00
111 Los Angeles Dodgers 2.50 1.00
114 New York Mets 2.50 1.00
115 New York Yankees 4.00 1.60
120 Washington Senators 2.50 1.00

1967 Topps

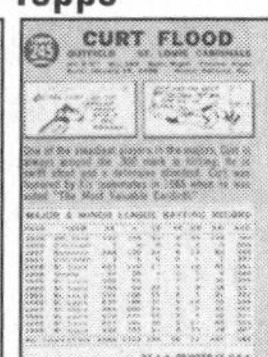

he cards in this 609-card set measure 2 1/2" by 1/2". The 1967 Topps series is considered by ome collectors to be one of the company's inest accomplishments in baseball card producion. Excellent color photographs are combined vith easy-to-read backs. Cards 458 to 533 are lightly harder to find than numbers 1 to 457, nd the inevitable high series (534 to 609) xists. Each checklist card features a small ciular picture of a popular player included in that eries. Printing discrepancies resulted in some igh series cards being in shorter supply. The hecklist below identifies (by DP) 22 doublerinted high numbers; of the 76 cards in the last eries, 54 cards were short printed and the other 2 cards are much more plentiful. Featured subets within this set include World Series cards 151-155) and League Leaders (233-244). A limted number of "proof" Roger Maris cards were roduced. These cards are blank backed and Maris is listed as a New York Yankee on it. Some ob Bolin cards: (number 252) have a white mear in between his names. Another tough ariation that has been recently discovered volves card number 58 Paul Schaal. The tough ersion has a green bat above his name. The key ookie Cards in the set are high number cards of od Carew and Tom Seaver. Confirmed methods f selling these cards include five-card nickel vax packs. Although rarely seen, there exists a alesman's sample panel of three cards that picures Earl Battey, Manny Mota, and Gene rabender with ad information on the back about he "new" Topps cards.

	NM	Ex
OMPLETE SET (609)	5000.00	2000.00
OMMON CARD (1-109)	1.50	.60
OMMON (110-283)	2.00	.80
OMMON (284-370)	2.50	1.00
OMMON (371-457)	4.00	1.60
OMMON (458-533)	6.00	2.40
OMMON (534-609)	15.00	6.00
OMMON DP (534-609)	8.00	3.20
VRAPPER (5-CENT)	25.00	10.00

Frank Robinson 25.00 7.50
Hank Bauer MG
Brooks Robinson DP
Jack Hamilton 1.50 .60
Duke Sims 1.50 .60
Hal Lanier 1.50 .60
Whitey Ford UER 20.00 8.00
(1953 listed as
1933 in stats on back)
Dick Simpson 1.50 .60
Don McMahon 1.50 .60
Chuck Harrison 1.50 .60
Ron Hansen 1.50 .60
0 Matty Alou 4.00 1.60
1 Barry Moore 1.50 .60
2 Jim Campanis 4.00 1.60
Bill Singer
3 Joe Sparma 1.50 .60
4 Phil Linz 4.00 1.60
5 Earl Battey 1.50 .60
6 Bill Hands 1.50 .60
7 Jim Gosger 1.50 .60
8 Gene Oliver 1.50 .60
9 Jim McGlothlin 1.50 .60
0 Orlando Cepeda 8.00 3.20
1 Dave Bristol MG 1.50 .60
2 Gene Brabender 1.50 .60
3 Larry Elliot 1.50 .60
4 Bob Allen 1.50 .60
5 Elston Howard 4.00 1.60
6A Bob Priddy NTR 30.00 12.00
6B Bob Priddy TR 4.00 1.60
7 Bob Saverine 1.50 .60
8 Barry Latman 1.50 .60
9 Tom McCraw 1.50 .60
0 Al Kaline DP 20.00 8.00
1 Jim Brewer 1.50 .60
2 Bob Bailey 4.00 1.60
3 Sal Bando RC 6.00 2.40
Randy Schwartz
4 Pete Cimino 1.50 .60
5 Rico Carty 4.00 1.60
6 Bob Tillman 1.50 .60
7 Rick Wise 4.00 1.60
38 Bob Johnson 1.50 .60
39 Curt Simmons 4.00 1.60
40 Rick Reichardt 1.50 .60
41 Joe Hoerner 1.50 .60
42 Mets Team 10.00 4.00
43 Chico Salmon 1.50 .60
44 Joe Nuxhall 4.00 1.60
45 Roger Maris 50.00 20.00
45A Roger Maris 1000.00 400.00
Yankees listed as team
Blank Back
46 Lindy McDaniel 4.00 1.60
47 Ken McMullen 1.50 .60
48 Bill Freehan 4.00 1.60
49 Roy Face 4.00 1.60
50 Tony Oliva 6.00 2.40
51 Dave Adlesh 1.50 .60
Wes Bales
52 Dennis Higgins 1.50 .60
53 Clay Dalrymple 1.50 .60
54 Dick Green 1.50 .60
55 Don Drysdale 15.00 6.00
56 Jose Tartabull 4.00 1.60
57 Pat Jarvis RC 4.00 1.60
58A Paul Schaal 20.00 8.00
Green Bat
58B Paul Schaal 1.50 .60
Normal Colored Bat
59 Ralph Terry 4.00 1.60
60 Luis Aparicio 8.00 3.20
61 Gordy Coleman 1.50 .60
62 Frank Robinson CL 8.00 1.60
63 Lou Brock 8.00 3.20
Curt Flood
64 Fred Valentine 1.50 .60
65 Tom Haller 4.00 1.60
66 Manny Mota 4.00 1.60
67 Ken Berry 1.50 .60
68 Bob Buhl 4.00 1.60
69 Vic Davalillo 1.50 .60
70 Ron Santo 6.00 2.40
71 Camilo Pascual 4.00 1.60
72 George Korince 1.50 .60
(Photo actually
James Murray Brown)
John (Tom) Matchick
73 Rusty Staub 6.00 2.40
74 Wes Stock 1.50 .60
75 George Scott 4.00 1.60
76 Jim Barbieri 1.50 .60
77 Dooley Womack 4.00 1.60
78 Pat Corrales 1.50 .60
79 Bubba Morton 1.50 .60
80 Jim Maloney 4.00 1.60
81 Eddie Stanky MG 4.00 1.60
82 Steve Barber 1.50 .60
83 Ollie Brown 1.50 .60
84 Tommie Sisk 1.50 .60
85 Johnny Callison 4.00 1.60
86A Mike McCormick NTR 30.00 12.00
(Senators on front
and Senators on back)
86B Mike McCormick TR 4.00 1.60
(Traded line
at end of bio;
Senators on front,
but Giants on back)
87 George Altman 1.50 .60
88 Mickey Lolich 4.00 1.60
89 Felix Millan 4.00 1.60
90 Jim Nash 1.50 .60
91 Johnny Lewis 1.50 .60
92 Ray Washburn 1.50 .60
93 Stan Bahnsen RC 4.00 1.60
Bobby Murcer
94 Ron Fairly 4.00 1.60
95 Sonny Siebert 1.50 .60
96 Art Shamsky 1.50 .60
97 Mike Cuellar 4.00 1.60
98 Rich Rollins 1.50 .60
99 Lee Stange 1.50 .60
100 Frank Robinson DP 15.00 6.00
101 Ken Johnson 1.50 .60
102 Philadelphia Phillies 4.00 1.60
Team Card
103 Mickey Mantle CL 20.00 4.00
104 Minnie Rojas 1.50 .60
105 Ken Boyer 6.00 2.40
106 Randy Hundley 4.00 1.60
107 Joel Horlen 1.50 .60
108 Alex Johnson 4.00 1.60
109 Rocky Colavito 6.00 2.40
Leon Wagner
110 Jack Aker 4.00 1.60
111 John Kennedy 2.00 .80
112 Dave Wickersham 2.00 .80
113 Dave Nicholson 2.00 .80
114 Jack Baldschun 2.00 .80
115 Paul Casanova 2.00 .80
116 Herman Franks MG 2.00 .80
117 Darrell Brandon 2.00 .80
118 Bernie Allen 2.00 .80
119 Wade Blasingame 2.00 .80
120 Floyd Robinson 2.00 .80
121 Eddie Bressoud 2.00 .80
122 George Brunet 2.00 .80
123 Jim Price 4.00 1.60
Luke Walker
124 Jim Stewart 2.00 .80
125 Moe Drabowsky 4.00 1.60
126 Tony Taylor 2.00 .80
127 John O'Donoghue 2.00 .80
128 Ed Spiezio 2.00 .80
129 Phil Roof 2.00 .80
130 Phil Regan 4.00 1.60
131 Yankees Team 10.00 4.00
132 Ozzie Virgil 2.00 .80
133 Ron Kline 2.00 .80
134 Gates Brown 6.00 2.40
135 Deron Johnson 4.00 1.60
136 Carroll Sembera 2.00 .80
137 Ron Clark 2.00 .80
Jim Ollum
138 Dick Kelley 2.00 .80
139 Dalton Jones 4.00 1.60
140 Willie Stargell 20.00 8.00
141 John Miller 2.00 .80
142 Jackie Brandt 2.00 .80
143 Pete Ward 2.00 .80
Don Buford
144 Bill Hepler 2.00 .80
145 Larry Brown 2.00 .80
146 Steve Carlton 50.00 20.00
147 Tom Egan 2.00 .80
148 Adolfo Phillips 2.00 .80
149 Joe Moeller 2.00 .80
150 Mickey Mantle 300.00 100.00
151 Moe Drabowsky WS 5.00 2.00
152 Jim Palmer WS 8.00 3.20
153 Paul Blair WS 5.00 2.00
154 Brooks Robinson WS 5.00 2.00
Dave McNally
155 WS Summary 5.00 2.00
Winners celebrate
156 Ron Herbel 2.00 .80
157 Danny Cater 2.00 .80
158 Jimmie Coker 2.00 .80
159 Bruce Howard 2.00 .80
160 Willie Davis 4.00 1.60
161 Dick Williams MG 4.00 1.60
162 Billy O'Dell 2.00 .80
163 Vic Roznovsky 2.00 .80
164 Dwight Siebler UER 2.00 .80
(Last line of stats
shows 1960 Minnesota)
165 Cleon Jones 4.00 1.60
166 Eddie Mathews 15.00 6.00
167 Joe Coleman 2.00 .80
Tim Cullen
168 Ray Culp 2.00 .80
169 Horace Clarke 4.00 1.60
170 Dick McAuliffe 4.00 1.60
171 Cal Koonce 2.00 .80
172 Bill Heath 2.00 .80
173 St. Louis Cardinals 4.00 1.60
Team Card
174 Dick Radatz 4.00 1.60
175 Bobby Knoop 2.00 .80
176 Sammy Ellis 2.00 .80
177 Tito Fuentes 1.50 .60
178 John Buzhardt 2.00 .80
179 Charles Vaughan 4.00 1.60
Cecil Upshaw
180 Curt Blefary 2.00 .80
181 Terry Fox 2.00 .80
182 Ed Charles 2.00 .80
183 Jim Pagliaroni 2.00 .80
184 George Thomas 2.00 .80
185 Ken Holtzman RC 4.00 1.60
186 Ed Kranepool 4.00 1.60
Ron Swoboda
187 Pedro Ramos 2.00 .80
188 Ken Harrelson 4.00 1.60
189 Chuck Hinton 2.00 .80
190 Turk Farrell 2.00 .80
191A Willie Mays CL 10.00 2.00
214 Tom Kelley
191B Willie Mays CL 12.00 2.40
214 Dick Kelley
192 Fred Gladding 2.00 .80
193 Jose Cardenal 4.00 1.60
194 Bob Allison 4.00 1.60
195 Al Jackson 2.00 .80
196 Johnny Romano 2.00 .80
197 Ron Perranoski 4.00 1.60
198 Chuck Hiller 2.00 .80
199 Billy Hitchcock MG 2.00 .80
200 Willie Mays UER 100.00 40.00
('63 Sna Francisco
on card back stats)
201 Hal Reniff 4.00 1.60
202 Johnny Edwards 2.00 .80
203 Al McBean 2.00 .80
204 Mike Epstein 6.00 2.40
Tom Phoebus
205 Dick Groat 4.00 1.60
206 Dennis Bennett 2.00 .80
207 John Orsino 2.00 .80
208 Jack Lamabe 2.00 .80
209 Joe Nossek 2.00 .80
210 Bob Gibson 20.00 8.00
211 Twins Team 4.00 1.60
212 Chris Zachary 2.00 .80
213 Jay Johnstone RC 4.00 1.60
214 Dick Kelley 2.00 .80
215 Ernie Banks 20.00 8.00
216 Norm Cash 8.00 3.20
Al Kaline
217 Rob Gardner 2.00 .80
218 Wes Parker 4.00 1.60
219 Clay Carroll 4.00 1.60
220 Jim Ray Hart 4.00 1.60
221 Woody Fryman 4.00 1.60
222 Darrell Osteen 4.00 1.60
Lee May
223 Mike Ryan 4.00 1.60
224 Walt Bond 2.00 .80
225 Mel Stottlemyre 6.00 2.40
226 Julian Javier 4.00 1.60
227 Paul Lindblad 2.00 .80
228 Gil Hodges MG 6.00 2.40
229 Larry Jackson 2.00 .80
230 Boog Powell 6.00 2.40
231 John Bateman 2.00 .80
232 Don Buford 2.00 .80
233 Gary Peters 4.00 1.60
Joel Horlen
Steve Hargan LL
234 Sandy Koufax 15.00 6.00
Mike Cuellar
Juan Marichal LL
235 Jim Kaat 6.00 2.40
Denny McLain
Earl Wilson LL
236 Sandy Koufax 25.00 10.00
Juan Marichal
Bob Gibson
Gaylord Perry LL
237 Sam McDowell 6.00 2.40
Jim Kaat
Earl Wilson LL
238 Sandy Koufax 12.00 4.80
Jim Bunning
Bob Veale LL
239 Frank Robinson 10.00 4.00
Tony Oliva
Al Kaline LL
240 Matty Alou 6.00 2.40
Felipe Alou
Rico Carty LL
241 Frank Robinson 10.00 4.00
Harmon Killebrew
Boog Powell LL
242 Hank Aaron 25.00 10.00
Bob Clemente
Richie Allen LL
243 Frank Robinson 10.00 4.00
Harmon Killebrew
Boog Powell LL
244 Hank Aaron 20.00 8.00
Richie Allen
Willie Mays LL
245 Curt Flood 6.00 2.40
246 Jim Perry 4.00 1.60
247 Jerry Lumpe 2.00 .80
248 Gene Mauch MG 4.00 1.60
249 Nick Willhite 2.00 .80
250 Hank Aaron UER 80.00 32.00
(Second 1961 in stats
should be 1962)
251 Woody Held 2.00 .80
252 Bob Bolin 2.00 .80
253 Bill Davis 2.00 .80
Gus Gil
254 Milt Pappas 4.00 1.60
(No facsimile auto-
graph on card front)
255 Frank Howard 4.00 1.60
256 Bob Hendley 2.00 .80
257 Charlie Smith 2.00 .80
258 Lee Maye 2.00 .80
259 Don Dennis 2.00 .80
260 Jim Lefebvre 4.00 1.60
261 John Wyatt 2.00 .80
262 Athletics Team 4.00 1.60
263 Hank Aguirre 2.00 .80
264 Ron Swoboda 4.00 1.60
265 Lou Burdette 4.00 1.60
266 Willie Stargell 4.00 1.60
Donn Clendenon
267 Don Schwall 2.00 .80
268 Johnny Briggs 2.00 .80
269 Don Nottebart 2.00 .80
270 Zoilo Versalles 2.00 .80
271 Eddie Watt 2.00 .80
272 Bill Connors RC 4.00 1.60
Dave Dowling
273 Dick Lines 2.00 .80
274 Bob Aspromonte 2.00 .80
275 Fred Whitfield 2.00 .80
276 Bruce Brubaker 2.00 .80
277 Steve Whitaker 6.00 2.40
278 Jim Kaat CL 8.00 1.60
279 Frank Linzy 2.00 .80
280 Tony Conigliaro 8.00 3.20
281 Bob Rodgers 2.00 .80
282 John Odom 2.00 .80
283 Gene Alley 4.00 1.60
284 Johnny Podres 4.00 1.60
285 Lou Brock 20.00 8.00
286 Wayne Causey 2.50 1.00
287 Greg Goossen 2.50 1.00
Bart Shirley
288 Denny Lemaster 2.50 1.00
289 Tom Tresh 5.00 2.00
290 Bill White 5.00 2.00
291 Jim Hannan 2.50 1.00
292 Don Pavletich 2.50 1.00
293 Ed Kirkpatrick 2.50 1.00
294 Walter Alston MG 8.00 3.20
295 Sam McDowell 5.00 2.00
296 Glenn Beckert 5.00 2.00
297 Dave Morehead 5.00 2.00
298 Ron Davis 2.50 1.00
299 Norm Siebern 2.50 1.00
300 Jim Kaat 5.00 2.00
301 Jesse Gonder 2.50 1.00
302 Orioles Team 8.00 3.20
303 Gil Blanco 2.50 1.00
304 Phil Gagliano 2.50 1.00
305 Earl Wilson 5.00 2.00
306 Bud Harrelson RC 5.00 2.00
307 Jim Beauchamp 2.50 1.00
308 Al Downing 5.00 2.00
309 Johnny Callison 5.00 2.00
Richie Allen
310 Gary Peters 2.50 1.00
311 Ed Brinkman 2.50 1.00
312 Don Mincher 2.50 1.00
313 Bob Lee 2.50 1.00
314 Mike Andrews 8.00 3.20
Reggie Smith RC
315 Billy Williams 15.00 6.00
316 Jack Kralick 2.50 1.00
317 Cesar Tovar 2.50 1.00
318 Dave Giusti 2.50 1.00
319 Paul Blair 5.00 2.00
320 Gaylord Perry 15.00 6.00
321 Mayo Smith MG 2.50 1.00
322 Jose Pagan 2.50 1.00
323 Mike Hershberger 2.50 1.00
324 Hal Woodeshick 2.50 1.00
325 Chico Cardenas 5.00 2.00
326 Bob Uecker 10.00 4.00
327 California Angels 8.00 3.20
Team Card
328 Clete Boyer UER 5.00 2.00
(Stats only go up
through 1965)
329 Charlie Lau 5.00 2.00
330 Claude Osteen 5.00 2.00
331 Joe Foy 5.00 2.00
332 Jesus Alou 2.50 1.00
333 Fergie Jenkins 20.00 8.00
334 Bob Allison 10.00 4.00
Harmon Killebrew
335 Bob Veale 5.00 2.00
336 Joe Azcue 2.50 1.00
337 Joe Morgan 15.00 6.00
338 Bob Locker 2.50 1.00
339 Chico Ruiz 2.50 1.00
340 Joe Pepitone 8.00 3.20
341 Dick Dietz 2.50 1.00
Bill Sorrell
342 Hank Fischer 2.50 1.00
343 Tom Satriano 2.50 1.00
344 Ossie Chavarria 2.50 1.00
345 Stu Miller 5.00 2.00
346 Jim Hickman 2.50 1.00
347 Grady Hatton MG 2.50 1.00
348 Tug McGraw 5.00 2.00
349 Bob Chance 2.50 1.00
350 Joe Torre 8.00 3.20
351 Vern Law 5.00 2.00
352 Ray Oyler 2.50 1.00
353 Bill McCool 2.50 1.00
354 Cubs Team 8.00 3.20
355 Carl Yastrzemski 60.00 24.00
356 Larry Jaster 2.50 1.00
357 Bill Skowron 5.00 2.00
358 Ruben Amaro 2.50 1.00
359 Dick Ellsworth 2.50 1.00
360 Leon Wagner 2.50 1.00
361 Roberto Clemente CL 15.00 3.00
362 Darold Knowles 2.50 1.00
363 Davey Johnson 5.00 2.00
364 Claude Raymond 2.50 1.00
365 John Roseboro 5.00 2.00
366 Andy Kosco 2.50 1.00
367 Bill Kelso 2.50 1.00
Don Wallace
368 Jack Hiatt 2.50 1.00
369 Jim Hunter 15.00 6.00
370 Tommy Davis 5.00 2.00
371 Jim Lonborg 8.00 3.20
372 Mike de la Hoz 4.00 1.60
373 Duane Josephson 4.00 1.60
Fred Klages DP
374A Mel Queen ERR DP 20.00 8.00
(Incomplete stat
line on back)
374B Mel Queen COR DP 4.00 1.60
(Complete stat
line on back)
375 Jake Gibbs 8.00 3.20
376 Don Lock DP 4.00 1.60
377 Luis Tiant 8.00 3.20
378 Detroit Tigers 8.00 3.20
Team Card UER
(Willie Horton with
262 RBI's in 1966)
379 Jerry May DP 4.00 1.60
380 Dean Chance DP 4.00 1.60
381 Dick Schofield DP 4.00 1.60
382 Dave McNally 8.00 3.20
383 Ken Henderson DP 4.00 1.60
384 Jim Cosman 4.00 1.60
Dick Hughes
385 Jim Fregosi 8.00 3.20
(Batting wrong)
386 Dick Selma DP 4.00 1.60
387 Cap Peterson DP 4.00 1.60
388 Arnold Earley DP 4.00 1.60
389 Alvin Dark MG DP 8.00 3.20
390 Jim Wynn DP 8.00 3.20
391 Wilbur Wood DP 8.00 3.20
392 Tommy Harper DP 8.00 3.20
393 Jim Bouton DP 8.00 3.20
394 Jake Wood DP 4.00 1.60
395 Chris Short 8.00 3.20
396 Denis Menke 4.00 1.60
Tony Cloninger
397 Willie Smith DP 4.00 1.60
398 Jeff Torborg 8.00 3.20
399 Al Worthington DP 4.00 1.60
400 Bob Clemente DP 100.00 40.00
401 Jim Coates 4.00 1.60
402A Phillies Rookies DP 20.00 8.00
Grant Jackson
Billy Wilson
Incomplete stat line
402B Phillies Rookies DP 8.00 3.20
Grant Jackson
Billy Wilson
403 Dick Nen 4.00 1.60
404 Nelson Briles 8.00 3.20
405 Russ Snyder 4.00 1.60
406 Lee Elia DP 4.00 1.60
407 Reds Team 8.00 3.20
408 Jim Northrup DP 8.00 3.20
409 Ray Sadecki 4.00 1.60
410 Lou Johnson DP 4.00 1.60
411 Dick Howser DP 4.00 1.60
412 Norm Miller 8.00 3.20
Doug Rader RC
413 Jerry Grote 4.00 1.60
414 Casey Cox 4.00 1.60
415 Sonny Jackson 4.00 1.60
416 Roger Repoz 4.00 1.60
417A Bob Bruce ERR DP 30.00 12.00
(RBAVES on back)
417B Bob Bruce COR DP 4.00 1.60
418 Sam Mele MG 4.00 1.60
419 Don Kessinger DP 8.00 3.20
420 Denny McLain 12.00 4.80
421 Dal Maxvill DP 4.00 1.60
422 Hoyt Wilhelm 15.00 6.00
423 Willie Mays 25.00 10.00
Willie McCovey DP
424 Pedro Gonzalez 4.00 1.60
425 Pete Mikkelsen 4.00 1.60
426 Lou Clinton 4.00 1.60
427A R.Gomez ERR DP 20.00 8.00
Incomplete stat
line on back
427B R.Gomez COR DP 4.00 1.60
Complete stat
line on back
428 Tom Hutton RC 8.00 3.20
Gene Michael DP
429 Garry Roggenburk DP 4.00 1.60
430 Pete Rose 100.00 40.00
431 Ted Uhlaender 4.00 1.60
432 Jimmie Hall DP 4.00 1.60
433 Al Luplow DP 4.00 1.60
434 Eddie Fisher DP 4.00 1.60
435 Mack Jones DP 4.00 1.60
436 Pete Ward 4.00 1.60
437 Senators Team 8.00 3.20
438 Chuck Dobson 4.00 1.60
439 Byron Browne 4.00 1.60
440 Steve Hargan 4.00 1.60
441 Jim Davenport 4.00 1.60
442 Bill Robinson RC 8.00 3.20
Joe Verbanic DP
443 Tito Francona DP 4.00 1.60
444 George Smith 4.00 1.60
445 Don Sutton 25.00 10.00
446 Russ Nixon DP 4.00 1.60
447A Bo Belinsky ERR DP 5.00 2.00

(Incomplete stat
line on back)
447B Bo Belinsky COR DP......... 8.00 3.20
(Complete stat
line on back)
448 Harry Walker DP MG 4.00 1.60
449 Orlando Pena 4.00 1.60
450 Richie Allen........................ 8.00 3.20
451 Fred Newman DP 4.00 1.60
452 Ed Kranepool 8.00 3.20
453 A.Monteagudo DP................ 4.00 1.60
454A Juan Marichal CL............ 12.00 2.40
Missing left ear
454B Juan Marichal CL............ 12.00 2.40
left ear showing
455 Tommie Agee 8.00 3.20
456 Phil Niekro 15.00 6.00
457 Andy Etchebarren DP........... 8.00 3.20
458 Lee Thomas 6.00 2.40
459 Dick Bosman RC 6.00 2.40
Pete Craig
460 Harmon Killebrew 60.00 24.00
461 Bob Miller 12.00 4.80
462 Bob Barton........................... 6.00 2.40
463 Sam McDowell..................... 12.00 4.80
Sonny Siebert
464 Dan Coombs 6.00 2.40
465 Willie Horton..................... 12.00 4.80
466 Bobby Wine 6.00 2.40
467 Jim O'Toole.......................... 6.00 2.40
468 Ralph Houk MG 6.00 2.40
469 Len Gabrielson..................... 6.00 2.40
470 Bob Shaw............................. 6.00 2.40
471 Rene Lachemann 6.00 2.40
472 John Gelnar 6.00 2.40
George Spriggs
473 Jose Santiago 6.00 2.40
474 Bob Tolan............................ 6.00 2.40
475 Jim Palmer 80.00 32.00
476 Tony Perez SP.................... 60.00 24.00
477 Braves Team 15.00 6.00
478 Bob Humphreys 6.00 2.40
479 Gary Bell 6.00 2.40
480 Willie McCovey 40.00 16.00
481 Leo Durocher MG 20.00 8.00
482 Bill Monbouquette................ 6.00 2.40
483 Jim Landis 6.00 2.40
484 Jerry Adair 6.00 2.40
485 Tim McCarver 25.00 10.00
486 Rich Reese........................... 6.00 2.40
Bill Whitby
487 Tommie Reynolds 6.00 2.40
488 Gerry Arrigo......................... 6.00 2.40
489 Doug Clemens 6.00 2.40
490 Tony Cloninger..................... 6.00 2.40
491 Sam Bowens......................... 6.00 2.40
492 Pittsburgh Pirates 15.00 6.00
Team Card
493 Phil Ortega 6.00 2.40
494 Bill Rigney MG 6.00 2.40
495 Fritz Peterson....................... 6.00 2.40
496 Orlando McFarlane................ 6.00 2.40
497 Ron Campbell 6.00 2.40
498 Larry Dierker 12.00 4.80
499 George Culver 6.00 2.40
Jose Vidal
500 Juan Marichal 25.00 10.00
501 Jerry Zimmerman 6.00 2.40
502 Derrell Griffith 6.00 2.40
503 Los Angeles Dodgers......... 20.00 8.00
Team Card
504 Orlando Martinez 6.00 2.40
505 Tommy Helms.................... 12.00 4.80
506 Smoky Burgess..................... 6.00 2.40
507 Ed Barnowski........................ 6.00 2.40
Larry Haney RC
508 Dick Hall............................... 6.00 2.40
509 Jim King................................ 6.00 2.40
510 Bill Mazeroski 25.00 10.00
511 Don Wert 6.00 2.40
512 Red Schoendienst MG 25.00 10.00
513 Marcelino Lopez................... 6.00 2.40
514 John Werhas......................... 6.00 2.40
515 Bert Campaneris 12.00 4.80
516 Giants Team 15.00 6.00
517 Fred Talbot 12.00 4.80
518 Denis Menke 6.00 2.40
519 Ted Davidson 6.00 2.40
520 Max Alvis 6.00 2.40
521 Boog Powell...................... 12.00 4.80
Curt Blefary
522 John Stephenson 6.00 2.40
523 Jim Merritt............................ 6.00 2.40
524 Felix Mantilla 6.00 2.40
525 Ron Hunt 6.00 2.40
526 Pat Dobson RC 6.00 2.40
George Korince
(See 67T-72)
527 Dennis Ribant 6.00 2.40
528 Rico Petrocelli.................... 20.00 8.00
529 Gary Wagner......................... 6.00 2.40
530 Felipe Alou 12.00 4.80
531 Brooks Robinson CL 15.00 3.00
532 Jim Hicks 6.00 2.40
533 Jack Fisher........................... 6.00 2.40
534 Hank Bauer MG DP............... 8.00 3.20
535 Donn Clendenon 25.00 10.00
536 Joe Niekro RC.................... 50.00 20.00
Paul Popovich
537 Chuck Estrada DP 8.00 3.20
538 J.C. Martin 15.00 6.00
539 Dick Egan DP........................ 8.00 3.20
540 Norm Cash......................... 50.00 20.00
541 Joe Gibbon......................... 15.00 6.00
542 Rick Monday RC 15.00 6.00
Tony Pierce DP
543 Dan Schneider 15.00 6.00
544 Cleveland Indians............... 30.00 12.00
Team Card
545 Jim Grant............................ 25.00 10.00
546 Woody Woodward 25.00 10.00
547 Russ Gibson 8.00 3.20
Bill Rohr DP
548 Tony Gonzalez DP 8.00 3.20
549 Jack Sanford 15.00 6.00
550 Vada Pinson DP 10.00 4.00
551 Doug Camilli DP.................... 8.00 3.20
552 Ted Savage......................... 25.00 10.00
553 Mike Hegan RC 40.00 16.00
Thad Tillotson
554 Andre Rodgers DP 8.00 3.20
555 Don Cardwell 25.00 10.00
556 Al Weis DP............................ 8.00 3.20
557 Al Ferrara 25.00 10.00
558 Mark Belanger RC 50.00 20.00
Bill Dillman
559 Dick Tracewski DP 8.00 3.20
560 Jim Bunning 60.00 24.00
561 Sandy Alomar 40.00 16.00
562 Steve Blass DP...................... 8.00 3.20
563 Joe Adcock 40.00 16.00
564 Alonzo Harris 8.00 3.20
Aaron Pointer
565 Lew Krausse 25.00 10.00
566 Gary Geiger DP 8.00 3.20
567 Steve Hamilton.................... 40.00 16.00
568 John Sullivan 40.00 16.00
569 Rod Carew RC 250.00 80.00
Hank Allen DP
570 Maury Wills 80.00 32.00
571 Larry Sherry....................... 25.00 10.00
572 Don Demeter...................... 25.00 10.00
573 Chicago White Sox............. 30.00 12.00
Team Card UER
(Indians team
stats on back)
574 Jerry Buchek 25.00 10.00
575 Dave Boswell 15.00 6.00
576 Ramon Hernandez 40.00 16.00
Norm Gigon RC
577 Bill Short............................ 15.00 6.00
578 John Boccabella.................. 15.00 6.00
579 Bill Henry 15.00 6.00
580 Rocky Colavito 125.00 50.00
581 Bill Denehy..................... 500.00 200.00
Tom Seaver RC
582 Jim Owens DP 8.00 3.20
583 Ray Barker 40.00 16.00
584 Jimmy Piersall 40.00 16.00
585 Wally Bunker....................... 25.00 10.00
586 Manny Jimenez 15.00 6.00
587 Don Shaw 40.00 16.00
Gary Sutherland RC
588 Johnny Klippstein DP............ 8.00 3.20
589 Dave Ricketts DP 8.00 3.20
590 Pete Richert 15.00 6.00
591 Ty Cline 25.00 10.00
592 Jim Shellenback.................. 25.00 10.00
Ron Willis RC
593 Wes Westrum MG............... 50.00 20.00
594 Dan Osinski......................... 40.00 16.00
595 Cookie Rojas 25.00 10.00
596 Galen Cisco DP 8.00 3.20
597 Ted Abernathy..................... 15.00 6.00
598 Walt Williams...................... 25.00 10.00
Ed Stroud
599 Bob Duliba DP 8.00 3.20
600 Brooks Robinson 250.00 100.00
601 Bill Bryan DP......................... 8.00 3.20
602 Juan Pizarro 40.00 16.00
603 Tim Talton.......................... 25.00 10.00
Ramon Webster
604 Red Sox Team.................. 125.00 50.00
605 Mike Shannon 50.00 20.00
606 Ron Taylor........................... 25.00 10.00
607 Mickey Stanley.................... 50.00 20.00
608 Rich Nye 8.00 3.20
John Upham DP
609 Tommy John 80.00 27.00

1967 Topps Posters Inserts

The wrappers of the 1967 Topps cards have this 32-card set advertised as follows: "Extra -- All Star Pin-Up Inside." Printed on (5" by 7") paper in full color, these "All-Star" inserts have fold lines which are generally not very noticeable when stored carefully. They are numbered, blank-backed, and carry a facsimile autograph.

	NM	Ex
COMPLETE SET (32)	60.00	24.00
1 Boog Powell	2.00	.80
2 Bert Campaneris	1.50	.60
3 Brooks Robinson	4.00	1.60
4 Tommie Agee	1.00	.40
5 Carl Yastrzemski	5.00	2.00
6 Mickey Mantle	20.00	8.00
7 Frank Howard	1.50	.60
8 Sam McDowell	1.50	.60
9 Orlando Cepeda	3.00	1.20
10 Chico Cardenas	1.00	.40
11 Roberto Clemente	10.00	4.00
12 Willie Mays	8.00	3.20
13 Cleon Jones	1.00	.40
14 Johnny Callison	1.50	.60
15 Hank Aaron	6.00	2.40
16 Don Drysdale	3.00	1.20
17 Bobby Knoop	1.00	.40
18 Tony Oliva	2.00	.80
19 Frank Robinson	3.00	1.20
20 Denny McLain	2.00	.80
21 Al Kaline	4.00	1.60
22 Joe Pepitone	1.50	.60
23 Harmon Killebrew	4.00	1.60
24 Leon Wagner	1.00	.40
25 Joe Morgan	3.00	1.20
26 Ron Santo	2.00	.80
27 Joe Torre	2.00	.80
28 Juan Marichal	2.00	.80
29 Matty Alou	1.00	.40
30 Felipe Alou	1.50	.60
31 Ron Hunt	1.00	.40
32 Willie McCovey	3.00	1.20

1968 Topps

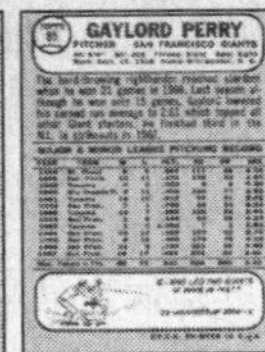

The cards in this 598-card set measure 2 1/2" by 3 1/2". The 1968 Topps set includes Sporting News All-Star Selections as card numbers 361 to 380. Other subsets in the set include League Leaders (1-12) and World Series cards (151-158). The front of each checklist card features a picture of a popular player inside a circle. Higher numbers 458 to 598 are slightly more difficult to obtain. The first series looks different from the other series, as it has a lighter, wider mesh background on the card front. The later series all had a much darker, finer mesh pattern. Among other fashions, cards were issued in five-card nickel packs. Those five cent packs were issued 24 packs to a box. Thirty-Sox card rack packs with an SRP of 29 cents were also issued. The key Rookie Cards in the set are Johnny Bench and Nolan Ryan. Lastly, some cards were also issued along with the "Win-A-Card" board game from Milton Bradley that included cards from the 1965 Topps Hot Rods and 1967 Topps football card sets. This version of these cards is somewhat difficult to distinguish, but are often found with a slight touch of the 1967 football set white border on the front top or bottom edge as well as a brighter yellow card back instead of the darker yellow or gold color. The known cards from this product include card numbers 16, 20, 34, 45, 108, and 149.

NM Ex
COMPLETE SET (598)........... 3000.00 1200.00
COMMON CARD (1-457) .... 2.00 .80
COMMON (458-598)................. 4.00 1.60
WRAPPER (5-CENT)............... 25.00 10.00
1 Roberto Clemente 30.00 12.00
Tony Gonzalez
Matty Alou LL
2 Carl Yastrzemski 15.00 6.00
Frank Robinson
Al Kaline LL
3 Orlando Cepeda 20.00 8.00
Roberto Clemente
Hank Aaron LL
4 Carl Yastrzemski 15.00 6.00
Harmon Killebrew
Frank Robinson LL
5 Hank Aaron 8.00 3.20
Jim Wynn
Ron Santo
Willie McCovey LL
6 Carl Yastrzemski 8.00 3.20
Harmon Killebrew
Frank Howard LL
7 Phil Niekro 4.00 1.60
Jim Bunning
Chris Short LL
8 Joel Horlen 4.00 1.60
Gary Peters
Sonny Siebert LL
9 Mike McCormick................... 4.00 1.60
Ferguson Jenkins
Jim Bunning
Claude Osteen LL
10A Jim Lonborg ERR 4.00 1.60
(Misspelled Lonberg
on card back)
Earl Wilson
Dean Chance LL
10B Jim Lonborg COR............... 4.00 1.60
Earl Wilson
Dean Chance LL
11 Jim Bunning........................ 6.00 2.40
Ferguson Jenkins
Gaylord Perry LL
12 Jim Lonborg UER 4.00 1.60
(Misspelled Longberg
on card back)
Sam McDowell
Dean Chance LL
13 Chuck Hartenstein............... 2.00 .80
14 Jerry McNertney .... 2.00 .80
15 Ron Hunt .... 2.00 .80
16 Lou Piniella 6.00 2.40
Richie Scheinblum
17 Dick Hall.............................. 2.00 .80
18 Mike Hershberger .... 2.00 .80
19 Juan Pizarro......................... 2.00 .80
20 Brooks Robinson 25.00 10.00
21 Ron Davis .... 2.00 .80
22 Pat Dobson 4.00 1.60
23 Chico Cardenas.................... 4.00 1.60
24 Bobby Locke .... 2.00 .80
25 Julian Javier......................... 4.00 1.60
26 Darrell Brandon.................... 2.00 .80
27 Gil Hodges MG..................... 8.00 3.20
28 Ted Uhlaender .... 2.00 .80
29 Joe Verbanic .... 2.00 .80
30 Joe Torre.............................. 6.00 2.40
31 Ed Stroud .... 2.00 .80
32 Joe Gibbon........................... 2.00 .80
33 Pete Ward .... 2.00 .80
34 Al Ferrara .... 2.00 .80
35 Steve Hargan .... 2.00 .80
36 Bob Moose........................... 4.00 1.60
Bob Robertson
37 Billy Williams 8.00 3.20
38 Tony Pierce .... 2.00 .80
39 Cookie Rojas .... 2.00 .80
40 Denny McLain....................... 8.00 3.20
41 Julio Gotay........................... 2.00 .80
42 Larry Haney .... 2.00 .80
43 Gary Bell .... 2.00 .80
44 Frank Kostro .... 2.00 .80
45 Tom Seaver........................ 50.00 20.00
46 Dave Ricketts....................... 2.00 .80
47 Ralph Houk MG 4.00 1.60
48 Ted Davidson........................ 2.00 .80
49A Eddie Brinkman .... 2.00 .80
(White team name)
49B Eddie Brinkman 50.00 20.00
(Yellow team name)
50 Willie Mays 60.00 24.00
51 Bob Locker............................ 2.00 .80
52 Hawk Taylor .... 2.00 .80
53 Gene Alley............................ 4.00 1.60
54 Stan Williams........................ 2.00 .80
55 Felipe Alou 4.00 1.60
56 Dave Leonhard...................... 2.00 .80
Dave May RC
57 Dan Schneider .... 2.00 .80
58 Eddie Mathews.................... 15.00 6.00
59 Don Lock .... 2.00 .80
60 Ken Holtzman........................ 4.00 1.60
61 Reggie Smith 4.00 1.60
62 Chuck Dobson .... 2.00 .80
63 Dick Kenworthy..................... 2.00 .80
64 Jim Merritt............................ 2.00 .80
65 John Roseboro 4.00 1.60
66A Casey Cox .... 2.00 .80
(White team name)
66B Casey Cox 100.00 40.00
(Yellow team name)
67 Jim Kaat CL 6.00 1.20
68 Ron Willis .... 2.00 .80
69 Tom Tresh 4.00 1.60
70 Bob Veale 4.00 1.60
71 Vern Fuller............................ 2.00 .80
72 Tommy John 6.00 2.40
73 Jim Ray Hart......................... 4.00 1.60
74 Milt Pappas 4.00 1.60
75 Don Mincher .... 2.00 .80
76 Jim Britton............................ 4.00 1.60
Ron Reed
77 Don Wilson 4.00 1.60
78 Jim Northrup 6.00 2.40
79 Ted Kubiak .... 2.00 .80
80 Rod Carew......................... 50.00 20.00
81 Larry Jackson .... 2.00 .80
82 Sam Bowens......................... 2.00 .80
83 John Stephenson.................. 2.00 .80
84 Bob Tolan............................. 2.00 .80
85 Gaylord Perry....................... 8.00 3.20
86 Willie Stargell....................... 8.00 3.20
87 Dick Williams MG 4.00 1.60
88 Phil Regan 4.00 1.60
89 Jake Gibbs............................ 4.00 1.60
90 Vada Pinson 4.00 1.60
91 Jim Ollom .... 2.00 .80
92 Ed Kranepool 4.00 1.60
93 Tony Cloninger..................... 2.00 .80
94 Lee Maye .... 2.00 .80
95 Bob Aspromonte................... 2.00 .80
96 Frank Coggins...................... 2.00 .80
Dick Nold
97 Tom Phoebus .... 2.00 .80
98 Gary Sutherland .... 2.00 .80
99 Rocky Colavito 8.00 3.20
100 Bob Gibson 25.00 10.00
101 Glenn Beckert.................... 4.00 1.60
102 Jose Cardenal 4.00 1.60
103 Don Sutton......................... 8.00 3.20
104 Dick Dietz........................... 2.00 .80
105 Al Downing 4.00 1.60
106 Dalton Jones .... 2.00 .80
107A Juan Marichal CL.............. 6.00 1.20
Tan wide mesh
107B Juan Marichal CL.............. 6.00 1.20
Brown fine mesh
108 Don Pavletich...................... 2.00 .80
109 Bert Campaneris 4.00 1.60
110 Hank Aaron 60.00 24.00
111 Rich Reese.......................... 2.00 .80
112 Woody Fryman.................... 2.00 .80
113 Tom Matchick 4.00 1.60
Daryl Patterson
114 Ron Swoboda 4.00 1.60
115 Sam McDowell.................... 4.00 1.60
116 Ken McMullen..................... 2.00 .80
117 Larry Jaster......................... 2.00 .80
118 Mark Belanger..................... 4.00 1.60
119 Ted Savage......................... 2.00 .80
120 Mel Stottlemyre 4.00 1.60
121 Jimmie Hall......................... 2.00 .80
122 Gene Mauch MG 4.00 1.60
123 Jose Santiago .... 2.00 .80
124 Nate Oliver .... 2.00 .80
125 Joel Horlen.......................... 2.00 .80
126 Bobby Etheridge.................. 2.00 .80
127 Paul Lindblad .... 2.00 .80
128 Tom Dukes.......................... 2.00 .80
Alonzo Harris
129 Mickey Stanley.................... 6.00 2.40
130 Tony Perez 8.00 3.20
131 Frank Bertaina .... 2.00 .80
132 Bud Harrelson..................... 4.00 1.60
133 Fred Whitfield...................... 2.00 .80
134 Pat Jarvis............................ 2.00 .80
135 Paul Blair 4.00 1.60
136 Randy Hundley.................... 4.00 1.60
137 Twins Team 4.00 1.60
138 Ruben Amaro .... 2.00 .80
139 Chris Short.......................... 2.00 .80
140 Tony Conigliaro................... 8.00 3.20
141 Dal Maxvill .... 2.00 .80
142 Buddy Bradford................... 2.00 .80
Bill Voss
143 Pete Cimino .... 2.00 .80
144 Joe Morgan...................... 12.00 4.80
145 Don Drysdale.................... 12.00 4.80
146 Sal Bando 4.00 1.60
147 Frank Linzy......................... 2.00 .80
148 Dave Bristol MG.................. 2.00 .80
149 Bob Saverine....................... 2.00 .80
150 Roberto Clemente............. 80.00 32.00
151 Lou Brock WS.................. 10.00 4.00
152 Carl Yastrzemski WS......... 10.00 4.00
153 Nellie Briles WS.................. 5.00 2.00
154 Bob Gibson WS 10.00 4.00
155 Jim Lonborg WS.................. 5.00 2.00
156 Rico Petrocelli WS............... 5.00 2.00
157 World Series Game 7........... 5.00 2.00
St. Louis wins it
158 WS Summary 5.00 2.00
Cardinals celebrate
159 Don Kessinger 4.00 1.60
160 Earl Wilson.......................... 4.00 1.60
161 Norm Miller......................... 2.00 .80
162 Hal Gilson 4.00 1.60
Mike Torrez
163 Gene Brabender .... 2.00 .80
164 Ramon Webster .... 2.00 .80
165 Tony Oliva 6.00 2.40
166 Claude Raymond.................. 2.00 .80
167 Elston Howard 6.00 2.40
168 Dodgers Team...................... 4.00 1.60
169 Bob Bolin .... 2.00 .80
170 Jim Fregosi 4.00 1.60
171 Don Nottebart .... 2.00 .80
172 Walt Williams....................... 2.00 .80
173 John Boozer......................... 2.00 .80
174 Bob Tillman.......................... 2.00 .80
175 Maury Wills.......................... 6.00 2.40
176 Bob Allen .... 2.00 .80
177 Jerry Koosman RC 500.00 200.00
Nolan Ryan RC
178 Don Wert 4.00 1.60
179 Bill Stoneman....................... 2.00 .80
180 Curt Flood 6.00 2.40
181 Jerry Zimmerman .... 2.00 .80
182 Dave Giusti.......................... 2.00 .80
183 Bob Kennedy MG 4.00 1.60
184 Lou Johnson .... 2.00 .80
185 Tom Haller........................... 2.00 .80
186 Eddie Watt .... 2.00 .80
187 Sonny Jackson..................... 2.00 .80
188 Cap Peterson .... 2.00 .80
189 Bill Landis .... 2.00 .80
190 Bill White 4.00 1.60
191 Dan Frisella .... 2.00 .80
192A Carl Yastrzemski CL........... 8.00 1.60
Special Baseball Playing Card
192B Carl Yastrzemski CL........... 8.00 1.60
Special Baseball
Playing Card Game
193 Jack Hamilton .... 2.00 .80
194 Don Buford .... 2.00 .80
195 Joe Pepitone 4.00 1.60
196 Gary Nolan 4.00 1.60
197 Larry Brown .... 2.00 .80
198 Roy Face 4.00 1.60
199 Roberto Rodriquez............... 2.00 .80
Darrell Osteen
200 Orlando Cepeda 8.00 3.20
201 Mike Marshall RC................. 4.00 1.60
202 Adolfo Phillips...................... 2.00 .80
203 Dick Kelley .... 2.00 .80
204 Andy Etchebarren................. 2.00 .80
205 Juan Marichal 8.00 3.20
206 Cal Ermer MG .... 2.00 .80
207 Carroll Sembera .... 2.00 .80
208 Willie Davis 4.00 1.60
209 Tim Cullen............................ 2.00 .80
210 Gary Peters .... 2.00 .80
211 J.C. Martin .... 2.00 .80
212 Dave Morehead .... 2.00 .80
213 Chico Ruiz............................ 2.00 .80
214 Stan Bahnsen 4.00 1.60
Frank Fernandez
215 Jim Bunning......................... 8.00 3.20
216 Bubba Morton .... 2.00 .80
217 Dick Farrell.......................... 2.00 .80
218 Ken Suarez .... 2.00 .80
219 Rob Gardner .... 2.00 .80
220 Harmon Killebrew 15.00 6.00
221 Braves Team 4.00 1.60
222 Jim Hardin .... 2.00 .80
223 Ollie Brown .... 2.00 .80
224 Jack Aker .... 2.00 .80
225 Richie Allen.......................... 6.00 2.40
226 Jimmie Price .... 2.00 .80
227 Joe Hoerner .... 2.00 .80
228 Jack Billingham.................... 4.00 1.60
Jim Fairey
229 Fred Klages .... 2.00 .80
230 Pete Rose......................... 60.00 24.00
231 Dave Baldwin .... 2.00 .80
232 Denis Menke .... 2.00 .80
233 George Scott........................ 4.00 1.60
234 Bill Monbouquette................. 2.00 .80
235 Ron Santo 8.00 3.20
236 Tug McGraw......................... 6.00 2.40
237 Alvin Dark MG...................... 4.00 1.60
238 Tom Satriano .... 2.00 .80
239 Bill Henry .... 2.00 .80
240 Al Kaline 40.00 16.00
241 Felix Millan.......................... 2.00 .80
242 Moe Drabowsky 4.00 1.60
243 Rich Rollins 4.00 1.60
244 John Donaldson.................... 2.00 .80
245 Tony Gonzalez .... 2.00 .80
246 Fritz Peterson 4.00 1.60
247 Johnny Bench RC 125.00 50.00
Ron Tompkins
248 Fred Valentine .... 2.00 .80
249 Bill Singer .... 2.00 .80
250 Carl Yastrzemski 30.00 12.00
251 Manny Sanguillen RC........... 6.00 2.40
252 Angels Team 4.00 1.60
253 Dick Hughes......................... 2.00 .80
254 Cleon Jones 4.00 1.60
255 Dean Chance 4.00 1.60
256 Norm Cash........................... 6.00 2.40
257 Phil Niekro 8.00 3.20
258 Jose Arcia .... 2.00 .80
Bill Schlesinger
259 Ken Boyer 6.00 2.40
260 Jim Wynn............................. 4.00 1.60
261 Dave Duncan........................ 4.00 1.60
262 Rick Wise 4.00 1.60
263 Horace Clarke....................... 4.00 1.60
264 Ted Abernathy .... 2.00 .80
265 Tommy Davis 4.00 1.60
266 Paul Popovich .... 2.00 .80
267 Herman Franks MG............... 2.00 .80
268 Bob Humphreys.................... 2.00 .80
269 Bob Tiefenauer..................... 2.00 .80
270 Matty Alou 4.00 1.60
271 Bobby Knoop .... 2.00 .80
272 Ray Culp .... 2.00 .80
273 Dave Johnson 4.00 1.60
274 Mike Cuellar......................... 4.00 1.60
275 Tim McCarver 6.00 2.40
276 Jim Roland........................... 2.00 .80
277 Jerry Buchek........................ 2.00 .80
278 Orlando Cepeda CL 6.00 1.20
279 Bill Hands............................. 2.00 .80
280 Mickey Mantle 250.00 100.00
281 Jim Campanis .... 2.00 .80
282 Rick Monday 4.00 1.60

283 Mel Queen 2.00 .80
284 Johnny Briggs 2.00 .80
285 Dick McAuliffe 6.00 2.40
286 Cecil Upshaw 2.00 .80
287 Mickey Abarbanel 2.00 .80
Cisco Carlos
288 Dave Wickersham 2.00 .80
289 Woody Held 2.00 .80
290 Willie McCovey 12.00 4.80
291 Dick Lines 2.00 .80
292 Art Shamsky 2.00 .80
293 Bruce Howard 2.00 .80
294 Red Schoendienst MG 6.00 2.40
295 Sonny Siebert 2.00 .80
296 Byron Browne 2.00 .80
297 Russ Gibson 2.00 .80
298 Jim Brewer 2.00 .80
299 Gene Michael 4.00 1.60
300 Rusty Staub 4.00 1.60
301 George Mitterwald 2.00 .80
Rick Renick
302 Gerry Arrigo 2.00 .80
303 Dick Green 4.00 1.60
304 Sandy Valdespino 2.00 .80
305 Minnie Rojas 2.00 .80
306 Mike Ryan 2.00 .80
307 John Hiller 4.00 1.60
308 Pirates Team 4.00 1.60
309 Ken Henderson 2.00 .80
310 Luis Aparicio 8.00 3.20
311 Jack Lamabe 2.00 .80
312 Curt Blefary 2.00 .80
313 Al Weis 2.00 .80
314 Bill Rohr 2.00 .80
George Spriggs
315 Zoilo Versalles 2.00 .80
316 Steve Barber 2.00 .80
317 Ron Brand 2.00 .80
318 Chico Salmon 2.00 .80
319 George Culver 2.00 .80
320 Frank Howard 4.00 1.60
321 Leo Durocher MG 6.00 2.40
322 Dave Boswell 2.00 .80
323 Deron Johnson 4.00 1.60
324 Jim Nash 2.00 .80
325 Manny Mota 4.00 1.60
326 Dennis Ribant 2.00 .80
327 Tony Taylor 4.00 1.60
328 Chuck Vinson 2.00 .80
Jim Weaver
329 Duane Josephson 2.00 .80
330 Roger Maris 50.00 20.00
331 Dan Osinski 2.00 .80
332 Doug Rader 4.00 1.60
333 Ron Herbel 2.00 .80
334 Orioles Team 4.00 1.60
335 Bob Allison 4.00 1.60
336 John Purdin 2.00 .80
337 Bill Robinson 4.00 1.60
338 Bob Johnson 2.00 .80
339 Rich Nye 2.00 .80
340 Max Alvis 2.00 .80
341 Jim Lemon MG 2.00 .80
342 Ken Johnson 2.00 .80
343 Jim Gosger 2.00 .80
344 Donn Clendenon 4.00 1.60
345 Bob Hendley 2.00 .80
346 Jerry Adair 2.00 .80
347 George Brunet 2.00 .80
348 Larry Colton 2.00 .80
Dick Thoenen
349 Ed Spiezio 4.00 1.60
350 Hoyt Wilhelm 8.00 3.20
351 Bob Barton 2.00 .80
352 Jackie Hernandez 2.00 .80
353 Mack Jones 2.00 .80
354 Pete Richert 2.00 .80
355 Ernie Banks 25.00 10.00
356A Ken Holtzman CL 6.00 1.20
Head centered within circle
356B Ken Holtzman 6.00 1.20
Head shifted right
within circle
357 Len Gabrielson 2.00 .80
358 Mike Epstein 2.00 .80
359 Joe Moeller 2.00 .80
360 Willie Horton 6.00 2.40
361 Harmon Killebrew AS 8.00 3.20
362 Orlando Cepeda AS 6.00 2.40
363 Rod Carew AS 8.00 3.20
364 Joe Morgan AS 8.00 3.20
365 Brooks Robinson AS 8.00 3.20
366 Ron Santo AS 6.00 2.40
367 Jim Fregosi AS 4.00 1.60
368 Gene Alley AS 4.00 1.60
369 Carl Yastrzemski AS 10.00 4.00
370 Hank Aaron AS 20.00 8.00
371 Tony Oliva AS 6.00 2.40
372 Lou Brock AS 8.00 3.20
373 Frank Robinson AS 8.00 3.20
374 Bob Clemente AS 30.00 12.00
375 Bill Freehan AS 4.00 1.60
376 Tim McCarver AS 4.00 1.60
377 Joel Horlen AS 4.00 1.60
378 Bob Gibson AS 8.00 3.20
379 Gary Peters AS 4.00 1.60
380 Ken Holtzman AS 4.00 1.60
381 Boog Powell 4.00 1.60
382 Ramon Hernandez 2.00 .80
383 Steve Whitaker 2.00 .80
384 Bill Henry 6.00 2.40
Hal McRae RC
385 Jim Hunter 10.00 4.00
386 Greg Goossen 2.00 .80
387 Joe Foy 2.00 .80
388 Ray Washburn 2.00 .80
389 Jay Johnstone 4.00 1.60
390 Bill Mazeroski 8.00 3.20
391 Bob Priddy 2.00 .80
392 Grady Hatton MG 2.00 .80
393 Jim Perry 4.00 1.60
394 Tommie Aaron 6.00 2.40
395 Camilo Pascual 4.00 1.60
396 Bobby Wine 2.00 .80
397 Vic Davalillo 2.00 .80
398 Jim Grant 2.00 .80
399 Ray Oyler 4.00 1.60
400A Mike McCormick 4.00 1.60
(Yellow letters)
400B Mike McCormick 150.00 60.00
(Team name in
white letters)
401 Mets Team 4.00 1.60
402 Mike Hegan 4.00 1.60
403 John Buzhardt 2.00 .80
404 Floyd Robinson 2.00 .80
405 Tommy Helms 4.00 1.60
406 Dick Ellsworth 2.00 .80
407 Gary Kolb 2.00 .80
408 Steve Carlton 30.00 12.00
409 Frank Peters 2.00 .80
Ron Stone
410 Ferguson Jenkins 10.00 4.00
411 Ron Hansen 2.00 .80
412 Clay Carroll 4.00 1.60
413 Tom McCraw 2.00 .80
414 Mickey Lolich 8.00 3.20
415 Johnny Callison 4.00 1.60
416 Bill Rigney MG 2.00 .80
417 Willie Crawford 2.00 .80
418 Eddie Fisher 2.00 .80
419 Jack Hiatt 2.00 .80
420 Cesar Tovar 2.00 .80
421 Ron Taylor 2.00 .80
422 Rene Lachemann 2.00 .80
423 Fred Gladding 2.00 .80
424 Chicago White Sox 4.00 1.60
Team Card
425 Jim Maloney 4.00 1.60
426 Hank Allen 2.00 .80
427 Dick Calmus 2.00 .80
428 Vic Roznovsky 2.00 .80
429 Tommie Sisk 2.00 .80
430 Rico Petrocelli 4.00 1.60
431 Dooley Womack 2.00 .80
432 Bill Davis 2.00 .80
Jose Vidal
433 Bob Rodgers 2.00 .80
434 Ricardo Joseph 2.00 .80
435 Ron Perranoski 4.00 1.60
436 Hal Lanier 2.00 .80
437 Don Cardwell 2.00 .80
438 Lee Thomas 4.00 1.60
439 Lum Harris MG 2.00 .80
440 Claude Osteen 4.00 1.60
441 Alex Johnson 4.00 1.60
442 Dick Bosman 2.00 .80
443 Joe Azcue 2.00 .80
444 Jack Fisher 2.00 .80
445 Mike Shannon 4.00 1.60
446 Ron Kline 2.00 .80
447 George Korince 4.00 1.60
Fred Lasher
448 Gary Wagner 2.00 .80
449 Gene Oliver 2.00 .80
450 Jim Kaat 6.00 2.40
451 Al Spangler 2.00 .80
452 Jesus Alou 2.00 .80
453 Sammy Ellis 2.00 .80
454A Frank Robinson CL 8.00 1.60
Cap complete within circle
454B Frank Robinson CL 8.00 1.60
Cap partially within circle
455 Rico Carty 4.00 1.60
456 John O'Donoghue 2.00 .80
457 Jim Lefebvre 4.00 1.60
458 Lew Krausse 6.00 2.40
459 Dick Simpson 4.00 1.60
460 Jim Lonborg 6.00 2.40
461 Chuck Hiller 4.00 1.60
462 Barry Moore 4.00 1.60
463 Jim Schaffer 4.00 1.60
464 Don McMahon 4.00 1.60
465 Tommie Agee 10.00 4.00
466 Bill Dillman 4.00 1.60
467 Dick Howser 10.00 4.00
468 Larry Sherry 4.00 1.60
469 Ty Cline 4.00 1.60
470 Bill Freehan 10.00 4.00
471 Orlando Pena 4.00 1.60
472 Walter Alston MG 6.00 2.40
473 Al Worthington 4.00 1.60
474 Paul Schaal 4.00 1.60
475 Joe Niekro 6.00 2.40
476 Woody Woodward 4.00 1.60
477 Philadelphia Phillies 8.00 3.20
Team Card
478 Dave McNally 6.00 2.40
479 Phil Gagliano 6.00 2.40
480 Tony Oliva 80.00 32.00
Chico Cardenas
Bob Clemente
481 John Wyatt 4.00 1.60
482 Jose Pagan 4.00 1.60
483 Darold Knowles 4.00 1.60
484 Phil Roof 4.00 1.60
485 Ken Berry 6.00 2.40
486 Cal Koonce 4.00 1.60
487 Lee May 10.00 4.00
488 Dick Tracewski 6.00 2.40
489 Wally Bunker 4.00 1.60
490 Harmon Killebrew 150.00 60.00
Willie Mays
Mickey Mantle
491 Denny Lemaster 4.00 1.60
492 Jeff Torborg 6.00 2.40
493 Jim McGlothlin 4.00 1.60
494 Ray Sadecki 4.00 1.60
495 Leon Wagner 4.00 1.60
496 Steve Hamilton 6.00 2.40
497 Cardinals Team 8.00 3.20
498 Bill Bryan 6.00 2.40
499 Steve Blass 6.00 2.40
500 Frank Robinson 30.00 12.00
501 John Odom 6.00 2.40
502 Mike Andrews 4.00 1.60
503 Al Jackson 6.00 2.40
504 Russ Snyder 4.00 1.60
505 Joe Sparma 10.00 4.00
506 Clarence Jones RC 4.00 1.60
507 Wade Blasingame 4.00 1.60
508 Duke Sims 4.00 1.60
509 Dennis Higgins 4.00 1.60
510 Ron Fairly 10.00 4.00
511 Bill Kelso 4.00 1.60
512 Grant Jackson 4.00 1.60
513 Hank Bauer MG 6.00 2.40
514 Al McBean 4.00 1.60
515 Russ Nixon 4.00 1.60
516 Pete Mikkelsen 4.00 1.60
517 Diego Segui 6.00 2.40
518A Clete Boyer CL ERR 12.00 2.40
539 AL Rookies
518B Clete Boyer CL COR 12.00 2.40
539 ML Rookies
519 Jerry Stephenson 4.00 1.60
520 Lou Brock 25.00 10.00
521 Don Shaw 4.00 1.60
522 Wayne Causey 4.00 1.60
523 John Tsitouris 4.00 1.60
524 Andy Kosco 6.00 2.40
525 Jim Davenport 4.00 1.60
526 Bill Denehy 4.00 1.60
527 Tito Francona 4.00 1.60
528 Tigers Team 60.00 24.00
529 Bruce Von Hoff 4.00 1.60
530 Brooks Robinson 40.00 16.00
Frank Robinson
531 Chuck Hinton 4.00 1.60
532 Luis Tiant 6.00 2.40
533 Wes Parker 6.00 2.40
534 Bob Miller 6.00 2.40
535 Danny Cater 6.00 2.40
536 Bill Short 4.00 1.60
537 Norm Siebern 6.00 2.40
538 Manny Jimenez 6.00 2.40
539 Jim Ray 4.00 1.60
Mike Ferraro
540 Nelson Briles 6.00 2.40
541 Sandy Alomar 6.00 2.40
542 John Boccabella 4.00 1.60
543 Bob Lee 4.00 1.60
544 Mayo Smith MG 12.00 4.80
545 Lindy McDaniel 6.00 2.40
546 Roy White 6.00 2.40
547 Dan Coombs 4.00 1.60
548 Bernie Allen 4.00 1.60
549 Curt Motton 4.00 1.60
Roger Nelson
550 Clete Boyer 6.00 2.40
551 Darrell Sutherland 4.00 1.60
552 Ed Kirkpatrick 4.00 1.60
553 Hank Aguirre 4.00 1.60
554 A's Team 10.00 4.00
555 Jose Tartabull 6.00 2.40
556 Dick Selma 4.00 1.60
557 Frank Quilici 6.00 2.40
558 Johnny Edwards 4.00 1.60
559 Carl Taylor 4.00 1.60
Luke Walker
560 Paul Casanova 4.00 1.60
561 Lee Elia 4.00 1.60
562 Jim Bouton 6.00 2.40
563 Ed Charles 4.00 1.60
564 Eddie Stanky MG 6.00 2.40
565 Larry Dierker 6.00 2.40
566 Ken Harrelson 6.00 2.40
567 Clay Dalrymple 4.00 1.60
568 Willie Smith 4.00 1.60
569 Ivan Murrell 4.00 1.60
Les Rohr
570 Rick Reichardt 4.00 1.60
571 Tony LaRussa 12.00 4.80
572 Don Bosch 4.00 1.60
573 Joe Coleman 4.00 1.60
574 Cincinnati Reds 10.00 4.00
Team Card
575 Jim Palmer 40.00 16.00
576 Dave Adlesh 4.00 1.60
577 Fred Talbot 4.00 1.60
578 Orlando Martinez 4.00 1.60
579 Larry Hisle RC 10.00 4.00
Mike Lum
580 Bob Bailey 4.00 1.60
581 Garry Roggenburk 4.00 1.60
582 Jerry Grote 10.00 4.00
583 Gates Brown 10.00 4.00
584 Larry Shepard MG 4.00 1.60
585 Wilbur Wood 6.00 2.40
586 Jim Pagliaroni 6.00 2.40
587 Roger Repoz 4.00 1.60
588 Dick Schofield 4.00 1.60
589 Ron Clark 4.00 1.60
Moe Ogier
590 Tommy Harper 6.00 2.40
591 Dick Nen 4.00 1.60
592 John Bateman 4.00 1.60
593 Lee Stange 4.00 1.60
594 Phil Linz 6.00 2.40
595 Phil Ortega 4.00 1.60
596 Charlie Smith 4.00 1.60
597 Bill McCool 4.00 1.60
598 Jerry May 6.00 1.85

1968 Topps Game Card Inserts

The cards in this 33-card set measure approximately 2 1/4" by 3 1/4". This "Game" card set of players, issued as inserts with the regular third series 1968 Topps baseball cards, was patterned directly after the Red Back and Blue Back sets of 1951. Each card has a color player photo set upon a pure white background, with a facsimile autograph underneath the picture. The cards have blue backs, and were also sold in boxed sets on a limited basis.

	NM	Ex
COMPLETE SET (33)	125.00	50.00
COMP.FACT SET (33)	125.00	50.00
1 Matty Alou	2.00	.80
2 Mickey Mantle	40.00	16.00
3 Carl Yastrzemski	8.00	3.20
4 Hank Aaron	15.00	6.00
5 Harmon Killebrew	8.00	3.20
6 Roberto Clemente	25.00	10.00
7 Frank Robinson	5.00	2.00
8 Willie Mays	15.00	6.00
9 Brooks Robinson	8.00	3.20
10 Tommy Davis	2.00	.80
11 Bill Freehan	2.00	.80
12 Claude Osteen	2.00	.80
13 Gary Peters	2.00	.80
14 Jim Lonborg	2.00	.80
15 Steve Hargan	2.00	.80
16 Dean Chance	2.00	.80
17 Mike McCormick	2.00	.80
18 Tim McCarver	2.00	.80
19 Ron Santo	3.00	1.20
20 Tony Gonzalez	2.00	.80
21 Frank Howard	2.00	.80
22 George Scott	2.00	.80
23 Richie Allen	3.00	1.20
24 Jim Wynn	2.00	.80
25 Gene Alley	2.00	.80
26 Rick Monday	2.00	.80
27 Al Kaline	8.00	3.20
28 Rusty Staub	2.00	.80
29 Rod Carew	5.00	2.00
30 Pete Rose	15.00	6.00
31 Joe Torre	3.00	1.20
32 Orlando Cepeda	3.00	1.20
33 Jim Fregosi	2.00	.80

1969 Topps

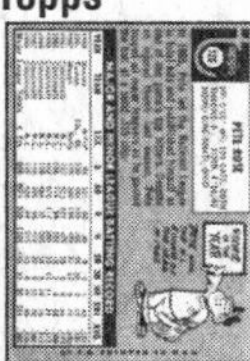

The cards in this 664-card set measure 2 1/2" by 3 1/2". The 1969 Topps set includes Sporting News All-Star Selections as card numbers 416 to 435. Other popular subsets within this set include League Leaders (1-12) and World Series cards (162-169). The fifth series contains several variations; the more difficult variety consists of cards with the player's first name, last name, and/or position in white letters instead of lettering in some other color. These are designated in the checklist below by WL (white letters). Each checklist card features a different popular player's picture inside a circle on the front of the checklist card. Two different team identifications of Clay Dalrymple and Donn Clendenon exist, as indicated in the checklist. The key Rookie Cards in this set are Rollie Fingers, Reggie Jackson, and Graig Nettles. This was the last year that Topps issued multi-player special star cards, ending a 13-year tradition, which they had begun in 1957. There were cropping differences in checklist cards 57, 214, and 412, due to their each being printed with two different series. The differences are difficult to explain and have not been greatly sought by collectors; hence they are not listed explicitly in the list below. The All-Star cards 426-435, when turned over and placed together, form a puzzle back of Pete Rose. This would turn out to be the final year that Topps issued cards in five-card nickel wax packs.

	NM	Ex
COMP. MASTER (695)	5000.00	2000.00
COMPLETE SET (664)	2800.00	1100.00
COMMON (1-218/328-512)	1.50	.60
COMMON (219-327)	2.50	1.00
COMMON (513-588)	2.00	.80
COMMON (589-664)	3.00	1.20
WRAPPER (5-CENT)	20.00	8.00

1 Carl Yastrzemski 15.00 5.25
Danny Cater
Tony Oliva LL
2 Pete Rose 8.00 3.20
Matty Alou
Felipe Alou LL
3 Ken Harrelson 4.00 1.60
Frank Howard
Jim Northrup LL
4 Willie McCovey 6.00 2.40
Ron Santo
Billy Williams LL
5 Frank Howard 4.00 1.60
Willie Horton
Ken Harrelson LL
6 Willie McCovey 6.00 2.40
Richie Allen
Ernie Banks LL
7 Luis Tiant 4.00 1.60
Sam McDowell
Dave McNally LL
8 Bob Gibson 6.00 2.40
Bobby Bolin
Bob Veale LL
9 Denny McLain 4.00 1.60
Dave McNally
Luis Tiant
Mel Stottlemyre LL
10 Juan Marichal 8.00 3.20
Bob Gibson
Fergie Jenkins LL
11 Sam McDowell 4.00 1.60
Denny McLain
Luis Tiant LL
12 Bob Gibson 4.00 1.60
Fergie Jenkins
Bill Singer LL
13 Mickey Stanley 2.50 1.00
14 Al McBean 1.50 .60
15 Boog Powell 4.00 1.60
16 Cesar Gutierrez 1.50 .60
Rich Robertson
17 Mike Marshall 2.50 1.00
18 Dick Schofield 1.50 .60
19 Ken Suarez 1.50 .60
20 Ernie Banks 20.00 8.00
21 Jose Santiago 1.50 .60
22 Jesus Alou 2.50 1.00
23 Lew Krausse 1.50 .60
24 Walt Alston MG 4.00 1.60
25 Roy White 2.50 1.00
26 Clay Carroll 2.50 1.00
27 Bernie Allen 1.50 .60
28 Mike Ryan 1.50 .60
29 Dave Morehead 1.50 .60
30 Bob Allison 2.50 1.00
31 Gary Gentry RC 2.50 1.00
Amos Otis RC
32 Sammy Ellis 1.50 .60
33 Wayne Causey 1.50 .60
34 Gary Peters 1.50 .60
35 Joe Morgan 10.00 4.00
36 Luke Walker 1.50 .60
37 Curt Motton 1.50 .60
38 Zoilo Versalles 2.50 1.00
39 Dick Hughes 1.50 .60
40 Mayo Smith MG 1.50 .60
41 Bob Barton 1.50 .60
42 Tommy Harper 2.50 1.00
43 Joe Niekro 2.50 1.00
44 Danny Cater 1.50 .60
45 Maury Wills 2.50 1.00
46 Fritz Peterson 2.50 1.00
47A Paul Popovich 2.50 1.00
No helmet emblem, thick airbrushing
47B Paul Popovich 2.50 1.00
No helmet emblem, light airbrushing
47C Paul Popovich 25.00 10.00
(C emblem on helmet)
48 Brant Alyea 1.50 .60
49A Royals Rookies ERR 25.00 10.00
Steve Jones
E. Rodriquez
49B Royals Rookies COR 1.50 .60
Steve Jones
E. Rodriguez
50 Roberto Clemente UER 60.00 24.00
Bats Right listed twice
51 Woody Fryman 2.50 1.00
52 Mike Andrews 1.50 .60
53 Sonny Jackson 1.50 .60
54 Cisco Carlos 1.50 .60
55 Jerry Grote 2.50 1.00
56 Rich Reese 1.50 .60
57 Denny McLain CL 6.00 1.20
58 Fred Gladding 1.50 .60
59 Jay Johnstone 2.50 1.00
60 Nelson Briles 2.50 1.00
61 Jimmie Hall 1.50 .60
62 Chico Salmon 1.50 .60
63 Jim Hickman 2.50 1.00
64 Bill Monbouquette 1.50 .60
65 Willie Davis 2.50 1.00
66 Mike Adamson 1.50 .60
Merv Rettenmund
67 Bill Stoneman 2.50 1.00
68 Dave Duncan 2.50 1.00
69 Steve Hamilton 2.50 1.00
70 Tommy Helms 2.50 1.00
71 Steve Whitaker 2.50 1.00
72 Ron Taylor 1.50 .60
73 Johnny Briggs 1.50 .60
74 Preston Gomez MG 2.50 1.00
75 Luis Aparicio 6.00 2.40
76 Norm Miller 1.50 .60
77A Ron Perranoski 2.50 1.00
(No emblem on cap)
77B Ron Perranoski 25.00 10.00
(LA on cap)
78 Tom Satriano 1.50 .60
79 Milt Pappas 2.50 1.00
80 Norm Cash 2.50 1.00
81 Mel Queen 1.50 .60
82 Rich Hebner RC 8.00 3.20
Al Oliver RC
83 Mike Ferraro 2.50 1.00
84 Bob Humphreys 1.50 .60
85 Lou Brock 20.00 8.00
86 Pete Richert 1.50 .60
87 Horace Clarke 2.50 1.00
88 Rich Nye 1.50 .60
89 Russ Gibson 1.50 .60
90 Jerry Koosman 2.50 1.00
91 Alvin Dark MG 2.50 1.00
92 Jack Billingham 2.50 1.00
93 Joe Foy 2.50 1.00
94 Hank Aguirre 1.50 .60
95 Johnny Bench 50.00 20.00
96 Denny Lemaster 1.50 .60
97 Buddy Bradford 1.50 .60
98 Dave Giusti 1.50 .60
99A Twins Rookies 15.00 6.00
Danny Morris
Graig Nettles RC
(No loop)
99B Twins Rookies 15.00 6.00
Danny Morris
Graig Nettles RC
(Errant loop in
upper left corner
of obverse)
100 Hank Aaron 50.00 20.00
101 Daryl Patterson 1.50 .60
102 Jim Davenport 1.50 .60
103 Roger Repoz 1.50 .60
104 Steve Blass 1.50 .60
105 Rick Monday 2.50 1.00
106 Jim Hannan 1.50 .60
107A Bob Gibson CL ERR 6.00 1.20
161 Jim Purdin
107B Bob Gibson CL COR 8.00 1.60
161 John Purdin
108 Tony Taylor 2.50 1.00
109 Jim Lonborg 2.50 1.00
110 Mike Shannon 2.50 1.00
111 John Morris RC 1.50 .60
112 J.C. Martin 2.50 1.00
113 Dave May 1.50 .60
114 Alan Closter 2.50 1.00
John Cumberland
115 Bill Hands 1.50 .60
116 Chuck Harrison 1.50 .60
117 Jim Fairey 2.50 1.00
118 Stan Williams 1.50 .60
119 Doug Rader 2.50 1.00
120 Pete Rose 50.00 20.00
121 Joe Grzenda 1.50 .60
122 Ron Fairly 2.50 1.00
123 Wilbur Wood 2.50 1.00
124 Hank Bauer MG 2.50 1.00
125 Ray Sadecki 1.50 .60

126 Dick Tracewski 1.50 .60
127 Kevin Collins 2.50 1.00
128 Tommie Aaron 2.50 1.00
129 Bill McCool 1.50 .60
130 Carl Yastrzemski 20.00 8.00
131 Chris Cannizzaro 1.50 .60
132 Dave Baldwin 1.50 .60
133 Johnny Callison 2.50 1.00
134 Jim Weaver 1.50 .60
135 Tommy Davis 2.50 1.00
136 Steve Huntz 1.50 .60
Mike Torrez
137 Wally Bunker 1.50 .60
138 John Bateman 1.50 .60
139 Andy Kosco 1.50 .60
140 Jim Lefebvre 2.50 1.00
141 Bill Dillman 1.50 .60
142 Woody Woodward 1.50 .60
143 Joe Nossek 1.50 .60
144 Bob Hendley 2.50 1.00
145 Max Alvis 1.50 .60
146 Jim Perry 2.50 1.00
147 Leo Durocher MG 4.00 1.60
148 Lee Stange 1.50 .60
149 Ollie Brown 2.50 1.00
150 Denny McLain 4.00 1.60
151A Clay Dalrymple 1.50 .60
Portrait, Orioles
151B Clay Dalrymple 15.00 6.00
Catching, Phillies
152 Tommie Sisk 1.50 .60
153 Ed Brinkman 1.50 .60
154 Jim Britton 1.50 .60
155 Pete Ward 1.50 .60
156 Hal Gilson 1.50 .60
Leon McFadden
157 Bob Rodgers 2.50 1.00
158 Joe Gibbon 1.50 .60
159 Jerry Adair 1.50 .60
160 Vada Pinson 2.50 1.00
161 John Purdin 1.50 .60
162 Bob Gibson WS 8.00 3.20
Fans 17
163 Willie Horton WS 6.00 2.40
164 Tim McCarver WS 12.00 4.80
Roger Maris
165 Lou Brock WS 8.00 3.20
166 Al Kaline WS 8.00 3.20
167 Jim Northrup WS 6.00 2.40
168 Mickey Lolich WS 8.00 3.20
Bob Gibson
169 Dick McAuliffe WS 6.00 2.40
Denny McLain
Willie Horton
170 Frank Howard 2.50 1.00
171 Glenn Beckert 2.50 1.00
172 Jerry Stephenson 1.50 .60
173 Bob Christian 1.50 .60
Gerry Nyman
174 Grant Jackson 1.50 .60
175 Jim Bunning 6.00 2.40
176 Joe Azcue 1.50 .60
177 Ron Reed 1.50 .60
178 Ray Oyler 2.50 1.00
179 Don Pavletich 1.50 .60
180 Willie Horton 2.50 1.00
181 Mel Nelson 1.50 .60
182 Bill Rigney MG 1.50 .60
183 Don Shaw 2.50 1.00
184 Roberto Pena 1.50 .60
185 Tom Phoebus 1.50 .60
186 Johnny Edwards 1.50 .60
187 Leon Wagner 1.50 .60
188 Rick Wise 2.50 1.00
189 Joe Lahoud 1.50 .60
John Thibodeau
190 Willie Mays 80.00 32.00
191 Lindy McDaniel 2.50 1.00
192 Jose Pagan 1.50 .60
193 Don Cardwell 2.50 1.00
194 Ted Uhlaender 1.50 .60
195 John Odom 1.50 .60
196 Lum Harris MG 1.50 .60
197 Dick Selma 1.50 .60
198 Willie Smith 1.50 .60
199 Jim French 1.50 .60
200 Bob Gibson 12.00 4.80
201 Russ Snyder 1.50 .60
202 Don Wilson 2.50 1.00
203 Dave Johnson 2.50 1.00
204 Jack Hiatt 1.50 .60
205 Rick Reichardt 1.50 .60
206 Larry Hisle 2.50 1.00
Barry Lersch
207 Roy Face 2.50 1.00
208A Donn Clendenon 2.50 1.00
Houston
208B Donn Clendenon 15.00 6.00
Expos
209 Larry Haney UER 1.50 .60
(Reverse negative)
210 Felix Millan 1.50 .60
211 Galen Cisco 1.50 .60
212 Tom Tresh 2.50 1.00
213 Gerry Arrigo 1.50 .60
214 Checklist 3 6.00 1.20
With 69T deckle CL
on back (no player)
215 Rico Petrocelli 2.50 1.00
216 Don Sutton 6.00 2.40
217 John Donaldson 1.50 .60
218 John Roseboro 2.50 1.00
219 Freddie Patek RC 4.00 1.60
220 Sam McDowell 4.00 1.60
221 Art Shamsky 4.00 1.60
222 Duane Josephson 2.50 1.00
223 Tom Dukes 4.00 1.60
224 Bill Harrelson 2.50 1.00
Steve Kealey
225 Don Kessinger 4.00 1.60
226 Bruce Howard 2.50 1.00
227 Frank Johnson 2.50 1.00
228 Dave Leonhard 2.50 1.00
229 Don Lock 2.50 1.00
230 Rusty Staub UER 4.00 1.60
For 1966 stats, Houston spelled Huoston
231 Pat Dobson 4.00 1.60
232 Dave Ricketts 2.50 1.00
233 Steve Barber 4.00 1.60
234 Dave Bristol MG 2.50 1.00
235 Jim Hunter 10.00 4.00
236 Manny Mota 4.00 1.60
237 Bobby Cox RC 10.00 4.00
238 Ken Johnson 2.50 1.00
239 Bob Taylor 4.00 1.60
240 Ken Harrelson 4.00 1.60
241 Jim Brewer 2.50 1.00
242 Frank Kostro 2.50 1.00
243 Ron Kline 2.50 1.00
244 Ray Fosse RC 4.00 1.60
George Woodson
245 Ed Charles 4.00 1.60
246 Joe Coleman 2.50 1.00
247 Gene Oliver 2.50 1.00
248 Bob Priddy 2.50 1.00
249 Ed Spiezio 4.00 1.60
250 Frank Robinson 20.00 8.00
251 Ron Herbel 2.50 1.00
252 Chuck Cottier 2.50 1.00
253 Jerry Johnson 2.50 1.00
254 Joe Schultz MG 4.00 1.60
255 Steve Carlton 30.00 12.00
256 Gates Brown 4.00 1.60
257 Jim Ray 2.50 1.00
258 Jackie Hernandez 4.00 1.60
259 Bill Short 2.50 1.00
260 Reggie Jackson RC 250.00 80.00
261 Bob Johnson 2.50 1.00
262 Mike Kekich 4.00 1.60
263 Jerry May 2.50 1.00
264 Bill Landis 2.50 1.00
265 Chico Cardenas 4.00 1.60
266 Tom Hutton 4.00 1.60
Alan Foster
267 Vicente Romo 2.50 1.00
268 Al Spangler 2.50 1.00
269 Al Weis 4.00 1.60
270 Mickey Lolich 4.00 1.60
271 Larry Stahl 4.00 1.60
272 Ed Stroud 2.50 1.00
273 Ron Willis 2.50 1.00
274 Clyde King MG 2.50 1.00
275 Vic Davalillo 2.50 1.00
276 Gary Wagner 2.50 1.00
277 Elrod Hendricks RC 2.50 1.00
278 Gary Geiger UER 2.50 1.00
(Batting wrong)
279 Roger Nelson 4.00 1.60
280 Alex Johnson 4.00 1.60
281 Ted Kubiak 2.50 1.00
282 Pat Jarvis 2.50 1.00
283 Sandy Alomar 4.00 1.60
284 Jerry Robertson 4.00 1.60
Mike Wegener
285 Don Mincher 4.00 1.60
286 Dock Ellis RC 4.00 1.60
287 Jose Tartabull 4.00 1.60
288 Ken Holtzman 4.00 1.60
289 Bart Shirley 2.50 1.00
290 Jim Kaat 4.00 1.60
291 Vern Fuller 2.50 1.00
292 Al Downing 4.00 1.60
293 Dick Dietz 2.50 1.00
294 Jim Lemon MG 2.50 1.00
295 Tony Perez 12.00 4.80
296 Andy Messersmith RC 4.00 1.60
297 Deron Johnson 2.50 1.00
298 Dave Nicholson 2.50 1.00
299 Mark Belanger 4.00 1.60
300 Felipe Alou 4.00 1.60
301 Darrell Brandon 4.00 1.60
302 Jim Pagliaroni 2.50 1.00
303 Cal Koonce 4.00 1.60
304 Bill Davis 6.00 2.40
Clarence Gaston RC
305 Dick McAuliffe 4.00 1.60
306 Jim Grant 4.00 1.60
307 Gary Kolb 2.50 1.00
308 Wade Blasingame 2.50 1.00
309 Walt Williams 2.50 1.00
310 Tom Haller 2.50 1.00
311 Sparky Lyle RC 10.00 4.00
312 Lee Elia 2.50 1.00
313 Bill Robinson 4.00 1.60
314 Don Drysdale CL 6.00 1.20
315 Eddie Fisher 2.50 1.00
316 Hal Lanier 2.50 1.00
317 Bruce Look 2.50 1.00
318 Jack Fisher 2.50 1.00
319 Ken McMullen UER 2.50 1.00
(Headings on back
are for a pitcher)
320 Dal Maxvill 2.50 1.00
321 Jim McAndrew 4.00 1.60
322 Jose Vidal 4.00 1.60
323 Larry Miller 2.50 1.00
324 Les Cain 4.00 1.60
Dave Campbell RC
325 Jose Cardenal 4.00 1.60
326 Gary Sutherland 4.00 1.60
327 Willie Crawford 2.50 1.00
328 Joel Horlen 1.50 .60
329 Rick Joseph 1.50 .60
330 Tony Conigliaro 4.00 1.60
331 Gil Garrido 2.50 1.00
Tom House RC
332 Fred Talbot 1.50 .60
333 Ivan Murrell 1.50 .60
334 Phil Roof 1.50 .60
335 Bill Mazeroski 6.00 2.40
336 Jim Roland 1.50 .60
337 Marty Martinez 1.50 .60
338 Del Unser 1.50 .60
339 Steve Mingori 1.50 .60
Jose Pena
340 Dave McNally 2.50 1.00
341 Dave Adlesh 1.50 .60
342 Bubba Morton 1.50 .60
343 Dan Frisella 1.50 .60
344 Tom Matchick 1.50 .60
345 Frank Linzy 1.50 .60
346 Wayne Comer 1.50 .60
347 Randy Hundley 2.50 1.00
348 Steve Hargan 1.50 .60
349 Dick Williams MG 2.50 1.00
350 Richie Allen 4.00 1.60
351 Carroll Sembera 1.50 .60
352 Paul Schaal 2.50 1.00
353 Jeff Torborg 2.50 1.00
354 Nate Oliver 1.50 .60
355 Phil Niekro 6.00 2.40
356 Frank Quilici 1.50 .60
357 Carl Taylor 1.50 .60
358 George Lauzerique 1.50 .60
Roberto Rodriquez
359 Dick Kelley 1.50 .60
360 Jim Wynn 2.50 1.00
361 Gary Holman 1.50 .60
362 Jim Maloney 2.50 1.00
363 Russ Nixon 1.50 .60
364 Tommie Agee 4.00 1.60
365 Jim Fregosi 2.50 1.00
366 Bo Belinsky 2.50 1.00
367 Lou Johnson 2.50 1.00
368 Vic Roznovsky 1.50 .60
369 Bob Skinner MG 2.50 1.00
370 Juan Marichal 8.00 3.20
371 Sal Bando 2.50 1.00
372 Adolfo Phillips 1.50 .60
373 Fred Lasher 1.50 .60
374 Bob Tillman 1.50 .60
375 Harmon Killebrew 15.00 6.00
376 Mike Fiore 1.50 .60
Jim Rooker RC
377 Gary Bell 2.50 1.00
378 Jose Herrera 1.50 .60
379 Ken Boyer 2.50 1.00
380 Stan Bahnsen 2.50 1.00
381 Ed Kranepool 2.50 1.00
382 Pat Corrales 2.50 1.00
383 Casey Cox 1.50 .60
384 Larry Shepard MG 1.50 .60
385 Orlando Cepeda 6.00 2.40
386 Jim McGlothlin 1.50 .60
387 Bobby Klaus 1.50 .60
388 Tom McCraw 1.50 .60
389 Dan Coombs 1.50 .60
390 Bill Freehan 2.50 1.00
391 Ray Culp 1.50 .60
392 Bob Burda 1.50 .60
393 Gene Brabender 2.50 1.00
394 Lou Piniella 6.00 2.40
Marv Staehle
395 Chris Short 1.50 .60
396 Jim Campanis 1.50 .60
397 Chuck Dobson 1.50 .60
398 Tito Francona 1.50 .60
399 Bob Bailey 2.50 1.00
400 Don Drysdale 15.00 6.00
401 Jake Gibbs 2.50 1.00
402 Ken Boswell 2.50 1.00
403 Bob Miller 1.50 .60
404 Vic LaRose 2.50 1.00
Gary Ross
405 Lee May 2.50 1.00
406 Phil Ortega 1.50 .60
407 Tom Egan 1.50 .60
408 Nate Colbert 1.50 .60
409 Bob Moose 1.50 .60
410 Al Kaline 25.00 10.00
411 Larry Dierker 2.50 1.00
412 Mickey Mantle CL DP 15.00 3.00
413 Roland Sheldon 2.50 1.00
414 Duke Sims 1.50 .60
415 Ray Washburn 1.50 .60
416 Willie McCovey AS 8.00 3.20
417 Ken Harrelson AS 3.00 1.20
418 Tommy Helms AS 3.00 1.20
419 Rod Carew AS 10.00 4.00
420 Ron Santo AS 4.00 1.60
421 Brooks Robinson AS 8.00 3.20
422 Don Kessinger AS 3.00 1.20
423 Bert Campaneris AS 4.00 1.60
424 Pete Rose AS 15.00 6.00
425 Carl Yastrzemski AS 10.00 4.00
426 Curt Flood AS 4.00 1.60
427 Tony Oliva AS 4.00 1.60
428 Lou Brock AS 6.00 2.40
429 Willie Horton AS 3.00 1.20
430 Johnny Bench AS 10.00 4.00
431 Bill Freehan AS 4.00 1.60
432 Bob Gibson AS 6.00 2.40
433 Denny McLain AS 3.00 1.20
434 Jerry Koosman AS 3.00 1.20
435 Sam McDowell AS 3.00 1.20
436 Gene Alley 2.50 1.00
437 Luis Alcaraz 1.50 .60
438 Gary Waslewski 1.50 .60
439 Ed Herrmann 1.50 .60
Dan Lazar
440A Willie McCovey 15.00 6.00
440B Willie McCovey WL 100.00 40.00
(McCovey white)
441A Dennis Higgins 1.50 .60
441B Dennis Higgins WL 25.00 10.00
(Higgins white)
442 Ty Cline 1.50 .60
443 Don Wert 1.50 .60
444A Joe Moeller 1.50 .60
444B Joe Moeller WL 25.00 10.00
(Moeller white)
445 Bobby Knoop 1.50 .60
446 Claude Raymond 1.50 .60
447A Ralph Houk MG 2.50 1.00
447B Ralph Houk WL 25.00 10.00
MG (Houk white)
448 Bob Tolan 2.50 1.00
449 Paul Lindblad 1.50 .60
450 Billy Williams 8.00 3.20
451A Rich Rollins 2.50 1.00
451B Rich Rollins WL 25.00 10.00
(Rich and 3B white)
452A Al Ferrara 1.50 .60
452B Al Ferrara WL 25.00 10.00
(Al and OF white)
453 Mike Cuellar 2.50 1.00
454A Phillies Rookies 2.50 1.00
Larry Colton
Don Money
454B Phillies Rookies WL 25.00 10.00
Larry Colton
Don Money
(Names in white)
455 Sonny Siebert 1.50 .60
456 Bud Harrelson 2.50 1.00
457 Dalton Jones 1.50 .60
458 Curt Blefary 1.50 .60
459 Dave Boswell 1.50 .60
460 Joe Torre 4.00 1.60
461A Mike Epstein 1.50 .60
461B Mike Epstein WL 25.00 10.00
(Epstein white)
462 Red Schoendienst 2.50 1.00
MG
463 Dennis Ribant 1.50 .60
464A Dave Marshall 1.50 .60
464B Dave Marshall WL 25.00 10.00
(Marshall white)
465 Tommy John 4.00 1.60
466 John Boccabella 2.50 1.00
467 Tommie Reynolds 1.50 .60
468A Pirates Rookies 1.50 .60
Bruce Dal Canton
Bob Robertson
468B Pirates Rookies WL 25.00 10.00
Bruce Dal Canton
Bob Robertson
(Names in white)
469 Chico Ruiz 1.50 .60
470A Mel Stottlemyre 2.50 1.00
470B Mel Stottlemyre WL 30.00 12.00
(Stottlemyre white)
471A Ted Savage 1.50 .60
471B Ted Savage WL 25.00 10.00
(Savage white)
472 Jim Price 1.50 .60
473A Jose Arcia 1.50 .60
473B Jose Arcia WL 25.00 10.00
(Jose and 2B white)
474 Tom Murphy 1.50 .60
475 Tim McCarver 4.00 1.60
476A Boston Rookies 3.00 1.20
Ken Brett RC
Gerry Moses
476B Boston Rookies WL 30.00 12.00
Ken Brett RC
Gerry Moses
(Names in white)
477 Jeff James 1.50 .60
478 Don Buford 1.50 .60
479 Richie Scheinblum 1.50 .60
480 Tom Seaver 80.00 32.00
481 Bill Melton 2.50 1.00
482A Jim Gosger 1.50 .60
482B Jim Gosger WL 25.00 10.00
(Jim and OF white)
483 Ted Abernathy 1.50 .60
484 Joe Gordon MG 2.50 1.00
485A Gaylord Perry 10.00 4.00
485B Gaylord Perry WL 80.00 32.00
(Perry white)
486A Paul Casanova 1.50 .60
486B Paul Casanova WL 25.00 10.00
(Casanova white)
487 Denis Menke 1.50 .60
488 Joe Sparma 1.50 .60
489 Clete Boyer 2.50 1.00
490 Matty Alou 2.50 1.00
491A Twins Rookies 1.50 .60
Jerry Crider
George Mitterwald
491B Twins Rookies WL 25.00 10.00
Jerry Crider
George Mitterwald
(Names in white)
492 Tony Cloninger 1.50 .60
493A Wes Parker 2.50 1.00
493B Wes Parker WL 25.00 10.00
(Parker white)
494 Ken Berry 1.50 .60
495 Bert Campaneris 2.50 1.00
496 Larry Jaster 1.50 .60
497 Julian Javier 2.50 1.00
498 Juan Pizarro 2.50 1.00
499 Don Bryant 1.50 .60
Steve Shea
500A Mickey Mantle UER 300.00 120.00
(No Topps copy-
right on card back)
500B Mickey Mantle WL 2000.00 800.00
(Mantle in white;
no Topps copyright
on card back) UER
501A Tony Gonzalez 2.50 1.00
501B Tony Gonzalez WL 25.00 10.00
(Tony and OF white)
502 Minnie Rojas 1.50 .60
503 Larry Brown 1.50 .60
504 Brooks Robinson CL 8.00 1.60
505A Bobby Bolin 1.50 .60
505B Bobby Bolin WL 25.00 10.00
(Bolin white)
506 Paul Blair 2.50 1.00
507 Cookie Rojas 2.50 1.00
508 Moe Drabowsky 2.50 1.00
509 Manny Sanguillen 2.50 1.00
510 Rod Carew 40.00 16.00
511A Diego Segui 2.50 1.00
511B Diego Segui WL 25.00 10.00
(Diego and P white)
512 Cleon Jones 2.50 1.00
513 Camilo Pascual 3.00 1.20
514 Mike Lum 2.00 .80
515 Dick Green 2.00 .80
516 Earl Weaver RC MG 20.00 8.00
517 Mike McCormick 3.00 1.20
518 Fred Whitfield 2.00 .80
519 Jerry Kenney 2.00 .80
Len Boehmer
520 Bob Veale 3.00 1.20
521 George Thomas 2.00 .80
522 Joe Hoerner 2.00 .80
523 Bob Chance 2.00 .80
524 Jose Laboy 3.00 1.20
Floyd Wicker
525 Earl Wilson 3.00 1.20
526 Hector Torres 2.00 .80
527 Al Lopez MG 5.00 2.00
528 Claude Osteen 3.00 1.20
529 Ed Kirkpatrick 3.00 1.20
530 Cesar Tovar 2.00 .80
531 Dick Farrell 2.00 .80
532 Tom Phoebus 3.00 1.20
Jim Hardin
Dave McNally
Mike Cuellar
533 Nolan Ryan 200.00 100.00
534 Jerry McNertney 3.00 1.20
535 Phil Regan 3.00 1.20
536 Danny Breeden 2.00 .80
Dave Roberts
537 Mike Paul 2.00 .80
538 Charlie Smith 2.00 .80
539 Mike Epstein 12.00 4.80
Ted Williams MG
540 Curt Flood 3.00 1.20
541 Joe Verbanic 2.00 .80
542 Bob Aspromonte 2.00 .80
543 Fred Newman 2.00 .80
544 Mike Kilkenny 2.00 .80
Ron Woods
545 Willie Stargell 12.00 4.80
546 Jim Nash 2.00 .80
547 Billy Martin MG 5.00 2.00
548 Bob Locker 2.00 .80
549 Ron Brand 2.00 .80
550 Brooks Robinson 30.00 12.00
551 Wayne Granger 2.00 .80
552 Ted Sizemore RC 3.00 1.20
Bill Sudakis
553 Ron Davis 2.00 .80
554 Frank Bertaina 2.00 .80
555 Jim Ray Hart 3.00 1.20
556 Sal Bando 3.00 1.20
Bert Campaneris
Danny Cater
557 Frank Fernandez 2.00 .80
558 Tom Burgmeier 3.00 1.20
559 Joe Hague 2.00 .80
Jim Hicks
560 Luis Tiant 3.00 1.20
561 Ron Clark 2.00 .80
562 Bob Watson RC 8.00 3.20
563 Marty Pattin 3.00 1.20
564 Gil Hodges MG 10.00 4.00
565 Hoyt Wilhelm 8.00 3.20
566 Ron Hansen 2.00 .80
567 Elvio Jimenez 2.00 .80
Jim Shellenback
568 Cecil Upshaw 2.00 .80
569 Billy Harris 1.50 .60
570 Ron Santo 8.00 3.20
571 Cap Peterson 2.00 .80
572 Willie McCovey 15.00 6.00
Juan Marichal
573 Jim Palmer 30.00 12.00
574 George Scott 3.00 1.20
575 Bill Singer 3.00 1.20
576 Ron Stone 2.00 .80
Bill Wilson
577 Mike Hegan 3.00 1.20
578 Don Bosch 2.00 .80
579 Dave Nelson 2.00 .80
580 Jim Northrup 3.00 1.20
581 Gary Nolan 3.00 1.20
582A Tony Oliva CL 6.00 1.20
White circle on back
582B Tony Oliva CL 8.00 1.60
Red circle on back
583 Clyde Wright 2.00 .80
584 Don Mason 2.00 .80
585 Ron Swoboda 3.00 1.20
586 Tim Cullen 2.00 .80
587 Joe Rudi RC 8.00 3.20
588 Bill White 3.00 1.20
589 Joe Pepitone 5.00 2.00
590 Rico Carty 5.00 2.00
591 Mike Hedlund 3.00 1.20
592 Rafael Robles 5.00 2.00
Al Santorini
593 Don Nottebart 3.00 1.20
594 Dooley Womack 3.00 1.20
595 Lee Maye 3.00 1.20
596 Chuck Hartenstein 3.00 1.20
597 Bob Floyd 40.00 16.00
Larry Burchart
Rollie Fingers RC
598 Ruben Amaro 3.00 1.20
599 John Boozer 3.00 1.20
600 Tony Oliva 8.00 3.20
601 Tug McGraw 8.00 3.20
602 Alec Distaso 5.00 2.00
Don Young
Jim Qualls
603 Joe Keough 3.00 1.20
604 Bobby Etheridge 3.00 1.20
605 Dick Ellsworth 3.00 1.20
606 Gene Mauch MG 5.00 2.00
607 Dick Bosman 3.00 1.20
608 Dick Simpson 3.00 1.20
609 Phil Gagliano 3.00 1.20
610 Jim Hardin 3.00 1.20
611 Bob Didier 5.00 2.00
Walt Hriniak RC
Gary Neibauer
612 Jack Aker 5.00 2.00
613 Jim Beauchamp 3.00 1.20
614 Tom Griffin 3.00 1.20
Skip Guinn
615 Len Gabrielson 3.00 1.20
616 Don McMahon 3.00 1.20
617 Jesse Gonder 3.00 1.20
618 Ramon Webster 3.00 1.20
619 Bill Butler 5.00 2.00
Pat Kelly
Juan Rios
620 Dean Chance 5.00 2.00
621 Bill Voss 3.00 1.20
622 Dan Osinski 3.00 1.20
623 Hank Allen 3.00 1.20
624 Darrel Chaney 5.00 2.00
Duffy Dyer RC
Terry Harmon
625 Mack Jones UER 5.00 2.00
(Batting wrong)
626 Gene Michael 5.00 2.00
627 George Stone 3.00 1.20
628 Bill Conigliaro RC 5.00 2.00
Syd O'Brien
Fred Wenz
629 Jack Hamilton 3.00 1.20
630 Bobby Bonds RC 30.00 12.00
631 John Kennedy 5.00 2.00
632 Jon Warden 3.00 1.20
633 Harry Walker MG 3.00 1.20
634 Andy Etchebarren 3.00 1.20
635 George Culver 3.00 1.20
636 Woody Held 3.00 1.20
637 Jerry DaVanon 5.00 2.00
Frank Reberger

Clay Kirby
638 Ed Sprague RC 3.00 1.20
639 Barry Moore 3.00 1.20
640 Ferguson Jenkins 20.00 8.00
641 Bobby Darwin 5.00 2.00
John Miller
Tommy Dean
642 John Hiller 3.00 1.20
643 Billy Cowan 3.00 1.20
644 Chuck Hinton 3.00 1.20
645 George Brunet 3.00 1.20
646 Dan McGinn 5.00 2.00
Carl Morton
647 Dave Wickersham 3.00 1.20
648 Bobby Wine 5.00 2.00
649 Al Jackson 3.00 1.20
650 Ted Williams MG 20.00 8.00
651 Gus Gil 5.00 2.00
652 Eddie Watt 3.00 1.20
653 A.Rodriguez RC UER 5.00 2.00
Photo actually
Angels' batboy
654 Carlos May RC 5.00 2.00
Don Secrist
Rich Morales
655 Mike Hershberger 3.00 1.20
656 Dan Schneider 3.00 1.20
657 Bobby Murcer 8.00 3.20
658 Tom Hall 3.00 1.20
Bill Burbach
Jim Miles
659 Johnny Podres 5.00 2.00
660 Reggie Smith 5.00 2.00
661 Jim Merritt 3.00 1.20
662 Dick Drago 5.00 2.00
George Spriggs
Bob Oliver
663 Dick Radatz 5.00 2.00
664 Ron Hunt 5.00 1.35

1969 Topps Decals Inserts

The 1969 Topps Decal Inserts are a set of 48 unnumbered decals issued as inserts in packages of 1969 Topps regular issue cards. Each decal is approximately 1" by 1 1/2" although including the plain backing the measurement is 1 3/4" by 2 1/8". The decals appear to be miniature versions of the Topps regular issue of that year. The copyright notice on the side indicates that these decals were produced in the United Kingdom. Most of the players on the decals are stars.

NM Ex
COMPLETE SET (48) 500.00 200.00
1 Hank Aaron 50.00 20.00
2 Richie Allen 8.00 3.20
3 Felipe Alou 5.00 2.00
4 Matty Alou 5.00 2.00
5 Luis Aparicio 8.00 3.20
6 Roberto Clemente 60.00 24.00
7 Donn Clendenon 3.00 1.20
8 Tommy Davis 5.00 2.00
9 Don Drysdale 10.00 4.00
10 Joe Foy 3.00 1.20
11 Jim Fregosi 5.00 2.00
12 Bob Gibson 10.00 4.00
13 Tony Gonzalez 3.00 1.20
14 Tom Haller 3.00 1.20
15 Ken Harrelson 5.00 2.00
16 Tommy Helms 3.00 1.20
17 Willie Horton 5.00 2.00
18 Frank Howard 5.00 2.00
19 Reggie Jackson 50.00 20.00
20 Ferguson Jenkins 8.00 3.20
21 Harmon Killebrew 15.00 6.00
22 Jerry Koosman 5.00 2.00
23 Mickey Mantle 100.00 47.50
24 Willie Mays 50.00 20.00
25 Tim McCarver 5.00 2.00
26 Willie McCovey 10.00 4.00
27 Sam McDowell 5.00 2.00
28 Denny McLain 5.00 2.00
29 Dave McNally 5.00 2.00
30 Don Mincher 3.00 1.20
31 Rick Monday 5.00 2.00
32 Tony Oliva 8.00 3.20
33 Camilo Pascual 3.00 1.20
34 Rick Reichardt 3.00 1.20
35 Frank Robinson 10.00 4.00
36 Pete Rose 50.00 12.00
37 Ron Santo 8.00 3.20
38 Tom Seaver 30.00 12.00
39 Dick Selma 3.00 1.20
40 Chris Short 3.00 1.20
41 Rusty Staub 8.00 3.20
42 Mel Stottlemyre 5.00 2.00
43 Luis Tiant 5.00 2.00
44 Pete Ward 3.00 1.20
45 Hoyt Wilhelm 8.00 3.20
46 Maury Wills 8.00 3.20
47 Jim Wynn 5.00 2.00
48 Carl Yastrzemski 20.00 8.00

1969 Topps Deckle Inserts

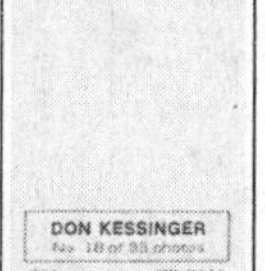

The cards in this 33-card set measure approximately 2 1/4" by 3 1/4". This unusual black and white insert set derives its name from the serrated border, or edge, of the cards. The cards were included as inserts in the regularly issued Topps baseball third series of 1969. Card number 11 is found with either Hoyt Wilhelm or Jim Wynn, and number 22 with either Rusty Staub or Joe Foy. The set price below does include all variations. The set numbering is arranged in team order by league except for cards 11 and 22.

NM Ex
COMPLETE SET (35) 100.00 40.00
1 Brooks Robinson 6.00 2.40
2 Boog Powell 2.50 1.00
3 Ken Harrelson 1.00 .40
4 Carl Yastrzemski 8.00 3.20
5 Jim Fregosi 1.50 .60
6 Luis Aparicio 2.50 1.00
7 Luis Tiant 1.50 .60
8 Denny McLain 2.50 1.00
9 Willie Horton 1.50 .60
10 Bill Freehan 1.50 .60
11A Hoyt Wilhelm 8.00 3.20
11B Jim Wynn 15.00 6.00
12 Rod Carew 4.00 1.60
13 Mel Stottlemyre 1.50 .60
14 Rick Monday 1.00 .40
15 Tommy Davis 1.50 .60
16 Frank Howard 1.50 .60
17 Felipe Alou 1.50 .60
18 Don Kessinger 1.00 .40
19 Ron Santo 2.50 1.00
20 Tommy Helms 1.00 .40
21 Pete Rose 12.00 4.00
22A Rusty Staub 1.50 .60
22B Joe Foy 12.00 4.80
23 Tom Haller 1.00 .40
24 Maury Wills 2.50 1.00
25 Jerry Koosman 1.50 .60
26 Richie Allen 4.00 1.60
27 Roberto Clemente 20.00 8.00
28 Curt Flood 2.50 1.00
29 Bob Gibson 4.00 1.60
30 Al Ferrara 1.00 .40
31 Willie McCovey 4.00 1.60
32 Juan Marichal 2.50 1.00
33 Willie Mays 12.00 4.80

1969 Topps Super

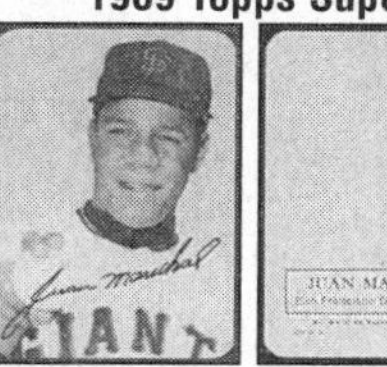

The cards in this 66-card set measure approximately 2 1/4" by 3 1/4". This beautiful Topps set was released independently of the regular baseball series of 1969. It is referred to as "Super Baseball" on the back of the card, a title which was also used for the postcard-size cards issued in 1970 and 1971. Complete sheets, and cards with square corners cut from these sheets, are sometimes encountered. The set numbering is in alphabetical order by teams within league. Cards from the far right of each row are usually found with a white line on the right edge. Although rarely seen, this set was issued in three-card cello packs. The set features Reggie Jackson in his Rookie Card year.

NM Ex
COMPLETE SET (66) 6000.00 2400.00
1 Dave McNally 15.00 6.00
2 Frank Robinson 200.00 80.00
3 Brooks Robinson 200.00 80.00
4 Ken Harrelson 20.00 8.00
5 Carl Yastrzemski 250.00 100.00
6 Ray Culp 15.00 6.00
7 Jim Fregosi 20.00 8.00
8 Rick Reichardt 15.00 6.00
9 Vic Davalillo 15.00 6.00
10 Luis Aparicio 80.00 32.00
11 Pete Ward 15.00 6.00
12 Joel Horlen 15.00 6.00
13 Luis Tiant 20.00 8.00
14 Sam McDowell 15.00 6.00
15 Jose Cardenal 15.00 6.00
16 Willie Horton 20.00 8.00
17 Denny McLain 25.00 10.00
18 Bill Freehan 20.00 8.00
19 Harmon Killebrew 150.00 60.00
20 Tony Oliva 30.00 12.00
21 Dean Chance 15.00 6.00
22 Joe Foy 15.00 6.00
23 Roger Nelson 15.00 6.00
24 Mickey Mantle 1000.00 400.00
25 Mel Stottlemyre 20.00 8.00
26 Roy White 20.00 8.00
27 Rick Monday 15.00 6.00
28 Reggie Jackson 500.00 200.00
29 Bert Campaneris 20.00 8.00
30 Frank Howard 25.00 10.00
31 Camilo Pascual 15.00 6.00
32 Tommy Davis 20.00 8.00
33 Don Mincher 15.00 6.00
34 Hank Aaron 500.00 200.00
35 Felipe Alou 25.00 10.00
36 Joe Torre 40.00 16.00
37 Ferguson Jenkins 80.00 32.00
38 Ron Santo 30.00 12.00
39 Billy Williams 80.00 32.00
40 Tommy Helms 15.00 6.00
41 Pete Rose 400.00 160.00
42 Joe Morgan 120.00 47.50
43 Jim Wynn 15.00 6.00
44 Curt Blefary 15.00 6.00
45 Willie Davis 15.00 6.00
46 Don Drysdale 100.00 40.00
47 Tom Haller 15.00 6.00
48 Rusty Staub 25.00 10.00
49 Maury Wills 30.00 12.00
50 Cleon Jones 15.00 6.00
51 Jerry Koosman 25.00 10.00
52 Tom Seaver 400.00 160.00
53 Richie Allen 25.00 10.00
54 Chris Short 15.00 6.00
55 Cookie Rojas 15.00 6.00
56 Matty Alou 15.00 6.00
57 Steve Blass 15.00 6.00
58 Roberto Clemente 600.00 240.00
59 Curt Flood 25.00 10.00
60 Bob Gibson 150.00 60.00
61 Tim McCarver 30.00 12.00
62 Dick Selma 15.00 6.00
63 Ollie Brown 15.00 6.00
64 Juan Marichal 100.00 40.00
65 Willie Mays 500.00 200.00
66 Willie McCovey 100.00 40.00

1970 Topps

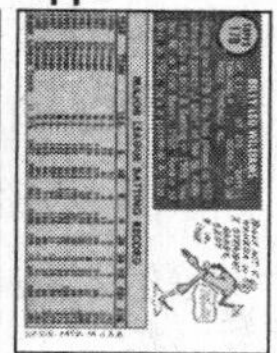

The cards in this 720-card set measure 2 1/2" by 3 1/2". The Topps set for 1970 has color photos surrounded by white frame lines and gray borders. The backs have a blue biographical section and a yellow record section. All-Star selections are featured on cards 450 to 469. Other topical subsets within this set include League Leaders (61-72), Playoffs cards (195-202), and World Series cards (305-310). There are graduations of scarcity, terminating in the high series (634-720), which are outlined in the value summary. Cards were issued in ten-card dime packs as well as thirty-three card cello packs quarter back encased in a small Topps box. The key Rookie Card in this set is Thurman Munson.

NM Ex
COMPLETE SET (720) 2000.00 1000.00
COMMON CARD (1-132) .75 .30
COMMON (373-459) 1.00 .40
COMMON CARD (373-459) 1.50 .60
COMMON (460-546) 2.00 .80
COMMON (547-633) 4.00 1.60
COMMON (634-720) 10.00 4.00
WRAPPER (10-CENT) 20.00 8.00
1 New York Mets 30.00 9.50
Team Card
2 Diego Segui 1.00 .40
3 Darrel Chaney .75 .30
4 Tom Egan .75 .30
5 Wes Parker 1.00 .40
6 Grant Jackson .75 .30
7 Gary Boyd .75 .30
Russ Nagelson
8 Jose Martinez .75 .30
9 Checklist 1 12.00 2.40
10 Carl Yastrzemski 20.00 8.00
11 Nate Colbert .75 .30
12 John Hiller .75 .30
13 Jack Hiatt .75 .30
14 Hank Allen .75 .30
15 Larry Dierker .75 .30
16 Charlie Metro MG .75 .30
17 Hoyt Wilhelm 4.00 1.60
18 Carlos May 1.00 .40
19 John Boccabella .75 .30
20 Dave McNally 1.00 .40
21 Vida Blue RC 4.00 1.60
Gene Tenace RC
22 Ray Washburn .75 .30
23 Bill Robinson 1.00 .40
24 Dick Selma .75 .30
25 Cesar Tovar .75 .30
26 Tug McGraw 2.00 .80
27 Chuck Hinton .75 .30
28 Billy Wilson .75 .30
29 Sandy Alomar 1.00 .40
30 Matty Alou 1.00 .40
31 Marty Pattin 1.00 .40
32 Harry Walker MG .75 .30
33 Don Wert .75 .30
34 Willie Crawford .75 .30
35 Joel Horlen .75 .30
36 Danny Breeden 1.00 .40
Bernie Carbo
37 Dick Drago .75 .30
38 Mack Jones .75 .30
39 Mike Nagy .75 .30
40 Rich Allen 2.00 .80
41 George Lauzerique .75 .30
42 Tito Fuentes .75 .30
43 Jack Aker .75 .30
44 Roberto Pena .75 .30
45 Dave Johnson 1.00 .40
46 Ken Rudolph .75 .30
47 Bob Miller .75 .30
48 Gil Garrido .75 .30
49 Tim Cullen .75 .30
50 Tommie Agee 1.00 .40
51 Bob Christian .75 .30
52 Bruce Dal Canton .75 .30
53 John Kennedy .75 .30
54 Jeff Torborg 1.00 .40
55 John Odom .75 .30
56 Joe Lis .75 .30
Scott Reid
57 Pat Kelly .75 .30
58 Dave Marshall .75 .30
59 Dick Ellsworth .75 .30
60 Jim Wynn 1.00 .40
61 Pete Rose 12.00 4.80
Bob Clemente
Cleon Jones LL
62 Rod Carew 2.00 .80
Reggie Smith
Tony Oliva LL
63 Willie McCovey 2.00 .80
Ron Santo
Tony Perez LL
64 Harmon Killebrew 4.00 1.60
Boog Powell
Reggie Jackson LL
65 Willie McCovey 4.00 1.60
Hank Aaron
Lee May LL
66 Harmon Killebrew 4.00 1.60
Frank Howard
Reggie Jackson LL
67 Juan Marichal 4.00 1.60
Steve Carlton
Bob Gibson LL
68 Dick Bosman 1.00 .40
Jim Palmer
Mike Cuellar LL
69 Tom Seaver 4.00 1.60
Phil Niekro
Fergie Jenkins
Juan Marichal LL
70 Dennis McLain 1.00 .40
Mike Cuellar
Dave Boswell
Dave McNally
Jim Perry
Mel Stottlemyre LL
71 Fergie Jenkins 2.00 .80
Bob Gibson
Bill Singer LL
72 Sam McDowell 1.00 .40
Mickey Lolich
Andy Messersmith LL
73 Wayne Granger .75 .30
74 Greg Washburn .75 .30
Wally Wolf
75 Jim Kaat 1.00 .40
76 Carl Taylor .75 .30
77 Frank Linzy .75 .30
78 Joe Lahoud .75 .30
79 Clay Kirby .75 .30
80 Don Kessinger 1.00 .40
81 Dave May .75 .30
82 Frank Fernandez .75 .30
83 Don Cardwell .75 .30
84 Paul Casanova .75 .30
85 Max Alvis .75 .30
86 Lum Harris MG .75 .30
87 Steve Renko RC .75 .30
88 Miguel Fuentes 1.00 .40
Dick Baney
89 Juan Rios .75 .30
90 Tim McCarver 1.00 .40
91 Rich Morales .75 .30
92 George Culver .75 .30
93 Rick Renick .75 .30
94 Freddie Patek 1.00 .40
95 Earl Wilson 1.00 .40
96 Leron Lee 1.00 .40
Jerry Reuss RC
97 Joe Moeller .75 .30
98 Gates Brown 1.00 .40
99 Bobby Pfeil .75 .30
100 Mel Stottlemyre 1.00 .40
101 Bobby Floyd .75 .30
102 Joe Rudi 1.00 .40
103 Frank Reberger .75 .30
104 Gerry Moses .75 .30
105 Tony Gonzalez .75 .30
106 Darold Knowles .75 .30
107 Bobby Etheridge .75 .30
108 Tom Burgmeier .75 .30
109 Garry Jestadt .75 .30
Carl Morton
110 Bob Moose .75 .30
111 Mike Hegan 1.00 .40
112 Dave Nelson .75 .30
113 Jim Ray .75 .30
114 Gene Michael 1.00 .40
115 Alex Johnson 1.00 .40
116 Sparky Lyle 1.00 .40
117 Don Young .75 .30
118 George Mitterwald .75 .30
119 Chuck Taylor .75 .30
120 Sal Bando 1.00 .40
121 Fred Beene .75 .30
Terry Crowley
122 George Stone .75 .30
123 Don Gutteridge MG .75 .30
124 Larry Jaster .75 .30
125 Deron Johnson .75 .30
126 Marty Martinez .75 .30
127 Joe Coleman .75 .30
128A Checklist 2 ERR 6.00 1.20
(226 R Perranoski)
128B Checklist 2 COR 6.00 1.20
(226 R. Perranoski)
129 Jimmie Price .75 .30
130 Ollie Brown .75 .30
131 Ray Lamb .75 .30
Bob Stinson
132 Jim McGlothlin .75 .30
133 Clay Carroll 1.00 .40
134 Danny Walton 1.00 .40
135 Dick Dietz 1.00 .40
136 Steve Hargan 1.00 .40
137 Art Shamsky 1.00 .40
138 Joe Foy 1.00 .40
139 Rich Nye 1.00 .40
140 Reggie Jackson 50.00 20.00
141 Dave Cash RC 1.50 .60
Johnny Jeter
142 Fritz Peterson 1.00 .40
143 Phil Gagliano 1.00 .40
144 Ray Culp 1.00 .40
145 Rico Carty 1.50 .60
146 Danny Murphy 1.00 .40
147 Angel Hermoso 1.00 .40
148 Earl Weaver MG 3.00 1.20
149 Billy Champion 1.00 .40
150 Harmon Killebrew 8.00 3.20
151 Dave Roberts 1.00 .40
152 Ike Brown 1.00 .40
153 Gary Gentry 1.00 .40
154 Jim Miles 1.00 .40
Jan Dukes
155 Denis Menke 1.00 .40
156 Eddie Fisher 1.00 .40
157 Manny Mota 1.50 .60
158 Jerry McNertney 1.50 .60
159 Tommy Helms 1.50 .60
160 Phil Niekro 5.00 2.00
161 Richie Scheinblum 1.00 .40
162 Jerry Johnson 1.00 .40
163 Syd O'Brien 1.00 .40
164 Ty Cline 1.00 .40
165 Ed Kirkpatrick 1.00 .40
166 Al Oliver 3.00 1.20
167 Bill Burbach 1.00 .40
168 Dave Watkins 1.00 .40
169 Tom Hall 1.00 .40
170 Billy Williams 5.00 2.00
171 Jim Nash 1.00 .40
172 Garry Hill 1.50 .60
Ralph Garr RC
173 Jim Hicks 1.00 .40
174 Ted Sizemore 1.50 .60
175 Dick Bosman 1.00 .40
176 Jim Ray Hart 1.50 .60
177 Jim Northrup 1.50 .60
178 Denny Lemaster 1.00 .40
179 Ivan Murrell 1.00 .40
180 Tommy John 1.50 .60
181 Sparky Anderson MG 5.00 2.00
182 Dick Hall 1.00 .40
183 Jerry Grote 1.50 .60
184 Ray Fosse 1.00 .40
185 Don Mincher 1.50 .60
186 Rick Joseph 1.00 .40
187 Mike Hedlund 1.00 .40
188 Manny Sanguillen 1.50 .60
189 Thurman Munson RC 80.00 32.00
Dave McDonald
190 Joe Torre 3.00 1.20
191 Vicente Romo 1.00 .40
192 Jim Qualls 1.00 .40
193 Mike Wegener 1.00 .40
194 Chuck Manuel 1.00 .40
195 Tom Seaver NLCS 15.00 6.00
196 Ken Boswell NLCS 2.00 .80
197 Nolan Ryan NLCS 30.00 12.00
198 NL Playoff Summary 15.00 6.00
Mets celebrate
(Nolan Ryan)
199 Mike Cuellar ALCS 2.00 .80
200 Boog Powell ALCS 3.00 1.20
201 Boog Powell ALCS 2.00 .80
Andy Etchebarren)
202 AL Playoff Summary 2.00 .80
Orioles celebrate
203 Rudy May 1.00 .40
204 Len Gabrielson 1.00 .40
205 Bert Campaneris 1.50 .60
206 Clete Boyer 1.50 .60
207 Norman McRae 1.00 .40
Bob Reed
208 Fred Gladding 1.00 .40
209 Ken Suarez 1.00 .40
210 Juan Marichal 5.00 2.00
211 Ted Williams MG UER 15.00 6.00
Throwing information on back incorrect
212 Al Santorini 1.00 .40
213 Andy Etchebarren 1.00 .40
214 Ken Boswell 1.00 .40
215 Reggie Smith 1.50 .60
216 Chuck Hartenstein 1.00 .40
217 Ron Hansen 1.00 .40
218 Ron Stone 1.00 .40
219 Jerry Kenney 1.00 .40
220 Steve Carlton 15.00 6.00
221 Ron Brand 1.00 .40
222 Jim Rooker 1.00 .40
223 Nate Oliver 1.00 .40
224 Steve Barber 1.50 .60
225 Lee May 1.50 .60
226 Ron Perranoski 1.00 .40
227 John Mayberry RC 1.50 .60
Bob Watkins
228 Aurelio Rodriguez 1.00 .40
229 Rich Robertson 1.00 .40
230 Brooks Robinson 15.00 6.00
231 Luis Tiant 1.50 .60
232 Bob Didier 1.00 .40
233 Lew Krausse 1.00 .40
234 Tommy Dean 1.00 .40
235 Mike Epstein 1.00 .40
236 Bob Veale 1.00 .40
237 Russ Gibson 1.00 .40
238 Jose Laboy 1.00 .40
239 Ken Berry 1.00 .40
240 Ferguson Jenkins 5.00 2.00
241 Al Fitzmorris 1.00 .40
Scott Northey
242 Walter Alston MG 3.00 1.20
243 Joe Sparma 1.00 .40
244A Checklist 3 6.00 1.20
(Red bat on front)
244B Checklist 3 6.00 1.20
(Brown bat on front)
245 Leo Cardenas 1.00 .40
246 Jim McAndrew 1.00 .40
247 Lou Klimchock 1.00 .40
248 Jesus Alou 1.00 .40
249 Bob Locker 1.00 .40
250 Willie McCovey UER 10.00 4.00
(1963 San Francisci)
251 Dick Schofield 1.00 .40
252 Lowell Palmer 1.00 .40
253 Ron Woods 1.00 .40
254 Camilo Pascual 1.00 .40
255 Jim Spencer 1.00 .40
256 Vic Davalillo 1.00 .40
257 Dennis Higgins 1.00 .40
258 Paul Popovich 1.00 .40
259 Tommie Reynolds 1.00 .40
260 Claude Osteen 1.00 .40
261 Curt Motton 1.00 .40
262 Jerry Morales 1.00 .40
Jim Williams
263 Duane Josephson 1.00 .40
264 Rich Hebner 1.00 .40
265 Randy Hundley 1.00 .40
266 Wally Bunker 1.00 .40
267 Herman Hill 1.00 .40
Paul Ratliff
268 Claude Raymond 1.00 .40
269 Cesar Gutierrez 1.00 .40
270 Chris Short 1.00 .40
271 Greg Goossen 1.50 .60
272 Hector Torres 1.50 .60
273 Ralph Houk MG 1.50 .60
274 Gerry Arrigo 1.00 .40
275 Duke Sims 1.00 .40

276 Ron Hunt 1.00 .40
277 Paul Doyle 1.00 .40
278 Tommie Aaron 1.00 .40
279 Bill Lee RC 1.50 .60
280 Donn Clendenon 1.50 .60
281 Casey Cox 1.00 .40
282 Steve Huntz 1.00 .40
283 Angel Bravo 1.00 .40
284 Jack Baldschun 1.00 .40
285 Paul Blair 1.50 .60
286 Jack Jenkins 5.00 2.00
Bill Buckner RC
287 Fred Talbot 1.00 .40
288 Larry Hisle 1.50 .60
289 Gene Brabender 1.00 .40
290 Rod Carew 15.00 6.00
291 Leo Durocher MG 3.00 1.20
292 Eddie Leon 1.00 .40
293 Bob Bailey 1.50 .60
294 Jose Azcue 1.00 .40
295 Cecil Upshaw 1.00 .40
296 Woody Woodward 1.00 .40
297 Curt Blefary 1.00 .40
298 Ken Henderson 1.00 .40
299 Buddy Bradford 1.00 .40
300 Tom Seaver 30.00 12.00
301 Chico Salmon 1.00 .40
302 Jeff James 1.00 .40
303 Brant Alyea 1.00 .40
304 Bill Russell RC 5.00 2.00
305 Don Buford WS 4.00 1.60
306 Donn Clendenon WS 4.00 1.60
307 Tommie Agee WS 4.00 1.60
308 J.C. Martin WS 4.00 1.60
309 Jerry Koosman WS 4.00 1.60
310 WS Summary 5.00 2.00
Mets whoop it up
311 Dick Green 1.00 .40
312 Mike Torrez 1.00 .40
313 Mayo Smith MG 1.00 .40
314 Bill McCool 1.00 .40
315 Luis Aparicio 5.00 2.00
316 Skip Guinn 1.00 .40
317 Billy Conigliaro 1.50 .60
Luis Alvarado
318 Willie Smith 1.00 .40
319 Clay Dalrymple 1.00 .40
320 Jim Maloney 1.50 .60
321 Lou Piniella 1.50 .60
322 Luke Walker 1.00 .40
323 Wayne Comer 1.00 .40
324 Tony Taylor 1.50 .60
325 Dave Boswell 1.00 .40
326 Bill Voss 1.00 .40
327 Hal King 1.00 .40
328 George Brunet 1.00 .40
329 Chris Cannizzaro 1.00 .40
330 Lou Brock 10.00 4.00
331 Chuck Dobson 1.00 .40
332 Bobby Wine 1.00 .40
333 Bobby Murcer 1.50 .60
334 Phil Regan 1.00 .40
335 Bill Freehan 1.50 .60
336 Del Unser 1.00 .40
337 Mike McCormick 1.50 .60
338 Paul Schaal 1.00 .40
339 Johnny Edwards 1.00 .40
340 Tony Conigliaro 3.00 1.20
341 Bill Sudakis 1.00 .40
342 Wilbur Wood 1.50 .60
343A Checklist 4 6.00 1.20
(Red bat on front)
343B Checklist 4 6.00 1.20
(Brown bat on front)
344 Marcelino Lopez 1.00 .40
345 Al Ferrara 1.00 .40
346 Red Schoendienst MG 1.50 .60
347 Russ Snyder 1.00 .40
348 Mike Jorgensen 1.50 .60
Jesse Hudson
349 Steve Hamilton 1.00 .40
350 Roberto Clemente 60.00 24.00
351 Tom Murphy 1.00 .40
352 Bob Barton 1.00 .40
353 Stan Williams 1.00 .40
354 Amos Otis 1.50 .60
355 Doug Rader 1.00 .40
356 Fred Lasher 1.00 .40
357 Bob Burda 1.00 .40
358 Pedro Borbon RC 1.50 .60
359 Phil Roof 1.00 .40
360 Curt Flood 1.50 .60
361 Ray Jarvis 1.00 .40
362 Joe Hague 1.00 .40
363 Tom Shopay 1.00 .40
364 Dan McGinn 1.00 .40
365 Zoilo Versalles 1.00 .40
366 Barry Moore 1.00 .40
367 Mike Lum 1.00 .40
368 Ed Herrmann 1.00 .40
369 Alan Foster 1.00 .40
370 Tommy Harper 1.50 .60
371 Rod Gaspar 1.00 .40
372 Dave Giusti 1.00 .40
373 Roy White 2.00 .80
374 Tommie Sisk 1.00 .40
375 Johnny Callison 2.00 .80
376 Lefty Phillips MG 1.50 .60
377 Bill Butler 1.50 .60
378 Jim Davenport 1.50 .60
379 Tom Tischinski 1.50 .60
380 Tony Perez 6.00 2.40
381 Bobby Brooks 1.50 .60
Mike Olivo
382 Jack DiLauro 1.50 .60
383 Mickey Stanley 2.00 .80
384 Gary Neibauer 1.50 .60
385 George Scott 2.00 .80
386 Bill Dillman 1.50 .60
387 Baltimore Orioles 3.00 1.20
Team Card
388 Byron Browne 1.50 .60
389 Jim Shellenback 1.50 .60
390 Willie Davis 2.00 .80
391 Larry Brown 1.50 .60
392 Walt Hriniak 2.00 .80
393 John Gelnar 1.50 .60
394 Gil Hodges MG 4.00 1.60
395 Walt Williams 1.50 .60
396 Steve Blass 2.00 .80
397 Roger Repoz 1.50 .60
398 Bill Stoneman 1.50 .60
399 New York Yankees 3.00 1.20
Team Card
400 Denny McLain 4.00 1.60
401 John Harrell 1.50 .60
Bernie Williams
402 Ellie Rodriguez 1.50 .60
403 Jim Bunning 6.00 2.40
404 Rich Reese 1.50 .60
405 Bill Hands 1.50 .60
406 Mike Andrews 1.50 .60
407 Bob Watson 2.00 .80
408 Paul Lindblad 1.50 .60
409 Bob Tolan 1.50 .60
410 Boog Powell 4.00 1.60
411 Los Angeles Dodgers 3.00 1.20
Team Card
412 Larry Burchart 1.50 .60
413 Sonny Jackson 1.50 .60
414 Paul Edmondson 1.50 .60
415 Julian Javier 2.00 .80
416 Joe Verbanic 1.50 .60
417 John Bateman 1.50 .60
418 John Donaldson 1.50 .60
419 Ron Taylor 1.50 .60
420 Ken McMullen 2.00 .80
421 Pat Dobson 2.00 .80
422 Royals Team 3.00 1.20
423 Jerry May 1.50 .60
424 Mike Kilkenny 1.50 .60
(Inconsistent design
card number in
white circle)
425 Bobby Bonds 6.00 2.40
426 Bill Rigney MG 1.50 .60
427 Fred Norman 1.50 .60
428 Don Buford 1.50 .60
429 Randy Bobb 1.50 .60
Jim Cosman
430 Andy Messersmith 2.00 .80
431 Ron Swoboda 2.00 .80
432A Checklist 5 6.00 1.20
(Baseball in
yellow letters)
432B Checklist 5 6.00 1.20
(Baseball in
white letters)
433 Ron Bryant 1.50 .60
434 Felipe Alou 2.00 .80
435 Nelson Briles 2.00 .80
436 Philadelphia Phillies 3.00 1.20
Team Card
437 Danny Cater 1.50 .60
438 Pat Jarvis 1.50 .60
439 Lee Maye 1.50 .60
440 Bill Mazeroski 6.00 2.40
441 John O'Donoghue 1.50 .60
442 Gene Mauch MG 2.00 .80
443 Al Jackson 1.50 .60
444 Billy Farmer 1.50 .60
John Matias
445 Vada Pinson 2.00 .80
446 Billy Grabarkewitz 1.50 .60
447 Lee Stange 1.50 .60
448 Houston Astros 3.00 1.20
Team Card
449 Jim Palmer 12.00 4.80
450 Willie McCovey AS 6.00 2.40
451 Boog Powell AS 4.00 1.60
452 Felix Millan AS 2.00 .80
453 Rod Carew AS 6.00 2.40
454 Ron Santo AS 4.00 1.60
455 Brooks Robinson AS 6.00 2.40
456 Don Kessinger AS 2.00 .80
457 Rico Petrocelli AS 4.00 1.60
458 Pete Rose AS 15.00 6.00
459 Reggie Jackson AS 12.00 4.80
460 Matty Alou AS 3.00 1.20
461 Carl Yastrzemski AS 10.00 4.00
462 Hank Aaron AS 15.00 6.00
463 Frank Robinson AS 8.00 3.20
464 Johnny Bench AS 15.00 6.00
465 Bill Freehan AS 3.00 1.20
466 Juan Marichal AS 5.00 2.00
467 Denny McLain AS 3.00 1.20
468 Jerry Koosman AS 3.00 1.20
469 Sam McDowell AS 3.00 1.20
470 Willie Stargell 10.00 4.00
471 Chris Zachary 2.00 .80
472 Braves Team 4.00 1.60
473 Don Bryant 2.00 .80
474 Dick Kelley 2.00 .80
475 Dick McAuliffe 3.00 1.20
476 Don Shaw 2.00 .80
477 Al Severinsen 2.00 .80
Roger Freed
478 Bobby Heise 2.00 .80
479 Dick Woodson 2.00 .80
480 Glenn Beckert 3.00 1.20
481 Jose Tartabull 2.00 .80
482 Tom Hilgendorf 2.00 .80
483 Gail Hopkins 2.00 .80
484 Gary Nolan 3.00 1.20
485 Jay Johnstone 3.00 1.20
486 Terry Harmon 2.00 .80
487 Cisco Carlos 2.00 .80
488 J.C. Martin 2.00 .80
489 Eddie Kasko MG 2.00 .80
490 Bill Singer 3.00 1.20
491 Graig Nettles 5.00 2.00
492 Keith Lampard 2.00 .80
Scipio Spinks
493 Lindy McDaniel 3.00 1.20
494 Larry Stahl 2.00 .80
495 Dave Morehead 2.00 .80
496 Steve Whitaker 2.00 .80
497 Eddie Watt 2.00 .80
498 Al Weis 2.00 .80
499 Skip Lockwood 3.00 1.20
500 Hank Aaron 50.00 20.00
501 Chicago White Sox 4.00 1.60
Team Card
502 Rollie Fingers 10.00 4.00
503 Dal Maxvill 2.00 .80
504 Don Pavletich 2.00 .80
505 Ken Holtzman 3.00 1.20
506 Ed Stroud 2.00 .80
507 Pat Corrales 2.00 .80
508 Joe Niekro 3.00 1.20
509 Montreal Expos 4.00 1.60
Team Card
510 Tony Oliva 5.00 2.00
511 Joe Hoerner 2.00 .80
512 Billy Harris 2.00 .80
513 Preston Gomez MG 2.00 .80
514 Steve Hovley 2.00 .80
515 Don Wilson 3.00 1.20
516 John Ellis 2.00 .80
Jim Lyttle
517 Joe Gibbon 2.00 .80
518 Bill Melton 2.00 .80
519 Don McMahon 2.00 .80
520 Willie Horton 3.00 1.20
521 Cal Koonce 2.00 .80
522 Angels Team 4.00 1.60
523 Jose Pena 2.00 .80
524 Alvin Dark MG 3.00 1.20
525 Jerry Adair 2.00 .80
526 Ron Herbel 2.00 .80
527 Don Bosch 2.00 .80
528 Elrod Hendricks 2.00 .80
529 Bob Aspromonte 2.00 .80
530 Bob Gibson 15.00 6.00
531 Ron Clark 2.00 .80
532 Danny Murtaugh MG 3.00 1.20
533 Buzz Stephen 2.00 .80
534 Minnesota Twins 4.00 1.60
Team Card
535 Andy Kosco 2.00 .80
536 Mike Kekich 2.00 .80
537 Joe Morgan 10.00 4.00
538 Bob Humphreys 2.00 .80
539 Denny Doyle 8.00 3.20
Larry Bowa RC
540 Gary Peters 2.00 .80
541 Bill Heath 2.00 .80
542 Checklist 6 6.00 1.20
543 Clyde Wright 2.00 .80
544 Cincinnati Reds 4.00 1.60
Team Card
545 Ken Harrelson 3.00 1.20
546 Ron Reed 2.00 .80
547 Rick Monday 6.00 2.40
548 Howie Reed 4.00 1.60
549 St. Louis Cardinals 6.00 2.40
Team Card
550 Frank Howard 6.00 2.40
551 Dock Ellis 6.00 2.40
552 Don O'Riley 4.00 1.60
Dennis Paepke
Fred Rico
553 Jim Lefebvre 6.00 2.40
554 Tom Timmermann 4.00 1.60
555 Orlando Cepeda 12.00 4.80
556 Dave Bristol MG 6.00 2.40
557 Ed Kranepool 6.00 2.40
558 Vern Fuller 4.00 1.60
559 Tommy Davis 6.00 2.40
560 Gaylord Perry 12.00 4.80
561 Tom McCraw 4.00 1.60
562 Ted Abernathy 4.00 1.60
563 Boston Red Sox 6.00 2.40
Team Card
564 Johnny Briggs 4.00 1.60
565 Jim Hunter 12.00 4.80
566 Gene Alley 6.00 2.40
567 Bob Oliver 4.00 1.60
568 Stan Bahnsen 6.00 2.40
569 Cookie Rojas 6.00 2.40
570 Jim Fregosi 6.00 2.40
White Chevy Pick-Up in Background
571 Jim Brewer 4.00 1.60
572 Frank Quilici 4.00 1.60
573 Mike Corkins 4.00 1.60
Rafael Robles
Ron Slocum
574 Bobby Bolin 6.00 2.40
575 Cleon Jones 6.00 2.40
576 Milt Pappas 6.00 2.40
577 Bernie Allen 4.00 1.60
578 Tom Griffin 4.00 1.60
579 Detroit Tigers 6.00 2.40
Team Card
580 Pete Rose 60.00 24.00
581 Tom Satriano 4.00 1.60
582 Mike Paul 4.00 1.60
583 Hal Lanier 4.00 1.60
584 Al Downing 6.00 2.40
585 Rusty Staub 8.00 3.20
586 Rickey Clark 4.00 1.60
587 Jose Arcia 4.00 1.60
588A Checklist 7 ERR 8.00 1.60
(666 Adolfo)
588B Checklist 7 COR 6.00 1.20
(666 Adolpho)
589 Joe Keough 4.00 1.60
590 Mike Cuellar 6.00 2.40
591 Mike Ryan UER 4.00 1.60
(Pitching Record
header on card back)
592 Daryl Patterson 4.00 1.60
593 Chicago Cubs 8.00 3.20
Team Card
594 Jake Gibbs 4.00 1.60
595 Maury Wills 8.00 3.20
596 Mike Hershberger 6.00 2.40
597 Sonny Siebert 4.00 1.60
598 Joe Pepitone 6.00 2.40
599 Dick Stelmaszek 4.00 1.60
Gene Martin
Dick Such
600 Willie Mays 80.00 32.00
601 Pete Richert 4.00 1.60
602 Ted Savage 4.00 1.60
603 Ray Oyler 4.00 1.60
604 Clarence Gaston 6.00 2.40
605 Rick Wise 6.00 2.40
606 Chico Ruiz 4.00 1.60
607 Gary Waslewski 4.00 1.60
608 Pittsburgh Pirates 6.00 2.40
Team Card
609 Buck Martinez RC 6.00 2.40
(Inconsistent design
card number in
white circle)
610 Jerry Koosman 8.00 3.20
611 Norm Cash 6.00 2.40
612 Jim Hickman 6.00 2.40
613 Dave Baldwin 6.00 2.40
614 Mike Shannon 6.00 2.40
615 Mark Belanger 6.00 2.40
616 Jim Merritt 4.00 1.60
617 Jim French 4.00 1.60
618 Billy Wynne 4.00 1.60
619 Norm Miller 4.00 1.60
620 Jim Perry 6.00 2.40
621 Mike McQueen 12.00 4.80
Darrell Evans RC
Rick Kester
622 Don Sutton 12.00 4.80
623 Horace Clarke 6.00 2.40
624 Clyde King MG 4.00 1.60
625 Dean Chance 4.00 1.60
626 Dave Ricketts 4.00 1.60
627 Gary Wagner 4.00 1.60
628 Wayne Garrett 4.00 1.60
629 Merv Rettenmund 4.00 1.60
630 Ernie Banks 50.00 20.00
631 Oakland Athletics 6.00 2.40
Team Card
632 Gary Sutherland 4.00 1.60
633 Roger Nelson 4.00 1.60
634 Bud Harrelson 15.00 6.00
635 Bob Allison 15.00 6.00
636 Jim Stewart 10.00 4.00
637 Cleveland Indians 12.00 4.80
Team Card
638 Frank Bertaina 10.00 4.00
639 Dave Campbell 15.00 6.00
640 Al Kaline 50.00 20.00
641 Al McBean 10.00 4.00
642 Greg Garrett 10.00 4.00
Gordon Lund
Jarvis Tatum
643 Jose Pagan 10.00 4.00
644 Gerry Nyman 10.00 4.00
645 Don Money 15.00 6.00
646 Jim Britton 10.00 4.00
647 Tom Matchick 10.00 4.00
648 Larry Haney 10.00 4.00
649 Jimmie Hall 10.00 4.00
650 Sam McDowell 15.00 6.00
651 Jim Gosger 10.00 4.00
652 Rich Rollins 15.00 6.00
653 Moe Drabowsky 10.00 4.00
654 Oscar Gamble RC 15.00 6.00
Boots Day
Angel Mangual
655 John Roseboro 15.00 6.00
656 Jim Hardin 10.00 4.00
657 San Diego Padres 12.00 4.80
Team Card
658 Ken Tatum 10.00 4.00
659 Pete Ward 10.00 4.00
660 Johnny Bench 80.00 32.00
661 Jerry Robertson 10.00 4.00
662 Frank Lucchesi MG 10.00 4.00
663 Tito Francona 10.00 4.00
664 Bob Robertson 10.00 4.00
665 Jim Lonborg 15.00 6.00
666 Adolpho Phillips 10.00 4.00
667 Bob Meyer 15.00 6.00
668 Bob Tillman 10.00 4.00
669 Bart Johnson 10.00 4.00
Dan Lazar
Mickey Scott
670 Ron Santo 15.00 6.00
671 Jim Campanis 10.00 4.00
672 Leon McFadden 10.00 4.00
673 Ted Uhlaender 10.00 4.00
674 Dave Leonhard 10.00 4.00
675 Jose Cardenal 15.00 6.00
676 Washington Senators 12.00 4.80
Team Card
677 Woodie Fryman 10.00 4.00
678 Dave Duncan 15.00 6.00
679 Ray Sadecki 10.00 4.00
680 Rico Petrocelli 15.00 6.00
681 Bob Garibaldi 10.00 4.00
682 Dalton Jones 10.00 4.00
683 Vern Geishert 15.00 6.00
Hal McRae
Wayne Simpson
684 Jack Fisher 10.00 4.00
685 Tom Haller 10.00 4.00
686 Jackie Hernandez 10.00 4.00
687 Bob Priddy 10.00 4.00
688 Ted Kubiak 15.00 6.00
689 Frank Tepedino 15.00 6.00
690 Ron Fairly 15.00 6.00
691 Joe Grzenda 10.00 4.00
692 Duffy Dyer 10.00 4.00
693 Bob Johnson 10.00 4.00
694 Gary Ross 10.00 4.00
695 Bobby Knoop 10.00 4.00
696 San Francisco Giants 12.00 4.80
Team Card
697 Jim Hannan 10.00 4.00
698 Tom Tresh 15.00 6.00
699 Hank Aguirre 10.00 4.00
700 Frank Robinson 50.00 20.00
701 Jack Billingham 10.00 4.00
702 Bob Johnson 10.00 4.00
Ron Klimkowski
Bill Zepp
703 Lou Marone 10.00 4.00
704 Frank Baker 10.00 4.00
705 Tony Cloninger UER 10.00 4.00
(Batter headings
on card back)
706 John McNamara MG 10.00 4.00
707 Kevin Collins 10.00 4.00
708 Jose Santiago 10.00 4.00
709 Mike Fiore 10.00 4.00
710 Felix Millan 10.00 4.00
711 Ed Brinkman 10.00 4.00
712 Nolan Ryan 200.00 80.00
713 Seattle Pilots 25.00 10.00
Team Card
714 Al Spangler 10.00 4.00
715 Mickey Lolich 15.00 6.00
716 Sal Campisi 15.00 6.00
Reggie Cleveland
Santiago Guzman
717 Tom Phoebus 10.00 4.00
718 Ed Spiezio 10.00 4.00
719 Jim Roland 10.00 4.00
720 Rick Reichardt 15.00 5.00

1970 Topps Booklets

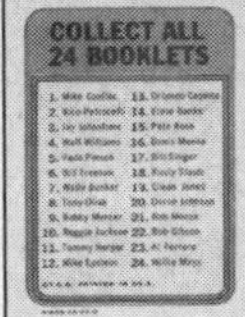

Inserted into packages of the 1970 Topps (and O-Pee-Chee) regular issue of cards, there are 24 miniature biographies of ballplayers in the set. Each numbered paper booklet contains six pages of comic book style story and a checklist of the booklet is available on the back page. These little booklets measure approximately 2 1/2" by 3 7/16".

	NM	Ex
COMPLETE SET (24)	40.00	16.00
COMMON CARD (1-16)	1.00	.40
COMMON CARD (17-24)	1.00	.01
1 Mike Cuellar	1.00	.40
2 Rico Petrocelli	1.00	.40
3 Jay Johnstone	1.00	.40
4 Walt Williams	1.00	.40
5 Vada Pinson	1.00	.40
6 Bill Freehan	1.00	.40
7 Wally Bunker	1.00	.40
8 Tony Oliva	1.50	.60
9 Bobby Murcer	1.00	.40
10 Reggie Jackson	6.00	2.40
11 Tommy Harper	1.00	.40
12 Mike Epstein	1.00	.40
13 Orlando Cepeda	1.50	.60
14 Ernie Banks	4.00	1.60
15 Pete Rose	6.00	2.40
16 Denis Menke	1.00	.40
17 Bill Singer	1.00	.40
18 Rusty Staub	1.50	.60
19 Cleon Jones	1.00	.40
20 Deron Johnson	1.00	.40
21 Bob Moose	1.00	.40
22 Bob Gibson	2.50	1.00
23 Al Ferrara	1.00	.40
24 Willie Mays	8.00	3.20

1970 Topps Posters Inserts

In 1970 Topps raised its price per package of cards to ten cents, and a series of 24 color posters was included as a bonus to the collector. Each thin-paper poster is numbered and features a large portrait and a smaller black and white action pose. It was folded five times to fit in the packaging. Each poster measures 8 11/16" by 9 5/8".

	NM	Ex
COMPLETE SET (24)	60.00	24.00
1 Joe Horlen	1.50	.60
2 Phil Niekro	2.00	.80
3 Willie Davis	1.50	.60
4 Lou Brock	5.00	2.00
5 Ron Santo	3.00	1.20
6 Ken Harrelson	1.50	.60
7 Willie McCovey	5.00	2.00
8 Rick Wise	1.50	.60
9 Andy Messersmith	1.50	.60
10 Ron Fairly	1.50	.60
11 Johnny Bench	10.00	4.00
12 Frank Robinson	5.00	2.00
13 Tommie Agee	1.50	.60
14 Roy White	1.50	.60
15 Larry Dierker	1.50	.60
16 Rod Carew	5.00	2.00
17 Don Mincher	1.50	.60
18 Ollie Brown	1.50	.60
19 Ed Kirkpatrick	1.50	.60
20 Reggie Smith	2.00	.80
21 Roberto Clemente	20.00	8.00
22 Frank Howard	2.00	.80
23 Bert Campaneris	2.00	.80
24 Denny McLain	2.00	.80

1970 Topps Scratchoffs

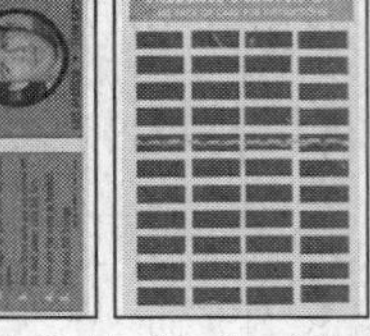

The 1970 Topps Scratch-off inserts are heavy cardboard, folded inserts issued with the regular card series of those years. Unfolded, they form a game board upon which a baseball game is played by means of rubbing off black ink from the playing squares to reveal moves. Inserts with white centers were issued in 1970 and inserts with red centers in 1971. Unfolded, these inserts measure 3 3/8" by 5". Obviously, a card which has been scratched off can be considered to be in no better than vg condition.

	NM	Ex
COMPLETE SET (24)	50.00	20.00
COMMON CARD (1-24)	1.00	.40
MINOR STARS	1.50	.60
SEMISTARS	2.50	1.00
1 Hank Aaron	8.00	3.20

2 Rich Allen 1.50 .60
3 Luis Aparicio 2.50 1.00
4 Sal Bando 1.50 .60
5 Glenn Beckert 1.00 .40
6 Dick Bosman 1.00 .40
7 Nate Colbert 1.00 .40
8 Mike Hegan 1.00 .40
9 Mack Jones 1.00 .40
10 Al Kaline 5.00 2.00
11 Harmon Killebrew 5.00 2.00
12 Juan Marichal 2.50 1.00
13 Tim McCarver 1.50 .60
14 Sam McDowell 1.50 .60
15 Claude Osteen 1.00 .40
16 Tony Perez 2.50 1.00
17 Lou Piniella 1.50 .60
18 Boog Powell 2.50 1.00
19 Tom Seaver 5.00 2.00
20 Jim Spencer 1.00 .40
21 Willie Stargell 4.00 1.60
22 Mel Stottlemyre 1.50 .60
23 Jim Wynn 1.50 .60
24 Carl Yastrzemski 6.00 2.40

1970 Topps Super

The cards in this 42-card set measure approximately 3 1/8" by 5 1/4". The 1970 Topps Super set was a separate Topps issue printed on heavy stock and marketed in its own wrapper with gum. The blue and yellow backs are identical to the respective player's backs in the 1970 Topps regular issue. Cards 38, Boog Powell, is the key card of the set; other short print run cards are listed in the checklist with SP. The obverse pictures are borderless and contain a facsimile autograph. The set was issued in three-card wax packs which came 24 packs to a box and 24 boxes to a case.

NM Ex
COMPLETE SET (42) 250.00 100.00
COMMON CARD (1-42) 2.00 .80
WRAPPER (10-CENT)
COMMON SP 4.00 1.60
1 Claude Osteen SP 4.00 1.60
2 Sal Bando SP 4.00 1.60
3 Luis Aparicio SP 5.00 2.00
4 Harmon Killebrew 5.00 2.00
5 Tom Seaver SP 25.00 10.00
6 Larry Dierker 2.50 1.00
7 Bill Freehan 2.50 1.00
8 Johnny Bench 15.00 6.00
9 Tommy Harper 2.00 .80
10 Sam McDowell 2.00 .80
11 Lou Brock 5.00 2.00
12 Roberto Clemente 30.00 12.00
13 Willie McCovey 5.00 2.00
14 Rico Petrocelli 2.00 .80
15 Phil Niekro 4.00 1.60
16 Frank Howard 2.50 1.00
17 Denny McLain 2.50 1.00
18 Willie Mays 20.00 8.00
19 Willie Stargell 5.00 2.00
20 Joel Horlen 2.00 .80
21 Ron Santo 3.00 1.20
22 Dick Bosman 2.00 .80
23 Tim McCarver 3.00 1.20
24 Hank Aaron 20.00 8.00
25 Andy Messersmith 2.00 .80
26 Tony Oliva 3.00 1.20
27 Mel Stottlemyre 2.50 1.00
28 Reggie Jackson 15.00 6.00
29 Carl Yastrzemski 15.00 6.00
30 Jim Fregosi 2.50 1.00
31 Vada Pinson 2.50 1.00
32 Lou Piniella 3.00 1.20
33 Bob Gibson 5.00 2.00
34 Pete Rose 20.00 8.00
35 Jim Wynn 2.50 1.00
36 Ollie Brown SP 6.00 2.40
37 Frank Robinson SP 20.00 8.00
38 Boog Powell SP 50.00 20.00
39 Willie Davis SP 4.00 1.60
40 Billy Williams SP 10.00 4.00
41 Rusty Staub 3.00 1.20
42 Tommie Agee 2.50 1.00

1971 Topps

The cards in this 752-card set measure 2 1/2" by 3 1/2". The 1971 Topps set is a challenge to complete in strict mint condition because the black obverse border is easily scratched and damaged. An unusual feature of this set is that the player is also pictured in black and white on the back of the card. Featured subsets within this set include League Leaders (61-72), Playoffs cards (195-202), and World Series cards (327-332). Cards 524-643 and the last series (644-752) are somewhat scarce. The last series was printed in two sheets of 132. On the printing sheets 44 cards were printed in 50 percent greater quantity than the other 66 cards. These 66 (slightly) shorter-printed numbers are identified in the checklist below by SP. The key Rookie Cards in this set are the multi-player Rookie Card of Dusty Baker and Don Baylor and the individual cards of Bert Blyleven, Dave Concepcion, Steve Garvey, and Ted Simmons. The Jim Northrup and Jim Nash cards have been seen with our without printing "blotches" on the card. There is still debate on whether those two cards are just printing issues or legitimate variations.

NM Ex
COMPLETE SET (752) 2500.00 1000.00
COMMON CARD (1-393) 1.50 .60
COMMON (394-523) 2.50 1.00
COMMON (524-643) 4.00 1.60
COMMON (644-752) 8.00 3.20
COMMON SP (644-752) 12.00 4.80
WRAPPER (10-CENT) 15.00 6.00
1 Baltimore Orioles 20.00 6.75
Team Card
2 Dock Ellis 1.50 .60
3 Dick McAuliffe 2.00 .80
4 Vic Davalillo 1.50 .60
5 Thurman Munson 100.00 24.00
6 Ed Spiezio 1.50 .60
7 Jim Holt 1.50 .60
8 Mike McQueen 1.50 .60
9 George Scott 2.00 .80
10 Claude Osteen 2.00 .80
11 Elliott Maddox 1.50 .60
12 Johnny Callison 2.00 .80
13 Charlie Brinkman 1.50 .60
Dick Moloney
14 Dave Concepcion RC 15.00 6.00
15 Andy Messersmith 2.00 .80
16 Ken Singleton RC 4.00 1.60
17 Billy Sorrell 1.50 .60
18 Norm Miller 1.50 .60
19 Skip Pitlock 1.50 .60
20 Reggie Jackson 50.00 20.00
21 Dan McGinn 1.50 .60
22 Phil Roof 1.50 .60
23 Oscar Gamble 1.50 .60
24 Rich Hand 1.50 .60
25 Clarence Gaston 2.00 .80
26 Bert Blyleven RC 20.00 8.00
27 Fred Cambria 1.50 .60
Gene Clines
28 Ron Klimkowski 1.50 .60
29 Don Buford 1.50 .60
30 Phil Niekro 6.00 2.40
31 Eddie Kasko MG 1.50 .60
32 Jerry DaVanon 1.50 .60
33 Del Unser 1.50 .60
34 Sandy Vance 1.50 .60
35 Lou Piniella 2.00 .80
36 Dean Chance 2.00 .80
37 Rich McKinney 1.50 .60
38 Jim Colborn 1.50 .60
39 Lerrin LaGrow 2.00 .80
Gene Lamont RC
40 Lee May 2.00 .80
41 Rick Austin 1.50 .60
42 Boots Day 1.50 .60
43 Steve Kealey 1.50 .60
44 Johnny Edwards 1.50 .60
45 Jim Hunter 6.00 2.40
46 Dave Campbell 2.00 .80
47 Johnny Jeter 1.50 .60
48 Dave Baldwin 1.50 .60
49 Don Money 1.50 .60
50 Willie McCovey 10.00 4.00
51 Steve Kline 1.50 .60
52 Oscar Brown 1.50 .60
Earl Williams RC
53 Paul Blair 2.00 .80
54 Checklist 1 10.00 2.00
55 Steve Carlton 20.00 8.00
56 Duane Josephson 1.50 .60
57 Von Joshua 1.50 .60
58 Bill Lee 2.00 .80
59 Gene Mauch MG 2.00 .80
60 Dick Bosman 1.50 .60
61 Alex Johnson 4.00 1.60
Carl Yastrzemski
Tony Oliva LL
62 Rico Carty 2.00 .80
Joe Torre
Manny Sanguillen LL
63 Frank Howard 4.00 1.60
Tony Conigliaro
Boog Powell LL
64 Johnny Bench 6.00 2.40
Tony Perez
Billy Williams LL
65 Frank Howard 4.00 1.60
Harmon Killebrew
Carl Yastrzemski LL
66 Johnny Bench 6.00 2.40
Billy Williams
Tony Perez LL
67 Diego Segui 4.00 1.60
Jim Palmer
Clyde Wright LL
68 Tom Seaver 4.00 1.60
Wayne Simpson
Luke Walker LL
69 Mike Cuellar 2.00 .80
Dave McNally
Jim Perry LL
70 Bob Gibson 6.00 2.40
Gaylord Perry
Fergie Jenkins LL
71 Sam McDowell 2.00 .80
Mickey Lolich
Bob Johnson LL
72 Tom Seaver 6.00 2.40
Bob Gibson
Fergie Jenkins LL
73 George Brunet 1.50 .60
74 Pete Hamm 1.50 .60
Jim Nettles
75 Gary Nolan 2.00 .80
76 Ted Savage 1.50 .60
77 Mike Compton 1.50 .60
78 Jim Spencer 1.50 .60
79 Wade Blasingame 1.50 .60
80 Bill Melton 1.50 .60
81 Felix Millan 1.50 .60
82 Casey Cox 1.50 .60
83 Tim Foli RC 2.00 .80
Randy Bobb
84 Marcel Lachemann RC 1.50 .60
85 Billy Grabarkewitz 1.50 .60
86 Mike Kilkenny 1.50 .60
87 Jack Heidemann 1.50 .60
88 Hal King 1.50 .60
89 Ken Brett 1.50 .60
90 Joe Pepitone 2.00 .80
91 Bob Lemon MG 2.00 .80
92 Fred Wenz 1.50 .60
93 Norm McRae 1.50 .60
Denny Riddleberger
94 Don Hahn 1.50 .60
95 Luis Tiant 2.00 .80
96 Joe Hague 1.50 .60
97 Floyd Wicker 1.50 .60
98 Joe Decker 1.50 .60
99 Mark Belanger 2.00 .80
100 Pete Rose 80.00 32.00
101 Les Cain 1.50 .60
102 Ken Forsch 2.00 .80
Larry Howard
103 Rich Severson 1.50 .60
104 Dan Frisella 1.50 .60
105 Tony Conigliaro 2.00 .80
106 Tom Dukes 1.50 .60
107 Roy Foster 1.50 .60
108 John Cumberland 1.50 .60
109 Steve Hovley 1.50 .60
110 Bill Mazeroski 6.00 2.40
111 Loyd Colson 1.50 .60
Bobby Mitchell
112 Manny Mota 2.00 .80
113 Jerry Crider 1.50 .60
114 Billy Conigliaro 2.00 .80
115 Donn Clendenon 2.00 .80
116 Ken Sanders 1.50 .60
117 Ted Simmons RC 8.00 3.20
118 Cookie Rojas 2.00 .80
119 Frank Lucchesi MG 1.50 .60
120 Willie Horton 2.00 .80
121 Jim Dunegan 1.50 .60
Roe Skidmore
122 Eddie Watt 1.50 .60
123A Checklist 2 10.00 2.00
(Card number
at bottom right)
123B Checklist 2 10.00 2.00
(Card number
centered)
124 Don Gullett RC 2.00 .80
125 Ray Fosse 1.50 .60
126 Danny Coombs 1.50 .60
127 Danny Thompson 2.00 .80
128 Frank Johnson 1.50 .60
129 Aurelio Monteagudo 1.50 .60
130 Denis Menke 1.50 .60
131 Curt Blefary 1.50 .60
132 Jose Laboy 1.50 .60
133 Mickey Lolich 2.00 .80
134 Jose Arcia 1.50 .60
135 Rick Monday 2.00 .80
136 Duffy Dyer 1.50 .60
137 Marcelino Lopez 1.50 .60
138 Joe Lis 2.00 .80
Willie Montanez
139 Paul Casanova 1.50 .60
140 Gaylord Perry 6.00 2.40
141 Frank Quilici 1.50 .60
142 Mack Jones 1.50 .60
143 Steve Blass 2.00 .80
144 Jackie Hernandez 1.50 .60
145 Bill Singer 2.00 .80
146 Ralph Houk MG 2.00 .80
147 Bob Priddy 1.50 .60
148 John Mayberry 2.00 .80
149 Mike Hershberger 1.50 .60
150 Sam McDowell 2.00 .80
151 Tommy Davis 2.00 .80
152 Lloyd Allen 1.50 .60
Winston Llenas
153 Gary Ross 1.50 .60
154 Cesar Gutierrez 1.50 .60
155 Ken Henderson 1.50 .60
156 Bart Johnson 1.50 .60
157 Bob Bailey 2.00 .80
158 Jerry Reuss 2.00 .80
159 Jarvis Tatum 1.50 .60
160 Tom Seaver 30.00 12.00
161 Coin Checklist 10.00 2.00
162 Jack Billingham 1.50 .60
163 Buck Martinez 2.00 .80
164 Frank Duffy 2.00 .80
Milt Wilcox
165 Cesar Tovar 1.50 .60
166 Joe Hoerner 1.50 .60
167 Tom Grieve RC 2.00 .80
168 Bruce Dal Canton 1.50 .60
169 Ed Herrmann 1.50 .60
170 Mike Cuellar 2.00 .80
171 Bobby Wine 1.50 .60
172 Duke Sims 1.50 .60
173 Gil Garrido 1.50 .60
174 Dave LaRoche 1.50 .60
175 Jim Hickman 1.50 .60
176 Bob Montgomery RC 2.00 .80
Doug Griffin
177 Hal McRae 2.00 .80
178 Dave Duncan 2.00 .80
179 Mike Corkins 1.50 .60
180 Al Kaline UER 20.00 8.00
(Home instead
of Birth)
181 Hal Lanier 1.50 .60
182 Al Downing 2.00 .80
183 Gil Hodges MG 4.00 1.60
184 Stan Bahnsen 1.50 .60
185 Julian Javier 1.50 .60
186 Bob Spence 1.50 .60
187 Ted Abernathy 1.50 .60
188 Bob Valentine RC 6.00 2.40
Mike Strahler
189 George Mitterwald 1.50 .60
190 Bob Tolan 1.50 .60
191 Mike Andrews 1.50 .60
192 Billy Wilson 1.50 .60
193 Bob Grich RC 4.00 1.60
194 Mike Lum 1.50 .60
195 Boog Powell ALCS 2.00 .80
196 Dave McNally ALCS 2.00 .80
197 Jim Palmer ALCS 4.00 1.60
198 AL Playoff Summary 2.00 .80
Orioles celebrate
199 Ty Cline NLCS 2.00 .80
200 Bobby Tolan NLCS 2.00 .80
201 Ty Cline NLCS 2.00 .80
202 NL Playoff Summary 2.00 .80
Reds celebrate
203 Larry Gura 2.00 .80
204 Bernie Smith 1.50 .60
George Kopacz
205 Gerry Moses 1.50 .60
206 Checklist 3 10.00 2.00
207 Alan Foster 1.50 .60
208 Billy Martin MG 4.00 1.60
209 Steve Renko 1.50 .60
210 Rod Carew 15.00 6.00
211 Phil Hennigan 1.50 .60
212 Rich Hebner 2.00 .80
213 Frank Baker 1.50 .60
214 Al Ferrara 1.50 .60
215 Diego Segui 1.50 .60
216 Reggie Cleveland 1.50 .60
Luis Melendez
217 Ed Stroud 1.50 .60
218 Tony Cloninger 1.50 .60
219 Elrod Hendricks 1.50 .60
220 Ron Santo 4.00 1.60
221 Dave Morehead 1.50 .60
222 Bob Watson 2.00 .80
223 Cecil Upshaw 1.50 .60
224 Alan Gallagher 1.50 .60
225 Gary Peters 1.50 .60
226 Bill Russell 2.00 .80
227 Floyd Weaver 1.50 .60
228 Wayne Garrett 1.50 .60
229 Jim Hannan 1.50 .60
230 Willie Stargell 15.00 6.00
231 Vince Colbert 2.00 .80
John Lowenstein RC
232 John Strohmayer 1.50 .60
233 Larry Bowa 2.00 .80
234 Jim Lyttle 1.50 .60
235 Nate Colbert 1.50 .60
236 Bob Humphreys 1.50 .60
237 Cesar Cedeno RC 2.00 .80
238 Chuck Dobson 1.50 .60
239 Red Schoendienst MG 2.00 .80
240 Clyde Wright 1.50 .60
241 Dave Nelson 1.50 .60
242 Jim Ray 1.50 .60
243 Carlos May 1.50 .60
244 Bob Tillman 1.50 .60
245 Jim Kaat 2.00 .80
246 Tony Taylor 1.50 .60
247 Jerry Cram 2.00 .80
Paul Splittorff
248 Hoyt Wilhelm 6.00 2.40
249 Chico Salmon 1.50 .60
250 Johnny Bench 50.00 20.00
251 Frank Reberger 1.50 .60
252 Eddie Leon 1.50 .60
253 Bill Sudakis 1.50 .60
254 Cal Koonce 1.50 .60
255 Bob Robertson 2.00 .80
256 Tony Gonzalez 1.50 .60
257 Nelson Briles 1.50 .60
258 Dick Green 1.50 .60
259 Dave Marshall 1.50 .60
260 Tommy Harper 2.00 .80
261 Darold Knowles 1.50 .60
262 Jim Williams 1.50 .60
Dave Robinson
263 John Ellis 1.50 .60
264 Joe Morgan 8.00 3.20
265 Jim Northrup 2.00 .80
266 Bill Stoneman 1.50 .60
267 Rich Morales 1.50 .60
268 Philadelphia Phillies 4.00 1.60
Team Card
269 Gail Hopkins 1.50 .60
270 Rico Carty 2.00 .80
271 Bill Zepp 1.50 .60
272 Tommy Helms 2.00 .80
273 Pete Richert 1.50 .60
274 Ron Slocum 1.50 .60
275 Vada Pinson 2.00 .80
276 Mike Davison 8.00 3.20
George Foster RC
277 Gary Waslewski 1.50 .60
278 Jerry Grote 2.00 .80
279 Lefty Phillips MG 1.50 .60
280 Ferguson Jenkins 6.00 2.40
281 Danny Walton 1.50 .60
282 Jose Pagan 1.50 .60
283 Dick Such 1.50 .60
284 Jim Gosger 1.50 .60
285 Sal Bando 2.00 .80
286 Jerry McNertney 1.50 .60
287 Mike Fiore 1.50 .60
288 Joe Moeller 1.50 .60
289 Chicago White Sox 4.00 1.60
Team Card
290 Tony Oliva 4.00 1.60
291 George Culver 1.50 .60
292 Jay Johnstone 2.00 .80
293 Pat Corrales 2.00 .80
294 Steve Dunning 1.50 .60
295 Bobby Bonds 4.00 1.60
296 Tom Timmermann 1.50 .60
297 Johnny Briggs 1.50 .60
298 Jim Nelson 1.50 .60
299 Ed Kirkpatrick 1.50 .60
300 Brooks Robinson 20.00 8.00
301 Earl Wilson 1.50 .60
302 Phil Gagliano 1.50 .60
303 Lindy McDaniel 2.00 .80
304 Ron Brand 1.50 .60
305 Reggie Smith 2.00 .80
306 Jim Nash 1.50 .60
307 Don Wert 1.50 .60
308 St. Louis Cardinals 4.00 1.60
Team Card
309 Dick Ellsworth 1.50 .60
310 Tommie Agee 2.00 .80
311 Lee Stange 1.50 .60
312 Harry Walker MG 1.50 .60
313 Tom Hall 1.50 .60
314 Jeff Torborg 2.00 .80
315 Ron Fairly 2.00 .80
316 Fred Scherman 1.50 .60
317 Jim Driscoll 1.50 .60
Angel Mangual
318 Rudy May 1.50 .60
319 Ty Cline 1.50 .60
320 Dave McNally 2.00 .80
321 Tom Matchick 1.50 .60
322 Jim Beauchamp 1.50 .60
323 Billy Champion 1.50 .60
324 Graig Nettles 2.00 .80
325 Juan Marichal 8.00 3.20
326 Richie Scheinblum 1.50 .60
327 Boog Powell WS 2.00 .80
328 Don Buford WS 2.00 .80
329 Frank Robinson WS 4.00 1.60
330 World Series Game 4 2.00 .80
Reds stay alive
331 Brooks Robinson WS 6.00 2.40
commits robbery
332 WS Summary 2.00 .80
Orioles celebrate
333 Clay Kirby 1.50 .60
334 Roberto Pena 1.50 .60
335 Jerry Koosman 2.00 .80
336 Detroit Tigers 4.00 1.60
Team Card
337 Jesus Alou 1.50 .60
338 Gene Tenace 2.00 .80
339 Wayne Simpson 1.50 .60
340 Rico Petrocelli 2.00 .80
341 Steve Garvey RC 40.00 16.00
342 Frank Tepedino 2.00 .80
343 Ed Acosta 2.00 .80
Milt May RC
344 Ellie Rodriguez 1.50 .60
345 Joel Horlen 1.50 .60
346 Lum Harris MG 1.50 .60
347 Ted Uhlaender 1.50 .60
348 Fred Norman 1.50 .60
349 Rich Reese 1.50 .60
350 Billy Williams 6.00 2.40
351 Jim Shellenback 1.50 .60
352 Denny Doyle 1.50 .60
353 Carl Taylor 1.50 .60
354 Don McMahon 1.50 .60
355 Bud Harrelson 4.00 1.60
(Nolan Ryan in photo)
356 Bob Locker 1.50 .60
357 Cincinnati Reds 4.00 1.60
Team Card
358 Danny Cater 1.50 .60
359 Ron Reed 1.50 .60
360 Jim Fregosi 2.00 .80
361 Don Sutton 6.00 2.40
362 Mike Adamson 1.50 .60
Roger Freed
363 Mike Nagy 1.50 .60
364 Tommy Dean 1.50 .60
365 Bob Johnson 1.50 .60
366 Ron Stone 1.50 .60
367 Dalton Jones 1.50 .60
368 Bob Veale 2.00 .80
369 Checklist 4 10.00 2.00
370 Joe Torre 4.00 1.60
371 Jack Hiatt 1.50 .60
372 Lew Krausse 1.50 .60
373 Tom McCraw 1.50 .60
374 Clete Boyer 2.00 .80
375 Steve Hargan 1.50 .60
376 Clyde Mashore 1.50 .60
Ernie McAnally
377 Greg Garrett 1.50 .60
378 Tito Fuentes 1.50 .60
379 Wayne Granger 1.50 .60
380 Ted Williams MG 12.00 4.80
381 Fred Gladding 1.50 .60
382 Jake Gibbs 1.50 .60
383 Rod Gaspar 1.50 .60
384 Rollie Fingers 6.00 2.40
385 Maury Wills 4.00 1.60
386 Boston Red Sox 2.00 .80
Team Card
387 Ron Herbel 1.50 .60
388 Al Oliver 4.00 1.60
389 Ed Brinkman 1.50 .60
390 Glenn Beckert 1.50 .60
391 Steve Brye 2.00 .80
Cotton Nash
392 Grant Jackson 1.50 .60
393 Merv Rettenmund 2.00 .80
394 Clay Carroll 2.50 1.00
395 Roy White 4.00 1.60
396 Dick Schofield 2.50 1.00
397 Alvin Dark MG 2.50 1.00
398 Howie Reed 2.50 1.00
399 Jim French 2.50 1.00
400 Hank Aaron 60.00 24.00
401 Tom Murphy 2.50 1.00
402 Los Angeles Dodgers 6.00 2.40
Team Card
403 Joe Coleman 2.50 1.00
404 Buddy Harris 2.50 1.00
Roger Metzger
405 Leo Cardenas 2.50 1.00
406 Ray Sadecki 2.50 1.00
407 Joe Rudi 4.00 1.60
408 Rafael Robles 2.50 1.00
409 Don Pavletich 2.50 1.00
410 Ken Holtzman 4.00 1.60
411 George Spriggs 2.50 1.00
412 Jerry Johnson 2.50 1.00
413 Pat Kelly 2.50 1.00
414 Woodie Fryman 2.50 1.00
415 Mike Hegan 2.50 1.00
416 Gene Alley 2.50 1.00
417 Dick Hall 2.50 1.00
418 Adolfo Phillips 2.50 1.00
419 Ron Hansen 2.50 1.00
420 Jim Merritt 2.50 1.00
421 John Stephenson 2.50 1.00
422 Frank Bertaina 2.50 1.00
423 Dennis Saunders 2.50 1.00
Tim Marting
424 Roberto Rodriquez 2.50 1.00
425 Doug Rader 4.00 1.60
426 Chris Cannizzaro 2.50 1.00
427 Bernie Allen 2.50 1.00
428 Jim McAndrew 2.50 1.00
429 Chuck Hinton 2.50 1.00
430 Wes Parker 4.00 1.60
431 Tom Burgmeier 2.50 1.00

432 Bob Didier 2.50 1.00
433 Skip Lockwood 2.50 1.00
434 Gary Sutherland 2.50 1.00
435 Jose Cardenal 4.00 1.60
436 Wilbur Wood 4.00 1.60
437 Danny Murtaugh MG 4.00 1.60
438 Mike McCormick 4.00 1.60
439 Greg Luzinski RC 6.00 2.40
Scott Reid
440 Bert Campaneris 4.00 1.60
441 Milt Pappas 4.00 1.60
442 California Angels 4.00 1.60
Team Card
443 Rich Robertson 2.50 1.00
444 Jimmie Price 2.50 1.00
445 Art Shamsky 2.50 1.00
446 Bobby Bolin 2.50 1.00
447 Cesar Geronimo 4.00 1.60
448 Dave Roberts 2.50 1.00
449 Brant Alyea 2.50 1.00
450 Bob Gibson 15.00 6.00
451 Joe Keough 2.50 1.00
452 John Boccabella 2.50 1.00
453 Terry Crowley 2.50 1.00
454 Mike Paul 2.50 1.00
455 Don Kessinger 4.00 1.60
456 Bob Meyer 2.50 1.00
457 Willie Smith 2.50 1.00
458 Ron Lolich 2.50 1.00
Dave Lemonds
459 Jim Lefebvre 2.50 1.00
460 Fritz Peterson 2.50 1.00
461 Jim Ray Hart 2.50 1.00
462 Washington Senators 6.00 2.40
Team Card
463 Tom Kelley 2.50 1.00
464 Aurelio Rodriguez 2.50 1.00
465 Tim McCarver 6.00 2.40
466 Ken Berry 2.50 1.00
467 Al Santorini 2.50 1.00
468 Frank Fernandez 2.50 1.00
469 Bob Aspromonte 2.50 1.00
470 Bob Oliver 2.50 1.00
471 Tom Griffin 2.50 1.00
472 Ken Rudolph 2.50 1.00
473 Gary Wagner 2.50 1.00
474 Jim Fairey 2.50 1.00
475 Ron Perranoski 2.50 1.00
476 Dal Maxvill 2.50 1.00
477 Earl Weaver MG 6.00 2.40
478 Bernie Carbo 2.50 1.00
479 Dennis Higgins 2.50 1.00
480 Manny Sanguillen 4.00 1.60
481 Daryl Patterson 2.50 1.00
482 San Diego Padres 6.00 2.40
Team Card
483 Gene Michael 2.50 1.00
484 Don Wilson 2.50 1.00
485 Ken McMullen 2.50 1.00
486 Steve Huntz 2.50 1.00
487 Paul Schaal 2.50 1.00
488 Jerry Stephenson 2.50 1.00
489 Luis Alvarado 2.50 1.00
490 Deron Johnson 2.50 1.00
491 Jim Hardin 2.50 1.00
492 Ken Boswell 2.50 1.00
493 Dave May 2.50 1.00
494 Ralph Garr 4.00 1.60
Rick Kester
495 Felipe Alou 4.00 1.60
496 Woody Woodward 2.50 1.00
497 Horacio Pina 2.50 1.00
498 John Kennedy 2.50 1.00
499 Checklist 5 10.00 2.00
500 Jim Perry 4.00 1.60
501 Andy Etchebarren 2.50 1.00
502 Chicago Cubs 6.00 2.40
Team Card
503 Gates Brown 4.00 1.60
504 Ken Wright 2.50 1.00
505 Ollie Brown 2.50 1.00
506 Bobby Knoop 2.50 1.00
507 George Stone 2.50 1.00
508 Roger Repoz 2.50 1.00
509 Jim Grant 2.50 1.00
510 Ken Harrelson 4.00 1.60
511 Chris Short 4.00 1.60
(Pete Rose leading off second)
512 Dick Mills 2.50 1.00
Mike Garman
513 Nolan Ryan 150.00 60.00
514 Ron Woods 2.50 1.00
515 Carl Morton 2.50 1.00
516 Ted Kubiak 2.50 1.00
517 Charlie Fox MG 2.50 1.00
518 Joe Grzenda 2.50 1.00
519 Willie Crawford 2.50 1.00
520 Tommy John 6.00 2.40
521 Leron Lee 2.50 1.00
522 Minnesota Twins 6.00 2.40
Team Card
523 John Odom 2.50 1.00
524 Mickey Stanley 6.00 2.40
525 Ernie Banks 50.00 20.00
526 Ray Jarvis 4.00 1.60
527 Cleon Jones 6.00 2.40
528 Wally Bunker 4.00 1.60
529 Enzo Hernandez 6.00 2.40
Bill Buckner
Marty Perez
530 Carl Yastrzemski 30.00 12.00
531 Mike Torrez 4.00 1.60
532 Bill Rigney MG 4.00 1.60
533 Mike Ryan 4.00 1.60
534 Luke Walker 4.00 1.60
535 Curt Flood 6.00 2.40
536 Claude Raymond 4.00 1.60
537 Tom Egan 4.00 1.60
538 Angel Bravo 4.00 1.60
539 Larry Brown 4.00 1.60
540 Larry Dierker 6.00 2.40
541 Bob Burda 4.00 1.60
542 Bob Miller 4.00 1.60
543 New York Yankees 10.00 4.00
Team Card
544 Vida Blue 6.00 2.40
545 Dick Dietz 4.00 1.60
546 John Matias 4.00 1.60
547 Pat Dobson 6.00 2.40
548 Don Mason 4.00 1.60
549 Jim Brewer 6.00 2.40
550 Harmon Killebrew 25.00 10.00
551 Frank Linzy 4.00 1.60
552 Buddy Bradford 4.00 1.60
553 Kevin Collins 4.00 1.60
554 Lowell Palmer 4.00 1.60
555 Walt Williams 4.00 1.60
556 Jim McGlothlin 4.00 1.60
557 Tom Satriano 4.00 1.60
558 Hector Torres 4.00 1.60
559 Terry Cox 4.00 1.60
Bill Gogolewski
Gary Jones
560 Rusty Staub 6.00 2.40
561 Syd O'Brien 4.00 1.60
562 Dave Giusti 4.00 1.60
563 San Francisco Giants 8.00 3.20
Team Card
564 Al Fitzmorris 4.00 1.60
565 Jim Wynn 6.00 2.40
566 Tim Cullen 4.00 1.60
567 Walt Alston MG 8.00 3.20
568 Sal Campisi 4.00 1.60
569 Ivan Murrell 4.00 1.60
570 Jim Palmer 30.00 12.00
571 Ted Sizemore 4.00 1.60
572 Jerry Kenney 4.00 1.60
573 Ed Kranepool 6.00 2.40
574 Jim Bunning 8.00 3.20
575 Bill Freehan 6.00 2.40
576 Adrian Garrett 4.00 1.60
Brock Davis
Garry Jestadt
577 Jim Lonborg 6.00 2.40
578 Ron Hunt 4.00 1.60
579 Marty Pattin 4.00 1.60
580 Tony Perez 20.00 8.00
581 Roger Nelson 4.00 1.60
582 Dave Cash 6.00 2.40
583 Ron Cook 4.00 1.60
584 Cleveland Indians 8.00 3.20
Team Card
585 Willie Davis 6.00 2.40
586 Dick Woodson 4.00 1.60
587 Sonny Jackson 4.00 1.60
588 Tom Bradley 4.00 1.60
589 Bob Barton 4.00 1.60
590 Alex Johnson 6.00 2.40
591 Jackie Brown 4.00 1.60
592 Randy Hundley 6.00 2.40
593 Jack Aker 4.00 1.60
594 Bob Chlupsa 6.00 2.40
Bob Stinson
Al Hrabosky RC
595 Dave Johnson 6.00 2.40
596 Mike Jorgensen 4.00 1.60
597 Ken Suarez 4.00 1.60
598 Rick Wise 6.00 2.40
599 Norm Cash 6.00 2.40
600 Willie Mays 100.00 40.00
601 Ken Tatum 4.00 1.60
602 Marty Martinez 4.00 1.60
603 Pittsburgh Pirates 8.00 3.20
Team Card
604 John Gelnar 4.00 1.60
605 Orlando Cepeda 8.00 3.20
606 Chuck Taylor 4.00 1.60
607 Paul Ratliff 4.00 1.60
608 Mike Wegener 4.00 1.60
609 Leo Durocher MG 8.00 3.20
610 Amos Otis 6.00 2.40
611 Tom Phoebus 4.00 1.60
612 Lou Camilli 4.00 1.60
Ted Ford
Steve Mingori
613 Pedro Borbon 4.00 1.60
614 Billy Cowan 4.00 1.60
615 Mel Stottlemyre 6.00 2.40
616 Larry Hisle 6.00 2.40
617 Clay Dalrymple 4.00 1.60
618 Tug McGraw 6.00 2.40
619A Checklist 6 ERR 10.00 2.00
(No copyright)
619B Checklist 6 COR 6.00 1.20
(Copyright on back)
620 Frank Howard 6.00 2.40
621 Ron Bryant 4.00 1.60
622 Joe Lahoud 4.00 1.60
623 Pat Jarvis 4.00 1.60
624 Oakland Athletics 8.00 3.20
Team Card
625 Lou Brock 30.00 12.00
626 Freddie Patek 6.00 2.40
627 Steve Hamilton 4.00 1.60
628 John Bateman 4.00 1.60
629 John Hiller 6.00 2.40
630 Roberto Clemente 150.00 60.00
631 Eddie Fisher 4.00 1.60
632 Darrel Chaney 4.00 1.60
633 Bobby Brooks 4.00 1.60
Pete Koegel
Scott Northey
634 Phil Regan 4.00 1.60
635 Bobby Murcer 6.00 2.40
636 Denny Lemaster 4.00 1.60
637 Dave Bristol MG 4.00 1.60
638 Stan Williams 4.00 1.60
639 Tom Haller 4.00 1.60
640 Frank Robinson 40.00 16.00
641 New York Mets 15.00 6.00
Team Card
642 Jim Roland 4.00 1.60
643 Rick Reichardt 4.00 1.60
644 Jim Stewart SP 12.00 4.80
645 Jim Maloney SP 15.00 6.00
646 Bobby Floyd SP 12.00 4.80
647 Juan Pizarro 8.00 3.20
648 Rich Folkers 25.00 10.00
Ted Martinez
John Matlack RC SP
649 Sparky Lyle SP 15.00 6.00
650 Rich Allen SP 30.00 12.00
651 Jerry Robertson SP 12.00 4.80
652 Atlanta Braves 12.00 4.80
Team Card
653 Russ Snyder SP 12.00 4.80
654 Don Shaw SP 12.00 4.80
655 Mike Epstein SP 12.00 4.80
656 Gerry Nyman SP 12.00 4.80
657 Jose Azcue 8.00 3.20
658 Paul Lindblad SP 12.00 4.80
659 Byron Browne SP 12.00 4.80
660 Ray Culp 8.00 3.20
661 Chuck Tanner MG SP 15.00 6.00
662 Mike Hedlund SP 12.00 4.80
663 Marv Staehle 8.00 3.20
664 Archie Reynolds 12.00 4.80
Bob Reynolds
Ken Reynolds SP
665 Ron Swoboda SP 15.00 6.00
666 Gene Brabender SP 12.00 4.80
667 Pete Ward 8.00 3.20
668 Gary Neibauer 8.00 3.20
669 Ike Brown SP 12.00 4.80
670 Bill Hands 8.00 3.20
671 Bill Voss SP 12.00 4.80
672 Ed Crosby SP 12.00 4.80
673 Gerry Janeski SP 12.00 4.80
674 Montreal Expos 12.00 4.80
Team Card
675 Dave Boswell 8.00 3.20
676 Tommie Reynolds 8.00 3.20
677 Jack DiLauro SP 12.00 4.80
678 George Thomas 8.00 3.20
679 Don O'Riley 8.00 3.20
680 Don Mincher SP 12.00 4.80
681 Bill Butler 8.00 3.20
682 Terry Harmon 8.00 3.20
683 Bill Burbach SP 12.00 4.80
684 Curt Motton 8.00 3.20
685 Moe Drabowsky 8.00 3.20
686 Chico Ruiz SP 12.00 4.80
687 Ron Taylor SP 12.00 4.80
688 S.Anderson MG SP 30.00 12.00
689 Frank Baker 8.00 3.20
690 Bob Moose 8.00 3.20
691 Bobby Heise 8.00 3.20
692 Hal Haydel 12.00 4.80
Rogelio Moret
Wayne Twitchell SP
693 Jose Pena SP 12.00 4.80
694 Rick Renick SP 12.00 4.80
695 Joe Niekro 12.00 4.80
696 Jerry Morales 8.00 3.20
697 Rickey Clark SP 12.00 4.80
698 M. Brewers SP 20.00 8.00
Team Card
699 Jim Britton 8.00 3.20
700 Boog Powell SP 25.00 10.00
701 Bob Garibaldi 8.00 3.20
702 Milt Ramirez 8.00 3.20
703 Mike Kekich 8.00 3.20
704 J.C. Martin SP 12.00 4.80
705 Dick Selma SP 12.00 4.80
706 Joe Foy SP 12.00 4.80
707 Fred Lasher 8.00 3.20
708 Russ Nagelson SP 12.00 4.80
709 Dusty Baker RC 80.00 32.00
Don Baylor RC
Tom Paciorek RC SP
710 Sonny Siebert 8.00 3.20
711 Larry Stahl SP 12.00 4.80
712 Jose Martinez 8.00 3.20
713 Mike Marshall SP 15.00 6.00
714 Dick Williams MG SP 15.00 6.00
715 Horace Clarke SP 15.00 6.00
716 Dave Leonhard 8.00 3.20
717 Tommie Aaron SP 12.00 4.80
718 Billy Wynne 8.00 3.20
719 Jerry May SP 12.00 4.80
720 Matty Alou 12.00 4.80
721 John Morris 8.00 3.20
722 Houston Astros SP 20.00 8.00
Team Card
723 Vicente Romo SP 12.00 4.80
724 Tom Tischinski SP 12.00 4.80
725 Gary Gentry SP 12.00 4.80
726 Paul Popovich 8.00 3.20
727 Ray Lamb SP 12.00 4.80
728 Wayne Redmond 8.00 3.20
Keith Lampard
Bernie Williams
729 Dick Billings 8.00 3.20
730 Jim Rooker 8.00 3.20
731 Jim Qualls SP 12.00 4.80
732 Bob Reed 8.00 3.20
733 Lee Maye SP 12.00 4.80
734 Rob Gardner SP 12.00 4.80
735 Mike Shannon SP 15.00 6.00
736 Mel Queen SP 12.00 4.80
737 P.Gomez SP MG 12.00 4.80
738 Russ Gibson SP 12.00 4.80
739 Barry Lersch SP 12.00 4.80
740 Luis Aparicio SP UER 30.00 12.00
(Led AL in steals
from 1965 to 1964,
should be 1956 to 1964)
741 Skip Guinn 8.00 3.20
742 Kansas City Royals 12.00 4.80
Team Card
743 John O'Donoghue SP 12.00 4.80
744 Chuck Manuel SP 12.00 4.80
745 Sandy Alomar SP 12.00 4.80
746 Andy Kosco 8.00 3.20
747 Al Severinsen 8.00 3.20
Scipio Spinks
Balor Moore
748 John Purdin SP 12.00 4.80
749 Ken Sztotkiewicz 8.00 3.20
750 Denny McLain SP 25.00 10.00
751 Al Weis SP 15.00 6.00
752 Dick Drago 12.00 2.90

1971 Topps Coins Inserts

This full-color set of 153 coins, which were inserted into packs, contains the photo of the player surrounded by a colored band, which contains the player's name, his team, his position and several stars. The backs contain the coin number, short biographical data and the line "Collect the entire set of 153 coins." The set was evidently produced in three groups of 51 as coins 1-51 have brass backs, coins 52-102 have chrome backs and coins 103-153 have blue backs. In fact it has been verified that the coins were printed in three sheets of 51 coins comprised of three rows of 17 coins. Each coin measures approximately 1 1/2" in diameter.

NM Ex
COMPLETE SET (153) 350.00 140.00
1 Clarence Gaston 1.50 .60
2 Dave Johnson 1.50 .60
3 Jim Bunning 2.50 1.00
4 Jim Spencer 1.00 .40
5 Felix Millan 1.00 .40
6 Gerry Moses 1.00 .40
7 Ferguson Jenkins 2.50 1.00
8 Felipe Alou 1.50 .60
9 Jim McGlothlin 1.00 .40
10 Dick McAuliffe 1.00 .40
11 Joe Torre 2.50 1.00
12 Jim Perry 1.50 .60
13 Bobby Bonds 2.50 1.00
14 Danny Cater 1.00 .40
15 Bill Mazeroski 2.50 1.00
16 Luis Aparicio 2.50 1.00
17 Doug Rader 1.00 .40
18 Vada Pinson 2.50 1.00
19 John Bateman 1.00 .40
20 Lew Krausse 1.00 .40
21 Billy Grabarkewitz 1.00 .40
22 Frank Howard 2.50 1.00
23 Jerry Koosman 2.50 1.00
24 Rod Carew 4.00 1.60
25 Al Ferrara 1.00 .40
26 Dave McNally 1.50 .60
27 Jim Hickman 1.00 .40
28 Sandy Alomar 1.50 .60
29 Lee May 1.50 .60
30 Rico Petrocelli 1.50 .60
31 Don Money 1.00 .40
32 Jim Rooker 1.00 .40
33 Dick Dietz 1.00 .40
34 Roy White 1.50 .60
35 Carl Morton 1.00 .40
36 Walt Williams 1.00 .40
37 Phil Niekro 1.50 .60
38 Bill Freehan 1.50 .60
39 Julian Javier 1.00 .40
40 Rick Monday 1.50 .60
41 Don Wilson 1.00 .40
42 Ray Fosse 1.50 .60
43 Art Shamsky 1.00 .40
44 Ted Savage 1.00 .40
45 Claude Osteen 1.50 .60
46 Ed Brinkman 1.00 .40
47 Matty Alou 1.50 .60
48 Bob Oliver 1.00 .40
49 Danny Coombs 1.00 .40
50 Frank Robinson 4.00 1.60
51 Randy Hundley 1.00 .40
52 Cesar Tovar 1.50 .60
53 Wayne Simpson 1.00 .40
54 Bobby Murcer 2.50 1.00
55 Carl Taylor 1.00 .40
56 Tommy John 1.50 .60
57 Willie McCovey 4.00 1.60
58 Carl Yastrzemski 10.00 4.00
59 Bob Bailey 1.00 .40
60 Clyde Wright 1.00 .40
61 Orlando Cepeda 2.50 1.00
62 Al Kaline 8.00 3.20
63 Bob Gibson 4.00 1.60
64 Bert Campaneris 1.50 .60
65 Ted Sizemore 1.00 .40
66 Duke Sims 1.00 .40
67 Bud Harrelson 1.00 .40
68 Gerald McNertney 1.00 .40
69 Jim Wynn 1.50 .60
70 Dick Bosman 1.00 .40
71 Roberto Clemente 25.00 10.00
72 Rich Reese 1.00 .40
73 Gaylord Perry 2.50 1.00
74 Boog Powell 2.50 1.00
75 Billy Williams 2.50 1.00
76 Bill Melton 1.00 .40
77 Nate Colbert 1.00 .40
78 Reggie Smith 1.50 .60
79 Deron Johnson 1.00 .40
80 Jim Hunter 2.50 1.00
81 Bobby Tolan 1.50 .60
82 Jim Northrup 1.50 .60
83 Ron Fairly 1.50 .60
84 Alex Johnson 1.50 .60
85 Pat Jarvis 1.00 .40
86 Sam McDowell 1.50 .60
87 Lou Brock 4.00 1.60
88 Danny Walton 1.00 .40
89 Denis Menke 1.00 .40
90 Jim Palmer 2.50 1.00
91 Tommy Agee 1.50 .60
92 Duane Josephson 1.00 .40
93 Willie Davis 1.50 .60
94 Mel Stottlemyre 1.50 .60
95 Ron Santo 2.50 1.00
96 Amos Otis 1.50 .60
97 Ken Henderson 1.00 .40
98 George Scott 1.50 .60
99 Dock Ellis 1.50 .60
100 Harmon Killebrew 8.00 3.20
101 Pete Rose 15.00 6.00
102 Rick Reichardt 1.00 .40
103 Cleon Jones 1.00 .40
104 Ron Perranoski 1.00 .40
105 Tony Perez 2.50 1.00
106 Mickey Lolich 1.50 .60
107 Tim McCarver 2.50 1.00
108 Reggie Jackson 12.00 4.80
109 Chris Cannizzaro 1.00 .40
110 Steve Hargan 1.00 .40
111 Rusty Staub 1.50 .60
112 Andy Messersmith 1.50 .60
113 Rico Carty 1.50 .60
114 Brooks Robinson 8.00 3.20
115 Steve Carlton 4.00 1.60
116 Mike Hegan 1.00 .40
117 Joe Morgan 2.50 1.00
118 Thurman Munson 10.00 4.00
119 Don Kessinger 1.00 .40
120 Joel Horlen 1.00 .40
121 Wes Parker 1.50 .60
122 Sonny Siebert 1.00 .40
123 Willie Stargell 4.00 1.60
124 Ellie Rodriguez 1.00 .40
125 Juan Marichal 2.50 1.00
126 Mike Epstein 1.00 .40
127 Tom Seaver 10.00 4.80
128 Tony Oliva 2.50 1.00
129 Jim Merritt 1.00 .40
130 Willie Horton 1.50 .60
131 Rick Wise 1.50 .60
132 Sal Bando 1.50 .60
133 Ollie Brown 1.00 .40
134 Ken Harrelson 1.50 .60
135 Mack Jones 1.00 .40
136 Jim Fregosi 1.50 .60
137 Hank Aaron 15.00 6.00
138 Fritz Peterson 1.00 .40
139 Joe Hague 1.00 .40
140 Tommy Harper 1.00 .40
141 Larry Dierker 1.50 .60
142 Tony Conigliaro 2.50 1.00
143 Glenn Beckert 1.00 .40
144 Carlos May 1.00 .40
145 Don Sutton 1.50 .60
146 Paul Casanova 1.00 .40
147 Bob Moose 1.00 .40
148 Chico Cardenas 1.00 .40
149 Johnny Bench 12.00 4.80
150 Mike Cuellar 1.50 .60
151 Donn Clendenon 1.00 .40
152 Lou Piniella 2.50 1.00
153 Willie Mays 20.00 8.00

1971 Topps Scratchoffs

These pack inserts featured the same players are the 1970 Topps Scratchoffs. However, the only difference is that the center of the game is red rather than black.

NM Ex
COMPLETE SET (24) 40.00 16.00
1 Hank Aaron 8.00 3.20
2 Rich Allen 1.50 .60
3 Luis Aparicio 4.00 1.60
4 Sal Bando 1.00 .40
5 Glenn Beckert 1.00 .40
6 Dick Bosman 1.00 .40
7 Nate Colbert 1.00 .40
8 Mike Hegan 1.00 .40
9 Mack Jones 1.00 .40
10 Al Kaline 5.00 2.00
11 Harmon Killebrew 5.00 2.00
12 Juan Marichal 4.00 1.60
13 Tim McCarver 2.00 .80
14 Sam McDowell 1.25 .50
15 Claude Osteen 1.00 .40
16 Tony Perez 3.00 1.20
17 Lou Piniella 1.50 .60
18 Boog Powell 1.50 .60
19 Tom Seaver 6.00 2.40
20 Jim Spencer 1.00 .40
21 Willie Stargell 5.00 2.00
22 Mel Stottlemyre 1.25 .50
23 Jim Wynn 1.25 .50
24 Carl Yastrzemski 5.00 2.00

1971 Topps Greatest Moments

The cards in this 55-card set measure 2 1/2" by 4 3/4". The 1971 Topps Greatest Moments set contains numbered cards depicting specific career highlights of current players. The obverses are black bordered and contain a small cameo picture of the left side; a deckle-bordered black and white action photo dominates the rest of the card. The backs are designed in newspaper style. Sometimes found in uncut sheets, this test set was retailed in gum packs on a very limited basis. Double prints (DP) are listed in the checklist below; there were 22 double prints and 33 single prints.

NM Ex
COMPLETE SET (55) 1500.00 600.00
COMMON CARD (1-55) 20.00 8.00
COMMON DP 8.00 3.20
1 Thurman Munson DP 40.00 16.00
2 Hoyt Wilhelm 25.00 10.00
3 Rico Carty 20.00 8.00
4 Carl Morton DP 8.00 3.20
5 Sal Bando DP 10.00 4.00
6 Bert Campaneris DP 10.00 4.00
7 Jim Kaat 25.00 10.00
8 Harmon Killebrew 80.00 32.00
9 Brooks Robinson 80.00 32.00
10 Jim Perry 20.00 8.00
11 Tony Oliva 30.00 12.00
12 Vada Pinson 25.00 10.00
13 Johnny Bench 125.00 50.00
14 Tony Perez 30.00 12.00
15 Pete Rose DP 80.00 32.00
16 Jim Fregosi DP 10.00 4.00
17 Alex Johnson DP 8.00 3.20
18 Clyde Wright DP 8.00 3.20
19 Al Kaline DP 40.00 16.00
20 Denny McLain 30.00 12.00
21 Jim Northrup 20.00 8.00
22 Bill Freehan 20.00 8.00
23 Mickey Lolich 25.00 10.00
24 Bob Gibson DP 30.00 12.00
25 Tim McCarver DP 8.00 3.20
26 Orlando Cepeda DP 20.00 8.00
27 Lou Brock DP 30.00 12.00
28 Nate Colbert DP 8.00 3.20
29 Maury Wills 30.00 12.00
30 Wes Parker 20.00 8.00

31 Jim Wynn 25.00 10.00
32 Larry Dierker 25.00 10.00
33 Bill Melton 20.00 8.00
34 Joe Morgan 30.00 12.00
35 Rusty Staub 25.00 10.00
36 Ernie Banks DP 40.00 16.00
37 Billy Williams 30.00 12.00
38 Lou Piniella 25.00 10.00
39 Rico Petrocelli DP 10.00 4.00
40 Carl Yastrzemski DP 50.00 20.00
41 Willie Mays DP 100.00 40.00
42 Tommy Harper 20.00 8.00
43 Jim Bunning DP 10.00 4.00
44 Fritz Peterson 25.00 10.00
45 Roy White 25.00 10.00
46 Bobby Murcer 30.00 12.00
47 Reggie Jackson 200.00 80.00
48 Frank Howard 25.00 10.00
49 Dick Bosman 20.00 8.00
50 Sam McDowell DP 10.00 4.00
51 Luis Aparicio DP 10.00 4.00
52 Willie McCovey DP 30.00 12.00
53 Joe Pepitone 25.00 10.00
54 Jerry Grote 25.00 10.00
55 Bud Harrelson 20.00 8.00

1971 Topps Super

The cards in this 63-card set measure 3 1/8" by 5 1/4". The obverse format of the Topps Super set of 1971 is identical to that of the 1970 set, that is, a borderless color photograph with a facsimile autograph printed on it. The backs are enlargements of the respective player's cards of the 1971 regular baseball issue. There are no reported scarcities in the set. Just as in 1970, this set was issued in three-card wax packs.

NM Ex
COMPLETE SET (63) 250.00 100.00
WRAPPER (10-CENT)
1 Reggie Smith 2.00 .80
2 Gaylord Perry 4.00 1.60
3 Ted Savage 1.50 .60
4 Donn Clendenon 1.50 .60
5 Boog Powell 2.50 1.00
6 Tony Perez 4.00 1.60
7 Dick Bosman 1.50 .60
8 Alex Johnson 1.50 .60
9 Rusty Staub 2.50 1.00
10 Mel Stottlemyre 2.50 1.00
11 Tony Oliva 2.50 1.00
12 Bill Freehan 2.00 .80
13 Fritz Peterson 1.50 .60
14 Wes Parker 2.00 .80
15 Cesar Cedeno 2.00 .80
16 Sam McDowell 2.00 .80
17 Frank Howard 2.00 .80
18 Dave McNally 2.00 .80
19 Rico Petrocelli 2.00 .80
20 Pete Rose 25.00 10.00
21 Luke Walker 1.50 .60
22 Nate Colbert 1.50 .60
23 Luis Aparicio 4.00 1.60
24 Jim Perry 2.00 .80
25 Lou Brock 5.00 2.00
26 Roy White 2.00 .80
27 Claude Osteen 1.50 .60
28 Carl Morton 1.50 .60
29 Rico Carty 2.00 .80
30 Larry Dierker 1.50 .60
31 Bert Campaneris 2.00 .80
32 Johnny Bench 15.00 6.00
33 Felix Millan 1.50 .60
34 Tim McCarver 2.50 1.00
35 Ron Santo 2.50 1.00
36 Tommie Agee 2.00 .80
37 Roberto Clemente 30.00 12.00
38 Reggie Jackson 15.00 6.00
39 Clyde Wright 1.50 .60
40 Rich Allen 2.50 1.00
41 Curt Flood 2.00 .80
42 Ferguson Jenkins 4.00 1.60
43 Willie Stargell 4.00 1.60
44 Hank Aaron 15.00 6.00
45 Amos Otis 2.00 .80
46 Willie McCovey 5.00 2.00
47 Bill Melton 1.50 .60
48 Bob Gibson 5.00 2.00
49 Carl Yastrzemski 10.00 4.00
50 Glenn Beckert 1.50 .60
51 Ray Fosse 1.50 .60
52 Cito Gaston 2.00 .80
53 Tom Seaver 10.00 4.00
54 Al Kaline 8.00 3.20
55 Jim Northrup 2.00 .80
56 Willie Mays 18.00 7.25
57 Sal Bando 2.00 .80
58 Deron Johnson 1.50 .60
59 Brooks Robinson 8.00 3.20
60 Harmon Killebrew 5.00 2.00
61 Joe Torre 4.00 1.60
62 Lou Piniella 2.50 1.00
63 Tommy Harper 1.50 .60

1972 Topps

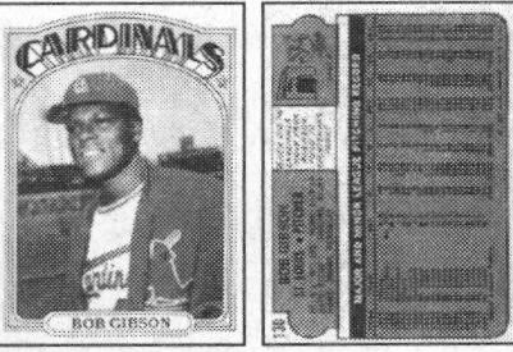

The cards in this 787-card set measure 2 1/2" by 3 1/2". The 1972 Topps set contained the most cards ever for a Topps set to that point in time. Features appearing for the first time were "Boyhood Photos" (341-348/491-498), Awards and Trophy cards (621-626), "In Action" (distributed throughout the set), and "Traded Cards" (751-757). Other subsets included League Leaders (85-96), Playoffs cards (221-222), and World Series cards (223-230). The curved lines of the color picture are a departure from the rectangular designs of other years. There is a series of intermediate scarcity (526-656) and the usual high numbers (657-787). The backs of cards 692, 694, 696, 700, 706 and 710 form a picture back of Tom Seaver. The backs of cards 698, 702, 704, 708, 712, 714 form a picture back of Tony Oliva. As in previous years, cards were issued in a variety of ways including ten-card wax packs which cost a dime and 28 card cello packs which cost a quarter. The 10 cents wax packs were issued 24 packs to a box while the cello packs were also issued 24 packs to a box. Rookie Cards in this set include Ron Cey and Carlton Fisk.

NM Ex
COMPLETE SET (787) 1500.00 700.00
COMMON CARD (1-132) .60 .24
COMMON (133-263) 1.00 .40
COMMON (264-394) 1.25 .50
COMMON (395-525) 1.50 .60
COMMON (526-656) 4.00 1.60
COMMON (657-787) 12.00 4.80
WRAPPER (10-CENT) 15.00 6.00
1 Pittsburgh Pirates 8.00 2.90
Team Card
2 Ray Culp .60 .24
3 Bob Tolan .60 .24
4 Checklist 1-132 6.00 1.20
5 John Bateman .60 .24
6 Fred Scherman .60 .24
7 Enzo Hernandez .60 .24
8 Ron Swoboda 1.25 .50
9 Stan Williams .60 .24
10 Amos Otis 1.25 .50
11 Bobby Valentine 1.25 .50
12 Jose Cardenal .60 .24
13 Joe Grzenda .60 .24
14 Pete Koegel .60 .24
Mike Anderson
Wayne Twitchell
15 Walt Williams .60 .24
16 Mike Jorgensen .60 .24
17 Dave Duncan 1.25 .50
18A Juan Pizarro .60 .24
(Yellow underline
C and S of Cubs)
18B Juan Pizarro 5.00 2.00
(Green underline
C and S of Cubs)
19 Billy Cowan .60 .24
20 Don Wilson .60 .24
21 Atlanta Braves 1.50 .60
Team Card
22 Rob Gardner .60 .24
23 Ted Kubiak .60 .24
24 Ted Ford .60 .24
25 Bill Singer .60 .24
26 Andy Etchebarren .60 .24
27 Bob Johnson .60 .24
28 Bob Gebhard .60 .24
Steve Brye
Hal Haydel
29A Bill Bonham .60 .24
(Yellow underline
C and S of Cubs)
29B Bill Bonham 5.00 2.00
(Green underline
C and S of Cubs)
30 Rico Petrocelli 1.25 .50
31 Cleon Jones 1.25 .50
32 Cleon Jones IA .60 .24
33 Billy Martin MG 4.00 1.60
34 Billy Martin IA 2.50 1.00
35 Jerry Johnson .60 .24
36 Jerry Johnson IA .60 .24
37 Carl Yastrzemski 10.00 4.00
38 Carl Yastrzemski IA 8.00 2.40
39 Bob Barton .60 .24
40 Bob Barton IA .60 .24
41 Tommy Davis 1.25 .50
42 Tommy Davis IA .60 .24
43 Rick Wise 1.25 .50
44 Rick Wise IA .60 .24
45A Glenn Beckert 1.25 .50
(Yellow underline
C and S of Cubs)
45B Glenn Beckert 5.00 2.00
(Green underline
C and S of Cubs)
46 Glenn Beckert IA .60 .24
47 John Ellis .60 .24
48 John Ellis IA .60 .24
49 Willie Mays 40.00 16.00
50 Willie Mays IA 20.00 8.00
51 Harmon Killebrew 8.00 3.20
52 Harmon Killebrew IA 4.00 1.60
53 Bud Harrelson 1.25 .50
54 Bud Harrelson IA .60 .24
55 Clyde Wright .60 .24
56 Rich Chiles .60 .24
57 Bob Oliver .60 .24
58 Ernie McAnally .60 .24
59 Fred Stanley .60 .24
60 Manny Sanguillen 1.25 .50
61 Burt Hooton RC 1.25 .50
Gene Hiser
Earl Stephenson
62 Angel Mangual .60 .24
63 Duke Sims .60 .24
64 Pete Broberg .60 .24
65 Cesar Cedeno 1.25 .50
66 Ray Corbin .60 .24
67 Red Schoendienst MG 2.50 1.00
68 Jim York .60 .24
69 Roger Freed .60 .24
70 Mike Cuellar 1.25 .50
71 California Angels 1.50 .60
Team Card
72 Bruce Kison RC .60 .24
73 Steve Huntz .60 .24
74 Cecil Upshaw .60 .24
75 Bert Campaneris 1.25 .50
76 Don Carrithers .60 .24
77 Ron Theobald .60 .24
78 Steve Arlin .60 .24
79 Mike Garman 50.00 20.00
Cecil Cooper RC
Carlton Fisk RC
80 Tony Perez 4.00 1.60
81 Mike Hedlund .60 .24
82 Ron Woods .60 .24
83 Dalton Jones .60 .24
84 Vince Colbert .60 .24
85 Joe Torre 2.50 1.00
Ralph Garr
Glenn Beckert LL
86 Tony Oliva 2.50 1.00
Bobby Murcer
Merv Rettenmund LL
87 Joe Torre 4.00 1.60
Willie Stargell
Hank Aaron LL
88 Harmon Killebrew 4.00 1.60
Frank Robinson
Reggie Smith LL
89 Willie Stargell 2.50 1.00
Hank Aaron
Lee May LL
90 Bill Melton 2.50 1.00
Norm Cash
Reggie Jackson LL
91 Tom Seaver 2.50 1.00
Dave Roberts UER
(Photo actually
Danny Coombs)
Don Wilson LL
92 Vida Blue 2.50 1.00
Wilbur Wood
Jim Palmer LL
93 Fergie Jenkins 4.00 1.60
Steve Carlton
Al Downing
Tom Seaver LL
94 Mickey Lolich 2.50 1.00
Vida Blue
Wilbur Wood LL
95 Tom Seaver 4.00 1.60
Fergie Jenkins
Bill Stoneman LL
96 Mickey Lolich 2.50 1.00
Vida Blue
Joe Coleman LL
97 Tom Kelley .60 .24
98 Chuck Tanner MG 1.25 .50
99 Ross Grimsley .60 .24
100 Frank Robinson 8.00 3.20
101 Bill Greif 2.50 1.00
J.R. Richard RC
Ray Busse
102 Lloyd Allen .60 .24
103 Checklist 133-263 6.00 1.20
104 Toby Harrah RC 1.25 .50
105 Gary Gentry .60 .24
106 Milwaukee Brewers 1.50 .60
Team Card
107 Jose Cruz RC 1.25 .50
108 Gary Waslewski .60 .24
109 Jerry May .60 .24
110 Ron Hunt .60 .24
111 Jim Grant .60 .24
112 Greg Luzinski 1.25 .50
113 Rogelio Moret .60 .24
114 Bill Buckner 1.25 .50
115 Jim Fregosi 1.25 .50
116 Ed Farmer .60 .24
117A Cleo James .60 .24
(Yellow underline
C and S of Cubs)
117B Cleo James 5.00 2.00
(Green underline
C and S of Cubs)
118 Skip Lockwood .60 .24
119 Marty Perez .60 .24
120 Bill Freehan 1.25 .50
121 Ed Sprague .60 .24
122 Larry Biittner .60 .24
123 Ed Acosta .60 .24
124 Alan Closter .60 .24
Rusty Torres
Roger Hambright
125 Dave Cash 1.25 .50
126 Bart Johnson .60 .24
127 Duffy Dyer .60 .24
128 Eddie Watt .60 .24
129 Charlie Fox MG .60 .24
130 Bob Gibson 8.00 3.20
131 Jim Nettles .60 .24
132 Joe Morgan 6.00 2.40
133 Joe Keough 1.00 .40
134 Carl Morton 1.00 .40
135 Vada Pinson 2.00 .80
136 Darrel Chaney 1.00 .40
137 Dick Williams MG 2.00 .80
138 Mike Kekich 1.00 .40
139 Tim McCarver 2.00 .80
140 Pat Dobson 2.00 .80
141 Buzz Capra 2.00 .80
Lee Stanton
Jon Matlack
142 Chris Chambliss RC 4.00 1.60
143 Garry Jestadt 1.00 .40
144 Marty Pattin 1.00 .40
145 Don Kessinger 2.00 .80
146 Steve Kealey 1.00 .40
147 Dave Kingman RC 6.00 2.40
148 Dick Billings 1.00 .40
149 Gary Neibauer 1.00 .40
150 Norm Cash 2.00 .80
151 Jim Brewer 1.00 .40
152 Gene Clines 1.00 .40
153 Rick Auerbach 1.00 .40
154 Ted Simmons 4.00 1.60
155 Larry Dierker 1.00 .40
156 Minnesota Twins 2.00 .80
Team Card
157 Don Gullett 1.00 .40
158 Jerry Kenney 1.00 .40
159 John Boccabella 1.00 .40
160 Andy Messersmith 2.00 .80
161 Brock Davis 1.00 .40
162 Jerry Bell 2.00 .80
Darrell Porter RC
Bob Reynolds UER
(Porter and Bell
photos switched)
163 Tug McGraw 4.00 1.60
164 Tug McGraw IA 2.00 .80
165 Chris Speier RC 2.00 .80
166 Chris Speier IA 1.00 .40
167 Deron Johnson 1.00 .40
168 Deron Johnson IA 1.00 .40
169 Vida Blue 4.00 1.60
170 Vida Blue IA 2.00 .80
171 Darrell Evans 4.00 1.60
172 Darrell Evans IA 2.00 .80
173 Clay Kirby 1.00 .40
174 Clay Kirby IA 1.00 .40
175 Tom Haller 1.00 .40
176 Tom Haller IA 1.00 .40
177 Paul Schaal 1.00 .40
178 Paul Schaal IA 1.00 .40
179 Dock Ellis 1.00 .40
180 Dock Ellis IA 1.00 .40
181 Ed Kranepool 2.00 .80
182 Ed Kranepool IA 1.00 .40
183 Bill Melton 1.00 .40
184 Bill Melton IA 1.00 .40
185 Ron Bryant 1.00 .40
186 Ron Bryant IA 1.00 .40
187 Gates Brown 1.00 .40
188 Frank Lucchesi MG 1.00 .40
189 Gene Tenace 2.00 .80
190 Dave Giusti 1.00 .40
191 Jeff Burroughs RC 4.00 1.60
192 Chicago Cubs 2.00 .80
Team Card
193 Kurt Bevacqua 1.00 .40
194 Fred Norman 1.00 .40
195 Orlando Cepeda 6.00 2.40
196 Mel Queen 1.00 .40
197 Johnny Briggs 1.00 .40
198 Charlie Hough RC 6.00 2.40
Bob O'Brien
Mike Strahler
199 Mike Fiore 1.00 .40
200 Lou Brock 8.00 3.20
201 Phil Roof 1.00 .40
202 Scipio Spinks 1.00 .40
203 Ron Blomberg 1.00 .40
204 Tommy Helms 1.00 .40
205 Dick Drago 1.00 .40
206 Dal Maxvill 1.00 .40
207 Tom Egan 1.00 .40
208 Milt Pappas 2.00 .80
209 Joe Rudi 2.00 .80
210 Denny McLain 2.00 .80
211 Gary Sutherland 1.00 .40
212 Grant Jackson 1.00 .40
213 Billy Parker 1.00 .40
Art Kusnyer
Tom Silverio
214 Mike McQueen 1.00 .40
215 Alex Johnson 2.00 .80
216 Joe Niekro 2.00 .80
217 Roger Metzger 1.00 .40
218 Eddie Kasko MG 1.00 .40
219 Rennie Stennett 2.00 .80
220 Jim Perry 2.00 .80
221 NL Playoffs 2.00 .80
Bucs champs
222 Br. Robinson ALCS 4.00 1.60
223 Dave McNally WS 2.00 .80
224 Dave Johnson WS 2.00 .80
Mark Belanger
225 Manny Sanguillen WS 2.00 .80
226 Roberto Clemente WS 8.00 3.20
227 Nellie Briles WS 2.00 .80
228 Frank Robinson WS 2.00 .80
Manny Sanguillen
229 Steve Blass WS 2.00 .80
230 WS Summary 2.00 .80
Pirates celebrate
231 Casey Cox 1.00 .40
232 Chris Arnold 1.00 .40
Jim Barr
Dave Rader
233 Jay Johnstone 2.00 .80
234 Ron Taylor 1.00 .40
235 Merv Rettenmund 1.00 .40
236 Jim McGlothlin 1.00 .40
237 New York Yankees 2.00 .80
Team Card
238 Leron Lee 1.00 .40
239 Tom Timmermann 1.00 .40
240 Rich Allen 2.00 .80
241 Rollie Fingers 6.00 2.40
242 Don Mincher 1.00 .40
243 Frank Linzy 1.00 .40
244 Steve Braun 1.00 .40
245 Tommie Agee 2.00 .80
246 Tom Burgmeier 1.00 .40
247 Milt May 1.00 .40
248 Tom Bradley 1.00 .40
249 Harry Walker MG 1.00 .40
250 Boog Powell 2.00 .80
251 Checklist 264-394 6.00 1.20
252 Ken Reynolds 1.00 .40
253 Sandy Alomar 2.00 .80
254 Boots Day 1.00 .40
255 Jim Lonborg 2.00 .80
256 George Foster 2.00 .80
257 Jim Foor 1.00 .40
Tim Hosley
Paul Jata
258 Randy Hundley 1.00 .40
259 Sparky Lyle 2.00 .80
260 Ralph Garr 2.00 .80
261 Steve Mingori 1.00 .40
262 San Diego Padres 2.00 .80
Team Card
263 Felipe Alou 2.00 .80
264 Tommy John 2.00 .80
265 Wes Parker 2.00 .80
266 Bobby Bolin 1.25 .50
267 Dave Concepcion 4.00 1.60
268 Dwain Anderson 1.25 .50
Chris Floethe
269 Don Hahn 1.25 .50
270 Jim Palmer 8.00 3.20
271 Ken Rudolph 1.25 .50
272 Mickey Rivers RC 2.00 .80
273 Bobby Floyd 1.25 .50
274 Al Severinsen 1.25 .50
275 Cesar Tovar 1.25 .50
276 Gene Mauch MG 2.00 .80
277 Elliott Maddox 1.25 .50
278 Dennis Higgins 1.25 .50
279 Larry Brown 1.25 .50
280 Willie McCovey 6.00 2.40
281 Bill Parsons 1.25 .50
282 Houston Astros 2.00 .80
Team Card
283 Darrell Brandon 1.25 .50
284 Ike Brown 1.25 .50
285 Gaylord Perry 6.00 2.40
286 Gene Alley 1.25 .50
287 Jim Hardin 1.25 .50
288 Johnny Jeter 1.25 .50
289 Syd O'Brien 1.25 .50
290 Sonny Siebert 1.25 .50
291 Hal McRae 2.00 .80
292 Hal McRae IA 1.25 .50
293 Dan Frisella 1.25 .50
294 Dan Frisella IA 1.25 .50
295 Dick Dietz 1.25 .50
296 Dick Dietz IA 1.25 .50
297 Claude Osteen 2.00 .80
298 Claude Osteen IA 1.25 .50
299 Hank Aaron 40.00 16.00
300 Hank Aaron IA 20.00 8.00
301 George Mitterwald 1.25 .50
302 George Mitterwald IA 1.25 .50
303 Joe Pepitone 2.00 .80
304 Joe Pepitone IA 1.25 .50
305 Ken Boswell 1.25 .50
306 Ken Boswell IA 1.25 .50
307 Steve Renko 1.25 .50
308 Steve Renko IA 1.25 .50
309 Roberto Clemente 50.00 20.00
310 Roberto Clemente IA 25.00 10.00
311 Clay Carroll 1.25 .50
312 Clay Carroll IA 1.25 .50
313 Luis Aparicio 6.00 2.40
314 Luis Aparicio IA 2.00 .80
315 Paul Splittorff 1.25 .50
316 Jim Bibby 2.00 .80
Jorge Roque
Santiago Guzman
317 Rich Hand 1.25 .50
318 Sonny Jackson 1.25 .50
319 Aurelio Rodriguez 1.25 .50
320 Steve Blass 2.00 .80
321 Joe Lahoud 1.25 .50
322 Jose Pena 1.25 .50
323 Earl Weaver MG 4.00 1.60
324 Mike Ryan 1.25 .50
325 Mel Stottlemyre 2.00 .80
326 Pat Kelly 1.25 .50
327 Steve Stone RC 2.00 .80
328 Boston Red Sox 2.00 .80
Team Card
329 Roy Foster 1.25 .50
330 Jim Hunter 6.00 2.40
331 Stan Swanson 1.25 .50
332 Buck Martinez 1.25 .50
333 Steve Barber 1.25 .50
334 Bill Fahey 1.25 .50
Jim Mason
Tom Ragland
335 Bill Hands 1.25 .50
336 Marty Martinez 1.25 .50
337 Mike Kilkenny 1.25 .50
338 Bob Grich 2.00 .80
339 Ron Cook 1.25 .50
340 Roy White 2.00 .80
341 Joe Torre KP 1.25 .50
342 Wilbur Wood KP 1.25 .50
343 Willie Stargell KP 2.00 .80
344 Dave McNally KP 1.25 .50
345 Rick Wise KP 1.25 .50
346 Jim Fregosi KP 1.25 .50
347 Tom Seaver KP 4.00 1.60
348 Sal Bando KP 1.25 .50
349 Al Fitzmorris 1.25 .50
350 Frank Howard 2.00 .80
351 Tom House 2.00 .80
Rick Kester
Jimmy Britton
352 Dave LaRoche 1.25 .50
353 Art Shamsky 1.25 .50
354 Tom Murphy 1.25 .50
355 Bob Watson 2.00 .80
356 Gerry Moses 1.25 .50
357 Woody Fryman 1.25 .50
358 Sparky Anderson MG 4.00 1.60
359 Don Pavletich 1.25 .50
360 Dave Roberts 1.25 .50
361 Mike Andrews 1.25 .50
362 New York Mets 2.00 .80
Team Card
363 Ron Klimkowski 1.25 .50
364 Johnny Callison 2.00 .80
365 Dick Bosman 2.00 .80
366 Jimmy Rosario 1.25 .50
367 Ron Perranoski 1.25 .50
368 Danny Thompson 1.25 .50
369 Jim Lefebvre 2.00 .80
370 Don Buford 1.25 .50
371 Denny Lemaster 1.25 .50
372 Lance Clemons 1.25 .50
Monty Montgomery
373 John Mayberry 2.00 .80
374 Jack Heidemann 1.25 .50
375 Reggie Cleveland 1.25 .50
376 Andy Kosco 1.25 .50
377 Terry Harmon 1.25 .50
378 Checklist 395-525 6.00 1.20
379 Ken Berry 1.25 .50
380 Earl Williams 1.25 .50
381 Chicago White Sox 2.00 .80
Team Card
382 Joe Gibbon 1.25 .50
383 Brant Alyea 1.25 .50
384 Dave Campbell 2.00 .80
385 Mickey Stanley 2.00 .80
386 Jim Colborn 1.25 .50
387 Horace Clarke 2.00 .80
388 Charlie Williams 1.25 .50
389 Bill Rigney MG 1.25 .50

390 Willie Davis 2.00 .80
391 Ken Sanders 1.25 .50
392 Fred Cambria 2.00 .80
Richie Zisk RC
393 Curt Motton 1.25 .50
394 Ken Forsch 2.00 .80
395 Matty Alou 2.00 .80
396 Paul Lindblad 1.50 .60
397 Philadelphia Phillies 2.00 .80
Team Card
398 Larry Hisle 2.00 .80
399 Milt Wilcox 2.00 .80
400 Tony Oliva 4.00 1.60
401 Jim Nash 1.50 .60
402 Bobby Heise 1.50 .60
403 John Cumberland 1.50 .60
404 Jeff Torborg 2.00 .80
405 Ron Fairly 2.00 .80
406 George Hendrick RC 2.00 .80
407 Chuck Taylor 1.50 .60
408 Jim Northrup 2.00 .80
409 Frank Baker 1.50 .60
410 Ferguson Jenkins 6.00 2.40
411 Bob Montgomery 1.50 .60
412 Dick Kelley 1.50 .60
413 Don Eddy 1.50 .60
Dave Lemonds
414 Bob Miller 1.50 .60
415 Cookie Rojas 2.00 .80
416 Johnny Edwards 1.50 .60
417 Tom Hall 1.50 .60
418 Tom Shopay 1.50 .60
419 Jim Spencer 1.50 .60
420 Steve Carlton 20.00 8.00
421 Ellie Rodriguez 1.50 .60
422 Ray Lamb 1.50 .60
423 Oscar Gamble 2.00 .80
424 Bill Gogolewski 1.50 .60
425 Ken Singleton 2.00 .80
426 Ken Singleton IA 1.50 .60
427 Tito Fuentes 1.50 .60
428 Tito Fuentes IA 1.50 .60
429 Bob Robertson 1.50 .60
430 Bob Robertson IA 1.50 .60
431 Clarence Gaston 2.00 .80
432 Clarence Gaston IA 2.00 .80
433 Johnny Bench 25.00 10.00
434 Johnny Bench IA 15.00 6.00
435 Reggie Jackson 30.00 12.00
436 Reggie Jackson IA 12.00 4.80
437 Maury Wills 2.00 .80
438 Maury Wills IA 2.00 .80
439 Billy Williams 6.00 2.40
440 Billy Williams IA 4.00 1.60
441 Thurman Munson 15.00 6.00
442 Thurman Munson IA 8.00 3.20
443 Ken Henderson 1.50 .60
444 Ken Henderson IA 1.50 .60
445 Tom Seaver 30.00 12.00
446 Tom Seaver IA 15.00 6.00
447 Willie Stargell 8.00 3.20
448 Willie Stargell IA 4.00 1.60
449 Bob Lemon MG 2.00 .80
450 Mickey Lolich 2.00 .80
451 Tony LaRussa 4.00 1.60
452 Ed Herrmann 1.50 .60
453 Barry Lersch 1.50 .60
454 Oakland A's 2.00 .80
Team Card
455 Tommy Harper 2.00 .80
456 Mark Belanger 2.00 .80
457 Darcy Fast 1.50 .60
Derrel Thomas
Mike Ivie
458 Aurelio Monteagudo 1.50 .60
459 Rick Renick 1.50 .60
460 Al Downing 1.50 .60
461 Tim Cullen 1.50 .60
462 Rickey Clark 1.50 .60
463 Bernie Carbo 1.50 .60
464 Jim Roland 1.50 .60
465 Gil Hodges MG 4.00 1.60
466 Norm Miller 1.50 .60
467 Steve Kline 1.50 .60
468 Richie Scheinblum 1.50 .60
469 Ron Herbel 1.50 .60
470 Ray Fosse 1.50 .60
471 Luke Walker 1.50 .60
472 Phil Gagliano 1.50 .60
473 Dan McGinn 1.50 .60
474 Don Baylor 15.00 6.00
Roric Harrison
Johnny Oates RC
475 Gary Nolan 2.00 .80
476 Lee Richard 1.50 .60
477 Tom Phoebus 1.50 .60
478 Checklist 526-656 6.00 1.20
479 Don Shaw 1.50 .60
480 Lee May 2.00 .80
481 Billy Conigliaro 2.00 .80
482 Joe Hoerner 1.50 .60
483 Ken Suarez 1.50 .60
484 Lum Harris MG 1.50 .60
485 Phil Regan 2.00 .80
486 John Lowenstein 1.50 .60
487 Detroit Tigers 2.00 .80
Team Card
488 Mike Nagy 1.50 .60
489 Terry Humphrey 1.50 .60
Keith Lampard
490 Dave McNally 2.00 .80
491 Lou Piniella KP 2.00 .80
492 Mel Stottlemyre KP 2.00 .80
493 Bob Bailey KP 2.00 .80
494 Willie Horton KP 2.00 .80
495 Bill Melton KP 2.00 .80
496 Bud Harrelson KP 2.00 .80
497 Jim Perry KP 2.00 .80
498 Brooks Robinson KP 4.00 1.60
499 Vicente Romo 1.50 .60
500 Joe Torre 4.00 1.60
501 Pete Hamm 1.50 .60
502 Jackie Hernandez 1.50 .60
503 Gary Peters 1.50 .60
504 Ed Spiezio 1.50 .60
505 Mike Marshall 2.00 .80
506 Terry Ley 1.50 .60
Jim Moyer
Dick Tidrow RC
507 Fred Gladding 1.50 .60
508 Elrod Hendricks 1.50 .60
509 Don McMahon 1.50 .60
510 Ted Williams MG 12.00 4.80
511 Tony Taylor 2.00 .80
512 Paul Popovich 1.50 .60
513 Lindy McDaniel 2.00 .80
514 Ted Sizemore 1.50 .60
515 Bert Blyleven 4.00 1.60
516 Oscar Brown 1.50 .60
517 Ken Brett 1.50 .60
518 Wayne Garrett 1.50 .60
519 Ted Abernathy 1.50 .60
520 Larry Bowa 2.00 .80
521 Alan Foster 1.50 .60
522 Los Angeles Dodgers 2.00 .80
Team Card
523 Chuck Dobson 1.50 .60
524 Ed Armbrister 1.50 .60
Mel Behney
525 Carlos May 2.00 .80
526 Bob Bailey 6.00 2.40
527 Dave Leonhard 4.00 1.60
528 Ron Stone 4.00 1.60
529 Dave Nelson 4.00 1.60
530 Don Sutton 12.00 4.80
531 Freddie Patek 6.00 2.40
532 Fred Kendall 4.00 1.60
533 Ralph Houk MG 6.00 2.40
534 Jim Hickman 6.00 2.40
535 Ed Brinkman 4.00 1.60
536 Doug Rader 6.00 2.40
537 Bob Locker 4.00 1.60
538 Charlie Sands 4.00 1.60
539 Terry Forster RC 6.00 2.40
540 Felix Millan 4.00 1.60
541 Roger Repoz 4.00 1.60
542 Jack Billingham 4.00 1.60
543 Duane Josephson 4.00 1.60
544 Ted Martinez 4.00 1.60
545 Wayne Granger 4.00 1.60
546 Joe Hague 4.00 1.60
547 Cleveland Indians 8.00 3.20
Team Card
548 Frank Reberger 4.00 1.60
549 Dave May 4.00 1.60
550 Brooks Robinson 25.00 10.00
551 Ollie Brown 4.00 1.60
552 Ollie Brown IA 4.00 1.60
553 Wilbur Wood 6.00 2.40
554 Wilbur Wood IA 6.00 2.40
555 Ron Santo 8.00 3.20
556 Ron Santo IA 6.00 2.40
557 John Odom 4.00 1.60
558 John Odom IA 4.00 1.60
559 Pete Rose 50.00 20.00
560 Pete Rose IA 25.00 10.00
561 Leo Cardenas 4.00 1.60
562 Leo Cardenas IA 4.00 1.60
563 Ray Sadecki 4.00 1.60
564 Ray Sadecki IA 4.00 1.60
565 Reggie Smith 6.00 2.40
566 Reggie Smith IA 4.00 1.60
567 Juan Marichal 12.00 4.80
568 Juan Marichal IA 6.00 2.40
569 Ed Kirkpatrick 4.00 1.60
570 Ed Kirkpatrick IA 4.00 1.60
571 Nate Colbert 4.00 1.60
572 Nate Colbert IA 4.00 1.60
573 Fritz Peterson 4.00 1.60
574 Fritz Peterson IA 4.00 1.60
575 Al Oliver 8.00 3.20
576 Leo Durocher MG 6.00 2.40
577 Mike Paul 4.00 1.60
578 Billy Grabarkewitz 4.00 1.60
579 Doyle Alexander RC 6.00 2.40
580 Lou Piniella 6.00 2.40
581 Wade Blasingame 4.00 1.60
582 Montreal Expos 8.00 3.20
Team Card
583 Darold Knowles 4.00 1.60
584 Jerry McNertney 4.00 1.60
585 George Scott 6.00 2.40
586 Denis Menke 4.00 1.60
587 Billy Wilson 4.00 1.60
588 Jim Holt 4.00 1.60
589 Hal Lanier 4.00 1.60
590 Graig Nettles 8.00 3.20
591 Paul Casanova 4.00 1.60
592 Lew Krausse 4.00 1.60
593 Rich Morales 4.00 1.60
594 Jim Beauchamp 4.00 1.60
595 Nolan Ryan 80.00 40.00
596 Manny Mota 6.00 2.40
597 Jim Magnuson 4.00 1.60
598 Hal King 6.00 2.40
599 Billy Champion 4.00 1.60
600 Al Kaline 25.00 10.00
601 George Stone 4.00 1.60
602 Dave Bristol MG 4.00 1.60
603 Jim Ray 4.00 1.60
604A Checklist 657-787 12.00 2.40
(Copyright on back
bottom right)
604B Checklist 657-787 12.00 2.40
(Copyright on back
bottom left)
605 Nelson Briles 6.00 2.40
606 Luis Melendez 4.00 1.60
607 Frank Duffy 4.00 1.60
608 Mike Corkins 4.00 1.60
609 Tom Grieve 6.00 2.40
610 Bill Stoneman 6.00 2.40
611 Rich Reese 4.00 1.60
612 Joe Decker 4.00 1.60
613 Mike Ferraro 4.00 1.60
614 Ted Uhlaender 4.00 1.60
615 Steve Hargan 4.00 1.60
616 Joe Ferguson RC 6.00 2.40
617 Kansas City Royals 8.00 3.20
Team Card
618 Rich Robertson 4.00 1.60
619 Rich McKinney 4.00 1.60
620 Phil Niekro 12.00 4.80
621 Comm. Award 8.00 3.20
622 MVP Award 8.00 3.20
623 Cy Young Award 8.00 3.20
624 Minor League Player 8.00 3.20
of the Year
625 Rookie of the Year 8.00 3.20
626 Babe Ruth Award 8.00 3.20
627 Moe Drabowsky 4.00 1.60
628 Terry Crowley 4.00 1.60
629 Paul Doyle 4.00 1.60
630 Rich Hebner 6.00 2.40
631 John Strohmayer 4.00 1.60
632 Mike Hegan 4.00 1.60
633 Jack Hiatt 4.00 1.60
634 Dick Woodson 4.00 1.60
635 Don Money 6.00 2.40
636 Bill Lee 6.00 2.40
637 Preston Gomez MG 4.00 1.60
638 Ken Wright 4.00 1.60
639 J.C. Martin 4.00 1.60
640 Joe Coleman 4.00 1.60
641 Mike Lum 4.00 1.60
642 Dennis Riddleberger 4.00 1.60
643 Russ Gibson 4.00 1.60
644 Bernie Allen 4.00 1.60
645 Jim Maloney 6.00 2.40
646 Chico Salmon 4.00 1.60
647 Bob Moose 4.00 1.60
648 Jim Lyttle 4.00 1.60
649 Pete Richert 4.00 1.60
650 Sal Bando 6.00 2.40
651 Cincinnati Reds 8.00 3.20
Team Card
652 Marcelino Lopez 4.00 1.60
653 Jim Fairey 4.00 1.60
654 Horacio Pina 6.00 2.40
655 Jerry Grote 4.00 1.60
656 Rudy May 4.00 1.60
657 Bobby Wine 12.00 4.80
658 Steve Dunning 12.00 4.80
659 Bob Aspromonte 12.00 4.80
660 Paul Blair 15.00 6.00
661 Bill Virdon MG 12.00 4.80
662 Stan Bahnsen 12.00 4.80
663 Fran Healy 15.00 6.00
664 Bobby Knoop 12.00 4.80
665 Chris Short 12.00 4.80
666 Hector Torres 12.00 4.80
667 Ray Newman 12.00 4.80
668 Texas Rangers 30.00 12.00
Team Card
669 Willie Crawford 12.00 4.80
670 Ken Holtzman 15.00 6.00
671 Donn Clendenon 15.00 6.00
672 Archie Reynolds 12.00 4.80
673 Dave Marshall 12.00 4.80
674 John Kennedy 12.00 4.80
675 Pat Jarvis 12.00 4.80
676 Danny Cater 12.00 4.80
677 Ivan Murrell 12.00 4.80
678 Steve Luebber 12.00 4.80
679 Bob Fenwick 12.00 4.80
Bob Stinson
680 Dave Johnson 15.00 6.00
681 Bobby Pfeil 12.00 4.80
682 Mike McCormick 15.00 6.00
683 Steve Hovley 12.00 4.80
684 Hal Breeden 12.00 4.80
685 Joel Horlen 12.00 4.80
686 Steve Garvey 40.00 16.00
687 Del Unser 12.00 4.80
688 St. Louis Cardinals 20.00 8.00
Team Card
689 Eddie Fisher 12.00 4.80
690 Willie Montanez 15.00 6.00
691 Curt Blefary 12.00 4.80
692 Curt Blefary IA 12.00 4.80
693 Alan Gallagher 12.00 4.80
694 Alan Gallagher IA 12.00 4.80
695 Rod Carew 50.00 20.00
696 Rod Carew IA 30.00 12.00
697 Jerry Koosman 15.00 6.00
698 Jerry Koosman IA 15.00 6.00
699 Bobby Murcer 15.00 6.00
700 Bobby Murcer IA 15.00 6.00
701 Jose Pagan 12.00 4.80
702 Jose Pagan IA 12.00 4.80
703 Doug Griffin 12.00 4.80
704 Doug Griffin IA 12.00 4.80
705 Pat Corrales 15.00 6.00
706 Pat Corrales IA 12.00 4.80
707 Tim Foli 12.00 4.80
708 Tim Foli IA 12.00 4.80
709 Jim Kaat 15.00 6.00
710 Jim Kaat IA 15.00 6.00
711 Bobby Bonds 20.00 8.00
712 Bobby Bonds IA 15.00 6.00
713 Gene Michael 20.00 8.00
714 Gene Michael IA 15.00 6.00
715 Mike Epstein 12.00 4.80
716 Jesus Alou 12.00 4.80
717 Bruce Dal Canton 12.00 4.80
718 Del Rice MG 12.00 4.80
719 Cesar Geronimo 12.00 4.80
720 Sam McDowell 15.00 6.00
721 Eddie Leon 12.00 4.80
722 Bill Sudakis 12.00 4.80
723 Al Santorini 12.00 4.80
724 John Curtis 12.00 4.80
Rich Hinton
Mickey Scott RC
725 Dick McAuliffe 15.00 6.00
726 Dick Selma 12.00 4.80
727 Jose Laboy 12.00 4.80
728 Gail Hopkins 12.00 4.80
729 Bob Veale 15.00 6.00
730 Rick Monday 15.00 6.00
731 Baltimore Orioles 20.00 8.00
Team Card
732 George Culver 12.00 4.80
733 Jim Ray Hart 15.00 6.00
734 Bob Burda 12.00 4.80
735 Diego Segui 12.00 4.80
736 Bill Russell 15.00 6.00
737 Len Randle 15.00 6.00
738 Jim Merritt 12.00 4.80
739 Don Mason 12.00 4.80
740 Rico Carty 15.00 6.00
741 Tom Hutton 15.00 6.00
John Milner
Rick Miller RC
742 Jim Rooker 12.00 4.80
743 Cesar Gutierrez 12.00 4.80
744 Jim Slaton 12.00 4.80
745 Julian Javier 15.00 6.00
746 Lowell Palmer 12.00 4.80
747 Jim Stewart 12.00 4.80
748 Phil Hennigan 12.00 4.80
749 Walter Alston MG 20.00 8.00
750 Willie Horton 15.00 6.00
751 Steve Carlton TR 40.00 16.00
752 Joe Morgan TR 40.00 16.00
753 Denny McLain TR 20.00 8.00
754 Frank Robinson TR 40.00 16.00
755 Jim Fregosi TR 15.00 6.00
756 Rick Wise TR 15.00 6.00
757 Jose Cardenal TR 15.00 6.00
758 Gil Garrido 12.00 4.80
759 Chris Cannizzaro 12.00 4.80
760 Bill Mazeroski 25.00 10.00
761 Ben Oglivie RC 25.00 10.00
Ron Cey RC
Bernie Williams
762 Wayne Simpson 12.00 4.80
763 Ron Hansen 12.00 4.80
764 Dusty Baker 20.00 8.00
765 Ken McMullen 12.00 4.80
766 Steve Hamilton 12.00 4.80
767 Tom McCraw 15.00 6.00
768 Denny Doyle 12.00 4.80
769 Jack Aker 12.00 4.80
770 Jim Wynn 15.00 6.00
771 San Francisco Giants 20.00 8.00
Team Card
772 Ken Tatum 12.00 4.80
773 Ron Brand 12.00 4.80
774 Luis Alvarado 12.00 4.80
775 Jerry Reuss 15.00 6.00
776 Bill Voss 12.00 4.80
777 Hoyt Wilhelm 25.00 10.00
778 Vic Albury 20.00 8.00
Rick Dempsey RC
Jim Strickland
779 Tony Cloninger 12.00 4.80
780 Dick Green 12.00 4.80
781 Jim McAndrew 12.00 4.80
782 Larry Stahl 12.00 4.80
783 Les Cain 12.00 4.80
784 Ken Aspromonte 12.00 4.80
785 Vic Davalillo 12.00 4.80
786 Chuck Brinkman 12.00 4.80
787 Ron Reed 15.00 5.25

1973 Topps

The cards in this 660-card set measure 2 1/2" by 3 1/2". The 1973 Topps set marked the last year in which Topps marketed baseball cards in consecutive series. The last series (529-660) is more difficult to obtain. In some parts of the country, however, all five series were distributed together. Beginning in 1974, all Topps cards were printed at the same time, thus eliminating the "high number" factor. The set features team leader cards with small individual pictures of the coaching staff members and a larger picture of the manager. The "background" variations below with respect to these leader cards are subtle and are best understood after a side-by-side comparison of the two varieties. An "All-Time Leaders" series (471-478) appeared for the first time in this set. Kid Pictures appeared again for the second year in a row (341-346). Other topical subsets within the set included League Leaders (61-68), Playoffs cards (201-202), World Series cards (203-210), and Rookie Prospects (601-616). For the fourth and final time, cards were issued in ten-card dime packs, cards were also released in 54-card rack packs. The key Rookie Cards in this set are all in the Rookie Prospect series: Bob Boone, Dwight Evans, and Mike Schmidt.

	NM	Ex
COMPLETE SET (660)	700.00	275.00
COMMON CARD (1-264)	.50	.20
COMMON (265-396)	.75	.30
COMMON (397-528)	1.25	.50
COMMON (529-660)	3.00	1.20
WRAP. (10-CENT, BAT)	15.00	6.00
WRAPPER (10-CENT)	15.00	6.00

1 Babe Ruth 714 40.00 11.50
Hank Aaron 673
Willie Mays 654 ATL
2 Rich Hebner 1.50 .60
3 Jim Lonborg 1.50 .60
4 John Milner .50 .20
5 Ed Brinkman .50 .20
6 Mac Scarce .50 .20
7 Texas Rangers 2.00 .80
Team Card
8 Tom Hall .50 .20
9 Johnny Oates 1.50 .60
10 Don Sutton 4.00 1.60
11 Chris Chambliss 1.50 .60
12A Don Zimmer MG 3.00 1.20
Dave Garcia CO
Johnny Podres CO
Bob Skinner CO
Whitey Wietelmann CO
(Podres no right ear)
12B Padres Leaders .75 .30
(Podres has right ear)
13 George Hendrick 1.50 .60
14 Sonny Siebert .50 .20
15 Ralph Garr 1.50 .60
16 Steve Braun .50 .20
17 Fred Gladding .50 .20
18 Leroy Stanton .50 .20
19 Tim Foli .50 .20
20 Stan Bahnsen .50 .20
21 Randy Hundley 1.50 .60
22 Ted Abernathy .50 .20
23 Dave Kingman 1.50 .60
24 Al Santorini .50 .20
25 Roy White 1.50 .60
26 Pittsburgh Pirates 2.00 .80
Team Card
27 Bill Gogolewski .50 .20
28 Hal McRae 1.50 .60
29 Tony Taylor 1.50 .60
30 Tug McGraw 1.50 .60
31 Buddy Bell RC 2.50 1.00
32 Fred Norman .50 .20
33 Jim Breazeale .50 .20
34 Pat Dobson .50 .20
35 Willie Davis 1.50 .60
36 Steve Barber .50 .20
37 Bill Robinson 1.50 .60
38 Mike Epstein .50 .20
39 Dave Roberts .50 .20
40 Reggie Smith 1.50 .60
41 Tom Walker .50 .20
42 Mike Andrews .50 .20
43 Randy Moffitt .50 .20
44 Rick Monday 1.50 .60
45 Ellie Rodriguez UER .50 .20
(Photo actually
John Felske)
46 Lindy McDaniel 1.50 .60
47 Luis Melendez .50 .20
48 Paul Splittorff .50 .20
49A Frank Quilici MG 3.00 1.20
Vern Morgan CO
Bob Rodgers CO
Ralph Rowe CO
Al Worthington CO
(Solid backgrounds)
49B Twins Leaders .75 .30
(Natural backgrounds)
50 Roberto Clemente 40.00 16.00
51 Chuck Seelbach .50 .20
52 Denis Menke .50 .20
53 Steve Dunning .50 .20
54 Checklist 1-132 3.00 .60
55 Jon Matlack 1.50 .60
56 Merv Rettenmund .50 .20
57 Derrel Thomas .50 .20
58 Mike Paul .50 .20
59 Steve Yeager RC 1.50 .60
60 Ken Holtzman 1.50 .60
61 Billy Williams 2.50 1.00
Rod Carew LL
62 Johnny Bench 2.50 1.00
Dick Allen LL
Home Run Leaders
63 Johnny Bench 2.50 1.00
Dick Allen
RBI Leaders
64 Lou Brock 1.50 .60
Bert Campaneris LL
65 Steve Carlton 1.50 .60
Luis Tiant LL
66 Steve Carlton 1.50 .60
Gaylord Perry
Wilbur Wood LL
67 Steve Carlton 25.00 10.00
Nolan Ryan LL
68 Clay Carroll 1.50 .60
Sparky Lyle LL
69 Phil Gagliano .50 .20
70 Milt Pappas 1.50 .60
71 Johnny Briggs .50 .20
72 Ron Reed .50 .20
73 Ed Herrmann .50 .20
74 Billy Champion .50 .20
75 Vada Pinson 1.50 .60
76 Doug Rader .50 .20
77 Mike Torrez 1.50 .60
78 Richie Scheinblum .50 .20
79 Jim Willoughby .50 .20
80 Tony Oliva UER 2.50 1.00
(Minnseota on front)
81A Whitey Lockman MG 1.50 .60
Hank Aguirre CO
Ernie Banks CO
Larry Jansen CO
Pete Reiser CO
(Solid backgrounds)
81B Cubs Leaders 1.50 .60
(Natural backgrounds)
82 Fritz Peterson .50 .20
83 Leron Lee .50 .20
84 Rollie Fingers 4.00 1.60
85 Ted Simmons 1.50 .60
86 Tom McCraw .50 .20
87 Ken Boswell .50 .20
88 Mickey Stanley 1.50 .60
89 Jack Billingham .50 .20
90 Brooks Robinson 8.00 3.20
91 Los Angeles Dodgers 2.00 .80
Team Card
92 Jerry Bell .50 .20
93 Jesus Alou .50 .20
94 Dick Billings .50 .20
95 Steve Blass 1.50 .60
96 Doug Griffin .50 .20
97 Willie Montanez 1.50 .60
98 Dick Woodson .50 .20
99 Carl Taylor .50 .20
100 Hank Aaron 40.00 16.00
101 Ken Henderson .50 .20
102 Rudy May .50 .20
103 Celerino Sanchez .50 .20
104 Reggie Cleveland .50 .20
105 Carlos May .50 .20
106 Terry Humphrey .50 .20
107 Phil Hennigan .50 .20
108 Bill Russell 1.50 .60
109 Doyle Alexander 1.50 .60
110 Bob Watson 1.50 .60
111 Dave Nelson .50 .20
112 Gary Ross .50 .20
113 Jerry Grote 1.50 .60
114 Lynn McGlothen .50 .20
115 Ron Santo 1.50 .60
116A Ralph Houk MG 3.00 1.20
Jim Hegan CO
Elston Howard CO
Dick Howser CO
Jim Turner CO
(Solid backgrounds)
116B Yankees Leaders .75 .30
(Natural backgrounds)
117 Ramon Hernandez .50 .20
118 John Mayberry 1.50 .60

9 Larry Bowa 1.50 .60
0 Joe Coleman .50 .20
1 Dave Rader .50 .20
2 Jim Strickland .50 .20
3 Sandy Alomar 1.50 .60
4 Jim Hardin .50 .20
5 Ron Fairly 1.50 .60
6 Jim Brewer .50 .20
7 Milwaukee Brewers 2.00 .80
Team Card
8 Ted Sizemore .50 .20
9 Terry Forster 1.50 .60
0 Pete Rose 30.00 12.00
1A Eddie Kasko MG 3.00 1.20
Doug Camilli CO
Don Lenhardt CO
Eddie Popowski CO
(No right ear)
Lee Stange CO
1B Red Sox Leaders 1.50 .60
(Popowski has right
ear showing)
2 Matty Alou 1.50 .60
3 Dave Roberts RC .50 .20
4 Milt Wilcox .50 .20
5 Lee May UER 1.50 .60
(Career average .000)
6A Earl Weaver MG 2.00 .80
George Bamberger CO
Jim Frey CO
Billy Hunter CO
George Staller CO
(Orange backgrounds)
6B Orioles Leaders 3.00 1.20
(Dark pale
backgrounds)
7 Jim Beauchamp .50 .20
8 Horacio Pina .50 .20
9 Carmen Fanzone .50 .20
0 Lou Piniella 2.50 1.00
1 Bruce Kison .50 .20
2 Thurman Munson 8.00 3.20
3 John Curtis .50 .20
4 Marty Perez .50 .20
5 Bobby Bonds 2.50 1.00
6 Woodie Fryman .50 .20
7 Mike Anderson .50 .20
8 Dave Goltz .50 .20
9 Ron Hunt .50 .20
0 Wilbur Wood 1.50 .60
1 Wes Parker 1.50 .60
2 Dave May .50 .20
3 Al Hrabosky 1.50 .60
4 Jeff Torborg 1.50 .60
5 Sal Bando 1.50 .60
6 Cesar Geronimo .50 .20
7 Denny Riddleberger .50 .20
8 Houston Astros 2.00 .80
Team Card
9 Clarence Gaston 1.50 .60
0 Jim Palmer 6.00 2.40
1 Ted Martinez .50 .20
2 Pete Broberg .50 .20
3 Vic Davalillo .50 .20
4 Monty Montgomery .50 .20
5 Luis Aparicio 4.00 1.60
6 Terry Harmon .50 .20
7 Steve Stone 1.50 .60
68 Jim Northrup 1.50 .60
69 Ron Schueler RC 1.50 .60
70 Harmon Killebrew 5.00 2.00
71 Bernie Carbo .50 .20
72 Steve Kline .50 .20
73 Hal Breeden .50 .20
74 Goose Gossage RC 6.00 2.40
75 Frank Robinson 6.00 2.40
76 Chuck Taylor .50 .20
77 Bill Plummer .50 .20
78 Don Rose .50 .20
79A Dick Williams MG 4.00 1.60
Jerry Adair CO
Vern Hoscheit CO
Irv Noren CO
Wes Stock CO
(Hoscheit left ear
showing)
79B A's Leaders 1.50 .60
(Hoscheit left ear
not showing)
80 Ferguson Jenkins 4.00 1.60
81 Jack Brohamer .50 .20
82 Mike Caldwell RC 1.50 .60
83 Don Buford .50 .20
84 Jerry Koosman 1.50 .60
85 Jim Wynn 1.50 .60
86 Bill Fahey .50 .20
87 Luke Walker .50 .20
88 Cookie Rojas 1.50 .60
89 Greg Luzinski 2.50 1.00
90 Bob Gibson 8.00 3.20
91 Detroit Tigers 2.50 1.00
Team Card
92 Pat Jarvis .50 .20
93 Carlton Fisk 10.00 4.00
94 Jorge Orta .50 .20
95 Clay Carroll .50 .20
96 Ken McMullen .50 .20
97 Ed Goodson .50 .20
98 Horace Clarke .50 .20
99 Bert Blyleven 2.50 1.00
200 Billy Williams 4.00 1.60
201 G. Hendrick ALCS 1.50 .60
202 George Foster NLCS 1.50 .60
203 Gene Tenace WS 1.50 .60
204 World Series Game 2 1.50 .60
A's two straight
205 Tony Perez WS 2.50 1.00
206 Gene Tenace WS 1.50 .60
207 Blue Moon Odom WS 1.50 .60
208 Johnny Bench WS6 5.00 2.00
209 Bert Campaneris WS 1.50 .60
210 W.S. Summary .50 .20
World champions:
A's Win
211 Balor Moore .50 .20
212 Joe Lahoud .50 .20
213 Steve Garvey 5.00 2.00
214 Dave Hamilton .50 .20
215 Dusty Baker 2.50 1.00
216 Toby Harrah 1.50 .60
217 Don Wilson .50 .20
218 Aurelio Rodriguez .50 .20
219 St. Louis Cardinals 2.50 1.00
Team Card
220 Nolan Ryan 50.00 24.00
221 Fred Kendall .50 .20
222 Rob Gardner .50 .20
223 Bud Harrelson 1.50 .60
224 Bill Lee 1.50 .60
225 Al Oliver 1.50 .60
226 Ray Fosse .50 .20
227 Wayne Twitchell .50 .20
228 Bobby Darwin .50 .20
229 Roric Harrison .50 .20
230 Joe Morgan 6.00 2.40
231 Bill Parsons .50 .20
232 Ken Singleton 1.50 .60
233 Ed Kirkpatrick .50 .20
234 Bill North .50 .20
235 Jim Hunter 4.00 1.60
236 Tito Fuentes .50 .20
237A Eddie Mathews MG 2.00 .80
Lew Burdette CO
Jim Busby CO
Roy Hartsfield CO
Ken Silvestri CO
(Burdette right ear
showing)
237B Braves Leaders 3.00 1.20
(Burdette right ear
not showing)
238 Tony Muser .50 .20
239 Pete Richert .50 .20
240 Bobby Murcer 1.50 .60
241 Dwain Anderson .50 .20
242 George Culver .50 .20
243 California Angels 2.50 1.00
Team Card
244 Ed Acosta .50 .20
245 Carl Yastrzemski 10.00 4.00
246 Ken Sanders .50 .20
247 Del Unser .50 .20
248 Jerry Johnson .50 .20
249 Larry Biittner .50 .20
250 Manny Sanguillen 1.50 .60
251 Roger Nelson .50 .20
252A Charlie Fox MG 4.00 1.60
Joe Amalfitano CO
Andy Gilbert CO
Don McMahon CO
John McNamara CO
(Orange backgrounds)
252B Giants Leaders 1.50 .60
(Dark pale
backgrounds)
253 Mark Belanger 1.50 .60
254 Bill Stoneman .50 .20
255 Reggie Jackson 15.00 6.00
256 Chris Zachary .50 .20
257A Yogi Berra MG 3.00 1.20
Roy McMillan CO
Joe Pignatano CO
Rube Walker CO
Eddie Yost CO
(Orange backgrounds)
257B Mets Leaders 5.00 2.00
(Dark pale
backgrounds)
258 Tommy John 1.50 .60
259 Jim Holt .50 .20
260 Gary Nolan 1.50 .60
261 Pat Kelly .50 .20
262 Jack Aker .50 .20
263 George Scott 1.50 .60
264 Checklist 133-264 1.50 .60
265 Gene Michael 1.50 .60
266 Mike Lum .75 .30
267 Lloyd Allen .75 .30
268 Jerry Morales .75 .30
269 Tim McCarver 1.50 .60
270 Luis Tiant 1.50 .60
271 Tom Hutton .75 .30
272 Ed Farmer .75 .30
273 Chris Speier .75 .30
274 Darold Knowles .75 .30
275 Tony Perez 4.00 1.60
276 Joe Lovitto .75 .30
277 Bob Miller .75 .30
278 Baltimore Orioles 1.50 .60
Team Card
279 Mike Strahler .75 .30
280 Al Kaline 8.00 3.20
281 Mike Jorgensen .75 .30
282 Steve Hovley .75 .30
283 Ray Sadecki .75 .30
284 Glenn Borgmann .75 .30
285 Don Kessinger 1.50 .60
286 Frank Linzy .75 .30
287 Eddie Leon .75 .30
288 Gary Gentry .75 .30
289 Bob Oliver .75 .30
290 Cesar Cedeno 1.50 .60
291 Rogelio Moret .75 .30
292 Jose Cruz 1.50 .60
293 Bernie Allen .75 .30
294 Steve Arlin .75 .30
295 Bert Campaneris 1.50 .60
296 Sparky Anderson MG 2.50 1.00
Alex Grammas CO
Ted Kluszewski CO
George Scherger CO
Larry Shepard CO
297 Walt Williams .75 .30
298 Ron Bryant .75 .30
299 Ted Ford .75 .30
300 Steve Carlton 10.00 4.00
301 Billy Grabarkewitz .75 .30
302 Terry Crowley .75 .30
303 Nelson Briles .75 .30
304 Duke Sims .75 .30
305 Willie Mays 40.00 16.00
306 Tom Burgmeier .75 .30
307 Boots Day .75 .30
308 Skip Lockwood .75 .30
309 Paul Popovich .75 .30
310 Dick Allen 1.50 .60
311 Joe Decker .75 .30
312 Oscar Brown .75 .30
313 Jim Ray .75 .30
314 Ron Swoboda 1.50 .60
315 John Odom .75 .30
316 San Diego Padres 1.50 .60
Team Card
317 Danny Cater .75 .30
318 Jim McGlothlin .75 .30
319 Jim Spencer .75 .30
320 Lou Brock 8.00 3.20
321 Rich Hinton .75 .30
322 Garry Maddox RC 1.50 .60
323 Billy Martin MG 1.50 .60
Art Fowler CO
Charlie Silvera CO
Dick Tracewski CO
Joe Schultz CO ERR
Schult's name not printed on card
324 Al Downing .75 .30
325 Boog Powell 1.50 .60
326 Darrell Brandon .75 .30
327 John Lowenstein .75 .30
328 Bill Bonham .75 .30
329 Ed Kranepool 1.50 .60
330 Rod Carew 8.00 3.20
331 Carl Morton .75 .30
332 John Felske .75 .30
333 Gene Clines .75 .30
334 Freddie Patek .75 .30
335 Bob Tolan .75 .30
336 Tom Bradley .75 .30
337 Dave Duncan 1.50 .60
338 Checklist 265-396 3.00 .60
339 Dick Tidrow .75 .30
340 Nate Colbert .75 .30
341 Jim Palmer KP 2.50 1.00
342 Sam McDowell KP .75 .30
343 Bobby Murcer KP .75 .30
344 Jim Hunter KP 2.50 1.00
345 Chris Speier KP .75 .30
346 Gaylord Perry KP 1.50 .60
347 Kansas City Royals 1.50 .60
Team Card
348 Rennie Stennett .75 .30
349 Dick McAuliffe .75 .30
350 Tom Seaver 12.00 4.80
351 Jimmy Stewart .75 .30
352 Don Stanhouse .75 .30
353 Steve Brye .75 .30
354 Billy Parker .75 .30
355 Mike Marshall 1.50 .60
356 Chuck Tanner MG 4.00 1.60
Joe Lonnett CO
Jim Mahoney CO
Al Monchak CO
Johnny Sain CO
357 Ross Grimsley .75 .30
358 Jim Nettles .75 .30
359 Cecil Upshaw .75 .30
360 Joe Rudi UER 1.50 .60
(Photo actually
Gene Tenace)
361 Fran Healy .75 .30
362 Eddie Watt .75 .30
363 Jackie Hernandez .75 .30
364 Rick Wise .75 .30
365 Rico Petrocelli 1.50 .60
366 Brock Davis .75 .30
367 Burt Hooton 1.50 .60
368 Bill Buckner 1.50 .60
369 Lerrin LaGrow .75 .30
370 Willie Stargell 5.00 2.00
371 Mike Kekich .75 .30
372 Oscar Gamble .75 .30
373 Clyde Wright .75 .30
374 Darrell Evans 1.50 .60
375 Larry Dierker 1.50 .60
376 Frank Duffy .75 .30
377 Gene Mauch MG 4.00 1.60
Dave Bristol CO
Larry Doby CO
Cal McLish CO
Jerry Zimmerman CO
378 Len Randle .75 .30
379 Cy Acosta .75 .30
380 Johnny Bench 12.00 4.80
381 Vicente Romo .75 .30
382 Mike Hegan .75 .30
383 Diego Segui .75 .30
384 Don Baylor 4.00 1.60
385 Jim Perry 1.50 .60
386 Don Money .75 .30
387 Jim Barr .75 .30
388 Ben Oglivie 1.50 .60
389 New York Mets 4.00 1.60
Team Card
390 Mickey Lolich 1.50 .60
391 Lee Lacy RC 1.50 .60
392 Dick Drago .75 .30
393 Jose Cardenal .75 .30
394 Sparky Lyle 1.50 .60
395 Roger Metzger .75 .30
396 Grant Jackson .75 .30
397 Dave Cash 1.25 .50
398 Rich Hand 1.25 .50
399 George Foster 2.00 .80
400 Gaylord Perry 5.00 2.00
401 Clyde Mashore 1.25 .50
402 Jack Hiatt 1.25 .50
403 Sonny Jackson 1.25 .50
404 Chuck Brinkman 1.25 .50
405 Cesar Tovar 1.25 .50
406 Paul Lindblad 1.25 .50
407 Felix Millan 1.25 .50
408 Jim Colborn 1.25 .50
409 Ivan Murrell 1.25 .50
410 Willie McCovey 6.00 2.40
(Bench behind plate)
411 Ray Corbin 1.25 .50
412 Manny Mota 2.00 .80
413 Tom Timmermann 1.25 .50
414 Ken Rudolph 1.25 .50
415 Marty Pattin 1.25 .50
416 Paul Schaal 1.25 .50
417 Scipio Spinks 1.25 .50
418 Bob Grich 2.00 .80
419 Casey Cox 1.25 .50
420 Tommie Agee 1.25 .50
421A Bobby Winkles MG 1.50 .60
Tom Morgan CO
Salty Parker CO
Jimmie Reese CO
John Roseboro CO
(Orange backgrounds)
421B Angels Leaders 3.00 1.20
(Dark pale
backgrounds)
422 Bob Robertson 1.25 .50
423 Johnny Jeter 1.25 .50
424 Denny Doyle 1.25 .50
425 Alex Johnson 1.25 .50
426 Dave LaRoche 1.25 .50
427 Rick Auerbach 1.25 .50
428 Wayne Simpson 1.25 .50
429 Jim Fairey 1.25 .50
430 Vida Blue 2.00 .80
431 Gerry Moses 1.25 .50
432 Dan Frisella 1.25 .50
433 Willie Horton 2.00 .80
434 San Francisco Giants 3.00 1.20
Team Card
435 Rico Carty 2.00 .80
436 Jim McAndrew 1.25 .50
437 John Kennedy 1.25 .50
438 Enzo Hernandez 1.25 .50
439 Eddie Fisher 1.25 .50
440 Glenn Beckert 1.25 .50
441 Gail Hopkins 1.25 .50
442 Dick Dietz 1.25 .50
443 Danny Thompson 1.25 .50
444 Ken Brett 1.25 .50
445 Ken Berry 1.25 .50
446 Jerry Reuss 2.00 .80
447 Joe Hague 1.25 .50
448 John Hiller 1.25 .50
449A Ken Aspromonte MG 4.00 1.60
Rocky Colavito CO
Joe Lutz CO
Warren Spahn CO
(Spahn's right
ear pointed)
449B Indians Leaders 4.00 1.60
(Spahn's right
ear round)
450 Joe Torre 3.00 1.20
451 John Vukovich 1.25 .50
452 Paul Casanova 1.25 .50
453 Checklist 397-528 3.00 .60
454 Tom Haller 1.25 .50
455 Bill Melton 1.25 .50
456 Dick Green 1.25 .50
457 John Strohmayer 1.25 .50
458 Jim Mason 1.25 .50
459 Jimmy Howarth 1.25 .50
460 Bill Freehan 2.00 .80
461 Mike Corkins 1.25 .50
462 Ron Blomberg 1.25 .50
463 Ken Tatum 1.25 .50
464 Chicago Cubs 3.00 1.20
Team Card
465 Dave Giusti 1.25 .50
466 Jose Arcia 1.25 .50
467 Mike Ryan 1.25 .50
468 Tom Griffin 1.25 .50
469 Dan Monzon 1.25 .50
470 Mike Cuellar 2.00 .80
471 Ty Cobb ATL 10.00 4.00
4191 Hits
472 Lou Gehrig ATL 15.00 6.00
23 Grand Slams
473 Hank Aaron ATL 10.00 4.00
6172 Total Bases
474 Babe Ruth ATL 20.00 8.00
2209 RBI
475 Ty Cobb ATL 8.00 3.20
.367 Batting Average
476 Walter Johnson ATL 3.00 1.20
113 Shutouts
477 Cy Young ATL 3.00 1.20
511 Victories
478 Walter Johnson ATL 3.00 1.20
3508 Strikeouts
479 Hal Lanier 1.25 .50
480 Juan Marichal 5.00 2.00
481 Chicago White Sox 3.00 1.20
Team Card
482 Rick Reuschel RC 3.00 1.20
483 Dal Maxvill 1.25 .50
484 Ernie McAnally 1.25 .50
485 Norm Cash 2.00 .80
486A Danny Ozark MG 1.50 .60
Carroll Beringer CO
Billy DeMars CO
Ray Rippelmeyer CO
Bobby Wine CO
(Orange backgrounds)
486B Phillies Leaders 3.00 1.20
(Dark pale
backgrounds)
487 Bruce Dal Canton 1.25 .50
488 Dave Campbell 2.00 .80
489 Jeff Burroughs 2.00 .80
490 Claude Osteen 2.00 .80
491 Bob Montgomery 1.25 .50
492 Pedro Borbon 1.25 .50
493 Duffy Dyer 1.25 .50
494 Rich Morales 1.25 .50
495 Tommy Helms 1.25 .50
496 Ray Lamb 1.25 .50
497A Red Schoendienst MG 2.00 .80
Vern Benson CO
George Kissell CO
Barney Schultz CO
(Orange backgrounds)
497B Cardinals Leaders 3.00 1.20
(Dark pale
backgrounds)
498 Graig Nettles 3.00 1.20
499 Bob Moose 1.25 .50
500 Oakland A's 3.00 1.20
Team Card
501 Larry Gura 1.25 .50
502 Bobby Valentine 3.00 1.20
503 Phil Niekro 5.00 2.00
504 Earl Williams 1.25 .50
505 Bob Bailey 1.25 .50
506 Bart Johnson 1.25 .50
507 Darrel Chaney 1.25 .50
508 Gates Brown 1.25 .50
509 Jim Nash 1.25 .50
510 Amos Otis 2.00 .80
511 Sam McDowell 2.00 .80
512 Dalton Jones 1.25 .50
513 Dave Marshall 1.25 .50
514 Jerry Kenney 1.25 .50
515 Andy Messersmith 2.00 .80
516 Danny Walton 1.25 .50
517A Bill Virdon MG 1.50 .60
Don Leppert CO
Bill Mazeroski CO
Dave Ricketts CO
Mel Wright CO
(Mazeroski has
no right ear)
517B Pirates Leaders 3.00 1.20
(Mazeroski has
right ear)
518 Bob Veale 1.25 .50
519 Johnny Edwards 1.25 .50
520 Mel Stottlemyre 2.00 .80
521 Atlanta Braves 3.00 1.20
Team Card
522 Leo Cardenas 1.25 .50
523 Wayne Granger 1.25 .50
524 Gene Tenace 2.00 .80
525 Jim Fregosi 2.00 .80
526 Ollie Brown 1.25 .50
527 Dan McGinn 1.25 .50
528 Paul Blair 1.25 .50
529 Milt May 3.00 1.20
530 Jim Kaat 5.00 2.00
531 Ron Woods 3.00 1.20
532 Steve Mingori 3.00 1.20
533 Larry Stahl 3.00 1.20
534 Dave Lemonds 3.00 1.20
535 Johnny Callison 5.00 2.00
536 Philadelphia Phillies 6.00 2.40
Team Card
537 Bill Slayback 3.00 1.20
538 Jim Ray Hart 5.00 2.00
539 Tom Murphy 3.00 1.20
540 Cleon Jones 5.00 2.00
541 Bob Bolin 3.00 1.20
542 Pat Corrales 5.00 2.00
543 Alan Foster 3.00 1.20
544 Von Joshua 3.00 1.20
545 Orlando Cepeda 8.00 3.20
546 Jim York 3.00 1.20
547 Bobby Heise 3.00 1.20
548 Don Durham 3.00 1.20
549 Whitey Herzog MG 5.00 2.00
Chuck Estrada CO
Chuck Hiller CO
Jackie Moore CO
550 Dave Johnson 5.00 2.00
551 Mike Kilkenny 3.00 1.20
552 J.C. Martin 3.00 1.20
553 Mickey Scott 3.00 1.20
554 Dave Concepcion 5.00 2.00
555 Bill Hands 3.00 1.20
556 New York Yankees 8.00 3.20
Team Card
557 Bernie Williams 3.00 1.20
558 Jerry May 3.00 1.20
559 Barry Lersch 3.00 1.20
560 Frank Howard 5.00 2.00
561 Jim Geddes 3.00 1.20
562 Wayne Garrett 3.00 1.20
563 Larry Haney 3.00 1.20
564 Mike Thompson 3.00 1.20
565 Jim Hickman 3.00 1.20
566 Lew Krausse 3.00 1.20
567 Bob Fenwick 3.00 1.20
568 Ray Newman 3.00 1.20
569 Walt Alston MG 8.00 3.20
Red Adams CO
Monty Basgall CO
Jim Gilliam CO
Tom Lasorda CO
570 Bill Singer 5.00 2.00
571 Rusty Torres 3.00 1.20
572 Gary Sutherland 3.00 1.20
573 Fred Beene 3.00 1.20
574 Bob Didier 3.00 1.20
575 Dock Ellis 3.00 1.20
576 Montreal Expos 6.00 2.40
Team Card
577 Eric Soderholm 3.00 1.20
578 Ken Wright 3.00 1.20
579 Tom Grieve 5.00 2.00
580 Joe Pepitone 5.00 2.00
581 Steve Kealey 3.00 1.20
582 Darrell Porter 5.00 2.00
583 Bill Grief 3.00 1.20
584 Chris Arnold 3.00 1.20
585 Joe Niekro 5.00 2.00
586 Bill Sudakis 3.00 1.20
587 Rich McKinney 3.00 1.20
588 Checklist 529-660 20.00 4.00
589 Ken Forsch 3.00 1.20
590 Deron Johnson 3.00 1.20
591 Mike Hedlund 3.00 1.20
592 John Boccabella 3.00 1.20
593 Jack McKeon MG 4.00 1.60
Galen Cisco CO
Harry Dunlop CO
Charlie Lau CO
594 Vic Harris 3.00 1.20
595 Don Gullett 5.00 2.00
596 Boston Red Sox 6.00 2.40
Team Card
597 Mickey Rivers 5.00 2.00
598 Phil Roof 3.00 1.20
599 Ed Crosby 3.00 1.20
600 Dave McNally 5.00 2.00
601 Sergio Robles 5.00 2.00
George Pena
Rick Stelmaszek
602 Mel Behney 5.00 2.00
Ralph Garcia
Doug Rau
603 Terry Hughes 5.00 2.00
Bill McNulty
Ken Reitz RC
604 Jesse Jefferson 5.00 2.00
Dennis O'Toole
Bob Strampe
605 Enos Cabell RC 5.00 2.00
Pat Bourque
Gonzalo Marquez
606 Gary Matthews RC 5.00 2.00
Tom Paciorek
Jorge Roque

607 Pepe Frias 5.00 2.00
Ray Busse
Mario Guerrero
608 Steve Busby RC 5.00 2.00
Dick Colpaert
George Medich RC
609 Larvell Blanks 5.00 2.00
Pedro Garcia
Dave Lopes RC
610 Jimmy Freeman 5.00 2.00
Charlie Hough
Hank Webb
611 Rich Coggins 5.00 2.00
Jim Wohlford
Richie Zisk
612 Steve Lawson 5.00 2.00
Bob Reynolds
Brent Strom
613 Bob Boone RC 15.00 6.00
Skip Jutze
Mike Ivie
614 Al Bumbry RC 20.00 8.00
Dwight Evans RC
Charlie Spikes
615 Ron Cey 150.00 60.00
John Hilton
Mike Schmidt RC
616 Norm Angelini 5.00 2.00
Steve Blateric
Mike Garman
617 Rich Chiles 3.00 1.20
618 Andy Etchebarren 3.00 1.20
619 Billy Wilson 3.00 1.20
620 Tommy Harper 5.00 2.00
621 Joe Ferguson 5.00 2.00
622 Larry Hisle 5.00 2.00
623 Steve Renko 3.00 1.20
624 Leo Durocher MG 5.00 2.00
Preston Gomez CO
Grady Hatton CO
Hub Kittle CO
Jim Owens CO
625 Angel Mangual 3.00 1.20
626 Bob Barton 3.00 1.20
627 Luis Alvarado 3.00 1.20
628 Jim Slaton 3.00 1.20
629 Cleveland Indians 6.00 2.40
Team Card
630 Denny McLain 8.00 3.20
631 Tom Matchick 3.00 1.20
632 Dick Selma 3.00 1.20
633 Ike Brown 3.00 1.20
634 Alan Closter 3.00 1.20
635 Gene Alley 5.00 2.00
636 Rickey Clark 3.00 1.20
637 Norm Miller 3.00 1.20
638 Ken Reynolds 3.00 1.20
639 Willie Crawford 3.00 1.20
640 Dick Bosman 3.00 1.20
641 Cincinnati Reds 6.00 2.40
Team Card
642 Jose Laboy 3.00 1.20
643 Al Fitzmorris 3.00 1.20
644 Jack Heidemann 3.00 1.20
645 Bob Locker 3.00 1.20
646 Del Crandall MG 4.00 1.60
Harvey Kuenn CO
Joe Nossek CO
Bob Shaw CO
Jim Walton CO
647 George Stone 3.00 1.20
648 Tom Egan 3.00 1.20
649 Rich Folkers 3.00 1.20
650 Felipe Alou 5.00 2.00
651 Don Carrithers 3.00 1.20
652 Ted Kubiak 3.00 1.20
653 Joe Hoerner 3.00 1.20
654 Minnesota Twins 6.00 2.40
Team Card
655 Clay Kirby 3.00 1.20
656 John Ellis 3.00 1.20
657 Bob Johnson 3.00 1.20
658 Elliott Maddox 3.00 1.20
659 Jose Pagan 3.00 1.20
660 Fred Scherman 5.00 1.95

1973 Topps Blue Team Checklists

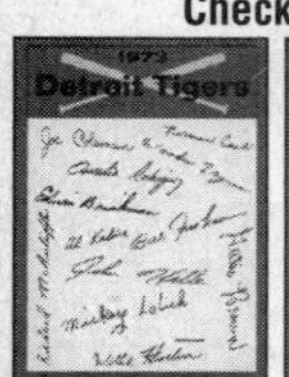

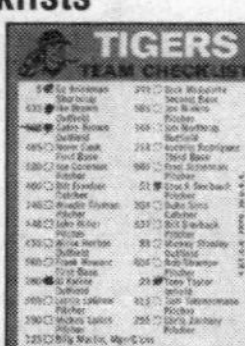

This 24-card standard-size set is rather difficult to find. These blue-bordered team checklist cards are very similar in design to the mass produced red trim team checklist cards issued by Topps the next year. Reportedly these were inserts only found in the test packs that included all series. In addition, a collector could mail in 25 cents and receive a full uncut sheet of these cards. This offer was somewhat limited in terms of collectors mailing in for them.

	NM	Ex
COMPLETE SET (24)	175.00	52.50
COMMON TEAM (1-24)	8.00	2.40
16 New York Mets	10.00	3.00
17 New York Yankees	10.00	3.00

1974 Topps

The cards in this 660-card set measure 2 1/2" by 3 1/2". This year marked the first time Topps issued all the cards of its baseball set at the same time rather than in series. Among other methods, cards were issued in eight-card dime wax packs and 42 card rack packs. The ten cent packs were issued 36 to a box. For the first time, factory sets were issued through the JC Penny's catalog. Sales were probably disappointing for it would be several years before factory sets were

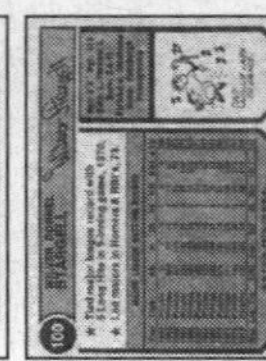

issued again. Some interesting variations were created by the rumored move of the San Diego Padres to Washington. Fifteen cards (13 players, the team card, and the rookie card (599) of the Padres were printed either as "San Diego" (SD) or "Washington." The latter are the scarcer variety and are denoted in the checklist below by WAS. Each team's manager and his coaches again have a combined card with small pictures of each coach below the larger photo of the team's manager. The first six cards in the set (1-6) feature Hank Aaron and his illustrious career. Other topical subsets included in the set are League Leaders (201-208), All-Star selections (331-339), Playoffs cards (470-471), World Series cards (472-479), and Rookie Prospects (596-608). The card backs for the All-Stars (331-339) have no statistics, but form a picture puzzle of Bobby Bonds, the 1973 All-Star Game MVP. The key Rookie Cards in this set are Ken Griffey Sr., Dave Parker and Dave Winfield.

	NM	Ex
COMPLETE SET (660)	400.00	160.00
COMP.FACT.SET (660)	600.00	240.00
WRAPPERS (10-CENTS)	10.00	4.00

1 Hank Aaron 715 40.00 12.00
2 Hank Aaron 54-57 8.00 3.20
3 Hank Aaron 58-61 8.00 3.20
4 Hank Aaron 62-65 8.00 3.20
5 Hank Aaron 66-69 8.00 3.20
6 Hank Aaron 70-73 8.00 3.20
7 Jim Hunter 4.00 1.60
8 George Theodore .50 .20
9 Mickey Lolich 1.00 .40
10 Johnny Bench 15.00 6.00
11 Jim Bibby .50 .20
12 Dave May .50 .20
13 Tom Hilgendorf .50 .20
14 Paul Popovich .50 .20
15 Joe Torre 2.00 .80
16 Baltimore Orioles 1.00 .40
Team Card
17 Doug Bird .50 .20
18 Gary Thomasson .50 .20
19 Gerry Moses .50 .20
20 Nolan Ryan 40.00 16.00
21 Bob Gallagher .50 .20
22 Cy Acosta .50 .20
23 Craig Robinson .50 .20
24 John Hiller 1.00 .40
25 Ken Singleton 1.00 .40
26 Bill Campbell .50 .20
27 George Scott 1.00 .40
28 Manny Sanguillen 1.00 .40
29 Phil Niekro 3.00 1.20
30 Bobby Bonds 2.00 .80
31 Preston Gomez MG 1.00 .40
Roger Craig CO
Hub Kittle CO
Grady Hatton CO
Bob Lillis CO
32A Johnny Grubb SD 1.00 .40
32B Johnny Grubb WASH 4.00 1.60
33 Don Newhauser .50 .20
34 Andy Kosco .50 .20
35 Gaylord Perry 3.00 1.20
36 St. Louis Cardinals 1.00 .40
Team Card
37 Dave Sells .50 .20
38 Don Kessinger 1.00 .40
39 Ken Suarez .50 .20
40 Jim Palmer 8.00 3.20
41 Bobby Floyd .50 .20
42 Claude Osteen 1.00 .40
43 Jim Wynn 1.00 .40
44 Mel Stottlemyre 1.00 .40
45 Dave Johnson 1.00 .40
46 Pat Kelly .50 .20
47 Dick Ruthven .50 .20
48 Dick Sharon .50 .20
49 Steve Renko .50 .20
50 Rod Carew 8.00 3.20
51 Bobby Heise .50 .20
52 Al Oliver 1.00 .40
53A Fred Kendall SD 1.00 .40
53B Fred Kendall WASH 4.00 1.60
54 Elias Sosa .50 .20
55 Frank Robinson 8.00 3.20
56 New York Mets 1.00 .40
Team Card
57 Darold Knowles .50 .20
58 Charlie Spikes .50 .20
59 Ross Grimsley .50 .20
60 Lou Brock 6.00 2.40
61 Luis Aparicio 3.00 1.20
62 Bob Locker .50 .20
63 Bill Sudakis .50 .20
64 Doug Rau .50 .20
65 Amos Otis 1.00 .40
66 Sparky Lyle 1.00 .40
67 Tommy Helms .50 .20
68 Grant Jackson .50 .20
69 Del Unser .50 .20
70 Dick Allen 2.00 .80
71 Dan Frisella .50 .20
72 Aurelio Rodriguez .50 .20
73 Mike Marshall 2.00 .80
74 Minnesota Twins 1.00 .40
Team Card
75 Jim Colborn .50 .20
76 Mickey Rivers 1.00 .40
77A Rich Troedson SD 1.00 .40
77B Rich Troedson WASH 4.00 1.60
78 Charlie Fox MG 1.00 .40
John McNamara CO
Joe Amalfitano CO
Andy Gilbert CO
Don McMahon CO
79 Gene Tenace 1.00 .40
80 Tom Seaver 12.00 4.80
81 Frank Duffy .50 .20
82 Dave Giusti .50 .20
83 Orlando Cepeda 3.00 1.20
84 Rick Wise .50 .20
85 Joe Morgan 8.00 3.20
86 Joe Ferguson 1.00 .40
87 Fergie Jenkins 3.00 1.20
88 Freddie Patek 1.00 .40
89 Jackie Brown .50 .20
90 Bobby Murcer 1.00 .40
91 Ken Forsch .50 .20
92 Paul Blair 1.00 .40
93 Rod Gilbreath .50 .20
94 Detroit Tigers 1.00 .40
Team Card
95 Steve Carlton 8.00 3.20
96 Jerry Hairston .50 .20
97 Bob Bailey .50 .20
98 Bert Blyleven 2.00 .80
99 Del Crandall MG 1.00 .40
Harvey Kuenn CO
Joe Nossek CO
Jim Walton CO
Al Widmar CO
100 Willie Stargell 6.00 2.40
101 Bobby Valentine 1.00 .40
102A Bill Greif SD 1.00 .40
102B Bill Greif WASH 4.00 1.60
103 Sal Bando 1.00 .40
104 Ron Bryant .50 .20
105 Carlton Fisk 12.00 4.80
106 Harry Parker .50 .20
107 Alex Johnson .50 .20
108 Al Hrabosky 1.00 .40
109 Bob Grich 1.00 .40
110 Billy Williams 3.00 1.20
111 Clay Carroll .50 .20
112 Dave Lopes 2.00 .80
113 Dick Drago .50 .20
114 Angels Team 1.00 .40
115 Willie Horton 1.00 .40
116 Jerry Reuss 1.00 .40
117 Ron Blomberg .50 .20
118 Bill Lee 1.00 .40
119 Danny Ozark MG 1.00 .40
Ray Ripplemeyer CO
Bobby Wine CO
Carroll Beringer CO
Billy DeMars CO
120 Wilbur Wood .50 .20
121 Larry Lintz .50 .20
122 Jim Holt .50 .20
123 Nelson Briles 1.00 .40
124 Bobby Coluccio .50 .20
125A Nate Colbert SD 1.00 .40
125B Nate Colbert WASH 4.00 1.60
126 Checklist 1-132 3.00 .60
127 Tom Paciorek 1.00 .40
128 John Ellis .50 .20
129 Chris Speier .50 .20
130 Reggie Jackson 15.00 6.00
131 Bob Boone 2.00 .80
132 Felix Millan .50 .20
133 David Clyde 1.00 .40
134 Denis Menke .50 .20
135 Roy White 1.00 .40
136 Rick Reuschel 1.00 .40
137 Al Bumbry 1.00 .40
138 Eddie Brinkman .50 .20
139 Aurelio Monteagudo .50 .20
140 Darrell Evans 2.00 .80
141 Pat Bourque .50 .20
142 Pedro Garcia .50 .20
143 Dick Woodson .50 .20
144 Walter Alston MG 3.00 1.20
Tom Lasorda CO
Jim Gilliam CO
Red Adams CO
Monty Basgall CO
145 Dock Ellis .50 .20
146 Ron Fairly 1.00 .40
147 Bart Johnson .50 .20
148A Dave Hilton SD 1.00 .40
148B Dave Hilton WASH 4.00 1.60
149 Mac Scarce .50 .20
150 John Mayberry 1.00 .40
151 Diego Segui .50 .20
152 Oscar Gamble 1.00 .40
153 Jon Matlack 1.00 .40
154 Houston Astros 1.00 .40
Team Card
155 Bert Campaneris 1.00 .40
156 Randy Moffitt .50 .20
157 Vic Harris .50 .20
158 Jack Billingham .50 .20
159 Jim Ray Hart .50 .20
160 Brooks Robinson 8.00 3.20
161 Ray Burris UER 1.00 .40
(Card number is
printed sideways)
162 Bill Freehan 1.00 .40
163 Ken Berry .50 .20
164 Tom House .50 .20
165 Willie Davis 1.00 .40
166 Jack McKeon MG 1.00 .40
Charlie Lau CO
Harry Dunlop CO
Galen Cisco CO
167 Luis Tiant 2.00 .80
168 Danny Thompson .50 .20
169 Steve Rogers RC 2.00 .80
170 Bill Melton .50 .20
171 Eduardo Rodriguez .50 .20
172 Gene Clines .50 .20
173A Randy Jones SD RC 2.00 .80
173B Randy Jones WASH 5.00 2.00
174 Bill Robinson 1.00 .40
175 Reggie Cleveland .50 .20
176 John Lowenstein .50 .20
177 Dave Roberts .50 .20
178 Garry Maddox 1.00 .40
179 Yogi Berra MG 5.00 2.00
Rube Walker CO
Eddie Yost CO
Roy McMillan CO
Joe Pignatano CO
180 Ken Holtzman 1.00 .40
181 Cesar Geronimo .50 .20
182 Lindy McDaniel 1.00 .40
183 Johnny Oates 1.00 .40
184 Texas Rangers 1.00 .40
Team Card
185 Jose Cardenal .50 .20
186 Fred Scherman .50 .20
187 Don Baylor 2.00 .80
188 Rudy Meoli .50 .20
189 Jim Brewer .50 .20
190 Tony Oliva 2.00 .80
191 Al Fitzmorris .50 .20
192 Mario Guerrero .50 .20
193 Tom Walker .50 .20
194 Darrell Porter 1.00 .40
195 Carlos May .50 .20
196 Jim Fregosi 1.00 .40
197A Vicente Romo SD 1.00 .40
197B V.Romo WASH 4.00 1.60
198 Dave Cash .50 .20
199 Mike Kekich .50 .20
200 Cesar Cedeno 1.00 .40
201 Rod Carew 6.00 2.40
Pete Rose LL
202 Reggie Jackson 5.00 2.00
Willie Stargell LL
203 Reggie Jackson 5.00 2.00
Willie Stargell LL
204 Tommy Harper 2.00 .80
Lou Brock LL
205 Wilbur Wood 1.00 .40
Ron Bryant LL
206 Jim Palmer 5.00 2.00
Tom Seaver LL
207 Nolan Ryan 12.00 4.80
Tom Seaver LL
208 John Hiller 1.00 .40
Mike Marshall LL
209 Ted Sizemore .50 .20
210 Bill Singer .50 .20
211 Chicago Cubs 1.00 .40
Team Card
212 Rollie Fingers 3.00 1.20
213 Dave Rader .50 .20
214 Billy Grabarkewitz .50 .20
215 Al Kaline UER 10.00 4.00
(No copyright on back)
216 Ray Sadecki .50 .20
217 Tim Foli .50 .20
218 Johnny Briggs .50 .20
219 Doug Griffin .50 .20
220 Don Sutton 3.00 1.20
221 Chuck Tanner MG 1.00 .40
Jim Mahoney CO
Alex Monchak CO
Johnny Sain CO
Joe Lonnett CO
222 Ramon Hernandez .50 .20
223 Jeff Burroughs 2.00 .80
224 Roger Metzger .50 .20
225 Paul Splittorff .50 .20
226A San Diego Padres 2.00 .80
Team Card San Diego Variation
226B San Diego Padres 8.00 3.20
Team Card Washington Variation
227 Mike Lum .50 .20
228 Ted Kubiak .50 .20
229 Fritz Peterson .50 .20
230 Tony Perez 4.00 1.60
231 Dick Tidrow .50 .20
232 Steve Brye .50 .20
233 Jim Barr .50 .20
234 John Milner .50 .20
235 Dave McNally 1.00 .40
236 Red Schoendienst MG 3.00 1.20
Barney Schultz CO
George Kissell CO
Johnny Lewis CO
Vern Benson CO
237 Ken Brett .50 .20
238 Fran Healy HOR .50 .20
(Munson sliding
in background)
239 Bill Russell 1.00 .40
240 Joe Coleman .50 .20
241A Glenn Beckert SD 1.00 .40
241B G.Beckert WASH 4.00 1.60
242 Bill Gogolewski .50 .20
243 Bob Oliver .50 .20
244 Carl Morton .50 .20
245 Cleon Jones .50 .20
246 Oakland Athletics 2.00 .80
Team Card
247 Rick Miller .50 .20
248 Tom Hall .50 .20
249 George Mitterwald .50 .20
250A Willie McCovey SD 8.00 3.20
250B W.McCovey WASH 25.00 10.00
251 Graig Nettles 2.00 .80
252 Dave Parker RC 10.00 4.00
253 John Boccabella .50 .20
254 Stan Bahnsen .50 .20
255 Larry Bowa 1.00 .40
256 Tom Griffin .50 .20
257 Buddy Bell 2.00 .80
258 Jerry Morales .50 .20
259 Bob Reynolds .50 .20
260 Ted Simmons 2.00 .80
261 Jerry Bell .50 .20
262 Ed Kirkpatrick .50 .20
263 Checklist 133-264 3.00 .60
264 Joe Rudi 1.00 .40
265 Tug McGraw 2.00 .80
266 Jim Northrup 1.00 .40
267 Andy Messersmith 1.00 .40
268 Tom Grieve 1.00 .40
269 Bob Johnson .50 .20
270 Ron Santo 2.00 .80
271 Bill Hands .50 .20
272 Paul Casanova .50 .20
273 Checklist 265-396 3.00 .60
274 Fred Beene .50 .20
275 Ron Hunt .50 .20
276 Bobby Winkles MG 1.00 .40
John Roseboro CO
Tom Morgan CO
Jimmie Reese CO
Salty Parker CO
277 Gary Nolan 1.00 .40
278 Cookie Rojas 1.00 .40
279 Jim Crawford .50 .20
280 Carl Yastrzemski 12.00 4.80
281 San Francisco Giants 1.00 .40
Team Card
282 Doyle Alexander 1.00 .40
283 Mike Schmidt 20.00 8.00
284 Dave Duncan 1.00 .40
285 Reggie Smith 1.00 .40
286 Tony Muser .50 .20
287 Clay Kirby .50 .20
288 Gorman Thomas RC 2.00 .80
289 Rick Auerbach .50 .20
290 Vida Blue 1.00 .40
291 Don Hahn .50 .20
292 Chuck Seelbach .50 .20
293 Milt May .50 .20
294 Steve Foucault .50 .20
295 Rick Monday 1.00 .40
296 Ray Corbin .50 .20
297 Hal Breeden .50 .20
298 Roric Harrison .50 .20
299 Gene Michael .50 .20
300 Pete Rose 25.00 10.00
301 Bob Montgomery .50 .20
302 Rudy May .50 .20
303 George Hendrick 1.00 .40
304 Don Wilson .50 .20
305 Tito Fuentes .50 .20
306 Earl Weaver MG 3.00 1.20
Jim Frey CO
George Bamberger CO
Billy Hunter CO
George Staller CO
307 Luis Melendez .50 .20
308 Bruce Dal Canton .50 .20
309A Dave Roberts SD 1.00 .40
309B Dave Roberts WASH 6.00 2.40
310 Terry Forster 1.00 .40
311 Jerry Grote 1.00 .40
312 Deron Johnson .50 .20
313 Barry Lersch .50 .20
314 Milwaukee Brewers 1.00 .40
Team Card
315 Ron Cey 2.00 .80
316 Jim Perry 1.00 .40
317 Richie Zisk 1.00 .40
318 Jim Merritt .50 .20
319 Randy Hundley .50 .20
320 Dusty Baker 2.00 .80
321 Steve Braun .50 .20
322 Ernie McAnally .50 .20
323 Richie Scheinblum .50 .20
324 Steve Kline .50 .20
325 Tommy Harper 1.00 .40
326 Sparky Anderson MG 3.00 1.20
Larry Shepard CO
George Scherger CO
Alex Grammas CO
Ted Kluszewski CO
327 Tom Timmermann .50 .20
328 Skip Jutze .50 .20
329 Mark Belanger 1.00 .40
330 Juan Marichal 5.00 2.00
331 Carlton Fisk 5.00 2.00
Johnny Bench AS
332 Dick Allen 8.00 3.20
Hank Aaron AS
333 Rod Carew 4.00 1.60
Joe Morgan AS
334 Brooks Robinson 2.00 .80
Ron Santo AS
335 Bert Campaneris 1.00 .40
Chris Speier AS
336 Bobby Murcer 5.00 2.00
Pete Rose AS
337 Amos Otis 1.00 .40
Cesar Cedeno AS
338 Reggie Jackson 5.00 2.00
Billy Williams AS
339 Jim Hunter 3.00 1.20
Rick Wise AS
340 Thurman Munson 8.00 3.20
341 Dan Driessen RC 1.00 .40
342 Jim Lonborg 1.00 .40
343 Royals Team 1.00 .40
344 Mike Caldwell .50 .20
345 Bill North .50 .20
346 Ron Reed .50 .20
347 Sandy Alomar 1.00 .40
348 Pete Richert .50 .20
349 John Vukovich .50 .20
350 Bob Gibson 8.00 3.20
351 Dwight Evans 3.00 1.20
352 Bill Stoneman .50 .20
353 Rich Coggins .50 .20
354 Whitey Lockman MG 1.00 .40
J.C. Martin CO
Hank Aguirre CO
Al Spangler CO
Jim Marshall CO
355 Dave Nelson .50 .20
356 Jerry Koosman 1.00 .40
357 Buddy Bradford .50 .20
358 Dal Maxvill .50 .20
359 Brent Strom .50 .20
360 Greg Luzinski 2.00 .80
361 Don Carrithers .50 .20
362 Hal King .50 .20
363 New York Yankees 2.00 .80
Team Card
364A Cito Gaston SD 2.00 .80
364B Cito Gaston WASH 8.00 3.20
365 Steve Busby 1.00 .40
366 Larry Hisle 1.00 .40
367 Norm Cash 2.00 .80
368 Manny Mota 1.00 .40
369 Paul Lindblad .50 .20
370 Bob Watson 1.00 .40
371 Jim Slaton .50 .20
372 Ken Reitz .50 .20
373 John Curtis .50 .20
374 Marty Perez .50 .20
375 Earl Williams .50 .20
376 Jorge Orta .50 .20
377 Ron Woods .50 .20
378 Burt Hooton 1.00 .40
379 Billy Martin MG 2.00 .80
Frank Lucchesi CO
Art Fowler CO
Charlie Silvera CO

Jackie Moore CO
80 Bud Harrelson 1.00 .40
81 Charlie Sands .50 .20
82 Bob Moose .50 .20
83 Philadelphia Phillies 1.00 .40
Team Card
84 Chris Chambliss 1.00 .40
85 Don Gullett 1.00 .40
86 Gary Matthews 2.00 .80
87A Rich Morales SD 1.00 .40
87B Rich Morales WASH 6.00 2.40
88 Phil Roof .50 .20
89 Gates Brown .50 .20
90 Lou Piniella 2.00 .80
91 Billy Champion .50 .20
92 Dick Green .50 .20
93 Orlando Pena .50 .20
94 Ken Henderson .50 .20
95 Doug Rader .50 .20
96 Tommy Davis 1.00 .40
97 George Stone .50 .20
98 Duke Sims .50 .20
99 Mike Paul .50 .20
00 Harmon Killebrew 6.00 2.40
01 Elliott Maddox .50 .20
02 Jim Rooker .50 .20
03 Darrell Johnson MG 1.00 .40
Eddie Popowski CO
Lee Stange CO
Don Zimmer CO
Don Bryant CO
404 Jim Howarth .50 .20
405 Ellie Rodriguez .50 .20
406 Steve Arlin .50 .20
407 Jim Wohlford .50 .20
408 Charlie Hough 1.00 .40
409 Ike Brown .50 .20
410 Pedro Borbon .50 .20
411 Frank Baker .50 .20
412 Chuck Taylor .50 .20
413 Don Money 1.00 .40
414 Checklist 397-528 3.00 .60
415 Gary Gentry .50 .20
416 Chicago White Sox 1.00 .40
Team Card
417 Rich Folkers .50 .20
418 Walt Williams .50 .20
419 Wayne Twitchell .50 .20
420 Ray Fosse .50 .20
421 Dan Fife .50 .20
422 Gonzalo Marquez .50 .20
423 Fred Stanley .50 .20
424 Jim Beauchamp .50 .20
425 Pete Broberg .50 .20
426 Rennie Stennett .50 .20
427 Bobby Bolin .50 .20
428 Gary Sutherland .50 .20
429 Dick Lange .50 .20
430 Matty Alou 1.00 .40
431 Gene Garber RC 1.00 .40
432 Chris Arnold .50 .20
433 Lerrin LaGrow .50 .20
434 Ken McMullen .50 .20
435 Dave Concepcion 2.00 .80
436 Don Hood .50 .20
437 Jim Lyttle .50 .20
438 Ed Herrmann .50 .20
439 Norm Miller .50 .20
440 Jim Kaat 2.00 .80
441 Tom Ragland .50 .20
442 Alan Foster .50 .20
443 Tom Hutton .50 .20
444 Vic Davalillo .50 .20
445 George Medich .50 .20
446 Len Randle .50 .20
447 Frank Quilici MG 1.00 .40
Ralph Rowe CO
Bob Rodgers CO
Vern Morgan CO
448 Ron Hodges .50 .20
449 Tom McCraw .50 .20
450 Rich Hebner 1.00 .40
451 Tommy John 2.00 .80
452 Gene Hiser .50 .20
453 Balor Moore .50 .20
454 Kurt Bevacqua .50 .20
455 Tom Bradley .50 .20
456 Dave Winfield RC 40.00 16.00
457 Chuck Goggin .50 .20
458 Jim Ray .50 .20
459 Cincinnati Reds 2.00 .80
Team Card
460 Boog Powell 2.00 .80
461 John Odom .50 .20
462 Luis Alvarado .50 .20
463 Pat Dobson .50 .20
464 Jose Cruz 2.00 .80
465 Dick Bosman .50 .20
466 Dick Billings .50 .20
467 Winston Llenas .50 .20
468 Pepe Frias .50 .20
469 Joe Decker .50 .20
470 Reggie Jackson ALCS 5.00 2.00
471 Jon Matlack NLCS 1.00 .40
472 Darold Knowles WS1 1.00 .40
473 Willie Mays WS 8.00 3.20
474 Bert Campaneris WS3 1.00 .40
475 Rusty Staub WS4 1.00 .40
476 Cleon Jones WS5 1.00 .40
477 Reggie Jackson WS 5.00 2.00
478 Bert Campaneris WS7 1.00 .40
479 WS Summary 1.00 .40
A's celebrate; win
2nd consecutive
championship
480 Willie Crawford .50 .20
481 Jerry Terrell .50 .20
482 Bob Didier .50 .20
483 Atlanta Braves 1.00 .40
Team Card
484 Carmen Fanzone .50 .20
485 Felipe Alou 2.00 .80
486 Steve Stone 1.00 .40
487 Ted Martinez .50 .20
488 Andy Etchebarren .50 .20
489 Danny Murtaugh MG 1.00 .40
Don Osborn CO
Don Leppert CO
Bill Mazeroski CO
Bob Skinner CO
490 Vada Pinson 2.00 .80
491 Roger Nelson .50 .20
492 Mike Rogodzinski .50 .20
493 Joe Hoerner .50 .20
494 Ed Goodson .50 .20
495 Dick McAuliffe 1.00 .40
496 Tom Murphy .50 .20
497 Bobby Mitchell .50 .20
498 Pat Corrales .50 .20
499 Rusty Torres .50 .20
500 Lee May 1.00 .40
501 Eddie Leon .50 .20
502 Dave LaRoche .50 .20
503 Eric Soderholm .50 .20
504 Joe Niekro 1.00 .40
505 Bill Buckner 1.00 .40
506 Ed Farmer .50 .20
507 Larry Stahl .50 .20
508 Montreal Expos 1.00 .40
Team Card
509 Jesse Jefferson .50 .20
510 Wayne Garrett .50 .20
511 Toby Harrah 1.00 .40
512 Joe Lahoud .50 .20
513 Jim Campanis .50 .20
514 Paul Schaal .50 .20
515 Willie Montanez .50 .20
516 Horacio Pina .50 .20
517 Mike Hegan .50 .20
518 Derrel Thomas .50 .20
519 Bill Sharp .50 .20
520 Tim McCarver 2.00 .80
521 Ken Aspromonte MG 1.00 .40
Clay Bryant CO
Tony Pacheco CO
522 J.R. Richard 2.00 .80
523 Cecil Cooper 2.00 .80
524 Bill Plummer .50 .20
525 Clyde Wright .50 .20
526 Frank Tepedino 1.00 .40
527 Bobby Darwin .50 .20
528 Bill Bonham .50 .20
529 Horace Clarke 1.00 .40
530 Mickey Stanley 1.00 .40
531 Gene Mauch MG 1.00 .40
Dave Bristol CO
Cal McLish CO
Larry Doby CO
Jerry Zimmerman CO
532 Skip Lockwood .50 .20
533 Mike Phillips .50 .20
534 Eddie Watt .50 .20
535 Bob Tolan .50 .20
536 Duffy Dyer .50 .20
537 Steve Mingori .50 .20
538 Cesar Tovar .50 .20
539 Lloyd Allen .50 .20
540 Bob Robertson .50 .20
541 Cleveland Indians 1.00 .40
Team Card
542 Goose Gossage 2.00 .80
543 Danny Cater .50 .20
544 Ron Schueler .50 .20
545 Billy Conigliaro 1.00 .40
546 Mike Corkins .50 .20
547 Glenn Borgmann .50 .20
548 Sonny Siebert .50 .20
549 Mike Jorgensen .50 .20
550 Sam McDowell 1.00 .40
551 Von Joshua .50 .20
552 Denny Doyle .50 .20
553 Jim Willoughby .50 .20
554 Tim Johnson .50 .20
555 Woodie Fryman .50 .20
556 Dave Campbell 1.00 .40
557 Jim McGlothlin .50 .20
558 Bill Fahey .50 .20
559 Darrel Chaney .50 .20
560 Mike Cuellar 1.00 .40
561 Ed Kranepool 1.00 .40
562 Jack Aker .50 .20
563 Hal McRae 1.00 .40
564 Mike Ryan .50 .20
565 Milt Wilcox .50 .20
566 Jackie Hernandez .50 .20
567 Boston Red Sox 1.00 .40
Team Card
568 Mike Torrez 1.00 .40
569 Rick Dempsey 1.00 .40
570 Ralph Garr 1.00 .40
571 Rich Hand .50 .20
572 Enzo Hernandez .50 .20
573 Mike Adams .50 .20
574 Bill Parsons .50 .20
575 Steve Garvey 3.00 1.20
576 Scipio Spinks .50 .20
577 Mike Sadek .50 .20
578 Ralph Houk MG 1.00 .40
579 Cecil Upshaw .50 .20
580 Jim Spencer .50 .20
581 Fred Norman .50 .20
582 Bucky Dent RC 5.00 2.00
583 Marty Pattin .50 .20
584 Ken Rudolph .50 .20
585 Merv Rettenmund .50 .20
586 Jack Brohamer .50 .20
587 Larry Christenson .50 .20
588 Hal Lanier .50 .20
589 Boots Day .50 .20
590 Roger Moret .50 .20
591 Sonny Jackson .50 .20
592 Ed Bane .50 .20
593 Steve Yeager 1.00 .40
594 Leroy Stanton .50 .20
595 Steve Blass 1.00 .40
596 Wayne Garland .50 .20
Fred Holdsworth
Mark Littell
Dick Pole
597 Dave Chalk 1.00 .40
John Gamble
Pete MacKanin
Manny Trillo RC
598 Dave Augustine 12.00 4.80
Ken Griffey RC
Steve Ontiveros
Jim Tyrone
599A Rookie Pitchers WAS 2.00 .80
Ron Diorio
Dave Freisleben
Frank Riccelli
Greg Shanahan
599B Rookie Pitchers SD 3.00 1.20
(SD in large print)
599C Rookie Pitchers SD 6.00 2.40
(SD in small print)
600 Ron Cash 5.00 2.00
Jim Cox
Bill Madlock RC
Reggie Sanders
601 Ed Armbrister 3.00 1.20
Rich Bladt
Brian Downing RC
Bake McBride RC
602 Glen Abbott 1.00 .40
Rick Henninger
Craig Swan
Dan Vossler
603 Barry Foote 1.00 .40
Tom Lundstedt
Charlie Moore RC
Sergio Robles
604 Terry Hughes 5.00 2.00
John Knox
Andre Thornton RC
Frank White RC
605 Vic Albury 4.00 1.60
Ken Frailing
Kevin Kobel
Frank Tanana RC
606 Jim Fuller 1.00 .40
Wilbur Howard
Tommy Smith
Otto Velez
607 Leo Foster 1.00 .40
Tom Heintzelman
Dave Rosello
Frank Taveras RC
608A Rookie Pitchers ERR 2.00 .80
Bob Apodaco (sic)
Dick Baney
John D'Acquisto
Mike Wallace
608B Rookie Pitchers COR 1.00 .40
Bob Apodaca
Dick Baney
John D'Acquisto
Mike Wallace
609 Rico Petrocelli 1.00 .40
610 Dave Kingman 2.00 .80
611 Rich Stelmaszek .50 .20
612 Luke Walker .50 .20
613 Dan Monzon .50 .20
614 Adrian Devine .50 .20
615 Johnny Jeter UER .50 .20
(Misspelled Johnnie
on card back)
616 Larry Gura .50 .20
617 Ted Ford .50 .20
618 Jim Mason .50 .20
619 Mike Anderson .50 .20
620 Al Downing .50 .20
621 Bernie Carbo .50 .20
622 Phil Gagliano .50 .20
623 Celerino Sanchez .50 .20
624 Bob Miller .50 .20
625 Ollie Brown .50 .20
626 Pittsburgh Pirates 1.00 .40
Team Card
627 Carl Taylor .50 .20
628 Ivan Murrell .50 .20
629 Rusty Staub 2.00 .80
630 Tommie Agee 1.00 .40
631 Steve Barber .50 .20
632 George Culver .50 .20
633 Dave Hamilton .50 .20
634 Eddie Mathews MG 3.00 1.20
Herm Starrette CO
Connie Ryan CO
Jim Busby CO
Ken Silvestri CO
635 Johnny Edwards .50 .20
636 Dave Goltz .50 .20
637 Checklist 529-660 3.00 .60
638 Ken Sanders .50 .20
639 Joe Lovitto .50 .20
640 Milt Pappas 1.00 .40
641 Chuck Brinkman .50 .20
642 Terry Harmon .50 .20
643 Dodgers Team 1.00 .40
644 Wayne Granger .50 .20
645 Ken Boswell .50 .20
646 George Foster 2.00 .80
647 Juan Beniquez .50 .20
648 Terry Crowley .50 .20
649 Fernando Gonzalez RC .50 .20
650 Mike Epstein .50 .20
651 Leron Lee .50 .20
652 Gail Hopkins .50 .20
653 Bob Stinson .50 .20
654A Jesus Alou ERR 4.00 1.60
(No position)
654B Jesus Alou COR 1.00 .40
(Outfield)
655 Mike Tyson .50 .20
656 Adrian Garrett .50 .20
657 Jim Shellenback .50 .20
658 Lee Lacy .50 .20
659 Joe Lis .50 .20
660 Larry Dierker .50 .20

1974 Topps Traded

The cards in this 44-card set measure 2 1/2" by 3 1/2". The 1974 Topps Traded set contains 43 player cards and one unnumbered checklist card. The fronts have the word "traded" in block letters and the backs are designed in newspaper style. Card numbers are the same as in the regular set except they are followed by a "T." No known scarcities exist for this set. The cards were inserted in all packs toward the end of the production run. They were produced in large enough quantity that they are no scarcer than the regular Topps cards.

	NM	Ex
COMPLETE SET (44)	20.00	8.00
23T Craig Robinson	.50	.20
42T Claude Osteen	.75	.30
43T Jim Wynn	.75	.30
51T Bobby Heise	.50	.20
59T Ross Grimsley	.50	.20
62T Bob Locker	.50	.20
63T Bill Sudakis	.50	.20
73T Mike Marshall	.75	.30
123T Nelson Briles	.75	.30
139T Aurelio Monteagudo	.50	.20
151T Diego Segui	.50	.20
165T Willie Davis	.75	.30
175T Reggie Cleveland	.50	.20
182T Lindy McDaniel	.75	.30
186T Fred Scherman	.50	.20
249T George Mitterwald	.50	.20
262T Ed Kirkpatrick	.50	.20
269T Bob Johnson	.50	.20
270T Ron Santo	1.00	.40
313T Barry Lersch	.50	.20
319T Randy Hundley	.75	.30
330T Juan Marichal	2.00	.80
348T Pete Richert	.50	.20
373T John Curtis	.50	.20
390T Lou Piniella	1.00	.40
428T Gary Sutherland	.50	.20
454T Kurt Bevacqua	.50	.20
458T Jim Ray	.50	.20
485T Felipe Alou	1.00	.40
486T Steve Stone	.75	.30
496T Tom Murphy	.50	.20
516T Horacio Pina	.50	.20
534T Eddie Watt	.50	.20
538T Cesar Tovar	.50	.20
544T Ron Schueler	.50	.20
579T Cecil Upshaw	.50	.20
585T Merv Rettenmund	.50	.20
612T Luke Walker	.50	.20
616T Larry Gura	.75	.30
618T Jim Mason	.50	.20
630T Tommie Agee	.75	.30
648T Terry Crowley	.50	.20
649T Fernando Gonzalez	.50	.20
NNO Traded Checklist	1.50	.30

1974 Topps Team Checklists

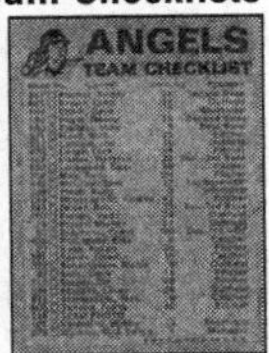

The cards in this 24-card set measure 2 1/2" by 3 1/2". The 1974 series of checklists was issued in packs with the regular cards for that year. The cards are unnumbered (arbitrarily numbered below alphabetically by team name) and have bright red borders. The year and team name appear in a green panel decorated by a crossed bats design, below which is a white area containing facsimile autographs of various players. The mustard-yellow and gray-colored backs list team members alphabetically, along with their card number, uniform number and position. Uncut sheets of these cards were also available through a wrapper mail-in offer. The uncut sheet value in NR/Mt or better condition is approximately $150.

	NM	Ex
COMPLETE SET (24)	20.00	6.00
COMMON TEAM (1-24)	1.00	.30

1975 Topps

The 1975 Topps set consists of 660 standard size cards. The design was radically different in appearance from sets of the preceding years. The most prominent change was the use of a two-color frame surrounding the picture area rather than a single, subdued color. A facsimile autograph appears on the picture, and the backs are printed in red and green on gray. Cards were released in ten-card wax packs, 18-card cello packs as well as in 42-card rack packs. The cello packs were issued 24 to a box. Cards 189-212 depict the MVP's of both leagues from 1951 through 1974. The first seven cards (1-7) feature players (listed in alphabetical order) breaking records or achieving milestones during the previous season. Cards 306-313 picture league leaders in various statistical categories. Cards 459-466 depict the results of post-season action. Team cards feature a checklist back for players on that team and show a small inset photo of the manager on the front. The following players' regular issue cards are explicitly denoted as All-Stars, 1, 50, 80, 140, 170, 180, 260, 320, 350, 390, 400, 420, 440, 470, 530, 570, and 600. This set is quite popular with collectors, at least in part due to the fact that the Rookie Cards of George Brett, Gary Carter, Keith Hernandez, Fred Lynn, Jim Rice and Robin Yount are all in the set.

NM Ex
COMPLETE SET (660) 500.00 200.00
WRAPPER (15-CENT) 8.00 3.20
1 Hank Aaron HL 30.00 10.00
2 Lou Brock HL 3.00 1.20
3 Bob Gibson HL 3.00 1.20
4 Al Kaline HL 6.00 2.40
5 Nolan Ryan HL 15.00 6.00
6 Mike Marshall HL 1.00 .40
7 Steve Busby HL 8.00 3.20
Dick Bosman
Nolan Ryan
8 Rogelio Moret .50 .20
9 Frank Tepedino 1.00 .40
10 Willie Davis 1.00 .40
11 Bill Melton .50 .20
12 David Clyde .50 .20
13 Gene Locklear RC 1.00 .40
14 Milt Wilcox .50 .20
15 Jose Cardenal 1.00 .40
16 Frank Tanana 2.00 .80
17 Dave Concepcion 2.00 .80
18 Tigers Team CL 2.00 .40
Ralph Houk MG
19 Jerry Koosman 1.00 .40
20 Thurman Munson 8.00 3.20
21 Rollie Fingers 3.00 1.20
22 Dave Cash .50 .20
23 Bill Russell 1.00 .40
24 Al Fitzmorris .50 .20
25 Lee May 1.00 .40
26 Dave McNally 1.00 .40
27 Ken Reitz .50 .20
28 Tom Murphy .50 .20
29 Dave Parker 3.00 1.20
30 Bert Blyleven 2.00 .80
31 Dave Rader .50 .20
32 Reggie Cleveland .50 .20
33 Dusty Baker 2.00 .80
34 Steve Renko .50 .20
35 Ron Santo 1.00 .40
36 Joe Lovitto .50 .20
37 Dave Freisleben .50 .20
38 Buddy Bell 2.00 .80
39 Andre Thornton 1.00 .40
40 Bill Singer .50 .20
41 Cesar Geronimo 1.00 .40
42 Joe Coleman .50 .20
43 Cleon Jones 1.00 .40
44 Pat Dobson .50 .20
45 Joe Rudi 1.00 .40
46 Phillies Team CL 2.00 .40
Danny Ozark MG UER
Terry Harmon listed as 339
instead of 399
47 Tommy John 2.00 .80
48 Freddie Patek 1.00 .40
49 Larry Dierker 1.00 .40
50 Brooks Robinson 8.00 3.20
51 Bob Forsch RC 1.00 .40
52 Darrell Porter 1.00 .40
53 Dave Giusti .50 .20
54 Eric Soderholm .50 .20
55 Bobby Bonds 2.00 .80
56 Rick Wise 1.00 .40
57 Dave Johnson 1.00 .40
58 Chuck Taylor .50 .20
59 Ken Henderson .50 .20
60 Fergie Jenkins 3.00 1.20
61 Dave Winfield 15.00 6.00
62 Fritz Peterson .50 .20
63 Steve Swisher .50 .20
64 Dave Chalk .50 .20
65 Don Gullett 1.00 .40
66 Willie Horton 1.00 .40
67 Tug McGraw 1.00 .40
68 Ron Blomberg .50 .20
69 John Odom .50 .20
70 Mike Schmidt 20.00 8.00
71 Charlie Hough 1.00 .40
72 Royals Team CL 2.00 .40
Jack McKeon MG
73 J.R. Richard 1.00 .40
74 Mark Belanger 1.00 .40
75 Ted Simmons 2.00 .80
76 Ed Sprague .50 .20
77 Richie Zisk 1.00 .40
78 Ray Corbin .50 .20
79 Gary Matthews 1.00 .40
80 Carlton Fisk 8.00 3.20
81 Ron Reed .50 .20
82 Pat Kelly .50 .20
83 Jim Merritt .50 .20
84 Enzo Hernandez .50 .20
85 Bill Bonham .50 .20
86 Joe Lis .50 .20
87 George Foster 2.00 .80
88 Tom Egan .50 .20
89 Jim Ray .50 .20
90 Rusty Staub 2.00 .80
91 Dick Green .50 .20
92 Cecil Upshaw .50 .20
93 Dave Lopes 2.00 .80
94 Jim Lonborg 1.00 .40
95 John Mayberry 1.00 .40
96 Mike Cosgrove .50 .20
97 Earl Williams .50 .20
98 Rich Folkers .50 .20
99 Mike Hegan .50 .20
100 Willie Stargell 4.00 1.60
101 Expos Team CL 2.00 .40
Gene Mauch MG
102 Joe Decker .50 .20
103 Rick Miller .50 .20
104 Bill Madlock 2.00 .80
105 Buzz Capra .50 .20
106 M. Hargrove RC UER 3.00 1.20
Gastonia At-bats are wrong
107 Jim Barr .50 .20
108 Tom Hall .50 .20
109 George Hendrick 1.00 .40
110 Wilbur Wood .50 .20
111 Wayne Garrett .50 .20
112 Larry Hardy .50 .20
113 Elliott Maddox .50 .20
114 Dick Lange .50 .20
115 Joe Ferguson .50 .20
116 Lerrin LaGrow .50 .20

117 Orioles Team CL 3.00 .60
Earl Weaver MG
118 Mike Anderson .50 .20
119 Tommy Helms .50 .20
120 Steve Busby UER 1.00 .40
(Photo actually
Fran Healy)
121 Bill North .50 .20
122 Al Hrabosky 1.00 .40
123 Johnny Briggs .50 .20
124 Jerry Reuss 1.00 .40
125 Ken Singleton 1.00 .40
126 Checklist 1-132 3.00 .60
127 Glenn Borgmann .50 .20
128 Bill Lee 1.00 .40
129 Rick Monday 1.00 .40
130 Phil Niekro 3.00 1.20
131 Toby Harrah 1.00 .40
132 Randy Moffitt .50 .20
133 Dan Driessen 1.00 .40
134 Ron Hodges .50 .20
135 Charlie Spikes .50 .20
136 Jim Mason .50 .20
137 Terry Forster 1.00 .40
138 Del Unser .50 .20
139 Horacio Pina .50 .20
140 Steve Garvey 3.00 1.20
141 Mickey Stanley 1.00 .40
142 Bob Reynolds .50 .20
143 Cliff Johnson 1.00 .40
144 Jim Wohlford .50 .20
145 Ken Holtzman 1.00 .40
146 Padres Team CL 2.00 .40
John McNamara MG
147 Pedro Garcia .50 .20
148 Jim Rooker .50 .20
149 Tim Foli .50 .20
150 Bob Gibson 6.00 2.40
151 Steve Brye .50 .20
152 Mario Guerrero .50 .20
153 Rick Reuschel 1.00 .40
154 Mike Lum .50 .20
155 Jim Bibby .50 .20
156 Dave Kingman 2.00 .80
157 Pedro Borbon 1.00 .40
158 Jerry Grote .50 .20
159 Steve Arlin .50 .20
160 Graig Nettles 2.00 .80
161 Stan Bahnsen .50 .20
162 Willie Montanez .50 .20
163 Jim Brewer .50 .20
164 Mickey Rivers 1.00 .40
165 Doug Rader 1.00 .40
166 Woodie Fryman .50 .20
167 Rich Coggins .50 .20
168 Bill Greif .50 .20
169 Cookie Rojas .50 .20
170 Bert Campaneris 1.00 .40
171 Ed Kirkpatrick .50 .20
172 Red Sox Team CL 3.00 .60
Darrell Johnson MG
173 Steve Rogers 1.00 .40
174 Bake McBride 1.00 .40
175 Don Money 1.00 .40
176 Burt Hooton 1.00 .40
177 Vic Correll .50 .20
178 Cesar Tovar .50 .20
179 Tom Bradley .50 .20
180 Joe Morgan 6.00 2.40
181 Fred Beene .50 .20
182 Don Hahn .50 .20
183 Mel Stottlemyre 1.00 .40
184 Jorge Orta .50 .20
185 Steve Carlton 8.00 3.20
186 Willie Crawford .50 .20
187 Denny Doyle .50 .20
188 Tom Griffin .50 .20
189 Larry (Yogi) Berra 4.00 1.60
Roy Campanella MVP
Campanella card never issued
190 Bobby Shantz 2.00 .80
Hank Sauer MVP
191 Al Rosen 2.00 .80
Roy Campanella MVP
192 Yogi Berra 4.00 1.60
Willie Mays MVP
193 Yogi Berra 3.00 1.20
Roy Campanella MVP
Campanella card never issued
he is pictured with LA cap
194 Mickey Mantle 10.00 4.00
Don Newcombe MVP
195 Mickey Mantle 12.00 4.80
Hank Aaron MVP
196 Jackie Jensen 3.00 1.20
Ernie Banks MVP
197 Nellie Fox 2.00 .80
Ernie Banks MVP
198 Roger Maris 2.00 .80
Dick Groat MVP
199 Roger Maris 3.00 1.20
Frank Robinson MVP
200 Mickey Mantle 10.00 4.00
Maury Wills MVP
(Wills card never issued)
201 Elston Howard 2.00 .80
Sandy Koufax MVP
202 Brooks Robinson 1.00 .40
Ken Boyer MVP
203 Zoilo Versalles 2.00 .80
Willie Mays MVP
204 Frank Robinson 6.00 2.40
Bob Clemente MVP
205 Carl Yastrzemski 2.00 .80
Orlando Cepeda MVP
206 Denny McLain UER 2.00 .80
Bob Gibson MVP
On the back McLain is spelled McClain
207 Harmon Killebrew 1.00 .40
Willie McCovey MVP
208 Boog Powell 2.00 .80
Johnny Bench MVP
209 Vida Blue 2.00 .80
Joe Torre MVP
210 Rich Allen 2.00 .80
Johnny Bench MVP
211 Reggie Jackson 5.00 2.00
Pete Rose MVP
212 Jeff Burroughs 2.00 .80
Steve Garvey MVP
213 Oscar Gamble 1.00 .40
214 Harry Parker .50 .20
215 Bobby Valentine 1.00 .40
216 Giants Team CL 2.00 .40
Wes Westrum MG
217 Lou Piniella 2.00 .80
218 Jerry Johnson .50 .20
219 Ed Herrmann .50 .20
220 Don Sutton 3.00 1.20
221 Aurelio Rodriguez .50 .20
222 Dan Spillner .50 .20
223 Robin Yount RC 50.00 20.00
224 Ramon Hernandez .50 .20
225 Bob Grich 1.00 .40
226 Bill Campbell .50 .20
227 Bob Watson 1.00 .40
228 George Brett RC 80.00 32.00
229 Barry Foote .50 .20
230 Jim Hunter 4.00 1.60
231 Mike Tyson .50 .20
232 Diego Segui .50 .20
233 Billy Grabarkewitz .50 .20
234 Tom Grieve 1.00 .40
235 Jack Billingham 1.00 .40
236 Angels Team CL 2.00 .40
Dick Williams MG
237 Carl Morton 1.00 .40
238 Dave Duncan 1.00 .40
239 George Stone .50 .20
240 Garry Maddox 1.00 .40
241 Dick Tidrow .50 .20
242 Jay Johnstone 1.00 .40
243 Jim Kaat 2.00 .80
244 Bill Buckner 1.00 .40
245 Mickey Lolich 2.00 .80
246 Cardinals Team CL 2.00 .40
Red Schoendienst MG
247 Enos Cabell .50 .20
248 Randy Jones 2.00 .80
249 Danny Thompson .50 .20
250 Ken Brett .50 .20
251 Fran Healy .50 .20
252 Fred Scherman .50 .20
253 Jesus Alou .50 .20
254 Mike Torrez 1.00 .40
255 Dwight Evans 2.00 .80
256 Billy Champion .50 .20
257 Checklist: 133-264 3.00 .60
258 Dave LaRoche .50 .20
259 Len Randle .50 .20
260 Johnny Bench 15.00 6.00
261 Andy Hassler .50 .20
262 Rowland Office .50 .20
263 Jim Perry 1.00 .40
264 John Milner .50 .20
265 Ron Bryant .50 .20
266 Sandy Alomar 1.00 .40
267 Dick Ruthven .50 .20
268 Hal McRae 1.00 .40
269 Doug Rau .50 .20
270 Ron Fairly 1.00 .40
271 Gerry Moses .50 .20
272 Lynn McGlothen .50 .20
273 Steve Braun .50 .20
274 Vicente Romo .50 .20
275 Paul Blair 1.00 .40
276 White Sox Team CL 2.00 .40
Chuck Tanner MG
277 Frank Taveras .50 .20
278 Paul Lindblad .50 .20
279 Milt May .50 .20
280 Carl Yastrzemski 12.00 4.80
281 Jim Slaton .50 .20
282 Jerry Morales .50 .20
283 Steve Foucault .50 .20
284 Ken Griffey 4.00 1.60
285 Ellie Rodriguez .50 .20
286 Mike Jorgensen .50 .20
287 Roric Harrison .50 .20
288 Bruce Ellingsen .50 .20
289 Ken Rudolph .50 .20
290 Jon Matlack .50 .20
291 Bill Sudakis .50 .20
292 Ron Schueler .50 .20
293 Dick Sharon .50 .20
294 Geoff Zahn .50 .20
295 Vada Pinson 2.00 .80
296 Alan Foster .50 .20
297 Craig Kusick .50 .20
298 Johnny Grubb .50 .20
299 Bucky Dent 2.00 .80
300 Reggie Jackson 15.00 6.00
301 Dave Roberts .50 .20
302 Rick Burleson 1.00 .40
303 Grant Jackson .50 .20
304 Pirates Team CL 2.00 .40
Danny Murtaugh MG
305 Jim Colborn .50 .20
306 Rod Carew 2.00 .80
Ralph Garr LL
307 Dick Allen 4.00 1.60
Mike Schmidt LL
308 Jeff Burroughs 2.00 .80
Johnny Bench LL
309 Bill North 2.00 .80
Lou Brock LL
310 Jim Hunter 2.00 .80
Fergie Jenkins
Andy Messersmith
Phil Niekro LL
311 Jim Hunter 2.00 .80
Buzz Capra LL
312 Nolan Ryan 12.00 4.80
Steve Carlton LL
313 Terry Forster 1.00 .40
Mike Marshall LL
314 Buck Martinez .50 .20
315 Don Kessinger 1.00 .40
316 Jackie Brown .50 .20
317 Joe Lahoud .50 .20
318 Ernie McAnally .50 .20
319 Johnny Oates 1.00 .40
320 Pete Rose 30.00 12.00
321 Rudy May .50 .20
322 Ed Goodson .50 .20
323 Fred Holdsworth .50 .20
324 Ed Kranepool 1.00 .40
325 Tony Oliva 2.00 .80
326 Wayne Twitchell .50 .20
327 Jerry Hairston .50 .20
328 Sonny Siebert .50 .20
329 Ted Kubiak .50 .20
330 Mike Marshall 1.00 .40
331 Indians Team CL 2.00 .40
Frank Robinson MG
332 Fred Kendall .50 .20
333 Dick Drago .50 .20
334 Greg Gross .50 .20
335 Jim Palmer 6.00 2.40
336 Rennie Stennett .50 .20
337 Kevin Kobel .50 .20
338 Rich Stelmaszek .50 .20
339 Jim Fregosi 1.00 .40
340 Paul Splittorff .50 .20
341 Hal Breeden .50 .20
342 Leroy Stanton .50 .20
343 Danny Frisella .50 .20
344 Ben Oglivie 1.00 .40
345 Clay Carroll 1.00 .40
346 Bobby Darwin .50 .20
347 Mike Caldwell .50 .20
348 Tony Muser .50 .20
349 Ray Sadecki .50 .20
350 Bobby Murcer 1.00 .40
351 Bob Boone 2.00 .80
352 Darold Knowles .50 .20
353 Luis Melendez .50 .20
354 Dick Bosman .50 .20
355 Chris Cannizzaro .50 .20
356 Rico Petrocelli 1.00 .40
357 Ken Forsch UER .50 .20
Forsch is misspelled in blurb
358 Al Bumbry 1.00 .40
359 Paul Popovich .50 .20
360 George Scott 1.00 .40
361 Dodgers Team CL 2.00 .40
Walter Alston MG
362 Steve Hargan .50 .20
363 Carmen Fanzone .50 .20
364 Doug Bird .50 .20
365 Bob Bailey .50 .20
366 Ken Sanders .50 .20
367 Craig Robinson .50 .20
368 Vic Albury .50 .20
369 Merv Rettenmund .50 .20
370 Tom Seaver 12.00 4.80
371 Gates Brown .50 .20
372 John D'Acquisto .50 .20
373 Bill Sharp .50 .20
374 Eddie Watt .50 .20
375 Roy White 1.00 .40
376 Steve Yeager 1.00 .40
377 Tom Hilgendorf .50 .20
378 Derrel Thomas .50 .20
379 Bernie Carbo .50 .20
380 Sal Bando 1.00 .40
381 John Curtis .50 .20
382 Don Baylor 2.00 .80
383 Jim York .50 .20
384 Brewers Team 2.00 .40
Del Crandall MG
385 Dock Ellis .50 .20
386 Checklist: 265-396 UER 3.00 .60
Dick Sharon's name is misspelled
387 Jim Spencer .50 .20
388 Steve Stone 1.00 .40
389 Tony Solaita .50 .20
390 Ron Cey 2.00 .80
391 Don DeMola .50 .20
392 Bruce Bochte RC 1.00 .40
393 Gary Gentry .50 .20
394 Larvell Blanks .50 .20
395 Bud Harrelson 1.00 .40
396 Fred Norman 1.00 .40
397 Bill Freehan 1.00 .40
398 Elias Sosa .50 .20
399 Terry Harmon .50 .20
400 Dick Allen 2.00 .80
401 Mike Wallace .50 .20
402 Bob Tolan .50 .20
403 Tom Buskey .50 .20
404 Ted Sizemore .50 .20
405 John Montague .50 .20
406 Bob Gallagher .50 .20
407 Herb Washington RC 2.00 .80
408 Clyde Wright UER .50 .20
Listed with wrong 1974 team
409 Bob Robertson .50 .20
410 Mike Cueller UER 1.00 .40
Sic, Cuellar
411 George Mitterwald .50 .20
412 Bill Hands .50 .20
413 Marty Pattin .50 .20
414 Manny Mota 1.00 .40
415 John Hiller 1.00 .40
416 Larry Lintz .50 .20
417 Skip Lockwood .50 .20
418 Leo Foster .50 .20
419 Dave Goltz .50 .20
420 Larry Bowa 2.00 .80
421 Mets Team CL 3.00 .60
Yogi Berra MG
422 Brian Downing 1.00 .40
423 Clay Kirby .50 .20
424 John Lowenstein .50 .20
425 Tito Fuentes .50 .20
426 George Medich .50 .20
427 Clarence Gaston 1.00 .40
428 Dave Hamilton .50 .20
429 Jim Dwyer .50 .20
430 Luis Tiant 2.00 .80
431 Rod Gilbreath .50 .20
432 Ken Berry .50 .20
433 Larry Demery .50 .20
434 Bob Locker .50 .20
435 Dave Nelson .50 .20
436 Ken Frailing .50 .20
437 Al Cowens 1.00 .40
438 Don Carrithers .50 .20
439 Ed Brinkman .50 .20
440 Andy Messersmith 1.00 .40
441 Bobby Heise .50 .20
442 Maximino Leon .50 .20
443 Twins Team CL 2.00 .40
Frank Quilici MG
444 Gene Garber 1.00 .40
445 Felix Millan .50 .20
446 Bart Johnson .50 .20
447 Terry Crowley .50 .20
448 Frank Duffy .50 .20
449 Charlie Williams .50 .20
450 Willie McCovey 6.00 2.40
451 Rick Dempsey 1.00 .40
452 Angel Mangual .50 .20
453 Claude Osteen 1.00 .40
454 Doug Griffin .50 .20
455 Don Wilson .50 .20
456 Bob Coluccio .50 .20
457 Mario Mendoza .50 .20
458 Ross Grimsley .50 .20
459 1974 AL Champs 1.00 .40
A's over Orioles
(Second base action
pictured)
460 Steve Garvey NLCS 2.00 .80
Frank Taveras
461 Reggie Jackson WS 5.00 2.00
462 World Series Game 2 1.00 .40
(Dodger dugout)
463 Rollie Fingers WS 2.00 .80
464 World Series Game 4 1.00 .40
(A's batter)
465 Joe Rudi WS5 1.00 .40
466 WS Summary 2.00 .80
A's do it again;
win third straight
A's group picture
467 Ed Halicki .50 .20
468 Bobby Mitchell .50 .20
469 Tom Dettore .50 .20
470 Jeff Burroughs 1.00 .40
471 Bob Stinson .50 .20
472 Bruce Dal Canton .50 .20
473 Ken McMullen .50 .20
474 Luke Walker .50 .20
475 Darrell Evans 1.00 .40
476 Ed Figueroa .50 .20
477 Tom Hutton .50 .20
478 Tom Burgmeier .50 .20
479 Ken Boswell .50 .20
480 Carlos May .50 .20
481 Will McEnaney 1.00 .40
482 Tom McCraw .50 .20
483 Steve Ontiveros .50 .20
484 Glenn Beckert 1.00 .40
485 Sparky Lyle 1.00 .40
486 Ray Fosse .50 .20
487 Astros Team CL 2.00 .40
Preston Gomez MG
488 Bill Travers .50 .20
489 Cecil Cooper 2.00 .80
490 Reggie Smith 1.00 .40
491 Doyle Alexander 1.00 .40
492 Rich Hebner 1.00 .40
493 Don Stanhouse .50 .20
494 Pete LaCock .50 .20
495 Nelson Briles 1.00 .40
496 Pepe Frias .50 .20
497 Jim Nettles .50 .20
498 Al Downing .50 .20
499 Marty Perez .50 .20
500 Nolan Ryan 50.00 20.00
501 Bill Robinson 1.00 .40
502 Pat Bourque .50 .20
503 Fred Stanley .50 .20
504 Buddy Bradford .50 .20
505 Chris Speier .50 .20
506 Leron Lee .50 .20
507 Tom Carroll .50 .20
508 Bob Hansen .50 .20
509 Dave Hilton .50 .20
510 Vida Blue 1.00 .40
511 Rangers Team CL 2.00 .40
Billy Martin MG
512 Larry Milbourne .50 .20
513 Dick Pole .50 .20
514 Jose Cruz 2.00 .80
515 Manny Sanguillen 1.00 .40
516 Don Hood .50 .20
517 Checklist: 397-528 3.00 .60
518 Leo Cardenas .50 .20
519 Jim Todd .50 .20
520 Amos Otis 1.00 .40
521 Dennis Blair .50 .20
522 Gary Sutherland .50 .20
523 Tom Paciorek 1.00 .40
524 John Doherty .50 .20
525 Tom House .50 .20
526 Larry Hisle 1.00 .40
527 Mac Scarce .50 .20
528 Eddie Leon .50 .20
529 Gary Thomasson .50 .20
530 Gaylord Perry 3.00 1.20
531 Reds Team CL 5.00 1.00
Sparky Anderson MG
532 Gorman Thomas 1.00 .40
533 Rudy Meoli .50 .20
534 Alex Johnson .50 .20
535 Gene Tenace 1.00 .40
536 Bob Moose .50 .20
537 Tommy Harper 1.00 .40
538 Duffy Dyer .50 .20
539 Jesse Jefferson .50 .20
540 Lou Brock 6.00 2.40
541 Roger Metzger .50 .20
542 Pete Broberg .50 .20
543 Larry Biittner .50 .20
544 Steve Mingori .50 .20
545 Billy Williams 3.00 1.20
546 John Knox .50 .20
547 Von Joshua .50 .20
548 Charlie Sands .50 .20
549 Bill Butler .50 .20
550 Ralph Garr 1.00 .40
551 Larry Christenson .50 .20
552 Jack Brohamer .50 .20
553 John Boccabella .50 .20
554 Goose Gossage 2.00 .80
555 Al Oliver 2.00 .80
556 Tim Johnson .50 .20
557 Larry Gura .50 .20
558 Dave Roberts .50 .20
559 Bob Montgomery .50 .20
560 Tony Perez 4.00 1.60
561 A's Team CL 2.00 .40
Alvin Dark MG
562 Gary Nolan 1.00 .40
563 Wilbur Howard .50 .20
564 Tommy Davis 1.00 .40
565 Joe Torre 2.00 .80
566 Ray Burris .50 .20
567 Jim Sundberg RC 2.00 .80
568 Dale Murray .50 .20
569 Frank White 1.00 .40
570 Jim Wynn 1.00 .40
571 Dave Lemanczyk .50 .20
572 Roger Nelson .50 .20
573 Orlando Pena .50 .20
574 Tony Taylor .50 .20
575 Gene Clines .50 .20
576 Phil Roof .50 .20
577 John Morris .50 .20
578 Dave Tomlin .50 .20
579 Skip Pitlock .50 .20
580 Frank Robinson 6.00 2.40
581 Darrel Chaney .50 .20
582 Eduardo Rodriguez .50 .20
583 Andy Etchebarren .50 .20
584 Mike Garman .50 .20
585 Chris Chambliss 1.00 .40
586 Tim McCarver 2.00 .80
587 Chris Ward .50 .20
588 Rick Auerbach .50 .20
589 Braves Team CL 2.00 .40
Clyde King MG
590 Cesar Cedeno 1.00 .40
591 Glenn Abbott .50 .20
592 Balor Moore .50 .20
593 Gene Lamont .50 .20
594 Jim Fuller .50 .20
595 Joe Niekro 1.00 .40
596 Ollie Brown .50 .20
597 Winston Llenas .50 .20
598 Bruce Kison .50 .20
599 Nate Colbert .50 .20
600 Rod Carew 8.00 3.20
601 Juan Beniquez .50 .20
602 John Vukovich .50 .20
603 Lew Krausse .50 .20
604 Oscar Zamora .50 .20
605 John Ellis .50 .20
606 Bruce Miller .50 .20
607 Jim Holt .50 .20
608 Gene Michael .50 .20
609 Elrod Hendricks .50 .20
610 Ron Hunt .50 .20
611 Yankees Team CL 2.00 .40
Bill Virdon MG
612 Terry Hughes .50 .20
613 Bill Parsons .50 .20
614 Jack Kucek 1.00 .40
Dyar Miller
Vern Ruhle
Paul Siebert
615 Pat Darcy 2.00 .80
Dennis Leonard RC
Tom Underwood
Hank Webb
616 Dave Augustine 15.00 6.00
Pepe Mangual
Jim Rice RC
John Scott
617 Mike Cubbage 2.00 .80
Doug DeCinces RC
Reggie Sanders
Manny Trillo
618 Jamie Easterly 1.00 .40
Tom Johnson
Scott McGregor RC
Rick Rhoden RC
619 Benny Ayala 1.00 .40
Nyls Nyman
Tommy Smith
Jerry Turner
620 Gary Carter RC 15.00 6.00
Marc Hill
Danny Meyer
Leon Roberts
621 John Denny RC 2.00 .80
Rawly Eastwick
Jim Kern
Juan Veintidos
622 Ed Armbrister 8.00 3.20
Fred Lynn RC
Tom Poquette
Terry Whitfield UER
(Listed as Ney York)
623 Phil Garner 10.00 4.00
Keith Hernandez RC UER
(Sic, bats right)
Bob Sheldon
Tom Veryzer
624 Doug Konieczny 1.00 .40
Gary Lavelle
Jim Otten
Eddie Solomon
625 Boog Powell 2.00 .80
626 Larry Haney UER .50 .20
Photo actually
Dave Duncan
627 Tom Walker .50 .20
628 Ron LeFlore RC 1.00 .40
629 Joe Hoerner .50 .20
630 Greg Luzinski 2.00 .80
631 Lee Lacy .50 .20
632 Morris Nettles .50 .20
633 Paul Casanova .50 .20
634 Cy Acosta .50 .20
635 Chuck Dobson .50 .20
636 Charlie Moore .50 .20
637 Ted Martinez .50 .20
638 Cubs Team CL 2.00 .40
Jim Marshall MG
639 Steve Kline .50 .20
640 Harmon Killebrew 6.00 2.40
641 Jim Northrup 1.00 .40
642 Mike Phillips .50 .20
643 Brent Strom .50 .20
644 Bill Fahey .50 .20
645 Danny Cater .50 .20
646 Checklist: 529-660 3.00 .60
647 Cl. Washington RC 2.00 .80
648 Dave Pagan .50 .20
649 Jack Heidemann .50 .20
650 Dave May .50 .20
651 John Morlan .50 .20
652 Lindy McDaniel 1.00 .40
653 Lee Richard UER .50 .20
(Listed as Richards
on card front)

654 Jerry Terrell .50 .20
655 Rico Carty 1.00 .40
656 Bill Plummer .50 .20
657 Bob Oliver .50 .20
658 Vic Harris .50 .20
659 Bob Apodaca .50 .20
660 Hank Aaron 30.00 9.00

1975 Topps Mini

This set is a parallel to the regular 1975 Topps set. Each card measures 2 1/4" by 3 1/8" and the set was regionally issued. Michigan and California were among the two areas to receive this issue. These cards were also sporadically distributed in other areas as collectors have recalled getting them in their local areas other than those mentioned above. The cards are currently valued the same as the regular 75 Topps cards and have proven not to have remained as popular as the regular 1975 issue. These cards were issued in 10 card packs which cost 15 cents on issue and were packed 36 to a box.

NM Ex
COMPLETE SET (660) 600.00 240.00
*MINI STARS: .75X TO 1.5X BASIC CARDS
*MINI RC'S: .5X TO 1X BASIC ROOKIE CARDS

1976 Topps

The 1976 Topps set of 660 standard-size cards is known for its sharp color photographs and interesting presentation of subjects. Cards were issued in ten-card wax packs, 42-card rack packs as well as cello packs and other options. Team cards feature a checklist back for players on that team and show a small inset photo of the manager on the front. A "Father and Son" series (66-70) spotlights five Major Leaguers whose fathers also made the "Big Show." Other subseries include "All Time All Stars" (341-350), "Record Breakers" from the previous season (1-6), League Leaders (191-205), Post-season cards (461-462), and Rookie Prospects (589-599). The following players' regular issue cards are explicitly denoted as All-Stars, 10, 48, 60, 140, 150, 165, 169, 240, 300, 370, 380, 395, 400, 420, 475, 500, 580, and 650. The key Rookie Cards in this set are Dennis Eckersley, Ron Guidry, and Willie Randolph. We've heard recent reports that this set was also issued in seven-card wax packs which cost a dime. Confirmation of that information would be appreciated.

NM Ex
COMPLETE SET (660) 250.00 100.00
1 Hank Aaron RB 15.00 4.70
2 Bobby Bonds RB 1.50 .60
3 Mickey Lolich RB .75 .30
4 Dave Lopes RB .75 .30
5 Tom Seaver RB 5.00 2.00
6 Rennie Stennett RB .75 .30
7 Jim Umbarger .40 .16
8 Tito Fuentes .40 .16
9 Paul Lindblad .40 .16
10 Lou Brock 5.00 2.00
11 Jim Hughes .40 .16
12 Richie Zisk .75 .30
13 John Wockenfuss .40 .16
14 Gene Garber .75 .30
15 George Scott .75 .30
16 Bob Apodaca .40 .16
17 New York Yankees 1.50 .30
Team Card CL
Billy Martin MG
18 Dale Murray .40 .16
19 George Brett 30.00 12.00
20 Bob Watson .75 .30
21 Dave LaRoche .40 .16
22 Bill Russell .75 .30
23 Brian Downing .40 .16
24 Cesar Geronimo .75 .30
25 Mike Torrez .75 .30
26 Andre Thornton .75 .30
27 Ed Figueroa .40 .16
28 Dusty Baker 1.50 .60
29 Rick Burleson .75 .30
30 John Montefusco .75 .30
31 Len Randle .40 .16
32 Danny Frisella .40 .16
33 Bill North .40 .16
34 Mike Garman .40 .16
35 Tony Oliva 1.50 .60
36 Frank Taveras .40 .16
37 John Hiller .75 .30
38 Garry Maddox .75 .30
39 Pete Broberg .40 .16
40 Dave Kingman 1.50 .60
41 Tippy Martinez .75 .30
42 Barry Foote .40 .16
43 Paul Splittorff .40 .16
44 Doug Rader .75 .30
45 Boog Powell 1.50 .60
46 Los Angeles Dodgers 1.50 .30
Team Card CL
Walter Alston MG
47 Jesse Jefferson .40 .16
48 Dave Concepcion 1.50 .60
49 Dave Duncan .75 .30
50 Fred Lynn 1.50 .60
51 Ray Burris .40 .16
52 Dave Chalk .40 .16
53 Mike Beard .40 .16
54 Dave Rader .40 .16
55 Gaylord Perry 2.50 1.00
56 Bob Tolan .40 .16
57 Phil Garner .75 .30
58 Ron Reed .40 .16
59 Larry Hisle .75 .30
60 Jerry Reuss .75 .30
61 Ron LeFlore .75 .30
62 Johnny Oates .75 .30
63 Bobby Darwin .40 .16
64 Jerry Koosman .75 .30
65 Chris Chambliss .75 .30
66 Gus Bell FS .75 .30
Buddy Bell
67 Ray Boone FS .75 .30
Bob Boone
68 Joe Coleman FS .40 .16
Joe Coleman Jr.
69 Jim Hegan FS .40 .16
Mike Hegan
70 Roy Smalley FS .75 .30
Roy Smalley Jr.
71 Steve Rogers .75 .30
72 Hal McRae .75 .30
73 Baltimore Orioles 1.50 .30
Team Card CL
Earl Weaver MG
74 Oscar Gamble .75 .30
75 Larry Dierker .75 .30
76 Willie Crawford .40 .16
77 Pedro Borbon .75 .30
78 Cecil Cooper .75 .30
79 Jerry Morales .40 .16
80 Jim Kaat 1.50 .60
81 Darrell Evans .75 .30
82 Von Joshua .40 .16
83 Jim Spencer .40 .16
84 Brent Strom .40 .16
85 Mickey Rivers .75 .30
86 Mike Tyson .40 .16
87 Tom Burgmeier .40 .16
88 Duffy Dyer .40 .16
89 Vern Ruhle .40 .16
90 Sal Bando .75 .30
91 Tom Hutton .40 .16
92 Eduardo Rodriguez .40 .16
93 Mike Phillips .40 .16
94 Jim Dwyer .40 .16
95 Brooks Robinson 6.00 2.40
96 Doug Bird .40 .16
97 Wilbur Howard .40 .16
98 Dennis Eckersley RC 25.00 10.00
99 Lee Lacy .40 .16
100 Jim Hunter 3.00 1.20
101 Pete LaCock .40 .16
102 Jim Willoughby .40 .16
103 Biff Pocoroba .40 .16
104 Cincinnati Reds 2.50 .50
Team Card CL
Sparky Anderson MG
105 Gary Lavelle .40 .16
106 Tom Grieve .75 .30
107 Dave Roberts .40 .16
108 Don Kirkwood .40 .16
109 Larry Lintz .40 .16
110 Carlos May .40 .16
111 Danny Thompson .40 .16
112 Kent Tekulve RC 1.50 .60
113 Gary Sutherland .40 .16
114 Jay Johnstone .75 .30
115 Ken Holtzman .75 .30
116 Charlie Moore .40 .16
117 Mike Jorgensen .40 .16
118 Boston Red Sox 1.50 .30
Team Card CL
Darrell Johnson MG
119 Checklist 1-132 1.50 .30
120 Rusty Staub .75 .30
121 Tony Solaita .40 .16
122 Mike Cosgrove .40 .16
123 Walt Williams .40 .16
124 Doug Rau .40 .16
125 Don Baylor 1.50 .60
126 Tom Dettore .40 .16
127 Larvell Blanks .40 .16
128 Ken Griffey Sr. 2.50 1.00
129 Andy Etchebarren .40 .16
130 Luis Tiant 1.50 .60
131 Bill Stein .40 .16
132 Don Hood .40 .16
133 Gary Matthews .75 .30
134 Mike Ivie .40 .16
135 Bake McBride .75 .30
136 Dave Goltz .40 .16
137 Bill Robinson .75 .30
138 Lerrin LaGrow .40 .16
139 Gorman Thomas .75 .30
140 Vida Blue .75 .30
141 Larry Parrish RC 1.50 .60
142 Dick Drago .40 .16
143 Jerry Grote .40 .16
144 Al Fitzmorris .40 .16
145 Larry Bowa .75 .30
146 George Medich .40 .16
147 Houston Astros 1.50 .30
Team Card CL
Bill Virdon MG
148 Stan Thomas .40 .16
149 Tommy Davis .75 .30
150 Steve Garvey 2.50 1.00
151 Bill Bonham .40 .16
152 Leroy Stanton .40 .16
153 Buzz Capra .40 .16
154 Bucky Dent .75 .30
155 Jack Billingham .75 .30
156 Rico Carty .75 .30
157 Mike Caldwell .40 .16
158 Ken Reitz .40 .16
159 Jerry Terrell .40 .16
160 Dave Winfield 10.00 4.00
161 Bruce Kison .40 .16
162 Jack Pierce .40 .16
163 Jim Slaton .40 .16
164 Pepe Mangual .40 .16
165 Gene Tenace .75 .30
166 Skip Lockwood .40 .16
167 Freddie Patek .75 .30
168 Tom Hilgendorf .40 .16
169 Graig Nettles 1.50 .60
170 Rick Wise .40 .16
171 Greg Gross .40 .16
172 Texas Rangers 1.50 .30
Team Card CL
Frank Lucchesi MG
173 Steve Swisher .40 .16
174 Charlie Hough .75 .30
175 Ken Singleton .75 .30
176 Dick Lange .40 .16
177 Marty Perez .40 .16
178 Tom Buskey .40 .16
179 George Foster 1.50 .60
180 Goose Gossage 1.50 .60
181 Willie Montanez .40 .16
182 Harry Rasmussen .40 .16
183 Steve Braun .40 .16
184 Bill Greif .40 .16
185 Dave Parker 1.50 .60
186 Tom Walker .40 .16
187 Pedro Garcia .40 .16
188 Fred Scherman .40 .16
189 Claudell Washington .75 .30
190 Jon Matlack .40 .16
191 Bill Madlock .75 .30
Ted Simmons
Manny Sanguillen LL
192 Rod Carew 2.50 1.00
Fred Lynn
Thurman Munson LL
193 Mike Schmidt 3.00 1.20
Dave Kingman
Greg Luzinski LL
194 Reggie Jackson 3.00 1.20
George Scott
John Mayberry LL
195 Greg Luzinski 1.50 .60
Johnny Bench
Tony Perez LL
196 George Scott .75 .30
John Mayberry
Fred Lynn LL
197 Dave Lopes 1.50 .60
Joe Morgan
Lou Brock LL
198 Mickey Rivers .75 .30
Claudell Washington
Amos Otis LL
199 Tom Seaver 2.50 1.00
Randy Jones
Andy Messersmith LL
200 Jim Hunter 1.50 .60
Jim Palmer
Vida Blue LL
201 Randy Jones 1.50 .60
Andy Messersmith
Tom Seaver LL
202 Jim Palmer 3.00 1.20
Jim Hunter
Dennis Eckersley LL
203 Tom Seaver 2.50 1.00
John Montefusco
Andy Messersmith LL
204 Frank Tanana .75 .30
Bert Blyleven
Gaylord Perry LL
205 Al Hrabosky .75 .30
Rich Gossage LL
206 Manny Trillo .40 .16
207 Andy Hassler .40 .16
208 Mike Lum .40 .16
209 Alan Ashby .75 .30
210 Lee May .75 .30
211 Clay Carroll .75 .30
212 Pat Kelly .40 .16
213 Dave Heaverlo .40 .16
214 Eric Soderholm .40 .16
215 Reggie Smith .75 .30
216 Montreal Expos 1.50 .30
Team Card CL
Karl Kuehl MG
217 Dave Freisleben .40 .16
218 John Knox .40 .16
219 Tom Murphy .40 .16
220 Manny Sanguillen .75 .30
221 Jim Todd .40 .16
222 Wayne Garrett .40 .16
223 Ollie Brown .40 .16
224 Jim York .40 .16
225 Roy White .75 .30
226 Jim Sundberg .75 .30
227 Oscar Zamora .40 .16
228 John Hale .40 .16
229 Jerry Remy .40 .16
230 Carl Yastrzemski 10.00 4.00
231 Tom House .40 .16
232 Frank Duffy .40 .16
233 Grant Jackson .40 .16
234 Mike Sadek .40 .16
235 Bert Blyleven 1.50 .60
236 Kansas City Royals 1.50 .30
Team Card CL
Whitey Herzog MG
237 Dave Hamilton .40 .16
238 Larry Biittner .40 .16
239 John Curtis .40 .16
240 Pete Rose 25.00 10.00
241 Hector Torres .40 .16
242 Dan Meyer .40 .16
243 Jim Rooker .40 .16
244 Bill Sharp .40 .16
245 Felix Millan .40 .16
246 Cesar Tovar .40 .16
247 Terry Harmon .40 .16
248 Dick Tidrow .40 .16
249 Cliff Johnson .75 .30
250 Fergie Jenkins 2.50 1.00
251 Rick Monday .75 .30
252 Tim Nordbrook .40 .16
253 Bill Buckner .75 .30
254 Rudy Meoli .40 .16
255 Fritz Peterson .40 .16
256 Rowland Office .40 .16
257 Ross Grimsley .40 .16
258 Nyls Nyman .40 .16
259 Darrel Chaney .40 .16
260 Steve Busby .40 .16
261 Gary Thomasson .40 .16
262 Checklist 133-264 1.50 .30
263 Lyman Bostock RC 1.50 .60
264 Steve Renko .40 .16
265 Willie Davis .75 .30
266 Alan Foster .40 .16
267 Aurelio Rodriguez .40 .16
268 Del Unser .40 .16
269 Rick Austin .40 .16
270 Willie Stargell 3.00 1.20
271 Jim Lonborg .75 .30
272 Rick Dempsey .75 .30
273 Joe Niekro .75 .30
274 Tommy Harper .75 .30
275 Rick Manning .40 .16
276 Mickey Scott .40 .16
277 Chicago Cubs 1.50 .30
Team Card CL
Jim Marshall MG
278 Bernie Carbo .40 .16
279 Roy Howell .40 .16
280 Burt Hooton .75 .30
281 Dave May .40 .16
282 Dan Osborn .40 .16
283 Merv Rettenmund .40 .16
284 Steve Ontiveros .40 .16
285 Mike Cuellar .75 .30
286 Jim Wohlford .40 .16
287 Pete Mackanin .40 .16
288 Bill Campbell .40 .16
289 Enzo Hernandez .40 .16
290 Ted Simmons .75 .30
291 Ken Sanders .40 .16
292 Leon Roberts .40 .16
293 Bill Castro .40 .16
294 Ed Kirkpatrick .40 .16
295 Dave Cash .40 .16
296 Pat Dobson .40 .16
297 Roger Metzger .40 .16
298 Dick Bosman .40 .16
299 Champ Summers .40 .16
300 Johnny Bench 12.00 4.80
301 Jackie Brown .40 .16
302 Rick Miller .40 .16
303 Steve Foucault .40 .16
304 California Angels 1.50 .30
Team Card CL
Dick Williams MG
305 Andy Messersmith .75 .30
306 Rod Gilbreath .40 .16
307 Al Bumbry .75 .30
308 Jim Barr .40 .16
309 Bill Melton .40 .16
310 Randy Jones .75 .30
311 Cookie Rojas .40 .16
312 Don Carrithers .40 .16
313 Dan Ford .40 .16
314 Ed Kranepool .40 .16
315 Al Hrabosky .75 .30
316 Robin Yount 15.00 6.00
317 John Candelaria RC 1.50 .60
318 Bob Boone 1.50 .60
319 Larry Gura .40 .16
320 Willie Horton .75 .30
321 Jose Cruz 1.50 .60
322 Glenn Abbott .40 .16
323 Rob Sperring .40 .16
324 Jim Bibby .40 .16
325 Tony Perez 3.00 1.20
326 Dick Pole .40 .16
327 Dave Moates .40 .16
328 Carl Morton .40 .16
329 Joe Ferguson .40 .16
330 Nolan Ryan 25.00 10.00
331 San Diego Padres 1.50 .30
Team Card CL
John McNamara MG
332 Charlie Williams .40 .16
333 Bob Coluccio .40 .16
334 Dennis Leonard .75 .30
335 Bob Grich .75 .30
336 Vic Albury .40 .16
337 Bud Harrelson .75 .30
338 Bob Bailey .40 .16
339 John Denny .75 .30
340 Jim Rice 4.00 1.60
341 Lou Gehrig ATG 12.00 4.80
342 Rogers Hornsby ATG 3.00 1.20
343 Pie Traynor ATG 1.50 .60
344 Honus Wagner ATG 5.00 2.00
345 Babe Ruth ATG 15.00 6.00
346 Ty Cobb ATG 12.00 4.80
347 Ted Williams ATG 12.00 4.80
348 Mickey Cochrane ATG 1.50 .60
349 Walter Johnson ATG 5.00 2.00
350 Lefty Grove ATG 1.50 .60
351 Randy Hundley .75 .30
352 Dave Giusti .40 .16
353 Sixto Lezcano .75 .30
354 Ron Blomberg .40 .16
355 Steve Carlton 6.00 2.40
356 Ted Martinez .40 .16
357 Ken Forsch .40 .16
358 Buddy Bell .75 .30
359 Rick Reuschel .75 .30
360 Jeff Burroughs .75 .30
361 Detroit Tigers 1.50 .30
Team Card CL
Ralph Houk MG
362 Will McEnaney .75 .30
363 Dave Collins RC .75 .30
364 Elias Sosa .40 .16
365 Carlton Fisk 6.00 2.40
366 Bobby Valentine .75 .30
367 Bruce Miller .40 .16
368 Wilbur Wood .40 .16
369 Frank White .75 .30
370 Ron Cey .75 .30
371 Elrod Hendricks .40 .16
372 Rick Baldwin .40 .16
373 Johnny Briggs .40 .16
374 Dan Warthen .40 .16
375 Ron Fairly .75 .30
376 Rich Hebner .75 .30
377 Mike Hegan .40 .16
378 Steve Stone .75 .30
379 Ken Boswell .40 .16
380 Bobby Bonds 1.50 .60
381 Denny Doyle .40 .16
382 Matt Alexander .40 .16
383 John Ellis .40 .16
384 Philadelphia Phillies 1.50 .30
Team Card CL
Danny Ozark MG
385 Mickey Lolich .75 .30
386 Ed Goodson .40 .16
387 Mike Miley .40 .16
388 Stan Perzanowski .40 .16
389 Glenn Adams .40 .16
390 Don Gullett .75 .30
391 Jerry Hairston .40 .16
392 Checklist 265-396 1.50 .30
393 Paul Mitchell .40 .16
394 Fran Healy .40 .16
395 Jim Wynn .75 .30
396 Bill Lee .40 .16
397 Tim Foli .40 .16
398 Dave Tomlin .40 .16
399 Luis Melendez .40 .16
400 Rod Carew 6.00 2.40
401 Ken Brett .40 .16
402 Don Money .75 .30
403 Geoff Zahn .40 .16
404 Enos Cabell .40 .16
405 Rollie Fingers 2.50 1.00
406 Ed Herrmann .40 .16
407 Tom Underwood .40 .16
408 Charlie Spikes .40 .16
409 Dave Lemanczyk .40 .16
410 Ralph Garr .75 .30
411 Bill Singer .40 .16
412 Toby Harrah .75 .30
413 Pete Varney .40 .16
414 Wayne Garland .40 .16
415 Vada Pinson 1.50 .60
416 Tommy John 1.50 .60
417 Gene Clines .40 .16
418 Jose Morales RC .40 .16
419 Reggie Cleveland .40 .16
420 Joe Morgan 5.00 2.00
421 Oakland A's 1.50 .30
Team Card CL
(No MG on front
422 Johnny Grubb .40 .16
423 Ed Halicki .40 .16
424 Phil Roof .40 .16
425 Rennie Stennett .40 .16
426 Bob Forsch .40 .16
427 Kurt Bevacqua .40 .16
428 Jim Crawford .40 .16
429 Fred Stanley .40 .16
430 Jose Cardenal .75 .30
431 Dick Ruthven .40 .16
432 Tom Veryzer .40 .16
433 Rick Waits .40 .16
434 Morris Nettles .40 .16
435 Phil Niekro 2.50 1.00
436 Bill Fahey .40 .16
437 Terry Forster .40 .16
438 Doug DeCinces .75 .30
439 Rick Rhoden .75 .30
440 John Mayberry .75 .30
441 Gary Carter 4.00 1.60
442 Hank Webb .40 .16
443 San Francisco Giants 1.50 .30
Team Card CL
(No MG on front
444 Gary Nolan .75 .30
445 Rico Petrocelli .75 .30
446 Larry Haney .40 .16
447 Gene Locklear .75 .30
448 Tom Johnson .40 .16
449 Bob Robertson .40 .16
450 Jim Palmer 5.00 2.00
451 Buddy Bradford .40 .16
452 Tom Hausman .40 .16
453 Lou Piniella 1.50 .60
454 Tom Griffin .40 .16
455 Dick Allen 1.50 .60
456 Joe Coleman .40 .16
457 Ed Crosby .40 .16
458 Earl Williams .40 .16
459 Jim Brewer .40 .16
460 Cesar Cedeno .75 .30
461 NL and AL Champs .75 .30
Reds sweep Bucs,
Bosox surprise A's
462 '75 World Series .75 .30
Reds Champs
463 Steve Hargan .40 .16
464 Ken Henderson .40 .16
465 Mike Marshall .75 .30
466 Bob Stinson .40 .16
467 Woodie Fryman .40 .16
468 Jesus Alou .40 .16
469 Rawly Eastwick .75 .30
470 Bobby Murcer .75 .30
471 Jim Burton .40 .16
472 Bob Davis .40 .16
473 Paul Blair .75 .30
474 Ray Corbin .40 .16
475 Joe Rudi .75 .30
476 Bob Moose .40 .16
477 Cleveland Indians 1.50 .30
Team Card CL
Frank Robinson MG
478 Lynn McGlothen .40 .16
479 Bobby Mitchell .40 .16
480 Mike Schmidt 15.00 6.00
481 Rudy May .40 .16
482 Tim Hosley .40 .16
483 Mickey Stanley .40 .16
484 Eric Raich .40 .16
485 Mike Hargrove .75 .30
486 Bruce Dal Canton .40 .16
487 Leron Lee .40 .16
488 Claude Osteen .75 .30
489 Skip Jutze .40 .16
490 Frank Tanana .75 .30
491 Terry Crowley .40 .16
492 Marty Pattin .40 .16
493 Derrel Thomas .40 .16
494 Craig Swan .75 .30
495 Nate Colbert .40 .16
496 Juan Beniquez .40 .16
497 Joe McIntosh .40 .16
498 Glenn Borgmann .40 .16
499 Mario Guerrero .40 .16
500 Reggie Jackson 12.00 4.80
501 Billy Champion .40 .16
502 Tim McCarver 1.50 .60
503 Elliott Maddox .40 .16
504 Pittsburgh Pirates 1.50 .30
Team Card CL
Danny Murtaugh MG
505 Mark Belanger .75 .30
506 George Mitterwald .40 .16
507 Ray Bare .40 .16
508 Duane Kuiper .40 .16
509 Bill Hands .40 .16

510 Amos Otis .75 .30
511 Jamie Easterley .40 .16
512 Ellie Rodriguez .40 .16
513 Bart Johnson .40 .16
514 Dan Driessen .75 .30
515 Steve Yeager .75 .30
516 Wayne Granger .40 .16
517 John Milner .40 .16
518 Doug Flynn .40 .16
519 Steve Brye .40 .16
520 Willie McCovey 5.00 2.00
521 Jim Colborn .40 .16
522 Ted Sizemore .40 .16
523 Bob Montgomery .40 .16
524 Pete Falcone .40 .16
525 Billy Williams 2.50 1.00
526 Checklist 397-528 1.50 .30
527 Mike Anderson .40 .16
528 Dock Ellis .40 .16
529 Deron Johnson .40 .16
530 Don Sutton 2.50 1.00
531 New York Mets 1.50 .30
Team Card CL
Joe Frazier MG
532 Milt May .40 .16
533 Lee Richard .40 .16
534 Stan Bahnsen .40 .16
535 Dave Nelson .40 .16
536 Mike Thompson .40 .16
537 Tony Muser .40 .16
538 Pat Darcy .40 .16
539 John Balaz .40 .16
540 Bill Freehan .75 .30
541 Steve Mingori .40 .16
542 Keith Hernandez .75 .30
543 Wayne Twitchell .40 .16
544 Pepe Frias .40 .16
545 Sparky Lyle .75 .30
546 Dave Rosello .40 .16
547 Roric Harrison .40 .16
548 Manny Mota .75 .30
549 Randy Tate .40 .16
550 Hank Aaron 25.00 10.00
551 Jerry DaVanon .40 .16
552 Terry Humphrey .40 .16
553 Randy Moffitt .40 .16
554 Ray Fosse .40 .16
555 Dyar Miller .40 .16
556 Minnesota Twins 1.50 .30
Team Card CL
Gene Mauch MG
557 Dan Spillner .40 .16
558 Clarence Gaston .75 .30
559 Clyde Wright .40 .16
560 Jorge Orta .40 .16
561 Tom Carroll .40 .16
562 Adrian Garrett .40 .16
563 Larry Demery .40 .16
564 Bubble Gum Champ 1.50 .60
Kurt Bevacqua
565 Tug McGraw .75 .30
566 Ken McMullen .40 .16
567 George Stone .40 .16
568 Rob Andrews .40 .16
569 Nelson Briles .75 .30
570 George Hendrick .75 .30
571 Don DeMola .40 .16
572 Rich Coggins .40 .16
573 Bill Travers .40 .16
574 Don Kessinger .75 .30
575 Dwight Evans 1.50 .60
576 Maximino Leon .40 .16
577 Marc Hill .40 .16
578 Ted Kubiak .40 .16
579 Clay Kirby .40 .16
580 Bert Campaneris .75 .30
581 St. Louis Cardinals 1.50 .30
Team Card CL
Red Schoendienst MG
582 Mike Kekich .40 .16
583 Tommy Helms .40 .16
584 Stan Wall .40 .16
585 Joe Torre 1.50 .60
586 Ron Schueler .40 .16
587 Leo Cardenas .40 .16
588 Kevin Kobel .40 .16
589 Santo Alcala 1.50 .60
Mike Flanagan RC
Joe Pactwa
Pablo Torrealba
590 Henry Cruz .75 .30
Chet Lemon RC
Ellis Valentine
Terry Whitfield
591 Steve Grilli .75 .30
Craig Mitchell
Jose Sosa
George Throop
592 Willie Randolph RC 5.00 2.00
Dave McKay
Jerry Royster
Roy Staiger
593 Larry Anderson .75 .30
Ken Crosby
Mark Littell
Butch Metzger
594 Andy Merchant .75 .30
Ed Ott
Royle Stillman
Jerry White
595 Art DeFillipis .75 .30
Randy Lerch
Sid Monge
Steve Barr
596 Craig Reynolds .75 .30
Lamar Johnson
Johnnie LeMaster
Jerry Manuel RC
597 Don Aase .75 .30
Jack Kucek
Frank LaCorte
Mike Pazik
598 Hector Cruz .75 .30
Jamie Quirk
Jerry Turner
Joe Wallis
599 Rob Dressler 8.00 3.20
Ron Guidry RC
Bob McClure
Pat Zachry
600 Tom Seaver 10.00 4.00
601 Ken Rudolph .40 .16
602 Doug Konieczny .40 .16
603 Jim Holt .40 .16
604 Joe Lovitto .40 .16
605 Al Downing .40 .16
606 Milwaukee Brewers 1.50 .30
Team Card CL
Alex Grammas MG
607 Rich Hinton .40 .16
608 Vic Correll .40 .16
609 Fred Norman .40 .16
610 Greg Luzinski 1.50 .60
611 Rich Folkers .40 .16
612 Joe Lahoud .40 .16
613 Tim Johnson .40 .16
614 Fernando Arroyo .40 .16
615 Mike Cubbage .40 .16
616 Buck Martinez .40 .16
617 Darold Knowles .40 .16
618 Jack Brohamer .40 .16
619 Bill Butler .40 .16
620 Al Oliver .75 .30
621 Tom Hall .40 .16
622 Rick Auerbach .40 .16
623 Bob Allietta .40 .16
624 Tony Taylor .40 .16
625 J.R. Richard .75 .30
626 Bob Sheldon .40 .16
627 Bill Plummer .40 .16
628 John D'Acquisto .40 .16
629 Sandy Alomar .75 .30
630 Chris Speier .40 .16
631 Atlanta Braves 1.50 .30
Team Card CL
Dave Bristol MG
632 Rogelio Moret .40 .16
633 John Stearns RC .75 .30
634 Larry Christenson .40 .16
635 Jim Fregosi .75 .30
636 Joe Decker .40 .16
637 Bruce Bochte .40 .16
638 Doyle Alexander .75 .30
639 Fred Kendall .40 .16
640 Bill Madlock 1.50 .60
641 Tom Paciorek .75 .30
642 Dennis Blair .40 .16
643 Checklist 529-660 1.50 .30
644 Tom Bradley .40 .16
645 Darrell Porter .75 .30
646 John Lowenstein .40 .16
647 Ramon Hernandez .40 .16
648 Al Cowens .40 .16
649 Dave Roberts .40 .16
650 Thurman Munson 6.00 2.40
651 John Odom .40 .16
652 Ed Armbrister .40 .16
653 Mike Norris RC .75 .30
654 Doug Griffin .40 .16
655 Mike Vail .40 .16
656 Chicago White Sox 1.50 .30
Team Card CL
Chuck Tanner MG
657 Roy Smalley RC .75 .30
658 Jerry Johnson .40 .16
659 Ben Oglivie .75 .30
660 Dave Lopes 1.50 .60

1976 Topps Traded

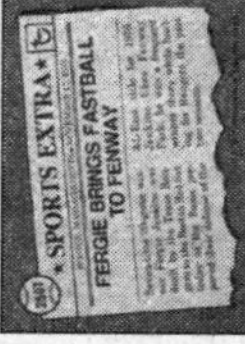

The cards in this 44-card set measure 2 1/2" by 3 1/2". The 1976 Topps Traded set contains 43 players and one unnumbered checklist card. The individuals pictured were traded after the Topps regular set was printed. A "Sports Extra" heading design is found on each picture and is also used to introduce the biographical section of the reverse. Each card is numbered according to the player's regular 1976 card with the addition of "T" to indicate his new status. As in 1974, the cards were inserted in all packs toward the end of the production run. According to published reports at the time, they were not released until April, 1976. Because they were produced in large quantities, they are no scarcer than the basic cards. Reports at the time indicated that a dealer could make approximately 35 sets from a vending case. The vending cases included both regular and traded cards.

NM Ex
COMPLETE SET (44) 30.00 12.00
27T Ed Figueroa .40 .16
28T Dusty Baker 1.50 .60
44T Doug Rader .75 .30
58T Ron Reed .40 .16
74T Oscar Gamble 1.50 .60
80T Jim Kaat 1.50 .60
83T Jim Spencer .40 .16
85T Mickey Rivers .75 .30
99T Lee Lacy .75 .30
120T Rusty Staub .75 .30
127T Larvell Blanks .40 .16
146T George Medich .40 .16
158T Ken Reitz .40 .16
208T Mike Lum .40 .16
211T Clay Carroll .40 .16
231T Tom House .40 .16
250T Fergie Jenkins 3.00 1.20
259T Darrel Chaney .40 .16
292T Leon Roberts .40 .16
296T Pat Dobson .40 .16
309T Bill Melton .40 .16
338T Bob Bailey .40 .16
380T Bobby Bonds 1.50 .60
383T John Ellis .40 .16
385T Mickey Lolich .75 .30
401T Ken Brett .40 .16
410T Ralph Garr .40 .16
411T Bill Singer .40 .16
428T Jim Crawford .40 .16
434T Morris Nettles .40 .16
464T Ken Henderson .40 .16
497T Joe McIntosh .40 .16
524T Pete Falcone .40 .16
527T Mike Anderson .40 .16
528T Dock Ellis .40 .16
532T Milt May .40 .16
554T Ray Fosse .40 .16
579T Clay Kirby .40 .16
583T Tommy Helms .40 .16
592T Willie Randolph 5.00 2.00
618T Jack Brohamer .40 .16
632T Rogelio Moret .40 .16
649T Dave Roberts .40 .16
NNO Traded Checklist 2.00 .40

1977 Topps

In 1977 for the fifth consecutive year, Topps produced a 660-card standard-size baseball set. Among other fashions, this set was released in 10-card wax packs as well as thirty-nine card rack packs. The player's name, team affiliation, and his position are compactly arranged over the picture area and a facsimile autograph appears on the photo. Team cards feature a checklist of that team's players in the set and a small picture of the manager on the front of the card. Appearing for the first time are the series "Brothers" (631-634) and "Turn Back the Clock" (433-437). Other subseries in the set are League Leaders (1-8), Record Breakers (231-234), Playoffs cards (276-277), World Series cards (411-413), and Rookie Prospects (472-479/487-494). The following players' regular issue cards are explicitly denoted as All-Stars, 30, 70, 100, 120, 170, 210, 240, 265, 301, 347, 400, 420, 450, 500, 521, 550, 560, and 580. The key Rookie Cards in the set are Jack Clark, Andre Dawson, Mark "The Bird" Fidrych, Dennis Martinez and Dale Murphy. Cards numbered 23 or lower, that feature Yankees and do not follow the numbering checklisted below, are not necessarily error cards. Those cards were issued in the NY area and distributed by Burger King. There was an aluminum version of the Dale Murphy rookie card number 476 produced (legally) in the early '80s; proceeds from the sales originally priced at 10.00) of this "card" went to the Huntington's Disease Foundation.

NM Ex
COMPLETE SET (660) 225.00 90.00
1 George Brett 8.00 2.30
Bill Madlock LL
2 Graig Nettles 2.50 1.00
Mike Schmidt LL
3 Lee May 1.50 .60
George Foster LL
4 Bill North .75 .30
Dave Lopes LL
5 Jim Palmer 1.50 .60
Randy Jones LL
6 Nolan Ryan 15.00 6.00
Tom Seaver LL
7 Mark Fidrych .75 .30
John Denny LL
8 Bill Campbell .75 .30
Rawly Eastwick LL
9 Doug Rader .30 .12
10 Reggie Jackson 10.00 4.00
11 Rob Dressler .30 .12
12 Larry Haney .30 .12
13 Luis Gomez .30 .12
14 Tommy Smith .30 .12
15 Don Gullett .75 .30
16 Bob Jones .30 .12
17 Steve Stone .75 .30
18 Indians Team CL 1.50 .30
Frank Robinson MG
19 John D'Acquisto .30 .12
20 Graig Nettles 1.50 .60
21 Ken Forsch .30 .12
22 Bill Freehan .75 .30
23 Dan Driessen .30 .12
24 Carl Morton .30 .12
25 Dwight Evans 1.50 .60
26 Ray Sadecki .30 .12
27 Bill Buckner .75 .30
28 Woodie Fryman .30 .12
29 Bucky Dent .75 .30
30 Greg Luzinski 1.50 .60
31 Jim Todd .30 .12
32 Checklist 1-132 1.50 .30
33 Wayne Garland .30 .12
34 Angels Team CL 1.50 .30
Norm Sherry MG
35 Rennie Stennett .30 .12
36 John Ellis .30 .12
37 Steve Hargan .30 .12
38 Craig Kusick .30 .12
39 Tom Griffin .30 .12
40 Bobby Murcer .75 .30
41 Jim Kern .30 .12
42 Jose Cruz .75 .30
43 Ray Bare .30 .12
44 Bud Harrelson .75 .30
45 Rawly Eastwick .30 .12
46 Buck Martinez .30 .12
47 Lynn McGlothen .30 .12
48 Tom Paciorek .75 .30
49 Grant Jackson .30 .12
50 Ron Cey .75 .30
51 Brewers Team CL 1.50 .30
Alex Grammas MG
52 Ellis Valentine .30 .12
53 Paul Mitchell .30 .12
54 Sandy Alomar .75 .30
55 Jeff Burroughs .75 .30
56 Rudy May .30 .12
57 Marc Hill .30 .12
58 Chet Lemon .75 .30
59 Larry Christenson .30 .12
60 Jim Rice 2.50 1.00
61 Manny Sanguillen .75 .30
62 Eric Raich .30 .12
63 Tito Fuentes .30 .12
64 Larry Biittner .30 .12
65 Skip Lockwood .30 .12
66 Roy Smalley .75 .30
67 Joaquin Andujar RC .75 .30
68 Bruce Bochte .30 .12
69 Jim Crawford .30 .12
70 Johnny Bench 10.00 4.00
71 Dock Ellis .30 .12
72 Mike Anderson .30 .12
73 Charlie Williams .30 .12
74 A's Team CL 1.50 .30
Jack McKeon MG
75 Dennis Leonard .75 .30
76 Tim Foli .30 .12
77 Dyar Miller .30 .12
78 Bob Davis .30 .12
79 Don Money .75 .30
80 Andy Messersmith .75 .30
81 Juan Beniquez .30 .12
82 Jim Rooker .30 .12
83 Kevin Bell .30 .12
84 Ollie Brown .30 .12
85 Duane Kuiper .30 .12
86 Pat Zachry .30 .12
87 Glenn Borgmann .30 .12
88 Stan Wall .30 .12
89 Butch Hobson RC .75 .30
90 Cesar Cedeno .75 .30
91 John Verhoeven .30 .12
92 Dave Rosello .30 .12
93 Tom Poquette .30 .12
94 Craig Swan .30 .12
95 Keith Hernandez .75 .30
96 Lou Piniella .75 .30
97 Dave Heaverlo .30 .12
98 Milt May .30 .12
99 Tom Hausman .30 .12
100 Joe Morgan 4.00 1.60
101 Dick Bosman .30 .12
102 Jose Morales .30 .12
103 Mike Bacsik .30 .12
104 Omar Moreno .75 .30
105 Steve Yeager .75 .30
106 Mike Flanagan .75 .30
107 Bill Melton .30 .12
108 Alan Foster .30 .12
109 Jorge Orta .30 .12
110 Steve Carlton 5.00 2.00
111 Rico Petrocelli .75 .30
112 Bill Greif .30 .12
113 Blue Jays Leaders 1.50 .30
Roy Hartsfield MG
Don Leppert CO
Bob Miller CO
Jackie Moore CO
Harry Warner CO
114 Bruce Dal Canton .30 .12
115 Rick Manning .30 .12
116 Joe Niekro .75 .30
117 Frank White .75 .30
118 Rick Jones .30 .12
119 John Stearns .30 .12
120 Rod Carew 5.00 2.00
121 Gary Nolan .30 .12
122 Ben Oglivie .75 .30
123 Fred Stanley .30 .12
124 George Mitterwald .30 .12
125 Bill Travers .30 .12
126 Rod Gilbreath .30 .12
127 Ron Fairly .75 .30
128 Tommy John 1.50 .60
129 Mike Sadek .30 .12
130 Al Oliver .75 .30
131 Orlando Ramirez .30 .12
132 Chip Lang .30 .12
133 Ralph Garr .75 .30
134 Padres Team CL 1.50 .30
John McNamara MG
135 Mark Belanger .75 .30
136 Jerry Mumphrey .75 .30
137 Jeff Terpko .30 .12
138 Bob Stinson .30 .12
139 Fred Norman .30 .12
140 Mike Schmidt 12.00 4.80
141 Mark Littell .30 .12
142 Steve Dillard .30 .12
143 Ed Herrmann .30 .12
144 Bruce Sutter RC 5.00 2.00
145 Tom Veryzer .30 .12
146 Dusty Baker 1.50 .60
147 Jackie Brown .30 .12
148 Fran Healy .30 .12
149 Mike Cubbage .30 .12
150 Tom Seaver 8.00 3.20
151 Johnny LeMaster .30 .12
152 Gaylord Perry 2.50 1.00
153 Ron Jackson RC .30 .12
154 Dave Giusti .30 .12
155 Joe Rudi .75 .30
156 Pete Mackanin .30 .12
157 Ken Brett .30 .12
158 Ted Kubiak .30 .12
159 Bernie Carbo .30 .12
160 Will McEnaney .30 .12
161 Garry Templeton RC 1.50 .60
162 Mike Cuellar .75 .30
163 Dave Hilton .30 .12
164 Tug McGraw .75 .30
165 Jim Wynn .75 .30
166 Bill Campbell .30 .12
167 Rich Hebner .75 .30
168 Charlie Spikes .30 .12
169 Darold Knowles .30 .12
170 Thurman Munson 5.00 2.00
171 Ken Sanders .30 .12
172 John Milner .30 .12
173 Chuck Scrivener .30 .12
174 Nelson Briles .75 .30
175 Butch Wynegar .75 .30
176 Bob Robertson .30 .12
177 Bart Johnson .30 .12
178 Bombo Rivera .30 .12
179 Paul Hartzell .30 .12
180 Dave Lopes .75 .30
181 Ken McMullen .30 .12
182 Dan Spillner .30 .12
183 Cardinals Team CL 1.50 .30
Vern Rapp MG
184 Bo McLaughlin .30 .12
185 Sixto Lezcano .30 .12
186 Doug Flynn .30 .12
187 Dick Pole .30 .12
188 Bob Tolan .30 .12
189 Rick Dempsey .75 .30
190 Ray Burris .30 .12
191 Doug Griffin .30 .12
192 Clarence Gaston .75 .30
193 Larry Gura .30 .12
194 Gary Matthews .75 .30
195 Ed Figueroa .30 .12
196 Len Randle .30 .12
197 Ed Ott .30 .12
198 Wilbur Wood .30 .12
199 Pepe Frias .30 .12
200 Frank Tanana .75 .30
201 Ed Kranepool .30 .12
202 Tom Johnson .30 .12
203 Ed Armbrister .30 .12
204 Jeff Newman .30 .12
205 Pete Falcone .30 .12
206 Boog Powell 1.50 .60
207 Glenn Abbott .30 .12
208 Checklist 133-264 1.50 .30
209 Rob Andrews .30 .12
210 Fred Lynn .75 .15
211 Giants Team CL 1.50 .60
Joe Altobelli MG
212 Jim Mason .30 .12
213 Maximino Leon .30 .12
214 Darrell Porter .75 .30
215 Butch Metzger .30 .12
216 Doug DeCinces .75 .30
217 Tom Underwood .30 .12
218 John Wathan RC .75 .30
219 Joe Coleman .30 .12
220 Chris Chambliss .75 .30
221 Bob Bailey .30 .12
222 Francisco Barrios .30 .12
223 Earl Williams .30 .12
224 Rusty Torres .30 .12
225 Bob Apodaca .30 .12
226 Leroy Stanton .75 .30
227 Joe Sambito .75 .30
228 Twins Team CL 1.50 .30
Gene Mauch MG
229 Don Kessinger .75 .30
230 Vida Blue .75 .30
231 George Brett RB 8.00 3.20
232 Minnie Minoso RB .75 .30
233 Jose Morales RB .30 .12
234 Nolan Ryan RB 15.00 6.00
235 Cecil Cooper .75 .30
236 Tom Buskey .30 .12
237 Gene Clines .30 .12
238 Tippy Martinez .30 .12
239 Bill Plummer .30 .12
240 Ron LeFlore .75 .30
241 Dave Tomlin .30 .12
242 Ken Henderson .30 .12
243 Ron Reed .30 .12
244 John Mayberry .75 .30
(Cartoon mentions
T206 Wagner)
245 Rick Rhoden .75 .30
246 Mike Vail .30 .12
247 Chris Knapp .30 .12
248 Wilbur Howard .30 .12
249 Pete Redfern .30 .12
250 Bill Madlock .75 .30
251 Tony Muser .30 .12
252 Dale Murray .30 .12
253 John Hale .30 .12
254 Doyle Alexander .30 .12
255 George Scott .75 .30
256 Joe Hoerner .30 .12
257 Mike Miley .30 .12
258 Luis Tiant .75 .30
259 Mets Team CL 1.50 .30
Joe Frazier MG
260 J.R. Richard .75 .30
261 Phil Garner .75 .30
262 Al Cowens .30 .12
263 Mike Marshall .75 .30
264 Tom Hutton .30 .12
265 Mark Fidrych RC 3.00 1.20
266 Derrel Thomas .30 .12
267 Ray Fosse .30 .12
268 Rick Sawyer .30 .12
269 Joe Lis .30 .12
270 Dave Parker 1.50 .60
271 Terry Forster .30 .12
272 Lee Lacy .30 .12
273 Eric Soderholm .30 .12
274 Don Stanhouse .30 .12
275 Mike Hargrove .75 .30
276 C.Chambliss ALCS 1.50 .60
homer decides it
277 Pete Rose NLCS 5.00 2.00
278 Danny Frisella .30 .12
279 Joe Wallis .30 .12
280 Jim Hunter 2.50 1.00
281 Roy Staiger .30 .12
282 Sid Monge .30 .12
283 Jerry DaVanon .30 .12
284 Mike Norris .30 .12
285 Brooks Robinson 5.00 2.00
286 Johnny Grubb .30 .06
287 Reds Team CL 1.50 .60
Sparky Anderson MG
288 Bob Montgomery .30 .12
289 Gene Garber .75 .30
290 Amos Otis .75 .30
291 Jason Thompson RC .75 .30
292 Rogelio Moret .30 .12
293 Jack Brohamer .30 .12
294 George Medich .30 .12
295 Gary Carter 2.50 1.00
296 Don Hood .30 .12
297 Ken Reitz .30 .12
298 Charlie Hough .75 .30

299 Otto Velez .75 .30
300 Jerry Koosman .75 .30
301 Toby Harrah .75 .30
302 Mike Garman .30 .12
303 Gene Tenace .75 .30
304 Jim Hughes .30 .12
305 Mickey Rivers .75 .30
306 Rick Waits .30 .12
307 Gary Sutherland .30 .12
308 Gene Pentz .30 .12
309 Red Sox Team CL 1.50 .30
Don Zimmer MG
310 Larry Bowa .75 .30
311 Vern Ruhle .30 .12
312 Rob Belloir .30 .12
313 Paul Blair .75 .30
314 Steve Mingori .30 .12
315 Dave Chalk .30 .12
316 Steve Rogers .30 .12
317 Kurt Bevacqua .30 .12
318 Duffy Dyer .30 .12
319 Goose Gossage 1.50 .60
320 Ken Griffey Sr. 1.50 .60
321 Dave Goltz .30 .12
322 Bill Russell .75 .30
323 Larry Lintz .30 .12
324 John Curtis .30 .12
325 Mike Ivie .30 .12
326 Jesse Jefferson .30 .12
327 Astros Team CL 1.50 .30
Bill Virdon MG
328 Tommy Boggs .30 .12
329 Ron Hodges .30 .12
330 George Hendrick .75 .30
331 Jim Colborn .30 .12
332 Elliott Maddox .30 .12
333 Paul Reuschel .30 .12
334 Bill Stein .30 .12
335 Bill Robinson .75 .30
336 Denny Doyle .30 .12
337 Ron Schueler .30 .12
338 Dave Duncan .75 .30
339 Adrian Devine .30 .12
340 Hal McRae .75 .30
341 Joe Kerrigan .30 .12
342 Jerry Remy .30 .12
343 Ed Halicki .30 .12
344 Brian Downing .75 .30
345 Reggie Smith .75 .30
346 Bill Singer .30 .12
347 George Foster 1.50 .60
348 Brent Strom .30 .12
349 Jim Holt .30 .12
350 Larry Dierker .75 .30
351 Jim Sundberg .75 .30
352 Mike Phillips .30 .12
353 Stan Thomas .30 .12
354 Pirates Team CL 1.50 .30
Chuck Tanner MG
355 Lou Brock 4.00 1.60
356 Checklist 265-396 1.50 .30
357 Tim McCarver 1.50 .60
358 Tom House .30 .12
359 Willie Randolph 1.50 .60
360 Rick Monday .75 .30
361 Eduardo Rodriguez .30 .12
362 Tommy Davis .75 .30
363 Dave Roberts .30 .12
364 Vic Correll .30 .12
365 Mike Torrez .75 .30
366 Ted Sizemore .30 .12
367 Dave Hamilton .30 .12
368 Mike Jorgensen .30 .12
369 Terry Humphrey .30 .12
370 John Montefusco .30 .12
371 Royals Team CL 1.50 .30
Whitey Herzog MG
372 Rich Folkers .30 .12
373 Bert Campaneris .75 .30
374 Kent Tekulve .75 .30
375 Larry Hisle .75 .30
376 Nino Espinosa .30 .12
377 Dave McKay .30 .12
378 Jim Umbarger .30 .12
379 Larry Cox .30 .12
380 Lee May .75 .30
381 Bob Forsch .30 .12
382 Charlie Moore .30 .12
383 Stan Bahnsen .30 .12
384 Darrel Chaney .30 .12
385 Dave LaRoche .30 .12
386 Manny Mota .75 .30
387 Yankees Team CL 2.50 .50
Billy Martin MG
388 Terry Harmon .30 .12
389 Ken Kravec .30 .12
390 Dave Winfield 6.00 2.40
391 Dan Warthen .30 .12
392 Phil Roof .30 .12
393 John Lowenstein .30 .12
394 Bill Laxton .30 .12
395 Manny Trillo .30 .12
396 Tom Murphy .30 .12
397 Larry Herndon RC .75 .30
398 Tom Burgmeier .30 .12
399 Bruce Boisclair .30 .12
400 Steve Garvey 2.50 1.00
401 Mickey Scott .30 .12
402 Tommy Helms .30 .12
403 Tom Grieve .75 .30
404 Eric Rasmussen .30 .12
405 Claudell Washington .75 .30
406 Tim Johnson .30 .12
407 Dave Freisleben .30 .12
408 Cesar Tovar .30 .12
409 Pete Broberg .30 .12
410 Willie Montanez .30 .12
411 Joe Morgan WS 2.50 1.00
Johnny Bench
412 Johnny Bench WS 2.50 1.00
413 WS Summary .75 .30
Cincy wins 2nd
straight series
414 Tommy Harper .75 .30
415 Jay Johnstone .75 .30
416 Chuck Hartenstein .30 .12
417 Wayne Garrett .30 .12
418 White Sox Team CL 1.50 .30
Bob Lemon MG
419 Steve Swisher .30 .12

420 Rusty Staub 1.50 .60
421 Doug Rau .30 .12
422 Freddie Patek .75 .30
423 Gary Lavelle .30 .12
424 Steve Brye .30 .12
425 Joe Torre 1.50 .60
426 Dick Drago .30 .12
427 Dave Rader .30 .12
428 Rangers Team CL 1.50 .30
Frank Lucchesi
429 Ken Boswell .30 .12
430 Fergie Jenkins 2.50 1.00
431 Dave Collins UER .75 .30
(Photo actually
Bobby Jones)
432 Buzz Capra .30 .12
433 Nate Colbert TBC .30 .12
(5 HR, 13 RBI)
434 Carl Yastrzemski TBC 1.50 .60
'67 Triple Crown
435 Maury Wills TBC .75 .30
104 steals
436 Bob Keegan TBC .30 .12
Majors' only no-hitter
437 Ralph Kiner TBC 1.50 .60
Leads NL in HR's
7th straight year
438 Marty Perez .30 .12
439 Gorman Thomas .75 .30
440 Jon Matlack .30 .12
441 Larvell Blanks .30 .12
442 Braves Team CL 1.50 .30
Dave Bristol MG
443 Lamar Johnson .30 .12
444 Wayne Twitchell .30 .12
445 Ken Singleton .75 .30
446 Bill Bonham .30 .12
447 Jerry Turner .30 .12
448 Ellie Rodriguez .30 .12
449 Al Fitzmorris .30 .12
450 Pete Rose 20.00 8.00
451 Checklist 397-528 1.50 .30
452 Mike Caldwell .30 .12
453 Pedro Garcia .30 .12
454 Andy Etchebarren .30 .12
455 Rick Wise .30 .12
456 Leon Roberts .30 .12
457 Steve Luebber .30 .12
458 Leo Foster .30 .12
459 Steve Foucault .30 .12
460 Willie Stargell 2.50 1.00
461 Dick Tidrow .30 .12
462 Don Baylor 1.50 .60
463 Jamie Quirk .30 .12
464 Randy Moffitt .30 .12
465 Rico Carty .75 .30
466 Fred Holdsworth .30 .12
467 Phillies Team CL 1.50 .30
Danny Ozark MG
468 Ramon Hernandez .30 .12
469 Pat Kelly .30 .12
470 Ted Simmons .75 .30
471 Del Unser .30 .12
472 Don Aase .30 .12
Bob McClure
Gil Patterson
Dave Wehrmeister
Sheldon Gill pictured instead of Gil
Patterson
473 Andre Dawson RC 20.00 8.00
Gene Richards
John Scott
Denny Walling
474 Bob Bailor .75 .30
Kiko Garcia
Craig Reynolds
Alex Taveras
475 Chris Batton .75 .30
Rick Camp
Scott McGregor
Manny Sarmiento
476 Gary Alexander 20.00 8.00
Rick Cerone
Dale Murphy RC
Kevin Pasley
477 Doug Ault .75 .30
Rich Dauer
Orlando Gonzalez
Phil Mankowski
478 Jim Gideon .75 .30
Leon Hooten
Dave Johnson
Mark Lemongello
479 Brian Asselstine .75 .30
Wayne Gross
Sam Mejias
Alvis Woods
480 Carl Yastrzemski 8.00 3.20
481 Roger Metzger .30 .12
482 Tony Solaita .30 .12
483 Richie Zisk .30 .12
484 Burt Hooton .75 .30
485 Roy White .75 .30
486 Ed Bane .30 .12
487 Larry Anderson .75 .30
Ed Glynn
Joe Henderson
Greg Terlecky
488 Jack Clark RC 3.00 1.20
Ruppert Jones RC
Lee Mazzilli RC
Dan Thomas
489 Len Barker RC .75 .30
Randy Lerch
Greg Minton
Mike Overy
490 Billy Almon .75 .30
Mickey Klutts
Tommy McMillan
Mark Wagner
491 Mike Dupree 3.00 1.20
Dennis Martinez RC
Craig Mitchell
Bob Sykes
492 Tony Armas RC .75 .30
Steve Kemp RC
Carlos Lopez
Gary Woods
493 Mike Krukow .75 .30
Jim Otten

Gary Wheelock
Mike Willis
494 Juan Bernhardt 1.50 .60
Mike Champion
Jim Gantner RC
Bump Wills
495 Al Hrabosky .30 .12
496 Gary Thomasson .30 .12
497 Clay Carroll .30 .12
498 Sal Bando .75 .30
499 Pablo Torrealba .30 .12
500 Dave Kingman 1.50 .60
501 Jim Bibby .30 .12
502 Randy Hundley .30 .12
503 Bill Lee .30 .12
504 Dodgers Team CL 1.50 .30
Tom Lasorda MG
505 Oscar Gamble .75 .30
506 Steve Grilli .30 .12
507 Mike Hegan .30 .12
508 Dave Pagan .30 .12
509 Cookie Rojas .75 .30
510 John Candelaria .30 .12
511 Bill Fahey .30 .12
512 Jack Billingham .30 .12
513 Jerry Terrell .30 .12
514 Cliff Johnson .30 .12
515 Chris Speier .30 .12
516 Bake McBride .75 .30
517 Pete Vuckovich RC .75 .30
518 Cubs Team CL 1.50 .30
Herman Franks MG
519 Don Kirkwood .30 .12
520 Garry Maddox .30 .12
521 Bob Grich .75 .30
Only card in set with no date of birth
522 Enzo Hernandez .30 .12
523 Rollie Fingers 2.50 1.00
524 Rowland Office .30 .12
525 Dennis Eckersley 5.00 2.00
526 Larry Parrish .75 .30
527 Dan Meyer .75 .30
528 Bill Castro .30 .12
529 Jim Essian .30 .12
530 Rick Reuschel .75 .30
531 Lyman Bostock .75 .30
532 Jim Willoughby .30 .12
533 Mickey Stanley .30 .12
534 Paul Splittorff .30 .12
535 Cesar Geronimo .30 .12
536 Vic Albury .30 .12
537 Dave Roberts .30 .12
538 Frank Taveras .30 .12
539 Mike Wallace .30 .12
540 Bob Watson .75 .30
541 John Denny .75 .30
542 Frank Duffy .30 .12
543 Ron Blomberg .30 .12
544 Gary Ross .30 .12
545 Bob Boone .75 .30
546 Oriole Team CL 1.50 .30
Earl Weaver MG
547 Willie McCovey 4.00 1.60
548 Joel Youngblood .30 .12
549 Jerry Royster .30 .12
550 Randy Jones .30 .12
551 Bill North .30 .12
552 Pepe Mangual .30 .12
553 Jack Heidemann .30 .12
554 Bruce Kimm .30 .12
555 Dan Ford .30 .12
556 Doug Bird .30 .12
557 Jerry White .30 .12
558 Elias Sosa .30 .12
559 Alan Bannister .30 .12
560 Dave Concepcion 1.50 .60
561 Pete LaCock .30 .12
562 Checklist 529-660 1.50 .30
563 Bruce Kison .30 .12
564 Alan Ashby .75 .30
565 Mickey Lolich .75 .30
566 Rick Miller .30 .12
567 Enos Cabell .30 .12
568 Carlos May .30 .12
569 Jim Lonborg .75 .30
570 Bobby Bonds 1.50 .60
571 Darrell Evans .75 .30
572 Ross Grimsley .30 .12
573 Joe Ferguson .30 .12
574 Aurelio Rodriguez .30 .12
575 Dick Ruthven .30 .12
576 Fred Kendall .30 .12
577 Jerry Augustine .30 .12
578 Bob Randall .30 .12
579 Don Carrithers .30 .12
580 George Brett 15.00 6.00
581 Pedro Borbon .30 .12
582 Ed Kirkpatrick .30 .12
583 Paul Lindblad .30 .12
584 Ed Goodson .30 .12
585 Rick Burleson .75 .30
586 Steve Renko .30 .12
587 Rick Baldwin .30 .12
588 Dave Moates .30 .12
589 Mike Cosgrove .30 .12
590 Buddy Bell .75 .30
591 Chris Arnold .30 .12
592 Dan Briggs .30 .12
593 Dennis Blair .30 .12
594 Biff Pocoroba .30 .12
595 John Hiller .30 .12
596 Jerry Martin .30 .12
597 Mariners Leaders CL 1.50 .30
Darrell Johnson MG
Don Bryant CO
Jim Busby CO
Vada Pinson CO
Wes Stock CO
598 Sparky Lyle .75 .30
599 Mike Tyson .30 .12
600 Jim Palmer 4.00 1.60
601 Mike Lum .30 .12
602 Andy Hassler .30 .12
603 Willie Davis .75 .30
604 Jim Slaton .30 .12
605 Felix Millan .30 .12
606 Steve Braun .30 .12
607 Larry Demery .30 .12
608 Roy Howell .30 .12
609 Jim Barr .30 .12

610 Jose Cardenal .75 .30
611 Dave Lemanczyk .30 .12
612 Barry Foote .30 .12
613 Reggie Cleveland .30 .12
614 Greg Gross .30 .12
615 Phil Niekro 2.50 1.00
616 Tommy Sandt .30 .12
617 Bobby Darwin .30 .12
618 Pat Dobson .30 .12
619 Johnny Oates .75 .30
620 Don Sutton 2.50 1.00
621 Tigers Team CL 1.50 .30
Ralph Houk MG
622 Jim Wohlford .30 .12
623 Jack Kucek .30 .12
624 Hector Cruz .30 .12
625 Ken Holtzman .75 .30
626 Al Bumbry .75 .30
627 Bob Myrick .30 .12
628 Mario Guerrero .30 .12
629 Bobby Valentine .75 .30
630 Bert Blyleven 1.50 .60
631 George Brett 6.00 2.40
Ken Brett
632 Bob Forsch .75 .30
Ken Forsch
633 Lee May .75 .30
Carlos May
634 Paul Reuschel .75 .30
Rick Reuschel UER
(Photos switched)
635 Robin Yount 8.00 3.20
636 Santo Alcala .30 .12
637 Alex Johnson .30 .12
638 Jim Kaat 1.50 .60
639 Jerry Morales .30 .12
640 Carlton Fisk 5.00 2.00
641 Dan Larson .30 .12
642 Willie Crawford .30 .12
643 Mike Pazik .30 .12
644 Matt Alexander .30 .12
645 Jerry Reuss .75 .30
646 Andres Mora .30 .12
647 Expos Team CL 1.50 .30
Dick Williams MG
648 Jim Spencer .30 .12
649 Dave Cash .30 .12
650 Nolan Ryan 30.00 12.00
651 Von Joshua .30 .12
652 Tom Walker .30 .12
653 Diego Segui .75 .30
654 Ron Pruitt .30 .12
655 Tony Perez 2.50 1.00
656 Ron Guidry 1.50 .60
657 Mick Kelleher .30 .12
658 Marty Pattin .30 .12
659 Merv Rettenmund .30 .12
660 Willie Horton 1.50 .30

1977 Topps Cloth Stickers

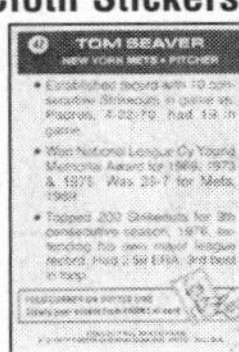

The "cards" in this 73-card set measure 2 1/2" by 3 1/2". The 1977 Cloth Stickers series was issued as a test set separately from the regular baseball series of that year. The packs of these cards contained two stickers as well as one "checklist puzzle" piece. The obverse pictures are identical to those appearing in the regular set, but the backs are completely different. There are 55 player cards and 18 unnumbered checklists, the latter bearing the title "Baseball Patches". The player cards are sequenced in alphabetical order. The checklists are puzzle pieces which, when properly arranged, form pictures of the A.L. and N.L. All-Star teams. Puzzle pieces are coded below by U (Upper), M (Middle), B (Bottom), L (left), C (Center), and R (Right). Cards marked with an SP in the checklist are in shorter supply than all others in the set. Even though we have assigned numbers 56 through 73 in our checklist for the puzzle cards, they are in fact all unnumbered.

	NM	Ex
COMPLETE SET (73)	125.00	50.00
COMMON CARD (1-55)	.25	.10
COMMON SP (1-55)	1.00	.40
COM.PUZZLE (56-73)	.10	.04

1 Alan Ashby .25 .10
2 Buddy Bell SP 1.25 .50
3 Johnny Bench 4.00 1.60
4 Vida Blue .75 .30
5 Bert Blyleven .75 .30
6 Steve Braun SP 1.00 .40
7 George Brett 10.00 4.00
8 Lou Brock 3.00 1.20
9 Jose Cardenal .25 .10
10 Rod Carew SP 6.00 2.40
11 Steve Carlton 4.00 1.60
12 Dave Cash .25 .10
13 Cesar Cedeno SP 1.25 .50
14 Ron Cey .75 .30
15 Mark Fidrych 5.00 2.00
16 Dan Ford .25 .10
17 Wayne Garland .25 .10
18 Ralph Garr .25 .10
19 Steve Garvey 3.00 1.20
20 Mike Hargrove .75 .30
21 Jim Hunter 2.00 .80
22 Reggie Jackson 4.00 1.60
23 Randy Jones .25 .10
24 Dave Kingman SP 1.25 .50
25 Bill Madlock .75 .30
26 Lee May SP 1.25 .50
27 John Mayberry .25 .10
28 John(Andy)Messersmith .25 .10
29 Willie Montanez .25 .10
30 John Montefusco SP 1.00 .40
31 Joe Morgan 2.00 .80

32 Thurman Munson 2.00 .80
33 Bobby Murcer .75 .30
34 Al Oliver SP 1.25 .50
35 Dave Pagan .25 .10
36 Jim Palmer SP 3.00 1.20
37 Tony Perez 2.00 .80
38 Pete Rose SP 12.00 4.80
39 Joe Rudi .50 .20
40 Nolan Ryan SP 60.00 24.00
41 Mike Schmidt 10.00 4.00
42 Tom Seaver 5.00 2.00
43 Ted Simmons .75 .30
44 Bill Singer .25 .10
45 Willie Stargell 3.00 1.20
46 Rusty Staub .75 .30
47 Don Sutton 2.00 .80
48 Luis Tiant .75 .30
49 Bill Travers .25 .10
50 Claudell Washington .75 .30
51 Bob Watson .75 .30
52 Dave Winfield 6.00 2.40
53 Carl Yastrzemski 4.00 1.60
54 Robin Yount 6.00 2.40
55 Richie Zisk .25 .10
56 AL Puzzle UL .10 .04
57 AL Puzzle UC .10 .04
58 AL Puzzle UR .10 .04
59 AL Puzzle ML .10 .04
60 AL Puzzle MC .10 .04
61 AL Puzzle MR .10 .04
62 AL Puzzle BL SP .20 .08
63 AL Puzzle BC SP .20 .08
64 AL Puzzle BR SP .20 .08
65 NL Puzzle UL .10 .04
66 NL Puzzle UC .10 .04
67 NL Puzzle UR .10 .04
68 NL Puzzle ML .10 .04
69 NL Puzzle MC .10 .04
70 NL Puzzle MR .10 .04
71 NL Puzzle BL .10 .04
72 NL Puzzle BC .10 .04
73 NL Puzzle BR .10 .04

1978 Topps

The cards in this 726-card set measure 2 1/2" by 3 1/2". As in previous years, this set was issued in many different ways: some of them include 14-card wax packs and 39-card rack packs. The 1978 Topps set experienced an increase in number of cards from the previous five regular issue sets of 660. Card numbers 1 through 7 feature Record Breakers (RB) of the 1977 season. Other subsets within this set include League Leaders (201-208), Post-season cards (411-413), and Rookie Prospects (701-711). The key Rookie Cards in this set are the multi-player Rookie Card of Paul Molitor and Alan Trammell, Jack Morris, Eddie Murray, Lance Parrish, and Lou Whitaker. Many of the Molitor/Trammell cards are found with black printing smudges. The manager cards in the set feature a "then and now" format on the card front showing the manager as he looked during his playing days. While no scarcities exist, 66 of the cards are more abundant in supply, as they were "double printed." These 66 double-printed cards are noted in the checklist by DP. Team cards again feature a checklist of that team's players in the set on the back. Cards numbered 23 or lower, that feature Astros, Rangers, Tigers, or Yankees and do not follow the numbering checklisted below, are not necessarily error cards. They are undoubtedly Burger King cards, separate sets with their own pricing and mass distribution. The Bump Wills card has been seen with either no black mark or a major black mark on the front of the card. We will continue to investigate this card and see whether or not it should be considered a variation.

	NM	Ex
COMPLETE SET (726)	200.00	80.00
COMMON CARD (1-726)	.25	.10
COMMON CARD DP	.15	.06

1 Lou Brock RB 3.00 .90
2 Sparky Lyle RB .60 .24
3 Willie McCovey RB 2.50 1.00
4 Brooks Robinson RB 1.25 .50
5 Pete Rose RB 8.00 3.20
6 Nolan Ryan RB 15.00 6.00
7 Reggie Jackson RB 4.00 1.60
8 Mike Sadek .25 .10
9 Doug DeCinces .60 .24
10 Phil Niekro 2.50 1.00
11 Rick Manning .25 .10
12 Don Aase .25 .10
13 Art Howe RC .60 .24
14 Lerrin LaGrow .25 .10
15 Tony Perez DP 1.25 .50
16 Roy White .60 .24
17 Mike Krukow .25 .10
18 Bob Grich .60 .24
19 Darrell Porter .60 .24
20 Pete Rose DP 12.00 4.80
21 Steve Kemp .25 .10
22 Charlie Hough .60 .24
23 Bump Wills .25 .10
24 Don Money DP .15 .06
25 Jon Matlack .25 .10
26 Rich Hebner .60 .24
27 Geoff Zahn .25 .10
28 Ed Ott .25 .10
29 Bob Lacey .25 .10
30 George Hendrick .60 .24
31 Glenn Abbott .25 .10
32 Garry Templeton .60 .24
33 Dave Lemanczyk .25 .10
34 Willie McCovey 3.00 1.20
35 Sparky Lyle .60 .24

1978 Topps

36 Eddie Murray RC 60.00 24.00
37 Rick Waits .25 .10
38 Willie Montanez .25 .10
39 Floyd Bannister RC .25 .10
40 Carl Yastrzemski 6.00 2.40
41 Burt Hooton .60 .24
42 Jorge Orta .25 .10
43 Bill Atkinson .25 .10
44 Toby Harrah .60 .24
45 Mark Fidrych 2.50 1.00
46 Al Cowens .25 .10
47 Jack Billingham .25 .10
48 Don Baylor 1.25 .50
49 Ed Kranepool .60 .24
50 Rick Reuschel .60 .24
51 Charlie Moore DP .15 .06
52 Jim Lonborg .60 .24
53 Phil Garner DP .25 .10
54 Tom Johnson .25 .10
55 Mitchell Page .25 .10
56 Randy Jones .25 .10
57 Dan Meyer .25 .10
58 Bob Forsch .25 .10
59 Otto Velez .25 .10
60 Thurman Munson 4.00 1.60
61 Larvell Blanks .25 .10
62 Jim Barr .25 .10
63 Don Zimmer MG .60 .24
64 Gene Pentz .25 .10
65 Ken Singleton .60 .24
66 Chicago White Sox 1.25 .25
Team Card CL
67 Claudell Washington .60 .24
68 Steve Foucault DP .15 .06
69 Mike Vail .25 .10
70 Goose Gossage 1.25 .50
71 Terry Humphrey .25 .10
72 Andre Dawson 4.00 1.60
73 Andy Hassler .25 .10
74 Checklist 1-121 1.25 .25
75 Dick Ruthven .25 .10
76 Steve Ontiveros .25 .10
77 Ed Kirkpatrick .25 .10
78 Pablo Torrealba .25 .10
79 Da.Johnson DP MG .15 .06
80 Ken Griffey Sr. 1.25 .50
81 Pete Redfern .25 .10
82 San Francisco Giants 1.25 .25
Team Card CL
83 Bob Montgomery .25 .10
84 Kent Tekulve .60 .24
85 Ron Fairly .60 .24
86 Dave Tomlin .25 .10
87 John Lowenstein .25 .10
88 Mike Phillips .25 .10
89 Ken Clay .25 .10
90 Larry Bowa 1.25 .50
91 Oscar Zamora .25 .10
92 Adrian Devine .25 .10
93 Bobby Cox DP .15 .06
94 Chuck Scrivener .25 .10
95 Jamie Quirk .25 .10
96 Baltimore Orioles 1.25 .25
Team Card CL
97 Stan Bahnsen .25 .10
98 Jim Essian .60 .24
99 Willie Hernandez RC 1.25 .50
100 George Brett 15.00 6.00
101 Sid Monge .25 .10
102 Matt Alexander .25 .10
103 Tom Murphy .25 .10
104 Lee Lacy .25 .10
105 Reggie Cleveland .25 .10
106 Bill Plummer .25 .10
107 Ed Halicki .25 .10
108 Von Joshua .25 .10
109 Joe Torre MG .60 .24
110 Richie Zisk .25 .10
111 Mike Tyson .25 .10
112 Houston Astros 1.25 .25
Team Card CL
113 Don Carrithers .25 .10
114 Paul Blair .60 .24
115 Gary Nolan .25 .10
116 Tucker Ashford .25 .10
117 John Montague .25 .10
118 Terry Harmon .25 .10
119 Dennis Martinez 2.50 1.00
120 Gary Carter 2.50 1.00
121 Alvis Woods .25 .10
122 Dennis Eckersley 3.00 1.20
123 Manny Trillo .25 .10
124 Dave Rozema RC .25 .10
125 George Scott .60 .24
126 Paul Moskau .25 .10
127 Chet Lemon .60 .24
128 Bill Russell .60 .24
129 Jim Colborn .25 .10
130 Jeff Burroughs .60 .24
131 Bert Blyleven 1.25 .50
132 Enos Cabell .25 .10
133 Jerry Augustine .25 .10
134 Steve Henderson .25 .10
135 Ron Guidry DP 1.25 .50
136 Ted Sizemore .25 .10
137 Craig Kusick .25 .10
138 Larry Demery .25 .10
139 Wayne Gross .25 .10
140 Rollie Fingers 2.50 1.00
141 Ruppert Jones .25 .10
142 John Montefusco .25 .10
143 Keith Hernandez .60 .24
144 Jesse Jefferson .25 .10
145 Rick Monday .60 .24
146 Doyle Alexander .60 .24
147 Lee Mazzilli .25 .10
148 Andre Thornton .60 .24
149 Dale Murray .25 .10
150 Bobby Bonds 1.25 .50
151 Milt Wilcox .25 .10
152 Ivan DeJesus .25 .10
153 Steve Stone .60 .24
154 Cecil Cooper DP .25 .10
155 Butch Hobson .25 .10
156 Andy Messersmith .60 .24
157 Pete LaCock DP .15 .06
158 Joaquin Andujar .60 .24
159 Lou Piniella .60 .24
160 Jim Palmer 3.00 1.20
161 Bob Boone 1.25 .50

162 Paul Thormodsgard .25 .10
163 Bill North .25 .10
164 Bob Owchinko .25 .10
165 Rennie Stennett .25 .10
166 Carlos Lopez .25 .10
167 Tim Foli .25 .10
168 Reggie Smith .60 .24
169 Jerry Johnson .25 .10
170 Lou Brock 3.00 1.20
171 Pat Zachry .25 .10
172 Mike Hargrove .60 .24
173 Robin Yount UER 5.00 2.00
(Played for Newark
in 1973, not 1971)
174 Wayne Garland .25 .10
175 Jerry Morales .25 .10
176 Milt May .25 .10
177 Gene Garber DP .25 .10
178 Dave Chalk .25 .10
179 Dick Tidrow .25 .10
180 Dave Concepcion 1.25 .50
181 Ken Forsch .25 .10
182 Jim Spencer .25 .10
183 Doug Bird .25 .10
184 Checklist 122-242 1.25 .25
185 Ellis Valentine .25 .10
186 Bob Stanley DP .15 .06
187 Jerry Royster DP .15 .06
188 Al Bumbry .60 .24
189 Tom Lasorda MG 2.50 1.00
190 John Candelaria .60 .24
191 Rodney Scott .25 .10
192 San Diego Padres 1.25 .25
Team Card CL
193 Rich Chiles .25 .10
194 Derrel Thomas .25 .10
195 Larry Dierker .60 .24
196 Bob Bailor .25 .10
197 Nino Espinosa .25 .10
198 Ron Pruitt .25 .10
199 Craig Reynolds .25 .10
200 Reggie Jackson 8.00 3.20
201 Dave Parker 1.25 .50
Rod Carew LL
202 George Foster .60 .24
Jim Rice LL DP
203 George Foster .60 .24
Larry Hisle LL
204 Frank Taveras .25 .10
Freddie Patek LL DP
205 Steve Carlton 2.50 1.00
Dave Goltz
Dennis Leonard
Jim Palmer LL
206 Phil Niekro 6.00 2.40
Nolan Ryan LL DP
207 John Candelaria .60 .24
Frank Tanana LL DP
208 Rollie Fingers 1.25 .50
Bill Campbell LL
209 Dock Ellis .25 .10
210 Jose Cardenal .25 .10
211 Earl Weaver MG DP 1.25 .50
212 Mike Caldwell .25 .10
213 Alan Bannister .25 .10
214 California Angels 1.25 .25
Team Card CL
215 Darrell Evans .60 .24
216 Mike Paxton .25 .10
217 Rod Gilbreath .25 .10
218 Marty Pattin .25 .10
219 Mike Cubbage .25 .10
220 Pedro Borbon .25 .10
221 Chris Speier .25 .10
222 Jerry Martin .25 .10
223 Bruce Kison .25 .10
224 Jerry Tabb .25 .10
225 Don Gullett DP .25 .10
226 Joe Ferguson .25 .10
227 Al Fitzmorris .25 .10
228 Manny Mota DP .25 .10
229 Leo Foster .25 .10
230 Al Hrabosky .25 .10
231 Wayne Nordhagen .25 .10
232 Mickey Stanley .25 .10
233 Dick Pole .25 .10
234 Herman Franks MG .25 .10
235 Tim McCarver .60 .24
236 Terry Whitfield .25 .10
237 Rich Dauer .25 .10
238 Juan Beniquez .25 .10
239 Dyar Miller .25 .10
240 Gene Tenace .60 .24
241 Pete Vuckovich .60 .24
242 Barry Bonnell DP .15 .06
243 Bob McClure .25 .10
244 Montreal Expos .60 .12
Team Card CL DP
245 Rick Burleson .60 .24
246 Dan Driessen .25 .10
247 Larry Christenson .25 .10
248 Frank White DP .60 .24
249 Dave Goltz DP .15 .06
250 Graig Nettles DP .60 .24
251 Don Kirkwood .25 .10
252 Steve Swisher DP .15 .06
253 Jim Kern .25 .10
254 Dave Collins .60 .24
255 Jerry Reuss .60 .24
256 Joe Altobelli MG .25 .10
257 Hector Cruz .25 .10
258 John Hiller .25 .10
259 Los Angeles Dodgers 1.25 .25
Team Card CL
260 Bert Campaneris .60 .24
261 Tim Hosley .25 .10
262 Rudy May .25 .10
263 Danny Walton .25 .10
264 Jamie Easterly .25 .10
265 Sal Bando DP .60 .24
266 Bob Shirley .25 .10
267 Doug Ault .25 .10
268 Gil Flores .25 .10
269 Wayne Twitchell .25 .10
270 Carlton Fisk 4.00 1.60
271 Randy Lerch DP .15 .06
272 Royle Stillman .25 .10
273 Fred Norman .25 .10
274 Freddie Patek .60 .24
275 Dan Ford .25 .10

276 Bill Bonham DP .15 .06
277 Bruce Boisclair .25 .10
278 Enrique Romo .25 .10
279 Bill Virdon MG .25 .10
280 Buddy Bell .60 .24
281 Eric Rasmussen DP .15 .06
282 New York Yankees 2.50 .50
Team Card CL
283 Omar Moreno .25 .10
284 Randy Moffitt .25 .10
285 Steve Yeager DP .60 .24
286 Ben Oglivie .60 .24
287 Kiko Garcia .25 .10
288 Dave Hamilton .25 .10
289 Checklist 243-363 1.25 .25
290 Willie Horton .60 .24
291 Gary Ross .25 .10
292 Gene Richards .25 .10
293 Mike Willis .25 .10
294 Larry Parrish .60 .24
295 Bill Lee .25 .10
296 Biff Pocoroba .25 .10
297 Warren Brusstar DP .15 .06
298 Tony Armas .60 .24
299 Whitey Herzog MG .60 .24
300 Joe Morgan 3.00 1.20
301 Buddy Schultz .25 .10
302 Chicago Cubs 1.25 .25
Team Card CL
303 Sam Hinds .25 .10
304 John Milner .25 .10
305 Rico Carty .60 .24
306 Joe Niekro .60 .24
307 Glenn Borgmann .25 .10
308 Jim Rooker .25 .10
309 Cliff Johnson .25 .10
310 Don Sutton 2.50 1.00
311 Jose Baez DP .15 .06
312 Greg Minton .25 .10
313 Andy Etchebarren .25 .10
314 Paul Lindblad .25 .10
315 Mark Belanger .60 .24
316 Henry Cruz DP .15 .06
317 Dave Johnson .25 .10
318 Tom Griffin .25 .10
319 Alan Ashby .25 .10
320 Fred Lynn .60 .24
321 Santo Alcala .25 .10
322 Tom Paciorek .60 .24
323 Jim Fregosi DP .25 .10
324 Vern Rapp MG .25 .10
325 Bruce Sutter 1.25 .50
326 Mike Lum DP .15 .06
327 Rick Langford DP .15 .06
328 Milwaukee Brewers 1.25 .25
Team Card CL
329 John Verhoeven .25 .10
330 Bob Watson .60 .24
331 Mark Littell .25 .10
332 Duane Kuiper .25 .10
333 Jim Todd .25 .10
334 John Stearns .25 .10
335 Bucky Dent .60 .24
336 Steve Busby .25 .10
337 Tom Grieve .60 .24
338 Dave Heaverlo .25 .10
339 Mario Guerrero .25 .10
340 Bake McBride .60 .24
341 Mike Flanagan .60 .24
342 Aurelio Rodriguez .25 .10
343 John Wathan DP .15 .06
344 Sam Ewing .25 .10
345 Luis Tiant .60 .24
346 Larry Biittner .25 .10
347 Terry Forster .25 .10
348 Del Unser .25 .10
349 Rick Camp DP .15 .06
350 Steve Garvey 2.50 1.00
351 Jeff Torborg .60 .24
352 Tony Scott .25 .10
353 Doug Bair .25 .10
354 Cesar Geronimo .25 .10
355 Bill Travers .25 .10
356 New York Mets 1.25 .25
Team Card CL
357 Tom Poquette .25 .10
358 Mark Lemongello .25 .10
359 Marc Hill .25 .10
360 Mike Schmidt 10.00 4.00
361 Chris Knapp .25 .10
362 Dave May .25 .10
363 Bob Randall .25 .10
364 Jerry Turner .25 .10
365 Ed Figueroa .25 .10
366 Larry Milbourne DP .15 .06
367 Rick Dempsey .60 .24
368 Balor Moore .25 .10
369 Tim Nordbrook .25 .10
370 Rusty Staub 1.25 .50
371 Ray Burris .25 .10
372 Brian Asselstine .25 .10
373 Jim Willoughby .25 .10
374 Jose Morales .25 .10
375 Tommy John 1.25 .50
376 Jim Wohlford .25 .10
377 Manny Sarmiento .25 .10
378 Bobby Winkles MG .25 .10
379 Skip Lockwood .25 .10
380 Ted Simmons .60 .24
381 Philadelphia Phillies 1.25 .25
Team Card CL
382 Joe Lahoud .25 .10
383 Mario Mendoza .25 .10
384 Jack Clark 1.25 .50
385 Tito Fuentes .25 .10
386 Bob Gorinski .25 .10
387 Ken Holtzman .60 .24
388 Bill Fahey DP .15 .06
389 Julio Gonzalez .25 .10
390 Oscar Gamble .60 .24
391 Larry Haney .25 .10
392 Billy Almon .25 .10
393 Tippy Martinez .60 .24
394 Roy Howell DP .15 .06
395 Jim Hughes .25 .10
396 Bob Stinson DP .15 .06
397 Greg Gross .25 .10
398 Don Hood .25 .10
399 Pete Mackanin .25 .10
400 Nolan Ryan 25.00 10.00

401 Sparky Anderson MG .60 .24
402 Dave Campbell .25 .10
403 Bud Harrelson .60 .24
404 Detroit Tigers 1.25 .25
Team Card CL
405 Rawly Eastwick .25 .10
406 Mike Jorgensen .25 .10
407 Odell Jones .25 .10
408 Joe Zdeb .25 .10
409 Ron Schueler .25 .10
410 Bill Madlock .60 .24
411 Mickey Rivers ALCS .60 .24
412 Davey Lopes NLCS .60 .24
413 Reggie Jackson WS 4.00 1.60
414 Darold Knowles DP .15 .06
415 Ray Fosse .25 .10
416 Jack Brohamer .25 .10
417 Mike Garman DP .15 .06
418 Tony Muser .25 .10
419 Jerry Garvin .25 .10
420 Greg Luzinski 1.25 .50
421 Junior Moore .25 .10
422 Steve Braun .25 .10
423 Dave Rosello .25 .10
424 Boston Red Sox 1.25 .25
Team Card CL
425 Steve Rogers DP .25 .10
426 Fred Kendall .25 .10
427 Mario Soto RC .60 .24
428 Joel Youngblood .25 .10
429 Mike Barlow .25 .10
430 Al Oliver .60 .24
431 Butch Metzger .25 .10
432 Terry Bulling .25 .10
433 Fernando Gonzalez .25 .10
434 Mike Norris .25 .10
435 Checklist 364-484 1.25 .25
436 Vic Harris DP .15 .06
437 Bo McLaughlin .25 .10
438 John Ellis .25 .10
439 Ken Kravec .25 .10
440 Dave Lopes .60 .24
441 Larry Gura .25 .10
442 Elliott Maddox .25 .10
443 Darrel Chaney .25 .10
444 Roy Hartsfield MG .25 .10
445 Mike Ivie .25 .10
446 Tug McGraw .60 .24
447 Leroy Stanton .25 .10
448 Bill Castro .25 .10
449 Tim Blackwell DP .15 .06
450 Tom Seaver 6.00 2.40
451 Minnesota Twins 1.25 .25
Team Card CL
452 Jerry Mumphrey .25 .10
453 Doug Flynn .25 .10
454 Dave LaRoche .25 .10
455 Bill Robinson .60 .24
456 Vern Ruhle .25 .10
457 Bob Bailey .25 .10
458 Jeff Newman .25 .10
459 Charlie Spikes .25 .10
460 Jim Hunter 2.50 1.00
461 Rob Andrews DP .15 .06
462 Rogelio Moret .25 .10
463 Kevin Bell .25 .10
464 Jerry Grote .25 .10
465 Hal McRae .60 .24
466 Dennis Blair .25 .10
467 Alvin Dark MG .60 .24
468 Warren Cromartie RC .60 .24
469 Rick Cerone .60 .24
470 J.R. Richard .60 .24
471 Roy Smalley .60 .24
472 Ron Reed .25 .10
473 Bill Buckner .60 .24
474 Jim Slaton .25 .10
475 Gary Matthews .60 .24
476 Bill Stein .25 .10
477 Doug Capilla .25 .10
478 Jerry Remy .25 .10
479 St. Louis Cardinals 1.25 .25
Team Card CL
480 Ron LeFlore .60 .24
481 Jackson Todd .25 .10
482 Rick Miller .25 .10
483 Ken Macha RC .25 .10
484 Jim Norris .25 .10
485 Chris Chambliss .60 .24
486 John Curtis .25 .10
487 Jim Tyrone .25 .10
488 Dan Spillner .25 .10
489 Rudy Meoli .25 .10
490 Amos Otis .60 .24
491 Scott McGregor .60 .24
492 Jim Sundberg .60 .24
493 Steve Renko .25 .10
494 Chuck Tanner MG .60 .24
495 Dave Cash .60 .24
496 Jim Clancy DP .15 .06
497 Glenn Adams .25 .10
498 Joe Sambito .25 .10
499 Seattle Mariners 1.25 .25
Team Card CL
500 George Foster 1.25 .50
501 Dave Roberts .25 .10
502 Pat Rockett .25 .10
503 Ike Hampton .25 .10
504 Roger Freed .25 .10
505 Felix Millan .25 .10
506 Ron Blomberg .25 .10
507 Willie Crawford .25 .10
508 Johnny Oates .60 .24
509 Brent Strom .25 .10
510 Willie Stargell 2.50 1.00
511 Frank Duffy .25 .10
512 Larry Herndon .25 .10
513 Barry Foote .25 .10
514 Rob Sperring .25 .10
515 Tim Corcoran .25 .10
516 Gary Beare .25 .10
517 Andres Mora .25 .10
518 Tommy Boggs DP .15 .06
519 Brian Downing .60 .24
520 Larry Hisle .25 .10
521 Steve Staggs .25 .10
522 Dick Williams MG .60 .24
523 Donnie Moore RC .25 .10
524 Bernie Carbo .25 .10
525 Jerry Terrell .25 .10

526 Cincinnati Reds 1.25 .25
Team Card CL
527 Vic Correll .25 .10
528 Rob Picciolo .25 .10
529 Paul Hartzell .25 .10
530 Dave Winfield 4.00 1.60
531 Tom Underwood .25 .10
532 Skip Jutze .25 .10
533 Sandy Alomar .60 .24
534 Wilbur Howard .25 .10
535 Checklist 485-605 1.25 .25
536 Roric Harrison .25 .10
537 Bruce Bochte .25 .10
538 Johnny LeMaster .25 .10
539 Vic Davalillo DP .15 .06
540 Steve Carlton 4.00 1.60
541 Larry Cox .25 .10
542 Tim Johnson .25 .10
543 Larry Harlow DP .15 .06
544 Len Randle DP .15 .06
545 Bill Campbell .25 .10
546 Ted Martinez .25 .10
547 John Scott .25 .10
548 Billy Hunter DP MG .15 .06
549 Joe Kerrigan .25 .10
550 John Mayberry .60 .24
551 Atlanta Braves 1.25 .25
Team Card CL
552 Francisco Barrios .25 .10
553 Terry Puhl .60 .24
554 Joe Coleman .25 .10
555 Butch Wynegar .25 .10
556 Ed Armbrister .25 .10
557 Tony Solaita .25 .10
558 Paul Mitchell .25 .10
559 Phil Mankowski .25 .10
560 Dave Parker 1.25 .50
561 Charlie Williams .25 .10
562 Glenn Burke .25 .10
563 Dave Rader .25 .10
564 Mick Kelleher .25 .10
565 Jerry Koosman .60 .24
566 Merv Rettenmund .25 .10
567 Dick Drago .25 .10
568 Tom Hutton .25 .10
569 Lary Sorensen .25 .10
570 Dave Kingman 1.25 .50
571 Buck Martinez .25 .10
572 Rick Wise .25 .10
573 Luis Gomez .25 .10
574 Bob Lemon MG 1.25 .50
575 Pat Dobson .25 .10
576 Sam Mejias .25 .10
577 Oakland A's 1.25 .25
Team Card CL
578 Buzz Capra .25 .10
579 Rance Mulliniks .25 .10
580 Rod Carew 4.00 1.60
581 Lynn McGlothen .25 .10
582 Fran Healy .25 .10
583 George Medich .25 .10
584 John Hale .25 .10
585 Woodie Fryman DP .15 .06
586 Ed Goodson .25 .10
587 John Urrea .25 .10
588 Jim Mason .25 .10
589 Bob Knepper .25 .10
590 Bobby Murcer .60 .24
591 George Zeber .25 .10
592 Bob Apodaca .25 .10
593 Dave Skaggs .25 .10
594 Dave Freisleben .25 .10
595 Sixto Lezcano .25 .10
596 Gary Wheelock .25 .10
597 Steve Dillard .25 .10
598 Eddie Solomon .25 .10
599 Gary Woods .25 .10
600 Frank Tanana .60 .24
601 Gene Mauch MG .60 .24
602 Eric Soderholm .25 .10
603 Will McEnaney .25 .10
604 Earl Williams .25 .10
605 Rick Rhoden .60 .24
606 Pittsburgh Pirates 1.25 .25
Team Card CL
607 Fernando Arroyo .25 .10
608 Johnny Grubb .25 .10
609 John Denny .25 .10
610 Garry Maddox .60 .24
611 Pat Scanlon .25 .10
612 Ken Henderson .25 .10
613 Marty Perez .25 .10
614 Joe Wallis .25 .10
615 Clay Carroll .25 .10
616 Pat Kelly .25 .10
617 Joe Nolan .25 .10
618 Tommy Helms .25 .10
619 Thad Bosley DP .15 .06
620 Willie Randolph 1.25 .50
621 Craig Swan DP .15 .06
622 Champ Summers .25 .10
623 Eduardo Rodriguez .25 .10
624 Gary Alexander DP .15 .06
625 Jose Cruz .60 .24
626 Toronto Blue Jays 1.25 .25
Team Card CL DP
627 David Johnson .25 .10
628 Ralph Garr .60 .24
629 Don Stanhouse .25 .10
630 Ron Cey 1.25 .50
631 Danny Ozark MG .25 .10
632 Rowland Office .25 .10
633 Tom Veryzer .25 .10
634 Len Barker .25 .10
635 Joe Rudi .60 .24
636 Jim Bibby .25 .10
637 Duffy Dyer .25 .10
638 Paul Splittorff .25 .10
639 Gene Clines .25 .10
640 Lee May DP .25 .10
641 Doug Rau .25 .10
642 Denny Doyle .25 .10
643 Tom House .25 .10
644 Jim Dwyer .25 .10
645 Mike Torrez .60 .24
646 Rick Auerbach DP .15 .06
647 Steve Dunning .25 .10
648 Gary Thomasson .25 .10
649 Moose Haas .25 .10
650 Cesar Cedeno .60 .24

651 Doug Rader .25 .10
652 Checklist 606-726 1.25 .25
653 Ron Hodges DP .15 .06
654 Pepe Frias .25 .10
655 Lyman Bostock .60 .24
656 Dave Garcia MG .25 .10
657 Bombo Rivera .25 .10
658 Manny Sanguillen .60 .24
659 Texas Rangers 1.25 .25
Team Card CL
660 Jason Thompson .60 .24
661 Grant Jackson .25 .10
662 Paul Dade .25 .10
663 Paul Reuschel .25 .10
664 Fred Stanley .25 .10
665 Dennis Leonard .60 .24
666 Billy Smith RC .25 .10
667 Jeff Byrd .25 .10
668 Dusty Baker 1.25 .50
669 Pete Falcone .25 .10
670 Jim Rice 1.25 .50
671 Gary Lavelle .25 .10
672 Don Kessinger .60 .24
673 Steve Brye .25 .10
674 Ray Knight RC 2.50 1.00
675 Jay Johnstone .60 .24
676 Bob Myrick .25 .10
677 Ed Herrmann .25 .10
678 Tom Burgmeier .25 .10
679 Wayne Garrett .25 .10
680 Vida Blue .60 .24
681 Rob Belloir .25 .10
682 Ken Brett .25 .10
683 Mike Champion .25 .10
684 Ralph Houk MG .60 .24
685 Frank Taveras .25 .10
686 Gaylord Perry 2.50 1.00
687 Julio Cruz RC .25 .10
688 George Mitterwald .25 .10
689 Cleveland Indians 1.25 .25
Team Card CL
690 Mickey Rivers .60 .24
691 Ross Grimsley .25 .10
692 Ken Reitz .25 .10
693 Lamar Johnson .25 .10
694 Elias Sosa .25 .10
695 Dwight Evans 1.25 .50
696 Steve Mingori .25 .10
697 Roger Metzger .25 .10
698 Juan Bernhardt .25 .10
699 Jackie Brown .25 .10
700 Johnny Bench 8.00 3.20
701 Tom Hume .60 .24
Larry Landreth
Steve McCatty
Bruce Taylor
702 Bill Nahorodny .60 .24
Kevin Pasley
Rick Sweet
Don Werner
703 Larry Andersen 5.00 2.00
Tim Jones
Mickey Mahler
Jack Morris RC DP
704 Garth Iorg 8.00 3.20
Dave Oliver
Sam Perlozzo
Lou Whitaker RC
705 Dave Bergman 1.25 .50
Miguel Dilone
Clint Hurdle
Willie Norwood
706 Wayne Cage .60 .24
Ted Cox
Pat Putnam
Dave Revering
707 Mickey Klutts 50.00 20.00
Paul Molitor RC
Alan Trammell RC
U.L. Washington
708 Bo Diaz 4.00 1.60
Dale Murphy
Lance Parrish RC
Ernie Whitt
709 Steve Burke .60 .24
Matt Keough
Lance Rautzhan
Dan Schatzeder
710 Dell Alston 1.25 .50
Rick Bosetti
Mike Easler RC
Keith Smith
711 Cardell Camper .25 .10
Dennis Lamp
Craig Mitchell
Roy Thomas DP
712 Bobby Valentine .60 .24
713 Bob Davis .25 .10
714 Mike Anderson .25 .10
715 Jim Kaat 1.25 .50
716 Clarence Gaston .60 .24
717 Nelson Briles .25 .10
718 Ron Jackson .25 .10
719 Randy Elliott .25 .10
720 Fergie Jenkins 2.50 1.00
721 Billy Martin MG 1.25 .50
722 Pete Broberg .25 .10
723 John Wockenfuss .25 .10
724 Kansas City Royals 1.25 .25
Team Card CL
725 Kurt Bevacqua .25 .10
726 Wilbur Wood 1.25 .30

1979 Topps

The cards in this 726-card set measure 2 1/2" by 3 1/2". Topps continued with the same number of cards as in 1978. As in previous years, this set was released in many different formats, among them are 12-card wax packs and 39-card rack packs. Various series spotlight League Leaders (1-8), "Season and Career Record Holders" (411-418), "Record Breakers" (201-206), and one "Prospects" card for each team (701-726). Team cards feature a checklist on back of that team's players in the set and a small picture of the manager on the front of the card. There are 66 cards that were double printed and these are noted in the checklist by the abbreviation DP. Bump Wills (369) was initially depicted in a Ranger uniform but with a Blue Jays affiliation; later printings correctly labeled him with Texas. The set price includes either Wills card. The key Rookie Cards in this set are Pedro Guerrero, Carney Lansford, Ozzie Smith, Bob Welch and Willie Wilson. Cards numbered 23 or lower, which feature Phillies or Yankees and do not follow the numbering checklisted below, are not necessarily error cards. They are undoubtedly Burger King cards, separate sets for each team with their own pricing and mass distribution.

NM Ex
COMPLETE SET (726) 175.00 70.00
COMMON CARD (1-726) .25 .10
COMMON CARD DP .15 .06
1 Rod Carew 2.50 .50
Dave Parker LL
2 Jim Rice 1.00 .40
George Foster LL
3 Jim Rice 1.00 .40
George Foster LL
4 Ron LeFlore .50 .20
Omar Moreno LL
5 Ron Guidry .50 .20
Gaylord Perry LL
6 Nolan Ryan 5.00 2.00
J.R. Richard LL
7 Ron Guidry .50 .20
Craig Swan LL
8 Rich Gossage 1.00 .40
Rollie Fingers LL
9 Dave Campbell .25 .10
10 Lee May .50 .20
11 Marc Hill .25 .10
12 Dick Drago .25 .10
13 Paul Dade .25 .10
14 Rafael Landestoy .25 .10
15 Ross Grimsley .25 .10
16 Fred Stanley .25 .10
17 Donnie Moore .25 .10
18 Tony Solaita .25 .10
19 Larry Gura DP .15 .06
20 Joe Morgan DP 2.00 .80
21 Kevin Kobel .25 .10
22 Mike Jorgensen .25 .10
23 Terry Forster .25 .10
24 Paul Molitor 10.00 4.00
25 Steve Carlton 3.00 1.20
26 Jamie Quirk .25 .10
27 Dave Goltz .25 .10
28 Steve Brye .25 .10
29 Rick Langford .25 .10
30 Dave Winfield 4.00 1.60
31 Tom House DP .15 .06
32 Jerry Mumphrey .25 .10
33 Dave Rozema .25 .10
34 Rob Andrews .25 .10
35 Ed Figueroa .25 .10
36 Alan Ashby .25 .10
37 Joe Kerrigan DP .15 .06
38 Bernie Carbo .25 .10
39 Dale Murphy 3.00 1.20
40 Dennis Eckersley 2.00 .80
41 Twins Team CL 1.00 .20
Gene Mauch MG
42 Ron Blomberg .25 .10
43 Wayne Twitchell .25 .10
44 Kurt Bevacqua .25 .10
45 Al Hrabosky .25 .10
46 Ron Hodges .25 .10
47 Fred Norman .25 .10
48 Merv Rettenmund .25 .10
49 Vern Ruhle .25 .10
50 Steve Garvey DP 1.00 .40
51 Ray Fosse DP .15 .06
52 Randy Lerch .25 .10
53 Mick Kelleher .25 .10
54 Dell Alston DP .15 .06
55 Willie Stargell 2.00 .80
56 John Hale .25 .10
57 Eric Rasmussen .25 .10
58 Bob Randall DP .15 .06
59 John Denny DP .25 .10
60 Mickey Rivers .50 .20
61 Bo Diaz .25 .10
62 Randy Moffitt .25 .10
63 Jack Brohamer .25 .10
64 Tom Underwood .25 .10
65 Mark Belanger .50 .20
66 Tigers Team CL 1.00 .20
Les Moss MG
67 Jim Mason DP .15 .06
68 Joe Niekro DP .25 .10
69 Elliott Maddox .25 .10
70 John Candelaria .50 .20
71 Brian Downing .50 .20
72 Steve Mingori .25 .10
73 Ken Henderson .25 .10
74 Shane Rawley .25 .10
75 Steve Yeager .50 .20
76 Warren Cromartie .50 .20
77 Dan Briggs DP .15 .06
78 Elias Sosa .25 .10
79 Ted Cox .25 .10
80 Jason Thompson .50 .20
81 Roger Erickson .25 .10
82 Mets Team CL 1.00 .20
Joe Torre MG
83 Fred Kendall .25 .10
84 Greg Minton .25 .10
85 Gary Matthews .50 .20
86 Rodney Scott .25 .10
87 Pete Falcone .25 .10
88 Bob Molinaro .25 .10
89 Dick Tidrow .25 .10
90 Bob Boone 1.00 .40
91 Terry Crowley .25 .10
92 Jim Bibby .25 .10
93 Phil Mankowski .25 .10
94 Len Barker .25 .10
95 Robin Yount 5.00 2.00
96 Indians Team CL 1.00 .20
Jeff Torborg
97 Sam Mejias .25 .10
98 Ray Burris .25 .10
99 John Wathan .50 .20
100 Tom Seaver DP 4.00 1.60
101 Roy Howell .25 .10
102 Mike Anderson .25 .10
103 Jim Todd .25 .10
104 Johnny Oates DP .25 .10
105 Rick Camp DP .15 .06
106 Frank Duffy .25 .10
107 Jesus Alou DP .15 .06
108 Eduardo Rodriguez .25 .10
109 Joel Youngblood .25 .10
110 Vida Blue .50 .20
111 Roger Freed .25 .10
112 Phillies Team 1.00 .20
Danny Ozark MG
113 Pete Redfern .25 .10
114 Cliff Johnson .25 .10
115 Nolan Ryan 20.00 8.00
116 Ozzie Smith RC 60.00 24.00
117 Grant Jackson .25 .10
118 Bud Harrelson .50 .20
119 Don Stanhouse .25 .10
120 Jim Sundberg .50 .20
121 Checklist 1-121 DP .50 .10
122 Mike Paxton .25 .10
123 Lou Whitaker 2.50 1.00
124 Dan Schatzeder .25 .10
125 Rick Burleson .25 .10
126 Doug Bair .25 .10
127 Thad Bosley .25 .10
128 Ted Martinez .25 .10
129 Marty Pattin DP .15 .06
130 Bob Watson DP .25 .10
131 Jim Clancy .25 .10
132 Rowland Office .25 .10
133 Bill Castro .25 .10
134 Alan Bannister .25 .10
135 Bobby Murcer .50 .20
136 Jim Kaat .50 .20
137 Larry Wolfe DP .15 .06
138 Mark Lee RC .25 .10
139 Luis Pujols .25 .10
140 Don Gullett .50 .20
141 Tom Paciorek .50 .20
142 Charlie Williams .25 .10
143 Tony Scott .25 .10
144 Sandy Alomar .50 .20
145 Rick Rhoden .50 .20
146 Duane Kuiper .25 .10
147 Dave Hamilton .25 .10
148 Bruce Boisclair .25 .10
149 Manny Sarmiento .25 .10
150 Wayne Cage .25 .10
151 John Hiller .25 .10
152 Rick Cerone .25 .10
153 Dennis Lamp .25 .10
154 Jim Gantner DP .25 .10
155 Dwight Evans 1.00 .40
156 Buddy Solomon .25 .10
157 U.L. Washington UER .25 .10
(Sic, bats left,
should be right)
158 Joe Sambito .25 .10
159 Roy White .50 .20
160 Mike Flanagan 1.00 .40
161 Barry Foote .25 .10
162 Tom Johnson .25 .10
163 Glenn Burke .25 .10
164 Mickey Lolich .50 .20
165 Frank Taveras .25 .10
166 Leon Roberts .25 .10
167 Roger Metzger DP .15 .06
168 Dave Freisleben .25 .10
169 Bill Nahorodny .25 .10
170 Don Sutton 2.00 .80
171 Gene Clines .25 .10
172 Mike Bruhert .25 .10
173 John Lowenstein .25 .10
174 Rick Auerbach .25 .10
175 George Hendrick 1.00 .40
176 Aurelio Rodriguez .25 .10
177 Ron Reed .25 .10
178 Alvis Woods .25 .10
179 Jim Beattie DP .15 .06
180 Larry Hisle .25 .10
181 Mike Garman .25 .10
182 Tim Johnson .25 .10
183 Paul Splittorff .25 .10
184 Darrel Chaney .25 .10
185 Mike Torrez .50 .20
186 Eric Soderholm .25 .10
187 Mark Lemongello .25 .10
188 Pat Kelly .25 .10
189 Eddie Whitson RC .25 .10
190 Ron Cey .50 .20
191 Mike Norris .25 .10
192 Cardinals Team CL 1.00 .20
Ken Boyer MG
193 Glenn Adams .25 .10
194 Randy Jones .25 .10
195 Bill Madlock .50 .20
196 Steve Kemp DP .25 .10
197 Bob Apodaca .25 .10
198 Johnny Grubb .25 .10
199 Larry Milbourne .25 .10
200 Johnny Bench DP 5.00 2.00
201 Mike Edwards RB .25 .10
202 Ron Guidry RB .50 .20
203 J.R. Richard RB .25 .10
204 Pete Rose RB 5.00 2.00
205 John Stearns RB .25 .10
206 Sammy Stewart RB .25 .10
207 Dave Lemanczyk .25 .10
208 Clarence Gaston .25 .10
209 Reggie Cleveland .25 .10
210 Larry Bowa .50 .20
211 Denny Martinez 2.00 .80
212 Carney Lansford RC 1.00 .40
213 Bill Travers .25 .10
214 Red Sox Team CL 1.00 .20
Don Zimmer MG
215 Willie McCovey 2.50 1.00
216 Wilbur Wood .25 .10
217 Steve Dillard .25 .10
218 Dennis Leonard .50 .20
219 Roy Smalley .50 .20
220 Cesar Geronimo .25 .10
221 Jesse Jefferson .25 .10
222 Bob Beall .25 .10
223 Kent Tekulve .50 .20
224 Dave Revering .25 .10
225 Goose Gossage 1.00 .40
226 Ron Pruitt .25 .10
227 Steve Stone .50 .20
228 Vic Davalillo .25 .10
229 Doug Flynn .25 .10
230 Bob Forsch .25 .10
231 John Wockenfuss .25 .10
232 Jimmy Sexton .25 .10
233 Paul Mitchell .25 .10
234 Toby Harrah .50 .20
235 Steve Rogers .25 .10
236 Jim Dwyer .25 .10
237 Billy Smith .25 .10
238 Balor Moore .25 .10
239 Willie Horton .50 .20
240 Rick Reuschel .50 .20
241 Checklist 122-242 DP .50 .10
242 Pablo Torrealba .25 .10
243 Buck Martinez DP .15 .06
244 Pirates Team CL 1.00 .20
Chuck Tanner MG
245 Jeff Burroughs .50 .20
246 Darrell Jackson .25 .10
247 Tucker Ashford DP .15 .06
248 Pete LaCock .25 .10
249 Paul Thormodsgard .25 .10
250 Willie Randolph .50 .20
251 Jack Morris 2.00 .80
252 Bob Stinson .25 .10
253 Rick Wise .25 .10
254 Luis Gomez .25 .10
255 Tommy John 1.00 .40
256 Mike Sadek .25 .10
257 Adrian Devine .25 .10
258 Mike Phillips .25 .10
259 Reds Team CL 1.00 .20
Sparky Anderson MG
260 Richie Zisk .25 .10
261 Mario Guerrero .25 .10
262 Nelson Briles .25 .10
263 Oscar Gamble .50 .20
264 Don Robinson RC .25 .10
265 Don Money .25 .10
266 Jim Willoughby .25 .10
267 Joe Rudi .50 .20
268 Julio Gonzalez .25 .10
269 Woodie Fryman .25 .10
270 Butch Hobson .50 .20
271 Rawly Eastwick .25 .10
272 Tim Corcoran .25 .10
273 Jerry Terrell .25 .10
274 Willie Norwood .25 .10
275 Junior Moore .25 .10
276 Jim Colborn .25 .10
277 Tom Grieve .50 .20
278 Andy Messersmith .50 .20
279 Jerry Grote DP .15 .06
280 Andre Thornton .50 .20
281 Vic Correll DP .15 .06
282 Blue Jays Team CL .50 .10
Roy Hartsfield MG
283 Ken Kravec .25 .10
284 Johnnie LeMaster .25 .10
285 Bobby Bonds 1.00 .40
286 Duffy Dyer .25 .10
287 Andres Mora .25 .10
288 Milt Wilcox .25 .10
289 Jose Cruz 1.00 .40
290 Dave Lopes .50 .20
291 Tom Griffin .25 .10
292 Don Reynolds .25 .10
293 Jerry Garvin .25 .10
294 Pepe Frias .25 .10
295 Mitchell Page .25 .10
296 Preston Hanna .25 .10
297 Ted Sizemore .25 .10
298 Rich Gale .25 .10
299 Steve Ontiveros .25 .10
300 Rod Carew 3.00 1.20
301 Tom Hume .25 .10
302 Braves Team CL 1.00 .20
Bobby Cox MG
303 Lary Sorensen DP .15 .06
304 Steve Swisher .25 .10
305 Willie Montanez .25 .10
306 Floyd Bannister .25 .10
307 Larvell Blanks .25 .10
308 Bert Blyleven 1.00 .40
309 Ralph Garr .50 .20
310 Thurman Munson 3.00 1.20
311 Gary Lavelle .25 .10
312 Bob Robertson .25 .10
313 Dyar Miller .25 .10
314 Larry Harlow .25 .10
315 Jon Matlack .25 .10
316 Milt May .25 .10
317 Jose Cardenal .50 .20
318 Bob Welch RC 2.00 .80
319 Wayne Garrett .25 .10
320 Carl Yastrzemski 5.00 2.00
321 Gaylord Perry 2.00 .80
322 Danny Goodwin .25 .10
323 Lynn McGlothen .25 .10
324 Mike Tyson .25 .10
325 Cecil Cooper .50 .20
326 Pedro Borbon .25 .10
327 Art Howe DP .25 .10
328 A's Team CL 1.00 .20
Jack McKeon MG
329 Joe Coleman .25 .10
330 George Brett 10.00 4.00
331 Mickey Mahler .25 .10
332 Gary Alexander .25 .10
333 Chet Lemon .50 .20
334 Craig Swan .50 .20
335 Chris Chambliss .50 .20
336 Bobby Thompson .25 .10
337 John Montague .25 .10
338 Vic Harris .25 .10
339 Ron Jackson .25 .10
340 Jim Palmer 2.50 1.00
341 Willie Upshaw .50 .20
342 Dave Roberts .25 .10
343 Ed Glynn .25 .10
344 Jerry Royster .25 .10
345 Tug McGraw .50 .20
346 Bill Buckner .50 .20
347 Doug Rau .25 .10
348 Andre Dawson 3.00 1.20
349 Jim Wright .25 .10
350 Garry Templeton .50 .20
351 Wayne Nordhagen DP .15 .06
352 Steve Renko .25 .10
353 Checklist 243-363 1.00 .20
354 Bill Bonham .25 .10
355 Lee Mazzilli .25 .10
356 Giants Team CL 1.00 .20
Joe Altobelli MG
357 Jerry Augustine .25 .10
358 Alan Trammell 3.00 1.20
359 Dan Spillner DP .15 .06
360 Amos Otis .50 .20
361 Tom Dixon .25 .10
362 Mike Cubbage .25 .10
363 Craig Skok .25 .10
364 Gene Richards .25 .10
365 Sparky Lyle .50 .20
366 Juan Bernhardt .25 .10
367 Dave Skaggs .25 .10
368 Don Aase .25 .10
369A Bump Wills ERR 3.00 1.20
(Blue Jays)
369B Bump Wills COR 3.00 1.20
(Rangers)
370 Dave Kingman 1.00 .40
371 Jeff Holly .25 .10
372 Lamar Johnson .25 .10
373 Lance Rautzhan .25 .10
374 Ed Herrmann .25 .10
375 Bill Campbell .25 .10
376 Gorman Thomas .50 .20
377 Paul Moskau .25 .10
378 Rob Picciolo DP .15 .06
379 Dale Murray .25 .10
380 John Mayberry .50 .20
381 Astros Team CL 1.00 .20
Bill Virdon MG
382 Jerry Martin .25 .10
383 Phil Garner .50 .20
384 Tommy Boggs .25 .10
385 Dan Ford .25 .10
386 Francisco Barrios .25 .10
387 Gary Thomasson .25 .10
388 Jack Billingham .25 .10
389 Joe Zdeb .25 .10
390 Rollie Fingers 2.00 .80
391 Al Oliver .50 .20
392 Doug Ault .25 .10
393 Scott McGregor .50 .20
394 Randy Stein .25 .10
395 Dave Cash .25 .10
396 Bill Plummer .25 .10
397 Sergio Ferrer .25 .10
398 Ivan DeJesus .25 .10
399 David Clyde .25 .10
400 Jim Rice 1.00 .40
401 Ray Knight .50 .20
402 Paul Hartzell .25 .10
403 Tim Foli .25 .10
404 White Sox Team CL 1.00 .20
Don Kessinger MG
405 Butch Wynegar DP .15 .06
406 Joe Wallis DP .15 .06
407 Pete Vuckovich .50 .20
408 Charlie Moore DP .15 .06
409 Willie Wilson RC 1.00 .40
410 Darrell Evans 1.00 .40
411 George Sisler ATL 2.50 1.00
Ty Cobb
412 Hack Wilson ATL 2.50 1.00
Hank Aaron
413 Roger Maris ATL 4.00 1.60
Hank Aaron
414 Rogers Hornsby ATL 2.50 1.00
Ty Cobb
415 Lou Brock ATL 1.00 .40
416 Jack Chesbro ATL .50 .20
Cy Young
417 Nolan Ryan ATL DP 5.00 2.00
Walter Johnson
418 D.Leonard ATL DP .25 .10
Walter Johnson
419 Dick Ruthven .25 .10
420 Ken Griffey Sr. .50 .20
421 Doug DeCinces .50 .20
422 Ruppert Jones .25 .10
423 Bob Montgomery .25 .10
424 Angels Team CL 1.00 .20
Jim Fregosi MG
425 Rick Manning .25 .10
426 Chris Speier .25 .10
427 Andy Replogle .25 .10
428 Bobby Valentine .50 .20
429 John Urrea DP .15 .06
430 Dave Parker .50 .20
431 Glenn Borgmann .25 .10
432 Dave Heaverlo .25 .10
433 Larry Biittner .25 .10
434 Ken Clay .25 .10
435 Gene Tenace .50 .20
436 Hector Cruz .25 .10
437 Rick Williams .25 .10
438 Horace Speed .25 .10
439 Frank White .50 .20
440 Rusty Staub 1.00 .40
441 Lee Lacy .25 .10
442 Doyle Alexander .25 .10
443 Bruce Bochte .25 .10
444 Aurelio Lopez .25 .10
445 Steve Henderson .25 .10
446 Jim Lonborg .50 .20
447 Manny Sanguillen .50 .20
448 Moose Haas .25 .10
449 Bombo Rivera .25 .10
450 Dave Concepcion 1.00 .40
451 Royals Team CL 1.00 .20
Whitey Herzog MG
452 Jerry Morales .25 .10
453 Chris Knapp .25 .10
454 Len Randle .25 .10
455 Bill Lee DP .15 .06
456 Chuck Baker .25 .10

457 Bruce Sutter .50 .20
458 Jim Essian .25 .10
459 Sid Monge .25 .10
460 Graig Nettles 1.00 .40
461 Jim Barr DP .15 .06
462 Otto Velez .25 .10
463 Steve Comer .25 .10
464 Joe Nolan .25 .10
465 Reggie Smith .50 .20
466 Mark Littell .25 .10
467 Don Kessinger DP .25 .10
468 Stan Bahnsen DP .15 .06
469 Lance Parrish 1.00 .40
470 Garry Maddox DP .25 .10
471 Joaquin Andujar .50 .20
472 Craig Kusick .25 .10
473 Dave Roberts .25 .10
474 Dick Davis .25 .10
475 Dan Driessen .25 .10
476 Tom Poquette .25 .10
477 Bob Grich .50 .20
478 Juan Beniquez .25 .10
479 Padres Team CL 1.00 .20
Roger Craig MG
480 Fred Lynn .50 .20
481 Skip Lockwood .25 .10
482 Craig Reynolds .25 .10
483 Checklist 364-484 DP .50 .10
484 Rick Waits .25 .10
485 Bucky Dent .50 .20
486 Bob Knepper .25 .10
487 Miguel Dilone .25 .10
488 Bob Owchinko .25 .10
489 Larry Cox UER .25 .10
(Photo actually
Dave Rader)
490 Al Cowens .25 .10
491 Tippy Martinez .25 .10
492 Bob Bailor .25 .10
493 Larry Christenson .25 .10
494 Jerry White .25 .10
495 Tony Perez 2.00 .80
496 Barry Bonnell DP .15 .06
497 Glenn Abbott .25 .10
498 Rich Chiles .25 .10
499 Rangers Team CL 1.00 .20
Pat Corrales MG
500 Ron Guidry .50 .20
501 Junior Kennedy .25 .10
502 Steve Braun .25 .10
503 Terry Humphrey .25 .10
504 Larry McWilliams .25 .10
505 Ed Kranepool .25 .10
506 John D'Acquisto .25 .10
507 Tony Armas .50 .20
508 Charlie Hough .50 .20
509 Mario Mendoza UER .25 .10
(Career BA .278,
should say .204)
510 Ted Simmons 1.00 .40
511 Paul Reuschel DP .15 .06
512 Jack Clark .50 .20
513 Dave Johnson .50 .20
514 Mike Proly .25 .10
515 Enos Cabell .25 .10
516 Champ Summers DP .15 .06
517 Al Bumbry .50 .20
518 Jim Umbarger .25 .10
519 Ben Oglivie .50 .20
520 Gary Carter 1.00 .40
521 Sam Ewing .25 .10
522 Ken Holtzman .50 .20
523 John Milner .25 .10
524 Tom Burgmeier .25 .10
525 Freddie Patek .25 .10
526 Dodgers Team CL 1.00 .20
Tom Lasorda MG
527 Lerrin LaGrow .25 .10
528 Wayne Gross DP .15 .06
529 Brian Asselstine .25 .10
530 Frank Tanana .50 .20
531 Fernando Gonzalez .25 .10
532 Buddy Schultz .25 .10
533 Leroy Stanton .25 .10
534 Ken Forsch .25 .10
535 Ellis Valentine .25 .10
536 Jerry Reuss .50 .20
537 Tom Veryzer .25 .10
538 Mike Ivie DP .15 .06
539 John Ellis .25 .10
540 Greg Luzinski .50 .20
541 Jim Slaton .25 .10
542 Rick Bosetti .25 .10
543 Kiko Garcia .25 .10
544 Fergie Jenkins 2.00 .80
545 John Stearns .25 .10
546 Bill Russell .50 .20
547 Clint Hurdle .25 .10
548 Enrique Romo .25 .10
549 Bob Bailey .25 .10
550 Sal Bando .50 .20
551 Cubs Team CL 1.00 .20
Herman Franks MG
552 Jose Morales .25 .10
553 Denny Walling .25 .10
554 Matt Keough .25 .10
555 Biff Pocoroba .25 .10
556 Mike Lum .25 .10
557 Ken Brett .25 .10
558 Jay Johnstone .50 .20
559 Greg Pryor .25 .10
560 John Montefusco .25 .10
561 Ed Ott .25 .10
562 Dusty Baker 1.00 .40
563 Roy Thomas .25 .10
564 Jerry Turner .25 .10
565 Rico Carty .50 .20
566 Nino Espinosa .25 .10
567 Richie Hebner .50 .20
568 Carlos Lopez .25 .10
569 Bob Sykes .25 .10
570 Cesar Cedeno .50 .20
571 Darrell Porter .50 .20
572 Rod Gilbreath .25 .10
573 Jim Kern .25 .10
574 Claudell Washington .50 .20
575 Luis Tiant .50 .20
576 Mike Parrott .25 .10
577 Brewers Team CL 1.00 .20
George Bamberger MG
578 Pete Broberg .25 .10
579 Greg Gross .25 .10
580 Ron Fairly .50 .20
581 Darold Knowles .25 .10
582 Paul Blair .50 .20
583 Julio Cruz .25 .10
584 Jim Rooker .25 .10
585 Hal McRae 1.00 .40
586 Bob Horner RC 1.00 .40
587 Ken Reitz .25 .10
588 Tom Murphy .25 .10
589 Terry Whitfield .25 .10
590 J.R. Richard .50 .20
591 Mike Hargrove .50 .20
592 Mike Krukow .25 .10
593 Rick Dempsey .50 .20
594 Bob Shirley .25 .10
595 Phil Niekro 2.00 .80
596 Jim Wohlford .25 .10
597 Bob Stanley .25 .10
598 Mark Wagner .25 .10
599 Jim Spencer .25 .10
600 George Foster .50 .20
601 Dave LaRoche .25 .10
602 Checklist 485-605 1.00 .20
603 Rudy May .25 .10
604 Jeff Newman .25 .10
605 Rick Monday DP .25 .10
606 Expos Team CL 1.00 .20
Dick Williams MG
607 Omar Moreno .25 .10
608 Dave McKay .25 .10
609 Silvio Martinez .25 .10
610 Mike Schmidt 8.00 3.20
611 Jim Norris .25 .10
612 Rick Honeycutt RC .50 .20
613 Mike Edwards .25 .10
614 Willie Hernandez .50 .20
615 Ken Singleton .50 .20
616 Billy Almon .25 .10
617 Terry Puhl .25 .10
618 Jerry Remy .25 .10
619 Ken Landreaux .50 .20
620 Bert Campaneris .50 .20
621 Pat Zachry .25 .10
622 Dave Collins .50 .20
623 Bob McClure .25 .10
624 Larry Herndon .25 .10
625 Mark Fidrych 2.00 .80
626 Yankees Team CL 1.00 .20
Bob Lemon MG
627 Gary Serum .25 .10
628 Del Unser .25 .10
629 Gene Garber .50 .20
630 Bake McBride .50 .20
631 Jorge Orta .25 .10
632 Don Kirkwood .25 .10
633 Rob Wilfong DP .15 .06
634 Paul Lindblad .25 .10
635 Don Baylor 1.00 .40
636 Wayne Garland .25 .10
637 Bill Robinson .50 .20
638 Al Fitzmorris .25 .10
639 Manny Trillo .25 .10
640 Eddie Murray 12.00 4.80
641 Bobby Castillo .25 .10
642 Wilbur Howard DP .15 .06
643 Tom Hausman .25 .10
644 Manny Mota .50 .20
645 George Scott DP .25 .10
646 Rick Sweet .25 .10
647 Bob Lacey .25 .10
648 Lou Piniella .50 .20
649 John Curtis .25 .10
650 Pete Rose 12.00 4.80
651 Mike Caldwell .25 .10
652 Stan Papi .25 .10
653 Warren Brusstar DP .15 .06
654 Rick Miller .25 .10
655 Jerry Koosman .50 .20
656 Hosken Powell .25 .10
657 George Medich .25 .10
658 Taylor Duncan .25 .10
659 Mariners Team CL 1.00 .20
Darrell Johnson MG
660 Ron LeFlore DP .25 .10
661 Bruce Kison .25 .10
662 Kevin Bell .25 .10
663 Mike Vail .25 .10
664 Doug Bird .25 .10
665 Lou Brock 2.50 1.00
666 Rich Dauer .25 .10
667 Don Hood .25 .10
668 Bill North .25 .10
669 Checklist 606-726 1.00 .20
670 Jim Hunter DP 1.00 .40
671 Joe Ferguson DP .15 .06
672 Ed Halicki .25 .10
673 Tom Hutton .25 .10
674 Dave Tomlin .25 .10
675 Tim McCarver 1.00 .40
676 Johnny Sutton .25 .10
677 Larry Parrish .50 .20
678 Geoff Zahn .25 .10
679 Derrel Thomas .25 .10
680 Carlton Fisk 3.00 1.20
681 John Henry Johnson .25 .10
682 Dave Chalk .25 .10
683 Dan Meyer DP .15 .06
684 Jamie Easterly DP .15 .06
685 Sixto Lezcano .25 .10
686 Ron Schueler DP .15 .06
687 Rennie Stennett .25 .10
688 Mike Willis .25 .10
689 Orioles Team CL 1.00 .20
Earl Weaver MG
690 Buddy Bell DP .25 .10
691 Dock Ellis DP .15 .06
692 Mickey Stanley .25 .10
693 Dave Rader .25 .10
694 Burt Hooton .50 .20
695 Keith Hernandez .50 .20
696 Andy Hassler .25 .10
697 Dave Bergman .25 .10
698 Bill Stein .25 .10
699 Hal Dues .25 .10
700 Reggie Jackson DP 5.00 2.00
701 Mark Corey .50 .20
John Flinn
Sammy Stewart
702 Joel Finch .50 .20
Garry Hancock
Allen Ripley
703 Jim Anderson .50 .20
Dave Frost
Bob Slater
704 Ross Baumgarten .50 .20
Mike Colbern
Mike Squires
705 Alfredo Griffin RC 1.00 .40
Tim Norrid
Dave Oliver
706 Dave Stegman .50 .20
Dave Tobik
Kip Young
707 Randy Bass RC 1.00 .40
Jim Gaudet
Randy McGilberry
708 Kevin Bass RC 1.00 .40
Eddie Romero
Ned Yost RC
709 Sam Perlozzo .50 .20
Rick Sofield
Kevin Stanfield
710 Brian Doyle .50 .20
Mike Heath
Dave Rajsich
711 Dwayne Murphy RC 1.00 .40
Bruce Robinson
Alan Wirth
712 Bud Anderson .50 .20
Greg Biercevicz
Byron McLaughlin
713 Danny Darwin RC 1.00 .40
Pat Putnam
Billy Sample
714 Victor Cruz .50 .20
Pat Kelly
Ernie Whitt
715 Bruce Benedict 1.00 .40
Glenn Hubbard RC
Larry Whisenton
716 Dave Geisel .50 .20
Karl Pagel
Scot Thompson
717 Mike LaCoss .50 .20
Ron Oester RC
Harry Spilman
718 Bruce Bochy .50 .20
Mike Fischlin
Don Pisker
719 Pedro Guerrero RC 1.00 .40
Rudy Law
Joe Simpson
720 Jerry Fry 1.00 .40
Jerry Pirtle
Scott Sanderson RC
721 Juan Berenguer .50 .20
Dwight Bernard
Dan Norman
722 Jim Morrison 1.00 .40
Lonnie Smith RC
Jim Wright
723 Dale Berra RC .50 .20
Eugenio Cotes
Ben Wiltbank
724 Tom Bruno 1.00 .40
George Frazier
Terry Kennedy RC
725 Jim Beswick .50 .20
Steve Mura
Broderick Perkins
726 Greg Johnston .50 .10
Joe Strain
John Tamargo

1980 Topps

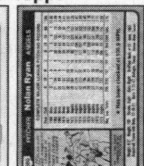

The cards in this 726-card set measure the standard size. In 1980 Topps released another set of the same size and number of cards as the previous two years. Distribution for these cards included 15-card wax packs as well as 42-card rack packs. A special experiment in 1980 was the issuance of a 28-card cello pack with a three-pack of gum at the bottom so no cards would be damaged. As with those sets, Topps again produced 66 double-printed cards in the set; they are noted by DP in the checklist below. The player's name appears over the picture and his position and team are found in pennant design. Every card carries a facsimile autograph. Team cards feature a team checklist of players in the set on the back and the manager's name on the front. Cards 1-6 show Highlights (HL) of the 1979 season, cards 201-207 are League Leaders, and cards 661-686 feature American and National League rookie "Future Stars," one card for each team showing three young prospects. The key Rookie Card in this set is Rickey Henderson; other Rookie Cards included in this set are Dan Quisenberry, Dave Stieb and Rick Sutcliffe.

NM Ex
COMPLETE SET (726) 120.00 47.50
COMMON CARD (1-726) .25 .10
COMMON DP .25 .10
1 Lou Brock HL 2.50 .50
Carl Yastrzemski
2 Willie McCovey HL .75 .30
3 Manny Mota HL .25 .10
4 Pete Rose HL 3.00 1.20
5 Garry Templeton HL .25 .10
6 Del Unser HL .25 .10
7 Mike Lum .25 .10
8 Craig Swan .25 .10
9 Steve Braun .25 .10
10 Dennis Martinez .75 .30
11 Jimmy Sexton .25 .10
12 John Curtis DP .25 .10
13 Ron Pruitt .25 .10
14 Dave Cash .75 .30
15 Bill Campbell .25 .10
16 Jerry Narron .25 .10
17 Bruce Sutter .75 .30
18 Ron Jackson .25 .10
19 Balor Moore .25 .10
20 Dan Ford .25 .10
21 Manny Sarmiento .25 .10
22 Pat Putnam .25 .10
23 Derrel Thomas .25 .10
24 Jim Slaton .25 .10
25 Lee Mazzilli .75 .30
26 Marty Pattin .25 .10
27 Del Unser .25 .10
28 Bruce Kison .25 .10
29 Mark Wagner .25 .10
30 Vida Blue .75 .30
31 Jay Johnstone .25 .10
32 Julio Cruz DP .25 .10
33 Tony Scott .25 .10
34 Jeff Newman DP .25 .10
35 Luis Tiant .75 .30
36 Rusty Torres .25 .10
37 Kiko Garcia .25 .10
38 Dan Spillner DP .25 .10
39 Rowland Office .25 .10
40 Carlton Fisk 2.50 1.00
41 Rangers Team CL .75 .15
Pat Corrales MG
42 David Palmer .25 .10
43 Bombo Rivera .25 .10
44 Bill Fahey .25 .10
45 Frank White .75 .30
46 Rico Carty .75 .30
47 Bill Bonham DP .25 .10
48 Rick Miller .25 .10
49 Mario Guerrero .25 .10
50 J.R. Richard .75 .30
51 Joe Ferguson DP .25 .10
52 Warren Brusstar .25 .10
53 Ben Oglivie .75 .30
54 Dennis Lamp .25 .10
55 Bill Madlock .75 .30
56 Bobby Valentine .75 .30
57 Pete Vuckovich .25 .10
58 Doug Flynn .25 .10
59 Eddy Putman .25 .10
60 Bucky Dent .75 .30
61 Gary Serum .25 .10
62 Mike Ivie .25 .10
63 Bob Stanley .25 .10
64 Joe Nolan .25 .10
65 Al Bumbry .75 .30
66 Royals Team CL .75 .15
Jim Frey MG
67 Doyle Alexander .25 .10
68 Larry Harlow .25 .10
69 Rick Williams .25 .10
70 Gary Carter 1.50 .60
71 John Milner DP .25 .10
72 Fred Howard DP .25 .10
73 Dave Collins .25 .10
74 Sid Monge .25 .10
75 Bill Russell .75 .30
76 John Stearns .25 .10
77 Dave Stieb RC 1.50 .60
78 Ruppert Jones .25 .10
79 Bob Owchinko .25 .10
80 Ron LeFlore .75 .30
81 Ted Sizemore .25 .10
82 Astros Team CL .75 .15
Bill Virdon MG
83 Steve Trout .25 .10
84 Gary Lavelle .25 .10
85 Ted Simmons .75 .30
86 Dave Hamilton .25 .10
87 Pepe Frias .25 .10
88 Ken Landreaux .25 .10
89 Don Hood .25 .10
90 Manny Trillo .75 .30
91 Rick Dempsey .75 .30
92 Rick Rhoden .25 .10
93 Dave Roberts DP .25 .10
94 Neil Allen .25 .10
95 Cecil Cooper .75 .30
96 A's Team CL .75 .15
Jim Marshall MG
97 Bill Lee .75 .30
98 Jerry Terrell .25 .10
99 Victor Cruz .25 .10
100 Johnny Bench 3.00 1.20
101 Aurelio Lopez .25 .10
102 Rich Dauer .25 .10
103 Bill Caudill .25 .10
104 Manny Mota .75 .30
105 Frank Tanana .75 .30
106 Jeff Leonard RC 1.50 .60
107 Francisco Barrios .25 .10
108 Bob Horner .75 .30
109 Bill Travers .25 .10
110 Fred Lynn DP .50 .20
111 Bob Knepper .25 .10
112 White Sox Team CL .75 .15
Tony LaRussa MG
113 Geoff Zahn .25 .10
114 Juan Beniquez .25 .10
115 Sparky Lyle .75 .30
116 Larry Cox .25 .10
117 Dock Ellis .25 .10
118 Phil Garner .75 .30
119 Sammy Stewart .25 .10
120 Greg Luzinski .75 .30
121 Checklist 1-121 .75 .15
122 Dave Rosello DP .25 .10
123 Lynn Jones .25 .10
124 Dave Lemanczyk .25 .10
125 Tony Perez .75 .30
126 Dave Tomlin .25 .10
127 Gary Thomasson .25 .10
128 Tom Burgmeier .25 .10
129 Craig Reynolds .25 .10
130 Amos Otis .75 .30
131 Paul Mitchell .25 .10
132 Biff Pocoroba .25 .10
133 Jerry Turner .25 .10
134 Matt Keough .25 .10
135 Bill Buckner .75 .30
136 Dick Ruthven .25 .10
137 John Castino .25 .10
138 Ross Baumgarten .25 .10
139 Dane Iorg .25 .10
140 Rich Gossage .75 .30
141 Gary Alexander .25 .10
142 Phil Huffman .25 .10
143 Bruce Bochte DP .25 .10
144 Steve Comer .25 .10
145 Darrell Evans .75 .30
146 Bob Welch .75 .30
147 Terry Puhl .25 .10
148 Manny Sanguillen .75 .30
149 Tom Hume .25 .10
150 Jason Thompson .25 .10
151 Tom Hausman DP .25 .10
152 John Fulgham .25 .10
153 Tim Blackwell .25 .10
154 Lary Sorensen .25 .10
155 Jerry Remy .25 .10
156 Tony Brizzolara .25 .10
157 Willie Wilson DP .50 .20
158 Rob Picciolo DP .25 .10
159 Ken Clay .25 .10
160 Eddie Murray 5.00 2.00
161 Larry Christenson .25 .10
162 Bob Randall .25 .10
163 Steve Swisher .25 .10
164 Greg Pryor .25 .10
165 Omar Moreno .25 .10
166 Glenn Abbott .25 .10
167 Jack Clark .75 .30
168 Rick Waits .25 .10
169 Luis Gomez .25 .10
170 Burt Hooton .75 .30
171 Fernando Gonzalez .25 .10
172 Ron Hodges .25 .10
173 John Henry Johnson .25 .10
174 Ray Knight .75 .30
175 Rick Reuschel .75 .30
176 Champ Summers .25 .10
177 Dave Heaverlo .25 .10
178 Tim McCarver .75 .30
179 Ron Davis .25 .10
180 Warren Cromartie .25 .10
181 Moose Haas .25 .10
182 Ken Reitz .25 .10
183 Jim Anderson DP .25 .10
184 Steve Renko DP .25 .10
185 Hal McRae .75 .30
186 Junior Moore .25 .10
187 Alan Ashby .25 .10
188 Terry Crowley .25 .10
189 Kevin Kobel .25 .10
190 Buddy Bell .75 .30
191 Ted Martinez .25 .10
192 Braves Team CL .75 .15
Bobby Cox MG
193 Dave Goltz .25 .10
194 Mike Easler .25 .10
195 John Montefusco .75 .30
196 Lance Parrish .75 .30
197 Byron McLaughlin .25 .10
198 Dell Alston DP .25 .10
199 Mike LaCoss .25 .10
200 Jim Rice .75 .30
201 Keith Hernandez .75 .30
Fred Lynn LL
202 Dave Kingman 1.50 .60
Gorman Thomas LL
203 Dave Winfield 1.50 .60
Don Baylor LL
204 Omar Moreno .75 .30
Willie Wilson LL
205 Joe Niekro .75 .30
Phil Niekro
Mike Flanagan LL
206 J.R. Richard 5.00 2.00
Nolan Ryan LL
207 J.R. Richard .75 .30
Ron Guidry LL
208 Wayne Cage .25 .10
209 Von Joshua .25 .10
210 Steve Carlton 1.50 .60
211 Dave Skaggs DP .25 .10
212 Dave Roberts .25 .10
213 Mike Jorgensen DP .25 .10
214 Angels Team CL .75 .15
Jim Fregosi MG
215 Sixto Lezcano .25 .10
216 Phil Mankowski .25 .10
217 Ed Halicki .25 .10
218 Jose Morales .25 .10
219 Steve Mingori .25 .10
220 Dave Concepcion .75 .30
221 Joe Cannon .25 .10
222 Ron Hassey .25 .10
223 Bob Sykes .25 .10
224 Willie Montanez .25 .10
225 Lou Piniella .75 .30
226 Bill Stein .25 .10
227 Len Barker .75 .30
228 Johnny Oates .75 .30
229 Jim Bibby .25 .10
230 Dave Winfield 1.50 .60
231 Steve McCatty .25 .10
232 Alan Trammell 1.50 .60
233 LaRue Washington .25 .10
234 Vern Ruhle .25 .10
235 Andre Dawson 1.50 .60
236 Marc Hill .25 .10
237 Scott McGregor .75 .30
238 Rob Wilfong .25 .10
239 Don Aase .25 .10
240 Dave Kingman .75 .30
241 Checklist 122-242 .75 .15
242 Lamar Johnson .25 .10
243 Jerry Augustine .25 .10
244 Cardinals Team CL .75 .15
Ken Boyer MG
245 Phil Niekro .75 .30
246 Tim Foli DP .25 .10
247 Frank Riccelli .25 .10
248 Jamie Quirk .25 .10
249 Jim Clancy .25 .10
250 Jim Kaat .75 .30
251 Kip Young .25 .10
252 Ted Cox .25 .10
253 John Montague .25 .10
254 Paul Dade DP .25 .10
255 Dusty Baker DP .50 .20

256 Roger Erickson .25 .10
257 Larry Herndon .25 .10
258 Paul Moskau .25 .10
259 Mets Team CL 1.50 .30
Joe Torre MG
260 Al Oliver .75 .30
261 Dave Chalk .25 .10
262 Benny Ayala .25 .10
263 Dave LaRoche DP .25 .10
264 Bill Robinson .25 .10
265 Robin Yount 3.00 1.20
266 Bernie Carbo .25 .10
267 Dan Schatzeder .25 .10
268 Rafael Landestoy .25 .10
269 Dave Tobik .25 .10
270 Mike Schmidt DP 3.00 1.20
271 Dick Drago DP .25 .10
272 Ralph Garr .75 .30
273 Eduardo Rodriguez .25 .10
274 Dale Murphy 2.50 1.00
275 Jerry Koosman .75 .30
276 Tom Veryzer .25 .10
277 Rick Bosetti .25 .10
278 Jim Spencer .25 .10
279 Rob Andrews .25 .10
280 Gaylord Perry .75 .30
281 Paul Blair .75 .30
282 Mariners Team CL .75 .15
Darrell Johnson MG
283 John Ellis .25 .10
284 Larry Murray DP .25 .10
285 Don Baylor .75 .30
286 Darold Knowles DP .25 .10
287 John Lowenstein .25 .10
288 Dave Rozema .25 .10
289 Bruce Bochy .25 .10
290 Steve Garvey 1.50 .60
291 Randy Scarberry .25 .10
292 Dale Berra .25 .10
293 Elias Sosa .25 .10
294 Charlie Spikes .25 .10
295 Larry Gura .25 .10
296 Dave Rader .25 .10
297 Tim Johnson .25 .10
298 Ken Holtzman .75 .30
299 Steve Henderson .25 .10
300 Ron Guidry .75 .30
301 Mike Edwards .25 .10
302 Dodgers Team CL 1.50 .30
Tom Lasorda MG
303 Bill Castro .25 .10
304 Butch Wynegar .25 .10
305 Randy Jones .75 .30
306 Denny Walling .25 .10
307 Rick Honeycutt .25 .10
308 Mike Hargrove .75 .30
309 Larry McWilliams .25 .10
310 Dave Parker .75 .30
311 Roger Metzger .25 .10
312 Mike Barlow .25 .10
313 Johnny Grubb .25 .10
314 Tim Stoddard .25 .10
315 Steve Kemp .75 .30
316 Bob Lacey .25 .10
317 Mike Anderson DP .25 .10
318 Jerry Reuss .75 .30
319 Chris Speier .25 .10
320 Dennis Eckersley 1.50 .60
321 Keith Hernandez .75 .30
322 Claudell Washington .25 .10
323 Mick Kelleher .25 .10
324 Tom Underwood .25 .10
325 Dan Driessen .25 .10
326 Bo McLaughlin .25 .10
327 Ray Fosse DP .50 .20
328 Twins Team CL .75 .15
Gene Mauch MG
329 Bert Roberge .25 .10
330 Al Cowens .25 .10
331 Richie Hebner .25 .10
332 Enrique Romo .25 .10
333 Jim Norris DP .25 .10
334 Jim Beattie .25 .10
335 Willie McCovey 1.50 .60
336 George Medich .25 .10
337 Carney Lansford .75 .30
338 John Wockenfuss .25 .10
339 John D'Acquisto .25 .10
340 Ken Singleton .75 .30
341 Jim Essian .25 .10
342 Odell Jones .25 .10
343 Mike Vail .25 .10
344 Randy Lerch .25 .10
345 Larry Parrish .75 .30
346 Buddy Solomon .25 .10
347 Harry Chappas .25 .10
348 Checklist 243-363 .75 .15
349 Jack Brohamer .25 .10
350 George Hendrick .75 .30
351 Bob Davis .25 .10
352 Dan Briggs .25 .10
353 Andy Hassler .25 .10
354 Rick Auerbach .25 .10
355 Gary Matthews .75 .30
356 Padres Team CL .75 .15
Jerry Coleman MG
357 Bob McClure .25 .10
358 Lou Whitaker .75 .30
359 Randy Moffitt .25 .10
360 Darrell Porter DP .50 .20
361 Wayne Garland .25 .10
362 Danny Goodwin .25 .10
363 Wayne Gross .25 .10
364 Ray Burris .25 .10
365 Bobby Murcer .75 .30
366 Rob Dressler .25 .10
367 Billy Smith .25 .10
368 Willie Aikens .25 .10
369 Jim Kern .25 .10
370 Cesar Cedeno .75 .30
371 Jack Morris .75 .30
372 Joel Youngblood .25 .10
373 Dan Petry DP RC .75 .30
374 Jim Gantner .75 .30
375 Ross Grimsley .25 .10
376 Gary Allenson .25 .10
377 Junior Kennedy .25 .10
378 Jerry Mumphrey .25 .10
379 Kevin Bell .25 .10
380 Garry Maddox .75 .30
381 Cubs Team CL .75 .15
Preston Gomez MG
382 Dave Freisleben .25 .10
383 Ed Ott .25 .10
384 Joey McLaughlin .25 .10
385 Enos Cabell .25 .10
386 Darrell Jackson .25 .10
387A Fred Stanley YL 2.00 .80
387B Fred Stanley .25 .10
(Red name on front)
388 Mike Paxton .25 .10
389 Pete LaCock .25 .10
390 Fergie Jenkins .75 .30
391 Tony Armas DP .50 .20
392 Milt Wilcox .25 .10
393 Ozzie Smith 10.00 4.00
394 Reggie Cleveland .25 .10
395 Ellis Valentine .25 .10
396 Dan Meyer .25 .10
397 Roy Thomas DP .25 .10
398 Barry Foote .25 .10
399 Mike Proly DP .25 .10
400 George Foster .75 .30
401 Pete Falcone .25 .10
402 Merv Rettenmund .25 .10
403 Pete Redfern DP .25 .10
404 Orioles Team CL .75 .15
Earl Weaver MG
405 Dwight Evans .75 .30
406 Paul Molitor 4.00 1.60
407 Tony Solaita .25 .10
408 Bill North .25 .10
409 Paul Splittorff .25 .10
410 Bobby Bonds .75 .30
411 Frank LaCorte .25 .10
412 Thad Bosley .25 .10
413 Allen Ripley .25 .10
414 George Scott .75 .30
415 Bill Atkinson .25 .10
416 Tom Brookens .25 .10
417 Craig Chamberlain DP .25 .10
418 Roger Freed DP .25 .10
419 Vic Correll .25 .10
420 Butch Hobson .25 .10
421 Doug Bird .25 .10
422 Larry Milbourne .25 .10
423 Dave Frost .25 .10
424 Yankees Team CL .75 .15
Dick Howser MG
424A Yankees Team CL
Billy Martin MG
Card is believed to be a pre-production issue
425 Mark Belanger .75 .30
426 Grant Jackson .25 .10
427 Tom Hutton DP .25 .10
428 Pat Zachry .25 .10
429 Duane Kuiper .25 .10
430 Larry Hisle DP .25 .10
431 Mike Krukow .25 .10
432 Willie Norwood .25 .10
433 Rich Gale .25 .10
434 Johnnie LeMaster .25 .10
435 Don Gullett .75 .30
436 Billy Almon .25 .10
437 Joe Niekro .75 .30
438 Dave Revering .25 .10
439 Mike Phillips .25 .10
440 Don Sutton .75 .30
441 Eric Soderholm .25 .10
442 Jorge Orta .25 .10
443 Mike Parrott .25 .10
444 Alvis Woods .25 .10
445 Mark Fidrych .75 .30
446 Duffy Dyer .25 .10
447 Nino Espinosa .25 .10
448 Jim Wohlford .25 .10
449 Doug Bair .25 .10
450 George Brett 8.00 3.20
451 Indians Team CL .75 .15
Dave Garcia MG
452 Steve Dillard .25 .10
453 Mike Bacsik .25 .10
454 Tom Donohue .25 .10
455 Mike Torrez .75 .30
456 Frank Taveras .25 .10
457 Bert Blyleven .75 .30
458 Billy Sample .25 .10
459 Mickey Lolich DP .50 .20
460 Willie Randolph .75 .30
461 Dwayne Murphy .25 .10
462 Mike Sadek DP .25 .10
463 Jerry Royster .25 .10
464 John Denny .75 .30
465 Rick Monday .75 .30
466 Mike Squires .25 .10
467 Jesse Jefferson .25 .10
468 Aurelio Rodriguez .25 .10
469 Randy Niemann DP .25 .10
470 Bob Boone .75 .30
471 Hosken Powell DP .25 .10
472 Willie Hernandez .75 .30
473 Bump Wills .25 .10
474 Steve Busby .75 .30
475 Cesar Geronimo .75 .30
476 Bob Shirley .25 .10
477 Buck Martinez .25 .10
478 Gil Flores .25 .10
479 Expos Team CL .75 .15
Dick Williams MG
480 Bob Watson .75 .30
481 Tom Paciorek .75 .30
482 R.Henderson RC UER 60.00 24.00
7 steals at Modesto,
should be at Fresno
483 Bo Diaz .25 .10
484 Checklist 364-484 .75 .15
485 Mickey Rivers .75 .30
486 Mike Tyson DP .25 .10
487 Wayne Nordhagen .25 .10
488 Roy Howell .25 .10
489 Preston Hanna DP .25 .10
490 Lee May .75 .30
491 Steve Mura DP .25 .10
492 Todd Cruz .25 .10
493 Jerry Martin .25 .10
494 Craig Minetto .25 .10
495 Bake McBride .75 .30
496 Silvio Martinez .25 .10
497 Jim Mason .25 .10
498 Danny Darwin .25 .10
499 Giants Team CL .75 .15
Dave Bristol MG
500 Tom Seaver 3.00 1.20
501 Rennie Stennett .25 .10
502 Rich Wortham DP .25 .10
503 Mike Cubbage .25 .10
504 Gene Garber .25 .10
505 Bert Campaneris .75 .30
506 Tom Buskey .25 .10
507 Leon Roberts .25 .10
508 U.L. Washington .25 .10
509 Ed Glynn .25 .10
510 Ron Cey .75 .30
511 Eric Wilkins .25 .10
512 Jose Cardenal .25 .10
513 Tom Dixon DP .25 .10
514 Steve Ontiveros .25 .10
515 Mike Caldwell UER .25 .10
1979 loss total reads
96 instead of 6
516 Hector Cruz .25 .10
517 Don Stanhouse .25 .10
518 Nelson Norman .25 .10
519 Steve Nicosia .25 .10
520 Steve Rogers .75 .30
521 Ken Brett .25 .10
522 Jim Morrison .25 .10
523 Ken Henderson .25 .10
524 Jim Wright DP .25 .10
525 Clint Hurdle .25 .10
526 Phillies Team CL .75 .15
Dallas Green MG
527 Doug Rau DP .25 .10
528 Adrian Devine .25 .10
529 Jim Barr .25 .10
530 Jim Sundberg DP .50 .20
531 Eric Rasmussen .25 .10
532 Willie Horton .75 .30
533 Checklist 485-605 .75 .15
534 Andre Thornton .75 .30
535 Bob Forsch .25 .10
536 Lee Lacy .25 .10
537 Alex Trevino .25 .10
538 Joe Strain .25 .10
539 Rudy May .25 .10
540 Pete Rose 8.00 3.20
541 Miguel Dilone .25 .10
542 Joe Coleman .25 .10
543 Pat Kelly .25 .10
544 Rick Sutcliffe RC 1.50 .60
545 Jeff Burroughs .75 .30
546 Rick Langford .25 .10
547 John Wathan .25 .10
548 Dave Rajsich .25 .10
549 Larry Wolfe .25 .10
550 Ken Griffey Sr. .75 .30
551 Pirates Team CL .75 .15
Chuck Tanner MG
552 Bill Nahorodny .25 .10
553 Dick Davis .25 .10
554 Art Howe .75 .30
555 Ed Figueroa .25 .10
556 Joe Rudi .75 .30
557 Mark Lee .25 .10
558 Alfredo Griffin .25 .10
559 Dale Murray .25 .10
560 Dave Lopes .75 .30
561 Eddie Whitson .25 .10
562 Joe Wallis .25 .10
563 Will McEnaney .25 .10
564 Rick Manning .25 .10
565 Dennis Leonard .25 .10
566 Bud Harrelson .75 .30
567 Skip Lockwood .25 .10
568 Gary Roenicke .25 .10
569 Terry Kennedy .25 .10
570 Roy Smalley .75 .30
571 Joe Sambito .25 .10
572 Jerry Morales DP .25 .10
573 Kent Tekulve .75 .30
574 Scot Thompson .25 .10
575 Ken Kravec .25 .10
576 Jim Dwyer .25 .10
577 Blue Jays Team CL .75 .15
Bobby Mattick MG
578 Scott Sanderson .25 .10
579 Charlie Moore .25 .10
580 Nolan Ryan 15.00 6.00
581 Bob Bailor .25 .10
582 Brian Doyle .25 .10
583 Bob Stinson .25 .10
584 Kurt Bevacqua .25 .10
585 Al Hrabosky .75 .30
586 Mitchell Page .25 .10
587 Garry Templeton .75 .30
588 Greg Minton .25 .10
589 Chet Lemon .75 .30
590 Jim Palmer 1.50 .60
591 Rick Cerone .25 .10
592 Jon Matlack .75 .30
593 Jesus Alou .25 .10
594 Dick Tidrow .25 .10
595 Don Money .25 .10
596 Rick Matula .25 .10
597 Tom Poquette .25 .10
598 Fred Kendall DP .25 .10
599 Mike Norris .25 .10
600 Reggie Jackson 3.00 1.20
601 Buddy Schultz .25 .10
602 Brian Downing .75 .30
603 Jack Billingham DP .25 .10
604 Glenn Adams .25 .10
605 Terry Forster .75 .30
606 Reds Team CL .75 .15
John McNamara MG
607 Woodie Fryman .25 .10
608 Alan Bannister .25 .10
609 Ron Reed .25 .10
610 Willie Stargell 1.50 .60
611 Jerry Garvin DP .25 .10
612 Cliff Johnson .25 .10
613 Randy Stein .25 .10
614 John Hiller .25 .10
615 Doug DeCinces .75 .30
616 Gene Richards .25 .10
617 Joaquin Andujar .75 .30
618 Bob Montgomery DP .25 .10
619 Sergio Ferrer .25 .10
620 Richie Zisk .75 .30
621 Bob Grich .75 .30
622 Mario Soto .75 .30
623 Gorman Thomas .75 .30
624 Lerrin LaGrow .25 .10
625 Chris Chambliss .75 .30
626 Tigers Team CL .75 .15
Sparky Anderson MG
627 Pedro Borbon .25 .10
628 Doug Capilla .25 .10
629 Jim Todd .25 .10
630 Larry Bowa .75 .30
631 Mark Littell .25 .10
632 Barry Bonnell .25 .10
633 Bob Apodaca .25 .10
634 Glenn Borgmann DP .25 .10
635 John Candelaria .75 .30
636 Toby Harrah .75 .30
637 Joe Simpson .25 .10
638 Mark Clear .25 .10
639 Larry Biittner .25 .10
640 Mike Flanagan .75 .30
641 Ed Kranepool .75 .30
642 Ken Forsch DP .25 .10
643 John Mayberry .75 .30
644 Charlie Hough .75 .30
645 Rick Burleson .75 .30
646 Checklist 606-726 .75 .15
647 Milt May .25 .10
648 Roy White .75 .30
649 Tom Griffin .25 .10
650 Joe Morgan 1.50 .60
651 Rollie Fingers .75 .30
652 Mario Mendoza .25 .10
653 Stan Bahnsen .25 .10
654 Bruce Boisclair DP .25 .10
655 Tug McGraw .75 .30
656 Larvell Blanks .25 .10
657 Dave Edwards .25 .10
658 Chris Knapp .25 .10
659 Brewers Team CL .75 .15
George Bamberger MG
660 Rusty Staub .75 .30
661 Mark Corey .25 .10
Dave Ford
Wayne Krenchicki
662 Joel Finch .25 .10
Mike O'Berry
Chuck Rainey
663 Ralph Botting .75 .30
Bob Clark
Dickie Thon RC
664 Mike Colbern .25 .10
Guy Hoffman
Dewey Robinson
665 Larry Andersen .25 .10
Bobby Cuellar
Sandy Wihtol
666 Mike Chris .25 .10
Al Greene
Bruce Robbins
667 Renie Martin .75 .30
Bill Paschall
Dan Quisenberry RC
668 Danny Boitano .25 .10
Willie Mueller
Lenn Sakata
669 Dan Graham .75 .30
Rick Sofield
Gary Ward RC
670 Bobby Brown .25 .10
Brad Gulden
Darryl Jones
671 Derek Bryant .75 .30
Brian Kingman
Mike Morgan RC
672 Charlie Beamon .25 .10
Rodney Craig
Rafael Vasquez
673 Brian Allard .25 .10
Jerry Don Gleaton
Greg Mahlberg
674 Butch Edge .25 .10
Pat Kelly
Ted Wilborn
675 Bruce Benedict .25 .10
Larry Bradford
Eddie Miller
676 Dave Geisel .25 .10
Steve Macko
Karl Pagel
677 Art DeFreites .25 .10
Frank Pastore
Harry Spilman
678 Reggie Baldwin .25 .10
Alan Knicely
Pete Ladd
679 Joe Beckwith .75 .30
Mickey Hatcher RC
Dave Patterson
680 Tony Bernazard .25 .10
Randy Miller
John Tamargo
681 Dan Norman 1.50 .60
Jesse Orosco RC
Mike Scott RC
682 Ramon Aviles .25 .10
Dickie Noles
Kevin Saucier
683 Dorian Boyland .25 .10
Alberto Lois
Harry Saferight
684 George Frazier .75 .30
Tom Herr RC
Dan O'Brien
685 Tim Flannery .25 .10
Brian Greer
Jim Wilhelm
686 Greg Johnston .25 .10
Dennis Littlejohn
Phil Nastu
687 Mike Heath DP .25 .10
688 Steve Stone .75 .30
689 Red Sox Team CL .75 .15
Don Zimmer MG
690 Tommy John .75 .30
691 Ivan DeJesus .25 .10
692 Rawly Eastwick DP .50 .20
693 Craig Kusick .25 .10
694 Jim Rooker .25 .10
695 Reggie Smith .75 .30
696 Julio Gonzalez .25 .10
697 David Clyde .25 .10
698 Oscar Gamble .75 .30
699 Floyd Bannister .25 .10
700 Rod Carew DP .75 .30
701 Ken Oberkfell .25 .10
702 Ed Farmer .25 .10
703 Otto Velez .25 .10
704 Gene Tenace .75 .30
705 Freddie Patek .75 .30
706 Tippy Martinez .25 .10
707 Elliott Maddox .25 .10
708 Bob Tolan .25 .10
709 Pat Underwood .25 .10
710 Graig Nettles .75 .30
711 Bob Galasso .25 .10
712 Rodney Scott .25 .10
713 Terry Whitfield .25 .10
714 Fred Norman .25 .10
715 Sal Bando .75 .30
716 Lynn McGlothen .25 .10
717 Mickey Klutts DP .25 .10
718 Greg Gross .25 .10
719 Don Robinson .75 .30
720 Carl Yastrzemski DP 2.00 .80
721 Paul Hartzell .25 .10
722 Jose Cruz .75 .30
723 Shane Rawley .25 .10
724 Jerry White .25 .10
725 Rick Wise .25 .10
726 Steve Yeager .75 .15

1981 Topps

The cards in this 726-card set measure the standard size. This set was issued primarily in 15-card wax packs and 50-card rack packs. League Leaders (1-8), Record Breakers (201-208), and Post-season cards (401-404) are the topical subsets. The team cards are all grouped together (661-686) and feature team checklist backs and a very small photo of the team's manager in the upper right corner of the obverse. The obverses carry the player's position and team in a baseball cap design, and the company name is printed in a small baseball. The backs are red and gray. The 66 double-printed cards are noted in the checklist by DP. Notable Rookie Cards in the set include Harold Baines, Kirk Gibson, Tim Raines, Jeff Reardon, and Fernando Valenzuela. During 1981, a promotion existed where collectors could order complete set in sheet form from Topps for $24.

Nm-Mt Ex-Mt
COMPLETE SET (726) 50.00 20.00
COMMON CARD (1-726) .15 .06
COMMON CARD DP .15 .06
1 George Brett 3.00 1.20
Bill Buckner LL
2 Reggie Jackson 1.50 .60
Ben Oglivie
Mike Schmidt LL
3 Cecil Cooper 1.50 .60
Mike Schmidt LL
4 Rickey Henderson 3.00 1.20
Ron LeFlore LL
5 Steve Stone .40 .16
Steve Carlton LL
6 Len Barker .40 .16
Steve Carlton LL
7 Rudy May .40 .16
Don Sutton LL
8 Dan Quisenberry .40 .16
Rollie Fingers
Tom Hume LL
9 Pete LaCock DP .15 .06
10 Mike Flanagan .15 .06
11 Jim Wohlford DP .15 .06
12 Mark Clear .15 .06
13 Joe Charboneau RC 1.50 .60
14 John Tudor RC 1.50 .60
15 Larry Parrish .15 .06
16 Ron Davis .15 .06
17 Cliff Johnson .15 .06
18 Glenn Adams .15 .06
19 Jim Clancy .15 .06
20 Jeff Burroughs .40 .16
21 Ron Oester .15 .06
22 Danny Darwin .15 .06
23 Alex Trevino .15 .06
24 Don Stanhouse .15 .06
25 Sixto Lezcano .15 .06
26 U.L. Washington .15 .06
27 Champ Summers DP .15 .06
28 Enrique Romo .15 .06
29 Gene Tenace .40 .16
30 Jack Clark .40 .16
31 Checklist 1-121 DP .25 .10
32 Ken Oberkfell .15 .06
33 Rick Honeycutt .15 .06
34 Aurelio Rodriguez .15 .06
35 Mitchell Page .15 .06
36 Ed Farmer .15 .06
37 Gary Roenicke .15 .06
38 Win Remmerswaal .15 .06
39 Tom Veryzer .15 .06
40 Tug McGraw .40 .16
41 Bob Babcock .25 .10
John Butcher
Jerry Don Gleaton
42 Jerry White DP .15 .06
43 Jose Morales .15 .06
44 Larry McWilliams .15 .06
45 Enos Cabell .15 .06
46 Rick Bosetti .15 .06
47 Ken Brett .15 .06
48 Dave Skaggs .15 .06
49 Bob Shirley .15 .06

50 Dave Lopes .40 .16
51 Bill Robinson DP .15 .06
52 Hector Cruz .15 .06
53 Kevin Saucier .15 .06
54 Ivan DeJesus .15 .06
55 Mike Norris .15 .06
56 Buck Martinez .15 .06
57 Dave Roberts .15 .06
58 Joel Youngblood .15 .06
59 Dan Petry .15 .06
60 Willie Randolph .40 .16
61 Butch Wynegar .15 .06
62 Joe Pettini .15 .06
63 Steve Renko DP .15 .06
64 Brian Asselstine .15 .06
65 Scott McGregor .15 .06
66 Manny Castillo .25 .10
Tim Ireland
Mike Jones
67 Ken Kravec .15 .06
68 Matt Alexander DP .15 .06
69 Ed Halicki .15 .06
70 Al Oliver DP .25 .10
71 Hal Dues .15 .06
72 Barry Evans DP .15 .06
73 Doug Bair .15 .06
74 Mike Hargrove .15 .06
75 Reggie Smith .40 .16
76 Mario Mendoza .15 .06
77 Mike Barlow .15 .06
78 Steve Dillard .15 .06
79 Bruce Robbins .15 .06
80 Rusty Staub .40 .16
81 Dave Stapleton .15 .06
82 Danny Heep .25 .10
Alan Knicely
Bobby Sprowl
83 Mike Proly .15 .06
84 Johnnie LeMaster .15 .06
85 Mike Caldwell .15 .06
86 Wayne Gross .15 .06
87 Rick Camp .15 .06
88 Joe Lefebvre .15 .06
89 Darrell Jackson .15 .06
90 Bake McBride .40 .16
91 Tim Stoddard DP .15 .06
92 Mike Easler .15 .06
93 Ed Glynn DP .15 .06
94 Harry Spilman DP .15 .06
95 Jim Sundberg .40 .16
96 Dave Beard .25 .10
Ernie Camacho
Pat Dempsey
97 Chris Speier .15 .06
98 Clint Hurdle .15 .06
99 Eric Wilkins .15 .06
100 Rod Carew .75 .30
101 Benny Ayala .15 .06
102 Dave Tobik .15 .06
103 Jerry Martin .15 .06
104 Terry Forster .40 .16
105 Jose Cruz .40 .16
106 Don Money .15 .06
107 Rich Wortham .15 .06
108 Bruce Benedict .15 .06
109 Mike Scott .40 .16
110 Carl Yastrzemski 2.50 1.00
111 Greg Minton .15 .06
112 Rusty Kuntz .25 .10
Fran Mullins
Leo Sutherland
113 Mike Phillips .15 .06
114 Tom Underwood .15 .06
115 Roy Smalley .40 .16
116 Joe Simpson .15 .06
117 Pete Falcone .15 .06
118 Kurt Bevacqua .15 .06
119 Tippy Martinez .15 .06
120 Larry Bowa .40 .16
121 Larry Harlow .15 .06
122 John Denny .15 .06
123 Al Cowens .15 .06
124 Jerry Garvin .15 .06
125 Andre Dawson .75 .30
126 Charlie Leibrandt RC .75 .30
127 Rudy Law .15 .06
128 Gary Allenson DP .15 .06
129 Art Howe .15 .06
130 Larry Gura .15 .06
131 Keith Moreland .15 .06
132 Tommy Boggs .15 .06
133 Jeff Cox .15 .06
134 Steve Mura .15 .06
135 Gorman Thomas .40 .16
136 Doug Capilla .15 .06
137 Hosken Powell .15 .06
138 Rich Dotson DP .15 .06
139 Oscar Gamble .15 .06
140 Bob Forsch .15 .06
141 Miguel Dilone .15 .06
142 Jackson Todd .15 .06
143 Dan Meyer .15 .06
144 Allen Ripley .15 .06
145 Mickey Rivers .15 .06
146 Bobby Castillo .15 .06
147 Dale Berra .15 .06
148 Randy Niemann .15 .06
149 Joe Nolan .15 .06
150 Mark Fidrych .40 .16
151 Claudell Washington .15 .06
152 John Urrea .15 .06
153 Tom Poquette .15 .06
154 Rick Langford .15 .06
155 Chris Chambliss .40 .16
156 Bob McClure .15 .06
157 John Wathan .15 .06
158 Fergie Jenkins .40 .16
159 Brian Doyle .15 .06
160 Garry Maddox .15 .06
161 Dan Graham .15 .06
162 Doug Corbett .15 .06
163 Bill Almon .15 .06
164 LaMarr Hoyt RC .75 .30
165 Tony Scott .15 .06
166 Floyd Bannister .15 .06
167 Terry Whitfield .15 .06
168 Don Robinson DP .15 .06
169 John Mayberry .15 .06
170 Ross Grimsley .15 .06
171 Gene Richards .15 .06
172 Gary Woods .15 .06
173 Bump Wills .15 .06
174 Doug Rau .15 .06
175 Dave Collins .15 .06
176 Mike Krukow .15 .06
177 Rick Peters .15 .06
178 Jim Essian DP .15 .06
179 Rudy May .15 .06
180 Pete Rose 5.00 2.00
181 Elias Sosa .15 .06
182 Bob Grich .40 .16
183 Dick Davis DP .15 .06
184 Jim Dwyer .15 .06
185 Dennis Leonard .15 .06
186 Wayne Nordhagen .15 .06
187 Mike Parrott .15 .06
188 Doug DeCinces .15 .06
189 Craig Swan .15 .06
190 Cesar Cedeno .40 .16
191 Rick Sutcliffe .40 .16
192 Terry Harper .25 .10
Ed Miller
Rafael Ramirez
193 Pete Vuckovich .15 .06
194 Rod Scurry .15 .06
195 Rich Murray .15 .06
196 Duffy Dyer .15 .06
197 Jim Kern .15 .06
198 Jerry Dybzinski .15 .06
199 Chuck Rainey .15 .06
200 George Foster .40 .16
201 Johnny Bench RB .75 .30
202 Steve Carlton RB .40 .16
203 Bill Gullickson RB .15 .06
204 Ron LeFlore RB .40 .16
Rodney Scott
205 Pete Rose RB 1.50 .60
206 Mike Schmidt RB 1.50 .60
207 Ozzie Smith RB 2.00 .80
208 Willie Wilson RB .15 .06
209 Dickie Thon DP .15 .06
210 Jim Palmer .75 .30
211 Derrel Thomas .15 .06
212 Steve Nicosia .15 .06
213 Al Holland .15 .06
214 Ralph Botting .25 .10
Jim Dorsey
John Harris
215 Larry Hisle .15 .06
216 John Henry Johnson .15 .06
217 Rich Hebner .15 .06
218 Paul Splittorff .15 .06
219 Ken Landreaux .15 .06
220 Tom Seaver 1.50 .60
221 Bob Davis .15 .06
222 Jorge Orta .15 .06
223 Roy Lee Jackson .15 .06
224 Pat Zachry .15 .06
225 Ruppert Jones .15 .06
226 Manny Sanguillen DP .25 .10
227 Fred Martinez .15 .06
228 Tom Paciorek .15 .06
229 Rollie Fingers .40 .16
230 George Hendrick .40 .16
231 Joe Beckwith .15 .06
232 Mickey Klutts .15 .06
233 Skip Lockwood .15 .06
234 Lou Whitaker .75 .30
235 Scott Sanderson .15 .06
236 Mike Ivie .15 .06
237 Charlie Moore .15 .06
238 Willie Hernandez .15 .06
239 Rick Miller DP .15 .06
240 Nolan Ryan 8.00 3.20
241 Checklist 122-242 DP .25 .10
242 Chet Lemon .40 .16
243 Sal Butera .15 .06
244 Tito Landrum .25 .10
Al Olmsted
Andy Rincon
245 Ed Figueroa .15 .06
246 Ed Ott DP .15 .06
247 Glenn Hubbard DP .15 .06
248 Joey McLaughlin .15 .06
249 Larry Cox .15 .06
250 Ron Guidry .40 .16
251 Tom Brookens .15 .06
252 Victor Cruz .15 .06
253 Dave Bergman .15 .06
254 Ozzie Smith 5.00 2.00
255 Mark Littell .15 .06
256 Bombo Rivera .15 .06
257 Rennie Stennett .15 .06
258 Joe Price .15 .06
259 Juan Berenguer 2.50 1.00
Hubie Brooks RC
Mookie Wilson
260 Ron Cey .40 .16
261 Rickey Henderson 10.00 4.00
262 Sammy Stewart .15 .06
263 Brian Downing .40 .16
264 Jim Norris .15 .06
265 John Candelaria .40 .16
266 Tom Herr .15 .06
267 Stan Bahnsen .15 .06
268 Jerry Royster .15 .06
269 Ken Forsch .15 .06
270 Greg Luzinski .40 .16
271 Bill Castro .15 .06
272 Bruce Kimm .15 .06
273 Stan Papi .15 .06
274 Craig Chamberlain .15 .06
275 Dwight Evans .75 .30
276 Dan Spillner .15 .06
277 Alfredo Griffin .15 .06
278 Rick Sofield .15 .06
279 Bob Knepper .40 .16
280 Ken Griffey .40 .16
281 Fred Stanley .15 .06
282 Rick Anderson .25 .10
Greg Biercevicz
Rodney Craig
283 Billy Sample .15 .06
284 Brian Kingman .15 .06
285 Jerry Turner .15 .06
286 Dave Frost .15 .06
287 Lenn Sakata .15 .06
288 Bob Clark .15 .06
289 Mickey Hatcher .15 .06
290 Bob Boone DP .25 .10
291 Aurelio Lopez .15 .06
292 Mike Squires .15 .06
293 Charlie Lea .15 .06
294 Mike Tyson DP .15 .06
295 Hal McRae .40 .16
296 Bill Nahorodny DP .15 .06
297 Bob Bailor .15 .06
298 Buddy Solomon .15 .06
299 Elliott Maddox .15 .06
300 Paul Molitor 1.50 .60
301 Matt Keough .15 .06
302 Jack Perconte 5.00 2.00
Mike Scioscia RC
Fernando Valenzuela RC
303 Johnny Oates .40 .16
304 John Castino .15 .06
305 Ken Clay .15 .06
306 Juan Beniquez DP .15 .06
307 Gene Garber .15 .06
308 Rick Manning .15 .06
309 Luis Salazar RC .75 .30
310 Vida Blue DP .25 .10
311 Freddie Patek .15 .06
312 Rick Rhoden .15 .06
313 Luis Pujols .15 .06
314 Rich Dauer .15 .06
315 Kirk Gibson RC 3.00 1.20
316 Craig Minetto .15 .06
317 Lonnie Smith .40 .16
318 Steve Yeager .40 .16
319 Rowland Office .15 .06
320 Tom Burgmeier .15 .06
321 Leon Durham RC .75 .30
322 Neil Allen .15 .06
323 Jim Morrison DP .15 .06
324 Mike Willis .15 .06
325 Ray Knight .40 .16
326 Biff Pocoroba .15 .06
327 Moose Haas .15 .06
328 Dave Engle .25 .10
Greg Johnston
Gary Ward
329 Joaquin Andujar .40 .16
330 Frank White .40 .16
331 Dennis Lamp .15 .06
332 Lee Lacy DP .15 .06
333 Sid Monge .15 .06
334 Dane Iorg .15 .06
335 Rick Cerone .15 .06
336 Eddie Whitson .15 .06
337 Lynn Jones .15 .06
338 Checklist 243-363 .40 .16
339 John Ellis .15 .06
340 Bruce Kison .15 .06
341 Dwayne Murphy .15 .06
342 Eric Rasmussen DP .15 .06
343 Frank Taveras .15 .06
344 Byron McLaughlin .15 .06
345 Warren Cromartie .15 .06
346 Larry Christenson DP .15 .06
347 Harold Baines RC 5.00 2.00
348 Bob Sykes .15 .06
349 Glenn Hoffman .15 .06
350 J.R. Richard .40 .16
351 Otto Velez .15 .06
352 Dick Tidrow DP .15 .06
353 Terry Kennedy .15 .06
354 Mario Soto .40 .16
355 Bob Horner .40 .16
356 George Stablein .25 .10
Craig Stimac
Tom Tellmann
357 Jim Slaton .15 .06
358 Mark Wagner .15 .06
359 Tom Hausman .15 .06
360 Willie Wilson .40 .16
361 Joe Strain .15 .06
362 Bo Diaz .15 .06
363 Geoff Zahn .15 .06
364 Mike Davis RC .25 .10
365 Graig Nettles DP .25 .10
366 Mike Ramsey RC .25 .10
367 Dennis Martinez .40 .16
368 Leon Roberts .15 .06
369 Frank Tanana .40 .16
370 Dave Winfield .75 .30
371 Charlie Hough .40 .16
372 Jay Johnstone .15 .06
373 Pat Underwood .15 .06
374 Tommy Hutton .15 .06
375 Dave Concepcion .40 .16
376 Ron Reed .15 .06
377 Jerry Morales .15 .06
378 Dave Rader .15 .06
379 Lary Sorensen .15 .06
380 Willie Stargell .75 .30
381 Carlos Lezcano .25 .10
Steve Macko
Randy Martz
382 Paul Mirabella .15 .06
383 Eric Soderholm DP .15 .06
384 Mike Sadek .15 .06
385 Joe Sambito .15 .06
386 Dave Edwards .15 .06
387 Phil Niekro .40 .16
388 Andre Thornton .40 .16
389 Marty Pattin .15 .06
390 Cesar Geronimo .15 .06
391 Dave Lemanczyk DP .15 .06
392 Lance Parrish .40 .16
393 Broderick Perkins .15 .06
394 Woodie Fryman .15 .06
395 Scot Thompson .15 .06
396 Bill Campbell .15 .06
397 Julio Cruz .15 .06
398 Ross Baumgarten .15 .06
399 Mike Boddicker RC 1.50 .60
Mark Corey
Floyd Rayford
400 Reggie Jackson 1.50 .60
401 George Brett ALCS 2.50 1.00
402 NL Champs .75 .30
Phillies squeak
past Astros
(Phillies celebrating)
403 Larry Bowa WS .75 .30
404 Tug McGraw WS .75 .30
405 Nino Espinosa .15 .06
406 Dickie Noles .15 .06
407 Ernie Whitt .15 .06
408 Fernando Arroyo .15 .06
409 Larry Herndon .15 .06
410 Bert Campaneris .40 .16
411 Terry Puhl .15 .06
412 Britt Burns .15 .06
413 Tony Bernazard .15 .06
414 John Pacella DP .15 .06
415 Ben Oglivie .40 .16
416 Gary Alexander .15 .06
417 Dan Schatzeder .15 .06
418 Bobby Brown .15 .06
419 Tom Hume .15 .06
420 Keith Hernandez .40 .16
421 Bob Stanley .15 .06
422 Dan Ford .15 .06
423 Shane Rawley .15 .06
424 Tim Lollar .25 .10
Bruce Robinson
Dennis Werth
425 Al Bumbry .15 .06
426 Warren Brusstar .15 .06
427 John D'Acquisto .15 .06
428 John Stearns .15 .06
429 Mick Kelleher .15 .06
430 Jim Bibby .15 .06
431 Dave Roberts .15 .06
432 Len Barker .40 .16
433 Rance Mulliniks .15 .06
434 Roger Erickson .15 .06
435 Jim Spencer .15 .06
436 Gary Lucas .15 .06
437 Mike Heath DP .15 .06
438 John Montefusco .15 .06
439 Denny Walling .15 .06
440 Jerry Reuss .15 .06
441 Ken Reitz .15 .06
442 Ron Pruitt .15 .06
443 Jim Beattie DP .15 .06
444 Garth Iorg .15 .06
445 Ellis Valentine .15 .06
446 Checklist 364-484 .40 .16
447 Junior Kennedy DP .15 .06
448 Tim Corcoran .15 .06
449 Paul Mitchell .15 .06
450 Dave Kingman DP .25 .10
451 Chris Bando .25 .10
Tom Brennan
Sandy Wihtol
452 Renie Martin .15 .06
453 Rob Wilfong DP .15 .06
454 Andy Hassler .15 .06
455 Rick Burleson .15 .06
456 Jeff Reardon RC 1.50 .60
457 Mike Lum .15 .06
458 Randy Jones .40 .16
459 Greg Gross .15 .06
460 Rich Gossage .40 .16
461 Dave McKay .15 .06
462 Jack Brohamer .15 .06
463 Milt May .15 .06
464 Adrian Devine .15 .06
465 Bill Russell .40 .16
466 Bob Molinaro .15 .06
467 Dave Stieb .40 .16
468 John Wockenfuss .15 .06
469 Jeff Leonard .40 .16
470 Manny Trillo .15 .06
471 Mike Vail .15 .06
472 Dyar Miller DP .15 .06
473 Jose Cardenal .15 .06
474 Mike LaCoss .15 .06
475 Buddy Bell .40 .16
476 Jerry Koosman .40 .16
477 Luis Gomez .15 .06
478 Juan Eichelberger .15 .06
479 Tim Raines RC 2.50 1.00
Roberto Ramos
Bobby Pate
480 Carlton Fisk .75 .30
481 Bob Lacey DP .15 .06
482 Jim Gantner .15 .06
483 Mike Griffin RC .25 .10
484 Max Venable DP .15 .06
485 Garry Templeton .40 .16
486 Marc Hill .15 .06
487 Dewey Robinson .15 .06
488 Damaso Garcia .15 .06
489 John Littlefield .15 .06
Photo on card believed to be Mark Riggins
490 Eddie Murray 2.50 1.00
491 Gordy Pladson .15 .06
492 Barry Foote .15 .06
493 Dan Quisenberry .15 .06
494 Bob Walk RC .75 .30
495 Dusty Baker .40 .16
496 Paul Dade .15 .06
497 Fred Norman .15 .06
498 Pat Putnam .15 .06
499 Frank Pastore .15 .06
500 Jim Rice .40 .16
501 Tim Foli DP .15 .06
502 Chris Bourjos .25 .10
Al Hargesheimer
Mike Rowland
503 Steve McCatty .15 .06
504 Dale Murphy .75 .30
505 Jason Thompson .15 .06
506 Phil Huffman .15 .06
507 Jamie Quirk .15 .06
508 Rob Dressler .15 .06
509 Pete Mackanin .15 .06
510 Lee Mazzilli .40 .16
511 Wayne Garland .15 .06
512 Gary Thomasson .15 .06
513 Frank LaCorte .15 .06
514 George Riley .15 .06
515 Robin Yount 2.50 1.00
516 Doug Bird .15 .06
517 Richie Zisk .15 .06
518 Grant Jackson .15 .06
519 John Tamargo DP .15 .06
520 Steve Stone .15 .06
521 Sam Mejias .15 .06
522 Mike Colbern .15 .06
523 John Fulgham .15 .06
524 Willie Aikens .15 .06
525 Mike Torrez .15 .06
526 Marty Bystrom .25 .10
Jay Loviglio
Jim Wright
527 Danny Goodwin .15 .06
528 Gary Matthews .40 .16
529 Dave LaRoche .15 .06
530 Steve Garvey .75 .30
531 John Curtis .15 .06
532 Bill Stein .15 .06
533 Jesus Figueroa .15 .06
534 Dave Smith RC .75 .30
535 Omar Moreno .15 .06
536 Bob Owchinko DP .15 .06
537 Ron Hodges .15 .06
538 Tom Griffin .15 .06
539 Rodney Scott .15 .06
540 Mike Schmidt DP 2.00 .80
541 Steve Swisher .15 .06
542 Larry Bradford DP .15 .06
543 Terry Crowley .15 .06
544 Rich Gale .15 .06
545 Johnny Grubb .15 .06
546 Paul Moskau .15 .06
547 Mario Guerrero .15 .06
548 Dave Goltz .15 .06
549 Jerry Remy .15 .06
550 Tommy John .40 .16
551 Vance Law 1.50 .60
Tony Pena RC
Pascual Perez RC
552 Steve Trout .15 .06
553 Tim Blackwell .15 .06
554 Bert Blyleven UER .40 .16
(1 is missing from
1980 on card back)
555 Cecil Cooper .40 .16
556 Jerry Mumphrey .15 .06
557 Chris Knapp .15 .06
558 Barry Bonnell .15 .06
559 Willie Montanez .15 .06
560 Joe Morgan .75 .30
561 Dennis Littlejohn .15 .06
562 Checklist 485-605 .40 .16
563 Jim Kaat .40 .16
564 Ron Hassey DP .15 .06
565 Burt Hooton .15 .06
566 Del Unser .15 .06
567 Mark Bomback .15 .06
568 Dave Revering .15 .06
569 Al Williams DP .15 .06
570 Ken Singleton .40 .16
571 Todd Cruz .15 .06
572 Jack Morris .75 .30
573 Phil Garner .40 .16
574 Bill Caudill .15 .06
575 Tony Perez .75 .30
576 Reggie Cleveland .15 .06
577 Luis Leal .25 .10
Brian Milner
Ken Schrom
578 Bill Gullickson RC .75 .30
579 Tim Flannery .15 .06
580 Don Baylor .40 .16
581 Roy Howell .15 .06
582 Gaylord Perry .40 .16
583 Larry Milbourne .15 .06
584 Randy Lerch .15 .06
585 Amos Otis .40 .16
586 Silvio Martinez .15 .06
587 Jeff Newman .15 .06
588 Gary Lavelle .15 .06
589 Lamar Johnson .15 .06
590 Bruce Sutter .40 .16
591 John Lowenstein .15 .06
592 Steve Comer .15 .06
593 Steve Kemp .15 .06
594 Preston Hanna DP .15 .06
595 Butch Hobson .15 .06
596 Jerry Augustine .15 .06
597 Rafael Landestoy .15 .06
598 George Vukovich DP .15 .06
599 Dennis Kinney .15 .06
600 Johnny Bench 1.50 .60
601 Don Aase .15 .06
602 Bobby Murcer .40 .16
603 John Verhoeven .15 .06
604 Rob Picciolo .15 .06
605 Don Sutton .40 .16
606 Bruce Berenyi .25 .10
Geoff Combe
Paul Householder
607 David Palmer .15 .06
608 Greg Pryor .15 .06
609 Lynn McGlothen .15 .06
610 Darrell Porter .15 .06
611 Rick Matula DP .15 .06
612 Duane Kuiper .15 .06
613 Jim Anderson .15 .06
614 Dave Rozema .15 .06
615 Rick Dempsey .15 .06
616 Rick Wise .15 .06
617 Craig Reynolds .15 .06
618 John Milner .15 .06
619 Steve Henderson .15 .06
620 Dennis Eckersley .75 .30
621 Tom Donohue .15 .06
622 Randy Moffitt .15 .06
623 Sal Bando .40 .16
624 Bob Welch .40 .16
625 Bill Buckner .40 .16
626 Dave Steffen .25 .10
Jerry Ujdur
Roger Weaver
627 Luis Tiant .40 .16
628 Vic Correll .15 .06
629 Tony Armas .15 .06
630 Steve Carlton .75 .30
631 Ron Jackson .15 .06
632 Alan Bannister .15 .06
633 Bill Lee .40 .16
634 Doug Flynn .15 .06
635 Bobby Bonds .40 .16
636 Al Hrabosky .40 .16
637 Jerry Narron .15 .06
638 Checklist 606-726 .40 .16
639 Carney Lansford .40 .16
640 Dave Parker .40 .16
641 Mark Belanger .15 .06
642 Vern Ruhle .15 .06
643 Lloyd Moseby RC .75 .30
644 Ramon Aviles DP .15 .06
645 Rick Reuschel .40 .16

646 Marvis Foley .15 .06
647 Dick Drago .15 .06
648 Darrell Evans .40 .16
649 Manny Sarmiento .15 .06
650 Bucky Dent .40 .16
651 Pedro Guerrero .40 .16
652 John Montague .15 .06
653 Bill Fahey .15 .06
654 Ray Burris .15 .06
655 Dan Driessen .15 .06
656 Jon Matlack .15 .06
657 Mike Cubbage DP .15 .06
658 Milt Wilcox .15 .06
659 John Flinn .75 .30
Ed Romero
Ned Yost
660 Gary Carter .75 .30
661 Orioles Team CL .40 .16
Earl Weaver MG
662 Red Sox Team CL .40 .16
Ralph Houk MG
663 Angels Team CL .40 .16
Jim Fregosi MG
664 White Sox CL .40 .16
Tony LaRussa MG
665 Indians Team CL .40 .16
Dave Garcia MG
666 Tigers Team CL .40 .16
Sparky Anderson MG
667 Royals Team CL .40 .16
Jim Frey MG
668 Brewers Team CL .40 .16
Bob Rodgers MG
669 Twins Team CL .40 .16
John Goryl MG
670 Yankees Team CL .40 .16
Gene Michael MG
671 A's Team CL .75 .30
Billy Martin MG
672 Mariners Team CL .40 .16
Maury Wills MG
673 Rangers Team CL .40 .16
Don Zimmer MG
674 Blue Jays Team CL .40 .16
Bobby Mattick MG
675 Braves Team CL .40 .16
Bobby Cox MG
676 Cubs Team CL .40 .16
Joe Amalfitano MG
677 Reds Team CL .40 .16
John McNamara MG
678 Astros Team CL .40 .16
Bill Virdon MG
679 Dodgers Team CL .75 .30
Tom Lasorda MG
680 Expos Team CL .40 .16
Dick Williams MG
681 Mets Team CL .75 .30
Joe Torre MG
682 Phillies Team CL .40 .16
Dallas Green MG
683 Pirates Team CL .40 .16
Chuck Tanner MG
684 Cardinals Team CL .40 .16
Whitey Herzog MG
685 Padres Team CL .40 .16
Frank Howard MG
686 Giants Team CL .40 .16
Dave Bristol MG
687 Jeff Jones .15 .06
688 Kiko Garcia .15 .06
689 Bruce Hurst RC 1.50 .60
Keith MacWhorter
Reid Nichols
690 Bob Watson .15 .06
691 Dick Ruthven .15 .06
692 Lenny Randle .15 .06
693 Steve Howe RC .25 .10
694 Bud Harrelson DP .25 .10
695 Kent Tekulve .15 .06
696 Alan Ashby .15 .06
697 Rick Waits .15 .06
698 Mike Jorgensen .15 .06
699 Glenn Abbott .15 .06
700 George Brett 4.00 1.60
701 Joe Rudi .40 .16
702 George Medich .15 .06
703 Alvis Woods .15 .06
704 Bill Travers DP .15 .06
705 Ted Simmons .40 .16
706 Dave Ford .15 .06
707 Dave Cash .15 .06
708 Doyle Alexander .15 .06
709 Alan Trammell DP .50 .20
710 Ron LeFlore DP .25 .10
711 Joe Ferguson .15 .06
712 Bill Bonham .15 .06
713 Bill North .15 .06
714 Pete Redfern .15 .06
715 Bill Madlock .40 .16
716 Glenn Borgmann .15 .06
717 Jim Barr DP .15 .06
718 Larry Biittner .15 .06
719 Sparky Lyle .40 .16
720 Fred Lynn .40 .16
721 Toby Harrah .40 .16
722 Joe Niekro .15 .06
723 Bruce Bochte .15 .06
724 Lou Piniella .40 .16
725 Steve Rogers .40 .16
726 Rick Monday .40 .16

1981 Topps Traded

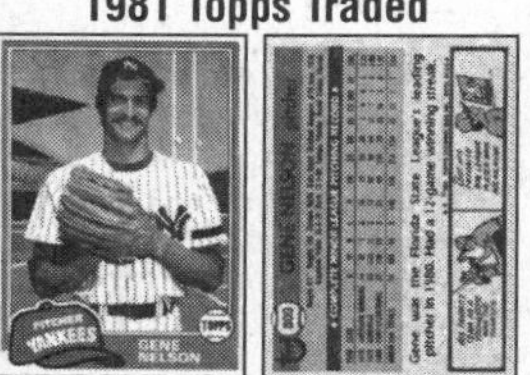

For the first time since 1976, Topps issued a 132-card factory boxed "traded" set in 1981, issued exclusively through hobby dealers. This set was sequentially numbered, alphabetically, from 727 to 858 and carries the same design as the regular issue 1981 Topps set. There are no key Rookie Cards in this set although Tim Raines, Jeff Reardon, and Fernando Valenzuela are depicted in their rookie year for cards. The key extended Rookie Card in the set is Danny Ainge.

Nm-Mt Ex-Mt
COMP.FACT.SET (132) 25.00 10.00
727 Danny Ainge XRC 3.00 1.20
728 Doyle Alexander .25 .10
729 Gary Alexander .25 .10
730 Bill Almon .25 .10
731 Joaquin Andujar 1.00 .40
732 Bob Bailor .25 .10
733 Juan Beniquez .25 .10
734 Dave Bergman .25 .10
735 Tony Bernazard .25 .10
736 Larry Biittner .25 .10
737 Doug Bird .25 .10
738 Bert Blyleven 1.00 .40
739 Mark Bomback .25 .10
740 Bobby Bonds 1.00 .40
741 Rick Bosetti .25 .10
742 Hubie Brooks 2.00 .80
743 Rick Burleson .25 .10
744 Ray Burris .25 .10
745 Jeff Burroughs 1.00 .40
746 Enos Cabell .25 .10
747 Ken Clay .25 .10
748 Mark Clear .25 .10
749 Larry Cox .25 .10
750 Hector Cruz .25 .10
751 Victor Cruz .25 .10
752 Mike Cubbage .25 .10
753 Dick Davis .25 .10
754 Brian Doyle .25 .10
755 Dick Drago .25 .10
756 Leon Durham 1.00 .40
757 Jim Dwyer .25 .10
758 Dave Edwards UER .25 .10
No birthdate on card
759 Jim Essian .25 .10
760 Bill Fahey .25 .10
761 Rollie Fingers 1.00 .40
762 Carlton Fisk 2.00 .80
763 Barry Foote .25 .10
764 Ken Forsch .25 .10
765 Kiko Garcia .25 .10
766 Cesar Geronimo .25 .10
767 Gary Gray .25 .10
768 Mickey Hatcher .25 .10
769 Steve Henderson .25 .10
770 Marc Hill .25 .10
771 Butch Hobson .25 .10
772 Rick Honeycutt .25 .10
773 Roy Howell .25 .10
774 Mike Ivie .25 .10
775 Roy Lee Jackson .25 .10
776 Cliff Johnson .25 .10
777 Randy Jones 1.00 .40
778 Ruppert Jones .25 .10
779 Mick Kelleher .25 .10
780 Terry Kennedy .25 .10
781 Dave Kingman 1.00 .40
782 Bob Knepper .25 .10
783 Ken Kravec .25 .10
784 Bob Lacey .25 .10
785 Dennis Lamp .25 .10
786 Rafael Landestoy .25 .10
787 Ken Landreaux .25 .10
788 Carney Lansford 1.00 .40
789 Dave LaRoche .25 .10
790 Joe Lefebvre .25 .10
791 Ron LeFlore 1.00 .40
792 Randy Lerch .25 .10
793 Sixto Lezcano .25 .10
794 John Littlefield .25 .10
795 Mike Lum .25 .10
796 Greg Luzinski 1.00 .40
797 Fred Lynn 1.00 .40
798 Jerry Martin .25 .10
799 Buck Martinez .25 .10
800 Gary Matthews 1.00 .40
801 Mario Mendoza .25 .10
802 Larry Milbourne .25 .10
803 Rick Miller .25 .10
804 John Montefusco .25 .10
805 Jerry Morales .25 .10
806 Jose Morales .25 .10
807 Joe Morgan 2.00 .80
808 Jerry Mumphrey .25 .10
809 Gene Nelson .25 .10
810 Ed Ott .25 .10
811 Bob Owchinko .25 .10
812 Gaylord Perry 1.00 .40
813 Mike Phillips .25 .10
814 Darrell Porter .25 .10
815 Mike Proly .25 .10
816 Tim Raines 3.00 1.20
817 Lenny Randle .25 .10
818 Doug Rau .25 .10
819 Jeff Reardon 2.00 .80
820 Ken Reitz .25 .10
821 Steve Renko .25 .10
822 Rick Reuschel 1.00 .40
823 Dave Revering .25 .10
824 Dave Roberts .25 .10
825 Leon Roberts .25 .10
826 Joe Rudi 1.00 .40
827 Kevin Saucier .25 .10
828 Tony Scott .25 .10
829 Bob Shirley .25 .10
830 Ted Simmons 1.00 .40
831 Lary Sorensen .25 .10
832 Jim Spencer .25 .10
833 Harry Spilman .25 .10
834 Fred Stanley .25 .10
835 Rusty Staub 1.00 .40
836 Bill Stein .25 .10
837 Joe Strain .25 .10
838 Bruce Sutter 1.00 .40
839 Don Sutton 1.00 .40
840 Steve Swisher .25 .10
841 Frank Tanana 1.00 .40
842 Gene Tenace 1.00 .40
843 Jason Thompson .25 .10
844 Dickie Thon .25 .10
845 Bill Travers .25 .10
846 Tom Underwood .25 .10
847 John Urrea .25 .10
848 Mike Vail .25 .10
849 Ellis Valentine .25 .10
850 Fernando Valenzuela 5.00 2.00
851 Pete Vuckovich .25 .10
852 Mark Wagner .25 .10
853 Bob Walk 1.00 .40
854 Claudell Washington .25 .10
855 Dave Winfield 2.00 .80
856 Geoff Zahn .25 .10
857 Richie Zisk .25 .10
858 Checklist 727-858 .25 .10

1982 Topps

The cards in this 792-card set measure the standard size. Cards were primarily distributed in 15-card wax packs and 51-card rack packs. The 1982 baseball series was the first of the largest sets Topps issued at one printing. The 66-card increase from the previous year's total eliminated the "double print" practice, that had occurred in every regular issue since 1978. Cards 1-6 depict Highlights of the strike-shortened 1981 season, cards 161-168 picture League Leaders, and there are subsets of AL (547-557) and NL (337-347) All-Stars (AS). The abbreviation "SA" in the checklist is given for the 40 "Super Action" cards introduced in this set. The team cards are actually Team Leader (TL) cards picturing the batting average and ERA leader for that team with a checklist back. All 26 of these cards were available from Topps on a perforated sheet through an offer on wax pack wrappers. Notable Rookie Cards include Brett Butler, Chili Davis, Cal Ripken Jr., Lee Smith, and Dave Stewart. Be careful when purchasing blank-back Cal Ripken Jr. Rookie Cards. Those cards are extremely likely to be counterfeit.

Nm-Mt Ex-Mt
COMPLETE SET (792) 80.00 32.00
1 Steve Carlton HL .30 .12
2 Ron Davis HL .15 .06
3 Tim Raines HL .30 .12
4 Pete Rose HL .60 .24
5 Nolan Ryan HL 3.00 1.20
6 Fernando Valenzuela HL .60 .24
7 Scott Sanderson .15 .06
8 Rich Dauer .15 .06
9 Ron Guidry .30 .12
10 Ron Guidry SA .15 .06
11 Gary Alexander .15 .06
12 Moose Haas .15 .06
13 Lamar Johnson .15 .06
14 Steve Howe .15 .06
15 Ellis Valentine .15 .06
16 Steve Comer .15 .06
17 Darrell Evans .30 .12
18 Fernando Arroyo .15 .06
19 Ernie Whitt .15 .06
20 Garry Maddox .15 .06
21 Bob Bonner 50.00 20.00
Cal Ripken RC
Jeff Schneider
Birthdate for Jeff Scheider is wrong
22 Jim Beattie .15 .06
23 Willie Hernandez .15 .06
24 Dave Frost .15 .06
25 Jerry Remy .15 .06
26 Jorge Orta .15 .06
27 Tom Herr .15 .06
28 John Urrea .15 .06
29 Dwayne Murphy .15 .06
30 Tom Seaver 1.25 .50
31 Tom Seaver SA .30 .12
32 Gene Garber .15 .06
33 Jerry Morales .15 .06
34 Joe Sambito .15 .06
35 Willie Aikens .15 .06
36 Al Oliver .60 .24
Doc Medich TL
37 Dan Graham .15 .06
38 Charlie Lea .15 .06
39 Lou Whitaker .30 .12
40 Dave Parker .30 .12
41 Dave Parker SA .15 .06
42 Rick Sofield .15 .06
43 Mike Cubbage .15 .06
44 Britt Burns .15 .06
45 Rick Cerone .15 .06
46 Jerry Augustine .15 .06
47 Jeff Leonard .15 .06
48 Bobby Castillo .15 .06
49 Alvis Woods .15 .06
50 Buddy Bell .30 .12
51 Jay Howell RC .75 .30
Carlos Lezcano
Ty Waller
52 Larry Andersen .15 .06
53 Greg Gross .15 .06
54 Ron Hassey .15 .06
55 Rick Burleson .15 .06
56 Mark Littell .15 .06
57 Craig Reynolds .15 .06
58 John D'Acquisto .15 .06
59 Rich Gedman .75 .30
60 Tony Armas .30 .12
61 Tommy Boggs .15 .06
62 Mike Tyson .15 .06
63 Mario Soto .30 .12
64 Lynn Jones .15 .06
65 Terry Kennedy .15 .06
66 Art Howe 2.00 .80
Nolan Ryan TL
67 Rich Gale .15 .06
68 Roy Howell .15 .06
69 Al Williams .15 .06
70 Tim Raines .60 .24
71 Roy Lee Jackson .15 .06
72 Rick Auerbach .15 .06
73 Buddy Solomon .15 .06
74 Bob Clark .15 .06
75 Tommy John .30 .12
76 Greg Pryor .15 .06
77 Miguel Dilone .15 .06
78 George Medich .15 .06
79 Bob Bailor .15 .06
80 Jim Palmer .30 .12
81 Jim Palmer SA .15 .06
82 Bob Welch .30 .12
83 Steve Balboni RC .75 .30
Andy McGaffigan
Andre Robertson
84 Rennie Stennett .15 .06
85 Lynn McGlothen .15 .06
86 Dane Iorg .15 .06
87 Matt Keough .15 .06
88 Biff Pocoroba .15 .06
89 Steve Henderson .15 .06
90 Nolan Ryan 6.00 2.40
91 Carney Lansford .30 .12
92 Brad Havens .15 .06
93 Larry Hisle .15 .06
94 Andy Hassler .15 .06
95 Ozzie Smith 2.50 1.00
96 George Brett 1.25 .50
Larry Gura TL
97 Paul Moskau .15 .06
98 Terry Bulling .15 .06
99 Barry Bonnell .15 .06
100 Mike Schmidt 3.00 1.20
101 Mike Schmidt SA 1.25 .50
102 Dan Briggs .15 .06
103 Bob Lacey .15 .06
104 Rance Mulliniks .15 .06
105 Kirk Gibson 1.25 .50
106 Enrique Romo .15 .06
107 Wayne Krenchicki .15 .06
108 Bob Sykes .15 .06
109 Dave Revering .15 .06
110 Carlton Fisk .60 .24
111 Carlton Fisk SA .30 .12
112 Billy Sample .15 .06
113 Steve McCatty .15 .06
114 Ken Landreaux .15 .06
115 Gaylord Perry .30 .12
116 Jim Wohlford .15 .06
117 Rawly Eastwick .30 .12
118 Terry Francona RC 2.50 1.00
Brad Mills
Bryn Smith RC
119 Joe Pittman .15 .06
120 Gary Lucas .15 .06
121 Ed Lynch .15 .06
122 Jamie Easterly UER .15 .06
(Photo actually
Reggie Cleveland)
123 Danny Goodwin .15 .06
124 Reid Nichols .15 .06
125 Danny Ainge .30 .12
126 Claudell Washington .60 .24
Rick Mahler TL
127 Lonnie Smith .15 .06
128 Frank Pastore .15 .06
129 Checklist 1-132 .30 .12
130 Julio Cruz .15 .06
131 Stan Bahnsen .15 .06
132 Lee May .15 .06
133 Pat Underwood .15 .06
134 Dan Ford .15 .06
135 Andy Rincon .15 .06
136 Lenn Sakata .15 .06
137 George Cappuzzello .15 .06
138 Tony Pena .30 .12
139 Jeff Jones .15 .06
140 Ron LeFlore .30 .12
141 Chris Bando .75 .30
Tom Brennan
Von Hayes RC
142 Dave LaRoche .15 .06
143 Mookie Wilson .30 .12
144 Fred Breining .15 .06
145 Bob Horner .30 .12
146 Mike Griffin .15 .06
147 Denny Walling .15 .06
148 Mickey Klutts .15 .06
149 Pat Putnam .15 .06
150 Ted Simmons .30 .12
151 Dave Edwards .15 .06
152 Ramon Aviles .15 .06
153 Roger Erickson .15 .06
154 Dennis Werth .15 .06
155 Otto Velez .15 .06
156 Rickey Henderson 1.25 .50
Steve McCatty TL
157 Steve Crawford .15 .06
158 Brian Downing .30 .12
159 Larry Biittner .15 .06
160 Luis Tiant .30 .12
161 Bill Madlock .30 .12
Carney Lansford LL
162 Mike Schmidt 1.25 .50
Tony Armas
Dwight Evans
Bobby Grich
Eddie Murray LL
163 Mike Schmidt 1.25 .50
Eddie Murray LL
164 Tim Raines 1.25 .50
Rickey Henderson LL
165 Tom Seaver .30 .12
Denny Martinez
Steve McCatty
Jack Morris
Pete Vuckovich LL
166 Fernando Valenzuela .30 .12
Len Barker LL
167 Nolan Ryan 2.00 .80
Steve McCatty LL
168 Bruce Sutter .30 .12
Rollie Fingers LL
169 Charlie Leibrandt .15 .06
170 Jim Bibby .15 .06
171 Bob Brenly RC 1.50 .60
Chili Davis RC
Bob Tufts
172 Bill Gullickson .15 .06
173 Jamie Quirk .15 .06
174 Dave Ford .15 .06
175 Jerry Mumphrey .15 .06
176 Dewey Robinson .15 .06
177 John Ellis .15 .06
178 Dyar Miller .15 .06
179 Steve Garvey .30 .12
180 Steve Garvey SA .15 .06
181 Silvio Martinez .15 .06
182 Larry Herndon .15 .06
183 Mike Proly .15 .06
184 Mick Kelleher .15 .06
185 Phil Niekro .30 .12
186 Keith Hernandez .30 .12
Bob Forsch TL
187 Jeff Newman .15 .06
188 Randy Martz .15 .06
189 Glenn Hoffman .15 .06
190 J.R. Richard .30 .12
191 Tim Wallach RC 1.50 .60
192 Broderick Perkins .15 .06
193 Darrell Jackson .15 .06
194 Mike Vail .15 .06
195 Paul Molitor .60 .24
196 Willie Upshaw .75 .30
197 Shane Rawley .15 .06
198 Chris Speier .15 .06
199 Don Aase .15 .06
200 George Brett 3.00 1.20
201 George Brett SA 1.50 .60
202 Rick Manning .15 .06
203 Jesse Barfield RC 1.50 .60
Brian Milner
Boomer Wells
204 Gary Roenicke .15 .06
205 Neil Allen .15 .06
206 Tony Bernazard .15 .06
207 Rod Scurry .15 .06
208 Bobby Murcer .30 .12
209 Gary Lavelle .15 .06
210 Keith Hernandez .30 .12
211 Dan Petry .15 .06
212 Mario Mendoza .15 .06
213 Dave Stewart RC 2.50 1.00
214 Brian Asselstine .15 .06
215 Mike Krukow .15 .06
216 Chet Lemon .60 .24
Dennis Lamp TL
217 Bo McLaughlin .15 .06
218 Dave Roberts .15 .06
219 John Curtis .15 .06
220 Manny Trillo .15 .06
221 Jim Slaton .15 .06
222 Butch Wynegar .15 .06
223 Lloyd Moseby .15 .06
224 Bruce Bochte .15 .06
225 Mike Torrez .15 .06
226 Checklist 133-264 .60 .24
227 Ray Burris .15 .06
228 Sam Mejias .15 .06
229 Geoff Zahn .15 .06
230 Willie Wilson .30 .12
231 Mark Davis RC .75 .30
Bob Dernier
Ozzie Virgil
232 Terry Crowley .15 .06
233 Duane Kuiper .15 .06
234 Ron Hodges .15 .06
235 Mike Easler .15 .06
236 John Martin RC .25 .10
237 Rusty Kuntz .15 .06
238 Kevin Saucier .15 .06
239 Jon Matlack .15 .06
240 Bucky Dent .30 .12
241 Bucky Dent SA .15 .06
242 Milt May .15 .06
243 Bob Owchinko .15 .06
244 Rufino Linares .15 .06
245 Ken Reitz .15 .06
246 Hubie Brooks .60 .24
Mike Scott TL
247 Pedro Guerrero .30 .12
248 Frank LaCorte .15 .06
249 Tim Flannery .15 .06
250 Tug McGraw .30 .12
251 Fred Lynn .30 .12
252 Fred Lynn SA .15 .06
253 Chuck Baker .15 .06
254 Jorge Bell RC 1.50 .60
255 Tony Perez .60 .24
256 Tony Perez SA .30 .12
257 Larry Harlow .15 .06
258 Bo Diaz .15 .06
259 Rodney Scott .15 .06
260 Bruce Sutter .30 .12
261 Howard Bailey .15 .06
Marty Castillo
Dave Rucker UER
(Rucker photo actually Roger Weaver)
262 Doug Bair .15 .06
263 Victor Cruz .15 .06
264 Dan Quisenberry .15 .06
265 Al Bumbry .15 .06
266 Rick Leach .15 .06
267 Kurt Bevacqua .15 .06
268 Rickey Keeton .15 .06
269 Jim Essian .15 .06
270 Rusty Staub .30 .12
271 Larry Bradford .15 .06
272 Bump Wills .15 .06
273 Doug Bird .15 .06
274 Bob Ojeda RC .75 .30
275 Bob Watson .15 .06
276 Rod Carew .60 .24
Ken Forsch TL
277 Terry Puhl .15 .06
278 John Littlefield .15 .06
279 Bill Russell .30 .12
280 Ben Oglivie .30 .12
281 John Verhoeven .15 .06
282 Ken Macha .15 .06
283 Brian Allard .15 .06
284 Bobby Grich .30 .12
285 Sparky Lyle .30 .12
286 Bill Fahey .15 .06
287 Alan Bannister .15 .06
288 Garry Templeton .30 .12
289 Bob Stanley .15 .06
290 Ken Singleton .30 .12
291 Vance Law .30 .12

Bob Long
Johnny Ray RC
292 David Palmer .15 .06
293 Rob Picciolo .15 .06
294 Mike LaCoss .15 .06
295 Jason Thompson .15 .06
296 Bob Walk .15 .06
297 Clint Hurdle .15 .06
298 Danny Darwin .15 .06
299 Steve Trout .15 .06
300 Reggie Jackson .60 .24
301 Reggie Jackson SA .30 .12
302 Doug Flynn .15 .06
303 Bill Caudill .15 .06
304 Johnnie LeMaster .15 .06
305 Don Sutton .30 .12
306 Don Sutton SA .15 .06
307 Randy Bass RC .75 .30
308 Charlie Moore .15 .06
309 Pete Redfern .15 .06
310 Mike Hargrove .15 .06
311 Dusty Baker .30 .12
Burt Hooton TL
312 Lenny Randle .15 .06
313 John Harris .15 .06
314 Buck Martinez .15 .06
315 Burt Hooton .15 .06
316 Steve Braun .15 .06
317 Dick Ruthven .15 .06
318 Mike Heath .15 .06
319 Dave Rozema .15 .06
320 Chris Chambliss .30 .12
321 Chris Chambliss SA .15 .06
322 Garry Hancock .15 .06
323 Bill Lee .30 .12
324 Steve Dillard .15 .06
325 Jose Cruz .30 .12
326 Pete Falcone .15 .06
327 Joe Nolan .15 .06
328 Ed Farmer .15 .06
329 U.L. Washington .15 .06
330 Rick Wise .15 .06
331 Benny Ayala .15 .06
332 Don Robinson .15 .06
333 Frank DiPino .15 .06
Marshall Edwards
Chuck Porter
334 Aurelio Rodriguez .15 .06
335 Jim Sundberg .30 .12
336 Tom Paciorek .60 .24
Glenn Abbott TL
337 Pete Rose AS .60 .24
338 Dave Lopes AS .15 .06
339 Mike Schmidt AS 1.25 .50
340 Dave Concepcion AS .15 .06
341 Andre Dawson AS .15 .06
342A George Foster AS .30 .12
(With autograph)
342B George Foster AS 1.25 .50
(W/o autograph)
343 Dave Parker AS .15 .06
344 Gary Carter AS .15 .06
345 F. Valenzuela AS .60 .24
346 Tom Seaver AS ERR .30 .12
("t ed")
346B Tom Seaver AS COR .30 .12
("tied")
347 Bruce Sutter AS .15 .06
348 Derrel Thomas .15 .06
349 George Frazier .15 .06
350 Thad Bosley .15 .06
351 Scott Brown .15 .06
Geoff Combe
Paul Householder
352 Dick Davis .15 .06
353 Jack O'Connor .15 .06
354 Roberto Ramos .15 .06
355 Dwight Evans .30 .12
356 Denny Lewallyn .15 .06
357 Butch Hobson .15 .06
358 Mike Parrott .15 .06
359 Jim Dwyer .15 .06
360 Len Barker .15 .06
361 Rafael Landestoy .15 .06
362 Jim Wright UER .15 .06
(Wrong Jim Wright
pictured)
363 Bob Molinaro .15 .06
364 Doyle Alexander .15 .06
365 Bill Madlock .30 .12
366 Luis Salazar .60 .24
Juan Eichelberger TL
367 Jim Kaat .30 .12
368 Alex Trevino .15 .06
369 Champ Summers .15 .06
370 Mike Norris .15 .06
371 Jerry Don Gleaton .15 .06
372 Luis Gomez .15 .06
373 Gene Nelson .15 .06
374 Tim Blackwell .15 .06
375 Dusty Baker .30 .12
376 Chris Welsh .15 .06
377 Kiko Garcia .15 .06
378 Mike Caldwell .15 .06
379 Rob Wilfong .15 .06
380 Dave Stieb .30 .12
381 Bruce Hurst .15 .06
Dave Schmidt
Julio Valdez
382 Joe Simpson .15 .06
383A Pascual Perez ERR 40.00 16.00
(No position
on front)
383B Pascual Perez COR .30 .12
384 Keith Moreland .15 .06
385 Ken Forsch .15 .06
386 Jerry White .15 .06
387 Tom Veryzer .15 .06
388 Joe Rudi .30 .12
389 George Vukovich .15 .06
390 Eddie Murray 1.25 .50
391 Dave Tobik .15 .06
392 Rick Bosetti .15 .06
393 Al Hrabosky .15 .06
394 Checklist 265-396 .60 .24
395 Omar Moreno .15 .06
396 John Castino .60 .24
Fernando Arroyo TL
397 Ken Brett .15 .06
398 Mike Squires .15 .06
399 Pat Zachry .15 .06
400 Johnny Bench 1.25 .50
401 Johnny Bench SA .60 .24
402 Bill Stein .15 .06
403 Jim Tracy .30 .12
404 Dickie Thon .30 .12
405 Rick Reuschel .30 .12
406 Al Holland .15 .06
407 Danny Boone .15 .06
408 Ed Romero .15 .06
409 Don Cooper .15 .06
410 Ron Cey .30 .12
411 Ron Cey SA .15 .06
412 Luis Leal .15 .06
413 Dan Meyer .15 .06
414 Elias Sosa .15 .06
415 Don Baylor .30 .12
416 Marty Bystrom .15 .06
417 Pat Kelly .15 .06
418 John Butcher .15 .06
Bobby Johnson
Dave Schmidt
419 Steve Stone .15 .06
420 George Hendrick .30 .12
421 Mark Clear .15 .06
422 Cliff Johnson .15 .06
423 Stan Papi .15 .06
424 Bruce Benedict .15 .06
425 John Candelaria .15 .06
426 Eddie Murray .60 .24
Sammy Stewart
427 Ron Oester .15 .06
428 LaMarr Hoyt .15 .06
429 John Wathan .15 .06
430 Vida Blue .30 .12
431 Vida Blue SA .15 .06
432 Mike Scott .30 .12
433 Alan Ashby .15 .06
434 Joe Lefebvre .15 .06
435 Robin Yount 2.00 .80
436 Joe Strain .15 .06
437 Juan Berenguer .15 .06
438 Pete Mackanin .15 .06
439 Dave Righetti RC 2.50 1.00
440 Jeff Burroughs .15 .06
441 Danny Heep .15 .06
Billy Smith
Bobby Sprowl
442 Bruce Kison .15 .06
443 Mark Wagner .15 .06
444 Terry Forster .30 .12
445 Larry Parrish .15 .06
446 Wayne Garland .15 .06
447 Darrell Porter .15 .06
448 Darrell Porter SA .15 .06
449 Luis Aguayo .15 .06
450 Jack Morris .30 .12
451 Ed Miller .15 .06
452 Lee Smith RC 3.00 1.20
453 Art Howe .15 .06
454 Rick Langford .15 .06
455 Tom Burgmeier .15 .06
456 Bill Buckner .30 .12
Randy Martz TL
457 Tim Stoddard .15 .06
458 Willie Montanez .15 .06
459 Bruce Berenyi .15 .06
460 Jack Clark .30 .12
461 Rich Dotson .15 .06
462 Dave Chalk .15 .06
463 Jim Kern .15 .06
464 Juan Bonilla RC .25 .10
465 Lee Mazzilli .15 .06
466 Randy Lerch .15 .06
467 Mickey Hatcher .15 .06
468 Floyd Bannister .15 .06
469 Ed Ott .15 .06
470 John Mayberry .15 .06
471 Atlee Hammaker .15 .06
Mike Jones
Darryl Motley
472 Oscar Gamble .15 .06
473 Mike Stanton .15 .06
474 Ken Oberkfell .15 .06
475 Alan Trammell .30 .12
476 Brian Kingman .15 .06
477 Steve Yeager .30 .12
478 Ray Searage .15 .06
479 Rowland Office .15 .06
480 Steve Carlton .60 .24
481 Steve Carlton SA .30 .12
482 Glenn Hubbard .15 .06
483 Gary Woods .15 .06
484 Ivan DeJesus .15 .06
485 Kent Tekulve .15 .06
486 Jerry Mumphrey .30 .12
Tommy John TL
487 Bob McClure .15 .06
488 Ron Jackson .15 .06
489 Rick Dempsey .15 .06
490 Dennis Eckersley .60 .24
491 Checklist 397-528 .60 .24
492 Joe Price .15 .06
493 Chet Lemon .30 .12
494 Hubie Brooks .15 .06
495 Dennis Leonard .15 .06
496 Johnny Grubb .15 .06
497 Jim Anderson .15 .06
498 Dave Bergman .15 .06
499 Paul Mirabella .15 .06
500 Rod Carew .60 .24
501 Rod Carew SA .30 .12
502 Steve Bedrosian RC UER 1.50 .60
Photo actually Larry Owen)
Brett Butler RC
Larry Owen
503 Julio Gonzalez .15 .06
504 Rick Peters .15 .06
505 Graig Nettles .30 .12
506 Graig Nettles SA .15 .06
507 Terry Harper .15 .06
508 Jody Davis .15 .06
509 Harry Spilman .15 .06
510 Fernando Valenzuela 1.25 .50
511 Ruppert Jones .15 .06
512 Jerry Dybzinski .15 .06
513 Rick Rhoden .15 .06
514 Joe Ferguson .15 .06
515 Larry Bowa .30 .12
516 Larry Bowa SA .15 .06
517 Mark Brouhard .15 .06
518 Garth Iorg .15 .06
519 Glenn Adams .15 .06
520 Mike Flanagan .15 .06
521 Bill Almon .15 .06
522 Chuck Rainey .15 .06
523 Gary Gray .15 .06
524 Tom Hausman .15 .06
525 Ray Knight .30 .12
526 Warren Cromartie .60 .24
Bill Gullickson TL
527 John Henry Johnson .15 .06
528 Matt Alexander .15 .06
529 Allen Ripley .15 .06
530 Dickie Noles .15 .06
531 Rich Bordi .15 .06
Mark Budaska
Kelvin Moore
532 Toby Harrah .30 .12
533 Joaquin Andujar .30 .12
534 Dave McKay .15 .06
535 Lance Parrish .30 .12
536 Rafael Ramirez .15 .06
537 Doug Capilla .15 .06
538 Lou Piniella .30 .12
539 Vern Ruhle .15 .06
540 Andre Dawson .30 .12
541 Barry Evans .15 .06
542 Ned Yost .15 .06
543 Bill Robinson .15 .06
544 Larry Christenson .15 .06
545 Reggie Smith .30 .12
546 Reggie Smith SA .15 .06
547 Rod Carew AS .30 .12
548 Willie Randolph AS .15 .06
549 George Brett AS 1.50 .60
550 Bucky Dent AS .15 .06
551 Reggie Jackson AS .30 .12
552 Ken Singleton AS .15 .06
553 Dave Winfield AS .15 .06
554 Carlton Fisk AS .30 .12
555 Scott McGregor AS .15 .06
556 Jack Morris AS .15 .06
557 Rich Gossage AS .15 .06
558 John Tudor .30 .12
559 Mike Hargrove .30 .12
Bert Blyleven TL
560 Doug Corbett .15 .06
561 Glenn Brummer .15 .06
Luis DeLeon
Gene Roof
562 Mike O'Berry .15 .06
563 Ross Baumgarten .15 .06
564 Doug DeCinces .15 .06
565 Jackson Todd .15 .06
566 Mike Jorgensen .15 .06
567 Bob Babcock .15 .06
568 Joe Pettini .15 .06
569 Willie Randolph .30 .12
570 Willie Randolph SA .15 .06
571 Glenn Abbott .15 .06
572 Juan Beniquez .15 .06
573 Rick Waits .15 .06
574 Mike Ramsey .15 .06
575 Al Cowens .15 .06
576 Milt May .60 .24
Vida Blue TL
577 Rick Monday .30 .12
578 Shooty Babitt .15 .06
579 Rick Mahler .15 .06
580 Bobby Bonds .30 .12
581 Ron Reed .15 .06
582 Luis Pujols .15 .06
583 Tippy Martinez .15 .06
584 Hosken Powell .15 .06
585 Rollie Fingers .30 .12
586 Rollie Fingers SA .15 .06
587 Tim Lollar .15 .06
588 Dale Berra .15 .06
589 Dave Stapleton .15 .06
590 Al Oliver .30 .12
591 Al Oliver SA .15 .06
592 Craig Swan .15 .06
593 Billy Smith .15 .06
594 Renie Martin .15 .06
595 Dave Collins .15 .06
596 Damaso Garcia .15 .06
597 Wayne Nordhagen .15 .06
598 Bob Galasso .15 .06
599 Jay Loviglio .15 .06
Reggie Patterson
Leo Sutherland
600 Dave Winfield .30 .12
601 Sid Monge .15 .06
602 Freddie Patek .15 .06
603 Rich Hebner .15 .06
604 Orlando Sanchez .15 .06
605 Steve Rogers .30 .12
606 John Mayberry .30 .12
Dave Stieb TL
607 Leon Durham .15 .06
608 Jerry Royster .15 .06
609 Rick Sutcliffe .30 .12
610 Rickey Henderson 4.00 1.60
611 Joe Niekro .15 .06
612 Gary Ward .15 .06
613 Jim Gantner .15 .06
614 Juan Eichelberger .15 .06
615 Bob Boone .30 .12
616 Bob Boone SA .15 .06
617 Scott McGregor .15 .06
618 Tim Foli .15 .06
619 Bill Campbell .15 .06
620 Ken Griffey .30 .12
621 Ken Griffey SA .15 .06
622 Dennis Lamp .15 .06
623 Ron Gardenhire RC .75 .30
Terry Leach
Tim Leary RC
624 Fergie Jenkins .30 .12
625 Hal McRae .30 .12
626 Randy Jones .15 .06
627 Enos Cabell .15 .06
628 Bill Travers .15 .06
629 John Wockenfuss .15 .06
630 Joe Charboneau .30 .12
631 Gene Tenace .30 .12
632 Bryan Clark RC .25 .10
633 Mitchell Page .15 .06
634 Checklist 529-660 .60 .24
635 Ron Davis .15 .06
636 Pete Rose 1.25 .50
Steve Carlton TL
637 Rick Camp .15 .06
638 John Milner .15 .06
639 Ken Kravec .15 .06
640 Cesar Cedeno .30 .12
641 Steve Mura .15 .06
642 Mike Scioscia .30 .12
643 Pete Vuckovich .15 .06
644 John Castino .15 .06
645 Frank White .30 .12
646 Frank White SA .15 .06
647 Warren Brusstar .15 .06
648 Jose Morales .15 .06
649 Ken Clay .15 .06
650 Carl Yastrzemski 2.00 .80
651 Carl Yastrzemski SA 1.25 .50
652 Steve Nicosia .15 .06
653 Tom Brunansky RC 1.50 .60
Luis Sanchez
Daryl Sconiers
654 Jim Morrison .15 .06
655 Joel Youngblood .15 .06
656 Eddie Whitson .15 .06
657 Tom Poquette .15 .06
658 Tito Landrum .15 .06
659 Fred Martinez .15 .06
660 Dave Concepcion .30 .12
661 Dave Concepcion SA .15 .06
662 Luis Salazar .15 .06
663 Hector Cruz .15 .06
664 Dan Spillner .15 .06
665 Jim Clancy .15 .06
666 Steve Kemp .60 .24
Dan Petry TL
667 Jeff Reardon .30 .12
668 Dale Murphy .60 .24
669 Larry Milbourne .15 .06
670 Steve Kemp .15 .06
671 Mike Davis .15 .06
672 Bob Knepper .15 .06
673 Keith Drumwright .15 .06
674 Dave Goltz .15 .06
675 Cecil Cooper .30 .12
676 Sal Butera .15 .06
677 Alfredo Griffin .15 .06
678 Tom Paciorek .15 .06
679 Sammy Stewart .15 .06
680 Gary Matthews .30 .12
681 Mike Marshall RC 1.50 .60
Ron Roenicke
Steve Sax RC
682 Jesse Jefferson .15 .06
683 Phil Garner .30 .12
684 Harold Baines .30 .12
685 Bert Blyleven .30 .12
686 Gary Allenson .15 .06
687 Greg Minton .15 .06
688 Leon Roberts .15 .06
689 Larry Sorensen .15 .06
690 Dave Kingman .30 .12
691 Dan Schatzeder .15 .06
692 Wayne Gross .15 .06
693 Cesar Geronimo .15 .06
694 Dave Wehrmeister .15 .06
695 Warren Cromartie .15 .06
696 Bill Madlock .60 .24
Eddie Solomon TL
697 John Montefusco .15 .06
698 Tony Scott .15 .06
699 Dick Tidrow .15 .06
700 George Foster .30 .12
701 George Foster SA .15 .06
702 Steve Renko .15 .06
703 Cecil Cooper .60 .24
Pete Vuckovich TL
704 Mickey Rivers .15 .06
705 Mickey Rivers SA .15 .06
706 Barry Foote .15 .06
707 Mark Bomback .15 .06
708 Gene Richards .15 .06
709 Don Money .15 .06
710 Jerry Reuss .15 .06
711 Dave Edler .75 .30
Dave Henderson RC
Reggie Walton
712 Dennis Martinez .30 .12
713 Del Unser .15 .06
714 Jerry Koosman .30 .12
715 Willie Stargell .60 .24
716 Willie Stargell SA .30 .12
717 Rick Miller .15 .06
718 Charlie Hough .30 .12
719 Jerry Narron .15 .06
720 Greg Luzinski .30 .12
721 Greg Luzinski SA .15 .06
722 Jerry Martin .15 .06
723 Junior Kennedy .15 .06
724 Dave Rosello .15 .06
725 Amos Otis .30 .12
726 Amos Otis SA .15 .06
727 Sixto Lezcano .15 .06
728 Aurelio Lopez .15 .06
729 Jim Spencer .15 .06
730 Gary Carter .30 .12
731 Mike Armstrong .15 .06
Doug Gwosdz
Fred Kuhaulua
732 Mike Lum .15 .06
733 Larry McWilliams .15 .06
734 Mike Ivie .15 .06
735 Rudy May .15 .06
736 Jerry Turner .15 .06
737 Reggie Cleveland .15 .06
738 Dave Engle .15 .06
739 Joey McLaughlin .15 .06
740 Dave Lopes .30 .12
741 Dave Lopes SA .15 .06
742 Dick Drago .15 .06
743 John Stearns .15 .06
744 Mike Witt .75 .30
745 Bake McBride .15 .06
746 Andre Thornton .15 .06
747 John Lowenstein .15 .06
748 Marc Hill .15 .06
749 Bob Shirley .15 .06
750 Jim Rice .30 .12
751 Rick Honeycutt .15 .06
752 Lee Lacy .15 .06
753 Tom Brookens .15 .06
754 Joe Morgan .30 .12
755 Joe Morgan SA .15 .06
756 Ken Griffey .30 .12
Tom Seaver TL
757 Tom Underwood .15 .06
758 Claudell Washington .15 .06
759 Paul Splittorff .15 .06
760 Bill Buckner .30 .12
761 Dave Smith .15 .06
762 Mike Phillips .15 .06
763 Tom Hume .15 .06
764 Steve Swisher .15 .06
765 Gorman Thomas .30 .12
766 Lenny Faedo 1.50 .60
Kent Hrbek RC
Tim Laudner
767 Roy Smalley .15 .06
768 Jerry Garvin .15 .06
769 Richie Zisk .15 .06
770 Rich Gossage .30 .12
771 Rich Gossage SA .15 .06
772 Bert Campaneris .30 .12
773 John Denny .15 .06
774 Jay Johnstone .15 .06
775 Bob Forsch .15 .06
776 Mark Belanger .15 .06
777 Tom Griffin .15 .06
778 Kevin Hickey RC .25 .10
779 Grant Jackson .15 .06
780 Pete Rose 4.00 1.60
781 Pete Rose SA 1.25 .50
782 Frank Taveras .15 .06
783 Greg Harris RC .25 .10
784 Milt Wilcox .15 .06
785 Dan Driessen .15 .06
786 Carney Lansford .60 .24
Mike Torrez TL
787 Fred Stanley .15 .06
788 Woodie Fryman .15 .06
789 Checklist 661-792 .60 .24
790 Larry Gura .15 .06
791 Bobby Brown .15 .06
792 Frank Tanana .30 .12

1982 Topps Traded

The cards in this 132-card set measure the standard size. The 1982 Topps Traded or extended series is distinguished by a "T" printed after the number (located on the reverse). This was the first time Topps began a tradition of newly numbering (and alphabetizing) their traded series from 1T to 132T. All 131 player photos used in the set are completely new. Of this total, 112 individuals are seen in the uniform of their new team, 11 youngsters have been elevated to single card status from multi-player "Future Stars" cards, and eight more are entirely new to the 1982 Topps lineup. The backs are almost completely red in color with black print. There are no key Rookie Cards in this set. Although the Cal Ripken card is this set's most valuable card, it is not his Rookie Card since he had already been included in the 1982 regular set, albeit on a multi-player card.

Nm-Mt Ex-Mt
COMP.FACT.SET (132) 150.00 60.00
1T Doyle Alexander .50 .20
2T Jesse Barfield 3.00 1.20
3T Ross Baumgarten .50 .20
4T Steve Bedrosian 1.50 .60
5T Mark Belanger .50 .20
6T Kurt Bevacqua .50 .20
7T Tim Blackwell .50 .20
8T Vida Blue 1.00 .40
9T Bob Boone 1.00 .40
10T Larry Bowa 1.00 .40
11T Dan Briggs .50 .20
12T Bobby Brown .50 .20
13T Tom Brunansky 3.00 1.20
14T Jeff Burroughs .50 .20
15T Enos Cabell .50 .20
16T Bill Campbell .50 .20
17T Bobby Castillo .50 .20
18T Bill Caudill .50 .20
19T Cesar Cedeno 1.00 .40
20T Dave Collins .50 .20
21T Doug Corbett .50 .20
22T Al Cowens .50 .20
23T Chili Davis 3.00 1.20
24T Dick Davis .50 .20
25T Ron Davis .50 .20
26T Doug DeCinces .50 .20
27T Ivan DeJesus .50 .20
28T Bob Dernier .50 .20
29T Bo Diaz .50 .20
30T Roger Erickson .50 .20
31T Jim Essian .50 .20
32T Ed Farmer .50 .20
33T Doug Flynn .50 .20
34T Tim Foli .50 .20
35T Dan Ford .50 .20
36T George Foster 1.00 .40
37T Dave Frost .50 .20
38T Rich Gale .50 .20
39T Ron Gardenhire 1.50 .60
40T Ken Griffey 1.00 .40
41T Greg Harris .50 .20
42T Von Hayes 1.50 .60
43T Larry Herndon .50 .20
44T Kent Hrbek 3.00 1.20
45T Mike Ivie .50 .20
46T Grant Jackson .50 .20
47T Reggie Jackson 2.00 .80
48T Ron Jackson .50 .20
49T Fergie Jenkins 1.00 .40
50T Lamar Johnson .50 .20

51T Randy Johnson .50 .20
52T Jay Johnstone .50 .20
53T Mick Kelleher .50 .20
54T Steve Kemp .50 .20
55T Junior Kennedy .50 .20
56T Jim Kern .50 .20
57T Ray Knight 1.00 .40
58T Wayne Krenchicki .50 .20
59T Mike Krukow .50 .20
60T Duane Kuiper .50 .20
61T Mike LaCoss .50 .20
62T Chet Lemon 1.00 .40
63T Sixto Lezcano .50 .20
64T Dave Lopes 1.00 .40
65T Jerry Martin .50 .20
66T Renie Martin .50 .20
67T John Mayberry .50 .20
68T Lee Mazzilli 1.00 .40
69T Bake McBride 1.00 .40
70T Dan Meyer .50 .20
71T Larry Milbourne .50 .20
72T Eddie Milner .50 .20
73T Sid Monge .50 .20
74T John Montefusco .50 .20
75T Jose Morales .50 .20
76T Keith Moreland .50 .20
77T Jim Morrison .50 .20
78T Rance Mulliniks .50 .20
79T Steve Mura .50 .20
80T Gene Nelson .50 .20
81T Joe Nolan .50 .20
82T Dickie Noles .50 .20
83T Al Oliver 1.00 .40
84T Jorge Orta .50 .20
85T Tom Paciorek .50 .20
86T Larry Parrish .50 .20
87T Jack Perconte .50 .20
88T Gaylord Perry 1.00 .40
89T Rob Picciolo .50 .20
90T Joe Pittman .50 .20
91T Hosken Powell .50 .20
92T Mike Proly .50 .20
93T Greg Pryor .50 .20
94T Charlie Puleo .50 .20
95T Shane Rawley .50 .20
96T Johnny Ray XRC 1.50 .60
97T Dave Revering .50 .20
98T Cal Ripken 120.00 47.50
99T Allen Ripley .50 .20
100T Bill Robinson .50 .20
101T Aurelio Rodriguez .50 .20
102T Joe Rudi 1.00 .40
103T Steve Sax 3.00 1.20
104T Dan Schatzeder .50 .20
105T Bob Shirley .50 .20
106T Eric Show XRC 1.50 .60
107T Roy Smalley .50 .20
108T Lonnie Smith .50 .20
109T Ozzie Smith 15.00 6.00
110T Reggie Smith 1.00 .40
111T Lary Sorensen .50 .20
112T Elias Sosa .50 .20
113T Mike Stanton .50 .20
114T Steve Stroughter .50 .20
115T Champ Summers .50 .20
116T Rick Sutcliffe 1.00 .40
117T Frank Tanana 1.00 .40
118T Frank Taveras .50 .20
119T Garry Templeton 1.00 .40
120T Alex Trevino .50 .20
121T Jerry Turner .50 .20
122T Ed VandeBerg .50 .20
123T Tom Veryzer .50 .20
124T Ron Washington .50 .20
125T Bob Watson .50 .20
126T Dennis Werth .50 .20
127T Eddie Whitson .50 .20
128T Rob Wilfong .50 .20
129T Bump Wills .50 .20
130T Gary Woods .50 .20
131T Butch Wynegar .50 .20
132T Checklist: 1-132 .50 .20

1983 Topps

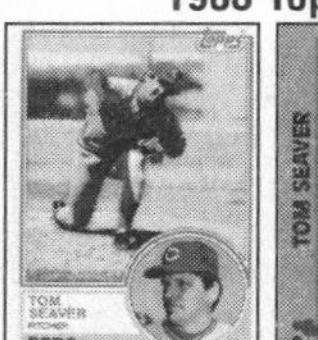

The cards in this 792-card set measure the standard size. Cards were primarily issued in 15-card wax packs and 51-card rack packs. The wax packs had 15 cards in each pack with an 30 cent SRP and were packed 36 packs to a box and 20 boxes to a case. Each player card front features a large action shot with a small cameo portrait at bottom right. There are special series for AL and NL All Stars (386-407), League Leaders (701-708), and Record Breakers (1-6). In addition, there are 34 "Super Veteran" (SV) cards and six numbered checklist cards. The Super Veteran cards are oriented horizontally and show two pictures of the featured player, a recent picture and a picture showing the player as a rookie. The team cards are actually Team Leader (TL) cards picturing the batting and pitching leader for that team with a checklist back. Notable Rookie Cards include Wade Boggs, Tony Gwynn and Ryne Sandberg. In each wax pack a game card was included which included prizes all the way up to a trip and tickets to the World Series. Card prizes possible from these cards included the 1983 Topps League Leaders sheet as well as with enough run accumulation, ordering of a part of the 1983 Topps Mail-Away glossy set. The factory sets were available in JC Penney's Christmas Catalog for $15.99.

Nm-Mt Ex-Mt
COMPLETE SET (792) 80.00 32.00
1 Tony Armas RB .30 .12
2 Rickey Henderson RB 1.25 .50
3 Greg Minton RB .15 .06
4 Lance Parrish RB .15 .06
5 Manny Trillo RB .15 .06
6 John Wathan RB .15 .06
7 Gene Richards .15 .06
8 Steve Balboni .15 .06
9 Joey McLaughlin .15 .06
10 Gorman Thomas .30 .12
11 Billy Gardner MG .15 .06
12 Paul Mirabella .15 .06
13 Larry Herndon .15 .06
14 Frank LaCorte .15 .06
15 Ron Cey .30 .12
16 George Vukovich .15 .06
17 Kent Tekulve .15 .06
18 Kent Tekulve SV .15 .06
19 Oscar Gamble .15 .06
20 Carlton Fisk .60 .24
21 Eddie Murray .60 .24
Jim Palmer TL
22 Randy Martz .15 .06
23 Mike Heath .15 .06
24 Steve Mura .15 .06
25 Hal McRae .30 .12
26 Jerry Royster .15 .06
27 Doug Corbett .15 .06
28 Bruce Bochte .15 .06
29 Randy Jones .15 .06
30 Jim Rice .30 .12
31 Bill Gullickson .15 .06
32 Dave Bergman .15 .06
33 Jack O'Connor .15 .06
34 Paul Householder .15 .06
35 Rollie Fingers .30 .12
36 Rollie Fingers SV .15 .06
37 Darrell Johnson MG .15 .06
38 Tim Flannery .15 .06
39 Terry Puhl .15 .06
40 Fernando Valenzuela .30 .12
41 Jerry Turner .15 .06
42 Dale Murray .15 .06
43 Bob Dernier .15 .06
44 Don Robinson .15 .06
45 John Mayberry .15 .06
46 Richard Dotson .15 .06
47 Dave McKay .15 .06
48 Lary Sorensen .15 .06
49 Willie McGee RC 1.50 .60
50 Bob Horner UER .30 .12
('82 RBI total 7)
51 Leon Durham .15 .06
Fergie Jenkins TL
52 Onix Concepcion .15 .06
53 Mike Witt .15 .06
54 Jim Maler .15 .06
55 Mookie Wilson .30 .12
56 Chuck Rainey .15 .06
57 Tim Blackwell .15 .06
58 Al Holland .15 .06
59 Benny Ayala .15 .06
60 Johnny Bench 1.25 .50
61 Johnny Bench SV .60 .24
62 Bob McClure .15 .06
63 Rick Monday .30 .12
64 Bill Stein .15 .06
65 Jack Morris .30 .12
66 Bob Lillis MG .15 .06
67 Sal Butera .15 .06
68 Eric Show RC .75 .30
69 Lee Lacy .15 .06
70 Steve Carlton .60 .24
71 Steve Carlton SV .30 .12
72 Tom Paciorek .15 .06
73 Allen Ripley .15 .06
74 Julio Gonzalez .15 .06
75 Amos Otis .30 .12
76 Rick Mahler .15 .06
77 Hosken Powell .15 .06
78 Bill Caudill .15 .06
79 Mick Kelleher .15 .06
80 George Foster .30 .12
81 Jerry Mumphrey .30 .12
Dave Righetti TL
82 Bruce Hurst .15 .06
83 Ryne Sandberg RC 15.00 6.00
84 Milt May .15 .06
85 Ken Singleton .30 .12
86 Tom Hume .15 .06
87 Joe Rudi .30 .12
88 Jim Gantner .15 .06
89 Leon Roberts .15 .06
90 Jerry Reuss .15 .06
91 Larry Milbourne .15 .06
92 Mike LaCoss .15 .06
93 John Castino .15 .06
94 Dave Edwards .15 .06
95 Alan Trammell .30 .12
96 Dick Howser MG .15 .06
97 Ross Baumgarten .15 .06
98 Vance Law .15 .06
99 Dickie Noles .15 .06
100 Pete Rose 4.00 1.60
101 Pete Rose SV 1.25 .50
102 Dave Beard .15 .06
103 Darrell Porter .15 .06
104 Bob Walk .15 .06
105 Don Baylor .30 .12
106 Gene Nelson .15 .06
107 Mike Jorgensen .15 .06
108 Glenn Hoffman .15 .06
109 Luis Leal .15 .06
110 Ken Griffey .30 .12
111 Al Oliver .30 .12
Steve Rogers TL
112 Bob Shirley .15 .06
113 Ron Roenicke .15 .06
114 Jim Slaton .15 .06
115 Chili Davis .30 .12
116 Dave Schmidt .15 .06
117 Alan Knicely .15 .06
118 Chris Welsh .15 .06
119 Tom Brookens .15 .06
120 Len Barker .15 .06
121 Mickey Hatcher .15 .06
122 Jimmy Smith .15 .06
123 George Frazier .15 .06
124 Marc Hill .15 .06
125 Leon Durham .15 .06
126 Joe Torre MG .60 .24
127 Preston Hanna .15 .06
128 Mike Ramsey .15 .06
129 Checklist: 1-132 .30 .12
130 Dave Stieb .30 .12
131 Ed Ott .15 .06
132 Todd Cruz .15 .06
133 Jim Barr .15 .06
134 Hubie Brooks .15 .06
135 Dwight Evans .30 .12
136 Willie Aikens .15 .06
137 Woodie Fryman .15 .06
138 Rick Dempsey .15 .06
139 Bruce Berenyi .15 .06
140 Willie Randolph .30 .12
141 Toby Harrah .30 .12
Rick Sutcliffe TL
142 Mike Caldwell .15 .06
143 Joe Pettini .15 .06
144 Mark Wagner .15 .06
145 Don Sutton .30 .12
146 Don Sutton SV .15 .06
147 Rick Leach .15 .06
148 Dave Roberts .15 .06
149 Johnny Ray .15 .06
150 Bruce Sutter .30 .12
151 Bruce Sutter SV .15 .06
152 Jay Johnstone .15 .06
153 Jerry Koosman .30 .12
154 Johnnie LeMaster .15 .06
155 Dan Quisenberry .15 .06
156 Billy Martin MG .60 .24
157 Steve Bedrosian .15 .06
158 Rob Wilfong .15 .06
159 Mike Stanton .15 .06
160 Dave Kingman .30 .12
161 Dave Kingman SV .15 .06
162 Mark Clear .15 .06
163 Cal Ripken 10.00 4.00
164 David Palmer .15 .06
165 Dan Driessen .15 .06
166 John Pacella .15 .06
167 Mark Brouhard .15 .06
168 Juan Eichelberger .15 .06
169 Doug Flynn .15 .06
170 Steve Howe .15 .06
171 Joe Morgan .30 .12
Bill Laskey TL
172 Vern Ruhle .15 .06
173 Jim Morrison .15 .06
174 Jerry Ujdur .15 .06
175 Bo Diaz .15 .06
176 Dave Righetti .30 .12
177 Harold Baines .30 .12
178 Luis Tiant .30 .12
179 Luis Tiant SV .15 .06
180 Rickey Henderson 2.50 1.00
181 Terry Felton .15 .06
182 Mike Fischlin .15 .06
183 Ed VandeBerg .15 .06
184 Bob Clark .15 .06
185 Tim Lollar .15 .06
186 Whitey Herzog MG .30 .12
187 Terry Leach .15 .06
188 Rick Miller .15 .06
189 Dan Schatzeder .15 .06
190 Cecil Cooper .30 .12
191 Joe Price .15 .06
192 Floyd Rayford .15 .06
193 Harry Spilman .15 .06
194 Cesar Geronimo .15 .06
195 Bob Stoddard .15 .06
196 Bill Fahey .15 .06
197 Jim Eisenreich RC .75 .30
198 Kiko Garcia .15 .06
199 Marty Bystrom .15 .06
200 Rod Carew .60 .24
201 Rod Carew SV .30 .12
202 Damaso Garcia .30 .12
Dave Stieb TL
203 Mike Morgan .15 .06
204 Junior Kennedy .15 .06
205 Dave Parker .30 .12
206 Ken Oberkfell .15 .06
207 Rick Camp .15 .06
208 Dan Meyer .15 .06
209 Mike Moore RC .75 .30
210 Jack Clark .30 .12
211 John Denny .15 .06
212 John Stearns .15 .06
213 Tom Burgmeier .15 .06
214 Jerry White .15 .06
215 Mario Soto .30 .12
216 Tony LaRussa MG .30 .12
217 Tim Stoddard .15 .06
218 Roy Howell .15 .06
219 Mike Armstrong .15 .06
220 Dusty Baker .30 .12
221 Joe Niekro .15 .06
222 Damaso Garcia .15 .06
223 John Montefusco .15 .06
224 Mickey Rivers .15 .06
225 Enos Cabell .15 .06
226 Enrique Romo .15 .06
227 Chris Bando .15 .06
228 Joaquin Andujar .30 .12
229 Bo Diaz .15 .06
Steve Carlton TL
230 Fergie Jenkins .30 .12
231 Fergie Jenkins SV .15 .06
232 Tom Brunansky .30 .12
233 Wayne Gross .15 .06
234 Larry Andersen .15 .06
235 Claudell Washington .15 .06
236 Steve Renko .15 .06
237 Dan Norman .15 .06
238 Bud Black RC .75 .30
239 Dave Stapleton .15 .06
240 Rich Gossage .30 .12
241 Rich Gossage SV .15 .06
242 Joe Nolan .15 .06
243 Duane Walker .15 .06
244 Dwight Bernard .15 .06
245 Steve Sax .30 .12
246 G.Bamberger MG .15 .06
247 Dave Smith .15 .06
248 Bake McBride .30 .12
249 Checklist: 133-264 .30 .12
250 Bill Buckner .30 .12
251 Alan Wiggins .15 .06
252 Luis Aguayo .15 .06
253 Larry McWilliams .15 .06
254 Rick Cerone .15 .06
255 Gene Garber .15 .06
256 Gene Garber SV .15 .06
257 Jesse Barfield .30 .12
258 Manny Castillo .15 .06
259 Jeff Jones .15 .06
260 Steve Kemp .15 .06
261 Larry Herndon .30 .12
Dan Petry TL
262 Ron Jackson .15 .06
263 Renie Martin .15 .06
264 Jamie Quirk .15 .06
265 Joel Youngblood .15 .06
266 Paul Boris .15 .06
267 Terry Francona .30 .12
268 Storm Davis RC .75 .30
269 Ron Oester .15 .06
270 Dennis Eckersley .60 .24
271 Ed Romero .15 .06
272 Frank Tanana .30 .12
273 Mark Belanger .15 .06
274 Terry Kennedy .15 .06
275 Ray Knight .30 .12
276 Gene Mauch MG .15 .06
277 Rance Mulliniks .15 .06
278 Kevin Hickey .15 .06
279 Greg Gross .30 .12
280 Bert Blyleven .30 .12
281 Andre Robertson .15 .06
282 Reggie Smith 1.25 .50
(Ryne Sandberg
ducking back)
283 Reggie Smith SV .15 .06
284 Jeff Lahti .15 .06
285 Lance Parrish .30 .12
286 Rick Langford .15 .06
287 Bobby Brown .15 .06
288 Joe Cowley .15 .06
289 Jerry Dybzinski .15 .06
290 Jeff Reardon .30 .12
291 Bill Madlock .30 .12
John Candelaria TL
292 Craig Swan .15 .06
293 Glenn Gulliver .15 .06
294 Dave Engle .15 .06
295 Jerry Remy .15 .06
296 Greg Harris .15 .06
297 Ned Yost .15 .06
298 Floyd Chiffer .15 .06
299 George Wright RC .75 .30
300 Mike Schmidt 3.00 1.20
301 Mike Schmidt SV 1.25 .50
302 Ernie Whitt .30 .12
303 Miguel Dilone .15 .06
304 Dave Rucker .15 .06
305 Larry Bowa .30 .12
306 Tom Lasorda MG .60 .24
307 Lou Piniella .30 .12
308 Jesus Vega .15 .06
309 Jeff Leonard .15 .06
310 Greg Luzinski .30 .12
311 Glenn Brummer .15 .06
312 Brian Kingman .15 .06
313 Gary Gray .15 .06
314 Ken Dayley .15 .06
315 Rick Burleson .15 .06
316 Paul Splittorff .15 .06
317 Gary Rajsich .15 .06
318 John Tudor .30 .12
319 Lenn Sakata .15 .06
320 Steve Rogers .30 .12
321 Robin Yount 1.25 .50
Pete Vuckovich TL
322 Dave Van Gorder .15 .06
323 Luis DeLeon .15 .06
324 Mike Marshall .30 .12
325 Von Hayes .15 .06
326 Garth Iorg .15 .06
327 Bobby Castillo .15 .06
328 Craig Reynolds .15 .06
329 Randy Niemann .15 .06
330 Buddy Bell .30 .12
331 Mike Krukow .15 .06
332 Glenn Wilson .75 .30
333 Dave LaRoche .15 .06
334 Dave LaRoche SV .15 .06
335 Steve Henderson .15 .06
336 Rene Lachemann MG .15 .06
337 Tito Landrum .15 .06
338 Bob Owchinko .15 .06
339 Terry Harper .15 .06
340 Larry Gura .15 .06
341 Doug DeCinces .15 .06
342 Atlee Hammaker .15 .06
343 Bob Bailor .15 .06
344 Roger LaFrancois .30 .12
345 Jim Clancy .15 .06
346 Joe Pittman .15 .06
347 Sammy Stewart .15 .06
348 Alan Bannister .15 .06
349 Checklist: 265-396 .30 .12
350 Robin Yount 2.00 .80
351 Cesar Cedeno .30 .12
Mario Soto TL
352 Mike Scioscia .30 .12
353 Steve Comer .15 .06
354 Randy Johnson .15 .06
355 Jim Bibby .15 .06
356 Gary Woods .15 .06
357 Len Matuszek .15 .06
358 Jerry Garvin .15 .06
359 Dave Collins .15 .06
360 Nolan Ryan 6.00 2.40
361 Nolan Ryan SV 3.00 1.20
362 Bill Almon .15 .06
363 John Stuper .15 .06
364 Brett Butler .30 .12
365 Dave Lopes .30 .12
366 Dick Williams MG .15 .06
367 Bud Anderson .15 .06
368 Richie Zisk .15 .06
369 Jesse Orosco .30 .12
370 Gary Carter .30 .12
371 Mike Richardt .15 .06
372 Terry Crowley .15 .06
373 Kevin Saucier .15 .06
374 Wayne Krenchicki .15 .06
375 Pete Vuckovich .15 .06
376 Ken Landreaux .15 .06
377 Lee May .15 .06
378 Lee May SV .15 .06
379 Guy Sularz .15 .06
380 Ron Davis .15 .06
381 Jim Rice .30 .12
Bob Stanley TL
382 Bob Knepper .15 .06
383 Ozzie Virgil .15 .06
384 Dave Dravecky RC 1.50 .60
385 Mike Easler .15 .06
386 Rod Carew AS .30 .12
387 Bob Grich AS .15 .06
388 George Brett AS 1.50 .60
389 Robin Yount AS 1.25 .50
390 Reggie Jackson AS .30 .12
391 Rickey Henderson AS 1.25 .50
392 Fred Lynn AS .15 .06
393 Carlton Fisk AS .30 .12
394 Pete Vuckovich AS .15 .06
395 Larry Gura AS .15 .06
396 Dan Quisenberry AS .15 .06
397 Pete Rose AS .60 .24
398 Manny Trillo AS .15 .06
399 Mike Schmidt AS 1.25 .50
400 Dave Concepcion AS .15 .06
401 Dale Murphy AS .30 .12
402 Andre Dawson AS .15 .06
403 Tim Raines AS .15 .06
404 Gary Carter AS .15 .06
405 Steve Rogers AS .15 .06
406 Steve Carlton AS .30 .12
407 Bruce Sutter AS .15 .06
408 Rudy May .15 .06
409 Marvis Foley .15 .06
410 Phil Niekro .30 .12
411 Phil Niekro SV .15 .06
412 Buddy Bell .30 .12
Charlie Hough TL
413 Matt Keough .15 .06
414 Julio Cruz .15 .06
415 Bob Forsch .15 .06
416 Joe Ferguson .15 .06
417 Tom Hausman .15 .06
418 Greg Pryor .15 .06
419 Steve Crawford .15 .06
420 Al Oliver .30 .12
421 Al Oliver SV .15 .06
422 George Cappuzzello .15 .06
423 Tom Lawless .15 .06
424 Jerry Augustine .15 .06
425 Pedro Guerrero .30 .12
426 Earl Weaver MG .30 .12
427 Roy Lee Jackson .15 .06
428 Champ Summers .15 .06
429 Eddie Whitson .15 .06
430 Kirk Gibson .30 .12
431 Gary Gaetti RC 1.50 .60
432 Porfirio Altamirano .15 .06
433 Dale Berra .15 .06
434 Dennis Lamp .15 .06
435 Tony Armas .30 .12
436 Bill Campbell .15 .06
437 Rick Sweet .15 .06
438 Dave LaPoint .15 .06
439 Rafael Ramirez .15 .06
440 Ron Guidry .30 .12
441 Ray Knight .30 .12
Joe Niekro TL
442 Brian Downing .30 .12
443 Don Hood .15 .06
444 Wally Backman .15 .06
445 Mike Flanagan .15 .06
446 Reid Nichols .15 .06
447 Bryn Smith .15 .06
448 Darrell Evans .30 .12
449 Eddie Milner .15 .06
450 Ted Simmons .30 .12
451 Ted Simmons SV .15 .06
452 Lloyd Moseby .15 .06
453 Lamar Johnson .15 .06
454 Bob Welch .30 .12
455 Sixto Lezcano .15 .06
456 Lee Elia MG .15 .06
457 Milt Wilcox .15 .06
458 Ron Washington .15 .06
459 Ed Farmer .15 .06
460 Roy Smalley .15 .06
461 Steve Trout .15 .06
462 Steve Nicosia .15 .06
463 Gaylord Perry .30 .12
464 Gaylord Perry SV .15 .06
465 Lonnie Smith .15 .06
466 Tom Underwood .15 .06
467 Rufino Linares .15 .06
468 Dave Goltz .15 .06
469 Ron Gardenhire .15 .06
470 Greg Minton .15 .06
471 Willie Wilson .30 .12
Vida Blue TL
472 Gary Allenson .15 .06
473 John Lowenstein .15 .06
474 Ray Burris .15 .06
475 Cesar Cedeno .30 .12
476 Rob Picciolo .15 .06
477 Tom Niedenfuer .15 .06
478 Phil Garner .30 .12
479 Charlie Hough .30 .12
480 Toby Harrah .30 .12
481 Scot Thompson .15 .06
482 Tony Gwynn UER RC 25.00 10.00
No Topps logo under
card number on back
483 Lynn Jones .15 .06
484 Dick Ruthven .15 .06
485 Omar Moreno .15 .06
486 Clyde King MG .15 .06
487 Jerry Hairston .15 .06
488 Alfredo Griffin .15 .06
489 Tom Herr .15 .06
490 Jim Palmer .30 .12
491 Jim Palmer SV .30 .12
492 Paul Serna .15 .06
493 Steve McCatty .15 .06
494 Bob Brenly .15 .06
495 Warren Cromartie .15 .06
496 Tom Veryzer .15 .06
497 Rick Sutcliffe .30 .12
498 Wade Boggs RC 12.00 4.80
499 Jeff Little .15 .06
500 Reggie Jackson .60 .24
501 Reggie Jackson SV .30 .12
502 Dale Murphy .60 .24

Phil Niekro TL
503 Moose Haas .15 .06
504 Don Werner .15 .06
505 Garry Templeton .30 .12
506 Jim Gott RC .75 .30
507 Tony Scott .15 .06
508 Tom Filer .15 .06
509 Lou Whitaker .30 .12
510 Tug McGraw .30 .12
511 Tug McGraw SV .15 .06
512 Doyle Alexander .15 .06
513 Fred Stanley .15 .06
514 Rudy Law .15 .06
515 Gene Tenace .30 .12
516 Bill Virdon MG .15 .06
517 Gary Ward .15 .06
518 Bill Laskey .15 .06
519 Terry Bulling .15 .06
520 Fred Lynn .30 .12
521 Bruce Benedict .15 .06
522 Pat Zachry .15 .06
523 Carney Lansford .30 .12
524 Tom Brennan .15 .06
525 Frank White .30 .12
526 Checklist: 397-528 .30 .12
527 Larry Biittner .15 .06
528 Jamie Easterly .15 .06
529 Tim Laudner .15 .06
530 Eddie Murray 1.25 .50
531 Rickey Henderson 1.25 .50
Rick Langford TL
532 Dave Stewart .30 .12
533 Luis Salazar .15 .06
534 John Butcher .15 .06
535 Manny Trillo .15 .06
536 John Wockenfuss .15 .06
537 Rod Scurry .15 .06
538 Danny Heep .15 .06
539 Roger Erickson .15 .06
540 Ozzie Smith 2.00 .80
541 Britt Burns .15 .06
542 Jody Davis .15 .06
543 Alan Fowlkes .15 .06
544 Larry Whisenton .15 .06
545 Floyd Bannister .15 .06
546 Dave Garcia MG .15 .06
547 Geoff Zahn .15 .06
548 Brian Giles .15 .06
549 Charlie Puleo .15 .06
550 Carl Yastrzemski 2.00 .80
551 Carl Yastrzemski SV 1.25 .50
552 Tim Wallach .30 .12
553 Dennis Martinez .30 .12
554 Mike Vail .15 .06
555 Steve Yeager .30 .12
556 Willie Upshaw .15 .06
557 Rick Honeycutt .15 .06
558 Dickie Thon .15 .06
559 Pete Redfern .15 .06
560 Ron LeFlore .30 .12
561 Lonnie Smith .30 .12
Joaquin Andujar TL
562 Dave Rozema .15 .06
563 Juan Bonilla .15 .06
564 Sid Monge .15 .06
565 Bucky Dent .30 .12
566 Manny Sarmiento .15 .06
567 Joe Simpson .15 .06
568 Willie Hernandez .15 .06
569 Jack Perconte .15 .06
570 Vida Blue .30 .12
571 Mickey Klutts .15 .06
572 Bob Watson .15 .06
573 Andy Hassler .15 .06
574 Glenn Adams .15 .06
575 Neil Allen .15 .06
576 Frank Robinson MG .60 .24
577 Luis Aponte .15 .06
578 David Green RC .75 .30
579 Rich Dauer .15 .06
580 Tom Seaver 1.25 .50
581 Tom Seaver SV .30 .12
582 Marshall Edwards .15 .06
583 Terry Forster .30 .12
584 Dave Hostetler .15 .06
585 Jose Cruz .30 .12
586 Frank Viola RC 2.50 1.00
587 Ivan DeJesus .15 .06
588 Pat Underwood .15 .06
589 Alvis Woods .15 .06
590 Tony Pena .15 .06
591 Greg Luzinski .30 .12
LaMarr Hoyt TL
592 Shane Rawley .15 .06
593 Broderick Perkins .15 .06
594 Eric Rasmussen .15 .06
595 Tim Raines .30 .12
596 Randy Johnson .15 .06
597 Mike Proly .15 .06
598 Dwayne Murphy .15 .06
599 Don Aase .15 .06
600 George Brett 3.00 1.20
601 Ed Lynch .15 .06
602 Rich Gedman .15 .06
603 Joe Morgan .30 .12
604 Joe Morgan SV .15 .06
605 Gary Roenicke .15 .06
606 Bobby Cox MG .30 .12
607 Charlie Leibrandt .15 .06
608 Don Money .15 .06
609 Danny Darwin .15 .06
610 Steve Garvey .30 .12
611 Bert Roberge .15 .06
612 Steve Swisher .15 .06
613 Mike Ivie .15 .06
614 Ed Glynn .15 .06
615 Garry Maddox .15 .06
616 Bill Nahorodny .15 .06
617 Butch Wynegar .15 .06
618 LaMarr Hoyt .15 .06
619 Keith Moreland .15 .06
620 Mike Norris .15 .06
621 Mookie Wilson .30 .12
Craig Swan TL
622 Dave Edler .15 .06
623 Luis Sanchez .15 .06
624 Glenn Hubbard .15 .06
625 Ken Forsch .15 .06
626 Jerry Martin .15 .06
627 Doug Bair .15 .06
628 Julio Valdez .15 .06
629 Charlie Lea .15 .06
630 Paul Molitor .60 .24
631 Tippy Martinez .15 .06
632 Alex Trevino .15 .06
633 Vicente Romo .15 .06
634 Max Venable .15 .06
635 Graig Nettles .30 .12
636 Graig Nettles SV .15 .06
637 Pat Corrales MG .15 .06
638 Dan Petry .15 .06
639 Art Howe .15 .06
640 Andre Thornton .15 .06
641 Billy Sample .15 .06
642 Checklist: 529-660 .30 .12
643 Bump Wills .15 .06
644 Joe Lefebvre .15 .06
645 Bill Madlock .30 .12
646 Jim Essian .15 .06
647 Bobby Mitchell .15 .06
648 Jeff Burroughs .15 .06
649 Tommy Boggs .15 .06
650 George Hendrick .30 .12
651 Rod Carew .30 .12
Mike Witt TL
652 Butch Hobson .15 .06
653 Ellis Valentine .15 .06
654 Bob Ojeda .15 .06
655 Al Bumbry .15 .06
656 Dave Frost .15 .06
657 Mike Gates .15 .06
658 Frank Pastore .15 .06
659 Charlie Moore .15 .06
660 Mike Hargrove .15 .06
661 Bill Russell .30 .12
662 Joe Sambito .15 .06
663 Tom O'Malley .15 .06
664 Bob Molinaro .15 .06
665 Jim Sundberg .30 .12
666 Sparky Anderson MG .30 .12
667 Dick Davis .15 .06
668 Larry Christenson .15 .06
669 Mike Squires .15 .06
670 Jerry Mumphrey .15 .06
671 Lenny Faedo .15 .06
672 Jim Kaat .30 .12
673 Jim Kaat SV .15 .06
674 Kurt Bevacqua .15 .06
675 Jim Beattie .15 .06
676 Biff Pocoroba .15 .06
677 Dave Revering .15 .06
678 Juan Beniquez .15 .06
679 Mike Scott .30 .12
680 Andre Dawson .30 .12
681 Pedro Guerrero .30 .12
Fernando Valenzuela TL
682 Bob Stanley .15 .06
683 Dan Ford .15 .06
684 Rafael Landestoy .15 .06
685 Lee Mazzilli .30 .12
686 Randy Lerch .15 .06
687 U.L. Washington .15 .06
688 Jim Wohlford .15 .06
689 Ron Hassey .15 .06
690 Kent Hrbek .30 .12
691 Dave Tobik .15 .06
692 Denny Walling .15 .06
693 Sparky Lyle .30 .12
694 Sparky Lyle SV .15 .06
695 Ruppert Jones .15 .06
696 Chuck Tanner MG .15 .06
697 Barry Foote .15 .06
698 Tony Bernazard .15 .06
699 Lee Smith .60 .24
700 Keith Hernandez .30 .12
701 Willie Wilson .30 .12
Al Oliver LL
702 Reggie Jackson .30 .12
Gorman Thomas
Dave Kingman LL
703 Hal McRae .60 .24
Dale Murphy
Al Oliver LL
704 Rickey Henderson 1.25 .50
Tim Raines LL
705 LaMarr Hoyt .30 .12
Steve Carlton LL
706 Floyd Bannister .30 .12
Steve Carlton LL
707 Rick Sutcliffe .30 .12
Steve Rogers LL
708 Dan Quisenberry .30 .12
Bruce Sutter LL
709 Jimmy Sexton .15 .06
710 Willie Wilson .30 .12
711 Bruce Bochte .30 .12
Jim Beattie TL
712 Bruce Kison .15 .06
713 Ron Hodges .15 .06
714 Wayne Nordhagen .15 .06
715 Tony Perez .60 .24
716 Tony Perez SV .30 .12
717 Scott Sanderson .15 .06
718 Jim Dwyer .15 .06
719 Rich Gale .15 .06
720 Dave Concepcion .30 .12
721 John Martin .15 .06
722 Jorge Orta .15 .06
723 Randy Moffitt .15 .06
724 Johnny Grubb .15 .06
725 Dan Spillner .15 .06
726 Harvey Kuenn MG .15 .06
727 Chet Lemon .30 .12
728 Ron Reed .15 .06
729 Jerry Morales .15 .06
730 Jason Thompson .15 .06
731 Al Williams .15 .06
732 Dave Henderson .15 .06
733 Buck Martinez .15 .06
734 Steve Braun .15 .06
735 Tommy John .30 .12
736 Tommy John SV .15 .06
737 Mitchell Page .15 .06
738 Tim Foli .15 .06
739 Rick Ownbey .15 .06
740 Rusty Staub .30 .12
741 Rusty Staub SV .15 .06
742 Terry Kennedy .30 .12
Tim Lollar
743 Mike Torrez .15 .06

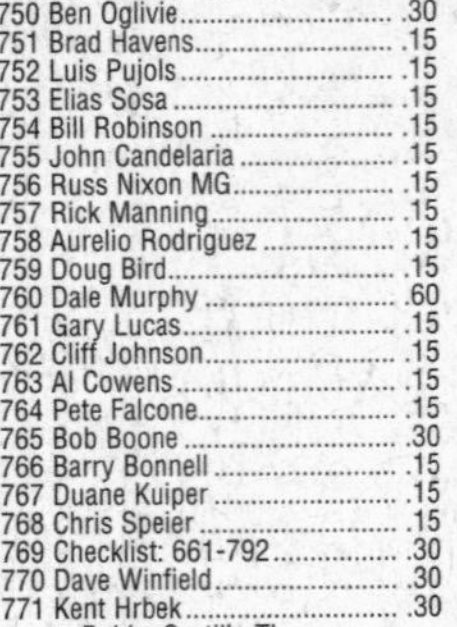
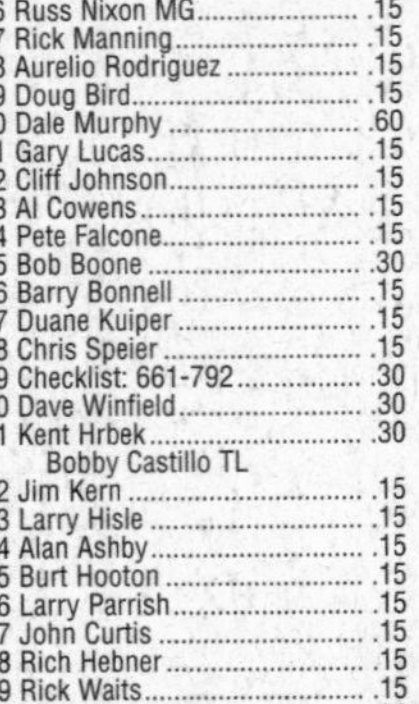

744 Brad Mills .15 .06
745 Scott McGregor .15 .06
746 John Wathan .15 .06
747 Fred Breining .15 .06
748 Derrel Thomas .15 .06
749 Jon Matlack .15 .06
750 Ben Oglivie .30 .12
751 Brad Havens .15 .06
752 Luis Pujols .15 .06
753 Elias Sosa .15 .06
754 Bill Robinson .15 .06
755 John Candelaria .15 .06
756 Russ Nixon MG .15 .06
757 Rick Manning .15 .06
758 Aurelio Rodriguez .15 .06
759 Doug Bird .15 .06
760 Dale Murphy .60 .24
761 Gary Lucas .15 .06
762 Cliff Johnson .15 .06
763 Al Cowens .15 .06
764 Pete Falcone .15 .06
765 Bob Boone .30 .12
766 Barry Bonnell .15 .06
767 Duane Kuiper .15 .06
768 Chris Speier .15 .06
769 Checklist: 661-792 .30 .12
770 Dave Winfield .30 .12
771 Kent Hrbek .30 .12
Bobby Castillo TL
772 Jim Kern .15 .06
773 Larry Hisle .15 .06
774 Alan Ashby .15 .06
775 Burt Hooton .15 .06
776 Larry Parrish .15 .06
777 John Curtis .15 .06
778 Rich Hebner .15 .06
779 Rick Waits .15 .06
780 Gary Matthews .30 .12
781 Rick Rhoden .15 .06
782 Bobby Murcer .30 .12
783 Bobby Murcer SV .15 .06
784 Jeff Newman .15 .06
785 Dennis Leonard .15 .06
786 Ralph Houk MG .15 .06
787 Dick Tidrow .15 .06
788 Dane Iorg .15 .06
789 Bryan Clark .15 .06
790 Bob Grich .30 .12
791 Gary Lavelle .15 .06
792 Chris Chambliss .30 .12
XX Game Insert Card .10 .04

1983 Topps Glossy Send-Ins

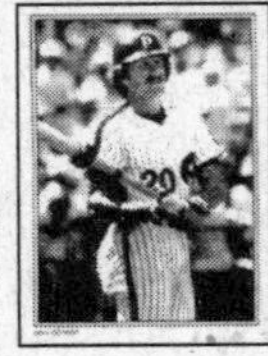

The cards in this 40-card set measure the standard size. The 1983 Topps "Collector's Edition" or "All-Star Set" (popularly known as "Glossies") consists of color ballplayer picture cards with shiny, glazed surfaces. The player's name appears in small print outside the frame line at bottom left. The backs contain no biography or record and list only the set titles, the player's name, team, position, and the card number.

Nm-Mt Ex-Mt
COMPLETE SET (40) 15.00 6.00
1 Carl Yastrzemski 1.25 .50
2 Mookie Wilson .20 .08
3 Andre Thornton .20 .08
4 Keith Hernandez .20 .08
5 Robin Yount 1.25 .50
6 Terry Kennedy .10 .04
7 Dave Winfield 1.25 .50
8 Mike Schmidt 1.50 .60
9 Buddy Bell .20 .08
10 Fernando Valenzuela .30 .12
11 Rich Gossage .20 .08
12 Bob Horner .20 .08
13 Toby Harrah .10 .04
14 Pete Rose 1.50 .60
15 Cecil Cooper .20 .08
16 Dale Murphy .50 .20
17 Carlton Fisk 1.25 .50
18 Ray Knight .10 .04
19 Jim Palmer 1.00 .40
20 Gary Carter 1.00 .40
21 Richie Zisk .10 .04
22 Dusty Baker .20 .08
23 Willie Wilson .10 .04
24 Bill Buckner .20 .08
25 Dave Stieb .10 .04
26 Bill Madlock .10 .04
27 Lance Parrish .20 .08
28 Nolan Ryan 5.00 2.00
29 Rod Carew 1.00 .40
30 Al Oliver .20 .08
31 George Brett 2.50 1.00
32 Jack Clark .10 .04
33 Rickey Henderson 2.00 .80
34 Dave Concepcion .20 .08
35 Kent Hrbek .20 .08
36 Steve Carlton 1.00 .40
37 Eddie Murray 1.25 .50
38 Ruppert Jones .10 .04
39 Reggie Jackson 1.25 .50
40 Bruce Sutter .20 .08

1983 Topps Traded

For the third year in a row, Topps issued a 132-card standard-size Traded (or extended) set featuring some of the year's top rookies and players who had changed teams during the year. The cards were available through hobby dealers only in factory set form and were printed in Ireland by the Topps affiliate in that country. The set is numbered alphabetically by player. The Darryl Strawberry card number 108 can be found with either one or two asterisks (in the lower left corner of the reverse). There is no difference in value for either version. The key (extended) Rookie Cards in this set include Julio Franco, Tony Phillips and Darryl Strawberry.

Nm-Mt Ex-Mt
COMP.FACT.SET (132) 40.00 16.00
1T Neil Allen .25 .10
2T Bill Almon .25 .10
3T Joe Altobelli MG .25 .10
4T Tony Armas 1.00 .40
5T Doug Bair .25 .10
6T Steve Baker .25 .10
7T Floyd Bannister .25 .10
8T Don Baylor 1.00 .40
9T Tony Bernazard .25 .10
10T Larry Biittner .25 .10
11T Dann Bilardello .25 .10
12T Doug Bird .25 .10
13T Steve Boros MG .25 .10
14T Greg Brock .25 .10
15T Mike C. Brown .25 .10
16T Tom Burgmeier .25 .10
17T Randy Bush .25 .10
18T Bert Campaneris 1.00 .40
19T Ron Cey 1.00 .40
20T Chris Codiroli .25 .10
21T Dave Collins .25 .10
22T Terry Crowley .25 .10
23T Julio Cruz .25 .10
24T Mike Davis .25 .10
25T Frank DiPino .25 .10
26T Bill Doran XRC 1.00 .40
27T Jerry Dybzinski .25 .10
28T Jamie Easterly .25 .10
29T Juan Eichelberger .25 .10
30T Jim Essian .25 .10
31T Pete Falcone .25 .10
32T Mike Ferraro MG .25 .10
33T Terry Forster 1.00 .40
34T Julio Franco XRC 4.00 1.60
35T Rich Gale .25 .10
36T Kiko Garcia .25 .10
37T Steve Garvey 1.00 .40
38T Johnny Grubb .25 .10
39T Mel Hall XRC* 1.00 .40
40T Von Hayes .25 .10
41T Danny Heep .25 .10
42T Steve Henderson .25 .10
43T Keith Hernandez 1.00 .40
44T Leo Hernandez .25 .10
45T Willie Hernandez .25 .10
46T Al Holland .25 .10
47T Frank Howard MG 1.00 .40
48T Bobby Johnson .25 .10
49T Cliff Johnson .25 .10
50T Odell Jones .25 .10
51T Mike Jorgensen .25 .10
52T Bob Kearney .25 .10
53T Steve Kemp .25 .10
54T Matt Keough .25 .10
55T Ron Kittle XRC* 2.00 .80
56T Mickey Klutts .25 .10
57T Alan Knicely .25 .10
58T Mike Krukow .25 .10
59T Rafael Landestoy .25 .10
60T Carney Lansford 1.00 .40
61T Joe Lefebvre .25 .10
62T Bryan Little .25 .10
63T Aurelio Lopez .25 .10
64T Mike Madden .25 .10
65T Rick Manning .25 .10
66T Billy Martin MG 2.00 .80
67T Lee Mazzilli 1.00 .40
68T Andy McGaffigan .25 .10
69T Craig McMurtry .25 .10
70T John McNamara MG .25 .10
71T Orlando Mercado .25 .10
72T Larry Milbourne .25 .10
73T Randy Moffitt .25 .10
74T Sid Monge .25 .10
75T Jose Morales .25 .10
76T Omar Moreno .25 .10
77T Joe Morgan 1.00 .40
78T Mike Morgan .25 .10
79T Dale Murray .25 .10
80T Jeff Newman .25 .10
81T Pete O'Brien XRC 1.00 .40
82T Jorge Orta .25 .10
83T Alejandro Pena XRC 2.00 .80
84T Pascual Perez .25 .10
85T Tony Perez 2.00 .80
86T Broderick Perkins .25 .10
87T Tony Phillips XRC 2.00 .80
88T Charlie Puleo .25 .10
89T Pat Putnam .25 .10
90T Jamie Quirk .25 .10
91T Doug Rader MG .25 .10
92T Chuck Rainey .25 .10
93T Bobby Ramos .25 .10
94T Gary Redus XRC 1.00 .40
95T Steve Renko .25 .10
96T Leon Roberts .25 .10
97T Aurelio Rodriguez .25 .10
98T Dick Ruthven .25 .10
99T Daryl Sconiers .25 .10
100T Mike Scott 1.00 .40
101T Tom Seaver 2.00 .80
102T John Shelby .25 .10
103T Bob Shirley .25 .10
104T Joe Simpson .25 .10
105T Doug Sisk .25 .10
106T Mike Smithson .25 .10
107T Elias Sosa .25 .10
108T D.Strawberry XRC 10.00 4.00
109T Tom Tellmann .25 .10
110T Gene Tenace 1.00 .40
111T Gorman Thomas 1.00 .40
112T Dick Tidrow .25 .10
113T Dave Tobik .25 .10
114T Wayne Tolleson .25 .10
115T Mike Torrez .25 .10
116T Manny Trillo .25 .10
117T Steve Trout .25 .10
118T Lee Tunnell .25 .10
119T Mike Vail .25 .10
120T Ellis Valentine .25 .10
121T Tom Veryzer .25 .10
122T George Vukovich .25 .10
123T Rick Waits .25 .10
124T Greg Walker 1.00 .40
125T Chris Welsh .25 .10
126T Len Whitehouse .25 .10
127T Eddie Whitson .25 .10
128T Jim Wohlford .25 .10
129T Matt Young XRC 1.00 .40
130T Joel Youngblood .25 .10
131T Pat Zachry .25 .10
132T Checklist 1T-132T .25 .10

1984 Topps

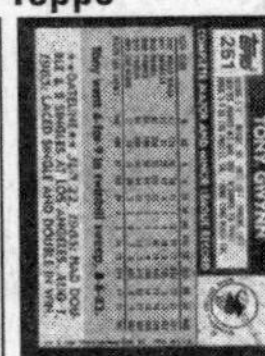

The cards in this 792-card set measure the standard size. Cards were primarily distributed in 15-card wax packs and 54-card rack packs. For the second year in a row, Topps utilized a dual picture on the front of the card. A portrait is shown in a square insert and an action shot is featured in the main photo. Card numbers 1-6 feature 1983 Highlights (HL), cards 131-138 depict League Leaders, card numbers 386-407 feature All-Stars, and card numbers 701-718 feature active Major League career leaders in various statistical categories. Each team leader (TL) card features the team's leading hitter and pitcher pictured on the front with a team checklist back. There are six numerical checklist cards in the set. The player cards feature team logos in the upper right corner of the reverse. The key Rookie Cards in this set are Don Mattingly and Darryl Strawberry. Topps tested a special send-in offer in Michigan and a few other states whereby collectors could obtain direct from Topps ten cards of their choice. Needless to say most people ordered the key (most valuable) players necessitating the printing of a special sheet to keep up with the demand. The special sheet had five cards of Darryl Strawberry, three cards of Don Mattingly, etc. The test was apparently a failure in Topps' eyes as they have never tried it again.

Nm-Mt Ex-Mt
COMPLETE SET (792) 50.00 20.00
1 Steve Carlton HL .25 .10
2 Rickey Henderson HL .60 .24
3 Dan Quisenberry HL .15 .06
4 Nolan Ryan HL 1.00 .40
Steve Carlton
Gaylord Perry
5 Dave Righetti HL .25 .10
Bob Forsch
Mike Warren
6 Johnny Bench HL .40 .16
Gaylord Perry
Carl Yastrzemski
7 Gary Lucas .15 .06
8 Don Mattingly RC 15.00 6.00
9 Jim Gott .15 .06
10 Robin Yount 1.00 .40
11 Kent Hrbek .25 .10
Ken Schrom TL
12 Billy Sample .15 .06
13 Scott Holman .15 .06
14 Tom Brookens .25 .10
15 Burt Hooton .15 .06
16 Omar Moreno .15 .06
17 John Denny .15 .06
18 Dale Berra .15 .06
19 Ray Fontenot .15 .06
20 Greg Luzinski .25 .10
21 Joe Altobelli MG .15 .06
22 Bryan Clark .15 .06
23 Keith Moreland .15 .06
24 John Martin .15 .06
25 Glenn Hubbard .15 .06
26 Bud Black .15 .06
27 Daryl Sconiers .15 .06
28 Frank Viola .40 .16
29 Danny Heep .15 .06
30 Wade Boggs 1.50 .60
31 Andy McGaffigan .15 .06
32 Bobby Ramos .15 .06
33 Tom Burgmeier .15 .06
34 Eddie Milner .15 .06
35 Don Sutton .25 .10
36 Denny Walling .15 .06
37 Buddy Bell .25 .10
Rick Honeycutt TL
38 Luis DeLeon .15 .06
39 Garth Iorg .15 .06
40 Dusty Baker .15 .06
41 Tony Bernazard .15 .06
42 Johnny Grubb .15 .06
43 Ron Reed .15 .06
44 Jim Morrison .15 .06
45 Jerry Mumphrey .15 .06
46 Ray Smith .15 .06
47 Rudy Law .15 .06
48 Julio Franco .40 .16
49 John Stuper .15 .06
50 Chris Chambliss .25 .10
51 Jim Frey MG .15 .06
52 Paul Splittorff .15 .06
53 Juan Beniquez .15 .06
54 Jesse Orosco .15 .06
55 Dave Concepcion .25 .10
56 Gary Allenson .15 .06

57 Dan Schatzeder .15 .06
58 Max Venable .15 .06
59 Sammy Stewart .15 .06
60 Paul Molitor UER .40 .16
('83 stats .272, 613, 167; should be .270, 608, 164)
61 Chris Codiroli .15 .06
62 Dave Hostetler .15 .06
63 Ed VandeBerg .15 .06
64 Mike Scioscia .25 .10
65 Kirk Gibson .25 .10
66 Jose Cruz 1.00 .40
Nolan Ryan TL
67 Gary Ward .15 .06
68 Luis Salazar .15 .06
69 Rod Scurry .15 .06
70 Gary Matthews .25 .10
71 Leo Hernandez .15 .06
72 Mike Squires .15 .06
73 Jody Davis .15 .06
74 Jerry Martin .15 .06
75 Bob Forsch .15 .06
76 Alfredo Griffin .15 .06
77 Brett Butler .25 .10
78 Mike Torrez .15 .06
79 Rob Wilfong .15 .06
80 Steve Rogers .25 .10
81 Billy Martin MG .40 .16
82 Doug Bird .15 .06
83 Richie Zisk .15 .06
84 Lenny Faedo .15 .06
85 Atlee Hammaker .15 .06
86 John Shelby .15 .06
87 Frank Pastore .15 .06
88 Rob Picciolo .15 .06
89 Mike Smithson .15 .06
90 Pedro Guerrero .25 .10
91 Dan Spillner .15 .06
92 Lloyd Moseby .15 .06
93 Bob Knepper .15 .06
94 Mario Ramirez .15 .06
95 Aurelio Lopez .25 .10
96 Hal McRae .25 .10
Larry Gura TL
97 LaMarr Hoyt .15 .06
98 Steve Nicosia .15 .06
99 Craig Lefferts RC .15 .06
100 Reggie Jackson .40 .16
101 Porfirio Altamirano .15 .06
102 Ken Oberkfell .15 .06
103 Dwayne Murphy .15 .06
104 Ken Dayley .15 .06
105 Tony Armas .25 .10
106 Tim Stoddard .15 .06
107 Ned Yost .15 .06
108 Randy Moffitt .15 .06
109 Brad Wellman .15 .06
110 Ron Guidry .25 .10
111 Bill Virdon MG .15 .06
112 Tom Niedenfuer .15 .06
113 Kelly Paris .15 .06
114 Checklist 1-132 .25 .10
115 Andre Thornton .15 .06
116 George Bjorkman .15 .06
117 Tom Veryzer .15 .06
118 Charlie Hough .25 .10
119 John Wockenfuss .15 .06
120 Keith Hernandez .25 .10
121 Pat Sheridan .15 .06
122 Cecilio Guante .15 .06
123 Butch Wynegar .15 .06
124 Damaso Garcia .15 .06
125 Britt Burns .15 .06
126 Dale Murphy .40 .16
Craig McMurtry TL
127 Mike Madden .15 .06
128 Rick Manning .15 .06
129 Bill Laskey .15 .06
130 Ozzie Smith 1.00 .40
131 Bill Madlock .60 .24
Wade Boggs LL
132 Mike Schmidt .60 .24
Jim Rice LL
133 Dale Murphy .40 .16
Cecil Cooper
Jim Rice LL
134 Tim Raines .60 .24
Rickey Henderson LL
135 John Denny .60 .24
LaMarr Hoyt LL
136 Steve Carlton .25 .10
Jack Morris LL
137 Atlee Hammaker .25 .10
Rick Honeycutt LL
138 Al Holland .25 .10
Dan Quisenberry LL
139 Bert Campaneris .25 .10
140 Storm Davis .15 .06
141 Pat Corrales MG .15 .06
142 Rich Gale .15 .06
143 Jose Morales .15 .06
144 Brian Harper RC .40 .16
145 Gary Lavelle .15 .06
146 Ed Romero .15 .06
147 Dan Petry .25 .10
148 Joe Lefebvre .15 .06
149 Jon Matlack .15 .06
150 Dale Murphy .40 .16
151 Steve Trout .15 .06
152 Glenn Brummer .15 .06
153 Dick Tidrow .15 .06
154 Dave Henderson .25 .10
155 Frank White .25 .10
156 Rickey Henderson .60 .24
Tim Conroy TL
157 Gary Gaetti .40 .16
158 John Curtis .15 .06
159 Darryl Cias .15 .06
160 Mario Soto .25 .10
161 Junior Ortiz .15 .06
162 Bob Ojeda .15 .06
163 Lorenzo Gray .15 .06
164 Scott Sanderson .15 .06
165 Ken Singleton .25 .10
166 Jamie Nelson .15 .06
167 Marshall Edwards .15 .06
168 Juan Bonilla .15 .06
169 Larry Parrish .15 .06
170 Jerry Reuss .15 .06
171 Frank Robinson MG .40 .16
172 Frank DiPino .15 .06
173 Marvell Wynne .40 .16
174 Juan Berenguer .15 .06
175 Graig Nettles .25 .10
176 Lee Smith .25 .10
177 Jerry Hairston .15 .06
178 Bill Krueger RC .15 .06
179 Buck Martinez .15 .06
180 Manny Trillo .15 .06
181 Roy Thomas .15 .06
182 Darryl Strawberry RC 2.00 .80
183 Al Williams .15 .06
184 Mike O'Berry .15 .06
185 Sixto Lezcano .15 .06
186 Lonnie Smith .25 .10
John Stuper TL
187 Luis Aponte .15 .06
188 Bryan Little .15 .06
189 Tim Conroy .15 .06
190 Ben Oglivie .25 .10
191 Mike Boddicker .15 .06
192 Nick Esasky .15 .06
193 Darrell Brown .15 .06
194 Domingo Ramos .15 .06
195 Jack Morris .25 .10
196 Don Slaught .25 .10
197 Garry Hancock .15 .06
198 Bill Doran RC* .40 .16
199 Willie Hernandez .15 .06
200 Andre Dawson .25 .10
201 Bruce Kison .15 .06
202 Bobby Cox MG .25 .10
203 Matt Keough .15 .06
204 Bobby Meacham .15 .06
205 Greg Minton .15 .06
206 Andy Van Slyke RC .75 .30
207 Donnie Moore .15 .06
208 Jose Oquendo RC .40 .16
209 Manny Sarmiento .15 .06
210 Joe Morgan .25 .10
211 Rick Sweet .15 .06
212 Broderick Perkins .15 .06
213 Bruce Hurst .15 .06
214 Paul Householder .15 .06
215 Tippy Martinez .15 .06
216 Carlton Fisk .25 .10
Richard Dotson TL
217 Alan Ashby .15 .06
218 Rick Waits .15 .06
219 Joe Simpson .15 .06
220 Fernando Valenzuela .25 .10
221 Cliff Johnson .15 .06
222 Rick Honeycutt .15 .06
223 Wayne Krenchicki .15 .06
224 Sid Monge .15 .06
225 Lee Mazzilli .25 .10
226 Juan Eichelberger .15 .06
227 Steve Braun .15 .06
228 John Rabb .15 .06
229 Paul Owens MG .15 .06
230 Rickey Henderson 1.00 .40
231 Gary Woods .15 .06
232 Tim Wallach .15 .06
233 Checklist 133-264 .25 .10
234 Rafael Ramirez .15 .06
235 Matt Young RC .40 .16
236 Ellis Valentine .15 .06
237 John Castino .15 .06
238 Reid Nichols .15 .06
239 Jay Howell .15 .06
240 Eddie Murray .60 .24
241 Bill Almon .15 .06
242 Alex Trevino .15 .06
243 Pete Ladd .15 .06
244 Candy Maldonado .15 .06
245 Rick Sutcliffe .25 .10
246 Mookie Wilson .25 .10
Tom Seaver TL
247 Onix Concepcion .15 .06
248 Bill Dawley .15 .06
249 Jay Johnstone .15 .06
250 Bill Madlock .25 .10
251 Tony Gwynn 2.50 1.00
252 Larry Christenson .15 .06
253 Jim Wohlford .15 .06
254 Shane Rawley .15 .06
255 Bruce Benedict .15 .06
256 Dave Geisel .15 .06
257 Julio Cruz .15 .06
258 Luis Sanchez .15 .06
259 Sparky Anderson MG .25 .10
260 Scott McGregor .15 .06
261 Bobby Brown .15 .06
262 Tom Candiotti RC .75 .30
263 Jack Fimple .15 .06
264 Doug Frobel RC .15 .06
265 Donnie Hill .15 .06
266 Steve Lubratich .15 .06
267 Carmelo Martinez .15 .06
268 Jack O'Connor .15 .06
269 Aurelio Rodriguez .15 .06
270 Jeff Russell RC .40 .16
271 Moose Haas .15 .06
272 Rick Dempsey .15 .06
273 Charlie Puleo .15 .06
274 Rick Monday .25 .10
275 Len Matuszek .15 .06
276 Rod Carew .25 .10
Geoff Zahn TL
277 Eddie Whitson .15 .06
278 Jorge Bell .25 .10
279 Ivan DeJesus .15 .06
280 Floyd Bannister .15 .06
281 Larry Milbourne .15 .06
282 Jim Barr .15 .06
283 Larry Biittner .15 .06
284 Howard Bailey .15 .06
285 Darrell Porter .15 .06
286 Lary Sorensen .15 .06
287 Warren Cromartie .15 .06
288 Jim Beattie .15 .06
289 Randy Johnson .15 .06
290 Dave Dravecky .15 .06
291 Chuck Tanner MG .15 .06
292 Tony Scott .15 .06
293 Ed Lynch .15 .06
294 U.L. Washington .15 .06
295 Mike Flanagan .15 .06
296 Jeff Newman .15 .06
297 Bruce Berenyi .15 .06
298 Jim Gantner .15 .06
299 John Butcher .15 .06
300 Pete Rose 2.00 .80
301 Frank LaCorte .15 .06
302 Barry Bonnell .15 .06
303 Marty Castillo .15 .06
304 Warren Brusstar .15 .06
305 Roy Smalley .15 .06
306 Pedro Guerrero .25 .10
Bob Welch TL
307 Bobby Mitchell .15 .06
308 Ron Hassey .15 .06
309 Tony Phillips RC .75 .30
310 Willie McGee .25 .10
311 Jerry Koosman .25 .10
312 Jorge Orta .15 .06
313 Mike Jorgensen .15 .06
314 Orlando Mercado .15 .06
315 Bobby Grich .25 .10
316 Mark Bradley .15 .06
317 Greg Pryor .15 .06
318 Bill Gullickson .15 .06
319 Al Bumbry .15 .06
320 Bob Stanley .15 .06
321 Harvey Kuenn MG .15 .06
322 Ken Schrom .15 .06
323 Alan Knicely .15 .06
324 Alejandro Pena RC* .75 .30
325 Darrell Evans .25 .10
326 Bob Kearney .15 .06
327 Ruppert Jones .15 .06
328 Vern Ruhle .15 .06
329 Pat Tabler .15 .06
330 John Candelaria .15 .06
331 Bucky Dent .25 .10
332 Kevin Gross RC .40 .16
333 Larry Herndon .25 .10
334 Chuck Rainey .15 .06
335 Don Baylor .25 .10
336 Pat Putnam .25 .10
Matt Young TL
337 Kevin Hagen .15 .06
338 Mike Warren .15 .06
339 Roy Lee Jackson .15 .06
340 Hal McRae .25 .10
341 Dave Tobik .15 .06
342 Tim Foli .15 .06
343 Mark Davis .15 .06
344 Rick Miller .15 .06
345 Kent Hrbek .25 .10
346 Kurt Bevacqua .15 .06
347 Allan Ramirez .15 .06
348 Toby Harrah .25 .10
349 Bob L. Gibson RC .15 .06
350 George Foster .25 .10
351 Russ Nixon MG .15 .06
352 Dave Stewart .25 .10
353 Jim Anderson .15 .06
354 Jeff Burroughs .15 .06
355 Jason Thompson .15 .06
356 Glenn Abbott .15 .06
357 Ron Cey .25 .10
358 Bob Dernier .15 .06
359 Jim Acker .15 .06
360 Willie Randolph .25 .10
361 Dave Smith .15 .06
362 David Green .15 .06
363 Tim Laudner .15 .06
364 Scott Fletcher .15 .06
365 Steve Bedrosian .15 .06
366 Terry Kennedy .25 .10
Dave Dravecky TL
367 Jamie Easterly .15 .06
368 Hubie Brooks .15 .06
369 Steve McCatty .15 .06
370 Tim Raines .25 .10
371 Dave Gumpert .15 .06
372 Gary Roenicke .15 .06
373 Bill Scherrer .15 .06
374 Don Money .15 .06
375 Dennis Leonard .15 .06
376 Dave Anderson RC .15 .06
377 Danny Darwin .15 .06
378 Bob Brenly .15 .06
379 Checklist 265-396 .25 .10
380 Steve Garvey .25 .10
381 Ralph Houk MG .15 .06
382 Chris Nyman .15 .06
383 Terry Puhl .15 .06
384 Lee Tunnell .15 .06
385 Tony Perez .40 .16
386 George Hendrick AS .15 .06
387 Johnny Ray AS .15 .06
388 Mike Schmidt AS .60 .24
389 Ozzie Smith AS .60 .24
390 Tim Raines AS .15 .06
391 Dale Murphy AS .25 .10
392 Andre Dawson AS .15 .06
393 Gary Carter AS .15 .06
394 Steve Rogers AS .15 .06
395 Steve Carlton AS .25 .10
396 Jesse Orosco AS .15 .06
397 Eddie Murray AS .40 .16
398 Lou Whitaker AS .15 .06
399 George Brett AS .60 .24
400 Cal Ripken AS 2.00 .80
401 Jim Rice AS .15 .06
402 Dave Winfield AS .15 .06
403 Lloyd Moseby AS .15 .06
404 Ted Simmons AS .15 .06
405 LaMarr Hoyt AS .15 .06
406 Ron Guidry AS .15 .06
407 Dan Quisenberry AS .15 .06
408 Lou Piniella .25 .10
409 Juan Agosto .15 .06
410 Claudell Washington .15 .06
411 Houston Jimenez .15 .06
412 Doug Rader MG .15 .06
413 Spike Owen RC .40 .16
414 Mitchell Page .15 .06
415 Tommy John .25 .10
416 Dane Iorg .15 .06
417 Mike Armstrong .15 .06
418 Ron Hodges .15 .06
419 John Henry Johnson .15 .06
420 Cecil Cooper .25 .10
421 Charlie Lea .15 .06
422 Jose Cruz .25 .10
423 Mike Morgan .15 .06
424 Dann Bilardello .15 .06
425 Steve Howe .15 .06
426 Cal Ripken 1.50 .60
Mike Boddicker TL
427 Rick Leach .15 .06
428 Fred Breining .15 .06
429 Randy Bush .15 .06
430 Rusty Staub .25 .10
431 Chris Bando .15 .06
432 Charles Hudson .15 .06
433 Rich Hebner .15 .06
434 Harold Baines .25 .10
435 Neil Allen .15 .06
436 Rick Peters .15 .06
437 Mike Proly .15 .06
438 Biff Pocoroba .15 .06
439 Bob Stoddard .15 .06
440 Steve Kemp .15 .06
441 Bob Lillis MG .15 .06
442 Byron McLaughlin .15 .06
443 Benny Ayala .15 .06
444 Steve Renko .15 .06
445 Jerry Remy .15 .06
446 Luis Pujols .15 .06
447 Tom Brunansky .15 .06
448 Ben Hayes .15 .06
449 Joe Pettini .15 .06
450 Gary Carter .25 .10
451 Bob Jones .15 .06
452 Chuck Porter .15 .06
453 Willie Upshaw .15 .06
454 Joe Beckwith .15 .06
455 Terry Kennedy .15 .06
456 Keith Moreland .15 .06
Fergie Jenkins TL
457 Dave Rozema .15 .06
458 Kiko Garcia .15 .06
459 Kevin Hickey .15 .06
460 Dave Winfield .25 .10
461 Jim Maler .15 .06
462 Lee Lacy .15 .06
463 Dave Engle .15 .06
464 Jeff A. Jones .15 .06
465 Mookie Wilson .25 .10
466 Gene Garber .15 .06
467 Mike Ramsey .15 .06
468 Geoff Zahn .15 .06
469 Tom O'Malley .15 .06
470 Nolan Ryan 3.00 1.20
471 Dick Howser MG .15 .06
472 Mike G. Brown RC .15 .06
473 Jim Dwyer .15 .06
474 Greg Bargar .15 .06
475 Gary Redus RC* .40 .16
476 Tom Tellmann .15 .06
477 Rafael Landestoy .15 .06
478 Alan Bannister .15 .06
479 Frank Tanana .25 .10
480 Ron Kittle .15 .06
481 Mark Thurmond .15 .06
482 Enos Cabell .15 .06
483 Fergie Jenkins .25 .10
484 Ozzie Virgil .15 .06
485 Rick Rhoden .15 .06
486 Don Baylor .25 .10
Ron Guidry TL
487 Ricky Adams .15 .06
488 Jesse Barfield .25 .10
489 Dave Von Ohlen .15 .06
490 Cal Ripken 4.00 1.60
491 Bobby Castillo .15 .06
492 Tucker Ashford .15 .06
493 Mike Norris .15 .06
494 Chili Davis .25 .10
495 Rollie Fingers .25 .10
496 Terry Francona .25 .10
497 Bud Anderson .15 .06
498 Rich Gedman .15 .06
499 Mike Witt .15 .06
500 George Brett 1.50 .60
501 Steve Henderson .15 .06
502 Joe Torre MG .40 .16
503 Elias Sosa .15 .06
504 Mickey Rivers .15 .06
505 Pete Vuckovich .15 .06
506 Ernie Whitt .15 .06
507 Mike LaCoss .15 .06
508 Mel Hall .25 .10
509 Brad Havens .15 .06
510 Alan Trammell .25 .10
511 Marty Bystrom .15 .06
512 Oscar Gamble .15 .06
513 Dave Beard .15 .06
514 Floyd Rayford .15 .06
515 Gorman Thomas .25 .10
516 Al Oliver .25 .10
Charlie Lea TL
517 John Moses .15 .06
518 Greg Walker .40 .16
519 Ron Davis .15 .06
520 Bob Boone .25 .10
521 Pete Falcone .15 .06
522 Dave Bergman .15 .06
523 Glenn Hoffman .15 .06
524 Carlos Diaz .15 .06
525 Willie Wilson .25 .10
526 Ron Oester .15 .06
527 Checklist 397-528 .25 .10
528 Mark Brouhard .15 .06
529 Keith Atherton .15 .06
530 Dan Ford .15 .06
531 Steve Boros MG .15 .06
532 Eric Show .15 .06
533 Ken Landreaux .15 .06
534 Pete O'Brien RC* .40 .16
535 Bo Diaz .15 .06
536 Doug Bair .15 .06
537 Johnny Ray .15 .06
538 Kevin Bass .15 .06
539 George Frazier .15 .06
540 George Hendrick .25 .10
541 Dennis Lamp .15 .06
542 Duane Kuiper .15 .06
543 Craig McMurtry .15 .06
544 Cesar Geronimo .15 .06
545 Bill Buckner .25 .10
546 Mike Hargrove .25 .10
Lary Sorensen TL
547 Mike Moore .15 .06
548 Ron Jackson .15 .06
549 Walt Terrell .15 .06
550 Jim Rice .25 .10
551 Scott Ullger .15 .06
552 Ray Burris .15 .06
553 Joe Nolan .15 .06
554 Ted Power .15 .06
555 Greg Brock .15 .06
556 Joey McLaughlin .15 .06
557 Wayne Tolleson .15 .06
558 Mike Davis .15 .06
559 Mike Scott .25 .10
560 Carlton Fisk .40 .16
561 Whitey Herzog MG .25 .10
562 Manny Castillo .15 .06
563 Glenn Wilson .25 .10
564 Al Holland .15 .06
565 Leon Durham .15 .06
566 Jim Bibby .15 .06
567 Mike Heath .15 .06
568 Pete Filson .15 .06
569 Bake McBride .25 .10
570 Dan Quisenberry .15 .06
571 Bruce Bochy .15 .06
572 Jerry Royster .15 .06
573 Dave Kingman .25 .10
574 Brian Downing .25 .10
575 Jim Clancy .15 .06
576 Jeff Leonard .25 .10
Atlee Hammaker TL
577 Mark Clear .15 .06
578 Lenn Sakata .15 .06
579 Bob James .15 .06
580 Lonnie Smith .15 .06
581 Jose DeLeon RC .40 .16
582 Bob McClure .15 .06
583 Derrel Thomas .15 .06
584 Dave Schmidt .15 .06
585 Dan Driessen .15 .06
586 Joe Niekro .15 .06
587 Von Hayes .15 .06
588 Milt Wilcox .15 .06
589 Mike Easler .15 .06
590 Dave Stieb .25 .10
591 Tony LaRussa MG .25 .10
592 Andre Robertson .15 .06
593 Jeff Lahti .15 .06
594 Gene Richards .15 .06
595 Jeff Reardon .25 .10
596 Ryne Sandberg 2.50 1.00
597 Rick Camp .15 .06
598 Rusty Kuntz .15 .06
599 Doug Sisk .15 .06
600 Rod Carew .40 .16
601 John Tudor .25 .10
602 John Wathan .15 .06
603 Renie Martin .15 .06
604 John Lowenstein .15 .06
605 Mike Caldwell .15 .06
606 Lloyd Moseby .25 .10
Dave Stieb TL
607 Tom Hume .15 .06
608 Bobby Johnson .15 .06
609 Dan Meyer .15 .06
610 Steve Sax .15 .06
611 Chet Lemon .25 .10
612 Harry Spilman .15 .06
613 Greg Gross .15 .06
614 Len Barker .15 .06
615 Garry Templeton .25 .10
616 Don Robinson .15 .06
617 Rick Cerone .15 .06
618 Dickie Noles .15 .06
619 Jerry Dybzinski .15 .06
620 Al Oliver .25 .10
621 Frank Howard MG .25 .10
622 Al Cowens .15 .06
623 Ron Washington .15 .06
624 Terry Harper .15 .06
625 Larry Gura .15 .06
626 Bob Clark .15 .06
627 Dave LaPoint .15 .06
628 Ed Jurak .15 .06
629 Rick Langford .15 .06
630 Ted Simmons .25 .10
631 Dennis Martinez .25 .10
632 Tom Foley .15 .06
633 Mike Krukow .15 .06
634 Mike Marshall .25 .10
635 Dave Righetti .25 .10
636 Pat Putnam .15 .06
637 Gary Matthews .25 .10
John Denny TL
638 George Vukovich .15 .06
639 Rick Lysander .15 .06
640 Lance Parrish .40 .16
641 Mike Richardt .15 .06
642 Tom Underwood .15 .06
643 Mike C. Brown .15 .06
644 Tim Lollar .15 .06
645 Tony Pena .15 .06
646 Checklist 529-660 .25 .10
647 Ron Roenicke .15 .06
648 Len Whitehouse .15 .06
649 Tom Herr .15 .06
650 Phil Niekro .25 .10
651 John McNamara MG .15 .06
652 Rudy May .15 .06
653 Dave Stapleton .15 .06
654 Bob Bailor .15 .06
655 Amos Otis .25 .10
656 Bryn Smith .15 .06
657 Thad Bosley .15 .06
658 Jerry Augustine .15 .06
659 Duane Walker .15 .06
660 Ray Knight .25 .10
661 Steve Yeager .25 .10
662 Tom Brennan .15 .06
663 Johnnie LeMaster .15 .06
664 Dave Stegman .15 .06
665 Buddy Bell .25 .10
666 Lou Whitaker .25 .10
Jack Morris TL
667 Vance Law .15 .06
668 Larry McWilliams .15 .06
669 Dave Lopes .25 .10
670 Rich Gossage .25 .10
671 Jamie Quirk .15 .06
672 Ricky Nelson .15 .06
673 Mike Walters .15 .06
674 Tim Flannery .15 .06

675 Pascual Perez .15 .06
676 Brian Giles .15 .06
677 Doyle Alexander .15 .06
678 Chris Speier .15 .06
679 Art Howe .15 .06
680 Fred Lynn .25 .10
681 Tom Lasorda MG .40 .16
682 Dan Morogiello .15 .06
683 Marty Barrett RC .40 .16
684 Bob Shirley .15 .06
685 Willie Aikens .15 .06
686 Joe Price .15 .06
687 Roy Howell .15 .06
688 George Wright .15 .06
689 Mike Fischlin .15 .06
690 Jack Clark .25 .10
691 Steve Lake .15 .06
692 Dickie Thon .15 .06
693 Alan Wiggins .15 .06
694 Mike Stanton .15 .06
695 Lou Whitaker .25 .10
696 Bill Madlock .25 .10
Rick Rhoden TL
697 Dale Murray .15 .06
698 Marc Hill .15 .06
699 Dave Rucker .15 .06
700 Mike Schmidt 1.50 .60
701 Bill Madlock .60 .24
Pete Rose
Dave Parker LL
702 Pete Rose .60 .24
Rusty Staub
Tony Perez LL
703 Mike Schmidt .60 .24
Tony Perez
Dave Kingman LL
704 Tony Perez .25 .10
Rusty Staub
Al Oliver LL
705 Joe Morgan .40 .16
Cesar Cedeno
Larry Bowa LL
706 Steve Carlton .25 .10
Fergie Jenkins
Tom Seaver LL
707 Steve Carlton 1.50 .60
Nolan Ryan
Tom Seaver LL
708 Tom Seaver .25 .10
Steve Carlton
Steve Rogers LL
709 Bruce Sutter .25 .10
Tug McGraw
Gene Garber LL
710 Rod Carew .40 .16
George Brett
Cecil Cooper LL
711 Rod Carew .25 .10
Bert Campaneris
Reggie Jackson LL
712 Reggie Jackson .25 .10
Graig Nettles
Greg Luzinski LL
713 Reggie Jackson .25 .10
Ted Simmons
Graig Nettles LL
714 Bert Campaneris .25 .10
Dave Lopes
Omar Moreno LL
715 Jim Palmer .25 .10
Don Sutton
Tommy John LL
716 Don Sutton .40 .16
Bert Blyleven
Jerry Koosman LL
717 Jim Palmer .25 .10
Rollie Fingers
Ron Guidry LL
718 Rollie Fingers .25 .10
Rich Gossage
Dan Quisenberry LL
719 Andy Hassler .15 .06
720 Dwight Evans .25 .10
721 Del Crandall MG .15 .06
722 Bob Welch .25 .10
723 Rich Dauer .15 .06
724 Eric Rasmussen .15 .06
725 Cesar Cedeno .25 .10
726 Ted Simmons .25 .10
Moose Haas TL
727 Joel Youngblood .15 .06
728 Tug McGraw .25 .10
729 Gene Tenace .25 .10
730 Bruce Sutter .25 .10
731 Lynn Jones .15 .06
732 Terry Crowley .15 .06
733 Dave Collins .15 .06
734 Odell Jones .15 .06
735 Rick Burleson .15 .06
736 Dick Ruthven .15 .06
737 Jim Essian .15 .06
738 Bill Schroeder .15 .06
739 Bob Watson .15 .06
740 Tom Seaver .60 .24
741 Wayne Gross .15 .06
742 Dick Williams MG .15 .06
743 Don Hood .15 .06
744 Jamie Allen .15 .06
745 Dennis Eckersley .40 .16
746 Mickey Hatcher .15 .06
747 Pat Zachry .15 .06
748 Jeff Leonard .15 .06
749 Doug Flynn .15 .06
750 Jim Palmer .25 .10
751 Charlie Moore .15 .06
752 Phil Garner .25 .10
753 Doug Gwosdz .15 .06
754 Kent Tekulve .15 .06
755 Garry Maddox .15 .06
756 Ron Oester .25 .10
Mario Soto TL
757 Larry Bowa .25 .10
758 Bill Stein .15 .06
759 Richard Dotson .15 .06
760 Bob Horner .25 .10
761 John Montefusco .15 .06
762 Rance Mulliniks .15 .06
763 Craig Swan .15 .06
764 Mike Hargrove .15 .06
765 Ken Forsch .15 .06
766 Mike Vail .15 .06
767 Carney Lansford .25 .10
768 Champ Summers .15 .06
769 Bill Caudill .15 .06
770 Ken Griffey .25 .10
771 Billy Gardner MG .15 .06
772 Jim Slaton .15 .06
773 Todd Cruz .15 .06
774 Tom Gorman .15 .06
775 Dave Parker .25 .10
776 Craig Reynolds .15 .06
777 Tom Paciorek .15 .06
778 Andy Hawkins .15 .06
779 Jim Sundberg .25 .10
780 Steve Carlton .40 .16
781 Checklist 661-792 .25 .10
782 Steve Balboni .15 .06
783 Luis Leal .15 .06
784 Leon Roberts .15 .06
785 Joaquin Andujar .25 .10
786 Wade Boggs .40 .16
Bob Ojeda TL
787 Bill Campbell .15 .06
788 Milt May .15 .06
789 Bert Blyleven .25 .10
790 Doug DeCinces .15 .06
791 Terry Forster .25 .10
792 Bill Russell .25 .10

1984 Topps Tiffany

This 792 card standard-size set was issued by Topps as a parallel to their regular issue. Printed in their Ireland facility, these cards are differentiated from the regular cards by the glossy fronts and pure white stock. These sets were available only through Topps' dealer network and sold only in factory set form. According to information from the time of issue, 10,000 of these sets were produced.

Nm-Mt Ex-Mt
COMP.FACT.SET (792) 200.00 80.00
*STARS: 3X TO 8X BASIC CARDS
*ROOKIES: 2.5X TO 6X BASIC CARDS

1984 Topps Glossy All-Stars

The cards in this 22-card set measure the standard size. Unlike the 1983 Topps Glossy set which was not distributed with its regular baseball cards, the 1984 Topps Glossy set was distributed as inserts in Topps Rak-Paks. The set features the nine American and National League All-Stars who started in the 1983 All Star game in Chicago. The managers and team captains (Yastrzemski and Bench) complete the set. The cards are numbered on the back and are ordered by position within league (AL: 1-11 and NL: 12-22).

Nm-Mt Ex-Mt
COMPLETE SET (22) 5.00 2.00
1 Harvey Kuenn MG .05 .02
2 Rod Carew .50 .20
3 Manny Trillo .05 .02
4 George Brett 1.00 .40
5 Robin Yount .50 .20
6 Jim Rice .10 .04
7 Fred Lynn .10 .04
8 Dave Winfield .50 .20
9 Ted Simmons .10 .04
10 Dave Stieb .05 .02
11 Carl Yastrzemski CAPT .50 .20
12 Whitey Herzog MG .05 .02
13 Al Oliver .10 .04
14 Steve Sax .10 .04
15 Mike Schmidt .75 .30
16 Ozzie Smith 1.00 .40
17 Tim Raines .15 .06
18 Andre Dawson .25 .10
19 Dale Murphy .25 .10
20 Gary Carter .40 .16
21 Mario Soto .05 .02
22 Johnny Bench CAPT .50 .20

1984 Topps Glossy Send-Ins

The cards in this 40-card set measure the standard size. Similar to last year's glossy set, this set was issued as a bonus prize to Topps All-Star Baseball Game cards found in wax packs. Twenty-five bonus runs from the game cards were necessary to obtain a five card subset of the series. There were eight different subsets of five cards. The cards are numbered and the set contains 20 stars from each league.

Nm-Mt Ex-Mt
COMPLETE SET (40) 12.00 4.80
1 Pete Rose 1.25 .50
2 Lance Parrish .20 .08
3 Steve Rogers .10 .04
4 Eddie Murray 1.00 .40
5 Johnny Ray .10 .04
6 Rickey Henderson 2.00 .80
7 Atlee Hammaker .10 .04
8 Wade Boggs 1.50 .60
9 Gary Carter 1.25 .50
10 Jack Morris .20 .08
11 Darrell Evans .20 .08
12 George Brett 2.50 1.00
13 Bob Horner .10 .04
14 Ron Guidry .20 .08
15 Nolan Ryan 5.00 2.00
16 Dave Winfield 1.00 .40
17 Ozzie Smith 2.00 .80
18 Ted Simmons .20 .08
19 Bill Madlock .10 .04
20 Tony Armas .10 .04
21 Al Oliver .20 .08
22 Jim Rice .20 .08
23 George Hendrick .10 .04
24 Dave Stieb .10 .04
25 Pedro Guerrero .10 .04
26 Rod Carew 1.00 .40
27 Steve Carlton .50 .20
28 Dave Righetti .20 .08
29 Darryl Strawberry .20 .08
30 Lou Whitaker .20 .08
31 Dale Murphy .30 .12
32 LaMarr Hoyt .10 .04
33 Jesse Orosco .20 .08
34 Cecil Cooper .20 .08
35 Andre Dawson .50 .20
36 Robin Yount 1.25 .50
37 Tim Raines .30 .12
38 Dan Quisenberry .10 .04
39 Mike Schmidt 2.00 .80
40 Carlton Fisk 1.50 .60

1984 Topps Traded

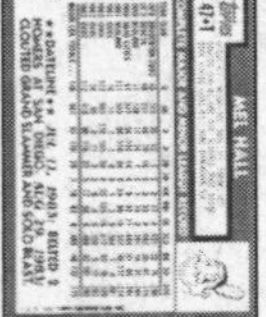

In now standard procedure, Topps issued its standard-size Traded (or extended) set for the fourth year in a row. Several of 1984's top rookies not contained in the regular set are pictured in the Traded set. Extended Rookie Cards in this set include Dwight Gooden, Jimmy Key, Mark Langston, Jose Rijo, and Bret Saberhagen. Again this year, the Topps affiliate in Ireland printed the cards, and the cards were available through hobby channels only in factory set form. The set numbering is in alphabetical order by player's name.

Nm-Mt Ex-Mt
COMP.FACT.SET (132) 30.00 12.00
1T Willie Aikens .40 .16
2T Luis Aponte .40 .16
3T Mike Armstrong .40 .16
4T Bob Bailor .40 .16
5T Dusty Baker .60 .24
6T Steve Balboni .40 .16
7T Alan Bannister .40 .16
8T Dave Beard .40 .16
9T Joe Beckwith .40 .16
10T Bruce Berenyi .40 .16
11T Dave Bergman .40 .16
12T Tony Bernazard .40 .16
13T Yogi Berra MG 1.50 .60
14T Barry Bonnell .40 .16
15T Phil Bradley 1.00 .40
16T Fred Breining .40 .16
17T Bill Buckner .60 .24
18T Ray Burris .40 .16
19T John Butcher .40 .16
20T Brett Butler .60 .24
21T Enos Cabell .40 .16
22T Bill Campbell .40 .16
23T Bill Caudill .40 .16
24T Bob Clark .40 .16
25T Bryan Clark .40 .16
26T Jaime Cocanower .40 .16
27T Ron Darling XRC* 2.00 .80
28T Alvin Davis XRC 1.00 .40
29T Ken Dayley .40 .16
30T Jeff Dedmon .40 .16
31T Bob Dernier .40 .16
32T Carlos Diaz .40 .16
33T Mike Easler .40 .16
34T Dennis Eckersley 1.00 .40
35T Jim Essian .40 .16
36T Darrell Evans .60 .24
37T Mike Fitzgerald .40 .16
38T Tim Foli .40 .16
39T George Frazier .40 .16
40T Rich Gale .40 .16
41T Barbaro Garbey .40 .16
42T Dwight Gooden XRC 5.00 2.00
43T Rich Gossage .60 .24
44T Wayne Gross .40 .16
45T Mark Gubicza XRC 1.00 .40
46T Jackie Gutierrez .40 .16
47T Mel Hall .60 .24
48T Toby Harrah .60 .24
49T Ron Hassey .40 .16
50T Rich Hebner .40 .16
51T Willie Hernandez .60 .24
52T Ricky Horton .40 .16
53T Art Howe .40 .16
54T Dane Iorg .40 .16
55T Brook Jacoby 1.00 .40
56T Mike Jeffcoat XRC .50 .20
57T Dave Johnson MG .40 .16
58T Lynn Jones .40 .16
59T Ruppert Jones .40 .16
60T Mike Jorgensen .40 .16
61T Bob Kearney .40 .16
62T Jimmy Key XRC 2.00 .80
63T Dave Kingman .60 .24
64T Jerry Koosman .60 .24
65T Wayne Krenchicki .40 .16
66T Rusty Kuntz .40 .16
67T Rene Lachemann MG .40 .16
68T Frank LaCorte .40 .16
69T Dennis Lamp .40 .16
70T Mark Langston XRC 2.00 .80
71T Rick Leach .40 .16
72T Craig Lefferts .50 .20
73T Gary Lucas .40 .16
74T Jerry Martin .40 .16
75T Carmelo Martinez .40 .16
76T Mike Mason XRC .50 .20
77T Gary Matthews .60 .24
78T Andy McGaffigan .40 .16
79T Larry Milbourne .40 .16
80T Sid Monge .40 .16
81T Jackie Moore MG .40 .16
82T Joe Morgan .60 .24
83T Graig Nettles .60 .24
84T Phil Niekro .60 .24
85T Ken Oberkfell .40 .16
86T Mike O'Berry .40 .16
87T Al Oliver .60 .24
88T Jorge Orta .40 .16
89T Amos Otis .60 .24
90T Dave Parker .60 .24
91T Tony Perez 1.00 .40
92T Gerald Perry 1.00 .40
93T Gary Pettis .40 .16
94T Rob Picciolo .40 .16
95T Vern Rapp MG .40 .16
96T Floyd Rayford .40 .16
97T Randy Ready XRC 1.00 .40
98T Ron Reed .40 .16
99T Gene Richards .40 .16
100T Jose Rijo XRC 2.00 .80
101T Jeff D. Robinson .40 .16
102T Ron Romanick .40 .16
103T Pete Rose 5.00 2.00
104T B.Saberhagen XRC 3.00 1.20
105T Juan Samuel XRC* 2.00 .80
106T Scott Sanderson .40 .16
107T Dick Schofield XRC* 1.00 .40
108T Tom Seaver 1.50 .60
109T Jim Slaton .40 .16
110T Mike Smithson .40 .16
111T Lary Sorensen .40 .16
112T Tim Stoddard .40 .16
113T Champ Summers .40 .16
114T Jim Sundberg .60 .24
115T Rick Sutcliffe .60 .24
116T Craig Swan .40 .16
117T Tim Teufel XRC* 1.00 .40
118T Derrel Thomas .40 .16
119T Gorman Thomas .60 .24
120T Alex Trevino .40 .16
121T Manny Trillo .40 .16
122T John Tudor .60 .24
123T Tom Underwood .40 .16
124T Mike Vail .40 .16
125T Tom Waddell .40 .16
126T Gary Ward .40 .16
127T Curtis Wilkerson .40 .16
128T Frank Williams .40 .16
129T Glenn Wilson .60 .24
130T John Wockenfuss .40 .16
131T Ned Yost .40 .16
132T Checklist 1T-132T .40 .16

1984 Topps Traded Tiffany

This 132-card standard-size set was issued by Topps as a premium parallel to their regular issue. This set was printed in the Topps Ireland factory and are differentiated from the regular cards by their glossy sheen and clean backs. These sets were only available through the Topps hobby distribution system. Topps issued these sets only if a dealer ordered the regular Tiffany sets, therefore approximately 10,000 of these sets were produced as well.

Nm-Mt Ex-Mt
COMP.FACT.SET (132) 60.00 24.00
*STARS: .6X TO 1.5X BASIC CARDS..
*ROOKIES: 1X TO 2.5X BASIC CARDS

1985 Topps

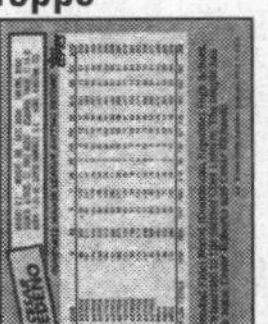

The 1985 Topps set contains 792 standard-size full-color cards. Cards were primarily distributed in 15-card wax packs, 51-card rack packs and factory (usually available through retail catalogs) sets. The wax packs were issued with an 35 cent SRP and were packaged 36 packs to a box and 20 boxes to a case. Manager cards feature the team checklist on the reverse. Full color card fronts feature both the Topps and team logos along with the team name, player's name, and his position. The first ten cards (1-10) are Record Breakers, cards 131-143 are Father and Sons, and cards 701 to 722 portray All-Star selections. Cards 271-282 represent "First Draft Picks" still active in professional baseball and cards 389-404 feature selected members of the 1984 U.S. Olympic Baseball Team. Rookie Cards include Roger Clemens, Eric Davis, Shawon Dunston, Dwight Gooden, Orel Hershiser, Jimmy Key, Mark Langston, Mark McGwire, Terry Pendleton, Kirby Puckett and Bret Saberhagen.

Nm-Mt Ex-Mt
COMPLETE SET (792) 100.00 40.00
COMP.FACT.SET (792) 150.00 60.00
1 Carlton Fisk RB .25 .10
2 Steve Garvey RB .15 .06
3 Dwight Gooden RB .60 .24
4 Cliff Johnson RB .15 .06
5 Joe Morgan RB .15 .06
6 Pete Rose RB .40 .16
7 Nolan Ryan RB 1.50 .60
8 Juan Samuel RB .15 .06
9 Bruce Sutter RB .15 .06
10 Don Sutton RB .15 .06
11 Ralph Houk MG .15 .06
12 Dave Lopes .25 .10
13 Tim Lollar .15 .06
14 Chris Bando .15 .06
15 Jerry Koosman .25 .10
16 Bobby Meacham .15 .06
17 Mike Scott .25 .10
18 Mickey Hatcher .15 .06
19 George Frazier .15 .06
20 Chet Lemon .25 .10
21 Lee Tunnell .15 .06
22 Duane Kuiper .15 .06
23 Bret Saberhagen RC 1.00 .40
24 Jesse Barfield .25 .10
25 Steve Bedrosian .15 .06
26 Roy Smalley .15 .06
27 Bruce Berenyi .15 .06
28 Dann Bilardello .15 .06
29 Odell Jones .15 .06
30 Cal Ripken 2.50 1.00
31 Terry Whitfield .15 .06
32 Chuck Porter .15 .06
33 Tito Landrum .15 .06
34 Ed Nunez .15 .06
35 Graig Nettles .25 .10
36 Fred Breining .15 .06
37 Reid Nichols .15 .06
38 Jackie Moore MG .15 .06
39 John Wockenfuss .15 .06
40 Phil Niekro .25 .10
41 Mike Fischlin .15 .06
42 Luis Sanchez .15 .06
43 Andre David .15 .06
44 Dickie Thon .15 .06
45 Greg Minton .15 .06
46 Gary Woods .15 .06
47 Dave Rozema .15 .06
48 Tony Fernandez .25 .10
49 Butch Davis .15 .06
50 John Candelaria .15 .06
51 Bob Watson .15 .06
52 Jerry Dybzinski .15 .06
53 Tom Gorman .15 .06
54 Cesar Cedeno .25 .10
55 Frank Tanana .25 .10
56 Jim Dwyer .15 .06
57 Pat Zachry .15 .06
58 Orlando Mercado .15 .06
59 Rick Waits .15 .06
60 George Hendrick .25 .10
61 Curt Kaufman .15 .06
62 Mike Ramsey .15 .06
63 Steve McCatty .15 .06
64 Mark Bailey .15 .06
65 Bill Buckner .25 .10
66 Dick Williams MG .15 .06
67 Rafael Santana .15 .06
68 Von Hayes .15 .06
69 Jim Winn .15 .06
70 Don Baylor .25 .10
71 Tim Laudner .15 .06
72 Rick Sutcliffe .25 .10
73 Rusty Kuntz .15 .06
74 Mike Krukow .15 .06
75 Willie Upshaw .15 .06
76 Alan Bannister .15 .06
77 Joe Beckwith .15 .06
78 Scott Fletcher .15 .06
79 Rick Mahler .15 .06
80 Keith Hernandez .25 .10
81 Lenn Sakata .15 .06
82 Joe Price .15 .06
83 Charlie Moore .15 .06
84 Spike Owen .15 .06
85 Mike Marshall .15 .06
86 Don Aase .15 .06
87 David Green .15 .06
88 Bryn Smith .15 .06
89 Jackie Gutierrez .15 .06
90 Rich Gossage .25 .10
91 Jeff Burroughs .15 .06
92 Paul Owens MG .15 .06
93 Don Schulze .15 .06
94 Toby Harrah .25 .10
95 Jose Cruz .25 .10
96 Johnny Ray .15 .06
97 Pete Filson .15 .06
98 Steve Lake .15 .06
99 Milt Wilcox .15 .06
100 George Brett 1.50 .60
101 Jim Acker .15 .06
102 Tommy Dunbar .15 .06
103 Randy Lerch .15 .06
104 Mike Fitzgerald .15 .06
105 Ron Kittle .15 .06
106 Pascual Perez .15 .06
107 Tom Foley .15 .06
108 Darnell Coles .15 .06
109 Gary Roenicke .15 .06
110 Alejandro Pena .15 .06
111 Doug DeCinces .15 .06
112 Tom Tellmann .15 .06
113 Tom Herr .15 .06
114 Bob James .15 .06
115 Rickey Henderson .75 .30
116 Dennis Boyd .15 .06
117 Greg Gross .15 .06
118 Eric Show .15 .06
119 Pat Corrales MG .15 .06
120 Steve Kemp .15 .06
121 Checklist: 1-132 .15 .06
122 Tom Brunansky .15 .06
123 Dave Smith .15 .06
124 Rich Hebner .15 .06
125 Kent Tekulve .15 .06
126 Ruppert Jones .15 .06
127 Mark Gubicza RC* .40 .16
128 Ernie Whitt .15 .06
129 Gene Garber .15 .06
130 Al Oliver .25 .10
131 Buddy Bell FS .25 .10
Gus Bell
132 Dale Berra FS .60 .24
Yogi Berra
133 Bob Boone FS .15 .06
Ray Boone
134 Terry Francona FS .25 .10
Tito Francona
135 Terry Kennedy FS .15 .06
Bob Kennedy
136 Jeff Kunkel FS .15 .06
Bill Kunkel

137 Vance Law FS .25 .10
Vern Law
138 Dick Schofield FS .15 .06
Dick Schofield
139 Joel Skinner FS .15 .06
Bob Skinner
140 Roy Smalley Jr. FS .15 .06
Roy Smalley
141 Mike Stenhouse FS .15 .06
Dave Stenhouse
142 Steve Trout FS .15 .06
Dizzy Trout
143 Ozzie Virgil FS .15 .06
Ossie Virgil
144 Ron Gardenhire .15 .06
145 Alvin Davis RC* .40 .16
146 Gary Redus .15 .06
147 Bill Swaggerty .15 .06
148 Steve Yeager .25 .10
149 Dickie Noles .15 .06
150 Jim Rice .25 .10
151 Moose Haas .15 .06
152 Steve Braun .15 .06
153 Frank LaCorte .15 .06
154 Angel Salazar .15 .06
155 Yogi Berra MG .60 .24
156 Craig Reynolds .15 .06
157 Tug McGraw .25 .10
158 Pat Tabler .15 .06
159 Carlos Diaz .15 .06
160 Lance Parrish .25 .10
161 Ken Schrom .15 .06
162 Benny Distefano .15 .06
163 Dennis Eckersley .40 .16
164 Jorge Orta .15 .06
165 Dusty Baker .25 .10
166 Keith Atherton .15 .06
167 Rufino Linares .15 .06
168 Garth Iorg .15 .06
169 Dan Spillner .15 .06
170 George Foster .25 .10
171 Bill Stein .15 .06
172 Jack Perconte .15 .06
173 Mike Young .15 .06
174 Rick Honeycutt .15 .06
175 Dave Parker .25 .10
176 Bill Schroeder .15 .06
177 Dave Von Ohlen .15 .06
178 Miguel Dilone .15 .06
179 Tommy John .25 .10
180 Dave Winfield .25 .10
181 Roger Clemens RC 25.00 10.00
182 Tim Flannery .15 .06
183 Larry McWilliams .15 .06
184 Carmen Castillo .15 .06
185 Al Holland .15 .06
186 Bob Lillis MG .15 .06
187 Mike Walters .15 .06
188 Greg Pryor .15 .06
189 Warren Brusstar .15 .06
190 Rusty Staub .25 .10
191 Steve Nicosia .15 .06
192 Howard Johnson .25 .10
193 Jimmy Key RC .75 .30
194 Dave Stegman .15 .06
195 Glenn Hubbard .15 .06
196 Pete O'Brien .15 .06
197 Mike Warren .15 .06
198 Eddie Milner .15 .06
199 Dennis Martinez .25 .10
200 Reggie Jackson .40 .16
201 Burt Hooton .15 .06
202 Gorman Thomas .25 .10
203 Bob McClure .15 .06
204 Art Howe .15 .06
205 Steve Rogers .25 .10
206 Phil Garner .25 .10
207 Mark Clear .15 .06
208 Champ Summers .15 .06
209 Bill Campbell .15 .06
210 Gary Matthews .25 .10
211 Clay Christiansen .15 .06
212 George Vukovich .15 .06
213 Billy Gardner MG .15 .06
214 John Tudor .25 .10
215 Bob Brenly .15 .06
216 Jerry Don Gleaton .15 .06
217 Leon Roberts .15 .06
218 Doyle Alexander .15 .06
219 Gerald Perry .15 .06
220 Fred Lynn .25 .10
221 Ron Reed .15 .06
222 Hubie Brooks .15 .06
223 Tom Hume .15 .06
224 Al Cowens .15 .06
225 Mike Boddicker .15 .06
226 Juan Beniquez .15 .06
227 Danny Darwin .15 .06
228 Dion James .15 .06
229 Dave LaPoint .15 .06
230 Gary Carter .25 .10
231 Dwayne Murphy .15 .06
232 Dave Beard .15 .06
233 Ed Jurak .15 .06
234 Jerry Narron .15 .06
235 Garry Maddox .15 .06
236 Mark Thurmond .15 .06
237 Julio Franco .25 .10
238 Jose Rijo RC .75 .30
239 Tim Teufel .15 .06
240 Dave Stieb .25 .10
241 Jim Frey MG .15 .06
242 Greg Harris .15 .06
243 Barbaro Garbey .15 .06
244 Mike Jones .15 .06
245 Chili Davis .25 .10
246 Mike Norris .15 .06
247 Wayne Tolleson .15 .06
248 Terry Forster .25 .10
249 Harold Baines .25 .10
250 Jesse Orosco .15 .06
251 Brad Gulden .15 .06
252 Dan Ford .15 .06
253 Sid Bream RC .40 .16
254 Pete Vuckovich .15 .06
255 Lonnie Smith .15 .06
256 Mike Stanton .15 .06
257 Bryan Little UER .15 .06
Name spelled Brian on front
258 Mike C. Brown .15 .06
259 Gary Allenson .15 .06
260 Dave Righetti .25 .10
261 Checklist: 133-264 .15 .06
262 Greg Booker .15 .06
263 Mel Hall .15 .06
264 Joe Sambito .15 .06
265 Juan Samuel .15 .06
266 Frank Viola .25 .10
267 Henry Cotto RC .15 .06
268 Chuck Tanner MG .15 .06
269 Doug Baker .15 .06
270 Dan Quisenberry .15 .06
271 Tim Foli FDP .15 .06
272 Jeff Burroughs FDP .15 .06
273 Bill Almon FDP .15 .06
274 F.Bannister FDP76 .15 .06
275 Harold Baines FDP77 .15 .06
276 Bob Horner FDP .15 .06
277 Al Chambers FDP .15 .06
278 Darryl Strawberry .40 .16
FDP80
279 Mike Moore FDP .15 .06
280 S.Dunston FDP82 RC .75 .30
281 T.Belcher RC FDP83 .40 .16
282 Shawn Abner FDP RC .15 .06
283 Fran Mullins .15 .06
284 Marty Bystrom .15 .06
285 Dan Driessen .15 .06
286 Rudy Law .15 .06
287 Walt Terrell .15 .06
288 Jeff Kunkel .15 .06
289 Tom Underwood .15 .06
290 Cecil Cooper .25 .10
291 Bob Welch .25 .10
292 Brad Komminsk .15 .06
293 Curt Young .15 .06
294 Tom Nieto .15 .06
295 Joe Niekro .15 .06
296 Ricky Nelson .15 .06
297 Gary Lucas .15 .06
298 Marty Barrett .15 .06
299 Andy Hawkins .15 .06
300 Rod Carew .40 .16
301 John Montefusco .15 .06
302 Tim Corcoran .15 .06
303 Mike Jeffcoat .15 .06
304 Gary Gaetti .25 .10
305 Dale Berra .15 .06
306 Rick Reuschel .25 .10
307 Sparky Anderson MG .25 .10
308 John Wathan .15 .06
309 Mike Witt .15 .06
310 Manny Trillo .15 .06
311 Jim Gott .15 .06
312 Marc Hill .15 .06
313 Dave Schmidt .15 .06
314 Ron Oester .15 .06
315 Doug Sisk .15 .06
316 John Lowenstein .15 .06
317 Jack Lazorko .15 .06
318 Ted Simmons .25 .10
319 Jeff Jones .15 .06
320 Dale Murphy .40 .16
321 Ricky Horton .15 .06
322 Dave Stapleton .15 .06
323 Andy McGaffigan .15 .06
324 Bruce Bochy .15 .06
325 John Denny .15 .06
326 Kevin Bass .15 .06
327 Brook Jacoby .15 .06
328 Bob Shirley .15 .06
329 Ron Washington .15 .06
330 Leon Durham .15 .06
331 Bill Laskey .15 .06
332 Brian Harper .15 .06
333 Willie Hernandez .15 .06
334 Dick Howser MG .15 .06
335 Bruce Benedict .15 .06
336 Rance Mulliniks .15 .06
337 Billy Sample .15 .06
338 Britt Burns .15 .06
339 Danny Heep .15 .06
340 Robin Yount 1.00 .40
341 Floyd Rayford .15 .06
342 Ted Power .15 .06
343 Bill Russell .25 .10
344 Dave Henderson .15 .06
345 Charlie Lea .15 .06
346 Terry Pendleton RC .75 .30
347 Rick Langford .15 .06
348 Bob Boone .25 .10
349 Domingo Ramos .15 .06
350 Wade Boggs .60 .24
351 Juan Agosto .15 .06
352 Joe Morgan .25 .10
353 Julio Solano .15 .06
354 Andre Robertson .15 .06
355 Bert Blyleven .25 .10
356 Dave Meier .15 .06
357 Rich Bordi .15 .06
358 Tony Pena .15 .06
359 Pat Sheridan .15 .06
360 Steve Carlton .25 .10
361 Alfredo Griffin .15 .06
362 Craig McMurtry .15 .06
363 Ron Hodges .15 .06
364 Richard Dotson .15 .06
365 Danny Ozark MG .15 .06
366 Todd Cruz .15 .06
367 Keefe Cato .15 .06
368 Dave Bergman .15 .06
369 R.J. Reynolds .15 .06
370 Bruce Sutter .25 .10
371 Mickey Rivers .15 .06
372 Roy Howell .15 .06
373 Mike Moore .15 .06
374 Brian Downing .25 .10
375 Jeff Reardon .25 .10
376 Jeff Newman .15 .06
377 Checklist: 265-396 .15 .06
378 Alan Wiggins .15 .06
379 Charles Hudson .15 .06
380 Ken Griffey .25 .10
381 Roy Smith .15 .06
382 Denny Walling .15 .06
383 Rick Lysander .15 .06
384 Jody Davis .15 .06
385 Jose DeLeon .15 .06
386 Dan Gladden RC .40 .16
387 Buddy Biancalana .15 .06
388 Bert Roberge .15 .06
389 Rod Dedeaux OLY CO .25 .10
390 Sid Akins OLY RC .15 .06
391 Flavio Alfaro OLY RC .15 .06
392 Don August OLY RC .15 .06
393 S.Bankhead RC OLY .15 .06
394 Bob Caffrey OLY RC .15 .06
395 Mike Dunne OLY RC .15 .06
396 Gary Green OLY RC .15 .06
397 John Hoover OLY RC .15 .06
398 Shane Mack RC OLY .40 .16
399 John Marzano OLY RC .15 .06
400 O.McDowell RC OLY .40 .16
401 M.McGwire OLY RC 40.00 16.00
402 Pat Pacillo OLY RC .15 .06
403 Cory Snyder OLY RC .75 .30
404 Billy Swift OLY RC .40 .16
405 Tom Veryzer .15 .06
406 Len Whitehouse .15 .06
407 Bobby Ramos .15 .06
408 Sid Monge .15 .06
409 Brad Wellman .15 .06
410 Bob Horner .25 .10
411 Bobby Cox MG .25 .10
412 Bud Black .15 .06
413 Vance Law .15 .06
414 Gary Ward .15 .06
415 Ron Darling UER .25 .10
(No trivia answer)
416 Wayne Gross .15 .06
417 John Franco RC .75 .30
418 Ken Landreaux .15 .06
419 Mike Caldwell .15 .06
420 Andre Dawson .25 .10
421 Dave Rucker .15 .06
422 Carney Lansford .25 .10
423 Barry Bonnell .15 .06
424 Al Nipper .15 .06
425 Mike Hargrove .15 .06
426 Vern Ruhle .15 .06
427 Mario Ramirez .15 .06
428 Larry Andersen .15 .06
429 Rick Cerone .15 .06
430 Ron Davis .15 .06
431 U.L. Washington .15 .06
432 Thad Bosley .15 .06
433 Jim Morrison .15 .06
434 Gene Richards .15 .06
435 Dan Petry .15 .06
436 Willie Aikens .15 .06
437 Al Jones .15 .06
438 Joe Torre MG .40 .16
439 Junior Ortiz .15 .06
440 Fernando Valenzuela .25 .10
441 Duane Walker .15 .06
442 Ken Forsch .15 .06
443 George Wright .15 .06
444 Tony Phillips .15 .06
445 Tippy Martinez .15 .06
446 Jim Sundberg .25 .10
447 Jeff Lahti .15 .06
448 Derrel Thomas .15 .06
449 Phil Bradley .40 .16
450 Steve Garvey .25 .10
451 Bruce Hurst .15 .06
452 John Castino .15 .06
453 Tom Waddell .15 .06
454 Glenn Wilson .15 .06
455 Bob Knepper .15 .06
456 Tim Foli .15 .06
457 Cecilio Guante .15 .06
458 Randy Johnson .15 .06
459 Charlie Leibrandt .15 .06
460 Ryne Sandberg 1.25 .50
461 Marty Castillo .15 .06
462 Gary Lavelle .15 .06
463 Dave Collins .15 .06
464 Mike Mason RC .15 .06
465 Bobby Grich .25 .10
466 Tony LaRussa MG .25 .10
467 Ed Lynch .15 .06
468 Wayne Krenchicki .15 .06
469 Sammy Stewart .15 .06
470 Steve Sax .15 .06
471 Pete Ladd .15 .06
472 Jim Essian .15 .06
473 Tim Wallach .15 .06
474 Kurt Kepshire .15 .06
475 Andre Thornton .15 .06
476 Jeff Stone .15 .06
477 Bob Ojeda .15 .06
478 Kurt Bevacqua .15 .06
479 Mike Madden .15 .06
480 Lou Whitaker .25 .10
481 Dale Murray .15 .06
482 Harry Spilman .15 .06
483 Mike Smithson .15 .06
484 Larry Bowa .25 .10
485 Matt Young .15 .06
486 Steve Balboni .15 .06
487 Frank Williams .15 .06
488 Joel Skinner .15 .06
489 Bryan Clark .15 .06
490 Jason Thompson .15 .06
491 Rick Camp .15 .06
492 Dave Johnson MG .15 .06
493 Orel Hershiser RC 1.00 .40
494 Rich Dauer .15 .06
495 Mario Soto .25 .10
496 Donnie Scott .15 .06
497 Gary Pettis UER .15 .06
(Photo actually
Gary's little
brother Lynn)
498 Ed Romero .15 .06
499 Danny Cox .15 .06
500 Mike Schmidt 1.50 .60
501 Dan Schatzeder .15 .06
502 Rick Miller .15 .06
503 Tim Conroy .15 .06
504 Jerry Willard .15 .06
505 Jim Beattie .15 .06
506 Franklin Stubbs .15 .06
507 Ray Fontenot .15 .06
508 John Shelby .15 .06
509 Milt May .15 .06
510 Kent Hrbek .25 .10
511 Lee Smith .25 .10
512 Tom Brookens .15 .06
513 Lynn Jones .15 .06
514 Jeff Cornell .15 .06
515 Dave Concepcion .25 .10
516 Roy Lee Jackson .15 .06
517 Jerry Martin .15 .06
518 Chris Chambliss .25 .10
519 Doug Rader MG .15 .06
520 LaMarr Hoyt .15 .06
521 Rick Dempsey .15 .06
522 Paul Molitor .40 .16
523 Candy Maldonado .15 .06
524 Rob Wilfong .15 .06
525 Darrell Porter .15 .06
526 David Palmer .15 .06
527 Checklist: 397-528 .15 .06
528 Bill Krueger .15 .06
529 Rich Gedman .15 .06
530 Dave Dravecky .15 .06
531 Joe Lefebvre .15 .06
532 Frank DiPino .15 .06
533 Tony Bernazard .15 .06
534 Brian Dayett .15 .06
535 Pat Putnam .15 .06
536 Kirby Puckett RC 5.00 2.00
537 Don Robinson .15 .06
538 Keith Moreland .15 .06
539 Aurelio Lopez .15 .06
540 Claudell Washington .15 .06
541 Mark Davis .15 .06
542 Don Slaught .15 .06
543 Mike Squires .15 .06
544 Bruce Kison .15 .06
545 Lloyd Moseby .15 .06
546 Brent Gaff .15 .06
547 Pete Rose MG .40 .16
548 Larry Parrish .15 .06
549 Mike Scioscia .25 .10
550 Scott McGregor .15 .06
551 Andy Van Slyke .25 .10
552 Chris Codiroli .15 .06
553 Bob Clark .15 .06
554 Doug Flynn .15 .06
555 Bob Stanley .15 .06
556 Sixto Lezcano .15 .06
557 Len Barker .15 .06
558 Carmelo Martinez .15 .06
559 Jay Howell .15 .06
560 Bill Madlock .25 .10
561 Darryl Motley .15 .06
562 Houston Jimenez .15 .06
563 Dick Ruthven .15 .06
564 Alan Ashby .15 .06
565 Kirk Gibson .25 .10
566 Ed VandeBerg .15 .06
567 Joel Youngblood .15 .06
568 Cliff Johnson .15 .06
569 Ken Oberkfell .15 .06
570 Darryl Strawberry .60 .24
571 Charlie Hough .25 .10
572 Tom Paciorek .15 .06
573 Jay Tibbs .15 .06
574 Joe Altobelli MG .15 .06
575 Pedro Guerrero .25 .10
576 Jaime Cocanower .15 .06
577 Chris Speier .15 .06
578 Terry Francona .25 .10
579 Ron Romanick .15 .06
580 Dwight Evans .25 .10
581 Mark Wagner .15 .06
582 Ken Phelps .15 .06
583 Bobby Brown .15 .06
584 Kevin Gross .15 .06
585 Butch Wynegar .15 .06
586 Bill Scherrer .15 .06
587 Doug Frobel .15 .06
588 Bobby Castillo .15 .06
589 Bob Dernier .15 .06
590 Ray Knight .25 .10
591 Larry Herndon .25 .10
592 Jeff D. Robinson .15 .06
593 Rick Leach .15 .06
594 Curt Wilkerson .15 .06
595 Larry Gura .15 .06
596 Jerry Hairston .15 .06
597 Brad Lesley .15 .06
598 Jose Oquendo .15 .06
599 Storm Davis .15 .06
600 Pete Rose 1.50 .60
601 Tom Lasorda MG .40 .16
602 Jeff Dedmon .15 .06
603 Rick Manning .15 .06
604 Daryl Sconiers .15 .06
605 Ozzie Smith 1.00 .40
606 Rich Gale .15 .06
607 Bill Almon .15 .06
608 Craig Lefferts .15 .06
609 Broderick Perkins .15 .06
610 Jack Morris .25 .10
611 Ozzie Virgil .15 .06
612 Mike Armstrong .15 .06
613 Terry Puhl .15 .06
614 Al Williams .15 .06
615 Marvell Wynne .15 .06
616 Scott Sanderson .15 .06
617 Willie Wilson .25 .10
618 Pete Falcone .15 .06
619 Jeff Leonard .15 .06
620 Dwight Gooden RC 1.25 .50
621 Marvis Foley .15 .06
622 Luis Leal .15 .06
623 Greg Walker .15 .06
624 Benny Ayala .15 .06
625 Mark Langston RC .75 .30
626 German Rivera .15 .06
627 Eric Davis RC 1.00 .40
628 Rene Lachemann MG .15 .06
629 Dick Schofield .15 .06
630 Tim Raines .25 .10
631 Bob Forsch .15 .06
632 Bruce Bochte .15 .06
633 Glenn Hoffman .15 .06
634 Bill Dawley .15 .06
635 Terry Kennedy .15 .06
636 Shane Rawley .15 .06
637 Brett Butler .25 .10
638 Mike Pagliarulo .15 .06
639 Ed Hodge .15 .06
640 Steve Henderson .15 .06
641 Rod Scurry .15 .06
642 Dave Owen .15 .06
643 Johnny Grubb .15 .06
644 Mark Huismann .15 .06
645 Damaso Garcia .15 .06
646 Scot Thompson .15 .06
647 Rafael Ramirez .15 .06
648 Bob Jones .15 .06
649 Sid Fernandez .25 .10
650 Greg Luzinski .25 .10
651 Jeff Russell .15 .06
652 Joe Nolan .15 .06
653 Mark Brouhard .15 .06
654 Dave Anderson .15 .06
655 Joaquin Andujar .25 .10
656 Chuck Cottier MG .15 .06
657 Jim Slaton .15 .06
658 Mike Stenhouse .15 .06
659 Checklist: 529-660 .15 .06
660 Tony Gwynn 1.25 .50
661 Steve Crawford .15 .06
662 Mike Heath .15 .06
663 Luis Aguayo .15 .06
664 Steve Farr RC .40 .16
665 Don Mattingly 2.50 1.00
666 Mike LaCoss .15 .06
667 Dave Engle .15 .06
668 Steve Trout .15 .06
669 Lee Lacy .15 .06
670 Tom Seaver .40 .16
671 Dane Iorg .15 .06
672 Juan Berenguer .15 .06
673 Buck Martinez .15 .06
674 Atlee Hammaker .15 .06
675 Tony Perez .40 .16
676 Albert Hall .15 .06
677 Wally Backman .15 .06
678 Joey McLaughlin .15 .06
679 Bob Kearney .15 .06
680 Jerry Reuss .15 .06
681 Ben Oglivie .25 .10
682 Doug Corbett .15 .06
683 Whitey Herzog MG .25 .10
684 Bill Doran .15 .06
685 Bill Caudill .15 .06
686 Mike Easler .15 .06
687 Bill Gullickson .15 .06
688 Len Matuszek .15 .06
689 Luis DeLeon .15 .06
690 Alan Trammell .25 .10
691 Dennis Rasmussen .15 .06
692 Randy Bush .15 .06
693 Tim Stoddard .15 .06
694 Joe Carter .60 .24
695 Rick Rhoden .15 .06
696 John Rabb .15 .06
697 Onix Concepcion .15 .06
698 Jorge Bell .25 .10
699 Donnie Moore .15 .06
700 Eddie Murray .60 .24
701 Eddie Murray AS .40 .16
702 Damaso Garcia AS .15 .06
703 George Brett AS .60 .24
704 Cal Ripken AS 1.50 .60
705 Dave Winfield AS .15 .06
706 Rickey Henderson AS .40 .16
707 Tony Armas AS .15 .06
708 Lance Parrish AS .15 .06
709 Mike Boddicker AS .15 .06
710 Frank Viola AS .15 .06
711 Dan Quisenberry AS .15 .06
712 Keith Hernandez AS .15 .06
713 Ryne Sandberg AS .60 .24
714 Mike Schmidt AS .60 .24
715 Ozzie Smith AS .60 .24
716 Dale Murphy AS .25 .10
717 Tony Gwynn AS 1.00 .40
718 Jeff Leonard AS .15 .06
719 Gary Carter AS .15 .06
720 Rick Sutcliffe AS .15 .06
721 Bob Knepper AS .15 .06
722 Bruce Sutter AS .15 .06
723 Dave Stewart .25 .10
724 Oscar Gamble .15 .06
725 Floyd Bannister .15 .06
726 Al Bumbry .15 .06
727 Frank Pastore .15 .06
728 Bob Bailor .15 .06
729 Don Sutton .25 .10
730 Dave Kingman .25 .10
731 Neil Allen .15 .06
732 John McNamara MG .15 .06
733 Tony Scott .15 .06
734 John Henry Johnson .15 .06
735 Garry Templeton .25 .10
736 Jerry Mumphrey .15 .06
737 Bo Diaz .15 .06
738 Omar Moreno .15 .06
739 Ernie Camacho .15 .06
740 Jack Clark .25 .10
741 John Butcher .15 .06
742 Ron Hassey .15 .06
743 Frank White .25 .10
744 Doug Bair .15 .06
745 Buddy Bell .25 .10
746 Jim Clancy .15 .06
747 Alex Trevino .15 .06
748 Lee Mazzilli .25 .10
749 Julio Cruz .15 .06
750 Rollie Fingers .25 .10
751 Kelvin Chapman .15 .06
752 Bob Owchinko .15 .06
753 Greg Brock .15 .06
754 Larry Milbourne .15 .06
755 Ken Singleton .25 .10
756 Rob Picciolo .15 .06
757 Willie McGee .25 .10
758 Ray Burris .15 .06
759 Jim Fanning MG .15 .06
760 Nolan Ryan 3.00 1.20
761 Jerry Remy .15 .06
762 Eddie Whitson .15 .06
763 Kiko Garcia .15 .06
764 Jamie Easterly .15 .06
765 Willie Randolph .25 .10
766 Paul Mirabella .15 .06
767 Darrell Brown .15 .06
768 Ron Cey .25 .10
769 Joe Cowley .15 .06
770 Carlton Fisk .40 .16
771 Geoff Zahn .15 .06
772 Johnnie LeMaster .15 .06
773 Hal McRae .25 .10

774 Dennis Lamp .15 .06
775 Mookie Wilson .25 .10
776 Jerry Royster .15 .06
777 Ned Yost .15 .06
778 Mike Davis .15 .06
779 Nick Esasky .15 .06
780 Mike Flanagan .15 .06
781 Jim Gantner .15 .06
782 Tom Niedenfuer .15 .06
783 Mike Jorgensen .15 .06
784 Checklist: 661-792 .15 .06
785 Tony Armas .25 .10
786 Enos Cabell .15 .06
787 Jim Wohlford .15 .06
788 Steve Comer .15 .06
789 Luis Salazar .15 .06
790 Ron Guidry .25 .10
791 Ivan DeJesus .15 .06
792 Darrell Evans .25 .10

1985 Topps Tiffany

For the second year, Topps issued a special glossy set through their hobby dealers. This set is a direct parallel to the regular Topps issue. These 792 cards are differentiated from the regular issue by their glossy fronts and very clear backs. These sets were only available through Topps' hobby dealers. According to original reports in 1985, only 5,000 of these sets were produced.

Nm-Mt Ex-Mt
COMP.FACT.SET (792) 600.00 240.00
*STARS: 3X TO 8X BASIC CARDS
*ROOKIES: 2.5X TO 6X BASIC CARDS

1985 Topps Glossy All-Stars

The cards in this 22-card set the standard size. Similar in design, both front and back, to last year's Glossy set, this edition features the managers, starting nine players and honorary captains of the National and American League teams in the 1984 All-Star game. The set is numbered on the reverse with players essentially ordered by position within league, NL: 1-11 and AL: 12-22.

Nm-Mt Ex-Mt
COMPLETE SET (22) 5.00 2.00
1 Paul Owens MG .05 .02
2 Steve Garvey .15 .06
3 Ryne Sandberg 1.00 .40
4 Mike Schmidt .75 .30
5 Ozzie Smith 1.00 .40
6 Tony Gwynn 1.25 .50
7 Dale Murphy .20 .08
8 Darryl Strawberry .10 .04
9 Gary Carter .50 .20
10 Charlie Lea .05 .02
11 Willie McCovey CAPT .10 .04
12 Joe Altobelli MG .05 .02
13 Rod Carew .50 .20
14 Lou Whitaker .10 .04
15 George Brett 1.00 .40
16 Cal Ripken 2.00 .80
17 Dave Winfield .50 .20
18 Chet Lemon .05 .02
19 Reggie Jackson .50 .20
20 Lance Parrish .05 .02
21 Dave Stieb .05 .02
22 Hank Greenberg CAPT .10 .04

1985 Topps Glossy Send-Ins

The cards in this 40-card set measure the standard size. Similar to last year's glossy set, this set was issued as a bonus prize to Topps All-Star Baseball Game cards found in wax packs. The set could be obtained by sending in the "Bonus Runs" from the "Winning Pitch" game insert cards. For 25 runs and 75 cents, a collector could send in for one of the eight different five card series plus automatically be entered in the Grand Prize Sweepstakes for a chance at a free trip to the All-Star game. The cards are numbered and contain 20 stars from each league.

Nm-Mt Ex-Mt
COMPLETE SET (40) 10.00 4.00
1 Dale Murphy .30 .12
2 Jesse Orosco .20 .08
3 Bob Brenly .20 .08
4 Mike Boddicker .10 .04
5 Dave Kingman .20 .08
6 Jim Rice .20 .08
7 Frank Viola .20 .08
8 Alvin Davis .10 .04
9 Rick Sutcliffe .10 .04
10 Pete Rose 1.25 .50
11 Leon Durham .10 .04
12 Joaquin Andujar .10 .04
13 Keith Hernandez .20 .08
14 Dave Winfield .75 .30
15 Reggie Jackson .75 .30
16 Alan Trammell .30 .12
17 Bert Blyleven .20 .08
18 Tony Armas .10 .04
19 Rich Gossage .20 .08
20 Jose Cruz .20 .08
21 Ryne Sandberg 2.00 .80
22 Bruce Sutter .20 .08
23 Mike Schmidt 1.25 .50
24 Cal Ripken 5.00 2.00
25 Dan Petry .10 .04
26 Jack Morris .20 .08
27 Don Mattingly 2.50 1.00
28 Eddie Murray 1.00 .40
29 Tony Gwynn 2.50 1.00
30 Charlie Lea .10 .04
31 Juan Samuel .10 .04
32 Phil Niekro .75 .30
33 Alejandro Pena .10 .04
34 Harold Baines .20 .08
35 Dan Quisenberry .10 .04
36 Gary Carter .75 .30
37 Mario Soto .10 .04
38 Dwight Gooden .50 .20
39 Tom Brunansky .10 .04
40 Dave Stieb .10 .04

1985 Topps Traded

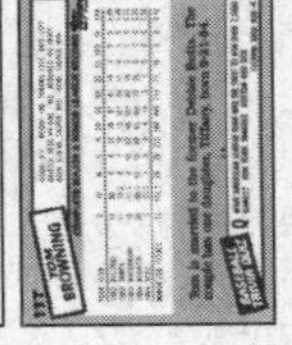

In its now standard procedure, Topps issued its standard-size Traded (or extended) set for the fifth year in a row. In addition to the typical factory set hobby distribution, Topps tested the limited issuance of these Traded cards in wax packs. Card design is identical to the regular-issue 1985 Topps set except for whiter card stock and T-suffixed numbering on back. The set numbering is in alphabetical order by player's name. The key extended Rookie Cards in this set include Vince Coleman, Ozzie Guillen, and Mickey Tettleton.

Nm-Mt Ex-Mt
COMP.FACT.SET (132) 6.00 2.40
1T Don Aase .15 .06
2T Bill Almon .15 .06
3T Benny Ayala .15 .06
4T Dusty Baker .40 .16
5T George Bamberger MG .15 .06
6T Dale Berra .15 .06
7T Rich Bordi .15 .06
8T Daryl Boston XRC* .25 .10
9T Hubie Brooks .15 .06
10T Chris Brown .25 .10
11T Tom Browning XRC* .50 .20
12T Al Bumbry .15 .06
13T Ray Burris .15 .06
14T Jeff Burroughs .15 .06
15T Bill Campbell .15 .06
16T Don Carman .15 .06
17T Gary Carter .40 .16
18T Bobby Castillo .15 .06
19T Bill Caudill .15 .06
20T Rick Cerone .15 .06
21T Bryan Clark .15 .06
22T Jack Clark .40 .16
23T Pat Clements .15 .06
24T Vince Coleman XRC 1.00 .40
25T Dave Collins .15 .06
26T Danny Darwin .15 .06
27T Jim Davenport MG .15 .06
28T Jerry Davis .15 .06
29T Brian Dayett .15 .06
30T Ivan DeJesus .15 .06
31T Ken Dixon .15 .06
32T Mariano Duncan XRC .50 .20
33T John Felske MG .15 .06
34T Mike Fitzgerald .15 .06
35T Ray Fontenot .15 .06
36T Greg Gagne XRC* .50 .20
37T Oscar Gamble .15 .06
38T Scott Garrelts .15 .06
39T Bob L. Gibson .15 .06
40T Jim Gott .15 .06
41T David Green .15 .06
42T Alfredo Griffin .15 .06
43T Ozzie Guillen XRC .50 .20
44T Eddie Haas MG .15 .06
45T Terry Harper .15 .06
46T Toby Harrah .40 .16
47T Greg Harris .15 .06
48T Ron Hassey .15 .06
49T Rickey Henderson 2.50 1.00
50T Steve Henderson .15 .06
51T George Hendrick .40 .16
52T Joe Hesketh .15 .06
53T Teddy Higuera XRC .50 .20
54T Donnie Hill .15 .06
55T Al Holland .15 .06
56T Burt Hooton .15 .06
57T Jay Howell .15 .06
58T Ken Howell .15 .06
59T LaMarr Hoyt .15 .06
60T Tim Hulett XRC* .25 .10
61T Bob James .15 .06
62T Steve Jeltz XRC .25 .10
63T Cliff Johnson .15 .06
64T Howard Johnson .40 .16
65T Ruppert Jones .15 .06
66T Steve Kemp .15 .06
67T Bruce Kison .15 .06
68T Alan Knicely .15 .06
69T Mike LaCoss .15 .06
70T Lee Lacy .15 .06
71T Dave LaPoint .15 .06
72T Gary Lavelle .15 .06
73T Vance Law .15 .06
74T Johnnie LeMaster .15 .06
75T Sixto Lezcano .15 .06
76T Tim Lollar .15 .06
77T Fred Lynn .40 .16
78T Billy Martin MG .75 .30
79T Ron Mathis .15 .06
80T Len Matuszek .15 .06
81T Gene Mauch MG .15 .06
82T Oddibe McDowell .50 .20
83T Roger McDowell XRC .50 .20
84T John McNamara MG .15 .06
85T Donnie Moore .15 .06
86T Gene Nelson .15 .06
87T Steve Nicosia .15 .06
88T Al Oliver .40 .16
89T Joe Orsulak XRC .50 .20
90T Rob Picciolo .15 .06
91T Chris Pittaro .15 .06
92T Jim Presley .50 .20
93T Rick Reuschel .40 .16
94T Bert Roberge .15 .06
95T Bob Rodgers MG .15 .06
96T Jerry Royster .15 .06
97T Dave Rozema .15 .06
98T Dave Rucker .15 .06
99T Vern Ruhle .15 .06
100T Paul Runge XRC .25 .10
101T Mark Salas .15 .06
102T Luis Salazar .15 .06
103T Joe Sambito .15 .06
104T Rick Schu .15 .06
105T Donnie Scott .15 .06
106T Larry Sheets XRC .25 .10
107T Don Slaught .15 .06
108T Roy Smalley .15 .06
109T Lonnie Smith .15 .06
110T Nate Snell UER .15 .06
(Headings on back for a batter)
111T Chris Speier .15 .06
112T Mike Stenhouse .15 .06
113T Tim Stoddard .15 .06
114T Jim Sundberg .40 .16
115T Bruce Sutter .40 .16
116T Don Sutton .40 .16
117T Kent Tekulve .15 .06
118T Tom Tellmann .15 .06
119T Walt Terrell .15 .06
120T M.Tettleton XRC .50 .20
121T Derrel Thomas .15 .06
122T Rich Thompson .15 .06
123T Alex Trevino .15 .06
124T John Tudor .40 .16
125T Jose Uribe .15 .06
126T Bobby Valentine MG .40 .16
127T Dave Von Ohlen .15 .06
128T U.L. Washington .15 .06
129T Earl Weaver MG .40 .16
130T Eddie Whitson .15 .06
131T Herm Winningham .15 .06
132T Checklist 1-132 .15 .06

1985 Topps Traded Tiffany

Just as in 1984, Topps issued an glossy update set. The 132-card standard-size set is a parallel to the Topps update issue. These sets were issued to the hobby through Topps dealer network and were printed in Ireland. Again -- similar to the regular Tiffany issue -- it is believed that 5,000 of these sets were produced.

Nm-Mt Ex-Mt
COMP.FACT.SET (132) 50.00 20.00
*STARS: 1.5X TO 4X BASIC CARDS
*ROOKIES: 1.5X TO 4X BASIC CARDS

1986 Topps

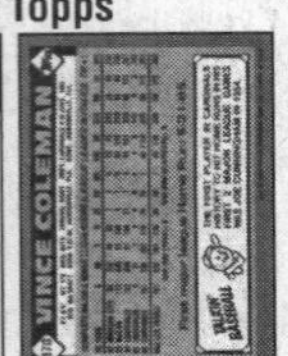

This set consists of 792 standard-size cards. Cards were primarily distributed in 15-card wax packs, 48-card rack packs and factors sets. This was also the first year Topps offered a factory set to hobby dealers. Standard card fronts feature a black and white split border framing a color photo with team name on top and player name on bottom. Subsets include Pete Rose tribute (1-7), Record Breakers (201-207), Turn Back the Clock (401-405), All-Stars (701-722) and Team Leaders (seeded throughout the set). Manager cards feature the team checklist on the reverse. There are two uncorrected errors involving misnumbered cards; see card numbers 51, 57, 141, and 171 in the checklist below. The key Rookie Cards in this set are Darren Daulton, Len Dykstra, Cecil Fielder, and Mickey Tettleton.

Nm-Mt Ex-Mt
COMPLETE SET (792) 25.00 10.00
COMP.X-MAS.SET (792) 120.00 47.50
1 Pete Rose 2.00 .80
2 Pete Rose 63-66 .25 .10
3 Pete Rose 67-70 .25 .10
4 Pete Rose 71-74 .25 .10
5 Pete Rose 75-78 .25 .10
6 Pete Rose 79-82 .25 .10
7 Pete Rose 83-85 .25 .10
8 Dwayne Murphy .10 .04
9 Roy Smith .10 .04
10 Tony Gwynn .60 .24
11 Bob Ojeda .10 .04
12 Jose Uribe .10 .04
13 Bob Kearney .10 .04
14 Julio Cruz .10 .04
15 Eddie Whitson .10 .04
16 Rick Schu .10 .04
17 Mike Stenhouse .10 .04
18 Brent Gaff .10 .04
19 Rich Hebner .10 .04
20 Lou Whitaker .15 .06
21 George Bamberger MG .10 .04
22 Duane Walker .10 .04
23 Manny Lee RC* .10 .04
24 Len Barker .10 .04
25 Willie Wilson .15 .06
26 Frank DiPino .10 .04
27 Ray Knight .15 .06
28 Eric Davis .25 .10
29 Tony Phillips .10 .04
30 Eddie Murray .40 .16
31 Jamie Easterly .10 .04
32 Steve Yeager .15 .06
33 Jeff Lahti .10 .04
34 Ken Phelps .10 .04
35 Jeff Reardon .15 .06
36 Lance Parrish TL .15 .06
37 Mark Thurmond .10 .04
38 Glenn Hoffman .10 .04
39 Dave Rucker .10 .04
40 Ken Griffey .15 .06
41 Brad Wellman .10 .04
42 Geoff Zahn .10 .04
43 Dave Engle .10 .04
44 Lance McCullers .10 .04
45 Damaso Garcia .10 .04
46 Billy Hatcher .10 .04
47 Juan Berenguer .10 .04
48 Bill Almon .10 .04
49 Rick Manning .10 .04
50 Dan Quisenberry .10 .04
51 Bobby Wine MG ERR .10 .04
Number of card on back is actually 57)
52 Chris Welsh .10 .04
53 Len Dykstra RC .75 .30
54 John Franco .15 .06
55 Fred Lynn .15 .06
56 Tom Niedenfuer .10 .04
57 Bill Doran .10 .04
(See also 51)
58 Bill Krueger .10 .04
59 Andre Thornton .10 .04
60 Dwight Evans .15 .06
61 Karl Best .10 .04
62 Bob Boone .15 .06
63 Ron Roenicke .10 .04
64 Floyd Bannister .10 .04
65 Dan Driessen .10 .04
66 Bob Forsch TL .10 .04
67 Carmelo Martinez .10 .04
68 Ed Lynch .10 .04
69 Luis Aguayo .10 .04
70 Dave Winfield .15 .06
71 Ken Schrom .10 .04
72 Shawon Dunston .15 .06
73 Randy O'Neal .10 .04
74 Rance Mulliniks .10 .04
75 Jose DeLeon .10 .04
76 Dion James .10 .04
77 Charlie Leibrandt .10 .04
78 Bruce Benedict .10 .04
79 Dave Schmidt .10 .04
80 Darryl Strawberry .25 .10
81 Gene Mauch MG .10 .04
82 Tippy Martinez .10 .04
83 Phil Garner .15 .06
84 Curt Young .10 .04
85 Tony Perez .15 .06
(Eric Davis also shown on card)
86 Tom Waddell .10 .04
87 Candy Maldonado .10 .04
88 Tom Nieto .10 .04
89 Randy St.Claire .10 .04
90 Garry Templeton .15 .06
91 Steve Crawford .10 .04
92 Al Cowens .10 .04
93 Scot Thompson .10 .04
94 Rich Bordi .10 .04
95 Ozzie Virgil .10 .04
96 Jim Clancy TL .10 .04
97 Gary Gaetti .15 .06
98 Dick Ruthven .10 .04
99 Buddy Biancalana .10 .04
100 Nolan Ryan 2.00 .80
101 Dave Bergman .10 .04
102 Joe Orsulak RC* .25 .10
103 Luis Salazar .10 .04
104 Sid Fernandez .10 .04
105 Gary Ward .10 .04
106 Ray Burris .10 .04
107 Rafael Ramirez .10 .04
108 Ted Power .10 .04
109 Len Matuszek .10 .04
110 Scott McGregor .10 .04
111 Roger Craig MG .15 .06
112 Bill Campbell .10 .04
113 U.L. Washington .10 .04
114 Mike C. Brown .10 .04
115 Jay Howell .10 .04
116 Brook Jacoby .10 .04
117 Bruce Kison .10 .04
118 Jerry Royster .10 .04
119 Barry Bonnell .10 .04
120 Steve Carlton .15 .06
121 Nelson Simmons .10 .04
122 Pete Filson .10 .04
123 Greg Walker .10 .04
124 Luis Sanchez .10 .04
125 Dave Lopes .15 .06
126 Mookie Wilson TL .10 .04
127 Jack Howell .10 .04
128 John Wathan .10 .04
129 Jeff Dedmon .10 .04
130 Alan Trammell .15 .06
131 Checklist: 1-132 .15 .06
132 Razor Shines .10 .04
133 Andy McGaffigan .10 .04
134 Carney Lansford .15 .06
135 Joe Niekro .10 .04
136 Mike Hargrove .10 .04
137 Charlie Moore .10 .04
138 Mark Davis .10 .04
139 Daryl Boston .10 .04
140 John Candelaria .10 .04
141 Chuck Cottier MG .10 .04
See also 171
142 Bob Jones .10 .04
143 Dave Van Gorder .10 .04
144 Doug Sisk .10 .04
145 Pedro Guerrero .15 .06
146 Jack Perconte .10 .04
147 Larry Sheets .10 .04
148 Mike Heath .10 .04
149 Brett Butler .15 .06
150 Joaquin Andujar .15 .06
151 Dave Stapleton .10 .04
152 Mike Morgan .10 .04
153 Ricky Adams .10 .04
154 Bert Roberge .10 .04
155 Bobby Grich .15 .06
156 Richard Dotson TL .10 .04
157 Ron Hassey .10 .04
158 Derrel Thomas .10 .04
159 Orel Hershiser UER .25 .10
(82 Alburquerque)
160 Chet Lemon .15 .06
161 Lee Tunnell .10 .04
162 Greg Gagne .10 .04
163 Pete Ladd .10 .04
164 Steve Balboni .10 .04
165 Mike Davis .10 .04
166 Dickie Thon .10 .04
167 Zane Smith .10 .04
168 Jeff Burroughs .10 .04
169 George Wright .10 .04
170 Gary Carter .15 .06
171 Bob Rodgers MG ERR .10 .04
Number of card on back actually 141)
172 Jerry Reed .10 .04
173 Wayne Gross .10 .04
174 Brian Snyder .10 .04
175 Steve Sax .10 .04
176 Jay Tibbs .10 .04
177 Joel Youngblood .10 .04
178 Ivan DeJesus .10 .04
179 Stu Cliburn .10 .04
180 Don Mattingly 1.25 .50
181 Al Nipper .10 .04
182 Bobby Brown .10 .04
183 Larry Andersen .10 .04
184 Tim Laudner .10 .04
185 Rollie Fingers .15 .06
186 Jose Cruz TL .10 .04
187 Scott Fletcher .10 .04
188 Bob Dernier .10 .04
189 Mike Mason .10 .04
190 George Hendrick .15 .06
191 Wally Backman .10 .04
192 Milt Wilcox .10 .04
193 Daryl Sconiers .10 .04
194 Craig McMurtry .10 .04
195 Dave Concepcion .15 .06
196 Doyle Alexander .10 .04
197 Enos Cabell .10 .04
198 Ken Dixon .10 .04
199 Dick Howser MG .10 .04
200 Mike Schmidt 1.00 .40
201 Vince Coleman RB .15 .06
202 Dwight Gooden RB .25 .10
203 Keith Hernandez RB .15 .06
204 Phil Niekro RB .15 .06
205 Tony Perez RB .15 .06
206 Pete Rose RB .40 .16
207 F. Valenzuela RB .10 .04
208 Ramon Romero .10 .04
209 Randy Ready .10 .04
210 Calvin Schiraldi .10 .04
211 Ed Wojna .10 .04
212 Chris Speier .10 .04
213 Bob Shirley .10 .04
214 Randy Bush .10 .04
215 Frank White .15 .06
216 Dwayne Murphy TL .10 .04
217 Bill Scherrer .10 .04
218 Randy Hunt .10 .04
219 Dennis Lamp .10 .04
220 Bob Horner .15 .06
221 Dave Henderson .10 .04
222 Craig Gerber .10 .04
223 Atlee Hammaker .10 .04
224 Cesar Cedeno .15 .06
225 Ron Darling .15 .06
226 Lee Lacy .10 .04
227 Al Jones .10 .04
228 Tom Lawless .10 .04
229 Bill Gullickson .10 .04
230 Terry Kennedy .10 .04
231 Jim Frey MG .10 .04
232 Rick Rhoden .10 .04
233 Steve Lyons .10 .04
234 Doug Corbett .10 .04
235 Butch Wynegar .10 .04
236 Frank Eufemia .10 .04
237 Ted Simmons .15 .06
238 Larry Parrish .10 .04
239 Joel Skinner .10 .04
240 Tommy John .15 .06
241 Tony Fernandez .10 .04
242 Rich Thompson .10 .04
243 Johnny Grubb .10 .04
244 Craig Lefferts .10 .04
245 Jim Sundberg .15 .06
246 Steve Carlton TL .15 .06
247 Terry Harper .10 .04
248 Spike Owen .10 .04
249 Rob Deer .10 .04
250 Dwight Gooden .40 .16
251 Rich Dauer .10 .04
252 Bobby Castillo .10 .04
253 Dann Bilardello .10 .04
254 Ozzie Guillen RC* .25 .10
255 Tony Armas .15 .06
256 Kurt Kepshire .10 .04
257 Doug DeCinces .10 .04
258 Tim Burke .10 .04
259 Dan Pasqua .10 .04
260 Tony Pena .10 .04
261 Bobby Valentine MG .15 .06
262 Mario Ramirez .10 .04
263 Checklist: 133-264 .15 .06
264 Darren Daulton RC .50 .20
265 Ron Davis .10 .04
266 Keith Moreland .10 .04
267 Paul Molitor .25 .10
268 Mike Scott .15 .06
269 Dane Iorg .10 .04
270 Jack Morris .15 .06
271 Dave Collins .10 .04
272 Tim Tolman .10 .04
273 Jerry Willard .10 .04
274 Ron Gardenhire .10 .04
275 Charlie Hough .15 .06
276 Willie Randolph TL .15 .06
277 Jaime Cocanower .10 .04

278 Sixto Lezcano .10 .04
279 Al Pardo .10 .04
280 Tim Raines .15 .06
281 Steve Mura .10 .04
282 Jerry Mumphrey .10 .04
283 Mike Fischlin .10 .04
284 Brian Dayett .10 .04
285 Buddy Bell .15 .06
286 Luis DeLeon .10 .04
287 John Christensen .10 .04
288 Don Aase .10 .04
289 Johnnie LeMaster .10 .04
290 Carlton Fisk .25 .10
291 Tom Lasorda MG .25 .10
292 Chuck Porter .10 .04
293 Chris Chambliss .15 .06
294 Danny Cox .10 .04
295 Kirk Gibson .15 .06
296 Geno Petralli .10 .04
297 Tim Lollar .10 .04
298 Craig Reynolds .10 .04
299 Bryn Smith .10 .04
300 George Brett 1.00 .40
301 Dennis Rasmussen .10 .04
302 Greg Gross .10 .04
303 Curt Wardle .10 .04
304 Mike Gallego RC .10 .04
305 Phil Bradley .10 .04
306 Terry Kennedy TL .10 .04
307 Dave Sax .10 .04
308 Ray Fontenot .10 .04
309 John Shelby .10 .04
310 Greg Minton .10 .04
311 Dick Schofield .10 .04
312 Tom Filer .10 .04
313 Joe DeSa .10 .04
314 Frank Pastore .10 .04
315 Mookie Wilson .15 .06
316 Sammy Khalifa .10 .04
317 Ed Romero .10 .04
318 Terry Whitfield .10 .04
319 Rick Camp .10 .04
320 Jim Rice .15 .06
321 Earl Weaver MG .15 .06
322 Bob Forsch .10 .04
323 Jerry Davis .10 .04
324 Dan Schatzeder .10 .04
325 Juan Beniquez .10 .04
326 Kent Tekulve .10 .04
327 Mike Pagliarulo .10 .04
328 Pete O'Brien .10 .04
329 Kirby Puckett .75 .30
330 Rick Sutcliffe .15 .06
331 Alan Ashby .10 .04
332 Darryl Motley .10 .04
333 Tom Henke .15 .06
334 Ken Oberkfell .10 .04
335 Don Sutton .15 .06
336 Andre Thornton TL .15 .06
337 Darnell Coles .10 .04
338 Jorge Bell .15 .06
339 Bruce Berenyi .10 .04
340 Cal Ripken 1.50 .60
341 Frank Williams .10 .04
342 Gary Redus .10 .04
343 Carlos Diaz .10 .04
344 Jim Wohlford .10 .04
345 Donnie Moore .10 .04
346 Bryan Little .10 .04
347 Teddy Higuera RC* .25 .10
348 Cliff Johnson .10 .04
349 Mark Clear .10 .04
350 Jack Clark .15 .06
351 Chuck Tanner MG .10 .04
352 Harry Spilman .10 .04
353 Keith Atherton .10 .04
354 Tony Bernazard .10 .04
355 Lee Smith .15 .06
356 Mickey Hatcher .10 .04
357 Ed VandeBerg .10 .04
358 Rick Dempsey .10 .04
359 Mike LaCoss .10 .04
360 Lloyd Moseby .10 .04
361 Shane Rawley .10 .04
362 Tom Paciorek .10 .04
363 Terry Forster .15 .06
364 Reid Nichols .10 .04
365 Mike Flanagan .10 .04
366 Dave Concepcion TL .15 .06
367 Aurelio Lopez .10 .04
368 Greg Brock .10 .04
369 Al Holland .10 .04
370 Vince Coleman RC* .50 .20
371 Bill Stein .10 .04
372 Ben Oglivie .15 .06
373 Urbano Lugo .10 .04
374 Terry Francona .15 .06
375 Rich Gedman .10 .04
376 Bill Dawley .10 .04
377 Joe Carter .15 .06
378 Bruce Bochte .10 .04
379 Bobby Meacham .10 .04
380 LaMarr Hoyt .10 .04
381 Ray Miller MG .10 .04
382 Ivan Calderon RC* .25 .10
383 Chris Brown .10 .04
384 Steve Trout .10 .04
385 Cecil Cooper .15 .06
386 Cecil Fielder RC .75 .30
387 Steve Kemp .10 .04
388 Dickie Noles .10 .04
389 Glenn Davis .10 .04
390 Tom Seaver .25 .10
391 Julio Franco .15 .06
392 John Russell .10 .04
393 Chris Pittaro .10 .04
394 Checklist: 265-396 .15 .06
395 Scott Garrelts .10 .04
396 Dwight Evans TL .15 .06
397 Steve Buechele RC .25 .10
398 Earnie Riles .10 .04
399 Bill Swift .10 .04
400 Rod Carew .25 .10
401 Fernando Valenzuela TBC '81 .10 .04
402 Tom Seaver TBC '76 .15 .06
403 Willie Mays TBC '71 .40 .16
404 Frank Robinson TBC '66 .15 .06
405 Roger Maris TBC '61 .40 .16
406 Scott Sanderson .10 .04
407 Sal Butera .10 .04
408 Dave Smith .10 .04
409 Paul Runge RC .10 .04
410 Dave Kingman .15 .06
411 Sparky Anderson MG .15 .06
412 Jim Clancy .10 .04
413 Tim Flannery .10 .04
414 Tom Gorman .10 .04
415 Hal McRae .15 .06
416 Dennis Martinez .15 .06
417 R.J. Reynolds .10 .04
418 Alan Knicely .10 .04
419 Frank Wills .10 .04
420 Von Hayes .10 .04
421 David Palmer .10 .04
422 Mike Jorgensen .10 .04
423 Dan Spillner .10 .04
424 Rick Miller .10 .04
425 Larry McWilliams .10 .04
426 Charlie Moore TL .10 .04
427 Joe Cowley .10 .04
428 Max Venable .10 .04
429 Greg Booker .10 .04
430 Kent Hrbek .15 .06
431 George Frazier .10 .04
432 Mark Bailey .10 .04
433 Chris Codiroli .10 .04
434 Curt Wilkerson .10 .04
435 Bill Caudill .10 .04
436 Doug Flynn .10 .04
437 Rick Mahler .10 .04
438 Clint Hurdle .10 .04
439 Rick Honeycutt .10 .04
440 Alvin Davis .10 .04
441 Whitey Herzog MG .25 .10
442 Ron Robinson .10 .04
443 Bill Buckner .15 .06
444 Alex Trevino .10 .04
445 Bert Blyleven .15 .06
446 Lenn Sakata .10 .04
447 Jerry Don Gleaton .10 .04
448 Herm Winningham .10 .04
449 Rod Scurry .10 .04
450 Graig Nettles .15 .06
451 Mark Brown .10 .04
452 Bob Clark .10 .04
453 Steve Jeltz .10 .04
454 Burt Hooton .10 .04
455 Willie Randolph .15 .06
456 Dale Murphy TL .25 .10
457 Mickey Tettleton RC .25 .10
458 Kevin Bass .10 .04
459 Luis Leal .10 .04
460 Leon Durham .10 .04
461 Walt Terrell .10 .04
462 Domingo Ramos .10 .04
463 Jim Gott .10 .04
464 Ruppert Jones .10 .04
465 Jesse Orosco .10 .04
466 Tom Foley .10 .04
467 Bob James .10 .04
468 Mike Scioscia .15 .06
469 Storm Davis .10 .04
470 Bill Madlock .15 .06
471 Bobby Cox MG .15 .06
472 Joe Hesketh .10 .04
473 Mark Brouhard .10 .04
474 John Tudor .15 .06
475 Juan Samuel .10 .04
476 Ron Mathis .10 .04
477 Mike Easler .10 .04
478 Andy Hawkins .10 .04
479 Bob Melvin .10 .04
480 Oddibe McDowell .10 .04
481 Scott Bradley .10 .04
482 Rick Lysander .10 .04
483 George Vukovich .10 .04
484 Donnie Hill .10 .04
485 Gary Matthews .15 .06
486 Bobby Grich TL .10 .04
487 Bret Saberhagen .15 .06
488 Lou Thornton .10 .04
489 Jim Winn .10 .04
490 Jeff Leonard .10 .04
491 Pascual Perez .10 .04
492 Kelvin Chapman .10 .04
493 Gene Nelson .10 .04
494 Gary Roenicke .10 .04
495 Mark Langston .15 .06
496 Jay Johnstone .10 .04
497 John Stuper .10 .04
498 Tito Landrum .10 .04
499 Bob L. Gibson .10 .04
500 Rickey Henderson .40 .16
501 Dave Johnson MG .10 .04
502 Glen Cook .10 .04
503 Mike Fitzgerald .10 .04
504 Denny Walling .10 .04
505 Jerry Koosman .15 .06
506 Bill Russell .15 .06
507 Steve Ontiveros RC .10 .04
508 Alan Wiggins .10 .04
509 Ernie Camacho .10 .04
510 Wade Boggs .25 .10
511 Ed Nunez .10 .04
512 Thad Bosley .10 .04
513 Ron Washington .10 .04
514 Mike Jones .10 .04
515 Darrell Evans .15 .06
516 Greg Minton TL .10 .04
517 Milt Thompson RC .25 .10
518 Buck Martinez .10 .04
519 Danny Darwin .10 .04
520 Keith Hernandez .15 .06
521 Nate Snell .10 .04
522 Bob Bailor .10 .04
523 Joe Price .10 .04
524 Darrell Miller .10 .04
525 Marvell Wynne .10 .04
526 Charlie Lea .10 .04
527 Checklist: 397-528 .15 .06
528 Terry Pendleton .15 .06
529 Marc Sullivan .10 .04
530 Rich Gossage .15 .06
531 Tony LaRussa MG .15 .06
532 Don Carman .10 .04
533 Billy Sample .10 .04
534 Jeff Calhoun .10 .04
535 Toby Harrah .15 .06
536 Jose Rijo .15 .06
537 Mark Salas .10 .04
538 Dennis Eckersley .25 .10
539 Glenn Hubbard .10 .04
540 Dan Petry .10 .04
541 Jorge Orta .10 .04
542 Don Schulze .10 .04
543 Jerry Narron .10 .04
544 Eddie Milner .10 .04
545 Jimmy Key .15 .06
546 Dave Henderson TL .10 .04
547 Roger McDowell RC* .25 .10
548 Mike Young .10 .04
549 Bob Welch .15 .06
550 Tom Herr .10 .04
551 Dave LaPoint .10 .04
552 Marc Hill .10 .04
553 Jim Morrison .10 .04
554 Paul Householder .10 .04
555 Hubie Brooks .10 .04
556 John Denny .10 .04
557 Gerald Perry .10 .04
558 Tim Stoddard .10 .04
559 Tommy Dunbar .10 .04
560 Dave Righetti .15 .06
561 Bob Lillis MG .10 .04
562 Joe Beckwith .10 .04
563 Alejandro Sanchez .10 .04
564 Warren Brusstar .10 .04
565 Tom Brunansky .10 .04
566 Alfredo Griffin .10 .04
567 Jeff Barkley .10 .04
568 Donnie Scott .10 .04
569 Jim Acker .10 .04
570 Rusty Staub .15 .06
571 Mike Jeffcoat .10 .04
572 Paul Zuvella .10 .04
573 Tom Hume .10 .04
574 Ron Kittle .10 .04
575 Mike Boddicker .10 .04
576 Andre Dawson TL .10 .04
577 Jerry Reuss .10 .04
578 Lee Mazzilli .15 .06
579 Jim Slaton .10 .04
580 Willie McGee .15 .06
581 Bruce Hurst .10 .04
582 Jim Gantner .10 .04
583 Al Bumbry .10 .04
584 Brian Fisher RC .10 .04
585 Garry Maddox .10 .04
586 Greg Harris .10 .04
587 Rafael Santana .10 .04
588 Steve Lake .10 .04
589 Sid Bream .10 .04
590 Bob Knepper .10 .04
591 Jackie Moore MG .10 .04
592 Frank Tanana .15 .06
593 Jesse Barfield .15 .06
594 Chris Bando .10 .04
595 Dave Parker .15 .06
596 Onix Concepcion .10 .04
597 Sammy Stewart .10 .04
598 Jim Presley .10 .04
599 Rick Aguilera RC .25 .10
600 Dale Murphy .25 .10
601 Gary Lucas .10 .04
602 Mariano Duncan RC* .25 .10
603 Bill Laskey .10 .04
604 Gary Pettis .10 .04
605 Dennis Boyd .10 .04
606 Hal McRae TL .15 .06
607 Ken Dayley .10 .04
608 Bruce Bochy .10 .04
609 Barbaro Garbey .10 .04
610 Ron Guidry .15 .06
611 Gary Woods .10 .04
612 Richard Dotson .10 .04
613 Roy Smalley .10 .04
614 Rick Waits .10 .04
615 Johnny Ray .10 .04
616 Glenn Brummer .10 .04
617 Lonnie Smith .10 .04
618 Jim Pankovits .10 .04
619 Danny Heep .10 .04
620 Bruce Sutter .15 .06
621 John Felske MG .10 .04
622 Gary Lavelle .10 .04
623 Floyd Rayford .10 .04
624 Steve McCatty .10 .04
625 Bob Brenly .10 .04
626 Roy Thomas .10 .04
627 Ron Oester .10 .04
628 Kirk McCaskill RC .25 .10
629 Mitch Webster .10 .04
630 Fernando Valenzuela .15 .06
631 Steve Braun .10 .04
632 Dave Von Ohlen .10 .04
633 Jackie Gutierrez .10 .04
634 Roy Lee Jackson .10 .04
635 Jason Thompson .10 .04
636 Lee Smith TL .10 .04
637 Rudy Law .10 .04
638 John Butcher .10 .04
639 Bo Diaz .10 .04
640 Jose Cruz .15 .06
641 Wayne Tolleson .10 .04
642 Ray Searage .10 .04
643 Tom Brookens .10 .04
644 Mark Gubicza .10 .04
645 Dusty Baker .15 .06
646 Mike Moore .10 .04
647 Mel Hall .10 .04
648 Steve Bedrosian .10 .04
649 Ronn Reynolds .10 .04
650 Dave Stieb .15 .06
651 Billy Martin MG .25 .10
652 Tom Browning .10 .04
653 Jim Dwyer .10 .04
654 Ken Howell .10 .04
655 Manny Trillo .10 .04
656 Brian Harper .10 .04
657 Juan Agosto .10 .04
658 Rob Wilfong .10 .04
659 Checklist: 529-660 .15 .06
660 Steve Garvey .15 .06
661 Roger Clemens 1.50 .60
662 Bill Schroeder .10 .04
663 Neil Allen .10 .04
664 Tim Corcoran .10 .04
665 Alejandro Pena .10 .04
666 Charlie Hough TL .15 .06
667 Tim Teufel .10 .04
668 Cecilio Guante .10 .04
669 Ron Cey .15 .06
670 Willie Hernandez .10 .04
671 Lynn Jones .10 .04
672 Rob Picciolo .10 .04
673 Ernie Whitt .10 .04
674 Pat Tabler .10 .04
675 Claudell Washington .10 .04
676 Matt Young .10 .04
677 Nick Esasky .10 .04
678 Dan Gladden .10 .04
679 Britt Burns .10 .04
680 George Foster .15 .06
681 Dick Williams MG .10 .04
682 Junior Ortiz .10 .04
683 Andy Van Slyke .15 .06
684 Bob McClure .10 .04
685 Tim Wallach .10 .04
686 Jeff Stone .10 .04
687 Mike Trujillo .10 .04
688 Larry Herndon .10 .04
689 Dave Stewart .15 .06
690 Ryne Sandberg UER .75 .30
(No Topps logo on front)
691 Mike Madden .10 .04
692 Dale Berra .10 .04
693 Tom Tellmann .10 .04
694 Garth Iorg .10 .04
695 Mike Smithson .10 .04
696 Bill Russell TL .15 .06
697 Bud Black .10 .04
698 Brad Komminsk .10 .04
699 Pat Corrales MG .10 .04
700 Reggie Jackson .25 .10
701 Keith Hernandez AS .10 .04
702 Tom Herr AS .10 .04
703 Tim Wallach AS .10 .04
704 Ozzie Smith AS .40 .16
705 Dale Murphy AS .15 .06
706 Pedro Guerrero AS .10 .04
707 Willie McGee AS .10 .04
708 Gary Carter AS .10 .04
709 Dwight Gooden AS .25 .10
710 John Tudor AS .10 .04
711 Jeff Reardon AS .10 .04
712 Don Mattingly AS .60 .24
713 Damaso Garcia AS .10 .04
714 George Brett AS .40 .16
715 Cal Ripken AS .40 .16
716 Rickey Henderson AS .25 .10
717 Dave Winfield AS .10 .04
718 George Bell AS .10 .04
719 Carlton Fisk AS .15 .06
720 Bret Saberhagen AS .10 .04
721 Ron Guidry AS .10 .04
722 Dan Quisenberry AS .10 .04
723 Marty Bystrom .10 .04
724 Tim Hulett .10 .04
725 Mario Soto .15 .06
726 Rick Dempsey TL .15 .06
727 David Green .10 .04
728 Mike Marshall .10 .04
729 Jim Beattie .10 .04
730 Ozzie Smith .60 .24
731 Don Robinson .10 .04
732 Floyd Youmans .10 .04
733 Ron Romanick .10 .04
734 Marty Barrett .10 .04
735 Dave Dravecky .10 .04
736 Glenn Wilson .10 .04
737 Pete Vuckovich .10 .04
738 Andre Robertson .10 .04
739 Dave Rozema .10 .04
740 Lance Parrish .15 .06
741 Pete Rose MG .40 .16
742 Frank Viola .15 .06
743 Pat Sheridan .10 .04
744 Lary Sorensen .10 .04
745 Willie Upshaw .10 .04
746 Denny Gonzalez .10 .04
747 Rick Cerone .10 .04
748 Steve Henderson .10 .04
749 Ed Jurak .10 .04
750 Gorman Thomas .15 .06
751 Howard Johnson .15 .06
752 Mike Krukow .10 .04
753 Dan Ford .10 .04
754 Pat Clements .10 .04
755 Harold Baines .15 .06
756 Rick Rhoden TL .10 .04
757 Darrell Porter .10 .04
758 Dave Anderson .10 .04
759 Moose Haas .10 .04
760 Andre Dawson .15 .06
761 Don Slaught .10 .04
762 Eric Show .10 .04
763 Terry Puhl .10 .04
764 Kevin Gross .10 .04
765 Don Baylor .15 .06
766 Rick Langford .10 .04
767 Jody Davis .10 .04
768 Vern Ruhle .10 .04
769 Harold Reynolds RC .75 .30
770 Vida Blue .15 .06
771 John McNamara MG .10 .04
772 Brian Downing .15 .06
773 Greg Pryor .10 .04
774 Terry Leach .10 .04
775 Al Oliver .15 .06
776 Gene Garber .10 .04
777 Wayne Krenchicki .10 .04
778 Jerry Hairston .10 .04
779 Rick Reuschel .15 .06
780 Robin Yount .60 .24
781 Joe Nolan .10 .04
782 Ken Landreaux .10 .04
783 Ricky Horton .10 .04
784 Alan Bannister .10 .04
785 Bob Stanley .10 .04
786 Mickey Hatcher TL .10 .04
787 Vance Law .10 .04
788 Marty Castillo .10 .04
789 Kurt Bevacqua .10 .04
790 Phil Niekro .15 .06
791 Checklist: 661-792 .15 .06
792 Charles Hudson .10 .04

1986 Topps Tiffany

These 792 cards form a parallel to the regular Topps set. These cards, available only through the Topps dealer network were issued in factory sealed boxes. These cards have a "glossy" front and a very clear back. These cards were printed in the Topps Ireland plant. Reports within the hobby indicate that it is believed that 5,000 of these sets were produced.

Nm-Mt Ex-Mt
COMP.FACT.SET (792) 150.00 60.00
*STARS: 5X TO 12X BASIC CARDS
*ROOKIES: 5X TO 12X BASIC CARDS

1986 Topps Glossy All-Stars

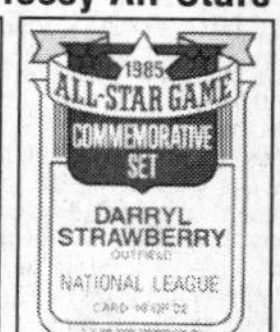

This 22-card standard-size set was distributed as an insert, one card per rak pack. The players featured are the starting lineups of the 1985 All-Star Game played in Minnesota. The cards are very colorful and have a high gloss finish.

Nm-Mt Ex-Mt
COMPLETE SET (22) 5.00 2.00
1 Sparky Anderson MG .05 .02
2 Eddie Murray .50 .20
3 Lou Whitaker .10 .04
4 George Brett 1.00 .40
5 Cal Ripken 2.00 .80
6 Jim Rice .10 .04
7 Rickey Henderson .50 .20
8 Dave Winfield .50 .20
9 Carlton Fisk .40 .16
10 Jack Morris .10 .04
11 AL Team Photo .05 .02
12 Dick Williams MG .05 .02
13 Steve Garvey .10 .04
14 Tom Herr .05 .02
15 Graig Nettles .10 .04
16 Ozzie Smith 1.00 .40
17 Tony Gwynn 1.00 .40
18 Dale Murphy .20 .08
19 Darryl Strawberry .10 .04
20 Terry Kennedy .05 .02
21 LaMarr Hoyt .05 .02
22 NL Team Photo .05 .02

1986 Topps Glossy Send-Ins

This 60-card glossy standard-size set was produced by Topps and distributed ten cards at a time based on the offer found on the wax packs. Each series of ten cards was available by sending in 1.00 plus six "special offer" cards inserted one per wax pack. The card backs are printed in red and blue on white card stock. The card fronts feature a white border and a green frame surrounding a full-color photo of the player.

Nm-Mt Ex-Mt
COMPLETE SET (60) 12.00 4.80
1 Oddibe McDowell .10 .04
2 Reggie Jackson .75 .30
3 Fernando Valenzuela .20 .08
4 Jack Clark .10 .04
5 Rickey Henderson 1.25 .50
6 Steve Balboni .10 .04
7 Keith Hernandez .20 .08
8 Lance Parrish .20 .08
9 Willie McGee .20 .08
10 Chris Brown .10 .04
11 Darryl Strawberry .20 .08
12 Ron Guidry .20 .08
13 Dave Parker .20 .08
14 Cal Ripken 4.00 1.60
15 Tim Raines .20 .08
16 Rod Carew .75 .30
17 Mike Schmidt 1.00 .40
18 George Brett 2.00 .80
19 Joe Hesketh .10 .04
20 Dan Pasqua .10 .04
21 Vince Coleman .20 .08
22 Tom Seaver .75 .30
23 Gary Carter .75 .30
24 Orel Hershiser .20 .08
25 Pedro Guerrero .10 .04
26 Wade Boggs .75 .30
27 Bret Saberhagen .20 .08
28 Carlton Fisk .75 .30
29 Kirk Gibson .20 .08
30 Brian Fisher .10 .04
31 Don Mattingly 2.00 .80
32 Tom Herr .10 .04
33 Eddie Murray .75 .30
34 Ryne Sandberg 1.50 .60
35 Dan Quisenberry .20 .08
36 Jim Rice .20 .08
37 Dale Murphy .30 .12
38 Steve Garvey .20 .08
39 Roger McDowell .10 .04
40 Earnie Riles .10 .04
41 Dwight Gooden .20 .08
42 Dave Winfield .60 .24
43 Dave Stieb .10 .04
44 Bob Horner .10 .04
45 Nolan Ryan 4.00 1.60

1986 Topps Glossy Send-Ins

Card	Nm-Mt	Ex-Mt
46 Ozzie Smith	2.00	.80
47 George Bell	.10	.04
48 Gorman Thomas	.10	.04
49 Tom Browning	.10	.04
50 Larry Sheets	.10	.04
51 Pete Rose	1.00	.40
52 Brett Butler	.20	.08
53 John Tudor	.10	.04
54 Phil Bradley	.10	.04
55 Jeff Reardon	.20	.08
56 Rich Gossage	.20	.08
57 Tony Gwynn	2.00	.80
58 Ozzie Guillen	.30	.12
59 Glenn Davis	.10	.04
60 Darrell Evans	.10	.04

1986 Topps Wax Box Cards

Topps printed cards (each measuring the standard 2 1/2" by 3 1/2") on the bottoms of their wax pack boxes for their regular issue cards; there are four different boxes, each with four cards. These sixteen cards ("numbered" A through P) are listed below; they are not considered an integral part of the regular set but are considered a separate set. The order of the set is alphabetical by player's name. These wax box cards are styled almost exactly like the 1986 Topps regular issue cards. Complete boxes would be worth an additional 25 percent premium over the prices below. The card lettering is sequenced in alphabetical order.

	Nm-Mt	Ex-Mt
COMPLETE SET (16)	8.00	3.20
A George Bell	.20	.08
B Wade Boggs	1.00	.40
C George Brett	2.00	.80
D Vince Coleman	.40	.16
E Carlton Fisk	1.00	.40
F Dwight Gooden	.40	.16
G Pedro Guerrero	.40	.16
H Ron Guidry	.40	.16
I Reggie Jackson	1.00	.40
J Don Mattingly	2.00	.80
K Oddibe McDowell	.20	.08
L Willie McGee	.40	.16
M Dale Murphy	.60	.24
N Pete Rose	1.25	.50
O Bret Saberhagen	.40	.16
P Fernando Valenzuela	.40	.16

1986 Topps Traded

This 132-card standard-size Traded set was distributed in factory set form in a red and white box through hobby dealers. The cards are identical in style to regular-issue 1986 Topps cards except for whiter stock and t-suffixed numbering. The key extended Rookie Cards in this set are Barry Bonds, Bobby Bonilla, Jose Canseco, Will Clark, Andres Galarraga, Bo Jackson, Wally Joyner, John Kruk, and Kevin Mitchell.

	Nm-Mt	Ex-Mt
COMP.FACT.SET (132)	50.00	20.00
1T Andy Allanson	.10	.04
2T Neil Allen	.10	.04
3T Joaquin Andujar	.15	.06
4T Paul Assenmacher	.25	.10
5T Scott Bailes	.10	.04
6T Don Baylor	.15	.06
7T Steve Bedrosian	.10	.04
8T Juan Beniquez	.10	.04
9T Juan Berenguer	.10	.04
10T Mike Bielecki	.10	.04
11T Barry Bonds XRC	40.00	16.00
12T Bobby Bonilla XRC	.50	.20
13T Juan Bonilla	.10	.04
14T Rich Bordi	.10	.04
15T Steve Boros MG	.10	.04
16T Rick Burleson	.10	.04
17T Bill Campbell	.10	.04
18T Tom Candiotti	.10	.04
19T John Cangelosi	.10	.04
20T Jose Canseco XRC	1.50	.60
21T Carmen Castillo	.10	.04
22T Rick Cerone	.10	.04
23T John Cerutti	.10	.04
24T Will Clark XRC	1.50	.60
25T Mark Clear	.10	.04
26T Darnell Coles	.10	.04
27T Dave Collins	.10	.04
28T Tim Conroy	.10	.04
29T Joe Cowley	.10	.04
30T Joel Davis	.10	.04
31T Rob Deer	.10	.04
32T John Denny	.10	.04
33T Mike Easler	.10	.04
34T Mark Eichhorn	.10	.04
35T Steve Farr	.10	.04
36T Scott Fletcher	.10	.04
37T Terry Forster	.15	.06
38T Terry Francona	.15	.06
39T Jim Fregosi MG	.10	.04
40T Andres Galarraga XRC	.75	.30
41T Ken Griffey	.15	.06
42T Bill Gullickson	.10	.04
43T Jose Guzman XRC *	.10	.04
44T Moose Haas	.10	.04
45T Billy Hatcher	.10	.04
46T Mike Heath	.10	.04
47T Tom Hume	.10	.04
48T Pete Incaviglia XRC	.25	.10
49T Dane Iorg	.10	.04
50T Bo Jackson XRC	1.50	.60
51T Wally Joyner XRC	.50	.20
52T Charlie Kerfeld	.10	.04
53T Eric King	.10	.04
54T Bob Kipper	.10	.04
55T Wayne Krenchicki	.10	.04
56T John Kruk XRC	.75	.30
57T Mike LaCoss	.10	.04
58T Pete Ladd	.10	.04
59T Mike Laga	.10	.04
60T Hal Lanier MG	.10	.04
61T Dave LaPoint	.10	.04
62T Rudy Law	.10	.04
63T Rick Leach	.10	.04
64T Tim Leary	.10	.04
65T Dennis Leonard	.10	.04
66T Jim Leyland MG XRC	.25	.10
67T Steve Lyons	.10	.04
68T Mickey Mahler	.10	.04
69T Candy Maldonado	.10	.04
70T Roger Mason XRC *	.10	.04
71T Bob McClure	.10	.04
72T Andy McGaffigan	.10	.04
73T Gene Michael MG	.10	.04
74T Kevin Mitchell XRC	.50	.20
75T Omar Moreno	.10	.04
76T Jerry Mumphrey	.10	.04
77T Phil Niekro	.15	.06
78T Randy Niemann	.10	.04
79T Juan Nieves	.10	.04
80T Otis Nixon XRC*	.25	.10
81T Bob Ojeda	.10	.04
82T Jose Oquendo	.10	.04
83T Tom Paciorek	.10	.04
84T David Palmer	.10	.04
85T Frank Pastore	.10	.04
86T Lou Piniella MG	.15	.06
87T Dan Plesac	.25	.10
88T Darrell Porter	.10	.04
89T Rey Quinones	.10	.04
90T Gary Redus	.10	.04
91T Bip Roberts XRC	.25	.10
92T Billy Joe Robidoux	.10	.04
93T Jeff D. Robinson	.10	.04
94T Gary Roenicke	.10	.04
95T Ed Romero	.10	.04
96T Angel Salazar	.10	.04
97T Joe Sambito	.10	.04
98T Billy Sample	.10	.04
99T Dave Schmidt	.10	.04
100T Ken Schrom	.10	.04
101T Tom Seaver	.25	.10
102T Ted Simmons	.15	.06
103T Sammy Stewart	.10	.04
104T Kurt Stillwell	.10	.04
105T Franklin Stubbs	.10	.04
106T Dale Sveum	.10	.04
107T Chuck Tanner MG	.10	.04
108T Danny Tartabull	.15	.06
109T Tim Teufel	.10	.04
110T Bob Tewksbury XRC	.25	.10
111T Andres Thomas	.10	.04
112T Milt Thompson	.25	.10
113T R.Thompson XRC	.25	.10
114T Jay Tibbs	.10	.04
115T Wayne Tolleson	.10	.04
116T Alex Trevino	.10	.04
117T Manny Trillo	.10	.04
118T Ed VandeBerg	.10	.04
119T Ozzie Virgil	.10	.04
120T Bob Walk	.10	.04
121T Gene Walter	.10	.04
122T Claudell Washington	.10	.04
123T Bill Wegman XRC *	.10	.04
124T Dick Williams MG	.10	.04
125T Mitch Williams XRC	.25	.10
126T Bobby Witt XRC	.25	.10
127T Todd Worrell XRC *	.25	.10
128T George Wright	.10	.04
129T Ricky Wright	.10	.04
130T Steve Yeager	.15	.06
131T Paul Zuvella	.10	.04
132T Checklist 1T-132T	.10	.04

1986 Topps Traded Tiffany

For the third consecutive season, Topps issued a Tiffany Update issue to go with their regular issue. These 132 cards feature the same players as in the regular set but have a "glossy" front and very clear back. These cards, released through Topps hobby dealers, were sent out only if the dealer ordered the regular Tiffany set. These cards were printed in Topps' Ireland plant. Again, similar to the regular set, it is believed that 5,000 of these sets were produced.

	Nm-Mt	Ex-Mt
COMP.FACT.SET (132)	1000.00	400.00

*STARS: 5X TO 12X BASIC CARDS
*ROOKIES: 5X TO 12X BASIC CARDS
FACTORY SET PRICE IS FOR SEALED SETS
OPENED SETS SELL FOR 50-60% OF SEALED

1987 Topps

This set consists of 792 standard-size cards. Cards were primarily issued in 17-card wax packs, 50-card rack packs and factory sets. Card fronts feature wood grain borders encasing a color photo (reminiscent of Topps' classic 1962 baseball set). Subsets include Record Breakers (1-7), Turn Back the Clock (311-315), All-Star selections (595-616) and Team Leaders (scattered throughout the set). The manager cards contain a team checklist on back. The key Rookie Cards in this set are Barry Bonds, Bobby Bonilla, Will Clark, Bo Jackson, Wally Joyner, John Kruk, Barry Larkin, Rafael Palmiero, Ruben Sierra, and Devon White.

	Nm-Mt	Ex-Mt
COMPLETE SET (792)	25.00	10.00
COMP.FACT SET (792)	25.00	10.00
COMP.HOBBY SET (792)	40.00	16.00
COMP.X-MAS.SET (792)	40.00	16.00
1 Roger Clemens RB	.25	.10
2 Jim Deshaies RB	.05	.02
3 Dwight Evans RB	.10	.04
4 Davey Lopes RB	.05	.02
5 Dave Righetti RB	.05	.02
6 Ruben Sierra RB	.25	.10
7 Todd Worrell RB	.05	.02
8 Terry Pendleton	.10	.04
9 Jay Tibbs	.05	.02
10 Cecil Cooper	.10	.04
11 Indians Team (Mound conference)	.05	.02
12 Jeff Sellers	.05	.02
13 Nick Esasky	.05	.02
14 Dave Stewart	.10	.04
15 Claudell Washington	.05	.02
16 Pat Clements	.05	.02
17 Pete O'Brien	.05	.02
18 Dick Howser MG	.05	.02
19 Matt Young	.05	.02
20 Gary Carter	.10	.04
21 Mark Davis	.05	.02
22 Doug DeCinces	.05	.02
23 Lee Smith	.10	.04
24 Tony Walker	.05	.02
25 Bert Blyleven	.10	.04
26 Greg Brock	.05	.02
27 Joe Cowley	.05	.02
28 Rick Dempsey	.05	.02
29 Jimmy Key	.10	.04
30 Tim Raines	.10	.04
31 Braves Team (Glenn Hubbard and Rafael Ramirez)	.05	.02
32 Tim Leary	.05	.02
33 Andy Van Slyke	.10	.04
34 Jose Rijo	.10	.04
35 Sid Bream	.05	.02
36 Eric King	.05	.02
37 Marvell Wynne	.05	.02
38 Dennis Leonard	.05	.02
39 Marty Barrett	.05	.02
40 Dave Righetti	.10	.04
41 Bo Diaz	.05	.02
42 Gary Redus	.05	.02
43 Gene Michael MG	.05	.02
44 Greg Harris	.05	.02
45 Jim Presley	.05	.02
46 Dan Gladden	.05	.02
47 Dennis Powell	.05	.02
48 Wally Backman	.05	.02
49 Terry Harper	.05	.02
50 Dave Smith	.05	.02
51 Mel Hall	.05	.02
52 Keith Atherton	.05	.02
53 Ruppert Jones	.05	.02
54 Bill Dawley	.05	.02
55 Tim Wallach	.05	.02
56 Brewers Team (Mound conference)	.05	.02
57 Scott Nielsen	.05	.02
58 Thad Bosley	.05	.02
59 Ken Dayley	.05	.02
60 Tony Pena	.05	.02
61 Bobby Thigpen RC	.25	.10
62 Bobby Meacham	.05	.02
63 Fred Toliver	.05	.02
64 Harry Spilman	.05	.02
65 Tom Browning	.05	.02
66 Marc Sullivan	.05	.02
67 Bill Swift	.05	.02
68 Tony LaRussa MG	.10	.04
69 Lonnie Smith	.05	.02
70 Charlie Hough	.10	.04
71 Mike Aldrete	.05	.02
72 Walt Terrell	.05	.02
73 Dave Anderson	.05	.02
74 Dan Pasqua	.05	.02
75 Ron Darling	.10	.04
76 Rafael Ramirez	.05	.02
77 Bryan Oelkers	.05	.02
78 Tom Foley	.05	.02
79 Juan Nieves	.05	.02
80 Wally Joyner RC	.40	.16
81 Padres Team (Andy Hawkins and Terry Kennedy)	.05	.02
82 Rob Murphy	.05	.02
83 Mike Davis	.05	.02
84 Steve Lake	.05	.02
85 Kevin Bass	.05	.02
86 Nate Snell	.05	.02
87 Mark Salas	.05	.02
88 Ed Wojna	.05	.02
89 Ozzie Guillen	.10	.04
90 Dave Stieb	.10	.04
91 Harold Reynolds	.10	.04
92A Urbano Lugo ERR (no trademark)	.15	.06
92B Urbano Lugo COR	.05	.02
93 Jim Leyland MG/TC RC*	.25	.10
94 Calvin Schiraldi	.05	.02
95 Oddibe McDowell	.05	.02
96 Frank Williams	.05	.02
97 Glenn Wilson	.05	.02
98 Bill Scherrer	.05	.02
99 Darryl Motley (Now with Braves on card front)	.05	.02
100 Steve Garvey	.10	.04
101 Carl Willis RC	.10	.04
102 Paul Zuvella	.05	.02
103 Rick Aguilera	.10	.04
104 Billy Sample	.05	.02
105 Floyd Youmans	.05	.02
106 Blue Jays Team (George Bell and Jesse Barfield)	.05	.02
107 John Butcher	.05	.02
108 Jim Gantner UER (Brewers logo reversed)	.05	.02
109 R.J. Reynolds	.05	.02
110 John Tudor	.10	.04
111 Alfredo Griffin	.05	.02
112 Alan Ashby	.05	.02
113 Neil Allen	.05	.02
114 Billy Beane	.10	.04
115 Donnie Moore	.05	.02
116 Bill Russell	.10	.04
117 Jim Beattie	.05	.02
118 Bobby Valentine MG	.10	.04
119 Ron Robinson	.05	.02
120 Eddie Murray	.25	.10
121 Kevin Romine	.05	.02
122 Jim Clancy	.05	.02
123 John Kruk RC*	.50	.20
124 Ray Fontenot	.05	.02
125 Bob Brenly	.05	.02
126 Mike Loynd RC	.10	.04
127 Vance Law	.05	.02
128 Checklist 1-132	.05	.02
129 Rick Cerone	.05	.02
130 Dwight Gooden	.10	.04
131 Pirates Team (Sid Bream and Tony Pena)	.05	.02
132 Paul Assenmacher	.25	.10
133 Jose Oquendo	.05	.02
134 Rich Yett	.05	.02
135 Mike Easler	.05	.02
136 Ron Romanick	.05	.02
137 Jerry Willard	.05	.02
138 Roy Lee Jackson	.05	.02
139 Devon White RC	.40	.16
140 Bret Saberhagen	.10	.04
141 Herm Winningham	.05	.02
142 Rick Sutcliffe	.10	.04
143 Steve Boros MG	.05	.02
144 Mike Scioscia	.10	.04
145 Charlie Kerfeld	.05	.02
146 Tracy Jones	.05	.02
147 Randy Niemann	.05	.02
148 Dave Collins	.05	.02
149 Ray Searage	.05	.02
150 Wade Boggs	.15	.06
151 Mike LaCoss	.05	.02
152 Toby Harrah	.10	.04
153 Duane Ward RC *	.25	.10
154 Tom O'Malley	.05	.02
155 Eddie Whitson	.05	.02
156 Mariners Team (Mound conference)	.05	.02
157 Danny Darwin	.05	.02
158 Tim Teufel	.05	.02
159 Ed Olwine	.05	.02
160 Julio Franco	.10	.04
161 Steve Ontiveros	.05	.02
162 Mike LaValliere RC *	.25	.10
163 Kevin Gross	.05	.02
164 Sammy Khalifa	.05	.02
165 Jeff Reardon	.10	.04
166 Bob Boone	.10	.04
167 Jim Deshaies RC *	.10	.04
168 Lou Piniella MG	.10	.04
169 Ron Washington	.05	.02
170 Bo Jackson RC	1.00	.40
171 Chuck Cary	.05	.02
172 Ron Oester	.05	.02
173 Alex Trevino	.05	.02
174 Henry Cotto	.05	.02
175 Bob Stanley	.05	.02
176 Steve Buechele	.05	.02
177 Keith Moreland	.05	.02
178 Cecil Fielder	.10	.04
179 Bill Wegman	.05	.02
180 Chris Brown	.05	.02
181 Cardinals Team (Mound conference)	.05	.02
182 Lee Lacy	.05	.02
183 Andy Hawkins	.05	.02
184 Bobby Bonilla RC	.40	.16
185 Roger McDowell	.05	.02
186 Bruce Benedict	.05	.02
187 Mark Huismann	.05	.02
188 Tony Phillips	.05	.02
189 Joe Hesketh	.05	.02
190 Jim Sundberg	.10	.04
191 Charles Hudson	.05	.02
192 Cory Snyder	.05	.02
193 Roger Craig MG	.10	.04
194 Kirk McCaskill	.05	.02
195 Mike Pagliarulo	.05	.02
196 Randy O'Neal UER (Wrong ML career W-L totals)	.05	.02
197 Mark Bailey	.05	.02
198 Lee Mazzilli	.10	.04
199 Mariano Duncan	.05	.02
200 Pete Rose	.60	.24
201 John Cangelosi	.05	.02
202 Ricky Wright	.05	.02
203 Mike Kingery RC	.10	.04
204 Sammy Stewart	.05	.02
205 Graig Nettles	.10	.04
206 Twins Team (Frank Viola and Tim Laudner)	.05	.02
207 George Frazier	.05	.02
208 John Shelby	.05	.02
209 Rick Schu	.05	.02
210 Lloyd Moseby	.05	.02
211 John Morris	.05	.02
212 Mike Fitzgerald	.05	.02
213 Randy Myers RC	.40	.16
214 Omar Moreno	.05	.02
215 Mark Langston	.05	.02
216 B.J. Surhoff RC	.40	.16
217 Chris Codiroli	.05	.02
218 Sparky Anderson MG	.10	.04
219 Cecilio Guante	.05	.02
220 Joe Carter	.10	.04
221 Vern Ruhle	.05	.02
222 Denny Walling	.05	.02
223 Charlie Leibrandt	.05	.02
224 Wayne Tolleson	.05	.02
225 Mike Smithson	.05	.02
226 Max Venable	.05	.02
227 Jamie Moyer RC	.50	.20
228 Curt Wilkerson	.05	.02
229 Mike Birkbeck	.10	.04
230 Don Baylor	.10	.04
231 Giants Team (Bob Brenly and Jim Gott)	.05	.02
232 Reggie Williams	.05	.02
233 Russ Morman	.05	.02
234 Pat Sheridan	.05	.02
235 Alvin Davis	.05	.02
236 Tommy John	.10	.04
237 Jim Morrison	.05	.02
238 Bill Krueger	.05	.02
239 Juan Espino	.05	.02
240 Steve Balboni	.05	.02
241 Danny Heep	.05	.02
242 Rick Mahler	.05	.02
243 Whitey Herzog MG	.10	.04
244 Dickie Noles	.05	.02
245 Willie Upshaw	.05	.02
246 Jim Dwyer	.05	.02
247 Jeff Reed	.05	.02
248 Gene Walter	.05	.02
249 Jim Pankovits	.05	.02
250 Teddy Higuera	.05	.02
251 Rob Wilfong	.05	.02
252 Dennis Martinez	.10	.04
253 Eddie Milner	.05	.02
254 Bob Tewksbury RC *	.25	.10
255 Juan Samuel	.05	.02
256 Royals Team (George Brett and Frank White)	.15	.06
257 Bob Forsch	.05	.02
258 Steve Yeager	.10	.04
259 Mike Greenwell RC	.25	.10
260 Vida Blue	.10	.04
261 Ruben Sierra RC	.50	.20
262 Jim Winn	.05	.02
263 Stan Javier	.05	.02
264 Checklist 133-264	.05	.02
265 Darrell Evans	.10	.04
266 Jeff Hamilton	.05	.02
267 Howard Johnson	.10	.04
268 Pat Corrales MG	.05	.02
269 Cliff Speck	.05	.02
270 Jody Davis	.05	.02
271 Mike G. Brown	.05	.02
272 Andres Galarraga	.10	.04
273 Gene Nelson	.05	.02
274 Jeff Hearron UER (Duplicate 1986 stat line on back)	.05	.02
275 LaMarr Hoyt	.05	.02
276 Jackie Gutierrez	.05	.02
277 Juan Agosto	.05	.02
278 Gary Pettis	.05	.02
279 Dan Plesac	.05	.02
280 Jeff Leonard	.05	.02
281 Reds Team Pete Rose, Bo Diaz and Bill Gullickson	.25	.10
282 Jeff Calhoun	.05	.02
283 Doug Drabek RC*	.40	.16
284 John Moses	.05	.02
285 Dennis Boyd	.05	.02
286 Mike Woodard	.05	.02
287 Dave Von Ohlen	.05	.02
288 Tito Landrum	.05	.02
289 Bob Kipper	.05	.02
290 Leon Durham	.05	.02
291 Mitch Williams RC *	.25	.10
292 Franklin Stubbs	.05	.02
293 Bob Rodgers MG	.05	.02
294 Steve Jeltz	.05	.02
295 Len Dykstra	.10	.04
296 Andres Thomas	.05	.02
297 Don Schulze	.05	.02
298 Larry Herndon	.05	.02
299 Joel Davis	.05	.02
300 Reggie Jackson	.15	.06
301 Luis Aquino UER (No trademark never corrected)	.05	.02
302 Bill Schroeder	.05	.02
303 Juan Berenguer	.05	.02
304 Phil Garner	.10	.04
305 John Franco	.10	.04
306 Red Sox Team (Tom Seaver, John McNamara MG, and Rich Gedman)	.10	.04
307 Lee Guetterman	.05	.02
308 Don Slaught	.05	.02
309 Mike Young	.05	.02
310 Frank Viola	.10	.04
311 Rickey Henderson TBC '82	.15	.06
312 Reggie Jackson TBC '77	.10	.04
313 Roberto Clemente TBC '72	.25	.10
314 Carl Yastrzemski UER TBC '67 (Sic, 112 RBI's on back)	.25	.10
315 Maury Wills TBC '62	.10	.04
316 Brian Fisher	.05	.02
317 Clint Hurdle	.05	.02
318 Jim Fregosi MG	.05	.02
319 Greg Swindell RC	.25	.10
320 Barry Bonds RC	15.00	6.00
321 Mike Laga	.05	.02
322 Chris Bando	.05	.02
323 Al Newman	.05	.02
324 David Palmer	.05	.02
325 Garry Templeton	.10	.04
326 Mark Gubicza	.05	.02
327 Dale Sveum	.05	.02
328 Bob Welch	.10	.04
329 Ron Roenicke	.05	.02
330 Mike Scott	.10	.04
331 Mets Team (Gary Carter and Darryl Strawberry)	.10	.04
332 Joe Price	.05	.02
333 Ken Phelps	.05	.02
334 Ed Correa	.05	.02
335 Candy Maldonado	.05	.02
336 Allan Anderson	.05	.02
337 Darrell Miller	.05	.02
338 Tim Conroy	.05	.02
339 Donnie Hill	.05	.02
340 Roger Clemens	.50	.20
341 Mike C. Brown	.05	.02
342 Bob James	.05	.02
343 Hal Lanier MG	.05	.02
344A Joe Niekro (Copyright inside righthand border)	.05	.02
344B Joe Niekro	.05	.02

(Copyright outside righthand border)
345 Andre Dawson .10 .04
346 Shawon Dunston .05 .02
347 Mickey Brantley .05 .02
348 Carmelo Martinez .05 .02
349 Storm Davis .05 .02
350 Keith Hernandez .10 .04
351 Gene Garber .05 .02
352 Mike Felder .05 .02
353 Ernie Camacho .05 .02
354 Jamie Quirk .05 .02
355 Don Carman .05 .02
356 White Sox Team .05 .02
(Mound conference)
357 Steve Fireovid .05 .02
358 Sal Butera .05 .02
359 Doug Corbett .05 .02
360 Pedro Guerrero .10 .04
361 Mark Thurmond .05 .02
362 Luis Quinones .05 .02
363 Jose Guzman .05 .02
364 Randy Bush .05 .02
365 Rick Rhoden .05 .02
366 Mark McGwire 4.00 1.60
367 Jeff Lahti .05 .02
368 John McNamara MG .05 .02
369 Brian Dayett .05 .02
370 Fred Lynn .10 .04
371 Mark Eichhorn .05 .02
372 Jerry Mumphrey .05 .02
373 Jeff Dedmon .05 .02
374 Glenn Hoffman .05 .02
375 Ron Guidry .10 .04
376 Scott Bradley .05 .02
377 John Henry Johnson .05 .02
378 Rafael Santana .05 .02
379 John Russell .05 .02
380 Rich Gossage .10 .04
381 Expos Team .05 .02
(Mound conference)
382 Rudy Law .05 .02
383 Ron Davis .05 .02
384 Johnny Grubb .05 .02
385 Orel Hershiser .10 .04
386 Dickie Thon .05 .02
387 T.R. Bryden .05 .02
388 Geno Petralli .05 .02
389 Jeff D. Robinson .05 .02
390 Gary Matthews .10 .04
391 Jay Howell .05 .02
392 Checklist 265-396 .05 .02
393 Pete Rose MG .15 .06
394 Mike Bielecki .05 .02
395 Damaso Garcia .05 .02
396 Tim Lollar .05 .02
397 Greg Walker .05 .02
398 Brad Havens .05 .02
399 Curt Ford .05 .02
400 George Brett .60 .24
401 Billy Joe Robidoux .05 .02
402 Mike Trujillo .05 .02
403 Jerry Royster .05 .02
404 Doug Sisk .05 .02
405 Brook Jacoby .05 .02
406 Yankees Team .50 .20
(Rickey Henderson and Don Mattingly)
407 Jim Acker .05 .02
408 John Mizerock .05 .02
409 Milt Thompson .05 .02
410 Fernando Valenzuela .10 .04
411 Darnell Coles .05 .02
412 Eric Davis .15 .06
413 Moose Haas .05 .02
414 Joe Orsulak .05 .02
415 Bobby Witt RC .25 .10
416 Tom Nieto .05 .02
417 Pat Perry .05 .02
418 Dick Williams MG .05 .02
419 Mark Portugal RC * .25 .10
420 Will Clark RC 1.00 .40
421 Jose DeLeon .05 .02
422 Jack Howell .05 .02
423 Jaime Cocanower .05 .02
424 Chris Speier .05 .02
425 Tom Seaver UER .15 .06
Earned Runs amount is wrong
For 86 Red Sox and Career
Also the ERA is wrong for 86 and career
426 Floyd Rayford .05 .02
427 Edwin Nunez .05 .02
428 Bruce Bochy .05 .02
429 Tim Pyznarski .05 .02
430 Mike Schmidt .50 .20
431 Dodgers Team .05 .02
(Mound conference)
432 Jim Slaton .05 .02
433 Ed Hearn .05 .02
434 Mike Fischlin .05 .02
435 Bruce Sutter .10 .04
436 Andy Allanson .05 .02
437 Ted Power .05 .02
438 Kelly Downs RC .10 .04
439 Karl Best .05 .02
440 Willie McGee .10 .04
441 Dave Leiper .05 .02
442 Mitch Webster .05 .02
443 John Felske MG .05 .02
444 Jeff Russell .05 .02
445 Dave Lopes .10 .04
446 Chuck Finley RC .40 .16
447 Bill Almon .05 .02
448 Chris Bosio RC .25 .10
449 Pat Dodson .10 .04
450 Kirby Puckett .25 .10
451 Joe Sambito .05 .02
452 Dave Henderson .05 .02
453 Scott Terry RC .10 .04
454 Luis Salazar .05 .02
455 Mike Boddicker .05 .02
456 A's Team .05 .02
(Mound conference)
457 Len Matuszek .05 .02
458 Kelly Gruber .05 .02
459 Dennis Eckersley .15 .06
460 Darryl Strawberry .10 .04
461 Craig McMurtry .05 .02
462 Scott Fletcher .05 .02
463 Tom Candiotti .05 .02
464 Butch Wynegar .05 .02
465 Todd Worrell .05 .02
466 Kal Daniels .05 .02
467 Randy St.Claire .05 .02
468 G.Bamberger MG .05 .02
469 Mike Diaz .05 .02
470 Dave Dravecky .05 .02
471 Ronn Reynolds .05 .02
472 Bill Doran .05 .02
473 Steve Farr .05 .02
474 Jerry Narron .05 .02
475 Scott Garrelts .05 .02
476 Danny Tartabull .05 .02
477 Ken Howell .05 .02
478 Tim Laudner .05 .02
479 Bob Sebra .05 .02
480 Jim Rice .10 .04
481 Phillies Team .05 .02
(Glenn Wilson Juan Samuel and Von Hayes)
482 Daryl Boston .05 .02
483 Dwight Lowry .05 .02
484 Jim Traber .05 .02
485 Tony Fernandez .05 .02
486 Otis Nixon .05 .02
487 Dave Gumpert .05 .02
488 Ray Knight .10 .04
489 Bill Gullickson .05 .02
490 Dale Murphy .15 .06
491 Ron Karkovice RC .25 .10
492 Mike Heath .05 .02
493 Tom Lasorda MG .15 .06
494 Barry Jones .05 .02
495 Gorman Thomas .10 .04
496 Bruce Bochte .05 .02
497 Dale Mohorcic .05 .02
498 Bob Kearney .05 .02
499 Bruce Ruffin RC .10 .04
500 Don Mattingly .60 .24
501 Craig Lefferts .05 .02
502 Dick Schofield .05 .02
503 Larry Andersen .05 .02
504 Mickey Hatcher .05 .02
505 Bryn Smith .05 .02
506 Orioles Team .05 .02
(Mound conference)
507 Dave L. Stapleton .05 .02
508 Scott Bankhead .05 .02
509 Enos Cabell .05 .02
510 Tom Henke .05 .02
511 Steve Lyons .05 .02
512 Dave Magadan RC .25 .10
513 Carmen Castillo .05 .02
514 Orlando Mercado .05 .02
515 Willie Hernandez .05 .02
516 Ted Simmons .10 .04
517 Mario Soto .10 .04
518 Gene Mauch MG .05 .02
519 Curt Young .05 .02
520 Jack Clark .10 .04
521 Rick Reuschel .10 .04
522 Checklist 397-528 .05 .02
523 Earnie Riles .05 .02
524 Bob Shirley .05 .02
525 Phil Bradley .05 .02
526 Roger Mason .05 .02
527 Jim Wohlford .05 .02
528 Ken Dixon .05 .02
529 Alvaro Espinoza RC .10 .04
530 Tony Gwynn .30 .12
531 Astros Team .10 .04
(Yogi Berra conference)
532 Jeff Stone .05 .02
533 Angel Salazar .05 .02
534 Scott Sanderson .05 .02
535 Tony Armas .10 .04
536 Terry Mulholland RC .25 .10
537 Rance Mulliniks .05 .02
538 Tom Niedenfuer .05 .02
539 Reid Nichols .05 .02
540 Terry Kennedy .05 .02
541 Rafael Belliard RC .25 .10
542 Ricky Horton .05 .02
543 Dave Johnson MG .05 .02
544 Zane Smith .05 .02
545 Buddy Bell .10 .04
546 Mike Morgan .05 .02
547 Rob Deer .05 .02
548 Bill Mooneyham .05 .02
549 Bob Melvin .05 .02
550 Pete Incaviglia RC * .25 .10
551 Frank Wills .05 .02
552 Larry Sheets .05 .02
553 Mike Maddux .05 .02
554 Buddy Biancalana .05 .02
555 Dennis Rasmussen .05 .02
556 Angels Team .05 .02
(Rene Lachemann CO, Mike Witt, and Bob Boone)
557 John Cerutti .05 .02
558 Greg Gagne .05 .02
559 Lance McCullers .05 .02
560 Glenn Davis .05 .02
561 Rey Quinones .05 .02
562 Bryan Clutterbuck .05 .02
563 John Stefero .05 .02
564 Larry McWilliams .05 .02
565 Dusty Baker .10 .04
566 Tim Hulett .05 .02
567 Greg Mathews .05 .02
568 Earl Weaver MG .10 .04
569 Wade Rowdon .05 .02
570 Sid Fernandez .05 .02
571 Ozzie Virgil .05 .02
572 Pete Ladd .05 .02
573 Hal McRae .10 .04
574 Manny Lee .05 .02
575 Pat Tabler .05 .02
576 Frank Pastore .05 .02
577 Dann Bilardello .05 .02
578 Billy Hatcher .05 .02
579 Rick Burleson .05 .02
580 Mike Krukow .05 .02
581 Cubs Team .05 .02
(Ron Cey and Steve Trout)
582 Bruce Berenyi .05 .02
583 Junior Ortiz .05 .02
584 Ron Kittle .05 .02
585 Scott Bailes .05 .02
586 Ben Oglivie .10 .04
587 Eric Plunk .05 .02
588 Wallace Johnson .05 .02
589 Steve Crawford .05 .02
590 Vince Coleman .05 .02
591 Spike Owen .05 .02
592 Chris Welsh .05 .02
593 Chuck Tanner MG .05 .02
594 Rick Anderson .05 .02
595 Keith Hernandez AS .05 .02
596 Steve Sax AS .05 .02
597 Mike Schmidt AS .25 .10
598 Ozzie Smith AS .25 .10
599 Tony Gwynn AS .15 .06
600 Dave Parker AS .05 .02
601 Darryl Strawberry AS .05 .02
602 Gary Carter AS .05 .02
603A D.Gooden AS .05 .02
ERR no trademark
603B D.Gooden AS COR .05 .02
604 F.Valenzuela AS .05 .02
605 Todd Worrell AS .05 .02
606 D.Mattingly AS COR .30 .12
606A Don Mattingly AS 1.00 .40
ERR (no trademark)
607 Tony Bernazard AS .05 .02
608 Wade Boggs AS .10 .04
609 Cal Ripken AS .25 .10
610 Jim Rice AS .05 .02
611 Kirby Puckett AS .15 .06
612 George Bell AS .05 .02
613 Lance Parrish AS UER .05 .02
(Pitcher heading on back)
614 Roger Clemens AS .25 .10
615 Teddy Higuera AS .05 .02
616 Dave Righetti AS .05 .02
617 Al Nipper .05 .02
618 Tom Kelly MG .05 .02
619 Jerry Reed .05 .02
620 Jose Canseco .25 .10
621 Danny Cox .05 .02
622 Glenn Braggs RC .10 .04
623 Kurt Stillwell .05 .02
624 Tim Burke .05 .02
625 Mookie Wilson .10 .04
626 Joel Skinner .05 .02
627 Ken Oberkfell .05 .02
628 Bob Walk .05 .02
629 Larry Parrish .05 .02
630 John Candelaria .05 .02
631 Tigers Team .05 .02
(Mound conference)
632 Rob Woodward .05 .02
633 Jose Uribe .05 .02
634 Rafael Palmeiro RC 2.00 .80
635 Ken Schrom .05 .02
636 Darren Daulton .10 .04
637 Bip Roberts RC* .25 .10
638 Rich Bordi .05 .02
639 Gerald Perry .05 .02
640 Mark Clear .05 .02
641 Domingo Ramos .05 .02
642 Al Pulido .05 .02
643 Ron Shepherd .05 .02
644 John Denny .05 .02
645 Dwight Evans .10 .04
646 Mike Mason .05 .02
647 Tom Lawless .05 .02
648 Barry Larkin RC 1.00 .40
649 Mickey Tettleton .10 .04
650 Hubie Brooks .05 .02
651 Benny Distefano .05 .02
652 Terry Forster .05 .02
653 Kevin Mitchell RC * .40 .16
654 Checklist 529-660 .05 .02
655 Jesse Barfield .10 .04
656 Rangers Team .05 .02
(Bobby Valentine MG and Ricky Wright)
657 Tom Waddell .05 .02
658 R.Thompson RC* .25 .10
659 Aurelio Lopez .05 .02
660 Bob Horner .10 .04
661 Lou Whitaker .10 .04
662 Frank DiPino .05 .02
663 Cliff Johnson .05 .02
664 Mike Marshall .05 .02
665 Rod Scurry .05 .02
666 Von Hayes .05 .02
667 Ron Hassey .05 .02
668 Juan Bonilla .05 .02
669 Bud Black .05 .02
670 Jose Cruz .10 .04
671A Ray Soff ERR .05 .02
(No D* before copyright line)
671B Ray Soff COR .05 .02
(D* before copyright line)
672 Chili Davis .10 .04
673 Don Sutton .10 .04
674 Bill Campbell .05 .02
675 Ed Romero .05 .02
676 Charlie Moore .05 .02
677 Bob Grich .10 .04
678 Carney Lansford .10 .04
679 Kent Hrbek .10 .04
680 Ryne Sandberg .40 .16
681 George Bell .10 .04
682 Jerry Reuss .05 .02
683 Gary Roenicke .05 .02
684 Kent Tekulve .05 .02
685 Jerry Hairston .05 .02
686 Doyle Alexander .05 .02
687 Alan Trammell .10 .04
688 Juan Beniquez .05 .02
689 Darrell Porter .05 .02
690 Dane Iorg .05 .02
691 Dave Parker .10 .04
692 Frank White .10 .04
693 Terry Puhl .05 .02
694 Phil Niekro .10 .04
695 Chico Walker .05 .02
696 Gary Lucas .05 .02
697 Ed Lynch .05 .02
698 Ernie Whitt .05 .02
699 Ken Landreaux .05 .02
700 Dave Bergman .05 .02
701 Willie Randolph .10 .04
702 Greg Gross .05 .02
703 Dave Schmidt .05 .02
704 Jesse Orosco .05 .02
705 Bruce Hurst .05 .02
706 Rick Manning .05 .02
707 Bob McClure .05 .02
708 Scott McGregor .05 .02
709 Dave Kingman .10 .04
710 Gary Gaetti .10 .04
711 Ken Griffey .10 .04
712 Don Robinson .05 .02
713 Tom Brookens .05 .02
714 Dan Quisenberry .05 .02
715 Bob Dernier .05 .02
716 Rick Leach .05 .02
717 Ed VandeBerg .05 .02
718 Steve Carlton .10 .04
719 Tom Hume .05 .02
720 Richard Dotson .05 .02
721 Tom Herr .05 .02
722 Bob Knepper .05 .02
723 Brett Butler .10 .04
724 Greg Minton .05 .02
725 George Hendrick .10 .04
726 Frank Tanana .10 .04
727 Mike Moore .05 .02
728 Tippy Martinez .05 .02
729 Tom Paciorek .05 .02
730 Eric Show .05 .02
731 Dave Concepcion .10 .04
732 Manny Trillo .05 .02
733 Bill Caudill .05 .02
734 Bill Madlock .10 .04
735 Rickey Henderson .25 .10
736 Steve Bedrosian .05 .02
737 Floyd Bannister .05 .02
738 Jorge Orta .05 .02
739 Chet Lemon .10 .04
740 Rich Gedman .05 .02
741 Paul Molitor .15 .06
742 Andy McGaffigan .05 .02
743 Dwayne Murphy .05 .02
744 Roy Smalley .05 .02
745 Glenn Hubbard .05 .02
746 Bob Ojeda .05 .02
747 Johnny Ray .05 .02
748 Mike Flanagan .05 .02
749 Ozzie Smith .40 .16
750 Steve Trout .05 .02
751 Garth Iorg .05 .02
752 Dan Petry .05 .02
753 Rick Honeycutt .05 .02
754 Dave LaPoint .05 .02
755 Luis Aguayo .05 .02
756 Carlton Fisk .15 .06
757 Nolan Ryan 1.00 .40
758 Tony Bernazard .05 .02
759 Joel Youngblood .05 .02
760 Mike Witt .05 .02
761 Greg Pryor .05 .02
762 Gary Ward .05 .02
763 Tim Flannery .05 .02
764 Bill Buckner .10 .04
765 Kirk Gibson .10 .04
766 Don Aase .05 .02
767 Ron Cey .10 .04
768 Dennis Lamp .05 .02
769 Steve Sax .05 .02
770 Dave Winfield .10 .04
771 Shane Rawley .05 .02
772 Harold Baines .10 .04
773 Robin Yount .40 .16
774 Wayne Krenchicki .05 .02
775 Joaquin Andujar .10 .04
776 Tom Brunansky .05 .02
777 Chris Chambliss .10 .04
778 Jack Morris .10 .04
779 Craig Reynolds .05 .02
780 Andre Thornton .05 .02
781 Atlee Hammaker .05 .02
782 Brian Downing .10 .04
783 Willie Wilson .10 .04
784 Cal Ripken .75 .30
785 Terry Francona .10 .04
786 Jimy Williams MG .05 .02
787 Alejandro Pena .05 .02
788 Tim Stoddard .05 .02
789 Dan Schatzeder .05 .02
790 Julio Cruz .05 .02
791 Lance Parrish .10 .04
792 Checklist 661-792 .05 .02

1987 Topps Tiffany

These 792 standard-size cards were a parallel to the regular Topps issue. These cards feature "glossy" fronts and easy to read backs. These cards are in the same style as the regular Topps issue. This set was printed in Ireland and was issued only in factory set form. Unlike previous years, a significantly higher amount of these cards were produced. Therefore, the values of these cards are a much lower mulitplier to the regular cards than previous years. It is believed that as many as 30,000 of these sets were produced. This increase was probably in response to increased dealer interest.

Nm-Mt Ex-Mt
COMP.FACT.SET (792) 150.00 60.00
*STARS: 2.5X TO 6X BASIC CARDS...
*ROOKIES: 4X TO 10X BASIC CARDS

1987 Topps Glossy All-Stars

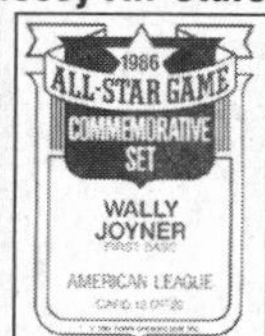

This set of 22 glossy cards was inserted one per rack pack. Players selected for the set are the starting players (plus manager and two pitchers) in the 1986 All-Star Game in Houston. Cards measure the standard size and the backs feature red and blue printing on a white card stock.

Nm-Mt Ex-Mt
COMPLETE SET (22) 5.00 2.00
1 Whitey Herzog MG .10 .04
2 Keith Hernandez .10 .04
3 Ryne Sandberg 1.00 .40
4 Mike Schmidt .50 .20
5 Ozzie Smith 1.00 .40
6 Tony Gwynn 1.00 .40
7 Dale Murphy .20 .08
8 Darryl Strawberry .10 .04
9 Gary Carter .50 .20
10 Dwight Gooden .15 .06
11 Fernando Valenzuela .10 .04
12 Dick Howser MG .05 .02
13 Wally Joyner .10 .04
14 Lou Whitaker .10 .04
15 Wade Boggs .50 .20
16 Cal Ripken 2.00 .80
17 Dave Winfield .20 .08
18 Rickey Henderson .60 .24
19 Kirby Puckett .50 .20
20 Lance Parrish .10 .04
21 Roger Clemens 1.00 .40
22 Teddy Higuera .05 .02

1987 Topps Glossy Send-Ins

Topps issued this set through a mail-in offer explained and advertised on the wax packs. This 60-card set features glossy fronts with each card measuring the standard size. The offer provided your choice of any one of the six 10-card subsets (1-10, 11-20, etc.) for 1.00 plus six of the Special Offer ("Spring Fever Baseball") insert cards, which were found one per wax pack. The last two players (numerically) in each ten-card subset are actually "Hot Prospects." This set is highlighted by an early Barry Bonds card.

Nm-Mt Ex-Mt
COMPLETE SET (60) 25.00 10.00
1 Don Mattingly 2.00 .80
2 Tony Gwynn 1.00 .40
3 Gary Gaetti .30 .12
4 Glenn Davis .20 .08
5 Roger Clemens 2.00 .80
6 Dale Murphy .75 .30
7 Lou Whitaker .30 .12
8 Roger McDowell .20 .08
9 Cory Snyder .20 .08
10 Todd Worrell .30 .12
11 Gary Carter .30 .12
12 Eddie Murray .75 .30
13 Bob Knepper .20 .08
14 Harold Baines .30 .12
15 Jeff Reardon .30 .12
16 Joe Carter .30 .12
17 Dave Parker .30 .12
18 Wade Boggs .50 .20
19 Danny Tartabull .20 .08
20 Jim Deshaies .20 .08
21 Rickey Henderson .75 .30
22 Rob Deer .20 .08
23 Ozzie Smith 1.25 .50
24 Dave Righetti .30 .12
25 Kent Hrbek .30 .12
26 Keith Hernandez .30 .12
27 Don Baylor .30 .12
28 Mike Schmidt 1.50 .60
29 Pete Incaviglia .30 .12
30 Barry Bonds 15.00 6.00
31 George Brett 2.00 .80
32 Darryl Strawberry .30 .12
33 Mike Witt .20 .08
34 Kevin Bass .20 .08
35 Jesse Barfield .20 .08
36 Bob Ojeda .20 .08
37 Cal Ripken 2.50 1.00
38 Vince Coleman .20 .08
39 Wally Joyner .50 .20
40 Robby Thompson .30 .12
41 Pete Rose 2.00 .80
42 Jim Rice .30 .12
43 Tony Bernazard .20 .08
44 Eric Davis .30 .12
45 George Bell .20 .08
46 Hubie Brooks .20 .08
47 Jack Morris .30 .12
48 Tim Raines .30 .12
49 Mark Eichhorn .20 .08
50 Kevin Mitchell .30 .12
51 Dwight Gooden .30 .12
52 Doug DeCinces .20 .08
53 Fernando Valenzuela .30 .12
54 Reggie Jackson .50 .20
55 Johnny Ray .20 .08
56 Mike Pagliarulo .20 .08
57 Kirby Puckett .75 .30
58 Lance Parrish .30 .12
59 Jose Canseco .75 .30
60 Greg Mathews .20 .08

1987 Topps Rookies

Inserted in each supermarket jumbo pack is a card from this series of 22 of 1986's best rookies as determined by Topps. Jumbo packs consisted of 100 (regular issue 1987 Topps baseball) cards with a stick of gum plus the insert "Rookie" card. The card fronts are in full color and measure the standard size. The card backs are printed in red and blue on white card stock and are numbered at the bottom essentially by alphabetical order.

	Nm-Mt	Ex-Mt
COMPLETE SET (22)	12.00	4.80
1 Andy Allanson	.25	.10
2 John Cangelosi	.25	.10
3 Jose Canseco	1.00	.40
4 Will Clark	2.50	1.00
5 Mark Eichhorn	.25	.10
6 Pete Incaviglia	.50	.20
7 Wally Joyner	.75	.30
8 Eric King	.25	.10
9 Dave Magadan	.50	.20
10 John Morris	.25	.10
11 Juan Nieves	.25	.10
12 Rafael Palmeiro	6.00	2.40
13 Billy Joe Robidoux	.25	.10
14 Bruce Ruffin	.25	.10
15 Ruben Sierra	1.00	.40
16 Cory Snyder	.25	.10
17 Kurt Stillwell	.25	.10
18 Dale Sveum	.25	.10
19 Danny Tartabull	.25	.10
20 Andres Thomas	.25	.10
21 Robby Thompson	.50	.20
22 Todd Worrell	.50	.20

1987 Topps Wax Box Cards

This set of eight cards is really four different sets of two smaller (approximately 2 1/8" by 3") cards which were printed on the side of the wax pack box; these eight cards are lettered A through H and are very similar in design to the Topps regular issue cards. The order of the set is alphabetical by player's name. Complete boxes would be worth an additional 25 percent premium over the prices below. The card backs are done in a newspaper headline style describing something about that player that happened the previous season. The card backs feature blue and yellow ink on gray card stock.

	Nm-Mt	Ex-Mt
COMPLETE SET (8)	3.00	1.20
A Don Baylor	.25	.10
B Steve Carlton	.75	.30
C Ron Cey	.25	.10
D Cecil Cooper	.10	.04
E Rickey Henderson	.75	.30
F Jim Rice	.25	.10
G Don Sutton	.75	.30
H Dave Winfield	.75	.30

1987 Topps Traded

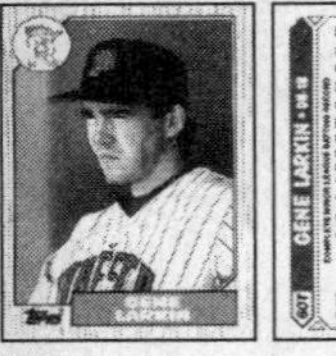

This 132-card standard-size Traded set was distributed exclusively in factory set form in a special green and white box through hobby dealers. The card fronts are identical in style to the Topps regular issue except for whiter stock and t-suffixed numbering on back. The cards are ordered alphabetically by player's last name. The key extended Rookie Cards in this set are Ellis Burks, David Cone, Greg Maddux, Fred McGriff and Matt Williams.

	Nm-Mt	Ex-Mt
COMP.FACT.SET (132)	10.00	4.00
1T Bill Almon	.05	.02
2T Scott Bankhead	.05	.02
3T Eric Bell	.10	.04
4T Juan Beniquez	.05	.02
5T Juan Berenguer	.05	.02
6T Greg Booker	.05	.02
7T Thad Bosley	.05	.02
8T Larry Bowa MG	.10	.04
9T Greg Brock	.05	.02
10T Bob Brower	.05	.02
11T Jerry Browne	.10	.04
12T Ralph Bryant	.05	.02
13T DeWayne Buice	.05	.02
14T Ellis Burks XRC	.50	.20
15T Ivan Calderon	.05	.02
16T Jeff Calhoun	.05	.02
17T Casey Candaele	.05	.02
18T John Cangelosi	.05	.02
19T Steve Carlton	.10	.04
20T Juan Castillo	.10	.04
21T Rick Cerone	.05	.02
22T Ron Cey	.10	.04
23T John Christensen	.05	.02
24T David Cone XRC	.75	.30
25T Chuck Crim	.05	.02
26T Storm Davis	.05	.02
27T Andre Dawson	.10	.04
28T Rick Dempsey	.05	.02
29T Doug Drabek	.50	.20
30T Mike Dunne	.05	.02
31T Dennis Eckersley	.15	.06
32T Lee Elia MG	.05	.02
33T Brian Fisher	.05	.02
34T Terry Francona	.10	.04
35T Willie Fraser	.10	.04
36T Billy Gardner MG	.05	.02
37T Ken Gerhart	.05	.02
38T Dan Gladden	.05	.02
39T Jim Gott	.05	.02
40T Cecilio Guante	.05	.02
41T Albert Hall	.05	.02
42T Terry Harper	.05	.02
43T Mickey Hatcher	.05	.02
44T Brad Havens	.05	.02
45T Neal Heaton	.05	.02
46T Mike Henneman XRC	.25	.10
47T Donnie Hill	.05	.02
48T Guy Hoffman	.05	.02
49T Brian Holton	.05	.02
50T Charles Hudson	.05	.02
51T Danny Jackson	.05	.02
52T Reggie Jackson	.15	.06
53T Chris James XRC *	.10	.04
54T Dion James	.05	.02
55T Stan Jefferson	.05	.02
56T Joe Johnson	.05	.02
57T Terry Kennedy	.05	.02
58T Mike Kingery	.10	.04
59T Ray Knight	.10	.04
60T Gene Larkin XRC	.25	.10
61T Mike LaValliere	.25	.10
62T Jack Lazorko	.05	.02
63T Terry Leach	.05	.02
64T Tim Leary	.05	.02
65T Jim Lindeman	.10	.04
66T Steve Lombardozzi	.05	.02
67T Bill Long	.05	.02
68T Barry Lyons	.05	.02
69T Shane Mack	.05	.02
70T Greg Maddux XRC	5.00	2.00
71T Bill Madlock	.10	.04
72T Joe Magrane XRC	.10	.04
73T Dave Martinez XRC *	.25	.10
74T Fred McGriff	.60	.24
75T Mark McLemore	.10	.04
76T Kevin McReynolds	.05	.02
77T Dave Meads	.05	.02
78T Eddie Milner	.05	.02
79T Greg Minton	.05	.02
80T John Mitchell XRC	.10	.04
81T Kevin Mitchell	.15	.06
82T Charlie Moore	.05	.02
83T Jeff Musselman	.05	.02
84T Gene Nelson	.05	.02
85T Graig Nettles	.10	.04
86T Al Newman	.05	.02
87T Reid Nichols	.05	.02
88T Tom Niedenfuer	.05	.02
89T Joe Niekro	.05	.02
90T Tom Nieto	.05	.02
91T Matt Nokes XRC	.25	.10
92T Dickie Noles	.05	.02
93T Pat Pacillo	.05	.02
94T Lance Parrish	.10	.04
95T Tony Pena	.05	.02
96T Luis Polonia XRC	.25	.10
97T Randy Ready	.05	.02
98T Jeff Reardon	.10	.04
99T Gary Redus	.05	.02
100T Jeff Reed	.05	.02
101T Rick Rhoden	.05	.02
102T Cal Ripken Sr. MG	.05	.02
103T Wally Ritchie	.05	.02
104T Jeff M. Robinson	.05	.02
105T Gary Roenicke	.05	.02
106T Jerry Royster	.05	.02
107T Mark Salas	.05	.02
108T Luis Salazar	.05	.02
109T Benny Santiago	.10	.04
110T Dave Schmidt	.05	.02
111T Kevin Seitzer XRC*	.25	.10
112T John Shelby	.05	.02
113T Steve Shields	.05	.02
114T John Smiley XRC	.25	.10
115T Chris Speier	.05	.02
116T Mike Stanley XRC*	.25	.10
117T Terry Steinbach XRC	.50	.20
118T Les Straker	.05	.02
119T Jim Sundberg	.10	.04
120T Danny Tartabull	.05	.02
121T Tom Trebelhorn MG	.05	.02
122T Dave Valle XRC **	.10	.04
123T Ed VandeBerg	.05	.02
124T Andy Van Slyke	.10	.04
125T Gary Ward	.05	.02
126T Alan Wiggins	.05	.02
127T Bill Wilkinson	.05	.02
128T Frank Williams	.05	.02
129T Matt Williams XRC	1.00	.40
130T Jim Winn	.05	.02
131T Matt Young	.05	.02
132T Checklist 1T-132T	.05	.02

1987 Topps Traded Tiffany

Since the update Tiffany cards were issued in the same quantities as the regular cards, again these cards are not valued as high as a multiplier as the previous years. These 132 standard-size cards parallel the regular cards but have glossy fronts and easy to read backs. These cards were issued in factory set form only. These sets, believed to be issued in the range of 30,000, are among the easiest of the Tiffany sets to find in the secondary market.

	Nm-Mt	Ex-Mt
COMP.FACT.SET (132)	40.00	16.00
*STARS: 2X TO 5X BASIC CARDS		
*ROOKIES: 2X TO 5X BASIC CARDS		

1988 Topps

This set consists of 792 standard-size cards. The cards were primarily issued in 15-card wax packs, 42-card rack packs and factory sets. Card fronts feature white borders encasing a color photo with team name running across the top and player name diagonally across the bottom. Subsets include Record Breakers (1-7), All-Stars (386-407), Turn Back the Clock (661-665), and Team Leaders (scattered throughout the set). The manager cards contain a team checklist on back. The key Rookie Cards in this set are Ellis Burks, Ken Caminiti, Tom Glavine, and Matt Williams.

	Nm-Mt	Ex-Mt
COMPLETE SET (792)	15.00	6.00
COMP.FACT SET (792)	15.00	6.00
COMP.X-MAS.SET (792)	40.00	16.00
1 Vince Coleman RB	.05	.02
2 Don Mattingly RB	.30	.12
3 Mark McGwire RB Rookie Homer Record (No white spot)	.75	.30
3A Mark McGwire RB Rookie Homer Record (White spot behind left foot)	.20	.08
4 Eddie Murray RB Switch Home Runs, Two Straight Games (No caption on front)	.15	.06
4A Eddie Murray RB Switch Home Runs, Two Straight Games (Caption in box on card front)	.50	.20
5 Phil Niekro Joe Niekro RB	.10	.04
6 Nolan Ryan RB	.40	.16
7 Benito Santiago RB	.05	.02
8 Kevin Elster	.05	.02
9 Andy Hawkins	.05	.02
10 Ryne Sandberg	.40	.16
11 Mike Young	.05	.02
12 Bill Schroeder	.05	.02
13 Andres Thomas	.05	.02
14 Sparky Anderson MG	.10	.04
15 Chili Davis	.10	.04
16 Kirk McCaskill	.05	.02
17 Ron Oester	.05	.02
18A Al Leiter RC ERR (Photo actually Steve George, right ear visible)	.50	.20
18B Al Leiter RC COR (Left ear visible)	.50	.20
19 Mark Davidson	.05	.02
20 Kevin Gross	.05	.02
21 Wade Boggs Spike Owen TL	.10	.04
22 Greg Swindell	.05	.02
23 Ken Landreaux	.05	.02
24 Jim Deshaies	.05	.02
25 Andres Galarraga	.10	.04
26 Mitch Williams	.05	.02
27 R.J. Reynolds	.05	.02
28 Jose Nunez	.05	.02
29 Angel Salazar	.05	.02
30 Sid Fernandez	.05	.02
31 Bruce Bochy	.05	.02
32 Mike Morgan	.05	.02
33 Rob Deer	.05	.02
34 Ricky Horton	.05	.02
35 Harold Baines	.10	.04
36 Jamie Moyer	.10	.04
37 Ed Romero	.05	.02
38 Jeff Calhoun	.05	.02
39 Gerald Perry	.05	.02
40 Orel Hershiser	.10	.04
41 Bob Melvin	.05	.02
42 Bill Landrum	.05	.02
43 Dick Schofield	.05	.02
44 Lou Piniella MG	.10	.04
45 Kent Hrbek	.10	.04
46 Darnell Coles	.05	.02
47 Joaquin Andujar	.10	.04
48 Alan Ashby	.05	.02
49 Dave Clark	.05	.02
50 Hubie Brooks	.05	.02
51 Eddie Murray Cal Ripken TL	.40	.16
52 Don Robinson	.05	.02
53 Curt Wilkerson	.05	.02
54 Jim Clancy	.05	.02
55 Phil Bradley	.05	.02
56 Ed Hearn	.05	.02
57 Tim Crews RC	.25	.10
58 Dave Magadan	.05	.02
59 Danny Cox	.05	.02
60 Rickey Henderson	.20	.08
61 Mark Knudson	.05	.02
62 Jeff Hamilton	.05	.02
63 Jimmy Jones	.05	.02
64 Ken Caminiti RC	.75	.30
65 Leon Durham	.05	.02
66 Shane Rawley	.05	.02
67 Ken Oberkfell	.05	.02
68 Dave Dravecky	.05	.02
69 Mike Hart	.05	.02
70 Roger Clemens	.50	.20
71 Gary Pettis	.05	.02
72 Dennis Eckersley	.15	.06
73 Randy Bush	.05	.02
74 Tom Lasorda MG	.15	.06
75 Joe Carter	.10	.04
76 Dennis Martinez	.10	.04
77 Tom O'Malley	.05	.02
78 Dan Petry	.05	.02
79 Ernie Whitt	.05	.02
80 Mark Langston	.05	.02
81 Ron Robinson John Franco TL	.05	.02
82 Darrel Akerfelds	.05	.02
83 Jose Oquendo	.05	.02
84 Cecilio Guante	.05	.02
85 Howard Johnson	.10	.04
86 Ron Karkovice	.05	.02
87 Mike Mason	.05	.02
88 Earnie Riles	.05	.02
89 Gary Thurman	.05	.02
90 Dale Murphy	.15	.06
91 Joey Cora RC	.25	.10
92 Len Matuszek	.05	.02
93 Bob Sebra	.05	.02
94 Chuck Jackson	.05	.02
95 Lance Parrish	.10	.04
96 Todd Benzinger RC*	.25	.10
97 Scott Garrelts	.05	.02
98 Rene Gonzales RC	.10	.04
99 Chuck Finley	.10	.04
100 Jack Clark	.10	.04
101 Allan Anderson	.05	.02
102 Barry Larkin	.15	.06
103 Curt Young	.05	.02
104 Dick Williams MG	.05	.02
105 Jesse Orosco	.05	.02
106 Jim Walewander	.05	.02
107 Scott Bailes	.05	.02
108 Steve Lyons	.05	.02
109 Joel Skinner	.05	.02
110 Teddy Higuera	.05	.02
111 Hubie Brooks Vance Law TL	.05	.02
112 Les Lancaster	.05	.02
113 Kelly Gruber	.05	.02
114 Jeff Russell	.05	.02
115 Johnny Ray	.05	.02
116 Jerry Don Gleaton	.05	.02
117 James Steels	.05	.02
118 Bob Welch	.10	.04
119 Robbie Wine	.05	.02
120 Kirby Puckett	.20	.08
121 Checklist 1-132	.05	.02
122 Tony Bernazard	.05	.02
123 Tom Candiotti	.05	.02
124 Ray Knight	.10	.04
125 Bruce Hurst	.05	.02
126 Steve Jeltz	.05	.02
127 Jim Gott	.05	.02
128 Johnny Grubb	.05	.02
129 Greg Minton	.05	.02
130 Buddy Bell	.10	.04
131 Don Schulze	.05	.02
132 Donnie Hill	.05	.02
133 Greg Mathews	.05	.02
134 Chuck Tanner MG	.05	.02
135 Dennis Rasmussen	.05	.02
136 Brian Dayett	.05	.02
137 Chris Bosio	.05	.02
138 Mitch Webster	.05	.02
139 Jerry Browne	.05	.02
140 Jesse Barfield	.10	.04
141 George Brett Bret Saberhagen TL	.20	.08
142 Andy Van Slyke	.10	.04
143 Mickey Tettleton	.05	.02
144 Don Gordon	.05	.02
145 Bill Madlock	.10	.04
146 Donell Nixon	.05	.02
147 Bill Buckner	.10	.04
148 Carmelo Martinez	.05	.02
149 Ken Howell	.05	.02
150 Eric Davis	.10	.04
151 Bob Knepper	.05	.02
152 Jody Reed RC	.25	.10
153 John Habyan	.05	.02
154 Jeff Stone	.05	.02
155 Bruce Sutter	.10	.04
156 Gary Matthews	.10	.04
157 Atlee Hammaker	.05	.02
158 Tim Hulett	.05	.02
159 Brad Arnsberg	.05	.02
160 Willie McGee	.10	.04
161 Bryn Smith	.05	.02
162 Mark McLemore	.05	.02
163 Dale Mohorcic	.05	.02
164 Dave Johnson MG	.05	.02
165 Robin Yount	.30	.12
166 Rick Rodriquez	.05	.02
167 Rance Mulliniks	.05	.02
168 Barry Jones	.05	.02
169 Ross Jones	.05	.02
170 Rich Gossage	.10	.04
171 Shawon Dunston Manny Trillo TL	.05	.02
172 Lloyd McClendon RC	.25	.10
173 Eric Plunk	.05	.02
174 Phil Garner	.10	.04
175 Kevin Bass	.05	.02
176 Jeff Reed	.05	.02
177 Frank Tanana	.10	.04
178 Dwayne Henry	.05	.02
179 Charlie Puleo	.05	.02
180 Terry Kennedy	.05	.02
181 David Cone	.10	.04
182 Ken Phelps	.05	.02
183 Tom Lawless	.05	.02
184 Ivan Calderon	.05	.02
185 Rick Rhoden	.05	.02
186 Rafael Palmeiro	.40	.16
187 Steve Kiefer	.05	.02
188 John Russell	.05	.02
189 Wes Gardner	.05	.02
190 Candy Maldonado	.05	.02
191 John Cerutti	.05	.02
192 Devon White	.10	.04
193 Brian Fisher	.05	.02
194 Tom Kelly MG	.05	.02
195 Dan Quisenberry	.05	.02
196 Dave Engle	.05	.02
197 Lance McCullers	.05	.02
198 Franklin Stubbs	.05	.02
199 Dave Meads	.05	.02
200 Wade Boggs	.15	.06
201 Bobby Valentine MG Pete O'Brien Pete Incaviglia Steve Buechele TL	.05	.02
202 Glenn Hoffman	.05	.02
203 Fred Toliver	.05	.02
204 Paul O'Neill	.15	.06
205 Nelson Liriano	.05	.02
206 Domingo Ramos	.05	.02
207 John Mitchell RC	.10	.04
208 Steve Lake	.05	.02
209 Richard Dotson	.05	.02
210 Willie Randolph	.10	.04
211 Frank DiPino	.05	.02
212 Greg Brock	.05	.02
213 Albert Hall	.05	.02
214 Dave Schmidt	.05	.02
215 Von Hayes	.05	.02
216 Jerry Reuss	.05	.02
217 Harry Spilman	.05	.02
218 Dan Schatzeder	.05	.02
219 Mike Stanley	.05	.02
220 Tom Henke	.05	.02
221 Rafael Belliard	.05	.02
222 Steve Farr	.05	.02
223 Stan Jefferson	.05	.02
224 Tom Trebelhorn MG	.05	.02
225 Mike Scioscia	.10	.04
226 Dave Lopes	.10	.04
227 Ed Correa	.05	.02
228 Wallace Johnson	.05	.02
229 Jeff Musselman	.05	.02
230 Pat Tabler	.05	.02
231 Barry Bonds Bobby Bonilla TL	.50	.20
232 Bob James	.05	.02
233 Rafael Santana	.05	.02
234 Ken Dayley	.05	.02
235 Gary Ward	.05	.02
236 Ted Power	.05	.02
237 Mike Heath	.05	.02
238 Luis Polonia RC*	.25	.10
239 Roy Smalley	.05	.02
240 Lee Smith	.10	.04
241 Damaso Garcia	.05	.02
242 Tom Niedenfuer	.05	.02
243 Mark Ryal	.05	.02
244 Jeff D. Robinson	.05	.02
245 Rich Gedman	.05	.02
246 Mike Campbell	.05	.02
247 Thad Bosley	.05	.02
248 Storm Davis	.05	.02
249 Mike Marshall	.05	.02
250 Nolan Ryan	1.00	.40
251 Tom Foley	.05	.02
252 Bob Brower	.05	.02
253 Checklist 133-264	.05	.02
254 Lee Elia MG	.05	.02
255 Mookie Wilson	.10	.04
256 Ken Schrom	.05	.02
257 Jerry Royster	.05	.02
258 Ed Nunez	.05	.02
259 Ron Kittle	.05	.02
260 Vince Coleman	.05	.02
261 Giants TL (Five players)	.05	.02
262 Drew Hall	.05	.02
263 Glenn Braggs	.05	.02
264 Les Straker	.05	.02
265 Bo Diaz	.05	.02
266 Paul Assenmacher	.05	.02
267 Billy Bean RC	.10	.04
268 Bruce Ruffin	.05	.02
269 Ellis Burks RC	.40	.16
270 Mike Witt	.05	.02
271 Ken Gerhart	.05	.02
272 Steve Ontiveros	.05	.02
273 Garth Iorg	.05	.02
274 Junior Ortiz	.05	.02
275 Kevin Seitzer	.05	.02
276 Luis Salazar	.05	.02
277 Alejandro Pena	.05	.02
278 Jose Cruz	.10	.04
279 Randy St.Claire	.05	.02
280 Pete Incaviglia	.05	.02
281 Jerry Hairston	.05	.02
282 Pat Perry	.05	.02
283 Phil Lombardi	.05	.02
284 Larry Bowa MG	.10	.04
285 Jim Presley	.05	.02
286 Chuck Crim	.05	.02
287 Manny Trillo	.05	.02
288 Pat Pacillo (Chris Sabo in background of photo)	.05	.02
289 Dave Bergman	.05	.02
290 Tony Fernandez	.05	.02
291 Billy Hatcher Kevin Bass TL	.05	.02
292 Carney Lansford	.10	.04
293 Doug Jones RC	.25	.10
294 Al Pedrique	.05	.02
295 Bert Blyleven	.10	.04
296 Floyd Rayford	.05	.02
297 Zane Smith	.05	.02
298 Milt Thompson	.05	.02
299 Steve Crawford	.05	.02
300 Don Mattingly	.60	.24
301 Bud Black	.05	.02
302 Jose Uribe	.05	.02
303 Eric Show	.05	.02
304 George Hendrick	.10	.04
305 Steve Sax	.05	.02
306 Billy Hatcher	.05	.02
307 Mike Trujillo	.05	.02
308 Lee Mazzilli	.10	.04
309 Bill Long	.05	.02
310 Tom Herr	.05	.02
311 Scott Sanderson	.05	.02
312 Joey Meyer	.05	.02
313 Bob McClure	.05	.02
314 Jimy Williams MG	.05	.02
315 Dave Parker	.10	.04
316 Jose Rijo	.10	.04
317 Tom Nieto	.05	.02
318 Mel Hall	.05	.02
319 Mike Loynd	.05	.02
320 Alan Trammell	.10	.04
321 Harold Baines Carlton Fisk TL	.10	.04
322 Vicente Palacios	.05	.02
323 Rick Leach	.05	.02
324 Danny Jackson	.05	.02
325 Glenn Hubbard	.05	.02
326 Al Nipper	.05	.02
327 Larry Sheets	.05	.02
328 Greg Cadaret	.05	.02
329 Chris Speier	.05	.02
330 Eddie Whitson	.05	.02
331 Brian Downing	.10	.04
332 Jerry Reed	.05	.02
333 Wally Backman	.05	.02
334 Dave LaPoint	.05	.02
335 Claudell Washington	.05	.02
336 Ed Lynch	.05	.02
337 Jim Gantner	.05	.02
338 Brian Holton UER 1987 ERA .389, should be 3.89	.05	.02
339 Kurt Stillwell	.05	.02
340 Jack Morris	.10	.04
341 Carmen Castillo	.05	.02
342 Larry Andersen	.05	.02

343 Greg Gagne .05 .02
344 Tony LaRussa MG .10 .04
345 Scott Fletcher .05 .02
346 Vance Law .05 .02
347 Joe Johnson .05 .02
348 Jim Eisenreich .05 .02
349 Bob Walk .05 .02
350 Will Clark .20 .08
351 Red Schoendienst CO .10 .04
Tony Pena TL
352 Bill Ripken RC* .05 .02
353 Ed Olwine .05 .02
354 Marc Sullivan .05 .02
355 Roger McDowell .05 .02
356 Luis Aguayo .05 .02
357 Floyd Bannister .05 .02
358 Rey Quinones .05 .02
359 Tim Stoddard .05 .02
360 Tony Gwynn .30 .12
361 Greg Maddux 1.00 .40
362 Juan Castillo .05 .02
363 Willie Fraser .05 .02
364 Nick Esasky .05 .02
365 Floyd Youmans .05 .02
366 Chet Lemon .10 .04
367 Tim Leary .05 .02
368 Gerald Young .05 .02
369 Greg Harris .05 .02
370 Jose Canseco .20 .08
371 Joe Hesketh .05 .02
372 Matt Williams RC .75 .30
373 Checklist 265-396 .05 .02
374 Doc Edwards MG .05 .02
375 Tom Brunansky .05 .02
376 Bill Wilkinson .05 .02
377 Sam Horn RC .10 .04
378 Todd Frohwirth .05 .02
379 Rafael Ramirez .05 .02
380 Joe Magrane RC* .05 .02
381 Wally Joyner .10 .04
Jack Howell TL
382 Keith A. Miller RC .25 .10
383 Eric Bell .05 .02
384 Neil Allen .05 .02
385 Carlton Fisk .15 .06
386 Don Mattingly AS .30 .12
387 Willie Randolph AS .05 .02
388 Wade Boggs AS .10 .04
389 Alan Trammell AS .05 .02
390 George Bell AS .05 .02
391 Kirby Puckett AS .15 .06
392 Dave Winfield AS .05 .02
393 Matt Nokes AS .05 .02
394 Roger Clemens AS .20 .08
395 Jimmy Key AS .05 .02
396 Tom Henke AS .05 .02
397 Jack Clark AS .05 .02
398 Juan Samuel AS .05 .02
399 Tim Wallach AS .05 .02
400 Ozzie Smith AS .20 .08
401 Andre Dawson AS .05 .02
402 Tony Gwynn AS .15 .06
403 Tim Raines AS .05 .02
404 Benny Santiago AS .05 .02
405 Dwight Gooden AS .05 .02
406 Shane Rawley AS .05 .02
407 Steve Bedrosian AS .05 .02
408 Dion James .05 .02
409 Joel McKeon .05 .02
410 Tony Pena .05 .02
411 Wayne Tolleson .05 .02
412 Randy Myers .10 .04
413 John Christensen .05 .02
414 John McNamara MG .05 .02
415 Don Carman .05 .02
416 Keith Moreland .05 .02
417 Mark Ciardi .05 .02
418 Joel Youngblood .05 .02
419 Scott McGregor .05 .02
420 Wally Joyner .10 .04
421 Ed VandeBerg .05 .02
422 Dave Concepcion .10 .04
423 John Smiley RC* .25 .10
424 Dwayne Murphy .05 .02
425 Jeff Reardon .10 .04
426 Randy Ready .05 .02
427 Paul Kilgus .05 .02
428 John Shelby .05 .02
429 Alan Trammell .10 .04
Kirk Gibson TL
430 Glenn Davis .05 .02
431 Casey Candaele .05 .02
432 Mike Moore .05 .02
433 Bill Pecota RC* .05 .02
434 Rick Aguilera .05 .02
435 Mike Pagliarulo .05 .02
436 Mike Bielecki .05 .02
437 Fred Manrique .05 .02
438 Rob Ducey .05 .02
439 Dave Martinez .05 .02
440 Steve Bedrosian .05 .02
441 Rick Manning .05 .02
442 Tom Bolton .05 .02
443 Ken Griffey .10 .04
444 C.Ripken Sr. MG UER .05 .02
two copyrights
445 Mike Krukow .05 .02
446 Doug DeCinces .05 .02
(Now with Cardinals
on card front)
447 Jeff Montgomery RC .25 .10
448 Mike Davis .05 .02
449 Jeff M. Robinson .05 .02
450 Barry Bonds 2.00 .80
451 Keith Atherton .05 .02
452 Willie Wilson .10 .04
453 Dennis Powell .05 .02
454 Marvell Wynne .05 .02
455 Shawn Hillegas .05 .02
456 Dave Anderson .05 .02
457 Terry Leach .05 .02
458 Ron Hassey .05 .02
459 Dave Winfield .05 .02
Willie Randolph TL
460 Ozzie Smith .30 .12
461 Danny Darwin .05 .02
462 Don Slaught .05 .02
463 Fred McGriff .20 .08
464 Jay Tibbs .05 .02
465 Paul Molitor .15 .06
466 Jerry Mumphrey .05 .02
467 Don Aase .05 .02
468 Darren Daulton .10 .04
469 Jeff Dedmon .05 .02
470 Dwight Evans .10 .04
471 Donnie Moore .05 .02
472 Robby Thompson .05 .02
473 Joe Niekro .05 .02
474 Tom Brookens .05 .02
475 Pete Rose MG .50 .20
476 Dave Stewart .10 .04
477 Jamie Quirk .05 .02
478 Sid Bream .05 .02
479 Brett Butler .10 .04
480 Dwight Gooden .10 .04
481 Mariano Duncan .05 .02
482 Mark Davis .05 .02
483 Rod Booker .05 .02
484 Pat Clements .05 .02
485 Harold Reynolds .10 .04
486 Pat Keedy .05 .02
487 Jim Pankovits .05 .02
488 Andy McGaffigan .05 .02
489 Pedro Guerrero .05 .02
Fernando Valenzuela TL
490 Larry Parrish .05 .02
491 B.J. Surhoff .10 .04
492 Doyle Alexander .05 .02
493 Mike Greenwell .05 .02
494 Wally Ritchie .05 .02
495 Eddie Murray .20 .08
496 Guy Hoffman .05 .02
497 Kevin Mitchell .10 .04
498 Bob Boone .10 .04
499 Eric King .05 .02
500 Andre Dawson .10 .04
501 Tim Birtsas .05 .02
502 Dan Gladden .05 .02
503 Junior Noboa .05 .02
504 Bob Rodgers MG .05 .02
505 Willie Upshaw .05 .02
506 John Cangelosi .05 .02
507 Mark Gubicza .05 .02
508 Tim Teufel .05 .02
509 Bill Dawley .05 .02
510 Dave Winfield .10 .04
511 Joel Davis .05 .02
512 Alex Trevino .05 .02
513 Tim Flannery .05 .02
514 Pat Sheridan .05 .02
515 Juan Nieves .05 .02
516 Jim Sundberg .10 .04
517 Ron Robinson .05 .02
518 Greg Gross .05 .02
519 Harold Reynolds .05 .02
Phil Bradley TL
520 Dave Smith .05 .02
521 Jim Dwyer .05 .02
522 Bob Patterson .05 .02
523 Gary Roenicke .05 .02
524 Gary Lucas .05 .02
525 Marty Barrett .05 .02
526 Juan Berenguer .05 .02
527 Steve Henderson .05 .02
528A Checklist 397-528 .15 .06
ERR (455 S. Carlton)
528B Checklist 397-528 .10 .04
COR (455 S. Hillegas)
529 Tim Burke .05 .02
530 Gary Carter .10 .04
531 Rich Yett .05 .02
532 Mike Kingery .05 .02
533 John Farrell RC .10 .04
534 John Wathan MG .05 .02
535 Ron Guidry .10 .04
536 John Morris .05 .02
537 Steve Buechele .05 .02
538 Bill Wegman .05 .02
539 Mike LaValliere .05 .02
540 Bret Saberhagen .10 .04
541 Juan Beniquez .05 .02
542 Paul Noce .05 .02
543 Kent Tekulve .05 .02
544 Jim Traber .05 .02
545 Don Baylor .10 .04
546 John Candelaria .05 .02
547 Felix Fermin .05 .02
548 Shane Mack .05 .02
549 Albert Hall .10 .04
Dale Murphy
Ken Griffey
Dion James TL
550 Pedro Guerrero .10 .04
551 Terry Steinbach .10 .04
552 Mark Thurmond .05 .02
553 Tracy Jones .05 .02
554 Mike Smithson .05 .02
555 Brook Jacoby .05 .02
556 Stan Clarke .05 .02
557 Craig Reynolds .05 .02
558 Bob Ojeda .05 .02
559 Ken Williams RC .05 .02
560 Tim Wallach .05 .02
561 Rick Cerone .05 .02
562 Jim Lindeman .05 .02
563 Jose Guzman .05 .02
564 Frank Lucchesi MG .05 .02
565 Lloyd Moseby .05 .02
566 Charlie O'Brien .05 .02
567 Mike Diaz .05 .02
568 Chris Brown .05 .02
569 Charlie Leibrandt .05 .02
570 Jeffrey Leonard .05 .02
571 Mark Williamson .05 .02
572 Chris James .05 .02
573 Bob Stanley .05 .02
574 Graig Nettles .10 .04
575 Don Sutton .10 .04
576 Tommy Hinzo .05 .02
577 Tom Browning .05 .02
578 Gary Gaetti .10 .04
579 Gary Carter .05 .02
Kevin McReynolds TL
580 Mark McGwire 1.50 .60
581 Tito Landrum .05 .02
582 Mike Henneman RC* .25 .10
583 Dave Valle .05 .02
584 Steve Trout .05 .02
585 Ozzie Guillen .05 .02
586 Bob Forsch .05 .02
587 Terry Puhl .05 .02
588 Jeff Parrett .05 .02
589 Geno Petralli .05 .02
590 George Bell .10 .04
591 Doug Drabek .05 .02
592 Dale Sveum .05 .02
593 Bob Tewksbury .05 .02
594 Bobby Valentine MG .10 .04
595 Frank White .10 .04
596 John Kruk .10 .04
597 Gene Garber .05 .02
598 Lee Lacy .05 .02
599 Calvin Schiraldi .05 .02
600 Mike Schmidt .50 .20
601 Jack Lazorko .05 .02
602 Mike Aldrete .05 .02
603 Rob Murphy .05 .02
604 Chris Bando .05 .02
605 Kirk Gibson .20 .08
606 Moose Haas .05 .02
607 Mickey Hatcher .05 .02
608 Charlie Kerfeld .05 .02
609 Gary Gaetti .10 .04
Kent Hrbek TL
610 Keith Hernandez .10 .04
611 Tommy John .10 .04
612 Curt Ford .05 .02
613 Bobby Thigpen .05 .02
614 Herm Winningham .05 .02
615 Jody Davis .05 .02
616 Jay Aldrich .05 .02
617 Oddibe McDowell .05 .02
618 Cecil Fielder .10 .04
619 Mike Dunne .05 .02
Inconsistent design,
black name on front
620 Cory Snyder .05 .02
621 Gene Nelson .05 .02
622 Kal Daniels .05 .02
623 Mike Flanagan .05 .02
624 Jim Leyland MG .10 .04
625 Frank Viola .10 .04
626 Glenn Wilson .05 .02
627 Joe Boever .05 .02
628 Dave Henderson .05 .02
629 Kelly Downs .05 .02
630 Darrell Evans .10 .04
631 Jack Howell .05 .02
632 Steve Shields .05 .02
633 Barry Lyons .05 .02
634 Jose DeLeon .05 .02
635 Terry Pendleton .10 .04
636 Charles Hudson .05 .02
637 Jay Bell RC .40 .16
638 Steve Balboni .05 .02
639 Glenn Braggs .05 .02
Tony Muser CO TL
640 Garry Templeton .10 .04
(Inconsistent design,
green border)
641 Rick Honeycutt .05 .02
642 Bob Dernier .05 .02
643 Rocky Childress .05 .02
644 Terry McGriff .05 .02
645 Matt Nokes RC* .25 .10
646 Checklist 529-660 .05 .02
647 Pascual Perez .05 .02
648 Al Newman .05 .02
649 DeWayne Buice .05 .02
650 Cal Ripken .75 .30
651 Mike Jackson RC* .25 .10
652 Bruce Benedict .05 .02
653 Jeff Sellers .05 .02
654 Roger Craig MG .10 .04
655 Len Dykstra .10 .04
656 Lee Guetterman .05 .02
657 Gary Redus .05 .02
658 Tim Conroy .05 .02
(Inconsistent design,
name in white)
659 Bobby Meacham .05 .02
660 Rick Reuschel .10 .04
661 Nolan Ryan TBC '83 .50 .20
662 Jim Rice TBC .05 .02
663 Ron Blomberg TBC .05 .02
664 Bob Gibson TBC '68 .25 .10
665 Stan Musial TBC '63 .20 .08
666 Mario Soto .10 .04
667 Luis Quinones .05 .02
668 Walt Terrell .05 .02
669 Lance Parrish .05 .02
Mike Ryan CO TL
670 Dan Plesac .05 .02
671 Tim Laudner .05 .02
672 John Davis .05 .02
673 Tony Phillips .05 .02
674 Mike Fitzgerald .05 .02
675 Jim Rice .10 .04
676 Ken Dixon .05 .02
677 Eddie Milner .05 .02
678 Jim Acker .05 .02
679 Darrell Miller .05 .02
680 Charlie Hough .10 .04
681 Bobby Bonilla .10 .04
682 Jimmy Key .10 .04
683 Julio Franco .10 .04
684 Hal Lanier MG .05 .02
685 Ron Darling .10 .04
686 Terry Francona .10 .04
687 Mickey Brantley .05 .02
688 Jim Winn .05 .02
689 Tom Pagnozzi RC .10 .04
690 Jay Howell .05 .02
691 Dan Pasqua .05 .02
692 Mike Birkbeck .05 .02
693 Benito Santiago .10 .04
694 Eric Nolte .05 .02
695 Shawon Dunston .10 .04
696 Duane Ward .05 .02
697 Steve Lombardozzi .05 .02
698 Brad Havens .05 .02
699 Benito Santiago .10 .04
Tony Gwynn TL
700 George Brett .50 .20
701 Sammy Stewart .05 .02
702 Mike Gallego .05 .02
703 Bob Brenly .05 .02
704 Dennis Boyd .05 .02
705 Juan Samuel .05 .02
706 Rick Mahler .05 .02
707 Fred Lynn .10 .04
708 Gus Polidor .05 .02
709 George Frazier .05 .02
710 Darryl Strawberry .10 .04
711 Bill Gullickson .05 .02
712 John Moses .05 .02
713 Willie Hernandez .05 .02
714 Jim Fregosi MG .05 .02
715 Todd Worrell .05 .02
716 Lenn Sakata .05 .02
717 Jay Baller .05 .02
718 Mike Felder .05 .02
719 Denny Walling .05 .02
720 Tim Raines .10 .04
721 Pete O'Brien .05 .02
722 Manny Lee .05 .02
723 Bob Kipper .05 .02
724 Danny Tartabull .05 .02
725 Mike Boddicker .05 .02
726 Alfredo Griffin .05 .02
727 Greg Booker .05 .02
728 Andy Allanson .05 .02
729 George Bell .10 .04
Fred McGriff TL
730 John Franco .10 .04
731 Rick Schu .05 .02
732 David Palmer .05 .02
733 Spike Owen .05 .02
734 Craig Lefferts .05 .02
735 Kevin McReynolds .05 .02
736 Matt Young .05 .02
737 Butch Wynegar .05 .02
738 Scott Bankhead .05 .02
739 Daryl Boston .05 .02
740 Rick Sutcliffe .10 .04
741 Mike Easler .05 .02
742 Mark Clear .05 .02
743 Larry Herndon .05 .02
744 Whitey Herzog MG .10 .04
745 Bill Doran .05 .02
746 Gene Larkin RC* .25 .10
747 Bobby Witt .05 .02
748 Reid Nichols .05 .02
749 Mark Eichhorn .05 .02
750 Bo Jackson .20 .08
751 Jim Morrison .05 .02
752 Mark Grant .05 .02
753 Danny Heep .05 .02
754 Mike LaCoss .05 .02
755 Ozzie Virgil .05 .02
756 Mike Maddux .05 .02
757 John Marzano .05 .02
758 Eddie Williams RC .10 .04
759 Mark McGwire .75 .30
Jose Canseco TL UER
(two copyrights)
760 Mike Scott .10 .04
761 Tony Armas .10 .04
762 Scott Bradley .05 .02
763 Doug Sisk .05 .02
764 Greg Walker .05 .02
765 Neal Heaton .05 .02
766 Henry Cotto .05 .02
767 Jose Lind RC .25 .10
768 Dickie Noles .05 .02
(Now with Tigers
on card front)
769 Cecil Cooper .10 .04
770 Lou Whitaker .10 .04
771 Ruben Sierra .10 .04
772 Sal Butera .05 .02
773 Frank Williams .05 .02
774 Gene Mauch MG .05 .02
775 Dave Stieb .10 .04
776 Checklist 661-792 .05 .02
777 Lonnie Smith .05 .02
778A Keith Comstock ERR 2.00 .80
(White "Padres")
778B Keith Comstock COR .05 .02
(Blue "Padres")
779 Tom Glavine RC 1.50 .60
780 Fernando Valenzuela .10 .04
781 Keith Hughes .05 .02
782 Jeff Ballard .05 .02
783 Ron Roenicke .05 .02
784 Joe Sambito .05 .02
785 Alvin Davis .05 .02
786 Joe Price .05 .02
Inconsistent design,
orange team name
787 Bill Almon .05 .02
788 Ray Searage .05 .02
789 Joe Carter .05 .02
Cory Snyder TL
790 Dave Righetti .10 .04
791 Ted Simmons .10 .04
792 John Tudor .10 .04

1988 Topps Tiffany

This was the fifth year that Topps issued a "Tiffany" set. These 792 standard-size cards parallel the regular Topps cards. These cards were issued in factory set form only, produced in Topps Irish facility, and only available through Topps hobby dealers. These cards were again produced in relatively large quantities and the mulitplier value is reduced compared to pre-1987 levels. It is believed that as many as 25,000 of these sets were produced.

Nm-Mt Ex-Mt
COMP.FACT.SET (792) 60.00 24.00
*STARS: 4X TO 10X BASIC CARDS
*ROOKIES: 4X TO 10X BASIC CARDS

1988 Topps Glossy All-Stars

This set of 22 glossy cards was inserted one per rack pack. Players selected for the set are the starting players (plus manager and honorary captain) in the 1987 All-Star Game in Oakland. Cards measure the standard size and the backs feature red and blue printing on a white card stock.

Nm-Mt Ex-Mt
COMPLETE SET (22) 4.00 1.60
1 John McNamara MG .05 .02
2 Don Mattingly 1.00 .40
3 Willie Randolph .10 .04
4 Wade Boggs .50 .20
5 Cal Ripken 2.00 .80
6 George Bell .05 .02
7 Rickey Henderson .75 .30
8 Dave Winfield .40 .16
9 Terry Kennedy .05 .02
10 Bret Saberhagen .10 .04
11 Jim Hunter CAPT .10 .04
12 Dave Johnson MG .10 .04
13 Jack Clark .10 .04
14 Ryne Sandberg 1.00 .40
15 Mike Schmidt .50 .20
16 Ozzie Smith 1.00 .40
17 Eric Davis .10 .04
18 Andre Dawson .20 .08
19 Darryl Strawberry .10 .04
20 Gary Carter .40 .16
21 Mike Scott .05 .02
22 Billy Williams CAPT .10 .04

1988 Topps Glossy Send-Ins

Topps issued this set through a mail-in offer explained and advertised on the wax packs. This 60-card set features glossy fronts with each card measuring the standard size. The offer provided your choice of any one of the six 10-card subsets (1-10, 11-20, etc.) for 1.25 plus six of the Special Offer ("Spring Fever Baseball") insert cards, which were found one per wax pack. One complete set was obtainable by sending 7.50 plus 18 special offer cards. The last two players (numerically) in each ten-card subset are actually "Hot Prospects."

Nm-Mt Ex-Mt
COMPLETE SET (60) 10.00 4.00
1 Andre Dawson .40 .16
2 Jesse Barfield .10 .04
3 Mike Schmidt 1.00 .40
4 Ruben Sierra .20 .08
5 Mike Scott .10 .04
6 Cal Ripken 4.00 1.60
7 Gary Carter .75 .30
8 Kent Hrbek .20 .08
9 Kevin Seitzer .10 .04
10 Mike Henneman .20 .08
11 Don Mattingly 2.00 .80
12 Tim Raines .20 .08
13 Roger Clemens 2.00 .80
14 Ryne Sandberg 1.50 .60
15 Tony Fernandez .20 .08
16 Eric Davis .20 .08
17 Jack Morris .20 .08
18 Tim Wallach .10 .04
19 Mike Dunne .10 .04
20 Mike Greenwell .10 .04
21 Dwight Evans .20 .08
22 Darryl Strawberry .20 .08
23 Cory Snyder .10 .04
24 Pedro Guerrero .10 .04
25 Rickey Henderson 1.25 .50
26 Dale Murphy .40 .16
27 Kirby Puckett .75 .30
28 Steve Bedrosian .10 .04
29 Devon White .20 .08
30 Benito Santiago .20 .08
31 George Bell .10 .04
32 Keith Hernandez .20 .08
33 Dave Stewart .20 .08
34 Dave Parker .20 .08
35 Tom Henke .10 .04
36 Willie McGee .20 .08
37 Alan Trammell .30 .12
38 Tony Gwynn 2.00 .80
39 Mark McGwire 3.00 1.20
40 Joe Magrane .10 .04
41 Jack Clark .20 .08
42 Willie Randolph .20 .08
43 Juan Samuel .10 .04
44 Joe Carter .30 .12
45 Shane Rawley .10 .04
46 Dave Winfield .50 .20
47 Ozzie Smith 2.00 .80
48 Wally Joyner .20 .08
49 B.J. Surhoff .20 .08
50 Ellis Burks .75 .30
51 Wade Boggs .75 .30
52 Howard Johnson .10 .04
53 George Brett 2.00 .80
54 Dwight Gooden .20 .08
55 Jose Canseco 1.00 .40
56 Lee Smith .20 .08
57 Paul Molitor .75 .30
58 Andres Galarraga .40 .16
59 Matt Nokes .10 .04
60 Casey Candaele .10 .04

1988 Topps Rookies

Inserted in each supermarket jumbo pack is a card from this series of 22 of 1987's best rookies as determined by Topps. Jumbo packs consisted of 100 (regular issue 1988 Topps baseball) cards with a stick of gum plus the insert "Rookie" card. The card fronts are in full color and measure the standard size. The card backs

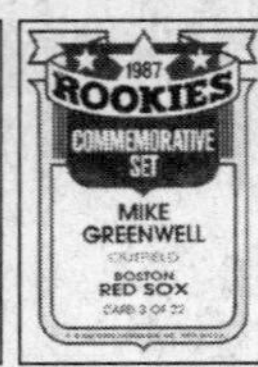

are printed in red and blue on white card stock and are numbered at the bottom.

Nm-Mt Ex-Mt
COMPLETE SET (22) 25.00 10.00
1 Bill Ripken .25 .10
2 Ellis Burks 1.00 .40
3 Mike Greenwell .25 .10
4 DeWayne Buice .25 .10
5 Devon White .50 .20
6 Fred Manrique .25 .10
7 Mike Henneman .50 .20
8 Matt Nokes .25 .10
9 Kevin Seitzer .50 .20
10 B.J. Surhoff .50 .20
11 Casey Candaele .25 .10
12 Randy Myers .75 .30
13 Mark McGwire 15.00 6.00
14 Luis Polonia .25 .10
15 Terry Steinbach .50 .20
16 Mike Dunne .25 .10
17 Al Pedrique .25 .10
18 Benito Santiago .50 .20
19 Kelly Downs .25 .10
20 Joe Magrane .25 .10
21 Jerry Browne .25 .10
22 Jeff Musselman .25 .10

1988 Topps Wax Box Cards

The cards in this 16-card set measure the standard size. Cards have essentially the same design as the 1988 Topps regular issue set. The cards were printed on the bottoms of the regular issue wax pack boxes. These 16 cards, "lettered" A through P, are considered a separate set in their own right and are not typically included in a complete set of the regular issue 1988 Topps cards. The value of the panels uncut is slightly greater, perhaps by 25 percent greater, than the value of the individual cards cut up carefully. The card lettering is sequenced alphabetically by player's name.

Nm-Mt Ex-Mt
COMPLETE SET (16) 5.00 2.00
A Don Baylor .20 .08
B Steve Bedrosian .10 .04
C Juan Beniquez .10 .04
D Bob Boone .20 .08
E Darrell Evans .20 .08
F Tony Gwynn 1.25 .50
G John Kruk .20 .08
H Marvell Wynne .10 .04
I Joe Carter .40 .16
J Eric Davis .20 .08
K Howard Johnson .10 .04
L Darryl Strawberry .20 .08
M Rickey Henderson 1.00 .40
N Nolan Ryan 2.50 1.00
O Mike Schmidt .75 .30
P Kent Tekulve .10 .04

1988 Topps Traded

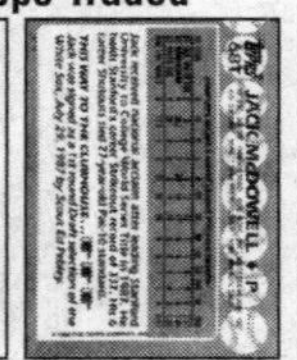

This standard-size 132-card Traded set was distributed exclusively in factory set form in blue and white taped boxes through hobby dealers. The cards are identical in style to the Topps regular issue except for whiter stock and t-suffixed numbering on back. Cards are ordered alphabetically by player's last name. This set generated additional interest upon release due to the inclusion of members of the 1988 U.S. Olympic baseball team. These Olympians are indicated in the checklist below by OLY. The key extended Rookie Cards in this set are Jim Abbott, Roberto Alomar, Brady Anderson, Andy Benes, Jay Buhner, Ron Gant, Mark Grace, Tino Martinez, Charles Nagy, Robin Ventura and Walt Weiss.

Nm-Mt Ex-Mt
COMP.FACT.SET (132) 8.00 3.20
1T Jim Abbott OLY XRC 1.00 .40
2T Juan Agosto .10 .04
3T Luis Alicea XRC .50 .20
4T Roberto Alomar XRC 2.00 .80
5T Brady Anderson XRC .75 .30
6T Jack Armstrong XRC .50 .20
7T Don August .10 .04
8T Floyd Bannister .10 .04
9T Bret Barberie OLY XRC .25 .10
10T Jose Bautista XRC .25 .10
11T Don Baylor .20 .08
12T Tim Belcher .10 .04
13T Buddy Bell .20 .08
14T Andy Benes OLY XRC .75 .30
15T Damon Berryhill XRC .50 .20
16T Bud Black .10 .04
17T Pat Borders XRC .50 .20
18T Phil Bradley .10 .04
19T J.Branson XRC OLY .50 .20
20T Tom Brunansky .10 .04
21T Jay Buhner XRC 1.00 .40
22T Brett Butler .20 .08
23T Jim Campanis OLY .10 .04
24T Sil Campusano .10 .04
25T John Candelaria .10 .04
26T Jose Cecena .10 .04
27T Rick Cerone .10 .04
28T Jack Clark .20 .08
29T Kevin Coffman .10 .04
30T Pat Combs OLY XRC .25 .10
31T Henry Cotto .10 .04
32T Chili Davis .20 .08
33T Mike Davis .10 .04
34T Jose DeLeon .10 .04
35T Richard Dotson .10 .04
36T Cecil Espy .10 .04
37T Tom Filer .10 .04
38T Mike Fiore OLY .10 .04
39T Ron Gant XRC .75 .30
40T Kirk Gibson .50 .20
41T Rich Gossage .20 .08
42T Mark Grace XRC 1.50 .60
43T Alfredo Griffin .10 .04
44T Ty Griffin OLY .10 .04
45T Bryan Harvey XRC .50 .20
46T Ron Hassey .10 .04
47T Ray Hayward .10 .04
48T Dave Henderson .10 .04
49T Tom Herr .10 .04
50T Bob Horner .20 .08
51T Ricky Horton .10 .04
52T Jay Howell .10 .04
53T Glenn Hubbard .10 .04
54T Jeff Innis .10 .04
55T Danny Jackson .10 .04
56T Darrin Jackson XRC* .25 .10
57T Roberto Kelly XRC* .50 .20
58T Ron Kittle .10 .04
59T Ray Knight .20 .08
60T Vance Law .10 .04
61T Jeffrey Leonard .10 .04
62T Mike Macfarlane XRC .50 .20
63T Scotti Madison .10 .04
64T Kirt Manwaring .10 .04
65T M.Marquess OLY CO .10 .04
66T T.Martinez OLY XRC 1.50 .60
67T Billy Masse OLY XRC .25 .10
68T Jack McDowell XRC .75 .30
69T Jack McKeon MG .20 .08
70T Larry McWilliams .10 .04
71T M.Morandini OLY XRC .50 .20
72T Keith Moreland .10 .04
73T Mike Morgan .10 .04
74T C.Nagy OLY XRC .50 .20
75T Al Nipper .10 .04
76T Russ Nixon MG .10 .04
77T Jesse Orosco .10 .04
78T Joe Orsulak .10 .04
79T Dave Palmer .10 .04
80T Mark Parent .10 .04
81T Dave Parker .20 .08
82T Dan Pasqua .10 .04
83T Melido Perez XRC* .50 .20
84T Steve Peters .10 .04
85T Dan Petry .10 .04
86T Gary Pettis .10 .04
87T Jeff Pico .10 .04
88T Jim Poole OLY XRC .25 .10
89T Ted Power .10 .04
90T Rafael Ramirez .10 .04
91T Dennis Rasmussen .10 .04
92T Jose Rijo .20 .08
93T Ernie Riles .10 .04
94T Luis Rivera .10 .04
95T D.Robbins XRC OLY .25 .10
96T Frank Robinson MG .30 .12
97T Cookie Rojas MG .10 .04
98T Chris Sabo XRC .75 .30
99T Mark Salas .10 .04
100T Luis Salazar .10 .04
101T Rafael Santana .10 .04
102T Nelson Santovenia .10 .04
103T Mackey Sasser XRC .50 .20
104T Calvin Schiraldi .10 .04
105T Mike Schooler .10 .04
106T S.Servais XRC OLY .50 .20
107T D.Silvestri XRC OLY .25 .10
108T Don Slaught .10 .04
109T J.Slusarski XRC OLY .25 .10
110T Lee Smith .20 .08
111T Pete Smith XRC* .25 .10
112T Jim Snyder MG .10 .04
113T E.Sprague OLY XRC .50 .20
114T Pete Stanicek .10 .04
115T Kurt Stillwell .10 .04
116T T.Stottlemyre XRC .50 .20
117T Bill Swift .10 .04
118T Pat Tabler .10 .04
119T Scott Terry .10 .04
120T Mickey Tettleton .10 .04
121T Dickie Thon .10 .04
122T Jeff Treadway XRC* .50 .20
123T Willie Upshaw .10 .04
124T R.Ventura OLY XRC 1.50 .60
125T Ron Washington .10 .04
126T Walt Weiss XRC* .75 .30
127T Bob Welch .20 .08
128T David Wells XRC 1.50 .60
129T Glenn Wilson .10 .04
130T Ted Wood OLY XRC .25 .10
131T Don Zimmer MG .20 .08
132T Checklist 1T-132T .10 .04

1988 Topps Traded Tiffany

As a bonus for those dealers who ordered the regular Tiffany sets, they received an equivalent number of Tiffany update sets. These 132 standard-size cards parallel the regular traded issue. Again issued in the Topps Irish facility, these cards feature glossy fronts and easy to read backs. These sets were only issued in complete factory form.

Nm-Mt Ex-Mt
COMP.FACT.SET (132) 40.00 16.00
*STARS: 1.5X TO 4X BASIC CARDS
*ROOKIES: 3X TO 8X BASIC CARDS

1989 Topps

This set consists of 792 standard-size cards. Cards were primarily issued in 15-card wax packs, 42-card rack packs and factory sets. Subsets in the set include Record Breakers (1-7), Turn Back the Clock (661-665), All-Star selections (386-407) and First Draft Picks,

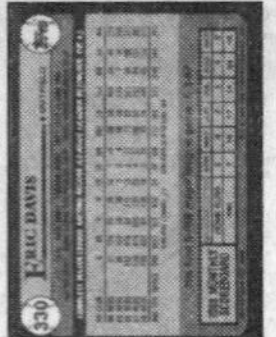

Future Stars and Team Leaders (all scattered throughout the set). The manager cards contain a team checklist on back. The key Rookie Cards in this set are Jim Abbott, Sandy Alomar Jr., Brady Anderson, Steve Avery, Andy Benes, Dante Bichette, Craig Biggio, Randy Johnson, Ramon Martinez, Gary Sheffield, John Smoltz, and Robin Ventura.

Nm-Mt Ex-Mt
COMPLETE SET (792) 20.00 8.00
COMP.FACT SET (792) 20.00 8.00
COMP.X-MAS.SET (792) 25.00 10.00
1 George Bell RB .05 .02
Slams 3 HR on Opening Day
2 Wade Boggs RB .10 .04
3 Gary Carter RB .05 .02
Sets Record for Career Putouts
4 Andre Dawson RB .05 .02
Logs Double Figures in HR and SB
5 Orel Hershiser RB .05 .02
Pitches 59 Scoreless Innings
6 Doug Jones RB UER .05 .02
Earns His 15th Straight Save
Photo actually Chris Codiroli
7 Kevin McReynolds RB .05 .02
Steals 21 Without Being Caught
8 Dave Eiland .05 .02
9 Tim Teufel .05 .02
10 Andre Dawson .10 .04
11 Bruce Sutter .10 .04
12 Dale Sveum .05 .02
13 Doug Sisk .05 .02
14 Tom Kelly MG .05 .02
15 Robby Thompson .05 .02
16 Ron Robinson .05 .02
17 Brian Downing .10 .04
18 Rick Rhoden .05 .02
19 Greg Gagne .05 .02
20 Steve Bedrosian .05 .02
21 Greg Walker TL .05 .02
22 Tim Crews .05 .02
23 Mike Fitzgerald .05 .02
24 Larry Andersen .05 .02
25 Frank White .10 .04
26 Dale Mohorcic .05 .02
27A Orestes Destrade .10 .04
(F* next to copyright) RC*
27B Orestes Destrade .10 .04
(E*F* next to copyright) RC*
28 Mike Moore .05 .02
29 Kelly Gruber .05 .02
30 Dwight Gooden .10 .04
31 Terry Francona .10 .04
32 Dennis Rasmussen .05 .02
33 B.J. Surhoff .10 .04
34 Ken Williams .05 .02
35 John Tudor UER .10 .04
(With Red Sox in '84,should be Pirates)
36 Mitch Webster .05 .02
37 Bob Stanley .05 .02
38 Paul Runge .05 .02
39 Mike Maddux .05 .02
40 Steve Sax .05 .02
41 Terry Mulholland .05 .02
42 Jim Eppard .05 .02
43 Guillermo Hernandez .05 .02
44 Jim Snyder MG .05 .02
45 Kal Daniels .05 .02
46 Mark Portugal .05 .02
47 Carney Lansford .10 .04
48 Tim Burke .05 .02
49 Craig Biggio RC .75 .30
50 George Bell .05 .02
51 Mark McLemore TL .05 .02
52 Bob Brenly .05 .02
53 Ruben Sierra .10 .04
54 Steve Trout .05 .02
55 Julio Franco .10 .04
56 Pat Tabler .05 .02
57 Alejandro Pena .05 .02
58 Lee Mazzilli .10 .04
59 Mark Davis .05 .02
60 Tom Brunansky .05 .02
61 Neil Allen .05 .02
62 Alfredo Griffin .05 .02
63 Mark Clear .05 .02
64 Alex Trevino .05 .02
65 Rick Reuschel .10 .04
66 Manny Trillo .05 .02
67 Dave Palmer .05 .02
68 Darrell Miller .05 .02
69 Jeff Ballard .05 .02
70 Mark McGwire 1.00 .40
71 Mike Boddicker .05 .02
72 John Moses .05 .02
73 Pascual Perez .05 .02
74 Nick Leyva MG .05 .02
75 Tom Henke .05 .02
76 Terry Blocker .05 .02
77 Doyle Alexander .05 .02
78 Jim Sundberg .10 .04
79 Scott Bankhead .05 .02
80 Cory Snyder .05 .02
81 Tim Raines TL .05 .02
82 Dave Leiper .05 .02
83 Jeff Blauser .05 .02
84 Bill Bene FDP .05 .02
85 Kevin McReynolds .05 .02
86 Al Nipper .05 .02
87 Larry Owen .05 .02
88 Darryl Hamilton RC * .25 .10
89 Dave LaPoint .05 .02
90 Vince Coleman UER .05 .02
(Wrong birth year)
91 Floyd Youmans .05 .02
92 Jeff Kunkel .05 .02
93 Ken Howell .05 .02
94 Chris Speier .05 .02
95 Gerald Young .05 .02
96 Rick Cerone .05 .02
97 Greg Mathews .05 .02
98 Larry Sheets .05 .02
99 Sherman Corbett .05 .02
100 Mike Schmidt .50 .20
101 Les Straker .05 .02
102 Mike Gallego .05 .02
103 Tim Birtsas .05 .02
104 Dallas Green MG .05 .02
105 Ron Darling .10 .04
106 Willie Upshaw .05 .02
107 Jose DeLeon .05 .02
108 Fred Manrique .05 .02
109 Hipolito Pena .05 .02
110 Paul Molitor .15 .06
111 Eric Davis TL .05 .02
112 Jim Presley .05 .02
113 Lloyd Moseby .05 .02
114 Bob Kipper .05 .02
115 Jody Davis .05 .02
116 Jeff Montgomery .05 .02
117 Dave Anderson .05 .02
118 Checklist 1-132 .05 .02
119 Terry Puhl .05 .02
120 Frank Viola .10 .04
121 Garry Templeton .10 .04
122 Lance Johnson .05 .02
123 Spike Owen .05 .02
124 Jim Traber .05 .02
125 Mike Krukow .05 .02
126 Sid Bream .05 .02
127 Walt Terrell .05 .02
128 Milt Thompson .05 .02
129 Terry Clark .05 .02
130 Gerald Perry .05 .02
131 Dave Otto .05 .02
132 Curt Ford .05 .02
133 Bill Long .05 .02
134 Don Zimmer MG .10 .04
135 Jose Rijo .10 .04
136 Joey Meyer .05 .02
137 Geno Petralli .05 .02
138 Wallace Johnson .05 .02
139 Mike Flanagan .05 .02
140 Shawon Dunston .05 .02
141 Brook Jacoby TL .05 .02
142 Mike Diaz .05 .02
143 Mike Campbell .05 .02
144 Jay Bell .10 .04
145 Dave Stewart .10 .04
146 Gary Pettis .05 .02
147 DeWayne Buice .05 .02
148 Bill Pecota .05 .02
149 Doug Dascenzo .05 .02
150 Fernando Valenzuela .10 .04
151 Terry McGriff .05 .02
152 Mark Thurmond .05 .02
153 Jim Pankovits .05 .02
154 Don Carman .05 .02
155 Marty Barrett .05 .02
156 Dave Gallagher .05 .02
157 Tom Glavine .25 .10
158 Mike Aldrete .05 .02
159 Pat Clements .05 .02
160 Jeffrey Leonard .05 .02
161 G. Olson RC FDP UER .25 .10
Born Scribner, NE, should be Omaha, NE
162 John Davis .05 .02
163 Bob Forsch .05 .02
164 Hal Lanier MG .05 .02
165 Mike Dunne .05 .02
166 Doug Jennings .05 .02
167 Steve Searcy FS .05 .02
168 Willie Wilson .10 .04
169 Mike Jackson .05 .02
170 Tony Fernandez .05 .02
171 Andres Thomas TL .05 .02
172 Frank Williams .05 .02
173 Mel Hall .05 .02
174 Todd Burns .05 .02
175 John Shelby .05 .02
176 Jeff Parrett .05 .02
177 Monty Fariss FDP .05 .02
178 Mark Grant .05 .02
179 Ozzie Virgil .05 .02
180 Mike Scott .10 .04
181 Craig Worthington .05 .02
182 Bob McClure .05 .02
183 Oddibe McDowell .05 .02
184 John Costello .05 .02
185 Claudell Washington .05 .02
186 Pat Perry .05 .02
187 Darren Daulton .10 .04
188 Dennis Lamp .05 .02
189 Kevin Mitchell .10 .04
190 Mike Witt .05 .02
191 Sil Campusano .05 .02
192 Paul Mirabella .05 .02
193 Sparky Anderson MG .10 .04
UER (553 Salazer)
194 Greg W. Harris RC .10 .04
195 Ozzie Guillen .05 .02
196 Denny Walling .05 .02
197 Neal Heaton .05 .02
198 Danny Heep .05 .02
199 Mike Schooler RC * .10 .04
200 George Brett .60 .24
201 Kelly Gruber TL .05 .02
202 Brad Moore .05 .02
203 Rob Ducey .05 .02
204 Brad Havens .05 .02
205 Dwight Evans .10 .04
206 Roberto Alomar .25 .10
207 Terry Leach .05 .02
208 Tom Pagnozzi .05 .02
209 Jeff Bittiger .05 .02
210 Dale Murphy .15 .06
211 Mike Pagliarulo .05 .02
212 Scott Sanderson .05 .02
213 Rene Gonzales .05 .02
214 Charlie O'Brien .05 .02
215 Kevin Gross .05 .02
216 Jack Howell .05 .02
217 Joe Price .05 .02
218 Mike LaValliere .05 .02
219 Jim Clancy .05 .02
220 Gary Gaetti .10 .04
221 Cecil Espy .05 .02
222 Mark Lewis FDP RC .25 .10
223 Jay Buhner .10 .04
224 Tony LaRussa MG .10 .04
225 Ramon Martinez RC .25 .10
226 Bill Doran .05 .02
227 John Farrell .05 .02
228 Nelson Santovenia .05 .02
229 Jimmy Key .10 .04
230 Ozzie Smith .40 .16
231 Roberto Alomar TL .25 .10
(Gary Carter at plate)
232 Ricky Horton .05 .02
233 Gregg Jefferies FS .05 .02
234 Tom Browning .05 .02
235 John Kruk .10 .04
236 Charles Hudson .05 .02
237 Glenn Hubbard .05 .02
238 Eric King .05 .02
239 Tim Laudner .05 .02
240 Greg Maddux .50 .20
241 Brett Butler .10 .04
242 Ed VandeBerg .05 .02
243 Bob Boone .10 .04
244 Jim Acker .05 .02
245 Jim Rice .10 .04
246 Rey Quinones .05 .02
247 Shawn Hillegas .05 .02
248 Tony Phillips .05 .02
249 Tim Leary .05 .02
250 Cal Ripken .75 .30
251 John Dopson .05 .02
252 Billy Hatcher .05 .02
253 Jose Alvarez RC .10 .04
254 Tom Lasorda MG .15 .06
255 Ron Guidry .10 .04
256 Benny Santiago .10 .04
257 Rick Aguilera .05 .02
258 Checklist 133-264 .05 .02
259 Larry McWilliams .05 .02
260 Dave Winfield .10 .04
261 Tom Brunansky .05 .02
Luis Alicea TL
262 Jeff Pico .05 .02
263 Mike Felder .05 .02
264 Rob Dibble RC .50 .20
265 Kent Hrbek .10 .04
266 Luis Aquino .05 .02
267 Jeff M. Robinson .05 .02
268 Keith Miller RC .25 .10
269 Tom Bolton .05 .02
270 Wally Joyner .10 .04
271 Jay Tibbs .05 .02
272 Ron Hassey .05 .02
273 Jose Lind .05 .02
274 Mark Eichhorn .05 .02
275 Danny Tartabull UER .05 .02
(Born San Juan, PR should be Miami, FL)
276 Paul Kilgus .05 .02
277 Mike Davis .05 .02
278 Andy McGaffigan .05 .02
279 Scott Bradley .05 .02
280 Bob Knepper .05 .02
281 Gary Redus .05 .02
282 Cris Carpenter RC * .10 .04
283 Andy Allanson .05 .02
284 Jim Leyland MG .10 .04
285 John Candelaria .05 .02
286 Darrin Jackson .10 .04
287 Juan Nieves .05 .02
288 Pat Sheridan .05 .02
289 Ernie Whitt .05 .02
290 John Franco .10 .04
291 Darryl Strawberry .05 .02
Keith Hernandez
Kevin McReynolds TL
292 Jim Corsi .05 .02
293 Glenn Wilson .05 .02
294 Juan Berenguer .05 .02
295 Scott Fletcher .05 .02
296 Ron Gant .10 .04
297 Oswald Peraza .05 .02
298 Chris James .05 .02
299 Steve Ellsworth .05 .02
300 Darryl Strawberry .10 .04
301 Charlie Leibrandt .05 .02
302 Gary Ward .05 .02
303 Felix Fermin .05 .02
304 Joel Youngblood .05 .02
305 Dave Smith .05 .02
306 Tracy Woodson .05 .02
307 Lance McCullers .05 .02
308 Ron Karkovice .05 .02
309 Mario Diaz .05 .02
310 Rafael Palmeiro .25 .10
311 Chris Bosio .05 .02
312 Tom Lawless .05 .02
313 Dennis Martinez .10 .04
314 Bobby Valentine MG .10 .04
315 Greg Swindell .05 .02
316 Walt Weiss .05 .02
317 Jack Armstrong RC * .25 .10
318 Gene Larkin .05 .02
319 Greg Booker .05 .02
320 Lou Whitaker .10 .04
321 Jody Reed TL .05 .02
322 John Smiley .05 .02
323 Gary Thurman .05 .02
324 Bob Milacki .05 .02
325 Jesse Barfield .10 .04
326 Dennis Boyd .05 .02
327 Mark Lemke RC .40 .16
328 Rick Honeycutt .05 .02
329 Bob Melvin .05 .02
330 Eric Davis .10 .04
331 Curt Wilkerson .05 .02
332 Tony Armas .10 .04
333 Bob Ojeda .05 .02
334 Steve Lyons .05 .02
335 Dave Righetti .10 .04
336 Steve Balboni .05 .02

337 Calvin Schiraldi .05 .02
338 Jim Adduci .05 .02
339 Scott Bailes .05 .02
340 Kirk Gibson .10 .04
341 Jim Deshaies .05 .02
342 Tom Brookens .05 .02
343 Gary Sheffield FS RC 1.50 .60
344 Tom Trebelhorn MG .05 .02
345 Charlie Hough .10 .04
346 Rex Hudler .05 .02
347 John Cerutti .05 .02
348 Ed Hearn .05 .02
349 Ron Jones .10 .04
350 Andy Van Slyke .10 .04
351 Bob Melvin .05 .02
Bill Fahey CO TL
352 Rick Schu .05 .02
353 Marvell Wynne .05 .02
354 Larry Parrish .05 .02
355 Mark Langston .05 .02
356 Kevin Elster .05 .02
357 Jerry Reuss .05 .02
358 Ricky Jordan RC * .25 .10
359 Tommy John .10 .04
360 Ryne Sandberg .40 .16
361 Kelly Downs .05 .02
362 Jack Lazorko .05 .02
363 Rich Yett .05 .02
364 Rob Deer .05 .02
365 Mike Henneman .05 .02
366 Herm Winningham .05 .02
367 Johnny Paredes .05 .02
368 Brian Holton .05 .02
369 Ken Caminiti .10 .04
370 Dennis Eckersley .15 .06
371 Manny Lee .05 .02
372 Craig Lefferts .05 .02
373 Tracy Jones .05 .02
374 John Wathan MG .05 .02
375 Terry Pendleton .10 .04
376 Steve Lombardozzi .05 .02
377 Mike Smithson .05 .02
378 Checklist 265-396 .05 .02
379 Tim Flannery .05 .02
380 Rickey Henderson .25 .10
381 Larry Sheets TL .05 .02
382 John Smoltz RC 1.00 .40
383 Howard Johnson .10 .04
384 Mark Salas .05 .02
385 Von Hayes .05 .02
386 Andres Galarraga AS .05 .02
387 Ryne Sandberg AS .25 .10
388 Bobby Bonilla AS .05 .02
389 Ozzie Smith AS .25 .10
390 Darryl Strawberry AS .05 .02
391 Andre Dawson AS .05 .02
392 Andy Van Slyke AS .05 .02
393 Gary Carter AS .05 .02
394 Orel Hershiser AS .05 .02
395 Danny Jackson AS .05 .02
396 Kirk Gibson AS .05 .02
397 Don Mattingly AS .30 .12
398 Julio Franco AS .05 .02
399 Wade Boggs AS .10 .04
400 Alan Trammell AS .05 .02
401 Jose Canseco AS .15 .06
402 Mike Greenwell AS .05 .02
403 Kirby Puckett AS .15 .06
404 Bob Boone AS .05 .02
405 Roger Clemens AS .25 .10
406 Frank Viola AS .05 .02
407 Dave Winfield AS .05 .02
408 Greg Walker .05 .02
409 Ken Dayley .05 .02
410 Jack Clark .10 .04
411 Mitch Williams .05 .02
412 Barry Lyons .05 .02
413 Mike Kingery .05 .02
414 Jim Fregosi MG .05 .02
415 Rich Gossage .10 .04
416 Fred Lynn .10 .04
417 Mike LaCoss .05 .02
418 Bob Dernier .05 .02
419 Tom Filer .05 .02
420 Joe Carter .10 .04
421 Kirk McCaskill .05 .02
422 Bo Diaz .05 .02
423 Brian Fisher .05 .02
424 Luis Polonia UER .05 .02
(Wrong birthdate)
425 Jay Howell .05 .02
426 Dan Gladden .05 .02
427 Eric Show .05 .02
428 Craig Reynolds .05 .02
429 Greg Gagne TL .05 .02
430 Mark Gubicza .05 .02
431 Luis Rivera .05 .02
432 Chad Kreuter RC .25 .10
433 Albert Hall .05 .02
434 Ken Patterson .05 .02
435 Len Dykstra .10 .04
436 Bobby Meacham .05 .02
437 Andy Benes FDP RC .40 .16
438 Greg Gross .05 .02
439 Frank DiPino .05 .02
440 Bobby Bonilla .10 .04
441 Jerry Reed .05 .02
442 Jose Oquendo .05 .02
443 Rod Nichols .05 .02
444 Moose Stubing MG .05 .02
445 Matt Nokes .05 .02
446 Rob Murphy .05 .02
447 Donell Nixon .05 .02
448 Eric Plunk .05 .02
449 Carmelo Martinez .05 .02
450 Roger Clemens .50 .20
451 Mark Davidson .05 .02
452 Israel Sanchez .05 .02
453 Tom Prince .05 .02
454 Paul Assenmacher .05 .02
455 Johnny Ray .05 .02
456 Tim Belcher .05 .02
457 Mackey Sasser .05 .02
458 Donn Pall .05 .02
459 Dave Valle TL .05 .02
460 Dave Stieb .10 .04
461 Buddy Bell .10 .04
462 Jose Guzman .05 .02
463 Steve Lake .05 .02
464 Bryn Smith .05 .02
465 Mark Grace .25 .10
466 Chuck Crim .05 .02
467 Jim Walewander .05 .02
468 Henry Cotto .05 .02
469 Jose Bautista RC .10 .04
470 Lance Parrish .10 .04
471 Steve Curry .05 .02
472 Brian Harper .05 .02
473 Don Robinson .05 .02
474 Bob Rodgers MG .05 .02
475 Dave Parker .10 .04
476 Jon Perlman .05 .02
477 Dick Schofield .05 .02
478 Doug Drabek .05 .02
479 Mike Macfarlane RC * .25 .10
480 Keith Hernandez .10 .04
481 Chris Brown .05 .02
482 Steve Peters .05 .02
483 Mickey Hatcher .05 .02
484 Steve Shields .05 .02
485 Hubie Brooks .05 .02
486 Jack McDowell .10 .04
487 Scott Lusader .05 .02
488 Kevin Coffman .05 .02
Now with Cubs
489 Mike Schmidt TL .15 .06
490 Chris Sabo RC * .40 .16
491 Mike Birkbeck .05 .02
492 Alan Ashby .05 .02
493 Todd Benzinger .05 .02
494 Shane Rawley .05 .02
495 Candy Maldonado .05 .02
496 Dwayne Henry .05 .02
497 Pete Stanicek .05 .02
498 Dave Valle .05 .02
499 Don Heinkel .05 .02
500 Jose Canseco .25 .10
501 Vance Law .05 .02
502 Duane Ward .05 .02
503 Al Newman .05 .02
504 Bob Walk .05 .02
505 Pete Rose MG .50 .20
506 Kirt Manwaring .05 .02
507 Steve Farr .05 .02
508 Wally Backman .05 .02
509 Bud Black .05 .02
510 Bob Horner .10 .04
511 Richard Dotson .05 .02
512 Donnie Hill .05 .02
513 Jesse Orosco .05 .02
514 Chet Lemon .10 .04
515 Barry Larkin .15 .06
516 Eddie Whitson .05 .02
517 Greg Brock .05 .02
518 Bruce Ruffin .05 .02
519 Willie Randolph TL .05 .02
520 Rick Sutcliffe .10 .04
521 Mickey Tettleton .05 .02
522 Randy Kramer .05 .02
523 Andres Thomas .05 .02
524 Checklist 397-528 .05 .02
525 Chili Davis .10 .04
526 Wes Gardner .05 .02
527 Dave Henderson .05 .02
528 Luis Medina .05 .02
(Lower left front
has white triangle)
529 Tom Foley .05 .02
530 Nolan Ryan 1.00 .40
531 Dave Hengel .05 .02
532 Jerry Browne .05 .02
533 Andy Hawkins .05 .02
534 Doc Edwards MG .05 .02
535 Todd Worrell UER .05 .02
(4 wins in '88,
should be 5)
536 Joel Skinner .05 .02
537 Pete Smith .05 .02
538 Juan Castillo .05 .02
539 Barry Jones .05 .02
540 Bo Jackson .25 .10
541 Cecil Fielder .10 .04
542 Todd Frohwirth .05 .02
543 Damon Berryhill .05 .02
544 Jeff Sellers .05 .02
545 Mookie Wilson .10 .04
546 Mark Williamson .05 .02
547 Mark McLemore .05 .02
548 Bobby Witt .05 .02
549 Jamie Moyer TL .05 .02
550 Orel Hershiser .10 .04
551 Randy Ready .05 .02
552 Greg Cadaret .05 .02
553 Luis Salazar .05 .02
554 Nick Esasky .05 .02
555 Bert Blyleven .10 .04
556 Bruce Fields .05 .02
557 Keith A. Miller .05 .02
558 Dan Pasqua .05 .02
559 Juan Agosto .05 .02
560 Tim Raines .10 .04
561 Luis Aguayo .05 .02
562 Danny Cox .05 .02
563 Bill Schroeder .05 .02
564 Russ Nixon MG .05 .02
565 Jeff Russell .05 .02
566 Al Pedrique .05 .02
567 David Wells UER .10 .04
(Complete Pitching
Recor)
568 Mickey Brantley .05 .02
569 German Jimenez .05 .02
570 Tony Gwynn UER .30 .12
('88 average should
be italicized as
league leader)
571 Billy Ripken .05 .02
572 Atlee Hammaker .05 .02
573 Jim Abbott FDP RC* .50 .20
574 Dave Clark .05 .02
575 Juan Samuel .05 .02
576 Greg Minton .05 .02
577 Randy Bush .05 .02
578 John Morris .05 .02
579 Glenn Davis TL .05 .02
580 Harold Reynolds .10 .04
581 Gene Nelson .05 .02
582 Mike Marshall .05 .02
583 Paul Gibson .05 .02
584 Randy Velarde UER .05 .02
(Signed 1935,
should be 1985)
585 Harold Baines .10 .04
586 Joe Boever .05 .02
587 Mike Stanley .05 .02
588 Luis Alicea RC * .25 .10
589 Dave Meads .05 .02
590 Andres Galarraga .10 .04
591 Jeff Musselman .05 .02
592 John Cangelosi .05 .02
593 Drew Hall .05 .02
594 Jimy Williams MG .05 .02
595 Teddy Higuera .05 .02
596 Kurt Stillwell .05 .02
597 Terry Taylor RC .10 .04
598 Ken Gerhart .05 .02
599 Tom Candiotti .05 .02
600 Wade Boggs .15 .06
601 Dave Dravecky .05 .02
602 Devon White .10 .04
603 Frank Tanana .10 .04
604 Paul O'Neill .15 .06
605A Bob Welch ERR 2.00 .80
(Missing line on back
Complete M.L. Pitching Record
605B Bob Welch COR .10 .04
606 Rick Dempsey .05 .02
607 Willie Ansley FDP RC .10 .04
608 Phil Bradley .05 .02
609 Frank Tanana .05 .02
Alan Trammell
Mike Heath TL
610 Randy Myers .10 .04
611 Don Slaught .05 .02
612 Dan Quisenberry .05 .02
613 Gary Varsho .05 .02
614 Joe Hesketh .05 .02
615 Robin Yount .40 .16
616 Steve Rosenberg .05 .02
617 Mark Parent .05 .02
618 Rance Mulliniks .05 .02
619 Checklist 529-660 .05 .02
620 Barry Bonds 1.25 .50
621 Rick Mahler .05 .02
622 Stan Javier .05 .02
623 Fred Toliver .05 .02
624 Jack McKeon MG .10 .04
625 Eddie Murray .25 .10
626 Jeff Reed .05 .02
627 Greg A. Harris .05 .02
628 Matt Williams .25 .10
629 Pete O'Brien .05 .02
630 Mike Greenwell .05 .02
631 Dave Bergman .05 .02
632 Bryan Harvey RC * .25 .10
633 Daryl Boston .05 .02
634 Marvin Freeman .05 .02
635 Willie Randolph .10 .04
636 Bill Wilkinson .05 .02
637 Carmen Castillo .05 .02
638 Floyd Bannister .05 .02
639 Walt Weiss TL .05 .02
640 Willie McGee .10 .04
641 Curt Young .05 .02
642 Angel Salazar .05 .02
643 Louie Meadows .05 .02
644 Lloyd McClendon .05 .02
645 Jack Morris .10 .04
646 Kevin Bass .05 .02
647 Randy Johnson RC 4.00 1.20
648 Sandy Alomar FS RC .40 .16
649 Stu Cliburn .05 .02
650 Kirby Puckett .25 .10
651 Tom Niedenfuer .05 .02
652 Rich Gedman .05 .02
653 Tommy Barrett .05 .02
654 Whitey Herzog MG .10 .04
655 Dave Magadan .05 .02
656 Ivan Calderon .05 .02
657 Joe Magrane .05 .02
658 R.J. Reynolds .05 .02
659 Al Leiter .25 .10
660 Will Clark .25 .10
661 D.Gooden TBC84 .05 .02
662 Lou Brock TBC79 .10 .04
663 Hank Aaron TBC74 .25 .10
664 Gil Hodges TBC 69 .10 .04
665A Tony Oliva TBC64 2.00 .80
ERR (fabricated card
is enlarged version
of Oliva's 64T card;
Topps copyright
missing)
665B Tony Oliva TBC 64 .10 .04
COR (fabricated
card)
666 Randy St.Claire .05 .02
667 Dwayne Murphy .05 .02
668 Mike Bielecki .05 .02
669 Orel Hershiser .10 .04
Mike Scioscia TL
670 Kevin Seitzer .05 .02
671 Jim Gantner .05 .02
672 Allan Anderson .05 .02
673 Don Baylor .10 .04
674 Otis Nixon .05 .02
675 Bruce Hurst .05 .02
676 Ernie Riles .05 .02
677 Dave Schmidt .05 .02
678 Dion James .05 .02
679 Willie Fraser .05 .02
680 Gary Carter .10 .04
681 Jeff D. Robinson .05 .02
682 Rick Leach .05 .02
683 Jose Cecena .05 .02
684 Dave Johnson MG .05 .02
685 Jeff Treadway .05 .02
686 Scott Terry .05 .02
687 Alvin Davis .05 .02
688 Zane Smith .05 .02
689A Stan Jefferson .05 .02
(Pink triangle on
front bottom left)
689B Stan Jefferson .05 .02
(Violet triangle on
front bottom left)
690 Doug Jones .05 .02
691 Roberto Kelly UER .05 .02
(83 Oneonita)
692 Steve Ontiveros .05 .02
693 Pat Borders RC * .25 .10
694 Les Lancaster .05 .02
695 Carlton Fisk .15 .06
696 Don August .05 .02
697A Franklin Stubbs .05 .02
(Team name on front
in white)
697B Franklin Stubbs .05 .02
(Team name on front
in gray)
698 Keith Atherton .05 .02
699 Al Pedrique TL .05 .02
Tony Gwynn sliding
700 Don Mattingly .60 .24
701 Storm Davis .05 .02
702 Jamie Quirk .05 .02
703 Scott Garrelts .05 .02
704 Carlos Quintana RC .10 .04
705 Terry Kennedy .05 .02
706 Pete Incaviglia .05 .02
707 Steve Jeltz .05 .02
708 Chuck Finley .10 .04
709 Tom Herr .05 .02
710 David Cone .10 .04
711 Candy Sierra .05 .02
712 Bill Swift .05 .02
713 Ty Griffin FDP .05 .02
714 Joe Morgan MG .10 .04
715 Tony Pena .05 .02
716 Wayne Tolleson .05 .02
717 Jamie Moyer .10 .04
718 Glenn Braggs .05 .02
719 Danny Darwin .05 .02
720 Tim Wallach .05 .02
721 Ron Tingley .05 .02
722 Todd Stottlemyre .05 .02
723 Rafael Belliard .05 .02
724 Jerry Don Gleaton .05 .02
725 Terry Steinbach .10 .04
726 Dickie Thon .05 .02
727 Joe Orsulak .05 .02
728 Charlie Puleo .05 .02
729 Steve Buechele TL .05 .02
(Inconsistent design,
team name on front
surrounded by black,
should be white)
730 Danny Jackson .05 .02
731 Mike Young .05 .02
732 Steve Buechele .05 .02
733 Randy Bockus .05 .02
734 Jody Reed .05 .02
735 Roger McDowell .05 .02
736 Jeff Hamilton .05 .02
737 Norm Charlton RC .25 .10
738 Darnell Coles .05 .02
739 Brook Jacoby .05 .02
740 Dan Plesac .05 .02
741 Ken Phelps .05 .02
742 Mike Harkey FS RC .10 .04
743 Mike Heath .05 .02
744 Roger Craig MG .10 .04
745 Fred McGriff .15 .06
746 G.Gonzalez UER .05 .02
Wrong birthdate
747 Wil Tejada .05 .02
748 Jimmy Jones .05 .02
749 Rafael Ramirez .05 .02
750 Bret Saberhagen .10 .04
751 Ken Oberkfell .05 .02
752 Jim Gott .05 .02
753 Jose Uribe .05 .02
754 Bob Brower .05 .02
755 Mike Scioscia .10 .04
756 Scott Medvin .05 .02
757 Brady Anderson RC .40 .16
758 Gene Walter .05 .02
759 Rob Deer TL .05 .02
760 Lee Smith .10 .04
761 Dante Bichette RC .40 .16
762 Bobby Thigpen .05 .02
763 Dave Martinez .05 .02
764 Robin Ventura FDP RC .75 .30
765 Glenn Davis .05 .02
766 Cecilio Guante .05 .02
767 Mike Capel .05 .02
768 Bill Wegman .05 .02
769 Junior Ortiz .05 .02
770 Alan Trammell .10 .04
771 Ron Kittle .05 .02
772 Ron Oester .05 .02
773 Keith Moreland .05 .02
774 Frank Robinson MG .15 .06
775 Jeff Reardon .10 .04
776 Nelson Liriano .05 .02
777 Ted Power .05 .02
778 Bruce Benedict .05 .02
779 Craig McMurtry .05 .02
780 Pedro Guerrero .10 .04
781 Greg Briley .10 .04
782 Checklist 661-792 .05 .02
783 Trevor Wilson RC .10 .04
784 Steve Avery FDP RC .25 .10
785 Ellis Burks .10 .04
786 Melido Perez .05 .02
787 Dave West RC .10 .04
788 Mike Morgan .05 .02
789 Bo Jackson TL .25 .10
790 Sid Fernandez .05 .02
791 Jim Lindeman .05 .02
792 Rafael Santana .05 .02

1989 Topps Tiffany

Again, Topps issed a standard-size "Glossy" parallel to their regular set. These cards, printed in the Topps Irish facility, have 792 standard-size cards and were issued in complete set form only. These cards have a "shiny" front as well as an easy to read back. These cards were issued only through Topps hobby dealers. With the "glut" of the previous two years Tiffany sets in the marketplace, it seems that approximately 15,000 of these sets were produced in 1989.

	Nm-Mt	Ex-Mt
COMP.FACT.SET (792)	120.00	47.50

*STARS: 5X TO 12X BASIC CARDS....
*ROOKIES: 5X TO 12X BASIC CARDS

1989 Topps Batting Leaders

The 1989 Topps Batting Leaders set contains 22 standard-size glossy cards. The fronts are bright red. The set depicts the 22 veterans with the highest lifetime batting averages. The cards were distributed one per Topps blister pack. These blister packs were sold exclusively through K-Mart stores. The cards in the set were numbered by K-Mart essentially in order of highest active career batting average entering the 1989 season.

	Nm-Mt	Ex-Mt
COMPLETE SET (22)	100.00	40.00
1 Wade Boggs	10.00	4.00
2 Tony Gwynn	20.00	8.00
3 Don Mattingly	20.00	8.00
4 Kirby Puckett	10.00	4.00
5 George Brett	20.00	8.00
6 Pedro Guerrero	.50	.20
7 Tim Raines	1.00	.40
8 Keith Hernandez	1.00	.40
9 Jim Rice	1.00	.40
10 Paul Molitor	8.00	3.20
11 Eddie Murray	8.00	3.20
12 Willie McGee	1.00	.40
13 Dave Parker	1.00	.40
14 Julio Franco	1.00	.40
15 Rickey Henderson	12.00	4.80
16 Kent Hrbek	1.00	.40
17 Willie Wilson	.50	.20
18 Johnny Ray	.50	.20
19 Pat Tabler	.50	.20
20 Carney Lansford	.50	.20
21 Robin Yount	8.00	3.20
22 Alan Trammell	2.00	.80

1989 Topps Glossy All-Stars

These glossy cards were inserted with Topps rack packs and honor the starting line-ups, managers, and honorary captains of the 1988 National and American League All-Star teams. The standard size cards are very similar in design to what Topps has used since 1984. The backs are printed in red and blue on white card stock.

	Nm-Mt	Ex-Mt
COMPLETE SET (22)	3.00	1.20
1 Tom Kelly MG	.05	.02
2 Mark McGwire	1.25	.50
3 Paul Molitor	.40	.16
4 Wade Boggs	.30	.12
5 Cal Ripken	1.50	.60
6 Jose Canseco	.25	.10
7 Rickey Henderson	.60	.24
8 Dave Winfield	.40	.16
9 Terry Steinbach	.05	.02
10 Frank Viola	.05	.02
11 Bobby Doerr CAPT	.10	.04
12 Whitey Herzog MG	.05	.02
13 Will Clark	.20	.08
14 Ryne Sandberg	.50	.20
15 Bobby Bonilla	.10	.04
16 Ozzie Smith	.50	.20
17 Vince Coleman	.05	.02
18 Andre Dawson	.20	.08
19 Darryl Strawberry	.10	.04
20 Gary Carter	.40	.16
21 Dwight Gooden	.10	.04
22 Willie Stargell CAPT	.15	.06

1989 Topps Glossy Send-Ins

The 1989 Topps Glossy Send-In set contains 60 standard-size cards. The fronts have color photos with white borders; the backs are light blue. The cards were distributed through the mail by Topps in six groups of ten cards. The last two cards out of each group of ten are young players or prospects.

	Nm-Mt	Ex-Mt
COMPLETE SET (60)	10.00	4.00
1 Kirby Puckett	.75	.30
2 Eric Davis	.20	.08
3 Joe Carter	.20	.08
4 Andy Van Slyke	.10	.04
5 Wade Boggs	.60	.24
6 David Cone	.20	.08
7 Kent Hrbek	.20	.08
8 Darryl Strawberry	.20	.08
9 Jay Buhner	.20	.08
10 Ron Gant	.20	.08
11 Will Clark	.40	.16

12 Jose Canseco .75 .30
13 Juan Samuel .10 .04
14 George Brett 1.50 .60
15 Benito Santiago .20 .08
16 Dennis Eckersley .60 .24
17 Gary Carter .60 .24
18 Frank Viola .10 .04
19 Roberto Alomar 1.50 .60
20 Paul Gibson .10 .04
21 Dave Winfield .60 .24
22 Howard Johnson .10 .04
23 Roger Clemens 1.50 .60
24 Bobby Bonilla .20 .08
25 Alan Trammell .30 .12
26 Kevin McReynolds .10 .04
27 George Bell .10 .04
28 Bruce Hurst .10 .04
29 Mark Grace .75 .30
30 Tim Belcher .10 .04
31 Mike Greenwell .10 .04
32 Glenn Davis .10 .04
33 Gary Gaetti .20 .08
34 Ryne Sandberg 1.50 .60
35 Rickey Henderson 1.00 .40
36 Dwight Evans .20 .08
37 Dwight Gooden .20 .08
38 Robin Yount .60 .24
39 Damon Berryhill .10 .04
40 Chris Sabo .10 .04
41 Mark McGwire 2.50 1.00
42 Ozzie Smith 1.50 .60
43 Paul Molitor .60 .24
44 Andres Galarraga .40 .16
45 Dave Stewart .20 .08
46 Tom Browning .10 .04
47 Cal Ripken 3.00 1.20
48 Orel Hershiser .20 .08
49 Dave Gallagher .10 .04
50 Walt Weiss .10 .04
51 Don Mattingly 1.50 .60
52 Tony Fernandez .10 .04
53 Tim Raines .20 .08
54 Jeff Reardon .20 .08
55 Kirk Gibson .20 .08
56 Jack Clark .10 .04
57 Danny Jackson .10 .04
58 Tony Gwynn 1.50 .60
59 Cecil Espy .10 .04
60 Jody Reed .10 .04

1989 Topps Rookies

Inserted in each supermarket jumbo pack is a card from this series of 22 of 1988's best rookies as determined by Topps. Jumbo packs consisted of 100 (regular issue 1989 Topps baseball) cards with a stick of gum plus the insert "Rookie" card. The card fronts are in full color and measure the standard size. The card backs are printed in red and blue on white card stock and are numbered at the bottom. The order of the set is alphabetical by player's name.

Nm-Mt Ex-Mt
COMPLETE SET (22) 12.00 4.80
1 Roberto Alomar 2.50 1.00
2 Brady Anderson .75 .30
3 Tim Belcher .25 .10
4 Damon Berryhill .25 .10
5 Jay Buhner 1.00 .40
6 Kevin Elster .25 .10
7 Cecil Espy .25 .10
8 Dave Gallagher .25 .10
9 Ron Gant 1.00 .40
10 Paul Gibson .25 .10
11 Mark Grace 2.00 .80
12 Darrin Jackson .25 .10
13 Gregg Jefferies .50 .20
14 Ricky Jordan .25 .10
15 Al Leiter 1.00 .40
16 Melido Perez .25 .10
17 Chris Sabo .25 .10
18 Nelson Santovenia .25 .10
19 Mackey Sasser .25 .10
20 Gary Sheffield 3.00 1.20
21 Walt Weiss .25 .10
22 David Wells 2.00 .80

1989 Topps Wax Box Cards

The cards in this 16-card set measure the standard size. Cards have essentially the same design as the 1989 Topps regular issue set. The cards were printed on the bottoms of the regular issue wax pack boxes. These 16 cards, "lettered" A through P, are considered a separate set in their own right and are not typically included in a complete set of the regular issue 1989 Topps cards. The order of the set is alphabetical by player's name. The value of the panels uncut is slightly greater, perhaps by 25 percent greater, than the value of the individual cards cut up carefully. The sixteen cards in this set honor players (and one manager) who reached career milestones during the 1988 season.

Nm-Mt Ex-Mt
COMPLETE SET (16) 8.00 3.20
A George Brett 1.00 .40
B Bill Buckner .20 .08
C Darrell Evans .20 .08
D Rich Gossage .20 .08
E Greg Gross .10 .04
F Rickey Henderson .75 .30
G Keith Hernandez .20 .08
H Tom Lasorda MG .40 .16
I Jim Rice .20 .08
J Cal Ripken 2.00 .80
K Nolan Ryan 2.00 .80
L Mike Schmidt .75 .30
M Bruce Sutter .20 .08
N Don Sutton .50 .20
O Kent Tekulve .10 .04
P Dave Winfield .50 .20

1989 Topps Traded

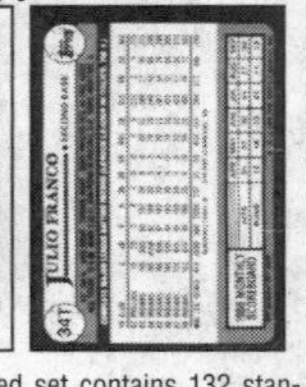

The 1989 Topps Traded set contains 132 standard-size cards. The cards were distributed exclusively in factory set form in red and white taped boxes through hobby dealers. The cards are identical to the 1989 Topps regular issue cards except for whiter stock and t-suffixed numbering on back. Rookie Cards in this set include Ken Griffey Jr., Deion Sanders and Omar Vizquel.

Nm-Mt Ex-Mt
COMP.FACT.SET (132) 15.00 6.00
1T Don Aase .05 .02
2T Jim Abbott .25 .10
3T Kent Anderson .05 .02
4T Keith Atherton .05 .02
5T Wally Backman .05 .02
6T Steve Balboni .05 .02
7T Jesse Barfield .10 .04
8T Steve Bedrosian .05 .02
9T Todd Benzinger .05 .02
10T Geronimo Berroa .05 .02
11T Bert Blyleven .10 .04
12T Bob Boone .10 .04
13T Phil Bradley .05 .02
14T Jeff Brantley RC .25 .10
15T Kevin Brown .25 .10
16T Jerry Browne .05 .02
17T Chuck Cary .05 .02
18T Carmen Castillo .05 .02
19T Jim Clancy .05 .02
20T Jack Clark .10 .04
21T Bryan Clutterbuck .05 .02
22T Jody Davis .05 .02
23T Mike Devereaux .05 .02
24T Frank DiPino .05 .02
25T Benny Distefano .05 .02
26T John Dopson .05 .02
27T Len Dykstra .10 .04
28T Jim Eisenreich .05 .02
29T Nick Esasky .05 .02
30T Alvaro Espinoza .05 .02
31T Darrell Evans UER .10 .04
(Stat headings on back are for a pitcher)
32T Junior Felix RC .10 .04
33T Felix Fermin .05 .02
34T Julio Franco .10 .04
35T Terry Francona .10 .04
36T Cito Gaston MG .05 .02
37T Bob Geren RC UER .05 .02
(Photo actually Mike Fennell)
38T Tom Gordon RC .40 .16
39T Tommy Gregg .05 .02
40T Ken Griffey Sr. .10 .04
41T Ken Griffey Jr. RC 8.00 3.20
42T Kevin Gross .05 .02
43T Lee Guetterman .05 .02
44T Mel Hall .05 .02
45T Erik Hanson RC .25 .10
46T Gene Harris RC .10 .04
47T Andy Hawkins .05 .02
48T Rickey Henderson .25 .10
49T Tom Herr .05 .02
50T Ken Hill RC .25 .10
51T Brian Holman RC * .10 .04
52T Brian Holton .05 .02
53T Art Howe MG .05 .02
54T Ken Howell .05 .02
55T Bruce Hurst .05 .02
56T Chris James .05 .02
57T Randy Johnson 2.50 .80
58T Jimmy Jones .05 .02
59T Terry Kennedy .05 .02
60T Paul Kilgus .05 .02
61T Eric King .05 .02
62T Ron Kittle .05 .02
63T John Kruk .10 .04
64T Randy Kutcher .05 .02
65T Steve Lake .05 .02
66T Mark Langston .05 .02
67T Dave LaPoint .05 .02
68T Rick Leach .05 .02
69T Terry Leach .05 .02
70T Jim Lefebvre MG .05 .02
71T Al Leiter .25 .10
72T Jeffrey Leonard .05 .02
73T Derek Lilliquist RC .10 .04
74T Rick Mahler .05 .02
75T Tom McCarthy .05 .02
76T Lloyd McClendon .05 .02
77T Lance McCullers .05 .02
78T Oddibe McDowell .05 .02
79T Roger McDowell .05 .02
80T Larry McWilliams .05 .02
81T Randy Milligan .05 .02
82T Mike Moore .05 .02
83T Keith Moreland .05 .02
84T Mike Morgan .05 .02
85T Jamie Moyer .10 .04
86T Rob Murphy .05 .02
87T Eddie Murray .25 .10
88T Pete O'Brien .05 .02
89T Gregg Olson .25 .10
90T Steve Ontiveros .05 .02
91T Jesse Orosco .05 .02
92T Spike Owen .05 .02
93T Rafael Palmeiro .25 .10
94T Clay Parker .05 .02
95T Jeff Parrett .05 .02
96T Lance Parrish .10 .04
97T Dennis Powell .05 .02
98T Rey Quinones .05 .02
99T Doug Rader MG .05 .02
100T Willie Randolph .10 .04
101T Shane Rawley .05 .02
102T Randy Ready .05 .02
103T Bip Roberts .05 .02
104T Kenny Rogers RC .75 .30
105T Ed Romero .05 .02
106T Nolan Ryan 1.50 .60
107T Luis Salazar .05 .02
108T Juan Samuel .05 .02
109T Alex Sanchez .05 .02
110T Deion Sanders RC 1.00 .40
111T Steve Sax .05 .02
112T Rick Schu .05 .02
113T Dwight Smith RC .25 .10
114T Lonnie Smith .05 .02
115T Billy Spiers RC .25 .10
116T Kent Tekulve .05 .02
117T Walt Terrell .05 .02
118T Milt Thompson .05 .02
119T Dickie Thon .05 .02
120T Jeff Torborg MG .05 .02
121T Jeff Treadway .05 .02
122T Omar Vizquel RC .75 .30
123T Jerome Walton RC .25 .10
124T Gary Ward .05 .02
125T Claudell Washington .05 .02
126T Curt Wilkerson .05 .02
127T Eddie Williams .05 .02
128T Frank Williams .05 .02
129T Ken Williams .05 .02
130T Mitch Williams .05 .02
131T Steve Wilson RC .10 .04
132T Checklist 1T-132T .05 .02

1989 Topps Traded Tiffany

For each set of regular Tiffany cards ordered, dealers received an update set. These 132 standard-size cards update the regular Topps issue. Again, these cards feature "glossy" fronts as well as easy to read backs. This set was issued only in complete form from the company. Again, the Topps Ireland printing facility produced these cards. Again, approximately 15,000 of these sets were produced.

Nm-Mt Ex-Mt
COMP.FACT.SET (132) 120.00 47.50
*STARS: 4X TO 10X BASIC CARDS
*ROOKIES: 5X TO 12X BASIC CARDS

1990 Topps

The 1990 Topps set contains 792 standard-size cards. Cards were issued primarily in wax packs, rack packs and hobby and retail Christmas factory sets. Card fronts feature various colored borders with the player's name at the bottom and team name at top. Subsets include All-Stars (385-407), Turn Back the Clock (661-665) and Draft Picks (scattered throughout the set). The key Rookie Cards in this set are Juan Gonzalez, Marquis Grissom, Sammy Sosa, Frank Thomas, Larry Walker and Bernie Williams. The Thomas card (414A) was printed without his name on front creating a scarce variation. The card is rarely seen and, for a newer issue, has experienced unprecedented growth as far as value. Be careful when purchasing this card as counterfeits have been produced. A very few cards of President George Bush made their ways into packs. While these cards were supposed to be never issued, a few collectors did receive these cards when opening packs. Since this card is thinly traded, no pricing is provided.

Nm-Mt Ex-Mt
COMPLETE SET (792) 20.00 6.00
COMP.FACT.SET (792) 25.00 7.50
COMP.X-MAS.SET (792) 40.00 12.00
1 Nolan Ryan 1.00 .30
2 Nolan Ryan Mets .50 .15
3 Nolan Ryan Angels .50 .15
4 Nolan Ryan Astros .50 .15
5 N.Ryan Rangers UER .50 .15
(Says Texas Stadium rather than Arlington Stadium)
6 Vince Coleman RB .05 .02
7 Rickey Henderson RB .15 .04
8 Cal Ripken RB .25 .07
9 Eric Plunk .05 .02
10 Barry Larkin .15 .04
11 Paul Gibson .05 .02
12 Joe Girardi .15 .04
13 Mark Williamson .05 .02
14 Mike Fetters RC .25 .07
15 Teddy Higuera .05 .02
16 Kent Anderson .05 .02
17 Kelly Downs .05 .02
18 Carlos Quintana .05 .02
19 Al Newman .05 .02
20 Mark Gubicza .05 .02
21 Jeff Torborg MG .05 .02
22 Bruce Ruffin .05 .02
23 Randy Velarde .05 .02
24 Joe Hesketh .05 .02
25 Willie Randolph .10 .03
26 Don Slaught .05 .02
27 Rick Leach .05 .02
28 Duane Ward .05 .02
29 John Cangelosi .05 .02
30 David Cone .10 .03
31 Henry Cotto .05 .02
32 John Farrell .05 .02
33 Greg Walker .05 .02
34 Tony Fossas .05 .02
35 Benito Santiago .10 .03
36 John Costello .05 .02
37 Domingo Ramos .05 .02
38 Wes Gardner .05 .02
39 Curt Ford .05 .02
40 Jay Howell .05 .02
41 Matt Williams .10 .03
42 Jeff M. Robinson .05 .02
43 Dante Bichette .25 .07
44 Roger Salkeld FDP RC .10 .03
45 Dave Parker UER .10 .03
(Born in Jackson, not Calhoun)
46 Rob Dibble .10 .03
47 Brian Harper .05 .02
48 Zane Smith .05 .02
49 Tom Lawless .05 .02
50 Glenn Davis .05 .02
51 Doug Rader MG .05 .02
52 Jack Daugherty .05 .02
53 Mike LaCoss .05 .02
54 Joel Skinner .05 .02
55 Darrell Evans UER .10 .03
(HR total should be 414, not 424)
56 Franklin Stubbs .05 .02
57 Greg Vaughn .05 .02
58 Keith Miller .05 .02
59 Ted Power .05 .02
60 George Brett .60 .18
61 Deion Sanders .25 .07
62 Ramon Martinez .05 .02
63 Mike Pagliarulo .05 .02
64 Danny Darwin .05 .02
65 Devon White .10 .03
66 Greg Litton .05 .02
67 Scott Sanderson .05 .02
68 Dave Henderson .05 .02
69 Todd Frohwirth .05 .02
70 Mike Greenwell .05 .02
71 Allan Anderson .05 .02
72 Jeff Huson RC .10 .03
73 Bob Milacki .05 .02
74 Jeff Jackson FDP RC .10 .03
75 Doug Jones .05 .02
76 Dave Valle .05 .02
77 Dave Bergman .05 .02
78 Mike Flanagan .05 .02
79 Ron Kittle .05 .02
80 Jeff Russell .05 .02
81 Bob Rodgers MG .05 .02
82 Scott Terry .05 .02
83 Hensley Meulens .05 .02
84 Ray Searage .05 .02
85 Juan Samuel .05 .02
86 Paul Kilgus .05 .02
87 Rick Luecken .05 .02
88 Glenn Braggs .05 .02
89 Clint Zavaras .05 .02
90 Jack Clark .10 .03
91 Steve Frey .05 .02
92 Mike Stanley .05 .02
93 Shawn Hillegas .05 .02
94 Herm Winningham .05 .02
95 Todd Worrell .05 .02
96 Jody Reed .05 .02
97 Curt Schilling 1.00 .30
98 Jose Gonzalez .05 .02
99 Rich Monteleone .05 .02
100 Will Clark .25 .07
101 Shane Rawley .05 .02
102 Stan Javier .05 .02
103 Marvin Freeman .05 .02
104 Bob Knepper .05 .02
105 Randy Myers .10 .03
106 Charlie O'Brien .05 .02
107 Fred Lynn .05 .02
108 Rod Nichols .05 .02
109 Roberto Kelly .05 .02
110 Tommy Helms MG .05 .02
111 Ed Whited .05 .02
112 Glenn Wilson .05 .02
113 Manny Lee .05 .02
114 Mike Bielecki .05 .02
115 Tony Pena .05 .02
116 Floyd Bannister .05 .02
117 Mike Sharperson .05 .02
118 Erik Hanson .05 .02
119 Billy Hatcher .05 .02
120 John Franco .10 .03
121 Robin Ventura .25 .07
122 Shawn Abner .05 .02
123 Rich Gedman .05 .02
124 Dave Dravecky .10 .03
125 Kent Hrbek .10 .03
126 Randy Kramer .05 .02
127 Mike Devereaux .05 .02
128 Checklist 1 .05 .02
129 Ron Jones .05 .02
130 Bert Blyleven .10 .03
131 Matt Nokes .05 .02
132 Lance Blankenship .05 .02
133 Ricky Horton .05 .02
134 E.Cunningham FDP RC .10 .03
135 Dave Magadan .05 .02
136 Kevin Brown .10 .03
137 Marty Pevey .05 .02
138 Al Leiter .25 .07
139 Greg Brock .05 .02
140 Andre Dawson .10 .03
141 John Hart MG .05 .02
142 Jeff Wetherby .05 .02
143 Rafael Belliard .05 .02
144 Bud Black .05 .02
145 Terry Steinbach .05 .02
146 Rob Richie .05 .02
147 Chuck Finley .10 .03
148 Edgar Martinez .15 .04
149 Steve Farr .05 .02
150 Kirk Gibson .10 .03
151 Rick Mahler .05 .02
152 Lonnie Smith .05 .02
153 Randy Milligan .05 .02
154 Mike Maddux .05 .02
155 Ellis Burks .15 .04
156 Ken Patterson .05 .02
157 Craig Biggio .15 .04
158 Craig Lefferts .05 .02
159 Mike Felder .05 .02
160 Dave Righetti .05 .02
161 Harold Reynolds .10 .03
162 Todd Zeile .10 .03
163 Phil Bradley .05 .02
164 Jeff Juden FDP RC .10 .03
165 Walt Weiss .05 .02
166 Bobby Witt .05 .02
167 Kevin Appier .10 .03
168 Jose Lind .05 .02
169 Richard Dotson .05 .02
170 George Bell .05 .02
171 Russ Nixon MG .05 .02
172 Tom Lampkin .05 .02
173 Tim Belcher .05 .02
174 Jeff Kunkel .05 .02
175 Mike Moore .05 .02
176 Luis Quinones .05 .02
177 Mike Henneman .05 .02
178 Chris James .05 .02
179 Brian Holton .05 .02
180 Tim Raines .10 .03
181 Juan Agosto .05 .02
182 Mookie Wilson .10 .03
183 Steve Lake .05 .02
184 Danny Cox .05 .02
185 Ruben Sierra .05 .02
186 Dave LaPoint .05 .02
187 Rick Wrona .05 .02
188 Mike Smithson .05 .02
189 Dick Schofield .05 .02
190 Rick Reuschel .05 .02
191 Pat Borders .05 .02
192 Don August .05 .02
193 Andy Benes .10 .03
194 Glenallen Hill .05 .02
195 Tim Burke .05 .02
196 Gerald Young .05 .02
197 Doug Drabek .05 .02
198 Mike Marshall .05 .02
199 Sergio Valdez .05 .02
200 Don Mattingly .60 .18
201 Cito Gaston MG .05 .02
202 Mike Macfarlane .05 .02
203 Mike Roesler .05 .02
204 Bob Dernier .05 .02
205 Mark Davis .05 .02
206 Nick Esasky .05 .02
207 Bob Ojeda .05 .02
208 Brook Jacoby .05 .02
209 Greg Mathews .05 .02
210 Ryne Sandberg .40 .12
211 John Cerutti .05 .02
212 Joe Orsulak .05 .02
213 Scott Bankhead .05 .02
214 Terry Francona .10 .03
215 Kirk McCaskill .05 .02
216 Ricky Jordan .05 .02
217 Don Robinson .05 .02
218 Wally Backman .05 .02
219 Donn Pall .05 .02
220 Barry Bonds .60 .18
221 Gary Mielke .05 .02
222 Kurt Stillwell UER .05 .02
(Graduate misspelled as gradute)
223 Tommy Gregg .05 .02
224 Delino DeShields RC .25 .07
225 Jim Deshaies .05 .02
226 Mickey Hatcher .05 .02
227 Kevin Tapani RC .25 .07
228 Dave Martinez .05 .02
229 David Wells .10 .03
230 Keith Hernandez .10 .03
231 Jack McKeon MG .05 .02
232 Darnell Coles .05 .02
233 Ken Hill .10 .03
234 Mariano Duncan .05 .02
235 Jeff Reardon .10 .03
236 Hal Morris .05 .02
237 Kevin Ritz .05 .02
238 Felix Jose .05 .02
239 Eric Show .05 .02
240 Mark Grace .15 .04
241 Mike Krukow .05 .02
242 Fred Manrique .05 .02
243 Barry Jones .05 .02
244 Bill Schroeder .05 .02
245 Roger Clemens .50 .15
246 Jim Eisenreich .05 .02
247 Jerry Reed .05 .02
248 Dave Anderson .05 .02
249 Mike (Texas) Smith .05 .02
250 Jose Canseco .25 .07
251 Jeff Blauser .05 .02
252 Otis Nixon .05 .02
253 Mark Portugal .05 .02
254 Francisco Cabrera .05 .02
255 Bobby Thigpen .05 .02
256 Marvell Wynne .05 .02
257 Jose DeLeon .05 .02
258 Barry Lyons .05 .02
259 Lance McCullers .05 .02
260 Eric Davis .10 .03
261 Whitey Herzog MG .10 .03
262 Checklist 2 .05 .02
263 Mel Stottlemyre Jr. .05 .02
264 Bryan Clutterbuck .05 .02
265 Pete O'Brien .05 .02
266 German Gonzalez .05 .02
267 Mark Davidson .05 .02
268 Rob Murphy .05 .02
269 Dickie Thon .05 .02
270 Dave Stewart .10 .03
271 Chet Lemon .05 .02
272 Bryan Harvey .05 .02
273 Bobby Bonilla .10 .03
274 Mauro Gozzo .05 .02
275 Mickey Tettleton .05 .02
276 Gary Thurman .05 .02
277 Lenny Harris .05 .02
278 Pascual Perez .05 .02
279 Steve Buechele .05 .02
280 Lou Whitaker .10 .03
281 Kevin Bass .05 .02
282 Derek Lilliquist .05 .02
283 Joey Belle .25 .07
284 Mark Gardner RC .10 .03
285 Willie McGee .10 .03
286 Lee Guetterman .05 .02
287 Vance Law .05 .02
288 Greg Briley .05 .02

289 Norm Charlton .05 .02
290 Robin Yount .40 .12
291 Dave Johnson MG .10 .03
292 Jim Gott .05 .02
293 Mike Gallego .05 .02
294 Craig McMurtry .05 .02
295 Fred McGriff .25 .07
296 Jeff Ballard .05 .02
297 Tommy Herr .05 .02
298 Dan Gladden .05 .02
299 Adam Peterson .05 .02
300 Bo Jackson .25 .07
301 Don Aase .05 .02
302 Marcus Lawton .05 .02
303 Rick Cerone .05 .02
304 Marty Clary .05 .02
305 Eddie Murray .25 .07
306 Tom Niedenfuer .05 .02
307 Bip Roberts .05 .02
308 Jose Guzman .05 .02
309 Eric Yelding .05 .02
310 Steve Bedrosian .05 .02
311 Dwight Smith .05 .02
312 Dan Quisenberry .05 .02
313 Gus Polidor .05 .02
314 Donald Harris FDP .05 .02
315 Bruce Hurst .05 .02
316 Carney Lansford .10 .03
317 Mark Guthrie .05 .02
318 Wallace Johnson .05 .02
319 Dion James .05 .02
320 Dave Stieb .10 .03
321 Joe Morgan MG .05 .02
322 Junior Ortiz .05 .02
323 Willie Wilson .05 .02
324 Pete Harnisch .05 .02
325 Robby Thompson .05 .02
326 Tom McCarthy .05 .02
327 Ken Williams .05 .02
328 Curt Young .05 .02
329 Oddibe McDowell .05 .02
330 Ron Darling .05 .02
331 Juan Gonzalez RC 1.50 .45
332 Paul O'Neill .15 .04
333 Bill Wegman .05 .02
334 Johnny Ray .05 .02
335 Andy Hawkins .05 .02
336 Ken Griffey Jr. .75 .23
337 Lloyd McClendon .05 .02
338 Dennis Lamp .05 .02
339 Dave Clark .05 .02
340 Fernando Valenzuela .10 .03
341 Tom Foley .05 .02
342 Alex Trevino .05 .02
343 Frank Tanana .05 .02
344 George Canale .05 .02
345 Harold Baines .10 .03
346 Jim Presley .05 .02
347 Junior Felix .05 .02
348 Gary Wayne .05 .02
349 Steve Finley .10 .03
350 Bret Saberhagen .10 .03
351 Roger Craig MG .05 .02
352 Bryn Smith .05 .02
353 Sandy Alomar Jr. .10 .03
(Not listed as Jr.
on card front)
354 Stan Belinda RC .10 .03
355 Marty Barrett .05 .02
356 Randy Ready .05 .02
357 Dave West .05 .02
358 Andres Thomas .05 .02
359 Jimmy Jones .05 .02
360 Paul Molitor .15 .04
361 Randy McCament .05 .02
362 Damon Berryhill .05 .02
363 Dan Petry .05 .02
364 Rolando Roomes .05 .02
365 Ozzie Guillen .05 .02
366 Mike Heath .05 .02
367 Mike Morgan .05 .02
368 Bill Doran .05 .02
369 Todd Burns .05 .02
370 Tim Wallach .05 .02
371 Jimmy Key .10 .03
372 Terry Kennedy .05 .02
373 Alvin Davis .05 .02
374 Steve Cummings RC .05 .02
375 Dwight Evans .10 .03
376 Checklist 3 UER .05 .02
(Higuera misalphabet-
ized in Brewer list)
377 Mickey Weston .05 .02
378 Luis Salazar .05 .02
379 Steve Rosenberg .05 .02
380 Dave Winfield .10 .03
381 Frank Robinson MG .15 .04
382 Jeff Musselman .05 .02
383 John Morris .05 .02
384 Pat Combs .05 .02
385 Fred McGriff AS .10 .03
386 Julio Franco AS .05 .02
387 Wade Boggs AS .10 .03
388 Cal Ripken AS .40 .12
389 Robin Yount AS .25 .07
390 Ruben Sierra AS .05 .02
391 Kirby Puckett AS .15 .04
392 Carlton Fisk AS .10 .03
393 Bret Saberhagen AS .05 .02
394 Jeff Ballard AS .05 .02
395 Jeff Russell AS .05 .02
396 A.Bartlett Giamatti .25 .07
COMM MEM
397 Will Clark AS .10 .03
398 Ryne Sandberg AS .25 .07
399 Howard Johnson AS .05 .02
400 Ozzie Smith AS .25 .07
401 Kevin Mitchell AS .05 .02
402 Eric Davis AS .05 .02
403 Tony Gwynn AS .15 .04
404 Craig Biggio AS .10 .03
405 Mike Scott AS .05 .02
406 Joe Magrane AS .05 .02
407 Mark Davis AS .05 .02
408 Trevor Wilson .05 .02
409 Tom Brunansky .05 .02
410 Joe Boever .05 .02
411 Ken Phelps .05 .02
412 Jamie Moyer .10 .03
413 Brian DuBois .05 .02
414A Frank Thomas FDP 500.00 150.00
ERR (Name missing
on card front)
414B F.Thomas COR RC 2.00 .60
415 Shawon Dunston .05 .02
416 Dave Johnson (P) .05 .02
417 Jim Gantner .05 .02
418 Tom Browning .05 .02
419 Beau Allred RC .05 .02
420 Carlton Fisk .15 .04
421 Greg Minton .05 .02
422 Pat Sheridan .05 .02
423 Fred Toliver .05 .02
424 Jerry Reuss .05 .02
425 Bill Landrum .05 .02
426 Jeff Hamilton UER .05 .02
(Stats say he fanned
197 times in 1987, but
he only had 147 at bats)
427 Carmen Castillo .05 .02
428 Steve Davis .05 .02
429 Tom Kelly MG .05 .02
430 Pete Incaviglia .05 .02
431 Randy Johnson .50 .12
432 Damaso Garcia .05 .02
433 Steve Olin RC .25 .07
434 Mark Carreon .05 .02
435 Kevin Seitzer .05 .02
436 Mel Hall .05 .02
437 Les Lancaster .05 .02
438 Greg Myers .05 .02
439 Jeff Parrett .05 .02
440 Alan Trammell .10 .03
441 Bob Kipper .05 .02
442 Jerry Browne .05 .02
443 Cris Carpenter .05 .02
444 Kyle Abbott FDP .05 .02
445 Danny Jackson .05 .02
446 Dan Pasqua .05 .02
447 Atlee Hammaker .05 .02
448 Greg Gagne .05 .02
449 Dennis Rasmussen .05 .02
450 Rickey Henderson .25 .07
451 Mark Lemke .05 .02
452 Luis DeLosSantos .05 .02
453 Jody Davis .05 .02
454 Jeff King .05 .02
455 Jeffrey Leonard .05 .02
456 Chris Gwynn .05 .02
457 Gregg Jefferies .10 .03
458 Bob McClure .05 .02
459 Jim Lefebvre MG .05 .02
460 Mike Scott .05 .02
461 Carlos Martinez .05 .02
462 Denny Walling .05 .02
463 Drew Hall .05 .02
464 Jerome Walton .05 .02
465 Kevin Gross .05 .02
466 Rance Mulliniks .05 .02
467 Juan Nieves .05 .02
468 Bill Ripken .05 .02
469 John Kruk .10 .03
470 Frank Viola .05 .02
471 Mike Brumley .05 .02
472 Jose Uribe .05 .02
473 Joe Price .05 .02
474 Rich Thompson .05 .02
475 Bob Welch .05 .02
476 Brad Komminsk .05 .02
477 Willie Fraser .05 .02
478 Mike LaValliere .05 .02
479 Frank White .10 .03
480 Sid Fernandez .05 .02
481 Garry Templeton .05 .02
482 Steve Carter .05 .02
483 Alejandro Pena .05 .02
484 Mike Fitzgerald .05 .02
485 John Candelaria .05 .02
486 Jeff Treadway .05 .02
487 Steve Searcy .05 .02
488 Ken Oberkfell .05 .02
489 Nick Leyva MG .05 .02
490 Dan Plesac .05 .02
491 Dave Cochrane RC .05 .02
492 Ron Oester .05 .02
493 Jason Grimsley RC .10 .03
494 Terry Puhl .05 .02
495 Lee Smith .10 .03
496 Cecil Espy UER .05 .02
('88 stats have 3
SB's, should be 33)
497 Dave Schmidt .05 .02
498 Rick Schu .05 .02
499 Bill Long .05 .02
500 Kevin Mitchell .05 .02
501 Matt Young .05 .02
502 Mitch Webster .05 .02
503 Randy St.Claire .05 .02
504 Tom O'Malley .05 .02
505 Kelly Gruber .05 .02
506 Tom Glavine .15 .04
507 Gary Redus .05 .02
508 Terry Leach .05 .02
509 Tom Pagnozzi .05 .02
510 Dwight Gooden .10 .03
511 Clay Parker .05 .02
512 Gary Pettis .05 .02
513 Mark Eichhorn .05 .02
514 Andy Allanson .05 .02
515 Len Dykstra .10 .03
516 Tim Leary .05 .02
517 Roberto Alomar .15 .04
518 Bill Krueger .05 .02
519 Bucky Dent MG .05 .02
520 Mitch Williams .05 .02
521 Craig Worthington .05 .02
522 Mike Dunne .05 .02
523 Jay Bell .10 .03
524 Daryl Boston .05 .02
525 Wally Joyner .10 .03
526 Checklist 4 .05 .02
527 Ron Hassey .05 .02
528 Kevin Wickander UER .05 .02
(Monthly scoreboard
strikeout total was 2.2,
that was his innings
pitched total)
529 Greg A. Harris .05 .02
530 Mark Langston .05 .02
531 Ken Caminiti .10 .03
532 Cecilio Guante .05 .02
533 Tim Jones .05 .02
534 Louie Meadows .05 .02
535 John Smoltz .25 .07
536 Bob Geren .05 .02
537 Mark Grant .05 .02
538 Bill Spiers UER .05 .02
(Photo actually
George Canale)
539 Neal Heaton .05 .02
540 Danny Tartabull .05 .02
541 Pat Perry .05 .02
542 Darren Daulton .10 .03
543 Nelson Liriano .05 .02
544 Dennis Boyd .05 .02
545 Kevin McReynolds .05 .02
546 Kevin Hickey .05 .02
547 Jack Howell .05 .02
548 Pat Clements .05 .02
549 Don Zimmer MG .05 .02
550 Julio Franco .10 .03
551 Tim Crews .05 .02
552 Mike(Miss.) Smith .05 .02
553 Scott Scudder UER .05 .02
(Cedar Rap1ds)
554 Jay Buhner .10 .03
555 Jack Morris .10 .03
556 Gene Larkin .05 .02
557 Jeff Innis .05 .02
558 Rafael Ramirez .05 .02
559 Andy McGaffigan .05 .02
560 Steve Sax .05 .02
561 Ken Dayley .05 .02
562 Chad Kreuter .05 .02
563 Alex Sanchez .05 .02
564 T.Houston FDP RC .25 .07
565 Scott Fletcher .05 .02
566 Mark Knudson .05 .02
567 Ron Gant .10 .03
568 John Smiley .05 .02
569 Ivan Calderon .05 .02
570 Cal Ripken .75 .23
571 Brett Butler .10 .03
572 Greg W. Harris .05 .02
573 Danny Heep .05 .02
574 Bill Swift .05 .02
575 Lance Parrish .05 .02
576 Mike Dyer RC .05 .02
577 Charlie Hayes .05 .02
578 Joe Magrane .05 .02
579 Art Howe MG .05 .02
580 Joe Carter .10 .03
581 Ken Griffey Sr. .10 .03
582 Rick Honeycutt .05 .02
583 Bruce Benedict .05 .02
584 Phil Stephenson .05 .02
585 Kal Daniels .05 .02
586 Edwin Nunez .05 .02
587 Lance Johnson .05 .02
588 Rick Rhoden .05 .02
589 Mike Aldrete .05 .02
590 Ozzie Smith .40 .12
591 Todd Stottlemyre .10 .03
592 R.J. Reynolds .05 .02
593 Scott Bradley .05 .02
594 Luis Sojo .05 .02
595 Greg Swindell .05 .02
596 Jose DeJesus .05 .02
597 Chris Bosio .05 .02
598 Brady Anderson .10 .03
599 Frank Williams .05 .02
600 Darryl Strawberry .10 .03
601 Luis Rivera .05 .02
602 Scott Garrelts .05 .02
603 Tony Armas .05 .02
604 Ron Robinson .05 .02
605 Mike Scioscia .05 .02
606 Storm Davis .05 .02
607 Steve Jeltz .05 .02
608 Eric Anthony RC .10 .03
609 Sparky Anderson MG .10 .03
610 Pedro Guerrero .05 .02
611 Walt Terrell .05 .02
612 Dave Gallagher .05 .02
613 Jeff Pico .05 .02
614 Nelson Santovenia .05 .02
615 Rob Deer .05 .02
616 Brian Holman .05 .02
617 Geronimo Berroa .05 .02
618 Ed Whitson .05 .02
619 Rob Ducey .05 .02
620 Tony Castillo .05 .02
621 Melido Perez .05 .02
622 Sid Bream .05 .02
623 Jim Corsi .05 .02
624 Darrin Jackson .05 .02
625 Roger McDowell .05 .02
626 Bob Melvin .05 .02
627 Jose Rijo .05 .02
628 Candy Maldonado .05 .02
629 Eric Hetzel .05 .02
630 Gary Gaetti .10 .03
631 John Wetteland .25 .07
632 Scott Lusader .05 .02
633 Dennis Cook .05 .02
634 Luis Polonia .05 .02
635 Brian Downing .05 .02
636 Jesse Orosco .05 .02
637 Craig Reynolds .05 .02
638 Jeff Montgomery .10 .03
639 Tony LaRussa MG .10 .03
640 Rick Sutcliffe .10 .03
641 Doug Strange .05 .02
642 Jack Armstrong .05 .02
643 Alfredo Griffin .05 .02
644 Paul Assenmacher .05 .02
645 Jose Oquendo .05 .02
646 Checklist 5 .05 .02
647 Rex Hudler .05 .02
648 Jim Clancy .05 .02
649 Dan Murphy RC .10 .03
650 Mike Witt .05 .02
651 Rafael Santana .05 .02
652 Mike Boddicker .05 .02
653 John Moses .05 .02
654 Paul Coleman FDP RC .05 .02
655 Gregg Olson .10 .03
656 Mackey Sasser .05 .02
657 Terry Mulholland .05 .02
658 Donell Nixon .05 .02
659 Greg Cadaret .05 .02
660 Vince Coleman .05 .02
661 Dick Howser TBC'85 .05 .02
UER (Seaver's 300th
on 7/11/85, should
be 8/4/85)
662 Mike Schmidt TBC'80 .25 .07
663 Fred Lynn TBC'75 .05 .02
664 Johnny Bench TBC'70 .15 .04
665 Sandy Koufax TBC'65 .50 .15
666 Brian Fisher .05 .02
667 Curt Wilkerson .05 .02
668 Joe Oliver .05 .02
669 Tom Lasorda MG .25 .07
670 Dennis Eckersley .10 .03
671 Bob Boone .10 .03
672 Roy Smith .05 .02
673 Joey Meyer .05 .02
674 Spike Owen .05 .02
675 Jim Abbott .15 .04
676 Randy Kutcher .05 .02
677 Jay Tibbs .05 .02
678 Kirt Manwaring UER .05 .02
('88 Phoenix stats
repeated)
679 Gary Ward .05 .02
680 Howard Johnson .05 .02
681 Mike Schooler .05 .02
682 Dann Bilardello .05 .02
683 Kenny Rogers .10 .03
684 Julio Machado .05 .02
685 Tony Fernandez .05 .02
686 Carmelo Martinez .05 .02
687 Tim Birtsas .05 .02
688 Milt Thompson .05 .02
689 Rich Yett .05 .02
690 Mark McGwire .60 .18
691 Chuck Cary .05 .02
692 Sammy Sosa RC 5.00 1.50
693 Calvin Schiraldi .05 .02
694 Mike Stanton RC .25 .07
695 Tom Henke .05 .02
696 B.J. Surhoff .10 .03
697 Mike Davis .05 .02
698 Omar Vizquel .25 .07
699 Jim Leyland MG .05 .02
700 Kirby Puckett .25 .07
701 Bernie Williams RC 1.00 .30
702 Tony Phillips .05 .02
703 Jeff Brantley .05 .02
704 Chip Hale .05 .02
705 Claudell Washington .05 .02
706 Geno Petralli .05 .02
707 Luis Aquino .05 .02
708 Larry Sheets .05 .02
709 Juan Berenguer .05 .02
710 Von Hayes .05 .02
711 Rick Aguilera .10 .03
712 Todd Benzinger .05 .02
713 Tim Drummond .05 .02
714 Marquis Grissom RC .40 .12
715 Greg Maddux .40 .12
716 Steve Balboni .05 .02
717 Ron Karkovice .05 .02
718 Gary Sheffield .25 .07
719 Wally Whitehurst .05 .02
720 Andres Galarraga .10 .03
721 Lee Mazzilli .05 .02
722 Felix Fermin .05 .02
723 Jeff D. Robinson .05 .02
724 Juan Bell .05 .02
725 Terry Pendleton .10 .03
726 Gene Nelson .05 .02
727 Pat Tabler .05 .02
728 Jim Acker .05 .02
729 Bobby Valentine MG .05 .02
730 Tony Gwynn .30 .09
731 Don Carman .05 .02
732 Ernest Riles .05 .02
733 John Dopson .05 .02
734 Kevin Elster .05 .02
735 Charlie Hough .10 .03
736 Rick Dempsey .05 .02
737 Chris Sabo .05 .02
738 Gene Harris .05 .02
739 Dale Sveum .05 .02
740 Jesse Barfield .05 .02
741 Steve Wilson .05 .02
742 Ernie Whitt .05 .02
743 Tom Candiotti .05 .02
744 Kelly Mann .05 .02
745 Hubie Brooks .05 .02
746 Dave Smith .05 .02
747 Randy Bush .05 .02
748 Doyle Alexander .05 .02
749 Mark Parent UER .05 .02
('87 BA .80,
should be .080)
750 Dale Murphy .25 .07
751 Steve Lyons .05 .02
752 Tom Gordon .10 .03
753 Chris Speier .05 .02
754 Bob Walk .05 .02
755 Rafael Palmeiro .15 .04
756 Ken Howell .05 .02
757 Larry Walker RC 1.00 .30
758 Mark Thurmond .05 .02
759 Tom Trebelhorn MG .05 .02
760 Wade Boggs .15 .04
761 Mike Jackson .05 .02
762 Doug Dascenzo .05 .02
763 Dennis Martinez .10 .03
764 Tim Teufel .05 .02
765 Chili Davis .10 .03
766 Brian Meyer .05 .02
767 Tracy Jones .05 .02
768 Chuck Crim .05 .02
769 Greg Hibbard RC .10 .03
770 Cory Snyder .05 .02
771 Pete Smith .05 .02
772 Jeff Reed .05 .02
773 Dave Leiper .05 .02
774 Ben McDonald RC .25 .07
775 Andy Van Slyke .10 .03
776 Charlie Leibrandt .05 .02
777 Tim Laudner .05 .02
778 Mike Jeffcoat .05 .02
779 Lloyd Moseby .05 .02
780 Orel Hershiser .10 .03
781 Mario Diaz .05 .02
782 Jose Alvarez .05 .02
783 Checklist 6 .05 .02
784 Scott Bailes .05 .02
785 Jim Rice .10 .03
786 Eric King .05 .02
787 Rene Gonzales .05 .02
788 Frank DiPino .05 .02
789 John Wathan MG .05 .02
790 Gary Carter .10 .03
791 Alvaro Espinoza .05 .02
792 Gerald Perry .05 .02
XX George Bush PRES

1990 Topps Tiffany

For the seventh year, Topps issued through its hobby dealer network a special "Tiffany" set. These sets which parallel the regular cards consist of 792 standard-size cards. These cards were only issued in complete set form. Since the number of cards produced is similar to the 1989 issue, it is believed that approximately 15,000 of these sets were produced.

Nm-Mt Ex-Mt
COMP.FACT.SET (792) 200.00 60.00
*STARS: 6X TO 15X BASIC CARDS
*ROOKIES: 6X TO 15X BASIC CARDS

1990 Topps Batting Leaders

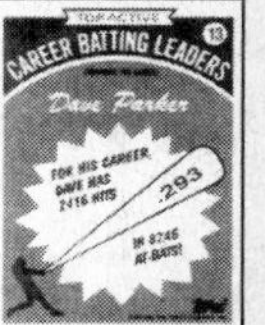

The 1990 Topps Batting Leaders set contains 22 standard-size cards. The front borders are emerald green, and the backs are white, blue and evergreen. This set, like the 1989 set of the same name, depicts the 22 major leaguers with the highest lifetime batting averages (minimum 765 games). The card numbers correspond to the player's rank in terms of career batting average. Many of the photos are the same as those from the 1989 set. The cards were distributed one per special 100-card Topps blister pack available only at K-Mart stores and were produced by Topps. The K-Mart logo does not appear anywhere on the cards themselves, although there is a Topps logo on the front and back of each card.

Nm-Mt Ex-Mt
COMPLETE SET (22) 100.00 30.00
1 Wade Boggs 10.00 3.00
2 Tony Gwynn 20.00 6.00
3 Kirby Puckett 10.00 3.00
4 Don Mattingly 20.00 6.00
5 George Brett 20.00 6.00
6 Pedro Guerrero .50 .15
7 Tim Raines 1.00 .30
8 Paul Molitor 8.00 2.40
9 Jim Rice 1.00 .30
10 Keith Hernandez 1.00 .30
11 Julio Franco 1.00 .30
12 Carney Lansford 1.00 .30
13 Dave Parker 1.00 .30
14 Willie McGee 1.00 .30
15 Robin Yount 8.00 2.40
16 Tony Fernandez 1.00 .30
17 Eddie Murray 8.00 2.40
18 Johnny Ray .50 .15
19 Lonnie Smith .50 .15
20 Phil Bradley .50 .15
21 Rickey Henderson 12.00 3.60
22 Kent Hrbek 1.00 .30

1990 Topps Glossy All-Stars

The 1990 Topps Glossy All-Star set contains 22 standard-size glossy cards. The front and back borders are white, and other design elements are red, blue and yellow. This set is almost identical to previous year sets of the same name. One card was included in each 1990 Topps rack pack. The players selected for the set were the starters, managers, and honorary captains in the previous year's All-Star Game.

Nm-Mt Ex-Mt
COMPLETE SET (22) 3.00 .90
1 Tom Lasorda MG .20 .06
2 Will Clark .20 .06
3 Ryne Sandberg .50 .15
4 Howard Johnson .05 .02
5 Ozzie Smith .60 .18
6 Kevin Mitchell .05 .02
7 Eric Davis .10 .03
8 Tony Gwynn .75 .23
9 Benito Santiago .10 .03
10 Rick Reuschel .05 .02
11 Don Drysdale CAPT .15 .04
12 Tony LaRussa MG .05 .02
13 Mark McGwire 1.25 .35
14 Julio Franco .10 .03
15 Wade Boggs .40 .12
16 Cal Ripken 1.50 .45
17 Bo Jackson .20 .06
18 Kirby Puckett .30 .09
19 Ruben Sierra .10 .03
20 Terry Steinbach .05 .02
21 Dave Stewart .10 .03
22 Carl Yastrzemski CAPT .20 .06

1990 Topps Glossy Send-Ins

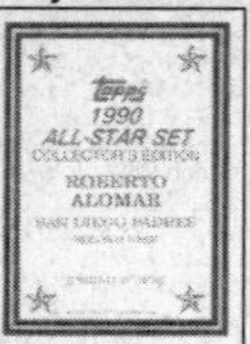

The 1990 Topps Glossy 60 set was issued as a mailaway by Topps for the eighth straight year. This standard-size, 60-card set features two young players among every ten players as Topps again broke down these cards into six series of ten cards each.

	Nm-Mt	Ex-Mt
COMPLETE SET (60)	12.00	3.60
1 Ryne Sandberg	1.50	.45
2 Nolan Ryan	5.00	1.50
3 Glenn Davis	.10	.03
4 Dave Stewart	.20	.06
5 Barry Larkin	.40	.12
6 Carney Lansford	.20	.06
7 Darryl Strawberry	.20	.06
8 Steve Sax	.10	.03
9 Carlos Martinez	.10	.03
10 Gary Sheffield	.50	.15
11 Don Mattingly	2.50	.75
12 Mark Grace	1.00	.30
13 Bret Saberhagen	.20	.06
14 Mike Scott	.10	.03
15 Robin Yount	.50	.15
16 Ozzie Smith	1.50	.45
17 Jeff Ballard	.10	.03
18 Rick Reuschel	.10	.03
19 Greg Briley	.10	.03
20 Ken Griffey Jr.	3.00	.90
21 Kevin Mitchell	.10	.03
22 Wade Boggs	.75	.23
23 Dwight Gooden	.20	.06
24 George Bell	.10	.03
25 Eric Davis	.20	.06
26 Ruben Sierra	.20	.06
27 Roberto Alomar	.75	.23
28 Gary Gaetti	.20	.06
29 Gregg Olson	.10	.03
30 Tom Gordon	.20	.06
31 Jose Canseco	.75	.23
32 Pedro Guerrero	.10	.03
33 Joe Carter	.20	.06
34 Mike Scioscia	.20	.06
35 Julio Franco	.20	.06
36 Joe Magrane	.10	.03
37 Rickey Henderson	1.00	.30
38 Tim Raines	.20	.06
39 Jerome Walton	.10	.03
40 Bob Geren	.10	.03
41 Andre Dawson	.40	.12
42 Mark McGwire	4.00	1.20
43 Howard Johnson	.10	.03
44 Bo Jackson	.40	.12
45 Shawon Dunston	.10	.03
46 Carlton Fisk	.50	.15
47 Mitch Williams	.10	.03
48 Kirby Puckett	.75	.23
49 Craig Worthington	.10	.03
50 Jim Abbott	.50	.15
51 Cal Ripken	5.00	1.50
52 Will Clark	.40	.12
53 Dennis Eckersley	.50	.15
54 Craig Biggio	.30	.09
55 Fred McGriff	.40	.12
56 Tony Gwynn	2.00	.60
57 Mickey Tettleton	.20	.06
58 Mark Davis	.10	.03
59 Omar Vizquel	.40	.12
60 Gregg Jefferies	.10	.03

1990 Topps Rookies

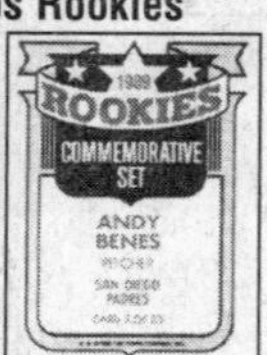

The 1990 Topps Jumbo Rookies set contains 33 standard-size glossy cards. The front and back borders are white, and other design elements are red, blue and yellow. This set is almost identical to previous year sets of the same name except that it contains 33 cards rather than only 22. One card was included in each 1990 Topps "jumbo" pack. The cards are numbered in alphabetical order. Sets of these cards were issued and stamped with various colors so Topps could test for colors of foil stamping.

	Nm-Mt	Ex-Mt
COMPLETE SET (33)	25.00	7.50
1 Jim Abbott	.75	.23
2 Albert Belle	1.00	.30
3 Andy Benes	.50	.15
4 Greg Briley	.25	.07
5 Kevin Brown	.50	.15
6 Mark Carreon	.25	.07
7 Mike Devereaux	.25	.07
8 Junior Felix	.25	.07
9 Bob Geren	.25	.07
10 Tom Gordon	.50	.15
11 Ken Griffey Jr.	5.00	1.50
12 Pete Harnisch	.25	.07
13 Greg W. Harris	.25	.07
14 Greg Hibbard	.25	.07
15 Ken Hill	.25	.07
16 Gregg Jefferies	.25	.07
17 Jeff King	.25	.07
18 Derek Lilliquist	.25	.07
19 Carlos Martinez	.25	.07
20 Ramon Martinez	.25	.07
21 Bob Milacki	.25	.07
22 Gregg Olson	.25	.07
23 Donn Pall	.25	.07
24 Kenny Rogers	.50	.15
25 Gary Sheffield	1.00	.30
26 Dwight Smith	.25	.07
27 Billy Spiers	.25	.07
28 Omar Vizquel	1.00	.30
29 Jerome Walton	.25	.07
30 Dave West	.25	.07
31 John Wetteland	.50	.15
32 Steve Wilson	.25	.07
33 Craig Worthington	.25	.07

1990 Topps Wax Box Cards

The 1990 Topps wax box cards comprise four different box bottoms with four cards each, for a total of 16 standard-size cards. The front borders are green. The vertically oriented backs are yellowish green. These cards depict various career milestones achieved during the 1989 season. The card numbers are actually the letters A through P. The card ordering is alphabetical by player's name.

	Nm-Mt	Ex-Mt
COMPLETE SET (16)	8.00	2.40
A Wade Boggs	.50	.15
B George Brett	1.00	.30
C Andre Dawson	.40	.12
D Darrell Evans	.20	.06
E Dwight Gooden	.20	.06
F Rickey Henderson	.75	.23
G Tom Lasorda MG	.30	.09
H Fred Lynn	.10	.03
I Mark McGwire	2.00	.60
J Dave Parker	.20	.06
K Jeff Reardon	.20	.06
L Rick Reuschel	.10	.03
M Jim Rice	.20	.06
N Cal Ripken	2.50	.75
O Nolan Ryan	2.50	.75
P Ryne Sandberg	.50	.15

1990 Topps Traded

The 1990 Topps Traded Set was the tenth consecutive year Topps issued a 132-card standard-size set at the end of the year. For the first time, Topps not only issued the set in factory set form but also distributed (on a significant basis) the set via seven-card wax packs. Unlike the factory set cards (which feature the whiter paper stock typical of the previous years Traded sets), the wax pack cards feature gray paper stock. Gray and white stock cards are equally valued. This set was arranged alphabetically by player and includes a mix of traded players and rookies for whom Topps did not include a card in the regular set. The key Rookie Cards in this set are Travis Fryman, Todd Hundley and Dave Justice.

	Nm-Mt	Ex-Mt
COMPLETE SET (132)	3.00	.90
COMP.FACT.SET (132)	2.50	.75
1T Darrel Akerfelds	.05	.02
2T Sandy Alomar Jr.	.10	.03
3T Brad Arnsberg	.05	.02
4T Steve Avery	.05	.02
5T Wally Backman	.05	.02
6T Carlos Baerga RC	.25	.07
7T Kevin Bass	.05	.02
8T Willie Blair RC	.10	.03
9T Mike Blowers RC	.25	.07
10T Shawn Boskie RC	.10	.03
11T Daryl Boston	.05	.02
12T Dennis Boyd	.05	.02
13T Glenn Braggs	.05	.02
14T Hubie Brooks	.05	.02
15T Tom Brunansky	.05	.02
16T John Burkett	.05	.02
17T Casey Candaele	.05	.02
18T John Candelaria	.05	.02
19T Gary Carter	.10	.03
20T Joe Carter	.10	.03
21T Rick Cerone	.05	.02
22T Scott Coolbaugh	.05	.02
23T Bobby Cox MG	.10	.03
24T Mark Davis	.05	.02
25T Storm Davis	.05	.02
26T Edgar Diaz	.05	.02
27T Wayne Edwards	.05	.02
28T Mark Eichhorn	.05	.02
29T Scott Erickson RC	.25	.07
30T Nick Esasky	.05	.02
31T Cecil Fielder	.10	.03
32T John Franco	.10	.03
33T Travis Fryman RC	.40	.12
34T Bill Gullickson	.05	.02
35T Darryl Hamilton	.05	.02
36T Mike Harkey	.05	.02
37T Bud Harrelson MG	.05	.02
38T Billy Hatcher	.05	.02
39T Keith Hernandez	.10	.03
40T Joe Hesketh	.05	.02
41T Dave Hollins RC	.25	.07
42T Sam Horn	.05	.02
43T Steve Howard	.05	.02
44T Todd Hundley RC	.25	.07
45T Jeff Huson	.05	.02
46T Chris James	.05	.02
47T Stan Javier	.05	.02
48T Dave Justice RC	.50	.15
49T Jeff Kaiser	.05	.02
50T Dana Kiecker	.05	.02
51T Joe Klink	.05	.02
52T Brent Knackert RC	.10	.03
53T Brad Komminsk	.05	.02
54T Mark Langston	.05	.02
55T Tim Layana	.05	.02
56T Rick Leach	.05	.02
57T Terry Leach	.05	.02
58T Tim Leary	.05	.02
59T Craig Lefferts	.05	.02
60T Charlie Leibrandt	.05	.02
61T Jim Leyritz RC	.25	.07
62T Fred Lynn	.05	.02
63T Kevin Maas RC	.25	.07
64T Shane Mack	.05	.02
65T Candy Maldonado	.05	.02
66T Fred Manrique	.05	.02
67T Mike Marshall	.05	.02
68T Carmelo Martinez	.05	.02
69T John Marzano	.05	.02
70T Ben McDonald	.05	.02
71T Jack McDowell	.05	.02
72T John McNamara MG	.05	.02
73T Orlando Mercado	.05	.02
74T Stump Merrill MG	.05	.02
75T Alan Mills RC	.10	.03
76T Hal Morris	.05	.02
77T Lloyd Moseby	.05	.02
78T Randy Myers	.10	.03
79T Tim Naehring RC	.10	.03
80T Junior Noboa	.05	.02
81T Matt Nokes	.05	.02
82T Pete O'Brien	.05	.02
83T John Olerud RC	.50	.15
84T Greg Olson RC	.10	.03
85T Junior Ortiz	.05	.02
86T Dave Parker	.10	.03
87T Rick Parker	.05	.02
88T Bob Patterson	.05	.02
89T Alejandro Pena	.05	.02
90T Tony Pena	.05	.02
91T Pascual Perez	.05	.02
92T Gerald Perry	.05	.02
93T Dan Petry	.05	.02
94T Gary Pettis	.05	.02
95T Tony Phillips	.05	.02
96T Lou Piniella MG	.10	.03
97T Luis Polonia	.05	.02
98T Jim Presley	.05	.02
99T Scott Radinsky RC	.10	.03
100T Willie Randolph	.10	.03
101T Jeff Reardon	.10	.03
102T Greg Riddoch MG	.05	.02
103T Jeff Robinson	.05	.02
104T Ron Robinson	.05	.02
105T Kevin Romine	.05	.02
106T Scott Ruskin	.05	.02
107T John Russell	.05	.02
108T Bill Sampen	.05	.02
109T Juan Samuel	.05	.02
110T Scott Sanderson	.05	.02
111T Jack Savage	.05	.02
112T Dave Schmidt	.05	.02
113T R.Schoendienst MG	.25	.07
114T Terry Shumpert	.05	.02
115T Matt Sinatro	.05	.02
116T Don Slaught	.05	.02
117T Bryn Smith	.05	.02
118T Lee Smith	.10	.03
119T Paul Sorrento RC	.25	.07
120T Franklin Stubbs UER ('84 says '99 and has the same stats as '89, '83 stats are missing)	.05	.02
121T Russ Swan RC	.10	.03
122T Bob Tewksbury	.05	.02
123T Wayne Tolleson	.05	.02
124T John Tudor	.05	.02
125T Randy Veres	.05	.02
126T Hector Villanueva RC	.10	.03
127T Mitch Webster	.05	.02
128T Ernie Whitt	.05	.02
129T Frank Wills	.05	.02
130T Dave Winfield	.10	.03
131T Matt Young	.05	.02
132T Checklist 1T-132T	.05	.02

1990 Topps Traded Tiffany

Again, one of these sets were issued for each regular Tiffany set produced. These 132 standard-size cards parallel the regular Traded issue and feature Glossy fronts and clearer backs. These cards were issued in complete set form only and were distributed through Topps hobby network. Similar to the regular Topps Tiffany set, it is believed that 15,000 of these sets were produced.

	Nm-Mt	Ex-Mt
COMP.FACT.SET (132)	30.00	9.00

*STARS: 6X TO 15X BASIC CARDS....
*ROOKIES: 6X TO 15X BASIC CARDS

1990 Topps Big

The 1990 Topps Big set contains 330 cards each measuring a slightly over-sized 2 5/8" by 3 3/4". In 1989 Topps had issued two oversize sets (Bigs and Bowmans), but in 1990 only the Topps Big were issued by Topps as an oversize set. The set was issued in three series of 110 cards. Some dealers believe the third series was distributed in far less quantity than the first two series. An early card of slugger Sammy Sosa was included in this set.

	Nm-Mt	Ex-Mt
COMPLETE SET (330)	25.00	7.50
1 Dwight Evans	.30	.09
2 Kirby Puckett	.75	.23
3 Kevin Gross	.20	.06
4 Ron Hassey	.20	.06
5 Lloyd McClendon	.20	.06
6 Bo Jackson	.75	.23
7 Lonnie Smith	.20	.06
8 Alvaro Espinoza	.20	.06
9 Roberto Alomar	.50	.15
10 Glenn Braggs	.20	.06
11 David Cone	.30	.09
12 Claudell Washington	.20	.06
13 Pedro Guerrero	.20	.06
14 Todd Benzinger	.20	.06
15 Jeff Russell	.20	.06
16 Terry Kennedy	.20	.06
17 Kelly Gruber	.20	.06
18 Alfredo Griffin	.20	.06
19 Mark Grace	.50	.15
20 Dave Winfield	.30	.09
21 Bret Saberhagen	.30	.09
22 Roger Clemens	1.50	.45
23 Bob Walk	.20	.06
24 Dave Magadan	.20	.06
25 Spike Owen	.20	.06
26 Jody Davis	.20	.06
27 Kent Hrbek	.30	.09
28 Mark McGwire	2.00	.60
29 Eddie Murray	.75	.23
30 Paul O'Neill	.50	.15
31 Jose DeLeon	.20	.06
32 Steve Lyons	.20	.06
33 Dan Plesac	.20	.06
34 Jack Howell	.20	.06
35 Greg Briley	.20	.06
36 Andy Hawkins	.20	.06
37 Cecil Espy	.20	.06
38 Rick Sutcliffe	.30	.09
39 Jack Clark	.30	.09
40 Dale Murphy	.75	.23
41 Mike Henneman	.20	.06
42 Rick Honeycutt	.20	.06
43 Willie Randolph	.30	.09
44 Marty Barrett	.20	.06
45 Willie Wilson	.20	.06
46 Wallace Johnson	.20	.06
47 Greg Brock	.20	.06
48 Tom Browning	.20	.06
49 Gerald Young	.20	.06
50 Dennis Eckersley	.30	.09
51 Scott Garrelts	.20	.06
52 Gary Redus	.20	.06
53 Al Newman	.20	.06
54 Daryl Boston	.20	.06
55 Ron Oester	.20	.06
56 Danny Tartabull	.20	.06
57 Gregg Jefferies	.30	.09
58 Tom Foley	.20	.06
59 Robin Yount	1.25	.35
60 Pat Borders	.20	.06
61 Mike Greenwell	.20	.06
62 Shawon Dunston	.20	.06
63 Steve Buechele	.20	.06
64 Dave Stewart	.30	.09
65 Jose Oquendo	.20	.06
66 Ron Gant	.30	.09
67 Mike Scioscia	.20	.06
68 Randy Velarde	.20	.06
69 Von Hayes	.20	.06
70 Tim Wallach	.20	.06
71 Eric Show	.20	.06
72 Eric Davis	.30	.09
73 Mike Gallego	.20	.06
74 Rob Deer	.20	.06
75 Ryne Sandberg	1.25	.35
76 Kevin Seitzer	.20	.06
77 Wade Boggs	.50	.15
78 Greg Gagne	.20	.06
79 John Smiley	.20	.06
80 Ivan Calderon	.20	.06
81 Pete Incaviglia	.20	.06
82 Orel Hershiser	.30	.09
83 Carney Lansford	.30	.09
84 Mike Fitzgerald	.20	.06
85 Don Mattingly	2.00	.60
86 Chet Lemon	.20	.06
87 Rolando Roomes	.20	.06
88 Billy Spiers	.20	.06
89 Pat Tabler	.20	.06
90 Danny Heep	.20	.06
91 Andre Dawson	.30	.09
92 Randy Bush	.20	.06
93 Tony Gwynn	1.00	.30
94 Tom Brunansky	.20	.06
95 Johnny Ray	.20	.06
96 Matt Williams	.30	.09
97 Barry Lyons	.20	.06
98 Jeff Hamilton	.20	.06
99 Tom Glavine	.50	.15
100 Ken Griffey Sr.	.30	.09
101 Tom Henke	.20	.06
102 Dave Righetti	.20	.06
103 Paul Molitor	.50	.15
104 Mike LaValliere	.20	.06
105 Frank White	.30	.09
106 Bob Welch	.20	.06
107 Ellis Burks	.50	.15
108 Andres Galarraga	.30	.09
109 Mitch Williams	.20	.06
110 Checklist 1-110	.20	.06
111 Craig Biggio	.50	.15
112 Dave Stieb	.30	.09
113 Ron Darling	.20	.06
114 Bert Blyleven	.30	.09
115 Dickie Thon	.20	.06
116 Carlos Martinez	.20	.06
117 Jeff King	.20	.06
118 Terry Steinbach	.20	.06
119 Frank Tanana	.20	.06
120 Mark Lemke	.20	.06
121 Chris Sabo	.20	.06
122 Glenn Davis	.20	.06
123 Mel Hall	.20	.06
124 Jim Gantner	.20	.06
125 Benito Santiago	.30	.09
126 Milt Thompson	.20	.06
127 Rafael Palmeiro	.50	.15
128 Barry Bonds	2.00	.60
129 Mike Bielecki	.20	.06
130 Lou Whitaker	.30	.09
131 Bob Ojeda	.20	.06
132 Dion James	.20	.06
133 Dennis Martinez	.30	.09
134 Fred McGriff	.75	.23
135 Terry Pendleton	.30	.09
136 Pat Combs	.20	.06
137 Kevin Mitchell	.20	.06
138 Marquis Grissom	.75	.23
139 Chris Bosio	.20	.06
140 Omar Vizquel	.75	.23
141 Steve Sax	.20	.06
142 Nelson Liriano	.20	.06
143 Kevin Elster	.20	.06
144 Dan Pasqua	.20	.06
145 Dave Smith	.20	.06
146 Craig Worthington	.20	.06
147 Dan Gladden	.20	.06
148 Oddibe McDowell	.20	.06
149 Bip Roberts	.20	.06
150 Randy Ready	.20	.06
151 Dwight Smith	.20	.06
152 Eddie Whitson	.20	.06
153 George Bell	.20	.06
154 Tim Raines	.30	.09
155 Sid Fernandez	.20	.06
156 Henry Cotto	.20	.06
157 Harold Baines	.30	.09
158 Willie McGee	.30	.09
159 Bill Doran	.20	.06
160 Steve Balboni	.20	.06
161 Pete Smith	.20	.06
162 Frank Viola	.20	.06
163 Gary Sheffield	.75	.23
164 Bill Landrum	.20	.06
165 Tony Fernandez	.20	.06
166 Mike Heath	.20	.06
167 Jody Reed	.20	.06
168 Wally Joyner	.30	.09
169 Robby Thompson	.20	.06
170 Ken Caminiti	.30	.09
171 Nolan Ryan	3.00	.90
172 Ricky Jordan	.20	.06
173 Lance Blankenship	.20	.06
174 Dwight Gooden	.30	.09
175 Ruben Sierra	.20	.06
176 Carlton Fisk	.50	.15
177 Garry Templeton	.20	.06
178 Mike Devereaux	.20	.06
179 Mookie Wilson	.30	.09
180 Jeff Blauser	.20	.06
181 Scott Bradley	.20	.06
182 Luis Salazar	.20	.06
183 Rafael Ramirez	.20	.06
184 Vince Coleman	.20	.06
185 Doug Drabek	.20	.06
186 Darryl Strawberry	.30	.09
187 Tim Burke	.20	.06
188 Jesse Barfield	.20	.06
189 Barry Larkin	.50	.15
190 Alan Trammell	.30	.09
191 Steve Lake	.20	.06
192 Derek Lilliquist	.20	.06
193 Don Robinson	.20	.06
194 Kevin McReynolds	.20	.06
195 Melido Perez	.20	.06
196 Jose Lind	.20	.06
197 Eric Anthony	.20	.06
198 B.J. Surhoff	.30	.09
199 John Olerud	1.00	.30
200 Mike Moore	.20	.06
201 Mark Gubicza	.20	.06
202 Phil Bradley	.20	.06
203 Ozzie Smith	1.25	.35
204 Greg Maddux	1.25	.35
205 Julio Franco	.30	.09
206 Tom Herr	.20	.06
207 Scott Fletcher	.20	.06
208 Bobby Bonilla	.30	.09
209 Bob Geren	.20	.06
210 Junior Felix	.20	.06
211 Dick Schofield	.20	.06
212 Jim Deshaies	.20	.06
213 Jose Uribe	.20	.06
214 John Kruk	.30	.09
215 Ozzie Guillen	.20	.06
216 Howard Johnson	.20	.06
217 Andy Van Slyke	.30	.09
218 Tim Laudner	.20	.06
219 Manny Lee	.20	.06
220 Checklist 111-220	.20	.06
221 Cory Snyder	.20	.06
222 Billy Hatcher	.20	.06
223 Bud Black	.20	.06
224 Will Clark	.75	.23
225 Kevin Tapani	.75	.23
226 Mike Pagliarulo	.20	.06
227 Dave Parker	.30	.09
228 Ben McDonald	.20	.06
229 Carlos Baerga	.30	.09
230 Roger McDowell	.20	.06
231 Delino DeShields	.75	.23
232 Mark Langston	.20	.06
233 Wally Backman	.20	.06
234 Jim Eisenreich	.20	.06
235 Mike Schooler	.20	.06
236 Kevin Bass	.20	.06
237 John Farrell	.20	.06
238 Kal Daniels	.20	.06
239 Tony Phillips	.20	.06
240 Todd Stottlemyre	.30	.09
241 Greg Olson	.20	.06
242 Charlie Hough	.30	.09
243 Mariano Duncan	.20	.06
244 Bill Ripken	.20	.06
245 Joe Carter	.30	.09
246 Tim Belcher	.20	.06
247 Roberto Kelly	.20	.06
248 Candy Maldonado	.20	.06
249 Mike Scott	.20	.06
250 Ken Griffey Jr.	3.00	.90
251 Nick Esasky	.20	.06
252 Tom Gordon	.30	.09
253 John Tudor	.20	.06
254 Gary Gaetti	.30	.09
255 Neal Heaton	.20	.06
256 Jerry Browne	.20	.06
257 Jose Rijo	.20	.06
258 Mike Boddicker	.20	.06
259 Brett Butler	.30	.09
260 Andy Benes	.30	.09
261 Kevin Brown	.30	.09
262 Hubie Brooks	.20	.06
263 Randy Milligan	.20	.06
264 John Franco	.30	.09
265 Sandy Alomar Jr.	.30	.09

266 Dave Valle .20 .06
267 Jerome Walton .20 .06
268 Bob Boone .30 .09
269 Ken Howell .20 .06
270 Jose Canseco .75 .23
271 Joe Magrane .20 .06
272 Brian DuBois .20 .06
273 Carlos Quintana .20 .06
274 Lance Johnson .20 .06
275 Steve Bedrosian .20 .06
276 Brook Jacoby .20 .06
277 Fred Lynn UER .20 .06
(Pirates logo
on card front)
278 Jeff Ballard .20 .06
279 Otis Nixon .20 .06
280 Chili Davis .30 .09
281 Joe Oliver .20 .06
282 Brian Holman .20 .06
283 Juan Samuel .20 .06
284 Rick Aguilera .30 .09
285 Jeff Reardon .30 .09
286 Sammy Sosa 10.00 3.00
287 Carmelo Martinez .20 .06
288 Greg Swindell .20 .06
289 Erik Hanson .20 .06
290 Tony Pena .20 .06
291 Pascual Perez .20 .06
292 Rickey Henderson .75 .23
293 Kurt Stillwell .20 .06
294 Todd Zeile .30 .09
295 Bobby Thigpen .20 .06
296 Larry Walker 1.50 .45
297 Rob Murphy .20 .06
298 Mitch Webster .20 .06
299 Devon White .30 .09
300 Len Dykstra .30 .09
301 Keith Hernandez .30 .09
302 Gene Larkin .20 .06
303 Jeffrey Leonard .20 .06
304 Jim Presley .20 .06
305 Lloyd Moseby .20 .06
306 John Smoltz .75 .23
307 Sam Horn .20 .06
308 Greg Litton .20 .06
309 Dave Henderson .20 .06
310 Mark McLemore .20 .06
311 Gary Pettis .20 .06
312 Mark Davis .20 .06
313 Cecil Fielder .30 .09
314 Jack Armstrong .20 .06
315 Alvin Davis .20 .06
316 Doug Jones .20 .06
317 Eric Yelding .20 .06
318 Joe Orsulak .20 .06
319 Chuck Finley .30 .09
320 Glenn Wilson .20 .06
321 Harold Reynolds .30 .09
322 Teddy Higuera .20 .06
323 Lance Parrish .20 .06
324 Bruce Hurst .20 .06
325 Dave West .20 .06
326 Kirk Gibson .30 .09
327 Cal Ripken 2.50 .75
328 Rick Reuschel .20 .06
329 Jim Abbott .50 .15
330 Checklist 221-330 .20 .06

1990 Topps Debut '89

The 1990 Topps Major League Debut Set is a 152-card, standard-size set arranged in alphabetical order by player's name. Each card front features the date of the player's first major league appearance. Strangely enough, even though the set commemorates the 1989 Major League debuts, the set was not issued until the 1990 season had almost begun. Key cards in this set include Joey (Albert) Belle, Juan Gonzalez, Ken Griffey, Jr., David Justice, Deion Sanders and Sammy Sosa (pictured as a member of the Texas Rangers).

Nm-Mt Ex-Mt
COMP.FACT.SET (152) 15.00 4.50
1 Jim Abbott .50 .15
2 Beau Allred .15 .04
3 Wilson Alvarez .25 .07
4 Kent Anderson .15 .04
5 Eric Anthony .15 .04
6 Kevin Appier .25 .07
7 Larry Arndt .15 .04
8 John Barfield .15 .04
9 Billy Bates .15 .04
10 Kevin Batiste .15 .04
11 Blaine Beatty .15 .04
12 Stan Belinda .15 .04
13 Juan Bell .15 .04
14 Joey Belle .75 .23
(Now known as Albert)
15 Andy Benes .25 .07
16 Mike Benjamin .15 .04
17 Geronimo Berroa .15 .04
18 Mike Blowers .25 .07
19 Brian Brady .15 .04
20 Francisco Cabrera .15 .04
21 George Canale .15 .04
22 Jose Cano .15 .04
23 Steve Carter .15 .04
24 Pat Combs .15 .04
25 Scott Coolbaugh .15 .04
26 Steve Cummings .15 .04
27 Pete Dalena .15 .04
28 Jeff Datz .15 .04
29 Bobby Davidson .15 .04
30 Drew Denson .15 .04
31 Gary DiSarcina .25 .07
32 Brian DuBois .15 .04
33 Mike Dyer .15 .04
34 Wayne Edwards .15 .04
35 Junior Felix .15 .04
36 Mike Fetters .15 .04
37 Steve Finley .25 .07
38 Darrin Fletcher .25 .07
39 LaVel Freeman .15 .04
40 Steve Frey .15 .04
41 Mark Gardner .15 .04
42 Joe Girardi .25 .07
43 Juan Gonzalez 2.50 .75
44 Goose Gozzo .15 .04
45 Tommy Greene .15 .04
46 Ken Griffey Jr. 5.00 1.50
47 Jason Grimsley .15 .04
48 Marquis Grissom .75 .23
49 Mark Guthrie .15 .04
50 Chip Hale .15 .04
51 Jack Hardy .15 .04
52 Gene Harris .15 .04
53 Mike Hartley .15 .04
54 Scott Hemond .15 .04
55 Xavier Hernandez .15 .04
56 Eric Hetzel .15 .04
57 Greg Hibbard .15 .04
58 Mark Higgins .15 .04
59 Glenallen Hill .15 .04
60 Chris Hoiles .25 .07
61 Shawn Holman .15 .04
62 Dann Howitt .15 .04
63 Mike Huff .15 .04
64 Terry Jorgensen .15 .04
65 David Justice 1.00 .30
66 Jeff King .15 .04
67 Matt Kinzer .15 .04
68 Joe Kraemer .15 .04
69 Marcus Lawton .15 .04
70 Derek Lilliquist .15 .04
71 Scott Little .15 .04
72 Greg Litton .15 .04
73 Rick Luecken .15 .04
74 Julio Machado .15 .04
75 Tom Magrann .15 .04
76 Kelly Mann .15 .04
77 Randy McCament .15 .04
78 Ben McDonald .15 .04
79 Chuck McElroy .15 .04
80 Jeff McKnight .15 .04
81 Kent Mercker .15 .04
82 Matt Merullo .15 .04
83 Hensley Meulens .15 .04
84 Kevin Mmahat .15 .04
85 Mike Munoz .15 .04
86 Dan Murphy .15 .04
87 Jaime Navarro .15 .04
88 Randy Nosek .15 .04
89 John Olerud 1.00 .30
90 Steve Olin .25 .07
91 Joe Oliver .15 .04
92 Francisco Oliveras .15 .04
93 Gregg Olson .25 .07
94 John Orton .15 .04
95 Dean Palmer .50 .15
96 Ramon Pena .15 .04
97 Jeff Peterek .15 .04
98 Marty Pevey .15 .04
99 Rusty Richards .15 .04
100 Jeff Richardson .15 .04
101 Rob Richie .15 .04
102 Kevin Ritz .15 .04
103 Rosario Rodriguez .15 .04
104 Mike Roesler .15 .04
105 Kenny Rogers .25 .07
106 Bobby Rose .15 .04
107 Alex Sanchez .15 .04
108 Deion Sanders .75 .23
109 Jeff Schaefer .15 .04
110 Jeff Schulz .15 .04
111 Mike Schwabe .15 .04
112 Dick Scott .15 .04
113 Scott Scudder .15 .04
114 Rudy Seanez .15 .04
115 Joe Skalski .15 .04
116 Dwight Smith .15 .04
117 Greg Smith .15 .04
118 Mike Smith .15 .04
119 Paul Sorrento .25 .07
120 Sammy Sosa 8.00 2.40
121 Billy Spiers .15 .04
122 Mike Stanton .15 .04
123 Phil Stephenson .15 .04
124 Doug Strange .15 .04
125 Russ Swan .15 .04
126 Kevin Tapani .25 .07
127 Stu Tate .15 .04
128 Greg Vaughn .15 .04
129 Robin Ventura .75 .23
130 Randy Veres .15 .04
131 Jose Vizcaino .25 .07
132 Omar Vizquel .75 .23
133 Larry Walker 2.50 .75
134 Jerome Walton .15 .04
135 Gary Wayne .15 .04
136 Lenny Webster .15 .04
137 Mickey Weston .15 .04
138 Jeff Wetherby .15 .04
139 John Wetteland .50 .15
140 Ed Whited .15 .04
141 Wally Whitehurst .15 .04
142 Kevin Wickander .15 .04
143 Dean Wilkins .15 .04
144 Dana Williams .15 .04
145 Paul Wilmet .15 .04
146 Craig Wilson .15 .04
147 Matt Winters .15 .04
148 Eric Yelding .15 .04
149 Clint Zavaras .15 .04
150 Todd Zeile .50 .15
151 Checklist Card .15 .04
152 Checklist Card .15 .04

1991 Topps

This set marks Topps tenth consecutive year of issuing a 792-card standard-size set. Cards were primarily issued in wax packs, rack packs and factory sets. The fronts feature a full color player photo with a white border. Topps also commemorated their fortieth anniversary by including a "Topps 40" logo on the front and back of each card. Virtually all of the cards have been discovered without the 40th logo on the back. Subsets include Record Breakers (2-8) and All-Stars (386-407). In addition, First Draft Picks and Future Stars subset cards are scattered throughout the set. The key Rookie Cards include Chipper Jones and Brian McRae. As a special promotion Topps inserted (randomly) into their wax packs one of every previous card they ever issued.

Nm-Mt Ex-Mt
COMPLETE SET (792) 20.00 6.00
COMP.FACT.SET (792) 25.00 7.50
1 Nolan Ryan 1.00 .30
2 George Brett RB .30 .09
3 Carlton Fisk RB .10 .03
4 Kevin Maas RB .05 .02
5 Cal Ripken RB .40 .12
6 Nolan Ryan RB .50 .15
7 Ryne Sandberg RB .25 .07
8 Bobby Thigpen RB .05 .02
9 Darrin Fletcher .05 .02
10 Gregg Olson .05 .02
11 Roberto Kelly .05 .02
12 Paul Assenmacher .05 .02
13 Mariano Duncan .05 .02
14 Dennis Lamp .05 .02
15 Von Hayes .05 .02
16 Mike Heath .05 .02
17 Jeff Brantley .05 .02
18 Nelson Liriano .05 .02
19 Jeff D. Robinson .05 .02
20 Pedro Guerrero .10 .03
21 Joe Morgan MG .05 .02
22 Storm Davis .05 .02
23 Jim Gantner .05 .02
24 Dave Martinez .05 .02
25 Tim Belcher .05 .02
26 Luis Sojo UER .05 .02
(Born in Barquisimento,
not Carquis)
27 Bobby Witt .05 .02
28 Alvaro Espinoza .05 .02
29 Bob Walk .05 .02
30 Gregg Jefferies .05 .02
31 Colby Ward .05 .02
32 Mike Simms .05 .02
33 Barry Jones .05 .02
34 Atlee Hammaker .05 .02
35 Greg Maddux .40 .12
36 Donnie Hill .05 .02
37 Tom Bolton .05 .02
38 Scott Bradley .05 .02
39 Jim Neidlinger .05 .02
40 Kevin Mitchell .05 .02
41 Ken Dayley .05 .02
42 Chris Hoiles .05 .02
43 Roger McDowell .05 .02
44 Mike Felder .05 .02
45 Chris Sabo .05 .02
46 Tim Drummond .05 .02
47 Brook Jacoby .05 .02
48 Dennis Boyd .05 .02
49A Pat Borders ERR .25 .07
(40 steals at
Kinston in '86)
49B Pat Borders COR .05 .02
(0 steals at
Kinston in '86)
50 Bob Welch .05 .02
51 Art Howe MG .05 .02
52 Francisco Oliveras .05 .02
53 Mike Sharperson UER .05 .02
(Born in 1961, not 1960)
54 Gary Mielke .05 .02
55 Jeffrey Leonard .05 .02
56 Jeff Parrett .05 .02
57 Jack Howell .05 .02
58 Mel Stottlemyre Jr. .05 .02
59 Eric Yelding .05 .02
60 Frank Viola .10 .03
61 Stan Javier .05 .02
62 Lee Guetterman .05 .02
63 Milt Thompson .05 .02
64 Tom Herr .05 .02
65 Bruce Hurst .05 .02
66 Terry Kennedy .05 .02
67 Rick Honeycutt .05 .02
68 Gary Sheffield .10 .03
69 Steve Wilson .05 .02
70 Ellis Burks .10 .03
71 Jim Acker .05 .02
72 Junior Ortiz .05 .02
73 Craig Worthington .05 .02
74 Shane Andrews RC .25 .07
75 Jack Morris .10 .03
76 Jerry Browne .05 .02
77 Drew Hall .05 .02
78 Geno Petralli .05 .02
79 Frank Thomas .25 .07
80A Fernando Valenzuela .40 .12
ERR (104 earned runs
in '90 tied for
league lead)
80B Fernando Valenzuela .10 .03
COR (104 earned runs
in '90 led league, 20
CG's in 1986 now
italicized)
81 Cito Gaston MG .05 .02
82 Tom Glavine .15 .04
83 Daryl Boston .05 .02
84 Bob McClure .05 .02
85 Jesse Barfield .05 .02
86 Les Lancaster .05 .02
87 Tracy Jones .05 .02
88 Bob Tewksbury .05 .02
89 Darren Daulton .10 .03
90 Danny Tartabull .05 .02
91 Greg Colbrunn RC .25 .07
92 Danny Jackson .05 .02
93 Ivan Calderon .05 .02
94 John Dopson .05 .02
95 Paul Molitor .15 .04
96 Trevor Wilson .05 .02
97A Brady Anderson ERR .40 .12
(September, 2 RBI and
3 hits, should be 3
RBI and 14 hits
97B Brady Anderson COR .10 .03
98 Sergio Valdez .05 .02
99 Chris Gwynn .05 .02
100 Don Mattingly COR .60 .18
(101 hits in 1990)
100A Don Mattingly ERR 2.00 .60
(10 hits in 1990)
101 Rob Ducey .05 .02
102 Gene Larkin .05 .02
103 Tim Costo RC .05 .02
104 Don Robinson .05 .02
105 Kevin McReynolds .05 .02
106 Ed Nunez .05 .02
107 Luis Polonia .05 .02
108 Matt Young .05 .02
109 Greg Riddoch MG .05 .02
110 Tom Henke .05 .02
111 Andres Thomas .05 .02
112 Frank DiPino .05 .02
113 Carl Everett RC .40 .12
114 Lance Dickson RC .10 .03
115 Hubie Brooks .05 .02
116 Mark Davis .05 .02
117 Dion James .05 .02
118 Tom Edens .05 .02
119 Carl Nichols .05 .02
120 Joe Carter .10 .03
121 Eric King .05 .02
122 Paul O'Neill .15 .04
123 Greg A. Harris .05 .02
124 Randy Bush .05 .02
125 Steve Bedrosian .05 .02
126 Bernard Gilkey .05 .02
127 Joe Price .05 .02
128 Travis Fryman .10 .03
(Front has SS
back has SS-3B)
129 Mark Eichhorn .05 .02
130 Ozzie Smith .40 .12
131A Checklist 1 ERR .25 .07
727 Phil Bradley
131B Checklist 1 COR .05 .02
717 Phil Bradley
132 Jamie Quirk .05 .02
133 Greg Briley .05 .02
134 Kevin Elster .05 .02
135 Jerome Walton .05 .02
136 Dave Schmidt .05 .02
137 Randy Ready .05 .02
138 Jamie Moyer .10 .03
139 Jeff Treadway .05 .02
140 Fred McGriff .15 .04
141 Nick Leyva MG .05 .02
142 Curt Wilkerson .05 .02
143 John Smiley .05 .02
144 Dave Henderson .05 .02
145 Lou Whitaker .10 .03
146 Dan Plesac .05 .02
147 Carlos Baerga .05 .02
148 Rey Palacios .05 .02
149 Al Osuna UER .10 .03
(Shown throwing right,
but bio says lefty)
150 Cal Ripken .75 .23
151 Tom Browning .05 .02
152 Mickey Hatcher .05 .02
153 Bryan Harvey .05 .02
154 Jay Buhner .10 .03
155A Dwight Evans ERR .40 .12
(Led league with
162 games in '82)
155B Dwight Evans COR .10 .03
(Tied for lead with
162 games in '82)
156 Carlos Martinez .05 .02
157 John Smoltz .15 .04
158 Jose Uribe .05 .02
159 Joe Boever .05 .02
160 Vince Coleman UER .05 .02
(Wrong birth year,
born 9/22/60)
161 Tim Leary .05 .02
162 Ozzie Canseco .05 .02
163 Dave Johnson .05 .02
164 Edgar Diaz .05 .02
165 Sandy Alomar Jr. .05 .02
166 Harold Baines .10 .03
167A R.Tomlin RC ERR .25 .07
Harriburg
167B R.Tomlin RC COR .10 .03
Harrisburg
168 John Olerud .10 .03
169 Luis Aquino .05 .02
170 Carlton Fisk .15 .04
171 Tony LaRussa MG .10 .03
172 Pete Incaviglia .05 .02
173 Jason Grimsley .05 .02
174 Ken Caminiti .10 .03
175 Jack Armstrong .05 .02
176 John Orton .05 .02
177 Reggie Harris .05 .02
178 Dave Valle .05 .02
179 Pete Harnisch .05 .02
180 Tony Gwynn .30 .09
181 Duane Ward .05 .02
182 Junior Noboa .05 .02
183 Clay Parker .05 .02
184 Gary Green .05 .02
185 Joe Magrane .05 .02
186 Rod Booker .05 .02
187 Greg Cadaret .05 .02
188 Damon Berryhill .05 .02
189 Daryl Irvine .05 .02
190 Matt Williams .10 .03
191 Willie Blair .05 .02
192 Rob Deer .05 .02
193 Felix Fermin .05 .02
194 Xavier Hernandez .05 .02
195 Wally Joyner .10 .03
196 Jim Vatcher .05 .02
197 Chris Nabholz .05 .02
198 R.J. Reynolds .05 .02
199 Mike Hartley .05 .02
200 Darryl Strawberry .10 .03
201 Tom Kelly MG .05 .02
202 Jim Leyritz .05 .02
203 Gene Harris .05 .02
204 Herm Winningham .05 .02
205 Mike Perez RC .10 .03
206 Carlos Quintana .05 .02
207 Gary Wayne .05 .02
208 Willie Wilson .05 .02
209 Ken Howell .05 .02
210 Lance Parrish .10 .03
211 Brian Barnes RC .05 .02
212 Steve Finley .10 .03
213 Frank Wills .05 .02
214 Joe Girardi .05 .02
215 Dave Smith .05 .02
216 Greg Gagne .05 .02
217 Chris Bosio .05 .02
218 Rick Parker .05 .02
219 Jack McDowell .05 .02
220 Tim Wallach .05 .02
221 Don Slaught .05 .02
222 Brian McRae RC .25 .07
223 Allan Anderson .05 .02
224 Juan Gonzalez .15 .04
225 Randy Johnson .30 .09
226 Alfredo Griffin .05 .02
227 Steve Avery UER .05 .02
(Pitched 13 games for
Durham in 1989, not 2)
228 Rex Hudler .05 .02
229 Rance Mulliniks .05 .02
230 Sid Fernandez .05 .02
231 Doug Rader MG .05 .02
232 Jose DeJesus .05 .02
233 Al Leiter .10 .03
234 Scott Erickson .05 .02
235 Dave Parker .10 .03
236A Frank Tanana ERR .25 .07
(Tied for lead with
269 K's in '75)
236B Frank Tanana COR .05 .02
(Led league with
269 K's in '75)
237 Rick Cerone .05 .02
238 Mike Dunne .05 .02
239 Darren Lewis .05 .02
240 Mike Scott .05 .02
241 Dave Clark UER .05 .02
(Career totals 19 HR
and 5 3B, should
be 22 and 3)
242 Mike LaCoss .05 .02
243 Lance Johnson .05 .02
244 Mike Jeffcoat .05 .02
245 Kal Daniels .05 .02
246 Kevin Wickander .05 .02
247 Jody Reed .05 .02
248 Tom Gordon .05 .02
249 Bob Melvin .05 .02
250 Dennis Eckersley .10 .03
251 Mark Lemke .05 .02
252 Mel Rojas .05 .02
253 Garry Templeton .05 .02
254 Shawn Boskie .05 .02
255 Brian Downing .05 .02
256 Greg Hibbard .05 .02
257 Tom O'Malley .05 .02
258 Chris Hammond .05 .02
259 Hensley Meulens .05 .02
260 Harold Reynolds .10 .03
261 Bud Harrelson MG .05 .02
262 Tim Jones .05 .02
263 Checklist 2 .05 .02
264 Dave Hollins .05 .02
265 Mark Gubicza .05 .02
266 Carmelo Castillo .05 .02
267 Mark Knudson .05 .02
268 Tom Brookens .05 .02
269 Joe Hesketh .05 .02
270 Mark McGwire COR .60 .18
(1987 Slugging Pctg.
listed as .618)
270A Mark McGwire ERR 2.00 .60
(1987 Slugging Pctg.
listed as 618)
271 Omar Olivares RC .10 .03
272 Jeff King .05 .02
273 Johnny Ray .05 .02
274 Ken Williams .05 .02
275 Alan Trammell .10 .03
276 Bill Swift .05 .02
277 Scott Coolbaugh .05 .02
278 Alex Fernandez UER .05 .02
(No '90 White Sox stats)
279A Jose Gonzalez ERR .25 .07
(Photo actually
Billy Bean)
279B Jose Gonzalez COR .05 .02
280 Bret Saberhagen .10 .03
281 Larry Sheets .05 .02
282 Don Carman .05 .02
283 Marquis Grissom .10 .03
284 Billy Spiers .05 .02
285 Jim Abbott .15 .04
286 Ken Oberkfell .05 .02
287 Mark Grant .05 .02
288 Derrick May .05 .02
289 Tim Birtsas .05 .02
290 Steve Sax .05 .02
291 John Wathan MG .05 .02
292 Bud Black .05 .02
293 Jay Bell .10 .03
294 Mike Moore .05 .02
295 Rafael Palmeiro .15 .04
296 Mark Williamson .05 .02
297 Manny Lee .05 .02
298 Omar Vizquel .15 .04
299 Scott Radinsky .05 .02
300 Kirby Puckett .25 .07
301 Steve Farr .05 .02
302 Tim Teufel .05 .02
303 Mike Boddicker .05 .02
304 Kevin Reimer .05 .02
305 Mike Scioscia .05 .02
306A Lonnie Smith ERR .40 .12

(136 games in '90)
306B Lonnie Smith COR .05 .02
(135 games in '90)
307 Andy Benes .05 .02
308 Tom Pagnozzi .05 .02
309 Norm Charlton .05 .02
310 Gary Carter .10 .03
311 Jeff Pico .05 .02
312 Charlie Hayes .05 .02
313 Ron Robinson .05 .02
314 Gary Pettis .05 .02
315 Roberto Alomar .15 .04
316 Gene Nelson .05 .02
317 Mike Fitzgerald .05 .02
318 Rick Aguilera .10 .03
319 Jeff McKnight .05 .02
320 Tony Fernandez .05 .02
321 Bob Rodgers MG .05 .02
322 Terry Shumpert .05 .02
323 Cory Snyder .05 .02
324A Ron Kittle ERR .40 .12
(Set another standard ...)
324B Ron Kittle COR .05 .02
(Tied another standard ...)
325 Brett Butler .10 .03
326 Ken Patterson .05 .02
327 Ron Hassey .05 .02
328 Walt Terrell .05 .02
329 Dave Justice UER .10 .03
(Drafted third round on card, should say fourth pick)
330 Dwight Gooden .10 .03
331 Eric Anthony .05 .02
332 Kenny Rogers .10 .03
333 C.Jones FDP RC 4.00 1.20
334 Todd Benzinger .05 .02
335 Mitch Williams .05 .02
336 Matt Nokes .05 .02
337A Keith Comstock ERR .25 .07
(Cubs logo on front)
337B Keith Comstock COR .05 .02
(Mariners logo on front)
338 Luis Rivera .05 .02
339 Larry Walker .25 .07
340 Ramon Martinez .05 .02
341 John Moses .05 .02
342 Mickey Morandini .05 .02
343 Jose Oquendo .05 .02
344 Jeff Russell .05 .02
345 Len Dykstra .10 .03
346 Jesse Orosco .05 .02
347 Greg Vaughn .05 .02
348 Todd Stottlemyre .05 .02
349 Dave Gallagher .05 .02
350 Glenn Davis .05 .02
351 Joe Torre MG .10 .03
352 Frank White .10 .03
353 Tony Castillo .05 .02
354 Sid Bream .05 .02
355 Chili Davis .10 .03
356 Mike Marshall .05 .02
357 Jack Savage .05 .02
358 Mark Parent .05 .02
359 Chuck Cary .05 .02
360 Tim Raines .10 .03
361 Scott Garrelts .05 .02
362 Hector Villenueva .05 .02
363 Rick Mahler .05 .02
364 Dan Pasqua .05 .02
365 Mike Schooler .05 .02
366A Checklist 3 ERR .25 .07
19 Carl Nichols
366B Checklist 3 COR .05 .02
119 Carl.Nichols
367 Dave Walsh RC .05 .02
368 Felix Jose .05 .02
369 Steve Searcy .05 .02
370 Kelly Gruber .05 .02
371 Jeff Montgomery .05 .02
372 Spike Owen .05 .02
373 Darrin Jackson .05 .02
374 Larry Casian .05 .02
375 Tony Pena .05 .02
376 Mike Harkey .05 .02
377 Rene Gonzales .05 .02
378A Wilson Alvarez ERR .25 .07
('89 Port Charlotte and '90 Birmingham stat lines omitted)
378B Wilson Alvarez COR .05 .02
Text still says 143 K's in 1988, whereas stats say 134
379 Randy Velarde .05 .02
380 Willie McGee .10 .03
381 Jim Leyland MG .05 .02
382 Mackey Sasser .05 .02
383 Pete Smith .05 .02
384 Gerald Perry .05 .02
385 Mickey Tettleton .05 .02
386 Cecil Fielder AS .05 .02
387 Julio Franco AS .05 .02
388 Kelly Gruber AS .05 .02
389 Alan Trammell AS .10 .03
390 Jose Canseco AS .10 .03
391 Rickey Henderson AS .15 .04
392 Ken Griffey Jr. AS .40 .12
393 Carlton Fisk AS .10 .03
394 Bob Welch AS .05 .02
395 Chuck Finley AS .05 .02
396 Bobby Thigpen AS .05 .02
397 Eddie Murray AS .15 .04
398 Ryne Sandberg AS .25 .07
399 Matt Williams AS .05 .02
400 Barry Larkin AS .10 .03
401 Barry Bonds AS .40 .12
402 Darryl Strawbery AS .05 .02
403 Bobby Bonilla AS .05 .02
404 Mike Scioscia AS .05 .02
405 Doug Drabek AS .05 .02
406 Frank Viola AS .05 .02
407 John Franco AS .05 .02
408 Earnest Riles .05 .02
409 Mike Stanley .05 .02
410 Dave Righetti .10 .03
411 Lance Blankenship .05 .02
412 Dave Bergman .05 .02
413 Terry Mulholland .05 .02
414 Sammy Sosa .50 .15
415 Rick Sutcliffe .10 .03
416 Randy Milligan .05 .02
417 Bill Krueger .05 .02
418 Nick Esasky .05 .02
419 Jeff Reed .05 .02
420 Bobby Thigpen .05 .02
421 Alex Cole .05 .02
422 Rick Reuschel .05 .02
423 Rafael Ramirez UER .05 .02
(Born 1959, not 1958)
424 Calvin Schiraldi .05 .02
425 Andy Van Slyke .10 .03
426 Joe Grahe RC .10 .03
427 Rick Dempsey .05 .02
428 John Barfield .05 .02
429 Stump Merrill MG .05 .02
430 Gary Gaetti .10 .03
431 Paul Gibson .05 .02
432 Delino DeShields .10 .03
433 Pat Tabler .05 .02
434 Julio Machado .05 .02
435 Kevin Maas .05 .02
436 Scott Bankhead .05 .02
437 Doug Dascenzo .05 .02
438 Vicente Palacios .05 .02
439 Dickie Thon .05 .02
440 George Bell .05 .02
441 Zane Smith .05 .02
442 Charlie O'Brien .05 .02
443 Jeff Innis .05 .02
444 Glenn Braggs .05 .02
445 Greg Swindell .05 .02
446 Craig Grebeck .05 .02
447 John Burkett .05 .02
448 Craig Lefferts .05 .02
449 Juan Berenguer .05 .02
450 Wade Boggs .15 .04
451 Neal Heaton .05 .02
452 Bill Schroeder .05 .02
453 Lenny Harris .05 .02
454A Kevin Appier ERR .40 .12
('90 Omaha stat line omitted)
454B Kevin Appier COR .10 .03
455 Walt Weiss .05 .02
456 Charlie Leibrandt .05 .02
457 Todd Hundley .05 .02
458 Brian Holman .05 .02
459 T.Trebelhorn MG UER .05 .02
Pitching and batting columns switched
460 Dave Stieb .05 .02
461 Robin Ventura .10 .03
462 Steve Frey .05 .02
463 Dwight Smith .05 .02
464 Steve Buechele .05 .02
465 Ken Griffey Sr. .10 .03
466 Charles Nagy .05 .02
467 Dennis Cook .05 .02
468 Tim Hulett .05 .02
469 Chet Lemon .05 .02
470 Howard Johnson .05 .02
471 Mike Lieberthal RC .40 .12
472 Kirt Manwaring .05 .02
473 Curt Young .05 .02
474 Phil Plantier RC .10 .03
475 Ted Higuera .05 .02
476 Glenn Wilson .05 .02
477 Mike Fetters .05 .02
478 Kurt Stillwell .05 .02
479 Bob Patterson UER .05 .02
(Has a decimal point between 7 and 9)
480 Dave Magadan .05 .02
481 Eddie Whitson .05 .02
482 Tino Martinez .15 .04
483 Mike Aldrete .05 .02
484 Dave LaPoint .05 .02
485 Terry Pendleton .10 .03
486 Tommy Greene .05 .02
487 Rafael Belliard .05 .02
488 Jeff Manto .05 .02
489 Bobby Valentine MG .05 .02
490 Kirk Gibson .10 .03
491 Kurt Miller RC .05 .02
492 Ernie Whitt .05 .02
493 Jose Rijo .05 .02
494 Chris James .05 .02
495 Charlie Hough .10 .03
496 Marty Barrett .05 .02
497 Ben McDonald .05 .02
498 Mark Salas .05 .02
499 Melido Perez .05 .02
500 Will Clark .25 .07
501 Mike Bielecki .05 .02
502 Carney Lansford .10 .03
503 Roy Smith .05 .02
504 Julio Valera .05 .02
505 Chuck Finley .10 .03
506 Darnell Coles .05 .02
507 Steve Jeltz .05 .02
508 Mike York .05 .02
509 Glenallen Hill .05 .02
510 John Franco .10 .03
511 Steve Balboni .05 .02
512 Jose Mesa .05 .02
513 Jerald Clark .05 .02
514 Mike Stanton .05 .02
515 Alvin Davis .05 .02
516 Karl Rhodes .05 .02
517 Joe Oliver .05 .02
518 Cris Carpenter .05 .02
519 Sparky Anderson MG .10 .03
520 Mark Grace .15 .04
521 Joe Orsulak .05 .02
522 Stan Belinda .05 .02
523 Rodney McCray .05 .02
524 Darrel Akerfelds .05 .02
525 Willie Randolph .10 .03
526A Moises Alou ERR .40 .12
(37 runs in 2 games for '90 Pirates)
526B Moises Alou COR .10 .03
(0 runs in 2 games for '90 Pirates)
527A Checklist 4 ERR .25 .07
105 Keith Miller
719 Kevin McReynolds
527B Checklist 4 COR .05 .02
105 Kevin McReynolds
719 Keith Miller
528 Dennis Martinez .10 .03
529 Marc Newfield RC .10 .03
530 Roger Clemens .50 .15
531 Dave Rohde .05 .02
532 Kirk McCaskill .05 .02
533 Oddibe McDowell .05 .02
534 Mike Jackson .05 .02
535 Ruben Sierra UER .05 .02
(Back reads 100 Runs amd 100 RBI's)
536 Mike Witt .05 .02
537 Jose Lind .05 .02
538 Bip Roberts .05 .02
539 Scott Terry .05 .02
540 George Brett .60 .18
541 Domingo Ramos .05 .02
542 Rob Murphy .05 .02
543 Junior Felix .05 .02
544 Alejandro Pena .05 .02
545 Dale Murphy .25 .07
546 Jeff Ballard .05 .02
547 Mike Pagliarulo .05 .02
548 Jaime Navarro .05 .02
549 John McNamara MG .05 .02
550 Eric Davis .10 .03
551 Bob Kipper .05 .02
552 Jeff Hamilton .05 .02
553 Joe Klink .05 .02
554 Brian Harper .05 .02
555 Turner Ward RC .10 .03
556 Gary Ward .05 .02
557 Wally Whitehurst .05 .02
558 Otis Nixon .05 .02
559 Adam Peterson .05 .02
560 Greg Smith .05 .02
561 Tim McIntosh .05 .02
562 Jeff Kunkel .05 .02
563 Brent Knackert .05 .02
564 Dante Bichette .10 .03
565 Craig Biggio .15 .04
566 Craig Wilson .05 .02
567 Dwayne Henry .05 .02
568 Ron Karkovice .05 .02
569 Curt Schilling .25 .07
570 Barry Bonds .75 .23
571 Pat Combs .05 .02
572 Dave Anderson .05 .02
573 Rich Rodriguez UER .05 .02
(Stats say drafted 4th, but bio says 9th round)
574 John Marzano .05 .02
575 Robin Yount .40 .12
576 Jeff Kaiser .05 .02
577 Bill Doran .05 .02
578 Dave West .05 .02
579 Roger Craig MG .05 .02
580 Dave Stewart .10 .03
581 Luis Quinones .05 .02
582 Marty Clary .05 .02
583 Tony Phillips .05 .02
584 Kevin Brown .10 .03
585 Pete O'Brien .05 .02
586 Fred Lynn .05 .02
587 Jose Offerman UER .05 .02
(Text says he signed 7/24/86, but bio says 1988)
588 Mark Whiten .05 .02
589 Scott Ruskin .05 .02
590 Eddie Murray .25 .07
591 Ken Hill .05 .02
592 B.J. Surhoff .05 .02
593A Mike Walker ERR .25 .07
('90 Canton-Akron stat line omitted)
593B Mike Walker COR .05 .02
594 Rich Garces RC .10 .03
595 Bill Landrum .05 .02
596 Ronnie Walden RC .10 .03
597 Jerry Don Gleaton .05 .02
598 Sam Horn .05 .02
599A Greg Myers ERR .25 .07
('90 Syracuse stat line omitted)
599B Greg Myers COR .05 .02
600 Bo Jackson .25 .07
601 Bob Ojeda .05 .02
602 Casey Candaele .05 .02
603A W.Chamberlain RC ERR .40 .12
Photo actually Louie Meadows
603B Wes Chamberlain RC COR .10 .03
604 Billy Hatcher .05 .02
605 Jeff Reardon .10 .03
606 Jim Gott .05 .02
607 Edgar Martinez .15 .04
608 Todd Burns .05 .02
609 Jeff Torborg MG .05 .02
610 Andres Galarraga .10 .03
611 Dave Eiland .05 .02
612 Steve Lyons .05 .02
613 Eric Show .05 .02
614 Luis Salazar .05 .02
615 Bert Blyleven .10 .03
616 Todd Zeile .05 .02
617 Bill Wegman .05 .02
618 Sil Campusano .05 .02
619 David Wells .10 .03
620 Ozzie Guillen .05 .02
621 Ted Power .05 .02
622 Jack Daugherty .05 .02
623 Jeff Blauser .05 .02
624 Tom Candiotti .05 .02
625 Terry Steinbach .05 .02
626 Gerald Young .05 .02
627 Tim Layana .05 .02
628 Greg Litton .05 .02
629 Wes Gardner .05 .02
630 Dave Winfield .10 .03
631 Mike Morgan .05 .02
632 Lloyd Moseby .05 .02
633 Kevin Tapani .05 .02
634 Henry Cotto .05 .02
635 Andy Hawkins .05 .02
636 Geronimo Pena .05 .02
637 Bruce Ruffin .05 .02
638 Mike Macfarlane .05 .02
639 Frank Robinson MG .15 .04
640 Andre Dawson .10 .03
641 Mike Henneman .05 .02
642 Hal Morris .05 .02
643 Jim Presley .05 .02
644 Chuck Crim .05 .02
645 Juan Samuel .05 .02
646 Andujar Cedeno .05 .02
647 Mark Portugal .05 .02
648 Lee Stevens .05 .02
649 Bill Sampen .05 .02
650 Jack Clark .10 .03
651 Alan Mills .05 .02
652 Kevin Romine .05 .02
653 Anthony Telford .05 .02
654 Paul Sorrento .05 .02
655 Erik Hanson .05 .02
656A Checklist 5 ERR .25 .07
348 Vicente Palacios
381 Jose Lind
537 Mike LaValliere
665 Jim Leyland
656B Checklist 5 ERR .25 .07
433 Vicente Palacios
(Palacios should be 438)
537 Jose Lind
665 Mike LaValliere
381 Jim Leyland
656C Checklist 5 COR .05 .02
438 Vicente Palacios
537 Jose Lind
665 Mike LaValliere
381 Jim Leyland
657 Mike Kingery .05 .02
658 Scott Aldred .05 .02
659 Oscar Azocar .05 .02
660 Lee Smith .10 .03
661 Steve Lake .05 .02
662 Ron Dibble .10 .03
663 Greg Brock .05 .02
664 John Farrell .05 .02
665 Mike LaValliere .05 .02
666 Danny Darwin .05 .02
667 Kent Anderson .05 .02
668 Bill Long .05 .02
669 Lou Piniella MG .10 .03
670 Rickey Henderson .25 .07
671 Andy McGaffigan .05 .02
672 Shane Mack .05 .02
673 Greg Olson UER .05 .02
(6 RBI in '88 at Tidewater and 2 RBI in '87, should be 48 and 15)
674A Kevin Gross ERR .25 .07
(89 BB with Phillies in '88 tied for league lead)
674B Kevin Gross COR .05 .02
(89 BB with Phillies in '88 led league)
675 Tom Brunansky .05 .02
676 Scott Chiamparino .05 .02
677 Billy Ripken .05 .02
678 Mark Davidson .05 .02
679 Bill Bathe .05 .02
680 David Cone .10 .03
681 Jeff Schaefer .05 .02
682 Ray Lankford .05 .02
683 Derek Lilliquist .05 .02
684 Milt Cuyler .05 .02
685 Doug Drabek .05 .02
686 Mike Gallego .05 .02
687A John Cerutti ERR .25 .07
(4.46 ERA in '90)
687B John Cerutti COR .05 .02
(4.76 ERA in '90)
688 Rosario Rodriguez .05 .02
689 John Kruk .10 .03
690 Orel Hershiser .10 .03
691 Mike Blowers .05 .02
692A Efrain Valdez ERR .25 .07
(Born 6/11/66)
692B Efrain Valdez COR .05 .02
(Born 7/11/66 and two lines of text added)
693 Francisco Cabrera .05 .02
694 Randy Veres .05 .02
695 Kevin Seitzer .05 .02
696 Steve Olin .05 .02
697 Shawn Abner .05 .02
698 Mark Guthrie .05 .02
699 Jim Lefebvre MG .05 .02
700 Jose Canseco .25 .07
701 Pascual Perez .05 .02
702 Tim Naehring .05 .02
703 Juan Agosto .05 .02
704 Devon White .10 .03
705 Robby Thompson .05 .02
706A Brad Arnsberg ERR .25 .07
(68.2 IP in '90)
706B Brad Arnsberg COR .05 .02
(62.2 IP in '90)
707 Jim Eisenreich .05 .02
708 John Mitchell .05 .02
709 Matt Sinatro .05 .02
710 Kent Hrbek .10 .03
711 Jose DeLeon .05 .02
712 Ricky Jordan .05 .02
713 Scott Scudder .05 .02
714 Marvell Wynne .05 .02
715 Tim Burke .05 .02
716 Bob Geren .05 .02
717 Phil Bradley .05 .02
718 Steve Crawford .05 .02
719 Keith Miller .05 .02
720 Cecil Fielder .10 .03
721 Mark Lee RC .05 .02
722 Wally Backman .05 .02
723 Candy Maldonado .05 .02
724 David Segui .05 .02
725 Ron Gant .10 .03
726 Phil Stephenson .05 .02
727 Mookie Wilson .10 .03
728 Scott Sanderson .05 .02
729 Don Zimmer MG .10 .03
730 Barry Larkin .15 .04
731 Jeff Gray .05 .02
732 Franklin Stubbs .05 .02
733 Kelly Downs .05 .02
734 John Russell .05 .02
735 Ron Darling .05 .02
736 Dick Schofield .05 .02
737 Tim Crews .05 .02
738 Mel Hall .05 .02
739 Russ Swan .05 .02
740 Ryne Sandberg .40 .12
741 Jimmy Key .10 .03
742 Tommy Gregg .05 .02
743 Bryn Smith .05 .02
744 Nelson Santovenia .05 .02
745 Doug Jones .05 .02
746 John Shelby .05 .02
747 Tony Fossas .05 .02
748 Al Newman .05 .02
749 Greg W. Harris .05 .02
750 Bobby Bonilla .10 .03
751 Wayne Edwards .05 .02
752 Kevin Bass .05 .02
753 Paul Marak UER .05 .02
(Stats say drafted in Jan. but bio says May)
754 Bill Pecota .05 .02
755 Mark Langston .05 .02
756 Jeff Huson .05 .02
757 Mark Gardner .05 .02
758 Mike Devereaux .05 .02
759 Bobby Cox MG .05 .02
760 Benny Santiago .10 .03
761 Larry Andersen .05 .02
762 Mitch Webster .05 .02
763 Dana Kiecker .05 .02
764 Mark Carreon .05 .02
765 Shawon Dunston .05 .02
766 Jeff Robinson .05 .02
767 Dan Wilson RC .25 .07
768 Don Pall .05 .02
769 Tim Sherrill .05 .02
770 Jay Howell .05 .02
771 Gary Redus UER .05 .02
(Born in Tanner, should say Athens)
772 Kent Mercker UER .05 .02
(Born in Indianapolis, should say Dublin, Ohio)
773 Tom Foley .05 .02
774 Dennis Rasmussen .05 .02
775 Julio Franco .10 .03
776 Brent Mayne .05 .02
777 John Candelaria .05 .02
778 Dan Gladden .05 .02
779 Carmelo Martinez .05 .02
780A Randy Myers ERR .40 .12
(15 career losses)
780B Randy Myers COR .05 .02
(19 career losses)
781 Darryl Hamilton .05 .02
782 Jim Deshaies .05 .02
783 Joel Skinner .05 .02
784 Willie Fraser .05 .02
785 Scott Fletcher .05 .02
786 Eric Plunk .05 .02
787 Checklist 6 .05 .02
788 Bob Milacki .05 .02
789 Tom Lasorda MG .25 .07
790 Ken Griffey Jr. .75 .23
791 Mike Benjamin .05 .02
792 Mike Greenwell .05 .02

1991 Topps Desert Shield

These 792 standard-size cards are parallel to the regular Topps issue. These cards were issued in special packs available only to servicepeople serving in the Desert Shield (later to be Desert Storm) campaign. The cards are differentiated by a "Desert Shield" logo in the upper right corner. There were many different types of forgeries created for these cards so some caution is urged in purchasing any expensive cards from the set.

Nm-Mt Ex-Mt
*STARS: 40X TO 100X BASIC CARDS
*ROOKIES: 15X TO 40X BASIC CARDS

1991 Topps Tiffany

This 792 standard-size set proved to be the final time Topps issued their Tiffany sets. These cards again parallel the regular issue and have "glossy" fronts and easy to read backs. These cards were issued in complete set form only. Since a limited amount of these sets were produced, the multiplier is one of the highest for any of these Topps sets. While no production number is guessed at for these sets, it is perceived in the hobby to be among the shortest printed Tiffany sets.

Nm-Mt Ex-Mt
COMP.FACT.SET (792) 200.00 60.00
*STARS: 12.5X TO 30X BASIC CARDS
*ROOKIES: 6X TO 15X BASIC CARDS

1991 Topps Rookies

This set contains 33 standard-size cards and were distributed at a rate of one per retail jumbo pack. The front and back borders are white and other design elements are red, blue, and yellow. This set is identical to the previous year's set. Topps also commemorated its 40th anniversary by including a "Topps 40" logo on the front. The cards are unnumbered and checklisted below in alphabetical order.

Nm-Mt Ex-Mt
COMPLETE SET (33) 20.00 6.00
1 Sandy Alomar .50 .15
2 Kevin Appier .50 .15
3 Steve Avery .25 .07
4 Carlos Baerga .50 .15

John Burkett .25 .07
Alex Cole .25 .07
Pat Combs .25 .07
Delino DeShields .50 .15
Travis Fryman 1.00 .30
0 Marquis Grissom .50 .15
1 Mike Harkey .25 .07
2 Glenallen Hill .25 .07
3 Jeff Huson .25 .07
4 Felix Jose .25 .07
5 Dave Justice 1.50 .45
6 Jim Leyritz .25 .07
7 Kevin Maas .25 .07
8 Ben McDonald .25 .07
9 Kent Mercker .25 .07
0 Hal Morris .25 .07
1 Chris Nabholz .25 .07
2 Tim Naehring .25 .07
3 Jose Offerman .25 .07
4 John Olerud 2.00 .60
5 Scott Radinsky .25 .07
6 Scott Ruskin .25 .07
7 Kevin Tapani .25 .07
8 Frank Thomas 8.00 2.40
9 Randy Tomlin .25 .07
0 Greg Vaughn 1.50 .45
1 Robin Ventura 1.50 .45
2 Larry Walker 1.50 .45
3 Todd Zeile 1.00 .30

1991 Topps Wax Box Cards

opps again in 1991 issued cards on the bottom f their wax pack boxes. There are four different oxes, each with four cards and a checklist on ne side. These standard-size cards have yellow orders rather than the white borders of the reg- lar issue cards, and they have different photos f the players. The backs are printed in pink and lue on gray cardboard stock and feature out- tanding achievements of the players. The cards re numbered by letter on the back. The cards ave the typical Topps 1991 design on the front f the card. The set was ordered in alphabetical rder and lettered A-P.

Nm-Mt Ex-Mt
OMPLETE SET (16) 6.00 1.80
Bert Blyleven .20 .06
George Brett 1.00 .30
Brett Butler .10 .03
Andre Dawson .50 .15
Dwight Evans .20 .06
Carlton Fisk .60 .18
Alfredo Griffin .10 .03
Rickey Henderson .60 .18
Willie McGee .20 .06
Dale Murphy .50 .15
Eddie Murray .60 .18
Dave Parker .20 .06
Jeff Reardon .20 .06
Nolan Ryan 2.50 .75
Juan Samuel .10 .03
Robin Yount .60 .18

1991 Topps Traded

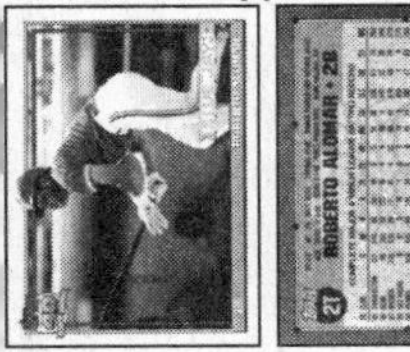

he 1991 Topps Traded set contains 132 stan- ard-size cards. The cards were issued primari- y in factory set form through hobby dealers but were also made available on a limited basis in wax packs. The cards in the wax packs (gray acks) and collated factory sets (white backs) re from different card stock. Both versions are alued equally. The card design is identical to the egular issue 1991 Topps cards except for the whiter stock (for factory set cards) and T-suf- ixed numbering. The set is numbered in alpha- etical order. The set includes a Team U.S.A. ubset, featuring 25 of America's top collegiate layers. The key Rookie Cards in this set are Jeff Bagwell, Jason Giambi, Luis Gonzalez, Charles Johnson and Ivan Rodriguez.

Nm-Mt Ex-Mt
COMPLETE SET (132) 10.00 3.00
COMP.FACT.SET (132) 10.00 3.00
T Juan Agosto .05 .02
T Roberto Alomar .15 .04
3T Wally Backman .05 .02
4T Jeff Bagwell RC 1.50 .45
5T Skeeter Barnes .05 .02
6T Steve Bedrosian .05 .02
7T Derek Bell .10 .03
8T George Bell .05 .02
9T Rafael Belliard .05 .02
0T Dante Bichette .10 .03
1T Bud Black .05 .02
2T Mike Boddicker .05 .02
3T Sid Bream .05 .02
4T Hubie Brooks .05 .02
5T Brett Butler .10 .03
6T Ivan Calderon .05 .02
7T John Candelaria .05 .02
8T Tom Candiotti .05 .02
9T Gary Carter .10 .03
20T Joe Carter .10 .03
21T Rick Cerone .05 .02
22T Jack Clark .10 .03
23T Vince Coleman .05 .02
24T Scott Coolbaugh .05 .02
25T Danny Cox .05 .02
26T Danny Darwin .05 .02
27T Chili Davis .10 .03
28T Glenn Davis .05 .02
29T Steve Decker .05 .02
30T Rob Deer .05 .02
31T Rich DeLucia .05 .02
32T John Dettmer USA RC .25 .07
33T Brian Downing .05 .02
34T D.Dreifort USA RC .50 .15
35T K.Dressendorfer RC .05 .02
36T Jim Essian MG .05 .02
37T Dwight Evans .10 .03
38T Steve Farr .05 .02
39T Jeff Fassero RC .25 .07
40T Junior Felix .05 .02
41T Tony Fernandez .05 .02
42T Steve Finley .10 .03
43T Jim Fregosi MG .05 .02
44T Gary Gaetti .10 .03
45T Jason Giambi USA RC 4.00 1.20
46T Kirk Gibson .10 .03
47T Leo Gomez .05 .02
48T Luis Gonzalez RC .50 .15
49T Jeff Granger USA RC .25 .07
50T Todd Greene USA RC .50 .15
51T J.Hammonds USA RC .50 .15
52T Mike Hargrove MG .05 .02
53T Pete Harnisch .05 .02
54T Rick Helling RC .50 .15
USA UER
Misspelled Hellings on card back
55T Glenallen Hill .05 .02
56T Charlie Hough .10 .03
57T Pete Incaviglia .05 .02
58T Bo Jackson .25 .07
59T Danny Jackson .05 .02
60T Reggie Jefferson .05 .02
61T C.Johnson USA RC .75 .23
62T Jeff Johnson .05 .02
63T T.Johnson USA RC .25 .07
64T Barry Jones .05 .02
65T Chris Jones RC .10 .03
66T Scott Kamieniecki RC .10 .03
67T Pat Kelly RC .10 .03
68T Darryl Kile .10 .03
69T Chuck Knoblauch .10 .03
70T Bill Krueger .05 .02
71T Scott Leius .05 .02
72T D.Leshnock USA RC .25 .07
73T Mark Lewis .05 .02
74T Candy Maldonado .05 .02
75T J.McDonald USA RC .25 .07
76T Willie McGee .10 .03
77T Fred McGriff .15 .04
78T B.McMillon USA RC .25 .07
79T Hal McRae MG .10 .03
80T D.Melendez USA RC .25 .07
81T Orlando Merced RC .10 .03
82T Jack Morris .10 .03
83T Phil Nevin USA RC 1.00 .30
84T Otis Nixon .05 .02
85T Johnny Oates MG .05 .02
86T Bob Ojeda .05 .02
87T Mike Pagliarulo .05 .02
88T Dean Palmer .10 .03
89T Dave Parker .10 .03
90T Terry Pendleton .10 .03
91T T.Phillips (P) USA RC .25 .07
92T Doug Piatt .05 .02
93T Ron Polk USA CO .25 .07
94T Tim Raines .10 .03
95T Willie Randolph .10 .03
96T Dave Righetti .10 .03
97T Ernie Riles .05 .02
98T C.Roberts USA RC .25 .07
99T Jeff D. Robinson .05 .02
100T Jeff M. Robinson .05 .02
101T Ivan Rodriguez RC 2.00 .60
102T S.Rodriguez USA RC .25 .07
103T Tom Runnells MG .05 .02
104T Scott Sanderson .05 .02
105T Bob Scanlan .05 .02
106T Pete Schourek RC .10 .03
107T Gary Scott .05 .02
108T Paul Shuey USA RC .50 .15
109T Doug Simons .05 .02
110T Dave Smith .05 .02
111T Cory Snyder .05 .02
112T Luis Sojo .05 .02
113T K.Steenstra USA RC .25 .07
114T Darryl Strawberry .10 .03
115T Franklin Stubbs .05 .02
116T Todd Taylor USA RC .25 .07
117T Wade Taylor .05 .02
118T Garry Templeton .05 .02
119T Mickey Tettleton .05 .02
120T Tim Teufel .05 .02
121T Mike Timlin RC .40 .12
122T David Tuttle USA RC .25 .07
123T Mo Vaughn .10 .03
124T Jeff Ware USA RC .25 .07
125T Devon White .10 .03
126T Mark Whiten .05 .02
127T Mitch Williams .05 .02
128T C.Wilson USA RC .25 .07
129T Willie Wilson .05 .02
130T C.Wimmer USA RC .25 .07
131T Ivan Zweig USA RC .25 .07
132T Checklist 1T-132T .05 .02

1991 Topps Traded Tiffany

In the final Tiffany relase, this 132-card standard-size set was released as a parallel issue to the regular Topps Traded issue. These cards were released in very limited quantities and the multiplier for these cards is higher than many previous Tiffany issues. These cards were issued in complete factory set form only. The set is considered to be among the shortest print of the Tiffany run and these cards are rarely seen in the secondary market.

Nm-Mt Ex-Mt
COMP.FACT.SET (132) 200.00 60.00
*STARS: 12.5X TO 30X BASIC CARDS
*ROOKIES: 10X TO 25X BASIC CARDS
*USA ROOKIES: 6X TO 15X BASIC CARDS

1991 Topps Debut '90

The 1991 Topps Major League Debut Set contains 171 standard-size cards. Although the checklist card is arranged chronologically in order of first major league appearance in 1990, the player cards are arranged alphabetically by the player's last name. Carlos Baerga and Frank Thomas are among the more prominent players featured in this set.

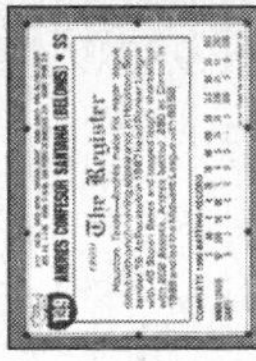

Nm-Mt Ex-Mt
COMP. FACT SET (171) 20.00 6.00
1 Paul Abbott .75 .23
2 Steve Adkins .15 .04
3 Scott Aldred .15 .04
4 Gerald Alexander .15 .04
5 Moises Alou .75 .23
6 Steve Avery .15 .04
7 Oscar Azocar .15 .04
8 Carlos Baerga .15 .04
9 Kevin Baez .15 .04
10 Jeff Baldwin .15 .04
11 Brian Barnes .15 .04
12 Kevin Bearse .15 .04
13 Kevin Belcher .15 .04
14 Mike Bell .15 .04
15 Sean Berry .75 .23
16 Joe Bitker .15 .04
17 Willie Blair .15 .04
18 Brian Bohanon .15 .04
19 Mike Bordick .75 .23
20 Shawn Boskie .15 .04
21 Rod Brewer .15 .04
22 Kevin D. Brown .15 .04
23 Dave Burba .75 .23
24 Jim Campbell .15 .04
25 Ozzie Canseco .15 .04
26 Chuck Carr .15 .04
27 Larry Casian .15 .04
28 Andujar Cedeno .15 .04
29 Wes Chamberlain .15 .04
30 Scott Chiamparino .15 .04
31 Steve Chitren .15 .04
32 Pete Coachman .15 .04
33 Alex Cole .15 .04
34 Jeff Conine .75 .23
35 Scott Cooper .15 .04
36 Milt Cuyler .15 .04
37 Steve Decker .15 .04
38 Rich DeLucia .15 .04
39 Delino DeShields .75 .23
40 Mark Dewey .15 .04
41 Carlos Diaz .15 .04
42 Lance Dickson .15 .04
43 Narciso Elvira .15 .04
44 Luis Encarnacion .15 .04
45 Scott Erickson .15 .04
46 Paul Faries .15 .04
47 Howard Farmer .15 .04
48 Alex Fernandez .15 .04
49 Travis Fryman .75 .23
50 Rich Garces .15 .04
51 Carlos Garcia .15 .04
52 Mike Gardiner .15 .04
53 Bernard Gilkey .15 .04
54 Tom Gilles .15 .04
55 Jerry Goff .15 .04
56 Leo Gomez .15 .04
57 Luis Gonzalez 3.00 .90
58 Joe Grahe .15 .04
59 Craig Grebeck .15 .04
60 Kip Gross .15 .04
61 Eric Gunderson .15 .04
62 Chris Hammond .15 .04
63 Dave Hansen .15 .04
64 Reggie Harris .15 .04
65 Bill Haselman .15 .04
66 Randy Hennis .15 .04
67 Carlos Hernandez .15 .04
68 Howard Hilton .15 .04
69 Dave Hollins .15 .04
70 Darren Holmes .75 .23
71 John Hoover .15 .04
72 Steve Howard .15 .04
73 Thomas Howard .15 .04
74 Todd Hundley .15 .04
75 Daryl Irvine .15 .04
76 Chris Jelic .15 .04
77 Dana Kiecker .15 .04
78 Brent Knackert .15 .04
79 Jimmy Kremers .15 .04
80 Jerry Kutzler .15 .04
81 Ray Lankford .15 .04
82 Tim Layana .15 .04
83 Terry Lee .15 .04
84 Mark Leiter .15 .04
85 Scott Leius .15 .04
86 Mark Leonard .15 .04
87 Darren Lewis .15 .04
88 Scott Lewis .15 .04
89 Jim Leyritz .15 .04
90 Dave Liddell .15 .04
91 Luis Lopez .15 .04
92 Kevin Maas .15 .04
93 Bob MacDonald .15 .04
94 Carlos Maldonado .15 .04
95 Chuck Malone .15 .04
96 Ramon Manon .15 .04
97 Jeff Manto .15 .04
98 Paul Marak .15 .04
99 Tino Martinez 1.50 .45
100 Derrick May .15 .04
101 Brent Mayne .15 .04
102 Paul McClellan .15 .04
103 Rodney McCray .15 .04
104 Tim McIntosh .15 .04
105 Brian McRae .75 .23
106 Jose Melendez .15 .04
107 Orlando Merced .15 .04
108 Alan Mills .15 .04
109 Gino Minutelli .15 .04
110 Mickey Morandini .15 .04
111 Pedro Munoz .15 .04
112 Chris Nabholz .15 .04
113 Tim Naehring .15 .04
114 Charles Nagy .15 .04
115 Jim Neidlinger .15 .04
116 Rafael Novoa .15 .04
117 Jose Offerman .15 .04
118 Omar Olivares .75 .23
119 Javier Ortiz .15 .04
120 Al Osuna .15 .04
121 Rick Parker .15 .04
122 Dave Pavlas .15 .04
123 Geronimo Pena .15 .04
124 Mike Perez .15 .04
125 Phil Plantier .15 .04
126 Jim Poole .15 .04
127 Tom Quinlan .15 .04
128 Scott Radinsky .15 .04
129 Darren Reed .15 .04
130 Karl Rhodes .15 .04
131 Jeff Richardson .15 .04
132 Rich Rodriguez .15 .04
133 Dave Rohde .15 .04
134 Mel Rojas .15 .04
135 Vic Rosario .15 .04
136 Rich Rowland .15 .04
137 Scott Ruskin .15 .04
138 Bill Sampen .15 .04
139 Andres Santana .15 .04
140 David Segui .15 .04
141 Jeff Shaw .15 .04
142 Tim Sherrill .15 .04
143 Terry Shumpert .15 .04
144 Mike Simms .15 .04
145 Daryl Smith .15 .04
146 Luis Sojo .15 .04
147 Steve Springer .15 .04
148 Ray Stephens .15 .04
149 Lee Stevens .15 .04
150 Mel Stottlemyre Jr. .15 .04
151 Glenn Sutko .15 .04
152 Anthony Telford .15 .04
153 Frank Thomas 5.00 1.50
154 Randy Tomlin .15 .04
155 Brian Traxler .15 .04
156 Efrain Valdez .15 .04
157 Rafael Valdez .15 .04
158 Julio Valera .15 .04
159 Jim Vatcher .15 .04
160 Hector Villanueva .15 .04
161 Hector Wagner .15 .04
162 Dave Walsh .15 .04
163 Steve Wapnick .15 .04
164 Colby Ward .15 .04
165 Turner Ward .75 .23
166 Terry Wells .15 .04
167 Mark Whiten .15 .04
168 Mike York .15 .04
169 Cliff Young .15 .04
170 Checklist Card .15 .04
171 Checklist Card .15 .04

1991 Topps Glossy All-Stars

These 22 glossy standard-size cards were inserted one per Topps rack packs and honor the starting lineup, managers and honorary captains of the 1990 National and American League All-Star teams. This would be the final year that this insert set was issued and the design is similar to what Topps produced each year since 1984.

Nm-Mt Ex-Mt
COMPLETE SET (22) 10.00 3.00
1 Tony LaRussa MG .20 .06
2 Mark McGwire 2.50 .75
3 Steve Sax .10 .03
4 Wade Boggs .50 .15
5 Cal Ripken Jr 3.00 .90
6 Rickey Henderson .75 .23
7 Ken Griffey, Jr. 2.00 .60
8 Jose Canseco .50 .15
9 Sandy Alomar Jr. .20 .06
10 Bob Welch .10 .03
11 Al Lopez CAPT .20 .06
12 Roger Craig MG .10 .03
13 Will Clark .50 .15
14 Ryne Sandberg .75 .23
15 Chris Sabo .10 .03
16 Ozzie Smith 1.00 .30
17 Kevin Mitchell .10 .03
18 Len Dykstra .20 .06
19 Andre Dawson .50 .15
20 Mike Scioscia .20 .06
21 Jack Armstrong .10 .03
22 Juan Marichal CAPT .30 .09

1992 Topps

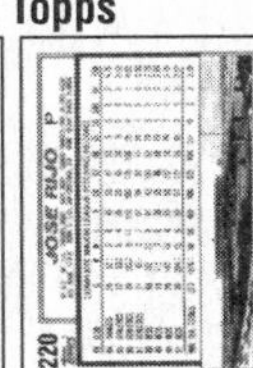

The 1992 Topps set contains 792 standard-size cards. Cards were distributed in plastic wrap packs, jumbo packs, rack packs and factory sets. The fronts have either posed or action color player photos on a white card face. Different color stripes frame the pictures, and the player's name and team name appear in two short color stripes respectively at the bottom. Special subsets included are Record Breakers (2-5), Prospects (58, 126, 179, 473, 551, 591, 618, 656, 676), and All-Stars (386-407). The key Rookie Cards in this set are Shawn Green and Manny Ramirez.

Nm-Mt Ex-Mt
COMPLETE SET (792) 25.00 7.50
COMP.FACT.SET (802) 25.00 7.50
COMP.HOLIDAY (811) 40.00 12.00
1 Nolan Ryan 1.00 .30
2 Ricky Henderson RB .15 .04
Most career SB's
(Some cards have print marks that show 1.991 on the front)
3 Jeff Reardon RB .05 .02
4 Nolan Ryan RB .50 .15
5 Dave Winfield RB .05 .02
6 Brien Taylor RC .25 .07
7 Jim Olander .05 .02
8 Bryan Hickerson RC .10 .03
9 Jon Farrell RC .10 .03
10 Wade Boggs .15 .04
11 Jack McDowell .05 .02
12 Luis Gonzalez .10 .03
13 Mike Scioscia .05 .02
14 Wes Chamberlain .05 .02
15 Dennis Martinez .10 .03
16 Jeff Montgomery .05 .02
17 Randy Milligan .05 .02
18 Greg Cadaret .05 .02
19 Jamie Quirk .05 .02
20 Bip Roberts .05 .02
21 Buck Rodgers MG .05 .02
22 Bill Wegman .05 .02
23 Chuck Knoblauch .10 .03
24 Randy Myers .05 .02
25 Ron Gant .10 .03
26 Mike Bielecki .05 .02
27 Juan Gonzalez .15 .04
28 Mike Schooler .05 .02
29 Mickey Tettleton .05 .02
30 John Kruk .10 .03
31 Bryn Smith .05 .02
32 Chris Nabholz .05 .02
33 Carlos Baerga .05 .02
34 Jeff Juden .05 .02
35 Dave Righetti .10 .03
36 Scott Ruffcorn RC .10 .03
37 Luis Polonia .05 .02
38 Tom Candiotti .05 .02
39 Greg Olson .05 .02
40 Cal Ripken 2.00 .60
41 Craig Lefferts .05 .02
42 Mike Macfarlane .05 .02
43 Jose Lind .05 .02
44 Rick Aguilera .10 .03
45 Gary Carter .10 .03
46 Steve Farr .05 .02
47 Rex Hudler .05 .02
48 Scott Scudder .05 .02
49 Damon Berryhill .05 .02
50 Ken Griffey Jr. .40 .12
51 Tom Runnells MG .05 .02
52 Juan Bell .05 .02
53 Tommy Gregg .05 .02
54 David Wells .10 .03
55 Rafael Palmeiro .15 .04
56 Charlie O'Brien .05 .02
57 Donn Pall .05 .02
58 Brad Ausmus RC .25 .07
Jim Campanis Jr.
Dave Nilsson
Doug Robbins
59 Mo Vaughn .10 .03
60 Tony Fernandez .05 .02
61 Paul O'Neill .15 .04
62 Gene Nelson .05 .02
63 Randy Ready .05 .02
64 Bob Kipper .05 .02
65 Willie McGee .10 .03
66 Scott Stahoviak RC .10 .03
67 Luis Salazar .05 .02
68 Marvin Freeman .05 .02
69 Kenny Lofton .15 .04
70 Gary Gaetti .10 .03
71 Erik Hanson .05 .02
72 Eddie Zosky .05 .02
73 Brian Barnes .05 .02
74 Scott Leius .05 .02
75 Bret Saberhagen .10 .03
76 Mike Gallego .05 .02
77 Jack Armstrong .05 .02
78 Ivan Rodriguez .25 .07
79 Jesse Orosco .05 .02
80 David Justice .10 .03
81 Ced Landrum .05 .02
82 Doug Simons .05 .02
83 Tommy Greene .05 .02
84 Leo Gomez .05 .02
85 Jose DeLeon .05 .02
86 Steve Finley .10 .03
87 Bob MacDonald .05 .02
88 Darrin Jackson .05 .02
89 Neal Heaton .05 .02
90 Robin Yount .40 .12
91 Jeff Reed .05 .02
92 Lenny Harris .05 .02
93 Reggie Jefferson .05 .02
94 Sammy Sosa .40 .12
95 Scott Bailes .05 .02
96 Tom McKinnon RC .10 .03
97 Luis Rivera .05 .02
98 Mike Harkey .05 .02
99 Jeff Treadway .05 .02
100 Jose Canseco .25 .07
101 Omar Vizquel .15 .04
102 Scott Kamieniecki .05 .02
103 Ricky Jordan .05 .02
104 Jeff Ballard .05 .02
105 Felix Jose .05 .02
106 Mike Boddicker .05 .02
107 Dan Pasqua .05 .02
108 Mike Timlin .05 .02
109 Roger Craig MG .05 .02
110 Ryne Sandberg .40 .12
111 Mark Carreon .05 .02
112 Oscar Azocar .05 .02
113 Mike Greenwell .05 .02
114 Mark Portugal .05 .02
115 Terry Pendleton .10 .03
116 Willie Randolph .10 .03
117 Scott Terry .05 .02

118 Chili Davis .10 .03
119 Mark Gardner .05 .02
120 Alan Trammell .10 .03
121 Derek Bell .10 .03
122 Gary Varsho .05 .02
123 Bob Ojeda .05 .02
124 Shawn Livsey RC .10 .03
125 Chris Hoiles .05 .02
126 Ryan Klesko .25 .07
John Jaha RC
Rico Brogna
Dave Staton
127 Carlos Quintana .05 .02
128 Kurt Stillwell .05 .02
129 Melido Perez .05 .02
130 Alvin Davis .05 .02
131 Checklist 1-132 .05 .02
132 Eric Show .05 .02
133 Rance Mulliniks .05 .02
134 Darryl Kile .10 .03
135 Von Hayes .05 .02
136 Bill Doran .05 .02
137 Jeff D. Robinson .05 .02
138 Monty Fariss .05 .02
139 Jeff Innis .05 .02
140 Mark Grace UER .15 .04
Home Calie., should be Calif.
141 Jim Leyland MG UER .10 .03
(No closed parenthesis after East in 1991)
142 Todd Van Poppel .05 .02
143 Paul Gibson .05 .02
144 Bill Swift .05 .02
145 Danny Tartabull .05 .02
146 Al Newman .05 .02
147 Cris Carpenter .05 .02
148 Anthony Young .05 .02
149 Brian Bohanon .05 .02
150 Roger Clemens UER .50 .15
(League leading ERA in 1990 not italicized)
151 Jeff Hamilton .05 .02
152 Charlie Leibrandt .05 .02
153 Ron Karkovice .05 .02
154 Hensley Meulens .05 .02
155 Scott Bankhead .05 .02
156 Manny Ramirez RC 2.50 .75
157 Keith Miller .05 .02
158 Todd Frohwirth .05 .02
159 Darrin Fletcher .05 .02
160 Bobby Bonilla .10 .03
161 Casey Candaele .05 .02
162 Paul Faries .05 .02
163 Dana Kiecker .05 .02
164 Shane Mack .05 .02
165 Mark Langston .05 .02
166 Geronimo Pena .05 .02
167 Andy Allanson .05 .02
168 Dwight Smith .05 .02
169 Chuck Crim .05 .02
170 Alex Cole .05 .02
171 Bill Plummer MG .05 .02
172 Juan Berenguer .05 .02
173 Brian Downing .05 .02
174 Steve Frey .05 .02
175 Orel Hershiser .10 .03
176 Ramon Garcia .05 .02
177 Dan Gladden .05 .02
178 Jim Acker .05 .02
179 Bobby DeJardin .05 .02
Cesar Bernhardt
Armando Moreno
Andy Stankiewicz
180 Kevin Mitchell .05 .02
181 Hector Villanueva .05 .02
182 Jeff Reardon .10 .03
183 Brent Mayne .05 .02
184 Jimmy Jones .05 .02
185 Benito Santiago .10 .03
186 Cliff Floyd RC .40 .12
187 Ernie Riles .05 .02
188 Jose Guzman .05 .02
189 Junior Felix .05 .02
190 Glenn Davis .05 .02
191 Charlie Hough .10 .03
192 Dave Fleming .05 .02
193 Omar Olivares .05 .02
194 Eric Karros .10 .03
195 David Cone .10 .03
196 Frank Castillo .05 .02
197 Glenn Braggs .05 .02
198 Scott Aldred .05 .02
199 Jeff Blauser .05 .02
200 Len Dykstra .10 .03
201 B.Showalter RC MG .25 .07
202 Rick Honeycutt .05 .02
203 Greg Myers .05 .02
204 Trevor Wilson .05 .02
205 Jay Howell .05 .02
206 Luis Sojo .05 .02
207 Jack Clark .10 .03
208 Julio Machado .05 .02
209 Lloyd McClendon .05 .02
210 Ozzie Guillen .05 .02
211 Jeremy Hernandez RC .10 .03
212 Randy Velarde .05 .02
213 Les Lancaster .05 .02
214 Andy Mota .05 .02
215 Rich Gossage .10 .03
216 Brent Gates RC .10 .03
217 Brian Harper .05 .02
218 Mike Flanagan .05 .02
219 Jerry Browne .05 .02
220 Jose Rijo .05 .02
221 Skeeter Barnes .05 .02
222 Jaime Navarro .05 .02
223 Mel Hall .05 .02
224 Bret Barberie .05 .02
225 Roberto Alomar .15 .04
226 Pete Smith .05 .02
227 Daryl Boston .05 .02
228 Eddie Whitson .05 .02
229 Shawn Boskie .05 .02
230 Dick Schofield .05 .02
231 Brian Drahman .05 .02
232 John Smiley .05 .02
233 Mitch Webster .05 .02
234 Terry Steinbach .05 .02
235 Jack Morris .10 .03
236 Bill Pecota .05 .02
237 Jose Hernandez RC .40 .12
238 Greg Litton .05 .02
239 Brian Holman .05 .02
240 Andres Galarraga .10 .03
241 Gerald Young .05 .02
242 Mike Mussina .25 .07
243 Alvaro Espinoza .05 .02
244 Darren Daulton .10 .03
245 John Smoltz .15 .04
246 Jason Pruitt RC .10 .03
247 Chuck Finley .10 .03
248 Jim Gantner .05 .02
249 Tony Fossas .05 .02
250 Ken Griffey Sr. .10 .03
251 Kevin Elster .05 .02
252 Dennis Rasmussen .05 .02
253 Terry Kennedy .05 .02
254 Ryan Bowen .05 .02
255 Robin Ventura .10 .03
256 Mike Aldrete .05 .02
257 Jeff Russell .05 .02
258 Jim Lindeman .05 .02
259 Ron Darling .05 .02
260 Devon White .10 .03
261 Tom Lasorda MG .10 .03
262 Terry Lee .05 .02
263 Bob Patterson .05 .02
264 Checklist 133-264 .05 .02
265 Teddy Higuera .05 .02
266 Roberto Kelly .05 .02
267 Steve Bedrosian .05 .02
268 Brady Anderson .10 .03
269 Ruben Amaro .05 .02
270 Tony Gwynn .30 .09
271 Tracy Jones .05 .02
272 Jerry Don Gleaton .05 .02
273 Craig Grebeck .05 .02
274 Bob Scanlan .05 .02
275 Todd Zeile .05 .02
276 Shawn Green RC 1.50 .45
277 Scott Chiamparino .05 .02
278 Darryl Hamilton .05 .02
279 Jim Clancy .05 .02
280 Carlos Martinez .05 .02
281 Kevin Appier .10 .03
282 John Wehner .05 .02
283 Reggie Sanders .05 .02
284 Gene Larkin .05 .02
285 Bob Welch .05 .02
286 Gilberto Reyes .05 .02
287 Pete Schourek .05 .02
288 Andujar Cedeno .05 .02
289 Mike Morgan .05 .02
290 Bo Jackson .25 .07
291 Phil Garner MG .05 .02
292 Ray Lankford .05 .02
293 Mike Henneman .05 .02
294 Dave Valle .05 .02
295 Alonzo Powell .05 .02
296 Tom Brunansky .05 .02
297 Kevin Brown .10 .03
298 Kelly Gruber .05 .02
299 Charles Nagy .05 .02
300 Don Mattingly .60 .18
301 Kirk McCaskill .05 .02
302 Joey Cora .05 .02
303 Dan Plesac .05 .02
304 Joe Oliver .05 .02
305 Tom Glavine .15 .04
306 Al Shirley RC .10 .03
307 Bruce Ruffin .05 .02
308 Craig Shipley .05 .02
309 Dave Martinez .05 .02
310 Jose Mesa .05 .02
311 Henry Cotto .05 .02
312 Mike LaValliere .05 .02
313 Kevin Tapani .05 .02
314 Jeff Huson .05 .02
(Shows Jose Canseco sliding into second)
315 Juan Samuel .05 .02
316 Curt Schilling .15 .04
317 Mike Bordick .05 .02
318 Steve Howe .05 .02
319 Tony Phillips .05 .02
320 George Bell .05 .02
321 Lou Piniella MG .10 .03
322 Tim Burke .05 .02
323 Milt Thompson .05 .02
324 Danny Darwin .05 .02
325 Joe Orsulak .05 .02
326 Eric King .05 .02
327 Jay Buhner .10 .03
328 Joel Johnston .05 .02
329 Franklin Stubbs .05 .02
330 Will Clark .25 .07
331 Steve Lake .05 .02
332 Chris Jones .05 .02
333 Pat Tabler .05 .02
334 Kevin Gross .05 .02
335 Dave Henderson .05 .02
336 Greg Anthony RC .10 .03
337 Alejandro Pena .05 .02
338 Shawn Abner .05 .02
339 Tom Browning .05 .02
340 Otis Nixon .05 .02
341 Bob Geren .05 .02
342 Tim Spehr .05 .02
343 John Vander Wal .05 .02
344 Jack Daugherty .05 .02
345 Zane Smith .05 .02
346 Rheal Cormier .05 .02
347 Kent Hrbek .10 .03
348 Rick Wilkins .05 .02
349 Steve Lyons .05 .02
350 Gregg Olson .05 .02
351 Greg Riddoch MG .05 .02
352 Ed Nunez .05 .02
353 Braulio Castillo .05 .02
354 Dave Bergman .05 .02
355 Warren Newson .05 .02
356 Luis Quinones .05 .02
357 Mike Witt .05 .02
358 Ted Wood .05 .02
359 Mike Moore .05 .02
360 Lance Parrish .05 .02
361 Barry Jones .05 .02
362 Javier Ortiz .05 .02
363 John Candelaria .05 .02
364 Glenallen Hill .05 .02
365 Duane Ward .05 .02
366 Checklist 265-396 .05 .02
367 Rafael Belliard .05 .02
368 Bill Krueger .05 .02
369 Steve Whitaker RC .10 .03
370 Shawon Dunston .05 .02
371 Dante Bichette .10 .03
372 Kip Gross .05 .02
373 Don Robinson .05 .02
374 Bernie Williams .15 .04
375 Bert Blyleven .10 .03
376 Chris Donnels .05 .02
377 Bob Zupcic RC .10 .03
378 Joel Skinner .05 .02
379 Steve Chitren .05 .02
380 Barry Bonds .60 .18
381 Sparky Anderson MG .10 .03
382 Sid Fernandez .05 .02
383 Dave Hollins .05 .02
384 Mark Lee .05 .02
385 Tim Wallach .05 .02
386 Will Clark AS .10 .03
387 Ryne Sandberg AS .25 .07
388 Howard Johnson AS .05 .02
389 Barry Larkin AS .10 .03
390 Barry Bonds AS .30 .09
391 Ron Gant AS .05 .02
392 Bobby Bonilla AS .05 .02
393 Craig Biggio AS .10 .03
394 Dennis Martinez AS .05 .02
395 Tom Glavine AS .10 .03
396 Lee Smith AS .05 .02
397 Cecil Fielder AS .05 .02
398 Julio Franco AS .05 .02
399 Wade Boggs AS .10 .03
400 Cal Ripken AS .40 .12
401 Jose Canseco AS .25 .07
402 Joe Carter AS .05 .02
403 Ruben Sierra AS .05 .02
404 Matt Nokes AS .05 .02
405 Roger Clemens AS .25 .07
406 Jim Abbott AS .10 .03
407 Bryan Harvey AS .05 .02
408 Bob Milacki .05 .02
409 Geno Petralli .05 .02
410 Dave Stewart .10 .03
411 Mike Jackson .05 .02
412 Luis Aquino .05 .02
413 Tim Teufel .05 .02
414 Jeff Ware .05 .02
415 Jim Deshaies .05 .02
416 Ellis Burks .10 .03
417 Allan Anderson .05 .02
418 Alfredo Griffin .05 .02
419 Wally Whitehurst .05 .02
420 Sandy Alomar Jr. .05 .02
421 Juan Agosto .05 .02
422 Sam Horn .05 .02
423 Jeff Fassero .05 .02
424 Paul McClellan .05 .02
425 Cecil Fielder .10 .03
426 Tim Raines .10 .03
427 Eddie Taubensee RC .25 .07
428 Dennis Boyd .05 .02
429 Tony LaRussa MG .10 .03
430 Steve Sax .05 .02
431 Tom Gordon .05 .02
432 Billy Hatcher .05 .02
433 Cal Eldred .05 .02
434 Wally Backman .05 .02
435 Mark Eichhorn .05 .02
436 Mookie Wilson .10 .03
437 Scott Servais .05 .02
438 Mike Maddux .05 .02
439 Chico Walker .05 .02
440 Doug Drabek .05 .02
441 Rob Deer .05 .02
442 Dave West .05 .02
443 Spike Owen .05 .02
444 Tyrone Hill RC .10 .03
445 Matt Williams .10 .03
446 Mark Lewis .05 .02
447 David Segui .05 .02
448 Tom Pagnozzi .05 .02
449 Jeff Johnson .05 .02
450 Mark McGwire .60 .18
451 Tom Henke .05 .02
452 Wilson Alvarez .05 .02
453 Gary Redus .05 .02
454 Darren Holmes .05 .02
455 Pete O'Brien .05 .02
456 Pat Combs .05 .02
457 Hubie Brooks .05 .02
458 Frank Tanana .05 .02
459 Tom Kelly MG .05 .02
460 Andre Dawson .10 .03
461 Doug Jones .05 .02
462 Rich Rodriguez .05 .02
463 Mike Simms .05 .02
464 Mike Jeffcoat .05 .02
465 Barry Larkin .15 .04
466 Stan Belinda .05 .02
467 Lonnie Smith .05 .02
468 Greg Harris .05 .02
469 Jim Eisenreich .05 .02
470 Pedro Guerrero .10 .03
471 Jose DeJesus .05 .02
472 Rich Rowland RC .10 .03
473 Frank Bolick .05 .02
Craig Paquette
Tom Redington
Paul Russo UER
(Line around top border)
474 Mike Rossiter RC .10 .03
475 Robby Thompson .05 .02
476 Randy Bush .05 .02
477 Greg Hibbard .05 .02
478 Dale Sveum .05 .02
479 Chito Martinez .05 .02
480 Scott Sanderson .05 .02
481 Tino Martinez .15 .04
482 Jimmy Key .10 .03
483 Terry Shumpert .05 .02
484 Mike Hartley .05 .02
485 Chris Sabo .05 .02
486 Bob Walk .05 .02
487 John Cerutti .05 .02
488 Scott Cooper .05 .02
489 Bobby Cox MG .10 .03
490 Julio Franco .10 .03
491 Jeff Brantley .05 .02
492 Mike Devereaux .05 .02
493 Jose Offerman .05 .02
494 Gary Thurman .05 .02
495 Carney Lansford .10 .03
496 Joe Grahe .05 .02
497 Andy Ashby .05 .02
498 Gerald Perry .05 .02
499 Dave Otto .05 .02
500 Vince Coleman .05 .02
501 Rob Mallicoat .05 .02
502 Greg Briley .05 .02
503 Pascual Perez .05 .02
504 Aaron Sele RC .40 .12
505 Bobby Thigpen .05 .02
506 Todd Benzinger .05 .02
507 Candy Maldonado .05 .02
508 Bill Gullickson .05 .02
509 Doug Dascenzo .05 .02
510 Frank Viola .10 .03
511 Kenny Rogers .10 .03
512 Mike Heath .05 .02
513 Kevin Bass .05 .02
514 Kim Batiste .05 .02
515 Delino DeShields .05 .02
516 Ed Sprague .05 .02
517 Jim Gott .05 .02
518 Jose Melendez .05 .02
519 Hal McRae MG .10 .03
520 Jeff Bagwell .25 .07
521 Joe Hesketh .05 .02
522 Milt Cuyler .05 .02
523 Shawn Hillegas .05 .02
524 Don Slaught .05 .02
525 Randy Johnson .25 .07
526 Doug Piatt .05 .02
527 Checklist 397-528 .05 .02
528 Steve Foster .05 .02
529 Joe Girardi .05 .02
530 Jim Abbott .15 .04
531 Larry Walker .15 .04
532 Mike Huff .05 .02
533 Mackey Sasser .05 .02
534 Benji Gil RC .25 .07
535 Dave Stieb .05 .02
536 Willie Wilson .05 .02
537 Mark Leiter .05 .02
538 Jose Uribe .05 .02
539 Thomas Howard .05 .02
540 Ben McDonald .05 .02
541 Jose Tolentino .05 .02
542 Keith Mitchell .05 .02
543 Jerome Walton .05 .02
544 Cliff Brantley .05 .02
545 Andy Van Slyke .10 .03
546 Paul Sorrento .05 .02
547 Herm Winningham .05 .02
548 Mark Guthrie .05 .02
549 Joe Torre MG .10 .03
550 Darryl Strawberry .10 .03
551 Wilfredo Cordero .25 .07
Chipper Jones
Manny Alexander
Alex Arias UER
(No line around top border)
552 Dave Gallagher .05 .02
553 Edgar Martinez .15 .04
554 Donald Harris .05 .02
555 Frank Thomas .25 .07
556 Storm Davis .05 .02
557 Dickie Thon .05 .02
558 Scott Garrelts .05 .02
559 Steve Olin .05 .02
560 Rickey Henderson .25 .07
561 Jose Vizcaino .05 .02
562 Wade Taylor .05 .02
563 Pat Borders .05 .02
564 Jimmy Gonzalez RC .10 .03
565 Lee Smith .10 .03
566 Bill Sampen .05 .02
567 Dean Palmer .10 .03
568 Bryan Harvey .05 .02
569 Tony Pena .05 .02
570 Lou Whitaker .10 .03
571 Randy Tomlin .05 .02
572 Greg Vaughn .05 .02
573 Kelly Downs .05 .02
574 Steve Avery UER .05 .02
(Should be 13 games for Durham in 1989)
575 Kirby Puckett .25 .07
576 Heathcliff Slocumb .05 .02
577 Kevin Seitzer .05 .02
578 Lee Guetterman .05 .02
579 Johnny Oates MG .05 .02
580 Greg Maddux .40 .12
581 Stan Javier .05 .02
582 Vicente Palacios .05 .02
583 Mel Rojas .05 .02
584 Wayne Rosenthal RC .10 .03
585 Lenny Webster .05 .02
586 Rod Nichols .05 .02
587 Mickey Morandini .05 .02
588 Russ Swan .05 .02
589 Mariano Duncan .05 .02
590 Howard Johnson .05 .02
591 Jeromy Burnitz .10 .03
Jacob Brumfield
Alan Cockrell
D.J. Dozier
592 Denny Neagle .10 .03
593 Steve Decker .05 .02
594 Brian Barber RC .10 .03
595 Bruce Hurst .05 .02
596 Kent Mercker .05 .02
597 Mike Magnante RC .10 .03
598 Jody Reed .05 .02
599 Steve Searcy .05 .02
600 Paul Molitor .15 .04
601 Dave Smith .05 .02
602 Mike Fetters .05 .02
603 Luis Mercedes .05 .02
604 Chris Gwynn .05 .02
605 Scott Erickson .05 .02
606 Brook Jacoby .05 .02
607 Todd Stottlemyre .05 .02
608 Scott Bradley .05 .02
609 Mike Hargrove MG .10 .03
610 Eric Davis .10 .03
611 Brian Hunter .05 .02
612 Pat Kelly .05 .02
613 Pedro Munoz .05 .02
614 Al Osuna .05 .02
615 Matt Merullo .05 .02
616 Larry Andersen .05 .02
617 Junior Ortiz .05 .02
618 Cesar Hernandez .05 .02
Steve Hosey
Jeff McNeely
Dan Peltier
619 Danny Jackson .05 .02
620 George Brett .60 .18
621 Dan Gakeler .05 .02
622 Steve Buechele .05 .02
623 Bob Tewksbury .05 .02
624 Shawn Estes RC .25 .07
625 Kevin McReynolds .05 .02
626 Chris Haney .05 .02
627 Mike Sharperson .05 .02
628 Mark Williamson .05 .02
629 Wally Joyner .10 .03
630 Carlton Fisk .15 .04
631 Armando Reynoso RC .25 .07
632 Felix Fermin .05 .02
633 Mitch Williams .05 .02
634 Manuel Lee .05 .02
635 Harold Baines .10 .03
636 Greg Harris .05 .02
637 Orlando Merced .05 .02
638 Chris Bosio .05 .02
639 Wayne Housie .05 .02
640 Xavier Hernandez .05 .02
641 David Howard .05 .02
642 Tim Crews .05 .02
643 Rick Cerone .05 .02
644 Terry Leach .05 .02
645 Deion Sanders .15 .04
646 Craig Wilson .05 .02
647 Marquis Grissom .10 .03
648 Scott Fletcher .05 .02
649 Norm Charlton .05 .02
650 Jesse Barfield .05 .02
651 Joe Slusarski .05 .02
652 Bobby Rose .05 .02
653 Dennis Lamp .05 .02
654 Allen Watson RC .10 .03
655 Brett Butler .10 .03
656 Rudy Pemberton .10 .03
Henry Rodriguez
Lee Tinsley RC
Gerald Williams
657 Dave Johnson .05 .02
658 Checklist 529-660 .05 .02
659 Brian McRae .05 .02
660 Fred McGriff .15 .04
661 Bill Landrum .05 .02
662 Juan Guzman .05 .02
663 Greg Gagne .05 .02
664 Ken Hill .05 .02
665 Dave Haas .05 .02
666 Tom Foley .05 .02
667 Roberto Hernandez .05 .02
668 Dwayne Henry .05 .02
669 Jim Fregosi MG .05 .02
670 Harold Reynolds .10 .03
671 Mark Whiten .05 .02
672 Eric Plunk .05 .02
673 Todd Hundley .05 .02
674 Mo Sanford .05 .02
675 Bobby Witt .05 .02
676 Sam Militello .25 .07
Pat Mahomes RC
Turk Wendell
Roger Salkeld
677 John Marzano .05 .02
678 Joe Klink .05 .02
679 Pete Incaviglia .05 .02
680 Dale Murphy .25 .07
681 Rene Gonzales .05 .02
682 Andy Benes .05 .02
683 Jim Poole .05 .02
684 Trever Miller RC .10 .03
685 Scott Livingstone .05 .02
686 Rich DeLucia .05 .02
687 Harvey Pulliam .05 .02
688 Tim Belcher .05 .02
689 Mark Lemke .05 .02
690 John Franco .10 .03
691 Walt Weiss .05 .02
692 Scott Ruskin .05 .02
693 Jeff King .05 .02
694 Mike Gardiner .05 .02
695 Gary Sheffield .10 .03
696 Joe Boever .05 .02
697 Mike Felder .05 .02
698 John Habyan .05 .02
699 Cito Gaston MG .05 .02
700 Ruben Sierra .05 .02
701 Scott Radinsky .05 .02
702 Lee Stevens .05 .02
703 Mark Wohlers .05 .02
704 Curt Young .05 .02
705 Dwight Evans .10 .03
706 Rob Murphy .05 .02
707 Gregg Jefferies .05 .02
708 Tom Bolton .05 .02
709 Chris James .05 .02
710 Kevin Maas .05 .02
711 Ricky Bones .05 .02
712 Curt Wilkerson .05 .02
713 Roger McDowell .05 .02
714 Pokey Reese RC .40 .12
715 Craig Biggio .15 .04
716 Kirk Dressendorfer .05 .02
717 Ken Dayley .05 .02
718 B.J. Surhoff .10 .03
719 Terry Mulholland .05 .02
720 Kirk Gibson .10 .03
721 Mike Pagliarulo .05 .02
722 Walt Terrell .05 .02
723 Jose Oquendo .05 .02
724 Kevin Morton .05 .02
725 Dwight Gooden .10 .03
726 Kirt Manwaring .05 .02
727 Chuck McElroy .05 .02
728 Dave Burba .05 .02
729 Art Howe MG .05 .02
730 Ramon Martinez .05 .02

731 Donnie Hill .05 .02
732 Nelson Santovenia .05 .02
733 Bob Melvin .05 .02
734 Scott Hatteberg RC .25 .07
735 Greg Swindell .05 .02
736 Lance Johnson .05 .02
737 Kevin Reimer .05 .02
738 Dennis Eckersley .10 .03
739 Rob Ducey .05 .02
740 Ken Caminiti .10 .03
741 Mark Gubicza .05 .02
742 Bill Spiers .05 .02
743 Darren Lewis .05 .02
744 Chris Hammond .05 .02
745 Dave Magadan .05 .02
746 Bernard Gilkey .05 .02
747 Willie Banks .05 .02
748 Matt Nokes .05 .02
749 Jerald Clark .05 .02
750 Travis Fryman .10 .03
751 Steve Wilson .05 .02
752 Billy Ripken .05 .02
753 Paul Assenmacher .05 .02
754 Charlie Hayes .05 .02
755 Alex Fernandez .05 .02
756 Gary Pettis .05 .02
757 Rob Dibble .10 .03
758 Tim Naehring .05 .02
759 Jeff Torborg MG .05 .02
760 Ozzie Smith .40 .12
761 Mike Fitzgerald .05 .02
762 John Burkett .05 .02
763 Kyle Abbott .05 .02
764 Tyler Green RC .10 .03
765 Pete Harnisch .05 .02
766 Mark Davis .05 .02
767 Kal Daniels .05 .02
768 Jim Thome .25 .07
769 Jack Howell .05 .02
770 Sid Bream .05 .02
771 Arthur Rhodes .05 .02
772 Garry Templeton UER .05 .02
(Stat heading in for pitchers)
773 Hal Morris .05 .02
774 Bud Black .05 .02
775 Ivan Calderon .05 .02
776 Doug Henry RC .10 .03
777 John Olerud .10 .03
778 Tim Leary .05 .02
779 Jay Bell .10 .03
780 Eddie Murray .25 .07
781 Paul Abbott .05 .02
782 Phil Plantier .05 .02
783 Joe Magrane .05 .02
784 Ken Patterson .05 .02
785 Albert Belle .10 .03
786 Royce Clayton .05 .02
787 Checklist 661-792 .05 .02
788 Mike Stanton .05 .02
789 Bobby Valentine MG .05 .02
790 Joe Carter .10 .03
791 Danny Cox .05 .02
792 Dave Winfield .10 .03

1992 Topps Gold

Topps produced a 792-card Topps Gold factory set packaged in a foil display box. Only this set contained an additional card of Brien Taylor, numbered 793 and hand signed by him. The production run was 12,000 sets. The Topps Gold cards were also available in regular series packs. According to Topps, on average collectors would find one Topps Gold card in every 36 wax packs, one in every 18 cello packs, one in every 12 rak packs, five per Vending box, one in every six jumbo packs, and ten per regular factory set. The checklist cards in the regular set were replaced with six individual Rookie player cards (131, 264, 366, 527, 658, 787) in the gold set. There were a number of uncorrected errors in the Gold set. Steve Finley (86) has gold band indicating he is Mark Davidson of the Astros. Andujar Cedeno (288) is listed as a member of the New York Yankees. Mike Huff (532) is listed as a member of the Boston Red Sox. Barry Larkin (465) is listed as a member of the Houston Astros but is correctly listed as a member of the Cincinnati Reds on his Gold Winners cards. Typically the individual cards are sold at a multiple of the player's respective value in the regular set.

Nm-Mt Ex-Mt
COMPLETE SET (792) 80.00 24.00
COMP.FACT.SET (793) 80.00 24.00
*STARS: 6X TO 15X BASIC CARDS
*ROOKIES: 4X TO 10X BASIC CARDS
131 Terry Mathews .75 .23
264 Rod Beck .75 .23
366 Tony Perezchica .75 .23
527 Terry McDaniel .75 .23
658 John Ramos .75 .23
787 Brian Williams .75 .23
793 B. Taylor AU/12000 15.00 4.50

1992 Topps Gold Winners

The 1992 Topps baseball card packs featured "Match-the-Stats" game cards in which the consumer could save "Runs". For 2.00 and every 100 Runs saved in this game, the consumer could receive through a mail-in offer ten Topps Gold cards. These particular Topps Gold cards carry the word "Winner" in gold foil on the card front. The checklist cards in the regular set were replaced with six individual Rookie player cards (131, 264, 366, 527, 658, 787) in the gold set. Typically the individual cards are sold at a multiple of the player's respective value in the regular set. The Gold winner promotion was very popular and the cards are in noticably larger supply than the basic Gold parallels. It did not hurt the supply of Winnner cards collectors could hold their cards up to the light to see which were the correct answers. Later printing of 1992 game cards were fixed so collectors could not cheat to get the answers.

Nm-Mt Ex-Mt
COMPLETE SET (792) 40.00 12.00
*STARS: 1.25X TO 3X BASIC CARDS
*ROOKIES: 1.25X TO 3X BASIC CARDS

131 Terry Mathews .15 .04
264 Rod Beck .15 .04
366 Tony Perezchica .15 .04
527 Terry McDaniel .15 .04
658 John Ramos .15 .04
787 Brian Williams .15 .04

1992 Topps Traded

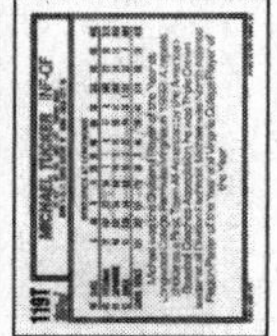

The 1992 Topps Traded set comprises 132 standard-size cards. The set was distributed exclusively in factory set form through hobby dealers. As in past editions, the set focuses on promising rookies, new managers, and players who changed teams. The set also includes a Team U.S.A. subset, featuring 25 of America's top college players and the Team U.S.A. coach. Card design is identical to the regular issue 1992 Topps cards except for the T-suffixed numbering. The cards are arranged in alphabetical order by player's last name. The key Rookie Cards in this set are Nomar Garciaparra, Brian Jordan and Jason Varitek.

Nm-Mt Ex-Mt
COMP.FACT.SET (132) 60.00 18.00
1T Willie Adams USA RC .25 .07
2T Jeff Alkire USA RC .25 .07
3T Felipe Alou MG .20 .06
4T Moises Alou .20 .06
5T Ruben Amaro .10 .03
6T Jack Armstrong .10 .03
7T Scott Bankhead .10 .03
8T Tim Belcher .10 .03
9T George Bell .10 .03
10T Freddie Benavides .10 .03
11T Todd Benzinger .10 .03
12T Joe Boever .10 .03
13T Ricky Bones .10 .03
14T Bobby Bonilla .20 .06
15T Hubie Brooks .10 .03
16T Jerry Browne .10 .03
17T Jim Bullinger .10 .03
18T Dave Burba .10 .03
19T Kevin Campbell .10 .03
20T Tom Candiotti .10 .03
21T Mark Carreon .10 .03
22T Gary Carter .20 .06
23T Archi Cianfrocco RC .10 .03
24T Phil Clark .10 .03
25T Chad Curtis RC .40 .12
26T Eric Davis .20 .06
27T Tim Davis USA RC .25 .07
28T Gary DiSarcina .10 .03
29T Darren Dreifort USA .10 .03
30T Mariano Duncan .10 .03
31T Mike Fitzgerald .10 .03
32T John Flaherty .10 .03
33T Darrin Fletcher .10 .03
34T Scott Fletcher .10 .03
35T R.Fraser CO USA RC .25 .07
36T Andres Galarraga .20 .06
37T Dave Gallagher .10 .03
38T Mike Gallego .10 .03
39T Nomar Garciaparra 50.00 15.00
USA RC
40T Jason Giambi USA 1.00 .30
41T Danny Gladden .10 .03
42T Rene Gonzales .10 .03
43T Jeff Granger USA .10 .03
44T Rick Greene USA RC .25 .07
45T J.Hammonds USA .20 .06
46T Charlie Hayes .10 .03
47T Von Hayes .10 .03
48T Rick Helling USA .10 .03
49T Butch Henry RC .10 .03
50T Carlos Hernandez .10 .03
51T Ken Hill .10 .03
52T Butch Hobson .10 .03
53T Vince Horsman .10 .03
54T Pete Incaviglia .10 .03
55T Gregg Jefferies .10 .03
56T Charles Johnson USA .20 .06
57T Doug Jones .10 .03
58T Brian Jordan RC .75 .23
59T Wally Joyner .20 .06
60T D.Kirkreit USA RC .25 .07
61T Bill Krueger .10 .03
62T Gene Lamont MG .10 .03
63T Jim Lefebvre MG .10 .03
64T Danny Leon .10 .03
65T Pat Listach RC .40 .12
66T Kenny Lofton .30 .09
67T Dave Martinez .10 .03
68T Derrick May .10 .03
69T Kirk McCaskill .10 .03
70T C.McConnell USA RC .25 .07
71T Kevin McReynolds .10 .03
72T Rusty Meacham .10 .03
73T Keith Miller .10 .03
74T Kevin Mitchell .10 .03
75T Jason Moler USA RC .25 .07
76T Mike Morgan .10 .03
77T Jack Morris .20 .06
78T C.Murray USA RC .75 .23
79T Eddie Murray .50 .15
80T Randy Myers .10 .03
81T Denny Neagle .20 .06
82T Phil Nevin USA .30 .09
83T Dave Nilsson .10 .03
84T Junior Ortiz .10 .03
85T Donovan Osborne .10 .03
86T Bill Pecota .10 .03
87T Melido Perez .10 .03
88T Mike Perez .10 .03
89T Hipolito Pichardo RC .10 .03
90T Willie Randolph .20 .06
91T Darren Reed .10 .03
92T Bip Roberts .10 .03
93T Chris Roberts USA .10 .03
94T Steve Rodriguez USA .10 .03
95T Bruce Ruffin .10 .03
96T Scott Ruskin .10 .03
97T Bret Saberhagen .20 .06
98T Rey Sanchez RC .40 .12
99T Steve Sax .10 .03
100T Curt Schilling .30 .09
101T Dick Schofield .10 .03
102T Gary Scott .10 .03
103T Kevin Seitzer .10 .03
104T Frank Seminara RC .10 .03
105T Gary Sheffield .20 .06
106T John Smiley .10 .03
107T Cory Snyder .10 .03
108T Paul Sorrento .10 .03
109T Sammy Sosa 1.50 .45
110T Matt Stairs RC .50 .15
111T Andy Stankiewicz .10 .03
112T Kurt Stillwell .10 .03
113T Rick Sutcliffe .20 .06
114T Bill Swift .10 .03
115T Jeff Tackett .10 .03
116T Danny Tartabull .10 .03
117T Eddie Taubensee .20 .06
118T Dickie Thon .10 .03
119T M.Tucker USA RC 1.50 .45
120T Scooter Tucker .10 .03
121T Marc Valdes USA RC .25 .07
122T Julio Valera .10 .03
123T J.Varitek USA RC 8.00 2.40
124T Ron Villone USA RC .25 .07
125T Frank Viola .20 .06
126T B.J. Wallace USA RC .25 .07
127T Dan Walters .10 .03
128T Craig Wilson USA .10 .03
129T Chris Wimmer USA .10 .03
130T Dave Winfield .20 .06
131T Herm Winningham .10 .03
132T Checklist 1T-132T .10 .03

1992 Topps Traded Gold

This 132 card standard-size set parallels the regular 1992 Topps Traded set. It was only issued through the Topps dealer network. Six thousand of these sets were produced and the only player difference is that Kerry Woodson replaces the checklist card

Nm-Mt Ex-Mt
COMP.FACT.SET (132) 100.00 30.00
*GOLD STARS: 1.5X TO 4X BASIC CARDS
*GOLD RC's: .75X TO 2X BASIC CARDS

1992 Topps Debut '91

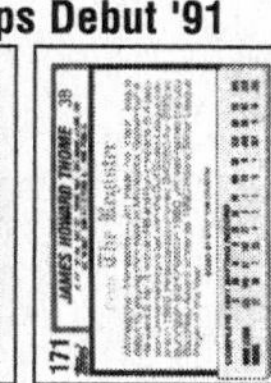

The 1991 Topps Debut '91 set contains 194 standard-size cards. The fronts feature a mix of either posed or action glossy color player photos, framed with two color border stripes on a white card face. Future MVP's Jeff Bagwell, Ivan Rodriguez and Mo Vaughn along with Vinny Castilla and Mike Mussina are among the featured players in the set.

Nm-Mt Ex-Mt
COMP.FACT.SET (194) 15.00 4.50
1 Kyle Abbott .25 .07
2 Dana Allison .25 .07
3 Rich Amaral .25 .07
4 Ruben Amaro .25 .07
5 Andy Ashby .25 .07
6 Jim Austin .25 .07
7 Jeff Bagwell 2.00 .60
8 Jeff Banister .25 .07
9 Willie Banks .25 .07
10 Bret Barberie .25 .07
11 Kim Batiste .25 .07
12 Chris Beasley .25 .07
13 Rod Beck .50 .15
14 Derek Bell .50 .15
15 Esteban Beltre .25 .07
16 Freddie Benavides .25 .07
17 Ricky Bones .25 .07
18 Denis Boucher .25 .07
19 Ryan Bowen .25 .07
20 Cliff Brantley .25 .07
21 John Briscoe .25 .07
22 Scott Brosius 2.00 .60
23 Terry Bross .25 .07
24 Jarvis Brown .25 .07
25 Scott Bullett .25 .07
26 Kevin Campbell .25 .07
27 Amalio Carreno .25 .07
28 Matias Carrillo .25 .07
29 Jeff Carter .25 .07
30 Vinny Castilla 2.50 .75
31 Braulio Castillo .25 .07
32 Frank Castillo .25 .07
33 Darrin Chapin .25 .07
34 Mike Christopher .25 .07
35 Mark Clark .50 .15
36 Royce Clayton .25 .07
37 Stu Cole .25 .07
38 Gary Cooper .25 .07
39 Archie Corbin .25 .07
40 Rheal Cormier .25 .07
41 Chris Cron .25 .07
42 Mike Dalton .25 .07
43 Mark Davis .25 .07
44 Francisco de la Rosa .25 .07
45 Chris Donnels .25 .07
46 Brian Drahman .25 .07
47 Tom Drees .25 .07
48 Kirk Dressendorfer .25 .07
49 Bruce Egloff .25 .07
50 Cal Eldred .25 .07
51 Jose Escobar .25 .07
52 Tony Eusebio .50 .15
53 Hector Fajardo .25 .07
54 Monty Fariss .25 .07
55 Jeff Fassero .25 .07
56 Dave Fleming .25 .07
57 Kevin Flora .25 .07
58 Steve Foster .25 .07
59 Dan Gakeler .25 .07
60 Ramon Garcia .25 .07
61 Chris Gardner .25 .07
62 Jeff Gardner .25 .07
63 Chris George .25 .07
64 Ray Giannelli .25 .07
65 Tom Goodwin .25 .07
66 Mark Grater .25 .07
67 Johnny Guzman .25 .07
68 Juan Guzman .25 .07
69 Dave Haas .25 .07
70 Chris Haney .25 .07
71 Shawn Hare .25 .07
72 Donald Harris .25 .07
73 Doug Henry .25 .07
74 Pat Hentgen .25 .07
75 Gil Heredia .50 .15
76 Jeremy Hernandez .25 .07
77 Jose Hernandez 1.00 .30
78 Roberto Hernandez .25 .07
79 Bryan Hickerson .25 .07
80 Milt Hill .25 .07
81 Vince Horsman .25 .07
82 Wayne Housie .25 .07
83 Chris Howard .25 .07
84 David Howard .25 .07
85 Mike Humphreys .25 .07
86 Brian Hunter .25 .07
87 Jim Hunter .25 .07
88 Mike Ignasiak .25 .07
89 Reggie Jefferson .25 .07
90 Jeff Johnson .25 .07
91 Joel Johnston .25 .07
92 Calvin Jones .25 .07
93 Chris Jones .25 .07
94 Stacy Jones .25 .07
95 Jeff Juden .25 .07
96 Scott Kamieniecki .25 .07
97 Eric Karros .50 .15
98 Pat Kelly .25 .07
99 John Kiely .25 .07
100 Darryl Kile .50 .15
101 Wayne Kirby .25 .07
102 Garland Kiser .25 .07
103 Chuck Knoblauch .50 .15
104 Randy Knorr .25 .07
105 Tom Kramer .25 .07
106 Ced Landrum .25 .07
107 Patrick Lennon .25 .07
108 Jim Lewis .25 .07
109 Mark Lewis .25 .07
110 Doug Lindsey .25 .07
111 Scott Livingstone .25 .07
112 Kenny Lofton 1.00 .30
113 Ever Magallanes .25 .07
114 Mike Magnante .25 .07
115 Barry Manuel .25 .07
116 Josias Manzanillo .25 .07
117 Chito Martinez .25 .07
118 Terry Mathews .25 .07
119 Rob Maurer .25 .07
120 Tim Mauser .25 .07
121 Terry McDaniel .25 .07
122 Rusty Meacham .25 .07
123 Luis Mercedes .25 .07
124 Paul Miller .25 .07
125 Keith Mitchell .25 .07
126 Bobby Moore .25 .07
127 Kevin Morton .25 .07
128 Andy Mota .25 .07
129 Jose Mota .25 .07
130 Mike Mussina 2.00 .60
131 Jeff Mutis .25 .07
132 Denny Neagle .50 .15
133 Warren Newson .25 .07
134 Jim Olander .25 .07
135 Erik Pappas .25 .07
136 Jorge Pedre .25 .07
137 Yorkis Perez .25 .07
138 Mark Petkovsek .25 .07
139 Doug Piatt .25 .07
140 Jeff Plympton .25 .07
141 Harvey Pulliam .25 .07
142 John Ramos .25 .07
143 Mike Remlinger .25 .07
144 Laddie Renfroe .25 .07
145 Armando Reynoso .50 .15
146 Arthur Rhodes .25 .07
147 Pat Rice .25 .07
148 Nikco Riesgo .25 .07
149 Carlos Rodriguez .25 .07
150 Ivan Rodriguez 2.00 .60
151 Wayne Rosenthal .25 .07
152 Rico Rossy .25 .07
153 Stan Royer .25 .07
154 Rey Sanchez .50 .15
155 Reggie Sanders .25 .07
156 Mo Sanford .25 .07
157 Bob Scanlan .25 .07
158 Pete Schourek .25 .07
159 Gary Scott .25 .07
160 Tim Scott .25 .07
161 Tony Scruggs .25 .07
162 Scott Servais .25 .07
163 Doug Simons .25 .07
164 Heathcliff Slocumb .25 .07
165 Joe Slusarski .25 .07
166 Tim Spehr .25 .07
167 Ed Sprague .25 .07
168 Jeff Tackett .25 .07
169 Eddie Taubensee .50 .15
170 Wade Taylor .25 .07
171 Jim Thome 2.00 .60
172 Mike Timlin .25 .07
173 Jose Tolentino .25 .07
174 John Vander Wal .25 .07
175 Todd Van Poppel .25 .07
176 Mo Vaughn .50 .15
177 Dave Wainhouse .25 .07
178 Don Wakamatsu .25 .07
179 Bruce Walton .25 .07
180 Kevin Ward .25 .07
181 Dave Weathers .25 .07
182 Eric Wedge .25 .07
183 John Wehner .25 .07
184 Rick Wilkins .25 .07
185 Bernie Williams 1.00 .30
186 Brian Williams .25 .07
187 Ron Witmeyer .25 .07
188 Mark Wohlers .25 .07
189 Ted Wood .25 .07
190 Anthony Young .25 .07
191 Eddie Zosky .25 .07
192 Bob Zupcic .25 .07
193 Checklist 1 .25 .07
194 Checklist 2 .25 .07

1993 Topps

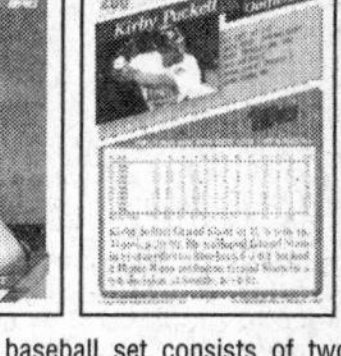

The 1993 Topps baseball set consists of two series, respectively, of 396 and 429 standard-size cards. A Topps Gold card was inserted in every 15-card pack. In addition, hobby and retail factory sets were produced. The fronts feature color action player photos with white borders. The player's name appears in a stripe at the bottom of the picture, and this stripe and two short diagonal stripes at the bottom corners of the picture are team color-coded. The backs are colorful and carry a color head shot, biography, complete statistical information, with a career highlight if space permitted. Cards 401-411 comprise an All-Star subset. Rookie Cards in this set include Jim Edmonds, Derek Jeter and Jason Kendall.

Nm-Mt Ex-Mt
COMPLETE SET (825) 40.00 12.00
COMP.HOBBY.SET (847) 50.00 15.00
COMP.RETAIL.SET (838) 40.00 12.00
COMP. SERIES 1 (396) 20.00 6.00
COMP.SERIES 2 (429) 20.00 6.00
1 Robin Yount .75 .23
2 Barry Bonds 1.25 .35
3 Ryne Sandberg .75 .23
4 Roger Clemens 1.00 .30
5 Tony Gwynn .60 .18
6 Jeff Tackett .10 .03
7 Pete Incaviglia .10 .03
8 Mark Wohlers .10 .03
9 Kent Hrbek .20 .06
10 Will Clark .50 .15
11 Eric Karros .20 .06
12 Lee Smith .20 .06
13 Esteban Beltre .10 .03
14 Greg Briley .10 .03
15 Marquis Grissom .20 .06
16 Dan Plesac .10 .03
17 Dave Hollins .10 .03
18 Terry Steinbach .10 .03
19 Ed Nunez .10 .03
20 Tim Salmon .30 .09
21 Luis Salazar .10 .03
22 Jim Eisenreich .10 .03
23 Todd Stottlemyre .10 .03
24 Tim Naehring .10 .03
25 John Franco .20 .06
26 Skeeter Barnes .10 .03
27 Carlos Garcia .10 .03
28 Joe Orsulak .10 .03
29 Dwayne Henry .10 .03
30 Fred McGriff .30 .09
31 Derek Lilliquist .10 .03
32 Don Mattingly 1.25 .35
33 B.J. Wallace .10 .03
34 Juan Gonzalez .30 .09
35 John Smoltz .30 .09
36 Scott Servais .10 .03
37 Lenny Webster .10 .03
38 Chris James .10 .03
39 Roger McDowell .10 .03
40 Ozzie Smith .75 .23
41 Alex Fernandez .10 .03
42 Spike Owen .10 .03
43 Ruben Amaro .10 .03
44 Kevin Seitzer .10 .03
45 Dave Fleming .10 .03
46 Eric Fox .10 .03
47 Bob Scanlan .10 .03
48 Bert Blyleven .20 .06
49 Brian McRae .10 .03
50 Roberto Alomar .30 .09
51 Mo Vaughn .20 .06
52 Bobby Bonilla .20 .06
53 Frank Tanana .10 .03
54 Mike LaValliere .10 .03
55 Mark McLemore .10 .03
56 Chad Mottola RC .10 .03
57 Norm Charlton .10 .03
58 Jose Melendez .10 .03
59 Carlos Martinez .10 .03
60 Roberto Kelly .10 .03
61 Gene Larkin .10 .03
62 Rafael Belliard .10 .03
63 Al Osuna .10 .03
64 Scott Chiamparino .10 .03
65 Brett Butler .20 .06
66 John Burkett .10 .03
67 Felix Jose .10 .03
68 Omar Vizquel .30 .09
69 John Vander Wal .10 .03
70 Roberto Hernandez .10 .03
71 Ricky Bones .10 .03
72 Jeff Grotewold .10 .03
73 Mike Moore .10 .03
74 Steve Buechele .10 .03
75 Juan Guzman .10 .03
76 Kevin Appier .20 .06
77 Junior Felix .10 .03
78 Greg W. Harris .10 .03
79 Dick Schofield .10 .03
80 Cecil Fielder .20 .06
81 Lloyd McClendon .10 .03

82 David Segui .10 .03
83 Reggie Sanders .10 .03
84 Kurt Stillwell .10 .03
85 Sandy Alomar Jr. .10 .03
86 John Habyan .10 .03
87 Kevin Reimer .10 .03
88 Mike Stanton .10 .03
89 Eric Anthony .10 .03
90 Scott Erickson .10 .03
91 Craig Colbert .10 .03
92 Tom Pagnozzi .10 .03
93 Pedro Astacio .10 .03
94 Lance Johnson .10 .03
95 Larry Walker .30 .09
96 Russ Swan .10 .03
97 Scott Fletcher .10 .03
98 Derek Jeter RC 10.00 3.00
99 Mike Williams .10 .03
100 Mark McGwire 1.25 .35
101 Jim Bullinger .10 .03
102 Brian Hunter .10 .03
103 Jody Reed .10 .03
104 Mike Butcher .10 .03
105 Gregg Jefferies .10 .03
106 Howard Johnson .10 .03
107 John Kiely .10 .03
108 Jose Lind .10 .03
109 Sam Horn .10 .03
110 Barry Larkin .30 .09
111 Bruce Hurst .10 .03
112 Brian Barnes .10 .03
113 Thomas Howard .10 .03
114 Mel Hall .10 .03
115 Robby Thompson .10 .03
116 Mark Lemke .10 .03
117 Eddie Taubensee .10 .03
118 David Hulse RC .10 .03
119 Pedro Munoz .10 .03
120 Ramon Martinez .10 .03
121 Todd Worrell .10 .03
122 Joey Cora .10 .03
123 Moises Alou .20 .06
124 Franklin Stubbs .10 .03
125 Pete O'Brien .10 .03
126 Bob Ayrault .10 .03
127 Carney Lansford .20 .06
128 Kal Daniels .10 .03
129 Joe Grahe .10 .03
130 Jeff Montgomery .10 .03
131 Dave Winfield .20 .06
132 Preston Wilson RC .50 .15
133 Steve Wilson .10 .03
134 Lee Guetterman .10 .03
135 Mickey Tettleton .10 .03
136 Jeff King .10 .03
137 Alan Mills .10 .03
138 Joe Oliver .10 .03
139 Gary Gaetti .20 .06
140 Gary Sheffield .20 .06
141 Dennis Cook .10 .03
142 Charlie Hayes .10 .03
143 Jeff Huson .10 .03
144 Kent Mercker .10 .03
145 Eric Young .10 .03
146 Scott Leius .10 .03
147 Bryan Hickerson .10 .03
148 Steve Finley .20 .06
149 Rheal Cormier .10 .03
150 Frank Thomas UER .50 .15
(Categories leading
league are italicized
but not printed in red)
151 Archi Cianfrocco .10 .03
152 Rich DeLucia .10 .03
153 Greg Vaughn .10 .03
154 Wes Chamberlain .10 .03
155 Dennis Eckersley .20 .06
156 Sammy Sosa .75 .23
157 Gary DiSarcina .10 .03
158 Kevin Koslofski .10 .03
159 Doug Linton .10 .03
160 Lou Whitaker .20 .06
161 Chad McConnell .10 .03
162 Joe Hesketh .10 .03
163 Tim Wakefield .50 .15
164 Leo Gomez .10 .03
165 Jose Rijo .10 .03
166 Tim Scott .10 .03
167 Steve Olin UER .10 .03
(Born 10/4/65
should say 10/10/65)
168 Kevin Maas .10 .03
169 Kenny Rogers .20 .06
170 David Justice .20 .06
171 Doug Jones .10 .03
172 Jeff Reboulet .10 .03
173 Andres Galarraga .20 .06
174 Randy Velarde .10 .03
175 Kirk McCaskill .10 .03
176 Darren Lewis .10 .03
177 Lenny Harris .10 .03
178 Jeff Fassero .10 .03
179 Ken Griffey Jr. .75 .23
180 Darren Daulton .20 .06
181 John Jaha .10 .03
182 Ron Darling .10 .03
183 Greg Maddux .75 .23
184 Damion Easley .10 .03
185 Jack Morris .20 .06
186 Mike Magnante .10 .03
187 John Dopson .10 .03
188 Sid Fernandez .10 .03
189 Tony Phillips .10 .03
190 Doug Drabek .10 .03
191 Sean Lowe RC .10 .03
192 Bob Milacki .10 .03
193 Steve Foster .10 .03
194 Jerald Clark .10 .03
195 Pete Harnisch .10 .03
196 Pat Kelly .10 .03
197 Jeff Frye .10 .03
198 Alejandro Pena .10 .03
199 Junior Ortiz .10 .03
200 Kirby Puckett .50 .15
201 Jose Uribe .10 .03
202 Mike Scioscia .10 .03
203 Bernard Gilkey .10 .03
204 Dan Pasqua .10 .03
205 Gary Carter .20 .06
206 Henry Cotto .10 .03
207 Paul Molitor .30 .09
208 Mike Hartley .10 .03
209 Jeff Parrett .10 .03
210 Mark Langston .10 .03
211 Doug Dascenzo .10 .03
212 Rick Reed .10 .03
213 Candy Maldonado .10 .03
214 Danny Darwin .10 .03
215 Pat Howell .10 .03
216 Mark Leiter .10 .03
217 Kevin Mitchell .10 .03
218 Ben McDonald .10 .03
219 Bip Roberts .10 .03
220 Benny Santiago .20 .06
221 Carlos Baerga .10 .03
222 Bernie Williams .30 .09
223 Roger Pavlik .10 .03
224 Sid Bream .10 .03
225 Matt Williams .20 .06
226 Willie Banks .10 .03
227 Jeff Bagwell .30 .09
228 Tom Goodwin .10 .03
229 Mike Perez .10 .03
230 Carlton Fisk .30 .09
231 John Wetteland .20 .06
232 Tino Martinez .30 .09
233 Rick Greene .10 .03
234 Tim McIntosh .10 .03
235 Mitch Williams .10 .03
236 Kevin Campbell .10 .03
237 Jose Vizcaino .10 .03
238 Chris Donnels .10 .03
239 Mike Boddicker .10 .03
240 John Olerud .20 .06
241 Mike Gardiner .10 .03
242 Charlie O'Brien .10 .03
243 Rob Deer .10 .03
244 Denny Neagle .20 .06
245 Chris Sabo .10 .03
246 Gregg Olson .10 .03
247 Frank Seminara UER .10 .03
(Acquired 12/3/98)
248 Scott Scudder .10 .03
249 Tim Burke .10 .03
250 Chuck Knoblauch .20 .06
251 Mike Bielecki .10 .03
252 Xavier Hernandez .10 .03
253 Jose Guzman .10 .03
254 Cory Snyder .10 .03
255 Orel Hershiser .20 .06
256 Wil Cordero .10 .03
257 Luis Alicea .10 .03
258 Mike Schooler .10 .03
259 Craig Grebeck .10 .03
260 Duane Ward .10 .03
261 Bill Wegman .10 .03
262 Mickey Morandini .10 .03
263 Vince Horsman .10 .03
264 Paul Sorrento .10 .03
265 Andre Dawson .20 .06
266 Rene Gonzales .10 .03
267 Keith Miller .10 .03
268 Derek Bell .10 .03
269 Todd Steverson RC .10 .03
270 Frank Viola .20 .06
271 Wally Whitehurst .10 .03
272 Kurt Knudsen .10 .03
273 Dan Walters .10 .03
274 Rick Sutcliffe .20 .06
275 Andy Van Slyke .20 .06
276 Paul O'Neill .30 .09
277 Mark Whiten .10 .03
278 Chris Nabholz .10 .03
279 Todd Burns .10 .03
280 Tom Glavine .30 .09
281 Butch Henry .10 .03
282 Shane Mack .10 .03
283 Mike Jackson .10 .03
284 Henry Rodriguez .10 .03
285 Bob Tewksbury .10 .03
286 Ron Karkovice .10 .03
287 Mike Gallego .10 .03
288 Dave Cochrane .10 .03
289 Jesse Orosco .10 .03
290 Dave Stewart .20 .06
291 Tommy Greene .10 .03
292 Rey Sanchez .10 .03
293 Rob Ducey .10 .03
294 Brent Mayne .10 .03
295 Dave Stieb .10 .03
296 Luis Rivera .10 .03
297 Jeff Innis .10 .03
298 Scott Livingstone .10 .03
299 Bob Patterson .10 .03
300 Cal Ripken 1.50 .45
301 Cesar Hernandez .10 .03
302 Randy Myers .10 .03
303 Brook Jacoby .10 .03
304 Melido Perez .10 .03
305 Rafael Palmeiro .30 .09
306 Damon Berryhill .10 .03
307 Dan Serafini RC .10 .03
308 Darryl Kile .20 .06
309 J.T. Bruett .10 .03
310 Dave Righetti .20 .06
311 Jay Howell .10 .03
312 Geronimo Pena .10 .03
313 Greg Hibbard .10 .03
314 Mark Gardner .10 .03
315 Edgar Martinez .30 .09
316 Dave Nilsson .10 .03
317 Kyle Abbott .10 .03
318 Willie Wilson .10 .03
319 Paul Assenmacher .10 .03
320 Tim Fortugno .10 .03
321 Rusty Meacham .10 .03
322 Pat Borders .10 .03
323 Mike Greenwell .10 .03
324 Willie Randolph .20 .06
325 Bill Gullickson .10 .03
326 Gary Varsho .10 .03
327 Tim Hulett .10 .03
328 Scott Ruskin .10 .03
329 Mike Maddux .10 .03
330 Danny Tartabull .10 .03
331 Kenny Lofton .20 .06
332 Geno Petralli .10 .03
333 Otis Nixon .10 .03
334 Jason Kendall RC .50 .15
335 Mark Portugal .10 .03
336 Mike Pagliarulo .10 .03
337 Kirt Manwaring .10 .03
338 Bob Ojeda .10 .03
339 Mark Clark .10 .03
340 John Kruk .20 .06
341 Mel Rojas .10 .03
342 Erik Hanson .10 .03
343 Doug Henry .10 .03
344 Jack McDowell .10 .03
345 Harold Baines .20 .06
346 Chuck McElroy .10 .03
347 Luis Sojo .10 .03
348 Andy Stankiewicz .10 .03
349 Hipolito Pichardo .10 .03
350 Joe Carter .20 .06
351 Ellis Burks .20 .06
352 Pete Schourek .10 .03
353 Buddy Groom .10 .03
354 Jay Bell .20 .06
355 Brady Anderson .20 .06
356 Freddie Benavides .10 .03
357 Phil Stephenson .10 .03
358 Kevin Wickander .10 .03
359 Mike Stanley .10 .03
360 Ivan Rodriguez .50 .15
361 Scott Bankhead .10 .03
362 Luis Gonzalez .20 .06
363 John Smiley .10 .03
364 Trevor Wilson .10 .03
365 Tom Candiotti .10 .03
366 Craig Wilson .10 .03
367 Steve Sax .10 .03
368 Delino DeShields .10 .03
369 Jaime Navarro .10 .03
370 Dave Valle .10 .03
371 Mariano Duncan .10 .03
372 Rod Nichols .10 .03
373 Mike Morgan .10 .03
374 Julio Valera .10 .03
375 Wally Joyner .20 .06
376 Tom Henke .10 .03
377 Herm Winningham .10 .03
378 Orlando Merced .10 .03
379 Mike Munoz .10 .03
380 Todd Hundley .10 .03
381 Mike Flanagan .10 .03
382 Tim Belcher .10 .03
383 Jerry Browne .10 .03
384 Mike Benjamin .10 .03
385 Jim Leyritz .10 .03
386 Ray Lankford .10 .03
387 Devon White .20 .06
388 Jeremy Hernandez .10 .03
389 Brian Harper .10 .03
390 Wade Boggs .30 .09
391 Derrick May .10 .03
392 Travis Fryman .20 .06
393 Ron Gant .20 .06
394 Checklist 1-132 .10 .03
395 CL 133-264 UER .10 .03
Eckersley
396 Checklist 265-396 .10 .03
397 George Brett 1.25 .35
398 Bobby Witt .10 .03
399 Daryl Boston .10 .03
400 Bo Jackson .50 .15
401 Fred McGriff .30 .09
Frank Thomas AS
402 Ryne Sandberg .50 .15
Carlos Baerga AS
403 Gary Sheffield .20 .06
Edgar Martinez AS
404 Barry Larkin .20 .06
Travis Fryman AS
405 Andy Van Slyke .50 .15
Ken Griffey Jr. AS
406 Larry Walker .30 .09
Kirby Puckett AS
407 Barry Bonds .60 .18
Joe Carter AS
408 Darren Daulton .20 .06
Brian Harper AS
409 Greg Maddux .50 .15
Roger Clemens AS
410 Tom Glavine .20 .06
Dave Fleming AS
411 Lee Smith .20 .06
Dennis Eckersley AS
412 Jamie McAndrew .10 .03
413 Pete Smith .10 .03
414 Juan Guerrero .10 .03
415 Todd Frohwirth .10 .03
416 Randy Tomlin .10 .03
417 B.J. Surhoff .20 .06
418 Jim Gott .10 .03
419 Mark Thompson RC .10 .03
420 Kevin Tapani .10 .03
421 Curt Schilling .20 .06
422 J.T. Snow RC .40 .12
423 Ryan Klesko .20 .06
Ivan Cruz
Bubba Smith
Larry Sutton RC
424 John Valentin .10 .03
425 Joe Girardi .10 .03
426 Nigel Wilson .10 .03
427 Bob MacDonald .10 .03
428 Todd Zeile .10 .03
429 Milt Cuyler .10 .03
430 Eddie Murray .50 .15
431 Rich Amaral .10 .03
432 Pete Young .10 .03
433 Roger Bailey RC .10 .03
Tom Schmidt
434 Jack Armstrong .10 .03
435 Willie McGee .20 .06
436 Greg W. Harris .10 .03
437 Chris Hammond .10 .03
438 Ritchie Moody RC .10 .03
439 Bryan Harvey .10 .03
440 Ruben Sierra .10 .03
441 Don Lemon .10 .03
Todd Pridy RC
442 Kevin McReynolds .10 .03
443 Terry Leach .10 .03
444 David Nied .10 .03
445 Dale Murphy .50 .15
446 Luis Mercedes .10 .03
447 Keith Shepherd RC .10 .03
448 Ken Caminiti .20 .06
449 Jim Austin .10 .03
450 Darryl Strawberry .20 .06
451 Ramon Caraballo .25 .07
Jon Shave RC
Brent Gates
Quinton McCracken
452 Bob Wickman .10 .03
453 Victor Cole .10 .03
454 John Johnstone RC .10 .03
455 Chili Davis .20 .06
456 Scott Taylor .10 .03
457 Tracy Woodson .10 .03
458 David Wells .20 .06
459 Derek Wallace RC .10 .03
460 Randy Johnson .50 .15
461 Steve Reed RC .10 .03
462 Felix Fermin .10 .03
463 Scott Aldred .10 .03
464 Greg Colbrunn .10 .03
465 Tony Fernandez .10 .03
466 Mike Felder .10 .03
467 Lee Stevens .10 .03
468 Matt Whiteside RC .10 .03
469 Dave Hansen .10 .03
470 Rob Dibble .20 .06
471 Dave Gallagher .10 .03
472 Chris Gwynn .10 .03
473 Dave Henderson .10 .03
474 Ozzie Guillen .10 .03
475 Jeff Reardon .20 .06
476 Mark Voisard .10 .03
Will Scalzitti RC
477 Jimmy Jones .10 .03
478 Greg Cadaret .10 .03
479 Todd Pratt RC .10 .03
480 Pat Listach .10 .03
481 Ryan Luzinski RC .10 .03
482 Darren Reed .10 .03
483 Brian Griffiths RC .10 .03
484 John Wehner .10 .03
485 Glenn Davis .10 .03
486 Eric Wedge RC .10 .03
487 Jesse Hollins .10 .03
488 Manuel Lee .10 .03
489 Scott Fredrickson RC .10 .03
490 Omar Olivares .10 .03
491 Shawn Hare .10 .03
492 Tom Lampkin .10 .03
493 Jeff Nelson .10 .03
494 Kevin Young .10 .03
Adell Davenport
Eduardo Perez
Lou Lucca RC
495 Ken Hill .10 .03
496 Reggie Jefferson .10 .03
497 Matt Petersen .10 .03
Willie Brown RC
498 Bud Black .10 .03
499 Chuck Crim .10 .03
500 Jose Canseco .50 .15
501 Johnny Oates MG .20 .06
Bobby Cox MG
502 Butch Hobson MG .10 .03
Jim Lefebvre MG
503 Buck Rodgers MG .20 .06
Tony Perez MG
504 Gene Lamont MG .20 .06
Don Baylor MG
505 Mike Hargrove MG .20 .06
Rene Lachemann MG
506 Sparky Anderson MG .20 .06
Art Howe MG
507 Hal McRae MG .20 .06
Tom Lasorda MG
508 Phil Garner MG .20 .06
Felipe Alou MG
509 Tom Kelly MG .10 .03
Jeff Torborg MG
510 Buck Showalter MG .20 .06
Jim Fregosi MG
511 Tony LaRussa MG .20 .06
Jim Leyland MG
512 Lou Piniella MG .20 .06
Joe Torre MG
513 Kevin Kennedy MG .10 .03
Jim Riggleman MG
514 Cito Gaston MG .20 .06
Dusty Baker MG
515 Greg Swindell .10 .03
516 Alex Arias .10 .03
517 Bill Pecota .10 .03
518 Benji Grigsby RC UER .10 .03
(Misspelled Bengi
on card front)
519 David Howard .10 .03
520 Charlie Hough .20 .06
521 Kevin Flora .10 .03
522 Shane Reynolds .10 .03
523 Doug Bochtler RC .10 .03
524 Chris Hoiles .10 .03
525 Scott Sanderson .10 .03
526 Mike Sharperson .10 .03
527 Mike Fetters .10 .03
528 Paul Quantrill .10 .03
529 Dave Silvestri .50 .15
Chipper Jones
Benji Gil
Jeff Patzke
530 Sterling Hitchcock RC .25 .07
531 Joe Millette .10 .03
532 Tom Brunansky .10 .03
533 Frank Castillo .10 .03
534 Randy Knorr .10 .03
535 Jose Oquendo .10 .03
536 Dave Haas .10 .03
537 Jason Hutchins RC .10 .03
Ryan Turner
538 Jimmy Baron RC .10 .03
539 Kerry Woodson .10 .03
540 Ivan Calderon .10 .03
541 Denis Boucher .10 .03
542 Royce Clayton .10 .03
543 Reggie Williams .10 .03
544 Steve Decker .10 .03
545 Dean Palmer .20 .06
546 Hal Morris .10 .03
547 Ryan Thompson .10 .03
548 Lance Blankenship .10 .03
549 Hensley Meulens .10 .03
550 Scott Radinsky .10 .03
551 Eric Young .10 .03
552 Jeff Blauser .10 .03
553 Andujar Cedeno .10 .03
554 Arthur Rhodes .10 .03
555 Terry Mulholland .10 .03
556 Darryl Hamilton .10 .03
557 Pedro Martinez 1.00 .30
558 Ryan Whitman RC .10 .03
Mark Skeels
559 Jamie Arnold RC .10 .03
560 Zane Smith .10 .03
561 Matt Nokes .10 .03
562 Bob Zupcic .10 .03
563 Shawn Boskie .10 .03
564 Mike Timlin .10 .03
565 Jerald Clark .10 .03
566 Rod Brewer .10 .03
567 Mark Carreon .10 .03
568 Andy Benes .10 .03
569 Shawn Barton RC .10 .03
570 Tim Wallach .10 .03
571 Dave Mlicki .10 .03
572 Trevor Hoffman .20 .06
573 John Patterson .10 .03
574 De Shawn Warren RC .10 .03
575 Monty Fariss .10 .03
576 Darrell Sherman .20 .06
Damon Buford
Cliff Floyd
Michael Moore
577 Tim Costo .10 .03
578 Dave Magadan .10 .03
579 Neil Garret .10 .03
Jason Bates RC
580 Walt Weiss .10 .03
581 Chris Haney .10 .03
582 Shawn Abner .10 .03
583 Marvin Freeman .10 .03
584 Casey Candaele .10 .03
585 Ricky Jordan .10 .03
586 Jeff Tabaka RC .10 .03
587 Manny Alexander .10 .03
588 Mike Trombley .10 .03
589 Carlos Hernandez .10 .03
590 Cal Eldred .10 .03
591 Alex Cole .10 .03
592 Phil Plantier .10 .03
593 Brett Merriman RC .10 .03
594 Jerry Nielsen .10 .03
595 Shawon Dunston .10 .03
596 Jimmy Key .20 .06
597 Gerald Perry .10 .03
598 Rico Brogna .10 .03
599 Clemente Nunez .10 .03
Daniel Robinson
600 Bret Saberhagen .20 .06
601 Craig Shipley .10 .03
602 Henry Mercedes .10 .03
603 Jim Thome .50 .15
604 Rod Beck .10 .03
605 Chuck Finley .20 .06
606 J. Owens RC .10 .03
607 Dan Smith .10 .03
608 Bill Doran .10 .03
609 Lance Parrish .20 .06
610 Dennis Martinez .20 .06
611 Tom Gordon .10 .03
612 Byron Mathews RC .10 .03
613 Joel Adamson RC .10 .03
614 Brian Williams .10 .03
615 Steve Avery .10 .03
616 Matt Mieske .10 .03
Tracy Sanders
Midre Cummings RC
Ryan Freeburg
617 Craig Lefferts .10 .03
618 Tony Pena .10 .03
619 Billy Spiers .10 .03
620 Todd Benzinger .10 .03
621 Mike Kotarski .10 .03
Greg Boyd RC
622 Ben Rivera .10 .03
623 Al Martin .10 .03
624 Sam Militello UER .10 .03
(Profile says drafted
in 1988, bio says
drafted in 1990)
625 Rick Aguilera .10 .03
626 Dan Gladden .10 .03
627 Andres Berumen RC .10 .03
628 Kelly Gruber .10 .03
629 Cris Carpenter .10 .03
630 Mark Grace .30 .09
631 Jeff Brantley .10 .03
632 Chris Widger RC .25 .07
633 Three Russians UER .10 .03
Rudolf Razjigaev
Eugneyi Puchkov
Ilya Bogatyrev
Bogatyrev is a shortstop,
card has pitching header
634 Mo Sanford .10 .03
635 Albert Belle .20 .06
636 Tim Teufel .10 .03
637 Greg Myers .10 .03
638 Brian Bohanon .10 .03
639 Mike Bordick .10 .03
640 Dwight Gooden .20 .06
641 Pat Leahy .10 .03
Gavin Baugh RC
642 Milt Hill .10 .03
643 Luis Aquino .10 .03
644 Dante Bichette .20 .06
645 Bobby Thigpen .10 .03
646 Rich Scheid RC .10 .03
647 Brian Sackinsky RC .10 .03
648 Ryan Hawblitzel .10 .03
649 Tom Marsh .10 .03
650 Terry Pendleton .20 .06
651 Rafael Bournigal .10 .03
652 Dave West .10 .03
653 Steve Hosey .10 .03
654 Gerald Williams .10 .03
655 Scott Cooper .10 .03
656 Gary Scott .10 .03
657 Mike Harkey .10 .03
658 Jeromy Burnitz .20 .06
Melvin Nieves
Rich Becker
Shon Walker RC

659 Ed Sprague .10 .03
660 Alan Trammell .20 .06
661 Garvin Alston RC .10 .03
Michael Case
662 Donovan Osborne .10 .03
663 Jeff Gardner .10 .03
664 Calvin Jones .10 .03
665 Darrin Fletcher .10 .03
666 Glenallen Hill .10 .03
667 Jim Rosenbohm RC .10 .03
668 Scott Lewis .10 .03
669 Kip Yaughn RC .10 .03
670 Julio Franco .20 .06
671 Dave Martinez .10 .03
672 Kevin Bass .10 .03
673 Todd Van Poppel .10 .03
674 Mark Gubicza .10 .03
675 Tim Raines .20 .06
676 Rudy Seanez .10 .03
677 Charlie Leibrandt .10 .03
678 Randy Milligan .10 .03
679 Kim Batiste .10 .03
680 Craig Biggio .30 .09
681 Darren Holmes .10 .03
682 John Candelaria .10 .03
683 Jerry Stafford .10 .03
Eddie Christian RC
684 Pat Mahomes .10 .03
685 Bob Walk .10 .03
686 Russ Springer .10 .03
687 Tony Sheffield RC .10 .03
688 Dwight Smith .10 .03
689 Eddie Zosky .10 .03
690 Bien Figueroa .10 .03
691 Jim Tatum RC .10 .03
692 Chad Kreuter .10 .03
693 Rich Rodriguez .10 .03
694 Shane Turner .10 .03
695 Kent Bottenfield .10 .03
696 Jose Mesa .10 .03
697 Darrell Whitmore RC .10 .03
698 Ted Wood .10 .03
699 Chad Curtis .10 .03
700 Nolan Ryan 2.00 .60
701 Mike Piazza 1.50 .45
Brook Fordyce
Carlos Delgado
Donnie Leshnock
702 Tim Pugh RC .10 .03
703 Jeff Kent .50 .15
704 Jon Goodrich .10 .03
Danny Figueroa RC
705 Bob Welch .10 .03
706 S.Clinkscales RC .10 .03
707 Donn Pall .10 .03
708 Greg Olson .10 .03
709 Jeff Juden .10 .03
710 Mike Mussina .30 .09
711 Scott Chiamparino .10 .03
712 Stan Javier .10 .03
713 John Doherty .10 .03
714 Kevin Gross .10 .03
715 Greg Gagne .10 .03
716 Steve Cooke .10 .03
717 Steve Farr .10 .03
718 Jay Buhner .20 .06
719 Butch Henry .10 .03
720 David Cone .20 .06
721 Rick Wilkins .10 .03
722 Chuck Carr .10 .03
723 Kenny Felder RC .10 .03
724 Guillermo Velasquez .10 .03
725 Billy Hatcher .10 .03
726 Mike Veneziale RC .10 .03
Ken Kendrena
727 Jonathan Hurst .10 .03
728 Steve Frey .10 .03
729 Mark Leonard .10 .03
730 Charles Nagy .10 .03
731 Donald Harris .10 .03
732 Travis Buckley RC .10 .03
733 Tom Browning .10 .03
734 Anthony Young .10 .03
735 Steve Shifflett .10 .03
736 Jeff Russell .10 .03
737 Wilson Alvarez .10 .03
738 Lance Painter RC .10 .03
739 Dave Weathers .10 .03
740 Len Dykstra .20 .06
741 Mike Devereaux .10 .03
742 Rene Arocha .50 .15
Alan Embree
Brien Taylor
Tim Crabtree
743 Dave Landaker RC .10 .03
744 Chris George .10 .03
745 Eric Davis .20 .06
746 Mark Strittmatter .10 .03
Lamarr Rogers RC
747 Carl Willis .10 .03
748 Stan Belinda .10 .03
749 Scott Kamieniecki .10 .03
750 Rickey Henderson .50 .15
751 Eric Hillman .10 .03
752 Pat Hentgen .10 .03
753 Jim Corsi .10 .03
754 Brian Jordan .20 .06
755 Bill Swift .10 .03
756 Mike Henneman .10 .03
757 Harold Reynolds .20 .06
758 Sean Berry .10 .03
759 Charlie Hayes .10 .03
760 Luis Polonia .10 .03
761 Darrin Jackson .10 .03
762 Mark Lewis .10 .03
763 Rob Maurer .10 .03
764 Willie Greene .10 .03
765 Vince Coleman .10 .03
766 Todd Revenig .10 .03
767 Rich Ireland RC .10 .03
768 Mike Macfarlane .10 .03
769 Francisco Cabrera .10 .03
770 Robin Ventura .20 .06
771 Kevin Ritz .10 .03
772 Chito Martinez .10 .03
773 Cliff Brantley .10 .03
774 Curt Leskanic RC .10 .03
775 Chris Bosio .10 .03
776 Jose Offerman .10 .03
777 Mark Guthrie .10 .03
778 Don Slaught .10 .03
779 Rich Monteleone .10 .03
780 Jim Abbott .30 .09
781 Jack Clark .20 .06
782 Reynol Mendoza .10 .03
Dan Roman RC
783 Heathcliff Slocumb .10 .03
784 Jeff Branson .10 .03
785 Kevin Brown .20 .06
786 Mike Christopher .10 .03
Ken Ryan
Aaron Taylor
Gus Gandarillas RC
787 Mike Matthews RC .10 .03
788 Mackey Sasser .10 .03
789 Jeff Conine UER .20 .06
No inclusion of 1990
RBI stats in career total
790 George Bell .10 .03
791 Pat Rapp .10 .03
792 Joe Boever .10 .03
793 Jim Poole .10 .03
794 Andy Ashby .10 .03
795 Deion Sanders .30 .09
796 Scott Brosius .20 .06
797 Brad Pennington .10 .03
798 Greg Blosser .10 .03
799 Jim Edmonds RC 3.00 .90
800 Shawn Jeter .10 .03
801 Jesse Levis .10 .03
802 Phil Clark UER .10 .03
(Word "a" is missing in
sentence beginning
with "In 1992 ...")
803 Ed Pierce RC .10 .03
804 Jose Valentin RC .40 .12
805 Terry Jorgensen .10 .03
806 Mark Hutton .10 .03
807 Troy Neel .10 .03
808 Bret Boone .30 .09
809 Cris Colon .10 .03
810 Domingo Martinez RC .10 .03
811 Javier Lopez .30 .09
812 Matt Walbeck RC .10 .03
813 Dan Wilson .20 .06
814 Scooter Tucker .10 .03
815 Billy Ashley .10 .03
816 Tim Laker RC .10 .03
817 Bobby Jones .20 .06
818 Brad Brink .10 .03
819 William Pennyfeather .10 .03
820 Stan Royer .10 .03
821 Doug Brocail .10 .03
822 Kevin Rogers .10 .03
823 Checklist 397-540 .10 .03
824 Checklist 541-691 .10 .03
825 Checklist 692-825 .10 .03

1993 Topps Gold

Several insertion schemes were devised for these 825 standard-size cards. Gold cards were inserted one per wax pack, three per rack pack, five per jumbo pack, and ten per factory set. The cards are identical to the regular-issue 1993 Topps baseball cards except that the gold-foil Topps Gold logo appears in an upper corner, and the team color-coded stripe at the bottom of the front, which carried the player's name, has been replaced with an embossed gold-foil stripe. The checklist cards (394-396, 823-825) have been replaced by player cards.

	Nm-Mt	Ex-Mt
COMP.GOLD SET (825)	60.00	18.00
COMP.SERIES 1 (396)	40.00	12.00
COMP.SERIES 2 (429)	25.00	7.50
COMMON (1G-825G)	.30	.09

*STARS: 1X TO 2.5X BASIC CARDS...
*ROOKIES: 1.25X TO 3X BASIC CARDS
394 Bernardo Brito .25 .07
395 Jim McNamara .25 .07
396 Rich Sauveur .25 .07
823 Keith Brown .25 .07
824 Russ McGinnis .25 .07
825 Mike Walker UER .25 .07
(Card has 1993 Mariner
stats, should be 1992)

1993 Topps Inaugural Marlins

These 825-card standard-size sets were issued by Topps to commemorate the debut seasons of the Colorado Rockies and Florida Marlins. Gold foil Marlins or Rockies logos distinguish these from regular issue cards. These cards were only issued in factory set form. 5,000 Rockies sets and 4,000 Marlins sets were initially printed, but each team had the option of receiving a maximum of 10,000 sets. The Rockies sets were distributed through the four team-owned stores and at Mile High Stadium. The Marlins sets were distributed through FMI and Joe Robbie Stadium.

	Nm-Mt	Ex-Mt
COMP.FACT.SET (825)	100.00	30.00

*STARS: 2.5X TO 6X BASIC CARDS...
*ROOKIES: 2.5X TO 6X BASIC CARDS

1993 Topps Inaugural Rockies

Similar to the Marlins set. This was a 1993 set with the Rockies logo imprinted on the card. They were only issued in factory set form. They were distributed through four Rockie owned stores and at Mile High Stadium. They are valued slightly less than the Marlins card as 1,000 more sets of Rockies were produced

	Nm-Mt	Ex-Mt
COMP.FACT.SET (825)	100.00	30.00

*STARS: 2.5X TO 6X BASIC CARDS...
*ROOKIES: 2.5X TO 6X BASIC CARDS

1993 Topps Black Gold

Topps Black Gold cards 1-22 were randomly inserted in series I packs while card numbers 23-44 were featured in series II packs. They were also inserted three per factory set. In the packs, the cards were inserted one everry 72 hobby or retail packs; one every 12 jumbo packs and one every 24 rack packs. Hobbyists could obtain the set by collecting individual random

insert cards or receive 11, 22, or 44 Black Gold cards by mail when they sent in special "You've Just Won" cards, which were randomly inserted in packs. Series I packs featured three different "You've Just Won" cards, entitling the holder to receive Group A (cards 1-11), Group B (cards 12-22), or Groups A and B (Cards 1-22). In a similar fashion, four "You've Just Won" cards were inserted in series II packs and entitled the holder to receive Group C (23-33), Group D (34-44), Groups C and D (23-44), or Groups A-D (1-44). By returning the "You've Just Won" card with 1.50 for postage and handling, the collector received not only the Black Gold cards won but also a special "You've Just Won" card and a congratulatory letter informing the collector that his/her name has been entered into a drawing for one of 500 uncut sheets of all 44 Topps Black Gold cards in a leatherette frame. These standard-size cards feature different color player photos than either the 1993 Topps regular issue or the Topps Gold issue. The player pictures are cut out and superimposed on a black gloss background. Inside white borders, gold refractory foil edges the top and bottom of the card face. On a black-and-gray pinstripe pattern inside white borders, the horizontal backs have a a second cut out player photo and a player profile on a blue panel. The player's name appears in gold foil lettering on a blue-and-gray geometric shape. The first 22 cards are National Leaguers while the second 22 cards are American Leaguers. Winner cards C and D were both originally produced erroneously and later corrected; the error versions show the players from Winner A and B on the respective fronts of Winner cards Cand D. There is no value difference in the variations at this time. The winner cards were redeemable until January 31, 1994.

	Nm-Mt	Ex-Mt
COMPLETE SET (44)	10.00	3.00
COMPLETE SERIES 1 (22)	4.00	1.20
COMPLETE SERIES 2 (22)	6.00	1.80

1 Barry Bonds 2.00 .60
2 Will Clark .75 .23
3 Darren Daulton .30 .09
4 Andre Dawson .30 .09
5 Delino DeShields .15 .04
6 Tom Glavine .50 .15
7 Marquis Grissom .30 .09
8 Tony Gwynn 1.00 .30
9 Eric Karros .30 .09
10 Ray Lankford .15 .04
11 Barry Larkin .50 .15
12 Greg Maddux 1.25 .35
13 Fred McGriff .50 .15
14 Joe Oliver .15 .04
15 Terry Pendleton .30 .09
16 Bip Roberts .15 .04
17 Ryne Sandberg 1.25 .35
18 Gary Sheffield .30 .09
19 Lee Smith .30 .09
20 Ozzie Smith 1.25 .35
21 Andy Van Slyke .30 .09
22 Larry Walker .50 .15
23 Roberto Alomar .50 .15
24 Brady Anderson .30 .09
25 Carlos Baerga .15 .04
26 Joe Carter .30 .09
27 Roger Clemens 1.50 .45
28 Mike Devereaux .15 .04
29 Dennis Eckersley .30 .09
30 Cecil Fielder .30 .09
31 Travis Fryman .30 .09
32 Juan Gonzalez UER .50 .15
(No copyright or
licensing on card)
33 Ken Griffey Jr. 1.25 .35
34 Brian Harper .15 .04
35 Pat Listach .15 .04
36 Kenny Lofton .30 .09
37 Edgar Martinez .50 .15
38 Jack McDowell .15 .04
39 Mark McGwire 2.00 .60
40 Kirby Puckett .75 .23
41 Mickey Tettleton .15 .04
42 Frank Thomas UER .75 .23
(No copyright or
licensing on card)
43 Robin Ventura .30 .09
44 Dave Winfield .30 .09

1993 Topps Traded

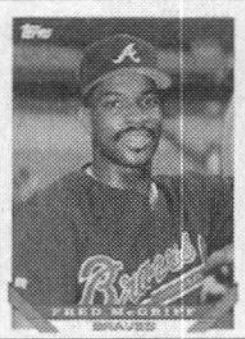

This 132-card standard-size set focuses on promising rookies, new managers, free agents, and players who changed teams. The set also includes 22 members of Team USA. The set has the same design on the front as the regular 1993 Topps issue. The backs are also the same design and carry a head shot, biography, stats, and career highlights. Rookie Cards in this set include Todd Helton.

	Nm-Mt	Ex-Mt
COMP.FACT.SET (132)	40.00	12.00

1T Barry Bonds 1.25 .35
2T Rich Renteria .10 .03
3T Aaron Sele .10 .03
4T C.Loewer USA RC .25 .07
5T Erik Pappas .10 .03
6T Greg McMichael RC .25 .07
7T Freddie Benavides .10 .03
8T Kirk Gibson .20 .06
9T Tony Fernandez .10 .03
10T Jay Gainer RC .25 .07
11T Orestes Destrade .10 .03
12T A.J. Hinch USA RC .50 .15
13T Bobby Munoz .10 .03
14T Tom Henke .10 .03
15T Rob Butler .10 .03
16T Gary Wayne .10 .03
17T David McCarty .10 .03
18T Walt Weiss .10 .03
19T Todd Helton USA RC 25.00 7.50
20T Mark Whiten .10 .03
21T Ricky Gutierrez .10 .03
22T D.Hermanson USA RC .50 .15
23T Sherman Obando RC .25 .07
24T Mike Piazza 1.50 .45
25T Jeff Russell .10 .03
26T Jason Bere .10 .03
27T Jack Voigt RC .25 .07
28T Chris Bosio .10 .03
29T Phil Hiatt .10 .03
30T M.Beaumont USA RC .25 .07
31T Andres Galarraga .20 .06
32T Greg Swindell .10 .03
33T Vinny Castilla .20 .06
34T P.Clougherty RC USA .25 .07
35T Greg Briley .10 .03
36T Dallas Green MG .10 .03
Davey Johnson MG
37T Tyler Green .10 .03
38T Craig Paquette .10 .03
39T Danny Sheaffer RC .25 .07
40T Jim Converse RC .25 .07
41T Terry Harvey USA RC .25 .07
42T Phil Plantier .10 .03
43T Doug Saunders RC .25 .07
44T Benny Santiago .20 .06
45T Dante Powell USA RC .25 .07
46T Jeff Parrett .10 .03
47T Wade Boggs .30 .09
48T Paul Molitor .30 .09
49T Turk Wendell .10 .03
50T David Wells .20 .06
51T Gary Sheffield .20 .06
52T Kevin Young .20 .06
53T Nelson Liriano .10 .03
54T Greg Maddux .75 .23
55T Derek Bell .10 .03
56T Matt Turner RC .25 .07
57T C.Nelson RC USA .20 .06
58T Mike Hampton .20 .06
59T Troy O'Leary RC .50 .15
60T Benji Gil .10 .03
61T Mitch Lyden RC .25 .07
62T J.T. Snow .30 .09
63T Damon Buford .10 .03
64T Gene Harris .10 .03
65T Randy Myers .10 .03
66T Felix Jose .10 .03
67T Todd Dunn USA RC .25 .07
68T Jimmy Key .20 .06
69T Pedro Castellano .10 .03
70T Mark Merila USA RC .25 .07
71T Rich Rodriguez .10 .03
72T Matt Mieske .10 .03
73T Pete Incaviglia .10 .03
74T Carl Everett .20 .06
75T Jim Abbott .30 .09
76T Luis Aquino .10 .03
77T Rene Arocha .20 .06
78T Jon Shave .10 .03
79T Todd Walker USA RC 1.00 .30
80T Jack Armstrong .10 .03
81T Jeff Richardson .10 .03
82T Blas Minor .10 .03
83T Dave Winfield .20 .06
84T Paul O'Neill .30 .09
85T Steve Reich USA RC .25 .07
86T Chris Hammond .10 .03
87T Hilly Hathaway RC .25 .07
88T Fred McGriff .30 .09
89T Dave Telgheder RC .25 .07
90T Richie Lewis RC .25 .07
91T Brent Gates .10 .03
92T Andre Dawson .20 .06
93T Andy Barkett USA RC .25 .07
94T Doug Drabek .10 .03
95T Joe Klink .10 .03
96T Willie Blair .10 .03
97T D.Graves USA RC 1.00 .30
98T Pat Meares RC .50 .15
99T Mike Lansing RC .50 .15
100T Marcos Armas RC .25 .07
101T D.Grass RC USA .25 .07
102T Chris Jones .10 .03
103T Ken Ryan RC .25 .07
104T Ellis Burks .20 .06
105T Roberto Kelly .10 .03
106T Dave Magadan .10 .03
107T Paul Wilson USA RC 1.00 .30
108T Rob Natal .10 .03
109T Paul Wagner .10 .03
110T Jeromy Burnitz .20 .06
111T Monty Fariss .10 .03
112T Kevin Mitchell .10 .03
113T Scott Pose RC .25 .07
114T Dave Stewart .20 .06
115T R.Johnson USA RC .25 .07
116T Armando Reynoso .10 .03
117T Geronimo Berroa .10 .03
118T Woody Williams RC 1.00 .30
119T Tim Bogar RC .25 .07
120T Bob Scafa USA RC .25 .07
121T Henry Cotto .10 .03
122T Gregg Jefferies .10 .03
123T Norm Charlton .10 .03
124T B.Wagner USA RC .25 .07
125T David Cone .20 .06
126T Daryl Boston .10 .03
127T Tim Wallach .10 .03
128T Mike Martin USA RC .25 .07
129T John Cummings RC .25 .07
130T Ryan Bowen .10 .03
131T John Powell USA RC .25 .07
132T Checklist 1-132 .10 .03

1994 Topps

These 792 standard-size cards were issued in two series of 396. Two types of factory sets were also issued. One features the 792 basic cards, ten Topps Gold, three Black Gold and three Finest Pre-Production cards for a total of 808. The other factory set (Bakers Dozen) includes the 792 basic cards, ten Topps Gold, three Black Gold, ten 1995 Topps Pre-Production cards and a sample pack of three special Topps cards for a total of 818. The standard cards feature glossy color player photos with white borders on the fronts. The player's name is in white cursive lettering at the bottom left, with the team name and player's position printed on a team color-coded bar. There is an inner multicolored border along the left side that extends obliquely across the bottom. The horizontal backs carry an action shot of the player with biography, statistics and highlights. Subsets include Draft Picks (201-210/739-762), All-Stars (384-394) and Stat Twins (601-609). Rookie Cards include Billy Wagner.

	Nm-Mt	Ex-Mt
COMPLETE SET (792)	50.00	15.00
COMP.FACT.SET (808)	60.00	18.00
COMP.BAKER SET (818)	60.00	18.00
COMP. SERIES 1 (396)	25.00	7.50
COMP. SERIES 2 (396)	25.00	7.50

1 Mike Piazza 1.00 .30
2 Bernie Williams .30 .09
3 Kevin Rogers .10 .03
4 Paul Carey .10 .03
5 Ozzie Guillen .10 .03
6 Derrick May .10 .03
7 Jose Mesa .10 .03
8 Todd Hundley .10 .03
9 Chris Haney .10 .03
10 John Olerud .20 .06
11 Andujar Cedeno .10 .03
12 John Smiley .10 .03
13 Phil Plantier .10 .03
14 Willie Banks .10 .03
15 Jay Bell .20 .06
16 Doug Henry .10 .03
17 Lance Blankenship .10 .03
18 Greg W. Harris .10 .03
19 Scott Livingstone .10 .03
20 Bryan Harvey .10 .03
21 Wil Cordero .10 .03
22 Roger Pavlik .10 .03
23 Mark Lemke .10 .03
24 Jeff Nelson .10 .03
25 Todd Zeile .10 .03
26 Billy Hatcher .10 .03
27 Joe Magrane .10 .03
28 Tony Longmire .10 .03
29 Omar Daal .10 .03
30 Kirt Manwaring .10 .03
31 Melido Perez .10 .03
32 Tim Hulett .10 .03
33 Jeff Schwarz .10 .03
34 Nolan Ryan 2.00 .60
35 Jose Guzman .10 .03
36 Felix Fermin .10 .03
37 Jeff Innis .10 .03
38 Brett Mayne .10 .03
39 Huck Flener RC .10 .03
40 Jeff Bagwell .30 .09
41 Kevin Wickander .10 .03
42 Ricky Gutierrez .10 .03
43 Pat Mahomes .10 .03
44 Jeff King .10 .03
45 Cal Eldred .10 .03
46 Craig Paquette .10 .03
47 Richie Lewis .10 .03
48 Tony Phillips .10 .03
49 Armando Reynoso .10 .03
50 Moises Alou .20 .06
51 Manuel Lee .10 .03
52 Otis Nixon .10 .03
53 Billy Ashley .10 .03
54 Mark Whiten .10 .03
55 Jeff Russell .10 .03
56 Chad Curtis .10 .03
57 Kevin Stocker .10 .03
58 Mike Jackson .10 .03
59 Matt Nokes .10 .03
60 Chris Bosio .10 .03
61 Damon Buford .10 .03
62 Tim Belcher .10 .03
63 Glenallen Hill .10 .03
64 Bill Wertz .10 .03
65 Eddie Murray .50 .15
66 Tom Gordon .10 .03
67 Alex Gonzalez .10 .03
68 Eddie Taubensee .10 .03
69 Jacob Brumfield .10 .03
70 Andy Benes .10 .03
71 Rich Becker .10 .03
72 Steve Cooke .10 .03
73 Billy Spiers .10 .03
74 Scott Brosius .20 .06
75 Alan Trammell .20 .06
76 Luis Aquino .10 .03
77 Jerald Clark .10 .03
78 Mel Rojas .10 .03
79 Billy Masse .10 .03
Stanton Cameron
Tim Clark
Craig McClure RC
80 Jose Canseco .50 .15
81 Greg McMichael .10 .03

82 Brian Turang RC .10 .03
83 Tom Urbani .10 .03
84 Garret Anderson .50 .15
85 Tony Pena .10 .03
86 Ricky Jordan .10 .03
87 Jim Gott .10 .03
88 Pat Kelly .10 .03
89 Bud Black .10 .03
90 Robin Ventura .20 .06
91 Rick Sutcliffe .20 .06
92 Jose Bautista .10 .03
93 Bob Ojeda .10 .03
94 Phil Hiatt .10 .03
95 Tim Pugh .10 .03
96 Randy Knorr .10 .03
97 Todd Jones .10 .03
98 Ryan Thompson .10 .03
99 Tim Mauser .10 .03
100 Kirby Puckett .50 .15
101 Mark Dewey .10 .03
102 B.J. Surhoff .20 .06
103 Sterling Hitchcock .10 .03
104 Alex Arias .10 .03
105 David Wells .20 .06
106 Daryl Boston .10 .03
107 Mike Stanton .10 .03
108 Gary Redus .10 .03
109 Delino DeShields .10 .03
110 Lee Smith .20 .06
111 Greg Litton .10 .03
112 Frankie Rodriguez .10 .03
113 Russ Springer .10 .03
114 Mitch Williams .10 .03
115 Eric Karros .20 .06
116 Jeff Brantley .10 .03
117 Jack Voigt .10 .03
118 Jason Bere .10 .03
119 Kevin Roberson .10 .03
120 Jimmy Key .20 .06
121 Reggie Jefferson .10 .03
122 Jeromy Burnitz .20 .06
123 Billy Brewer .10 .03
124 Willie Canate .10 .03
125 Greg Swindell .10 .03
126 Hal Morris .10 .03
127 Brad Ausmus .10 .03
128 George Tsamis .10 .03
129 Denny Neagle .20 .06
130 Pat Listach .10 .03
131 Steve Karsay .10 .03
132 Bret Barberie .10 .03
133 Mark Leiter .10 .03
134 Greg Colbrunn .10 .03
135 David Nied .10 .03
136 Dean Palmer .20 .06
137 Steve Avery .10 .03
138 Bill Haselman .10 .03
139 Tripp Cromer .10 .03
140 Frank Viola .20 .06
141 Rene Gonzales .10 .03
142 Curt Schilling .20 .06
143 Tim Wallach .10 .03
144 Bobby Munoz .10 .03
145 Brady Anderson .20 .06
146 Rod Beck .10 .03
147 Mike LaValliere .10 .03
148 Greg Hibbard .10 .03
149 Kenny Lofton .20 .06
150 Dwight Gooden .20 .06
151 Greg Gagne .10 .03
152 Ray McDavid .10 .03
153 Chris Donnels .10 .03
154 Dan Wilson .10 .03
155 Todd Stottlemyre .10 .03
156 David McCarty .10 .03
157 Paul Wagner .10 .03
158 Orlando Miller 1.50 .45
Brandon Wilson
Derek Jeter
Mike Neal
159 Mike Fetters .10 .03
160 Scott Lydy .10 .03
161 Darrell Whitmore .10 .03
162 Bob MacDonald .10 .03
163 Vinny Castilla .20 .06
164 Denis Boucher .10 .03
165 Ivan Rodriguez .50 .15
166 Ron Gant .20 .06
167 Tim Davis .10 .03
168 Steve Dixon .10 .03
169 Scott Fletcher .10 .03
170 Terry Mulholland .10 .03
171 Greg Myers .10 .03
172 Brett Butler .20 .06
173 Bob Wickman .10 .03
174 Dave Martinez .10 .03
175 Fernando Valenzuela .20 .06
176 Craig Grebeck .10 .03
177 Shawn Boskie .10 .03
178 Albie Lopez .10 .03
179 Butch Huskey .10 .03
180 George Brett 1.25 .35
181 Juan Guzman .10 .03
182 Eric Anthony .10 .03
183 Rob Dibble .20 .06
184 Craig Shipley .10 .03
185 Kevin Tapani .10 .03
186 Marcus Moore .10 .03
187 Graeme Lloyd .10 .03
188 Mike Bordick .10 .03
189 Chris Hammond .10 .03
190 Cecil Fielder .20 .06
191 Curt Leskanic .10 .03
192 Lou Frazier .10 .03
193 Steve Dreyer RC .10 .03
194 Javier Lopez .20 .06
195 Edgar Martinez .30 .09
196 Allen Watson .10 .03
197 John Flaherty .10 .03
198 Kurt Stillwell .10 .03
199 Danny Jackson .10 .03
200 Cal Ripken 1.50 .45
201 Mike Bell FDP RC .10 .03
202 Alan Benes FDP RC .25 .07
203 Matt Farner FDP RC .10 .03
204 Jeff Granger .10 .03
205 B.Kieschnick FDP RC .25 .07
206 Jeremy Lee FDP RC .10 .03
207 C.Peterson FDP RC .10 .03
208 Alan Rice FDP RC .10 .03
209 Billy Wagner FDP RC .50 .15
210 Kelly Wunsch FDP RC .25 .07
211 Tom Candiotti .10 .03
212 Domingo Jean .10 .03
213 John Burkett .10 .03
214 George Bell .10 .03
215 Dan Plesac .10 .03
216 Manny Ramirez .30 .09
217 Mike Maddux .10 .03
218 Kevin McReynolds .10 .03
219 Pat Borders .10 .03
220 Doug Drabek .10 .03
221 Larry Luebbers RC .10 .03
222 Trevor Hoffman .20 .06
223 Pat Meares .10 .03
224 Danny Miceli .10 .03
225 Greg Vaughn .10 .03
226 Scott Hemond .10 .03
227 Pat Rapp .10 .03
228 Kirk Gibson .20 .06
229 Lance Painter .10 .03
230 Larry Walker .30 .09
231 Benji Gil .10 .03
232 Mark Wohlers .10 .03
233 Rich Amaral .10 .03
234 Eric Pappas .10 .03
235 Scott Cooper .10 .03
236 Mike Butcher .10 .03
237 Curtis Pride .50 .15
Shawn Green
Mark Sweeney
Eddie Davis
238 Kim Batiste .10 .03
239 Paul Assenmacher .10 .03
240 Will Clark .50 .15
241 Jose Offerman .10 .03
242 Todd Frohwirth .10 .03
243 Tim Raines .20 .06
244 Rick Wilkins .10 .03
245 Bret Saberhagen .20 .06
246 Thomas Howard .10 .03
247 Stan Belinda .10 .03
248 Rickey Henderson .50 .15
249 Brian Williams .10 .03
250 Barry Larkin .30 .09
251 Jose Valentin .10 .03
252 Lenny Webster .10 .03
253 Blas Minor .10 .03
254 Tim Teufel .10 .03
255 Bobby Witt .10 .03
256 Walt Weiss .10 .03
257 Chad Kreuter .10 .03
258 Roberto Mejia .10 .03
259 Cliff Floyd .20 .06
260 Julio Franco .20 .06
261 Rafael Belliard .10 .03
262 Marc Newfield .10 .03
263 Gerald Perry .10 .03
264 Ken Ryan .10 .03
265 Chili Davis .20 .06
266 Dave West .10 .03
267 Royce Clayton .10 .03
268 Pedro Martinez .50 .15
269 Mark Hutton .10 .03
270 Frank Thomas .50 .15
271 Brad Pennington .10 .03
272 Mike Harkey .10 .03
273 Sandy Alomar Jr. .10 .03
274 Dave Gallagher .10 .03
275 Wally Joyner .20 .06
276 Ricky Trlicek .10 .03
277 Al Osuna .10 .03
278 Pokey Reese .10 .03
279 Kevin Higgins .10 .03
280 Rick Aguilera .10 .03
281 Orlando Merced .10 .03
282 Mike Mohler .10 .03
283 John Jaha .10 .03
284 Robb Nen .20 .06
285 Travis Fryman .20 .06
286 Mark Thompson .10 .03
287 Mike Lansing .10 .03
288 Craig Lefferts .10 .03
289 Damon Berryhill .10 .03
290 Randy Johnson .50 .15
291 Jeff Reed .10 .03
292 Danny Darwin .10 .03
293 J.T. Snow .20 .06
294 Tyler Green .10 .03
295 Chris Hoiles .10 .03
296 Roger McDowell .10 .03
297 Spike Owen .10 .03
298 Salomon Torres .10 .03
299 Wilson Alvarez .10 .03
300 Ryne Sandberg .75 .23
301 Derek Lilliquist .10 .03
302 Howard Johnson .10 .03
303 Greg Cadaret .10 .03
304 Pat Hentgen .10 .03
305 Craig Biggio .30 .09
306 Scott Service .10 .03
307 Melvin Nieves .10 .03
308 Mike Trombley .10 .03
309 Carlos Garcia .10 .03
310 Robin Yount UER .75 .23
(listed with 111 triples in 1988; should be 11)
311 Marcos Armas .10 .03
312 Rich Rodriguez .10 .03
313 Justin Thompson .10 .03
314 Danny Sheaffer .10 .03
315 Ken Hill .10 .03
316 Chad Ogea .10 .03
Duff Brumley
Terrell Wade RC
Chris Michalak
317 Cris Carpenter .10 .03
318 Jeff Blauser .10 .03
319 Ted Power .10 .03
320 Ozzie Smith .75 .23
321 John Dopson .10 .03
322 Chris Turner .10 .03
323 Pete Incaviglia .10 .03
324 Alan Mills .10 .03
325 Jody Reed .10 .03
326 Rich Monteleone .10 .03
327 Mark Carreon .10 .03
328 Donn Pall .10 .03
329 Matt Walbeck .10 .03
330 Charles Nagy .10 .03
331 Jeff McKnight .10 .03
332 Jose Lind .10 .03
333 Mike Timlin .10 .03
334 Doug Jones .10 .03
335 Kevin Mitchell .10 .03
336 Luis Lopez .10 .03
337 Shane Mack .10 .03
338 Randy Tomlin .10 .03
339 Matt Mieske .10 .03
340 Mark McGwire 1.25 .35
341 Nigel Wilson .10 .03
342 Danny Gladden .10 .03
343 Mo Sanford .10 .03
344 Sean Berry .10 .03
345 Kevin Brown .20 .06
346 Greg Olson .10 .03
347 Dave Magadan .10 .03
348 Rene Arocha .10 .03
349 Carlos Quintana .10 .03
350 Jim Abbott .30 .09
351 Gary DiSarcina .10 .03
352 Ben Rivera .10 .03
353 Carlos Hernandez .10 .03
354 Darren Lewis .10 .03
355 Harold Reynolds .20 .06
356 Scott Ruffcorn .10 .03
357 Mark Gubicza .10 .03
358 Paul Sorrento .10 .03
359 Anthony Young .10 .03
360 Mark Grace .30 .09
361 Rob Butler .10 .03
362 Kevin Bass .10 .03
363 Eric Helfand .10 .03
364 Derek Bell .10 .03
365 Scott Erickson .10 .03
366 Al Martin .10 .03
367 Ricky Bones .10 .03
368 Jeff Branson .10 .03
369 Luis Ortiz .50 .15
David Bell RC
Jason Giambi
George Arias
370 Benito Santiago .20 .06
(See also 379)
371 John Doherty .10 .03
372 Joe Girardi .10 .03
373 Tim Scott .10 .03
374 Marvin Freeman .10 .03
375 Deion Sanders .30 .09
376 Roger Salkeld .10 .03
377 Bernard Gilkey .10 .03
378 Tony Fossas .10 .03
379 Mark McLemore UER .10 .03
(Card number is 370)
380 Darren Daulton .20 .06
381 Chuck Finley .20 .06
382 Mitch Webster .10 .03
383 Gerald Williams .10 .03
384 Frank Thomas AS .30 .09
Fred McGriff AS
385 Roberto Alomar AS .20 .06
Robby Thompson AS
386 Wade Boggs AS .20 .06
Matt Williams AS
387 Cal Ripken AS .50 .15
Jeff Blauser AS
388 Ken Griffey Jr. AS .50 .15
Len Dykstra AS
389 Juan Gonzalez AS .20 .06
David Justice AS
390 George Belle AS .60 .18
Bobby Bonds AS
391 Mike Stanley AS .50 .15
Mike Piazza AS
392 Jack McDowell AS .30 .09
Greg Maddux AS
393 Jimmy Key AS .20 .06
Tom Glavine AS
394 Jeff Montgomery AS .10 .03
Randy Myers AS
395 Checklist 1-198 .10 .03
396 Checklist 199-396 .10 .03
397 Tim Salmon .30 .09
398 Todd Benzinger .10 .03
399 Frank Castillo .10 .03
400 Ken Griffey Jr. .75 .23
401 John Kruk .20 .06
402 Dave Telgheder .10 .03
403 Gary Gaetti .20 .06
404 Jim Edmonds .50 .15
405 Don Slaught .10 .03
406 Jose Oquendo .10 .03
407 Bruce Ruffin .10 .03
408 Phil Clark .10 .03
409 Joe Klink .10 .03
410 Lou Whitaker .20 .06
411 Kevin Seitzer .10 .03
412 Darrin Fletcher .10 .03
413 Kenny Rogers .20 .06
414 Bill Pecota .10 .03
415 Dave Fleming .10 .03
416 Luis Alicea .10 .03
417 Paul Quantrill .10 .03
418 Damion Easley .10 .03
419 Wes Chamberlain .10 .03
420 Harold Baines .20 .06
421 Scott Radinsky .10 .03
422 Rey Sanchez .10 .03
423 Junior Ortiz .10 .03
424 Jeff Kent .20 .06
425 Brian McRae .10 .03
426 Ed Sprague .10 .03
427 Tom Edens .10 .03
428 Willie Greene .10 .03
429 Bryan Hickerson .10 .03
430 Dave Winfield .20 .06
431 Pedro Astacio .10 .03
432 Mike Gallego .10 .03
433 Dave Burba .10 .03
434 Bob Walk .10 .03
435 Darryl Hamilton .10 .03
436 Vince Horsman .10 .03
437 Bob Natal .10 .03
438 Mike Henneman .10 .03
439 Willie Blair .10 .03
440 Dennis Martinez .20 .06
441 Dan Peltier .10 .03
442 Tony Tarasco .10 .03
443 John Cummings .10 .03
444 Geronimo Pena .10 .03
445 Aaron Sele .10 .03
446 Stan Javier .10 .03
447 Mike Williams .10 .03
448 Greg Pirkl .10 .03
Roberto Petagine
D.J.Boston
Shawn Wooten RC
449 Jim Poole .10 .03
450 Carlos Baerga .10 .03
451 Bob Scanlan .10 .03
452 Lance Johnson .10 .03
453 Eric Hillman .10 .03
454 Keith Miller .10 .03
455 Dave Stewart .20 .06
456 Pete Harnisch .10 .03
457 Roberto Kelly .10 .03
458 Tim Worrell .10 .03
459 Pedro Munoz .10 .03
460 Orel Hershiser .20 .06
461 Randy Velarde .10 .03
462 Trevor Wilson .10 .03
463 Jerry Goff .10 .03
464 Bill Wegman .10 .03
465 Dennis Eckersley .20 .06
466 Jeff Conine .20 .06
467 Joe Boever .10 .03
468 Dante Bichette .20 .06
469 Jeff Shaw .10 .03
470 Rafael Palmeiro .30 .09
471 Phil Leftwich RC .10 .03
472 Jay Buhner .20 .06
473 Bob Tewksbury .10 .03
474 Tim Naehring .10 .03
475 Tom Glavine .30 .09
476 Dave Hollins .10 .03
477 Arthur Rhodes .10 .03
478 Joey Cora .10 .03
479 Mike Morgan .10 .03
480 Albert Belle .20 .06
481 John Franco .20 .06
482 Hipolito Pichardo .10 .03
483 Duane Ward .10 .03
484 Luis Gonzalez .20 .06
485 Joe Oliver .10 .03
486 Wally Whitehurst .10 .03
487 Mike Benjamin .10 .03
488 Eric Davis .20 .06
489 Scott Kamieniecki .10 .03
490 Kent Hrbek .20 .06
491 John Hope RC .10 .03
492 Jesse Orosco .10 .03
493 Troy Neel .10 .03
494 Ryan Bowen .10 .03
495 Mickey Tettleton .10 .03
496 Chris Jones .10 .03
497 John Wetteland .20 .06
498 David Hulse .10 .03
499 Greg Maddux .75 .23
500 Bo Jackson .50 .15
501 Donovan Osborne .10 .03
502 Mike Greenwell .10 .03
503 Steve Frey .10 .03
504 Jim Eisenreich .10 .03
505 Robby Thompson .10 .03
506 Leo Gomez .10 .03
507 Dave Staton .10 .03
508 Wayne Kirby .10 .03
509 Tim Bogar .10 .03
510 David Cone .20 .06
511 Devon White .20 .06
512 Xavier Hernandez .10 .03
513 Tim Costo .10 .03
514 Gene Harris .10 .03
515 Jack McDowell .10 .03
516 Kevin Gross .10 .03
517 Scott Leius .10 .03
518 Lloyd McClendon .10 .03
519 Alex Diaz RC .10 .03
520 Wade Boggs .30 .09
521 Bob Welch .10 .03
522 Henry Cotto .10 .03
523 Mike Moore .10 .03
524 Tim Laker .10 .03
525 Andres Galarraga .20 .06
526 Jamie Moyer .20 .06
527 Norberto Martin .10 .03
Ruben Santana
Jason Hardtke
Chris Sexton RC
528 Sid Bream .10 .03
529 Erik Hanson .10 .03
530 Ray Lankford .10 .03
531 Rob Deer .10 .03
532 Rod Correia .10 .03
533 Roger Mason .10 .03
534 Mike Devereaux .10 .03
535 Jeff Montgomery .10 .03
536 Dwight Smith .10 .03
537 Jeremy Hernandez .10 .03
538 Ellis Burks .20 .06
539 Bobby Jones .10 .03
540 Paul Molitor .30 .09
541 Jeff Juden .10 .03
542 Chris Sabo .10 .03
543 Larry Casian .10 .03
544 Jeff Gardner .10 .03
545 Ramon Martinez .10 .03
546 Paul O'Neill .30 .09
547 Steve Hosey .10 .03
548 Dave Nilsson .10 .03
549 Ron Darling .10 .03
550 Matt Williams .20 .06
551 Jack Armstrong .10 .03
552 Bill Krueger .10 .03
553 Freddie Benavides .10 .03
554 Jeff Fassero .10 .03
555 Chuck Knoblauch .20 .06
556 Guillermo Velasquez .10 .03
557 Joel Johnston .10 .03
558 Tom Lampkin .10 .03
559 Todd Van Poppel .10 .03
560 Gary Sheffield .20 .06
561 Skeeter Barnes .10 .03
562 Darren Holmes .10 .03
563 John Vander Wal .10 .03
564 Mike Ignasiak .10 .03
565 Fred McGriff .30 .09
566 Luis Polonia .10 .03
567 Mike Perez .10 .03
568 John Valentin .10 .03
569 Mike Felder .10 .03
570 Tommy Greene .10 .03
571 David Segui .10 .03
572 Roberto Hernandez .10 .03
573 Steve Wilson .10 .03
574 Willie McGee .20 .06
575 Randy Myers .10 .03
576 Darrin Jackson .10 .03
577 Eric Plunk .10 .03
578 Mike Macfarlane .10 .03
579 Doug Brocail .10 .03
580 Steve Finley .20 .06
581 John Roper .10 .03
582 Danny Cox .10 .03
583 Chip Hale .10 .03
584 Scott Bullett .10 .03
585 Kevin Reimer .10 .03
586 Brent Gates .10 .03
587 Matt Turner .10 .03
588 Rich Rowland .10 .03
589 Kent Bottenfield .10 .03
590 Marquis Grissom .20 .06
591 Doug Strange .10 .03
592 Jay Howell .10 .03
593 Omar Vizquel .30 .09
594 Rheal Cormier .10 .03
595 Andre Dawson .20 .06
596 Hilly Hathaway .10 .03
597 Todd Pratt .10 .03
598 Mike Mussina .30 .09
599 Alex Fernandez .10 .03
600 Don Mattingly 1.25 .35
601 Frank Thomas MOG .30 .09
602 Ryne Sandberg MOG .50 .15
603 Wade Boggs MOG .20 .06
604 Cal Ripken MOG .75 .23
605 Barry Bonds MOG .60 .18
606 Ken Griffey Jr. MOG .50 .15
607 Kirby Puckett MOG .30 .09
608 Darren Daulton MOG .10 .03
609 Paul Molitor MOG .20 .06
610 Terry Steinbach .10 .03
611 Todd Worrell .10 .03
612 Jim Thome .50 .15
613 Chuck McElroy .10 .03
614 John Habyan .10 .03
615 Sid Fernandez .10 .03
616 Eddie Zambrano .10 .03
Glenn Murray
Chad Mottola
Jermaine Allensworth RC
617 Steve Bedrosian .10 .03
618 Rob Ducey .10 .03
619 Tom Browning .10 .03
620 Tony Gwynn .60 .18
621 Carl Willis .10 .03
622 Kevin Young .10 .03
623 Rafael Novoa .10 .03
624 Jerry Browne .10 .03
625 Charlie Hough .20 .06
626 Chris Gomez .10 .03
627 Steve Reed .10 .03
628 Kirk Rueter .20 .06
629 Matt Whiteside .10 .03
630 David Justice .20 .06
631 Brad Holman .10 .03
632 Brian Jordan .20 .06
633 Scott Bankhead .10 .03
634 Torey Lovullo .10 .03
635 Len Dykstra .20 .06
636 Ben McDonald .10 .03
637 Steve Howe .10 .03
638 Jose Vizcaino .10 .03
639 Bill Swift .10 .03
640 Darryl Strawberry .20 .06
641 Steve Farr .10 .03
642 Tom Kramer .10 .03
643 Joe Orsulak .10 .03
644 Tom Henke .10 .03
645 Joe Carter .20 .06
646 Ken Caminiti .20 .06
647 Reggie Sanders .20 .06
648 Andy Ashby .10 .03
649 Derek Parks .10 .03
650 Andy Van Slyke .20 .06
651 Juan Bell .10 .03
652 Roger Smithberg .10 .03
653 Chuck Carr .10 .03
654 Bill Gullickson .10 .03
655 Charlie Hayes .10 .03
656 Chris Nabholz .10 .03
657 Karl Rhodes .10 .03
658 Pete Smith .10 .03
659 Bret Boone .20 .06
660 Gregg Jefferies .10 .03
661 Bob Zupcic .10 .03
662 Steve Sax .10 .03
663 Mariano Duncan .10 .03
664 Jeff Tackett .10 .03
665 Mark Langston .10 .03
666 Steve Buechele .10 .03
667 Candy Maldonado .10 .03
668 Woody Williams .20 .06
669 Tim Wakefield .20 .06
670 Danny Tartabull .10 .03
671 Charlie O'Brien .10 .03
672 Felix Jose .10 .03
673 Bobby Ayala .10 .03
674 Scott Servais .10 .03
675 Roberto Alomar .30 .09
676 Pedro A.Martinez RC .10 .03
677 Eddie Guardado .10 .03
678 Mark Lewis .10 .03
679 Jaime Navarro .10 .03
680 Ruben Sierrra .10 .03
681 Rick Renteria .10 .03
682 Storm Davis .10 .03
683 Cory Snyder .10 .03
684 Ron Karkovice .10 .03
685 Juan Gonzalez .30 .09
686 Chris Howard .30 .09
Carlos Delgado
Jason Kendall
Paul Bako
687 John Smoltz .30 .09
688 Brian Dorsett .10 .03
689 Omar Olivares .10 .03
690 Mo Vaughn .20 .06
691 Joe Grahe .10 .03
692 Mickey Morandini .10 .03

693 Tino Martinez .30 .09
694 Brian Barnes .10 .03
695 Mike Stanley .10 .03
696 Mark Clark .10 .03
697 Dave Hansen .10 .03
698 Willie Wilson .10 .03
699 Pete Schourek .10 .03
700 Barry Bonds 1.25 .35
701 Kevin Appier .20 .06
702 Tony Fernandez .10 .03
703 Darryl Kile .20 .06
704 Archi Cianfrocco .10 .03
705 Jose Rijo .10 .03
706 Brian Harper .10 .03
707 Zane Smith .10 .03
708 Dave Henderson .10 .03
709 Angel Miranda UER .10 .03
(no Topps logo on back)
710 Orestes Destrade .10 .03
711 Greg Gohr .10 .03
712 Eric Young .10 .03
713 Todd Williams .10 .03
Ron Watson
Kirk Bullinger
Mike Welch
714 Tim Spehr .10 .03
715 Hank Aaron 715 HR .50 .15
716 Nate Minchey .10 .03
717 Mike Blowers .10 .03
718 Kent Mercker .10 .03
719 Tom Pagnozzi .10 .03
720 Roger Clemens 1.00 .30
721 Eduardo Perez .10 .03
722 Milt Thompson .10 .03
723 Gregg Olson .10 .03
724 Kirk McCaskill .10 .03
725 Sammy Sosa .75 .23
726 Alvaro Espinoza .10 .03
727 Henry Rodriguez .10 .03
728 Jim Leyritz .10 .03
729 Steve Scarsone .10 .03
730 Bobby Bonilla .20 .06
731 Chris Gwynn .10 .03
732 Al Leiter .20 .06
733 Bip Roberts .10 .03
734 Mark Portugal .10 .03
735 Terry Pendleton .20 .06
736 Dave Valle .10 .03
737 Paul Kilgus .10 .03
738 Greg A. Harris .10 .03
739 Jon Ratliff DP RC .10 .03
740 Kirk Presley DP RC .10 .03
741 Josue Estrada DP RC .10 .03
742 Wayne Gomes DP RC .10 .03
743 Pat Watkins DP RC .10 .03
744 Jamey Wright DP RC .25 .07
745 Jay Powell DP RC .10 .03
746 Ryan McGuire DP RC .10 .03
747 Marc Barcelo DP RC .10 .03
748 Sloan Smith DP RC .10 .03
749 John Wasdin DP RC .10 .03
750 Marc Vlades DP .10 .03
751 Dan Ehler DP RC .10 .03
752 Andre King DP RC .10 .03
753 Greg Keagle DP RC .10 .03
754 Jason Myers DP RC .10 .03
755 Dax Winslett DP RC .10 .03
756 Casey Whitten DP RC .10 .03
757 Tony Fuduric DP RC .10 .03
758 Greg Norton DP RC .25 .07
759 Jeff D'Amico DP RC .25 .07
760 Ryan Hancock DP RC .10 .03
761 David Cooper DP RC .10 .03
762 Kevin Orie DP RC .10 .03
763 John O'Donoghue .10 .03
Mike Oquist
764 Cory Bailey RC .10 .03
Scott Hatteberg
765 Mark Holzemer .10 .03
Paul Swingle RC
766 James Baldwin .10 .03
Rod Bolton
767 Jerry Di Poto .25 .07
Julian Tavarez RC
768 Danny Bautista .10 .03
Sean Bergman
769 Bob Hamelin .10 .03
Joe Vitiello
770 Mark Kiefer .10 .03
Troy O'Leary
771 Denny Hocking .10 .03
Oscar Munoz RC
772 Russ Davis .10 .03
Brien Taylor
773 Kyle Abbott RC .25 .07
Miguel Jimenez
774 Kevin King .10 .03
Eric Plantenberg RC
775 Jon Shave .10 .03
Desi Wilson
776 Domingo Cedeno .10 .03
Paul Spoljaric
777 Chipper Jones .50 .15
Ryan Klesko
778 Steve Trachsel .10 .03
Turk Wendell
779 Johnny Ruffin .10 .03
Jerry Spradlin RC
780 Jason Bates .10 .03
John Burke
781 Carl Everett .20 .06
Dave Weathers
782 Gary Mota .10 .03
James Mouton
783 Raul Mondesi .20 .06
Ben Van Ryn
784 Gabe White .20 .06
Rondell White
785 Brook Fordyce .20 .06
Bill Pulsipher
786 Kevin Foster RC .10 .03
Gene Schall
787 Rich Aude RC .10 .03
Midre Cummings
788 Brian Barber .10 .03
Rich Batchelor
789 Brian Johnson RC .10 .03
Scott Sanders
790 Ricky Faneyte .10 .03
J.R. Phillips
791 Checklist 3 .10 .03
792 Checklist 4 .10 .03

1994 Topps Gold

The 1994 Topps Gold set is parallel to the basic issue. They were inserted one per wax or mini pack, two per mini jumbo, three per rack pack, four per jumbo, five per jumbo rack and ten per factory set. The only difference between the Gold issue and the basic cards is gold foil on the player's name and the Topps logo. As in previous Gold Sets, player cards (cards 395-96 and 791-92) replace the Checklist cards.

	Nm-Mt	Ex-Mt
COMPLETE SET (792)	80.00	24.00
COMP.SERIES 1 (396)	40.00	12.00
COMP.SERIES 2 (396)	40.00	12.00

*STARS: 1.5X to 4X BASIC CARDS
*ROOKIES: 1.25X to 3X BASIC CARDS
395 Bill Brennan .40 .12
396 Jeff Bronkey .40 .12
791 Mike Cook .40 .12
792 Dan Pasqua .40 .12

1994 Topps Black Gold

Randomly inserted one in every 72 packs, this 44-card standard-size set was issued in two series of 22. Cards were also issued three per 1994 Topps factory set. Collectors had a chance, through redemption cards to receive all or part of the set. There are seven Winner redemption cards for a total 51 cards associated with this set. The set is considered complete with the 44 player cards. Card fronts feature color player action photos. The player's name at bottom and the team name at top are screened in gold foil. The backs contain a player photo and statistical rankings. The winner cards were redeemable until January 31, 1995

	Nm-Mt	Ex-Mt
COMPLETE SET (44)	25.00	7.50
COMPLETE SERIES 1 (22)	15.00	4.50
COMPLETE SERIES 2 (22)	10.00	3.00

1 Roberto Alomar .60 .18
2 Carlos Baerga .20 .06
3 Albert Belle .40 .12
4 Joe Carter .40 .12
5 Cecil Fielder .40 .12
6 Travis Fryman .40 .12
7 Juan Gonzalez .60 .18
8 Ken Griffey Jr. 1.50 .45
9 Chris Hoiles .20 .06
10 Randy Johnson 1.00 .30
11 Kenny Lofton .40 .12
12 Jack McDowell .20 .06
13 Paul Molitor .60 .18
14 Jeff Montgomery .20 .06
15 John Olerud .40 .12
16 Rafael Palmeiro .60 .18
17 Kirby Puckett 1.00 .30
18 Cal Ripken 3.00 .90
19 Tim Salmon .60 .18
20 Mike Stanley .20 .06
21 Frank Thomas 1.00 .30
22 Robin Ventura .40 .12
23 Jeff Bagwell .60 .18
24 Jay Bell .40 .12
25 Craig Biggio .60 .18
26 Jeff Blauser .20 .06
27 Barry Bonds 2.50 .75
28 Darren Daulton .40 .12
29 Len Dykstra .40 .12
30 Andres Galarraga .40 .12
31 Ron Gant .40 .12
32 Tom Glavine .60 .18
33 Mark Grace .60 .18
34 Marquis Grissom .40 .12
35 Gregg Jefferies .20 .06
36 David Justice .40 .12
37 John Kruk .40 .12
38 Greg Maddux 1.50 .45
39 Fred McGriff .60 .18
40 Randy Myers .20 .06
41 Mike Piazza 2.00 .60
42 Sammy Sosa 1.50 .45
43 Robby Thompson .20 .06
44 Matt Williams .40 .12
A Winner A 1-11 .20 .06
B Winner B 12-22 .20 .06
C Winner C 23-33 .20 .06
D Winner D 34-44 .20 .06
AB Winner AB 1-22 .20 .06
CD Winner CD 23-44 .20 .06
ABCD Winner ABCD 1-44 .20 .06

1994 Topps Traded

This set consists of 132 standard-size cards featuring traded players in their new uniforms, rookies and draft choices. Factory sets consisted of 140 cards including a set of eight Topps Finest cards. Card fronts feature a player photo with the player's name, team and position at the bottom. The horizontal backs have a player photo to the left with complete career statisics and highlights. Rookie Cards include Rusty Greer, Ben Grieve, Paul Konerko Terrence Long and Chan Ho Park.

	Nm-Mt	Ex-Mt
COMP.FACT.SET (140)	30.00	9.00

1T Paul Wilson .20 .06
2T Bill Taylor RC 1.00 .30
3T Dan Wilson .10 .03
4T Mark Smith .10 .03
5T Toby Borland RC .25 .07
6T Dave Clark .10 .03
7T Dennis Martinez .20 .06
8T Dave Gallagher .10 .03
9T Josias Manzanillo .10 .03
10T Brian Anderson RC 1.00 .30
11T Damon Berryhill .10 .03
12T Alex Cole .10 .03
13T Jacob Shumate RC .25 .07
14T Oddibe McDowell .10 .03
15T Willie Banks .10 .03
16T Jerry Browne .10 .03
17T Donnie Elliott .10 .03
18T Ellis Burks .20 .06
19T Chuck McElroy .10 .03
20T Luis Polonia .10 .03
21T Brian Harper .10 .03
22T Mark Portugal .10 .03
23T Dave Henderson .10 .03
24T Mark Acre RC .25 .07
25T Julio Franco .20 .06
26T Darren Hall RC .25 .07
27T Eric Anthony .10 .03
28T Sid Fernandez .10 .03
29T Rusty Greer RC 1.50 .45
30T Riccardo Ingram RC .25 .07
31T Gabe White .10 .03
32T Tim Belcher .10 .03
33T Terrence Long RC 1.50 .45
34T Mark Dalesandro RC .25 .07
35T Mike Kelly .10 .03
36T Jack Morris .20 .06
37T Jeff Brantley .10 .03
38T Larry Barnes RC .25 .07
39T Brian R. Hunter .10 .03
40T Otis Nixon .10 .03
41T Bret Wagner .10 .03
42T Pedro Martinez TR .50 .15
Delino Deshields
43T Heathcliff Slocumb .10 .03
44T Ben Grieve RC 1.50 .45
45T John Hudek RC .25 .07
46T Shawon Dunston .10 .03
47T Greg Colbrunn .10 .03
48T Joey Hamilton .10 .03
49T Marvin Freeman .10 .03
50T Terry Mulholland .10 .03
51T Keith Mitchell .10 .03
52T Dwight Smith .10 .03
53T Shawn Boskie .10 .03
54T Kevin Witt RC 1.00 .30
55T Ron Gant .20 .06
56T Trenidad Hubbard RC 10.00 3.00
Jason Schmidt RC
Larry Sutton
Stephen Larkin RC
57T Jody Reed .10 .03
58T Rick Helling .10 .03
59T John Powell .10 .03
60T Eddie Murray .50 .15
61T Joe Hall RC .25 .07
62T Jorge Fabregas .10 .03
63T Mike Mordecai RC .25 .07
64T Ed Vosberg .10 .03
65T Rickey Henderson .50 .15
66T Tim Grieve RC .25 .07
67T Jon Lieber .10 .03
68T Chris Howard .10 .03
69T Matt Walbeck .10 .03
70T Chan Ho Park RC 1.50 .45
71T Bryan Eversgerd RC .25 .07
72T John Dettmer .10 .03
73T Erik Hanson .10 .03
74T Mike Thurman RC .25 .07
75T Bobby Ayala .10 .03
76T Rafael Palmeiro .30 .09
77T Bret Boone .20 .06
78T Paul Shuey .10 .03
79T Kevin Foster RC .25 .07
80T Dave Magadan .10 .03
81T Bip Roberts .10 .03
82T Howard Johnson .10 .03
83T Xavier Hernandez .10 .03
84T Ross Powell RC .25 .07
85T Doug Million RC .25 .07
86T Geronimo Berroa .10 .03
87T Mark Farris RC .25 .07
88T Butch Henry .10 .03
89T Junior Felix .10 .03
90T Bo Jackson .50 .15
91T Hector Carrasco .10 .03
92T Charlie O'Brien .10 .03
93T Omar Vizquel .30 .09
94T David Segui .10 .03
95T Dustin Hermanson .20 .06
96T Gar Finnvold RC .25 .07
97T Dave Stevens .10 .03
98T Corey Pointer RC .25 .07
99T Felix Fermin .10 .03
100T Lee Smith .20 .06
101T Reid Ryan RC 1.00 .30
102T Bobby Munoz .10 .03
103T Deion Sanders TR .30 .09
Roberto Kelly
104T Turner Ward .10 .03
105T W.VanLandingham RC .25 .07
106T Vince Coleman .10 .03
107T Stan Javier .10 .03
108T Darrin Jackson .10 .03
109T C.J. Nitkowski RC .25 .07
110T Anthony Young .10 .03
111T Kurt Miller .10 .03
112T Paul Konerko RC 5.00 1.50
113T Walt Weiss .10 .03
114T Daryl Boston .10 .03
115T Will Clark .50 .15
116T Matt Smith RC .25 .07
117T Mark Leiter .10 .03
118T Gregg Olson .10 .03
119T Tony Pena .10 .03
120T Jose Vizcaino .10 .03
121T Rick White RC .25 .07
122T Rich Rowland .10 .03
123T Jeff Reboulet .10 .03
124T Greg Hibbard .10 .03
125T Chris Sabo .10 .03
126T Doug Jones .10 .03
127T Tony Fernandez .10 .03
128T Carlos Reyes RC .25 .07
129T Kevin L.Brown RC 1.00 .30
130T Ryne Sandberg 1.25 .35
Farewell
131T Ryne Sandberg 1.25 .35
Farewell
132T Checklist 1-132 .10 .03

1994 Topps Traded Finest Inserts

Each Topps Traded factory set contained a complete eight card set of Finest Inserts. These cards are numbered separately and designed differently from the base cards. Each Finest Insert features a action shot of a player set against purple chrome background. The set highlights the top performers midway through the 1994 season, detailing their performances through July. The cards are numbered on back "X of 8".

	Nm-Mt	Ex-Mt
COMPLETE SET (8)	5.00	1.50

1 Greg Maddux .75 .23
2 Mike Piazza 1.00 .30
3 Matt Williams .20 .06
4 Raul Mondesi .20 .06
5 Ken Griffey Jr. .75 .23
6 Kenny Lofton .20 .06
7 Frank Thomas .50 .15
8 Manny Ramirez .30 .09

1995 Topps

These 660 standard-size cards feature color action player photos with white borders on the fronts. This set was released in two series. The first series contained 396 cards while the second series had 264 cards. Cards were distributed in 11-card packs (SRP $1.29), jumbo packs and factory sets. One "Own The Game" instant winner card has been inserted in every 120 packs. Rookie cards in this set include Rey Ordonez. Due to the 1994 baseball strike, it was publicly announced that production for this set was the lowest print run since 1966.

	Nm-Mt	Ex-Mt
COMPLETE SET (660)	80.00	24.00
COMP.HOBBY SET (677)	120.00	36.00
COMP.RETAIL SET (677)	120.00	36.00
COMP.SERIES 1 (396)	40.00	12.00
COMP.SERIES 2 (264)	40.00	12.00

1 Frank Thomas .75 .23
2 Mickey Morandini .15 .04
3 Babe Ruth 100th B-Day 2.00 .60
4 Scott Cooper .15 .04
5 David Cone .30 .09
6 Jacob Shumate .15 .04
7 Trevor Hoffman .30 .09
8 Shane Mack .15 .04
9 Delino DeShields .15 .04
10 Matt Williams .30 .09
11 Sammy Sosa 1.25 .35
12 Gary DiSarcina .15 .04
13 Kenny Rogers .30 .09
14 Jose Vizcaino .15 .04
15 Lou Whitaker .30 .09
16 Ron Darling .15 .04
17 Dave Nilsson .15 .04
18 Chris Hammond .15 .04
19 Sid Bream .15 .04
20 Denny Martinez .30 .09
21 Orlando Merced .15 .04
22 John Wetteland .30 .09
23 Mike Devereaux .15 .04
24 Rene Arocha .15 .04
25 Jay Buhner .30 .09
26 Darren Holmes .15 .04
27 Hal Morris .15 .04
28 Brian Buchanan RC .15 .04
29 Keith Miller .15 .04
30 Paul Molitor .50 .15
31 Dave West .15 .04
32 Tony Tarasco .15 .04
33 Scott Sanders .15 .04
34 Eddie Zambrano .15 .04
35 Ricky Bones .15 .04
36 John Valentin .15 .04
37 Kevin Tapani .15 .04
38 Tim Wallach .15 .04
39 Darren Lewis .15 .04
40 Travis Fryman .30 .09
41 Mark Leiter .15 .04
42 Jose Bautista .15 .04
43 Pete Smith .15 .04
44 Bret Barberie .15 .04
45 Dennis Eckersley .30 .09
46 Ken Hill .15 .04
47 Chad Ogea .15 .04
48 Pete Harnisch .15 .04
49 James Baldwin .15 .04
50 Mike Mussina .50 .15
51 Al Martin .15 .04
52 Mark Thompson .15 .04
53 Matt Smith .15 .04
54 Joey Hamilton .15 .04
55 Edgar Martinez .50 .15
56 John Smiley .15 .04
57 Rey Sanchez .15 .04
58 Mike Timlin .15 .04
59 Ricky Bottalico .15 .04
60 Jim Abbott .50 .15
61 Mike Kelly .15 .04
62 Brian Jordan .30 .09
63 Ken Ryan .15 .04
64 Matt Mieske .15 .04
65 Rick Aguilera .15 .04
66 Ismael Valdes .15 .04
67 Royce Clayton .15 .04
68 Junior Felix .15 .04
69 Harold Reynolds .30 .09
70 Juan Gonzalez .50 .15
71 Kelly Stinnett .15 .04
72 Carlos Reyes .15 .04
73 Dave Weathers .15 .04
74 Mel Rojas .15 .04
75 Doug Drabek .15 .04
76 Charles Nagy .15 .04
77 Tim Raines .30 .09
78 Midre Cummings .15 .04
79 Gene Schall .15 .04
Scott Talanoa
Harold Williams
Ray Brown RC
80 Rafael Palmeiro .50 .15
81 Charlie Hayes .15 .04
82 Ray Lankford .15 .04
83 Tim Davis .15 .04
84 C.J. Nitkowski .15 .04
85 Andy Ashby .15 .04
86 Gerald Williams .15 .04
87 Terry Shumpert .15 .04
88 Heathcliff Slocumb .15 .04
89 Domingo Cedeno .15 .04
90 Mark Grace .50 .15
91 Brad Woodall RC .15 .04
92 Gar Finnvold .15 .04
93 Jaime Navarro .15 .04
94 Carlos Hernandez .15 .04
95 Mark Langston .15 .04
96 Chuck Carr .15 .04
97 Mike Gardiner .15 .04
98 Dave McCarty .15 .04
99 Cris Carpenter .15 .04
100 Barry Bonds 2.00 .60
101 David Segui .15 .04
102 Scott Brosius .30 .09
103 Mariano Duncan .15 .04
104 Kenny Lofton .30 .09
105 Ken Caminiti .30 .09
106 Darrin Jackson .15 .04
107 Jim Poole .15 .04
108 Wil Cordero .15 .04
109 Danny Miceli .15 .04
110 Walt Weiss .15 .04
111 Tom Pagnozzi .15 .04
112 Terrence Long .30 .09
113 Bret Boone .30 .09
114 Daryl Boston .15 .04
115 Wally Joyner .30 .09
116 Rob Butler .15 .04
117 Rafael Belliard .15 .04
118 Luis Lopez .15 .04
119 Tony Fossas .15 .04
120 Len Dykstra .30 .09
121 Mike Morgan .15 .04
122 Denny Hocking .15 .04
123 Kevin Gross .15 .04
124 Todd Benzinger .15 .04
125 John Doherty .15 .04
126 Eduardo Perez .15 .04
127 Dan Smith .15 .04
128 Joe Orsulak .15 .04
129 Brent Gates .15 .04
130 Jeff Conine .30 .09
131 Doug Henry .15 .04
132 Paul Sorrento .15 .04
133 Mike Hampton .30 .09
134 Tim Spehr .15 .04
135 Julio Franco .30 .09
136 Mike Dyer .15 .04
137 Chris Sabo .15 .04
138 Rheal Cormier .15 .04
139 Paul Konerko .30 .09
140 Dante Bichette .30 .09
141 Chuck McElroy .15 .04
142 Mike Stanley .15 .04
143 Bob Hamelin .15 .04
144 Tommy Greene .15 .04
145 John Smoltz .50 .15
146 Ed Sprague .15 .04
147 Ray McDavid .15 .04
148 Otis Nixon .15 .04
149 Turk Wendell .15 .04
150 Chris James .15 .04
151 Derek Parks .15 .04
152 Jose Offerman .15 .04
153 Tony Clark .15 .04
154 Chad Curtis .15 .04
155 Mark Portugal .15 .04
156 Bill Pulsipher .15 .04
157 Troy Neel .15 .04
158 Dave Winfield .30 .09
159 Bill Wegman .15 .04
160 Benito Santiago .30 .09
161 Jose Mesa .15 .04
162 Luis Gonzalez .30 .09
163 Alex Fernandez .15 .04
164 Freddie Benavides .15 .04
165 Ben McDonald .15 .04
166 Blas Minor .15 .04
167 Bret Wagner .15 .04
168 Mac Suzuki .15 .04
169 Roberto Mejia .15 .04
170 Wade Boggs .50 .15
171 Pokey Reese .15 .04
172 Hipolito Pichardo .15 .04
173 Kim Batiste .15 .04
174 Darren Hall .15 .04

175 Tom Glavine .50 .15
176 Phil Plantier .15 .04
177 Chris Howard .15 .04
178 Karl Rhodes .15 .04
179 LaTroy Hawkins .15 .04
180 Raul Mondesi .30 .09
181 Jeff Reed .15 .04
182 Milt Cuyler .15 .04
183 Jim Edmonds .50 .15
184 Hector Fajardo .15 .04
185 Jeff Kent .30 .09
186 Wilson Alvarez .15 .04
187 Geronimo Berroa .15 .04
188 Billy Spiers .15 .04
189 Derek Lilliquist .15 .04
190 Craig Biggio .50 .15
191 Roberto Hernandez .15 .04
192 Bob Natal .15 .04
193 Bobby Ayala .15 .04
194 Travis Miller RC .15 .04
195 Bob Tewksbury .15 .04
196 Rondell White .30 .09
197 Steve Cooke .15 .04
198 Jeff Branson .15 .04
199 Derek Jeter 2.00 .60
200 Tim Salmon .50 .15
201 Steve Frey .15 .04
202 Kent Mercker .15 .04
203 Randy Johnson .75 .23
204 Todd Worrell .15 .04
205 Mo Vaughn .30 .09
206 Howard Johnson .15 .04
207 John Wasdin .15 .04
208 Eddie Williams .15 .04
209 Tim Belcher .15 .04
210 Jeff Montgomery .15 .04
211 Kirt Manwaring .15 .04
212 Ben Grieve .30 .09
213 Pat Hentgen .15 .04
214 Shawon Dunston .15 .04
215 Mike Greenwell .15 .04
216 Alex Diaz .15 .04
217 Pat Mahomes .15 .04
218 Dave Hansen .15 .04
219 Kevin Rogers .15 .04
220 Cecil Fielder .30 .09
221 Andrew Lorraine .15 .04
222 Jack Armstrong .15 .04
223 Todd Hundley .15 .04
224 Mark Acre .15 .04
225 Darrell Whitmore .15 .04
226 Randy Milligan .15 .04
227 Wayne Kirby .15 .04
228 Darryl Kile .30 .09
229 Bob Zupcic .15 .04
230 Jay Bell .30 .09
231 Dustin Hermanson .15 .04
232 Harold Baines .30 .09
233 Alan Benes .15 .04
234 Felix Fermin .15 .04
235 Ellis Burks .30 .09
236 Jeff Brantley .15 .04
237 Brian Hunter .40 .12
Jose Malave
Karim Garcia RC
Shane Pullen
238 Matt Nokes .15 .04
239 Ben Rivera .15 .04
240 Joe Carter .30 .09
241 Jeff Granger .15 .04
242 Terry Pendleton .30 .09
243 Melvin Nieves .15 .04
244 Frankie Rodriguez .15 .04
245 Darryl Hamilton .15 .04
246 Brooks Kieschnick .15 .04
247 Todd Hollandsworth .15 .04
248 Joe Rosselli .15 .04
249 Bill Gullickson .15 .04
250 Chuck Knoblauch .30 .09
251 Kurt Miller .15 .04
252 Bobby Jones .15 .04
253 Lance Blankenship .15 .04
254 Matt Whiteside .15 .04
255 Darrin Fletcher .15 .04
256 Eric Plunk .15 .04
257 Shane Reynolds .15 .04
258 Norberto Martin .15 .04
259 Mike Thurman .15 .04
260 Andy Van Slyke .30 .09
261 Dwight Smith .15 .04
262 Allen Watson .15 .04
263 Dan Wilson .15 .04
264 Brent Mayne .15 .04
265 Bip Roberts .15 .04
266 Sterling Hitchcock .15 .04
267 Alex Gonzalez .15 .04
268 Greg Harris .15 .04
269 Ricky Jordan .15 .04
270 Johnny Ruffin .15 .04
271 Mike Stanton .15 .04
272 Rich Rowland .15 .04
273 Steve Trachsel .15 .04
274 Pedro Munoz .15 .04
275 Ramon Martinez .15 .04
276 Dave Henderson .15 .04
277 Chris Gomez .15 .04
278 Joe Grahe .15 .04
279 Rusty Greer .30 .09
280 John Franco .30 .09
281 Mike Bordick .15 .04
282 Jeff D'Amico .15 .04
283 Dave Magadan .15 .04
284 Tony Pena .15 .04
285 Greg Swindell .15 .04
286 Doug Million .15 .04
287 Gabe White .15 .04
288 Trey Beamon .15 .04
289 Arthur Rhodes .15 .04
290 Juan Guzman .15 .04
291 Jose Oquendo .15 .04
292 Willie Blair .15 .04
293 Eddie Taubensee .15 .04
294 Steve Howe .15 .04
295 Greg Maddux 1.25 .35
296 Mike Macfarlane .15 .04
297 Curt Schilling .30 .09
298 Phil Clark .15 .04
299 Woody Williams .15 .04
300 Jose Canseco .75 .23
301 Aaron Sele .15 .04
302 Carl Willis .15 .04
303 Steve Buechele .15 .04
304 Dave Burba .15 .04
305 Orel Hershiser .30 .09
306 Damion Easley .15 .04
307 Mike Henneman .15 .04
308 Josias Manzanillo .15 .04
309 Kevin Seitzer .15 .04
310 Ruben Sierra .15 .04
311 Bryan Harvey .15 .04
312 Jim Thome .75 .23
313 Ramon Castro RC .40 .12
314 Lance Johnson .15 .04
315 Marquis Grissom .30 .09
316 Terrell Wade .15 .04
Juan Acevedo
Matt Arrandale
Eddie Priest RC
317 Paul Wagner .15 .04
318 Jamie Moyer .30 .09
319 Todd Zeile .15 .04
320 Chris Bosio .15 .04
321 Steve Reed .15 .04
322 Erik Hanson .15 .04
323 Luis Polonia .15 .04
324 Ryan Klesko .30 .09
325 Kevin Appier .30 .09
326 Jim Eisenreich .15 .04
327 Randy Knorr .15 .04
328 Craig Shipley .15 .04
329 Tim Naehring .15 .04
330 Randy Myers .15 .04
331 Alex Cole .15 .04
332 Jim Gott .15 .04
333 Mike Jackson .15 .04
334 John Flaherty .15 .04
335 Chili Davis .30 .09
336 Benji Gil .15 .04
337 Jason Jacome .15 .04
338 Stan Javier .15 .04
339 Mike Fetters .15 .04
340 Rich Renteria .15 .04
341 Kevin Witt .15 .04
342 Scott Servais .15 .04
343 Craig Grebeck .15 .04
344 Kirk Rueter .15 .04
345 Don Slaught .15 .04
346 Armando Benitez .30 .09
347 Ozzie Smith 1.25 .35
348 Mike Blowers .15 .04
349 Armando Reynoso .15 .04
350 Barry Larkin .50 .15
351 Mike Williams .15 .04
352 Scott Kamieniecki .15 .04
353 Gary Gaetti .30 .09
354 Todd Stottlemyre .15 .04
355 Fred McGriff .50 .15
356 Tim Mauser .15 .04
357 Chris Gwynn .15 .04
358 Frank Castillo .15 .04
359 Jeff Reboulet .15 .04
360 Roger Clemens 1.50 .45
361 Mark Carreon .15 .04
362 Chad Kreuter .15 .04
363 Mark Farris .15 .04
364 Bob Welch .15 .04
365 Dean Palmer .30 .09
366 Jeromy Burnitz .30 .09
367 B.J. Surhoff .30 .09
368 Mike Butcher .15 .04
369 Brad Clontz .15 .04
Steve Phoenix
Scott Gentile
Bucky Buckles RC
370 Eddie Murray .75 .23
371 Orlando Miller .15 .04
372 Ron Karkovice .15 .04
373 Richie Lewis .15 .04
374 Lenny Webster .15 .04
375 Jeff Tackett .15 .04
376 Tom Urbani .15 .04
377 Tino Martinez .50 .15
378 Mark Dewey .15 .04
379 Charles O'Brien .15 .04
380 Terry Mulholland .15 .04
381 Thomas Howard .15 .04
382 Chris Haney .15 .04
383 Billy Hatcher .15 .04
384 Jeff Bagwell AS .50 .15
Frank Thomas AS
385 Bret Boone AS .30 .09
Carlos Baerga AS
386 Matt Williams AS .30 .09
Wade Boggs AS
387 Wil Cordero AS .75 .23
Cal Ripken AS
388 Barry Bonds AS 1.00 .30
Ken Griffey AS
389 Tony Gwynn AS .30 .09
Albert Belle AS
390 Dante Bichette AS .50 .15
Kirby Puckett AS
391 Mike Piazza AS .75 .23
Mike Stanley AS
392 Greg Maddux AS .75 .23
David Cone AS
393 Danny Jackson AS .15 .04
Jimmy Key AS
394 John Franco AS .15 .04
Lee Smith AS
395 Checklist 1-198 .15 .04
396 Checklist 199-396 .15 .04
397 Ken Griffey Jr. 1.25 .35
398 Rick Heiserman RC .15 .04
399 Don Mattingly 2.00 .60
400 Henry Rodriguez .15 .04
401 Lenny Harris .15 .04
402 Ryan Thompson .15 .04
403 Darren Oliver .15 .04
404 Omar Vizquel .50 .15
405 Jeff Bagwell .50 .15
406 Doug Webb RC .15 .04
407 Todd Van Poppel .15 .04
408 Leo Gomez .15 .04
409 Mark Whiten .15 .04
410 Pedro A.Martinez .15 .04
411 Reggie Sanders .15 .04
412 Kevin Foster .15 .04
413 Danny Tartabull .15 .04
414 Jeff Blauser .15 .04
415 Mike Magnante .15 .04
416 Tom Candiotti .15 .04
417 Rod Beck .15 .04
418 Jody Reed .15 .04
419 Vince Coleman .15 .04
420 Danny Jackson .15 .04
421 Ryan Nye RC .15 .04
422 Larry Walker .50 .15
423 Russ Johnson DP .15 .04
424 Pat Borders .15 .04
425 Lee Smith .30 .09
426 Paul O'Neill .50 .15
427 Devon White .30 .09
428 Jim Bullinger .15 .04
429 Greg Hansell .15 .04
Brian Sackinsky
Carey Paige
Rob Welch RC
430 Steve Avery .15 .04
431 Tony Gwynn 1.00 .30
432 Pat Meares .15 .04
433 Bill Swift .15 .04
434 David Wells .30 .09
435 John Briscoe .15 .04
436 Roger Pavlik .15 .04
437 Jayson Peterson RC .15 .04
438 Roberto Alomar .50 .15
439 Billy Brewer .15 .04
440 Gary Sheffield .30 .09
441 Lou Frazier .15 .04
442 Terry Steinbach .15 .04
443 Jay Payton RC .75 .23
444 Jason Bere .15 .04
445 Denny Neagle .30 .09
446 Andres Galarraga .30 .09
447 Hector Carrasco .15 .04
448 Bill Risley .15 .04
449 Andy Benes .15 .04
450 Jim Leyritz .15 .04
451 Jose Oliva .15 .04
452 Greg Vaughn .15 .04
453 Rich Monteleone .15 .04
454 Tony Eusebio .15 .04
455 Chuck Finley .30 .09
456 Kevin Brown .30 .09
457 Joe Boever .15 .04
458 Bobby Munoz .15 .04
459 Bret Saberhagen .30 .09
460 Kurt Abbott .15 .04
461 Bobby Witt .15 .04
462 Cliff Floyd .30 .09
463 Mark Clark .15 .04
464 Andujar Cedeno .15 .04
465 Marvin Freeman .15 .04
466 Mike Piazza 1.25 .35
467 Willie Greene .15 .04
468 Pat Kelly .15 .04
469 Carlos Delgado .30 .09
470 Willie Banks .15 .04
471 Matt Walbeck .15 .04
472 Mark McGwire 2.00 .60
473 M.Christensen RC .15 .04
474 Alan Trammell .30 .09
475 Tom Gordon .15 .04
476 Greg Colbrunn .15 .04
477 Darren Daulton .30 .09
478 Albie Lopez .15 .04
479 Robin Ventura .30 .09
480 Eddie Perez RC .40 .12
Jason Kendall
Einar Diaz
Bret Hemphill
481 Bryan Eversgerd .15 .04
482 Dave Fleming .15 .04
483 Scott Livingstone .15 .04
484 Pete Schourek .15 .04
485 Bernie Williams .50 .15
486 Mark Lemke .15 .04
487 Eric Karros .30 .09
488 Scott Ruffcorn .15 .04
489 Billy Ashley .15 .04
490 Rico Brogna .15 .04
491 John Burkett .15 .04
492 Cade Gaspar RC .15 .04
493 Jorge Fabregas .15 .04
494 Greg Gagne .15 .04
495 Doug Jones .15 .04
496 Troy O'Leary .15 .04
497 Pat Rapp .15 .04
498 Butch Henry .15 .04
499 John Olerud .30 .09
500 John Hudek .15 .04
501 Jeff King .15 .04
502 Bobby Bonilla .30 .09
503 Albert Belle .30 .09
504 Rick Wilkins .15 .04
505 John Jaha .15 .04
506 Nigel Wilson .15 .04
507 Sid Fernandez .15 .04
508 Deion Sanders .50 .15
509 Gil Heredia .15 .04
510 Scott Elarton RC .40 .12
511 Melido Perez .15 .04
512 Greg McMichael .15 .04
513 Rusty Meacham .15 .04
514 Shawn Green .30 .09
515 Carlos Garcia .15 .04
516 Dave Stevens .15 .04
517 Eric Young .15 .04
518 Omar Daal .15 .04
519 Kirk Gibson .30 .09
520 Spike Owen .15 .04
521 Jacob Cruz RC .30 .09
522 Sandy Alomar Jr. .15 .04
523 Steve Bedrosian .15 .04
524 Ricky Gutierrez .15 .04
525 Dave Veres .15 .04
526 Gregg Jefferies .15 .04
527 Jose Valentin .15 .04
528 Robb Nen .30 .09
529 Jose Rijo .15 .04
530 Sean Berry .15 .04
531 Mike Gallego .15 .04
532 Roberto Kelly .15 .04
533 Kevin Stocker .15 .04
534 Kirby Puckett .75 .23
535 Chipper Jones .75 .23
536 Russ Davis .15 .04
537 Jon Lieber .15 .04
538 Trey Moore RC .15 .04
539 Joe Girardi .15 .04
540 Quilvio Veras .40 .12
Arquimedez Pozo
Miguel Cairo RC
Jason Camilli
541 Tony Phillips .15 .04
542 Brian Anderson .15 .04
543 Ivan Rodriguez .75 .23
544 Jeff Cirillo .15 .04
545 Joey Cora .15 .04
546 Chris Hoiles .15 .04
547 Bernard Gilkey .15 .04
548 Mike Lansing .15 .04
549 Jimmy Key .30 .09
550 Mark Wohlers .15 .04
551 Chris Clemons RC .15 .04
552 Vinny Castilla .30 .09
553 Mark Guthrie .15 .04
554 Mike Lieberthal .30 .09
555 Tommy Davis RC .15 .04
556 Robby Thompson .15 .04
557 Danny Bautista .15 .04
558 Will Clark .75 .23
559 Rickey Henderson .75 .23
560 Todd Jones .15 .04
561 Jack McDowell .15 .04
562 Carlos Rodriguez .15 .04
563 Mark Eichhorn .15 .04
564 Jeff Nelson .15 .04
565 Eric Anthony .15 .04
566 Randy Velarde .15 .04
567 Javier Lopez .30 .09
568 Kevin Mitchell .15 .04
569 Steve Karsay .15 .04
570 Brian Meadows RC .15 .04
571 Rey Ordonez RC .75 .23
Mike Metcalfe
Kevin Orie
Ray Holbert
572 John Kruk .30 .09
573 Scott Leius .15 .04
574 John Patterson .15 .04
575 Kevin Brown .30 .09
576 Mike Moore .15 .04
577 Manny Ramirez .50 .15
578 Jose Lind .15 .04
579 Derrick May .15 .04
580 Cal Eldred .15 .04
581 David Bell .75 .23
Joel Chelmis
Lino Diaz
Aaron Boone RC
582 J.T. Snow .30 .09
583 Luis Sojo .15 .04
584 Moises Alou .30 .09
585 Dave Clark .15 .04
586 Dave Hollins .15 .04
587 Nomar Garciaparra 2.00 .60
588 Cal Ripken 2.50 .75
589 Pedro Astacio .15 .04
590 J.R. Phillips .15 .04
591 Jeff Frye .15 .04
592 Bo Jackson .75 .23
593 Steve Ontiveros .15 .04
594 David Nied .15 .04
595 Brad Ausmus .15 .04
596 Carlos Baerga .15 .04
597 James Mouton .15 .04
598 Ozzie Guillen .15 .04
599 Ozzie Timmons .75 .23
Curtis Goodwin
Johnny Damon
Jeff Abbott RC
600 Yorkis Perez .15 .04
601 Rich Rodriguez .15 .04
602 Mark McLemore .15 .04
603 Jeff Fassero .15 .04
604 John Roper .15 .04
605 Mark Johnson RC .40 .12
606 Wes Chamberlain .15 .04
607 Felix Jose .15 .04
608 Tony Longmire .15 .04
609 Duane Ward .15 .04
610 Brett Butler .30 .09
611 W.VanLandingham .15 .04
612 Mickey Tettleton .15 .04
613 Brady Anderson .30 .09
614 Reggie Jefferson .15 .04
615 Mike Kingery .15 .04
616 Derek Bell .15 .04
617 Scott Erickson .15 .04
618 Bob Wickman .15 .04
619 Phil Leftwich .15 .04
620 David Justice .30 .09
621 Paul Wilson .15 .04
622 Pedro Martinez .75 .23
623 Terry Mathews .15 .04
624 Brian McRae .15 .04
625 Bruce Ruffin .15 .04
626 Steve Finley .30 .09
627 Ron Gant .30 .09
628 Rafael Bournigal .15 .04
629 Darryl Strawberry .30 .09
630 Luis Alicea .15 .04
631 Mark Smith .15 .04
Scott Klingenbeck
632 Cory Bailey .15 .04
Scott Hatteberg
633 Todd Greene .30 .09
Troy Percival
634 Rod Bolton .15 .04
Olmedo Saenz
635 Steve Kline .15 .04
Herb Perry
636 Sean Bergman .15 .04
Shannon Penn
637 Joe Randa .15 .04
Joe Vitiello
638 Jose Mercedes .15 .04
Duane Singleton
639 Marc Barcelo .15 .04
Marty Cordova
640 Andy Pettitte .30 .09
Ruben Rivera
641 Willie Adams .15 .04
Scott Spiezio
642 Eddy Diaz RC .15 .04
Desi Relaford
643 Terrell Lowery .15 .04
Jon Shave
644 Angel Martinez .15 .04
Paul Spoljaric
645 Tony Graffanino .15 .04
Damon Hollins
646 Darron Cox .15 .04
Doug Glanville
647 Tim Belk .15 .04
Pat Watkins
648 Rod Pedraza .15 .04
Phil Schneider
649 Vic Darensbourg .15 .04
Marc Valdes
650 Rick Huisman .15 .04
Roberto Petagine
651 Roger Cedeno .40 .12
Ron Coomer RC
652 Shane Andrews .40 .12
Carlos Perez RC
653 Jason Isringhausen .30 .09
Chris Roberts
654 Wayne Gomes .15 .04
Kevin Jordan
655 Esteban Loaiza .15 .04
Steve Pegues
656 Terry Bradshaw .15 .04
John Frascatore
657 Andres Berumen .15 .04
Bryce Florie
658 Dan Carlson .15 .04
Keith Williams
659 Checklist .15 .04
660 Checklist .15 .04

1995 Topps Cyberstats

The 396-card Cyberstats insert set was issued one per pack and three per jumbo pack. Each 1995 Topps series had 198 Cyberstat cards. The idea was to present prorated statistics for the 1994 strike shortened season. The photos on front are the same as the basic issue. The difference is that the photo is given a glossy or metallic finish. The backs contain yearly and career statistics, including the prorated 1994 numbers.

	Nm-Mt	Ex-Mt
COMPLETE SET (396)	60.00	18.00
COMP.SERIES 1 (198)	25.00	7.50
COMP.SERIES 2 (198)	40.00	12.00

*STARS: 1X TO 2.5X BASIC CARDS...

1995 Topps Finest Inserts

This 15-card standard-size set was inserted one every 36 Topps series two packs. This set featured the top 15 players in total bases from the 1994 season. The fronts feature a player photo, with his team identification and name on the bottom of the card. The horizontal backs feature another player photo along with a breakdown of how many of each type of hit each player got on the way to their season total. The set is sequenced in order of how they finished in the majors for the 1994 season.

	Nm-Mt	Ex-Mt
COMPLETE SET (15)	60.00	18.00
1 Jeff Bagwell	3.00	.90
2 Albert Belle	2.00	.60
3 Ken Griffey Jr.	8.00	2.40
4 Frank Thomas	5.00	1.50
5 Matt Williams	2.00	.60
6 Dante Bichette	2.00	.60
7 Barry Bonds	12.00	3.60
8 Moises Alou	2.00	.60
9 Andres Galarraga	2.00	.60
10 Kenny Lofton	2.00	.60
11 Rafael Palmeiro	3.00	.90
12 Tony Gwynn	6.00	1.80
13 Kirby Puckett	5.00	1.50
14 Jose Canseco	5.00	1.50
15 Jeff Conine	2.00	.60

1995 Topps League Leaders

Randomly inserted in jumbo packs at a rate of one in three and retail packs at a rate of one in six, this 50-card standard-size set showcases those that were among league leaders in various categories. Card fronts feature a player photo with a black background. The player's name appears in gold foil at the bottom and the category with which he led the league or was among the leaders is in yellow letters up the right side. The backs contain various graphs and where the player placed among the leaders.

	Nm-Mt	Ex-Mt
COMPLETE SET (50)	50.00	15.00
COMPLETE SERIES 1 (25)	20.00	6.00
COMPLETE SERIES 2 (25)	30.00	9.00
LL1 Albert Belle	.60	.18
LL2 Kevin Mitchell	.30	.09
LL3 Wade Boggs	1.00	.30
LL4 Tony Gwynn	2.00	.60
LL5 Moises Alou	.60	.18
LL6 Andres Galarraga	.60	.18
LL7 Matt Williams	.60	.18
LL8 Barry Bonds	4.00	1.20

LL9 Frank Thomas 1.50 .45
LL10 Jose Canseco 1.50 .45
LL11 Jeff Bagwell 1.00 .30
LL12 Kirby Puckett 1.50 .45
LL13 Julio Franco .60 .18
LL14 Albert Belle .60 .18
LL15 Fred McGriff 1.00 .30
LL16 Kenny Lofton .60 .18
LL17 Otis Nixon .30 .09
LL18 Brady Anderson .60 .18
LL19 Deion Sanders 1.00 .30
LL20 Chuck Carr .30 .09
LL21 Pat Hentgen .30 .09
LL22 Andy Benes .30 .09
LL23 Roger Clemens 3.00 .90
LL24 Greg Maddux 2.50 .75
LL25 Pedro Martinez .30 .09
LL26 Paul O'Neill 1.00 .30
LL27 Jeff Bagwell 1.00 .30
LL28 Frank Thomas 1.50 .45
LL29 Hal Morris .30 .09
LL30 Kenny Lofton .60 .18
LL31 Ken Griffey Jr. 2.50 .75
LL32 Jeff Bagwell 1.00 .30
LL33 Albert Belle .60 .18
LL34 Fred McGriff 1.00 .30
LL35 Cecil Fielder .60 .18
LL36 Matt Williams .60 .18
LL37 Joe Carter .60 .18
LL38 Dante Bichette .60 .18
LL39 Frank Thomas 1.50 .45
LL40 Mike Piazza 2.50 .75
LL41 Craig Biggio 1.00 .30
LL42 Vince Coleman .30 .09
LL43 Marquis Grissom .60 .18
LL44 Chuck Knoblauch .60 .18
LL45 Darren Lewis .30 .09
LL46 Randy Johnson 1.50 .45
LL47 Jose Rijo .30 .09
LL48 Chuck Finley .60 .18
LL49 Bret Saberhagen .60 .18
LL50 Kevin Appier .60 .18

1995 Topps Traded

This set contains 165 standard-size cards and was sold in 11-card packs for $1.29. The set features rookies, draft picks and players who had been traded. The fronts contain a photo with a white border. The backs have a player picture in a scoreboard and his statistics and information. Subsets featured are: At the Break (1T-10T) and All-Stars (156T-164T). Rookie Cards in this set include Michael Barrett, Carlos Beltran, Ben Davis, Hideo Nomo and Richie Sexson.

Nm-Mt Ex-Mt
COMPLETE SET (165) 60.00 18.00
1T Frank Thomas ATB .60 .18
2T Ken Griffey Jr. ATB 1.00 .30
3T Barry Bonds ATB 1.25 .35
4T Albert Belle ATB .40 .12
5T Cal Ripken ATB 1.50 .45
6T Mike Piazza ATB 1.00 .30
7T Tony Gwynn ATB .60 .18
8T Jeff Bagwell ATB .40 .12
9T Mo Vaughn ATB .20 .06
10T Matt Williams ATB .20 .06
11T Ray Durham .40 .12
12T Juan LeBron 10.00 3.00
Card pictures Carlos Beltran instead of Juan LeBron RC
13T Shawn Green .40 .12
14T Kevin Gross .20 .06
15T Jon Nunnally .20 .06
16T Brian Maxcy RC .25 .07
17T Mark Kiefer .20 .06
18T Carlos Beltran UER 30.00 9.00
Card pictures Juan LeBron instead of Carlos Beltran RC.
19T Mike Mimbs RC .25 .07
20T Larry Walker .60 .18
21T Chad Curtis .20 .06
22T Jeff Barry .20 .06
23T Joe Oliver .20 .06
24T Tomas Perez RC .25 .07
25T Michael Barrett RC 1.00 .30
26T Brian McRae .20 .06
27T Derek Bell .20 .06
28T Ray Durham .40 .12
29T Todd Williams .20 .06
30T Ryan Jaroncyk RC .25 .07
31T Todd Steverson .20 .06
32T Mike Devereaux .20 .06
33T Rheal Cormier .20 .06
34T Benny Santiago .40 .12
35T Bobby Higginson RC 1.00 .30
36T Jack McDowell .20 .06
37T Mike Macfarlane .20 .06
38T Tony McKnight RC .25 .07
39T Brian Hunter .20 .06
40T Hideo Nomo RC 3.00 .90
41T Brett Butler .40 .12
42T Donovan Osborne .20 .06
43T Scott Karl .20 .06
44T Tony Phillips .20 .06
45T Marty Cordova .20 .06
46T Dave Mlicki .20 .06
47T Bronson Arroyo RC 5.00 1.50
48T John Burkett .20 .06
49T J.D. Smart RC .25 .07
50T Mickey Tettleton .20 .06
51T Todd Stottlemyre .20 .06
52T Mike Perez .20 .06
53T Terry Mulholland .20 .06
54T Edgardo Alfonzo .40 .12
55T Zane Smith .20 .06
56T Jacob Brumfield .20 .06
57T Andujar Cedeno .20 .06
58T Jose Parra .20 .06
59T Manny Alexander .20 .06
60T Tony Tarasco .20 .06
61T Orel Hershiser .40 .12
62T Tim Scott .20 .06
63T Felix Rodriguez RC .50 .15
64T Ken Hill .20 .06
65T Marquis Grissom .40 .12
66T Lee Smith .40 .12
67T Jason Bates .20 .06
68T Felipe Lira .20 .06
69T Alex Hernandez RC .25 .07
70T Tony Fernandez .20 .06
71T Scott Radinsky .20 .06
72T Jose Canseco 1.00 .30
73T Mark Grudzielanek RC .50 .15
74T Ben Davis RC .50 .15
75T Jim Abbott .60 .18
76T Roger Bailey .20 .06
77T Gregg Jefferies .20 .06
78T Erik Hanson .20 .06
79T Brad Radke RC 1.00 .30
80T Jaime Navarro .20 .06
81T John Wetteland .40 .12
82T Chad Fonville RC .25 .07
83T John Mabry .20 .06
84T Glenallen Hill .20 .06
85T Ken Caminiti .40 .12
86T Tom Goodwin .20 .06
87T Darren Bragg .20 .06
88T Pat Ahearne .25 .07
Gary Rath
Larry Wimberly
Robbie Bell RC
89T Jeff Russell .20 .06
90T Dave Gallagher .20 .06
91T Steve Finley .40 .12
92T Vaughn Eshelman .20 .06
93T Kevin Jarvis .20 .06
94T Mark Gubicza .20 .06
95T Tim Wakefield .40 .12
96T Bob Tewksbury .20 .06
97T Sid Roberson RC .25 .07
98T Tom Henke .20 .06
99T Michael Tucker .20 .06
100T Jason Bates .20 .06
101T Otis Nixon .20 .06
102T Mark Whiten .20 .06
103T Dilson Torres RC .25 .07
104T Melvin Bunch RC .25 .07
105T Terry Pendleton .40 .12
106T Corey Jenkins RC .25 .07
107T Glenn Dishman RC .25 .07
Rob Grable
108T Reggie Taylor RC .50 .15
109T Curtis Goodwin .20 .06
110T David Cone .40 .12
111T Antonio Osuna .20 .06
112T Paul Shuey .20 .06
113T Doug Jones .20 .06
114T Mark McLemore .20 .06
115T Kevin Ritz .20 .06
116T John Kruk .40 .12
117T Trevor Wilson .20 .06
118T Jerald Clark .20 .06
119T Julian Tavarez .20 .06
120T Tim Pugh .20 .06
121T Todd Zeile .20 .06
122T Mark Sweeney UER 3.00 .90
George Arias
Richie Sexson RC
Brian Schneider
123T Bobby Witt .20 .06
124T Hideo Nomo 1.00 .30
125T Joey Cora .20 .06
126T Jim Scharrer RC .25 .07
127T Paul Quantrill .20 .06
128T Chipper Jones ROY .60 .18
129T Kenny James RC .25 .07
130T Lyle Mouton .60 .18
Mariano Rivera
131T Tyler Green .20 .06
132T Brad Clontz .20 .06
133T Jon Nunnally .20 .06
134T Dave Magadan .20 .06
135T Al Leiter .40 .12
136T Bret Barberie .20 .06
137T Bill Swift .20 .06
138T Scott Cooper .20 .06
139T Roberto Kelly .20 .06
140T Charlie Hayes .20 .06
141T Pete Harnisch .20 .06
142T Rich Amaral .20 .06
143T Rudy Seanez .20 .06
144T Pat Listach .20 .06
145T Quilvio Veras .20 .06
146T Jose Olmeda RC .25 .07
147T Roberto Petagine .20 .06
148T Kevin Brown .40 .12
149T Phil Plantier .20 .06
150T Carlos Perez .40 .12
151T Pat Borders .20 .06
152T Tyler Green .20 .06
153T Stan Belinda .20 .06
154T Dave Stewart .40 .12
155T Andre Dawson .40 .12
156T Frank Thomas AS .60 .18
Fred McGriff UER
(McGriff's team shown as Blue Jays)
157T Carlos Baerga AS .40 .12
Craig Biggio
158T Wade Boggs AS .40 .12
Matt Williams
159T Cal Ripken AS 1.00 .30
Ozzie Smith
160T Ken Griffey Jr. AS 1.00 .30
Tony Gwynn
161T Albert Belle AS 1.25 .35
Barry Bonds
162T Kirby Puckett .60 .18
Len Dykstra
163T Ivan Rodriguez AS 1.00 .30
Mike Piazza
164T Randy Johnson AS 1.25 .35
Hideo Nomo
165T Checklist .20 .06

1995 Topps Traded Power Boosters

This 10-card standard-size set was inserted in packs at a rate of one in 36. The set is comprised of parallel cards for the first 10 cards of the regular Topps Traded set which was the "At the Break" subset. The cards are done on extra-thick stock. The fronts have an action photo on a "Power Boosted" background, which is similar to diffraction technology, with the words "at the break" on the left side. The backs have a head shot and player information including his mid-season statistics for 1995 and previous years.

Nm-Mt Ex-Mt
COMPLETE SET (10) 80.00 24.00
1 Frank Thomas 10.00 3.00
2 Ken Griffey Jr. 15.00 4.50
3 Barry Bonds 20.00 6.00
4 Albert Belle 6.00 1.80
5 Cal Ripken 25.00 7.50
6 Mike Piazza 15.00 4.50
7 Tony Gwynn 10.00 3.00
8 Jeff Bagwell 6.00 1.80
9 Mo Vaughn 3.00 .90
10 Matt Williams 3.00 .90

1996 Topps

This set consists of 440 standard-size cards. These cards were issued in 12-card foil packs with a suggested retail price of $1.29. The fronts feature full-color photos surrounded by a white background. Information on the backs includes a player photo, season and career stats and text. First series subsets include Star Power (1-6, 8-12), Draft Picks (13-26), AAA Stars (101-104), and Future Stars (210-219). A special Mickey Mantle card was issued as card number 7 (his uniform number) and became the last card to be issued as card number 7 in the Topps brand set. Rookie Cards in this set include Sean Casey, Geoff Jenkins and Daryle Ward.

Nm-Mt Ex-Mt
COMPLETE SET (440) 40.00 12.00
COMP.HOBBY SET (449) 40.00 12.00
COMP.CEREAL SET (444) 60.00 18.00
COMP.SERIES 1 (220) 20.00 6.00
COMP.SERIES 2 (220) 20.00 6.00
COMMON CARD (1-440) .20 .06
COMMON RC .25 .07
1 Tony Gwynn STP .30 .09
2 Mike Piazza STP .50 .15
3 Greg Maddux STP .50 .15
4 Jeff Bagwell STP .20 .06
5 Larry Walker STP .20 .06
6 Barry Larkin STP .20 .06
7 Mickey Mantle 4.00 1.20
8 Tom Glavine STP UER .20 .06
Won 21 games in June 95
9 Craig Biggio STP .20 .06
10 Barry Bonds STP .50 .15
11 H.Slocumb STP .20 .06
12 Matt Williams STP .20 .06
13 Todd Helton 1.00 .30
14 Mark Redman .25 .07
15 Michael Barrett .25 .07
16 Ben Davis .25 .07
17 Juan LeBron .25 .07
18 Tony McKnight .25 .07
19 Ryan Jaroncyk .25 .07
20 Corey Jenkins .25 .07
21 Jim Scharrer .25 .07
22 Mark Bellhorn RC 3.00 .90
23 Jarrod Washburn RC .60 .18
24 Geoff Jenkins RC 1.00 .30
25 Sean Casey RC 4.00 1.20
26 Brett Tomko RC .40 .12
27 Tony Fernandez .20 .06
28 Rich Becker .20 .06
29 Andujar Cedeno .20 .06
30 Paul Molitor .30 .09
31 Brent Gates .20 .06
32 Glenallen Hill .20 .06
33 Mike Macfarlane .20 .06
34 Manny Alexander .20 .06
35 Todd Zeile .20 .06
36 Joe Girardi .20 .06
37 Tony Tarasco .20 .06
38 Tim Belcher .20 .06
39 Tom Goodwin .20 .06
40 Orel Hershiser .20 .06
41 Tripp Cromer .20 .06
42 Sean Bergman .20 .06
43 Troy Percival .20 .06
44 Kevin Stocker .20 .06
45 Albert Belle .20 .06
46 Tony Eusebio .20 .06
47 Sid Roberson .20 .06
48 Todd Hollandsworth .20 .06
49 Mark Wohlers .20 .06
50 Kirby Puckett .50 .15
51 Darren Holmes .20 .06
52 Ron Karkovice .20 .06
53 Al Martin .20 .06
54 Pat Rapp .20 .06
55 Mark Grace .30 .09
56 Greg Gagne .20 .06
57 Stan Javier .20 .06
58 Scott Sanders .20 .06
59 J.T. Snow .20 .06
60 David Justice .20 .06
61 Royce Clayton .20 .06
62 Kevin Foster .20 .06
63 Tim Naehring .20 .06
64 Orlando Miller .20 .06
65 Mike Mussina .30 .09
66 Jim Eisenreich .20 .06
67 Felix Fermin .20 .06
68 Bernie Williams .30 .09
69 Robb Nen .20 .06
70 Ron Gant .20 .06
71 Felipe Lira .20 .06
72 Jacob Brumfield .20 .06
73 John Mabry .20 .06
74 Mark Carreon .20 .06
75 Carlos Baerga .20 .06
76 Jim Dougherty .20 .06
77 Ryan Thompson .20 .06
78 Scott Leius .20 .06
79 Roger Pavlik .20 .06
80 Gary Sheffield .20 .06
81 Julian Tavarez .20 .06
82 Andy Ashby .20 .06
83 Mark Lemke .20 .06
84 Omar Vizquel .30 .09
85 Darren Daulton .20 .06
86 Mike Lansing .20 .06
87 Rusty Greer .20 .06
88 Dave Stevens .20 .06
89 Jose Offerman .20 .06
90 Tom Henke .20 .06
91 Troy O'Leary .20 .06
92 Michael Tucker .20 .06
93 Marvin Freeman .20 .06
94 Alex Diaz .20 .06
95 John Wetteland .20 .06
96 Cal Ripken 2131 2.00 .60
97 Mike Mimbs .20 .06
98 Bobby Higginson .20 .06
99 Edgardo Alfonzo .20 .06
100 Frank Thomas .50 .15
101 Steve Gibralter .20 .06
Bob Abreu
102 Brian Givens .25 .07
T.J. Mathews
103 Chris Pritchett .25 .07
Trenidad Hubbard
104 Eric Owens .25 .07
Butch Huskey
105 Doug Drabek .20 .06
106 Tomas Perez .20 .06
107 Mark Leiter .20 .06
108 Joe Oliver .20 .06
109 Tony Castillo .20 .06
110 Checklist (1-110) .20 .06
111 Kevin Seitzer .20 .06
112 Pete Schourek .20 .06
113 Sean Berry .20 .06
114 Todd Stottlemyre .20 .06
115 Joe Carter .20 .06
116 Jeff King .20 .06
117 Dan Wilson .20 .06
118 Kurt Abbott .20 .06
119 Lyle Mouton .20 .06
120 Jose Rijo .20 .06
121 Curtis Goodwin .20 .06
122 Jose Valentin .20 .06
123 Ellis Burks .20 .06
124 David Cone .20 .06
125 Eddie Murray .50 .15
126 Brian Jordan .20 .06
127 Darrin Fletcher .20 .06
128 Curt Schilling .20 .06
129 Ozzie Guillen .20 .06
130 Kenny Rogers .20 .06
131 Tom Pagnozzi .20 .06
132 Garret Anderson .20 .06
133 Bobby Jones .20 .06
134 Chris Gomez .20 .06
135 Mike Stanley .20 .06
136 Hideo Nomo .50 .15
137 Jon Nunnally .20 .06
138 Tim Wakefield .20 .06
139 Steve Finley .20 .06
140 Ivan Rodriguez .50 .15
141 Quilvio Veras .20 .06
142 Mike Fetters .20 .06
143 Mike Greenwell .20 .06
144 Bill Pulsipher .20 .06
145 Mark McGwire 1.25 .35
146 Frank Castillo .20 .06
147 Greg Vaughn .20 .06
148 Pat Hentgen .20 .06
149 Walt Weiss .20 .06
150 Randy Johnson .50 .15
151 David Segui .20 .06
152 Benji Gil .20 .06
153 Tom Candiotti .20 .06
154 Geronimo Berroa .20 .06
155 John Franco .20 .06
156 Jay Bell .20 .06
157 Mark Gubicza .20 .06
158 Hal Morris .20 .06
159 Wilson Alvarez .20 .06
160 Derek Bell .20 .06
161 Ricky Bottalico .20 .06
162 Bret Boone .20 .06
163 Brad Radke .20 .06
164 John Valentin .20 .06
165 Steve Avery .20 .06
166 Mark McLemore .20 .06
167 Danny Jackson .20 .06
168 Tino Martinez .30 .09
169 Shane Reynolds .20 .06
170 Terry Pendleton .20 .06
171 Jim Edmonds .20 .06
172 Esteban Loaiza .20 .06
173 Ray Durham .20 .06
174 Carlos Perez .20 .06
175 Raul Mondesi .20 .06
176 Steve Ontiveros .20 .06
177 Chipper Jones .50 .15
178 Otis Nixon .20 .06
179 John Burkett .20 .06
180 Gregg Jefferies .20 .06
181 Denny Martinez .20 .06
182 Ken Caminiti .20 .06
183 Doug Jones .20 .06
184 Brian McRae .20 .06
185 Don Mattingly 1.25 .35
186 Mel Rojas .20 .06
187 Marty Cordova .20 .06
188 Vinny Castilla .20 .06
189 John Smoltz .30 .09
190 Travis Fryman .20 .06
191 Chris Hoiles .20 .06
192 Chuck Finley .20 .06
193 Ryan Klesko .20 .06
194 Alex Fernandez .20 .06
195 Dante Bichette .20 .06
196 Eric Karros .20 .06
197 Roger Clemens 1.00 .30
198 Randy Myers .20 .06
199 Tony Phillips .20 .06
200 Cal Ripken 1.50 .45
201 Rod Beck .20 .06
202 Chad Curtis .20 .06
203 Jack McDowell .20 .06
204 Gary Gaetti .20 .06
205 Ken Griffey Jr. .75 .23
206 Ramon Martinez .20 .06
207 Jeff Kent .20 .06
208 Brad Ausmus .20 .06
209 Devon White .20 .06
210 Jason Giambi .20 .06
211 Nomar Garciaparra .75 .23
212 Billy Wagner .20 .06
213 Todd Greene .20 .06
214 Paul Wilson .20 .06
215 Johnny Damon .30 .09
216 Alan Benes .20 .06
217 Karim Garcia .20 .06
218 Dustin Hermanson .20 .06
219 Derek Jeter 1.25 .35
220 Checklist (111-220) .20 .06
221 Kirby Puckett STP .30 .09
222 Cal Ripken STP .75 .23
223 Albert Belle STP .20 .06
224 Randy Johnson STP .30 .09
225 Wade Boggs STP .20 .06
226 Carlos Baerga STP .20 .06
227 Ivan Rodriguez STP .30 .09
228 Mike Mussina STP .20 .06
229 Frank Thomas STP .30 .09
230 Ken Griffey Jr. STP .50 .15
231 Jose Mesa STP .20 .06
232 Matt Morris RC 1.50 .45
233 Craig Wilson RC 1.50 .45
234 Alvie Shepherd .25 .07
235 Randy Winn RC .60 .18
236 David Yocum RC .25 .07
237 Jason Brester RC .25 .07
238 Shane Monahan RC .25 .07
239 Brian McNichol RC .25 .07
240 Reggie Taylor .25 .07
241 Garrett Long .25 .07
242 Jonathan Johnson .25 .07
243 Jeff Liefer RC .25 .07
244 Brian Powell .25 .07
245 Brian Buchanan RC .25 .07
246 Mike Piazza .75 .23
247 Edgar Martinez .30 .09
248 Chuck Knoblauch .20 .06
249 Andres Galarraga .20 .06
250 Tony Gwynn .60 .18
251 Lee Smith .20 .06
252 Sammy Sosa .75 .23
253 Jim Thome .50 .15
254 Frank Rodriguez .20 .06
255 Charlie Hayes .20 .06
256 Bernard Gilkey .20 .06
257 John Smiley .20 .06
258 Brady Anderson .20 .06
259 Rico Brogna .20 .06
260 Kirt Manwaring .20 .06
261 Len Dykstra .20 .06
262 Tom Glavine .30 .09
263 Vince Coleman .20 .06
264 John Olerud .20 .06
265 Orlando Merced .20 .06
266 Kent Mercker .20 .06
267 Terry Steinbach .20 .06
268 Brian L. Hunter .20 .06
269 Jeff Fassero .20 .06
270 Jay Buhner .20 .06
271 Jeff Brantley .20 .06
272 Tim Raines .20 .06
273 Jimmy Key .20 .06
274 Mo Vaughn .20 .06
275 Andre Dawson .20 .06
276 Jose Mesa .20 .06
277 Brett Butler .20 .06
278 Luis Gonzalez .20 .06
279 Steve Sparks .20 .06
280 Chili Davis .20 .06
281 Carl Everett .20 .06
282 Jeff Cirillo .20 .06
283 Thomas Howard .20 .06
284 Paul O'Neill .30 .09
285 Pat Meares .20 .06
286 Mickey Tettleton .20 .06
287 Rey Sanchez .20 .06
288 Bip Roberts .20 .06
289 Roberto Alomar .30 .09
290 Ruben Sierra .20 .06
291 John Flaherty .20 .06
292 Bret Saberhagen .20 .06
293 Barry Larkin .30 .09
294 Sandy Alomar Jr. .20 .06
295 Ed Sprague .20 .06
296 Gary DiSarcina .20 .06
297 Marquis Grissom .20 .06
298 John Frascatore .20 .06
299 Will Clark .50 .15
300 Barry Bonds 1.25 .35
301 Ozzie Smith UER .75 .23
Padres is listed as Padre
302 Dave Nilsson .20 .06
303 Pedro Martinez .50 .15
304 Joey Cora .20 .06
305 Rick Aguilera .20 .06
306 Craig Biggio .30 .09
307 Jose Vizcaino .20 .06
308 Jeff Montgomery .20 .06
309 Moises Alou .20 .06
310 Robin Ventura .20 .06
311 David Wells .20 .06
312 Delino DeShields .20 .06
313 Trevor Hoffman .20 .06
314 Andy Benes .20 .06
315 Deion Sanders .30 .09
316 Jim Bullinger .20 .06
317 John Jaha .20 .06
318 Greg Maddux .75 .23
319 Tim Salmon .30 .09
320 Ben McDonald .20 .06

321 Sandy Martinez	.20	.06
322 Dan Miceli	.20	.06
323 Wade Boggs	.30	.09
324 Ismael Valdes	.20	.06
325 Juan Gonzalez	.30	.09
326 Charles Nagy	.20	.06
327 Ray Lankford	.20	.06
328 Mark Portugal	.20	.06
329 Bobby Bonilla	.20	.06
330 Reggie Sanders	.20	.06
331 Jamie Brewington RC	.25	.07
332 Aaron Sele	.20	.06
333 Pete Harnisch	.20	.06
334 Cliff Floyd	.20	.06
335 Cal Eldred	.20	.06
336 Jason Bates	.20	.06
337 Tony Clark	.20	.06
338 Jose Herrera	.20	.06
339 Alex Ochoa	.20	.06
340 Mark Loretta	.20	.06
341 Donne Wall	.20	.06
342 Jason Kendall	.20	.06
343 Shannon Stewart	.20	.06
344 Brooks Kieschnick	.20	.06
345 Chris Snopek	.20	.06
346 Ruben Rivera	.20	.06
347 Jeff Suppan	.20	.06
348 Phil Nevin	.20	.06
349 John Wasdin	.20	.06
350 Jay Payton	.20	.06
351 Tim Crabtree	.20	.06
352 Rick Krivda	.20	.06
353 Bob Wolcott	.20	.06
354 Jimmy Haynes	.20	.06
355 Herb Perry	.20	.06
356 Ryne Sandberg	.75	.23
357 Harold Baines	.20	.06
358 Chad Ogea	.20	.06
359 Lee Tinsley	.20	.06
360 Matt Williams	.20	.06
361 Randy Velarde	.20	.06
362 Jose Canseco	.50	.15
363 Larry Walker	.30	.09
364 Kevin Appier	.20	.06
365 Darryl Hamilton	.20	.06
366 Jose Lima	.20	.06
367 Javy Lopez	.20	.06
368 Dennis Eckersley	.20	.06
369 Jason Isringhausen	.20	.06
370 Mickey Morandini	.20	.06
371 Scott Cooper	.20	.06
372 Jim Abbott	.30	.09
373 Paul Sorrento	.20	.06
374 Chris Hammond	.20	.06
375 Lance Johnson	.20	.06
376 Kevin Brown	.20	.06
377 Luis Alicea	.20	.06
378 Andy Pettitte	.30	.09
379 Dean Palmer	.20	.06
380 Jeff Bagwell	.30	.09
381 Jaime Navarro	.20	.06
382 Rondell White	.20	.06
383 Erik Hanson	.20	.06
384 Pedro Munoz	.20	.06
385 Heathcliff Slocumb	.20	.06
386 Wally Joyner	.20	.06
387 Bob Tewksbury	.20	.06
388 David Bell	.20	.06
389 Fred McGriff	.30	.09
390 Mike Henneman	.20	.06
391 Robby Thompson	.20	.06
392 Norm Charlton	.20	.06
393 Cecil Fielder	.20	.06
394 Benito Santiago	.20	.06
395 Rafael Palmeiro	.30	.09
396 Ricky Bones	.20	.06
397 Rickey Henderson	.50	.15
398 C.J. Nitkowski	.20	.06
399 Shawon Dunston	.20	.06
400 Manny Ramirez	.30	.09
401 Bill Swift	.20	.06
402 Chad Fonville	.20	.06
403 Joey Hamilton	.20	.06
404 Alex Gonzalez	.20	.06
405 Roberto Hernandez	.20	.06
406 Jeff Blauser	.20	.06
407 LaTroy Hawkins	.20	.06
408 Greg Colbrunn	.20	.06
409 Todd Hundley	.20	.06
410 Glenn Dishman	.20	.06
411 Joe Vitiello	.20	.06
412 Todd Worrell	.20	.06
413 Wil Cordero	.20	.06
414 Ken Hill	.20	.06
415 Carlos Garcia	.20	.06
416 Bryan Rekar	.20	.06
417 Shawn Green	.20	.06
418 Tyler Green	.20	.06
419 Mike Blowers	.20	.06
420 Kenny Lofton	.20	.06
421 Denny Neagle	.20	.06
422 Jeff Conine	.20	.06
423 Mark Langston	.20	.06
424 Steve Cox Jesse Ibarra Derrek Lee Ron Wright RC	.40	.12
425 Jim Bonnici Billy Owens Richie Sexson Daryle Ward RC	.40	.12
426 Kevin Jordan Bobby Morris Desi Relaford Adam Riggs RC	.25	.07
427 Tim Harkrider Rey Ordonez Neifi Perez Enrique Wilson	.25	.07
428 Bartolo Colon Doug Million Rafael Orellano Ray Ricken	.20	.06
429 Jeff D'Amico Marty Janzen RC Gary Rath Clint Sodowsky	.25	.07
430 Matt Drews Rich Hunter RC Matt Ruebel Bret Wagner	.25	.07
431 Jaime Bluma David Coggin Steve Montgomery Brandon Reed RC	.25	.07
432 Mike Figga Raul Ibanez Paul Konerko Julio Mosquera	.60	.18
433 Brian Barber Marc Kroon Marc Valdes Don Wengert	.20	.06
434 George Arias Chris Haas RC Scott Rolen Scott Spiezio	.50	.15
435 Brian Banks Vladimir Guerrero Andruw Jones Billy McMillon	2.00	.60
436 Roger Cedeno Derrick Gibson Ben Grieve Shane Spencer RC	.60	.18
437 Anton French Demond Smith DaRond Stovall RC Keith Williams	.25	.07
438 Michael Coleman RC Jacob Cruz Richard Hidalgo Charles Peterson	.25	.07
439 Trey Beamon Yamil Benitez Jermaine Dye Angel Echevarria	.20	.06
440 Checklist	.20	.06
F7 M.Mantle Last Day	5.00	1.50
NNO Mickey Mantle TRIB Promotes the Mantle Foundation Black and White Photo	3.00	.90

1996 Topps Classic Confrontations

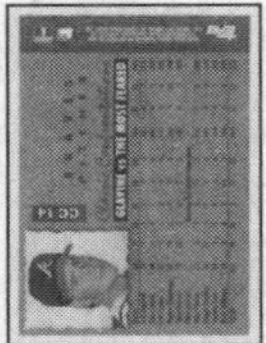

These cards were inserted at a rate of one in every five-card Series one retail pack sold at Walmart. The first ten cards showcase hitters, while the last five cards feature pitchers. Inside white borders, the fronts show player cutouts on a brownish rock background featuring a shadow image of the player. The player's name is gold foil stamped across the bottom. The horizontal backs of the hitters' cards are aqua and present headshots and statistics. The backs of the pitchers cards are purple and present the same information.

	Nm-Mt	Ex-Mt
COMPLETE SET (15)	6.00	1.80
CC1 Ken Griffey Jr.	.60	.18
CC2 Cal Ripken	1.25	.35
CC3 Edgar Martinez	.25	.07
CC4 Kirby Puckett	.40	.12
CC5 Frank Thomas	.40	.12
CC6 Barry Bonds	1.00	.30
CC7 Reggie Sanders	.15	.04
CC8 Andres Galarraga	.15	.04
CC9 Tony Gwynn	.50	.15
CC10 Mike Piazza	.60	.18
CC11 Randy Johnson	.40	.12
CC12 Mike Mussina	.25	.07
CC13 Roger Clemens	.75	.23
CC14 Tom Glavine	.25	.07
CC15 Greg Maddux	.60	.18

1996 Topps Mantle

Randomly inserted in Series one packs at a rate of one in nine hobby packs, one in six retail packs and one in two jumbo packs; these cards are reprints of the original Mickey Mantle cards issued from 1951 through 1969. The fronts look the same except for a commemorative stamp, while the backs clearly state that they are "Mickey Mantle Commemorative" cards and have a 1996 copyright date. These cards honor Yankee great Mickey Mantle, who passed away in August 1995 after a gallant battle against cancer. Based on evidence from an uncut sheet auctioned off at the 1996 Kit Young Hawaii Trade Show, some collectors/dealers believe that cards 15 through 19 were slightly shorter printed in relation to the other 14 cards.

	Nm-Mt	Ex-Mt
COMPLETE SET (19)	100.00	30.00
COMMON MANTLE (3-14)	8.00	2.40
COM.MANTLE SP (15-19)	10.00	3.00
SER.1 ODDS 1:9 HOB, 1:6 RET, 1:2 JUM		
FOUR PER CEREAL FACT.SET		
CARDS 15-19 SHORTPRINTED BY 20%		
1 Mickey Mantle 1951 Bowman	30.00	9.00
2 Mickey Mantle 1952 Topps	30.00	9.00

1996 Topps Masters of the Game

Cards from this 20-card standard-size set were randomly inserted into first-series hobby packs at a rate of one in 18. In addition, every factory set contained two Masters of the Game cards. The cards are numbered with a "MG" prefix in the lower left corner.

	Nm-Mt	Ex-Mt
COMPLETE SET (20)	30.00	9.00
1 Dennis Eckersley	1.00	.30
2 Denny Martinez	1.00	.30
3 Eddie Murray	2.50	.75
4 Paul Molitor	1.50	.45
5 Ozzie Smith	4.00	1.20
6 Rickey Henderson	2.50	.75
7 Tim Raines	1.00	.30
8 Lee Smith	1.00	.30
9 Cal Ripken	8.00	2.40
10 Chili Davis	1.00	.30
11 Wade Boggs	1.50	.45
12 Tony Gwynn	3.00	.90
13 Don Mattingly	6.00	1.80
14 Bret Saberhagen	1.00	.30
15 Kirby Puckett	2.50	.75
16 Joe Carter	1.00	.30
17 Roger Clemens	5.00	1.50
18 Barry Bonds	6.00	1.80
19 Greg Maddux	4.00	1.20
20 Frank Thomas	2.50	.75

1996 Topps Mystery Finest

Randomly inserted in first-series packs at a rate of one in 36 hobby and retail packs and one in eight jumbo packs, this 26-card standard-size set features a bit of a mystery. The fronts have opaque coating that must be removed before the player can be identified. After the opaque coating is removed, the fronts feature a player photo surrounded by silver borders. The backs feature a choice of players along with a corresponding mystery finest trivia fact. Some of these cards were also issued with refractor fronts.

	Nm-Mt	Ex-Mt
COMPLETE SET (26)	120.00	36.00
*REF: 1.25X TO 3X BASIC MYSTERY FINEST		
REF.SER.1 ODDS 1:216 HOB/RET, 1:36 JUM		
M1 Hideo Nomo	5.00	1.50
M2 Greg Maddux	8.00	2.40
M3 Randy Johnson	5.00	1.50
M4 Chipper Jones	5.00	1.50
M5 Marty Cordova	2.00	.60
M6 Garret Anderson	2.00	.60
M7 Cal Ripken	15.00	4.50
M8 Kirby Puckett	5.00	1.50
M9 Tony Gwynn	6.00	1.80
M10 Manny Ramirez	3.00	.90
M11 Jim Edmonds	2.00	.60
M12 Mike Piazza	8.00	2.40
M13 Barry Bonds	12.00	3.60
M14 Raul Mondesi	2.00	.60
M15 Sammy Sosa	8.00	2.40
M16 Ken Griffey Jr.	8.00	2.40
M17 Albert Belle	2.00	.60
M18 Dante Bichette	2.00	.60
M19 Mo Vaughn	2.00	.60
M20 Jeff Bagwell	3.00	.90
M21 Frank Thomas	5.00	1.50
M22 Hideo Nomo	5.00	1.50
M23 Cal Ripken	15.00	4.50
M24 Mike Piazza	8.00	2.40
M25 Ken Griffey Jr.	8.00	2.40
M26 Frank Thomas	5.00	1.50

1996 Topps Power Boosters

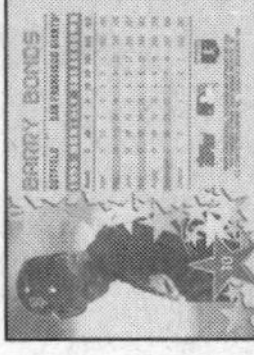

Randomly inserted into packs, these cards are a metallic version of 25 of the first 26 cards from the basic Topps set. Card numbers 1-6 and 8-12 were issued at a rate of one every 36 first series retail packs, while numbers 13-26 were issued in hobby packs at a rate of one in 36. Inserted in place of two basic cards, they are printed on 28 point stock and the fronts have prismatic foil printing. Card number 7, which is Mickey Mantle in the regular set, was not issued in a Power Booster form. A first year card of Sean Casey highlights this set.

	Nm-Mt	Ex-Mt
COMP. STAR POWER SET (11)	50.00	15.00
COMMON (1-6/8-12)	2.00	.60
COMP. DRAFT PICKS SET (14)	3.00	.90
COMMON (12-26)	2.00	.60
1 Tony Gwynn	6.00	1.80
2 Mike Piazza	8.00	2.40
3 Greg Maddux	8.00	2.40
4 Jeff Bagwell	3.00	.90
5 Larry Walker	3.00	.90
6 Barry Larkin	3.00	.90
8 Tom Glavine	3.00	.90
9 Craig Biggio	3.00	.90
10 Barry Bonds	12.00	3.60
11 Heathcliff Slocumb	2.00	.60
12 Matt Williams	2.00	.60
13 Todd Helton	10.00	3.00
14 Mark Redman	2.00	.60
15 Michael Barrett	2.00	.60
16 Ben Davis	2.00	.60
17 Juan LeBron	2.00	.60
18 Tony McKnight	2.00	.60
19 Ryan Jaroncyk	2.00	.60
20 Corey Jenkins	2.00	.60
21 Jim Scharrer	2.00	.60
22 Mark Bellhorn	10.00	3.00
23 Jarrod Washburn	5.00	1.50
24 Geoff Jenkins	8.00	2.40
25 Sean Casey	25.00	7.50
26 Brett Tomko	5.00	1.50

1996 Topps Profiles

Randomly inserted into Series one and two packs at a rate of one in 12 hobby and retail packs, one in six jumbo packs and one in eight ANCO packs;, this 20-card standard-size set features 10 players from each league. One card from the first series and two from the second series were also included in all Topps factory sets. Topps spokesmen Kirby Puckett (AL) and Tony Gwynn (NL) give opinions on players within their league. The fronts feature a player photo set against a silver-foil background. The player's name is on the bottom. A photo of either Gwynn or Puckett as well as the words "Profiles by ..." is on the right. The backs feature a player photo, some career data as well as Gwynn's or Puckett's opinion about the featured player. The cards are numbered with either an "AL or NL" prefix on the back depending on the player's league. The cards are sequenced in alphabetical order within league.

	Nm-Mt	Ex-Mt
COMPLETE SET (40)	40.00	12.00
COMPLETE SERIES 1 (20)	30.00	9.00
COMPLETE SERIES 2 (20)	10.00	3.00
AL1 Roberto Alomar	.75	.23
AL2 Carlos Baerga	.50	.15
AL3 Albert Belle	.50	.15
AL4 Cecil Fielder	.50	.15
AL5 Ken Griffey Jr.	2.00	.60
AL6 Randy Johnson	1.25	.35
AL7 Paul O'Neill	.75	.23
AL8 Cal Ripken	4.00	1.20
AL9 Frank Thomas	1.25	.35
AL10 Mo Vaughn	.50	.15
AL11 Jay Buhner	.50	.15
AL12 Marty Cordova	.50	.15
AL13 Jim Edmonds	.50	.15
AL14 Juan Gonzalez	.75	.23
AL15 Kenny Lofton	.50	.15
AL16 Edgar Martinez	.75	.23
AL17 Don Mattingly	3.00	.90
AL18 Mark McGwire	3.00	.90
AL19 Rafael Palmeiro	.75	.23
AL20 Tim Salmon	.75	.23
NL1 Jeff Bagwell	.75	.23
NL2 Derek Bell	.50	.15
NL3 Barry Bonds	3.00	.90
NL4 Greg Maddux	2.00	.60
NL5 Fred McGriff	.75	.23
NL6 Raul Mondesi	.50	.15
NL7 Mike Piazza	2.00	.60
NL8 Reggie Sanders	.50	.15
NL9 Sammy Sosa	2.00	.60
NL10 Larry Walker	.75	.23
NL11 Dante Bichette	.50	.15
NL12 Andres Galarraga	.50	.15
NL13 Ron Gant	.50	.15
NL14 Tom Glavine	.75	.23
NL15 Chipper Jones	1.25	.35
NL16 David Justice	.50	.15
NL17 Barry Larkin	.75	.23
NL18 Hideo Nomo	1.25	.35
NL19 Gary Sheffield	.50	.15
NL20 Matt Williams	.50	.15

1996 Topps Road Warriors

This 20-card set was inserted only into Series two WalMart packs at a rate of one per pack and featured leading hitters of the majors. The set is sequenced in alphabetical order.

	Nm-Mt	Ex-Mt
COMPLETE SET (20)	12.00	3.60
RW1 Derek Bell	.40	.12
RW2 Albert Belle	.40	.12
RW3 Craig Biggio	.60	.18
RW4 Barry Bonds	2.50	.75
RW5 Jay Buhner	.40	.12
RW6 Jim Edmonds	.40	.12
RW7 Gary Gaetti	.40	.12
RW8 Ron Gant	.40	.12
RW9 Edgar Martinez	.60	.18
RW10 Tino Martinez	.60	.18
RW11 Mark McGwire	2.50	.75
RW12 Mike Piazza	1.50	.45
RW13 Manny Ramirez	.60	.18
RW14 Tim Salmon	.60	.18
RW15 Reggie Sanders	.40	.12
RW16 Frank Thomas	1.00	.30
RW17 John Valentin	.40	.12
RW18 Mo Vaughn	.40	.12
RW19 Robin Ventura	.40	.12
RW20 Matt Williams	.40	.12

1996 Topps Wrecking Crew

Randomly inserted in Series two hobby packs at a rate of one in 18, this 15-card set honors some of the hottest home run producers in the League. One card from this set was also inserted into Topps Hobby Factory sets. The cards feature color action player photos with foil stamping.

	Nm-Mt	Ex-Mt
COMPLETE SET (15)	60.00	18.00
WC1 Jeff Bagwell	3.00	.90
WC2 Albert Belle	2.00	.60
WC3 Barry Bonds	12.00	3.60
WC4 Jose Canseco	5.00	1.50
WC5 Joe Carter	2.00	.60
WC6 Cecil Fielder	2.00	.60
WC7 Ron Gant	2.00	.60
WC8 Juan Gonzalez	3.00	.90
WC9 Ken Griffey Jr	8.00	2.40
WC10 Fred McGriff	3.00	.90
WC11 Mark McGwire	12.00	3.60
WC12 Mike Piazza	8.00	2.40
WC13 Frank Thomas	5.00	1.50
WC14 Mo Vaughn	2.00	.60
WC15 Matt Williams	2.00	.60

1996 Topps Team Topps

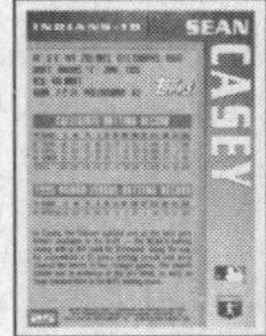

Parallel cards from nine selected teams were issued by Topps in 1996 and distributed in team set form to commemorate their superior performances in 1995. The team sets were issued with the "Big Topps cards" in special packaging for retail stores. Each team set carried an SRP of $4.99. Please note, alphabetical prefixes have been added to the card numbers below for easier checklisting purposes. The actual cards do not carry these prefixes. The Cubs, Orioles, Rangers, White Sox and Yankees cards carry a "Team Topps" logo on each card front. The four other teams carry logos on the card fronts as follows: Braves - "World Champions", Dodgers - "35 Seasons", Indians - "1995 American League Champions" and Mariners - "1995 AL West Champions". It's interesting to note that a parallel version of star first basemen Sean Casey's Rookie Card was included within the Indians team set.

	Nm-Mt	Ex-Mt
COMPLETE SET (150)	100.00	30.00
B3 Greg Maddux STAR	3.00	.90
B8 Tom Glavine STAR	1.25	.35
B12 Jim Scharrer	.25	.07
B49 Mark Wohlers	.25	.07
B60 David Justice	1.00	.30
B83 Mark Lemke	.25	.07
B165 Steve Avery	.25	.07
B177 Chipper Jones	3.00	.90
B189 John Smoltz	.50	.15
B193 Ryan Klesko	.50	.15
B262 Tom Glavine	1.25	.35
B266 Kent Mercker	.25	.07
B297 Marquis Grissom	.25	.07
B318 Greg Maddux	3.00	.90
B367 Javy Lopez	.50	.15
B389 Fred McGriff	.75	.23
B406 Jeff Blauser	.25	.07
C35 Todd Zeile	.50	.15
C55 Mark Grace	1.00	.30
C62 Kevin Foster	.25	.07
C146 Frank Castillo	.25	.07
C184 Brian McRae	.25	.07
C198 Randy Myers	.25	.07
C239 Brian McNichol	.25	.07
C252 Sammy Sosa	2.50	.75
C278 Luis Gonzalez	1.00	.30
C287 Rey Sanchez	.25	.07
C316 Jim Bullinger	.25	.07
C344 Brooks Kieschnick	.25	.07
C356 Ryne Sandberg	1.25	.35
C381 Jaime Navarro	.25	.07
C399 Shawon Dunston	.25	.07

D2 Mike Piazza UER 3.00 .90
Basic card front, Star Power subset back
D48 Todd Hollandsworth .25 .07
D89 Jose Offerman .25 .07
D136 Hideo Nomo 1.25 .35
D153 Tom Candiotti .50 .15
D175 Raul Mondesi .50 .15
D196 Eric Karros .50 .15
D206 Ramon Martinez .25 .07
D217 Karim Garcia 1.00 .30
D236 David Yocum .25 .07
D246 M.Piazza STAR UER 3.00 .90
Star Power subset front, basic issue card back
D277 Brett Butler .50 .15
D312 Delino DeShields .50 .15
D324 Ismael Valdes .25 .07
D402 Chad Fonville .25 .07
D412 Todd Worrell .25 .07
I25 Sean Casey 5.00 1.50
I40 Orel Hershiser .50 .15
I45 Albert Belle .50 .15
I75 Carlos Baerga .50 .15
I81 Julian Tavarez .25 .07
I84 Omar Vizquel 1.00 .30
I125 Eddie Murray 1.25 .35
I181 Denny Martinez .50 .15
I223 Albert Belle STAR .50 .15
I226 Carlos Baerga STAR .50 .15
I231 Jose Mesa STAR .50 .15
I253 Jim Thome 1.00 .30
I276 Jose Mesa .50 .15
I294 Sandy Alomar Jr. .50 .15
I326 Charles Nagy .25 .07
I355 Herb Perry .25 .07
I358 Chad Ogea .25 .07
I373 Paul Sorrento .25 .07
I400 Manny Ramirez 1.25 .35
I414 Ken Hill .25 .07
I420 Kenny Lofton .75 .23
M38 Tim Belcher .25 .07
M67 Felix Fermin .25 .07
M94 Alex Diaz .25 .07
M117 Dan Wilson .25 .07
M150 Randy Johnson 1.25 .35
M168 Tino Martinez .50 .15
M205 Ken Griffey Jr. 3.00 .90
M224 R.Johnson STAR 1.25 .35
M230 K.Griffey Jr. STAR 3.00 .90
M238 Shane Monahan .25 .07
M247 Edgar Martinez .75 .23
M263 Vince Coleman .25 .07
M270 Jay Buhner .50 .15
M304 Joey Cora .25 .07
M314 Andy Benes .25 .07
M353 Bob Wolcott .25 .07
M392 Norm Charlton .25 .07
M419 Mike Blowers .25 .07
O34 Manny Alexander .25 .07
O65 M.Mussina STAR UER 1.00 .30
Star Power card front, basic issue card back
O96 Cal Ripken 2131 5.00 1.50
O121 Curtis Goodwin .25 .07
O183 Doug Jones .25 .07
O191 Chris Hoiles .25 .07
O200 Cal Ripken 5.00 1.50
O222 Cal Ripken STAR 5.00 1.50
O228 M.Mussina UER 1.00 .30
Basic issue card front, Star Power subset card back
O234 Alvie Shepherd .25 .07
O258 Brady Anderson .50 .15
O320 Ben McDonald .25 .07
O329 Bobby Bonilla .25 .07
O352 Rick Krivda .25 .07
O354 Jimmy Haynes .25 .07
O357 Harold Baines .50 .15
O376 Kevin Brown .75 .23
O395 Rafael Palmeiro 1.00 .30
R79 Roger Pavlik .25 .07
R87 Rusty Greer .50 .15
R130 Kenny Rogers .25 .07
R140 Ivan Rodriguez 1.25 .35
R152 Benji Gil .25 .07
R166 Mark McLemore .50 .15
R178 Otis Nixon .25 .07
R227 I.Rodriguez STAR 1.25 .35
R242 Jonathan Johnson .25 .07
R286 Mickey Tettleton .25 .07
R299 Will Clark 1.00 .30
R325 Juan Gonzalez 1.25 .35
R379 Dean Palmer .50 .15
R387 Bob Tewksbury .25 .07
W52 Ron Karkovice .25 .07
W100 Frank Thomas 2.00 .60
W119 Lyle Mouton .25 .07
W129 Ozzie Guillen .50 .15
W159 Wilson Alvarez .25 .07
W173 Ray Durham .50 .15
W194 Alex Fernandez .25 .07
W229 F.Thomas STAR 2.00 .60
W243 Jeff Liefer .25 .07
W272 Tim Raines .50 .15
W310 Robin Ventura 1.00 .30
W345 Chris Snopek .25 .07
W375 Lance Johnson .25 .07
W405 Roberto Hernandez .25 .07
Y7 Mickey Mantle 10.00 3.00
Y27 Tony Fernandez .50 .15
Y68 Bernie Williams 1.00 .30
Y95 John Wetteland .50 .15
Y124 David Cone .75 .23
Y135 Mike Stanley .25 .07
Y185 Don Mattingly 2.50 .75
Y203 Jack McDowell .25 .07
Y219 Derek Jeter 5.00 1.50
Y225 Wade Boggs STAR 1.25 .35
Y245 Brian Buchanan .25 .07
Y273 Jimmy Key .50 .15
Y284 Paul O'Neill 1.00 .30
Y290 Ruben Sierra .50 .15
Y323 Wade Boggs 1.25 .35
Y346 Ruben Rivera .25 .07
Y361 Randy Velarde .25 .07
Y378 Andy Pettitte .50 .15

1997 Topps

This 495-card set was primarily distributed in first and second series 11-card packs with a suggested retail price of $1.29. In addition, eight-card retail packs, 40-card jumbo packs and 504-card factory sets (containing the complete 495-card set plus a random selection of eight insert cards and one hermetically sealed Willie Mays or Mickey Mantle Reprint insert) were made available. The card fronts feature a color action player photo with a gloss coating and a spot matte finish on the outside border with gold foil stamping. The backs carry another player photo, player information and statistics. The set includes the following subsets: Season Highlights (100-104, 462-466), Prospects (200-207, 487-494), the first ever expansion team cards of the Arizona Diamondbacks (249-251,468-469 and the Tampa Bay Devil Rays (252-253, 470-472) and Draft Picks (269-274, 477-483). Card 42 is a special Jackie Robinson tribute card commemorating the 50th anniversary of his contribution to baseball history and numbered for his Dodgers uniform number. Card number 7 does not exist because it was retired in honor of Mickey Mantle. Card number 84 does not exist because Mike Fetters' card was incorrectly numbered 61. Card number 277 does not exist because Chipper Jones' card was incorrectly numbered 276. Rookie Cards include Kris Benson and Eric Chavez. The Derek Jeter autograph card found at the end of our checklist was seeded one every 576 second series packs.

	Nm-Mt	Ex-Mt
COMPLETE SET (495)	80.00	24.00
COMP.SERIES 1 (275)	40.00	12.00
COMP.SERIES 2 (220)	40.00	12.00

1 Barry Bonds 1.25 .35
2 Tom Pagnozzi .20 .06
3 Terrell Wade .20 .06
4 Jose Valentin .20 .06
5 Mark Clark .20 .06
6 Brady Anderson .20 .06
8 Wade Boggs .30 .09
9 Scott Stahoviak .20 .06
10 Andres Galarraga .20 .06
11 Steve Avery .20 .06
12 Rusty Greer .20 .06
13 Derek Jeter 1.25 .35
14 Ricky Bottalico .20 .06
15 Andy Ashby .20 .06
16 Paul Shuey .20 .06
17 F.P. Santangelo .20 .06
18 Royce Clayton .20 .06
19 Mike Mohler .20 .06
20 Mike Piazza .75 .23
21 Jaime Navarro .20 .06
22 Billy Wagner .20 .06
23 Mike Timlin .20 .06
24 Garret Anderson .20 .06
25 Ben McDonald .20 .06
26 Mel Rojas .20 .06
27 John Burkett .20 .06
28 Jeff King .20 .06
29 Reggie Jefferson .20 .06
30 Kevin Appier .20 .06
31 Felipe Lira .20 .06
32 Kevin Tapani .20 .06
33 Mark Portugal .20 .06
34 Carlos Garcia .20 .06
35 Joey Cora .20 .06
36 David Segui .20 .06
37 Mark Grace .30 .09
38 Erik Hanson .20 .06
39 Jeff D'Amico .20 .06
40 Jay Buhner .20 .06
41 B.J. Surhoff .20 .06
42 Jackie Robinson TRIB .50 .15
43 Roger Pavlik .20 .06
44 Hal Morris .20 .06
45 Mariano Duncan .20 .06
46 Harold Baines .20 .06
47 Jorge Fabregas .20 .06
48 Jose Herrera .20 .06
49 Jeff Cirillo .20 .06
50 Tom Glavine .30 .09
51 Pedro Astacio .20 .06
52 Mark Gardner .20 .06
53 Arthur Rhodes .20 .06
54 Troy O'Leary .20 .06
55 Bip Roberts .20 .06
56 Mike Lieberthal .20 .06
57 Shane Andrews .20 .06
58 Scott Karl .20 .06
59 Gary DiSarcina .20 .06
60 Andy Pettitte .30 .09
61 Kevin Elster .20 .06
61B Mike Fetters UER .20 .06
Card was intended as number 84
62 Mark McGwire 1.25 .35
63 Dan Wilson .20 .06
64 Mickey Morandini .20 .06
65 Chuck Knoblauch .20 .06
66 Tim Wakefield .20 .06
67 Raul Mondesi .20 .06
68 Todd Jones .20 .06
69 Albert Belle .20 .06
70 Trevor Hoffman .20 .06
71 Eric Young .20 .06
72 Robert Perez .20 .06
73 Butch Huskey .20 .06
74 Brian McRae .20 .06
75 Jim Edmonds .20 .06
76 Mike Henneman .20 .06
77 Frank Rodriguez .20 .06
78 Danny Tartabull .20 .06
79 Robb Nen .20 .06
80 Reggie Sanders .20 .06
81 Ron Karkovice .20 .06
82 Benito Santiago .20 .06
83 Mike Lansing .20 .06
85 Craig Biggio .30 .09
86 Mike Bordick .20 .06
87 Ray Lankford .20 .06
88 Charles Nagy .20 .06
89 Paul Wilson .20 .06
90 John Wetteland .20 .06
91 Tom Candiotti .20 .06
92 Carlos Delgado .20 .06
93 Derek Bell .20 .06
94 Mark Lemke .20 .06
95 Edgar Martinez .30 .09
96 Rickey Henderson .50 .15
97 Greg Myers .20 .06
98 Jim Leyritz .20 .06
99 Mark Johnson .20 .06
100 Dwight Gooden HL .20 .06
101 Al Leiter HL .20 .06
102 John Mabry HL .20 .06
103 Alex Ochoa HL .20 .06
104 Mike Piazza HL .50 .15
105 Jim Thome .50 .15
106 Ricky Otero .20 .06
107 Jamey Wright .20 .06
108 Frank Thomas .50 .15
109 Jody Reed .20 .06
110 Orel Hershiser .20 .06
111 Terry Steinbach .20 .06
112 Mark Loretta .20 .06
113 Turk Wendell .20 .06
114 Marvin Benard .20 .06
115 Kevin Brown .20 .06
116 Robert Person .20 .06
117 Joey Hamilton .20 .06
118 Francisco Cordova .20 .06
119 John Smiley .20 .06
120 Travis Fryman .20 .06
121 Jimmy Key .20 .06
122 Tom Goodwin .20 .06
123 Mike Greenwell .20 .06
124 Juan Gonzalez .30 .09
125 Pete Harnisch .20 .06
126 Roger Cedeno .20 .06
127 Ron Gant .20 .06
128 Mark Langston .20 .06
129 Tim Crabtree .20 .06
130 Greg Maddux .75 .23
131 W.VanLandingham .20 .06
132 Wally Joyner .20 .06
133 Randy Myers .20 .06
134 John Valentin .20 .06
135 Bret Boone .20 .06
136 Bruce Ruffin .20 .06
137 Chris Snopek .20 .06
138 Paul Molitor .30 .09
139 Mark McLemore .20 .06
140 Rafael Palmeiro .30 .09
141 Herb Perry .20 .06
142 Luis Gonzalez .20 .06
143 Doug Drabek .20 .06
144 Ken Ryan .20 .06
145 Todd Hundley .20 .06
146 Ellis Burks .20 .06
147 Ozzie Guillen .20 .06
148 Rich Becker .20 .06
149 Sterling Hitchcock .20 .06
150 Bernie Williams .30 .09
151 Mike Stanley .20 .06
152 Roberto Alomar .30 .09
153 Jose Mesa .20 .06
154 Steve Trachsel .20 .06
155 Alex Gonzalez .20 .06
156 Troy Percival .20 .06
157 John Smoltz .30 .09
158 Pedro Martinez .50 .15
159 Jeff Conine .20 .06
160 Bernard Gilkey .20 .06
161 Jim Eisenreich .20 .06
162 Mickey Tettleton .20 .06
163 Justin Thompson .20 .06
164 Jose Offerman .20 .06
165 Tony Phillips .20 .06
166 Ismael Valdes .20 .06
167 Ryne Sandberg UER .75 .23
Card has him with 252 homers in 1996
168 Matt Mieske .20 .06
169 Geronimo Berroa .20 .06
170 Otis Nixon .20 .06
171 John Mabry .20 .06
172 Shawon Dunston .20 .06
173 Omar Vizquel .30 .09
174 Chris Hoiles .20 .06
175 Dwight Gooden .20 .06
176 Wilson Alvarez .20 .06
177 Todd Hollandsworth .20 .06
178 Roger Salkeld .20 .06
179 Rey Sanchez .20 .06
180 Rey Ordonez .20 .06
181 Denny Martinez .20 .06
182 Ramon Martinez .20 .06
183 Dave Nilsson .20 .06
184 Marquis Grissom .20 .06
185 Randy Velarde .20 .06
186 Ron Coomer .20 .06
187 Tino Martinez .30 .09
188 Jeff Brantley .20 .06
189 Steve Finley .20 .06
190 Andy Benes .20 .06
191 Terry Adams .20 .06
192 Mike Blowers .20 .06
193 Russ Davis .20 .06
194 Darryl Hamilton .20 .06
195 Jason Kendall .20 .06
196 Johnny Damon .30 .09
197 Dave Martinez .20 .06
198 Mike Macfarlane .20 .06
199 Norm Charlton .20 .06
200 Doug Million RC .25 .07
Damian Moss
Bobby Rodgers
201 Geoff Jenkins .20 .06
Raul Ibanez
Mike Cameron
202 Sean Casey .20 .06
Jim Bonnici
Dmitri Young
203 Jed Hansen .20 .06
Homer Bush
Felipe Crespo
204 Kevin Orie .20 .06
Gabe Alvarez
Aaron Boone
205 Ben Davis .20 .06
Kevin Brown
Bobby Estalella
206 Billy McMillon RC .40 .12
Bubba Trammell
Dante Powell
207 Jarrod Washburn .20 .06
Marc Wilkins RC
Glendon Rusch
208 Brian Hunter .20 .06
209 Jason Giambi .20 .06
210 Henry Rodriguez .20 .06
211 Edgar Renteria .20 .06
212 Edgardo Alfonzo .20 .06
213 Fernando Vina .20 .06
214 Shawn Green .20 .06
215 Ray Durham .20 .06
216 Joe Randa .20 .06
217 Armando Reynoso .20 .06
218 Eric Davis .20 .06
219 Bob Tewksbury .20 .06
220 Jacob Cruz .20 .06
221 Glenallen Hill .20 .06
222 Gary Gaetti .20 .06
223 Donne Wall .20 .06
224 Brad Clontz .20 .06
225 Marty Janzen .20 .06
226 Todd Worrell .20 .06
227 John Franco .20 .06
228 David Wells .20 .06
229 Gregg Jefferies .20 .06
230 Tim Naehring .20 .06
231 Thomas Howard .20 .06
232 Roberto Hernandez .20 .06
233 Kevin Ritz .20 .06
234 Julian Tavarez .20 .06
235 Ken Hill .20 .06
236 Greg Gagne .20 .06
237 Bobby Chouinard .20 .06
238 Joe Carter .20 .06
239 Jermaine Dye .20 .06
240 Antonio Osuna .20 .06
241 Julio Franco .20 .06
242 Mike Grace .20 .06
243 Aaron Sele .20 .06
244 David Justice .20 .06
245 Sandy Alomar Jr. .20 .06
246 Jose Canseco .50 .15
247 Paul O'Neill .30 .09
248 Sean Berry .20 .06
249 Nick Bierbrodt .25 .07
Kevin Sweeney RC
250 Larry Rodriguez RC .25 .07
Vladimir Nunez RC
251 Ron Hartman .25 .07
David Hayman RC
252 Alex Sanchez .50 .15
Matthew Quatraro RC
253 Ronni Seberino RC .25 .07
Pablo Ortego RC
254 Rex Hudler .20 .06
255 Orlando Miller .20 .06
256 Mariano Rivera .30 .09
257 Brad Radke .20 .06
258 Bobby Higginson .20 .06
259 Jay Bell .20 .06
260 Mark Grudzielanek .20 .06
261 Lance Johnson .20 .06
262 Ken Caminiti .20 .06
263 J.T. Snow .20 .06
264 Gary Sheffield .20 .06
265 Darrin Fletcher .20 .06
266 Eric Owens .20 .06
267 Luis Castillo .20 .06
268 Scott Rolen .50 .15
269 Todd Noel .25 .07
John Oliver RC
270 Robert Stratton RC .40 .12
Corey Lee RC
271 Gil Meche RC .50 .15
Matt Halloran RC
272 Eric Milton RC .75 .23
Dee Brown RC
273 Josh Garrett .25 .07
Chris Reitsma RC
274 A.J.Zapp RC .75 .23
Jason Marquis
275 Checklist .20 .06
276 Checklist .20 .06
277 Chipper Jones UER .50 .15
incorrectly numbered 276
278 Orlando Merced .20 .06
279 Ariel Prieto .20 .06
280 Al Leiter .20 .06
281 Pat Meares .20 .06
282 Darryl Strawberry .20 .06
283 Jamie Moyer .20 .06
284 Scott Servais .20 .06
285 Delino DeShields .20 .06
286 Danny Graves .20 .06
287 Gerald Williams .20 .06
288 Todd Greene .20 .06
289 Rico Brogna .20 .06
290 Derrick Gibson .20 .06
291 Joe Girardi .20 .06
292 Darren Lewis .20 .06
293 Nomar Garciaparra .75 .23
294 Greg Colbrunn .20 .06
295 Jeff Bagwell .30 .09
296 Brent Gates .20 .06
297 Jose Vizcaino .20 .06
298 Alex Ochoa .20 .06
299 Sid Fernandez .20 .06
300 Ken Griffey Jr. .75 .23
301 Chris Gomez .20 .06
302 Wendell Magee .20 .06
303 Darren Oliver .20 .06
304 Mel Nieves .20 .06
305 Sammy Sosa .75 .23
306 George Arias .20 .06
307 Jack McDowell .20 .06
308 Stan Javier .20 .06
309 Kimera Bartee .20 .06
310 James Baldwin .20 .06
311 Rocky Coppinger .20 .06
312 Keith Lockhart .20 .06
313 C.J. Nitkowski .20 .06
314 Allen Watson .20 .06
315 Darryl Kile .20 .06
316 Amaury Telemaco .20 .06
317 Jason Isringhausen .20 .06
318 Manny Ramirez .30 .09
319 Terry Pendleton .20 .06
320 Tim Salmon .30 .09
321 Eric Karros .20 .06
322 Mark Whiten .20 .06
323 Rick Krivda .20 .06
324 Brett Butler .20 .06
325 Randy Johnson .50 .15
326 Eddie Taubensee .20 .06
327 Mark Leiter .20 .06
328 Kevin Gross .20 .06
329 Ernie Young .20 .06
330 Pat Hentgen .20 .06
331 Rondell White .20 .06
332 Bobby Witt .20 .06
333 Eddie Murray .50 .15
334 Tim Raines .20 .06
335 Jeff Fassero .20 .06
336 Chuck Finley .20 .06
337 Willie Adams .20 .06
338 Chan Ho Park .20 .06
339 Jay Powell .20 .06
340 Ivan Rodriguez .50 .15
341 Jermaine Allensworth .20 .06
342 Jay Payton .20 .06
343 T.J. Mathews .20 .06
344 Tony Batista .20 .06
345 Ed Sprague .20 .06
346 Jeff Kent .20 .06
347 Scott Erickson .20 .06
348 Jeff Suppan .20 .06
349 Pete Schourek .20 .06
350 Kenny Lofton .20 .06
351 Alan Benes .20 .06
352 Fred McGriff .30 .09
353 Charlie O'Brien .20 .06
354 Darren Bragg .20 .06
355 Alex Fernandez .20 .06
356 Al Martin .20 .06
357 Bob Wells .20 .06
358 Chad Mottola .20 .06
359 Devon White .20 .06
360 David Cone .20 .06
361 Bobby Jones .20 .06
362 Scott Sanders .20 .06
363 Karim Garcia .20 .06
364 Kirt Manwaring .20 .06
365 Chili Davis .20 .06
366 Mike Hampton .20 .06
367 Chad Ogea .20 .06
368 Curt Schilling .20 .06
369 Phil Nevin .20 .06
370 Roger Clemens 1.00 .30
371 Willie Greene .20 .06
372 Kenny Rogers .20 .06
373 Jose Rijo .20 .06
374 Bobby Bonilla .20 .06
375 Mike Mussina .30 .09
376 Curtis Pride .20 .06
377 Todd Walker .20 .06
378 Jason Bere .20 .06
379 Heathcliff Slocumb .20 .06
380 Dante Bichette .20 .06
381 Carlos Baerga .20 .06
382 Livan Hernandez .20 .06
383 Jason Schmidt .20 .06
384 Kevin Stocker .20 .06
385 Matt Williams .20 .06
386 Bartolo Colon .20 .06
387 Will Clark .50 .15
388 Dennis Eckersley .20 .06
389 Brooks Kieschnick .20 .06
390 Ryan Klesko .20 .06
391 Mark Carreon .20 .06
392 Tim Worrell .20 .06
393 Dean Palmer .20 .06
394 Wil Cordero .20 .06
395 Javy Lopez .20 .06
396 Rich Aurilia .20 .06
397 Greg Vaughn .20 .06
398 Vinny Castilla .20 .06
399 Jeff Montgomery .20 .06
400 Cal Ripken 1.50 .45
401 Walt Weiss .20 .06
402 Brad Ausmus .20 .06
403 Ruben Rivera .20 .06
404 Mark Wohlers .20 .06
405 Rick Aguilera .20 .06
406 Tony Clark .20 .06
407 Lyle Mouton .20 .06
408 Bill Pulsipher .20 .06
409 Jose Rosado .20 .06
410 Tony Gwynn .60 .18
411 Cecil Fielder .20 .06
412 John Flaherty .20 .06
413 Lenny Dykstra .20 .06
414 Ugueth Urbina .20 .06
415 Brian Jordan .20 .06
416 Bob Abreu .20 .06
417 Craig Paquette .20 .06
418 Sandy Martinez .20 .06
419 Jeff Blauser .20 .06
420 Barry Larkin .30 .09
421 Kevin Seitzer .20 .06
422 Tim Belcher .20 .06
423 Paul Sorrento .20 .06
424 Cal Eldred .20 .06
425 Robin Ventura .20 .06
426 John Olerud .20 .06
427 Bob Wolcott .20 .06
428 Matt Lawton .20 .06
429 Rod Beck .20 .06
430 Shane Reynolds .20 .06
431 Mike James .20 .06
432 Steve Wojciechowski .20 .06
433 Vladimir Guerrero .50 .15
434 Dustin Hermanson .20 .06
435 Marty Cordova .20 .06
436 Marc Newfield .20 .06
437 Todd Stottlemyre .20 .06
438 Jeffrey Hammonds .20 .06
439 Dave Stevens .20 .06
440 Hideo Nomo .50 .15

441 Mark Thompson .20 .06
442 Mark Lewis .20 .06
443 Quinton McCracken .20 .06
444 Cliff Floyd .20 .06
445 Denny Neagle .20 .06
446 John Jaha .20 .06
447 Mike Sweeney .20 .06
448 John Wasdin .20 .06
449 Chad Curtis .20 .06
450 Mo Vaughn .20 .06
451 Donovan Osborne .20 .06
452 Ruben Sierra .20 .06
453 Michael Tucker .20 .06
454 Kurt Abbott .20 .06
455 Andruw Jones UER .20 .06
Birthdate is incorrectly listed
as 1-22-67, should be 1-22-77
456 Shannon Stewart .20 .06
457 Scott Brosius .20 .06
458 Juan Guzman .20 .06
459 Ron Villone .20 .06
460 Moises Alou .20 .06
461 Larry Walker .30 .09
462 Eddie Murray SH .30 .09
463 Paul Molitor SH .20 .06
464 Hideo Nomo SH .20 .06
465 Barry Bonds SH .50 .15
466 Todd Hundley SH .20 .06
467 Rheal Cormier .20 .06
468 Jason Conti RC .25 .07
Jhensy Sandoval
469 Rod Barajas 1.50 .45
Jackie Rexrode RC
470 Cedric Bowers RC .25 .07
Jared Sandberg RC
471 Chei Gunner RC .25 .07
Paul Wilder
472 Mike Decelle .25 .07
Marcus McCain RC
473 Todd Zeile .20 .06
474 Neifi Perez .20 .06
475 Jeromy Burnitz .20 .06
476 Trey Beamon .20 .06
477 Braden Looper RC .40 .12
John Patterson
478 Danny Peoples .75 .23
Jake Westbrook RC
479 Eric Chavez 1.25 .35
Adam Eaton RC
480 Joe Lawrence RC .25 .07
Pete Tucci
481 Kris Benson .75 .23
Billy Koch RC
482 John Nicholson .25 .07
Andy Prater RC
483 Mark Johnson RC .75 .23
Mark Kotsay
484 Armando Benitez .20 .06
485 Mike Matheny .20 .06
486 Jeff Reed .20 .06
487 Mark Bellhorn .20 .06
Russ Johnson
Enrique Wilson
488 Ben Grieve .20 .06
Richard Hidalgo
Scott Morgan RC
489 Paul Konerko .20 .06
Derrek Lee UER
spelled Derek on back
Ron Wright
490 Wes Helms RC 3.00 .90
Bill Mueller
Brad Seitzer
491 Jeff Abbott .20 .06
Shane Monahan
Edgard Velazquez
492 Jimmy Anderson RC .25 .07
Ron Blazier
Gerald Witasick
493 Darin Blood .75 .06
Heath Murray
Carl Pavano
494 Nelson Figueroa RC .25 .07
Mark Redman
Mike Villano
495 Checklist .20 .06
496 Checklist .20 .06
NNO Derek Jeter AU 150.00 45.00

1997 Topps All-Stars

Randomly inserted in Series one hobby and retail packs at a rate of one in 18 and one in every six jumbo packs, this 22-card set printed on rainbow foilboard features the top 11 players from each league and from each position as voted by the Topps Sports Department. The fronts carry a photo of a "first team" all-star player while the backs carry a different photo of that player alongside the "second team" and "third team" selections. Only the "first team" players are checklisted listed below.

	Nm-Mt	Ex-Mt
COMPLETE SET (22)	25.00	7.50
AS1 Ivan Rodriguez	1.50	.45
AS2 Todd Hundley	.60	.18
AS3 Frank Thomas	1.50	.45
AS4 Andres Galarraga	.60	.18
AS5 Chuck Knoblauch	.60	.18
AS6 Eric Young	.60	.18
AS7 Jim Thome	1.50	.45
AS8 Chipper Jones	1.50	.45
AS9 Cal Ripken	5.00	1.50
AS10 Barry Larkin	1.00	.30
AS11 Albert Belle	.60	.18
AS12 Barry Bonds	4.00	1.20
AS13 Ken Griffey Jr.	2.50	.75
AS14 Ellis Burks	.60	.18
AS15 Juan Gonzalez	1.00	.30
AS16 Gary Sheffield	.60	.18
AS17 Andy Pettitte	1.00	.30
AS18 Tom Glavine	1.00	.30
AS19 Pat Hentgen	.60	.18
AS20 John Smoltz	1.00	.30
AS21 Roberto Hernandez	.60	.18
AS22 Mark Wohlers	.60	.18

1997 Topps Awesome Impact

Randomly inserted in second series 11-card retail packs at a rate of 1:18, cards from this 20-card set feature a selection of top young stars and prospects. Each card front features a color player action shot cut out against a silver prismatic background.

	Nm-Mt	Ex-Mt
COMPLETE SET (20)	100.00	30.00
AI1 Jaime Bluma	3.00	.90
AI2 Tony Clark	3.00	.90
AI3 Jermaine Dye	3.00	.90
AI4 Nomar Garciaparra	12.00	3.60
AI5 Vladimir Guerrero	8.00	2.40
AI6 Todd Hollandsworth	3.00	.90
AI7 Derek Jeter	20.00	6.00
AI8 Andruw Jones	3.00	.90
AI9 Chipper Jones	8.00	2.40
AI10 Jason Kendall	3.00	.90
AI11 Brooks Kieschnick	3.00	.90
AI12 Alex Ochoa	3.00	.90
AI13 Rey Ordonez	3.00	.90
AI14 Neifi Perez	3.00	.90
AI15 Edgar Renteria	3.00	.90
AI16 Mariano Rivera	5.00	1.50
AI17 Ruben Rivera	3.00	.90
AI18 Scott Rolen	8.00	2.40
AI19 Billy Wagner	3.00	.90
AI20 Todd Walker	3.00	.90

1997 Topps Hobby Masters

Randomly inserted in first and second series hobby packs at a rate of one in 36, cards from this 10-card set honor twenty players picked by hobby dealers from across the country as their all-time favorites. Cards 1-10 were issued in first series packs and 11-20 in second series. Printed on 28-point diffraction foilboard, one card replaces two regular cards when inserted in packs. The fronts feature borderless color player photos on a background of the player's profile. The backs carry player information.

	Nm-Mt	Ex-Mt
COMPLETE SET (20)	80.00	24.00
COMPLETE SERIES 1 (10)	40.00	12.00
COMPLETE SERIES 2 (10)	40.00	12.00
HM1 Ken Griffey Jr.	6.00	1.80
HM2 Cal Ripken	12.00	3.60
HM3 Greg Maddux	6.00	1.80
HM4 Albert Belle	1.50	.45
HM5 Tony Gwynn	5.00	1.50
HM6 Jeff Bagwell	2.50	.75
HM7 Randy Johnson	4.00	1.20
HM8 Raul Mondesi	1.50	.45
HM9 Juan Gonzalez	2.50	.75
HM10 Kenny Lofton	1.50	.45
HM11 Frank Thomas	4.00	1.20
HM12 Mike Piazza	6.00	1.80
HM13 Chipper Jones	4.00	1.20
HM14 Brady Anderson	1.50	.45
HM15 Ken Caminiti	1.50	.45
HM16 Barry Bonds	10.00	3.00
HM17 Mo Vaughn	1.50	.45
HM18 Derek Jeter	10.00	3.00
HM19 Sammy Sosa	6.00	1.80
HM20 Andres Galarraga	1.50	.45

1997 Topps Inter-League Finest

Randomly inserted in Series one hobby and retail packs at a rate of one in 36 and jumbo packs at a rate of one in 10; this 14-card set features top individual match-ups from inter-league rivalries. One player from each major league team is represented on each side of this double-sided set with a color photo and is covered with the patented Finest clear protector.

	Nm-Mt	Ex-Mt
COMPLETE SET (14)	60.00	18.00
*REF.: 1X TO 2.5X BASIC INTER-LG	4.00	1.20
REF.SER.1 ODDS 1:216 HOB/RET, 1:56 JUM		
ILM1 Mark McGwire / Barry Bonds	10.00	3.00
ILM2 Tim Salmon / Mike Piazza	6.00	1.80
ILM3 Ken Griffey Jr. / Dante Bichette	6.00	1.80
ILM4 Juan Gonzalez / Tony Gwynn	5.00	1.50
ILM5 Frank Thomas / Sammy Sosa	6.00	1.80
ILM6 Albert Belle / Barry Larkin	1.50	.45
ILM7 Johnny Damon / Brian Jordan	1.50	.45
ILM8 Paul Molitor / Jeff King	2.50	.75
ILM9 John Jaha / Jeff Bagwell	2.50	.75
ILM10 Bernie Williams / Todd Hundley	2.50	.75
ILM11 Joe Carter / Henry Rodriguez	1.50	.45
ILM12 Cal Ripken / Gregg Jefferies	12.00	3.60
ILM13 Mo Vaughn / Chipper Jones	4.00	1.20
ILM14 Travis Fryman / Gary Sheffield	1.50	.45

1997 Topps Mantle

Randomly inserted at the rate of one in 12 Series one hobby/retail packs and one every three jumbo packs, this 16-card set features authentic reprints of Topps Mickey Mantle cards that were not reprinted last year. Each card is stamped with the commemorative gold foil logo.

	Nm-Mt	Ex-Mt
COMPLETE SET (16)	100.00	30.00
COMMON (21-36)	8.00	2.40
COMMON FINEST (21-36)	8.00	2.40
FINEST SER.2 1:24 HOB/RET, 1:6 JUM		
COMMON REF. (21-36)	30.00	9.00
REF.SER.2 1:216 HOB/RET,1:60 JUM .		

1997 Topps Mays

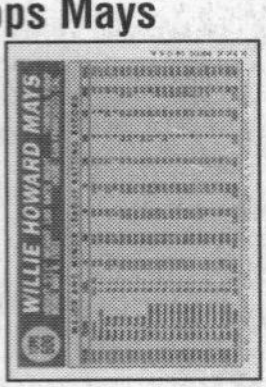

Randomly inserted at the rate of one in eight first series hobby/retail packs and one every two jumbo packs; cards from this 27-card set feature reprints of both the Topps and Bowman vintage Mays cards . Each card front is highlighted by a special commemorative gold foil stamp. Randomly inserted in first series hobby packs only (at the rate of one in 2,400) are personally signed cards. A special 4 1/4" by 5 3/4" jumbo reprint of the 1952 Topps Willie Mays card was made available exclusively in special series one Wal-Mart boxes. Each box (shaped much like a cereal box) contained ten eight-card retail packs and the aforementioned jumbo card and retailed for $10.

	Nm-Mt	Ex-Mt
COMPLETE SET (27)	100.00	30.00
COMMON MAYS (3-27)	4.00	1.20
COMMON FINEST (1-27)	4.00	1.20
*'51-'52 FINEST: .4X TO 1X BASIC MAYS REPRINTS		
FINEST SER.2 1:20 HOB/RET,1:4 JUM		
COMMON REF. (1-27)	10.00	3.00
*'51-'52 REF: 1X TO 2.5X BASIC MAYS REPRINTS		
REF.SER.2 1:180 HOB/RET,1:48 JUM .		
1 Willie Mays 1951 Bowman	8.00	2.40
2 Willie Mays 1952 Topps	6.00	1.80
J261 W.Mays 1952 Jumbo	8.00	1.80

1997 Topps Mays Autographs

Acording to Topps, Mays signed about 65 each of the following cards: 51B, 52T, 53T, 55B, 55T, 57T, 58T, 60T, 60T AS, 61T, 61T AS, 63T, 64T, 65T, 66T, 69T, 70T, 72T, 73T. The cards all have a "Certified Topps Autograph" stamp on them.

	Nm-Mt	Ex-Mt
COMMON CARD (1953-1958)	120.00	36.00
COMMON CARD (1960-1973)	120.00	36.00
1 Willie Mays 1951 Bowman	200.00	60.00
2 Willie Mays 1952 Topps	200.00	60.00

1997 Topps Season's Best

This 25-card set was randomly inserted into Topps Series two packs at a rate of one every six hobby/retail packs and one per jumbo pack; this set features five top players from each of the following five statistical categories: Leading Looters (top base stealers), Bleacher Reachers (top home run hitters), Hill Toppers (most wins), Number Crunchers (most RBI's), Kings of Swings (top slugging percentages). The fronts display color player photos printed on prismatic illusion foilboard. The backs carry another player photo and statistics.

	Nm-Mt	Ex-Mt
COMPLETE SET (25)	25.00	7.50
SB1 Tony Gwynn	2.50	.75
SB2 Frank Thomas	2.00	.60
SB3 Ellis Burks	.75	.23
SB4 Paul Molitor	1.25	.35
SB5 Chuck Knoblauch	.75	.23
SB6 Mark McGwire	5.00	1.50
SB7 Brady Anderson	.75	.23
SB8 Ken Griffey Jr.	3.00	.90
SB9 Albert Belle	.75	.23
SB10 Andres Galarraga	.75	.23
SB11 Andres Galarraga	.75	.23
SB12 Albert Belle	.75	.23
SB13 Juan Gonzalez	1.25	.35
SB14 Mo Vaughn	.75	.23
SB15 Rafael Palmeiro	1.25	.35
SB16 John Smoltz	1.25	.35
SB17 Andy Pettitte	1.25	.35
SB18 Pat Hentgen	.75	.23
SB19 Mike Mussina	1.25	.35
SB20 Andy Benes	.75	.23
SB21 Kenny Lofton	.75	.23
SB22 Tom Goodwin	.75	.23
SB23 Otis Nixon	.75	.23
SB24 Eric Young	.75	.23
SB25 Lance Johnson	.75	.23

1997 Topps Sweet Strokes

This 15-card retail only set was randomly inserted in series one retail packs at a rate of one in 12. Printed on Rainbow foilboard, the set features color photos of some of Baseball's top hitters.

	Nm-Mt	Ex-Mt
COMPLETE SET (15)	40.00	12.00
SS1 Roberto Alomar	1.50	.45
SS2 Jeff Bagwell	1.50	.45
SS3 Albert Belle	1.00	.30
SS4 Barry Bonds	6.00	1.80
SS5 Mark Grace	1.50	.45
SS6 Ken Griffey Jr.	4.00	1.20
SS7 Tony Gwynn	3.00	.90
SS8 Chipper Jones	2.50	.75
SS9 Edgar Martinez	1.50	.45
SS10 Mark McGwire	6.00	1.80
SS11 Rafael Palmeiro	1.50	.45
SS12 Mike Piazza	4.00	1.20
SS13 Gary Sheffield	1.00	.30
SS14 Frank Thomas	2.50	.75
SS15 Mo Vaughn	1.00	.30

1997 Topps Team Timber

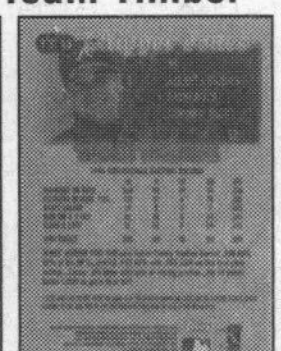

Randomly inserted into all second series hobby/retail packs at a rate of 1:36 and second series Hobby Collector (jumbo) packs at a rate of 1:8, cards from this 16-card set highlight a selection of baseball's top sluggers. Each card features a simulated wood-grain stock, but the fronts are UV-coated, making the cards bow noticeably.

	Nm-Mt	Ex-Mt
COMPLETE SET (16)	40.00	12.00
TT1 Ken Griffey Jr.	4.00	1.20
TT2 Ken Caminiti	1.00	.30
TT3 Bernie Williams	1.50	.45
TT4 Jeff Bagwell	1.50	.45
TT5 Frank Thomas	2.50	.75
TT6 Andres Galarraga	1.00	.30
TT7 Barry Bonds	6.00	1.80
TT8 Rafael Palmeiro	1.50	.45
TT9 Brady Anderson	1.00	.30
TT10 Juan Gonzalez	1.50	.45
TT11 Mo Vaughn	1.00	.30
TT12 Mark McGwire	6.00	1.80
TT13 Gary Sheffield	1.00	.30
TT14 Albert Belle	1.00	.30
TT15 Chipper Jones	2.50	.75
TT16 Mike Piazza	4.00	1.20

1998 Topps

This 503-card set was distributed in two separate series: 282 cards in first series and 221 cards in second series. 11-card packs carried a suggested retail price of $1.29. Cards were also distributed in Home Team Advantage jumbo packs and hobby, retail and Christmas factory sets. Card fronts feature color action player photos printed on 16 pt. stock with player information and career statistics on the back. Card number 7 was permanently retired in 1996 to honor Mickey Mantle. Series one contains the following subsets: Draft Picks (245-249), Prospects (250-259), Season Highlights (265-269), Interleague (270-274) Checklists (275-276) and World Series (277-283). Series two contains Season Highlights (474-478), Interleague (479-483), Prospects (484-495/498-501) and Checklists (502-503). Rookie Cards of note include Ryan Anderson, Michael Cuddyer, Jack Cust and Troy Glaus. This set also features Topps long-awaited first regular-issue Alex Rodriguez card (504). The superstar shortstop was left out of all Topps sets for the first four years of his career due to a problem between Topps and Rodriguez's agent Scott Boras. Finally, as part of an agreement with the Baseball Hall of Fame, Topps produced commemorative admission tickets featuring Roberto Clemente memorabilia from the Hall in the form of a Topps card. These were the standard admission tickets for the shrine, and were also included one per case in 1998 Topps series two baseball.

	Nm-Mt	Ex-Mt
COMPLETE SET (503)	80.00	24.00
COMP.HOBBY SET (511)	100.00	30.00
COMP.RETAIL SET (511)	100.00	30.00
COMP.SERIES 1 (282)	40.00	12.00
COMP.SERIES 2 (221)	40.00	12.00
1 Tony Gwynn	.60	.18
2 Larry Walker	.30	.09
3 Billy Wagner	.20	.06
4 Denny Neagle	.20	.06
5 Vladimir Guerrero	.50	.15
6 Kevin Brown	.30	.09
8 Mariano Rivera	.30	.09
9 Tony Clark	.20	.06
10 Deion Sanders	.30	.09
11 Francisco Cordova	.20	.06
12 Matt Williams	.20	.06
13 Carlos Baerga	.20	.06
14 Mo Vaughn	.20	.06
15 Bobby Witt	.20	.06
16 Matt Stairs	.20	.06
17 Chan Ho Park	.20	.06
18 Mike Bordick	.20	.06
19 Michael Tucker	.20	.06
20 Frank Thomas	.50	.15
21 Roberto Clemente	1.00	.30
22 Dmitri Young	.20	.06
23 Steve Trachsel	.20	.06
24 Jeff Kent	.20	.06
25 Scott Rolen	.50	.15
26 John Thomson	.20	.06
27 Joe Vitiello	.20	.06
28 Eddie Guardado	.20	.06
29 Charlie Hayes	.20	.06
30 Juan Gonzalez	.30	.09
31 Garret Anderson	.20	.06
32 John Jaha	.20	.06
33 Omar Vizquel	.30	.09
34 Brian Hunter	.20	.06
35 Jeff Bagwell	.30	.09
36 Mark Lemke	.20	.06
37 Doug Glanville	.20	.06
38 Dan Wilson	.20	.06
39 Steve Cooke	.20	.06
40 Chili Davis	.20	.06
41 Mike Cameron	.20	.06
42 F.P. Santangelo	.20	.06
43 Brad Ausmus	.20	.06
44 Gary DiSarcina	.20	.06
45 Pat Hentgen	.20	.06
46 Wilton Guerrero	.20	.06
47 Devon White	.20	.06
48 Danny Patterson	.20	.06
49 Pat Meares	.20	.06
50 Rafael Palmeiro	.30	.09
51 Mark Gardner	.20	.06
52 Jeff Blauser	.20	.06
53 Dave Hollins	.20	.06
54 Carlos Garcia	.20	.06
55 Ben McDonald	.20	.06
56 John Mabry	.20	.06
57 Trevor Hoffman	.20	.06
58 Tony Fernandez	.20	.06
59 Rich Loiselle	.20	.06
60 Mark Leiter	.20	.06
61 Pat Kelly	.20	.06
62 John Flaherty	.20	.06
63 Roger Bailey	.20	.06
64 Tom Gordon	.20	.06
65 Ryan Klesko	.20	.06
66 Darryl Hamilton	.20	.06
67 Jim Eisenreich	.20	.06
68 Butch Huskey	.20	.06
69 Mark Grudzielanek	.20	.06
70 Marquis Grissom	.20	.06
71 Mark McLemore	.20	.06
72 Gary Gaetti	.20	.06
73 Greg Gagne	.20	.06
74 Lyle Mouton	.20	.06
75 Jim Edmonds	.20	.06
76 Shawn Green	.20	.06

77 Greg Vaughn .20 .06
78 Terry Adams .20 .06
79 Kevin Polcovich .20 .06
80 Troy O'Leary .20 .06
81 Jeff Shaw .20 .06
82 Rich Becker .20 .06
83 David Wells .20 .06
84 Steve Karsay .20 .06
85 Charles Nagy .20 .06
86 B.J. Surhoff .20 .06
87 Jamey Wright .20 .06
88 James Baldwin .20 .06
89 Edgardo Alfonzo .20 .06
90 Jay Buhner .20 .06
91 Brady Anderson .20 .06
92 Scott Servais .20 .06
93 Edgar Renteria .20 .06
94 Mike Lieberthal .20 .06
95 Rick Aguilera .20 .06
96 Walt Weiss .20 .06
97 Deivi Cruz .20 .06
98 Kurt Abbott .20 .06
99 Henry Rodriguez .20 .06
100 Mike Piazza .75 .23
101 Bill Taylor .20 .06
102 Todd Zeile .20 .06
103 Rey Ordonez .20 .06
104 Willie Greene .20 .06
105 Tony Womack .20 .06
106 Mike Sweeney .20 .06
107 Jeffrey Hammonds .20 .06
108 Kevin Orie .20 .06
109 Alex Gonzalez .20 .06
110 Jose Canseco .50 .15
111 Paul Sorrento .20 .06
112 Joey Hamilton .20 .06
113 Brad Radke .20 .06
114 Steve Avery .20 .06
115 Esteban Loaiza .20 .06
116 Stan Javier .20 .06
117 Chris Gomez .20 .06
118 Royce Clayton .20 .06
119 Orlando Merced .20 .06
120 Kevin Appier .20 .06
121 Mel Nieves .20 .06
122 Joe Girardi .20 .06
123 Rico Brogna .20 .06
124 Kent Mercker .20 .06
125 Manny Ramirez .30 .09
126 Jeromy Burnitz .20 .06
127 Kevin Foster .20 .06
128 Matt Morris .20 .06
129 Jason Dickson .20 .06
130 Tom Glavine .30 .09
131 Wally Joyner .20 .06
132 Rick Reed .20 .06
133 Todd Jones .20 .06
134 Dave Martinez .20 .06
135 Sandy Alomar Jr. .20 .06
136 Mike Lansing .20 .06
137 Sean Berry .20 .06
138 Doug Jones .20 .06
139 Todd Stottlemyre .20 .06
140 Jay Bell .20 .06
141 Jaime Navarro .20 .06
142 Chris Hoiles .20 .06
143 Joey Cora .20 .06
144 Scott Spiezio .20 .06
145 Joe Carter .20 .06
146 Jose Guillen .20 .06
147 Damion Easley .20 .06
148 Lee Stevens .20 .06
149 Alex Fernandez .20 .06
150 Randy Johnson .50 .15
151 J.T. Snow .20 .06
152 Chuck Finley .20 .06
153 Bernard Gilkey .20 .06
154 David Segui .20 .06
155 Dante Bichette .20 .06
156 Kevin Stocker .20 .06
157 Carl Everett .20 .06
158 Jose Valentin .20 .06
159 Pokey Reese .20 .06
160 Derek Jeter 1.25 .35
161 Roger Pavlik .20 .06
162 Mark Wohlers .20 .06
163 Ricky Bottalico .20 .06
164 Ozzie Guillen .20 .06
165 Mike Mussina .30 .09
166 Gary Sheffield .20 .06
167 Hideo Nomo .50 .15
168 Mark Grace .30 .09
169 Aaron Sele .20 .06
170 Darryl Kile .20 .06
171 Shawn Estes .20 .06
172 Vinny Castilla .20 .06
173 Ron Coomer .20 .06
174 Jose Rosado .20 .06
175 Kenny Lofton .20 .06
176 Jason Giambi .20 .06
177 Hal Morris .20 .06
178 Darren Bragg .20 .06
179 Orel Hershiser .20 .06
180 Ray Lankford .20 .06
181 Hideki Irabu .20 .06
182 Kevin Young .20 .06
183 Javy Lopez .20 .06
184 Jeff Montgomery .20 .06
185 Mike Holtz .20 .06
186 George Williams .20 .06
187 Cal Eldred .20 .06
188 Tom Candiotti .20 .06
189 Glenallen Hill .20 .06
190 Brian Giles .20 .06
191 Dave Mlicki .20 .06
192 Garrett Stephenson .20 .06
193 Jeff Frye .20 .06
194 Joe Oliver .20 .06
195 Bob Hamelin .20 .06
196 Luis Sojo .20 .06
197 LaTroy Hawkins .20 .06
198 Kevin Elster .20 .06
199 Jeff Reed .20 .06
200 Dennis Eckersley .20 .06
201 Bill Mueller .20 .06
202 Russ Davis .20 .06
203 Armando Benitez .20 .06
204 Quilvio Veras .20 .06
205 Tim Naehring .20 .06
206 Quinton McCracken .20 .06
207 Raul Casanova .20 .06
208 Matt Lawton .20 .06
209 Luis Alicea .20 .06
210 Luis Gonzalez .20 .06
211 Allen Watson .20 .06
212 Gerald Williams .20 .06
213 David Bell .20 .06
214 Todd Hollandsworth .20 .06
215 Wade Boggs .30 .09
216 Jose Mesa .20 .06
217 Jamie Moyer .20 .06
218 Darren Daulton .20 .06
219 Mickey Morandini .20 .06
220 Rusty Greer .20 .06
221 Jim Bullinger .20 .06
222 Jose Offerman .20 .06
223 Matt Karchner .20 .06
224 Woody Williams .20 .06
225 Mark Loretta .20 .06
226 Mike Hampton .20 .06
227 Willie Adams .20 .06
228 Scott Hatteberg .20 .06
229 Rich Amaral .20 .06
230 Terry Steinbach .20 .06
231 Glendon Rusch .20 .06
232 Bret Boone .20 .06
233 Robert Person .20 .06
234 Jose Hernandez .20 .06
235 Doug Drabek .20 .06
236 Jason McDonald .20 .06
237 Chris Widger .20 .06
238 Tom Martin .20 .06
239 Dave Burba .20 .06
240 Pete Rose Jr. .20 .06
241 Bobby Ayala .20 .06
242 Tim Wakefield .20 .06
243 Dennis Springer .20 .06
244 Tim Belcher .20 .06
245 Jon Garland .20 .06
Geoff Goetz
246 Glenn Davis .40 .12
Lance Berkman
247 Vernon Wells .30 .09
Aaron Akin
248 Adam Kennedy .20 .06
Jason Romano
249 Jason Dellaero .20 .06
Troy Cameron
250 Alex Sanchez .20 .06
Jared Sandberg
251 Pablo Ortega .20 .06
James Manias
252 Jason Conti RC .20 .06
Mike Stoner
253 John Patterson .20 .06
Larry Rodriguez
254 Adrian Beltre .50 .15
Ryan Minor RC
Aaron Boone
255 Ben Grieve .20 .06
Brian Buchanan
Dermal Brown
256 Kerrry Wood .50 .15
Carl Pavano
Gil Meche
257 David Ortiz 1.00 .30
Daryle Ward
Richie Sexson
258 Randy Winn .20 .06
Juan Encarnacion
Andrew Vessel
259 Kris Benson .20 .06
Travis Smith
Courtney Duncan RC
260 Chad Hermansen .20 .06
Brent Butler
Warren Morris RC
261 Ben Davis .20 .06
Eli Marrero
Ramon Hernandez
262 Eric Chavez .30 .09
Russell Branyan
Russ Johnson
263 Todd Dunwoody RC .20 .06
John Barnes
Ryan Jackson
264 Matt Clement .20 .06
Roy Halladay
Brian Fuentes RC
265 Randy Johnson SH .30 .09
266 Kevin Brown SH .20 .06
267 Ricardo Rincon SH .20 .06
Francisco Cordova
268 N.Garciaparra SH .50 .15
269 Tino Martinez SH .20 .06
270 Chuck Knoblauch IL .20 .06
271 Pedro Martinez IL .30 .09
272 Denny Neagle IL .20 .06
273 Juan Gonzalez IL .20 .06
274 Andres Galarraga IL .20 .06
275 Checklist .20 .06
276 Checklist .20 .06
277 Moises Alou WS .20 .06
278 Sandy Alomar Jr. WS .20 .06
279 Gary Sheffield WS .20 .06
280 Matt Williams WS .20 .06
281 Livan Hernandez WS .20 .06
282 Chad Ogea WS .20 .06
283 Marlins Champs .20 .06
284 Tino Martinez .30 .09
285 Roberto Alomar .30 .09
286 Jeff King .20 .06
287 Brian Jordan .20 .06
288 Darin Erstad .20 .06
289 Ken Caminiti .20 .06
290 Jim Thome .50 .15
291 Paul Molitor .30 .09
292 Ivan Rodriguez .50 .15
293 Bernie Williams .30 .09
294 Todd Hundley .20 .06
295 Andres Galarraga .20 .06
296 Greg Maddux .75 .23
297 Edgar Martinez .30 .09
298 Ron Gant .20 .06
299 Derek Bell .20 .06
300 Roger Clemens 1.00 .30
301 Rondell White .20 .06
302 Barry Larkin .30 .09
303 Robin Ventura .20 .06
304 Jason Kendall .20 .06
305 Chipper Jones .50 .15
306 John Franco .20 .06
307 Sammy Sosa .75 .23
308 Troy Percival .20 .06
309 Chuck Knoblauch .20 .06
310 Ellis Burks .20 .06
311 Al Martin .20 .06
312 Tim Salmon .30 .09
313 Moises Alou .20 .06
314 Lance Johnson .20 .06
315 Justin Thompson .20 .06
316 Will Clark .50 .15
317 Barry Bonds 1.25 .35
318 Craig Biggio .30 .09
319 John Smoltz .30 .09
320 Cal Ripken 1.50 .45
321 Ken Griffey Jr. .75 .23
322 Paul O'Neill .30 .09
323 Todd Helton .30 .09
324 John Olerud .20 .06
325 Mark McGwire 1.25 .35
326 Jose Cruz Jr. .20 .06
327 Jeff Cirillo .20 .06
328 Dean Palmer .20 .06
329 John Wetteland .20 .06
330 Steve Finley .20 .06
331 Albert Belle .20 .06
332 Curt Schilling .20 .06
333 Raul Mondesi .20 .06
334 Andruw Jones .20 .06
335 Nomar Garciaparra .75 .23
336 David Justice .20 .06
337 Andy Pettitte .30 .09
338 Pedro Martinez .50 .15
339 Travis Miller .20 .06
340 Chris Stynes .20 .06
341 Gregg Jefferies .20 .06
342 Jeff Fassero .20 .06
343 Craig Counsell .20 .06
344 Wilson Alvarez .20 .06
345 Bip Roberts .20 .06
346 Kelvim Escobar .20 .06
347 Mark Bellhorn .20 .06
348 Cory Lidle RC .30 .09
349 Fred McGriff .30 .09
350 Chuck Carr .20 .06
351 Bob Abreu .20 .06
352 Juan Guzman .20 .06
353 Fernando Vina .20 .06
354 Andy Benes .20 .06
355 Dave Nilsson .20 .06
356 Bobby Bonilla .20 .06
357 Ismael Valdes .20 .06
358 Carlos Perez .20 .06
359 Kirk Rueter .20 .06
360 Bartolo Colon .20 .06
361 Mel Rojas .20 .06
362 Johnny Damon .30 .09
363 Geronimo Berroa .20 .06
364 Reggie Sanders .20 .06
365 Jermaine Allensworth .20 .06
366 Orlando Cabrera .20 .06
367 Jorge Fabregas .20 .06
368 Scott Stahoviak .20 .06
369 Ken Cloude .20 .06
370 Donovan Osborne .20 .06
371 Roger Cedeno .20 .06
372 Neifi Perez .20 .06
373 Chris Holt .20 .06
374 Cecil Fielder .20 .06
375 Marty Cordova .20 .06
376 Tom Goodwin .20 .06
377 Jeff Suppan .20 .06
378 Jeff Brantley .20 .06
379 Mark Langston .20 .06
380 Shane Reynolds .20 .06
381 Mike Fetters .20 .06
382 Todd Greene .20 .06
383 Ray Durham .20 .06
384 Carlos Delgado .20 .06
385 Jeff D'Amico .20 .06
386 Brian McRae .20 .06
387 Alan Benes .20 .06
388 Heathcliff Slocumb .20 .06
389 Eric Young .20 .06
390 Travis Fryman .20 .06
391 David Cone .20 .06
392 Otis Nixon .20 .06
393 Jeremi Gonzalez .20 .06
394 Jeff Juden .20 .06
395 Jose Vizcaino .20 .06
396 Ugueth Urbina .20 .06
397 Ramon Martinez .20 .06
398 Robb Nen .20 .06
399 Harold Baines .20 .06
400 Delino DeShields .20 .06
401 John Burkett .20 .06
402 Sterling Hitchcock .20 .06
403 Mark Clark .20 .06
404 Terrell Wade .20 .06
405 Scott Brosius .20 .06
406 Chad Curtis .20 .06
407 Brian Johnson .20 .06
408 Roberto Kelly .20 .06
409 Dave Dellucci RC .40 .12
410 Michael Tucker .20 .06
411 Mark Kotsay .20 .06
412 Mark Lewis .20 .06
413 Ryan McGuire .20 .06
414 Shawon Dunston .20 .06
415 Brad Rigby .20 .06
416 Scott Erickson .20 .06
417 Bobby Jones .20 .06
418 Darren Oliver .20 .06
419 John Smiley .20 .06
420 T.J. Mathews .20 .06
421 Dustin Hermanson .20 .06
422 Mike Timlin .20 .06
423 Willie Blair .20 .06
424 Manny Alexander .20 .06
425 Bob Tewksbury .20 .06
426 Pete Schourek .20 .06
427 Reggie Jefferson .20 .06
428 Ed Sprague .20 .06
429 Jeff Conine .20 .06
430 Roberto Hernandez .20 .06
431 Tom Pagnozzi .20 .06
432 Jaret Wright .30 .09
433 Livan Hernandez .20 .06
434 Andy Ashby .20 .06
435 Todd Dunn .20 .06
436 Bobby Higginson .20 .06
437 Rod Beck .20 .06
438 Jim Leyritz .20 .06
439 Matt Williams .20 .06
440 Brett Tomko .20 .06
441 Joe Randa .20 .06
442 Chris Carpenter .20 .06
443 Dennis Reyes .20 .06
444 Al Leiter .20 .06
445 Jason Schmidt .20 .06
446 Ken Hill .20 .06
447 Shannon Stewart .20 .06
448 Enrique Wilson .20 .06
449 Fernando Tatis .20 .06
450 Jimmy Key .20 .06
451 Darrin Fletcher .20 .06
452 John Valentin .20 .06
453 Kevin Tapani .20 .06
454 Eric Karros .20 .06
455 Jay Bell .20 .06
456 Walt Weiss .20 .06
457 Devon White .20 .06
458 Carl Pavano .30 .06
459 Mike Lansing .20 .06
460 John Flaherty .20 .06
461 Richard Hidalgo .20 .06
462 Quinton McCracken .20 .06
463 Karim Garcia .20 .06
464 Miguel Cairo .20 .06
465 Edwin Diaz .20 .06
466 Bobby Smith .20 .06
467 Yamil Benitez .20 .06
468 Rich Butler .20 .06
469 Ben Ford RC .20 .06
470 Bubba Trammell .20 .06
471 Brent Brede .20 .06
472 Brooks Kieschnick .20 .06
473 Carlos Castillo .20 .06
474 Brad Radke SH .20 .06
475 Roger Clemens SH .50 .15
476 Curt Schilling SH .20 .06
477 John Olerud SH .20 .06
478 Mark McGwire SH .60 .18
479 Mike Piazza .50 .15
Ken Griffey Jr. IL
480 Jeff Bagwell .30 .09
Frank Thomas IL
481 Chipper Jones .30 .09
Nomar Garciaparra IL
482 Larry Walker .20 .06
Juan Gonzalez IL
483 Gary Sheffield .20 .06
Tino Martinez IL
484 Derrick Gibson .20 .06
Michael Coleman
Norm Hutchins
485 Braden Looper .20 .06
Cliff Politte
Brian Rose
486 Eric Milton .20 .06
Jason Marquis
Corey Lee
487 A.J.Hinch .30 .09
Mark Osborne
Robert Fick RC
488 Aramis Ramirez .30 .09
Alex Gonzalez
Sean Casey
489 Donnie Bridges .20 .06
Tim Drew RC
490 Ntema Ndungidi RC .20 .06
Darnell McDonald
491 Ryan Anderson RC .30 .09
Mark Mangum
492 J.J.Davis 1.50 .45
Troy Glaus RC
493 Jayson Werth RC .20 .06
Dan Reichert
494 John Curtice RC .40 .12
Michael Cuddyer RC
495 Jack Cust RC .30 .09
Jason Standridge
496 Brian Anderson .20 .06
497 Tony Saunders .20 .06
498 Vladimir Nunez .20 .06
Jhensy Sandoval
499 Brad Penny .30 .09
Nick Bierbrodt
500 Dustin Carr .20 .06
Luis Cruz RC
501 Cedric Bowers .20 .06
Marcus McCain
502 Checklist .20 .06
503 Checklist .20 .06
504 Alex Rodriguez 2.00 .60

1998 Topps Minted in Cooperstown

Randomly inserted in first and second series packs at the rate of one in eight, this 503 card set is a parallel version of the base set. The set is distinguished by the special "Minted in Cooperstown" logo stamped on each card. Similar to the regular set, card number 7 does not exist.

Nm-Mt Ex-Mt
*STARS: 5X TO 12X BASIC CARDS...
*ROOKIES: 6X TO 15X BASIC CARDS

1998 Topps Inaugural Devil Rays

This 503 card set was issued by Topps only in factory set form. Just as for the teams which began play in 1993, special sets with a Devil Rays logo was issued. The sets were sold only through retail outlets. These sets apparently did not sell well enough at the stadium and were later closed out to one of the home shopping networks. The logo is in gold foil and is in the middle of the card.

Nm-Mt Ex-Mt
COMP.FACT.SET (503) 120.00 36.00
*STARS: 1.5X TO 4X BASIC CARDS...
*ROOKIES: 2.5X TO 6X BASIC CARDS

1998 Topps Inaugural Diamondbacks

Similar to the Devil Rays set, Topps issued a factory set with the Diamond Backs logo to honor the first season the Arizona Diamondbacks played. The sets were issued in factory form and were only available through the Diamondback retail outlet.

Nm-Mt Ex-Mt
COMP.FACT.SET (503) 120.00 36.00
*STARS: 1.5X TO 4X BASIC CARDS...
*ROOKIES: 2.5X TO 6X BASIC CARDS

1998 Topps Baby Boomers

Randomly inserted in retail packs only at the rate of one in 36, this 15-card set features color photos of young players who have already made their mark in the game dispite less than three years in the majors.

	Nm-Mt	Ex-Mt
COMPLETE SET (15)	50.00	15.00
BB1 Derek Jeter	12.00	3.60
BB2 Scott Rolen	5.00	1.50
BB3 Nomar Garciaparra	8.00	2.40
BB4 Jose Cruz Jr.	2.00	.60
BB5 Darin Erstad	2.00	.60
BB6 Todd Helton	3.00	.90
BB7 Tony Clark	2.00	.60
BB8 Jose Guillen	2.00	.60
BB9 Andruw Jones	2.00	.60
BB10 Vladimir Guerrero	5.00	1.50
BB11 Mark Kotsay	2.00	.60
BB12 Todd Greene	2.00	.60
BB13 Andy Pettitte	3.00	.90
BB14 Justin Thompson	2.00	.60
BB15 Alan Benes	2.00	.60

1998 Topps Clemente

Randomly inserted in first and second series packs at the rate of one in 18, cards from this 19-card set honor the memory of Roberto Clemente on the 25th anniversary of his untimely death with conventional reprints of his Topps cards. All odd numbered cards were seeded in first series packs. All even numbered cards were seeded in second series packs.

	Nm-Mt	Ex-Mt
COMPLETE SET (19)	120.00	36.00
COMPLETE SERIES 1 (10)	60.00	18.00
COMPLETE SERIES 2 (9)	60.00	18.00
COMMON CARD (2-19)	8.00	2.40
1 Roberto Clemente 1955	15.00	4.50

1998 Topps Clemente Finest

Randomly inserted in first and second series packs at the rate of one in 72, cards from this nineteen-card set honor the memory of Roberto Clemente on the 25th anniversary of his untimely death with Finest reprints of his Topps cards. First series packs contained only even numbered cards. Second series packs contained only odd numbered cards.

	Nm-Mt	Ex-Mt
COMPLETE SET (19)	150.00	45.00
COMPLETE SERIES 1 (9)	80.00	24.00
COMPLETE SERIES 2 (10)	80.00	24.00
COMMON CARD (2-19)	10.00	3.00
COMMON REF. (1-19)		
*REFRACTOR: .75X TO 2X FINEST		
REFRACTOR STATED ODDS 1:288		
1 Roberto Clemente 1955	20.00	6.00

1998 Topps Clemente Memorabilia Madness

As a major promotion for 1998 Topps series one, Topps created 46 different Roberto Clemente exchange cards for a total of 854 prizes. All 46 prizes (including the quantity available of each prize) is detailed explicitly in the listings below. The quantity is noted immediately after the prize. All 854 exchange cards looked identical to each other on front and almost identical to each other on back. Card fronts feature a blue, purple and white dot matrix head shot of Clemente surrounded by burgundy borders. Card backs featured extensive guidelines and rules for the exchange program. The only difference for each card were the few sentences on back detailing which specific prize each of the 46 different cards could be exchanged for. Lucky collectors that got their hands on these scarce exchange cards had until August 31st, 1998 to redeem their prizes. Odds for pulling one of these cards was approximately 1:3,708 hobby packs and approximately 1:1,020 hobby collector packs. Prices for almost all of these exchange cards have been excluded due to scarcity and lack of market information.

	Nm-Mt	Ex-Mt
COMMON CARD (1-46)	80.00	24.00
NNO Wild Card	1.00	.30

1998 Topps Clemente Tribute

Randomly inserted in packs at the rate of one in 12, this five-card set honors the memory of Roberto Clemente on the 25th anniversay of his untimely death and features color photos printed on mirror foilboard on newly designed cards.

	Nm-Mt	Ex-Mt
COMPLETE SET (5)	8.00	2.40
COMMON (RC1-RC5)	2.00	.60

1998 Topps Clout Nine

Randomly inserted in Topps Series two packs at the rate of one in 72, this nine-card set features color photos of the top players statiscally at each of the nine playing positions.

	Nm-Mt	Ex-Mt
COMPLETE SET (9)	40.00	12.00
C1 Edgar Martinez	4.00	1.20
C2 Mike Piazza	10.00	3.00
C3 Frank Thomas	6.00	1.80
C4 Craig Biggio	4.00	1.20
C5 Vinny Castilla	2.50	.75
C6 Jeff Blauser	2.50	.75
C7 Barry Bonds	15.00	4.50
C8 Ken Griffey Jr.	10.00	3.00
C9 Larry Walker	4.00	1.20

1998 Topps Etch-A-Sketch

Randomly inserted in Topps Series one packs at the rate of one in 36, this nine-card set features drawings by artist George Vlosich III of some of baseball's hottest superstars using an Etch A Sketch as a canvas.

	Nm-Mt	Ex-Mt
COMPLETE SET (9)	30.00	9.00
ES1 Albert Belle	1.25	.35
ES2 Barry Bonds	8.00	2.40
ES3 Ken Griffey Jr.	5.00	1.50
ES4 Greg Maddux	5.00	1.50
ES5 Hideo Nomo	3.00	.90
ES6 Mike Piazza	5.00	1.50
ES7 Cal Ripken	10.00	3.00
ES8 Frank Thomas	3.00	.90
ES9 Mo Vaughn	1.25	.35

1998 Topps Flashback

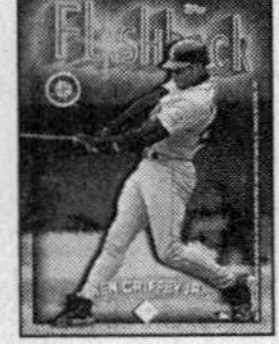

Randomly inserted in Topps Series one packs at the rate of one in 72, these two-sided cards of top players feature photographs of how they looked "then" as rookies on one side and how they look "now" as stars on the other.

	Nm-Mt	Ex-Mt
COMPLETE SET (10)	80.00	24.00
FB1 Barry Bonds	20.00	6.00
FB2 Ken Griffey Jr.	12.00	3.60
FB3 Paul Molitor	5.00	1.50
FB4 Randy Johnson	8.00	2.40
FB5 Cal Ripken	25.00	7.50
FB6 Tony Gwynn	10.00	3.00
FB7 Kenny Lofton	3.00	.90
FB8 Gary Sheffield	3.00	.90
FB9 Deion Sanders	5.00	1.50
FB10 Brady Anderson	3.00	.90

1998 Topps Focal Points

Randomly inserted in Topps Series two hobby packs only at the rate of one in 36, this 15-card set features color photos of current superstars with a special focus on the skills that have put them at the top.

	Nm-Mt	Ex-Mt
COMPLETE SET (15)	80.00	24.00
FP1 Juan Gonzalez	3.00	.90
FP2 Nomar Garciaparra	8.00	2.40
FP3 Jose Cruz Jr.	2.00	.60
FP4 Cal Ripken	15.00	4.50
FP5 Ken Griffey Jr.	8.00	2.40
FP6 Ivan Rodriguez	5.00	1.50
FP7 Larry Walker	3.00	.90
FP8 Barry Bonds	12.00	3.60
FP9 Roger Clemens	10.00	3.00
FP10 Frank Thomas	5.00	1.50
FP11 Chuck Knoblauch	2.00	.60
FP12 Mike Piazza	8.00	2.40
FP13 Greg Maddux	8.00	2.40
FP14 Vladimir Guerrero	5.00	1.50
FP15 Andruw Jones	2.00	.60

1998 Topps HallBound

Randomly inserted in Topps Series one hobby packs only at the rate of one in 36, this 15-card set features color photos of top stars who are bound for the Hall of Fame printed on foil mirrorboard cards.

	Nm-Mt	Ex-Mt
COMPLETE SET (15)	80.00	24.00
HB1 Paul Molitor	3.00	.90
HB2 Tony Gwynn	6.00	1.80
HB3 Wade Boggs	3.00	.90
HB4 Roger Clemens	10.00	3.00
HB5 Dennis Eckersley	2.00	.60
HB6 Cal Ripken	15.00	4.50
HB7 Greg Maddux	8.00	2.40
HB8 Rickey Henderson	3.00	.90
HB9 Ken Griffey Jr.	8.00	2.40
HB10 Frank Thomas	5.00	1.50
HB11 Mark McGwire	12.00	3.60
HB12 Barry Bonds	12.00	3.60
HB13 Mike Piazza	8.00	2.40
HB14 Juan Gonzalez	3.00	.90
HB15 Randy Johnson	5.00	1.50

1998 Topps Milestones

Randomly inserted in Topps Series two retail packs only at the rate of one in 36, this ten-card set features color photos of players with the ability to set new records in the sport.

	Nm-Mt	Ex-Mt
COMPLETE SET (10)	50.00	15.00
MS1 Barry Bonds	10.00	3.00
MS2 Roger Clemens	8.00	2.40
MS3 Dennis Eckersley	1.50	.45
MS4 Juan Gonzalez	2.50	.75
MS5 Ken Griffey Jr.	6.00	1.80
MS6 Tony Gwynn	5.00	1.50
MS7 Greg Maddux	6.00	1.80
MS8 Mark McGwire	10.00	3.00
MS9 Cal Ripken	12.00	3.60
MS10 Frank Thomas	4.00	1.20

1998 Topps Mystery Finest

Randomly inserted in first series packs at the rate of one in 36, this 20-card set features color action player photos which showcase five of the 1997 season's most intriguing inter-league matchups.

	Nm-Mt	Ex-Mt
COMPLETE SET (20)	80.00	24.00
*REFRACTOR: 1X TO 2.5X BASIC MYS.FIN.		
REFRACTOR SER.1 STATED ODDS: 1:144		
ILM1 Chipper Jones	5.00	1.50
ILM2 Cal Ripken	15.00	4.50
ILM3 Greg Maddux	8.00	2.40
ILM4 Rafael Palmeiro	3.00	.90
ILM5 Todd Hundley	2.00	.60
ILM6 Derek Jeter	12.00	3.60
ILM7 John Olerud	2.00	.60
ILM8 Tino Martinez	3.00	.90
ILM9 Larry Walker	3.00	.90
ILM10 Ken Griffey Jr.	8.00	2.40
ILM11 Andres Galarraga	2.00	.60
ILM12 Randy Johnson	5.00	1.50
ILM13 Mike Piazza	8.00	2.40
ILM14 Jim Edmonds	2.00	.60
ILM15 Eric Karros	2.00	.60
ILM16 Tim Salmon	3.00	.90
ILM17 Sammy Sosa	8.00	2.40
ILM18 Frank Thomas	5.00	1.50
ILM19 Mark Grace	3.00	.90
ILM20 Albert Belle	2.00	.60

1998 Topps Mystery Finest Bordered

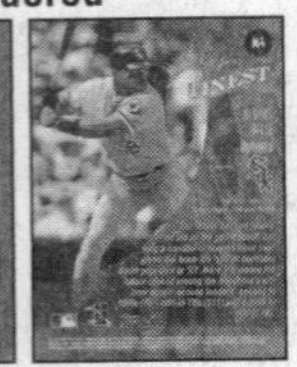

Randomly inserted in Topps Series two packs at the rate of one in 36, this 20-card set features bordered color player photos of current hot players.

	Nm-Mt	Ex-Mt
COMPLETE SET (20)	100.00	30.00
*BORDERED REF: .75X TO 2X BORDERED		
BORDERED REF.SER.2 ODDS 1:108 ...		
*BORDERLESS: .6X TO 1.5X BORDERED		
BORDERLESS SER.2 ODDS 1:72		
*BORDERLESS REF: 1.25X TO 3X BORDERED		
BORDERLESS REF.SER.2 ODDS 1:288		
M1 Nomar Garciaparra	8.00	2.40
M2 Chipper Jones	5.00	1.50
M3 Scott Rolen	5.00	1.50
M4 Albert Belle	2.00	.60
M5 Mo Vaughn	2.00	.60
M6 Jose Cruz Jr.	2.00	.60
M7 Mark McGwire	12.00	3.60
M8 Derek Jeter	12.00	3.60
M9 Tony Gwynn	6.00	1.80
M10 Frank Thomas	5.00	1.50
M11 Tino Martinez	3.00	.90
M12 Greg Maddux	8.00	2.40
M13 Juan Gonzalez	3.00	.90
M14 Larry Walker	3.00	.90
M15 Mike Piazza	8.00	2.40
M16 Cal Ripken	15.00	4.50
M17 Jeff Bagwell	3.00	.90
M18 Andruw Jones	2.00	.60
M19 Barry Bonds	12.00	3.60
M20 Ken Griffey Jr.	8.00	2.40

1998 Topps Rookie Class

Randomly inserted in Topps Series two packs at the rate of one in 12, this 10-card set features color photos of top young stars with less than one year's playing time in the Majors. The backs carry player information.

	Nm-Mt	Ex-Mt
COMPLETE SET (10)	6.00	1.80
R1 Travis Lee	.75	.23
R2 Richard Hidalgo	.75	.23
R3 Todd Helton	1.25	.35
R4 Paul Konerko	.75	.23
R5 Mark Kotsay	.75	.23
R6 Derrek Lee	.75	.23
R7 Eli Marrero	.75	.23
R8 Fernando Tatis	.75	.23
R9 Juan Encarnacion	.75	.23
R10 Ben Grieve	.75	.23

1999 Topps

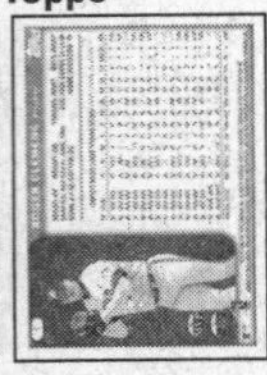

The 1999 Topps set consisted of 462 standard-size cards. Each 11 card pack carried a suggested retail price of $1.29 per pack. Cards were also distributed in 40-card Home Team advantage jumbo packs, hobby, retail and Christmas factory sets. The Mark McGwire number 220 card was issued in 70 different varieties to honor his record setting season. The Sammy Sosa number 461 card was issued in 66 different varieties to honor his 1998 season. Basic sets are considered complete with any one of the 70 McGwire and 66 Sosa variations. A.J. Burnett, Pat Burrell, and Alex Escobar are the most notable Rookie Cards in the set. Card number 7 was not issued as Topps continues to honor the memory of Mickey Mantle. The Christmas factory set contains one Nolan Ryan finest reprint card as an added bonus, while the hobby and retail factory sets just contained the regular sets in a factory box.

	Nm-Mt	Ex-Mt
COMPLETE SET (462)	80.00	24.00
COMP.HOBBY SET (462)	80.00	24.00
COMP.X-MAS SET (463)	80.00	24.00
COMP. SERIES 1 (241)	40.00	12.00
COMP. SERIES 2 (221)	40.00	12.00
COMP.MAC HR SET (70)	400.00	120.00
COMP.SOSA HR SET (66)	200.00	60.00
1 Roger Clemens	1.00	.30
2 Andres Galarraga	.20	.06
3 Scott Brosius	.20	.06
4 John Flaherty	.20	.06
5 Jim Leyritz	.20	.06
6 Ray Durham	.20	.06
8 Jose Vizcaino	.20	.06
9 Will Clark	.50	.15
10 David Wells	.20	.06
11 Jose Guillen	.20	.06
12 Scott Hatteberg	.20	.06
13 Edgardo Alfonzo	.20	.06
14 Mike Bordick	.20	.06
15 Manny Ramirez	.30	.09
16 Greg Maddux	.75	.23
17 David Segui	.20	.06
18 Darryl Strawberry	.20	.06
19 Brad Radke	.20	.06
20 Kerry Wood	.50	.15
21 Matt Anderson	.20	.06
22 Derrek Lee	.20	.06
23 Mickey Morandini	.20	.06
24 Paul Konerko	.20	.06
25 Travis Lee	.20	.06
26 Ken Hill	.20	.06
27 Kenny Rogers	.20	.06
28 Paul Sorrento	.20	.06
29 Quilvio Veras	.20	.06
30 Todd Walker	.20	.06
31 Ryan Jackson	.20	.06
32 John Olerud	.20	.06
33 Doug Glanville	.20	.06
34 Nolan Ryan	2.00	.60
35 Ray Lankford	.20	.06
36 Mark Loretta	.20	.06
37 Jason Dickson	.20	.06
38 Sean Bergman	.20	.06
39 Quinton McCracken	.20	.06
40 Bartolo Colon	.20	.06
41 Brady Anderson	.20	.06
42 Chris Stynes	.20	.06
43 Jorge Posada	.30	.09
44 Justin Thompson	.20	.06
45 Johnny Damon	.30	.09
46 Armando Benitez	.20	.06
47 Brant Brown	.20	.06
48 Charlie Hayes	.20	.06
49 Darren Dreifort	.20	.06
50 Juan Gonzalez	.30	.09
51 Chuck Knoblauch	.20	.06
52 Todd Helton	.30	.09
53 Rick Reed	.20	.06
54 Chris Gomez	.20	.06
55 Gary Sheffield	.20	.06
56 Rod Beck	.20	.06
57 Rey Sanchez	.20	.06
58 Garret Anderson	.20	.06
59 Jimmy Haynes	.20	.06
60 Steve Woodard	.20	.06
61 Rondell White	.20	.06
62 Vladimir Guerrero	.50	.15
63 Eric Karros	.20	.06
64 Russ Davis	.20	.06
65 Mo Vaughn	.20	.06
66 Sammy Sosa	.75	.23
67 Troy Percival	.20	.06
68 Kenny Lofton	.20	.06
69 Bill Taylor	.20	.06
70 Mark McGwire	1.25	.35
71 Roger Cedeno	.20	.06
72 Javy Lopez	.20	.06
73 Damion Easley	.20	.06
74 Andy Pettitte	.30	.09
75 Tony Gwynn	.60	.18
76 Ricardo Rincon	.20	.06
77 F.P. Santangelo	.20	.06
78 Jay Bell	.20	.06
79 Scott Servais	.20	.06
80 Jose Canseco	.50	.15
81 Roberto Hernandez	.20	.06
82 Todd Dunwoody	.20	.06
83 John Wetteland	.20	.06
84 Mike Caruso	.20	.06
85 Derek Jeter	1.25	.35
86 Aaron Sele	.20	.06
87 Jose Lima	.20	.06
88 Ryan Christenson	.20	.06
89 Jeff Cirillo	.20	.06
90 Jose Hernandez	.20	.06
91 Mark Kotsay	.20	.06
92 Darren Bragg	.20	.06
93 Albert Belle	.20	.06
94 Matt Lawton	.20	.06
95 Pedro Martinez	.50	.15
96 Greg Vaughn	.20	.06
97 Neifi Perez	.20	.06
98 Gerald Williams	.20	.06
99 Derek Bell	.20	.06
100 Ken Griffey Jr.	.75	.23
101 David Cone	.20	.06
102 Brian Johnson	.20	.06
103 Dean Palmer	.20	.06
104 Javier Valentin	.20	.06
105 Trevor Hoffman	.20	.06
106 Butch Huskey	.20	.06
107 Dave Martinez	.20	.06
108 Billy Wagner	.20	.06
109 Shawn Green	.20	.06
110 Ben Grieve	.20	.06
111 Tom Goodwin	.20	.06
112 Jaret Wright	.20	.06
113 Aramis Ramirez	.20	.06
114 Dmitri Young	.20	.06
115 Hideki Irabu	.20	.06
116 Roberto Kelly	.20	.06
117 Jeff Fassero	.20	.06
118 Mark Clark UER	.20	.06
1997 and Career Victory totals are wrong		
119 Jason McDonald	.20	.06
120 Matt Williams	.20	.06
121 Dave Burba	.20	.06
122 Bret Saberhagen	.20	.06
123 Deivi Cruz	.20	.06
124 Chad Curtis	.20	.06
125 Scott Rolen	.50	.15
126 Lee Stevens	.20	.06
127 J.T. Snow	.20	.06
128 Rusty Greer	.20	.06
129 Brian Meadows	.20	.06
130 Jim Edmonds	.20	.06
131 Ron Gant	.20	.06
132 A.J. Hinch UER	.20	.06
Photo is a reverse negative		
133 Shannon Stewart	.20	.06
134 Brad Fullmer	.20	.06
135 Cal Eldred	.20	.06
136 Matt Walbeck	.20	.06
137 Carl Everett	.20	.06
138 Walt Weiss	.20	.06
139 Fred McGriff	.30	.09
140 Darin Erstad	.20	.06
141 Dave Nilsson	.20	.06
142 Eric Young	.20	.06
143 Dan Wilson	.20	.06
144 Jeff Reed	.20	.06
145 Brett Tomko	.20	.06
146 Terry Steinbach	.20	.06
147 Seth Greisinger	.20	.06
148 Pat Meares	.20	.06
149 Livan Hernandez	.20	.06
150 Jeff Bagwell	.30	.09
151 Bob Wickman	.20	.06
152 Omar Vizquel	.30	.09
153 Eric Davis	.20	.06
154 Larry Sutton	.20	.06
155 Magglio Ordonez	.20	.06
156 Eric Milton	.20	.06
157 Darren Lewis	.20	.06
158 Rick Aguilera	.20	.06
159 Mike Lieberthal	.20	.06
160 Robb Nen	.20	.06
161 Brian Giles	.20	.06
162 Jeff Brantley	.20	.06
163 Gary DiSarcina	.20	.06
164 John Valentin	.20	.06
165 David Dellucci	.20	.06
166 Chan Ho Park	.20	.06
167 Masato Yoshii	.20	.06
168 Jason Schmidt	.20	.06
169 LaTroy Hawkins	.20	.06
170 Bret Boone	.20	.06
171 Jerry DiPoto	.20	.06
172 Mariano Rivera	.30	.09
173 Mike Cameron	.20	.06
174 Scott Erickson	.20	.06
175 Charles Johnson	.20	.06
176 Bobby Jones	.20	.06
177 Francisco Cordova	.20	.06
178 Todd Jones	.20	.06
179 Jeff Montgomery	.20	.06
180 Mike Mussina	.30	.09
181 Bob Abreu	.20	.06
182 Ismael Valdes	.20	.06
183 Andy Fox	.20	.06
184 Woody Williams	.20	.06
185 Denny Neagle	.20	.06
186 Jose Valentin	.20	.06
187 Darrin Fletcher	.20	.06
188 Gabe Alvarez	.20	.06
189 Eddie Taubensee	.20	.06
190 Edgar Martinez	.30	.09
191 Jason Kendall	.20	.06
192 Darryl Kile	.20	.06
193 Jeff King	.20	.06
194 Rey Ordonez	.20	.06
195 Andruw Jones	.20	.06
196 Tony Fernandez	.20	.06
197 Jamey Wright	.20	.06
198 B.J. Surhoff	.20	.06
199 Vinny Castilla	.20	.06
200 David Wells HL	.20	.06
201 Mark McGwire HL	.60	.18
202 Sammy Sosa HL	.50	.15
203 Roger Clemens HL	.50	.15
204 Kerry Wood HL	.30	.09
205 Lance Berkman Mike Frank Gabe Kapler	.40	.12
206 Alex Escobar RC Ricky Ledee Mike Stoner	.40	.12
207 Peter Bergeron RC Jeremy Giambi George Lombard	.40	.12
208 Michael Barrett Ben Davis Robert Fick	.25	.07
209 Pat Cline Ramon Hernandez Jayson Werth	.25	.07
210 Bruce Chen Chris Enochs Ryan Anderson	.25	.07
211 Mike Lincoln Octavio Dotel Brad Penny	.25	.07
212 Chuck Abbott RC Brent Butler Danny Klassen	.25	.07
213 Chris C.Jones Jeff Urban RC	.25	.07
214 Arturo McDowell RC Tony Torcato	.25	.07
215 Josh McKinley RC Jason Tyner	.40	.12
216 Matt Burch Seth Etheron RC UER back Etherton	.25	.07
217 Mamon Tucker RC Rick Elder	.40	.12
218 J.M.Gold Ryan Mills RC	.25	.07
219 Adam Brown Choo Freeman RC	.25	.07
220A Mark McGwire HR 1	40.00	12.00
220B Mark McGwire HR 2	15.00	4.50

220C Mark McGwire HR 3 15.00 4.50
220D Mark McGwire HR 4 15.00 4.50
220E Mark McGwire HR 5 15.00 4.50
220F Mark McGwire HR 6 15.00 4.50
220G Mark McGwire HR 7 15.00 4.50
220H Mark McGwire HR 8 15.00 4.50
220I Mark McGwire HR 9 15.00 4.50
220J M.McGwire HR 10 15.00 4.50
220K M.McGwire HR 11 15.00 4.50
220L M.McGwire HR 12 15.00 4.50
220M M.McGwire HR 13 15.00 4.50
220N M.McGwire HR 14 15.00 4.50
220O M.McGwire HR 15 15.00 4.50
220P M.McGwire HR 16 15.00 4.50
220Q M.McGwire HR 17 15.00 4.50
220R M.McGwire HR 18 15.00 4.50
220S M.McGwire HR 19 15.00 4.50
220T M.McGwire HR 20 15.00 4.50
220U M.McGwire HR 21 15.00 4.50
220V M.McGwire HR 22 15.00 4.50
220W M.McGwire HR 23 15.00 4.50
220X M.McGwire HR 24 15.00 4.50
220Y M.McGwire HR 25 15.00 4.50
220Z M.McGwire HR 26 15.00 4.50
220AA M.McGwire HR 27 15.00 4.50
220AB M.McGwire HR 28 15.00 4.50
220AC M.McGwire HR 29 15.00 4.50
220AD M.McGwire HR 30 15.00 4.50
220AE M.McGwire HR 31 15.00 4.50
220AF M.McGwire HR 32 15.00 4.50
220AG M.McGwire HR 33 15.00 4.50
220AH M.McGwire HR 34 15.00 4.50
220AI M.McGwire HR 35 15.00 4.50
220AJ M.McGwire HR 36 15.00 4.50
220AK M.McGwire HR 37 15.00 4.50
220AL M.McGwire HR 38 15.00 4.50
220AM M.McGwire HR 39 15.00 4.50
220AN M.McGwire HR 40 15.00 4.50
220AO M.McGwire HR 41 15.00 4.50
220AP M.McGwire HR 42 15.00 4.50
220AQ M.McGwire HR 43 15.00 4.50
220AR M.McGwire HR 44 15.00 4.50
220AS M.McGwire HR 45 15.00 4.50
220AT M.McGwire HR 46 15.00 4.50
220AU M.McGwire HR 47 15.00 4.50
220AV M.McGwire HR 48 15.00 4.50
220AW M.McGwire HR 49 15.00 4.50
220AX M.McGwire HR 50 15.00 4.50
220AY M.McGwire HR 51 15.00 4.50
220AZ M.McGwire HR 52 15.00 4.50
220BB M.McGwire HR 53 15.00 4.50
220CC M.McGwire HR 54 15.00 4.50
220DD M.McGwire HR 55 15.00 4.50
220EE M.McGwire HR 56 15.00 4.50
220FF M.McGwire HR 57 15.00 4.50
220GG M.McGwire HR 58 15.00 4.50
220HH M.McGwire HR 59 15.00 4.50
220II M.McGwire HR 60 15.00 4.50
220JJ M.McGwire HR 61 30.00 9.00
220KK M.McGwire HR 62 40.00 12.00
220LL M.McGwire HR 63 15.00 4.50
220MM M.McGwire HR 64 15.00 4.50
220NN M.McGwire HR 65 15.00 4.50
220OO M.McGwire HR 66 15.00 4.50
220PP M.McGwire HR 67 15.00 4.50
220QQ M.McGwire HR 68 15.00 4.50
220RR M.McGwire HR 69 15.00 4.50
220SS M.McGwire HR 70 80.00 24.00
221 Larry Walker LL .20 .06
222 Bernie Williams LL .20 .06
223 Mark McGwire LL .60 .18
224 Ken Griffey Jr. LL .50 .15
225 Sammy Sosa LL .50 .15
226 Juan Gonzalez LL .20 .06
227 Dante Bichette LL .20 .06
228 Alex Rodriguez LL .50 .15
229 Sammy Sosa LL .50 .15
230 Derek Jeter LL .60 .18
231 Greg Maddux LL .50 .15
232 Roger Clemens LL .50 .15
233 Ricky Ledee WS .20 .06
234 Chuck Knoblauch WS .20 .06
235 Bernie Williams WS .20 .06
236 Tino Martinez WS .20 .06
237 Orl. Hernandez WS .20 .06
238 Scott Brosius WS .20 .06
239 Andy Pettitte WS .20 .06
240 Mariano Rivera WS .20 .06
241 Checklist 1 .20 .06
242 Checklist 2 .20 .06
243 Tom Glavine .30 .09
244 Andy Benes .20 .06
245 Sandy Alomar Jr. .20 .06
246 Wilton Guerrero .20 .06
247 Alex Gonzalez .20 .06
248 Roberto Alomar .30 .09
249 Ruben Rivera .20 .06
250 Eric Chavez .20 .06
251 Ellis Burks .20 .06
252 Richie Sexson .20 .06
253 Steve Finley .20 .06
254 Dwight Gooden .20 .06
255 Dustin Hermanson .20 .06
256 Kirk Rueter .20 .06
257 Steve Trachsel .20 .06
258 Gregg Jefferies .20 .06
259 Matt Stairs .20 .06
260 Shane Reynolds .20 .06
261 Gregg Olson .20 .06
262 Kevin Tapani .20 .06
263 Matt Morris .20 .06
264 Carl Pavano .20 .06
265 Nomar Garciaparra .75 .23
266 Kevin Young .20 .06
267 Rick Helling .20 .06
268 Matt Franco .20 .06
269 Brian McRae .20 .06
270 Cal Ripken 1.50 .45
271 Jeff Abbott .20 .06
272 Tony Batista .20 .06
273 Bill Simas .20 .06
274 Brian Hunter .20 .06
275 John Franco .20 .06
276 Devon White .20 .06
277 Rickey Henderson .50 .15
278 Chuck Finley .20 .06
279 Mike Blowers .20 .06
280 Mark Grace .30 .09
281 Randy Winn .20 .06
282 Bobby Bonilla .20 .06
283 David Justice .20 .06
284 Shane Monahan .20 .06
285 Kevin Brown .30 .09
286 Todd Zeile .20 .06
287 Al Martin .20 .06
288 Troy O'Leary .20 .06
289 Darryl Hamilton .20 .06
290 Tino Martinez .30 .09
291 David Ortiz .30 .09
292 Tony Clark .20 .06
293 Ryan Minor .20 .06
294 Mark Leiter .20 .06
295 Wally Joyner .20 .06
296 Cliff Floyd .20 .06
297 Shawn Estes .20 .06
298 Pat Hentgen .20 .06
299 Scott Elarton .20 .06
300 Alex Rodriguez .75 .23
301 Ozzie Guillen .20 .06
302 Hideo Nomo .50 .15
303 Ryan McGuire .20 .06
304 Brad Ausmus .20 .06
305 Alex Gonzalez .20 .06
306 Brian Jordan .20 .06
307 John Jaha .20 .06
308 Mark Grudzielanek .20 .06
309 Juan Guzman .20 .06
310 Tony Womack .20 .06
311 Dennis Reyes .20 .06
312 Marty Cordova .20 .06
313 Ramiro Mendoza .20 .06
314 Robin Ventura .20 .06
315 Rafael Palmeiro .30 .09
316 Ramon Martinez .20 .06
317 Pedro Astacio .20 .06
318 Dave Hollins .20 .06
319 Tom Candiotti .20 .06
320 Al Leiter .20 .06
321 Rico Brogna .20 .06
322 Reggie Jefferson .20 .06
323 Bernard Gilkey .20 .06
324 Jason Giambi .20 .06
325 Craig Biggio .30 .09
326 Troy Glaus .20 .06
327 Delino DeShields .20 .06
328 Fernando Vina .20 .06
329 John Smoltz .30 .09
330 Jeff Kent .20 .06
331 Roy Halladay .20 .06
332 Andy Ashby .20 .06
333 Tim Wakefield .20 .06
334 Roger Clemens 1.00 .30
335 Bernie Williams .30 .09
336 Desi Relaford .20 .06
337 John Burkett .20 .06
338 Mike Hampton .20 .06
339 Royce Clayton .20 .06
340 Mike Piazza .75 .23
341 Jeremi Gonzalez .20 .06
342 Mike Lansing .20 .06
343 Jamie Moyer .20 .06
344 Ron Coomer .20 .06
345 Barry Larkin .30 .09
346 Fernando Tatis .20 .06
347 Chili Davis .20 .06
348 Bobby Higginson .20 .06
349 Hal Morris .20 .06
350 Larry Walker .30 .09
351 Carlos Guillen .20 .06
352 Miguel Tejada .20 .06
353 Travis Fryman .20 .06
354 Jarrod Washburn .20 .06
355 Chipper Jones .50 .15
356 Todd Stottlemyre .20 .06
357 Henry Rodriguez .20 .06
358 Eli Marrero .20 .06
359 Alan Benes .20 .06
360 Tim Salmon .30 .09
361 Luis Gonzalez .20 .06
362 Scott Spiezio .20 .06
363 Chris Carpenter .20 .06
364 Bobby Howry .20 .06
365 Raul Mondesi .20 .06
366 Ugueth Urbina .20 .06
367 Tom Evans .20 .06
368 Kerry Ligtenberg RC .25 .07
369 Adrian Beltre .20 .06
370 Ryan Klesko .30 .09
371 Wilson Alvarez .20 .06
372 John Thomson .20 .06
373 Tony Saunders .20 .06
374 Dave Mlicki .20 .06
375 Ken Caminiti .20 .06
376 Jay Buhner .20 .06
377 Bill Mueller .20 .06
378 Jeff Blauser .20 .06
379 Edgar Renteria .20 .06
380 Jim Thome .50 .15
381 Joey Hamilton .20 .06
382 Calvin Pickering .20 .06
383 Marquis Grissom .20 .06
384 Omar Daal .20 .06
385 Curt Schilling .20 .06
386 Jose Cruz Jr. .20 .06
387 Chris Widger .20 .06
388 Pete Harnisch .20 .06
389 Charles Nagy .20 .06
390 Tom Gordon .20 .06
391 Bobby Smith .20 .06
392 Derrick Gibson .20 .06
393 Jeff Conine .20 .06
394 Carlos Perez .20 .06
395 Barry Bonds 1.25 .35
396 Mark McLemore .20 .06
397 Juan Encarnacion .20 .06
398 Wade Boggs .30 .09
399 Ivan Rodriguez .50 .15
400 Moises Alou .20 .06
401 Jeromy Burnitz .20 .06
402 Sean Casey .20 .06
403 Jose Offerman .20 .06
404 Joe Fontenot .20 .06
405 Kevin Millwood .20 .06
406 Lance Johnson .20 .06
407 Richard Hidalgo .20 .06
408 Mike Jackson .20 .06
409 Brian Anderson .20 .06
410 Jeff Shaw .20 .06
411 Preston Wilson .20 .06
412 Todd Hundley .20 .06
413 Jim Parque .20 .06
414 Justin Baughman .20 .06
415 Dante Bichette .20 .06
416 Paul O'Neill .30 .09
417 Miguel Cairo .20 .06
418 Randy Johnson .50 .15
419 Jesus Sanchez .20 .06
420 Carlos Delgado .20 .06
421 Ricky Ledee .20 .06
422 Orlando Hernandez .20 .06
423 Frank Thomas .50 .15
424 Pokey Reese .20 .06
425 Carlos Lee .40 .12
Mike Lowell
Kit Pellow RC
426 Michael Cuddyer .25 .07
Mark DeRosa
Jerry Hairston Jr.
427 Marlon Anderson .40 .12
Ron Belliard
Orlando Cabrera
428 Micah Bowie .25 .07
Phil Norton RC
Randy Wolf
429 Jack Cressend RC .25 .07
Jason Rakers
John Rocker
430 Ruben Mateo .25 .07
Scott Morgan
Mike Zywica RC
431 Jason LaRue .25 .07
Matt LeCroy
Mitch Meluskey
432 Gabe Kapler .25 .07
Armando Rios
Fernando Seguignol
433 Adam Kennedy .25 .07
Mickey Lopez RC
Jackie Rexrode
434 Jose Fernandez RC .25 .07
Jeff Liefer
Chris Truby
435 Corey Koskie .75 .23
Doug Mientkiewicz RC
Damon Minor
436 Roosevelt Brown RC .40 .12
Dernell Stenson
Vernon Wells
437 A.J. Burnett RC .75 .23
Billy Koch
John Nicholson
438 Matt Belisle .25 .07
Matt Roney RC
439 Austin Kearns 2.00 .60
Chris George RC
440 Nate Bump RC .40 .12
Nate Cornejo
441 Brad Lidge 1.50 .45
Mike Nannini RC
442 Matt Holliday .75 .23
Jeff Winchester RC
443 Adam Everett .50 .15
Chip Ambres RC
444 Pat Burrell 1.25 .35
Eric Valent RC
445 Roger Clemens SK .50 .15
446 Kerry Wood SK .30 .09
447 Curt Schilling SK .20 .06
448 Randy Johnson SK .30 .09
449 Pedro Martinez SK .30 .09
450 Jeff Bagwell AT .50 .15
Andres Galarraga
Mark McGwire
451 John Olerud AT .20 .06
Jim Thome
Tino Martinez
452 Alex Rodriguez AT .60 .18
Nomar Garciaparra
Derek Jeter
453 Vinny Castilla AT .30 .09
Chipper Jones
Scott Rolen
454 Sammy Sosa AT .50 .15
Ken Griffey Jr.
Juan Gonzalez
455 Barry Bonds AT .50 .15
Manny Ramirez
Larry Walker
456 Frank Thomas AT .50 .15
Tim Salmon
David Justice
457 Travis Lee AT .20 .06
Todd Helton
Ben Grieve
458 Vladimir Guerrero AT .20 .06
Greg Vaughn
Bernie Williams
459 Mike Piazza AT .50 .15
Ivan Rodriguez
Jason Kendall
460 Roger Clemens AT .50 .15
Kerry Wood
Greg Maddux
461A Sammy Sosa HR 1 20.00 6.00
461B Sammy Sosa HR 2 8.00 2.40
461C Sammy Sosa HR 3 8.00 2.40
461D Sammy Sosa HR 4 8.00 2.40
461E Sammy Sosa HR 5 8.00 2.40
461F Sammy Sosa HR 6 8.00 2.40
461G Sammy Sosa HR 7 8.00 8.75
461H Sammy Sosa HR 8 8.00 2.40
461I Sammy Sosa HR 9 8.00 2.40
461J Sammy Sosa HR 10 8.00 2.40
461K Sammy Sosa HR 11 8.00 2.40
461L Sammy Sosa HR 12 8.00 2.40
461M Sammy Sosa HR 13 8.00 2.40
461N Sammy Sosa HR 14 8.00 2.40
461O Sammy Sosa HR 15 8.00 2.40
461P Sammy Sosa HR 16 8.00 2.40
461Q Sammy Sosa HR 17 8.00 2.40
461R Sammy Sosa HR 18 8.00 2.40
461S Sammy Sosa HR 19 8.00 2.40
461T Sammy Sosa HR 20 8.00 2.40
461U Sammy Sosa HR 21 8.00 2.40
461V Sammy Sosa HR 22 8.00 2.40
461W Sammy Sosa HR 23 8.00 2.40
461X Sammy Sosa HR 24 8.00 2.40
461Y Sammy Sosa HR 25 8.00 2.40
461Z Sammy Sosa HR 26 8.00 2.40
461AA S.Sosa HR 27 8.00 2.40
461AB S.Sosa HR 28 8.00 2.40
461AC S.Sosa HR 29 8.00 2.40
461AD S.Sosa HR 30 8.00 2.40
461AE S.Sosa HR 31 8.00 2.40
461AF S.Sosa HR 32 8.00 2.40
461AG S.Sosa HR 33 8.00 2.40
461AH S.Sosa HR 34 8.00 2.40
461AI S.Sosa HR 35 8.00 2.40
461AJ S.Sosa HR 36 8.00 2.40
461AK S.Sosa HR 37 8.00 2.40
461AL S.Sosa HR 38 8.00 2.40
461AM S.Sosa HR 39 8.00 2.40
461AN S.Sosa HR 40 8.00 2.40
461AO S.Sosa HR 41 8.00 2.40
461AP S.Sosa HR 42 8.00 2.40
461AR S.Sosa HR 43 8.00 2.40
461AS S.Sosa HR 44 8.00 2.40
461AT S.Sosa HR 45 8.00 2.40
461AU S.Sosa HR 46 8.00 2.40
461AV S.Sosa HR 47 8.00 2.40
461AW S.Sosa HR 48 8.00 2.40
461AX S.Sosa HR 49 8.00 2.40
461AY S.Sosa HR 50 8.00 2.40
461AZ S.Sosa HR 51 8.00 2.40
461BB S.Sosa HR 52 8.00 2.40
461CC S.Sosa HR 53 8.00 2.40
461DD S.Sosa HR 54 8.00 2.40
461EE S.Sosa HR 55 8.00 2.40
461FF S.Sosa HR 56 8.00 2.40
461GG S.Sosa HR 57 8.00 2.40
461HH S.Sosa HR 58 8.00 2.40
461II S.Sosa HR 59 8.00 2.40
461JJ S.Sosa HR 60 8.00 2.40
461KK S.Sosa HR 61 20.00 6.00
461LL S.Sosa HR 62 25.00 7.50
461MM S.Sosa HR 63 10.00 3.00
461NN S.Sosa HR 64 10.00 3.00
461OO S.Sosa HR 65 10.00 3.00
461PP S.Sosa HR 66 30.00 9.00
462 Checklist .20 .06
463 Checklist .20 .06

1999 Topps MVP Promotion

This is a partial parallel to the regular Topps set. Draft pick and Prospect cards were not included in series one but were included in series two. The front of the card features the same photo as the basic issue card but is adorned with a bold gold foil MVP Promotion logo. The back features contest guidelines for the Topps MVP Promotion. If the featured player was awarded player of the week status (as determined by Topps) his card was then redeemable at season's end for a special set of all the weekly winners. Only 100 of each MVP Promotion card was produced. Stated odds were as follows: series 1 hobby packs 1:515, series 1 Home Team Advantage packs 1:142 and series 2 hobby packs 1:504, Series 2 Home Team Advantage 1:139 and series 2 retail 1:504. The exchange deadline to redeem winning cards was December 31st, 1999. Winning prize cards were mailed out between February 15th, 2000 and April 30th, 2000. The winning cards were the following numbers (which correspond to the regular Topps set): 35, 52, 70, 96, 101, 125, 127, 139, 159, 198, 248, 265, 290, 292, 300, 315, 340, 346, 350, 352, 355, 360, 365, 416, and 418. Since Topps destroyed these Winner exchange cards once they received them, they're in noticeably shorter supply than other cards from this set. Despite this fact, no noticeable premiums in secondary trading levels have been detected for these cards.

Nm-Mt Ex-Mt
*STARS: 20X TO 50X BASIC CARDS
*ROOKIES: 10X TO 25X BASIC CARDS
35 Ray Lankford W 10.00 3.00
52 Todd Helton W 15.00 4.50
70 Mark McGwire W 60.00 18.00
96 Greg Vaughn W 10.00 3.00
101 David Cone W 10.00 3.00
125 Scott Rolen W 25.00 7.50
127 J.T. Snow W 10.00 3.00
139 Fred McGriff W 15.00 4.50
159 Mike Lieberthal W 10.00 3.00
198 B.J. Surhoff W 10.00 3.00
248 Roberto Alomar W 15.00 4.50
265 Nomar Garciaparra W 40.00 12.00
290 Tino Martinez W 15.00 4.50
292 Tony Clark W 10.00 3.00
300 Alex Rodriguez W 40.00 12.00
315 Rafael Palmeiro W 15.00 4.50
340 Mike Piazza W 40.00 12.00
346 Fernando Tatis W 10.00 3.00
350 Larry Walker W 15.00 4.50
352 Miguel Tejada W 10.00 3.00
355 Chipper Jones W 25.00 7.50
360 Tim Salmon W 15.00 4.50
365 Raul Mondesi W 10.00 3.00
416 Paul O'Neill W 15.00 4.50
418 Randy Johnson W 25.00 7.50

1999 Topps MVP Promotion Exchange

This 25-card set was available only to those lucky collectors who obtained one of the twenty-five winning player cards from the 1999 Topps MVP Promotion parallel set. Each week, throughout the 1999 season, Topps named a new Player of the Week, and that player's Topps MVP Promotion parallel card was made redeemable for this 25-card set. The deadline to exchange the winning cards was December 31st, 1999. The exchange cards shipped out in mid-February, 2000.

Nm-Mt Ex-Mt
COMP.FACT.SET (25) 50.00 15.00
MVP1 Raul Mondesi 1.50 .45
MVP2 Tim Salmon 2.50 .75
MVP3 Fernando Tatis 1.50 .45
MVP4 Larry Walker 2.50 .75
MVP5 Fred McGriff 2.50 .75
MVP6 Nomar Garciaparra 6.00 1.80
MVP7 Rafael Palmeiro 2.50 .75
MVP8 Randy Johnson 4.00 1.20
MVP9 Mike Lieberthal 1.50 .45
MVP10 B.J. Surhoff 1.50 .45
MVP11 Todd Helton 2.50 .75
MVP12 Tino Martinez 2.50 .75
MVP13 Scott Rolen 4.00 1.20
MVP14 Mike Piazza 6.00 1.80
MVP15 David Cone 1.50 .45
MVP16 Tony Clark 1.50 .45
MVP17 Roberto Alomar 2.50 .75
MVP18 Miguel Tejada 1.50 .45
MVP19 Alex Rodriguez 6.00 1.80
MVP20 J.T. Snow 1.50 .45
MVP21 Ray Lankford 1.50 .45
MVP22 Greg Vaughn 1.50 .45
MVP23 Paul O'Neill 2.50 .75
MVP24 Chipper Jones 4.00 1.20
MVP25 Mark McGwire 10.00 3.00

1999 Topps Oversize

Inserted one per Home Team Advantage and one per Hobby box, these cards feature sixteen of the leading players in an oversize version. The photos are the same as the regular Topps cards. We have numbered the cards with A and B prefixes to denote series one versus series two distribution, although Topps decided to number each series 1 through 8.

Nm-Mt Ex-Mt
COMPLETE SERIES 1 (8) 15.00 4.50
COMPLETE SERIES 2 (8) 15.00 4.50

1999 Topps All-Matrix

This 30-card insert set consists of three thematic subsets (Club 40 are numbers 1-13, '99 Rookie Rush are number's 14-23 and Club K are numbers 24-30). All 30-cards feature silver foil dot-matrix technology. Cards were seeded exclusively into series 2 packs as follows: 1:18 hobby, 1:18 retail and 1:5 Home Team Advantage.

Nm-Mt Ex-Mt
COMPLETE SET (30) 80.00 24.00
AM1 Mark McGwire 10.00 3.00
AM2 Sammy Sosa 6.00 1.80
AM3 Ken Griffey Jr. 6.00 1.80
AM4 Greg Vaughn 1.50 .45
AM5 Albert Belle 1.50 .45
AM6 Vinny Castilla 1.50 .45
AM7 Jose Canseco 4.00 1.20
AM8 Juan Gonzalez 2.50 .75
AM9 Manny Ramirez 2.50 .75
AM10 Andres Galarraga 1.50 .45
AM11 Rafael Palmeiro 2.50 .75
AM12 Alex Rodriguez 6.00 1.80
AM13 Mo Vaughn 1.50 .45
AM14 Eric Chavez 1.50 .45
AM15 Gabe Kapler 3.00 .90
AM16 Calvin Pickering 1.50 .45
AM17 Ruben Mateo 2.00 .60
AM18 Roy Halladay 1.50 .45
AM19 Jeremy Giambi 1.50 .45
AM20 Alex Gonzalez 1.50 .45
AM21 Ron Belliard 3.00 .90
AM22 Marlon Anderson 3.00 .90
AM23 Carlos Lee 3.00 .90
AM24 Kerry Wood 4.00 1.20
AM25 Roger Clemens 8.00 2.40
AM26 Curt Schilling 1.50 .45
AM27 Kevin Brown 2.50 .75
AM28 Randy Johnson 4.00 1.20
AM29 Pedro Martinez 4.00 1.20
AM30 Orlando Hernandez 1.50 .45

1999 Topps All-Topps Mystery Finest

Randomly inserted in Topps Series two packs at the the rate of one in 36, this 33-card set features 11 three-player positional parallels of the All-Topps subset printed using Finest technology. All three players are printed on the back, but the collector has to peel off the opaque protector to reveal who is on the front.

	Nm-Mt	Ex-Mt
COMPLETE SET (33)	250.00	75.00

*REFRACTORS: 1X TO 2.5X BASIC ATMF
SER.2 REF.ODDS 1:144 HOB/RET, 1:32 HTA

	Nm-Mt	Ex-Mt
M1 Jeff Bagwell	5.00	1.50
M2 Andres Galarraga	3.00	.90
M3 Mark McGwire	20.00	6.00
M4 John Olerud	3.00	.90
M5 Jim Thome	8.00	2.40
M6 Tino Martinez	5.00	1.50
M7 Alex Rodriguez	12.00	3.60
M8 Nomar Garciaparra	12.00	3.60
M9 Derek Jeter	20.00	6.00
M10 Vinny Castilla	3.00	.90
M11 Chipper Jones	8.00	2.40
M12 Scott Rolen	8.00	2.40
M13 Sammy Sosa	12.00	3.60
M14 Ken Griffey Jr.	12.00	3.60
M15 Juan Gonzalez	5.00	1.50
M16 Barry Bonds	20.00	6.00
M17 Manny Ramirez	5.00	1.50
M18 Larry Walker	5.00	1.50
M19 Frank Thomas	8.00	2.40
M20 Tim Salmon	5.00	1.50
M21 Dave Justice	3.00	.90
M22 Travis Lee	3.00	.90
M23 Todd Helton	5.00	1.50
M24 Ben Grieve	3.00	.90
M25 Vladimir Guerrero	8.00	2.40
M26 Greg Vaughn	3.00	.90
M27 Bernie Williams	5.00	1.50
M28 Mike Piazza	12.00	3.60
M29 Ivan Rodriguez	8.00	2.40
M30 Jason Kendall	3.00	.90
M31 Roger Clemens	15.00	4.50
M32 Kerry Wood	8.00	2.40
M33 Greg Maddux	12.00	3.60

1999 Topps Autographs

Inserted one in every 532 first series hobby packs, one in every 146 first series Home Team Advantage packs,d one in every 501 second series hobby packs and one in every 138 second seriesHome Team Advantage packs, these cards feature an assortment of young and old players affixing their signature to these cards. Cards A1-A8 were distributed exclusively in first series packs and cards A9-A16 were distributed exclusively in second series packs. The fronts feature a player photo with the authentic autograph on the bottom.

	Nm-Mt	Ex-Mt
A1 Roger Clemens	100.00	30.00
A2 Chipper Jones	50.00	15.00
A3 Scott Rolen	40.00	12.00
A4 Alex Rodriguez	80.00	24.00
A5 Andres Galarraga	15.00	4.50
A6 Rondell White	15.00	4.50
A7 Ben Grieve	10.00	3.00
A8 Troy Glaus	15.00	4.50
A9 Moises Alou	15.00	4.50
A10 Barry Bonds	250.00	75.00
A11 Vladimir Guerrero	40.00	12.00
A12 Andruw Jones	15.00	4.50
A13 Darin Erstad	15.00	4.50
A14 Shawn Green	15.00	4.50
A15 Eric Chavez	15.00	4.50
A16 Pat Burrell	20.00	6.00

1999 Topps Hall of Fame Collection

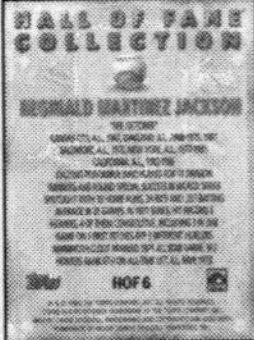

This 10 card set features Hall of Famers with photos of the plaques and a silhoutted photo. These cards were inserted one every 12 hobby packs and one every three HTA packs.

	Nm-Mt	Ex-Mt
COMPLETE SET (10)	20.00	6.00
HOF1 Mike Schmidt	4.00	1.20
HOF2 Brooks Robinson	2.00	.60
HOF3 Stan Musial	3.00	.90
HOF4 Willie McCovey	2.00	.60
HOF5 Eddie Mathews	2.00	.60
HOF6 Reggie Jackson	2.00	.60
HOF7 Ernie Banks	2.00	.60
HOF8 Whitey Ford	2.00	.60
HOF9 Bob Feller	2.00	.60
HOF10 Yogi Berra	2.00	.60

1999 Topps Lords of the Diamond

This die-cut insert set was inserted one every 18 hobby packs and one every five HTA packs. The words "Lords of the Diamond" are printed on the top while the players name is at the bottom. The middle of the card has the players photo.

	Nm-Mt	Ex-Mt
COMPLETE SET (15)	50.00	15.00
LD1 Ken Griffey Jr.	4.00	1.20
LD2 Chipper Jones	2.50	.75
LD3 Sammy Sosa	4.00	1.20
LD4 Frank Thomas	2.50	.75
LD5 Mark McGwire	6.00	1.80
LD6 Jeff Bagwell	1.50	.45
LD7 Alex Rodriguez	4.00	1.20
LD8 Juan Gonzalez	1.50	.45
LD9 Barry Bonds	6.00	1.80
LD10 Nomar Garciaparra	4.00	1.20
LD11 Darin Erstad	1.00	.30
LD12 Tony Gwynn	3.00	.90
LD13 Andres Galarraga	1.00	.30
LD14 Mike Piazza	4.00	1.20
LD15 Greg Maddux	4.00	1.20

1999 Topps New Breed

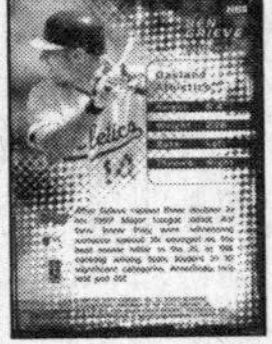

Fifteen of the young stars of the game are featured in this insert set. The cards were seeded into the 99 Topps packs at a rate of one every 18 hobby packs and one every five HTA packs.

	Nm-Mt	Ex-Mt
COMPLETE SET (15)	25.00	7.50
NB1 Darin Erstad	.75	.23
NB2 Brad Fullmer	.75	.23
NB3 Kerry Wood	2.00	.60
NB4 Nomar Garciaparra	3.00	.90
NB5 Travis Lee	.75	.23
NB6 Scott Rolen	2.00	.60
NB7 Todd Helton	1.25	.35
NB8 Vladimir Guerrero	2.00	.60
NB9 Derek Jeter	5.00	1.50
NB10 Alex Rodriguez	3.00	.90
NB11 Ben Grieve	.75	.23
NB12 Andruw Jones	.75	.23
NB13 Paul Konerko	.75	.23
NB14 Aramis Ramirez	.75	.23
NB15 Adrian Beltre	1.25	.35

1999 Topps Picture Perfect

This 10 card insert set was inserted one every eight hobby packs and one every two HTA packs. These cards all contain a minor, very difficult to determine mistake and part of the charm is to figure out what the error is in the card.

	Nm-Mt	Ex-Mt
COMPLETE SET (10)	15.00	4.50
P1 Ken Griffey Jr.	1.50	.45
P2 Kerry Wood	1.00	.30
P3 Pedro Martinez	1.00	.30
P4 Mark McGwire	2.50	.75
P5 Greg Maddux	1.50	.45
P6 Sammy Sosa	1.50	.45
P7 Greg Vaughn	.40	.12
P8 Juan Gonzalez	.60	.18
P9 Jeff Bagwell	.60	.18
P10 Derek Jeter	2.50	.75

1999 Topps Power Brokers

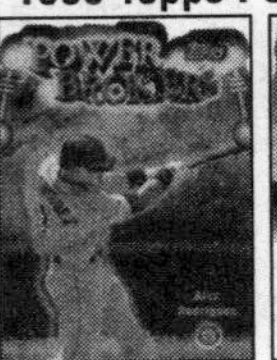

This 20 card set features leading baseball players. They were inserted at a seeded rate of one every 36 hobby/retail packs and one every eight HTA packs.

	Nm-Mt	Ex-Mt
COMPLETE SET (20)	120.00	36.00

*REFRACTORS: 1X TO 2.5X BASIC BROKERS
SER.1 REF.ODDS 1:144 HOB/RET, 1:32 HTA

	Nm-Mt	Ex-Mt
PB1 Mark McGwire	12.00	3.60
PB2 Andres Galarraga	2.00	.60
PB3 Ken Griffey Jr.	8.00	2.40
PB4 Sammy Sosa	8.00	2.40
PB5 Juan Gonzalez	3.00	.90
PB6 Alex Rodriguez	8.00	2.40
PB7 Frank Thomas	5.00	1.50
PB8 Jeff Bagwell	3.00	.90
PB9 Vinny Castilla	2.00	.60
PB10 Mike Piazza	8.00	2.40
PB11 Greg Vaughn	2.00	.60
PB12 Barry Bonds	12.00	3.60
PB13 Mo Vaughn	2.00	.60
PB14 Jim Thome	5.00	1.50
PB15 Larry Walker	3.00	.90
PB16 Chipper Jones	5.00	1.50
PB17 Nomar Garciaparra	8.00	2.40
PB18 Manny Ramirez	3.00	.90
PB19 Roger Clemens	10.00	3.00
PB20 Kerry Wood	5.00	1.50

1999 Topps Record Numbers

Randomly inserted in Series two hobby and retail packs at the rate of one in eight and HTA packs at a rate of one in two, this 10-card set features action color photos of record-setting players with silver foil highlights.

	Nm-Mt	Ex-Mt
COMPLETE SET (10)	15.00	4.50
RN1 Mark McGwire	2.50	.75
RN2 Mike Piazza	1.50	.45
RN3 Curt Schilling	.40	.12
RN4 Ken Griffey Jr.	1.50	.45
RN5 Sammy Sosa	1.50	.45
RN6 Nomar Garciaparra	1.50	.45
RN7 Kerry Wood	1.00	.30
RN8 Roger Clemens	2.00	.60
RN9 Cal Ripken	3.00	.90
RN10 Mark McGwire	2.50	.75

1999 Topps Record Numbers Gold

Randomly seeded in series two packs, these scarce gold-foiled cards parallel the more common "silver-foiled" Record Numbers inserts. The print run for each card was based upon the statistic specified on the card. Erroneous stated odds for these Gold cards were unfortunately printed on all series two wrappers. According to sources at Topps the correct pack odds are as follows: RN1 1:151,320 hob, 1:38,016 HTA, 1:138,567 ret, RN2 1:28,317 hob, 1:7,797 HTA, 1:28,340 ret, RN3 1:32,134 hob, 1:8,848 HTA, 1:32,160 ret, RN4 1:29,288 hob, 1:8,064 HTA, 1:29,312 ret, RN5 1:907,920 hob, 1:133,056 HTA, 1:1,524,420 ret, RN6 1:605,280 hob, 1:88,704 HTA, 1:1,016,280 ret, RN7 1:907,920 hob, 1:133,056 HTA, 1:1,524,420 ret, RN8 1:907,920 hob, 1:133,056 HTA, 1:1,524,420 ret, RN9 1:3891 hob, 1:1069 HTA, 1:3888 ret, RN10 1:63,312 hob, 1:17,741 HTA, 1:63,510 ret.

	Nm-Mt	Ex-Mt
RN1 Mark McGwire/70	100.00	30.00
RN2 Mike Piazza/362	15.00	4.50
RN3 Curt Schilling/319	8.00	2.40
RN4 Ken Griffey Jr./350	20.00	6.00
RN5 Sammy Sosa/20		
RN6 N.Garciaparra/30	120.00	36.00
RN7 Kerry Wood/20		
RN8 Roger Clemens/20		
RN9 Cal Ripken/2632	15.00	4.50
RN10 Mark McGwire/162	40.00	12.00

1999 Topps Ryan

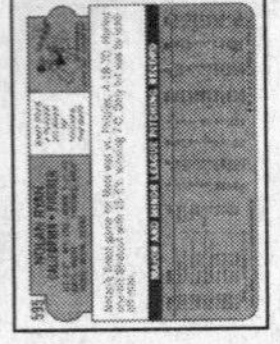

These cards reflect the Nolan Ryan Reprints of earlier Topps cards featuring the pitcher known for "Texas Heat". These cards are replicas of Ryan's cards and have a commemorative sticker placed on them as well. The cards were seeded one every 18 hobby/retail packs and one every five HTA packs. Odd-numbered cards (i.e. 1, 3, 5 etc.) were distributed in first series packs and even numbered cards were distributed in second series packs.

	Nm-Mt	Ex-Mt
COMPLETE SET (27)	80.00	24.00
COMPLETE SERIES 1 (14)	40.00	12.00
COMPLETE SERIES 2 (13)	40.00	12.00
COMMON CARD (1-27)	5.00	1.50
1 Nolan Ryan 1968	10.00	3.00

1999 Topps Ryan Autographs

Nolan Ryan signed a selection of all 27 cards for this reprint set. The autographed cards were issued one every 4,250 series one hobby packs, one in every 5,007 series two hobby packs and one every 1,176 series one HTA packs.

	Nm-Mt	Ex-Mt
COMMON CARD (1-13)	200.00	60.00
COMMON CARD (14-27)	200.00	60.00
1 Nolan Ryan 1968	350.00	105.00

1999 Topps Traded

This set contains 121 cards and was distributed as factory boxed sets only. The fronts feature color action player photo. The backs carry player information. Rookie Cards include Sean Burroughs, Josh Hamilton, Corey Patterson and Alfonso Soriano.

	Nm-Mt	Ex-Mt
COMP.FACT.SET (122)	40.00	12.00
COMPLETE SET (121)	25.00	7.50
T1 Seth Etherton	.20	.06
T2 Mark Harriger RC	.25	.07
T3 Matt Wise RC	.25	.07
T4 Carlos E. Hernandez RC	.25	.07
T5 Julio Lugo RC	.25	.07
T6 Mike Nannini	.20	.06
T7 Justin Bowles RC	.25	.07
T8 Mark Mulder RC	1.50	.35
T9 Roberto Vaz RC	.25	.07
T10 Felipe Lopez RC	.25	.07
T11 Matt Belisle	.20	.06
T12 Micah Bowie	.20	.06
T13 Ruben Quevedo RC	.25	.07
T14 Jose Garcia RC	.25	.07
T15 David Kelton RC	.25	.07
T16 Phil Norton	.20	.06
T17 Corey Patterson RC	1.50	.45
T18 Ron Walker RC	.25	.07
T19 Paul Hoover RC	.25	.07
T20 Ryan Rupe RC	.25	.07
T21 J.D. Closser RC	.40	.12
T22 Rob Ryan RC	.25	.07
T23 Steve Colyer RC	.25	.07
T24 Bubba Crosby RC	.40	.12
T25 Luke Prokopec RC	.25	.07
T26 Matt Blank RC	.25	.07
T27 Josh McKinley	.20	.06
T28 Nate Bump	.20	.06
T29 G.Chiaramonte RC	.25	.07
T30 Arturo McDowell	.20	.06
T31 Tony Torcato	.20	.06
T32 Dave Roberts RC	.40	.12
T33 C.C. Sabathia RC	.75	.23
T34 Sean Spencer RC	.25	.07
T35 Chip Ambres	.20	.06
T36 A.J. Burnett	.60	.18
T37 Mo Bruce RC	.25	.07
T38 Jason Tyner	.20	.06
T39 Mamon Tucker	.20	.06
T40 Sean Burroughs RC	1.00	.30
T41 Kevin Eberwein RC	.25	.07
T42 Junior Herndon RC	.25	.07
T43 Bryan Wolff RC	.25	.07
T44 Pat Burrell	1.00	.30
T45 Eric Valent	.20	.06
T46 Carlos Pena RC	.40	.12
T47 Mike Zywica	.20	.06
T48 Adam Everett	.30	.09
T49 Juan Pena RC	.25	.07
T50 Adam Dunn RC	3.00	.90
T51 Austin Kearns	1.50	.45
T52 Jacobo Sequea RC	.25	.07
T53 Choo Freeman	.20	.06
T54 Jeff Winchester	.20	.06
T55 Matt Burch	.20	.06
T56 Chris George	.20	.06
T57 Scott Mullen RC	.25	.07
T58 Kit Pellow	.20	.06
T59 Mark Quinn RC	.25	.07
T60 Nate Cornejo	.25	.07
T61 Ryan Mills	.20	.06
T62 Kevin Beirne RC	.25	.07
T63 Kip Wells RC	.40	.12
T64 Juan Rivera RC	.25	.07
T65 Alfonso Soriano RC	4.00	1.20
T66 Josh Hamilton RC	.40	.12
T67 Josh Girdley RC	.25	.07
T68 Kyle Snyder RC	.25	.07
T69 Mike Paradis RC	.25	.07
T70 Jason Jennings RC	.40	.12
T71 David Walling RC	.25	.07
T72 Omar Ortiz RC	.25	.07
T73 Jay Gehrke RC	.25	.07
T74 Casey Burns RC	.25	.07
T75 Carl Crawford RC	1.25	.35
T76 Reggie Sanders	.20	.06
T77 Will Clark	.50	.15
T78 David Wells	.20	.06
T79 Paul Konerko	.20	.06
T80 Armando Benitez	.20	.06
T81 Brant Brown	.20	.06
T82 Mo Vaughn	.20	.06
T83 Jose Canseco	.50	.15
T84 Albert Belle	.20	.06
T85 Dean Palmer	.20	.06
T86 Greg Vaughn	.20	.06
T87 Mark Clark	.20	.06
T88 Pat Meares	.20	.06
T89 Eric Davis	.20	.06
T90 Brian Giles	.20	.06
T91 Jeff Brantley	.20	.06
T92 Bret Boone	.20	.06
T93 Ron Gant	.20	.06
T94 Mike Cameron	.20	.06
T95 Charles Johnson	.20	.06
T96 Denny Neagle	.20	.06
T97 Brian Hunter	.20	.06
T98 Jose Hernandez	.20	.06
T99 Rick Aguilera	.20	.06
T100 Tony Batista	.20	.06
T101 Roger Cedeno	.20	.06
T102 C.Gubanich RC	.25	.07
T103 Tim Belcher	.20	.06
T104 Bruce Aven	.20	.06
T105 Brian Daubach RC	.25	.07
T106 Ed Sprague	.20	.06
T107 Michael Tucker	.20	.06
T108 Homer Bush	.20	.06
T109 Armando Reynoso	.20	.06
T110 Brook Fordyce	.20	.06
T111 Matt Mantei	.20	.06
T112 Dave Mlicki	.20	.06
T113 Kenny Rogers	.20	.06
T114 Livan Hernandez	.20	.06
T115 Butch Huskey	.20	.06
T116 David Segui	.20	.06
T117 Darryl Hamilton	.20	.06
T118 Terry Mulholland	.20	.06
T119 Randy Velarde	.20	.06
T120 Bill Taylor	.20	.06
T121 Kevin Appier	.20	.06

1999 Topps Traded Autographs

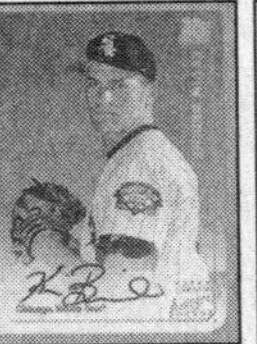

Inserted one per factory box set, this 75-card set features autographed parallel version of the first 75 cards of the basic 1999 Topps Traded set. The card fronts have a light faded image on the base to accentuate the signature.

	Nm-Mt	Ex-Mt
COMPLETE SET (75)	700.00	210.00
T1 Seth Etherton	5.00	1.50
T2 Mark Harriger	10.00	3.00
T3 Matt Wise	10.00	3.00
T4 Carlos E. Hernandez	10.00	3.00
T5 Julio Lugo	10.00	3.00
T6 Mike Nannini	5.00	1.50
T7 Justin Bowles	10.00	3.00
T8 Mark Mulder	50.00	15.00
T9 Roberto Vaz	10.00	3.00
T10 Felipe Lopez	10.00	3.00
T11 Matt Belisle	5.00	1.50
T12 Micah Bowie	5.00	1.50
T13 Ruben Quevedo	5.00	1.50
T14 Jose Garcia	10.00	3.00
T15 David Kelton	10.00	3.00
T16 Phil Norton	10.00	3.00
T17 Corey Patterson	50.00	15.00
T18 Ron Walker	5.00	1.50
T19 Paul Hoover	10.00	3.00
T20 Ryan Rupe	5.00	1.50
T21 J.D. Closser	15.00	4.50
T22 Rob Ryan	5.00	1.50
T23 Steve Colyer	10.00	3.00
T24 Bubba Crosby	15.00	4.50
T25 Luke Prokopec	5.00	1.50
T26 Matt Blank	10.00	3.00
T27 Josh McKinley	10.00	3.00
T28 Nate Bump	10.00	3.00
T29 G.Chiaramonte	5.00	1.50
T30 Arturo McDowell	5.00	1.50
T31 Tony Torcato	10.00	3.00
T32 Dave Roberts	15.00	4.50
T33 C.C. Sabathia	40.00	12.00
T34 Sean Spencer	5.00	1.50
T35 Chip Ambres	5.00	1.50
T36 A.J. Burnett	25.00	7.50
T37 Mo Bruce	5.00	1.50
T38 Jason Tyner	5.00	1.50
T39 Mamon Tucker	5.00	1.50
T40 Sean Burroughs	30.00	9.00
T41 Kevin Eberwein	5.00	1.50
T42 Junior Herndon	10.00	3.00
T43 Bryan Wolff	10.00	3.00
T44 Pat Burrell	40.00	12.00
T45 Eric Valent	10.00	3.00
T46 Carlos Pena	15.00	4.50
T47 Mike Zywica	10.00	3.00
T48 Adam Everett	25.00	7.50
T49 Juan Pena	10.00	3.00
T50 Adam Dunn	100.00	30.00
T51 Austin Kearns	50.00	15.00
T52 Jacobo Sequea	5.00	1.50
T53 Choo Freeman	10.00	3.00
T54 Jeff Winchester	5.00	1.50
T55 Matt Burch	10.00	3.00
T56 Chris George	10.00	3.00
T57 Scott Mullen	5.00	1.50
T58 Kit Pellow	5.00	1.50
T59 Mark Quinn	10.00	3.00
T60 Nate Cornejo	10.00	3.00
T61 Ryan Mills	5.00	1.50
T62 Kevin Beirne	10.00	3.00
T63 Kip Wells	15.00	4.50
T64 Juan Rivera	10.00	3.00
T65 Alfonso Soriano	120.00	36.00
T66 Josh Hamilton	25.00	7.50
T67 Josh Girdley	5.00	1.50
T68 Kyle Snyder	5.00	1.50
T69 Mike Paradis	5.00	1.50
T70 Jason Jennings	15.00	4.50
T71 David Walling	5.00	1.50
T72 Omar Ortiz	10.00	3.00
T73 Jay Gehrke	10.00	3.00
T74 Casey Burns	10.00	3.00
T75 Carl Crawford	40.00	12.00

2000 Topps

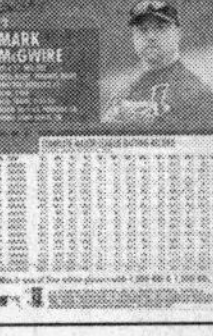

This 478 card set was issued in two separate series. The first series (containing cards 1-239) was released in December, 1999. The second series (containing cards 240-479) was released in April, 2000. The cards were issued in various formats including an eleven card hobby or retail pack with an SRP of $1.29 and a 40 card HomeTeam Advantage jumbo pack. Cards 1-200 and 240-440 are individual player cards with subsets as follows: Prospects (201-208/441-448), Draft Picks (209-220/449-455), Season Highlights (217-221/456-460), Post Season Highlights (222-228), 20th Century's Best (229-235/468-474), Magic Moments (236-240/475-479) and League Leaders (461-467). After the success Topps had with the multiple versions of Mark McGwire 220 and Sammy Sosa 461 in 1999, they made five versions each of the Magic Moments cards this year. Each Magic Moment variation featured different gold foil text on front commemorating a specific achievement in the featured player's career. Please note, that basic hand-collected sets are considered complete with the inclusion of any one of each of these Magic Moment cards. A reprint of the 1985 Mark McGwire Rookie Card was inserted one every 36 hobby and retail first series packs and one every eight HTA first series packs. Card number 7 was not issued as Topps continues to honor the memory of Mickey Mantle who wore that number during his career. Players with notable Rookie Cards in this set include Ben Sheets and Barry Zito.

	Nm-Mt	Ex-Mt
COMPLETE SET (478)	50.00	15.00
COMP.HOBBY SET (478)	50.00	15.00
COMP. SERIES 1 (239)	25.00	7.50
COMP. SERIES 2 (240)	25.00	7.50
MCGWIRE MM SET (5)	12.00	3.60
AARON MM SET (5)	10.00	3.00
RIPKEN MM SET (5)	15.00	4.50
BOGGS MM SET (5)	3.00	.90
GWYNN MM SET (5)	6.00	1.80
GRIFFEY MM SET (5)	8.00	2.40
BONDS MM SET (5)	12.00	3.60
SOSA MM SET (5)	8.00	2.40
JETER MM SET (5)	12.00	3.60
A.ROD MM SET (5)	8.00	2.40
1 Mark McGwire	1.25	.35
2 Tony Gwynn	.60	.18
3 Wade Boggs	.30	.09
4 Cal Ripken	1.50	.45
5 Matt Williams	.20	.06
6 Jay Buhner	.20	.06
8 Jeff Conine	.20	.06
9 Todd Greene	.20	.06
10 Mike Lieberthal	.20	.06
11 Steve Avery	.20	.06
12 Bret Saberhagen	.20	.06
13 Magglio Ordonez	.20	.06
14 Brad Radke	.20	.06
15 Derek Jeter	1.25	.35
16 Javy Lopez	.20	.06
17 Russ Davis	.20	.06
18 Armando Benitez	.20	.06
19 B.J. Surhoff	.20	.06
20 Darryl Kile	.20	.06
21 Mark Lewis	.20	.06
22 Mike Williams	.20	.06
23 Mark McLemore	.20	.06
24 Sterling Hitchcock	.20	.06
25 Darin Erstad	.20	.06
26 Ricky Gutierrez	.20	.06
27 John Jaha	.20	.06
28 Homer Bush	.20	.06
29 Darrin Fletcher	.20	.06
30 Mark Grace	.30	.09
31 Fred McGriff	.30	.09
32 Omar Daal	.20	.06
33 Eric Karros	.20	.06
34 Orlando Cabrera	.20	.06
35 J.T. Snow	.20	.06
36 Luis Castillo	.20	.06
37 Rey Ordonez	.20	.06
38 Bob Abreu	.20	.06
39 Warren Morris	.20	.06
40 Juan Gonzalez	.30	.09
41 Mike Lansing	.20	.06
42 Chili Davis	.20	.06
43 Dean Palmer	.20	.06
44 Hank Aaron	.75	.23
45 Jeff Bagwell	.30	.09
46 Jose Valentin	.20	.06
47 Shannon Stewart	.20	.06
48 Kent Bottenfield	.20	.06
49 Jeff Shaw	.20	.06
50 Sammy Sosa	.75	.23
51 Randy Johnson	.50	.15
52 Benny Agbayani	.20	.06
53 Dante Bichette	.20	.06
54 Pete Harnisch	.20	.06
55 Frank Thomas	.50	.15
56 Jorge Posada	.30	.09
57 Todd Walker	.20	.06
58 Juan Encarnacion	.20	.06
59 Mike Sweeney	.20	.06
60 Pedro Martinez	.50	.15
61 Lee Stevens	.20	.06
62 Brian Giles	.20	.06
63 Chad Ogea	.20	.06
64 Ivan Rodriguez	.50	.15
65 Roger Cedeno	.20	.06
66 David Justice	.20	.06
67 Steve Trachsel	.20	.06
68 Eli Marrero	.20	.06
69 Dave Nilsson	.20	.06
70 Ken Caminiti	.20	.06
71 Tim Raines	.20	.06
72 Brian Jordan	.20	.06
73 Jeff Blauser	.20	.06
74 Bernard Gilkey	.20	.06
75 John Flaherty	.20	.06
76 Brent Mayne	.20	.06
77 Jose Vidro	.20	.06
78 David Bell	.20	.06
79 Bruce Aven	.20	.06
80 John Olerud	.20	.06
81 Pokey Reese	.20	.06
82 Woody Williams	.20	.06
83 Ed Sprague	.20	.06
84 Joe Girardi	.20	.06
85 Barry Larkin	.30	.09
86 Mike Caruso	.20	.06
87 Bobby Higginson	.20	.06
88 Roberto Kelly	.20	.06
89 Edgar Martinez	.30	.09
90 Mark Kotsay	.20	.06
91 Paul Sorrento	.20	.06
92 Eric Young	.20	.06
93 Carlos Delgado	.20	.06
94 Troy Glaus	.20	.06
95 Ben Grieve	.20	.06
96 Jose Lima	.20	.06
97 Garret Anderson	.20	.06
98 Luis Gonzalez	.20	.06
99 Carl Pavano	.20	.06
100 Alex Rodriguez	.75	.23
101 Preston Wilson	.20	.06
102 Ron Gant	.20	.06
103 Brady Anderson	.20	.06
104 Rickey Henderson	.50	.15
105 Gary Sheffield	.20	.06
106 Mickey Morandini	.20	.06
107 Jim Edmonds	.20	.06
108 Kris Benson	.20	.06
109 Adrian Beltre	.30	.09
110 Alex Fernandez	.20	.06
111 Dan Wilson	.20	.06
112 Mark Clark	.20	.06
113 Greg Vaughn	.20	.06
114 Neifi Perez	.20	.06
115 Paul O'Neill	.30	.09
116 Jermaine Dye	.20	.06
117 Todd Jones	.20	.06
118 Terry Steinbach	.20	.06
119 Greg Norton	.20	.06
120 Curt Schilling	.20	.06
121 Todd Zeile	.20	.06
122 Edgardo Alfonzo	.20	.06
123 Ryan McGuire	.20	.06
124 Rich Aurilia	.20	.06
125 John Smoltz	.30	.09
126 Bob Wickman	.20	.06
127 Richard Hidalgo	.20	.06
128 Chuck Finley	.20	.06
129 Billy Wagner	.20	.06
130 Todd Hundley	.20	.06
131 Dwight Gooden	.20	.06
132 Russ Ortiz	.20	.06
133 Mike Lowell	.20	.06
134 Reggie Sanders	.20	.06
135 John Valentin	.20	.06
136 Brad Ausmus	.20	.06
137 Chad Kreuter	.20	.06
138 David Cone	.20	.06
139 Brook Fordyce	.20	.06
140 Roberto Alomar	.30	.09
141 Charles Nagy	.20	.06
142 Brian Hunter	.20	.06
143 Mike Mussina	.30	.09
144 Robin Ventura	.30	.09
145 Kevin Brown	.30	.09
146 Pat Hentgen	.20	.06
147 Ryan Klesko	.20	.06
148 Derek Bell	.20	.06
149 Andy Sheets	.20	.06
150 Larry Walker	.30	.09
151 Scott Williamson	.20	.06
152 Jose Offerman	.20	.06
153 Doug Mientkiewicz	.20	.06
154 John Snyder RC	.40	.12
155 Sandy Alomar Jr.	.20	.06
156 Joe Nathan	.20	.06
157 Lance Johnson	.20	.06
158 Odalis Perez	.20	.06
159 Hideo Nomo	.50	.15
160 Steve Finley	.20	.06
161 Dave Martinez	.20	.06
162 Matt Walbeck	.20	.06
163 Bill Spiers	.20	.06
164 Fernando Tatis	.20	.06
165 Kenny Lofton	.20	.06
166 Paul Byrd	.20	.06
167 Aaron Sele	.20	.06
168 Eddie Taubensee	.20	.06
169 Reggie Jefferson	.20	.06
170 Roger Clemens	1.00	.30
171 Francisco Cordova	.20	.06
172 Mike Bordick	.20	.06
173 Wally Joyner	.20	.06
174 Marvin Benard	.20	.06
175 Jason Kendall	.20	.06
176 Mike Stanley	.20	.06
177 Chad Allen	.20	.06
178 Carlos Beltran	.30	.09
179 Deivi Cruz	.20	.06
180 Chipper Jones	.50	.15
181 Vladimir Guerrero	.50	.15
182 Dave Burba	.20	.06
183 Tom Goodwin	.20	.06
184 Brian Daubach	.20	.06
185 Jay Bell	.20	.06
186 Roy Halladay	.20	.06
187 Miguel Tejada	.20	.06
188 Armando Rios	.20	.06
189 Fernando Vina	.20	.06
190 Eric Davis	.20	.06
191 Henry Rodriguez	.20	.06
192 Joe McEwing	.20	.06
193 Jeff Kent	.20	.06
194 Mike Jackson	.20	.06
195 Mike Morgan	.20	.06
196 Jeff Montgomery	.20	.06
197 Jeff Zimmerman	.20	.06
198 Tony Fernandez	.20	.06
199 Jason Giambi	.20	.06
200 Jose Canseco	.50	.15
201 Alex Gonzalez	.20	.06
202 Jack Cust	.40	.12
Mike Colangelo		
Dee Brown		
203 Felipe Lopez	.50	.15
Alfonso Soriano		
Pablo Ozuna		
204 Erubiel Durazo	.40	.12
Pat Burrell		
Nick Johnson		
205 John Sneed RC	.40	.12
Kip Wells		
Matt Blank		
206 Josh Kalinowski	.40	.12
Michael Tejera		
Chris Mears RC		
207 Roosevelt Brown	.40	.12
Corey Patterson		
Lance Berkman		
208 Kit Pellow	.40	.12
Kevin Barker		
Russ Branyan		
209 B.J. Garbe	.75	.23
Larry Bigbie RC		
210 Eric Munson	.40	.12
Bobby Bradley RC		
211 Josh Girdley	.40	.12
Kyle Snyder		
212 Chance Caple RC	.40	.12
Jason Jennings		
213 Ryan Christianson	.50	.15
Brett Myers RC		
214 Jason Stumm	.40	.12
Rob Purvis RC		
215 David Walling	.40	.12
Mike Paradis		
216 Omar Ortiz	.40	.12
Jay Gehrke		
217 David Cone HL	.20	.06
218 Jose Jimenez HL	.20	.06
219 Chris Singleton HL	.20	.06
220 Fernando Tatis HL	.20	.06
221 Todd Helton HL	.20	.06
222 Kevin Millwood DIV	.20	.06
223 Todd Pratt DIV	.20	.06
224 Orl.Hernandez DIV	.20	.06
225 Pedro Martinez DIV	.30	.09
226 Tom Glavine LCS	.20	.06
227 Bernie Williams LCS	.20	.06
228 Mariano Rivera WS	.20	.06
229 Tony Gwynn 20CB	.60	.18
230 Wade Boggs 20CB	.30	.09
231 Lance Johnson CB	.20	.06
232 Mark McGwire 20CB	1.25	.35
233 R.Henderson 20CB	.50	.15
234 R.Henderson 20CB	.50	.15
235 Roger Clemens 20CB	1.00	.30
236A M.McGwire MM	3.00	.90
1st HR		
236B M.McGwire MM	3.00	.90
1987 ROY		
236C M.McGwire MM	3.00	.90
62nd HR		
236D M.McGwire MM	3.00	.90
70th HR		
236E M.McGwire MM	3.00	.90
500th HR		
237A H.Aaron MM	2.00	.60
1st Career HR		
237B H.Aaron MM	2.00	.60
1957 MVP		
237C H.Aaron MM	2.00	.60
3000th Hit		
237D H.Aaron MM	2.00	.60
715th HR		
237E H.Aaron MM	2.00	.60
755th HR		
238A C.Ripken MM	4.00	1.20
1982 ROY		
238B C.Ripken MM	4.00	1.20
1991 MVP		
238C C.Ripken MM	4.00	1.20
2131 Game		
238D C.Ripken MM	4.00	1.20
Streak Ends		
238E C.Ripken MM	4.00	1.20
400th HR		
239A W.Boggs MM	.75	.23
1983 Batting		
239B W.Boggs MM	.75	.23
1988 Batting		
239C W.Boggs MM	.75	.23
2000th Hit		
239D W.Boggs MM	.75	.23
1996 Champs		
239E W.Boggs MM	.75	.23
3000th Hit		
240A T.Gwynn MM	1.50	.45
1984 Batting		
240B T.Gwynn MM	1.50	.45
1984 NLCS		
240C T.Gwynn MM	1.50	.45
1995 Batting		
240D T.Gwynn MM	1.50	.45
1998 NLCS		
240E T.Gwynn MM	1.50	.45
3000th Hit		
241 Tom Glavine	.30	.09
242 David Wells	.20	.06
243 Kevin Appier	.20	.06
244 Troy Percival	.20	.06
245 Ray Lankford	.20	.06
246 Marquis Grissom	.20	.06
247 Randy Winn	.20	.06
248 Miguel Batista	.20	.06
249 Darren Dreifort	.20	.06
250 Barry Bonds	1.25	.35
251 Harold Baines	.20	.06
252 Cliff Floyd	.20	.06
253 Freddy Garcia	.20	.06
254 Kenny Rogers	.20	.06
255 Ben Davis	.20	.06
256 Charles Johnson	.20	.06
257 Bubba Trammell	.20	.06
258 Desi Relaford	.20	.06
259 Al Martin	.20	.06
260 Andy Pettitte	.30	.09
261 Carlos Lee	.20	.06
262 Matt Lawton	.20	.06
263 Andy Fox	.20	.06
264 Chan Ho Park	.20	.06
265 Billy Koch	.20	.06
266 Dave Roberts	.20	.06
267 Carl Everett	.20	.06
268 Orel Hershiser	.20	.06
269 Trot Nixon	.20	.06
270 Rusty Greer	.20	.06
271 Will Clark	.50	.15
272 Quilvio Veras	.20	.06
273 Rico Brogna	.20	.06
274 Devon White	.20	.06
275 Tim Hudson	.20	.06
276 Mike Hampton	.20	.06
277 Miguel Cairo	.20	.06
278 Darren Oliver	.20	.06
279 Jeff Cirillo	.20	.06
280 Al Leiter	.20	.06
281 Shane Andrews	.20	.06
282 Carlos Febles	.20	.06
283 Pedro Astacio	.20	.06
284 Juan Guzman	.20	.06
285 Orlando Hernandez	.20	.06
286 Paul Konerko	.20	.06
287 Tony Clark	.20	.06
288 Aaron Boone	.20	.06
289 Ismael Valdes	.20	.06
290 Moises Alou	.20	.06
291 Kevin Tapani	.20	.06
292 John Franco	.20	.06
293 Todd Zeile	.20	.06
294 Jason Schmidt	.20	.06
295 Johnny Damon	.30	.09
296 Scott Brosius	.20	.06
297 Travis Fryman	.20	.06
298 Jose Vizcaino	.20	.06
299 Eric Chavez	.20	.06
300 Mike Piazza	.75	.23
301 Matt Clement	.20	.06
302 Cristian Guzman	.20	.06
303 C.J. Nitkowski	.20	.06
304 Michael Tucker	.20	.06
305 Brett Tomko	.20	.06
306 Mike Lansing	.20	.06
307 Eric Owens	.20	.06
308 Livan Hernandez	.20	.06
309 Rondell White	.20	.06
310 Todd Stottlemyre	.20	.06
311 Chris Carpenter	.20	.06
312 Ken Hill	.20	.06
313 Mark Loretta	.20	.06
314 John Rocker	.20	.06
315 Richie Sexson	.20	.06
316 Ruben Mateo	.20	.06
317 Joe Randa	.20	.06
318 Mike Sirotka	.20	.06
319 Jose Rosado	.20	.06
320 Matt Mantei	.20	.06
321 Kevin Millwood	.20	.06
322 Gary DiSarcina	.20	.06
323 Dustin Hermanson	.20	.06
324 Mike Stanton	.20	.06
325 Kirk Rueter	.20	.06
326 Damian Miller RC	.40	.12
327 Doug Glanville	.20	.06
328 Scott Rolen	.50	.15
329 Ray Durham	.20	.06
330 Butch Huskey	.20	.06
331 Mariano Rivera	.30	.09
332 Darren Lewis	.20	.06
333 Mike Timlin	.20	.06
334 Mark Grudzielanek	.20	.06
335 Mike Cameron	.20	.06
336 Kelvim Escobar	.20	.06
337 Bret Boone	.20	.06
338 Mo Vaughn	.20	.06
339 Craig Biggio	.30	.09
340 Michael Barrett	.20	.06
341 Marlon Anderson	.20	.06
342 Bobby Jones	.20	.06
343 John Halama	.20	.06
344 Todd Ritchie	.20	.06
345 Chuck Knoblauch	.20	.06
346 Rick Reed	.20	.06
347 Kelly Stinnett	.20	.06
348 Tim Salmon	.30	.09
349 A.J. Hinch	.20	.06
350 Jose Cruz Jr.	.20	.06
351 Roberto Hernandez	.20	.06
352 Edgar Renteria	.20	.06
353 Jose Hernandez	.20	.06
354 Brad Fullmer	.20	.06
355 Trevor Hoffman	.20	.06
356 Troy O'Leary	.20	.06
357 Justin Thompson	.20	.06
358 Kevin Young	.20	.06
359 Hideki Irabu	.20	.06
360 Jim Thome	.50	.15
361 Steve Karsay	.20	.06
362 Octavio Dotel	.20	.06
363 Omar Vizquel	.30	.09
364 Raul Mondesi	.20	.06
365 Shane Reynolds	.20	.06
366 Bartolo Colon	.20	.06
367 Chris Widger	.20	.06
368 Gabe Kapler	.20	.06
369 Bill Simas	.20	.06
370 Tino Martinez	.30	.09
371 John Thomson	.20	.06
372 Delino DeShields	.20	.06
373 Carlos Perez	.20	.06
374 Eddie Perez	.20	.06
375 Jeromy Burnitz	.20	.06
376 Jimmy Haynes	.20	.06
377 Travis Lee	.20	.06
378 Darryl Hamilton	.20	.06
379 Jamie Moyer	.20	.06
380 Alex Gonzalez	.20	.06
381 John Wetteland	.20	.06
382 Vinny Castilla	.20	.06
383 Jeff Suppan	.20	.06
384 Jim Leyritz	.20	.06
385 Robb Nen	.20	.06
386 Wilson Alvarez	.20	.06
387 Andres Galarraga	.20	.06
388 Mike Remlinger	.20	.06
389 Geoff Jenkins	.20	.06
390 Matt Stairs	.20	.06
391 Bill Mueller	.20	.06
392 Mike Lowell	.20	.06
393 Andy Ashby	.20	.06
394 Ruben Rivera	.20	.06
395 Todd Helton	.30	.09
396 Bernie Williams	.30	.09
397 Royce Clayton	.20	.06
398 Manny Ramirez	.30	.09
399 Kerry Wood	.50	.15
400 Ken Griffey Jr.	.75	.23
401 Enrique Wilson	.20	.06
402 Joey Hamilton	.20	.06
403 Shawn Estes	.20	.06
404 Ugueth Urbina	.20	.06
405 Albert Belle	.20	.06
406 Rick Helling	.20	.06
407 Steve Parris	.20	.06
408 Eric Milton	.20	.06
409 Dave Mlicki	.20	.06
410 Shawn Green	.20	.06
411 Jaret Wright	.20	.06
412 Tony Womack	.20	.06
413 Vernon Wells	.20	.06
414 Ron Belliard	.20	.06
415 Ellis Burks	.20	.06
416 Scott Erickson	.20	.06
417 Rafael Palmeiro	.30	.09
418 Damion Easley	.20	.06
419 Jamey Wright	.20	.06
420 Corey Koskie	.20	.06
421 Bobby Howry	.20	.06
422 Ricky Ledee	.20	.06
423 Dmitri Young	.20	.06
424 Sidney Ponson	.20	.06
425 Greg Maddux	.75	.23
426 Jose Guillen	.20	.06
427 Jon Lieber	.20	.06
428 Andy Benes	.20	.06
429 Randy Velarde	.20	.06
430 Sean Casey	.20	.06
431 Torii Hunter	.20	.06
432 Ryan Rupe	.20	.06
433 David Segui	.20	.06
434 Todd Pratt	.20	.06
435 Nomar Garciaparra	.75	.23
436 Denny Neagle	.20	.06
437 Ron Coomer	.20	.06
438 Chris Singleton	.20	.06
439 Tony Batista	.20	.06
440 Andruw Jones	.20	.06
441 Aubrey Huff	.20	.06
Sean Burroughs		
Adam Piatt		
442 Rafael Furcal	.40	.12
Travis Dawkins		
Jason Dellaero		
443 Mike Lamb RC	.40	.12
Joe Crede		
Wilton Veras		
444 Julio Zuleta RC	.40	.12
Jorge Toca		
Dernell Stenson		
445 Garry Maddox Jr. RC	.40	.12
Gary Matthews Jr.		
Tim Raines Jr.		
446 Mark Mulder	.40	.12
C.C. Sabathia		
Matt Riley		
447 Scott Downs RC	.40	.12
Chris George		
Matt Belisle		
448 Doug Mirabelli	.40	.12
Ben Petrick		
Jayson Werth		
449 Josh Hamilton	.40	.12
Corey Myers RC		
450 Ben Christensen RC	.40	.12
Richard Stahl RC		
451 Ben Sheets RC	2.00	.60
Barry Zito		
452 Kurt Ainsworth	.40	.12
Ty Howington RC		
453 Vince Faison RC	.40	.12
Rick Asadoorian		
454 Keith Reed RC	.40	.12
Jeff Heaverlo		
455 Mike MacDougal	.40	.12
Brad Baker RC		
456 Mark McGwire SH	.60	.18
457 Cal Ripken SH	.75	.23
458 Wade Boggs SH	.20	.06
459 Tony Gwynn SH	.30	.09
460 Jesse Orosco SH	.20	.06
461 Larry Walker	.30	.09
Nomar Garciaparra LL		
462 Ken Griffey Jr.	.50	.15
Mark McGwire LL		
463 Manny Ramirez	.50	.15
Mark McGwire LL		
464 Pedro Martinez	.30	.09
Randy Johnson LL		
465 Pedro Martinez	.30	.09
Randy Johnson LL		
466 Derek Jeter	.50	.15
Luis Gonzalez LL		
467 Larry Walker	.20	.06
Manny Ramirez LL		
468 Tony Gwynn 20CB	.60	.18
469 Mark McGwire 20CB	1.25	.35
470 Frank Thomas 20CB	.50	.15
471 Harold Baines 20CB	.20	.06
472 Roger Clemens 20CB	1.00	.30
473 John Franco 20CB	.20	.06
474 John Franco 20CB	.20	.06
475A K.Griffey Jr. MM	2.00	.60
350th HR		
475B K.Griffey Jr. MM	2.00	.60
1997 MVP		
475C K.Griffey Jr. MM	2.00	.60
HR Dad		
475D K.Griffey Jr. MM	2.00	.60
1992 AS MVP		
475E K.Griffey Jr. MM	2.00	.60
50 HR 1997		
476A B.Bonds MM	3.00	.90
400HR/400SB		
476B B.Bonds MM	3.00	.90
40HR/40SB		
476C B.Bonds MM	3.00	.90
1993 MVP		
476D B.Bonds MM	3.00	.90
1990 MVP		
476E B.Bonds MM	3.00	.90
1992 MVP		
477A S.Sosa MM	2.00	.60
20 HR June		
477B S.Sosa MM	2.00	.60
66 HR 1998		
477C S.Sosa MM	2.00	.60
60 HR 1999		
477D S.Sosa MM	2.00	.60
1998 MVP		
477E S.Sosa MM HR's	2.00	.60
61/62		
478A D.Jeter MM	3.00	.90
1996 ROY		

Card	Nm-Mt	Ex-Mt
478B D.Jeter MM Wins 1999 WS	3.00	.90
478C D.Jeter MM Wins 1998 WS	3.00	.90
478D D.Jeter MM Wins 1996 WS	3.00	.90
478E D.Jeter MM 17 GM Hit Streak	3.00	.90
479A A.Rodriguez MM 40HR/40SB	2.00	.60
479B A.Rodriguez MM 100th HR	2.00	.60
479C A.Rodriguez MM 1996 POY	2.00	.60
479D A.Rodriguez MM Wins 1 Million	2.00	.60
479E A.Rodriguez MM 1996 Batting Leader	2.00	.60
NNO M. McGwire 85 Reprint	5.00	1.50

2000 Topps 20th Century Best Sequential

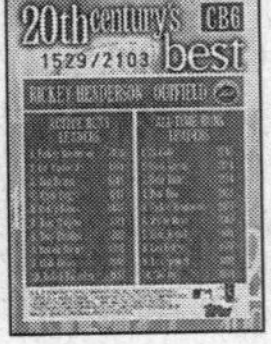

Inserted into first series hobby packs at an overall rate of one in 869 and one in 239 HTA packs, and into series two hobby packs at one in 362 and one in 100 HTA packs, these cards parallel the Century's Best subset within the base 2000 Topps set (cards 229-235/468-474). These insert cards, unlike the regular cards, feature "CB" prefixed numbering on back and have dramatic sparkling foil-coated fronts. Each card is sequentially numbered to the featured players highlighted career statistic.

Card	Nm-Mt	Ex-Mt
CB1 T.Gwynn AVG/339	40.00	12.00
CB2 W.Boggs 2B/578	20.00	6.00
CB3 L.Johnson 3B/117	25.00	7.50
CB4 M.McGwire HR/522	50.00	15.00
CB5 Rickey Henderson SB/1334	15.00	4.50
CB6 Rickey Henderson RUN/2103	15.00	4.50
CB7 R.Clemens WIN/247	60.00	18.00
CB8 Tony Gwynn HIT/3067	15.00	4.50
CB9 Mark McGwire SLG/587	50.00	15.00
CB10 Frank Thomas OBP/440	30.00	9.00
CB11 Harold Baines RBI/1583	8.00	2.40
CB12 Roger Clemens K's/3316	25.00	7.50
CB13 John Franco ERA/264	12.00	3.60
CB14 John Franco SV/416	12.00	3.60

2000 Topps Home Team Advantage

These cards were distributed exclusively in a 479-card factory set. Each set contained the 478-card base issue 2000 Topps set plus one Hank Aaron Chrome Reprint card. All of the base cards within Home Team Advantage factory sets were stamped with a special "HTA" gold foil logo on the card front. Oddly, cards 222-228 (Divisional Playoffs), 229-235 (20th Century's Best), 236-240 (Magic Moments), 461-467 (League Leaders) and 468-474 (20th Century Best) did NOT feature the gold-foil HTA tag. Thus, those cards are identical to basic issue Topps cards and are not included within our checklist for this set (though they are included within the complete factory set).

	Nm-Mt	Ex-Mt
COMP.FACT.SET (479)	80.00	24.00
*HTA: .75X TO 2X BASIC CARDS		

2000 Topps MVP Promotion

Inserted one in every 510 first series hobby and retail packs and one in every 140 first series HTA packs, this set is an almost complete parallel of the regular Topps set. The cards in the first series parallel cards number 1 through 201 and second series parallels cards 241-440. Card numbers 7 and 44 were never produced for this set. Each MVP Promotion parallel card has a prominent gold foil MVP logo on the front and contest rules and guidelines on back. Only 100 of each of these cards were printed and a new winner was announced each week throughout the 2000 season as Topps selected their top player of the week. Winning cards could be redeemed for a complete set of exchnage cards featuring every weekly winning player. Winning cards were verified through either calling 1-888-Go-Topps or checking on the Topps web site prior to the deadline. The exchange deadline for these cards was December 31st, 2000. The winning cards were the following numbers (in correspondence with the basic issue 2000 Topps card): 13, 15, 45, 50, 53, 55, 60, 72, 87, 90, 93, 107, 109, 116, 148, 165, 180, 199, 250, 271, 350, 395, 398, 403 and 427. Since Topps destroyed these Winner exchange cards once they received them, they're in noticeably shorter supply than other cards from this set. Despite this fact, no noticeable premiums in secondary trading levels have been detected for these cards.

Card	Nm-Mt	Ex-Mt
*STARS: 30X TO 60X BASIC CARDS..		
13 Magglio Ordonez W	12.00	3.60
15 Derek Jeter W	80.00	24.00
45 Jeff Bagwell W	20.00	6.00
50 Sammy Sosa W	50.00	15.00
53 Dante Bichette W	12.00	3.60
55 Frank Thomas W	30.00	9.00
60 Pedro Martinez W	30.00	9.00
72 Brian Jordan W	12.00	3.60
87 Bobby Higginson W	12.00	3.60
90 Mark Kotsay W	12.00	3.60
93 Carlos Delgado W	12.00	3.60
107 Jim Edmonds W	12.00	3.60
109 Adrian Beltre W	20.00	6.00
116 Jermaine Dye W	12.00	3.60
148 Derek Bell W	12.00	3.60
165 Kenny Lofton W	12.00	3.60
180 Chipper Jones W	30.00	9.00
199 Jason Giambi W	12.00	3.60
250 Barry Bonds W	80.00	24.00
271 Will Clark W	30.00	9.00
350 Jose Cruz Jr. W	12.00	3.60
395 Todd Helton W	20.00	6.00
398 Manny Ramirez W	20.00	6.00
403 Shawn Estes W	12.00	3.60
427 Jon Lieber W	12.00	3.60

2000 Topps MVP Promotion Exchange

This 25-card set was available only to those lucky collectors who obtained one of the twenty-five winning player cards from the 2000 Topps MVP Promotion parallel set. Each week, throughout the 2000 season, Topps named a new Player of the Week, and that player's Topps MVP Promotion parallel card was made redeemable for this 25-card set. The deadline to exchange the winning cards was 12/31/00.

Card	Nm-Mt	Ex-Mt
COMPLETE SET (25)	50.00	15.00
MVP1 Pedro Martinez	4.00	1.20
MVP2 Jim Edmonds	1.50	.45
MVP3 Derek Bell	1.50	.45
MVP4 Jermaine Dye	1.50	.45
MVP5 Jose Cruz Jr.	1.50	.45
MVP6 Todd Helton	2.50	.75
MVP7 Brian Jordan	1.50	.45
MVP8 Shawn Estes	1.50	.45
MVP9 Dante Bichette	1.50	.45
MVP10 Carlos Delgado	1.50	.45
MVP11 Bobby Higginson	1.50	.45
MVP12 Mark Kotsay	1.50	.45
MVP13 Magglio Ordonez	1.50	.45
MVP14 Jon Lieber	1.50	.45
MVP15 Frank Thomas	4.00	1.20
MVP16 Manny Ramirez	2.50	.75
MVP17 Sammy Sosa	6.00	1.80
MVP18 Will Clark	4.00	1.20
MVP19 Jeff Bagwell	2.50	.75
MVP20 Derek Jeter	10.00	3.00
MVP21 Adrian Beltre	2.50	.75
MVP22 Kenny Lofton	1.50	.45
MVP23 Barry Bonds	10.00	3.00
MVP24 Jason Giambi	1.50	.45
MVP25 Chipper Jones	4.00	1.20

2000 Topps Oversize

Each 2000 Topps hobby and Home Team Advantage box has one of these cards as a chiptopper. A chiptopper is a card that lies on top of the packs within the sealed box. These cards are exact parallels of their corresponding base issue card except, of course, for their larger size (3" by 5") and 1-8 numbering on back. Please note, for checklisting purposes, we've added "A" and "B" prefixes to each card number to signify which cards were seeded in first versus second series packs.

Card	Nm-Mt	Ex-Mt
COMPLETE SERIES 1 (8)	20.00	6.00
COMPLETE SERIES 2 (8)	15.00	4.50
A1 Mark McGwire	3.00	.90
A2 Hank Aaron	2.00	.60
A3 Derek Jeter	3.00	.90
A4 Sammy Sosa	2.00	.60
A5 Alex Rodriguez	2.00	.60
A6 Chipper Jones	1.25	.35
A7 Cal Ripken	4.00	1.20
A8 Pedro Martinez	1.25	.35
B1 Barry Bonds	3.00	.90
B2 Orlando Hernandez	.50	.15
B3 Mike Piazza	2.00	.60
B4 Manny Ramirez	.75	.23
B5 Ken Griffey Jr.	2.00	.60
B6 Rafael Palmeiro	.75	.23
B7 Greg Maddux	2.00	.60
B8 Nomar Garciaparra	2.00	.60

2000 Topps 21st Century

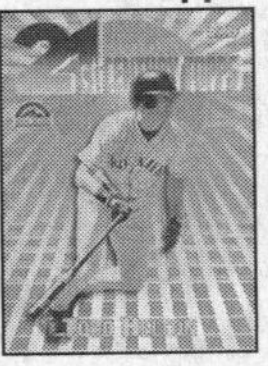

Inserted one every 18 first series hobby and retail packs and one every five first series HTA packs, these 10 cards feature players who are among those expected to be among the best players in the first part of the 21st century.

Card	Nm-Mt	Ex-Mt
COMPLETE SET (10)	10.00	3.00
C1 Ben Grieve	.40	.12
C2 Alex Gonzalez	.40	.12
C3 Derek Jeter	2.50	.75
C4 Sean Casey	.40	.12
C5 Nomar Garciaparra	1.50	.45
C6 Alex Rodriguez	1.50	.45
C7 Scott Rolen	1.00	.30
C8 Andruw Jones	.40	.12
C9 Vladimir Guerrero	1.00	.30
C10 Todd Helton	.60	.18

2000 Topps Aaron

For their year 2000 product, Topps chose to reprint cards of All-Time Home Run King, Hank Aaron. The cards were inserted one every 18 hobby and retail pack and one every five HTA packs in both first and second series. The even year cards were released in the first series and the odd year cards were issued in the second series. Each card can be easily detected from the original cards issued from the 1950-70s by the large gold foil logo on front and the glossy card stock.

Card	Nm-Mt	Ex-Mt
COMMON CARD (1-23)	5.00	1.50
1 Hank Aaron 1954	10.00	3.00

2000 Topps Aaron Autographs

Due to the fact that Topps could not obtain actual signed Hank Aaron cards prior to pack out for first series in December, 2000 - Topps inserted into first series packs at a rate of one in 4361 hobby and retail and 1 in 1199 first series HTA packs exchange cards of which were redeemable (prior to the May 31st, 2000 deadline) for a signed Hank Aaron Reprint card. The 12 exchange cards distributed in series one were redeemable exclusively for specific even year Reprint cards. The 11 odd year Autographs were obtained by Topps well in time for the second series release in April, 2000 and thus those actual autographed cards were seeded directly into the series two packs.

Card	Nm-Mt	Ex-Mt
COMMON CARD (2-23)	200.00	60.00
1 Hank Aaron 1954	250.00	75.00

2000 Topps All-Star Rookie Team

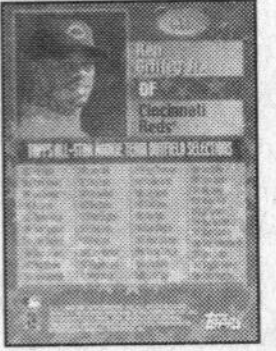

Randomly inserted into packs at one in 36 HOB/RET packs and one in eight HTA packs, this 10-card insert set features players that had break-through seasons their first year. Card backs carry a "RT" prefix.

Card	Nm-Mt	Ex-Mt
COMPLETE SET (10)	25.00	7.50
RT1 Mark McGwire	5.00	1.50
RT2 Chuck Knoblauch	.75	.23
RT3 Chipper Jones	2.00	.60
RT4 Cal Ripken	6.00	1.80
RT5 Manny Ramirez	1.25	.35
RT6 Jose Canseco	2.00	.60
RT7 Ken Griffey Jr.	3.00	.90
RT8 Mike Piazza	3.00	.90
RT9 Dwight Gooden	.75	.23
RT10 Billy Wagner UER Les Cain's name is spelled Less	.75	.23

2000 Topps All-Topps

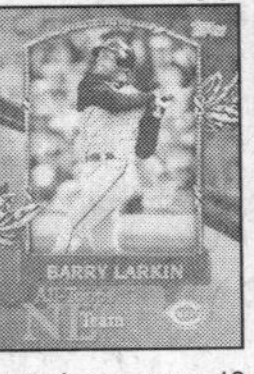

Inserted one every 12 first series hobby and retail packs and one every three first series HTA packs, this set features 10 star National Leaguers, 10 star American Leaguers, and a comparision to Hall of Famers at their respective position. Each card is printed on silver foil-board with select metalization. The National League players were issued in series one, while the American League players were issued in series two.

Card	Nm-Mt	Ex-Mt
COMPLETE SET (20)	20.00	6.00
COMPLETE N.L.(10)	10.00	3.00
COMPLETE A.L. (10)	10.00	3.00
AT1 Greg Maddux	1.50	.45
AT2 Mike Piazza	1.50	.45
AT3 Mark McGwire	2.50	.75
AT4 Craig Biggio	.60	.18
AT5 Chipper Jones	1.00	.30
AT6 Barry Larkin	.60	.18
AT7 Barry Bonds	2.50	.75
AT8 Andruw Jones	.40	.12
AT9 Sammy Sosa	1.50	.45
AT10 Larry Walker	.60	.18
AT11 Pedro Martinez	1.00	.30
AT12 Ivan Rodriguez	1.00	.30
AT13 Rafael Palmeiro	.60	.18
AT14 Roberto Alomar	.60	.18
AT15 Cal Ripken	3.00	.90
AT16 Derek Jeter	2.50	.75
AT17 Albert Belle	.40	.12
AT18 Ken Griffey Jr.	1.50	.45
AT19 Manny Ramirez	.60	.18
AT20 Jose Canseco	1.00	.30

2000 Topps Autographs

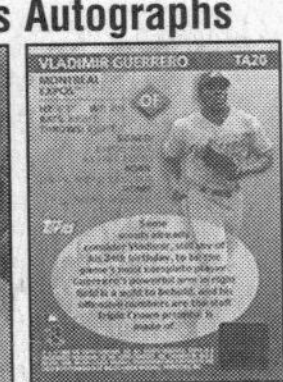

Inserted at various level of difficulty, these players signed autographs for the 2000 Topps product. Group A players were inserted one every 7589 first series hobby and retail packs and one every 2087 first series HTA packs. Group A players were issued at a rate of one in every 5840 second series hobby and retail packs, and one every 1607 HTA packs. Group B players were inserted one every 4553 first series hobby and retail packs and one every 1252 first series HTA packs. Group B players were inserted at a rate of one every 2337 second series hobby and retail packs, and one every 643 HTA packs. Group C players were inserted one every 1518 first series hobby and retail packs and one every 417 first series HTA packs. Group C players were inserted one every 1169 second series hobby and retail packs, and one in every 321 HTA packs. Group D players were inserted one every 911 first series hobby and retails packs and one every 250 first series HTA packs. Group D players were inserted one in every 701 second series hobby and retail packs, and one in every 193 HTA packs. Group E autographs were issued one every 1138 first series hobby and retail and one every 313 first series HTA packs. Group E players were inserted one in every 1754 second series hobby and retail packs, and one in every 482 HTA packs. Originally intended to be a straight numerical run of TA1-TA15 for series one, cards TA 4 (Sean Casey) and TA 15 (Carlos Beltran) were dropped and replaced with TA 20 (Vladimir Guerrero) and TA 27 (Mike Sweeney).

Card	Nm-Mt	Ex-Mt
TA1 Alex Rodriguez A	120.00	36.00
TA2 Tony Gwynn A	60.00	18.00
TA3 Vinny Castilla B	25.00	7.50
TA4 Sean Casey B	40.00	12.00
TA5 Shawn Green C	25.00	7.50
TA6 Rey Ordonez C	15.00	4.50
TA7 Matt Lawton C	15.00	4.50
TA8 Tony Womack C	15.00	4.50
TA9 Gabe Kapler D	15.00	4.50
TA10 Pat Burrell D	25.00	7.50
TA11 Preston Wilson D	25.00	7.50
TA12 Troy Glaus D	25.00	7.50
TA13 Carlos Beltran D	50.00	15.00
TA14 Josh Girdley E	15.00	4.50
TA15 B.J. Garbe E	15.00	4.50
TA16 Derek Jeter A	150.00	45.00
TA17 Cal Ripken A	200.00	60.00
TA18 Ivan Rodriguez B	50.00	15.00
TA19 Rafael Palmeiro B	60.00	18.00
TA20 Vladimir Guerrero B	50.00	15.00
TA21 Raul Mondesi C	25.00	7.50
TA22 Scott Rolen C	50.00	15.00
TA23 Billy Wagner C	40.00	12.00
TA24 Fernando Tatis C	15.00	4.50
TA25 Ruben Mateo D	15.00	4.50
TA26 Carlos Febles D	15.00	4.50
TA27 Mike Sweeney D	25.00	7.50
TA28 Alex Gonzalez D	15.00	4.50
TA29 Miguel Tejada D	25.00	7.50
TA30 Josh Hamilton E	15.00	4.50

2000 Topps Combos

Randomly inserted into packs at one in 18 hobby and retail packs, and one in every five HTA packs, this 10-card insert set showcases player groupings unified by a common theme, such as Home Run Kings, and features artist renderings of each player reminiscent of Topps' classic 1959 set. Card backs carry a "TC" prefix.

Card	Nm-Mt	Ex-Mt
COMPLETE SET (10)	25.00	7.50
TC1 Roberto Alomar Manny Ramirez Kenny Lofton Jim Thome	1.50	.45
TC2 Tom Glavine Greg Maddux John Smoltz	3.00	.90
TC3 Derek Jeter Bernie Williams Tino Martinez	4.00	1.20
TC4 Ivan Rodriguez Mike Piazza	2.50	.75
TC5 Nomar Garciaparra Alex Rodriguez Derek Jeter	2.50	.75
TC6 Sammy Sosa Mark McGwire	3.00	.90
TC7 Pedro Martinez Randy Johnson	1.50	.45
TC8 Barry Bonds Ken Griffey Jr.	4.00	1.20
TC9 Chipper Jones Ivan Rodriguez	1.50	.45
TC10 Cal Ripken Tony Gwynn Wade Boggs	1.50	.45

2000 Topps Hands of Gold

Inserted on every 18 first series hobby and retail packs and one every five first series HTA packs, this seven card set features players who have won at least five Gold Gloves. Each card is foil-stamped, die-cut and specially embossed.

Card	Nm-Mt	Ex-Mt
COMPLETE SET (7)	8.00	2.40
HG1 Barry Bonds	2.50	.75
HG2 Ivan Rodriguez	1.00	.30
HG3 Ken Griffey Jr.	1.50	.45
HG4 Roberto Alomar	.60	.18
HG5 Tony Gwynn	1.25	.35
HG6 Omar Vizquel	.60	.18
HG7 Greg Maddux	1.50	.45

2000 Topps Own the Game

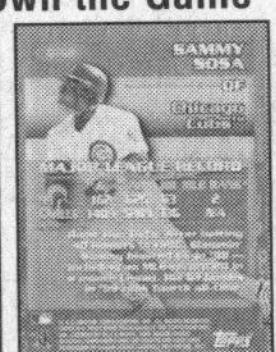

Randomly inserted into series two hobby and retail packs at a rate one in every 12, and one in every three series two HTA packs, this 30-card insert set features the top statistical leaders in major league baseball. Card backs carry an "OTG" prefix.

Card	Nm-Mt	Ex-Mt
COMPLETE SET (30)	50.00	15.00
OTG1 Derek Jeter	5.00	1.50
OTG2 B.J. Surhoff	.75	.23
OTG3 Luis Gonzalez	.75	.23
OTG4 Manny Ramirez	1.25	.35
OTG5 Rafael Palmeiro	1.25	.35
OTG6 Mark McGwire	5.00	1.50
OTG7 Mark McGwire	5.00	1.50
OTG8 Sammy Sosa	3.00	.90
OTG9 Ken Griffey Jr.	3.00	.90
OTG10 Larry Walker	1.25	.35
OTG11 Nomar Garciaparra	3.00	.90
OTG12 Derek Jeter	5.00	1.50
OTG13 Larry Walker	1.25	.35
OTG14 Mark McGwire	5.00	1.50
OTG15 Manny Ramirez	1.25	.35
OTG16 Pedro Martinez	2.00	.60
OTG17 Randy Johnson	2.00	.60
OTG18 Kevin Millwood	.75	.23
OTG19 Randy Johnson	2.00	.60
OTG20 Pedro Martinez	2.00	.60
OTG21 Kevin Brown	1.25	.35
OTG22 Chipper Jones	2.00	.60
OTG23 Ivan Rodriguez	2.00	.60
OTG24 Mariano Rivera	1.25	.35
OTG25 Scott Williamson	.75	.23
OTG26 Carlos Beltran	1.25	.35
OTG27 Randy Johnson	2.00	.60
OTG28 Pedro Martinez	2.00	.60
OTG29 Sammy Sosa	3.00	.90
OTG30 Manny Ramirez	1.25	.35

2000 Topps Perennial All-Stars

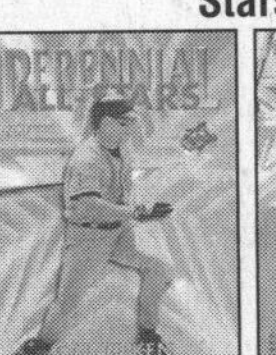

This set is inserted into first series hobby and retail packs at a rate of one in 18 and first series HTA packs at a rate of one every five packs.

These 10 cards feature players who consistently achieve All-Star recognition.

	Nm-Mt	Ex-Mt
COMPLETE SET (10)	20.00	6.00
PA1 Ken Griffey Jr.	1.50	.45
PA2 Derek Jeter	2.50	.75
PA3 Sammy Sosa	1.50	.45
PA4 Cal Ripken	3.00	.90
PA5 Mike Piazza	1.50	.45
PA6 Nomar Garciaparra	1.50	.45
PA7 Jeff Bagwell	.60	.18
PA8 Barry Bonds	2.50	.75
PA9 Alex Rodriguez	1.50	.45
PA10 Mark McGwire	2.50	.75

2000 Topps Power Players

Inserted into hobby and retail first series packs at a rate of one in eight and first series HTA packs at a rate one every other pack, this set features 20 of the best sluggers in baseball.

	Nm-Mt	Ex-Mt
COMPLETE SET (20)	25.00	7.50
P1 Juan Gonzalez	.60	.18
P2 Ken Griffey Jr.	1.50	.45
P3 Mark McGwire	2.50	.75
P4 Nomar Garciaparra	1.50	.45
P5 Barry Bonds	2.50	.75
P6 Mo Vaughn	.40	.12
P7 Larry Walker	.60	.18
P8 Alex Rodriguez	1.50	.45
P9 Jose Canseco	1.00	.30
P10 Jeff Bagwell	.60	.18
P11 Manny Ramirez	.60	.18
P12 Albert Belle	.40	.12
P13 Frank Thomas	1.00	.30
P14 Mike Piazza	1.50	.45
P15 Chipper Jones	1.00	.30
P16 Sammy Sosa	1.50	.45
P17 Vladimir Guerrero	1.00	.30
P18 Scott Rolen	1.00	.30
P19 Raul Mondesi	.40	.12
P20 Derek Jeter	2.50	.75

2000 Topps Stadium Autograph Relics

Exclusively inserted into first series HTA jumbo packs at a rate of one in 165 first series packs, and one in every 135 second series HTA packs, these cards feature a piece of a major league stadium (mostly infield bases) as well as as a photo and an autograph of the featured superstar who played there. Among the venerable ballparks included in this set are Wrigley Field, Fenway Park and Yankee Stadium.

	Nm-Mt	Ex-Mt
SR1 Don Mattingly	150.00	45.00
SR2 Carl Yastrzemski	120.00	36.00
SR3 Ernie Banks	80.00	24.00
SR4 Johnny Bench	80.00	24.00
SR5 Willie Mays	200.00	60.00
SR6 Mike Schmidt	120.00	36.00
SR7 Lou Brock	50.00	15.00
SR8 Al Kaline	80.00	24.00
SR9 Paul Molitor	50.00	15.00
SR10 Eddie Mathews	80.00	24.00

2000 Topps Limited

These parallel cards were issued exclusively in factory set form (an attractive black box with a glossy teal overlay) and offered collectors the chance to get an upgraded premium version of the basic 2000 Topps. Each factory set contained a total of 619 cards including the complete 478 card basic Topps set plus the following insert sets: 21st Century Topps, Aaron Reprints, All-Star Rookie Team, All-Topps, Combos, Hands of Gold, Own the Game, Perennial All-Stars, Power Players and the Mark McGwire 1985 Reprint. Collectors received only one of five different variations of the Magic Moments subset cards (236-240/475-479) per factory set. Each card has thick gloss and features a "Limited Edition" gold foil stamp on front. Stated print run was originally 6000 serial numbered sets but actual production turned out to be 4,000 sets (with only 800 copies of each of the Magic Moments variation subset cards). Each factory box is serial numbered x/4000 but the individual cards are not numbered in any way. The sets were distributed in late September, 2000.

	Nm-Mt	Ex-Mt
COMP.FACT.SET (619)	150.00	45.00
COMPLETE SET (478)	100.00	30.00
STARS: 2.5X TO 6X BASIC CARDS...		
ROOKIES: 3X TO 8X BASIC CARDS..		
MAGIC MOMENTS: 1.25X TO 3X BASIC MM		

2000 Topps Traded

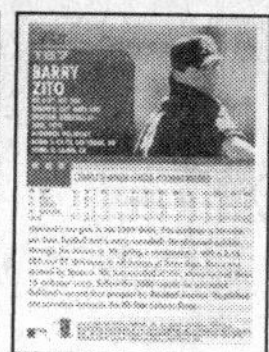

The 2000 Topps Traded sets were released in October, 2000 and featured a 135-card base set, and one additional autograph card. The set carried a suggested retail price of $29.99. Please note that each card in the base set carried a "T" prefix before the card number. Topps announced that due to the unavailability of certain players previously scheduled to sign autographs, Topps will include a small quantity of autographed cards from the 2000 Topps Baseball Rookies/Traded set into its 2000 Bowman Baseball Draft Picks and Prospects set. Notable Rookie Cards include Cristian Guerrero and J.R. House.

	Nm-Mt	Ex-Mt
COMP.FACT.SET (136)	50.00	15.00
COMPLETE SET (135)	25.00	7.50
FACT.SET PRICE IS FOR SEALED SETS		
T1 Mike MacDougal	.30	.09
T2 Andy Tracy RC	.30	.09
T3 Brandon Phillips RC	.50	.15
T4 Brandon Inge RC	.30	.09
T5 Robbie Morrison RC	.30	.09
T6 Josh Pressley RC	.30	.09
T7 Todd Moser RC	.30	.09
T8 Rob Purvis	.30	.09
T9 Chance Caple	.20	.06
T10 Ben Sheets	1.25	.35
T11 Russ Jacobson RC	.30	.09
T12 Brian Cole RC	.30	.09
T13 Brad Baker	.30	.09
T14 Alex Cintron RC	.30	.09
T15 Lyle Overbay RC	1.25	.35
T16 Mike Edwards RC	.30	.09
T17 Sean McGowan RC	.30	.09
T18 Jose Molina	.20	.06
T19 Marcos Castillo RC	.30	.09
T20 Josue Espada RC	.30	.09
T21 Alex Gordon RC	.30	.09
T22 Rob Pugmire RC	.30	.09
T23 Jason Stumm	.20	.06
T24 Ty Howington	.30	.09
T25 Brett Myers	.50	.15
T26 Maicer Izturis RC	.50	.15
T27 John McDonald	.20	.06
T28 W.Rodriguez RC	.30	.09
T29 Carlos Zambrano RC	3.00	.90
T30 Alejandro Diaz RC	.30	.09
T31 Geraldo Guzman RC	.30	.09
T32 J.R. House RC	.30	.09
T33 Elvin Nina RC	.30	.09
T34 Juan Pierre RC	.75	.23
T35 Ben Johnson RC	.30	.09
T36 Jeff Bailey RC	.30	.09
T37 Miguel Olivo RC	.50	.15
T38 F.Rodriguez RC	2.00	.60
T39 Tony Pena Jr. RC	.30	.09
T40 Miguel Cabrera RC	15.00	4.50
T41 Asdrubal Oropeza RC	.30	.09
T42 Junior Zamora RC	.30	.09
T43 Jovanny Cedeno RC	.30	.09
T44 John Sneed	.30	.09
T45 Josh Kalinowski	.30	.09
T46 Mike Young RC	4.00	1.20
T47 Rico Washington RC	.30	.09
T48 Chad Durbin RC	.30	.09
T49 Junior Brignac RC	.30	.09
T50 Carlos Hernandez RC	.30	.09
T51 Cesar Izturis RC	.75	.23
T52 Oscar Salazar RC	.30	.09
T53 Pat Strange RC	.30	.09
T54 Rick Asadoorian	.30	.09
T55 Keith Reed	.30	.09
T56 Leo Estrella RC	.30	.09
T57 Wascar Serrano RC	.30	.09
T58 Richard Gomez RC	.30	.09
T59 Ramon Santiago RC	.30	.09
T60 Jovanny Sosa RC	.30	.09
T61 Aaron Rowand RC	1.25	.35
T62 Junior Guerrero RC	.30	.09
T63 Luis Terrero RC	.75	.23
T64 Brian Sanches RC	.30	.09
T65 Scott Sobkowiak RC	.30	.09
T66 Gary Majewski RC	.50	.15
T67 Barry Zito	1.25	.35
T68 Ryan Christianson	.30	.09
T69 Cristian Guerrero RC	.30	.09
T70 T.De La Rosa RC	.30	.09
T71 Andrew Beinbrink RC	.30	.09
T72 Ryan Knox RC	.30	.09
T73 Alex Graman RC	.30	.09
T74 Juan Guzman RC	.30	.09
T75 Ruben Salazar RC	.30	.09
T76 Luis Matos RC	.30	.09
T77 Tony Mota RC	.30	.09
T78 Doug Davis	.20	.06
T79 Ben Christensen	.20	.06
T80 Mike Lamb	.50	.15
T81 Adrian Gonzalez RC	1.25	.35
T82 Mike Stodolka RC	.30	.09
T83 Adam Johnson RC	.30	.09
T84 Matt Wheatland RC	.30	.09
T85 Corey Smith RC	.30	.09
T86 Rocco Baldelli RC	3.00	.90
T87 Keith Bucktrot RC	.30	.09
T88 Adam Wainwright RC	.75	.23
T89 Scott Thorman RC	.30	.09
T90 Tripper Johnson RC	.30	.09
T91 Jim Edmonds	.30	.09
T92 Masato Yoshii	.20	.06
T93 Adam Kennedy	.20	.06
T94 Darryl Kile	.20	.06
T95 Mark McLemore	.20	.06
T96 Ricky Gutierrez	.20	.06
T97 Juan Gonzalez	.50	.15
T98 Melvin Mora	.30	.09
T99 Dante Bichette	.30	.09
T100 Lee Stevens	.20	.06
T101 Roger Cedeno	.20	.06
T102 John Olerud	.30	.09
T103 Eric Young	.20	.06
T104 Mickey Morandini	.20	.06
T105 Travis Lee	.20	.06
T106 Greg Vaughn	.20	.06
T107 Todd Zeile	.30	.09
T108 Chuck Finley	.30	.09
T109 Ismael Valdes	.20	.06
T110 Reggie Sanders	.20	.06
T111 Pat Hentgen	.20	.06
T112 Ryan Klesko	.30	.09
T113 Derek Bell	.20	.06
T114 Hideo Nomo	.75	.23
T115 Aaron Sele	.20	.06
T116 Fernando Vina	.20	.06
T117 Wally Joyner	.30	.09
T118 Brian Hunter	.20	.06
T119 Joe Girardi	.20	.06
T120 Omar Daal	.20	.06
T121 Brook Fordyce	.20	.06
T122 Jose Valentin	.20	.06
T123 Curt Schilling	.30	.09
T124 B.J. Surhoff	.30	.09
T125 Henry Rodriguez	.20	.06
T126 Mike Bordick	.20	.06
T127 David Justice	.30	.09
T128 Charles Johnson	.30	.09
T129 Will Clark	.75	.23
T130 Dwight Gooden	.30	.09
T131 David Segui	.20	.06
T132 Denny Neagle	.30	.09
T133 Jose Canseco	.75	.23
T134 Bruce Chen	.20	.06
T135 Jason Bere	.20	.06

2000 Topps Traded Autographs

Randomly inserted into 2000 Topps Traded sets at a rate of one per sealed factory set, this 80-card set features autographed cards of some of the Major League's most talented prospects. Card backs carry a "TTA" prefix.

	Nm-Mt	Ex-Mt
TTA1 Mike MacDougal	10.00	3.00
TTA2 Andy Tracy	5.00	1.50
TTA3 Brandon Phillips	15.00	4.50
TTA4 Brandon Inge	10.00	3.00
TTA5 Robbie Morrison	5.00	1.50
TTA6 Josh Pressley	5.00	1.50
TTA7 Todd Moser	5.00	1.50
TTA8 Rob Purvis	10.00	3.00
TTA9 Chance Caple	5.00	1.50
TTA10 Ben Sheets	50.00	15.00
TTA11 Russ Jacobson	5.00	1.50
TTA12 Brian Cole	5.00	1.50
TTA13 Brad Baker	10.00	3.00
TTA14 Alex Cintron	10.00	3.00
TTA15 Lyle Overbay	40.00	12.00
TTA16 Mike Edwards	5.00	1.50
TTA17 Sean McGowan	5.00	1.50
TTA18 Jose Molina	5.00	1.50
TTA19 Marcos Castillo	5.00	1.50
TTA20 Josue Espada	5.00	1.50
TTA21 Alex Gordon	5.00	1.50
TTA22 Rob Pugmire	5.00	1.50
TTA23 Jason Stumm	5.00	1.50
TTA24 Ty Howington	10.00	3.00
TTA25 Brett Myers	15.00	4.50
TTA26 Maicer Izturis	15.00	4.50
TTA27 John McDonald	5.00	1.50
TTA28 Wilfredo Rodriguez	5.00	1.50
TTA29 Carlos Zambrano	100.00	30.00
TTA30 Alejandro Diaz	5.00	1.50
TTA31 Geraldo Guzman	5.00	1.50
TTA32 J.R. House	10.00	3.00
TTA33 Elvin Nina	5.00	1.50
TTA34 Juan Pierre	25.00	7.50
TTA35 Ben Johnson	5.00	1.50
TTA36 Jeff Bailey	5.00	1.50
TTA37 Miguel Olivo	15.00	4.50
TTA38 F.Rodriguez	60.00	18.00
TTA39 Tony Pena Jr.	10.00	3.00
TTA40 Miguel Cabrera	250.00	75.00
TTA41 Asdrubal Oropeza	5.00	1.50
TTA42 Junior Zamora	5.00	1.50
TTA43 Jovanny Cedeno	5.00	1.50
TTA44 John Sneed	5.00	1.50
TTA45 Josh Kalinowski	10.00	3.00
TTA46 Mike Young	80.00	24.00
TTA47 Rico Washington	5.00	1.50
TTA48 Chad Durbin	5.00	1.50
TTA49 Junior Brignac	5.00	1.50
TTA50 Carlos Hernandez	10.00	3.00
TTA51 Cesar Izturis	25.00	7.50
TTA52 Oscar Salazar	5.00	1.50
TTA53 Pat Strange	5.00	1.50
TTA54 Rick Asadoorian	10.00	3.00
TTA55 Keith Reed	10.00	3.00
TTA56 Leo Estrella	5.00	1.50
TTA57 Wascar Serrano	5.00	1.50
TTA58 Richard Gomez	5.00	1.50
TTA59 Ramon Santiago	10.00	3.00
TTA60 Jovanny Sosa	10.00	3.00
TTA61 Aaron Rowand	40.00	12.00
TTA62 Junior Guerrero	5.00	1.50
TTA63 Luis Terrero	25.00	7.50
TTA64 Brian Sanches	5.00	1.50
TTA65 Scott Sobkowiak	5.00	1.50
TTA66 Gary Majewski	15.00	4.50
TTA67 Barry Zito	50.00	15.00
TTA68 Ryan Christianson	10.00	3.00
TTA69 Cristian Guerrero	10.00	3.00
TTA70 Tomas De La Rosa	5.00	1.50
TTA71 Andrew Beinbrink	10.00	3.00
TTA72 Ryan Knox	5.00	1.50
TTA73 Alex Graman	5.00	1.50
TTA74 Juan Guzman	5.00	1.50
TTA75 Ruben Salazar	5.00	1.50
TTA76 Luis Matos	10.00	3.00
TTA77 Tony Mota	5.00	1.50
TTA78 Doug Davis	5.00	1.50
TTA79 Ben Christensen	5.00	1.50
TTA80 Mike Lamb	10.00	3.00

2001 Topps

The 2001 Topps set featured 790 cards and was issued over two series. The set looks to bring back some of the heritage that Topps established in the past by bringing back Manager cards, dual-player prospect cards, and the 2000 season highlight cards. Notable Rookie Cards include Hee Seop Choi. Please note that some cards have been discovered with nothing printed on front but blank white except for the players name and 50th Topps anniversary logo printed in Gold. Factory sets include five special cards inserted specifically in those sets. Card number 7 was not issued as Topps continued to honor the memory of Mickey Mantle.

	Nm-Mt	Ex-Mt
COMPLETE SET (790)	80.00	24.00
COMP.FACT.BLUE SET (795)	100.00	30.00
COMP.SERIES 1 (405)	40.00	12.00
COMP. SERIES 2 (385)	40.00	12.00
COMMON (1-6/8-791)	.20	.06
COMMON (352-376/727-751)	.25	.07
1 Cal Ripken	1.50	.45
2 Chipper Jones	.50	.15
3 Roger Cedeno	.20	.06
4 Garret Anderson	.20	.06
5 Robin Ventura	.20	.06
6 Daryle Ward	.20	.06
7 Does Not Exist		
8 Craig Paquette	.20	.06
9 Phil Nevin	.20	.06
10 Jermaine Dye	.20	.06
11 Chris Singleton	.20	.06
12 Mike Stanton	.20	.06
13 Brian Hunter	.20	.06
14 Mike Redmond	.20	.06
15 Jim Thome	.50	.15
16 Brian Jordan	.20	.06
17 Joe Girardi	.20	.06
18 Steve Woodard	.20	.06
19 Dustin Hermanson	.20	.06
20 Shawn Green	.20	.06
21 Todd Stottlemyre	.20	.06
22 Dan Wilson	.20	.06
23 Todd Pratt	.20	.06
24 Derek Lowe	.20	.06
25 Juan Gonzalez	.30	.09
26 Clay Bellinger	.20	.06
27 Jeff Fassero	.20	.06
28 Pat Meares	.20	.06
29 Eddie Taubensee	.20	.06
30 Paul O'Neill	.30	.09
31 Jeffrey Hammonds	.20	.06
32 Pokey Reese	.20	.06
33 Mike Mussina	.30	.09
34 Rico Brogna	.20	.06
35 Jay Buhner	.20	.06
36 Steve Cox	.20	.06
37 Quilvio Veras	.20	.06
38 Marquis Grissom	.20	.06
39 Shigetoshi Hasegawa	.20	.06
40 Shane Reynolds	.20	.06
41 Adam Piatt	.20	.06
42 Luis Polonia	.20	.06
43 Brook Fordyce	.20	.06
44 Preston Wilson	.20	.06
45 Ellis Burks	.20	.06
46 Armando Rios	.20	.06
47 Chuck Finley	.20	.06
48 Dan Plesac	.20	.06
49 Shannon Stewart	.20	.06
50 Mark McGwire	1.25	.35
51 Mark Loretta	.20	.06
52 Gerald Williams	.20	.06
53 Eric Young	.20	.06
54 Peter Bergeron	.20	.06
55 Dave Hansen	.20	.06
56 Arthur Rhodes	.20	.06
57 Bobby Jones	.20	.06
58 Matt Clement	.20	.06
59 Mike Benjamin	.20	.06
60 Pedro Martinez	.50	.15
61 Jose Canseco	.50	.15
62 Matt Anderson	.20	.06
63 Torii Hunter	.20	.06
64 Carlos Lee UER	.20	.06
1999 Charlotte Games Played are wrong		
65 David Cone	.20	.06
66 Rey Sanchez	.20	.06
67 Eric Chavez	.20	.06
68 Rick Helling	.20	.06
69 Manny Alexander	.20	.06
70 John Franco	.20	.06
71 Mike Bordick	.20	.06
72 Andres Galarraga	.20	.06
73 Jose Cruz Jr.	.20	.06
74 Mike Matheny	.20	.06
75 Randy Johnson	.50	.15
76 Richie Sexson	.20	.06
77 Vladimir Nunez	.20	.06
78 Harold Baines	.20	.06
79 Aaron Boone	.20	.06
80 Darin Erstad	.20	.06
81 Alex Gonzalez	.20	.06
82 Gil Heredia	.20	.06
83 Shane Andrews	.20	.06
84 Todd Hundley	.20	.06
85 Bill Mueller	.20	.06
86 Mark McLemore	.20	.06
87 Scott Spiezio	.20	.06
88 Kevin McGlinchy	.20	.06
89 Bubba Trammell	.20	.06
90 Manny Ramirez	.30	.09
91 Mike Lamb	.20	.06
92 Scott Karl	.20	.06
93 Brian Buchanan	.20	.06
94 Chris Turner	.20	.06
95 Mike Sweeney	.20	.06
96 John Wetteland	.20	.06
97 Rob Bell	.20	.06
98 Pat Rapp	.20	.06
99 John Burkett	.20	.06
100 Derek Jeter	1.25	.35
101 J.D. Drew	.20	.06
102 Jose Offerman	.20	.06
103 Rick Reed	.20	.06
104 Will Clark	.50	.15
105 Rickey Henderson	.50	.15
106 Dave Berg	.20	.06
107 Kirk Rueter	.20	.06
108 Lee Stevens	.20	.06
109 Jay Bell	.20	.06
110 Fred McGriff	.30	.09
111 Julio Zuleta	.20	.06
112 Brian Anderson	.20	.06
113 Orlando Cabrera	.20	.06
114 Alex Fernandez	.20	.06
115 Derek Bell	.20	.06
116 Eric Owens	.20	.06
117 Brian Bohanon	.20	.06
118 Dennys Reyes	.20	.06
119 Mike Stanley	.20	.06
120 Jorge Posada	.30	.09
121 Rich Becker	.20	.06
122 Paul Konerko	.20	.06
123 Mike Remlinger	.20	.06
124 Travis Lee	.20	.06
125 Ken Caminiti	.20	.06
126 Kevin Barker	.20	.06
127 Paul Quantrill	.20	.06
128 Ozzie Guillen	.20	.06
129 Kevin Tapani	.20	.06
130 Mark Johnson	.20	.06
131 Randy Wolf	.20	.06
132 Michael Tucker	.20	.06
133 Darren Lewis	.20	.06
134 Joe Randa	.20	.06
135 Jeff Cirillo	.20	.06
136 David Ortiz	.30	.09
137 Herb Perry	.20	.06
138 Jeff Nelson	.20	.06
139 Chris Stynes	.20	.06
140 Johnny Damon	.30	.09
141 Jeff Reboulet	.20	.06
142 Jason Schmidt	.20	.06
143 Charles Johnson	.20	.06
144 Pat Burrell	.20	.06
145 Gary Sheffield	.20	.06
146 Tom Glavine	.30	.09
147 Jason Isringhausen	.20	.06
148 Chris Carpenter	.20	.06
149 Jeff Suppan	.20	.06
150 Ivan Rodriguez	.50	.15
151 Luis Sojo	.20	.06
152 Ron Villone	.20	.06
153 Mike Sirotka	.20	.06
154 Chuck Knoblauch	.20	.06
155 Jason Kendall	.20	.06
156 Dennis Cook	.20	.06
157 Bobby Estalella	.20	.06
158 Jose Guillen	.20	.06
159 Thomas Howard	.20	.06
160 Carlos Delgado	.20	.06
161 Benji Gil	.20	.06
162 Tim Bogar	.20	.06
163 Kevin Elster	.20	.06
164 Einar Diaz	.20	.06
165 Andy Benes	.20	.06
166 Adrian Beltre	.30	.09
167 David Bell	.20	.06
168 Turk Wendell	.20	.06
169 Pete Harnisch	.20	.06
170 Roger Clemens	1.00	.30
171 Scott Williamson	.20	.06
172 Kevin Jordan	.20	.06
173 Brad Penny	.20	.06
174 John Flaherty	.20	.06
175 Troy Glaus	.20	.06
176 Kevin Appier	.20	.06
177 Walt Weiss	.20	.06
178 Tyler Houston	.20	.06
179 Michael Barrett	.20	.06
180 Mike Hampton	.20	.06
181 Francisco Cordova	.20	.06
182 Mike Jackson	.20	.06
183 David Segui	.20	.06
184 Carlos Febles	.20	.06
185 Roy Halladay	.20	.06
186 Seth Etherton	.20	.06
187 Charlie Hayes	.20	.06
188 Fernando Tatis	.20	.06
189 Steve Trachsel	.20	.06
190 Livan Hernandez	.20	.06
191 Joe Oliver	.20	.06
192 Stan Javier	.20	.06
193 B.J. Surhoff	.20	.06
194 Rob Ducey	.20	.06
195 Barry Larkin	.30	.09
196 Danny Patterson	.20	.06
197 Bobby Howry	.20	.06
198 Dmitri Young	.20	.06
199 Brian Hunter	.20	.06
200 Alex Rodriguez	.75	.23
201 Hideo Nomo	.50	.15
202 Luis Alicea	.20	.06
203 Warren Morris	.20	.06
204 Antonio Alfonseca	.20	.06
205 Edgardo Alfonzo	.20	.06
206 Mark Grudzielanek	.20	.06
207 Fernando Vina	.20	.06
208 Willie Greene	.20	.06
209 Homer Bush	.20	.06
210 Jason Giambi	.20	.06
211 Mike Morgan	.20	.06
212 Steve Karsay	.20	.06
213 Matt Lawton	.20	.06
214 Wendell Magee Jr.	.20	.06
215 Rusty Greer	.20	.06
216 Keith Lockhart	.20	.06
217 Billy Koch	.20	.06
218 Todd Hollandsworth	.20	.06

219 Raul Ibanez .20 .06
220 Tony Gwynn .60 .18
221 Carl Everett .20 .06
222 Hector Carrasco .20 .06
223 Jose Valentin .20 .06
224 Deivi Cruz .20 .06
225 Bret Boone .20 .06
226 Kurt Abbott .20 .06
227 Melvin Mora .20 .06
228 Danny Graves .20 .06
229 Jose Jimenez .20 .06
230 James Baldwin .20 .06
231 C.J. Nitkowski .20 .06
232 Jeff Zimmerman .20 .06
233 Mike Lowell .20 .06
234 Hideki Irabu .20 .06
235 Greg Vaughn .20 .06
236 Omar Daal .20 .06
237 Darren Dreifort .20 .06
238 Gil Meche .20 .06
239 Damian Jackson .20 .06
240 Frank Thomas .50 .15
241 Travis Miller .20 .06
242 Jeff Frye .20 .06
243 Dave Magadan .20 .06
244 Luis Castillo .20 .06
245 Bartolo Colon .20 .06
246 Steve Kline .20 .06
247 Shawon Dunston .20 .06
248 Rick Aguilera .20 .06
249 Omar Olivares .20 .06
250 Craig Biggio .30 .09
251 Scott Schoeneweis .20 .06
252 Dave Veres .20 .06
253 Ramon Martinez .20 .06
254 Jose Vidro .20 .06
255 Todd Helton .30 .09
256 Greg Norton .20 .06
257 Jacque Jones .20 .06
258 Jason Grimsley .20 .06
259 Dan Reichert .20 .06
260 Robb Nen .20 .06
261 Mark Clark .20 .06
262 Scott Hatteberg .20 .06
263 Doug Brocail .20 .06
264 Mark Johnson .20 .06
265 Eric Davis .20 .06
266 Terry Shumpert .20 .06
267 Kevin Millar .20 .06
268 Ismael Valdes .20 .06
269 Richard Hidalgo .20 .06
270 Randy Velarde .20 .06
271 Bengie Molina .20 .06
272 Tony Womack .20 .06
273 Enrique Wilson .20 .06
274 Jeff Brantley .20 .06
275 Rick Ankiel .20 .06
276 Terry Mulholland .20 .06
277 Ron Belliard .20 .06
278 Terrence Long .20 .06
279 Alberto Castillo .20 .06
280 Royce Clayton .20 .06
281 Joe McEwing .20 .06
282 Jason McDonald .20 .06
283 Ricky Bottalico .20 .06
284 Keith Foulke .20 .06
285 Brad Radke .20 .06
286 Gabe Kapler .20 .06
287 Pedro Astacio .20 .06
288 Armando Reynoso .20 .06
289 Darryl Kile .20 .06
290 Reggie Sanders .20 .06
291 Esteban Yan .20 .06
292 Joe Nathan .20 .06
293 Jay Payton .20 .06
294 Francisco Cordero .20 .06
295 Gregg Jefferies .20 .06
296 LaTroy Hawkins .20 .06
297 Jeff Tam RC .40 .12
298 Jacob Cruz .20 .06
299 Chris Holt .20 .06
300 Vladimir Guerrero .50 .15
301 Marvin Benard .20 .06
302 Alex Ramirez .20 .06
303 Mike Williams .20 .06
304 Sean Bergman .20 .06
305 Juan Encarnacion .20 .06
306 Russ Davis .20 .06
307 Hanley Frias .20 .06
308 Ramon Hernandez .20 .06
309 Matt Walbeck .20 .06
310 Bill Spiers .20 .06
311 Bob Wickman .20 .06
312 Sandy Alomar Jr. .20 .06
313 Eddie Guardado .20 .06
314 Shane Halter .20 .06
315 Geoff Jenkins .20 .06
316 Brian Meadows .20 .06
317 Damian Miller .20 .06
318 Darrin Fletcher .20 .06
319 Rafael Furcal .20 .06
320 Mark Grace .30 .09
321 Mark Mulder .20 .06
322 Joe Torre MG .20 .06
323 Bobby Cox MG .20 .06
324 Mike Scioscia MG .20 .06
325 Mike Hargrove MG .20 .06
326 Jimy Williams MG .20 .06
327 Jerry Manuel MG .20 .06
328 Buck Showalter MG .20 .06
329 Charlie Manuel MG .20 .06
330 Don Baylor MG .20 .06
331 Phil Garner MG .20 .06
332 Jack McKeon MG .20 .06
333 Tony Muser MG .20 .06
334 Buddy Bell MG .20 .06
335 Tom Kelly MG .20 .06
336 John Boles MG .20 .06
337 Art Howe MG .20 .06
338 Larry Dierker MG .20 .06
339 Lou Piniella MG .20 .06
340 Davey Johnson MG .20 .06
341 Larry Rothschild MG .20 .06
342 Davey Lopes MG .20 .06
343 Johnny Oates MG .20 .06
344 Felipe Alou MG .20 .06
345 Jim Fregosi MG .20 .06
346 Bobby Valentine MG .20 .06
347 Terry Francona MG .20 .06
348 Gene Lamont MG .20 .06
349 Tony LaRussa MG .20 .06
350 Bruce Bochy MG .20 .06
351 Dusty Baker MG .20 .06
352 Adrian Gonzalez .40 .12
Adam Johnson
353 Matt Wheatland .25 .07
Bryan Digby
354 Tripper Johnson .25 .07
Scott Thorman
355 Phil Dumatrait .25 .07
Adam Wainwright
356 Scott Heard .40 .12
David Parrish RC
357 Rocco Baldelli .50 .15
Mark Folsom RC
358 Dominic Rich RC .40 .12
Aaron Herr
359 Mike Stodolka .25 .07
Sean Burnett
360 Derek Thompson .25 .07
Corey Smith
361 Danny Borrell RC .40 .12
Jason Bourgeois RC
362 Chin-Feng Chen .40 .12
Corey Patterson
Josh Hamilton
363 Ryan Anderson .50 .15
Barry Zito
C.C. Sabathia
364 Scott Sobkowiak .50 .15
David Walling
Ben Sheets
365 Ty Howington .25 .07
Josh Kalinowski
Josh Girdley
366 Hee Seop Choi RC .75 .23
Aaron McNeal
Jason Hart
367 Bobby Bradley .40 .12
Kurt Ainsworth
Chin-Hui Tsao
368 Mike Glendenning .25 .07
Kenny Kelly
Juan Silvestre
369 J.R. House .25 .07
Ramon Castro
Ben Davis
370 Chance Caple .50 .15
Rafael Soriano RC
Pasqual Coco
371 Travis Hafner RC 1.50 .45
Eric Munson
Bucky Jacobsen
372 Jason Conti .25 .07
Chris Wakeland
Brian Cole
373 Scott Seabol .40 .12
Aubrey Huff
Joe Crede
374 Adam Everett .25 .07
Jose Ortiz
Keith Ginter
375 Carlos Hernandez .25 .07
Geraldo Guzman
Adam Eaton
376 Bobby Kielty .25 .07
Milton Bradley
Juan Rivera
377 Mark McGwire GM .60 .18
378 Don Larsen GM .20 .06
379 Bobby Thomson GM .20 .06
380 Bill Mazeroski GM .20 .06
381 Reggie Jackson GM .30 .09
382 Kirk Gibson GM .20 .06
383 Roger Maris GM .30 .09
384 Cal Ripken GM .75 .23
385 Hank Aaron GM .50 .15
386 Joe Carter GM .20 .06
387 Cal Ripken SH 1.50 .45
388 Randy Johnson SH .30 .09
389 Ken Griffey Jr. SH .75 .23
390 Troy Glaus SH .20 .06
391 Kazuhiro Sasaki SH .20 .06
392 Sammy Sosa LL .30 .09
Troy Glaus
393 Todd Helton LL .20 .06
Edgar Martinez
394 Todd Helton LL .50 .15
Nomar Garicaparra
395 Barry Bonds LL .50 .15
Jason Giambi
396 Todd Helton LL .20 .06
Manny Ramirez
397 Todd Helton LL .20 .06
Darin Erstad
398 Kevin Brown LL .30 .09
Pedro Martinez
399 Randy Johnson LL .30 .09
Pedro Martinez
400 Will Clark HL .50 .15
401 New York Mets HL .50 .15
402 New York Yankees HL .75 .23
403 Seattle Mariners HL .20 .06
404 Mike Hampton HL .20 .06
405 New York Yankees HL 1.00 .30
406 N.Y. Yankees Champs 2.00 .60
407 Jeff Bagwell .30 .09
408 Brant Brown .20 .06
409 Brad Fullmer .20 .06
410 Dean Palmer .20 .06
411 Greg Zaun .20 .06
412 Jose Vizcaino .20 .06
413 Jeff Abbott .20 .06
414 Travis Fryman .20 .06
415 Mike Cameron .20 .06
416 Matt Mantei .20 .06
417 Alan Benes .20 .06
418 Mickey Morandini .20 .06
419 Troy Percival .20 .06
420 Eddie Perez .20 .06
421 Vernon Wells .20 .06
422 Ricky Gutierrez .20 .06
423 Carlos Hernandez .20 .06
424 Chan Ho Park .20 .06
425 Armando Benitez .20 .06
426 Sidney Ponson .20 .06
427 Adrian Brown .20 .06
428 Ruben Mateo .20 .06
429 Alex Ochoa .20 .06
430 Jose Rosado .20 .06
431 Masato Yoshii .20 .06
432 Corey Koskie .20 .06
433 Andy Pettitte .30 .09
434 Brian Daubach .20 .06
435 Sterling Hitchcock .20 .06
436 Timo Perez .20 .06
437 Shawn Estes .20 .06
438 Tony Armas Jr. .20 .06
439 Danny Bautista .20 .06
440 Randy Winn .20 .06
441 Wilson Alvarez .20 .06
442 Rondell White .20 .06
443 Jeromy Burnitz .20 .06
444 Kelvim Escobar .20 .06
445 Paul Bako .20 .06
446 Javier Vazquez .20 .06
447 Eric Gagne .50 .15
448 Kenny Lofton .20 .06
449 Mark Kotsay .20 .06
450 Jamie Moyer .20 .06
451 Delino DeShields .20 .06
452 Rey Ordonez .20 .06
453 Russ Ortiz .20 .06
454 Dave Burba .20 .06
455 Eric Karros .20 .06
456 Felix Martinez .20 .06
457 Tony Batista .20 .06
458 Bobby Higginson .20 .06
459 Jeff D'Amico .20 .06
460 Shane Spencer .20 .06
461 Brent Mayne .20 .06
462 Glendon Rusch .20 .06
463 Chris Gomez .20 .06
464 Jeff Shaw .20 .06
465 Damon Buford .20 .06
466 Mike DiFelice .20 .06
467 Jimmy Haynes .20 .06
468 Billy Wagner .20 .06
469 A.J. Hinch .20 .06
470 Gary DiSarcina .20 .06
471 Tom Lampkin .20 .06
472 Adam Eaton .20 .06
473 Brian Giles .20 .06
474 John Thomson .20 .06
475 Cal Eldred .20 .06
476 Ramiro Mendoza .20 .06
477 Scott Sullivan .20 .06
478 Scott Rolen .50 .15
479 Todd Ritchie .20 .06
480 Pablo Ozuna .20 .06
481 Carl Pavano .20 .06
482 Matt Morris .20 .06
483 Matt Stairs .20 .06
484 Tim Belcher .20 .06
485 Lance Berkman .20 .06
486 Brian Meadows .20 .06
487 Bob Abreu .20 .06
488 John VanderWal .20 .06
489 Donnie Sadler .20 .06
490 Damion Easley .20 .06
491 David Justice .20 .06
492 Ray Durham .20 .06
493 Todd Zeile .20 .06
494 Desi Relaford .20 .06
495 Cliff Floyd .20 .06
496 Scott Downs .20 .06
497 Barry Bonds 1.25 .35
498 Jeff D'Amico .20 .06
499 Octavio Dotel .20 .06
500 Kent Mercker .20 .06
501 Craig Grebeck .20 .06
502 Roberto Hernandez .20 .06
503 Matt Williams .20 .06
504 Bruce Aven .20 .06
505 Brett Tomko .20 .06
506 Kris Benson .20 .06
507 Neifi Perez .20 .06
508 Alfonso Soriano .30 .09
509 Keith Osik .20 .06
510 Matt Franco .20 .06
511 Steve Finley .20 .06
512 Olmedo Saenz .20 .06
513 Esteban Loaiza .20 .06
514 Adam Kennedy .20 .06
515 Scott Elarton .20 .06
516 Moises Alou .20 .06
517 Bryan Rekar .20 .06
518 Darryl Hamilton .20 .06
519 Osvaldo Fernandez .20 .06
520 Kip Wells .20 .06
521 Bernie Williams .30 .09
522 Mike Darr .20 .06
523 Marlon Anderson .20 .06
524 Derrek Lee .20 .06
525 Ugueth Urbina .20 .06
526 Vinny Castilla .20 .06
527 David Wells .20 .06
528 Jason Marquis .20 .06
529 Orlando Palmeiro .20 .06
530 Carlos Perez .20 .06
531 J.T. Snow .20 .06
532 Al Leiter .20 .06
533 Jimmy Anderson .20 .06
534 Brett Laxton .20 .06
535 Butch Huskey .20 .06
536 Orlando Hernandez .20 .06
537 Magglio Ordonez .20 .06
538 Willie Blair .20 .06
539 Kevin Sefcik .20 .06
540 Chad Curtis .20 .06
541 John Halama .20 .06
542 Andy Fox .20 .06
543 Juan Guzman .20 .06
544 Frank Menechino RC .20 .06
545 Raul Mondesi .20 .06
546 Tim Salmon .30 .09
547 Ryan Rupe .20 .06
548 Jeff Reed .20 .06
549 Mike Mordecai .20 .06
550 Jeff Kent .20 .06
551 Wiki Gonzalez .20 .06
552 Kenny Rogers .20 .06
553 Kevin Young .20 .06
554 Brian Johnson .20 .06
555 Tom Goodwin .20 .06
556 Tony Clark UER .20 .06
0 games, 208 At-Bats
557 Mac Suzuki .20 .06
558 Brian Moehler .20 .06
559 Jim Parque .20 .06
560 Mariano Rivera .30 .09
561 Trot Nixon .20 .06
562 Mike Mussina .30 .09
563 Nelson Figueroa .20 .06
564 Alex Gonzalez .20 .06
565 Benny Agbayani .20 .06
566 Ed Sprague .20 .06
567 Scott Erickson .20 .06
568 Abraham Nunez .20 .06
569 Jerry DiPoto .20 .06
570 Sean Casey .20 .06
571 Wilton Veras .20 .06
572 Joe Mays .20 .06
573 Bill Simas .20 .06
574 Doug Glanville .20 .06
575 Scott Sauerbeck .20 .06
576 Ben Davis .20 .06
577 Jesus Sanchez .20 .06
578 Ricardo Rincon .20 .06
579 John Olerud .20 .06
580 Curt Schilling .20 .06
581 Alex Cora .20 .06
582 Pat Hentgen .20 .06
583 Javy Lopez .20 .06
584 Ben Grieve .20 .06
585 Frank Castillo .20 .06
586 Kevin Stocker .20 .06
587 Mark Sweeney .20 .06
588 Ray Lankford .20 .06
589 Turner Ward .20 .06
590 Felipe Crespo .20 .06
591 Omar Vizquel .30 .09
592 Mike Lieberthal .20 .06
593 Ken Griffey Jr. .75 .23
594 Troy O'Leary .20 .06
595 Dave Mlicki .20 .06
596 Manny Ramirez .30 .09
597 Mike Lansing .20 .06
598 Rich Aurilia .20 .06
599 Russell Branyan .20 .06
600 Russ Johnson .20 .06
601 Greg Colbrunn .20 .06
602 Andruw Jones .20 .06
603 Henry Blanco .20 .06
604 Jarrod Washburn .20 .06
605 Tony Eusebio .20 .06
606 Aaron Sele .20 .06
607 Charles Nagy .20 .06
608 Ryan Klesko .20 .06
609 Dante Bichette .20 .06
610 Bill Haselman .20 .06
611 Jerry Spradlin .20 .06
612 A. Rodriguez Rangers .75 .23
613 Jose Silva .20 .06
614 Darren Oliver .20 .06
615 Pat Mahomes .20 .06
616 Roberto Alomar .30 .09
617 Edgar Renteria .20 .06
618 Jon Lieber .20 .06
619 John Rocker .20 .06
620 Miguel Tejada .20 .06
621 Mo Vaughn .20 .06
622 Jose Lima .20 .06
623 Kerry Wood .50 .15
624 Mike Timlin .20 .06
625 Wil Cordero .20 .06
626 Albert Belle .20 .06
627 Bobby Jones .20 .06
628 Doug Mirabelli .20 .06
629 Jason Tyner .20 .06
630 Andy Ashby .20 .06
631 Jose Hernandez .20 .06
632 Devon White .20 .06
633 Ruben Rivera .20 .06
634 Steve Parris .20 .06
635 David McCarty .20 .06
636 Jose Canseco .50 .15
637 Todd Walker .20 .06
638 Stan Spencer .20 .06
639 Wayne Gomes .20 .06
640 Freddy Garcia .20 .06
641 Jeremy Giambi .20 .06
642 Luis Lopez .20 .06
643 John Smoltz .30 .09
644 Kelly Stinnett .20 .06
645 Kevin Brown .20 .06
646 Wilton Guerrero .20 .06
647 Al Martin .20 .06
648 Woody Williams .20 .06
649 Brian Rose .20 .06
650 Rafael Palmeiro .30 .09
651 Pete Schourek .20 .06
652 Kevin Jarvis .20 .06
653 Mark Redman .20 .06
654 Ricky Ledee .20 .06
655 Larry Walker .30 .09
656 Paul Byrd .20 .06
657 Jason Bere .20 .06
658 Rick White .20 .06
659 Calvin Murray .20 .06
660 Greg Maddux .75 .23
661 Ron Gant .20 .06
662 Eli Marrero .20 .06
663 Graeme Lloyd .20 .06
664 Trevor Hoffman .20 .06
665 Nomar Garciaparra .75 .23
666 Glenallen Hill .20 .06
667 Matt LeCroy .20 .06
668 Justin Thompson .20 .06
669 Brady Anderson .20 .06
670 Miguel Batista .20 .06
671 Erubiel Durazo .20 .06
672 Kevin Millwood .20 .06
673 Mitch Meluskey .20 .06
674 Luis Gonzalez .20 .06
675 Edgar Martinez .30 .09
676 Robert Person .20 .06
677 Benito Santiago .20 .06
678 Todd Jones .20 .06
679 Tino Martinez .30 .09
680 Carlos Beltran .30 .09
681 Gabe White .20 .06
682 Bret Saberhagen .20 .06
683 Jeff Conine .20 .06
684 Jaret Wright .20 .06
685 Bernard Gilkey .20 .06
686 Garrett Stephenson .20 .06
687 Jamey Wright .20 .06
688 Sammy Sosa .75 .23
689 John Jaha .20 .06
690 Ramon Martinez .20 .06
691 Robert Fick .20 .06
692 Eric Milton .20 .06
693 Denny Neagle .20 .06
694 Ron Coomer .20 .06
695 John Valentin .20 .06
696 Placido Polanco .20 .06
697 Tim Hudson .20 .06
698 Marty Cordova .20 .06
699 Chad Kreuter .20 .06
700 Frank Catalanotto .20 .06
701 Tim Wakefield .20 .06
702 Jim Edmonds .20 .06
703 Michael Tucker .20 .06
704 Cristian Guzman .20 .06
705 Joey Hamilton .20 .06
706 Mike Piazza .75 .23
707 Dave Martinez .20 .06
708 Mike Hampton .20 .06
709 Bobby Bonilla .20 .06
710 Juan Pierre .20 .06
711 John Parrish .20 .06
712 Kory DeHaan .20 .06
713 Brian Tollberg .20 .06
714 Chris Truby .20 .06
715 Emil Brown .20 .06
716 Ryan Dempster .20 .06
717 Rich Garces .20 .06
718 Mike Myers .20 .06
719 Luis Ordaz .20 .06
720 Kazuhiro Sasaki .20 .06
721 Mark Quinn .20 .06
722 Ramon Ortiz .20 .06
723 Kerry Ligtenberg .20 .06
724 Rolando Arrojo .20 .06
725 Tsuyoshi Shinjo RC .50 .15
726 Ichiro Suzuki RC 15.00 4.50
727 Roy Oswalt .50 .15
Pat Strange
Jon Rauch
728 Phil Wilson RC 2.00 .60
Jake Peavy RC
Darwin Cubillan RC
729 Steve Smyth RC .25 .07
Mike Bynum
Nathan Haynes
730 Michael Cuddyer .25 .07
Joe Lawrence
Choo Freeman
731 Carlos Pena .25 .07
Larry Barnes
DeWayne Wise
732 Travis Dawkins .40 .12
Erick Almonte
Felipe Lopez
733 Alex Escobar .25 .07
Eric Valent
Brad Wilkerson
734 Toby Hall .25 .07
Rod Barajas
Jeff Goldbach
735 Jason Romano .40 .12
Marcus Giles
Pablo Ozuna
736 Dee Brown .40 .12
Jack Cust
Vernon Wells
737 David Espinosa .40 .12
Luis Montanez RC
738 Anthony Pluta RC .40 .12
Justin Wayne RC
739 Josh Axelson RC .40 .12
Carmen Cali RC
740 Shaun Boyd RC .40 .12
Chris Morris RC
741 Tommy Arko RC .40 .12
Dan Moylan RC
742 Luis Cotto RC .25 .07
Luis Escobar
743 Brandon Mims RC .40 .12
Blake Williams RC
744 Chris Russ RC .25 .07
Bryan Edwards
745 Joe Torres .25 .07
Ben Diggins
746 Hugh Quattlebaum RC .50 .15
Edwin Encarnacion RC
747 Brian Bass RC .40 .12
Odannis Ayala RC
748 Jason Kaanoi .25 .07
Michael Matthews RC UER
name misspelled Mathews
749 Stuart McFarland RC .40 .12
Adam Sterrett RC
750 David Krynzel .75 .23
Grady Sizemore
751 Keith Bucktrot .25 .07
Dane Sardinha
752 Anaheim Angels TC .20 .06
753 Ariz. Diamondbacks TC .20 .06
754 Atlanta Braves TC .20 .06
755 Baltimore Orioles TC .20 .06
756 Boston Red Sox TC .20 .06
757 Chicago Cubs TC .20 .06
758 Chicago White Sox TC .20 .06
759 Cincinnati Reds TC .20 .06
760 Cleveland Indians TC .20 .06
761 Colorado Rockies TC .20 .06
762 Detroit Tigers TC .20 .06
763 Florida Marlins TC .20 .06
764 Houston Astros TC .20 .06
765 K.C. Royals TC .20 .06
766 L.A. Dodgers TC .20 .06
767 Milw. Brewers TC .20 .06
768 Minnesota Twins TC .20 .06
769 Montreal Expos TC .20 .06
770 New York Mets TC .20 .06
771 New York Yankees TC 1.00 .30
772 Oakland Athletics TC .20 .06
773 Phil. Phillies TC .20 .06
774 Pittsburgh Pirates TC .20 .06
775 San Diego Padres TC .20 .06
776 San Francisco Giants TC .20 .06
777 Seattle Mariners TC .20 .06
778 St. Louis Cardinals TC .20 .06
779 T.B. Devil Rays TC .20 .06
780 Texas Rangers TC .20 .06
781 Toronto Blue Jays TC .20 .06
782 Bucky Dent GM .20 .06
783 Jackie Robinson GM .50 .15

784 Roberto Clemente GM
785 Nolan Ryan GM
786 Kerry Wood GM
787 Rickey Henderson GM
788 Lou Brock GM
789 David Wells GM
790 Andruw Jones GM
791 Carlton Fisk GM
TK Bo Jackson
Deion Sanders Bat
NNO Bobby Thomson
Ralph Branca
1991 Bowman Autograph

2001 Topps Gold

Randomly inserted into first series packs at a rate of 1:17 Hobby/Retail and 1:4 HTA and second series packs at a rate of 1:14 Hobby/Retail and 1:3 HTA, this 790-card set is a complete parallel of the 2001 Topps base set. These cards were produced with a special gold-foil border on front and were individually serial numbered to 2001 on back. Please note that card number 7 does not exist.

*STARS: 10X TO 25X BASIC CARDS..
*PROSPECTS 352-376/725/751: 4X TO 10X
*ROOKIES 352-376/725-751: 4X TO 10X

2001 Topps Home Team Advantage

This factory-sealed 790-card set was issued exclusively to Topps network of Home Team Advantage baseball card shops. The sets were packaged in attractive gold foil boxes and each card features a distinctive "HTA" foil stamp on front.

COMP.HTA.GOLD SET (790) ... 120.00 36.00
*HTA: .75X TO 2X BASIC CARDS ......

2001 Topps Limited

These attractive cards parallel the basic 2001 Topps set. The product was distributed exclusively in factory set format. Each set contained the 790-card basic set plus five Topps Archives Reserve Future Rookie Reprints chrome inserts wrapped together in a plastic cello pack. The sets were distributed through hobby dealers in attractive wood boxes and carried a suggested retail price of $173. Each Topps Limited card was printed on 20 pt. stock paper featuring glossy fronts and backs and a "Limited Edition" gold foil logo on front. Though the cards lack individual serial-numbering, Topps announced production at 3,805 sets. Each set states that total on the bottom of the wooden box.

COMP.FACT.SET (790) 200.00 60.00
*STARS: 2X TO 5X BASIC CARDS......
*ROOKIES: 1.25X TO 3X BASIC CARDS

2001 Topps A Look Ahead

Randomly inserted into packs at 1:25 Hobby/Retail and 1:5 HTA, this 10-card insert takes a look a players that are on their way to Cooperstown. Card backs carry a "LA" prefix.

COMPLETE SET (10) 30.00 9.00
LA1 Vladimir Guerrero
LA2 Derek Jeter
LA3 Todd Helton
LA4 Alex Rodriguez
LA5 Ken Griffey Jr.
LA6 Nomar Garciaparra
LA7 Chipper Jones
LA8 Ivan Rodriguez
LA9 Pedro Martinez
LA10 Rick Ankiel

2001 Topps A Tradition Continues

Randomly inserted into packs at 1:17 Hobby/Retail and 1:5 HTA, this 30-card insert features players that look to carry the tradition of Major League Baseball well into the 21st century. Card backs carry a "TRC" prefix.

COMPLETE SET (30) 100.00 30.00
TRC1 Chipper Jones
TRC2 Cal Ripken
TRC3 Mike Piazza
TRC4 Ken Griffey Jr.
TRC5 Randy Johnson
TRC6 Derek Jeter
TRC7 Scott Rolen
TRC8 Nomar Garciaparra
TRC9 Roberto Alomar
TRC10 Greg Maddux
TRC11 Ivan Rodriguez
TRC12 Jeff Bagwell
TRC13 Alex Rodriguez
TRC14 Pedro Martinez
TRC15 Sammy Sosa
TRC16 Jim Edmonds
TRC17 Mo Vaughn
TRC18 Barry Bonds
TRC19 Larry Walker
TRC20 Mark McGwire
TRC21 Vladimir Guerrero
TRC22 Andruw Jones
TRC23 Todd Helton
TRC24 Kevin Brown
TRC25 Tony Gwynn
TRC26 Manny Ramirez
TRC27 Roger Clemens
TRC28 Frank Thomas
TRC29 Shawn Green
TRC30 Jim Thome

2001 Topps Base Hit Autograph Relics

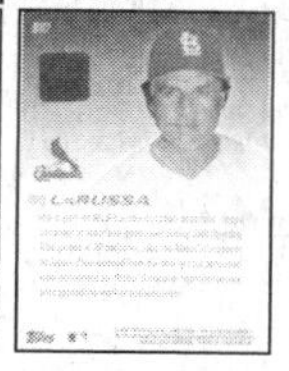

Inserted in series two packs at a rate of one in 1,1462 hobby or retail packs and one in 325 HTA packs, these 28 cards features managers along with a game-used memorabilia piece and an autograph.

BH1 Mike Scioscia
BH2 Larry Dierker
BH3 Art Howe
BH4 Jim Fregosi
BH5 Bobby Cox
BH6 Davey Lopes
BH7 Tony LaRussa
BH8 Don Baylor
BH9 Larry Rothschild
BH10 Buck Showalter
BH11 Davey Johnson
BH12 Felipe Alou
BH13 Charlie Manuel
BH14 Lou Piniella
BH15 John Boles
BH16 Bobby Valentine
BH17 Mike Hargrove
BH18 Bruce Bochy
BH19 Terry Francona
BH20 Gene Lamont
BH21 Johnny Oates
BH22 Jimy Williams
BH23 Jack McKeon
BH24 Buddy Bell
BH25 Tony Muser
BH26 Phil Garner
BH27 Tom Kelly
BH28 Jerry Manuel

2001 Topps Before There Was Topps

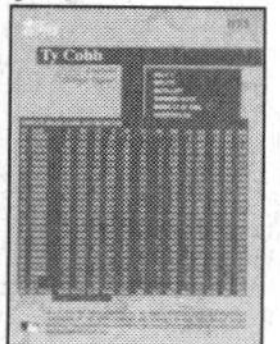

Issued in series two packs at a rate of one in 25 hobby/retail packs and one in five HTA packs; these 10 cards feature superstars who concluded their career before Topps started their dominance of the card market.

COMPLETE SET (10) 40.00 12.00
BT1 Lou Gehrig
BT2 Babe Ruth
BT3 Cy Young
BT4 Walter Johnson
BT5 Ty Cobb
BT6 Rogers Hornsby
BT7 Honus Wagner
BT8 Christy Mathewson
BT9 Grover Alexander
BT10 Joe DiMaggio

2001 Topps Combos

Randomly inserted into packs at a rate of 1:12 Hobby/Retail and 1:4 HTA, this 20-card insert set pairs up players that have put up similar statistics throughout their carrers. Card backs carry a "TC" prefix. Instead of having photographs, these cards feature drawings of the featured players.

COMPLETE SET (20) 60.00 18.00
COMPLETE SERIES 1 (10) 30.00 9.00
COMPLETE SERIES 2 (10) 30.00 9.00
TC1 Derek Jeter
Yogi Berra
Whitey Ford
Don Mattingly
Reggie Jackson
TC2 Chipper Jones
Mike Schmidt
TC3 Brooks Robinson
Cal Ripken
TC4 Bob Gibson
Pedro Martinez
TC5 Ivan Rodriguez
Johnny Bench
TC6 Ernie Banks
Alex Rodriguez
TC7 Joe Morgan
Ken Griffey Jr.
Barry Larkin
Johnny Bench
TC8 Vladimir Guerrero
Roberto Clemente
TC9 Ken Griffey Jr.
Hank Aaron
TC10 Casey Stengel MG
Joe Torre MG
TC11 Kevin Brown
Sandy Koufax
Don Drysdale UER
Card states the Dodgers swept the 1965 World Series
They won the Series in 7 games
TC12 Mark McGwire
Sammy Sosa
Roger Maris
Babe Ruth
TC13 Ted Williams
Carl Yastrzemski
Nomar Garciaparra
TC14 Greg Maddux
Roger Clemens
Cy Young
TC15 Tony Gwynn
Ted Williams
TC16 Cal Ripken
Lou Gehrig
TC17 Sandy Koufax
Randy Johnson
Warren Spahn
Steve Carlton
TC18 Mike Piazza
Josh Gibson
TC19 Barry Bonds
Willie Mays
TC20 Jackie Robinson
Larry Doby

2001 Topps Golden Anniversary

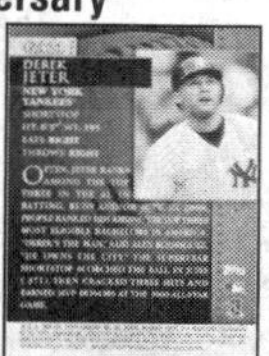

Randomly inserted into packs at 1:10 Hobby/Retail and 1:1 HTA, this 50-card insert celibrates Topps's 50th Anniversary by taking a look at some of the all-time greats. Card backs carry a "GA" prefix.

COMPLETE SET (50) 80.00 24.00
GA1 Hank Aaron
GA2 Ernie Banks
GA3 Mike Schmidt
GA4 Willie Mays
GA5 Johnny Bench
GA6 Tom Seaver
GA7 Frank Robinson
GA8 Sandy Koufax
GA9 Bob Gibson
GA10 Ted Williams
GA11 Cal Ripken
GA12 Tony Gwynn
GA13 Mark McGwire
GA14 Ken Griffey Jr.
GA15 Greg Maddux
GA16 Roger Clemens
GA17 Barry Bonds
GA18 Rickey Henderson
GA19 Mike Piazza
GA20 Jose Canseco
GA21 Derek Jeter
GA22 N.Garciaparra UER
Card has incorrect bat and throw information
Garciaparra bats and throws righthanded
GA23 Alex Rodriguez
GA24 Sammy Sosa
GA25 Ivan Rodriguez
GA26 Vladimir Guerrero
GA27 Chipper Jones
GA28 Jeff Bagwell
GA29 Pedro Martinez
GA30 Randy Johnson
GA31 Pat Burrell
GA32 Josh Hamilton
GA33 Ryan Anderson
GA34 Corey Patterson
GA35 Eric Munson
GA36 Sean Burroughs
GA37 C.C. Sabathia
GA38 Chin-Feng Chen
GA39 Barry Zito
GA40 Adrian Gonzalez
GA41 Mark McGwire
GA42 Nomar Garciaparra
GA43 Todd Helton
GA44 Matt Williams
GA45 Troy Glaus
GA46 Geoff Jenkins
GA47 Frank Thomas
GA48 Mo Vaughn
GA49 Barry Larkin
GA50 J.D. Drew

2001 Topps Golden Anniversary Autographs

Randomly inserted into packs, this 98-card insert features authentic autographs of both modern day and former greats. Card backs carry a "GAA" prefix followed by the players initials. Please note that the Andy Pafko, Lou Brock, Rafael Furcal and Todd Zeile cards all packed out in series one packs as exchange cards with a redemption deadline of November 30th, 2001. In addition, Carlos Silva, Eddy Furniss, Phil Merrell and Carlos Silva packed out as exchange cards in series two packs with a redemption deadline of April 30th, 2003.

GAA-AG A.Gonzalez G
GAA-AH Aaron Herr I2
GAA-AJ A. Johnson G1-I2
GAA-AO Augie Ojeda B2
GAA-AP Andy Pafko C1
GAA-BB Barry Bonds B2
GAA-BE Brian Esposito I2
GAA-BG Bob Gibson C2
GAA-BK Bobby Kielty I2
GAA-BO Ben Oglivie D2
GAA-BR B.Robinson B
GAA-BT Brian Tollberg I2
GAA-CC Chris Clapinski I2
GAA-CD Chad Durbin I2
GAA-CE Carl Erskine D2
GAA-CJ Chipper Jones B1
GAA-CL Colby Lewis I2
GAA-CR Chris Richard I2
GAA-CS Carlos Silva I2
GAA-CY C. Yastrzemski C2
GAA-DA Dick Allen C1
GAA-DA Denny Abreu I2
GAA-DG Dick Groat D2
GAA-DT D. Thompson I2
GAA-EB Ernie Banks B1
GAA-EB Eric Byrnes I2
GAA-EF Eddy Furniss I2
GAA-EM Eric Munson G2
GAA-ER E. Ramirez I2
GAA-GB George Bell D2
GAA-GG G. Guzman I2
GAA-GM G. Matthews Jr. D2
GAA-GS G. Sizemore I2
GAA-GT G.Templeton C
GAA-HA Hank Aaron B1
GAA-JB Johnny Bench C2
GAA-JC Jorge Cantu I2
GAA-JL John Lackey I2
GAA-JM J. Marquis G1
GAA-JR Joe Rudi C1
GAA-JR Juan Rincon I2
GAA-JS Juan Salas I2
GAA-JV Jose Vidro F1
GAA-JW Justin Wayne H2
GAA-KG Kevin Gregg B2
GAA-KH Ken Holtzman D2
GAA-KT Kent Tekulve D2
GAA-LB Lou Brock B1
GAA-LM L. Montanez H2
GAA-LR Luis Rivas I2
GAA-MB M. Bradley G2
GAA-MC Mike Cuellar C1
GAA-MG M. Glendenning I2
GAA-ML Matt Lawton F2
GAA-ML Mike Lamb G1
GAA-MO M.Ordonez B
GAA-MS Mike Schmidt B1
GAA-MS Mike Sweeney F2
GAA-MS Mike Stodolka I2
GAA-MW M.Wheatland G
GAA-MW M. Wenner I2
GAA-NG Nick Green I2
GAA-NJ Neil Jenkins I2
GAA-NR Nolan Ryan A2
GAA-PB Pat Burrell G1
GAA-PM Phil Merrell I2
GAA-RA Rick Ankiel D1
GAA-RB R. Baldelli G1-I2
GAA-RC Rod Carew B1
GAA-RF Rafael Furcal G1
GAA-RJ R. Jackson A2
GAA-RS Ron Swoboda C1
GAA-SH Scott Heard G1
GAA-SK Sandy Koufax A1
GAA-SM Stan Musial A2
GAA-SR Scott Rolen F2
GAA-ST Scott Thorman I2
GAA-TA Tony Alvarez I2
GAA-TH Todd Helton B2
GAA-TJ T. Johnson I2
GAA-TS Tom Seaver A2
GAA-VL Vernon Law C1
GAA-WD Willie Davis D2
GAA-WF Whitey Ford C2
GAA-WH W.Hernandez C
GAA-WM Willie Mays A1
GAA-WW Wilbur Wood D2
GAA-YB Yogi Berra B1
GAA-YH Yamid Haad I2
GAA-YT Y. Torrealba I2
GAA-CCS Corey Smith I2
GAA-GHB George Brett A2
GAA-JDD J.D. Drew E2
GAA-MAB Mike Bynum I2
GAA-MFL M. Lockwood I2
GAA-MJS M. Stodolka G1
GAA-MJW M. Wheatland I2
GAA-TDLR T. De la Rosa I2

2001 Topps Hit Parade Relics

Issued in retail packs at odds of one in 2,607 these six cards feature players who have achieved major career milestones along with a piece of memorabilia.

HP1 Reggie Jackson
HP2 Dave Winfield
HP3 Eddie Murray
HP4 Rickey Henderson
HP5 Robin Yount
HP6 Carl Yastrzemski

2001 Topps King of Kings Relics

Randomly inserted into packs at 1:2056 Hobby/Retail and 1:457 HTA, this four-card insert features game-used memorabilia from Nolan Ryan, Rickey Henderson, and Hank Aaron. Please note that a special fourth card containing game-used memorabila of all three were inserted into HTA packs at 1:8903. Card backs carry a "KKG" prefix.

KKR1 Hank Aaron
KKR2 Nolan Ryan
KKR3 Rickey Henderson
KKR4 Mark McGwire B
KKR5 Bob Gibson A
KKR6 Nolan Ryan B
KKGE Hank Aaron
Nolan Ryan
Rickey Henderson
KKLE2 Mark Mcgwire
Bob Gibson
Nolan Ryan

2001 Topps Noteworthy

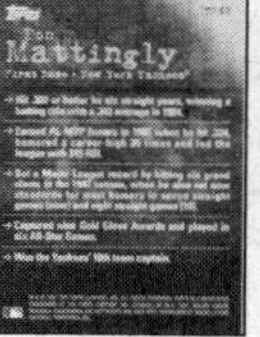

Inserted in hobby/retail packs at a rate of one in eight and HTA packs at a rate of one per pack; this 50-card set feature a mix of active and retired players who achieved significant feats during their career.

COMPLETE SET (50) 80.00 24.00
TN1 Mark McGwire
TN2 Derek Jeter
TN3 Sammy Sosa
TN4 Todd Helton
TN5 Alex Rodriguez
TN6 Chipper Jones
TN7 Barry Bonds
TN8 Ken Griffey Jr.
TN9 Nomar Garciaparra
TN10 Frank Thomas
TN11 Randy Johnson
TN12 Cal Ripken
TN13 Mike Piazza
TN14 Ivan Rodriguez
TN15 Jeff Bagwell
TN16 Vladimir Guerrero
TN17 Greg Maddux
TN18 Tony Gwynn
TN19 Larry Walker
TN20 Juan Gonzalez
TN21 Scott Rolen
TN22 Jason Giambi
TN23 Jeff Kent
TN24 Pat Burrell
TN25 Pedro Martinez
TN26 Willie Mays
TN27 Whitey Ford
TN28 Jackie Robinson
TN29 Ted Williams UER
Card has wrong year for his last at-bat
TN30 Babe Ruth
TN31 Warren Spahn
TN32 Nolan Ryan
TN33 Yogi Berra
TN34 Mike Schmidt
TN35 Steve Carlton
TN36 Brooks Robinson
TN37 Bob Gibson
TN38 Reggie Jackson
TN39 Johnny Bench
TN40 Ernie Banks
TN41 Eddie Mathews

TN42 Don Mattingly 5.00 1.50
TN43 Duke Snider 1.00 .30
TN44 Hank Aaron 4.00 1.20
TN45 Roberto Clemente 5.00 1.50
TN46 Harmon Killebrew 1.50 .45
TN47 Frank Robinson 1.00 .30
TN48 Stan Musial 3.00 .90
TN49 Lou Brock 1.00 .30
TN50 Joe Morgan 1.00 .30

2001 Topps Originals Relics

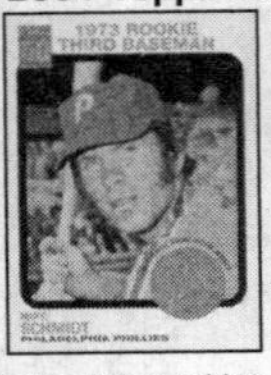

Randomly inserted into packs at different rates depening which series these cards were inserted in, this ten-card insert set features game-used jersey cards of players like Roberto Clemente and Carl Yastrzemski. Please note that the Willie Mays card is actually a game-used jacket.

Nm-Mt Ex-Mt
SER.1 STATED ODDS 1:1172 H/R, 1:260 HTA
SER.2 STATED ODDS 1:1023 H/R, 1:227 HTA
1 Roberto Clemente 55 100.00 30.00
2 Carl Yastrzemski 60 40.00 12.00
3 Mike Schmidt 73 40.00 12.00
4 Wade Boggs 83 25.00 7.50
5 Chipper Jones 91 25.00 7.50
6 Willie Mays 52 50.00 15.00
7 Lou Brock 62 25.00 7.50
8 Dave Parker 74 15.00 4.50
9 Barry Bonds 86 50.00 15.00
10 Alex Rodriguez 98 25.00 7.50

2001 Topps Team Topps Legends Autographs

These signed cards were inserted into various 2001-2003 Topps products. As these cards were inserted into different products and some were exchange cards. Most players in this set were featured on reprinted versions of their classic Topps "rookie" and "final" cards. The checklist was originally comprised of cards TT1-TT50 (with each player having an R and F suffix (i.e. Willie Mays is featured on TT1F with his 1973 card and TT1R with his 1952 card). In late 2002 and throughout 2003, additional players were added to the set with checklist numbering outside of the TT1-TT50 schematic. The numbering for these late additions was based on player's initials (i.e. Lou Brock's card is TT-LB) and only reprints of their rookie-year cards were produced.

Nm-Mt Ex-Mt
RANDOM INSERTS IN 01-03 TOPPS BRANDS
TOPPS AMER.PIE EXCH.DEADLINE 11/01/03
TOPPS GALLERY EXCH.DEADLINE 06/30/03
02 TOPPS EXCH.DEADLINE 12/01/03.
TT1F Willie Mays 73 120.00 36.00
T'02-TA'02/A
TT1R Willie Mays 52 150.00 45.00
AP
TT2F Hank Aaron 76
TT2R Hank Aaron 54
TT3F Stan Musial 63
TT3R Stan Musial 58 AS 60.00 18.00
TT4F Ernie Banks 71
TT4R Ernie Banks 54
TT5F Yogi Berra 65
TT5R Yogi Berra 52
TT6F Whitey Ford 67 25.00 7.50
TT/A-T10'02
TT6R Whitey Ford 53 25.00 7.50
T'02/F-TA'02/B
TT7F Nolan Ryan 94
TT7R Nolan Ryan 68 250.00 75.00
T206'02/A-TA'02/A
TT8F Carl Yastrzemski 83 50.00 15.00
TT8R Carl Yastrzemski 60 60.00 18.00
AP-T'02/A-TA'02/B-T10'02
TT9F Brooks Robinson 77
TT9R Brooks Robinson 57 50.00 15.00
TT10F Frank Robinson 75 25.00 7.50
BH5-TH'02/2
TT10R Frank Robinson 57 40.00 12.00
GL-T'02/A-TA'02/B
TT11F Tom Seaver 87
TT11R Tom Seaver 67 80.00 24.00
TA'02/A
TT12F Duke Snider 64
TT12R Duke Snider 52 40.00 12.00
TT13F Warren Spahn 65 40.00 12.00
BH1-TT-T'02/B-TA'02/B
TT13R Warren Spahn 52 40.00 12.00
AP-BB/A-TT/C
TT14F Johnny Bench 83 50.00 15.00
TT14R Johnny Bench 68 100.00 30.00
AP
TT15F Reggie Jackson 87
TT15R Reggie Jackson 69 100.00 30.00
AP-TA'02/A
TT16F Al Kaline 74
TT16R Al Kaline 54 50.00 15.00
TT17F Willie McCovey 80
TT17R Willie McCovey 60
TT18F Bob Gibson 75 25.00 7.50
AP'02
TT18R Bob Gibson 59 40.00 12.00
AP-BB/A-T'02/A
TT19F Mike Schmidt 89
TT19R Mike Schmidt 73 120.00 36.00
TT20F Harmon Killebrew 75
TT20R Harmon Killebrew 55 60.00 18.00
TT21F Bob Feller 56
TT21R Bob Feller 52 BH2 15.00 4.50
TT23F Gil McDougald 60 15.00 4.50
GL-TA'02/B
TT23R Gil McDougald 52 15.00 4.50
BB/B
TT24F Jimmy Piersall 67
TT24R Jimmy Piersall 56
TT25F Luis Tiant 83 15.00 4.50
GL EXCH
TT25R Luis Tiant 65 15.00 4.50
AP-BB/B-'02 TA/B
TT26F Minnie Minoso 64
TT26R Minnie Minoso 52
TT27F Andy Pafko 59 25.00 7.50
GL
TT27R Andy Pafko 52 25.00 7.50
BB/B-BH/3-GL
TT28F Herb Score 62 15.00 4.50
BB/B-GL-TT/B
TT28R Herb Score 56 15.00 4.50
BB/B-TA'02/B
TT29F Bill Skowron 67 15.00 4.50
TT29R Bill Skowron 54 15.00 4.50
AP-BB/A-T206'02/C
TT30F Maury Wills 72
TT30R Maury Wills 67
TT31F Clete Boyer 71 15.00 4.50
TA'02/B
TT31R Clete Boyer 57 15.00 4.50
AP-BB/B
TT32F Hank Bauer 61
TT32R Hank Bauer 52
TT33F Vida Blue 87 15.00 4.50
T'02/C/TR
TT33R Vida Blue 70 15.00 4.50
AP-T206'02/B-TH'02/4
TT34F Don Larsen 65
TT34R Don Larsen 56 25.00 7.50
TT35F Joe Pepitone 73 10.00 3.00
TT/A
TT35R Joe Pepitone 62 10.00 3.00
AP
TT36F Enos Slaughter 59 25.00 7.50
BH4-TT/A
TT36R Enos Slaughter 52 25.00 7.50
TAR'02
TT37F Tug McGraw 85 25.00 7.50
BB/B
TT37R Tug McGraw 65 40.00 12.00
AP-BB/B-TT/B
TT38F Fergie Jenkins 84
TT38R Fergie Jenkins 66 15.00 4.50
TT39F Willie Hernandez 89
TT39R Willie Hernandez 78
TT40F Gaylord Perry 83
TT40R Gaylord Perry 62 15.00 4.50
TT41F Carlton Fisk 93
TT41R Carlton Fisk 72
TT42F Kirk Gibson 95
TT42R Kirk Gibson 81
TT43F Bobby Thomson 60 15.00 4.50
TT-TH'02/3
TT43R Bobby Thomson 52 15.00 4.50
AP-TT/D-T'02/B-T10'02
TT44F Juan Marichal 74
TT44R Juan Marichal 61
TT45F Dom DiMaggio 53
TT45R Dom DiMaggio 52
TT46F Robin Roberts 66 T'02/E 25.00 7.50
TT46R Robin Roberts 52
TT47F Frank Howard 73 15.00 4.50
TT/A-TH'02/1
TT47R Frank Howard 60 15.00 4.50
AP-T'02/D-TA'02/B
TT48F Bobby Richardson 66 15.00 4.50
TT/A-T'02/B-T10'02
TT48R Bobby Richardson 57 15.00 4.50
AP-BB/B
TT49F Tony Kubek 65
TT49R Tony Kubek 57 60.00 18.00
AP-TA/B
TT50F Mickey Lolich 80 15.00 4.50
TT/A
TT50R Mickey Lolich 64 15.00 4.50
AP-T'02/C-TA'02/B-TH'02/1
TT51RF Ralph Branca 52 15.00 4.50
TT/D-T'02/E
TT-GC Gary Carter 75 15.00 4.50
TT-GG Goose Gossage 73 15.00 4.50
TAR'02
TT-GN Craig Nettles 69 15.00 4.50
02 'TAR
TT-JB Jim Bunning 65 40.00 12.00
TT-JM Joe Morgan 65 40.00 12.00
TT-JP Jim Palmer 66 15.00 4.50
TAR '02
TT-JS Johnny Sain 52 15.00 4.50
TT-LA Luis Aparicio 56 15.00 4.50
TT-LB Lou Brock 62 40.00 12.00
TT-PB Paul Blair 65 10.00 3.00
TT-RY Robin Yount 75 80.00 24.00
TT-VL Vern Law 52 15.00 4.50

2001 Topps Through the Years Reprints

Randomly inserted into packs at 1:8 Hobby/Retail and 1:1 HTA, this 50-card set takes a look at some of the best players to every make it onto a Topps trading card.

Nm-Mt Ex-Mt
COMPLETE SET (50) 120.00 36.00
1 Yogi Berra '57 3.00 .90
2 Roy Campanella '56 3.00 .90
3 Willie Mays '53 5.00 1.50
4 Andy Pafko '52 3.00 .90
5 Jackie Robinson '52 3.00 .90
6 Stan Musial '59 4.00 1.20
7 Duke Snider '56 3.00 .90
8 Warren Spahn '56 3.00 .90
9 Ted Williams '54 UER 8.00 2.40
Williams is spelled William
Also wrong birthdate
10 Eddie Mathews '55 3.00 .90
11 Willie McCovey '60 3.00 .90
12 Frank Robinson '69 3.00 .90
13 Ernie Banks '66 3.00 .90
14 Hank Aaron '65 5.00 1.50
15 Sandy Koufax '61 6.00 1.80
16 Bob Gibson '68 3.00 .90
17 Harmon Killebrew '67 3.00 .90
18 Whitey Ford '64 3.00 .90
19 Roberto Clemente '63 8.00 2.40
20 Juan Marichal '62 3.00 .90
21 Johnny Bench '70 3.00 .90
22 Willie Stargell '73 3.00 .90
23 Joe Morgan '74 3.00 .90
24 Carl Yastrzemski '71 4.00 1.20
25 Reggie Jackson '76 3.00 .90
26 Tom Seaver '78 3.00 .90
27 Steve Carlton '77 3.00 .90
28 Jim Palmer '79 3.00 .90
29 Rod Carew '72 3.00 .90
30 George Brett '75 8.00 2.40
31 Roger Clemens '85 6.00 1.80
32 Don Mattingly '84 10.00 3.00
33 Ryne Sandberg '89 5.00 1.50
34 Mike Schmidt '81 5.00 1.50
35 Cal Ripken '82 10.00 3.00
36 Tony Gwynn '83 4.00 1.20
37 Ozzie Smith '87 5.00 1.50
38 Wade Boggs '88 3.00 .90
39 Nolan Ryan '80 6.00 1.80
40 Robin Yount '86 5.00 1.50
41 Mark McGwire '99 6.00 1.80
42 Ken Griffey Jr. '92 4.00 1.20
43 Sammy Sosa '90 4.00 1.20
44 Alex Rodriguez '98 4.00 1.20
45 Barry Bonds '94 6.00 1.80
46 Mike Piazza '95 4.00 1.20
47 Chipper Jones '91 3.00 .90
48 Greg Maddux '96 4.00 1.20
49 Nomar Garciaparra '97 4.00 1.20
50 Derek Jeter '93 8.00 2.40

2001 Topps What Could Have Been

Inserted at a rate of one in 25 hobby/retail packs or one in five HTA packs, these 10 cards feature stars of the Negro leagues who never got to play in the majors while they were at their peak.

Nm-Mt Ex-Mt
COMPLETE SET (10) 25.00 7.50
WCB1 Josh Gibson 5.00 1.50
WCB2 Satchel Paige 3.00 .90
WCB3 Buck Leonard 2.00 .60
WCB4 James Bell 3.00 .90
WCB5 Rube Foster 3.00 .90
WCB6 Martin DiHigo 2.00 .60
WCB7 William Johnson 2.00 .60
WCB8 Mule Suttles 2.00 .60
WCB9 Ray Dandridge 2.00 .60
WCB10 John Lloyd 2.00 .60

2001 Topps Traded

The 2001 Topps Traded product was released in October 2001, and features a 265-card base set. The 2001 Topps Traded and the 2001 Topps Chrome Traded were combined and sold together. Each pack contained eight 2001 Topps Traded and two 2001 Topps Chrome Traded cards for a total of ten cards in each pack. The 265-card set is broken down as follows: 99 cards highlighting player deals made during the 2000 off-season and 2001 season; 60 future stars who have never appeared alone on a Topps card; 55 rookies who make their premiere on a Topps card; six managers (T145-T150) who've either switched teams or were newly hired for the 2001 season and 45 traded repints (T100 through T144) of rookie cards featured in past Topps Traded sets. The packs carried a 3.00 per pack SRP and came 24 packs to a box.

Nm-Mt Ex-Mt
COMPLETE SET (265) 100.00 30.00
COMMON (T1-T99/T145-T265) .40 .12
COMMON (100-144) 1.00 .30
T1 Sandy Alomar Jr. .40 .12
T2 Kevin Appier .50 .15
T3 Brad Ausmus .40 .12
T4 Derek Bell .40 .12
T5 Bret Boone .50 .15
T6 Rico Brogna .40 .12
T7 Ellis Burks .50 .15
T8 Ken Caminiti .50 .15
T9 Roger Cedeno .40 .12
T10 Royce Clayton .40 .12
T11 Enrique Wilson .40 .12
T12 Rheal Cormier .40 .12
T13 Eric Davis .50 .15
T14 Shawon Dunston .40 .12
T15 Andres Galarraga .50 .15
T16 Tom Gordon .40 .12
T17 Mark Grace .75 .23
T18 Jeffrey Hammonds .40 .12
T19 Dustin Hermanson .40 .12
T20 Quinton McCracken .40 .12
T21 Todd Hundley .40 .12
T22 Charles Johnson .50 .15
T23 Marquis Grissom .50 .15
T24 Jose Mesa .40 .12
T25 Brian Boehringer .40 .12
T26 John Rocker .40 .12
T27 Jeff Frye .40 .12
T28 Reggie Sanders .40 .12
T29 David Segui .40 .12
T30 Mike Sirotka .40 .12
T31 Fernando Tatis .40 .12
T32 Steve Trachsel .40 .12
T33 Ismael Valdes .40 .12
T34 Randy Velarde .40 .12
T35 Ryan Kohlmeier .40 .12
T36 Mike Bordick .50 .15
T37 Kent Bottenfield .40 .12
T38 Pat Rapp .40 .12
T39 Jeff Nelson .40 .12
T40 Ricky Bottalico .40 .12
T41 Luke Prokopec .40 .12
T42 Hideo Nomo 1.25 .35
T43 Bill Mueller .50 .15
T44 Roberto Kelly .40 .12
T45 Chris Holt .40 .12
T46 Mike Jackson .40 .12
T47 Devon White .50 .15
T48 Gerald Williams .40 .12
T49 Eddie Taubensee .40 .12
T50 Brian Hunter UER .40 .12
Brian R Hunter pictured
Brian L Hunter stats
T51 Nelson Cruz .40 .12
T52 Jeff Fassero .40 .12
T53 Bubba Trammell .40 .12
T54 Bo Porter .40 .12
T55 Greg Norton .40 .12
T56 Benito Santiago .50 .15
T57 Ruben Rivera .40 .12
T58 Dee Brown .40 .12
T59 Jose Canseco UER 1.25 .35
2000 strikeout totals are wrong
T60 Chris Michalak .40 .12
T61 Tim Worrell .40 .12
T62 Matt Clement .40 .12
T63 Bill Pulsipher .40 .12
T64 Troy Brohawn RC .40 .12
T65 Mark Kotsay .40 .12
T66 Jimmy Rollins .50 .15
T67 Shea Hillenbrand .50 .15
T68 Ted Lilly .40 .12
T69 Jermaine Dye .50 .15
T70 Jerry Hairston Jr. .40 .12
T71 John Mabry .40 .12
T72 Kurt Abbott .40 .12
T73 Eric Owens .40 .12
T74 Jeff Brantley .40 .12
T75 Roy Oswalt .75 .23
T76 Doug Mientkiewicz .50 .15
T77 Rickey Henderson 1.25 .35
T78 Jason Grimsley .40 .12
T79 Christian Parker RC .40 .12
T80 Donne Wall .40 .12
T81 Alex Arias .40 .12
T82 Willis Roberts .40 .12
T83 Ryan Minor .40 .12
T84 Jason LaRue .40 .12
T85 Ruben Sierra .40 .12
T86 Johnny Damon .75 .23
T87 Juan Gonzalez .75 .23
T88 C.C. Sabathia .50 .15
T89 Tony Batista .50 .15
T90 Jay Witasick .40 .12
T91 Brent Abernathy .40 .12
T92 Paul LoDuca .50 .15
T93 Wes Helms .40 .12
T94 Mark Wohlers .40 .12
T95 Rob Bell .40 .12
T96 Tim Redding .40 .12
T97 Bud Smith RC .40 .12
T98 Adam Dunn .75 .23
T99 Ichiro Suzuki 20.00 6.00
Albert Pujols ROY
T100 Carlton Fisk 81 1.25 .35
T101 Tim Raines 81 1.00 .30
T102 Juan Marichal 74 1.00 .30
T103 Dave Winfield 81 1.00 .30
T104 Reggie Jackson 82 1.25 .35
T105 Cal Ripken 82 6.00 1.80
T106 Ozzie Smith 82 3.00 .90
T107 Tom Seaver 83 1.25 .35
T108 Lou Piniella 74 1.00 .30
T109 Dwight Gooden 84 1.00 .30
T110 Bret Saberhagen 84 1.00 .30
T111 Gary Carter 85 1.00 .30
T112 Jack Clark 85 1.00 .30
T113 R. Henderson 85 2.00 .60
T114 Barry Bonds 86 5.00 1.50
T115 Bobby Bonilla 86 1.00 .30
T116 Jose Canseco 86 2.00 .60
T117 Will Clark 86 1.00 .30
T118 Andres Galarraga 86 1.00 .30
T119 Bo Jackson 86 2.00 .60
T120 Wally Joyner 86 1.00 .30
T121 Ellis Burks 87 1.00 .30
T122 David Cone 87 1.00 .30
T123 Greg Maddux 87 3.00 .90
T124 Willie Randolph 76 1.00 .30
T125 Dennis Eckersley 87 1.00 .30
T126 Matt Williams 87 1.00 .30
T127 Joe Morgan 81 1.00 .30
T128 Fred McGriff 87 1.25 .35
T129 Roberto Alomar 88 1.25 .35
T130 Lee Smith 88 1.00 .30
T131 David Wells 88 1.00 .30
T132 Ken Griffey Jr. 89 3.00 .90
T133 Deion Sanders 89 1.25 .35
T134 Nolan Ryan 89 4.00 1.20
T135 David Justice 90 1.00 .30
T136 Joe Carter 91 1.00 .30
T137 Jack Morris 92 1.00 .30
T138 Mike Piazza 93 3.00 .90
T139 Barry Bonds 93 5.00 1.50
T140 Terrence Long 94 1.00 .30
T141 Ben Grieve 94 1.00 .30
T142 Richie Sexson 95 1.00 .30
George Arias
Mark Sweeney
Brian Schneider
T143 Sean Burroughs 99 1.00 .30
T144 Alfonso Soriano 99 1.25 .35
T145 Bob Boone MG .50 .15
T146 Larry Bowa MG .50 .15
T147 Bob Brenly MG .40 .12
T148 Buck Martinez MG .40 .12
T149 L. McClendon MG .40 .12
T150 Jim Tracy MG .40 .12
T151 Jared Abruzzo RC .40 .12
T152 Kurt Ainsworth .40 .12
T153 Willie Bloomquist .50 .15
T154 Ben Broussard .40 .12
T155 Bobby Bradley .40 .12
T156 Mike Bynum .40 .12
T157 A.J. Hinch .40 .12
T158 Ryan Christianson .40 .12
T159 Carlos Silva .40 .12
T160 Joe Crede .40 .12
T161 Jack Cust .40 .12
T162 Ben Diggins .40 .12
T163 Phil Dumatrait .40 .12
T164 Alex Escobar .40 .12
T165 Miguel Olivo .40 .12
T166 Chris George .40 .12
T167 Marcus Giles .50 .15
T168 Keith Ginter .40 .12
T169 Josh Girdley .40 .12
T170 Tony Alvarez .40 .12
T171 Scott Seabol .40 .12
T172 Josh Hamilton .40 .12
T173 Jason Hart .40 .12
T174 Israel Alcantara .40 .12
T175 Jake Peavy 1.25 .35
T176 Stubby Clapp RC .40 .12
T177 D'Angelo Jimenez .40 .12
T178 Nick Johnson .40 .12
T179 Ben Johnson .40 .12
T180 Larry Bigbie .40 .12
T181 Allen Levrault .40 .12
T182 Felipe Lopez .40 .12
T183 Sean Burnett .40 .12
T184 Nick Neugebauer .40 .12
T185 Austin Kearns .50 .15
T186 Corey Patterson .50 .15
T187 Carlos Pena .40 .12
T188 R. Rodriguez RC .40 .12
T189 Juan Rivera .40 .12
T190 Grant Roberts .40 .12
T191 Adam Pettyjohn RC .40 .12
T192 Jared Sandberg .40 .12
T193 Xavier Nady .40 .12
T194 Dane Sardinha .40 .12
T195 Shawn Sonnier .40 .12
T196 Rafael Soriano .50 .15
T197 Brian Specht RC .40 .12
T198 Aaron Myette .40 .12
T199 Juan Uribe RC .50 .15
T200 Jayson Werth .40 .12
T201 Brad Wilkerson .40 .12
T202 Horacio Estrada .40 .12
T203 Joel Pineiro 1.25 .35
T204 Matt LeCroy .40 .12
T205 Michael Coleman .40 .12
T206 Ben Sheets .75 .23
T207 Eric Byrnes .40 .12
T208 Sean Burroughs .50 .15
T209 Ken Harvey .40 .12
T210 Travis Hafner 2.00 .60
T211 Erick Almonte .40 .12
T212 Jason Belcher RC .40 .12
T213 Wilson Betemit RC .40 .12
T214 Hank Blalock RC 6.00 1.80
T215 Danny Borrell .40 .12
T216 John Buck RC .50 .15
T217 Freddie Bynum RC .40 .12
T218 Noel Devarez RC .40 .12
T219 Juan Diaz RC .40 .12
T220 Felix Diaz RC .40 .12
T221 Josh Fogg RC .40 .12
T222 Matt Ford RC .40 .12
T223 Scott Heard .40 .12
T224 Ben Hendrickson RC .50 .15
T225 Cody Ross RC .40 .12
T226 A. Hernandez RC .40 .12
T227 Alfredo Amezaga RC .40 .12
T228 Bob Keppel RC .50 .15
T229 Ryan Madson RC .75 .23
T230 Octavio Martinez RC .40 .12
T231 Hee Seop Choi .75 .23
T232 Thomas Mitchell .40 .12
T233 Luis Montanez .40 .12
T234 Andy Morales RC .40 .12
T235 Justin Morneau RC 6.00 1.80
T236 Toe Nash RC .40 .12
T237 V. Pascucci RC .40 .12
T238 Roy Smith RC .40 .12
T239 Antonio Perez RC .40 .12
T240 Chad Petty RC .40 .12
T241 Steve Smyth .40 .12
T242 Jose Reyes RC 3.00 .90
T243 Eric Reynolds RC .40 .12
T244 Dominic Rich .40 .12
T245 J. Richardson RC .40 .12
T246 Ed Rogers RC .40 .12
T247 Albert Pujols RC 40.00 12.00
T248 Esix Snead RC .40 .12
T249 Luis Torres RC .40 .12
T250 Matt White RC .40 .12
T251 Blake Williams .40 .12
T252 Chris Russ .40 .12
T253 Joe Kennedy RC .50 .15
T254 Jeff Randazzo RC .40 .12
T255 Beau Hale RC .40 .12
T256 Brad Hennessey RC 2.00 .60
T257 Jake Gautreau RC .40 .12
T258 Jeff Mathis RC 1.50 .45

T259 Aaron Heilman RC .40 .12
T260 B. Sardinha RC .75 .23
T261 Irvin Guzman RC 4.00 1.20
T262 Gabe Gross RC .50 .15
T263 J.D. Martin RC .40 .12
T264 Chris Smith RC .40 .12
T265 Kenny Baugh RC .40 .12

2001 Topps Traded Gold

This set is a parallel to the 2001 Topps Traded set. Inserted into the 2001 Topps Traded at a rate of one in three, these cards are serial numbered to 2001 have have a gold foil border.

Nm-Mt Ex-Mt
*STARS: 4X TO 10X BASIC CARDS....
*REPRINTS: 1.5X TO 4X BASIC..........
*ROOKIES: 1X TO 2.5X BASIC............

2001 Topps Traded Autographs

Inserted at a rate of one in 626, these cards share the same design as the 2001 Topps Golden Anniversary Autographs. The only difference is the front bottom of the card reads "Golden Anniversary Traded Star". The cards carry a 'TTA' prefix.

Nm-Mt Ex-Mt
TTA-JD Johnny Damon 25.00 7.50
TTA-MM Mike Mussina 25.00 7.50

2001 Topps Traded Dual Relics

Inserted at a rate of one in 376, these cards highlight a player who has switched teams and feature a swatch of game-used jersey from both his former and current teams. The cards carry a 'TRR' prefix.

Nm-Mt Ex-Mt
TTR-BG Ben Grieve EXCH 15.00 4.50
TTR-DH D. Hermanson 15.00 4.50
TTR-FT Fernando Tatis 15.00 4.50
TTR-MR Manny Ramirez 20.00 6.00

2001 Topps Traded Farewell Dual Relic

Inserted at a rate of one in 4693, this card features bat pieces from both Cal Ripken and Tony Gwynn and is a farewell tribute to both players. The card carries a 'FR' prefix.

Nm-Mt Ex-Mt
FR-RG Cal Ripken 120.00 36.00
Tony Gwynn

2001 Topps Traded Hall of Fame Bat Relic

nserted at a rate of one in 2796, this card features bat pieces from both Kirby Puckett and Dave Winfield and commemorates their entrance n Cooperstown. The card carries a 'HFR' prefix.

Nm-Mt Ex-Mt
HFR-PW Kirby Puckett 50.00 15.00
Dave Winfield

2001 Topps Traded Relics

nserted at a rate of one in 29, this 33-card set eatures game used bats or jersey swatches for players who have switched teams this season. All jersey swatches represent each player's new eam. The cards carry a 'TTR' prefix. An exchange card for a Matt Stairs Jersey card was packed out.

Nm-Mt Ex-Mt
G A. Galarraga Bat 10.00 3.00
B1 Bobby Bonilla Bat 10.00 3.00

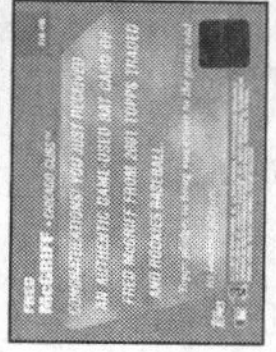

BB2 Bret Boone Jsy 10.00 3.00
BM Bill Mueller Jsy 10.00 3.00
CJ C. Johnson Jsy 10.00 3.00
DB Derek Bell Bat 10.00 3.00
DN Denny Neagle Jsy 10.00 3.00
DW David Wells Jsy 10.00 3.00
ED Eric Davis Bat 10.00 3.00
EW E. Wilson Bat 10.00 3.00
FM Fred McGriff Bat 15.00 4.50
GW G. Williams Bat 10.00 3.00
HR Hideo Nomo Jsy 50.00 15.00
JC Jose Canseco Bat 15.00 4.50
JD J. Dye Bat SP 10.00 3.00
JD1 J. Damon Bat 15.00 4.50
JD2 Johnny Damon Jsy 15.00 4.50
JG Juan Gonzalez Bat 15.00 4.50
JH J. Hammonds Jsy 10.00 3.00
KC Ken Caminiti Bat 10.00 3.00
KS K. Stinnett Bat SP 10.00 3.00
MG1 Mark Grace Bat 15.00 4.50
MG2 M. Grissom Bat 10.00 3.00
MH M. Hampton Jsy 10.00 3.00
MS M. Stairs Jsy EXCH 10.00 3.00
NP Neifi Perez Bat 10.00 3.00
RB Rico Brogna Jsy 10.00 3.00
RG Ron Gant Bat 10.00 3.00
ROC R. Cedeno Jsy 10.00 3.00
RS Ruben Sierra Bat 10.00 3.00
RSC R. Clayton Bat 10.00 3.00
SA S. Alomar Jr. Bat 10.00 3.00
TH Todd Hundley Jsy 10.00 3.00
TR Tim Raines Jsy 10.00 3.00

2001 Topps Traded Rookie Relics

Inserted at a rate of one in 91, this 18-card set features bat pieces or jersey swatches for rookies. The cards carry a 'TRR' prefix. An exchange card for the Ed Rogers Bat card was seeded into packs.

Nm-Mt Ex-Mt
TRR-AB Angel Berroa Jsy 10.00 3.00
TRR-AP A. Pujols Bat SP 40.00 12.00
TRR-BO Bill Ortega Jsy 8.00 2.40
TRR-ER E.Rogers Bat SP EXCH 10.00 3.00
TRR-HC H. Cota Jsy 8.00 2.40
TRR-JL Jason Lane Jsy 8.00 2.40
TRR-JS Jae Seo Jsy 8.00 2.40
TRR-JS Jamal Strong Jsy 8.00 2.40
TRR-JV Jose Valverde Jsy 10.00 3.00
TRR-JY Jason Young Jsy 8.00 2.40
TRR-NC Nate Cornejo Jsy 8.00 2.40
TRR-NN N. Neugebauer Jsy 8.00 2.40
TRR-PF P. Feliz Jsy SP 8.00 2.40
TRR-RS Richard Stahl Jsy 8.00 2.40
TRR-SB S. Burroughs Jsy 8.00 2.40
TRR-TS T. Shinjo Bat SP 10.00 3.00
TRR-WB W. Betemit Bat 8.00 2.40
TRR-WR Wilkin Ruan Jsy 8.00 2.40

2001 Topps Traded Who Would Have Thought

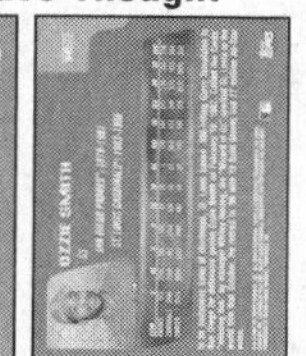

Inserted at a rate of one in eight, this 20-card set portrays players who fans thought would never be traded. The cards carry a 'WWHT' prefix.

Nm-Mt Ex-Mt
COMPLETE SET (20) 40.00 12.00
WWHT1 Nolan Ryan 6.00 1.80
WWHT2 Ozzie Smith 4.00 1.20
WWHT3 Tom Seaver 1.50 .45
WWHT4 Steve Carlton 1.50 .45
WWHT5 Reggie Jackson 1.50 .45
WWHT6 Frank Robinson 1.50 .45
WWHT7 Keith Hernandez 1.50 .45
WWHT8 Andre Dawson 1.50 .45
WWHT9 Lou Brock 1.50 .45
WWHT10 D. Eckersley 1.50 .45
WWHT11 Dave Winfield 1.50 .45
WWHT12 Rod Carew 1.50 .45
WWHT13 Willie Randolph 1.50 .45
WWHT14 Dwight Gooden 1.50 .45
WWHT15 Carlton Fisk 1.50 .45
WWHT16 Dale Murphy 2.50 .75
WWHT17 Paul Molitor 1.50 .45
WWHT18 Gary Carter 1.50 .45
WWHT19 Wade Boggs 1.50 .45
WWHT20 Willie Mays 5.00 1.50

2002 Topps

The complete set of 2002 Topps consists of 718 cards issued in two separate series. The first series of 364 cards was distributed in November, 2001 and the second series of 354 cards followed up in April, 2002. Please note, the first series is numbered 1-365, but card number seven does not exist (the number was "retired" in 1996 by Topps to honor Mickey Mantle). Similar to the 1999 McGwire and Sosa home run cards, Barry Bonds is featured on card number 365 with 73 different versions to commemorate each of the homers he smashed during the 2001 season. The first series set is considered complete with any "one" of these variations. The cards were issued either in 10 card hobby/retail packs with an SRP of $1.29 or 37 card HTA packs with an SRP of $5 per pack. The hobby packs were issued 36 to a box and 12 boxes to a case. The HTA packs were issued 12 to a box and eight to a case. Cards numbered 277-305 feature managers; cards numbered 307-325/671-690 feature leading prospects; cards numbered 326-331/691-695 feature 2001 draft picks; cards numbered 332-336 feature leading highlights of the 2001 season; cards numbered 337-348 feature league leaders; cards numbered 349-356 feature the eight teams which made the playoffs; cards numbered 357-364 feature major league baseball's stirring tribute to the events of September 11, 2001; cards 641-670 feature Team Cards; 696-713 are Gold Glove subsets, 714-715 are Cy Young subsets, 716-717 are MVP subsets and 718-719 are Rookie of the Year subsets. Notable Rookie Cards include Joe Mauer and Kazhuisa Ishii. Also, Topps repurchased more than 21,000 actual vintage Topps cards and randomly seeded them into packs as follows - Ser.1 Home Team Advantage 1:169, ser.1 retail 1:tbd, ser.2 hobby 1:431, ser.2 Home Team Advantage 1:113 and ser.2 retail 1:331. Brown-boxed hobby factory sets were issued in May, 2002 containing the full 718-card basic set and five Topps Archives Reprints inserts. Green-boxed retail factory sets were issued in late August, 2002 containing the full 718-card basic set and cards 1-5 of a 10-card Draft Picks set. There has been a recently discovered variation of card 160 in which there is a correct back picture for Albert Pujols (#160). While Topps has confirmed this variation, it is unknown what percent of the print run has the correct back photo.

Nm-Mt Ex-Mt
COMPLETE SET (718) 80.00 24.00
COMP.FACT.BROWN SET (723) 80.00 24.00
COMP.FACT.GREEN SET (723) 80.00 24.00
COMP. SERIES 1 (365) 40.00 12.00
COMPLETE SERIES 2 (354) 40.00 12.00
COMMON CARD (1-6/8-719) .20 .06
COMMON (307-331) .50 .15
COMMON CARD (332-364) .50 .15
1 Pedro Martinez .50 .15
2 Mike Stanton .20 .06
3 Brad Penny .20 .06
4 Mike Matheny .20 .06
5 Johnny Damon .30 .09
6 Bret Boone .20 .06
7 Does Not Exist
8 Chris Truby .20 .06
9 B.J. Surhoff .20 .06
10 Mike Hampton .20 .06
11 Juan Pierre .20 .06
12 Mark Buehrle .20 .06
13 Bob Abreu .20 .06
14 David Cone .20 .06
15 Aaron Sele UER .20 .06
Card lists him as being born in New Mexico
He was born in Minnesota
16 Fernando Tatis .20 .06
17 Bobby Jones .20 .06
18 Rick Helling .20 .06
19 Dmitri Young .20 .06
20 Mike Mussina UER .30 .09
Career win total is wrong
21 Mike Sweeney .20 .06
22 Cristian Guzman .20 .06
23 Ryan Kohlmeier .20 .06
24 Adam Kennedy .20 .06
25 Larry Walker .30 .09
26 Eric Davis UER .20 .06
2000 Stolen Base totals are wrong
27 Jason Tyner .20 .06
28 Eric Young .20 .06
29 Jason Marquis .20 .06
30 Luis Gonzalez .20 .06
31 Kevin Tapani .20 .06
32 Orlando Cabrera .20 .06
33 Marty Cordova UER .20 .06
Career homer total, 1003
34 Brad Ausmus .20 .06
35 Livan Hernandez .20 .06
36 Alex Gonzalez .20 .06
37 Edgar Renteria .20 .06
38 Bengie Molina .20 .06
39 Frank Menechino .20 .06
40 Rafael Palmeiro .30 .09
41 Brad Fullmer .20 .06
42 Julio Zuleta .20 .06
43 Darren Dreifort .20 .06
44 Trot Nixon .20 .06
45 Trevor Hoffman .20 .06
46 Vladimir Nunez .20 .06
47 Mark Kotsay .20 .06
48 Kenny Rogers .20 .06
49 Ben Petrick .20 .06
50 Jeff Bagwell .30 .09
51 Juan Encarnacion .20 .06
52 Ramiro Mendoza .20 .06
53 Brian Meadows .20 .06
54 Chad Curtis .20 .06
55 Aramis Ramirez .20 .06
56 Mark McLemore .20 .06
57 Dante Bichette .20 .06
58 Scott Schoeneweis .20 .06
59 Jose Cruz Jr. .20 .06
60 Roger Clemens 1.00 .30
61 Jose Guillen .20 .06
62 Darren Oliver .20 .06
63 Chris Reitsma .20 .06
64 Jeff Abbott .20 .06
65 Robin Ventura .20 .06
66 Denny Neagle .20 .06
67 Al Martin .20 .06
68 Benito Santiago .20 .06
69 Roy Oswalt .20 .06
70 Juan Gonzalez .30 .09
71 Garret Anderson .20 .06
72 Bobby Bonilla .20 .06
73 Danny Bautista .20 .06
74 J.T. Snow .20 .06
75 Derek Jeter 1.25 .35
76 John Olerud .20 .06
77 Kevin Appier .20 .06
78 Phil Nevin .20 .06
79 Sean Casey .20 .06
80 Troy Glaus .20 .06
81 Joe Randa .20 .06
82 Jose Valentin .20 .06
83 Ricky Bottalico .20 .06
84 Todd Zeile .20 .06
85 Barry Larkin .30 .09
86 Bob Wickman .20 .06
87 Jeff Shaw .20 .06
88 Greg Vaughn .20 .06
89 Fernando Vina .20 .06
90 Mark Mulder .20 .06
91 Paul Bako .20 .06
92 Aaron Boone .20 .06
93 Esteban Loaiza .20 .06
94 Richie Sexson .20 .06
95 Alfonso Soriano .30 .09
96 Tony Womack .20 .06
97 Paul Shuey .20 .06
98 Melvin Mora .20 .06
99 Tony Gwynn .60 .18
100 Vladimir Guerrero .50 .15
101 Keith Osik .20 .06
102 Bud Smith .20 .06
103 Scott Williamson .20 .06
104 Daryle Ward .20 .06
105 Doug Mientkiewicz .20 .06
106 Stan Javier .20 .06
107 Russ Ortiz .20 .06
108 Wade Miller .20 .06
109 Luke Prokopec .20 .06
110 Andruw Jones UER .20 .06
Careel SB total, 1442
111 Ron Coomer .20 .06
112 Dan Wilson UER .20 .06
Career SB total, 1245
113 Luis Castillo .20 .06
114 Derek Bell .20 .06
115 Gary Sheffield .20 .06
116 Ruben Rivera .20 .06
117 Paul O'Neill .30 .09
118 Craig Paquette .20 .06
119 Kelvin Escobar .20 .06
120 Brad Radke .20 .06
121 Jorge Fabregas .20 .06
122 Randy Winn .20 .06
123 Tom Goodwin .20 .06
124 Jaret Wright .20 .06
125 Manny Ramirez .30 .09
126 Al Leiter .20 .06
127 Ben Davis .20 .06
128 Frank Catalanotto .20 .06
129 Jose Cabrera .20 .06
130 Magglio Ordonez .20 .06
131 Jose Macias .20 .06
132 Ted Lilly .20 .06
133 Chris Holt .20 .06
134 Eric Milton .20 .06
135 Shannon Stewart .20 .06
136 Omar Olivares .20 .06
137 David Segui .20 .06
138 Jeff Nelson .20 .06
139 Matt Williams .20 .06
140 Ellis Burks .20 .06
141 Jason Bere .20 .06
142 Jimmy Haynes .20 .06
143 Ramon Hernandez .20 .06
144 Craig Counsell UER .20 .06
Card pictures Greg Colbrunn
Some vital stats are wrong as well
145 John Smoltz .30 .09
146 Homer Bush .20 .06
147 Quilvio Veras .20 .06
148 Esteban Yan .20 .06
149 Ramon Ortiz .20 .06
150 Carlos Delgado .20 .06
151 Lee Stevens .20 .06
152 Wil Cordero .20 .06
153 Mike Bordick .20 .06
154 John Flaherty .20 .06
155 Omar Daal .20 .06
156 Todd Ritchie .20 .06
157 Carl Everett .20 .06
158 Scott Sullivan .20 .06
159 Deivi Cruz .20 .06
160 Albert Pujols UER 1.00 .30
Placido Polanco pictured on back
160A Albert Pujols
Pujols correctly pictured on back
161 Royce Clayton .20 .06
162 Jeff Suppan .20 .06
163 C.C. Sabathia .20 .06
164 Jimmy Rollins .20 .06
165 Rickey Henderson .50 .15
166 Rey Ordonez .20 .06
167 Shawn Estes .20 .06
168 Reggie Sanders .20 .06
169 Jon Lieber .20 .06
170 Armando Benitez .20 .06
171 Mike Remlinger .20 .06
172 Billy Wagner .20 .06
173 Troy Percival .20 .06
174 Devon White .20 .06
175 Ivan Rodriguez .50 .15
176 Dustin Hermanson .20 .06
177 Brian Anderson .20 .06
178 Graeme Lloyd .20 .06
179 Russel Branyan .20 .06
180 Bobby Higginson .20 .06
181 Alex Gonzalez .20 .06
182 John Franco .20 .06
183 Sidney Ponson .20 .06
184 Jose Mesa .20 .06
185 Todd Hollandsworth .20 .06
186 Kevin Young .20 .06
187 Tim Wakefield .20 .06
188 Craig Biggio .30 .09
189 Jason Isringhausen .20 .06
190 Mark Quinn .20 .06
191 Glendon Rusch .20 .06
192 Damian Miller .20 .06
193 Sandy Alomar Jr. .20 .06
194 Scott Brosius .20 .06
195 Dave Martinez .20 .06
196 Danny Graves .20 .06
197 Shea Hillenbrand .20 .06
198 Jimmy Anderson .20 .06
199 Travis Lee .20 .06
200 Randy Johnson .50 .15
201 Carlos Beltran .30 .09
202 Jerry Hairston .20 .06
203 Jesus Sanchez .20 .06
204 Eddie Taubensee .20 .06
205 David Wells .20 .06
206 Russ Davis .20 .06
207 Michael Barrett .20 .06
208 Marquis Grissom .20 .06
209 Byung-Hyun Kim .20 .06
210 Hideo Nomo .50 .15
211 Ryan Rupe .20 .06
212 Ricky Gutierrez .20 .06
213 Darryl Kile .20 .06
214 Rico Brogna .20 .06
215 Terrence Long .20 .06
216 Mike Jackson .20 .06
217 Jamey Wright .20 .06
218 Adrian Beltre .30 .09
219 Benny Agbayani .20 .06
220 Chuck Knoblauch .20 .06
221 Randy Wolf .20 .06
222 Andy Ashby .20 .06
223 Corey Koskie .20 .06
224 Roger Cedeno .20 .06
225 Ichiro Suzuki .75 .23
226 Keith Foulke .20 .06
227 Ryan Minor .20 .06
228 Shawon Dunston .20 .06
229 Alex Cora .20 .06
230 Jeromy Burnitz .20 .06
231 Mark Grace .30 .09
232 Aubrey Huff .20 .06
233 Jeffrey Hammonds .20 .06
234 Olmedo Saenz .20 .06
235 Brian Jordan .20 .06
236 Jeremy Giambi .20 .06
237 Joe Girardi .20 .06
238 Eric Gagne .50 .15
239 Masato Yoshii .20 .06
240 Greg Maddux .75 .23
241 Bryan Rekar .20 .06
242 Ray Durham .20 .06
243 Torii Hunter .20 .06
244 Derrek Lee .20 .06
245 Jim Edmonds .20 .06
246 Einar Diaz .20 .06
247 Brian Bohanon .20 .06
248 Ron Belliard .20 .06
249 Mike Lowell .20 .06
250 Sammy Sosa .75 .23
251 Richard Hidalgo .20 .06
252 Bartolo Colon .20 .06
253 Jorge Posada .30 .09
254 LaTroy Hawkins .20 .06
255 Paul LoDuca .20 .06
256 Carlos Febles .20 .06
257 Nelson Cruz .20 .06
258 Edgardo Alfonzo .20 .06
259 Joey Hamilton .20 .06
260 Cliff Floyd .20 .06
261 Wes Helms .20 .06
262 Jay Bell .20 .06
263 Mike Cameron .20 .06
264 Paul Konerko .20 .06
265 Jeff Kent .20 .06
266 Robert Fick .20 .06
267 Allen Levrault .20 .06
268 Placido Polanco .20 .06
269 Marlon Anderson .20 .06
270 Mariano Rivera .30 .09
271 Chan Ho Park .20 .06
272 Jose Vizcaino .20 .06
273 Jeff D'Amico .20 .06
274 Mark Gardner .20 .06
275 Travis Fryman .20 .06
276 Darren Lewis .20 .06
277 Bruce Bochy MG .20 .06
278 Jerry Manuel MG .20 .06
279 Bob Brenly MG .20 .06
280 Don Baylor MG .20 .06
281 Davey Lopes MG .20 .06
282 Jerry Narron MG .20 .06
283 Tony Muser MG .20 .06
284 Hal McRae MG .20 .06
285 Bobby Cox MG .20 .06
286 Larry Dierker MG .20 .06
287 Phil Garner MG .20 .06
288 Joe Kerrigan MG .20 .06
289 Bobby Valentine MG .20 .06
290 Dusty Baker MG .20 .06
291 Lloyd McClendon MG .20 .06
292 Mike Scioscia MG .20 .06
293 Buck Martinez MG .20 .06
294 Larry Bowa MG .20 .06
295 Tony LaRussa MG .20 .06
296 Jeff Torborg MG .20 .06
297 Tom Kelly MG .20 .06
298 Mike Hargrove MG .20 .06
299 Art Howe MG .20 .06
300 Lou Piniella MG .20 .06
301 Charlie Manuel MG .20 .06
302 Buddy Bell MG .20 .06

303 Tony Perez MG .20 .06
304 Bob Boone MG .20 .06
305 Joe Torre MG .50 .15
306 Jim Tracy MG .20 .06
307 Jason Lane PROS .50 .15
308 Chris George PROS .50 .15
309 Hank Blalock PROS UER 1.00 .30
Bio has him throwing lefty
310 Joe Borchard PROS .50 .15
311 Marlon Byrd PROS .50 .15
312 R. Cabrera PROS RC .50 .15
313 F. Sanchez PROS RC .50 .15
314 S. Wiggins PROS RC .50 .15
315 J. Maule PROS RC .50 .15
316 D. Cesar PROS RC .50 .15
317 Boof Bonser PROS .50 .15
318 J. Tolentino PROS RC .50 .15
319 Earl Snyder PROS RC .50 .15
320 T. Wade PROS RC .50 .15
321 N. Calzado PROS RC .50 .15
322 Eric Glaser PROS RC .50 .15
323 C. Kuzmic PROS RC .50 .15
324 Nic Jackson PROS RC .50 .15
325 Mike Rivera PROS .50 .15
326 Jason Bay PROS RC 2.50 .75
327 Chris Smith DP .50 .15
328 Jake Gautreau DP .50 .15
329 Gabe Gross DP .50 .15
330 Kenny Baugh DP .50 .15
331 J.D. Martin DP .50 .15
332 Barry Bonds HL 1.25 .35
500th Homer
333 Rickey Henderson HL .50 .15
Sets record for career walks
334 Bud Smith HL .50 .15
335 R. Henderson HL 3000 .50 .15
336 Barry Bonds HL 1.25 .35
73 homers in a season
337 Ichiro Suzuki .50 .15
Jason Giambi
Roberto Alomar LL
338 Alex Rodriguez .50 .15
Ichiro Suzuki
Bret Boone LL
339 Alex Rodriguez .50 .15
Jim Thome
Rafael Palmeiro LL
340 Bret Boone .50 .15
Juan Gonzalez
Alex Rodriguez LL
341 Freddy Garcia .50 .15
Mike Mussina
Joe Mays LL
342 Hideo Nomo .50 .15
Mike Mussina
Roger Clemens LL
343 Larry Walker .50 .15
Todd Helton
Moises Alou
Lance Berkman LL
344 Sammy Sosa .50 .15
Todd Helton
Barry Bonds LL
345 Barry Bonds .50 .15
Sammy Sosa
Luis Gonzalez LL
346 Sammy Sosa .50 .15
Todd Helton
Luis Gonzalez LL
347 Randy Johnson .50 .15
Curt Schilling
John Burkett LL
348 Randy Johnson .50 .15
Curt Schilling
Chan Ho Park LL
349 Seattle Mariners PB .50 .15
350 Oakland Athletics PB .50 .15
351 New York Yankees PB .50 .15
352 Cleveland Indians PB .50 .15
353 Ariz. Diamondbacks PB .50 .15
354 Atlanta Braves PB .50 .15
355 St. Louis Cardinals PB .50 .15
356 Houston Astros PB .50 .15
357 Ariz.Diamondbacks .50 .15
Colorado Rockies UWS
358 Mike Piazza UWS .50 .15
359 Braves-Phillies UWS .50 .15
360 Curt Schilling UWS .50 .15
361 Roger Clemens .50 .15
Lee Mazzilli UWS
362 Sammy Sosa UWS .50 .15
363 Tom Lampkin .50 .15
Ichiro Suzuki
Bret Boone UWS
364 Barry Bonds .50 .15
Jeff Bagwell UWS
365 Barry Bonds HR 1 15.00 4.50
365 Barry Bonds HR 2 10.00 3.00
365 Barry Bonds HR 3 10.00 3.00
365 Barry Bonds HR 4 10.00 3.00
365 Barry Bonds HR 5 10.00 3.00
365 Barry Bonds HR 6 10.00 3.00
365 Barry Bonds HR 7 10.00 3.00
365 Barry Bonds HR 8 10.00 3.00
365 Barry Bonds HR 9 10.00 3.00
365 Barry Bonds HR 10 10.00 3.00
365 Barry Bonds HR 11 10.00 3.00
365 Barry Bonds HR 12 10.00 3.00
365 Barry Bonds HR 13 10.00 3.00
365 Barry Bonds HR 14 10.00 3.00
365 Barry Bonds HR 15 10.00 3.00
365 Barry Bonds HR 16 10.00 3.00
365 Barry Bonds HR 17 10.00 3.00
365 Barry Bonds HR 18 10.00 3.00
365 Barry Bonds HR 19 10.00 3.00
365 Barry Bonds HR 20 10.00 3.00
365 Barry Bonds HR 21 10.00 3.00
365 Barry Bonds HR 22 10.00 3.00
365 Barry Bonds HR 23 10.00 3.00
365 Barry Bonds HR 24 10.00 3.00
365 Barry Bonds HR 25 10.00 3.00
365 Barry Bonds HR 26 10.00 3.00
365 Barry Bonds HR 27 10.00 3.00
365 Barry Bonds HR 28 10.00 3.00
365 Barry Bonds HR 29 10.00 3.00
365 Barry Bonds HR 30 10.00 3.00
365 Barry Bonds HR 31 10.00 3.00
365 Barry Bonds HR 32 UER 10.00 3.00
No pitcher is listed on this card
365 Barry Bonds HR 33 10.00 3.00
365 Barry Bonds HR 34 10.00 3.00
365 Barry Bonds HR 35 10.00 3.00
365 Barry Bonds HR 36 10.00 3.00
365 Barry Bonds HR 37 10.00 3.00
365 Barry Bonds HR 38 10.00 3.00
365 Barry Bonds HR 39 10.00 3.00
365 Barry Bonds HR 40 10.00 3.00
365 Barry Bonds HR 41 10.00 3.00
365 Barry Bonds HR 42 10.00 3.00
365 Barry Bonds HR 43 10.00 3.00
365 Barry Bonds HR 44 10.00 3.00
365 Barry Bonds HR 45 10.00 3.00
365 Barry Bonds HR 46 10.00 3.00
365 Barry Bonds HR 47 10.00 3.00
365 Barry Bonds HR 48 10.00 3.00
365 Barry Bonds HR 49 10.00 3.00
365 Barry Bonds HR 50 10.00 3.00
365 Barry Bonds HR 51 10.00 3.00
365 Barry Bonds HR 52 10.00 3.00
365 Barry Bonds HR 53 10.00 3.00
365 Barry Bonds HR 54 10.00 3.00
365 Barry Bonds HR 55 10.00 3.00
365 Barry Bonds HR 56 10.00 3.00
365 Barry Bonds HR 57 10.00 3.00
365 Barry Bonds HR 58 10.00 3.00
365 Barry Bonds HR 59 10.00 3.00
365 Barry Bonds HR 60 10.00 3.00
365 Barry Bonds HR 61 15.00 4.50
365 Barry Bonds HR 62 10.00 3.00
365 Barry Bonds HR 63 10.00 3.00
365 Barry Bonds HR 64 10.00 3.00
365 Barry Bonds HR 65 10.00 3.00
365 Barry Bonds HR 66 10.00 3.00
365 Barry Bonds HR 67 10.00 3.00
365 Barry Bonds HR 68 10.00 3.00
365 Barry Bonds HR 69 10.00 3.00
365 Barry Bonds HR 70 15.00 4.50
365 Barry Bonds HR 71 10.00 3.00
365 Barry Bonds HR 72 10.00 3.00
365 Barry Bonds HR 73 50.00 15.00
366 Pat Meares .20 .06
367 Mike Lieberthal .20 .06
368 Larry Bigbie .20 .06
369 Ron Gant .20 .06
370 Moises Alou .20 .06
371 Chad Kreuter .20 .06
372 Willis Roberts .20 .06
373 Toby Hall .20 .06
374 Miguel Batista .20 .06
375 John Burkett .20 .06
376 Cory Lidle .20 .06
377 Nick Neugebauer .20 .06
378 Jay Payton .20 .06
379 Steve Karsay .20 .06
380 Eric Chavez .20 .06
381 Kelly Stinnett .20 .06
382 Jarrod Washburn .20 .06
383 Rick White .20 .06
384 Jeff Conine .20 .06
385 Fred McGriff .30 .09
386 Marvin Benard .20 .06
387 Joe Crede .20 .06
388 Dennis Cook .20 .06
389 Rick Reed .20 .06
390 Tom Glavine .30 .09
391 Rondell White .20 .06
392 Matt Morris .20 .06
393 Pat Rapp .20 .06
394 Robert Person .20 .06
395 Omar Vizquel .30 .09
396 Jeff Cirillo .20 .06
397 Dave Mlicki .20 .06
398 Jose Ortiz .20 .06
399 Ryan Dempster .20 .06
400 Curt Schilling .20 .06
401 Peter Bergeron .20 .06
402 Kyle Lohse .20 .06
403 Craig Wilson UER .20 .06
Homer totals are wrong
404 David Justice .20 .06
405 Darin Erstad .20 .06
406 Jose Mercedes .20 .06
407 Carl Pavano .20 .06
408 Albie Lopez .20 .06
409 Alex Ochoa .20 .06
410 Chipper Jones .50 .15
411 Tyler Houston .20 .06
412 Dean Palmer .20 .06
413 Damian Jackson .20 .06
414 Josh Towers .20 .06
415 Rafael Furcal .20 .06
416 Mike Morgan .20 .06
417 Herb Perry .20 .06
418 Mike Sirotka .20 .06
419 Mark Wohlers .20 .06
420 Nomar Garciaparra .75 .23
421 Felipe Lopez .20 .06
422 Joe McEwing .20 .06
423 Jacque Jones .20 .06
424 Julio Franco .20 .06
425 Frank Thomas .50 .15
426 So Taguchi RC .75 .23
427 Kazuhisa Ishii RC 1.50 .45
428 D'Angelo Jimenez .20 .06
429 Chris Stynes .20 .06
430 Kerry Wood .50 .15
431 Chris Singleton .20 .06
432 Erubiel Durazo .20 .06
433 Matt Lawton .20 .06
434 Bill Mueller .20 .06
435 Jose Canseco .50 .15
436 Ben Grieve .20 .06
437 Terry Mulholland .20 .06
438 David Bell .20 .06
439 A.J. Pierzynski .20 .06
440 Adam Dunn .30 .09
441 Jon Garland .20 .06
442 Jeff Fassero .20 .06
443 Julio Lugo .20 .06
444 Carlos Guillen .20 .06
445 Orlando Hernandez .20 .06
446 Mark Loretta UER .20 .06
Photo is Curtis Leskanic
447 Scott Spiezio .20 .06
448 Kevin Millwood .20 .06
449 Jamie Moyer .20 .06
450 Todd Helton .30 .09
451 Todd Walker .20 .06
452 Jose Lima .20 .06
453 Brook Fordyce .20 .06
454 Aaron Rowand .20 .06
455 Barry Zito .20 .06
456 Eric Owens .20 .06
457 Charles Nagy .20 .06
458 Raul Ibanez .20 .06
459 Joe Mays .20 .06
460 Jim Thome .50 .15
461 Adam Eaton .20 .06
462 Felix Martinez .20 .06
463 Vernon Wells .20 .06
464 Donnie Sadler .20 .06
465 Tony Clark .20 .06
466 Jose Hernandez .20 .06
467 Ramon Martinez .20 .06
468 Rusty Greer .20 .06
469 Rod Barajas .20 .06
470 Lance Berkman .20 .06
471 Brady Anderson .20 .06
472 Pedro Astacio .20 .06
473 Shane Halter .20 .06
474 Bret Prinz .20 .06
475 Edgar Martinez .30 .09
476 Steve Trachsel .20 .06
477 Gary Matthews Jr. .20 .06
478 Ismael Valdes .20 .06
479 Juan Uribe .20 .06
480 Shawn Green .20 .06
481 Kirk Rueter .20 .06
482 Damion Easley .20 .06
483 Chris Carpenter .20 .06
484 Kris Benson .20 .06
485 Antonio Alfonseca .20 .06
486 Kyle Farnsworth .20 .06
487 Brandon Lyon .20 .06
488 Hideki Irabu .20 .06
489 David Ortiz .30 .09
490 Mike Piazza .75 .23
491 Derek Lowe .20 .06
492 Chris Gomez .20 .06
493 Mark Johnson .20 .06
494 John Rocker .20 .06
495 Eric Karros .20 .06
496 Bill Haselman .20 .06
497 Dave Veres .20 .06
498 Pete Harnisch .20 .06
499 Tomokazu Ohka .20 .06
500 Barry Bonds 1.25 .35
501 David Dellucci .20 .06
502 Wendell Magee .20 .06
503 Tom Gordon .20 .06
504 Javier Vazquez .20 .06
505 Ben Sheets .20 .06
506 Wilton Guerrero .20 .06
507 John Halama .20 .06
508 Mark Redman .20 .06
509 Jack Wilson .20 .06
510 Bernie Williams .30 .09
511 Miguel Cairo .20 .06
512 Denny Hocking .20 .06
513 Tony Batista .20 .06
514 Mark Grudzielanek .20 .06
515 Jose Vidro .20 .06
516 Sterling Hitchcock .20 .06
517 Billy Koch .20 .06
518 Matt Clement .20 .06
519 Bruce Chen .20 .06
520 Roberto Alomar .30 .09
521 Orlando Palmeiro .20 .06
522 Steve Finley .20 .06
523 Danny Patterson .20 .06
524 Terry Adams .20 .06
525 Tino Martinez .30 .09
526 Tony Armas Jr. .20 .06
527 Geoff Jenkins .20 .06
528 Kerry Robinson .20 .06
529 Corey Patterson .20 .06
530 Brian Giles .20 .06
531 Jose Jimenez .20 .06
532 Joe Kennedy .20 .06
533 Armando Rios .20 .06
534 Osvaldo Fernandez .20 .06
535 Ruben Sierra .20 .06
536 Octavio Dotel .20 .06
537 Luis Sojo .20 .06
538 Brent Butler .20 .06
539 Pablo Ozuna UER .20 .06
Games played for Portland is wrong for 2002
540 Freddy Garcia .20 .06
541 Chad Durbin .20 .06
542 Orlando Merced .20 .06
543 Michael Tucker .20 .06
544 Roberto Hernandez .20 .06
545 Pat Burrell .20 .06
546 A.J. Burnett .20 .06
547 Bubba Trammell .20 .06
548 Scott Elarton .20 .06
549 Mike Darr .20 .06
550 Ken Griffey Jr. .75 .23
551 Ugueth Urbina .20 .06
552 Todd Jones .20 .06
553 Delino Deshields .20 .06
554 Adam Piatt .20 .06
555 Jason Kendall .20 .06
556 Hector Ortiz .20 .06
557 Turk Wendell .20 .06
558 Rob Bell .20 .06
559 Sun Woo Kim .20 .06
560 Raul Mondesi .20 .06
561 Brent Abernathy .20 .06
562 Seth Etherton .20 .06
563 Shawn Wooten .20 .06
564 Jay Buhner .20 .06
565 Andres Galarraga .20 .06
566 Shane Reynolds .20 .06
567 Rod Beck .20 .06
568 Dee Brown .20 .06
569 Pedro Feliz .20 .06
570 Ryan Klesko .20 .06
571 John Vander Wal UER .20 .06
Home Run Total in 1999 was 64
572 Nick Bierbrodt .20 .06
573 Joe Nathan .20 .06
574 James Baldwin .20 .06
575 J.D. Drew .20 .06
576 Greg Colbrunn .20 .06
577 Doug Glanville .20 .06
578 Brandon Duckworth .20 .06
579 Shawn Chacon .20 .06
580 Rich Aurilia .20 .06
581 Chuck Finley .20 .06
582 Abraham Nunez .20 .06
583 Kenny Lofton .20 .06
584 Brian Daubach .20 .06
585 Miguel Tejada .20 .06
586 Nate Cornejo .20 .06
587 Kazuhiro Sasaki .20 .06
588 Chris Richard .20 .06
589 Armando Reynoso .20 .06
590 Tim Hudson .20 .06
591 Neifi Perez .20 .06
592 Steve Cox .20 .06
593 Henry Blanco .20 .06
594 Ricky Ledee .20 .06
595 Tim Salmon .30 .09
596 Luis Rivas .20 .06
597 Jeff Zimmerman .20 .06
598 Matt Stairs .20 .06
599 Preston Wilson .20 .06
600 Mark McGwire 1.25 .35
601 Timo Perez UER .20 .06
Biographical Information is that of Aaron Rowand's
602 Matt Anderson .20 .06
603 Todd Hundley .20 .06
604 Rick Ankiel .20 .06
605 Tsuyoshi Shinjo .20 .06
606 Woody Williams .20 .06
607 Jason LaRue .20 .06
608 Carlos Lee .20 .06
609 Russ Johnson .20 .06
610 Scott Rolen .50 .15
611 Brent Mayne .20 .06
612 Darrin Fletcher .20 .06
613 Ray Lankford .20 .06
614 Troy O'Leary .20 .06
615 Javier Lopez .20 .06
616 Randy Velarde .20 .06
617 Vinny Castilla .20 .06
618 Milton Bradley .20 .06
619 Ruben Mateo .20 .06
620 Jason Giambi Yankees .20 .06
621 Andy Benes .20 .06
622 Joe Mauer RC 5.00 1.50
623 Andy Pettitte .30 .09
624 Jose Offerman .20 .06
625 Mo Vaughn .20 .06
626 Steve Sparks .20 .06
627 Mike Matthews .20 .06
628 Robb Nen .20 .06
629 Kip Wells .20 .06
630 Kevin Brown .20 .06
631 Arthur Rhodes .20 .06
632 Gabe Kapler .20 .06
633 Jermaine Dye .20 .06
634 Josh Beckett .20 .06
635 Pokey Reese .20 .06
636 Benji Gil .20 .06
637 Marcus Giles .20 .06
638 Julian Tavarez .20 .06
639 Jason Schmidt .20 .06
640 Alex Rodriguez .75 .23
641 Anaheim Angels TC .20 .06
642 Arizona Diamondbacks TC .30 .09
643 Atlanta Braves TC .20 .06
644 Baltimore Orioles TC .20 .06
645 Boston Red Sox TC .20 .06
646 Chicago Cubs TC .20 .06
647 Chicago White Sox TC .20 .06
648 Cincinnati Reds TC .20 .06
649 Cleveland Indians TC .20 .06
650 Colorado Rockies TC .20 .06
651 Detroit Tigers TC .20 .06
652 Florida Marlins TC .20 .06
653 Houston Astros TC .20 .06
654 Kansas City Royals TC .20 .06
655 Los Angeles Dodgers TC .20 .06
656 Milwaukee Brewers TC .20 .06
657 Minnesota Twins TC .20 .06
658 Montreal Expos TC .20 .06
659 New York Mets TC .20 .06
660 New York Yankees TC .50 .15
661 Oakland Athletics TC .20 .06
662 Philadelphia Phillies TC .20 .06
663 Pittsburgh Pirates TC .20 .06
664 San Diego Padres TC .20 .06
665 San Francisco Giants TC .20 .06
666 Seattle Mariners TC .30 .09
667 St. Louis Cardinals TC .20 .06
668 T.B. Devil Rays TC .20 .06
669 Texas Rangers TC .20 .06
670 Toronto Blue Jays TC .20 .06
671 Juan Cruz PROS .50 .15
672 Kevin Cash PROS RC .50 .15
673 Jimmy Gobble PROS RC .75 .23
674 Mike Hill PROS RC .50 .15
675 T.Buchholz PROS RC .50 .15
676 Bill Hall PROS .50 .15
677 B.Roneberg PROS RC .50 .15
678 R.Huffman PROS RC .50 .15
679 Chris Tritle PROS RC .50 .15
680 Nate Espy PROS RC .50 .15
681 Nick Alvarez PROS RC .50 .15
682 Jason Botts PROS RC .75 .23
683 Ryan Gripp PROS RC .50 .15
684 Dan Phillips PROS RC .50 .15
685 Pablo Arias PROS RC .50 .15
686 J.Rodriguez PROS RC .50 .15
687 Rich Harden PROS RC 4.00 1.20
688 Neal Frendling PROS RC .50 .15
689 Rich Thompson PROS RC .50 .15
690 G.Montalbano PROS RC .50 .15
691 Len Dinardo DP RC .50 .15
692 Ryan Raburn DP RC .50 .15
693 Josh Barfield DP RC 1.50 .45
694 David Bacani DP RC .50 .15
695 Dan Johnson DP RC .75 .23
696 Mike Mussina GG .20 .06
697 Ivan Rodriguez GG .50 .15
698 Doug Mientkiewicz GG .20 .06
699 Roberto Alomar GG .20 .06
700 Eric Chavez GG .20 .06
701 Omar Vizquel GG .20 .06
702 Mike Cameron GG .20 .06
703 Torii Hunter GG .20 .06
704 Ichiro Suzuki GG .50 .15
705 Greg Maddux GG .50 .15
706 Brad Ausmus GG .20 .06
707 Todd Helton GG .20 .06
708 Fernando Vina GG .20 .06
709 Scott Rolen GG .30 .09
710 Orlando Cabrera GG .20 .06
711 Andruw Jones GG .20 .06
712 Jim Edmonds GG .20 .06
713 Larry Walker GG .20 .06
714 Roger Clemens CY .50 .15
715 Randy Johnson CY .30 .09
716 Ichiro Suzuki MVP .50 .15
717 Barry Bonds MVP .50 .15
718 Ichiro Suzuki ROY .50 .15
719 Albert Pujols ROY .50 .15

2002 Topps Gold

Inserted one per 19 first series hobby packs, one per 15 first series retail packs, one per 5 first series HTA packs, one per 12 second series hobby packs, one per 9 second series retail packs and one per three second series HTA packs, this set parallels cards 1-330 and 366-695 of the 2002 Topps set. Each card features bold, gold-foil borders on front and 2002 serial-numbered sets were produced.

Nm-Mt Ex-Mt
*GOLD 1-306/366-670: 8X TO 20X BASIC
*GOLD 307-330/671-695: 3X TO 8X BASIC
*GOLD 426-427: 2X TO 5X BASIC......

2002 Topps Home Team Advantage

This is a parallel to the Topps set. Each of these cards, which were available only in the blue factory sets have the words "Home Team Advantage" stamped on them.

Nm-Mt Ex-Mt
COMP.FACT.SET (685) 70.00 21.00
*HTA: .75X TO 2X BASIC
*BONDS HR 70: .2X TO .5X BASIC HR 70

2002 Topps Limited

This 790 card factory set was issued in October, 2002. It had a SRP of $150 and parallels the regular Topps set except for the reprinting of all 73 Barry Bonds 365 cards. These cards can be differentiated from the regular cards by their "glossy" finish on the front.

Nm-Mt Ex-Mt
COMP.FACT.SET (790) 200.00 60.00
*LTD STARS: 2X TO 5X BASIC CARDS
*307-331/426-427/622/671-695: 1.5X TO 4X
*BONDS HR: .2X TO .5X BASIC BONDS HR

2002 Topps 1952 Reprints

Inserted at a rate of one in 25 hobby, one in five HTA packs and one in 16 retail packs, these nineteen reprint cards feature players who participated in the 1952 World Series which was won by the New York Yankees.

Nm-Mt Ex-Mt
COMPLETE SET (19) 50.00 15.00
COMPLETE SERIES 1 (9) 25.00 7.50
COMPLETE SERIES 2 (10) 25.00 7.50
52R-1 Roy Campanella 5.00 1.50
52R-2 Duke Snider 4.00 1.20
52R-3 Carl Erskine 4.00 1.20
52R-4 Andy Pafko 4.00 1.20
52R-5 Johnny Mize 4.00 1.20
52R-6 Billy Martin 5.00 1.50
52R-7 Phil Rizzuto 5.00 1.50
52R-8 Gil McDougald 4.00 1.20
52R-9 Allie Reynolds 4.00 1.20
52R-10 Jackie Robinson 5.00 1.50
52R-11 Preacher Roe 4.00 1.20
52R-12 Gil Hodges 5.00 1.50
52R-13 Billy Cox 4.00 1.20
52R-14 Yogi Berra 5.00 1.50
52R-15 Gene Woodling 4.00 1.20
52R-16 Johnny Sain 4.00 1.20
52R-17 Ralph Houk 4.00 1.20
52R-18 Joe Collins 4.00 1.20
52R-19 Hank Bauer 4.00 1.20

2002 Topps 1952 Reprints Autographs

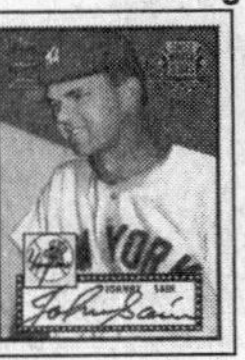
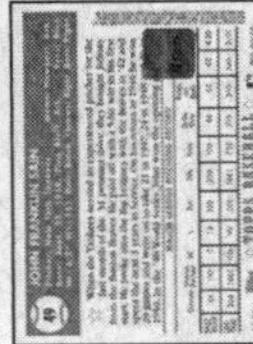

Inserted in series one packs at a rate of one in 10,268 hobby packs, one in 2826 HTA packs and one in 8,005 retail packs and series two packs at a rate of 1:7524 hobby, one in 1985 HTA packs and one in 5839 retail packs these eleven cards feature signed copies of the 1952 reprints. Phil Rizzuto did not return his cards in time for inclusion in this product and those cards could be redeemed until December 1st, 2003. Due to scarcity, no pricing is provided for these cards. These cards were released in different series and we have notated that information next to the player's name in our checklist.

Nm-Mt Ex-Mt
AP-A Andy Pafko S1 150.00 45.00
CE-A Carl Erskine S1 100.00 30.00
DS-A Duke Snider S1 150.00 45.00

GM-A Gil McDougald S1 .... 100.00 30.00
HB-A Hank Bauer S2
JB-A Joe Black S1 .... 100.00 30.00
JS-A Johnny Sain S2
PR-A Preacher Roe S2
PR-A Phil Rizzuto S1 .... 150.00 45.00
RH-A Ralph Houk S2
YB-A Yogi Berra S2

2002 Topps 1952 World Series Highlights

Inserted in first and second series packs at a rate of one in 25 hobby, one in five HTA and one in 16 retail packs, these eleven cards feature highlights of the 1952 World Series. Next to the card, we have notated whether they were released in the first or second series.

Nm-Mt Ex-Mt
COMPLETE SET (7) 10.00 3.00
COMPLETE SERIES 1 (3) 4.00 1.20
COMPLETE SERIES 2 (4) 6.00 1.80
52WS-1 Dodgers Line Up 1 .... 2.00 .60
52WS-2 Billy Martin's Homer 2 .. 2.00 .60
52WS-3 Dodgers Celebrate 1 ..... 2.00 .60
52WS-4 Yanks Slip Dodgers 2 .... 2.00 .60
52WS-5 Carl Erskine 1 .... 2.00 .60
52WS-6 Casey Stengel MG .... 2.00 .60
Allie Reynolds 2
52WS-7 Allie Reynolds .... 2.00 .60
Relieves Ed Lopat 2

2002 Topps 5-Card Stud Aces Relics

nserted into second series packs at a rate of one n 1180 hobby, one in 293 HTA and one in 966 retail, these five cards feature some of the best pitchers in baseball along with a game jersey swatch "relic".

Nm-Mt Ex-Mt
5A-GM Greg Maddux Jsy 40.00 12.00
5A-MH Mike Hampton Jsy 15.00 4.50
5A-MM Mark Mulder Jsy 15.00 4.50
5A-PM Pedro Martinez Jsy 25.00 7.50
5A-RJ Randy Johnson Jsy 25.00 7.50

2002 Topps 5-Card Stud Deuces are Wild Relics

nserted into second series packs at an overall rate of one in 1962 hobby, one in 487 HTA and one in 1609 retail, these five cards feature memorabilia game bat and game jersey relics from two of the stars from the same team. These cards were issued in different odds depending on which series they were from and we have notated which group next to the card in the checklist.

Nm-Mt Ex-Mt
SER.2 A ODDS 1:3078 H, 1:796 HTA, 1:2422 R
SER.2 B ODDS 1:5410 H, 1:1254 HTA, 1:4827 R
5D-BG Bret Boone Jsy 25.00 7.50
Freddy Garcia Jsy A
5D-BK Barry Bonds Jsy 50.00 15.00
Jeff Kent Jsy A
5D-JG Randy Johnson Jsy 40.00 12.00
Luis Gonzalez Bat B
5D-TA Jim Thome Jsy 40.00 12.00
Roberto Alomar Bat B
5D-WH Larry Walker Bat 40.00 12.00
Todd Helton Bat B

2002 Topps 5-Card Stud Jack of All Trades Relics

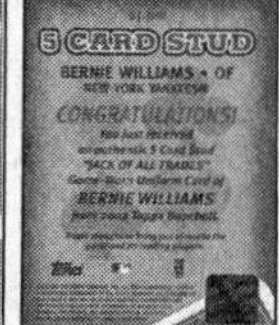

serted into second series packs at an overall rate of one in 1350 Hobby packs, one in 333 HTA packs and one on 1119 retail packs, these five cards feature some of the best five-tool players in the field along with a game-used memorabilia relic from their career. These cards were issued at different odds depending on the player and we have notated that information in our checklist.

Nm-Mt Ex-Mt
5J-AJ Andruw Jones A 15.00 4.50
5J-BB Barry Bonds A 40.00 12.00
5J-BW Bernie Williams A 25.00 7.50
5J-IR Ivan Rodriguez A 25.00 7.50
5J-RO Roberto Alomar B

2002 Topps 5-Card Stud Kings of the Clubhouse Relics

Inserted into packs at an overall rate of one in 1449 hobby packs, one in 334 HTA packs and one in 1119 retail packs, these five cards feature some of the most effective and highly driven clubhouse leaders along with a game-used memorabilia relic from their career. Depending on the player, these cards were issued in two groups and we have notated that information in our checklist.

Nm-Mt Ex-Mt
SER.2 A ODDS 1:1570 H, 1:358 HTA, 1:1211 R
SER.2B ODDS 1:18883 H,1:4943 HTA,1:14736 R
5K-EM Edgar Martinez A 25.00 7.50
5K-PO Paul O'Neill B
5K-RJ Randy Johnson A 25.00 7.50
5K-TG Tom Glavine A 25.00 7.50
5K-TH Todd Helton A 25.00 7.50

2002 Topps 5-Card Stud Three of a Kind Relics

Inserted into packs at an overall rate of one in 2039 Hobby packs, one in 524 HTA packs and one in retail 1609 packs, these five cards feature memorabilia relics from three stars from the same team. Depending on the card, these cards were issued as part of two groups, and we have notated that information next to the card in our checklist

Nm-Mt Ex-Mt
SER.2 A ODDS 1:3078 H, 1:796 HTA, 1:2422 R
SER.2 B ODDS 1:6043 H, 1:1532 HTA, 1:4827 R
5TBDB A.J. Burnett 60.00 18.00
Ryan Dempster
Josh Beckett A
5TFBJ Rafael Furcal 60.00 18.00
Wilson Betemit
Andruw Jones B
5TLOC Carlos Lee 80.00 24.00
Magglio Ordonez
Jose Canseco B
5TPSW Jorge Posada 80.00 24.00
Alfonso Soriano
Bernie Williams B
5TSPA Tsuyoshi Shinjo 80.00 24.00
Mike Piazza
Edgardo Alfonzo A

2002 Topps All-World Team

Inserted into second series packs at a rate of one in 12 packs and one in 4 HTA packs, these 25 cards feature an international mix of upper-echelon stars. These cards are extremely thick as well.

Nm-Mt Ex-Mt
COMPLETE SET (25) 60.00 18.00
AW-1 Ichiro Suzuki .... 3.00 .90
AW-2 Barry Bonds 5.00 1.50
AW-3 Pedro Martinez .... 2.00 .60
AW-4 Juan Gonzalez .... 1.50 .45
AW-5 Larry Walker .... 1.50 .45
AW-6 Sammy Sosa .... 3.00 .90
AW-7 Mariano Rivera .... 1.50 .45
AW-8 Vladimir Guerrero .... 2.00 .60
AW-9 Alex Rodriguez .... 3.00 .90
AW-10 Albert Pujols 4.00 1.20
AW-11 Luis Gonzalez .... 1.50 .45
AW-12 Ken Griffey Jr. .... 3.00 .90
AW-13 Kazuhiro Sasaki .... 1.50 .45
AW-14 Bob Abreu .... 1.50 .45
AW-15 Todd Helton .... 1.50 .45
AW-16 Nomar Garciaparra .... 3.00 .90
AW-17 Miguel Tejada .... 1.50 .45
AW-18 Roger Clemens 4.00 1.20
AW-19 Mike Piazza .... 3.00 .90
AW-20 Carlos Delgado .... 1.50 .45
AW-21 Derek Jeter 5.00 1.50
AW-22 Hideo Nomo .... 2.00 .60
AW-23 Randy Johnson .... 2.00 .60
AW-24 Ivan Rodriguez .... 2.00 .60
AW-25 Chan Ho Park .... 1.50 .45

2002 Topps Autographs

Inserted at varying odds, these 40 cards feature authentic autographs. Alex Rodriguez, Barry Bonds and Xavier Nady did not return their cards in time for series one packout, thus exchange cards were seeded into packs. Those cards could be redeemed until December 1st, 2003. First series cards have a numerical card number on back (i.e. TA-1) and series two cards have card numbering based on player's initials (i.e. TA-AB).

Nm-Mt Ex-Mt
SER.1 A 1:15,402 H, 1:4256 HTA, 1:12,008 R
SER.2 A 1:10,071 H, 1:2404, 1:7702 R
SER.1 B 1:49,599 H, 1:12,312 HTA, 1:46,944 R
SER.2 B 1:1867 H, 1:487 HTA, 1:1449 R
SER.1 C 1:4104 H, 1:1130 HTA, 1:3238 R
SER.2 C 1:10,071 H, 1:2646 HTA, 1:7702 R
SER.1 D 1:9853 H, 1:2714 HTA, 1:7284 R
SER.2 D 1:1885 H, 1:496 HTA, 1:1449 R
SER.1 E 1:4104 H, 1:1130 HTA, 1:3238 R
SER.2 E 1:5023 H, 1:1323 HTA, 1:3851 R
SER.1 F 1:985 H, 1:271 HTA, 1:776 R
SER.2 F 1:940 H, 1:247 HTA, 1:725 R
SER.2 G 1:3017 H, 1:794 HTA, 1:2327 R
NO A1/B1 PRICING DUE TO SCARCITY
TA-1 Carlos Delgado B1 .... 40.00 12.00
TA-2 Ivan Rodriguez A1 .... 60.00 18.00
TA-3 Miguel Tejada C1 .... 25.00 7.50
TA-4 Geoff Jenkins E1 .... 15.00 4.50
TA-5 Johnny Damon A1 .... 50.00 15.00
TA-6 Tim Hudson C1 .... 30.00 9.00
TA-7 Terrence Long E1 .... 15.00 4.50
TA-8 Gabe Kapler C1 .... 15.00 4.50
TA-9 Magglio Ordonez C1 .... 25.00 7.50
TA-10 Barry Bonds A1 .... 350.00 105.00
TA-11 Pat Burrell C1 .... 25.00 7.50
TA-12 Mike Mussina A1 .... 50.00 15.00
TA-13 Eric Valent F1 .... 10.00 3.00
TA-14 Xavier Nady F1 .... 10.00 3.00
TA-15 Cristian Guerrero F1 .... 10.00 3.00
TA-16 Ben Sheets F1 .... 15.00 4.50
TA-17 Corey Patterson C1 .... 25.00 7.50
TA-18 Carlos Pena F1 .... 10.00 3.00
TA-19 Alex Rodriguez 120.00 36.00
D1/A2 EXCH
TA-AB Adrian Beltre B2 .... 50.00 15.00
TA-AE Alex Escobar F2 .... 15.00 4.50
TA-BG Brian Giles B2 .... 30.00 9.00
TA-BW Brad Wilkerson G2 .... 10.00 3.00
TA-BGR Ben Grieve B2 .... 30.00 9.00
TA-CF Cliff Floyd C2 .... 25.00 7.50
TA-CG Cristian Guzman B2 .... 30.00 9.00
TA-JD Jermaine Dye D2 .... 25.00 7.50
TA-JH Josh Hamilton E2 .... 15.00 4.50
TA-JO Jose Ortiz D2 .... 15.00 4.50
TA-JR Jimmy Rollins D2 .... 25.00 7.50
TA-JW Justin Wayne D2 .... 15.00 4.50
TA-KG Keith Ginter F2 .... 10.00 3.00
TA-MS Mike Sweeney B2 .... 30.00 9.00
TA-NJ Nick Johnson F2 .... 10.00 3.00
TA-RF Rafael Furcal B2 .... 30.00 9.00
TA-RK Ryan Klesko B2 .... 30.00 9.00
TA-RO Roy Oswalt F2 .... 15.00 4.50
TA-RP Rafael Palmeiro A2 .... 60.00 18.00
TA-RS Richie Sexson B2 .... 30.00 9.00
TA-TG Troy Glaus A2 .... 40.00 12.00

2002 Topps Coaches Collection Relics

Inserted at overall odds of one in 236 retail packs, these 26 cards feature memorabilia from either a coach or a manager currently involved in major league baseball. The Billy Williams jersey card was not available when these cards were packed and that card could be redeemed until April 30th, 2004.

Nm-Mt Ex-Mt
SER.2 BAT ODDS 1:404 RETAIL
SER.2 UNIFORM ODDS 1:565 RETAIL
CC-AH Art Howe Bat 25.00 7.50
CC-AT Alan Trammell Bat 40.00 12.00
CC-BB Bruce Bochy Bat 25.00 7.50
CC-BM Buck Martinez Bat 25.00 7.50
CC-BV Bobby Valentine Bat 40.00 12.00
CC-BW Billy Williams Jsy 40.00 12.00
CC-BBE Buddy Bell Bat 40.00 12.00
CC-BBR Bob Brenly Bat 40.00 12.00
CC-DB Dusty Baker Bat 40.00 12.00
CC-DL Davey Lopes Bat 40.00 12.00
CC-DBA Don Baylor Bat 40.00 12.00
CC-EH Elrod Hendricks Bat 25.00 7.50
CC-EM Eddie Murray Bat 60.00 18.00
CC-FW Frank White Bat 40.00 12.00
CC-HM Hal McRae Jsy 10.00 3.00
CC-JT Joe Torre Jsy 15.00 4.50
CC-KG Ken Griffey Sr. Jsy 10.00 3.00
CC-LB Larry Bowa Bat 40.00 12.00
CC-LP Lance Parrish Bat 40.00 12.00
CC-MH Mike Hargrove Bat 40.00 12.00
CC-MS Mike Scioscia Bat 40.00 12.00
CC-MW Mookie Wilson Bat 40.00 12.00
CC-PG Phil Garner Bat 25.00 7.50
CC-PM Paul Molitor Bat 50.00 15.00
CC-TP Tony Perez Jsy 10.00 3.00
CC-WR Willie Randolph Bat 40.00 12.00

2002 Topps Draft Picks

This 10-card set was distributed in two separate cello-wrapped five-card packets. Cards 1-5 were distributed in late August, 2002 as a bonus in green-boxed 2002 Topps retail factory sets. Cards 6-10 were distributed in November, 2002 within 2002 Topps Holiday factory sets. The cards are designed in the same manner as the Draft Picks and Prospects subsets from the basic 2002 Topps set and feature a selection of players chosen in the 2002 MLB Draft.

Nm-Mt Ex-Mt
COMPLETE SET (10) 50.00 15.00
COMP.SERIES 1 SET (5) 25.00 7.50
COMP.SERIES 2 SET (5) 25.00 7.50
1 Scott Moore 8.00 2.40
2 Val Majewski 10.00 3.00
3 Brian Slocum 5.00 1.50
4 Chris Gruler 8.00 2.40
5 Mark Schramek 8.00 2.40
6 Joe Saunders 5.00 1.50
7 Jeff Francis 10.00 3.00
8 Royce Ring 8.00 2.40
9 Greg Miller 10.00 3.00
10 Brandon Weeden 5.00 1.50

2002 Topps East Meets West

Issued at a rate of one in 24, these eight cards feature Masanori Murakami along with eight other Japanese players who have also played in the major leagues.

Nm-Mt Ex-Mt
COMPLETE SET (8) 15.00 4.50
EWHI Hideki Irabu .... 2.00 .60
Masanori Murakami
EWHN Hideo Nomo .... 2.00 .60
Masanori Murakami
EWKS Kazuhiro Sasaki .... 2.00 .60
Masanori Murakami
EWMS Mac Suzuki .... 2.00 .60
Masanori Murakami
EWMY Masato Yoshii .... 2.00 .60
Masanori Murakami
EWSH S. Hasagawa .... 2.00 .60
Masanori Murakami
EWTO Tomo Ohka .... 2.00 .60
Masanori Murakami
EWTS Tsuyoshi Shinjo .... 2.00 .60
Masanori Murakami

2002 Topps East Meets West Relics

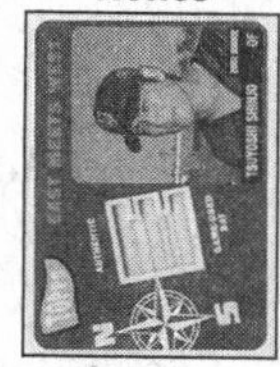

Inserted in packs at different odds depending on whether it is a bat or jersey card, these three cards feature game-used relics from Japanese born players.

Nm-Mt Ex-Mt
SR1 BAT 1:12296 H,1:3380 HTA,1:9606 R
SER.1 JSY 1:3419 H, 1:939 HTA, 1:2685 R
EWR-HN Hideo Nomo Jsy 50.00 15.00
EWR-KS K. Sasaki Jsy 25.00 7.50
EWR-TS T. Shinjo Bat 25.00 7.50

2002 Topps Ebbets Field Seat Relics

Inserted at a rate of one in 9,116 hobby packs, one in 2516 HTA packs and one in 7,222 retail packs, these nine cards feature not only the player but a slice of a seat used at Brooklyn's Ebbets Field.

Nm-Mt Ex-Mt
EFR-AP Andy Pafko 120.00 36.00
EFR-BC Billy Cox 120.00 36.00
EFR-CF Carl Furillo 120.00 36.00
EFR-DS Duke Snider 150.00 45.00
EFR-GH Gil Hodges 150.00 45.00
EFR-JB Joe Black 120.00 36.00
EFR-JR Jackie Robinson 250.00 75.00
EFR-RC Roy Campanella 200.00 60.00
EFR-PWR Pee Wee Reese 150.00 45.00

2002 Topps Ebbets Field/Yankee Stadium Seat Dual Relics

Featuring a slice of a seat from both Ebbets Field and from Yankee Stadium, these cards feature a selection of leading players from the 1952 World Series paired up with actual pieces of stadium seats taken from the historic Ebbets Field and Yankee Stadium ballparks. The Snider/Berra card was inserted at a rate of one in 86,070 series one hobby packs and the Rizzuto/Pafko card was inserted ata rate of one in 59,511 series two hobby packs. Only 52 copies of each card were produced. Both cards were intended to be hand-numbered (i.e. 1/52, 2/52 etc.) but due to production errors only the Snider/Berra card packed out as such.

Nm-Mt Ex-Mt
RP Phil Rizzuto
Andy Pafko
SB Duke Snider
Yogi Berra

2002 Topps Ebbets Field/Yankee Stadium Seat Dual Relics Autographs

Inserted into first series packs at stated odds of one in 15,670 HTA packs and second series packs at a rate of one in 11,908 HTA packs, these cards feature a stadium seat along with an autograph of both featured players on these cards. Each card was issued to 25 serial numbered sets and due to market scarcity, no pricing is provided. The Rizzuto/Pafko card from series two was seeded into packs as an exchange card with a deadline of April 30th, 2004.

Nm-Mt Ex-Mt
RP Phil Rizzuto
Andy Pafko 2
SB Duke Snider
Yogi Berra 1

2002 Topps Hall of Fame Vintage BuyBacks AutoProofs

In one of the most ambitious efforts put forth by a manufacturer in hobby history, Topps went into the secondary market and bought more than 3,500 vintage Topps cards (including an amazing selection from the 1950's and 1960's) featuring almost two dozen Hall of Famers (including stars such as Nolan Ryan, Yogi Berra and Carl Yastrzemski) for this far-reaching AutoProofs promotion. In most cases, 100 count lots of each vintage card were used (a staggering figure considering the scarcity of many of the 1950's and 1960's cards) with a few of the more common cards from the early 1980's tallying 200 or 300 count lots. After repurchase, each card was signed by the featured athlete, serial-numbered to a specific amount (exact print runs provided in our checklist) and affixed with a Topps hologram of authenticity on back. The cards were distributed across many 2002 Topps products - starting off with 2002 Topps series one baseball in November, 2001. Odds for finding these cards in packs is as follows: series 1 - 1:2341 hobby and 1:1841 retail; series 2 - 1:2341 hobby, 1:tbd retail.

Nm-Mt Ex-Mt
BR17 B.Robinson 82 KM/200 ... 40.00 12.00
EW10 Earl Weaver 87/100 .... 25.00 7.50
FJ33 F.Jenkins 84/100 .... 25.00 7.50
GP26 G.Perry 82/100 .... 25.00 7.50
GP29 G.Perry 83/100 .... 25.00 7.50
GP30 G.Perry 83 SV/200 .... 25.00 7.50
OC2 Orl Cepeda 82 KM/200 ..... 25.00 7.50
RF15 R.Fingers 81/300 .... 25.00 7.50
RF16 R.Fingers 81 LL/100 .... 25.00 7.50
RF18 R.Fingers 82/100 .... 25.00 7.50
RF19 Rollie Fingers 82 IA/200 .. 25.00 7.50
RF21 Rollie Fingers 82 KM/300 25.00 7.50
RF22 Rollie Fingers 83/200 ...... 25.00 7.50
RF24 Rollie Fingers 84/200 ...... 25.00 7.50
RF27 R.Fingers 85/300 .... 25.00 7.50

RF28 Rollie Fingers 86/100 ...... 25.00 7.50
SC7 S.Carlton 84 LL V/100 ...... 40.00 12.00
SC8 Steve Carlton 85/200 ...... 40.00 12.00
SC10 Steve Carlton 87/200 ...... 40.00 12.00

2002 Topps Hobby Masters

Inserted at a rate of one in 25 hobby and one in 16 retail packs, these 20 cards feature some of the leading players in the game.

Nm-Mt Ex-Mt
COMPLETE SET (20) 80.00 24.00
HM1 Mark McGwire 8.00 2.40
HM2 Derek Jeter 8.00 2.40
HM3 Chipper Jones ...... 3.00 .90
HM4 Roger Clemens 6.00 1.80
HM5 Vladimir Guerrero ...... 3.00 .90
HM6 Ichiro Suzuki 5.00 1.50
HM7 Todd Helton ...... 3.00 .90
HM8 Alex Rodriguez 5.00 1.50
HM9 Albert Pujols 6.00 1.80
HM10 Sammy Sosa 5.00 1.50
HM11 Ken Griffey Jr. 5.00 1.50
HM12 Randy Johnson ...... 3.00 .90
HM13 Nomar Garciaparra 5.00 1.50
HM14 Ivan Rodriguez ...... 3.00 .90
HM15 Manny Ramirez ...... 3.00 .90
HM16 Barry Bonds 8.00 2.40
HM17 Mike Piazza 5.00 1.50
HM18 Pedro Martinez ...... 3.00 .90
HM19 Jeff Bagwell ...... 3.00 .90
HM20 Luis Gonzalez ...... 3.00 .90

2002 Topps Like Father Like Son Relics

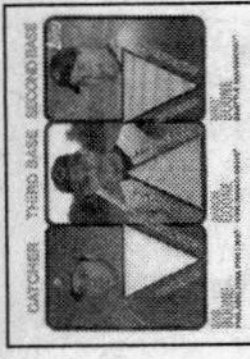
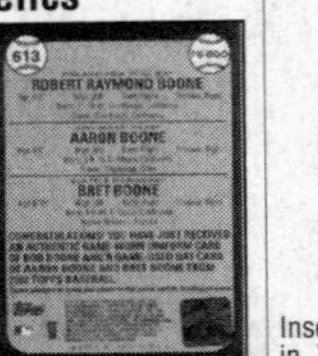

These combination memorabilia cards feature famous baseball families with two generations of fathers and sons. The card designs are each based upon the original Topps design of the father's rookie card season (aka The Boone Family card features a 1973 Topps style to honor the year Bob Boone had his Rookie Card issued). The cards were seeded exclusively into retail packs at a rate of 1:1304.

Nm-Mt Ex-Mt
FS-AL Sandy Alomar Sr. Bat 80.00 24.00
Sandy Alomar Jr. Bat
Roberto Alomar Bat
FS-BE Yogi Berra Jsy 80.00 24.00
Dale Berra Jsy
FS-BON Bobby Bonds 120.00 36.00
Barry Bonds
FS-BOO Bob Boone Jsy 80.00 24.00
Aaron Boone Jsy
Bret Boone Bat
FS-CR Jose Cruz Sr. 80.00 24.00
Jose Cruz Jr.

2002 Topps Own the Game

Issued at a rate of one in 12 hobby packs and one in eight retail packs, these 30 cards feature players who are among the league leaders for their position.

Nm-Mt Ex-Mt
COMPLETE SET (30) 40.00 12.00
OG1 Moises Alou ...... 1.00 .30
OG2 Roberto Alomar ...... 1.50 .45
OG3 Luis Gonzalez ...... 1.00 .30
OG4 Bret Boone ...... 1.00 .30
OG5 Barry Bonds 6.00 1.80
OG6 Jim Thome ...... 2.50 .75
OG7 Jimmy Rollins ...... 1.00 .30
OG8 Cristian Guzman ...... 1.00 .30
OG9 Lance Berkman ...... 1.00 .30
OG10 Mike Sweeney ...... 1.00 .30
OG11 Rich Aurilia ...... 1.00 .30
OG12 Ichiro Suzuki 4.00 1.20
OG13 Luis Gonzalez ...... 1.00 .30
OG14 Ichiro Suzuki 4.00 1.20
OG15 Jimmy Rollins ...... 1.00 .30
OG16 Roger Cedeno ...... 1.00 .30
OG17 Barry Bonds 6.00 1.80
OG18 Jim Thome ...... 2.50 .75
OG19 Curt Schilling ...... 1.00 .30
OG20 Roger Clemens 5.00 1.50
OG21 Curt Schilling ...... 1.00 .30
OG22 Brad Radke ...... 1.00 .30
OG23 Greg Maddux 4.00 1.20
OG24 Mark Mulder ...... 1.00 .30
OG25 Jeff Shaw ...... 1.00 .30
OG26 Mariano Rivera ...... 1.50 .45
OG27 Randy Johnson ...... 2.50 .75
OG28 Pedro Martinez ...... 2.50 .75
OG29 John Burkett ...... 1.00 .30
OG30 Tim Hudson ...... 1.00 .30

2002 Topps Prime Cuts Autograph Relics

Inserted into first series packs at a rate of one in 88,678 hobby and one in 24,624 HTA and second series packs at one in 8927 hobby and one in 2360 HTA packs, these eight cards feature both a memorabilia relic from the player's career as well as their autograph. Cards from series one were issued to a stated print run of 60 serial numbered sets while cards from series two were issued to a stated print run of 50 serial numbered sets. We have notated next to the players name which series the card was issued in.

Nm-Mt Ex-Mt
NO PRICING DUE TO SCARCITY ......
PCA-AE Alex Escobar S2 ......
PCA-BB Barry Bonds S1 ......
PCA-JH Josh Hamilton S2 ......
PCA-NJ Nick Johnson S2 ......
PCA-TH Toby Hall S2 ......
PCA-WB Wilson Betemit S2 ......
PCA-XN Xavier Nady S2 ......
PCA-CPE Carlos Pena S2 ......

2002 Topps Prime Cuts Barrel Relics

Inserted in second series packs at a rate of one in 7824 hobby packs and one in 2063 HTA packs, these eight cards feature a piece from the selected player bat barrel. These cards were issued to a stated print run of 50 serial numbered sets.

Nm-Mt Ex-Mt
NO PRICING DUE TO SCARCITY ......
PCA-AD Adam Dunn ......
PCA-AG Alexis Gomez ......
PCA-AR Aaron Rowand ......
PCA-CP Corey Patterson ......
PCA-JC Joe Crede ......
PCA-MG Marcus Giles ......
PCA-RS Ruben Salazar ......
PCA-SB Sean Burroughs ......

2002 Topps Prime Cuts Pine Tar Relics

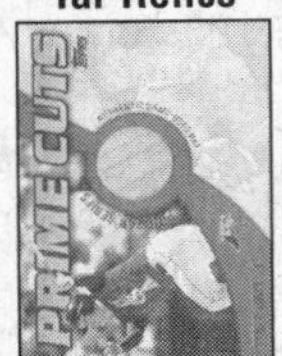

Inserted in packs at stated odds of one in 4,420 hobby packs and one in 1214 HTA packs for first series packs and one in 1043 hobby and one in 275 HTA packs for second series packs, these 20 cards feature pieces from the pine tar section of the player's bat. We have notated which series the player was issued in next to his name in our checklist. These cards have a stated print run of 200 serial numbered sets.

Nm-Mt Ex-Mt
PCP-AD Adam Dunn 2 ...... 40.00 12.00
PCP-AE Alex Escobar 2 ...... 25.00 7.50
PCP-AG Alexis Gomez 2 ...... 25.00 7.50
PCP-AP Albert Pujols 1 ...... 60.00 18.00
PCP-AR Aaron Rowand 2 ...... 25.00 7.50
PCP-BB Barry Bonds 1 ...... 80.00 24.00
PCP-CP Corey Patterson 2 ...... 25.00 7.50
PCP-JC Joe Crede 2 ...... 25.00 7.50
PCP-JH Josh Hamilton 2 ...... 25.00 7.50
PCP-LG Luis Gonzalez 1 ...... 25.00 7.50
PCP-MG Marcus Giles 2 ...... 25.00 7.50
PCP-NJ Nick Johnson 2 ...... 25.00 7.50
PCP-RS Ruben Salazar 2 ...... 25.00 7.50
PCP-SB Sean Burroughs 2 ...... 25.00 7.50
PCP-TG Tony Gwynn 1 ...... 50.00 15.00
PCP-TH Todd Helton 1 ...... 40.00 12.00
PCP-TH Toby Hall 2 ...... 25.00 7.50
PCP-WB Wilson Betemit 2 ...... 25.00 7.50
PCP-XN Xavier Nady 2 ...... 25.00 7.50
PCP-CPE Carlos Pena 2 ...... 25.00 7.50

2002 Topps Prime Cuts Trademark Relics

Issued in first series packs at a rate of one in 8,868 hobby and one in 2428 HTA packs and second series packs at a rate of one in 2087 hobby and one in 549 HTA packs, these cards

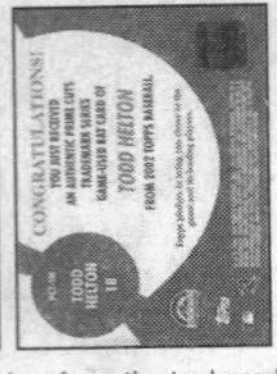

feature a slice of bat taken from the trademark section of a game used bat. Only 100 serial numbered copies of each card were produced. First and second series distribution information is detailed after the player's name in our set checklist.

Nm-Mt Ex-Mt
PCT-AD Adam Dunn 2 ...... 60.00 18.00
PCT-AE Alex Escobar 2 ...... 40.00 12.00
PCT-AG Alexis Gomez 2 ...... 40.00 12.00
PCT-AP Albert Pujols 1 ...... 100.00 30.00
PCT-AR Aaron Rowand 2 ...... 40.00 12.00
PCT-BB Barry Bonds 1 ...... 120.00 36.00
PCT-CP Corey Patterson 2 ...... 40.00 12.00
PCT-JC Joe Crede 2 ...... 40.00 12.00
PCT-JH Josh Hamilton 2 ...... 40.00 12.00
PCT-LG Luis Gonzalez 1 ...... 40.00 12.00
PCT-MG Marcus Giles 2 ...... 40.00 12.00
PCT-NJ Nick Johnson 2 ...... 40.00 12.00
PCT-RS Ruben Salazar 2 ...... 40.00 12.00
PCT-SB Sean Burroughs 2 ...... 40.00 12.00
PCT-TG Tony Gwynn 1 ...... 80.00 24.00
PCT-TH Todd Helton 1 ...... 60.00 18.00
PCT-TH Toby Hall 2 ...... 40.00 12.00
PCT-WB Wilson Betemit 2 ...... 40.00 12.00
PCT-XN Xavier Nady 2 ...... 40.00 12.00
PCT-CPE Carlos Pena 2 ...... 40.00 12.00

2002 Topps Ring Masters

Issued at a rate of one in 25 hobby packs and one in 16 retail packs, these 10 cards feature players who have earned World Series rings in their career.

Nm-Mt Ex-Mt
COMPLETE SET (10) 25.00 7.50
RM1 Derek Jeter 5.00 1.50
RM2 Mark McGwire 5.00 1.50
RM3 Mariano Rivera ...... 1.50 .45
RM4 Gary Sheffield ...... 1.50 .45
RM5 Al Leiter ...... 1.50 .45
RM6 Chipper Jones ...... 2.00 .60
RM7 Roger Clemens 4.00 1.20
RM8 Greg Maddux ...... 3.00 .90
RM9 Roberto Alomar ...... 1.50 .45
RM10 Paul O'Neill ...... 1.50 .45

2002 Topps Summer School Battery Mates Relics

Issued at a rate of one in 4,4401 hobby packs and one in 3,477 retail packs, these two cards feature a pitcher and catcher from the same team.

Nm-Mt Ex-Mt
BM-LP Al Leiter 40.00 12.00
Mike Piazza
BM-ML Greg Maddux 40.00 12.00
Javy Lopez

2002 Topps Summer School Heart of the Order Relics

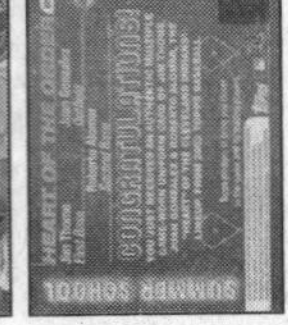

Issued at an overall rate of one in 4,247 hobby packs and one in 3,325 retail packs, these four cards feature relics from three key players from a team's lineup.

Nm-Mt Ex-Mt
SER.1 A 1:8,220 H, 1:2253 HTA, 1:6452 R
SER.1 B 1:8,778 H, 1:2411 HTA, 1:6862 R
HTO-ARB Bob Abreu 80.00 24.00
Scott Rolen
Pat Burrell A
HTO-KBA Jeff Kent 100.00 30.00
Barry Bonds
Rich Aurilia A
HTO-OWM Paul O'Neill 80.00 24.00
Bernie Williams
Tino Martinez
HTO-TGA Jim Thome 80.00 24.00
Juan Gonzalez
Roberto Alomar

2002 Topps Summer School Hit and Run Relics

Issued at an overall rate of one in 4,241 hobby packs and one in 3,325 HTA packs, these three cards feature relics from some of the leading young stars in baseball.

Nm-Mt Ex-Mt
SER.1 A 1:24591 H, 1:6760 HTA, 1:19649 R
SER.1 B 1:12296 H, 1:3380 HTA, 1:9606 R
SER.1 C 1:8788 H, 1:2411 HTA, 1:6862 R
HRR-DE Darin Erstad 15.00 4.50
UER BAT B
Name spelled Darrin on front
HRR-JD J.Damon Bat A 25.00 7.50
HRR-RF R.Furcal Jsy C 15.00 4.50

2002 Topps Summer School Turn Two Relics

Issued at a rate of one in 4,401 hobby packs and one in 3,477 retail packs, these two cards feature relics from two of the best double play combination in baseball's history.

Nm-Mt Ex-Mt
TTR-TW Alan Trammell 50.00 15.00
Lou Whitaker
TTR-VA Omar Vizquel 50.00 15.00
Roberto Alomar

2002 Topps Summer School Two Bagger Relics

Issued at an overall rate of one in 3,733 hobby packs and one in 2,941 retail packs, these three cards feature game-used relics from leading hitters in the game.

Nm-Mt Ex-Mt
SER.1 A 1:4401 H, 1:1210 HTA, 1:3477 R
SER.1 B 1:24591 H,1:6760 HTA,1:19649 R
2B-SR Scott Rolen Jsy A 25.00 7.50
2B-TG Tony Gwynn Bat B 40.00 12.00
2B-TH Todd Helton Jsy A 25.00 7.50

2002 Topps Yankee Stadium Seat Relics

Inserted into second series packs at a stated rate of one in 579 Hobby, one in 1472 HTA and one in 4313 Retail, these nine cards feature retired Yankee greats along with a piece of a seat used in the originaly Yankee Stadium.

Nm-Mt Ex-Mt
YSR-AR Allie Reynolds 120.00 36.00
YSR-BM Billy Martin 150.00 45.00
YSR-GM Gil McDougald 120.00 36.00
YSR-GW Gene Woodling 120.00 36.00
YSR-HB Hank Bauer 120.00 36.00
YSR-JC Joe Collins 120.00 36.00
YSR-JM Johnny Mize 120.00 36.00
YSR-PR Phil Rizzuto 150.00 45.00
YSR-YB Yogi Berra 200.00 60.00

2002 Topps Traded

This 275 card set was released in October, 2002. These cards were issued in 10 card hobby packs which were issued 24 packs to a box and 12 boxes to a case with an SRP of $3 per pack. In addition, this product was also issued in 35 count HTA packs. Cards numbered 1 to 100 were issued one per pack. Cards from previous traded sets were repurchased by Topps and were issued at a stated rate of one in 24 Hobby and Retail Packs and one in 10 HTA packs. However,

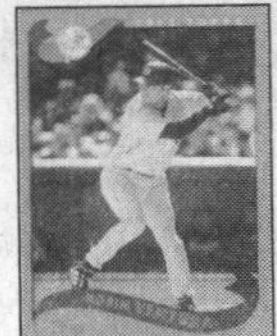

there is no way of being able to identify that these cards are anything but original cards as no marking or stamping is on these cards.

Nm-Mt Ex-Mt
COMPLETE SET (275) 180.00 55.00
COMMON CARD (T1-T110) ...... 1.50 .45
COMMON CARD (T111-T275) ...... .40 .12
T1 Jeff Weaver ...... 1.50 .45
T2 Jay Powell ...... 1.50 .45
T3 Alex Gonzalez ...... 1.50 .45
T4 Jason Isringhausen ...... 1.50 .45
T5 Tyler Houston ...... 1.50 .45
T6 Ben Broussard ...... 1.50 .45
T7 Chuck Knoblauch ...... 1.50 .45
T8 Brian L. Hunter ...... 1.50 .45
T9 Dustan Mohr ...... 1.50 .45
T10 Eric Hinske ...... 1.50 .45
T11 Roger Cedeno ...... 1.50 .45
T12 Eddie Perez ...... 1.50 .45
T13 Jeromy Burnitz ...... 1.50 .45
T14 Bartolo Colon ...... 1.50 .45
T15 Rick Helling ...... 1.50 .45
T16 Dan Plesac ...... 1.50 .45
T17 Scott Strickland ...... 1.50 .45
T18 Antonio Alfonseca ...... 1.50 .45
T19 Ricky Gutierrez ...... 1.50 .45
T20 John Valentin ...... 1.50 .45
T21 Raul Mondesi ...... 1.50 .45
T22 Ben Davis ...... 1.50 .45
T23 Nelson Figueroa ...... 1.50 .45
T24 Earl Snyder ...... 1.50 .45
T25 Robin Ventura ...... 1.50 .45
T26 Jimmy Haynes ...... 1.50 .45
T27 Kenny Kelly ...... 1.50 .45
T28 Morgan Ensberg ...... 1.50 .45
T29 Reggie Sanders ...... 1.50 .45
T30 Shigetoshi Hasegawa ...... 1.50 .45
T31 Mike Timlin ...... 1.50 .45
T32 Russell Branyan ...... 1.50 .45
T33 Alan Embree ...... 1.50 .45
T34 D'Angelo Jimenez ...... 1.50 .45
T35 Kent Mercker ...... 1.50 .45
T36 Jesse Orosco ...... 1.50 .45
T37 Gregg Zaun ...... 1.50 .45
T38 Reggie Taylor ...... 1.50 .45
T39 Andres Galarraga ...... 1.50 .45
T40 Chris Truby ...... 1.50 .45
T41 Bruce Chen ...... 1.50 .45
T42 Darren Lewis ...... 1.50 .45
T43 Ryan Kohlmeier ...... 1.50 .45
T44 John McDonald ...... 1.50 .45
T45 Omar Daal ...... 1.50 .45
T46 Matt Clement ...... 1.50 .45
T47 Glendon Rusch ...... 1.50 .45
T48 Chan Ho Park ...... 1.50 .45
T49 Benny Agbayani ...... 1.50 .45
T50 Juan Gonzalez ...... 2.50 .75
T51 Carlos Baerga ...... 1.50 .45
T52 Tim Raines ...... 1.50 .45
T53 Kevin Appier ...... 1.50 .45
T54 Marty Cordova ...... 1.50 .45
T55 Jeff D'Amico ...... 1.50 .45
T56 Dmitri Young ...... 1.50 .45
T57 Roosevelt Brown ...... 1.50 .45
T58 Dustin Hermanson ...... 1.50 .45
T59 Jose Rijo ...... 1.50 .45
T60 Todd Ritchie ...... 1.50 .45
T61 Lee Stevens ...... 1.50 .45
T62 Placido Polanco ...... 1.50 .45
T63 Eric Young ...... 1.50 .45
T64 Chuck Finley ...... 1.50 .45
T65 Dicky Gonzalez ...... 1.50 .45
T66 Jose Macias ...... 1.50 .45
T67 Gabe Kapler ...... 1.50 .45
T68 Sandy Alomar Jr. ...... 1.50 .45
T69 Henry Blanco ...... 1.50 .45
T70 Julian Tavarez ...... 1.50 .45
T71 Paul Bako ...... 1.50 .45
T72 Scott Rolen 4.00 1.20
T73 Brian Jordan ...... 1.50 .45
T74 Rickey Henderson 4.00 1.20
T75 Kevin Mench ...... 1.50 .45
T76 Hideo Nomo 4.00 1.20
T77 Jeremy Giambi ...... 1.50 .45
T78 Brad Fullmer ...... 1.50 .45
T79 Carl Everett ...... 1.50 .45
T80 David Wells ...... 1.50 .45
T81 Aaron Sele ...... 1.50 .45
T82 Todd Hollandsworth ...... 1.50 .45
T83 Vicente Padilla ...... 1.50 .45
T84 Kenny Lofton ...... 1.50 .45
T85 Corky Miller ...... 1.50 .45
T86 Josh Fogg ...... 1.50 .45
T87 Cliff Floyd ...... 1.50 .45
T88 Craig Paquette ...... 1.50 .45
T89 Jay Payton ...... 1.50 .45
T90 Carlos Pena ...... 1.50 .45
T91 Juan Encarnacion ...... 1.50 .45
T92 Rey Sanchez ...... 1.50 .45
T93 Ryan Dempster ...... 1.50 .45
T94 Mario Encarnacion ...... 1.50 .45
T95 Jorge Julio ...... 1.50 .45
T96 John Mabry ...... 1.50 .45
T97 Todd Zeile ...... 1.50 .45
T98 Johnny Damon Sox 4.00 1.20
T99 Deivi Cruz ...... 1.50 .45
T100 Gary Sheffield ...... 1.50 .45
T101 Ted Lilly ...... 1.50 .45
T102 Todd Van Poppel ...... 1.50 .45
T103 Shawn Estes ...... 1.50 .45
T104 Cesar Izturis ...... 1.50 .45
T105 Ron Coomer ...... 1.50 .45
T106 Grady Little MG RC ...... 1.50 .45
T107 Jimy Williams MG ...... 1.50 .45
T108 Tony Pena MG ...... 1.50 .45
T109 Frank Robinson MG ...... 2.50 .75
T110 Ron Gardenhire MG ...... 1.50 .45

T111 Dennis Tankersley .40 .12
T112 Alejandro Cadena RC .40 .12
T113 Justin Reid RC .40 .12
T114 Nate Field RC .40 .12
T115 Rene Reyes RC .40 .12
T116 Nelson Castro RC .40 .12
T117 Miguel Olivo .40 .12
T118 David Espinosa .40 .12
T119 Chris Bootcheck RC .40 .12
T120 Rob Henkel RC .40 .12
T121 Steve Bechler RC .40 .12
T122 Mark Outlaw RC .40 .12
T123 Henry Pichardo RC .40 .12
T124 Michael Floyd RC .40 .12
T125 Richard Lane RC .40 .12
T126 Pete Zamora RC .40 .12
T127 Javier Colina .40 .12
T128 Greg Sain RC .50 .15
T129 Ronnie Merrill .40 .12
T130 Gavin Floyd RC 2.50 .75
T131 Josh Bonifay RC .40 .12
T132 Tommy Marx RC .40 .12
T133 Gary Cates Jr. RC .40 .12
T134 Neal Cotts RC 1.00 .30
T135 Angel Berroa .40 .12
T136 Elio Serrano RC .40 .12
T137 J.J. Putz RC .40 .12
T138 Ruben Gotay RC .40 .12
T139 Eddie Rogers .40 .12
T140 Wily Mo Pena .40 .12
T141 Tyler Yates RC .50 .15
T142 Colin Young RC .40 .12
T143 Chance Caple .40 .12
T144 Ben Howard RC .40 .12
T145 Ryan Bukvich RC .40 .12
T146 Cliff Bartosh RC .40 .12
T147 Brandon Claussen .40 .12
T148 Cristian Guerrero .40 .12
T149 Derrick Lewis .40 .12
T150 Eric Miller RC .40 .12
T151 Justin Huber RC .75 .23
T152 Adrian Gonzalez .40 .12
T153 Brian West RC .40 .12
T154 Chris Baker RC .40 .12
T155 Drew Henson .40 .12
T156 Scott Hairston RC 1.50 .45
T157 Jason Simontacchi RC .40 .12
T158 Jason Arnold RC .75 .23
T159 Brandon Phillips .40 .12
T160 Adam Roller RC .40 .12
T161 Scotty Layfield RC .40 .12
T162 Freddie Money RC .40 .12
T163 Noochie Varner RC .40 .12
T164 Terrance Hill RC .40 .12
T165 Jeremy Hill RC .40 .12
T166 Carlos Cabrera RC .40 .12
T167 Jose Morban RC .40 .12
T168 Kevin Frederick RC .40 .12
T169 Mark Teixeira .60 .18
T170 Brian Rogers .40 .12
T171 Anastacio Martinez RC .40 .12
T172 Bobby Jenks RC .75 .23
T173 David Gil RC .40 .12
T174 Andres Torres .40 .12
T175 James Barrett RC .40 .12
T176 Jimmy Journell .40 .12
T177 Brett Kay RC .40 .12
T178 Jason Young RC .40 .12
T179 Mark Hamilton RC .40 .12
T180 Jose Bautista RC .50 .15
T181 Blake McGinley RC .40 .12
T182 Ryan Mottl RC .40 .12
T183 Jeff Austin RC .40 .12
T184 Xavier Nady .40 .12
T185 Kyle Kane RC .40 .12
T186 Travis Foley RC .40 .12
T187 Nathan Kaup RC .40 .12
T188 Eric Cyr .40 .12
T189 Josh Cisneros RC .40 .12
T190 Brad Nelson RC 1.25 .35
T191 Clint Weibl RC .40 .12
T192 Ron Calloway RC .40 .12
T193 Jung Bong .40 .12
T194 Rolando Viera RC .40 .12
T195 Jason Bulger RC .40 .12
T196 Chone Figgins RC .75 .23
T197 Jimmy Alvarez RC .40 .12
T198 Joel Crump RC .40 .12
T199 Ryan Doumit RC .50 .15
T200 Demetrius Heath RC .40 .12
T201 John Ennis RC .40 .12
T202 Doug Sessions RC .40 .12
T203 Clinton Hosford RC .40 .12
T204 Chris Narveson RC .40 .12
T205 Ross Peeples RC .40 .12
T206 Alex Requena RC .40 .12
T207 Matt Erickson RC .40 .12
T208 Brian Forystek RC .40 .12
T209 Dewon Brazelton .40 .12
T210 Nathan Haynes .40 .12
T211 Jack Cust .40 .12
T212 Jesse Foppert RC 1.00 .30
T213 Jesus Cota RC .40 .12
T214 Juan M. Gonzalez RC .40 .12
T215 Tim Kalita RC .40 .12
T216 Manny Delcarmen RC .40 .12
T217 Jim Kavourias RC .40 .12
T218 C.J. Wilson RC .40 .12
T219 Edwin Yan RC .40 .12
T220 Andy Van Hekken .40 .12
T221 Michael Cuddyer .40 .12
T222 Jeff Verplancke RC .40 .12
T223 Mike Wilson RC .40 .12
T224 Corwin Malone RC .40 .12
T225 Chris Snelling RC .40 .12
T226 Joe Rogers RC .40 .12
T227 Jason Bay 2.50 .75
T228 Ezequiel Astacio RC .40 .12
T229 Joey Hammond RC .40 .12
T230 Chris Duffy RC .40 .12
T231 Mark Prior 2.50 .75
T232 Hansel Izquierdo RC .40 .12
T233 Franklyn German RC .40 .12
T234 Alexis Gomez .40 .12
T235 Jorge Padilla RC .40 .12
T236 Ryan Snare RC .40 .12
T237 Deivis Santos .40 .12
T238 Taggert Bozied RC .75 .23
T239 Mike Peeples RC .40 .12
T240 Ronald Acuna RC .40 .12
T241 Koyie Hill .40 .12
T242 Garrett Guzman RC .40 .12
T243 Ryan Church RC .75 .23
T244 Tony Fontana RC .40 .12
T245 Keto Anderson RC .40 .12
T246 Brad Bouras RC .40 .12
T247 Jason Dubois RC 1.25 .35
T248 Angel Guzman RC 3.00 .90
T249 Joel Hanrahan RC .75 .23
T250 Joe Jiannetti RC .40 .12
T251 Sean Pierce RC .40 .12
T252 Jake Mauer RC .40 .12
T253 Marshall McDougall RC .40 .12
T254 Edwin Almonte RC .40 .12
T255 Shawn Riggans RC .40 .12
T256 Steven Shell RC .40 .12
T257 Kevin Hooper RC .40 .12
T258 Michael Frick RC .40 .12
T259 Travis Chapman RC .40 .12
T260 Tim Hummel RC .40 .12
T261 Adam Morrissey RC .40 .12
T262 Dontrelle Willis RC 3.00 .90
T263 Justin Sherrod RC .40 .12
T264 Gerald Smiley RC .40 .12
T265 Tony Miller RC .40 .12
T266 Nolan Ryan WW 2.50 .75
T267 Reggie Jackson WW .60 .18
T268 Steve Garvey WW .40 .12
T269 Wade Boggs WW .60 .18
T270 Sammy Sosa WW 1.50 .45
T271 Curt Schilling WW .40 .12
T272 Mark Grace WW .60 .18
T273 Jason Giambi WW .40 .12
T274 Ken Griffey Jr. WW 1.50 .45
T275 Roberto Alomar WW .60 .18

2002 Topps Traded Gold

Inserted at a stated rate of one in three hobby and retail and one per HTA pack, this is a paralle of the 2002 Topps Traded set. Each card has "gold" borders and were issued to a stated print run of 2002 serial numbered sets.

Nm-Mt Ex-Mt
*GOLD 1-110: .6X TO 1.5X BASIC......
*GOLD 111-275: 2.5X TO 6X BASIC...
*GOLD RC'S 111-275: 1.5X TO 4X BASIC RC'S

2002 Topps Traded Farewell Relic

Inserted at a stated rate of one in 590 Hobby, one in 169 HTA and in 595 Retail packs, this one card set features one-time MVP Jose Canseco along with a game-used bat piece from his career. Canseco had announced his retirement during the 2002 season in an failed attempt to return to the majors.

Nm-Mt Ex-Mt
FW-JC Jose Canseco Bat 15.00 4.50

2002 Topps Traded Hall of Fame Relic

Inserted at a stated rate of one in 1533 Hobby Packs, one in 439 HTA packs and one in 1574 Retail packs, this one card set features Ozzie Smith along with a game-used bat piece from his career. Ozzie Smith was inducted into the HOF in 2002.

Nm-Mt Ex-Mt
HOF-OS Ozzie Smith Bat 30.00 9.00

2002 Topps Traded Signature Moves

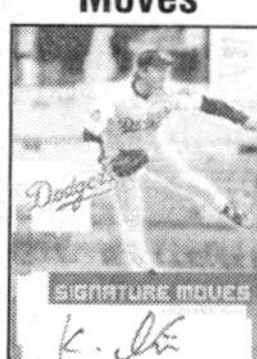

Inserted at overall odds of one in 91 Hobby or Retail packs and one in 26 HTA packs, these 26 cards feature a mix of basically prospects along with a couple of stars who moved to new teams for 2002 and signed these cards for inclusion in the Topps Traded set. Since there were nine different insertion odds for these cards we have notated both the insertion odds for each group along with which group the player belong to.

Nm-Mt Ex-Mt
A ODDS 1:15,292 H, 1:4288 HTA, 1:22,032 R
B ODDS 1:3846 H, 1:1105 HTA, 1:3840 R
C ODDS 1:6147 H, 1:1778 HTA, 1:6418 R
D ODDS 1:1917 H, 1:548 HTA, 1:1953 R
E ODDS 1:341 H, 1:97 HTA, 1:342 R ..
F ODDS 1:2247 H, 1:645 HTA, 1:2261 R
G ODDS 1:568 H, 1:162 HTA, 1:571 R
GROUP H ODDS 1:256 H/R, 1:73 HTA
I ODDS 1:1023 H, 1:293 HTA, 1:1025 R
OVERALL ODDS 1:91 HOB/RET, 1:26 HTA
AC Antoine Cameron D 15.00 4.50
AM Andy Morales H 8.00 2.40
BB Boof Bonser E 10.00 3.00
BC Brandon Claussen E 10.00 3.00
CS Chris Smith G 8.00 2.40
CU Chase Utley E 25.00 7.50
CW Corwin Malone H 10.00 3.00
DT Dennis Tankersley F 10.00 3.00
FJ Forrest Johnson E 10.00 3.00
JD Johnny Damon Sox B 40.00 12.00
JD Jeff DaVanon I 8.00 2.40
JM Jake Mauer G 10.00 3.00
JM Justin Morneau H 25.00 7.50
JP Juan Pena E 10.00 3.00
JS Juan Silvestre D 10.00 3.00
JW Justin Wayne E 10.00 3.00
KI Kazuhisa Ishii A 50.00 15.00
MC Matt Cooper E 10.00 3.00
MO Moises Alou B 15.00 4.50
MT Marcus Thames G 8.00 2.40
RA Roberto Alomar C 30.00 9.00
RH Ryan Hannaman E 10.00 3.00
RM Ramon Moreta H 10.00 3.00
TB Tony Blanco E 10.00 3.00
TL Todd Linden H 20.00 6.00
VD Victor Diaz H 25.00 7.50

2002 Topps Traded Tools of the Trade Dual Relics

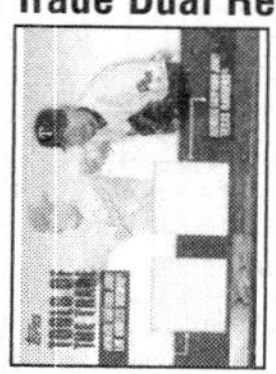

Inserted at overall odds of one in 539 Hobby, one in 155 HTA and one in 542 Retail packs, these three cards feature two game-used relics from the featured players. As these cards were issued in different insertion ratios, we have notated that information as to the player's specific group next to their name in our checklist.

Nm-Mt Ex-Mt
A ODDS 1:3407 H, 1:972 HTA, 1:3672 R
B ODDS 1:639 H, 1:183 HTA, 1:642 R
DTRR-CP Chan Ho Park B 15.00 4.50
DTRR-HN Hideo Nomo A 50.00 15.00
DTRR-MO Moises Alou B 15.00 4.50

2002 Topps Traded Tools of the Trade Relics

Inserted at overall odds for bats of one in 34 Hobby and Retail and one in 10 HTA and for jerseys at one in 426 Hobby, one in 122 HTA and one in 427 retail, these 35 cards feature players who switched teams for the 2002 season along with a game-used memorabilia piece. We have notated in our checklist what type of memorabilia piece on each player's card. In addition, since the bat cards were inserted at three different odds, we have notated that information as to the card's group next to their name in our checklist.

Nm-Mt Ex-Mt
BAT A 1:1203 H, 1:344 HTA, 1:1224 R
BAT B 1:1807 H, 1:517 HTA, 1:1836 R
BAT C 1:35 H/R, 1:10 HTA
AB Roberto Alomar Bat C 10.00 3.00
AG Andres Galarraga Bat C 8.00 2.40
BF Brad Fullmer Bat C 8.00 2.40
BJ Brian Jordan Bat C 8.00 2.40
CE Carl Everett Bat C 8.00 2.40
CK Chuck Knoblauch Bat C 8.00 2.40
CP Carlos Pena Bat A 10.00 3.00
DB David Bell Bat C 8.00 2.40
DJ Dave Justice Bat C 8.00 2.40
EY Eric Young Bat C 8.00 2.40
GS Gary Sheffield Bat C 8.00 2.40
HB Rickey Henderson Bat C 10.00 3.00
JBU Jeromy Burnitz Bat C 8.00 2.40
JCI Jeff Cirillo Bat B 8.00 2.40
JDB Johnny Damon Sox Bat C . 10.00 3.00
JG Juan Gonzalez Jsy 10.00 3.00
JP Josh Phelps Jsy 8.00 2.40
JV John Vander Wal Bat C 8.00 2.40
KL Kenny Lofton Bat C 8.00 2.40
MA Moises Alou Bat C 8.00 2.40
MLB Matt Lawton Bat C 8.00 2.40
MT Michael Tucker Bat C 8.00 2.40
MVB Mo Vaughn Bat C 8.00 2.40
MVJ Mo Vaughn Jsy 8.00 2.40
PP Placido Polanco Bat A 10.00 3.00
RS Reggie Sanders Bat C 8.00 2.40
RV Robin Ventura Bat C 8.00 2.40
RW Rondell White Bat C 8.00 2.40
SI Ruben Sierra Bat C 8.00 2.40
SR Scott Rolen Bat A 25.00 7.50
TC Tony Clark Bat C 8.00 2.40
TM Tino Martinez Bat C 10.00 3.00
TR Tim Raines Bat C 8.00 2.40
TS Tsuyoshi Shinjo Bat C 8.00 2.40
VC Vinny Castilla Bat C 8.00 2.40

2003 Topps

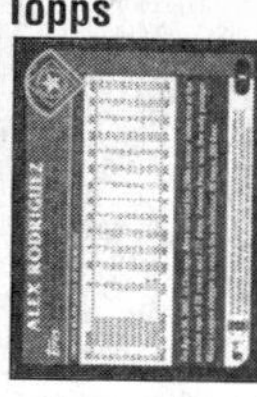

The first series of 366 cards was released in November, 2002. The second series of 354 cards were released in April, 2003. The set was issued either in 10 card hobby packs or 36 card HTA packs. The regular packs were issued 36 packs to a box and 12 boxes to a case with an SRP of $1.59. The HTA packs were issued 12 packs to a box and eight boxes to a case with an SRP of $5 per pack. The following subsets were issued in the first series: 262 through 291 basically featured current managers, cards numbered 292 through 321 featured players in their first year on a Topps card, cards numbered 322 through 331 featured two players who were expected to be major rookies during the 2003 season, cards numbered 332 through 336 honored players who achieved major feats during 2002, cards numbered 337 through 352 featured league leaders, cards 354 and 355 had post season highlights and cards 356 through 367 honored the best players in the American League. Second series subsets included Team Checklists (630-659); Draft Picks (660-674); Prospects (675-684); Award Winners (685-708) All-Stars (709-719) and World Series (720-721). As has been Topps tradition since 1997, there was no card number 7 issued in honor of the memory of Mickey Mantle.

Nm-Mt Ex-Mt
COMPLETE SET (720) 80.00 24.00
COMPLETE SERIES 1 (366) 40.00 12.00
COMPLETE SERIES 2 (354) 40.00 12.00
COMMON CARD (1-6/8-721) .20 .06
COMMON (292-331/660-684) .50 .15
1 Alex Rodriguez .75 .23
2 Dan Wilson .20 .06
3 Jimmy Rollins .20 .06
4 Jermaine Dye .20 .06
5 Steve Karsay .20 .06
6 Timo Perez .20 .06
7 Does Not Exist
8 Jose Vidro .20 .06
9 Eddie Guardado .20 .06
10 Mark Prior .50 .15
11 Curt Schilling .20 .06
12 Dennis Cook .20 .06
13 Andruw Jones .20 .06
14 David Segui .20 .06
15 Trot Nixon .20 .06
16 Kerry Wood .50 .15
17 Magglio Ordonez .20 .06
18 Jason LaRue .20 .06
19 Danys Baez .20 .06
20 Todd Helton .30 .09
21 Denny Neagle .20 .06
22 Dave Mlicki .20 .06
23 Roberto Hernandez .20 .06
24 Odalis Perez .20 .06
25 Nick Neugebauer .20 .06
26 David Ortiz .30 .09
27 Andres Galarraga .20 .06
28 Edgardo Alfonzo .20 .06
29 Chad Bradford .20 .06
30 Jason Giambi .20 .06
31 Brian Giles .20 .06
32 Deivi Cruz .20 .06
33 Robb Nen .20 .06
34 Jeff Nelson .20 .06
35 Edgar Renteria .20 .06
36 Aubrey Huff .20 .06
37 Brandon Duckworth .20 .06
38 Juan Gonzalez .30 .09
39 Sidney Ponson .20 .06
40 Eric Hinske .20 .06
41 Kevin Appier .20 .06
42 Danny Bautista .20 .06
43 Javier Lopez .20 .06
44 Jeff Conine .20 .06
45 Carlos Baerga .20 .06
46 Ugueth Urbina .20 .06
47 Mark Buehrle .20 .06
48 Aaron Boone .20 .06
49 Jason Simontacchi .20 .06
50 Sammy Sosa .75 .23
51 Jose Jimenez .20 .06
52 Bobby Higginson .20 .06
53 Luis Castillo .20 .06
54 Orlando Merced .20 .06
55 Brian Jordan .20 .06
56 Eric Young .20 .06
57 Bobby Kielty .20 .06
58 Luis Rivas .20 .06
59 Brad Wilkerson .20 .06
60 Roberto Alomar .30 .09
61 Roger Clemens 1.00 .30
62 Scott Hatteberg .20 .06
63 Andy Ashby .20 .06
64 Mike Williams .20 .06
65 Ron Gant .20 .06
66 Benito Santiago .20 .06
67 Bret Boone .20 .06
68 Matt Morris .20 .06
69 Troy Glaus .20 .06
70 Austin Kearns .20 .06
71 Jim Thome .50 .15
72 Rickey Henderson .50 .15
73 Luis Gonzalez .20 .06
74 Brad Fullmer .20 .06
75 Herbert Perry .20 .06
76 Randy Wolf .20 .06
77 Miguel Tejada .20 .06
78 Jimmy Anderson .20 .06
79 Ramon Martinez .20 .06
80 Ivan Rodriguez .50 .15
81 John Flaherty .20 .06
82 Shannon Stewart .20 .06
83 Orlando Palmeiro .20 .06
84 Rafael Furcal .20 .06
85 Kenny Rogers .20 .06
86 Terry Adams .20 .06
87 Mo Vaughn .20 .06
88 Jose Cruz Jr. .20 .06
89 Mike Matheny .20 .06
90 Alfonso Soriano .30 .09
91 Orlando Cabrera .20 .06
92 Jeffrey Hammonds .20 .06
93 Hideo Nomo .50 .15
94 Carlos Febles .20 .06
95 Billy Wagner .20 .06
96 Alex Gonzalez .20 .06
97 Todd Zeile .20 .06
98 Omar Vizquel .30 .09
99 Jose Rijo .20 .06
100 Ichiro Suzuki .75 .23
101 Steve Cox .20 .06
102 Hideki Irabu .20 .06
103 Roy Halladay .20 .06
104 David Eckstein .20 .06
105 Greg Maddux .75 .23
106 Jay Gibbons .20 .06
107 Travis Driskill .20 .06
108 Fred McGriff .30 .09
109 Frank Thomas .50 .15
110 Shawn Green .20 .06
111 Ruben Quevedo .20 .06
112 Jacque Jones .20 .06
113 Tomo Ohka .20 .06
114 Joe McEwing .20 .06
115 Ramiro Mendoza .20 .06
116 Mark Mulder .20 .06
117 Mike Lieberthal .20 .06
118 Jack Wilson .20 .06
119 Randall Simon .20 .06
120 Bernie Williams .30 .09
121 Marvin Benard .20 .06
122 Jamie Moyer .20 .06
123 Andy Benes .20 .06
124 Tino Martinez .30 .09
125 Esteban Yan .20 .06
126 Juan Uribe .20 .06
127 Jason Isringhausen .20 .06
128 Chris Carpenter .20 .06
129 Mike Cameron .20 .06
130 Gary Sheffield .20 .06
131 Geronimo Gil .20 .06
132 Brian Daubach .20 .06
133 Corey Patterson .20 .06
134 Aaron Rowand .20 .06
135 Chris Reitsma .20 .06
136 Bob Wickman .20 .06
137 Cesar Izturis .20 .06
138 Jason Jennings .20 .06
139 Brandon Inge .20 .06
140 Larry Walker .30 .09
141 Ramon Santiago .20 .06
142 Vladimir Nunez .20 .06
143 Jose Vizcaino .20 .06
144 Mark Quinn .20 .06
145 Michael Tucker .20 .06
146 Darren Dreifort .20 .06
147 Ben Sheets .20 .06
148 Corey Koskie .20 .06
149 Tony Armas Jr. .20 .06
150 Kazuhisa Ishii .20 .06
151 Al Leiter .20 .06
152 Steve Trachsel .20 .06
153 Mike Stanton .20 .06
154 David Justice .20 .06
155 Marlon Anderson .20 .06
156 Jason Kendall .20 .06
157 Brian Lawrence .20 .06
158 J.T. Snow .20 .06
159 Edgar Martinez .30 .09
160 Pat Burrell .20 .06
161 Kerry Robinson .20 .06
162 Greg Vaughn .20 .06
163 Carl Everett .20 .06
164 Vernon Wells .20 .06
165 Jose Mesa .20 .06
166 Troy Percival .20 .06
167 Erubiel Durazo .20 .06
168 Jason Marquis .20 .06
169 Jerry Hairston Jr. .20 .06
170 Vladimir Guerrero .50 .15
171 Byung-Hyun Kim .20 .06
172 Marcus Giles .20 .06
173 Johnny Damon .50 .15
174 Jon Lieber .20 .06
175 Terrence Long .20 .06
176 Sean Casey .20 .06
177 Adam Dunn .30 .09
178 Juan Pierre .20 .06
179 Wendell Magee .20 .06
180 Barry Zito .20 .06
181 Aramis Ramirez .20 .06
182 Pokey Reese .20 .06
183 Jeff Kent .20 .06
184 Russ Ortiz .20 .06
185 Ruben Sierra .20 .06
186 Brent Abernathy .20 .06
187 Ismael Valdes UER .20 .06
Card does not include 2002 Rangers stats
188 Tom Wilson .20 .06
189 Craig Counsell .20 .06
190 Mike Mussina .30 .09
191 Ramon Hernandez .20 .06
192 Adam Kennedy .20 .06
193 Tony Womack .20 .06
194 Wes Helms .20 .06
195 Tony Batista .20 .06
196 Rolando Arrojo .20 .06
197 Kyle Farnsworth .20 .06
198 Gary Bennett .20 .06
199 Scott Sullivan .20 .06
200 Albert Pujols 1.00 .30
201 Kirk Rueter .20 .06
202 Phil Nevin .20 .06
203 Kip Wells .20 .06
204 Ron Coomer .20 .06
205 Jeromy Burnitz .20 .06
206 Kyle Lohse .20 .06
207 Mike DeJean .20 .06
208 Paul Lo Duca .20 .06
209 Carlos Beltran .30 .09

210 Roy Oswalt .20 .06
211 Mike Lowell .20 .06
212 Robert Fick .20 .06
213 Todd Jones .20 .06
214 C.C. Sabathia .20 .06
215 Danny Graves .20 .06
216 Todd Hundley .20 .06
217 Tim Wakefield .20 .06
218 Derek Lowe .20 .06
219 Kevin Millwood .20 .06
220 Jorge Posada .30 .09
221 Bobby J. Jones .20 .06
222 Carlos Guillen .20 .06
223 Fernando Vina .20 .06
224 Ryan Rupe .20 .06
225 Kelvim Escobar .20 .06
226 Ramon Ortiz .20 .06
227 Junior Spivey .20 .06
228 Juan Cruz .20 .06
229 Melvin Mora .20 .06
230 Lance Berkman .20 .06
231 Brent Butler .20 .06
232 Shane Halter .20 .06
233 Derrek Lee .20 .06
234 Matt Lawton .20 .06
235 Chuck Knoblauch .20 .06
236 Eric Gagne .50 .15
237 Alex Sanchez .20 .06
238 Denny Hocking .20 .06
239 Eric Milton .20 .06
240 Rey Ordonez .20 .06
241 Orlando Hernandez .20 .06
242 Robert Person .20 .06
243 Sean Burroughs .20 .06
244 Jeff Cirillo .20 .06
245 Mike Lamb .20 .06
246 Jose Valentin .20 .06
247 Ellis Burks .20 .06
248 Shawn Chacon .20 .06
249 Josh Beckett .20 .06
250 Nomar Garciaparra .75 .23
251 Craig Biggio .30 .09
252 Joe Randa .20 .06
253 Mark Grudzielanek .20 .06
254 Glendon Rusch .20 .06
255 Michael Barrett .20 .06
256 Omar Daal .20 .06
257 Elmer Dessens .20 .06
258 Wade Miller .20 .06
259 Adrian Beltre .30 .09
260 Vicente Padilla .20 .06
261 Kazuhiro Sasaki .20 .06
262 Mike Scioscia MG .20 .06
263 Bobby Cox MG .20 .06
264 Mike Hargrove MG .20 .06
265 Grady Little MG RC .20 .06
266 Alex Gonzalez UER .20 .06
2002 stats are listed as all zero's
267 Jerry Manuel MG .20 .06
268 Bob Boone MG .20 .06
269 Joel Skinner MG .20 .06
270 Clint Hurdle MG .20 .06
271 Miguel Batista UER .20 .06
All 2002 Stats are 0's
272 Bob Brenly MG .20 .06
273 Jeff Torborg MG .20 .06
274 Jimy Williams MG UER .20 .06
Career managerial record is wrong
275 Tony Pena MG .20 .06
276 Jim Tracy MG .20 .06
277 Jerry Royster MG .20 .06
278 Ron Gardenhire MG .20 .06
279 Frank Robinson MG .30 .09
280 John Halama .20 .06
281 Joe Torre MG .30 .09
282 Art Howe MG .20 .06
283 Larry Bowa MG .20 .06
284 Lloyd McClendon MG .20 .06
285 Bruce Bochy MG .20 .06
286 Dusty Baker MG .20 .06
287 Lou Piniella MG .20 .06
288 Tony LaRussa MG .20 .06
289 Todd Walker .20 .06
290 Jerry Narron MG .20 .06
291 Carlos Tosca MG .20 .06
292 Chris Duncan FY RC .50 .15
293 Franklin Gutierrez FY RC 2.00 .60
294 Adam LaRoche FY .50 .15
295 Manuel Ramirez FY RC .50 .15
296 Il Kim FY RC .50 .15
297 Wayne Lydon FY RC .50 .15
298 Daryl Clark FY RC .50 .15
299 Sean Pierce FY .50 .15
300 Andy Marte FY RC 2.50 .75
301 Matthew Peterson FY RC .50 .15
302 Gonzalo Lopez FY RC .50 .15
303 Bernie Castro FY RC .50 .15
304 Cliff Lee FY .50 .15
305 Jason Perry FY RC .75 .23
306 Jaime Bubela FY RC .50 .15
307 Alexis Rios FY .50 .15
308 Brendan Harris FY RC .50 .15
309 R.Nivar-Martinez FY RC .75 .23
310 Terry Tiffee FY RC .75 .23
311 Kevin Youkilis FY RC 1.50 .45
312 Ruddy Lugo FY RC .50 .15
313 C.J. Wilson FY .50 .15
314 Mike McNutt FY RC .50 .15
315 Jeff Clark FY RC .50 .15
316 Mark Malaska FY RC .50 .15
317 Doug Waechter FY RC .50 .15
318 Derell McCall FY RC .50 .15
319 Scott Tyler FY RC .50 .15
320 Craig Brazell FY RC .50 .15
321 Walter Young FY .50 .15
322 Marlon Byrd .50 .15
Jorge Padilla FS
323 Chris Snelling .50 .15
Shin-Soo Choo FS
324 Hank Blalock .50 .15
Mark Teixeira FS
325 Josh Hamilton .50 .15
Carl Crawford FS
326 Orlando Hudson .50 .15
Josh Phelps FS
327 Jack Cust .50 .15
Rene Reyes FS
328 Angel Berroa .50 .15
Alexis Gomez FS
329 Michael Cuddyer .50 .15
Michael Restovich FS
330 Juan Rivera .50 .15
Marcus Thames FS
331 Brandon Puffer .50 .15
Jung Bong FS
332 Mike Cameron SH .20 .06
333 Shawn Green SH .20 .06
334 Oakland A's SH .20 .06
335 Jason Giambi SH .20 .06
336 Derek Lowe SH .20 .06
337 Manny Ramirez .50 .15
Mike Sweeney
Bernie Williams LL
338 Alfonso Soriano .30 .09
Alex Rodriguez
Derek Jeter LL
339 Alex Rodriguez .50 .15
Jim Thome
Rafael Palmeiro LL
340 Alex Rodriguez .50 .15
Maggio Ordonez
Miguel Tejada LL
341 Pedro Martinez .20 .06
Derek Lowe
Barry Zito LL
342 Pedro Martinez .30 .09
Roger Clemens
Mike Mussina LL
343 Larry Walker .50 .15
Vladimir Guerrero
Todd Helton LL
344 Sammy Sosa .50 .15
Albert Pujols
Shawn Green LL
345 Sammy Sosa .50 .15
Lance Berkman
Shawn Green LL
346 Lance Berkman .20 .06
Albert Pujols
Pat Burrell LL
347 Randy Johnson .30 .09
Greg Maddux
Tom Glavine LL
348 Randy Johnson .30 .09
Curt Schilling
Kerry Wood LL
349 Francisco Rodriguez .20 .06
Darin Erstad
Tim Salmon
AL Division Series
350 Minnesota Twins .30 .09
St Louis Cardinals
AL and NL Division Series
351 Anaheim Angels .30 .09
San Francisco Giants
AL and NL Division Series
352 Jim Edmonds .30 .09
Scott Rolen
NL Division Series
353 Adam Kennedy ALCS .20 .06
354 J.T. Snow WS .30 .09
355 David Bell NLCS .30 .09
356 Jason Giambi AS .20 .06
357 Alfonso Soriano AS .20 .06
358 Alex Rodriguez AS .50 .15
359 Eric Chavez AS .20 .06
360 Torii Hunter AS .20 .06
361 Bernie Williams AS .20 .06
362 Garret Anderson AS .20 .06
363 Jorge Posada AS .20 .06
364 Derek Lowe AS .20 .06
365 Barry Zito AS .20 .06
366 Manny Ramirez AS .20 .06
367 Mike Scioscia AS .20 .06
368 Francisco Rodriguez .20 .06
369 Chris Hammond .20 .06
370 Chipper Jones .50 .15
371 Chris Singleton .20 .06
372 Cliff Floyd .20 .06
373 Bobby Hill .20 .06
374 Antonio Osuna .20 .06
375 Barry Larkin .30 .09
376 Charles Nagy .20 .06
377 Denny Stark .20 .06
378 Dean Palmer .20 .06
379 Eric Owens .20 .06
380 Randy Johnson .50 .15
381 Jeff Suppan .20 .06
382 Eric Karros .20 .06
383 Luis Vizcaino .20 .06
384 Johan Santana .30 .09
385 Javier Vazquez .20 .06
386 John Thomson .20 .06
387 Nick Johnson .20 .06
388 Mark Ellis .20 .06
389 Doug Glanville .20 .06
390 Ken Griffey Jr. .75 .23
391 Bubba Trammell .20 .06
392 Livan Hernandez .20 .06
393 Desi Relaford .20 .06
394 Eli Marrero .20 .06
395 Jared Sandberg .20 .06
396 Barry Bonds 1.25 .35
397 Esteban Loaiza .20 .06
398 Aaron Sele .20 .06
399 Geoff Blum .20 .06
400 Derek Jeter 1.25 .35
401 Eric Byrnes .20 .06
402 Mike Timlin .20 .06
403 Mark Kotsay .20 .06
404 Rich Aurilia .20 .06
405 Joel Pineiro .20 .06
406 Chuck Finley .20 .06
407 Bengie Molina .20 .06
408 Steve Finley .20 .06
409 Julio Franco .20 .06
410 Marty Cordova .20 .06
411 Shea Hillenbrand .20 .06
412 Mark Bellhorn .20 .06
413 Jon Garland .20 .06
414 Reggie Taylor .20 .06
415 Milton Bradley .20 .06
416 Carlos Pena .20 .06
417 Andy Fox .20 .06
418 Brad Ausmus .20 .06
419 Brent Mayne .20 .06
420 Paul Quantrill .20 .06
421 Carlos Delgado .20 .06
422 Kevin Mench .20 .06
423 Joe Kennedy .20 .06
424 Mike Crudale .20 .06
425 Mark McLemore .20 .06
426 Bill Mueller .20 .06
427 Rob Mackowiak .20 .06
428 Ricky Ledee .20 .06
429 Ted Lilly .20 .06
430 Sterling Hitchcock .20 .06
431 Scott Strickland .20 .06
432 Damion Easley .20 .06
433 Torii Hunter .20 .06
434 Brad Radke .20 .06
435 Geoff Jenkins .20 .06
436 Paul Byrd .20 .06
437 Morgan Ensberg .20 .06
438 Mike Maroth .20 .06
439 Mike Hampton .20 .06
440 Adam Hyzdu .20 .06
441 Vance Wilson .20 .06
442 Todd Ritchie .20 .06
443 Tom Gordon .20 .06
444 John Burkett .20 .06
445 Rodrigo Lopez .20 .06
446 Tim Spooneybarger .20 .06
447 Quinton Mccracken .20 .06
448 Tim Salmon .30 .09
449 Jarrod Washburn .20 .06
450 Pedro Martinez .50 .15
451 Dustan Mohr .20 .06
452 Julio Lugo .20 .06
453 Scott Stewart .20 .06
454 Armando Benitez .20 .06
455 Raul Mondesi .20 .06
456 Robin Ventura .20 .06
457 Bobby Abreu .20 .06
458 Josh Fogg .20 .06
459 Ryan Klesko .20 .06
460 Tsuyoshi Shinjo .20 .06
461 Jim Edmonds .20 .06
462 Cliff Politte .20 .06
463 Chan Ho Park .20 .06
464 John Mabry .20 .06
465 Woody Williams .20 .06
466 Jason Michaels .20 .06
467 Scott Schoeneweis .20 .06
468 Brian Anderson .20 .06
469 Brett Tomko .20 .06
470 Scott Erickson .20 .06
471 Kevin Millar Sox .20 .06
472 Danny Wright .20 .06
473 Jason Schmidt .20 .06
474 Scott Williamson .20 .06
475 Einar Diaz .20 .06
476 Jay Payton .20 .06
477 Juan Acevedo .20 .06
478 Ben Grieve .20 .06
479 Raul Ibanez .20 .06
480 Richie Sexson .20 .06
481 Rick Reed .20 .06
482 Pedro Astacio .20 .06
483 Adam Platt .20 .06
484 Bud Smith .20 .06
485 Tomas Perez .20 .06
486 Adam Eaton .20 .06
487 Rafael Palmeiro .30 .09
488 Jason Tyner .20 .06
489 Scott Rolen .50 .15
490 Randy Winn .20 .06
491 Ryan Jensen .20 .06
492 Trevor Hoffman .20 .06
493 Craig Wilson .20 .06
494 Jeremy Giambi .20 .06
495 Daryle Ward .20 .06
496 Shane Spencer .20 .06
497 Andy Pettitte .30 .09
498 John Franco .20 .06
499 Felipe Lopez .20 .06
500 Mike Piazza .75 .23
501 Cristian Guzman .20 .06
502 Jose Hernandez .20 .06
503 Octavio Dotel .20 .06
504 Brad Penny .20 .06
505 Dave Veres .20 .06
506 Ryan Dempster .20 .06
507 Joe Crede .20 .06
508 Chad Hermansen .20 .06
509 Gary Matthews Jr. .20 .06
510 Matt Franco .20 .06
511 Ben Weber .20 .06
512 Dave Berg .20 .06
513 Michael Young .30 .09
514 Frank Catalanotto .20 .06
515 Darin Erstad .20 .06
516 Matt Williams .20 .06
517 B.J. Surhoff .20 .06
518 Kerry Ligtenberg .20 .06
519 Mike Bordick .20 .06
520 Arthur Rhodes .20 .06
521 Joe Girardi .20 .06
522 D'Angelo Jimenez .20 .06
523 Paul Konerko .20 .06
524 Jose Macias .20 .06
525 Joe Mays .20 .06
526 Marquis Grissom .20 .06
527 Neifi Perez .20 .06
528 Preston Wilson .20 .06
529 Jeff Weaver .20 .06
530 Eric Chavez .20 .06
531 Placido Polanco .20 .06
532 Matt Mantei .20 .06
533 James Baldwin .20 .06
534 Toby Hall .20 .06
535 Brendan Donnelly .20 .06
536 Benji Gil .20 .06
537 Damian Moss .20 .06
538 Jorge Julio .20 .06
539 Matt Clement .20 .06
540 Brian Moehler .20 .06
541 Lee Stevens .20 .06
542 Jimmy Haynes .20 .06
543 Terry Mulholland .20 .06
544 Dave Roberts .20 .06
545 J.C. Romero .20 .06
546 Bartolo Colon .20 .06
547 Roger Cedeno .20 .06
548 Mariano Rivera .30 .09
549 Billy Koch .20 .06
550 Manny Ramirez .30 .09
551 Travis Lee .20 .06
552 Oliver Perez .20 .06
553 Tim Worrell .20 .06
554 Rafael Soriano .20 .06
555 Damian Miller .20 .06
556 John Smoltz .30 .09
557 Willis Roberts .20 .06
558 Tim Hudson .20 .06
559 Moises Alou .20 .06
560 Gary Glover .20 .06
561 Corky Miller .20 .06
562 Ben Broussard .20 .06
563 Gabe Kapler .20 .06
564 Chris Woodward .20 .06
565 Paul Wilson .20 .06
566 Todd Hollandsworth .20 .06
567 So Taguchi .20 .06
568 John Olerud .20 .06
569 Reggie Sanders .20 .06
570 Jake Peavy .20 .06
571 Kris Benson .20 .06
572 Todd Pratt .20 .06
573 Ray Durham .20 .06
574 Boomer Wells .20 .06
575 Chris Widger .20 .06
576 Shawn Wooten .20 .06
577 Tom Glavine .30 .09
578 Antonio Alfonseca .20 .06
579 Keith Foulke .20 .06
580 Shawn Estes .20 .06
581 Mark Grace .30 .09
582 Dmitri Young .20 .06
583 A.J. Burnett .20 .06
584 Richard Hidalgo .20 .06
585 Mike Sweeney .20 .06
586 Alex Cora .20 .06
587 Matt Stairs .20 .06
588 Doug Mientkiewicz .20 .06
589 Fernando Tatis .20 .06
590 David Weathers .20 .06
591 Cory Lidle .20 .06
592 Dan Plesac .20 .06
593 Jeff Bagwell .30 .09
594 Steve Sparks .20 .06
595 Sandy Alomar Jr. .20 .06
596 John Lackey .20 .06
597 Rick Helling .20 .06
598 Mark DeRosa .20 .06
599 Carlos Lee .20 .06
600 Garret Anderson .20 .06
601 Vinny Castilla .20 .06
602 Ryan Drese .20 .06
603 LaTroy Hawkins .20 .06
604 David Bell .20 .06
605 Freddy Garcia .20 .06
606 Miguel Cairo .20 .06
607 Scott Spiezio .20 .06
608 Mike Remlinger .20 .06
609 Tony Graffanino .20 .06
610 Russell Branyan .20 .06
611 Chris Magruder .20 .06
612 Jose Contreras RC 1.00 .30
613 Carl Pavano .20 .06
614 Kevin Brown .20 .06
615 Tyler Houston .20 .06
616 A.J. Pierzynski .20 .06
617 Tony Fiore .20 .06
618 Peter Bergeron .20 .06
619 Rondell White .20 .06
620 Brett Myers .20 .06
621 Kevin Young .20 .06
622 Kenny Lofton .20 .06
623 Ben Davis .20 .06
624 J.D. Drew .20 .06
625 Chris Gomez .20 .06
626 Karim Garcia .20 .06
627 Ricky Gutierrez .20 .06
628 Mark Redman .20 .06
629 Juan Encarnacion .20 .06
630 Anaheim Angels TC .30 .09
631 Ariz.Diamondbacks TC .20 .06
632 Atlanta Braves TC .20 .06
633 Baltimore Orioles TC .20 .06
634 Boston Red Sox TC .20 .06
635 Chicago Cubs TC .20 .06
636 Chicago White Sox TC .20 .06
637 Cincinnati Reds TC .20 .06
638 Cleveland Indians TC .20 .06
639 Colorado Rockies TC .20 .06
640 Detroit Tigers TC .20 .06
641 Florida Marlins TC .20 .06
642 Houston Astros TC .20 .06
643 Kansas City Royals TC .20 .06
644 Los Angeles Dodgers TC .20 .06
645 Milwaukee Brewers TC .20 .06
646 Minnesota Twins TC .20 .06
647 Montreal Expos TC .20 .06
648 New York Mets TC .20 .06
649 New York Yankees TC .30 .09
650 Oakland Athletics TC .20 .06
651 Philadelphia Phillies TC .20 .06
652 Pittsburgh Pirates TC .20 .06
653 San Diego Padres TC .20 .06
654 San Francisco Giants TC .20 .06
655 Seattle Mariners TC .20 .06
656 St. Louis Cardinals TC .20 .06
657 T.B. Devil Rays TC .20 .06
658 Texas Rangers TC .20 .06
659 Toronto Blue Jays TC .20 .06
660 Bryan Bullington DP RC 1.25 .35
661 Jeremy Guthrie DP .50 .15
662 Joey Gomes DP RC .50 .15
663 E.Bastida-Martinez DP RC .50 .15
664 Brian Wright DP RC .50 .15
665 B.J. Upton DP 1.00 .30
666 Jeff Francis DP .50 .15
667 Drew Meyer DP .50 .15
668 Jeremy Hermida DP .50 .15
669 Khalil Greene DP 2.00 .60
670 Darrell Rasner DP RC .50 .15
671 Cole Hamels DP .50 .15
672 James Loney DP .50 .15
673 Sergio Santos DP .50 .15
674 Jason Pridie DP .50 .15
675 Brandon Phillips .50 .15
Victor Martinez
676 Hee Seop Choi .50 .15
Nic Jackson
677 Dontrelle Willis .50 .15
Jason Stokes
678 Chad Tracy .50 .15
Lyle Overbay
679 Joe Borchard .50 .15
Corwin Malone
680 Joe Mauer .75 .23
Justin Morneau
681 Drew Henson .50 .15
Brandon Claussen
682 Chase Utley .50 .15
Gavin Floyd
683 Taggert Bozied .50 .15
Xavier Nady
684 Aaron Heilman .50 .15
Jose Reyes
685 Kenny Rogers AW .20 .06
686 Bengie Molina AW .20 .06
687 John Olerud AW .20 .06
688 Bret Boone AW .20 .06
689 Eric Chavez AW .20 .06
690 Alex Rodriguez AW .50 .15
691 Darin Erstad AW .20 .06
692 Ichiro Suzuki AW .50 .15
693 Torii Hunter AW .20 .06
694 Greg Maddux AW .50 .15
695 Brad Ausmus AW .20 .06
696 Todd Helton AW .20 .06
697 Fernando Vina AW .20 .06
698 Scott Rolen AW .30 .09
699 Edgar Renteria AW .20 .06
700 Andruw Jones AW .20 .06
701 Larry Walker AW .20 .06
702 Jim Edmonds AW .20 .06
703 Barry Zito AW .20 .06
704 Randy Johnson AW .30 .09
705 Miguel Tejada AW .20 .06
706 Barry Bonds AW .60 .18
707 Eric Hinske AW .20 .06
708 Jason Jennings AW .20 .06
709 Todd Helton AS .20 .06
710 Jeff Kent AS .20 .06
711 Edgar Renteria AS .20 .06
712 Scott Rolen AS .30 .09
713 Barry Bonds AS .60 .18
714 Sammy Sosa AS .50 .15
715 Vladimir Guerrero AS .30 .09
716 Mike Piazza AS .50 .15
717 Curt Schilling AS .20 .06
718 Randy Johnson AS .30 .09
719 Bobby Cox AS .20 .06
720 Anaheim Angels WS .30 .09
721 Anaheim Angels WS .50 .15

2003 Topps Black

Inserted at a stated rate of one in 16 HTA series one packs and one in 10 HTA series 2 packs, this is a partial parallel to the Topps set. Only cards numbered from 1 through 331 were printed (though card number 7 does not exist, thus 330 cards comprise the series one set). However, the second series was issued in complete parallel form. These cards were issued to a stated print run of 52 serial numbered sets.

Nm-Mt Ex-Mt
*BLACK 1-291/368-659/685-721: 30X TO 80X
*BLACK 292-331/660-684: 20X TO 50X
*BLK RC 292-331/612/660-684: 15X TO 40X

2003 Topps Box Bottoms

These cards were issued as a four-card sheet on the bottom of first and second series Home Team Advantage boxes. The sheets were not perforated, but did include dotted lines between each card indicating where the cards should be cut if they were to be separated. The cards are identical parallels to the basic issue 2003 Topps cards (including the same checklist numbers on the card backs). The key difference is the readily noticeable plain cardboard stock used for these Box Bottom parallels as averse to the high gloss card stock used for the basic issue cards.

Nm-Mt Ex-Mt
*BOX BOTTOM CARDS: 1X TO 2.5X BASIC
1 Alex Rodriguez 1 2.00 .60
10 Mark Prior 4 1.25 .35
11 Curt Schilling 1 .50 .15
20 Todd Helton 1 .75 .23
50 Sammy Sosa 2 2.00 .60
73 Luis Gonzalez 1 .50 .15
77 Miguel Tejada 4 .50 .15
80 Ivan Rodriguez 4 1.25 .35
90 Alfonso Soriano 2 .75 .23
150 Kazuhisa Ishii 2 .50 .15
160 Pat Burrell 4 .50 .15
177 Adam Dunn 3 .75 .23
180 Barry Zito 3 .50 .15
200 Albert Pujols 2 2.50 .75
230 Lance Berkman 3 .50 .15
250 Nomar Garciaparra 3 2.00 .60
368 Francisco Rodriguez 5 .50 .15
370 Chipper Jones 8 1.25 .35
380 Randy Johnson 8 1.25 .35
387 Nick Johnson 7 .50 .15
390 Ken Griffey Jr. 6 2.00 .60
396 Barry Bonds 5 3.00 .90
433 Torii Hunter 5 .50 .15
450 Pedro Martinez 6 1.25 .35
489 Scott Rolen 8 1.25 .35
500 Mike Piazza 6 2.00 .60
530 Eric Chavez 6 .50 .15
550 Manny Ramirez 7 .75 .23
558 Tim Hudson 7 .50 .15
585 Mike Sweeney 8 .50 .15
593 Jeff Bagwell 5 .75 .23
600 Garret Anderson 7 .50 .15

2003 Topps Gold

Inserted at a stated rate of one in 16 first series hobby packs and one in five first series HTA packs, this is a partial parallel to the first series set. For the first series, nly cards numbered from 1 through 331 were printed. The second series was issued in its totality for this parallel. The second series cards were also issued at a stated rate of one in seven hobby packs, one in two HTA packs and one in five retail packs. All gold cards were issued to a stated print run of 2003 serial numbered sets.

Nm-Mt Ex-Mt
*GOLD 1-291/368-659/685-721: 6X TO 15X
*GOLD: 292-331/660-684: 3X TO 8X
*GOLD RC's: 292-331/612/660-684: 3X TO 8X

2003 Topps All-Stars

Issued at a stated rate of one in 15 second series hobby packs and one in five second series HTA packs, this 20 card set features most of the leading players in baseball.

	Nm-Mt	Ex-Mt
COMPLETE SET (20)	50.00	15.00
1 Alfonso Soriano	2.00	.60
2 Barry Bonds	6.00	1.80
3 Ichiro Suzuki	4.00	1.20
4 Alex Rodriguez	4.00	1.20
5 Miguel Tejada	2.00	.60
6 Nomar Garciaparra	4.00	1.20
7 Jason Giambi	2.00	.60
8 Manny Ramirez	2.00	.60
9 Derek Jeter	6.00	1.80
10 Garret Anderson	2.00	.60
11 Barry Zito	2.00	.60
12 Sammy Sosa	4.00	1.20
13 Adam Dunn	2.00	.60
14 Vladimir Guerrero	2.50	.75
15 Mike Piazza	4.00	1.20
16 Shawn Green	2.00	.60
17 Luis Gonzalez	2.00	.60
18 Todd Helton	2.00	.60
19 Torii Hunter	2.00	.60
20 Curt Schilling	2.00	.60

2003 Topps Autographs

Issued at varying stated odds, these 38 cards feature a mix of prospect and starts who signed cards for inclusion in the 2003 Topps product. The following players did not return their cards in time for inclusion in series 1 packs and these cards could be redeemed until November 30, 2004: Darin Erstad and Scott Rolen.

	Nm-Mt	Ex-Mt
GROUP A1 SER.1 1:8910 H, 1: 2533 HTA		
GROUP B1 SER.1 1:24,710 H, 1:7037 HTA		
GROUP C1 SER.1 1:11,097 H, 1:5758 HTA		
GROUP D1 SER.1 1:20,144 H, 1:5758 HTA		
GROUP E1 SER.1 1:11,730 H, 1:3333 HTA		
GROUP F1 SER.1 1:2209 H, 1:395 HTA		
GROUP G1 SER.1 1:3471 H, 1:460 HTA		
GROUP A2 1:31,408 H, 1:8808 HTA, 1:26,208 R		
GROUP B2 1:5188 H, 1:1460 HTA, 1:4368 R		
GROUP C2 1:864 H, 1:232 HTA, 1:708 R		
GROUP D2 1:790 H, 1:214 HTA, 1:647 R		
AJ Andruw Jones A1		
AK1 Austin Kearns F1	15.00	4.50
AK2 Austin Kearns C2	15.00	4.50
AP Albert Pujols B2	150.00	45.00
AS Alfonso Soriano A1		
BH Brad Hawpe D2	10.00	3.00
BS Ben Sheets E1	15.00	4.50
BU B.J. Upton D2	30.00	9.00
BZ Barry Zito C2	40.00	12.00
CE Clint Everts D2	15.00	4.50
CF Cliff Floyd C2	25.00	7.50
DE Darin Erstad B1	25.00	7.50
DW Dontrelle Willis D2	40.00	12.00
EC Eric Chavez A1	40.00	12.00
EH Eric Hinske C2	15.00	4.50
EM Eric Milton C1	15.00	4.50
HB Hank Blalock F1	25.00	7.50
JB Josh Beckett C2	40.00	12.00
JDM J.D. Martin G1	10.00	3.00
JL Jason Lane G1	10.00	3.00
JM Joe Mauer F1	25.00	7.50
JPH Josh Phelps C2	15.00	4.50
JV Jose Vidro C2	15.00	4.50
LB Lance Berkman A2	60.00	18.00
MB Mark Buehrle C1	25.00	7.50
MO Maggio Ordonez B2	25.00	7.50
MP Mark Prior F1	60.00	18.00
MTE Mark Teixeira F1	25.00	7.50
MTH Marcus Thames G1	10.00	3.00
MT1 Miguel Tejada A1		
MT2 Miguel Tejada C2	25.00	7.50
NN Nick Neugebauer D1	15.00	4.50
OH Orlando Hudson G1	10.00	3.00
PK Paul Konerko C2	25.00	7.50
PL1 Paul Lo Duca F1	15.00	4.50
PL2 Paul Lo Duca C2	25.00	7.50
SR Scott Rolen A1	80.00	24.00
TH Torii Hunter C2	25.00	7.50

2003 Topps Blue Backs

Issued in the style of the 1951 Topps Blue Back set, these 40 cards were inserted into first series packs at a stated rate of one in 12 hobby packs and one in four HTA packs.

	Nm-Mt	Ex-Mt
BB1 Albert Pujols	4.00	1.20
BB2 Ichiro Suzuki	3.00	.90
BB3 Sammy Sosa	3.00	.90
BB4 Kazuhisa Ishii	2.00	.60
BB5 Alex Rodriguez	3.00	.90
BB6 Derek Jeter	5.00	1.50
BB7 Vladimir Guerrero	2.00	.60
BB8 Ken Griffey Jr.	3.00	.90
BB9 Jason Giambi	2.00	.60
BB10 Todd Helton	2.00	.60
BB11 Mike Piazza	3.00	.90
BB12 Nomar Garciaparra	3.00	.90
BB13 Chipper Jones	2.00	.60
BB14 Ivan Rodriguez	2.00	.60
BB15 Luis Gonzalez	2.00	.60
BB16 Pat Burrell	2.00	.60
BB17 Mark Prior	2.00	.60
BB18 Adam Dunn	2.00	.60
BB19 Jeff Bagwell	2.00	.60
BB20 Austin Kearns	2.00	.60
BB21 Alfonso Soriano	2.00	.60
BB22 Jim Thome	2.00	.60
BB23 Bernie Williams	2.00	.60
BB24 Pedro Martinez	2.00	.60
BB25 Lance Berkman	2.00	.60
BB26 Randy Johnson	2.00	.60
BB27 Rafael Palmeiro	2.00	.60
BB28 Richie Sexson	2.00	.60
BB29 Troy Glaus	2.00	.60
BB30 Shawn Green	2.00	.60
BB31 Larry Walker	2.00	.60
BB32 Eric Hinske	2.00	.60
BB33 Andruw Jones	2.00	.60
BB34 Barry Bonds	5.00	1.50
BB35 Curt Schilling	2.00	.60
BB36 Greg Maddux	3.00	.90
BB37 Jimmy Rollins	2.00	.60
BB38 Eric Chavez	2.00	.60
BB39 Scott Rolen	2.00	.60
BB40 Mike Sweeney	2.00	.60

2003 Topps Draft Picks

	MINT	NRMT
COMPLETE SERIES 1 (5)	25.00	11.00
COMPLETE SERIES 2 (5)	25.00	11.00
1-5 ISSUED IN RETAIL SETS		
6-10 DISTRIBUTED IN HOLIDAY SETS		
1 Brandon Wood	6.00	2.70
2 Ryan Wagner	5.00	2.20
3 Sean Rodriguez	6.00	2.70
4 Chris Lubanski	8.00	3.60
5 Chad Billingsley	6.00	2.70
6 Javi Herrera	5.00	2.20
7 Brian McFall	5.00	2.20
8 Nick Markakis	5.00	2.20
9 Adam Miller	8.00	3.60
10 Daric Barton	15.00	6.75

2003 Topps Farewell to Riverfront Stadium Relics

Issued at a stated rate of one in 37 second series HTA packs, this 10 card set featured leading current and retired Cincinnati Reds players since 1970 as well as a piece of Riverfront Stadium.

	Nm-Mt	Ex-Mt
AD Adam Dunn	25.00	7.50
AK Austin Kearns	25.00	7.50
BL Barry Larkin	25.00	7.50
DC Dave Concepcion	25.00	7.50
JB Johnny Bench	40.00	12.00
JM Joe Morgan	25.00	7.50
KG Ken Griffey Jr.	25.00	7.50
PO Paul O'Neill	25.00	7.50
TP Tony Perez	25.00	7.50
TS Tom Seaver	25.00	7.50

2003 Topps First Year Player Bonus

Issued as five card bonus "packs" these 10 cards featured players in their first year on a Topps card. Cards number 1 through 5 were issued in a sealed clear cello pack within the "red" hobby factory sets while cards number 6-10 were issued in the "blue" Sears/JC Penney factory sets.

	Nm-Mt	Ex-Mt
COMP.HOBBY SET (5)		
1 Ismael Castro		
2 Branden Florence		
3 Michael Garciaparra	5.00	1.50
4 Hanley Ramirez		
5 Pete LaForest	5.00	1.50
6 Rajai Davis		
7 Gary Schneidmiller		
8 Corey Shafer		
9 Thomari Story-Harden		
10 Bryan Grace		

2003 Topps Flashback

This set, featuring basically retired players, was inserted at a stated rate of one in 12 HTA first series packs. Only Mike Piazza and Randy Johnson were active at the time this set was issued.

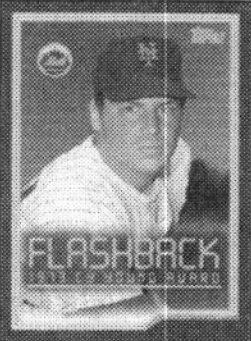

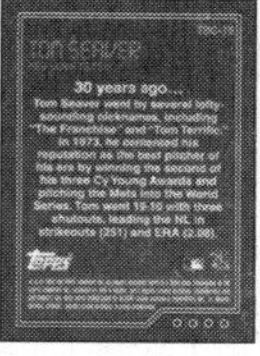

	Nm-Mt	Ex-Mt
AR Al Rosen	5.00	1.50
BM Bill Madlock	5.00	1.50
CY Carl Yastrzemski	12.00	3.60
DM Dale Murphy	6.00	1.80
EM Eddie Mathews	6.00	1.80
GB George Brett	15.00	4.50
HK Harmon Killebrew	6.00	1.80
JP Jim Palmer	5.00	1.50
LD Lenny Dykstra	5.00	1.50
MP Mike Piazza	10.00	3.00
NR Nolan Ryan	15.00	4.50
RJ Randy Johnson	6.00	1.80
RR Robin Roberts	5.00	1.50
TS Tom Seaver	5.00	1.50
WS Warren Spahn	5.00	1.50

2003 Topps Hit Parade

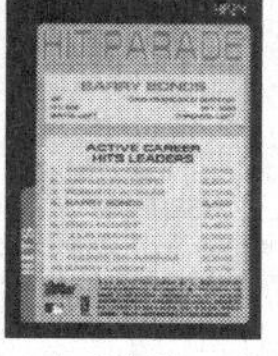

Issued at a stated rate of one in 15 hobby packs, one in 5 HTA packs and one in 10 retail packs, this 30 card set feature active players in the top 10 of home runs, runs batted in or hits.

	Nm-Mt	Ex-Mt
COMPLETE SET (30)	60.00	18.00
1 Barry Bonds	5.00	1.50
2 Sammy Sosa	3.00	.90
3 Rafael Palmeiro	2.00	.60
4 Fred McGriff	2.00	.60
5 Ken Griffey Jr.	3.00	.90
6 Juan Gonzalez	2.00	.60
7 Andres Galarraga	2.00	.60
8 Jeff Bagwell	2.00	.60
9 Frank Thomas	2.00	.60
10 Matt Williams	2.00	.60
11 Barry Bonds	5.00	1.50
12 Rafael Palmeiro	2.00	.60
13 Fred McGriff	2.00	.60
14 Andres Galarraga	2.00	.60
15 Ken Griffey Jr.	3.00	.90
16 Sammy Sosa	3.00	.90
17 Jeff Bagwell	2.00	.60
18 Juan Gonzalez	2.00	.60
19 Frank Thomas	2.00	.60
20 Matt Williams	2.00	.60
21 Rickey Henderson	2.00	.60
22 Rafael Palmeiro	2.00	.60
23 Roberto Alomar	2.00	.60
24 Barry Bonds	5.00	1.50
25 Mark Grace	2.00	.60
26 Fred McGriff	2.00	.60
27 Julio Franco	2.00	.60
28 Craig Biggio	2.00	.60
29 Andres Galarraga	2.00	.60
30 Barry Larkin	2.00	.60

2003 Topps Hobby Masters

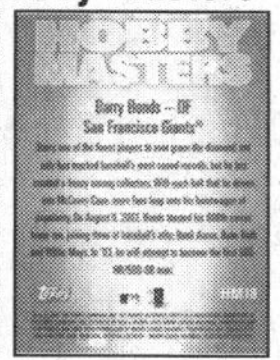

Inserted into first series packs at stated odds of one in 18 Hobby packs and one in six HTA packs, these 20 cards feature some of the most popular players in the hobby.

	Nm-Mt	Ex-Mt
COMPLETE SET (20)	40.00	12.00
HM1 Ichiro Suzuki	3.00	.90
HM2 Kazuhisa Ishii	2.00	.60
HM3 Derek Jeter	5.00	1.50
HM4 Sammy Sosa	3.00	.90
HM5 Alex Rodriguez	3.00	.90
HM6 Mike Piazza	3.00	.90
HM7 Chipper Jones	2.00	.60
HM8 Vladimir Guerrero	2.00	.60
HM9 Nomar Garciaparra	3.00	.90
HM10 Todd Helton	2.00	.60
HM11 Jason Giambi	2.00	.60
HM12 Ken Griffey Jr.	3.00	.90
HM13 Albert Pujols	4.00	1.20
HM14 Ivan Rodriguez	2.00	.60
HM15 Mark Prior	2.00	.60
HM16 Adam Dunn	2.00	.60
HM17 Randy Johnson	2.00	.60
HM18 Barry Bonds	5.00	1.50
HM19 Alfonso Soriano	2.00	.60
HM20 Pat Burrell	2.00	.60

2003 Topps Own the Game

Inserted into first series packs at stated odds of one in 12 hobby and one in four HTA, these 30 cards feature players who put up big numbers during the 2002 season.

	Nm-Mt	Ex-Mt
OG1 Ichiro Suzuki	3.00	.90
OG2 Todd Helton	2.00	.60
OG3 Larry Walker	2.00	.60
OG4 Mike Sweeney	2.00	.60
OG5 Sammy Sosa	3.00	.90
OG6 Lance Berkman	2.00	.60
OG7 Alex Rodriguez	3.00	.90
OG8 Jim Thome	2.00	.60
OG9 Shawn Green	2.00	.60
OG10 Nomar Garciaparra	3.00	.90
OG11 Miguel Tejada	2.00	.60
OG12 Jason Giambi	2.00	.60
OG13 Magglio Ordonez	2.00	.60
OG14 Manny Ramirez	2.00	.60
OG15 Alfonso Soriano	2.00	.60
OG16 Johnny Damon	2.00	.60
OG17 Derek Jeter	5.00	1.50
OG18 Albert Pujols	4.00	1.20
OG19 Luis Castillo	2.00	.60
OG20 Barry Bonds	5.00	1.50
OG21 Garret Anderson	2.00	.60
OG22 Jimmy Rollins	2.00	.60
OG23 Curt Schilling	2.00	.60
OG24 Barry Zito	2.00	.60
OG25 Randy Johnson	2.00	.60
OG26 Tom Glavine	2.00	.60
OG27 Roger Clemens	4.00	1.20
OG28 Pedro Martinez	2.00	.60
OG29 Derek Lowe	2.00	.60
OG30 John Smoltz	2.00	.60

2003 Topps Prime Cuts Relics

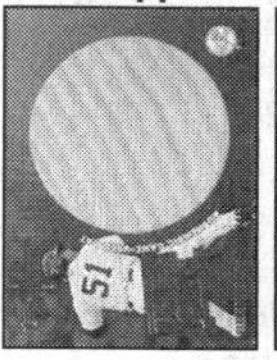

Inserted into first series packs at a stated rate of one in 37,066 hobby packs and one in 5067 HTA packs and second series packs at a rate of one in 116,208 hobby, one in 1480 HTA and one in 4368 retail packs, these 31 cards featured game-used bat pieces taken from the barrel of the bat. Each of these cards were issued to a stated print run of 50 serial numbered sets.

	Nm-Mt	Ex-Mt
AD1 Adam Dunn 1	80.00	24.00
AD2 Adam Dunn 2	80.00	24.00
AP Albert Pujols 1	120.00	36.00
AR1 Alex Rodriguez 1	80.00	24.00
AR2 Alex Rodriguez 2	80.00	24.00
AS Alfonso Soriano 2	80.00	24.00
BBO Barry Bonds 2	120.00	36.00
BW Bernie Williams 1	80.00	24.00
CD Carlos Delgado 2	50.00	15.00
EC Eric Chavez 2	50.00	15.00
EM Edgar Martinez 2	80.00	24.00
FT Frank Thomas 1	80.00	24.00
HB Hank Blalock 2	80.00	24.00
IR Ivan Rodriguez 1	80.00	24.00
JG Juan Gonzalez 1	80.00	24.00
JP Jorge Posada 2	80.00	24.00
LB Lance Berkman 1	50.00	15.00
LG Luis Gonzalez 2	50.00	15.00
MP Mike Piazza 1	80.00	24.00
MP Mark Prior 2	80.00	24.00
MV Mo Vaughn 1	50.00	15.00
NG1 Nomar Garciaparra 1	100.00	30.00
NG2 Nomar Garciaparra 2	100.00	30.00
RA1 Roberto Alomar 1	80.00	24.00
RA2 Roberto Alomar 2	80.00	24.00
RH Rickey Henderson 2	80.00	24.00
RJ Randy Johnson 2	80.00	24.00
RP Rafael Palmeiro 2	80.00	24.00
TG Tony Gwynn 2	80.00	24.00
TH Todd Helton 1	80.00	24.00
TM Tino Martinez 2	80.00	24.00

2003 Topps Prime Cuts Autograph Relics

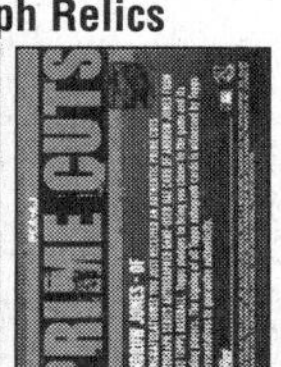

Inserted into first series packs at stated odds of one in 27,661 hobby and one in 7,917 HTA packs or second series packs, one in 8808 HTA packs or 232,416 hobb packs, one in 8808 HTA packs or one in 28,598 retail packs, these ten cards feature players who signed the relics cut from the barrel of the bat they used in a game. These cards were issued to a stated print run of 50 serial numbered sets.

	Nm-Mt	Ex-Mt
AJ Andruw Jones 1	150.00	45.00
AP Albert Pujols 2		
CJ Chipper Jones 1	200.00	60.00
DE Darin Erstad 1		
EC Eric Chavez 1	150.00	45.00
LB Lance Berkman 2	150.00	45.00
MO Maggio Ordonez 2	150.00	45.00
MT Miguel Tejada 1	150.00	45.00
RP Rafael Palmeiro 1		
SR Scott Rolen 1		

2003 Topps Prime Cuts Pine Tar Relics

Inserted into first series packs at a stated rate of one in 9266 hobby packs and one in 1267 HTA packs and second series packs at a rate of one in 4288 hobby, one in 587 HTA and one in 928 retail, these 42 cards featured game-used bat pieces taken from the handle of the bat. Each of these cards were issued to a stated print run of 200 serial numbered sets.

	Nm-Mt	Ex-Mt
AD1 Adam Dunn 1	40.00	12.00
AD2 Adam Dunn 2	40.00	12.00
AJ Andruw Jones 1	25.00	7.50
AP1 Albert Pujols 1	60.00	18.00
AP2 Albert Pujols 2	60.00	18.00
AR1 Alex Rodriguez 1	40.00	12.00
AR2 Alex Rodriguez 2	40.00	12.00
AS1 Alfonso Soriano 1	40.00	12.00
AS2 Alfonso Soriano 2	40.00	12.00
BBO Barry Bonds 2	60.00	18.00
BW Bernie Williams 1	40.00	12.00
CD Carlos Delgado 2	25.00	7.50
CJ Chipper Jones 1	40.00	12.00
DE Darin Erstad 1	25.00	7.50
EC1 Eric Chavez 1	25.00	7.50
EC2 Eric Chavez 2	25.00	7.50
EM Edgar Martinez 2	40.00	12.00
FT Frank Thomas 1	40.00	12.00
HB Hank Blalock 2	40.00	12.00
IR Ivan Rodriguez 1	40.00	12.00
JG Juan Gonzalez 1	40.00	12.00
JP Jorge Posada 2	40.00	12.00
LB1 Lance Berkman 1	25.00	7.50
LB2 Lance Berkman 2	25.00	7.50
LG Luis Gonzalez 2	25.00	7.50
MO Magglio Ordonez 2	25.00	7.50
MP Mike Piazza 1	40.00	12.00
MP Mark Prior 2	40.00	12.00
MT Miguel Tejada 1	25.00	7.50
MV Mo Vaughn 1	25.00	7.50
NG1 Nomar Garciaparra 1	50.00	15.00
NG2 Nomar Garciaparra 2	50.00	15.00
RA1 Roberto Alomar 1	40.00	12.00
RA2 Roberto Alomar 2	40.00	12.00
RH Rickey Henderson 2	40.00	12.00
RJ Randy Johnson 2	40.00	12.00
RP1 Rafael Palmeiro 1	40.00	12.00
RP2 Rafael Palmeiro 2	40.00	12.00
SR Scott Rolen 1	40.00	12.00
TG Tony Gwynn 2	40.00	12.00
TH Todd Helton 1	40.00	12.00
TM Tino Martinez 2	40.00	12.00

2003 Topps Prime Cuts Trademark Relics

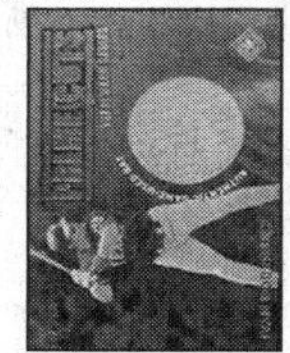

Inserted into first series packs at a stated rate of one in 18,533 hobby packs and one in 2533 HTA packs or second series packs at a rate of one in 12,912 hobby, one in 881 HTA or one in 1857 retail; these 42 cards featured game-used bat pieces taken from the middle of the bat. Each of these cards were issued to a stated print run of 100 serial numbered sets.

	Nm-Mt	Ex-Mt
AD1 Adam Dunn 1	50.00	15.00
AD2 Adam Dunn 2	50.00	15.00
AJ Andruw Jones 1	40.00	12.00
AP1 Albert Pujols 1	100.00	30.00
AP2 Albert Pujols 2	100.00	30.00
AR1 Alex Rodriguez 1	60.00	18.00
AR2 Alex Rodriguez 2	60.00	18.00
AS1 Alfonso Soriano 1	50.00	15.00
AS2 Alfonso Soriano 2	50.00	15.00
BBO Barry Bonds 2	100.00	30.00
BW Bernie Williams 1	50.00	15.00
CD Carlos Delgado 2	40.00	12.00
CJ Chipper Jones 1	50.00	15.00
DE Darin Erstad 1	40.00	12.00
EC1 Eric Chavez 1	40.00	12.00
EC2 Eric Chavez 2	40.00	12.00
EM Edgar Martinez 2	50.00	15.00
FT Frank Thomas 1	50.00	15.00
HB Hank Blalock 2	50.00	15.00
IR Ivan Rodriguez 1	50.00	15.00
JG Juan Gonzalez 1	50.00	15.00
JP Jorge Posada 2	50.00	15.00
LB1 Lance Berkman 1	40.00	12.00
LB2 Lance Berkman 2	40.00	12.00
LG Luis Gonzalez 2	40.00	12.00
MO Magglio Ordonez 2	40.00	12.00
MP Mike Piazza 1	80.00	24.00
MP Mark Prior 2	50.00	15.00
MT Miguel Tejada 1	40.00	12.00
MV Mo Vaughn 1	40.00	12.00
NG1 Nomar Garciaparra 1	80.00	24.00
NG2 Nomar Garciaparra 2	80.00	24.00
RA1 Roberto Alomar 1	50.00	15.00
RA2 Roberto Alomar 2	50.00	15.00
RH Rickey Henderson 2	50.00	15.00
RJ Randy Johnson 2	50.00	15.00
RP1 Rafael Palmeiro 1	50.00	15.00

RP2 Rafael Palmeiro 2 .... 50.00 15.00
SR Scott Rolen 1 .... 50.00 15.00
TG Tony Gwynn 2 .... 50.00 15.00
TH Todd Helton 1 .... 50.00 15.00
TM Tino Martinez 2 .... 50.00 15.00

2003 Topps Record Breakers

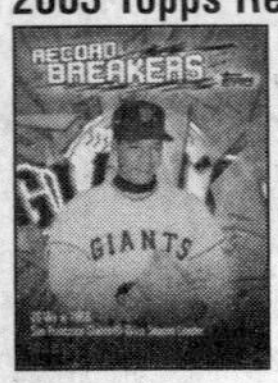

Inserted into packs at a stated rate of one in six hobby, one in two HTA and one in four retail, these 101 cards feature a mix of active and retired players who hold some sort of season, team, league or major league record.

Nm-Mt Ex-Mt
COMPLETE SET (100) 120.00 36.00
COMPLETE SERIES 1 (50) 60.00 18.00
COMPLETE SERIES 2 (50) 60.00 18.00
AG Andres Galarraga 1 .... 1.50 .45
AR1 Alex Rodriguez 1 .... 2.50 .75
AR2 Alex Rodriguez 2 .... 2.50 .75
BB1 Barry Bonds 1 .... 4.00 1.20
BB2 Barry Bonds 2 .... 4.00 1.20
BF Bob Feller 2 .... 1.50 .45
BG Bob Gibson 1 .... 1.50 .45
CB Craig Biggio 2 .... 1.50 .45
CD1 Carlos Delgado 1 .... 1.50 .45
CD2 Carlos Delgado 2 .... 1.50 .45
CF Cliff Floyd 1 .... 1.50 .45
CJ Chipper Jones 1 .... 1.50 .45
CK Chuck Klein 1 .... 1.50 .45
CS Curt Schilling 1 .... 1.50 .45
DE Darin Erstad 2 .... 1.50 .45
DG Dwight Gooden 2 .... 1.50 .45
DM Don Mattingly 1 .... 5.00 1.50
EM Edgar Martinez 2 .... 1.50 .45
EM Eddie Mathews 1 .... 2.00 .60
FJ Fergie Jenkins 1 .... 1.50 .45
FM Fred McGriff 1 .... 1.50 .45
FR1 Frank Robinson 1 .... 2.00 .60
FR2 Frank Robinson 2 .... 2.00 .60
FT Frank Thomas 2 .... 1.50 .45
GA Garret Anderson 2 .... 1.50 .45
GB1 George Brett 1 .... 5.00 1.50
GB2 George Brett 2 .... 5.00 1.50
GF1 George Foster 1 .... 1.50 .45
GF2 George Foster 2 .... 1.50 .45
GM Greg Maddux 2 .... 2.50 .75
GS Gary Sheffield 1 .... 1.50 .45
HG Hank Greenberg 1 .... 2.00 .60
HK Harmon Killebrew 1 .... 2.00 .60
HW Hack Wilson 1 .... 2.00 .60
IS Ichiro Suzuki 2 .... 2.50 .75
JB1 Jeff Bagwell 1 .... 1.50 .45
JB2 Jeff Bagwell 2 .... 1.50 .45
JD Johnny Damon 2 .... 1.50 .45
JG Jason Giambi 1 .... 1.50 .45
JK Jeff Kent 2 .... 1.50 .45
JME Jose Mesa 2 .... 1.50 .45
JM1 Juan Marichal 1 .... 1.50 .45
JM2 Juan Marichal 2 .... 1.50 .45
JO John Olerud 1 .... 1.50 .45
JP Jim Palmer 2 .... 1.50 .45
JR Jim Rice 2 .... 1.50 .45
JS John Smoltz 2 .... 1.50 .45
JT Jim Thome 2 .... 1.50 .45
KG1 Ken Griffey Jr. 1 .... 2.50 .75
KG2 Ken Griffey Jr. 2 .... 2.50 .75
LA Luis Aparicio 2 .... 1.50 .45
LBR1 Lou Brock 1 .... 2.00 .60
LBR2 Lou Brock 2 .... 2.00 .60
LB1 Lance Berkman 1 .... 1.50 .45
LB2 Lance Berkman 2 .... 1.50 .45
LC Luis Castillo 1 .... 1.50 .45
LD Lenny Dykstra 2 .... 1.50 .45
LG1 Luis Gonzalez 1 .... 1.50 .45
LG2 Luis Gonzalez 2 .... 1.50 .45
LW Larry Walker 2 .... 1.50 .45
MP Mike Piazza 1 .... 2.50 .75
MR Manny Ramirez 2 .... 1.50 .45
MS Mike Sweeney 1 .... 1.50 .45
MSC Mike Schmidt 1 .... 4.00 1.20
NG Nomar Garciaparra 2 .... 2.50 .75
NR Nolan Ryan 1 .... 5.00 1.50
PM Pedro Martinez 1 .... 1.50 .45
PM Paul Molitor 2 .... 2.00 .60
PW Preston Wilson 1 .... 1.50 .45
RA Roberto Alomar 2 .... 1.50 .45
RC Roger Clemens 1 .... 3.00 .90
RCA Rod Carew 1 .... 2.00 .60
RG Ron Guidry 1 .... 1.50 .45
RH1 Rickey Henderson 1 .... 1.50 .45
RH2 Rickey Henderson 2 .... 1.50 .45
RJ1 Randy Johnson 1 .... 1.50 .45
RJ2 Randy Johnson 2 .... 1.50 .45
RP Rafael Palmeiro 1 .... 1.50 .45
RS1 Richie Sexson 1 .... 1.50 .45
RS2 Richie Sexson 2 .... 1.50 .45
RY1 Robin Yount 1 .... 3.00 .90
RY2 Robin Yount 2 .... 3.00 .90
SG1 Shawn Green 1 .... 1.50 .45
SG2 Shawn Green 2 .... 1.50 .45
SS1 Sammy Sosa 1 .... 2.50 .75
SS2 Sammy Sosa 2 .... 2.50 .75
TG Troy Glaus 1 .... 1.50 .45
TG1 Tony Gwynn 1 .... 2.50 .75
TG2 Tony Gwynn 2 .... 2.50 .75
TH1 Todd Helton 1 .... 1.50 .45
TH2 Todd Helton 2 .... 1.50 .45
TK Ted Kluszewski 2 .... 2.00 .60
TR Tim Raines 2 .... 1.50 .45
TS1 Tom Seaver 1 .... 2.00 .60
TS2 Tom Seaver 2 .... 2.00 .60
VG1 Vladimir Guerrero 1 .... 1.50 .45
VG2 Vladimir Guerrero 2 .... 1.50 .45
WB Wade Boggs 2 .... 2.00 .60
WM Willie Mays 2 .... 5.00 1.50
WS Willie Stargell 2 .... 2.00 .60

2003 Topps Record Breakers Autographs

This 19 card set partially parallels the Record Breaker insert set. Most of the cards, except for Luis Gonzalez, were inserted into first series packs at a stated rate of one in 6941 hobby packs and one in 1178 HTA packs. The second series cards were issued at a stated rate of one in 2218 hobby, one in 634 HTA and one in 1850 retail packs.

Nm-Mt Ex-Mt
GROUP A1 SER.1 1:6941 H, 1:1178 HTA
GROUP B1 SER.1 1:34,320 H, 1:9744 HTA
GRP 2 SER.2 1:2218 H, 1:634 HTA, 1:1850 R
CF Cliff Floyd A1 .... 25.00 7.50
CJ Chipper Jones A1 .... 100.00 30.00
DM Don Mattingly 2 .... 150.00 45.00
FJ Fergie Jenkins A1 .... 40.00 12.00
GF George Foster 2 .... 40.00 12.00
HK Harmon Killebrew A1 .... 80.00 24.00
JM Juan Marichal 2 .... 60.00 18.00
LA Luis Aparicio 2 .... 40.00 12.00
LB Lance Berkman 2 .... 60.00 18.00
LBR Lou Brock 2 .... 60.00 18.00
LG Luis Gonzalez B1 .... 40.00 12.00
MS Mike Schmidt A1 .... 120.00 36.00
RP Rafael Palmeiro A1 .... 80.00 24.00
RS Richie Sexson A1 .... 40.00 12.00
RY Robin Yount A1 .... 80.00 24.00
SG Shawn Green A1 ....
SW Mike Sweeney A1 .... 40.00 12.00
TG Troy Glaus A1 ....
WM Willie Mays 2 .... 150.00 45.00

2003 Topps Record Breakers Relics

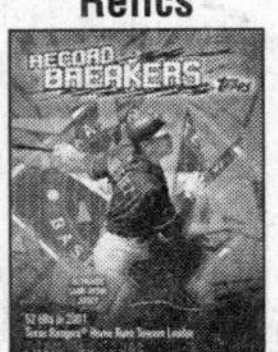

This 40 card set partially parallels the Record Breaker insert set. These cards, depending on the group they belonged to, were inserted into first and second series packs at different rates and we have noted all that information in our headers.

Nm-Mt Ex-Mt
BAT A1 SER.1 ODDS 1:13,528 H, 1:4872 HTA
BAT B1 SER.1 ODDS 1:9058 H, 1:1689 HTA
BAT C1 SER.1 ODDS 1:743 H, 1:90 HTA
UNI A1 SER.1 ODDS 1:6178 H, 1:700 HTA
UNI B1 SER.1 ODDS 1:355 H, 1:51 HTA
BAT 2 SER.2 ODDS 1:191 H, 1:59 HTA
UNI A2 SER.2 ODDS 1:5235, 1:400 HTA
UNI B2 SER.2 ODDS 1:418, 1:176 HTA
UNI C2 SER.2 ODDS 1:1151, 1:87 HTA
AR1 Alex Rodriguez Uni B1 .... 15.00 4.50
AR2 Alex Rodriguez Uni B2 .... 15.00 4.50
CD1 Carlos Delgado Uni B1 .... 10.00 3.00
CD2 Carlos Delgado Uni B2 .... 10.00 3.00
CJ Chipper Jones Uni B1 .... 15.00 4.50
DE Darin Erstad Uni A2 .... 10.00 3.00
DG Dwight Gooden Uni B2 .... 10.00 3.00
DM Don Mattingly Bat C1 .... 40.00 12.00
EM Edgar Martinez Bat 2 .... 15.00 4.50
FR1 Frank Robinson Bat C1 .... 15.00 4.50
FR2 Frank Robinson Bat 2 .... 15.00 4.50
FT Frank Thomas Bat 2 .... 15.00 4.50
GB1 George Brett Bat C1 .... 25.00 7.50
GB2 George Brett Bat 2 .... 25.00 7.50
HG Hank Greenberg Bat B1 .... 40.00 12.00
HW Hack Wilson Bat A1 .... 50.00 15.00
JB Jeff Bagwell Uni B1 .... 15.00 4.50
JR Jim Rice Uni B2 .... 10.00 3.00
LBE Lance Berkman Bat C1 .... 10.00 3.00
LC Luis Castillo Bat C1 .... 10.00 3.00
LG Luis Gonzalez Bat 2 .... 10.00 3.00
LGO Luis Gonzalez Uni B1 .... 10.00 3.00
MP Mike Piazza Bat C1 .... 25.00 7.50
MS Mike Sweeney Bat C1 .... 10.00 3.00
NR Nolan Ryan Uni A1 .... 50.00 15.00
NRA Nolan Ryan Uni C2 .... 40.00 12.00
PM Pedro Martinez Uni B1 .... 15.00 4.50
RH Rickey Henderson Bat C1 .... 15.00 4.50
RHO Rogers Hornsby Bat 2 .... 40.00 12.00
RS Richie Sexson Uni C2 .... 10.00 3.00
RY1 Robin Yount Uni B1 .... 15.00 4.50
RY2 Robin Yount Bat 2 .... 15.00 4.50
SG Shawn Green Uni B1 .... 10.00 3.00
TG Tony Gwynn 2B Bat 2 .... 15.00 4.50
TG2 Tony Gwynn Avg Bat 2 .... 15.00 4.50
TH1 Todd Helton Uni B1 .... 15.00 4.50
TH2 Todd Helton Uni B2 .... 15.00 4.50
TK Ted Kluszewski Bat 2 .... 15.00 4.50
TR Tim Raines Bat 2 .... 15.00 4.50
WB Wade Boggs Bat 2 .... 15.00 4.50

2003 Topps Record Breakers Nolan Ryan

Inserted at a stated rate of one in two HTA packs, this seven card set features all-time strikeout king Nolan Ryan. Each of these cards commemorate one of his record setting seven no-hitters.

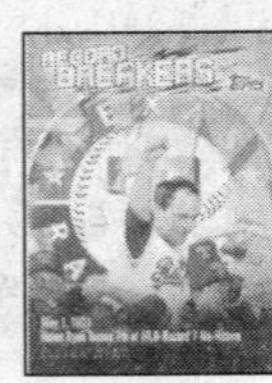

Nm-Mt Ex-Mt
COMPLETE SET (7) 60.00 18.00
COMMON CARD (NR1-NR7) 10.00 3.00

2003 Topps Record Breakers Nolan Ryan Autographs

Inserted at a stated rate of one in 1894 HTA packs, this three card set honors Nolan Ryan and the teams he tossed no-hitters for.

Nm-Mt Ex-Mt
COMMON CARD 250.00 75.00

2003 Topps Red Backs

Inserted in second series packs at a stated rate of one in 12 hobby and one in eight retail; this 40-card set features leading players in the style of the 1951 Topps Red Back set.

Nm-Mt Ex-Mt
COMPLETE SET (40) 100.00 30.00
1 Nomar Garciaparra 4.00 1.20
2 Ichiro Suzuki 4.00 1.20
3 Alex Rodriguez 4.00 1.20
4 Sammy Sosa 4.00 1.20
5 Barry Bonds 6.00 1.80
6 Vladimir Guerrero .... 2.50 .75
7 Derek Jeter 6.00 1.80
8 Miguel Tejada .... 2.00 .60
9 Alfonso Soriano .... 2.00 .60
10 Manny Ramirez .... 2.00 .60
11 Adam Dunn .... 2.00 .60
12 Jason Giambi .... 2.00 .60
13 Mike Piazza 4.00 1.20
14 Scott Rolen .... 2.50 .75
15 Shawn Green .... 2.00 .60
16 Randy Johnson .... 2.50 .75
17 Todd Helton .... 2.00 .60
18 Garret Anderson .... 2.00 .60
19 Curt Schilling .... 2.00 .60
20 Albert Pujols 5.00 1.50
21 Chipper Jones .... 2.50 .75
22 Luis Gonzalez .... 2.00 .60
23 Mark Prior .... 2.50 .75
24 Jim Thome .... 2.50 .75
25 Ivan Rodriguez .... 2.50 .75
26 Torii Hunter .... 2.00 .60
27 Lance Berkman .... 2.00 .60
28 Troy Glaus .... 2.00 .60
29 Andruw Jones .... 2.00 .60
30 Barry Zito .... 2.00 .60
31 Jeff Bagwell .... 2.00 .60
32 Magglio Ordonez .... 2.00 .60
33 Pat Burrell .... 2.00 .60
34 Mike Sweeney .... 2.00 .60
35 Rafael Palmeiro .... 2.00 .60
36 Larry Walker .... 2.00 .60
37 Carlos Delgado .... 2.00 .60
38 Brian Giles .... 2.00 .60
39 Pedro Martinez .... 2.50 .75
40 Greg Maddux 4.00 1.20

2003 Topps Team Topps Legends Autographs

Nm-Mt Ex-Mt
SEE 2001 TOPPS TEAM TOPPS FOR PRICING

2003 Topps Turn Back the Clock Autographs

This five card set was inserted at a stated rate of one in 134 HTA packs except for Bill Madlock who signed fewer cards and his card was inserted at a stated rate of one in 268 HTA packs.

Nm-Mt Ex-Mt
GROUP A SER.1 ODDS 1:134 HTA ....
GROUP B SER.1 ODDS 1:268 HTA ....
BM Bill Madlock B 15.00 4.50
DM Dale Murphy A 40.00 12.00
HK Harmon Killebrew A ....
JP Jim Palmer A 20.00 6.00
LD Lenny Dykstra A 20.00 6.00

2003 Topps Traded

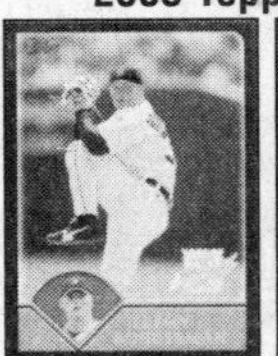

This 275 card-set was released in October, 2003. The set was issued in 10 card packs with an $3 SRP which came 24 packs to a box and 12 boxes to a case. Cards numbered 1 through 115 feature veterans who were traded while cards 116 through 120 feature managers. Cards numbered 121 through 165 featured prospects and cards 166 through 275 feature Rookie Cards. All of these cards were issued with a "T" prefix.

MINT NRMT
COMPLETE SET (275) 50.00 22.00
COMMON CARD (T1-T120) .... .20 .09
COMMON CARD (121-165) .... .40 .18
T1 Juan Pierre .... .20 .09
T2 Mark Grudzielanek .... .20 .09
T3 Tanyon Sturtze .... .20 .09
T4 Greg Vaughn .... .20 .09
T5 Greg Myers .... .20 .09
T6 Randall Simon .... .20 .09
T7 Todd Hundley .... .20 .09
T8 Marlon Anderson .... .20 .09
T9 Jeff Reboulet .... .20 .09
T10 Alex Sanchez .... .20 .09
T11 Mike Rivera .... .20 .09
T12 Todd Walker .... .20 .09
T13 Ray King .... .20 .09
T14 Shawn Estes .... .20 .09
T15 Gary Matthews Jr. .... .20 .09
T16 Jaret Wright .... .20 .09
T17 Edgardo Alfonzo .... .20 .09
T18 Omar Daal .... .20 .09
T19 Ryan Rupe .... .20 .09
T20 Tony Clark .... .20 .09
T21 Jeff Suppan .... .20 .09
T22 Mike Stanton .... .20 .09
T23 Ramon Martinez .... .20 .09
T24 Armando Rios .... .20 .09
T25 Johnny Estrada .... .20 .09
T26 Joe Girardi .... .20 .09
T27 Ivan Rodriguez .... .50 .23
T28 Robert Fick .... .20 .09
T29 Rick White .... .20 .09
T30 Robert Person .... .20 .09
T31 Alan Benes .... .20 .09
T32 Chris Carpenter .... .20 .09
T33 Chris Widger .... .20 .09
T34 Travis Hafner .... .20 .09
T35 Mike Venafro .... .20 .09
T36 Jon Lieber .... .20 .09
T37 Orlando Hernandez .... .20 .09
T38 Aaron Myette .... .20 .09
T39 Paul Bako .... .20 .09
T40 Erubiel Durazo .... .20 .09
T41 Mark Guthrie .... .20 .09
T42 Steve Avery .... .20 .09
T43 Damian Jackson .... .20 .09
T44 Rey Ordonez .... .20 .09
T45 John Flaherty .... .20 .09
T46 Byung-Hyun Kim .... .20 .09
T47 Tom Goodwin .... .20 .09
T48 Elmer Dessens .... .20 .09
T49 Al Martin .... .20 .09
T50 Gene Kingsale .... .20 .09
T51 Lenny Harris .... .20 .09
T52 David Ortiz Sox .... .50 .23
T53 Jose Lima .... .20 .09
T54 Mike Difelice .... .20 .09
T55 Jose Hernandez .... .20 .09
T56 Todd Zeile .... .20 .09
T57 Roberto Hernandez .... .20 .09
T58 Albie Lopez .... .20 .09
T59 Roberto Alomar .... .30 .14
T60 Russ Ortiz .... .20 .09
T61 Brian Daubach .... .20 .09
T62 Carl Everett .... .20 .09
T63 Jeromy Burnitz .... .20 .09
T64 Mark Bellhorn .... .20 .09
T65 Ruben Sierra .... .20 .09
T66 Mike Fetters .... .20 .09
T67 Armando Benitez .... .20 .09
T68 Deivi Cruz .... .20 .09
T69 Jose Cruz Jr. .... .20 .09
T70 Jeremy Fikac .... .20 .09
T71 Jeff Kent .... .20 .09
T72 Andres Galarraga .... .20 .09
T73 Rickey Henderson .... .50 .23
T74 Royce Clayton .... .20 .09
T75 Troy O'Leary .... .20 .09
T76 Ron Coomer .... .20 .09
T77 Greg Colbrunn .... .20 .09
T78 Wes Helms .... .20 .09
T79 Kevin Millwood .... .20 .09
T80 Damion Easley .... .20 .09
T81 Bobby Kielty .... .20 .09
T82 Keith Osik .... .20 .09
T83 Ramiro Mendoza .... .20 .09
T84 Shea Hillenbrand .... .20 .09
T85 Shannon Stewart .... .20 .09
T86 Eddie Perez .... .20 .09
T87 Ugueth Urbina .... .20 .09
T88 Orlando Palmeiro .... .20 .09
T89 Graeme Lloyd .... .20 .09
T90 John Vander Wal .... .20 .09
T91 Gary Bennett .... .20 .09
T92 Shane Reynolds .... .20 .09
T93 Steve Parris .... .20 .09
T94 Julio Lugo .... .20 .09
T95 John Halama .... .20 .09
T96 Carlos Baerga .... .20 .09
T97 Jim Parque .... .20 .09
T98 Mike Williams .... .20 .09
T99 Fred McGriff .... .30 .14
T100 Kenny Rogers .... .20 .09
T101 Matt Herges .... .20 .09
T102 Jay Bell .... .20 .09
T103 Esteban Yan .... .20 .09
T104 Eric Owens .... .20 .09
T105 Aaron Fultz .... .20 .09
T106 Rey Sanchez .... .20 .09
T107 Jim Thome .... .50 .23
T108 Aaron Boone .... .20 .09
T109 Raul Mondesi .... .20 .09
T110 Kenny Lofton .... .20 .09
T111 Jose Guillen .... .20 .09
T112 Aramis Ramirez .... .20 .09
T113 Sidney Ponson .... .20 .09
T114 Scott Williamson .... .20 .09
T115 Robin Ventura .... .20 .09
T116 Dusty Baker MG .... .20 .09
T117 Felipe Alou MG .... .20 .09
T118 Buck Showalter MG .... .20 .09
T119 Jack McKeon MG .... .20 .09
T120 Art Howe MG .... .20 .09
T121 Bobby Crosby PROS .... .60 .25
T122 Adrian Gonzalez PROS .... .40 .18
T123 Kevin Cash PROS .... .40 .18
T124 Shin-Soo Choo PROS .... .40 .18
T125 Chin-Feng Chen PROS .... 1.00 .45
T126 Miguel Cabrera PROS .... 1.00 .45
T127 Jason Young PROS .... .40 .18
T128 Alex Herrera PROS .... .40 .18
T129 Jason Dubois PROS .... .40 .18
T130 Jeff Mathis PROS .... .40 .18
T131 Casey Kotchman PROS .... .60 .25
T132 Ed Rogers PROS .... .40 .18
T133 Wilson Betemit PROS .... .40 .18
T134 Jim Kavourias PROS .... .40 .18
T135 Taylor Buchholz PROS .... .40 .18
T136 Adam LaRoche PROS .... .40 .18
T137 D.McPherson PROS .... 1.00 .45
T138 Jesus Cota PROS .... .40 .18
T139 Clint Nageotte PROS .... .40 .18
T140 Boof Bonser PROS .... .40 .18
T141 Walter Young PROS .... .40 .18
T142 Joe Crede PROS .... .40 .18
T143 Denny Bautista PROS .... .40 .18
T144 Victor Diaz PROS .... .40 .18
T145 Chris Narveson PROS .... .40 .18
T146 Gabe Gross PROS .... .40 .18
T147 Jimmy Journell PROS .... .40 .18
T148 Rafael Soriano PROS .... .40 .18
T149 Jerome Williams PROS .... .40 .18
T150 Aaron Cook PROS .... .40 .18
T151 An. Martinez PROS .... .40 .18
T152 Scott Hairston PROS .... .40 .18
T153 John Buck PROS .... .40 .18
T154 Ryan Ludwick PROS .... .40 .18
T155 Chris Bootcheck PROS .... .40 .18
T156 John Rheinecker PROS .... .40 .18
T157 Jason Lane PROS .... .40 .18
T158 Shelley Duncan PROS .... .40 .18
T159 Adam Wainwright PROS .... .40 .18
T160 Jason Arnold PROS .... .40 .18
T161 Jonny Gomes PROS .... .40 .18
T162 James Loney PROS .... .40 .18
T163 Mike Fontenot PROS .... .40 .18
T164 Khalil Greene PROS .... 2.00 .90
T165 Sean Burnett PROS .... .40 .18
T166 David Martinez FY RC .... .40 .18
T167 Felix Pie FY RC .... 2.00 .90
T168 Joe Valentine FY RC .... .40 .18
T169 Brandon Webb FY RC .... 1.00 .45
T170 Matt Diaz FY RC .... .50 .23
T171 Lew Ford FY RC .... 1.25 .55
T172 Jeremy Griffiths FY RC .... .50 .23
T173 Matt Hensley FY RC .... .40 .18
T174 Charlie Manning FY RC .... .40 .18
T175 Elizardo Ramirez FY RC .... .75 .35
T176 Greg Aquino FY RC .... .40 .18
T177 Felix Sanchez FY RC .... .40 .18
T178 Kelly Shoppach FY RC .... 1.00 .45
T179 Bubba Nelson FY RC .... .50 .23
T180 Mike O'Keefe FY RC .... .40 .18
T181 Hanley Ramirez FY RC .... 2.00 .90
T182 T.Wellemeyer FY RC .... .50 .23
T183 Dustin Moseley FY RC .... .50 .23
T184 Eric Crozier FY RC .... .50 .23
T185 Ryan Shealy FY RC .... .75 .35
T186 Jer. Bonderman FY RC .... .75 .35
T187 T.Story-Harden FY RC .... .40 .18
T188 Dusty Brown FY RC .... .40 .18
T189 Rob Hammock FY RC .... .50 .23
T190 Jorge Piedra FY RC .... .50 .23
T191 Chris De La Cruz FY RC .... .40 .18
T192 Eli Whiteside FY RC .... .40 .18
T193 Jason Kubel FY RC .... 2.00 .90
T194 Jon Schuerholz FY RC .... .40 .18
T195 St. Randolph FY RC .... .40 .18
T196 Andy Sisco FY RC .... 1.00 .45
T197 Sean Smith FY RC .... .50 .23
T198 Jon-Mark Sprowl FY RC .... .75 .35
T199 Matt Kata FY RC .... .75 .35
T200 Robinson Cano FY RC .... 1.00 .45
T201 Nook Logan FY RC .... .40 .18
T202 Ben Francisco FY RC .... .50 .23
T203 Arnie Munoz FY RC .... .40 .18
T204 Ozzie Chavez FY RC .... .40 .18
T205 Eric Riggs FY RC .... .50 .23
T206 Beau Kemp FY RC .... .40 .18
T207 Travis Wong FY RC .... .50 .23
T208 Dustin Yount FY RC .... .50 .23
T209 Brian McCann FY RC .... .75 .35
T210 Wilton Reynolds FY RC .... .50 .23
T211 Matt Bruback FY RC .... .40 .18
T212 Andrew Brown FY RC .... .50 .23
T213 Edgar Gonzalez FY RC .... .40 .18
T214 Eider Torres FY RC .... .40 .18
T215 Aquilino Lopez FY RC .... .40 .18
T216 Bobby Basham FY RC .... .50 .23
T217 Tim Olson FY RC .... .50 .23
T218 Nathan Panther FY RC .... .75 .35
T219 Bryan Grace FY RC .... .40 .18
T220 Dusty Gomon FY RC .... .50 .23
T221 Wil Ledezma FY RC .... .50 .23
T222 Josh Willingham FY RC .... .50 .23
T223 David Cash FY RC .... .40 .18
T224 Oscar Villarreal FY RC .... .40 .18
T225 Jeff Duncan FY RC .... .50 .23
T226 Kade Johnson FY RC .... .40 .18
T227 L.Steidlmayer FY RC .... .40 .18
T228 Brandon Watson FY RC .... .40 .18

T229 Jose Morales FY RC .40 .18
T230 Mike Gallo FY RC .40 .18
T231 Tyler Adamczyk FY RC .40 .18
T232 Adam Stern FY RC .40 .18
T233 Brennan King FY RC .40 .18
T234 Dan Haren FY RC .75 .35
T235 Mi. Hernandez FY RC .40 .18
T236 Ben Fritz FY RC .40 .18
T237 Clay Hensley FY RC .40 .18
T238 Tyler Johnson FY RC .40 .18
T239 Pete LaForest FY RC .50 .23
T240 Tyler Martin FY RC .40 .18
T241 J.D. Durbin FY RC .75 .35
T242 Shane Victorino FY RC .40 .18
T243 Rajai Davis FY RC .50 .23
T244 Ismael Castro FY RC .40 .18
T245 C.Wang FY RC 1.25 .55
T246 Travis Ishikawa FY RC .40 .18
T247 Corey Shafer FY RC .50 .23
T248 G.Schneidmiller FY RC .40 .18
T249 Dave Pember FY RC .40 .18
T250 Keith Stamler FY RC .40 .18
T251 Tyson Graham FY RC .40 .18
T252 Ryan Cameron FY RC .40 .18
T253 E.Eckenstahler FY RC .40 .18
T254 Ma. Peterson FY RC .40 .18
T255 D. McGowan FY RC .75 .35
T256 Pr. Redman FY RC .40 .18
T257 Haj Turay FY RC .50 .23
T258 Carlos Guzman FY RC .50 .23
T259 Matt DeMarco FY RC .40 .18
T260 Derek Michaelis FY RC .40 .18
T261 Brian Burgamy FY RC .40 .18
T262 Jay Sitzman FY RC .40 .18
T263 Chris Fallon FY RC .40 .18
T264 Mike Adams FY RC .40 .18
T265 Clint Barmes FY RC .50 .23
T266 Eric Reed FY RC .75 .35
T267 Willie Eyre FY RC .40 .18
T268 Carlos Duran FY RC .40 .18
T269 Nick Trzesniak FY RC .40 .18
T270 Ferdin Tejeda FY RC .40 .18
T271 Mi. Garciaparra FY RC .75 .35
T272 Michael Hinckley FY RC 1.00 .45
T273 Br. Florence FY RC .40 .18
T274 Trent Oeltjen FY RC .50 .23
T275 Mike Neu FY RC .40 .18

2003 Topps Traded Gold

MINT NRMT
GOLD 1-120: 5X TO 12X BASIC
GOLD 121-165: 2.5X TO 6X BASIC
GOLD 166-275: 1.5X TO 4X BASIC
TATED ODDS 1:2 HOB/RET, 1:1 HTA
TATED PRINT RUN 2003 SERIAL #'d SETS

2003 Topps Traded Future Phenoms Relics

MINT NRMT
ROUP A ODDS 1:2330 HOB/RET, 1:669 HTA
ROUP B ODDS 1:505 HOB/RET, 1:144 HTA
ROUP C ODDS 1:101 HOB/RET, 1:29 HTA
P Brandon Phillips Bat B 8.00 3.60
C Chin-Feng Chen Jsy C 25.00 11.00
DC Carl Crawford Bat C 8.00 3.60
S Chris Snelling Bat C 8.00 3.60
B Hank Blalock Bat C 10.00 4.50
M Justin Morneau Bat C 10.00 4.50
T Joe Thurston Jsy C 8.00 3.60
B Marlon Byrd Bat C 8.00 3.60
R Michael Restovich Bat B 8.00 3.60
T Mark Teixeira Bat B 8.00 3.60
B Rocco Baldelli Bat B 8.00 3.60
AH Trey Hodges Jsy C 8.00 3.60
H Travis Hafner Bat C 8.00 3.60
B Wilson Betemit Bat C 8.00 3.60
PB Willie Bloomquist Bat A 15.00 6.75

2003 Topps Traded Hall of Fame Relics

MINT NRMT
TATED ODDS 1:1009 HOB/RET, 1:289 HTA
M Eddie Murray Bat 25.00 11.00
C Gary Carter Uni 15.00 6.75

2003 Topps Traded Hall of Fame Dual Relic

MINT NRMT
STATED ODDS 1:2015 HOB/RET, 1:578 HTA
CM Gary Carter Uni 30.00 13.50
Eddie Murray Bat

2003 Topps Traded Signature Moves Autographs

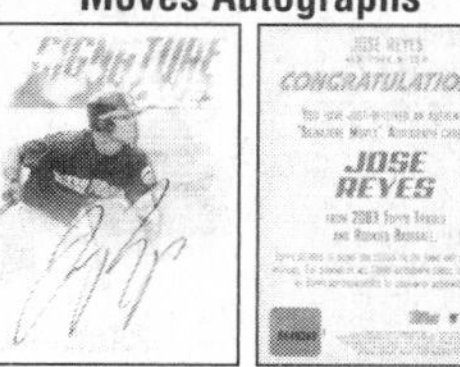

MINT NRMT
GROUP A ODDS 1:280 HOB/RET, 1:80 HTA
GROUP B ODDS 1:114 HOB/RET, 1:33 HTA
BC Bartolo Colon A 15.00 6.75
BU B.J. Upton B 30.00 13.50
CF Cliff Floyd A 15.00 6.75
DB David Bell A 15.00 6.75
EA Erick Almonte B 10.00 4.50
ER Elizardo Ramirez B 15.00 6.75
FP Felix Pie B 25.00 11.00
IR Robert Fick A 10.00 4.50
JB Joe Borchard B 10.00 4.50
JC Jose Cruz Jr. A 10.00 4.50
JF Jesse Foppert B 15.00 6.75
JG Joey Gomes B 10.00 4.50
JJC Jack Cust A 10.00 4.50
JL James Loney B 10.00 4.50
JR Jose Reyes B 15.00 6.75
JS Jason Stokes A 25.00 11.00
KG Khalil Greene A 50.00 22.00
MT Mark Teixeira A 25.00 11.00
VM Victor Martinez B 25.00 11.00
WY Walter Young B 10.00 4.50

2003 Topps Traded Topps Blue Chips Autographs

MINT NRMT
STATED ODDS 1:631
SEE 03 TEAM TOPPS BLUE CHIP FOR PRICES

2003 Topps Traded Transactions Bat Relics

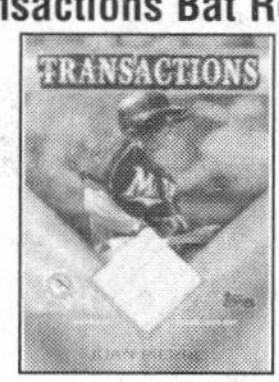

MINT NRMT
GROUP A ODDS 1:168 HOB/RET, 1:48 HTA
GROUP B ODDS 1:78 HOB/RET, 1:22 HTA
AG Andres Galarraga A 8.00 3.60
CF Cliff Floyd B 8.00 3.60
DB David Bell B 8.00 3.60
EA Edgardo Alfonzo B 8.00 3.60
ED Erubiel Durazo B 8.00 3.60
EK Eric Karros B 10.00 4.50
FL Felipe Lopez A 8.00 3.60
FM Fred McGriff B 10.00 4.50
JC Jose Cruz Jr. B 8.00 3.60
JG Jeremy Giambi A 8.00 3.60
JK Jeff Kent B 8.00 3.60
JP Juan Pierre B 8.00 3.60
JT Jim Thome A 10.00 4.50
KL Kenny Lofton A 15.00 6.75
KMO Kevin Millar Sox B 20.00 9.00
PW Preston Wilson A 8.00 3.60
RD Ray Durham A 8.00 3.60
RF Robert Fick A 8.00 3.60
RO Rey Ordonez B 8.00 3.60
RS Ruben Sierra A 8.00 3.60
RW Rondell White B 8.00 3.60
SH Tsuyoshi Shinjo B 8.00 3.60
SS Shane Spencer A 8.00 3.60
TG Tom Glavine A 10.00 4.50
TZ Todd Zeile A 8.00 3.60

2003 Topps Traded Transactions Dual Relics

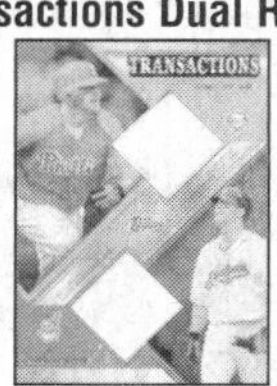

MINT NRMT
STATED ODDS 1:421 HOB/RET, 1:120 HTA
IR Ivan Rodriguez Marlins-Rgr 20.00 9.00
JT Jim Thome Phils-Indians 20.00 9.00
KM Kevin Millwood Phils-Braves 15.00 6.75

2004 Topps

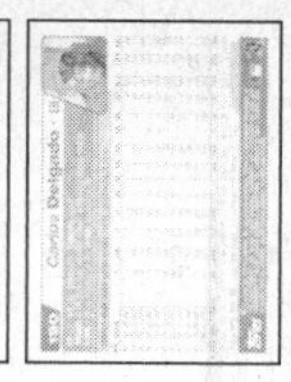

This 366-card standard-size first series was released in November, 2003. In addition, a 366-card second series was released in April, 2004. The cards were issued in 10-card hobby or retail packs with an $1.59 SRP which came 36 packs to a box and 12 boxes to a case. In addition, these cards were also issued in 35-card HTA packs with an $5 SRP which came 12 packs to a box and eight boxes to a case. Please note that insert cards were issued in different rates in retail packs as they were in hobby packs. In addition, to continuing honoring the memory of Mickey Mantle, there was no card number 7 issued in this set. Both cards numbered 267 and 274 are numbered as 267 and thus no card number 274 exists. Please note the following subsets were issued: Managers (268-296); First Year Cards (297-326); Future Stars (327-331); Highlights (332-336); League Leaders (337-348); Post-Season Play (349-355); American League All-Stars (356-367). The second series had the following subsets: Team Card (638-667), Draft Picks (668-687), Prospects (688-692), Combo Cards (693-695), Gold Gloves (696-713), Award Winners (714-718), National League All-Stars (719-729) and World Series Highlights (730-733).

MINT NRMT
COMP.HOBBY SET (737) 80.00 36.00
COMP.HOLIDAY SET (742) 80.00 36.00
COMP.RETAIL SET (737) 80.00 36.00
COMP.ASTROS SET (737) 80.00 36.00
COMP.CUBS SET (737) 80.00 36.00
COMP.RED SOX SET (737) 80.00 36.00
COMP.YANKEES SET (737) 80.00 36.00
COMPLETE SET (732) 80.00 36.00
COMPLETE SERIES 1 (366) 40.00 18.00
COMPLETE SERIES 2 (366) 40.00 18.00
COMMON CARD (1-6/8-732) .20 .09
COMMON (297-326/668-687) .50 .23
COMMON (327-331/688-692) .50 .23
1 Jim Thome .50 .23
2 Reggie Sanders .20 .09
3 Mark Kotsay .20 .09
4 Edgardo Alfonzo .20 .09
5 Ben Davis .20 .09
6 Mike Matheny .20 .09
8 Marlon Anderson .20 .09
9 Chan Ho Park .20 .09
10 Ichiro Suzuki .75 .35
11 Kevin Millwood .20 .09
12 Bengie Molina .20 .09
13 Tom Glavine .30 .14
14 Junior Spivey .20 .09
15 Marcus Giles .20 .09
16 David Segui .20 .09
17 Kevin Millar .20 .09
18 Corey Patterson .20 .09
19 Aaron Rowand .20 .09
20 Derek Jeter 1.00 .45
21 Jason LaRue .20 .09
22 Chris Hammond .20 .09
23 Jay Payton .20 .09
24 Bobby Higginson .20 .09
25 Lance Berkman .20 .09
26 Juan Pierre .20 .09
27 Brent Mayne .20 .09
28 Fred McGriff .30 .14
29 Richie Sexson .20 .09
30 Tim Hudson .20 .09
31 Mike Piazza .75 .35
32 Brad Radke .20 .09
33 Jeff Weaver .20 .09
34 Ramon Hernandez .20 .09
35 David Bell .20 .09
36 Craig Wilson .20 .09
37 Jake Peavy .20 .09
38 Tim Worrell .20 .09
39 Gil Meche .20 .09
40 Albert Pujols 1.00 .45
41 Michael Young .20 .09
42 Josh Phelps .20 .09
43 Brendan Donnelly .20 .09
44 Steve Finley .20 .09
45 John Smoltz .30 .14
46 Jay Gibbons .20 .09
47 Trot Nixon .20 .09
48 Carl Pavano .20 .09
49 Frank Thomas .50 .23
50 Mark Prior .50 .23
51 Danny Graves .20 .09
52 Milton Bradley UER .20 .09
53 Jose Jimenez .20 .09
54 Shane Halter .20 .09
55 Mike Lowell .20 .09
56 Geoff Blum .20 .09
57 Michael Tucker UER .20 .09
Dee Brown pictured
58 Paul Lo Duca .20 .09
59 Vicente Padilla .20 .09
60 Jacque Jones .20 .09
61 Fernando Tatis .20 .09
62 Ty Wigginton .20 .09
63 Pedro Astacio .20 .09
64 Andy Pettitte .30 .14
65 Terrence Long .20 .09
66 Cliff Floyd .20 .09
67 Mariano Rivera .30 .14
68 Carlos Silva .20 .09
69 Marlon Byrd .20 .09
70 Mark Mulder .20 .09
71 Kerry Ligtenberg .20 .09
72 Carlos Guillen .20 .09
73 Fernando Vina .20 .09
74 Lance Carter .20 .09
75 Hank Blalock .20 .09
76 Jimmy Rollins .20 .09
77 Francisco Rodriguez .20 .09
78 Javy Lopez .20 .09
79 Jerry Hairston Jr. .20 .09
80 Andruw Jones .20 .09
81 Rodrigo Lopez .20 .09
82 Johnny Damon .50 .23
83 Hee Seop Choi .20 .09
84 Miguel Olivo .20 .09
85 Jon Garland .20 .09
86 Matt Lawton .20 .09
87 Juan Uribe .20 .09
88 Steve Sparks .20 .09
89 Tim Spooneybarger .20 .09
90 Jose Vidro .20 .09
91 Luis Rivas .20 .09
92 Hideo Nomo .50 .23
93 Javier Vazquez .20 .09
94 Al Leiter .20 .09
95 Darren Dreifort .20 .09
96 Alex Cintron .20 .09
97 Zach Day .20 .09
98 Jorge Posada .30 .14
99 John Halama .20 .09
100 Alex Rodriguez .75 .35
101 Orlando Palmeiro .20 .09
102 Dave Berg .20 .09
103 Brad Fullmer .20 .09
104 Mike Hampton .20 .09
105 Willis Roberts .20 .09
106 Ramiro Mendoza .20 .09
107 Juan Cruz .20 .09
108 Esteban Loaiza .20 .09
109 Russell Branyan .20 .09
110 Todd Helton .30 .14
111 Braden Looper .20 .09
112 Octavio Dotel .20 .09
113 Mike MacDougal .20 .09
114 Cesar Izturis .20 .09
115 Johan Santana .30 .14
116 Jose Contreras .20 .09
117 Placido Polanco .20 .09
118 Jason Phillips .20 .09
119 Adam Eaton .20 .09
120 Vernon Wells .20 .09
121 Ben Grieve .20 .09
122 Randy Winn .20 .09
123 Ismael Valdes .20 .09
124 Eric Owens .20 .09
125 Curt Schilling .20 .09
126 Russ Ortiz .20 .09
127 Mark Buehrle .20 .09
128 Danys Baez .20 .09
129 Dmitri Young .20 .09
130 Kazuhisa Ishii .20 .09
131 A.J. Pierzynski .20 .09
132 Michael Barrett .20 .09
133 Joe McEwing .20 .09
134 Alex Cora .20 .09
135 Tom Wilson .20 .09
136 Carlos Zambrano .20 .09
137 Brett Tomko .20 .09
138 Shigetoshi Hasegawa .20 .09
139 Jarrod Washburn .20 .09
140 Greg Maddux .75 .35
141 Craig Counsell .20 .09
142 Reggie Taylor .20 .09
143 Omar Vizquel .30 .14
144 Alex Gonzalez .20 .09
145 Billy Wagner .20 .09
146 Brian Jordan .20 .09
147 Wes Helms .20 .09
148 Kyle Lohse .20 .09
149 Timo Perez .20 .09
150 Jason Giambi .20 .09
151 Erubiel Durazo .20 .09
152 Mike Lieberthal .20 .09
153 Jason Kendall .20 .09
154 Xavier Nady .20 .09
155 Kirk Rueter .20 .09
156 Mike Cameron .20 .09
157 Miguel Cairo .20 .09
158 Woody Williams .20 .09
159 Toby Hall .20 .09
160 Bernie Williams .30 .14
161 Darin Erstad .20 .09
162 Matt Mantei .20 .09
163 Geronimo Gil .20 .09
164 Bill Mueller .20 .09
165 Damian Miller .20 .09
166 Tony Graffanino .20 .09
167 Sean Casey .20 .09
168 Brandon Phillips .20 .09
169 Mike Remlinger .20 .09
170 Adam Dunn .30 .14
171 Carlos Lee .20 .09
172 Juan Encarnacion .20 .09
173 Angel Berroa .20 .09
174 Desi Relaford .20 .09
175 Paul Quantrill .20 .09
176 Ben Sheets .20 .09
177 Eddie Guardado .20 .09
178 Rocky Biddle .20 .09
179 Mike Stanton .20 .09
180 Eric Chavez .20 .09
181 Jason Michaels .20 .09
182 Terry Adams .20 .09
183 Kip Wells .20 .09
184 Brian Lawrence .20 .09
185 Bret Boone .20 .09
186 Tino Martinez .30 .14
187 Aubrey Huff .20 .09
188 Kevin Mench .20 .09
189 Tim Salmon .30 .14
190 Carlos Delgado .20 .09
191 John Lackey .20 .09
192 Oscar Villarreal .20 .09
193 Luis Matos .20 .09
194 Derek Lowe .20 .09
195 Mark Grudzielanek .20 .09
196 Tom Gordon .20 .09
197 Matt Clement .20 .09
198 Byung-Hyun Kim .20 .09
199 Brandon Inge .20 .09
200 Nomar Garciaparra .75 .35
201 Antonio Osuna .20 .09
202 Jose Mesa .20 .09
203 Bo Hart .20 .09
204 Jack Wilson .20 .09
205 Ray Durham .20 .09
206 Freddy Garcia .20 .09
207 J.D. Drew .20 .09
208 Einar Diaz .20 .09
209 Roy Halladay .20 .09
210 David Eckstein UER .20 .09
Adam Kennedy pictured
211 Jason Marquis .20 .09
212 Jorge Julio .20 .09
213 Tim Wakefield .20 .09
214 Moises Alou .20 .09
215 Bartolo Colon .20 .09
216 Jimmy Haynes .20 .09
217 Preston Wilson .20 .09
218 Luis Castillo .20 .09
219 Richard Hidalgo .20 .09
220 Manny Ramirez .30 .14
221 Mike Mussina .30 .14
222 Randy Wolf .20 .09
223 Kris Benson .20 .09
224 Ryan Klesko .20 .09
225 Rich Aurilia .20 .09
226 Kelvim Escobar .20 .09
227 Francisco Cordero .20 .09
228 Kazuhiro Sasaki .20 .09
229 Danny Bautista .20 .09
230 Rafael Furcal .20 .09
231 Travis Driskill .20 .09
232 Kyle Farnsworth .20 .09
233 Jose Valentin .20 .09
234 Felipe Lopez .20 .09
235 C.C. Sabathia .20 .09
236 Brad Penny .20 .09
237 Brad Ausmus .20 .09
238 Raul Ibanez .20 .09
239 Adrian Beltre .30 .14
240 Rocco Baldelli .20 .09
241 Orlando Hudson .20 .09
242 Dave Roberts .20 .09
243 Doug Mientkiewicz .20 .09
244 Brad Wilkerson .20 .09
245 Scott Strickland .20 .09
246 Ryan Franklin .20 .09
247 Chad Bradford .20 .09
248 Gary Bennett .20 .09
249 Jose Cruz Jr. .20 .09
250 Jeff Kent .20 .09
251 Josh Beckett .20 .09
252 Ramon Ortiz .20 .09
253 Miguel Batista .20 .09
254 Jung Bong .20 .09
255 Deivi Cruz .20 .09
256 Alex Gonzalez .20 .09
257 Shawn Chacon .20 .09
258 Runelvys Hernandez .20 .09
259 Joe Mays .20 .09
260 Eric Gagne .50 .23
261 Dustan Mohr UER .20 .09
1998 Kinston stats are wrong
262 Tomokazu Ohka .20 .09
263 Eric Byrnes .20 .09
264 Frank Catalanotto .20 .09
265 Cristian Guzman .20 .09
266 Orlando Cabrera .20 .09
267A Juan Castro .20 .09
267B M.Scioscia MG UER 274 .20 .09
268 Bob Brenly MG .20 .09
269 Bobby Cox MG .20 .09
270 Mike Hargrove MG .20 .09
271 Grady Little MG .20 .09
272 Dusty Baker MG .20 .09
273 Jerry Manuel MG .20 .09
275 Eric Wedge MG .20 .09
276 Clint Hurdle MG .20 .09
277 Alan Trammell MG .20 .09
278 Jack McKeon MG .20 .09
279 Jimy Williams MG .20 .09
280 Tony Pena MG .20 .09
281 Jim Tracy MG .20 .09
282 Ned Yost MG .20 .09
283 Ron Gardenhire MG .20 .09
284 Frank Robinson MG .30 .14
285 Art Howe MG .20 .09
286 Joe Torre MG .30 .14
287 Ken Macha MG .20 .09
288 Larry Bowa MG .20 .09
289 Lloyd McClendon MG .20 .09
290 Bruce Bochy MG .20 .09
291 Felipe Alou MG .20 .09
292 Bob Melvin MG .20 .09
293 Tony LaRussa MG .20 .09
294 Lou Piniella MG .20 .09
295 Buck Showalter MG .20 .09
296 Carlos Tosca MG .20 .09
297 Anthony Acevedo FY RC .50 .23
298 Anthony Lerew FY RC .75 .35
299 Blake Hawksworth FY RC .50 .23
300 Brayan Pena FY RC .50 .23
301 Casey Myers FY RC .50 .23
302 Craig Ansman FY RC .50 .23
303 David Murphy FY RC 1.00 .45
304 Dave Crouthers FY RC .50 .23
305 Dioner Navarro FY RC 1.25 .55
306 Donald Levinski FY RC .50 .23
307 Jesse Roman FY RC .50 .23
308 Sung Jung FY RC .50 .23
309 Jon Knott FY RC .50 .23
310 Josh Labandeira FY RC .50 .23
311 Kenny Perez FY RC .50 .23
312 Khalid Ballouli FY RC .50 .23
313 Kyle Davies FY RC .75 .35
314 Marcus McBeth FY RC .50 .23
315 Matt Creighton FY RC .50 .23
316 Chris O'Riordan FY RC .50 .23
317 Mike Gosling FY RC .50 .23
318 Nic Ungs FY RC .50 .23
319 Omar Falcon FY RC .50 .23
320 Rodney Choy Foo FY RC .50 .23
321 Tim Frend FY RC .50 .23
322 Todd Self FY RC .50 .23
323 Tydus Meadows FY RC .50 .23
324 Yadier Molina FY RC 1.00 .45
325 Zach Duke FY RC 1.50 .70
326 Zach Miner FY RC .50 .23
327 Bernie Castro .50 .23
Khalil Greene FS
328 Ryan Madson .50 .23
Elizardo Ramirez FS
329 Rich Harden .50 .23
Bobby Crosby FS
330 Zack Greinke .50 .23
Jimmy Gobble FS
331 Bobby Jenks .50 .23
Casey Kotchman FS
332 Sammy Sosa HL .50 .23
333 Kevin Millwood HL .20 .09
334 Rafael Palmeiro HL .20 .09
335 Roger Clemens HL .50 .23
336 Eric Gagne HL .30 .14
337 Bill Mueller .50 .23
Manny Ramirez
Derek Jeter

AL Batting Avg LL
338 Vernon Wells .50 .23
Ichiro Suzuki
Michael Young
AL Hits LL
339 Alex Rodriguez .50 .23
Frank Thomas
Carlos Delgado
AL Home Runs LL
340 Carlos Delgado .50 .23
Alex Rodriguez
Bret Boone
AL RBI's LL
341 Pedro Martinez .30 .14
Tim Hudson
Esteban Loaiza
AL ERA LL
342 Esteban Loaiza .30 .14
Pedro Martinez
Roy Halladay
AL Strikeouts LL
343 Albert Pujols .50 .23
Todd Helton
Edgar Renteria
NL Batting Avg LL
344 Albert Pujols .50 .23
Todd Helton
Juan Pierre
NL Hits LL
345 Jim Thome .30 .14
Richie Sexson
Javy Lopez
NL Home Runs LL
346 Preston Wilson .30 .14
Gary Sheffield
Jim Thome
NL RBI's LL
347 Jason Schmidt .30 .14
Kevin Brown
Mark Prior
NL ERA LL
348 Kerry Wood .30 .14
Mark Prior
Javier Vazquez
NL Strikeouts LL
349 Roger Clemens .50 .23
David Wells ALDS
350 Kerry Wood .30 .14
Mark Prior NLDS
351 Josh Beckett .30 .14
Miguel Cabrera
Ivan Rodriguez NLCS
352 Jason Giambi .50 .23
Mariano Rivera
Aaron Boone ALCS
353 Derek Lowe .50 .23
Ivan Rodriguez AL/NLDS
354 Pedro Martinez .50 .23
Jorge Posada
Roger Clemens ALCS
355 Juan Pierre WS .20 .09
356 Carlos Delgado AS .20 .09
357 Bret Boone AS .20 .09
358 Alex Rodriguez AS .50 .23
359 Bill Mueller AS .20 .09
360 Vernon Wells AS .20 .09
361 Garret Anderson AS .20 .09
362 Magglio Ordonez AS .20 .09
363 Jorge Posada AS .20 .09
364 Roy Halladay AS .20 .09
365 Andy Pettitte AS .20 .09
366 Frank Thomas AS .30 .14
367 Jody Gerut AS .20 .09
368 Sammy Sosa .75 .35
369 Joe Crede .20 .09
370 Gary Sheffield .20 .09
371 Coco Crisp .20 .09
372 Torii Hunter .20 .09
373 Derrek Lee .20 .09
374 Adam Everett .20 .09
375 Miguel Tejada .20 .09
376 Jeremy Affeldt .20 .09
377 Robin Ventura .20 .09
378 Scott Podsednik .20 .09
379 Matthew LeCroy .20 .09
380 Vladimir Guerrero .50 .23
381 Tike Redman .20 .09
382 Jeff Nelson .20 .09
383 Cliff Lee .20 .09
384 Bobby Abreu .20 .09
385 Josh Fogg .20 .09
386 Trevor Hoffman .20 .09
387 Jesse Foppert .20 .09
388 Edgar Martinez .30 .14
389 Edgar Renteria .20 .09
390 Chipper Jones .50 .23
391 Eric Munson .20 .09
392 Dewon Brazelton .20 .09
393 John Thomson .20 .09
394 Chris Woodward .20 .09
395 Adam LaRoche .20 .09
396 Elmer Dessens .20 .09
397 Johnny Estrada .20 .09
398 Damian Moss .20 .09
399 Gabe Kapler .20 .09
400 Dontrelle Willis .20 .09
401 Troy Glaus .20 .09
402 Raul Mondesi .20 .09
403 Shane Reynolds .20 .09
404 Kurt Ainsworth .20 .09
405 Pedro Martinez .50 .23
406 Eric Karros .20 .09
407 Billy Koch .20 .09
408 Scott Schoeneweis .20 .09
409 Paul Wilson .20 .09
410 Mike Sweeney .20 .09
411 Jason Bay .20 .09
412 Mark Redman .20 .09
413 Jason Jennings .20 .09
414 Rondell White .20 .09
415 Todd Hundley .20 .09
416 Shannon Stewart .20 .09
417 Jae Weong Seo .20 .09
418 Livan Hernandez .20 .09
419 Mark Ellis .20 .09
420 Pat Burrell .20 .09
421 Mark Loretta .20 .09
422 Robb Nen .20 .09
423 Joel Pineiro .20 .09
424 Jason Simontacchi .20 .09
425 Sterling Hitchcock .20 .09
426 Rey Ordonez .20 .09
427 Greg Myers .20 .09
428 Shane Spencer .20 .09
429 Carlos Baerga .20 .09
430 Garret Anderson .20 .09
431 Horacio Ramirez .20 .09
432 Brian Roberts .20 .09
433 Damian Jackson .20 .09
434 Doug Glanville .20 .09
435 Brian Daubach .20 .09
436 Alex Escobar .20 .09
437 Alex Sanchez .20 .09
438 Jeff Bagwell .30 .14
439 Darrell May .20 .09
440 Shawn Green .20 .09
441 Geoff Jenkins .20 .09
442 Endy Chavez .20 .09
443 Nick Johnson .20 .09
444 Jose Guillen .20 .09
445 Tomas Perez .20 .09
446 Phil Nevin .20 .09
447 Jason Schmidt .20 .09
448 Julio Mateo .20 .09
449 So Taguchi .20 .09
450 Randy Johnson .50 .23
451 Paul Byrd .20 .09
452 Chone Figgins .20 .09
453 Larry Bigbie .20 .09
454 Scott Williamson .20 .09
455 Ramon Martinez .20 .09
456 Roberto Alomar .30 .14
457 Ryan Dempster .20 .09
458 Ryan Ludwick .20 .09
459 Ramon Santiago .20 .09
460 Jeff Conine .20 .09
461 Brad Lidge .20 .09
462 Ken Harvey .20 .09
463 Guillermo Mota .20 .09
464 Rick Reed .20 .09
465 Joey Eischen .20 .09
466 Wade Miller .20 .09
467 Steve Karsay .20 .09
468 Chase Utley .20 .09
469 Matt Stairs .20 .09
470 Yorvit Torrealba .20 .09
471 Joe Kennedy .20 .09
472 Reed Johnson .20 .09
473 Victor Zambrano .20 .09
474 Jeff Davanon .20 .09
475 Luis Gonzalez .20 .09
476 Eli Marrero .20 .09
477 Ray King .20 .09
478 Jack Cust .20 .09
479 Omar Daal .20 .09
480 Todd Walker .20 .09
481 Shawn Estes .20 .09
482 Chris Reitsma .20 .09
483 Jake Westbrook .20 .09
484 Jeremy Bonderman .20 .09
485 A.J. Burnett .20 .09
486 Roy Oswalt .20 .09
487 Kevin Brown .20 .09
488 Eric Milton .20 .09
489 Claudio Vargas .20 .09
490 Roger Cedeno .20 .09
491 David Wells .20 .09
492 Scott Hatteberg .20 .09
493 Ricky Ledee .20 .09
494 Eric Young .20 .09
495 Armando Benitez .20 .09
496 Dan Haren .20 .09
497 Carl Crawford .20 .09
498 Laynce Nix .20 .09
499 Eric Hinske .20 .09
500 Ivan Rodriguez .50 .23
501 Scot Shields .20 .09
502 Brandon Webb .20 .09
503 Mark DeRosa .20 .09
504 Jhonny Peralta .20 .09
505 Adam Kennedy .20 .09
506 Tony Batista .20 .09
507 Jeff Suppan .20 .09
508 Kenny Lofton .20 .09
509 Scott Sullivan .20 .09
510 Ken Griffey Jr. .75 .35
511 Billy Traber .20 .09
512 Larry Walker .30 .14
513 Mike Maroth .20 .09
514 Todd Hollandsworth .20 .09
515 Kirk Saarloos .20 .09
516 Carlos Beltran .30 .14
517 Juan Rivera .20 .09
518 Roger Clemens 1.00 .45
519 Karim Garcia .20 .09
520 Jose Reyes .20 .09
521 Brandon Duckworth .20 .09
522 Brian Giles .20 .09
523 J.T. Snow .20 .09
524 Jamie Moyer .20 .09
525 Jason Isringhausen .20 .09
526 Julio Lugo .20 .09
527 Mark Teixeira .20 .09
528 Cory Lidle .20 .09
529 Lyle Overbay .20 .09
530 Troy Percival .20 .09
531 Robby Hammock .20 .09
532 Robert Fick .20 .09
533 Jason Johnson .20 .09
534 Brandon Lyon .20 .09
535 Antonio Alfonseca .20 .09
536 Tom Goodwin .20 .09
537 Paul Konerko .20 .09
538 D'Angelo Jimenez .20 .09
539 Ben Broussard .20 .09
540 Magglio Ordonez .20 .09
541 Ellis Burks .20 .09
542 Carlos Pena .20 .09
543 Chad Fox .20 .09
544 Jeriome Robertson .20 .09
545 Travis Hafner .20 .09
546 Joe Randa .20 .09
547 Wil Cordero .20 .09
548 Brady Clark .20 .09
549 Ruben Sierra .20 .09
550 Barry Zito .20 .09
551 Brett Myers .20 .09
552 Oliver Perez .20 .09
553 Trey Hodges .20 .09
554 Benito Santiago .20 .09
555 David Ross .20 .09
556 Ramon Vazquez .20 .09
557 Joe Nathan .20 .09
558 Dan Wilson .20 .09
559 Joe Mauer .30 .14
560 Jim Edmonds .20 .09
561 Shawn Wooten .20 .09
562 Matt Kata .20 .09
563 Vinny Castilla .20 .09
564 Marty Cordova .20 .09
565 Aramis Ramirez .20 .09
566 Carl Everett .20 .09
567 Ryan Freel .20 .09
568 Jason Davis .20 .09
569 Mark Bellhorn Sox .30 .14
570 Craig Monroe .20 .09
571 Roberto Hernandez .20 .09
572 Tim Redding .20 .09
573 Kevin Appier .20 .09
574 Jeromy Burnitz .20 .09
575 Miguel Cabrera .30 .14
576 Ramon Nivar .20 .09
577 Casey Blake .20 .09
578 Aaron Boone .20 .09
579 Jermaine Dye .20 .09
580 Jerome Williams .20 .09
581 John Olerud .20 .09
582 Scott Rolen .50 .23
583 Bobby Kielty .20 .09
584 Travis Lee .20 .09
585 Jeff Cirillo .20 .09
586 Scott Spiezio .20 .09
587 Stephen Randolph .20 .09
588 Melvin Mora .20 .09
589 Mike Timlin .20 .09
590 Kerry Wood .50 .23
591 Tony Womack .20 .09
592 Jody Gerut .20 .09
593 Franklyn German .20 .09
594 Morgan Ensberg .20 .09
595 Odalis Perez .20 .09
596 Michael Cuddyer .20 .09
597 Jon Lieber .20 .09
598 Mike Williams .20 .09
599 Jose Hernandez .20 .09
600 Alfonso Soriano .30 .14
601 Marquis Grissom .20 .09
602 Matt Morris .20 .09
603 Damian Rolls .20 .09
604 Juan Gonzalez .30 .14
605 Aquilino Lopez .20 .09
606 Jose Valverde .20 .09
607 Kenny Rogers .20 .09
608 Joe Borowski .20 .09
609 Josh Bard .20 .09
610 Austin Kearns .20 .09
611 Chin-Hui Tsao .20 .09
612 Wil Ledezma .20 .09
613 Aaron Guiel .20 .09
614 LaTroy Hawkins .20 .09
615 Tony Armas Jr. .20 .09
616 Steve Trachsel .20 .09
617 Ted Lilly .20 .09
618 Todd Pratt .20 .09
619 Sean Burroughs .20 .09
620 Rafael Palmeiro .30 .14
621 Jeremi Gonzalez .20 .09
622 Quinton McCracken .20 .09
623 David Ortiz .50 .23
624 Randall Simon .20 .09
625 Wily Mo Pena .20 .09
626 Nate Cornejo .20 .09
627 Brian Anderson .20 .09
628 Corey Koskie .20 .09
629 Keith Foulke Sox .30 .14
630 Rheal Cormier .20 .09
631 Sidney Ponson .20 .09
632 Gary Matthews Jr. .20 .09
633 Herbert Perry .20 .09
634 Shea Hillenbrand .20 .09
635 Craig Biggio .30 .14
636 Barry Larkin .30 .14
637 Arthur Rhodes .20 .09
638 Anaheim Angels TC .20 .09
639 Arizona Diamondbacks TC .20 .09
640 Atlanta Braves TC .20 .09
641 Baltimore Orioles TC .20 .09
642 Boston Red Sox TC .30 .14
643 Chicago Cubs TC .20 .09
644 Chicago White Sox TC .20 .09
645 Cincinnati Reds TC .20 .09
646 Cleveland Indians TC .20 .09
647 Colorado Rockies TC .20 .09
648 Detroit Tigers TC .20 .09
649 Florida Marlins TC .20 .09
650 Houston Astros TC .20 .09
651 Kansas City Royals TC .20 .09
652 Los Angeles Dodgers TC .20 .09
653 Milwaukee Brewers TC .20 .09
654 Minnesota Twins TC .20 .09
655 Montreal Expos TC .20 .09
656 New York Mets TC .20 .09
657 New York Yankees TC .50 .23
658 Oakland Athletics TC .20 .09
659 Philadelphia Phillies TC .20 .09
660 Pittsburgh Pirates TC .20 .09
661 San Diego Padres TC .20 .09
662 San Francisco Giants TC .20 .09
663 Seattle Mariners TC .20 .09
664 St. Louis Cardinals TC .20 .09
665 Tampa Bay Devil Rays TC .20 .09
666 Texas Rangers TC .20 .09
667 Toronto Blue Jays TC .20 .09
668 Kyle Sleeth DP RC 1.00 .45
669 Bradley Sullivan DP RC .50 .23
670 Carlos Quentin DP RC 2.00 .90
671 Conor Jackson DP RC 2.00 .90
672 Jeffrey Allison DP RC .50 .23
673 Matthew Moses DP RC 1.00 .45
674 Tim Stauffer DP RC .75 .35
675 Estee Harris DP RC .50 .23
676 David Aardsma DP RC .50 .23
677 Omar Quintanilla DP RC 1.00 .45
678 Aaron Hill DP .50 .23
679 Tony Richie DP RC .50 .23
680 Lastings Milledge DP RC 2.00 .90
681 Brad Snyder DP RC 1.00 .45
682 Jason Hirsh DP RC .50 .23
683 Logan Kensing DP RC .50 .23
684 Chris Lubanski DP .50 .23
685 Ryan Harvey DP .50 .23
686 Ryan Wagner DP .50 .23
687 Rickie Weeks DP .50 .23
688 Grady Sizemore .50 .23
Jeremy Guthrie
689 Edwin Jackson .50 .23
Greg Miller
690 Jeremy Reed .50 .23
Neal Cotts
691 Adam Loewen .50 .23
Nick Markakis
692 B.J. Upton .50 .23
Delmon Young
693 Kings of New York 1.50 .70
Alex Rodriguez
Derek Jeter
694 Fan Favorites 1.00 .45
Ichiro Suzuki
Albert Pujols
695 South Philly Sluggers 1.00 .45
Jim Thome
Mike Schmidt
696 Mike Mussina GG .20 .09
697 Bengie Molina GG .20 .09
698 John Olerud GG .20 .09
699 Bret Boone GG .20 .09
700 Eric Chavez GG .20 .09
701 Alex Rodriguez GG .50 .23
702 Mike Cameron GG UER .20 .09
Pictures Randy Winn
703 Ichiro Suzuki GG .50 .23
704 Torii Hunter GG .20 .09
705 Mike Hampton GG .20 .09
706 Mike Matheny GG .20 .09
707 Derrek Lee GG .20 .09
708 Luis Castillo GG .20 .09
709 Scott Rolen GG .30 .14
710 Edgar Renteria GG .20 .09
711 Andruw Jones GG .20 .09
712 Jose Cruz Jr. GG .20 .09
713 Jim Edmonds GG .20 .09
714 Roy Halladay CY .20 .09
715 Eric Gagne CY .30 .14
716 Alex Rodriguez MVP .50 .23
717 Angel Berroa ROY .20 .09
718 Dontrelle Willis ROY .20 .09
719 Todd Helton AS .20 .09
720 Marcus Giles AS .20 .09
721 Edgar Renteria AS .20 .09
722 Scott Rolen AS .30 .14
723 Albert Pujols AS .50 .23
724 Gary Sheffield AS .20 .09
725 Javy Lopez AS .20 .09
726 Eric Gagne AS .30 .14
727 Randy Wolf AS .20 .09
728 Bobby Cox AS .20 .09
729 Scott Podsednik AS .20 .09
730 Alex Gonzalez WS .30 .14
731 Brad Penny WS .30 .14
732 Josh Beckett .30 .14
Ivan Rodriguez
Alex Gonzalez WS
733 Josh Beckett WS MVP .30 .14

2004 Topps Black

MINT NRMT
*BLACK 1-296/368-: 20X TO 50X
*BLACK 297-326/668-: 10X TO 25X
*BLACK 327-331/688-692: 20X TO 50X
SERIES 1 ODDS 1:13 HTA
SERIES 2 ODDS 1:12 HTA
STATED PRINT RUN 53 SERIAL #'d SETS
CARDS 7 AND 274 DO NOT EXIST
SCIOSCIA AND J.CASTRO NUMBERED 267

2004 Topps Box Bottoms

The player list in our checklist has the player's name as well as what sheet his card is located on. Sheets 1-4 were issued on the bottom of first series HTA boxes and sheets 5-8 on second series.

MINT NRMT
*BOX BOTTOM CARDS: 1X TO 2.5X BASIC
ONE 4-CARD SHEET PER HTA BOX

2004 Topps Gold

MINT NRMT
*GOLD 1-296/368-: 6X TO 15X
*GOLD 297-326/668-687: 2X TO 5X
*GOLD 327-331/688-692: 2X TO 5X
SERIES 1 ODDS 1:11 HOB, 1:3 HTA, 1:10 RET
SERIES 2 ODDS 1:8 HOB, 1:2 HTA, 1:8 RET
STATED PRINT RUN 2004 SERIAL #'d SETS
CARDS 7 AND 274 DO NOT EXIST
SCIOSCIA AND J.CASTRO NUMBERED 267

2004 Topps All-Star Patch Relics

Nm-Mt Ex-Mt
SER.2 ODDS 1:7698 H, 1:2208 HTA, 1:7819 R
STATED PRINT RUN 15 SETS
CARDS ARE NOT SERIAL-NUMBERED
PRINT RUN INFO PROVIDED BY TOPPS
NO PRICING DUE TO SCARCITY
AB Aaron Boone
AJ Andruw Jones
AP Albert Pujols
AR Alex Rodriguez
BB Bret Boone
BD Brendan Donnelly
BW Billy Wagner
CD Carlos Delgado
CE Carl Everett
EG Eddie Guardado
EGA Eric Gagne
EL Esteban Loaiza
EM Edgar Martinez
ER Edgar Renteria
GA Garret Anderson
HB Hank Blalock
JE Jim Edmonds
JG Jason Giambi
JL Javy Lopez
JM Jamie Moyer
JP Jorge Posada
JS Jason Schmidt
JV Jose Vidro
KF Keith Foulke
KW Kerry Wood
ML Mike Lowell
MM Mark Mulder
MMO Melvin Mora
NG Nomar Garciaparra
PL Paul Lo Duca
PW Preston Wilson
RF Rafael Furcal
RH Ramon Hernandez
RO Russ Ortiz
RS Richie Sexson
RW Randy Wolf
RWH Rondell White
SH Shigetoshi Hasegawa
SR Scott Rolen
TG Troy Glaus
TH Todd Helton
VW Vernon Wells
WW Woody Williams

2004 Topps 1st Edition

MINT NRMT
*1ST ED 1-296: 1.25X TO 3X BASIC
*1ST ED 297-RC'S: X TO X BASIC
*1ST ED 327-331/688-: 1.25X TO 3X BASIC
DISTRIBUTED IN 1ST EDITION BOXES
CARDS 7 AND 274 DO NOT EXIST
SCIOSCIA AND J.CASTRO NUMBERED 267

2004 Topps All-Star Stitches Jersey Relics

MINT NRMT
SERIES 1 ODDS 1:137 HOB/RET, 1:39 HTA
AB Aaron Boone 10.00 4.50
AJ Andruw Jones 10.00 4.50
AR Alex Rodriguez 15.00 6.75
BD Brendan Donnelly 10.00 4.50
BW Billy Wagner 10.00 4.50
CE Carl Everett 10.00 4.50
EG Eddie Guardado 10.00 4.50
EGA Eric Gagne 10.00 4.50
EL Esteban Loaiza 10.00 4.50
EM Edgar Martinez 10.00 4.50
ER Edgar Renteria 10.00 4.50
HB Hank Blalock 10.00 4.50
JL Javy Lopez 10.00 4.50
JM Jamie Moyer 10.00 4.50
JP Jorge Posada 10.00 4.50
JS Jason Schmidt 10.00 4.50
JV Jose Vidro 10.00 4.50
KF Keith Foulke 10.00 4.50
KW Kerry Wood 10.00 4.50
ML Mike Lowell 10.00 4.50
MM Mark Mulder 10.00 4.50
MMO Melvin Mora 10.00 4.50
NG Nomar Garciaparra 15.00 6.75
PL Paul Lo Duca 10.00 4.50
PW Preston Wilson 10.00 4.50
RF Rafael Furcal 10.00 4.50
RH Ramon Hernandez 10.00 4.50
RO Russ Ortiz 10.00 4.50
RW Randy Wolf 10.00 4.50
RWH Rondell White 10.00 4.50
SH Shigetoshi Hasegawa 10.00 4.50
SR Scott Rolen 10.00 4.50
TG Troy Glaus 10.00 4.50
TH Todd Helton 10.00 4.50
VW Vernon Wells 10.00 4.50
WW Woody Williams 10.00 4.50

2004 Topps All-Stars

Nm-Mt Ex-Mt
COMPLETE SET (20) 40.00 12.00
SERIES 2 ODDS 1:16 H, 1:4 HTA
TAS1 Jason Giambi 2.00 .60
TAS2 Ichiro Suzuki 3.00 .90
TAS3 Alex Rodriguez 3.00 .90
TAS4 Albert Pujols 4.00 1.20
TAS5 Alfonso Soriano 2.00 .60
TAS6 Nomar Garciaparra 3.00 .90
TAS7 Andruw Jones 2.00 .60
TAS8 Carlos Delgado 2.00 .60
TAS9 Gary Sheffield 2.00 .60
TAS10 Jorge Posada 2.00 .60
TAS11 Magglio Ordonez 2.00 .60
TAS12 Kerry Wood 2.00 .60
TAS13 Garret Anderson 2.00 .60
TAS14 Bret Boone 2.00 .60

TAS15 Hank Blalock 2.00 .60
TAS16 Mike Lowell 2.00 .60
TAS17 Todd Helton 2.00 .60
TAS18 Vernon Wells 2.00 .60
TAS19 Roger Clemens 4.00 1.20
TAS20 Scott Rolen 2.00 .60

2004 Topps American Treasures Presidential Signatures

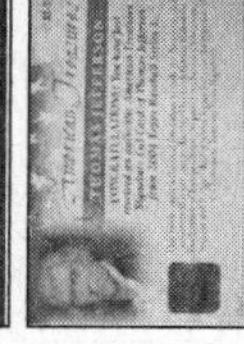

Randomly inserted into packs, this set features a "cut" signature from each of the United State Presidents. Each of these cards feature the cut signature against a United States flag background while the back features an informational blurb about that president.

MINT NRMT
SER.1 ODDS 1:175,770 HOBBY, 1:52,080 HTA
SER.1 ODDS 1:138,240 RETAIL
STATED PRINT RUN 1 SERIAL #'d SET
NO PRICING DUE TO SCARCITY
AJ Andrew Jackson
AJO Andrew Johnson
AL Abraham Lincoln
BC Bill Clinton
BH Benjamin Harrison
CA Chester A. Arthur
CC Calvin Coolidge
DE Dwight D. Eisenhower
FP Franklin Pierce
FR Franklin D. Roosevelt
GB George W. Bush
GC Grover Cleveland
GF Gerald Ford
GHB George H.W. Bush
GW George Washington
HH Herbert Hoover
HT Harry S. Truman
JA John Adams
JB James Buchanan
JC Jimmy Carter
JG James Garfield
JK John F. Kennedy
JM James Madison
JMO James Monroe
JP James K. Polk
JQA John Quincy Adams
JT John Tyler
LJ Lyndon B. Johnson
MF Millard Fillmore
MV Martin Van Buren
RH Rutherford B. Hayes
RN Richard Nixon
RR Ronald Reagan
TJ Thomas Jefferson
TR Theodore Roosevelt
UG Ulysses S. Grant
WH Warren Harding
WHH William H. Harrison
WM William McKinley
WT William Howard Taft
WW Woodrow Wilson
ZT Zachary Taylor

2004 Topps American Treasures Presidential Signatures Dual

This card is similar to the basic American Treasures Presidential Cut Signatures but feature two signatures from George H. Bush and his son George W. Bush. Only one copy of this card was produced and it was seeded exclusively into first series Home Team Advantage packs.

Nm-Mt Ex-Mt
SERIES 1 ODDS 1:208,320 HTA
STATED PRINT RUN 1 SERIAL #'d CARD
NO PRICING DUE TO SCARCITY
GB2 George H.W. Bush
George W. Bush

2004 Topps American Treasures Signatures

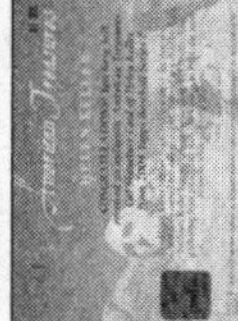

Building on the popularity and interest the first series Presidential Autographs gave this product, Topps issed 17 signed cards of famed Americans past and present as very tough inserts (one in 658,152 hobby, one in 98,256 HTA and one in 1,156,384 retail packs). Each of these cards were issued to a stated print run of one serial numbered set.

Nm-Mt Ex-Mt
SER.2 ODDS 1:658,152 HOBBY, 1:98,256 HTA
SER.2 ODDS 1:156,384 RETAIL
STATED PRINT RUN 1 SERIAL #'d SET
NO PRICING DUE TO SCARCITY
AB Alexander Graham Bell
ABU Aaron Burr
AE Albert Einstein
CL Charles Lindbergh
DM Douglas MacArthur
DW Daniel Webster
GP George S. Patton
HK Helen Keller
JS Jonas Salk
MT Mark Twain
NA Neil Armstrong
OW Orville Wright
PH Patrick Henry
RK Robert F. Kennedy
TE Thomas A. Edison
WD Walt Disney
WH William Randolph Hearst

2004 Topps American Treasures Signatures Dual

This card which was issued at a stated rate of one in 1,196,512 HTA packs feature signatures of Mark Twain/Samuel Clemens. Samuel Clemens, who wrote under the pseudonym of Mark Twain, signed items both ways during his lifetime and Topps found one type of each signature to put on this card. This card was issued to a stated print run of one serial numbered set.

Nm-Mt Ex-Mt
SERIES 2 STATED ODDS 1:196,512 HTA
STATED PRINT RUN 1 SERIAL #'d CARD
NO PRICING DUE TO SCARCITY
MT Mark Twain
Samuel Clemens

2004 Topps Autographs

Please note Josh Beckett, Mike Lowell, Mark Prior, Ivan Rodriguez and Scott Rolen did not return their cards in time for inclusion into packs and the exchange date for these cards were November 30th, 2005 for Series one exchange cards and April 30th, 2006 for Series two exchange cards. Cards issued in first series packs carry a "1" and cards from series 2 carry a "2" after their group seeding notes within our checklist.

MINT NRMT
SER.1 B 1:7362 H, 1:1911 HTA, 1:7472 R
SER.1 C 1:10,900 H, 1:2741 HTA, 1:11,059 R
SER.1 D 1:1053 H, 1:273 HTA, 1:1055 R
SER.1 E 1:6278 H, 1:1640 HTA, 1:6284 R
SER.1 F 1:1229 H, 1:318 HTA, 1:1229 R
SER.1 G 1:2340 H, 1:668 HTA, 1:2336 R
SER.1 H 1:1167 H, 1:351 HTA, 1:1229 R
SER.2 A 1:10,530 H, 1:2848 HTA, 1:9774 R
SER.2 B 1:1504 H, 1:391 HTA, 1:1422 R
SER.2 C 1:1319 H, 1:333 HTA, 1:1303 R
AB Aaron Boone B2 40.00 18.00
AH Aubrey Huff B2 15.00 6.75
AK Austin Kearns B1 25.00 11.00
BB Bobby Brownlie C2 25.00 11.00
BS Benito Santiago D1 25.00 11.00
BU B.J. Upton F1 25.00 11.00
CF Cliff Floyd D1 15.00 6.75
DM Dustin McGowan C2 10.00 4.50
DW Dontrelle Willis B2 15.00 6.75
EH Eric Hinske H1 8.00 3.60
ER Elizardo Ramirez H1 8.00 3.60
GA Garret Anderson B2 25.00 11.00
HB Hank Blalock D1 15.00 6.75
IR Ivan Rodriguez B2 EXCH 60.00 27.00
JB Josh Beckett B1 EXCH 30.00 13.50
JG Jay Gibbons A1 15.00 6.75
JP1 Josh Phelps G1 8.00 3.60
JP2 Jorge Posada B2 25.00 11.00
JV Jose Vidro F1 8.00 3.60
KG Khalil Greene H1 30.00 13.50
LB Lance Berkman A2 30.00 13.50
MC Miguel Cabrera C2 25.00 11.00
ML Mike Lowell F1 EXCH 10.00 4.50
MO Magglio Ordonez F1 25.00 11.00
MP Mark Prior D1 EXCH 60.00 27.00
MS Mike Sweeney D1 15.00 6.75
MT Mark Teixeira D1 25.00 11.00
PK Paul Konerko G1 10.00 4.50
PL Paul Lo Duca E1 15.00 6.75
SP Scott Podsednik B2 15.00 6.75
SR Scott Rolen A2 EXCH 50.00 22.00
TH Torii Hunter C1 15.00 6.75
VM Victor Martinez D1 15.00 6.75
ZG Zack Greinke C2 15.00 6.75

2004 Topps Derby Digs Jersey Relics

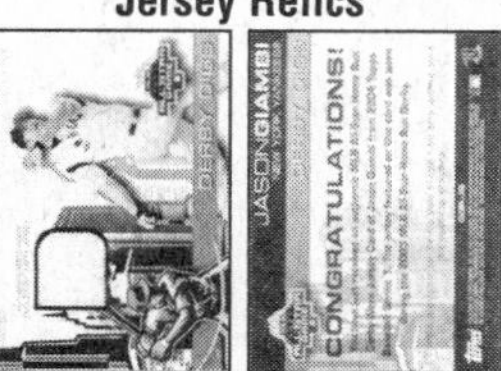

MINT NRMT
SERIES 1 ODDS 1:585 H, 1:167 HTA, 1:586 R
AP Albert Pujols 25.00 11.00
BB Bret Boone 10.00 4.50
CD Carlos Delgado 10.00 4.50
GA Garret Anderson 10.00 4.50
JE Jim Edmonds 10.00 4.50
JG Jason Giambi 10.00 4.50
RS Richie Sexson 10.00 4.50

2004 Topps Draft Pick Bonus

Nm-Mt Ex-Mt
COMP.RETAIL SET (5) 15.00 4.50
COMP.HOLIDAY SET (10) 25.00 7.50
1-5 ISSUED IN BLUE RETAIL FACT.SET
6-15 ISSUED IN GREEN HOLIDAY FACT.SET
1 Josh Johnson 5.00 1.50
2 Donny Lucy 4.00 1.20
3 Greg Golson 5.00 1.50
4 K.C. Herren 5.00 1.50
5 Jeff Marquez 5.00 1.50
6 Mark Rogers 6.00 1.80
7 Eric Hurley 5.00 1.50
8 Gio Gonzalez 5.00 1.50
9 Thomas Diamond 5.00 1.50
10 Matt Bush 8.00 2.40
11 Kyle Waldrop 5.00 1.50
12 Neil Walker 5.00 1.50
13 Mike Ferris 5.00 1.50
14 Ray Liotta 5.00 1.50
15 Phillip Hughes 5.00 1.50

2004 Topps Fall Classic Covers

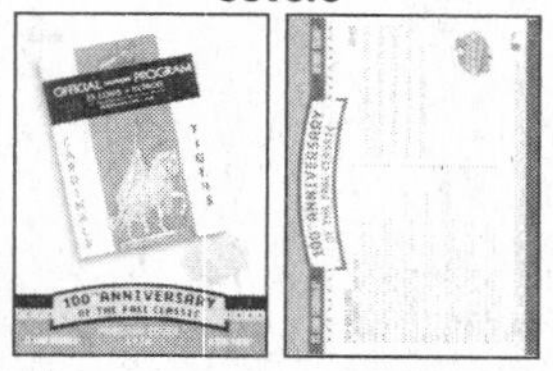

MINT NRMT
COMPLETE SET (99) 240.00 110.00
COMPLETE SERIES 1 (48) 120.00 55.00
COMPLETE SERIES 2 (51) 120.00 55.00
COMMON CARD 4.00 1.80
SERIES 1 ODDS 1:12 HOB/RET, 1:4 HTA
SERIES 2 ODDS 1:12 HOB/RET, 1:5 HTA
EVEN YEARS DISTRIBUTED IN SERIES 1
ODD YEARS DISTRIBUTED IN SERIES 2

2004 Topps First Year Player Bonus

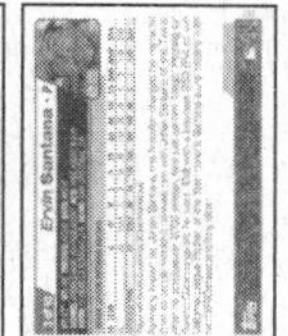

Nm-Mt Ex-Mt
COMPLETE SERIES 1 (5) 15.00 4.50
COMPLETE SERIES 2 (5) 15.00 4.50
1-5 ISSUED IN BROWN HOBBY FACT.SETS
6-10 ISSUED IN JC PENNEY FACT.SETS
1 Travis Blackley 5.00 1.50
2 Rudy Guillen 5.00 1.50
3 Ervin Santana 5.00 1.50
4 Wanell Severino 4.00 1.20
5 Kevin Kouzmanoff 5.00 1.50
6 Alberto Callaspo 5.00 1.50
7 Bobby Brownlie 5.00 1.50
8 Travis Hanson 4.00 1.20
9 Joaquin Arias 4.00 1.20
10 Merkin Valdez 5.00 1.50

2004 Topps Hit Parade

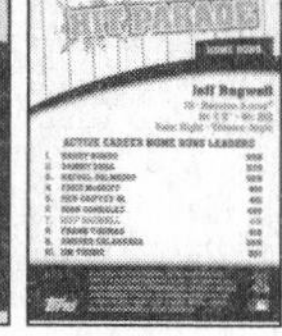

Nm-Mt Ex-Mt
COMPLETE SET (30) 40.00 12.00
SERIES 2 ODDS 1:7 HOB, 1:2 HTA, 1:9 RET
HP1 Sammy Sosa HR 3.00 .90
HP2 Rafael Palmeiro HR 2.00 .60
HP3 Fred McGriff HR 2.00 .60
HP4 Ken Griffey Jr. HR 3.00 .90
HP5 Juan Gonzalez HR 2.00 .60
HP6 Frank Thomas HR 2.00 .60
HP7 Andres Galarraga HR 2.00 .60
HP8 Jim Thome HR 2.00 .60
HP9 Jeff Bagwell HR 2.00 .60
HP10 Gary Sheffield HR 2.00 .60
HP11 Rafael Palmeiro RBI 2.00 .60
HP12 Sammy Sosa RBI 3.00 .90
HP13 Fred McGriff RBI 2.00 .60
HP14 Andres Galarraga RBI 2.00 .60
HP15 Juan Gonzalez RBI 2.00 .60
HP16 Frank Thomas RBI 2.00 .60
HP17 Jeff Bagwell RBI 2.00 .60
HP18 Ken Griffey Jr. RBI 3.00 .90
HP19 Ruben Sierra RBI 2.00 .60
HP20 Gary Sheffield RBI 2.00 .60
HP21 Rafael Palmeiro Hits 2.00 .60
HP22 Roberto Alomar Hits 2.00 .60
Card number in Blue
HP22A Roberto Alomar Hits 2.00 .60
Card number in White
HP23 Julio Franco Hits 2.00 .60
HP24 Andres Galarraga Hits 2.00 .60
HP25 Fred McGriff Hits 2.00 .60
HP26 Craig Biggio Hits 2.00 .60
HP27 Barry Larkin Hits 2.00 .60
HP28 Steve Finley Hits 2.00 .60
HP29 B.J. Surhoff Hits 2.00 .60
HP30 Jeff Bagwell Hits 2.00 .60

2004 Topps Hobby Masters

MINT NRMT
COMPLETE SET (20) 40.00 18.00
SERIES 1 ODDS 1:12 HOBBY, 1:4 HTA
1 Albert Pujols 4.00 1.80
2 Mark Prior 2.00 .90
3 Alex Rodriguez 3.00 1.35
4 Nomar Garciaparra 3.00 1.35
5 Barry Bonds 5.00 2.20
6 Sammy Sosa 3.00 1.35
7 Alfonso Soriano 2.00 .90
8 Ichiro Suzuki 3.00 1.35
9 Derek Jeter 4.00 1.80
10 Jim Thome 2.00 .90
11 Jason Giambi 2.00 .90
12 Mike Piazza 3.00 1.35
13 Barry Zito 2.00 .90
14 Randy Johnson 2.00 .90
15 Adam Dunn 2.00 .90
16 Vladimir Guerrero 2.00 .90
17 Gary Sheffield 2.00 .90
18 Carlos Delgado 2.00 .90
19 Chipper Jones 2.00 .90
20 Dontrelle Willis 2.00 .90

2004 Topps Own the Game

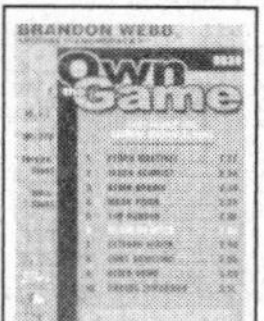

MINT NRMT
COMPLETE SET (30) 60.00 27.00
SERIES 1 ODDS 1:18 HOB/RET, 1:6 HTA
1 Jim Thome 2.00 .90
2 Albert Pujols 4.00 1.80
3 Alex Rodriguez 3.00 1.35
4 Barry Bonds 5.00 2.20
5 Ichiro Suzuki 3.00 1.35
6 Derek Jeter 4.00 1.80
7 Nomar Garciaparra 3.00 1.35
8 Alfonso Soriano 2.00 .90
9 Gary Sheffield 2.00 .90
10 Jason Giambi 2.00 .90
11 Todd Helton 2.00 .90
12 Garret Anderson 2.00 .90
13 Carlos Delgado 2.00 .90
14 Manny Ramirez 2.00 .90
15 Richie Sexson 2.00 .90
16 Vernon Wells 2.00 .90
17 Preston Wilson 2.00 .90
18 Frank Thomas 2.00 .90
19 Shawn Green 2.00 .90
20 Rafael Furcal 2.00 .90
21 Juan Pierre 2.00 .90
22 Javy Lopez 2.00 .90
23 Edgar Renteria 2.00 .90
24 Mark Prior 2.00 .90
25 Pedro Martinez 2.00 .90
26 Kerry Wood 2.00 .90
27 Curt Schilling 2.00 .90
28 Roy Halladay 2.00 .90
29 Eric Gagne 2.00 .90
30 Brandon Webb 2.00 .90

2004 Topps Presidential First Pitch Seat Relics

Nm-Mt Ex-Mt
SERIES 2 ODDS 1:592 H, 1:169 HTA, 1:592 R
BC Bill Clinton 50.00 15.00
CC Calvin Coolidge 25.00 7.50
DE Dwight Eisenhower 25.00 7.50
FR Franklin D. Roosevelt 40.00 12.00
GB George W. Bush 50.00 15.00
GF Gerald Ford 40.00 12.00
HH Herbert Hoover 25.00 7.50
HT Harry Truman 25.00 7.50
JK John F. Kennedy 50.00 15.00
LJ Lyndon B. Johnson 25.00 7.50
RN Richard Nixon 50.00 15.00
RR Ronald Reagan 60.00 18.00
WH Warren Harding 25.00 7.50
WT William Taft 25.00 7.50
WW Woodrow Wilson 25.00 7.50
GHB George H.W. Bush 40.00 12.00

2004 Topps Presidential Pastime

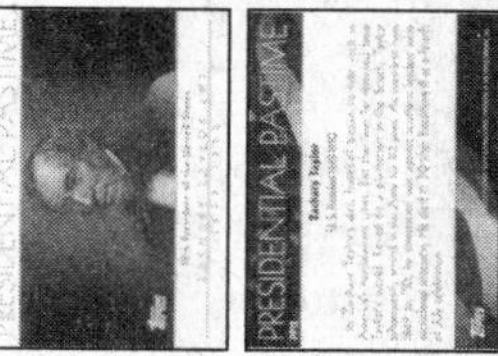

Nm-Mt Ex-Mt
COMPLETE SET (42) 100.00 30.00
SERIES 2 ODDS 1:6 HOB, 1:2 HTA, 1:6 RET
PP1 George Washington 5.00 1.50
PP2 John Adams 3.00 .90
PP3 Thomas Jefferson 5.00 1.50
PP4 James Madison 3.00 .90
PP5 James Monroe 3.00 .90
PP6 John Quincy Adams 3.00 .90
PP7 Andrew Jackson 3.00 .90
PP8 Martin Van Buren 3.00 .90
PP9 William Harrison 3.00 .90
PP10 John Tyler 3.00 .90
PP11 James Polk 3.00 .90
PP12 Zachary Taylor 3.00 .90
PP13 Millard Fillmore 3.00 .90
PP14 Franklin Pierce 3.00 .90
PP15 James Buchanan 3.00 .90
PP16 Abraham Lincoln 5.00 1.50
PP17 Andrew Johnson 3.00 .90
PP18 Ulysses S. Grant 4.00 1.20
PP19 Rutherford B. Hayes 3.00 .90
PP20 James Garfield 3.00 .90
PP21 Chester Arthur 3.00 .90
PP22 Grover Cleveland 3.00 .90
PP23 Benjamin Harrison 3.00 .90
PP24 William McKinley 3.00 .90
PP25 Theodore Roosevelt 4.00 1.20
PP26 William Taft 3.00 .90
PP27 Woodrow Wilson 3.00 .90
PP28 Warren Harding 3.00 .90
PP29 Calvin Coolidge 3.00 .90
PP30 Herbert Hoover 3.00 .90
PP31 Franklin D. Roosevelt 4.00 1.20
PP32 Harry Truman 3.00 .90
PP33 Dwight Eisenhower 3.00 .90
PP34 John F. Kennedy 4.00 1.20
PP35 Lyndon B. Johnson 3.00 .90
PP36 Richard Nixon 4.00 1.20
PP37 Gerald Ford 4.00 1.20
PP38 Jimmy Carter 3.00 .90
PP39 Ronald Reagan 10.00 3.00
PP40 George H.W. Bush 4.00 1.20
PP41 Bill Clinton 5.00 1.50
PP42 George W. Bush 5.00 1.50

2004 Topps Prospect Bonus

Nm-Mt Ex-Mt
COMP.ASTROS SET (5) 15.00 4.50
COMP.CUBS SET (5) 15.00 4.50
COMP.RED SOX SET (5) 15.00 4.50
COMP.YANKEES SET (5) 15.00 4.50
A1-A5 ISSUED IN ASTROS FACTORY SET
C1-C5 ISSUED IN CUBS FACTORY SET
R1-R5 ISSUED IN RED SOX FACTORY SET
Y1-Y5 ISSUED IN YANKEES FACTORY SET
A1 Brooks Conrad 4.00 1.20
A2 Hector Gimenez 4.00 1.20
A3 Kevin Davidson 4.00 1.20
A4 Chris Burke 4.00 1.20
A5 John Buck 4.00 1.20
C1 Bobby Brownlie 5.00 1.50
C2 Felix Pie 4.00 1.20
C3 Jon Connolly 5.00 1.50
C4 David Kelton 4.00 1.20
C5 Ricky Nolasco 4.00 1.20
R1 David Murphy 5.00 1.50
R2 Kevin Youkilis 4.00 1.20
R3 Juan Cedeno 4.00 1.20
R4 Matt Murton 4.00 1.20
R5 Kenny Perez 4.00 1.20
Y1 Rudy Guillen 5.00 1.50
Y2 David Parrish 4.00 1.20
Y3 Brad Halsey 5.00 1.50
Y4 Hector Made 5.00 1.50
Y5 Robinson Cano 5.00 1.50

2004 Topps Series Seats Relics

Nm-Mt Ex-Mt
SERIES 2 ODDS 1:316 HOB/RET, 1:89 HTA
AK Al Kaline 25.00 7.50

BF Bob Feller 15.00 4.50
BM Bill Mazeroski 25.00 7.50
BP Boog Powell 15.00 4.50
BR Brooks Robinson 15.00 4.50
FR Frank Robinson 15.00 4.50
HK Harmon Killebrew 25.00 7.50
JP Jim Palmer 15.00 4.50
LA Luis Aparicio 15.00 4.50
LP Lou Piniella 15.00 4.50
PM Paul Molitor 15.00 4.50
RJ Reggie Jackson 15.00 4.50
RY Robin Yount 25.00 7.50
WM Willie Mays 40.00 12.00
WS Warren Spahn 15.00 4.50

2004 Topps Series Stitches Relics

Nm-Mt Ex-Mt
SER.2 GROUP A 1:829 H, 1:236 HTA, 1:832 R
SER.2 GROUP B 1:980 H, 1:280 HTA, 1:984 R
SER.2 GROUP C 1:686 H, 1:196 HTA, 1:686 R
AS Alfonso Soriano Bat B 25.00 7.50
CJ Chipper Jones Jsy C 15.00 4.50
DG Dwight Gooden Jsy A 10.00 3.00
DJ David Justice Bat B 15.00 4.50
FR Frank Robinson Bat A 15.00 4.50
GB George Brett Bat A 40.00 12.00
GC Gary Carter Jkt C 10.00 3.00
HK Harmon Killebrew Bat A 40.00 12.00
JB Johnny Bench Bat A 25.00 7.50
JBE Josh Beckett Jsy C 10.00 3.00
JC Joe Carter Bat B 15.00 4.50
JCA Jose Canseco Bat C 25.00 7.50
KG Kirk Gibson Bat B 15.00 4.50
KP Kirby Puckett Bat B 25.00 7.50
LD Lenny Dykstra Bat A 15.00 4.50
MS Mike Schmidt Uni A 40.00 12.00
PO Paul O'Neill Bat A 25.00 7.50
RC Roger Clemens Uni C 20.00 6.00
RJ Randy Johnson Jsy A 15.00 4.50
RJA Reggie Jackson Bat B 25.00 7.50
RY Robin Yount Uni A 25.00 7.50
SG Steve Garvey Bat B 15.00 4.50
TS Tom Seaver Uni A 15.00 4.50
WM Willie Mays Bat A 50.00 15.00

2004 Topps Legends Autographs

MINT NRMT
ISSUED IN VARIOUS 03-04 TOPPS BRANDS
SER.1 ODDS 1:1399 H, 1:421 HTA, 1:1494 R
SER.2 ODDS 1:766 H, 1:216 HTA, 1:802 R
01 APARICIO/CARTER AU'S DIST.IN 04 PACKS
SEE 01 TOPPS FOR APARICIO/CARTER
AD Andre Dawson 15.00 6.75
BC Bert Campaneris 15.00 6.75
BP Boog Powell 15.00 6.75
CE Carl Erskine 15.00 6.75
DE Dwight Evans 25.00 11.00
DJ Davey Johnson 10.00 4.50
JP Jim Piersall 15.00 6.75
JP Johnny Podres 15.00 6.75
JR Joe Rudi 15.00 6.75
LD Lenny Dykstra
NR Nolan Ryan
SA Sparky Anderson 15.00 6.75
SG Steve Garvey 15.00 6.75
WM Willie Mays 150.00 70.00

2004 Topps World Series Highlights

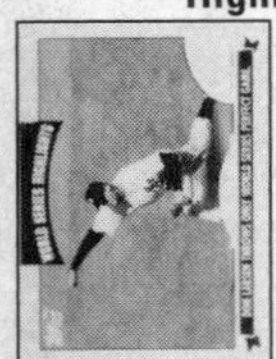

MINT NRMT
COMPLETE SET (30) 80.00 36.00
COMPLETE SERIES 1 (15) 40.00 18.00
COMPLETE SERIES 2 (15) 40.00 18.00
SERIES 1 ODDS 1:18 HOB/RET, 1:6 HTA
SERIES 2 ODDS 1:18 HOB/RET, 1:7 HTA
AJ Andruw Jones 2 2.00 .90
AK Al Kaline 2 3.00 1.35
BM Bill Mazeroski 1 3.00 1.35
BR Brooks Robinson 1 3.00 1.35
BT Bobby Thomson 2 2.00 .90
CF Carlton Fisk 1 3.00 1.35
CY Carl Yastrzemski 1 4.00 1.80
DB Dusty Baker 2 2.00 .90
DJ David Justice 2 2.00 .90
DL Don Larsen 1 2.00 .90
DS Duke Snider 2 3.00 1.35
FR Frank Robinson 2 2.00 .90
JB Johnny Bench 2 3.00 1.35
JC Joe Carter 2 2.00 .90
JCA Jose Canseco 2 3.00 1.35
JP1 Jim Palmer 1 2.00 .90
JP2 Johnny Podres 2 2.00 .90
KG Kirk Gibson 1 2.00 .90
KP Kirby Puckett 1 3.00 1.35
LB Lou Brock 1 3.00 1.35
LG Luis Gonzalez 2 2.00 .90
MS Mike Schmidt 1 5.00 2.20
OS Ozzie Smith 2 4.00 1.80
RJ Reggie Jackson 1 3.00 1.35
RY Robin Yount 1 4.00 1.80
SM Stan Musial 1 4.00 1.80
TS Tom Seaver 1 3.00 1.35
WF Whitey Ford 2 3.00 1.35
WM1 Willie Mays 1 5.00 2.20
WM2 Willie McCovey 2 2.00 .90

2004 Topps World Series Highlights Autographs

MINT NRMT
SERIES 1 ODDS 1:74 HTA
SERIES 2 ODDS 1:69 HTA
AK Al Kaline 2 40.00 18.00
BM Bill Mazeroski 1 40.00 18.00
BR Brooks Robinson 1 40.00 18.00
BT Bobby Thomson 2 25.00 11.00
CF Carlton Fisk 1 80.00 36.00
DB Dusty Baker 2 25.00 11.00
DJ David Justice 2 25.00 11.00
DL Don Larsen 1 40.00 18.00
DS Duke Snider 2 40.00 18.00
HK Harmon Killebrew 1 40.00 18.00
JB Johnny Bench 2 60.00 27.00
JP1 Jim Palmer 1 25.00 11.00
JP2 Johnny Podres 2 25.00 11.00
KG Kirk Gibson 1 40.00 18.00
LB Lou Brock 1 40.00 18.00
MS Mike Schmidt 1 60.00 27.00
RJ Reggie Jackson 2 60.00 27.00
RY Robin Yount 1 50.00 22.00
SM Stan Musial 2 80.00 36.00
WF Whitey Ford 2 40.00 18.00

2004 Topps Traded

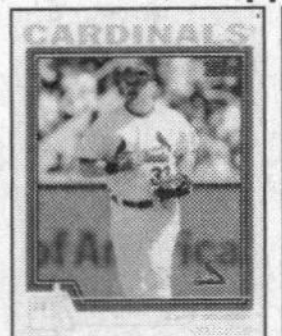

This 220-card set was released in October, 2004. The set was issued in 11-card hobby and retail packs (including one puzzle piece) which had an $3 SRP and which came 24 packs to a box and 12 boxes to a case. Cards numbered 1-65 feature players who were traded, while cards numbered 66 through 70 feature managers who took over teams after the basic set was issued and cards 71 through 90 are high draft picks, cards numbered 91 through 110 are prospect cards and cards numbered 111-220 feature Rookie Cards.

Nm-Mt Ex-Mt
COMPLETE SET (220) 50.00 15.00
COMMON CARD (1-70) .20 .06
COMMON CARD (71-90) .50 .15
COMMON CARD (91-110) .40 .12
COMMON CARD (111-220) .40 .12
PLATE ODDS 1:1151 H, 1:1173 R, 1:327 HTA
PLATE PRINT RUN 1 SET PER COLOR
BLACK-CYAN-MAGENTA-YELLOW ISSUED
NO PLATE PRICING DUE TO SCARCITY
T1 Pokey Reese .20 .06
T2 Tony Womack .20 .06
T3 Richard Hidalgo .20 .06
T4 Juan Uribe .20 .06
T5 J.D. Drew .20 .06
T6 Alex Gonzalez .20 .06
T7 Carlos Guillen .20 .06
T8 Doug Mientkiewicz .20 .06
T9 Fernando Vina .20 .06
T10 Milton Bradley .20 .06
T11 Kelvim Escobar .20 .06
T12 Ben Grieve .20 .06
T13 Brian Jordan .20 .06
T14 A.J. Pierzynski .20 .06
T15 Billy Wagner .20 .06
T16 Terrence Long .20 .06
T17 Carlos Beltran .30 .09
T18 Carl Everett .20 .06
T19 Reggie Sanders .20 .06
T20 Javy Lopez .20 .06
T21 Jay Payton .20 .06
T22 Octavio Dotel .20 .06
T23 Eddie Guardado .20 .06
T24 Andy Pettitte .30 .09
T25 Richie Sexson .20 .06
T26 Ronnie Belliard .20 .06
T27 Michael Tucker .20 .06
T28 Brad Fullmer .20 .06
T29 Freddy Garcia .20 .06
T30 Bartolo Colon .20 .06
T31 Larry Walker .30 .09
T32 Mark Kotsay .20 .06
T33 Jason Marquis .20 .06
T34 Dustan Mohr .20 .06
T35 Javier Vazquez .20 .06
T36 Nomar Garciaparra .75 .23
T37 Tino Martinez .30 .09
T38 Hee Seop Choi .20 .06
T39 Damian Miller .20 .06
T40 Jose Lima .20 .06
T41 Ty Wigginton .20 .06
T42 Raul Ibanez .20 .06
T43 Danys Baez .20 .06
T44 Tony Clark .20 .06
T45 Greg Maddux .75 .23
T46 Victor Zambrano .20 .06
T47 Orlando Cabrera Sox .20 .06
T48 Jose Cruz Jr. .20 .06
T49 Kris Benson .20 .06
T50 Alex Rodriguez 1.00 .30
T51 Steve Finley .20 .06
T52 Ramon Hernandez .20 .06
T53 Esteban Loaiza .20 .06
T54 Ugueth Urbina .20 .06
T55 Jeff Weaver .20 .06
T56 Flash Gordon .20 .06
T57 Jose Contreras .20 .06
T58 Paul Lo Duca .20 .06
T59 Junior Spivey .20 .06
T60 Curt Schilling .50 .15
T61 Brad Penny .20 .06
T62 Braden Looper .20 .06
T63 Miguel Cairo .20 .06
T64 Juan Encarnacion .20 .06
T65 Miguel Batista .20 .06
T66 Terry Francona MG .20 .06
T67 Lee Mazzilli MG .20 .06
T68 Al Pedrique MG .20 .06
T69 Ozzie Guillen MG .20 .06
T70 Phil Garner MG .20 .06
T71 Matt Bush DP RC 2.50 .75
T72 Homer Bailey DP RC 2.00 .60
T73 Greg Golson DP RC 1.50 .45
T74 Kyle Waldrop DP RC 1.25 .35
T75 Richie Robnett DP RC 1.25 .35
T76 Jay Rainville DP RC 1.25 .35
T77 Bill Bray DP RC .50 .15
T78 Phillip Hughes DP RC 1.25 .35
T79 Scott Elbert DP RC 1.25 .35
T80 Josh Fields DP RC 2.00 .60
T81 Justin Orenduff DP RC 1.25 .35
T82 Dan Putnam DP RC 1.25 .35
T83 Chris Nelson DP RC 2.50 .75
T84 Blake DeWitt DP RC 2.50 .75
T85 J.P. Howell DP RC 1.25 .35
T86 Huston Street DP RC 1.25 .35
T87 Kurt Suzuki DP RC 1.50 .45
T88 Erick San Pedro DP RC .50 .15
T89 Matt Tuiasosopo DP RC 4.00 1.20
T90 Matt Macri DP RC 1.25 .35
T91 Chad Tracy PROS .40 .12
T92 Scott Hairston PROS .40 .12
T93 Jonny Gomes PROS .40 .12
T94 Chin-Feng Chen PROS .40 .12
T95 Chien-Ming Wang PROS .40 .12
T96 Dustin McGowan PROS .40 .12
T97 Chris Burke PROS .40 .12
T98 Denny Bautista PROS .40 .12
T99 Preston Larrison PROS .40 .12
T100 Kevin Youkilis PROS .40 .12
T101 John Maine PROS .40 .12
T102 Guillermo Quiroz PROS .40 .12
T103 Dave Krynzel PROS .40 .12
T104 David Kelton PROS .40 .12
T105 Edwin Encarnacion PROS .40 .12
T106 Chad Gaudin PROS .40 .12
T107 Sergio Mitre PROS .40 .12
T108 Laynce Nix PROS .40 .12
T109 David Parrish PROS .40 .12
T110 Brandon Claussen PROS .40 .12
T111 Frank Francisco FY RC .40 .12
T112 Brian Dallimore FY RC .40 .12
T113 Jim Crowell FY RC .50 .15
T114 Andres Blanco FY RC .40 .12
T115 Eduardo Villacis FY RC .40 .12
T116 Kazuhito Tadano FY RC .50 .15
T117 Aarom Baldiris FY RC .50 .15
T118 Justin Germano FY RC .40 .12
T119 Joey Gathright FY RC 1.25 .35
T120 Franklyn Gracesqui FY RC .40 .12
T121 Chin-Lung Hu FY RC 1.00 .30
T122 Scott Olsen FY RC 1.25 .35
T123 Tyler Davidson FY RC .50 .15
T124 Fausto Carmona FY RC .75 .23
T125 Tim Hutting FY RC .40 .12
T126 Ryan Meaux FY RC .40 .12
T127 Jon Connolly FY RC 1.00 .30
T128 Hector Made FY RC .75 .23
T129 Jamie Brown FY RC .40 .12
T130 Paul McAnulty FY RC .75 .23
T131 Chris Saenz FY RC .40 .12
T132 Marland Williams FY RC .50 .15
T133 Mike Huggins FY RC .40 .12
T134 Jesse Crain FY RC .75 .23
T135 Chad Bentz FY RC .40 .12
T136 Kazuo Matsui FY RC 1.50 .45
T137 Paul Maholm FY RC .75 .23
T138 Brock Jacobsen FY RC .40 .12
T139 Casey Daigle FY RC .40 .12
T140 Nyjer Morgan FY RC .40 .12
T141 Tom Mastny FY RC .40 .12
T142 Kody Kirkland FY RC .75 .23
T143 Jose Capellan FY RC 1.50 .45
T144 Felix Hernandez FY RC 3.00 .90
T145 Shawn Hill FY RC .40 .12
T146 Danny Gonzalez FY RC .40 .12
T147 Scott Dohmann FY RC .40 .12
T148 Tommy Murphy FY RC .40 .12
T149 Akinori Otsuka FY RC .40 .12
T150 Miguel Perez FY RC .40 .12
T151 Mike Rouse FY RC .40 .12
T152 Ramon Ramirez FY RC .40 .12
T153 Luke Hughes FY RC .40 .12
T154 Howie Kendrick FY RC .75 .23
T155 Ryan Budde FY RC .40 .12
T156 Charlie Zink FY RC .40 .12
T157 Warner Madrigal FY RC .75 .23
T158 Jason Szuminski FY RC .40 .12
T159 Chad Chop FY RC .40 .12
T160 Shingo Takatsu FY RC 1.00 .30
T161 Matt Lemanczyk FY RC .40 .12
T162 Wardell Starling FY RC .40 .12
T163 Nick Gorneault FY RC .50 .15
T164 Scott Proctor FY RC .50 .15
T165 Brooks Conrad FY RC .50 .15
T166 Hector Gimenez FY RC .40 .12
T167 Kevin Howard FY RC .50 .15
T168 Vince Perkins FY RC .50 .15
T169 Brock Peterson FY RC .40 .12
T170 Chris Shelton FY RC .75 .23
T171 Erick Aybar FY RC 1.25 .35
T172 Paul Bacot FY RC .50 .15
T173 Matt Capps FY RC .40 .12
T174 Kory Casto FY RC .40 .12
T175 Juan Cedeno FY RC .40 .12
T176 Vito Chiaravalloti FY RC .75 .23
T177 Alec Zumwalt FY RC .40 .12
T178 J.J. Furmaniak FY RC .75 .23
T179 Lee Gwaltney FY RC .40 .12
T180 Donald Kelly FY RC .40 .12
T181 Benji DeQuin FY RC .40 .12
T182 Brant Colamarino FY RC .75 .23
T183 Juan Gutierrez FY RC .40 .12
T184 Carl Loadenthal FY RC .50 .15
T185 Ricky Nolasco FY RC .40 .12
T186 Jeff Salazar FY RC 1.00 .30
T187 Rob Tejeda FY RC .40 .12
T188 Alex Romero FY RC .40 .12
T189 Yoann Torrealba FY RC .40 .12
T190 Carlos Sosa FY RC .40 .12
T191 Tim Bittner FY RC .40 .12
T192 Chris Aguila FY RC .40 .12
T193 Jason Frasor FY RC .40 .12
T194 Reid Gorecki FY RC .40 .12
T195 Dustin Nippert FY RC .40 .12
T196 Javier Guzman FY RC .50 .15
T197 Harvey Garcia FY RC .40 .12
T198 Ivan Ochoa FY RC .40 .12
T199 David Wallace FY RC .50 .15
T200 Joel Zumaya FY RC .75 .23
T201 Casey Kopitzke FY RC .40 .12
T202 Lincoln Holdzkom FY RC .40 .12
T203 Chad Santos FY RC .40 .12
T204 Brian Pilkington FY RC .40 .12
T205 Terry Jones FY RC .50 .15
T206 Jerome Gamble FY RC .40 .12
T207 Brad Eldred FY RC 1.25 .35
T208 David Pauley FY RC .40 .12
T209 Kevin Davidson FY RC .40 .12
T210 Damaso Espino FY RC .40 .12
T211 Tom Farmer FY RC .40 .12
T212 Michael Mooney FY RC .40 .12
T213 James Tomlin FY RC .40 .12
T214 Greg Thissen FY RC .40 .12
T215 Calvin Hayes FY RC .50 .15
T216 Fernando Cortez FY RC .40 .12
T217 Sergio Silva FY RC .40 .12
T218 Jon de Vries FY RC .40 .12
T219 Don Sutton FY RC 1.00 .30
T220 Leo Nunez FY RC .40 .12

2004 Topps Traded Blue

Nm-Mt Ex-Mt
ODDS 1:4574 H, 1:4925 R, 1:1238 HTA
STATED PRINT RUN 1 SERIAL #'d SET
NO PRICING DUE TO SCARCITY

2004 Topps Traded Gold

Nm-Mt Ex-Mt
*GOLD 1-70: 5X TO 12X BASIC
*GOLD 71-90: 1X TO 2.5X BASIC
*GOLD 91-110: 2.5X TO 6X BASIC
*GOLD 111-220: 1.5X TO 4X BASIC
STATED ODDS 1:2 HOB/RET, 1:1 HTA
STATED PRINT RUN 2004 SERIAL #'d SETS

2004 Topps Traded Future Phenoms Relics

Nm-Mt Ex-Mt
GROUP A ODDS 1:184 H/R, 1:53 HTA
GROUP B ODDS 1:65 H/R, 1:27 HTA
AG Adrian Gonzalez Bat A 10.00 3.00
BC Bobby Crosby Bat A 15.00 4.50
BU B.J. Upton Bat A 15.00 4.50
DN Dioner Navarro Bat B 8.00 2.40
DY Delmon Young Bat A 15.00 4.50
ED Eric Duncan Bat B 5.00 1.50
EJ Edwin Jackson Jsy B 5.00 1.50
JH J.J. Hardy Bat B 5.00 1.50
JM Justin Morneau Bat A 10.00 3.00
JW Jayson Werth Bat A 15.00 4.50
KC Kevin Cash Bat B 5.00 1.50
KM Kazuo Matsui Bat A 15.00 4.50
LM Lastings Milledge Bat B 8.00 2.40
MM Mark Malaska Jsy A 8.00 2.40
NG Nick Green Bat A 10.00 3.00
RN Ramon Nivar Bat A 8.00 2.40
VM Victor Martinez Bat A 10.00 3.00

2004 Topps Traded Hall of Fame Relics

Nm-Mt Ex-Mt
A ODDS 1:3388 H, 1:3518 R, 1:966 HTA
B ODDS 1:1011 H, 1:1026 R, 1:289 HTA
DE Dennis Eckersley Jsy B 15.00 4.50
PM Paul Molitor Bat A 25.00 7.50

2004 Topps Traded Hall of Fame Dual Relic

Nm-Mt Ex-Mt
ODDS 1:3388 H, 1:3518 R, 1:966 HTA
ME Paul Molitor Bat 40.00 12.00
Dennis Eckersley Jsy

2004 Topps Traded Puzzle

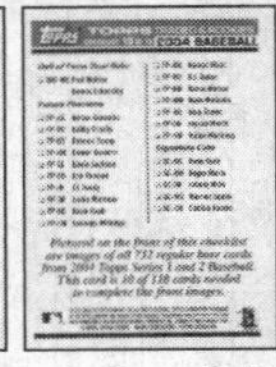

Nm-Mt Ex-Mt
COMPLETE PUZZLE (110) 50.00 15.00
COMMON PIECE (1-110) .50 .15
ONE PER PACK

2004 Topps Traded Signature Cuts

Nm-Mt Ex-Mt
STATED ODDS 1:91,472 HOB, 1:39,600 HTA
STATED PRINT RUN 1 SERIAL #'d SET
NO PRICING DUE TO SCARCITY
BR Babe Ruth
CH Catfish Hunter
JM Johnny Mize
RM Roger Maris
WS Warren Spahn

2004 Topps Traded Signature Moves

Nm-Mt Ex-Mt
A ODDS 1:675 H, 1:684 R, 1:193 HTA
B ODDS 1:169 H/R, 1:48 HTA
EXCHANGE DEADLINE 12/31/06
AR Alex Rodriguez A 150.00 45.00
AW Adam Wainwright B 15.00 4.50
EM Eli Marrero B 10.00 3.00
FV Fernando Vina B 10.00 3.00
IR Ivan Rodriguez A EXCH 30.00 9.00
JV Javier Vazquez A 15.00 4.50
MB Milton Bradley B 15.00 4.50
MK Mark Kotsay B 15.00 4.50
MN Mike Neu B 10.00 3.00

2004 Topps Traded Transactions Relics

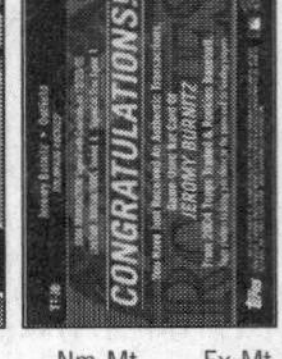

Nm-Mt Ex-Mt
STATED ODDS 1:106 H, 1:107 R, 1:30 HTA
AP Andy Pettitte Bat 10.00 3.00
AR Alex Rodriguez Yanks Jsy 25.00 7.50
BJ Brian Jordan Bat 8.00 2.40
CE Carl Everett Bat 8.00 2.40
GS Gary Sheffield Bat 10.00 3.00
HC Hee Seop Choi Bat 8.00 2.40
IR Ivan Rodriguez Bat 10.00 3.00
JB Jeromy Burnitz Bat 8.00 2.40
JG Juan Gonzalez Bat 10.00 3.00
JL Javy Lopez Bat 8.00 2.40
KL Kenny Lofton Bat 8.00 2.40
KM Kazuo Matsui Bat 15.00 4.50
MT Miguel Tejada Bat 8.00 2.40
RA Roberto Alomar Bat 10.00 3.00
RC Roger Clemens Bat 15.00 4.50
RLS Richie Sexson Bat 8.00 2.40
RP Rafael Palmeiro Bat 10.00 3.00
RS Reggie Sanders Bat 8.00 2.40
RW Rondell White Bat 8.00 2.40
VG Vladimir Guerrero Bat 10.00 3.00

2004 Topps Traded Transactions Dual Relics

Nm-Mt Ex-Mt
STATED ODDS 1:562 H, 1:563 R, 1:160 HTA
AR Alex Rodriguez Rgr-Yanks 25.00 7.50
CS Curt Schilling D'backs-Sox 20.00 6.00
RP Rafael Palmeiro O's-Rgr 15.00 4.50

2005 Topps

Nm-Mt Ex-Mt
COMPLETE SERIES 1 (367)...... 40.00 12.00
COMMON (1-6/8-296) .20 .06
COMMON CARD (297-326) .50 .15
COMMON CARD 327- .50 .15
COMMON (349-355/368) 1.00 .30
CARD NUMBER 7 DOES NOT EXIST...
OVERALL PLATE SER.1 ODDS 1:154 HTA
PLATE PRINT RUN 1 SET PER COLOR
BLACK-CYAN-MAGENTA-YELLOW ISSUED
NO PLATE PRICING DUE TO SCARCITY
1 Alex Rodriguez .75 .23
2 Placido Polanco .20 .06
3 Torii Hunter .20 .06
4 Lyle Overbay .20 .06
5 Johnny Damon .50 .15
6 Johnny Estrada .20 .06
7 Does Not Exist
8 Francisco Rodriguez .20 .06
9 Jason LaRue .20 .06
10 Sammy Sosa .75 .23
11 Randy Wolf .20 .06
12 Jason Bay .20 .06
13 Tom Glavine .30 .09
14 Michael Tucker .20 .06
15 Brian Giles .20 .06
16 Dan Wilson .20 .06
17 Jim Edmonds .20 .06
18 Danys Baez .20 .06
19 Roy Halladay .20 .06
20 Hank Blalock .20 .06
21 Darin Erstad .20 .06
22 Robby Hammock .20 .06
23 Mike Hampton .20 .06
24 Mark Bellhorn .30 .09
25 Jim Thome .50 .15
26 Scott Schoeneweis .20 .06
27 Jody Gerut .20 .06
28 Vinny Castilla .20 .06
29 Luis Castillo .20 .06
30 Ivan Rodriguez .50 .15
31 Craig Biggio .30 .09
32 Joe Randa .20 .06
33 Adrian Beltre .30 .09
34 Scott Podsednik .20 .06
35 Cliff Floyd .20 .06
36 Livan Hernandez .20 .06
37 Eric Byrnes .20 .06
38 Gabe Kapler .20 .06
39 Jack Wilson .20 .06
40 Gary Sheffield .20 .06
41 Chan Ho Park .20 .06
42 Carl Crawford .20 .06
43 Miguel Batista .20 .06
44 David Bell .20 .06
45 Jeff DaVanon .20 .06
46 Brandon Webb .20 .06
47 Bronson Arroyo .20 .06
48 Melvin Mora .20 .06
49 David Ortiz .50 .15
50 Andruw Jones .20 .06
51 Chone Figgins .20 .06
52 Danny Graves .20 .06
53 Preston Wilson .20 .06
54 Jeremy Bonderman .20 .06
55 Chad Fox .20 .06
56 Dan Miceli .20 .06
57 Jimmy Gobble .20 .06
58 Darren Dreifort .20 .06
59 Matt LeCroy .20 .06
60 Jose Vidro .20 .06
61 Al Leiter .20 .06
62 Javier Vazquez .20 .06
63 Erubiel Durazo .20 .06
64 Doug Glanville .20 .06
65 Scot Shields .20 .06
66 Edgardo Alfonzo .20 .06
67 Ryan Franklin .20 .06
68 Francisco Cordero .20 .06
69 Brett Myers .20 .06
70 Curt Schilling .50 .15
71 Matt Kata .20 .06
72 Mark DeRosa .20 .06
73 Rodrigo Lopez .20 .06
74 Tim Wakefield .30 .09
75 Frank Thomas .50 .15
76 Jimmy Rollins .20 .06
77 Barry Zito .20 .06
78 Hideo Nomo .50 .15
79 Brad Wilkerson .20 .06
80 Adam Dunn .30 .09
81 Billy Traber .20 .06
82 Fernando Vina .20 .06
83 Nate Robertson .20 .06
84 Brad Ausmus .20 .06
85 Mike Sweeney .20 .06
86 Kip Wells .20 .06
87 Chris Reitsma .20 .06
88 Zach Day .20 .06
89 Tony Clark .20 .06
90 Bret Boone .20 .06
91 Mark Loretta .20 .06
92 Jerome Williams .20 .06
93 Randy Winn .20 .06
94 Marlon Anderson .20 .06
95 Aubrey Huff .20 .06
96 Kevin Mench .20 .06
97 Frank Catalanotto .20 .06
98 Flash Gordon .20 .06
99 Scott Hatteberg .20 .06
100 Albert Pujols 1.00 .30
101 Jose/Bengie Molina .20 .06
102 Oscar Villarreal .20 .06
103 Jay Gibbons .20 .06
104 Byung-Hyun Kim .20 .06
105 Joe Borowski .20 .06
106 Mark Grudzielanek .20 .06
107 Mark Buehrle .20 .06
108 Paul Wilson .20 .06
109 Ronnie Belliard .20 .06
110 Reggie Sanders .20 .06
111 Tim Redding .20 .06
112 Brian Lawrence .20 .06
113 Darrell May .20 .06
114 Jose Hernandez .20 .06
115 Ben Sheets .20 .06
116 Johan Santana .30 .09
117 Billy Wagner .20 .06
118 Mariano Rivera .30 .09
119 Steve Trachsel .20 .06
120 Akinori Otsuka .20 .06
121 Bobby Kielty .20 .06
122 Orlando Hernandez .20 .06
123 Raul Ibanez .20 .06
124 Mike Matheny .20 .06
125 Vernon Wells .20 .06
126 Jason Isringhausen .20 .06
127 Jose Guillen .20 .06
128 Danny Bautista .20 .06
129 Marcus Giles .20 .06
130 Javy Lopez .20 .06
131 Kevin Millar .30 .09
132 Kyle Farnsworth .20 .06
133 Carl Pavano .20 .06
134 D'Angelo Jimenez .20 .06
135 Casey Blake .20 .06
136 Matt Holliday .20 .06
137 Bobby Higginson .20 .06
138 Nate Field .20 .06
139 Alex Gonzalez .20 .06
140 Jeff Kent .20 .06
141 Aaron Guiel .20 .06
142 Shawn Green .20 .06
143 Bill Hall .20 .06
144 Shannon Stewart .20 .06
145 Juan Rivera .20 .06
146 Coco Crisp .20 .06
147 Mike Mussina .30 .09
148 Eric Chavez .20 .06
149 Jon Lieber .20 .06
150 Vladimir Guerrero .50 .15
151 Alex Cintron .20 .06
152 Horacio Ramirez .20 .06
153 Sidney Ponson .20 .06
154 Trot Nixon .30 .09
155 Greg Maddux .75 .23
156 Edgar Renteria .20 .06
157 Ryan Freel .20 .06
158 Matt Lawton .20 .06
159 Shawn Chacon .20 .06
160 Josh Beckett .20 .06
161 Ken Harvey .20 .06
162 Juan Cruz .20 .06
163 Juan Encarnacion .20 .06
164 Wes Helms .20 .06
165 Brad Radke .20 .06
166 Claudio Vargas .20 .06
167 Mike Cameron .20 .06
168 Billy Koch .20 .06
169 Bobby Crosby .20 .06
170 Mike Lieberthal .20 .06
171 Rob Mackowiak .20 .06
172 Sean Burroughs .20 .06
173 J.T. Snow Jr. .20 .06
174 Paul Konerko .20 .06
175 Luis Gonzalez .20 .06
176 John Lackey .20 .06
177 Antonio Alfonseca .20 .06
178 Brian Roberts .20 .06
179 Bill Mueller .30 .09
180 Carlos Lee .20 .06
181 Corey Patterson .20 .06
182 Sean Casey .20 .06
183 Cliff Lee .20 .06
184 Jason Jennings .20 .06
185 Dmitri Young .20 .06
186 Juan Uribe .20 .06
187 Andy Pettitte .30 .09
188 Juan Gonzalez .30 .09
189 Pokey Reese .20 .06
190 Jason Phillips .20 .06
191 Rocky Biddle .20 .06
192 Lew Ford .20 .06
193 Mark Mulder .20 .06
194 Bobby Abreu .20 .06
195 Jason Kendall .20 .06
196 Terrence Long .20 .06
197 A.J. Pierzynski .20 .06
198 Eddie Guardado .20 .06
199 So Taguchi .20 .06
200 Jason Giambi .20 .06
201 Tony Batista .20 .06
202 Kyle Lohse .20 .06
203 Trevor Hoffman .20 .06
204 Tike Redman .20 .06
205 Matt Herges .20 .06
206 Gil Meche .20 .06
207 Chris Carpenter .20 .06
208 Ben Broussard .20 .06
209 Eric Young .20 .06
210 Doug Waechter .20 .06
211 Jarrod Washburn .20 .06
212 Chad Tracy .20 .06
213 John Smoltz .30 .09
214 Jorge Julio .20 .06
215 Todd Walker .20 .06
216 Shingo Takatsu .20 .06
217 Jose Acevedo .20 .06
218 David Riske .20 .06
219 Shawn Estes .20 .06
220 Lance Berkman .20 .06
221 Carlos Guillen .20 .06
222 Jeremy Affeldt .20 .06
223 Cesar Izturis .20 .06
224 Scott Sullivan .20 .06
225 Kazuo Matsui .30 .09
226 Josh Fogg .20 .06
227 Jason Schmidt .20 .06
228 Jason Marquis .20 .06
229 Scott Spiezio .20 .06
230 Miguel Tejada .20 .06
231 Bartolo Colon .20 .06
232 Jose Valverde .20 .06
233 Derrek Lee .20 .06
234 Scott Williamson .20 .06
235 Joe Crede .20 .06
236 John Thomson .20 .06
237 Mike MacDougal .20 .06
238 Eric Gagne .50 .15
239 Alex Sanchez .20 .06
240 Miguel Cabrera .30 .09
241 Luis Rivas .20 .06
242 Adam Everett .20 .06
243 Jason Johnson .20 .06
244 Travis Hafner .20 .06
245 Jose Valentin .20 .06
246 Stephen Randolph .20 .06
247 Rafael Furcal .20 .06
248 Adam Kennedy .20 .06
249 Luis Matos .20 .06
250 Mark Prior .50 .15
251 Angel Berroa .20 .06
252 Phil Nevin .20 .06
253 Oliver Perez .20 .06
254 Orlando Hudson .20 .06
255 Braden Looper .20 .06
256 Khalil Greene .30 .09
257 Tim Worrell .20 .06
258 Carlos Zambrano .20 .06
259 Odalis Perez .20 .06
260 Gerald Laird .20 .06
261 Jose Cruz Jr. .20 .06
262 Michael Barrett .20 .06
263 Michael Young .20 .06
264 Toby Hall .20 .06
265 Woody Williams .20 .06
266 Rich Harden .20 .06
267 Mike Scioscia MG .20 .06
268 Al Pedrique MG .20 .06
269 Bobby Cox MG .20 .06
270 Lee Mazzilli MG .20 .06
271 Terry Francona MG .30 .09
272 Dusty Baker MG .20 .06
273 Ozzie Guillen MG .20 .06
274 Dave Miley MG .20 .06
275 Eric Wedge MG .20 .06
276 Clint Hurdle MG .20 .06
277 Alan Trammell MG .30 .09
278 Jack McKeon MG .20 .06
279 Phil Garner MG .20 .06
280 Tony Pena MG .20 .06
281 Jim Tracy MG .20 .06
282 Ned Yost MG .20 .06
283 Ron Gardenhire MG .20 .06
284 Frank Robinson MG .30 .09
285 Art Howe MG .20 .06
286 Joe Torre MG .30 .09
287 Ken Macha MG .20 .06
288 Larry Bowa MG .20 .06
289 Lloyd McClendon MG .20 .06
290 Bruce Bochy MG .20 .06
291 Felipe Alou MG .20 .06
292 Bob Melvin MG .20 .06
293 Tony LaRussa MG .20 .06
294 Lou Piniella MG .20 .06
295 Buck Showalter MG .20 .06
296 John Gibbons MG .20 .06
297 Steve Doetsch FY RC .50 .15
298 Melky Cabrera FY RC 1.00 .30
299 Luis Ramirez FY RC .50 .15
300 Chris Seddon FY RC .50 .15
301 Nate Schierholtz FY .75 .23
302 Ian Kinsler FY RC 1.00 .30
303 Brandon Moss FY RC 1.00 .30
304 Chadd Blasko FY RC .50 .15
305 Jeremy West FY RC 1.00 .30
306 Sean Marshall FY RC .50 .15
307 Matt DeSalvo FY RC .50 .15
308 Ryan Sweeney FY RC 1.00 .30
309 Matthew Lindstrom FY RC .50 .15
310 Ryan Goleski FY RC .75 .23
311 Brett Harper FY RC .50 .15
312 Chris Roberson FY RC .50 .15
313 Andre Ethier FY RC .75 .23
314 Chris Denorfia FY RC .50 .15
315 Ian Bladergroen FY RC 1.00 .30
316 Darren Fenster FY RC .50 .15
317 Kevin West FY RC .75 .23
318 Chaz Lytle FY RC .75 .23
319 James Jurries FY RC .50 .15
320 Matt Rogelstad FY RC .50 .15
321 Wade Robinson FY RC .50 .15
322 Jake Dittler FY .50 .15
323 Brian Stavisky FY RC .50 .15
324 Kole Strayhorn FY RC .50 .15
325 Jose Vaquedano FY RC .50 .15
326 Elvys Quezada FY RC .50 .15
327 John Maine .50 .15
Val Majewski FS
328 Rickie Weeks .50 .15
J.J. Hardy FS
329 Gabe Gross .50 .15
Guillermo Quiroz FS
330 David Wright 3.00 .90
Craig Brazell FS
331 Dallas McPherson .50 .15
Jeff Mathis FS
332 Randy Johnson SH .30 .09
333 Randy Johnson SH .30 .09
334 Ichiro Suzuki SH .50 .15
335 Ken Griffey Jr. SH .50 .15
336 Greg Maddux SH .50 .15
337 Ichiro Suzuki .50 .15
Melvin Mora
Vladimir Guerrero LL
338 Ichiro Suzuki .50 .15
Michael Young
Vladimir Guerrero LL
339 Manny Ramirez .50 .15
Paul Konerko
David Ortiz LL
340 Miguel Tejada .50 .15
David Ortiz
Manny Ramirez LL
341 Johan Santana .50 .15
Curt Schilling
Jake Westbrook LL
342 Johan Santana .50 .15
Pedro Martinez
Curt Schilling LL
343 Todd Helton .30 .09
Mark Loretta
Adrian Beltre LL
344 Juan Pierre .20 .06
Mark Loretta
Jack Wilson LL
345 Adrian Beltre .50 .15
Adam Dunn
Albert Pujols LL
346 Vinny Castilla .50 .15
Scott Rolen
Albert Pujols LL
347 Jake Peavy .30 .09
Randy Johnson
Ben Sheets LL
348 Randy Johnson .30 .09
Ben Sheets
Jason Schmidt LL
349 Alex Rodriguez 1.00 .30
Ruben Sierra ALDS
350 Larry Walker 1.00 .30
Albert Pujols NLDS
351 Curt Schilling 1.00 .30
David Ortiz ALDS
352 Curt Schilling WS2 1.00 .30
353 Sox Celebration 1.00 .30
David Ortiz
Curt Schilling ALCS
354 Cards Celebration 1.00 .30
Albert Pujols
Jim Edmonds NLCS
355 Mark Bellhorn WS1 1.00 .30
356 Paul Konerko AS .20 .06
357 Alfonso Soriano AS .20 .06
358 Miguel Tejada AS .20 .06
359 Melvin Mora AS .20 .06
360 Vladimir Guerrero AS .30 .09
361 Ichiro Suzuki AS .50 .15
362 Manny Ramirez AS .20 .06
363 Ivan Rodriguez AS .30 .09
364 Johan Santana AS .20 .06
365 Paul Konerko AS .20 .06
366 David Ortiz AS .30 .09
367 Bobby Crosby AS .20 .06
368 Sox Celebration 2.00 .60
Manny Ramirez
Derek Lowe WS4

2005 Topps 1st Edition

Nm-Mt Ex-Mt
*1st ED 1-296/332-348
*1st ED 297-326: 1.25X TO 3X
*1st ED 327-331: 1.25X TO 3X
*1st ED 349-
DISTRIBUTED IN 1ST EDITION BOXES
CARD NUMBER 7 DOES NOT EXIST...

2005 Topps Black

Nm-Mt Ex-Mt
*1st ED 1-296/332-348
*1st ED 297-326: 15X TO 40X
*1st ED 327-331: 20X TO 50X
SERIES 1 ODDS 1:13 HTA
STATED PRINT RUN 54 SERIAL #'d SETS
CARD NUMBER 7 DOES NOT EXIST...
330 David Wright 50.00 15.00
Craig Brazell FS

2005 Topps Box Bottoms

Nm-Mt Ex-Mt
A.Rod/Vlad/Sosa/Shef 4.00 1.20
Thome/Giambi/Blal/Dunn 4.00 1.20
Pujols/I.Rod/Teja/Cabrera 4.00 1.20
Kaz/Shingo/Otsuka/Nomo 4.00 1.20
*BOX BOTTOM CARDS: 1X TO 2.5X BASIC
ONE 4-CARD SHEET PER HTA BOX...

2005 Topps Gold

Nm-Mt Ex-Mt
*1st ED 1-296/332-348
*1st ED 297-326: 2X TO 5X
*1st ED 327-331: 2X TO 5X
SERIES 1 ODDS 1:8 HOB, 1:3 HTA, 1:10 RET
STATED PRINT RUN 2005 SERIAL #'d SETS
CARD NUMBER 7 DOES NOT EXIST...
330 David Wright 8.00 2.40
Craig Brazell FS

2005 Topps All-Star Stitches Relics

Nm-Mt Ex-Mt
SERIES 1 ODDS 1:96 H, 1:27 HTA, 1:80 R
AP Albert Pujols 20.00 6.00
AS Alfonso Soriano 10.00 3.00
BA Bobby Abreu 10.00 3.00
BL Barry Larkin 10.00 3.00
BS Ben Sheets 10.00 3.00
CB Carlos Beltran 10.00 3.00
CC Carl Crawford 10.00 3.00
CP Carl Pavano 10.00 3.00
CS C.C. Sabathia 10.00 3.00
CZ Carlos Zambrano 10.00 3.00
DK Danny Kolb 10.00 3.00
DO David Ortiz 10.00 3.00
EL Esteban Loaiza 10.00 3.00
ER Edgar Renteria 10.00 3.00
FG Tom Gordon 10.00 3.00
FR Francisco Rodriguez 10.00 3.00
GS Gary Sheffield 10.00 3.00
HB Hank Blalock 10.00 3.00
IR Ivan Rodriguez 10.00 3.00
JE Johnny Estrada 10.00 3.00
JG Jason Giambi 10.00 3.00
JK Jeff Kent 10.00 3.00
JN Joe Nathan 10.00 3.00
JT Jim Thome 10.00 3.00
JW Jack Wilson 10.00 3.00
KH Ken Harvey 10.00 3.00
LB Lance Berkman 10.00 3.00
MA Moises Alou 10.00 3.00
MC Miguel Cabrera 10.00 3.00
ML Mike Lowell 10.00 3.00
MLA Matt Lawton 10.00 3.00
MLO Mark Loretta 10.00 3.00
MM Mark Mulder 10.00 3.00
MP Mike Piazza 15.00 4.50
MR Manny Ramirez 10.00 3.00
MRI Mariano Rivera 10.00 3.00
MT Miguel Tejada 10.00 3.00
MY Michael Young 10.00 3.00
PL Paul Lo Duca 10.00 3.00
RB Ronnie Belliard 10.00 3.00
SR Scott Rolen 10.00 3.00
SS Sammy Sosa 15.00 4.50
TG Tom Glavine 10.00 3.00
TH Todd Helton 10.00 3.00
TL Ted Lilly 10.00 3.00
VG Vladimir Guerrero 10.00 3.00
VM Victor Martinez 10.00 3.00

2005 Topps Autographs

Carlos Beltran and Zack Greinke did not return their cards in time to be included within first series packs, thus exchange cards with a deadline redemption date of November 30th, 2006 were placed into packs in their place.

Nm-Mt Ex-Mt
SER.1 A 1:2683 H, 1:767 HTA, 1:2238 R
SER.1 B 1:3950 H, 1:1129 HTA, 1:3300 R
SER.1 C 1:305 H, 1:87 HTA, 1:254 R
SER.1 D 1:2913 H, 1:833 HTA, 1:2432 R
SER.1 EXCH.DEADLINE 11/30/06
AR Alex Rodriguez A 175.00 52.50
ARI Alexis Rios C 25.00 7.50
CB Carlos Beltran A EXCH 60.00 18.00
CK Casey Kotchman C 25.00 7.50
CT Chad Tracy C 15.00 4.50
DD David DeJesus C 15.00 4.50
DM Dallas McPherson D 25.00 7.50
DW David Wright C 60.00 18.00
EC Eric Chavez A 25.00 7.50
JC Jose Capellan B 25.00 7.50
JM Justin Morneau C 25.00 7.50
JMA John Maine C 15.00 4.50
JSM Jeff Mathis C 15.00 4.50
MC Miguel Cabrera C 40.00 12.00
MH Matt Holliday C 15.00 4.50
TH Torii Hunter A 25.00 7.50
VW Vernon Wells A 25.00 7.50
ZG Zack Greinke C EXCH 15.00 4.50

2005 Topps Celebrity Threads Jersey Relics

Nm-Mt Ex-Mt
SERIES 1 ODDS 1:562 H, 1:161 HTA, 1:468 R
RELICS ARE FROM CELEBRITY AS EVENT
CC Cesar Cedeno 10.00 3.00
CF Cecil Fielder 15.00 4.50
DW Dave Winfield 10.00 3.00
GG Goose Gossage 10.00 3.00
HR Harold Reynolds 10.00 3.00
MS Mike Scott 10.00 3.00
OS Ozzie Smith 20.00 6.00
RF Rollie Fingers 10.00 3.00

2005 Topps Dem Bums

Nm-Mt Ex-Mt
COMPLETE SET (21) 40.00 12.00
SERIES 1 ODDS 1:12 H, 1:4 HTA, 1:12 R
BB Bob Borkowski 2.50 .75
CE Carl Erskine 2.50 .75
CF Carl Furillo 2.50 .75
CL Clem Labine 2.50 .75
DH Don Hoak 2.50 .75
DN Don Newcombe 2.50 .75
DS Duke Snider 4.00 1.20
DZ Don Zimmer 2.50 .75
ER Ed Roebuck 2.50 .75
GS George Shuba 2.50 .75
JB Joe Black 2.50 .75
JG Jim Gilliam 2.50 .75
JH Jim Hughes 2.50 .75
JP Johnny Podres 2.50 .75
JR Jackie Robinson 5.00 1.50
KS Karl Spooner 2.50 .75
RC Roy Campanella 5.00 1.50
RCR Roger Craig 2.50 .75
RM Russ Meyer 2.50 .75
RW Rube Walker 2.50 .75
WA Walter Alston 2.50 .75

2005 Topps Dem Bums Autographs

Nm-Mt Ex-Mt
SERIES 1 ODDS 1:150 HTA
CE Carl Erskine 25.00 7.50
CL Clem Labine 25.00 7.50
DS Duke Snider 50.00 15.00
DZ Don Zimmer 40.00 12.00
JP Johnny Podres 25.00 7.50

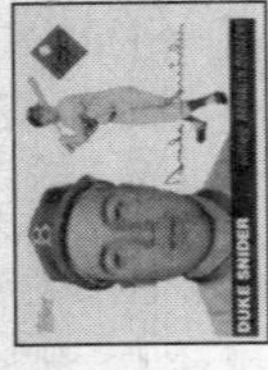
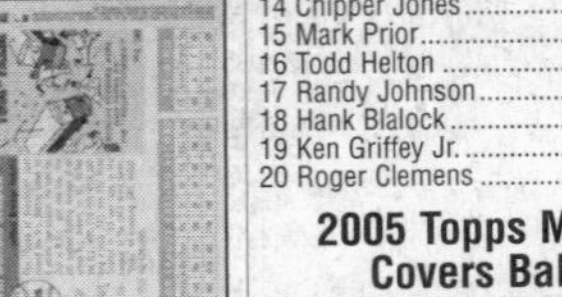

2005 Topps Dem Bums Cut Signatures

Nm-Mt Ex-Mt
SER.1 ODDS 1:347,438 H, 1:71,104 HTA
SER.1 ODDS 1:436,320 R
STATED PRINT RUN 1 SERIAL #'d SET
NO PRICING DUE TO SCARCITY
BB Bob Borkowski
CE Carl Erskine
CF Carl Furillo
CL Clem Labine
DN Don Newcombe
DS Duke Snider
DZ Don Zimmer
ER Ed Roebuck
JB Joe Black
JG Jim Gilliam
RM Russ Meyer
SA Sandy Amoros

2005 Topps Derby Digs Jersey Relics

Nm-Mt Ex-Mt
SER.1 ODDS 1:11,208 HOBBY, 1:3232 HTA
SER.1 ODDS 1:9630 RETAIL
STATED PRINT RUN 100 SERIAL #'d SETS
DO David Ortiz 40.00 12.00
HB Hank Blalock
JT Jim Thome 40.00 12.00
LB Lance Berkman 25.00 7.50
MT Miguel Tejada
SS Sammy Sosa 40.00 12.00

2005 Topps Grudge Match

Nm-Mt Ex-Mt
COMPLETE SET (10) 20.00 6.00
SERIES 1 ODDS 1:24 H, 1:8 HTA, 1:18 R
1 Jorge Posada 2.00 .60
Pedro Martinez
2 Mike Piazza 3.00 .90
Roger Clemens
3 Mariano Rivera 2.00 .60
Luis Gonzalez
4 Jim Edmonds 2.00 .60
Carlos Zambrano
5 Aaron Boone 2.00 .60
Tim Wakefield
6 Manny Ramirez 3.00 .90
Roger Clemens
7 Michael Tucker 2.00 .60
Eric Gagne
8 Ivan Rodriguez 2.00 .60
J.T. Snow
9 Alex Rodriguez 3.00 .90
Bronson Arroyo
10 Corky Miller 3.00 .90
Sammy Sosa

2005 Topps Hobby Masters

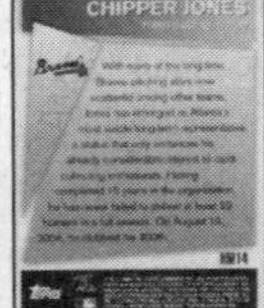

Nm-Mt Ex-Mt
COMPLETE SET (20) 40.00 12.00
SERIES 1 ODDS 1:18 HOBBY, 1:6 HTA
1 Alex Rodriguez 3.00 .90
2 Sammy Sosa 3.00 .90
3 Ichiro Suzuki 3.00 .90
4 Albert Pujols 4.00 1.20
5 Derek Jeter 4.00 1.20
6 Jim Thome 2.00 .60
7 Vladimir Guerrero 2.00 .60
8 Nomar Garciaparra 3.00 .90
9 Mike Piazza 3.00 .90
10 Jason Giambi 2.00 .60
11 Ivan Rodriguez 2.00 .60
12 Alfonso Soriano 2.00 .60
13 Dontrelle Willis 2.00 .60
14 Chipper Jones 2.00 .60
15 Mark Prior 2.00 .60
16 Todd Helton 2.00 .60
17 Randy Johnson 2.00 .60
18 Hank Blalock 2.00 .60
19 Ken Griffey Jr. 3.00 .90
20 Roger Clemens 4.00 1.20

2005 Topps Midsummer Covers Ball Relics

Nm-Mt Ex-Mt
SER.1 ODDS 1:46,325 H, 1:3333 HTA
STATED PRINT RUN 10 SERIAL #'d SETS
NO PRICING DUE TO SCARCITY
AP Albert Pujols
AR Alex Rodriguez
AS Alfonso Soriano
IR Ivan Rodriguez
JG Jason Giambi
JT Jim Thome
RC Roger Clemens
RJ Randy Johnson
SS Sammy Sosa
VG Vladimir Guerrero

2005 Topps Own the Game

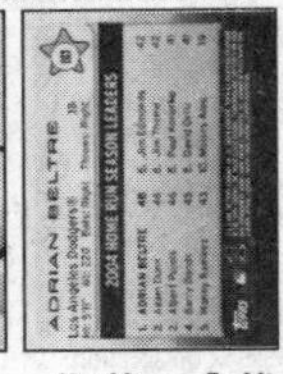

Nm-Mt Ex-Mt
COMPLETE SET (30) 50.00 15.00
SERIES 1 ODDS 1:12 H, 1:4 HTA, 1:12 R
1 Ichiro Suzuki 3.00 .90
2 Todd Helton 2.00 .60
3 Adrian Beltre 2.00 .60
4 Albert Pujols 4.00 1.20
5 Adam Dunn 2.00 .60
6 Jim Thome 2.00 .60
7 Miguel Tejada 2.00 .60
8 David Ortiz 2.00 .60
9 Manny Ramirez 2.00 .60
10 Scott Rolen 2.00 .60
11 Gary Sheffield 2.00 .60
12 Vladimir Guerrero 2.00 .60
13 Jim Edmonds 2.00 .60
14 Ivan Rodriguez 2.00 .60
15 Lance Berkman 2.00 .60
16 Michael Young 2.00 .60
17 Juan Pierre 2.00 .60
18 Craig Biggio 2.00 .60
19 Johnny Damon 2.00 .60
20 Jimmy Rollins 2.00 .60
21 Scott Podsednik 2.00 .60
22 Bobby Abreu 2.00 .60
23 Lyle Overbay 2.00 .60
24 Carl Crawford 2.00 .60
25 Mark Loretta 2.00 .60
26 Vinny Castilla 2.00 .60
27 Curt Schilling 2.00 .60
28 Johan Santana 2.00 .60
29 Randy Johnson 2.00 .60
30 Pedro Martinez 2.00 .60

2005 Topps Spokesman Jersey Relic

Nm-Mt Ex-Mt
SER.1 ODDS 1:5627 H, 1:1604 HTA, 1:4692 R
RELIC IS EVENT WORN
AR Alex Rodriguez 50.00 15.00

2005 Topps Touch Em All Base Relics

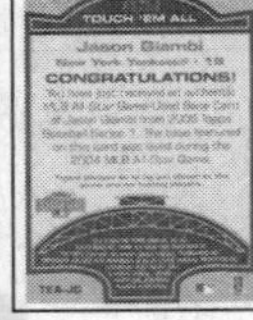

Nm-Mt Ex-Mt
SER.1 ODDS 1:13,493 HOBBY, 1:3878 HTA
SER.1 ODDS 1:11,440 RETAIL
STATED PRINT RUN 50 SERIAL #'d SETS
AP Albert Pujols
AR Alex Rodriguez
AS Alfonso Soriano
CB Carlos Beltran
IR Ivan Rodriguez
JG Jason Giambi
JT Jim Thome
SR Scott Rolen
SS Sammy Sosa
VG Vladimir Guerrero

2005 Topps World Treasures Cut Signatures

Nm-Mt Ex-Mt
SER.1 ODDS 1:135,475 HOB, 1:42,662 HTA
SER.1 ODDS 1:109,080 RETAIL
STATED PRINT RUN 1 SERIAL #'d SET
NO PRICING DUE TO SCARCITY
AP Alexander Papagos
BC Bill Clinton
BJ Benito Juarez
BY Boris Yeltsin
CD Charles de Gaulle
CG Che Guevara
CK Chiang Kai-shek
CP Czar Paul I
DG David Ben-Gurion
FB Fulgencio Batista
FM Ferdinand Marcos
FR Franklin D. Roosevelt
GAN Gamal Abdel Nasser
HT Harry S. Truman
JC Jimmy Carter
JK John F. Kennedy
JN Jawaharlal Nehru
JP Juan Peron
KE King Edward VII
KF King Frederick the Great
KFU King Fuad I
KG King George III
KGV King George V
KH King Hussein of Jordan
KW Kaiser Wilhelm II
LB Leonid Brezhnev
LH Lord Henry Palmerston
LW Lech Walesa
MB Menachem Begin
MD Moshe Dayan
MG Mikhail Gorbachev
MT Margaret Thatcher
MTE Mother Teresa
MTI Marshal Tito
NB Napoleon Bonaparte
NM Nelson Mandela
PD Princess Diana
PG Princess Grace of Monaco
a.k.a. Grace Kelly
PJP Pope John Paul II
PT Pierre Trudeau
QN Queen Noor of Jordan
RFK Robert F. Kennedy
RR Ronald Reagan
SP Shimon Peres
TM Thurgood Marshall
WC Winston Churchill
WG William Gladstone
YR Yitzhak Rabin

2005 Topps World Treasures Dual Signatures

Nm-Mt Ex-Mt
SERIES 1 ODDS 1:213,312 HTA
STATED PRINT RUN 1 SERIAL #'d SET
NO PRICING DUE TO SCARCITY
BC George W. Bush
Dick Cheney
BK George W. Bush
John Kerry
CE Dick Cheney
John Edwards
KE John Kerry
John Edwards

2003 Topps 205

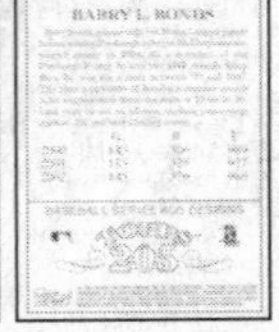

This 165 card series one set was released in July, 2003. The 175 card series two set was released several months later in February, 204. These cards were issued in eight-card packs which came 20 packs to a box and 10 boxes to a case. Cards number 1 through 120 feature veterans. Please note that 15 of these cards were issued with variations and we have notated the differences in these cards in our checklist. Cards number 121 through 130 feature propsects who were about ready to jump into the majors. Cards numbered 131 through 144 feature some players in their first year of cards. Card number 145 features Louis Sockalexis who was supposedly the player the Cleveland Indians named their team in honor of. (This supposition has been buttressed by recently rediscovered newspaper clippings from 1897). Cards numbered 146 to 150 feature various "reprints" of some of the tougher T-205 cards. Also randomly inserted in packs were cards featuring "repurchased" tobacco cards. Those cards were inserted at a stated rate of one in 336 for 1st series cards and one in 295 for second series cards. The second series featured the following subsets: T205 Reprints from cards 151 through 154, retired players from card 155 through 160; prospects from cards 161 through 169. First year players from cards 170 through 192. In addition, 10 players had 2 variations in the second series and we have notated this information along with some players who were issued in shorter quantity we have put an SP next to that player's name.

Nm-Mt Ex-Mt
COMPLETE SERIES 1 (165) 40.00 12.00
COMPLETE SERIES 2 (175) 125.00 38.00
COMP.SERIES 2 w/o SP's (155) 40.00 12.00
COM (1-130/161-169/193-315) .50 .15
COMMON (131-145/170-192) .50 .15
COMMON (146-150) 1.00 .30
COMMON SP 2.50 .75
SERIES 2 SP STATED ODDS 1:5
1A Barry Bonds w/Cap 3.00 .90
1B Barry Bonds w/Helmet 3.00 .90
2 Bret Boone .50 .15
3A Albert Pujols Clear Logo 2.50 .75
3B Albert Pujols White Logo 2.50 .75
4 Carl Crawford .50 .15
5 Bartolo Colon .50 .15
6 Cliff Floyd .50 .15
7 John Olerud .50 .15
8A Jason Giambi Full Jkt .50 .15
8B Jason Giambi Partial Jkt .50 .15
9 Edgardo Alfonzo .50 .15
10 Ivan Rodriguez 1.25 .35
11 Jim Edmonds .50 .15
12A Mike Piazza Orange 2.00 .60
12B Mike Piazza Yellow 2.00 .60
13 Greg Maddux 2.00 .60
14 Jose Vidro .50 .15
15A Vlad Guerrero Clear Logo 1.25 .35
15B V.Guerrero White Logo 1.25 .35
16 Bernie Williams .75 .23
17 Roger Clemens 2.50 .75
18A Miguel Tejada Blue .50 .15
18B Miguel Tejada Green .50 .15
19 Carlos Delgado .50 .15
20A Alfonso Soriano w/Bat .75 .23
20B Alf. Soriano Sunglasses .75 .23
21 Bobby Cox MG .50 .15
22 Mike Scioscia .50 .15
23 John Smoltz .75 .23
24 Luis Gonzalez .50 .15
25 Shawn Green .50 .15
26 Raul Ibanez .50 .15
27 Andruw Jones .50 .15
28 Josh Beckett .50 .15
29 Derek Lowe .50 .15
30 Todd Helton .75 .23
31 Barry Larkin .75 .23
32 Jason Jennings .50 .15
33 Darin Erstad .50 .15
34 Magglio Ordonez .50 .15
35 Mike Sweeney .50 .15
36 Kazuhisa Ishii .50 .15
37 Ron Gardenhire MG .50 .15
38 Tim Hudson .50 .15
39 Tim Salmon .75 .23
40A Pat Burrell Black Bat .50 .15
40B Pat Burrell Brown Bat .50 .15
41 Manny Ramirez .75 .23
42 Nick Johnson .50 .15
43 Tom Glavine .75 .23
44 Mark Mulder .50 .15
45 Brian Jordan .50 .15
46 Rafael Palmeiro .75 .23
47 Vernon Wells .50 .15
48 Bob Brenly MG .50 .15
49 C.C. Sabathia .50 .15
50A A.Rodriguez Look Ahead 2.00 .60
50B A.Rodriguez Look Away 2.00 .60
51A Sammy Sosa Head Duck 2.00 .60
51B Sammy Sosa Head Left 2.00 .60
52 Paul Konerko .50 .15
53 Craig Biggio .75 .23
54 Moises Alou .50 .15
55 Johnny Damon 1.25 .35
56 Torii Hunter .50 .15
57 Omar Vizquel .75 .23
58 Orlando Hernandez .50 .15
59 Barry Zito .50 .15
60 Lance Berkman .50 .15
61 Carlos Beltran .75 .23
62 Edgar Renteria .50 .15
63 Ben Sheets .50 .15
64 Doug Mientkiewicz .50 .15
65 Troy Glaus .50 .15
66 Preston Wilson .50 .15
67 Kerry Wood 1.25 .35
68 Frank Thomas 1.25 .35
69 Jimmy Rollins .50 .15
70 Brian Giles .50 .15
71 Bobby Higginson .50 .15
72 Larry Walker .75 .23
73 Randy Johnson 1.25 .35
74 Tony LaRussa MG .50 .15
75A Derek Jeter w/Gold Trim 3.00 .90
75B D.Jeter w/o Gold Trim 3.00 .90
76 Bobby Abreu .50 .15
77A A.Dunn Closed Mouth .75 .23
77B Adam Dunn Open Mouth .75 .23
78 Ryan Klesko .50 .15
79 Francisco Rodriguez .50 .15
80 Scott Rolen 1.25 .35
81 Roberto Alomar .75 .23
82 Joe Torre MG .75 .23
83 Jim Thome 1.25 .35
84 Kevin Millwood .50 .15
85 J.T. Snow .50 .15
86 Trevor Hoffman .50 .15
87 Jay Gibbons .50 .15
88A Mark Prior New Logo 1.25 .35
88B Mark Prior Old Logo 1.25 .35
89 Rich Aurilia .50 .15
90 Chipper Jones 1.25 .35
91 Richie Sexson .50 .15
92 Gary Sheffield .50 .15
93 Pedro Martinez 1.25 .35
94 Rodrigo Lopez .50 .15
95 Al Leiter .50 .15
96 Jorge Posada .75 .23
97 Luis Castillo .50 .15
98 Aubrey Huff .50 .15
99 A.J. Pierzynski .50 .15
100A I.Suzuki Look Ahead 2.00 .60
100B Ichiro Suzuki Look Right 2.00 .60
101 Eric Chavez .50 .15
102 Brett Myers .50 .15
103 Jason Kendall .50 .15
104 Jeff Kent .50 .15
105 Eric Hinske .50 .15
106 Jacque Jones .50 .15
107 Phil Nevin .50 .15
108 Roy Oswalt .50 .15
109 Curt Schilling .50 .15
110A N.Garciaparra w/Gold Trim 2.00 .60
110B N.Garciaparra w/o Gold Trim 2.00 .60
111 Garret Anderson .50 .15
112 Eric Gagne 1.25 .35
113 Javier Vazquez .50 .15
114 Jeff Bagwell .75 .23
115 Mike Lowell .50 .15
116 Carlos Pena .50 .15
117 Ken Griffey Jr. 2.00 .60
118 Tony Batista .50 .15
119 Edgar Martinez .75 .23
120 Austin Kearns .50 .15
121 Jason Stokes PROS .75 .23
122 Jose Reyes PROS .50 .15
123 Rocco Baldelli PROS .50 .15
124 Joe Borchard PROS .50 .15
125 Joe Mauer PROS 1.25 .35
126 Gavin Floyd PROS .50 .15
127 Mark Teixeira PROS .50 .15
128 Jeremy Guthrie PROS .50 .15
129 B.J. Upton PROS 1.50 .45
130 Khalil Greene PROS 2.50 .75
131 Hanley Ramirez FY RC 2.50 .75
132 Andy Marte FY RC 3.00 .90
133 J.D. Durbin FY RC 1.00 .30
134 Jason Kubel FY RC 2.50 .75
135 Craig Brazell FY RC .60 .18
136 Bryan Bullington FY RC 1.50 .45
137 Jose Contreras FY RC 1.25 .35
138 Brian Burgamy FY RC .50 .15
139 E.Bastida-Martinez FY RC .50 .15
140 Joey Gomes FY RC .50 .15
141 Ismael Castro FY RC .60 .18
142 Travis Wong FY RC .60 .18
143 Mi.Garciaparra FY RC 1.00 .30
144 Arnaldo Munoz FY RC .50 .15
145 Louis Sockalexis FY XRC .50 .15
146 Richard Hoblitzell REP 1.00 .30
147 George Graham REP 1.00 .30
148 Hal Chase REP 1.00 .30
149 John McGraw REP 1.50 .45
150 Bobby Wallace REP 1.00 .30
151 David Shean REP 1.00 .30
152 Richard Hoblitzell REP SP 2.50 .75
153 Hal Chase REP 1.00 .30
154 Hooks Wiltse REP 1.00 .30
155 George Brett RET 4.00 1.20
156 Willie Mays RET 3.00 .90
157 Honus Wagner RET SP 10.00 3.00
158 Nolan Ryan RET 4.00 1.20
159 Reggie Jackson RET 1.50 .45
160 Mike Schmidt RET 3.00 .90
161 Josh Barfield PROS .50 .15
162 Grady Sizemore PROS .50 .15
163 Justin Morneau PROS .75 .23
164 Laynce Nix PROS .50 .15
165 Zack Greinke PROS .75 .23
166 Victor Martinez PROS .75 .23
167 Jeff Mathis PROS .50 .15
168 Casey Kotchman PROS .75 .23
169 Gabe Gross PROS .50 .15
170 Edwin Jackson FY RC 3.00 .90
171 Delmon Young FY SP RC 12.00 3.60
172 Eric Duncan FY SP RC 6.00 1.80
173 Brian Snyder FY SP RC 5.00 1.50
174 Chris Lubanski FY SP RC 6.00 1.80
175 Ryan Harvey FY SP RC 6.00 1.80
176 Nick Markakis FY SP RC 5.00 1.50
177 Chad Billingsley FY SP RC 6.00 1.80
178 Elizardo Ramirez FY RC 1.00 .30
179 Ben Francisco FY RC .60 .18
180 Franklin Gutierrez FY SP RC 8.00 2.40
181 Aaron Hill FY SP RC 5.00 1.50
182 Kevin Correia FY RC .50 .15
183 Kelly Shoppach FY RC 1.25 .35
184 Felix Pie FY SP RC 8.00 2.40
185 Adam Loewen FY SP RC 5.00 1.50
186 Danny Garcia FY RC .50 .15
187 Rickie Weeks FY SP RC 10.00 3.00
188 Robby Hammock FY SP RC 5.00 1.50
189 Ryan Wagner FY SP RC 5.00 1.50
190 Matt Kata FY SP RC 5.00 1.50
191 Bo Hart FY SP RC 5.00 1.50
192 Brandon Webb FY SP RC 5.00 1.50
193 Bengie Molina .50 .15
194 Junior Spivey .50 .15
195 Gary Sheffield .50 .15
196 Jason Johnson .50 .15
197 David Ortiz .75 .23
198 Roberto Alomar .75 .23
199 Wily Mo Pena .50 .15
200 Sammy Sosa 2.00 .60
201 Jay Payton .50 .15
202 Dmitri Young .50 .15
203 Derrek Lee .50 .15
204A Jeff Bagwell w/Hat .75 .23
204B Jeff Bagwell w/o Hat .75 .23
205 Runelvys Hernandez .50 .15
206 Kevin Brown .50 .15
207 Wes Helms .50 .15
208 Eddie Guardado .50 .15
209 Orlando Cabrera .50 .15
210 Alfonso Soriano .75 .23
211 Ty Wigginton .50 .15
212A Rich Harden Look Left .75 .23
212B Rich Harden Look Right .75 .23
213 Mike Lieberthal .50 .15
214 Brian Giles .50 .15
215 Jason Schmidt .50 .15
216 Jamie Moyer .50 .15
217 Matt Morris .50 .15
218 Victor Zambrano .50 .15
219 Roy Halladay .50 .15
220 Mike Hampton .50 .15

221 Kevin Millar Sox .50 .15
222 Hideo Nomo 1.25 .35
223 Milton Bradley .50 .15
224 Jose Guillen .50 .15
225 Derek Jeter 3.00 .90
226 Rondell White .50 .15
227A Hank Blalock Blue Jsy .75 .23
227B Hank Blalock White Jsy .75 .23
228 Shigetoshi Hasegawa .50 .15
229 Mike Mussina .75 .23
230 Cristian Guzman .50 .15
231A Todd Helton Blue .75 .23
231B Todd Helton Green .75 .23
232 Kenny Lofton .50 .15
233 Carl Everett .50 .15
234 Shea Hillenbrand .50 .15
235 Brad Fullmer .50 .15
236 Bernie Williams .75 .23
237 Vicente Padilla .50 .15
238 Tim Worrell .50 .15
239 Juan Gonzalez .75 .23
240 Ichiro Suzuki 2.00 .60
241 Aaron Boone .50 .15
242 Shannon Stewart .50 .15
243A Barry Zito Blue .50 .15
243B Barry Zito Green .50 .15
244 Reggie Sanders .50 .15
245 Scott Podsednik .50 .15
246 Miguel Cabrera 1.25 .35
247 Angel Berroa .50 .15
248 Carlos Zambrano .50 .15
249 Marlon Byrd .50 .15
250 Mark Prior 1.25 .35
251 Esteban Loaiza .50 .15
252 David Eckstein .50 .15
253 Alex Cintron .50 .15
254 Melvin Mora .50 .15
255 Russ Ortiz .50 .15
256 Carlos Lee .50 .15
257 Tino Martinez .75 .23
258 Randy Wolf .50 .15
259 Jason Phillips .50 .15
260 Vladimir Guerrero 1.25 .35
261 Brad Wilkerson .50 .15
262 Ivan Rodriguez 1.25 .35
263 Matt Lawton .50 .15
264 Adam Dunn .75 .23
265 Joe Borowski .50 .15
266 Jody Gerut .50 .15
267 Alex Rodriguez 2.00 .60
268 Brendan Donnelly .50 .15
269A Randy Johnson Grey 1.25 .35
269B Randy Johnson Pink 1.25 .35
270 Nomar Garciaparra 2.00 .60
271 Javy Lopez .50 .15
272 Travis Hafner .50 .15
273 Juan Pierre .50 .15
274 Morgan Ensberg .50 .15
275 Albert Pujols 2.50 .75
276 Jason LaRue .50 .15
277 Paul Lo Duca .50 .15
278 Andy Pettitte .75 .23
279 Mike Piazza 2.00 .60
280A Jim Thome Blue 1.25 .35
280B Jim Thome Green 1.25 .35
281 Marquis Grissom .50 .15
282 Woody Williams .50 .15
283A Curt Schilling Look Ahead .50 .15
283B Curt Schilling Look Right .50 .15
284A Chipper Jones Blue 1.25 .35
284B Chipper Jones Yellow 1.25 .35
285 Deivi Cruz .50 .15
286 Johnny Damon 1.25 .35
287 Chin-Hui Tsao .50 .15
288 Alex Gonzalez .50 .15
289 Billy Wagner .50 .15
290 Jason Giambi .50 .15
291 Keith Foulke .50 .15
292 Jerome Williams .50 .15
293 Livan Hernandez .50 .15
294 Aaron Guiel .50 .15
295 Randall Simon .50 .15
296 Byung-Hyun Kim .50 .15
297 Jorge Julio .50 .15
298 Miguel Batista .50 .15
299 Rafael Furcal .50 .15
300A Dontrelle Willis No Smile .75 .23
300B Dontrelle Willis Smile SP 4.00 1.20
301 Alex Sanchez .50 .15
302 Shawn Chacon .50 .15
303 Matt Clement .50 .15
304 Luis Matos .50 .15
305 Steve Finley .50 .15
306 Marcus Giles .50 .15
307 Boomer Wells .50 .15
308 Jeromy Burnitz .50 .15
309 Mike MacDougal .50 .15
310 Mariano Rivera .75 .23
311 Adrian Beltre .75 .23
312 Mark Loretta .50 .15
313 Ugueth Urbina .50 .15
314 Bill Mueller .50 .15
315 Johan Santana .75 .23
NNO Vintage Buyback

2003 Topps 205 American Beauty

Nm-Mt Ex-Mt
*AMER.BTY: 1.25X TO 3X BASIC
RANDOM INSERTS IN PACKS
*AMER.BTY PURPLE: 4X TO 10X BASIC
PURPLE CARDS ARE 10% OF PRINT RUN
CL: 1/20/50/51/100/146-150

2003 Topps 205 Bazooka Blue

Nm-Mt Ex-Mt
SERIES 2 STATED ODDS 1:2744 PACKS
SERIES 2 STATED ODDS 1:208 MINI BOXES
STATED PRINT RUN 1 SET
NO PRICING DUE TO SCARCITY

2003 Topps 205 Bazooka Red

Nm-Mt Ex-Mt
SERIES 1 STATED ODDS 1:1573 PACKS
SERIES 2 STATED ODDS 1:691 PACKS
SERIES 2 STATED ODDS 1:52 MINI BOXES
SERIES 1 STATED PRINT RUN 5 SETS
SERIES 2 STATED PRINT RUN 4 SETS
NO PRICING DUE TO SCARCITY

2003 Topps 205 Brooklyn

Nm-Mt Ex-Mt
*BROOKLYN C 1-130: .75X TO 2X BASIC
*BROOKLYN U 1-130: 1.25X TO 3X BASIC
*BROOKLYN U 131-144: 1.25X TO 3X BASIC
*BROOKLYN R 1-130: 2X TO 5X BASIC
*BROOKLYN R 131-144: 2X TO 5X BASIC
BROOKLYN 5 PRINT RUN 5 SETS
NO BROOKLYN 5 PRICING DUE TO SCARCITY
1-150 RANDOM INSERTS IN SER.1 PACKS
SEE BECKETT.COM FOR C/U/R/5 SCHEMATIC
SCHEMATIC IS IN OPG SUBSCRIPTION AREA
*BRKLYN 151-315: 2X TO 5X BASIC
*BRKLYN 151-315: .6X TO 1.5X BASIC SP
151-315 SERIES 2 STATED ODDS 1:12
151-315 STATED PRINT RUN 205 SETS
151-315 ARE NOT SERIAL-NUMBERED
151-315 PRINT RUN PROVIDED BY TOPPS

2003 Topps 205 Brooklyn Exclusive Pose

Nm-Mt Ex-Mt
*BROOKLYN EP: 1X TO 2.5X POLAR EP
OVERALL BROOKLYN SERIES 2 ODDS 1:12
STATED PRINT RUN 205 SETS
CARDS ARE NOT SERIAL-NUMBERED
PRINT RUN PROVIDED BY TOPPS

2003 Topps 205 Cycle

Nm-Mt Ex-Mt
*CYCLE 121-145: 1.25X TO 3X BASIC
RANDOM INSERTS IN PACKS
*CYCLE PURPLE 121-130: 4X TO 10X BASIC
*CYCLE PURPLE 131-145: 3X TO 8X BASIC
PURPLE CARDS ARE 10% OF PRINT RUN

2003 Topps 205 Drum

Nm-Mt Ex-Mt
*DRUM: 2X TO 5X BASIC
*DRUM: .6X TO 1.5X BASIC SP
RANDOM INSERTS IN PACKS

2003 Topps 205 Drum Exclusive Pose

Nm-Mt Ex-Mt
*DRUM EP: 1X TO 2.5X POLAR EP
RANDOM INSERTS IN SERIES 2 PACKS

2003 Topps 205 Honest

Nm-Mt Ex-Mt
*HONEST: 1.25X TO 3X BASIC
RANDOM INSERTS IN PACKS
*HONEST PURPLE: 4X TO 10X BASIC
PURPLE CARDS ARE 10% OF PRINT RUN
CL: 1/3/8/12/15/18/20/40/50/51/75/77/88
CL: 100/110

2003 Topps 205 Piedmont

Nm-Mt Ex-Mt
*PIEDMONT: 1.25X TO 3X BASIC
RANDOM INSERTS IN PACKS
*PIEDMONT PURPLE: 4X TO 10X BASIC
PURPLE CARDS ARE 10% OF PRINT RUN
CL: 2-19/21-49/

2003 Topps 205 Polar Bear

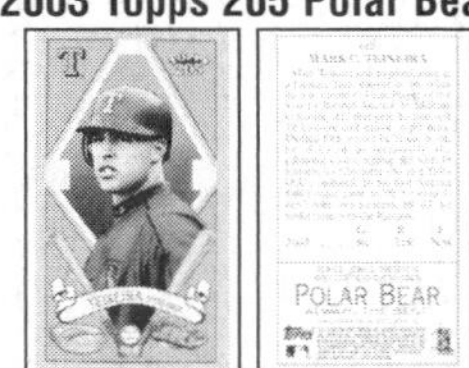

Nm-Mt Ex-Mt
*POLAR BEAR: .75X TO 2X BASIC
*POLAR BEAR: .25X TO .6X BASIC SP
RANDOM INSERTS IN PACKS

2003 Topps 205 Polar Bear Exclusive Pose

Nm-Mt Ex-Mt
RANDOM INSERTS IN SERIES 2 PACKS
316 Willie Mays EP 6.00 1.80
317 Delmon Young EP 8.00 2.40
318 Rickie Weeks EP 6.00 1.80
319 Ryan Wagner EP 2.00 .60
320 Brandon Webb EP 2.50 .75
321 Chris Lubanski EP 4.00 1.20
322 Ryan Harvey EP 4.00 1.20
323 Nick Markakis EP 2.50 .75
324 Chad Billingsley EP 3.00 .90
325 Aaron Hill EP 2.50 .75
326 Brian Snyder EP 2.00 .60
327 Eric Duncan EP 3.00 .90
328 Sammy Sosa EP 4.00 1.20
329 Alfonso Soriano EP 2.00 .60
330 Ichiro Suzuki EP 4.00 1.20
331 Alex Rodriguez EP 4.00 1.20
332 Nomar Garciaparra EP 4.00 1.20
333 Albert Pujols EP 5.00 1.50
334 Jim Thome EP 2.50 .75
335 Dontrelle Willis EP 2.00 .60

2003 Topps 205 Sovereign

Nm-Mt Ex-Mt
*SOVEREIGN: 1.25X TO 3X BASIC
*SOVEREIGN: .4X TO 1X BASIC SP
RANDOM INSERTS IN PACKS
*SOV.GREEN: 2.5X TO 6X BASIC
*SOV.GREEN: 1.25X TO 3X BASIC SP
SOV.GREEN CARDS ARE 25% OF PRINT RUN

2003 Topps 205 Sovereign Exclusive Pose

Nm-Mt Ex-Mt
*SOVEREIGN EP: .6X TO 1.5X POLAR EP
RANDOM INSERTS IN SERIES 2 PACKS
*SOV.GREEN EP: 1.25X TO 3X POLAR EP
SOV.GREEN CARDS ARE 25% OF PRINT RUN

2003 Topps 205 Sweet Caporal

Nm-Mt Ex-Mt
*SWEET CAP: 1.25X TO 3X BASIC
RANDOM INSERTS IN PACKS
*SWEET CAP PURPLE: 4X TO 10X BASIC
PURPLE CARDS ARE 10% OF PRINT RUN
CL: 70-99/101-120

2003 Topps 205 Autographs

These cards feature autographs of leading players. These cards were inserted at varying odds and we have noted what group the player belongs to in our checklist. Though lacking serial numbering, representatives at Topps publicly announced only 50 copies of Hank Aaron's card were produced - making it, by far, the scarcest card in this set.

Nm-Mt Ex-Mt
SER.1 GROUP A1 ODDS 1:2434
SER.1 GROUP B1 ODDS 1:608
SER.1 GROUP C1 ODDS 1:1460
SER.1 GROUP D1 ODDS 1:122
SER.2 GROUP A2 ODDS 1:5816
SER.2 GROUP B2 ODDS 1:646
SER.2 GROUP C2 ODDS 1:49
A2 STATED PRINT RUN 50 CARDS
A2 IS NOT SERIAL-NUMBERED
A2 PRINT RUN PROVIDED BY TOPPS
CF Cliff Floyd B1 20.00 6.00
DW Dontrelle Willis C2 25.00 7.50
ED Eric Duncan C2 20.00 6.00
FP Felix Pie C2 25.00 7.50
HA Hank Aaron A2 SP/50
JR Jose Reyes D1 15.00 4.50
JW Jerome Williams B2 25.00 7.50
LB Lance Berkman B1 30.00 9.00
LC Luis Castillo C2 10.00 3.00
MB Marlon Byrd D1 10.00 3.00
MO Maggio Ordonez C1 25.00 7.50
MS Mike Sweeney B1 25.00 7.50
PL Paul Lo Duca D1 15.00 4.50
RH Rich Harden C2 25.00 7.50
RWA Ryan Wagner C2 15.00 4.50
SR Scott Rolen A1 50.00 15.00
TH Torii Hunter D1 15.00 4.50

2003 Topps 205 Relics

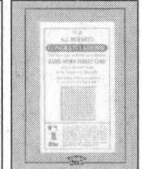

Randomly inserted into packs, these 43 cards feature game-used memorabilia pieces of the featured players. Please note that many of these cards were inserted in different rates and we have noted both the insert ratio as well as the group the player belongs to in our checklisting information.

Nm-Mt Ex-Mt
COM.UNI A1/RELIC A2 15.00 4.50
COM.BAT B-D1/UNI E1/RELIC B2 10.00 3.00
COMMON BAT E-H1/UNI F-M1 8.00 2.40
SER.1 BAT GROUP A1 ODDS 1:1216
SER.1 BAT GROUP B1 ODDS 1:972
SER.1 BAT GROUP C1 ODDS 1:270
SER.1 BAT GROUP D1 ODDS 1:365
SER.1 BAT GROUP E1 ODDS 1:561
SER.1 BAT GROUP F1 ODDS 1:486
SER.1 BAT GROUP G1 ODDS 1:91
SER.1 BAT GROUP H1 ODDS 1:203
SER.1 UNI GROUP A1 ODDS 1:4884
SER.1 UNI GROUP B1 ODDS 1:456
SER.1 UNI GROUP C1 ODDS 1:1460
SER.1 UNI GROUP D1 ODDS 1:1216
SER.1 UNI GROUP E1 ODDS 1:973
SER.1 UNI GROUP F1 ODDS 1:608
SER.1 UNI GROUP G1 ODDS 1:61
SER.1 UNI GROUP H1 ODDS 1:183
SER.1 UNI GROUP I1 ODDS 1:83
SER.1 UNI GROUP J1 ODDS 1:324
SER.1 UNI GROUP K1 ODDS 1:317
SER.1 UNI GROUP L1 ODDS 1:243
SER.1 UNI GROUP M1 ODDS 1:221
SER.2 RELIC GROUP A ODDS 1:79
SER.2 RELIC GROUP B ODDS 1:16
AB A.J. Burnett Jsy G1 8.00 2.40
AD Adam Dunn Bat G1 10.00 3.00
AJ Andruw Jones Jsy B2 UER 15.00 4.50
Chipper Jones is pictured
AL Al Leiter Jsy I1 8.00 2.40
APB Albert Pujols Bat A2 25.00 7.50
AP1 Albert Pujols Uni E1 20.00 6.00
AP2 Albert Pujols Hat A2 25.00 7.50
ARA Aramis Ramirez Bat B2 10.00 3.00
AR1 Alex Rodriguez Jsy H1 15.00 4.50
AR2 Alex Rodriguez Bat B2 15.00 4.50
AS1 Alfonso Soriano Uni G1 10.00 3.00
AS2 Alfonso Soriano Bat A2 20.00 6.00
BB1 Barry Bonds Uni B1 25.00 7.50
BB2 Bret Boone Bat A2 15.00 4.50
BD Brandon Duckworth Jsy B2 10.00 3.00
BG1 Brian Giles Bat G1 8.00 2.40
BG2 Brian Giles Bat A2 15.00 4.50
BP Brad Penny Jsy B2 10.00 3.00
BW1 Bernie Williams Bat D1 15.00 4.50
BW2 Bernie Williams Jsy A2 20.00 6.00
BZ Barry Zito Jsy K1 8.00 2.40
CB Craig Biggio Uni B2 15.00 4.50
CD Carlos Delgado Jsy B2 10.00 3.00
CG Cristian Guzman Jsy B2 10.00 3.00
CJB Chipper Jones Bat A2 20.00 6.00
CP Corey Patterson Bat A2 15.00 4.50
CS1 Curt Schilling Jsy B1 10.00 3.00
CS2 Curt Schilling Bat B2 10.00 3.00
DE Darin Erstad Uni A2 15.00 4.50
DL Derek Lowe Hat A1 15.00 4.50
DW Dontrelle Willis Uni B2 15.00 4.50
EC Eric Chavez Bat G1 8.00 2.40
EG Eric Gagne Jsy G1 10.00 3.00
EMA Edgar Martinez Jsy B2 15.00 4.50
EMU Eddie Murray Bat A2 25.00 7.50
FM Fred McGriff Bat B2 15.00 4.50
FR Frank Robinson Bat A2 20.00 6.00
FT Frank Thomas Jsy B2 15.00 4.50
GA Garret Anderson Uni L1 8.00 2.40
GB George Brett Jsy A2 40.00 12.00
GC Gary Carter Bat A2 15.00 4.50
GM1 Greg Maddux Jsy B1 15.00 4.50
GM2 Greg Maddux Bat A2 20.00 6.00
GS Gary Sheffield Bat B2 10.00 3.00
HB Hank Blalock Bat B2 15.00 4.50
IR Ivan Rodriguez Bat A2 20.00 6.00
JB1 Jeff Bagwell Uni G1 10.00 3.00
JB2 Jeff Bagwell Bat A2 20.00 6.00
JC Jose Canseco Bat B2 15.00 4.50
JD Johnny Damon Bat B1 15.00 4.50
JE Jim Edmonds Jsy A2 15.00 4.50
JG Jason Giambi Bat A2 15.00 4.50
JGI Jeremy Giambi Jsy B2 10.00 3.00
JGO Juan Gonzalez Bat B2 15.00 4.50
JJ Jason Jennings Jsy G1 8.00 2.40
JK Jeff Kent Bat C1 10.00 3.00
JO John Olerud Jsy B2 10.00 3.00
JP Jorge Posada Bat A2 20.00 6.00
JS John Smoltz Jsy B1 15.00 4.50
JT Jim Thome Bat F1 10.00 3.00
KB Kevin Brown Jsy B2 10.00 3.00
KI Kazuhisa Ishii Jsy I1 8.00 2.40
KL1 Kenny Lofton Bat G1 8.00 2.40
KL2 Kenny Lofton Uni B2 10.00 3.00
LB Lance Berkman Bat C1 10.00 3.00
LC Luis Castillo Jsy G1 8.00 2.40
LG1 Luis Gonzalez Jsy J1 8.00 2.40
LG2 Luis Gonzalez Bat A2 15.00 4.50
LW Larry Walker Jsy B2 15.00 4.50
MC Mike Cameron Jsy B2 10.00 3.00
MG Mark Grace Bat A2 20.00 6.00
MGR Marquis Grissom Bat B2 10.00 3.00
MM Mark Mulder Uni A2 15.00 4.50
MO Maggio Ordonez Jsy M1 8.00 2.40
MP1 Mike Piazza Bat C1 15.00 4.50
MP2 Mike Piazza Bat A2 20.00 6.00
MR Manny Ramirez Bat H1 10.00 3.00
MSC Mike Schmidt Bat A2 30.00 9.00
MSW Mike Sweeney Bat H1 8.00 2.40
MTE Miguel Tejada Bat B2 10.00 3.00
MTI Mark Teixeira Bat B2 10.00 3.00
MV Mo Vaughn Jsy I1 8.00 2.40
NG1 Nomar Garciaparra Jsy G1 15.00 4.50
NG2 Nomar Garciaparra Bat A2 20.00 6.00
NJ Nick Johnson Bat D1 10.00 3.00
NR Nolan Ryan Uni A2 60.00 18.00
PM1 Pedro Martinez Jsy F1 10.00 3.00
PM2 Pedro Martinez Jsy A2 20.00 6.00
PO Paul O'Neill Uni B2 15.00 4.50
RA1 Roberto Alomar Bat G1 10.00 3.00
RA2 Roberto Alomar Uni B2 15.00 4.50
RBB Rocco Baldelli Bat B2 10.00 3.00
RBJ Rocco Baldelli Jsy B2 10.00 3.00
RC Roger Clemens Uni A2 20.00 6.00
RF1 Rafael Furcal Bat E1 8.00 2.40
RF2 Rafael Furcal Bat A2 15.00 4.50
RH Rickey Henderson Bat B2 15.00 4.50
RJ1 Randy Johnson Jsy C1 15.00 4.50
RJ2 Randy Johnson Jsy A2 20.00 6.00
RO Roy Oswalt Jsy I1 8.00 2.40
RP1 Rafael Palmeiro Jsy H1 10.00 3.00
RP2 Rafael Palmeiro Bat A2 20.00 6.00
RV Robin Ventura Bat B2 10.00 3.00
SB Sean Burroughs Bat B2 10.00 3.00
SR1 Scott Rolen Bat A1 15.00 4.50
SR2 Scott Rolen Uni A2 20.00 6.00
SS Sammy Sosa Jsy A2 20.00 6.00
SST Shannon Stewart Bat B2 10.00 3.00
TG Troy Glaus Uni A2 15.00 4.50
TH Todd Helton Jsy D1 15.00 4.50
TM Tino Martinez Bat B2 15.00 4.50
TP Troy Percival Uni G1 8.00 2.40
TS Tsuyoshi Shinjo Bat B2 10.00 3.00
VG Vladimir Guerrero Bat A2 20.00 6.00
VW Vernon Wells Jsy A2 15.00 4.50
WB Wade Boggs Bat A2 20.00 6.00

2003 Topps 205 Team Topps Legends Autographs

Nm-Mt Ex-Mt
SER.1 GROUP A1 ODDS 1:1461
SER.1 GROUP B1 ODDS 1:2433
SER.1 GROUP C1 ODDS 1:609
SER.2 STATED ODDS 1:20,581
SEE 2001 TOPPS TEAM TOPPS FOR PRICING
SEE 2003 TOPPS TEAM TOPPS FOR PRICING

2003 Topps 205 Triple Folder Polar Bear

Nm-Mt Ex-Mt
COMPLETE SET (100) 50.00 15.00
COMPLETE SERIES 1 (50) 25.00 7.50
COMPLETE SERIES 2 (50) 25.00 7.50
ONE PER PACK
*BROOKLYN: 3X TO 8X BASIC
SERIES 1 BROOKLYN ODDS 1:72
SERIES 2 BROOKLYN ODDS 1:29

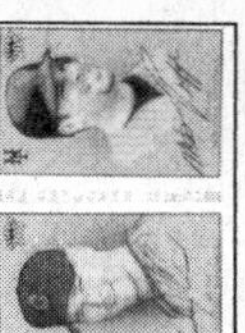

TF1 Barry Bonds 2.50 .75
Jason LaRue
TF2 Alfonso Soriano 2.50 .75
Derek Jeter
TF3 Alex Rodriguez 1.50 .45
Miguel Tejada
TF4 Nomar Garciaparra 2.50 .75
Derek Jeter
TF5 Omar Vizquel 1.50 .45
Alex Rodriguez
TF6 Paul Konerko 1.00 .30
Omar Vizquel
TF7 Paul Konerko 1.00 .30
Magglio Ordonez
TF8 Doug Mientkiewicz 1.00 .30
Darin Erstad
TF9 Jason Kendall 1.00 .30
Jimmy Rollins
TF10 Shawn Green 1.00 .30
Roberto Alomar
TF11 Derek Jeter 2.50 .75
Roberto Alomar
TF12 Bobby Abreu 1.00 .30
Luis Castillo
TF13 Randy Johnson 1.00 .30
Curt Schilling
TF14 Mike Piazza 1.50 .45
Kerry Wood
TF15 Roger Clemens 2.00 .60
Jorge Posada
TF16 Ichiro Suzuki 1.50 .45
Ryan Klesko
TF17 Alfonso Soriano 1.00 .30
Chipper Jones
TF18 Barry Bonds 2.50 .75
Nick Johnson
TF19 Chipper Jones 1.00 .30
Andruw Jones
TF20 Bobby Abreu 1.00 .30
Paul Konerko
TF21 Rafael Palmeiro 1.50 .45
Alex Rodriguez
TF22 Eric Hinske 1.00 .30
Carlos Delgado
TF23 Nomar Garciaparra 1.50 .45
Jay Gibbons
TF24 Mike Piazza 1.50 .45
Luis Gonzalez
TF25 J.T. Snow 1.00 .30
Vladimir Guerrero
TF26 Jason Giambi 1.00 .30
Bernie Williams
TF27 Miguel Tejada 1.00 .30
Richie Sexson
TF28 Doug Mientkiewicz 1.00 .30
Jimmy Rollins
TF29 Eric Chavez 2.50 .75
Derek Jeter
TF30 Alfonso Soriano 1.00 .30
Bret Boone
TF31 Chipper Jones 1.50 .45
Mike Piazza
TF32 Ichiro Suzuki 1.50 .45
Bret Boone
TF33 Bobby Abreu 1.50 .45
Mike Piazza
TF34 Jimmy Rollins 1.00 .30
Pat Burell
TF35 Ichiro Suzuki 1.50 .45
Miguel Tejada
TF36 Jason LaRue 2.50 .75
Barry Bonds
TF37 Derek Jeter 2.50 .75
Alfonso Soriano
TF38 Miguel Tejada 1.50 .45
Alex Rodriguez
TF39 Derek Jeter 2.50 .75
Nomar Garciaparra
TF40 Alex Rodriguez 1.50 .45
Omar Vizquel
TF41 Curt Schilling 1.00 .30
Randy Johnson
TF42 Jorge Posada 2.00 .60
Roger Clemens
TF43 Ryan Klesko 1.50 .45
Ichiro Suzuki
TF44 Nick Johnson 2.50 .75
Barry Bonds
TF45 Alex Rodriguez 1.50 .45
Rafael Palmeiro
TF46 Vladimir Guerrero 1.00 .30
J.T. Snow
TF47 Derek Jeter 2.50 .75
Eric Chavez
TF48 Bret Boone 1.50 .45
Ichiro Suzuki
TF49 Mike Piazza 1.50 .45
Bobby Abreu
TF50 Miguel Tejada 1.50 .45
Ichiro Suzuki
TF51 Juan Pierre 1.00 .30
Jim Thome
TF52 Kevin Millwood 1.00 .30
Jim Thome
TF53 Hank Blalock 1.00 .30
Jorge Posada
TF54 Deivi Cruz 1.00 .30
Hank Blalock
TF55 Rafael Furcal 1.00 .30
Ty Wigginton
TF56 Jim Thome 1.50 .45
Nomar Garciaparra
TF57 Craig Biggio 1.00 .30
Jason Giambi
TF58 Aaron Boone 1.00 .30
Jason Giambi
TF59 Jason Giambi 1.00 .30

Bernie Williams
TF60 Cristian Guzman 1.00 .30
Jody Gerut
TF61 Todd Helton 1.00 .30
Jose Reyes
TF62 Derek Jeter 2.50 .75
Hank Blalock
TF63 Mike Piazza 1.50 .45
Jimmy Rollins
TF64 Bernie Williams 2.50 .75
Derek Jeter
TF65 Andruw Jones 1.00 .30
Rafael Furcal
TF66 Mike Piazza 1.50 .45
Andruw Jones
TF67 Mike Piazza 1.50 .45
Cliff Floyd
TF68 Jason Kendall 2.00 .60
Albert Pujols
TF69 Nomar Garciaparra 1.50 .45
Manny Ramirez
TF70 Jorge Posada 1.50 .45
Alex Rodriguez
TF71 Derek Jeter 2.50 .75
Alex Rodriguez
TF72 Mike Sweeney 1.50 .45
Alex Rodriguez
TF73 Marquis Grissom 1.00 .30
Ivan Rodriguez
TF74 Jason Phillips 1.00 .30
Gary Sheffield
TF75 Chipper Jones 1.00 .30
Gary Sheffield
TF76 Junior Spivey 1.00 .30
Gary Sheffield
TF77 Al Leiter 1.50 .45
Ichiro Suzuki
TF78 Jose Vidro 1.00 .30
Jim Thome
TF79 Jimmy Rollins 1.00 .30
Paul Lo Duca
TF80 Alex Rodriguez 1.50 .45
Rafael Palmeiro
TF81 Albert Pujols 2.00 .60
Jim Edmonds
TF82 Eric Chavez 1.00 .30
Mike Sweeney
TF83 Cristian Guzman 1.00 .30
Jimmy Rollins
TF84 Alfonso Soriano 1.00 .30
Bernie Williams
TF85 Ichiro Suzuki 2.00 .60
Derek Jeter
TF86 Jimmy Rollins 1.00 .30
Derrek Lee
TF87 Shawn Green 1.00 .30
Paul Lo Duca
TF88 Carlos Delgado 1.00 .30
Jorge Posada
TF89 Dmitri Young 1.00 .30
C.C. Sabathia
TF90 Dontrelle Willis 1.00 .30
Shawn Chacon
TF91 Edgar Martinez 1.50 .45
Alex Rodriguez
TF92 Edgar Martinez 1.00 .30
Carlos Delgado
TF93 Edgar Martinez 1.00 .30
Esteban Loaiza
TF94 Roy Halladay 1.00 .30
C.C. Sabathia
TF95 Ichiro Suzuki 1.50 .45
Albert Pujols
TF96 Ichiro Suzuki 1.50 .45
Shigetoshi Hasegawa
TF97 Geoff Jenkins 1.00 .30
Aaron Boone
TF98 Nomar Garciaparra 1.50 .45
Alfonso Soriano
TF99 Jorge Posada 1.00 .30
Alfonso Soriano
TF100 Vernon Wells 1.00 .30
Garret Anderson

2003 Topps 205 Triple Folder Autographs

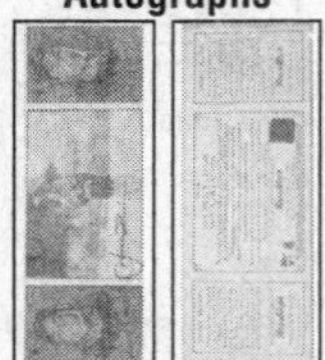

Nm-Mt Ex-Mt
SERIES 2 STATED ODDS 1:355 HOBBY
STATED PRINT RUN 205 SETS
CARDS ARE NOT SERIAL-NUMBERED
PRINT RUN PROVIDED BY TOPPS
DW Dontrelle Willis 50.00 15.00
JW Jerome Williams 40.00 12.00
RH Rich Harden 50.00 15.00
RW Ryan Wagner 50.00 15.00

2003 Topps 205 World Series Line-Ups

Nm-Mt Ex-Mt
SERIES 2 ODDS 1:27,440 PACKS
SERIES 2 ODDS 1:1960 MINI BOXES.
STATED PRINT RUN 1 SET
NO PRICING DUE TO SCARCITY
AL1 David Wells
AL2 Jorge Posada
AL3 Nick Johnson
AL4 Alfonso Soriano
AL5 Aaron Boone
AL6 Derek Jeter
AL7 Juan Rivera
AL8 Bernie Williams
AL9 Karim Garcia
AL10 Jason Giambi
NL1 Brad Penny
NL2 Ivan Rodriguez
NL3 Derrek Lee
NL4 Luis Castillo
NL5 Mike Lowell
NL6 Alex Gonzalez
NL7 Miguel Cabrera
NL8 Juan Pierre
NL9 Juan Encarnacion
NL10 Jeff Conine

2002 Topps 206

Issued in three separate series this 526-card set featured a mix of veterans, rookies and retired greats in the general style of the classic T-206 set issued more than 90 years prior. Series one consists of cards 1-180 and went live in February, 2002, series two consists of cards 181-307 - including 96 variations - and went live in early August, 2002 and series three consists of cards 308-456 - including 15 variations and a total of 55 short prints seeded at a rate of one per pack - and went live in January, 2003. Each pack contained eight cards with an SRP of $4. Packs were issued 20 per box and each case had 10 boxes. The following subsets were issued as part of the set: Prospects (131-140/261-270/399-418); First Year Players (141-155/271-285/419-432), Retired Stars (156-170/286-298/433-448) and Reprints (171-180/299-307/449-456). The First Year Player subset cards 141-155 and 277-285 were inserted at stated odds of one in two packs making them short-prints in comparison to other cards in the set. According to press release notes, Topps purchased more than 4,000 original Tobacco cards and also randomly inserted those in packs. They created a "holder" for these smaller cards inside the standard-size cards of the Topps 206 set. Stated pack odds for these "repurchased" Tobacco cards was 1:110 for series one, 1:179 for series two and 1:101 for series three.

Nm-Mt Ex-Mt
COMPLETE SET (525) 220.00 65.00
COMPLETE SERIES 1 (180) 60.00 18.00
COMPLETE SERIES 2 (180) 60.00 18.00
COMPLETE SERIES 3 (165) 100.00 30.00
COM(1-140/181-260/308-418) .50 .15
COMMON (141-155/271-285) .50 .15
COMMON RC (308-418) .50 .15
COMMON SP (308-398) 2.00 .60
COMMON FYP SP (1.00 .30
COMMON RET SP (433-447) 2.00 .60
1 Vladimir Guerrero 1.25 .35
2 Sammy Sosa 2.00 .60
3 Garret Anderson .50 .15
4 Rafael Palmeiro .75 .23
5 Juan Gonzalez .75 .23
6 John Smoltz .75 .23
7 Mark Mulder .50 .15
8 Jon Lieber .50 .15
9 Greg Maddux 2.00 .60
10 Moises Alou .50 .15
11 Joe Randa .50 .15
12 Bobby Abreu .50 .15
13 Juan Pierre .50 .15
14 Kerry Wood 1.25 .35
15 Craig Biggio .75 .23
16 Curt Schilling .50 .15
17 Brian Jordan .50 .15
18 Edgardo Alfonzo .50 .15
19 Darren Dreifort .50 .15
20 Todd Helton .75 .23
21 Ramon Ortiz .50 .15
22 Ichiro Suzuki 2.00 .60
23 Jimmy Rollins .50 .15
24 Darin Erstad .50 .15
25 Shawn Green .50 .15
26 Tino Martinez .75 .23
27 Bret Boone .50 .15
28 Alfonso Soriano .75 .23
29 Chan Ho Park .50 .15
30 Roger Clemens 2.50 .75
31 Cliff Floyd .50 .15
32 Johnny Damon .75 .23
33 Frank Thomas 1.25 .35
34 Barry Bonds 3.00 .90
35 Luis Gonzalez .50 .15
36 Carlos Lee .50 .15
37 Roberto Alomar .75 .23
38 Carlos Delgado .50 .15
39 Nomar Garciaparra 2.00 .60
40 Jason Kendall .50 .15
41 Scott Rolen 1.25 .35
42 Tom Glavine .75 .23
43 Ryan Klesko .50 .15
44 Brian Giles .50 .15
45 Bud Smith .50 .15
46 Charles Nagy .50 .15
47 Tony Gwynn 1.50 .45
48 C.C. Sabathia UER .50 .15
Credited with incorrect victory total in 2001
49 Frank Catalanotto .50 .15
50 Jerry Hairston .50 .15
51 Jeromy Burnitz .50 .15
52 David Justice .50 .15
53 Bartolo Colon .50 .15
54 Andres Galarraga .50 .15
55 Jeff Weaver .50 .15
56 Terrence Long .50 .15
57 Tsuyoshi Shinjo .50 .15
58 Barry Zito .50 .15
59 Mariano Rivera .75 .23
60 John Olerud .50 .15
61 Randy Johnson 1.25 .35
62 Kenny Lofton .50 .15
63 Jermaine Dye .50 .15
64 Troy Glaus .50 .15
65 Larry Walker .75 .23
66 Hideo Nomo 1.25 .35
67 Mike Mussina .75 .23
68 Paul LoDuca .50 .15
69 Magglio Ordonez .50 .15
70 Paul O'Neill .75 .23
71 Sean Casey .50 .15
72 Lance Berkman .50 .15
73 Adam Dunn .75 .23
74 Aramis Ramirez .50 .15
75 Rafael Furcal .50 .15
76 Gary Sheffield .50 .15
77 Todd Hollandsworth .50 .15
78 Chipper Jones 1.25 .35
79 Bernie Williams .75 .23
80 Richard Hidalgo .50 .15
81 Eric Chavez .50 .15
82 Mike Piazza 2.00 .60
83 J.D. Drew .50 .15
84 Ken Griffey Jr. 2.00 .60
85 Joe Kennedy .50 .15
86 Joel Pineiro .50 .15
87 Josh Towers .50 .15
88 Andruw Jones .50 .15
89 Carlos Beltran .75 .23
90 Mike Cameron .50 .15
91 Albert Pujols 2.50 .75
92 Alex Rodriguez 2.00 .60
93 Omar Vizquel .75 .23
94 Juan Encarnacion .50 .15
95 Jeff Bagwell .75 .23
96 Jose Canseco 1.25 .35
97 Ben Sheets .50 .15
98 Mark Grace .75 .23
99 Mike Sweeney .50 .15
100 Mark McGwire 3.00 .90
101 Ivan Rodriguez 1.25 .35
102 Rich Aurilia .50 .15
103 Cristian Guzman .50 .15
104 Roy Oswalt .50 .15
105 Tim Hudson .50 .15
106 Brent Abernathy .50 .15
107 Mike Hampton .50 .15
108 Miguel Tejada .50 .15
109 Bobby Higginson .50 .15
110 Edgar Martinez .75 .23
111 Jorge Posada .75 .23
112 Jason Giambi Yankees .50 .15
113 Pedro Astacio .50 .15
114 Kazuhiro Sasaki .50 .15
115 Preston Wilson .50 .15
116 Jason Bere .50 .15
117 Mark Quinn .50 .15
118 Pokey Reese .50 .15
119 Derek Jeter 3.00 .90
120 Shannon Stewart .50 .15
121 Jeff Kent .50 .15
122 Jeremy Giambi .50 .15
123 Pat Burrell .50 .15
124 Jim Edmonds .50 .15
125 Mark Buehrle .50 .15
126 Kevin Brown .50 .15
127 Raul Mondesi .50 .15
128 Pedro Martinez 1.25 .35
129 Jim Thome 1.25 .35
130 Russ Ortiz .50 .15
131 Br.Duckworth PROS .50 .15
132 Ryan Jamison PROS .50 .15
133 Brandon Inge PROS .50 .15
134 Felipe Lopez PROS .50 .15
135 Jason Lane PROS .50 .15
136 F.Johnson PROS RC .50 .15
137 Greg Nash PROS .50 .15
138 Covelli Crisp PROS .50 .15
139 Nick Neugebauer PROS .50 .15
140 Dustan Mohr PROS .50 .15
141 Freddy Sanchez FYP RC .50 .15
142 Justin Backsmeyer FYP RC .50 .15
143 Jorge Julio FYP .50 .15
144 Ryan Mottl FYP RC .50 .15
145 Chris Tritle FYP RC .50 .15
146 Noochie Varner FYP RC .50 .15
147 Brian Rogers FYP .50 .15
148 Michael Hill FYP RC .50 .15
149 Luis Pineda FYP .50 .15
150 Rich Thompson FYP RC .50 .15
151 Bill Hall FYP .50 .15
152 Juan Dominguez FYP RC 1.00 .30
153 Justin Woodrow FYP .50 .15
154 Nic Jackson FYP RC 1.00 .30
155 Laynce Nix FYP RC 3.00 .90
156 Hank Aaron RET 5.00 1.50
157 Ernie Banks RET 2.50 .75
158 Johnny Bench RET 2.50 .75
159 George Brett RET 6.00 1.80
160 Carlton Fisk RET 1.50 .45
161 Bob Gibson RET 1.50 .45
162 Reggie Jackson RET 1.50 .45
163 Don Mattingly RET 6.00 1.80
164 Kirby Puckett RET 2.50 .75
165 Frank Robinson RET 1.50 .45
166 Nolan Ryan RET 6.00 1.80
167 Tom Seaver RET 1.50 .45
168 Mike Schmidt RET 5.00 1.50
169 Dave Winfield RET 1.00 .30
170 Carl Yastrzemski RET 3.00 .90
171 Frank Chance REP 1.00 .30
172 Ty Cobb REP 5.00 1.50
173 Sam Crawford REP 1.00 .30
174 Johnny Evers REP 1.00 .30
175 John McGraw REP 2.50 .75
176 Eddie Plank REP 2.50 .75
177 Tris Speaker REP 2.50 .75
178 Joe Tinker REP 1.00 .30
179 H.Wagner Orange REP 8.00 2.40
180 Cy Young REP 2.50 .75
181 Javier Vazquez .50 .15
182A Mark Mulder Green Jsy .50 .15
182B Mark Mulder White Jsy .50 .15
183A R.Clemens Blue Jsy 2.50 .75
183B R.Clemens Pinstripes 2.50 .75
184 Kazuhisa Ishii RC 1.25 .35
185 Roberto Alomar .75 .23
186 Lance Berkman .50 .15
187A A.Dunn Arms Folded .75 .23
187B Adam Dunn w/Bat .75 .23
188A Aramis Ramirez w/Bat .50 .15
188B Aramis Ramirez w/o Bat .50 .15
189 Chuck Knoblauch .50 .15
190 Nomar Garciaparra 2.00 .60
191 Brad Penny .50 .15
192A Gary Sheffield w/Bat .50 .15
192B Gary Sheffield w/o Bat .50 .15
193 Alfonso Soriano .75 .23
194 Andruw Jones .50 .15
195A R.Johnson Black Jsy 1.25 .35
195B R.Johnson Purple Jsy 1.25 .35
196A C.Patterson Blue Jsy .50 .15
196B C.Patterson Pinstripes .50 .15
197 Milton Bradley .50 .15
198A J.Damon Blue Jsy/Cap 1.25 .35
198B J.Damon Blue Jsy/Hlmt 1.25 .35
198C J.Damon White Jsy 1.25 .35
199A Paul Lo Duca Blue Jsy .50 .15
199B Paul Lo Duca White Jsy .50 .15
200A Albert Pujols Red Jsy 2.50 .75
200B Albert Pujols Running 2.50 .75
200C Albert Pujols w/Bat 2.50 .75
201 Scott Rolen 1.25 .35
202A J.D. Drew Running .50 .15
202B J.D. Drew w/Bat .50 .15
202C J.D. Drew White Jsy .50 .15
203 Vladimir Guerrero 1.25 .35
204A Jason Giambi Blue Jsy .50 .15
204B Jason Giambi Grey Jsy .50 .15
204C Jason Giambi Pinstripes .50 .15
205A Moises Alou Grey Jsy .50 .15
205B Moises Alou Pinstripes .50 .15
206A Mag. Ordonez Signing .50 .15
206B Magglio Ordonez w/Bat .50 .15
207 Carlos Febles .50 .15
208 So Taguchi RC .75 .23
209A Raf. Palmeiro One Hand .75 .23
209B Raf. Palmeiro Two Hands .75 .23
210 David Wells .50 .15
211 Orlando Cabrera .50 .15
212 Sammy Sosa 2.00 .60
213 Armando Benitez .50 .15
214 Wes Helms .50 .15
215A Mar. Rivera Arms Folded .75 .23
215B Mar. Rivera Holding Ball .75 .23
216 Jimmy Rollins .50 .15
217 Matt Lawton .50 .15
218A Shawn Green w/Bat .50 .15
218B Shawn Green w/o Bat .50 .15
219A Bernie Williams w/Bat .75 .23
219B Bernie Williams w/o Bat .75 .23
220A Bret Boone Blue Jsy .50 .15
220B Bret Boone White Jsy .50 .15
221A Alex Rodriguez Blue Jsy 2.00 .60
221B Alex Rodriguez One Hand 2.00 .60
221C Alex Rodriguez Two Hands 2.00 .60
222 Roger Cedeno .50 .15
223 Marty Cordova .50 .15
224 Fred McGriff .75 .23
225A Chipper Jones Batting 1.25 .35
225B Chipper Jones Running 1.25 .35
226 Kerry Wood 1.25 .35
227A Larry Walker Grey Jsy .75 .23
227B Larry Walker Purple Jsy .75 .23
228 Robin Ventura .50 .15
229 Robert Fick .50 .15
230A Tino Martinez Black Glove .75 .23
230B Tino Martinez Throwing .75 .23
230C Tino Martinez w/Bat .75 .23
231 Ben Petrick .50 .15
232 Neifi Perez .50 .15
233 Pedro Martinez 1.25 .35
234A Brian Jordan Grey Jsy .50 .15
234B Brian Jordan White Jsy .50 .15
235 Freddy Garcia .50 .15
236A Derek Jeter Batting 3.00 .90
236B Derek Jeter Blue Jsy 3.00 .90
236C Derek Jeter Kneeling 3.00 .90
237 Ben Grieve .50 .15
238A Barry Bonds Black Jsy 3.00 .90
238B B.Bonds w/Wrist Band 3.00 .90
238C B.Bonds w/o Wrist Band 3.00 .90
239 Luis Gonzalez .50 .15
240 Shane Halter .50 .15
241A Brian Giles Black Jsy .50 .15
241B Brian Giles Grey Jsy .50 .15
242 Bud Smith .50 .15
243 Richie Sexson .50 .15
244A Barry Zito Green Jsy .50 .15
244B Barry Zito White Jsy .50 .15
245 Eric Milton .50 .15
246A Ivan Rodriguez Blue Jsy 1.25 .35
246B I.Rodriguez Grey Jsy 1.25 .35
246C I.Rodriguez White Jsy 1.25 .35
247 Toby Hall .50 .15
248A Mike Piazza Black Jsy 2.00 .60
248B Mike Piazza Grey Jsy 2.00 .60
249 Ruben Sierra .50 .15
250A Tsuyoshi Shinjo Cap .50 .15
250B Tsuyoshi Shinjo Helmet .50 .15
251A Jer. Dye Green Jsy .50 .15
251B Jermaine Dye White Jsy .50 .15
252 Roy Oswalt .50 .15
253 Todd Helton .75 .23
254 Adrian Beltre .75 .23
255 Doug Mientkiewicz .50 .15
256A Ichiro Suzuki Blue Jsy 2.00 .60
256B Ichiro Suzuki w/Bat 2.00 .60
256C Ichiro Suzuki White Jsy 2.00 .60
257A C.C. Sabathia Blue Jsy .50 .15
257B C.C. Sabathia White Jsy .50 .15
258 Paul Konerko .50 .15
259 Ken Griffey Jr. 2.00 .60
260A Jeromy Burnitz w/Bat .50 .15
260B Jeromy Burnitz w/o Bat .50 .15
261 Hank Blalock PROS 1.25 .35
262 Mark Prior PROS 2.00 .60
263 Josh Beckett PROS .50 .15
264 Carlos Pena PROS .50 .15
265 Sean Burroughs PROS .50 .15
266 Austin Kearns PROS .50 .15
267 Chin-Hui Tsao PROS .50 .15
268 Dewon Brazelton PROS .50 .15
269 J.D. Martin PROS .50 .15
270 Marlon Byrd PROS .50 .15
271 Joe Mauer FYP RC 5.00 1.50
272 Jason Botts FYP RC .75 .23
273 Mauricio Lara FYP RC .50 .15
274 Jonny Gomes FYP RC .75 .23
275 Gavin Floyd FYP RC 2.50 .75
276 Alex Requena FYP RC .50 .15
277 Jimmy Gobble FYP RC .75 .23
278 Chris Duffy FYP RC .50 .15
279 Colt Griffin FYP RC .75 .23
280 Ryan Church FYP RC .75 .23
281 Beltran Perez FYP RC .50 .15
282 Clint Nageotte FYP RC 1.25 .35
283 Justin Schuda FYP RC .50 .15
284 Scott Hairston FYP RC 1.50 .45
285 Mario Ramos FYP RC .50 .15
286 Tom Seaver White Sox RET 1.50 .45
286 Tom Seaver Mets RET 1.50 .45
287 H.Aaron White Jsy RET 5.00 1.50
287 H.Aaron Blue Jsy RET 5.00 1.50
288 Mike Schmidt RET 5.00 1.50
289A R.Yount Blue Jsy RET 4.00 1.20
289B R.Yount P'stripes RET 4.00 1.20
290 Joe Morgan RET 1.00 .30
291 Frank Robinson RET 1.50 .45
292A Reggie Jackson A's RET 1.50 .45
292B Reggie Jackson Yanks RET 1.50 .45
293A Nolan Ryan Astros RET 6.00 1.80
293B N.Ryan Rangers RET 6.00 1.80
294 Dave Winfield RET 1.00 .30
295 Willie Mays RET 5.00 1.50
296 Brooks Robinson RET 1.50 .45
297A Mark McGwire A's RET 6.00 1.80
297B M.McGwire Cards RET 6.00 1.80
298 Honus Wagner RET 2.50 .75
299A Sherry Magee REP 1.00 .30
299B Sherry Magie UER REP 1.00 .30
300 Frank Chance REP 1.00 .30
301A Joe Doyle NY REP 1.00 .30
301B Joe Doyle NY Nat'l REP 1.00 .30
302 John McGraw REP 2.50 .75
303 Jimmy Collins REP 1.00 .30
304 Buck Herzog REP 1.00 .30
305 Sam Crawford REP 1.00 .30
306 Cy Young REP 2.50 .75
307 Honus Wagner Blue REP 8.00 2.40
308A A.Rodriguez Blue Jsy SP 4.00 1.20
308B A.Rodriguez White Jsy 2.00 .60
309 Vernon Wells .50 .15
310A B.Bonds w/Elbow Pad 3.00 .90
310B B.Bonds w/o Elbow Pad SP 6.00 1.80
311 Vicente Padilla .50 .15
312A A.Soriano w/Wristband .75 .23
312B A.Soriano w/o Wristband SP 2.00 .60
313 Mike Piazza 2.00 .60
314 Jacque Jones .50 .15
315 Shawn Green SP 2.00 .60
316 Paul Byrd .50 .15
317 Lance Berkman .50 .15
318 Larry Walker .75 .23
319 Ken Griffey Jr. SP 4.00 1.20
320 Shea Hillenbrand .50 .15
321 Jay Gibbons .50 .15
322 Andruw Jones .50 .15
323 Luis Gonzalez SP 2.00 .60
324 Garret Anderson .50 .15
325 Roy Halladay .50 .15
326 Randy Winn .50 .15
327 Matt Morris .50 .15
328 Robb Nen .50 .15
329 Trevor Hoffman .50 .15
330 Kip Wells .50 .15
331 Orlando Hernandez .50 .15
332 Rey Ordonez .50 .15
333 Torii Hunter .50 .15
334 Geoff Jenkins .50 .15
335 Eric Karros .50 .15
336 Mike Lowell .50 .15
337 Nick Johnson .50 .15
338 Randall Simon .50 .15
339 Ellis Burks .50 .15
340A S.Sosa Blue Jsy SP 4.00 1.20
340B Sammy Sosa White Jsy 2.00 .60
341 Pedro Martinez 1.25 .35
342 Junior Spivey .50 .15
343 Vinny Castilla .50 .15
344 Randy Johnson SP 2.50 .75
345 Chipper Jones SP 2.50 .75
346 Orlando Hudson .50 .15
347 Albert Pujols SP 5.00 1.50
348 Rondell White .50 .15
349 Vladimir Guerrero 1.25 .35
350A Mark Prior Red SP 4.00 1.20
350B Mark Prior Yellow 2.00 .60
351 Eric Gagne 1.25 .35
352 Todd Zeile .50 .15
353 Manny Ramirez SP 2.00 .60
354 Kevin Millwood .50 .15
355 Troy Percival .50 .15
356A Jason Giambi Batting SP 2.00 .60
356B Jason Giambi Throwing .50 .15
357 Bartolo Colon .50 .15
358 Jeremy Giambi .50 .15
359 Jose Cruz Jr. .50 .15
360A I.Suzuki Blue Jsy SP 4.00 1.20
360B I.Suzuki White Jsy 2.00 .60
361 Eddie Guardado .50 .15
362 Ivan Rodriguez 1.25 .35
363 Carl Crawford .50 .15
364 Jason Simontacchi RC .50 .15
365 Kenny Lofton .50 .15
366 Raul Mondesi .50 .15
367 A.J. Pierzynski .50 .15
368 Ugueth Urbina .50 .15
369 Rodrigo Lopez .50 .15
370A N.Garciaparra One Bat SP 4.00 1.20
370B N.Garciaparra Two Bats 2.00 .60
371 Craig Counsell .50 .15
372 Barry Larkin .75 .23
373 Carlos Pena .50 .15
374 Luis Castillo .50 .15
375 Raul Ibanez .50 .15
376 Kazuhisa Ishii SP 2.50 .75
377 Derek Lowe .50 .15
378 Curt Schilling .50 .15
379 Jim Thome Phillies 1.25 .35
380A Derek Jeter Blue SP 6.00 1.80
380B Derek Jeter Seats 3.00 .90
381 Pat Burrell .50 .15
382 Jamie Moyer .50 .15
383 Eric Hinske .50 .15
384 Scott Rolen 1.25 .35
385 Miguel Tejada SP 2.00 .60
386 Andy Pettitte .75 .23
387 Mike Lieberthal .50 .15
388 Al Leiter .50 .15
389 Todd Helton SP 2.00 .60
390A Adam Dunn Bat SP 2.00 .60
390B Adam Dunn Glove .75 .23
391 Cliff Floyd .50 .15

392 Tim Salmon .75 .23
393 Joe Torre MG .75 .23
394 Bobby Cox MG .50 .15
395 Tony LaRussa MG .50 .15
396 Art Howe MG .50 .15
397 Bob Brenly MG .50 .15
398 Ron Gardenhire MG .50 .15
399 Mike Cuddyer PROS .50 .15
400 Joe Mauer PROS 5.00 1.50
401 Mark Teixeira PROS .75 .23
402 Hee Seop Choi PROS .50 .15
403 Angel Berroa PROS .50 .15
404 Jesse Foppert PROS RC 1.00 .30
405 Bobby Crosby PROS 1.25 .35
406 Jose Reyes PROS .75 .23
407 C.Kotchman PROS RC 3.00 .90
408 Aaron Heilman PROS .50 .15
409 Adrian Gonzalez PROS .50 .15
410 Delwyn Young PROS RC 1.25 .35
411 Brett Myers PROS .50 .15
412 Justin Huber PROS RC .75 .23
413 Drew Henson PROS .50 .15
414 T.Bozied PROS RC .75 .23
415 Dontrelle Willis PROS RC 3.00 .90
416 Rocco Baldelli PROS .50 .15
417 Jason Stokes PROS RC 3.00 .90
418 Brandon Phillips PROS .50 .15
419 Jake Blalock FYP RC 1.50 .45
420 Micah Schilling FYP RC 1.00 .30
421 Denard Span FYP RC 1.00 .30
422A J.Loney Red FYP RC 2.00 .60
422B J.Loney w/Sky FYP RC 2.00 .60
423A W.Bankston Blue FYP RC 1.25 .35
423B W.Bankston w/Sky FYP RC 1.25 .35
424 Jeremy Hermida FYP RC 2.00 .60
425 C.Granderson FYP RC 1.50 .45
426A J.Pridie Red FYP RC 1.00 .30
426B J.Pridie w/Sky FYP RC 1.00 .30
427 Larry Broadway FYP RC 1.00 .30
428A K.Greene Green FYP RC 10.00 3.00
428B K.Greene Red FYP RC 10.00 3.00
429 Joey Votto FYP RC 1.25 .35
430A B.Upton Grey FYP RC 8.00 2.40
430B B.Upton w/People FYP RC 8.00 2.40
431A S.Santos Gold FYP RC 2.00 .60
431B S.Santos Grey FYP RC 2.00 .60
432 Brian Dopirak FYP RC 3.00 .90
433 Ozzie Smith RET SP 4.00 1.20
434 Wade Boggs RET SP 2.50 .75
435 Yogi Berra RET SP 4.00 1.20
436 Al Kaline RET SP 4.00 1.20
437 Robin Roberts RET SP 2.00 .60
438 Rob. Clemente RET SP 8.00 2.40
439 Gary Carter RET SP 2.00 .60
440 Fergie Jenkins RET SP 2.00 .60
441 Orlando Cepeda RET SP 2.00 .60
442 Rod Carew RET SP 2.50 .75
443 Ha. Killebrew RET SP 4.00 1.20
444 Duke Snider RET SP 2.50 .75
445 Stan Musial RET SP 6.00 1.80
446 Hank Greenberg RET SP 4.00 1.20
447 Lou Brock RET SP 2.50 .75
448 Jim Palmer RET 1.00 .30
449 John McGraw REP 1.00 .30
450 Mordecai Brown REP 1.00 .30
451 Christy Mathewson REP 1.50 .45
452 Sam Crawford REP 1.00 .30
453 Bill O'Hara REP 1.00 .30
454 Joe Tinker REP 1.00 .30
455 Nap Lajoie REP 1.50 .45
456 Honus Wagner Red REP 8.00 2.40
NNO Repurchased Tobacco Card

2002 Topps 206 American Beauty

Inserted into third series packs as a stated rate of one in 15,316 these five cards were issued with the very scarce American Beauty back. These cards were issued to a stated print run of five sets so no pricing is provided due to scarcity.

Nm-Mt Ex-Mt
308 A.Rodriguez White Jsy
310 B.Bonds w/Elbow Pad
312 A.Soriano w/Wristband
370 N.Garciaparra Two Bats
456 Honus Wagner Red REP

2002 Topps 206 Bazooka

This quasi-parallel skip-numbered set was inserted at stated odds of one 1185 first series packs, one in 1989 second series packs and one in 825 third series packs. Though the cards are not serial-numbered in any manner, officials at Topps did publicly release a statement verifying that only 30 copies of each card were produced. This set was limited to 15 key players from each series of the 206 set making the set complete at 45 cards. These cards feature a "Bazooka" back, which is the only back on these parallel cards which was not a tobacco producer during the original tobacco card era. Due to market scarcity, no pricing is currently provided.

Nm-Mt Ex-Mt
22 Ichiro Suzuki Portrait
23 Jimmy Rollins
34 Barry Bonds
47 Tony Gwynn
57 Tsuyoshi Shinjo
73 Adam Dunn
91 Albert Pujols
100 Mark McGwire
104 Roy Oswalt
112 Jason Giambi Yankees
119 Derek Jeter
131 Brandon Duckworth PROS
154 Nic Jackson FYP
166 Nolan Ryan RET
172 Ty Cobb REP
185 Roberto Alomar
190 Nomar Garciaparra
203 Vladimir Guerrero
212 Sammy Sosa
221B A.Rodriguez One Hand
233 Pedro Martinez
244B Barry Zito White Jsy
248A Mike Piazza Black Jsy
253 Todd Helton
259 Ken Griffey Jr.
262 Mark Prior Blue PROS
271 Joe Mauer FYP
288 Mike Schmidt RET
306 Cy Young REP
307 Honus Wagner Blue REP
308 A.Rodriguez White Jsy
310 B.Bonds w/Elbow Pad
312 A.Soriano w/Wristband
315 Shawn Green
337 Nick Johnson
350 Mark Prior Yellow
360 Ichiro Suzuki White Jsy
381 Pat Burrell
385 Miguel Tejada
393 Joe Torre MG
413 Drew Henson PROS
430 B.J. Upton Grey FYP
438 Roberto Clemente RET
454 Joe Tinker REP
456 Honus Wagner Red REP

2002 Topps 206 Carolina Brights

Randomly inserted in second series packs and using the "Carolina Brights" backs, these cards parallel the Topps 206 second series cards.

Nm-Mt Ex-Mt
*CAROLINA 181-270: 3X TO 8X BASIC
*CAROLINA RC's 181-270: 1X TO 2.5X
*CAROLINA 271-285: 1.25X TO 3X BASIC
*CAROLINA 286-307: 2X TO 5X BASIC

2002 Topps 206 Cycle

Randomly inserted in first series packs and using the "Cycle" backs, this is a complete parallel of the Topps 206 first series.

Nm-Mt Ex-Mt
*CYCLE 1-140: 5X TO 12X BASIC CARDS
*CYCLE 141-155: 1.25X TO 3X BASIC
*CYCLE 156-180: 3X TO 8X BASIC

2002 Topps 206 Drum

Issued at a stated rate of one in 3711 third series packs, these five cards feature "Drum" backs. These cards have a stated print run of 20 sets and no pricing is provided due to market scarcity.

Nm-Mt Ex-Mt
324 Garret Anderson
356 Jason Giambi Batting
360 I.Suzuki White Jsy
390 Adam Dunn Glove
400 Joe Mauer PROS

2002 Topps 206 Lenox

Issued at a stated rate of one in 7422 third series packs, these five cards feature "Lenox" backs. These cards have a stated print run of 10 sets and no pricing is provided due to market scarcity.

Nm-Mt Ex-Mt
308 A.Rodriguez Blue Jsy
340 Sammy Sosa White Jsy
349 Vladimir Guerrero
353 Manny Ramirez
416 Rocco Baldelli PROS

2002 Topps 206 Piedmont Black

Randomly inserted in second series packs and using the "Piedmont" backs, these cards parallel the Topps 206 second series cards. The words on the back are in black ink and thus these cards are called Piedmont Black

Nm-Mt Ex-Mt
*P'MONT.BLACK 181-270: 1.5X TO 4X BASIC
*P'MONT.BLACK RC's 181-270: .5X TO 1.2X
*P'MONT.BLACK 271-285: .6X TO 1.5X
*P'MONT.BLACK 286-307: 1X TO 2.5X

2002 Topps 206 Piedmont Red

Randomly inserted in second series packs and using the "Piedmont" backs, these cards parallel the Topps 206 second series cards. The words on the back are in black ink and thus these cards are called Piedmont Red.

Nm-Mt Ex-Mt
*P'MONT.RED 181-270: 3X TO 8X BASIC
*P'MONT.RED RC's 181-270: 1X TO 2.5X
*P'MONT.RED 271-285: 1.25X TO 3X
*P'MONT.RED 286-307: 2X TO 5X BASIC

2002 Topps 206 Polar Bear

Randomly inserted into approximately two out of every three packs and using the "Polar Bear" backs, this is a complete parallel of the Topps 206 set. Cards 1-180 were distributed in first series packs, 181-307 in second series packs and 308-456 in third series packs. The set is actually complete at 525 cards, but the checklist runs from 1-307 with 96 variations intermingled within.

Nm-Mt Ex-Mt
*POLAR 1-140/181-270/308-418: 1.25X TO 3X
*RC 1-140/181-270/308-418: .5X TO 1.2X
*FYP 141-155/271-285: .5X TO 1.2X
*SP 308-418: .6X TO 1.5X SP
*FYP 419-432: .5X TO 1.2X
*RT/RP 156-180/286-307/448-456: .75X TO 2X
*RET 443-447: .75X TO 2X

2002 Topps 206 Sweet Caporal Black

Randomly inserted into packs, this is a parallel to the T206 third series. These cards have the words "Sweet Caporal" in black on the back.

Nm-Mt Ex-Mt
*BLACK 308-418: 2.5X TO 6X BASIC
*BLACK SP 308-418: 1.25X TO 3X BASIC
*BLACK RC 308-418: 1X TO 2.5X BASIC
*BLACK 419-432: 1.25X TO 3X BASIC
*BLACK 433-447: .75X TO 2X BASIC
*BLACK 448-456: 1.5X TO 4X BASIC

2002 Topps 206 Sweet Caporal Blue

Randomly inserted into packs, this is a parallel to the T206 third series. These cards have the words "Sweet Caporal" in blue on the back.

Nm-Mt Ex-Mt
*BLUE 308-418: 2X TO 5X BASIC
*BLUE SP 308-418: 1X TO 2.5X BASIC
*BLUE RC 308-418: .75X TO 2X BASIC
*BLUE 419-432: 1X TO 2.5X BASIC
*BLUE 433-447: .6X TO 1.5X BASIC
*BLUE 448-456: 1.25X TO 3X BASIC

2002 Topps 206 Sweet Caporal Red

Randomly inserted into packs, this is a parallel to the T206 third series. These cards have the words "Sweet Caporal" in blue on the back.

Nm-Mt Ex-Mt
*RED 308-418: 1.5X TO 4X BASIC
*RED SP 308-418: .75X TO 2X BASIC
*RED RC 308-418: .6X TO 1.5X BASIC
*RED 419-432: .75X TO 2X BASIC
*RED 433-447: .5X TO 1.2X BASIC
*RED 448-456: 1X TO 2.5X BASIC

2002 Topps 206 Tolstoi

Randomly inserted in first series packs and using the "Tolstoi" backs, this is a complete parallel of the Topps 206 first series.

Nm-Mt Ex-Mt
*TOLSTOI 1-140: 1.5X TO 4X BASIC
*TOLSTOI 141-155: .4X TO 1X BASIC
*TOLSTOI 156-180: 1X TO 2.5X BASIC

2002 Topps 206 Tolstoi Red

Randomly inserted in packs and using the "Tolstoi" backs, this is a complete parallel of the Topps 206 first series. These cards are differentiated from the more common Tolstoi backs as the color on the back is red. These cards were printed at a stated rate of 25 percent of the total Tolstoi run.

Nm-Mt Ex-Mt
*TOLSTOI RED 1-140: 3X TO 8X BASIC
*TOLSTOI RED 141-155: .6X TO 1.5X BASIC
*TOLSTOI RED 156-180: 2X TO 5X BASIC

2002 Topps 206 Uzit

Randomly inserted into packs, this is a parallel to the T206 third series. These cards have "Uzit" on the back.

Nm-Mt Ex-Mt
*UZIT 308-418: 3X TO 8X BASIC
*UZIT SP 308-418: 1.5X TO 4X BASIC
*UZIT RC 308-418: 1.5X TO 4X BASIC
*UZIT 419-432: 1.5X TO 4X BASIC
*UZIT 433-447: 1X TO 2.5X BASIC
*UZIT 448-456: 2X TO 5X BASIC

2002 Topps 206 Autographs

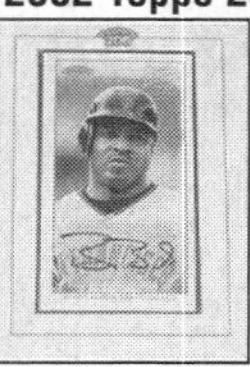

Inserted at an overall stated rate of one in 41 series one packs, one in 55 series two packs and varying group specific odds in series three packs (see details below), these cards feature a mix of young players and veteran stars who autographed cards for the T206 product.

Nm-Mt Ex-Mt
SER.1 GROUP A1 ODDS 1:1067
SER.1 GROUP B1 ODDS 1:1122
SER.1 GROUP C1 ODDS 1:532
SER.1 GROUP D1 ODDS 1:444
SER.1 GROUP E1 ODDS 1:532
SER.1 GROUP F1 ODDS 1:121
SER.1 GROUP G1 ODDS 1:118
SER.2 GROUP A2 ODDS 1:511
SER.2 GROUP B2 ODDS 1:893
SER.2 GROUP C2 ODDS 1:1557
SER.2 GROUP D2 ODDS 1:106
SER.2 GROUP E2 ODDS 1:638
SER.2 GROUP F2 ODDS 1:596
SER.2 GROUP G2 ODDS 1:526
SER.3 GROUP A3 ODDS 1:810
SER.3 GROUP B3 ODDS 1:442
SER.3 GROUP C3 ODDS 1:411
SER.3 GROUP D3 ODDS 1:393
SER.3 GROUP E3 ODDS 1:393
SER.3 GROUP F3 ODDS 1:384
SER.3 GROUP G3 ODDS 1:383
AP Albert Pujols A2 175.00 52.50
AR Alex Rodriguez A1 150.00 45.00
BB Barry Bonds A1 300.00 90.00
BG Brian Giles G1 15.00 4.50
BI Brandon Inge D1 15.00 4.50
BS Ben Sheets E2 15.00 4.50
BSM Bud Smith B2 15.00 4.50
BZ Barry Zito D1 30.00 9.00
CG Cristian Guzman G1 10.00 3.00
CT Chris Tritle G2 15.00 4.50
DB Dewon Brazelton D2 10.00 3.00
DE David Eckstein G3 10.00 3.00
DH Drew Henson D3 20.00 6.00
EC Eric Chavez A2 30.00 9.00
FJ Forrest Johnson F1 10.00 3.00
FL Felipe Lopez C1 15.00 4.50
GF Gavin Floyd D2 25.00 7.50
GN Greg Nash F1 10.00 3.00
HB Hank Blalock D2 25.00 7.50
JC Jose Cruz Jr. A3 15.00 4.50
JD Johnny Damon Sox B2 40.00 12.00
JDM J.D. Martin D2 10.00 3.00
JE Jim Edmonds C1 40.00 12.00
JJ Jorge Julio F1 10.00 3.00
JM Joe Mauer D2 50.00 15.00
JR Jimmy Rollins G1 15.00 4.50
JV Jose Vidro B3 10.00 3.00
KI Kazuhisa Ishii A2 50.00 15.00
LB Lance Berkman A2 40.00 12.00
LG Luis Gonzalez C2 25.00 7.50
MA Moises Alou A2 15.00 4.50
MB Milton Bradley C3 15.00 4.50
MB Marlon Byrd D2 10.00 3.00
ML Mike Lamb F3 10.00 3.00
MO Magglio Ordonez E1 20.00 6.00
MP Mark Prior D2 60.00 18.00
MT Marcus Thames E3 10.00 3.00
RC Roger Clemens B1 150.00 45.00
RJ Ryan Jamison F1 10.00 3.00
RS Richie Sexson F2 15.00 4.50
SR Scott Rolen A2 50.00 15.00
ST So Taguchi A2 40.00 12.00

2002 Topps 206 Relics

Issued in first series packs at overall stated odds of one in 11 and second series packs at overall stated odds of one in 12 and third series packs at various odds, these 109 cards feature either a bat sliver or a jersey/uniform swatch. Representatives at Topps announced that only 25 copies of the Honus Wagner blue Bat and Honus Wagner Red Bat and 100 copies of the Ty Cobb Bat card (both seeded into second series packs) were produced. Please note, all first series Relics feature light yellow frames (surrounding the mini-sized card), all second series Relics feature light blue frames and third series Relics feature light pink frames.

Nm-Mt Ex-Mt
SER.1 BAT GROUP A1 ODDS 1:166
SER.1 BAT GROUP B1 ODDS 1:1780
SER.2 BAT GROUP A2 ODDS 1:35,217
SER.2 BAT GROUP B2 ODDS 1:8991
SER.2 BAT GROUP C2 ODDS 1:2097
SER.2 BAT GROUP D2 ODDS 1:75
SER.2 BAT GROUP E2 ODDS 1:1377
SER.2 BAT GROUP F2 ODDS 1:893
SER.2 BAT GROUP G2 ODDS 1:248
SER.2 BAT GROUP H2 ODDS 1:319
SER.2 BAT GROUP I2 ODDS 1:447
SER.2 BAT OVERALL ODDS 1:40
SER.3 BAT GROUP A3 ODDS 1:15,316
SER.3 BAT GROUP B3 ODDS 1:390
SER.3 BAT GROUP C3 ODDS 1:370
SER.3 BAT GROUP D3 ODDS 1:34
SER.3 BAT GROUP E3 ODDS 1:187
SER.3 BAT GROUP F3 ODDS 1:185
SER.1 UNI GROUP A1 ODDS 1:14
SER.1 UNI GROUP B1 ODDS 1:74
SER.2 UNI GROUP A2 ODDS 1:372
SER.2 UNI GROUP B2 ODDS 1:27
SER.2 UNI GROUP C2 ODDS 1:62
SER.2 UNI GROUP D2 ODDS 1:447
SER.2 UNI OVERALL ODDS 1:18
SER.3 UNI GROUP A3 ODDS 1:247
SER.3 UNI GROUP B3 ODDS 1:185
SER.3 UNI GROUP C3 ODDS 1:62
SER.3 UNI GROUP D3 ODDS 1:187
SER.3 UNI GROUP E3 ODDS 1:27
SER.3 UNI GROUP F3 ODDS 1:176
AB A.J. Burnett Jsy B2 8.00 2.40
AD2 Adam Dunn Bat D2 15.00 4.50
AD3 Adam Dunn Bat C3 15.00 4.50
AJ1 Andruw Jones Jsy A1 8.00 2.40
AJ2 Andruw Jones Jsy C2 8.00 2.40
AJ3 Andruw Jones Uni E3 8.00 2.40
AP1 Albert Pujols Bat A1 20.00 6.00
AP2 Albert Pujols Jsy B2 20.00 6.00
AP3 Albert Pujols Bat D3 20.00 6.00
ARA Aramis Ramirez Bat D2 15.00 4.50
AR2 Alex Rodriguez Bat D2 20.00 6.00
AR3 Alex Rodriguez Bat D3 15.00 4.50
AS1 Alfonso Soriano Bat A1 15.00 4.50
AS2 Alfonso Soriano Bat I2 10.00 3.00
AS3 Alfonso Soriano Bat D3 10.00 3.00
BB1 Barry Bonds Jsy A1 25.00 7.50
BB2 Barry Bonds Uni C2 25.00 7.50
BD Brandon Duckworth Jsy B2 8.00 2.40
BH Buck Herzog Bat G2 40.00 12.00
BL Barry Larkin Jsy B2 10.00 3.00
BP Brad Penny Jsy B2 8.00 2.40
BW1 Bernie Williams Jsy A1 10.00 3.00
BW2 Bernie Williams Jsy B2 10.00 3.00
BW3 Bernie Williams Uni A3 15.00 4.50
BZ1 Barry Zito Jsy A1 8.00 2.40
BZ3 Barry Zito Uni C3 8.00 2.40
CB Craig Biggio Jsy B1 10.00 3.00
CD Carlos Delgado Jsy A1 8.00 2.40
CF1 Cliff Floyd Jsy A1 8.00 2.40
CF2 Cliff Floyd Jsy B2 8.00 2.40
CG Cristian Guzman Jsy B2 8.00 2.40
CJ1 Chipper Jones Jsy A1 15.00 4.50
CJ2 Chipper Jones Jsy B2 15.00 4.50
CJ3 Chipper Jones Uni B3 15.00 4.50
CL Carlos Lee Jsy A1 8.00 2.40
CP Corey Patterson Bat F3 8.00 2.40
CS2 Curt Schilling Bat D2 15.00 4.50
CS3 Curt Schilling Bat D3 8.00 2.40
DE Darin Erstad Jsy B2 8.00 2.40
DM Doug Mientkiewicz Uni D3 8.00 2.40
EC2 Eric Chavez Bat H2 8.00 2.40
EC3 Eric Chavez Uni E3 8.00 2.40
EM1 Edgar Martinez Jsy A1 10.00 3.00
EM2 Edgar Martinez Jsy B2 10.00 3.00
FM Fred McGriff Bat D2 15.00 4.50
FT1 Frank Thomas Jsy A1 15.00 4.50
FT2 Frank Thomas Jsy B2 15.00 4.50
FT3 Frank Thomas Uni C3 15.00 4.50
GM1 Greg Maddux Jsy A1 15.00 4.50
GM2 Greg Maddux Jsy C2 15.00 4.50
GS2 Gary Sheffield Bat D2 15.00 4.50
GS3 Gary Sheffield Bat B3 15.00 4.50
HW1 H.Wag Orange Bat B1 400.00 120.00
HW2 H.Wagner Blue Bat A2 SP/25
HW3 H.Wagner Red Bat A3 SP/25
IR1 Ivan Rodriguez Jsy A1 15.00 4.50
IR2 Ivan Rodriguez Uni A2 15.00 4.50
IR3 Ivan Rodriguez Bat D3 15.00 4.50
JB1 Jeff Bagwell Jsy A1 10.00 3.00
JB2 Jeff Bagwell Uni C2 10.00 3.00
JB3 Jeff Bagwell Bat D3 10.00 3.00
JD J.Damon Sox Bat D2 20.00 6.00
JE1 Jim Edmonds Jsy A1 8.00 2.40
JE3 Jim Edmonds Uni F3 8.00 2.40
JG Juan Gonzalez Bat D2 15.00 4.50
JH Josh Hamilton Bat D2 10.00 3.00
JJ Jason Jennings Jsy B2 8.00 2.40
JK Jeff Kent Uni B2 8.00 2.40
JO1 John Olerud Jsy A1 8.00 2.40
JO2 John Olerud Jsy B2 8.00 2.40
JT Joe Tinker Bat G2 60.00 18.00
JW Jeff Weaver Jsy A1 8.00 2.40
KB Kevin Brown Jsy B2 8.00 2.40
KL Kenny Lofton Jsy B1 8.00 2.40
LG Luis Gonzalez Uni E3 8.00 2.40
LW1 Larry Walker Jsy A1 10.00 3.00
LW2 Larry Walker Jsy B2 10.00 3.00
MC Mike Cameron Jsy A1 8.00 2.40
MG Mark Grace Bat D2 15.00 4.50
MO Magglio Ordonez Jsy A1 8.00 2.40
MP1 Mike Piazza Jsy A1 15.00 4.50
MP2 Mike Piazza Uni C2 15.00 4.50
MP3 Mike Piazza Uni C3 15.00 4.50
MT2 Miguel Tejada Bat H2 8.00 2.40
MT3 Miguel Tejada Uni E3 8.00 2.40
MV2 Mo Vaughn Bat D2 15.00 4.50
MV3 Mo Vaughn Uni E3 8.00 2.40
MW Matt Williams Jsy B2 8.00 2.40
NG Nomar Garciaparra Bat C3 20.00 6.00
NJ Nick Johnson Bat E3 8.00 2.40
PB Pat Burrell Bat B3 15.00 4.50
PM Pedro Martinez Uni A3 20.00 6.00
PO Paul O'Neill Jsy A1 10.00 3.00
PW Preston Wilson Jsy B2 10.00 3.00
RA1 Roberto Alomar Jsy A1 10.00 3.00
RA2 Roberto Alomar Bat D2 15.00 4.50
RA3 Roberto Alomar Bat D3 10.00 3.00
RD Ryan Dempster Jsy B2 8.00 2.40
RH2 Rickey Henderson Bat D2 20.00 6.00
RH3 Rickey Henderson Bat D3 15.00 4.50
RJ1 Randy Johnson Jsy A1 15.00 4.50
RJ2 Randy Johnson Jsy C2 15.00 4.50
RJ3 Randy Johnson Uni A3 20.00 6.00
RP2 Rafael Palmeiro Jsy B2 10.00 3.00
RP3 Rafael Palmeiro Uni B3 10.00 3.00
RV Robin Ventura Bat D2 15.00 4.50
SB Sean Burroughs Bat D2 15.00 4.50
SC Sam Crawford Bat A1 60.00 18.00
SCR Sam Crawford Bat C2 60.00 18.00
SG1 Shawn Green Jsy A1 8.00 2.40
SG2 Shawn Green Jsy C2 8.00 2.40
SR Scott Rolen Bat D3 15.00 4.50
SS Shannon Stewart Bat A1 15.00 4.50
TC Ty Cobb Bat B2 SP/100 500.00 150.00
TL Travis Lee Bat D2 10.00 3.00
TM1 Tino Martinez Jsy A1 10.00 3.00
TM2 Tino Martinez Bat D2 15.00 4.50
WB Wilson Betemit Bat D3 8.00 2.40
BBO1 Bret Boone Jsy B1 8.00 2.40
BBO2 Bret Boone Jsy D2 8.00 2.40
CHP Chan Ho Park Bat A1 15.00 4.50
JCA Jose Canseco Bat A1 20.00 6.00
JCO Jimmy Collins Bat F2 60.00 18.00
JEV1 Johnny Evers Jsy A1 60.00 18.00
JEV2 Johnny Evers Bat G2 60.00 18.00
JMA Joe Mays Jsy B2 8.00 2.40
JMC1 John McGraw Bat A1 80.00 24.00
JMC2 John McGraw Bat E2 80.00 24.00
JTH1 Jim Thome Jsy A1 15.00 4.50
JTH2 Jim Thome Bat D2 20.00 6.00
JTH3 Jim Thome Uni C3 15.00 4.50
TGL1 Tom Glavine Jsy A1 10.00 3.00
TGL2 Tom Glavine Jsy A2 10.00 3.00
TGW1 Tony Gwynn Jsy A1 15.00 4.50
TGW2 Tony Gwynn Jsy B2 15.00 4.50
TGW3 Tony Gwynn Uni E3 15.00 4.50
THA Toby Hall Jsy B2 8.00 2.40
THE1 Todd Helton Jsy A1 10.00 3.00
THE2 Todd Helton Jsy C2 10.00 3.00
THE3 Todd Helton Uni E3 10.00 3.00
TSH2 Tsuyoshi Shinjo Bat D2 15.00 4.50
TSH3 Tsuyoshi Shinjo Bat D3 8.00 2.40
TSP Tris Speaker Bat A1 100.00 30.00
JAGI Jason Giambi Jsy A1 8.00 2.40
JEGI Jeremy Giambi Jsy A1 8.00 2.40

2002 Topps 206 Team 206 Series 1

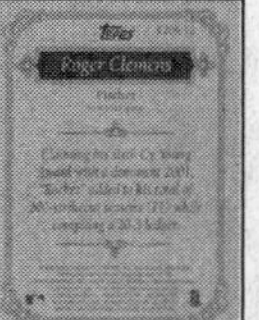

Inserted at an approximate rate of one per pack (only not in a pack when an autograph or relic card was inserted), these 20 cards feature the leading players from the 206 first series in a more modern design.

Nm-Mt Ex-Mt
COMPLETE SET (20) 15.00 4.50
T206-1 Barry Bonds 2.50 .75
T206-2 Ivan Rodriguez 1.00 .30
T206-3 Luis Gonzalez .50 .15
T206-4 Jason Giambi Yankees .50 .15
T206-5 Pedro Martinez 1.00 .30
T206-6 Larry Walker .60 .18
T206-7 Bob Abreu .50 .15
T206-8 Derek Jeter 2.50 .75
T206-9 Bret Boone .50 .15
T206-10 Mike Piazza 1.50 .45
T206-11 Alex Rodriguez 1.50 .45
T206-12 Roger Clemens 2.00 .60
T206-13 Albert Pujols 2.00 .60
T206-14 Randy Johnson 1.00 .30
T206-15 Sammy Sosa 1.50 .45
T206-16 Cristian Guzman .50 .15
T206-17 Shawn Green .50 .15
T206-18 Curt Schilling .50 .15
T206-19 Ichiro Suzuki 1.50 .45
T206-20 Chipper Jones 1.00 .30

2002 Topps 206 Team 206 Series 2

Inserted at an approximate rate of one per pack (only not in a pack when an autograph or relic card was inserted), these 20 cards feature the leading players from the 206 second series in a more modern design.

Nm-Mt Ex-Mt
COMPLETE SET (25) 15.00 4.50
T206-1 Alex Rodriguez 1.50 .45
T206-2 Sammy Sosa 1.50 .45
T206-3 Jason Giambi .50 .15
T206-4 Nomar Garciaparra 1.50 .45
T206-5 Ichiro Suzuki 1.50 .45
T206-6 Chipper Jones 1.00 .30
T206-7 Derek Jeter 2.50 .75
T206-8 Barry Bonds 2.50 .75
T206-9 Mike Piazza 1.50 .45
T206-10 Randy Johnson 1.00 .30
T206-11 Shawn Green .50 .15
T206-12 Todd Helton .60 .18
T206-13 Luis Gonzalez .50 .15
T206-14 Albert Pujols 2.00 .60
T206-15 Curt Schilling .50 .15
T206-16 Scott Rolen 1.00 .30
T206-17 Ivan Rodriguez 1.00 .30
T206-18 Roberto Alomar .60 .18
T206-19 Cristian Guzman .50 .15
T206-20 Bret Boone .50 .15
T206-21 Barry Zito .50 .15
T206-22 Larry Walker .60 .18
T206-23 Eric Chavez .50 .15
T206-24 Roger Clemens 2.00 .60
T206-25 Pedro Martinez 1.00 .30

2002 Topps 206 Team 206 Series 3

Inserted at an approximate rate of one per pack (only not in a pack when an autograph or relic card was inserted), these 30 cards feature the leading players from the 206 third series in a more modern design.

Nm-Mt Ex-Mt
COMPLETE SET (30) 15.00 4.50
1 Ichiro Suzuki 1.50 .45
2 Kazuhisa Ishii .50 .15
3 Alex Rodriguez 1.50 .45
4 Mark Prior 1.50 .45
5 Derek Jeter 2.50 .75
6 Sammy Sosa 1.50 .45
7 Nomar Garciaparra 1.50 .45
8 Mike Piazza 1.50 .45
9 Jason Giambi .50 .15
10 Vladimir Guerrero 1.00 .30
11 Curt Schilling .50 .15
12 Jim Thome Phillies 1.00 .30
13 Adam Dunn .60 .18
14 Albert Pujols 2.00 .60
15 Pat Burrell .50 .15
16 Chipper Jones 1.00 .30
17 Randy Johnson 1.00 .30
18 Todd Helton .60 .18
19 Luis Gonzalez .50 .15
20 Alfonso Soriano .60 .18
21 Shawn Green .50 .15
22 Pedro Martinez 1.00 .30
23 Lance Berkman .50 .15
24 Ivan Rodriguez 1.00 .30
25 Larry Walker .60 .18
26 Andruw Jones .50 .15
27 Ken Griffey Jr. 1.50 .45
28 Manny Ramirez .60 .18
29 Barry Bonds 2.50 .75
30 Miguel Tejada .50 .15

2002 Topps 206 Team 206 Series 2

2003 Topps All-Time Fan Favorites

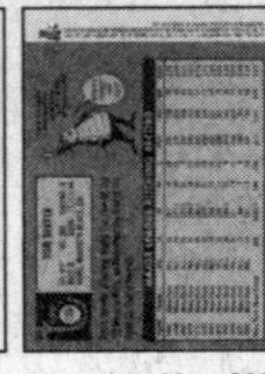

This 150-card set was released in May, 2003. This set was issued in six card packs with an $3 SRP which came 24 packs to a box and eight boxes to a case. These cards were issued in different styles with photos purporting to be from that era in which the faux card was issued. While most of the photos are close to the era they are supposed to be from, some photos such as the 64 Brooks Robinson design and the 54 Tom Lasorda are obviously not from the correct time period. The Monte Irvin card was issued in equal quantities with or without the facsmile autograph. A set is considered complete with only one of the Irvin cards. A notable card in this set is the first mainstream card of legendary broadcaster Ernie Harwell who was the Tigers announcers for more than 30 years.

Nm-Mt Ex-Mt
COMPLETE SET (150) 50.00 15.00
1 Willie Mays 3.00 .90
2 Whitey Ford 1.00 .30
3 Stan Musial 2.50 .75
4 Paul Blair .60 .18
5 Harold Reynolds .60 .18
6 Bob Friend .60 .18
7 Rod Carew 1.00 .30
8 Kirk Gibson .60 .18
9 Graig Nettles .60 .18
10 Ozzie Smith 2.50 .75
11 Tony Perez .60 .18
12 Tim Wallach .60 .18
13 Bert Campaneris .60 .18
14 Cory Snyder .60 .18
15 Dave Parker .60 .18
16 Darrell Evans .60 .18
17 Joe Pepitone .60 .18
18 Don Sutton .60 .18
19 Dale Murphy 1.50 .45
20 George Brett 4.00 1.20
21 Carlton Fisk 1.00 .30
22 Bob Watson .60 .18
23 Wally Joyner .60 .18
24 Paul Molitor 1.00 .30
25 Keith Hernandez .60 .18
26 Jerry Koosman .60 .18
27 George Bell .60 .18
28 Boog Powell 1.00 .30
29 Bruce Sutter .60 .18
30 Ernie Banks 1.50 .45
31 Steve Lyons .60 .18
32 Earl Weaver .60 .18
33 Dave Stieb .60 .18
34 Alan Trammell .60 .18
35 Bret Saberhagen .60 .18
36 J.R. Richard .60 .18
37 Mickey Rivers .60 .18
38 Juan Marichal .60 .18
39 Gaylord Perry .60 .18
40 Don Mattingly 4.00 1.20
41 Bob Grich .60 .18
42 Steve Sax .60 .18
43 Sparky Anderson .60 .18
44 Luis Aparicio .60 .18
45 Fergie Jenkins .60 .18
46 Jim Palmer .60 .18
47 Howard Johnson .60 .18
48 Dwight Evans .60 .18
49 Bill Buckner .60 .18
50 Cal Ripken 5.00 1.50
51 Jose Cruz .60 .18
52 Tony Oliva .60 .18
53 Bobby Richardson .60 .18
54 Luis Tiant .60 .18
55 Warren Spahn 1.00 .30
56 Phil Rizzuto 1.00 .30
57 Eric Davis .60 .18
58 Vida Blue .60 .18
59 Steve Balboni .60 .18
60 Mike Schmidt 3.00 .90
61 Ken Griffey Sr. .60 .18
62 Jim Abbott 1.00 .30
63 Whitey Herzog .60 .18
64 Rich Gossage .60 .18
65 Tony Armas .60 .18
66 Bill Skowron 1.00 .30
67 Don Newcombe .60 .18
68 Bill Madlock .60 .18
69 Lance Parrish .60 .18
70 Reggie Jackson 1.00 .30
71 Willie Wilson .60 .18
72 Terry Pendleton .60 .18
73 Jim Piersall .60 .18
74 George Foster .60 .18
75 Bob Horner .60 .18
76 Chris Sabo .60 .18
77 Fred Lynn .60 .18
78 Jim Rice .60 .18
79 Maury Wills .60 .18
80 Yogi Berra 1.50 .45
81 Johnny Sain 1.00 .30
82 Tom Lasorda .60 .18
83 Bill Mazeroski 1.00 .30
84 John Kruk .60 .18
85 Bob Feller .60 .18
86 Frank Robinson 1.00 .30
87 Red Schoendienst .60 .18
88 Gary Carter .60 .18
89 Andre Dawson .60 .18
90 Tim McCarver .60 .18
91 Robin Yount 2.50 .75
92 Phil Niekro .60 .18
93 Joe Morgan .60 .18
94 Darren Daulton .60 .18
95 Bobby Thomson .60 .18
96 Alvin Davis .60 .18
97 Robin Roberts 1.00 .30
98 Kirby Puckett 1.50 .45
99 Jack Clark .60 .18
100 Hank Aaron 3.00 .90
101 Orlando Cepeda .60 .18
102 Vern Law .60 .18
103 Cecil Cooper .60 .18
104 Don Larsen .60 .18
105 Mario Mendoza .60 .18
106 Tony Gwynn 2.00 .60
107 Ernie Tekulve .60 .18
108A Monte Irvin .60 .18
108B Monte Irvin NO AU ERR .60 .18
109 Tommy John .60 .18
110 Rollie Fingers .60 .18
111 Johnny Podres .60 .18
112 Jeff Reardon .60 .18
113 Buddy Bell .60 .18
114 Dwight Gooden .60 .18
115 Garry Templeton .60 .18
116 Johnny Bench 1.50 .45
117 Joe Rudi .60 .18
118 Ron Guidry .60 .18
119 Vince Coleman .60 .18
120 Al Kaline 1.50 .45
121 Carl Yastrzemski 2.50 .75
122 Hank Bauer .60 .18
123 Mark Fidrych .60 .18
124 Paul O'Neill 1.00 .30
125 Ron Cey .60 .18
126 Willie McGee .60 .18
127 Harmon Killebrew 1.50 .45
128 Dave Concepcion .60 .18
129 Harold Baines .60 .18
130 Lou Brock 1.00 .30
131 Lee Smith .60 .18
132 Willie McCovey .60 .18
133 Steve Garvey .60 .18
134 Kent Tekulve .60 .18
135 Tom Seaver 1.00 .30
136 Bo Jackson 1.50 .45
137 Walt Weiss .60 .18
138 Brook Jacoby .60 .18
139 Dennis Eckersley .60 .18
140 Duke Snider 1.00 .30
141 Lenny Dykstra .60 .18
142 Greg Luzinski .60 .18
143 Jim Bunning .60 .18
144 Jose Canseco 1.50 .45
145 Ron Santo 1.00 .30
146 Bert Blyleven .60 .18
147 Wade Boggs 1.00 .30
148 Brooks Robinson 1.00 .30
149 Ray Knight .60 .18
150 Nolan Ryan 4.00 1.20

2003 Topps All-Time Fan Favorites Chrome Refractors

Inserted at a stated rate of one in 18, this is a parallel to the basic set. These cards were produced using the Topps Chrome technology and were issued to a stated print run of 299 serial numbered sets.

Nm-Mt Ex-Mt
*CHROME REF: 3X TO 8X BASIC

2003 Topps All-Time Fan Favorites Archives Autographs

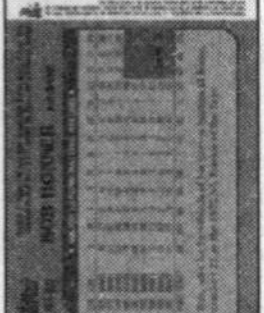

This 165-card set was issued at different odds depending on what group the player belonged to. Please note that exchange cards with a redemption deadline of April 30th, 2005, were seeded into packs for the following players: Dave Concepcion, Bob Feller, Tug McGraw, Paul O'Neill and Kirby Puckett. In addition, exchange cards were produced for a small percentage of Eric Davis cards (though the bulk of his real autographs did make pack out).

Nm-Mt Ex-Mt
GROUP A STATED ODDS 1:218
GROUP B STATED ODDS 1:759
GROUP C STATED ODDS 1:116
GROUP D STATED ODDS 1:45
GROUP E STATED ODDS 1:87
GROUP F STATED ODDS 1:1028
GROUP G STATED ODDS 1:838
GROUP H STATED ODDS 1:818
GROUP I STATED ODDS 1:796
GROUP J STATED ODDS 1:111
GROUP K STATED ODDS 1:759
GROUP L STATED ODDS 1:744
AD Alvin Davis D 10.00 3.00
ADA Andre Dawson A 60.00 18.00
AK Al Kaline A 150.00 45.00
AO Al Oliver D 10.00 3.00
AT Alan Trammell C 25.00 7.50
BB Bert Blyleven D 15.00 4.50
BBE Buddy Bell C 15.00 4.50
BBI Buddy Biancalana D 10.00 3.00
BBU Bill Buckner C 15.00 4.50
BC Bert Campaneris E 10.00 3.00
BF Bob Feller C EXCH 15.00 4.50
BFR Bob Friend D 10.00 3.00
BGR Bob Grich D 10.00 3.00
BH Bob Horner J 10.00 3.00
BJ Bo Jackson A 150.00 45.00
BJA Brook Jacoby E 10.00 3.00
BL Bill Lee D 10.00 3.00
BMA Bill Madlock D 10.00 3.00
BMZ Bill Mazeroski A 100.00 30.00
BP Boog Powell D 15.00 4.50
BRO Brooks Robinson A 100.00 30.00
BS Bill Skowron D 15.00 4.50
BSA Bret Saberhagen A 60.00 18.00
BSU Bruce Sutter C 15.00 4.50
BT Bobby Thomson A 60.00 18.00
BW Bob Watson C 15.00 4.50
CC Cecil Cooper E 10.00 3.00
CF Carlton Fisk A 100.00 30.00
CL Carney Lansford C 15.00 4.50
CLE Chet Lemon D 10.00 3.00
CN Cory Snyder C 15.00 4.50
CR Cal Ripken A 300.00 90.00
CS Chris Sabo H 10.00 3.00
CSP Chris Speier C 15.00 4.50
CY Carl Yastrzemski A 200.00 60.00
DC Dave Concepcion A EXCH 60.00 18.00
DD Darren Daulton C 15.00 4.50
DDE Doug DeCinces C 15.00 4.50
DE Darrell Evans D 10.00 3.00
DEC Dennis Eckersley A 100.00 30.00
DEV Dwight Evans A 60.00 18.00
DG Dwight Gooden A 60.00 18.00
DL Don Larsen D 15.00 4.50
DM Dale Murphy A 100.00 30.00
DN Don Newcombe A 60.00 18.00
DON Don Mattingly A 150.00 45.00
DP Dave Parker A 60.00 18.00
DS Dave Stieb C 25.00 7.50
DSN Duke Snider A 100.00 30.00
DSU Don Sutton A 60.00 18.00
EB Ernie Banks A 150.00 45.00
ED Eric Davis I 15.00 4.50
EH Ernie Harwell C 60.00 18.00
EW Earl Weaver D 10.00 3.00
FJ Fergie Jenkins C 15.00 4.50
FL Fred Lynn A 60.00 18.00
FR Frank Robinson A 100.00 30.00
GB George Bell D 10.00 3.00
GBR George Brett A 250.00 75.00
GC Gary Carter A 60.00 18.00
GF George Foster D 10.00 3.00
GL Greg Luzinski C 15.00 4.50
GN Graig Nettles D 15.00 4.50
GP Gaylord Perry B 25.00 7.50
GT Garry Templeton C 15.00 4.50
HA Hank Aaron A 300.00 90.00
HB Hank Bauer A 60.00 18.00
HBA Harold Baines C 15.00 4.50
HJ Howard Johnson K 10.00 3.00
HK Harmon Killebrew A 150.00 45.00
HR Harold Reynolds A 60.00 18.00
JA Jim Abbott D 15.00 4.50
JB Jim Bunning A 150.00 45.00
JBE Johnny Bench A 150.00 45.00
JC Jack Clark B 25.00 7.50
JCA Joe Carter A 60.00 18.00
JCR Jose Cruz D 10.00 3.00
JK Jerry Koosman F 25.00 7.50
JKR John Kruk A 100.00 30.00
JM Joe Morgan A 60.00 18.00
JMA Juan Marichal A 100.00 30.00
JMO John Montefusco D 10.00 3.00
JOS Jose Canseco A 100.00 30.00
JP Jim Palmer A 100.00 30.00
JPE Joe Pepitone E 10.00 3.00
JR J.R. Richard E 10.00 3.00
JRE Jeff Reardon D 10.00 3.00
JRI Jim Rice A 60.00 18.00
JRU Joe Rudi E 10.00 3.00
KG Ken Griffey Sr. A 60.00 18.00
KGI Kirk Gibson A 100.00 30.00
KH Keith Hernandez A 60.00 18.00
KM Kevin Mitchell L 10.00 3.00
KP Kirby Puckett A EXCH 80.00 24.00
KS Kevin Seitzer D 10.00 3.00
KT Kent Tekulve C 15.00 4.50
LA Luis Aparicio D 10.00 3.00
LB Lou Brock A 100.00 30.00
LD Lenny Dykstra G 10.00 3.00
LDU Leon Durham D 10.00 3.00
LP Lance Parrish D 10.00 3.00
LS Lee Smith J 10.00 3.00
LT Luis Tiant A 60.00 18.00
MCG Willie McGee A 100.00 30.00
MF Mark Fidrych J 10.00 3.00
MI Monte Irvin A 60.00 18.00
MM Mario Mendoza E 10.00 3.00
MP Mike Pagliarulo E 10.00 3.00
MR Mickey Rivers E 10.00 3.00
MS Mike Schmidt A 250.00 75.00
MW Maury Wills E 10.00 3.00
NR Nolan Ryan A 300.00 90.00
OC Orlando Cepeda A 100.00 30.00
OS Ozzie Smith A 150.00 45.00
PB Paul Blair J 10.00 3.00
PM Paul Molitor A 100.00 30.00
PN Phil Niekro A 60.00 18.00
PO Paul O'Neill A EXCH 100.00 30.00
PR Phil Rizzuto A 100.00 30.00
RCA Rod Carew A 100.00 30.00
RCE Ron Cey D 10.00 3.00
RD Rob Dibble C 25.00 7.50
RDA Ron Darling C 15.00 4.50
RF Rollie Fingers A 60.00 18.00
RG Rich Gossage A 60.00 18.00
RGU Ron Guidry C 15.00 4.50
RJ Reggie Jackson A 150.00 45.00
RK Ralph Kiner A 100.00 30.00
RKI Ron Kittle D 10.00 3.00
RR Robin Roberts B 25.00 7.50
RS Red Schoendienst C 15.00 4.50
RSA Ron Santo D 25.00 7.50
RY Ray Knight J 10.00 3.00
RYO Robin Yount A 150.00 45.00
SA Sparky Anderson A 60.00 18.00
SB Steve Balboni E 10.00 3.00
SG Steve Garvey B 25.00 7.50
SL Steve Lyons C 15.00 4.50
SM Stan Musial A 200.00 60.00
SS Steve Sax D 10.00 3.00
SY Steve Yeager E 10.00 3.00
TA Tony Armas D 10.00 3.00
TG Tony Gwynn A 150.00 45.00
TH Tom Herr D 10.00 3.00
TJ Tommy John B 15.00 4.50
TL Tom Lasorda A 60.00 18.00
TM Tim McCarver A 60.00 18.00
TMC Tug McGraw D EXCH 25.00 7.50
TP Terry Pendleton B 15.00 4.50
TPE Tony Perez A 100.00 30.00
TSE Tom Seaver A 150.00 45.00
TW Tim Wallach E 10.00 3.00
VB Vida Blue C 15.00 4.50
VC Vince Coleman J 10.00 3.00
WB Wade Boggs A 100.00 30.00
WF Whitey Ford A 150.00 45.00
WH Whitey Herzog C 25.00 7.50
WHE Willie Hernandez D 10.00 3.00
WJ Wally Joyner J 10.00 3.00
WM Willie Mays A 300.00 90.00
WMC Willie McCovey A 100.00 30.00
WS Warren Spahn D 40.00 12.00
WW Walt Weiss D 10.00 3.00
WWI Willie Wilson A 60.00 18.00
YB Yogi Berra A 150.00 45.00

2003 Topps All-Time Fan Favorites Best Seat in the House Relics

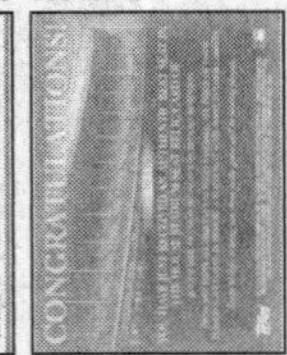

Inserted at a stated rate of one in 13 special relic packs, these five cards feature a group of stars from a team along with a piece of a set from a now retired ballpark.

Nm-Mt Ex-Mt
BS1 Brooks Robinson 25.00 7.50
Frank Robinson
Jim Palmer
BS2 Bob Grich 25.00 7.50
Rod Carew
Wally Joyner
BS3 Dave Parker 25.00 7.50
Kent Tekulve
Willie Stargell
Phil Garner
BS4 Paul Molitor 40.00 12.00
Robin Yount
Rollie Fingers
BS5 Bob Horner 25.00 7.50
Dale Murphy
Phil Niekro

2003 Topps All-Time Fan Favorites Relics

Issued one per special "relic" box-topper pack, these 43 cards feature players from the basic set along with a game-used memorabilia piece.

Nm-Mt Ex-Mt
ADA Andre Dawson Bat 10.00 3.00
AT Alan Trammell Bat 10.00 3.00
BFR Bob Friend Jsy 10.00 3.00
BH Bob Horner Bat 10.00 3.00
BJ Bo Jackson Bat 25.00 7.50
BR Bobby Richardson Bat 15.00 4.50
CF Curt Flood Bat 10.00 3.00
CS Chris Sabo Bat 10.00 3.00
DEC Dennis Eckersley Uni 10.00 3.00
DM Dale Murphy Bat 25.00 7.50
DON Don Mattingly Bat 40.00 12.00
DP Dave Parker Bat 10.00 3.00
FL Fred Lynn Bat 10.00 3.00
GBR George Brett Uni 30.00 9.00
GC Gary Carter Bat 10.00 3.00
GF George Foster Bat 10.00 3.00
GL Greg Luzinski Bat 10.00 3.00
HBA Harold Baines Bat 15.00 4.50
HR Harold Reynolds Bat 10.00 3.00
JCR Jose Cruz Bat 10.00 3.00
JM Joe Morgan Bat 10.00 3.00
JOS Jose Canseco Bat 15.00 4.50
JRI Jim Rice Bat 10.00 3.00
JRU Joe Rudi Bat 10.00 3.00
KGI Kirk Gibson Bat 10.00 3.00
KH Keith Hernandez Bat 10.00 3.00
KM Kevin Mitchell Bat 10.00 3.00
KP Kirby Puckett Bat 25.00 7.50
LD Lenny Dykstra Bat 10.00 3.00
LP Lance Parrish Bat 15.00 4.50
MCG Willie McGee Bat 15.00 4.50
MS Mike Schmidt Bat 30.00 9.00
MW Maury Wills Bat 10.00 3.00
NC Norm Cash Jsy 50.00 15.00
PO Paul O'Neill Bat 15.00 4.50
RCA Rod Carew Bat 15.00 4.50
RDA Ron Darling Jsy 10.00 3.00
SG Steve Garvey Bat 10.00 3.00
TMC Tug McGraw Jsy 10.00 3.00
VC Vince Coleman Bat 10.00 3.00
WHE Willie Hernandez Jsy 10.00 3.00
WJ Wally Joyner Bat 10.00 3.00
WS Willie Stargell Bat 15.00 4.50

2003 Topps All-Time Fan Favorites Team Topps Legends Autographs

Nm-Mt Ex-Mt
SEE 2001 TOPPS TEAM TOPPS FOR PRICING

2003 Topps All-Time Fan Favorites Don Zimmer AutoProofs

Inserted at a stated rate of one in 4971, these 13 cards feature authentic signed versions of Don Zimmer's cards issued between 1955 and 1978. We have notated the print run next to the player's name in our checklist and note that due to market scarcity there is no pricing.

Nm-Mt Ex-Mt
1 Don Zimmer 55 Bow/1
2 Don Zimmer 55/5
3 Don Zimmer 56/9
4 Don Zimmer 58/5
5 Don Zimmer 59/17
6 Don Zimmer 60/14
7 Don Zimmer 61/24
8 Don Zimmer 62/1
9 Don Zimmer 63/29
10 Don Zimmer 64/14
11 Don Zimmer 65/14
12 Don Zimmer 73 MG/3
13 Don Zimmer 78 MG/11

2004 Topps All-Time Fan Favorites

This 150-card set was released in June, 2004. This set was issued in six card packs with an $5 SRP which came 24 packs to a box and 10 boxes to a case. This set has several noticable 1st cards including former commissioners Peter Ueberroth and Fay Vincent, long-time umpire Eric Gregg and long time Yankee Stadium public address announcer legend Bob Shepard.

Nm-Mt Ex-Mt
COMPLETE SET (150) 50.00 15.00
1 Willie Mays 3.00 .90
2 Bob Gibson 1.00 .30
3 Dave Stieb .60 .18
4 Tim McCarver .60 .18
5 Reggie Jackson 1.00 .30
6 John Candelaria .60 .18
7 Lenny Dykstra .60 .18
8 Tony Oliva .60 .18
9 Frank Viola .60 .18
10 Don Mattingly 4.00 1.20
11 Garry Maddox .60 .18
12 Randy Jones .60 .18
13 Joe Carter .60 .18
14 Orlando Cepeda .60 .18
15 Bob Sheppard ANC 1.00 .30
16 Bobby Grich .60 .18
17 George Scott .60 .18
18 Mickey Rivers .60 .18
19 Ron Santo 1.00 .30
20 Mike Schmidt 3.00 .90
21 Luis Aparicio .60 .18
22 Cesar Geronimo .60 .18
23 Jack Morris .60 .18
24 Jeffrey Loria OWNER .60 .18
25 George Brett 4.00 1.20
26 Paul O'Neill 1.00 .30
27 Reggie Smith .60 .18
28 Robin Yount 2.50 .75
29 Andre Dawson .60 .18
30 Whitey Ford 1.00 .30
31 Ralph Kiner .60 .18
32 Will Clark 1.50 .45
33 Keith Hernandez .60 .18
34 Tony Fernandez .60 .18
35 Willie McGee .60 .18
36 Harmon Killebrew 1.50 .45
37 Dave Kingman .60 .18
38 Kirk Gibson 1.00 .30
39 Terry Steinbach .60 .18
40 Frank Robinson .60 .18
41 Chet Lemon .60 .18
42 Mike Cuellar .60 .18
43 Darrell Evans .60 .18
44 Don Kessinger .60 .18
45 Dave Concepcion .60 .18
46 Sparky Anderson .60 .18
47 Bret Saberhagen .60 .18
48 Brett Butler .60 .18
49 Kent Hrbek .60 .18
50 Hank Aaron 3.00 .90
51 Rudolph Giuliani 1.50 .45
52 Clete Boyer .60 .18
53 Mookie Wilson .60 .18
54 Dave Stewart .60 .18
55 Gary Matthews Sr. .60 .18
56 Roy Face .60 .18
57 Vida Blue .60 .18
58 Jimmy Key 1.00 .30
59 Al Hrabosky .60 .18
60 Al Kaline 1.50 .45
61 Mike Scott .60 .18
62 Jack McDowell .60 .18
63 Reggie Jackson 1.00 .30
64 Earl Weaver .60 .18
65 Ernie Harwell ANC 1.00 .30
66 David Justice .60 .18
67 Wilbur Wood .60 .18
68 Mike Boddicker .60 .18
69 Don Zimmer .60 .18
70 Jim Palmer .60 .18
71 Doug DeCinces .60 .18
72 Ryne Sandberg 3.00 .90
73 Don Newcombe .60 .18
74 Denny Martinez .60 .18
75 Carl Yastrzemski 2.50 .75
76 Bake McBride .60 .18
77 Andy Van Slyke .60 .18
78 Bruce Sutter .60 .18
79 Bobby Valentine .60 .18
80 Johnny Bench 1.50 .45
81 Orel Hershiser .60 .18
82 Cecil Fielder .60 .18
83 Lou Whitaker .60 .18
84 Alan Trammell .60 .18
85 Sam McDowell .60 .18
86 Ray Knight .60 .18
87 Gregg Jefferies .60 .18
88 Ben Oglivie .60 .18
89 Billy Beane .60 .18
90 Yogi Berra 1.50 .45
91 Jose Canseco 1.50 .45
92 Bobby Bonilla .60 .18
93 Darren Daulton .60 .18
94 Harold Reynolds .60 .18
95 Lou Brock 1.00 .30
96 Pete Incaviglia .60 .18
97 Eric Gregg UMP .60 .18
98 Devon White .60 .18
99 Kelly Gruber .60 .18
100 Nolan Ryan 4.00 1.20
101 Carlton Fisk 1.00 .30
102 George Foster .60 .18
103 Dennis Eckersley 1.00 .30
104 Rick Sutcliffe .60 .18
105 Cal Ripken 5.00 1.50
106 Norm Cash .60 .18
107 Charlie Hough .60 .18
108 Paul Molitor 1.00 .30
109 Maury Wills .60 .18
110 Tom Seaver 1.00 .30
111 Brooks Robinson 1.00 .30
112 Jim Rice .60 .18
113 Dwight Gooden .60 .18
114 Harold Baines .60 .18
115 Tim Raines .60 .18
116 Roy Smalley .60 .18
117 Richie Allen .60 .18
118 Ron Swoboda .60 .18
119 Ron Guidry 1.00 .30
120 Duke Snider 1.00 .30
121 Ferguson Jenkins .60 .18
122 Mark Fidrych UER .60 .18
Posing as a lefty
123 Buddy Bell .60 .18
124 Bo Jackson 1.50 .45
125 Stan Musial 2.50 .75
126 Jesse Barfield .60 .18
127 Tony Gwynn 2.00 .60
128 Phil Garner .60 .18
129 Dale Murphy 1.00 .30
130 Wade Boggs 1.00 .30
131 Sid Fernandez .60 .18
132 Monte Irvin .60 .18
133 Peter Ueberroth COM .60 .18
134 Gary Gaetti .60 .18
135 Gorman Thomas .60 .18
136 Dave Lopes .60 .18
137 Sy Berger .60 .18
138 Buck O'Neil UER .60 .18
Wrong birth year on back
139 Herb Score .60 .18
140 Rod Carew 1.00 .30
141 Joe Buck ANC 1.00 .30
142 Willie Horton .60 .18
143 Hal McRae .60 .18
144 Rollie Fingers .60 .18
145 Tom Brunansky .60 .18
146 Fay Vincent COM .60 .18
147 Gary Carter .60 .18
148 Bobby Richardson .60 .18
149 Steve Garvey .60 .18
150 Don Larsen .60 .18

2004 Topps All-Time Fan Favorites Refractors

Nm-Mt Ex-Mt
*REFRACTORS: 3X TO 8X BASIC
STATED ODDS 1:19
STATED PRINT RUN 299 SERIAL #'d SETS

2004 Topps All-Time Fan Favorites Autographs

A few players did not return their autograph in time for inclusion in packs and those autographs could be redeemed until May 31, 2006.

Nm-Mt Ex-Mt
GROUP A ODDS 1:69,360
GROUP B ODDS 1:648
GROUP C ODDS 1:102
GROUP D ODDS 1:5662
GROUP E ODDS 1:181
GROUP F ODDS 1:208
GROUP G ODDS 1:509
GROUP H ODDS 1:356
GROUP I ODDS 1:58
GROUP J ODDS 1:148
GROUP K ODDS 1:128
GROUP L ODDS 1:135
GROUP M ODDS 1:104
GROUP N ODDS 1:228
OVERALL AUTO ODDS 1:12
GROUP A PRINT RUN 10 CARDS
GROUP B PRINT RUN 50 SETS
GROUP C PRINT RUN 100 SETS
GROUP D PRINT RUN 150 CARDS
CARDS ARE NOT SERIAL-NUMBERED
PRINT RUNS PROVIDED BY TOPPS
NO GROUP A PRICING DUE TO SCARCITY
AD Andre Dawson C 40.00 12.00
AH Al Hrabosky L 15.00 4.50
AK Al Kaline B 120.00 36.00
AT Alan Trammell C 40.00 12.00
AV Andy Van Slyke C 60.00 18.00
BB Billy Beane C 25.00 7.50
BBE Buddy Bell N 25.00 7.50
BG Bob Gibson C 60.00 18.00
BGR Bobby Grich I 10.00 3.00
BJ Bo Jackson B 120.00 36.00
BMB Bobby Bonilla C EXCH 25.00 7.50
BO Ben Oglivie I 10.00 3.00
BON Buck O'Neil K 15.00 4.50
BR Bobby Richardson F 25.00 7.50
BRO Brooks Robinson B 80.00 24.00
BS Bob Sheppard A/10 EXCH
BSA Bret Saberhagen C 40.00 12.00
BSU Bruce Sutter F 25.00 7.50
BV Bobby Valentine C 40.00 12.00
CF Carlton Fisk B 80.00 24.00
CG Cesar Geronimo C 40.00 12.00
CH Charlie Hough G 15.00 4.50
CL Chet Lemon M 10.00 3.00
CR Cal Ripken B 300.00 90.00
CY Carl Yastrzemski B 200.00 60.00
DC Dave Concepcion C 40.00 12.00
DD Darren Daulton L 15.00 4.50
DDE Doug DeCinces E 15.00 4.50
DE Darrell Evans I 15.00 4.50
DEC Dennis Eckersley C 60.00 18.00
DG Dwight Gooden B 50.00 15.00
DJ David Justice E 25.00 7.50
DK Dave Kingman E 40.00 12.00
DKE Don Kessinger M 15.00 4.50
DL Dave Lopes M 10.00 3.00
DLA Don Larsen L 25.00 7.50
DM Dale Murphy B 80.00 24.00
DON Don Mattingly B 150.00 45.00
DS Dave Stewart H EXCH 15.00 4.50
DSN Duke Snider C 60.00 18.00
DST Dave Stieb J 15.00 4.50
DZ Don Zimmer I 25.00 7.50
EG Eric Gregg I 10.00 3.00
EH Ernie Harwell E 25.00 7.50
EW Earl Weaver M 15.00 4.50
FJ Ferguson Jenkins F 25.00 7.50
FR Frank Robinson C 60.00 18.00
FVI Fay Vincent C 60.00 18.00
FVI1 Frank Viola I 15.00 4.50
GB George Brett B 200.00 60.00
GC Gary Carter B 50.00 15.00
GF George Foster I 10.00 3.00
GMA Gary Matthews Sr. J 10.00 3.00
GS George Scott K EXCH 15.00 4.50
HA Hank Aaron B 300.00 90.00
HB Harold Baines C 40.00 12.00
HK Harmon Killebrew C 100.00 30.00
HR Harold Reynolds C 40.00 12.00
JB Jesse Barfield J 10.00 3.00
JB1 Joe Buck C 40.00 12.00
JBE Johnny Bench C 120.00 36.00
JC Joe Carter C 40.00 12.00
JCA Jose Canseco C 60.00 18.00
JKE Jimmy Key C 40.00 12.00
JM Jack McDowell K 10.00 3.00
JMO Jack Morris K 10.00 3.00
JP Jim Palmer B 80.00 24.00
JR Jim Rice C 40.00 12.00
KG Kirk Gibson B 80.00 24.00
KH Keith Hernandez B 50.00 15.00
LA Luis Aparicio C 40.00 12.00
LB Lou Brock C 60.00 18.00
LD Lenny Dykstra C 25.00 7.50
MB Mike Boddicker J 10.00 3.00
MF Mark Fidrych C 40.00 12.00
MI Monte Irvin C 40.00 12.00
MR Mickey Rivers M 10.00 3.00
MS Mike Schmidt B
MSC Mike Scott M 10.00 3.00
MW Maury Wills I 15.00 4.50
MWI Mookie Wilson L 10.00 3.00
NR Nolan Ryan D 200.00 60.00
OC Orlando Cepeda C 60.00 18.00
OH Orel Hershiser E 40.00 12.00
PI Pete Incaviglia E 15.00 4.50
PM Paul Molitor B 80.00 24.00
PO Paul O'Neill B 80.00 24.00
PU Peter Ueberroth C 120.00 36.00
RA Richie Allen I EXCH 15.00 4.50
RC Rod Carew C 60.00 18.00
RF Rollie Fingers C 40.00 12.00
RG Ron Guidry C 40.00 12.00
RJO Randy Jones L 10.00 3.00
RJ2 Reggie Jackson C 100.00 30.00
RK Ralph Kiner G 40.00 12.00
RKN Ray Knight C 25.00 7.50
RS Ron Santo I 25.00 7.50
RSU Rick Sutcliffe C 40.00 12.00
RSW Ron Swoboda N 15.00 4.50
RY Robin Yount B 150.00 45.00
RYN Ryne Sandberg C 150.00 45.00
SA Sparky Anderson C 40.00 12.00
SB Sy Berger H 25.00 7.50
SF Sid Fernandez C 40.00 12.00
SG Steve Garvey C 40.00 12.00
SM Stan Musial C 150.00 45.00
SM1 Sam McDowell C 40.00 12.00
TB Tom Brunansky C 40.00 12.00
TF Tony Fernandez F 15.00 4.50
TG Tony Gwynn B 150.00 45.00
TM Tim McCarver E 15.00 4.50
TO Tony Oliva E 40.00 12.00
TR Tim Raines E 40.00 12.00
TSE Tom Seaver B 120.00 36.00
VB Vida Blue F 15.00 4.50
WB Wade Boggs B 80.00 24.00
WF Whitey Ford C 80.00 24.00
WH Willie Horton K 15.00 4.50
WM Willie Mays B
WMC Willie McGee C 40.00 12.00
WW Wilbur Wood I 15.00 4.50
YB Yogi Berra C 100.00 30.00

2004 Topps All-Time Fan Favorites Best Seat in the House Relics

Nm-Mt Ex-Mt
STATED ODDS 1:10 RELIC PACKS
BS1 Tom Seaver 25.00 7.50
George Foster
Johnny Bench
BS2 Frank Robinson 15.00 4.50
Jim Palmer
Brooks Robinson
BS3 Dave Parker 15.00 4.50
Bill Madlock
Bill Mazeroski
BS4 Kent Hrbek 25.00 7.50
Rod Carew
Harmon Killebrew

2004 Topps All-Time Fan Favorites Relics

Nm-Mt Ex-Mt
ONE PER RELIC PACK
BR Brooks Robinson Bat 10.00 3.00
BS Bret Saberhagen Jsy 8.00 2.40
CF Carlton Fisk Bat 10.00 3.00
CY Carl Yastrzemski Bat 25.00 7.50
DE Dennis Eckersley Uni 10.00 3.00
DJ David Justice Bat 8.00 2.40
DP Dave Parker Uni 8.00 2.40
DS Darryl Strawberry Bat 8.00 2.40
EW Earl Weaver Jsy 8.00 2.40
FR Frank Robinson Jsy 8.00 2.40
FRB Frank Robinson Bat 8.00 2.40
GB George Brett Uni 25.00 7.50
GC Gary Carter Jsy 8.00 2.40
GF George Foster Bat 8.00 2.40
GN Graig Nettles Bat 8.00 2.40
HK Harmon Killebrew Jsy 25.00 7.50
HR Harold Reynolds Bat 8.00 2.40
JC Jose Canseco Jsy 15.00 4.50
JCB Jose Canseco Bat 15.00 4.50
JM Joe Morgan Bat 8.00 2.40
JP Jim Palmer Uni 8.00 2.40
JR Jim Rice Jsy 8.00 2.40
KG Kirk Gibson Bat 10.00 3.00
KH Keith Hernandez Bat 8.00 2.40
KP Kirby Puckett Jsy 15.00 4.50
LB Lou Brock Jsy 10.00 3.00
MS Mike Schmidt Bat 20.00 6.00
MW Maury Wills Jsy 8.00 2.40
NR Nolan Ryan Jsy 40.00 12.00
RC Rod Carew Bat 10.00 3.00
RJ Reggie Jackson Bat 10.00 3.00
TP Tony Perez Bat 8.00 2.40
WB Wade Boggs Uni 10.00 3.00
WM Willie Mays Uni 50.00 15.00

2001 Topps American Pie

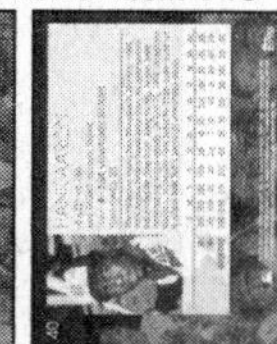

This 150-card set captured the essence of America at the height of the Baby Boomers Era of the '60's and '70's. Cards 1-115 features major leaguers, 116-140 features historic events and 141-150 features American icons of the '60's and '70's. The cards were issued in five card packs with an SRP of $4.00/pack. These packs were issued 24 to a box.

Nm-Mt Ex-Mt
COMPLETE SET (150) 40.00 12.00
1 Al Kaline 1.25 .35
2 Al Oliver .50 .15
3 Andre Dawson .50 .15
4 Bert Blyleven .50 .15
5 Bill Buckner .50 .15
6 Bill Mazeroski .75 .23
7 Bob Gibson .75 .23
8 Bill Freehan .50 .15
9 Bobby Grich .50 .15
10 Bobby Murcer .50 .15
11 Bobby Richardson .50 .15
12 Boog Powell .75 .23
13 Brooks Robinson .75 .23
14 Carl Yastrzemski 2.00 .60
15 Carlton Fisk .75 .23
16 Clete Boyer .30 .09
17 Curt Flood .50 .15
18 Dale Murphy 1.25 .35
19 Tony Conigliaro .75 .23
20 Dave Parker .50 .15
21 Dave Winfield .50 .15
22 Dick Allen .50 .15
23 Dick Groat .50 .15
24 Don Drysdale 1.25 .35
25 Don Sutton .50 .15
26 Dwight Evans .50 .15
27 Eddie Mathews 1.25 .35
28 Elston Howard .75 .23
29 Frank Howard .50 .15
30 Frank Robinson .75 .23
31 Fred Lynn .50 .15
32 Gary Carter .50 .15
33 Gaylord Perry .50 .15
34 Norm Cash .50 .15
35 George Brett 3.00 .90
36 George Foster .50 .15
37 Goose Gossage .50 .15
38 Graig Nettles .50 .15
39 Greg Luzinski .50 .15
40 Hank Aaron 2.50 .75
41 Harmon Killebrew 1.25 .35
42 Jack Clark .50 .15
43 Jack Morris .50 .15
44 Jim Wynn .50 .15
45 Jim Kaat .50 .15
46 Jim Palmer .50 .15
47 Joe Pepitone .30 .09
48 Joe Rudi .30 .09
49 Johnny Bench 1.25 .35
50 Juan Marichal .50 .15
51 Keith Hernandez .50 .15
52 Bucky Dent .50 .15
53 Lou Brock .75 .23
54 Ron Cey .50 .15
55 Luis Aparicio .50 .15
56 Luis Tiant .50 .15
57 Mark Fidrych .50 .15
58 Maury Wills .50 .15
59 Mickey Lolich .50 .15
60 Mickey Rivers .30 .09
61 Mike Schmidt 2.50 .75
62 Moose Skowron .50 .15
63 Nolan Ryan 3.00 .90
64 Orlando Cepeda .50 .15
65 Ozzie Smith 2.00 .60
66 Phil Niekro .50 .15
67 Reggie Jackson .75 .23
68 Reggie Smith .50 .15
69 Rico Carty .30 .09
70 Roberto Clemente 3.00 .90
71 Robin Yount 2.00 .60
72 Roger Maris 1.25 .35
73 Rollie Fingers .50 .15
74 Ron Guidry .50 .15
75 Ron Santo .75 .23
76 Ron Swoboda .50 .15
77 Sal Bando .50 .15
78 Sam McDowell .50 .15
79 Steve Carlton .50 .15
80 Thurman Munson 1.25 .35
81 Tim McCarver .50 .15
82 Tom Seaver .75 .23
83 Mike Cuellar .50 .15
84 Tony Kubek .75 .23
85 Tommy John .50 .15
86 Tony Perez .50 .15
87 Tug McGraw .50 .15
88 Vida Blue .50 .15
89 Warren Spahn .75 .23
90 Whitey Ford .75 .23
91 Willie Mays 2.50 .75
92 Willie McCovey .50 .15
93 Willie Stargell .75 .23
94 Yogi Berra 1.25 .35
95 Stan Musial 2.00 .60
96 Jim Piersall .50 .15
97 Duke Snider .75 .23
98 Bruce Sutter .50 .15
99 Dave Concepcion .50 .15
100 Darrell Evans .50 .15
101 Dennis Eckersley .50 .15
102 Hoyt Wilhelm .50 .15
103 Minnie Minoso .50 .15
104 Don Newcombe .50 .15
105 Richie Ashburn .75 .23
106 Alan Trammell .50 .15
107 Jim Hunter .75 .23
108 Lou Whitaker .50 .15
109 Johnny Podres .50 .15
110 Denny Martinez .50 .15
111 Willie Horton .50 .15
112 Dean Chance .30 .09
113 Fergie Jenkins .50 .15
114 Cecil Cooper .50 .15
115 Rick Reuschel .30 .09
116 Civil Rights .30 .09
117 Bay of Pigs .30 .09
118 Cuban Missile Crisis .30 .09
119 N.Y. World's Fair .30 .09
120 Atomic Bomb .30 .09
Test Ban Treaty
121 John F. Kennedy 1.25 .35
Assassination
122 Lyndon Johnson .30 .09
123 The Motown Sound .30 .09
124 British Music Invasion .50 .15
125 U.S.Troops .30 .09
in Vietnam
126 Space Race .30 .09
127 Robert F. Kennedy .50 .15
128 Peace Movement .30 .09
129 Man On The Moon .50 .15
130 Woodstock .30 .09
131 Flower Power .30 .09
132 Women's Lib .30 .09
133 Vietnam Cease Fire .30 .09
134 U.S. Gas Shortage .30 .09
135 Watergate .50 .15
136 Nixon Resigns .50 .15
137 Bicentennial .30 .09
138 Disco .30 .09
139 Three Mile Island .30 .09
140 Iran Hostage Crisis .30 .09
141 John F. Kennedy 2.00 .60
142 Marilyn Monroe 2.00 .60
143 Elvis Presley 2.00 .60
144 Jimi Hendrix 1.25 .35
145 Arthur Ashe .50 .15
146 Richard Nixon 1.25 .35
147 James Dean 1.25 .35

148 Janis Joplin .50 .15
149 Frank Sinatra 1.25 .35
150 Malcolm X .50 .15

2001 Topps American Pie Decade Leaders

Inserted at a rate of one in 12, this 10-card set features players who led the Majors in different categories for the entire decades of the '60's and '70's. These cards contained a 'DL' prefix in the numbering.

	Nm-Mt	Ex-Mt
COMPLETE SET (10)	30.00	9.00
DL1 Willie Stargell	1.50	.45
DL2 Harmon Killebrew	2.50	.75
DL3 Johnny Bench	2.50	.75
DL4 Hank Aaron	5.00	1.50
DL5 Rod Carew	1.50	.45
DL6 Roberto Clemente	6.00	1.80
DL7 Nolan Ryan	6.00	1.80
DL8 Bob Gibson	1.50	.45
DL9 Jim Palmer	1.50	.45
DL10 Juan Marichal	1.50	.45

2001 Topps American Pie Entertainment Star Autographs

Inserted at a rate of one in 1,071, this three card set features T.V. personalities who've signed original Topps non-sports cards from the 60's and '70's. Many different cards were signed by each person, but all carry equal value. Each card displays a sequentially numbered Topps "Genuine Issue" sticker.

	Nm-Mt	Ex-Mt
1 Danny Bonaduce	80.00	24.00
2 Lou Ferrigno	120.00	36.00
3 Adam West	100.00	30.00

2001 Topps American Pie Profiles in Courage

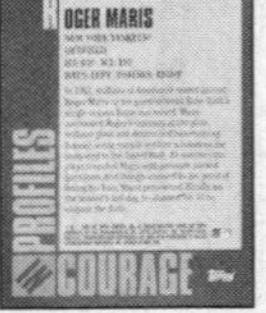

Inserted at a rate of one in eight, this 20-card set profiled major leaguers who possessed unparalleled tenacity. The cards carry a 'PIC' prefix. The term "Profiles in Courage" comes from a book authored by John F. Kennedy before he became President.

	Nm-Mt	Ex-Mt
COMPLETE SET (20)	50.00	15.00
PIC1 Roger Maris	3.00	.90
PIC2 Lou Brock	2.00	.60
PIC3 Brooks Robinson	2.00	.60
PIC4 Carl Yastrzemski	4.00	1.20
PIC5 Mike Schmidt	6.00	1.80
PIC6 Hank Aaron	6.00	1.80
PIC7 Tom Seaver	2.00	.60
PIC8 Willie Mays	6.00	1.80
PIC9 Graig Nettles	1.50	.45
PIC10 Frank Robinson	2.00	.60
PIC11 Rollie Fingers	1.50	.45
PIC12 Tony Perez	1.50	.45
PIC13 George Brett	8.00	2.40
PIC14 Robin Yount	5.00	1.50
PIC15 Nolan Ryan	8.00	2.40
PIC16 Warren Spahn	2.00	.60
PIC17 Johnny Bench	3.00	.90
PIC18 Vida Blue	1.50	.45
PIC19 Roberto Clemente	8.00	2.40
PIC20 Thurman Munson	3.00	.90

2001 Topps American Pie Relics

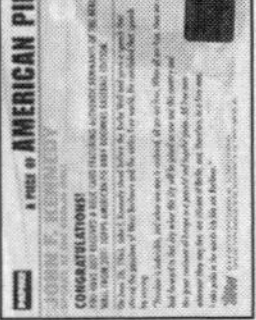

Inserted at a rate of one in 29, this four card set featured memorabilia from pop culture icons of the '60's and '70's. The cards carry a 'PAPM' prefix.

	Nm-Mt	Ex-Mt
PAPM1 F. Sinatra Jacket	50.00	15.00
PAPM2 John F. Kennedy Berlin Wall	20.00	6.00
PAPM3 E. Presley Jacket	120.00	36.00
PAPM4 Janis Joplin Dress	80.00	24.00

2001 Topps American Pie Rookie Reprint Relics

Inserted at a rate of one in 116, this 20-card set featured jersey swatches and bat pieces inserted into the players' reprinted rookie cards. The cards carry a 'BBRR' prefix.

	Nm-Mt	Ex-Mt
BBRR-AD A.Dawson Bat	15.00	4.50
BBRR-AO Al Oliver Jsy	15.00	4.50
BBRR-BG Bobby Grich Jsy	15.00	4.50
BBRR-BM B.Murcer Bat	40.00	12.00
BBRR-BP Boog Powell Bat	25.00	7.50
BBRR-DE D.Eckersley Bat	15.00	4.50
BBRR-DS Don Sutton Jsy	15.00	4.50
BBRR-DW D.Winfield Bat	15.00	4.50
BBRR-GB G.Brett Jsy	40.00	12.00
BBRR-GC Gary Carter Bat	15.00	4.50
BBRR-JB J. Bench Bat	25.00	7.50
BBRR-JK Jim Kaat Bat	15.00	4.50
BBRR-JM Joe Morgan Jsy	15.00	4.50
BBRR-MF M. Fidrych Jsy	15.00	4.50
BBRR-OS Ozzie Smith Bat	25.00	7.50
BBRR-RJ R. Jackson Jsy	25.00	7.50
BBRR-RY R. Yount Jsy	25.00	7.50
BBRR-SC S. Carlton Bat	15.00	4.50
BBRR-TM T. McCarver Bat	15.00	4.50
BBRR-TM T.Munson Jsy	40.00	12.00

2001 Topps American Pie Timeless Classics Relics

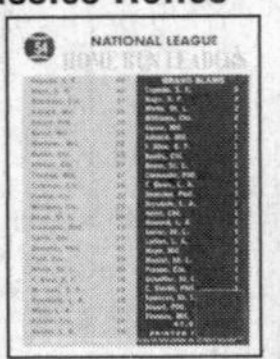

Inserted at a rate of one in 80, this 45-card set contains game-used bat or game-used uniform reprint leader cards depicting ballplayers who led the league during some of the game's most memorable seasons. The cards carry a 'BBTC' prefix.

	Nm-Mt	Ex-Mt
BBTC1 S.McDowell 66 Jsy	15.00	4.50
BBTC2 S.McDowell 70 Jsy	15.00	4.50
BBTC3 F.Howard 60 Jsy	15.00	4.50
BBTC4 Dick Groat 61 Bat	15.00	4.50
BBTC5 R.Maris 62 Bat	60.00	18.00
BBTC6 O.Cepeda 62 Jsy	15.00	4.50
BBTC7 Willie Mays 63 Jsy	50.00	15.00
BBTC8 Carl Yastrzemski 64 Jsy	40.00	12.00
BBTC9 R.Clemente 65 Bat	80.00	24.00
BBTC10 Harmon Killebrew 65 Bat	25.00	7.50
BBTC11 Brooks Robinson 65 Jsy	25.00	7.50
BBTC12 W. Mays 66 Jsy	50.00	15.00
BBTC13 T. Conigliaro 66 Jsy	25.00	7.50
BBTC14 F.Robinson 66 Jsy	25.00	7.50
BBTC15 Carl Yastrzemski 68 HR Jsy	40.00	12.00
BBTC16 Carl Yastrzemski 68 RBI Jsy	40.00	12.00
BBTC17 Carl Yastrzemski 68 BA Jsy	40.00	12.00
BBTC18 H.Aaron 66 Bat	50.00	15.00
BBTC19 F.Howard 69 Bat	15.00	4.50
BBTC20 Carl Yastrzemski 69 Bat	40.00	12.00
BBTC21 Willie McCovey 70 Jsy	15.00	4.50
BBTC22 Rico Carty 71 Bat	15.00	4.50
BBTC23 F.Howard 71 Bat	15.00	4.50
BBTC24 J.Bench 71 Bat	25.00	7.50
BBTC25 W.Stargell 72 Bat	25.00	7.50
BBTC26 S.Carlton 73 Jsy	15.00	4.50
BBTC27 N.Cash 62 Jsy	25.00	7.50
BBTC28 R.Jackson 74 Jsy	25.00	7.50
BBTC29 W.Stargell 74 Jsy	25.00	7.50
BBTC30 Mike Schmidt 75 Jsy	40.00	12.00
BBTC31 Mike Schmidt 76 Jsy	40.00	12.00
BBTC32 M. Rivers 76 Bat	15.00	4.50
BBTC33 T. Seaver 77 Jsy	25.00	7.50
BBTC34 G. Brett 77 Bat	40.00	12.00
BBTC35 G. Foster 77 Bat	15.00	4.50
BBTC36 G. Nettles 77 Bat	15.00	4.50
BBTC37 N. Ryan 77 Jsy	60.00	18.00
BBTC38 N. Ryan 79 Jsy	60.00	18.00
BBTC39 D. Parker 78 Bat	15.00	4.50
BBTC40 G. Foster 78 Bat	15.00	4.50
BBTC41 Dick Allen 73 Bat	15.00	4.50
BBTC42 D.Parker 79 Bat	15.00	4.50
BBTC43 Fred Lynn 80 Jsy	15.00	4.50
BBTC44 Keith Hernandez 80 Bat	15.00	4.50
BBTC45 D. Winfield 80 Bat	15.00	4.50

2001 Topps American Pie Woodstock Relics

Inserted at an overall rate of one in 138, this 25 card set featured 24 game used bat cards and one card featuring mud from Yasgur's farm. Yasgur's farm was the location of the Woodstock festival in 1969. The odds for bat cards were one in 167, while the odds for the mud was one in 806.

	Nm-Mt	Ex-Mt
BBWM-BB B. Buckner Bat	15.00	4.50
BBWM-BF Bill Freehan Bat	15.00	4.50
BBWM-BR Brooks Robinson Bat	25.00	7.50
BBWM-CF Carlton Fisk Bat	25.00	7.50
BBWM-CY Carl Yastrzemski Bat	40.00	12.00
BBWM-DE Dw. Evans Bat	15.00	4.50
BBWM-DG Dick Groat Bat	15.00	4.50
BBWM-DS D. Snider Bat	25.00	7.50
BBWM-DW Dave Winfield Bat	15.00	4.50
BBWM-FL Fred Lynn Bat	15.00	4.50
BBWM-FR Frank Robinson Bat	25.00	7.50
BBWM-GB G. Brett Bat	40.00	12.00
BBWM-JP J. Piersall Bat	15.00	4.50
BBWM-JR Joe Rudi Bat	15.00	4.50
BBWM-JW Jim Wynn Bat	15.00	4.50
BBWM-MW M. Wills Bat	15.00	4.50
BBWM-OC O. Cepeda Bat	15.00	4.50
BBWM-RJ R. Jackson Bat	25.00	7.50
BBWM-RY R. Yount Bat	25.00	7.50
BBWM-SM S. Musial Bat	50.00	15.00
BBWM-TK Ted Kluszewski Bat	25.00	7.50
BBWM-TP Tony Perez Bat	15.00	4.50
BBWM-WM W. Mays Bat	50.00	15.00
BBWM-WS Woodstock	15.00	4.50
BBWM-WS Willie Stargell Bat	25.00	7.50

2002 Topps American Pie

This set was released in May, 2002. These cards were issued in seven card packs with a $4 SRP and were issued 24 packs to a box and 10 boxes to a case. This set has an eclectic mix between baseball players and celebrities and events of the past.

	Nm-Mt	Ex-Mt
COMPLETE SET (150)	40.00	12.00
1 Warren Spahn	.75	.23
2 Reggie Jackson	.75	.23
3 Bill Mazeroski	.75	.23
4 Carl Yastrzemski	2.00	.60
5 Whitey Ford	.75	.23
6 Ralph Houk	.50	.15
7 Rod Carew	.75	.23
8 Kirk Gibson	.50	.15
9 Bobby Thomson	.50	.15
10 Don Newcombe	.50	.15
11 Gaylord Perry	.50	.15
12 Bruce Sutter	.50	.15
13 Bob Gibson	.75	.23
14 Brooks Robinson	.75	.23
15 Steve Carlton	.50	.15
16 Robin Yount	2.00	.60
17 Ernie Banks	1.25	.35
18 Lou Brock	.75	.23
19 Al Kaline	1.25	.35
20 Carlton Fisk	.75	.23
21 Frank Robinson	.75	.23
22 Bobby Bonds	.50	.15
23 Andre Dawson	.50	.15
24 Goose Gossage	.50	.15
25 Fred Lynn	.50	.15
26 Keith Hernandez	.50	.15
27 Rollie Fingers	.50	.15
28 Juan Marichal	.50	.15
29 Maury Wills	.50	.15
30 Dave Winfield	.50	.15
31 Frank Howard	.50	.15
32 Tony Gwynn	1.50	.45
33 Jim Palmer	.50	.15
34 Mike Schmidt	2.50	.75
35 Bo Jackson	1.25	.35
36 Ferguson Jenkins	.50	.15
37 Bobby Richardson	.50	.15
38 Harmon Killebrew	1.25	.35
39 Monte Irvin	.50	.15
40 Jim Abbott	.75	.23
41 Wade Boggs	.75	.23
42 Jackie Robinson	1.25	.35
43 Ralph Branca	.50	.15
44 Minnie Minoso	.50	.15
45 Tug McGraw	.50	.15
46 Willie Mays	2.50	.75
47 Nolan Ryan	3.00	.90
48 Duke Snider	.75	.23
49 Tom Seaver	.75	.23
50 Casey Stengel	.75	.23
51 D-Day	.50	.15
52 Gulf War	.50	.15
53 Vietnam War	.50	.15
54 Korean War	.50	.15
55 Secret Service	.50	.15
56 Crayons	.50	.15
57 Hoover Dam	.50	.15
58 Penicillin	.50	.15
59 Polio Vaccine	.50	.15
60 Empire State Building	.50	.15
61 Television	.50	.15
62 Duke Ellington	.75	.23
63 Voyager Mission	.50	.15
64 Space Shuttle	.50	.15
65 Ellis Island	.50	.15
66 Statue Of Liberty	.50	.15
67 Battle Of The Bulge	.50	.15
68 Battle Of Midway	.50	.15
69 Iwo Jima	.50	.15
70 Panama Canal	.50	.15
71 Charles Lindbergh Spirit Of St. Louis	.50	.15
72 Civil Rights We Shall Overcome	.50	.15
73 Space Race	.50	.15
74 Alaska Pipeline	.50	.15
75 Teddy Bear	.50	.15
76 Seabiscuit	.50	.15
77 Bazooka Joe	.50	.15
78 Mt. Rushmore	.50	.15
79 Yellowstone Park	.50	.15
80 Niagara Falls	.50	.15
81 Grand Canyon	.50	.15
82 Hoola Hoop	.50	.15
83 George Patton	.75	.23
84 Florence Griffith Joyner	.50	.15
85 Amelia Earhart	.50	.15
86 Glen Miller	.50	.15
87 Rick Monday	.50	.15
88 Buzz Aldrin	.50	.15
89 Rosa Parks	.50	.15
90 Edward R. Murrow	.50	.15
91 Susan B. Anthony	.50	.15
92 Bobby Kennedy	.50	.15
93 Gloria Steinem	.50	.15
94 Hank Greenberg	1.25	.35
95 Jimmy Doolittle	.50	.15
96 Thurgood Marshall	.50	.15
97 Ernest Hemingway	1.25	.35
98 Henry Ford	.75	.23
99 Wright Brothers	.50	.15
100 Thomas Edison	.50	.15
101 Albert Einstein	1.25	.35
102 Will Rogers	.50	.15
103 George Gershwin	.50	.15
104 Irving Berlin	.50	.15
105 Frank Lloyd Wright	.50	.15
106 Howard Hughes	.75	.23
107 George M. Cohan	.50	.15
108 Jack Kerouac	.75	.23
109 Harry Houdini	.75	.23
110 Helen Keller	.50	.15
111 John McCain	.50	.15
112 Andrew Carnegie	.50	.15
113 Sandra Day O'Connor	.50	.15
114 Brooklyn Bridge	.50	.15
115 Douglas MacArthur	.75	.23
116 Elvis Presley	2.00	.60
117 George Burns	.50	.15
118 Judy Garland	1.25	.35
119 Buddy Holly	.50	.15
120 Don McLean	.50	.15
121 Marilyn Monroe	2.00	.60
122 Humphrey Bogart	1.50	.45
123 Gary Cooper	.75	.23
124 The Andrews Sisters	.50	.15
125 Jim Thorpe	1.25	.35
126 Joe Louis	1.25	.35
127 Jesse Owens	.75	.23
128 Kate Smith	.50	.15
129 W.C. Fields	.50	.15
130 Bette Davis	.75	.23
131 Jayne Mansfield	.75	.23
132 William McKinley	.50	.15
133 Teddy Roosevelt	1.25	.35
134 William Taft	.50	.15
135 Woodrow Wilson	.50	.15
136 Warren Harding	.50	.15
137 Calvin Coolidge	.50	.15
138 Herbert Hoover	.50	.15
139 Franklin D. Roosevelt	.75	.23
140 Harry Truman	.75	.23
141 Dwight Eisenhower	.75	.23
142 John F. Kennedy	2.00	.60
143 Lyndon B. Johnson	.75	.23
144 Richard Nixon	1.25	.35
145 Gerald Ford	.75	.23
146 Jimmy Carter	.75	.23
147 Ronald Reagan	5.00	1.50
148 George H.W. Bush	.50	.15
149 Bill Clinton	3.00	.90
150 George W. Bush	3.00	.90

2002 Topps American Pie First Pitch Seat Relics

Inserted into packs at stated odds of one in 32 hobby and 1:56 retail, these cards feature pictures of presidents along with seats from a ball park in which they threw out a first pitch of a game.

	Nm-Mt	Ex-Mt
BC Bill Clinton	60.00	18.00
CC Calvin Coolidge	15.00	4.50
DE Dwight Eisenhower	25.00	7.50
FDR Franklin D. Roosevelt	25.00	7.50
GF Gerald Ford	40.00	12.00
GHWB George H.W. Bush	15.00	4.50
GWB George W. Bush	80.00	24.00
HH Herbert Hoover	15.00	4.50
HT Harry Truman	25.00	7.50
JFK John F. Kennedy	80.00	24.00
RN Richard Nixon	50.00	15.00
RR Ronald Reagan	60.00	18.00
WH Warren Harding	15.00	4.50
WT William Taft	15.00	4.50
WW Woodrow Wilson	15.00	4.50
LBJ Lyndon B. Johnson	25.00	7.50

2002 Topps American Pie Piece of American Pie

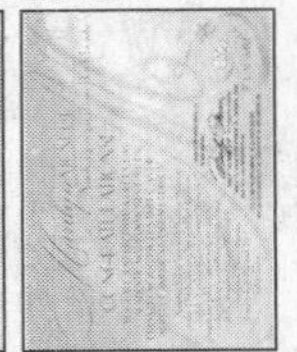

Inserted at different odds depending on the memorabilia item, these cards feature a cut swatch from an clothing item worn by a famous celebrity.

	Nm-Mt	Ex-Mt
H.BOGART SCARF ODDS 1:1074 H, 1:1930 R		
G.BURNS COAT ODDS 1:680 H, 1:1218 R		
G.COOPER SCARF ODDS 1:414 H, 1:739 R		
B.DAVIS JACKET ODDS 1:680 H, 1:1218 R		
J.GARLAND SCARF ODDS 1:680 H, 1:1218 R		
J.MANSFIELD PANTS ODDS 1:680 H, 11218 R		
M.MONROE DRESS ODDS 1:684 H, 1:1221 R		
E.PRESLEY COAT ODDS 1:684 H, 1:1221 R		
E.PRESLEY SHIRT ODDS 1:684 H, 1:1221 R		
R.REAGAN WALL ODDS 1:675 H, 1:1218 R		
BD Bette Davis Jacket	80.00	24.00
EP Elvis Presley Shirt	150.00	45.00
EP2 Elvis Presley Coat	150.00	45.00
GB George Burns Coat	60.00	18.00
GC Gary Cooper Scarf	60.00	18.00
HB H.Bogart Scarf	120.00	36.00
JD Judy Garland Scarf	80.00	24.00
JM Jayne Mansfield Shirt	100.00	30.00
MM Marilyn Monroe Dress	400.00	120.00
RR Ronald Reagan Wall	150.00	45.00

2002 Topps American Pie Sluggers Blue

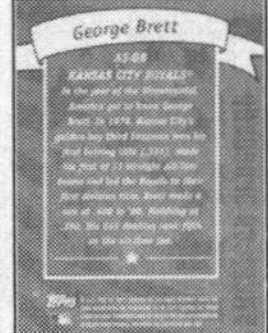

Inserted one per pack, these 25 cards feature famous sluggers born in America. These cards came in four different colored borders: Blue, Gold, Red and Silver. All four colors were produced in equal quantities.

	Nm-Mt	Ex-Mt
COMPLETE SET (25)	50.00	15.00
*RED/GOLD/SILVER: EQUAL VALUE...		
1 Rod Carew	2.50	.75
2 Brooks Robinson	2.50	.75
3 Mike Schmidt	8.00	2.40
4 Carlton Fisk	2.50	.75
5 Reggie Jackson	2.50	.75
6 Carl Yastrzemski	6.00	1.80
7 Kirk Gibson	1.50	.45
8 Al Kaline	4.00	1.20
9 Frank Robinson	2.50	.75
10 Fred Lynn	1.50	.45
11 Dave Winfield	1.50	.45
12 Harmon Killebrew	4.00	1.20
13 Monte Irvin	1.50	.45
14 Willie Mays	8.00	2.40
15 Duke Snider	2.50	.75
16 George Foster	1.50	.45
17 Joe Carter	1.50	.45
18 Eddie Mathews	4.00	1.20
19 George Brett	10.00	3.00
20 Frank Howard	1.50	.45
21 Andre Dawson	1.50	.45
22 Ted Kluszewski	2.50	.75
23 Ryne Sandberg	6.00	1.80
24 Jack Clark	1.50	.45
25 Cecil Cooper	1.50	.45

2002 Topps American Pie Through the Year Relics

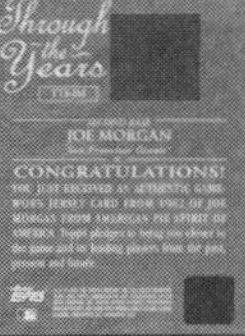

These 26 cards feature various memorabilia items from retired players career. These cards were inserted at differening odds depending on what type of memorabilia was attached to the card. All the cards in this set have a "TTY" prefix.

	Nm-Mt	Ex-Mt
BAT STATED ODDS 1:211 H, 1:377 R		
JERSEY STATED ODDS 1:32 H, 1:58 R		
UNIFORM STATED ODDS 1:60 H, 1:107 R		
AD Andre Dawson Bat	15.00	4.50
AL Al Oliver Jsy	15.00	4.50
BB Bill Buckner Jsy	15.00	4.50

CY Carl Yastrzemski Jsy 40.00 12.00
DA Dick Allen Bat 15.00 4.50
DM Don Mattingly Bat 50.00 15.00
DP Dave Parker Jsy 15.00 4.50
DS Darryl Strawberry Bat 15.00 4.50
DW Dave Winfield Bat 15.00 4.50
EM Eddie Mathews Uni. 25.00 7.50
FR Frank Robinson Jsy 20.00 6.00
GP Gaylord Perry Uniform 15.00 4.50
JA Jim Abbott Jsy 20.00 6.00
JB Johnny Bench Uniform 25.00 7.50
JC Jack Clark Jsy 15.00 4.50
JK Jim Kaat Uniform 15.00 4.50
JM Joe Morgan Jsy 15.00 4.50
JR Joe Rudi Jsy 15.00 4.50
MM Minnie Minoso Jsy 15.00 4.50
NR Nolan Ryan Uniform 50.00 15.00
RM Rick Monday Jsy 15.00 4.50
TM Thurman Munson Bat 40.00 12.00
TS Tom Seaver Jsy 20.00 6.00
WB Wade Boggs Jsy 20.00 6.00
WM Willie Mays Uniform 40.00 12.00
WS Willie Stargell Uniform 20.00 6.00

1991 Topps Archives 1953

The 1953 Topps Archive set is a reprint of the original 274-card 1953 Topps set. The only card missing from the reprint set is that of Billy Loes (174), who did not give Topps permission to reprint his card. Moreover, the set has been extended by 57 cards, with cards honoring Mrs. Eleanor Engle, Hoyt Wilhelm (who had already been included in the set as card number 151), 1953 HOF inductees Dizzy Dean and Al Simmons, and "prospect" Hank Aaron. Although the original cards measured 2 5/8" by 3 3/4", the reprint cards measure the modern standard size. Production quantities were supposedly limited to not more than 18,000 cases.

Nm-Mt Ex-Mt
COMPLETE SET (330) 60.00 18.00
COMMON CARD (1-220) .15 .04
COMMON (221-280) .25 .07
COMMON (281-337) .30 .09
1 Jackie Robinson .75 .23
2 Luke Easter .30 .09
3 George Crowe .15 .04
4 Ben Wade .15 .04
5 Joe Dobson .15 .04
6 Sam Jones .15 .04
7 Bob Borkowski .15 .04
8 Clem Koshorek .15 .04
9 Joe Collins .30 .09
10 Smoky Burgess .30 .09
11 Sal Yvars .15 .04
12 Howie Judson .15 .04
13 Conrado Marrero .15 .04
14 Clem Labine .50 .15
15 Bobo Newsom .30 .09
16 Peanuts Lowrey .15 .04
17 Billy Hitchcock .15 .04
18 Ted Lepcio .15 .04
19 Mel Parnell .15 .04
20 Hank Thompson .15 .04
21 Billy Johnson .15 .04
22 Howie Fox .15 .04
23 Toby Atwell .15 .04
24 Ferris Fain .15 .04
25 Ray Boone .15 .04
26 Dale Mitchell .30 .09
27 Roy Campanella .75 .23
28 Eddie Pellagrini .15 .04
29 Hal Jeffcoat .15 .04
30 Willard Nixon .15 .04
31 Ewell Blackwell .30 .09
32 Clyde Vollmer .15 .04
33 Bob Kennedy .15 .04
34 George Shuba .15 .04
35 Irv Noren .15 .04
36 Johnny Groth .15 .04
37 Eddie Mathews .75 .23
38 Jim Hearn .15 .04
39 Eddie Miksis .15 .04
40 John Lipon .15 .04
41 Enos Slaughter .30 .09
42 Gus Zernial .30 .09
43 Gil McDougald .30 .09
44 Ellis Kinder .15 .04
45 Grady Hatton .15 .04
46 Johnny Klippstein .15 .04
47 Bubba Church .15 .04
48 Bob Del Greco .15 .04
49 Faye Throneberry .15 .04
50 Chuck Dressen MG .15 .04
51 Frank Campos .15 .04
52 Ted Gray .15 .04
53 Sherm Lollar .30 .09
54 Bob Feller .30 .09
55 Maurice McDermott .15 .04
56 Gerry Staley .15 .04
57 Carl Scheib .15 .04
58 George Metkovich .15 .04
59 Karl Drews .15 .04
60 Cloyd Boyer .15 .04
61 Early Wynn .50 .15
62 Monte Irvin .30 .09
63 Gus Niarhos .15 .04
64 Dave Philley .15 .04
65 Earl Harrist .15 .04
66 Minnie Minoso .30 .09
67 Roy Sievers .30 .09
68 Del Rice .15 .04
69 Dick Brodowski .15 .04
70 Ed Yuhas .15 .04
71 Tony Bartirome .15 .04
72 Fred Hutchinson .30 .09
73 Eddie Robinson .15 .04
74 Joe Rossi .15 .04
75 Mike Garcia .30 .09
76 Pee Wee Reese .75 .23
77 Johnny Mize .30 .09
78 Red Schoendienst .30 .09
79 Johnny Wyrostek .15 .04
80 Jim Hegan .15 .04
81 Joe Black .30 .09
82 Mickey Mantle 20.00 6.00
83 Howie Pollet .15 .04
84 Bob Hooper .15 .04
85 Bobby Morgan .15 .04
86 Billy Martin .50 .15
87 Ed Lopat .30 .09
88 Willie Jones .15 .04
89 Chuck Stobbs .15 .04
90 Hank Edwards .15 .04
91 Ebba St.Claire .15 .04
92 Paul Minner .15 .04
93 Hal Rice .15 .04
94 Bill Kennedy .15 .04
95 Willard Marshall .15 .04
96 Virgil Trucks .15 .04
97 Don Kolloway .15 .04
98 Cal Abrams .15 .04
99 Dave Madison .15 .04
100 Bill Miller .15 .04
101 Ted Wilks .15 .04
102 Connie Ryan .15 .04
103 Joe Astroth .15 .04
104 Yogi Berra 2.50 .75
105 Joe Nuxhall .30 .09
106 Johnny Antonelli .30 .09
107 Danny O'Connell .15 .04
108 Bob Porterfield .15 .04
109 Alvin Dark .30 .09
110 Herman Wehmeier .15 .04
111 Hank Sauer .30 .09
112 Ned Garver .15 .04
113 Jerry Priddy .15 .04
114 Phil Rizzuto .75 .23
115 George Spencer .15 .04
116 Frank Smith .15 .04
117 Sid Gordon .15 .04
118 Gus Bell .30 .09
119 Johnny Sain .30 .09
120 Davey Williams .15 .04
121 Walt Dropo .15 .04
122 Elmer Valo .15 .04
123 Tommy Byrne .15 .04
124 Sibby Sisti .15 .04
125 Dick Williams .30 .09
126 Bill Connelly .15 .04
127 Clint Courtney .15 .04
128 Wilmer Mizell .30 .09
129 Keith Thomas .15 .04
130 Turk Lown .15 .04
131 Harry Byrd .15 .04
132 Tom Morgan .15 .04
133 Gil Coan .15 .04
134 Rube Walker .15 .04
135 Al Rosen .30 .09
136 Ken Heintzelman .15 .04
137 John Rutherford .15 .04
138 George Kell .50 .15
139 Sammy White .15 .04
140 Tommy Glaviano .15 .04
141 Allie Reynolds .75 .23
142 Vic Wertz .30 .09
143 Billy Pierce .30 .09
144 Bob Schultz .15 .04
145 Harry Dorish .15 .04
146 Granny Hamner .30 .09
147 Warren Spahn .50 .15
148 Mickey Grasso .15 .04
149 Dom DiMaggio .75 .23
150 Harry Simpson .15 .04
151 Hoyt Wilhelm .30 .09
152 Bob Adams .15 .04
153 Andy Seminick .30 .09
154 Dick Groat .30 .09
155 Dutch Leonard .15 .04
156 Jim Rivera .15 .04
157 Bob Addis .15 .04
158 Johnny Logan .30 .09
159 Wayne Terwilliger .15 .04
160 Bob Young .15 .04
161 Vern Bickford .15 .04
162 Ted Kluszewski .50 .15
163 Fred Hatfield .15 .04
164 Frank Shea .15 .04
165 Billy Hoeft .15 .04
166 Billy Hunter .15 .04
167 Art Schult .15 .04
168 Willard Schmidt .15 .04
169 Dizzy Trout .15 .04
170 Bill Werle .15 .04
171 Bill Glynn .15 .04
172 Rip Repulski .15 .04
173 Preston Ward .15 .04
174 Billy Loes
(Not printed)
175 Ron Kline .15 .04
176 Don Hoak .15 .04
177 Jim Dyck .15 .04
178 Jim Waugh .15 .04
179 Gene Hermanski .15 .04
180 Virgil Stallcup .15 .04
181 Al Zarilla .15 .04
182 Bobby Hofman .15 .04
183 Stu Miller .15 .04
184 Hal Brown .15 .04
185 Jim Pendleton .15 .04
186 Charlie Bishop .15 .04
187 Jim Fridley .15 .04
188 Andy Carey .30 .09
189 Ray Jablonski .15 .04
190 Dixie Walker CO .30 .09
191 Ralph Kiner .50 .15
192 Wally Westlake .15 .04
193 Mike Clark .15 .04
194 Eddie Kazak .15 .04
195 Ed McGhee .15 .04
196 Bob Keegan .15 .04
197 Del Crandall .30 .09
198 Forrest Main .15 .04
199 Marion Fricano .15 .04
200 Gordon Goldsberry .15 .04
201 Paul LaPalme .15 .04
202 Carl Sawatski .15 .04
203 Cliff Fannin .15 .04
204 Dick Bokelman .15 .04
205 Vern Benson .15 .04
206 Ed Bailey .15 .04
207 Whitey Ford .50 .15
208 Jim Wilson .15 .04
209 Jim Greengrass .15 .04
210 Bob Cerv .15 .04
211 J.W. Porter .15 .04
212 Jack Dittmer .15 .04
213 Ray Scarborough .15 .04
214 Bill Bruton .15 .04
215 Gene Conley .15 .04
216 Jim Hughes .15 .04
217 Murray Wall .15 .04
218 Les Fusselman .15 .04
219 Pete Runnels UER .30 .09
(Photo actually
Don Johnson)
220 Satchel Paige UER .75 .23
(Misspelled Satchell
on card front)
221 Bob Milliken .25 .07
222 Vic Janowicz .50 .15
223 Johnny O'Brien .50 .15
224 Lou Sleater .25 .07
225 Bobby Shantz .50 .15
226 Ed Erautt .25 .07
227 Morrie Martin .25 .07
228 Hal Newhouser .75 .23
229 Rocky Krsnich .25 .07
230 Johnny Lindell .25 .07
231 Solly Hemus .25 .07
232 Dick Kokos .25 .07
233 Al Aber .25 .07
234 Ray Murray .25 .07
235 John Hetki .25 .07
236 Harry Perkowski .25 .07
237 Bud Podbielan .25 .07
238 Cal Hogue .25 .07
239 Jim Delsing .25 .07
240 Fred Marsh .25 .07
241 Al Sima .25 .07
242 Charlie Silvera .50 .15
243 Carlos Bernier .25 .07
244 Willie Mays 12.00 3.60
245 Bill Norman CO .25 .07
246 Roy Face .50 .15
247 Mike Sandlock .25 .07
248 Gene Stephens .25 .07
249 Eddie O'Brien .50 .15
250 Bob Wilson .25 .07
251 Sid Hudson .25 .07
252 Hank Foiles .25 .07
253 Does not exist
254 Preacher Roe .50 .15
255 Dixie Howell .25 .07
256 Les Peden .25 .07
257 Bob Boyd .25 .07
258 Jim Gilliam .50 .15
259 Roy McMillan .50 .15
260 Sam Calderone .25 .07
261 Does not exist
262 Bob Oldis .25 .07
263 Johnny Podres .50 .15
264 Gene Woodling .50 .15
265 Jackie Jensen .50 .15
266 Bob Cain .25 .07
267 Does not exist
268 Does not exist
269 Duane Pillette .25 .07
270 Vern Stephens .50 .15
271 Does not exist
272 Bill Antonello .25 .07
273 Harvey Haddix .50 .15
274 John Riddle .25 .07
275 Does not exist
276 Ken Raffensberger .25 .07
277 Don Lund .25 .07
278 Willie Miranda .25 .07
279 Joe Coleman .25 .07
280 Milt Bolling .25 .07
281 Jimmie Dykes MG .50 .15
282 Ralph Houk .50 .15
283 Frank Thomas .50 .15
284 Bob Lemon 1.25 .35
285 Joe Adcock .50 .15
286 Jimmy Piersall .50 .15
287 Mickey Vernon .50 .15
288 Robin Roberts .50 .15
289 Rogers Hornsby MG .75 .23
290 Hank Bauer .50 .15
291 Hoot Evers .30 .09
292 Whitey Lockman .50 .15
293 Ralph Branca .50 .15
294 Wally Post .50 .15
295 Phil Cavarretta MG .50 .15
296 Gil Hodges 1.25 .35
297 Roy Smalley .30 .09
298 Bob Friend .50 .15
299 Dusty Rhodes .30 .09
300 Eddie Stanky .30 .09
301 Harvey Kuenn .50 .15
302 Marty Marion .30 .09
303 Sal Maglie .50 .15
304 Lou Boudreau MG .50 .15
305 Carl Furillo .75 .23
306 Bobo Holloman .30 .09
307 Steve O'Neill MG .30 .09
308 Carl Erskine .75 .23
309 Leo Durocher MG .50 .15
310 Lew Burdette .50 .15
311 Richie Ashburn .75 .23
312 Hoyt Wilhelm .50 .15
313 Bucky Harris MG .50 .15
314 Joe Garagiola .50 .15
315 Johnny Pesky .50 .15
316 Fred Haney MG .30 .09
317 Hank Aaron 10.00 3.00
318 Curt Simmons .50 .15
319 Ted Williams 10.00 3.00
320 Don Newcombe .50 .15
321 Charlie Grimm MG .50 .15
322 Paul Richards MG .50 .15
323 Wes Westrum .30 .09
324 Vern Law .30 .09
325 Casey Stengel MG 1.25 .35
326 Dizzy Dean and .75 .23
Al Simmons
(1953 HOF Inductees)
327 Duke Snider .50 .15
328 Bill Rigney .50 .15
329 Al Lopez MG .50 .15
330 Bobby Thomson .50 .15
331 Nellie Fox .75 .23
332 Eleanor Engle .50 .15
333 Larry Doby .50 .15
334 Billy Goodman .50 .15
335 Checklist 1-140 .30 .09
336 Checklist 141-280 .30 .09
337 Checklist 281-337 .30 .09

1994 Topps Archives 1954

The 1954 Archives set includes 248 reprint cards from the original set, plus eight specially created prospect cards (Roberto Clemente, Harmon Killebrew, Bob Grim, Camilo Pascual, Herb Score, Elston Howard, Bill Virdon, and Don Zimmer). No factory sets were sold. Randomly inserted were 1,954 redemption cards good for actual 1954 Topps cards; 1,954 Hank Aaron autographed gold cards; and 1,954 redemption cards for full sets of ToppsGold Archives cards. Each 12-card pack contains 11 Archives cards plus one ToppsGold Archives card. A random insert card replaced the gold card in every 2,210 packs. Ted Williams' cards numbers 1 and 250, as well as a new Mickey Mantle's card number 259, were issued as inserts in the 1994 Upper Deck All-Time Heroes series.

Nm-Mt Ex-Mt
COMPLETE SET (256) 150.00 45.00
COMMON CARD (2-249) .15 .04
COMMON (251-258) .15 .04
1 Not Issued
2 Gus Zernial .30 .09
3 Monte Irvin .30 .09
4 Hank Sauer .30 .09
5 Ed Lopat .30 .09
6 Pete Runnels .30 .09
7 Ted Kluszewski .50 .15
8 Bobby Young .15 .04
9 Harvey Haddix .30 .09
10 Jackie Robinson .75 .23
11 Paul Smith .15 .04
12 Del Crandall .30 .09
13 Billy Martin .50 .15
14 Preacher Roe .30 .09
15 Al Rosen .30 .09
16 Vic Janowicz .30 .09
17 Phil Rizzuto .75 .23
18 Walt Dropo .15 .04
19 Johnny Lipon .15 .04
20 Warren Spahn .50 .15
21 Bobby Shantz .30 .09
22 Jim Greengrass .15 .04
23 Luke Easter .30 .09
24 Granny Hamner .30 .09
25 Harvey Kuenn .30 .09
26 Ray Jablonski .15 .04
27 Ferris Fain .15 .04
28 Paul Minner .15 .04
29 Jim Hegan .15 .04
30 Ed Mathews .75 .23
31 Johnny Klippstein .15 .04
32 Duke Snider .50 .15
33 Johnny Schmitz .15 .04
34 Jim Rivera .15 .04
35 Jim Gilliam .30 .09
36 Hoyt Wilhelm .30 .09
37 Whitey Ford .50 .15
38 Eddie Stanky MG .30 .09
39 Sherm Lollar .30 .09
40 Mel Parnell .15 .04
41 Willie Jones .15 .04
42 Don Mueller .15 .04
43 Dick Groat .30 .09
44 Ned Garver .15 .04
45 Richie Ashburn .50 .15
46 Ken Raffensberger .15 .04
47 Ellis Kinder .15 .04
48 Billy Hunter .15 .04
49 Ray Murray .15 .04
50 Yogi Berra 1.50 .45
51 Johnny Lindell .15 .04
52 Vic Power .15 .04
53 Jack Dittmer .15 .04
54 Vern Stephens .30 .09
55 Phil Cavarretta MG .30 .09
56 Willie Miranda .15 .04
57 Luis Aloma .15 .04
58 Bob Wilson .15 .04
59 Gene Conley .15 .04
60 Frank Baumholtz .15 .04
61 Bob Cain .15 .04
62 Eddie Robinson .15 .04
63 Johnny Pesky .30 .09
64 Hank Thompson .15 .04
65 Bob Swift .15 .04
66 Ted Lepcio .15 .04
67 Jim Willis .15 .04
68 Sammy Calderone .15 .04
69 Bud Podbielan .15 .04
70 Larry Doby .30 .09
71 Frank Smith .15 .04
72 Preston Ward .15 .04
73 Wayne Terwilliger .15 .04
74 Bill Taylor .15 .04
75 Fred Haney MG .15 .04
76 Bob Scheffing CO .15 .04
77 Ray Boone .15 .04
78 Ted Kazanski .15 .04
79 Andy Pafko .30 .09
80 Jackie Jensen .30 .09
81 Dave Hoskins .15 .04
82 Milt Bolling .15 .04
83 Joe Collins .30 .09
84 Dick Cole .15 .04
85 Bob Turley .30 .09
86 Billy Herman CO .30 .09
87 Roy Face .30 .09
88 Matt Batts .15 .04
89 Howie Pollet .15 .04
90 Willie Mays 5.00 1.50
91 Bob Oldis .15 .04
92 Wally Westlake .15 .04
93 Sid Hudson .15 .04
94 Ernie Banks 3.00 .90
95 Hal Rice .15 .04
96 Charlie Silvera .30 .09
97 Jerry Lane .15 .04
98 Joe Black .30 .09
99 Bob Hofman .15 .04
100 Bob Keegan .15 .04
101 Gene Woodling .30 .09
102 Gil Hodges .75 .23
103 Jim Lemon .15 .04
104 Mike Sandlock .15 .04
105 Andy Carey .30 .09
106 Dick Kokos .15 .04
107 Duane Pillette .15 .04
108 Thornton Kipper .15 .04
109 Bill Bruton .15 .04
110 Harry Dorish .15 .04
111 Jim Delsing .15 .04
112 Bill Renna .15 .04
113 Bob Boyd .15 .04
114 Dean Stone .15 .04
115 Rip Repulski .15 .04
116 Steve Bilko .15 .04
117 Solly Hemus .15 .04
118 Carl Scheib .15 .04
119 Johnny Antonelli .30 .09
120 Roy McMillan .30 .09
121 Clem Labine .50 .15
122 Johnny Logan .30 .09
123 Bobby Adams .15 .04
124 Marion Fricano .15 .04
125 Harry Perkowski .15 .04
126 Ben Wade .15 .04
127 Steve O'Neill MG .15 .04
128 Henry Aaron 6.00 1.80
129 Forrest Jacobs .15 .04
130 Hank Bauer .30 .09
131 Reno Bertoia .15 .04
132 Tom Lasorda .50 .15
133 Del Baker CO .15 .04
134 Cal Hogue .15 .04
135 Joe Presko .15 .04
136 Connie Ryan .15 .04
137 Wally Moon .30 .09
138 Bob Borkowski .15 .04
139 Ed O'Brien .30 .09
Johnny O'Brien
140 Tom Wright .15 .04
141 Joe Jay .15 .04
142 Tom Poholsky .15 .04
143 Rollie Hemsley CO .15 .04
144 Bill Werle .15 .04
145 Elmer Valo .15 .04
146 Don Johnson .15 .04
147 John Riddle CO .15 .04
148 Bob Trice .15 .04
149 Jim Robertson .15 .04
150 Dick Kryhoski .15 .04
151 Alex Grammas .15 .04
152 Mike Blyzka .15 .04
153 Rube Walker .15 .04
154 Mike Fornieles .15 .04
155 Bob Kennedy .15 .04
156 Joe Coleman .15 .04
157 Don Lenhardt .15 .04
158 Peanuts Lowrey .15 .04
159 Dave Philley .15 .04
160 Red Kress CO .15 .04
161 John Hetki .15 .04
162 Herman Wehmeier .15 .04
163 Frank House .15 .04
164 Stu Miller .15 .04
165 Jim Pendleton .15 .04
166 Johnny Podres .30 .09
167 Don Lund .15 .04
168 Morrie Martin .15 .04
169 Jim Hughes .15 .04
170 Dusty Rhodes .15 .04
171 Leo Kiely .15 .04
172 Hal Brown .15 .04
173 Jack Harshman .15 .04
174 Tom Qualters .15 .04
175 Frank Leja .15 .04
176 Bob Keely .15 .04
177 Bob Milliken .15 .04
178 Bill Glynn .15 .04
179 Gair Allie .15 .04
180 Wes Westrum .15 .04
181 Mel Roach .15 .04
182 Chuck Harmon .15 .04
183 Earle Combs CO .75 .23
184 Ed Bailey .15 .04
185 Chuck Stobbs .15 .04
186 Karl Olson .15 .04
187 Heinie Manush CO .75 .23
188 Dave Jolly .15 .04
189 Bob Ross .15 .04
190 Ray Herbert .15 .04
191 Dick Schofield .15 .04
192 Cot Deal CO .15 .04
193 Johnny Hopp CO .15 .04
194 Bill Sarni .15 .04
195 Bill Consolo .15 .04
196 Stan Jok .15 .04
197 Schoolboy Rowe CO .30 .09
198 Carl Sawatski .15 .04
199 Rocky Nelson .15 .04
200 Larry Jansen .15 .04
201 Al Kaline 3.00 .90
202 Bob Purkey .15 .04
203 Harry Brecheen CO .15 .04
204 Angel Scull .15 .04
205 Johnny Sain .30 .09
206 Ray Crone .15 .04
207 Tom Oliver CO .15 .04
208 Grady Hatton .15 .04
209 Charlie Thompson .15 .04
210 Bob Buhl .15 .04
211 Don Hoak .15 .04
212 Mickey Micelotta .15 .04

213 John Fitzpatrick CO .15 .04
214 Arnold Portocarrero .15 .04
215 Ed McGhee .15 .04
216 Al Sima .15 .04
217 Paul Schreiber CO .15 .04
218 Fred Marsh .15 .04
219 Charlie Kress .15 .04
220 Ruben Gomez .15 .04
221 Dick Brodowski .15 .04
222 Bill Wilson .15 .04
223 Joe Haynes CO .15 .04
224 Dick Weik .15 .04
225 Don Liddle .15 .04
226 Jehosie Heard .15 .04
227 Buster Mills CO .15 .04
228 Gene Hermanski .15 .04
229 Bob Talbot .15 .04
230 Bob Kuzava .15 .04
231 Roy Smalley .15 .04
232 Lou Limmer .15 .04
233 Augie Galan .15 .04
234 Jerry Lynch .15 .04
235 Vern Law .15 .04
236 Paul Penson .15 .04
237 Mike Ryba .15 .04
238 Al Aber .15 .04
239 Bill Skowron .50 .15
240 Sam Mele .15 .04
241 Bob Miller .15 .04
242 Curt Roberts .15 .04
243 Ray Blades CO .15 .04
244 Leroy Wheat .15 .04
245 Roy Sievers .30 .09
246 Howie Fox .15 .04
247 Eddie Mayo CO .15 .04
248 Al Smith .15 .04
249 Wilmer Mizell .30 .09
250 Not Issued
251 Roberto Clemente 10.00 3.00
252 Bob Grim .15 .04
253 Elston Howard .50 .15
254 Harmon Killebrew .75 .23
255 Camilo Pascual .15 .04
256 Herb Score .30 .09
257 Bill Virdon .30 .09
258 Don Zimmer .30 .09
NNO Hank Aaron AU 200.00 60.00
NNO Gold Redem. Card Exp. 1.05

1994 Topps Archives 1954 Gold

This set parallels the 1994 Topps Archives 1954 reprint series. It has the same design as the regular issue reprint, except that the team logo and the facsimile autograph are gold-foil stamped on the fronts.

Nm-Mt Ex-Mt
*STARS: 1.5X TO 4X BASIC CARDS...

1995 Topps Archives Brooklyn Dodgers

This 165-card set measures the standard size and is a single series release. The set honors the Brooklyn Dodger teams of 1952-1956 and consists of 127 reprints of Topps and Bowman cards produced during that time. The cards "that never were" have been created for the players not featured on Topps and Bowman cards and replicate the design of the card for the year the player would have been pictured. Cards numbered 117-120 commemorate the four games the Dodgers won for the 1955 World Series Championship. Though the cards are numbered as they were originally issued, Topps renumbered them as a complete set and they are checklisted accordingly. Some dealers believe that cards numbered from 111 through 165 were printed in shorter supply than other cards in this set. A very limited amount of signed Sandy Koufax cards (number 102 and number 146) were signed and randomly inserted into packs.

Nm-Mt Ex-Mt
COMPLETE SET (165) 150.00 45.00
1 Andy Pafko .50 .15
2 Wayne Terwilliger .25 .07
3 Billy Loes .50 .15
4 Gil Hodges 2.00 .60
5 Duke Snider 1.00 .30
6 Jim Russell .25 .07
7 Chris Van Cuyk .25 .07
8 Preacher Roe .50 .15
9 Johnny Schmitz .25 .07
10 Bud Podbielan .25 .07
11 Phil Haugstad .25 .07
12 Clyde King .25 .07
13 Billy Cox .50 .15
14 Rocky Bridges .25 .07
15 Carl Erskine 1.00 .30
16 Erv Palica .25 .07
17 Ralph Branca .50 .15
18 Jackie Robinson 2.00 .60
19 Roy Campanella 2.00 .60
20 Rube Walker .25 .07
21 Johnny Rutherford .25 .07
22 Joe Black .50 .15
23 George Shuba .25 .07
24 Pee Wee Reese 2.00 .60
25 Clem Labine 1.00 .30
26 Bobby Morgan .25 .07
27 Cookie Lavagetto CO .25 .07
28 Chuck Dressen MG .25 .07
29 Ben Wade .25 .07
30 Rocky Nelson .25 .07
31 Billy Herman CO .50 .15
32 Jake Pitler CO .25 .07
33 Dick Williams .50 .15
34 Cal Abrams .25 .07
35 Carl Furillo 1.00 .30
36 Don Newcombe .50 .15
37 Jackie Robinson 2.00 .60
38 Ben Wade .25 .07
39 Clem Labine 1.00 .30
40 Roy Campanella 2.00 .60
41 George Shuba .25 .07
42 Chuck Dressen MG .25 .07
43 Pee Wee Reese 2.00 .60
44 Joe Black .50 .15
45 Bobby Morgan .25 .07
46 Dick Williams .50 .15
47 Rube Walker .25 .07
48 Johnny Rutherford .25 .07
49 Billy Loes .50 .15
50 Don Hoak .25 .07
51 Jim Hughes .25 .07
52 Bob Milliken .25 .07
53 Preacher Roe .50 .15
54 Dixie Howell .25 .07
55 Junior Gilliam 1.00 .30
56 Johnny Podres .50 .15
57 Bill Antonello .25 .07
58 Ralph Branca .50 .15
59 Gil Hodges 2.00 .60
60 Carl Furillo 1.00 .30
61 Carl Erskine 1.00 .30
62 Don Newcombe .50 .15
63 Duke Snider 1.00 .30
64 Billy Cox .50 .15
65 Russ Meyer .25 .07
66 Jackie Robinson 2.00 .60
67 Preacher Roe .50 .15
68 Duke Snider 1.00 .30
69 Junior Gilliam 1.00 .30
70 Billy Herman CO .50 .15
71 Joe Black .50 .15
72 Gil Hodges 2.00 .60
73 Clem Labine 1.00 .30
74 Ben Wade .25 .07
75 Tom Lasorda 1.00 .30
76 Rube Walker .25 .07
77 Johnny Podres .50 .15
78 Jim Hughes .25 .07
79 Bob Milliken .25 .07
80 Charlie Thompson .25 .07
81 Don Hoak .25 .07
82 Roberto Clemente 4.00 1.20
83 Don Zimmer .50 .15
84 Roy Campanella 2.00 .60
85 Billy Cox .50 .15
86 Carl Erskine 1.00 .30
87 Carl Furillo 1.00 .30
88 Don Newcombe .50 .15
89 Pee Wee Reese 2.00 .60
90 George Shuba .25 .07
91 Junior Gilliam 1.00 .30
92 Billy Herman CO .50 .15
93 Johnny Podres .50 .15
94 Don Hoak .25 .07
95 Jackie Robinson 2.00 .60
96 Jim Hughes .25 .07
97 Bob Borkowski .50 .15
98 Sandy Amoros .25 .07
99 Karl Spooner .50 .15
100 Don Zimmer .25 .07
101 Rube Walker .25 .07
102 Bob Milliken 4.00 1.20
103 Sandy Koufax .50 .15
104 Joe Black 1.00 .30
105 Clem Labine 2.00 .60
106 Gil Hodges .25 .07
107 Ed Roebuck .25 .07
108 Bert Hamrik 1.00 .30
109 Duke Snider 1.00 .30
110 Bob Borkowski .25 .07
111 Roger Craig .50 .15
112 Don Drysdale 2.00 .60
113 Dixie Howell .25 .07
114 Frank Kellert .25 .07
115 Tom Lasorda 1.00 .30
116 Chuck Templeton .25 .07
117 Jackie Robinson WS 1.00 .30
118 Gil Hodges WS 2.00 .60
119 Duke Snider WS 1.00 .30
120 Johnny Podres WS 2.00 .60
121 Don Hoak .25 .07
122 Roy Campanella 2.00 .60
123 Pee Wee Reese 2.00 .60
124 Bob Darnell .25 .07
125 Don Zimmer .50 .15
126 George Shuba .25 .07
127 Johnny Podres .50 .15
128 Junior Gilliam 1.00 .30
129 Don Newcombe .50 .15
130 Jim Hughes .25 .07
131 Gil Hodges 2.00 .60
132 Carl Furillo 1.00 .30
133 Carl Erskine 1.00 .30
134 Erv Palica .25 .07
135 Russ Meyer .25 .07
136 Billy Loes .50 .15
137 Walt Moryn .25 .07
138 Chico Fernandez .25 .07
139 Charlie Neal .25 .07
140 Ken Lehman .25 .07
141 Walter Alston MG 1.00 .30
142 Jackie Robinson 2.00 .60
143 Sandy Amoros .50 .15
144 Ed Roebuck .25 .07
145 Roger Craig .50 .15
146 Sandy Koufax 2.00 .60
147 Karl Spooner .25 .07
148 Don Zimmer .50 .15
149 Roy Campanella 2.00 .60
150 Gil Hodges 2.00 .60
151 Duke Snider 1.00 .30
152 Team Card 1.00 .30
153 Johnny Podres .50 .15
154 Don Bessent .25 .07
155 Carl Furillo 1.00 .30
156 Randy Jackson .25 .07
157 Carl Erskine 1.00 .30
158 Don Newcombe .50 .15
159 Pee Wee Reese 2.00 .60
160 Billy Loes .50 .15
161 Junior Gilliam 1.00 .30
162 Clem Labine 1.00 .30
163 Charlie Neal .25 .07
164 Rube Walker .25 .07
165 Checklist .25 .07
AU103 Sandy Koufax 103AU 500.00 120.00
AU146 Sandy Koufax 146 AU 500.00 150.00

2001 Topps Archives

Issued in two series of 225 cards, this 450 card set features some of the first and last cards of retired superstars and other retired star players. The cards were issued in eight card packs with an SRP of $4. These packs were issued 20 packs to a box and eight boxes to a case. A very annoying feature of this set was the checklist numbers were so small that it was very difficult to tell what the number of the card was if a collector was trying to build a set.

Nm-Mt Ex-Mt
COMPLETE SET (450) 160.00 47.50
COMP. SERIES 1 (225) 80.00 24.00
COMP. SERIES 2 (225) 80.00 24.00
1 Johnny Antonelli 52 1.00 .30
2 Yogi Berra 52 UER 2.50 .75
Berra's first card was 51 Topps Red Back
3 Dom DiMaggio 52 UER 1.00 .30
His first Topps card is 1951 Red Back
4 Carl Erskine 52 1.00 .30
5 Larry Doby 52 1.00 .30
6 Monte Irvin 52 1.00 .30
7 Vernon Law 52 1.00 .30
8 Eddie Mathews 52 2.50 .75
9 Willie Mays 52 5.00 1.50
10 Gil McDougald 52 1.00 .30
11 Andy Pafko 52 1.50 .45
12 Phil Rizzuto 52 2.50 .75
13 Preacher Roe 52 UER 1.00 .30
His first Topps card is 51 Topps Red Back
14 Hank Sauer 52 UER 1.00 .30
His first Topps card is 51 Topps Blue Back
15 Bobby Shantz 52 1.00 .30
16 Enos Slaughter 52 UER 1.00 .30
His first Topps card is 51 Topps Blue Back
17 Warren Spahn 52 UER 1.50 .45
His First Topps card was 1951 Topps Red Back
18 Mickey Vernon 52 UER 1.00 .30
His First Topps Card was 1951 Topps Blue Back
19 Early Wynn 52 UER 1.00 .30
His first Topps card is a 1951 Topps Red Back
20 Gaylord Perry 62 1.00 .30
21 Johnny Podres 53 1.00 .30
22 Ernie Banks 54 2.50 .75
23 Moose Skowron 54 1.00 .30
24 Harmon Killebrew 55 2.50 .75
25 Ted Williams 54 5.00 1.50
26 Jimmy Piersall 56 1.00 .30
27 Frank Thomas 56 1.00 .30
28 Bill Mazeroski 57 2.50 .75
29 Bobby Richardson 57 1.00 .30
30 Frank Robinson 57 1.50 .45
31 Stan Musial 58 4.00 1.20
32 Johnny Callison 59 1.00 .30
33 Bob Gibson 59 1.50 .45
34 Frank Howard 60 1.00 .30
35 Willie McCovey 60 1.00 .30
36 Carl Yastrzemski 60 4.00 1.20
37 Jim Maloney 61 1.00 .30
38 Ron Santo 61 1.50 .45
39 Lou Brock 62 1.50 .45
40 Tim McCarver 62 1.00 .30
41 Joe Pepitone 62 .50 .15
42 Boog Powell 62 1.50 .45
43 Bill Freehan 63 1.00 .30
44 Dick Allen 64 1.00 .30
45 Willie Horton 64 .50 .15
46 Mickey Lolich 64 1.00 .30
47 Wilbur Wood 64 .50 .15
48 Bert Campaneris 65 1.00 .30
49 Rod Carew 67 1.50 .45
50 Luis Aparicio 56 1.00 .30
51 Joe Morgan 65 1.00 .30
52 Luis Tiant 65 1.00 .30
53 Bobby Murcer 66 1.00 .30
54 Don Sutton 66 1.00 .30
55 Ken Holtzman 67 .50 .15
56 Reggie Smith 67 1.00 .30
57 Hal McRae 68 1.00 .30
58 Roy White 68 UER 1.00 .30
His Rookie Card is 66 Topps
59 Reggie Jackson 69 1.50 .45
60 Graig Nettles 69 1.00 .30
61 Joe Rudi 69 1.00 .30
62 Vida Blue 70 1.00 .30
63 Darrell Evans 70 1.00 .30
64 David Concepcion 71 1.00 .30
65 Bobby Grich 71 1.00 .30
66 Greg Luzinski 71 1.00 .30
67 Ron Cey 72 1.00 .30
68 George Hendrick 72 .50 .15
69 Dwight Evans 73 1.50 .45
70 Gary Matthews 73 .50 .15
71 Mike Schmidt 73 6.00 1.80
72 Jim Kaat 60 1.00 .30
73 Dave Winfield 74 1.00 .30
74 Gary Carter 75 1.50 .45
75 Dennis Eckersley 76 1.00 .30
76 Kent Tekulve 76 1.00 .30
77 Andre Dawson 77 1.50 .45
78 Denny Martinez 77 1.00 .30
79 Bruce Sutter 77 1.00 .30
80 Jack Morris 78 1.00 .30
81 Ozzie Smith 80 5.00 1.50
82 Lee Smith 82 1.00 .30
83 Don Mattingly 84 8.00 2.40
84 Joe Carter 85 1.00 .30
85 Kirby Puckett 85 2.50 .75
86 Joe Adcock 52 1.00 .30
87 Gus Bell 52 UER .50 .15
His first Topps card is 1951 Topps Red Back
88 Roy Campanella 52 2.50 .75
89 Jackie Jensen 52 1.00 .30
90 Johnny Mize 52 1.50 .45
91 Allie Reynolds 52 1.00 .30
92 Al Rosen 52 UER 1.00 .30
His first Topps card is a 1951 Topps Red Back
93 Hal Newhouser 53 1.00 .30
94 Harvey Kuenn 54 1.00 .30
95 Nellie Fox 56 2.50 .75
96 Elston Howard 56 1.50 .45
97 Sal Maglie 57 1.00 .30
98 Roger Maris 58 2.50 .75
99 Norm Cash 60 UER 1.00 .30
His Rookie Card was in 1959 Topps
100 Thurman Munson 70 2.50 .75
101 Roy Campanella 57 UER 2.50 .75
His first Topps card is in 1952
102 Larry Doby 59 1.00 .30
103 Dom Dimaggio 53 1.00 .30
104 Johnny Mize 53 1.00 .30
105 Allie Reynolds 53 1.00 .30
106 Preacher Roe 54 1.00 .30
107 Hal Newhouser 55 .50 .15
108 Monte Irvin 56 1.00 .30
109 Carl Erskine 59 1.00 .30
110 Enos Slaughter 59 1.00 .30
111 Gil McDougald 60 1.00 .30
112 Andy Pafko 59 1.00 .30
113 Sal Maglie 59 .50 .15
114 Johnny Antonelli 61 .50 .15
115 Phil Rizzuto 61 1.50 .45
116 Yogi Berra 62 2.50 .75
117 Jim Wynn 77 .50 .15
118 Mickey Vernon 63 .50 .15
119 Gus Bell 64 .50 .15
120 Ted Williams 58 3.00 .90
121 Frank Thomas 65 .50 .15
122 Bobby Richardson 66 1.00 .30
123 Gaylord Perry 83 1.00 .30
124 Vernon Law 67 .50 .15
125 Jimmy Piersall 67 .50 .15
126 Moose Skowron 67 1.00 .30
127 Joe Adcock 63 .50 .15
128 Johnny Podres 69 1.00 .30
129 Ernie Banks 71 2.50 .75
130 Jim Maloney 72 .50 .15
131 Johnny Callison 73 .50 .15
132 Eddie Mathews 68 1.50 .45
133 Joe Pepitone 73 .50 .15
134 Warren Spahn 65 1.50 .45
135 Bill Mazeroski 72 1.50 .45
136 Norm Cash 74 1.00 .30
137 Bob Gibson 75 1.50 .45
138 Harmon Killebrew 75 2.50 .75
139 Frank Robinson 75 1.50 .45
140 Ron Santo 75 1.00 .30
141 Hank Sauer 59 .50 .15
142 Bobby Shantz 64 .50 .15
143 Nellie Fox 65 1.50 .45
144 Elston Howard 68 1.50 .45
145 Jackie Jensen 61 1.00 .30
146 Al Rosen 56 1.00 .30
147 Dick Allen 76 .50 .15
148 Bill Freehan 77 1.00 .30
149 Boog Powell 77 1.00 .30
150 Lou Brock 79 UER 1.50 .45
Header for stats on back is for a pitcher
Brock was an outfielder
151 Rod Carew 86 1.50 .45
152 Wilbur Wood 79 .50 .15
153 Thurman Munson 79 2.50 .75
154 Ken Holtzman 80 .50 .15
155 Willie Horton 80 .50 .15
156 Mickey Lolich 80 .50 .15
157 Tim McCarver 80 .50 .15
158 Willie McCovey 80 1.00 .30
159 Roy White 80 .50 .15
160 Bobby Murcer 83 1.00 .30
161 Joe Rudi 83 .50 .15
162 Reggie Smith 83 .50 .15
163 Luis Tiant 83 .50 .15
164 Bert Campaneris 84 .50 .15
165 Frank Howard 73 .50 .15
166 Harvey Kuenn 66 .50 .15
167 Greg Luzinski 85 .50 .15
168 Luis Aparicio 74 1.00 .30
169 Willie Mays 73 3.00 .90
170 Roger Maris 68 2.50 .75
171 Vida Blue 87 .50 .15
172 Bobby Grich 87 .50 .15
173 Reggie Jackson 87 1.50 .45
174 Hal McRae 87 .50 .15
175 Carl Yastrzemski 83 2.50 .75
176 David Concepcion 88 .50 .15
177 Ron Cey 87 .50 .15
178 George Hendrick 88 .50 .15
179 Gary Matthews 88 .50 .15
180 Stan Musial 63 2.50 .75
181 Graig Nettles 88 .50 .15
182 Don Sutton 88 1.00 .30
183 Kent Tekulve 88 .50 .15
184 Bruce Sutter 89 1.00 .30
185 Darrell Evans 90 .50 .15
186 Mike Schmidt 89 2.50 .75
187 Jim Kaat 83 .50 .15
188 Dwight Evans 92 1.00 .30
189 Gary Carter 93 1.00 .30
190 Jack Morris 94 .50 .15
191 Joe Morgan 85 1.00 .30
192 Dave Winfield 95 1.00 .30
193 Andre Dawson 96 1.00 .30
194 Lee Smith 96 .50 .15
195 Ozzie Smith 96 4.00 1.20
196 Denny Martinez 97 .50 .15
197 Don Mattingly 96 4.00 1.20
198 Joe Carter 98 1.00 .30
199 Dennis Eckersley 98 1.00 .30
200 Kirby Puckett 96 2.50 .75
201 Walter Alston MG 56 1.00 .30
202 Casey Stengel MG 60 1.00 .30
203 S. Anderson MG 71 1.00 .30
204 T. Lasorda MG 88 1.00 .30
205 Whitey Herzog MG 88 .50 .15
206 AL HR Leaders 70 1.00 .30
Harmon Killebrew
Frank Howard
Reggie Jackson
207 NL HR Leaders 68 1.00 .30
Hank Aaron
Jim Wynn
Ron Santo
Willie McCovey
208 AL HR Leaders 67 2.50 .75
Brooks Robinson
Harmon Killebrew
Boog Powell
209 AL Batting Leaders 65 1.00 .30
Tony Oliva
Brooks Robinson
Elston Howard
210 NL HR Leaders 64 1.00 .30
Hank Aaron
Willie McCovey
Willie Mays
Orlando Cepeda
211 NL HR Leaders 63 1.00 .30
Hank Aaron
Frank Robinson
Willie Mays
Ernie Banks
Orlando Cepeda
212 AL HR Leaders 68 2.50 .75
Carl Yastrzemski
Harmon Killebrew
Frank Howard
213 Ernie Banks 59 Thrill 2.50 .75
214 Hank Aaron 59 Thrill 3.00 .90
215 Willie Mays 59 Thrill 3.00 .90
216 Al Kaline 59 Thrill 2.50 .75
217 Stan Musial 59 Thrill 2.50 .75
218 Duke Snider 59 Thrill 1.50 .45
219 The Champs 67 1.50 .45
Frank Robinson
Hank Bauer MG
Brooks Robinson UER
All Cards have a 1965 Leaders Back
220 Pride of the NL 63 2.50 .75
Willie Mays
Stan Musial
221 Whitey Ford WS 63 1.50 .45
222 Jerry Koosman WS 70 .50 .15
223 Bob Gibson WS 65 1.50 .45
224 Gil Hodges WS 60 1.50 .45
225 R. Jackson WS 78 1.50 .45
226 Hank Bauer 52 1.00 .30
227 Ralph Branca 52 1.00 .30
228 Joe Garagiola 52 1.00 .30
229 Bob Feller 52 1.00 .30
230 Dick Groat 52 1.00 .30
231 George Kell 52 1.50 .45
232 Bob Boone 73 1.00 .30
233 Minnie Minoso 52 1.00 .30
234 Billy Pierce 52 1.00 .30
235 Robin Roberts 52 1.00 .30
236 Johnny Sain 52 1.00 .30
237 Red Schoendienst 52 1.00 .30
238 Curt Simmons 52 1.00 .30
239 Duke Snider 52 1.50 .45
240 Bobby Thomson 52 1.50 .45
241 Hoyt Wilhelm 52 1.50 .45
242 Roy Face 53 1.00 .30
243 Ralph Kiner 53 1.00 .30
244 Hank Aaron 54 6.00 1.80
245 Al Kaline 54 2.50 .75
246 Don Larsen 56 1.00 .30
247 Tug McGraw 65 1.00 .30
248 Don Newcombe 56 1.50 .45
249 Herb Score 56 1.00 .30
250 Clete Boyer 57 1.00 .30
251 Lindy McDaniel 57 .50 .15
252 Brooks Robinson 57 1.50 .45
253 Orlando Cepeda 58 1.00 .30
254 Larry Bowa 70 1.00 .30
255 Mike Cuellar 59 1.00 .30
256 Jim Perry 59 1.00 .30
257 Dave Parker 74 1.00 .30
258 Maury Wills 60 1.00 .30
259 Willie Davis 61 .50 .15
260 Juan Marichal 61 1.00 .30
261 Jim Bouton 62 1.00 .30
262 Dean Chance 62 1.00 .30
263 Sam McDowell 62 1.00 .30
264 Whitey Ford 53 1.50 .45
265 Bob Uecker 62 1.50 .45
266 Willie Stargell 63 1.50 .45
267 Rico Carty 64 1.00 .30
268 Tommy John 64 1.00 .30
269 Phil Niekro 64 1.00 .30
270 Paul Blair 65 1.00 .30
271 Steve Carlton 65 3.00 .90
272 Jim Lonborg 65 1.00 .30
273 Tony Perez 65 1.00 .30
274 Ron Swoboda 65 1.00 .30
275 Fergie Jenkins 66 1.00 .30
276 Jim Palmer 66 1.00 .30
277 Sal Bando 67 1.00 .30
278 Tom Seaver 67 4.00 1.20
279 Johnny Bench 68 4.00 1.20
280 Nolan Ryan 68 6.00 1.80
281 Rollie Fingers 69 1.00 .30
282 Sparky Lyle 69 1.00 .30
283 Al Oliver 69 1.00 .30
284 Bob Watson 69 1.00 .30
285 Bill Buckner 70 1.00 .30
286 Bert Blyleven 71 1.50 .45
287 George Foster 71 1.00 .30
288 Al Hrabosky 71 .50 .15
289 Cecil Cooper 72 1.00 .30
290 Carlton Fisk 72 1.50 .45
291 Mickey Rivers 72 1.00 .30
292 Goose Gossage 73 1.00 .30
293 Rick Reuschel 73 1.00 .30
294 Bucky Dent 74 1.00 .30
295 Frank Tanana 74 1.00 .30
296 George Brett 75 8.00 2.40
297 Keith Hernandez 75 1.00 .30
298 Fred Lynn 75 1.00 .30
299 Robin Yount 75 5.00 1.50
300 Ron Guidry 76 1.00 .30
301 Jack Clark 77 1.00 .30

302 Mark Fidrych 77 .... 1.00 .30
303 Dale Murphy 77 .... 2.50 .75
304 Willie Hernandez 78 .... .50 .15
305 Lou Whitaker 78 .... 1.00 .30
306 Kirk Gibson 81 .... 1.50 .45
307 Wade Boggs 83 .... 1.50 .45
308 Ryne Sandberg 83 .... 6.00 1.80
309 Orel Hershiser 85 .... 1.00 .30
310 Jimmy Key 85 .... 1.00 .30
311 Richie Ashburn 52 .... 1.50 .45
312 Smoky Burgess 52 .... 1.00 .30
313 Gil Hodges 52 .... 2.50 .75
314 Ted Kluszewski 52 .... 1.50 .45
315 Pee Wee Reese 52 .... 2.50 .75
316 Jackie Robinson 52 .... 2.50 .75
317 Jim Wynn 64 .... .50 .15
318 Satchel Paige 53 .... 2.50 .75
319 Roberto Clemente 55 .... 6.00 1.80
320 Carl Furillo 56 .... 1.00 .30
321 Don Drysdale 57 .... 2.50 .75
322 Curt Flood 58 .... 1.00 .30
323 Bob Allison 59 .... 1.00 .30
324 Tony Conigliaro 64 .... 1.00 .30
325 Dan Quisenberry 80 .... 1.00 .30
326 Ralph Branca 52 .... .50 .15
327 Bob Feller 53 .... 1.00 .30
328 Satchel Paige 53 .... 2.50 .75
329 George Kell 58 .... 1.50 .45
330 Pee Wee Reese 58 .... 1.50 .45
331 Bobby Thomson 60 .... 1.00 .30
332 Carl Furillo 60 .... .50 .15
333 Hank Bauer 61 .... .50 .15
334 Herb Score 62 .... .50 .15
335 Richie Ashburn 63 .... 1.50 .45
336 Billy Pierce 64 .... .50 .15
337 Duke Snider 64 .... 1.50 .45
338 Early Wynn 62 .... .50 .15
339 Robin Roberts 66 .... 1.00 .30
340 Dick Groat 67 .... .50 .15
341 Curt Simmons 67 .... .50 .15
342 Bob Uecker 67 .... 1.50 .45
343 Smoky Burgess 67 .... .50 .15
344 Jim Bouton 68 .... .50 .15
345 Roy Face 69 .... .50 .15
346 Don Drysdale 69 .... 2.50 .75
347 Bob Allison 70 .... .50 .15
348 Clete Boyer 71 .... .50 .15
349 Dean Chance 71 .... .50 .15
350 Tony Conigliaro 71 .... .50 .15
351 Curt Flood 71 .... .50 .15
352 Hoyt Wilhelm 72 .... 1.00 .30
353 Ron Swoboda 73 .... .50 .15
354 Roberto Clemente 73 .... 4.00 1.20
355 Tug McGraw 85 .... .50 .15
356 Orlando Cepeda 74 .... 1.00 .30
357 Joe Garagiola 52 .... .50 .15
358 Juan Marichal 74 .... 1.00 .30
359 Sam McDowell 74 .... .50 .15
360 Johnny Sain 55 .... .50 .15
361 Ted Kluszewski 61 .... 1.00 .30
362 Al Kaline 74 .... 2.50 .75
363 Lindy McDaniel 75 .... .50 .15
364 Don Newcombe 60 .... 1.00 .30
365 Jim Perry 75 .... .50 .15
366 Hank Aaron 76 .... 4.00 1.20
367 Don Larsen 65 .... 1.00 .30
368 Mike Cuellar 77 .... .50 .15
369 Willie Davis 77 .... .50 .15
370 Ralph Kiner 53 .... 1.00 .30
371 Minnie Minoso 64 .... 1.00 .30
372 Larry Bowa 85 .... .50 .15
373 Brooks Robinson 77 .... 1.50 .45
374 Bob Boone 90 .... .50 .15
375 Jim Lonborg 79 .... .50 .15
376 Paul Blair 80 .... .50 .15
377 Rico Carty 80 .... .50 .15
378 Sal Bando 81 .... .50 .15
379 Mark Fidrych 81 .... .50 .15
380 Al Hrabosky 82 .... .50 .15
381 Willie Stargell 82 .... 1.50 .45
382 Johnny Bench 83 .... 2.50 .75
383 Dave Parker 91 .... .50 .15
384 Sparky Lyle 83 .... .50 .15
385 Fergie Jenkins 84 .... 1.00 .30
386 Jim Palmer 84 .... 1.00 .30
387 Whitey Ford 67 .... 1.50 .45
388 Tony Perez 86 .... 1.00 .30
389 Mickey Rivers 85 .... .50 .15
390 Bob Watson 85 .... .50 .15
391 Rollie Fingers 86 .... 1.00 .30
392 George Foster 86 .... .50 .15
393 Al Oliver 86 .... .50 .15
394 Tom Seaver 87 .... 1.50 .45
395 Maury Wills 72 .... .50 .15
396 Steve Carlton 87T .... 1.00 .30
397 Cecil Cooper 88 .... .50 .15
398 Bill Buckner 88 .... .50 .15
399 Phil Niekro 87 .... 1.00 .30
400 Red Schoendienst 62 .... 1.00 .30
401 Ron Guidry 89 .... .50 .15
402 Willie Hernandez 89 .... .50 .15
403 Tommy John 89 .... .50 .15
404 Gil Hodges 63 .... 2.50 .75
405 Bucky Dent 84 .... .50 .15
406 Keith Hernandez 90 .... 1.00 .30
407 Dan Quisenberry 90 .... .50 .15
408 Fred Lynn 91 .... .50 .15
409 Rick Reuschel 91 .... .50 .15
410 Jackie Robinson 56 .... 2.50 .75
411 Goose Gossage 92 .... .50 .15
412 Bert Blyleven 93 .... 1.00 .30
413 Jack Clark 93 .... .50 .15
414 Carlton Fisk 93 .... 1.50 .45
415 Dale Murphy 93 .... 1.50 .45
416 Frank Tanana 93 .... .50 .15
417 George Brett 94 .... 5.00 1.50
418 Robin Yount 94 .... 4.00 1.20
419 Kirk Gibson 95 .... 1.00 .30
420 Lou Whitaker 95 .... .50 .15
421 R. Sandberg 97 UER 5.00 1.50
Card lists 1996 homers as 252
422 Jimmy Key 98 .... 1.00 .30
423 Nolan Ryan 94 .... 4.00 1.20
424 Wade Boggs 00 .... 1.00 .30
425 Orel Hershiser 00 .... .50 .15
426 Billy Martin MG 84 .... 1.00 .30
427 Ralph Houk MG 62 .... 1.00 .30
428 Chuck Tanner MG 72 .... .50 .15
429 Earl Weaver MG 71 .... 1.00 .30
430 Leo Durocher MG 52 .... 1.00 .30
431 AL HR Leaders 66 .... 1.00 .30
Tony Conigliaro
Norm Cash
Willie Horton
432 NL HR Leaders 60 .... 2.50 .75
Ernie Banks
Hank Aaron
Eddie Mathews
Ken Boyer
433 AL Batting Leaders 62 .... 1.00 .30
Norm Cash
Elston Howard
Al Kaline
Jimmy Piersall
434 Leading Firemen 79 .... .50 .15
Goose Gossage
Rollie Fingers
435 Strikeout Leaders 77 .... 1.50 .45
Nolan Ryan
Tom Seaver
436 HR Leaders 74 .... 1.00 .30
Reggie Jackson
Willie Stargell
437 RBI Leaders 73 .... 1.50 .45
Johnny Bench
Dick Allen
438 Roger Maris .... 2.50 .75
Blasts 61st 62
439 Carl Yastrzemski .... 2.50 .75
World Series Game Two 68
440 Nolan Ryan RB 78 .... 4.00 1.20
441 Baltimore Orioles 70 .... 1.00 .30
442 Tony Perez RB 86 .... .50 .15
443 Steve Carlton RB 84 .... .50 .15
444 Wade Boggs RB 89 .... 1.00 .30
445 Andre Dawson RB 89 .... 1.00 .30
446 Whitey Ford WS 62 .... 1.50 .45
447 Hank Aaron WS 59 .... 4.00 1.20
448 Bob Gibson WS 69 .... 1.50 .45
449 R.Clemente WS 72 .... 4.00 1.20
450 Brooks Robinson .... 1.00 .30
Orioles/WS 71

2001 Topps Archives Autographs

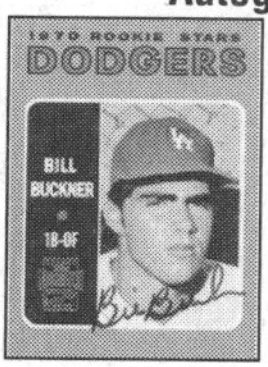

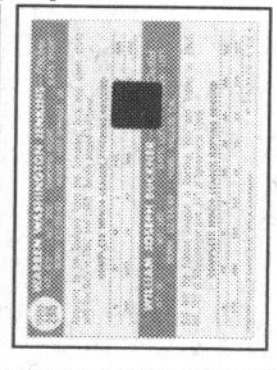

Inserted at overall odds of one in 20, these 159 cards feature the players signing their reprint cards. The set is checklisted TAA1-TAA170 but 11 cards do not exist as follows: 9, 15, 47, 72, 82, 84, 95, 105, 109, 159 and 161. The only first series exchange card was Keith Hernandez but unfortunately, Topps was unable to fulfill the card and sent collectors an array of other signed cards. The series two exchange card subjects were Juan Marichal, Jack Morris, Billy Pierce, Boog Powell, Ron Santo, Enos Slaughter, Ozzie Smith, Reggie Smith, Don Sutton, Bob Uecker, Jim Wynn and Robin Yount. Of these players, Juan Marichal, Ozzie Smith and Reggie Smith did not return any cards. The series one exchange date was April 30th, 2002 . The series two exchange deadline was exactly one year later - April 30th, 2003.

Nm-Mt Ex-Mt
SER.1 GROUP A ODDS 1:3049..........
SER.2 GROUP A ODDS 1:2904..........
SER.1 GROUP B ODDS 1:872..........
SER.2 GROUP B ODDS 1:480..........
SER.1 GROUP C ODDS 1:697..........
SER.2 GROUP C ODDS 1:4782..........
SER.1 GROUP D ODDS 1:122..........
SER.2 GROUP D ODDS 1:662..........
SER.1 GROUP E ODDS 1:26..........
SER.2 GROUP E ODDS 1:209..........
SER.1 GROUP F ODDS 1:6097..........
SER.2 GROUP F ODDS 1:1455..........
SER.2 GROUP G ODDS 1:320..........
SER.2 GROUP H ODDS 1:412..........
SER.2 GROUP I ODDS 1:192..........
SER.2 GROUP J ODDS 1:38..........
SER.2 GROUP K ODDS 1:329..........
TAA1 Johnny Antonelli E1 .... 15.00 4.50
TAA2 Hank Bauer E1 .... 25.00 7.50
TAA3 Yogi Berra A2 SP/50 .... 300.00 90.00
TAA4 Ralph Branca E1 .... 25.00 7.50
TAA5 Dom DiMaggio E1 .... 40.00 12.00
TAA6 Joe Garagiola E1 .... 40.00 12.00
TAA7 Carl Erskine D1 .... 30.00 9.00
TAA8 Bob Feller E1 .... 15.00 4.50
TAA9 Does Not Exist ....
TAA10 Dick Groat D1 .... 30.00 9.00
TAA11 Monte Irvin E1 .... 25.00 7.50
TAA12 George Kell E1 .... 25.00 7.50
TAA13 Vernon Law E1 .... 15.00 4.50
TAA14 Bob Boone E1 .... 15.00 4.50
TAA15 Does Not Exist ....
TAA16 W.Mays A2 SP/50 .... 400.00 120.00
TAA17 Gil McDougald E1 .... 25.00 7.50
TAA18 Minnie Minoso E1 .... 25.00 7.50
TAA19 Andy Pafko D2 .... 40.00 12.00
TAA20 Billy Pierce E2 .... 10.00 3.00
TAA21 P. Rizzuto B2 SP/200 .... 100.00 30.00
TAA22 Robin Roberts C1 .... 50.00 15.00
TAA23 Preacher Roe E1 .... 25.00 7.50
TAA24 Johnny Sain E1 .... 15.00 4.50
TAA25 Hank Sauer E1 .... 15.00 4.50
TAA26 R. Schoendienst E1 .... 15.00 4.50
TAA27 Bobby Shantz E1 .... 15.00 4.50
TAA28 Curt Simmons E1 .... 15.00 4.50
TAA29 Enos Slaughter E2 .... 25.00 7.50
TAA30 Duke Snider B1 .... 100.00 30.00
TAA31 Warren Spahn C2 .... 100.00 30.00
TAA32 B.Thomson E1 .... 25.00 7.50
TAA33 Mickey Vernon B2 .... 15.00 4.50
TAA34 Hoyt Wilhelm D1 .... 50.00 15.00
TAA35 Jim Wynn E2 .... 10.00 3.00
TAA36 Roy Face E1 .... 15.00 4.50
TAA37 Gaylord Perry C2 .... 60.00 18.00
TAA38 Ralph Kiner B1 .... 60.00 18.00
TAA39 Johnny Podres E2 .... 15.00 4.50
TAA40 H.Aaron A2 SP/50 .... 400.00 120.00
TAA41 E.Banks A2 SP/50 .... 300.00 90.00
TAA42 Al Kaline B1 .... 150.00 45.00
TAA43 Moose Skowron E1 .... 15.00 4.50
TAA44 D.Larsen A1 SP/50 .... 200.00 60.00
TAA45 H.Killebrew B1 .... 150.00 45.00
TAA46 Tug McGraw E1 .... 40.00 12.00
TAA47 Does Not Exist ....
TAA48 Don Newcombe E1 .... 15.00 4.50
TAA49 Jim Piersall E2 .... 15.00 4.50
TAA50 Herb Score E1 .... 15.00 4.50
TAA51 Frank Thomas E1 .... 15.00 4.50
TAA52 Clete Boyer D1 .... 20.00 6.00
TAA53 Bill Mazeroski C2 .... 60.00 18.00
TAA54 Lindy McDaniel E1 .... 15.00 4.50
TAA55 B. Richardson E2 .... 15.00 4.50
TAA56 B. Robinson A SP/50 .... 200.00 60.00
TAA57 Frank Robinson B1 .... 150.00 45.00
TAA58 Orlando Cepeda B1 .... 60.00 18.00
TAA59 S. Musial A1 SP/50 .... 300.00 90.00
TAA60 Larry Bowa D1 .... 30.00 9.00
TAA61 Johnny Callison E2 .... 10.00 3.00
TAA62 Mike Cuellar D1 .... 20.00 6.00
TAA63 B. Gibson A1 SP/50 .... 200.00 60.00
TAA64 Jim Perry E2 .... 10.00 3.00
TAA65 Frank Howard E1 .... 15.00 4.50
TAA66 Dave Parker E1 .... 15.00 4.50
TAA67 Willie McCovey D2 .... 100.00 30.00
TAA68 Maury Wills E1 .... 15.00 4.50
TAA69 C. Yastrzemski F1 .... 250.00 75.00
TAA70 Willie Davis E1 .... 15.00 4.50
TAA71 Jim Maloney E2 .... 10.00 3.00
TAA72 Does Not Exist ....
TAA73 Ron Santo E2 .... 40.00 12.00
TAA74 Jim Bouton D1 .... 30.00 9.00
TAA75 L. Brock A2 SP/50 .... 200.00 60.00
TAA76 Dean Chance E1 .... 15.00 4.50
TAA77 Tim McCarver 60.00 18.00
B2 SP/200
TAA78 Sam McDowell D1 .... 20.00 6.00
TAA79 Joe Pepitone E1 .... 15.00 4.50
TAA80 Whitey Ford F1 .... 100.00 30.00
TAA81 Boog Powell E2 .... 25.00 7.50
TAA82 Does Not Exist ....
TAA83 Bill Freehan D2 .... 15.00 4.50
TAA84 Does Not Exist ....
TAA85 Dick Allen B2 .... 40.00 12.00
TAA86 Rico Carty E1 .... 15.00 4.50
TAA87 Willie Horton E2 .... 10.00 3.00
TAA88 Tommy John E1 .... 15.00 4.50
TAA89 Mickey Lolich E2 .... 15.00 4.50
TAA90 Phil Niekro D1 .... 30.00 9.00
TAA91 Wilbur Wood E1 .... 15.00 4.50
TAA92 Paul Blair E1 .... 15.00 4.50
TAA93 B. Campaneris E2 .... 15.00 4.50
TAA94 Steve Carlton D1 .... 50.00 15.00
TAA95 Does Not Exist ....
TAA96 Jim Lonborg E1 .... 15.00 4.50
TAA97 Luis Aparicio B1 .... 60.00 18.00
TAA98 Tony Perez D1 .... 50.00 15.00
TAA99 J. Morgan B2 SP/200 .... 60.00 18.00
TAA100 Ron Swoboda D1 .... 30.00 9.00
TAA101 Luis Tiant E2 .... 15.00 4.50
TAA102 Fergie Jenkins D1 .... 30.00 9.00
TAA103 Bobby Murcer D2 .... 60.00 18.00
TAA104 Jim Palmer B1 .... 100.00 30.00
TAA105 Does Not Exist ....
TAA106 Sal Bando E2 .... 15.00 4.50
TAA107 Ken Holtzman B1 .... 60.00 18.00
TAA108 T.Seaver A2 SP/50 .... 200.00 60.00
TAA109 Does Not Exist ....
TAA110 J.Bench A1 SP/50 .... 250.00 75.00
TAA111 Hal McRae E2 .... 10.00 3.00
TAA112 Nolan Ryan A2 .... 400.00 120.00
TAA113 Roy White D2 .... 15.00 4.50
TAA114 Rollie Fingers C1 .... 30.00 9.00
TAA115 R.Jackson A2 SP/50 .... 300.00 90.00
TAA116 Sparky Lyle E1 .... 15.00 4.50
TAA117 Graig Nettles D2 .... 25.00 7.50
TAA118 Al Oliver E1 .... 15.00 4.50
TAA119 Joe Rudi B2 .... 15.00 4.50
TAA120 Bob Watson E1 .... 15.00 4.50
TAA121 Vida Blue E2 .... 10.00 3.00
TAA122 Bill Buckner E1 .... 15.00 4.50
TAA123 Darrell Evans E1 .... 15.00 4.50
TAA124 Bert Blyleven D1 .... 30.00 9.00
TAA125 D.Concepcion D2 .... 25.00 7.50
TAA126 George Foster E1 .... 15.00 4.50
TAA127 Bobby Grich E1 .... 15.00 4.50
TAA128 Al Hrabosky E1 .... 15.00 4.50
TAA129 Greg Luzinski D1 .... 30.00 9.00
TAA130 Cecil Cooper E1 .... 15.00 4.50
TAA131 Ron Cey E2 .... 10.00 3.00
TAA132 Carlton Fisk B1 .... 100.00 30.00
TAA133 G.Hendrick E2 .... 10.00 3.00
TAA134 Mickey Rivers E1 .... 15.00 4.50
TAA135 Dwight Evans D2 .... 25.00 7.50
TAA136 Rich Gossage E1 .... 15.00 4.50
TAA137 G. Matthews B2 .... 15.00 4.50
TAA138 Rick Reuschel E1 .... 15.00 4.50
TAA139 Mike Schmidt 300.00 90.00
A1 SP/50
TAA140 Bucky Dent D1 .... 30.00 9.00
TAA141 Jim Kaat B2 .... 25.00 7.50
TAA142 Frank Tanana E1 .... 15.00 4.50
TAA143 Dave Winfield 100.00 30.00
B2 SP/200
TAA144 G.Brett A1 SP/50 .... 300.00 90.00
TAA145 G.Carter B2 SP/200 .... 60.00 18.00
TAA146 Keith Hernandez D1 ....
TAA147 Fred Lynn C1 .... 30.00 9.00
TAA148 R.Yount B2 SP/200 .... 150.00 45.00
TAA149 Dennis Eckersley 100.00 30.00
B2 SP/200
TAA150 Ron Guidry E2 .... 25.00 7.50
TAA151 Kent Tekulve D1 .... 20.00 6.00
TAA152 Jack Clark E1 .... 15.00 4.50
TAA153 A.Dawson B2 SP/200 .... 60.00 18.00
TAA154 Mark Fidrych E1 .... 15.00 4.50
TAA155 Dennis Martinez 50.00 15.00
B2 SP/200
TAA156 Dale Murphy C1 .... 80.00 24.00
TAA157 Bruce Sutter D2 .... 25.00 7.50
TAA158 W.Hernandez D2 .... 15.00 4.50
TAA159 Does Not Exist ....
TAA160 Lou Whitaker D2 .... 25.00 7.50
TAA161 Does Not Exist ....
TAA162 Kirk Gibson E1 .... 25.00 7.50
TAA163 Lee Smith D2 .... 25.00 7.50
TAA164 Wade Boggs B1 .... 150.00 45.00
TAA165 Ryne Sandberg 150.00 45.00
B2 SP/200
TAA166 Don Mattingly D1 .... 120.00 36.00
TAA167 J.Carter B2 SP/200 .... 50.00 15.00
TAA168 Orel Hershiser D2 .... 40.00 12.00
TAA169 Kirby Puckett A2 .... 100.00 30.00
TAA170 Jimmy Key C1 .... 50.00 15.00

2001 Topps Archives AutoProofs

Inserted at a rate of one in 2,444 in series one and one in 2,391 in series two these 10 cards feature players signing their actual cards. Each of these cards are serial numbered to 100. Willie McCovey and Willie Mays were both first series exchange cards with a redemption deadline of April 30th, 2002. Carlton Fisk, Robin Roberts and Hoyt Wilhelm were series two exchange cards with a redemption deadline of April 30th, 2003.

Nm-Mt Ex-Mt
1 Wade Boggs 99 S1 .... 80.00 24.00
2 Carlton Fisk 93 S2 .... 100.00 30.00
3 Willie Mays 73 S1 .... 200.00 60.00
4 Willie McCovey 80 S1 .... 80.00 24.00
5 J.Palmer 82/84 EXCH S1 .... 60.00 18.00
6 Robin Roberts 66 S2 .... 80.00 24.00
7 Duke Snider 64 S2 .... 80.00 24.00
8 Warren Spahn 65 S2 .... 80.00 24.00
9 Hoyt Wilhelm 63 S2 .... 60.00 18.00
10 Carl Yastrzemski 83 S1 .... 150.00 45.00

2001 Topps Archives Bucks

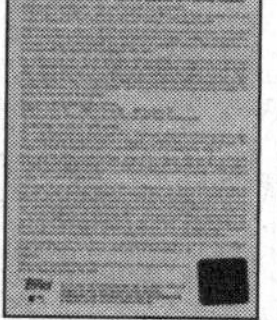

Randomly inserted in packs, these three cards issued in the style of the old Baseball Bucks were good for money toward Topps 50th anniversary merchandise.

Nm-Mt Ex-Mt
TB1 Willie Mays $1 .... 10.00 3.00
TB2 Roberto Clemente $5 .... 25.00 7.50
TB3 Jackie Robinson $10 .... 25.00 7.50

2001 Topps Archives Future Rookie Reprints

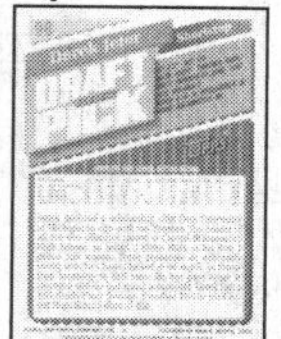

Issued five per sealed Topps factory and HTA sets, these 20 cardds feature Rookie Card reprints of today's leading players.

Nm-Mt Ex-Mt
COMPLETE SET (20) 50.00 15.00
1 Barry Bonds 87 .... 8.00 2.40
2 Chipper Jones 91 .... 3.00 .90
3 Cal Ripken 82 .... 10.00 3.00
4 Shawn Green 92 .... 1.25 .35
5 Frank Thomas 90 .... 3.00 .90
6 Derek Jeter 93 .... 8.00 2.40
7 Geoff Jenkins 96 .... 1.25 .35
8 Jim Edmonds 93 .... 1.25 .35
9 Bernie Williams 90 .... 2.00 .60
10 Sammy Sosa 90 .... 5.00 1.50
11 Rickey Henderson 80 .... 3.00 .90
12 Calvin Reese 92 .... 1.25 .35
13 Randy Johnson 89 .... 3.00 .90
14 Juan Gonzalez 90 .... 2.00 .60
15 Gary Sheffield 89 .... 1.25 .35
16 Manny Ramirez 92 .... 2.00 .60
17 Pokey Reese 92 .... 1.25 .35
18 Preston Wilson 93 .... 1.25 .35
19 Jay Payton 95 .... 1.25 .35
20 Rafael Palmeiro 87 .... 2.00 .60

2001 Topps Archives Rookie Reprint Bat Relics

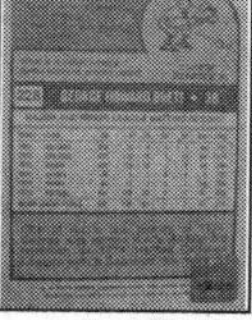

Inserted in series one packs at a rate of one in 1,356 and second series packs at a rate of one in 1,1307 these six cards feature not only the rookie reprint but also a game used bat slice.

Nm-Mt Ex-Mt
TARR1 Johnny Bench 25.00 7.50
TARR2 George Brett 50.00 15.00
TARR3 Fred Lynn 15.00 4.50
TARR4 Reggie Jackson 25.00 7.50
TARR5 Mike Schmidt 50.00 15.00
TARR6 Willie Stargell 25.00 7.50

2002 Topps Archives

This 200 card set was released in early April, 2002. These cards were issued in eight card packs which were issued in 20 pack boxes and were packed eight boxes to a case. The packs had an SRP of $4 per pack. This set was subtitled "Best Years" and it featured a reprint of the player's Topps card from their best year in the majors. Interestingly, Topps changed the backs of most of the cards to include the stats from that selected year. Also, in many of the cards, the text was changed to reflect the best year rather than using the original verbiage.

Nm-Mt Ex-Mt
COMPLETE SET (200) 100.00 30.00
1 Willie Mays 62 .... 5.00 1.50
2 Dale Murphy 83 .... 2.50 .75
3 Dave Winfield 79 .... 1.00 .30
4 Roger Maris 61 .... 2.50 .75
5 Ron Cey 77 .... 1.00 .30
6 Lee Smith 91 .... 1.00 .30
7 Len Dykstra 93 .... 1.00 .30
8 Ray Fosse 70 .... 1.00 .30
9 Warren Spahn 57 .... 1.50 .45
10 Herb Score 56 .... 1.00 .30
11 Jim Wynn 74 .... 1.00 .30
12 Sam McDowell 70 .... 1.00 .30
13 Fred Lynn 79 .... 1.00 .30
14 Yogi Berra 54 .... 2.50 .75
15 Ron Santo 64 .... 1.50 .45
16 Alvin Dark 53 .... 1.00 .30
17 Bill Buckner 85 .... 1.00 .30
18 Rollie Fingers 81 .... 1.00 .30
19 Tony Gwynn 97 .... 3.00 .90
20 Red Schoendienst 53 .... 1.00 .30
21 Gaylord Perry 72 .... 1.00 .30
22 Jose Cruz 83 .... 1.00 .30
23 Dennis Martinez 91 .... 1.00 .30
24 Dave McNally 68 .... 1.00 .30
25 Norm Cash 61 .... 1.00 .30
26 Ted Kluszewski 54 UER .... 1.50 .45
Card has Yogi Berra's stats on back
27 Rick Reuschel 77 .... 1.00 .30
28 Bruce Sutter 77 .... 1.00 .30
29 Don Larsen 56 .... 1.00 .30
30 Claudell Washington 82 .... 1.00 .30
31 Luis Aparicio 60 .... 1.00 .30
32 Clete Boyer 62 .... 1.00 .30
33 Goose Gossage 77 .... 1.00 .30
34 Ray Knight 79 .... 1.00 .30
35 Roy Campanella 53 .... 2.50 .75
36 Tug McGraw 71 .... 1.00 .30
37 Bob Lemon 52 .... 1.00 .30
38 Willie Stargell 71 .... 1.50 .45
39 Roberto Clemente 66 .... 5.00 1.50
40 Jim Fregosi 70 .... 1.00 .30
41 Reggie Smith 77 .... 1.00 .30
42 Dave Parker 78 .... 1.00 .30
43 Darrell Evans 73 .... 1.00 .30
44 Ryne Sandberg 90 .... 4.00 1.20
45 Manny Mota 72 .... 1.00 .30
46 Dennis Eckersley 92 .... 1.00 .30
47 Nellie Fox 59 .... 1.50 .45
48 Gil Hodges 54 .... 2.50 .75
49 Reggie Jackson 69 .... 1.50 .45
50 Bobby Shantz 52 .... 1.00 .30
51 Cecil Cooper 80 .... 1.00 .30
52 Jim Kaat 66 .... 1.00 .30
53 George Hendrick 80 .... 1.00 .30
54 Johnny Podres 61 .... 1.00 .30
55 Bob Gibson 68 .... 1.50 .45
56 Vern Law 60 .... 1.00 .30
57 Joe Adcock 56 .... 1.00 .30
58 Jack Clark 87 .... 1.00 .30
59 Bill Mazeroski 60 .... 1.50 .45
60 Carl Yastrzemski 67 .... 4.00 1.20
61 Bobby Murcer 71 .... 1.00 .30
62 Davey Johnson 73 .... 1.00 .30
63 Jim Palmer 75 .... 1.00 .30
64 Roy Face 59 .... 1.00 .30
65 Dean Chance 64 .... 1.00 .30
66 Moose Skowron 60 .... 1.50 .45
67 Dwight Evans 87 .... 1.00 .30
68 Kirk Gibson 88 .... 1.00 .30
69 Sal Bando 69 .... 1.00 .30
70 Mike Schmidt 80 .... 5.00 1.50
71 Bo Jackson 89 .... 2.50 .75
72 Chris Chambliss 76 .... 1.00 .30
73 Fergie Jenkins 71 .... 1.00 .30
74 Brooks Robinson 64 .... 1.50 .45
75 Bobby Richardson 62 .... 1.00 .30
76 Duke Snider 54 .... 1.50 .45
77 Allie Reynolds 52 .... 1.50 .45
78 Harmon Killebrew 66 .... 2.50 .75
79 Steve Carlton 72 .... 1.00 .30
80 Bert Blyleven 73 .... 1.00 .30
81 Phil Niekro 69 .... 1.00 .30
82 Lew Burdette 56 .... 1.00 .30
83 Hoyt Wilhelm 64 .... 1.00 .30
84 Curt Flood 65 .... 1.00 .30
85 Willie Hernandez 84 .... 1.00 .30
86 Robin Yount 82 .... 4.00 1.20
87 Robin Roberts 52 .... 1.00 .30
88 Whitey Ford 61 .... 1.50 .45
89 Tony Oliva 64 .... 1.00 .30

90 Don Newcombe 56 .... 1.00 .30
91 Al Oliver 82 .... 1.00 .30
92 Mike Cuellar 69 .... 1.00 .30
93 Mike Scott 86 .... 1.00 .30
94 Dick Allen 66 .... 1.00 .30
95 Jimmy Piersall 56 .... 1.00 .30
96 Bill Freehan 68 .... 1.00 .30
97 Willie Horton 65 .... 1.00 .30
98 Bob Friend 60 .... 1.00 .30
99 Ken Holtzman 73 .... 1.00 .30
100 Rico Carty 70 .... 1.00 .30
101 Gil McDougald 56 .... 1.00 .30
102 Lee May 69 .... 1.00 .30
103 Joe Pepitone 64 .... 1.00 .30
104 Gene Tenace 75 .... 1.00 .30
105 Gary Carter 85 .... 1.00 .30
106 Tim McCarver 67 .... 1.00 .30
107 Ernie Banks 58 .... 2.50 .75
108 George Foster 77 .... 1.00 .30
109 Lou Brock 74 .... 1.50 .45
110 Dick Groat 60 .... 1.00 .30
111 Graig Nettles 77 .... 1.00 .30
112 Boog Powell 69 .... 1.50 .45
113 Joe Carter 86 .... 1.00 .30
114 Juan Marichal 66 .... 1.00 .30
115 Larry Doby 54 .... 1.00 .30
116 Fernando Valenzuela 86 .... 1.00 .30
117 Luis Tiant 68 .... 1.00 .30
118 Early Wynn 59 .... 1.00 .30
119 Bill Madlock 75 .... 1.00 .30
120 Eddie Mathews 53 .... 2.50 .75
121 George Brett 80 .... 6.00 1.80
122 Al Kaline 55 .... 2.50 .75
123 Frank Howard 69 .... 1.00 .30
124 Mickey Lolich 71 .... 1.00 .30
125 Kirby Puckett 88 .... 2.50 .75
126 Bob Cerv 58 .... 1.00 .30
127 Will Clark 89 .... 2.50 .75
128 Vida Blue 71 .... 1.00 .30
129 Kevin Mitchell 89 .... 1.00 .30
130 Bucky Dent 80 .... 1.00 .30
131 Tom Seaver 69 .... 1.50 .45
132 Jerry Koosman 76 .... 1.00 .30
133 Orlando Cepeda 61 .... 1.00 .30
134 Nolan Ryan 73 .... 6.00 1.80
135 Tony Kubek 60 .... 1.50 .45
136 Don Drysdale 62 .... 2.50 .75
137 Paul Blair 69 .... 1.00 .30
138 Elston Howard 63 .... 1.50 .45
139 Joe Rudi 74 .... 1.00 .30
140 Tommie Agee 70 .... 1.00 .30
141 Richie Ashburn 58 .... 1.50 .45
142 Jim Bunning 65 .... 1.00 .30
143 Hank Sauer 52 .... 1.00 .30
144 Greg Luzinski 77 .... 1.00 .30
145 Ron Guidry 78 .... 1.00 .30
146 Rod Carew 77 .... 1.50 .45
147 Andre Dawson 87 .... 1.00 .30
148 Keith Hernandez 79 .... 1.00 .30
149 Carlton Fisk 77 .... 1.50 .45
150 Cleon Jones 69 .... 1.00 .30
151 Don Mattingly 85 .... 6.00 1.80
152 Vada Pinson 63 .... 1.00 .30
153 Ozzie Smith 87 .... 4.00 1.20
154 Dave Concepcion 79 .... 1.00 .30
155 Al Rosen 53 .... 1.00 .30
156 Tommy John 68 .... 1.00 .30
157 Bob Ojeda 86 .... 1.00 .30
158 Frank Robinson 66 .... 1.50 .45
159 Darryl Strawberry 87 .... 1.00 .30
160 Bobby Bonds 73 .... 1.00 .30
161 Bert Campaneris 70 .... 1.00 .30
162 Catfish Hunter 74 .... 1.50 .45
163 Bud Harrelson 70 .... 1.00 .30
164 Dwight Gooden 85 .... 1.00 .30
165 Wade Boggs 87 .... 1.50 .45
166 Joe Morgan 76 .... 1.00 .30
167 Ron Swoboda 67 .... 1.00 .30
168 Hank Aaron 57 .... 5.00 1.50
169 Steve Garvey 77 .... 1.00 .30
170 Mickey Rivers 77 .... 1.00 .30
171 Johnny Bench 70 .... 2.50 .75
172 Ralph Terry 62 .... 1.00 .30
173 Billy Pierce 56 .... 1.00 .30
174 Thurman Munson 76 .... 2.50 .75
175 Don Sutton 72 .... 1.00 .30
176 Sparky Anderson 84 MG .... 1.00 .30
177 Gil Hodges 69 MG .... 2.50 .75
178 Davey Johnson 86 MG .... 1.00 .30
179 Frank Robinson 89 MG .... 1.50 .45
180 Red Schoendienst 67 MG .... 1.00 .30
181 Roger Maris 61 AS .... 2.50 .75
182 Willie Mays 62 AS 5.00 1.50
183 Luis Aparicio 60 AS .... 1.00 .30
184 Nellie Fox 59 AS .... 1.50 .45
185 Ernie Banks 58 AS .... 2.50 .75
186 Orlando Cepeda 62 AS .... 1.00 .30
187 Whitey Ford 61 AS .... 1.50 .45
188 Bob Gibson 69 AS .... 1.50 .45
189 Bill Mazeroski 59 AS .... 1.50 .45
190 Hank Aaron 58 AS 5.00 1.50
191 1971 AL HR Leaders .... 1.00 .30
Frank Howard
Harmon Killebrew
Carl Yastrzemski
192 1962 NL HR Leaders .... 1.50 .45
Orlando Cepeda
Frank Robinson
Willie Mays
193 1967 NL RBI Leaders .... 2.50 .75
Hank Aaron
Roberto Clemente
Dick Allen
194 1970 NL Win Leaders .... 1.00 .30
Tom Seaver
Phil Niekro
Fergie Jenkins
Juan Marichal
195 1976 AL ERA Leaders .... 1.00 .30
Jim Palmer
Catfish Hunter
Dennis Eckersley
196 Hank Aaron 76 HL 5.00 1.50
197 Brooks Robinson 78 HL .... 1.50 .45
198 Tom Seaver 70 HL .... 1.00 .30
199 Jim Palmer 71 HL .... 1.00 .30
200 Lou Brock 75 HL .... 1.50 .45

2002 Topps Archives Autographs

Issued at overall stated odds of one in 22 hobby packs and 1:22 retail packs, these 59 cards feature many of the players featured in the 2002 Topps Archives set. Since there were so many groups that the different players belong to 12 different groups. We have notated the group that these players belong to next to their name in our checklist.

Nm-Mt Ex-Mt
GROUP A ODDS 1:19,803 HOB, 1:20,040 RET
GROUP B ODDS 1:12,872 HOB, 1:13,360 RET
GROUP C ODDS 1:11,193 HOB, 1:11,451 RET
GROUP D ODDS 1:8045 HOB, 1:8016 RET
GROUP E ODDS 1:753 HOB, 1:756 RET
GROUP F ODDS 1:3387 HOB, 1:3340 RET
GROUP G ODDS 1:1355 HOB, 1:1359 RET
GROUP H ODDS 1:1129 HOB, 1:1129 RET
GROUP K ODDS 1:748 HOB, 1:749 RET
GROUP L ODDS 1:45 HOB, 1:45 RET.
TAA-AD Alvin Dark 53 J 30.00 9.00
TAA-AK Al Kaline 55 E 150.00 45.00
TAA-BB Bobby Bonds 73 J 30.00 9.00
TAA-BC Bert Campaneris 70 L 15.00 4.50
TAA-BD Bucky Dent 80 J 20.00 6.00
TAA-BH Bud Harrelson 70 L 15.00 4.50
TAA-BJ Bo Jackson 89 F ....
TAA-BP Billy Pierce 56 J 15.00 4.50
TAA-BS Bruce Sutter 77 J 20.00 6.00
TAA-CC Chris Chambliss 76 J 20.00 6.00
TAA-DA Dick Allen 66 J 30.00 9.00
TAA-DG Dwight Gooden 85 G ....
TAA-DM Dave McNally 68 L 20.00 6.00
TAA-DN Don Newcombe 56 I 20.00 6.00
TAA-DP Dave Parker 78 H 20.00 6.00
TAA-DS Duke Snider 52 E ....
TAA-DW Dave Winfield 79 D ....
TAA-EB Ernie Banks 58 E 150.00 45.00
TAA-FJ Fergie Jenkins 71 J 20.00 6.00
TAA-FL Fred Lynn 79 J 20.00 6.00
TAA-GB George Brett 80 E 300.00 90.00
TAA-GC Gary Carter 85 E ....
TAA-GF George Foster 77 L 20.00 6.00
TAA-GH Willie Hernandez 84 L 15.00 4.50
TAA-GL Greg Luzinski 77 J 20.00 6.00
TAA-GP Gaylord Perry 72 J 20.00 6.00
TAA-HA Hank Aaron 57 E 250.00 75.00
TAA-HK Harmon Killebrew 69 E ....
TAA-HW Hoyt Wilhelm 64 L 20.00 6.00
TAA-JF Jim Fregosi 70 I 15.00 4.50
TAA-JK Jim Kaat 66 J 20.00 6.00
TAA-JP Jim Palmer 75 E ....
TAA-JR Joe Rudi 74 J 20.00 6.00
TAA-KH Keith Hernandez 79 J 40.00 12.00
TAA-KM Kevin Mitchell 89 J 20.00 6.00
TAA-KP Kirby Puckett 88 A ....
TAA-LB Lew Burdette 56 L 20.00 6.00
TAA-LD Len Dykstra 94 J 20.00 6.00
TAA-LS Lee Smith 91 H 20.00 6.00
TAA-MR Mickey Rivers 77 L 15.00 4.50
TAA-MS Mike Schmidt 80 B ....
TAA-RS Ron Santo 64 L 30.00 9.00
TAA-RT Ralph Terry 62 J 30.00 9.00
TAA-RY Robin Yount 82 C 100.00 30.00
TAA-SB Sal Bando 69 L 20.00 6.00
TAA-SG Steve Garvey 77 J 20.00 6.00
TAA-TJ Tommy John 68 L 20.00 6.00
TAA-TO Tony Oliva 64 J 40.00 12.00
TAA-BPO Boog Powell 69 J 30.00 9.00
TAA-BRO B.Robinson 64 E 150.00 45.00
TAA-DEV Darrell Evans 73 J 20.00 6.00
TAA-DGR Dick Groat 60 L 20.00 6.00
TAA-JBU Jim Bunning 65 L 50.00 15.00
TAA-JCR Jose Cruz 83 K 20.00 6.00
TAA-JKO Jerry Koosman 76 G ....
TAA-JPI Jimmy Piersall 56 J 20.00 6.00
TAA-JPO Johnny Podres 61 J 20.00 6.00
TAA-RCE Ron Cey 77 L 20.00 6.00
TAA-RSM Reggie Smith 77 L 20.00 6.00

2002 Topps Archives AutoProofs

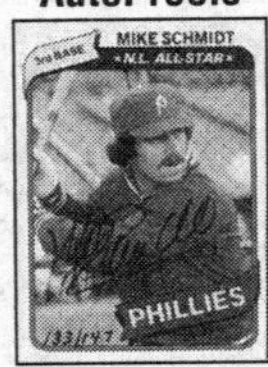

Randomly inserted into 1:616 hobby packs and 1:617 retail packs, these 10 cards feature original Topps cards which were repurchased by Topps on the secondary market and then signed by the featured player. Since each player signed a different amount of cards, we have notated those stated print runs next to the players name in our checklist. Cards with a print run of 40 or fewer are not priced due to market scarcity.

Nm-Mt Ex-Mt
GROUP A ODDS 1:128,720 H, 1:80,160 R
GROUP B ODDS 1:42,907 H, 1:40,080 R
GROUP C ODDS 1:17,163 H, 1:16,032 R
GROUP D ODDS 1:5254 H, 1:5344 R.
GROUP E ODDS 1:8305 H, 1:8016 R.
GROUP F ODDS 1:7151 H, 1:7287 R.
GROUP G ODDS 1:6436 H, 1:6680 R.
GROUP H ODDS 1:4597 H, 1:4453 R.
GROUP I ODDS 1:3731 H, 1:3817 R.
GROUP J ODDS 1:2258 H, 1:2290 R.
NO PRICING ON QTY 16 OR LESS
1 Gary Carter 85 E/80 .... 40.00 12.00
2 Jose Cruz 83 F/95 .... 40.00 12.00
3 Steve Garvey 77 A/5 ....
4 Bo Jackson 89 J/300 .... 60.00 18.00
5 Kevin Mitchell 89 D/65 .... 40.00 12.00
6 Kirby Puckett 88 D/65 .... 100.00 30.00
7 Mike Schmidt 80 H/147 .... 120.00 36.00
8 Ozzie Smith 87 G/105 .... 100.00 30.00
9 Darryl Strawberry 87 I/181 .... 40.00 12.00
10 Dave Winfield 79 B/16 ....
11 Robin Yount 82 C/39 .... 150.00 45.00

2002 Topps Archives Bat Relics

Randomly inserted into hobby and retail packs, these 19 cards feature players from the Archives set along with a game-used bat piece. Players in group A were inserted at stated odds of one in 106 while players in group B were inserted at stated odds of one in 282. We have notated what group each player is part of in our checklist.

Nm-Mt Ex-Mt
TBR-AD Andre Dawson 87 A 15.00 4.50
TBR-BF Bill Freehan 68 A 15.00 4.50
TBR-BR Brooks Robinson 64 A 20.00 6.00
TBR-CY Carl Yastrzemski 67 B 40.00 12.00
TBR-DE Dwight Evans 87 A 15.00 4.50
TBR-DM Don Mattingly 85 A 50.00 15.00
TBR-DP Dave Parker 78 A 15.00 4.50
TBR-GB George Brett 80 A 40.00 12.00
TBR-GC Gary Carter 85 A 15.00 4.50
TBR-JB Johnny Bench 70 A 25.00 7.50
TBR-JC Joe Carter 86 A 15.00 4.50
TBR-JM Joe Morgan 76 B 15.00 4.50
TBR-NC Norm Cash 61 A 15.00 4.50
TBR-RJ Reggie Jackson 69 A 20.00 6.00
TBR-RM Roger Maris 61 A 60.00 18.00
TBR-RS Ron Santo 64 A 20.00 6.00
TBR-RY Robin Yount 82 B 25.00 7.50
TBR-WH Willie Horton 65 A 15.00 4.50
TBR-WS Willie Stargell 71 A 20.00 6.00

2002 Topps Archives Reprints

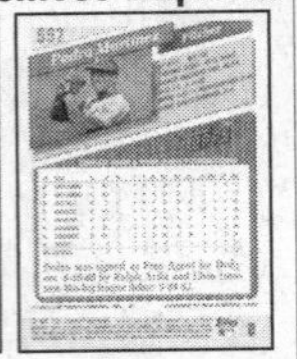

Issued at a stated rate of five per sealed 2002 Topps Factory set, these 10 cards feature reprints of first Topps cards of some of the leading superstars in baseball.

Nm-Mt Ex-Mt
COMPLETE SET (10) 25.00 7.50
1 Alex Rodriguez 98 .... 3.00 .90
2 Jason Giambi 94 .... 2.00 .60
3 Pedro Martinez 93 .... 2.00 .60
4 Ichiro Suzuki 01 .... 3.00 .90
5 Jeff Bagwell 91 .... 2.00 .60
6 Ivan Rodriguez 91 .... 2.00 .60
7 Mike Piazza 93 .... 3.00 .90
8 Nomar Garciaparra 95 .... 3.00 .90
9 Ken Griffey Jr. 89 .... 3.00 .90
10 Albert Pujols 01 .... 4.00 1.20

2002 Topps Archives Seat Relics

Randomly inserted into hobby and retail packs, these 19 cards feature a player from the Archives set along with a piece of a seat from a ballpark they played in. There were three different groups of players and they were inserted at odds ranging from one in 80 packs to one in 1636 packs.

Nm-Mt Ex-Mt
GROUP A ODDS 1:1629 HOB, 1:1636 RET
GROUP B ODDS 1:80 HOB, 1:80 RET.
GROUP C ODDS 1:1160 HOB, 1:1162 RET
TSR-BL Bob Lemon 52 B 15.00 4.50
TSR-DP Dave Parker 78 B 15.00 4.50
TSR-DS Duke Snider 54 B 20.00 6.00
TSR-EB Ernie Banks 58 B 25.00 7.50
TSR-EM Eddie Mathews 53 B 25.00 7.50
TSR-HS Herb Score 56 B 15.00 4.50
TSR-JB Jim Bunning 65 B 15.00 4.50
TSR-JC Joe Carter 86 B 15.00 4.50
TSR-JP Jim Palmer 75 B 15.00 4.50
TSR-ML Mickey Lolich 71 B 15.00 4.50
TSR-NF Nellie Fox 59 B 20.00 6.00
TSR-RA Richie Ashburn 58 B 20.00 6.00
TSR-RC Rod Carew 77 B 20.00 6.00
TSR-RG Ron Guidry 78 C 15.00 4.50
TSR-SA Sparky Anderson 84 B 15.00 4.50
TSR-SM Sam McDowell 70 B 15.00 4.50
TSR-TK Ted Kluszewski 54 B 20.00 6.00
TSR-WS Warren Spahn 57 B 20.00 6.00
TSR-YB Yogi Berra 54 A 25.00 7.50

2002 Topps Archives Uniform Relics

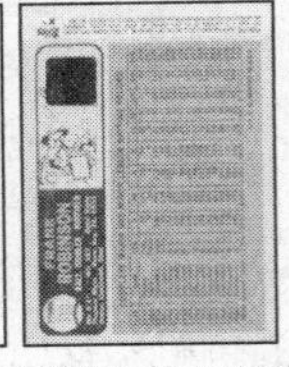

Inserted into hobby and retail packs at stated odds of one in 28, these 20 cards feature players from the Archives set along with a game-worn uniform swatch of that player.

Nm-Mt Ex-Mt
TUR-BB Bobby Bonds 73 .... 15.00 4.50
TUR-DC Dave Concepcion 79 .... 15.00 4.50
TUR-DE Dennis Eckersley 92 .... 15.00 4.50
TUR-DM Dale Murphy 83 .... 25.00 7.50
TUR-DS Don Sutton 72 .... 15.00 4.50
TUR-DW Dave Winfield 79 .... 15.00 4.50
TUR-FL Fred Lynn 79 .... 15.00 4.50
TUR-FR Frank Robinson 66 .... 20.00 6.00
TUR-GB George Brett 80 .... 40.00 12.00
TUR-GP Gaylord Perry 72 .... 15.00 4.50
TUR-KP Kirby Puckett 88 .... 25.00 7.50
TUR-NR Nolan Ryan 73 .... 50.00 15.00
TUR-OC Orlando Cepeda 61 .... 15.00 4.50
TUR-OS Ozzie Smith 87 .... 25.00 7.50
TUR-PN Phil Niekro 69 .... 15.00 4.50
TUR-RS Ryne Sandberg 90 .... 40.00 12.00
TUR-SA Sparky Anderson 84 .... 15.00 4.50
TUR-SG Steve Garvey 77 .... 15.00 4.50
TUR-WB Wade Boggs 87 .... 20.00 6.00
TUR-WC Will Clark 89 .... 25.00 7.50

2001 Topps Archives Reserve

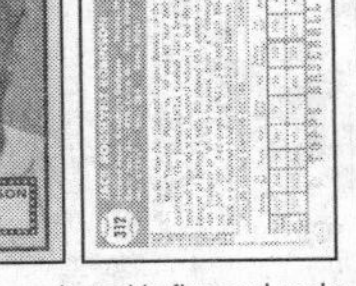

This 100 card set was issued in five card packs. These five card packs were issued in special display boxes which included one signed baseball per sealed box. These sealed boxes were issued six boxes to a case. The boxes (ball plus packs) had an SPR of $100 per box.

Nm-Mt Ex-Mt
COMPLETE SET (100) 100.00 30.00
1 Joe Adcock 52 .... 1.50 .45
2 Brooks Robinson 57 .... 2.50 .75
3 Luis Aparicio 56 .... 1.50 .45
4 Richie Ashburn 52 .... 2.50 .75
5 Hank Bauer 52 .... 1.50 .45
6 Johnny Bench 68 .... 6.00 1.80
7 Wade Boggs 83 .... 2.50 .75
8 Moose Skowron 54 .... 1.50 .45
9 George Brett 75 .... 12.00 3.60
10 Lou Brock 62 .... 2.50 .75
11 Roy Campanella 52 .... 4.00 1.20
12 Willie Hernandez 78 .... 1.50 .45
13 Steve Carlton 65 .... 5.00 1.50
14 Gary Carter 75 .... 2.50 .75
15 Hoyt Wilhelm 52 .... 2.50 .75
16 Orlando Cepeda 58 .... 1.50 .45
17 Roberto Clemente 55 .... 8.00 2.40
18 Dale Murphy 77 .... 4.00 1.20
19 Dave Concepcion 71 .... 1.50 .45
20 Dom DiMaggio 52 .... 1.50 .45
21 Larry Doby 52 .... 1.50 .45
22 Don Drysdale 57 .... 4.00 1.20
23 Dennis Eckersley 76 .... 1.50 .45
24 Bob Feller 52 .... 1.50 .45
25 Rollie Fingers 69 .... 1.50 .45
26 Carlton Fisk 72 .... 2.50 .75
27 Nellie Fox 56 .... 2.50 .75
28 Mickey Rivers 72 .... 1.50 .45
29 Tommy John 64 .... 1.50 .45
30 Johnny Sain 52 .... 1.50 .45
31 Keith Hernandez 75 .... 1.50 .45
32 Gil Hodges 52 .... 4.00 1.20
33 Elston Howard 56 .... 2.50 .75
34 Frank Howard 60 .... 1.50 .45
35 Bob Gibson 59 .... 2.50 .75
36 Fergie Jenkins 66 .... 1.50 .45
37 Jackie Jensen 52 .... 1.50 .45
38 Al Kaline 54 .... 4.00 1.20
39 Harmon Killebrew 55 .... 4.00 1.20
40 Ralph Kiner 53 .... 1.50 .45
41 Dick Groat 52 .... 1.50 .45
42 Don Larsen 56 .... 1.50 .45
43 Ralph Branca 52 .... 1.50 .45
44 Mickey Lolich 64 .... 1.50 .45
45 Juan Marichal 61 .... 1.50 .45
46 Roger Maris 58 .... 4.00 1.20
47 Bobby Thomson 52 .... 1.50 .45
48 Eddie Mathews 52 .... 4.00 1.20
49 Don Mattingly 84 .... 12.00 3.60
50 Willie McCovey 60 .... 1.50 .45
51 Gil McDougald 52 .... 1.50 .45
52 Tug McGraw 65 .... 1.50 .45
53 Billy Pierce 52 .... 1.50 .45
54 Minnie Minoso 52 .... 1.50 .45
55 Johnny Mize 52 .... 2.50 .75
56 Roy Face 53 .... 1.50 .45
57 Joe Morgan 65 .... 1.50 .45
58 Thurman Munson 70 .... 4.00 1.20
59 Stan Musial 58 .... 5.00 1.50
60 Phil Niekro 65 .... 1.50 .45
61 Paul Blair 65 .... 1.50 .45
62 Andy Pafko 52 .... 2.50 .75
63 Satchel Paige 53 .... 4.00 1.20
64 Tony Perez 65 .... 1.50 .45
65 Sal Bando 67 .... 1.50 .45
66 Jimmy Piersall 56 .... 1.50 .45
67 Kirby Puckett 85 .... 4.00 1.20
68 Phil Rizzuto 52 .... 4.00 1.20
69 Robin Roberts 52 .... 1.50 .45
70 Jackie Robinson 52 .... 4.00 1.20
71 Ryne Sandberg 83 .... 12.00 3.60
72 Mike Schmidt 73 .... 10.00 3.00
73 Red Schoendienst 52 .... 1.50 .45
74 Herb Score 56 .... 1.50 .45
75 Enos Slaughter 52 .... 1.50 .45
76 Ozzie Smith 80 .... 8.00 2.40
77 Warren Spahn 52 .... 2.50 .75
78 Don Sutton 66 .... 1.50 .45
79 Luis Tiant 65 .... 1.50 .45
80 Ted Kluszewski 52 .... 2.50 .75
81 Whitey Ford 53 .... 2.50 .75
82 Maury Wills 60 .... 1.50 .45
83 Dave Winfield 74 .... 1.50 .45
84 Early Wynn 52 .... 1.50 .45
85 Carl Yastrzemski 60 .... 5.00 1.50
86 Robin Yount 75 .... 8.00 2.40
87 Bob Allison 59 .... 1.50 .45
88 Clete Boyer 57 .... 1.50 .45
89 Reggie Jackson 69 .... 2.50 .75
90 Yogi Berra 52 .... 4.00 1.20
91 Willie Mays 52 .... 8.00 2.40
92 Jim Palmer 66 .... 1.50 .45
93 Pee Wee Reese 52 .... 4.00 1.20
94 Frank Robinson 57 .... 2.50 .75
95 Boog Powell 62 .... 2.50 .75
96 Willie Stargell 63 .... 2.50 .75
97 Nolan Ryan 68 .... 10.00 3.00
98 Tom Seaver 67 .... 6.00 1.80
99 Duke Snider 52 .... 2.50 .75
100 Bill Mazeroski 57 .... 4.00 1.20

2001 Topps Archives Reserve Autographed Baseballs

Issued one per sealed box, these 30 players signed baseballs for inclusion in this product. Each player signed an amount of ball between 100 and 1000 and we have included that information next to the player's name.

Nm-Mt Ex-Mt
1 Johnny Bench/100 .... 100.00 30.00
2 Paul Blair/1000 .... 20.00 6.00
3 Clete Boyer/1000 .... 25.00 7.50
4 Ralph Branca/400 .... 30.00 9.00
5 Roy Face/1000 .... 25.00 7.50
6 Bob Feller/1000 .... 25.00 7.50
7 Whitey Ford/100 .... 80.00 24.00
8 Bob Gibson/1000 .... 40.00 12.00
9 Dick Groat/1000 .... 25.00 7.50
10 Frank Howard/1000 .... 25.00 7.50
11 Reggie Jackson/100 .... 100.00 30.00
12 Don Larsen/100 .... 40.00 12.00
13 Mickey Lolich/500 .... 25.00 7.50
14 Willie Mays/100 .... 200.00 60.00
15 Gil McDougald/500 .... 30.00 9.00
16 Tug McGraw/100 .... 30.00 9.00
17 Minnie Minoso/1000 .... 25.00 7.50
18 Andy Pafko/500 .... 30.00 9.00
19 Joe Pepitone/1000 .... 20.00 6.00
20 Robin Roberts/1000 .... 30.00 9.00
21 Frank Robinson/100 .... 60.00 18.00
22 Nolan Ryan/100 .... 200.00 60.00
23 Herb Score/500 .... 25.00 7.50
24 Tom Seaver/100 .... 100.00 30.00
25 Moose Skowron/1000 .... 30.00 9.00
26 Warren Spahn/100 .... 80.00 24.00
27 Bobby Thomson/400 .... 30.00 9.00
28 Luis Tiant/500 .... 25.00 7.50
29 Carl Yastrzemski/100 .... 120.00 36.00
30 Maury Wills/1000 .... 25.00 7.50

2001 Topps Archives Reserve Future Rookie Reprints

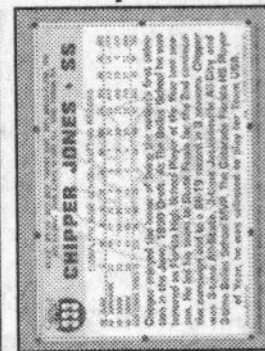

Issued five per Topps Limited factory set, these 20 cards are reprints of the featured players rookie card.

Nm-Mt Ex-Mt
COMPLETE SET (20) 120.00 36.00
1 Barry Bonds 87 .... 15.00 4.50
2 Chipper Jones 91 .... 6.00 1.80
3 Cal Ripken 82 .... 25.00 7.50
4 Shawn Green 92 .... 2.50 .75
5 Frank Thomas 90 .... 6.00 1.80
6 Derek Jeter 93 .... 20.00 6.00
7 Geoff Jenkins 96 .... 2.50 .75
8 Jim Edmonds 93 .... 2.50 .75
9 Bernie Williams 90 .... 4.00 1.20
10 Sammy Sosa 90 .... 10.00 3.00
11 Rickey Henderson 80 .... 6.00 1.80
12 Tony Gwynn 83 .... 8.00 2.40
13 Randy Johnson 89 .... 6.00 1.80
14 Juan Gonzalez 90 .... 4.00 1.20
15 Gary Sheffield 89 .... 2.50 .75
16 Manny Ramirez 92 .... 4.00 1.20
17 Pokey Reese 92 .... 2.50 .75
18 Preston Wilson 93 .... 2.50 .75

19 Jay Payton 95 .... 2.50 .75
20 Rafael Palmeiro 87 .... 4.00 1.20

2001 Topps Archives Reserve Rookie Reprint Autographs

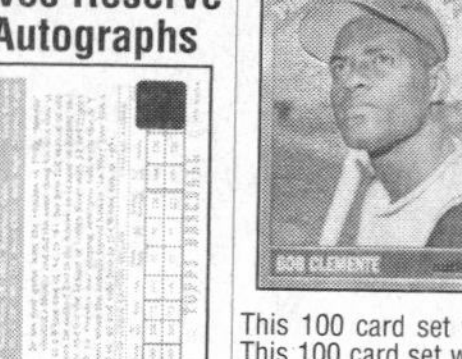

Inserted one per 10 packs, these 27 cards feature autographs of the players rookie reprint card. Each player signed a different amount of cards and those are notated by groups A, B or C in our checklist. Cards 15, 20, 22, 24, 28, 30, 31, and 35 do not exist. Willie Mays did not return his cards in time for inclusion in the packout. Those cards could be redeemed until July 31, 2003.

Nm-Mt Ex-Mt
ARA1 Willie Mays C 200.00 60.00
ARA2 Whitey Ford B 60.00 18.00
ARA3 Nolan Ryan A 200.00 60.00
ARA4 Carl Yastrzemski B 120.00 36.00
ARA5 Frank Robinson B 50.00 15.00
ARA6 Tom Seaver A 120.00 36.00
ARA7 Warren Spahn A 80.00 24.00
ARA8 Johnny Bench A 120.00 36.00
ARA9 Reggie Jackson A 120.00 36.00
ARA10 Bob Gibson B 50.00 15.00
ARA11 Bob Feller D 20.00 6.00
ARA12 Gil McDougald A 25.00 7.50
ARA13 Luis Tiant A 20.00 6.00
ARA14 Minnie Minoso D 20.00 6.00
ARA16 Herb Score B 20.00 6.00
ARA17 Moose Skowron C 25.00 7.50
ARA18 Maury Wills D 20.00 6.00
ARA19 Clete Boyer A 20.00 6.00
ARA21 Don Larsen A 25.00 7.50
ARA23 Tug McGraw C 30.00 9.00
ARA25 Robin Roberts C 25.00 7.50
ARA26 Frank Howard A 20.00 6.00
ARA27 Mickey Lolich D 20.00 6.00
ARA29 Tommy John C 20.00 6.00
ARA32 Dick Groat D 20.00 6.00
ARA33 Roy Face D 20.00 6.00
ARA34 Paul Blair D 15.00 4.50

2001 Topps Archives Reserve Rookie Reprint Relics

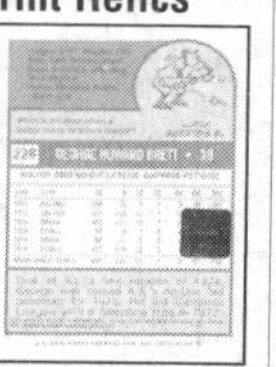

Issued at a rate of one in 10 packs, these 51 cards feature not only a rookie reprint of the featured player but also a memorabilia piece relating to their career.

Nm-Mt Ex-Mt
ARR1 B.Robinson Jsy 25.00 7.50
ARR2 Tony Conigliaro Jsy 25.00 7.50
ARR3 Frank Howard Jsy 15.00 4.50
ARR4 Don Sutton Jsy 15.00 4.50
ARR5 F.Jenkins Jsy 15.00 4.50
ARR6 Frank Robinson Jsy 25.00 7.50
ARR7 Don Mattingly Jsy 40.00 12.00
ARR8 Willie Stargell Jsy 25.00 7.50
ARR9 Moose Skowron Jsy 25.00 7.50
ARR10 Fred Lynn Jsy 15.00 4.50
ARR11 George Brett Jsy 40.00 12.00
ARR12 Nolan Ryan Jsy 50.00 15.00
ARR13 O.Cepeda Jsy 15.00 4.50
ARR14 R.Jackson Jsy 25.00 7.50
ARR15 Steve Carlton Jsy 15.00 4.50
ARR16 Tom Seaver Jsy 25.00 7.50
ARR17 T. Munson Jsy 40.00 12.00
ARR18 Yogi Berra Jsy 25.00 7.50
ARR19 W. McCovey Jsy 15.00 4.50
ARR20 Robin Yount Jsy 25.00 7.50
ARR21 Al Kaline Bat 25.00 7.50
ARR22 C. Yastrzemski Bat 40.00 12.00
ARR23 Carlton Fisk Bat 25.00 7.50
ARR24 Dale Murphy Bat 25.00 7.50
ARR25 Dave Winfield Bat 15.00 4.50
ARR26 Dick Groat Bat 15.00 4.50
ARR27 Dom DiMaggio Bat 25.00 7.50
ARR28 Don Mattingly Bat 40.00 12.00
ARR29 Gary Carter Bat 15.00 4.50
ARR30 George Kell Bat 25.00 7.50
ARR31 H. Killebrew Bat 25.00 7.50
ARR32 Jackie Jensen Bat 25.00 7.50
ARR33 J. Robinson Bat 80.00 24.00
ARR34 Jim Piersall Bat 15.00 4.50
ARR35 Joe Adcock Bat 15.00 4.50
ARR36 Joe Carter Bat 15.00 4.50
ARR37 Johnny Mize Bat 25.00 7.50
ARR38 Kirk Gibson Bat 15.00 4.50
ARR39 Mickey Vernon Bat 15.00 4.50
ARR40 Mike Schmidt Bat 40.00 12.00
ARR41 R. Sandberg Bat 40.00 12.00
ARR42 Ozzie Smith Bat 25.00 7.50
ARR43 T.Kluszewski Bat 25.00 7.50
ARR44 Wade Boggs Bat 25.00 7.50
ARR45 Willie Mays Bat 100.00 30.00
ARR46 Duke Snider Bat 25.00 7.50
ARR47 Harvey Kuenn Bat 15.00 4.50
ARR48 Robin Yount Bat 25.00 7.50
ARR49 R.Schoendienst Bat 15.00 4.50
ARR50 Elston Howard Bat 25.00 7.50
ARR51 Bob Allison Bat 15.00 4.50

2002 Topps Archives Reserve

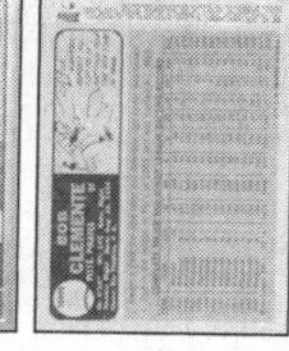

This 100 card set was released in June, 2002. This 100 card set was issued in four card packs which came 10 packs to a box and four boxes to a case. Each box also contined an autographed baseball.

Nm-Mt Ex-Mt
COMPLETE SET (100) 150.00 45.00
1 Lee Smith 91 .... 1.50 .45
2 Gaylord Perry 72 .... 1.50 .45
3 Al Oliver 82 .... 1.50 .45
4 Goose Gossage 77 .... 1.50 .45
5 Bill Madlock 75 .... 1.50 .45
6 Rod Carew 77 .... 2.50 .75
7 Fred Lynn 79 .... 1.50 .45
8 Frank Robinson 66 .... 2.50 .75
9 Al Kaline 55 .... 4.00 1.20
10 Len Dykstra 93 .... 1.50 .45
11 Carlton Fisk 77 .... 2.50 .75
12 Nellie Fox 59 .... 2.50 .75
13 Reggie Jackson 69 .... 2.50 .75
14 Bob Gibson 68 .... 2.50 .75
15 Bill Buckner 85 .... 1.50 .45
16 Harmon Killebrew 69 .... 4.00 1.20
17 Gary Carter 85 .... 1.50 .45
18 Dave Winfield 79 .... 1.50 .45
19 Ozzie Smith 87 .... 6.00 1.80
20 Dwight Evans 87 .... 1.50 .45
21 Dave Concepcion 79 .... 1.50 .45
22 Joe Morgan 76 .... 1.50 .45
23 Clete Boyer 62 .... 1.50 .45
24 Will Clark 89 .... 4.00 1.20
25 Lee May 69 .... 1.50 .45
26 Kevin Mitchell 89 .... 1.50 .45
27 Roger Maris 61 .... 4.00 1.20
28 Mickey Lolich 71 .... 1.50 .45
29 Luis Aparicio 60 .... 1.50 .45
30 George Foster 77 .... 1.50 .45
31 Don Mattingly 85 .... 10.00 3.00
32 Fernando Valenzuela 86 .... 1.50 .45
33 Bobby Bonds 73 .... 1.50 .45
34 Jim Palmer 75 .... 1.50 .45
35 Dennis Eckersley 92 .... 1.50 .45
36 Kirby Puckett 88 .... 4.00 1.20
37 Jose Cruz 83 .... 1.50 .45
38 Richie Ashburn 58 .... 2.50 .75
39 Whitey Ford 61 .... 2.50 .75
40 Robin Roberts 52 .... 1.50 .45
41 Don Newcombe 56 .... 1.50 .45
42 Roy Campanella 53 .... 4.00 1.20
43 Dennis Martinez 91 .... 1.50 .45
44 Larry Doby 54 .... 1.50 .45
45 Steve Garvey 77 .... 1.50 .45
46 Thurman Munson 76 .... 4.00 1.20
47 Dale Murphy 83 .... 4.00 1.20
48 Moose Skowron 60 .... 2.50 .75
49 Tom Seaver 69 .... 2.50 .75
50 Orlando Cepeda 61 .... 1.50 .45
51 Graig Nettles 77 .... 1.50 .45
52 Willie Stargell 71 .... 2.50 .75
53 Yogi Berra 54 .... 4.00 1.20
54 Steve Carlton 72 .... 1.50 .45
55 Don Sutton 72 .... 1.50 .45
56 Brooks Robinson 64 .... 2.50 .75
57 Vida Blue 71 .... 1.50 .45
58 Rollie Fingers 81 .... 1.50 .45
59 Jim Bunning 65 .... 1.50 .45
60 Nolan Ryan 73 .... 10.00 3.00
61 Hank Aaron 57 .... 8.00 2.40
62 Fergie Jenkins 71 .... 1.50 .45
63 Andre Dawson 87 .... 1.50 .45
64 Ernie Banks 58 .... 4.00 1.20
65 Early Wynn 59 .... 1.50 .45
66 Duke Snider 54 .... 2.50 .75
67 Red Schoendienst 53 .... 1.50 .45
68 Don Drysdale 62 .... 4.00 1.20
69 Catfish Hunter 74 .... 2.50 .75
70 George Brett 80 .... 10.00 3.00
71 Elston Howard 63 .... 2.50 .75
72 Wade Boggs 87 .... 2.50 .75
73 Keith Hernandez 79 .... 1.50 .45
74 Billy Pierce 56 .... 1.50 .45
75 Ted Kluszewski 54 .... 2.50 .75
76 Carl Yastrzemski 67 .... 6.00 1.80
77 Bert Blyleven 73 .... 1.50 .45
78 Tony Oliva 64 .... 1.50 .45
79 Joe Carter 86 .... 1.50 .45
80 Johnny Bench 70 .... 4.00 1.20
81 Tony Gwynn 97 .... 5.00 1.50
82 Mike Schmidt 80 .... 8.00 2.40
83 Phil Niekro 69 .... 1.50 .45
84 Juan Marichal 66 .... 1.50 .45
85 Eddie Mathews 53 .... 4.00 1.20
86 Boog Powell 69 .... 2.50 .75
87 Dwight Gooden 85 .... 1.50 .45
88 Darryl Strawberry 87 .... 1.50 .45
89 Roberto Clemente 66 .... 10.00 3.00
90 Ryne Sandberg 90 .... 8.00 2.40
91 Jack Clark 87 .... 1.50 .45
92 Willie Mays 62 .... 8.00 2.40
93 Ron Guidry 78 .... 1.50 .45
94 Kirk Gibson 88 .... 1.50 .45
95 Lou Brock 74 .... 2.50 .75
96 Robin Yount 82 .... 6.00 1.80
97 Bill Mazeroski 60 .... 2.50 .75
98 Dave Parker 78 .... 1.50 .45
99 Hoyt Wilhelm 64 .... 1.50 .45
100 Warren Spahn 57 .... 2.50 .75

2002 Topps Archives Reserve Autographed Baseballs

Inserted one per Archives Reserve box, these 21 autographed baseballs feature authentic signatures from some of baseball's best all-time players. Since the players signed a different amount

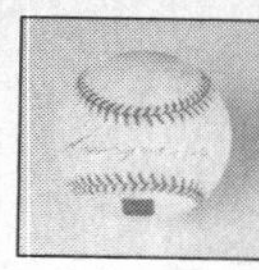

of cards, we have notated that information next to their name in our checklist.

Nm-Mt Ex-Mt
1 Luis Aparicio/1600 .... 25.00 7.50
2 Ernie Banks/50 ....
3 Yogi Berra/100 .... 120.00 36.00
4 Lou Brock/400 .... 50.00 15.00
5 Jim Bunning/500 .... 60.00 18.00
6 Gary Carter/500 .... 30.00 9.00
7 Goose Gossage/500 .... 30.00 9.00
8 Fergie Jenkins/1000 .... 25.00 7.50
9 Al Kaline/250 .... 100.00 30.00
10 Harmon Killebrew/250 .... 100.00 30.00
11 Willie Mays/50 ....
12 Joe Morgan/250 .... 50.00 15.00
13 Graig Nettles/1600 .... 25.00 7.50
14 Jim Palmer/400 .... 30.00 9.00
15 Gaylord Perry/500 .... 30.00 9.00
16 Brooks Robinson/500 .... 50.00 15.00
17 Mike Schmidt/250 .... 120.00 36.00
18 Duke Snider/100 .... 100.00 30.00
19 Dave Winfield/1650 .... 40.00 12.00
20 Robin Yount/250 .... 100.00 30.00
NNO Auto Ball Exchange Card .. 50.00 15.00

2002 Topps Archives Reserve Autographs

Inserted at overall stated odds of one in 15 hobby and one in 203 retail, these 17 cards feature the players signed the Archives reserve "reprint" of their key year card. Since the players all signed at a different rate based on their "group", we have listed their group affiliation next to their name in our checklist.

Nm-Mt Ex-Mt
GROUP A ODDS 1:1077 RET ....
GROUP B ODDS 1:1421 RET ....
GROUP C ODDS 1:947 RET ....
GROUP D ODDS 1:1421 RET ....
GROUP E ODDS 1:718 RET ....
TRA-AK Al Kaline 55 C 60.00 18.00
TRA-BR Brooks Robinson 64 B 30.00 9.00
TRA-DS Duke Snider 54 A 80.00 24.00
TRA-EB Ernie Banks 58 A 100.00 30.00
TRA-FJ Fergie Jenkins 71 E 15.00 4.50
TRA-GC Gary Carter 85 B 30.00 9.00
TRA-GN Graig Nettles 77 D 15.00 4.50
TRA-GP Gaylord Perry 72 C 20.00 6.00
TRA-HK Harmon Killebrew 69 C 60.00 18.00
TRA-JM Joe Morgan 76 B 30.00 9.00
TRA-LA Luis Aparicio 60 D 20.00 6.00
TRA-LB Lou Brock 74 B 30.00 9.00
TRA-LS Lee Smith 91 E 15.00 4.50
TRA-MS Mike Schmidt 80 A 120.00 36.00
TRA-RY Robin Yount 82 A 120.00 36.00
TRA-WM Willie Mays 62 A 150.00 45.00
TRA-YB Yogi Berra 54 A 100.00 30.00

2002 Topps Archives Reserve Bat Relics

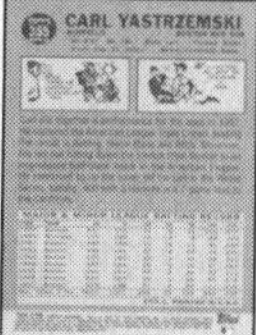

Inserted at stated odds of one in 22 hobby packs, these 10 cards feature not only the player's "best card" but also a game-used bat piece from each player. The players belonged to different groups in terms of scarcity and we have put that information next to their name in our checklist.

Nm-Mt Ex-Mt
TRR-CF Carlton Fisk 77 B 15.00 4.50
TRR-DW Dave Winfield 79 C 15.00 4.50
TRR-OC Orlando Cepeda 61 B .. 15.00 4.50
TRR-RM Roger Maris 61 A 100.00 30.00
TRR-TM Thurman Munson 76 B 40.00 12.00
TRR-CYB Carl Yastrzemski 67 B 40.00 12.00
TRR-DMB Don Mattingly 85 B .. 40.00 12.00
TRR-EMB Eddie Mathews 53 B. 20.00 6.00
TRR-GBB George Brett 80 B 25.00 7.50
TRR-HAB Hank Aaron 57 B 50.00 15.00

2002 Topps Archives Reserve Uniform Relics

Inserted at stated odds of one in seven hobby packs, these 15 cards feature not only the player's "best card" but also a game-used bat piece from each player. The players belonged to different groups in terms of scarcity and we have put that information next to their name in our checklist.

Nm-Mt Ex-Mt
BR Brooks Robinson 64 Uni D . 15.00 4.50
EB Ernie Banks 58 Uni C 25.00 7.50
GC Gary Carter 85 Jsy C 20.00 6.00

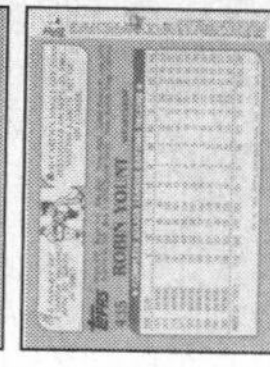

JB Johnny Bench 70 Uni D 15.00 4.50
JM Juan Marichal 66 Jsy A 20.00 6.00
KP Kirby Puckett 88 Jsy D 15.00 4.50
NF Nellie Fox 59 Uni C 20.00 6.00
NR Nolan Ryan 73 Jsy D 40.00 12.00
RS Red Schoendienst 53 Jsy B 15.00 4.50
RY Robin Yount 82 Uni D 15.00 4.50
TG Tony Gwynn 97 Jsy D 15.00 4.50
WB Wade Boggs 87 Jsy D 15.00 4.50
WC Will Clark 89 Jsy C 25.00 7.50
WM Willie Mays 62 Uni C 50.00 15.00
WS Willie Stargell 71 Uni D 15.00 4.50

1996 Topps Chrome

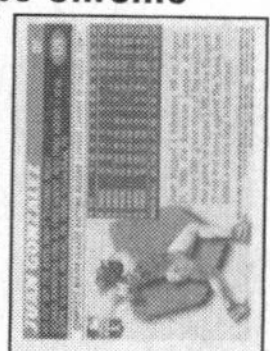

The 1996 Topps Chrome set was issued in one series totalling 165 cards and features a selection of players from the 1996 Topps regular set. The four-card packs retailed for $3.00 each. Each chromium card is a replica of its regular version with the exception of the Topps Chrome logo replacing the traditional logo. Included in the set is a Mickey Mantle number 7 Commemorative card and a Cal Ripken Tribute card.

Nm-Mt Ex-Mt
COMPLETE SET (165) 50.00 15.00
1 Tony Gwynn STP .... 1.25 .35
2 Mike Piazza STP .... 2.00 .60
3 Greg Maddux STP .... 2.00 .60
4 Jeff Bagwell STP .... .75 .23
5 Larry Walker STP .... .75 .23
6 Barry Larkin STP .... .75 .23
7 Mickey Mantle COMM 10.00 3.00
8 Tom Glavine STP .... .75 .23
9 Craig Biggio STP .... .75 .23
10 Barry Bonds STP .... 2.00 .60
11 H.Slocumb STP .... .75 .23
12 Matt Williams STP .... .75 .23
13 Todd Helton 4.00 1.20
14 Paul Molitor .... 1.25 .35
15 Glenallen Hill .... .75 .23
16 Troy Percival .... .75 .23
17 Albert Belle .... .75 .23
18 Mark Wohlers .... .75 .23
19 Kirby Puckett .... 2.00 .60
20 Mark Grace .... 1.25 .35
21 J.T. Snow .... .75 .23
22 David Justice .... .75 .23
23 Mike Mussina .... 1.25 .35
24 Bernie Williams .... 1.25 .35
25 Ron Gant .... .75 .23
26 Carlos Baerga .... .75 .23
27 Gary Sheffield .... .75 .23
28 Cal Ripken 2131 .... 6.00 1.80
29 Frank Thomas .... 2.00 .60
30 Kevin Seitzer .... .75 .23
31 Joe Carter .... .75 .23
32 Jeff King .... .75 .23
33 David Cone .... .75 .23
34 Eddie Murray .... 2.00 .60
35 Brian Jordan .... .75 .23
36 Garret Anderson .... .75 .23
37 Hideo Nomo .... 2.00 .60
38 Steve Finley .... .75 .23
39 Ivan Rodriguez .... 2.00 .60
40 Quilvio Veras .... .75 .23
41 Mark McGwire 5.00 1.50
42 Greg Vaughn .... .75 .23
43 Randy Johnson .... 2.00 .60
44 David Segui .... .75 .23
45 Derek Bell .... .75 .23
46 John Valentin .... .75 .23
47 Steve Avery .... .75 .23
48 Tino Martinez .... 1.25 .35
49 Shane Reynolds .... .75 .23
50 Jim Edmonds .... .75 .23
51 Raul Mondesi .... .75 .23
52 Chipper Jones .... 2.00 .60
53 Gregg Jefferies .... .75 .23
54 Ken Caminiti .... .75 .23
55 Brian McRae .... .75 .23
56 Don Mattingly 5.00 1.50
57 Marty Cordova .... .75 .23
58 Vinny Castilla .... .75 .23
59 John Smoltz .... 1.25 .35
60 Travis Fryman .... .75 .23
61 Ryan Klesko .... .75 .23
62 Alex Fernandez .... .75 .23
63 Dante Bichette .... .75 .23
64 Eric Karros .... .75 .23
65 Roger Clemens 4.00 1.20
66 Randy Myers .... .75 .23
67 Cal Ripken 6.00 1.80
68 Rod Beck .... .75 .23
69 Jack McDowell .... .75 .23
70 Ken Griffey Jr. .... 3.00 .90
71 Ramon Martinez .... .75 .23
72 Jason Giambi .... .75 .23
73 Nomar Garciaparra FS .... 3.00 .90
74 Billy Wagner .... .75 .23
75 Todd Greene .... .75 .23
76 Paul Wilson .... .75 .23
77 Johnny Damon .... 1.25 .35
78 Alan Benes .... .75 .23

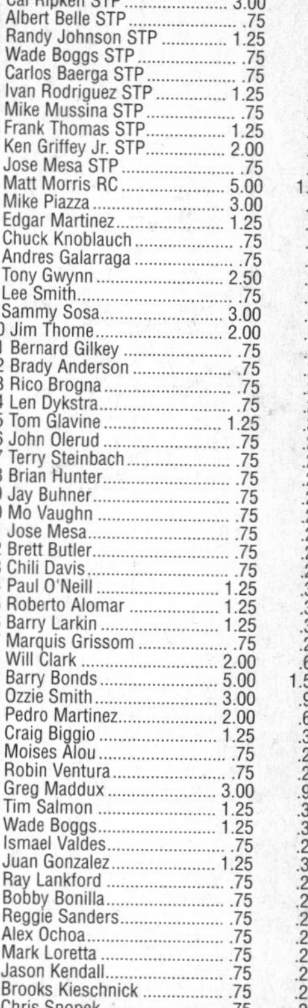

79 Karim Garcia FS .... .75 .23
80 Derek Jeter FS 5.00 1.50
81 Kirby Puckett STP .... 1.25 .35
82 Cal Ripken STP .... 3.00 .90
83 Albert Belle STP .... .75 .23
84 Randy Johnson STP .... 1.25 .35
85 Wade Boggs STP .... .75 .23
86 Carlos Baerga STP .... .75 .23
87 Ivan Rodriguez STP .... 1.25 .35
88 Mike Mussina STP .... .75 .23
89 Frank Thomas STP .... 1.25 .35
90 Ken Griffey Jr. STP .... 2.00 .60
91 Jose Mesa STP .... .75 .23
92 Matt Morris RC 5.00 1.50
93 Mike Piazza .... 3.00 .90
94 Edgar Martinez .... 1.25 .35
95 Chuck Knoblauch .... .75 .23
96 Andres Galarraga .... .75 .23
97 Tony Gwynn .... 2.50 .75
98 Lee Smith .... .75 .23
99 Sammy Sosa .... 3.00 .90
100 Jim Thome .... 2.00 .60
101 Bernard Gilkey .... .75 .23
102 Brady Anderson .... .75 .23
103 Rico Brogna .... .75 .23
104 Len Dykstra .... .75 .23
105 Tom Glavine .... 1.25 .35
106 John Olerud .... .75 .23
107 Terry Steinbach .... .75 .23
108 Brian Hunter .... .75 .23
109 Jay Buhner .... .75 .23
110 Mo Vaughn .... .75 .23
111 Jose Mesa .... .75 .23
112 Brett Butler .... .75 .23
113 Chili Davis .... .75 .23
114 Paul O'Neill .... 1.25 .35
115 Roberto Alomar .... 1.25 .35
116 Barry Larkin .... 1.25 .35
117 Marquis Grissom .... .75 .23
118 Will Clark .... 2.00 .60
119 Barry Bonds 5.00 1.50
120 Ozzie Smith .... 3.00 .90
121 Pedro Martinez .... 2.00 .60
122 Craig Biggio .... 1.25 .35
123 Moises Alou .... .75 .23
124 Robin Ventura .... .75 .23
125 Greg Maddux .... 3.00 .90
126 Tim Salmon .... 1.25 .35
127 Wade Boggs .... 1.25 .35
128 Ismael Valdes .... .75 .23
129 Juan Gonzalez .... 1.25 .35
130 Ray Lankford .... .75 .23
131 Bobby Bonilla .... .75 .23
132 Reggie Sanders .... .75 .23
133 Alex Ochoa .... .75 .23
134 Mark Loretta .... .75 .23
135 Jason Kendall .... .75 .23
136 Brooks Kieschnick .... .75 .23
137 Chris Snopek .... .75 .23
138 Ruben Rivera NOW .... .75 .23
139 Jeff Suppan .... .75 .23
140 John Wasdin .... .75 .23
141 Jay Payton .... .75 .23
142 Rick Krivda .... .75 .23
143 Jimmy Haynes .... .75 .23
144 Ryne Sandberg .... 3.00 .90
145 Matt Williams .... .75 .23
146 Jose Canseco .... 2.00 .60
147 Larry Walker .... 1.25 .35
148 Kevin Appier .... .75 .23
149 Javy Lopez .... .75 .23
150 Dennis Eckersley .... .75 .23
151 Jason Isringhausen .... .75 .23
152 Dean Palmer .... .75 .23
153 Jeff Bagwell .... 1.25 .35
154 Rondell White .... .75 .23
155 Wally Joyner .... .75 .23
156 Fred McGriff .... 1.25 .35
157 Cecil Fielder .... .75 .23
158 Rafael Palmeiro .... 1.25 .35
159 Rickey Henderson .... 2.00 .60
160 Shawon Dunston .... .75 .23
161 Manny Ramirez .... 1.25 .35
162 Alex Gonzalez .... .75 .23
163 Shawn Green .... .75 .23
164 Kenny Lofton .... .75 .23
165 Jeff Conine .... .75 .23

1996 Topps Chrome Refractors

Randomly inserted at the rate of one in every 12 packs, this 165-card set is parallel to the regular Chrome set. The difference in design is the refractive quality of the cards.

Nm-Mt Ex-Mt
*STARS: 2.5X TO 6X BASIC CARDS ...
*ROOKIES: 1.5X TO 4X BASIC CARDS

1996 Topps Chrome Masters of the Game

Randomly inserted in packs at a rate of one in 12, this 20-card set honors players who are masters of their playing positions. The fronts feature color action photography with brilliant color metallization.

Nm-Mt Ex-Mt
COMPLETE SET (20) 60.00 18.00
*REF: 1X TO 2.5X BASIC CHR.MASTERS
REF.STATED ODDS 1:36 HOBBY ....
1 Dennis Eckersley .... 2.00 .60
2 Denny Martinez .... 2.00 .60
3 Eddie Murray 5.00 1.50
4 Paul Molitor .... 3.00 .90
5 Ozzie Smith 8.00 2.40
6 Rickey Henderson 5.00 1.50

7 Tim Raines 2.00 .60
8 Lee Smith 2.00 .60
9 Cal Ripken 15.00 4.50
10 Chili Davis 2.00 .60
11 Wade Boggs 3.00 .90
12 Tony Gwynn 6.00 1.80
13 Don Mattingly 12.00 3.60
14 Bret Saberhagen 2.00 .60
15 Kirby Puckett 5.00 1.50
16 Joe Carter 2.00 .60
17 Roger Clemens 10.00 3.00
18 Barry Bonds 12.00 3.60
19 Greg Maddux 8.00 2.40
20 Frank Thomas 5.00 1.50

1996 Topps Chrome Wrecking Crew

Randomly inserted in packs at a rate of one in 24, this 15-card set features baseball's top hitters and is printed in color action photography with brilliant color metallization.

	Nm-Mt	Ex-Mt
COMPLETE SET (15)	80.00	24.00
*REF: 1X TO 2.5X BASIC CHR.WRECKING		
REF.STATED ODDS 1:72 HOBBY		
WC1 Jeff Bagwell	4.00	1.20
WC2 Albert Belle	2.50	.75
WC3 Barry Bonds	15.00	4.50
WC4 Jose Canseco	6.00	1.80
WC5 Joe Carter	2.50	.75
WC6 Cecil Fielder	2.50	.75
WC7 Ron Gant	2.50	.75
WC8 Juan Gonzalez	4.00	1.20
WC9 Ken Griffey Jr.	10.00	3.00
WC10 Fred McGriff	4.00	1.20
WC11 Mark McGwire	15.00	4.50
WC12 Mike Piazza	10.00	3.00
WC13 Frank Thomas	6.00	1.80
WC14 Mo Vaughn	2.50	.75
WC15 Matt Williams	2.50	.75

1997 Topps Chrome

The 1997 Topps Chrome set was issued in one series totalling 165 cards and was distributed in four-card packs with a suggested retail price of $3.00. Using Chromium technology to highlight the cards, this set features a metalized version of the cards of some of the best players from the 1997 regular Topps Series one and two. An attractive 8 1/2" by 11" chrome promo sheet was sent to dealers advertising this set.

	Nm-Mt	Ex-Mt
COMPLETE SET (165)	50.00	15.00
1 Barry Bonds	5.00	1.50
2 Jose Valentin	.75	.23
3 Brady Anderson	.75	.23
4 Wade Boggs	1.25	.35
5 Andres Galarraga	.75	.23
6 Rusty Greer	.75	.23
7 Derek Jeter	5.00	1.50
8 Ricky Bottalico	.75	.23
9 Mike Piazza	3.00	.90
10 Garret Anderson	.75	.23
11 Jeff King	.75	.23
12 Kevin Appier	.75	.23
13 Mark Grace	1.25	.35
14 Jeff D'Amico	.75	.23
15 Jay Buhner	.75	.23
16 Hal Morris	.75	.23
17 Harold Baines	.75	.23
18 Jeff Cirillo	.75	.23
19 Tom Glavine	1.25	.35
20 Andy Pettitte	1.25	.35
21 Mark McGwire	5.00	1.50
22 Chuck Knoblauch	.75	.23
23 Raul Mondesi	.75	.23
24 Albert Belle	.75	.23
25 Trevor Hoffman	.75	.23
26 Eric Young	.75	.23
27 Brian McRae	.75	.23
28 Jim Edmonds	.75	.23
29 Robb Nen	.75	.23
30 Reggie Sanders	.75	.23
31 Mike Lansing	.75	.23
32 Craig Biggio	1.25	.35
33 Ray Lankford	.75	.23
34 Charles Nagy	.75	.23
35 Paul Wilson	.75	.23
36 John Wetteland	.75	.23
37 Derek Bell	.75	.23
38 Edgar Martinez	1.25	.35
39 Rickey Henderson	2.00	.60
40 Jim Thome	2.00	.60
41 Frank Thomas	2.00	.60
42 Jackie Robinson	2.00	.60
43 Terry Steinbach	.75	.23
44 Kevin Brown	.75	.23
45 Joey Hamilton	.75	.23
46 Travis Fryman	.75	.23
47 Juan Gonzalez	1.25	.35
48 Ron Gant	.75	.23
49 Greg Maddux	3.00	.90
50 Wally Joyner	.75	.23
51 John Valentin	.75	.23
52 Bret Boone	.75	.23
53 Paul Molitor	1.25	.35
54 Rafael Palmeiro	1.25	.35
55 Todd Hundley	.75	.23
56 Ellis Burks	.75	.23
57 Bernie Williams	1.25	.35
58 Roberto Alomar	1.25	.35
59 Jose Mesa	.75	.23
60 Troy Percival	.75	.23
61 John Smoltz	1.25	.35
62 Jeff Conine	.75	.23
63 Bernard Gilkey	.75	.23
64 Mickey Tettleton	.75	.23
65 Justin Thompson	.75	.23
66 Tony Phillips	.75	.23
67 Ryne Sandberg	3.00	.90
68 Geronimo Berroa	.75	.23
69 Todd Hollandsworth	.75	.23
70 Rey Ordonez	.75	.23
71 Marquis Grissom	.75	.23
72 Tino Martinez	1.25	.35
73 Steve Finley	.75	.23
74 Andy Benes	.75	.23
75 Jason Kendall	.75	.23
76 Johnny Damon	1.25	.35
77 Jason Giambi	.75	.23
78 Henry Rodriguez	.75	.23
79 Edgar Renteria	.75	.23
80 Ray Durham	.75	.23
81 Gregg Jefferies	.75	.23
82 Roberto Hernandez	.75	.23
83 Joe Carter	.75	.23
84 Jermaine Dye	.75	.23
85 Julio Franco	.75	.23
86 David Justice	.75	.23
87 Jose Canseco	2.00	.60
88 Paul O'Neill	1.25	.35
89 Mariano Rivera	1.25	.35
90 Bobby Higginson	.75	.23
91 Mark Grudzielanek	.75	.23
92 Lance Johnson	.75	.23
93 Ken Caminiti	.75	.23
94 Gary Sheffield	.75	.23
95 Luis Castillo	.75	.23
96 Scott Rolen	2.00	.60
97 Chipper Jones	2.00	.60
98 Darryl Strawberry	.75	.23
99 Nomar Garciaparra	3.00	.90
100 Jeff Bagwell	1.25	.35
101 Ken Griffey Jr.	3.00	.90
102 Sammy Sosa	3.00	.90
103 Jack McDowell	.75	.23
104 James Baldwin	.75	.23
105 Rocky Coppinger	.75	.23
106 Manny Ramirez	1.25	.35
107 Tim Salmon	1.25	.35
108 Eric Karros	.75	.23
109 Brett Butler	.75	.23
110 Randy Johnson	2.00	.60
111 Pat Hentgen	.75	.23
112 Rondell White	.75	.23
113 Eddie Murray	2.00	.60
114 Ivan Rodriguez	2.00	.60
115 Jermaine Allensworth	.75	.23
116 Ed Sprague	.75	.23
117 Kenny Lofton	.75	.23
118 Alan Benes	.75	.23
119 Fred McGriff	1.25	.35
120 Alex Fernandez	.75	.23
121 Al Martin	.75	.23
122 Devon White	.75	.23
123 David Cone	.75	.23
124 Karim Garcia	.75	.23
125 Chili Davis	.75	.23
126 Roger Clemens	4.00	1.20
127 Bobby Bonilla	.75	.23
128 Mike Mussina	1.25	.35
129 Todd Walker	.75	.23
130 Dante Bichette	.75	.23
131 Carlos Baerga	.75	.23
132 Matt Williams	.75	.23
133 Will Clark	2.00	.60
134 Dennis Eckersley	.75	.23
135 Ryan Klesko	.75	.23
136 Dean Palmer	.75	.23
137 Javy Lopez	.75	.23
138 Greg Vaughn	.75	.23
139 Vinny Castilla	.75	.23
140 Cal Ripken	6.00	1.80
141 Ruben Rivera	.75	.23
142 Mark Wohlers	.75	.23
143 Tony Clark	.75	.23
144 Jose Rosado	.75	.23
145 Tony Gwynn	2.50	.75
146 Cecil Fielder	.75	.23
147 Brian Jordan	.75	.23
148 Bob Abreu	.75	.23
149 Barry Larkin	1.25	.35
150 Robin Ventura	.75	.23
151 John Olerud	.75	.23
152 Rod Beck	.75	.23
153 Vladimir Guerrero	2.00	.60
154 Marty Cordova	.75	.23
155 Todd Stottlemyre	.75	.23
156 Hideo Nomo	2.00	.60
157 Denny Neagle	.75	.23
158 John Jaha	.75	.23
159 Mo Vaughn	.75	.23
160 Andruw Jones	.75	.23
161 Moises Alou	.75	.23
162 Larry Walker	1.25	.35
163 Eddie Murray SH	1.25	.35
164 Paul Molitor SH	.75	.23
165 Checklist	.75	.23

1997 Topps Chrome Refractors

Randomly inserted in packs at a rate of one in 12, this 165-card set is a parallel version of the regular Topps Chrome set and is similar in design. The difference is found in the refractive quality of the cards.

	Nm-Mt	Ex-Mt
*STARS: 2.5X TO 6X BASE CARDS		

1997 Topps Chrome All-Stars

Randomly inserted in packs at a rate of one in 24, this 22-card set features color player photos printed on rainbow foilboard. The set showcases the top three players from each position from both the American and National leagues as voted on by the Topps Sports Department.

	Nm-Mt	Ex-Mt
COMPLETE SET (22)	100.00	30.00
*REF: 1X TO 2.5X BASIC CHROME AS		
REFRACTOR STATED ODDS 1:72		
AS1 Ivan Rodriguez	6.00	1.80
AS2 Todd Hundley	2.50	.75
AS3 Frank Thomas	6.00	1.80
AS4 Andres Galarraga	2.50	.75
AS5 Chuck Knoblauch	2.50	.75
AS6 Eric Young	2.50	.75
AS7 Jim Thome	6.00	1.80
AS8 Chipper Jones	6.00	1.80
AS9 Cal Ripken	20.00	6.00
AS10 Barry Larkin	4.00	1.20
AS11 Albert Belle	2.50	.75
AS12 Barry Bonds	15.00	4.50
AS13 Ken Griffey Jr.	10.00	3.00
AS14 Ellis Burks	2.50	.75
AS15 Juan Gonzalez	4.00	1.20
AS16 Gary Sheffield	2.50	.75
AS17 Andy Pettitte	4.00	1.20
AS18 Tom Glavine	4.00	1.20
AS19 Pat Hentgen	2.50	.75
AS20 John Smoltz	4.00	1.20
AS21 Roberto Hernandez	2.50	.75
AS22 Mark Wohlers	2.50	.75

1997 Topps Chrome Diamond Duos

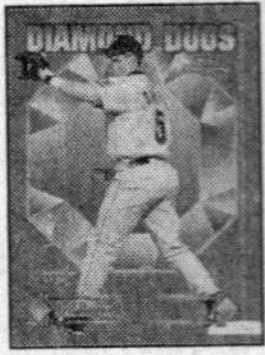

Randomly inserted in packs at a rate of one in 36, this 10-card set features color player photos of two superstar teammates on double sided chromium cards.

	Nm-Mt	Ex-Mt
COMPLETE SET (10)	50.00	15.00
*REF: 1X TO 2.5X BASIC DIAM.DUOS		
REFRACTOR STATED ODDS 1:108		
DD1 Chipper Jones / Andruw Jones	5.00	1.50
DD2 Derek Jeter / Bernie Williams	12.00	3.60
DD3 Ken Griffey Jr. / Jay Buhner	8.00	2.40
DD4 Kenny Lofton / Manny Ramirez	3.00	.90
DD5 Jeff Bagwell / Craig Biggio	3.00	.90
DD6 Juan Gonzalez / Ivan Rodriguez	5.00	1.50
DD7 Cal Ripken / Brady Anderson	15.00	4.50
DD8 Mike Piazza / Hideo Nomo	8.00	2.40
DD9 Andres Galarraga / Dante Bichette	2.00	.60
DD10 Frank Thomas / Albert Belle	5.00	1.50

1997 Topps Chrome Season's Best

Randomly inserted in packs at a rate of one in 18, this 25-card set features color player photos of the five top players from five statistical categories: most steals (Leading Looters), most home runs (Bleacher Reachers), most wins (Hill Toppers), most RBIs (Number Crunchers), and best slugging percentage (Kings of Swing).

	Nm-Mt	Ex-Mt
COMPLETE SET (25)	60.00	18.00
*REF: 1X TO 2.5X BASIC SEAS.BEST		
REFRACTOR STATED ODDS 1:54		
1 Tony Gwynn	6.00	1.80
2 Frank Thomas	5.00	1.50
3 Ellis Burks	2.00	.60
4 Paul Molitor	3.00	.90
5 Chuck Knoblauch	2.00	.60
6 Mark McGwire	12.00	3.60
7 Brady Anderson	2.00	.60
8 Ken Griffey Jr.	8.00	2.40
9 Albert Belle	2.00	.60
10 Andres Galarraga	2.00	.60
11 Andres Galarraga	2.00	.60
12 Albert Belle	2.00	.60
13 Juan Gonzalez	3.00	.90
14 Mo Vaughn	2.00	.60
15 Rafael Palmeiro	3.00	.90
16 John Smoltz	3.00	.90
17 Andy Pettitte	3.00	.90
18 Pat Hentgen	2.00	.60
19 Mike Mussina	3.00	.90
20 Andy Benes	2.00	.60
21 Kenny Lofton	2.00	.60
22 Tom Goodwin	2.00	.60
23 Otis Nixon	2.00	.60
24 Eric Young	2.00	.60
25 Lance Johnson	2.00	.60

1998 Topps Chrome

The 1998 Topps Chrome set was issued in two separate series of 282 and 221 cards respectively with design and content paralleling the base 1998 Topps set. Four-card packs carried a suggested retail price of $3 each. Card fronts feature color action player photos printed wtih Chromium technology on metalized cards. The backs carry player information. As is tradition with Topps sets since 1996, card number seven was excluded from the set in honor of Mickey Mantle. Subsets are as follows: Prospects/Draft Picks (245-264/484-501), Season Highlights (265-269/474-478), Inter-League (270-274/479-483), Checklists (275-276/502-503) and World Series (277-283). After four years of being excluded from Topps products, superstar Alex Rodriguez finally made his Topps debut as card number 504. Notable Rookie Cards include Ryan Anderson, Michael Cuddyer, Jack Cust and Troy Glaus.

	Nm-Mt	Ex-Mt
COMPLETE SET (503)	150.00	45.00
COMP. SERIES 1 (282)	80.00	24.00
COMP. SERIES 2 (221)	80.00	24.00
1 Tony Gwynn	2.50	.75
2 Larry Walker	1.25	.35
3 Billy Wagner	.75	.23
4 Denny Neagle	.75	.23
5 Vladimir Guerrero	2.00	.60
6 Kevin Brown	1.25	.35
8 Mariano Rivera	1.25	.35
9 Tony Clark	.75	.23
10 Deion Sanders	1.25	.35
11 Francisco Cordova	.75	.23
12 Matt Williams	.75	.23
13 Carlos Baerga	.75	.23
14 Mo Vaughn	.75	.23
15 Bobby Witt	.75	.23
16 Matt Stairs	.75	.23
17 Chan Ho Park	.75	.23
18 Mike Bordick	.75	.23
19 Michael Tucker	.75	.23
20 Frank Thomas	2.00	.60
21 Roberto Clemente	5.00	1.50
22 Dmitri Young	.75	.23
23 Steve Trachsel	.75	.23
24 Jeff Kent	.75	.23
25 Scott Rolen	2.00	.60
26 John Thomson	.75	.23
27 Joe Vitiello	.75	.23
28 Eddie Guardado	.75	.23
29 Charlie Hayes	.75	.23
30 Juan Gonzalez	1.25	.35
31 Garret Anderson	.75	.23
32 John Jaha	.75	.23
33 Omar Vizquel	1.25	.35
34 Brian Hunter	.75	.23
35 Jeff Bagwell	1.25	.35
36 Mark Lemke	.75	.23
37 Doug Glanville	.75	.23
38 Dan Wilson	.75	.23
39 Steve Cooke	.75	.23
40 Chili Davis	.75	.23
41 Mike Cameron	.75	.23
42 F.P. Santangelo	.75	.23
43 Brad Ausmus	.75	.23
44 Gary DiSarcina	.75	.23
45 Pat Hentgen	.75	.23
46 Wilton Guerrero	.75	.23
47 Devon White	.75	.23
48 Danny Patterson	.75	.23
49 Pat Meares	.75	.23
50 Rafael Palmeiro	1.25	.35
51 Mark Gardner	.75	.23
52 Jeff Blauser	.75	.23
53 Dave Hollins	.75	.23
54 Carlos Garcia	.75	.23
55 Ben McDonald	.75	.23
56 John Mabry	.75	.23
57 Trevor Hoffman	.75	.23
58 Tony Fernandez	.75	.23
59 Rich Loiselle RC	.75	.23
60 Mark Leiter	.75	.23
61 Pat Kelly	.75	.23
62 John Flaherty	.75	.23
63 Roger Bailey	.75	.23
64 Tom Gordon	.75	.23
65 Ryan Klesko	.75	.23
66 Darryl Hamilton	.75	.23
67 Jim Eisenreich	.75	.23
68 Butch Huskey	.75	.23
69 Mark Grudzielanek	.75	.23
70 Marquis Grissom	.75	.23
71 Mark McLemore	.75	.23
72 Gary Gaetti	.75	.23
73 Greg Gagne	.75	.23
74 Lyle Mouton	.75	.23
75 Jim Edmonds	.75	.23
76 Shawn Green	.75	.23
77 Greg Vaughn	.75	.23
78 Terry Adams	.75	.23
79 Kevin Polcovich	.75	.23
80 Troy O'Leary	.75	.23
81 Jeff Shaw	.75	.23
82 Rich Becker	.75	.23
83 David Wells	.75	.23
84 Steve Karsay	.75	.23
85 Charles Nagy	.75	.23
86 B.J. Surhoff	.75	.23
87 Jamey Wright	.75	.23
88 James Baldwin	.75	.23
89 Edgardo Alfonzo	.75	.23
90 Jay Buhner	.75	.23
91 Brady Anderson	.75	.23
92 Scott Servais	.75	.23
93 Edgar Renteria	.75	.23
94 Mike Lieberthal	.75	.23
95 Rick Aguilera	.75	.23
96 Walt Weiss	.75	.23
97 Deivi Cruz	.75	.23
98 Kurt Abbott	.75	.23
99 Henry Rodriguez	.75	.23
100 Mike Piazza	3.00	.90
101 Billy Taylor	.75	.23
102 Todd Zeile	.75	.23
103 Rey Ordonez	.75	.23
104 Willie Greene	.75	.23
105 Tony Womack	.75	.23
106 Mike Sweeney	.75	.23
107 Jeffrey Hammonds	.75	.23
108 Kevin Orie	.75	.23
109 Alex Gonzalez	.75	.23
110 Jose Canseco	2.00	.60
111 Paul Sorrento	.75	.23
112 Joey Hamilton	.75	.23
113 Brad Radke	.75	.23
114 Steve Avery	.75	.23
115 Esteban Loaiza	.75	.23
116 Stan Javier	.75	.23
117 Chris Gomez	.75	.23
118 Royce Clayton	.75	.23
119 Orlando Merced	.75	.23
120 Kevin Appier	.75	.23
121 Mel Nieves	.75	.23
122 Joe Girardi	.75	.23
123 Rico Brogna	.75	.23
124 Kent Mercker	.75	.23
125 Manny Ramirez	1.25	.35
126 Jeromy Burnitz	.75	.23
127 Kevin Foster	.75	.23
128 Matt Morris	.75	.23
129 Jason Dickson	.75	.23
130 Tom Glavine	1.25	.35
131 Wally Joyner	.75	.23
132 Rick Reed	.75	.23
133 Todd Jones	.75	.23
134 Dave Martinez	.75	.23
135 Sandy Alomar Jr.	.75	.23
136 Mike Lansing	.75	.23
137 Sean Berry	.75	.23
138 Doug Jones	.75	.23
139 Todd Stottlemyre	.75	.23
140 Jay Bell	.75	.23
141 Jaime Navarro	.75	.23
142 Chris Hoiles	.75	.23
143 Joey Cora	.75	.23
144 Scott Spiezio	.75	.23
145 Joe Carter	.75	.23
146 Jose Guillen	.75	.23
147 Damion Easley	.75	.23
148 Lee Stevens	.75	.23
149 Alex Fernandez	.75	.23
150 Randy Johnson	2.00	.60
151 J.T. Snow	.75	.23
152 Chuck Finley	.75	.23
153 Bernard Gilkey	.75	.23
154 David Segui	.75	.23
155 Dante Bichette	.75	.23
156 Kevin Stocker	.75	.23
157 Carl Everett	.75	.23
158 Jose Valentin	.75	.23
159 Pokey Reese	.75	.23
160 Derek Jeter	5.00	1.50
161 Roger Pavlik	.75	.23
162 Mark Wohlers	.75	.23
163 Ricky Bottalico	.75	.23
164 Ozzie Guillen	.75	.23
165 Mike Mussina	1.25	.35
166 Gary Sheffield	.75	.23
167 Hideo Nomo	2.00	.60
168 Mark Grace	1.25	.35
169 Aaron Sele	.75	.23
170 Darryl Kile	.75	.23
171 Shawn Estes	.75	.23
172 Vinny Castilla	.75	.23
173 Ron Coomer	.75	.23
174 Jose Rosado	.75	.23
175 Kenny Lofton	.75	.23
176 Jason Giambi	.75	.23
177 Hal Morris	.75	.23
178 Darren Bragg	.75	.23
179 Orel Hershiser	.75	.23
180 Ray Lankford	.75	.23
181 Hideki Irabu	.75	.23
182 Kevin Young	.75	.23
183 Javy Lopez	.75	.23
184 Jeff Montgomery	.75	.23
185 Mike Holtz	.75	.23
186 George Williams	.75	.23
187 Cal Eldred	.75	.23
188 Tom Candiotti	.75	.23
189 Glenallen Hill	.75	.23
190 Brian Giles	.75	.23
191 Dave Mlicki	.75	.23
192 Garrett Stephenson	.75	.23
193 Jeff Frye	.75	.23
194 Joe Oliver	.75	.23
195 Bob Hamelin	.75	.23
196 Luis Sojo	.75	.23
197 LaTroy Hawkins	.75	.23
198 Kevin Elster	.75	.23
199 Jeff Reed	.75	.23
200 Dennis Eckersley	.75	.23
201 Bill Mueller	.75	.23
202 Russ Davis	.75	.23
203 Armando Benitez	.75	.23
204 Quilvio Veras	.75	.23
205 Tim Naehring	.75	.23
206 Quinton McCracken	.75	.23
207 Raul Casanova	.75	.23

208 Matt Lawton .75 .23
209 Luis Alicea .75 .23
210 Luis Gonzalez .75 .23
211 Allen Watson .75 .23
212 Gerald Williams .75 .23
213 David Bell .75 .23
214 Todd Hollandsworth .75 .23
215 Wade Boggs 1.25 .35
216 Jose Mesa .75 .23
217 Jamie Moyer .75 .23
218 Darren Daulton .75 .23
219 Mickey Morandini .75 .23
220 Rusty Greer .75 .23
221 Jim Bullinger .75 .23
222 Jose Offerman .75 .23
223 Matt Karchner .75 .23
224 Woody Williams .75 .23
225 Mark Loretta .75 .23
226 Mike Hampton .75 .23
227 Willie Adams .75 .23
228 Scott Hatteberg .75 .23
229 Rich Amaral .75 .23
230 Terry Steinbach .75 .23
231 Glendon Rusch .75 .23
232 Bret Boone .75 .23
233 Robert Person .75 .23
234 Jose Hernandez .75 .23
235 Doug Drabek .75 .23
236 Jason McDonald .75 .23
237 Chris Widger .75 .23
238 Tom Martin .75 .23
239 Dave Burba .75 .23
240 Pete Rose Jr. RC .75 .23
241 Bobby Ayala .75 .23
242 Tim Wakefield .75 .23
243 Dennis Springer .75 .23
244 Tim Belcher .75 .23
245 Jon Garland 1.00 .30
Geoff Goetz
246 Glenn Davis 1.25 .35
Lance Berkman
247 Vernon Wells 1.00 .30
Aaron Akin
248 Adam Kennedy 1.00 .30
Jason Romano
249 Jason Dellaero 1.00 .30
Troy Cameron
250 Alex Sanchez 1.00 .30
Jared Sandberg
251 Pablo Ortega 1.00 .30
James Manias
252 Jason Conti RC 1.00 .30
Mike Stoner
253 John Patterson 1.00 .30
Larry Rodriguez
254 Adrian Beltre 1.50 .45
Ryan Minor RC
Aaron Boone
255 Ben Grieve 1.00 .30
Brian Buchanan
Dermal Brown
256 Kerrry Wood 2.00 .60
Carl Pavano
Gil Meche
257 David Ortiz 2.00 .60
Daryle Ward
Richie Sexson
258 Randy Winn 1.00 .30
Juan Encarnacion
Andrew Vessel
259 Kris Benson 1.00 .30
Travis Smith
Courtney Duncan RC
260 Chad Hermansen RC 1.00 .30
Brent Butler
Warren Morris
261 Ben Davis 1.00 .30
Eli Marrero
Ramon Hernandez
262 Eric Chavez 1.00 .30
Russell Branyan
Russ Johnson
263 Todd Dunwoody RC 1.00 .30
John Barnes
Ryan Jackson
264 Matt Clement 1.00 .30
Roy Halladay
Brian Fuentes RC
265 Randy Johnson SH 1.25 .35
266 Kevin Brown SH .75 .23
267 Ricardo Rincon SH .75 .23
268 N.Garciaparra SH 2.00 .60
269 Tino Martinez SH .75 .23
270 Chuck Knoblauch IL .75 .23
271 Pedro Martinez IL 1.25 .35
272 Denny Neagle IL .75 .23
273 Juan Gonzalez IL .75 .23
274 Andres Galarraga IL .75 .23
275 Checklist .75 .23
276 Checklist .75 .23
277 Moises Alou WS .75 .23
278 Sandy Alomar Jr. WS .75 .23
279 Gary Sheffield WS .75 .23
280 Matt Williams WS .75 .23
281 Livan Hernandez WS .75 .23
282 Chad Ogea WS .75 .23
283 Marlins Champs .75 .23
284 Tino Martinez 1.25 .35
285 Roberto Alomar 1.25 .35
286 Jeff King .75 .23
287 Brian Jordan .75 .23
288 Darin Erstad .75 .23
289 Ken Caminiti .75 .23
290 Jim Thome 2.00 .60
291 Paul Molitor 1.25 .35
292 Ivan Rodriguez 2.00 .60
293 Bernie Williams 1.25 .35
294 Todd Hundley .75 .23
295 Andres Galarraga .75 .23
296 Greg Maddux 3.00 .90
297 Edgar Martinez 1.25 .35
298 Ron Gant .75 .23
299 Derek Bell .75 .23
300 Roger Clemens 4.00 1.20
301 Rondell White .75 .23
302 Barry Larkin 1.25 .35
303 Robin Ventura .75 .23
304 Jason Kendall .75 .23
305 Chipper Jones 2.00 .60
306 John Franco .75 .23
307 Sammy Sosa 3.00 .90
308 Troy Percival .75 .23
309 Chuck Knoblauch .75 .23
310 Ellis Burks .75 .23
311 Al Martin .75 .23
312 Tim Salmon 1.25 .35
313 Moises Alou .75 .23
314 Lance Johnson .75 .23
315 Justin Thompson .75 .23
316 Will Clark 2.00 .60
317 Barry Bonds 5.00 1.50
318 Craig Biggio 1.25 .35
319 John Smoltz 1.25 .35
320 Cal Ripken 6.00 1.80
321 Ken Griffey Jr. 3.00 .90
322 Paul O'Neill 1.25 .35
323 Todd Helton 1.25 .35
324 John Olerud .75 .23
325 Mark McGwire 5.00 1.50
326 Jose Cruz Jr. .75 .23
327 Jeff Cirillo .75 .23
328 Dean Palmer .75 .23
329 John Wetteland .75 .23
330 Steve Finley .75 .23
331 Albert Belle .75 .23
332 Curt Schilling .75 .23
333 Raul Mondesi .75 .23
334 Andruw Jones .75 .23
335 Nomar Garciaparra 3.00 .90
336 David Justice .75 .23
337 Andy Pettitte 1.25 .35
338 Pedro Martinez 2.00 .60
339 Travis Miller .75 .23
340 Chris Stynes .75 .23
341 Gregg Jefferies .75 .23
342 Jeff Fassero .75 .23
343 Craig Counsell .75 .23
344 Wilson Alvarez .75 .23
345 Bip Roberts .75 .23
346 Kelvim Escobar .75 .23
347 Mark Bellhorn .75 .23
348 Cory Lidle RC 1.00 .30
349 Fred McGriff 1.25 .35
350 Chuck Carr .75 .23
351 Bob Abreu .75 .23
352 Juan Guzman .75 .23
353 Fernando Vina .75 .23
354 Andy Benes .75 .23
355 Dave Nilsson .75 .23
356 Bobby Bonilla .75 .23
357 Ismael Valdes .75 .23
358 Carlos Perez .75 .23
359 Kirk Rueter .75 .23
360 Bartolo Colon .75 .23
361 Mel Rojas .75 .23
362 Johnny Damon 1.25 .35
363 Geronimo Berroa .75 .23
364 Reggie Sanders .75 .23
365 Jermaine Allensworth .75 .23
366 Orlando Cabrera .75 .23
367 Jorge Fabregas .75 .23
368 Scott Stahoviak .75 .23
369 Ken Cloude .75 .23
370 Donovan Osborne .75 .23
371 Roger Cedeno .75 .23
372 Neifi Perez .75 .23
373 Chris Holt .75 .23
374 Cecil Fielder .75 .23
375 Marty Cordova .75 .23
376 Tom Goodwin .75 .23
377 Jeff Suppan .75 .23
378 Jeff Brantley .75 .23
379 Mark Langston .75 .23
380 Shane Reynolds .75 .23
381 Mike Fetters .75 .23
382 Todd Greene .75 .23
383 Ray Durham .75 .23
384 Carlos Delgado .75 .23
385 Jeff D'Amico .75 .23
386 Brian McRae .75 .23
387 Alan Benes .75 .23
388 Heathcliff Slocumb .75 .23
389 Eric Young .75 .23
390 Travis Fryman .75 .23
391 David Cone .75 .23
392 Otis Nixon .75 .23
393 Jeremi Gonzalez .75 .23
394 Jeff Juden .75 .23
395 Jose Vizcaino .75 .23
396 Ugueth Urbina .75 .23
397 Ramon Martinez .75 .23
398 Robb Nen .75 .23
399 Harold Baines .75 .23
400 Delino DeShields .75 .23
401 John Burkett .75 .23
402 Sterling Hitchcock .75 .23
403 Mark Clark .75 .23
404 Terrell Wade .75 .23
405 Scott Brosius .75 .23
406 Chad Curtis .75 .23
407 Brian Johnson .75 .23
408 Roberto Kelly .75 .23
409 Dave Dellucci RC 1.25 .35
410 Michael Tucker .75 .23
411 Mark Kotsay .75 .23
412 Mark Lewis .75 .23
413 Ryan McGuire .75 .23
414 Shawon Dunston .75 .23
415 Brad Rigby .75 .23
416 Scott Erickson .75 .23
417 Bobby Jones .75 .23
418 Darren Oliver .75 .23
419 John Smiley .75 .23
420 T.J. Mathews .75 .23
421 Dustin Hermanson .75 .23
422 Mike Timlin .75 .23
423 Willie Blair .75 .23
424 Manny Alexander .75 .23
425 Bob Tewksbury .75 .23
426 Pete Schourek .75 .23
427 Reggie Jefferson .75 .23
428 Ed Sprague .75 .23
429 Jeff Conine .75 .23
430 Roberto Hernandez .75 .23
431 Tom Pagnozzi .75 .23
432 Jaret Wright .75 .23
433 Livan Hernandez .75 .23
434 Andy Ashby .75 .23
435 Todd Dunn .75 .23
436 Bobby Higginson .75 .23
437 Rod Beck .75 .23
438 Jim Leyritz .75 .23
439 Matt Williams .75 .23
440 Brett Tomko .75 .23
441 Joe Randa .75 .23
442 Chris Carpenter .75 .23
443 Dennis Reyes .75 .23
444 Al Leiter .75 .23
445 Jason Schmidt .75 .23
446 Ken Hill .75 .23
447 Shannon Stewart .75 .23
448 Enrique Wilson .75 .23
449 Fernando Tatis .75 .23
450 Jimmy Key .75 .23
451 Darrin Fletcher .75 .23
452 John Valentin .75 .23
453 Kevin Tapani .75 .23
454 Eric Karros .75 .23
455 Jay Bell .75 .23
456 Walt Weiss .75 .23
457 Devon White .75 .23
458 Carl Pavano 1.25 .35
459 Mike Lansing .75 .23
460 John Flaherty .75 .23
461 Richard Hidalgo .75 .23
462 Quinton McCracken .75 .23
463 Karim Garcia .75 .23
464 Miguel Cairo .75 .23
465 Edwin Diaz .75 .23
466 Bobby Smith .75 .23
467 Yamil Benitez .75 .23
468 Rich Butler RC .75 .23
469 Ben Ford RC .75 .23
470 Bubba Trammell .75 .23
471 Brent Brede .75 .23
472 Brooks Kieschnick .75 .23
473 Carlos Castillo .75 .23
474 Brad Radke SH .75 .23
475 Roger Clemens SH 2.00 .60
476 Curt Schilling SH .75 .23
477 John Olerud SH .75 .23
478 Mark McGwire SH 2.50 .75
479 Mike Piazza IL 2.00 .60
Ken Griffey Jr.
480 Jeff Bagwell 1.25 .35
Frank Thomas
481 Chipper Jones 1.25 .35
Nomar Garciaparra IL
482 Larrry Walker IL .75 .23
Juan Gonzalez IL
483 Gary Sheffield IL .75 .23
Tino Martinez IL
484 Derrick Gibson 1.00 .30
Michael Coleman
Norm Hutchins
485 Braden Looper 1.00 .30
Cliff Politte
Brian Rose
486 Eric Milton 1.00 .30
Jason Marquis
Corey Lee
487 A.J.Hinch 1.00 .30
Mark Osborne RC
Robert Fick
488 Aramis Ramirez 1.00 .30
Alex Gonzalez
Sean Casey
489 Donnie Bridges 1.00 .30
Tim Drew RC
490 Ntema Ndungidi RC 1.00 .30
Darnell McDonald
491 Ryan Anderson RC 1.00 .30
Mark Mangum
492 J.J.Davis 5.00 1.50
Troy Glaus RC
493 Jayson Werth RC 1.00 .30
Dan Reichert
494 John Curtice RC 1.25 .35
Michael Cuddyer RC
495 Jack Cust RC 1.00 .30
Jason Standridge
496 Brian Anderson 1.00 .30
497 Tony Saunders 1.00 .30
498 Vladimir Nunez 1.00 .30
Jhensy Sandoval
499 Brad Penny 1.00 .30
Nick Bierbrodt
500 Dustin Carr 1.00 .30
Luis Cruz RC
501 Cedric Bowers 1.00 .30
Marcus McCain
502 Checklist .75 .23
503 Checklist .75 .23
504 Alex Rodriguez 4.00 1.20

1998 Topps Chrome Baby Boomers

Randomly inserted in first series packs at the rate of one in 24, this 15 card set features color action photos printed on metalized cards with Chromium technology of young players who have already made their mark in the game with less than three years in the majors.

	Nm-Mt	Ex-Mt
COMPLETE SET (15)	80.00	24.00

*REF: .75X TO 2X BASIC CHR.BOOMERS
REFRACTOR SER.1 STATED ODDS 1:72

BB1 Derek Jeter 15.00 4.50
BB2 Scott Rolen 6.00 1.80
BB3 Nomar Garciaparra 10.00 3.00
BB4 Jose Cruz Jr. 2.50 .75
BB5 Darin Erstad 2.50 .75
BB6 Todd Helton 4.00 1.20
BB7 Tony Clark 2.50 .75
BB8 Jose Guillen 2.50 .75
BB9 Andruw Jones 2.50 .75
BB10 Vladimir Guerrero 6.00 1.80
BB11 Mark Kotsay 2.50 .75
BB12 Todd Greene 2.50 .75
BB13 Andy Pettitte 4.00 1.20
BB14 Justin Thompson 2.50 .75
BB15 Alan Benes 2.50 .75

1998 Topps Chrome Clout Nine

Randomly seeded at a rate of one in 24 second series packs, cards from this nine-card set feature a selection of the league's top sluggers. The cards are a straight parallel of the previously released 1998 Topps Clout 9 set, except of course for the Chromium stock fronts.

	Nm-Mt	Ex-Mt
COMPLETE SET (9)	60.00	18.00

*REF: .75X TO 2X BASIC CHR.CLOUT
REFRACTOR SER.2 STATED ODDS 1:72

C1 Edgar Martinez 4.00 1.20
C2 Mike Piazza 10.00 3.00
C3 Frank Thomas 6.00 1.80
C4 Craig Biggio 4.00 1.20
C5 Vinny Castilla 2.50 .75
C6 Jeff Blauser 2.50 .75
C7 Barry Bonds 15.00 4.50
C8 Ken Griffey Jr. 10.00 3.00
C9 Larry Walker 4.00 1.20

1998 Topps Chrome Flashback

Randomly inserted in first series packs at the rate of one in 24, this 10-card set features two-sided cards with color action photos of top players printed on metalized cards with Chromium technology. One side displays how they looked "then" as rookies, while the other side shows how they look "now" as stars.

	Nm-Mt	Ex-Mt
COMPLETE SET (10)	80.00	24.00

*REF: .75X TO 2X BASIC CHR.FLASHBACK
REFRACTOR SER.1 STATED ODDS 1:72

FB1 Barry Bonds 15.00 4.50
FB2 Ken Griffey Jr. 10.00 3.00
FB3 Paul Molitor 4.00 1.20
FB4 Randy Johnson 6.00 1.80
FB5 Cal Ripken 20.00 6.00
FB6 Tony Gwynn 8.00 2.40
FB7 Kenny Lofton 2.50 .75
FB8 Gary Sheffield 2.50 .75
FB9 Deion Sanders 4.00 1.20
FB10 Brady Anderson 2.50 .75

1998 Topps Chrome HallBound

Randomly inserted in first series packs at the rate of one in 24, this 15-card set features color photos printed on metalized cards with Chromium technology of top stars who are bound for the Hall of Fame in Cooperstown, New York.

	Nm-Mt	Ex-Mt
COMPLETE SET (15)	150.00	45.00

*REF: .75X TO 2X BASIC HALLBOUND
REFRACTOR SER.1 STATED ODDS 1:72

HB1 Paul Molitor 5.00 1.50
HB2 Tony Gwynn 10.00 3.00
HB3 Wade Boggs 5.00 1.50
HB4 Roger Clemens 15.00 4.50
HB5 Dennis Eckersley 3.00 .90
HB6 Cal Ripken 25.00 7.50
HB7 Greg Maddux 12.00 3.60
HB8 Rickey Henderson 5.00 1.50
HB9 Ken Griffey Jr. 12.00 3.60
HB10 Frank Thomas 8.00 2.40
HB11 Mark McGwire 20.00 6.00
HB12 Barry Bonds 20.00 6.00
HB13 Mike Piazza 12.00 3.60
HB14 Juan Gonzalez 5.00 1.50
HB15 Randy Johnson 8.00 2.40

1998 Topps Chrome Milestones

Randomly seeded at a rate of one in every 24 second series packs, these 10 cards feature a selection of veteran stars that achieved specific career milestones in 1997. The cards are a

straight parallel from the previously released 1998 Topps Milestones inserts except, of course, for the Chromium finish on the fronts.

	Nm-Mt	Ex-Mt
COMPLETE SET (10)	120.00	36.00

*REF: .75X TO 2X BASIC CHR.MILE
REFRACTOR SER.2 STATED ODDS 1:72

MS1 Barry Bonds 12.00 3.60
MS2 Roger Clemens 10.00 3.00
MS3 Dennis Eckersley 2.00 .60
MS4 Juan Gonzalez 3.00 .90
MS5 Ken Griffey Jr. 8.00 2.40
MS6 Tony Gwynn 6.00 1.80
MS7 Greg Maddux 8.00 2.40
MS8 Mark McGwire 12.00 3.60
MS9 Cal Ripken 15.00 4.50
MS10 Frank Thomas 5.00 1.50

1998 Topps Chrome Rookie Class

Randomly seeded at a rate of one in 12 second series packs, cards from this 10-card set feature a selection of the league's top rookies for 1998. The cards are a straight parallel of the previously released 1998 Topps Rookie Class set, except of course for the Chromium stock fronts.

	Nm-Mt	Ex-Mt
COMPLETE SET (10)	20.00	6.00

*REF: .75X TO 2X BASIC CHR.RK.CLASS
REFRACTOR SER.2 STATED ODDS 1:24

R1 Travis Lee 2.00 .60
R2 Richard Hidalgo 2.00 .60
R3 Todd Helton 3.00 .90
R4 Paul Konerko 2.00 .60
R5 Mark Kotsay 2.00 .60
R6 Derrek Lee 2.00 .60
R7 Eli Marrero 2.00 .60
R8 Fernando Tatis 2.00 .60
R9 Juan Encarnacion 2.00 .60
R10 Ben Grieve 2.00 .60

1999 Topps Chrome

The 1999 Topps Chrome set totaled 462 cards (though is numbered 1-463 - card number 7 was never issued in honor of Mickey Mantle). The product was distributed in first and second series four-card packs each carrying a suggested retail price of $3. The first series cards were 1-6/8-242, second series cards 243-463. The card fronts feature action color player photos. The backs carry player information. The set contains the following subsets: Season Highlights (200-204), Prospects (205-212/425-437), Draft Picks (213-219/438-444), League Leaders (221-232), World Series (233-240), Strikeout Kings (445-449), All-Topps (450-460) and four Checklist Cards (241-242/462-463). The Mark McGwire Home Run Record Breaker card (220) was released in 70 different variations highlighting every home run that he hit in 1998. The Sammy Sosa Home Run Parade card (461) was issued in 66 different variations. A 462 card set of 1999 Topps Chrome is considered complete with any version of the McGwire 220 and Sosa 461. Rookie Cards of note include Pat Burrell and Alex Escobar

	Nm-Mt	Ex-Mt
COMPLETE SET (462)	120.00	36.00
COMP. SERIES 1 (241)	60.00	18.00
COMP. SERIES 2 (221)	60.00	18.00
COMMON (1-6/8-463)	.50	.15
COMMON (205-212/425-437)	1.00	.30

1 Roger Clemens 4.00 1.20
2 Andres Galarraga .75 .23
3 Scott Brosius .75 .23
4 John Flaherty .50 .15
5 Jim Leyritz .50 .15
6 Ray Durham .75 .23
8 Jose Vizcaino .50 .15
9 Will Clark 2.00 .60
10 David Wells .75 .23
11 Jose Guillen .75 .23
12 Scott Hatteberg .50 .15
13 Edgardo Alfonzo .50 .15
14 Mike Bordick .50 .15
15 Manny Ramirez 1.25 .35
16 Greg Maddux 3.00 .90
17 David Segui .50 .15
18 Darryl Strawberry .75 .23
19 Brad Radke .75 .23

20 Kerry Wood 2.00 .60
21 Matt Anderson .50 .15
22 Derrek Lee .75 .23
23 Mickey Morandini .50 .15
24 Paul Konerko .75 .23
25 Travis Lee .50 .15
26 Ken Hill .50 .15
27 Kenny Rogers .75 .23
28 Paul Sorrento .50 .15
29 Quilvio Veras .50 .15
30 Todd Walker .50 .15
31 Ryan Jackson .50 .15
32 John Olerud .75 .23
33 Doug Glanville .50 .15
34 Nolan Ryan 6.00 1.80
35 Ray Lankford .50 .15
36 Mark Loretta .75 .23
37 Jason Dickson .50 .15
38 Sean Bergman .50 .15
39 Quinton McCracken .50 .15
40 Bartolo Colon .75 .23
41 Brady Anderson .75 .23
42 Chris Stynes .50 .15
43 Jorge Posada 1.25 .35
44 Justin Thompson .50 .15
45 Johnny Damon 1.25 .35
46 Armando Benitez .50 .15
47 Brant Brown .50 .15
48 Charlie Hayes .50 .15
49 Darren Dreifort .50 .15
50 Juan Gonzalez 1.25 .35
51 Chuck Knoblauch .75 .23
52 Todd Helton 1.25 .35
53 Rick Reed .50 .15
54 Chris Gomez .50 .15
55 Gary Sheffield .75 .23
56 Rod Beck .50 .15
57 Rey Sanchez .50 .15
58 Garret Anderson .75 .23
59 Jimmy Haynes .50 .15
60 Steve Woodard .50 .15
61 Rondell White .75 .23
62 Vladimir Guerrero 2.00 .60
63 Eric Karros .75 .23
64 Russ Davis .50 .15
65 Mo Vaughn .75 .23
66 Sammy Sosa 3.00 .90
67 Troy Percival .75 .23
68 Kenny Lofton .75 .23
69 Bill Taylor .50 .15
70 Mark McGwire 5.00 1.50
71 Roger Cedeno .50 .15
72 Javy Lopez .75 .23
73 Damion Easley .50 .15
74 Andy Pettitte 1.25 .35
75 Tony Gwynn 2.50 .75
76 Ricardo Rincon .50 .15
77 F.P. Santangelo .50 .15
78 Jay Bell .75 .23
79 Scott Servais .50 .15
80 Jose Canseco 2.00 .60
81 Roberto Hernandez .50 .15
82 Todd Dunwoody .50 .15
83 John Wetteland .75 .23
84 Mike Caruso .50 .15
85 Derek Jeter 5.00 1.50
86 Aaron Sele .50 .15
87 Jose Lima .50 .15
88 Ryan Christenson .50 .15
89 Jeff Cirillo .50 .15
90 Jose Hernandez .50 .15
91 Mark Kotsay .50 .15
92 Darren Bragg .50 .15
93 Albert Belle .75 .23
94 Matt Lawton .50 .15
95 Pedro Martinez 2.00 .60
96 Greg Vaughn .50 .15
97 Neifi Perez .50 .15
98 Gerald Williams .50 .15
99 Derek Bell .50 .15
100 Ken Griffey Jr. 3.00 .90
101 David Cone .75 .23
102 Brian Johnson .50 .15
103 Dean Palmer .75 .23
104 Javier Valentin .50 .15
105 Trevor Hoffman .75 .23
106 Butch Huskey .50 .15
107 Dave Martinez .50 .15
108 Billy Wagner .75 .23
109 Shawn Green .75 .23
110 Ben Grieve .50 .15
111 Tom Goodwin .50 .15
112 Jaret Wright .50 .15
113 Aramis Ramirez .75 .23
114 Dmitri Young .75 .23
115 Hideki Irabu .50 .15
116 Roberto Kelly .50 .15
117 Jeff Fassero .50 .15
118 Mark Clark .50 .15
119 Jason McDonald .50 .15
120 Matt Williams .75 .23
121 Dave Burba .50 .15
122 Bret Saberhagen .75 .23
123 Deivi Cruz .50 .15
124 Chad Curtis .50 .15
125 Scott Rolen 2.00 .60
126 Lee Stevens .50 .15
127 J.T. Snow .75 .23
128 Rusty Greer .75 .23
129 Brian Meadows .50 .15
130 Jim Edmonds .75 .23
131 Ron Gant .75 .23
132 A.J. Hinch .50 .15
133 Shannon Stewart .75 .23
134 Brad Fullmer .50 .15
135 Cal Eldred .50 .15
136 Matt Walbeck .50 .15
137 Carl Everett .75 .23
138 Walt Weiss .50 .15
139 Fred McGriff 1.25 .35
140 Darin Erstad .75 .23
141 Dave Nilsson .50 .15
142 Eric Young .50 .15
143 Dan Wilson .50 .15
144 Jeff Reed .50 .15
145 Brett Tomko .50 .15
146 Terry Steinbach .50 .15
147 Seth Greisinger .50 .15
148 Pat Meares .50 .15
149 Livan Hernandez .50 .15
150 Jeff Bagwell 1.25 .35
151 Bob Wickman .50 .15
152 Omar Vizquel 1.25 .35
153 Eric Davis .50 .15
154 Larry Sutton .50 .15
155 Magglio Ordonez .75 .23
156 Eric Milton .50 .15
157 Darren Lewis .50 .15
158 Rick Aguilera .50 .15
159 Mike Lieberthal .75 .23
160 Robb Nen .75 .23
161 Brian Giles .75 .23
162 Jeff Brantley .50 .15
163 Gary DiSarcina .50 .15
164 John Valentin .50 .15
165 Dave Dellucci .50 .15
166 Chan Ho Park .75 .23
167 Masato Yoshii .50 .15
168 Jason Schmidt .75 .23
169 LaTroy Hawkins .50 .15
170 Bret Boone .75 .23
171 Jerry DiPoto .50 .15
172 Mariano Rivera 1.25 .35
173 Mike Cameron .75 .23
174 Scott Erickson .50 .15
175 Charles Johnson .75 .23
176 Bobby Jones .50 .15
177 Francisco Cordova .50 .15
178 Todd Jones .50 .15
179 Jeff Montgomery .50 .15
180 Mike Mussina 1.25 .35
181 Bob Abreu .75 .23
182 Ismael Valdes .50 .15
183 Andy Fox .50 .15
184 Woody Williams .50 .15
185 Denny Neagle .50 .15
186 Jose Valentin .50 .15
187 Darrin Fletcher .50 .15
188 Gabe Alvarez .50 .15
189 Eddie Taubensee .50 .15
190 Edgar Martinez 1.25 .35
191 Jason Kendall .75 .23
192 Darryl Kile .75 .23
193 Jeff King .50 .15
194 Rey Ordonez .50 .15
195 Andruw Jones .75 .23
196 Tony Fernandez .50 .15
197 Jamey Wright .50 .15
198 B.J. Surhoff .75 .23
199 Vinny Castilla .75 .23
200 David Wells HL .50 .15
201 Mark McGwire HL 2.50 .75
202 Sammy Sosa HL 2.00 .60
203 Roger Clemens HL 2.00 .60
204 Kerry Wood HL 1.25 .35
205 Gabe Kapler 1.00 .30
Lance Berkman
Mike Frank
206 Alex Escobar RC 1.00 .30
Ricky Ledee
Mike Stoner
207 Peter Bergeron RC 1.00 .30
Jeremy Giambi
George Lombard
208 Michael Barrett 1.00 .30
Ben Davis
Robert Fick
209 Jayson Werth 1.00 .30
Ramon Hernandez
Pat Cline
210 Ryan Anderson 1.00 .30
Bruce Chen
Chris Enochs
211 Brad Penny 1.00 .30
Octavio Dotel
Mike Lincoln
212 Chuck Abbott RC 1.00 .30
Brent Butler
Danny Klassen
213 Chris C.Jones 1.00 .30
Jeff Urban RC
214 Arturo McDowell RC 1.00 .30
Tony Torcato
215 Josh McKinley RC 1.00 .30
Jason Tyner
216 Matt Burch 1.00 .30
Seth Etherton RC
217 Mamon Tucker RC 1.00 .30
Rick Elder
218 J.M.Gold 1.00 .30
Ryan Mills RC
219 Andy Brown 1.00 .30
Choo Freeman RC
220A Mark McGwire HR 1 50.00 15.00
220B Mark McGwire HR 2 30.00 9.00
220C Mark McGwire HR 3 30.00 9.00
220D Mark McGwire HR 4 30.00 9.00
220E Mark McGwire HR 5 30.00 9.00
220F Mark McGwire HR 6 30.00 9.00
220G Mark McGwire HR 7 30.00 9.00
220H Mark McGwire HR 8 30.00 9.00
220I Mark McGwire HR 9 30.00 9.00
220J M.McGwire HR 10 30.00 9.00
220K M.McGwire HR 11 30.00 9.00
220L M.McGwire HR 12 30.00 9.00
220M M.McGwire HR 13 30.00 9.00
220N M.McGwire HR 14 30.00 9.00
220O M.McGwire HR 15 30.00 9.00
220P M.McGwire HR 16 30.00 9.00
220Q M.McGwire HR 17 30.00 9.00
220R M.McGwire HR 18 30.00 9.00
220S M.McGwire HR 19 30.00 9.00
220T M.McGwire HR 20 30.00 9.00
220U M.McGwire HR 21 30.00 9.00
220V M.McGwire HR 22 30.00 9.00
220W M.McGwire HR 23 30.00 9.00
220X M.McGwire HR 24 30.00 9.00
220Y M.McGwire HR 25 30.00 9.00
220Z M.McGwire HR 26 30.00 9.00
220AA M.McGwire HR 27 30.00 9.00
220AB M.McGwire HR 28 30.00 9.00
220AC M.McGwire HR 29 30.00 9.00
220AD M.McGwire HR 30 30.00 9.00
220AE M.McGwire HR 31 30.00 9.00
220AF M.McGwire HR 32 30.00 9.00
220AG M.McGwire HR 33 30.00 9.00
220AH M.McGwire HR 34 30.00 9.00
220AI M.McGwire HR 35 30.00 9.00
220AJ M.McGwire HR 36 30.00 9.00
220AK M.McGwire HR 37 30.00 9.00
220AL M.McGwire HR 38 30.00 9.00
220AM M.McGwire HR 39 30.00 9.00
220AN M.McGwire HR 40 30.00 9.00
220AO M.McGwire HR 41 30.00 9.00
220AP M.McGwire HR 42 30.00 9.00
220AQ M.McGwire HR 43 30.00 9.00
220AR M.McGwire HR 44 30.00 9.00
220AS M.McGwire HR 45 30.00 9.00
220AT M.McGwire HR 46 30.00 9.00
220AU M.McGwire HR 47 30.00 9.00
220AV M.McGwire HR 48 30.00 9.00
220AW M.McGwire HR 49 30.00 9.00
220AX M.McGwire HR 50 30.00 9.00
220AY M.McGwire HR 51 30.00 9.00
220AZ M.McGwire HR 52 30.00 9.00
220BB M.McGwire HR 53 30.00 9.00
220CC M.McGwire HR 54 30.00 9.00
220DD M.McGwire HR 55 30.00 9.00
220EE M.McGwire HR 56 30.00 9.00
220FF M.McGwire HR 57 30.00 9.00
220GG M.McGwire HR 58 30.00 9.00
220HH M.McGwire HR 59 30.00 9.00
220II M.McGwire HR 60 30.00 9.00
220JJ M.McGwire HR 61 50.00 15.00
220KK M.McGwire HR 62 80.00 24.00
220LL M.McGwire HR 63 50.00 15.00
220MM M.McGwire HR 64 50.00 15.00
220NN M.McGwire HR 65 50.00 15.00
220OO M.McGwire HR 66 50.00 15.00
220PP M.McGwire HR 67 50.00 15.00
220QQ M.McGwire HR 68 50.00 15.00
220RR M.McGwire HR 69 50.00 15.00
220SS M.McGwire HR 70 150.00 45.00
221 Larry Walker LL .75 .23
222 Bernie Williams LL .75 .23
223 Mark McGwire LL 2.50 .75
224 Ken Griffey Jr. LL 2.00 .60
225 Sammy Sosa LL 2.00 .60
226 Juan Gonzalez LL .75 .23
227 Dante Bichette LL .50 .15
228 Alex Rodriguez LL 2.00 .60
229 Sammy Sosa LL 2.00 .60
230 Derek Jeter LL 2.50 .75
231 Greg Maddux LL 2.00 .60
232 Roger Clemens LL 2.00 .60
233 Ricky Ledee WS .50 .15
234 Chuck Knoblauch WS .50 .15
235 Bernie Williams WS .75 .23
236 Tino Martinez WS .75 .23
237 Orl. Hernandez WS .50 .15
238 Scott Brosius WS .50 .15
239 Andy Pettitte WS .75 .23
240 Mariano Rivera WS .75 .23
241 Checklist .50 .15
242 Checklist .50 .15
243 Tom Glavine 1.25 .35
244 Andy Benes .50 .15
245 Sandy Alomar Jr. .50 .15
246 Wilton Guerrero .50 .15
247 Alex Gonzalez .50 .15
248 Roberto Alomar 1.25 .35
249 Ruben Rivera .50 .15
250 Eric Chavez .75 .23
251 Ellis Burks .75 .23
252 Richie Sexson .75 .23
253 Steve Finley .75 .23
254 Dwight Gooden .75 .23
255 Dustin Hermanson .50 .15
256 Kirk Rueter .50 .15
257 Steve Trachsel .50 .15
258 Gregg Jefferies .50 .15
259 Matt Stairs .50 .15
260 Shane Reynolds .50 .15
261 Gregg Olson .50 .15
262 Kevin Tapani .50 .15
263 Matt Morris .75 .23
264 Carl Pavano .75 .23
265 Nomar Garciaparra 3.00 .90
266 Kevin Young .75 .23
267 Rick Helling .50 .15
268 Matt Franco .50 .15
269 Brian McRae .50 .15
270 Cal Ripken 6.00 1.80
271 Jeff Abbott .50 .15
272 Tony Batista .75 .23
273 Bill Simas .50 .15
274 Brian Hunter .50 .15
275 John Franco .75 .23
276 Devon White .75 .23
277 Rickey Henderson 2.00 .60
278 Chuck Finley .75 .23
279 Mike Blowers .50 .15
280 Mark Grace 1.25 .35
281 Randy Winn .50 .15
282 Bobby Bonilla .75 .23
283 David Justice .75 .23
284 Shane Monahan .50 .15
285 Kevin Brown 1.25 .35
286 Todd Zeile .75 .23
287 Al Martin .50 .15
288 Troy O'Leary .50 .15
289 Darryl Hamilton .50 .15
290 Tino Martinez 1.25 .35
291 David Ortiz 1.25 .35
292 Tony Clark .50 .15
293 Ryan Minor .50 .15
294 Mark Leiter .50 .15
295 Wally Joyner .75 .23
296 Cliff Floyd .75 .23
297 Shawn Estes .50 .15
298 Pat Hentgen .50 .15
299 Scott Elarton .50 .15
300 Alex Rodriguez 3.00 .90
301 Ozzie Guillen .50 .15
302 Hideo Nomo 2.00 .60
303 Ryan McGuire .50 .15
304 Brad Ausmus .50 .15
305 Alex Gonzalez .50 .15
306 Brian Jordan .75 .23
307 John Jaha .50 .15
308 Mark Grudzielanek .50 .15
309 Juan Guzman .50 .15
310 Tony Womack .50 .15
311 Dennis Reyes .50 .15
312 Marty Cordova .50 .15
313 Ramiro Mendoza .50 .15
314 Robin Ventura .75 .23
315 Rafael Palmeiro 1.25 .35
316 Ramon Martinez .50 .15
317 Pedro Astacio .50 .15
318 Dave Hollins .50 .15
319 Tom Candiotti .50 .15
320 Al Leiter .75 .23
321 Rico Brogna .50 .15
322 Reggie Jefferson .50 .15
323 Bernard Gilkey .50 .15
324 Jason Giambi .75 .23
325 Craig Biggio 1.25 .35
326 Troy Glaus .75 .23
327 Delino DeShields .50 .15
328 Fernando Vina .50 .15
329 John Smoltz 1.25 .35
330 Jeff Kent .75 .23
331 Roy Halladay .50 .15
332 Andy Ashby .50 .15
333 Tim Wakefield .75 .23
334 Roger Clemens 4.00 1.20
335 Bernie Williams 1.25 .35
336 Desi Relaford .50 .15
337 John Burkett .50 .15
338 Mike Hampton .75 .23
339 Royce Clayton .50 .15
340 Mike Piazza 3.00 .90
341 Jeremi Gonzalez .50 .15
342 Mike Lansing .50 .15
343 Jamie Moyer .75 .23
344 Ron Coomer .50 .15
345 Barry Larkin 1.25 .35
346 Fernando Tatis .50 .15
347 Chili Davis .75 .23
348 Bobby Higginson .75 .23
349 Hal Morris .50 .15
350 Larry Walker 1.25 .35
351 Carlos Guillen .75 .23
352 Miguel Tejada .75 .23
353 Travis Fryman .75 .23
354 Jarrod Washburn .50 .15
355 Chipper Jones 2.00 .60
356 Todd Stottlemyre .50 .15
357 Henry Rodriguez .50 .15
358 Eli Marrero .50 .15
359 Alan Benes .50 .15
360 Tim Salmon 1.25 .35
361 Luis Gonzalez .75 .23
362 Scott Spiezio .50 .15
363 Chris Carpenter .50 .15
364 Bobby Howry .50 .15
365 Raul Mondesi .75 .23
366 Ugueth Urbina .50 .15
367 Tom Evans .50 .15
368 Kerry Ligtenberg RC .50 .15
369 Adrian Beltre 1.25 .35
370 Ryan Klesko .75 .23
371 Wilson Alvarez .50 .15
372 John Thomson .50 .15
373 Tony Saunders .50 .15
374 Dave Mlicki .50 .15
375 Ken Caminiti .75 .23
376 Jay Buhner .75 .23
377 Bill Mueller .75 .23
378 Jeff Blauser .50 .15
379 Edgar Renteria .75 .23
380 Jim Thome 2.00 .60
381 Joey Hamilton .50 .15
382 Calvin Pickering .50 .15
383 Marquis Grissom .75 .23
384 Omar Daal .50 .15
385 Curt Schilling .75 .23
386 Jose Cruz Jr. .50 .15
387 Chris Widger .50 .15
388 Pete Harnisch .50 .15
389 Charles Nagy .50 .15
390 Tom Gordon .50 .15
391 Bobby Smith .50 .15
392 Derrick Gibson .50 .15
393 Jeff Conine .75 .23
394 Carlos Perez .50 .15
395 Barry Bonds 5.00 1.50
396 Mark McLemore .50 .15
397 Juan Encarnacion .50 .15
398 Wade Boggs 1.25 .35
399 Ivan Rodriguez 2.00 .60
400 Moises Alou .75 .23
401 Jeromy Burnitz .75 .23
402 Sean Casey .75 .23
403 Jose Offerman .50 .15
404 Joe Fontenot .50 .15
405 Kevin Millwood .75 .23
406 Lance Johnson .50 .15
407 Richard Hidalgo .50 .15
408 Mike Jackson .50 .15
409 Brian Anderson .50 .15
410 Jeff Shaw .50 .15
411 Preston Wilson .75 .23
412 Todd Hundley .50 .15
413 Jim Parque .50 .15
414 Justin Baughman .50 .15
415 Dante Bichette .75 .23
416 Paul O'Neill 1.25 .35
417 Miguel Cairo .50 .15
418 Randy Johnson 2.00 .60
419 Jesus Sanchez .50 .15
420 Carlos Delgado .75 .23
421 Ricky Ledee .50 .15
422 Orlando Hernandez .50 .15
423 Frank Thomas 2.00 .60
424 Pokey Reese .50 .15
425 Carlos Lee 1.00 .30
Mike Lowell
Kit Pellow RC
426 Michael Cuddyer 1.00 .30
Mark DeRosa
Jerry Hairston Jr.
427 Marlon Anderson 1.00 .30
Ron Belliard
Orlando Cabrera
428 Micah Bowie 1.00 .30
Phil Norton RC
Randy Wolf
429 Jack Cressend RC 1.00 .30
Jason Rakers
John Rocker
430 Ruben Mateo 1.00 .30
Scott Morgan
Mike Zywica RC
431 Jason LaRue 1.00 .30
Matt LeCroy
Mitch Meluskey
432 Gabe Kapler 1.00 .30
Armando Rios
Fernando Seguignol
433 Adam Kennedy 1.00 .30
Mickey Lopez RC
Jackie Rexrode
434 Jose Fernandez RC 1.00 .30
Jeff Liefer
Chris Truby
435 Corey Koskie 2.00 .60
Doug Mientkiewicz RC
Damon Minor
436 Roosevelt Brown RC 1.00 .30
Dernell Stenson
Vernon Wells
437 A.J. Burnett RC 2.00 .60
Billy Koch
John Nicholson
438 Matt Belisle 1.00 .30
Matt Roney RC
439 Austin Kearns 4.00 1.20
Chris George RC
440 Nate Bump RC 1.00 .30
Nate Cornejo
441 Brad Lidge 4.00 1.20
Mike Nannini RC
442 Matt Holliday 2.00 .60
Jeff Winchester RC
443 Adam Everett 1.50 .45
Chip Ambres RC
444 Pat Burrell 2.50 .75
Eric Valent RC
445 Roger Clemens SK 2.00 .60
446 Kerry Wood SK 1.25 .35
447 Curt Schilling SK .50 .15
448 Randy Johnson SK 1.25 .35
449 Pedro Martinez SK 1.25 .35
450 Jeff Bagwell AT 2.00 .60
Andres Galarraga
Mark McGwire
451 John Olerud AT .75 .23
Jim Thome
Tino Martinez
452 Alex Rodriguez AT 2.50 .75
Nomar Garciaparra
Derek Jeter
453 Vinny Castilla AT 1.25 .35
Chipper Jones
Scott Rolen
454 Sammy Sosa AT 2.00 .60
Ken Griffey Jr.
Juan Gonzalez
455 Barry Bonds AT 2.00 .60
Manny Ramirez
Larry Walker
456 Frank Thomas AT 2.00 .60
Tim Salmon
David Justice
457 Travis Lee AT .75 .23
Todd Helton
Ben Grieve
458 Vladimir Guerrero AT .75 .23
Greg Vaughn
Bernie Williams
459 Mike Piazza AT 2.00 .60
Ivan Rodriguez
Jason Kendall
460 Roger Clemens AT 2.00 .60
Kerry Wood
Greg Maddux
461A Sammy Sosa HR 1 25.00 7.50
461B Sammy Sosa HR 2 15.00 4.50
461C Sammy Sosa HR 3 15.00 4.50
461D Sammy Sosa HR 4 15.00 4.50
461E Sammy Sosa HR 5 15.00 4.50
461F Sammy Sosa HR 6 15.00 4.50
461G Sammy Sosa HR 7 15.00 4.50
461H Sammy Sosa HR 8 15.00 4.50
461I Sammy Sosa HR 9 15.00 4.50
461J Sammy Sosa HR 10 15.00 4.50
461K Sammy Sosa HR 11 15.00 4.50
461L Sammy Sosa HR 12 15.00 4.50
461M Sammy Sosa HR 13 15.00 4.50
461N Sammy Sosa HR 14 15.00 4.50
461O Sammy Sosa HR 15 15.00 4.50
461P Sammy Sosa HR 16 15.00 4.50
461Q Sammy Sosa HR 17 15.00 4.50
461R Sammy Sosa HR 18 15.00 4.50
461S Sammy Sosa HR 19 15.00 4.50
461T Sammy Sosa HR 20 15.00 4.50
461U Sammy Sosa HR 21 15.00 4.50
461V Sammy Sosa HR 22 15.00 4.50
461W Sammy Sosa HR 23 15.00 4.50
461X Sammy Sosa HR 24 15.00 4.50
461Y Sammy Sosa HR 25 15.00 4.50
461Z Sammy Sosa HR 26 15.00 4.50
461AA S.Sosa HR 27 15.00 4.50
461AB S.Sosa HR 28 15.00 4.50
461AC S.Sosa HR 29 15.00 4.50
461AD S.Sosa HR 30 15.00 4.50
461AE S.Sosa HR 31 15.00 4.50
461AF S.Sosa HR 32 15.00 4.50
461AG S.Sosa HR 33 15.00 4.50
461AH S.Sosa HR 34 15.00 4.50
461AI S.Sosa HR 35 15.00 4.50
461AJ S.Sosa HR 36 15.00 4.50
461AK S.Sosa HR 37 15.00 4.50
461AL S.Sosa HR 38 15.00 4.50
461AM S.Sosa HR 39 15.00 4.50
461AN S.Sosa HR 40 15.00 4.50
461AO S.Sosa HR 41 15.00 4.50
461AP S.Sosa HR 42 15.00 4.50
461AR S.Sosa HR 43 15.00 4.50
461AS S.Sosa HR 44 15.00 4.50
461AT S.Sosa HR 45 15.00 4.50
461AU S.Sosa HR 46 15.00 4.50
461AV S.Sosa HR 47 15.00 4.50
461AW S.Sosa HR 48 15.00 4.50
461AX S.Sosa HR 49 15.00 4.50
461AY S.Sosa HR 50 15.00 4.50
461AZ S.Sosa HR 51 15.00 4.50
461BB S.Sosa HR 52 15.00 4.50
461CC S.Sosa HR 53 15.00 4.50
461DD S.Sosa HR 54 15.00 4.50
461EE S.Sosa HR 55 15.00 4.50
461FF S.Sosa HR 56 15.00 4.50
461GG S.Sosa HR 57 15.00 4.50
461HH S.Sosa HR 58 15.00 4.50
461II S.Sosa HR 59 15.00 4.50
461JJ S.Sosa HR 60 15.00 4.50
461KK S.Sosa HR 61 25.00 7.50
461LL S.Sosa HR 62 40.00 12.00

461MM S.Sosa HR 63 25.00 7.50
461NN S.Sosa HR 64 25.00 7.50
461OO S.Sosa HR 65 25.00 7.50
461PP S.Sosa HR 66 80.00 24.00
462 Checklist .50 .15
463 Checklist .50 .15

1999 Topps Chrome Refractors

Randomly inserted in packs at the rate of one in 12, this 462-card set is parallel to the base set and is similar in design. The difference is found in the refractive quality of the card. It's estimated that only around 15 to 25 of each McGwire number 220 refractor was produced.

Nm-Mt Ex-Mt
*STARS: 2.5X TO 6X BASIC CARDS
*ROOKIES: 1.5X TO 4X BASIC CARDS
MCGWIRE 220 HR 1 250.00 75.00
MCGWIRE 220 HR 2-60 120.00 36.00
MCGWIRE 220 HR 61 200.00 60.00
MCGWIRE 220 HR 62 300.00 90.00
MCGWIRE 220 HR 63-69 120.00 36.00
MCGWIRE 220 HR 70 400.00 120.00
SOSA 461 HR 1 80.00 24.00
SOSA 461 HR 2-60 40.00 12.00
SOSA 461 HR 61 60.00 18.00
SOSA 461 HR 62 100.00 30.00
SOSA 461 HR 63-65 40.00 12.00
SOSA 461 HR 66 150.00 45.00

1999 Topps Chrome All-Etch

Randomly inserted in Series two packs at the rate of one in six, this 30-card set features color player photos printed on All-Etch technology. A refractive parallel version of this set was also produced with an insertion rate of 1:24 packs.

Nm-Mt Ex-Mt
COMPLETE SET (30) 100.00 30.00
*REFRACTORS: .75X TO 2X BASIC ALL-ETCH
SER.2 REFRACTOR ODDS 1:24
AE1 Mark McGwire 12.00 3.60
AE2 Sammy Sosa 8.00 2.40
AE3 Ken Griffey Jr. 8.00 2.40
AE4 Greg Vaughn 1.25 .35
AE5 Albert Belle 2.00 .60
AE6 Vinny Castilla 2.00 .60
AE7 Jose Canseco 5.00 1.50
AE8 Juan Gonzalez 3.00 .90
AE9 Manny Ramirez 3.00 .90
AE10 Andres Galarraga 2.00 .60
AE11 Rafael Palmeiro 3.00 .90
AE12 Alex Rodriguez 8.00 2.40
AE13 Mo Vaughn 2.00 .60
AE14 Eric Chavez 2.00 .60
AE15 Gabe Kapler 2.50 .75
AE16 Calvin Pickering 1.25 .35
AE17 Ruben Mateo 2.50 .75
AE18 Roy Halladay 1.25 .35
AE19 Jeremy Giambi 1.25 .35
AE20 Alex Gonzalez 1.25 .35
AE21 Ron Belliard 2.50 .75
AE22 Marlon Anderson 2.50 .75
AE23 Carlos Lee 2.50 .75
AE24 Kerry Wood 5.00 1.50
AE25 Roger Clemens 10.00 3.00
AE26 Curt Schilling 2.00 .60
AE27 Kevin Brown 3.00 .90
AE28 Randy Johnson 5.00 1.50
AE29 Pedro Martinez 5.00 1.50
AE30 Orlando Hernandez 1.25 .35

1999 Topps Chrome Early Road to the Hall

Randomly inserted in Series one packs at the rate of one in 12, this 10-card set features color photos of ten players with less than 10 years in the Majors but are already headed towards the Hall of Fame in Cooperstown, New York.

Nm-Mt Ex-Mt
COMPLETE SET (10) 60.00 18.00
*REFRACTORS: 3X TO 8X BASIC ROAD
SER.1 REFRACTOR ODDS 1:944 HOBBY
REF.PRINT RUN 100 SERIAL #'d SETS
ER1 Nomar Garciaparra 8.00 2.40
ER2 Derek Jeter 12.00 3.60
ER3 Alex Rodriguez 8.00 2.40
ER4 Juan Gonzalez 3.00 .90
ER5 Ken Griffey Jr. 8.00 2.40
ER6 Chipper Jones 5.00 1.50
ER7 Vladimir Guerrero 5.00 1.50
ER8 Jeff Bagwell 3.00 .90
ER9 Ivan Rodriguez 5.00 1.50
ER10 Frank Thomas 5.00 1.50

1999 Topps Chrome Fortune 15

Randomly inserted into Series two packs at the rate of one in 12, this 15-card set features color photos of the League's most elite veteran and rookie players. A refractor parallel version of this set was also produced with an insertion rate of 1:627 packs and sequentially numnbered to 100.

Nm-Mt Ex-Mt
COMPLETE SET (15) 100.00 30.00
*REFRACTORS: 4X TO 8X BASIC FORT.15
SER.2 REFRACTOR ODDS 1:627
REF.PRINT RUN 100 SERIAL #'d SETS
FF1 Alex Rodriguez 8.00 2.40
FF2 Nomar Garciaparra 8.00 2.40
FF3 Derek Jeter 12.00 3.60
FF4 Troy Glaus 2.00 .60
FF5 Ken Griffey Jr. 8.00 2.40
FF6 Vladimir Guerrero 5.00 1.50
FF7 Kerry Wood 5.00 1.50
FF8 Eric Chavez 2.00 .60
FF9 Greg Maddux 8.00 2.40
FF10 Mike Piazza 8.00 2.40
FF11 Sammy Sosa 8.00 2.40
FF12 Mark McGwire 12.00 3.60
FF13 Ben Grieve 1.25 .35
FF14 Chipper Jones 5.00 1.50
FF15 Manny Ramirez 3.00 .90

1999 Topps Chrome Lords of the Diamond

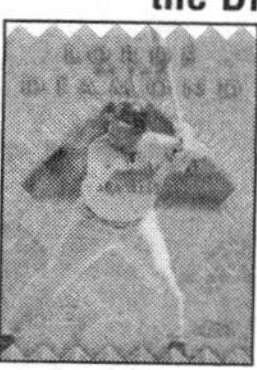

Randomly inserted in Series one packs at the rate of one in eight, this 15-card set features color photos of some of the true masters of the ballfield. A refractive parallel version of this set was also produced with an insertion rate of 1:24.

Nm-Mt Ex-Mt
COMPLETE SET (15) 50.00 15.00
*REFRACTORS: .6X TO 1.5X BASIC LORDS
SER.1 REFRACTOR ODDS 1:24
LD1 Ken Griffey Jr. 4.00 1.20
LD2 Chipper Jones 2.50 .75
LD3 Sammy Sosa 4.00 1.20
LD4 Frank Thomas 2.50 .75
LD5 Mark McGwire 6.00 1.80
LD6 Jeff Bagwell 1.50 .45
LD7 Alex Rodriguez 4.00 1.20
LD8 Juan Gonzalez 1.50 .45
LD9 Barry Bonds 6.00 1.80
LD10 Nomar Garciaparra 4.00 1.20
LD11 Darin Erstad 1.00 .30
LD12 Tony Gwynn 3.00 .90
LD13 Andres Galarraga 1.00 .30
LD14 Mike Piazza 4.00 1.20
LD15 Greg Maddux 4.00 1.20

1999 Topps Chrome New Breed

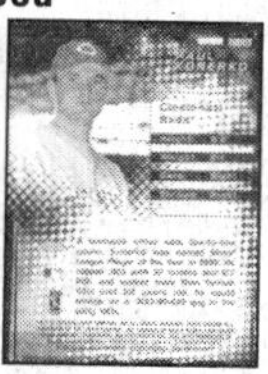

Randomly inserted in Series one packs at the rate of one in 24, this 15-card set features color photos of some of today's young stars in Major League Baseball. A refractive parallel version of this set was also produced with an insertion rate of 1:72.

Nm-Mt Ex-Mt
COMPLETE SET (15) 100.00 30.00
*REFRACTORS: .6X TO 1.5X BASIC BREED
SER.1 REFRACTOR ODDS 1:72
NB1 Darin Erstad 3.00 .90
NB2 Brad Fullmer 2.00 .60
NB3 Kerry Wood 8.00 2.40
NB4 Nomar Garciaparra 12.00 3.60
NB5 Travis Lee 2.00 .60
NB6 Scott Rolen 8.00 2.40
NB7 Todd Helton 5.00 1.50
NB8 Vladimir Guerrero 8.00 2.40
NB9 Derek Jeter 20.00 6.00
NB10 Alex Rodriguez 12.00 3.60
NB11 Ben Grieve 2.00 .60
NB12 Andruw Jones 3.00 .90
NB13 Paul Konerko 3.00 .90
NB14 Aramis Ramirez 3.00 .90
NB15 Adrian Beltre 5.00 1.50

1999 Topps Chrome Record Numbers

Randomly inserted in Series two packs at the rate of one in 36, this 10-card set features color photos of top Major League record-setters. A refractive parallel version of this set was also produced with an insertion rate of 1:144.

Nm-Mt Ex-Mt
COMPLETE SET (10) 150.00 45.00
*REFRACTORS: .75X TO 2X BASIC REC.NUM.
SER.2 REFRACTOR ODDS 1:144
RN1 Mark McGwire 20.00 6.00
RN2 Mike Piazza 12.00 3.60
RN3 Curt Schilling 3.00 .90
RN4 Ken Griffey Jr. 12.00 3.60
RN5 Sammy Sosa 12.00 3.60
RN6 Nomar Garciaparra 12.00 3.60
RN7 Kerry Wood 8.00 2.40
RN8 Roger Clemens 15.00 4.50
RN9 Cal Ripken 25.00 7.50
RN10 Mark McGwire 20.00 6.00

1999 Topps Chrome Traded

This 121-card set features color photos on Chromium cards of 46 of the most notable transactions of the 1999 season and 75 newcomers accented with the Topps "Rookie Card" logo. The set was distributed only in factory boxes. Due to a very late ship date (January, 2000) this set caused some commotion in the hobby as to its status as a 1999 or 2000 product. Notable Rookie Cards include Josh Hamilton and Corey Patterson.

Nm-Mt Ex-Mt
COMP.FACT SET (121) 80.00 24.00
T1 Seth Etherton .40 .12
T2 Mark Harriger RC .50 .15
T3 Matt Wise RC .50 .15
T4 Carlos E. Hernandez RC .75 .23
T5 Julio Lugo RC .50 .15
T6 Mike Nannini .40 .12
T7 Justin Bowles RC .50 .15
T8 Mark Mulder RC 5.00 1.20
T9 Roberto Vaz RC .50 .15
T10 Felipe Lopez RC .75 .23
T11 Matt Belisle .40 .12
T12 Micah Bowie .40 .12
T13 Ruben Quevedo RC .50 .15
T14 Jose Garcia RC .50 .15
T15 David Kelton RC .75 .23
T16 Phil Norton .40 .12
T17 Corey Patterson RC 5.00 1.50
T18 Ron Walker RC .50 .15
T19 Paul Hoover RC .50 .15
T20 Ryan Rupe RC .50 .15
T21 J.D. Closser RC 1.25 .35
T22 Rob Ryan RC .50 .15
T23 Steve Colyer RC .75 .23
T24 Bubba Crosby RC 1.25 .35
T25 Luke Prokopec RC .50 .15
T26 Matt Blank RC .50 .15
T27 Josh McKinley .60 .18
T28 Nate Bump .50 .15
T29 G.Chiaramonte RC .50 .15
T30 Arturo McDowell .40 .12
T31 Tony Torcato .60 .18
T32 Dave Roberts RC 1.25 .35
T33 C.C. Sabathia RC 2.50 .75
T34 Sean Spencer RC .50 .15
T35 Chip Ambres .40 .12
T36 A.J. Burnett 1.50 .45
T37 Mo Bruce RC .50 .15
T38 Jason Tyner .40 .12
T39 Mamon Tucker .40 .12
T40 Sean Burroughs RC 2.50 .75
T41 Kevin Eberwein RC .50 .15
T42 Junior Herndon RC .75 .23
T43 Bryan Wolff RC .50 .15
T44 Pat Burrell 2.50 .75
T45 Eric Valent .75 .23
T46 Carlos Pena RC 1.25 .35
T47 Mike Zywica .40 .12
T48 Adam Everett 1.00 .30
T49 Juan Pena RC .50 .15
T50 Adam Dunn RC 8.00 2.40
T51 Austin Kearns 4.00 1.20
T52 Jacobo Sequea RC .50 .15
T53 Choo Freeman .60 .18
T54 Jeff Winchester .40 .12
T55 Matt Burch .50 .15
T56 Chris George .60 .18
T57 Scott Mullen RC .50 .15
T58 Kit Pellow .50 .15
T59 Mark Quinn RC .75 .23
T60 Nate Cornejo .75 .23
T61 Ryan Mills .40 .12
T62 Kevin Beirne RC .75 .23
T63 Kip Wells RC 1.25 .35
T64 Juan Rivera RC .75 .23
T65 Alfonso Soriano RC 10.00 3.00
T66 Josh Hamilton RC 1.25 .35
T67 Josh Girdley RC .50 .15
T68 Kyle Snyder RC .50 .15
T69 Mike Paradis RC .50 .15
T70 Jason Jennings RC 1.25 .35
T71 David Walling RC .50 .15
T72 Omar Ortiz RC .50 .15
T73 Jay Gehrke RC .50 .15
T74 Casey Burns RC .50 .15
T75 Carl Crawford RC 3.00 .90
T76 Reggie Sanders .40 .12
T77 Will Clark 1.50 .45
T78 David Wells .60 .18
T79 Paul Konerko .60 .18
T80 Armando Benitez .40 .12
T81 Brant Brown .40 .12
T82 Mo Vaughn .60 .18
T83 Jose Canseco 1.50 .45
T84 Albert Belle .60 .18
T85 Dean Palmer .60 .18
T86 Greg Vaughn .40 .12
T87 Mark Clark .40 .12
T88 Pat Meares .40 .12
T89 Eric Davis .60 .18
T90 Brian Giles .60 .18
T91 Jeff Brantley .40 .12
T92 Bret Boone .60 .18
T93 Ron Gant .60 .18
T94 Mike Cameron .60 .18
T95 Charles Johnson .60 .18
T96 Denny Neagle .40 .12
T97 Brian Hunter .40 .12
T98 Jose Hernandez .40 .12
T99 Rick Aguilera .40 .12
T100 Tony Batista .60 .18
T101 Roger Cedeno .40 .12
T102 C.Gubanich RC .50 .15
T103 Tim Belcher .40 .12
T104 Bruce Aven .40 .12
T105 Brian Daubach RC .75 .23
T106 Ed Sprague .40 .12
T107 Michael Tucker .40 .12
T108 Homer Bush .40 .12
T109 Armando Reynoso .40 .12
T110 Brook Fordyce .40 .12
T111 Matt Mantei .40 .12
T112 Dave Mlicki .40 .12
T113 Kenny Rogers .60 .18
T114 Livan Hernandez .40 .12
T115 Butch Huskey .40 .12
T116 David Segui .40 .12
T117 Darryl Hamilton .40 .12
T118 Terry Mulholland .40 .12
T119 Randy Velarde .40 .12
T120 Bill Taylor .40 .12
T121 Kevin Appier .60 .18

2000 Topps Chrome

These cards parallel the regular Topps set and are issued using Topps' Chromium technology and color metallization. The first series product was released in February, 2000 and second series in May, 2000. Four card packs for each series carried an SRP of $3.00. Similar to the regular set, no card number 7 was issued and a Mark McGwire rookie reprint card was also inserted into packs. Also, like the base Topps set all of the Magic Moments subset cards (235-239 and 475-479) are available in five variations - each detailing a different highlight in the featured player's career. The base Chrome set is considered complete with any of the Magic Moments variations (for each player). Notable Rookie Cards include Rick Asadoorian, Ben Sheets and Barry Zito.

Nm-Mt Ex-Mt
COMPLETE SET (478) 160.00 47.50
COMP. SERIES 1 (240) 80.00 24.00
COMP. SERIES 2 (240) 80.00 24.00
MCGWIRE MM SET (5) 50.00 15.00
AARON MM SET (5) 40.00 12.00
RIPKEN MM SET (5) 60.00 18.00
BOGGS MM SET (5) 12.00 3.60
GWYNN MM SET (5) 25.00 7.50
GRIFFEY MM SET (5) 30.00 9.00
BONDS MM SET (5) 50.00 15.00
SOSA MM SET (5) 30.00 9.00
JETER MM SET (5) 50.00 15.00
A.ROD MM SET (5) 40.00 12.00
1 Mark McGwire 5.00 1.50
2 Tony Gwynn 2.50 .75
3 Wade Boggs 1.25 .35
4 Cal Ripken 6.00 1.80
5 Matt Williams .75 .23
6 Jay Buhner .75 .23
7 Does Not Exist
8 Jeff Conine .75 .23
9 Todd Greene .75 .23
10 Mike Lieberthal .75 .23
11 Steve Avery .75 .23
12 Bret Saberhagen .75 .23
13 Magglio Ordonez .75 .23
14 Brad Radke .75 .23
15 Derek Jeter 5.00 1.50
16 Javy Lopez .75 .23
17 Russ Davis .75 .23
18 Armando Benitez .75 .23
19 B.J. Surhoff .75 .23
20 Darryl Kile .75 .23
21 Mark Lewis .75 .23
22 Mike Williams .75 .23
23 Mark McLemore .75 .23
24 Sterling Hitchcock .75 .23
25 Darin Erstad .75 .23
26 Ricky Gutierrez .75 .23
27 John Jaha .75 .23
28 Homer Bush .75 .23
29 Darrin Fletcher .75 .23
30 Mark Grace 1.25 .35
31 Fred McGriff 1.25 .35
32 Omar Daal .75 .23
33 Eric Karros .75 .23
34 Orlando Cabrera .75 .23
35 J.T. Snow .75 .23
36 Luis Castillo .75 .23
37 Rey Ordonez .75 .23
38 Bob Abreu .75 .23
39 Warren Morris .75 .23
40 Juan Gonzalez 1.25 .35
41 Mike Lansing .75 .23
42 Chili Davis .75 .23
43 Dean Palmer .75 .23
44 Hank Aaron 4.00 1.20
45 Jeff Bagwell 1.25 .35
46 Jose Valentin .75 .23
47 Shannon Stewart .75 .23
48 Kent Bottenfield .75 .23
49 Jeff Shaw .75 .23
50 Sammy Sosa 3.00 .90
51 Randy Johnson 2.00 .60
52 Benny Agbayani .75 .23
53 Dante Bichette .75 .23
54 Pete Harnisch .75 .23
55 Frank Thomas 2.00 .60
56 Jorge Posada 1.25 .35
57 Todd Walker .75 .23
58 Juan Encarnacion .75 .23
59 Mike Sweeney .75 .23
60 Pedro Martinez 2.00 .60
61 Lee Stevens .75 .23
62 Brian Giles .75 .23
63 Chad Ogea .75 .23
64 Ivan Rodriguez 2.00 .60
65 Roger Cedeno .75 .23
66 David Justice .75 .23
67 Steve Trachsel .75 .23
68 Eli Marrero .75 .23
69 Dave Nilsson .75 .23
70 Ken Caminiti .75 .23
71 Tim Raines .75 .23
72 Brian Jordan .75 .23
73 Jeff Blauser .75 .23
74 Bernard Gilkey .75 .23
75 John Flaherty .75 .23
76 Brent Mayne .75 .23
77 Jose Vidro .75 .23
78 David Bell .75 .23
79 Bruce Aven .75 .23
80 John Olerud .75 .23
81 Pokey Reese .75 .23
82 Woody Williams .75 .23
83 Ed Sprague .75 .23
84 Joe Girardi .75 .23
85 Barry Larkin 1.25 .35
86 Mike Caruso .75 .23
87 Bobby Higginson .75 .23
88 Roberto Kelly .75 .23
89 Edgar Martinez 1.25 .35
90 Mark Kotsay .75 .23
91 Paul Sorrento .75 .23
92 Eric Young .75 .23
93 Carlos Delgado .75 .23
94 Troy Glaus .75 .23
95 Ben Grieve .75 .23
96 Jose Lima .75 .23
97 Garret Anderson .75 .23
98 Luis Gonzalez .75 .23
99 Carl Pavano .75 .23
100 Alex Rodriguez 3.00 .90
101 Preston Wilson .75 .23
102 Ron Gant .75 .23
103 Brady Anderson .75 .23
104 Rickey Henderson 2.00 .60
105 Gary Sheffield .75 .23
106 Mickey Morandini .75 .23
107 Jim Edmonds .75 .23
108 Kris Benson .75 .23
109 Adrian Beltre 1.25 .35
110 Alex Fernandez .75 .23
111 Dan Wilson .75 .23
112 Mark Clark .75 .23
113 Greg Vaughn .75 .23
114 Neifi Perez .75 .23
115 Paul O'Neill 1.25 .35
116 Jermaine Dye .75 .23
117 Todd Jones .75 .23
118 Terry Steinbach .75 .23
119 Greg Norton .75 .23
120 Curt Schilling .75 .23
121 Todd Zeile .75 .23
122 Edgardo Alfonzo .75 .23
123 Ryan McGuire .75 .23
124 Rich Aurilia .75 .23
125 John Smoltz 1.25 .35
126 Bob Wickman .75 .23
127 Richard Hidalgo .75 .23
128 Chuck Finley .75 .23
129 Billy Wagner .75 .23
130 Todd Hundley .75 .23
131 Dwight Gooden .75 .23
132 Russ Ortiz .75 .23
133 Mike Lowell .75 .23
134 Reggie Sanders .75 .23
135 John Valentin .75 .23
136 Brad Ausmus .75 .23
137 Chad Kreuter .75 .23
138 David Cone .75 .23
139 Brook Fordyce .75 .23
140 Roberto Alomar 1.25 .35
141 Charles Nagy .75 .23
142 Brian Hunter .75 .23
143 Mike Mussina 1.25 .35
144 Robin Ventura 1.25 .35
145 Kevin Brown 1.25 .35
146 Pat Hentgen .75 .23
147 Ryan Klesko .75 .23
148 Derek Bell .75 .23
149 Andy Sheets .75 .23
150 Larry Walker .75 .23
151 Scott Williamson .75 .23
152 Jose Offerman .75 .23
153 Doug Mientkiewicz .75 .23
154 John Snyder RC 1.00 .30
155 Sandy Alomar Jr. .75 .23
156 Joe Nathan .75 .23
157 Lance Johnson .75 .23
158 Odalis Perez .75 .23
159 Hideo Nomo 2.00 .60
160 Steve Finley .75 .23
161 Dave Martinez .75 .23
162 Matt Walbeck .75 .23
163 Bill Spiers .75 .23
164 Fernando Tatis .75 .23
165 Kenny Lofton .75 .23
166 Paul Byrd .75 .23
167 Aaron Sele .75 .23
168 Eddie Taubensee .75 .23
169 Reggie Jefferson .75 .23
170 Roger Clemens 4.00 1.20
171 Francisco Cordova .75 .23
172 Mike Bordick .75 .23

173 Wally Joyner .75 .23
174 Marvin Benard .75 .23
175 Jason Kendall .75 .23
176 Mike Stanley .75 .23
177 Chad Allen .75 .23
178 Carlos Beltran 1.25 .35
179 Deivi Cruz .75 .23
180 Chipper Jones 2.00 .60
181 Vladimir Guerrero 2.00 .60
182 Dave Burba .75 .23
183 Tom Goodwin .75 .23
184 Brian Daubach .75 .23
185 Jay Bell .75 .23
186 Roy Halladay .75 .23
187 Miguel Tejada .75 .23
188 Armando Rios .75 .23
189 Fernando Vina .75 .23
190 Eric Davis .75 .23
191 Henry Rodriguez .75 .23
192 Joe McEwing .75 .23
193 Jeff Kent .75 .23
194 Mike Jackson .75 .23
195 Mike Morgan .75 .23
196 Jeff Montgomery .75 .23
197 Jeff Zimmerman .75 .23
198 Tony Fernandez .75 .23
199 Jason Giambi .75 .23
200 Jose Canseco 2.00 .60
201 Alex Gonzalez .75 .23
202 Jack Cust 1.00 .30
Mike Colangelo
Dee Brown
203 Felipe Lopez 2.00 .60
Alfonso Soriano
Pablo Ozuna
204 Erubiel Durazo 1.50 .45
Pat Burrell
Nick Johnson
205 John Sneed RC 1.00 .30
Kip Wells
Matt Blank
206 Josh Kalinowski 1.00 .30
Michael Tejera
Chris Mears RC
207 Roosevelt Brown 1.50 .45
Corey Patterson
Lance Berkman
208 Kit Pellow 1.00 .30
Kevin Barker
Russ Branyan
209 B.J. Garbe 4.00 1.20
Larry Bigbie RC
210 Eric Munson 1.50 .45
Bobby Bradley RC
211 Josh Girdley 1.00 .30
Kyle Snyder
212 Chance Caple RC 1.00 .30
Jason Jennings
213 Ryan Christianson 2.50 .75
Brett Myers RC
214 Jason Stumm 1.00 .30
Rob Purvis RC
215 David Walling 1.00 .30
Mike Paradis
216 Omar Ortiz 1.00 .30
Jay Gehrke
217 David Cone HL .75 .23
218 Jose Jimenez HL .75 .23
219 Chris Singleton HL .75 .23
220 Fernando Tatis HL .75 .23
221 Todd Helton HL .75 .23
222 Kevin Millwood DIV .75 .23
223 Todd Pratt DIV .75 .23
224 Orl. Hernandez DIV .75 .23
225 Pedro Martinez DIV 1.25 .35
226 Tom Glavine LCS .75 .23
227 Bernie Williams LCS .75 .23
228 Mariano Rivera WS .75 .23
229 Tony Gwynn 20CB 2.50 .75
230 Wade Boggs 20CB 1.25 .35
231 Lance Johnson CB .75 .23
232 Mark McGwire 20CB 5.00 1.50
233 R.Henderson 20CB 2.00 .60
234 R.Henderson 20CB 2.00 .60
235 Roger Clemens 20CB 4.00 1.20
236A Mark McGwire MM 12.00 3.60
1st HR
236B Mark McGwire MM 12.00 3.60
1987 ROY
236C Mark McGwire MM 12.00 3.60
62nd HR
236D Mark McGwire MM 12.00 3.60
70th HR
236E Mark McGwire MM 12.00 3.60
500th HR
237A Hank Aaron MM 10.00 3.00
1st Career HR
237B Hank Aaron MM 10.00 3.00
1957 MVP
237C Hank Aaron MM 10.00 3.00
3000th Hit
237D Hank Aaron MM 10.00 3.00
715th HR
237E Hank Aaron 10.00 3.00
MM 755th HR
238A Cal Ripken MM 15.00 4.50
1982 ROY
238B Cal Ripken MM 15.00 4.50
1991 MVP
238C Cal Ripken MM 15.00 4.50
2131 Game
238D Cal Ripken MM 15.00 4.50
Streak Ends
238E Cal Ripken MM 15.00 4.50
400th HR
239A Wade Boggs MM 3.00 .90
1983 Batting
239B Wade Boggs MM 3.00 .90
1988 Batting
239C Wade Boggs MM 3.00 .90
2000th Hit
239D Wade Boggs MM 3.00 .90
1996 Champs
239E Wade Boggs MM 3.00 .90
3000th Hit
240A Tony Gwynn MM 6.00 1.80
1984 Batting
240B Tony Gwynn MM 6.00 1.80
1984 NLCS
240C Tony Gwynn MM 6.00 1.80
1995 Batting
240D Tony Gwynn MM 6.00 1.80
1998 NLCS
240E Tony Gwynn MM 6.00 1.80
3000th Hit
241 Tom Glavine 1.25 .35
242 David Wells .75 .23
243 Kevin Appier .75 .23
244 Troy Percival .75 .23
245 Ray Lankford .75 .23
246 Marquis Grissom .75 .23
247 Randy Winn .75 .23
248 Miguel Batista .75 .23
249 Darren Dreifort .75 .23
250 Barry Bonds 4.00 1.20
251 Harold Baines .75 .23
252 Cliff Floyd .75 .23
253 Freddy Garcia .75 .23
254 Kenny Rogers .75 .23
255 Ben Davis .75 .23
256 Charles Johnson .75 .23
257 Bubba Trammell .75 .23
258 Desi Relaford .75 .23
259 Al Martin .75 .23
260 Andy Pettitte 1.25 .35
261 Carlos Lee .75 .23
262 Matt Lawton .75 .23
263 Andy Fox .75 .23
264 Chan Ho Park .75 .23
265 Billy Koch .75 .23
266 Dave Roberts .75 .23
267 Carl Everett .75 .23
268 Orel Hershiser .75 .23
269 Trot Nixon .75 .23
270 Rusty Greer .75 .23
271 Will Clark 2.00 .60
272 Quilvio Veras .75 .23
273 Rico Brogna .75 .23
274 Devon White .75 .23
275 Tim Hudson .75 .23
276 Mike Hampton .75 .23
277 Miguel Cairo .75 .23
278 Darren Oliver .75 .23
279 Jeff Cirillo .75 .23
280 Al Leiter .75 .23
281 Shane Andrews .75 .23
282 Carlos Febles .75 .23
283 Pedro Astacio .75 .23
284 Juan Guzman .75 .23
285 Orlando Hernandez .75 .23
286 Paul Konerko .75 .23
287 Tony Clark .75 .23
288 Aaron Boone .75 .23
289 Ismael Valdes .75 .23
290 Moises Alou .75 .23
291 Kevin Tapani .75 .23
292 John Franco .75 .23
293 Todd Zeile .75 .23
294 Jason Schmidt .75 .23
295 Johnny Damon 1.25 .35
296 Scott Brosius .75 .23
297 Travis Fryman .75 .23
298 Jose Vizcaino .75 .23
299 Eric Chavez .75 .23
300 Mike Piazza 3.00 .90
301 Matt Clement .75 .23
302 Cristian Guzman .75 .23
303 C.J. Nitkowski .75 .23
304 Michael Tucker .75 .23
305 Brett Tomko .75 .23
306 Mike Lansing .75 .23
307 Eric Owens .75 .23
308 Livan Hernandez .75 .23
309 Rondell White .75 .23
310 Todd Stottlemyre .75 .23
311 Chris Carpenter .75 .23
312 Ken Hill .75 .23
313 Mark Loretta .75 .23
314 John Rocker .75 .23
315 Richie Sexson .75 .23
316 Ruben Mateo .75 .23
317 Joe Randa .75 .23
318 Mike Sirotka .75 .23
319 Jose Rosado .75 .23
320 Matt Mantei .75 .23
321 Kevin Millwood .75 .23
322 Gary DiSarcina .75 .23
323 Dustin Hermanson .75 .23
324 Mike Stanton .75 .23
325 Kirk Rueter .75 .23
326 Damian Miller RC 1.50 .45
327 Doug Glanville .75 .23
328 Scott Rolen 2.00 .60
329 Ray Durham .75 .23
330 Butch Huskey .75 .23
331 Mariano Rivera 1.25 .35
332 Darren Lewis .75 .23
333 Mike Timlin .75 .23
334 Mark Grudzielanek .75 .23
335 Mike Cameron .75 .23
336 Kelvim Escobar .75 .23
337 Bret Boone .75 .23
338 Mo Vaughn .75 .23
339 Craig Biggio 1.25 .35
340 Michael Barrett .75 .23
341 Marlon Anderson .75 .23
342 Bobby Jones .75 .23
343 John Halama .75 .23
344 Todd Ritchie .75 .23
345 Chuck Knoblauch .75 .23
346 Rick Reed .75 .23
347 Kelly Stinnett .75 .23
348 Tim Salmon 1.25 .35
349 A.J. Hinch .75 .23
350 Jose Cruz Jr. .75 .23
351 Roberto Hernandez .75 .23
352 Edgar Renteria .75 .23
353 Jose Hernandez .75 .23
354 Brad Fullmer .75 .23
355 Trevor Hoffman .75 .23
356 Troy O'Leary .75 .23
357 Justin Thompson .75 .23
358 Kevin Young .75 .23
359 Hideki Irabu .75 .23
360 Jim Thome 2.00 .60
361 Steve Karsay .75 .23
362 Octavio Dotel .75 .23
363 Omar Vizquel 1.25 .35
364 Raul Mondesi .75 .23
365 Shane Reynolds .75 .23
366 Bartolo Colon .75 .23
367 Chris Widger .75 .23
368 Gabe Kapler .75 .23
369 Bill Simas .75 .23
370 Tino Martinez 1.25 .35
371 John Thomson .75 .23
372 Delino DeShields .75 .23
373 Carlos Perez .75 .23
374 Eddie Perez .75 .23
375 Jeromy Burnitz .75 .23
376 Jimmy Haynes .75 .23
377 Travis Lee .75 .23
378 Darryl Hamilton .75 .23
379 Jamie Moyer .75 .23
380 Alex Gonzalez .75 .23
381 John Wetteland .75 .23
382 Vinny Castilla .75 .23
383 Jeff Suppan .75 .23
384 Jim Leyritz .75 .23
385 Robb Nen .75 .23
386 Wilson Alvarez .75 .23
387 Andres Galarraga .75 .23
388 Mike Remlinger .75 .23
389 Geoff Jenkins .75 .23
390 Matt Stairs .75 .23
391 Bill Mueller .75 .23
392 Mike Lowell .75 .23
393 Andy Ashby .75 .23
394 Ruben Rivera .75 .23
395 Todd Helton 1.25 .35
396 Bernie Williams 1.25 .35
397 Royce Clayton .75 .23
398 Manny Ramirez 1.25 .35
399 Kerry Wood 2.00 .60
400 Ken Griffey Jr. 3.00 .90
401 Enrique Wilson .75 .23
402 Joey Hamilton .75 .23
403 Shawn Estes .75 .23
404 Ugueth Urbina .75 .23
405 Albert Belle .75 .23
406 Rick Helling .75 .23
407 Steve Parris .75 .23
408 Eric Milton .75 .23
409 Dave Mlicki .75 .23
410 Shawn Green .75 .23
411 Jaret Wright .75 .23
412 Tony Womack .75 .23
413 Vernon Wells .75 .23
414 Ron Belliard .75 .23
415 Ellis Burks .75 .23
416 Scott Erickson .75 .23
417 Rafael Palmeiro 1.25 .35
418 Damion Easley .75 .23
419 Jamey Wright .75 .23
420 Corey Koskie .75 .23
421 Bobby Howry .75 .23
422 Ricky Ledee .75 .23
423 Dmitri Young .75 .23
424 Sidney Ponson .75 .23
425 Greg Maddux 3.00 .90
426 Jose Guillen .75 .23
427 Jon Lieber .75 .23
428 Andy Benes .75 .23
429 Randy Velarde .75 .23
430 Sean Casey .75 .23
431 Torii Hunter .75 .23
432 Ryan Rupe .75 .23
433 David Segui .75 .23
434 Todd Pratt .75 .23
435 Nomar Garciaparra 3.00 .90
436 Denny Neagle .75 .23
437 Ron Coomer .75 .23
438 Chris Singleton .75 .23
439 Tony Batista .75 .23
440 Andruw Jones .75 .23
441 Aubrey Huff .75 .23
Sean Burroughs
Adam Piatt
442 Rafael Furcal 1.50 .45
Travis Dawkins
Jason Dellaero
443 Mike Lamb RC 1.50 .45
Joe Crede
Wilton Veras
444 Julio Zuleta RC 1.00 .30
Jorge Toca
Dernell Stenson
445 Garry Maddox Jr. RC 1.00 .30
Gary Matthews Jr.
Tim Raines Jr.
446 Mark Mulder 1.50 .45
C.C. Sabathia
Matt Riley
447 Scott Downs RC 1.00 .30
Chris George
Matt Belisle
448 Doug Mirabelli 1.00 .30
Ben Petrick
Jayson Werth
449 Josh Hamilton 1.50 .45
Corey Myers RC
450 Ben Christensen RC 1.50 .45
Richard Stahl
451 Ben Sheets RC 6.00 1.80
Barry Zito RC
452 Kurt Ainsworth 1.50 .45
Ty Howington RC
453 Vince Faison RC 1.50 .45
Rick Asadoorian
454 Keith Reed RC 1.00 .30
Jeff Heaverlo
455 Mike MacDougal 1.50 .45
Brad Baker RC
456 Mark McGwire SH 2.50 .75
457 Cal Ripken SH 3.00 .90
458 Wade Boggs SH .75 .23
459 Tony Gwynn SH 1.25 .35
460 Jesse Orosco SH .75 .23
461 Larry Walker 1.25 .35
Nomar Garciaparra LL
462 Ken Griffey Jr. 2.00 .60
Mark McGwire LL
463 Manny Ramirez 2.00 .60
Mark McGwire LL
464 Pedro Martinez 1.25 .35
Randy Johnson LL
465 Pedro Martinez 1.25 .35
Randy Johnson LL
466 Derek Jeter 2.00 .60
Luis Gonzalez LL
467 Larry Walker .75 .23
Manny Ramirez LL
468 Tony Gwynn 20CB 2.50 .75
469 Mark McGwire 20CB 5.00 1.50
470 Frank Thomas 20CB 2.00 .60
471 Harold Baines 20CB .75 .23
472 Roger Clemens 20CB 4.00 1.20
473 John Franco 20CB .75 .23
474 John Franco 20CB .75 .23
475A Ken Griffey Jr. MM 8.00 2.40
350th HR
475B Ken Griffey Jr. MM 8.00 2.40
1997 MVP
475C Ken Griffey Jr. MM 8.00 2.40
HR Dad
475D Ken Griffey Jr. MM 8.00 2.40
1992 AS MVP
475E Ken Griffey Jr. MM 8.00 2.40
50 HR 1997
476A Barry Bonds MM 12.00 3.60
400HR/400SB
476B Barry Bonds MM 12.00 3.60
40HR/40SB
476C Barry Bonds MM 12.00 3.60
1993 MVP
476D Barry Bonds MM 12.00 3.60
1990 MVP
476E Barry Bonds MM 12.00 3.60
1992 MVP
477A Sammy Sosa 8.00 2.40
MM 20 HR June
477B Sammy Sosa MM 8.00 2.40
66 HR 1998
477C Sammy Sosa MM 8.00 2.40
60 HR 1999
477D Sammy Sosa MM 8.00 2.40
1998 MVP
477E Sammy Sosa MM 8.00 2.40
HR's 61/62
478A Derek Jeter MM 12.00 3.60
1996 ROY
478B Derek Jeter MM 12.00 3.60
Wins 1999 WS
478C Derek Jeter MM 12.00 3.60
Wins 1998 WS
478D Derek Jeter MM 12.00 3.60
Wins 1996 WS
478E Derek Jeter MM 12.00 3.60
17 GM Hit Streak
479A Alex Rodriguez MM 10.00 3.00
40HR/40SB
479B Alex Rodriguez MM 10.00 3.00
100th HR
479C Alex Rodriguez 10.00 3.00
MM 1996 POY
479D Alex Rodriguez 10.00 3.00
MM Wins 1 Million
479E Alex Rodriguez MM 10.00 3.00
1996 Batting Leader
NNO M.McGwire 85 Reprint 8.00 2.40

2000 Topps Chrome Refractors

These cards which parallel the regular Topps Chrome set were issued at a rate of one in 12 packs. The Mark McGwire rookie reprint card was issued at a rate of one in 12,116 first series packs and are serial numbered to 70.

Nm-Mt Ex-Mt
*STARS: 2.5X TO 6X BASIC CARDS...
*PROSPECTS 202-216: 2.5X TO 6X BASIC
*ROOKIES 202-216: 2X TO 5X BASIC
*PROSPECTS 441-455: 2.5X TO 6X BASIC
*ROOKIES 441-455: 2X TO 5X BASIC
MCGWIRE MM SET (5) 150.00 45.00
MCGWIRE MM (236A-236E) 40.00 12.00
AARON MM SET (5) 120.00 36.00
AARON MM (237A-237E) 30.00 9.00
RIPKEN MM SET (5) 200.00 60.00
RIPKEN MM (238A-238E) 50.00 15.00
BOGGS MM SET (5) 40.00 12.00
BOGGS MM (239A-239E) 10.00 3.00
GWYNN MM SET (5) 80.00 24.00
GWYNN MM (240A-240E) 20.00 6.00
GRIFFEY MM SET (5) 100.00 30.00
GRIFFEY MM (475A-475E) 25.00 7.50
BONDS MM SET (5) 150.00 45.00
BONDS MM (476A-476E) 40.00 12.00
SOSA MM SET (5) 100.00 30.00
SOSA MM (477A-477E) 25.00 7.50
JETER MM SET (5) 150.00 45.00
JETER MM (478A-478E) 40.00 12.00
A.ROD MM SET (5) 120.00 36.00
A.ROD MM (479A-479E) 30.00 9.00

2000 Topps Chrome 21st Century

Inserted at a rate of one in 16, this 10 cards feature players who are expected to be the best in the first part of the 21st century. Card backs carry a "C" prefix.

Nm-Mt Ex-Mt
COMPLETE SET (10) 40.00 12.00
*REF: 1X TO 2.5X BASIC 21ST CENT.
SER.1 REFRACTOR ODDS 1:80
C1 Ben Grieve 1.50 .45
C2 Alex Gonzalez 1.50 .45
C3 Derek Jeter 10.00 3.00
C4 Sean Casey 1.50 .45
C5 Nomar Garciaparra 6.00 1.80
C6 Alex Rodriguez 6.00 1.80
C7 Scott Rolen 4.00 1.20
C8 Andruw Jones 1.50 .45
C9 Vladimir Guerrero 4.00 1.20
C10 Todd Helton 2.50 .75

2000 Topps Chrome All-Star Rookie Team

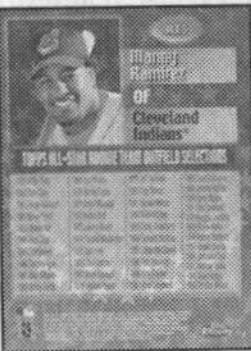

Randomly inserted into packs at one in 16, this 10-card insert set features players that made the All-Star game their rookie season. Card backs carry a "RT" prefix.

Nm-Mt Ex-Mt
COMPLETE SET (10) 50.00 15.00
*REF: 1X TO 2.5X BASIC ASR TEAM
REFRACTOR STATED ODDS 1:80
RT1 Mark McGwire 10.00 3.00
RT2 Chuck Knoblauch 1.50 .45
RT3 Chipper Jones 4.00 1.20
RT4 Cal Ripken 12.00 3.60
RT5 Manny Ramirez 2.50 .75
RT6 Jose Canseco 4.00 1.20
RT7 Ken Griffey Jr. 6.00 1.80
RT8 Mike Piazza 6.00 1.80
RT9 Dwight Gooden 1.50 .45
RT10 Billy Wagner 1.50 .45

2000 Topps Chrome All-Topps

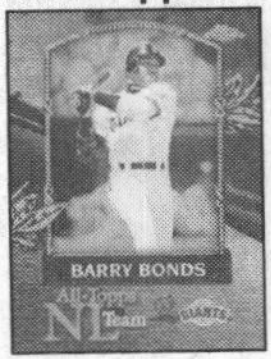

Inserted at a rate of one in 32 first and second series packs, these 10 cards feature the best players in the American and National Leagues. National League cards 91-10) were distributed in series one and American league (11-20) in series two. Card backs carry an "AT" prefix.

Nm-Mt Ex-Mt
COMPLETE SET (20) 160.00 47.50
COMPLETE N.L. (10) 80.00 24.00
COMPLETE A.L.(10) 80.00 24.00
*REFRACTORS: 1X TO 2.5X BASIC ALL NL
REFRACTOR ODDS 1:160
AT1 Greg Maddux 10.00 3.00
AT2 Mike Piazza 10.00 3.00
AT3 Mark McGwire 15.00 4.50
AT4 Craig Biggio 4.00 1.20
AT5 Chipper Jones 6.00 1.80
AT6 Barry Larkin 4.00 1.20
AT7 Barry Bonds 12.00 3.60
AT8 Andruw Jones 2.50 .75
AT9 Sammy Sosa 10.00 3.00
AT10 Larry Walker 2.50 .75
AT11 Pedro Martinez 6.00 1.80
AT12 Ivan Rodriguez 6.00 1.80
AT13 Rafael Palmeiro 4.00 1.20
AT14 Roberto Alomar 4.00 1.20
AT15 Cal Ripken 20.00 6.00
AT16 Derek Jeter 15.00 4.50
AT17 Albert Belle 2.50 .75
AT18 Ken Griffey Jr. 10.00 3.00
AT19 Manny Ramirez 4.00 1.20
AT20 Jose Canseco 6.00 1.80

2000 Topps Chrome Allegiance

This Topps Chrome exclusive set features 2 players who have spent their entire career wi just one team. The Allegiance cards were issue at a rate of one in 16 and have a "TA" prefix.

Nm-Mt Ex-Mt
COMPLETE SET (20) 120.00 36.0
*REF: 4X TO 10X BASIC ALLEGIANCE
SER.1 REFRACTOR ODDS 1:424 HOBBY
REFRACTOR PRINT RUN 100 SERIAL #'d SET
TA1 Derek Jeter 15.00 4.5
TA2 Ivan Rodriguez 6.00 1.8
TA3 Alex Rodriguez 10.00 3.0
TA4 Cal Ripken 20.00 6.0
TA5 Mark Grace 4.00 1.2
TA6 Tony Gwynn 8.00 2.4
TA7 Tom Glavine 4.00 1.2
TA8 Frank Thomas 6.00 1.8
TA9 Manny Ramirez 4.00 1.2
TA10 Barry Larkin 4.00 1.2
TA11 Bernie Williams 4.00 1.2
TA12 Eric Karros 2.50 .7
TA13 Vladimir Guerrero 6.00 1.8
TA14 Craig Biggio 4.00 1.2
TA15 Nomar Garciaparra 10.00 3.0
TA16 Andruw Jones 2.50 .7
TA17 Jim Thome 6.00 1.8
TA18 Scott Rolen 6.00 1.8
TA19 Chipper Jones 6.00 1.8
TA20 Ken Griffey Jr. 10.00 3.0

2000 Topps Chrome Combos

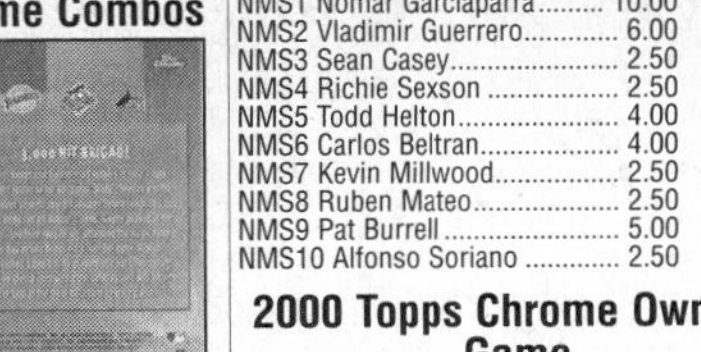

Randomly inserted into series two packs at one in 16, this 10-card insert features a variety of player combinations, such as the 1999 MVP's. Card backs carry a "TC" prefix.

	Nm-Mt	Ex-Mt
COMPLETE SET (10)	80.00	24.00
*REFRACTORS: 1X TO 2.5X BASIC COMBO		
REFRACTOR ODDS 1:80		
TC1 Roberto Alomar	2.50	.75
Manny Ramirez		
Kenny Lofton		
Jim Thome		
TC2 Tom Glavine	6.00	1.80
Greg Maddux		
John Smoltz		
TC3 Derek Jeter	10.00	3.00
Bernie Williams		
Tino Martinez		
TC4 Ivan Rodriguez	6.00	1.80
Mike Piazza		
TC5 Nomar Garciaparra	10.00	3.00
Alex Rodriguez		
Derek Jeter		
TC6 Sammy Sosa	10.00	3.00
Mark McGwire		
TC7 Pedro Martinez	4.00	1.20
Randy Johnson		
TC8 Barry Bonds	6.00	1.80
Ken Griffey Jr.		
TC9 Chipper Jones	4.00	1.20
Ivan Rodriguez		
TC10 Cal Ripken	12.00	3.60
Tony Gwynn		
Wade Boggs		

2000 Topps Chrome Kings

Randomly inserted into series two packs at one in 32, this 10-card insert features some of the greatest players in major league baseball. Card backs carry a "CK" prefix.

	Nm-Mt	Ex-Mt
COMPLETE SET (10)	80.00	24.00
CK1 Mark McGwire	15.00	4.50
CK2 Sammy Sosa	10.00	3.00
CK3 Ken Griffey Jr.	10.00	3.00
CK4 Mike Piazza	10.00	3.00
CK5 Alex Rodriguez	10.00	3.00
CK6 Manny Ramirez	4.00	1.20
CK7 Barry Bonds	12.00	3.60
CK8 Nomar Garciaparra	10.00	3.00
CK9 Chipper Jones	6.00	1.80
CK10 Vladimir Guerrero	6.00	1.80

2000 Topps Chrome Kings Refractors

Randomly inserted into series two packs at one in 514, this 10-card insert is a complete parallel of the Chrome Kings insert. Each card was serial numbered to the amount of homeruns that the individual players had after the 1999 season. Production runs are listed below. Card backs carry a "CK" prefix.

	Nm-Mt	Ex-Mt
COMPLETE SET (10)	300.00	90.00
CK1 Mark McGwire/522	30.00	9.00
CK2 Sammy Sosa/366	25.00	7.50
CK3 Ken Griffey Jr./398	25.00	7.50
CK4 Mike Piazza/240	25.00	7.50
CK5 Alex Rodriguez/148	50.00	15.00
CK6 Manny Ramirez/198	15.00	4.50
CK7 Barry Bonds/445	25.00	7.50
CK8 N.Garciaparra/96	50.00	15.00
CK9 Chipper Jones/153	20.00	6.00
CK10 V.Guerrero/92	40.00	12.00

2000 Topps Chrome New Millennium Stars

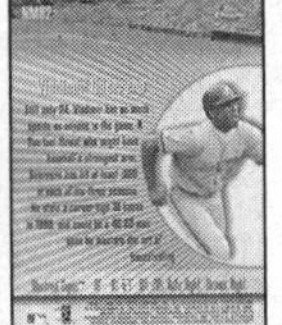

Randomly inserted into series two packs at one in 32, this 10-card insert features some of the major league's hottest young talent. Card backs carry a "NMS" prefix.

	Nm-Mt	Ex-Mt
COMPLETE SET (10)	40.00	12.00
*REFRACTORS: 1X TO 2.5X BASIC MILL.		
SER.2 REFRACTOR ODDS 1:160		
NMS1 Nomar Garciaparra	10.00	3.00
NMS2 Vladimir Guerrero	6.00	1.80
NMS3 Sean Casey	2.50	.75
NMS4 Richie Sexson	2.50	.75
NMS5 Todd Helton	4.00	1.20
NMS6 Carlos Beltran	4.00	1.20
NMS7 Kevin Millwood	2.50	.75
NMS8 Ruben Mateo	2.50	.75
NMS9 Pat Burrell	5.00	1.50
NMS10 Alfonso Soriano	2.50	.75

2000 Topps Chrome Own the Game

Randomly inserted into series two packs at one in 11, this 30-card insert features players that are amoung the major league's statistical leaders year after year. Card backs carry an "OTG" prefix.

	Nm-Mt	Ex-Mt
COMPLETE SET (30)	200.00	60.00
*REFRACTORS: 1X TO 2.5X BASIC OWN		
SER.2 REFRACTOR ODDS 1:55		
OTG1 Derek Jeter	15.00	4.50
OTG2 B.J. Surhoff	2.50	.75
OTG3 Luis Gonzalez	2.50	.75
OTG4 Manny Ramirez	4.00	1.20
OTG5 Rafael Palmeiro	4.00	1.20
OTG6 Mark McGwire	15.00	4.50
OTG7 Mark McGwire	15.00	4.50
OTG8 Sammy Sosa	10.00	3.00
OTG9 Ken Griffey Jr.	10.00	3.00
OTG10 Larry Walker	2.50	.75
OTG11 Nomar Garciaparra	10.00	3.00
OTG12 Derek Jeter	15.00	4.50
OTG13 Larry Walker	2.50	.75
OTG14 Mark McGwire	15.00	4.50
OTG15 Manny Ramirez	4.00	1.20
OTG16 Pedro Martinez	6.00	1.80
OTG17 Randy Johnson	6.00	1.80
OTG18 Kevin Millwood	2.50	.75
OTG19 Randy Johnson	6.00	1.80
OTG20 Pedro Martinez	6.00	1.80
OTG21 Kevin Brown	4.00	1.20
OTG22 Chipper Jones	6.00	1.80
OTG23 Ivan Rodriguez	6.00	1.80
OTG24 Mariano Rivera	4.00	1.20
OTG25 Scott Williamson	2.50	.75
OTG26 Carlos Beltran	4.00	1.20
OTG27 Randy Johnson	6.00	1.80
OTG28 Pedro Martinez	6.00	1.80
OTG29 Sammy Sosa	10.00	3.00
OTG30 Manny Ramirez	4.00	1.20

2000 Topps Chrome Power Players

This 20 card set, issued at a rate of one in eight packs, features players who are the leading power hitters in the majors. Card backs carry a "P" prefix.

	Nm-Mt	Ex-Mt
COMPLETE SET (20)	100.00	30.00
*REFRACTORS: 1X TO 2.5X BASIC POWER		
SER.1 REFRACTOR ODDS 1:40		
P1 Juan Gonzalez	2.50	.75
P2 Ken Griffey Jr.	6.00	1.80
P3 Mark McGwire	10.00	3.00
P4 Nomar Garciaparra	6.00	1.80
P5 Barry Bonds	8.00	2.40
P6 Mo Vaughn	1.50	.45
P7 Larry Walker	1.50	.45
P8 Alex Rodriguez	6.00	1.80
P9 Jose Canseco	4.00	1.20
P10 Jeff Bagwell	2.50	.75
P11 Manny Ramirez	2.50	.75
P12 Albert Belle	1.50	.45
P13 Frank Thomas	4.00	1.20
P14 Mike Piazza	6.00	1.80
P15 Chipper Jones	4.00	1.20
P16 Sammy Sosa	6.00	1.80
P17 Vladimir Guerrero	4.00	1.20
P18 Scott Rolen	4.00	1.20
P19 Raul Mondesi	1.50	.45
P20 Derek Jeter	10.00	3.00

2000 Topps Chrome Traded

The 2000 Topps Chrome Traded set was released in late November, 2000 and features a 135-card base set. The set is an exact parallel of the Topps Traded set.This set was produced using Topps' chrome technology. Please note that card backs carry a "T" prefix. Each set came with 135 cards and carried a $99.99 suggested retail price. Notable Rookie Cards include Cristian Guerrero and J.R. House.

	Nm-Mt	Ex-Mt
COMP.FACT.SET (135)	80.00	24.00
T1 Mike MacDougal	1.00	.30
T2 Andy Tracy RC	.50	.15
T3 Brandon Phillips RC	1.50	.45
T4 Brandon Inge RC	1.00	.30
T5 Robbie Morrison RC	.50	.15
T6 Josh Pressley RC	.50	.15
T7 Todd Moser RC	.50	.15
T8 Rob Purvis	.60	.18
T9 Chance Caple	.40	.12
T10 Ben Sheets	2.50	.75
T11 Russ Jacobson RC	.50	.15
T12 Brian Cole RC	.50	.15
T13 Brad Baker	.60	.18
T14 Alex Cintron RC	1.00	.30
T15 Lyle Overbay RC	4.00	1.20
T16 Mike Edwards RC	.50	.15
T17 Sean McGowan RC	.50	.15
T18 Jose Molina	.40	.12
T19 Marcos Castillo RC	.50	.15
T20 Josue Espada RC	.50	.15
T21 Alex Gordon RC	.50	.15
T22 Rob Pugmire RC	.50	.15
T23 Jason Stumm	.50	.15
T24 Ty Howington	.60	.18
T25 Brett Myers	1.00	.30
T26 Maicer Izturis RC	1.50	.45
T27 John McDonald	.40	.12
T28 W.Rodriguez RC	.50	.15
T29 Carlos Zambrano RC	8.00	2.40
T30 Alejandro Diaz RC	.50	.15
T31 Geraldo Guzman RC	.50	.15
T32 J.R. House RC	1.00	.30
T33 Elvin Nina RC	.50	.15
T34 Juan Pierre RC	2.50	.75
T35 Ben Johnson RC	.50	.15
T36 Jeff Bailey RC	.50	.15
T37 Miguel Olivo RC	1.50	.45
T38 F.Rodriguez RC	6.00	1.80
T39 Tony Pena Jr. RC	1.00	.30
T40 Miguel Cabrera RC	40.00	12.00
T41 Asdrubal Oropeza RC	.50	.15
T42 Junior Zamora RC	1.00	.30
T43 Jovanny Cedeno RC	.50	.15
T44 John Sneed	.60	.18
T45 Josh Kalinowski	.60	.18
T46 Mike Young RC	8.00	2.40
T47 Rico Washington RC	.50	.15
T48 Chad Durbin RC	.50	.15
T49 Junior Brignac RC	.50	.15
T50 Carlos Hernandez RC	1.00	.30
T51 Cesar Izturis RC	2.50	.75
T52 Oscar Salazar RC	.50	.15
T53 Pat Strange RC	.50	.15
T54 Rick Asadoorian	1.00	.30
T55 Keith Reed	.60	.18
T56 Leo Estrella RC	.50	.15
T57 Wascar Serrano RC	.50	.15
T58 Richard Gomez RC	.50	.15
T59 Ramon Santiago RC	1.00	.30
T60 Jovanny Sosa RC	1.00	.30
T61 Aaron Rowand RC	4.00	1.20
T62 Junior Guerrero RC	.50	.15
T63 Luis Terrero RC	2.50	.75
T64 Brian Sanches RC	.50	.15
T65 Scott Sobkowiak RC	.50	.15
T66 Gary Majewski RC	1.50	.45
T67 Barry Zito	2.50	.75
T68 Ryan Christianson	1.00	.30
T69 Cristian Guerrero RC	1.00	.30
T70 T.De La Rosa RC	.50	.15
T71 Andrew Beinbrink RC	.50	.15
T72 Ryan Knox RC	.50	.15
T73 Alex Graman RC	.50	.15
T74 Juan Guzman RC	.50	.15
T75 Ruben Salazar RC	.50	.15
T76 Luis Matos RC	1.00	.30
T77 Tony Mota RC	.50	.15
T78 Doug Davis	.40	.12
T79 Ben Christensen	.40	.12
T80 Mike Lamb	1.00	.30
T81 Adrian Gonzalez RC	4.00	1.20
T82 Mike Stodolka RC	.50	.15
T83 Adam Johnson RC	1.00	.30
T84 Matt Wheatland RC	.50	.15
T85 Corey Smith RC	1.00	.30
T86 Rocco Baldelli RC	8.00	2.40
T87 Keith Bucktrot RC	.50	.15
T88 Adam Wainwright RC	2.50	.75
T89 Scott Thorman RC	1.00	.30
T90 Tripper Johnson RC	1.00	.30
T91 Jim Edmonds	.60	.18
T92 Masato Yoshii	.40	.12
T93 Adam Kennedy	.40	.12
T94 Darryl Kile	.60	.18
T95 Mark McLemore	.40	.12
T96 Ricky Gutierrez	.40	.12
T97 Juan Gonzalez	1.00	.30
T98 Melvin Mora	.60	.18
T99 Dante Bichette	.60	.18
T100 Lee Stevens	.40	.12
T101 Roger Cedeno	.40	.12
T102 John Olerud	.60	.18
T103 Eric Young	.40	.12
T104 Mickey Morandini	.40	.12
T105 Travis Lee	.40	.12
T106 Greg Vaughn	.40	.12
T107 Todd Zeile	.60	.18
T108 Chuck Finley	.60	.18
T109 Ismael Valdes	.40	.12
T110 Reggie Sanders	.40	.12
T111 Pat Hentgen	.40	.12
T112 Ryan Klesko	.60	.18
T113 Derek Bell	.40	.12
T114 Hideo Nomo	1.50	.45
T115 Aaron Sele	.40	.12
T116 Fernando Vina	.40	.12
T117 Wally Joyner	.60	.18
T118 Brian Hunter	.40	.12
T119 Joe Girardi	.40	.12
T120 Omar Daal	.40	.12
T121 Brook Fordyce	.40	.12
T122 Jose Valentin	.40	.12
T123 Curt Schilling	.60	.18
T124 B.J. Surhoff	.60	.18
T125 Henry Rodriguez	.40	.12
T126 Mike Bordick	.40	.12
T127 David Justice	.60	.18
T128 Charles Johnson	.60	.18
T129 Will Clark	1.50	.45
T130 Dwight Gooden	.60	.18
T131 David Segui	.40	.12
T132 Denny Neagle	.60	.18
T133 Jose Canseco	1.50	.45
T134 Bruce Chen	.40	.12
T135 Jason Bere	.40	.12

2001 Topps Chrome

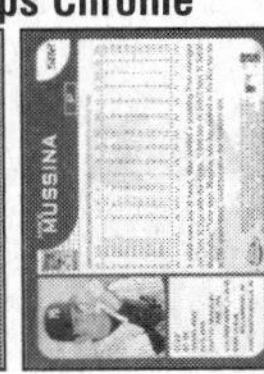

The 2001 Topps Chrome product was released in two separate series. The first series shipped in February 2001, and features a 331-card base set produced with Topps' special chrome technology. This set parallels the regular 2001 Topps base set in card design and photography but card numbering differs due to the fact that the manufacturer decided to select only the best 331 cards of the 405 card basic Topps set to be featured in this upgraded Chrome product. Each Topps Chrome pack contains four cards, and carried a suggested retail price of $2.99. Please note, card number 7 does not exist. The number was retired in Topps and Topps Chrome brands back in 1996 in honor of Yankees legend Mickey Mantle. Notable Rookie Cards include Hee Seop Choi.

	Nm-Mt	Ex-Mt
COMPLETE SET (661)	300.00	90.00
COMP. SERIES 1 (331)	150.00	45.00
COMP. SERIES 2 (330)	150.00	45.00
1 Cal Ripken	6.00	1.80
2 Chipper Jones	2.00	.60
3 Roger Cedeno	.50	.15
4 Garret Anderson	.75	.23
5 Robin Ventura	.75	.23
6 Daryle Ward	.50	.15
7 Does Not Exist		
8 Phil Nevin	.75	.23
9 Jermaine Dye	.75	.23
10 Chris Singleton	.50	.15
11 Mike Redmond	.50	.15
12 Jim Thome	2.00	.60
13 Brian Jordan	.75	.23
14 Dustin Hermanson	.50	.15
15 Shawn Green	.75	.23
16 Todd Stottlemyre	.50	.15
17 Dan Wilson	.50	.15
18 Derek Lowe	.75	.23
19 Juan Gonzalez	1.25	.35
20 Pat Meares	.50	.15
21 Paul O'Neill	1.25	.35
22 Jeffrey Hammonds	.50	.15
23 Pokey Reese	.50	.15
24 Mike Mussina	1.25	.35
25 Rico Brogna	.50	.15
26 Jay Buhner	.75	.23
27 Steve Cox	.50	.15
28 Quilvio Veras	.50	.15
29 Marquis Grissom	.75	.23
30 Shigetoshi Hasegawa	.75	.23
31 Shane Reynolds	.50	.15
32 Adam Piatt	.50	.15
33 Preston Wilson	.75	.23
34 Ellis Burks	.75	.23
35 Armando Rios	.50	.15
36 Chuck Finley	.75	.23
37 Shannon Stewart	.75	.23
38 Mark McGwire	5.00	1.50
39 Gerald Williams	.50	.15
40 Eric Young	.50	.15
41 Peter Bergeron	.50	.15
42 Arthur Rhodes	.50	.15
43 Bobby Jones	.50	.15
44 Matt Clement	.50	.15
45 Pedro Martinez	2.00	.60
46 Jose Canseco	2.00	.60
47 Matt Anderson	.50	.15
48 Torii Hunter	.75	.23
49 Carlos Lee	.75	.23
50 Eric Chavez	.75	.23
51 Rick Helling	.50	.15
52 John Franco	.75	.23
53 Mike Bordick	.75	.23
54 Andres Galarraga	.75	.23
55 Jose Cruz Jr.	.50	.15
56 Mike Matheny	.75	.23
57 Randy Johnson	2.00	.60
58 Richie Sexson	.75	.23
59 Vladimir Nunez	.50	.15
60 Aaron Boone	.75	.23
61 Darin Erstad	.75	.23
62 Alex Gonzalez	.50	.15
63 Gil Heredia	.50	.15
64 Shane Andrews	.50	.15
65 Todd Hundley	.50	.15
66 Bill Mueller	.75	.23
67 Mark McLemore	.50	.15
68 Scott Spiezio	.50	.15
69 Kevin McGlinchy	.50	.15
70 Manny Ramirez	1.25	.35
71 Mike Lamb	.50	.15
72 Brian Buchanan	.50	.15
73 Mike Sweeney	.75	.23
74 John Wetteland	.75	.23
75 Rob Bell	.50	.15
76 John Burkett	.50	.15
77 Derek Jeter	5.00	1.50
78 J.D. Drew	.75	.23
79 Jose Offerman	.50	.15
80 Rick Reed	.50	.15
81 Will Clark	2.00	.60
82 Rickey Henderson	2.00	.60
83 Kirk Rueter	.50	.15
84 Lee Stevens	.50	.15
85 Jay Bell	.75	.23
86 Fred McGriff	1.25	.35
87 Julio Zuleta	.50	.15
88 Brian Anderson	.50	.15
89 Orlando Cabrera	.75	.23
90 Alex Fernandez	.50	.15
91 Derek Bell	.50	.15
92 Eric Owens	.50	.15
93 Dennys Reyes	.50	.15
94 Mike Stanley	.50	.15
95 Jorge Posada	1.25	.35
96 Paul Konerko	.75	.23
97 Mike Remlinger	.50	.15
98 Travis Lee	.50	.15
99 Ken Caminiti	.75	.23
100 Kevin Barker	.50	.15
101 Ozzie Guillen	.50	.15
102 Randy Wolf	.50	.15
103 Michael Tucker	.50	.15
104 Darren Lewis	.50	.15
105 Joe Randa	.50	.15
106 Jeff Cirillo	.50	.15
107 David Ortiz	1.25	.35
108 Herb Perry	.50	.15
109 Jeff Nelson	.50	.15
110 Chris Stynes	.50	.15
111 Johnny Damon	1.25	.35
112 Jason Schmidt	.75	.23
113 Charles Johnson	.50	.15
114 Pat Burrell	.75	.23
115 Gary Sheffield	.75	.23
116 Tom Glavine	1.25	.35
117 Jason Isringhausen	.75	.23
118 Chris Carpenter	.50	.15
119 Jeff Suppan	.50	.15
120 Ivan Rodriguez	2.00	.60
121 Luis Sojo	.50	.15
122 Ron Villone	.50	.15
123 Mike Sirotka	.50	.15
124 Chuck Knoblauch	.75	.23
125 Jason Kendall	.75	.23
126 Bobby Estalella	.50	.15
127 Jose Guillen	.75	.23
128 Carlos Delgado	.75	.23
129 Benji Gil	.50	.15
130 Einar Diaz	.50	.15
131 Andy Benes	.50	.15
132 Adrian Beltre	1.25	.35
133 Roger Clemens	4.00	1.20
134 Scott Williamson	.50	.15
135 Brad Penny	.50	.15
136 Troy Glaus	.75	.23
137 Kevin Appier	.75	.23
138 Walt Weiss	.50	.15
139 Michael Barrett	.50	.15
140 Mike Hampton	.75	.23
141 Francisco Cordova	.50	.15
142 David Segui	.50	.15
143 Carlos Febles	.50	.15
144 Roy Halladay	.50	.15
145 Seth Etherton	.50	.15
146 Fernando Tatis	.50	.15
147 Livan Hernandez	.50	.15
148 B.J. Surhoff	.75	.23
149 Barry Larkin	1.25	.35
150 Bobby Howry	.50	.15
151 Dmitri Young	.75	.23
152 Brian Hunter	.50	.15
153 A.Rodriguez Rangers	3.00	.90
154 Hideo Nomo	2.00	.60
155 Warren Morris	.50	.15
156 Antonio Alfonseca	.50	.15
157 Edgardo Alfonzo	.50	.15
158 Mark Grudzielanek	.50	.15
159 Fernando Vina	.50	.15
160 Homer Bush	.50	.15
161 Jason Giambi	.75	.23
162 Steve Karsay	.50	.15
163 Matt Lawton	.50	.15
164 Rusty Greer	.75	.23
165 Billy Koch	.50	.15
166 Todd Hollandsworth	.50	.15
167 Raul Ibanez	.50	.15
168 Tony Gwynn	2.50	.75
169 Carl Everett	.75	.23
170 Hector Carrasco	.50	.15
171 Jose Valentin	.50	.15
172 Deivi Cruz	.50	.15
173 Bret Boone	.75	.23
174 Melvin Mora	.75	.23
175 Danny Graves	.50	.15
176 Jose Jimenez	.50	.15
177 James Baldwin	.50	.15
178 C.J. Nitkowski	.50	.15
179 Jeff Zimmerman	.50	.15
180 Mike Lowell	.75	.23
181 Hideki Irabu	.50	.15
182 Greg Vaughn	.50	.15
183 Omar Daal	.50	.15
184 Darren Dreifort	.50	.15
185 Gil Meche	.50	.15
186 Damian Jackson	.50	.15
187 Frank Thomas	2.00	.60
188 Luis Castillo	.50	.15
189 Bartolo Colon	.75	.23
190 Craig Biggio	1.25	.35
191 Scott Schoeneweis	.50	.15
192 Dave Veres	.50	.15
193 Ramon Martinez	.50	.15
194 Jose Vidro	.50	.15
195 Todd Helton	1.25	.35
196 Greg Norton	.50	.15
197 Jacque Jones	.75	.23
198 Jason Grimsley	.50	.15
199 Dan Reichert	.50	.15
200 Robb Nen	.75	.23
201 Scott Hatteberg	.50	.15
202 Terry Shumpert	.50	.15
203 Kevin Millar	.75	.23
204 Ismael Valdes	.50	.15
205 Richard Hidalgo	.50	.15
206 Randy Velarde	.50	.15
207 Bengie Molina	.50	.15
208 Tony Womack	.50	.15
209 Enrique Wilson	.50	.15
210 Jeff Brantley	.50	.15
211 Rick Ankiel	.50	.15
212 Terry Mulholland	.50	.15
213 Ron Belliard	.50	.15

214 Terrence Long .50 .15
215 Alberto Castillo .50 .15
216 Royce Clayton .50 .15
217 Joe McEwing .50 .15
218 Jason McDonald .50 .15
219 Ricky Bottalico .50 .15
220 Keith Foulke .75 .23
221 Brad Radke .75 .23
222 Gabe Kapler .50 .15
223 Pedro Astacio .50 .15
224 Armando Reynoso .50 .15
225 Darryl Kile .75 .23
226 Reggie Sanders .50 .15
227 Esteban Yan .50 .15
228 Joe Nathan .50 .15
229 Jay Payton .50 .15
230 Francisco Cordero .50 .15
231 Gregg Jefferies .50 .15
232 LaTroy Hawkins .50 .15
233 Jacob Cruz .50 .15
234 Chris Holt .50 .15
235 Vladimir Guerrero 2.00 .60
236 Marvin Benard .50 .15
237 Alex Ramirez .50 .15
238 Mike Williams .50 .15
239 Sean Bergman .50 .15
240 Juan Encarnacion .50 .15
241 Russ Davis .50 .15
242 Ramon Hernandez .50 .15
243 Sandy Alomar Jr. .50 .15
244 Eddie Guardado .50 .15
245 Shane Halter .50 .15
246 Geoff Jenkins .75 .23
247 Brian Meadows .50 .15
248 Damian Miller .50 .15
249 Darrin Fletcher .50 .15
250 Rafael Furcal .75 .23
251 Mark Grace 1.25 .35
252 Mark Mulder .75 .23
253 Joe Torre MG .75 .23
254 Bobby Cox MG .50 .15
255 Mike Scioscia MG .50 .15
256 Mike Hargrove MG .50 .15
257 Jimy Williams MG .50 .15
258 Jerry Manuel MG .50 .15
259 Charlie Manuel MG .50 .15
260 Don Baylor MG .75 .23
261 Phil Garner MG .50 .15
262 Tony Muser MG .50 .15
263 Buddy Bell MG .75 .23
264 Tom Kelly MG .50 .15
265 John Boles MG .50 .15
266 Art Howe MG .50 .15
267 Larry Dierker MG .50 .15
268 Lou Piniella MG .75 .23
269 Larry Rothschild MG .50 .15
270 Davey Lopes MG .75 .23
271 Johnny Oates MG .50 .15
272 Felipe Alou MG .50 .15
273 Bobby Valentine MG .50 .15
274 Tony LaRussa MG .50 .15
275 Bruce Bochy MG .50 .15
276 Dusty Baker MG .75 .23
277 Adrian Gonzalez 1.50 .45
Adam Johnson
278 Matt Wheatland 1.00 .30
Bryan Digby
279 Tripper Johnson 1.00 .30
Scott Thorman
280 Phil Dumatrait 1.00 .30
Adam Wainwright
281 Scott Heard 1.50 .45
David Parrish RC
282 Rocco Baldelli 2.00 .60
Mark Folsom
283 Dominic Rich RC 1.50 .45
Aaron Herr
284 Mike Stodolka 1.00 .30
Sean Burnett
285 Derek Thompson 1.00 .30
Corey Smith
286 Danny Borrell 1.50 .45
Jason Bourgeois RC
287 Chin-Feng Chen 1.50 .45
Corey Patterson
Josh Hamilton
288 Ryan Anderson 2.00 .60
Barry Zito
C.C. Sabathia
289 Scott Sobkowiak 2.00 .60
David Walling
Ben Sheets
290 Ty Howington 1.00 .30
Josh Kalinowski
Josh Girdley
291 Hee Seop Choi 3.00 .90
Aaron McNeal
Jason Hart
292 Bobby Bradley 1.50 .45
Kurt Ainsworth
Chin-Hui Tsao
293 Mike Glendenning 1.00 .30
Kenny Kelly
Juan Silvestre
294 J.R. House 1.00 .30
Ramon Castro
Ben Davis
295 Chance Caple 2.00 .60
Rafael Soriano
Pasqual Coco
296 Travis Hafner RC 6.00 1.80
Eric Munson
Bucky Jacobsen
297 Jason Conti 1.00 .30
Chris Wakeland
Brian Cole
298 Scott Seabol 1.50 .45
Aubrey Huff
Joe Crede
299 Adam Everett 1.00 .30
Jose Ortiz
Keith Ginter
300 Carlos Hernandez 1.00 .30
Geraldo Guzman
Adam Eaton
301 Bobby Kielty 1.00 .30
Milton Bradley
Juan Rivera
302 Mark McGwire GM 2.50 .75
303 Don Larsen GM .75 .23
304 Bobby Thomson GM .75 .23
305 Bill Mazeroski GM .75 .23
306 Reggie Jackson GM 1.25 .35
307 Kirk Gibson GM .75 .23
308 Roger Maris GM 1.25 .35
309 Cal Ripken GM 3.00 .90
310 Hank Aaron GM 2.00 .60
311 Joe Carter GM .75 .23
312 Cal Ripken SH 3.00 .90
313 Randy Johnson SH 1.25 .35
314 Ken Griffey Jr. SH 2.00 .60
315 Troy Glaus SH .75 .23
316 Kazuhiro Sasaki SH .75 .23
317 Sammy Sosa 1.25 .35
Troy Glaus LL
318 Todd Helton .75 .23
Edgar Martinez LL
319 Todd Helton 2.00 .60
Nomar Garicaparra LL
320 Barry Bonds 2.00 .60
Jason Giambi LL
321 Todd Helton .75 .23
Manny Ramirez LL
322 Todd Helton .75 .23
Darin Erstad LL
323 Kevin Brown 1.25 .35
Pedro Martinez LL
324 Randy Johnson 1.25 .35
Pedro Martinez LL
325 Will Clark HL 2.00 .60
326 New York Mets HL 2.00 .60
327 New York Yankees HL 3.00 .90
328 Seattle Mariners HL .75 .23
329 Mike Hampton HL .75 .23
330 New York Yankees HL 4.00 1.20
331 N.Y. Yankees Champs 8.00 2.40
332 Jeff Bagwell 1.25 .35
333 Andy Pettitte 1.25 .35
334 Tony Armas Jr. .50 .15
335 Jeromy Burnitz .75 .23
336 Javier Vazquez .75 .23
337 Eric Karros .75 .23
338 Brian Giles .75 .23
339 Scott Rolen 2.00 .60
340 David Justice .75 .23
341 Ray Durham .75 .23
342 Todd Zeile .75 .23
343 Cliff Floyd .75 .23
344 Barry Bonds 5.00 1.50
345 Matt Williams .75 .23
346 Steve Finley .75 .23
347 Scott Elarton .50 .15
348 Bernie Williams 1.25 .35
349 David Wells .75 .23
350 J.T. Snow .75 .23
351 Al Leiter .75 .23
352 Maggio Ordonez .75 .23
353 Raul Mondesi .75 .23
354 Tim Salmon 1.25 .35
355 Jeff Kent .75 .23
356 Mariano Rivera 1.25 .35
357 John Olerud .75 .23
358 Javy Lopez .75 .23
359 Ben Grieve .50 .15
360 Ray Lankford .50 .15
361 Ken Griffey Jr. 3.00 .90
362 Rich Aurilia .50 .15
363 Andruw Jones .75 .23
364 Ryan Klesko .75 .23
365 Roberto Alomar 1.25 .35
366 Miguel Tejada .75 .23
367 Mo Vaughn .75 .23
368 Albert Belle .75 .23
369 Jose Canseco 2.00 .60
370 Kevin Brown .75 .23
371 Rafael Palmeiro 1.25 .35
372 Mark Redman .50 .15
373 Larry Walker 1.25 .35
374 Greg Maddux 3.00 .90
375 Nomar Garciaparra 3.00 .90
376 Kevin Millwood .75 .23
377 Edgar Martinez 1.25 .35
378 Sammy Sosa 3.00 .90
379 Tim Hudson .75 .23
380 Jim Edmonds .75 .23
381 Mike Piazza 3.00 .90
382 Brant Brown .50 .15
383 Brad Fullmer .50 .15
384 Alan Benes .50 .15
385 Mickey Morandini .50 .15
386 Troy Percival .75 .23
387 Eddie Perez .50 .15
388 Vernon Wells .75 .23
389 Ricky Gutierrez .50 .15
390 Rondell White .75 .23
391 Kelvim Escobar .50 .15
392 Tony Batista .75 .23
393 Jimmy Haynes .50 .15
394 Billy Wagner .75 .23
395 A.J. Hinch .50 .15
396 Matt Morris .75 .23
397 Lance Berkman .75 .23
398 Jeff D'Amico .50 .15
399 Octavio Dotel .50 .15
400 Olmedo Saenz .50 .15
401 Esteban Loaiza .50 .15
402 Adam Kennedy .50 .15
403 Moises Alou .75 .23
404 Orlando Palmeiro .50 .15
405 Kevin Young .50 .15
406 Tom Goodwin .50 .15
407 Mac Suzuki .50 .15
408 Pat Hentgen .50 .15
409 Kevin Stocker .50 .15
410 Mark Sweeney .75 .23
411 Tony Eusebio .50 .15
412 Edgar Renteria .50 .15
413 John Rocker .50 .15
414 Jose Lima .50 .15
415 Kerry Wood 2.00 .60
416 Mike Timlin .50 .15
417 Jose Hernandez .50 .15
418 Jeremy Giambi .50 .15
419 Luis Lopez .50 .15
420 Mitch Meluskey .50 .15
421 Garrett Stephenson .50 .15
422 Jamey Wright .50 .15
423 John Jaha .50 .15
424 Placido Polanco .50 .15
425 Marty Cordova .50 .15
426 Joey Hamilton .50 .15
427 Travis Fryman .75 .23
428 Mike Cameron .75 .23
429 Matt Mantei .50 .15
430 Chan Ho Park .75 .23
431 Shawn Estes .50 .15
432 Danny Bautista .50 .15
433 Wilson Alvarez .50 .15
434 Kenny Lofton .75 .23
435 Russ Ortiz .75 .23
436 Dave Burba .50 .15
437 Felix Martinez .50 .15
438 Jeff Shaw .50 .15
439 Mike DiFelice .50 .15
440 Roberto Hernandez .50 .15
441 Bryan Rekar .50 .15
442 Ugueth Urbina .50 .15
443 Vinny Castilla .75 .23
444 Carlos Perez .50 .15
445 Juan Guzman .50 .15
446 Ryan Rupe .50 .15
447 Mike Mordecai .50 .15
448 Ricardo Rincon .50 .15
449 Curt Schilling .75 .23
450 Alex Cora .50 .15
451 Turner Ward .50 .15
452 Omar Vizquel 1.25 .35
453 Russ Branyan .50 .15
454 Russ Johnson .50 .15
455 Greg Colbrunn .50 .15
456 Charles Nagy .50 .15
457 Wil Cordero .50 .15
458 Jason Tyner .50 .15
459 Devon White .75 .23
460 Kelly Stinnett .50 .15
461 Wilton Guerrero .50 .15
462 Jason Bere .50 .15
463 Calvin Murray .50 .15
464 Miguel Batista .50 .15
466 Luis Gonzalez .75 .23
467 Jaret Wright .50 .15
468 Chad Kreuter .50 .15
469 Armando Benitez .75 .23
470 Erubiel Durazo .50 .15
470 Sidney Ponson .50 .15
471 Adrian Brown .50 .15
472 Sterling Hitchcock .50 .15
473 Timo Perez .50 .15
474 Jamie Moyer .75 .23
475 Delino DeShields .50 .15
476 Glendon Rusch .50 .15
477 Chris Gomez .50 .15
478 Adam Eaton .50 .15
479 Pablo Ozuna .50 .15
480 Bob Abreu .75 .23
481 Kris Benson .50 .15
482 Keith Osik .50 .15
483 Darryl Hamilton .50 .15
484 Marlon Anderson .50 .15
485 Jimmy Anderson .50 .15
486 John Halama .50 .15
487 Nelson Figueroa .50 .15
488 Alex Gonzalez .50 .15
489 Benny Agbayani .50 .15
490 Ed Sprague .50 .15
491 Scott Erickson .50 .15
492 Doug Glanville .50 .15
493 Jesus Sanchez .50 .15
494 Mike Lieberthal .75 .23
495 Aaron Sele .50 .15
496 Pat Mahomes .50 .15
497 Ruben Rivera .50 .15
498 Wayne Gomes .50 .15
499 Freddy Garcia .75 .23
500 Al Martin .50 .15
501 Woody Williams .50 .15
502 Paul Byrd .50 .15
503 Rick White .50 .15
504 Trevor Hoffman .75 .23
505 Brady Anderson .75 .23
506 Robert Person .50 .15
507 Jeff Conine .75 .23
508 Chris Truby .50 .15
509 Emil Brown .50 .15
510 Ryan Dempster .50 .15
511 Ruben Mateo .50 .15
512 Alex Ochoa .50 .15
513 Jose Rosado .50 .15
514 Masato Yoshii .50 .15
515 Brian Daubach .50 .15
516 Jeff D'Amico .50 .15
517 Brent Mayne .50 .15
518 John Thomson .50 .15
519 Todd Ritchie .50 .15
520 John VanderWal .50 .15
521 Neifi Perez .50 .15
522 Chad Curtis .50 .15
523 Kenny Rogers .75 .23
524 Trot Nixon .75 .23
525 Sean Casey .75 .23
526 Wilton Veras .50 .15
527 Troy O'Leary .50 .15
528 Dante Bichette .75 .23
529 Jose Silva .50 .15
530 Darren Oliver .50 .15
531 Steve Parris .50 .15
532 David McCarty .50 .15
533 Todd Walker .50 .15
534 Brian Rose .50 .15
535 Pete Schourek .50 .15
536 Ricky Ledee .50 .15
537 Justin Thompson .50 .15
538 Benito Santiago .50 .15
539 Carlos Beltran 1.25 .35
540 Gabe White .50 .15
541 Bret Saberhagen .75 .23
542 Ramon Martinez .50 .15
543 John Valentin .50 .15
544 Frank Catalanotto .50 .15
545 Tim Wakefield .75 .23
546 Michael Tucker .50 .15
547 Juan Pierre .75 .23
548 Rich Garces .50 .15
549 Luis Ordaz .50 .15
550 Jerry Spradlin .50 .15
551 Corey Koskie .75 .23
552 Cal Eldred .50 .15
553 Alfonso Soriano 1.25 .35
554 Kip Wells .50 .15
555 Orlando Hernandez .50 .15
556 Bill Simas .50 .15
557 Jim Parque .50 .15
558 Joe Mays .50 .15
559 Tim Belcher .50 .15
560 Shane Spencer .50 .15
561 Glenallen Hill .50 .15
562 Matt LeCroy .50 .15
563 Tino Martinez 1.25 .35
564 Eric Milton .50 .15
565 Ron Coomer .50 .15
566 Cristian Guzman .50 .15
567 Kazuhiro Sasaki .75 .23
568 Mark Quinn .50 .15
569 Eric Gagne 2.00 .60
570 Kerry Ligtenberg .50 .15
571 Rolando Arrojo .50 .15
572 Jon Lieber .50 .15
573 Jose Vizcaino .50 .15
574 Jeff Abbott .50 .15
575 Carlos Hernandez .50 .15
576 Scott Sullivan .50 .15
577 Matt Stairs .50 .15
578 Tom Lampkin .50 .15
579 Donnie Sadler .50 .15
580 Desi Relaford .50 .15
581 Scott Downs .50 .15
582 Mike Mussina 1.25 .35
583 Ramon Ortiz .50 .15
584 Mike Myers .50 .15
585 Frank Castillo .50 .15
586 Manny Ramirez 1.25 .35
587 Alex Rodriguez 3.00 .90
588 Andy Ashby .50 .15
589 Felipe Crespo .50 .15
590 Bobby Bonilla .75 .23
591 Denny Neagle .50 .15
592 Dave Martinez .50 .15
593 Mike Hampton .75 .23
594 Gary DiSarcina .50 .15
595 Tsuyoshi Shinjo RC 2.00 .60
596 Albert Pujols RC 60.00 18.00
597 Roy Oswalt 2.00 .60
Pat Strange
Jon Rauch
598 Phil Wilson RC 8.00 2.40
Jake Peavy RC
Darwin Cubillan RC
599 Nathan Haynes 1.00 .30
Steve Smyth RC
Mike Bynum
600 Joe Lawrence 1.00 .30
Choo Freeman
Michael Cuddyer
601 Larry Barnes 1.00 .30
DeWayne Wise
Carlos Pena
602 Felipe Lopez 1.50 .45
Gookie Dawkins
Eric Almonte RC
603 Brad Wilkerson 1.00 .30
Alex Escobar
Eric Valent
604 Jeff Goldbach 1.00 .30
Toby Hall
Rod Barajas
605 Marcus Giles 1.50 .45
Pablo Ozuna
Jason Romano
606 Vernon Wells 1.50 .45
Jack Cust
Dee Brown
607 Luis Montanez RC 1.50 .45
David Espinosa
608 Anthony Pluta RC 1.50 .45
Justin Wayne RC
609 Josh Axelson RC 1.50 .45
Carmen Cali RC
610 Shaun Boyd RC 1.50 .45
Chris Morris RC
611 Dan Moylan RC 1.50 .45
Tommy Arko RC
612 Luis Cotto RC 1.00 .30
Luis Escobar
613 Blake Williams RC 1.50 .45
Brandon Mims RC
614 Chris Russ RC 1.00 .30
Bryan Edwards
615 Joe Torres 1.00 .30
Ben Diggins
616 Hugh Quattlebaum RC 2.00 .60
Edwin Encarnacion RC
617 Brian Bass RC 1.50 .45
Odannis Ayala RC
618 Jason Kaanoi 1.00 .30
Michael Matthews RC UER
name misspelled Mathews
619 Stuart McFarland RC 1.50 .45
Adam Sterrett RC
620 David Krynzel 3.00 .90
Grady Sizemore
621 Keith Bucktrot 1.00 .30
Dane Sardinha
622 Anaheim Angels TC .75 .23
623 Ariz. Diamondbacks TC .75 .23
624 Atlanta Braves TC .75 .23
625 Baltimore Orioles TC .75 .23
626 Boston Red Sox TC .75 .23
627 Chicago Cubs TC .75 .23
628 Chicago White Sox TC .75 .23
629 Cincinnati Reds TC .75 .23
630 Cleveland Indians TC .75 .23
631 Colorado Rockies TC .75 .23
632 Detroit Tigers TC .75 .23
633 Florida Marlins TC .75 .23
634 Houston Astros TC .75 .23
635 K.C. Royals TC .75 .23
636 L.A. Dodgers TC .75 .23
637 Milw. Brewers TC .75 .23
638 Minnesota Twins TC .75 .23
639 Montreal Expos TC .75 .23
640 New York Mets TC .75 .23
641 New York Yankees TC 4.00 1.20
642 Oakland Athletics TC .75 .23
643 Phil. Phillies TC .75 .23
644 Pittsburgh Pirates TC .75 .23
645 San Diego Padres TC .75 .23
646 S.F. Giants TC .75 .23
647 Seattle Mariners TC .75 .23
648 St. Louis Cardinals TC .75 .23
649 T. Bay Devil Rays TC .75 .23
650 Texas Rangers TC .75 .23
651 Toronto Blue Jays TC .75 .23
652 Bucky Dent GM .50 .15
653 Jackie Robinson GM 2.00 .60
654 Roberto Clemente GM 2.50 .75
655 Nolan Ryan GM 3.00 .90
656 Kerry Wood GM 1.25 .35
657 Rickey Henderson GM 2.00 .60
658 Lou Brock GM 1.25 .35
659 David Wells GM .50 .15
660 Andruw Jones GM .50 .15
661 Carlton Fisk GM .75 .23

2001 Topps Chrome Retrofractors

Randomly inserted into packs at one in 12, this 661-card set is a complete parallel set of the 2001 Topps Chrome base set. Please note that these cards were produced with Topps Refractor technology.

Nm-Mt Ex-Mt
*STARS: 2.5X TO 6X BASIC CARDS...
*PROSPECTS 277-301/595-621: 2X TO 5X
*ROOKIES 277-301/595-621: 2X TO 5X

2001 Topps Chrome Before There Was Topps

This set parallels the regular Before There Was Topps insert cards. These cards were inserted at a rate of one in 20 2001 Topps Chrome series two hobby/retail packs.

Nm-Mt Ex-Mt
COMPLETE SET (10) 80.00 24.00
*REFRACTORS: 1.25X TO 3X BASIC BEFORE
SER.2 REFRACTOR ODDS 1:200 HOB/RET
BT1 Lou Gehrig 12.00 3.60
BT2 Babe Ruth 20.00 6.00
BT3 Cy Young 6.00 1.80
BT4 Walter Johnson 6.00 1.80
BT5 Ty Cobb 10.00 3.00
BT6 Rogers Hornsby 6.00 1.80
BT7 Honus Wagner 6.00 1.80
BT8 Christy Mathewson 6.00 1.80
BT9 Grover Alexander 6.00 1.80
BT10 Joe DiMaggio 12.00 3.60

2001 Topps Chrome Combos

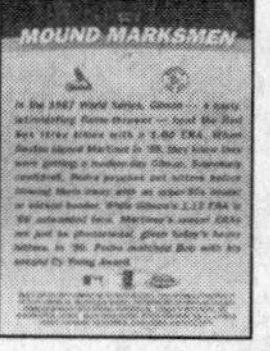

Randomly insert into packs at 1:12 Hobby/Retail and 1:4 HTA, this 10-card insert pairs up players that have put up similar statistics throughout their careers. Card backs carry a "TC" prefix. Please note that these cards feature Topps' special chrome technology.

Nm-Mt Ex-Mt
COMPLETE SET (20) 120.00 36.00
COMPLETE SERIES 1 (10) 60.00 18.00
COMPLETE SERIES 2 (10) 60.00 18.00
*REFRACTORS: 1.5X TO 4X BASIC COMBO
REFRACTOR ODDS 1:120 H/R
TC1 Derek Jeter 10.00 3.00
Yogi Berra
Whitey Ford
Don Mattingly
Reggie Jackson
TC2 Chipper Jones 3.00 .90
Mike Schmidt
TC3 Brooks Robinson 8.00 2.40
Cal Ripken
TC4 Bob Gibson 3.00 .90
Pedro Martinez
TC5 Ivan Rodriguez 3.00 .90
Johnny Bench
TC6 Ernie Banks 5.00 1.50
Alex Rodriguez
TC7 Joe Morgan 3.00 .90
Ken Griffey Jr.
Barry Larkin
Johnny Bench
TC8 Vladimir Guerrero 3.00 .90
Roberto Clemente
TC9 Ken Griffey Jr. 5.00 1.50
Hank Aaron
TC10 Casey Stengel MG 3.00 .90
Joe Torre
TC11 Kevin Brown 6.00 1.80
Sandy Koufax
Don Drysdale UER
Card states the Dodgers swept the 1965 World Series
They won the Series in 7 games
TC12 Mark McGwire 8.00 2.40
Sammy Sosa
Roger Maris
Babe Ruth
TC13 Ted Williams 5.00 1.50
Carl Yastrzemski
Nomar Garciaparra
TC14 Greg Maddux 5.00 1.50
Roger Clemens
Cy Young
TC15 Tony Gwynn 6.00 1.80
Ted Williams

TC16 Cal Ripken 10.00 3.00
Lou Gehrig
TC17 Sandy Koufax 10.00 3.00
Randy Johnson
Warren Spahn
Steve Carlton
TC18 Mike Piazza 4.00 1.20
Josh Gibson
TC19 Barry Bonds 8.00 2.40
Willie Mays
TC20 Jackie Robinson 3.00 .90
Larry Doby

2001 Topps Chrome Golden Anniversary

Randomly inserted into packs at 1:10 Hobby/Retail, this 50-card insert celibrates Topp's 50th Anniversary by taking a look at some of the all-time greats. Card backs carry a "GA" prefix. Please note that these cards feature Topps' special chrome technology.

Nm-Mt Ex-Mt
COMPLETE SET (50) 300.00 90.00
*REFRACTORS: 1.5X TO 4X BASIC ANNV.
SER.1 REFRACTOR ODDS 1:100
GA1 Hank Aaron 10.00 3.00
GA2 Ernie Banks 5.00 1.50
GA3 Mike Schmidt 10.00 3.00
GA4 Willie Mays 10.00 3.00
GA5 Johnny Bench 5.00 1.50
GA6 Tom Seaver 3.00 .90
GA7 Frank Robinson 3.00 .90
GA8 Sandy Koufax 15.00 4.50
GA9 Bob Gibson 3.00 .90
GA10 Ted Williams 10.00 3.00
GA11 Cal Ripken 15.00 4.50
GA12 Tony Gwynn 6.00 1.80
GA13 Mark McGwire 12.00 3.60
GA14 Ken Griffey Jr. 8.00 2.40
GA15 Greg Maddux 8.00 2.40
GA16 Roger Clemens 10.00 3.00
GA17 Barry Bonds 12.00 3.60
GA18 Rickey Henderson 5.00 1.50
GA19 Mike Piazza 8.00 2.40
GA20 Jose Canseco 5.00 1.50
GA21 Derek Jeter 12.00 3.60
GA22 Nomar Garciaparra 8.00 2.40
GA23 Alex Rodriguez 8.00 2.40
GA24 Sammy Sosa 8.00 2.40
GA25 Ivan Rodriguez 5.00 1.50
GA26 Vladimir Guerrero 5.00 1.50
GA27 Chipper Jones 5.00 1.50
GA28 Jeff Bagwell 3.00 .90
GA29 Pedro Martinez 5.00 1.50
GA30 Randy Johnson 5.00 1.50
GA31 Pat Burrell 2.00 .60
GA32 Josh Hamilton 2.00 .60
GA33 Ryan Anderson 2.00 .60
GA34 Corey Patterson 2.00 .60
GA35 Eric Munson 2.00 .60
GA36 Sean Burroughs 2.00 .60
GA37 C.C. Sabathia 2.00 .60
GA38 Chin-Feng Chen 2.00 .60
GA39 Barry Zito 3.00 .90
GA40 Adrian Gonzalez 2.00 .60
GA41 Mark McGwire 12.00 3.60
GA42 Nomar Garciaparra 8.00 2.40
GA43 Todd Helton 3.00 .90
GA44 Matt Williams 2.00 .60
GA45 Troy Glaus 2.00 .60
GA46 Geoff Jenkins 2.00 .60
GA47 Frank Thomas 5.00 1.50
GA48 Mo Vaughn 2.00 .60
GA49 Barry Larkin 3.00 .90
GA50 J.D. Drew 2.00 .60

2001 Topps Chrome King Of Kings

Randomly inserted into packs at 1:5,157 series one hobby and 1:5,209 series one retail and 1:6383 series two hobby and 1:6,520 series two retail, this seven-card insert features game-used memorabilia from major superstars. Please note that a special fourth card containing game-used memorabila of all three were inserted into Hobby packs at 1:59,220. Card backs carry a "KKR" prefix.

Nm-Mt Ex-Mt
KKR1 Hank Aaron 120.00 36.00
KKR2 Nolan Ryan Rangers 150.00 45.00
KKR3 Rickey Henderson 50.00 15.00
KKR4 Does Not Exist
KKR5 Bob Gibson 50.00 15.00
KKR6 Nolan Ryan Angels 150.00 45.00
KKGE Hank Aaron
Nolan Ryan
Rickey Henderson

2001 Topps Chrome King Of Kings Refractors

This insert is a complete parallel of the Chrome King of Kings insert set produced with Topps patented refractor technology. The first three cards were randomly inserted exclusively into first series hobby packs at 1:16,920. Cards 5 and 6 were randomly seeded exclusively into second series hobby packs at a rate of 1:23,022. Card number 4 in the set (intended to feature Mark McGwire) was never produced. Only ten of each card was printed and each is hand-numbered in their blue pen on back. Please note that a special "Golden Edition" card containing game-used memorabilia of Aaron, Ryan and Henderson was inserted into first series hobby packs at a rate of 1:212,169. Only 5 copies of this card were produced. Card backs carry a "KKR" prefix. Due to scarcity, no pricing is provided.

Nm-Mt Ex-Mt
KKR1 Hank Aaron/10
KKR2 Nolan Ryan Rangers/10
KKR3 Rickey Henderson/10
KKR4 Does Not Exist
KKR5 Bob Gibson/10
KKR6 Nolan Ryan Angels/10
KKGE Hank Aaron
Nolan Ryan
Rickey Henderson/5

2001 Topps Chrome Originals

Randomly inserted into Hobby packs at 1:1783 and Retail packs at 1:1788, this ten-card insert features game-used jersey cards of players like Roberto Clemente and Carl Yastrzemski produced with Topps patented chrome technology.

Nm-Mt Ex-Mt
REFRACT.1-5 SER.1 ODDS 1:9644 HOBBY
REFRACT.6-10 SER.2 ODDS 1:8372 HOBBY
REFRACTOR PRINT RUN 10 #'d SETS
NO REFRACTOR PRICE DUE TO SCARCITY
1 Roberto Clemente 300.00 90.00
2 Carl Yastrzemski 100.00 30.00
3 Mike Schmidt 100.00 30.00
4 Wade Boggs 40.00 12.00
5 Chipper Jones 60.00 18.00
6 Willie Mays 120.00 36.00
7 Lou Brock 40.00 12.00
8 Dave Parker 25.00 7.50
9 Barry Bonds 120.00 36.00
10 Alex Rodriguez 50.00 15.00

2001 Topps Chrome Past to Present

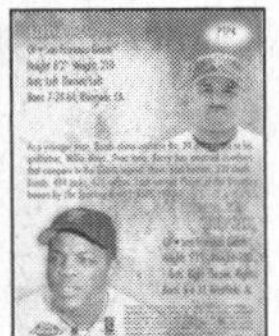

Randomly insert into packs at 1:18 Hobby/Retail, this 10-card insert pairs up players that have put up similar statistics throughout their careers. Card backs carry a "PTP" prefix. Please note that these cards feature Topps' special chrome technology.

Nm-Mt Ex-Mt
COMPLETE SET (10) 60.00 18.00
*REFRACTORS: 1.5X TO 4X BASIC PAST
SER.1 REFRACTOR ODDS 1:180
PTP1 Phil Rizzuto 12.00 3.60
Derek Jeter
PTP2 Warren Spahn 8.00 2.40
Greg Maddux
PTP3 Yogi Berra 10.00 3.00
Jorge Posada
PTP4 Willie Mays 20.00 6.00
Barry Bonds
PTP5 Red Schoendienst 4.00 1.20
Fernando Vina
PTP6 Duke Snider 4.00 1.20
Shawn Green
PTP7 Bob Feller 4.00 1.20
Bartolo Colon
PTP8 Johnny Mize 4.00 1.20
Tino Martinez
PTP9 Larry Doby 4.00 1.20
Manny Ramirez
PTP10 Eddie Mathews 5.00 1.50
Chipper Jones

2001 Topps Chrome Through the Years Reprints

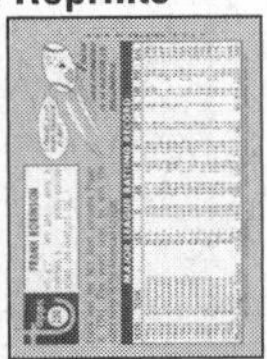

Randomly inserted into packs at 1:10 Hobby/Retail, this 50-card set takes a look at some of the best players to every make it onto a Topps trading card. Please note that these cards were produced with Topps chrome technology.

Nm-Mt Ex-Mt
COMPLETE SET (50) 300.00 90.00
*REFRACTORS: 1.5X TO 4X BASIC THROUGH
SER.1 REFRACTOR ODDS 1:100
1 Yogi Berra 57 6.00 1.80
2 Roy Campanella 56 6.00 1.80
3 Willie Mays 53 10.00 3.00
4 Andy Pafko 52 6.00 1.80
5 Jackie Robinson 52 6.00 1.80
6 Stan Musial 59 8.00 2.40
7 Duke Snider 56 5.00 1.50
8 Warren Spahn 56 5.00 1.50
9 Ted Williams 54 15.00 4.50
10 Eddie Mathews 55 6.00 1.80
11 Willie McCovey 60 5.00 1.50
12 Frank Robinson 69 5.00 1.50
13 Ernie Banks 66 6.00 1.80
14 Hank Aaron 65 10.00 3.00
15 Sandy Koufax 61 12.00 3.60
16 Bob Gibson 68 5.00 1.50
17 Harmon Killebrew 67 6.00 1.80
18 Whitey Ford 64 5.00 1.50
19 Roberto Clemente 63 15.00 4.50
20 Juan Marichal 61 5.00 1.50
21 Johnny Bench 70 6.00 1.80
22 Willie Stargell 73 5.00 1.50
23 Joe Morgan 74 5.00 1.50
24 Carl Yastrzemski 71 8.00 2.40
25 Reggie Jackson 76 5.00 1.50
26 Tom Seaver 78 5.00 1.50
27 Steve Carlton 77 5.00 1.50
28 Jim Palmer 79 5.00 1.50
29 Rod Carew 72 5.00 1.50
30 George Brett 75 20.00 6.00
31 Roger Clemens 85 12.00 3.60
32 Don Mattingly 84 20.00 6.00
33 Ryne Sandberg 89 10.00 3.00
34 Mike Schmidt 81 10.00 3.00
35 Cal Ripken 82 20.00 6.00
36 Tony Gwynn 83 8.00 2.40
37 Ozzie Smith 87 10.00 3.00
38 Wade Boggs 88 5.00 1.50
39 Nolan Ryan 80 15.00 4.50
40 Robin Yount 86 10.00 3.00
41 Mark McGwire 99 12.00 3.60
42 Ken Griffey Jr. 92 8.00 2.40
43 Sammy Sosa 90 8.00 2.40
44 Alex Rodriguez 98 8.00 2.40
45 Barry Bonds 94 12.00 3.60
46 Mike Piazza 95 8.00 2.40
47 Chipper Jones 91 6.00 1.80
48 Greg Maddux 96 8.00 2.40
49 Nomar Garciaparra 97 8.00 2.40
50 Derek Jeter 93 15.00 4.50

2001 Topps Chrome What Could Have Been

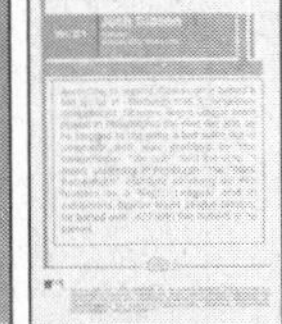

Inserted a rate of one in 30 hobby/retail packs, these 10 cards parallel the regular What Could Have Been retail set.

Nm-Mt Ex-Mt
COMPLETE SET (10) 40.00 12.00
*REFRACTORS: 1.5X TO 4X BASIC WHAT
SER.2 REFRACTOR ODDS 1:300 HOB/RET
WCB1 Josh Gibson 10.00 3.00
WCB2 Satchel Paige 4.00 1.20
WCB3 Buck Leonard 4.00 1.20
WCB4 James Bell 4.00 1.20
WCB5 Rube Foster 4.00 1.20
WCB6 Martin DiHigo 4.00 1.20
WCB7 William Johnson 4.00 1.20
WCB8 Mule Suttles 4.00 1.20
WCB9 Ray Dandridge 4.00 1.20
WCB10 John Lloyd 4.00 1.20

2001 Topps Chrome Traded

This set is a parallel to the 2001 Topps Traded set. Inserted into the 2001 Topps Traded at a rate of two per pack, these cards feature the patented "Chrome" technology which Topps uses.

Nm-Mt Ex-Mt
COMPLETE SET (266) 150.00 45.00
COMMON (1-99/145-266) .75 .23
COMMON (100-144) 1.25 .35
T1 Sandy Alomar Jr. .75 .23
T2 Kevin Appier 1.25 .35
T3 Brad Ausmus .75 .23
T4 Derek Bell .75 .23
T5 Bret Boone 1.25 .35
T6 Rico Brogna .75 .23
T7 Ellis Burks 1.25 .35
T8 Ken Caminiti 1.25 .35
T9 Roger Cedeno .75 .23
T10 Royce Clayton .75 .23
T11 Enrique Wilson .75 .23
T12 Rheal Cormier .75 .23
T13 Eric Davis 1.25 .35
T14 Shawon Dunston .75 .23
T15 Andres Galarraga 1.25 .35
T16 Tom Gordon .75 .23
T17 Mark Grace 2.00 .60
T18 Jeffrey Hammonds .75 .23
T19 Dustin Hermanson .75 .23
T20 Quinton McCracken .75 .23
T21 Todd Hundley .75 .23
T22 Charles Johnson 1.25 .35
T23 Marquis Grissom 1.25 .35
T24 Jose Mesa .75 .23
T25 Brian Boehringer .75 .23
T26 John Rocker .75 .23
T27 Jeff Frye .75 .23
T28 Reggie Sanders .75 .23
T29 David Segui .75 .23
T30 Mike Sirotka .75 .23
T31 Fernando Tatis .75 .23
T32 Steve Trachsel .75 .23
T33 Ismael Valdes .75 .23
T34 Randy Velarde .75 .23
T35 Ryan Kohlmeier .75 .23
T36 Mike Bordick 1.25 .35
T37 Kent Bottenfield .75 .23
T38 Pat Rapp .75 .23
T39 Jeff Nelson .75 .23
T40 Ricky Bottalico .75 .23
T41 Luke Prokopec .75 .23
T42 Hideo Nomo 3.00 .90
T43 Bill Mueller 1.25 .35
T44 Roberto Kelly .75 .23
T45 Chris Holt .75 .23
T46 Mike Jackson .75 .23
T47 Devon White 1.25 .35
T48 Gerald Williams .75 .23
T49 Eddie Taubensee .75 .23
T50 Brian Hunter UER .75 .23
Brian R Hunter pictured
Brian L Hunter stats
T51 Nelson Cruz .75 .23
T52 Jeff Fassero .75 .23
T53 Bubba Trammell .75 .23
T54 Bo Porter .75 .23
T55 Greg Norton .75 .23
T56 Benito Santiago 1.25 .35
T57 Ruben Rivera .75 .23
T58 Dee Brown .75 .23
T59 Jose Canseco 3.00 .90
T60 Chris Michalak .75 .23
T61 Tim Worrell .75 .23
T62 Matt Clement .75 .23
T63 Bill Pulsipher .75 .23
T64 Troy Brohawn RC 1.00 .30
T65 Mark Kotsay .75 .23
T66 Jimmy Rollins 1.25 .35
T67 Shea Hillenbrand 1.25 .35
T68 Ted Lilly .75 .23
T69 Jermaine Dye 1.25 .35
T70 Jerry Hairston Jr. .75 .23
T71 John Mabry .75 .23
T72 Kurt Abbott .75 .23
T73 Eric Owens .75 .23
T74 Jeff Brantley .75 .23
T75 Roy Oswalt 2.00 .60
T76 Doug Mientkiewicz 1.25 .35
T77 Rickey Henderson 3.00 .90
T78 Jason Grimsley .75 .23
T79 Christian Parker RC 1.00 .30
T80 Donne Wall .75 .23
T81 Alex Arias .75 .23
T82 Willis Roberts .75 .23
T83 Ryan Minor .75 .23
T84 Jason LaRue .75 .23
T85 Ruben Sierra .75 .23
T86 Johnny Damon 2.00 .60
T87 Juan Gonzalez 2.00 .60
T88 C.C. Sabathia 1.25 .35
T89 Tony Batista 1.25 .35
T90 Jay Witasick .75 .23
T91 Brent Abernathy .75 .23
T92 Paul LoDuca 1.25 .35
T93 Wes Helms .75 .23
T94 Mark Wohlers .75 .23
T95 Rob Bell .75 .23
T96 Tim Redding .75 .23
T97 Bud Smith RC 1.00 .30
T98 Adam Dunn 2.00 .60
T99 Ichiro Suzuki 25.00 7.50
Albert Pujols ROY
T100 Carlton Fisk 81 2.00 .60
T101 Tim Raines 81 1.25 .35
T102 Juan Marichal 74 1.25 .35
T103 Dave Winfield 81 1.25 .35
T104 Reggie Jackson 82 2.00 .60
T105 Cal Ripken 82 10.00 3.00
T106 Ozzie Smith 82 5.00 1.50
T107 Tom Seaver 83 2.00 .60
T108 Lou Piniella 74 1.25 .35
T109 Dwight Gooden 84 1.25 .35
T110 Bret Saberhagen 84 1.25 .35
T111 Gary Carter 85 1.25 .35
T112 Jack Clark 85 1.25 .35
T113 Rickey Henderson 85 3.00 .90
T114 Barry Bonds 86 8.00 2.40
T115 Bobby Bonilla 86 1.25 .35
T116 Jose Canseco 86 3.00 .90
T117 Will Clark 86 3.00 .90
T118 Andres Galarraga 86 1.25 .35
T119 Bo Jackson 86 3.00 .90
T120 Wally Joyner 86 1.25 .35
T121 Ellis Burks 87 1.25 .35
T122 David Cone 87 1.25 .35
T123 Greg Maddux 87 5.00 1.50
T124 Willie Randolph 76 1.25 .35
T125 Dennis Eckersley 87 1.25 .35
T126 Matt Williams 87 1.25 .35
T127 Joe Morgan 81 1.25 .35
T128 Fred McGriff 87 2.00 .60
T129 Roberto Alomar 88 2.00 .60
T130 Lee Smith 88 1.25 .35
T131 David Wells 88 1.25 .35
T132 Ken Griffey Jr. 89 5.00 1.50
T133 Deion Sanders 89 2.00 .60
T134 Nolan Ryan 89 8.00 2.40
T135 David Justice 90 1.25 .35
T136 Joe Carter 91 1.25 .35
T137 Jack Morris 92 1.25 .35
T138 Mike Piazza 93 5.00 1.50
T139 Barry Bonds 93 8.00 2.40
T140 Terrence Long 94 1.25 .35
T141 Ben Grieve 94 1.25 .35
T142 Richie Sexson 95 1.25 .35
George Arias
Mark Sweeney
Brian Schneider
T143 Sean Burroughs 99 1.25 .35
T144 Alfonso Soriano 99 2.00 .60
T145 Bob Boone MG 1.25 .35
T146 Larry Bowa MG 1.25 .35
T147 Bob Brenly MG .75 .23
T148 Buck Martinez MG .75 .23
T149 L. McClendon MG .75 .23
T150 Jim Tracy MG .75 .23
T151 Jared Abruzzo RC 1.00 .30
T152 Kurt Ainsworth .75 .23
T153 Willie Bloomquist 1.25 .35
T154 Ben Broussard .75 .23
T155 Bobby Bradley .75 .23
T156 Mike Bynum .75 .23
T157 A.J. Hinch .75 .23
T158 Ryan Christianson .75 .23
T159 Carlos Silva .75 .23
T160 Joe Crede .75 .23
T161 Jack Cust .75 .23
T162 Ben Diggins .75 .23
T163 Phil Dumatrait .75 .23
T164 Alex Escobar .75 .23
T165 Miguel Olivo .75 .23
T166 Chris George .75 .23
T167 Marcus Giles 1.25 .35
T168 Keith Ginter .75 .23
T169 Josh Girdley .75 .23
T170 Tony Alvarez .75 .23
T171 Scott Seabol .75 .23
T172 Josh Hamilton .75 .23
T173 Jason Hart .75 .23
T174 Israel Alcantara .75 .23
T175 Jake Peavy 5.00 1.50
T176 Stubby Clapp RC 1.00 .30
T177 D'Angelo Jimenez .75 .23
T178 Nick Johnson .75 .23
T179 Ben Johnson .75 .23
T180 Larry Bigbie .75 .23
T181 Allen Levrault .75 .23
T182 Felipe Lopez .75 .23
T183 Sean Burnett .75 .23
T184 Nick Neugebauer .75 .23
T185 Austin Kearns 1.25 .35
T186 Corey Patterson 1.25 .35
T187 Carlos Pena .75 .23
T188 R. Rodriguez RC 1.00 .30
T189 Juan Rivera .75 .23
T190 Grant Roberts .75 .23
T191 Adam Pettyjohn RC 1.00 .30
T192 Jared Sandberg .75 .23
T193 Xavier Nady .75 .23
T194 Dane Sardinha .75 .23
T195 Shawn Sonnier .75 .23
T196 Rafael Soriano 1.25 .35
T197 Brian Specht RC 1.00 .30
T198 Aaron Myette .75 .23
T199 Juan Uribe RC 1.25 .35
T200 Jayson Werth .75 .23
T201 Brad Wilkerson .75 .23
T202 Horacio Estrada .75 .23
T203 Joel Pineiro 3.00 .90
T204 Matt LeCroy .75 .23
T205 Michael Coleman .75 .23
T206 Ben Sheets 2.00 .60
T207 Eric Byrnes .75 .23
T208 Sean Burroughs 1.25 .35
T209 Ken Harvey .75 .23
T210 Travis Hafner 4.00 1.20
T211 Erick Almonte 1.00 .30
T212 Jason Belcher RC 1.00 .30
T213 Wilson Betemit RC 1.00 .30
T214 Hank Blalock RC 15.00 4.50
T215 Danny Borrell 1.00 .30
T216 John Buck RC 1.25 .35
T217 Freddie Bynum RC 1.00 .30
T218 Noel Devarez RC 1.00 .30
T219 Juan Diaz RC 1.00 .30
T220 Felix Diaz RC 1.00 .30
T221 Josh Fogg RC 1.00 .30
T222 Matt Ford RC 1.00 .30
T223 Scott Heard .75 .23
T224 Ben Hendrickson RC 1.25 .35
T225 Cody Ross RC 1.00 .30
T226 A. Hernandez RC 1.00 .30
T227 Alfredo Amezaga RC 1.00 .30
T228 Bob Keppel RC 1.25 .35
T229 Ryan Madson RC 2.00 .60
T230 Octavio Martinez RC 1.00 .30
T231 Hee Seop Choi 2.00 .60
T232 Thomas Mitchell .75 .23
T233 Luis Montanez 1.00 .30
T234 Andy Morales RC 1.00 .30
T235 Justin Morneau RC 15.00 4.50
T236 Toe Nash RC 1.00 .30
T237 V. Pascucci RC 1.00 .30
T238 Roy Smith RC 1.00 .30
T239 Antonio Perez RC 1.00 .30
T240 Chad Petty RC 1.00 .30
T241 Steve Smyth 1.00 .30
T242 Jose Reyes RC 8.00 2.40
T243 Eric Reynolds RC 1.00 .30
T244 Dominic Rich 1.00 .30
T245 J. Richardson RC 1.00 .30
T246 Ed Rogers RC 1.00 .30
T247 Albert Pujols 60.00 18.00
T248 Esix Snead RC 1.00 .30
T249 Luis Torres RC 1.00 .30
T250 Matt White RC 1.00 .30
T251 Blake Williams 1.00 .30
T252 Chris Russ 1.00 .30
T253 Joe Kennedy RC 1.25 .35
T254 Jeff Randazzo RC 1.00 .30
T255 Beau Hale RC 1.00 .30
T256 Brad Hennessey RC 3.00 .90
T257 Jake Gautreau RC 1.00 .30
T258 Jeff Mathis RC 4.00 1.20
T259 Aaron Heilman RC 1.00 .30
T260 B. Sardinha RC 2.00 .60
T261 Irvin Guzman RC 10.00 3.00
T262 Gabe Gross RC 1.25 .35
T263 J.D. Martin RC 1.00 .30
T264 Chris Smith RC 1.00 .30
T265 Kenny Baugh RC 1.00 .30
T266 Ichiro Suzuki RC 30.00 9.00

2001 Topps Chrome Traded Retrofractors

This set is a parallel to the 2001 Topps Chrome Traded set. Inserted into the 2001 Topps Traded at a rate of one in 12, these cards feature grayback card stock with refractor technology on the front.

Nm-Mt Ex-Mt
*STARS: 1.5X TO 4X BASIC CARDS...
*REPRINTS: 1X TO 2.5X BASIC.........
*ROOKIES: 1.25X TO 3X BASIC.........
T99 Ichiro Suzuki 100.00 30.00
Albert Pujols ROY
T214 Hank Blalock 50.00 15.00
T242 Jose Reyes 25.00 7.50
T247 Albert Pujols 175.00 52.50
T258 Jeff Mathis 50.00 15.00
T266 Ichiro Suzuki 100.00 30.00

2002 Topps Chrome

This product's first series, consisting of cards 1-6 and 8-331, was released in late January, 2002. The second series, consisting of cards 366-695, was released in early June, 2002. Both first and second series packs contained four cards and carried an SRP of $3. Sealed boxes contained 24 packs. The set parallels the 2002 Topps set except, of course, for the upgraded chrome card stock. Unlike the 1999 Topps Chrome product, featuring 70 variations of Mark McGwire's Home Run record card, the 2002 first series product did not include different variations of the Barry Bonds Home Run record cards. Please note, that just as in the basic 2002 Topps set there is no card number 7 as it is still retired in honor of Mickey Mantle. In addition, the foil-coated subset cards from the basic Topps set (cards 332-365 and 696-719) were NOT replicated for this Chrome set, thus it's considered complete at 660 cards. Notable Rookie Cards include Kazuhisa Ishii and Joe Mauer.

Nm-Mt Ex-Mt
COMPLETE SET (660) 300.00 90.00
COMPLETE SERIES 1 (330) 150.00 45.00
COMPLETE SERIES 2 (330) 150.00 45.00
COMMON (1-331/366-695) .50 .15
COMMON (307-326/671-690) 1.50 .45
COMMON (327-331/691-695) 1.50 .45
1 Pedro Martinez 2.50 .75
2 Mike Stanton .50 .15
3 Brad Penny .50 .15
4 Mike Matheny 1.00 .30
5 Johnny Damon 1.50 .45
6 Bret Boone 1.00 .30
7 Does Not Exist
8 Chris Truby .50 .15
9 B.J. Surhoff 1.00 .30
10 Mike Hampton 1.00 .30
11 Juan Pierre 1.00 .30
12 Mark Buehrle 1.00 .30
13 Bob Abreu 1.00 .30
14 David Cone 1.00 .30
15 Aaron Sele .50 .15
16 Fernando Tatis .50 .15
17 Bobby Jones .50 .15
18 Rick Helling .50 .15
19 Dmitri Young 1.00 .30
20 Mike Mussina 1.50 .45
21 Mike Sweeney 1.00 .30
22 Cristian Guzman .50 .15
23 Ryan Kohlmeier .50 .15
24 Adam Kennedy .50 .15
25 Larry Walker 1.50 .45
26 Eric Davis 1.00 .30
27 Jason Tyner .50 .15
28 Eric Young .50 .15
29 Jason Marquis .50 .15
30 Luis Gonzalez 1.00 .30
31 Kevin Tapani .50 .15
32 Orlando Cabrera 1.00 .30
33 Marty Cordova .50 .15
34 Brad Ausmus .50 .15
35 Livan Hernandez .50 .15
36 Alex Gonzalez .50 .15
37 Edgar Renteria 1.00 .30
38 Bengie Molina .50 .15
39 Frank Menechino .50 .15
40 Rafael Palmeiro 1.50 .45
41 Brad Fullmer .50 .15
42 Julio Zuleta .50 .15
43 Darren Dreifort .50 .15
44 Trot Nixon 1.00 .30
45 Trevor Hoffman 1.00 .30
46 Vladimir Nunez .50 .15
47 Mark Kotsay .50 .15
48 Kenny Rogers 1.00 .30
49 Ben Petrick .50 .15
50 Jeff Bagwell 1.50 .45
51 Juan Encarnacion .50 .15
52 Ramiro Mendoza .50 .15
53 Brian Meadows .50 .15
54 Chad Curtis .50 .15
55 Aramis Ramirez 1.00 .30
56 Mark McLemore .50 .15
57 Dante Bichette 1.00 .30
58 Scott Schoeneweis .50 .15
59 Jose Cruz Jr. .50 .15
60 Roger Clemens 5.00 1.50
61 Jose Guillen 1.00 .30
62 Darren Oliver .50 .15
63 Chris Reitsma .50 .15
64 Jeff Abbott .50 .15
65 Robin Ventura 1.00 .30
66 Denny Neagle .50 .15
67 Al Martin .50 .15
68 Benito Santiago 1.00 .30
69 Roy Oswalt 1.00 .30
70 Juan Gonzalez 1.50 .45
71 Garret Anderson 1.00 .30
72 Bobby Bonilla 1.00 .30
73 Danny Bautista .50 .15
74 J.T. Snow 1.00 .30
75 Derek Jeter 6.00 1.80
76 John Olerud 1.00 .30
77 Kevin Appier 1.00 .30
78 Phil Nevin 1.00 .30
79 Sean Casey 1.00 .30
80 Troy Glaus 1.00 .30
81 Joe Randa .50 .15
82 Jose Valentin .50 .15
83 Ricky Bottalico .50 .15
84 Todd Zeile 1.00 .30
85 Barry Larkin 1.50 .45
86 Bob Wickman .50 .15
87 Jeff Shaw .50 .15
88 Greg Vaughn .50 .15
89 Fernando Vina .50 .15
90 Mark Mulder 1.00 .30
91 Paul Bako .50 .15
92 Aaron Boone 1.00 .30
93 Esteban Loaiza .50 .15
94 Richie Sexson 1.00 .30
95 Alfonso Soriano 1.50 .45
96 Tony Womack .50 .15
97 Paul Shuey .50 .15
98 Melvin Mora 1.00 .30
99 Tony Gwynn 3.00 .90
100 Vladimir Guerrero 2.50 .75
101 Keith Osik .50 .15
102 Bud Smith .50 .15
103 Scott Williamson .50 .15
104 Daryle Ward .50 .15
105 Doug Mientkiewicz 1.00 .30
106 Stan Javier .50 .15
107 Russ Ortiz 1.00 .30
108 Wade Miller .50 .15
109 Luke Prokopec .50 .15
110 Andruw Jones 1.00 .30
111 Ron Coomer .50 .15
112 Dan Wilson .50 .15
113 Luis Castillo .50 .15
114 Derek Bell .50 .15
115 Gary Sheffield 1.00 .30
116 Ruben Rivera .50 .15
117 Paul O'Neill 1.50 .45
118 Craig Paquette .50 .15
119 Kelvim Escobar .50 .15
120 Brad Radke 1.00 .30
121 Jorge Fabregas .50 .15
122 Randy Winn .50 .15
123 Tom Goodwin .50 .15
124 Jaret Wright .50 .15
125 Barry Bonds HR 73 40.00 12.00
126 Al Leiter .50 .15
127 Ben Davis .50 .15
128 Frank Catalanotto .50 .15
129 Jose Cabrera .50 .15
130 Magglio Ordonez 1.00 .30
131 Jose Macias .50 .15
132 Ted Lilly .50 .15
133 Chris Holt .50 .15
134 Eric Milton .50 .15
135 Shannon Stewart 1.00 .30
136 Omar Olivares .50 .15
137 David Segui .50 .15
138 Jeff Nelson .50 .15
139 Matt Williams 1.00 .30
140 Ellis Burks 1.00 .30
141 Jason Bere .50 .15
142 Jimmy Haynes .50 .15
143 Ramon Hernandez .50 .15
144 Craig Counsell .50 .15
145 John Smoltz 1.50 .45
146 Homer Bush .50 .15
147 Quilvio Veras .50 .15
148 Esteban Yan .50 .15
149 Ramon Ortiz .50 .15
150 Carlos Delgado 1.00 .30
151 Lee Stevens .50 .15
152 Wil Cordero .50 .15
153 Mike Bordick 1.00 .30
154 John Flaherty .50 .15
155 Omar Daal .50 .15
156 Todd Ritchie .50 .15
157 Carl Everett 1.00 .30
158 Scott Sullivan .50 .15
159 Deivi Cruz .50 .15
160 Albert Pujols 5.00 1.50
161 Royce Clayton .50 .15
162 Jeff Suppan .50 .15
163 C.C. Sabathia 1.00 .30
164 Jimmy Rollins 1.00 .30
165 Rickey Henderson 2.50 .75
166 Rey Ordonez .50 .15
167 Shawn Estes .50 .15
168 Reggie Sanders .50 .15
169 Jon Lieber .50 .15
170 Armando Benitez 1.00 .30
171 Mike Remlinger .50 .15
172 Billy Wagner 1.00 .30
173 Troy Percival 1.00 .30
174 Devon White 1.00 .30
175 Ivan Rodriguez 2.50 .75
176 Dustin Hermanson .50 .15
177 Brian Anderson .50 .15
178 Graeme Lloyd .50 .15
179 Russell Branyan .50 .15
180 Bobby Higginson 1.00 .30
181 Alex Gonzalez .50 .15
182 John Franco 1.00 .30
183 Sidney Ponson .50 .15
184 Jose Mesa .50 .15
185 Todd Hollandsworth .50 .15
186 Kevin Young .50 .15
187 Tim Wakefield 1.00 .30
188 Craig Biggio 1.50 .45
189 Jason Isringhausen 1.00 .30
190 Mark Quinn .50 .15
191 Glendon Rusch .50 .15
192 Damian Miller .50 .15
193 Sandy Alomar Jr. .50 .15
194 Scott Brosius 1.00 .30
195 Dave Martinez .50 .15
196 Danny Graves .50 .15
197 Shea Hillenbrand 1.00 .30
198 Jimmy Anderson .50 .15
199 Travis Lee .50 .15
200 Randy Johnson 2.50 .75
201 Carlos Beltran 1.50 .45
202 Jerry Hairston .50 .15
203 Jesus Sanchez .50 .15
204 Eddie Taubensee .50 .15
205 David Wells 1.00 .30
206 Russ Davis .50 .15
207 Michael Barrett .50 .15
208 Marquis Grissom 1.00 .30
209 Byung-Hyun Kim 1.00 .30
210 Hideo Nomo 2.50 .75
211 Ryan Rupe .50 .15
212 Ricky Gutierrez .50 .15
213 Darryl Kile 1.00 .30
214 Rico Brogna .50 .15
215 Terrence Long .50 .15
216 Mike Jackson .50 .15
217 Jamey Wright .50 .15
218 Adrian Beltre 1.50 .45
219 Benny Agbayani .50 .15
220 Chuck Knoblauch 1.00 .30
221 Randy Wolf .50 .15
222 Andy Ashby .50 .15
223 Corey Koskie 1.00 .30
224 Roger Cedeno .50 .15
225 Ichiro Suzuki 4.00 1.20
226 Keith Foulke 1.00 .30
227 Ryan Minor .50 .15
228 Shawon Dunston .50 .15
229 Alex Cora .50 .15
230 Jeromy Burnitz 1.00 .30
231 Mark Grace 1.50 .45
232 Aubrey Huff 1.00 .30
233 Jeffrey Hammonds .50 .15
234 Olmedo Saenz .50 .15
235 Brian Jordan 1.00 .30
236 Jeremy Giambi .50 .15
237 Joe Girardi .50 .15
238 Eric Gagne 2.50 .75
239 Masato Yoshii .50 .15
240 Greg Maddux 4.00 1.20
241 Bryan Rekar .50 .15
242 Ray Durham 1.00 .30
243 Torii Hunter 1.00 .30
244 Derrek Lee 1.00 .30
245 Jim Edmonds 1.00 .30
246 Einar Diaz .50 .15
247 Brian Bohanon .50 .15
248 Ron Belliard .50 .15
249 Mike Lowell 1.00 .30
250 Sammy Sosa 4.00 1.20
251 Richard Hidalgo .50 .15
252 Bartolo Colon 1.00 .30
253 Jorge Posada 1.50 .45
254 Latroy Hawkins .50 .15
255 Paul LoDuca 1.00 .30
256 Carlos Febles .50 .15
257 Nelson Cruz .50 .15
258 Edgardo Alfonzo .50 .15
259 Joey Hamilton .50 .15
260 Cliff Floyd 1.00 .30
261 Wes Helms .50 .15
262 Jay Bell 1.00 .30
263 Mike Cameron 1.00 .30
264 Paul Konerko 1.00 .30
265 Jeff Kent 1.00 .30
266 Robert Fick .50 .15
267 Allen Levrault .50 .15
268 Placido Polanco .50 .15
269 Marlon Anderson .50 .15
270 Mariano Rivera 1.50 .45
271 Chan Ho Park 1.00 .30
272 Jose Vizcaino .50 .15
273 Jeff D'Amico .50 .15
274 Mark Gardner .50 .15
275 Travis Fryman 1.00 .30
276 Darren Lewis .50 .15
277 Bruce Bochy MG .50 .15
278 Jerry Manuel MG .50 .15
279 Bob Brenly MG .50 .15
280 Don Baylor MG 1.00 .30
281 Davey Lopes MG 1.00 .30
282 Jerry Narron MG .50 .15
283 Tony Muser MG .50 .15
284 Hal McRae MG 1.00 .30
285 Bobby Cox MG .50 .15
286 Larry Dierker MG .50 .15
287 Phil Garner MG .50 .15
288 Joe Kerrigan MG .50 .15
289 Bobby Valentine MG .50 .15
290 Dusty Baker MG 1.00 .30
291 Lloyd McClendon MG .50 .15
292 Mike Scioscia MG .50 .15
293 Buck Martinez MG .50 .15
294 Larry Bowa MG 1.00 .30
295 Tony LaRussa MG 1.00 .30
296 Jeff Torborg MG .50 .15
297 Tom Kelly MG .50 .15
298 Mike Hargrove MG .50 .15
299 Art Howe MG .50 .15
300 Lou Piniella MG 1.00 .30
301 Charlie Manuel MG .50 .15
302 Buddy Bell MG 1.00 .30
303 Tony Perez MG 1.00 .30
304 Bob Boone MG 1.00 .30
305 Joe Torre MG 2.50 .75
306 Jim Tracy MG .50 .15
307 Jason Lane PROS 1.50 .45
308 Chris George PROS 1.50 .45
309 Hank Blalock PROS 2.50 .75
310 Joe Borchard PROS 1.50 .45
311 Marlon Byrd PROS 1.50 .45
312 Ray. Cabrera PROS RC 1.50 .45
313 Fr. Sanchez PROS RC 1.50 .45
314 Scott Wiggins PROS RC 1.50 .45
315 Jason Maule PROS RC 1.50 .45
316 Dionys Cesar PROS RC 1.50 .45
317 Boof Bonser PROS 1.50 .45
318 Juan Tolentino PROS RC 1.50 .45
319 Earl Snyder PROS RC 2.50 .75
320 Travis Wade PROS RC 1.50 .45
321 Nap. Calzado PROS RC 1.50 .45
322 Eric Glaser PROS 1.50 .45
323 Craig Kuzmic PROS RC 1.50 .45
324 Nic Jackson PROS RC 1.50 .45
325 Mike Rivera PROS 1.50 .45
326 Jason Bay PROS RC 6.00 1.80
327 Chris Smith DP 1.50 .45
328 Jake Gautreau DP 1.50 .45
329 Gabe Gross DP 1.50 .45
330 Kenny Baugh DP 1.50 .45
331 J.D. Martin DP 1.50 .45
366 Pat Meares .50 .15
367 Mike Lieberthal 1.00 .30
368 Larry Bigbie .50 .15
369 Ron Gant 1.00 .30
370 Moises Alou 1.00 .30
371 Chad Kreuter .50 .15
372 Willis Roberts .50 .15
373 Toby Hall .50 .15
374 Miguel Batista .50 .15
375 John Burkett .50 .15
376 Cory Lidle .50 .15
377 Nick Neugebauer .50 .15
378 Jay Payton .50 .15
379 Steve Karsay .50 .15
380 Eric Chavez 1.00 .30
381 Kelly Stinnett .50 .15
382 Jarrod Washburn .50 .15
383 Rick White .50 .15
384 Jeff Conine 1.00 .30
385 Fred McGriff 1.50 .45
386 Marvin Benard .50 .15
387 Joe Crede .50 .15
388 Dennis Cook .50 .15
389 Rick Reed .50 .15
390 Tom Glavine 1.50 .45
391 Rondell White 1.00 .30
392 Matt Morris 1.00 .30
393 Pat Rapp .50 .15
394 Robert Person .50 .15
395 Omar Vizquel 1.50 .45
396 Jeff Cirillo .50 .15
397 Dave Mlicki .50 .15
398 Jose Ortiz .50 .15
399 Ryan Dempster .50 .15
400 Curt Schilling 1.00 .30
401 Peter Bergeron .50 .15
402 Kyle Lohse .50 .15
403 Craig Wilson 1.00 .30
404 David Justice 1.00 .30
405 Darin Erstad 1.00 .30
406 Jose Mercedes .50 .15
407 Carl Pavano 1.00 .30
408 Albie Lopez .50 .15
409 Alex Ochoa .50 .15
410 Chipper Jones 2.50 .75
411 Tyler Houston .50 .15
412 Dean Palmer 1.00 .30
413 Damian Jackson .50 .15
414 Josh Towers .50 .15
415 Rafael Furcal 1.00 .30
416 Mike Morgan .50 .15
417 Herb Perry .50 .15
418 Mike Sirotka .50 .15
419 Mark Wohlers .50 .15
420 Nomar Garciaparra 4.00 1.20
421 Felipe Lopez .50 .15
422 Joe McEwing .50 .15
423 Jacque Jones 1.00 .30
424 Julio Franco 1.00 .30
425 Frank Thomas 2.50 .75
426 So Taguchi RC 2.50 .75
427 Kazuhisa Ishii RC 5.00 1.50
428 D'Angelo Jimenez .50 .15
429 Chris Stynes .50 .15
430 Kerry Wood 2.50 .75
431 Chris Singleton .50 .15
432 Erubiel Durazo .50 .15
433 Matt Lawton .50 .15
434 Bill Mueller 1.00 .30
435 Jose Canseco 2.50 .75
436 Ben Grieve .50 .15
437 Terry Mulholland .50 .15
438 David Bell .50 .15
439 A.J. Pierzynski 1.00 .30
440 Adam Dunn 1.50 .45
441 Jon Garland .50 .15
442 Jeff Fassero .50 .15
443 Julio Lugo .50 .15
444 Carlos Guillen 1.00 .30
445 Orlando Hernandez .50 .15
446 Mark Loretta 1.00 .30
447 Scott Spiezio .50 .15
448 Kevin Millwood 1.00 .30
449 Jamie Moyer 1.00 .30
450 Todd Helton 1.50 .45
451 Todd Walker .50 .15
452 Jose Lima .50 .15
453 Brook Fordyce .50 .15
454 Aaron Rowand 1.00 .30
455 Barry Zito 1.00 .30
456 Eric Owens .50 .15
457 Charles Nagy .50 .15
458 Raul Ibanez .50 .15
459 Joe Mays .50 .15
460 Jim Thome 2.50 .75
461 Adam Eaton .50 .15
462 Felix Martinez .50 .15
463 Vernon Wells 1.00 .30
464 Donnie Sadler .50 .15
465 Tony Clark .50 .15
466 Jose Hernandez .50 .15
467 Ramon Martinez .50 .15
468 Rusty Greer 1.00 .30
469 Rod Barajas .50 .15
470 Lance Berkman 1.00 .30
471 Brady Anderson 1.00 .30
472 Pedro Astacio .50 .15
473 Shane Halter .50 .15
474 Bret Prinz .50 .15
475 Edgar Martinez 1.50 .45
476 Steve Trachsel .50 .15
477 Gary Matthews Jr. .50 .15
478 Ismael Valdes .50 .15
479 Juan Uribe .50 .15
480 Shawn Green 1.00 .30
481 Kirk Rueter .50 .15
482 Damion Easley .50 .15
483 Chris Carpenter .50 .15
484 Kris Benson .50 .15
485 Antonio Alfonseca .50 .15
486 Kyle Farnsworth .50 .15
487 Brandon Lyon .50 .15
488 Hideki Irabu .50 .15
489 David Ortiz 1.50 .45
490 Mike Piazza 4.00 1.20
491 Derek Lowe 1.00 .30
492 Chris Gomez .50 .15
493 Mark Johnson .50 .15
494 John Rocker .50 .15
495 Eric Karros 1.00 .30
496 Bill Haselman .50 .15
497 Dave Veres .50 .15
498 Pete Harnisch .50 .15
499 Tomokazu Ohka .50 .15
500 Barry Bonds 6.00 1.80
501 David Dellucci .50 .15
502 Wendell Magee .50 .15
503 Tom Gordon .50 .15
504 Javier Vazquez 1.00 .30
505 Ben Sheets .50 .15
506 Wilton Guerrero .50 .15
507 John Halama .50 .15
508 Mark Redman .50 .15
509 Jack Wilson 1.00 .30
510 Bernie Williams 1.50 .45
511 Miguel Cairo .50 .15
512 Denny Hocking .50 .15
513 Tony Batista 1.00 .30
514 Mark Grudzielanek .50 .15
515 Jose Vidro .50 .15
516 Sterling Hitchcock .50 .15
517 Billy Koch .50 .15
518 Matt Clement .50 .15
519 Bruce Chen .50 .15
520 Roberto Alomar 1.50 .45
521 Orlando Palmeiro .50 .15
522 Steve Finley 1.00 .30
523 Danny Patterson .50 .15
524 Terry Adams .50 .15
525 Tino Martinez 1.50 .45
526 Tony Armas Jr. UER .50 .15
Career stats do not include pre-2001
527 Geoff Jenkins 1.00 .30
528 Kerry Robinson .50 .15
529 Corey Patterson 1.00 .30
530 Brian Giles 1.00 .30
531 Jose Jimenez .50 .15
532 Joe Kennedy .50 .15
533 Armando Rios .50 .15
534 Osvaldo Fernandez .50 .15
535 Ruben Sierra .50 .15
536 Octavio Dotel .50 .15
537 Luis Sojo .50 .15
538 Brent Butler .50 .15
539 Pablo Ozuna .50 .15
540 Freddy Garcia 1.00 .30
541 Chad Durbin .50 .15
542 Orlando Merced .50 .15
543 Michael Tucker .50 .15
544 Roberto Hernandez .50 .15
545 Pat Burrell 1.00 .30
546 A.J. Burnett .50 .15
547 Bubba Trammell .50 .15
548 Scott Elarton .50 .15
549 Mike Darr .50 .15
550 Ken Griffey Jr. 4.00 1.20
551 Ugueth Urbina .50 .15
552 Todd Jones .50 .15
553 Delino Deshields .50 .15
554 Adam Piatt .50 .15
555 Jason Kendall 1.00 .30
556 Hector Ortiz .50 .15
557 Turk Wendell .50 .15
558 Rob Bell .50 .15
559 Sun Woo Kim .50 .15
560 Raul Mondesi 1.00 .30
561 Brent Abernathy .50 .15
562 Seth Etherton .50 .15
563 Shawn Wooten .50 .15
564 Jay Buhner 1.00 .30
565 Andres Galarraga 1.00 .30
566 Shane Reynolds .50 .15
567 Rod Beck .50 .15
568 Dee Brown .50 .15
569 Pedro Feliz .50 .15
570 Ryan Klesko 1.00 .30
571 John Vander Wal .50 .15
572 Nick Bierbrodt .50 .15
573 Joe Nathan .50 .15
574 James Baldwin .50 .15
575 J.D. Drew 1.00 .30
576 Greg Colbrunn .50 .15
577 Doug Glanville .50 .15
578 Brandon Duckworth .50 .15
579 Shawn Chacon .50 .15
580 Rich Aurilia .50 .15
581 Chuck Finley 1.00 .30
582 Abraham Nunez .50 .15
583 Kenny Lofton 1.00 .30
584 Brian Daubach .50 .15
585 Miguel Tejada 1.00 .30
586 Nate Cornejo .50 .15
587 Kazuhiro Sasaki 1.00 .30
588 Chris Richard .50 .15
589 Armando Reynoso .50 .15
590 Tim Hudson 1.00 .30
591 Neifi Perez .50 .15
592 Steve Cox .50 .15
593 Henry Blanco .50 .15
594 Ricky Ledee .50 .15
595 Tim Salmon 1.50 .45
596 Luis Rivas .50 .15
597 Jeff Zimmerman .50 .15
598 Matt Stairs .50 .15
599 Preston Wilson 1.00 .30
600 Mark McGwire 6.00 1.80
601 Timo Perez .50 .15
602 Matt Anderson .50 .15
603 Todd Hundley .50 .15
604 Rick Ankiel .50 .15
605 Tsuyoshi Shinjo 1.00 .30
606 Woody Williams .50 .15
607 Jason LaRue .50 .15
608 Carlos Lee 1.00 .30
609 Russ Johnson .50 .15
610 Scott Rolen 2.50 .75
611 Brent Mayne .50 .15
612 Darrin Fletcher .50 .15
613 Ray Lankford .50 .15
614 Troy O'Leary .50 .15
615 Javier Lopez 1.00 .30
616 Randy Velarde .50 .15
617 Vinny Castilla 1.00 .30
618 Milton Bradley 1.00 .30
619 Ruben Mateo .50 .15
620 Jason Giambi Yankees 1.00 .30
621 Andy Benes .50 .15
622 Joe Mauer RC 10.00 3.00
623 Andy Pettitte 1.50 .45
624 Jose Offerman 1.00 .30
625 Mo Vaughn 1.00 .30
626 Steve Sparks .50 .15
627 Mike Matthews .50 .15

628 Robb Nen 1.00 .30
629 Kip Wells .50 .15
630 Kevin Brown 1.00 .30
631 Arthur Rhodes .50 .15
632 Gabe Kapler .50 .15
633 Jermaine Dye 1.00 .30
634 Josh Beckett 1.00 .30
635 Pokey Reese .50 .15
636 Benji Gil .50 .15
637 Marcus Giles 1.00 .30
638 Julian Tavarez .50 .15
639 Jason Schmidt 1.00 .30
640 Alex Rodriguez 4.00 1.20
641 Anaheim Angels TC 1.00 .30
642 Ariz. Diamondbacks TC 1.50 .45
643 Atlanta Braves TC 1.00 .30
644 Baltimore Orioles TC 1.00 .30
645 Boston Red Sox TC 1.00 .30
646 Chicago Cubs TC 1.00 .30
647 Chicago White Sox TC 1.00 .30
648 Cincinnati Reds TC 1.00 .30
649 Cleveland Indians TC 1.00 .30
650 Colorado Rockies TC 1.00 .30
651 Detroit Tigers TC 1.00 .30
652 Florida Marlins TC 1.00 .30
653 Houston Astros TC 1.00 .30
654 Kansas City Royals TC 1.00 .30
655 Los Angeles Dodgers TC 1.00 .30
656 Milwaukee Brewers TC 1.00 .30
657 Minnesota Twins TC 1.00 .30
658 Montreal Expos TC 1.00 .30
659 New York Mets TC 1.00 .30
660 New York Yankees TC 2.50 .75
661 Oakland Athletics TC 1.00 .30
662 Philadelphia Phillies TC 1.00 .30
663 Pittsburgh Pirates TC 1.00 .30
664 San Diego Padres TC 1.00 .30
665 San Francisco Giants TC 1.00 .30
666 Seattle Mariners TC 1.50 .45
667 St. Louis Cardinals TC 1.00 .30
668 T.B. Devil Rays TC 1.00 .30
669 Texas Rangers TC 1.00 .30
670 Toronto Blue Jays TC 1.00 .30
671 Juan Cruz PROS 1.50 .45
672 Kevin Cash PROS RC 1.50 .45
673 Jimmy Gobble PROS RC 2.50 .75
674 Mike Hill PROS RC 1.50 .45
675 T.Buchholz PROS RC 1.50 .45
676 Bill Hall PROS 1.50 .45
677 B.Roneberg PROS RC 1.50 .45
678 R.Huffman PROS RC 1.50 .45
679 Chris Tritle PROS RC 1.50 .45
680 Nate Espy PROS 1.50 .45
681 Nick Alvarez PROS RC 1.50 .45
682 Jason Botts PROS RC 2.50 .75
683 Ryan Gripp PROS RC 1.50 .45
684 Dan Phillips PROS RC 1.50 .45
685 Pablo Arias PROS RC 1.50 .45
686 J.Rodriguez PROS RC 1.50 .45
687 Rich Harden PROS RC 10.00 3.00
688 Neal Frendling PROS RC 1.50 .45
689 R.Thompson PROS RC 1.50 .45
690 G.Montalbano PROS RC 1.50 .45
691 Len Dinardo DP RC 1.50 .45
692 Ryan Raburn DP RC 1.50 .45
693 Josh Barfield DP RC 4.00 1.20
694 David Bacani DP RC 1.50 .45
695 Dan Johnson DP RC 2.50 .75

2002 Topps Chrome Black Refractors

Issued in second series hobby packs at a stated rate of one in 21, these cards parallel the 2002 Topps Chrome set. Black Refractors can be differentiated from the regular cards by their black borders. In addition, each card was serial-numbered to 50 in thin gold foil on the card back.

Nm-Mt Ex-Mt
*BLACK: 6X TO 15X BASIC CARDS
*BLACK 307-331/671-695: 5X TO 12X BASIC
125 Barry Bonds HR 73 250.00 75.00

2002 Topps Chrome Gold Refractors

Inserted into first and second series packs at stated odds of one in four, these cards parallel the 2002 Topps Chrome set. The cards can be differentiated by their striking gold borders and refractive sheen on front.

Nm-Mt Ex-Mt
*GOLD: 2X TO 5X BASIC
*GOLD 307-331/671-695: 1.5X TO 4X BASIC

2002 Topps Chrome 1952 Reprints

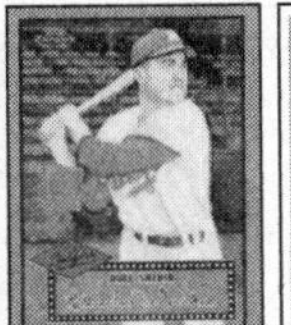

Issued in packs at stated odds of one in eight, these nineteen reprint cards feature players who participated in the 1952 World Series which was won by the New York Yankees.

Nm-Mt Ex-Mt
COMPLETE SET (19) 50.00 15.00
COMPLETE SERIES 1 (9) 25.00 7.50
COMPLETE SERIES 2 (10) 25.00 7.50
*REF: .75X TO 2X BASIC 52 REPRINTS
52R-1 Roy Campanella 5.00 1.50
52R-2 Duke Snider 4.00 1.20
52R-3 Carl Erskine 4.00 1.20
52R-4 Andy Pafko 4.00 1.20
52R-5 Johnny Mize 4.00 1.20
52R-6 Billy Martin 5.00 1.50
52R-7 Phil Rizzuto 5.00 1.50
52R-8 Gil McDougald 4.00 1.20
52R-9 Allie Reynolds 4.00 1.20
52R-10 Jackie Robinson 5.00 1.50
52R-11 Preacher Roe 4.00 1.20
52R-12 Gil Hodges 5.00 1.50
52R-13 Billy Cox 4.00 1.20
52R-14 Yogi Berra 5.00 1.50
52R-15 Gene Woodling 4.00 1.20
52R-16 Johnny Sain 4.00 1.20
52R-17 Ralph Houk 4.00 1.20
52R-18 Joe Collins 4.00 1.20
52R-19 Hank Bauer 4.00 1.20

2002 Topps Chrome 5-Card Stud Aces Relics

Inserted in second series packs at a stated rate of one in 140, these five cards feature leading pitchers along with a game-worn jersey swatch.

Nm-Mt Ex-Mt
5A-AL Al Leiter Jsy 15.00 4.50
5A-BZ Barry Zito Jsy 15.00 4.50
5A-CS Curt Schilling Jsy 15.00 4.50
5A-KB Kevin Brown Jsy 15.00 4.50
5A-TH Tim Hudson Jsy 15.00 4.50

2002 Topps Chrome 5-Card Stud Deuces are Wild Relics

Inserted in second series packs at an overall stated rate of one in 428, these three cards feature teammates as well as a piece of game-used memorabilia from each player.

Nm-Mt Ex-Mt
SER.2 BAT ODDS 1:1098
SER.2 UNIFORM ODDS 1:704
5D-BT Bernie Williams Bat
Tino Martinez Bat
5D-CA Chipper Jones Bat
Andruw Jones Bat
5D-RC Ryan Dempster Uni 15.00 4.50
Cliff Floyd Uni

2002 Topps Chrome 5-Card Stud Jack of all Trades Relics

Inserted in second series packs at a stated rate of one in 428, these three cards feature players who have all five tools along with a piece of game-used memorabilia of that player.

Nm-Mt Ex-Mt
SER.2 BAT ODDS 1:1098
SER.2 JERSEY ODDS 1:704
5J-AR Alex Rodriguez Bat
5J-CJ Chipper Jones Jsy 25.00 7.50
5J-MO Magglio Ordonez Bat

2002 Topps Chrome 5-Card Stud Kings of the Clubhouse Relics

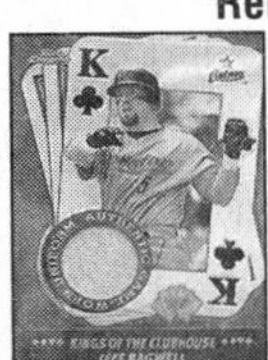

Inserted in second series packs at a stated rate of one in 303, these three cards feature three of the best team leaders along with a piece of game-used memorabilia from the featured player.

Nm-Mt Ex-Mt
SER.2 BAT ODDS 1:2204
SER.2 JERSEY ODDS 1:704
SER.2 UNIFORM ODDS 1:704
5K-AR Alex Rodriguez Bat
5K-JB Jeff Bagwell Uniform 20.00 6.00
5K-TG Tony Gwynn Jsy 30.00 9.00

2002 Topps Chrome 5-Card Stud Three of a Kind Relics

Inserted into second series packs at a stated rate of one in 689, these three cards feature a group of three teammates along with a piece of game-used memorabilia from each player.

Nm-Mt Ex-Mt
5TAIR Alex Rodriguez Bat 80.00 24.00
Ivan Rodriguez Jsy
Rafael Palmeiro Uni
5TBEJ Bret Boone Bat 80.00 24.00
Edgar Martinez Bat
John Olerud Bat
5TJCL Jeff Bagwell Uni 80.00 24.00
Craig Biggio Bat
Lance Berkman Bat

2002 Topps Chrome Summer School Like Father Like Son Relics

Issued in packs at stated odds of one in 790, this card features memorabilia from Preston and Mookie Wilson.

Nm-Mt Ex-Mt
FSC-WI Preston Wilson 15.00 4.50
Mookie Wilson

2002 Topps Chrome Summer School Battery Mates Relics

Inserted at overall odds of one in 349, these two cards feature memorabilia from a pitcher and catcher from the same team. The Hampton/Petrick card was seeded at a rate of 1:716 and the Glavine/Lopez at 1:681.

Nm-Mt Ex-Mt
BMC-GL Tom Glavine 25.00 7.50
Javier Lopez B
BMC-HP Mike Hampton 15.00 4.50
Ben Petrick A UER
Card has two jersey swatches on it

2002 Topps Chrome Summer School Top of the Order Relics

Inserted into packs at an overall rate of one in 106, these 12 cards featured players who lead off for their teams along with a memorabilia piece. Uniforms (a.k.a. pants), jerseys and bats were utilized for this set. Bat cards were seeded into five different groups at the following ratios: Group A 1:1383, Group B 1:1538, Group C 1:3170, Group D 1:2902, Group E 1:2544. Jersey cards were seeded into two groups as follows: Group A 1:790 and Group B 1:659. Uniform cards were seeded into three groups as follows: Group A 1:920, Group B 1:651 and Group C 1:614.

Nm-Mt Ex-Mt
TOC-BA Benny Agbayani Uni C 15.00 4.50
TOC-CB Craig Biggio Uni A 25.00 7.50
TOC-CK Chuck Knoblauch Bat E 15.00 4.50
TOC-JD Johnny Damon Bat B 25.00 7.50
TOC-JK Jason Kendall Bat D 15.00 4.50
TOC-JP Juan Pierre Bat A 15.00 4.50
TOC-KL Kenny Lofton Uni B 15.00 4.50
TOC-PB Peter Bergeron Jsy A 15.00 4.50
TOC-PL Paul LoDuca Bat A 15.00 4.50
TOC-RF Rafael Furcal Bat C 15.00 4.50
TOC-RH R.Henderson Bat B 25.00 7.50
TOC-SS Shannon Stewart Jsy B 15.00 4.50

2002 Topps Chrome Traded

Inserted at a stated rate of two per 2002 Topps Traded Hobby or Retail Pack and sever per 2002 Topps Traded HTA pack, this is a complete parallel of the 2002 Topps Traded set. Unlike the regular Topps Traded set, all cards are printed in equal quantities.

Nm-Mt Ex-Mt
COMPLETE SET (275) 120.00 36.00

Nm-Mt Ex-Mt
T1 Jeff Weaver .50 .15
T2 Jay Powell .50 .15
T3 Alex Gonzalez .50 .15
T4 Jason Isringhausen .75 .23
T5 Tyler Houston .50 .15
T6 Ben Broussard .50 .15
T7 Chuck Knoblauch .75 .23
T8 Brian L. Hunter .50 .15
T9 Dustan Mohr .50 .15
T10 Eric Hinske .50 .15
T11 Roger Cedeno .50 .15
T12 Eddie Perez .50 .15
T13 Jeromy Burnitz .50 .15
T14 Bartolo Colon .75 .23
T15 Rick Helling .50 .15
T16 Dan Plesac .50 .15
T17 Scott Strickland .50 .15
T18 Antonio Alfonseca .50 .15
T19 Ricky Gutierrez .50 .15
T20 John Valentin .50 .15
T21 Raul Mondesi .75 .23
T22 Ben Davis .50 .15
T23 Nelson Figueroa .50 .15
T24 Earl Snyder .50 .15
T25 Robin Ventura .75 .23
T26 Jimmy Haynes .50 .15
T27 Kenny Kelly .50 .15
T28 Morgan Ensberg .75 .23
T29 Reggie Sanders .50 .15
T30 Shigetoshi Hasegawa .75 .23
T31 Mike Timlin .50 .15
T32 Russell Branyan .50 .15
T33 Alan Embree .50 .15
T34 D'Angelo Jimenez .50 .15
T35 Kent Mercker .50 .15
T36 Jesse Orosco .50 .15
T37 Gregg Zaun .50 .15
T38 Reggie Taylor .50 .15
T39 Andres Galarraga .75 .23
T40 Chris Truby .50 .15
T41 Bruce Chen .50 .15
T42 Darren Lewis .50 .15
T43 Ryan Kohlmeier .50 .15
T44 John McDonald .50 .15
T45 Omar Daal .50 .15
T46 Matt Clement .50 .15
T47 Glendon Rusch .50 .15
T48 Chan Ho Park .75 .23
T49 Benny Agbayani .50 .15
T50 Juan Gonzalez 1.25 .35
T51 Carlos Baerga .50 .15
T52 Tim Raines .75 .23
T53 Kevin Appier .75 .23
T54 Marty Cordova .50 .15
T55 Jeff D'Amico .50 .15
T56 Dmitri Young .75 .23
T57 Roosevelt Brown .50 .15
T58 Dustin Hermanson .50 .15
T59 Jose Rijo .50 .15
T60 Todd Ritchie .50 .15
T61 Lee Stevens .50 .15
T62 Placido Polanco .50 .15
T63 Eric Young .50 .15
T64 Chuck Finley .75 .23
T65 Dicky Gonzalez .50 .15
T66 Jose Macias .50 .15
T67 Gabe Kapler .50 .15
T68 Sandy Alomar Jr. .50 .15
T69 Henry Blanco .50 .15
T70 Julian Tavarez .50 .15
T71 Paul Bako .50 .15
T72 Scott Rolen 2.00 .60
T73 Brian Jordan .75 .23
T74 Rickey Henderson 2.00 .60
T75 Kevin Mench .50 .15
T76 Hideo Nomo 2.00 .60
T77 Jeremy Giambi .50 .15
T78 Brad Fullmer .50 .15
T79 Carl Everett .75 .23
T80 David Wells .75 .23
T81 Aaron Sele .50 .15
T82 Todd Hollandsworth .50 .15
T83 Vicente Padilla .50 .15
T84 Kenny Lofton .75 .23
T85 Corky Miller .50 .15
T86 Josh Fogg .50 .15
T87 Cliff Floyd .75 .23
T88 Craig Paquette .50 .15
T89 Jay Payton .50 .15
T90 Carlos Pena .50 .15
T91 Juan Encarnacion .50 .15
T92 Rey Sanchez .50 .15
T93 Ryan Dempster .50 .15
T94 Mario Encarnacion .50 .15
T95 Jorge Julio .50 .15
T96 John Mabry .50 .15
T97 Todd Zeile .75 .23
T98 Johnny Damon 1.25 .35
T99 Deivi Cruz .50 .15
T100 Gary Sheffield .75 .23
T101 Ted Lilly .50 .15
T102 Todd Van Poppel .50 .15
T103 Shawn Estes .50 .15
T104 Cesar Izturis .50 .15
T105 Ron Coomer .50 .15
T106 Grady Little MG RC .50 .15
T107 Jimy Williams MGR .50 .15
T108 Tony Pena MGR .50 .15
T109 Frank Robinson MGR 1.25 .35
T110 Ron Gardenhire MGR .50 .15
T111 Dennis Tankersley .50 .15
T112 Alejandro Cadena RC 1.00 .30
T113 Justin Reid RC 1.00 .30
T114 Nate Field RC 1.00 .30
T115 Rene Reyes RC 1.00 .30
T116 Nelson Castro RC 1.00 .30
T117 Miguel Olivo .50 .15
T118 David Espinosa .50 .15
T119 Chris Bootcheck RC 1.00 .30
T120 Rob Henkel RC 1.00 .30
T121 Steve Bechler RC 1.00 .30
T122 Mark Outlaw RC 1.00 .30
T123 Henry Pichardo RC 1.00 .30
T124 Michael Floyd RC 1.00 .30
T125 Richard Lane RC 1.00 .30
T126 Pete Zamora RC 1.00 .30
T127 Javier Colina .50 .15
T128 Greg Sain RC 1.25 .35
T129 Ronnie Merrill .50 .15
T130 Gavin Floyd RC 6.00 1.80
T131 Josh Bonifay RC 1.00 .30
T132 Tommy Marx RC 1.00 .30
T133 Gary Cates Jr. RC 1.00 .30
T134 Neal Cotts RC 2.50 .75
T135 Angel Berroa .50 .15
T136 Elio Serrano RC 1.00 .30
T137 J.J. Putz RC 1.00 .30
T138 Ruben Gotay RC 1.00 .30
T139 Eddie Rogers .50 .15
T140 Wily Mo Pena .75 .23
T141 Tyler Yates RC 1.25 .35
T142 Colin Young RC .75 .23
T143 Chance Caple .50 .15
T144 Ben Howard RC 1.00 .30
T145 Ryan Bukvich RC 1.00 .30
T146 Cliff Bartosh RC 1.00 .30
T147 Brandon Claussen .50 .15
T148 Cristian Guerrero .50 .15
T149 Derrick Lewis .50 .15
T150 Eric Miller RC 1.00 .30
T151 Justin Huber RC 2.00 .60
T152 Adrian Gonzalez .75 .23
T153 Brian West RC 1.00 .30
T154 Chris Baker RC 1.00 .30
T155 Drew Henson .75 .23
T156 Scott Hairston RC 4.00 1.20
T157 Jason Simontacchi RC 1.00 .30
T158 Jason Arnold RC 2.00 .60
T159 Brandon Phillips .50 .15
T160 Adam Roller RC 1.00 .30
T161 Scotty Layfield RC 1.00 .30
T162 Freddie Money RC 1.00 .30
T163 Noochie Varner RC 1.00 .30
T164 Terrance Hill RC 1.00 .30
T165 Jeremy Hill RC 1.00 .30
T166 Carlos Cabrera RC 1.00 .30
T167 Jose Morban RC 1.00 .30
T168 Kevin Frederick RC 1.00 .30
T169 Mark Teixeira 1.25 .35
T170 Brian Rogers .50 .15
T171 Anastacio Martinez RC 1.00 .30
T172 Bobby Jenks RC 2.00 .60
T173 David Gil RC 1.00 .30
T174 Andres Torres .50 .15
T175 James Barrett RC 1.00 .30
T176 Jimmy Journell .50 .15
T177 Brett Kay RC 1.00 .30
T178 Jason Young RC 1.00 .30
T179 Mark Hamilton RC 1.00 .30
T180 Jose Bautista RC
T181 Blake McGinley RC 1.00 .30
T182 Ryan Mottl RC 1.00 .30
T183 Jeff Austin RC 1.00 .30
T184 Xavier Nady .50 .15
T185 Kyle Kane RC 1.00 .30
T186 Travis Foley RC 1.00 .30
T187 Nathan Kaup RC 1.00 .30
T188 Eric Cyr .50 .15
T189 Josh Cisneros RC 1.00 .30
T190 Brad Nelson RC 3.00 .90
T191 Clint Weibl RC 1.00 .30
T192 Ron Calloway RC 1.00 .30
T193 Jung Bong .50 .15
T194 Rolando Viera RC 1.00 .30
T195 Jason Bulger RC 1.00 .30
T196 Chone Figgins RC 2.00 .60
T197 Jimmy Alvarez RC 1.00 .30
T198 Joel Crump RC 1.00 .30
T199 Ryan Doumit RC 1.25 .35
T200 Demetrius Heath RC 1.00 .30
T201 John Ennis RC 1.00 .30
T202 Doug Sessions RC 1.00 .30
T203 Clinton Hosford RC 1.00 .30
T204 Chris Narveson RC 1.00 .30
T205 Ross Peeples RC 1.00 .30
T206 Alex Requena RC 1.00 .30
T207 Matt Erickson RC 1.00 .30
T208 Brian Forystek RC 1.00 .30
T209 Dewon Brazelton .50 .15
T210 Nathan Haynes .50 .15
T211 Jack Cust .50 .15
T212 Jesse Foppert RC 2.50 .75
T213 Jesus Cota RC 1.00 .30
T214 Juan M. Gonzalez RC 1.00 .30
T215 Tim Kalita RC 1.00 .30
T216 Manny Delcarmen RC 1.00 .30
T217 Jim Kavourias RC 1.00 .30
T218 C.J. Wilson RC 1.00 .30
T219 Edwin Yan RC 1.00 .30
T220 Andy Van Hekken .50 .15
T221 Michael Cuddyer .50 .15
T222 Jeff Verplancke RC 1.00 .30
T223 Mike Wilson RC 1.00 .30
T224 Corwin Malone RC 1.00 .30
T225 Chris Snelling RC 1.00 .30
T226 Joe Rogers RC 1.00 .30
T227 Jason Bay 6.00 1.80
T228 Ezequiel Astacio RC 1.00 .30
T229 Joey Hammond RC 1.00 .30
T230 Chris Duffy RC 1.00 .30
T231 Mark Prior 3.00 .90
T232 Hansel Izquierdo RC 1.00 .30
T233 Franklyn German RC 1.00 .30
T234 Alexis Gomez .50 .15
T235 Jorge Padilla RC 1.00 .30
T236 Ryan Snare RC 1.00 .30
T237 Deivis Santos .50 .15
T238 Taggert Bozied RC 2.00 .60
T239 Mike Peeples RC 1.00 .30
T240 Ronald Acuna RC 1.00 .30
T241 Koyie Hill .50 .15
T242 Garrett Guzman RC 1.00 .30
T243 Ryan Church RC 2.00 .60
T244 Tony Fontana RC 1.00 .30
T245 Keto Anderson RC 1.00 .30
T246 Brad Bouras RC 1.00 .30
T247 Jason Dubois RC 3.00 .90

T248 Angel Guzman RC 8.00 2.40
T249 Joel Hanrahan RC 2.00 .60
T250 Joe Jiannetti RC 1.00 .30
T251 Sean Pierce RC 1.00 .30
T252 Jake Mauer RC 1.00 .30
T253 Marshall McDougall RC 1.00 .30
T254 Edwin Almonte RC 1.00 .30
T255 Shawn Riggans RC 1.00 .30
T256 Steven Shell RC 1.00 .30
T257 Kevin Hooper RC 1.00 .30
T258 Michael Frick RC 1.00 .30
T259 Travis Chapman RC 1.00 .30
T260 Tim Hummel RC 1.00 .30
T261 Adam Morrissey RC 1.00 .30
T262 Dontrelle Willis RC 8.00 2.40
T263 Justin Sherrod RC 1.00 .30
T264 Gerald Smiley RC 1.00 .30
T265 Tony Miller RC 1.00 .30
T266 Nolan Ryan WW 5.00 1.50
T267 Reggie Jackson WW 1.25 .35
T268 Steve Garvey WW .75 .23
T269 Wade Boggs WW 1.25 .35
T270 Sammy Sosa WW 3.00 .90
T271 Curt Schilling WW .75 .23
T272 Mark Grace WW 1.25 .35
T273 Jason Giambi WW .50 .15
T274 Ken Griffey Jr. WW 3.00 .90
T275 Roberto Alomar WW 1.25 .35

2002 Topps Chrome Traded Black Refractors

Inserted at a stated rate of one in 56 Topps Traded hobby or retail packs and one in 16 HTA packs, this is a parallel of the Topps Chrome Traded set. These cards can be differentiated from the regular cards by their black borders and are printed to a stated print run of 100 serial numbered sets.

Nm-Mt Ex-Mt
*BLACK REF: 4X TO 10X BASIC
*BLACK REF RC'S: 4X TO 10X BASIC RC'S

2002 Topps Chrome Traded Refractors

nserted at a stated rate of one in 12 Topps Traded packs, this is a parallel of the Topps Chrome Traded set. These cards can be differentiated from the regular cards by their "refractive" sheen and are notated as refractors on the back of the card.

Nm-Mt Ex-Mt
*REF: 2X TO 5X BASIC
*REF RC'S: 1.5X TO 4X BASIC RC'S
STATED ODDS 1:12 HOB/RET, 1:12 HTA

2003 Topps Chrome

The first series of 2003 Topps Chrome was released in January, 2003. These cards were issued in four card packs which came 24 packs to a box and 10 boxes to a case with an SRP of $3 per pack. Cards numbered 201 through 220 feature players in their first year of Topps cards. The second series, which also consisted of 220 cards, was released in May, 2003. Cards number 421 through 430 were draft pick cards while cards 431 through 440 were two player prospect cards.

Nm-Mt Ex-Mt
COMPLETE SET (440) 200.00 60.00
COMPLETE SERIES 1 (220) 100.00 30.00
COMPLETE SERIES 2 (220) 100.00 30.00
COMMON (1-200/221-420) 1.00 .30
COMMON (201-220/421-440) 1.50 .45
1 Alex Rodriguez 4.00 1.20
2 Eddie Guardado 1.00 .30
3 Curt Schilling 1.00 .30
4 Andruw Jones 1.00 .30
5 Magglio Ordonez 1.00 .30
6 Todd Helton 1.50 .45
7 Odalis Perez 1.00 .30
8 Edgardo Alfonzo 1.00 .30
9 Eric Hinske 1.00 .30
10 Danny Bautista 1.00 .30
11 Sammy Sosa 4.00 1.20
12 Roberto Alomar 1.50 .45
13 Roger Clemens 5.00 1.50
14 Austin Kearns 1.00 .30
15 Luis Gonzalez 1.00 .30
16 Mo Vaughn 1.00 .30
17 Alfonso Soriano 1.50 .45
18 Orlando Cabrera 1.00 .30
19 Hideo Nomo 2.50 .75
20 Omar Vizquel 1.50 .45
21 Greg Maddux 4.00 1.20
22 Fred McGriff 1.50 .45
23 Frank Thomas 2.50 .75
24 Shawn Green 1.00 .30
25 Jacque Jones 1.00 .30
26 Bernie Williams 1.50 .45
27 Corey Patterson 1.00 .30
28 Cesar Izturis 1.00 .30
29 Larry Walker 1.50 .45
30 Darren Dreifort 1.00 .30
31 Al Leiter 1.00 .30
32 Jason Marquis 1.00 .30
33 Sean Casey 1.00 .30
34 Craig Counsell 1.00 .30
35 Albert Pujols 5.00 1.50
36 Kyle Lohse 1.00 .30
37 Paul Lo Duca 1.00 .30
38 Roy Oswalt 1.00 .30
39 Danny Graves 1.00 .30
40 Kevin Millwood 1.00 .30
41 Lance Berkman 1.00 .30
42 Denny Hocking 1.00 .30
43 Jose Valentin 1.00 .30
44 Josh Beckett 1.00 .30
45 Nomar Garciaparra 4.00 1.20
46 Craig Biggio 1.50 .45
47 Omar Daal 1.00 .30
48 Jimmy Rollins 1.00 .30
49 Jermaine Dye 1.00 .30
50 Edgar Renteria 1.00 .30
51 Brandon Duckworth 1.00 .30
52 Luis Castillo 1.00 .30
53 Andy Ashby 1.00 .30
54 Mike Williams 1.00 .30
55 Benito Santiago 1.00 .30
56 Bret Boone 1.00 .30
57 Randy Wolf 1.00 .30
58 Ivan Rodriguez 2.50 .75
59 Shannon Stewart 1.00 .30
60 Jose Cruz Jr. 1.00 .30
61 Billy Wagner 1.00 .30
62 Alex Gonzalez 1.00 .30
63 Ichiro Suzuki 4.00 1.20
64 Joe McEwing 1.00 .30
65 Mark Mulder 1.00 .30
66 Mike Cameron 1.00 .30
67 Corey Koskie 1.00 .30
68 Marlon Anderson 1.00 .30
69 Jason Kendall 1.00 .30
70 J.T. Snow 1.00 .30
71 Edgar Martinez 1.50 .45
72 Vernon Wells 1.00 .30
73 Vladimir Guerrero 2.50 .75
74 Adam Dunn 1.50 .45
75 Barry Zito 1.00 .30
76 Jeff Kent 1.00 .30
77 Russ Ortiz 1.00 .30
78 Phil Nevin 1.00 .30
79 Carlos Beltran 1.50 .45
80 Mike Lowell 1.00 .30
81 Bob Wickman 1.00 .30
82 Junior Spivey 1.00 .30
83 Melvin Mora 1.00 .30
84 Derrek Lee 1.00 .30
85 Chuck Knoblauch 1.00 .30
86 Eric Gagne 2.50 .75
87 Orlando Hernandez 1.00 .30
88 Robert Person 1.00 .30
89 Elmer Dessens 1.00 .30
90 Wade Miller 1.00 .30
91 Adrian Beltre 1.50 .45
92 Kazuhiro Sasaki 1.00 .30
93 Timo Perez 1.00 .30
94 Jose Vidro 1.00 .30
95 Geronimo Gil 1.00 .30
96 Trot Nixon 1.00 .30
97 Denny Neagle 1.00 .30
98 Roberto Hernandez 1.00 .30
99 David Ortiz 1.50 .45
100 Robb Nen 1.00 .30
101 Sidney Ponson 1.00 .30
102 Kevin Appier 1.00 .30
103 Javier Lopez 1.00 .30
104 Jeff Conine 1.00 .30
105 Mark Buehrle 1.00 .30
106 Jason Simontacchi 1.00 .30
107 Jose Jimenez 1.00 .30
108 Brian Jordan 1.00 .30
109 Brad Wilkerson 1.00 .30
110 Scott Hatteberg 1.00 .30
111 Matt Morris 1.00 .30
112 Miguel Tejada 1.00 .30
113 Rafael Furcal 1.00 .30
114 Steve Cox 1.00 .30
115 Roy Halladay 1.00 .30
116 David Eckstein 1.00 .30
117 Tomo Ohka 1.00 .30
118 Jack Wilson 1.00 .30
119 Randall Simon 1.00 .30
120 Jamie Moyer 1.00 .30
121 Andy Benes 1.00 .30
122 Tino Martinez 1.50 .45
123 Esteban Yan 1.00 .30
124 Jason Isringhausen 1.00 .30
125 Chris Carpenter 1.00 .30
126 Aaron Rowand 1.00 .30
127 Brandon Inge 1.00 .30
128 Jose Vizcaino 1.00 .30
129 Jose Mesa 1.00 .30
130 Troy Percival 1.00 .30
131 Jon Lieber 1.00 .30
132 Brian Giles 1.00 .30
133 Aaron Boone 1.00 .30
134 Bobby Higginson 1.00 .30
135 Luis Rivas 1.00 .30
136 Troy Glaus 1.00 .30
137 Jim Thome 2.50 .75
138 Ramon Martinez 1.00 .30
139 Jay Gibbons 1.00 .30
140 Mike Lieberthal 1.00 .30
141 Juan Uribe 1.00 .30
142 Gary Sheffield 1.00 .30
143 Ramon Santiago 1.00 .30
144 Ben Sheets 1.00 .30
145 Tony Armas Jr. 1.00 .30
146 Kazuhisa Ishii 1.00 .30
147 Erubiel Durazo 1.00 .30
148 Jerry Hairston Jr. 1.00 .30
149 Byung-Hyun Kim 1.00 .30
150 Marcus Giles 1.00 .30
151 Johnny Damon 2.50 .75
152 Terrence Long 1.00 .30
153 Juan Pierre 1.00 .30
154 Aramis Ramirez 1.00 .30
155 Brent Abernathy 1.00 .30
156 Ismael Valdes 1.00 .30
157 Mike Mussina 1.50 .45
158 Ramon Hernandez 1.00 .30
159 Adam Kennedy 1.00 .30
160 Tony Womack 1.00 .30
161 Tony Batista 1.00 .30
162 Kip Wells 1.00 .30
163 Jeromy Burnitz 1.00 .30
164 Todd Hundley 1.00 .30
165 Tim Wakefield 1.00 .30
166 Derek Lowe 1.00 .30
167 Jorge Posada 1.50 .45
168 Ramon Ortiz 1.00 .30
169 Brent Butler 1.00 .30
170 Shane Halter 1.00 .30
171 Matt Lawton 1.00 .30
172 Alex Sanchez 1.00 .30
173 Eric Milton 1.00 .30
174 Vicente Padilla 1.00 .30
175 Steve Karsay 1.00 .30
176 Mark Prior 2.50 .75
177 Kerry Wood 2.50 .75
178 Jason LaRue 1.00 .30
179 Danys Baez 1.00 .30
180 Nick Neugebauer 1.00 .30
181 Andres Galarraga 1.00 .30
182 Jason Giambi 1.00 .30
183 Aubrey Huff 1.00 .30
184 Juan Gonzalez 1.50 .45
185 Ugueth Urbina 1.00 .30
186 Rickey Henderson 2.50 .75
187 Brad Fullmer 1.00 .30
188 Todd Zeile 1.00 .30
189 Jason Jennings 1.00 .30
190 Vladimir Nunez 1.00 .30
191 David Justice 1.00 .30
192 Brian Lawrence 1.00 .30
193 Pat Burrell 1.00 .30
194 Pokey Reese 1.00 .30
195 Robert Fick 1.00 .30
196 C.C. Sabathia 1.00 .30
197 Fernando Vina 1.00 .30
198 Sean Burroughs 1.00 .30
199 Ellis Burks 1.00 .30
200 Joe Randa 1.00 .30
201 Chris Duncan FY RC 1.50 .45
202 Franklin Gutierrez FY RC 6.00 1.80
203 Adam LaRoche FY 1.50 .45
204 Manuel Ramirez FY RC 2.50 .75
205 Il Kim FY RC 1.50 .45
206 Daryl Clark FY RC 2.50 .75
207 Sean Pierce FY 1.50 .45
208 Andy Marte FY RC 8.00 2.40
209 Bernie Castro FY RC 1.50 .45
210 Jason Perry FY RC 2.50 .75
211 Jaime Bubela FY RC 1.50 .45
212 Alexis Rios FY 1.50 .45
213 Brendan Harris FY RC 2.50 .75
214 R.Nivar-Martinez FY RC 2.50 .75
215 Terry Tiffee FY RC 2.50 .75
216 Kevin Youkilis FY RC 5.00 1.50
217 Derell McCall FY RC 1.50 .45
218 Scott Tyler FY RC 2.50 .75
219 Craig Brazell FY RC 2.50 .75
220 Walter Young FY 1.50 .45
221 Francisco Rodriguez 1.00 .30
222 Chipper Jones 2.50 .75
223 Chris Singleton 1.00 .30
224 Cliff Floyd 1.00 .30
225 Bobby Hill 1.00 .30
226 Antonio Osuna 1.00 .30
227 Barry Larkin 1.50 .45
228 Dean Palmer 1.00 .30
229 Eric Owens 1.00 .30
230 Randy Johnson 2.50 .75
231 Jeff Suppan 1.00 .30
232 Eric Karros 1.00 .30
233 Johan Santana 1.50 .45
234 Javier Vazquez 1.00 .30
235 John Thomson 1.00 .30
236 Nick Johnson 1.00 .30
237 Mark Ellis 1.00 .30
238 Doug Glanville 1.00 .30
239 Ken Griffey Jr. 4.00 1.20
240 Bubba Trammell 1.00 .30
241 Livan Hernandez 1.00 .30
242 Desi Relaford 1.00 .30
243 Eli Marrero 1.00 .30
244 Jared Sandberg 1.00 .30
245 Barry Bonds 6.00 1.80
246 Aaron Sele 1.00 .30
247 Derek Jeter 6.00 1.80
248 Eric Byrnes 1.00 .30
249 Rich Aurilia 1.00 .30
250 Joel Pineiro 1.00 .30
251 Chuck Finley 1.00 .30
252 Bengie Molina 1.00 .30
253 Steve Finley 1.00 .30
254 Marty Cordova 1.00 .30
255 Shea Hillenbrand 1.00 .30
256 Milton Bradley 1.00 .30
257 Carlos Pena 1.00 .30
258 Brad Ausmus 1.00 .30
259 Carlos Delgado 1.00 .30
260 Kevin Mench 1.00 .30
261 Joe Kennedy 1.00 .30
262 Mark McLemore 1.00 .30
263 Bill Mueller 1.00 .30
264 Ricky Ledee 1.00 .30
265 Ted Lilly 1.00 .30
266 Sterling Hitchcock 1.00 .30
267 Scott Strickland 1.00 .30
268 Damion Easley 1.00 .30
269 Torii Hunter 1.00 .30
270 Brad Radke 1.00 .30
271 Geoff Jenkins 1.00 .30
272 Paul Byrd 1.00 .30
273 Morgan Ensberg 1.00 .30
274 Mike Maroth 1.00 .30
275 Mike Hampton 1.00 .30
276 Flash Gordon 1.00 .30
277 John Burkett 1.00 .30
278 Rodrigo Lopez 1.00 .30
279 Tim Spooneybarger 1.00 .30
280 Quinton McCracken 1.00 .30
281 Tim Salmon 1.50 .45
282 Jarrod Washburn 1.00 .30
283 Pedro Martinez 2.50 .75
284 Julio Lugo 1.00 .30
285 Armando Benitez 1.00 .30
286 Raul Mondesi 1.00 .30
287 Robin Ventura 1.00 .30
288 Bobby Abreu 1.00 .30
289 Josh Fogg 1.00 .30
290 Ryan Klesko 1.00 .30
291 Tsuyoshi Shinjo 1.00 .30
292 Jim Edmonds 1.00 .30
293 Chan Ho Park 1.00 .30
294 John Mabry 1.00 .30
295 Woody Williams 1.00 .30
296 Scott Schoeneweis 1.00 .30
297 Brian Anderson 1.00 .30
298 Brett Tomko 1.00 .30
299 Scott Erickson 1.00 .30
300 Kevin Millar Sox 1.00 .30
301 Danny Wright 1.00 .30
302 Jason Schmidt 1.00 .30
303 Scott Williamson 1.00 .30
304 Einar Diaz 1.00 .30
305 Jay Payton 1.00 .30
306 Juan Acevedo 1.00 .30
307 Ben Grieve 1.00 .30
308 Raul Ibanez 1.00 .30
309 Richie Sexson 1.00 .30
310 Rick Reed 1.00 .30
311 Pedro Astacio 1.00 .30
312 Bud Smith 1.00 .30
313 Tomas Perez 1.00 .30
314 Rafael Palmeiro 1.50 .45
315 Jason Tyner 1.00 .30
316 Scott Rolen 2.50 .75
317 Randy Winn 1.00 .30
318 Ryan Jensen 1.00 .30
319 Trevor Hoffman 1.00 .30
320 Craig Wilson 1.00 .30
321 Jeremy Giambi 1.00 .30
322 Andy Pettitte 1.50 .45
323 John Franco 1.00 .30
324 Felipe Lopez 1.00 .30
325 Mike Piazza 4.00 1.20
326 Cristian Guzman 1.00 .30
327 Jose Hernandez 1.00 .30
328 Octavio Dotel 1.00 .30
329 Brad Penny 1.00 .30
330 Dave Veres 1.00 .30
331 Ryan Dempster 1.00 .30
332 Joe Crede 1.00 .30
333 Chad Hermansen 1.00 .30
334 Gary Matthews Jr. 1.00 .30
335 Frank Catalanotto 1.00 .30
336 Darin Erstad 1.00 .30
337 Matt Williams 1.00 .30
338 B.J. Surhoff 1.00 .30
339 Kerry Ligtenberg 1.00 .30
340 Mike Bordick 1.00 .30
341 Joe Girardi 1.00 .30
342 D'Angelo Jimenez 1.00 .30
343 Paul Konerko 1.00 .30
344 Joe Mays 1.00 .30
345 Marquis Grissom 1.00 .30
346 Neifi Perez 1.00 .30
347 Preston Wilson 1.00 .30
348 Jeff Weaver 1.00 .30
349 Eric Chavez 1.00 .30
350 Placido Polanco 1.00 .30
351 Matt Mantei 1.00 .30
352 James Baldwin 1.00 .30
353 Toby Hall 1.00 .30
354 Benji Gil 1.00 .30
355 Damian Moss 1.00 .30
356 Jorge Julio 1.00 .30
357 Matt Clement 1.00 .30
358 Lee Stevens 1.00 .30
359 Dave Roberts 1.00 .30
360 J.C. Romero 1.00 .30
361 Bartolo Colon 1.00 .30
362 Roger Cedeno 1.00 .30
363 Mariano Rivera 1.50 .45
364 Billy Koch 1.00 .30
365 Manny Ramirez 1.50 .45
366 Travis Lee 1.00 .30
367 Oliver Perez 1.00 .30
368 Tim Worrell 1.00 .30
369 Damian Miller 1.00 .30
370 John Smoltz 1.50 .45
371 Willis Roberts 1.00 .30
372 Tim Hudson 1.00 .30
373 Moises Alou 1.00 .30
374 Corky Miller 1.00 .30
375 Ben Broussard 1.00 .30
376 Gabe Kapler 1.00 .30
377 Chris Woodward 1.00 .30
378 Todd Hollandsworth 1.00 .30
379 So Taguchi 1.00 .30
380 John Olerud 1.00 .30
381 Reggie Sanders 1.00 .30
382 Jake Peavy 1.00 .30
383 Kris Benson 1.00 .30
384 Ray Durham 1.00 .30
385 Boomer Wells 1.00 .30
386 Tom Glavine 1.50 .45
387 Antonio Alfonseca 1.00 .30
388 Keith Foulke 1.00 .30
389 Shawn Estes 1.00 .30
390 Mark Grace 1.50 .45
391 Dmitri Young 1.00 .30
392 A.J. Burnett 1.00 .30
393 Richard Hidalgo 1.00 .30
394 Mike Sweeney 1.00 .30
395 Doug Mientkiewicz 1.00 .30
396 Cory Lidle 1.00 .30
397 Jeff Bagwell 1.50 .45
398 Steve Sparks 1.00 .30
399 Sandy Alomar Jr. 1.00 .30
400 John Lackey 1.00 .30
401 Rick Helling 1.00 .30
402 Carlos Lee 1.00 .30
403 Garret Anderson 1.00 .30
404 Vinny Castilla 1.00 .30
405 David Bell 1.00 .30
406 Freddy Garcia 1.00 .30
407 Scott Spiezio 1.00 .30
408 Russell Branyan 1.00 .30
409 Jose Contreras RC 3.00 .90
410 Kevin Brown 1.00 .30
411 Tyler Houston 1.00 .30
412 A.J. Pierzynski 1.00 .30
413 Peter Bergeron 1.00 .30
414 Brett Myers 1.00 .30
415 Kenny Lofton 1.00 .30
416 Ben Davis 1.00 .30
417 J.D. Drew 1.00 .30
418 Ricky Gutierrez 1.00 .30
419 Mark Redman 1.00 .30
420 Juan Encarnacion 1.00 .30
421 Bryan Bullington DP RC 4.00 1.20
422 Jeremy Guthrie DP 1.50 .45
423 Joey Gomes DP RC 1.50 .45
424 E.Bastida-Martinez DP RC 1.50 .45
425 Brian Wright DP RC 1.50 .45
426 B.J. Upton DP 3.00 .90
427 Jeff Francis DP 1.50 .45
428 Jeremy Hermida DP 1.50 .45
429 Khalil Greene DP 5.00 1.50
430 Darrell Rasner DP RC 1.50 .45
431 Brandon Phillips 2.50 .75
Victor Martinez
432 Hee Seop Choi 1.50 .45
Nic Jackson
433 Dontrelle Willis 1.50 .45
Jason Stokes
434 Chad Tracy 1.50 .45
Lyle Overbay
435 Joe Borchard 1.50 .45
Corwin Malone
436 Joe Mauer 2.50 .75
Justin Morneau
437 Drew Henson 1.50 .45
Brandon Claussen
438 Chase Utley 1.50 .45
Gavin Floyd
439 Taggert Bozied 1.50 .45
Xavier Nady
440 Aaron Heilman 1.50 .45
Jose Reyes

2003 Topps Chrome Black Refractors

Issued at a stated rate of one in 20 for first series cards and one in 17 for second series cards, this is a parallel to the Topps Chrome set. These cards have black borders and were issued to a stated print run of 199 serial numbered sets.

Nm-Mt Ex-Mt
*BLACK 1-200/221-420: 2X TO 5X
*BLACK 201-220/409/421-440: 2.5X TO 6X

2003 Topps Chrome Gold Refractors

Issued at a stated rate of one in eight for first series cards and two in eight for second series cards, this is a parallel to the Topps Chrome set. These cards have gold borders and were issued to a stated print run of 449 serial numbered sets.

Nm-Mt Ex-Mt
*GOLD 1-200/221-420: 1.25X TO 3X
*GOLD 201-220/409/421-440: 1.5X TO 4X

2003 Topps Chrome Refractors

Issued at a stated rate of one in five, this is a parallel to the Topps Chrome set. These cards use the patented Topps Chrome technology and were issued to a stated print run of 699 serial numbered sets.

Nm-Mt Ex-Mt
*REF 1-200/201-420: 1X TO 2.5X
*REF 201-220/409/421-440: 1.25X TO 3X

2003 Topps Chrome Silver Refractors

Nm-Mt Ex-Mt
*SILVER REF 221-420: 1.25X TO 3X BASIC
*SILVER REF 421-440: 1.5X TO 4X BASIC
ONE PER SER.2 RETAIL EXCH.CARD
CARDS WERE ONLY PRODUCED FOR SER.2

2003 Topps Chrome Uncirculated X-Fractors

Issued at a box-topper, this is a parallel to the Topps Chrome set. Each of these cards were issued in a special case and each of these cards were issued to a stated print run of 50 serial numbered sets for first series cards and a stated print run of 57 serial numbered cards for second series cards.

Nm-Mt Ex-Mt
*X-FRACT 1-200/221-420: 4X TO 10X
*X-FRACT 201-220/409/421-440: 5X TO 12X

2003 Topps Chrome Blue Backs Relics

Randomly inserted into packs, these 20 cards are authentic game-used memorabilia attached to a card which was in 1951 Blue Back design. These cards were issued in three different odds and we have notated those odds as well as what group the player belonged to in our checklist.

Nm-Mt Ex-Mt
BAT ODDS 1:236 HOB/RET
UNI GROUP A ODDS 1:69 HOB/RET
UNI GROUP B ODDS 1:662 HOB/RET
AD Adam Dunn Uni B 15.00 4.50
AP Albert Pujols Uni A 25.00 7.50
AR Alex Rodriguez Bat 25.00 7.50
AS Alfonso Soriano Bat 15.00 4.50
BW Bernie Williams Bat 15.00 4.50
EC Eric Chavez Uni A 10.00 3.00
FT Frank Thomas Uni A 15.00 4.50
JB Josh Beckett Uni A 10.00 3.00
JBA Jeff Bagwell Uni A 10.00 3.00
JR Jimmy Rollins Uni A 10.00 3.00
KW Kerry Wood Uni A 15.00 4.50
LB Lance Berkman Bat 15.00 4.50
MO Magglio Ordonez Uni A 10.00 3.00
MP Mike Piazza Uni A 20.00 6.00
NG Nomar Garciaparra Bat 25.00 7.50
NJ Nick Johnson Bat 15.00 4.50
PK Paul Konerko Uni A 10.00 3.00
RA Roberto Alomar Bat 15.00 4.50
SG Shawn Green Uni A 10.00 3.00
TS Tsuyoshi Shinjo Bat 15.00 4.50

2003 Topps Chrome Record Breakers Relics

Randomly inserted into packs, these 40 cards feature a mix of active and retired players along with a game-used memorabilia piece. These cards were issued in a few different group and we have notated that information next to the player's name in our checklist.

	Nm-Mt	Ex-Mt
BAT 1 ODDS 1:364 HOB/RET............		
BAT 2 ODDS 1:131 HOB/RET............		
UNI GROUP A1 ODDS 1:413 HOB/RET		
UNI GROUP B1 ODDS 1:50 HOB/RET.		
UNI GROUP A2 ODDS 1:1707 HOB/RET		
UNI GROUP B2 ODDS 1:127 HOB/RET		
AR1 Alex Rodriguez Uni B1	15.00	4.50
AR2 Alex Rodriguez Bat 2	15.00	4.50
BB Barry Bonds Walks Uni B2	25.00	7.50
BB2 Barry Bonds Slg Uni B2	25.00	7.50
BB3 Barry Bonds Bat 2	25.00	7.50
CB Craig Biggio Uni B1	10.00	3.00
CD Carlos Delgado Uni B1	10.00	3.00
CF Cliff Floyd Bat 1	10.00	3.00
DE Darin Erstad Bat 2	10.00	3.00
DLE Dennis Eckersley Uni A2	15.00	4.50
DM Don Mattingly Bat 2	40.00	12.00
FT Frank Thomas Uni B1	15.00	4.50
HK Harmon Killebrew Uni B1	25.00	7.50
HR Harold Reynolds Bat 2	10.00	3.00
JB1 Jeff Bagwell Slg Uni B1	10.00	3.00
JB2 Jeff Bagwell RBI Uni B2	10.00	3.00
JC Jose Canseco Bat 2	15.00	4.50
JG Juan Gonzalez Uni B1	10.00	3.00
JM Joe Morgan Bat 1	10.00	3.00
JS John Smoltz Uni B2	10.00	3.00
KS Kazuhiro Sasaki Uni B1	10.00	3.00
LB Lou Brock Bat 1	20.00	6.00
LG1 Luis Gonzalez RBI Bat 1	10.00	3.00
LG2 Luis Gonzalez Avg Bat 2	10.00	3.00
LW Larry Walker Bat 1	15.00	4.50
MP Mike Piazza Uni B1	20.00	6.00
MR Manny Ramirez Bat 2	15.00	4.50
MS Mike Schmidt Uni A1	40.00	12.00
PM Paul Molitor Bat 2	15.00	4.50
RC Rod Carew Avg Bat 2	15.00	4.50
RC2 Rod Carew Hits Bat 2	15.00	4.50
RH1 R.Henderson A's Bat 1	15.00	4.50
RH2 R.Henderson Yanks Bat 2	15.00	4.50
RJ1 Randy Johnson ERA Uni B1	15.00	4.50
RJ2 Randy Johnson Wins Uni B2	15.00	4.50
RY Robin Yount Uni B1	25.00	7.50
SM Stan Musial Uni A1	50.00	15.00
SS Sammy Sosa Bat 2	20.00	6.00
TH Todd Helton Bat 1	15.00	4.50
TS Tom Seaver Uni B2	20.00	6.00

2003 Topps Chrome Red Backs Relics

Randomly inserted into packs, these 20 cards are authentic game-used memorabilia attached to a card which was in 1951 Red Back design. These cards were issued in three different odds and we have notated those odds as well as what group the player belonged to in our checklist.

	Nm-Mt	Ex-Mt
SERIES 2 BAT A ODDS 1:342 HOB/RET		
SERIES 2 BAT B ODDS 1:383 HOB/RET		
SERIES 2 JERSEY ODDS 1:49 HOB/RET		
AD Adam Dunn Jsy	10.00	3.00
AJ Andruw Jones Jsy	10.00	3.00
AP Albert Pujols Bat B	20.00	6.00
AR Alex Rodriguez Jsy	15.00	4.50
AS Alfonso Soriano Bat A	15.00	4.50
CJ Chipper Jones Jsy	15.00	4.50
CS Curt Schilling Jsy	10.00	3.00
GA Garrett Anderson Bat A	15.00	4.50
JB Jeff Bagwell Jsy	10.00	3.00
MP Mike Piazza Jsy	15.00	4.50
MR Manny Ramirez Bat B	10.00	3.00
MS Mike Sweeney Jsy	10.00	3.00
NG Nomar Garciaparra Bat A	25.00	7.50
PB Pat Burrell Bat A	15.00	4.50
PM Pedro Martinez Jsy	15.00	4.50
RA Roberto Alomar Jsy	10.00	3.00
RJ Randy Johnson Jsy	15.00	4.50
SR Scott Rolen Bat A	15.00	4.50
TH Todd Helton Jsy	10.00	3.00
TKH Torii Hunter Jsy	10.00	3.00

2003 Topps Chrome Traded

These cards were issued at a stated rate of two per 2003 Topps Traded pack. Cards numbered 1 through 115 feature veterans who were traded while cards 116 through 120 feature managers. Cards numbered 121 through 165 featured prospects and cards 166 through 275 feature Rookie Cards. All of these cards were issued with a "T" prefix.

	MINT	NRMT
COMPLETE SET (275)	120.00	55.00
COMMON CARD (1-120)	.75	.35
COMMON CARD (121-165)	1.00	.45
COMMON CARD (166-275)	1.00	.45
2 PER 2003 TOPPS TRADED HOBBY PACK		
2 PER 2003 TOPPS TRADED HTA PACK		
2 PER 2003 TOPPS TRADED RETAIL PACK		
T1 Juan Pierre	.75	.35
T2 Mark Grudzielanek	.75	.35
T3 Tanyon Sturtze	.75	.35
T4 Greg Vaughn	.75	.35
T5 Greg Myers	.75	.35
T6 Randall Simon	.75	.35
T7 Todd Hundley	.75	.35
T8 Marlon Anderson	.75	.35
T9 Jeff Reboulet	.75	.35
T10 Alex Sanchez	.75	.35
T11 Mike Rivera	.75	.35
T12 Todd Walker	.75	.35
T13 Ray King	.75	.35
T14 Shawn Estes	.75	.35
T15 Gary Matthews Jr.	.75	.35
T16 Jaret Wright	.75	.35
T17 Edgardo Alfonzo	.75	.35
T18 Omar Daal	.75	.35
T19 Ryan Rupe	.75	.35
T20 Tony Clark	.75	.35
T21 Jeff Suppan	.75	.35
T22 Mike Stanton	.75	.35
T23 Ramon Martinez	.75	.35
T24 Armando Rios	.75	.35
T25 Johnny Estrada	.75	.35
T26 Joe Girardi	.75	.35
T27 Ivan Rodriguez	2.00	.90
T28 Robert Fick	.75	.35
T29 Rick White	.75	.35
T30 Robert Person	.75	.35
T31 Alan Benes	.75	.35
T32 Chris Carpenter	.75	.35
T33 Chris Widger	.75	.35
T34 Travis Hafner	.75	.35
T35 Mike Venafro	.75	.35
T36 Jon Lieber	.75	.35
T37 Orlando Hernandez	.75	.35
T38 Aaron Myette	.75	.35
T39 Paul Bako	.75	.35
T40 Erubiel Durazo	.75	.35
T41 Mark Guthrie	.75	.35
T42 Steve Avery	.75	.35
T43 Damian Jackson	.75	.35
T44 Rey Ordonez	.75	.35
T45 John Flaherty	.75	.35
T46 Byung-Hyun Kim	.75	.35
T47 Tom Goodwin	.75	.35
T48 Elmer Dessens	.75	.35
T49 Al Martin	.75	.35
T50 Gene Kingsale	.75	.35
T51 Lenny Harris	.75	.35
T52 David Ortiz Sox	2.00	.90
T53 Jose Lima	.75	.35
T54 Mike Difelice	.75	.35
T55 Jose Hernandez	.75	.35
T56 Todd Zeile	.75	.35
T57 Roberto Hernandez	.75	.35
T58 Albie Lopez	.75	.35
T59 Roberto Alomar	1.25	.55
T60 Russ Ortiz	.75	.35
T61 Brian Daubach	.75	.35
T62 Carl Everett	.75	.35
T63 Jeromy Burnitz	.75	.35
T64 Mark Bellhorn	.75	.35
T65 Ruben Sierra	.75	.35
T66 Mike Fetters	.75	.35
T67 Armando Benitez	.75	.35
T68 Deivi Cruz	.75	.35
T69 Jose Cruz Jr.	.75	.35
T70 Jeremy Fikac	.75	.35
T71 Jeff Kent	.75	.35
T72 Andres Galarraga	.75	.35
T73 Rickey Henderson	2.00	.90
T74 Royce Clayton	.75	.35
T75 Troy O'Leary	.75	.35
T76 Ron Coomer	.75	.35
T77 Greg Colbrunn	.75	.35
T78 Wes Helms	.75	.35
T79 Kevin Millwood	.75	.35
T80 Damion Easley	.75	.35
T81 Bobby Kielty	.75	.35
T82 Keith Osik	.75	.35
T83 Ramiro Mendoza	.75	.35
T84 Shea Hillenbrand	.75	.35
T85 Shannon Stewart	.75	.35
T86 Eddie Perez	.75	.35
T87 Ugueth Urbina	.75	.35
T88 Orlando Palmeiro	.75	.35
T89 Graeme Lloyd	.75	.35
T90 John Vander Wal	.75	.35
T91 Gary Bennett	.75	.35
T92 Shane Reynolds	.75	.35
T93 Steve Parris	.75	.35
T94 Julio Lugo	.75	.35
T95 John Halama	.75	.35
T96 Carlos Baerga	.75	.35
T97 Jim Parque	.75	.35
T98 Mike Williams	.75	.35
T99 Fred McGriff	1.25	.55
T100 Kenny Rogers	.75	.35
T101 Matt Herges	.75	.35
T102 Jay Bell	.75	.35
T103 Esteban Yan	.75	.35
T104 Eric Owens	.75	.35
T105 Aaron Fultz	.75	.35
T106 Rey Sanchez	.75	.35
T107 Jim Thome	2.00	.90
T108 Aaron Boone	.75	.35
T109 Raul Mondesi	.75	.35
T110 Kenny Lofton	.75	.35
T111 Jose Guillen	.75	.35
T112 Aramis Ramirez	.75	.35
T113 Sidney Ponson	.75	.35
T114 Scott Williamson	.75	.35
T115 Robin Ventura	.75	.35
T116 Dusty Baker MG	.75	.35
T117 Felipe Alou MG	.75	.35
T118 Buck Showalter MG	.75	.35
T119 Jack McKeon MG	.75	.35
T120 Art Howe MG	.75	.35
T121 Bobby Crosby PROS	1.50	.70
T122 Adrian Gonzalez PROS	1.00	.45
T123 Kevin Cash PROS	1.00	.45
T124 Shin-Soo Choo PROS	1.00	.45
T125 Chin-Feng Chen PROS	2.50	1.10
T126 Miguel Cabrera PROS	2.50	1.10
T127 Jason Young PROS	1.00	.45
T128 Alex Herrera PROS	1.00	.45
T129 Jason Dubois PROS	1.00	.45
T130 Jeff Mathis PROS	1.00	.45
T131 Casey Kotchman PROS	1.50	.70
T132 Ed Rogers PROS	1.00	.45
T133 Wilson Betemit PROS	1.00	.45
T134 Jim Kavourias PROS	1.00	.45
T135 Taylor Buchholz PROS	1.00	.45
T136 Adam LaRoche PROS	1.00	.45
T137 D.McPherson PROS	2.50	1.10
T138 Jesus Cota PROS	1.00	.45
T139 Clint Nageotte PROS	1.00	.45
T140 Boof Bonser PROS	1.00	.45
T141 Walter Young PROS	1.00	.45
T142 Joe Crede PROS	1.00	.45
T143 Denny Bautista PROS	1.00	.45
T144 Victor Diaz PROS	1.00	.45
T145 Chris Narveson PROS	1.00	.45
T146 Gabe Gross PROS	1.00	.45
T147 Jimmy Journell PROS	1.00	.45
T148 Rafael Soriano PROS	1.00	.45
T149 Jerome Williams PROS	1.00	.45
T150 Aaron Cook PROS	1.00	.45
T151 An. Martinez PROS	1.00	.45
T152 Scott Hairston PROS	1.00	.45
T153 John Buck PROS	1.00	.45
T154 Ryan Ludwick PROS	1.00	.45
T155 Chris Bootcheck PROS	1.00	.45
T156 John Rheinecker PROS	1.00	.45
T157 Jason Lane PROS	1.00	.45
T158 Shelley Duncan PROS	1.00	.45
T159 Adam Wainwright PROS	1.00	.45
T160 Jason Arnold PROS	1.00	.45
T161 Jonny Gomes PROS	1.00	.45
T162 James Loney PROS	1.00	.45
T163 Mike Fontenot PROS	1.00	.45
T164 Khalil Greene PROS	5.00	2.20
T165 Sean Burnett PROS	1.00	.45
T166 David Martinez FY RC	1.00	.45
T167 Felix Pie FY RC	5.00	2.20
T168 Joe Valentine FY RC	1.00	.45
T169 Brandon Webb FY RC	2.50	1.10
T170 Matt Diaz FY RC	1.25	.55
T171 Lew Ford FY RC	3.00	1.35
T172 Jeremy Griffiths FY RC	1.25	.55
T173 Matt Hensley FY RC	1.00	.45
T174 Charlie Manning FY RC	1.00	.45
T175 Elizardo Ramirez FY RC	2.00	.90
T176 Greg Aquino FY RC	1.00	.45
T177 Felix Sanchez FY RC	1.00	.45
T178 Kelly Shoppach FY RC	2.50	1.10
T179 Bubba Nelson FY RC	1.25	.55
T180 Mike O'Keefe FY RC	1.00	.45
T181 Hanley Ramirez FY RC	5.00	2.20
T182 T.Wellemeyer FY RC	1.25	.55
T183 Dustin Moseley FY RC	1.25	.55
T184 Eric Crozier FY RC	1.25	.55
T185 Ryan Shealy FY RC	2.00	.90
T186 Jer. Bonderman FY RC	2.00	.90
T187 T.Story-Harden FY RC	1.00	.45
T188 Dusty Brown FY RC	1.00	.45
T189 Rob Hammock FY RC	1.25	.55
T190 Jorge Piedra FY RC	1.25	.55
T191 Chris De La Cruz FY RC	1.00	.45
T192 Eli Whiteside FY RC	1.00	.45
T193 Jason Kubel FY RC	5.00	2.20
T194 Jon Schuerholz FY RC	1.00	.45
T195 St. Randolph FY RC	1.00	.45
T196 Andy Sisco FY RC	2.50	1.10
T197 Sean Smith FY RC	1.25	.55
T198 Jon-Mark Sprowl FY RC	2.00	.90
T199 Matt Kata FY RC	2.00	.90
T200 Robinson Cano FY RC	2.50	1.10
T201 Nook Logan FY RC	1.00	.45
T202 Ben Francisco FY RC	1.25	.55
T203 Arnie Munoz FY RC	1.00	.45
T204 Ozzie Chavez FY RC	1.00	.45
T205 Eric Riggs FY RC	1.25	.55
T206 Beau Kemp FY RC	1.00	.45
T207 Travis Wong FY RC	1.25	.55
T208 Dustin Yount FY RC	1.25	.55
T209 Brian McCann FY RC	2.00	.90
T210 Wilton Reynolds FY RC	1.25	.55
T211 Matt Bruback FY RC	1.00	.45
T212 Andrew Brown FY RC	1.25	.55
T213 Edgar Gonzalez FY RC	1.00	.45
T214 Eider Torres FY RC	1.00	.45
T215 Aquilino Lopez FY RC	1.00	.45
T216 Bobby Basham FY RC	1.25	.55
T217 Tim Olson FY RC	1.25	.55
T218 Nathan Panther FY RC	2.00	.90
T219 Bryan Grace FY RC	1.00	.45
T220 Dusty Gomon FY RC	1.25	.55
T221 Wil Ledezma FY RC	1.25	.55
T222 Josh Willingham FY RC	1.25	.55
T223 David Cash FY RC	1.00	.45
T224 Oscar Villarreal FY RC	1.00	.45
T225 Jeff Duncan FY RC	1.25	.55
T226 Kade Johnson FY RC	1.00	.45
T227 L.Steidlmayer FY RC	1.00	.45
T228 Brandon Watson FY RC	1.00	.45
T229 Jose Morales FY RC	1.00	.45
T230 Mike Gallo FY RC	1.00	.45
T231 Tyler Adamczyk FY RC	1.00	.45
T232 Adam Stern FY RC	1.00	.45
T233 Brennan King FY RC	1.00	.45
T234 Dan Haren FY RC	2.00	.90
T235 Mi. Hernandez FY RC	1.00	.45
T236 Ben Fritz FY RC	1.00	.45
T237 Clay Hensley FY RC	1.00	.45
T238 Tyler Johnson FY RC	1.00	.45
T239 Pete LaForest FY RC	1.25	.55
T240 Tyler Martin FY RC	1.00	.45
T241 J.D. Durbin FY RC	2.00	.90
T242 Shane Victorino FY RC	1.00	.45
T243 Rajai Davis FY RC	1.25	.55
T244 Ismael Castro FY RC	1.00	.45
T245 C.Wang FY RC	2.50	1.10
T246 Travis Ishikawa FY RC	1.00	.45
T247 Corey Shafer FY RC	1.25	.55
T248 G.Schneidmiller FY RC	1.00	.45
T249 Dave Pember FY RC	1.00	.45
T250 Keith Stamler FY RC	1.00	.45
T251 Tyson Graham FY RC	1.00	.45
T252 Ryan Cameron FY RC	1.00	.45
T253 Eric Eckenstahler FY	1.00	.45
T254 Ma. Peterson FY RC	1.00	.45
T255 Dustin McGowan FY RC	2.00	.90
T256 Pr. Redman FY RC	1.00	.45
T257 Haj Turay FY RC	1.25	.55
T258 Carlos Guzman FY RC	1.25	.55
T259 Matt DeMarco FY RC	1.00	.45
T260 Derek Michaelis FY RC	1.00	.45
T261 Brian Burgamy FY RC	1.00	.45
T262 Jay Sitzman FY RC	1.00	.45
T263 Chris Fallon FY RC	1.00	.45
T264 Mike Adams FY RC	1.00	.45
T265 Clint Barmes FY RC	1.25	.55
T266 Eric Reed FY RC	2.00	.90
T267 Willie Eyre FY RC	1.00	.45
T268 Carlos Duran FY RC	1.00	.45
T269 Nick Trzesniak FY RC	1.00	.45
T270 Ferdin Tejeda FY RC	1.00	.45
T271 Mi. Garciaparra FY RC	2.00	.90
T272 Michael Hinckley FY RC	2.50	1.10
T273 Br. Florence FY RC	1.00	.45
T274 Trent Oeltjen FY RC	1.25	.55
T275 Mike Neu FY RC	1.00	.45

2003 Topps Chrome Traded Refractors

	MINT	NRMT
*REF 1-120: 2X TO 5X BASIC............		
*REF 121-165: 1.5X TO 4X BASIC......		
*REF 166-275: 1.5X TO 4X BASIC......		
STATED ODDS 1:12 HOB/RET, 1:4 HTA		

2003 Topps Chrome Traded Uncirculated X-Fractors

	MINT	NRMT
ONE PER TOPPS TRADED HTA BOX...		
STATED PRINT RUN 25 SERIAL #'d SETS		
NO PRICING DUE TO SCARCITY		

2004 Topps Chrome

This 233 card first series was released in January, 2004. A matching second series of 233 cards was released in May, 2004. This set was issued in four-card packs with an $3 SRP which came 20 packs to a box and 10 boxes to a case. The first 210 cards of the first series are veterans while the final 23 cards of the set feature first year cards. Please note that cards 221 through 233 were autographed by the featured players and those cards were issued to a stated rate of one in 21 hobby packs and one in 33 retail packs. In the second series cards nunbered 234 through 246 feature autographs of the rookie pictured and those cards were inserted at a stated rate of one in 22 hobby packs and one in 35 retail packs. Bradley Sullivan (#234) was issued with either the correct back or an incorrect back numbered to 345 which consistitued about 20 percent of the total press run.

	Nm-Mt	Ex-Mt
COMP.SERIES 1 w/o SP's (220)	80.00	24.00
COMP.SERIES 2 w/o SP's (220)	80.00	24.00
COMMON (1-210/257-466)	1.00	.30
COMMON (211-220/247-256)	1.00	.30
COMMON AU (221-233)	10.00	3.00
1 Jim Thome	2.50	.75
2 Reggie Sanders	1.00	.30
3 Mark Kotsay	1.00	.30
4 Edgardo Alfonzo	1.00	.30
5 Tim Wakefield	1.00	.30
6 Moises Alou	1.00	.30
7 Jorge Julio	1.00	.30
8 Bartolo Colon	1.00	.30
9 Chan Ho Park	1.00	.30
10 Ichiro Suzuki	4.00	1.20
11 Kevin Millwood	1.00	.30
12 Preston Wilson	1.00	.30
13 Tom Glavine	1.50	.45
14 Junior Spivey	1.00	.30
15 Marcus Giles	1.00	.30
16 David Segui	1.00	.30
17 Kevin Millar	1.00	.30
18 Corey Patterson	1.00	.30
19 Aaron Rowand	1.00	.30
20 Derek Jeter	5.00	1.50
21 Luis Castillo	1.00	.30
22 Manny Ramirez	1.50	.45
23 Jay Payton	1.00	.30
24 Bobby Higginson	1.00	.30
25 Lance Berkman	1.00	.30
26 Juan Pierre	1.00	.30
27 Mike Mussina	1.50	.45
28 Fred McGriff	1.50	.45
29 Richie Sexson	1.00	.30
30 Tim Hudson	1.00	.30
31 Mike Piazza	4.00	1.20
32 Brad Radke	1.00	.30
33 Jeff Weaver	1.00	.30
34 Ramon Hernandez	1.00	.30
35 David Bell	1.00	.30
36 Randy Wolf	1.00	.30
37 Jake Peavy	1.00	.30
38 Tim Worrell	1.00	.30
39 Gil Meche	1.00	.30
40 Albert Pujols	5.00	1.50
41 Michael Young	1.00	.30
42 Josh Phelps	1.00	.30
43 Brendan Donnelly	1.00	.30
44 Steve Finley	1.00	.30
45 John Smoltz	1.50	.45
46 Jay Gibbons	1.00	.30
47 Trot Nixon	1.00	.30
48 Carl Pavano	1.00	.30
49 Frank Thomas	2.50	.75
50 Mark Prior	2.50	.75
51 Danny Graves	1.00	.30
52 Milton Bradley	1.00	.30
53 Kris Benson	1.00	.30
54 Ryan Klesko	1.00	.30
55 Mike Lowell	1.00	.30
56 Geoff Blum	1.00	.30
57 Michael Tucker	1.00	.30
58 Paul Lo Duca	1.00	.30
59 Vicente Padilla	1.00	.30
60 Jacque Jones	1.00	.30
61 Fernando Tatis	1.00	.30
62 Ty Wigginton	1.00	.30
63 Rich Aurilia	1.00	.30
64 Andy Pettitte	1.50	.45
65 Terrence Long	1.00	.30
66 Cliff Floyd	1.00	.30
67 Mariano Rivera	1.50	.45
68 Kelvim Escobar	1.00	.30
69 Marlon Byrd	1.00	.30
70 Mark Mulder	1.00	.30
71 Francisco Cordero	1.00	.30
72 Carlos Guillen	1.00	.30
73 Fernando Vina	1.00	.30
74 Lance Carter	1.00	.30
75 Hank Blalock	1.00	.30
76 Jimmy Rollins	1.00	.30
77 Francisco Rodriguez	1.00	.30
78 Javy Lopez	1.00	.30
79 Jerry Hairston Jr.	1.00	.30
80 Andruw Jones	1.00	.30
81 Rodrigo Lopez	1.00	.30
82 Johnny Damon	2.50	.75
83 Hee Seop Choi	1.00	.30
84 Kazuhiro Sasaki	1.00	.30
85 Danny Bautista	1.00	.30
86 Matt Lawton	1.00	.30
87 Juan Uribe	1.00	.30
88 Rafael Furcal	1.00	.30
89 Kyle Farnsworth	1.00	.30
90 Jose Vidro	1.00	.30
91 Luis Rivas	1.00	.30
92 Hideo Nomo	2.50	.75
93 Javier Vazquez	1.00	.30
94 Al Leiter	1.00	.30
95 Jose Valentin	1.00	.30
96 Alex Cintron	1.00	.30
97 Zach Day	1.00	.30
98 Jorge Posada	1.50	.45
99 C.C. Sabathia	1.00	.30
100 Alex Rodriguez	4.00	1.20
101 Brad Penny	1.00	.30
102 Brad Ausmus	1.00	.30
103 Raul Ibanez	1.00	.30
104 Mike Hampton	1.00	.30
105 Adrian Beltre	1.50	.45
106 Ramiro Mendoza	1.00	.30
107 Rocco Baldelli	1.00	.30
108 Esteban Loaiza	1.00	.30
109 Russell Branyan	1.00	.30
110 Todd Helton	1.50	.45
111 Braden Looper	1.00	.30
112 Octavio Dotel	1.00	.30
113 Mike MacDougal	1.00	.30
114 Cesar Izturis	1.00	.30
115 Johan Santana	1.50	.45
116 Jose Contreras	1.00	.30
117 Placido Polanco	1.00	.30
118 Jason Phillips	1.00	.30
119 Orlando Hudson	1.00	.30
120 Vernon Wells	1.00	.30
121 Ben Grieve	1.00	.30
122 Dave Roberts	1.00	.30
123 Ismael Valdes	1.00	.30
124 Eric Owens	1.00	.30
125 Curt Schilling	1.00	.30
126 Russ Ortiz	1.00	.30
127 Mark Buehrle	1.00	.30
128 Doug Mientkiewicz	1.00	.30
129 Dmitri Young	1.00	.30
130 Kazuhisa Ishii	1.00	.30
131 A.J. Pierzynski	1.00	.30
132 Brad Wilkerson	1.00	.30
133 Joe McEwing	1.00	.30
134 Alex Cora	1.00	.30
135 Jose Cruz Jr.	1.00	.30
136 Carlos Zambrano	1.00	.30
137 Jeff Kent	1.00	.30
138 Shigetoshi Hasegawa	1.00	.30
139 Jarrod Washburn	1.00	.30
140 Greg Maddux	4.00	1.20
141 Josh Beckett	1.00	.30
142 Miguel Batista	1.00	.30
143 Omar Vizquel	1.50	.45
144 Alex Gonzalez	1.00	.30
145 Billy Wagner	1.00	.30
146 Brian Jordan	1.00	.30
147 Wes Helms	1.00	.30
148 Deivi Cruz	1.00	.30
149 Alex Gonzalez	1.00	.30
150 Jason Giambi	1.00	.30
151 Erubiel Durazo	1.00	.30
152 Mike Lieberthal	1.00	.30
153 Jason Kendall	1.00	.30
154 Xavier Nady	1.00	.30
155 Kirk Rueter	1.00	.30
156 Mike Cameron	1.00	.30
157 Miguel Cairo	1.00	.30
158 Woody Williams	1.00	.30
159 Toby Hall	1.00	.30
160 Bernie Williams	1.50	.45
161 Darin Erstad	1.00	.30
162 Matt Mantei	1.00	.30
163 Shawn Chacon	1.00	.30
164 Bill Mueller	1.00	.30
165 Damian Miller	1.00	.30
166 Tony Graffanino	1.00	.30
167 Sean Casey	1.00	.30
168 Brandon Phillips	1.00	.30
169 Runelvys Hernandez	1.00	.30

170 Adam Dunn 1.50 .45
171 Carlos Lee 1.00 .30
172 Juan Encarnacion 1.00 .30
173 Angel Berroa 1.00 .30
174 Desi Relaford 1.00 .30
175 Joe Mays 1.00 .30
176 Ben Sheets 1.00 .30
177 Eddie Guardado 1.00 .30
178 Rocky Biddle 1.00 .30
179 Eric Gagne 2.50 .75
180 Eric Chavez 1.00 .30
181 Jason Michaels 1.00 .30
182 Dustan Mohr 1.00 .30
183 Kip Wells 1.00 .30
184 Brian Lawrence 1.00 .30
185 Bret Boone 1.00 .30
186 Tino Martinez 1.50 .45
187 Aubrey Huff 1.00 .30
188 Kevin Mench 1.00 .30
189 Tim Salmon 1.50 .45
190 Carlos Delgado 1.00 .30
191 John Lackey 1.00 .30
192 Eric Byrnes 1.00 .30
193 Luis Matos 1.00 .30
194 Derek Lowe 1.00 .30
195 Mark Grudzielanek 1.00 .30
196 Tom Gordon 1.00 .30
197 Matt Clement 1.00 .30
198 Byung-Hyun Kim 1.00 .30
199 Brandon Inge 1.00 .30
200 Nomar Garciaparra 4.00 1.20
201 Frank Catalanotto 1.00 .30
202 Cristian Guzman 1.00 .30
203 Bo Hart 1.00 .30
204 Jack Wilson 1.00 .30
205 Ray Durham 1.00 .30
206 Freddy Garcia 1.00 .30
207 J.D. Drew 1.00 .30
208 Orlando Cabrera 1.00 .30
209 Roy Halladay 1.00 .30
210 David Eckstein 1.00 .30
211 Omar Falcon FY RC 1.00 .30
212 Todd Self FY RC 1.00 .30
213 David Murphy FY RC 2.50 .75
214 Dioner Navarro FY RC 3.00 .90
215 Marcus McBeth FY RC 1.00 .30
216 Chris O'Riordan FY RC 1.00 .30
217 Rodney Choy Foo FY RC 1.00 .30
218 Tim Frend FY RC 1.00 .30
219 Yadier Molina FY RC 2.50 .75
220 Zach Duke FY RC 4.00 1.20
221 Anthony Lerew FY AU RC 15.00 4.50
222 B.Hawksworth FY AU RC 15.00 4.50
223 Brayan Pena FY AU RC 10.00 3.00
224 Craig Ansman FY AU RC 10.00 3.00
225 Jon Knott FY AU RC 10.00 3.00
226 Josh Labandeira FY AU RC 10.00 3.00
227 Khalid Ballouli FY AU RC 10.00 3.00
228 Kyle Davies FY AU RC 15.00 4.50
229 Matt Creighton FY AU RC 10.00 3.00
230 Mike Gosling FY AU RC 10.00 3.00
231 Nic Ungs FY AU RC 10.00 3.00
232 Zach Miner FY AU RC 15.00 4.50
233 Donald Levinski FY AU RC 10.00 3.00
234A Bradley Sullivan FY AU RC 15.00 4.50
234B B.Sullivan FY AU ERR 345 25.00 7.50
235 Carlos Quentin FY AU RC 30.00 9.00
236 Conor Jackson FY AU RC 30.00 9.00
237 Estee Harris FY AU RC 10.00 3.00
238 Jeffrey Allison FY AU RC 15.00 4.50
239 Kyle Sleeth FY AU RC 15.00 4.50
240 Matthew Moses FY AU RC 15.00 4.50
241 Tim Stauffer FY AU RC 15.00 4.50
242 Brad Snyder FY AU RC 15.00 4.50
243 Jason Hirsh FY AU RC 10.00 3.00
244 L.Milledge FY AU RC 25.00 7.50
245 Logan Kensing FY AU RC 10.00 3.00
246 Kory Casto FY AU RC 10.00 3.00
247 David Aardsma FY RC 1.00 .30
248 Omar Quintanilla FY RC 2.50 .75
249 Ervin Santana FY RC 3.00 .90
250 Merkin Valdez FY RC 2.50 .75
251 Vito Chiaravalloti FY RC 2.00 .60
252 Travis Blackley FY RC 2.00 .60
253 Chris Shelton FY RC 2.00 .60
254 Rudy Guillen FY RC 2.50 .75
255 Bobby Brownlie FY RC 2.00 .60
256 Paul Maholm FY RC 2.00 .60
257 Roger Clemens 5.00 1.50
258 Laynce Nix 1.00 .30
259 Eric Hinske 1.00 .30
260 Ivan Rodriguez 2.50 .75
261 Brandon Webb 1.00 .30
262 Jhonny Peralta 1.00 .30
263 Adam Kennedy 1.00 .30
264 Tony Batista 1.00 .30
265 Jeff Suppan 1.00 .30
266 Kenny Lofton 1.00 .30
267 Scott Sullivan 1.00 .30
268 Ken Griffey Jr. 4.00 1.20
269 Juan Rivera 1.00 .30
270 Larry Walker 1.50 .45
271 Todd Hollandsworth 1.00 .30
272 Carlos Beltran 1.50 .45
273 Carl Crawford 1.00 .30
274 Karim Garcia 1.00 .30
275 Jose Reyes 1.00 .30
276 Brandon Duckworth 1.00 .30
277 Brian Giles 1.00 .30
278 J.T. Snow 1.00 .30
279 Jamie Moyer 1.00 .30
280 Julio Lugo 1.00 .30
281 Mark Teixeira 1.00 .30
282 Cory Lidle 1.00 .30
283 Lyle Overbay 1.00 .30
284 Troy Percival 1.00 .30
285 Robby Hammock 1.00 .30
286 Jason Johnson 1.00 .30
287 Damian Rolls 1.00 .30
288 Antonio Alfonseca 1.00 .30
289 Tom Goodwin 1.00 .30
290 Paul Konerko 1.00 .30
291 D'Angelo Jimenez 1.00 .30
292 Ben Broussard 1.00 .30
293 Magglio Ordonez 1.00 .30
294 Carlos Pena 1.00 .30
295 Chad Fox 1.00 .30
296 Jeriome Robertson 1.00 .30
297 Travis Hafner 1.00 .30
298 Joe Randa 1.00 .30
299 Brady Clark 1.00 .30
300 Barry Zito 1.00 .30
301 Ruben Sierra 1.00 .30
302 Brett Myers 1.00 .30
303 Oliver Perez 1.00 .30
304 Benito Santiago 1.00 .30
305 David Ross 1.00 .30
306 Joe Nathan 1.00 .30
307 Jim Edmonds 1.00 .30
308 Matt Kata 1.00 .30
309 Vinny Castilla 1.00 .30
310 Marty Cordova 1.00 .30
311 Aramis Ramirez 1.00 .30
312 Carl Everett 1.00 .30
313 Ryan Freel 1.00 .30
314 Mark Bellhorn Sox 1.50 .45
315 Joe Mauer 1.50 .45
316 Tim Redding 1.00 .30
317 Jeromy Burnitz 1.00 .30
318 Miguel Cabrera 1.50 .45
319 Ramon Nivar 1.00 .30
320 Casey Blake 1.00 .30
321 Adam LaRoche 1.00 .30
322 Jermaine Dye 1.00 .30
323 Jerome Williams 1.00 .30
324 John Olerud 1.00 .30
325 Scott Rolen 2.50 .75
326 Bobby Kielty 1.00 .30
327 Travis Lee 1.00 .30
328 Jeff Cirillo 1.00 .30
329 Scott Spiezio 1.00 .30
330 Melvin Mora 1.00 .30
331 Mike Timlin 1.00 .30
332 Kerry Wood 2.50 .75
333 Tony Womack 1.00 .30
334 Jody Gerut 1.00 .30
335 Morgan Ensberg 1.00 .30
336 Odalis Perez 1.00 .30
337 Michael Cuddyer 1.00 .30
338 Jose Hernandez 1.00 .30
339 LaTroy Hawkins 1.00 .30
340 Marquis Grissom 1.00 .30
341 Matt Morris 1.00 .30
342 Juan Gonzalez 1.50 .45
343 Jose Valverde 1.00 .30
344 Joe Borowski 1.00 .30
345 Josh Bard 1.00 .30
346 Austin Kearns 1.00 .30
347 Chin-Hui Tsao 1.00 .30
348 Wil Ledezma 1.00 .30
349 Aaron Guiel 1.00 .30
350 Alfonso Soriano 1.50 .45
351 Ted Lilly 1.00 .30
352 Sean Burroughs 1.00 .30
353 Rafael Palmeiro 1.50 .45
354 Quinton McCracken 1.00 .30
355 David Ortiz 2.50 .75
356 Randall Simon 1.00 .30
357 Wily Mo Pena 1.00 .30
358 Brian Anderson 1.00 .30
359 Corey Koskie 1.00 .30
360 Keith Foulke Sox 1.50 .45
361 Sidney Ponson 1.00 .30
362 Gary Matthews Jr. 1.00 .30
363 Herbert Perry 1.00 .30
364 Shea Hillenbrand 1.00 .30
365 Craig Biggio 1.50 .45
366 Barry Larkin 1.50 .45
367 Arthur Rhodes 1.00 .30
368 Sammy Sosa 4.00 1.20
369 Joe Crede 1.00 .30
370 Gary Sheffield 1.00 .30
371 Coco Crisp 1.00 .30
372 Torii Hunter 1.00 .30
373 Derrek Lee 1.00 .30
374 Adam Everett 1.00 .30
375 Miguel Tejada 1.00 .30
376 Jeremy Affeldt 1.00 .30
377 Robin Ventura 1.00 .30
378 Scott Podsednik 1.00 .30
379 Matthew LeCroy 1.00 .30
380 Vladimir Guerrero 2.50 .75
381 Steve Karsay 1.00 .30
382 Jeff Nelson 1.00 .30
383 Chase Utley 1.00 .30
384 Bobby Abreu 1.00 .30
385 Josh Fogg 1.00 .30
386 Trevor Hoffman 1.00 .30
387 Matt Stairs 1.00 .30
388 Edgar Martinez 1.50 .45
389 Edgar Renteria 1.00 .30
390 Chipper Jones 2.50 .75
391 Eric Munson 1.00 .30
392 Dewon Brazelton 1.00 .30
393 John Thomson 1.00 .30
394 Chris Woodward 1.00 .30
395 Joe Kennedy 1.00 .30
396 Reed Johnson 1.00 .30
397 Johnny Estrada 1.00 .30
398 Damian Moss 1.00 .30
399 Victor Zambrano 1.00 .30
400 Dontrelle Willis 1.00 .30
401 Troy Glaus 1.00 .30
402 Raul Mondesi 1.00 .30
403 Jeff Davanon 1.00 .30
404 Kurt Ainsworth 1.00 .30
405 Pedro Martinez 2.50 .75
406 Eric Karros 1.00 .30
407 Billy Koch 1.00 .30
408 Luis Gonzalez 1.00 .30
409 Jack Cust 1.00 .30
410 Mike Sweeney 1.00 .30
411 Jason Bay 1.00 .30
412 Mark Redman 1.00 .30
413 Jason Jennings 1.00 .30
414 Rondell White 1.00 .30
415 Todd Hundley 1.00 .30
416 Shannon Stewart 1.00 .30
417 Jae Weong Seo 1.00 .30
418 Livan Hernandez 1.00 .30
419 Mark Ellis 1.00 .30
420 Pat Burrell 1.00 .30
421 Mark Loretta 1.00 .30
422 Robb Nen 1.00 .30
423 Joel Pineiro 1.00 .30
424 Todd Walker 1.00 .30
425 Jeremy Bonderman 1.00 .30
426 A.J. Burnett 1.00 .30
427 Greg Myers 1.00 .30
428 Roy Oswalt 1.00 .30
429 Carlos Baerga 1.00 .30
430 Garret Anderson 1.00 .30
431 Horacio Ramirez 1.00 .30
432 Brian Roberts 1.00 .30
433 Kevin Brown 1.00 .30
434 Eric Milton 1.00 .30
435 Ramon Vazquez 1.00 .30
436 Alex Escobar 1.00 .30
437 Alex Sanchez 1.00 .30
438 Jeff Bagwell 1.50 .45
439 Claudio Vargas 1.00 .30
440 Shawn Green 1.00 .30
441 Geoff Jenkins 1.00 .30
442 David Wells 1.00 .30
443 Nick Johnson 1.00 .30
444 Jose Guillen 1.00 .30
445 Scott Hatteberg 1.00 .30
446 Phil Nevin 1.00 .30
447 Jason Schmidt 1.00 .30
448 Ricky Ledee 1.00 .30
449 So Taguchi 1.00 .30
450 Randy Johnson 2.50 .75
451 Eric Young 1.00 .30
452 Chone Figgins 1.00 .30
453 Larry Bigbie 1.00 .30
454 Scott Williamson 1.00 .30
455 Ramon Martinez 1.00 .30
456 Roberto Alomar 1.50 .45
457 Ryan Dempster 1.00 .30
458 Ryan Ludwick 1.00 .30
459 Ramon Santiago 1.00 .30
460 Jeff Conine 1.00 .30
461 Brad Lidge 1.00 .30
462 Ken Harvey 1.00 .30
463 Guillermo Mota 1.00 .30
464 Rick Reed 1.00 .30
465 Armando Benitez 1.00 .30
466 Wade Miller 1.00 .30

2004 Topps Chrome Black Refractors

Nm-Mt Ex-Mt
*BLACK 1-210/257-466: 1.5X TO 4X BASIC
*BLACK 211-220/247-256: 1.5X TO 4X BASIC
1-220 SERIES 1 ODDS 1:10 H, 1:20 R
247-466 SERIES 2 ODDS 1:19 H, 1:20 R
221-233 SERIES 1 ODDS 1:1527 H, 1:2480 R
234-246 SERIES 2 ODDS 1:1579 H, 1:2549 R
221-246 PRINT RUN 25 SERIAL #'d SETS
221-246 NO PRICING DUE TO SCARCITY

2004 Topps Chrome Gold Refractors

Nm-Mt Ex-Mt
*GOLD 1-210/257-466: 1.25X TO 3X BASIC
*GOLD 211-220/247-256: 1.25X TO 3X BASIC
1-220 SERIES 1 ODDS 1:5 H, 1:10 R
247-466 SERIES 2 ODDS 1:9 H, 1:10 R
*GOLD AU 221-246: 2X TO 4X BASIC AU
221-233 SERIES 1 ODDS 1:759 H, 1:1208 R
234-246 SERIES 2 ODDS 1:790 H, 1:1324 R
221-246 PRINT RUN 50 SERIAL #'d SETS

2004 Topps Chrome Red X-Fractors

Nm-Mt Ex-Mt
*RED XF 1-210/257-466: 3X TO 8X BASIC
*RED XF 211-220/247-256: 3X TO 8X BASIC
1-220 ONE PER SER.1 PARALLEL HOT PACK
247-466 1 PER SER.2 PARALLEL HOT PACK
ONE HOT PACK PER SEALED HOBBY BOX
1-220 STATED PRINT RUN 63 SETS
247-466 STATED PRINT RUN 61 SETS
1-220/247-466 ARE NOT SERIAL #'d.
1-220/247-466 PRINT RUN GIVEN BY TOPPS
221-233 SERIES 1 ODDS 1:21,371 HOBBY
234-246 SERIES 2 ODDS 1:20,800 HOBBY
221-246 PRINT RUN 1 SERIAL #'d SET
221-246 NO PRICING DUE TO SCARCITY

2004 Topps Chrome Refractors

Nm-Mt Ex-Mt
*REF 1-210/257-466: 1X TO 2.5X BASIC
*REF 211-220/247-256: 1X TO 2.5X BASIC
1-220 SERIES 1 ODDS 1:4 H/R
247-466 SERIES 2 ODDS 1:4 H/R
*REF AU 221-246: 1X TO 2.5X BASIC AU
221-233 SERIES 1 ODDS 1:380 H, 1:597 R
234-246 SERIES 2 ODDS 1:375 H, 1:680 R
221-246 PRINT RUN 100 SERIAL #'d SETS
244 Lastings Milledge FY AU 60.00 18.00

2004 Topps Chrome Fashionably Great Relics

Nm-Mt Ex-Mt
ONE RELIC PER SER.1 GU HOBBY PACK
GROUP A 1:59 SER.1 RETAIL
GROUP B 1:107 SER.1 RETAIL
AD Adam Dunn Jsy A 10.00 3.00
AJ Andruw Jones Uni A 8.00 2.40
AP Albert Pujols Jsy A 25.00 7.50
AR Alex Rodriguez Uni A 15.00 4.50
BM Brett Myers Jsy A 8.00 2.40
BW Billy Wagner Jsy B 8.00 2.40
CB Craig Biggio Uni A 10.00 3.00
CD Carlos Delgado Jsy A 8.00 2.40
CF Cliff Floyd Jsy A 8.00 2.40
CJ Chipper Jones Uni A 10.00 3.00
CS Curt Schilling Jsy A 8.00 2.40
DL Derek Lowe Uni B 8.00 2.40
EC Eric Chavez Uni B 8.00 2.40
FG Freddy Garcia Jsy A 8.00 2.40
FM Fred McGriff Jsy A 10.00 3.00
FT Frank Thomas Uni A 10.00 3.00
HB Hank Blalock Jsy A 8.00 2.40
IR Ivan Rodriguez Uni B 10.00 3.00
JB Jeff Bagwell Uni A 10.00 3.00
JBO Joe Borchard Jsy A 8.00 2.40
JO John Olerud Jsy A 8.00 2.40
JR Juan Rivera Jsy A 8.00 2.40
JS John Smoltz Uni A 10.00 3.00
JV Jose Vidro Jsy A 8.00 2.40
KB Kevin Brown Jsy B 8.00 2.40
MM Mark Mulder Uni A 8.00 2.40
MP Mike Piazza Uni A 15.00 4.50
MR Manny Ramirez Uni A 10.00 3.00
MS Mike Sweeney Uni A 8.00 2.40
NG Nomar Garciaparra Uni B 15.00 4.50
PM Pedro Martinez Jsy A 10.00 3.00
RP Rafael Palmeiro Jsy A 10.00 3.00
SS Sammy Sosa Jsy A 15.00 4.50
TH Tim Hudson Uni B 8.00 2.40
THO Trevor Hoffman Uni A 8.00 2.40
VW Vernon Wells Jsy B 8.00 2.40
WP Wily Mo Pena Jsy A 8.00 2.40

2004 Topps Chrome Handle With Care Bat Knob Relics

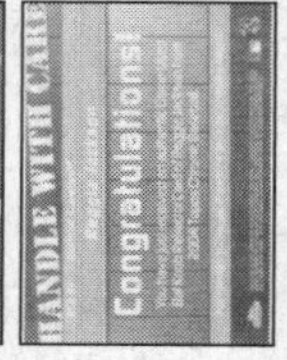

Nm-Mt Ex-Mt
STATED PRINT RUN 5 SERIAL #'d SETS
1 OF 1 PRINT RUN 1 SERIAL #'d SET
NO PRICING DUE TO SCARCITY
RANDOM IN SERIES 1 HOBBY RELIC PACKS
AK Al Kaline
AP Albert Pujols
AR Alex Rodriguez
AS Alfonso Soriano
BR Brooks Robinson
CF Carlton Fisk
CY Carl Yastrzemski
FR Frank Robinson
GB George Brett
HK Harmon Killebrew
JB Johnny Bench
JG Jason Giambi
JT Jim Thome
LB Lance Berkman
LBR Lou Brock
LG Luis Gonzalez
MT Miguel Tejada
NG Nomar Garciaparra
PM Paul Molitor
RJ Reggie Jackson
RY Robin Yount
TH Torii Hunter
WB Wade Boggs
WM Willie Mays
WS Willie Stargell

2004 Topps Chrome Presidential First Pitch Seat Relics

Nm-Mt Ex-Mt
SERIES 2 ODDS 1:15 BOX-LOADER HOBBY
SERIES 2 ODDS 1:633 HOBBY
STATED PRINT RUN 100 SETS
CARDS ARE NOT SERIAL-NUMBERED
PRINT RUN INFO PROVIDED BY TOPPS
BC Bill Clinton 50.00 15.00
CC Calvin Coolidge 25.00 7.50
DE Dwight Eisenhower 25.00 7.50
FR Franklin D. Roosevelt 40.00 12.00
GB George W. Bush 50.00 15.00
GF Gerald Ford 40.00 12.00
GHB George H.W. Bush 40.00 12.00
HH Herbert Hoover 25.00 7.50
HT Harry Truman 25.00 7.50
JK John F. Kennedy 50.00 15.00
LJ Lyndon B. Johnson 25.00 7.50
RN Richard Nixon 50.00 15.00
RR Ronald Reagan 60.00 18.00
WH Warren Harding 25.00 7.50
WT William Taft 25.00 7.50
WW Woodrow Wilson 25.00 7.50

2004 Topps Chrome Presidential Pastime Refractors

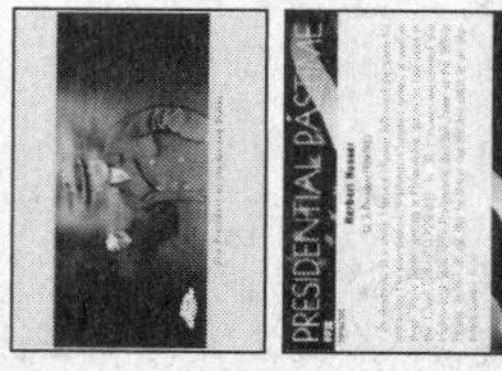

Nm-Mt Ex-Mt
COMPLETE SET (42) 120.00 36.00
SERIES 2 ODDS 1:9 HOBBY
*X-FRACTOR p/r 26-43: 2X TO 5X BASIC
X-FRACTOR SER.2 ODDS 1:400 H, 1:791 R
X-F PRINT RUNS B/WN 1-43 COPIES PER
NO X-F PRICING ON QTY OF 25 OR LESS
PP1 George Washington 6.00 1.80
PP2 John Adams 4.00 1.20
PP3 Thomas Jefferson 6.00 1.80
PP4 James Madison 4.00 1.20
PP5 James Monroe 4.00 1.20
PP6 John Quincy Adams 4.00 1.20
PP7 Andrew Jackson 4.00 1.20
PP8 Martin Van Buren 4.00 1.20
PP9 William Harrison 4.00 1.20
PP10 John Tyler 4.00 1.20
PP11 James Polk 4.00 1.20
PP12 Zachary Taylor 4.00 1.20
PP13 Millard Fillmore 4.00 1.20
PP14 Franklin Pierce 4.00 1.20
PP15 James Buchanan 4.00 1.20
PP16 Abraham Lincoln 6.00 1.80
PP17 Andrew Johnson 4.00 1.20
PP18 Ulysses S. Grant 5.00 1.50
PP19 Rutherford B. Hayes 4.00 1.20
PP20 James Garfield 4.00 1.20
PP21 Chester Arthur 4.00 1.20
PP22 Grover Cleveland 4.00 1.20
PP23 Benjamin Harrison 4.00 1.20
PP24 William McKinley 4.00 1.20
PP25 Theodore Roosevelt 5.00 1.50
PP26 William Taft 4.00 1.20
PP27 Woodrow Wilson 4.00 1.20
PP28 Warren Harding 4.00 1.20
PP29 Calvin Coolidge 4.00 1.20
PP30 Herbert Hoover 4.00 1.20
PP31 Franklin D. Roosevelt 5.00 1.50
PP32 Harry Truman 4.00 1.20
PP33 Dwight Eisenhower 4.00 1.20
PP34 John F. Kennedy 5.00 1.50
PP35 Lyndon B. Johnson 4.00 1.20
PP36 Richard Nixon 5.00 1.50
PP37 Gerald Ford 5.00 1.50
PP38 Jimmy Carter 4.00 1.20
PP39 Ronald Reagan 12.00 3.60
PP40 George H.W. Bush 5.00 1.50
PP41 Bill Clinton 6.00 1.80
PP42 George W. Bush 6.00 1.80

2004 Topps Chrome Town Heroes Relics

Nm-Mt Ex-Mt
SER.2 ODDS 1 PER HOBBY BOX-LOADER
SER.2 ODDS 1:48 RETAIL
AP Albert Pujols Bat 15.00 4.50
AR Alex Rodriguez Bat 15.00 4.50
BZ Barry Zito Uni 8.00 2.40
CJ Chipper Jones Jsy 10.00 3.00
EC Eric Chavez Uni 8.00 2.40
FT Frank Thomas Jsy 10.00 3.00
HN Hideo Nomo Jsy 10.00 3.00
JG Jason Giambi Uni 8.00 2.40
JR Jose Reyes Bat 8.00 2.40
KW Kerry Wood Jsy 10.00 3.00
LB Lance Berkman Jsy 8.00 2.40
MM Mark Mulder Uni 8.00 2.40
MP Mark Prior Bat 10.00 3.00
MR Manny Ramirez Bat 10.00 3.00
MT Miguel Tejada Bat 8.00 2.40
NG Nomar Garciaparra Bat 10.00 3.00
RH Rich Harden Uni 8.00 2.40
RP Rafael Palmeiro Jsy 10.00 3.00
SS Sammy Sosa Jsy 15.00 4.50
SST Shannon Stewart Jsy 8.00 2.40
TH Tim Hudson Uni 8.00 2.40

2004 Topps Chrome Traded

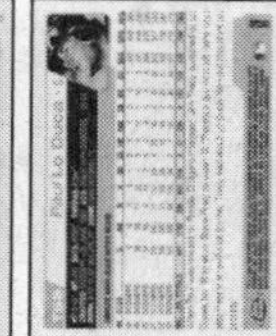

These cards were issued at a stated rate of two per 2004 Topps Traded pack. Cards numbered 1 through 65 feature veterans who were traded while cards 66 through 70 feature managers. Cards numbered 71 through 90 feature high draft picks, cards numbered 91 through 110 feature prospect and cards 111 through 220 feature Rookie Cards. All of these cards were issued with a "T" prefix.

Nm-Mt Ex-Mt
COMPLETE SET (220) 120.00 36.00
COMMON CARD (1-70) .75 .23
COMMON CARD (71-90) 1.25 .35
COMMON CARD (91-110) 1.00 .30
COMMON CARD (111-220) 1.00 .30
2 PER 2004 TOPPS TRADED HOBBY PACK
2 PER 2004 TOPPS TRADED HTA PACK
2 PER 2004 TOPPS TRADED RETAIL PACK
PLATE ODDS 1:1151 H, 1:1173 R, 1:327 HTA
PLATE PRINT RUN 1 SET PER COLOR
BLACK-CYAN-MAGENTA-YELLOW ISSUED
NO PLATE PRICING DUE TO SCARCITY
T1 Pokey Reese .75 .23
T2 Tony Womack .75 .23
T3 Richard Hidalgo .75 .23

T4 Juan Uribe .75 .23
T5 J.D. Drew .75 .23
T6 Alex Gonzalez .75 .23
T7 Carlos Guillen .75 .23
T8 Doug Mientkiewicz .75 .23
T9 Fernando Vina .75 .23
T10 Milton Bradley .75 .23
T11 Kelvim Escobar .75 .23
T12 Ben Grieve .75 .23
T13 Brian Jordan .75 .23
T14 A.J. Pierzynski .75 .23
T15 Billy Wagner .75 .23
T16 Terrence Long .75 .23
T17 Carlos Beltran 1.25 .35
T18 Carl Everett .75 .23
T19 Reggie Sanders .75 .23
T20 Javy Lopez .75 .23
T21 Jay Payton .75 .23
T22 Octavio Dotel .75 .23
T23 Eddie Guardado .75 .23
T24 Andy Pettitte 1.25 .35
T25 Richie Sexson .75 .23
T26 Ronnie Belliard .75 .23
T27 Michael Tucker .75 .23
T28 Brad Fullmer .75 .23
T29 Freddy Garcia .75 .23
T30 Bartolo Colon .75 .23
T31 Larry Walker 1.25 .35
T32 Mark Kotsay .75 .23
T33 Jason Marquis .75 .23
T34 Dustan Mohr .75 .23
T35 Javier Vazquez .75 .23
T36 Nomar Garciaparra 3.00 .90
T37 Tino Martinez 1.25 .35
T38 Hee Seop Choi .75 .23
T39 Damian Miller .75 .23
T40 Jose Lima .75 .23
T41 Ty Wigginton .75 .23
T42 Raul Ibanez .75 .23
T43 Danys Baez .75 .23
T44 Tony Clark .75 .23
T45 Greg Maddux 3.00 .90
T46 Victor Zambrano .75 .23
T47 Orlando Cabrera Sox .75 .23
T48 Jose Cruz Jr. .75 .23
T49 Kris Benson .75 .23
T50 Alex Rodriguez 4.00 1.20
T51 Steve Finley .75 .23
T52 Ramon Hernandez .75 .23
T53 Esteban Loaiza .75 .23
T54 Ugueth Urbina .75 .23
T55 Jeff Weaver .75 .23
T56 Flash Gordon .75 .23
T57 Jose Contreras .75 .23
T58 Paul Lo Duca .75 .23
T59 Junior Spivey .75 .23
T60 Curt Schilling 2.00 .60
T61 Brad Penny .75 .23
T62 Braden Looper .75 .23
T63 Miguel Cairo .75 .23
T64 Juan Encarnacion .75 .23
T65 Miguel Batista .75 .23
T66 Terry Francona MG .75 .23
T67 Lee Mazzilli MG .75 .23
T68 Al Pedrique MG .75 .23
T69 Ozzie Guillen MG .75 .23
T70 Phil Garner MG .75 .23
T71 Matt Bush DP RC 6.00 1.80
T72 Homer Bailey DP RC 5.00 1.50
T73 Greg Golson DP RC 4.00 1.20
T74 Kyle Waldrop DP RC 3.00 .90
T75 Richie Robnett DP RC 3.00 .90
T76 Jay Rainville DP RC 3.00 .90
T77 Bill Bray DP RC 1.25 .35
T78 Phillip Hughes DP RC 3.00 .90
T79 Scott Elbert DP RC 3.00 .90
T80 Josh Fields DP RC 5.00 1.50
T81 Justin Orenduff DP RC 3.00 .90
T82 Dan Putnam DP RC 3.00 .90
T83 Chris Nelson DP RC 6.00 1.80
T84 Blake DeWitt DP RC 6.00 1.80
T85 J.P. Howell DP RC 3.00 .90
T86 Huston Street DP RC 3.00 .90
T87 Kurt Suzuki DP RC 4.00 1.20
T88 Erick San Pedro DP RC 1.25 .35
T89 Matt Tuiasosopo DP RC 8.00 2.40
T90 Matt Macri DP RC 3.00 .90
T91 Chad Tracy PROS 1.00 .30
T92 Scott Hairston PROS 1.00 .30
T93 Jonny Gomes PROS 1.00 .30
T94 Chin-Feng Chen PROS 1.00 .30
T95 Chien-Ming Wang PROS 1.00 .30
T96 Dustin McGowan PROS 1.00 .30
T97 Chris Burke PROS 1.00 .30
T98 Denny Bautista PROS 1.00 .30
T99 Preston Larrison PROS 1.00 .30
T100 Kevin Youkilis PROS 1.00 .30
T101 John Maine PROS 1.00 .30
T102 Guillermo Quiroz PROS 1.00 .30
T103 Dave Krynzel PROS 1.00 .30
T104 David Kelton PROS 1.00 .30
T105 Edwin Encarnacion PROS 1.00 .30
T106 Chad Gaudin PROS 1.00 .30
T107 Sergio Mitre PROS 1.00 .30
T108 Laynce Nix PROS 1.00 .30
T109 David Parrish PROS 1.00 .30
T110 Brandon Claussen PROS 1.00 .30
T111 Frank Francisco FY RC 1.00 .30
T112 Brian Dallimore FY RC 1.00 .30
T113 Jim Crowell FY RC 1.25 .35
T114 Andres Blanco FY RC 1.00 .30
T115 Eduardo Villacis FY RC 1.00 .30
T116 Kazuhito Tadano FY RC 1.25 .35
T117 Aarom Baldiris FY RC 1.25 .35
T118 Justin Germano FY RC 1.00 .30
T119 Joey Gathright FY RC 3.00 .90
T120 Franklyn Gracesqui FY RC 1.00 .30
T121 Chin-Lung Hu FY RC 2.50 .75
T122 Scott Olsen FY RC 3.00 .90
T123 Tyler Davidson FY RC 1.25 .35
T124 Fausto Carmona FY RC 2.00 .60
T125 Tim Hutting FY RC 1.00 .30
T126 Ryan Meaux FY RC 1.00 .30
T127 Jon Connolly FY RC 2.50 .75
T128 Hector Made FY RC 2.00 .60
T129 Jamie Brown FY RC 1.00 .30
T130 Paul McAnulty FY RC 2.00 .60
T131 Chris Saenz FY RC 1.00 .30
T132 Marland Williams FY RC 1.25 .35
T133 Mike Huggins FY RC 1.00 .30

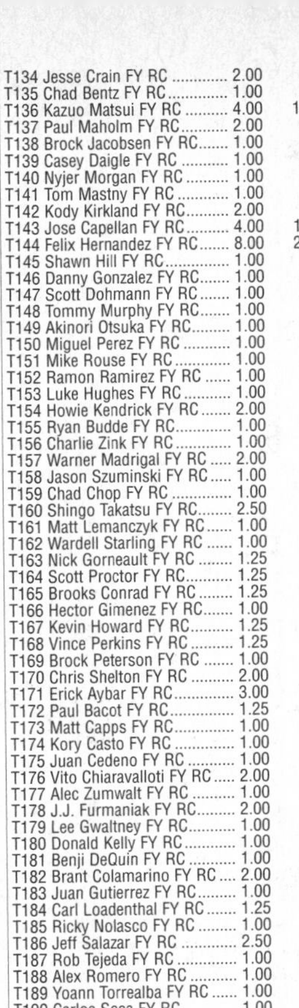

T134 Jesse Crain FY RC 2.00 .60
T135 Chad Bentz FY RC 1.00 .30
T136 Kazuo Matsui FY RC 4.00 1.20
T137 Paul Maholm FY RC 2.00 .60
T138 Brock Jacobsen FY RC 1.00 .30
T139 Casey Daigle FY RC 1.00 .30
T140 Nyjer Morgan FY RC 1.00 .30
T141 Tom Mastny FY RC 1.00 .30
T142 Kody Kirkland FY RC 2.00 .60
T143 Jose Capellan FY RC 4.00 1.20
T144 Felix Hernandez FY RC 8.00 2.40
T145 Shawn Hill FY RC 1.00 .30
T146 Danny Gonzalez FY RC 1.00 .30
T147 Scott Dohmann FY RC 1.00 .30
T148 Tommy Murphy FY RC 1.00 .30
T149 Akinori Otsuka FY RC 1.00 .30
T150 Miguel Perez FY RC 1.00 .30
T151 Mike Rouse FY RC 1.00 .30
T152 Ramon Ramirez FY RC 1.00 .30
T153 Luke Hughes FY RC 1.00 .30
T154 Howie Kendrick FY RC 2.00 .60
T155 Ryan Budde FY RC 1.00 .30
T156 Charlie Zink FY RC 1.00 .30
T157 Warner Madrigal FY RC 2.00 .60
T158 Jason Szuminski FY RC 1.00 .30
T159 Chad Chop FY RC 1.00 .30
T160 Shingo Takatsu FY RC 2.50 .75
T161 Matt Lemanczyk FY RC 1.00 .30
T162 Wardell Starling FY RC 1.00 .30
T163 Nick Gorneault FY RC 1.25 .35
T164 Scott Proctor FY RC 1.25 .35
T165 Brooks Conrad FY RC 1.25 .35
T166 Hector Gimenez FY RC 1.00 .30
T167 Kevin Howard FY RC 1.25 .35
T168 Vince Perkins FY RC 1.25 .35
T169 Brock Peterson FY RC 1.00 .30
T170 Chris Shelton FY RC 2.00 .60
T171 Erick Aybar FY RC 3.00 .90
T172 Paul Bacot FY RC 1.25 .35
T173 Matt Capps FY RC 1.00 .30
T174 Kory Casto FY RC 1.00 .30
T175 Juan Cedeno FY RC 1.00 .30
T176 Vito Chiaravalloti FY RC 2.00 .60
T177 Alec Zumwalt FY RC 1.00 .30
T178 J.J. Furmaniak FY RC 2.00 .60
T179 Lee Gwaltney FY RC 1.00 .30
T180 Donald Kelly FY RC 1.00 .30
T181 Benji DeQuin FY RC 1.00 .30
T182 Brant Colamarino FY RC 2.00 .60
T183 Juan Gutierrez FY RC 1.00 .30
T184 Carl Loadenthal FY RC 1.25 .35
T185 Ricky Nolasco FY RC 1.00 .30
T186 Jeff Salazar FY RC 2.50 .75
T187 Rob Tejeda FY RC 1.00 .30
T188 Alex Romero FY RC 1.00 .30
T189 Yoann Torrealba FY RC 1.00 .30
T190 Carlos Sosa FY RC 1.00 .30
T191 Tim Bittner FY RC 1.00 .30
T192 Chris Aguila FY RC 1.00 .30
T193 Jason Frasor FY RC 1.00 .30
T194 Reid Gorecki FY RC 1.00 .30
T195 Dustin Nippert FY RC 1.00 .30
T196 Javier Guzman FY RC 1.25 .35
T197 Harvey Garcia FY RC 1.00 .30
T198 Ivan Ochoa FY RC 1.00 .30
T199 David Wallace FY RC 1.25 .35
T200 Joel Zumaya FY RC 2.00 .60
T201 Casey Kopitzke FY RC 1.00 .30
T202 Lincoln Holdzkom FY RC 1.00 .30
T203 Chad Santos FY RC 1.00 .30
T204 Brian Pilkington FY RC 1.00 .30
T205 Terry Jones FY RC 1.25 .35
T206 Jerome Gamble FY RC 1.00 .30
T207 Brad Eldred FY RC 3.00 .90
T208 David Pauley FY RC 1.00 .30
T209 Kevin Davidson FY RC 1.00 .30
T210 Damaso Espino FY RC 1.00 .30
T211 Tom Farmer FY RC 1.00 .30
T212 Michael Mooney FY RC 1.00 .30
T213 James Tomlin FY RC 1.00 .30
T214 Greg Thissen FY RC 1.00 .30
T215 Calvin Hayes FY RC 1.25 .35
T216 Fernando Cortez FY RC 1.00 .30
T217 Sergio Silva FY RC 1.00 .30
T218 Jon de Vries FY RC 1.00 .30
T219 Don Sutton FY RC 2.50 .75
T220 Leo Nunez FY RC 1.00 .30

2004 Topps Chrome Traded Blue Refractors

Nm-Mt Ex-Mt
ODDS 1:4574 H, 1:4925 R, 1:1238 HTA
STATED PRINT RUN 1 SERIAL #'d SET
NO PRICING DUE TO SCARCITY

2004 Topps Chrome Traded Refractors

Nm-Mt Ex-Mt
*REF 1-70: 2X TO 5X BASIC
*REF 71-90: 1X TO 2.5X BASIC
*REF 91-110: 1.5X TO 4X BASIC
*REF 111-220: 1.5X TO 4X BASIC
STATED ODDS 1:12 HOB/RET, 1:4 HTA
STATED PRINT RUN 355 SETS
CARDS ARE NOT SERIAL-NUMBERED
PRINT RUN INFO PROVIDED BY TOPPS

2004 Topps Chrome Traded X-Fractors

Nm-Mt Ex-Mt
*XF 1-70: 8X TO 20X BASIC
*XF 91-110: 6X TO 15X BASIC
ONE XF PACK PER SEALED HTA BOX.
ONE XF CARD PER XF PACK.
STATED PRINT RUN 20 SERIAL #'d SETS
NO PRICING ON 71-90 DUE TO SCARCITY
NO PRICING ON 91-110 DUE TO SCARCITY

2004 Topps Clubhouse Relics

This 154-card set was released in August, 2004. The set was issued in two-card packs (both of which were game-used pieces) with an $30 SRP which came 10 packs to a box and six boxes to a case.

Nm-Mt Ex-Mt
TWO RELICS PER PACK

GROUP A CARDS NOT SERIAL-NUMBERED
GROUP A PRINT RUNS PROVIDED BY TOPPS
AB Armando Benitez Jsy C 5.00 1.50
AD Adam Dunn Jsy C 8.00 2.40
AG Adrian Gonzalez Jsy C 5.00 1.50
AJ Andruw Jones Jsy C 5.00 1.50
AK Al Kaline Jsy E 10.00 3.00
AL Al Leiter Jsy C 5.00 1.50
AP Albert Pujols Jsy C 15.00 4.50
AR Alex Rodriguez Bat C 12.00 3.60
ARA Aramis Ramirez Bat B 5.00 1.50
AS Alfonso Soriano Bat D 8.00 2.40
BA Bobby Abreu Jsy D 5.00 1.50
BB Bret Boone Jsy E 5.00 1.50
BF Brad Fullmer Bat A/200 8.00 2.40
BL Barry Larkin Bat A/200 12.00 3.60
BM Brett Myers Jsy D 5.00 1.50
BW Bernie Williams Uni C 8.00 2.40
BWA Billy Wagner Jsy C 5.00 1.50
BZ Barry Zito Jsy A/230 8.00 2.40
CCR Carl Crawford Bat B 5.00 1.50
CD Carlos Delgado Jsy A/200 8.00 2.40
CE Carl Everett Bat C 5.00 1.50
CFC Chin-Feng Chen Jsy E 10.00 3.00
CFL Cliff Floyd Uni B 5.00 1.50
CG Cristian Guzman Jsy B 5.00 1.50
CJ Chipper Jones Jsy E 8.00 2.40
CL Chris Lubanski Jsy A/209 8.00 2.40
CP Chan Ho Park Jsy E 5.00 1.50
CPA Corey Patterson Jsy A/267 8.00 2.40
CR Cal Ripken Jsy E 25.00 7.50
CS C.C. Sabathia Jsy E 5.00 1.50
CSC Curt Schilling Jsy C 5.00 1.50
CST Casey Stengel Uni A/217 15.00 4.50
CY Carl Yastrzemski Jsy E 15.00 4.50
DC Dave Concepcion Bat D 6.00 1.80
DE Dennis Eckersley Uni E 10.00 3.00
DJ Derek Jeter Bat C 15.00 4.50
DL Derek Lowe Jsy A/200 8.00 2.40
DP Dave Parker Bat A/292 10.00 3.00
DS Duke Snider Bat C 10.00 3.00
EA Edgardo Alfonzo Bat A/286 8.00 2.40
EC Eric Chavez Uni E 5.00 1.50
EG Eric Gagne Uni E 8.00 2.40
EH Estee Harris Jsy A/206 RC 8.00 2.40
EL Esteban Loaiza Jsy B 5.00 1.50
EM Eddie Mathews Jsy A/174 25.00 7.50
EMA Edgar Martinez Bat A/200 12.00 3.60
EMU Eddie Murray Bat B 12.00 3.60
FM Fred McGriff Bat E 8.00 2.40
FR Frank Robinson Uni B 8.00 2.40
FT Frank Thomas Bat C 8.00 2.40
FV Fern Valenzuela Bat A/288 10.00 3.00
GB George Brett Uni E 15.00 4.50
GC Gary Carter Jkt A/221 10.00 3.00
GM Greg Maddux Jsy B 12.00 3.60
GS Gary Sheffield Jsy D 5.00 1.50
HA Hank Aaron Bat A/113 50.00 15.00
HB Hank Bauer Bat B 8.00 2.40
HBL Hank Blalock Jsy E 5.00 1.50
HN Hideo Nomo Bat A/207 12.00 3.60
IR Ivan Rodriguez Jsy D 8.00 2.40
JB Jeff Bagwell Jsy A/200 12.00 3.60
JBE Johnny Bench Uni E 10.00 3.00
JBU Jeromy Burnitz Bat A/208 8.00 2.40
JC Jeff Cirillo Bat B 5.00 1.50
JCA Joe Carter Jsy A/259 10.00 3.00
JF Jonathan Fulton Jsy A/200 8.00 2.40
JG Jason Giambi Uni E 5.00 1.50
JGO Juan Gonzalez Bat B 8.00 2.40
JH James Houser Jsy A/182 8.00 2.40
JKE Jeff Kent Jsy A/200 8.00 2.40
JL Javy Lopez Jsy D 5.00 1.50
JO John Olerud Jsy B 5.00 1.50
JP Jorge Posada Jsy A/264 12.00 3.60
JPB Josh Beckett Jsy A/195 8.00 2.40
JR Jackie Robinson Bat A/262 50.00 15.00
JRE Jose Reyes Jsy E 5.00 1.50
JRO Jimmy Rollins Jsy E 5.00 1.50
JS Jay Sborz Jsy A/176 8.00 2.40
JSM John Smoltz Jsy E 8.00 2.40
JT Jim Thome Jsy C 8.00 2.40
JV Javier Vazquez Jsy A/283 8.00 2.40
JVI Jose Vidro Jsy A/275 8.00 2.40
KB Kevin Brown Uni A/168 8.00 2.40
KG Ken Griffey Jr. Jsy A/200 20.00 6.00
KI Kazuhisa Ishii Jsy C 5.00 1.50
KM Kevin Millwood Jsy E 5.00 1.50
LB Lance Berkman Jsy B 5.00 1.50
LG Luis Gonzalez Jsy B 5.00 1.50
LW Larry Walker Jsy C 8.00 2.40
MB Marlon Byrd Jsy B 5.00 1.50
MC Miguel Cabrera Jsy B 8.00 2.40
MDG Marquis Grissom Bat B 5.00 1.50
MG Mark Grace Jsy E 10.00 3.00
MH Mickey Hall Jsy A/217 8.00 2.40
MM Mark Mulder Uni E 5.00 1.50
MO Magglio Ordonez Bat B 5.00 1.50
MP Mike Piazza Jsy B 12.00 3.60
MR Manny Ramirez Jsy A/207 12.00 3.60
MRI Mariano Rivera Uni A/239 12.00 3.60
MS Mike Schmidt Jsy D 15.00 4.50
MSW Mike Sweeney Jsy E 5.00 1.50
MT Mark Teixeira Jsy D 5.00 1.50
MTE Miguel Tejada Uni B 5.00 1.50
NG Nomar Garciaparra Bat B 12.00 3.60
NR Nolan Ryan Uni E 20.00 6.00
OC Orlando Cepeda Bat B 8.00 2.40
OH Orel Hershiser Jsy E 6.00 1.80
OHU Orlando Hudson Jsy A/200 8.00 2.40
OS Ozzie Smith Jsy D 12.00 3.60
PB Pat Burrell Jsy E 5.00 1.50
PK Paul Konerko Bat B 5.00 1.50
PL Paul Lo Duca Uni B 5.00 1.50
PM Pedro Martinez Jsy A/200 12.00 3.60
PW Preston Wilson Jsy B 5.00 1.50
RA Roberto Alomar Uni E 8.00 2.40
RB Rocco Baldelli Jsy E 5.00 1.50
RC Roberto Clemente Bat B 50.00 15.00
RCE Ron Cey Bat B 8.00 2.40
RF Rafael Furcal Jsy E 5.00 1.50
RH Ramon Hernandez Jsy E 5.00 1.50
RHE Rickey Henderson Uni E 10.00 3.00
RJ Reggie Jackson Jsy D 10.00 3.00
RLC Roger Cedeno Bat B 5.00 1.50
RP Rafael Palmeiro Uni A/200 12.00 3.60
RS Richie Sexson Bat A/200 8.00 2.40
RSA Ryne Sandberg Bat E 15.00 4.50
RSI Ruben Sierra Bat B 5.00 1.50
RY Robin Yount Bat B 15.00 4.50
SF Steve Finley Jsy C 5.00 1.50
SG Shawn Green Jsy C 5.00 1.50
SL Steve Lerud Jsy A/213 8.00 2.40
SR Scott Rolen Bat B 8.00 2.40
SS Sammy Sosa Jsy E 12.00 3.60
TA Tony Armas Jr. Jsy C 5.00 1.50
TB Tony Batista Jsy E 5.00 1.50
TG Tom Glavine Jsy B 8.00 2.40
TGL Troy Glaus Jsy E 5.00 1.50
TGW Tony Gwynn Bat E 12.00 3.60
TH Tim Hudson Uni E 5.00 1.50
THE Todd Helton Bat C 8.00 2.40
THU Torii Hunter Jsy E 5.00 1.50
TM Tino Martinez Uni E 8.00 2.40
TP Tony Perez Uni B 8.00 2.40
TPE Troy Percival Uni B 5.00 1.50
TS Tim Salmon Uni C 8.00 2.40
VG Vladimir Guerrero Jsy E 8.00 2.40
VW Vernon Wells Bat A/200 8.00 2.40
WB Wade Boggs Jsy A/250 15.00 4.50
WC Will Clark Jsy E 10.00 3.00
WF Whitey Ford Uni A/296 15.00 4.50
WM Willie Mays Jsy D 40.00 12.00
WP Wily Mo Pena Jsy B 5.00 1.50
WS Willie Stargell Uni A/200 15.00 4.50
YB Yogi Berra Uni B 12.00 3.60

2004 Topps Clubhouse Black Relics

Nm-Mt Ex-Mt
*BLACK: 1.25X TO 3X ACTIVE GROUP C-E
*BLACK: 1X TO 2.5X RETIRED GROUP C-E
*BLACK: 1.25X TO 3X ACTIVE GROUP B
*BLACK: .75X TO 2X RETIRED GROUP B
*BLACK: .75X TO 2X ACTIVE GROUP A
*BLACK: .6X TO 1.5X RETIRED GROUP A
STATED ODDS 1:16
STATED PRINT RUN 25 SERIAL #'d SETS
NO RC YR PRICING DUE TO SCARCITY

2004 Topps Clubhouse Copper Relics

Nm-Mt Ex-Mt
*COPPER: .5X TO 1.2X ACTIVE C-E
*COPPER: .6X TO 1.5X RETIRED C-E
*COPPER: .5X TO 1.2X ACTIVE B
*COPPER: .5X TO 1.2X RETIRED B
*COPPER: .4X TO 1X ACTIVE A
*COPPER: .4X TO 1X RETIRED A
STATED ODDS 1:4
STATED PRINT RUN 99 SERIAL #'d SETS

2004 Topps Clubhouse Red Relics

Nm-Mt Ex-Mt
STATED ODDS 1:399
STATED PRINT RUN 1 SERIAL #'d SET
NO PRICING DUE TO SCARCITY

2004 Topps Clubhouse All-Star Appeal Relics Base

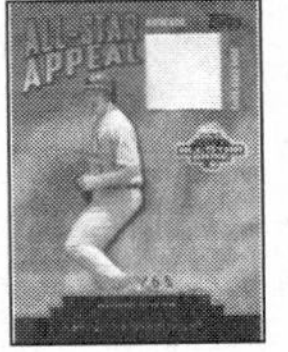

Nm-Mt Ex-Mt
*BASE: .5X TO 1.2X ON-DECK CIRCLE
STATED ODDS 1:36
STATED PRINT RUN 65 SERIAL #'d SETS
ER Edgar Renteria 10.00 3.00
RF Rafael Furcal 10.00 3.00

2004 Topps Clubhouse All-Star Appeal Relics On-Deck Circle

Nm-Mt Ex-Mt
STATED ODDS 1:26
STATED PRINT RUN 90 SERIAL #'d SETS
BALL STATED ODDS 1:237
BALL PRINT RUN 10 SERIAL #'d SETS
NO BALL PRICING DUE TO SCARCITY
AJ Andruw Jones 8.00 2.40
AP Albert Pujols 20.00 6.00
AR Alex Rodriguez 15.00 4.50
AS Alfonso Soriano 10.00 3.00
BB Bret Boone 8.00 2.40
CD Carlos Delgado 8.00 2.40
EM Edgar Martinez 10.00 3.00
GA Garret Anderson 8.00 2.40
GS Gary Sheffield 8.00 2.40
HB Hank Blalock 8.00 2.40
JE Jim Edmonds 8.00 2.40
JG Jason Giambi 8.00 2.40
JL Javy Lopez 8.00 2.40
JP Jorge Posada 10.00 3.00
JV Jose Vidro 8.00 2.40
LC Luis Castillo 8.00 2.40
LG Luis Gonzalez 8.00 2.40
ML Mike Lowell 8.00 2.40
MO Magglio Ordonez 8.00 2.40
NG Nomar Garciaparra 15.00 4.50
PW Preston Wilson 8.00 2.40
RS Richie Sexson 8.00 2.40
SR Scott Rolen 10.00 3.00
TG Troy Glaus 8.00 2.40
TH Todd Helton 10.00 3.00
VW Vernon Wells 8.00 2.40

2004 Topps Clubhouse All-Star Appeal Relics Autographs Ball

Nm-Mt Ex-Mt
STATED ODDS 1:510
STATED PRINT RUN 30 SERIAL #'d SETS
GA Garret Anderson 30.00 9.00
GS Gary Sheffield 50.00 15.00
HB Hank Blalock 30.00 9.00
JP Jorge Posada 60.00 18.00

2004 Topps Clubhouse All-Star Appeal Relics Autographs Base

Nm-Mt Ex-Mt
STATED ODDS 1:308
STATED PRINT RUN 50 SERIAL #'d SETS
GA Garret Anderson 25.00 7.50
GS Gary Sheffield 40.00 12.00
HB Hank Blalock 25.00 7.50
JP Jorge Posada 50.00 15.00

2004 Topps Clubhouse All-Star Appeal Relics Autographs On-Deck Circle

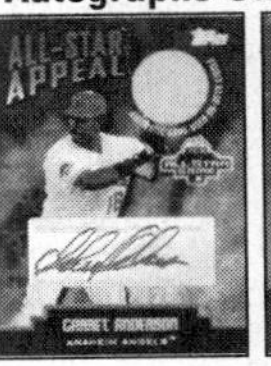

Nm-Mt Ex-Mt
GROUP A ODDS 1:363
GROUP B ODDS 1:192
GROUP C ODDS 1:146
GROUP D ODDS 1:67
PRINT RUNS B/WN 170-920 COPIES PER
GA Garret Anderson B/320 15.00 4.50
GS Gary Sheffield A/170 40.00 12.00
HB Hank Blalock D/920 10.00 3.00
JP Jorge Posada C/420 40.00 12.00

2004 Topps Clubhouse Career Legends Relics

 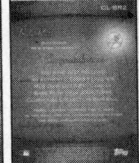

Nm-Mt Ex-Mt
STATED ODDS 1:46
PRINT RUNS B/WN 11-184 COPIES PER
NO PRICING ON QTY OF 12 OR LESS
BR1 Babe Ruth HR Bat/60 200.00 60.00
BR2 Babe Ruth RBI Bat/171 180.00 55.00
BR3 Babe Ruth 2B Bat/45 200.00 60.00
BR4 Babe Ruth 3B Bat/16 250.00 75.00
BR5 Babe Ruth SN Bat/22 250.00 75.00
EB1 Ernie Banks RBI Uni/143 15.00 4.50
EB2 Ernie Banks 2B Uni/34 25.00 7.50
EB3 Ernie Banks HR Jkt/47 20.00 6.00
EB4 Ernie Banks 3B Jkt/11
EB5 Ernie Banks SN Jkt/19 40.00 12.00
EB6 Ernie Banks BB Jkt/71 20.00 6.00
LG1 Lou Gehrig HR Bat/49 150.00 45.00

LG2 Lou Gehrig RBI Bat/184 120.00 36.00
LG3 Lou Gehrig 2B Bat/52 150.00 45.00
LG4 Lou Gehrig 3B Bat/20 200.00 60.00
LG5 Lou Gehrig SN Bat/17 200.00 60.00
TC1 Ty Cobb SN Bat/24 120.00 36.00
TC2 Ty Cobb HR Uni/12
TC3 Ty Cobb 2B Uni/47 120.00 36.00
TC4 Ty Cobb 3B Uni/24 150.00 45.00
WM1 Willie Mays HR Jsy/52 80.00 24.00
WM2 Willie Mays RBI Jsy/141 60.00 18.00
WM3 Willie Mays 2B Jsy/43 80.00 24.00
WM4 Willie Mays 3B Jsy/20 80.00 24.00
WM5 Willie Mays SN Jsy/22 80.00 24.00

2004 Topps Clubhouse Double Play Relics

Nm-Mt Ex-Mt
STATED ODDS 1:165
STATED PRINT RUN 75 SERIAL #'d SETS
B ='S BAT, J ='S JSY, U ='S UNI
CLE Brandon Phillips Jsy 25.00 7.50
Omar Vizquel Jsy
Travis Hafner Bat
NYM Jose Reyes Jsy 25.00 7.50
Ty Wigginton Uni
Mike Piazza Bat
NYY Derek Jeter Bat 50.00 15.00
Alex Rodriguez Bat
Jason Giambi Bat
PHI Jimmy Rollins Jsy 25.00 7.50
David Bell Bat
Jim Thome Bat
SDP Khalil Greene Jsy 25.00 7.50
Sean Burroughs Bat
Phil Nevin Jsy

2004 Topps Clubhouse Frozen Ropes Relics

Nm-Mt Ex-Mt
STATED ODDS 1:26
STATED PRINT RUN 50 SERIAL #'d SETS
AD Adam Dunn Jsy 15.00 4.50
ADA Andre Dawson Bat 10.00 3.00
AH Aubrey Huff Jsy 10.00 3.00
AP Albert Pujols Jsy 25.00 7.50
AR Alex Rodriguez Bat 20.00 6.00
AS Alfonso Soriano Bat 15.00 4.50
BA Bobby Abreu Jsy 10.00 3.00
BR Brooks Robinson Bat 15.00 4.50
BW Bernie Williams Uni 15.00 4.50
CB Craig Biggio Bat 15.00 4.50
CE Carl Everett Bat 10.00 3.00
CJ Chipper Jones Jsy 15.00 4.50
CY Carl Yastrzemski Jsy 30.00 9.00
DM Don Mattingly Jsy 40.00 12.00
DMU Dale Murphy Bat 15.00 4.50
DS Duke Snider Bat 15.00 4.50
EC Eric Chavez Jsy 10.00 3.00
EM Edgar Martinez Bat 15.00 4.50
GC Gary Carter Jkt 10.00 3.00
GS Gary Sheffield Jsy 10.00 3.00
HB Hank Blalock Jsy 10.00 3.00
IR Ivan Rodriguez Jsy 15.00 4.50
JB Jeff Bagwell Jsy 15.00 4.50
JBE Johnny Bench Uni 25.00 7.50
JG Jason Giambi Uni 10.00 3.00
JR Jose Reyes Jsy 10.00 3.00
JT Jim Thome Jsy 15.00 4.50
KP Kirby Puckett Uni 25.00 7.50
LB Lance Berkman Jsy 10.00 3.00
LG Luis Gonzalez Jsy 10.00 3.00
MO Magglio Ordonez Bat 10.00 3.00
MP Mike Piazza Jsy 20.00 6.00
MR Manny Ramirez Jsy 15.00 4.50
MS Mike Schmidt Jsy 40.00 12.00
MT Miguel Tejada Uni 10.00 3.00
OS Ozzie Smith Jsy 30.00 9.00
PK Paul Konerko Bat 10.00 3.00
PW Preston Wilson Jsy 10.00 3.00
RB Rocco Baldelli Jsy 10.00 3.00
RF Rafael Furcal Jsy 10.00 3.00
RP Rafael Palmeiro Jsy 15.00 4.50
RS Ryne Sandberg Bat 40.00 12.00
SG Shawn Green Jsy 10.00 3.00
SS Sammy Sosa Jsy 20.00 6.00
TH Todd Helton Bat 15.00 4.50
VG Vladimir Guerrero Jsy 15.00 4.50
WB Wade Boggs Jsy 15.00 4.50

2004 Topps Clubhouse Heart of the Lineup Relics

Nm-Mt Ex-Mt
STATED ODDS 1:52
STATED PRINT RUN 100 SERIAL #'d SETS
B ='s BAT, J ='s JSY, U ='s UNI
ARI Steve Finley Jsy 15.00 4.50
Richie Sexson Jsy
Luis Gonzalez Jsy
CHC Sammy Sosa Jsy 40.00 12.00
Moises Alou Uni
Aramis Ramirez Bat

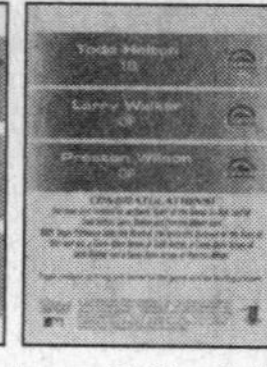

CHW Magglio Ordonez Jsy 25.00 7.50
Frank Thomas Jsy
Carlos Lee Bat
CIN Ken Griffey Jr. Jsy 40.00 12.00
Austin Kearns Jsy
Adam Dunn Jsy
COL Todd Helton Jsy 25.00 7.50
Larry Walker Jsy
Preston Wilson Jsy
HOU Jeff Bagwell Jsy 25.00 7.50
Jeff Kent Bat
Lance Berkman Bat
NYY Alex Rodriguez Bat 40.00 12.00
Jason Giambi Uni
Gary Sheffield Jsy
PHI Jim Thome Jsy 25.00 7.50
Pat Burrell Jsy
Bobby Abreu Jsy
SEA Edgar Martinez Jsy 25.00 7.50
Bret Boone Jsy
John Olerud Jsy
STL Albert Pujols Jsy 50.00 15.00
Jim Edmonds Jsy
Scott Rolen Bat
TEX Alfonso Soriano Bat 25.00 7.50
Mark Teixeira Jsy
Hank Blalock Jsy
TOR Vernon Wells Jsy 15.00 4.50
Carlos Delgado Jsy
Eric Hinske Bat

2004 Topps Clubhouse Patch Place Relics

Nm-Mt Ex-Mt
STATED ODDS 1:50
STATED PRINT RUN 25 SERIAL #'d SETS
AD Adam Dunn 25.00 7.50
ADA Andre Dawson 25.00 7.50
AP Albert Pujols 60.00 18.00
AR Alex Rodriguez 50.00 15.00
CB Craig Biggio 25.00 7.50
CD Carlos Delgado 15.00 4.50
CS Curt Schilling 15.00 4.50
CY Carl Yastrzemski 80.00 24.00
DE Darin Erstad 15.00 4.50
DM Dale Murphy 40.00 12.00
EG Eric Gagne 40.00 12.00
EM Eddie Mathews 80.00 24.00
FR Frank Robinson 25.00 7.50
GB George Brett 60.00 18.00
GC Gary Carter 25.00 7.50
HB Hank Blalock 15.00 4.50
IR Ivan Rodriguez 40.00 12.00
JB Jeff Bagwell 25.00 7.50
JBE Josh Beckett 15.00 4.50
JE Jim Edmonds 15.00 4.50
KI Kazuhisa Ishii 15.00 4.50
LB Lance Berkman 15.00 4.50
LBR Lou Brock 40.00 12.00
LG Luis Gonzalez 15.00 4.50
MM Mark Mulder 15.00 4.50
MP Mike Piazza 50.00 15.00
MR Manny Ramirez 25.00 7.50
MS Mike Schmidt 80.00 24.00
MT Mark Teixeira 15.00 4.50
MTE Miguel Tejada 15.00 4.50
NG Nomar Garciaparra 50.00 15.00
NR Nolan Ryan 80.00 24.00
PM Pedro Martinez 40.00 12.00
RB Rocco Baldelli 15.00 4.50
RH Rickey Henderson 40.00 12.00
RJ Randy Johnson 40.00 12.00
RJA Reggie Jackson 40.00 12.00
RP Rafael Palmeiro 25.00 7.50
RY Robin Yount 50.00 15.00
SG Shawn Green 15.00 4.50
SR Scott Rolen 40.00 12.00
SS Sammy Sosa 50.00 15.00
TG Tony Gwynn 50.00 15.00
TH Todd Helton 25.00 7.50
THU Torii Hunter 15.00 4.50
TS Tom Seaver 40.00 12.00
VG Vladimir Guerrero 40.00 12.00
WB Wade Boggs 40.00 12.00
WM Willie Mays 120.00 36.00

2004 Topps Clubhouse Power Pieces Relics

Nm-Mt Ex-Mt
STATED ODDS 1:62
PRINT RUNS B/WN 2-75 COPIES PER
NO PRICING ON QTY OF 14 OR LESS
AD Andre Dawson Bat/8
AJ Andruw Jones Jsy/25 12.00 3.60
AP Albert Pujols Jsy/5
AR Alex Rodriguez Bat/13
AS Alfonso Soriano Bat/12
BM Brett Myers Jsy/39 8.00 2.40
BP Brad Penny Jsy/31 12.00 3.60
BR Babe Ruth Bat/3
BRO Brooks Robinson Bat/5
BZ Barry Zito Uni/75 8.00 2.40
CD Carlos Delgado Jsy/25 12.00 3.60
CJ Chipper Jones Jsy/10
CP Corey Patterson Jsy/20 12.00 3.60
CS Curt Schilling Jsy/38 8.00 2.40
CY Carl Yastrzemski Jsy/8
DJ Derek Jeter Bat/2
DS Duke Snider Bat/4
EB Ernie Banks Jkt/14
FR Frank Robinson Uni/20 25.00 7.50
GB George Brett Uni/5
GC Gary Carter Jkt/8
HB Hank Blalock Jsy/9
HK Harmon Killebrew Jsy/4
JB Josh Beckett Jsy/61 8.00 2.40
JG Jason Giambi Uni/25 12.00 3.60
JK Jeff Kent Jsy/12
JP Jorge Posada Jsy/20 12.00 3.60
JPI Juan Pierre Bat/9
JT Jim Thome Jsy/25 25.00 7.50
KI Kazuhisa Ishii Jsy/17 15.00 4.50
KS Kazuhiro Sasaki Jsy/22 25.00 7.50
LG Lou Gehrig Bat/4
MC Miguel Cabrera Jsy/24 20.00 6.00
MM Mark Mulder Uni/20 12.00 3.60
MP Mike Piazza Jsy/31 40.00 12.00
MS Mike Schmidt Jsy/20 80.00 24.00
MT Mark Teixeira Jsy/23 12.00 3.60
NR Nolan Ryan Uni/34 80.00 24.00
OV Omar Vizquel Bat/13
PM Pedro Martinez Jsy/45 15.00 4.50
RB Rocco Baldelli Jsy/5
RJ Reggie Jackson Jsy/44 25.00 7.50
SR Scott Rolen Bat/27 25.00 7.50
SS Sammy Sosa Jsy/21 40.00 12.00
TG Troy Glaus Jsy/25 12.00 3.60
TH Tim Hudson Uni/15 15.00 4.50
THE Todd Helton Bat/17 25.00 7.50
THU Torii Hunter Jsy/48 8.00 2.40
WM Willie Mays Jsy/24 80.00 24.00

2004 Topps Cracker Jack

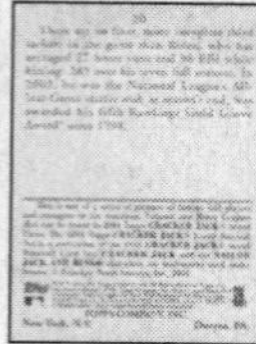

This 250 card set was released in April, 2004. The set was issued in nine-card packs which came 20 packs to a box and 10 boxes to a case. Please note that many cards in this set were issued in shorter supply than others (we have notated those cards with an SP) or have variation poses. In addition, to mirror the original Cracker Jack set the managers of the 2003 World Series were included as well as the Marlins Owner, Jeffrey Loria. In addition, to acknowledge the late trade of Alex Rodriguez to the Yankees a Rodriguez card in a Yankee uniform was a late addition to this set and was issued without a card number. In addition, 550 original cracker jacks were inserted into packs, those cards were issued at a stated rate of one in 2598 hobby and one in 3084 retail packs.

Nm-Mt Ex-Mt
COMPLETE SET (250) 200.00 60.00
COMP.SET w/o SP's (200) 40.00 12.00
COMMON CARD .40 .12
COMMON SP 4.00 1.20
COMMON SP RC 4.00 1.20
SP STATED ODDS 1:3
SP CL: 226/229B/232/236A-236B
1 Jose Reyes SP 4.00 1.20
2 Edgar Renteria .40 .12
3A Albert Pujols Portrait 2.00 .60
3B Albert Pujols Swinging SP 8.00 2.40
4 Garret Anderson .40 .12
5 Bobby Abreu .40 .12
6 Andruw Jones .40 .12
7 Jeff Kent .40 .12
8 Magglio Ordonez .40 .12
9 Kris Benson .40 .12
10 Luis Gonzalez .40 .12
11 Corey Patterson .40 .12
12 Connie Mack MG .40 .12
13 Vernon Wells SP 4.00 1.20
14 Jim Edmonds .40 .12
15 Bret Boone .40 .12
16 Travis Lee .40 .12
17 Alex Rodriguez Yanks SP 8.00 2.40
18 Erubiel Durazo .40 .12
19 Brett Myers .40 .12
20 Scott Rolen SP 5.00 1.50
21 Paul Lo Duca .40 .12
22 Geoff Jenkins .40 .12
23 Charles Comiskey .40 .12
24 Cliff Floyd .40 .12
25A Jim Thome Batting 1.00 .30
25B Jim Thome Fielding SP 5.00 1.50
26 Russ Ortiz .40 .12
27 Bill Mueller .40 .12
28 Kenny Lofton .40 .12
29 Jay Gibbons .40 .12
30 Ken Griffey Jr. 1.50 .45
31 Jeff Bagwell .60 .18
32 Jose Lima .40 .12
33 Brad Radke .40 .12
34 Ramon Hernandez .40 .12
35 Brian Giles SP 4.00 1.20
36 Jeremy Bonderman .40 .12
37 Jerome Williams .40 .12
38 Rafael Palmeiro .60 .18
39 Scott Podsednik .40 .12
40 Rafael Furcal .40 .12
41 Roy Oswalt .40 .12
42 Orlando Hudson .40 .12
43 Todd Helton .60 .18
44 Kerry Wood 1.00 .30
45 Tom Glavine .60 .18
46 David Eckstein .40 .12
47 Trot Nixon .40 .12
48 Preston Wilson .40 .12
49 Bernie Williams .60 .18
50 Eric Gagne SP 5.00 1.50
51 Ichiro Suzuki SP 6.00 1.80
52 Juan Gonzalez .60 .18
53 Torii Hunter .40 .12
54 Bartolo Colon .40 .12
55A Dick Hoblitzell ERR .40 .12
55B Dick Hoblitzell COR .40 .12
56 Al Leiter .40 .12
57 Johnny Damon 1.00 .30
58 Larry Walker .60 .18
59 Brian Jordan .40 .12
60 Richie Sexson SP 4.00 1.20
61 Orlando Cabrera .40 .12
62 Jason Phillips .40 .12
63 Phil Nevin .40 .12
64 John Olerud .40 .12
65 Miguel Tejada .40 .12
66A Nap La Joie ERR 1.00 .30
66B Nap Lajoie COR 1.00 .30
67 C.C. Sabathia .40 .12
68 Ty Wigginton .40 .12
69 Troy Glaus .40 .12
70 Mike Piazza 1.50 .45
71 Craig Biggio .60 .18
72 Cristian Guzman .40 .12
73 Dmitri Young .40 .12
74 Roger Clemens 2.00 .60
75 Runelvys Hernandez .40 .12
76 Nomar Garciaparra 1.50 .45
77 Mark Mulder .40 .12
78 Derek Lowe .40 .12
79 Paul Konerko .40 .12
80A Sammy Sosa SP 6.00 1.80
80B Felix Pie SP 4.00 1.20
81 Vladimir Guerrero 1.00 .30
82 Xavier Nady .40 .12
83 Joel Pineiro .40 .12
84 Chipper Jones 1.00 .30
85 Manny Ramirez .60 .18
86A Burt Shotten ERR .40 .12
86B Burt Shotton COR UER .40 .12
Began his playing career in 1997; should be 1907
87 Raul Ibanez SP 4.00 1.20
88 Eric Chavez .40 .12
89 Frank Catalanotto .40 .12
90 Dontrelle Willis .40 .12
91 Roy Halladay .40 .12
92 Jermaine Dye .40 .12
93 Jason Kendall .40 .12
94 Jacque Jones .40 .12
95A Gary Sheffield Braves .40 .12
95B Gary Sheffield Yanks SP 5.00 1.50
96 Mike Lieberthal .40 .12
97 Adam Dunn .60 .18
98 Carl Crawford .40 .12
99 Reggie Sanders .40 .12
100 Mark Prior SP 5.00 1.50
101 Luis Matos .40 .12
102 Barry Zito .40 .12
103 Randy Johnson 1.00 .30
104A Kevin Brown .40 .12
104B Edwin Jackson SP 4.00 1.20
105 Pat Burrell .40 .12
106 Steve Finley .40 .12
107 Moises Alou .40 .12
108 David Ortiz SP 5.00 1.50
109 Austin Kearns SP 4.00 1.20
110 Carlos Beltran .60 .18
111 Shawn Green .40 .12
112 Javier Vazquez .40 .12
113 Hideo Nomo 1.00 .30
114 Kazuhisa Ishii .40 .12
115 Corey Koskie .40 .12
116 Kevin Millwood .40 .12
117 Randy Wolf .40 .12
118 Darin Erstad .40 .12
119 Fernando Vina .40 .12
120 Pedro Martinez 1.00 .30
121 Melvin Mora .40 .12
122 Carl Everett .40 .12
123 Matt Morris .40 .12
124 Greg Maddux 1.50 .45
125 Jason Schmidt .40 .12
126 Mark Teixeira SP 4.00 1.20
127 Randy Winn .40 .12
128 Rich Aurilia .40 .12
129 Vicente Padilla .40 .12
130 Tim Hudson .40 .12
131 Marlon Byrd .40 .12
132 Jae Weong Seo .40 .12
133 Branch Rickey MG .40 .12
134 A.J. Pierzynski .40 .12
135 Ryan Klesko .40 .12
136 Eric Hinske .40 .12
137 Mike Cameron .40 .12
138 Roberto Alomar .60 .18
139 Jarrod Washburn .40 .12
140A Curt Schilling D'backs .40 .12
140B Curt Schilling Sox SP 5.00 1.50
141 Omar Vizquel .60 .18
142 Mike Sweeney .40 .12
143 Wade Miller .40 .12
144 Jose Vidro .40 .12
145 Rich Harden SP 4.00 1.20
146 Eric Munson .40 .12
147 Lance Berkman .40 .12
148 Mark Buehrle .40 .12
149 Carlos Delgado .40 .12
150 Sean Burroughs .40 .12
151 Kevin Millar .40 .12
152 Frank Thomas 1.00 .30
153 Adrian Beltre .60 .18
154 Shannon Stewart .40 .12
155 Johan Santana .60 .18
156 Edgardo Alfonzo .40 .12
157 Jose Cruz Jr. .40 .12
158 Sidney Ponson .40 .12
159 Edgar Martinez .60 .18
160 Jamie Moyer .40 .12
161 Tony Batista .40 .12
162 Wes Helms .40 .12
163 Brandon Webb SP 4.00 1.20
164 Gil Meche .40 .12
165 Marcus Giles SP 4.00 1.20
166 Angel Berroa SP 4.00 1.20
167 Rocco Baldelli SP 4.00 1.20
168 Michael Young .40 .12
169 Esteban Loaiza .40 .12
170 Casey Blake .40 .12
171 Jody Gerut .40 .12
172 Bo Hart SP 4.00 1.20
173 Kelvim Escobar .40 .12
174 Aaron Guiel .40 .12
175 Javy Lopez SP 4.00 1.20
176 Aubrey Huff .40 .12
177 Hank Blalock .40 .12
178 Edwin Jackson .40 .12
179 Delmon Young SP 5.00 1.50
180 Bobby Jenks .40 .12
181 Felix Pie .40 .12
182 Jeremy Reed SP 4.00 1.20
183 Aaron Hill .40 .12
184 Casey Kotchman SP 4.00 1.20
185 Grady Sizemore .40 .12
186 Joe Mauer SP 5.00 1.50
187 Ryan Harvey .40 .12
188 Neal Cotts .40 .12
189 Victor Martinez .40 .12
190 Rene Reyes .40 .12
191 Eric Duncan .40 .12
192 B.J. Upton SP 5.00 1.50
193 Khalil Greene SP 5.00 1.50
194 Bobby Crosby .60 .18
195 Rickie Weeks SP 4.00 1.20
196 Zack Greinke SP 4.00 1.20
197 Laynce Nix .40 .12
198 Vito Chiaravalloti SP RC 5.00 1.50
199 Estee Harris RC .50 .15
200 Jon Knott SP RC 4.00 1.20
201 Dioner Navarro RC 1.25 .35
202 Craig Ansman RC .50 .15
203 Travis Blackley RC .75 .23
204 Yadier Molina RC 1.00 .30
205 Rodney Choy Foo RC .50 .15
206 Kyle Sleeth SP RC 5.00 1.50
207 Jeff Allison RC .75 .23
208 Josh Labandeira RC .50 .15
209 Lastings Milledge SP RC 6.00 1.80
210 Rudy Guillen SP RC 5.00 1.50
211 Blake Hawksworth SP RC 5.00 1.50
212 David Aardsma RC .50 .15
213 Shawn Hill RC .50 .15
214 Erick Aybar SP RC 5.00 1.50
215 Ervin Santana RC 1.25 .35
216 Tim Stauffer SP RC 5.00 1.50
217 Merkin Valdez RC 1.00 .30
218 Jack McKeon MG .40 .12
219 Jeff Conine .40 .12
220 Josh Beckett SP 4.00 1.20
221 Luis Castillo .40 .12
222 Mike Lowell .40 .12
223 Juan Pierre .40 .12
224A Ivan Rodriguez Marlins 1.00 .30
224B Ivan Rodriguez Tigers SP 5.00 1.50
225 A.J. Burnett .40 .12
226 Miguel Cabrera SP 5.00 1.50
227 Jeffrey Loria .40 .12
228 Joe Torre MG .60 .18
229A Jason Giambi Portrait .40 .12
229B Jason Giambi Fielding SP 4.00 1.20
230 Aaron Boone .40 .12
231 Jose Contreras .40 .12
232 Derek Jeter SP 8.00 2.40
233 Ruben Sierra .40 .12
234 Mike Mussina .60 .18
235 Mariano Rivera .60 .18
236A Jorge Posada SP 5.00 1.50
236B Dioner Navarro SP 5.00 1.50
237 Alfonso Soriano .60 .18
NNO Alex Rodriguez Yanks 3.00 .90
VB Vintage Buyback

2004 Topps Cracker Jack Mini

Nm-Mt Ex-Mt
COMP.SET w/o SP's (200) 80.00 24.00
*MINI: .75X TO 2X BASIC
*MINI: .75X TO 2X BASIC RC
*MINI SP: .6X TO 1.5X BASIC SP
*MINI SP: .5X TO 1.2X BASIC SP RC
MINI STATED ODDS ONE PER PACK
MINI SP STATED ODDS 1:20
SP'S ARE SAME AS IN BASIC SET

2004 Topps Cracker Jack Mini Autographs

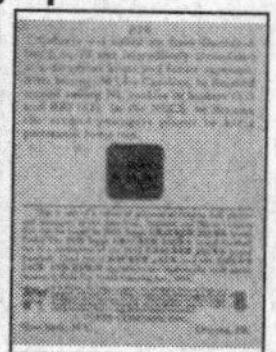

Luis Castillo did not return his cards in time for pack-out and those cards could be redeemed until March 31, 2006.

Nm-Mt Ex-Mt
STATED ODDS 1:258 HOBBY/RETAIL
SHEFFIELD PRINT RUN 50 CARDS
SHEFFIELD IS NOT SERIAL NUMBERED
SHEFFIELD INFO PROVIDED BY TOPPS
95 Gary Sheffield SP/50
112 Javier Vazquez 40.00 12.00
163 Brandon Webb 20.00 6.00
165 Marcus Giles 20.00 6.00
221 Luis Castillo EXCH 10.00 3.00
226 Miguel Cabrera 40.00 12.00

2004 Topps Cracker Jack Mini Blue

Nm-Mt Ex-Mt
*BLUE: 4X TO 10X BASIC
*BLUE: 2.5X TO 6X BASIC RC
*BLUE SP: 1.25X TO 3X BASIC SP
*BLUE SP: 1X TO 2.5X BASIC SP RC
BLUE STATED ODDS 1:10
BLUE SP STATED ODDS 1:60
SP'S ARE SAME AS IN BASIC SET

2004 Topps Cracker Jack Mini White

Nm-Mt Ex-Mt
STATED ODDS 1:6189 HOB, 1:6413 RET
STATED PRINT RUN 1 SET
CARDS ARE NOT SERIAL-NUMBERED
PRINT RUN INFO PROVIDED BY TOPPS
NO PRICING DUE TO SCARCITY

2004 Topps Cracker Jack Stickers

Nm-Mt Ex-Mt
*STICKERS: .75X TO 2X BASIC
*STICKERS: .75X TO 2X BASIC RC
*SP STICKERS: .4X TO 1X BASIC SP
*SP STICKERS: .4X TO 1X BASIC SP RC
ONE PER SURPRISE PACK
SP ODDS 1:10 SURPRISE PACKS
SP'S ARE SAME AS IN BASIC SET

2004 Topps Cracker Jack 1-2-3 Strikes You're Out Relics

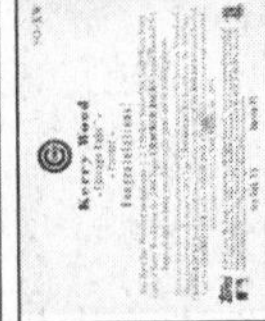

Nm-Mt Ex-Mt
GROUP A 1:5045 H, 1:5310 R SURPRISE
GROUP B 1:103 H, 1:109 R SURPRISE
GROUP C 1:177 H, 1:202 R SURPRISE
GROUP D 1:157 H, 1:191 R SURPRISE
BM Brett Myers Jsy C 8.00 2.40
BW Billy Wagner Jsy B 8.00 2.40
BZ Barry Zito Jsy B 8.00 2.40
CCS C.C. Sabathia Jsy C 8.00 2.40
CS Curt Schilling Jsy A 15.00 4.50
DL Derek Lowe Jsy B 8.00 2.40
EG Eric Gagne Jsy C 10.00 3.00
HN Hideo Nomo Jsy B 10.00 3.00
JB Josh Beckett Uni B 8.00 2.40
JS John Smoltz Jsy D 10.00 3.00
KB Kevin Brown Uni B 8.00 2.40
KM Kevin Millwood Jsy D 8.00 2.40
KW Kerry Wood Jsy C 10.00 3.00
MAM Mark Mulder Uni D 8.00 2.40
MM Mike Mussina Uni A 20.00 6.00
PM Pedro Martinez Jsy B 10.00 3.00
RH Rich Harden Jsy B 8.00 2.40
RJ Randy Johnson Jsy B 10.00 3.00

2004 Topps Cracker Jack Secret Surprise Signatures

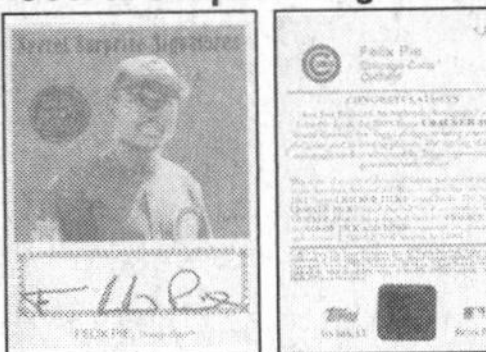
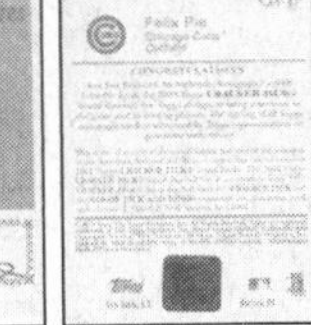

Scott Rolen did not return his cards in time for pack-out and those cards could be redeemed until March 31, 2006.

Nm-Mt Ex-Mt
GROUP A 1:1448 H, 1:1657 R SURPRISE
GROUP B 1:451 H, 1:524 R SURPRISE
GROUP C 1:323 H, 1:368 R SURPRISE
GROUP D 1:372 H, 1:404 R SURPRISE
AH Aubrey Huff B 15.00 4.50
BG Brian Giles D 15.00 4.50
CF Cliff Floyd B 15.00 4.50
DM Dustin McGowan B 10.00 3.00
DW Dontrelle Willis A 15.00 4.50
FP Felix Pie C 15.00 4.50
JW Jerome Williams A 15.00 4.50
ML Mike Lamb C 10.00 3.00
MV Merkin Valdez B 25.00 7.50
SP Scott Podsednik D 15.00 4.50
SR Scott Rolen C EXCH 40.00 12.00

2004 Topps Cracker Jack Take Me Out to the Ballgame Relics

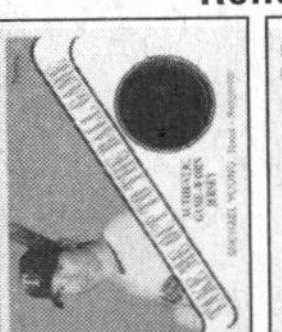
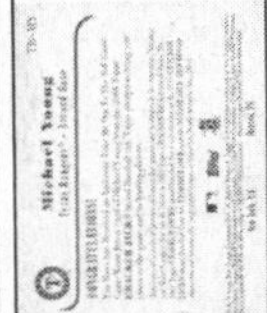

Nm-Mt Ex-Mt
GROUP A 1:654 SURPRISE
GROUP B 1:645 H, 1:645 R SURPRISE
GROUP C 1:152 H, 1:194 R SURPRISE
GROUP D 1:131 H, 1:223 R SURPRISE
GROUP E 1:99 H, 1:125 R SURPRISE
GROUP F 1:201 H, 1:264 R SURPRISE
GROUP G 1:211 H, 1:297 R SURPRISE
GROUP H 1:190 H, 1:226 R SURPRISE
GROUP I 1:126 H, 1:154 R SURPRISE
GROUP J 1:149 H, 1:189 R SURPRISE
GROUP K 1:89 H, 1:93 R SURPRISE
AB Angel Berroa Bat I 8.00 2.40
AD Adam Dunn Jsy C 10.00 3.00
AP Albert Pujols Uni G 15.00 4.50
AP2 Albert Pujols Bat C 15.00 4.50
AR Alex Rodriguez Jsy H 10.00 3.00
AR2 A.Rodriguez Yanks Bat C 20.00 6.00
AS Alfonso Soriano Uni G 10.00 3.00
AS2 Alfonso Soriano Bat A 15.00 4.50
BA Bob Abreu Jsy E 8.00 2.40
BB1 Bret Boone Bat C 8.00 2.40
BB2 Bret Boone Jsy K 8.00 2.40
CB Craig Biggio Jsy E 10.00 3.00
CJ Chipper Jones Jsy K 10.00 3.00
EC Eric Chavez Uni F 8.00 2.40
GA Garrett Anderson Bat B 10.00 3.00
HB Hank Blalock Bat C 8.00 2.40
IR Ivan Rodriguez Bat D 10.00 3.00
JB Jeff Bagwell Uni E 10.00 3.00
JE Jim Edmonds Jsy E 8.00 2.40
JGA Jason Giambi Jsy C 8.00 2.40
JGH Jason Giambi Uni F 8.00 2.40
JL Javy Lopez Jsy E 8.00 2.40
JL2 Javy Lopez Bat A 10.00 3.00
JR Jose Reyes Jsy D 8.00 2.40
JRO Jimmy Rollins Jsy E 8.00 2.40
JT Jim Thome Jsy I 10.00 3.00
KW Kerry Wood Jsy G 10.00 3.00
LB Lance Berkman Bat F 8.00 2.40
LB2 Lance Berkman Jsy K 8.00 2.40
LG Luis Gonzalez Jsy B 10.00 3.00
LW Larry Walker Jsy J 10.00 3.00
MA Moises Alou Jsy J 8.00 2.40
MC Miguel Cabrera Bat H 10.00 3.00
MCT Mark Teixeira Jsy I 8.00 2.40
MG Marcus Giles Jsy E 8.00 2.40
MP Mike Piazza Jsy F 10.00 3.00
MR Manny Ramirez Uni C 10.00 3.00
MS Mike Sweeney Jsy A 10.00 3.00
MT Miguel Tejada Bat K 8.00 2.40
MY Michael Young Jsy D 8.00 2.40
NG Nomar Garciaparra Jsy B 15.00 4.50
NG2 Nomar Garciaparra Bat A 15.00 4.50
PB Pat Burrell Jsy E 8.00 2.40
PL Paul Lo Duca Uni D 8.00 2.40
RB Rocco Baldelli Bat H 8.00 2.40
RF Rafael Furcal Jsy J 8.00 2.40
SG Shawn Green Uni D 8.00 2.40
SG2 Shawn Green Bat C 8.00 2.40
SS Sammy Sosa Bat D 15.00 4.50
SS2 Sammy Sosa Jsy E 15.00 4.50
TG Troy Glaus Jsy I 8.00 2.40
TH Todd Helton Jsy K 10.00 3.00
TKH Torii Hunter Jsy B 10.00 3.00
VW Vernon Wells Jsy D 8.00 2.40

1996 Topps Gallery

The 1996 Topps Gallery set was issued in one series totalling 180 cards. The eight-card packs retailed for $3.00 each. The set is divided into five themes: Classics (1-90), New Editions (91-108), Modernists (109-126), Futurists (127-144) and Masters (145-180). Each theme features a different design on front, but the bulk of the set has full-bleed, color action shots. A Mickey Mantle Masterpiece was inserted into these packs at a rate of one every 48 packs. It is priced at the bottom of these listings.

Nm-Mt Ex-Mt
COMPLETE SET (180) 40.00 12.00
1 Tom Glavine .75 .23
2 Carlos Baerga .50 .15
3 Dante Bichette .50 .15
4 Mark Langston .50 .15
5 Ray Lankford .50 .15
6 Moises Alou .50 .15
7 Marquis Grissom .50 .15
8 Ramon Martinez .50 .15
9 Steve Finley .50 .15
10 Todd Hundley .50 .15
11 Brady Anderson .50 .15
12 John Valentin .50 .15
13 Heathcliff Slocumb .50 .15
14 Ruben Sierra .50 .15
15 Jeff Conine .50 .15
16 Jay Buhner .50 .15
17 Sammy Sosa 2.00 .60
18 Doug Drabek .50 .15
19 Jose Mesa .50 .15
20 Jeff King .50 .15
21 Mickey Tettleton .50 .15
22 Jeff Montgomery .50 .15
23 Alex Fernandez .50 .15
24 Greg Vaughn .50 .15
25 Chuck Finley .50 .15
26 Terry Steinbach .50 .15
27 Rod Beck .50 .15
28 Jack McDowell .50 .15
29 Mark Wohlers .50 .15
30 Len Dykstra .50 .15
31 Bernie Williams .75 .23
32 Travis Fryman .50 .15
33 Jose Canseco 1.25 .35
34 Ken Caminiti .50 .15
35 Devon White .50 .15
36 Bobby Bonilla .50 .15
37 Paul Sorrento .50 .15
38 Ryne Sandberg 2.00 .60
39 Derek Bell .50 .15
40 Bobby Jones .50 .15
41 J.T. Snow .50 .15
42 Denny Neagle .50 .15
43 Tim Wakefield .50 .15
44 Andres Galarraga .50 .15
45 David Segui .50 .15
46 Lee Smith .50 .15
47 Mel Rojas .50 .15
48 John Franco .50 .15
49 Pete Schourek .50 .15
50 John Wetteland .50 .15
51 Paul Molitor .75 .23
52 Ivan Rodriguez 1.25 .35
53 Chris Hoiles .50 .15
54 Mike Greenwell .50 .15
55 Orel Hershiser .50 .15
56 Brian McRae .50 .15
57 Geronimo Berroa .50 .15
58 Craig Biggio .75 .23
59 David Justice .50 .15
60 Lance Johnson .50 .15
61 Andy Ashby .50 .15
62 Randy Myers .50 .15
63 Gregg Jefferies .50 .15
64 Kevin Appier .50 .15
65 Rick Aguilera .50 .15
66 Shane Reynolds .50 .15
67 John Smoltz .75 .23
68 Ron Gant .50 .15
69 Eric Karros .50 .15
70 Jim Thome 1.25 .35
71 Terry Pendleton .50 .15
72 Kenny Rogers .50 .15
73 Robin Ventura .50 .15
74 Dave Nilsson .50 .15
75 Brian Jordan .50 .15
76 Glenallen Hill .50 .15
77 Greg Colbrunn .50 .15
78 Roberto Alomar .75 .23
79 Rickey Henderson 1.25 .35
80 Carlos Garcia .50 .15
81 Dean Palmer .50 .15
82 Mike Stanley .50 .15
83 Hal Morris .50 .15
84 Wade Boggs .75 .23
85 Chad Curtis .50 .15
86 Roberto Hernandez .50 .15
87 John Olerud .50 .15
88 Frank Castillo .50 .15
89 Rafael Palmeiro .75 .23
90 Trevor Hoffman .50 .15
91 Marty Cordova .50 .15
92 Hideo Nomo 1.25 .35
93 Johnny Damon .75 .23
94 Bill Pulsipher .50 .15
95 Garret Anderson .50 .15
96 Ray Durham .50 .15
97 Ricky Bottalico .50 .15
98 Carlos Perez .50 .15
99 Troy Percival .50 .15
100 Chipper Jones 1.25 .35
101 Esteban Loaiza .50 .15
102 John Mabry .50 .15
103 Jon Nunnally .50 .15
104 Andy Pettitte .75 .23
105 Lyle Mouton .50 .15
106 Jason Isringhausen .50 .15
107 Brian L.Hunter .50 .15
108 Quilvio Veras .50 .15
109 Jim Edmonds .50 .15
110 Ryan Klesko .50 .15
111 Pedro Martinez 1.25 .35
112 Joey Hamilton .50 .15
113 Vinny Castilla .50 .15
114 Alex Gonzalez .50 .15
115 Raul Mondesi .50 .15
116 Rondell White .50 .15
117 Dan Miceli .50 .15
118 Tom Goodwin .50 .15
119 Bret Boone .50 .15
120 Shawn Green .50 .15
121 Jeff Cirillo .50 .15
122 Rico Brogna .50 .15
123 Chris Gomez .50 .15
124 Ismael Valdes .50 .15
125 Javy Lopez .50 .15
126 Manny Ramirez .75 .23
127 Paul Wilson .50 .15
128 Billy Wagner .50 .15
129 Eric Owens .50 .15
130 Todd Greene .50 .15
131 Karim Garcia .50 .15
132 Jimmy Haynes .50 .15
133 Michael Tucker .50 .15
134 John Wasdin .50 .15
135 Brooks Kieschnick .50 .15
136 Alex Ochoa .50 .15
137 Ariel Prieto .50 .15
138 Tony Clark .50 .15
139 Mark Loretta .50 .15
140 Rey Ordonez .50 .15
141 Chris Snopek .50 .15
142 Roger Cedeno .50 .15
143 Derek Jeter 3.00 .90
144 Jeff Suppan .50 .15
145 Greg Maddux 2.00 .60
146 Ken Griffey Jr. 2.00 .60
147 Tony Gwynn 1.50 .45
148 Darren Daulton .50 .15
149 Will Clark 1.25 .35
150 Mo Vaughn .50 .15
151 Reggie Sanders .50 .15
152 Kirby Puckett 1.25 .35
153 Paul O'Neill .75 .23
154 Tim Salmon .75 .23
155 Mark McGwire 3.00 .90
156 Barry Bonds 3.00 .90
157 Albert Belle .50 .15
158 Edgar Martinez .75 .23
159 Mike Mussina .75 .23
160 Cecil Fielder .50 .15
161 Kenny Lofton .50 .15
162 Randy Johnson 1.25 .35
163 Juan Gonzalez .75 .23
164 Jeff Bagwell .75 .23
165 Joe Carter .50 .15
166 Mike Piazza 2.00 .60
167 Eddie Murray 1.25 .35
168 Cal Ripken 4.00 1.20
169 Barry Larkin .75 .23
170 Chuck Knoblauch .50 .15
171 Chili Davis .50 .15
172 Fred McGriff .75 .23
173 Matt Williams .50 .15
174 Roger Clemens 2.50 .75
175 Frank Thomas 1.25 .35
176 Dennis Eckersley .50 .15
177 Gary Sheffield .50 .15
178 David Cone .50 .15
179 Larry Walker .75 .23
180 Mark Grace .75 .23
NNO M. Mantle Masterpiece 20.00 6.00

1996 Topps Gallery Players Private Issue

Randomly inserted in packs at a rate of one in 12, this 180-card parallel is foil stamped. The backs are sequentially numbered 0-999, with the first 100 cards (numbers 0-99) sent to the players and the balance inserted in packs. Topps released a statement at the end of the 1996 season, claiming that they destroyed 400 sets.

Nm-Mt Ex-Mt
*STARS: 6X TO 15X BASIC CARDS
*ROOKIES: 5X TO 12X BASIC CARDS

1996 Topps Gallery Expressionists

Randomly inserted in packs at a rate of one in 24, this 20-card set features leaders printed on triple foil stamped and texture embossed cards. Card backs contain a second photo and narrative about the player.

Nm-Mt Ex-Mt
COMPLETE SET (20) 80.00 24.00
1 Mike Piazza 8.00 2.40
2 J.T. Snow 2.00 .60
3 Ken Griffey Jr. 8.00 2.40
4 Kirby Puckett 5.00 1.50
5 Carlos Baerga 2.00 .60
6 Chipper Jones 5.00 1.50
7 Hideo Nomo 5.00 1.50
8 Mark McGwire 12.00 3.60
9 Gary Sheffield 2.00 .60
10 Randy Johnson 5.00 1.50
11 Ray Lankford 2.00 .60
12 Sammy Sosa 8.00 2.40
13 Denny Martinez 2.00 .60
14 Jose Canseco 5.00 1.50
15 Tony Gwynn 6.00 1.80
16 Edgar Martinez 3.00 .90
17 Reggie Sanders 2.00 .60
18 Andres Galarraga 2.00 .60
19 Albert Belle 2.00 .60
20 Barry Larkin 3.00 .90

1996 Topps Gallery Photo Gallery

Randomly inserted in packs at a rate of one in 30, this 15-card set features top photography chronicling baseball's biggest stars and greatest moments from last year. Each double foil stamped card is printed on 24 pt. stock with customized designs to accentuate the photography.

Nm-Mt Ex-Mt
COMPLETE SET (15) 80.00 24.00
PG1 Eddie Murray 6.00 1.80
PG2 Randy Johnson 6.00 1.80
PG3 Cal Ripken 20.00 6.00
PG4 Bret Boone 2.50 .75
PG5 Frank Thomas 6.00 1.80
PG6 Jeff Conine 2.50 .75
PG7 Johnny Damon 4.00 1.20
PG8 Roger Clemens 12.00 3.60
PG9 Albert Belle 2.50 .75
PG10 Ken Griffey Jr. 10.00 3.00
PG11 Kirby Puckett 6.00 1.80
PG12 David Justice 2.50 .75
PG13 Bobby Bonilla 2.50 .75
PG14 Colorado Rockies 2.50 .75
PG15 Atlanta Braves 2.50 .75

1997 Topps Gallery

The 1997 Topps Gallery set was issued in one series totalling 180 cards. The eight-card packs retailed for $4.00 each. This hobby only set is divided into four themes: Veterans, Prospects, Rising Stars and Young Stars. Printed on 24-point card stock with a high-gloss film and etch stamped with one or more foils, each theme features a different design on front with a variety of informative statistics and revealing player text on the back.

Nm-Mt Ex-Mt
COMPLETE SET (180) 50.00 15.00
1 Paul Molitor .75 .23
2 Devon White .50 .15
3 Andres Galarraga .50 .15
4 Cal Ripken 4.00 1.20
5 Tony Gwynn 1.50 .45
6 Mike Stanley .50 .15
7 Orel Hershiser .50 .15
8 Jose Canseco 1.25 .35
9 Chili Davis .50 .15
10 Harold Baines .50 .15
11 Rickey Henderson 1.25 .35
12 Darryl Strawberry .50 .15
13 Todd Worrell .50 .15
14 Cecil Fielder .50 .15
15 Gary Gaetti .50 .15
16 Bobby Bonilla .50 .15
17 Will Clark 1.25 .35
18 Kevin Brown .50 .15
19 Tom Glavine .75 .23
20 Wade Boggs .75 .23
21 Edgar Martinez .75 .23
22 Lance Johnson .50 .15
23 Gregg Jefferies .50 .15
24 Bip Roberts .50 .15
25 Tony Phillips .50 .15
26 Greg Maddux 2.00 .60
27 Mickey Tettleton .50 .15
28 Terry Steinbach .50 .15
29 Ryne Sandberg 2.00 .60
30 Wally Joyner .50 .15
31 Joe Carter .50 .15
32 Ellis Burks .50 .15
33 Fred McGriff .75 .23
34 Barry Larkin .75 .23
35 John Franco .50 .15
36 Rafael Palmeiro .75 .23
37 Mark McGwire 3.00 .90
38 Ken Caminiti .50 .15
39 David Cone .50 .15
40 Julio Franco .50 .15
41 Roger Clemens 2.50 .75
42 Barry Bonds 3.00 .90
43 Dennis Eckersley .50 .15
44 Eddie Murray 1.25 .35
45 Paul O'Neill .75 .23
46 Craig Biggio .75 .23
47 Roberto Alomar .75 .23
48 Mark Grace .75 .23
49 Matt Williams .50 .15
50 Jay Buhner .50 .15
51 John Smoltz .75 .23
52 Randy Johnson 1.25 .35
53 Ramon Martinez .50 .15
54 Curt Schilling .50 .15
55 Gary Sheffield .50 .15
56 Jack McDowell .50 .15
57 Brady Anderson .50 .15
58 Dante Bichette .50 .15
59 Ron Gant .50 .15
60 Alex Fernandez .50 .15
61 Moises Alou .50 .15
62 Travis Fryman .50 .15
63 Dean Palmer .50 .15
64 Todd Hundley .50 .15
65 Jeff Brantley .50 .15
66 Bernard Gilkey .50 .15
67 Geronimo Berroa .50 .15
68 John Wetteland .50 .15
69 Robin Ventura .50 .15
70 Ray Lankford .50 .15
71 Kevin Appier .50 .15
72 Larry Walker .75 .23
73 Juan Gonzalez .75 .23
74 Jeff King .50 .15
75 Greg Vaughn .50 .15
76 Steve Finley .50 .15
77 Brian McRae .50 .15
78 Paul Sorrento .50 .15
79 Ken Griffey Jr. 2.00 .60
80 Omar Vizquel .75 .23
81 Jose Mesa .50 .15
82 Albert Belle .50 .15
83 Glenallen Hill .50 .15
84 Sammy Sosa 2.00 .60
85 Andy Benes .50 .15
86 David Justice .50 .15
87 Marquis Grissom .50 .15
88 John Olerud .50 .15
89 Tino Martinez .75 .23
90 Frank Thomas 1.25 .35
91 Raul Mondesi .50 .15
92 Steve Trachsel .50 .15
93 Jim Edmonds .50 .15
94 Rusty Greer .50 .15
95 Joey Hamilton .50 .15
96 Ismael Valdes .50 .15
97 Dave Nilsson .50 .15
98 John Jaha .50 .15
99 Alex Gonzalez .50 .15
100 Javy Lopez .50 .15
101 Ryan Klesko .50 .15
102 Tim Salmon .75 .23
103 Bernie Williams .75 .23
104 Roberto Hernandez .50 .15
105 Chuck Knoblauch .50 .15
106 Mike Lansing .50 .15
107 Vinny Castilla .50 .15
108 Reggie Sanders .50 .15
109 Mo Vaughn .50 .15
110 Rondell White .50 .15
111 Ivan Rodriguez 1.25 .35
112 Mike Mussina .75 .23
113 Carlos Baerga .50 .15
114 Jeff Conine .50 .15
115 Jim Thome 1.25 .35
116 Manny Ramirez .75 .23
117 Kenny Lofton .50 .15
118 Wilson Alvarez .50 .15
119 Eric Karros .50 .15
120 Robb Nen .50 .15
121 Mark Wohlers .50 .15
122 Ed Sprague .50 .15

123 Pat Hentgen .50 .15
124 Juan Guzman .50 .15
125 Derek Bell .50 .15
126 Jeff Bagwell .75 .23
127 Eric Young .50 .15
128 John Valentin .50 .15
129 Al Martin UER .50 .15
Picture of Javy Lopez
130 Trevor Hoffman .50 .15
131 Henry Rodriguez .50 .15
132 Pedro Martinez 1.25 .35
133 Mike Piazza 2.00 .60
134 Brian Jordan .50 .15
135 Jose Valentin .50 .15
136 Jeff Cirillo .50 .15
137 Chipper Jones 1.25 .35
138 Ricky Bottalico .50 .15
139 Hideo Nomo 1.25 .35
140 Troy Percival .50 .15
141 Rey Ordonez .50 .15
142 Edgar Renteria .50 .15
143 Luis Castillo .50 .15
144 Vladimir Guerrero 1.25 .35
145 Jeff D'Amico .50 .15
146 Andruw Jones .50 .15
147 Darin Erstad .50 .15
148 Bob Abreu .50 .15
149 Carlos Delgado .50 .15
150 Jamey Wright .50 .15
151 Nomar Garciaparra 2.00 .60
152 Jason Kendall .50 .15
153 Jermaine Allensworth .50 .15
154 Scott Rolen 1.25 .35
155 Rocky Coppinger .50 .15
156 Paul Wilson .50 .15
157 Garret Anderson .50 .15
158 Mariano Rivera .75 .23
159 Ruben Rivera .50 .15
160 Andy Pettitte .75 .23
161 Derek Jeter 3.00 .90
162 Neifi Perez .50 .15
163 Ray Durham .50 .15
164 James Baldwin .50 .15
165 Marty Cordova .50 .15
166 Tony Clark .50 .15
167 Michael Tucker .50 .15
168 Mike Sweeney .50 .15
169 Johnny Damon .75 .23
170 Jermaine Dye .50 .15
171 Alex Ochoa .50 .15
172 Jason Isringhausen .50 .15
173 Mark Grudzielanek .50 .15
174 Jose Rosado .50 .15
175 Todd Hollandsworth .50 .15
176 Alan Benes .50 .15
177 Jason Giambi .50 .15
178 Billy Wagner .50 .15
179 Justin Thompson .50 .15
180 Todd Walker .50 .15

1997 Topps Gallery Gallery of Heroes

Randomly inserted in packs at a rate of one in 36, this 10-card set features color player photos designed to command the attention paid to works hanging in art museums. The backs carry player information.

Nm-Mt Ex-Mt
COMPLETE SET (10) 150.00 45.00
GH1 Derek Jeter 25.00 7.50
GH2 Chipper Jones 10.00 3.00
GH3 Frank Thomas 10.00 3.00
GH4 Ken Griffey Jr. 15.00 4.50
GH5 Cal Ripken 30.00 9.00
GH6 Mark McGwire 25.00 7.50
GH7 Mike Piazza 15.00 4.50
GH8 Jeff Bagwell 6.00 1.80
GH9 Tony Gwynn 12.00 3.60
GH10 Mo Vaughn 4.00 1.20

1997 Topps Gallery Peter Max Serigraphs

Randomly inserted in packs at a rate of one in 24, this 10-card set features painted renditions of ten superstars by the artist, Peter Max. The backs carry his commentary about the player.

Nm-Mt Ex-Mt
COMPLETE SET (10) 80.00 24.00
*AUTOS: 8X TO 20X BASIC SERIGRAPH
AUTOS RANDOM INSERTS IN PACKS
AUTOS PRINT RUN 40 SERIAL #'d SETS
AU'S SIGNED BY MAX BENEATH UV COATING
1 Derek Jeter 12.00 3.60
2 Albert Belle 2.00 .60
3 Ken Caminiti 2.00 .60
4 Chipper Jones 5.00 1.50
5 Ken Griffey Jr. 8.00 2.40
6 Frank Thomas 5.00 1.50
7 Cal Ripken 15.00 4.50
8 Mark McGwire 12.00 3.60
9 Barry Bonds 12.00 3.60
10 Mike Piazza 8.00 2.40

1997 Topps Gallery Photo Gallery

Randomly inserted in packs at a rate of one in 24, this 16-card set features color photos of some of baseball's hottest stars and their most memorable moments. Each card is enhanced by customized designs and double foil-stamping.

Nm-Mt Ex-Mt
COMPLETE SET (16) 100.00 30.00
PG1 John Wetteland 2.50 .75
PG2 Paul Molitor 4.00 1.20
PG3 Eddie Murray 6.00 1.80
PG4 Ken Griffey Jr. 10.00 3.00
PG5 Chipper Jones 6.00 1.80
PG6 Derek Jeter 15.00 4.50
PG7 Frank Thomas 6.00 1.80
PG8 Mark McGwire 15.00 4.50
PG9 Kenny Lofton 2.50 .75
PG10 Gary Sheffield 2.50 .75
PG11 Mike Piazza 10.00 3.00
PG12 Vinny Castilla 2.50 .75
PG13 Andres Galarraga 2.50 .75
PG14 Andy Pettitte 4.00 1.20
PG15 Robin Ventura 2.50 .75
PG16 Barry Larkin 4.00 1.20

1998 Topps Gallery

The 1998 Topps Gallery hobby-only set was issued in one series totalling 150 cards. The six-card packs retailed for $3.00 each. The set is divided by five subset groupings: Expressionists, Exhibitionists, Impressions, Portraits and Permanent Collection. Each theme features a different design with informative stats and text on each player.

Nm-Mt Ex-Mt
COMPLETE SET (150) 50.00 15.00
1 Andruw Jones .50 .15
2 Fred McGriff .75 .23
3 Wade Boggs .75 .23
4 Pedro Martinez 1.25 .35
5 Matt Williams .50 .15
6 Wilson Alvarez .50 .15
7 Henry Rodriguez .50 .15
8 Jay Bell .50 .15
9 Marquis Grissom .50 .15
10 Darryl Kile .50 .15
11 Chuck Knoblauch .50 .15
12 Kenny Lofton .50 .15
13 Quinton McCracken .50 .15
14 Andres Galarraga .50 .15
15 Brian Jordan .50 .15
16 Mike Lansing .50 .15
17 Travis Fryman .50 .15
18 Tony Saunders .50 .15
19 Moises Alou .50 .15
20 Travis Lee .50 .15
21 Garret Anderson .50 .15
22 Ken Caminiti .50 .15
23 Pedro Astacio .50 .15
24 Ellis Burks .50 .15
25 Albert Belle .50 .15
26 Alan Benes .50 .15
27 Jay Buhner .50 .15
28 Derek Bell .50 .15
29 Jeromy Burnitz .50 .15
30 Kevin Appier .50 .15
31 Jeff Cirillo .50 .15
32 Bernard Gilkey .50 .15
33 David Cone .50 .15
34 Jason Dickson .50 .15
35 Jose Cruz Jr. .50 .15
36 Marty Cordova .50 .15
37 Ray Durham .50 .15
38 Jaret Wright .50 .15
39 Billy Wagner .50 .15
40 Roger Clemens 2.50 .75
41 Juan Gonzalez .75 .23
42 Jeremi Gonzalez .50 .15
43 Mark Grudzielanek .50 .15
44 Tom Glavine .75 .23
45 Barry Larkin .75 .23
46 Lance Johnson .50 .15
47 Bobby Higginson .50 .15
48 Mike Mussina .75 .23
49 Al Martin .50 .15
50 Mark McGwire 3.00 .90
51 Todd Hundley .50 .15
52 Ray Lankford .50 .15
53 Jason Kendall .50 .15
54 Javy Lopez .50 .15
55 Ben Grieve .50 .15
56 Randy Johnson 1.25 .35
57 Jeff King .50 .15
58 Mark Grace .75 .23
59 Rusty Greer .50 .15
60 Greg Maddux 2.00 .60
61 Jeff Kent .50 .15
62 Rey Ordonez .50 .15
63 Hideo Nomo 1.25 .35
64 Charles Nagy .50 .15
65 Rondell White .50 .15
66 Todd Helton .75 .23
67 Jim Thome 1.25 .35
68 Denny Neagle .50 .15
69 Ivan Rodriguez 1.25 .35
70 Vladimir Guerrero 1.25 .35
71 Jorge Posada .75 .23
72 J.T. Snow .50 .15
73 Reggie Sanders .50 .15
74 Scott Rolen 1.25 .35
75 Robin Ventura .50 .15
76 Mariano Rivera .75 .23
77 Cal Ripken 4.00 1.20
78 Justin Thompson .50 .15
79 Mike Piazza 2.00 .60
80 Kevin Brown .75 .23
81 Sandy Alomar Jr. .50 .15
82 Craig Biggio .75 .23
83 Vinny Castilla .50 .15
84 Eric Young .50 .15
85 Bernie Williams .75 .23
86 Brady Anderson .50 .15
87 Bobby Bonilla .50 .15
88 Tony Clark .50 .15
89 Dan Wilson .50 .15
90 John Wetteland .50 .15
91 Barry Bonds 3.00 .90
92 Chan Ho Park .50 .15
93 Carlos Delgado .50 .15
94 David Justice .50 .15
95 Chipper Jones 1.25 .35
96 Shawn Estes .50 .15
97 Jason Giambi .50 .15
98 Ron Gant .50 .15
99 John Olerud .50 .15
100 Frank Thomas 1.25 .35
101 Jose Guillen .50 .15
102 Brad Radke .50 .15
103 Troy Percival .50 .15
104 John Smoltz .75 .23
105 Edgardo Alfonzo .50 .15
106 Dante Bichette .50 .15
107 Larry Walker .75 .23
108 John Valentin .50 .15
109 Roberto Alomar .75 .23
110 Mike Cameron .50 .15
111 Eric Davis .50 .15
112 Johnny Damon .75 .23
113 Darin Erstad .50 .15
114 Omar Vizquel .75 .23
115 Derek Jeter 3.00 .90
116 Tony Womack .50 .15
117 Edgar Renteria .50 .15
118 Raul Mondesi .50 .15
119 Tony Gwynn 1.50 .45
120 Ken Griffey Jr. 2.00 .60
121 Jim Edmonds .50 .15
122 Brian Hunter .50 .15
123 Neifi Perez .50 .15
124 Dean Palmer .50 .15
125 Alex Rodriguez 2.00 .60
126 Tim Salmon .75 .23
127 Curt Schilling .50 .15
128 Kevin Orie .50 .15
129 Andy Pettitte .75 .23
130 Gary Sheffield .50 .15
131 Jose Rosado .50 .15
132 Manny Ramirez .75 .23
133 Rafael Palmeiro .75 .23
134 Sammy Sosa 2.00 .60
135 Jeff Bagwell .75 .23
136 Delino DeShields .50 .15
137 Ryan Klesko .50 .15
138 Mo Vaughn .50 .15
139 Steve Finley .50 .15
140 Nomar Garciaparra 2.00 .60
141 Paul Molitor .75 .23
142 Pat Hentgen .50 .15
143 Eric Karros .50 .15
144 Bobby Jones .50 .15
145 Tino Martinez .75 .23
146 Matt Morris .50 .15
147 Livan Hernandez .50 .15
148 Edgar Martinez .75 .23
149 Paul O'Neill .75 .23
150 Checklist .50 .15

1998 Topps Gallery Gallery Proofs

Randomly inserted in packs at a rate of one in 34, this 150-card set is a parallel to the Topps Gallery base set. The set is sequentially numbered to 125.

Nm-Mt Ex-Mt
*STARS: 10X TO 25X BASIC CARDS..

1998 Topps Gallery Player's Private Issue

Randomly inserted in packs at a rate of one in 17, this 150-card set is a parallel to the Topps Gallery base set. The set is sequentially numbered to 250.

Nm-Mt Ex-Mt
*STARS: 5X TO 12X BASIC CARDS....

1998 Topps Gallery Player's Private Issue Auction

Seeded at a rate of one per pack, these standard-sized cards loosely parallel the far more scarce Player's Private Issue cards. Two glaring differences, however, are readily apparent: 1) The Auction cards are printed on thin paper stock (compared to the thick 20 pt board for PPI cards) and 2) The Auction card backs contain rules and guidelines for the auction promotion (compared to the normal statistics and player photo on the PPI cards). Collectors who obtained Auction cards were supposed to "bid" on a selection of ten different pieces of framed artwork (one for each of the following players: J.Gonzalez, M.McGwire, C.Ripken, M.Piazza, C.Jones, F.Thomas, D.Jeter, K.Griffey Jr., A.Rodriguez and N.Garciaparra). Bidding points were available in 25, 50, 75 and 100 point increments detailed at the top right corner of each Auction card back. Point totals were doubled, however, when the player featured on the Auction card was the same player actually being bid on. The auction period ran from July 4th, 1998 through October 16th, 1998. During that time period, collectors had to mail in their accumulated bid points and specify which of the ten pieces they were bidding upon. An "800" number was available for collectors to check upon the status of the current high bid, allowing them the opportunity to submit additional bid points prior to the October 16th closing date. Winners were notified 30 days after the closing date.

Nm-Mt Ex-Mt
COMPLETE SET (150) 100.00 30.00
*STARS: .75X TO 2X BASIC CARDS...

1998 Topps Gallery Awards Gallery

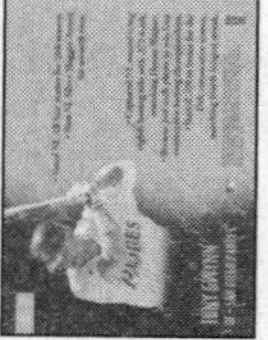

Randomly inserted in packs at a rate of one in 24, this 10-card set honors the achievements of the majors top stars.

Nm-Mt Ex-Mt
COMPLETE SET (10) 60.00 18.00
AG1 Ken Griffey Jr. 10.00 3.00
AG2 Larry Walker 4.00 1.20
AG3 Roger Clemens 12.00 3.60
AG4 Pedro Martinez 6.00 1.80
AG5 Nomar Garciaparra 10.00 3.00
AG6 Scott Rolen 6.00 1.80
AG7 Frank Thomas 6.00 1.80
AG8 Tony Gwynn 8.00 2.40
AG9 Mark McGwire 15.00 4.50
AG10 Livan Hernandez 2.50 .75

1998 Topps Gallery Gallery of Heroes

Randomly inserted in packs at a rate of one in 24, this 15-card set is an insert to the Topps Gallery base set. The fronts feature a translucent stain-glass design that helps showcase some of today's high performance players.

Nm-Mt Ex-Mt
COMPLETE SET (15) 150.00 45.00
*JUMBOS: .3X TO .8X BASIC HEROES
ONE JUMBO PER HOBBY BOX
GH1 Ken Griffey Jr. 12.00 3.60
GH2 Derek Jeter 20.00 6.00
GH3 Barry Bonds 20.00 6.00
GH4 Alex Rodriguez 12.00 3.60
GH5 Frank Thomas 8.00 2.40
GH6 Nomar Garciaparra 12.00 3.60
GH7 Mark McGwire 20.00 6.00
GH8 Mike Piazza 12.00 3.60
GH9 Cal Ripken 25.00 7.50
GH10 Jose Cruz Jr. 3.00 .90
GH11 Jeff Bagwell 5.00 1.50
GH12 Chipper Jones 8.00 2.40
GH13 Juan Gonzalez 5.00 1.50
GH14 Hideo Nomo 8.00 2.40
GH15 Greg Maddux 12.00 3.60

1999 Topps Gallery

The 1999 Topps Gallery set was issued in one series totalling 150 cards and was distributed in six-card packs for a suggested retail price of $3. The set features 100 veteran stars and 50 subset cards finely crafted and printed on 24-pt. stock, with serigraph textured frame, etched foil stamping, and spot UV finish. The set contains the following subsets: Masters (101-115), Artisans (116-127), and Apprentices (128-150). Rookie Cards inlcude Pat Burrell, Nick Johnson and Alfonso Soriano.

Nm-Mt Ex-Mt
COMPLETE SET (150) 50.00 15.00
COMP.SET w/o SP's (100) 25.00 7.50
COMMON CARD (1-100) .30 .09
COMMON (101-150) .75 .23
1 Mark McGwire 2.00 .60
2 Jim Thome .75 .23
3 Bernie Williams .50 .15
4 Larry Walker .50 .15
5 Juan Gonzalez .50 .15
6 Ken Griffey Jr. 1.25 .35
7 Raul Mondesi .30 .09
8 Sammy Sosa 1.25 .35
9 Greg Maddux 1.25 .35
10 Jeff Bagwell .50 .15
11 Vladimir Guerrero .75 .23
12 Scott Rolen .75 .23
13 Nomar Garciaparra 1.25 .35
14 Mike Piazza 1.25 .35
15 Travis Lee .30 .09
16 Carlos Delgado .30 .09
17 Darin Erstad .30 .09
18 David Justice .30 .09
19 Cal Ripken 2.50 .75
20 Derek Jeter 2.00 .60
21 Tony Clark .30 .09
22 Barry Larkin .50 .15
23 Greg Vaughn .30 .09
24 Jeff Kent .30 .09
25 Wade Boggs .50 .15
26 Andres Galarraga .30 .09
27 Ken Caminiti .30 .09
28 Jason Kendall .30 .09
29 Todd Helton .50 .15
30 Chuck Knoblauch .30 .09
31 Roger Clemens 1.50 .45
32 Jeromy Burnitz .30 .09
33 Javy Lopez .30 .09
34 Roberto Alomar .50 .15
35 Eric Karros .30 .09
36 Ben Grieve .30 .09
37 Eric Davis .30 .09
38 Rondell White .30 .09
39 Dmitri Young .30 .09
40 Ivan Rodriguez .75 .23
41 Paul O'Neill .50 .15
42 Jeff Cirillo .30 .09
43 Kerry Wood .75 .23
44 Albert Belle .30 .09
45 Frank Thomas .75 .23
46 Manny Ramirez .50 .15
47 Tom Glavine .50 .15
48 Mo Vaughn .30 .09
49 Jose Cruz Jr. .30 .09
50 Sandy Alomar Jr. .30 .09
51 Edgar Martinez .50 .15
52 John Olerud .30 .09
53 Todd Walker .30 .09
54 Tim Salmon .50 .15
55 Derek Bell .30 .09
56 Matt Williams .30 .09
57 Alex Rodriguez 1.25 .35
58 Rusty Greer .30 .09
59 Vinny Castilla .30 .09
60 Jason Giambi .30 .09
61 Mark Grace .50 .15
62 Jose Canseco .75 .23
63 Gary Sheffield .30 .09
64 Brad Fullmer .30 .09
65 Trevor Hoffman .30 .09
66 Mark Kotsay .30 .09
67 Mike Mussina .50 .15
68 Johnny Damon .30 .09
69 Tino Martinez .50 .15
70 Curt Schilling .30 .09
71 Jay Buhner .30 .09
72 Kenny Lofton .30 .09
73 Randy Johnson .75 .23
74 Kevin Brown .50 .15
75 Brian Jordan .30 .09
76 Craig Biggio .50 .15
77 Barry Bonds 2.00 .60
78 Tony Gwynn 1.00 .30
79 Jim Edmonds .30 .09
80 Shawn Green .30 .09
81 Todd Hundley .30 .09
82 Cliff Floyd .30 .09
83 Jose Guillen .30 .09
84 Dante Bichette .30 .09
85 Moises Alou .30 .09
86 Chipper Jones .75 .23
87 Ray Lankford .30 .09
88 Fred McGriff .50 .15
89 Rod Beck .30 .09
90 Dean Palmer .30 .09
91 Pedro Martinez .75 .23
92 Andruw Jones .30 .09
93 Robin Ventura .30 .09
94 Ugueth Urbina .30 .09
95 Orlando Hernandez .30 .35
96 Sean Casey .30 .09
97 Denny Neagle .30 .09
98 Troy Glaus .30 .09
99 John Smoltz .50 .15
100 Al Leiter .30 .09
101 Ken Griffey Jr. MAS 2.50 .75
102 Frank Thomas MAS 1.50 .45
103 Mark McGwire MAS 4.00 1.20
104 Sammy Sosa MAS 2.50 .75
105 Chipper Jones MAS 1.50 .45
106 Alex Rodriguez MAS 2.50 .75
107 N.Garciaparra MAS 2.50 .75
108 Juan Gonzalez MAS 1.00 .30
109 Derek Jeter MAS 4.00 1.20
110 Mike Piazza MAS 2.50 .75
111 Barry Bonds MAS 4.00 1.20
112 Tony Gwynn MAS 2.00 .40
113 Cal Ripken MAS 5.00 1.50
114 Greg Maddux MAS 2.50 .75
115 Roger Clemens MAS 3.00 .90
116 Brad Fullmer ART .75 .23
117 Kerry Wood ART 1.50 .45
118 Ben Grieve ART .75 .23
119 Todd Helton ART 1.00 .30
120 Kevin Millwood ART .75 .23
121 Sean Casey ART .75 .23
122 V.Guerrero ART 1.50 .45
123 Travis Lee ART .75 .23
124 Troy Glaus ART .75 .23
125 Bartolo Colon ART .75 .23
126 Andruw Jones ART .75 .23
127 Scott Rolen ART 1.50 .45
128 A.Soriano APP RC 5.00 1.50
129 Nick Johnson APP RC 1.50 .45
130 Matt Belisle APP RC .75 .23
131 Jorge Toca APP RC .75 .23
132 Masao Kida APP RC .75 .23
133 Carlos Pena APP RC 1.00 .30
134 Adrian Beltre APP 1.00 .30
135 Eric Chavez APP .75 .23
136 Carlos Beltran APP 1.00 .30
137 Alex Gonzalez APP .75 .23
138 Ryan Anderson APP .75 .23
139 Ruben Mateo APP .75 .23
140 Bruce Chen APP .75 .23
141 Pat Burrell APP RC 2.50 .75
142 Michael Barrett APP .75 .23
143 Carlos Lee APP .75 .23

Card	Nm-Mt	Ex-Mt
44 Mark Mulder APP RC	3.00	.75
45 C.Freeman APP RC	.75	.23
46 Gabe Kapler APP	.75	.23
47 J.Encarnacion APP	.75	.23
48 Jeremy Giambi APP	.75	.23
49 Jason Tyner APP RC	.75	.23
50 George Lombard APP	.75	.23

1999 Topps Gallery Player's Private Issue

Randomly inserted in packs at the rate of one in 17, this 150-card set is parallel to the base set with a "Players Private Issue" foil stamp and sequentially numbered to 250.

Nm-Mt Ex-Mt

*STARS 1-100: 8X TO 20X BASIC CARDS
*MASTERS 101-115: 4X TO 10X BASIC
*ARTISANS 116-127:3X TO 8X BASIC
*APPRENTICES 128-150: 3X TO 8X BASIC
*APP.RC'S 128-150: 2X TO 5X BASIC

1999 Topps Gallery Autographs

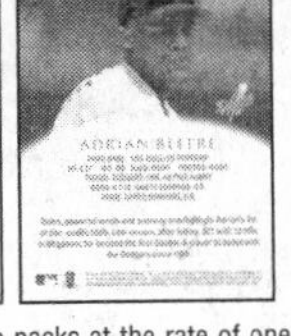

Randomly inserted into packs at the rate of one in 209, this three-card set features color photos of three of baseball's top prospects printed on 24-point stock with the "Topps Certified Autograph" foil stamp logo.

Card	Nm-Mt	Ex-Mt
GA1 Troy Glaus	15.00	4.50
GA2 Adrian Beltre	25.00	7.50
GA3 Eric Chavez	15.00	4.50

1999 Topps Gallery Awards Gallery

Randomly inserted into packs at the rate of one in 12, this 10-card set features color photos of the game's HR Champs, Cy Young award winners, RBI Leaders, MVP winnners, and Rookies of the year from 1998.

Card	Nm-Mt	Ex-Mt
COMPLETE SET (10)	30.00	9.00
AG1 Kerry Wood	3.00	.90
AG2 Ben Grieve	1.25	.35
AG3 Roger Clemens	6.00	1.80
AG4 Tom Glavine	2.00	.60
AG5 Juan Gonzalez	2.00	.60
AG6 Sammy Sosa	5.00	1.50
AG7 Ken Griffey Jr.	5.00	1.50
AG8 Mark McGwire	8.00	2.40
AG9 Bernie Williams	2.00	.60
AG10 Larry Walker	2.00	.60

1999 Topps Gallery Exhibitions

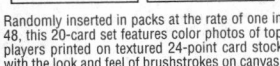

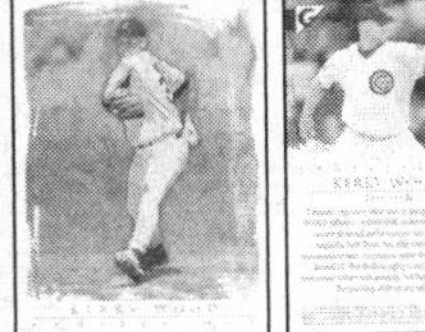

Randomly inserted in packs at the rate of one in 48, this 20-card set features color photos of top players printed on textured 24-point card stock with the look and feel of brushstrokes on canvas.

Card	Nm-Mt	Ex-Mt
COMPLETE SET (20)	200.00	60.00
E1 Sammy Sosa	12.00	3.60
E2 Mark McGwire	20.00	6.00
E3 Greg Maddux	12.00	3.60
E4 Roger Clemens	15.00	4.50
E5 Ben Grieve	3.00	.90
E6 Kerry Wood	8.00	2.40
E7 Ken Griffey Jr.	12.00	3.60
E8 Tony Gwynn	10.00	3.00
E9 Cal Ripken	25.00	7.50
E10 Frank Thomas	8.00	2.40
E11 Jeff Bagwell	5.00	1.50
E12 Derek Jeter	20.00	6.00
E13 Alex Rodriguez	12.00	3.60
E14 Nomar Garciaparra	12.00	3.60
E15 Manny Ramirez	5.00	1.50
E16 Vladimir Guerrero	8.00	2.40
E17 Darin Erstad	3.00	.90
E18 Scott Rolen	8.00	2.40
E19 Mike Piazza	12.00	3.60
E20 Andres Galarraga	3.00	.90

1999 Topps Gallery Gallery of Heroes

Randomly inserted into packs at the rate of one in 24, this 10-card set features some of the

game's top players depicted on clear Polycarbonate stock simulating the appearance of stained glass.

Card	Nm-Mt	Ex-Mt
COMPLETE SET (10)	80.00	24.00
GH1 Mark McGwire	12.00	3.60
GH2 Sammy Sosa	8.00	2.40
GH3 Ken Griffey Jr.	8.00	2.40
GH4 Mike Piazza	8.00	2.40
GH5 Derek Jeter	12.00	3.60
GH6 Nomar Garciaparra	8.00	2.40
GH7 Kerry Wood	5.00	1.50
GH8 Ben Grieve	2.00	.60
GH9 Chipper Jones	5.00	1.50
GH10 Alex Rodriguez	8.00	2.40

1999 Topps Gallery Heritage

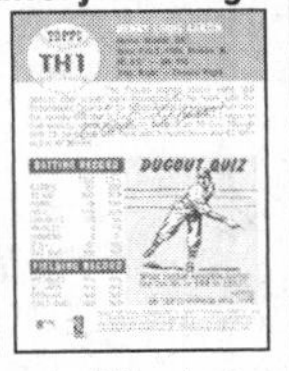

Randomly inserted into packs at the rate of one in 12, this 20-card set features color photos of legendary stars printed on 24-point conventional card stock depicting the 1953 Topps design. This was one of the most popular insert sets issued in 1999 as hobbyists responded well to the gorgeous 1953 retro art. Interestingly, the back of the Aaron card was written as if it were 1953 while the modern players were written about their current accomplishments.

Card	Nm-Mt	Ex-Mt
COMPLETE SET (20)	250.00	75.00
*PROOFS: .4X TO 1X BASIC HERITAGE		
PROOFS STATED ODDS 1:48		
TH1 Hank Aaron	30.00	9.00
TH2 Ben Grieve	8.00	2.40
TH3 Nomar Garciaparra	25.00	7.50
TH4 Roger Clemens	30.00	9.00
TH5 Travis Lee	8.00	2.40
TH6 Tony Gwynn	20.00	6.00
TH7 Alex Rodriguez	25.00	7.50
TH8 Ken Griffey Jr.	25.00	7.50
TH9 Derek Jeter	40.00	12.00
TH10 Sammy Sosa	25.00	7.50
TH11 Scott Rolen	15.00	4.50
TH12 Chipper Jones	15.00	4.50
TH13 Cal Ripken	50.00	15.00
TH14 Kerry Wood	15.00	4.50
TH15 Barry Bonds	40.00	12.00
TH16 Juan Gonzalez	10.00	3.00
TH17 Mike Piazza	25.00	7.50
TH18 Greg Maddux	25.00	7.50
TH19 Frank Thomas	15.00	4.50
TH20 Mark McGwire	50.00	15.00

2000 Topps Gallery

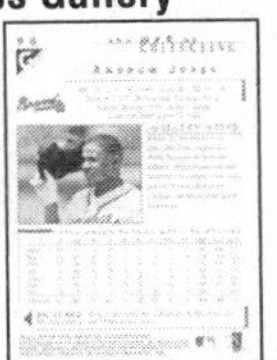

The 2000 Topps Gallery product was released in early June, 2000 as a 150-card set. The set features 100 player cards, a 20-card Masters of the Game subset, and a 30-card Students of the Game subset. Please note that cards 101-150 were issued at a rate of one per pack. Each pack contained six cards and carried a suggested retail price of $3.00. Notable Rookie Cards include Bobby Bradley.

Card	Nm-Mt	Ex-Mt
COMPLETE SET (150)	100.00	30.00
COMP.SET w/o SP's (100)	25.00	7.50
COMMON CARD (1-100)	.30	.09
COMMON (101-150)	1.00	.30
1 Nomar Garciaparra	1.25	.35
2 Kevin Millwood	.30	.09
3 Jay Bell	.30	.09
4 Rusty Greer	.30	.09
5 Bernie Williams	.50	.15
6 Barry Larkin	.50	.15
7 Carlos Beltran	.50	.15
8 Damion Easley	.30	.09
9 Magglio Ordonez	.30	.09
10 Matt Williams	.30	.09
11 Shannon Stewart	.30	.09
12 Ray Lankford	.30	.09
13 Vinny Castilla	.30	.09
14 Miguel Tejada	.30	.09
15 Craig Biggio	.50	.15
16 Chipper Jones	.75	.23
17 Albert Belle	.30	.09
18 Doug Glanville	.30	.09
19 Brian Giles	.30	.09
20 Shawn Green	.30	.09
21 Bret Boone	.30	.09
22 Luis Gonzalez	.30	.09
23 Carlos Delgado	.30	.09
24 J.D. Drew	.30	.09
25 Ivan Rodriguez	.75	.23
26 Tino Martinez	.50	.15
27 Erubiel Durazo	.30	.09
28 Scott Rolen	.75	.23
29 Gary Sheffield	.30	.09
30 Manny Ramirez	.50	.15
31 Luis Castillo	.30	.09
32 Fernando Tatis	.30	.09
33 Darin Erstad	.30	.09
34 Tim Hudson	.30	.09
35 Sammy Sosa	1.25	.35
36 Jason Kendall	.30	.09
37 Todd Walker	.30	.09
38 Orlando Hernandez	.30	.09
39 Pokey Reese	.30	.09
40 Mike Piazza	1.25	.35
41 B.J. Surhoff	.30	.09
42 Tony Gwynn	1.00	.30
43 Kevin Brown	.30	.09
44 Preston Wilson	.30	.09
45 Kenny Lofton	.30	.09
46 Rondell White	.30	.09
47 Frank Thomas	.75	.23
48 Neifi Perez	.30	.09
49 Edgardo Alfonzo	.15	.04
50 Ken Griffey Jr.	1.25	.35
51 Barry Bonds	2.00	.60
52 Brian Jordan	.30	.09
53 Raul Mondesi	.30	.09
54 Troy Glaus	.30	.09
55 Curt Schilling	.30	.09
56 Mike Mussina	.50	.15
57 Brian Daubach	.30	.09
58 Roger Clemens	1.50	.45
59 Carlos Febles	.30	.09
60 Todd Helton	.50	.15
61 Mark Grace	.50	.15
62 Randy Johnson	.75	.23
63 Jeff Bagwell	.50	.15
64 Tom Glavine	.50	.15
65 Adrian Beltre	.50	.15
66 Rafael Palmeiro	.50	.15
67 Paul O'Neill	.50	.15
68 Robin Ventura	.30	.09
69 Ray Durham	.30	.09
70 Mark McGwire	2.00	.60
71 Greg Vaughn	.30	.09
72 Javy Lopez	.30	.09
73 Ryan Klesko	.30	.09
74 Mike Lieberthal	.30	.09
75 Cal Ripken	2.50	.75
76 Juan Gonzalez	.50	.15
77 Sean Casey	.30	.09
78 Jermaine Dye	.30	.09
79 John Olerud	.30	.09
80 Jose Canseco	.75	.23
81 Eric Karros	.30	.09
82 Roberto Alomar	.50	.15
83 Ben Grieve	.30	.09
84 Greg Maddux	1.25	.35
85 Pedro Martinez	.75	.23
86 Tony Clark	.30	.09
87 Richie Sexson	.30	.09
88 Cliff Floyd	.30	.09
89 Eric Chavez	.30	.09
90 Andruw Jones	.30	.09
91 Vladimir Guerrero	.75	.23
92 Alex Gonzalez	.30	.09
93 Jim Thome	.75	.23
94 Bob Abreu	.30	.09
95 Derek Jeter	2.00	.60
96 Larry Walker	.50	.15
97 Mike Hampton	.30	.09
98 Mo Vaughn	.30	.09
99 Jason Giambi	.30	.09
100 Alex Rodriguez	1.25	.35
101 Mark McGwire MAS	4.00	1.20
102 Sammy Sosa MAS	2.50	.75
103 Alex Rodriguez MAS	2.50	.75
104 Derek Jeter MAS	4.00	1.20
105 Greg Maddux MAS	2.50	.75
106 Jeff Bagwell MAS	1.00	.30
107 N.Garciaparra MAS	2.50	.75
108 Mike Piazza MAS	2.50	.75
109 Pedro Martinez MAS	1.50	.45
110 Chipper Jones MAS	1.50	.45
111 Randy Johnson MAS	1.50	.45
112 Barry Bonds MAS	4.00	1.20
113 Ken Griffey Jr. MAS	2.50	.75
114 Manny Ramirez MAS	1.00	.30
115 Ivan Rodriguez MAS	1.50	.45
116 Juan Gonzalez MAS	1.00	.30
117 V.Guerrero MAS	1.50	.45
118 Tony Gwynn MAS	2.00	.60
119 Larry Walker MAS	1.00	.30
120 Cal Ripken MAS	5.00	1.50
121 Josh Hamilton SG	1.00	.30
122 Corey Patterson SG	1.00	.30
123 Pat Burrell SG	1.00	.30
124 Nick Johnson SG	1.00	.30
125 Adam Piatt SG	1.00	.30
126 Rick Ankiel SG	1.00	.30
127 A.J. Burnett SG	1.00	.30
128 Ben Petrick SG	1.00	.30
129 Rafael Furcal SG	1.00	.30
130 Alfonso Soriano SG	1.50	.45
131 Dee Brown SG	1.00	.30
132 Ruben Mateo SG	1.00	.30
133 Pablo Ozuna SG	1.00	.30
134 S.Burroughs SG UER Eric Munson's bio on back	1.00	.30
135 Mark Mulder SG	1.00	.30
136 Jason Jennings SG	1.00	.30
137 Eric Munson SG	1.00	.30
138 Vernon Wells SG	1.00	.30
139 Brett Myers SG RC	1.00	.30
140 B.Christensen SG RC	1.00	.30
141 Bobby Bradley SG RC	1.00	.30
142 Ruben Salazar SG RC	1.00	.30
143 R.Christianson SG RC	1.00	.30
144 Corey Myers SG RC	1.00	.30
145 Aaron Rowand SG RC	2.50	.75
146 Julio Zuleta SG RC	1.00	.30
147 Kurt Ainsworth SG RC	1.00	.30
148 Scott Downs SG RC	1.00	.30
149 Larry Bigbie SG RC	1.50	.45
150 Chance Caple SG RC	1.00	.30

2000 Topps Gallery Player's Private Issue

Randomly inserted into packs at one in 20, this 150-card set is a complete parallel of the Topps Gallery base set. Each card in the set is individually serial numbered to 250. The cards are serial numbered in gold foil on the back of the cards.

Nm-Mt Ex-Mt

*STARS 1-100: 6X TO 15X BASIC CARDS
*MASTERS 101-120: 3X TO 8X BASIC
*STUDENTS 121-138: 1.5X TO 4X BASIC
*STUDENTS RC's 139-150: 2X TO 5X BASIC

2000 Topps Gallery Autographs

Randomly inserted into packs at one in 153, this insert set features autographed cards from five of the major league's top prospects. Card backs are numbered using the players initials.

Card	Nm-Mt	Ex-Mt
BP Ben Petrick	10.00	3.00
CP Corey Patterson	15.00	4.50
RA Rick Ankiel	15.00	4.50
RM Ruben Mateo	10.00	3.00
VW Vernon Wells	15.00	4.50

2000 Topps Gallery Exhibits

Randomly inserted into packs at one in 18, this 30-card insert captures some of baseball's best on canvas texturing. Card backs carry a "GE" prefix.

Card	Nm-Mt	Ex-Mt
COMPLETE SET (30)	300.00	90.00
GE1 Mark McGwire	20.00	6.00
GE2 Jeff Bagwell	5.00	1.50
GE3 Mike Piazza	12.00	3.60
GE4 Alex Rodriguez	12.00	3.60
GE5 Nomar Garciaparra	12.00	3.60
GE6 Ivan Rodriguez	8.00	2.40
GE7 Chipper Jones	8.00	2.40
GE8 Cal Ripken	25.00	7.50
GE9 Tony Gwynn	10.00	3.00
GE10 Jose Canseco	8.00	2.40
GE11 Albert Belle	3.00	.90
GE12 Greg Maddux	12.00	3.60
GE13 Barry Bonds	20.00	6.00
GE14 Ken Griffey Jr.	12.00	3.60
GE15 Juan Gonzalez	5.00	1.50
GE16 Rickey Henderson	15.00	4.50
GE17 Craig Biggio	5.00	1.50
GE18 Vladimir Guerrero	8.00	2.40
GE19 Rey Ordonez	10.00	3.00
GE20 Roberto Alomar	5.00	1.50
GE21 Derek Jeter	20.00	6.00
GE22 Manny Ramirez	5.00	1.50
GE23 Shawn Green	3.00	.90
GE24 Sammy Sosa	12.00	3.60
GE25 Larry Walker	5.00	1.50
GE26 Pedro Martinez	8.00	2.40
GE27 Randy Johnson	8.00	2.40
GE28 Pat Burrell	3.00	.90
GE29 Josh Hamilton	3.00	.90
GE30 Corey Patterson	3.00	.90

2000 Topps Gallery Gallery of Heroes

Randomly inserted into packs at one in 24, this insert features ten celestial superstars on clear, die-cut polycarbonate stock, creating a stained glass effect. Card backs carry a "GH" prefix.

Card	Nm-Mt	Ex-Mt
COMPLETE SET (10)	80.00	24.00
GH1 Alex Rodriguez	8.00	2.40
GH2 Chipper Jones	5.00	1.50
GH3 Pedro Martinez	5.00	1.50
GH4 Sammy Sosa	8.00	2.40
GH5 Mark McGwire	12.00	3.60
GH6 Nomar Garciaparra	8.00	2.40
GH7 Vladimir Guerrero	5.00	1.50
GH8 Ken Griffey Jr.	8.00	2.40
GH9 Mike Piazza	8.00	2.40
GH10 Derek Jeter	12.00	3.60

2000 Topps Gallery Heritage

Randomly inserted into packs at one in 12, this 20-card insert set was influenced by the 1954 Topps set, the set features many of baseball's

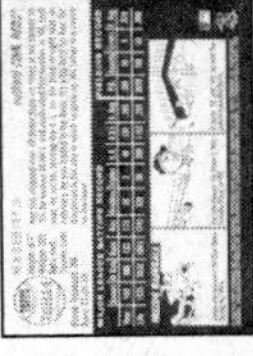

elite players as illustrated artist renderings. Card backs carry a "TGH" prefix.

Card	Nm-Mt	Ex-Mt
COMPLETE SET (20)	150.00	45.00
*PROOFS: .6X TO 1.5X BASIC HERITAGE		
PROOFS STATED ODDS 1:27		
TGH1 Mark McGwire	25.00	7.50
TGH2 Sammy Sosa	15.00	4.50
TGH3 Greg Maddux	15.00	4.50
TGH4 Mike Piazza	15.00	4.50
TGH5 Ivan Rodriguez	10.00	3.00
TGH6 Manny Ramirez	6.00	1.80
TGH7 Jeff Bagwell	6.00	1.80
TGH8 Sean Casey	4.00	1.20
TGH9 Orlando Hernandez	4.00	1.20
TGH10 Randy Johnson	10.00	3.00
TGH11 Pedro Martinez	10.00	3.00
TGH12 Vladimir Guerrero	10.00	3.00
TGH13 Shawn Green	4.00	1.20
TGH14 Ken Griffey Jr.	15.00	4.50
TGH15 Alex Rodriguez	15.00	4.50
TGH16 Nomar Garciaparra	15.00	4.50
TGH17 Derek Jeter	25.00	7.50
TGH18 Tony Gwynn	12.00	3.60
TGH19 Chipper Jones	10.00	3.00
TGH20 Cal Ripken	30.00	9.00

2000 Topps Gallery Proof Positive

Randomly insert into packs at one in 48, these ten cards couple one master of the game with one student of the game by way of positive and negative photography. Card backs carry a "P" prefix.

Card	Nm-Mt	Ex-Mt
COMPLETE SET (10)	100.00	30.00
P1 Ken Griffey Jr. Ruben Mateo	10.00	3.00
P2 Derek Jeter Alfonso Soriano	15.00	4.50
P3 Mark McGwire Pat Burrell	15.00	4.50
P4 Pedro Martinez A.J.Burnett	6.00	1.80
P5 Alex Rodriguez Rafael Furcal	10.00	3.00
P6 Sammy Sosa Corey Patterson	10.00	3.00
P7 Randy Johnson Rick Ankiel	6.00	1.80
P8 Chipper Jones Adam Piatt	6.00	1.80
P9 Nomar Garciaparra Pablo Ozuna	10.00	3.00
P10 Mike Piazza Eric Munson	10.00	3.00

2001 Topps Gallery

This 150 card set was issued in six card packs with an SRP of $3. The packs were issued 24 packs to a box with eight boxes to a case. Cards numbered 102-150 were short printed in these ratios: Prospects from 102-141 were issued one every 2.5 packs, rookies from 102-141 were issued one every 3.5 packs and cards numbered 142-150 were issued one every five packs. Card number 50 was supposedly only available to people who could show their dealers that that was the only card they were missing for the set. However, a retail version of that card was issued so many collectors did not get to share in the surprise of finding out the missing card was Willie Mays. In addition, a special Ichiro card was randomly included in packs, these cards were good for either an American or a Japanese version of what would become card number 151. The deadline to receive the Mays HTA version was October 24th, 2001 while the Ichiro exchange deadline was June 30th, 2003.

Card	Nm-Mt	Ex-Mt
COMPLETE SET (150)	80.00	24.00
COMP.SET w/o SP's (100)	40.00	12.00
COMMON (1-49/51-101)	.50	.15
COMMON (102-150)	3.00	.90
1 Darin Erstad	.50	.15
2 Chipper Jones	1.25	.35
3 Nomar Garciaparra	2.00	.60
4 Fernando Vina	.50	.15
5 Bartolo Colon	.50	.15
6 Bobby Higginson	.50	.15

	Nm-Mt	Ex-Mt
7 Antonio Alfonseca	.50	.15
8 Mike Sweeney	.50	.15
9 Kevin Brown	.50	.15
10 Jose Vidro	.50	.15
11 Derek Jeter	3.00	.90
12 Jason Giambi	.50	.15
13 Pat Burrell	.50	.15
14 Jeff Kent	.50	.15
15 Alex Rodriguez	2.00	.60
16 Rafael Palmeiro	.75	.23
17 Garret Anderson	.50	.15
18 Brad Fullmer	.50	.15
19 Doug Glanville	.50	.15
20 Mark Quinn	.50	.15
21 Mo Vaughn	.50	.15
22 Andruw Jones	.50	.15
23 Pedro Martinez	1.25	.35
24 Ken Griffey Jr.	2.00	.60
25 Roberto Alomar	.75	.23
26 Dean Palmer	.50	.15
27 Jeff Bagwell	.75	.23
28 Jermaine Dye	.50	.15
29 Chan Ho Park	.50	.15
30 Vladimir Guerrero	1.25	.35
31 Bernie Williams	.75	.23
32 Ben Grieve	.50	.15
33 Jason Kendall	.50	.15
34 Barry Bonds	3.00	.90
35 Jim Edmonds	.50	.15
36 Ivan Rodriguez	1.25	.35
37 Javy Lopez	.50	.15
38 J.T. Snow	.50	.15
39 Erubiel Durazo	.50	.15
40 Terrence Long	.50	.15
41 Tim Salmon	.75	.23
42 Greg Maddux	2.00	.60
43 Sammy Sosa	2.00	.60
44 Sean Casey	.50	.15
45 Jeff Cirillo	.50	.15
46 Juan Gonzalez	.75	.23
47 Richard Hidalgo	.50	.15
48 Shawn Green	.50	.15
49 Jeromy Burnitz	.50	.15
50 Willie Mays HTA N.Y. Giants	15.00	4.50
50 Willie Mays RETAIL S.F. Giants	40.00	12.00
51 David Justice	.50	.15
52 Tim Hudson	.50	.15
53 Brian Giles	.50	.15
54 Robb Nen	.50	.15
55 Fernando Tatis	.50	.15
56 Tony Batista	.50	.15
57 Pokey Reese	.50	.15
58 Ray Durham	.50	.15
59 Greg Vaughn	.50	.15
60 Kazuhiro Sasaki	.50	.15
61 Troy Glaus	.50	.15
62 Rafael Furcal	.50	.15
63 Magglio Ordonez	.50	.15
64 Jim Thome	1.25	.35
65 Todd Helton	.75	.23
66 Preston Wilson	.50	.15
67 Moises Alou	.50	.15
68 Gary Sheffield	.50	.15
69 Geoff Jenkins	.50	.15
70 Mike Piazza	2.00	.60
71 Jorge Posada	.75	.23
72 Bobby Abreu	.50	.15
73 Phil Nevin	.50	.15
74 John Olerud	.50	.15
75 Mark McGwire	3.00	.90
76 Jose Cruz Jr.	.50	.15
77 David Segui	.50	.15
78 Neifi Perez	.50	.15
79 Omar Vizquel	.75	.23
80 Rick Ankiel	.50	.15
81 Randy Johnson	1.25	.35
82 Albert Belle	.50	.15
83 Frank Thomas	1.25	.35
84 Manny Ramirez	.75	.23
85 Larry Walker	.75	.23
86 Luis Castillo	.50	.15
87 Johnny Damon	.75	.23
88 Adrian Beltre	.75	.23
89 Cristian Guzman	.50	.15
90 Jay Payton	.50	.15
91 Miguel Tejada	.50	.15
92 Scott Rolen	1.25	.35
93 Ryan Klesko	.50	.15
94 Edgar Martinez	.75	.23
95 Fred McGriff	.75	.23
96 Carlos Delgado	.50	.15
97 Barry Zito	.75	.23
98 Mike Lieberthal	.50	.15
99 Trevor Hoffman	.50	.15
100 Gabe Kapler	.50	.15
101 Edgardo Alfonzo	.50	.15
102 Corey Patterson	3.00	.90
103 Alfonso Soriano	.75	.23
104 Keith Ginter	3.00	.90
105 Keith Reed	3.00	.90
106 Nick Johnson	3.00	.90
107 Carlos Pena	3.00	.90
108 Vernon Wells	3.00	.90
109 Roy Oswalt	3.00	.90
110 Alex Escobar	3.00	.90
111 Adam Everett	3.00	.90
112 Jimmy Rollins	3.00	.90
113 Marcus Giles	3.00	.90
114 Jack Cust	3.00	.90
115 Chin-Feng Chen	3.00	.90
116 Pablo Ozuna	3.00	.90
117 Ben Sheets	3.00	.90
118 Adrian Gonzalez	3.00	.90
119 Ben Davis	3.00	.90
120 Eric Valent	3.00	.90
121 Scott Heard	3.00	.90
122 David Parrish RC	3.00	.90
123 Sean Burnett	3.00	.90
124 Derek Thompson	3.00	.90
125 Tim Christman RC	3.00	.90
126 Mike Jacobs RC	3.00	.90
127 Luis Montanez RC	3.00	.90
128 Chris Bass RC	3.00	.90
129 Will Smith RC	3.00	.90
130 Justin Wayne RC	3.00	.90
131 Shawn Fagan RC	3.00	.90
132 Chad Petty RC	3.00	.90
133 J.R. House	3.00	.90
134 Joel Pineiro	4.00	1.20
135 Albert Pujols RC	40.00	12.00
136 Carmen Cali RC	3.00	.90
137 Steve Smyth RC	3.00	.90
138 John Lackey	3.00	.90
139 Bob Keppel RC	3.00	.90
140 Dominic Rich RC	3.00	.90
141 Josh Hamilton	3.00	.90
142 Nolan Ryan	6.00	1.80
143 Tom Seaver	3.00	.90
144 Reggie Jackson	3.00	.90
145 Johnny Bench	4.00	1.20
146 Warren Spahn	3.00	.90
147 Brooks Robinson	3.00	.90
148 Carl Yastrzemski	5.00	1.50
149 Al Kaline	4.00	1.20
150 Bob Feller	3.00	.90
151A I. Suzuki English RC	25.00	7.50
151B I.Suzuki Japan RC	25.00	7.50

2001 Topps Gallery Press Plates

Randomly inserted into packs at one in 1347, this 150-card insert is a complete parallel of the base set. The set features the actual press plates used to make all of the 150-card base set. There are four colored press plates inserted for each player: black, cyan, magenta, and yellow.

	Nm-Mt	Ex-Mt
NO PRICING DUE TO SCARCITY		

2001 Topps Gallery Autographs

Inserted at overall odds of one in 232, these six cards feature cards signed by active professionals. All of these cards are all also the special painted cards for this product. Rick Ankiel did not return his cards in time for inclusion in this product. Those cards were redeemable until June 30, 2003.

	Nm-Mt	Ex-Mt
GROUP A STATED ODDS 1:1066		
GROUP B STATED ODDS 1:1144		
GROUP C STATED ODDS 1:400		
GA-AG Adrian Gonzalez B	20.00	6.00
GA-AR Alex Rodriguez A	150.00	45.00
GA-BB Barry Bonds A	300.00	90.00
GA-IR Ivan Rodriguez A	80.00	24.00
GA-PB Pat Burrell C	20.00	6.00
GA-RA R. Ankiel C EXCH	20.00	6.00

2001 Topps Gallery Bucks

Issued at a rate of one in 102, this "Buck" was good for $5 towards purchase of Topps Memorabilia.

	Nm-Mt	Ex-Mt
1 Johnny Bench $5	5.00	1.50

2001 Topps Gallery Heritage

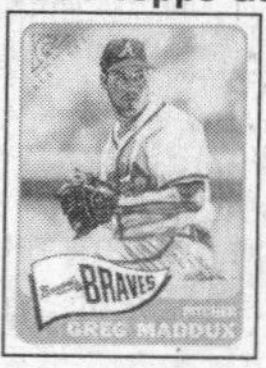

Inserted one per 12 packs, these 12 cards feature a mix of active and retired players in the design Topps used for their 1965 set.

	Nm-Mt	Ex-Mt
COMPLETE SET (10)	60.00	18.00
GH1 Todd Helton	3.00	.90
GH2 Greg Maddux	8.00	2.40
GH3 Pedro Martinez	5.00	1.50
GH4 Orlando Cepeda	3.00	.90
GH5 Willie McCovey	3.00	.90
GH6 Ken Griffey Jr.	8.00	2.40
GH7 Alex Rodriguez	8.00	2.40
GH8 Derek Jeter	12.00	3.60
GH9 Mark McGwire	12.00	3.60
GH10 Vladimir Guerrero	5.00	1.50

2001 Topps Gallery Heritage Game Jersey

Inserted at a rate of one in 133 packs, these five cards feature pieces of game-worn uniforms along with the Gallery Heritage design.

	Nm-Mt	Ex-Mt
GHR-GM Greg Maddux	25.00	7.50
GHR-MR Mystery Jersey	1.00	.30
GHR-OC Orlando Cepeda	15.00	4.50
GHR-PM Pedro Martinez	25.00	7.50
GHR-VG Vladimir Guerrero	25.00	7.50
GHR-WM Willie McCovey	15.00	4.50

2001 Topps Gallery Heritage Game Jersey Autographs

Issued at a rate of one in 16,313 these two cards feature not only the Heritage design and a game-worn jersey piece but they also feature an autograph by the featured player. Orlando Cepeda did not return his cards in time for inclusion in this set so those cards were redeemable until June 30, 2003. These cards are serial numbered to 25.

	Nm-Mt	Ex-Mt
GHRA-OC Orlando Cepeda		
GHRA-WM W.McCovey		

2001 Topps Gallery Originals Game Bat

Issued at a rate of one per 133 packs these 15 cards feature game-used bat cards from 15 leading active hitters today. These cards display the genuine issue sticker. Sammy Sosa and Jason Giambi were the two players made available through the Mystery Exchange redemption cards.

	Nm-Mt	Ex-Mt
GR-AG Adrian Gonzalez	10.00	3.00
GR-AJ Andruw Jones	10.00	3.00
GR-BW Bernie Williams	15.00	4.50
GR-DE Darin Erstad	10.00	3.00
GR-JD Jermaine Dye	10.00	3.00
GR-JG Jason Giambi	10.00	3.00
GR-JK Jason Kendall	10.00	3.00
GR-JFK Jeff Kent	10.00	3.00
GR-MR1 Mystery Relic	1.00	.30
GR-MR2 Mystery Relic	1.00	.30
GR-PR Pokey Reese	10.00	3.00
GR-PW Preston Wilson	10.00	3.00
GR-RA Roberto Alomar	15.00	4.50
GR-RP Rafael Palmeiro	15.00	4.50
GR-RV Robin Ventura	10.00	3.00
GR-SG Shawn Green	10.00	3.00
GR-SS Sammy Sosa	25.00	7.50

2001 Topps Gallery Star Gallery

Issued at a rate of one in eight, these 10 cards feature some of the most popular players in the game.

	Nm-Mt	Ex-Mt
COMPLETE SET (10)	40.00	12.00
SG1 Vladimir Guerrero	2.50	.75
SG2 Alex Rodriguez	4.00	1.20
SG3 Derek Jeter	6.00	1.80
SG4 Nomar Garciaparra	4.00	1.20
SG5 Ken Griffey Jr.	4.00	1.20
SG6 Mark McGwire	6.00	1.80
SG7 Chipper Jones	2.50	.75
SG8 Sammy Sosa	4.00	1.20
SG9 Barry Bonds	6.00	1.80
SG10 Mike Piazza	4.00	1.20

2002 Topps Gallery

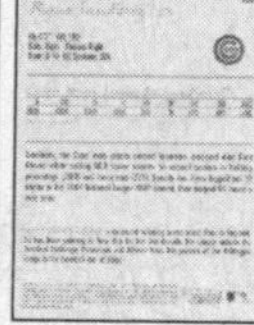

This 200 card set was released in June, 2002. The set was issued in five-card packs, with an SRP of $3, which came packaged 24 packs to a box and eight boxes to a case. The first 150 cards of this set featured veterans while cards 1511 through 190 featured rookies and cards 191-200 featured retired stars.

	Nm-Mt	Ex-Mt
COMPLETE SET (200)	100.00	30.00
COMMON CARD (1-150)	.50	.15
COMMON CARD (151-190)	1.00	.30
COMMON CARD (191-200)	2.00	.60
1 Jason Giambi	.50	.15
2 Mark Grace	.75	.23
3 Bret Boone	.50	.15
4 Antonio Alfonseca	.50	.15
5 Kevin Brown	.50	.15
6 Cristian Guzman	.50	.15
7 Magglio Ordonez	.50	.15
8 Luis Gonzalez	.50	.15
9 Jorge Posada	.75	.23
10 Roberto Alomar	.75	.23
11 Mike Sweeney	.50	.15
12 Jeff Kent	.50	.15
13 Matt Morris	.50	.15
14 Alfonso Soriano	.75	.23
15 Adam Dunn	.75	.23
16 Neifi Perez	.50	.15
17 Todd Walker	.50	.15
18 J.D. Drew	.50	.15
19 Eric Chavez	.50	.15
20 Alex Rodriguez	2.00	.60
21 Ray Lankford	.50	.15
22 Roger Cedeno	.50	.15
23 Chipper Jones	1.25	.35
24 Josh Beckett	.50	.15
25 Mike Piazza	2.00	.60
26 Freddy Garcia	.50	.15
27 Todd Helton	.75	.23
28 Tino Martinez	.75	.23
29 Kazuhiro Sasaki	.50	.15
30 Curt Schilling	.50	.15
31 Mark Buehrle	.50	.15
32 John Olerud	.50	.15
33 Brad Radke	.50	.15
34 Steve Sparks	.50	.15
35 Jason Tyner	.50	.15
36 Jeff Shaw	.50	.15
37 Mariano Rivera	.75	.23
38 Russ Ortiz	.50	.15
39 Richard Hidalgo	.50	.15
40 Carl Everett	.50	.15
41 John Burkett	.50	.15
42 Tim Hudson	.50	.15
43 Mike Hampton	.50	.15
44 Orlando Cabrera	.50	.15
45 Barry Zito	.50	.15
46 C.C. Sabathia	.50	.15
47 Chan Ho Park	.50	.15
48 Tom Glavine	.75	.23
49 Aramis Ramirez	.50	.15
50 Lance Berkman	.50	.15
51 Al Leiter	.50	.15
52 Phil Nevin	.50	.15
53 Javier Vazquez	.50	.15
54 Troy Glaus	.50	.15
55 Tsuyoshi Shinjo	.50	.15
56 Albert Pujols	2.50	.75
57 John Smoltz	.75	.23
58 Derek Jeter	3.00	.90
59 Robb Nen	.50	.15
60 Jason Kendall	.50	.15
61 Eric Gagne	1.25	.35
62 Vladimir Guerrero	1.25	.35
63 Corey Patterson	.50	.15
64 Rickey Henderson	1.25	.35
65 Jack Wilson	.50	.15
66 Jason LaRue	.50	.15
67 Sammy Sosa	2.00	.60
68 Ken Griffey Jr.	2.00	.60
69 Randy Johnson	1.25	.35
70 Nomar Garciaparra	2.00	.60
71 Ivan Rodriguez	1.25	.35
72 J.T. Snow	.50	.15
73 Darryl Kile	.50	.15
74 Andruw Jones	.50	.15
75 Brian Giles	.50	.15
76 Pedro Martinez	1.25	.35
77 Jeff Bagwell	.75	.23
78 Rafael Palmeiro	.75	.23
79 Ryan Dempster	.50	.15
80 Jeff Cirillo	.50	.15
81 Geoff Jenkins	.50	.15
82 Brandon Duckworth	.50	.15
83 Roger Clemens	2.50	.75
84 Fred McGriff	.75	.23
85 Hideo Nomo	1.25	.35
86 Larry Walker	.75	.23
87 Sean Casey	.50	.15
88 Trevor Hoffman	.50	.15
89 Robert Fick	.50	.15
90 Armando Benitez	.50	.15
91 Jeromy Burnitz	.50	.15
92 Bernie Williams	.75	.23
93 Carlos Delgado	.50	.15
94 Troy Percival	.50	.15
95 Nate Cornejo	.50	.15
96 Derrek Lee	.50	.15
97 Jose Ortiz	.50	.15
98 Brian Jordan	.50	.15
99 Jose Cruz Jr.	.50	.15
100 Ichiro Suzuki	2.00	.60
101 Jose Mesa	.50	.15
102 Tim Salmon	.75	.23
103 Bud Smith	.50	.15
104 Paul LoDuca	.50	.15
105 Juan Pierre	.50	.15
106 Ben Grieve	.50	.15
107 Russell Branyan	.50	.15
108 Bob Abreu	.50	.15
109 Moises Alou	.50	.15
110 Richie Sexson	.50	.15
111 Jerry Hairston Jr.	.50	.15
112 Marlon Anderson	.50	.15
113 Juan Gonzalez	.75	.23
114 Craig Biggio	.75	.23
115 Carlos Beltran	.75	.23
116 Eric Milton	.50	.15
117 Cliff Floyd	.50	.15
118 Rich Aurilia	.50	.15
119 Adrian Beltre	.75	.23
120 Jason Bere	.50	.15
121 Darin Erstad	.50	.15
122 Ben Sheets	.50	.15
123 Johnny Damon Sox	1.25	.35
124 Jimmy Rollins	.50	.15
125 Shawn Green	.50	.15
126 Greg Maddux	2.00	.60
127 Mark Mulder	.50	.15
128 Bartolo Colon	.50	.15
129 Shannon Stewart	.50	.15
130 Ramon Ortiz	.50	.15
131 Kerry Wood	1.25	.35
132 Ryan Klesko	.50	.15
133 Preston Wilson	.50	.15
134 Roy Oswalt	.50	.15
135 Rafael Furcal	.75	.23
136 Eric Karros	.50	.15
137 Nick Neugebauer	.50	.15
138 Doug Mientkiewicz	.50	.15
139 Paul Konerko	.50	.15
140 Bobby Higginson	.50	.15
141 Garret Anderson	.50	.15
142 Wes Helms	.50	.15
143 Brent Abernathy	.50	.15
144 Scott Rolen	1.25	.35
145 Dmitri Young	.50	.15
146 Jim Thome	1.25	.35
147 Raul Mondesi	.50	.15
148 Pat Burrell	.50	.15
149 Gary Sheffield	.50	.15
150 Miguel Tejada	.50	.15
151 Brandon Inge PROS	1.00	.30
152 Carlos Pena PROS	1.00	.30
153 Jason Lane PROS	1.00	.30
154 Nathan Haynes PROS	1.00	.30
155 Hank Blalock PROS	1.50	.45
156 Juan Cruz PROS	1.00	.30
157 Morgan Ensberg PROS	1.00	.30
158 Sean Burroughs PROS	1.00	.30
159 Ed Rogers PROS	1.00	.30
160 Nick Johnson PROS	1.00	.30
161 Orlando Hudson PROS	1.00	.30
162 A.Martinez PROS RC	1.00	.30
163 Jeremy Affeldt PROS	1.00	.30
164 Brandon Claussen PROS	1.00	.30
165 Deivis Santos PROS	1.00	.30
166 Mike Rivera PROS	1.00	.30
167 Carlos Silva PROS	1.00	.30
168 Val Pascucci PROS	1.00	.30
169 Xavier Nady PROS	1.00	.30
170 David Espinosa PROS	1.00	.30
171 Dan Phillips FYP RC	1.00	.30
172 Tony Fontana FYP RC	1.00	.30
173 Juan Silvestre FYP	1.00	.30
174 Henry Pichardo FYP RC	1.00	.30
175 Pablo Arias FYP RC	1.00	.30
176 Brett Roneberg FYP RC	1.00	.30
177 Chad Qualls FYP RC	1.00	.30
178 Greg Sain FYP RC	1.50	.45
179 Rene Reyes FYP RC	1.00	.30
180 So Taguchi FYP RC	1.50	.45
181 Dan Johnson FYP RC	1.50	.45
182 J.Backsmeyer FYP RC	1.00	.30
183 J.M. Gonzalez FYP RC	1.00	.30
184 Jason Ellison FYP RC	1.00	.30
185 Kazuhisa Ishii FYP RC	4.00	1.20
186 Joe Mauer FYP RC	8.00	2.40
187 James Shanks FYP RC	1.00	.30
188 Kevin Cash FYP RC	1.00	.30
189 J.J. Trujillo FYP RC	1.00	.30
190 Jorge Padilla FYP RC	1.00	.30
191 Nolan Ryan RET	6.00	1.80
192 George Brett RET	6.00	1.80
193 Ryne Sandberg RET	5.00	1.50
194 Robin Yount RET	4.00	1.20
195 Tom Seaver RET	2.00	.60
196 Mike Schmidt RET	5.00	1.50
197 Frank Robinson RET	2.00	.60
198 Harmon Killebrew RET	2.50	.75
199 Kirby Puckett RET	2.50	.75
200 Don Mattingly RET	6.00	1.80

2002 Topps Gallery Veteran Variation 1

Inserted at stated odds of one in 24, these 10 cards feature the most important players from the Gallery set featuring a variation from the regular issue cards. Since these were not announced until after the product went live, we have put the information about the variation next to the player's name.

	Nm-Mt	Ex-Mt
1 Jason Giambi Solid Blue	2.50	.75
20 Alex Rodriguez Grey Jsy	10.00	3.00
25 Mike Piazza Black Jsy	10.00	3.00
27 Todd Helton Solid Blue	4.00	1.20
56 Albert Pujols Red Hat	12.00	3.60
58 Derek Jeter Solid Blue	15.00	4.50
67 Sammy Sosa Black Bat	10.00	3.00
71 Ivan Rodriguez Blue Jsy	6.00	1.80
76 Pedro Martinez Red Shirt	6.00	1.80
100 Ichiro Suzuki Empty Dugout	10.00	3.00

2002 Topps Gallery Veteran Variation 2

Inserted at stated odds of one in 4065, these 10 cards feature the most important players from the Gallery set featuring a variation from the regular issue cards. Since these were not announced until after the product went live, we have put the information about the variation next to the player's name. Since these cards are so difficult, no pricing is available due to market scarcity.

	Nm-Mt	Ex-Mt
1 Jason Giambi White Btg Glv		
20 Alex Rodriguez Grass Stain		
25 Mike Piazza Solid Orange		
27 Todd Helton Black Bat		
56 Albert Pujols Blue Wrist		
58 Derek Jeter Solid Red		
67 Sammy Sosa Red Wrist		
71 Ivan Rodriguez No Wrist		
76 Pedro Martinez No Ball		
100 Ichiro Suzuki Brown Bat		

2002 Topps Gallery Autographs

Issued at overall stated odds of one in 240, these 10 cards feature players who have added their signature to these painted cards. The players belong to three different groups and we have put that information about their group next to their name in our checklist.

	Nm-Mt	Ex-Mt
GROUP A ODDS 1:815 HOB/RET........		
GROUP B ODDS 1:1017 HOB, 1:1023 RET		
GROUP C ODDS 1:509 HOB/RET........		
GA-BBO Bret Boone A	25.00	7.50
GA-JD J.D. Drew B	40.00	12.00
GA-JL Jason Lane C	10.00	3.00
GA-JP Jorge Posada A	50.00	15.00
GA-JS Juan Silvestre C	10.00	3.00
GA-LB Lance Berkman A	40.00	12.00
GA-LG Luis Gonzalez B	25.00	7.50
GA-MO Magglio Ordonez A	25.00	7.50
GA-SG Shawn Green A	25.00	7.50

2002 Topps Gallery Bucks

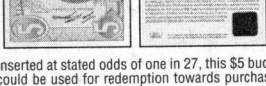

Inserted at stated odds of one in 27, this $5 buck could be used for redemption towards purchasing original Topps Gallery artwork.

	Nm-Mt	Ex-Mt
NNO Nolan Ryan $5	8.00	2.40

2002 Topps Gallery Heritage

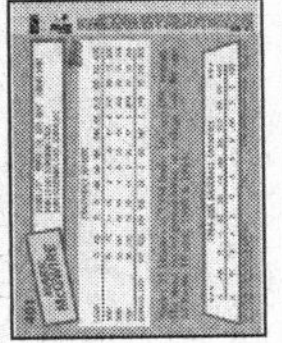

Inserted at stated odds of one in 12, these 25 cards feature drawings of players in the style of their Topps rookie card. We have put the year of the players "Topps" rookie card next to their name in our checklist.

	Nm-Mt	Ex-Mt
COMPLETE SET (25)	120.00	36.00
GH-AK Al Kaline 54	5.00	1.50
GH-AR Alex Rodriguez 98	8.00	2.40
GH-BR Brooks Robinson 57	3.00	.90
GH-BBO Bret Boone 93	3.00	.90
GH-CJ Chipper Jones 91	5.00	1.50
GH-CY Carl Yastrzemski 60	8.00	2.40
GH-GM Greg Maddux 87	8.00	2.40
GH-JG Jason Giambi 91	3.00	.90
GH-KG Ken Griffey Jr. 89	8.00	2.40
GH-LG Luis Gonzalez 91	3.00	.90
GH-MM Mark McGwire 85	15.00	4.50
GH-MP Mike Piazza 93	8.00	2.40
GH-MS Mike Schmidt 73	10.00	3.00
GH-NR Nolan Ryan 68	12.00	3.60
GH-PM Pedro Martinez 93	5.00	1.50
GH-RA Roberto Alomar 88	3.00	.90
GH-RC Roger Clemens 85	10.00	3.00
GH-RJ Reggie Jackson 69	3.00	.90
GH-RY Robin Yount 75	8.00	2.40
GH-SG Shawn Green 92	3.00	.90
GH-SM Stan Musial 58	8.00	2.40
GH-SS Sammy Sosa 90	8.00	2.40
GH-TG Tony Gwynn 83	6.00	1.80
GH-TS Tom Seaver 67	3.00	.90
GH-TSH Tsuyoshi Shinjo 01	3.00	.90

2002 Topps Gallery Heritage Autographs

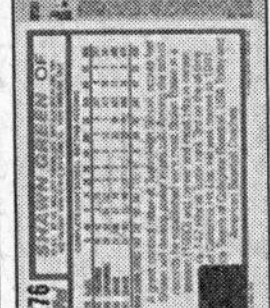

Inserted at stated odds of one in 13,595 hobby and one in 14,064 retail, these three cards feature authentic autographs of the featured players. These cards have a stated print run of 25 serial numbered sets and due to market scarcity, no pricing is provided for these cards.

	Nm-Mt	Ex-Mt
GHA-LG Luis Gonzalez 91		
GHA-SG Shawn Green 92		
GHA-BBO Bret Boone 93		

2002 Topps Gallery Heritage Uniform Relics

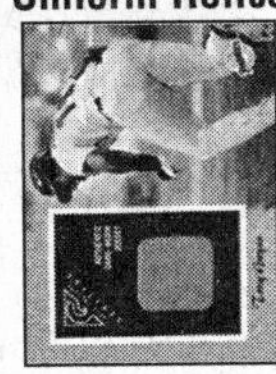

Inserted in packs at an overall stated rate of one in 85, these nine cards are a partial parallel to the Heritage insert set. Each card contains not only the player's photo but also a game-worn uniform piece. The players were broken up into two groups and we have notated the groups the player belonged to as well as their stated odds in our set information.

	Nm-Mt	Ex-Mt
GROUP A ODDS 1:106 HOB/RET........		
GROUP B ODDS 1:424 HOB/RET........		
GHR-AR Alex Rodriguez 98 A	20.00	6.00
GHR-CJ Chipper Jones 91 B	15.00	4.50
GHR-GM Greg Maddux 87 A	15.00	4.50
GHR-LG Luis Gonzalez 91 A	10.00	3.00
GHR-MP Mike Piazza 93 A	15.00	4.50
GHR-PM Pedro Martinez 93 A	15.00	4.50
GHR-TG Tony Gwynn 83 A	15.00	4.50
GHR-TS Tsuyoshi Shinjo 01 A	10.00	3.00
GHR-BBO Bret Boone 93 A	10.00	3.00

2002 Topps Gallery Original Bat Relics

Inserted at overall stated odds of one in 169, these 15 cards feature not only the player's photo featured but also a game-used bat piece.

	Nm-Mt	Ex-Mt
GO-AJ Andruw Jones	10.00	3.00
GO-AP Albert Pujols	40.00	12.00
GO-AR Alex Rodriguez	15.00	4.50
GO-AS Alfonso Soriano	15.00	4.50
GO-BW Bernie Williams	15.00	4.50
GO-BBO Bret Boone	10.00	3.00
GO-CD Carlos Delgado	10.00	3.00
GO-CJ Chipper Jones	15.00	4.50
GO-JC Jose Canseco	15.00	4.50
GO-JG Juan Gonzalez	15.00	4.50
GO-LG Luis Gonzalez	10.00	3.00
GO-MP Mike Piazza	25.00	7.50
GO-TG Tony Gwynn	20.00	6.00
GO-TH Todd Helton	15.00	4.50
GO-TM Tino Martinez	15.00	4.50

2003 Topps Gallery

This 200 card set was released in August, 2003. These cards were issued in four card packs with an $5 SRP which came 20 packs to a box and eight boxes to a case. Cards numbered 1 through 150 featured veterans while cards 151 through 167 featured first year cards, cards 168 through 190 featured leading prospects and cards numbered 191 through 200 featured legendary retired players. In addition, 20 variations (seeded at a stated rate of one in 20) were also included in this set.

	MINT	NRMT
COMP.SET w/o SP's (200)	100.00	45.00
COMMON (1-150/168-190)	.50	.23
COMMON CARD (151-167)	.60	.25
VARIATION STATED ODDS 1:20........		
COMMON CARD (191-200)	1.25	.55
1 Jason Giambi	.50	.23
1A Jason Giambi Blue Jsy	5.00	2.20
2 Miguel Tejada	.50	.23
3 Mike Lieberthal	.50	.23
4 Jason Kendall	.50	.23
5 Robb Nen	.50	.23
6 Freddy Garcia	.50	.23
7 Scott Rolen	1.25	.55
8 Boomer Wells	.50	.23
9 Rafael Palmeiro	.75	.35
10 Garret Anderson	.50	.23
11 Curt Schilling	.75	.35
12 Greg Maddux	2.00	.90
13 Rodrigo Lopez	.50	.23
14 Nomar Garciaparra	2.00	.90
14A N.Garciaparra Btg Glv	8.00	3.60
15 Kerry Wood	1.25	.55
16 Frank Thomas	1.25	.55
17 Ken Griffey Jr.	2.00	.90
18 Jim Thome	1.25	.55
19 Todd Helton	.75	.35
20 Lance Berkman	.50	.23
21 Robert Fick	.50	.23
22 Kevin Brown	.50	.23
23 Richie Sexson	.50	.23
24 Eddie Guardado	.50	.23
25 Vladimir Guerrero	1.25	.55
26 Mike Piazza	2.00	.90
27 Bernie Williams	.75	.35
28 Eric Chavez	.50	.23
29 Jimmy Rollins	.50	.23
30 Ichiro Suzuki	2.00	.90
30A I.Suzuki Black Sleeve	8.00	3.60
31 J.D. Drew	.50	.23
32 Nick Johnson	.50	.23
33 Shannon Stewart	.50	.23
34 Tim Salmon	.75	.35
35 Andruw Jones	.50	.23
36 Jay Gibbons	.50	.23
37 Johnny Damon	1.25	.55
38 Fred McGriff	.75	.35
39 Carlos Lee	.50	.23
40 Adam Dunn	.75	.35
40A Adam Dunn Red Sleeve	5.00	2.20
41 Jason Jennings	.50	.23
42 Mike Lowell	.50	.23
43 Mike Sweeney	.50	.23
44 Shawn Green	.50	.23
45 Doug Mientkiewicz	.50	.23
46 Bartolo Colon	.50	.23
47 Edgardo Alfonzo	.50	.23
48 Roger Clemens	2.50	1.10
49 Randy Wolf	.50	.23
50 Alex Rodriguez	2.00	.90
50A Alex Rodriguez Red Shirt	8.00	3.60
51 Vernon Wells	.50	.23
52 Kenny Lofton	.50	.23
53 Mariano Rivera	.75	.35
54 Brian Jordan	.50	.23
55 Roberto Alomar	.75	.35
56 Carlos Pena	.50	.23
57 Moises Alou	.50	.23
58 John Smoltz	.75	.35
59 Adam Kennedy	.50	.23
60 Randy Johnson	1.25	.55
61 Mark Buehrle	.50	.23
62 C.C. Sabathia	.50	.23
63 Craig Biggio	.75	.35
64 Eric Karros	.50	.23
65 Jose Vidro	.50	.23
66 Tim Hudson	.50	.23
67 Trevor Hoffman	.50	.23
68 Bret Boone	.50	.23
69 Carl Crawford	.50	.23
70 Derek Jeter	3.00	1.35
71 Troy Percival	.50	.23
72 Gary Sheffield	.50	.23
73 Rickey Henderson	1.25	.55
74 Paul Konerko	.50	.23
75 Larry Walker	.75	.35
76 Pat Burrell	.50	.23
77 Brian Giles	.50	.23
78 Jeff Kent	.50	.23
79 Kazuhiro Sasaki	.50	.23
80 Chipper Jones	1.25	.55
81 Darin Erstad	.50	.23
82 Sean Casey	.50	.23
83 Luis Gonzalez	.50	.23
84 Roy Oswalt	.50	.23
85 Dustan Mohr	.50	.23
86 Al Leiter	.50	.23
87 Mike Mussina	.75	.35
88 Vicente Padilla	.50	.23
89 Rich Aurilia	.50	.23
90 Albert Pujols	2.50	1.10
91 John Olerud	.50	.23
92 Ivan Rodriguez	1.25	.55
93 Eric Hinske	.50	.23
94 Phil Nevin	.50	.23
95 Barry Zito	.50	.23
96 Armando Benitez	.50	.23
97 Torii Hunter	.50	.23
98 Paul Lo Duca	.50	.23
99 Preston Wilson	.50	.23
100 Sammy Sosa	2.00	.90
100A Sammy Sosa Black Bat	8.00	3.60
101 Jarrod Washburn	.50	.23
102 Steve Finley	.50	.23
103 Cliff Floyd	.50	.23
104 Mark Prior	1.25	.55
105 Austin Kearns	.50	.23
106 Jeff Bagwell	.75	.35
107 A.J. Pierzynski	.50	.23
108 Pedro Martinez	1.25	.55
109 Orlando Cabrera	.50	.23
110 Raul Mondesi	.50	.23
111 Russ Ortiz	.50	.23
112 Ruben Sierra	.50	.23
113 Tino Martinez	.75	.35
114 Manny Ramirez	.75	.35
115 Troy Glaus	.75	.35
116 Magglio Ordonez	.50	.23
117 Omar Vizquel	.75	.35
118 Carlos Beltran	.75	.35
119 Jose Hernandez	.50	.23
120 Javier Vazquez	.50	.23
121 Jorge Posada	.75	.35
122 Aramis Ramirez	.50	.23
123 Jason Schmidt	.50	.23
124 Jamie Moyer	.50	.23
125 Jim Edmonds	.50	.23
126 Aubrey Huff	.50	.23
127 Carlos Delgado	.50	.23
128 Junior Spivey	.50	.23
129 Tom Glavine	.75	.35
130 Marty Cordova	.50	.23
131 Derek Lowe	.50	.23
132 Ellis Burks	.50	.23
133 Barry Bonds	3.00	1.35
134 Josh Beckett	.50	.23
135 Raul Ibanez	.50	.23
136 Kazuhisa Ishii	.50	.23
137 Geoff Jenkins	.50	.23
138 Eric Milton	.50	.23
139 Mo Vaughn	.50	.23
140 Mark Mulder	.50	.23
141 Bobby Abreu	.50	.23
142 Ryan Klesko	.50	.23
143 Tsuyoshi Shinjo	.50	.23
144 Jose Mesa	.50	.23
145 Shea Hillenbrand	.50	.23
146 Edgar Renteria	.50	.23
147 Juan Gonzalez	.75	.35
148 Edgar Martinez	.75	.35
149 Matt Morris	.50	.23
150 Alfonso Soriano	.75	.35
150A Alfonso Soriano No Pad	5.00	2.20
151 Bryan Bullington FY RC	2.50	1.10
151A B.Bullington Red Back FY	5.00	2.20
152 Andy Marte FY RC	5.00	2.20
152A A.Marte No Necklace FY	10.00	4.50
153 Brendan Harris FY RC	1.00	.45
154 Juan Camacho FY RC	.60	.25
155 Byron Gettis FY RC	.60	.25
156 Daryl Clark FY RC	1.00	.45
157 J.D. Durbin FY RC	1.50	.70
158 Craig Brazell FY RC	1.00	.45
158A Craig Brazell Black Jsy	5.00	2.20
159 Jason Kubel FY RC	4.00	1.80
160 Br. Roberson FY RC	.60	.25
161 Jose Contreras FY RC	2.00	.90
162 Hanley Ramirez FY RC	4.00	1.80
163 Jaime Bubela FY RC	.60	.25
164 Chris Duncan FY RC	.60	.25
165 Tyler Johnson FY RC	.60	.25
166 Joey Gomes FY RC	.60	.25
167 Ben Francisco FY RC	1.00	.45
168 Adam LaRoche PROS	.50	.23
169 Tommy Whiteman PROS	.50	.23
170 Trey Hodges PROS	.50	.23
171 Fr. Rodriguez PROS	.50	.23
172 Jason Arnold PROS	.50	.23
173 Brett Myers PROS	.50	.23
174 Rocco Baldelli PROS	2.00	.90
175 Adrian Gonzalez PROS	.50	.23
176 Dontrelle Willis PROS	.75	.35
177 Walter Young PROS	.50	.23
178 Marlon Byrd PROS	.50	.23
179 Aaron Heilman PROS	.50	.23
180 Casey Kotchman PROS	.75	.35
181 Miguel Cabrera PROS	1.25	.55
182 Hee Seop Choi PROS	.50	.23
183 Drew Henson PROS	.50	.23
184 Jose Reyes PROS	.50	.23
185 Michael Cuddyer PROS	.50	.23
186 Brandon Phillips PROS	.50	.23
187 Victor Martinez PROS	.75	.35
188 Joe Mauer PROS	1.25	.55
189 Hank Blalock PROS	.75	.35
190 Mark Teixeira PROS	.50	.23
191 Willie Mays RET	4.00	1.80
192 George Brett RET	5.00	2.20
193 Tony Gwynn RET	2.50	1.10
194 Carl Yastrzemski RET	3.00	1.35
195 Nolan Ryan RET	5.00	2.20
196 Reggie Jackson RET	1.25	.55
197 Mike Schmidt RET	4.00	1.80
198 Cal Ripken RET	6.00	2.70
199 Don Mattingly RET	5.00	2.20
200 Tom Seaver RET	1.25	.55

2003 Topps Gallery Artist's Proofs

	MINT	NRMT
*AP 1-150/168-190: .75X TO 2X BASIC		
*AP 151-167: .75X TO 2X BASIC........		
*AP 191-200: 1X TO 2.5X BASIC........		
ONE PER PACK........		
AP'S FEATURE SILVER HOLO-FOIL		

2003 Topps Gallery Press Plates

	MINT	NRMT
RANDOM INSERTS IN PACKS........		
STATED PRINT RUN 4 SERIAL #'d SETS		
NO PRICING DUE TO SCARCITY		

2003 Topps Gallery Bucks

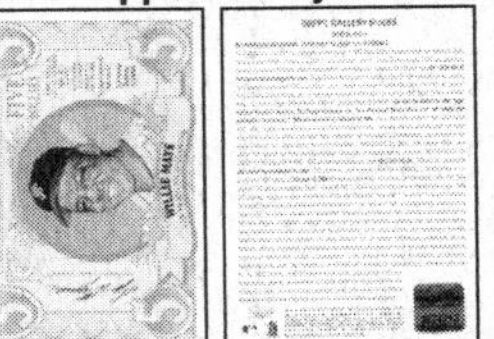

Inserted at a stated rate of one in 41, this one "card" insert set featured a photo of Willie Mays along with a $5 gift certificate good for Topps product.

	MINT	NRMT
5 Willie Mays $5	5.00	2.20

2003 Topps Gallery Currency Collection Coin Relics

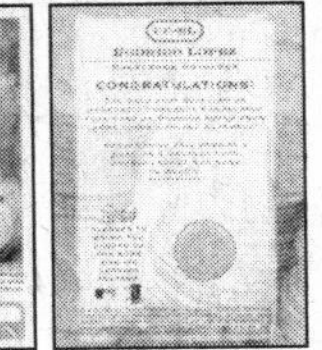

Inserted in each hobby box as a "box-topper" these 25 cards feature players from throughout the world along with a coin from their homeland.

	MINT	NRMT
AJ Andruw Jones	8.00	3.60
AP Albert Pujols	20.00	9.00
AS Alfonso Soriano	8.00	3.60
BA Bobby Abreu	8.00	3.60
BC Bartolo Colon	8.00	3.60
ER Edgar Renteria	8.00	3.60
FR Francisco Rodriguez	8.00	3.60
HC Hee Seop Choi	8.00	3.60
HN Hideo Nomo	10.00	4.50
IS Ichiro Suzuki	15.00	6.75
JR Jose Reyes	8.00	3.60
KI Kazuhisa Ishii	8.00	3.60
KS Kazuhiro Sasaki	8.00	3.60
LW Larry Walker	8.00	3.60
MO Magglio Ordonez	8.00	3.60
MR Manny Ramirez	8.00	3.60
MRI Mariano Rivera	8.00	3.60
OC Orlando Cabrera	8.00	3.60
OV Omar Vizquel	8.00	3.60
PM Pedro Martinez	10.00	4.50
RL Rodrigo Lopez	8.00	3.60
RM Raul Mondesi	8.00	3.60
SS Sammy Sosa	15.00	6.75
VG Vladimir Guerrero	10.00	4.50
VP Vicente Padilla	8.00	3.60

2003 Topps Gallery Heritage

	MINT	NRMT
STATED ODDS 1:10........		
AD Adam Dunn	5.00	2.20
AS Alfonso Soriano	5.00	2.20
BW Bernie Williams	5.00	2.20
CY Carl Yastrzemski	8.00	3.60
DJ Derek Jeter	12.00	5.50
DS Duke Snider	5.00	2.20
GB George Brett	10.00	4.50
HK Harmon Killebrew	5.00	2.20
HN Hideo Nomo	5.00	2.20
IR Ivan Rodriguez	5.00	2.20
IS Ichiro Suzuki	8.00	3.60
JC Jose Canseco	5.00	2.20
JT Jim Thome	5.00	2.20
KP Kirby Puckett	5.00	2.20
KR Jerry Koosman Nolan Ryan	15.00	6.75
MT Miguel Tejada	3.00	1.35
NG Nomar Garciaparra	8.00	3.60
RC Roger Clemens	10.00	4.50
RH Rickey Henderson	5.00	2.20
RJ Randy Johnson	5.00	2.20
SG Shawn Green	3.00	1.35
TG Tom Glavine	5.00	2.20
TGW Tony Gwynn	6.00	2.70
WB Wade Boggs	5.00	2.20
WM Willie Mays	10.00	4.50

2003 Topps Gallery Heritage Autograph Relics

Randomly inserted into packs, these four cards feature not only a game-used memorabilia piece but also an authentic autograph of the featured player. Each of these cards were issued to a stated print run of 25 copies and no pricing is available due to market scarcity.

	MINT	NRMT
NO PRICING DUE TO SCARCITY		
GB George Brett Bat		
KP Kirby Puckett Bat		
TG Tony Gwynn Jsy		
WB Wade Boggs Uni		

2003 Topps Gallery Heritage Relics

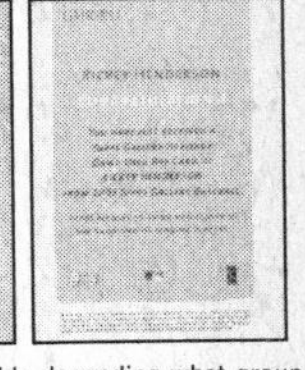

Inserted at varying odds depending what group the card belonged to, this 10 card set featured game-used memorabilia pieces of the featured player.

	MINT	NRMT
GROUP A ODDS 1:141........		
GROUP B ODDS 1:67........		
GB George Brett Bat A	25.00	11.00
HK Harmon Killebrew Bat A	25.00	11.00
HN Hideo Nomo Jsy A	15.00	6.75
JC Jose Canseco Bat B	10.00	4.50
KP Kirby Puckett Bat A	15.00	6.75
RC Roger Clemens Jsy A	15.00	6.75
RH Rickey Henderson Bat B	10.00	4.50
SG Shawn Green Jsy B	8.00	3.60
TG Tony Gwynn Bat B	15.00	6.75
WB Wade Boggs Uni B	10.00	4.50

2003 Topps Gallery Originals Bat Relics

MINT NRMT
GROUP A ODDS 1:131
GROUP B ODDS 1:81
GROUP C ODDS 1:15
AD Adam Dunn C 10.00 4.50
AJ Andruw Jones C 8.00 3.60
AP Albert Pujols B 20.00 9.00
AR Alex Rodriguez C 15.00 6.75
AS Alfonso Soriano B 10.00 4.50
BB Bret Boone C 8.00 3.60
BW Bernie Williams C 10.00 4.50
CJ Chipper Jones C 10.00 4.50
CY Carl Yastrzemski A 20.00 9.00
DH Drew Henson B 8.00 3.60
FT Frank Thomas C 10.00 4.50
GS Gary Sheffield C 8.00 3.60
IR Ivan Rodriguez C 10.00 4.50
JM Joe Mauer A 15.00 6.75
JT Jim Thome C 10.00 4.50
LB Lance Berkman C 8.00 3.60
LG Luis Gonzalez A 10.00 4.50
MA Moises Alou B 8.00 3.60
MO Magglio Ordonez C 8.00 3.60
MP Mike Piazza C 15.00 6.75
MR Manny Ramirez C 10.00 4.50
MT Miguel Tejada A 10.00 4.50
NG Nomar Garciaparra B 15.00 6.75
RA Roberto Alomar C 10.00 4.50
RH Rickey Henderson C 10.00 4.50
RP Rafael Palmeiro C 10.00 4.50
SG Shawn Green B 8.00 3.60
TG Tony Gwynn C 10.00 4.50
TH Todd Helton C 10.00 4.50
THU Torii Hunter A 10.00 4.50

2003 Topps Gallery HOF

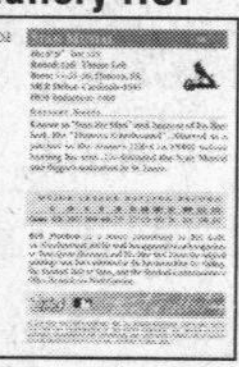

This set was released in April, 2003. Each card in the set was actually issued in different versions, some of each were easy to identify and others had far more subtle differences. This set was issued in five card packs with an $5 SRP. The packs were issued in 20 pack boxes which came six boxes to a case.

Nm-Mt Ex-Mt
COMPLETE SET (74) 40.00 12.00
COMMON CARD (1-74) .75 .23
COMMON VARIATION (1-74) 1.50 .45
1 Willie Mays Bleachers 3.00 .90
1B Willie Mays Gold 6.00 1.80
2 Al Kaline Stripes 1.50 .45
2B Al Kaline No Stripes 3.00 .90
3 Hank Aaron Black Hat 3.00 .90
3B Hank Aaron Blue Hat 6.00 1.80
4 Carl Yastrzemski Black Ltr 2.50 .75
4B Carl Yastrzemski Red Ltr 5.00 1.50
5 Luis Aparicio Wood Bat .75 .23
5B Luis Aparicio Black Bat 1.50 .45
6 Sam Crawford Grey Uni .75 .23
6B Sam Crawford Navy Uni 1.50 .45
7 Tom Lasorda Trees .75 .23
7B Tom Lasorda Red 1.50 .45
8 John McGraw MG No Logo .75 .23
8B J.McGraw MG NY Logo 1.50 .45
9 Edd Roush White C .75 .23
9B Edd Roush Red C 1.50 .45
10 Reggie Jackson Grass 1.00 .30
10B Reggie Jackson Red 2.00 .60
11 Catfish Hunter Yellow Jsy 1.00 .30
11B Catfish Hunter White Jsy 2.00 .60
12 Rob. Clemente White Uni 4.00 1.20
12B Rob. Clemente Yellow Uni 8.00 2.40
13 Eddie Collins Grey Uni .75 .23
13B Eddie Collins Navy Uni 1.50 .45
14 Frankie Frisch Olive .75 .23
14B Frankie Frisch Blue 1.50 .45
15 Nolan Ryan Leather Glv 4.00 1.20
15B Nolan Ryan Black Glv 8.00 2.40
16 Brooks Robinson Yellow 1.00 .30
16B Brooks Robinson Green 2.00 .60
17 Phil Niekro Black Hat .75 .23
17B Phil Niekro Blue Hat 1.50 .45
18 Joe Cronin Blue Sleeve .75 .23
18B Joe Cronin White Sleeve 1.50 .45
19 Joe Tinker White Hat .75 .23
19B Joe Tinker Blue Hat 1.50 .45
20 Johnny Bench Day 1.50 .45
20B Johnny Bench Night 3.00 .90
21 Harry Heilmann Day .75 .23
21B Harry Heilmann Night 1.50 .45
22 Ernie Harwell BRD Red Tie .75 .23
22B Ernie Harwell BRD Blue Tie 1.50 .45
23 Warren Spahn Patch 1.00 .30
23B Warren Spahn No Patch 2.00 .60
24 George Kelly Blue Bill .75 .23
24B George Kelly Red Bill 1.50 .45
25 Phil Rizzuto Bleachers 1.00 .30
25B Phil Rizzuto Green 2.00 .60
26 Robin Roberts Day .75 .23
26B Robin Roberts Night 1.50 .45
27 Ozzie Smith Red Sleeve 2.50 .75
27B Ozzie Smith Blue Sleeve 5.00 1.50
28 Jim Palmer White Hat .75 .23
28B Jim Palmer Black Hat 1.50 .45
29 Duke Snider No Patch 1.00 .30
29B Duke Snider Flag Patch 2.00 .60
30 Bob Feller White Uni .75 .23
30B Bob Feller Grey Uni 1.50 .45
31 Buck Leonard Bleachers .75 .23
31B Buck Leonard Red 1.50 .45
32 Kirby Puckett Wood Bat 1.50 .45
32B Kirby Puckett Black Bat 3.00 .90
33 Monte Irvin Black Sleeve .75 .23
33B Monte Irvin White Sleeve 1.50 .45
34 Chuck Klein Black Socks .75 .23
34B Chuck Klein Red Socks 1.50 .45
35 Willie Stargell Yellow Uni 1.00 .30
35B Willie Stargell White Uni 2.00 .60
36 Juan Marichal Ballpark .75 .23
36B Juan Marichal Gold 1.50 .45
37 Lou Brock Day 1.00 .30
37B Lou Brock Night 2.00 .60
38 Bucky Harris Black W .75 .23
38B Bucky Harris Red W 1.50 .45
39 Bobby Doerr Ballpark .75 .23
39B Bobby Doerr Red 1.50 .45
40 Lee MacPhail Blue Tie .75 .23
40B Lee MacPhail Red Tie 1.50 .45
41 H.Manush Grey Sleeve .75 .23
41B H.Manush Navy Sleeve 1.50 .45
42 George Brett Patch 4.00 1.20
42B George Brett No Patch 8.00 2.40
43 Harmon Killebrew Blue Hat 1.50 .45
43B Har. Killebrew Red Hat 3.00 .90
44 Whitey Ford Day 1.00 .30
44B Whitey Ford Night 2.00 .60
45 Eddie Mathews Day 1.50 .45
45B Eddie Mathews Night 3.00 .90
46 Gaylord Perry Leather Glv .75 .23
46B Gaylord Perry Black Glv 1.50 .45
47 Red Schoendienst Stripes .75 .23
47B R.Schoendienst No Stripes 1.50 .45
48 Earl Weaver MG Day .75 .23
48B Earl Weaver MG Night 1.50 .45
49 Joe Morgan Day .75 .23
49B Joe Morgan Night 1.50 .45
50 Mike Schmidt Grey Uni 3.00 .90
50B Mike Schmidt White Uni 6.00 1.80
51 Willie McCovey Wood Bat .75 .23
51B Willie McCovey Black Bat 1.50 .45
52 Stan Musial Day 2.50 .75
52B Stan Musial Night 5.00 1.50
53 Don Sutton Ballpark .75 .23
53B Don Sutton Gray 1.50 .45
54 Hank Greenberg w/Player 1.50 .45
54B H.Greenberg No Player 3.00 .90
55 Robin Yount w/Player 2.50 .75
55B Robin Yount No Player 5.00 1.50
56 Tom Seaver Leather Glv 1.00 .30
56B Tom Seaver Black Glv 2.00 .60
57 Tony Perez Wood Bat .75 .23
57B Tony Perez Black Bat 1.50 .45
58 George Sisler w/Ad .75 .23
58B George Sisler No Ad 1.50 .45
59 Jim Bottomley White Hat .75 .23
59B Jim Bottomley Red Hat 1.50 .45
60 Yogi Berra Leather Chest 1.50 .45
60B Yogi Berra Navy Chest 3.00 .90
61 Fred Lindstrom Blue Bill .75 .23
61B Fred Lindstrom Red Bill 1.50 .45
62 Napoleon Lajoie White Uni 1.50 .45
62B Nap. Lajoie Navy Uni 3.00 .90
63 Frank Robinson Wood Bat 1.00 .30
63B Fr. Robinson Black Bat 2.00 .60
64 Carlton Fisk Red Ltr 1.00 .30
64B Carlton Fisk Black Ltr 2.00 .60
65 Orlando Cepeda Blue Sky .75 .23
65B Orlando Cepeda Sunset 1.50 .45
66 Fergie Jenkins Leather Glv .75 .23
66B Fergie Jenkins Black Glv 1.50 .45
67 Ernie Banks Day 1.50 .45
67B Ernie Banks Night 3.00 .90
68 Bill Mazeroski No Sleeves 1.00 .30
68B Bill Mazeroski w/Sleeves 2.00 .60
69 Jim Bunning Grey Uni .75 .23
69B Jim Bunning White Uni 1.50 .45
70 Rollie Fingers Day .75 .23
70B Rollie Fingers Night 1.50 .45
71 Jimmie Foxx Black Sleeve 1.50 .45
71B Ji. Foxx White Sleeve 3.00 .90
72 Rod Carew Red Btg Glv 1.00 .30
72B Rod Carew Blue Btg Glv 2.00 .60
73 Sparky Anderson Blue Sky .75 .23
73B Sparky Anderson Yellow 1.50 .45
74 George Kell Red D .75 .23
74B George Kell White D 1.50 .45

2003 Topps Gallery HOF Artist's Proofs

Inserted in packs at a rate of one per for basic cards and one in 20 for variations cards, this is a complete parallel of the Topps Gallery set. The Artist Proof cards can be differentiated by the presence of silver foil and those are also much heavier than the regular cards.

Nm-Mt Ex-Mt
*ARTIST'S PROOFS: .75X TO 2X BASIC
*VARIATIONS: 2X TO 5X BASIC VAR .

2003 Topps Gallery HOF Accent Mark Autographs

Issued at various odds depending on who signed the cards, these six cards featured authentic autographs of the featured HOFer. Each person signed a different amount of cards and we have notated the group of the signed card next to their name in our checklist.

Nm-Mt Ex-Mt
GROUP A ODDS 1:3446
GROUP B ODDS 1:2074
GROUP C ODDS 1:1483
GROUP D ODDS 1:1149
GROUP E ODDS 1:941
GROUP F ODDS 1:545
ARTIST'S PROOFS ODDS 1:1723
ARTIST'S PROOFS PRINT RUN 25 #'d SETS
NO AP PRICING DUE TO SCARCITY
AP'S FEATURE SILVER HOLO-FOIL
BD Bobby Doerr B 40.00 12.00
LM Lee MacPhail D 40.00 12.00
RR Robin Roberts E 40.00 12.00
RS Red Schoendienst C 40.00 12.00
WS Warren Spahn F 30.00 9.00
YB Yogi Berra A 80.00 24.00

2003 Topps Gallery HOF ARTifact Relics

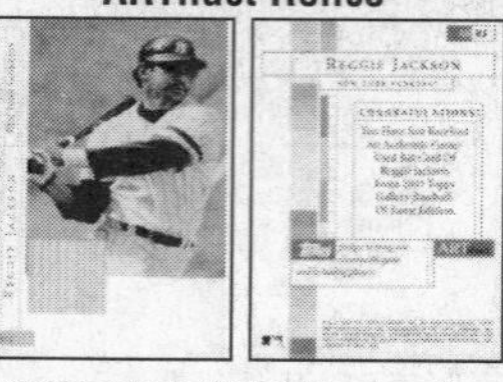

Inserted in packs at differing rates depending on what group the relic belongs to, this is a 57-card insert set featuring game-used relic pieces of various Hall of Famers. We have notated next to the player's name both the relic piece as well as what group the relic piece belonged to.

Nm-Mt Ex-Mt
BAT GROUP A ODDS 1:1812
BAT GROUP B ODDS 1:469
BAT GROUP C ODDS 1:242
BAT GROUP D ODDS 1:111
BAT GROUP E ODDS 1:96
BAT GROUP F ODDS 1:28
BAT GROUP G ODDS 1:62
JSY/UNI GROUP A ODDS 1:1812
JSY/UNI GROUP B ODDS 1:2353
JSY/UNI GROUP C ODDS 1:728
JSY/UNI GROUP D ODDS 1:151
JSY/UNI GROUP E ODDS 1:145
ARTIST'S PROOFS BAT ODDS 1:345
ARTIST'S PROOFS JSY/UNI ODDS 1:967
ARTIST'S PROOFS PRINT RUN 25 #'d SETS
NO AP PRICING DUE TO SCARCITY
AP'S FEATURE SILVER HOLO-FOIL
AK Al Kaline Bat F 15.00 4.50
BD Bobby Doerr Jsy D 10.00 3.00
BH Bucky Harris Bat F 15.00 4.50
BR Babe Ruth Bat B 180.00 55.00
BRO Brooks Robinson Bat D 15.00 4.50
CF Carlton Fisk Bat G 15.00 4.50
CK Chuck Klein Bat F 15.00 4.50
CY Carl Yastrzemski Bat F 20.00 6.00
DS Duke Snider Bat F 15.00 4.50
DSU Don Sutton Bat D 10.00 3.00
EB Ernie Banks Uni B 40.00 12.00
EC Eddie Collins Bat B 30.00 9.00
EM Eddie Mathews Jsy A
ER Edd Roush Bat B 30.00 9.00
FF Frankie Frisch Bat E 15.00 4.50
FR Frank Robinson Bat G 15.00 4.50
GB George Brett Jsy D 30.00 9.00
GK George Kelly Bat D 20.00 6.00
GP Gaylord Perry Uni E 10.00 3.00
GS George Sisler Bat F 15.00 4.50
HA Hank Aaron Bat F 25.00 7.50
HG Hank Greenberg Bat D 40.00 12.00
HH Harry Heilmann Bat B 20.00 6.00
HK Harmon Killebrew Jsy E 20.00 6.00
HM Heinie Manush Bat B 20.00 6.00
HW Honus Wagner Bat A
HWI Hoyt Wilhelm Uni D 10.00 3.00
JB Jim Bottomley Bat E 15.00 4.50
JBE Johnny Bench Bat G 15.00 4.50
JF Jimmie Foxx Bat A
JM Joe Morgan Bat E 10.00 3.00
JP Jim Palmer Jsy A
JR Jackie Robinson Bat C 50.00 15.00
JT Joe Tinker Bat E 25.00 7.50
KP Kirby Puckett Bat E 20.00 6.00
LA Luis Aparicio Bat A
LB Lou Brock Bat A
LG Lou Gehrig Bat C 150.00 45.00
MS Mike Schmidt Uni E 30.00 9.00
NR Nolan Ryan Bat C 60.00 18.00
OC Orlando Cepeda Bat F 10.00 3.00
OS Ozzie Smith Bat E 20.00 6.00
PN Phil Niekro Uni D 10.00 3.00
PW Paul Waner Bat C 25.00 7.50
RCA Rod Carew Jsy E 15.00 4.50
RJ Reggie Jackson Bat F 15.00 4.50
RY Robin Yount Bat F 20.00 6.00
SA Sparky Anderson Uni A
SC Sam Crawford Bat D 25.00 7.50
SM Stan Musial Bat D 30.00 9.00
TC Ty Cobb Bat C 120.00 36.00
TLA Tom Lasorda Jsy A
TP Tony Perez Bat F 10.00 3.00
TS Tom Seaver Bat C 20.00 6.00
WM Willie Mays Jsy C 50.00 15.00
WMC Willie McCovey Bat F 10.00 3.00
WS Willie Stargell Jsy C 20.00 6.00

2003 Topps Gallery HOF ARTifact Relics Autographs

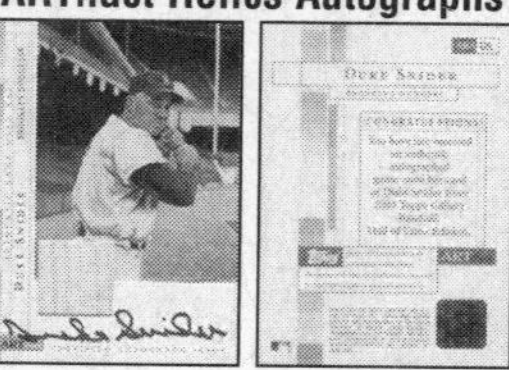

Inserted at different rates depending on which group the player belonged to, these 11 cards feature not only a game-used relic piece of the featured player but also an authentic autograph. We have notated next to the player's name not only what type of memorabilia piece but also what group the card belongs to.

Nm-Mt Ex-Mt
GROUP A ODDS 1:3446
GROUP B ODDS 1:691
GROUP C ODDS 1:691
ARTIST'S PROOFS ODDS 1:941
ARTIST'S PROOFS PRINT RUN 25 #'d SETS
NO AP PRICING DUE TO SCARCITY
AP'S FEATURE SILVER HOLO-FOIL
AK Al Kaline Bat C 100.00 30.00
BD Bobby Doerr Jsy C 50.00 15.00
BRO Brooks Robinson Bat C 80.00 24.00
DS Duke Snider Bat B 80.00 24.00
HK Harmon Killebrew Jsy B 80.00 24.00
JM Joe Morgan Bat B 50.00 15.00
JP Jim Palmer Jsy A
MS Mike Schmidt Uni B
OC Orlando Cepeda Bat B
RS Red Schoendienst Jsy A
RY Robin Yount Bat A

2003 Topps Gallery HOF Currency Connection Coin Relics

Issued as a box topper, these 12 cards feature not only a player but an authentic coin from a key point in their career.

Nm-Mt Ex-Mt
STATED ODDS ONE PER BOX
BF B.Feller 1945 Dime B 15.00 4.50
BR B.Ruth 1916 Dime A 80.00 24.00
EB E.Banks 1958 Penny B 25.00 7.50
HG H.Greenberg 1945 Nickel B 25.00 7.50
JR J.Robinson 1946 Dime B 25.00 7.50
LG L.Gehrig 1938 Nickel A 40.00 12.00
OC O.Cepeda 1958 Penny B 15.00 4.50
SM S.Musial 1943 Penny B 40.00 12.00
TC T.Cobb 1909 Penny A 50.00 15.00
WM W.Mays 1958 Penny B 25.00 7.50
WMA W.Mays 1954 Nickel B 25.00 7.50
WMC W.McCovey 1959 Penny B 15.00 4.50

2003 Topps Gallery HOF Paint by Number Patch Relics

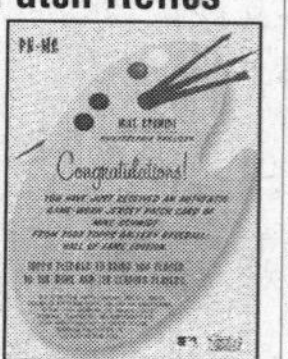

Inserted into packs at a stated rate of one in 1037, these 14 cards feature prime patch swatches of game-worn jerseys on specially designed art cards. These cards were issued to a stated print run of 25 serial numbered sets and no pricing is available due to market scarcity.

Nm-Mt Ex-Mt
CH Catfish Hunter
CY Carl Yastrzemski
DS Don Sutton
EM Eddie Mathews
FJ Fergie Jenkins
GB George Brett
HK Harmon Killebrew
JP Jim Palmer
MS Mike Schmidt
NR Nolan Ryan
OS Ozzie Smith
RY Robin Yount
TL Tom Lasorda
WM Willie McCovey

2003 Topps Gallery HOF Team Topps Legends Autographs

Nm-Mt Ex-Mt
SEE 2001 TEAM TOPPS FOR PRICING

2001 Topps Heritage

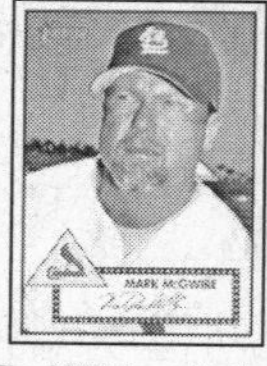
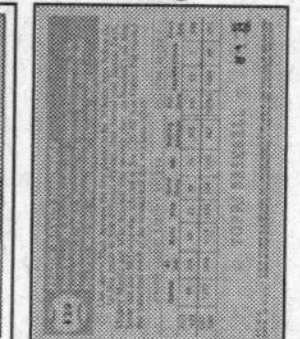

The 2001 Topps Heritage product was released in February 2001. Each pack contained eight cards and carried a $1.99 SRP. The base set features 407 cards. Please note that all low series cards 1-80, feature both red and black back variations and are in shorter supply than mid-series cards 81-310. Also, high series cards 311-407 are short-printed with an announced seeding ratio of 1:2 packs. Finally, the following mid-series cards were erroneously printed exclusively in black back format: 103, 159, 171, 176, 179, 188, 201, 212, 224 and 241. All told, a master set of all red and black variations consists of 487-cards (397 red backs and 90 black backs). Most collectors in pursuit of a 407-card complete set typically intermingle red and black back cards.

Nm-Mt Ex-Mt
COMP.MASTER SET (487) 400.00 120.00
COMPLETE SET (407) 300.00 90.00
COMP.SET w/o SP's (230) 60.00 18.00
COMMON CARD (81-310) .50 .15
COMMON CARD (1-80) 2.50 .75
COMMON (311-407) 5.00 1.50
1 Kris Benson 2.50 .75
1 Kris Benson Black 2.50 .75
2 Brian Jordan 2.50 .75
2 Brian Jordan Black 2.50 .75
3 Fernando Vina 2.50 .75
3 Fernando Vina Black 2.50 .75
4 Mike Sweeney 2.50 .75
4 Mike Sweeney Black 2.50 .75
5 Rafael Palmeiro 2.50 .75
5 Rafael Palmeiro Black 2.50 .75
6 Paul O'Neill 2.50 .75
6 Paul O'Neill Black 2.50 .75
7 Todd Helton 2.50 .75
7 Todd Helton Black 2.50 .75
8 Ramiro Mendoza 2.50 .75
8 Ramiro Mendoza Black 2.50 .75
9 Kevin Millwood 2.50 .75
9 Kevin Millwood Black 2.50 .75
10 Chuck Knoblauch 2.50 .75
10 Chuck Knoblauch Black 2.50 .75
11 Derek Jeter 10.00 3.00
11 Derek Jeter Black 10.00 3.00
12 A.Rodriguez Rangers 6.00 1.80
12 A.Rod Black Rangers 6.00 1.80
13 Geoff Jenkins 2.50 .75
13 Geoff Jenkins Black 2.50 .75
14 David Justice 2.50 .75
14 David Justice Black 2.50 .75
15 David Cone 2.50 .75
15 David Cone Black 2.50 .75
16 Andres Galarraga 2.50 .75
16 Andres Galarraga Black 2.50 .75
17 Garret Anderson 2.50 .75
17 Garret Anderson Black 2.50 .75
18 Roger Cedeno 2.50 .75
18 Roger Cedeno Black 2.50 .75
19 Randy Velarde 2.50 .75
19 Randy Velarde Black 2.50 .75
20 Carlos Delgado 2.50 .75
20 Carlos Delgado Black 2.50 .75
21 Quilvio Veras 2.50 .75
21 Quilvio Veras Black 2.50 .75
22 Jose Vidro 2.50 .75
22 Jose Vidro Black 2.50 .75
23 Corey Patterson 2.50 .75
23 Corey Patterson Black 2.50 .75
24 Jorge Posada 2.50 .75
24 Jorge Posada Black 2.50 .75
25 Eddie Perez 2.50 .75
25 Eddie Perez Black 2.50 .75
26 Jack Cust 2.50 .75
26 Jack Cust Black 2.50 .75
27 Sean Burroughs 2.50 .75
27 Sean Burroughs Black 2.50 .75
28 Randy Wolf 2.50 .75
28 Randy Wolf Black 2.50 .75
29 Mike Lamb 2.50 .75
29 Mike Lamb Black 2.50 .75
30 Rafael Furcal 2.50 .75
30 Rafael Furcal Black 2.50 .75
31 Barry Bonds 10.00 3.00
31 Barry Bonds Black 10.00 3.00
32 Tim Hudson 2.50 .75
32 Tim Hudson Black 2.50 .75
33 Tom Glavine 2.50 .75
33 Tom Glavine Black 2.50 .75
34 Javy Lopez 2.50 .75
34 Javy Lopez Black 2.50 .75
35 Aubrey Huff 2.50 .75
35 Aubrey Huff Black 2.50 .75
36 Wally Joyner 2.50 .75
36 Wally Joyner Black 2.50 .75
37 Magglio Ordonez 2.50 .75
37 Magglio Ordonez Black 2.50 .75
38 Matt Lawton 2.50 .75
38 Matt Lawton Black 2.50 .75
39 Mariano Rivera 2.50 .75
39 Mariano Rivera Black 2.50 .75
40 Andy Ashby 2.50 .75
40 Andy Ashby Black 2.50 .75
41 Mark Buehrle 2.50 .75
41 Mark Buehrle Black 2.50 .75
42 Esteban Loaiza 2.50 .75
42 Esteban Loaiza Black 2.50 .75
43 Mark Redman 2.50 .75
43 Mark Redman Black 2.50 .75
44 Mark Quinn 2.50 .75
44 Mark Quinn Black 2.50 .75
45 Tino Martinez 2.50 .75
45 Tino Martinez Black 2.50 .75
46 Joe Mays 2.50 .75
46 Joe Mays Black 2.50 .75
47 Walt Weiss 2.50 .75
47 Walt Weiss Black 2.50 .75
48 Roger Clemens 8.00 2.40
48 Roger Clemens Black 8.00 2.40
49 Greg Maddux 6.00 1.80
49 Greg Maddux Black 6.00 1.80
50 Richard Hidalgo 2.50 .75
50 Richard Hidalgo Black 2.50 .75
51 Orlando Hernandez 2.50 .75
51 O.Hernandez Black 2.50 .75
52 Chipper Jones 4.00 1.20
52 Chipper Jones Black 4.00 1.20
53 Ben Grieve 2.50 .75
53 Ben Grieve Black 2.50 .75
54 Jimmy Haynes 2.50 .75
54 Jimmy Haynes Black 2.50 .75
55 Ken Caminiti 2.50 .75
55 Ken Caminiti Black 2.50 .75
56 Tim Salmon 2.50 .75
56 Tim Salmon Black 2.50 .75
57 Andy Pettitte 2.50 .75
57 Andy Pettitte Black 2.50 .75
58 Darin Erstad 2.50 .75
58 Darin Erstad Black 2.50 .75
59 Marquis Grissom 2.50 .75
59 Marquis Grissom Black 2.50 .75
60 Raul Mondesi 2.50 .75
60 Raul Mondesi Black 2.50 .75
61 Bengie Molina 2.50 .75
61 Bengie Molina Black 2.50 .75
62 Miguel Tejada 2.50 .75
62 Miguel Tejada Black 2.50 .75
63 Jose Cruz Jr. 2.50 .75
63 Jose Cruz Jr. Black 2.50 .75
64 Billy Koch 2.50 .75
64 Billy Koch Black 2.50 .75
65 Troy Glaus 2.50 .75
65 Troy Glaus Black 2.50 .75

66 Cliff Floyd 2.50 .75
66 Cliff Floyd Black 2.50 .75
67 Tony Batista 2.50 .75
67 Tony Batista Black 2.50 .75
68 Jeff Bagwell 2.50 .75
68 Jeff Bagwell Black 2.50 .75
69 Billy Wagner 2.50 .75
69 Billy Wagner Black 2.50 .75
70 Eric Chavez 2.50 .75
70 Eric Chavez Black 2.50 .75
71 Troy Percival 2.50 .75
71 Troy Percival Black 2.50 .75
72 Andruw Jones 2.50 .75
72 Andruw Jones Black 2.50 .75
73 Shane Reynolds 2.50 .75
73 Shane Reynolds Black 2.50 .75
74 Barry Zito 2.50 .75
74 Barry Zito Black 2.50 .75
75 Roy Halladay 2.50 .75
75 Roy Halladay Black 2.50 .75
76 David Wells 2.50 .75
76 David Wells Black 2.50 .75
77 Jason Giambi 2.50 .75
77 Jason Giambi Black 2.50 .75
78 Scott Elarton 2.50 .75
78 Scott Elarton Black 2.50 .75
79 Moises Alou 2.50 .75
79 Moises Alou Black 2.50 .75
80 Adam Piatt 2.50 .75
80 Adam Piatt Black 2.50 .75
81 Wilton Veras .50 .15
82 Darryl Kile .60 .18
83 Johnny Damon 1.00 .30
84 Tony Armas Jr. .50 .15
85 Ellis Burks .60 .18
86 Jamey Wright .50 .15
87 Jose Vizcaino .50 .15
88 Bartolo Colon .60 .18
89 Carmen Cali RC .60 .18
90 Kevin Brown .60 .18
91 Josh Hamilton .50 .15
92 Jay Buhner .60 .18
93 Scott Pratt RC .60 .18
94 Alex Cora .50 .15
95 Luis Montanez RC .60 .18
96 Dmitri Young .60 .18
97 J.T. Snow .60 .18
98 Damion Easley .50 .15
99 Greg Norton .50 .15
100 Matt Wheatland .50 .15
101 Chin-Feng Chen .60 .18
102 Tony Womack .50 .15
103 Adam Kennedy Black .50 .15
104 J.D. Drew .60 .18
105 Carlos Febles .50 .15
106 Jim Thome 1.50 .45
107 Danny Graves .50 .15
108 Dave Mlicki .50 .15
109 Ron Coomer .50 .15
110 James Baldwin .50 .15
111 Shaun Boyd RC .60 .18
112 Brian Bohanon .50 .15
113 Jacque Jones .60 .18
114 Alfonso Soriano 1.00 .30
115 Tony Clark .50 .15
116 Terrence Long .50 .15
117 Todd Hundley .50 .15
118 Kazuhiro Sasaki .60 .18
119 Brian Sellier RC .60 .18
120 John Olerud .60 .18
121 Javier Vazquez .60 .18
122 Sean Burnett .50 .15
123 Matt LeCroy .50 .15
124 Erubiel Durazo .50 .15
125 Juan Encarnacion .50 .15
126 Pablo Ozuna .50 .15
127 Russ Ortiz .60 .18
128 David Segui .50 .15
129 Mark McGwire 4.00 1.20
130 Mark Grace 1.00 .30
131 Fred McGriff 1.00 .30
132 Carl Pavano .60 .18
133 Derek Thompson .50 .15
134 Shawn Green .60 .18
135 B.J. Surhoff .60 .18
136 Michael Tucker .50 .15
137 Jason Isringhausen .60 .18
138 Eric Milton .50 .15
139 Mike Stodolka .50 .15
140 Milton Bradley .60 .18
141 Curt Schilling .60 .18
142 Sandy Alomar Jr. .50 .15
143 Brent Mayne .50 .15
144 Todd Jones .50 .15
145 Charles Johnson .60 .18
146 Dean Palmer .60 .18
147 Masato Yoshii .50 .15
148 Edgar Renteria .60 .18
149 Joe Randa .50 .15
150 Adam Johnson .50 .15
151 Greg Vaughn .50 .15
152 Adrian Beltre 1.00 .30
153 Glenallen Hill .50 .15
154 David Parrish RC .60 .18
155 Neifi Perez .50 .15
156 Pete Harnisch .50 .15
157 Paul Konerko .60 .18
158 Dennys Reyes .50 .15
159 Jose Lima Black .50 .15
160 Eddie Taubensee .50 .15
161 Miguel Cairo .50 .15
162 Jeff Kent .60 .18
163 Dustin Hermanson .50 .15
164 Alex Gonzalez .50 .15
165 Hideo Nomo 1.50 .45
166 Sammy Sosa 2.50 .75
167 C.J. Nitkowski .50 .15
168 Cal Eldred .50 .15
169 Jeff Abbott .50 .15
170 Jim Edmonds .60 .18
171 Mark Mulder Black .60 .18
172 Dominic Rich RC .60 .18
173 Ray Lankford .50 .15
174 Danny Borrell RC .60 .18
175 Rick Aguilera .50 .15
176 S.Stewart Black .60 .18
177 Steve Finley .60 .18
178 Jim Parque .50 .15
179 Kevin Appier Black .60 .18
180 Adrian Gonzalez .60 .18
181 Tom Goodwin .50 .15
182 Kevin Tapani .50 .15
183 Fernando Tatis .50 .15
184 Mark Grudzielanek .50 .15
185 Ryan Anderson .50 .15
186 Jeffrey Hammonds .50 .15
187 Corey Koskie .60 .18
188 Brad Fullmer Black .50 .15
189 Rey Sanchez .50 .15
190 Michael Barrett .50 .15
191 Rickey Henderson 1.50 .45
192 Jermaine Dye .60 .18
193 Scott Brosius .60 .18
194 Matt Anderson .50 .15
195 Brian Buchanan .50 .15
196 Derrek Lee .60 .18
197 Larry Walker 1.00 .30
198 Dan Moylan RC .60 .18
199 Vinny Castilla .60 .18
200 Ken Griffey Jr. 2.50 .75
201 Matt Stairs Black .50 .15
202 Ty Howington .50 .15
203 Andy Benes .50 .15
204 Luis Gonzalez .60 .18
205 Brian Moehler .50 .15
206 Harold Baines .60 .18
207 Pedro Astacio .50 .15
208 Cristian Guzman .50 .15
209 Kip Wells .50 .15
210 Frank Thomas 1.50 .45
211 Jose Rosado .50 .15
212 Vernon Wells Black .60 .18
213 Bobby Higginson .60 .18
214 Juan Gonzalez 1.00 .30
215 Omar Vizquel 1.00 .30
216 Bernie Williams 1.00 .30
217 Aaron Sele .50 .15
218 Shawn Estes .50 .15
219 Roberto Alomar 1.00 .30
220 Rick Ankiel .50 .15
221 Josh Kalinowski .50 .15
222 David Bell .50 .15
223 Keith Foulke .60 .18
224 Craig Biggio Black 1.00 .30
225 Josh Axelson RC .60 .18
226 Scott Williamson .50 .15
227 Ron Belliard .50 .15
228 Chris Singleton .50 .15
229 Alex Serrano RC .60 .18
230 Deivi Cruz .50 .15
231 Eric Munson .50 .15
232 Luis Castillo .50 .15
233 Edgar Martinez 1.00 .30
234 Jeff Shaw .50 .15
235 Jeromy Burnitz .60 .18
236 Richie Sexson .60 .18
237 Will Clark 1.50 .45
238 Ron Villone .50 .15
239 Kerry Wood 1.50 .45
240 Rich Aurilia .50 .15
241 Mo Vaughn Black .60 .18
242 Travis Fryman .60 .18
243 M. Ramirez Red Sox 1.00 .30
244 Chris Stynes .50 .15
245 Ray Durham .60 .18
246 Juan Uribe RC 1.00 .30
247 Juan Guzman .50 .15
248 Lee Stevens .50 .15
249 Devon White .60 .18
250 Kyle Lohse RC 1.00 .30
251 Bryan Wolff .50 .15
252 Matt Galante RC .60 .18
253 Eric Young .50 .15
254 Freddy Garcia .60 .18
255 Jay Bell .60 .18
256 Steve Cox .50 .15
257 Torii Hunter .60 .18
258 Jose Canseco 1.50 .45
259 Brad Ausmus .50 .15
260 Jeff Cirillo .50 .15
261 Brad Penny .50 .15
262 Antonio Alfonseca .50 .15
263 Russ Branyan .50 .15
264 Chris Morris RC .60 .18
265 John Lackey .50 .15
266 Justin Wayne RC .60 .18
267 Brad Radke .60 .18
268 Todd Stottlemyre .50 .15
269 Mark Loretta .60 .18
270 Matt Williams .60 .18
271 Kenny Lofton .60 .18
272 Jeff D'Amico .50 .15
273 Jamie Moyer .60 .18
274 Darren Dreifort .50 .15
275 Denny Neagle .50 .15
276 Orlando Cabrera .60 .18
277 Chuck Finley .60 .18
278 Miguel Batista .60 .18
279 Carlos Beltran 1.00 .30
280 Eric Karros .60 .18
281 Mark Kotsay .50 .15
282 Ryan Dempster .50 .15
283 Barry Larkin 1.00 .30
284 Jeff Suppan .50 .15
285 Gary Sheffield .60 .18
286 Jose Valentin .50 .15
287 Robb Nen .60 .18
288 Chan Ho Park .60 .18
289 John Halama .50 .15
290 Steve Smyth RC .60 .18
291 Gerald Williams .50 .15
292 Preston Wilson .60 .18
293 Victor Hall RC .60 .18
294 Ben Sheets 1.00 .30
295 Eric Davis .60 .18
296 Kirk Rueter .50 .15
297 Chad Petty RC .60 .18
298 Kevin Millar .60 .18
299 Marvin Benard .50 .15
300 Vladimir Guerrero 1.50 .45
301 Livan Hernandez .50 .15
302 Travis Baptist RC .50 .15
303 Bill Mueller .60 .18
304 Mike Cameron .60 .18
305 Randy Johnson 1.50 .45
306 Alan Mahaffey RC .50 .15
307 Timo Perez UER .50 .15
No facsimile autograph on card
308 Pokey Reese .50 .15
309 Ryan Rupe .50 .15
310 Carlos Lee .60 .18
311 Doug Glanville SP 5.00 1.50
312 Jay Payton SP 5.00 1.50
313 Troy O'Leary SP 5.00 1.50
314 Francisco Cordero SP 5.00 1.50
315 Rusty Greer SP 5.00 1.50
316 Cal Ripken SP 25.00 7.50
317 Ricky Ledee SP 5.00 1.50
318 Brian Daubach SP 5.00 1.50
319 Robin Ventura SP 5.00 1.50
320 Todd Zeile SP 5.00 1.50
321 Francisco Cordova SP 5.00 1.50
322 Henry Rodriguez SP 5.00 1.50
323 Pat Meares SP 5.00 1.50
324 Glendon Rusch SP 5.00 1.50
325 Keith Osik SP 5.00 1.50
326 Robert Keppel SP RC 8.00 2.40
327 Bobby Jones SP 5.00 1.50
328 Alex Ramirez SP 5.00 1.50
329 Robert Person SP 5.00 1.50
330 Ruben Mateo SP 5.00 1.50
331 Rob Bell SP 5.00 1.50
332 Carl Everett SP 5.00 1.50
333 Jason Schmidt SP 5.00 1.50
334 Scott Rolen SP 8.00 2.40
335 Jimmy Anderson SP 5.00 1.50
336 Bret Boone SP 5.00 1.50
337 Delino DeShields SP 5.00 1.50
338 Trevor Hoffman SP 5.00 1.50
339 Bob Abreu SP 5.00 1.50
340 Mike Williams SP 5.00 1.50
341 Mike Hampton SP 5.00 1.50
342 John Wetteland SP 5.00 1.50
343 Scott Erickson SP 5.00 1.50
344 Enrique Wilson SP 5.00 1.50
345 Tim Wakefield SP 5.00 1.50
346 Mike Lowell SP 5.00 1.50
347 Todd Pratt SP 5.00 1.50
348 Brook Fordyce SP 5.00 1.50
349 Benny Agbayani SP 5.00 1.50
350 Gabe Kapler SP 5.00 1.50
351 Sean Casey SP 5.00 1.50
352 Darren Oliver SP 5.00 1.50
353 Todd Ritchie SP 5.00 1.50
354 Kenny Rogers SP 5.00 1.50
355 Jason Kendall SP 5.00 1.50
356 John Vander Wal SP 5.00 1.50
357 Ramon Martinez SP 5.00 1.50
358 Edgardo Alfonzo SP 5.00 1.50
359 Phil Nevin SP 5.00 1.50
360 Albert Belle SP 5.00 1.50
361 Ruben Rivera SP 5.00 1.50
362 Pedro Martinez SP 8.00 2.40
363 Derek Lowe SP 5.00 1.50
364 Pat Burrell SP 5.00 1.50
365 Mike Mussina SP 8.00 2.40
366 Brady Anderson SP 5.00 1.50
367 Darren Lewis SP 5.00 1.50
368 Sidney Ponson SP 5.00 1.50
369 Adam Eaton SP 5.00 1.50
370 Eric Owens SP 5.00 1.50
371 Aaron Boone SP 5.00 1.50
372 Matt Clement SP 5.00 1.50
373 Derek Bell SP 5.00 1.50
374 Trot Nixon SP 5.00 1.50
375 Travis Lee SP 5.00 1.50
376 Mike Benjamin SP 5.00 1.50
377 Jeff Zimmerman SP 5.00 1.50
378 Mike Lieberthal SP 5.00 1.50
379 Rick Reed SP 5.00 1.50
380 N.Garciaparra SP 12.00 3.60
381 Omar Daal SP 5.00 1.50
382 Ryan Klesko SP 5.00 1.50
383 Rey Ordonez SP 5.00 1.50
384 Kevin Young SP 5.00 1.50
385 Rick Helling SP 5.00 1.50
386 Brian Giles SP 5.00 1.50
387 Tony Gwynn SP 10.00 3.00
388 Ed Sprague SP 5.00 1.50
389 J.R. House SP 5.00 1.50
390 Scott Hatteberg SP 5.00 1.50
391 John Valentin SP 5.00 1.50
392 Melvin Mora SP 5.00 1.50
393 Royce Clayton SP 5.00 1.50
394 Jeff Fassero SP 5.00 1.50
395 Manny Alexander SP 5.00 1.50
396 John Franco SP 5.00 1.50
397 Luis Alicea SP 5.00 1.50
398 Ivan Rodriguez SP 8.00 2.40
399 Kevin Jordan SP 5.00 1.50
400 Jose Offerman SP 5.00 1.50
401 Jeff Conine SP 5.00 1.50
402 Seth Etherton SP 5.00 1.50
403 Mike Bordick SP 5.00 1.50
404 Al Leiter SP 5.00 1.50
405 Mike Piazza SP 12.00 3.60
406 Armando Benitez SP 5.00 1.50
407 Warren Morris SP 5.00 1.50
NNO 1952 Card Redemption EXCH
NNO Replica Hat-Jsy EXCH

2001 Topps Heritage Chrome

Randomly inserted into packs at one in 25 Hob/Ret, this 110-card insert is a partial parallel of the 2001 Topps Heritage base set. Each card was produced using Topps Chrome technology. Please note that each card is also individually serial numbered to 552.

Nm-Mt Ex-Mt
STATED ODDS 1:25 HOB/RET
STATED PRINT RUN 552 SERIAL #'d SETS
CP1 Cal Ripken 50.00 15.00
CP2 Jim Thome 15.00 4.50
CP3 Derek Jeter 40.00 12.00
CP4 Andres Galarraga 8.00 2.40
CP5 Carlos Delgado 8.00 2.40
CP6 Roberto Alomar 10.00 3.00
CP7 Tom Glavine 10.00 3.00
CP8 Gary Sheffield 8.00 2.40
CP9 Mo Vaughn 8.00 2.40
CP10 Preston Wilson 8.00 2.40
CP11 Mike Mussina 10.00 3.00
CP12 Greg Maddux 25.00 7.50
CP13 Ivan Rodriguez 15.00 4.50
CP14 Al Leiter 8.00 2.40
CP15 Seth Etherton 8.00 2.40
CP16 Edgardo Alfonzo 8.00 2.40
CP17 Richie Sexson 8.00 2.40
CP18 Andruw Jones 8.00 2.40
CP19 Bartolo Colon 8.00 2.40
CP20 Darin Erstad 8.00 2.40
CP21 Kevin Brown 8.00 2.40
CP22 Mike Sweeney 8.00 2.40
CP23 Mike Piazza 25.00 7.50
CP24 Rafael Palmeiro 10.00 3.00
CP25 Terrence Long 8.00 2.40
CP26 Kazuhiro Sasaki 8.00 2.40
CP27 John Olerud 8.00 2.40
CP28 Mark McGwire 40.00 12.00
CP29 Fred McGriff 10.00 3.00
CP30 Todd Helton 10.00 3.00
CP31 Curt Schilling 8.00 2.40
CP32 Alex Rodriguez 25.00 7.50
CP33 Jeff Kent 8.00 2.40
CP34 Pat Burrell 8.00 2.40
CP35 Jim Edmonds 8.00 2.40
CP36 Mark Mulder 8.00 2.40
CP37 Troy Glaus 8.00 2.40
CP38 Jay Payton 8.00 2.40
CP39 Jermaine Dye 8.00 2.40
CP40 Larry Walker 10.00 3.00
CP41 Ken Griffey Jr. 25.00 7.50
CP42 Jeff Bagwell 10.00 3.00
CP43 Rick Ankiel 8.00 2.40
CP44 Mark Redman 8.00 2.40
CP45 Edgar Martinez 10.00 3.00
CP46 Mike Hampton 8.00 2.40
CP47 Manny Ramirez 10.00 3.00
CP48 Ray Durham 8.00 2.40
CP49 Rafael Furcal 8.00 2.40
CP50 Sean Casey 8.00 2.40
CP51 Jose Canseco 15.00 4.50
CP52 Barry Bonds 40.00 12.00
CP53 Tim Hudson 8.00 2.40
CP54 Barry Zito 10.00 3.00
CP55 Chuck Finley 8.00 2.40
CP56 Magglio Ordonez 8.00 2.40
CP57 David Wells 8.00 2.40
CP58 Jason Giambi 8.00 2.40
CP59 Tony Gwynn 20.00 6.00
CP60 Vladimir Guerrero 15.00 4.50
CP61 Randy Johnson 15.00 4.50
CP62 Bernie Williams 10.00 3.00
CP63 Craig Biggio 10.00 3.00
CP64 Jason Kendall 8.00 2.40
CP65 Pedro Martinez 15.00 4.50
CP66 Mark Quinn 8.00 2.40
CP67 Frank Thomas 15.00 4.50
CP68 Nomar Garciaparra 25.00 7.50
CP69 Brian Giles 8.00 2.40
CP70 Shawn Green 8.00 2.40
CP71 Roger Clemens 30.00 9.00
CP72 Sammy Sosa 25.00 7.50
CP73 Juan Gonzalez 10.00 3.00
CP74 Orlando Hernandez 8.00 2.40
CP75 Chipper Jones 15.00 4.50
CP76 Josh Hamilton 8.00 2.40
CP77 Adam Johnson 8.00 2.40
CP78 Shaun Boyd 8.00 2.40
CP79 Alfonso Soriano 10.00 3.00
CP80 Derek Thompson 8.00 2.40
CP81 Adrian Gonzalez 8.00 2.40
CP82 Ryan Anderson 8.00 2.40
CP83 Corey Patterson 8.00 2.40
CP84 J.R. House 8.00 2.40
CP85 Sean Burroughs 8.00 2.40
CP86 Bryan Wolff 8.00 2.40
CP87 John Lackey 8.00 2.40
CP88 Ben Sheets 10.00 3.00
CP89 Timo Perez 8.00 2.40
CP90 Robert Keppel 10.00 3.00
CP91 Luis Montanez 8.00 2.40
CP92 Sean Burnett 8.00 2.40
CP93 Justin Wayne 8.00 2.40
CP94 Eric Munson 8.00 2.40
CP95 Steve Smyth 8.00 2.40
CP96 Matt Galante 8.00 2.40
CP97 Carmen Cali 8.00 2.40
CP98 Brian Sellier 8.00 2.40
CP99 David Parrish 8.00 2.40
CP100 Danny Borrell 8.00 2.40
CP101 Chad Petty 8.00 2.40
CP102 Dominic Rich 8.00 2.40
CP103 Josh Axelson 8.00 2.40
CP104 Alex Serrano 8.00 2.40
CP105 Juan Uribe 10.00 3.00
CP106 Travis Baptist 8.00 2.40
CP107 Alan Mahaffey 8.00 2.40
CP108 Kyle Lohse 10.00 3.00
CP109 Victor Hall 8.00 2.40
CP110 Scott Pratt 8.00 2.40

2001 Topps Heritage Autographs

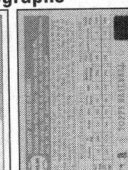

Randomly inserted into packs at one in 142 HOB/RET, this 51-card insert set features authentic autographs from many of the Major League's top players. Please note that a few of the players packed out as exchange cards, and must be redeemed by 1/31/02. Due to the untimely passing of Eddie Mathews, please note the exchange card issued for him went unredeemed. In addition, Larry Doby's card was originally seeded in packs as exchange cards (of which carried a January 31st, 2002 deadline).

Nm-Mt Ex-Mt
*RED INK: .75X TO 1.5X BASIC AU
RED INK ODDS 1:545 HOB, 1:546 RET
RED INK PRINT RUN 52 SERIAL #'d SETS
THAAH Aubrey Huff 50.00 15.00
THAAP Andy Pafko 80.00 24.00
THAAR Alex Rodriguez 200.00 60.00
THABB Barry Bonds 400.00 120.00
THABS Bobby Shantz 50.00 15.00
THABT Bobby Thomson 100.00 30.00
THACD Carlos Delgado 50.00 15.00
THACF Cliff Floyd 50.00 15.00
THACJ Chipper Jones 120.00 36.00
THACP Corey Patterson 50.00 15.00
THACS Curt Simmons 50.00 15.00
THADD Dom DiMaggio 120.00 36.00
THADG Dick Groat 50.00 15.00
THADS Duke Snider 150.00 45.00
THAEM Eddie Mathews EXCH .50 .15
THAES Enos Slaughter 100.00 30.00
THAFV Fernando Vina 30.00 9.00
THAGJ Geoff Jenkins 50.00 15.00
THAGM Gil McDougald 60.00 18.00
THAHB Hank Bauer 100.00 30.00
THAHS Hank Sauer 50.00 15.00
THAHW Hoyt Wilhelm 100.00 30.00
THAJG Joe Garagiola 80.00 24.00
THAJM Joe Mays 30.00 9.00
THAJS Johnny Sain 50.00 15.00
THAJV Jose Vidro 30.00 9.00
THAKB Kris Benson 30.00 9.00
THALD Larry Doby 120.00 36.00
THAMB Mark Buehrle 50.00 15.00
THAMI Monte Irvin 60.00 18.00
THAML Mike Lamb 30.00 9.00
THAML Matt Lawton 30.00 9.00
THAMM Minnie Minoso 100.00 30.00
THAMO Magglio Ordonez 50.00 15.00
THAMQ Mark Quinn 30.00 9.00
THAMR Mark Redman 30.00 9.00
THAMS Mike Sweeney 50.00 15.00
THAMV Mickey Vernon 50.00 15.00
THANG N.Garciaparra 150.00 45.00
THAPR Preacher Roe 120.00 36.00
THAPFR Phil Rizzuto 120.00 36.00
THARH Richard Hidalgo 30.00 9.00
THARR Robin Roberts 100.00 30.00
THARS Red Schoendienst 50.00 15.00
THARW Randy Wolf 50.00 15.00
THASPB Sean Burroughs 50.00 15.00
THATG Tom Glavine 100.00 30.00
THATH Todd Helton 60.00 18.00
THATL Terrence Long 30.00 9.00
THAVL Vernon Law 50.00 15.00
THAWM Willie Mays 250.00 75.00
THAWS Warren Spahn 100.00 30.00

2001 Topps Heritage AutoProofs

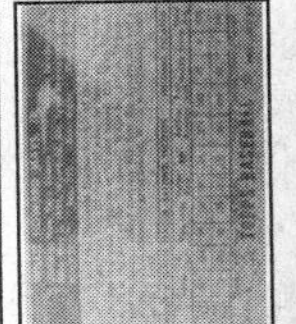

Randomly inserted at approximately 1 in every 5749 boxes, this card is an actual 1952 Topps Willie Mays card that was bought from the Topps Company, then individually autographed by Willie Mays, and distributed into packs. Please note that each card is individually serial numbered to 25.

Nm-Mt Ex-Mt
NO PRICING DUE TO SCARCITY
AUTOPROOF IS A REAL '52 TOPPS CARD
AP1 Willie Mays '52T AU/25

2001 Topps Heritage Classic Renditions

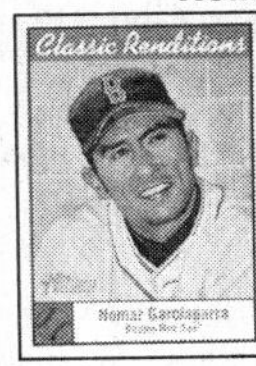

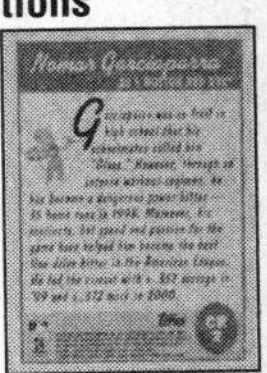

Randomly inserted into packs at one in 5 Hobby, and one in 9 Retail, this 10-card insert set features artist drawn sketches of some of the best modern day ballplayers. Card backs carry a "CR" prefix.

Nm-Mt Ex-Mt
COMPLETE SET (10) 20.00 6.00
CR1 Mark McGwire 4.00 1.20
CR2 Nomar Garciaparra 2.50 .75
CR3 Barry Bonds 4.00 1.20
CR4 Sammy Sosa 2.50 .75
CR5 Chipper Jones 1.50 .45
CR6 Pat Burrell 1.00 .30
CR7 Frank Thomas 1.50 .45
CR8 Manny Ramirez 1.00 .30
CR9 Derek Jeter 4.00 1.20
CR10 Ken Griffey Jr. 2.50 .75

2001 Topps Heritage Classic Renditions Autograph

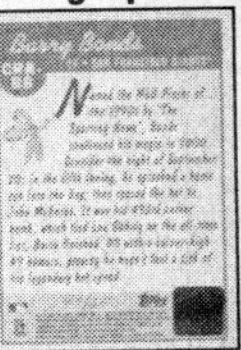

Randomly inserted into packs at one in 19,710 Hobby, and 1:20,926 Retail, this three-card insert set is a partial parallel of the Classic Renditions insert. Each of these cards have been autographed by the given player and are individually serial numbered to 25. Due to market scarcity, no pricing is provided.

	Nm-Mt	Ex-Mt
CRA-BB Barry Bonds		
CRA-CJ Chipper Jones		
CRA-NG Nomar Garciaparra		

2001 Topps Heritage Clubhouse Collection

Randomly inserted into packs, this 22-card insert features game-used memorabilia cards from past and present stars. Included in the set are game-used bat and jersey cards. Please note that a numbered of the players have autographed 25 of each of these cards. Also note that a few of the cards packed out as exchange cards, and must have been redeemed by 01/31/02. Common Bat cards were inserted at a rate of 1:590 and Jersey cards at 1:798 Hobby/1:799 Retail. Dual Bat cards were inserted at 1:5701 Hobby/1:5772 Retail. Dual Jersey cards were inserted into packs at 1:28,744 Hobby/1:29,820 Retail. Autographed Bat cards were inserted at 1:19,710 Hobby/1:20,928 Retail, and Autographed Jerseys at 1:62,714 Hobby/1:83,712 Retail. Exchange cards - with a deadline of Janury 31st, 2002 - were seeded into packs for the following cards: Eddie Mathews Bat, Duke Snider Bat AU and Willie Mays Bat AU.

	Nm-Mt	Ex-Mt
BB Barry Bonds Bat	80.00	24.00
CJ Chipper Jones Bat	50.00	15.00
DS Duke Snider Bat	50.00	15.00
EM Eddie Mathews Bat	50.00	15.00
FT Frank Thomas Jsy	50.00	15.00
FV Fernando Vina Bat	40.00	12.00
MM Minnie Minoso Jsy	40.00	12.00
RA Richie Ashburn Bat	50.00	15.00
RS Red Schoendienst Bat	40.00	12.00
SG Shawn Green Bat	40.00	12.00
SR Scott Rolen Bat	50.00	15.00
WM Willie Mays Bat	150.00	45.00
ADS Duke Snider Bat AU/25		
AMM Minnie Minoso Jsy AU/25		
ARS Red Schoendienst Bat AU/25		
AWM Willie Mays Bat AU/25		
DSSG Duke Snider	200.00	60.00
Shawn Green Bat/52		
EMCJ Eddie Mathews	150.00	45.00
Chipper Jones Bat/52		
MMFT Minnie Minoso	150.00	45.00
Frank Thomas Jsy/52		
RASR Richie Ashburn	200.00	60.00
Scott Rolen Bat/52		
RSFV Red Schoendienst	150.00	45.00
Fernando Vina Bat/52		
WMBB Willie Mays	300.00	90.00
Barry Bonds Bat/52		

2001 Topps Heritage Grandstand Glory

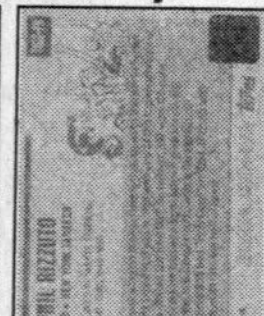

Randomly inserted into packs at 1:211 Hobby/Retail, this seven-card insert set features a swatch of original stadium seating. Card backs carry the player's initials as numbering.

	Nm-Mt	Ex-Mt
JR Jackie Robinson	50.00	15.00
NF Nellie Fox	25.00	7.50
PR Phil Rizzuto	40.00	12.00
RA Richie Ashburn	25.00	7.50
RR Robin Roberts	25.00	7.50
WM Willie Mays	80.00	24.00
YB Yogi Berra	40.00	12.00

2001 Topps Heritage New Age Performers

Randomly inserted into packs at 1:8 Hobby, 1:15 Retail, this 15-card insert set features players that have become the superstars of the future. Card backs carry a "NAP" prefix.

	Nm-Mt	Ex-Mt
COMPLETE SET (15)	50.00	15.00
NAP1 Mike Piazza	4.00	1.20
NAP2 Sammy Sosa	4.00	1.20
NAP3 Alex Rodriguez	4.00	1.20
NAP4 Barry Bonds	6.00	1.80
NAP5 Ken Griffey Jr.	4.00	1.20
NAP6 Chipper Jones	2.50	.75
NAP7 Randy Johnson	2.50	.75
NAP8 Derek Jeter	6.00	1.80
NAP9 Nomar Garciaparra	4.00	1.20
NAP10 Mark McGwire	6.00	1.80
NAP11 Jeff Bagwell	2.50	.75
NAP12 Pedro Martinez	2.50	.75
NAP13 Todd Helton	2.50	.75
NAP14 Vladimir Guerrero	2.50	.75
NAP15 Greg Maddux	4.00	1.20

2001 Topps Heritage Then and Now

Randomly inserted into Hobby packs at 1:8 and Retail packs at 1:15, this 10-card set pairs up modern day heroes with players from the past that compare statistically. Card backs carry a "TH" prefix.

	Nm-Mt	Ex-Mt
COMPLETE SET (10)	30.00	9.00
TH1 Yogi Berra	3.00	.90
Mike Piazza		
TH2 Duke Snider	3.00	.90
Sammy Sosa		
TH3 Willie Mays	4.00	1.20
Ken Griffey Jr.		
TH4 Phil Rizzuto	5.00	1.50
Derek Jeter		
TH5 Pee Wee Reese	3.00	.90
Nomar Garciaparra		
TH6 Jackie Robinson	3.00	.90
Alex Rodriguez		
TH7 Johnny Mize	5.00	1.50
Mark McGwire		
TH8 Bob Feller	2.00	.60
Pedro Martinez		
TH9 Robin Roberts	3.00	.90
Greg Maddux		
TH10 Warren Spahn	2.00	.60
Randy Johnson		

2001 Topps Heritage Time Capsule

This unique set features swatches of fabric taken from actual combat uniforms from the 1952 Korean War. It's important to note that though these cards do indeed feature patches of vintage Korean War uniforms, they were not worn by the athlete featured on the card. Stated odds for the four single-player cards was 1:369. Unlike the other cards in this set, the lone dual-player Willie Mays-Ted Williams card is hand-numbered on back. Only 52 copies of this card were produced, and each is marked by hand on back in black pen "X/52". The stated odds for this dual-player card is 1:28,744 packs.

	Nm-Mt	Ex-Mt
DN Don Newcombe	25.00	7.50
TW Ted Williams UER	100.00	30.00
Card says 525 career homers, Williams hit 521		
WF Whitey Ford	40.00	12.00
WM Willie Mays	100.00	30.00
WMTW Willie Mays	250.00	75.00
Ted Williams/52		

2002 Topps Heritage

Issued in early February 2002, this set was the second year that Topps used their Heritage brand and achieved success in the secondary market. These cards were issued in eight card packs which were packed 24 to a box and had a SRP of $3 per pack. The set consists of 440 cards with seven short prints among the low numbers as well as all cards from 364 through 446 as short prints. Those cards were all inserted at a rate of one in two packs. In addition, there was an unannounced variation in which 10 cards were printed in both day and night versions. The night versions were also inserted into packs at a rate of one in two.

	Nm-Mt	Ex-Mt
COMPLETE SET (440)	250.00	75.00
COMP.SET w/o SP's (350)	80.00	24.00
COMMON CARD (1-363)	.50	.15
COMMON SP (364-446)	5.00	1.50
1 Ichiro Suzuki SP	12.00	3.60
2 Darin Erstad	.60	.18
3 Rod Beck	.60	.18
4 Doug Mientkiewicz	.60	.18
5 Mike Sweeney	.60	.18
6 Roger Clemens	3.00	.90
7 Jason Tyner	.50	.15
8 Alex Gonzalez	.50	.15
9 Eric Young	.50	.15
10 Randy Johnson	1.50	.45
10N Randy Johnson Night SP	8.00	2.40
11 Aaron Sele	.50	.15
12 Tony Clark	.50	.15
13 C.C. Sabathia	.60	.18
14 Melvin Mora	.60	.18
15 Tim Hudson	.60	.18
16 Ben Petrick	.50	.15
17 Tom Glavine	1.00	.30
18 Jason Lane	.50	.15
19 Larry Walker	1.00	.30
20 Mark Mulder	.60	.18
21 Steve Finley	.60	.18
22 Bengie Molina	.50	.15
23 Rob Bell	.50	.15
24 Nathan Haynes	.50	.15
25 Rafael Furcal	.60	.18
25N Rafael Furcal Night SP	5.00	1.50
26 Mike Mussina	1.00	.30
27 Paul LoDuca	.60	.18
28 Torii Hunter	.60	.18
29 Carlos Lee	.60	.18
30 Jimmy Rollins	.60	.18
31 Arthur Rhodes	.50	.15
32 Ivan Rodriguez	1.50	.45
33 Wes Helms	.50	.15
34 Cliff Floyd	.60	.18
35 Julian Tavarez	.50	.15
36 Mark McGwire	4.00	1.20
37 Chipper Jones SP	8.00	2.40
38 Denny Neagle	.50	.15
39 Odalis Perez	.50	.15
40 Antonio Alfonseca	.50	.15
41 Edgar Renteria	.60	.18
42 Troy Glaus	.60	.18
43 Scott Brosius	.60	.18
44 Abraham Nunez	.50	.15
45 Jamey Wright	.50	.15
46 Bobby Bonilla	.60	.18
47 Ismael Valdes	.50	.15
48 Chris Reitsma	.50	.15
49 Neifi Perez	.50	.15
50 Juan Cruz	.50	.15
51 Kevin Brown	.60	.18
52 Ben Grieve	.50	.15
53 Alex Rodriguez SP	12.00	3.60
54 Charles Nagy	.50	.15
55 Reggie Sanders	.50	.15
56 Nelson Figueroa	.50	.15
57 Felipe Lopez	.50	.15
58 Bill Ortega	.50	.15
59 Jeffrey Hammonds	.60	.18
60 Johnny Estrada	.50	.15
61 Bob Wickman	.50	.15
62 Doug Glanville	.50	.15
63 Jeff Cirillo	.50	.15
63N Jeff Cirillo Night SP	5.00	1.50
64 Corey Patterson	.60	.18
65 Aaron Myette	.50	.15
66 Magglio Ordonez	.60	.18
67 Ellis Burks	.60	.18
68 Miguel Tejada	.60	.18
69 John Olerud	.60	.18
69N John Olerud Night SP	5.00	1.50
70 Greg Vaughn	.50	.15
71 Andy Pettitte	1.00	.30
72 Mike Matheny	.60	.18
73 Brandon Duckworth	.50	.15
74 Scott Schoeneweis	.50	.15
75 Mike Lowell	.60	.18
76 Einar Diaz	.50	.15
77 Tino Martinez	1.00	.30
78 Matt Williams	.60	.18
79 Jason Young RC	1.00	.30
80 Nate Cornejo	.50	.15
81 Andres Galarraga	.60	.18
82 Bernie Williams SP	8.00	2.40
83 Ryan Klesko	.60	.18
84 Dan Wilson	.50	.15
85 Henry Pichardo RC	1.00	.30
86 Ray Durham	.60	.18
87 Omar Daal	.50	.15
88 Derrek Lee	.60	.18
89 Al Leiter	.60	.18
90 Darrin Fletcher	.50	.15
91 Josh Beckett	.60	.18
92 Johnny Damon	1.00	.30
92N Johnny Damon Night SP	8.00	2.40
93 Abraham Nunez	.50	.15
94 Ricky Ledee	.50	.15
95 Richie Sexson	.60	.18
96 Adam Kennedy	.50	.15
97 Raul Mondesi	.60	.18
98 John Burkett	.60	.18
99 Ben Sheets	.60	.18
99N Ben Sheets Night SP	5.00	1.50
100 Preston Wilson	.60	.18
100N Pr. Wilson Night SP	5.00	1.50
101 Boof Bonser	.50	.15
102 Shigetoshi Hasegawa	.60	.18
103 Carlos Febles	.50	.15
104 Jorge Posada SP	8.00	2.40
105 Michael Tucker	.50	.15
106 Roberto Hernandez	.50	.15
107 John Rodriguez RC	1.00	.30
108 Danny Graves	.50	.15
109 Rich Aurilia	.50	.15
110 Jon Lieber	.50	.15
111 Tim Hummel RC	1.00	.30
112 J.T. Snow	.60	.18
113 Kris Benson	.50	.15
114 Derek Jeter	4.00	1.20
115 John Franco	.60	.18
116 Matt Stairs	.50	.15
117 Ben Davis	.50	.15
118 Darryl Kile	.60	.18
119 Mike Peeples RC	1.00	.30
120 Kevin Tapani	.50	.15
121 Armando Benitez	.60	.18
122 Damian Miller	.50	.15
123 Jose Jimenez	.50	.15
124 Pedro Astacio	.50	.15
125 Marlyn Tisdale RC	1.00	.30
126 Deivi Cruz	.50	.15
127 Paul O'Neill	1.00	.30
128 Jermaine Dye	.60	.18
129 Marcus Giles	.60	.18
130 Mark Loretta	.60	.18
131 Garret Anderson	.60	.18
132 Todd Ritchie	.50	.15
133 Joe Crede	.50	.15
134 Kevin Millwood	.60	.18
135 Shane Reynolds	.50	.15
136 Mark Grace	1.00	.30
137 Shannon Stewart	.60	.18
138 Nick Neugebauer	.50	.15
139 Nic Jackson RC	1.00	.30
140 Robb Nen UER	.60	.18
Name spelled Rob on front		
141 Dmitri Young	.60	.18
142 Kevin Appier	.60	.18
143 Jack Cust	.50	.15
144 Andres Torres	.50	.15
145 Frank Thomas	1.50	.45
146 Jason Kendall	.60	.18
147 Greg Maddux	2.50	.75
148 David Justice	.60	.18
149 Hideo Nomo	1.50	.45
150 Bret Boone	.60	.18
151 Wade Miller	.60	.18
152 Jeff Kent	.60	.18
153 Scott Williamson	.50	.15
154 Julio Lugo	.50	.15
155 Bobby Higginson	.60	.18
156 Geoff Jenkins	.60	.18
157 Darren Dreifort	.50	.15
158 Freddy Sanchez RC	1.00	.30
159 Bud Smith	.50	.15
160 Phil Nevin	.60	.18
161 Cesar Izturis	.50	.15
162 Sean Casey	.60	.18
163 Jose Ortiz	.50	.15
164 Brent Abernathy	.50	.15
165 Kevin Young	.50	.15
166 Daryle Ward	.60	.18
167 Trevor Hoffman	.60	.18
168 Rondell White	.60	.18
169 Kip Wells	.50	.15
170 John Vander Wal	.50	.15
171 Jose Lima	.50	.15
172 Wilton Guerrero	.50	.15
173 Aaron Dean RC	1.00	.30
174 Rick Helling	.50	.15
175 Juan Pierre	.60	.18
176 Jay Bell	.60	.18
177 Craig House	.50	.15
178 David Bell	.50	.15
179 Pat Burrell	.60	.18
180 Eric Gagne	1.50	.45
181 Adam Pettyjohn	.50	.15
182 Ugueth Urbina	.50	.15
183 Peter Bergeron	.50	.15
184 Adrian Gonzalez UER	.60	.18
Birthdate is wrong		
184N Adrian Gonzalez	5.00	1.50
Night SP UER		
Birthdate is wrong		
185 Damion Easley	.50	.15
186 Gookie Dawkins	.50	.15
187 Matt Lawton	.50	.15
188 Frank Catalanotto	.50	.15
189 David Wells	.60	.18
190 Roger Cedeno	.50	.15
191 Brian Giles	.60	.18
192 Julio Zuleta	.50	.15
193 Timo Perez	.50	.15
194 Billy Wagner	.60	.18
195 Craig Counsell	.50	.15
196 Bart Miadich	.50	.15
197 Gary Sheffield	.60	.18
198 Richard Hidalgo	.50	.15
199 Juan Uribe	.50	.15
200 Curt Schilling	.60	.18
201 Javy Lopez	.60	.18
202 Jimmy Haynes	.50	.15
203 Jim Edmonds	.60	.18
204 Pokey Reese	.50	.15
204N Pokey Reese Night SP	5.00	1.50
205 Matt Clement	.50	.15
206 Dean Palmer	.60	.18
207 Nick Johnson	.60	.18
208 Nate Espy RC	1.00	.30
209 Pedro Feliz	.50	.15
210 Aaron Rowand	.60	.18
211 Masato Yoshii	.50	.15
212 Jose Cruz Jr.	.50	.15
213 Paul Byrd	.50	.15
214 Mark Phillips RC	1.00	.30
215 Benny Agbayani	.50	.15
216 Frank Menechino	.50	.15
217 John Flaherty	.50	.15
218 Brian Boehringer	.50	.15
219 Todd Hollandsworth	.50	.15
220 Sammy Sosa SP	12.00	3.60
221 Steve Sparks	.50	.15
222 Homer Bush	.50	.15
223 Mike Hampton	.60	.18
224 Bobby Abreu	.60	.18
225 Barry Larkin	1.00	.30
226 Ryan Rupe	.50	.15
227 Bubba Trammell	.50	.15
228 Todd Zeile	.60	.18
229 Jeff Shaw	.50	.15
230 Alex Ochoa	.50	.15
231 Orlando Cabrera	.60	.18
232 Jeremy Giambi	.50	.15
233 Tomo Ohka	.50	.15
234 Luis Castillo	.50	.15
235 Chris Holt	.50	.15
236 Shawn Green	.60	.18
237 Sidney Ponson	.50	.15
238 Lee Stevens	.50	.15
239 Hank Blalock	1.50	.45
240 Randy Winn	.50	.15
241 Pedro Martinez	1.50	.45
242 Vinny Castilla	.60	.18
243 Steve Karsay	.50	.15
244 Barry Bonds SP	20.00	6.00
245 Jason Bere	.50	.15
246 Scott Rolen	1.50	.45
246N Scott Rolen Night SP	8.00	2.40
247 Ryan Kohlmeier	.50	.15
248 Kerry Wood	1.50	.45
249 Aramis Ramirez	.60	.18
250 Lance Berkman	.60	.18
251 Omar Vizquel	1.00	.30
252 Juan Encarnacion	.50	.15
253 Does Not Exist		
254 David Segui	.50	.15
255 Brian Anderson	.50	.15
256 Jay Payton	.50	.15
257 Mark Grudzielanek	.50	.15
258 Jimmy Anderson	.50	.15
259 Eric Valent	.50	.15
260 Chad Durbin	.50	.15
261 Does Not Exist		
262 Alex Gonzalez	.50	.15
263 Scott Dunn	.50	.15
264 Scott Elarton	.50	.15
265 Tom Gordon	.50	.15
266 Moises Alou	.60	.18
267 Does Not Exist		
268 Does Not Exist		
269 Mark Buehrle	.60	.18
270 Jerry Hairston	.50	.15
271 Does Not Exist		
272 Luke Prokopec	.50	.15
273 Graeme Lloyd	.50	.15
274 Bret Prinz	.50	.15
275 Does Not Exist		
276 Chris Carpenter	.50	.15
277 Ryan Minor	.50	.15
278 Jeff D'Amico	.50	.15
279 Raul Ibanez	.50	.15
280 Joe Mays	.50	.15
281 Livan Hernandez	.50	.15
282 Robin Ventura	.60	.18
283 Gabe Kapler	.50	.15
284 Tony Batista	.60	.18
285 Ramon Hernandez	.50	.15
286 Craig Paquette	.50	.15
287 Mark Kotsay	.50	.15
288 Mike Lieberthal	.60	.18
289 Joe Borchard	.50	.15
290 Cristian Guzman	.50	.15
291 Craig Biggio	1.00	.30
292 Joaquin Benoit	.50	.15
293 Ken Caminiti	.60	.18
294 Sean Burroughs	.60	.18
295 Eric Karros	.60	.18
296 Eric Chavez	.60	.18
297 LaTroy Hawkins	.50	.15
298 Alfonso Soriano	1.00	.30
299 John Smoltz	1.00	.30
300 Adam Dunn	1.00	.30
301 Ryan Dempster	.50	.15
302 Travis Hafner	.60	.18
303 Russell Branyan	.50	.15
304 Dustin Hermanson	.50	.15
305 Jim Thome	1.50	.45
306 Carlos Beltran	1.00	.30
307 Jason Botts RC	1.00	.30
308 David Cone	.60	.18
309 Ivanon Coffie	.50	.15
310 Brian Jordan	.60	.18
311 Todd Walker	.50	.15
312 Jeromy Burnitz	.60	.18
313 Tony Armas Jr.	.50	.15
314 Jeff Conine	.60	.18
315 Todd Jones	.50	.15
316 Roy Oswalt	.60	.18
317 Aubrey Huff	.60	.18
318 Josh Fogg	.50	.15
319 Jose Vidro	.50	.15
320 Jace Brewer	.50	.15
321 Mike Redmond	.50	.15
322 Noochie Varner RC	1.00	.30
323 Russ Ortiz	.60	.18
324 Edgardo Alfonzo	.50	.15
325 Ruben Sierra	.50	.15
326 Calvin Murray	.50	.15
327 Marlon Anderson	.50	.15
328 Albie Lopez	.50	.15
329 Chris Gomez	.50	.15
330 Fernando Tatis	.50	.15
331 Stubby Clapp	.50	.15
332 Rickey Henderson	1.50	.45
333 Brad Radke	.60	.18
334 Brent Mayne	.50	.15
335 Cory Lidle	.50	.15
336 Edgar Martinez	1.00	.30
337 Aaron Boone	.60	.18
338 Jay Witasick	.50	.15
339 Benito Santiago	.60	.18
340 Jose Mercedes	.50	.15
341 Fernando Vina	.50	.15
342 A.J. Pierzynski	.60	.18
343 Jeff Bagwell	1.00	.30
344 Brian Bohanon	.50	.15
345 Adrian Beltre	1.00	.30
346 Troy Percival	.60	.18
347 Napoleon Calzado RC	1.00	.30
348 Ruben Rivera	.50	.15
349 Rafael Soriano	.50	.15
350 Damian Jackson	.50	.15
351 Joe Randa	.50	.15
352 Chan Ho Park	.60	.18
353 Dante Bichette	.60	.18
354 Bartolo Colon	.60	.18
355 Jason Bay RC	3.00	.90
356 Shea Hillenbrand	.60	.18
357 Matt Morris	.60	.18
358 Brad Penny	.50	.15
359 Mark Quinn	.50	.15
360 Marquis Grissom	.60	.18
361 Henry Blanco	.50	.15
362 Billy Koch	.60	.18
363 Mike Cameron	.60	.18
364 Albert Pujols SP	15.00	4.50
365 Paul Konerko SP	5.00	1.50
366 Eric Milton SP	5.00	1.50
367 Nick Bierbrodt SP	5.00	1.50
368 Rafael Palmeiro SP	8.00	2.40
369 Jorge Padilla SP RC	5.00	1.50
370 Jason Giambi	5.00	1.50
Yankees SP		
Stats on back are Jeremy Giambi's		
371 Mike Piazza SP	12.00	3.60
372 Alex Cora SP	5.00	1.50
373 Todd Helton SP	8.00	2.40
374 Juan Gonzalez SP	8.00	2.40
375 Mariano Rivera SP	8.00	2.40
376 Jason LaRue SP	5.00	1.50
377 Tony Gwynn SP	10.00	3.00
378 Wilson Betemit SP	5.00	1.50

379 J.J. Trujillo SP RC 5.00 1.50
380 Brad Ausmus SP 5.00 1.50
381 Chris George SP 5.00 1.50
382 Jose Canseco SP 8.00 2.40
383 Ramon Ortiz SP 5.00 1.50
384 John Rocker SP 5.00 1.50
385 Rey Ordonez SP 5.00 1.50
386 Ken Griffey Jr. SP 12.00 3.60
387 Juan Pena SP 5.00 1.50
388 Michael Barrett SP 5.00 1.50
389 J.D. Drew SP 5.00 1.50
390 Corey Koskie SP 5.00 1.50
391 Vernon Wells SP 5.00 1.50
392 Juan Tolentino SP RC 5.00 1.50
393 Luis Gonzalez SP 5.00 1.50
394 Terrence Long SP 5.00 1.50
395 Travis Lee SP 5.00 1.50
396 Earl Snyder SP RC 8.00 2.40
397 Nomar Garciaparra SP 12.00 3.60
398 Jason Schmidt SP 5.00 1.50
399 David Espinosa SP 5.00 1.50
400 Steve Green SP 5.00 1.50
401 Jack Wilson SP 5.00 1.50
402 Chris Tritle SP RC 5.00 1.50
403 Angel Berroa SP 5.00 1.50
404 Josh Towers SP 5.00 1.50
405 Andruw Jones SP 5.00 1.50
406 Brent Butler SP 5.00 1.50
407 Craig Kuzmic SP 5.00 1.50
408 Derek Bell SP 5.00 1.50
409 Eric Glaser SP RC 5.00 1.50
410 Joel Pineiro SP 5.00 1.50
411 Alexis Gomez SP 5.00 1.50
412 Mike Rivera SP 5.00 1.50
413 Shawn Estes SP 5.00 1.50
414 Milton Bradley SP 5.00 1.50
415 Carl Everett SP 5.00 1.50
416 Kazuhiro Sasaki SP 5.00 1.50
417 Tony Fontana SP RC 5.00 1.50
418 Josh Pearce SP 5.00 1.50
419 Gary Matthews Jr. SP 5.00 1.50
420 Raymond Cabrera SP RC 5.00 1.50
421 Joe Kennedy SP 5.00 1.50
422 Jason Maule SP RC 5.00 1.50
423 Casey Fossum SP 5.00 1.50
424 Christian Parker SP 5.00 1.50
425 Laynce Nix SP RC 25.00 7.50
426 Byung-Hyun Kim SP 5.00 1.50
427 Freddy Garcia SP 5.00 1.50
428 Herbert Perry SP 5.00 1.50
429 Jason Marquis SP 5.00 1.50
430 Sandy Alomar Jr. SP 5.00 1.50
431 Roberto Alomar SP 8.00 2.40
432 Tsuyoshi Shinjo SP 5.00 1.50
433 Tim Wakefield SP 5.00 1.50
434 Robert Fick SP 5.00 1.50
435 Vladimir Guerrero SP 8.00 2.40
436 Jose Mesa SP 5.00 1.50
437 Scott Spiezio SP 5.00 1.50
438 Jose Hernandez SP 5.00 1.50
439 Jose Acevedo SP 5.00 1.50
440 Brian West SP RC 5.00 1.50
441 Barry Zito SP 5.00 1.50
442 Luis Maza SP 5.00 1.50
443 Marlon Byrd SP 5.00 1.50
444 A.J. Burnett SP 5.00 1.50
445 Dee Brown SP 5.00 1.50
446 Carlos Delgado SP 5.00 1.50
NNO 1953 Repurchased EXCH ....

2002 Topps Heritage Chrome

Inserted into packs at stated odds of one in 29, these 100 cards feature the "Chrome" technology and have a stated print run of 553 copies.

Nm-Mt Ex-Mt
THC1 Darin Erstad 8.00 2.40
THC2 Doug Mientkiewicz 8.00 2.40
THC3 Mike Sweeney 8.00 2.40
THC4 Roger Clemens 25.00 7.50
THC5 C.C. Sabathia 8.00 2.40
THC6 Tim Hudson 8.00 2.40
THC7 Jason Lane 8.00 2.40
THC8 Larry Walker 8.00 2.40
THC9 Mark Mulder 8.00 2.40
THC10 Mike Mussina 8.00 2.40
THC11 Paul LoDuca 8.00 2.40
THC12 Jimmy Rollins 8.00 2.40
THC13 Ivan Rodriguez 12.00 3.60
THC14 Mark McGwire 30.00 9.00
THC15 Edgar Renteria 8.00 2.40
THC16 Scott Brosius 8.00 2.40
THC17 Juan Cruz 8.00 2.40
THC18 Kevin Brown 8.00 2.40
THC19 Charles Nagy 8.00 2.40
THC20 Bill Ortega 8.00 2.40
THC21 Corey Patterson 8.00 2.40
THC22 Magglio Ordonez 8.00 2.40
THC23 Brandon Duckworth 8.00 2.40
THC24 Scott Schoeneweis 8.00 2.40
THC25 Tino Martinez 8.00 2.40
THC26 Jason Young 8.00 2.40
THC27 Nate Cornejo 8.00 2.40
THC28 Ryan Klesko 8.00 2.40
THC29 Omar Daal 8.00 2.40
THC30 Raul Mondesi 8.00 2.40
THC31 Boof Bonser 8.00 2.40
THC32 Rich Aurilia 8.00 2.40
THC33 Jon Lieber 8.00 2.40
THC34 Tim Hummel 8.00 2.40
THC35 J.T. Snow 8.00 2.40
THC36 Derek Jeter 30.00 9.00
THC37 Darryl Kile 8.00 2.40
THC38 Armando Benitez 8.00 2.40
THC39 Marlyn Tisdale 8.00 2.40
THC40 Shannon Stewart 8.00 2.40
THC41 Nic Jackson 8.00 2.40
THC42 Robb Nen UER 8.00 2.40
First name misspelled Rob
THC43 Dmitri Young 8.00 2.40
THC44 Greg Maddux 20.00 6.00
THC45 Hideo Nomo 12.00 3.60
THC46 Bret Boone 8.00 2.40
THC47 Wade Miller 8.00 2.40
THC48 Jeff Kent 8.00 2.40
THC49 Freddy Sanchez 8.00 2.40
THC50 Bud Smith 8.00 2.40
THC51 Sean Casey 8.00 2.40
THC52 Brent Abernathy 8.00 2.40
THC53 Trevor Hoffman 8.00 2.40
THC54 Aaron Dean 8.00 2.40
THC55 Juan Pierre 8.00 2.40
THC56 Pat Burrell 8.00 2.40
THC57 Gookie Dawkins 8.00 2.40
THC58 Roger Cedeno 8.00 2.40
THC59 Brian Giles 8.00 2.40
THC60 Jim Edmonds 8.00 2.40
THC61 Dean Palmer 8.00 2.40
THC62 Nick Johnson 8.00 2.40
THC63 Nate Espy 8.00 2.40
THC64 Aaron Rowand 8.00 2.40
THC65 Mark Phillips 10.00 3.00
THC66 Mike Hampton 8.00 2.40
THC67 Bobby Abreu 8.00 2.40
THC68 Alex Ochoa 8.00 2.40
THC69 Shawn Green 8.00 2.40
THC70 Hank Blalock 12.00 3.60
THC71 Pedro Martinez 12.00 3.60
THC72 Ryan Kohlmeier 8.00 2.40
THC73 Kerry Wood 12.00 3.60
THC74 Aramis Ramirez 8.00 2.40
THC75 Lance Berkman 8.00 2.40
THC76 Scott Dunn 8.00 2.40
THC77 Moises Alou 8.00 2.40
THC78 Mark Buehrle 8.00 2.40
THC79 Jerry Hairston 8.00 2.40
THC80 Joe Borchard 8.00 2.40
THC81 Cristian Guzman 8.00 2.40
THC82 Sean Burroughs 8.00 2.40
THC83 Alfonso Soriano 8.00 2.40
THC84 Adam Dunn 8.00 2.40
THC85 Jim Thome 12.00 3.60
THC86 Jason Botts 10.00 3.00
THC87 Jeromy Burnitz 8.00 2.40
THC88 Roy Oswalt 8.00 2.40
THC89 Russ Ortiz 8.00 2.40
THC90 Marlon Anderson 8.00 2.40
THC91 Stubby Clapp 8.00 2.40
THC92 Rickey Henderson 12.00 3.60
THC93 Brad Radke 8.00 2.40
THC94 Jeff Bagwell 8.00 2.40
THC95 Troy Percival 8.00 2.40
THC96 Napoleon Calzado 8.00 2.40
THC97 Joe Randa 8.00 2.40
THC98 Chan Ho Park 8.00 2.40
THC99 Jason Bay 15.00 4.50
THC100 Mark Quinn 8.00 2.40

2002 Topps Heritage Classic Renditions

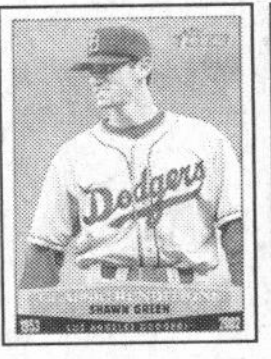
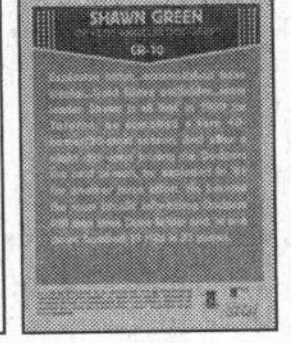

Inserted into packs at stated odds of one in 12, these 10 cards show how current players might look like if they played in their 1953 team uniforms. These cards are printed on grayback paper stock.

Nm-Mt Ex-Mt
COMPLETE SET (10) 20.00 6.00
CR1 Kerry Wood .... 2.50 .75
CR2 Brian Giles .... 2.00 .60
CR3 Roger Cedeno .... 2.00 .60
CR4 Jason Giambi .... 2.00 .60
CR5 Albert Pujols 5.00 1.50
CR6 Mark Buehrle .... 2.00 .60
CR7 Cristian Guzman .... 2.00 .60
CR8 Jimmy Rollins .... 2.00 .60
CR9 Jim Thome .... 2.50 .75
CR10 Shawn Green .... 2.00 .60

2002 Topps Heritage Classic Renditions Autographs

Partially paralleling the Classic Rendition set, these three cards were all autographed by the player and have a stated print run of 25 sets. Due to market scarcity, no pricing is provided for these cards.

Nm-Mt Ex-Mt
CRABG Brian Giles ....
CRACG Cristian Guzman ....
CRAJR Jimmy Rollins ....

2002 Topps Heritage Clubhouse Collection

Inserted into packs at a rate for jersey cards of one in 332 and bat cards at a rate of one in 498, these 12 cards feature a mix of active and retired players with a memorabilia swatch.

Nm-Mt Ex-Mt
CCAD Alvin Dark Bat 25.00 7.50
CCBB Barry Bonds Bat 80.00 24.00
CCCP Corey Patterson Bat 25.00 7.50
CCEM Eddie Mathews Jsy 40.00 12.00
CCGK George Kell Jsy 40.00 12.00
CCGM Greg Maddux Jsy 40.00 12.00
CCHS Hank Sauer Bat 25.00 7.50
CCJP Jorge Posada Bat 40.00 12.00
CCNG Nomar Garciaparra Bat ... 50.00 15.00
CCRA Rich Aurilia Bat 25.00 7.50
CCWM Willie Mays Bat 100.00 30.00
CCYB Yogi Berra Jsy 40.00 12.00

2002 Topps Heritage Clubhouse Collection Autographs

These four cards parallel the Clubhouse Collection insert set. These cards feature autographs from the noted players are are serial numbered to 25. Due to market scarcity, no pricing is provided for these players.

Nm-Mt Ex-Mt
CCAAD Alvin Dark Bat ....
CCAGK George Kell Jsy ....
CCAWM Willie Mays Bat ....
CCAYB Yogi Berra Jsy ....

2002 Topps Heritage Clubhouse Collection Duos

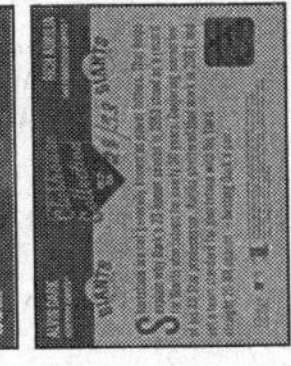

Inserted into packs at stated odds of one in 5016, these six cards feature one current player and one 1953 franchise alum from that same team with a relic from each player. These cards have a stated print run of 53 serial numbered sets. Due to market scarcity, no pricing is provided for these cards.

Nm-Mt Ex-Mt
CC2BP Yogi Berra Jsy 150.00 45.00
Jorge Posada Bat
CC2DA Alvin Dark Bat 100.00 30.00
Rich Aurilia Bat
CC2KR George Kell Jsy 150.00 45.00
Nomar Garciaparra Bat
CC2MB Willie Mays Bat 250.00 75.00
Barry Bonds Bat UER
Card states Bonds is Mays' godfather
It is the other way around
CC2SM Eddie Mathews Jsy 200.00 60.00
Greg Maddux Jsy
CC2SP Hank Sauer Bat 100.00 30.00
Corey Patterson Bat

2002 Topps Heritage Grandstand Glory

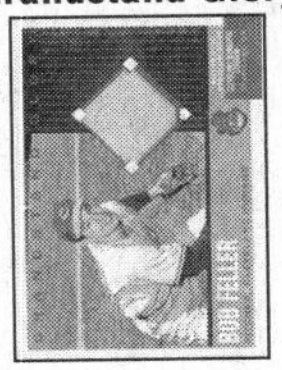

Inserted into packs at different rates depending on which grop the player is from, these 12 cards feature retired 1950's players along with an authentic relic from an historic 1950's stadium.

Nm-Mt Ex-Mt
GROUP A STATED ODDS 1:4115 ....
GROUP B STATED ODDS 1:531 ....
GROUP C STATED ODDS 1:1576 ....
GROUP D STATED ODDS 1:370 ....
GROUP E STATED ODDS 1:483 ....
GGBF Bob Feller E 25.00 7.50
GGBM Billy Martin B 40.00 12.00
GGBP Billy Pierce B 20.00 6.00
GGBS Bobby Shantz D 20.00 6.00
GGEW Early Wynn E 25.00 7.50
GGHN Hal Newhouser B 25.00 7.50
GGHS Hank Sauer C 20.00 6.00
GGRC Roy Campanella D 40.00 12.00
GGSP Satchel Paige A 60.00 18.00
GGTK Ted Kluszewski E 40.00 12.00
GGWF Whitey Ford D 25.00 7.50
GGWS Warren Spahn D 25.00 7.50

2002 Topps Heritage New Age Performers

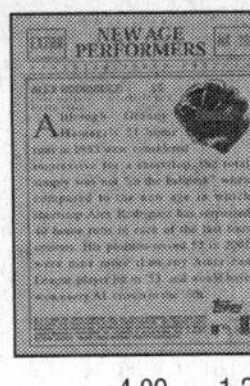

Inserted into packs at stated odds of one in 15, these 15 cards feature powerhouse players whose accomplishments have cemented their names in major league history.

Nm-Mt Ex-Mt
COMPLETE SET (15) 50.00 15.00
NA1 Luis Gonzalez .... 2.00 .60
NA2 Mark McGwire 6.00 1.80
NA3 Barry Bonds 6.00 1.80
NA4 Ken Griffey Jr. 4.00 1.20
NA5 Ichiro Suzuki 4.00 1.20
NA6 Sammy Sosa 4.00 1.20
NA7 Andruw Jones .... 2.00 .60
NA8 Derek Jeter 6.00 1.80
NA9 Todd Helton .... 2.00 .60
NA10 Alex Rodriguez 4.00 1.20
NA11 Jason Giambi Yankees .... 2.00 .60
NA12 Bret Boone .... 2.00 .60
NA13 Roberto Alomar .... 2.00 .60
NA14 Albert Pujols 5.00 1.50
NA15 Vladimir Guerrero .... 2.50 .75

2002 Topps Heritage Real One Autographs

Inserted into packs at different odds depending on which group the player belongs to, this 28 card set features a mix of authentic autographs between active players and those who were active in the 1953 season. Please note that the group whiche each player belongs to is listed next to their name in our checklist.

Nm-Mt Ex-Mt
GROUP 1 STATED ODDS 1:346 ....
GROUP 2 STATED ODDS 1:6363 ....
GROUP 3 STATED ODDS 1:4908 ....
GROUP 4 STATED ODDS 1:3196 ....
GROUP 5 STATED ODDS 1:498 ....
*RED INK: .75X TO 1.5X BASIC AUTO'S
RED INK ODDS 1:306 ....
RED INK PRINT RUN 53 SERIAL #'d SETS
RO-AC Andy Carey 1 .... 40.00 12.00
RO-AD Alvin Dark 1 .... 60.00 18.00
RO-AR Al Rosen 1 .... 100.00 30.00
RO-ARO Alex Rodriguez 2 ...... 150.00 45.00
RO-ASC Al Schoendienst 1 .... 60.00 18.00
RO-BF Bob Feller 1 .... 60.00 18.00
RO-BG Brian Giles 5 .... 25.00 7.50
RO-BS Bobby Shantz 1 .... 60.00 18.00
RO-CG Cristian Guzman 5 .... 15.00 4.50
RO-DD Dom DiMaggio 1 .... 100.00 30.00
RO-ES Enos Slaughter 1 .... 100.00 30.00
RO-GK George Kell 1 .... 60.00 18.00
RO-GM Gil McDougald 1 .... 100.00 30.00
RO-HW Hoyt Wilhelm 1 .... 60.00 18.00
RO-JB Joe Black 1 .... 60.00 18.00
RO-JE Jim Edmonds 4 .... 40.00 12.00
RO-JP John Podres 1 .... 60.00 18.00
RO-MI Monte Irvin 1 .... 60.00 18.00
RO-OM Minnie Minoso 1 .... 60.00 18.00
RO-PR Phil Rizzuto 1 .... 100.00 30.00
RO-PRO Preacher Roe 1 .... 60.00 18.00
RO-RB Ray Boone 1 .... 60.00 18.00
RO-RF Roy Face 1 .... 60.00 18.00
RO-RCL Roger Clemens 3 .... 150.00 45.00
RO-WF Whitey Ford 1 .... 100.00 30.00
RO-WM Willie Mays 1 .... 200.00 60.00
RO-WS Warren Spahn 1 .... 100.00 30.00
RO-YB Yogi Berra 1 .... 100.00 30.00

2002 Topps Heritage Then and Now

Inserted into packs at stated odds of one in 15, these 10 cards feature a 1953 player as well as a current stand-out. These cards offer statistical comparisions in major stat categories and are printed in greyback paper stock.

Nm-Mt Ex-Mt
COMPLETE SET (10) 30.00 9.00
TN1 Eddie Mathews 6.00 1.80
Barry Bonds
TN2 Al Rosen 4.00 1.20
Alex Rodriguez
TN3 Carl Furillo .... 2.00 .60
Larry Walker
TN4 Minnie Minoso 4.00 1.20
Ichiro Suzuki
TN5 Richie Ashburn .... 2.00 .60
Rich Aurilia
TN6 Al Rosen .... 2.00 .60
Bret Boone
TN7 Duke Snider 4.00 1.20
Sammy Sosa
TN8 Al Rosen 4.00 1.20
Alex Rodriguez
TN9 Robin Roberts .... 2.50 .75
Randy Johnson
TN10 Billy Pierce .... 2.50 .75
Hideo Nomo

2003 Topps Heritage

This 430-card set, which was designed to honor the 1954 Topps set, was released in February, 2003. These cards were issued in five card packs with an $3 SRP. These packs were issued in 24 pack boxes which came eight boxes to a case. In addition, many cards in the set were issued in two varieties. A few cards were issued featuring either a logo used today or a scarcer version in which the logo was used in the 1954 set. In addition, some cards were printed with either the originally designed version or a black background. The black background version is the tougher of the two versions of each card. A few cards between 1 and 363 were produced in less quantities and all cards from 364 on up were short printed as well. In a nod to the 1954 set, Alex Rodriguez had both cards 1 and 250; just as Ted Williams had in the original 1954 Topps set.

Nm-Mt Ex-Mt
COMPLETE SET (450) 400.00 120.00
COMP.SET w/o SP's (350) 80.00 24.00
COMMON CARD .... .50 .15
COMMON RC .... 1.00 .30
COMMON SP 5.00 1.50
COMMON SP RC 5.00 1.50
1A Alex Rodriguez Red .... 2.50 .75
1B Alex Rodriguez Black SP 12.00 3.60
2 Jose Cruz Jr. .... .50 .15
3 Ichiro Suzuki SP 12.00 3.60
4 Rich Aurilia .... .50 .15
5 Trevor Hoffman .... .60 .18
6A Brian Giles New Logo .... .60 .18
6B Brian Giles Old Logo SP 5.00 1.50
7A Albert Pujols Orange .... 3.00 .90
7B Albert Pujols Black SP 15.00 4.50
8 Vicente Padilla .... .50 .15
9 Bobby Crosby .... 1.00 .30
10A Derek Jeter New Logo 4.00 1.20
10B Derek Jeter Old Logo SP ... 15.00 4.50
11A Pat Burrell New Logo .... .60 .18
11B Pat Burrell Old Logo SP 5.00 1.50
12 Armando Benitez .... .60 .18
13 Javier Vazquez .... .60 .18
14 Justin Morneau .... 1.00 .30
15 Doug Mientkiewicz .... .60 .18
16 Kevin Brown .... .60 .18
17 Alexis Gomez .... .50 .15
18A Lance Berkman Blue .... .60 .18
18B Lance Berkman Black SP 5.00 1.50
19 Adrian Gonzalez .... .60 .18
20A Todd Helton Green .... 1.00 .30
20B Todd Helton Black SP 8.00 2.40
21 Carlos Pena .... .50 .15
22 Matt Lawton .... .50 .15
23 Elmer Dessens .... .50 .15
24 Hee Seop Choi .... .50 .15
25 Chris Duncan SP RC 5.00 1.50
26 Ugueth Urbina .... .50 .15
27A Rodrigo Lopez New Logo .... .50 .15
27B Ro. Lopez Old Logo SP 5.00 1.50
28 Damian Moss .... .50 .15
29 Steve Finley .... .60 .18
30A Sammy Sosa New Logo .... 2.50 .75
30B S.Sosa Old Logo SP 12.00 3.60
31 Kevin Cash .... .50 .15
32 Kenny Rogers .... .60 .18
33 Ben Grieve .... .50 .15
34 Jason Simontacchi .... .50 .15
35 Shin-Soo Choo .... .60 .18
36 Freddy Garcia .... .60 .18
37 Jesse Foppert .... .60 .18
38 Tony LaRussa MG .... .60 .18
39 Mark Kotsay .... .60 .18
40 Barry Zito .... .60 .18
41 Josh Fogg .... .50 .15
42 Marlon Byrd .... .50 .15
43 Marcus Thames .... .50 .15
44 Al Leiter .... .60 .18
45 Michael Barrett .... .50 .15
46 Jake Peavy .... .60 .18
47 Dustan Mohr .... .50 .15
48 Alex Sanchez .... .50 .15
49 Chin-Feng Chen .... .60 .18
50A Kazuhisa Ishii Blue .... .60 .18
50B Kazuhisa Ishii Black SP 5.00 1.50
51 Carlos Beltran .... 1.00 .30
52 Franklin Gutierrez RC .... 3.00 .90
53 Miguel Cabrera .... 1.50 .45
54 Roger Clemens .... 3.00 .90
55 Juan Cruz .... .50 .15
56 Jason Young .... .50 .15
57 Alex Herrera .... .50 .15
58 Aaron Boone .... .60 .18
59 Mark Buehrle .... .60 .18
60 Larry Walker .... 1.00 .30
61 Morgan Ensberg .... .50 .15
62 Barry Larkin .... 1.00 .30
63 Joe Borchard .... .50 .15
64 Jason Dubois .... .60 .18
65 Shea Hillenbrand .... .60 .18
66 Jay Gibbons .... .50 .15
67 Vinny Castilla .... .60 .18
68 Jeff Mathis .... .60 .18
69 Curt Schilling .... .60 .18
70 Garret Anderson .... .60 .18
71 Josh Phelps .... .50 .15
72 Chan Ho Park .... .60 .18
73 Edgar Renteria .... .60 .18
74 Kazuhiro Sasaki .... .60 .18
75 Lloyd McClendon MG .... .50 .15
76 Jon Lieber .... .50 .15
77 Rolando Viera .... .50 .15
78 Jeff Conine .... .60 .18
79 Kevin Millwood .... .60 .18
80A Randy Johnson Green .... 1.50 .45

80B Randy Johnson Black SP 12.00 3.60
81 Troy Percival .60 .18
82 Cliff Floyd .60 .18
83 Tony Graffanino .50 .15
84 Austin Kearns .60 .18
85 Manuel Ramirez SP RC 8.00 2.40
86 Jim Tracy MG .50 .15
87 Rondell White .60 .18
88 Trot Nixon .60 .18
89 Carlos Lee .60 .18
90 Mike Lowell .60 .18
91 Raul Ibanez .50 .15
92 Ricardo Rodriguez .50 .15
93 Ben Sheets .60 .18
94 Jason Perry SP RC 8.00 2.40
95 Mark Teixeira .60 .18
96 Brad Fullmer .50 .15
97 Casey Kotchman 1.00 .30
98 Craig Counsell .50 .15
99 Jason Marquis .50 .15
100A N.Garciaparra New Logo 2.50 .75
100B N.Garciaparra Old Logo SP 12.00 3.60
101 Ed Rogers .50 .15
102 Wilson Betemit .50 .15
103 Wayne Lydon RC 1.00 .30
104 Jack Cust .50 .15
105 Derrek Lee .60 .18
106 Jim Kavourias .50 .15
107 Joe Randa .50 .15
108 Taylor Buchholz .50 .15
109 Gabe Kapler .50 .15
110 Preston Wilson .60 .18
111 Craig Biggio 1.00 .30
112 Paul Lo Duca .60 .18
113 Eddie Guardado .50 .15
114 Andres Galarraga 1.00 .30
115 Edgardo Alfonzo .50 .15
116 Robin Ventura .60 .18
117 Jeremy Giambi .50 .15
118 Ray Durham .60 .18
119 Mariano Rivera 1.00 .30
120 Jimmy Rollins .60 .18
121 Dennis Tankersley .50 .15
122 Jason Schmidt .60 .18
123 Bret Boone .60 .18
124 Josh Hamilton .60 .18
125 Scott Rolen 1.50 .45
126 Steve Cox .50 .15
127 Larry Bowa MG .60 .18
128 Adam LaRoche SP 5.00 1.50
129 Ryan Klesko .60 .18
130 Tim Hudson .60 .18
131 Brandon Claussen .50 .15
132 Craig Brazell SP RC 8.00 2.40
133 Grady Little MG .50 .15
134 Jarrod Washburn .50 .15
135 Lyle Overbay .60 .18
136 John Burkett .50 .15
137 Daryl Clark RC 1.00 .30
138 Kirk Rueter .50 .15
139A Joe Mauer 1.50 .45
Jake Mauer Green
139B Joe Mauer 8.00 2.40
Jake Mauer Black SP
140 Troy Glaus .60 .18
141 Trey Hodges SP 5.00 1.50
142 Dallas McPherson 1.50 .45
143 Art Howe MG .50 .15
144 Jesus Cota .50 .15
145 J.R. House .50 .15
146 Reggie Sanders .50 .15
147 Clint Nageotte .50 .15
148 Jim Edmonds .60 .18
149 Carl Crawford .60 .18
150A Mike Piazza Blue 2.50 .75
150B Mike Piazza Black SP 12.00 3.60
151 Seung Song .50 .15
152 Roberto Hernandez .60 .18
153 Marquis Grissom .60 .18
154 Billy Wagner .60 .18
155 Josh Beckett .60 .18
156A R.Simon New Logo .50 .15
156B R.Simon Old Logo SP 5.00 1.50
157 Ben Broussard .50 .15
158 Russell Branyan .50 .15
159 Frank Thomas 1.50 .45
160 Alex Escobar .50 .15
161 Mark Bellhorn .50 .15
162 Melvin Mora .60 .18
163 Andruw Jones .60 .18
164 Danny Bautista .50 .15
165 Ramon Ortiz .50 .15
166 Wily Mo Pena .60 .18
167 Jose Jimenez .50 .15
168 Mark Redman .50 .15
169 Angel Berroa .50 .15
170 Andy Marte SP RC 15.00 4.50
171 Juan Gonzalez 1.00 .30
172 Fernando Vina .50 .15
173 Joel Pineiro .60 .18
174 Boof Bonser .50 .15
175 Bernie Castro SP RC 5.00 1.50
176 Bobby Cox MG .50 .15
177 Jeff Kent .60 .18
178 Oliver Perez .60 .18
179 Chase Utley .60 .18
180 Mark Mulder .60 .18
181 Bobby Abreu .60 .18
182 Ramiro Mendoza .50 .15
183 Aaron Heilman .50 .15
184 A.J. Pierzynski .60 .18
185 Eric Gagne 1.50 .45
186 Kirk Saarloos .50 .15
187 Ron Gardenhire MG .50 .15
188 Dmitri Young .60 .18
189 Todd Zeile .60 .18
190A Jim Thome New Logo 1.50 .45
190B Jim Thome Old Logo SP 8.00 2.40
191 Cliff Lee .50 .15
192 Matt Morris .60 .18
193 Robert Fick .50 .15
194 C.C. Sabathia .60 .18
195 Alexis Rios 1.00 .30
196 D'Angelo Jimenez .50 .15
197 Edgar Martinez 1.00 .30
198 Robb Nen .60 .18
199 Taggert Bozied .50 .15
200 Vladimir Guerrero SP 8.00 2.40
201 Walter Young SP 5.00 1.50
202 Brendan Harris RC 1.00 .30
203 Mike Hargrove MG .50 .15
204 Vernon Wells .60 .18
205 Hank Blalock 1.00 .30
206 Mike Cameron .60 .18
207 Tony Batista .60 .18
208 Matt Williams .60 .18
209 Tony Womack .50 .15
210 R.Nivar-Martinez RC 1.00 .30
211 Aaron Sele .50 .15
212 Mark Grace 1.00 .30
213 Joe Crede .50 .15
214 Ryan Dempster .50 .15
215 Omar Vizquel 1.00 .30
216 Juan Pierre .60 .18
217 Denny Bautista .60 .18
218 Chuck Knoblauch .60 .18
219 Eric Karros .60 .18
220 Victor Diaz .60 .18
221 Jacque Jones .60 .18
222 Jose Vidro .50 .15
223 Joe McEwing .50 .15
224 Nick Johnson .50 .15
225 Eric Chavez .60 .18
226 Jose Mesa .50 .15
227 Aramis Ramirez .60 .18
228 John Lackey .60 .18
229 David Bell .50 .15
230 John Olerud .60 .18
231 Tino Martinez 1.00 .30
232 Randy Winn .50 .15
233 Todd Hollandsworth .50 .15
234 Ruddy Lugo RC 1.00 .30
235 Carlos Delgado .60 .18
236 Chris Narveson .50 .15
237 Tim Salmon 1.00 .30
238 Orlando Palmeiro .50 .15
239 Jeff Clark SP RC 5.00 1.50
240 Byung-Hyun Kim .60 .18
241 Mike Remlinger .50 .15
242 Johnny Damon 1.50 .45
243 Corey Patterson .60 .18
244 Paul Konerko .60 .18
245 Danny Graves .50 .15
246 Ellis Burks .60 .18
247 Gavin Floyd .60 .18
248 Jaime Bubela RC 1.00 .30
249 Sean Burroughs .60 .18
250 Alex Rodriguez SP 12.00 3.60
251 Gabe Gross .50 .15
252 Rafael Palmeiro 1.00 .30
253 Dewon Brazelton .50 .15
254 Jimmy Journell .50 .15
255 Rafael Soriano .50 .15
256 Jerome Williams .60 .18
257 Xavier Nady .50 .15
258 Mike Williams .50 .15
259 Randy Wolf .50 .15
260A Miguel Tejada Orange .60 .18
260B Miguel Tejada Black SP 5.00 1.50
261 Juan Rivera .50 .15
262 Rey Ordonez .50 .15
263 Bartolo Colon .60 .18
264 Eric Milton .50 .15
265 Jeffrey Hammonds .50 .15
266 Odalis Perez .50 .15
267 Mike Sweeney .60 .18
268 Richard Hidalgo .50 .15
269 Alex Gonzalez .50 .15
270 Aaron Cook .50 .15
271 Earl Snyder .50 .15
272 Todd Walker .50 .15
273 Aaron Rowand .50 .15
274 Matt Clement .50 .15
275 Anastacio Martinez .50 .15
276 Mike Bordick .60 .18
277 John Smoltz 1.00 .30
278 Scott Hairston .60 .18
279 David Eckstein .50 .15
280 Shannon Stewart .60 .18
281 Carl Everett .60 .18
282 Aubrey Huff .60 .18
283 Mike Mussina 1.00 .30
284 Ruben Sierra .50 .15
285 Russ Ortiz .60 .18
286 Brian Lawrence .50 .15
287 Kip Wells .50 .15
288 Placido Polanco .50 .15
289 Ted Lilly .50 .15
290 Andy Pettitte 1.00 .30
291 John Buck .50 .15
292 Orlando Cabrera .50 .15
293 Cristian Guzman .50 .15
294 Ruben Quevedo .50 .15
295 Cesar Izturis .50 .15
296 Ryan Ludwick .50 .15
297 Roy Oswalt .60 .18
298 Jason Stokes 1.00 .30
299 Mike Hampton .60 .18
300 Pedro Martinez 1.50 .45
301 Nic Jackson .50 .15
302A Mag. Ordonez New Logo .60 .18
302B Mag. Ordonez Old Logo SP 5.00 1.50
303 Manny Ramirez 1.00 .30
304 Jorge Julio .50 .15
305 Javy Lopez .60 .18
306 Roy Halladay .50 .15
307 Kevin Mench .50 .15
308 Jason Isringhausen .60 .18
309 Carlos Guillen .60 .18
310 Tsuyoshi Shinjo .60 .18
311 Phil Nevin .60 .18
312 Pokey Reese .50 .15
313 Jorge Padilla .50 .15
314 Jermaine Dye .60 .18
315 David Wells .60 .18
316 Mo Vaughn .60 .18
317 Bernie Williams 1.00 .30
318 Michael Restovich .50 .15
319 Jose Hernandez .50 .15
320 Richie Sexson .60 .18
321 Daryle Ward .50 .15
322 Luis Castillo .50 .15
323 Rene Reyes .50 .15
324 Victor Martinez 1.00 .30
325A Adam Dunn New Logo 1.00 .30
325B Adam Dunn Old Logo SP 8.00 2.40
326 Corwin Malone .50 .15
327 Kerry Wood 1.50 .45
328 Rickey Henderson 1.50 .45
329 Marty Cordova .50 .15
330 Greg Maddux 2.50 .75
331 Miguel Batista .50 .15
332 Chris Bootcheck .50 .15
333 Carlos Baerga .50 .15
334 Antonio Alfonseca .50 .15
335 Shane Halter .50 .15
336 Juan Encarnacion .50 .15
337 Tom Gordon .50 .15
338 Hideo Nomo 1.50 .45
339 Torii Hunter .60 .18
340A Alfonso Soriano Yellow 1.00 .30
340B Alf. Soriano Black SP 8.00 2.40
341 Roberto Alomar 1.00 .30
342 David Justice .60 .18
343 Mike Lieberthal .60 .18
344 Jeff Weaver .60 .18
345 Timo Perez .50 .15
346 Travis Lee .50 .15
347 Sean Casey .60 .18
348 Willie Harris .50 .15
349 Derek Lowe .60 .18
350 Tom Glavine 1.00 .30
351 Eric Hinske .50 .15
352 Rocco Baldelli .60 .18
353 J.D. Drew .60 .18
354 Jamie Moyer .60 .18
355 Todd Linden .50 .15
356 Benito Santiago .60 .18
357 Brad Baker .50 .15
358 Alex Gonzalez .50 .15
359 Brandon Duckworth .50 .15
360 John Rheinecker .50 .15
361 Orlando Hernandez .50 .15
362 Pedro Astacio .50 .15
363 Brad Wilkerson .50 .15
364 David Ortiz SP 8.00 2.40
365 Geoff Jenkins SP 5.00 1.50
366 Brian Jordan SP 5.00 1.50
367 Paul Byrd SP 5.00 1.50
368 Jason Lane SP 5.00 1.50
369 Jeff Bagwell SP 8.00 2.40
370 Bobby Higginson SP 5.00 1.50
371 Juan Uribe SP 5.00 1.50
372 Lee Stevens SP 5.00 1.50
373 Jimmy Haynes SP 5.00 1.50
374 Jose Valentin SP 5.00 1.50
375 Ken Griffey Jr. SP 12.00 3.60
376 Barry Bonds SP 20.00 6.00
377 Gary Matthews Jr. SP 5.00 1.50
378 Gary Sheffield SP 5.00 1.50
379 Rick Helling SP 5.00 1.50
380 Junior Spivey SP 5.00 1.50
381 Francisco Rodriguez SP 5.00 1.50
382 Chipper Jones SP 8.00 2.40
383 Orlando Hudson SP 5.00 1.50
384 Ivan Rodriguez SP 8.00 2.40
385 Chris Snelling SP 5.00 1.50
386 Kenny Lofton SP 5.00 1.50
387 Eric Cyr SP 5.00 1.50
388 Jason Kendall SP 5.00 1.50
389 Marlon Anderson SP 5.00 1.50
390 Billy Koch SP 5.00 1.50
391 Shelley Duncan SP 5.00 1.50
392 Jose Reyes SP 5.00 1.50
393 Fernando Tatis SP 5.00 1.50
394 Michael Cuddyer SP 5.00 1.50
395 Mark Prior SP 8.00 2.40
396 Dontrelle Willis SP 8.00 2.40
397 Jay Payton SP 5.00 1.50
398 Brandon Phillips SP 5.00 1.50
399 Dustin Moseley SP RC 8.00 2.40
400 Jason Giambi SP 5.00 1.50
401 John Mabry SP 5.00 1.50
402 Ron Gant SP 5.00 1.50
403 J.T. Snow SP 5.00 1.50
404 Jeff Cirillo SP 5.00 1.50
405 Darin Erstad SP 5.00 1.50
406 Luis Gonzalez SP 5.00 1.50
407 Marcus Giles SP 5.00 1.50
408 Brian Daubach SP 5.00 1.50
409 Moises Alou SP 5.00 1.50
410 Raul Mondesi SP 5.00 1.50
411 Adrian Beltre SP 8.00 2.40
412 A.J. Burnett SP 5.00 1.50
413 Jason Jennings SP 5.00 1.50
414 Edwin Almonte SP 5.00 1.50
415 Fred McGriff SP 8.00 2.40
416 Tim Raines Jr. SP 5.00 1.50
417 Rafael Furcal SP 5.00 1.50
418 Erubiel Durazo SP 5.00 1.50
419 Drew Henson SP 5.00 1.50
420 Kevin Appier SP 5.00 1.50
421 Chad Tracy SP 5.00 1.50
422 Adam Wainwright SP 5.00 1.50
423 Choo Freeman SP 5.00 1.50
424 Sandy Alomar Jr. SP 5.00 1.50
425 Corey Koskie SP 5.00 1.50
426 Jeromy Burnitz SP 5.00 1.50
427 Jorge Posada SP 8.00 2.40
428 Jason Arnold SP 5.00 1.50
429 Brett Myers SP 5.00 1.50
430 Shawn Green SP 5.00 1.50

2003 Topps Heritage Chrome

Inserted at a stated rate of one in eight, this is a partial parallel to the basic Topps Heritage set. These cards feature Topps special Chrome technology and were printed to a stated print run of 1954 serial numbered sets.

Nm-Mt Ex-Mt
THC1 Alex Rodriguez 12.00 3.60
THC2 Ichiro Suzuki 12.00 3.60
THC3 Brian Giles 5.00 1.50
THC4 Albert Pujols 15.00 4.50
THC5 Derek Jeter 20.00 6.00
THC6 Pat Burrell 5.00 1.50
THC7 Lance Berkman 5.00 1.50
THC8 Todd Helton 5.00 1.50
THC9 Chris Duncan 5.00 1.50
THC10 Rodrigo Lopez 5.00 1.50
THC11 Sammy Sosa 12.00 3.60
THC12 Barry Zito 5.00 1.50
THC13 Marlon Byrd 5.00 1.50
THC14 Al Leiter 5.00 1.50
THC15 Kazuhisa Ishii 5.00 1.50
THC16 Franklin Gutierrez 12.00 3.60
THC17 Roger Clemens 15.00 4.50
THC18 Mark Buehrle 5.00 1.50
THC19 Larry Walker 5.00 1.50
THC20 Curt Schilling 5.00 1.50
THC21 Garret Anderson 5.00 1.50
THC22 Randy Johnson 8.00 2.40
THC23 Cliff Floyd 5.00 1.50
THC24 Austin Kearns 5.00 1.50
THC25 Manuel Ramirez 5.00 1.50
THC26 Raul Ibanez 5.00 1.50
THC27 Jason Perry 8.00 2.40
THC28 Mark Teixeira 5.00 1.50
THC29 Nomar Garciaparra 12.00 3.60
THC30 Wayne Lydon 5.00 1.50
THC31 Preston Wilson 5.00 1.50
THC32 Paul Lo Duca 5.00 1.50
THC33 Edgardo Alfonzo 5.00 1.50
THC34 Jeremy Giambi 5.00 1.50
THC35 Mariano Rivera 5.00 1.50
THC36 Jimmy Rollins 5.00 1.50
THC37 Bret Boone 5.00 1.50
THC38 Scott Rolen 8.00 2.40
THC39 Adam LaRoche 5.00 1.50
THC40 Tim Hudson 5.00 1.50
THC41 Craig Brazell 8.00 2.40
THC42 Daryl Clark 8.00 2.40
THC43 Joe Mauer 8.00 2.40
Jake Mauer
THC44 Troy Glaus 5.00 1.50
THC45 Trey Hodges 5.00 1.50
THC46 Carl Crawford 5.00 1.50
THC47 Mike Piazza 12.00 3.60
THC48 Josh Beckett 5.00 1.50
THC49 Randall Simon 5.00 1.50
THC50 Frank Thomas 8.00 2.40
THC51 Andruw Jones 5.00 1.50
THC52 Andy Marte 15.00 4.50
THC53 Bernie Castro 5.00 1.50
THC54 Jim Thome 8.00 2.40
THC55 Alexis Rios 5.00 1.50
THC56 Vladimir Guerrero 8.00 2.40
THC57 Walter Young 5.00 1.50
THC58 Hank Blalock 5.00 1.50
THC59 Ramon Nivar-Martinez 8.00 2.40
THC60 Jacque Jones 5.00 1.50
THC61 Nick Johnson 5.00 1.50
THC62 Ruddy Lugo 5.00 1.50
THC63 Carlos Delgado 5.00 1.50
THC64 Jeff Clark 5.00 1.50
THC65 Johnny Damon 8.00 2.40
THC66 Jaime Bubela 5.00 1.50
THC67 Alex Rodriguez 12.00 3.60
THC68 Rafael Palmeiro 5.00 1.50
THC69 Miguel Tejada 5.00 1.50
THC70 Bartolo Colon 5.00 1.50
THC71 Mike Sweeney 5.00 1.50
THC72 John Smoltz 5.00 1.50
THC73 Shannon Stewart 5.00 1.50
THC74 Mike Mussina 5.00 1.50
THC75 Roy Oswalt 5.00 1.50
THC76 Pedro Martinez 8.00 2.40
THC77 Magglio Ordonez 5.00 1.50
THC78 Manny Ramirez 5.00 1.50
THC79 David Wells 5.00 1.50
THC80 Richie Sexson 5.00 1.50
THC81 Adam Dunn 5.00 1.50
THC82 Greg Maddux 12.00 3.60
THC83 Alfonso Soriano 5.00 1.50
THC84 Roberto Alomar 5.00 1.50
THC85 Derek Lowe 5.00 1.50
THC86 Tom Glavine 5.00 1.50
THC87 Jeff Bagwell 5.00 1.50
THC88 Ken Griffey Jr. 12.00 3.60
THC89 Barry Bonds 20.00 6.00
THC90 Gary Sheffield 5.00 1.50
THC91 Chipper Jones 8.00 2.40
THC92 Orlando Hudson 5.00 1.50
THC93 Jose Cruz Jr. 5.00 1.50
THC94 Mark Prior 8.00 2.40
THC95 Jason Giambi 5.00 1.50
THC96 Luis Gonzalez 5.00 1.50
THC97 Drew Henson 5.00 1.50
THC98 Cristian Guzman 5.00 1.50
THC99 Shawn Green 5.00 1.50
THC100 Jose Vidro 5.00 1.50

2003 Topps Heritage Clubhouse Collection Relics

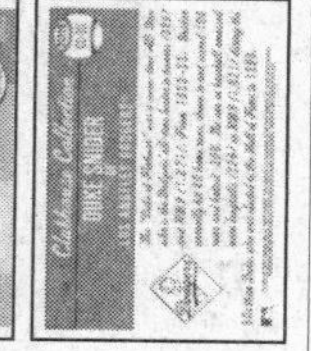

Inserted at different odds depending on the relic, these 12 cards feature a mix of active and retire players and various game-used relics used during their career.

Nm-Mt Ex-Mt
BAT A STATED ODDS 1:2569
BAT B STATED ODDS 1:2506
BAT C STATED ODDS 1:2464
BAT D STATED ODDS 1:1989
UNI A STATED ODDS 1:4223
UNI B STATED ODDS 1:1207
UNI C STATED ODDS 1:921
UNI D STATED ODDS 1:171
AD Adam Dunn Uni D 15.00 4.50
AK Al Kaline Bat D 30.00 9.00
AP Albert Pujols Uni D 20.00 6.00
AR Alex Rodriguez Uni D 20.00 6.00
CJ Chipper Jones Uni D 15.00 4.50
DS Duke Snider Uni A 40.00 12.00
EB Ernie Banks Bat C 30.00 9.00
EM Eddie Mathews Bat B 30.00 9.00
JG Jim Gilliam Uni B 15.00 4.50
KW Kerry Wood Uni D 15.00 4.50
SG Shawn Green Uni C 15.00 4.50
WM Willie Mays Bat A 50.00 15.00

2003 Topps Heritage Clubhouse Collection Autograph Relics

Inserted in packs at a stated rate of one in 15,424, these four cards feature not only a game used relic from the featured player but also an authentic autograph. These cards were issued to a stated print run of 25 serial numbered sets and no pricing is provided due to market scarcity.

Nm-Mt Ex-Mt
AK Al Kaline Bat
DS Duke Snider Uni
EB Ernie Banks Bat
WM Willie Mays Bat

2003 Topps Heritage Clubhouse Collection Dual Relics

Issued at a stated rate of one in 9,521, these three cards feature game-used relics from both a legendary player and a current star of the same franchise. These cards were issued to a stated print run of 54 serial numbered sets.

Nm-Mt Ex-Mt
BW Ernie Banks Bat
Kerry Wood Uni
MJ Eddie Mathews Bat
Chipper Jones Uni
SG Duke Snider Uni
Shawn Green Uni

2003 Topps Heritage Flashbacks

Inserted at a stated rate of one in 12, these 10 cards feature thrilling moments from the 1954 season.

Nm-Mt Ex-Mt
COMPLETE SET 10) 20.00 6.00
F1 Willie Mays 5.00 1.50
F2 Yogi Berra 2.50 .75
F3 Ted Kluszewski 2.00 .60
F4 Stan Musial 4.00 1.20
F5 Hank Aaron 5.00 1.50
F6 Duke Snider 2.00 .60
F7 Richie Ashburn 2.00 .60
F8 Robin Roberts 2.00 .60
F9 Mickey Vernon 2.00 .60
F10 Don Larsen 2.00 .60

2003 Topps Heritage Flashbacks Autographs

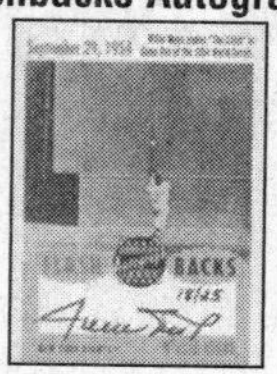

Inserted at a stated rate of one in 65,384 this card features an authentic autograph of Willie Mays. This card was issued to a stated print run of 25 serial numbered cards and no pricing is available due to market scarcity.

Nm-Mt Ex-Mt
WM Willie Mays

2003 Topps Heritage Grandstand Glory Stadium Relics

Inserted at different odds depending on the group, these 12 cards feature a player photo along with a seat relic from any of nine historic ballparks involved in their career.

Nm-Mt Ex-Mt
GROUP A ODDS 1:2804
GROUP B ODDS 1:514
GROUP C ODDS 1:1446
GROUP D ODDS 1:1356
GROUP E ODDS 1:654

ROUP F ODDS 1:214
K Al Kaline F 20.00 6.00
P Andy Pafko F 10.00 3.00
G Dick Groat D 15.00 4.50
S Duke Snider A 25.00 7.50
B Ernie Banks C 25.00 7.50
M Eddie Mathews F 15.00 4.50
R Phil Rizzuto E 20.00 6.00
A Richie Ashburn B 20.00 6.00
K Ted Kluszewski B 20.00 6.00
WM Willie Mays B 40.00 12.00
WS Warren Spahn F 15.00 4.50
B Yogi Berra E 25.00 7.50

2003 Topps Heritage New Age Performers

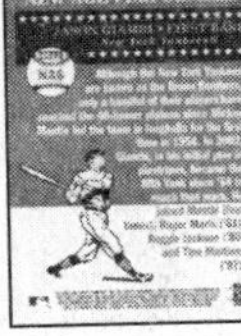

Issued at a stated rate of one in 15, these 15 cards feature prominent active players who have taken the game of baseball to new levels.

	Nm-Mt	Ex-Mt
NA1 Mike Piazza	4.00	1.20
NA2 Ichiro Suzuki	4.00	1.20
NA3 Derek Jeter	6.00	1.80
NA4 Alex Rodriguez	4.00	1.20
NA5 Sammy Sosa	4.00	1.20
NA6 Jason Giambi	2.00	.60
NA7 Vladimir Guerrero	2.50	.75
NA8 Albert Pujols	5.00	1.50
NA9 Todd Helton	2.00	.60
NA10 Nomar Garciaparra	4.00	1.20
NA11 Randy Johnson	2.50	.75
NA12 Jim Thome	2.50	.75
NA13 Barry Bonds	6.00	1.80
NA14 Miguel Tejada	2.00	.60
NA15 Alfonso Soriano	2.00	.60

2003 Topps Heritage Real One Autographs

Inserted at various odds depending on what group the player belonged to, these cards feature authentic autographs from the featured player. Topps made an effort to secure autographs from every person who was still living that was in the 1954 Topps set. Hank Aaron, Yogi Berra and Johnny Sain did not return their cards in time for inclusion in this set and a collector could redeem these cards until February 28, 2005.

	Nm-Mt	Ex-Mt
RETIRED ODDS 1:188		
ACTIVE A ODDS 1:6168		
ACTIVE B ODDS 1:1540		
ACTIVE C ODDS 1:2802		
*RED INK: 1X TO 2X BASIC RETIRED		
*RED INK: .75X TO 1.5X BASIC ACTIVE A		
*RED INK: .75X TO 1.5X BASIC ACTIVE B		
*RED INK: .75X TO 1.5X BASIC ACTIVE C		
RED INK STATED ODDS 1:696		
RED INK PRINT RUN 54 SERIAL #'d SETS		
AK Al Kaline	100.00	30.00
AP Andy Pafko	60.00	18.00
BR Bob Ross	25.00	7.50
BS Bill Skowron	40.00	12.00
BSH Bobby Shantz	40.00	12.00
BT Bob Talbot	25.00	7.50
BWE Bill Werle	25.00	7.50
CH Cal Hogue	25.00	7.50
CK Charlie Kress	25.00	7.50
CS Carl Scheib	25.00	7.50
DG Dick Groat	40.00	12.00
DK Dick Kryhoski	25.00	7.50
DL Don Lenhardt	25.00	7.50
DLU Don Lund	25.00	7.50
DS Duke Snider	100.00	30.00
EB Ernie Banks	150.00	45.00
EM Eddie Mayo	25.00	7.50
GH Gene Hermanski	25.00	7.50
HA Hank Aaron EXCH	250.00	75.00
HB Hank Bauer	40.00	12.00
JC Jose Cruz Jr. B	25.00	7.50
JP Joe Presko	25.00	7.50
JPO Johnny Podres	40.00	12.00
JR Jimmy Rollins C	25.00	7.50
JS Johnny Sain EXCH	40.00	12.00
JV Jose Vidro B	25.00	7.50
JW Jim Willis	25.00	7.50
LB Lance Berkman A	60.00	18.00
LJ Larry Jansen	40.00	12.00
LW Leroy Wheat	25.00	7.50
MB Matt Batts	25.00	7.50
MBL Mike Blyzka	25.00	7.50
MI Monte Irvin	60.00	18.00
MM Mickey Micelotta	25.00	7.50
MS Mike Sandlock	25.00	7.50
PP Paul Penson	25.00	7.50
PR Phil Rizzuto	60.00	18.00
PRO Preacher Roe	40.00	12.00
RF Roy Face	40.00	12.00
RM Ray Murray	25.00	7.50
TL Tom Lasorda	100.00	30.00
VL Vern Law	40.00	12.00
WF Whitey Ford	60.00	18.00
WM Willie Mays	200.00	60.00
YB Yogi Berra EXCH	100.00	30.00

2003 Topps Heritage Then and Now

Issued at a stated rate of one in 15, these 10 cards feature an 1954 star along with a current standout. The backs compare 10 league leaders of 1954 to the league leaders of 2002. Interestingly enough, Ted Kluszewski and Alex Rodriguez are on both the first two cards in this set.

	Nm-Mt	Ex-Mt
COMPLETE SET (10)	30.00	9.00
TN1 Ted Kluszewski Alex Rodriguez HR	4.00	1.20
TN2 Ted Kluszewski Alex Rodriguez RBI	4.00	1.20
TN3 Willie Mays Barry Bonds Batting	6.00	1.80
TN4 Don Mueller Alfonso Soriano	2.00	.60
TN5 Stan Musial Garret Anderson	4.00	1.20
TN6 Minnie Minoso Johnny Damon	2.50	.75
TN7 Willie Mays Barry Bonds Slugging	6.00	1.80
TN8 Duke Snider Alex Rodriguez	4.00	1.20
TN9 Robin Roberts Randy Johnson	2.50	.75
TN10 Johnny Antonelli Pedro Martinez	2.50	.75

2004 Topps Heritage

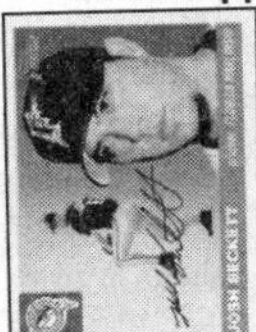

This 495 card set was released in February, 2004. As this was the fourth year this set was issued, the cards were designed in the style of the 1955 Topps set. This set was issued in eight card packs which came 24 packs to a box and eight boxes to a case. This set features a mix of cards printed to standard amounts as well as various Short Prints and then even some variation short prints. Any type of short printed card was issued to a stated rate of one in two. We have delineated in our checklist what the various variations are. In addition, all cards from 398 through 475 are SP's.

	Nm-Mt	Ex-Mt
COMPLETE SET (495)	400.00	120.00
COMP.SET w/o SP's (385)	50.00	15.00
SP STATED ODDS 1:2		
1A Jim Thome Fielding	1.50	.45
1B Jim Thome Hitting SP	8.00	2.40
2 Nomar Garciaparra SP	10.00	3.00
3 Aramis Ramirez	.60	.18
4 Rafael Palmeiro SP	8.00	2.40
5 Danny Graves	.50	.15
6 Casey Blake	.50	.15
7 Juan Uribe	.50	.15
8A Dmitri Young New Logo	.60	.18
8B Dmitri Young Old Logo SP	5.00	1.50
9 Billy Wagner	.60	.18
10A Jason Giambi Swinging	.60	.18
10B Jason Giambi Btg Stance SP	5.00	1.50
11 Carlos Beltran	1.00	.30
12 Chad Hermansen	.50	.15
13 B.J. Upton	1.50	.45
14 Dustan Mohr	.50	.15
15 Endy Chavez	.50	.15
16 Cliff Floyd	.60	.18
17 Bernie Williams	1.00	.30
18 Eric Chavez	.60	.18
19 Chase Utley	.60	.18
20 Randy Johnson	1.50	.45
21 Vernon Wells	.60	.18
22 Juan Gonzalez	1.00	.30
23 Joe Kennedy	.50	.15
24 Bengie Molina	.50	.15
25 Carlos Lee	.60	.18
26 Horacio Ramirez	.50	.15
27 Anthony Acevedo RC	1.00	.30
28 Sammy Sosa SP	10.00	3.00
29 Jon Garland	.50	.15
30A Adam Dunn Fielding	1.00	.30
30B Adam Dunn Hitting SP	8.00	2.40
31 Aaron Rowand	.60	.18
32 Jody Gerut	.50	.15
33 Chin-Hui Tsao	.60	.18
34 Alex Sanchez	.50	.15
35 A.J. Burnett	.50	.15
36 Brad Ausmus	.50	.15
37 Blake Hawksworth RC	1.00	.30
38 Francisco Rodriguez	.60	.18
39 Alex Cintron	.50	.15
40A Chipper Jones Pointing	1.50	.45
40B Chipper Jones Fielding SP	8.00	2.40
41 Deivi Cruz	.50	.15
42 Bill Mueller	.60	.18
43 Joe Borowski	.50	.15
44 Jimmy Haynes	.50	.15
45 Mark Loretta	.60	.18
46 Jerome Williams	.60	.18
47 Gary Sheffield Yanks SP	8.00	2.40
48 Richard Hidalgo	.50	.15
49A Jason Kendall New Logo	.60	.18
49B Jason Kendall Old Logo SP	5.00	1.50
50 Ichiro Suzuki SP	10.00	3.00
51 Jim Edmonds	.60	.18
52 Frank Catalanotto	.50	.15
53 Jose Contreras	.60	.18
54 Mo Vaughn	.60	.18
55 Brendan Donnelly	.50	.15
56 Luis Gonzalez	.60	.18
57 Robert Fick	.50	.15
58 Laynce Nix	.60	.18
59 Johnny Damon	1.50	.45
60A Magglio Ordonez Running	.60	.18
60B Magglio Ordonez Hitting SP	5.00	1.50
61 Matt Clement	.50	.15
62 Ryan Ludwick	.50	.15
63 Luis Castillo	.50	.15
64 Dave Crouthers RC	1.00	.30
65 Dave Berg	.50	.15
66 Kyle Davies RC	1.00	.30
67 Tim Salmon	1.00	.30
68 Marcus Giles	.60	.18
69 Marty Cordova	.50	.15
70A Todd Helton White Jsy	1.00	.30
70B Todd Helton Purple Jsy SP	8.00	2.40
71 Jeff Kent	.60	.18
72 Michael Tucker	.50	.15
73 Cesar Izturis	.50	.15
74 Paul Quantrill	.50	.15
75 Conor Jackson RC	2.00	.60
76 Placido Polanco	.50	.15
77 Adam Eaton	.50	.15
78 Ramon Hernandez	.60	.18
79 Edgardo Alfonzo	.50	.15
80 Dioner Navarro RC	1.25	.35
81 Woody Williams	.50	.15
82 Rey Ordonez	.50	.15
83 Randy Winn	.50	.15
84 Casey Myers RC	1.00	.30
85A R.Choy Foo New Logo RC	1.00	.30
85B R.Choy Foo Old Logo SP	5.00	1.50
86 Ray Durham	.60	.18
87 Sean Burroughs	.60	.18
88 Tim Frend RC	1.00	.30
89 Shigetoshi Hasegawa	.60	.18
90 Jeffrey Allison RC	1.00	.30
91 Orlando Hudson	.50	.15
92 Matt Creighton SP RC	5.00	1.50
93 Tim Worrell	.50	.15
94 Kris Benson	.50	.15
95 Mike Lieberthal	.60	.18
96 David Wells	.60	.18
97 Jason Phillips	.50	.15
98 Bobby Cox MGR	.50	.15
99 Johan Santana	1.00	.30
100A Alex Rodriguez Hitting	2.50	.75
100B Alex Rodriguez Throwing SP	10.00	3.00
101 John Vander Wal	.50	.15
102 Orlando Cabrera	.60	.18
103 Hideo Nomo	1.50	.45
104 Todd Walker	.50	.15
105 Jason Johnson	.50	.15
106 Matt Mantei	.50	.15
107 Jarrod Washburn	.50	.15
108 Preston Wilson	.60	.18
109 Carl Pavano	.60	.18
110 Geoff Blum	.50	.15
111 Eric Gagne	1.50	.45
112 Geoff Jenkins	.60	.18
113 Joe Torre MGR	1.00	.30
114 Jon Knott RC	1.00	.30
115 Hank Blalock	.60	.18
116 John Olerud	.60	.18
117A Pat Burrell New Logo	.60	.18
117B Pat Burrell Old Logo SP	5.00	1.50
118 Aaron Boone	.60	.18
119 Zach Day	.50	.15
120A Frank Thomas New Logo	1.50	.45
120B Frank Thomas Old Logo SP	8.00	2.40
121 Kyle Farnsworth	.50	.15
122 Derek Lowe	.60	.18
123 Zach Miner SP RC	8.00	2.40
124 Matthew Moses SP RC	8.00	2.40
125 Jesse Roman RC	1.00	.30
126 Josh Phelps	.50	.15
127 Nic Ungs RC	1.00	.30
128 Dan Haren	.50	.15
129 Kirk Rueter	.50	.15
130 Jack McKeon MGR	.60	.18
131 Keith Foulke	.60	.18
132 Garrett Stephenson	.50	.15
133 Wes Helms	.50	.15
134 Raul Ibanez	.50	.15
135 Morgan Ensberg	.60	.18
136 Jay Payton	.60	.18
137 Billy Koch	.50	.15
138 Mark Grudzielanek	.50	.15
139 Rodrigo Lopez	.50	.15
140 Corey Patterson	.60	.18
141 Troy Percival	.60	.18
142 Shea Hillenbrand	.60	.18
143 Brad Fullmer	.60	.18
144 Ricky Nolasco RC	1.00	.30
145 Mark Teixeira	.60	.18
146 Tydus Meadows RC	1.00	.30
147 Toby Hall	.50	.15
148 Orlando Palmeiro	.50	.15
149 Khalid Ballouli RC	1.00	.30
150 Grady Little MGR	.50	.15
151 David Eckstein	.50	.15
152 Kenny Perez RC	1.00	.30
153 Ben Grieve	.50	.15
154 Ismael Valdes	.50	.15
155 Bret Boone	.60	.18
156 Jesse Foppert	.50	.15
157 Vicente Padilla	.50	.15
158 Bobby Abreu	.60	.18
159 Scott Hatteberg	.50	.15
160 Carlos Quentin RC	2.00	.60
161 Anthony Lerew RC	1.00	.30
162 Lance Carter	.50	.15
163 Robb Nen	.60	.18
164 Zach Duke SP RC	8.00	2.40
165 Xavier Nady	.50	.15
166 Kip Wells	.50	.15
167 Kevin Millwood	.60	.18
168 Jon Lieber	.50	.15
169 Jose Reyes	.60	.18
170 Eric Byrnes	.50	.15
171 Paul Konerko	.60	.18
172 Chris Lubanski	.60	.18
173 Jae Weong Seo	.50	.15
174 Corey Koskie	.60	.18
175 Tim Stauffer RC	1.00	.30
176 John Lackey	.50	.15
177 Danny Bautista	.50	.15
178 Shane Reynolds	.50	.15
179 Jorge Julio	.50	.15
180A Manny Ramirez New Logo	1.00	.30
180B Manny Ramirez Old Logo SP	8.00	2.40
181 Alex Gonzalez	.50	.15
182A Moises Alou New Logo	.60	.18
182B Moises Alou Old Logo SP	5.00	1.50
183 Mark Buehrle	.60	.18
184 Carlos Guillen	.60	.18
185 Nate Cornejo	.50	.15
186 Billy Traber	.50	.15
187 Jason Jennings	.50	.15
188 Eric Munson	.50	.15
189 Braden Looper	.50	.15
190 Juan Encarnacion	.50	.15
191 Dusty Baker MGR	.60	.18
192 Travis Lee	.50	.15
193 Miguel Cairo	.50	.15
194 Rich Aurilia SP	5.00	1.50
195 Tom Gordon	.50	.15
196 Freddy Garcia	.60	.18
197 Brian Lawrence	.50	.15
198 Jorge Posada SP	8.00	2.40
199 Javier Vazquez	.60	.18
200A Albert Pujols New Logo	3.00	.90
200B Albert Pujols Old Logo SP	12.00	3.60
201 Victor Zambrano	.50	.15
202 Eli Marrero	.50	.15
203 Joel Pineiro	.60	.18
204 Rondell White	.60	.18
205 Craig Ansman RC	1.00	.30
206 Michael Young	.60	.18
207 Carlos Baerga	.50	.15
208 Andruw Jones	.60	.18
209 Jerry Hairston Jr.	.50	.15
210 Shawn Green SP	5.00	1.50
211 Ron Gardenhire MGR	.50	.15
212 Darin Erstad	.60	.18
213A Brandon Webb Glove Chest	.60	.18
213B Brandon Webb Glove Out SP	5.00	1.50
214 Greg Maddux	2.50	.75
215 Reed Johnson	.50	.15
216 John Thomson	.50	.15
217 Tino Martinez	1.00	.30
218 Mike Cameron	.60	.18
219 Edgar Martinez	1.00	.30
220 Eric Young	.50	.15
221 Reggie Sanders	.50	.15
222 Randy Wolf	.50	.15
223 Erubiel Durazo	.50	.15
224 Mike Mussina	1.00	.30
225 Tom Glavine	1.00	.30
226 Troy Glaus	.60	.18
227 Oscar Villarreal	.50	.15
228 David Segui	.50	.15
229 Jeff Suppan	.50	.15
230 Kenny Lofton	.60	.18
231 Esteban Loaiza	.50	.15
232 Felipe Lopez	.50	.15
233 Matt Lawton	.50	.15
234 Mark Bellhorn	.60	.18
235 Wil Ledezma	.50	.15
236 Todd Hollandsworth	.50	.15
237 Octavio Dotel	.50	.15
238 Darren Dreifort	.50	.15
239 Paul Lo Duca	.60	.18
240 Richie Sexson	.60	.18
241 Doug Mientkiewicz	.60	.18
242 Luis Rivas	.50	.15
243 Claudio Vargas	.50	.15
244 Mark Ellis	.50	.15
245 Brett Myers	.50	.15
246 Jake Peavy	.60	.18
247 Marquis Grissom	.60	.18
248 Armando Benitez	.60	.18
249 Ryan Franklin	.50	.15
250A Alfonso Soriano Throwing	1.00	.30
250B Alfonso Soriano Fielding SP	8.00	2.40
251 Tim Hudson	.60	.18
252 Shannon Stewart	.60	.18
253 A.J. Pierzynski	.60	.18
254 Runelvys Hernandez	.50	.15
255 Roy Oswalt	.60	.18
256 Shawn Chacon	.50	.15
257 Tony Graffanino	.50	.15
258 Tim Wakefield	.60	.18
259 Damian Miller	.50	.15
260 Joe Crede	.50	.15
261 Jason LaRue	.50	.15
262 Jose Jimenez	.50	.15
263 Juan Pierre	.60	.18
264 Wade Miller	.50	.15
265 Odalis Perez	.50	.15
266 Eddie Guardado	.50	.15
267 Rocky Biddle	.50	.15
268 Jeff Nelson	.50	.15
269 Terrence Long	.50	.15
270 Ramon Ortiz	.50	.15
271 Raul Mondesi	.60	.18
272 Ugueth Urbina	.50	.15
273 Jeromy Burnitz	.60	.18
274 Brad Radke	.60	.18
275 Jose Vidro	.50	.15
276 Bobby Jenks	.50	.15
277 Ty Wigginton	.50	.15
278 Jose Guillen	.50	.15
279 Delmon Young	1.00	.30
280 Brian Giles	.60	.18
281 Jason Schmidt	.60	.18
282 Nick Markakis	.60	.18
283 Felipe Alou MGR	.60	.18
284 Carl Crawford	.60	.18
285 Neifi Perez	.50	.15
286 Miguel Tejada	.60	.18
287 Victor Martinez	.60	.18
288 Adam Kennedy	.50	.15
289 Kerry Ligtenberg	.50	.15
290 Scott Williamson	.50	.15
291 Tony Womack	.50	.15
292 Travis Hafner	.60	.18
293 Bobby Crosby	1.00	.30
294 Chad Billingsley	.60	.18
295 Russ Ortiz	.60	.18
296 John Burkett	.50	.15
297 Carlos Zambrano	.60	.18
298 Randall Simon	.50	.15
299 Juan Castro	.50	.15
300 Mike Lowell	.60	.18
301 Fred McGriff	1.00	.30
302 Glendon Rusch	.50	.15
303 Sung Jung RC	1.00	.30
304 Rocco Baldelli	.60	.18
305 Fernando Vina	.50	.15
306 Gil Meche	.50	.15
307 Jose Cruz Jr.	.50	.15
308 Bernie Castro	.50	.15
309 Scott Spiezio	.50	.15
310 Paul Byrd	.50	.15
311A Jay Gibbons New Logo	.50	.15
311B Jay Gibbons Old Logo SP	5.00	1.50
312 Trot Nixon	.60	.18
313 Chris O'Riordan RC	1.00	.30
314 Julio Lugo	.50	.15
315 Ben Davis	.50	.15
316 Mike Williams	.50	.15
317 Trevor Hoffman	.60	.18
318 Andy Pettitte	1.00	.30
319 Orlando Hernandez	.50	.15
320 Juan Rivera	.50	.15
321 Elizardo Ramirez	.50	.15
322 Junior Spivey	.50	.15
323 Tony Batista	.60	.18
324 Mike Remlinger	.50	.15
325 Alex Gonzalez	.50	.15
326 Aaron Hill	.50	.15
327 Steve Finley	.60	.18
328 Vinny Castilla	.60	.18
329 Eric Duncan	.60	.18
330 Mike Gosling RC	1.00	.30
331 Eric Hinske	.50	.15
332 Scott Rolen	1.50	.45
333 Benito Santiago	.60	.18
334 Jimmy Gobble	.50	.15
335 Bobby Higginson	.60	.18
336 Kelvim Escobar	.50	.15
337 Mike DeJean	.50	.15
338 Sidney Ponson	.50	.15
339 Todd Self RC	1.00	.30
340 Jeff Cirillo	.50	.15
341 Jimmy Rollins	.60	.18
342A Barry Zito White Jsy	.60	.18
342B Barry Zito Green Jsy SP	5.00	1.50
343 Felix Pie	.60	.18
344 Matt Morris	.60	.18
345 Kazuhiro Sasaki	.60	.18
346 Jack Wilson	.60	.18
347 Nick Johnson	.50	.15
348 Wil Cordero	.50	.15
349 Ryan Madson	.50	.15
350 Torii Hunter	.60	.18
351 Andy Ashby	.50	.15
352 Aubrey Huff	.60	.18
353 Brad Lidge	.60	.18
354 Derrek Lee	.60	.18
355 Yadier Molina RC	1.25	.35
356 Paul Wilson	.50	.15
357 Omar Vizquel	1.00	.30
358 Rene Reyes	.50	.15
359 Marlon Anderson	.50	.15
360 Bobby Kielty	.50	.15
361A Ryan Wagner New Logo	.50	.15
361B Ryan Wagner Old Logo SP	5.00	1.50
362 Justin Morneau	.60	.18
363 Shane Spencer	.50	.15
364 David Bell	.50	.15
365 Matt Stairs	.50	.15
366 Joe Borchard	.50	.15
367 Mark Redman	.50	.15
368 Dave Roberts	.50	.15
369 Desi Relaford	.50	.15
370 Rich Harden	.60	.18
371 Fernando Tatis	.50	.15
372 Eric Karros	.60	.18
373 Eric Milton	.60	.18
374 Mike Sweeney	.60	.18
375 Brian Daubach	.50	.15
376 Brian Snyder	.50	.15
377 Chris Reitsma	.50	.15
378 Kyle Lohse	.50	.15
379 Livan Hernandez	.60	.18
380 Robin Ventura	.60	.18
381 Jacque Jones	.60	.18
382 Danny Kolb	.50	.15
383 Casey Kotchman	.60	.18
384 Cristian Guzman	.50	.15
385 Josh Beckett	.60	.18
386 Khalil Greene	1.50	.45
387 Greg Myers	.50	.15
388 Francisco Cordero	.50	.15
389 Donald Levinski RC	1.00	.30
390 Roy Halladay	.60	.18
391 J.D. Drew	.60	.18
392 Jamie Moyer	.60	.18
393 Ken Macha MGR	.50	.15
394 Jeff Davanon	.50	.15
395 Matt Kata	.50	.15
396 Jack Cust	.50	.15
397 Mike Timlin	.50	.15
398 Zack Greinke SP	5.00	1.50
399 Byung-Hyun Kim SP	5.00	1.50
400 Kazuhisa Ishii SP	5.00	1.50
401 Brayan Pena SP RC	5.00	1.50
402 Garret Anderson SP	5.00	1.50
403 Kyle Sleeth SP RC	8.00	2.40
404 Javy Lopez SP	5.00	1.50
405 Damian Moss SP	5.00	1.50
406 David Ortiz SP	8.00	2.40
407 Pedro Martinez SP	8.00	2.40

408 Hee Seop Choi SP 5.00 1.50
409 Carl Everett SP 5.00 1.50
410 Dontrelle Willis SP 5.00 1.50
411 Ryan Harvey SP 5.00 1.50
412 Russell Branyan SP 5.00 1.50
413 Milton Bradley SP 5.00 1.50
414 Marcus McBeth SP RC 5.00 1.50
415 Carlos Pena SP 5.00 1.50
416 Ivan Rodriguez SP 8.00 2.40
417 Craig Biggio SP 8.00 2.40
418 Angel Berroa SP 5.00 1.50
419 Brian Jordan SP 5.00 1.50
420 Scott Podsednik SP 5.00 1.50
421 Omar Falcon SP RC 5.00 1.50
422 Joe Mays SP 5.00 1.50
423 Brad Wilkerson SP 5.00 1.50
424 Al Leiter SP 5.00 1.50
425 Derek Jeter SP 12.00 3.60
426 Mark Mulder SP 5.00 1.50
427 Marlon Byrd SP 5.00 1.50
428 David Murphy SP RC 8.00 2.40
429 Phil Nevin SP 5.00 1.50
430 J.T. Snow SP 5.00 1.50
431 Brad Sullivan SP RC 8.00 2.40
432 Bo Hart SP 5.00 1.50
433 Josh Labandeira SP RC 5.00 1.50
434 Chan Ho Park SP 5.00 1.50
435 Carlos Delgado SP 5.00 1.50
436 Curt Schilling Sox SP 8.00 2.40
437 John Smoltz SP 8.00 2.40
438 Luis Matos SP 5.00 1.50
439 Mark Prior SP 8.00 2.40
440 Roberto Alomar SP 8.00 2.40
441 Coco Crisp SP 5.00 1.50
442 Austin Kearns SP 5.00 1.50
443 Larry Walker SP 8.00 2.40
444 Neal Cotts SP 5.00 1.50
445 Jeff Bagwell SP 8.00 2.40
446 Adrian Beltre SP 8.00 2.40
447 Grady Sizemore SP 5.00 1.50
448 Keith Ginter SP 5.00 1.50
449 Vladimir Guerrero SP 8.00 2.40
450 Lyle Overbay SP 5.00 1.50
451 Rafael Furcal SP 5.00 1.50
452 Melvin Mora SP 5.00 1.50
453 Kerry Wood SP 8.00 2.40
454 Jose Valentin SP 5.00 1.50
455 Ken Griffey Jr. SP 10.00 3.00
456 Brandon Phillips SP 5.00 1.50
457 Miguel Cabrera SP 8.00 2.40
458 Edwin Jackson SP 5.00 1.50
459 Eric Owens SP 5.00 1.50
460 Miguel Batista SP 5.00 1.50
461 Mike Hampton SP 5.00 1.50
462 Kevin Millar SP 5.00 1.50
463 Bartolo Colon SP 5.00 1.50
464 Sean Casey SP 5.00 1.50
465 C.C. Sabathia SP 5.00 1.50
466 Rickie Weeks SP 5.00 1.50
467 Brad Penny SP 5.00 1.50
468 Mike MacDougal SP 5.00 1.50
469 Kevin Brown SP 5.00 1.50
470 Lance Berkman SP 5.00 1.50
471 Ben Sheets SP 5.00 1.50
472 Mariano Rivera SP 8.00 2.40
473 Mike Piazza SP 10.00 3.00
474 Ryan Klesko SP 5.00 1.50
475 Edgar Renteria SP 5.00 1.50

2004 Topps Heritage Chrome

Nm-Mt Ex-Mt
STATED ODDS 1:7
STATED PRINT RUN 1955 SERIAL #'d SETS
1 Sammy Sosa 10.00 3.00
2 Nomar Garciaparra 10.00 3.00
3 Ichiro Suzuki 10.00 3.00
4 Rafael Palmeiro 6.00 1.80
5 Carlos Delgado 5.00 1.50
6 Troy Glaus 5.00 1.50
7 Jay Gibbons 5.00 1.50
8 Frank Thomas 6.00 1.80
9 Pat Burrell 5.00 1.50
10 Albert Pujols 12.00 3.60
11 Brandon Webb 5.00 1.50
12 Chipper Jones 6.00 1.80
13 Magglio Ordonez 5.00 1.50
14 Adam Dunn 6.00 1.80
15 Todd Helton 6.00 1.80
16 Jason Giambi 5.00 1.50
17 Alfonso Soriano 6.00 1.80
18 Barry Zito 5.00 1.50
19 Jim Thome 6.00 1.80
20 Alex Rodriguez 10.00 3.00
21 Hee Seop Choi 5.00 1.50
22 Pedro Martinez 6.00 1.80
23 Kerry Wood 6.00 1.80
24 Bartolo Colon 5.00 1.50
25 Austin Kearns 5.00 1.50
26 Ken Griffey Jr. 10.00 3.00
27 Coco Crisp 5.00 1.50
28 Larry Walker 6.00 1.80
29 Ivan Rodriguez 6.00 1.80
30 Dontrelle Willis 5.00 1.50
31 Miguel Cabrera 6.00 1.80
32 Jeff Bagwell 6.00 1.80
33 Lance Berkman 5.00 1.50
34 Shawn Green 5.00 1.50
35 Kevin Brown 5.00 1.50
36 Vladimir Guerrero 6.00 1.80
37 Mike Piazza 10.00 3.00
38 Derek Jeter 12.00 3.60
39 John Smoltz 6.00 1.80
40 Mark Prior 6.00 1.80
41 Gary Sheffield Yanks 5.00 1.50
42 Curt Schilling Sox 6.00 1.80
43 Randy Johnson 6.00 1.80
44 Luis Gonzalez 5.00 1.50
45 Andruw Jones 5.00 1.50
46 Greg Maddux 10.00 3.00
47 Tony Batista 5.00 1.50
48 Esteban Loaiza 5.00 1.50
49 Chin-Hui Tsao 5.00 1.50
50 Mike Lowell 5.00 1.50
51 Jeff Kent 5.00 1.50
52 Richie Sexson 5.00 1.50
53 Torii Hunter 5.00 1.50
54 Jose Vidro 5.00 1.50
55 Jose Reyes 5.00 1.50
56 Jimmy Rollins 5.00 1.50
57 Bret Boone 5.00 1.50
58 Rocco Baldelli 5.00 1.50
59 Hank Blalock 5.00 1.50
60 Rickie Weeks 5.00 1.50
61 Rodney Choy Foo 5.00 1.50
62 Zach Miner 5.00 1.50
63 Brayan Pena 5.00 1.50
64 David Murphy 5.00 1.50
65 Matt Creighton 5.00 1.50
66 Kyle Sleeth 5.00 1.50
67 Matthew Moses 5.00 1.50
68 Josh Labandeira 5.00 1.50
69 Grady Sizemore 5.00 1.50
70 Edwin Jackson 5.00 1.50
71 Marcus McBeth 5.00 1.50
72 Brad Sullivan 5.00 1.50
73 Zach Duke 6.00 1.80
74 Omar Falcon 5.00 1.50
75 Conor Jackson 8.00 2.40
76 Carlos Quentin 8.00 2.40
77 Craig Ansman 5.00 1.50
78 Mike Gosling 5.00 1.50
79 Kyle Davies 5.00 1.50
80 Anthony Lerew 5.00 1.50
81 Sung Jung 5.00 1.50
82 Dave Crouthers 5.00 1.50
83 Kenny Perez 5.00 1.50
84 Jeffrey Allison 5.00 1.50
85 Nic Ungs 5.00 1.50
86 Donald Levinski 5.00 1.50
87 Anthony Acevedo 5.00 1.50
88 Todd Self 5.00 1.50
89 Tim Frend 5.00 1.50
90 Tydus Meadows 5.00 1.50
91 Khalid Ballouli 5.00 1.50
92 Dioner Navarro 5.00 1.50
93 Casey Myers 5.00 1.50
94 Jon Knott 5.00 1.50
95 Tim Stauffer 5.00 1.50
96 Ricky Nolasco 5.00 1.50
97 Blake Hawksworth 5.00 1.50
98 Jesse Roman 5.00 1.50
99 Yadier Molina 5.00 1.50
100 Chris O'Riordan 5.00 1.50
101 Cliff Floyd 5.00 1.50
102 Nick Johnson 5.00 1.50
103 Edgar Martinez 6.00 1.80
104 Brett Myers 5.00 1.50
105 Francisco Rodriguez 5.00 1.50
106 Scott Rolen 6.00 1.80
107 Mark Teixeira 5.00 1.50
108 Miguel Tejada 5.00 1.50
109 Vernon Wells 5.00 1.50
110 Jerome Williams 5.00 1.50

2004 Topps Heritage Chrome Black Refractors

Nm-Mt Ex-Mt
*BLACK REF: 3X TO 6X CHROME
*BLACK REF: 4X TO 8X CHROME RC YR
STATED ODDS 1:251
STATED PRINT RUN 55 SERIAL #'d SETS

2004 Topps Heritage Chrome Refractors

Nm-Mt Ex-Mt
*REFRACTOR: .6X TO 1.5X CHROME
*REFRACTOR: .75X TO 2X CHROME RC YR
STATED ODDS 1:25
STATED PRINT RUN 555 SERIAL #'d SETS

2004 Topps Heritage Clubhouse Collection Relics

Nm-Mt Ex-Mt
GROUP A ODDS 1:3037
GROUP B ODDS 1:4142
GROUP C ODDS 1:138
GROUP D ODDS 1:92
GROUP A STATED PRINT RUN 100 SETS
GROUP A PRINT RUN PROVIDED BY TOPPS
GROUP A ARE NOT SERIAL-NUMBERED
AD Adam Dunn Jsy D 10.00 3.00
AJ Andruw Jones Jsy C 8.00 2.40
AK Al Kaline Bat A 50.00 15.00
AP Albert Pujols Uni C 15.00 4.50
AR Alex Rodriguez Jsy C 10.00 3.00
AS Alfonso Soriano Uni D 10.00 3.00
BA Bobby Abreu Jsy D 8.00 2.40
BB Bret Boone Jsy D 8.00 2.40
BM Brett Myers Jsy D 8.00 2.40
BZ Barry Zito Uni C 8.00 2.40
CJ Chipper Jones Jsy D 10.00 3.00
CS C.C. Sabathia Jsy D 8.00 2.40
DS Duke Snider Bat A 40.00 12.00
EC Eric Chavez Uni D 8.00 2.40
EG Eric Gagne Uni D 8.00 2.40
FM Fred McGriff Bat C 10.00 3.00
GM Greg Maddux Jsy C 15.00 4.50
GS Gary Sheffield Uni D 8.00 2.40
HB Hank Blalock Jsy D 8.00 2.40
HK Harmon Killebrew Jsy C 25.00 7.50
IR Ivan Rodriguez Bat C 10.00 3.00
JD Johnny Damon Uni D 10.00 3.00
JG Jason Giambi Uni D 8.00 2.40
JL Javy Lopez Jsy D 8.00 2.40
JR Jimmy Rollins Jsy D 8.00 2.40
JRE Jose Reyes Jsy D 8.00 2.40
JS John Smoltz Jsy C 10.00 3.00
JT Jim Thome Bat D 10.00 3.00
KB Kevin Brown Uni D 8.00 2.40
KI Kazuhisa Ishii Uni D 8.00 2.40
KW Kerry Wood Jsy D 10.00 3.00
LB Lance Berkman Jsy C 8.00 2.40
LG Luis Gonzalez Jsy D 8.00 2.40
MG Marcus Giles Jsy C 8.00 2.40
MM Mark Mulder Uni D 8.00 2.40
MR Manny Ramirez Jsy C 10.00 3.00
MS Mike Sweeney Jsy D 8.00 2.40
MT Miguel Tejada Uni D 8.00 2.40
MTB Miguel Tejada Bat C 8.00 2.40
MTE Mark Teixeira Jsy D 8.00 2.40
NG Nomar Garciaparra Uni C 15.00 4.50
PL Paul Lo Duca Uni C 8.00 2.40
PM Pedro Martinez Jsy D 10.00 3.00
RB Rocco Baldelli Jsy D 8.00 2.40
RC Roger Clemens Uni D 15.00 4.50
RF Rafael Furcal Jsy D 8.00 2.40
RJ Randy Johnson Jsy C 10.00 3.00
SG Shawn Green Uni C 8.00 2.40
SM Stan Musial Bat A 60.00 18.00
SR Scott Rolen Uni B 10.00 3.00
SRB Scott Rolen Bat C 10.00 3.00
SS Sammy Sosa Jsy C 15.00 4.50
TG Troy Glaus Uni C 8.00 2.40
TH Tim Hudson Uni D 8.00 2.40
THU Torii Hunter Bat C 8.00 2.40
VW Vernon Wells Jsy C 8.00 2.40
WM Willie Mays Uni A 100.00 30.00
YB Yogi Berra Jsy A 50.00 15.00

2004 Topps Heritage Clubhouse Collection Autograph Relics

Nm-Mt Ex-Mt
STATED ODDS 1:15,186
STATED PRINT RUN 25 SERIAL #'d SETS
NO PRICING DUE TO SCARCITY
AK Al Kaline Bat
DS Duke Snider Bat
EB Ernie Banks Uni
WM Willie Mays Uni

2004 Topps Heritage Clubhouse Collection Dual Relics

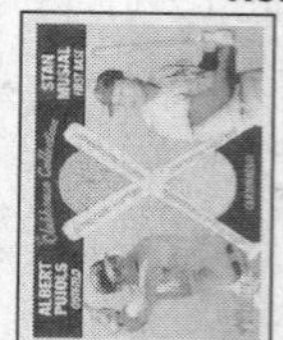

Nm-Mt Ex-Mt
STATED ODDS 1:9244
STATED PRINT RUN 55 SERIAL #'d SETS
BC Yogi Berra Uni 150.00 45.00
Roger Clemens Uni
GS Shawn Green Jsy 150.00 45.00
Duke Snider Uni
MP Albert Pujols Jsy 250.00 75.00
Stan Musial Uni

2004 Topps Heritage Doubleheader

Nm-Mt Ex-Mt
ONE PER SEALED HOBBY BOX
VINTAGE D-HEADERS RANDOMLY SEEDED
1-2 Alex Rodriguez 8.00 2.40
Nomar Garciaparra
3-4 Ichiro Suzuki 10.00 3.00
Albert Pujols
5-6 Sammy Sosa 10.00 3.00
Derek Jeter
7-8 Jim Thome 8.00 2.40
Adam Dunn
9-10 Jason Giambi 8.00 2.40
Ivan Rodriguez
11-12 Todd Helton 8.00 2.40
Luis Gonzalez
13-14 Jeff Bagwell 8.00 2.40
Lance Berkman
15-16 Alfonso Soriano 8.00 2.40
Dontrelle Willis
17-18 Mark Prior 8.00 2.40
Vladimir Guerrero
19-20 Mike Piazza 10.00 3.00
Roger Clemens
21-22 Randy Johnson 8.00 2.40
Curt Schilling
23-24 Gary Sheffield 8.00 2.40
Pedro Martinez
25-26 Carlos Delgado 5.00 1.50
Jimmy Rollins
27-28 Andruw Jones 8.00 2.40
Chipper Jones
29-30 Rocco Baldelli 5.00 1.50
Hank Blalock
NNO Vintage Buyback

2004 Topps Heritage Flashbacks

Nm-Mt Ex-Mt
COMPLETE SET (10) 15.00 4.50
STATED ODDS 1:12
F1 Duke Snider 3.00 .90
F2 Johnny Podres 2.00 .60
F3 Don Newcombe 2.00 .60
F4 Al Kaline 3.00 .90
F5 Willie Mays 5.00 1.50
F6 Stan Musial 4.00 1.20
F7 Harmon Killebrew 3.00 .90
F8 Herb Score 2.00 .60
F9 Whitey Ford 3.00 .90
F10 Robin Roberts 2.00 .60

2004 Topps Heritage Flashbacks Autographs

Nm-Mt Ex-Mt
STATED ODDS 1:30,373
STATED PRINT RUN 25 SERIAL #'d SETS
NO PRICING DUE TO SCARCITY
AK Al Kaline
NPS Don Newcombe
Johnny Podres
Duke Snider

2004 Topps Heritage Grandstand Glory Stadium Seat Relics

Nm-Mt Ex-Mt
GROUP A ODDS 1:27,731
GROUP A ODDS 1:606
GROUP A STATED PRINT RUN 55 CARDS
GROUP A PRINT RUN PROVIDED BY TOPPS
GROUP A IS NOT SERIAL-NUMBERED
AK Al Kaline B 25.00 7.50
HK Harmon Killebrew B 25.00 7.50
SM Stan Musial B 40.00 12.00
WM Willie Mays A 150.00 45.00
WS Warren Spahn B 20.00 6.00
YB Yogi Berra B 25.00 7.50

2004 Topps Heritage New Age Performers

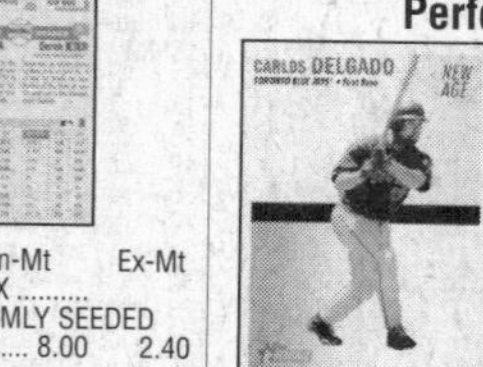

Nm-Mt Ex-Mt
COMPLETE SET (15) 30.00 9.00
STATED ODDS 1:15
NA1 Jason Giambi 2.00 .60
NA2 Ichiro Suzuki 4.00 1.20
NA3 Alex Rodriguez 4.00 1.20
NA4 Alfonso Soriano 2.00 .60
NA5 Albert Pujols 5.00 1.50
NA6 Nomar Garciaparra 4.00 1.20
NA7 Mark Prior 2.50 .75
NA8 Derek Jeter 5.00 1.50
NA9 Sammy Sosa 4.00 1.20
NA10 Carlos Delgado 2.00 .60
NA11 Jim Thome 2.50 .75
NA12 Todd Helton 2.00 .60
NA13 Gary Sheffield 2.00 .60
NA14 Vladimir Guerrero 2.50 .75
NA15 Josh Beckett 2.00 .60

2004 Topps Heritage Real One Autographs

These autograph cards feature a mix of players who are active today; players who had cards in the 1955 Topps set and Stan Musial signing cards as if he were in the 1955 set. Scott Rolen did not return his cards in time for pack out and those exchange cards could be redeemed until February 28, 2006.

Nm-Mt Ex-Mt
STATED ODDS 1:230
STATED PRINT RUN 200 SETS
PRINT RUN INFO PROVIDED BY TOPPS
BASIC AUTOS ARE NOT SERIAL-NUMBERED
*RED INK: .75X TO 1.5X RETIRED
*RED INK MAYS: 1.25X TO 2X BASIC MAYS
*RED INK: .75X TO 1.5X ACTIVE
RED INK ODDS 1:835
RED INK PRINT RUN 55 #'d SETS
RED INK ALSO CALLED SPECIAL EDITION
EXCHANGE DEADLINE 02/28/06
AH Aubrey Huff 40.00 12.00
AK Al Kaline 100.00 30.00
BB Bob Borkowski 50.00 15.00
BC Billy Consolo 60.00 18.00
BG Bill Glynn 50.00 15.00
BK Bob Kline 50.00 15.00
BM Bob Milliken 50.00 15.00
BW Bill Wilson 50.00 15.00
CF Cliff Floyd 40.00 12.00
DN Don Newcombe 60.00 18.00
DP Duane Pillette 50.00 15.00
DS Duke Snider 100.00 30.00
DW Dontrelle Willis 40.00 12.00
EB Ernie Banks 120.00 36.00
FS Frank Smith 50.00 15.00
GA Gair Allie 50.00 15.00
HE Harry Elliott 50.00 15.00
HK Harmon Killebrew 100.00 30.00
HP Harry Perkowski 50.00 15.00
HV Corky Valentine 50.00 15.00
JG Johnny Gray 50.00 15.00
JP Jim Pearce 50.00 15.00
JPO Johnny Podres 60.00 18.00
LL Lou Limmer 60.00 18.00
ML Mike Lowell 40.00 12.00
MO Magglio Ordonez 40.00 12.00
SK Steve Kraly 60.00 18.00
SM Stan Musial 120.00 36.00
SR Scott Rolen EXCH 60.00 18.00
TK Thornton Kipper 50.00 15.00
TW Tom Wright 50.00 15.00
VT Jake Thies 50.00 15.00
WM Willie Mays 200.00 60.00
YB Yogi Berra 100.00 30.00

2004 Topps Heritage Then and Now

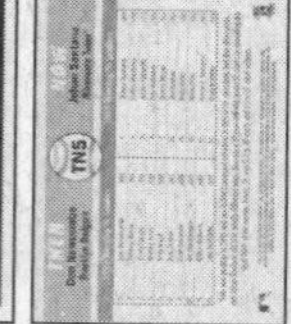

Nm-Mt Ex-Mt
COMPLETE SET (6) 10.00 3.00
STATED ODDS 1:15
TN1 Willie Mays 5.00 1.50
Jim Thome
TN2 Al Kaline 5.00 1.50
Albert Pujols
TN3 Duke Snider 3.00 .90
Carlos Delgado
TN4 Robin Roberts 2.00 .60
Roy Halladay
TN5 Don Newcombe 3.00 .90
Johan Santana
TN6 Herb Score 3.00 .90
Kerry Wood

1998 Topps Opening Day

This 165-card set is a parallel version of basic 1998 Topps cards and features 110 cards from Series 1 and 55 cards from Series 2. Cards were issued in special retail seven-card "Opening Day" packs carrying an SRP of $0.99. The cards are an exact parallel of the 1998 Topps base cards except, of course, for the bold Opening Day foil logo on front and the different numbering on back.

Nm-Mt Ex-Mt
COMPLETE SET (165) 50.00 15.00
*OPEN.DAY: .75X TO 2X BASIC TOPPS
ISSUED IN OPENING DAY PACKS

1999 Topps Opening Day

This 165-card set is a parallel version of basic 1999 Topps cards. Cards were issued in special retail seven-card "Opening Day" packs carrying an SRP of $0.99. The cards are an exact parallel of the 1999 Topps base cards except, of course, for the bold Opening Day foil logo on front and the different numbering on back. A Hank Aaron autograph card was inserted one every 29,462 packs.

Nm-Mt Ex-Mt
COMPLETE SET (165) 40.00 12.00
*OPEN.DAY: .75X TO 2X BASIC TOPPS
ISSUED IN OPENING DAY PACKS
AARON AUTO STATED ODDS 1:29,642
1 Hank Aaron 2.50 .75
NNO Hank Aaron AU 200.00 60.00

2000 Topps Opening Day

The Topps Opening Day set was released in March, 2000 as a retail only 165-card set that eatured 153 player cards, 10 Memorable Moments, 1 Hank Aaron 1954 reprint, and 1 checklist. Each pack contained seven cards and carried a suggested retail price of .99.

	Nm-Mt	Ex-Mt
COMPLETE SET (165)	40.00	12.00
*OPEN.DAY: .75X TO 2X BASIC TOPPS		
ISSUED IN OPENING DAY PACKS		
JER 110 AARON '54 REPRINT #'d 128		
NO MM VARIATIONS IN OPENING DAY		

2000 Topps Opening Day Autographs

Randomly inserted in packs, this insert set features autographs of five major league players. There were three levels of autographs. Level A were inserted into packs at one in 4207, Level B were inserted at one in 48074, Level C were inserted at one in 6280. Card backs carry an "ODA" prefix.

	Nm-Mt	Ex-Mt
ODA1 Edgardo Alfonzo A	25.00	7.50
ODA2 Wade Boggs A	80.00	24.00
ODA3 Robin Ventura A	40.00	12.00
ODA4 Josh Hamilton B	25.00	7.50
ODA5 Vernon Wells C	40.00	12.00

2001 Topps Opening Day

The 2001 Topps Opening Day product packed out in early March, 2001 and offers a 165-card base set. The base set features 150 Veteran players (1-150), four Prospects (151-154), 10 Golden Moments cards (155-164), and one checklist card (165). Each pack contained seven cards, and carries a suggested retail price of 1.99.

	Nm-Mt	Ex-Mt
COMPLETE SET (165)	40.00	12.00
*OPEN.DAY: .75X TO 2X BASIC TOPPS		
ISSUED IN OPENING DAY PACKS		

2001 Topps Opening Day Autographs

Randomly inserted into packs, this 4-card insert set features authentic autographs from four of the Major League's top players. The set is broken down into four groups: Group A is Chipper Jones (1:31,680), Group B is Todd Helton (1:15,020), Group C is Magglio Ordonez (1:10,004), and Group D is Corey Patterson (1:5,940). Card backs carry an "ODA" prefix followed by the player's initials.

	Nm-Mt	Ex-Mt
ODA-CJ Chipper Jones A	120.00	36.00
ODA-CP Corey Patterson D	30.00	9.00
ODA-MO Magglio Ordonez C	30.00	9.00
ODA-TH Todd Helton B	50.00	15.00

2002 Topps Opening Day

Released in early 2002, this 165 card set, which was issued in seven-card packs is a partial parallel of the 2002 Topps set. These cards all have an opening day logo on the front. The Barry Bonds card issued at card numbered 73 only featured the 73 home run logo. Unlike the regular set, this was the only version of that card issued.

	Nm-Mt	Ex-Mt
COMPLETE SET (165)	40.00	12.00
*OPEN.DAY: .75X TO X2 BASIC TOPPS		
ISSUED IN OPENING DAY PACKS		

2002 Topps Opening Day Autographs

Randomly inserted into packs, these three cards feature autographs of players in the Opening Day set. These cards were all inserted at differening odds and we have notated that information next to the player's name.

	Nm-Mt	Ex-Mt
GROUP A STATED ODDS 1:6069		
GROUP B STATED ODDS 1:3036		
GROUP C STATED ODDS 1:2014		
NO PRICING DUE TO SCARCITY		
ODA-BS Ben Sheets B		
ODA-GJ Geoff Jenkins A		
ODA-NJ Nick Johnson C		

2003 Topps Opening Day

This 165-card set was issued in February, 2003. These cards were issued in six card packs which came 22 packs to a box and 20 boxes to a case. These cards can be notated by the special Topps Opening Day logo printed on the front.

	Nm-Mt	Ex-Mt
COMPLETE SET (165)	40.00	12.00
*OPEN.DAY: .75X TO 2X BASIC TOPPS		
ISSUED IN OPENING DAY PACKS		

2003 Topps Opening Day Stickers

Issued one per pack, these 72 cards partially parallel the Opening Day set. Each of the fronts is designed exactly as the basic 2003 Topps card.

	Nm-Mt	Ex-Mt
*OD STICKERS: 1.5X TO 4X BASIC TOPPS 2.00 .60		
ONE PER PACK		

2003 Topps Opening Day Autographs

Inserted at different odds depending on which group the players were assigned to, these cards feature authentic autographs of the featured players.

	Nm-Mt	Ex-Mt
GROUP A ODDS 1:10,623		
GROUP B ODDS 1:3539		
GROUP C ODDS 1:2654		
JD Johnny Damon B	40.00	12.00
LB Lance Berkman A	40.00	12.00
RF Rafael Furcal C	25.00	7.50

2003 Topps Opening Day Team Topps Legends

	Nm-Mt	Ex-Mt
SEE 2001 TOPPS TEAM TOPPS FOR PRICING		

2004 Topps Opening Day

This 165-card set, which is a mini-parallel to the basic Topps set was released in February, 2004. The set was issued in six card packs which came 36 packs to a box and 20 boxes to a case. Each of these cards have a special "Opening Day" logo embossed on them.

	Nm-Mt	Ex-Mt
COMPLETE SET (165)	40.00	12.00
*OPEN.DAY 1-165: .75X TO 2X BASIC TOPPS		
ISSUED IN OPENING DAY PACKS		

2004 Topps Opening Day Autographs

	Nm-Mt	Ex-Mt
STATED ODDS 1:629		
AT Andres Torres	15.00	4.50
DW Dontrelle Willis	25.00	7.50
JD Jeff Duncan		
JW Jerome Williams	25.00	7.50
RH Rich Harden	25.00	7.50
RW Ryan Wagner	15.00	4.50

2004 Topps Opening Day Topps Autographs

	Nm-Mt	Ex-Mt
STATED ODDS 1:11,412		
SEE 04 TOPPS TEAM TOPPS FOR PRICING		

2004 Topps Originals Signature

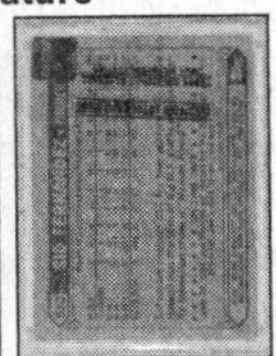

This 1179-card set was released in July, 2004. The set was released in one-card packs with an $50 SRP which came six packs to a box and 4 boxes to a case. All of the cards used in the set were original Topps cards which Topps bought back and the players signed. All of the players signed one copy of each of their rookie cards.

	Nm-Mt	Ex-Mt
ONE AUTO PER PACK		
PRINT RUNS B/WN 1-339 COPIES PER		
NO PRICING ON QTY OF 14 OR LESS		
AD1 Andre Dawson 77/1		
AD2 Andre Dawson 79/3		
AD3 Andre Dawson 80/27	30.00	9.00
AD4 Andre Dawson 81/37	20.00	6.00
AD5 Andre Dawson 82/55	20.00	6.00
AD6 Andre Dawson 83/47	20.00	6.00
AD7 Andre Dawson 84/25	30.00	9.00
AD8 Andre Dawson 85/22	30.00	9.00
AD9 Andre Dawson 86/24	30.00	9.00
AD10 Andre Dawson 88/9		
AH1 Al Hrabosky 71/1		
AH2 Al Hrabosky 74/2		
AH3 Al Hrabosky 75/1		
AH4 Al Hrabosky 76/5		
AH5 Al Hrabosky 77/5		
AH6 Al Hrabosky 78/20	25.00	7.50
AH7 Al Hrabosky 79/40	20.00	6.00
AH8 Al Hrabosky 80/61	20.00	6.00
AH9 Al Hrabosky 81/38	15.00	4.50
AH10 Al Hrabosky 82/62	15.00	4.50
AH11 Al Hrabosky 89 Sr./20	20.00	6.00
AK1 Al Kaline 54/1		
AK2 Al Kaline 59/1		
AK3 Al Kaline 60/1		
AK4 Al Kaline 60 AS/1		
AK5 Al Kaline 61/3		
AK6 Al Kaline 62/3		
AK7 Al Kaline 62 AS/2		
AK8 Al Kaline 64/4		
AK9 Al Kaline 66/1		
AK10 Al Kaline 67/18	120.00	36.00
AK11 Al Kaline 68/6		
AK12 Al Kaline 69/7		
AK13 Al Kaline 70/3		
AK14 Al Kaline 71/7		
AK15 Al Kaline 72/11		
AK16 Al Kaline 73/25	80.00	24.00
AK17 Al Kaline 74/11		
AK18 Al Kaline 75 HL/1		
AO1 Al Oliver 69/1		
AO2 Al Oliver 74/2		
AO3 Al Oliver 75/2		
AO4 Al Oliver 76/2		
AO5 Al Oliver 78/3		
AO6 Al Oliver 79/42	20.00	6.00
AO7 Al Oliver 80/6		
AO8 Al Oliver 81/54	15.00	4.50
AO9 Al Oliver 82/45	15.00	4.50
AO10 Al Oliver 83/50	15.00	4.50
AO11 Al Oliver 84/51	15.00	4.50
AO12 Al Oliver 85/46	15.00	4.50
AO13 Al Oliver 86/44	15.00	4.50
AT1 Alan Trammell 79/12		
AT2 Alan Trammell 80/17	40.00	12.00
AT3 Alan Trammell 81/26	25.00	7.50
AT4 Alan Trammell 82/40	20.00	6.00
AT5 Alan Trammell 83/21	30.00	9.00
AT6 Alan Trammell 84/57	20.00	6.00
AT7 Alan Trammell 85/39	20.00	6.00
AT8 Alan Trammell 86/23	30.00	9.00
AT9 Alan Trammell 87/15	40.00	12.00
AV1 Andy Van Slyke 84/1		
AV2 Andy Van Slyke 85/35	40.00	12.00
AV3 Andy Van Slyke 86/37	30.00	9.00
AV4 Andy Van Slyke 87/178	25.00	7.50
AV5 Andy Van Slyke 87 TR/130	25.00	7.50
BB1 Buddy Bell 73/1		
BB2 Buddy Bell 75/1		
BB3 Buddy Bell 76/1		
BB4 Buddy Bell 78/3		
BB5 Buddy Bell 79/135	15.00	4.50
BB6 Buddy Bell 80/10		
BB7 Buddy Bell 81/11		
BB8 Buddy Bell 82/34	15.00	4.50
BB9 Buddy Bell 83/83	10.00	3.00
BB10 Buddy Bell 84/22	20.00	6.00
BB11 Buddy Bell 85/13		
BB12 Buddy Bell 86/32	15.00	4.50
BBL1 Bert Blyleven 71/1		
BBL2 Bert Blyleven 75/1		
BBL3 Bert Blyleven 76/4		
BBL4 Bert Blyleven 79/45	30.00	9.00
BBL5 Bert Blyleven 80/12		
BBL6 Bert Blyleven 81/29	25.00	7.50
BBL7 Bert Blyleven 82 NNO/51	30.00	9.00
BBL8 Bert Blyleven 83/41	20.00	6.00
BBL9 Bert Blyleven 84/10		
BBL10 Bert Blyleven 85/40	20.00	6.00
BBL11 Bert Blyleven 86/62	20.00	6.00
BBL12 Bert Blyleven 87/54	20.00	6.00
BC1 Bert Campaneris 65/1		
BC2 Bert Campaneris 72/5		
BC3 Bert Campaneris 74/1		
BC4 Bert Campaneris 78/2		
BC5 Bert Campaneris 79/107	15.00	4.50
BC6 Bert Campaneris 80/6		
BC7 Bert Campaneris 84/28	15.00	4.50
BD1 Bucky Dent 74/1		
BD2 Bucky Dent 78/1		
BD3 Bucky Dent 79/14		
BD4 Bucky Dent 80/9		
BD5 Bucky Dent 81/16	40.00	12.00
BD6 Bucky Dent 82/49	20.00	6.00
BD7 Bucky Dent 83/92	10.00	3.00
BD8 Bucky Dent 84/63	15.00	4.50
BD9 Bucky Dent 90 MG/10		
BG1 Bob Grich 71/1		
BG2 Bob Grich 79/29	20.00	6.00
BG3 Bob Grich 80/70	15.00	4.50
BG4 Bob Grich 81/14		
BG5 Bob Grich 82/45	15.00	4.50
BG6 Bob Grich 83/85	10.00	3.00
BG7 Bob Grich 84/57	15.00	4.50
BG8 Bob Grich 85/36	15.00	4.50
BG9 Bob Grich 86/13		
BH1 Bob Horner 79/1		
BH2 Bob Horner 80/14		
BH3 Bob Horner 81/11		
BH4 Bob Horner 82/21	30.00	9.00
BH5 Bob Horner 83/69	15.00	4.50
BH6 Bob Horner 84/63	20.00	6.00
BH7 Bob Horner 85/15	40.00	12.00
BH8 Bob Horner 86/118	15.00	4.50
BH9 Bob Horner 87/38	20.00	6.00
BJ1 Bo Jackson 86 TR/1		
BJ2 Bo Jackson 87/100	60.00	18.00
BJA1 Brook Jacoby 85/1		
BJA2 Brook Jacoby 86/133	10.00	3.00
BJA3 Brook Jacoby 87/191	10.00	3.00
BJA4 Brook Jacoby 88/9		
BM1 Bill Madlock 74/1		
BM2 Bill Madlock 75/7		
BM3 Bill Madlock 76/4		
BM4 Bill Madlock 79/6		
BM5 Bill Madlock 80/11		
BM6 Bill Madlock 81/11		
BM7 Bill Madlock 82/26	15.00	4.50
BM8 Bill Madlock 83/55	15.00	4.50
BM9 Bill Madlock 84/69	10.00	3.00
BM10 Bill Madlock 85/60	15.00	4.50
BM11 Bill Madlock 86/63	15.00	4.50
BM12 Bill Madlock 87/42	15.00	4.50
BP1 Boog Powell 62/1		
BP2 Boog Powell 64/4		
BP3 Boog Powell 65/7		
BP4 Boog Powell 66/4		
BP5 Boog Powell 67/3		
BP6 Boog Powell 69/5		
BP7 Boog Powell 70/6		
BP8 Boog Powell 72/13		
BP9 Boog Powell 73/17	40.00	12.00
BP10 Boog Powell 74/7		
BP11 Boog Powell 75/19	40.00	12.00
BP12 Boog Powell 76/6		
BP13 Boog Powell 77/15	40.00	12.00
BR1 Brooks Robinson 57/1		
BR2 Brooks Robinson 59/1		
BR3 Brooks Robinson 60/2		
BR4 Brooks Robinson 61/1		
BR5 Brooks Robinson 69/6		
BR6 Brooks Robinson 69 AS/2		
BR7 Brooks Robinson 70/8		
BR8 Brooks Robinson 70 AS/3		
BR9 Brooks Robinson 72/6		
BR10 Brooks Robinson 73/14		
BR11 Brooks Robinson 74/20	60.00	18.00
BR12 Brooks Robinson 75/10		
BR13 Brooks Robinson 76/17	60.00	18.00
BR14 Brooks Robinson 77/13		
BS1 Bret Saberhagen 85/1		
BS2 Bret Saberhagen 86/23	30.00	9.00
BS3 Bret Saberhagen 87/230	15.00	4.50
BSU1 Bruce Sutter 77/1		
BSU2 Bruce Sutter 78/5		
BSU3 Bruce Sutter 79/8		
BSU4 Bruce Sutter 80/9		
BSU5 Bruce Sutter 81/11		
BSU6 Bruce Sutter 82/111	15.00	4.50
BSU7 Bruce Sutter 83/45	20.00	6.00
BSU8 Bruce Sutter 84/24	30.00	9.00
BSU9 Bruce Sutter 85/19	40.00	12.00
BSU10 Bruce Sutter 86/78	15.00	4.50
BSU11 Bruce Sutter 87/36	20.00	6.00
BU1 Bill Buckner 70/1		
BU2 Bill Buckner 74/5		
BU3 Bill Buckner 75/1		
BU4 Bill Buckner 76/1		
BU5 Bill Buckner 78/1		
BU6 Bill Buckner 79/11		
BU7 Bill Buckner 80/8		
BU8 Bill Buckner 81/39	20.00	6.00
BU9 Bill Buckner 82/38	20.00	6.00
BU10 Bill Buckner 83/47	20.00	6.00
BU11 Bill Buckner 84/31	25.00	7.50
BU12 Bill Buckner 84 TR/24	30.00	9.00
BU13 Bill Buckner 85/80	15.00	4.50
BU14 Bill Buckner 86/63	20.00	6.00
BW1 Bob Watson 69/1		
BW2 Bob Watson 74/1		
BW3 Bob Watson 79/77	15.00	4.50
BW4 Bob Watson 80/8		
BW5 Bob Watson 81/16	25.00	7.50
BW6 Bob Watson 82/23	20.00	6.00
BW7 Bob Watson 83/93	10.00	3.00
BW8 Bob Watson 84/64	15.00	4.50
BW9 Bob Watson 85/68	10.00	3.00
CF1 Cecil Fielder 86/1		
CF2 Cecil Fielder 87/208	25.00	7.50
CF3 Cecil Fielder 88/26	40.00	12.00
CF4 Cecil Fielder 89/16	60.00	18.00
CFI1 Carlton Fisk 72/1		
CFI2 Carlton Fisk 78/3		
CFI3 Carlton Fisk 79/24	60.00	18.00
CFI4 Carlton Fisk 80/32	50.00	15.00
CFI5 Carlton Fisk 81/14		
CFI6 Carlton Fisk 82/30	40.00	12.00
CG1 Cesar Geronimo 71/1		
CG2 Cesar Geronimo 74/1		
CG3 Cesar Geronimo 79/28	20.00	6.00
CG4 Cesar Geronimo 80/11		
CG5 Cesar Geronimo 81/21	20.00	6.00
CG6 Cesar Geronimo 82/52	15.00	4.50
CG7 Cesar Geronimo 83/67	10.00	3.00
CG8 Cesar Geronimo 84/70	10.00	3.00
CH1 Charlie Hough 72/1		
CH2 Charlie Hough 83/19	25.00	7.50
CH3 Charlie Hough 84/50	15.00	4.50
CH4 Charlie Hough 85/57	15.00	4.50
CH5 Charlie Hough 86/66	10.00	3.00
CH6 Charlie Hough 87/46	15.00	4.50
CH7 Charlie Hough 88/19	25.00	7.50
CH8 Charlie Hough 91 TR/70	10.00	3.00
CH9 Charlie Hough 92/25	20.00	6.00
CH10 Charlie Hough 94/8		
CL1 Carney Lansford 79/1		
CL2 Carney Lansford 80/12		
CL3 Carney Lansford 81/184	10.00	3.00
CL4 Carney Lansford 82/6		
CL5 Carney Lansford 83/40	15.00	4.50
CL6 Carney Lansford 85/35	15.00	4.50
CL7 Carney Lansford 86/76	10.00	3.00
CLE1 Chet Lemon 76/1		
CLE2 Chet Lemon 78/3		
CLE3 Chet Lemon 79/24	25.00	7.50
CLE4 Chet Lemon 80/16	25.00	7.50
CLE5 Chet Lemon 81/12		
CLE6 Chet Lemon 82/23	20.00	6.00
CLE7 Chet Lemon 83/35	15.00	4.50
CLE8 Chet Lemon 84/42	15.00	4.50
CLE9 Chet Lemon 85/32	15.00	4.50
CLE10 Chet Lemon 86/136	10.00	3.00
CLE11 Chet Lemon 87/27	15.00	4.50
CR1 Cal Ripken 82/1		
CR2 Cal Ripken 84/10		
CR3 Cal Ripken 85/15		
CR4 Cal Ripken 86/74	120.00	36.00
CS1 Cory Snyder 85 OLY/1		
CS2 Cory Snyder 87/291	10.00	3.00
CS3 Cory Snyder 91/39	15.00	4.50
CS4 Cory Snyder 91 TR/8		
CS5 Cory Snyder 93/8		
CS6 Cory Snyder 93 Gold/8		
CS7 Cory Snyder 94/10		
CY1 Carl Yastrzemski 60/1		
CY2 Carl Yastrzemski 78/3		
CY3 Carl Yastrzemski 79/2		
CY4 Carl Yastrzemski 80/60	100.00	30.00
CY5 Carl Yastrzemski 81/35	120.00	36.00
DC1 Dave Concepcion 71/1		
DC2 Dave Concepcion 75/2		
DC3 Dave Concepcion 76/1		
DC4 Dave Concepcion 78/3		
DC5 Dave Concepcion 79/3		
DC6 Dave Concepcion 80/21	40.00	12.00
DC7 Dave Concepcion 81/8		
DC8 Dave Concepcion 82/43	20.00	6.00
DC9 Dave Concepcion 83/34	25.00	7.50
DC10 Dave Concepcion 84/24	30.00	9.00
DC11 Dave Concepcion 85/41	20.00	6.00
DC12 Dave Concepcion 86/69	15.00	4.50
DD1 Darren Daulton 86/1		
DD2 Darren Daulton 87/269	10.00	3.00
DD3 Darren Daulton 90/8		
DD4 Darren Daulton 92/32	15.00	4.50
DD5 Darren Daulton 94/17	25.00	7.50
DD6 Darren Daulton 96/22	20.00	6.00
DDE1 Doug DeCinces 75/1		
DDE2 Doug DeCinces 79/38	20.00	6.00
DDE3 Doug DeCinces 80/24	25.00	7.50
DDE4 Doug DeCinces 81/24	20.00	6.00
DDE5 Doug DeCinces 82/42	15.00	4.50
DDE6 Doug DeCinces 83/75	10.00	3.00
DDE7 Doug DeCinces 84/19	25.00	7.50
DDE8 Doug DeCinces 85/54	15.00	4.50
DDE9 Doug DeCinces 86/74	10.00	3.00
DE1 Dennis Eckersley 76/1		
DE2 Dennis Eckersley 78/10		
DE3 Dennis Eckersley 79/44	50.00	15.00
DE4 Dennis Eckersley 80/40	50.00	15.00
DE5 Dennis Eckersley 81/9		
DEV1 Darrell Evans 70/1		
DEV2 Darrell Evans 74/5		
DEV3 Darrell Evans 75/3		
DEV4 Darrell Evans 78/2		
DEV5 Darrell Evans 79/19	25.00	7.50
DEV6 Darrell Evans 80/5		
DEV7 Darrell Evans 81/15	25.00	7.50
DEV8 Darrell Evans 82/25	20.00	6.00
DEV9 Darrell Evans 83/63	15.00	4.50
DEV10 Darrell Evans 84/81	10.00	3.00
DEV11 Darrell Evans 85/48	15.00	4.50
DEV12 Darrell Evans 86/82	10.00	3.00
DG1 Dwight Gooden 85/1		
DG2 Dwight Gooden 86/16	60.00	18.00
DG3 Dwight Gooden 87/52	30.00	9.00
DG4 Dwight Gooden 89/19	60.00	18.00
DJ1 David Justice 90 DB/69	15.00	4.50
DJ2 David Justice 90 TR/1		
DJ3 David Justice 93/32	25.00	7.50
DK1 Dave Kingman 72/1		
DK2 Dave Kingman 79/9		
DK3 Dave Kingman 80/8		
DK4 Dave Kingman 81/25	30.00	9.00
DK5 Dave Kingman 82/5		
DK6 Dave Kingman 83/32	25.00	7.50
DK7 Dave Kingman 86/25	30.00	9.00
DL1 Davey Lopes 73/1		
DL2 Davey Lopes 76/1		
DL3 Davey Lopes 78/1		
DL4 Davey Lopes 79/71	15.00	4.50
DL5 Davey Lopes 80/19	25.00	7.50
DL6 Davey Lopes 81/12		
DL7 Davey Lopes 82/17	25.00	7.50
DL8 Davey Lopes 83/65	15.00	4.50
DL9 Davey Lopes 84/15	25.00	7.50
DL10 Davey Lopes 85/24	20.00	6.00
DL11 Davey Lopes 86/40	15.00	4.50
DL12 Davey Lopes 01 MG/67	10.00	3.00
DL13 Davey Lopes 02 MG/19	25.00	7.50
DM1 Don Mattingly 84/1		
DM2 Don Mattingly 85/16		
DM3 Don Mattingly 87/84	100.00	30.00
DMU1 Dale Murphy 77/1		
DMU2 Dale Murphy 79/38	50.00	15.00
DMU3 Dale Murphy 80/11		
DMU4 Dale Murphy 82/1		
DMU5 Dale Murphy 83/10		
DMU6 Dale Murphy 84/29	40.00	12.00
DMU7 Dale Murphy 85/18	60.00	18.00
DMU8 Dale Murphy 86/25	50.00	15.00
DMU9 Dale Murphy 87/91	25.00	7.50
DMU10 Dale Murphy 88/11		
DMU11 Dale Murphy 89/14		
DP1 Dave Parker 74/1		
DP2 Dave Parker 75/2		
DP3 Dave Parker 79/6		
DP4 Dave Parker 80/9		
DP5 Dave Parker 81/19	60.00	18.00
DP6 Dave Parker 82/73	25.00	7.50
DP7 Dave Parker 83/30	40.00	12.00
DP8 Dave Parker 84/14		
DP9 Dave Parker 85/45	30.00	9.00
DP10 Dave Parker 86/29	40.00	12.00
DP11 Dave Parker 87/12		
DP12 Dave Parker 88/11		
DS1 Duke Snider 52/1		
DS2 Duke Snider 58/3		
DS3 Duke Snider 59/4		
DS4 Duke Snider 60/2		
DS5 Duke Snider 61/13		
DS6 Duke Snider 62/4		
DS7 Duke Snider 63/4		
DS8 Duke Snider 64/18	120.00	36.00
DSE1 Dave Stieb 80/1		
DSE2 Dave Stieb 81/21	50.00	15.00
DSE3 Dave Stieb 82/34	40.00	12.00
DSE4 Dave Stieb 83/70	25.00	7.50
DSE5 Dave Stieb 84/20	50.00	15.00
DSE6 Dave Stieb 85/55	30.00	9.00
DSE7 Dave Stieb 86/69	25.00	7.50
DSE8 Dave Stieb 87/75	25.00	7.50
DSE9 Dave Stieb 88/11		
DSR1 Darryl Strawberry 84/1		
DSR2 Darryl Strawberry 85/32	25.00	7.50
DSR3 Darryl Strawberry 86/24	30.00	9.00
DSR4 Darryl Strawberry 87/183	15.00	4.50
DSR5 Darryl Strawberry 87 AS/110	15.00	4.50
DSW1 Dave Stewart 82/1		
DSW2 Dave Stewart 83/41	15.00	4.50
DSW3 Dave Stewart 84/60	15.00	4.50
DSW4 Dave Stewart 85/24	20.00	6.00
DSW5 Dave Stewart 86/53	15.00	4.50
DSW6 Dave Stewart 87/171	10.00	3.00
EB1 Ernie Banks 54/1		
EB2 Ernie Banks 58 AS/1		
EB3 Ernie Banks 59/1		
EB4 Ernie Banks 59 AS/1		
EB5 Ernie Banks 60/2		
EB6 Ernie Banks 61/2		
EB7 Ernie Banks 61 MVP/7		
EB8 Ernie Banks 62/3		
EB9 Ernie Banks 64/5		
EB10 Ernie Banks 66/7		

EB11 Ernie Banks 67/4
EB12 Ernie Banks 68/7
EB13 Ernie Banks 69/7
EB14 Ernie Banks 70/2
ED1 Eric Davis 85/1
ED2 Eric Davis 86/13
ED3 Eric Davis 87/336 15.00 4.50
EW1 Earl Weaver 69 MG/1
EW2 Earl Weaver 72 MG/1
EW3 Earl Weaver 74 MG/1
EW4 Earl Weaver 78 MG/52 20.00 6.00
EW5 Earl Weaver 83 MG/38 15.00 4.50
EW6 Earl Weaver 85 TR MG/12
EW7 Earl Weaver 86 MG/107 10.00 3.00
EW8 Earl Weaver 87 MG/175 10.00 3.00
FJ1 Fergie Jenkins 66/1
FJ2 Fergie Jenkins 68/2
FJ3 Fergie Jenkins 70/1
FJ4 Fergie Jenkins 71/1
FJ5 Fergie Jenkins 72/4
FJ6 Fergie Jenkins 76/10
FJ7 Fergie Jenkins 77/11
FJ8 Fergie Jenkins 78/17 40.00 12.00
FJ9 Fergie Jenkins 79/9
FJ10 Fergie Jenkins 80/37 30.00 9.00
FJ11 Fergie Jenkins 81/32 25.00 7.50
FJ12 Fergie Jenkins 82/65 20.00 6.00
FJ13 Fergie Jenkins 83/22 30.00 9.00
FJ14 Fergie Jenkins 84/42 20.00 6.00
FR1 Frank Robinson 57/1
FR2 Frank Robinson 63/1
FR3 Frank Robinson 65/1
FR4 Frank Robinson 69/4
FR5 Frank Robinson 71/2
FR6 Frank Robinson 72/16 60.00 18.00
FR7 Frank Robinson 73/4
FR8 Frank Robinson 74/4
FR9 Frank Robinson 75/1
FR10 Frank Robinson 83 MG/13
FR11 Frank Robinson 84 MG/3
FV1 Frank Viola 83/1
FV2 Frank Viola 84/1
FV3 Frank Viola 85/25 30.00 9.00
FV4 Frank Viola 86/99 15.00 4.50
FV5 Frank Viola 87/209 15.00 4.50
FV6 Frank Viola 88/10
GB1 George Bell 82/1
GB2 George Bell 84/67 10.00 3.00
GB3 George Bell 85/32 15.00 4.50
GB4 George Bell 86/46 15.00 4.50
GB5 George Bell 87/204 10.00 3.00
GBR1 George Brett 75/1
GBR2 George Brett 79/16
GBR3 George Brett 80/9
GBR4 George Brett 81/19
GBR5 George Brett 82/6
GC1 Gary Carter 75/1
GC2 Gary Carter 78/9
GC3 Gary Carter 79/21 40.00 12.00
GC4 Gary Carter 80/24 40.00 12.00
GC5 Gary Carter 81/22 30.00 9.00
GC6 Gary Carter 82/12
GC7 Gary Carter 83/2
GC8 Gary Carter 84/9
GF1 George Foster 71/1
GF2 George Foster 74/5
GF3 George Foster 75/3
GF4 George Foster 76/1
GF5 George Foster 78/3
GF6 George Foster 79/20 25.00 7.50
GF7 George Foster 80/7
GF8 George Foster 81/10
GF9 George Foster 82/14
GF10 George Foster 83/39 15.00 4.50
GF11 George Foster 84/112 10.00 3.00
GF12 George Foster 85/76 10.00 3.00
GF13 George Foster 86/64 15.00 4.50
GL1 Greg Luzinski 71/1
GL2 Greg Luzinski 72/5
GL3 Greg Luzinski 75/6
GL4 Greg Luzinski 76/1
GL5 Greg Luzinski 78/5
GL6 Greg Luzinski 79/14
GL7 Greg Luzinski 80/21 40.00 12.00
GL8 Greg Luzinski 81/11
GL9 Greg Luzinski 82/34 25.00 7.50
GL10 Greg Luzinski 83/75 15.00 4.50
GL11 Greg Luzinski 84/85 15.00 4.50
GL12 Greg Luzinski 85/92 15.00 4.50
GM1 Gary Matthews Sr. 73/1
GM2 Gary Matthews Sr. 82/10
GM3 Gary Matthews Sr. 83/20 20.00 6.00
GM4 Gary Matthews Sr. 84/43 15.00 4.50
GM5 Gary Matthews Sr. 85/39 15.00 4.50
GM6 Gary Matthews Sr. 86/38 15.00 4.50
GM7 Gary Matthews Sr. 87/82 10.00 3.00
GM8 Gary Matthews Sr. 88/30 15.00 4.50
HA1 Hank Aaron 54/1
HA2 Hank Aaron 58 AS/2
HA3 Hank Aaron 59/1
HA4 Hank Aaron 60 AS/1
HA5 Hank Aaron 61/1
HA6 Hank Aaron 61 MVP/1
HA7 Hank Aaron 62 AS/1
HA8 Hank Aaron 65/1
HA9 Hank Aaron 68/1
HA10 Hank Aaron 69/1
HA11 Hank Aaron 70/6
HA12 Hank Aaron 70 AS/3
HA13 Hank Aaron 71/3
HA14 Hank Aaron 72/2
HA15 Hank Aaron 73/8
HA16 Hank Aaron 75/5
HA17 Hank Aaron 75 HL/1
HA18 Hank Aaron 76/12
HB1 Harold Baines 81/1
HB2 Harold Baines 82/31 25.00 7.50
HB3 Harold Baines 83/19 40.00 12.00
HB4 Harold Baines 84/5
HB5 Harold Baines 85/97 15.00 4.50
HB6 Harold Baines 86/93 15.00 4.50
HB7 Harold Baines 87/115 15.00 4.50
HK1 Harmon Killebrew 55/1
HK2 Harmon Killebrew 60/1
HK3 Harmon Killebrew 61/1
HK4 Harmon Killebrew 62/1
HK5 Harmon Killebrew 64/2
HK6 Harmon Killebrew 66/2
HK7 Harmon Killebrew 68/2
HK8 Harmon Killebrew 68 AS/2
HK9 Harmon Killebrew 69/5
HK10 Harmon Killebrew 70/3
HK11 Harmon Killebrew 71/3
HK12 Harmon Killebrew 72/12
HK13 Harmon Killebrew 73/4
HK14 Harmon Killebrew 74/6
HK15 Harmon Killebrew 75/9
HR1 Harold Reynolds 86/1
HR2 Harold Reynolds 87/255 15.00 4.50
JA1 Jim Abbott 88 TR/339 25.00 7.50
JA2 Jim Abbott 89/1
JA3 Jim Abbott 90 DB/50 30.00 9.00
JB1 Jesse Barfield 82/1
JB2 Jesse Barfield 83/45 15.00 4.50
JB3 Jesse Barfield 84/12
JB4 Jesse Barfield 85/60 15.00 4.50
JB5 Jesse Barfield 86/37 15.00 4.50
JB6 Jesse Barfield 87/180 10.00 3.00
JB7 Jesse Barfield 88/10
JBE1 Johnny Bench 68/1
JBE2 Johnny Bench 79/14
JBE3 Johnny Bench 80/10
JBE4 Johnny Bench 81/8
JBE5 Johnny Bench 82/16 80.00 24.00
JBE6 Johnny Bench 83/2
JC1 John Candelaria 76/1
JC2 John Candelaria 79/77 25.00 7.50
JC3 John Candelaria 80/8
JC4 John Candelaria 81/19 40.00 12.00
JC5 John Candelaria 82/42 20.00 6.00
JC6 John Candelaria 83/77 15.00 4.50
JC7 John Candelaria 84/18 40.00 12.00
JC8 John Candelaria 85/61 20.00 6.00
JC9 John Candelaria 86/36 20.00 6.00
JC10 John Candelaria 87/13
JCA1 Jose Canseco 86 TR/1
JCA2 Jose Canseco 87/99 50.00 15.00
JCR1 Joe Carter 85/1
JCR2 Joe Carter 86/24 50.00 15.00
JCR3 Joe Carter 87/23 50.00 15.00
JCR4 Joe Carter 90/2
JCU1 Jose Cruz Sr. 72/1
JCU2 Jose Cruz Sr. 74/2
JCU3 Jose Cruz Sr. 76/1
JCU4 Jose Cruz Sr. 78/5
JCU5 Jose Cruz Sr. 79/7
JCU6 Jose Cruz Sr. 80/14
JCU7 Jose Cruz Sr. 81/14
JCU8 Jose Cruz Sr. 82/28 15.00 4.50
JCU9 Jose Cruz Sr. 83/102 10.00 3.00
JCU10 Jose Cruz Sr. 84/67 10.00 3.00
JCU11 Jose Cruz Sr. 85/68 10.00 3.00
JCU12 Jose Cruz Sr. 86/31 15.00 4.50
JK1 Jimmy Key 85/1
JK2 Jimmy Key 86/21 30.00 9.00
JK3 Jimmy Key 87/263 15.00 4.50
JK4 Jimmy Key 88/15 40.00 12.00
JK5 Jimmy Key 92/37 20.00 6.00
JK6 Jimmy Key 94/11
JKR1 John Kruk 86 TR/1
JKR2 John Kruk 87/214 25.00 7.50
JKR3 John Kruk 92/22 50.00 15.00
JKR4 John Kruk 93/13
JL1 Jim Leyritz 90 TR/1
JL2 Jim Leyritz 91/38 15.00 4.50
JL3 Jim Leyritz 93/49 15.00 4.50
JL4 Jim Leyritz 94/16 25.00 7.50
JL5 Jim Leyritz 95/14
JL6 Jim Leyritz 97/62 15.00 4.50
JL7 Jim Leyritz 98/20 20.00 6.00
JL8 Jim Leyritz 99/124 10.00 3.00
JL9 Jim Leyritz 00/40 15.00 4.50
JM1 Jack McDowell 88 TR/1
JM2 Jack McDowell 89/36 15.00 4.50
JM3 Jack McDowell 90 TR/61 15.00 4.50
JM4 Jack McDowell 91/33 15.00 4.50
JM5 Jack McDowell 92/38 15.00 4.50
JM6 Jack McDowell 93/27 15.00 4.50
JM7 Jack McDowell 94/3
JM8 Jack McDowell 95/9
JM9 Jack McDowell 96/15 25.00 7.50
JM10 Jack McDowell 97/27 15.00 4.50
JMO1 Joe Morgan 65/1
JMO2 Joe Morgan 74/2
JMO3 Joe Morgan 75/1
JMO4 Joe Morgan 76/5
JMO5 Joe Morgan 77/6
JMO6 Joe Morgan 78/3
JMO7 Joe Morgan 79/4
JMO8 Joe Morgan 80/12
JMO9 Joe Morgan 81/32 25.00 7.50
JMO10 Joe Morgan 82/18 40.00 12.00
JMO11 Joe Morgan 83/49 20.00 6.00
JMO12 Joe Morgan 83 TR/4
JMO13 Joe Morgan 84/73 15.00 4.50
JMO14 Joe Morgan 85/40 20.00 6.00
JP1 Jim Palmer 66/1
JP2 Jim Palmer 79/4
JP3 Jim Palmer 80/33 30.00 9.00
JP4 Jim Palmer 81/23 30.00 9.00
JP5 Jim Palmer 82/24 30.00 9.00
JP6 Jim Palmer 83/7
JP7 Jim Palmer 84/9
JR1 Jim Rice 75/1
JR2 Jim Rice 76/2
JR3 Jim Rice 77/4
JR4 Jim Rice 78/3
JR5 Jim Rice 79/6
JR6 Jim Rice 80/9
JR7 Jim Rice 81/123 15.00 4.50
JR8 Jim Rice 82/24 30.00 9.00
JR9 Jim Rice 83/71 15.00 4.50
JR10 Jim Rice 84/12
JRU1 Joe Rudi 69/1
JRU2 Joe Rudi 72/2
JRU3 Joe Rudi 73/9
JRU4 Joe Rudi 74/6
JRU5 Joe Rudi 75/7
JRU6 Joe Rudi 76/4
JRU7 Joe Rudi 77/7
JRU8 Joe Rudi 78/14
JRU9 Joe Rudi 79/24 25.00 7.50
JRU10 Joe Rudi 80/45 20.00 6.00
JRU11 Joe Rudi 82/26 15.00 4.50
JRU12 Joe Rudi 83/75 10.00 3.00
KB1 Kevin Bass 79/1
KB2 Kevin Bass 84/71 10.00 3.00
KB3 Kevin Bass 85/30 15.00 4.50
KB4 Kevin Bass 86/44 15.00 4.50
KB5 Kevin Bass 87/74 10.00 3.00
KB6 Kevin Bass 90 TR/35 15.00 4.50
KG1 Ken Griffey Sr. 74/1
KG2 Ken Griffey Sr. 75/2
KG3 Ken Griffey Sr. 76/2
KG4 Ken Griffey Sr. 79/3
KG5 Ken Griffey Sr. 80/15 40.00 12.00
KG6 Ken Griffey Sr. 81/11
KG7 Ken Griffey Sr. 82/18 40.00 12.00
KG8 Ken Griffey Sr. 83/70 15.00 4.50
KG9 Ken Griffey Sr. 84/64 20.00 6.00
KG10 Ken Griffey Sr. 85/32 25.00 7.50
KG11 Ken Griffey Sr. 86 TR/32 25.00 7.50
KGI1 Kirk Gibson 81/1
KGI2 Kirk Gibson 82/35 25.00 7.50
KGI3 Kirk Gibson 83/35 25.00 7.50
KGI4 Kirk Gibson 84/5
KGI5 Kirk Gibson 85/44 20.00 6.00
KGI6 Kirk Gibson 86/44 20.00 6.00
KGI7 Kirk Gibson 87/65 20.00 6.00
KGI8 Kirk Gibson 89/14
KGI9 Kirk Gibson 90/12
KGU1 Kelly Gruber 87/1
KGU2 Kelly Gruber 88/77 10.00 3.00
KGU3 Kelly Gruber 89/44 15.00 4.50
KGU4 Kelly Gruber 90/86 10.00 3.00
KGU5 Kelly Gruber 91/52 15.00 4.50
KGU6 Kelly Gruber 92/55 15.00 4.50
KGU7 Kelly Gruber 93/26 15.00 4.50
KGU8 Kelly Gruber 93 Gold/9
KH1 Keith Hernandez 75/1
KH2 Keith Hernandez 79/8
KH3 Keith Hernandez 80/38 30.00 9.00
KH4 Keith Hernandez 81/19 40.00 12.00
KH5 Keith Hernandez 82/156 15.00 4.50
KH6 Keith Hernandez 83/17 40.00 12.00
KH7 Keith Hernandez 84/4
KH8 Keith Hernandez 86/7
KS1 Kevin Seitzer 87 TR/1
KS2 Kevin Seitzer 88/88 10.00 3.00
KS3 Kevin Seitzer 89/39 15.00 4.50
KS4 Kevin Seitzer 90/18 25.00 7.50
KS5 Kevin Seitzer 91/39 15.00 4.50
KS6 Kevin Seitzer 92/49 15.00 4.50
KS7 Kevin Seitzer 92 Gold/2
KS8 Kevin Seitzer 92 TR/9
KS9 Kevin Seitzer 93/38 15.00 4.50
KS10 Kevin Seitzer 94/22 20.00 6.00
KS11 Kevin Seitzer 95/16 25.00 7.50
KS12 Kevin Seitzer 96/9
KS13 Kevin Seitzer 97/24 20.00 6.00
KT1 Kent Tekulve 76/1
KT2 Kent Tekulve 78/2
KT3 Kent Tekulve 79/14
KT4 Kent Tekulve 80/6
KT5 Kent Tekulve 81/17 40.00 12.00
KT6 Kent Tekulve 82/36 20.00 6.00
KT7 Kent Tekulve 83/52 20.00 6.00
KT8 Kent Tekulve 84/71 15.00 4.50
KT9 Kent Tekulve 85/43 20.00 6.00
KT10 Kent Tekulve 86/57 20.00 6.00
KT11 Kent Tekulve 87/32 25.00 7.50
KT12 Kent Tekulve 88/20 30.00 9.00
LA1 Luis Aparicio 56/1
LA2 Luis Aparicio 60/1
LA3 Luis Aparicio 61/3
LA4 Luis Aparicio 62/2
LA5 Luis Aparicio 63/3
LA6 Luis Aparicio 66/3
LA7 Luis Aparicio 67/2
LA8 Luis Aparicio 68/14
LA9 Luis Aparicio 69/49 25.00 7.50
LA10 Luis Aparicio 70/2
LA11 Luis Aparicio 71/1
LA12 Luis Aparicio 72/15 40.00 12.00
LA13 Luis Aparicio 73/3
LA14 Luis Aparicio 74/3
LB1 Lou Brock 62/1
LB2 Lou Brock 66/1
LB3 Lou Brock 68/2
LB4 Lou Brock 70/20 60.00 18.00
LB5 Lou Brock 71/3
LB6 Lou Brock 72/3
LB7 Lou Brock 73/4
LB8 Lou Brock 74/5
LB9 Lou Brock 75/9
LB10 Lou Brock 76/5
LB11 Lou Brock 77/11
LB12 Lou Brock 78/11
LB13 Lou Brock 79/27 50.00 15.00
LD1 Leon Durham 81/1
LD2 Leon Durham 82/51 15.00 4.50
LD3 Leon Durham 83/52 15.00 4.50
LD4 Leon Durham 84/151 10.00 3.00
LD5 Leon Durham 85/1
LD6 Leon Durham 86/19 25.00 7.50
LD7 Leon Durham 87/87 10.00 3.00
LDY1 Len Dykstra 86/1
LDY2 Len Dykstra 87/200 15.00 4.50
LDY3 Len Dykstra 88/30 25.00 7.50
LDY4 Len Dykstra 89/17 40.00 12.00
LDY5 Len Dykstra 92/7
LS1 Lee Smith 82/1
LS2 Lee Smith 83/39 20.00 6.00
LS3 Lee Smith 84/6
LS4 Lee Smith 85/9
LS5 Lee Smith 86/29 25.00 7.50
LS6 Lee Smith 87/237 15.00 4.50
LS7 Lee Smith 88/27 25.00 7.50
LS8 Lee Smith 92/12
LT1 Luis Tiant 65/1
LT2 Luis Tiant 68/16 40.00 12.00
LT3 Luis Tiant 70/9
LT4 Luis Tiant 71/2
LT5 Luis Tiant 73/12
LT6 Luis Tiant 74/19 40.00 12.00
LT7 Luis Tiant 75/10
LT8 Luis Tiant 76/3
LT9 Luis Tiant 77/3
LT10 Luis Tiant 78/6
LT11 Luis Tiant 79/22 25.00 7.50
LT12 Luis Tiant 80/23 25.00 7.50
LT13 Luis Tiant 81/20 20.00 6.00
LT14 Luis Tiant 82/51 15.00 4.50
LT15 Luis Tiant 83/58 15.00 4.50
MB1 Mike Boddicker 81/1
MB2 Mike Boddicker 84/56 15.00 4.50
MB3 Mike Boddicker 85/139 10.00 3.00
MB4 Mike Boddicker 86/66 10.00 3.00
MB5 Mike Boddicker 87/88 10.00 3.00
MF1 Mark Fidrych 77/1
MF2 Mark Fidrych 78/3
MF3 Mark Fidrych 79/74 25.00 7.50
MF4 Mark Fidrych 80/16 40.00 12.00
MF5 Mark Fidrych 81/11
MR1 Mickey Rivers 72/1
MR2 Mickey Rivers 79/35 20.00 6.00
MR3 Mickey Rivers 80/14
MR4 Mickey Rivers 81/13
MR5 Mickey Rivers 82/49 15.00 4.50
MR6 Mickey Rivers 83/79 10.00 3.00
MR7 Mickey Rivers 84/91 10.00 3.00
MR8 Mickey Rivers 85/34 15.00 4.50
MS1 Mike Schmidt 73/1
MS2 Mike Schmidt 80/100 60.00 18.00
MSC1 Mike Scott 80/1
MSC2 Mike Scott 81/6
MSC3 Mike Scott 82/32 15.00 4.50
MSC4 Mike Scott 83/55 15.00 4.50
MSC5 Mike Scott 84/28 15.00 4.50
MSC6 Mike Scott 86/73 10.00 3.00
MSC7 Mike Scott 87/36 15.00 4.50
MSC8 Mike Scott 88/21 20.00 6.00
MT1 Paul Molitor
Alan Trammell 78/1
MW1 Mookie Wilson 81/1
MW2 Mookie Wilson 82/20 30.00 9.00
MW3 Mookie Wilson 83/41 20.00 6.00
MW4 Mookie Wilson 84/11
MW5 Mookie Wilson 85/51 20.00 6.00
MW6 Mookie Wilson 86/47 20.00 6.00
MW7 Mookie Wilson 87/67 15.00 4.50
MW8 Mookie Wilson 88/12
NR1 Nolan Ryan 68/1
NR2 Nolan Ryan 80/10
NR3 Nolan Ryan 81/13
NR4 Nolan Ryan 82/1
NR5 Nolan Ryan 83/23 175.00 52.50
NR6 Nolan Ryan 84/20 175.00 52.50
NR7 Nolan Ryan 85/4
NR8 Nolan Ryan 86/20 175.00 52.50
OH1 Orel Hershiser 85/1
OH2 Orel Hershiser 86/23 50.00 15.00
OH3 Orel Hershiser 87/218 25.00 7.50
OH4 Orel Hershiser 88/9
OS1 Ozzie Smith 79/1
OS2 Ozzie Smith 81/28 60.00 18.00
OS3 Ozzie Smith 82/27 60.00 18.00
OS4 Ozzie Smith 83/6
OS5 Ozzie Smith 84/19 80.00 24.00
OS6 Ozzie Smith 85/16 80.00 24.00
OS7 Ozzie Smith 86/3
PI1 Pete Incaviglia 86 TR/1
PI2 Pete Incaviglia 87/311 10.00 3.00
PM1 Paul Molitor 79/15 60.00 18.00
PM2 Paul Molitor 80/26 50.00 15.00
PM3 Paul Molitor 81/12
PM4 Paul Molitor 82/32 40.00 12.00
PM5 Paul Molitor 83/14
PO1 Paul O'Neill 88/1
PO2 Paul O'Neill 89/24 50.00 15.00
PO3 Paul O'Neill 90/18 60.00 18.00
PO4 Paul O'Neill 91/24 50.00 15.00
PO5 Paul O'Neill 97/33 40.00 12.00
RC1 Rod Carew 67/1
RC2 Rod Carew 70/10
RC3 Rod Carew 78/2
RC4 Rod Carew 79/29 50.00 15.00
RC5 Rod Carew 80/10
RC6 Rod Carew 81/21 50.00 15.00
RC7 Rod Carew 82/18 60.00 18.00
RC8 Rod Carew 84/9
RCE1 Ron Cey 72/1
RCE2 Ron Cey 75/4
RCE3 Ron Cey 79/55 20.00 6.00
RCE4 Ron Cey 80/8
RCE5 Ron Cey 81/16 25.00 7.50
RCE6 Ron Cey 82/34 15.00 4.50
RCE7 Ron Cey 83/87 10.00 3.00
RCE8 Ron Cey 83 TR/68 10.00 3.00
RCE9 Ron Cey 84/15 25.00 7.50
RCE10 Ron Cey 85/19 25.00 7.50
RCE11 Ron Cey 86/43 15.00 4.50
RD1 Ron Darling 85/1
RD2 Ron Darling 86/12
RD3 Ron Darling 87/224 15.00 4.50
RD4 Ron Darling 93/13
RDI1 Rob Dibble 89/1
RDI2 Rob Dibble 90/31 25.00 7.50
RDI3 Rob Dibble 91/62 20.00 6.00
RDI4 Rob Dibble 92/56 20.00 6.00
RDI5 Rob Dibble 92 Gold/17 40.00 12.00
RDI6 Rob Dibble 93/47 20.00 6.00
RDI7 Rob Dibble 94/37 20.00 6.00
RF1 Rollie Fingers 69/1
RF2 Rollie Fingers 78/6
RF3 Rollie Fingers 79/52 30.00 9.00
RF4 Rollie Fingers 80/15 40.00 12.00
RF5 Rollie Fingers 81/18 40.00 12.00
RF6 Rollie Fingers 82/8
RG1 Rich Gossage 73/1
RG2 Rich Gossage 74/6
RG3 Rich Gossage 76/3
RG4 Rich Gossage 78/2
RG5 Rich Gossage 79/11
RG6 Rich Gossage 80/15 40.00 12.00
RG7 Rich Gossage 81/21 20.00 6.00
RG8 Rich Gossage 82/30 25.00 7.50
RG9 Rich Gossage 83/34 25.00 7.50
RG10 Rich Gossage 84/90 15.00 4.50
RG11 Rich Gossage 85/7
RG12 Rich Gossage 86/30 25.00 7.50
RGU1 Ron Guidry 76/1
RGU2 Ron Guidry 78/9
RGU3 Ron Guidry 79/10
RGU4 Ron Guidry 80/22 40.00 12.00
RGU5 Ron Guidry 81/104 15.00 4.50
RGU6 Ron Guidry 82/53 20.00 6.00
RGU7 Ron Guidry 83/53 20.00 6.00
RGU8 Ron Guidry 84/40 20.00 6.00
RGU9 Ron Guidry 85/50 20.00 6.00
RGU10 Ron Guidry 86/15 40.00 12.00
RJ1 Reggie Jackson 69/1
RJ2 Reggie Jackson 73/3
RJ3 Reggie Jackson 75/1
RJ4 Reggie Jackson 76/2
RJ5 Reggie Jackson 79/2
RJ6 Reggie Jackson 80/7
RJ7 Reggie Jackson 81/12
RJ8 Reggie Jackson 82/21 60.00 18.00
RJ9 Reggie Jackson 83/14
RJ10 Reggie Jackson 84/3
RJ11 Reggie Jackson 85/17 80.00 24.00
RJ12 Reggie Jackson 86/17 80.00 24.00
RK1 Ron Kittle 84/1
RK2 Ron Kittle 85/86 10.00 3.00
RK3 Ron Kittle 86/55 15.00 4.50
RK4 Ron Kittle 87/201 10.00 3.00
RKN1 Ray Knight 78/1
RKN2 Ray Knight 79/10
RKN3 Ray Knight 80/5
RKN4 Ray Knight 81/7
RKN5 Ray Knight 82/25 30.00 9.00
RKN6 Ray Knight 83/36 20.00 6.00
RKN7 Ray Knight 84/26 25.00 7.50
RKN8 Ray Knight 85/68 15.00 4.50
RKN9 Ray Knight 86/80 15.00 4.50
RKN10 Ray Knight 87 TR/90 15.00 4.50
RM1 Reggie Smith 67/1
RM2 Reggie Smith 69/1
RM3 Reggie Smith 73/7
RM4 Reggie Smith 74/4
RM5 Reggie Smith 75/2
RM6 Reggie Smith 76/3
RM7 Reggie Smith 77/2
RM8 Reggie Smith 79/15 25.00 7.50
RM9 Reggie Smith 80/16 25.00 7.50
RM10 Reggie Smith 81/14
RM11 Reggie Smith 82/32 15.00 4.50
RM12 Reggie Smith 83/48 15.00 4.50
RS1 Ryne Sandberg 83/1
RS2 Ryne Sandberg 84/37 100.00 30.00
RS3 Ryne Sandberg 85/4
RS4 Ryne Sandberg 86/1
RS5 Ryne Sandberg 87/32 100.00 30.00
RS6 Ryne Sandberg 88/6
RS7 Ryne Sandberg 89/9
RS8 Ryne Sandberg 92/10
RSA1 Ron Santo 61/1
RSA2 Ron Santo 67/2
RSA3 Ron Santo 68/6
RSA4 Ron Santo 69/2
RSA5 Ron Santo 70/1
RSA6 Ron Santo 70 AS/1
RSA7 Ron Santo 71/2
RSA8 Ron Santo 72/2
RSA9 Ron Santo 72 IA/3
RSA10 Ron Santo 73/13
RSA11 Ron Santo 74/2
RSA12 Ron Santo 74 TR/1
RSA13 Ron Santo 75/12
RU1 Rick Sutcliffe 80/1
RU2 Rick Sutcliffe 81/9
RU3 Rick Sutcliffe 82/53 15.00 4.50
RU4 Rick Sutcliffe 83/43 15.00 4.50
RU5 Rick Sutcliffe 84/33 15.00 4.50
RU6 Rick Sutcliffe 85/82 10.00 3.00
RU7 Rick Sutcliffe 86/10
RU8 Rick Sutcliffe 87/19 25.00 7.50
RY1 Robin Yount 75/1
RY2 Robin Yount 77/1
RY3 Robin Yount 78/3
RY4 Robin Yount 79/1
RY5 Robin Yount 80/18 80.00 24.00
RY6 Robin Yount 81/23 80.00 24.00
RY7 Robin Yount 82/11
RY8 Robin Yount 83/2
RY9 Robin Yount 84/15 80.00 24.00
RY10 Robin Yount 85/5
RY11 Robin Yount 86/21 80.00 24.00
SA1 Sparky Anderson 59/1
SA2 Sparky Anderson 60/2
SA3 Sparky Anderson 74 MG/3
SA4 Sparky Anderson 78 MG/6
SA5 Sparky Anderson 83 MG/67 15.00 4.50
SA6 Sparky Anderson 84 MG/97 15.00 4.50
SA7 Sparky Anderson 85 MG/73 15.00 4.50
SA8 Sparky Anderson 86 MG/6
SF1 Sid Fernandez 85/1
SF2 Sid Fernandez 86/18 40.00 12.00
SF3 Sid Fernandez 87/211 15.00 4.50
SF4 Sid Fernandez 93/20 30.00 9.00
SG1 Steve Garvey 71/1
SG2 Steve Garvey 75/1
SG3 Steve Garvey 76/4
SG4 Steve Garvey 79/26 50.00 15.00
SG5 Steve Garvey 80/5
SG6 Steve Garvey 81/10
SG7 Steve Garvey 82/122 25.00 7.50
SG8 Steve Garvey 83/19 60.00 18.00
SG9 Steve Garvey 84/32 40.00 12.00
SG10 Steve Garvey 85/129 25.00 7.50
SM1 Stan Musial 58 AS/15 150.00 45.00
SM2 Stan Musial 59/1
SM3 Stan Musial 60/5
SM4 Stan Musial 61/13
SM5 Stan Musial 62/16 150.00 45.00
SM6 Stan Musial 63/1
SS1 Steve Sax 82/1
SS2 Steve Sax 83/34 15.00 4.50
SS3 Steve Sax 84/14
SS4 Steve Sax 85/33 15.00 4.50
SS5 Steve Sax 86/45 15.00 4.50
SS6 Steve Sax 87/215 10.00 3.00
SS7 Steve Sax 88/10
SY1 Steve Yeager 73/1
SY2 Steve Yeager 74/1
SY3 Steve Yeager 76/1
SY4 Steve Yeager 78/18 25.00 7.50
SY5 Steve Yeager 79/23 25.00 7.50
SY6 Steve Yeager 80/10
SY7 Steve Yeager 81/12
SY8 Steve Yeager 82/18 25.00 7.50
SY9 Steve Yeager 83/80 10.00 3.00
SY10 Steve Yeager 84/15 25.00 7.50
SY11 Steve Yeager 85/4
SY12 Steve Yeager 86/47 15.00 4.50
SY13 Steve Yeager 86 TR/100 10.00 3.00
TB1 Tom Brunansky 82/1
TB2 Tom Brunansky 83/27 15.00 4.50
TB3 Tom Brunansky 84/62 15.00 4.50
TB4 Tom Brunansky 85/13
TB5 Tom Brunansky 86/28 15.00 4.50
TB6 Tom Brunansky 87/193 10.00 3.00
TB7 Tom Brunansky 88/18 25.00 7.50
TB8 Tom Brunansky 90/8
TF1 Tony Fernandez 85/1
TF2 Tony Fernandez 86/41 15.00 4.50
TF3 Tony Fernandez 87/228 10.00 3.00
TF4 Tony Fernandez 88/10
TF5 Tony Fernandez 90/11

1 Tony Gwynn 83/1
2 Tony Gwynn 84/95 60.00 18.00
3 Tony Gwynn 85/4
1 Tom Herr 80/1
2 Tom Herr 81/22 20.00 6.00
3 Tom Herr 82/42 15.00 4.50
4 Tom Herr 83/80 10.00 3.00
5 Tom Herr 84/30 15.00 4.50
6 Tom Herr 85/17 25.00 7.50
7 Tom Herr 86/28 15.00 4.50
8 Tom Herr 87/134 10.00 3.00
1 Tim McCarver 62/1
2 Tim McCarver 76/5
3 Tim McCarver 77/8
4 Tim McCarver 78/12
5 Tim McCarver 79/22 25.00 7.50
6 Tim McCarver 80/4
1 Tony Oliva 63/1
2 Tony Oliva 68/1
3 Tony Oliva 69/4
4 Tony Oliva 69 AS/1
5 Tony Oliva 70/9
6 Tony Oliva 71/2
7 Tony Oliva 72/5
8 Tony Oliva 73/18 40.00 12.00
9 Tony Oliva 74/11
10 Tony Oliva 75/10
11 Tony Oliva 76/1
1 Tim Raines 81/1
2 Tim Raines 82/43 20.00 6.00
3 Tim Raines 83/26 25.00 7.50
4 Tim Raines 84/10
5 Tim Raines 85/43 20.00 6.00
6 Tim Raines 86/21 30.00 9.00
7 Tim Raines 87/211 15.00 4.50
S1 Tom Seaver 67/1
S2 Tom Seaver 79/44 60.00 18.00
S3 Tom Seaver 80/9
S4 Tom Seaver 81/16 80.00 24.00
S5 Tom Seaver 82/25 60.00 18.00
S6 Tom Seaver 83/4
S7 Tom Seaver 85/6
W1 Tim Wallach 82/1
W2 Tim Wallach 83/49 15.00 4.50
W3 Tim Wallach 84/13
W4 Tim Wallach 85/46 15.00 4.50
W5 Tim Wallach 86/44 15.00 4.50
W6 Tim Wallach 87/197 10.00 3.00
B1 Vida Blue 70/1
B2 Vida Blue 72/1
B3 Vida Blue 75/1
B4 Vida Blue 78/10
B5 Vida Blue 79/21 25.00 7.50
B6 Vida Blue 80/10
B7 Vida Blue 81/227 10.00 3.00
B8 Vida Blue 82/53 15.00 4.50
B9 Vida Blue 83/45 15.00 4.50
C1 Vince Coleman 85 TR/1
C2 Vince Coleman 87/299 15.00 4.50
C3 Vince Coleman 88/34 25.00 7.50
C4 Vince Coleman 91 TR/23 30.00 9.00
VB1 Wade Boggs 83/1
VB2 Wade Boggs 84/20 60.00 18.00
VB3 Wade Boggs 85/25 60.00 18.00
VB4 Wade Boggs 86/9
VB5 Wade Boggs 87/45 50.00 15.00
WF1 Whitey Ford 53/1
WF2 Whitey Ford 58/1
WF3 Whitey Ford 59/3
WF4 Whitey Ford 60/5
WF5 Whitey Ford 61/6
WF6 Whitey Ford 62/5
WF7 Whitey Ford 62 AS/2
WF8 Whitey Ford 62 WS/3
WF9 Whitey Ford 63/1
WF10 Whitey Ford 65/1
WF11 Whitey Ford 66/9
WF12 Whitey Ford 67/13
WH1 Whitey Herzog 57/1
WH2 Whitey Herzog 61/13
WH3 Whitey Herzog 62/1
WH4 Whitey Herzog 83 MG/63 15.00 4.50
WH5 Whitey Herzog 84 MG/85 10.00 3.00
WH6 Whitey Herzog 85 MG/75 10.00 3.00
WH7 Whitey Herzog 86 MG/66 10.00 3.00
WH8 Whitey Herzog 87 MG/29 15.00 4.50
WH9 Whitey Herzog 88 MG/35 15.00 4.50
WJ1 Wally Joyner 86 TR/1
WJ2 Wally Joyner 87/335 15.00 4.50
WJ3 Wally Joyner 94/14
WM1 Willie Mays 52/1
WM2 Willie Mays 60/1
WM3 Willie Mays 61/3
WM4 Willie Mays 61 MVP/4
WM5 Willie Mays 62/1
WM6 Willie Mays 62 AS/3
WM7 Willie Mays 69/1
WM8 Willie Mays 70/2
WM9 Willie Mays 72/25 300.00 90.00
WM10 Willie Mays 72 IA/5
WM11 Willie Mays 73/5
WMC1 Willie McGee 83/1
WMC2 Willie McGee 84/66 25.00 7.50
WMC3 Willie McGee 85/44 30.00 9.00
WMC4 Willie McGee 86/24 50.00 15.00
WMC5 Willie McGee 87/117 25.00 7.50
WW1 Walt Weiss 88 TR/1
WW2 Walt Weiss 89/34 15.00 4.50
WW3 Walt Weiss 91/30 15.00 4.50
WW4 Walt Weiss 92/71 10.00 3.00
WW5 Walt Weiss 93/10
WW6 Walt Weiss 94/21 20.00 6.00
WW7 Walt Weiss 97/49 15.00 4.50
WW8 Walt Weiss 98 Rockies/23 20.00 6.00
WW9 Walt Weiss 98 Braves/21 20.00 6.00
WW10 Walt Weiss 99/40 15.00 4.50
WW11 Walt Weiss 01/51 15.00 4.50
YB1 Yogi Berra 52/1
YB2 Yogi Berra 59/1
YB3 Yogi Berra 60/1
YB4 Yogi Berra 61/2
YB5 Yogi Berra 62/3
YB6 Yogi Berra 64 MG/3
YB7 Yogi Berra 65 CO/1
YB8 Yogi Berra 73 MG/5
YB9 Yogi Berra 74 MG/6
YB10 Yogi Berra 85 MG/27 80.00 24.00

2002 Topps Pristine

This 210 card set was issued in October, 2002. This set was issued in eight card packs with an $40 SRP which came five packs to a box and six boxes to a case. The first 140 cards feature active veterans stars while cards 141-150 feature retired greats and cards numbered 151-210 feature three different versions of each rookie. Each rookie has a common version, a uncommon version which has a print run of 1999 serial numbered sets and a rare version which has a stated print run of 799 serial numbered sets.

Nm-Mt Ex-Mt
COMMON CARD (1-140) 1.25 .35
COMMON CARD (141-150) 2.00 .60
COMMON C CARD (151-210) 1.25 .35
COMMON U CARD (151-210) 2.50 .75
COMMON R CARD (151-210) 4.00 1.20
1 Alex Rodriguez 5.00 1.50
2 Carlos Delgado 1.25 .35
3 Jimmy Rollins 1.25 .35
4 Jason Kendall 1.25 .35
5 John Olerud 1.25 .35
6 Albert Pujols 6.00 1.80
7 Curt Schilling 1.25 .35
8 Gary Sheffield 1.25 .35
9 Johnny Damon Sox 3.00 .90
10 Ichiro Suzuki 5.00 1.50
11 Pat Burrell 1.25 .35
12 Garret Anderson 1.25 .35
13 Andruw Jones 1.25 .35
14 Kerry Wood 3.00 .90
15 Kenny Lofton 1.25 .35
16 Adam Dunn 2.00 .60
17 Juan Pierre 1.25 .35
18 Josh Beckett 1.25 .35
19 Roy Oswalt 1.25 .35
20 Derek Jeter 8.00 2.40
21 Jose Vidro 1.25 .35
22 Richie Sexson 1.25 .35
23 Mike Sweeney 1.25 .35
24 Jeff Kent 1.25 .35
25 Jason Giambi 1.25 .35
26 Bret Boone 1.25 .35
27 J.D. Drew 1.25 .35
28 Shannon Stewart 1.25 .35
29 Miguel Tejada 1.25 .35
30 Barry Bonds 8.00 2.40
31 Randy Johnson 3.00 .90
32 Pedro Martinez 3.00 .90
33 Magglio Ordonez 1.25 .35
34 Todd Helton 2.00 .60
35 Craig Biggio 2.00 .60
36 Shawn Green 1.25 .35
37 Vladimir Guerrero 3.00 .90
38 Mo Vaughn 1.25 .35
39 Alfonso Soriano 2.00 .60
40 Barry Zito 1.25 .35
41 Aramis Ramirez 1.25 .35
42 Ryan Klesko 1.25 .35
43 Ruben Sierra 1.25 .35
44 Tino Martinez 2.00 .60
45 Toby Hall 1.25 .35
46 Ivan Rodriguez 3.00 .90
47 Raul Mondesi 1.25 .35
48 Carlos Pena 1.25 .35
49 Darin Erstad 1.25 .35
50 Sammy Sosa 5.00 1.50
51 Bartolo Colon 1.25 .35
52 Robert Fick 1.25 .35
53 Cliff Floyd 1.25 .35
54 Brian Jordan 1.25 .35
55 Torii Hunter 1.25 .35
56 Roberto Alomar 2.00 .60
57 Roger Clemens 6.00 1.80
58 Mark Mulder 1.25 .35
59 Brian Giles 1.25 .35
60 Mike Piazza 5.00 1.50
61 Rich Aurilia 1.25 .35
62 Freddy Garcia 1.25 .35
63 Jim Edmonds 1.25 .35
64 Eric Hinske 1.25 .35
65 Vicente Padilla 1.25 .35
66 Javier Vazquez 1.25 .35
67 Cristian Guzman 1.25 .35
68 Paul Lo Duca 1.25 .35
69 Bobby Abreu 1.25 .35
70 Nomar Garciaparra 5.00 1.50
71 Troy Glaus 1.25 .35
72 Chipper Jones 3.00 .90
73 Scott Rolen 3.00 .90
74 Lance Berkman 1.25 .35
75 C.C. Sabathia 1.25 .35
76 Bernie Williams 2.00 .60
77 Rafael Palmeiro 2.00 .60
78 Phil Nevin 1.25 .35
79 Kazuhiro Sasaki 1.25 .35
80 Eric Chavez 1.25 .35
81 Jorge Posada 2.00 .60
82 Edgardo Alfonzo 1.25 .35
83 Geoff Jenkins 1.25 .35
84 Preston Wilson 1.25 .35
85 Jim Thome 3.00 .90
86 Frank Thomas 3.00 .90
87 Jeff Bagwell 2.00 .60
88 Greg Maddux 5.00 1.50
89 Mark Prior 6.00 1.80
90 Larry Walker 2.00 .60
91 Luis Gonzalez 1.25 .35
92 Tim Hudson 1.25 .35
93 Tsuyoshi Shinjo 1.25 .35
94 Juan Gonzalez 2.00 .60
95 Shea Hillenbrand 1.25 .35
96 Paul Konerko 1.25 .35
97 Tom Glavine 2.00 .60
98 Marty Cordova 1.25 .35
99 Moises Alou 1.25 .35
100 Ken Griffey Jr. 5.00 1.50
101 Hank Blalock 3.00 .90
102 Matt Morris 1.25 .35
103 Robb Nen 1.25 .35
104 Mike Cameron 1.25 .35
105 Mark Buehrle 1.25 .35
106 Sean Burroughs 1.25 .35
107 Orlando Cabrera 1.25 .35
108 Jeromy Burnitz 1.25 .35
109 Juan Uribe 1.25 .35
110 Eric Milton 1.25 .35
111 Carlos Lee 1.25 .35
112 Jose Mesa 1.25 .35
113 Morgan Ensberg 1.25 .35
114 Derek Lowe 1.25 .35
115 Juan Cruz 1.25 .35
116 Mike Lieberthal 1.25 .35
117 Armando Benitez 1.25 .35
118 Vinny Castilla 1.25 .35
119 Russ Ortiz 1.25 .35
120 Mike Lowell 1.25 .35
121 Corey Patterson 1.25 .35
122 Mike Mussina 2.00 .60
123 Rafael Furcal 1.25 .35
124 Mark Grace 2.00 .60
125 Ben Sheets 1.25 .35
126 John Smoltz 2.00 .60
127 Fred McGriff 2.00 .60
128 Nick Johnson 1.25 .35
129 J.T. Snow 1.25 .35
130 Jeff Cirillo 1.25 .35
131 Trevor Hoffman 1.25 .35
132 Kevin Brown 1.25 .35
133 Mariano Rivera 2.00 .60
134 Marlon Anderson 1.25 .35
135 Al Leiter 1.25 .35
136 Doug Mientkiewicz 1.25 .35
137 Eric Karros 1.25 .35
138 Bobby Higginson 1.25 .35
139 Sean Casey 1.25 .35
140 Troy Percival 1.25 .35
141 Willie Mays 6.00 1.80
142 Carl Yastrzemski 5.00 1.50
143 Stan Musial 5.00 1.50
144 Harmon Killebrew 3.00 .90
145 Mike Schmidt 6.00 1.80
146 Duke Snider 2.00 .60
147 Brooks Robinson 2.00 .60
148 Frank Robinson 2.00 .60
149 Nolan Ryan 8.00 2.40
150 Reggie Jackson 2.00 .60
151 Joe Mauer C RC 10.00 3.00
152 Joe Mauer U 20.00 6.00
153 Joe Mauer R 30.00 9.00
154 Colt Griffin C RC 2.00 .60
155 Colt Griffin U 4.00 1.20
156 Colt Griffin R 6.00 1.80
157 Jason Simontacchi C RC 1.25 .35
158 Jason Simontacchi U 2.50 .75
159 Jason Simontacchi R 4.00 1.20
160 Casey Kotchman C RC 6.00 1.80
161 Casey Kotchman U 12.00 3.60
162 Casey Kotchman R 20.00 6.00
163 Greg Sain C RC 2.00 .60
164 Greg Sain U 4.00 1.20
165 Greg Sain R 6.00 1.80
166 David Wright C RC 15.00 4.50
167 David Wright U 25.00 7.50
168 David Wright R 40.00 12.00
169 Scott Hairston C RC 3.00 .90
170 Scott Hairston U 6.00 1.80
171 Scott Hairston R 10.00 3.00
172 Rolando Viera C RC 1.25 .35
173 Rolando Viera U 2.50 .75
174 Rolando Viera R 4.00 1.20
175 Tyrell Godwin C RC 1.25 .35
176 Tyrell Godwin U 2.50 .75
177 Tyrell Godwin R 4.00 1.20
178 Jesus Cota C RC 1.25 .35
179 Jesus Cota U 2.50 .75
180 Jesus Cota R 4.00 1.20
181 Dan Johnson C RC 2.00 .60
182 Dan Johnson U 4.00 1.20
183 Dan Johnson R 6.00 1.80
184 Mario Ramos C RC 1.25 .35
185 Mario Ramos U 2.50 .75
186 Mario Ramos R 4.00 1.20
187 Jason Dubois C RC 2.50 .75
188 Jason Dubois U 5.00 1.50
189 Jason Dubois R 8.00 2.40
190 Jonny Gomes C RC 2.00 .60
191 Jonny Gomes U 4.00 1.20
192 Jonny Gomes R 6.00 1.80
193 Chris Snelling C RC 1.25 .35
194 Chris Snelling U 2.50 .75
195 Chris Snelling R 4.00 1.20
196 Hansel Izquierdo C RC 1.25 .35
197 Hansel Izquierdo U 2.50 .75
198 Hansel Izquierdo R 4.00 1.20
199 So Taguchi C RC 2.00 .60
200 So Taguchi U 4.00 1.20
201 So Taguchi R 6.00 1.80
202 Kazuhisa Ishii C RC 2.50 .75
203 Kazuhisa Ishii U 5.00 1.50
204 Kazuhisa Ishii R 8.00 2.40
205 Jorge Padilla C RC 1.25 .35
206 Jorge Padilla U 2.50 .75
207 Jorge Padilla R 4.00 1.20
208 Earl Snyder C RC 2.00 .60
209 Earl Snyder U 4.00 1.20
210 Earl Snyder R 6.00 1.80

2002 Topps Pristine Gold Refractors

Inserted one per hobby box, this is a parallel of the regular set. Each card has a stated print run of 70 serial numbered sets.

Nm-Mt Ex-Mt
*GOLD 1-140: 2.5X TO 6X BASIC
*GOLD 141-150: 2.5X TO 6X BASIC
*GOLD C 151-210: 4X TO 10X BASIC C
*GOLD U 151-210: 2X TO 5X BASIC U
*GOLD R 151-210: 1.25X TO 3X BASIC R
166 David Wright C 120.00 45.00
167 David Wright U 120.00 36.00
168 David Wright R 120.00 36.00

2002 Topps Pristine Refractors

Issued at different odds depending on the card number, these cards parallel the regular pristine set. The veterans and retired players were issued to a stated print run of 149 serial numbered sets. The rookie cards were issued to stated print runs of 1999 for the common versions, 799 for the uncommon versions and 149 for the rare version.

Nm-Mt Ex-Mt
*REFRACTORS 1-140: 1.5X TO 4X
*REFRACTORS 141-150: 1.5X TO 4X.
1-150 STATED ODDS 1:4
*REFRACTORS C 151-210: 1X TO 2.5X
COMMON 151-210 STATED ODDS 1:2
*REFRACTORS U 151-210: .75X TO 2X
UNCOMMON 151-210 STATED ODDS 1:5
*REFRACTORS R 151-210: .75X TO 2X
RARE 151-210 STATED ODDS 1:27

2002 Topps Pristine Fall Memories

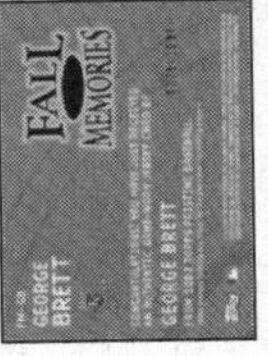

Issued at different odds depending on which group the insert card belonged to, these cards feature players who had participated in post-season play and a piece of game-used memorabilia pertaining to that player. We have listed the stated print run information for that player as well as what type of memorabilia next to the player's name in our checklist.

Nm-Mt Ex-Mt
GROUP A ODDS 1:21
GROUP B ODDS 1:8
GROUP C ODDS 1:49
GROUP A PRINT RUN 425 SERIAL #'d SETS
GROUP B PRINT RUN 1000 SERIAL #'d SETS
GROUP C PRINT RUN 1600 SERIAL #'d SETS
AJ Andruw Jones Uni B 8.00 2.40
AS Alfonso Soriano Bat B 10.00 3.00
BB Barry Bonds Bat A 40.00 12.00
BW Bernie Williams Bat B 10.00 3.00
CJ Chipper Jones Bat A 15.00 4.50
CS Curt Schilling Jsy B 8.00 2.40
EM Eddie Murray Bat A 15.00 4.50
GB George Brett Jsy B 25.00 7.50
GS Gary Sheffield Bat C 8.00 2.40
JB Johnny Bench Jsy B 15.00 4.50
JP Jorge Posada Bat B 10.00 3.00
KP Kirby Puckett Bat A 15.00 4.50
LG Luis Gonzalez Bat B 8.00 2.40
MG Mark Grace Bat A 15.00 4.50
RJ Reggie Jackson Bat A 15.00 4.50
SG Shawn Green Bat A 10.00 3.00
TG Tom Glavine Jsy B 10.00 3.00
TH Todd Helton Jsy B 10.00 3.00
TM Tino Martinez Bat A 15.00 4.50
WM Willie Mays Jsy A 40.00 12.00

2002 Topps Pristine In the Gap

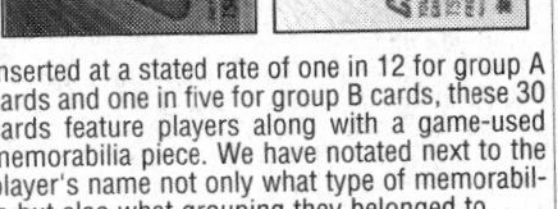

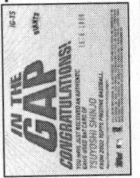

Inserted at a stated rate of one in 12 for group A cards and one in five for group B cards, these 30 cards feature players along with a game-used memorabilia piece. We have notated next to the player's name not only what type of memorabilia but also what grouping they belonged to.

Nm-Mt Ex-Mt
GROUP A PRINT RUN 425 SERIAL #'d SETS
GROUP B PRINT RUN 1000 SERIAL #'d SETS
AD Adam Dunn Jsy B 10.00 3.00
AJ Andruw Jones Jsy B 8.00 2.40
AP Albert Pujols Uni B 20.00 6.00
AR Alex Rodriguez Bat A 15.00 4.50
ARA Aramis Ramirez Bat A 10.00 3.00
AS Alfonso Soriano Bat A 15.00 4.50
BB Bret Boone Bat B 8.00 2.40
BBO Barry Bonds Uni B 30.00 9.00
BW Bernie Williams Bat B 15.00 4.50
CD Carlos Delgado Bat A 10.00 3.00
DE Darin Erstad Bat A 10.00 3.00
EC Eric Chavez Bat A 10.00 3.00
IR Ivan Rodriguez Bat A 15.00 4.50
JE Jim Edmonds Jsy B 8.00 2.40
JK Jeff Kent Jsy B 8.00 2.40
LB Lance Berkman Bat A 10.00 3.00
LW Larry Walker Jsy B 10.00 3.00
MP Mike Piazza Bat A 15.00 4.50
NG Nomar Garciaparra Bat A 15.00 4.50
PL Paul Lo Duca Bat A 10.00 3.00
PW Preston Wilson Jsy B 8.00 2.40
RA Roberto Alomar Bat B 10.00 3.00
RH Rickey Henderson Bat A 15.00 4.50
RK Ryan Klesko Bat A 10.00 3.00
RP Rafael Palmeiro Bat A 15.00 4.50
TG Tony Gwynn Jsy B 15.00 4.50
TH Todd Helton Bat B 10.00 3.00
TS Tsuyoshi Shinjo Bat B 8.00 2.40
WB Wade Boggs Uni B 10.00 3.00
WBE Wilson Betemit Bat B 8.00 2.40

2002 Topps Pristine Patches

Inserted at stated odds of one in 126, these 25 cards feature game-used patches of the featured player. Each of these cards were issued to a stated print run of 25 serial numbered sets and no pricing is provided due to scarcity.

Nm-Mt Ex-Mt
AD Adam Dunn
AJ Andruw Jones
AP Albert Pujols
AR Alex Rodriguez
BB Bret Boone
BBO Barry Bonds
CD Carlos Delgado
CJ Chipper Jones
CS Curt Schilling
DM Don Mattingly
EC Eric Chavez
FT Frank Thomas
GB George Brett
GM Greg Maddux
KS Kazuhiro Sasaki
LW Larry Walker
MP Mike Piazza
NG Nomar Garciaparra
PM Pedro Martinez
RP Rafael Palmeiro
SR Scott Rolen
TG Tony Gwynn
TGL Tom Glavine
TH Todd Helton
WB Wade Boggs

2002 Topps Pristine Personal Endorsements

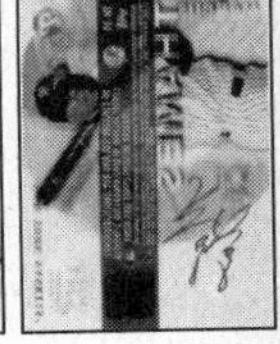

Inserted at different odds depending on the group the player belonged to, these cards feature authentic player autographs on a clear acrylic like card surface. We have notated what group the player belongs to next to their name in our checklist.

Nm-Mt Ex-Mt
GROUP A ODDS 1:396
GROUP B ODDS 1:63
GROUP C ODDS 1:79
GROUP D ODDS 1:33
GROUP E ODDS 1:9
GROUP F ODDS 1:53
AP Albert Pujols A 100.00 30.00
BB Barry Bonds E 200.00 60.00
BS Ben Sheets B 20.00 6.00
CG Cristian Guzman C 10.00 3.00
CK Casey Kotchman E 15.00 4.50
CM Corwin Malone E 10.00 3.00
DB Dewon Brazelton D 10.00 3.00
GF Gavin Floyd D 25.00 7.50
IG Irvin Guzman E 20.00 6.00
JD Johnny Damon Sox B 40.00 12.00
JL Jason Lane E 10.00 3.00
JR Jimmy Rollins C 15.00 4.50
JS Juan Silvestre E 10.00 3.00
KB Kenny Baugh F 10.00 3.00
KI Kazuhisa Ishii A 40.00 12.00
LB Lance Berkman B 30.00 9.00
MT Marcus Thames E 10.00 3.00
NN Nick Neugebauer E 10.00 3.00
OH Orlando Hudson D 10.00 3.00
RA Roberto Alomar B 30.00 9.00
ST So Taguchi B 30.00 9.00

2002 Topps Pristine Popular Demand

Inserted at a stated print run of one in four, these 20 cards feature some of the leading players in the game along with a game-used memorabilia piece. Each card was issued to a stated print run of 1000 serial numbered sets.

Nm-Mt Ex-Mt
AD Adam Dunn Jsy 10.00 3.00
AP Albert Pujols Jsy 20.00 6.00
AR Alex Rodriguez Bat 15.00 4.50
BB Bret Boone Jsy 8.00 2.40
BBO Barry Bonds Uni 30.00 9.00
CD Carlos Delgado Uni 8.00 2.40
CJ Chipper Jones Jsy 15.00 4.50
CS Curt Schilling Jsy 8.00 2.40
DM Don Mattingly Jsy 40.00 12.00
FT Frank Thomas Jsy 15.00 4.50
IR Ivan Rodriguez Uni 15.00 4.50

JB Jeff Bagwell Jsy 10.00 3.00
LW Larry Walker Jsy 10.00 3.00
MP Mike Piazza Jsy 15.00 4.50
NG Nomar Garciaparra Bat 15.00 4.50
RA Roberto Alomar Jsy 10.00 3.00
SG Shawn Green Jsy 8.00 2.40
TG Tony Gwynn Jsy 15.00 4.50
TH Todd Helton Jsy 10.00 3.00
WB Wade Boggs Jsy 10.00 3.00

2002 Topps Pristine Portions

Issued at different odds depending on which group the insert card belonged to, these cards feature some leading players along with a piece of game-used memorabilia pertaining to that player. We have listed the stated print run information for that player as well as what type of memorabilia next to the player's name in our checklist.

Nm-Mt Ex-Mt
GROUP A ODDS 1:21
GROUP B ODDS 1:4
GROUP C ODDS 1:33
GROUP A PRINT RUN 425 SERIAL #'d SETS
GROUP B PRINT RUN 1000 SERIAL #'d SETS
GROUP C PRINT RUN 2400 SERIAL #'d SETS
AD Adam Dunn Bat B 15.00 4.50
AP Albert Pujols Uni B 20.00 6.00
AR Alex Rodriguez Jsy B 15.00 4.50
BB Bret Boone Jsy B 10.00 3.00
BBO Barry Bonds Uni C 20.00 6.00
CB Craig Biggio Jsy B 15.00 4.50
CD Carlos Delgado Jsy B 10.00 3.00
CF Cliff Floyd Jsy B 10.00 3.00
CG Cristian Guzman Jsy B 8.00 2.40
EM Edgar Martinez Bat A 15.00 4.50
GM Greg Maddux Jsy A 15.00 4.50
IR Ivan Rodriguez Bat A 15.00 4.50
JB Jeff Bagwell Uni A 15.00 4.50
JP Jorge Posada Bat A 15.00 4.50
KS Kazuhiro Sasaki Jsy A 15.00 4.50
LB Lance Berkman Bat A 15.00 4.50
LD Paul Lo Duca Jsy B 10.00 3.00
MM Mike Mussina Uni B 15.00 4.50
MO Magglio Ordonez Jsy B 10.00 3.00
MP Mike Piazza Bat A 15.00 4.50
NG Nomar Garciaparra Jsy B 15.00 4.50
NJ Nick Johnson Bat B 8.00 2.40
NR Nolan Ryan Uni B 50.00 15.00
RA Roberto Alomar Bat A 15.00 4.50
RD Ryan Dempster Jsy B 8.00 2.40
RF Rafael Furcal Jsy B 10.00 3.00
RP Rafael Palmeiro Jsy B 15.00 4.50
TH Todd Helton Jsy B 15.00 4.50

2003 Topps Pristine

This 190 card pack was issued in special eight-card packs, which actually came as a few packs within a large pack. Each pack contained a mix of cards from the base set as well as an encased special. In the basic set, cards numbered 1 through 95 featured veterans, cards numbered 96 through 100 featured retired greats and cards 101 through 190 featured rookies. Each of the rookies were issued in three forms as "Common", "Uncommon" or "Rare". The "Uncommon" rookies were issued to a stated print run of 1499 serial numbered sets while the "rare" rookies were issued to a stated print run of 499 serial numbered sets.

MINT NRMT
COMMON CARD (1-100) 1.50 .70
COMMON C (101-190) 1.25 .55
C 101-190 APPX. 2X EASIER THAN 1-100
COMMON U (101-190) 2.50 1.10
UNCOMMON 101-190 STATED ODDS 1:2
UNCOMMON PRINT 1499 SERIAL #'d SETS
COMMON R (101-190) 5.00 2.20
RARE 101-190 STATED ODDS 1:6
RARE PRINT RUN 499 SERIAL #'d SETS
1 Pedro Martinez 4.00 1.80
2 Derek Jeter 10.00 4.50
3 Alex Rodriguez 6.00 2.70
4 Miguel Tejada 1.50 .70
5 Nomar Garciaparra 6.00 2.70
6 Austin Kearns 1.50 .70
7 Jose Vidro 1.50 .70
8 Bret Boone 1.50 .70
9 Scott Rolen 4.00 1.80
10 Mike Sweeney 1.50 .70
11 Jason Schmidt 1.50 .70
12 Alfonso Soriano 2.50 1.10
13 Tim Hudson 1.50 .70
14 A.J. Pierzynski 1.50 .70
15 Lance Berkman 1.50 .70
16 Frank Thomas 4.00 1.80
17 Gary Sheffield 1.50 .70
18 Jarrod Washburn 1.50 .70
19 Hideo Nomo 4.00 1.80
20 Barry Zito 1.50 .70
21 Kevin Millwood 1.50 .70
22 Matt Morris 1.50 .70
23 Carl Crawford 1.50 .70
24 Carlos Delgado 1.50 .70
25 Mike Piazza 6.00 2.70
26 Brad Radke 1.50 .70
27 Richie Sexson 1.50 .70
28 Kevin Brown 1.50 .70
29 Carlos Beltran 2.50 1.10
30 Curt Schilling 1.50 .70
31 Chipper Jones 4.00 1.80
32 Paul Konerko 1.50 .70
33 Larry Walker 2.50 1.10
34 Jeff Bagwell 2.50 1.10
35 Jason Giambi 1.50 .70
36 Mark Mulder 1.50 .70
37 Vicente Padilla 1.50 .70
38 Kris Benson 1.50 .70
39 Bernie Williams 2.50 1.10
40 Jim Thome 4.00 1.80
41 Roger Clemens 8.00 3.60
42 Roberto Alomar 2.50 1.10
43 Torii Hunter 1.50 .70
44 Bobby Abreu 1.50 .70
45 Jeff Kent 1.50 .70
46 Roy Oswalt 1.50 .70
47 Bartolo Colon 1.50 .70
48 Greg Maddux 6.00 2.70
49 Tom Glavine 2.50 1.10
50 Sammy Sosa 6.00 2.70
51 Ichiro Suzuki 6.00 2.70
52 Mark Prior 4.00 1.80
53 Manny Ramirez 2.50 1.10
54 Andruw Jones 1.50 .70
55 Randy Johnson 4.00 1.80
56 Garret Anderson 1.50 .70
57 Roy Halladay 1.50 .70
58 Rafael Palmeiro 2.50 1.10
59 Rocco Baldelli 1.50 .70
60 Albert Pujols 8.00 3.60
61 Edgar Renteria 1.50 .70
62 John Olerud 1.50 .70
63 Rich Aurilia 1.50 .70
64 Ryan Klesko 1.50 .70
65 Brian Giles 1.50 .70
66 Eric Chavez 1.50 .70
67 Jorge Posada 2.50 1.10
68 Cliff Floyd 1.50 .70
69 Vladimir Guerrero 4.00 1.80
70 Cristian Guzman 1.50 .70
71 Raul Ibanez 1.50 .70
72 Paul Lo Duca 1.50 .70
73 A.J. Burnett 1.50 .70
74 Ken Griffey Jr. 6.00 2.70
75 Mark Buehrle 1.50 .70
76 Moises Alou 1.50 .70
77 Adam Dunn 2.50 1.10
78 Tony Batista 1.50 .70
79 Troy Glaus 1.50 .70
80 Luis Gonzalez 1.50 .70
81 Shea Hillenbrand 1.50 .70
82 Kerry Wood 4.00 1.80
83 Magglio Ordonez 1.50 .70
84 Omar Vizquel 2.50 1.10
85 Bobby Higginson 1.50 .70
86 Mike Lowell 1.50 .70
87 Runelvys Hernandez 1.50 .70
88 Shawn Green 1.50 .70
89 Erubiel Durazo 1.50 .70
90 Pat Burrell 1.50 .70
91 Todd Helton 2.50 1.10
92 Jim Edmonds 1.50 .70
93 Aubrey Huff 1.50 .70
94 Eric Hinske 1.50 .70
95 Barry Bonds 10.00 4.50
96 Willie Mays 8.00 3.60
97 Bo Jackson 4.00 1.80
98 Carl Yastrzemski 6.00 2.70
99 Don Mattingly 10.00 4.50
100 Gary Carter 2.50 1.10
101 Jose Contreras C RC 2.00 .90
102 Jose Contreras U 4.00 1.80
103 Jose Contreras R 8.00 3.60
104 Dan Haren C RC 2.00 .90
105 Dan Haren U 4.00 1.80
106 Dan Haren R 8.00 3.60
107 Michel Hernandez C RC 1.25 .55
108 Michel Hernandez U 2.50 1.10
109 Michel Hernandez R 5.00 2.20
110 Bobby Basham C RC 1.25 .55
111 Bobby Basham U 2.50 1.10
112 Bobby Basham R 5.00 2.20
113 Bryan Bullington C RC 2.50 1.10
114 Bryan Bullington U 5.00 2.20
115 Bryan Bullington R 10.00 4.50
116 Bernie Castro C RC 1.25 .55
117 Bernie Castro U 2.50 1.10
118 Bernie Castro R 5.00 2.20
119 Chien-Ming Wang C RC 2.00 .90
120 Chien-Ming Wang U 4.00 1.80
121 Chien-Ming Wang R 8.00 3.60
122 Eric Crozier C RC 1.25 .55
123 Eric Crozier U 2.50 1.10
124 Eric Crozier R 5.00 2.20
125 Mi. Garciaparra C RC 2.00 .90
126 Michael Garciaparra U 4.00 1.80
127 Michael Garciaparra R 8.00 3.60
128 Joey Gomes C RC 1.25 .55
129 Joey Gomes U 2.50 1.10
130 Joey Gomes R 5.00 2.20
131 Wil Ledezma C RC 1.25 .55
132 Wil Ledezma U 2.50 1.10
133 Wil Ledezma R 5.00 2.20
134 Branden Florence C RC 1.25 .55
135 Branden Florence U 2.50 1.10
136 Branden Florence R 5.00 2.20
137 Jeremy Bonderman C RC 2.00 .90
138 Jeremy Bonderman U 4.00 1.80
139 Jeremy Bonderman R 8.00 3.60
140 Travis Ishikawa C RC 1.25 .55
141 Travis Ishikawa U 2.50 1.10
142 Travis Ishikawa R 5.00 2.20
143 Ben Francisco C RC 1.25 .55
144 Ben Francisco U 2.50 1.10
145 Ben Francisco R 5.00 2.20
146 Jason Kubel C RC 4.00 1.80
147 Jason Kubel U 8.00 3.60
148 Jason Kubel R 15.00 6.75
149 Tyler Martin C RC 1.25 .55
150 Tyler Martin U 2.50 1.10
151 Tyler Martin R 5.00 2.20
152 Jason Perry C RC 2.00 .90
153 Jason Perry U 4.00 1.80
154 Jason Perry R 8.00 3.60
155 Ryan Shealy C RC 2.00 .90
156 Ryan Shealy U 4.00 1.80
157 Ryan Shealy R 8.00 3.60
158 Hanley Ramirez C RC 4.00 1.80
159 Hanley Ramirez U 8.00 3.60
160 Hanley Ramirez R 15.00 6.75
161 Rajai Davis C RC 1.25 .55
162 Rajai Davis U 2.50 1.10
163 Rajai Davis R 5.00 2.20
164 Gary Schneidmiller C RC 1.25 .55
165 Gary Schneidmiller U 2.50 1.10
166 Gary Schneidmiller R 5.00 2.20
167 Haj Turay C RC 1.25 .55
168 Haj Turay U 2.50 1.10
169 Haj Turay R 5.00 2.20
170 Kevin Youkilis C RC 3.00 1.35
171 Kevin Youkilis U 6.00 2.70
172 Kevin Youkilis R 12.00 5.50
173 Shane Bazzell C RC 1.25 .55
174 Shane Bazzell U 2.50 1.10
175 Shane Bazzell R 5.00 2.20
176 Elizardo Ramirez C RC 2.00 .90
177 Elizardo Ramirez U 4.00 1.80
178 Elizardo Ramirez R 8.00 3.60
179 Robinson Cano C RC 2.00 .90
180 Robinson Cano U 4.00 1.80
181 Robinson Cano R 8.00 3.60
182 Nook Logan C RC 1.25 .55
183 Nook Logan U 2.50 1.10
184 Nook Logan R 5.00 2.20
185 Dustin McGowan C RC 2.00 .90
186 Dustin McGowan U 4.00 1.80
187 Dustin McGowan R 8.00 3.60
188 Ryan Howard C RC 5.00 2.20
189 Ryan Howard U 10.00 4.50
190 Ryan Howard R 20.00 9.00

2003 Topps Pristine Gold Refractors

MINT NRMT
*GOLD 1-95: 2.5X TO 6X BASIC
*GOLD 96-100: 2.5X TO 6X BASIC
*GOLD C 101-190: 4X TO 10X BASIC C
*GOLD U 101-190: 2X TO 5X BASIC U
*GOLD R 101-190: 1X TO 2.5X BASIC R
ONE PER SEALED HOBBY BOX
STATED PRINT RUN 69 SERIAL #'d SETS

2003 Topps Pristine Plates

MINT NRMT
STATED ODDS 1:83
STATED PRINT RUN 4 SETS
BLACK, CYAN, MAGENTA AND YELLOW EXIST
NO PRICING DUE TO SCARCITY

2003 Topps Pristine Refractors

MINT NRMT
*REFRACTORS 1-95: 2X TO 5X BASIC
*REFRACTORS 96-100: 2X TO 5X BASIC
REFRACTORS 1-100 ODDS 1:8
REFRACTORS 1-100 PRINT RUN 99 #'d SETS
*REFRACTORS C 101-190: .75X TO 2X
COMMON 101-190 RANDOM IN PACKS
COMMON 101-190 PRINT RUN 1599 #'d SETS
*REFRACTORS U 101-190: .75X TO 2X
UNCOMMON 101-190 ODDS 1:6
UNCOMMON 101-190 PRINT 499 #'d SETS
*REFRACTORS R 101-190: .75X TO 2X
RARE 101-190 ODDS 1:27
RARE 101-190 PRINT RUN 99 #'d SETS

2003 Topps Pristine Bonds Jersey Relics

MINT NRMT
REFRACTOR ODDS 1:787
REFRACTOR PRINT RUN 25 SERIAL #'d SETS
NO REFRACTOR PRICING DUE TO SCARCITY
BB Barry Bonds BB 40.00 18.00
GG Barry Bonds GG 40.00 18.00
HR Barry Bonds HR 40.00 18.00
MVP Barry Bonds MVP 40.00 18.00

2003 Topps Pristine Bonds Dual Relics

MINT NRMT
REFRACTOR STATED ODDS 1:787
REFRACTOR PRINT RUN 25 SERIAL #'d SETS
NO REFRACTOR PRICING DUE TO SCARCITY
BJ Barry Bonds Jsy 50.00 22.00
Randy Johnson Jsy
BM Willie Mays Jsy 120.00 55.00
Barry Bonds Jsy
BR Alex Rodriguez Jsy 50.00 22.00
Barry Bonds Jsy
BT Miguel Tejada Bat 50.00 22.00
Barry Bonds Bat

2003 Topps Pristine Bomb Squad Relics

MINT NRMT
GROUP A ODDS 1:3
GROUP B ODDS 1:5
GROUP C ODDS 1:9
REFRACTOR ODDS 1:59
REFRACTOR PRINT RUN 25 SERIAL #'d SETS
NO REFRACTOR PRICING DUE TO SCARCITY
AD Adam Dunn Jsy A 10.00 4.50
AJ Andruw Jones Bat B 10.00 4.50
AP1 Albert Pujols Bat A 20.00 9.00
AP2 Albert Pujols Uni B 25.00 11.00
AR1 Alex Rodriguez Bat C 10.00 4.50
AR2 Alex Rodriguez Jsy A 10.00 4.50
AS Alfonso Soriano Uni A 10.00 4.50
BB Barry Bonds Jsy B 25.00 11.00
CC Carl Crawford Bat C 8.00 3.60
CF Cliff Floyd Bat B 10.00 4.50
CJ Chipper Jones Bat B 15.00 6.75
DE1 Darin Erstad Uni B 10.00 4.50
DE2 Darin Erstad Jsy B 10.00 4.50
EC1 Eric Chavez Gray Uni A 8.00 3.60
EC2 Eric Chavez White Uni A 8.00 3.60
FT Frank Thomas Bat C 10.00 4.50
GA1 Garret Anderson Bat A 8.00 3.60
GA2 Garret Anderson Uni B 10.00 4.50
GB1 George Brett Jsy A 25.00 11.00
GB2 George Brett Bat B 30.00 13.50
GC Gary Carter Bat C 8.00 3.60
GS Gary Sheffield Bat A 8.00 3.60
HB Hank Blalock Bat B 15.00 6.75
JAG Juan Gonzalez Jsy B 15.00 6.75
JB Johnny Bench Bat A 10.00 4.50
JG Jason Giambi Bat A 8.00 3.60
JK Jeff Kent Bat B 10.00 4.50
JRB Jeff Bagwell Bat B 15.00 6.75
JT Jim Thome Bat B 15.00 6.75
LB1 Lance Berkman Jsy C 8.00 3.60
LB2 Lance Berkman Bat C 8.00 3.60
LG Luis Gonzalez Jsy B 10.00 4.50
MO Magglio Ordonez Jsy A 8.00 3.60
MO1 Moises Alou Uni A 8.00 3.60
MO2 Moises Alou Bat B 10.00 4.50
MP Mike Piazza Jsy B 15.00 6.75
MR Manny Ramirez Bat A 10.00 4.50
MS1 Mike Schmidt Bat A 20.00 9.00
MS2 Mike Schmidt Uni A 20.00 9.00
MT Miguel Tejada Bat B 10.00 4.50
NG1 Nomar Garciaparra Bat B 15.00 6.75
NG2 Nomar Garciaparra Jsy B 15.00 6.75
RH Rickey Henderson Bat B 15.00 6.75
RP Rafael Palmeiro Jsy B 15.00 6.75
SG Shawn Green Bat B 10.00 4.50
SS1 Sammy Sosa Bat B 15.00 6.75
SS2 Sammy Sosa Jsy A 15.00 6.75
TG1 Troy Glaus Bat A 8.00 3.60
TG2 Troy Glaus Uni B 10.00 4.50
TH Todd Helton Bat B 15.00 6.75
TS Tim Salmon Uni B 15.00 6.75
VG1 Vladimir Guerrero Jsy A 10.00 4.50
VG2 Vladimir Guerrero Bat A 10.00 4.50

2003 Topps Pristine Borders Relics

MINT NRMT
REFRACTOR ODDS 1:210
REFRACTOR PRINT RUN 25 SERIAL #'d SETS
NO REFRACTOR PRICING DUE TO SCARCITY
AJ Andruw Jones Uni 10.00 4.50
AP Albert Pujols Jsy 20.00 9.00
AS Alfonso Soriano Bat 10.00 4.50
BW Bernie Williams Bat 10.00 4.50
CC Chin Feng Chen Jsy 40.00 18.00
CG Cristian Guzman Bat 8.00 3.60
IR Ivan Rodriguez Bat 10.00 4.50
KI Kazuhisa Ishii Jsy 8.00 3.60
MO Magglio Ordonez Jsy 8.00 3.60
MR Manny Ramirez Jsy 10.00 4.50
MT Miguel Tejada Bat 8.00 3.60
PM Pedro Martinez Jsy 10.00 4.50
SS Sammy Sosa Jsy 15.00 6.75
TS Tsuyoshi Shinjo Bat 8.00 3.60
VG Vladimir Guerrero Jsy 10.00 4.50

2003 Topps Pristine Corners Relics

MINT NRMT
STATED ODDS 1:12
REFRACTOR ODDS 1:285
REFRACTOR PRINT RUN 25 SERIAL #'d SETS
NO REFRACTOR PRICING DUE TO SCARCITY
AS Edgardo Alfonzo Bat 10.00 4.50
J.T. Snow Bat
BK Sean Burroughs Jsy 10.00 4.50
Ryan Klesko Bat
BM Adrian Beltre Bat 15.00 6.75
Fred McGriff Bat
BT David Bell Bat 15.00 6.75
Jim Thome Bat
CD Eric Chavez Bat 10.00 4.50
Erubiel Durazo Bat
GS Troy Glaus Jsy 10.00 4.50
Scott Speizio Jsy
KM Corey Koskie Bat 15.00 6.75
Doug Mientkiewicz Bat
RM Scott Rolen Bat 25.00 11.00
Tino Martinez Bat
TP Mark Teixeira Bat 15.00 6.75
Rafael Palmeiro Bat
VG Robin Ventura Bat 10.00 4.50
Jason Giambi Bat
WG Matt Williams Bat 15.00 6.75
Mark Grace Bat

2003 Topps Pristine Factor Bat Relics

MINT NRMT
STATED ODDS 1:9
REFRACTOR ODDS 1:210
REFRACTOR PRINT RUN 25 SERIAL #'d SETS
NO REFRACTOR PRICING DUE TO SCARCITY
AD Adam Dunn 10.00 4.50
AR Alex Rodriguez 10.00 4.50
AS Alfonso Soriano 10.00 4.50
DE Darin Erstad 8.00 3.60
JG Jason Giambi 8.00 3.60
LB Lance Berkman 8.00 3.60
MO Magglio Ordonez 8.00 3.60
MP Mike Piazza 15.00 6.75
MR Manny Ramirez 10.00 4.50
NG Nomar Garciaparra 15.00 6.75
SS Sammy Sosa 15.00 6.75
TG Troy Glaus 8.00 3.60
TH Todd Helton 10.00 4.50
TKH Torii Hunter 8.00 3.60
VG Vladimir Guerrero 10.00 4.50

2003 Topps Pristine Mini

MINT NRMT
VETERAN STATED ODDS 1:8
ROOKIE STATED ODDS 1:16
AK Austin Kearns V 3.00 1.35
AR Alex Rodriguez V 10.00 4.50
AS Alfonso Soriano V 4.00 1.80
BB Barry Bonds V 15.00 6.75
BC Bernie Castro R 3.00 1.35
BG Brian Giles V 3.00 1.35
BPB Bryan Bullington R 10.00 4.50
BWB Bobby Basham R 4.00 1.80
CW Chien-Ming Wang R 8.00 3.60
DH Dan Haren R 5.00 2.20
DJ Derek Jeter V 15.00 6.75
DM Dustin McGowan R 8.00 3.60
EC Eric Chavez V 3.00 1.35
ELC Eric Crozier R 4.00 1.80
ER Elizardo Ramirez R 8.00 3.60
IS Ichiro Suzuki V 10.00 4.50
JB Jeremy Bonderman R 5.00 2.20
JC Jose Contreras R 8.00 3.60
JG Jason Giambi V 3.00 1.35
JJK Jason Kubel R 10.00 4.50
JK Jeff Kent V 3.00 1.35
JT Jim Thome V 6.00 2.70
KY Kevin Youkilis R 8.00 3.60
MH Michel Hernandez R 3.00 1.35
MJP Mike Piazza V 10.00 4.50
MO Magglio Ordonez V 3.00 1.35
MP Mark Prior V 6.00 2.70
MT Miguel Tejada V 3.00 1.35
NG Nomar Garciaparra V 10.00 4.50
NL Nook Logan R 3.00 1.35
RB Rocco Baldelli V 3.00 1.35
RC Roger Clemens V 12.00 5.50
RD Rajai Davis R 4.00 1.80
RH Ryan Howard R 10.00 4.50
RJC Robinson Cano R 6.00 2.70
RS Ryan Shealy R 5.00 2.20
SS Sammy Sosa V 10.00 4.50
TM Tyler Martin R 3.00 1.35
VG Vladimir Guerrero V 6.00 2.70
WL Wil Ledezma R 4.00 1.80

2003 Topps Pristine Mini Autograph

MINT NRMT
STATED ODDS 1:636
STATED PRINT RUN 100 CARDS
PRINT RUN INFO PROVIDED BY TOPPS

CARD IS NOT SERIAL-NUMBERED ....
RC Roger Clemens 120.00 55.00

2003 Topps Pristine Personal Endorsements

MINT NRMT
STATED ODDS 1:5
GOLD STATED ODDS 1:184
GOLD PRINT RUN 25 SERIAL #'d SETS
NO GOLD PRICING DUE TO SCARCITY
AB Andrew Brown 15.00 6.75
BM Brett Myers 10.00 4.50
DE David Eckstein 10.00 4.50
FS Felix Sanchez 10.00 4.50
FV Fernando Vina 10.00 4.50
JG Jay Gibbons 10.00 4.50
JP Josh Phelps 10.00 4.50
KH Ken Harvey 15.00 6.75
KS Kelly Shoppach 15.00 6.75
LF Lew Ford 15.00 6.75
ML Mike Lowell 15.00 6.75
MS Mike Sweeney 15.00 6.75
PK Paul Konerko 15.00 6.75
RJH Rich Harden 25.00 11.00
RYC Ryan Church 10.00 4.50
SR Scott Rolen 25.00 11.00
VM Victor Martinez 25.00 11.00

2003 Topps Pristine Primary Elements Patch Relics

MINT NRMT
STATED ODDS 1:45
STATED PRINT RUN 50 SETS
CARDS ARE NOT SERIAL-NUMBERED
PRINT RUN INFO PROVIDED BY TOPPS
NO PRICING DUE TO SCARCITY
REFRACTOR ODDS 1:224
REFRACTOR PRINT RUN 10 SERIAL #'d SETS
NO REFRACTOR PRICING DUE TO SCARCITY
AD Adam Dunn
AJ Andruw Jones
AP Albert Pujols
AR Alex Rodriguez
BB Barry Bonds
BRB Bret Boone
BZ Barry Zito
CD Carlos Delgado
CJ Chipper Jones
CR Cal Ripken
CS Curt Schilling
EC Eric Chavez
EG Eric Gagne
GM Greg Maddux
JB Jeff Bagwell
KI Kazuhisa Ishii
LB Lance Berkman
LG Luis Gonzalez
MM Mark Mulder
MO Magglio Ordonez
MP Mike Piazza
MR Manny Ramirez
MRO Moises Alou
MT Miguel Tejada
NG Nomar Garciaparra
PK Paul Konerko
PM Pedro Martinez
RJ Randy Johnson
RO Roy Oswalt
RP Rafael Palmeiro
SG Shawn Green
SS Sammy Sosa
TG Tony Gwynn
TH Todd Helton
TKH Torii Hunter

2004 Topps Pristine

This 190-card set was released in October, 2004. The set was issued, in what has been traditional for this product, in a pack within a pack concept. The "full" pack, is an eight card pack with an $30 SRP which came five packs to a box and six boxes to a case. Cards numbered 1 through 100 feature veterans while cards 101 through 190 feature three cards each of the same rookie with decreasing print runs for each card. The Common Rookie Cards were printed in the approximate same print run as the veterans while the uncommon cards were issued to a stated rate of one in two with a stated print run of 999 serial numbered sets and the rare rookies were issued with a stated print run of 499 serial numbered sets and were issued at a stated rate of one in four. There are some reports that the #168 and #169 Chris Saenz cards were never produced.

Nm-Mt Ex-Mt
COMMON CARD (1-100) .... 1.50 .45
COMMON C (101-190) .... 2.00 .60
C 101-190 APPROX.EQUAL TO 1-100
COMMON U (101-190) .... 3.00 .90
UNCOMMON 101-190 STATED ODDS 1:2
UNCOMMON 101-190 PRINT 999 #'d SETS
COMMON R (101-190) 5.00 1.50
RARE 101-190 STATED ODDS 1:4
RARE 101-190 PRINT RUN 499 #'d SETS
OVERALL PLATES ODDS 1:52 HOBBY
PLATE PRINT RUN 1 SET PER COLOR
BLACK-CYAN-MAGENTA-YELLOW ISSUED
NO PLATE PRICING DUE TO SCARCITY
1 Jim Thome 4.00 1.20
2 Ryan Klesko .... 1.50 .45
3 Ichiro Suzuki 6.00 1.80
4 Rocco Baldelli .... 1.50 .45
5 Vernon Wells .... 1.50 .45
6 Javier Vazquez .... 1.50 .45
7 Billy Wagner .... 1.50 .45
8 Jose Reyes .... 1.50 .45
9 Lance Berkman .... 1.50 .45
10 Alex Rodriguez 6.00 1.80
11 Pat Burrell .... 1.50 .45
12 Mark Mulder .... 1.50 .45
13 Mike Piazza 6.00 1.80
14 Miguel Cabrera .... 2.50 .75
15 Larry Walker .... 2.50 .75
16 Carlos Lee .... 1.50 .45
17 Mark Prior 4.00 1.20
18 Pedro Martinez 4.00 1.20
19 Melvin Mora .... 1.50 .45
20 Sammy Sosa 6.00 1.80
21 Bartolo Colon .... 1.50 .45
22 Luis Gonzalez .... 1.50 .45
23 Marcus Giles .... 1.50 .45
24 Ken Griffey Jr. 6.00 1.80
25 Ivan Rodriguez 4.00 1.20
26 Carlos Beltran .... 2.50 .75
27 Geoff Jenkins .... 1.50 .45
28 Nick Johnson .... 1.50 .45
29 Gary Sheffield .... 1.50 .45
30 Alfonso Soriano .... 2.50 .75
31 Scott Rolen 4.00 1.20
32 Garret Anderson .... 1.50 .45
33 Richie Sexson .... 1.50 .45
34 Curt Schilling 4.00 1.20
35 Greg Maddux 6.00 1.80
36 Adam Dunn .... 2.50 .75
37 Preston Wilson .... 1.50 .45
38 Josh Beckett .... 1.50 .45
39 Roy Oswalt .... 1.50 .45
40 Derek Jeter 8.00 2.40
41 Jason Kendall .... 1.50 .45
42 Bret Boone .... 1.50 .45
43 Torii Hunter .... 1.50 .45
44 Roy Halladay .... 1.50 .45
45 Edgar Renteria .... 1.50 .45
46 Troy Glaus .... 1.50 .45
47 Chipper Jones 4.00 1.20
48 Manny Ramirez .... 2.50 .75
49 C.C. Sabathia .... 1.50 .45
50 Albert Pujols 8.00 2.40
51 Randy Wolf .... 1.50 .45
52 Eric Chavez .... 1.50 .45
53 Kevin Brown .... 1.50 .45
54 Cliff Floyd .... 1.50 .45
55 Jeff Bagwell .... 2.50 .75
56 Frank Thomas 4.00 1.20
57 David Ortiz 4.00 1.20
58 Rafael Palmeiro .... 2.50 .75
59 Randy Johnson 4.00 1.20
60 Vladimir Guerrero 4.00 1.20
61 Carlos Delgado .... 1.50 .45
62 Hank Blalock .... 1.50 .45
63 Jim Edmonds .... 1.50 .45
64 Jason Schmidt .... 1.50 .45
65 Mike Lieberthal .... 1.50 .45
66 Tim Hudson .... 1.50 .45
67 Jorge Posada .... 2.50 .75
68 Jose Vidro .... 1.50 .45
69 Eric Gagne 4.00 1.20
70 Roger Clemens 8.00 2.40
71 Mike Lowell .... 1.50 .45
72 Dontrelle Willis .... 1.50 .45
73 Austin Kearns .... 1.50 .45
74 Kerry Wood 4.00 1.20
75 Miguel Tejada .... 1.50 .45
76 Bobby Abreu .... 1.50 .45
77 Edgar Martinez .... 2.50 .75
78 Joe Mauer .... 2.50 .75
79 Mike Sweeney .... 1.50 .45
80 Jason Giambi .... 1.50 .45
81 Mark Teixeira .... 1.50 .45
82 Aubrey Huff .... 1.50 .45
83 Brian Giles .... 1.50 .45
84 Barry Zito .... 1.50 .45
85 Mike Mussina .... 2.50 .75
86 Brandon Webb .... 1.50 .45
87 Andruw Jones .... 1.50 .45
88 Javy Lopez .... 1.50 .45
89 Bill Mueller .... 1.50 .45
90 Scott Podsednik .... 1.50 .45
91 Moises Alou .... 1.50 .45
92 Esteban Loaiza .... 1.50 .45
93 Magglio Ordonez .... 1.50 .45
94 Jeff Kent .... 1.50 .45
95 Todd Helton .... 2.50 .75
96 Juan Pierre .... 1.50 .45
97 Jody Gerut .... 1.50 .45
98 Angel Berroa .... 1.50 .45
99 Shawn Green .... 1.50 .45
100 Nomar Garciaparra 6.00 1.80
101 David Aardsma C RC .... 2.00 .60
102 David Aardsma U .... 3.00 .90
103 David Aardsma R 5.00 1.50
104 Erick Aybar C RC 4.00 1.20
105 Erick Aybar U 6.00 1.80
106 Erick Aybar R 10.00 3.00
107 Chad Bentz C RC .... 2.00 .60
108 Chad Bentz U .... 3.00 .90
109 Chad Bentz R 5.00 1.50
110 Travis Blackley C RC .... 2.00 .60
111 Travis Blackley U .... 3.00 .90
112 Travis Blackley R 5.00 1.50
113 Bobby Brownlie C RC .... 3.00 .90
114 Bobby Brownlie U 5.00 1.50
115 Bobby Brownlie R 8.00 2.40
116 Alberto Callaspo C RC .... 3.00 .90
117 Alberto Callaspo U 5.00 1.50
118 Alberto Callaspo R 8.00 2.40
119 Kazuo Matsui C RC 5.00 1.50
120 Kazuo Matsui U 8.00 2.40
121 Kazuo Matsui R 12.00 3.60
122 Jesse Crain C RC .... 3.00 .90
123 Jesse Crain U 5.00 1.50
124 Jesse Crain R 8.00 2.40
125 Howie Kendrick C RC .... 3.00 .90
126 Howie Kendrick U 5.00 1.50
127 Howie Kendrick R 8.00 2.40
128 Blake Hawksworth C RC .... 2.00 .60
129 Blake Hawksworth U .... 3.00 .90
130 Blake Hawksworth R 5.00 1.50
131 Conor Jackson C RC 6.00 1.80
132 Conor Jackson U 10.00 3.00
133 Conor Jackson R 15.00 4.50
134 Paul Maholm C RC .... 3.00 .90
135 Paul Maholm U 5.00 1.50
136 Paul Maholm R 8.00 2.40
137 Lastings Milledge C RC 6.00 1.80
138 Lastings Milledge U 10.00 3.00
139 Lastings Milledge R 15.00 4.50
140 Matt Moses C RC .... 3.00 .90
141 Matt Moses U 5.00 1.50
142 Matt Moses R 8.00 2.40
143 David Murphy C RC .... 3.00 .90
144 David Murphy U 5.00 1.50
145 David Murphy R 8.00 2.40
146 Dioner Navarro C RC 4.00 1.20
147 Dioner Navarro U 6.00 1.80
148 Dioner Navarro R 10.00 3.00
149 Dustin Nippert C RC .... 2.00 .60
150 Dustin Nippert U .... 3.00 .90
151 Dustin Nippert R 5.00 1.50
152 Vito Chiaravalloti C RC .... 3.00 .90
153 Vito Chiaravalloti U 5.00 1.50
154 Vito Chiaravalloti R 8.00 2.40
155 Akinori Otsuka C RC .... 2.00 .60
156 Akinori Otsuka U .... 3.00 .90
157 Akinori Otsuka R 5.00 1.50
158 Casey Daigle C RC .... 2.00 .60
159 Casey Daigle U .... 3.00 .90
160 Casey Daigle R 5.00 1.50
161 Carlos Quentin C RC 6.00 1.80
162 Carlos Quentin U 10.00 3.00
163 Carlos Quentin R 15.00 4.50
164 Omar Quintanilla C RC .... 3.00 .90
165 Omar Quintanilla U 5.00 1.50
166 Omar Quintanilla R 8.00 2.40
167 Chris Saenz C RC .... 2.00 .60
168 Chris Saenz U ....
169 Chris Saenz R ....
170 Ervin Santana C RC 4.00 1.20
171 Ervin Santana U 6.00 1.80
172 Ervin Santana R 10.00 3.00
173 Chris Shelton C RC .... 3.00 .90
174 Chris Shelton U 5.00 1.50
175 Chris Shelton R 8.00 2.40
176 Kyle Sleeth C RC .... 3.00 .90
177 Kyle Sleeth U 5.00 1.50
178 Kyle Sleeth R 8.00 2.40
179 Brad Snyder C RC .... 3.00 .90
180 Brad Snyder U 5.00 1.50
181 Brad Snyder R 8.00 2.40
182 Tim Stauffer C RC .... 3.00 .90
183 Tim Stauffer U 5.00 1.50
184 Tim Stauffer R 8.00 2.40
185 Shingo Takatsu C RC .... 3.00 .90
186 Shingo Takatsu U 5.00 1.50
187 Shingo Takatsu R 8.00 2.40
188 Merkin Valdez C RC .... 3.00 .90
189 Merkin Valdez U 5.00 1.50
190 Merkin Valdez R 8.00 2.40

2004 Topps Pristine Gold Refractors

Nm-Mt Ex-Mt
*GOLD 1-100: 2.5X TO 6X BASIC
*GOLD C 101-190: 2.5X TO 6X BASIC
*GOLD U 101-190: 1.5X TO 4X BASIC
*GOLD R 101-190: 1X TO 2.5X BASIC
ONE PER SEALED HOBBY BOX
STATED PRINT RUN 41 SERIAL #'d SETS
137 Lastings Milledge C 60.00 18.00
138 Lastings Milledge U 60.00 18.00
139 Lastings Milledge R 60.00 18.00

2004 Topps Pristine Refractors

Nm-Mt Ex-Mt
*REFRACTORS 1-100: 2.5X TO 6X BASIC
1-100 STATED ODDS 1:11
1-100 PRINT RUN 49 SERIAL #'d SETS
*REFRACTORS C 101-190: .6X TO 1.5X BASIC
COMMON 101-190 RANDOM IN PACKS
COMMON 101-190 PRINT RUN 999 #'d SETS
*REFRACTORS U 101-190: .6X TO 1.5X BASIC
UNCOMMON 101-190 ODDS 1:5
UNCOMMON 101-190 PRINT 399 #'d SETS
*REFRACTORS R 101-190: 1X TO 2.5X BASIC
RARE 101-190 ODDS 1:35
RARE 101-190 PRINT RUN 49 #'d SETS
137 Lastings Milledge C 10.00 3.00
138 Lastings Milledge U 15.00 4.50
139 Lastings Milledge R 60.00 18.00

2004 Topps Pristine 1-2-3 Triple Relics

Nm-Mt Ex-Mt
STATED ODDS 1:171
*REFRACTOR: X TO X BASIC
REFRACTOR ODDS 1:686
REFRACTOR PRINT RUN 25 #'d SETS
B ='S BAT; J ='S JSY
BOS Johnny Damon Bat 50.00 15.00
Bill Mueller Jsy
Nomar Garciaparra Jsy
CHC Mark Grudzielanek Bat 40.00 12.00
Alex Gonzalez Bat
Sammy Sosa Bat
NYY Kenny Lofton Bat 50.00 15.00
Derek Jeter Bat
Alex Rodriguez Bat

2004 Topps Pristine Fantasy Favorites Relics

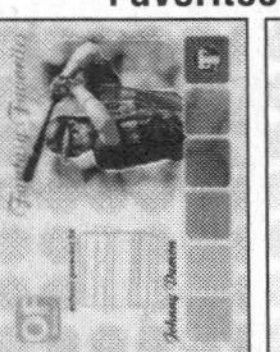
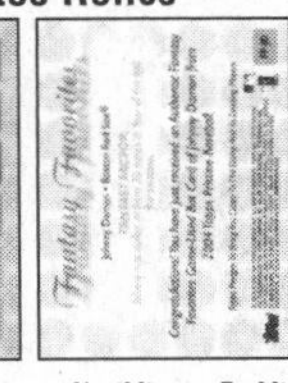

Nm-Mt Ex-Mt
RANDOM INSERTS IN PACKS
*REFRACTOR: 2X TO 5X BASIC
REFRACTOR STATED ODDS 1:59
REFRACTOR PRINT RUN 25 #'d SETS
AB Angel Berroa Bat 5.00 1.50
AJ Andruw Jones Jsy 5.00 1.50
AP Albert Pujols Jsy 15.00 4.50
AR Alex Rodriguez Bat 10.00 3.00
BB Bret Boone Jsy 5.00 1.50
BW Brandon Webb Uni 5.00 1.50
CD Carlos Delgado Jsy 5.00 1.50
CJ Chipper Jones Jsy 10.00 3.00
CK Corey Koskie Bat 5.00 1.50
DJ Derek Jeter Bat 20.00 6.00
EG Eric Gagne Jsy 10.00 3.00
FT Frank Thomas Jsy 10.00 3.00
JB Jeff Bagwell Uni 8.00 2.40
JD Johnny Damon Bat 10.00 3.00
JR Jimmy Rollins Jsy 5.00 1.50
JT Jim Thome Uni 10.00 3.00
JV Jose Vidro Bat 5.00 1.50
KL Kenny Lofton Bat 5.00 1.50
KW Kerry Wood Jsy 10.00 3.00
LW Larry Walker Jsy 8.00 2.40
MA Moises Alou Jsy 5.00 1.50
MG Mark Grudzielanek Bat 5.00 1.50
MP Mark Prior Jsy 10.00 3.00
MPI Mike Piazza Jsy 10.00 3.00
MT Mark Teixeira Bat 5.00 1.50
NG Nomar Garciaparra Jsy 10.00 3.00
PM Pedro Martinez Jsy 10.00 3.00
PW Preston Wilson Jsy 5.00 1.50
RB Rocco Baldelli Bat 5.00 1.50
RF Rafael Furcal Bat 5.00 1.50
RFJ Rafael Furcal Jsy 5.00 1.50
SG Shawn Green Jsy 5.00 1.50
TH Tim Hudson Jsy 5.00 1.50
THE Todd Helton Jsy 8.00 2.40
VG Vladimir Guerrero Bat 10.00 3.00

2004 Topps Pristine Going Going Gone Bat Relics

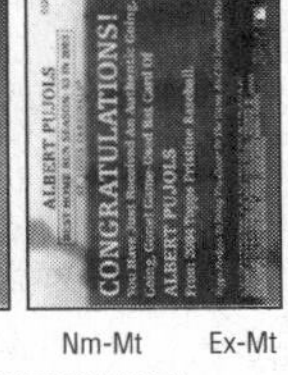

Nm-Mt Ex-Mt
GROUP A ODDS 1:6
GROUP B ODDS 1:11
*REFRACTOR: 2X TO 5X BASIC
REFRACTOR STATED ODDS 1:93
REFRACTOR PRINT RUN 25 #'d SETS
AD Adam Dunn B 8.00 2.40
AP Albert Pujols A 15.00 4.50
AR Alex Rodriguez A 10.00 3.00
AS Alfonso Soriano A 8.00 2.40
BB Bret Boone A 5.00 1.50
CJ Chipper Jones A 10.00 3.00
DO David Ortiz B 10.00 3.00
FT Frank Thomas B 10.00 3.00
JG Juan Gonzalez A 8.00 2.40
JJ Jacque Jones A 5.00 1.50
JK Jeff Kent A 5.00 1.50
JT Jim Thome A 10.00 3.00
LB Lance Berkman A 5.00 1.50
LG Luis Gonzalez A 5.00 1.50
MO Magglio Ordonez A 5.00 1.50
MP Mike Piazza B 10.00 3.00
MR Manny Ramirez B 8.00 2.40
RK Ryan Klesko B 5.00 1.50
SR Scott Rolen A 10.00 3.00
SS Sammy Sosa A 10.00 3.00
VG Vladimir Guerrero A 10.00 3.00
VW Vernon Wells A 5.00 1.50

2004 Topps Pristine Key Acquisition Bat Relics

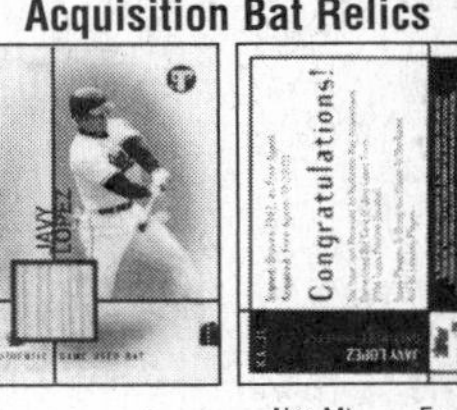

Nm-Mt Ex-Mt
STATED ODDS 1:8
*REFRACTOR: 2X TO 5X BASIC
REFRACTOR ODDS 1:256
REFRACTOR PRINT RUN 25 #'d SETS
AR Alex Rodriguez 10.00 3.00
AS Alfonso Soriano 8.00 2.40
GS Gary Sheffield 5.00 1.50
HC Hee Seop Choi 5.00 1.50
IR Ivan Rodriguez 10.00 3.00
JG Juan Gonzalez 8.00 2.40
JL Javy Lopez 5.00 1.50
VG Vladimir Guerrero 10.00 3.00

2004 Topps Pristine Mini

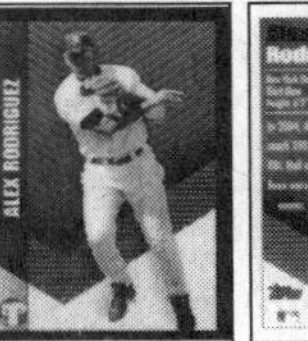

Nm-Mt Ex-Mt
STATED ODDS 1:5
AO Akinori Otsuka R .... 3.00 .90
AP Albert Pujols V 10.00 3.00
AR Alex Rodriguez V 8.00 2.40
BH Blake Hawksworth R .... 3.00 .90
CJ Chipper Jones V 5.00 1.50
CJA Conor Jackson R 8.00 2.40
DA David Aardsma R .... 3.00 .90
DJ Derek Jeter V 10.00 3.00
DM David Murphy R 4.00 1.20
DN Dioner Navarro R 5.00 1.50
DW Dontrelle Willis V .... 3.00 .90
EA Erick Aybar R 5.00 1.50
HK Howie Kendrick R 4.00 1.20
IS Ichiro Suzuki V 8.00 2.40
JG Jason Giambi V .... 3.00 .90
JT Jim Thome V 5.00 1.50
KM Kazuo Matsui R 6.00 1.80
KS Kyle Sleeth R 4.00 1.20
KW Kerry Wood V 5.00 1.50
LM Lastings Milledge R 8.00 2.40
MM Matt Moses R 4.00 1.20
MP Mark Prior V 5.00 1.50
MPI Mike Piazza V 8.00 2.40
MV Merkin Valdez R 4.00 1.20
NG Nomar Garciaparra V 8.00 2.40
SS Sammy Sosa V 8.00 2.40
ST Shingo Takatsu R 4.00 1.20
TS Tim Stauffer R 4.00 1.20
VC Vito Chiaravalloti R 4.00 1.20
VG Vladimir Guerrero V 5.00 1.50

2004 Topps Pristine Mini Relics

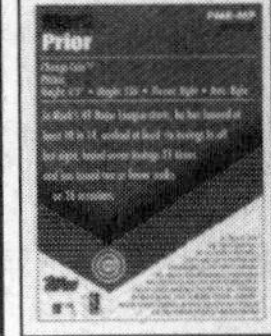

Nm-Mt Ex-Mt
STATED ODDS 1:51
STATED PRINT RUN 100 SETS
CARDS ARE NOT SERIAL-NUMBERED
PRINT RUN INFO PROVIDED BY TOPPS
AP Albert Pujols Jsy 25.00 7.50
CJ Chipper Jones Jsy 15.00 4.50
EG Eric Gagne Jsy 15.00 4.50
JB Jeff Bagwell Uni 12.00 3.60
KW Kerry Wood Jsy 15.00 4.50
MP Mark Prior Jsy 15.00 4.50
NG Nomar Garciaparra Jsy 15.00 4.50
PM Pedro Martinez Jsy 15.00 4.50
PW Preston Wilson Jsy 8.00 2.40
MPI Mike Piazza Jsy 15.00 4.50

2004 Topps Pristine Patch Place Relics

Nm-Mt Ex-Mt
GROUP A ODDS 1:30
GROUP B ODDS 1:34
REFRACTOR STATED ODDS 1:155

REFRACTOR PRINT RUN 10 #'d SETS
NO REF.PRICING DUE TO SCARCITY..
LISTED PRICES ARE SINGLE COLOR PATCH
*MULTI-COLOR: ADD 100% PREMIUM

AD Adam Dunn A 15.00 4.50
AJ Andruw Jones A 10.00 3.00
AK Austin Kearns A 10.00 3.00
AP Albert Pujols B 40.00 12.00
BB Bret Boone B 10.00 3.00
BZ Barry Zito A 10.00 3.00
CC Chin-Feng Chen A 40.00 12.00
CD Carlos Delgado A 10.00 3.00
CJ Chipper Jones B 15.00 4.50
DW Dontrelle Willis A 10.00 3.00
EG Eric Gagne A 15.00 4.50
FT Frank Thomas A 15.00 4.50
JB Jeff Bagwell B 15.00 4.50
JBE Josh Beckett B 10.00 3.00
JR Jose Reyes A 10.00 3.00
JS John Smoltz A 15.00 4.50
KW Kerry Wood A 15.00 4.50
LC Luis Castillo A 10.00 3.00
LG Luis Gonzalez B 10.00 3.00
ML Mike Lowell A 10.00 3.00
MP Mark Prior B 15.00 4.50
MPI Mike Piazza B 15.00 4.50
NG Nomar Garciaparra A 15.00 4.50
PL Paul Lo Duca A 10.00 3.00
PM Pedro Martinez B 15.00 4.50
PW Preston Wilson A 10.00 3.00
RB Rocco Baldelli A 10.00 3.00
RF Rafael Furcal A 10.00 3.00
RJ Randy Johnson B 15.00 4.50
SG Shawn Green A 10.00 3.00
SS Sammy Sosa A 15.00 4.50
TH Tim Hudson A 10.00 3.00
THE Todd Helton B 15.00 4.50

2004 Topps Pristine Personal Endorsements

Nm-Mt Ex-Mt
GROUP A ODDS 1:39
GROUP B ODDS 1:41
GROUP C ODDS 1:7
GOLD STATED ODDS 1:73
GOLD PRINT RUN 25 SERIAL #'d SETS
NO GOLD PRICING DUE TO SCARCITY

AH Aubrey Huff C 10.00 3.00
AR Alex Rodriguez A 150.00 45.00
BC Bobby Crosby C 15.00 4.50
BM Brett Myers A 10.00 3.00
BW Brandon Webb B 10.00 3.00
CJ Conor Jackson C 25.00 7.50
CL Chris Lubanski C 10.00 3.00
DA David Aardsma C 10.00 3.00
DM Dustin McGowan C 10.00 3.00
DY Delmon Young A 25.00 7.50
EH Estee Harris C 10.00 3.00
ES Ervin Santana C 15.00 4.50
GA Garret Anderson A 15.00 4.50
GS Gary Sheffield A 40.00 12.00
GSI Grady Sizemore C 15.00 4.50
HB Hank Blalock B 15.00 4.50
IR Ivan Rodriguez A 40.00 12.00
JF Jennie Finch A 150.00 45.00
JM Joe Mauer B 40.00 12.00
JP Jorge Posada A 40.00 12.00
JV Javier Vazquez A 15.00 4.50
LB Lance Berkman A 25.00 7.50
MC Miguel Cabrera B 25.00 7.50
MG Marcus Giles A 15.00 4.50
SP Scott Podsednik B 15.00 4.50
VC Vito Chiaravalloti C 15.00 4.50
VG Vladimir Guerrero A 40.00 12.00
WM Willie Mays A 200.00 60.00

2004 Topps Pristine Two of a Kind Dual Autographs

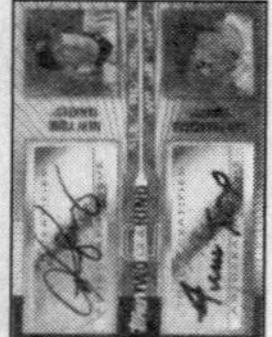

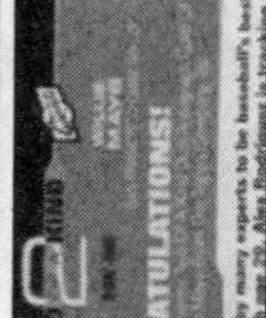

Nm-Mt Ex-Mt
STATED ODDS 1:3705
STATED PRINT RUN 13 SERIAL #'d CARDS
NO PRICING DUE TO SCARCITY
RM Alex Rodriguez
Willie Mays

2001 Topps Reserve

Issued in August, 2001, this 151 card set was issued in special boxes which included a signed baseball of a rookie/prospect and 10 packs.

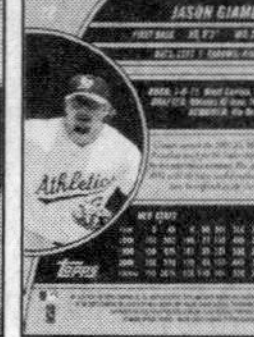

Cards numbered 101-151 were short printed. Cards numbered 101-145 and 151 were available at a rate of one in five hobby packs and one in 52 retail packs. Cards numbered 146-150 were inserted at a rate of one in 54 retail packs. Cards numbered 101-145 had a print run of 945 serial number sets, cards numbered 146-150 had a print run of 1170 sets and card number 151 had a print run of 1500 sets.

Nm-Mt Ex-Mt
COMP.SET w/o SP's (100) 100.00 30.00
COMMON CARD (1-100) 1.00 .30
COMMON (101-151) 8.00 2.40
1 Darin Erstad 1.00 .30
2 Moises Alou 1.00 .30
3 Tony Batista 1.00 .30
4 Andruw Jones 1.00 .30
5 Edgar Renteria 1.00 .30
6 Eric Young 1.00 .30
7 Steve Finley 1.00 .30
8 Adrian Beltre 1.50 .45
9 Vladimir Guerrero 2.50 .75
10 Barry Bonds 6.00 1.80
11 Juan Gonzalez 1.50 .45
12 Jay Buhner 1.00 .30
13 Luis Castillo 1.00 .30
14 Cal Ripken 8.00 2.40
15 Bob Abreu 1.00 .30
16 Ivan Rodriguez 2.50 .75
17 Nomar Garciaparra 4.00 1.20
18 Todd Helton 1.50 .45
19 Bobby Higginson 1.00 .30
20 Jorge Posada 1.50 .45
21 Tim Salmon 1.50 .45
22 Jason Giambi 1.00 .30
23 Jose Cruz Jr. 1.00 .30
24 Chipper Jones 2.50 .75
25 Jim Edmonds 1.00 .30
26 Gerald Williams 1.00 .30
27 Randy Johnson 2.50 .75
28 Gary Sheffield 1.00 .30
29 Jeff Kent 1.00 .30
30 Jim Thome 2.50 .75
31 John Olerud 1.00 .30
32 Cliff Floyd 1.00 .30
33 Mike Lowell 1.00 .30
34 Phil Nevin 1.00 .30
35 Scott Rolen 2.50 .75
36 Alex Rodriguez 4.00 1.20
37 Ken Griffey Jr. 4.00 1.20
38 Neifi Perez 1.00 .30
39 Cristian Guzman 1.00 .30
40 Mariano Rivera 1.50 .45
41 Troy Glaus 1.00 .30
42 Johnny Damon 1.50 .45
43 Rafael Furcal 1.00 .30
44 Jeromy Burnitz 1.00 .30
45 Mark McGwire 6.00 1.80
46 Fred McGriff 1.50 .45
47 Matt Williams 1.00 .30
48 Kevin Brown 1.00 .30
49 J.T. Snow 1.00 .30
50 Kenny Lofton 1.00 .30
51 Al Martin 1.00 .30
52 Antonio Alfonseca 1.00 .30
53 Edgardo Alfonzo 1.00 .30
54 Ryan Klesko 1.00 .30
55 Pat Burrell 1.00 .30
56 Rafael Palmeiro 1.50 .45
57 Sean Casey 1.00 .30
58 Jeff Cirillo 1.00 .30
59 Ray Durham 1.00 .30
60 Derek Jeter 6.00 1.80
61 Jeff Bagwell 1.50 .45
62 Carlos Delgado 1.00 .30
63 Tom Glavine 1.50 .45
64 Richie Sexson 1.00 .30
65 J.D. Drew 1.00 .30
66 Ben Grieve 1.00 .30
67 Mark Grace 1.50 .45
68 Shawn Green 1.00 .30
69 Robb Nen 1.00 .30
70 Omar Vizquel 1.50 .45
71 Edgar Martinez 1.50 .45
72 Preston Wilson 1.00 .30
73 Mike Piazza 4.00 1.20
74 Tony Gwynn 3.00 .90
75 Jason Kendall 1.00 .30
76 Manny Ramirez 1.50 .45
77 Pokey Reese 1.00 .30
78 Mike Sweeney 1.00 .30
79 Magglio Ordonez 1.00 .30
80 Bernie Williams 1.50 .45
81 Richard Hidalgo 1.00 .30
82 Brad Fullmer 1.00 .30
83 Greg Maddux 4.00 1.20
84 Geoff Jenkins 1.00 .30
85 Sammy Sosa 4.00 1.20
86 Luis Gonzalez 1.00 .30
87 Eric Karros 1.00 .30
88 Jose Vidro 1.00 .30
89 Rich Aurilia 1.00 .30
90 Roberto Alomar 1.50 .45
91 Mike Cameron 1.00 .30
92 Mike Mussina 1.50 .45
93 Barry Zito 1.50 .45
94 Mike Lieberthal 1.00 .30
95 Brian Giles 1.00 .30
96 Pedro Martinez 2.50 .75
97 Barry Larkin 1.50 .45
98 Jermaine Dye 1.00 .30
99 Frank Thomas 2.50 .75
100 David Justice 1.00 .30
101 Gary Johnson RC 8.00 2.40
102 Matt Ford RC 8.00 2.40
103 Albert Pujols RC 80.00 24.00
104 Brad Cresse 8.00 2.40
105 V. Pascucci RC 8.00 2.40
106 Bob Keppel RC 10.00 3.00
107 Luis Torres RC 8.00 2.40
108 Tony Blanco RC 10.00 3.00
109 Ronnie Corona RC 8.00 2.40
110 Phil Wilson RC 8.00 2.40
111 John Buck RC 10.00 3.00
112 Jim Journell RC 8.00 2.40
113 Victor Hall RC 8.00 2.40
114 Jeff Andra RC 8.00 2.40
115 Greg Nash RC 8.00 2.40
116 Travis Hafner RC 15.00 4.50
117 Casey Fossum RC 8.00 2.40
118 Miguel Olivo 8.00 2.40
119 Elpidio Guzman RC 8.00 2.40
120 Jason Belcher RC 8.00 2.40
121 Esix Snead RC 8.00 2.40
122 Joe Thurston RC 8.00 2.40
123 Rafael Soriano RC 10.00 3.00
124 Ed Rogers RC 8.00 2.40
125 Omar Beltre RC 8.00 2.40
126 Brett Gray RC 8.00 2.40
127 Deivi Mendez RC 8.00 2.40
128 Freddie Bynum RC 8.00 2.40
129 David Krynzel 8.00 2.40
130 Blake Williams RC 8.00 2.40
131 R. Abercrombie RC 8.00 2.40
132 Miguel Villilo RC 8.00 2.40
133 Ryan Madson RC 10.00 3.00
134 Matt Thompson RC 8.00 2.40
135 Mark Burnett RC 8.00 2.40
136 Andy Beal RC 8.00 2.40
137 Ryan Ludwick RC 8.00 2.40
138 Roberto Miniel RC 8.00 2.40
139 Steve Smyth RC 8.00 2.40
140 Ben Washburn RC 8.00 2.40
141 Marvin Seale RC 8.00 2.40
142 Reggie Griggs RC 8.00 2.40
143 Seung Song RC 10.00 3.00
144 Chad Petty RC 8.00 2.40
145 Noel Devarez RC 8.00 2.40
146 Matt Butler RC 8.00 2.40
147 Brett Evert RC 8.00 2.40
148 Cesar Izturis 8.00 2.40
149 Troy Farnsworth RC 8.00 2.40
150 Brian Schmitt RC 8.00 2.40
151 Ichiro Suzuki RC 50.00 15.00

2001 Topps Reserve Rookie Autographs

Inserted in retail packs, these 50 cards feature autographs from rookie/prospects in the Topps Reserve product. Cards numbered 1-45 have a stated print run of 160 sets while cards numbered 46-50 have a stated print run of 330 set. Group A cards were inserted at a rate of one in 155 while Group B cards were inserted at a rate of one in 252. Overall, the odds of getting an autograph card was one in 96 retail packs. These cards have a "TRA" prefix.

Nm-Mt Ex-Mt
TRA-1 Gary Johnson A 12.00 3.60
TRA-2 Matt Ford A 12.00 3.60
TRA-3 Albert Pujols A 250.00 75.00
TRA-4 Brad Cresse A 12.00 3.60
TRA-5 V. Pascucci A 12.00 3.60
TRA-6 Bob Keppel A 15.00 4.50
TRA-7 Luis Torres A 12.00 3.60
TRA-8 Tony Blanco A 20.00 6.00
TRA-9 Ronnie Corona A 12.00 3.60
TRA-10 Phil Wilson A 12.00 3.60
TRA-11 John Buck A 15.00 4.50
TRA-12 Jim Journell A 12.00 3.60
TRA-13 Victor Hall A 12.00 3.60
TRA-14 Jeff Andra A 12.00 3.60
TRA-15 Greg Nash A 12.00 3.60
TRA-16 Travis Hafner A 30.00 9.00
TRA-17 Casey Fossum A 12.00 3.60
TRA-18 Miguel Olivo A 12.00 3.60
TRA-19 Elpidio Guzman A 12.00 3.60
TRA-20 Jason Belcher A 12.00 3.60
TRA-21 Esix Snead A 12.00 3.60
TRA-22 Joe Thurston A 12.00 3.60
TRA-23 Rafael Soriano A 15.00 4.50
TRA-24 Ed Rogers A 12.00 3.60
TRA-25 Omar Beltre A 12.00 3.60
TRA-26 Brett Gray A 12.00 3.60
TRA-27 Deivi Mendez A 12.00 3.60
TRA-28 Freddie Bynum A 12.00 3.60
TRA-29 David Krynzel A 12.00 3.60
TRA-30 Blake Williams A 12.00 3.60
TRA-31 R. Abercrombie A 12.00 3.60
TRA-32 Miguel Villilo A 12.00 3.60
TRA-33 Ryan Madson A 20.00 6.00
TRA-34 Matt Thompson A 12.00 3.60
TRA-35 Mark Burnett A 12.00 3.60
TRA-36 Andy Beal A 12.00 3.60
TRA-37 Ryan Ludwick A 12.00 3.60
TRA-38 Roberto Miniel A 12.00 3.60
TRA-39 Steve Smyth A 12.00 3.60
TRA-40 Ben Washburn A 12.00 3.60
TRA-41 Marvin Seale A 12.00 3.60
TRA-42 Reggie Griggs A 12.00 3.60
TRA-43 Seung Song A 15.00 4.50
TRA-44 Chad Petty A 12.00 3.60
TRA-45 Noel Devarez A 12.00 3.60
TRA-46 Matt Butler B 12.00 3.60
TRA-47 Brett Evert B 12.00 3.60
TRA-48 Cesar Izturis B 12.00 3.60
TRA-49 Troy Farnsworth B 12.00 3.60
TRA-50 Brian Schmitt B 12.00 3.60

2001 Topps Reserve Rookie Autographs PSA Graded

Inserted one per hobby box, these cards were graded by PSA and included in the Topps Reserve product. 555 of each card was produced as a cumulative print run. The mystery exchange card had an exchange deadline of July 31, 2003.

Nm-Mt Ex-Mt
101 G.Johnson Mint 20.00 6.00
101 G.Johnson NmMt 12.00 3.60
102 M.Ford Mint 20.00 6.00
102 M.Ford NmMt 12.00 3.60
103 A.Pujols NmMt 250.00 75.00
104 B.Cresse Mint 20.00 6.00
104 B.Cresse NmMt 12.00 3.60
105 V.Pascucci Mint 20.00 6.00
105 V.Pascucci NmMt 12.00 3.60
106 B.Keppel Mint 25.00 7.50
106 B.Keppel NmMt 15.00 4.50
107 L.Torres Mint 20.00 6.00
107 L.Torres NmMt 12.00 3.60
108 T.Blanco NmMt 20.00 6.00
109 R.Corona Mint 20.00 6.00
109 R.Corona NmMt 12.00 3.60
110 P.Wilson NmMt 20.00 6.00
111 J.Buck NmMt 15.00 4.50
112 J.Journell NmMt 12.00 3.60
113 V.Hall Mint 20.00 6.00
113 V.Hall NmMt 12.00 3.60
114 J.Andra NmMt 20.00 6.00
115 G.Nash Mint 25.00 7.50
115 G.Nash NmMt 15.00 4.50
116 T.Hafner Mint 50.00 15.00
116 T.Hafner NmMt 30.00 9.00
117 C.Fossum Mint 20.00 6.00
117 C.Fossum NmMt 12.00 3.60
118 M.Olivo NmMt 12.00 3.60
119 E.Guzman Mint 20.00 6.00
119 E.Guzman NmMt 12.00 3.60
120 J.Belcher Mint 20.00 6.00
120 J.Belcher NmMt 12.00 3.60
121 E.Snead NmMt 12.00 3.60
122 J.Thurston Mint 20.00 6.00
122 J.Thurston NmMt 12.00 3.60
123 R.Soriano Mint 25.00 7.50
123 R.Soriano NmMt 15.00 4.50
124 E.Rogers Mint 20.00 6.00
124 E.Rogers NmMt 12.00 3.60
125 O.Beltre Mint 20.00 6.00
125 O.Beltre NmMt 12.00 3.60
126 B.Gray Mint 20.00 6.00
126 B.Gray NmMt 12.00 3.60
127 D.Mendez Mint 20.00 6.00
127 D.Mendez NmMt 12.00 3.60
128 F.Bynum Mint 20.00 6.00
128 F.Bynum NmMt 12.00 3.60
129 D.Krynzel Mint 20.00 6.00
129 D.Krynzel NmMt 12.00 3.60
130 B.Williams Mint 20.00 6.00
130 B.Williams NmMt 12.00 3.60
131 R.Abercrombie Mint 20.00 6.00
131 R.Abercrombie NmMt 12.00 3.60
132 M.Villilo Mint 20.00 6.00
132 M.Villilo NmMt 12.00 3.60
133 R.Madson NmMt 20.00 6.00
134 M.Thompson Mint 20.00 6.00
134 M.Thompson NmMt 12.00 3.60
135 M.Burnett Mint 20.00 6.00
135 M.Burnett NmMt 12.00 3.60
136 A.Beal Mint 20.00 6.00
136 A.Beal NmMt 12.00 3.60
137 R.Ludwick Mint 20.00 6.00
137 R.Ludwick NmMt 12.00 3.60
138 R.Miniel Mint 20.00 6.00
138 R.Miniel NmMt 12.00 3.60
139 S.Smyth Mint 20.00 6.00
139 S.Smyth NmMt 12.00 3.60
140 B.Washburn Mint 20.00 6.00
140 B.Washburn NmMt 12.00 3.60
141 M.Seale Mint 20.00 6.00
141 M.Seale NmMt 12.00 3.60
142 R.Griggs Mint 20.00 6.00
142 R.Griggs NmMt 12.00 3.60
143 S.Song Mint 20.00 6.00
143 S.Song NmMt 12.00 3.60
144 C.Petty Mint 20.00 6.00
144 C.Petty NmMt 12.00 3.60
145 N.Devarez Mint 20.00 6.00
145 N.Devarez NmMt 12.00 3.60
NNO Mystery Exchange .50 .15

2001 Topps Reserve Game Bats

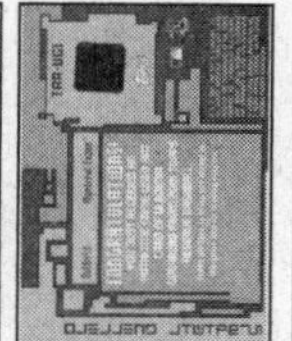

Randomly inserted in packs, these 14 cards feature bat relic cards from some of the leading hitters in the game.

Nm-Mt Ex-Mt
TRR-BW Bernie Williams 15.00 4.50
TRR-DE Darin Erstad 15.00 4.50
TRR-JB Jeff Bagwell 15.00 4.50
TRR-MP Mike Piazza 25.00 7.50
TRR-NG N.Garciaparra 40.00 12.00
TRR-VG Vladimir Guerrero 15.00 4.50
TRR-ARI Alex Rodriguez 25.00 7.50
TRR-BBI Barry Bonds 40.00 12.00
TRR-CDI Carlos Delgado 15.00 4.50
TRR-CJI Chipper Jones 15.00 4.50
TRR-IRI Ivan Rodriguez 15.00 4.50
TRR-JEI Jim Edmonds 10.00 3.00
TRR-RFI Rafael Furcal 10.00 3.00
TRR-TGI Tony Gwynn 15.00 4.50

2001 Topps Reserve Game Jerseys

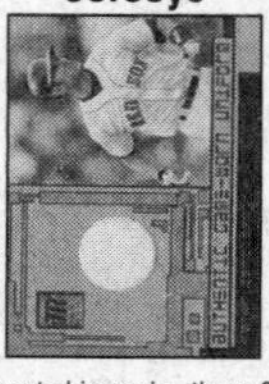

Randomly inserted in packs, these 20 cards feature game-worn uniform relics from some of the leading players in the game.

Nm-Mt Ex-Mt
TRR-AR Alex Rodriguez 25.00 7.50
TRR-BB Barry Bonds 30.00 9.00
TRR-CD Carlos Delgado 10.00 3.00
TRR-CJ Chipper Jones 15.00 4.50
TRR-DJ David Justice 10.00 3.00
TRR-FT Frank Thomas 15.00 4.50
TRR-GM Greg Maddux 15.00 4.50
TRR-IR Ivan Rodriguez 15.00 4.50
TRR-JE Jim Edmonds 10.00 3.00
TRR-JG Juan Gonzalez 15.00 4.50
TRR-NP N.Garciaparra 20.00 6.00
TRR-PM Pedro Martinez 15.00 4.50
TRR-RA Roberto Alomar 15.00 4.50
TRR-RJ Randy Johnson 15.00 4.50
TRR-RP Rafael Palmeiro 15.00 4.50
TRR-SG Shawn Green 10.00 3.00
TRR-SR Scott Rolen 15.00 4.50
TRR-TG Tony Gwynn 15.00 4.50
TRR-TH Todd Helton 15.00 4.50
TRR-VG Vladimir Guerrero 15.00 4.50

2001 Topps Reserve Rookie Baseballs

Inserted at a rate of one per box, these 45 baseballs were signed by the feature rookie/prospect. The Fernando Cabrera and Felix Lugo cards were only available in retail packs as an exchange. These signed balls were redeemable until July 31, 2003.

Nm-Mt Ex-Mt
1 Reggie Abercrombie 20.00 6.00
2 Jeff Andra 20.00 6.00
3 Andy Beal 20.00 6.00
4 Omar Beltre 20.00 6.00
5 Tony Blanco 25.00 7.50
6 Mark Burnett 20.00 6.00
7 Freddie Bynum 20.00 6.00
8 Fernando Cabrera 20.00 6.00
9 Ronnie Corona 20.00 6.00
10 Brad Cresse 20.00 6.00
11 Noel Devarez 20.00 6.00
12 Matt Ford 20.00 6.00
13 Casey Fossum 20.00 6.00
14 Brett Gray 20.00 6.00
15 Reggie Griggs 20.00 6.00
16 Elpidio Guzman 20.00 6.00
17 Travis Hafner 50.00 15.00
18 Victor Hall 20.00 6.00
19 Gary Johnson 20.00 6.00
20 Jim Journell 20.00 6.00
21 Bob Keppel 25.00 7.50
22 David Krynzel 20.00 6.00
23 Ryan Ludwick 20.00 6.00
24 Felix Lugo 20.00 6.00
25 Ryan Madson 25.00 7.50
26 Deivi Mendez 20.00 6.00
27 Roberto Miniel 20.00 6.00
28 Greg Nash 20.00 6.00
29 Miguel Olivo 20.00 6.00
30 Valentino Pascucci 20.00 6.00
31 Chad Petty 20.00 6.00
32 Albert Pujols 400.00 120.00
33 Ed Rogers 20.00 6.00
34 Marvin Seale 20.00 6.00
35 Steve Smyth 20.00 6.00
36 Esix Snead 20.00 6.00
37 Seung Song 25.00 7.50
38 Rafael Soriano 25.00 7.50
39 Matt Thompson 20.00 6.00
40 Joe Thurston 20.00 6.00
41 Luis Torres 20.00 6.00
42 Miguel Villilo 20.00 6.00
43 Ben Washburn 20.00 6.00
44 Blake Williams 20.00 6.00
45 Phil Wilson 20.00 6.00

2002 Topps Reserve

This 150 card set was released in late July, 2002. These cards were issued in five card packs which came 10 packs to a box and six boxes in a case. Each box also contained a autographed mini-helmet as an inducement to purchase the box. Cards number 1-135 featured veteran stars while cards 136 through 150 featured Rookie Cards which had a stated print run of 999 serial numbered sets.

	Nm-Mt	Ex-Mt
COMP.SET w/o SP's (135)	100.00	30.00
COMMON CARD (1-135)	1.00	.30
COMMON CARD (136-150)	5.00	1.50
1 Alex Rodriguez	4.00	1.20
2 Tsuyoshi Shinjo	1.00	.30
3 Craig Biggio	1.50	.45
4 Troy Glaus	1.00	.30
5 Mike Rivera	1.00	.30
6 Curt Schilling	1.00	.30
7 Garret Anderson	1.00	.30
8 Ben Sheets	1.00	.30
9 Todd Helton	1.50	.45
10 Paul Konerko	1.00	.30
11 Sammy Sosa	4.00	1.20
12 Bud Smith	1.00	.30
13 Jeff Bagwell	1.50	.45
14 Albert Pujols	5.00	1.50
15 Jose Vidro	1.00	.30
16 Carlos Delgado	1.00	.30
17 Torii Hunter	1.00	.30
18 Jerry Hairston	1.00	.30
19 Troy Percival	1.00	.30
20 Vladimir Guerrero	2.50	.75
21 Geoff Jenkins	1.00	.30
22 Carlos Pena	1.00	.30
23 Juan Gonzalez	1.50	.45
24 Raul Mondesi	1.00	.30
25 Jimmy Rollins	1.00	.30
26 Mariano Rivera	1.50	.45
27 Jorge Posada	1.50	.45
28 Magglio Ordonez	1.00	.30
29 Roberto Alomar	1.50	.45
30 Randy Johnson	2.50	.75
31 Xavier Nady	1.00	.30
32 Terrence Long	1.00	.30
33 Chipper Jones	2.50	.75
34 Rich Aurilia	1.00	.30
35 Aramis Ramirez	1.00	.30
36 Jim Thome	2.50	.75
37 Bret Boone	1.00	.30
38 Angel Berroa	1.00	.30
39 Jeff Conine	1.00	.30
40 Cliff Floyd	1.00	.30
41 Pedro Martinez	2.50	.75
42 J.D. Drew	1.00	.30
43 Kazuhiro Sasaki	1.00	.30
44 Jon Rauch	1.00	.30
45 Orlando Hudson	1.00	.30
46 Scott Rolen	2.50	.75
47 Rafael Furcal	1.00	.30
48 Brad Penny	1.00	.30
49 Miguel Tejada	1.00	.30
50 Orlando Cabrera	1.00	.30
51 Bob Abreu	1.00	.30
52 Darin Erstad	1.00	.30
53 Edgar Martinez	1.50	.45
54 Ben Grieve	1.00	.30
55 Shawn Green	1.00	.30
56 Ivan Rodriguez	2.50	.75
57 Josh Beckett	1.00	.30
58 Ray Durham	1.00	.30
59 Jason Hart	1.00	.30
60 Nathan Haynes	1.00	.30
61 Jason Giambi	1.00	.30
62 Eric Chavez	1.00	.30
63 Matt Morris	1.00	.30
64 Lance Berkman	1.00	.30
65 Jeff Kent	1.00	.30
66 Andruw Jones	1.00	.30
67 Brian Giles	1.00	.30
68 Morgan Ensberg	1.00	.30
69 Pat Burrell	1.00	.30
70 Ken Griffey Jr.	4.00	1.20
71 Carlos Beltran	1.50	.45
72 Ichiro Suzuki	4.00	1.20
73 Larry Walker	1.50	.45
74 J.J. Putz RC	1.00	.30
75 Mike Piazza	4.00	1.20
76 Rafael Palmeiro	1.50	.45
77 Mark Prior	4.00	1.20
78 Toby Hall	1.00	.30
79 Pokey Reese	1.00	.30
80 Mike Mussina	1.50	.45
81 Omar Vizquel	1.50	.45
82 Shannon Stewart	1.00	.30
83 Jeromy Burnitz	1.00	.30
84 Bernie Williams	1.50	.45
85 C.C. Sabathia	1.00	.30
86 Mike Hampton	1.00	.30
87 Kevin Brown	1.00	.30
88 Juan Cruz	1.00	.30
89 Jeff Weaver	1.00	.30
90 Jason Lane	1.00	.30
91 Adam Dunn	1.00	.45
92 Jose Cruz Jr.	1.00	.30
93 Marlon Anderson	1.00	.30
94 Jeff Cirillo	1.00	.30
95 Mark Buehrle	1.00	.30
96 Austin Kearns	1.00	.30
97 Tim Hudson	1.00	.30
98 Brian Jordan	1.00	.30
99 Phil Nevin	1.00	.30
100 Barry Bonds	6.00	1.80
101 Derek Jeter	6.00	1.80
102 Javier Vazquez	1.00	.30
103 Jason Kendall	1.00	.30
104 Jim Edmonds	1.00	.30
105 Kenny Kelly	1.00	.30
106 Juan Pena	1.00	.30
107 Mark Grace	1.50	.45
108 Roger Clemens	5.00	1.50
109 Barry Zito	1.00	.30
110 Greg Vaughn	1.00	.30
111 Greg Maddux	4.00	1.20
112 Richie Sexson	1.00	.30
113 Jermaine Dye	1.00	.30
114 Kerry Wood	2.50	.75
115 Matt Lawton	1.00	.30
116 Sean Casey	1.00	.30
117 Gary Sheffield	1.00	.30
118 Preston Wilson	1.00	.30
119 Cristian Guzman	1.00	.30
120 Mike Sweeney	1.00	.30
121 Neifi Perez	1.00	.30
122 Paul LoDuca	1.00	.30
123 Luis Gonzalez	1.00	.30
124 Ryan Klesko	1.00	.30
125 Alfonso Soriano	1.50	.45
126 Bobby Higginson	1.00	.30
127 Juan Pierre	1.00	.30
128 Moises Alou	1.00	.30
129 Roy Oswalt	1.00	.30
130 Nomar Garciaparra	4.00	1.20
131 Fred McGriff	1.50	.45
132 Edgardo Alfonzo	1.00	.30
133 Johnny Damon Sox	2.50	.75
134 Dewon Brazelton	1.00	.30
135 Mark Mulder	1.00	.30
136 So Taguchi FYP RC	8.00	2.40
137 Mario Ramos FYP RC	5.00	1.50
138 Dan Johnson FYP RC	8.00	2.40
139 Hansel Izquierdo FYP RC	5.00	1.50
140 Kazuhisa Ishii FYP RC	12.00	3.60
141 Jon Switzer FYP RC	5.00	1.50
142 Chris Tritle FYP RC	5.00	1.50
143 Chris Snelling FYP RC	5.00	1.50
144 Chone Figgins FYP RC	8.00	2.40
145 Dan Phillips FYP RC	5.00	1.50
146 John Rodriguez FYP RC	5.00	1.50
147 Colt Griffin FYP RC	8.00	2.40
148 Jonny Gomes FYP RC	8.00	2.40
149 Josh Barfield FYP RC	10.00	3.00
150 Joe Mauer FYP RC	30.00	9.00

2002 Topps Reserve Parallel

Inserted in packs at stated odds of one in 12, this is a parallel to the basic Reserve set. These cards are also printed to a stated print run of 150 serial numbered sets.

Nm-Mt Ex-Mt

*PARALLEL 1-135: 1.5X TO 4X BASIC
*PARALLEL 136-150: .6X TO 1.5X BASIC

2002 Topps Reserve Autograph Mini-Helmets

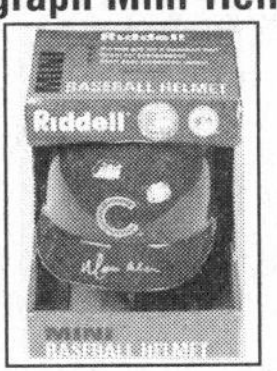

Topps got eighteen major league stars to sign Riddell mini-helmets. The helmets were inserted exclusively into hobby boxes at a rate of one per box. Each helmet is serial-numbered to either 225 (for group A), 475 (for group B) or 975 (for group C) on the outside back portion of the item. Oddly, the wrappers and boxes contradict one another when referencing the grouping manner these helmets were distributed in. Our checklist follows the groups detailed on the boxes (groups A-C). Please note, the wrapper confusingly references groups A-D in an effort to intermingle the scarce gold Autograph Mini-Helmets (of which feature gold ink signatures and are each serial-numbered to 25). For ease of use, we've transferred the wrapper stated odds to match the box. For example, the box lists Todd Helton and Luis Gonzalez as group A yet the wrapper references them as group B. In this instance, we've listed the wrapper odds for Helton and Gonzalez as group A to match up the checklist provided on the box.

	Nm-Mt	Ex-Mt
GROUP A ODDS 1:285		
GROUP B ODDS 1:39		
GROUP C ODDS 1:14		
ODDS ARE PER PACK NOT PER BOX		
GROUP A PRINT RUN 225 SERIAL #'d SETS		
GROUP B PRINT RUN 475 SERIAL #'d SETS		
GROUP C PRINT RUN 975 SERIAL #'d SETS		
GOLD ODDS 1:279		
GOLD ODDS ARE PER PACK NOT PER BOX		
GOLD PRINT RUN 25 SERIAL #'d SETS		
GOLD HELMETS FEATURE GOLD INK AUTO		
NO GOLD PRICING DUE TO SCARCITY		
1 Roberto Alomar C	30.00	9.00
2 Moises Alou C	25.00	7.50
3 Lance Berkman C	30.00	9.00
4 Bret Boone B	30.00	9.00
5 Eric Chavez B	30.00	9.00
6 Adam Dunn C	30.00	9.00
7 Cliff Floyd C	25.00	7.50
8 Troy Glaus B	30.00	9.00
9 Luis Gonzalez A	40.00	12.00
10 Todd Helton A	50.00	15.00
11 Magglio Ordonez C	25.00	7.50
12 Rafael Palmeiro B	60.00	18.00
13 Albert Pujols B	150.00	45.00
14 Alex Rodriguez B	150.00	45.00
15 Scott Rolen C	50.00	15.00
16 Jimmy Rollins C	25.00	7.50
17 Alfonso Soriano B	60.00	18.00
18 Barry Zito C	30.00	9.00

2002 Topps Reserve Baseball Relics

Issued at stated odds of one in 1761, these two cards feature cut up baseballs used in games by the featured players. Each card is printed to a stated print run of 100 serial numbered sets.

	Nm-Mt	Ex-Mt
AR Alex Rodriguez		
I Ichiro Suzuki		

2002 Topps Reserve Bat Relics

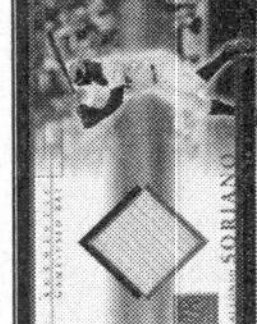

Inserted at overall stated odds of one in 12, these 20 cards feature game-used bat pieces from the featured player. These cards were inserted in packs at different odds depending on the featured player. We have listed each of the odds in our set information and put the group id for the player next to their name in our checklist.

	Nm-Mt	Ex-Mt
GROUP A ODDS 1:1563		
GROUP B ODDS 1:1180		
GROUP C ODDS 1:61		
GROUP D ODDS 1:219		
GROUP E ODDS 1:31		
GROUP F ODDS 1:179		
GROUP G ODDS 1:135		
GROUP H ODDS 1:46		
AJ Andruw Jones E	10.00	3.00
AP Albert Pujols F	15.00	4.50
AR Alex Rodriguez E	15.00	4.50
AS Alfonso Soriano E	10.00	3.00
BB Barry Bonds A	30.00	9.00
BW Bernie Williams E	10.00	3.00
CD Carlos Delgado C	10.00	3.00
CJ Chipper Jones C	10.00	3.00
FT Frank Thomas E	10.00	3.00
IR Ivan Rodriguez E	10.00	3.00
JB Jeff Bagwell E	10.00	3.00
JG Juan Gonzalez D	10.00	3.00
LG Luis Gonzalez C	10.00	3.00
MP Mike Piazza H	15.00	4.50
RA Roberto Alomar B	15.00	4.50
RH Rickey Henderson C	10.00	3.00
RP Rafael Palmeiro C	10.00	3.00
TG Tony Gwynn H	15.00	4.50
TM Tino Martinez C	10.00	3.00
TS Tsuyoshi Shinjo G	10.00	3.00

2002 Topps Reserve Patch Relics

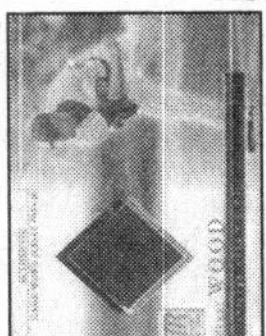

Inserted in packs at stated odds of one in 668, these 21 cards feature game worn uniform patches. These cards are serial numbered to a stated print run of 25 serial numbered sets and there is no pricing due to market scarcity.

	Nm-Mt	Ex-Mt
AJ Andruw Jones		
BB Barry Bonds		
CD Carlos Delgado		
CJ Chipper Jones		
CS Curt Schilling		
DE Darin Erstad		
FT Frank Thomas		
GM Greg Maddux		
IR Ivan Rodriguez		
JG Juan Gonzalez		
KS Kazuhiro Sasaki		
KW Kerry Wood		
LG Luis Gonzalez		
MO Magglio Ordonez		
MP Mike Piazza		
PM Pedro Martinez		
RJ Randy Johnson		
RP Rafael Palmeiro		
SR Scott Rolen		
TG Tony Gwynn		
TH Todd Helton		

2002 Topps Reserve Uniform Relics

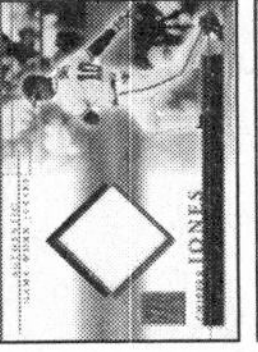

Inserted at overall stated odds of one in five, these 24 cards feature game-worn uniform swatches of the featured player. These cards were issued at differing odds depending on which group and we have included those odds in our set information. Our checklist also includes the information of what group the specific card belongs to.

	Nm-Mt	Ex-Mt
GROUP A ODDS 1:376		
GROUP B ODDS 1:179		
GROUP C ODDS 1:10		
GROUP D ODDS 1:14		
GROUP E ODDS 1:16		
AJ Andruw Jones D	10.00	3.00
AP Albert Pujols E	15.00	4.50
AR Alex Rodriguez C	15.00	4.50
BB Barry Bonds E	25.00	7.50
BBO Bret Boone C	10.00	3.00
CJ Chipper Jones C	10.00	3.00
CS Curt Schilling E	10.00	3.00
DE Darin Erstad D	10.00	3.00
FT Frank Thomas C	10.00	3.00
GM Greg Maddux C	15.00	4.50
IR Ivan Rodriguez D	10.00	3.00
KS Kazuhiro Sasaki C	10.00	3.00
KW Kerry Wood E	10.00	3.00
LG Luis Gonzalez C	10.00	3.00
MM Mark Mulder C	10.00	3.00
MO Magglio Ordonez D	10.00	3.00
MP Mike Piazza C	15.00	4.50
NG Nomar Garciaparra D	15.00	4.50
PM Pedro Martinez A	15.00	4.50
RJ Randy Johnson B	10.00	3.00
RP Rafael Palmeiro C	10.00	3.00
SR Scott Rolen C	10.00	3.00
TG Tony Gwynn E	15.00	4.50
TH Todd Helton C	10.00	3.00

2003 Topps Retired Signature

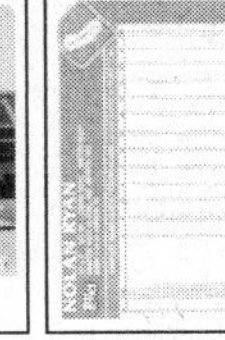

This 110-card set was released in July, 2003. The set was issued in five card packs with an $30 SRP which came five packs to a box and six boxes to a case.

	MINT	NRMT
COMPLETE SET (110)	200.00	90.00
1 Willie Mays	6.00	2.70
2 Tony Perez	1.25	.55
3 Tom Seaver	2.00	.90
4 Johnny Bench	3.00	1.35
5 Rod Carew	2.00	.90
6 Red Schoendienst	1.25	.55
7 Phil Rizzuto	2.00	.90
8 Ozzie Smith	5.00	2.20
9 Maury Wills	1.25	.55
10 Hank Aaron	6.00	2.70
11 Jim Palmer	1.25	.55
12 Jose Cruz Sr.	1.25	.55
13 Dave Parker	1.25	.55
14 Don Sutton	1.25	.55
15 Brooks Robinson	2.00	.90
16 Bo Jackson	3.00	1.35
17 Andre Dawson	1.25	.55
18 Fergie Jenkins	1.25	.55
19 George Foster	1.25	.55
20 George Brett	8.00	3.60
21 Jerry Koosman	1.25	.55
22 John Kruk	1.25	.55
23 Kent Tekulve	1.25	.55
24 Lee Smith	1.25	.55
25 Nolan Ryan	8.00	3.60
26 Paul O'Neill	1.25	.55
27 Rich Gossage	1.25	.55
28 Ron Santo	1.25	.55
29 Tom Lasorda	1.25	.55
30 Tony Gwynn	4.00	1.80
31 Vida Blue	1.25	.55
32 Whitey Herzog	1.25	.55
33 Willie McGee	1.25	.55
34 Bill Mazeroski	1.25	.55
35 Al Kaline	3.00	1.35
36 Bobby Richardson	1.25	.55
37 Carlton Fisk	2.00	.90
38 Darrell Evans	1.25	.55
39 Dave Concepcion	1.25	.55
40 Cal Ripken	10.00	4.50
41 Dwight Evans	1.25	.55
42 Earl Weaver	1.25	.55
43 Fred Lynn	1.25	.55
44 Greg Luzinski	1.25	.55
45 Duke Snider	2.00	.90
46 Hank Bauer	1.25	.55
47 Jim Rice	1.25	.55
48 Johnny Sain	1.25	.55
49 Lenny Dykstra	1.25	.55
50 Mike Schmidt	6.00	2.70
51 Orlando Cepeda	1.25	.55
52 Ralph Kiner	1.25	.55
53 Robin Roberts	1.25	.55
54 Ron Guidry	1.25	.55
55 Steve Garvey	1.25	.55
56 Tony Oliva	1.25	.55
57 Whitey Ford	2.00	.90
58 Willie McCovey	1.25	.55
59 Phil Niekro	1.25	.55
60 Stan Musial	5.00	2.20
61 Rollie Fingers	1.25	.55
62 Robin Yount	5.00	2.20
63 Alan Trammell	1.25	.55
64 Bill Buckner	1.25	.55
65 Bob Feller	1.25	.55
66 Bruce Sutter	1.25	.55
67 Dale Murphy	3.00	1.35
68 Dennis Eckersley	1.25	.55
69 Don Newcombe	1.25	.55
70 Don Mattingly	8.00	3.60
71 Dwight Gooden	1.25	.55
72 Frank Robinson	2.00	.90
73 Gary Carter	1.25	.55
74 Graig Nettles	1.25	.55
75 Harmon Killebrew	3.00	1.35
76 Jim Bunning	1.25	.55
77 Joe Morgan	1.25	.55
78 Joe Rudi	1.25	.55
79 Jose Canseco	3.00	1.35
80 Ernie Banks	3.00	1.35
81 Luis Aparicio	1.25	.55
82 Luis Tiant	1.25	.55
83 Mark Fidrych	1.25	.55
84 Kirk Gibson	1.25	.55
85 Lou Brock	2.00	.90
86 Juan Marichal	1.25	.55
87 Monte Irvin	1.25	.55
88 Paul Molitor	2.00	.90
89 Tommy John	1.25	.55
90 Warren Spahn	2.00	.90
91 Wade Boggs	2.00	.90
92 Reggie Jackson	2.00	.90
93 Kirby Puckett	3.00	1.35
94 Boog Powell	2.00	.90
95 Carl Yastrzemski	5.00	2.20
96 Bobby Thomson	1.25	.55
97 Bill Skowron	1.25	.55
98 Bill Madlock	1.25	.55
99 Sparky Anderson	1.25	.55
100 Yogi Berra	3.00	1.35
101 Bobby Doerr	1.25	.55
102 Gaylord Perry	1.25	.55
103 George Kell	1.25	.55
104 Harold Reynolds	1.25	.55
105 Joe Carter	1.25	.55
106 Johnny Podres	1.25	.55
107 Ron Cey	1.25	.55
108 Tim McCarver	1.25	.55
109 Tug McGraw	1.25	.55
110 Don Larsen	1.25	.55

2003 Topps Retired Signature Black

MINT NRMT

*BLACK: 2.5X TO 6X BASIC
STATED ODDS 1:8
STATED PRINT RUN 99 SERIAL #'d SETS

2003 Topps Retired Signature Autographs

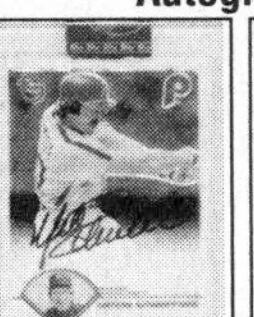

Inserted at a stated rate of one per pack, these 120 cards feature signatures from some of the most famous retired players. These cards were signed in different ratios and we have notated the insert odds as well as what group the player belonged to in our checklist.

	MINT	NRMT
ONE AUTOGRAPH PER PACK		
A-B PRINT RUNS PROVIDED BY TOPPS		
GROUPS A-B ARE NOT SERIAL-NUMBERED		
NO GROUP A PRICING DUE TO SCARCITY		
AD Andre Dawson D	20.00	9.00
AK Al Kaline C	100.00	45.00
AT Alan Trammell E	10.00	4.50
BB Bert Blyleven F	10.00	4.50
BBU Bill Buckner C	30.00	13.50
BD Bobby Doerr C	50.00	22.00
BF Bob Feller F	10.00	4.50
BGR Bobby Grich C	30.00	13.50
BH Bob Horner C	50.00	22.00
BJ Bo Jackson C	100.00	45.00
BM Bill Madlock G	10.00	4.50
BMA Bill Mazeroski C	60.00	27.00
BP Boog Powell G	15.00	6.75
BR Bobby Richardson G	10.00	4.50
BRO Brooks Robinson B/75	200.00	90.00
BS Bill Skowron G	15.00	6.75
BSA Bret Saberhagen C	50.00	22.00
BSU Bruce Sutter E	10.00	4.50
BT Bobby Thomson D	20.00	9.00
BW Bob Watson C	30.00	13.50
CF Carlton Fisk C	60.00	27.00
CR Cal Ripken A/25		
CY Carl Yastrzemski C	150.00	70.00
DE Darrell Evans F	10.00	4.50
DEC Dennis Eckersley C	60.00	27.00
DEV Dwight Evans B/78	200.00	90.00
DG Dwight Gooden C	50.00	22.00
DL Don Larsen G	15.00	6.75
DM Dale Murphy C	100.00	45.00
DN Don Newcombe C	30.00	13.50
DON Don Mattingly B/81	250.00	110.00
DP Dave Parker C	50.00	22.00
DS Dave Stieb C	50.00	22.00
DSN Duke Snider B/75	200.00	90.00
DSU Don Sutton C	50.00	22.00
EB Ernie Banks A/24		
EW Earl Weaver G	10.00	4.50
FJ Fergie Jenkins D	20.00	9.00
FL Fred Lynn C	50.00	22.00
FR Frank Robinson C	80.00	36.00
GB George Brett A/25		
GC Gary Carter B/77	150.00	70.00
GF George Foster G	10.00	4.50
GK George Kell C	50.00	22.00
GL Greg Luzinski D	20.00	9.00
GN Graig Nettles G	15.00	6.75
GP Gaylord Perry C	30.00	13.50
HA Hank Aaron A/30		
HB Harold Baines F	10.00	4.50
HBA Hank Bauer C	50.00	22.00
HK Harmon Killebrew B/76	200.00	90.00
HR Harold Reynolds C	30.00	13.50
JA Jim Abbott E	15.00	6.75
JB Jim Bunning B/76	200.00	90.00
JBE Johnny Bench C	80.00	36.00
JC Joe Carter C	50.00	22.00
JCA Jose Canseco C	80.00	36.00
JCR Jose Cruz Sr. D	15.00	6.75
JK Jerry Koosman C	30.00	13.50
JKR John Kruk C	50.00	22.00
JM Joe Morgan C	50.00	22.00
JMA Juan Marichal C	50.00	22.00
JP Jim Palmer C	60.00	27.00
JPI Jim Piersall G	15.00	6.75
JPO Johnny Podres G	10.00	4.50

JR Jim Rice C 50.00 22.00
JRU Joe Rudi F 10.00 4.50
KG Kirk Gibson C 50.00 22.00
KGR Ken Griffey Sr. C 50.00 22.00
KP Kirby Puckett B/75
KT Kent Tekulve C 30.00 13.50
LA Luis Aparicio G 15.00 6.75
LB Lou Brock B/76 200.00 90.00
LD Lenny Dykstra D 20.00 9.00
LP Lance Parrish G 10.00 4.50
LS Lee Smith E 10.00 4.50
LT Luis Tiant G 10.00 4.50
MF Mark Fidrych D 20.00 9.00
MI Monte Irvin C 60.00 27.00
MS Mike Schmidt B/83 250.00 110.00
MW Maury Wills F 10.00 4.50
NR Nolan Ryan B/77 300.00 135.00
OC Orlando Cepeda B/75 200.00 90.00
OS Ozzie Smith C 100.00 45.00
PM Paul Molitor C 60.00 27.00
PN Phil Niekro D 20.00 9.00
PO Paul O'Neill C 60.00 27.00
PR Phil Rizzuto B/77 200.00 90.00
RCA Rod Carew C 80.00 36.00
RCE Ron Cey F 10.00 4.50
RF Rollie Fingers C 50.00 22.00
RG Rich Gossage C 30.00 13.50
RGU Ron Guidry D 30.00 13.50
RJ Reggie Jackson C 100.00 45.00
RK Ralph Kiner B/80 200.00 90.00
RR Robin Roberts C 60.00 27.00
RS Red Schoendienst B/83 200.00 90.00
RSA Ron Santo G 15.00 6.75
RY Robin Yount A/25
SA Sparky Anderson C 30.00 13.50
SG Steve Garvey D 20.00 9.00
SM Stan Musial A/28
TG Tony Gwynn A/25
TJ Tommy John C 30.00 13.50
TL Tom Lasorda B/76 150.00 70.00
TM Tim McCarver C 50.00 22.00
TMC Tug McGraw D 50.00 22.00
TO Tony Oliva C 50.00 22.00
TP Tony Perez C 50.00 22.00
TPE Terry Pendleton D 15.00 6.75
TS Tom Seaver C 60.00 27.00
VB Vida Blue E 10.00 4.50
WB Wade Boggs B/77 200.00 90.00
WF Whitey Ford C 60.00 27.00
WH Whitey Herzog D 15.00 6.75
WM Willie Mays A/25
WMC Willie McCovey C 80.00 36.00
WMG Willie McGee D 20.00 9.00
WS Warren Spahn F 40.00 18.00
YB Yogi Berra A/25

2003 Topps Retired Signature Autographs Refractors

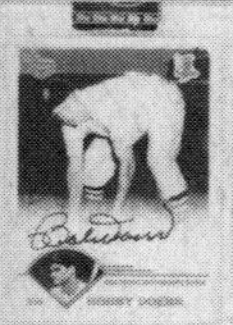

MINT NRMT
STATED ODDS 1:27
STATED PRINT RUN 25 SERIAL #'d SETS
NO PRICING DUE TO SCARCITY

2004 Topps Retired Signature

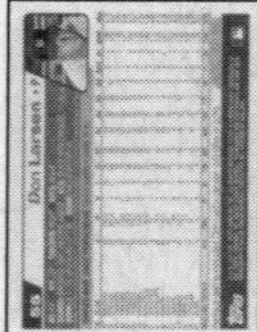

This 110-card set was released in September, 2004. The set was issued in four card packs (of which one card was autographed) with an $30 SRP which came five packs to a box and six boxes to a case.

Nm-Mt Ex-Mt
COMPLETE SET (110) 200.00 60.00
1 Willie Mays 6.00 1.80
2 Tony Gwynn 5.00 1.50
3 Dale Murphy 2.00 .60
4 Lenny Dykstra 1.25 .35
5 Johnny Bench 3.00 .90
6 Bill Buckner 1.25 .35
7 Ferguson Jenkins 1.25 .35
8 George Brett 6.00 1.80
9 Ralph Kiner 2.00 .60
10 Ernie Banks 3.00 .90
11 Hal McRae 1.25 .35
12 Lou Brock 2.00 .60
13 Keith Hernandez 1.25 .35
14 Jose Canseco 3.00 .90
15 Whitey Ford 2.00 .60
16 Dave Kingman 1.25 .35
17 Tim Raines 1.25 .35
18 Paul O'Neill 2.00 .60
19 Lou Whitaker 1.25 .35
20 Mike Schmidt 6.00 1.80
21 Wally Joyner 1.00 .30
22 Kirk Gibson 1.25 .35
23 Ryne Sandberg 6.00 1.80
24 Luis Tiant 1.25 .35
25 Al Kaline 3.00 .90
26 Brooks Robinson 2.00 .60
27 Don Zimmer 1.25 .35
28 Nolan Ryan 8.00 2.40
29 Maury Wills 1.25 .35
30 Stan Musial 5.00 1.50
31 Garry Maddox 1.00 .30
32 Tom Brunansky 1.00 .30
33 Don Mattingly 6.00 1.80
34 Earl Weaver 1.25 .35
35 Bobby Grich 1.25 .35
36 Orlando Cepeda 1.25 .35
37 Alan Trammell 1.25 .35
38 Al Hrabosky 1.00 .30
39 Dave Lopes 1.00 .30
40 Rod Carew 2.00 .60
41 Robin Yount 5.00 1.50
42 Dwight Gooden 1.25 .35
43 Andre Dawson 1.25 .35
44 Hank Aaron 6.00 1.80
45 Norm Cash 2.00 .60
46 Reggie Jackson 2.00 .60
47 Jim Rice 1.25 .35
48 Carlton Fisk 2.00 .60
49 Dave Parker 1.25 .35
50 Cal Ripken 10.00 3.00
51 Roy Face 1.00 .30
52 Bob Gibson 2.00 .60
53 Jimmy Key 1.25 .35
54 Al Oliver 1.00 .30
55 Don Larsen 1.25 .35
56 Tom Seaver 2.00 .60
57 Tony Armas 1.00 .30
58 Dave Stieb 1.25 .35
59 Will Clark 3.00 .90
60 Duke Snider 2.00 .60
61 Cesar Geronimo 1.00 .30
62 Ron Kittle 1.00 .30
63 Ron Santo 2.00 .60
64 Mickey Rivers 1.00 .30
65 Jim Piersall 1.25 .35
66 Ron Swoboda 1.25 .35
67 Kent Hrbek 1.00 .30
68 Dennis Eckersley 2.00 .60
69 Greg Luzinski 1.25 .35
70 Harmon Killebrew 3.00 .90
71 Ron Guidry 1.25 .35
72 Steve Garvey 1.25 .35
73 Andy Van Slyke 1.25 .35
74 Goose Gossage 1.25 .35
75 Ozzie Smith 5.00 1.50
76 Richie Allen 1.25 .35
77 Vida Blue 1.00 .30
78 Tony Oliva 1.25 .35
79 Darryl Strawberry 1.25 .35
80 Frank Robinson 1.25 .35
81 Bruce Sutter 1.25 .35
82 Dave Concepcion 1.25 .35
83 Darrell Evans 1.00 .30
84 Jack Morris 1.25 .35
85 Bo Jackson 3.00 .90
86 Orel Hershiser 1.25 .35
87 Rob Dibble 1.25 .35
88 Wade Boggs 2.00 .60
89 Fernando Valenzuela 1.25 .35
90 Jim Palmer 1.25 .35
91 George Foster 1.25 .35
92 Mike Scott 1.00 .30
93 Paul Molitor 2.00 .60
94 Gary Carter 1.25 .35
95 Bobby Richardson 1.25 .35
96 Rollie Fingers 1.25 .35
97 Tim McCarver 1.25 .35
98 John Candelaria 1.25 .35
99 Dave Winfield 1.25 .35
100 Yogi Berra 3.00 .90
101 Bill Madlock 1.25 .35
102 Jack McDowell 1.00 .30
103 Luis Aparicio 1.25 .35
104 Graig Nettles 1.25 .35
105 Dave Stewart 1.25 .35
106 Darren Daulton 1.25 .35
107 Gary Gaetti 1.25 .35
108 Tony Fernandez 1.00 .30
109 Buddy Bell 1.00 .30
110 Carl Yastrzemski 5.00 1.50

2004 Topps Retired Signature Black

Nm-Mt Ex-Mt
*BLACK: 2.5X TO 6X BASIC
STATED ODDS 1:7
STATED PRINT RUN 99 SERIAL #'d SETS

2004 Topps Retired Signature Autographs

Nm-Mt Ex-Mt
GROUP A ODDS 1:675
GROUP B ODDS 1:338
GROUP C ODDS 1:82
GROUP D ODDS 1:25
GROUP E ODDS 1:8
GROUP F ODDS 1:46
GROUP G ODDS 1:2
GROUP H ODDS 1:33
GROUP A PRINT RUN 25 SETS
GROUP B PRINT RUN 50 SETS
GROUP C PRINT RUN 75 SETS
GROUP A-C ARE NOT SERIAL-NUMBERED
A-C PRINT RUNS PROVIDED BY TOPPS
OVERALL PRESS PLATE ODDS 1:222
PLATE PRINT RUN 1 SET PER COLOR
BLACK-CYAN-MAGENTA-YELLOW ISSUED
NO PLATE PRICING DUE TO SCARCITY
AH Al Hrabosky E 10.00 3.00
AO Al Oliver G 15.00 4.50
AT Alan Trammell E 15.00 4.50
BB Bill Buckner G 15.00 4.50
BBE Buddy Bell E 10.00 3.00
BD Bucky Dent E 10.00 3.00
BG Bob Gibson C 80.00 24.00
BGR Bobby Grich G 10.00 3.00
BM Bill Madlock G 10.00 3.00
BR Bobby Richardson G 15.00 4.50
BRO Brooks Robinson C 150.00 45.00
BS Bruce Sutter G 15.00 4.50
CF Carlton Fisk D 40.00 12.00
CG Cesar Geronimo E 15.00 4.50
CR Cal Ripken A 400.00 120.00
CY Carl Yastrzemski A 200.00 60.00
DD Darren Daulton G 10.00 3.00
DE Darrell Evans G 10.00 3.00
DEC Dennis Eckersley E 25.00 7.50
DG Dwight Gooden C 50.00 15.00
DL Davey Lopes F 10.00 3.00
DM Don Mattingly C 150.00 45.00
DMU Dale Murphy G 25.00 7.50
DP Dave Parker E 15.00 4.50
DS Darryl Strawberry D 25.00 7.50
DSN Duke Snider B 120.00 36.00
DST Dave Stieb G 15.00 4.50
DZ Don Zimmer D 25.00 7.50
EB Ernie Banks B 200.00 60.00
EW Earl Weaver G 10.00 3.00
FJ Ferguson Jenkins G 15.00 4.50
FR Frank Robinson D 40.00 12.00
GC Gary Carter D 25.00 7.50
GF George Foster E 10.00 3.00
GG Goose Gossage E 15.00 4.50
GL Greg Luzinski E 10.00 3.00
GN Graig Nettles G 15.00 4.50
HA Hank Aaron B 300.00 90.00
JB Johnny Bench C 120.00 36.00
JC John Candelaria D 25.00 7.50
JCA Jose Canseco D 50.00 15.00
JK Jimmy Key G 10.00 3.00
JM Jack McDowell G 10.00 3.00
JP Jim Piersall E 10.00 3.00
KG Kirk Gibson E 25.00 7.50
LT Luis Tiant G 10.00 3.00
MS Mike Schmidt C 150.00 45.00
MW Maury Wills G 10.00 3.00
NR Nolan Ryan A 400.00 120.00
OC Orlando Cepeda G 15.00 4.50
OH Orel Hershiser E 15.00 4.50
OS Ozzie Smith C 100.00 30.00
PM Paul Molitor D 50.00 15.00
PO Paul O'Neill D 25.00 7.50
RC Rod Carew E 40.00 12.00
RD Rob Dibble E 10.00 3.00
RF Rollie Fingers E 15.00 4.50
RFA Roy Face H 15.00 4.50
RK Ralph Kiner D 40.00 12.00
RKI Ron Kittle G 10.00 3.00
RS Ron Swoboda G 10.00 3.00
RSA Ryne Sandberg D 60.00 18.00
RSN Ron Santo G 25.00 7.50
RY Robin Yount A 200.00 60.00
SM Stan Musial B 200.00 60.00
TA Tony Armas G 10.00 3.00
TB Tom Brunansky G 10.00 3.00
TF Tony Fernandez E 10.00 3.00
TG Tony Gwynn C 100.00 30.00
TO Tony Oliva E 25.00 7.50
TS Tom Seaver C 100.00 30.00
VB Vida Blue G 10.00 3.00
WB Wade Boggs D 50.00 15.00
WF Whitey Ford C 80.00 24.00
WJ Wally Joyner G 10.00 3.00
YB Yogi Berra C 150.00 45.00

1997 Topps Stars

The 1997 Topps Stars set was issued in one series totalling 125 cards and was distributed in seven-card packs with a suggested retail price of $3. A checklisted card was added to every fifth pack as an extra card. The set was available exclusively to Home Team Advantage members and features color player photos printed on super-thick, 20-point stock with matte gold foil stamping and a textured matte laminate and spot UV coating. The backs carry another photo of the same player with biographical information and career statistics. Rookie cards include Kris Benson, Lance Berkman, Vernon Wells and Kerry Wood.

Nm-Mt Ex-Mt
COMPLETE SET (125) 30.00 9.00
1 Larry Walker .50 .15
2 Tino Martinez .50 .15
3 Cal Ripken 2.50 .75
4 Ken Griffey Jr. 1.25 .35
5 Chipper Jones .75 .23
6 David Justice .30 .09
7 Mike Piazza 1.25 .35
8 Jeff Bagwell .50 .15
9 Ron Gant .30 .09
10 Sammy Sosa 1.25 .35
11 Tony Gwynn 1.00 .30
12 Carlos Baerga .30 .09
13 Frank Thomas .75 .23
14 Moises Alou .30 .09
15 Barry Larkin .50 .15
16 Ivan Rodriguez .75 .23
17 Greg Maddux 1.25 .35
18 Jim Edmonds .30 .09
19 Jose Canseco .75 .23
20 Rafael Palmeiro .50 .15
21 Paul Molitor .50 .15
22 Kevin Appier .30 .09
23 Raul Mondesi .30 .09
24 Lance Johnson .30 .09
25 Edgar Martinez .50 .15
26 Andres Galarraga .30 .09
27 Mo Vaughn .30 .09
28 Ken Caminiti .30 .09
29 Cecil Fielder .30 .09
30 Harold Baines .30 .09
31 Roberto Alomar .50 .15
32 Shawn Estes .30 .09
33 Tom Glavine .50 .15
34 Dennis Eckersley .30 .09
35 Manny Ramirez .50 .15
36 John Olerud .30 .09
37 Juan Gonzalez .50 .15
38 Chuck Knoblauch .30 .09
39 Albert Belle .30 .09
40 Vinny Castilla .30 .09
41 John Smoltz .50 .15
42 Barry Bonds 2.00 .60
43 Randy Johnson .75 .23
44 Brady Anderson .30 .09
45 Jeff Blauser .30 .09
46 Craig Biggio .50 .15
47 Jeff Conine .30 .09
48 Marquis Grissom .30 .09
49 Mark Grace .50 .15
50 Roger Clemens 1.50 .45
51 Mark McGwire 2.00 .60
52 Fred McGriff .50 .15
53 Gary Sheffield .30 .09
54 Bobby Jones .30 .09
55 Eric Young .30 .09
56 Robin Ventura .30 .09
57 Wade Boggs .50 .15
58 Joe Carter .30 .09
59 Ryne Sandberg 1.25 .35
60 Matt Williams .30 .09
61 Todd Hundley .30 .09
62 Dante Bichette .30 .09
63 Chili Davis .30 .09
64 Kenny Lofton .30 .09
65 Jay Buhner .30 .09
66 Will Clark .75 .23
67 Travis Fryman .30 .09
68 Pat Hentgen .30 .09
69 Ellis Burks .30 .09
70 Mike Mussina .50 .15
71 Hideo Nomo .75 .23
72 Sandy Alomar Jr. .30 .09
73 Bobby Bonilla .30 .09
74 Rickey Henderson .75 .23
75 David Cone .30 .09
76 Terry Steinbach .30 .09
77 Pedro Martinez .75 .23
78 Jim Thome .75 .23
79 Rod Beck .30 .09
80 Randy Myers .30 .09
81 Charles Nagy .30 .09
82 Mark Wohlers .30 .09
83 Paul O'Neill .50 .15
84 Curt Schilling .30 .09
85 Joey Cora .30 .09
86 John Franco .30 .09
87 Kevin Brown .30 .09
88 Benito Santiago .30 .09
89 Ray Lankford .30 .09
90 Bernie Williams .50 .15
91 Jason Dickson .30 .09
92 Jeff Cirillo .30 .09
93 Nomar Garciaparra 1.25 .35
94 Mariano Rivera .50 .15
95 Javy Lopez .30 .09
96 Tony Womack RC .75 .23
97 Jose Rosado .30 .09
98 Denny Neagle .30 .09
99 Darryl Kile .30 .09
100 Justin Thompson .30 .09
101 Juan Encarnacion .30 .09
102 Brad Fullmer .30 .09
103 Kris Benson RC 1.25 .35
104 Todd Helton .75 .23
105 Paul Konerko .30 .09
106 Travis Lee RC .50 .15
107 Todd Greene .30 .09
108 Mark Kotsay RC 1.25 .35
109 Carl Pavano 1.00 .30
110 Kerry Wood RC 10.00 3.00
111 Jason Romano RC .30 .09
112 Geoff Goetz RC .30 .09
113 Scott Hodges RC .30 .09
114 Aaron Akin RC .30 .09
115 Vernon Wells RC 2.00 .60
116 Chris Stowe RC .30 .09
117 Brett Caradonna RC .30 .09
118 Adam Kennedy RC .75 .23
119 Jayson Werth RC 1.25 .35
120 Glenn Davis RC .30 .09
121 Troy Cameron RC .30 .09
122 J.J. Davis RC .50 .15
123 Jason Dellaero RC .30 .09
124 Jason Standridge RC .50 .15
125 Lance Berkman RC 6.00 1.80
NNO Checklist .30 .09

1997 Topps Stars Always Mint

Randomly inserted in packs at the rate of one in 12, this 125-card set is parallel to the base set and is printed on double-chromed paper stock.

Nm-Mt Ex-Mt
*ALWAYS: 4X TO 10X BASIC
*ALWAYS: 2X TO 5X BASIC RC'S

1997 Topps Stars '97 All-Stars

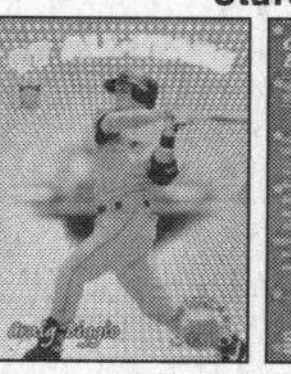
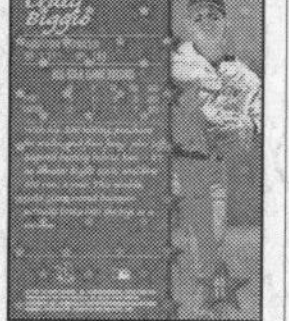

Randomly inserted in packs at the rate of one in 24, this 20-card set features color photos of players who represented their league in the 1997 All-Star Game in Cleveland and are printed on embossed uniluster.

Nm-Mt Ex-Mt
COMPLETE SET (20) 300.00 90.00
AS1 Greg Maddux 25.00 7.50
AS2 Randy Johnson 15.00 4.50
AS3 Tino Martinez 10.00 3.00
AS4 Jeff Bagwell 10.00 3.00
AS5 Ivan Rodriguez 15.00 4.50
AS6 Mike Piazza 25.00 7.50
AS7 Cal Ripken 50.00 15.00
AS8 Ken Caminiti 6.00 1.80
AS9 Tony Gwynn 20.00 6.00
AS10 Edgar Martinez 10.00 3.00
AS11 Craig Biggio 10.00 3.00
AS12 Roberto Alomar 10.00 3.00
AS13 Larry Walker 10.00 3.00
AS14 Brady Anderson 6.00 1.80
AS15 Barry Bonds 40.00 12.00
AS16 Ken Griffey Jr. 25.00 7.50
AS17 Ray Lankford 6.00 1.80
AS18 Paul O'Neill 10.00 3.00
AS19 Jeff Blauser 6.00 1.80
AS20 Sandy Alomar 6.00 1.80

1997 Topps Stars All-Star Memories

Randomly inserted in packs at the rate of one in 24, this 10-card set features color photos printed on laser-cut foilboard of the best performing all-star players.

Nm-Mt Ex-Mt
COMPLETE SET (10) 60.00 18.00
ASM1 Cal Ripken 20.00 6.00
ASM2 Jeff Conine 2.50 .75
ASM3 Mike Piazza 10.00 3.00
ASM4 Randy Johnson 6.00 1.80
ASM5 Ken Griffey Jr. 10.00 3.00
ASM6 Fred McGriff 4.00 1.20
ASM7 Moises Alou 2.50 .75
ASM8 Hideo Nomo 6.00 1.80
ASM9 Larry Walker 4.00 1.20
ASM10 Sandy Alomar 2.50 .75

1997 Topps Stars Future All-Stars

Randomly inserted in packs at the rate of one in 12, this 15-card set features color photos printed on prismatic rainbow diffraction foilboard of players who are candidates to be next year's all-stars.

Nm-Mt Ex-Mt
COMPLETE SET (15) 40.00 12.00
FAS1 Derek Jeter 12.00 3.60
FAS2 Andruw Jones 2.00 .60
FAS3 Vladimir Guerrero 4.00 1.20
FAS4 Scott Rolen 4.00 1.20
FAS5 Jose Guillen 2.00 .60
FAS6 Jose Cruz Jr. 2.50 .75
FAS7 Darin Erstad 2.00 .60
FAS8 Tony Clark 1.00 .30
FAS9 Scott Spiezio 1.00 .30
FAS10 Kevin Orie 1.00 .30
FAS11 Pokey Reese 1.00 .30
FAS12 Billy Wagner 2.00 .60
FAS13 Matt Morris 2.00 .60
FAS14 Jeremi Gonzalez 1.00 .30
FAS15 Hideki Irabu 2.00 .60

1997 Topps Stars Rookie Reprints

Randomly inserted in packs at the rate of one in six, this 15-card set features reprints of the rookie cards of 15 top Hall of Famers.

Nm-Mt Ex-Mt
COMPLETE SET (15) 50.00 15.00
1 Luis Aparicio 4.00 1.20
2 Richie Ashburn 4.00 1.20
3 Jim Bunning 4.00 1.20
4 Bob Feller 4.00 1.20
5 Rollie Fingers 4.00 1.20
6 Monte Irvin 4.00 1.20
7 Al Kaline 8.00 2.40
8 Ralph Kiner 4.00 1.20
9 Eddie Mathews 8.00 2.40
10 Hal Newhouser 4.00 1.20
11 Gaylord Perry 4.00 1.20
12 Robin Roberts 4.00 1.20
13 Brooks Robinson 4.00 1.20
14 Enos Slaughter 4.00 1.20
15 Earl Weaver 4.00 1.20

1997 Topps Stars Rookie Reprint Autographs

andomly inserted in packs at the rate of one in 0, this 14-card set is an autographed parallel ersion of the regular Topps Stars Rookie eprint set. The Topps Certified Issue Autograph tamp is printed on each card. Card No. 2 was upposed to be Richie Ashburn but he passed way before being able to sign his cards so this ard does not exist. This set is one of the more oteworthy issues from the late 1990's in that it tarted the popular trend of reprinted card autographed Rookie Cards heavily used by Topps for everal years thereafter.

	Nm-Mt	Ex-Mt
Luis Aparicio	25.00	7.50
Jim Bunning	50.00	15.00
Bob Feller	25.00	7.50
Rollie Fingers	25.00	7.50
Monte Irvin	40.00	12.00
Al Kaline	50.00	15.00
Ralph Kiner	25.00	7.50
Eddie Mathews	120.00	36.00
0 Hal Newhouser	80.00	24.00
1 Gaylord Perry	25.00	7.50
2 Robin Roberts	40.00	12.00
3 Brooks Robinson	40.00	12.00
4 Enos Slaughter	40.00	12.00
5 Earl Weaver	25.00	7.50

1998 Topps Stars

Distributed in six-card packs, this 150-card set features color action player photos printed on 20 pt. stock with red foil highlights, luminous diffraction, matte gold foil stamping, textured matte laminate, and spot UV coating. The pictured players are also grouped into five tool categories of baseball: Arm Strength, Hit for Average, Hit for Power, Defense, and Speed. A checklist card was added to every fifth pack as an extra card.

	Nm-Mt	Ex-Mt
COMP.RED SET (150)	80.00	24.00
1 Greg Maddux	3.00	.90
2 Darryl Kile	.75	.23
3 Rod Beck	.75	.23
4 Ellis Burks	.75	.23
5 Gary Sheffield	.75	.23
6 David Ortiz	2.00	.60
7 Marquis Grissom	.75	.23
8 Tony Womack	.75	.23
9 Mike Mussina	1.25	.35
10 Bernie Williams	1.25	.35
11 Andy Benes	.75	.23
12 Rusty Greer	.75	.23
13 Carlos Delgado	.75	.23
14 Jim Edmonds	.75	.23
15 Raul Mondesi	.75	.23
16 Andres Galarraga	.75	.23
17 Wade Boggs	1.25	.35
18 Paul O'Neill	1.25	.35
19 Edgar Renteria	.75	.23
20 Tony Clark	.75	.23
21 Vladimir Guerrero	2.00	.60
22 Moises Alou	.75	.23
23 Bernard Gilkey	.75	.23
24 Lance Johnson	.75	.23
25 Ben Grieve	.75	.23
26 Sandy Alomar Jr.	.75	.23
27 Ray Durham	.75	.23
28 Shawn Estes	.75	.23
29 David Segui	.75	.23
30 Javy Lopez	.75	.23
31 Steve Finley	.75	.23
32 Rey Ordonez	.75	.23
33 Derek Jeter	5.00	1.50
34 Henry Rodriguez	.75	.23
35 Mo Vaughn	.75	.23
36 Richard Hidalgo	.75	.23
37 Omar Vizquel	1.25	.35
38 Johnny Damon	1.25	.35
39 Brian Hunter	.75	.23
40 Matt Williams	.75	.23
41 Chuck Finley	.75	.23
42 Jeromy Burnitz	.75	.23
43 Livan Hernandez	.75	.23
44 Delino DeShields	.75	.23
45 Charles Nagy	.75	.23
46 Scott Rolen	2.00	.60
47 Neifi Perez	.75	.23
48 John Wetteland	.75	.23
49 Eric Milton	.75	.23
50 Mike Piazza	3.00	.90
51 Cal Ripken	6.00	1.80
52 Mariano Rivera	1.25	.35
53 Butch Huskey	.75	.23
54 Quinton McCracken	.75	.23
55 Jose Cruz Jr.	.75	.23
56 Brian Jordan	.75	.23
57 Hideo Nomo	2.00	.60
58 Masato Yoshii RC	1.25	.35
59 Cliff Floyd	.75	.23
60 Jose Guillen	.75	.23
61 Jeff Shaw	.75	.23
62 Edgar Martinez	1.25	.35
63 Rondell White	.75	.23
64 Hal Morris	.75	.23
65 Barry Larkin	1.25	.35
66 Eric Young	.75	.23
67 Ray Lankford	.75	.23
68 Derek Bell	.75	.23
69 Charles Johnson	.75	.23
70 Robin Ventura	.75	.23
71 Chuck Knoblauch	.75	.23
72 Kevin Brown	1.25	.35
73 Jose Valentin	.75	.23
74 Jay Buhner	.75	.23
75 Tony Gwynn	2.50	.75
76 Andy Pettitte	1.25	.35
77 Edgardo Alfonzo	.75	.23
78 Kerry Wood	2.00	.60
79 Darin Erstad	.75	.23
80 Paul Konerko	.75	.23
81 Jason Kendall	.75	.23
82 Tino Martinez	1.25	.35
83 Brad Radke	.75	.23
84 Jeff King	.75	.23
85 Travis Lee	.75	.23
86 Jeff Kent	.75	.23
87 Trevor Hoffman	.75	.23
88 David Cone	.75	.23
89 Jose Canseco	2.00	.60
90 Juan Gonzalez	1.25	.35
91 Todd Hundley	.75	.23
92 John Valentin	.75	.23
93 Sammy Sosa	3.00	.90
94 Jason Giambi	.75	.23
95 Chipper Jones	2.00	.60
96 Jeff Blauser	.75	.23
97 Brad Fullmer	.75	.23
98 Derrek Lee	.75	.23
99 Denny Neagle	.75	.23
100 Ken Griffey Jr.	3.00	.90
101 David Justice	.75	.23
102 Tim Salmon	1.25	.35
103 J.T. Snow	.75	.23
104 Fred McGriff	1.25	.35
105 Brady Anderson	.75	.23
106 Larry Walker	1.25	.35
107 Jeff Cirillo	.75	.23
108 Andruw Jones	.75	.23
109 Manny Ramirez	1.25	.35
110 Justin Thompson	.75	.23
111 Vinny Castilla	.75	.23
112 Chan Ho Park	.75	.23
113 Mark Grudzielanek	.75	.23
114 Mark Grace	1.25	.35
115 Ken Caminiti	.75	.23
116 Ryan Klesko	.75	.23
117 Rafael Palmeiro	1.25	.35
118 Pat Hentgen	.75	.23
119 Eric Karros	.75	.23
120 Randy Johnson	2.00	.60
121 Roberto Alomar	1.25	.35
122 John Olerud	.75	.23
123 Paul Molitor	1.25	.35
124 Dean Palmer	.75	.23
125 Nomar Garciaparra	3.00	.90
126 Curt Schilling	.75	.23
127 Jay Bell	.75	.23
128 Craig Biggio	1.25	.35
129 Marty Cordova	.75	.23
130 Ivan Rodriguez	2.00	.60
131 Todd Helton	1.25	.35
132 Jim Thome	2.00	.60
133 Albert Belle	.75	.23
134 Mike Lansing	.75	.23
135 Mark McGwire	5.00	1.50
136 Roger Clemens	4.00	1.20
137 Tom Glavine	1.25	.35
138 Ron Gant	.75	.23
139 Alex Rodriguez	3.00	.90
140 Jeff Bagwell	1.25	.35
141 John Smoltz	1.25	.35
142 Kenny Lofton	.75	.23
143 Dante Bichette	.75	.23
144 Pedro Martinez	2.00	.60
145 Barry Bonds	5.00	1.50
146 Travis Fryman	.75	.23
147 Bobby Jones	.75	.23
148 Bobby Higginson	.75	.23
149 Reggie Sanders	.75	.23
150 Frank Thomas	2.00	.60

1998 Topps Stars Bronze

Randomly inserted one in every pack, this 150-card set is a parallel version of the base set and is distinguished by bronze foil highlights. Only 9799 sets were produced and are serially numbered.

	Nm-Mt	Ex-Mt
COMPLETE SET (150)	80.00	24.00
*BRONZE: SAME VALUE AS RED		

1998 Topps Stars Gold

Randomly inserted in packs at the rate of one in two, this 150-card set is a parallel version of the base set and is distinguished by gold foil highlights. Only 2299 of this set were produced and serially numbered.

	Nm-Mt	Ex-Mt
COMPLETE SET (150)	300.00	90.00
*STARS: 1.25X TO 3X BASIC CARDS		

1998 Topps Stars Gold Rainbow

Randomly inserted in packs at the rate of one in 46, this 150-card set is a parallel version of the base set and is distinguished by its foil highlights. Only 99 sets were produced and and serially numbered.

	Nm-Mt	Ex-Mt
*STARS: 4X TO 10X BASIC CARDS		

1998 Topps Stars Silver

Randomly inserted in packs, this 150-card set is a parallel version of the base set and is distinguished by silver foil highlights. Only 4399 of this set were produced and serially numbered.

	Nm-Mt	Ex-Mt
COMPLETE SET (150)	200.00	60.00
*STARS: .75X TO 2X BASIC CARDS		

1998 Topps Stars Galaxy Bronze

Randomly inserted in packs at the rate of one in 818, this 10-card set features color images of players who possess all five of the tools of Baseball printed on a star galaxy background with bronze foil highlights. Only 100 of each card were produced and are sequentially numbered.

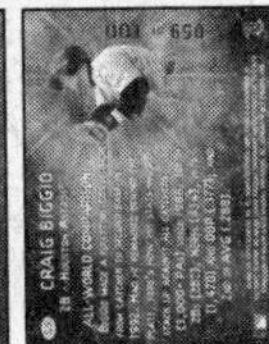

	Nm-Mt	Ex-Mt
*SILVER: .5X TO 1.2X BRONZE		
SILVER STATED ODDS 1:910		
SILVER PRINT RUN 75 SERIAL #'d SETS		
*GOLD: .6X TO 1.5X BRONZE		
GOLD STATED ODDS 1:1364		
GOLD PRINT RUN 50 SERIAL #'d SETS		
GOLD RAINBOW STATED ODDS 1:13643		
GOLD RBW.PRINT RUN 5 SERIAL #'d SETS		
GOLD RBW.NO PRICING DUE TO SCARCITY		
G1 Barry Bonds	60.00	18.00
G2 Jeff Bagwell	15.00	4.50
G3 Nomar Garciaparra	40.00	12.00
G4 Chipper Jones	25.00	7.50
G5 Ken Griffey Jr.	40.00	12.00
G6 Sammy Sosa	40.00	12.00
G7 Larry Walker	15.00	4.50
G8 Alex Rodriguez	40.00	12.00
G9 Craig Biggio	15.00	4.50
G10 Raul Mondesi	10.00	3.00

1998 Topps Stars Luminaries Bronze

Randomly inserted in packs at the rate of one in 545, this 15-card insert set features color photos of three of the top players from each of the five tools of Baseball with bronze foil highlights. Only 100 of each card were produced and are sequentially numbered.

	Nm-Mt	Ex-Mt
COMPLETE SET (15)	400.00	120.00
*SILVER: .5X TO 1.2X BRONZE		
SILVER STATED ODDS 1:606		
SILVER PRINT RUN 75 SERIAL #'d SETS		
*GOLD: .6X TO 1.5X BRONZE		
GOLD STATED ODDS 1:910		
GOLD PRINT RUN 50 SERIAL #'d SETS		
GOLD RAINBOW STATED ODDS 1:9095		
GOLD RBW.PRINT RUN 5 SERIAL #'d SETS		
GOLD RBW.NO PRICING DUE TO SCARCITY		
L1 Ken Griffey Jr.	40.00	12.00
L2 Mark McGwire	60.00	18.00
L3 Juan Gonzalez	15.00	4.50
L4 Tony Gwynn	30.00	9.00
L5 Frank Thomas	25.00	7.50
L6 Mike Piazza	40.00	12.00
L7 Chuck Knoblauch	10.00	3.00
L8 Kenny Lofton	10.00	3.00
L9 Barry Bonds	60.00	18.00
L10 Matt Williams	10.00	3.00
L11 Raul Mondesi	10.00	3.00
L12 Ivan Rodriguez	25.00	7.50
L13 Alex Rodriguez	40.00	12.00
L14 Nomar Garciaparra	40.00	12.00
L15 Ken Caminiti	10.00	3.00

1998 Topps Stars Rookie Reprints

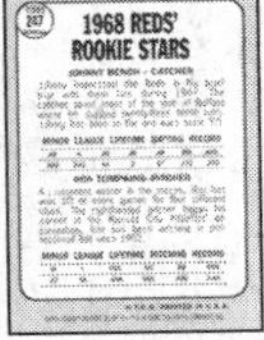

Randomly inserted in packs at the rate of one in 24, this five-card set features reprints of Topps rookie cards of five Hall of Famers.

	Nm-Mt	Ex-Mt
COMPLETE SET (5)	40.00	12.00
1 Johnny Bench	8.00	2.40
2 Whitey Ford	5.00	1.50
3 Joe Morgan	5.00	1.50
4 Mike Schmidt	12.00	3.60
5 Carl Yastrzemski	10.00	3.00

1998 Topps Stars Rookie Reprints Autographs

Randomly inserted in packs at the rate of one in 327, this five-card set is an autographed parallel version to the Topps Stars Rookie Reprints set. Each card carries the Certified Autograph Issue stamp.

	Nm-Mt	Ex-Mt
1 Johnny Bench	60.00	18.00
2 Whitey Ford	50.00	15.00
3 Joe Morgan	50.00	15.00
4 Mike Schmidt	80.00	24.00
5 Carl Yastrzemski	80.00	24.00

1998 Topps Stars Supernovas Bronze

Randomly inserted in packs at the rate of one in 818, this 10-card set features color images of players who dramatically excel in one or possess all five tools of Baseball printed on a star background with bronze foil highlights. Only 100 of each card were produced and are sequentially numbered.

	Nm-Mt	Ex-Mt
*SILVER: .5X TO 1.2X BRONZE		
SILVER STATED ODDS 1:910		
SILVER PRINT RUN 75 SERIAL #'d SETS		
*GOLD: .6X TO 1.5X BRONZE		
GOLD STATED ODDS 1:1364		
GOLD PRINT RUN 50 SERIAL #'d SETS		
GOLD RAINBOW STATED ODDS 1:13643		
GOLD RBW.PRINT RUN 5 SERIAL #'d SETS		
GOLD RBW.NO PRICING DUE TO SCARCITY		
S1 Ben Grieve	10.00	3.00
S2 Travis Lee	10.00	3.00
S3 Todd Helton	15.00	4.50
S4 Adrian Beltre	25.00	7.50
S5 Derrek Lee	10.00	3.00
S6 David Ortiz	25.00	7.50
S7 Brad Fullmer	10.00	3.00
S8 Mark Kotsay	10.00	3.00
S9 Paul Konerko	10.00	3.00
S10 Kerry Wood	25.00	7.50

1999 Topps Stars

The 1999 Topps Stars set was issued in one series for a total of 180 cards and distributed in six-card packs with a suggested retail price of $3. The set features action color player photos printed on 20-point card stock with foil-stamping, flood gloss, and metallic inks. The backs carry five-star player evaluation. The set features the following subsets: Luminaries (151-170) and Supernovas (171-180). Rookie Cards include Pat Burrell, Alex Escobar, Nick Johnson and Alfonso Soriano.

	Nm-Mt	Ex-Mt
COMPLETE SET (180)	50.00	15.00
1 Ken Griffey Jr.	2.00	.60
2 Chipper Jones	1.25	.35
3 Mike Piazza	2.00	.60
4 Nomar Garciaparra	2.00	.60
5 Derek Jeter	3.00	.90
6 Frank Thomas	1.25	.35
7 Ben Grieve	.50	.15
8 Mark McGwire	3.00	.90
9 Sammy Sosa	2.00	.60
10 Alex Rodriguez	2.00	.60
11 Troy Glaus	.50	.15
12 Eric Chavez	.50	.15
13 Kerry Wood	1.25	.35
14 Barry Bonds	3.00	.90
15 Vladimir Guerrero	1.25	.35
16 Albert Belle	.50	.15
17 Juan Gonzalez	.75	.23
18 Roger Clemens	2.50	.75
19 Ruben Mateo	.50	.15
20 Cal Ripken	4.00	1.20
21 Darin Erstad	.50	.15
22 Jeff Bagwell	.75	.23
23 Roy Halladay	.50	.15
24 Todd Helton	.75	.23
25 Michael Barrett	.50	.15
26 Manny Ramirez	.75	.23
27 Fernando Seguignol	.50	.15
28 Pat Burrell RC	1.50	.45
29 Andruw Jones	.50	.15
30 Randy Johnson	1.25	.35
31 Jose Canseco	1.25	.35
32 Brad Fullmer	.50	.15
33 Alex Escobar RC	.50	.15
34 Alfonso Soriano RC	5.00	1.50
35 Larry Walker	.75	.23
36 Matt Clement	.50	.15
37 Mo Vaughn	.50	.15
38 Bruce Chen	.50	.15
39 Travis Lee	.50	.15
40 Adrian Beltre	.75	.23
41 Alex Gonzalez	.50	.15
42 Jason Tyner RC	.50	.15
43 George Lombard	.50	.15
44 Scott Rolen	1.25	.35
45 Mark Mulder RC	2.00	.45
46 Gabe Kapler	.50	.15
47 Choo Freeman RC	.50	.15
48 Tony Gwynn	1.50	.45
49 A.J. Burnett RC	1.00	.30
50 Matt Belisle RC	.50	.15
51 Greg Maddux	2.00	.60
52 John Smoltz	.75	.23
53 Mark Grace	.75	.23
54 Wade Boggs	.75	.23
55 Bernie Williams	.75	.23
56 Pedro Martinez	1.25	.35
57 Barry Larkin	.75	.23
58 Orlando Hernandez	.50	.15
59 Jason Kendall	.50	.15
60 Mark Kotsay	.50	.15
61 Jim Thome	1.25	.35
62 Gary Sheffield	.50	.15
63 Preston Wilson	.50	.15
64 Rafael Palmeiro	.75	.23
65 David Wells	.50	.15
66 Shawn Green	.50	.15
67 Tom Glavine	.75	.23
68 Jeromy Burnitz	.50	.15
69 Kevin Brown	.75	.23
70 Rondell White	.50	.15
71 Roberto Alomar	.75	.23
72 Cliff Floyd	.50	.15
73 Craig Biggio	.75	.23
74 Greg Vaughn	.50	.15
75 Ivan Rodriguez	1.25	.35
76 Vinny Castilla	.50	.15
77 Todd Walker	.50	.15
78 Paul Konerko	.50	.15
79 Andy Brown RC	.50	.15
80 Todd Hundley	.50	.15
81 Dmitri Young	.50	.15
82 Tony Clark	.50	.15
83 Nick Johnson RC	1.00	.30
84 Mike Caruso	.50	.15
85 David Ortiz	.75	.23
86 Matt Williams	.50	.15
87 Raul Mondesi	.50	.15
88 Kenny Lofton	.50	.15
89 Miguel Tejada	.50	.15
90 Dante Bichette	.50	.15
91 Jorge Posada	.75	.23
92 Carlos Beltran	.75	.23
93 Carlos Delgado	.50	.15
94 Javy Lopez	.50	.15
95 Aramis Ramirez	.50	.15
96 Neifi Perez	.50	.15
97 Marlon Anderson	.50	.15
98 David Cone	.50	.15
99 Moises Alou	.50	.15
100 John Olerud	.50	.15
101 Tim Salmon	.75	.23
102 Jason Giambi	.50	.15
103 Sandy Alomar Jr.	.50	.15
104 Curt Schilling	.50	.15
105 Andres Galarraga	.50	.15
106 Rusty Greer	.50	.15
107 Bobby Seay RC	.50	.15
108 Eric Young	.50	.15
109 Brian Jordan	.50	.15
110 Eric Davis	.50	.15
111 Will Clark	1.25	.35
112 Andy Ashby	.50	.15
113 Edgardo Alfonzo	.50	.15
114 Paul O'Neill	.75	.23
115 Denny Neagle	.50	.15
116 Eric Karros	.50	.15
117 Ken Caminiti	.50	.15
118 Garret Anderson	.50	.15
119 Todd Stottlemyre	.50	.15
120 David Justice	.50	.15
121 Francisco Cordova	.50	.15
122 Robin Ventura	.50	.15
123 Mike Mussina	.75	.23
124 Hideki Irabu	.50	.15
125 Justin Thompson	.50	.15
126 Mariano Rivera	.75	.23
127 Delino DeShields	.50	.15
128 Steve Finley	.50	.15
129 Jose Cruz Jr.	.50	.15
130 Ray Lankford	.50	.15
131 Jim Edmonds	.50	.15
132 Charles Johnson	.50	.15
133 Al Leiter	.50	.15
134 Jose Offerman	.50	.15
135 Eric Milton	.50	.15
136 Dean Palmer	.50	.15
137 Johnny Damon	.75	.23
138 Andy Pettitte	.75	.23
139 Ray Durham	.50	.15
140 Ugueth Urbina	.50	.15
141 Marquis Grissom	.50	.15
142 Ryan Klesko	.50	.15
143 Brady Anderson	.50	.15
144 Bobby Higginson	.50	.15
145 Chuck Knoblauch	.50	.15
146 Rickey Henderson	1.25	.35
147 Kevin Millwood	.50	.15
148 Fred McGriff	.75	.23
149 Damion Easley	.50	.15
150 Tino Martinez	.75	.23
151 Greg Maddux LUM	1.25	.35
152 Scott Rolen LUM	.75	.23
153 Pat Burrell LUM	.60	.18
154 Roger Clemens LUM	1.25	.35
155 Albert Belle LUM	.50	.15
156 Troy Glaus LUM	.50	.15
157 Cal Ripken LUM	2.00	.60
158 Alfonso Soriano LUM	2.00	.60
159 Manny Ramirez LUM	.50	.15
160 Eric Chavez LUM	.50	.15
161 Kerry Wood LUM	.75	.23
162 Tony Gwynn LUM	.75	.23
163 Barry Bonds LUM	1.25	.35
164 Ruben Mateo LUM	.50	.15
165 Todd Helton LUM	.50	.15
166 Darin Erstad LUM	.50	.15
167 Jeff Bagwell LUM	.50	.15
168 Juan Gonzalez LUM	.50	.15
169 Mo Vaughn LUM	.50	.15
170 V.Guerrero LUM	.75	.23
171 N.Garciaparra SUP	1.25	.35
172 Derek Jeter SUP	1.50	.45
173 Alex Rodriguez SUP	1.25	.35
174 Ben Grieve SUP	.50	.15
175 Mike Piazza SUP	1.25	.35
176 Chipper Jones SUP	.75	.23
177 Frank Thomas SUP	.75	.23
178 Ken Griffey Jr. SUP	1.25	.35
179 Sammy Sosa SUP	1.25	.35
180 Mark McGwire SUP	1.50	.45

1999 Topps Stars Foil

Randomly inserted into packs at the rate of one in 15, this 180-card set is parallel to the base se, printed on heavy 20-point card stock treated with silver select metallization, and sequentially numbered to 299. This numbering is quite off is that it lacks gold foil. Instead, the cards are simply embossed with the serial number on back, making it easy to miss.

Nm-Mt Ex-Mt
*STARS: 3X TO 8X BASIC CARDS......
*ROOKIES: 1.5X TO 4X BASIC CARDS

1999 Topps Stars One Star

Inserted two per pack, this 100-card set features the game's top stars from the 150 veterans pictured on the base cards and printed with dark silver metallic inks and foil stamping. The backs outline the player's career highlights.

Nm-Mt Ex-Mt
COMPLETE SET (100) 40.00 12.00
1 Ken Griffey Jr. 1.50 .45
2 Chipper Jones 1.00 .30
3 Mike Piazza 1.50 .45
4 Nomar Garciaparra 1.50 .45
5 Derek Jeter 2.50 .75
6 Frank Thomas 1.00 .30
7 Ben Grieve .40 .12
8 Mark McGwire 2.50 .75
9 Sammy Sosa 1.50 .45
10 Alex Rodriguez 1.50 .45
11 Troy Glaus .40 .12
12 Eric Chavez .40 .12
13 Kerry Wood 1.00 .30
14 Barry Bonds 2.50 .75
15 Vladimir Guerrero 1.00 .30
16 Albert Belle .40 .12
17 Juan Gonzalez .60 .18
18 Roger Clemens 2.00 .60
19 Ruben Mateo .40 .12
20 Cal Ripken 3.00 .90
21 Darin Erstad .40 .12
22 Jeff Bagwell .60 .18
23 Roy Halladay .40 .12
24 Todd Helton .60 .18
25 Michael Barrett .40 .12
26 Manny Ramirez .60 .18
27 Fernando Seguignol .40 .12
28 Pat Burrell 1.00 .30
29 Andruw Jones .40 .12
30 Randy Johnson 1.00 .30
31 Jose Canseco 1.00 .30
32 Brad Fullmer .40 .12
33 Alex Escobar .30 .09
34 Alfonso Soriano 4.00 1.20
35 Larry Walker .60 .18
36 Matt Clement .40 .12
37 Mo Vaughn .40 .12
38 Bruce Chen .40 .12
39 Travis Lee .40 .12
40 Adrian Beltre .60 .18
41 Alex Gonzalez .40 .12
42 Jason Tyner .40 .12
43 George Lombard .40 .12
44 Scott Rolen 1.00 .30
45 Mark Mulder 1.50 .45
46 Gabe Kapler .40 .12
47 Choo Freeman .40 .12
48 Tony Gwynn 1.25 .35
49 A.J. Burnett .75 .23
50 Matt Belisle .40 .12
51 Greg Maddux 1.50 .45
52 John Smoltz .60 .18
53 Mark Grace .60 .18
54 Wade Boggs .60 .18
55 Bernie Williams .60 .18
56 Pedro Martinez 1.00 .30
57 Barry Larkin .60 .18
58 Orlando Hernandez .40 .12
59 Jason Kendall .40 .12
60 Mark Kotsay .40 .12
61 Jim Thome 1.00 .30
62 Gary Sheffield .40 .12
63 Preston Wilson .40 .12
64 Rafael Palmeiro .60 .18
65 David Wells .40 .12
66 Shawn Green .40 .12
67 Tom Glavine .60 .18
68 Jeromy Burnitz .40 .12
69 Kevin Brown .60 .18
70 Rondell White .40 .12
71 Roberto Alomar .60 .18
72 Cliff Floyd .40 .12
73 Craig Biggio .60 .18
74 Greg Vaughn .40 .12
75 Ivan Rodriguez 1.00 .30
76 Vinny Castilla .40 .12
77 Todd Walker .40 .12
78 Paul Konerko .40 .12
79 Andy Brown .40 .12
80 Todd Hundley .40 .12
81 Dmitri Young .40 .12
82 Tony Clark .40 .12
83 Nick Johnson .75 .23
84 Mike Caruso .40 .12
85 David Ortiz .60 .18
86 Matt Williams .40 .12
87 Raul Mondesi .40 .12
88 Kenny Lofton .40 .12
89 Miguel Tejada .40 .12
90 Dante Bichette .40 .12
91 Jorge Posada .60 .18
92 Carlos Beltran .60 .18
93 Carlos Delgado .40 .12
94 Javy Lopez .40 .12
95 Aramis Ramirez .40 .12
96 Neifi Perez .40 .12
97 Marlon Anderson .40 .12
98 David Cone .40 .12
99 Moises Alou .40 .12
100 John Olerud .40 .12

1999 Topps Stars One Star Foil

This 100-card set is parallel to the regular insert set and serially numbered to 249.

Nm-Mt Ex-Mt
*STARS: 5X TO 12X BASIC ONE STAR
*ROOKIES: 2.5X TO 6X BASIC ONE STAR

1999 Topps Stars Two Star

Inserted one per pack, this 50-card set features color photos of the game's top players printed with light gold metallic inks and foil stamping. The backs carry the player 1998 season highlights.

Nm-Mt Ex-Mt
COMPLETE SET (50) 30.00 9.00
1 Ken Griffey Jr. 1.50 .45
2 Chipper Jones 1.00 .30
3 Mike Piazza 1.50 .45
4 Nomar Garciaparra 1.50 .45
5 Derek Jeter 2.50 .75
6 Frank Thomas 1.00 .30
7 Ben Grieve .40 .12
8 Mark McGwire 2.50 .75
9 Sammy Sosa 1.50 .45
10 Alex Rodriguez 1.50 .45
11 Troy Glaus .40 .12
12 Eric Chavez .40 .12
13 Kerry Wood 1.00 .30
14 Barry Bonds 2.50 .75
15 Vladimir Guerrero 1.00 .30
16 Albert Belle .40 .12
17 Juan Gonzalez .60 .18
18 Roger Clemens 2.00 .60
19 Ruben Mateo .40 .12
20 Cal Ripken 3.00 .90
21 Darin Erstad .40 .12
22 Jeff Bagwell .60 .18
23 Roy Halladay .40 .12
24 Todd Helton .60 .18
25 Michael Barrett .40 .12
26 Manny Ramirez .60 .18
27 Fernando Seguignol .40 .12
28 Pat Burrell 1.00 .30
29 Andruw Jones .40 .12
30 Randy Johnson 1.00 .30
31 Jose Canseco 1.00 .30
32 Brad Fullmer .40 .12
33 Alex Escobar .30 .09
34 Alfonso Soriano 4.00 1.20
35 Larry Walker .60 .18
36 Matt Clement .40 .12
37 Mo Vaughn .40 .12
38 Bruce Chen .40 .12
39 Travis Lee .40 .12
40 Adrian Beltre .60 .18
41 Alex Gonzalez .40 .12
42 Jason Tyner .40 .12
43 George Lombard .40 .12
44 Scott Rolen 1.00 .30
45 Mark Mulder 1.50 .45
46 Gabe Kapler .40 .12
47 Choo Freeman .40 .12
48 Tony Gwynn 1.25 .35
49 A.J. Burnett .75 .23
50 Matt Belisle .40 .12

1999 Topps Stars Two Star Foil

Randomly inserted in packs at the rate of one in 82, this 50-card set is a gold select metallization parallel version of the regular insert set. Only 199 serial-numbered sets were produced.

Nm-Mt Ex-Mt
*STARS: 6X TO 15X BASIC TWO STAR
*ROOKIES: 4X TO 10X BASIC TWO STAR

1999 Topps Stars Three Star

Randomly inserted in packs at the rate of one in five, this 20-card set features color photos of the hottest stars in the game printed with refractive silver foil stamping along with gold metallic inks. The backs carry "Star Qualities" text indicating exactly what makes the player shine.

Nm-Mt Ex-Mt
COMPLETE SET (20) 50.00 15.00
1 Ken Griffey Jr. 2.50 .75
2 Chipper Jones 1.50 .45
3 Mike Piazza 2.50 .75
4 Nomar Garciaparra 2.50 .75
5 Derek Jeter 4.00 1.20
6 Frank Thomas 1.50 .45
7 Ben Grieve .60 .18
8 Mark McGwire 4.00 1.20
9 Sammy Sosa 2.50 .75
10 Alex Rodriguez 2.50 .75
11 Troy Glaus .60 .18
12 Eric Chavez .60 .18
13 Kerry Wood 1.50 .45
14 Barry Bonds 4.00 1.20
15 Vladimir Guerrero 1.50 .45
16 Albert Belle .60 .18
17 Juan Gonzalez 1.00 .30
18 Roger Clemens 3.00 .90
19 Ruben Mateo .60 .18
20 Cal Ripken 5.00 1.50

1999 Topps Stars Three Star Foil

Randomly inserted in packs at the rate of one in 410, this 20-card set is a gold select metallization parallel version of the regular insert set and sequentially numbered to 99.

Nm-Mt Ex-Mt
*STARS: 6X TO 15X BASIC THREE STAR

1999 Topps Stars Four Star

Randomly inserted in packs at the rate of one in 10, this 10-card set features color action photos of top rank players printed using dark gold metallic inks and refractive foil stamping on the fronts. The backs carry the player's honors and accolades.

Nm-Mt Ex-Mt
COMPLETE SET (10) 40.00 12.00
1 Ken Griffey Jr. 2.50 .75
2 Chipper Jones 1.50 .45
3 Mike Piazza 2.50 .75
4 Nomar Garciaparra 2.50 .75
5 Derek Jeter 4.00 1.20
6 Frank Thomas 1.50 .45
7 Ben Grieve .60 .18
8 Mark McGwire 4.00 1.20
9 Sammy Sosa 2.50 .75
10 Alex Rodriguez 2.50 .75

1999 Topps Stars Four Star Foil

Randomly inserted in packs at the rate of one in 1650, this 10-card set is a gold select metallization foil parallel version of the regular insert set. Only 49 serial-numbered sets were produced.

Nm-Mt Ex-Mt
*STARS: 8X TO 20X BASIC FOUR STAR

1999 Topps Stars Bright Futures

Randomly inserted in packs at the rate of one in 41, this 10-card set features action color photos of top rising prospects with foil stamping and sequentially numbered to 1999.

Nm-Mt Ex-Mt
COMPLETE SET (10) 40.00 12.00
*FOIL: 3X TO 8X BASIC BR.FUTURES
FOIL ODDS 1:2702
FOIL PRINT RUN 30 SERIAL #'d SETS
BF1 Troy Glaus 3.00 .90
BF2 Eric Chavez 3.00 .90
BF3 Adrian Beltre 5.00 1.50
BF4 Michael Barrett 3.00 .90
BF5 Gabe Kapler 3.00 .90
BF6 Alex Gonzalez 3.00 .90
BF7 Matt Clement 3.00 .90
BF8 Pat Burrell 2.50 .75
BF9 Ruben Mateo 3.00 .90
BF10 Alfonso Soriano 6.00 1.80

1999 Topps Stars Galaxy

Randomly inserted in packs at the rate of one in 41, this 10-card set features color action photos of top MLB stars printed with a foil stamp and sequentially numbered to 1999. Each card is serial numbered of 1999 on back.

Nm-Mt Ex-Mt
COMPLETE SET (10) 100.00 30.00
*FOIL: 4X TO 10X BASIC GALAXY
FOIL ODDS 1:2702
FOIL PRINT RUN 30 SERIAL #'d SETS
G1 Mark McGwire 15.00 4.50
G2 Roger Clemens 12.00 3.60
G3 Nomar Garciaparra 10.00 3.00
G4 Alex Rodriguez 10.00 3.00
G5 Kerry Wood 6.00 1.80
G6 Ben Grieve 2.50 .75
G7 Derek Jeter 15.00 4.50
G8 Vladimir Guerrero 6.00 1.80
G9 Ken Griffey Jr. 10.00 3.00
G10 Sammy Sosa 10.00 3.00

1999 Topps Stars Rookie Reprints

These five cards are reprints of famous vintage Rookie Cards issued by Topps from an era gone by. The cards are very detailed replicas of the actual vintage issues except, of course, for the modern era high end white card stock, glossy coatings and standard 2 1/2" by 3 1/2" size (the real Banks and Berra RC's were not made with those dimensions). The cards were randomly seeded into packs at a rate of 1:65. A total of 2,500 serial numbered sets were produced.

Nm-Mt Ex-Mt
COMPLETE SET (5) 80.00 24.00
1 Frank Robinson 15.00 4.50
2 Ernie Banks 20.00 6.00
3 Yogi Berra 20.00 6.00
4 Bob Gibson 15.00 4.50
5 Tom Seaver 15.00 4.50

1999 Topps Stars Rookie Reprints Autographs

These autographed cards are parallel issues to the more common Rookie Reprints inserts. Each card has been signed by the athlete and stamped as a "Topps Certified Autograph Issue". The cards are randomly seeded into packs at a rate of 1:406 except for the Ernie Banks card of which is seeded at 1:812. Judging from analysis of the total product print run, it appears that each athlete signed approximately 500 cards - except for

Banks of whom it appears signed around 1,000 cards.

Nm-Mt Ex-Mt
1 Frank Robinson 40.00 12.00
2 Ernie Banks DP 80.00 24.00
3 Yogi Berra 60.00 18.00
4 Bob Gibson 40.00 12.00
5 Tom Seaver 40.00 12.00

2000 Topps Stars

The 2000 Topps Stars product was released in July, 2000 and featured a 200-card base set. The base set was broken into tiers as follows: 135 Base Veterans (1-135), 15 Rookies (136-150), 50 Spotlights (151-200). Each pack contained six cards and carried a suggested retail price of $3.00. Notable Rookie Cards include Jose Ortiz (his first licensed Rookie Card on the market), Rick Asadoorian and Bobby Bradley.

Nm-Mt Ex-Mt
COMPLETE SET (200) 50.00 15.00
1 Vladimir Guerrero 1.25 .35
2 Eric Karros .50 .15
3 Omar Vizquel .75 .23
4 Ken Griffey Jr. 2.00 .60
5 Preston Wilson .50 .15
6 Albert Belle .50 .15
7 Ryan Klesko .50 .15
8 Bob Abreu .50 .15
9 Warren Morris .40 .12
10 Rafael Palmeiro .75 .23
11 Nomar Garciaparra 2.00 .60
12 Dante Bichette .50 .15
13 Jeff Cirillo .40 .12
14 Carlos Beltran .75 .23
15 Tony Clark .40 .12
16 Ray Durham .50 .15
17 Mark McGwire 3.00 .90
18 Jim Thome 1.25 .35
19 Todd Walker .40 .12
20 Richie Sexson .50 .15
21 Adrian Beltre .75 .23
22 Jay Bell .50 .15
23 Craig Biggio .75 .23
24 Ben Grieve .40 .12
25 Greg Maddux 2.00 .60
26 Fernando Tatis .40 .12
27 Jeromy Burnitz .50 .15
28 Vinny Castilla .50 .15
29 Mark Grace .75 .23
30 Derek Jeter 3.00 .90
31 Larry Walker .75 .23
32 Ivan Rodriguez 1.25 .35
33 Curt Schilling .50 .15
34 Mike Lamb RC .50 .15
35 Kevin Brown .50 .15
36 Andruw Jones .50 .15
37 Chris Mears RC .50 .15
38 Bartolo Colon .50 .15
39 Edgardo Alfonzo .40 .12
40 Brady Anderson .50 .15
41 Andres Galarraga .50 .15
42 Scott Rolen 1.25 .35
43 Manny Ramirez .75 .23
44 Carlos Delgado .50 .15
45 David Cone .50 .15
46 Carl Everett .50 .15
47 Chipper Jones 1.25 .35
48 Barry Bonds 3.00 .90
49 Dean Palmer .50 .15
50 Frank Thomas 1.25 .35
51 Paul O'Neill .75 .23
52 Mo Vaughn .50 .15
53 Todd Helton .75 .23
54 Jason Giambi .50 .15
55 Brian Jordan .50 .15
56 Luis Gonzalez .50 .15
57 Alex Rodriguez 2.00 .60
58 J.D. Drew .50 .15
59 Javy Lopez .50 .15
60 Tony Gwynn 1.50 .45
61 Jason Kendall .50 .15
62 Pedro Martinez 1.25 .35
63 Matt Williams .50 .15
64 Gary Sheffield .50 .15
65 Roberto Alomar .75 .23
66 Lyle Overbay RC 2.50 .75
67 Jeff Bagwell .75 .23
68 Tim Hudson .50 .15
69 Sammy Sosa 2.00 .60
70 Keith Reed RC .50 .15
71 Robin Ventura .50 .15
72 Cal Ripken 4.00 1.20
73 Alex Gonzalez .40 .12
74 Aaron McNeal RC .50 .15
75 Mike Lieberthal .50 .15
76 Brian Giles .50 .15
77 Kevin Millwood .50 .15
78 Troy O'Leary .40 .12
79 Raul Mondesi .50 .15
80 John Olerud .50 .15
81 David Justice .50 .15
82 Erubiel Durazo .40 .12
83 Shawn Green .50 .15
84 Tino Martinez .75 .23
85 Greg Vaughn .40 .12
86 Tom Glavine .75 .23
87 Jose Canseco 1.25 .35
88 Kenny Lofton .50 .15
89 Brian Daubach .40 .12
90 Mike Piazza 2.00 .60
91 Randy Johnson 1.25 .35
92 Pokey Reese .40 .12
93 Troy Glaus .50 .15
94 Kerry Wood 1.25 .35
95 Sean Casey .50 .15
96 Magglio Ordonez .50 .15
97 Bernie Williams .75 .23
98 Juan Gonzalez .75 .23
99 Barry Larkin .75 .23
100 Orlando Hernandez .40 .12
101 Roger Clemens 2.50 .75
102 Bob Gibson .75 .23
103 Gary Carter .50 .15
104 Willie Stargell .75 .23
105 Joe Morgan .50 .15
106 Brooks Robinson .75 .23
107 Ozzie Smith 2.00 .60
108 Carl Yastrzemski 2.00 .60
109 Al Kaline 1.25 .35
110 Frank Robinson .75 .23
111 Lance Berkman .50 .15
112 Adam Piatt .40 .12
113 Vernon Wells .50 .15
114 Rafael Furcal .50 .15
115 Rick Ankiel .50 .15
116 Corey Patterson .50 .15
117 Josh Hamilton .40 .12
118 Jack Cust .40 .12
119 Josh Girdley .40 .12
120 Pablo Ozuna .40 .12
121 Sean Burroughs .50 .15
122 Pat Burrell .50 .15
123 Chad Hermansen .40 .12
124 Ruben Mateo .40 .12
125 Ben Petrick .40 .12
126 Dee Brown .40 .12
127 Eric Munson .40 .12
128 Ruben Salazar RC .50 .15
129 Kip Wells .40 .12
130 Alfonso Soriano 1.25 .35
131 Mark Mulder .50 .15
132 Roosevelt Brown .40 .12
133 Nick Johnson .40 .12
134 Kyle Snyder .40 .12
135 David Walling .40 .12
136 Geraldo Guzman RC .50 .15
137 John Sneed RC .50 .15
138 Ben Christensen RC .50 .15
139 Corey Myers RC .50 .15
140 Jose Ortiz RC .50 .15
141 Ryan Christianson RC .50 .15
142 Brett Myers RC .75 .23
143 Bobby Bradley RC .50 .15
144 Rick Asadoorian RC .50 .15
145 Julio Zuleta RC .50 .15
146 Ty Howington RC .50 .15
147 Josh Kalinowski RC .50 .15
148 B.J. Garbe RC .50 .15
149 Scott Downs RC .50 .15
150 Dan Wright RC .50 .15
151 Jeff Bagwell SPOT .50 .15
152 V.Guerrero SPOT .75 .23
153 Mike Piazza SPOT 1.25 .35
154 Juan Gonzalez SPOT .50 .15
155 Ivan Rodriguez SPOT .75 .23
156 Manny Ramirez SPOT .50 .15
157 Sammy Sosa SPOT 1.25 .35
158 Chipper Jones SPOT .75 .23
159 Shawn Green SPOT .40 .12
160 Ken Griffey Jr. SPOT 1.25 .35
161 Cal Ripken SPOT 2.00 .60
162 N.Garciaparra SPOT 1.25 .35
163 Derek Jeter SPOT 1.50 .45
164 Barry Bonds SPOT 1.50 .45
165 Greg Maddux SPOT 1.25 .35
166 Mark McGwire SPOT 1.50 .45
167 Roberto Alomar SPOT .50 .15
168 Alex Rodriguez SPOT 1.25 .35
169 Randy Johnson SPOT .75 .23
170 Tony Gwynn SPOT .75 .23
171 Pedro Martinez SPOT .75 .23
172 Bob Gibson SPOT .50 .15
173 Gary Carter SPOT .40 .12
174 Willie Stargell SPOT .50 .15
175 Joe Morgan SPOT .40 .12
176 B.Robinson SPOT .50 .15
177 Ozzie Smith SPOT 1.25 .35
178 C.Yastrzemski SPOT 1.25 .35
179 Al Kaline SPOT .75 .23
180 Frank Robinson SPOT .50 .15
181 Adam Piatt SPOT .40 .12
182 Alfonso Soriano SPOT .75 .23
183 Corey Patterson SPOT .40 .12
184 Vernon Wells SPOT .40 .12
185 Pat Burrell SPOT .40 .12
186 Mark Mulder SPOT .40 .12
187 Eric Munson SPOT .40 .12
188 Rafael Furcal SPOT .40 .12
189 Rick Ankiel SPOT .50 .15
190 Ruben Mateo SPOT .40 .12
191 S.Burroughs SPOT .50 .15
192 Josh Hamilton SPOT .40 .12
193 Brett Myers SPOT .50 .15
194 B.Christensen SPOT .50 .15
195 Ty Howington SPOT .50 .15
196 R.Asadoorian SPOT .50 .15
197 J.Kalinowski SPOT .50 .15
198 Corey Myers SPOT .50 .15
199 R.Christianson SPOT .50 .15
200 John Sneed SPOT .50 .15

2000 Topps Stars Metallic Blue

Randomly inserted into packs, this 200-card set is a complete parallel of the 2000 Topps Stars base set that features a metallic blue foil lettering. The set is broken into two tiers as follows: Veterans (1-150) inserted one in 26, individually serial numbered to 299, Subset cards (151-200) inserted at one in 232, individually serial numbered to 99.

Nm-Mt Ex-Mt
COMMON CARD (1-150) 2.00 .60
*STARS 1-150: 3X TO 8X BASIC CARDS
*ROOKIES 1-150: 2.5X TO 6X BASIC CARDS
COMMON (151-200) 4.00 1.20
*STARS 151-180: 10X TO 25X BASIC
*ROOKIES 193-200: 8X TO 20X BASIC

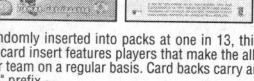

2000 Topps Stars All-Star Authority

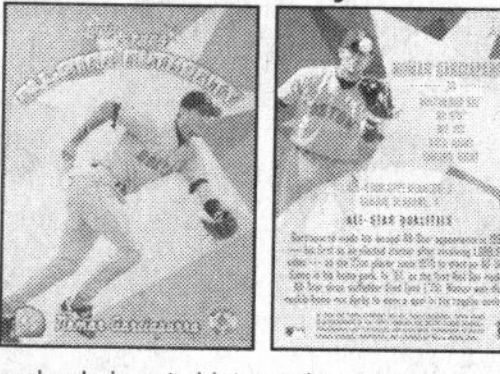

Randomly inserted into packs at one in 13, this 14-card insert features players that make the all-star team on a regular basis. Card backs carry an "AS" prefix.

	Nm-Mt	Ex-Mt
COMPLETE SET (14)	60.00	18.00
AS1 Mark McGwire	6.00	1.80
AS2 Sammy Sosa	4.00	1.20
AS3 Ken Griffey Jr.	4.00	1.20
AS4 Cal Ripken	8.00	2.40
AS5 Tony Gwynn	3.00	.90
AS6 Barry Bonds	6.00	1.80
AS7 Mike Piazza	4.00	1.20
AS8 Pedro Martinez	2.50	.75
AS9 Chipper Jones	2.50	.75
AS10 Manny Ramirez	1.50	.45
AS11 Alex Rodriguez	4.00	1.20
AS12 Derek Jeter	6.00	1.80
AS13 Nomar Garciaparra	4.00	1.20
AS14 Roberto Alomar	1.50	.45

2000 Topps Stars Autographs

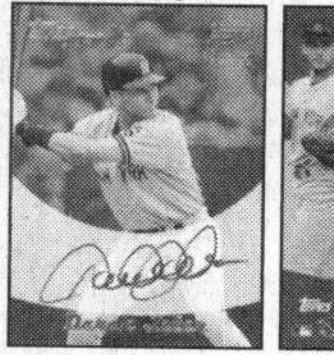
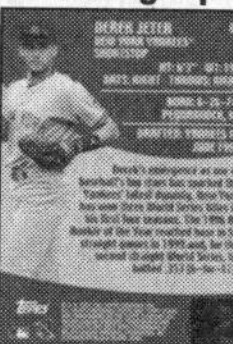

Randomly inserted into packs, this 13-card insert features autographed cards of past and present Major League stars. Please note that there are two tiers in this autograph set: Group A were inserted at a rate of one in 382, and Group B were inserted at a rate of one in 1636. Please note that these cards were numbered using the player's initials.

	Nm-Mt	Ex-Mt
AK Al Kaline B	50.00	15.00
BG Bob Gibson A	40.00	12.00
BR Brooks Robinson B	25.00	7.50
CY Carl Yastrzemski B	80.00	24.00
DJ Derek Jeter A	120.00	36.00
FR Frank Robinson B	25.00	7.50
GC Gary Carter B	15.00	4.50
JM Joe Morgan B	15.00	4.50
KM Kevin Millwood A	15.00	4.50
OS Ozzie Smith A	60.00	18.00
RA Rick Ankiel A	15.00	4.50
RF Rafael Furcal A	15.00	4.50
WS Willie Stargell B	60.00	18.00

2000 Topps Stars Game Gear Bats

Randomly inserted into packs, this 10-card insert features game-used bat cards of Major League prospects. Please note that there are three tiers in this bat set: Group A were inserted at a rate of one in 2289, and Group B were inserted at a rate of one in 1353, and Group C were inserted at one in 175. Card backs carry a "GGB" prefix. Chipper Jones and Mark Quinn were seeded into packs as exchange cards with a redemption deadline of May 30th, 2001.

	Nm-Mt	Ex-Mt
GGB1 Rafael Furcal C	10.00	3.00
GGB2 Sean Burroughs B	10.00	3.00
GGB3 Corey Patterson B	10.00	3.00
GGB4 Chipper Jones B	15.00	4.50
GGB5 Vernon Wells C	10.00	3.00
GGB6 Mark Quinn B	8.00	2.40
GGB7 Eric Munson C	8.00	2.40
GGB8 Ben Petrick B	8.00	2.40
GGB9 Dee Brown A	8.00	2.40
GGB10 Lance Berkman C	10.00	3.00

2000 Topps Stars Game Gear Jerseys

Randomly inserted into packs at one in 382, this three-card insert features game-used jersey cards of Kevin Millwood, Brad Penny and J.D. Drew. Please note that the Brad Penny was an exchange card with a deadline of 05/30/01. Card backs carry a "GGJ" prefix.

	Nm-Mt	Ex-Mt
GGJ1 Kevin Millwood	10.00	3.00
GGJ2 Brad Penny	10.00	3.00
GGJ3 J.D. Drew	10.00	3.00

2000 Topps Stars Progression

Randomly inserted into packs at one in 13, this nine-card insert set features a past star, a modern star, and a future star on each card. Card backs carry a "P" prefix.

	Nm-Mt	Ex-Mt
COMPLETE SET (9)	50.00	15.00
P1 Bob Gibson Pedro Martinez Rick Ankiel	3.00	.90
P2 Gary Carter Mike Piazza Ben Petrick	5.00	1.50
P3 Willie Stargell Mark McGwire Pat Burrell	8.00	2.40
P4 Joe Morgan Roberto Alomar Ruben Salazar	2.00	.60
P5 Brooks Robinson Chipper Jones Sean Burroughs	3.00	.90
P6 Ozzie Smith Derek Jeter Rafael Furcal	8.00	2.40
P7 Carl Yastrzemski Barry Bonds Josh Hamilton	8.00	2.40
P8 Al Kaline Ken Griffey Jr. Ruben Mateo	5.00	1.50
P9 Frank Robinson Manny Ramirez Corey Patterson	2.00	.60

2000 Topps Stars Walk of Fame

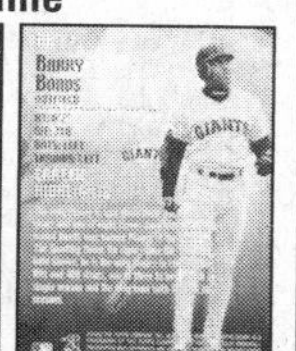

Randomly inserted into packs at one in eight, this 15-card insert features players that are on their way to the Hall of Fame. Card backs carry a "WF" prefix.

	Nm-Mt	Ex-Mt
COMPLETE SET (15)	50.00	15.00
WF1 Cal Ripken	6.00	1.80
WF2 Ken Griffey Jr.	3.00	.90
WF3 Mark McGwire	5.00	1.50
WF4 Sammy Sosa	3.00	.90
WF5 Alex Rodriguez	3.00	.90
WF6 Derek Jeter	5.00	1.50
WF7 Nomar Garciaparra	3.00	.90
WF8 Chipper Jones	2.00	.60
WF9 Manny Ramirez	1.25	.35
WF10 Mike Piazza	3.00	.90
WF11 Vladimir Guerrero	2.00	.60
WF12 Barry Bonds	5.00	1.50
WF13 Tony Gwynn	2.50	.75
WF14 Roberto Alomar	1.25	.35
WF15 Pedro Martinez	2.00	.60

2001 Topps Stars

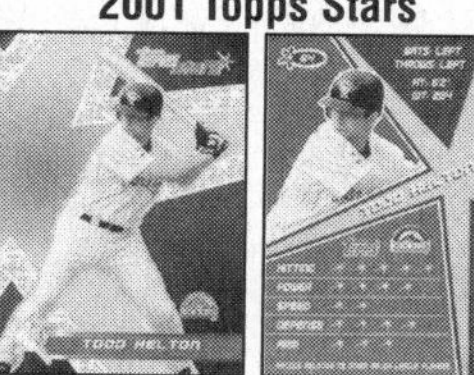

The 2001 Topps Stars product was released in June, 2001 and featured a 200-card base set that was broken into tiers as follows: Base Veterans (1-150), and Prospects/Rookies (151-200). Each pack contained six cards, and carried a suggested retail price of $3.00.

	Nm-Mt	Ex-Mt
COMPLETE SET (200)	50.00	15.00
1 Darin Erstad	.50	.15
2 Luis Gonzalez	.50	.15
3 Rafael Furcal	.50	.15
4 Dante Bichette	.50	.15
5 Sammy Sosa	2.00	.60
6 Ken Griffey Jr.	2.00	.60
7 Jim Thome	1.25	.35
8 Bobby Higginson	.50	.15
9 Cliff Floyd	.50	.15
10 Lance Berkman	.50	.15
11 Eric Karros	.50	.15
12 Jeromy Burnitz	.50	.15
13 Jose Vidro	.40	.12
14 Benny Agbayani	.40	.12
15 Jorge Posada	.75	.23
16 Ramon Hernandez	.40	.12
17 Jason Kendall	.50	.15
18 Jeff Kent	.50	.15
19 John Olerud	.50	.15
20 Al Martin	.40	.12
21 Gerald Williams	.40	.12
22 Gabe Kapler	.40	.12
23 Carlos Delgado	.50	.15
24 Mariano Rivera	.75	.23
25 Javy Lopez	.50	.15
26 Paul Konerko	.50	.15
27 Daryle Ward	.40	.12
28 Mike Lieberthal	.50	.15
29 Tom Goodwin	.40	.12
30 Garret Anderson	.50	.15
31 Steve Finley	.50	.15
32 Brian Jordan	.50	.15
33 Nomar Garciaparra	2.00	.60
34 Ray Durham	.50	.15
35 Sean Casey	.50	.15
36 Kenny Lofton	.50	.15
37 Dean Palmer	.50	.15
38 Jeff Bagwell	.75	.23
39 Mike Sweeney	.50	.15
40 Adrian Beltre	.75	.23
41 Richie Sexson	.50	.15
42 Vladimir Guerrero	1.25	.35
43 Derek Jeter	3.00	.90
44 Miguel Tejada	.50	.15
45 Doug Glanville	.40	.12
46 Brian Giles	.50	.15
47 Marvin Benard	.40	.12
48 Edgar Martinez	.75	.23
49 Edgar Renteria	.50	.15
50 Fred McGriff	.75	.23
51 Ivan Rodriguez	1.25	.35
52 Brad Fullmer	.40	.12
53 Antonio Alfonseca	.40	.12
54 Tom Glavine	.75	.23
55 Warren Morris	.40	.12
56 Johnny Damon	.75	.23
57 Dmitri Young	.50	.15
58 Mo Vaughn	.50	.15
59 Randy Johnson	1.25	.35
60 Greg Maddux	2.00	.60
61 Carl Everett	.50	.15
62 Magglio Ordonez	.50	.15
63 Pokey Reese	.40	.12
64 Todd Helton	.75	.23
65 Preston Wilson	.50	.15
66 Richard Hidalgo	.40	.12
67 Jermaine Dye	.50	.15
68 Gary Sheffield	.50	.15
69 Geoff Jenkins	.50	.15
70 Edgardo Alfonzo	.40	.12
71 Paul O'Neill	.75	.23
72 Terrence Long	.40	.12
73 Bob Abreu	.50	.15
74 Kevin Young	.40	.12
75 J.T. Snow	.50	.15
76 Alex Rodriguez	2.00	.60
77 Jim Edmonds	.50	.15
78 Mark McGwire	3.00	.90
79 Tony Batista	.50	.15
80 Darrin Fletcher	.40	.12
81 Robb Nen	.50	.15
82 Jose Offerman	.40	.12
83 Travis Fryman	.50	.15
84 Joe Randa	.40	.12
85 Omar Vizquel	.75	.23
86 Tim Salmon	.75	.23
87 Andruw Jones	.50	.15
88 Albert Belle	.50	.15
89 Manny Ramirez	.75	.23
90 Frank Thomas	1.25	.35
91 Barry Larkin	.75	.23
92 Neifi Perez	.40	.12
93 Luis Castillo	.40	.12
94 Moises Alou	.50	.15
95 Mark Quinn	.40	.12
96 Kevin Brown	.50	.15
97 Cristian Guzman	.40	.12
98 Mike Piazza	2.00	.60
99 Bernie Williams	.75	.23
100 Jason Giambi	.50	.15
101 Scott Rolen	1.25	.35
102 Phil Nevin	.50	.15
103 Rich Aurilia	.40	.12
104 Mike Cameron	.50	.15
105 Fernando Vina	.40	.12
106 Greg Vaughn	.40	.12
107 Jose Cruz Jr.	.40	.12
108 Raul Mondesi	.50	.15
109 Ben Molina	.40	.12
110 Pedro Martinez	1.25	.35
111 Todd Hollandsworth	.40	.12
112 Jacque Jones	.50	.15
113 Rickey Henderson	1.25	.35
114 Troy Glaus	.50	.15
115 Chipper Jones	1.25	.35
116 Delino DeShields	.40	.12
117 Eric Young	.40	.12
118 Jose Valentin	.40	.12
119 Roberto Alomar	.75	.23
120 Jeff Cirillo	.40	.12
121 Mike Lowell	.50	.15
122 Julio Lugo	.40	.12
123 Shawn Green	.50	.15
124 Marquis Grissom	.50	.15
125 Matt Lawton	.40	.12
126 Jay Payton	.40	.12
127 David Justice	.50	.15
128 Eric Chavez	.50	.15
129 Pat Burrell	.50	.15
130 Ryan Klesko	.50	.15
131 Barry Bonds	3.00	.90
132 Jay Buhner	.50	.15
133 J.D. Drew	.50	.15
134 Rafael Palmeiro	.75	.23
135 Shannon Stewart	.50	.15
136 Juan Gonzalez	.75	.23
137 Tony Womack	.40	.12
138 Carlos Lee	.50	.15
139 Derrek Lee	.50	.15
140 Ben Grieve	.40	.12
141 Ron Belliard	.40	.12
142 Stan Musial	2.00	.60
143 Ernie Banks	1.25	.35
144 Jim Palmer	.50	.15
145 Tony Perez	.50	.15
146 Duke Snider	.75	.23
147 Rod Carew	.75	.23
148 Warren Spahn	.75	.23
149 Yogi Berra	1.50	.45
150 Juan Marichal	.50	.15
151 Eric Munson	.40	.12
152 Carlos Pena	.40	.12
153 Joe Crede	.40	.12
154 Ryan Anderson	.40	.12
155 Milton Bradley	.50	.15
156 Sean Burroughs	.50	.15
157 Corey Patterson	.50	.15
158 C.C. Sabathia	.50	.15
159 Ben Petrick	.40	.12
160 Aubrey Huff	.50	.15
161 Gookie Dawkins	.40	.12
162 Ben Sheets	.75	.23
163 Pablo Ozuna	.40	.12
164 Eric Valent	.40	.12
165 Rod Barajas	.40	.12
166 Chin-Feng Chen	.50	.15
167 Josh Hamilton	.40	.12
168 Keith Ginter	.40	.12
169 Vernon Wells	.50	.15
170 Dernell Stenson	.40	.12
171 Alfonso Soriano	.75	.23
172 Jason Marquis	.40	.12
173 Nick Johnson	.40	.12
174 Adam Everett	.40	.12
175 Jimmy Rollins	.50	.15
176 Ben Diggins	.40	.12
177 John Lackey	.40	.12
178 Scott Heard	.40	.12
179 Brian Hitchcox RC	.60	.18
180 Odannis Ayala RC	.60	.18
181 Scott Pratt RC	.60	.18
182 Greg Runser RC	.60	.18
183 Chris Russ RC	.60	.18
184 Derek Thompson	.40	.12
185 Jason Jones RC	.60	.18
186 Dominic Rich RC	.60	.18
187 Chad Petty RC	.60	.18
188 Steve Smyth RC	.60	.18
189 Bryan Hebson RC	.60	.18
190 Danny Borrell RC	.60	.18
191 Bob Keppel RC	1.00	.30
192 Justin Wayne RC	.60	.18
193 R. Abercrombie RC	.60	.18
194 Travis Baptist RC	.40	.12
195 Shawn Fagan RC	.60	.18
196 Jose Reyes RC	5.00	1.50
197 Chris Bass RC	.60	.18
198 Albert Pujols RC	40.00	12.00
199 Luis Cotto RC	.60	.18
200 Jake Peavy RC	4.00	1.20

2001 Topps Stars Elimination

Randomly inserted into packs at one in 72, this insert set is actually a partial parallel of the 2001 Topps Stars base set. These cards are serial numbered to 100, and offer the collector a chance at winning two tickets to the 2002 All-Star Game. Winning cards must be exchanged by 10/19/01.

Nm-Mt Ex-Mt
*STARS: 6X TO 15X BASIC CARDS....

2001 Topps Stars Gold

Randomly inserted into packs at one in 9, this insert set is actually a complete parallel of the 2001 Topps Stars base set. These cards are serial numbered to 499, and feature a special gold-foil stamping on the card fronts.

Nm-Mt Ex-Mt
*STARS: 2X TO 5X BASIC CARDS......
*ROOKIES: 1.5X TO 4X BASIC CARDS

2001 Topps Stars Onyx

Randomly inserted into packs at one in 48, this insert set is actually a complete parallel of the 2001 Topps Stars base set. These cards are serial numbered to 99, and feature a special onyx-foil stamping on the card fronts.

Nm-Mt Ex-Mt
*STARS: 8X TO 20X BASIC CARDS....
*ROOKIES: 5X TO 12X BASIC CARDS

2001 Topps Stars Autographs

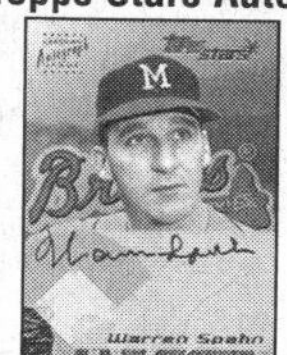

Randomly inserted into packs at one in 353, this insert set features 13 authentic autographs from award winning superstars. Card backs carry a "TSA" prefix followed by the player's initials. Exchange cards with a redemption deadline of April 30th, 2003 were seeded into packs for Ernie Banks, Yogi Berra, Rod Carew, Todd Helton, Juan Marichal, Tony Perez and Duke Snider.

	Nm-Mt	Ex-Mt
TSA-CD Carlos Delgado	25.00	7.50
TSA-DS Duke Snider	40.00	12.00
TSA-EB Ernie Banks	50.00	15.00
TSA-EM Eric Munson	15.00	4.50
TSA-IR Ivan Rodriguez	50.00	15.00
TSA-JM Juan Marichal	25.00	7.50
TSA-JP Jim Palmer	25.00	7.50
TSA-RC Rod Carew	40.00	12.00
TSA-SM Stan Musial	80.00	24.00
TSA-TH Todd Helton	40.00	12.00
TSA-TP Tony Perez	25.00	7.50
TSA-WS Warren Spahn	50.00	15.00
TSA-YB Yogi Berra	50.00	15.00

2001 Topps Stars Game Gear Autographs

Randomly inserted into packs, this five-card insert set features authentic swatches of memorabilia plus an authentic autograph from some of the younger talent in the Major Leagues. Card backs carry a "TSR" prefix followed by the player's initials. Please note that cards featuring a swatch of jersey were inserted at 1:19288, cards containing bat were inserted at 1:12240. Each card is individually serial numbered to 25. Due to market scarcity, no pricing is provided. Exchange cards with a redemption deadline of April 30th, 2003 were seeded into packs for Barry Bonds, Todd Helton and Corey Patterson.

Nm-Mt Ex-Mt
TSRABB Barry Bonds Jsy
TSRACP Cory Patterson Bat
TSRARF Rafael Furcal Bat
TSRATH Todd Helton Jsy
TSRATL Terrence Long Bat

2001 Topps Stars Game Gear Bats

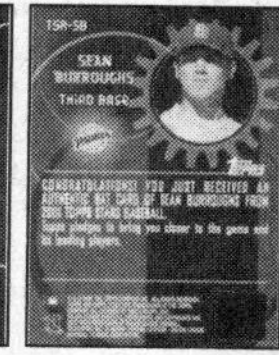

Randomly inserted into packs at one in 187, this insert set features swatches of actual game-used bats. Card backs carry a "TSR" prefix followed by the player's initials.

	Nm-Mt	Ex-Mt
TSRAB Adrian Beltre A	15.00	4.50
TSRAK Adam Kennedy A	10.00	3.00
TSRAP Adam Piatt A	10.00	3.00
TSRBD Ben Davis A	10.00	3.00
TSRCP Corey Patterson B	10.00	3.00
TSRED Erubiel Durazo A	10.00	3.00
TSREM Eric Munson A	10.00	3.00
TSRFL Felipe Lopez A	10.00	3.00
TSRFS F. Seguignol A	10.00	3.00
TSRGL George Lombard A	10.00	3.00
TSRGM G.Matthews Jr. A	10.00	3.00
TSRJE J.Encarnacion A	10.00	3.00
TSRJDD J.D. Drew A	10.00	3.00
TSRLB Lance Berkman A	10.00	3.00
TSRMC M. Cuddyer A	10.00	3.00
TSRNP Neifi Perez A	10.00	3.00
TSRRF Rafael Furcal B	10.00	3.00
TSRRS Richie Sexson A	10.00	3.00
TSRSB Sean Burroughs A	10.00	3.00
TSRSR Scott Rolen A	15.00	4.50
TSRTL Terrence Long B	10.00	3.00

2001 Topps Stars Game Gear Jerseys

Randomly inserted into packs at one in 61, this insert set features swatches of actual game-used jerseys. Card backs carry a "TSR" prefix followed by the player's initials.

	Nm-Mt	Ex-Mt
TSR-AJ Andruw Jones A	10.00	3.00
TSR-BB Barry Bonds B	30.00	9.00
TSR-CJ Chipper Jones A	15.00	4.50
TSR-EA E. Alfonzo A	10.00	3.00
TSR-EM Edgar Martinez A	15.00	4.50
TSR-FT Frank Thomas A	15.00	4.50
TSR-JV Jose Vidro A	10.00	3.00
TSR-LC Luis Castillo A	10.00	3.00
TSR-MO M. Ordonez A	10.00	3.00
TSR-MP Mike Piazza A	20.00	6.00
TSR-RA Roberto Alomar A	15.00	4.50
TSR-SS Sammy Sosa A	20.00	6.00
TSR-TG Tony Gwynn A	15.00	4.50
TSR-TH Todd Helton B	15.00	4.50
TSR-SHS S. Stewart A	10.00	3.00

2001 Topps Stars Player's Choice Awards

Inserted at a rate of one in 12, these 10 cards feature the three nominees for various honors at the MLBPA Player's Choice Award ceremony.

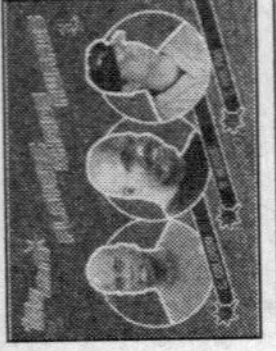

Nm-Mt Ex-Mt
COMPLETE SET (10) 30.00 9.00
PCA1 Barry Bonds 8.00 2.40
Todd Helton
Carlos Delgado
PCA2 Eric Davis 1.25 .35
Gary Sheffield
Turk Wendell
PCA3 Carlos Delgado 5.00 1.50
Alex Rodriguez
Frank Thomas
PCA4 Pedro Martinez 2.00 .60
David Wells
Andy Pettitte
PCA5 Kazuhiro Sasaki 1.25 .35
Mark Quinn
Terrence Long
PCA6 Frank Thomas 3.00 .90
Jay Buhner
Bobby Higginson
PCA7 Todd Helton 8.00 2.40
Barry Bonds
Jeff Kent
PCA8 Randy Johnson 5.00 1.50
Tom Glavine
Greg Maddux
PCA9 Rafael Furcal 1.25 .35
Rick Ankiel
Jay Payton
PCA10 Andres Galarraga 1.25 .35
Moises Alou
Jeff D'Amico

2001 Topps Stars Player's Choice Awards Relics

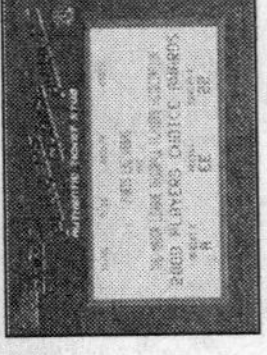
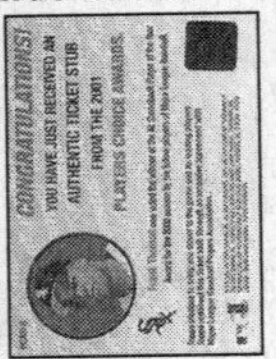

Inserted at a rate of one in 1,530 packs, these 10 cards feature pieces of memorabilia from 10 of the players nominated for various Player's Choice awards.

Nm-Mt Ex-Mt
PCAR1 Carlos Delgado 20.00 6.00
PCAR2 Eric Davis 20.00 6.00
PCAR3 Carlos Delgado 20.00 6.00
PCAR4 Pedro Martinez 30.00 9.00
PCAR5 Terrence Long 20.00 6.00
PCAR6 Frank Thomas 30.00 9.00
PCAR7 Todd Helton 30.00 9.00
PCAR8 Randy Johnson 30.00 9.00
PCAR9 Rafael Furcal 20.00 6.00
PCAR10 Andres Galarraga 20.00 6.00

2001 Topps Stars Progression

Randomly inserted into packs at one in 8, each card in the set features three players that are very similar statistically. Card backs carry a "P" prefix.

Nm-Mt Ex-Mt
COMPLETE SET (9) 15.00 4.50
P1 Ernie Banks 2.50 .75
Alex Rodriguez
Alfonso Soriano
P2 Yogi Berra 1.50 .45
Ivan Rodriguez
Ramon Hernandez
P3 Tony Perez 1.50 .45
Carlos Delgado
Eric Munson
P4 Rod Carew 1.50 .45
Roberto Alomar
Jose Ortiz
P5 Stan Musial 2.50 .75
Darin Erstad
Alex Escobar
P6 Jim Palmer 1.50 .45
Kevin Brown
Kurt Ainsworth
P7 Duke Snider 1.50 .45
Jim Edmonds
Vernon Wells
P8 Warren Spahn 1.50 .45
Randy Johnson
Ryan Anderson
P9 Juan Marichal 1.50 .45
Bartolo Colon
Bobby Bradley

2000 Topps Subway Series

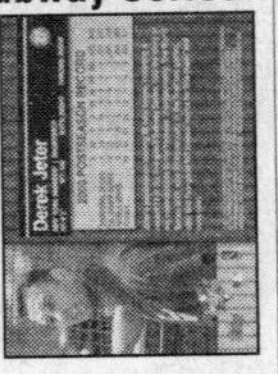

This 100 card standard-size set was issued by Topps to honor the first World Series played between two teams from NY since 1956. The sets were issued in a special box and included one "Fan-Fare Token" card inserted per set. A couple different tokens have been discovered for some players in this set. There is no value difference for whatever token in in this card. Please note that the complete rosters were included for each team as well as various cards featuring post-season highlights.

Nm-Mt Ex-Mt
COMP.FACT SET (101) 120.00 36.00
COMPLETE SET (100) 25.00 7.50
1 Mike Piazza 2.50 .75
2 Jay Payton .40 .12
3 Edgardo Alfonzo .40 .12
4 Todd Pratt .40 .12
5 Todd Zeile .60 .18
6 Mike Bordick .40 .12
7 Robin Ventura .60 .18
8 Benny Agbayani .40 .12
9 Timo Perez .60 .18
10 Kurt Abbott .40 .12
11 Matt Franco .40 .12
12 Bubba Trammell .40 .12
13 Darryl Hamilton .40 .12
14 Lenny Harris .40 .12
15 Joe McEwing .40 .12
16 Mike Hampton .60 .18
17 Al Leiter .60 .18
18 Rick Reed .40 .12
19 Bobby Jones .40 .12
20 Glendon Rusch .40 .12
21 Armando Benitez .60 .18
22 John Franco .60 .18
23 Rick White .40 .12
24 Dennis Cook .40 .12
25 Turk Wendell .40 .12
26 Bobby Valentine MG .40 .12
27 Derek Jeter 4.00 1.20
28 Chuck Knoblauch .60 .18
29 Tino Martinez 1.00 .30
30 Jorge Posada 1.00 .30
31 Luis Sojo .40 .12
32 Scott Brosius .60 .18
33 Chris Turner .40 .12
34 Bernie Williams 1.00 .30
35 David Justice .60 .18
36 Paul O'Neill 1.00 .30
37 Glenallen Hill .40 .12
38 Jose Vizcaino .40 .12
39 Luis Polonia .40 .12
40 Clay Bellinger .40 .12
41 Orlando Hernandez .40 .12
42 Roger Clemens 3.00 .90
43 Andy Pettitte 1.00 .30
44 Denny Neagle .40 .12
45 Dwight Gooden .60 .18
46 David Cone .60 .18
47 Mariano Rivera 1.00 .30
48 Jeff Nelson .40 .12
49 Mike Stanton .40 .12
50 Jason Grimsley .40 .12
51 Jose Canseco 1.50 .45
52 Joe Torre MG .60 .18
53 Edgardo Alfonzo .40 .12
54 Darryl Hamilton .40 .12
55 John Franco .60 .18
56 Benny Agbayani .40 .12
57 Bobby Jones .40 .12
58 New York Mets .60 .18
59 Bobby Valentine MG .60 .18
60 Mike Piazza 2.50 .75
61 Armando Benitez .60 .18
62 Mike Piazza 2.50 .75
63 Mike Piazza 2.50 .75
64 Todd Zeile .60 .18
65 Timo Perez .60 .18
66 Timo Perez .60 .18
67 Mike Hampton .60 .18
68 Andy Pettitte 1.00 .30
69 Tino Martinez 1.00 .30
70 Joe Torre MG .60 .18
71 New York Yankees .60 .18
72 Orlando Hernandez .40 .12
73 Bernie Williams 1.00 .30
74 Andy Pettitte 1.00 .30
75 Mariano Rivera 1.00 .30
76 New York Yankees .60 .18
77 Roger Clemens 3.00 .90
78 Derek Jeter 4.00 1.20
79 David Justice .60 .18
80 Mariano Rivera 1.00 .30
81 Tino Martinez 1.00 .30
82 New York Yankees .60 .18
83 Jorge Posada 1.00 .30
84 Chuck Knoblauch .60 .18
85 Jose Vizcaino .40 .12
86 Roger Clemens 3.00 .90
87 Mike Piazza 2.50 .75
88 Clay Bellinger .40 .12
89 Robin Ventura .60 .18
90 Benny Agbayani .40 .12
91 Orlando Hernandez .40 .12
92 Derek Jeter 4.00 1.20
93 Mike Piazza 2.50 .75
94 Mariano Rivera 1.00 .30
95 Derek Jeter 4.00 1.20
96 Luis Sojo .40 .12
97 New York Yankees .60 .18
98 Mike Hampton .60 .18
99 David Justice .60 .18
100 Derek Jeter 4.00 1.20
NNO New York Yankees
Promo card

2000 Topps Subway Series FanFare Tokens

Issued one per Topps Subway Series factory set, these cards featured the player photo next to an New York City subway token. The token embedded in the card were used by the MTA (Metropolitan Transportation Authority) in approximately 1953. These cards became very heavily sought after soon after release and have continued to be popular for their unique design.

Nm-Mt Ex-Mt
SSR1 Timo Perez 50.00 15.00
SSR2 Edgardo Alfonzo 50.00 15.00
SSR3 Mike Piazza 150.00 45.00
SSR4 Robin Ventura 50.00 15.00
SSR5 Todd Zeile 50.00 15.00
SSR6 Benny Agbayani 50.00 15.00
SSR7 Jay Payton 50.00 15.00
SSR8 Mike Bordick 50.00 15.00
SSR9 Matt Franco 50.00 15.00
SSR10 Mike Hampton 50.00 15.00
SSR11 Al Leiter 50.00 15.00
SSR12 Rick Reed 50.00 15.00
SSR13 Bobby Jones 50.00 15.00
SSR14 Glendon Rusch 50.00 15.00
SSR15 Darryl Hamilton 50.00 15.00
SSR16 Turk Wendell 50.00 15.00
SSR17 John Franco 50.00 15.00
SSR18 Armando Benitez 50.00 15.00
SSR19 Chuck Knoblauch 50.00 15.00
SSR20 Derek Jeter 250.00 75.00
SSR21 David Justice 80.00 24.00
SSR22 Bernie Williams 80.00 24.00
SSR23 Jorge Posada 80.00 24.00
SSR24 Paul O'Neill 80.00 24.00
SSR25 Tino Martinez 80.00 24.00
SSR26 Luis Sojo 50.00 15.00
SSR27 Scott Brosius 50.00 15.00
SSR28 Jose Canseco 100.00 30.00
SSR29 Orlando Hernandez 50.00 15.00
SSR30 Roger Clemens 200.00 60.00
SSR31 Andy Pettitte 80.00 24.00
SSR32 Denny Neagle 50.00 15.00
SSR33 David Cone 50.00 15.00
SSR34 Jeff Nelson 50.00 15.00
SSR35 Mike Stanton 50.00 15.00
SSR36 Mariano Rivera 80.00 24.00

2002 Topps Total

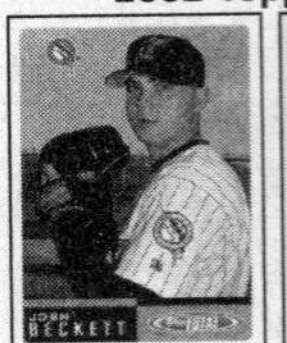

This 990 card set was issued in June, 2002. These cards were issued in 10 card packs which came 36 packs to a box and six boxes to a case. Each card was numbered not only in a numerical sequence but also in a team sequence.

Nm-Mt Ex-Mt
COMPLETE SET (990) 150.00 45.00
1 Joe Mauer RC 5.00 1.50
2 Derek Jeter 2.00 .60
3 Shawn Green .30 .09
4 Vladimir Guerrero .75 .23
5 Mike Piazza 1.25 .35
6 Brandon Duckworth .20 .06
7 Aramis Ramirez .30 .09
8 Josh Barfield RC 1.50 .45
9 Troy Glaus .30 .09
10 Sammy Sosa 1.25 .35
11 Rod Barajas .20 .06
12 Tsuyoshi Shinjo .30 .09
13 Larry Bigbie .20 .06
14 Tino Martinez .50 .15
15 Craig Biggio .50 .15
16 Anastacio Martinez RC .40 .12
17 John McDonald .20 .06
18 Kyle Kane RC .25 .07
19 Aubrey Huff .20 .06
20 Juan Cruz .20 .06
21 Doug Creek .20 .06
22 Luther Hackman .20 .06
23 Rafael Furcal .30 .09
24 Andres Torres .20 .06
25 Jason Giambi .30 .09
26 Jose Paniagua .20 .06
27 Jose Offerman .20 .06
28 Alex Arias .20 .06
29 J.M. Gold .20 .06
30 Jeff Bagwell .50 .15
31 Brent Cookson .20 .06
32 Kelly Wunsch .20 .06
33 Larry Walker .50 .15
34 Luis Gonzalez .30 .09
35 John Franco .30 .09
36 Roy Oswalt .30 .09
37 Tom Glavine .50 .15
38 C.C. Sabathia .30 .09
39 Jay Gibbons .30 .09
40 Wilson Betemit .20 .06
41 Tony Armas Jr. .20 .06
42 Mo Vaughn .30 .09
43 Gerard Oakes RC .40 .12
44 Dmitri Young .30 .09
45 Tim Salmon .50 .15
46 Barry Zito .30 .09
47 Adrian Gonzalez .30 .09
48 Joe Davenport .20 .06
49 Adrian Hernandez .20 .06
50 Randy Johnson .75 .23
52 Adam Pettyjohn .20 .06
53 Alex Escobar .20 .06
54 Stevenson Agosto RC .25 .07
55 Omar Daal .20 .06
56 Mike Buddie .20 .06
57 Dave Williams .20 .06
58 Marquis Grissom .30 .09
59 Pat Burrell .30 .09
60 Mark Prior 2.00 .60
61 Mike Bynum .20 .06
62 Mike Hill RC .40 .12
63 Brandon Backe RC .75 .23
64 Dan Wilson .20 .06
65 Nick Johnson .20 .06
66 Jason Grimsley .20 .06
67 Russ Johnson .20 .06
68 Todd Walker .20 .06
69 Kyle Farnsworth .20 .06
70 Ben Broussard .20 .06
71 Garrett Guzman RC .40 .12
72 Terry Mulholland .20 .06
73 Tyler Houston .20 .06
74 Jace Brewer .20 .06
75 Chris Baker RC .40 .12
76 Frank Catalanotto .20 .06
77 Mike Redmond .20 .06
78 Matt Wise .20 .06
79 Fernando Vina .20 .06
80 Kevin Brown .30 .09
81 Grant Balfour .20 .06
82 Clint Nageotte RC 1.00 .30
83 Jeff Tam .20 .06
84 Steve Trachsel .20 .06
85 Tomo Ohka .20 .06
86 Keith McDonald .20 .06
87 Jose Ortiz .20 .06
88 Rusty Greer .30 .09
89 Jeff Suppan .20 .06
90 Moises Alou .30 .09
91 Juan Encarnacion .20 .06
92 Tyler Yates RC .50 .15
93 Scott Strickland .20 .06
94 Brent Butler .20 .06
95 Jon Rauch .20 .06
96 Brian Mallette RC .25 .07
97 Joe Randa .20 .06
98 Cesar Crespo .20 .06
99 Felix Rodriguez .20 .06
100 Chipper Jones .75 .23
101 Victor Martinez .75 .23
102 Danny Graves .20 .06
103 Brandon Berger .20 .06
104 Carlos Garcia .20 .06
105 Alfonso Soriano .50 .15
106 Allan Simpson RC .25 .07
107 Brad Thomas .20 .06
108 Devon White .30 .09
109 Scott Chiasson .20 .06
110 Cliff Floyd .30 .09
111 Scott Williamson .20 .06
112 Julio Zuleta .20 .06
113 Terry Adams .20 .06
114 Zach Day .20 .06
115 Ben Grieve .20 .06
116 Mark Ellis .20 .06
117 Bobby Jenks RC .75 .23
118 LaTroy Hawkins .20 .06
119 Tim Raines Jr. .20 .06
120 Juan Uribe .20 .06
121 Bob Scanlan .20 .06
122 Brad Nelson RC 1.25 .35
123 Adam Johnson .20 .06
124 Raul Casanova .20 .06
125 Jeff D'Amico .20 .06
126 Aaron Cook RC .40 .12
127 Alan Benes .20 .06
128 Mark Little .20 .06
129 Randy Wolf .20 .06
130 Phil Nevin .30 .09
131 Guillermo Mota .20 .06
132 Nick Neugebauer .20 .06
133 Pedro Borbon Jr. .20 .06
134 Doug Mientkiewicz .30 .09
135 Edgardo Alfonzo .20 .06
136 Dustan Mohr .20 .06
137 Dan Reichert .20 .06
138 Dewon Brazelton .20 .06
139 Orlando Cabrera .30 .09
140 Todd Hollandsworth .20 .06
141 Darren Dreifort .20 .06
142 Jose Valentin .20 .06
143 Josh Kalinowski .20 .06
144 Randy Keisler .20 .06
145 Bret Boone .30 .09
146 Roosevelt Brown .20 .06
147 Brent Abernathy .20 .06
148 Jorge Julio .20 .06
149 Alex Gonzalez .20 .06
150 Juan Pierre .30 .09
151 Roger Cedeno .20 .06
152 Javier Vazquez .30 .09
153 Armando Benitez .30 .09
154 Dave Burba .20 .06
155 Brad Penny .20 .06
156 Ryan Jensen .20 .06
157 Jeromy Burnitz .30 .09
158 Matt Childers RC .40 .12
159 Wilmy Caceres .20 .06
160 Roger Clemens 1.50 .45
161 Jamie Cerda RC .40 .12
162 Jason Christiansen .20 .06
163 Pokey Reese .20 .06
164 Ivanon Coffie .20 .06
165 Joaquin Benoit .20 .06
166 Mike Matheny .30 .09
167 Eric Cammack .20 .06
168 Alex Graman .20 .06
169 Brook Fordyce .20 .06
170 Mike Lieberthal .30 .09
171 Giovanni Carrara .20 .06
172 Antonio Perez .20 .06
173 Fernando Tatis .20 .06
174 Jason Bay RC 2.50 .75
175 Jason Botts RC .75 .23
176 Danys Baez .20 .06
177 Shea Hillenbrand .30 .09
178 Jack Cust .20 .06
179 Clay Bellinger .20 .06
180 Roberto Alomar .50 .15
181 Graeme Lloyd .20 .06
182 Clint Weibl RC .25 .07
183 Royce Clayton .20 .06
184 Ben Davis .20 .06
185 Brian Adams RC .25 .07
186 Jack Wilson .30 .09
187 David Coggin .20 .06
188 Derrick Turnbow .20 .06
189 Vladimir Nunez .20 .06
190 Mariano Rivera .50 .15
191 Wilson Guzman .20 .06
192 Michael Barrett .20 .06
193 Corey Patterson .30 .09
194 Luis Sojo .20 .06
195 Scott Elarton .20 .06
196 Charles Thomas RC .40 .12
197 Ricky Bottalico .20 .06
198 Wilfredo Rodriguez .20 .06
199 Ricardo Rincon .20 .06
200 John Smoltz .50 .15
201 Travis Miller .20 .06
202 Ben Weber .20 .06
203 T.J. Tucker .20 .06
204 Terry Shumpert .20 .06
205 Bernie Williams .50 .15
206 Russ Ortiz .30 .09
207 Nate Rolison .20 .06
208 Jose Cruz Jr. .20 .06
209 Bill Ortega .20 .06
210 Carl Everett .30 .09
211 Luis Lopez .20 .06
212 Brian Wolfe RC .40 .12
213 Doug Davis .20 .06
214 Troy Mattes .20 .06
215 Al Leiter .30 .09
216 Joe Mays .20 .06
217 Bobby Smith .20 .06
218 J.J. Trujillo RC .40 .12
219 Hideo Nomo .75 .23
220 Jimmy Rollins .30 .09
221 Bobby Seay .20 .06
222 Mike Thurman .20 .06
223 Bartolo Colon .30 .09
224 Jesus Sanchez .20 .06
225 Ray Durham .30 .09
226 Juan Diaz .20 .06
227 Lee Stevens .20 .06
228 Ben Howard RC .40 .12
229 James Mouton .20 .06
230 Paul Quantrill .20 .06
231 Randy Knorr .20 .06
232 Abraham Nunez .20 .06
233 Mike Fetters .20 .06
234 Mario Encarnacion .20 .06
235 Jeremy Fikac .20 .06
236 Travis Lee .20 .06
237 Bob File .20 .06
238 Pete Harnisch .20 .06
239 Randy Galvez RC .40 .12
240 Geoff Goetz .20 .06
241 Gary Glover .20 .06
242 Troy Percival .30 .09
243 Len Dinardo RC .40 .12
244 Jonny Gomes RC .75 .23
245 Jesus Medrano RC .40 .12
246 Rey Ordonez .20 .06
247 Juan Gonzalez .50 .15
248 Jose Guillen .30 .09
249 Franklyn German RC .40 .12
250 Mike Mussina .50 .15
251 Ugueth Urbina .20 .06
252 Melvin Mora .30 .09
253 Gerald Williams .20 .06
254 Jared Sandberg .20 .06
255 Darrin Fletcher .20 .06
256 A.J. Pierzynski .30 .09
257 Lenny Harris .20 .06
258 Blaine Neal .20 .06
259 Denny Neagle .20 .06
260 Jason Hart .20 .06
261 Henry Mateo .20 .06
262 Rheal Cormier .20 .06
263 Luis Terrero .20 .06
264 Shigetoshi Hasegawa .30 .09
265 Bill Haselman .20 .06
266 Scott Hatteberg .20 .06
267 Adam Hyzdu .20 .06
268 Mike Williams .20 .06
269 Marlon Anderson .20 .06
270 Bruce Chen .20 .06
271 Eli Marrero .20 .06
272 Jimmy Haynes .20 .06
273 Bronson Arroyo .30 .09
274 Kevin Jordan .20 .06
275 Rick Helling .20 .06
276 Mark Loretta .30 .09
277 Dustin Hermanson .20 .06
278 Pablo Ozuna .20 .06
279 Keto Anderson RC .40 .12
280 Jermaine Dye .30 .09
281 Will Smith .20 .06
282 Brian Daubach .20 .06
283 Eric Hinske .20 .06
284 Joe Jiannetti RC .40 .12
285 Chan Ho Park .30 .09
286 Curtis Legendre RC .40 .12
287 Jeff Reboulet .20 .06
288 Scott Rolen .75 .23
289 Chris Richard .20 .06
290 Eric Chavez .30 .09
291 Scot Shields .20 .06
292 Donnie Sadler .20 .06
293 Dave Veres .20 .06
294 Craig Counsell .20 .06
295 Armando Reynoso .20 .06
296 Kyle Lohse .20 .06
297 Arthur Rhodes .20 .06
298 Sidney Ponson .20 .06
299 Trevor Hoffman .30 .09
300 Kerry Wood .75 .23
301 Danny Bautista .20 .06
302 Scott Sauerbeck .20 .06
303 Johnny Estrada .20 .06
304 Mike Timlin .20 .06
305 Orlando Hernandez .20 .06
306 Tony Clark .20 .06
307 Tomas Perez .20 .06
308 Marcus Giles .30 .09

309 Mike Bordick .30 .09
310 Jorge Posada .50 .15
311 Jason Conti .20 .06
312 Kevin Millar .30 .09
313 Paul Shuey .20 .06
314 Jake Mauer RC .40 .12
315 Luke Hudson .20 .06
316 Angel Berroa .20 .06
317 Fred Bastardo RC .40 .12
318 Shawn Estes .20 .06
319 Andy Ashby .20 .06
320 Ryan Klesko .30 .09
321 Kevin Appier .30 .09
322 Juan Pena .20 .06
323 Alex Herrera .20 .06
324 Robb Nen .30 .09
325 Orlando Hudson .20 .06
326 Lyle Overbay .30 .09
327 Ben Sheets .30 .09
328 Mike DiFelice .20 .06
329 Pablo Arias RC .40 .12
330 Mike Sweeney .30 .09
331 Rick Ankiel .20 .06
332 Tomas De La Rosa .20 .06
333 Kazuhisa Ishii RC 1.50 .45
334 Jose Reyes .50 .15
335 Jeremy Giambi .20 .06
336 Jose Mesa .20 .06
337 Ralph Roberts RC .40 .12
338 Jose Nunez .20 .06
339 Curt Schilling .30 .09
340 Sean Casey .30 .09
341 Bob Wells .20 .06
342 Carlos Beltran .50 .15
343 Alexis Gomez .20 .06
344 Brandon Claussen .20 .06
345 Buddy Groom .20 .06
346 Mark Phillips RC .75 .23
347 Francisco Cordova .20 .06
348 Joe Oliver .20 .06
349 Danny Patterson .20 .06
350 Joel Pineiro .30 .09
351 J.R. House .20 .06
352 Benny Agbayani .20 .06
353 Jose Vidro .20 .06
354 Reed Johnson RC .50 .15
355 Mike Lowell .30 .09
356 Scott Schoeneweis .20 .06
357 Brian Jordan .30 .09
358 Steve Finley .30 .09
359 Randy Choate .20 .06
360 Jose Lima .20 .06
361 Miguel Olivo .20 .06
362 Kenny Rogers .30 .09
363 David Justice .30 .09
364 Brandon Knight .20 .06
365 Joe Kennedy .20 .06
366 Eric Valent .20 .06
367 Nelson Cruz .20 .06
368 Brian Giles .30 .09
369 Charles Gipson RC .25 .07
370 Juan Pena .20 .06
371 Mark Redman .20 .06
372 Billy Koch .20 .06
373 Ted Lilly .20 .06
374 Craig Paquette .20 .06
375 Kevin Jarvis .20 .06
376 Scott Erickson .20 .06
377 Josh Paul .20 .06
378 Darwin Cubillan .20 .06
379 Nelson Figueroa .20 .06
380 Darin Erstad .30 .09
381 Jeremy Hill RC .40 .12
382 Elvin Nina .20 .06
383 David Wells .30 .09
384 Jay Caligiuri RC .40 .12
385 Freddy Garcia .30 .09
386 Damian Miller .20 .06
387 Bobby Higginson .30 .09
388 Alejandro Giron RC .40 .12
389 Ivan Rodriguez .75 .23
390 Ed Rogers .20 .06
391 Andy Benes .20 .06
392 Matt Blank .20 .06
393 Ryan Vogelsong .20 .06
394 Kelly Ramos RC .25 .07
395 Eric Karros .30 .09
396 Bobby J. Jones .20 .06
397 Omar Vizquel .50 .15
398 Matt Perisho .20 .06
399 Delino DeShields .20 .06
400 Carlos Hernandez .20 .06
401 Derrek Lee .30 .09
402 Kirk Rueter .20 .06
403 David Wright RC 10.00 3.00
404 Paul LoDuca .30 .09
405 Brian Schneider .20 .06
406 Milton Bradley .30 .09
407 Daryle Ward .30 .09
408 Cody Ransom .20 .06
409 Fernando Rodney .20 .06
410 John Suomi RC .40 .12
411 Joe Girardi .20 .06
412 Demetrius Heath RC .40 .12
413 John Foster RC .40 .12
414 Doug Glanville .20 .06
415 Ryan Kohlmeier .20 .06
416 Mike Matthews .20 .06
417 Craig Wilson .30 .09
418 Jay Witasick .20 .06
419 Jay Payton .20 .06
420 Andruw Jones .30 .09
421 Benji Gil .20 .06
422 Jeff Liefer .20 .06
423 Kevin Young .20 .06
424 Richie Sexson .30 .09
425 Cory Lidle .20 .06
426 Shane Halter .20 .06
427 Jesse Foppert RC 1.00 .30
428 Jose Molina .20 .06
429 Nick Alvarez RC .40 .12
430 Brian L. Hunter .20 .06
431 Cliff Bartosh RC .40 .12
432 Junior Spivey .20 .06
433 Eric Good RC .40 .12
434 Chin-Feng Chen .30 .09
435 T.J. Mathews .20 .06
436 Rich Rodriguez .20 .06
437 Bobby Abreu .30 .09
438 Joe McEwing .20 .06
439 Michael Tucker .20 .06
440 Preston Wilson .30 .09
441 Mike MacDougal .30 .09
442 Shannon Stewart .30 .09
443 Bob Howry .20 .06
444 Mike Benjamin .20 .06
445 Erik Hiljus .20 .06
446 Ryan Gripp RC .40 .12
447 Jose Vizcaino .20 .06
448 Shawn Wooten .20 .06
449 Steve Kent RC .40 .12
450 Ramiro Mendoza .20 .06
451 Jake Westbrook .20 .06
452 Joe Lawrence .20 .06
453 Jae Seo .20 .06
454 Ryan Fry RC .40 .12
455 Darren Lewis .20 .06
456 Brad Wilkerson .20 .06
457 Gustavo Chacin RC .50 .15
458 Adrian Brown .20 .06
459 Mike Cameron .30 .09
460 Bud Smith .20 .06
461 Derrick Lewis .20 .06
462 Derek Lowe .30 .09
463 Matt Williams .30 .09
464 Jason Jennings .20 .06
465 Albie Lopez .20 .06
466 Felipe Lopez .20 .06
467 Luke Allen .20 .06
468 Brian Anderson .20 .06
469 Matt Riley .20 .06
470 Ryan Dempster .20 .06
471 Matt Ginter .20 .06
472 David Ortiz .50 .15
473 Cole Barthel RC .40 .12
474 Damian Jackson .20 .06
475 Andy Van Hekken .20 .06
476 Doug Brocail .20 .06
477 Denny Hocking .20 .06
478 Sean Douglass .20 .06
479 Eric Owens .20 .06
480 Ryan Ludwick .20 .06
481 Todd Pratt .20 .06
482 Aaron Sele .20 .06
483 Edgar Renteria .30 .09
484 Raymond Cabrera RC .40 .12
485 Brandon Lyon .20 .06
486 Chase Utley .50 .15
487 Robert Fick .20 .06
488 Wilfredo Cordero .20 .06
489 Octavio Dotel .20 .06
490 Paul Abbott .20 .06
491 Jason Kendall .30 .09
492 Jarrod Washburn .20 .06
493 Dane Sardinha .20 .06
494 Jung Bong .20 .06
495 J.D. Drew .30 .09
496 Jason Schmidt .30 .09
497 Mike Magnante .20 .06
498 Jorge Padilla RC .40 .12
499 Eric Gagne .75 .23
500 Todd Helton .50 .15
501 Jeff Weaver .20 .06
502 Alex Sanchez .20 .06
503 Ken Griffey Jr. 1.25 .35
504 Abraham Nunez .20 .06
505 Reggie Sanders .20 .06
506 Casey Kotchman RC 3.00 .90
507 Jim Mann .20 .06
508 Matt LeCroy .20 .06
509 Frank Castillo .20 .06
510 Geoff Jenkins .30 .09
511 Jayson Durocher RC .25 .07
512 Ellis Burks .30 .09
513 Aaron Fultz .20 .06
514 Hiram Bocachica .20 .06
515 Nate Espy RC .40 .12
516 Placido Polanco .20 .06
517 Kerry Ligtenberg .20 .06
518 Doug Nickle .20 .06
519 Ramon Ortiz .20 .06
520 Greg Swindell .20 .06
521 J.J. Davis .20 .06
522 Sandy Alomar Jr. .20 .06
523 Chris Carpenter .20 .06
524 Vance Wilson .20 .06
525 Nomar Garciaparra 1.25 .35
526 Jim Mecir .20 .06
527 Taylor Buchholz RC .40 .12
528 Brent Mayne .20 .06
529 John Rodriguez RC .40 .12
530 David Segui .20 .06
531 Nate Cornejo .20 .06
532 Gil Heredia .20 .06
533 Esteban Loaiza .20 .06
534 Pat Mahomes .20 .06
535 Matt Morris .30 .09
536 Todd Stottlemyre .20 .06
537 Brian Lesher .20 .06
538 Arturo McDowell .20 .06
539 Felix Diaz .20 .06
540 Mark Mulder .30 .09
541 Kevin Frederick RC .40 .12
542 Andy Fox .20 .06
543 Dionys Cesar RC .25 .07
544 Justin Miller .20 .06
545 Keith Osik .20 .06
546 Shane Reynolds .20 .06
547 Mike Myers .20 .06
548 Raul Chavez RC .25 .07
549 Joe Nathan .20 .06
550 Ryan Anderson .20 .06
551 Jason Marquis .20 .06
552 Marty Cordova .20 .06
553 Kevin Tapani .20 .06
554 Jimmy Anderson .20 .06
555 Pedro Martinez .75 .23
556 Rocky Biddle .20 .06
557 Alex Ochoa .20 .06
558 D'Angelo Jimenez .20 .06
559 Wilkin Ruan .20 .06
560 Terrence Long .20 .06
561 Mark Lukasiewicz .20 .06
562 Jose Santiago .20 .06
563 Brad Fullmer .20 .06
564 Corky Miller .20 .06
565 Matt White .20 .06
566 Mark Grace .50 .15
567 Raul Ibanez .20 .06
568 Josh Towers .20 .06
569 Juan M. Gonzalez RC .40 .12
570 Brian Buchanan .20 .06
571 Ken Harvey .20 .06
572 Jeffrey Hammonds .20 .06
573 Wade Miller .20 .06
574 Elpidio Guzman .20 .06
575 Kevin Olsen .20 .06
576 Austin Kearns .30 .09
577 Tim Kalita RC .40 .12
578 David Dellucci .20 .06
579 Alex Gonzalez .20 .06
580 Joe Orloski RC .40 .12
581 Gary Matthews Jr. .20 .06
582 Ryan Mills .20 .06
583 Erick Almonte .20 .06
584 Jeremy Affeldt .20 .06
585 Chris Tritle RC .40 .12
586 Michael Cuddyer .20 .06
587 Kris Foster .20 .06
588 Russell Branyan .20 .06
589 Darren Oliver .20 .06
590 Freddie Money RC .40 .12
591 Carlos Lee .30 .09
592 Tim Wakefield .30 .09
593 Bubba Trammell .20 .06
594 John Koronka RC .40 .12
595 Geoff Blum .20 .06
596 Darryl Kile .30 .09
597 Neifi Perez .20 .06
598 Torii Hunter .30 .09
599 Luis Castillo .20 .06
600 Mark Buehrle .30 .09
601 Jeff Zimmerman .20 .06
602 Mike DeJean .20 .06
603 Julio Lugo .20 .06
604 Chad Hermansen .20 .06
605 Keith Foulke .30 .09
606 Lance Davis .20 .06
607 Jeff Austin RC .40 .12
608 Brandon Inge .20 .06
609 Orlando Merced .20 .06
610 Johnny Damon Sox .75 .23
611 Doug Henry .20 .06
612 Adam Kennedy .20 .06
613 Wiki Gonzalez .20 .06
614 Brian West RC .40 .12
615 Andy Pettitte .50 .15
616 Chone Figgins RC .75 .23
617 Matt Lawton .20 .06
618 Paul Rigdon .20 .06
619 Keith Lockhart .20 .06
620 Tim Redding .20 .06
621 John Parrish .20 .06
622 Homer Bush .20 .06
623 Todd Greene .20 .06
624 David Eckstein .20 .06
625 Greg Montalbano RC .40 .12
626 Joe Beimel .20 .06
627 Adrian Beltre .50 .15
628 Charles Nagy .20 .06
629 Cristian Guzman .20 .06
630 Toby Hall .20 .06
631 Jose Hernandez .20 .06
632 Jose Macias .30 .09
633 Jaret Wright .20 .06
634 Steve Parris .20 .06
635 Gene Kingsale .20 .06
636 Tim Worrell .20 .06
637 Billy Martin .20 .06
638 Jovanny Cedeno .20 .06
639 Curtis Leskanic .20 .06
640 Tim Hudson .30 .09
641 Juan Castro .20 .06
642 Rafael Soriano .20 .06
643 Juan Rincon .20 .06
644 Mark DeRosa .20 .06
645 Carlos Pena .20 .06
646 Robin Ventura .30 .09
647 Odalis Perez .20 .06
648 Damion Easley .20 .06
649 Benito Santiago .30 .09
650 Alex Rodriguez 1.25 .35
651 Aaron Rowand .30 .09
652 Alex Cora .20 .06
653 Bobby Kielty .20 .06
654 Jose Rodriguez RC .40 .12
655 Herbert Perry .20 .06
656 Jeff Urban .20 .06
657 Paul Bako .20 .06
658 Shane Spencer .20 .06
659 Pat Hentgen .20 .06
660 Jeff Kent .30 .09
661 Mark McLemore .20 .06
662 Chuck Knoblauch .30 .09
663 Blake Stein .20 .06
664 Brett Roneberg RC .40 .12
665 Josh Phelps .30 .09
666 Byung-Hyun Kim .30 .09
667 Dave Martinez .20 .06
668 Mike Maroth .20 .06
669 Shawn Chacon .20 .06
670 Billy Wagner .30 .09
671 Luis Alicea .20 .06
672 Sterling Hitchcock .20 .06
673 Adam Piatt .20 .06
674 Ryan Franklin .20 .06
675 Luke Prokopec .20 .06
676 Alfredo Amezaga .20 .06
677 Gookie Dawkins .20 .06
678 Eric Byrnes .20 .06
679 Barry Larkin .50 .15
680 Albert Pujols 1.50 .45
681 Edwards Guzman .20 .06
682 Jason Bere .20 .06
683 Adam Everett .20 .06
684 Greg Colbrunn .20 .06
685 Brandon Puffer RC .40 .12
686 Mark Kotsay .20 .06
687 Willie Bloomquist .20 .06
688 Hank Blalock .75 .23
689 Travis Hafner .30 .09
690 Lance Berkman .30 .09
691 Joe Crede .20 .06
692 Chuck Finley .30 .09
693 John Grabow .20 .06
694 Randy Winn .20 .06
695 Mike James .20 .06
696 Kris Benson .20 .06
697 Bret Prinz .20 .06
698 Jeff Williams .20 .06
699 Eric Munson .20 .06
700 Mike Hampton .30 .09
701 Ramon E. Martinez .20 .06
702 Hansel Izquierdo RC .40 .12
703 Nathan Haynes .20 .06
704 Eddie Taubensee .20 .06
705 Esteban German .20 .06
706 Ross Gload .20 .06
707 Matt Merricks RC .40 .12
708 Chris Piersoll RC .25 .07
709 Seth Greisinger .20 .06
710 Ichiro Suzuki 1.25 .35
711 Cesar Izturis .20 .06
712 Brad Cresse .20 .06
713 Carl Pavano .30 .09
714 Steve Sparks .20 .06
715 Dennis Tankersley .20 .06
716 Kelvim Escobar .20 .06
717 Jason LaRue .20 .06
718 Corey Koskie .30 .09
719 Vinny Castilla .30 .09
720 Tim Drew .20 .06
721 Chin-Hui Tsao .30 .09
722 Paul Byrd .20 .06
723 Alex Cintron .20 .06
724 Orlando Palmeiro .20 .06
725 Ramon Hernandez .20 .06
726 Mark Johnson .20 .06
727 B.J. Ryan .20 .06
728 Wendell Magee .20 .06
729 Michael Coleman .20 .06
730 Mario Ramos RC .40 .12
731 Mike Stanton .20 .06
732 Dee Brown .20 .06
733 Brad Ausmus .20 .06
734 Napoleon Calzado RC .40 .12
735 Woody Williams .20 .06
736 Paxton Crawford .20 .06
737 Jason Karnuth .20 .06
738 Michael Restovich .20 .06
739 Ramon Castro .20 .06
740 Magglio Ordonez .30 .09
741 Tom Gordon .20 .06
742 Mark Grudzielanek .20 .06
743 Jaime Moyer .30 .09
744 Marlyn Tisdale RC .40 .12
745 Steve Kline .20 .06
746 Adam Eaton .20 .06
747 Eric Glaser RC .40 .12
748 Sean DePaula .20 .06
749 Greg Norton .20 .06
750 Steve Reed .20 .06
751 Ricardo Aramboles .20 .06
752 Matt Mantei .20 .06
753 Gene Stechschulte .20 .06
754 Chuck McElroy .20 .06
755 Barry Bonds 2.00 .60
756 Matt Anderson .20 .06
757 Yorvit Torrealba .20 .06
758 Jason Standridge .20 .06
759 Desi Relaford .20 .06
760 Jolbert Cabrera .20 .06
761 Chris George .20 .06
762 Erubiel Durazo .20 .06
763 Paul Konerko .30 .09
764 Tike Redman .20 .06
765 Chad Ricketts RC .25 .07
766 Roberto Hernandez .20 .06
767 Mark Lewis .20 .06
768 Livan Hernandez .20 .06
769 Carlos Brackley RC .40 .12
770 Kazuhiro Sasaki .30 .09
771 Bill Hall .20 .06
772 Nelson Castro RC .40 .12
773 Eric Milton .20 .06
774 Tom Davey .20 .06
775 Todd Ritchie .20 .06
776 Seth Etherton .20 .06
777 Chris Singleton .20 .06
778 Robert Averette RC .25 .07
779 Robert Person .20 .06
780 Fred McGriff .50 .15
781 Richard Hidalgo .20 .06
782 Kris Wilson .20 .06
783 John Rocker .20 .06
784 Justin Kaye .20 .06
785 Glendon Rusch .20 .06
786 Greg Vaughn .20 .06
787 Mike Lamb .20 .06
788 Greg Myers .20 .06
789 Nate Field RC .40 .12
790 Jim Edmonds .30 .09
791 Olmedo Saenz .20 .06
792 Jason Johnson .20 .06
793 Mike Lincoln .20 .06
794 Todd Coffey RC .40 .12
795 Jesus Sanchez .20 .06
796 Aaron Myette .20 .06
797 Tony Womack .20 .06
798 Chad Kreuter .20 .06
799 Brady Clark .20 .06
800 Adam Dunn .50 .15
801 Jacque Jones .30 .09
802 Kevin Millwood .30 .09
803 Mike Rivera .20 .06
804 Jim Thome .75 .23
805 Jeff Conine .30 .09
806 Elmer Dessens .20 .06
807 Randy Velarde .20 .06
808 Carlos Delgado .30 .09
809 Steve Karsay .20 .06
810 Casey Fossum .20 .06
811 J.C. Romero .20 .06
812 Chris Truby .20 .06
813 Tony Graffanino .20 .06
814 Wascar Serrano .20 .06
815 Delvin James .20 .06
816 Pedro Feliz .20 .06
817 Damian Rolls .20 .06
818 Scott Linebrink .20 .06
819 Rafael Palmeiro .50 .15
820 Javy Lopez .30 .09
821 Larry Barnes .20 .06
822 Brian Lawrence .20 .06
823 Scotty Layfield RC .40 .12
824 Jeff Cirillo .20 .06
825 Willis Roberts .20 .06
826 Rich Harden RC 4.00 1.20
827 Chris Snelling RC .40 .12
828 Gary Sheffield .30 .09
829 Jeff Heaverlo .20 .06
830 Matt Clement .20 .06
831 Rich Garces .20 .06
832 Rondell White .30 .09
833 Henry Pichardo RC .40 .12
834 Aaron Boone .30 .09
835 Ruben Sierra .20 .06
836 Deivis Santos .20 .06
837 Tony Batista .30 .09
838 Rob Bell .20 .06
839 Frank Thomas .75 .23
840 Jose Silva .20 .06
841 Dan Johnson RC .75 .23
842 Steve Cox .20 .06
843 Jose Acevedo .20 .06
844 Jay Bell .30 .09
845 Mike Sirotka .20 .06
846 Garret Anderson .30 .09
847 James Shanks RC .40 .12
848 Trot Nixon .30 .09
849 Keith Ginter .20 .06
850 Tim Spooneybarger .20 .06
851 Matt Stairs .20 .06
852 Chris Stynes .20 .06
853 Marvin Benard .20 .06
854 Raul Mondesi .30 .09
855 Jeremy Owens .20 .06
856 Jon Garland .20 .06
857 Mitch Meluskey .20 .06
858 Chad Durbin .20 .06
859 John Burkett .20 .06
860 Jon Switzer RC .40 .12
861 Peter Bergeron .20 .06
862 Jesus Colome .20 .06
863 Todd Hundley .20 .06
864 Ben Petrick .20 .06
865 So Taguchi RC .50 .15
866 Ryan Drese .20 .06
867 Mike Trombley .20 .06
868 Rick Reed .20 .06
869 Mark Teixeira .50 .15
870 Corey Thurman RC .40 .12
871 Brian Roberts .20 .06
872 Mike Timlin .20 .06
873 Chris Reitsma .20 .06
874 Jeff Fassero .20 .06
875 Carlos Valderrama .20 .06
876 John Lackey .20 .06
877 Travis Fryman .30 .09
878 Ismael Valdes .20 .06
879 Rick White .20 .06
880 Edgar Martinez .50 .15
881 Dean Palmer .30 .09
882 Matt Allegra RC .40 .12
883 Greg Sain RC .50 .15
884 Carlos Silva .20 .06
885 Jose Valverde RC .50 .15
886 Dernell Stenson .20 .06
887 Todd Van Poppel .20 .06
888 Wes Anderson .20 .06
889 Bill Mueller .30 .09
890 Morgan Ensberg .30 .09
891 Marcus Thames .20 .06
892 Adam Walker RC .40 .12
893 John Halama .20 .06
894 Frank Menechino .20 .06
895 Greg Maddux 1.25 .35
896 Gary Bennett .20 .06
897 Mauricio Lara RC .40 .12
898 Mike Young .75 .23
899 Travis Phelps .20 .06
900 Rich Aurilia .20 .06
901 Henry Blanco .20 .06
902 Carlos Febles .20 .06
903 Scott MacRae .20 .06
904 Lou Merloni .20 .06
905 Dicky Gonzalez .20 .06
906 Jeff DaVanon .20 .06
907 A.J. Burnett .20 .06
908 Einar Diaz .20 .06
909 Julio Franco .30 .09
910 John Olerud .30 .09
911 Mark Hamilton RC .40 .12
912 David Riske .20 .06
913 Jason Tyner .20 .06
914 Britt Reames .20 .06
915 Vernon Wells .30 .09
916 Eddie Perez .20 .06
917 Edwin Almonte RC .40 .12
918 Enrique Wilson .20 .06
919 Chris Gomez .20 .06
920 Jayson Werth .20 .06
921 Jeff Nelson .20 .06
922 Freddy Sanchez RC .40 .12
923 John Vander Wal .20 .06
924 Chad Qualls RC .40 .12
925 Gabe White .20 .06
926 Chad Harville .20 .06
927 Ricky Gutierrez .20 .06
928 Carlos Guillen .30 .09
929 B.J. Surhoff .30 .09
930 Chris Woodward .20 .06
931 Ricardo Rodriguez .20 .06
932 Jimmy Gobble RC .75 .23
933 Jon Lieber .20 .06
934 Craig Kuzmic RC .40 .12
935 Eric Young .20 .06
936 Greg Zaun .20 .06
937 Miguel Batista .20 .06
938 Danny Wright .20 .06
939 Todd Zeile .30 .09
940 Chad Zerbe .20 .06
941 Jason Young RC .40 .12
942 Ronnie Belliard .20 .06
943 John Ennis RC .40 .12
944 John Flaherty .20 .06
945 Jerry Hairston Jr. .20 .06
946 Al Levine .20 .06
947 Antonio Alfonseca .20 .06
948 Brian Moehler .20 .06
949 Calvin Murray .20 .06
950 Nick Bierbrodt .20 .06
951 Sun Woo Kim .20 .06
952 Noochie Varner RC .40 .12
953 Luis Rivas .20 .06
954 Donnie Bridges .20 .06
955 Ramon Vazquez .20 .06
956 Luis Garcia .20 .06
957 Mark Quinn .20 .06
958 Armando Rios .20 .06

959 Chad Fox .20 .06
960 Hee Seop Choi .20 .06
961 Turk Wendell .20 .06
962 Adam Roller RC .40 .12
963 Grant Roberts .20 .06
964 Ben Molina .20 .06
965 Juan Rivera .20 .06
966 Matt Kinney .20 .06
967 Rod Beck .20 .06
968 Xavier Nady .20 .06
969 Masato Yoshii .20 .06
970 Miguel Tejada .30 .09
971 Danny Kolb .20 .06
972 Mike Remlinger .20 .06
973 Ray Lankford .20 .06
974 Ryan Minor .20 .06
975 J.T. Snow .30 .09
976 Brad Radke .30 .09
977 Jason Lane .20 .06
978 Jamey Wright .20 .06
979 Tom Goodwin .20 .06
980 Erik Bedard .20 .06
981 Gabe Kapler .20 .06
982 Brian Reith .20 .06
983 Nic Jackson RC .40 .12
984 Kurt Ainsworth .20 .06
985 Jason Isringhausen .30 .09
986 Willie Harris .20 .06
987 David Cone .30 .09
988 Bob Wickman .20 .06
989 Wes Helms .20 .06
990 Josh Beckett .30 .09

2002 Topps Total Award Winners

Issued at a stated rate of one in six, these 30 cards honored players who have won major awards during their career.

	Nm-Mt	Ex-Mt
COMPLETE SET (30)	40.00	12.00
AW1 Ichiro Suzuki	3.00	.90
AW2 Albert Pujols	4.00	1.20
AW3 Barry Bonds	5.00	1.50
AW4 Ichiro Suzuki	3.00	.90
AW5 Randy Johnson	2.00	.60
AW6 Roger Clemens	4.00	1.20
AW7 Jason Giambi A's	.75	.23
AW8 Bret Boone	.75	.23
AW9 Troy Glaus	.75	.23
AW10 Alex Rodriguez	3.00	.90
AW11 Juan Gonzalez	1.25	.35
AW12 Ichiro Suzuki	3.00	.90
AW13 Jorge Posada	1.25	.35
AW14 Edgar Martinez	1.25	.35
AW15 Todd Helton	1.25	.35
AW16 Jeff Kent	.75	.23
AW17 Albert Pujols	4.00	1.20
AW18 Rich Aurilia	.75	.23
AW19 Barry Bonds	5.00	1.50
AW20 Luis Gonzalez	.75	.23
AW21 Sammy Sosa	3.00	.90
AW22 Mike Piazza	3.00	.90
AW23 Mike Hampton	.75	.23
AW24 Ruben Sierra	.75	.23
AW25 Matt Morris	.75	.23
AW26 Curt Schilling	.75	.23
AW27 Alex Rodriguez	3.00	.90
AW28 Barry Bonds	5.00	1.50
AW29 Jim Thome	2.00	.60
AW30 Barry Bonds	5.00	1.50

2002 Topps Total Production

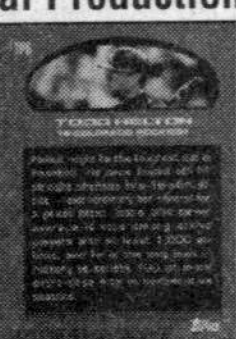

Issued at a stated rate of one in 12, these 10 cards feature players who are among the best in the game in producing large offensive numbers.

	Nm-Mt	Ex-Mt
COMPLETE SET (10)	20.00	6.00
TP1 Alex Rodriguez	3.00	.90
TP2 Barry Bonds	5.00	1.50
TP3 Ichiro Suzuki	3.00	.90
TP4 Edgar Martinez	1.25	.35
TP5 Jason Giambi	1.25	.35
TP6 Todd Helton	1.25	.35
TP7 Nomar Garciaparra	3.00	.90
TP8 Vladimir Guerrero	2.00	.60
TP9 Sammy Sosa	3.00	.90
TP10 Chipper Jones	2.00	.60

2002 Topps Total Team Checklists

Seeded at a rate of approximately two in every three packs, these 30 cards feature team checklists for the 990-card Topps Total set. The card fronts are identical to the corresponding basic issue Topps Total cards. But the card backs feature a checklist of players (unlike basic issue cards of which feature statistics and career information on the specific player pictured on front). In addition, unlike basic issue Topps Total cards, these Team Checklist cards do not feature glossy coating on front and back.

	Nm-Mt	Ex-Mt
COMPLETE SET (30)	10.00	3.00
TTC1 Troy Glaus	.20	.06
TTC2 Randy Johnson	.50	.15
TTC3 Chipper Jones	.50	.15
TTC4 Scott Erickson	.20	.06
TTC5 Nomar Garciaparra	.75	.23
TTC6 Sammy Sosa	.75	.23
TTC7 Magglio Ordonez	.20	.06
TTC8 Ken Griffey Jr.	.75	.23
TTC9 Jim Thome	.50	.15
TTC10 Todd Helton	.30	.09
TTC11 Bobby Higginson	.20	.06
TTC12 Josh Beckett	.20	.06
TTC13 Jeff Bagwell	.30	.09
TTC14 Mike Sweeney	.20	.06
TTC15 Shawn Green	.20	.06
TTC16 Geoff Jenkins	.20	.06
TTC17 Cristian Guzman	.20	.06
TTC18 Vladimir Guerrero	.50	.15
TTC19 Mike Piazza	.75	.23
TTC20 Derek Jeter	1.25	.35
TTC21 Eric Chavez	.20	.06
TTC22 Pat Burrell	.20	.06
TTC23 Brian Giles	.20	.06
TTC24 Phil Nevin	.20	.06
TTC25 Ichiro Suzuki	.75	.23
TTC26 Barry Bonds	1.25	.35
TTC27 J.D. Drew	.20	.06
TTC28 Carlos Delgado	.20	.06
TTC29 Toby Hall	.20	.06
TTC30 Alex Rodriguez		

2002 Topps Total Topps

Inserted in packs at a stated rate of one in three, these 50 cards feature some of the leading players in the game.

	Nm-Mt	Ex-Mt
COMPLETE SET (50)	50.00	15.00
TT1 Roberto Alomar	1.25	.35
TT2 Moises Alou	.75	.23
TT3 Jeff Bagwell	1.25	.35
TT4 Lance Berkman	.75	.23
TT5 Barry Bonds	5.00	1.50
TT6 Bret Boone	.75	.23
TT7 Kevin Brown	.75	.23
TT8 Eric Chavez	.75	.23
TT9 Roger Clemens	4.00	1.20
TT10 Carlos Delgado	.75	.23
TT11 Cliff Floyd	.75	.23
TT12 Nomar Garciaparra	3.00	.90
TT13 Jason Giambi	.75	.23
TT14 Brian Giles	.75	.23
TT15 Troy Glaus	.75	.23
TT16 Tom Glavine	1.25	.35
TT17 Luis Gonzalez	.75	.23
TT18 Juan Gonzalez	1.25	.35
TT19 Shawn Green	.75	.23
TT20 Ken Griffey Jr.	3.00	.90
TT21 Vladimir Guerrero	2.00	.60
TT22 Jorge Posada	1.25	.35
TT23 Todd Helton	1.25	.35
TT24 Tim Hudson	.75	.23
TT25 Derek Jeter	5.00	1.50
TT26 Randy Johnson	2.00	.60
TT27 Andruw Jones	.75	.23
TT28 Chipper Jones	2.00	.60
TT29 Jeff Kent	.75	.23
TT30 Greg Maddux	3.00	.90
TT31 Edgar Martinez	1.25	.35
TT32 Pedro Martinez	2.00	.60
TT33 Magglio Ordonez	.75	.23
TT34 Rafael Palmeiro	1.25	.35
TT35 Mike Piazza	3.00	.90
TT36 Albert Pujols	4.00	1.20
TT37 Aramis Ramirez	.75	.23
TT38 Mariano Rivera	1.25	.35
TT39 Alex Rodriguez	3.00	.90
TT40 Ivan Rodriguez	2.00	.60
TT41 Curt Schilling	.75	.23
TT42 Gary Sheffield	.75	.23
TT43 Sammy Sosa	3.00	.90
TT44 Ichiro Suzuki	3.00	.90
TT45 Miguel Tejada	.75	.23
TT46 Frank Thomas	2.00	.60
TT47 Jim Thome	2.00	.60
TT48 Larry Walker	1.25	.35
TT49 Bernie Williams	1.25	.35
TT50 Kerry Wood	2.00	.60

2003 Topps Total

For the second straight year, Topps issued this 990 card set which was designed to be a comprehensive look at who was in the majors at the time of issue. This set was released in May, 2003. This set was issued in 10 card packs with an 99 cent SRP which came 36 packs to a box and 6 boxes to a case.

	Nm-Mt	Ex-Mt
COMPLETE SET (990)	200.00	60.00
COMMON CARD (1-990)	.20	.06
COMMON RC	.25	.07
1 Brent Abernathy	.20	.06
2 Bobby Hill	.20	.06
3 Victor Martinez	.50	.15
4 Chip Ambres	.20	.06
5 Matt Anderson	.20	.06
6 Ricardo Aramboles	.20	.06
7 Carlos Pena	.20	.06
8 Aaron Guiel	.20	.06
9 Luke Allen	.20	.06
10 Francisco Rodriguez	.30	.09
11 Jason Marquis	.20	.06
12 Edwin Almonte	.20	.06
13 Grant Balfour	.20	.06
14 Adam Piatt	.20	.06
15 Andy Phillips	.20	.06
16 Adrian Beltre	.50	.15
17 Brandon Backe	.20	.06
18 Dave Berg	.20	.06
19 Brett Myers	.20	.06
20 Brian Meadows	.20	.06
21 Chin-Feng Chen	.30	.09
22 Blake Williams	.20	.06
23 Josh Bard	.20	.06
24 Josh Beckett	.30	.09
25 Tommy Whiteman	.20	.06
26 Matt Childers	.20	.06
27 Adam Everett	.20	.06
28 Mike Bordick	.30	.09
29 Antonio Alfonseca	.20	.06
30 Doug Creek	.20	.06
31 J.D. Drew	.30	.09
32 Milton Bradley	.30	.09
33 David Wells	.30	.09
34 Vance Wilson	.20	.06
35 Jeff Fassero	.20	.06
36 Sandy Alomar	.20	.06
37 Ryan Vogelsong	.20	.06
38 Roger Clemens	1.50	.45
39 Juan Gonzalez	.50	.15
40 Dustin Hermanson	.20	.06
41 Andy Ashby	.20	.06
42 Adam Hyzdu	.20	.06
43 Ben Broussard	.20	.06
44 Ryan Klesko	.30	.09
45 Chris Buglovsky FY RC	.40	.12
46 Bud Smith	.20	.06
47 Aaron Boone	.30	.09
48 Cliff Floyd	.30	.09
49 Alex Cora	.20	.06
50 Curt Schilling	.30	.09
51 Michael Cuddyer	.20	.06
52 Joe Valentine FY RC	.40	.12
53 Carlos Guillen	.30	.09
54 Angel Berroa	.20	.06
55 Eli Marrero	.20	.06
56 A.J. Burnett	.20	.06
57 Oliver Perez	.30	.09
58 Matt Morris	.30	.09
59 Valerio De Los Santos	.20	.06
60 Austin Kearns	.30	.09
61 Darren Dreifort	.20	.06
62 Jason Standridge	.20	.06
63 Carlos Silva	.20	.06
64 Moises Alou	.30	.09
65 Jason Anderson	.20	.06
66 Russell Branyan	.20	.06
67 B.J. Ryan	.20	.06
68 Cory Aldridge	.20	.06
69 Ellis Burks	.30	.09
70 Troy Glaus	.30	.09
71 Kelly Wunsch	.20	.06
72 Brad Wilkerson	.20	.06
73 Jayson Durocher	.20	.06
74 Tony Fiore	.20	.06
75 Brian Giles	.30	.09
76 Billy Wagner	.30	.09
77 Neifi Perez	.20	.06
78 Jose Valverde	.20	.06
79 Brent Butler	.20	.06
80 Mario Ramos	.20	.06
81 Kerry Robinson	.20	.06
82 Brent Mayne	.20	.06
83 Sean Casey	.30	.09
84 Danys Baez	.20	.06
85 Chase Utley	.30	.09
86 Jared Sandberg	.20	.06
87 Terrence Long	.20	.06
88 Kevin Walker	.20	.06
89 Royce Clayton	.20	.06
90 Shea Hillenbrand	.30	.09
91 Brad Lidge	.30	.09
92 Shawn Chacon	.20	.06
93 Kenny Rogers	.30	.09
94 Chris Snelling	.20	.06
95 Omar Vizquel	.50	.15
96 Joe Borchard	.20	.06
97 Matt Belisle	.20	.06
98 Steve Smyth	.20	.06
99 Raul Mondesi	.30	.09
100 Chipper Jones	.75	.23
101 Victor Alvarez	.20	.06
102 J.M. Gold	.20	.06
103 Willis Roberts	.20	.06
104 Eddie Guardado	.20	.06
105 Brad Voyles	.20	.06
106 Bronson Arroyo	.30	.09
107 Juan Castro	.20	.06
108 Dan Plesac	.20	.06
109 Ramon Castro	.20	.06
110 Tim Salmon	.50	.15
111 Gene Kingsale	.20	.06
112 J.D. Closser	.20	.06
113 Mark Buehrle	.30	.09
114 Steve Karsay	.20	.06
115 Cristian Guerrero	.20	.06
116 Brad Ausmus	.20	.06
117 Cristian Guzman	.20	.06
118 Dan Wilson	.20	.06
119 Jake Westbrook	.20	.06
120 Manny Ramirez	.50	.15
121 Jason Giambi	.30	.09
122 Bob Wickman	.20	.06
123 Aaron Cook	.20	.06
124 Alfredo Amezaga	.20	.06
125 Corey Thurman	.20	.06
126 Brandon Puffer	.20	.06
127 Hee Seop Choi	.20	.06
128 Javier Vazquez	.30	.09
129 Carlos Valderrama	.20	.06
130 Jerome Williams	.30	.09
131 Wilson Betemit	.20	.06
132 Luke Prokopec	.20	.06
133 Esteban Yan	.20	.06
134 Brandon Berger	.20	.06
135 Bill Hall	.20	.06
136 LaTroy Hawkins	.20	.06
137 Nate Cornejo	.20	.06
138 Jim Mecir	.20	.06
139 Joe Crede	.20	.06
140 Andres Galarraga	.30	.09
141 Reggie Sanders	.20	.06
142 Joey Eischen	.20	.06
143 Mike Timlin	.20	.06
144 Jose Cruz Jr.	.20	.06
145 Wes Helms	.20	.06
146 Brian Roberts	.20	.06
147 Bret Prinz	.20	.06
148 Brian Hunter	.20	.06
149 Chad Hermansen	.20	.06
150 Andruw Jones	.30	.09
151 Kurt Ainsworth	.20	.06
152 Cliff Bartosh	.20	.06
153 Kyle Lohse	.20	.06
154 Brian Jordan	.30	.09
155 Coco Crisp	.20	.06
156 Tomas Perez	.20	.06
157 Keith Foulke	.30	.09
158 Chris Carpenter	.20	.06
159 Mike Remlinger	.20	.06
160 Dewon Brazelton	.20	.06
161 Brook Fordyce	.20	.06
162 Rusty Greer	.30	.09
163 Scott Downs	.20	.06
164 Jason Dubois	.30	.09
165 David Coggin	.20	.06
166 Mike DeJean	.20	.06
167 Carlos Hernandez	.20	.06
168 Matt Williams	.30	.09
169 Rheal Cormier	.20	.06
170 Duaner Sanchez	.20	.06
171 Craig Counsell	.20	.06
172 Edgar Martinez	.50	.15
173 Zack Greinke	.50	.15
174 Pedro Feliz	.20	.06
175 Randy Choate	.20	.06
176 Jon Garland	.20	.06
177 Keith Ginter	.20	.06
178 Carlos Febles	.20	.06
179 Kerry Wood	.75	.23
180 Jack Cust	.20	.06
181 Koyie Hill	.20	.06
182 Ricky Gutierrez	.20	.06
183 Ben Grieve	.20	.06
184 Scott Eyre	.20	.06
185 Jason Isringhausen	.30	.09
186 Gookie Dawkins	.20	.06
187 Roberto Alomar	.50	.15
188 Eric Junge	.20	.06
189 Carlos Beltran	.50	.15
190 Denny Hocking	.20	.06
191 Jason Schmidt	.30	.09
192 Cory Lidle	.20	.06
193 Rob Mackowiak	.20	.06
194 Charlton Jimerson RC	.40	.12
195 Darin Erstad	.30	.09
196 Jason Davis	.20	.06
197 Luis Castillo	.20	.06
198 Juan Encarnacion	.20	.06
199 Jeffrey Hammonds	.20	.06
200 Nomar Garciaparra	1.25	.35
201 Ryan Christianson	.20	.06
202 Robert Person	.20	.06
203 Damian Moss	.20	.06
204 Chris Richard	.20	.06
205 Todd Hundley	.20	.06
206 Paul Bako	.20	.06
207 Adam Kennedy	.20	.06
208 Scott Hatteberg	.20	.06
209 Andy Pratt	.20	.06
210 Ken Griffey Jr.	1.25	.35
211 Chris George	.20	.06
212 Lance Niekro	.20	.06
213 Greg Colbrunn	.20	.06
214 Herbert Perry	.20	.06
215 Cody Ransom	.20	.06
216 Craig Biggio	.50	.15
217 Miguel Batista	.20	.06
218 Alex Escobar	.20	.06
219 Willie Harris	.20	.06
220 Scott Strickland	.20	.06
221 Felix Rodriguez	.20	.06
222 Torii Hunter	.30	.09
223 Tyler Houston	.20	.06
224 Darrell May	.20	.06
225 Benito Santiago	.30	.09
226 Ryan Dempster	.20	.06
227 Andy Fox	.20	.06
228 Jung Bong	.20	.06
229 Jose Macias	.20	.06
230 Shannon Stewart	.30	.09
231 Buddy Groom	.20	.06
232 Eric Valent	.20	.06
233 Scott Schoenweis	.20	.06
234 Corey Hart	.30	.09
235 Brett Tomko	.20	.06
236 Shane Bazzell RC	.40	.12
237 Tim Hummel	.20	.06
238 Matt Stairs	.20	.06
239 Pete Munro	.20	.06
240 Ismael Valdes	.20	.06
241 Brian Fuentes	.20	.06
242 Cesar Izturis	.20	.06
243 Mark Bellhorn	.30	.09
244 Geoff Jenkins	.30	.09
245 Derek Jeter	2.00	.60
246 Anderson Machado	.20	.06
247 Dave Roberts	.20	.06
248 Jaime Cerda	.20	.06
249 Woody Williams	.20	.06
250 Vernon Wells	.30	.09
251 Jon Lieber	.20	.06
252 Franklyn German	.20	.06
253 David Segui	.20	.06
254 Freddy Garcia	.30	.09
255 James Baldwin	.20	.06
256 Tony Alvarez	.20	.06
257 Walter Young	.20	.06
258 Alex Herrera	.20	.06
259 Robert Fick	.20	.06
260 Rob Bell	.20	.06
261 Ben Petrick	.20	.06
262 Dee Brown	.20	.06
263 Mike Bacsik	.20	.06
264 Corey Patterson	.30	.09
265 Marvin Benard	.20	.06
266 Eddie Rogers	.20	.06
267 Elio Serrano	.20	.06
268 D'Angelo Jimenez	.20	.06
269 Adam Johnson	.20	.06
270 Gregg Zaun	.20	.06
271 Nick Johnson	.20	.06
272 Geoff Goetz	.20	.06
273 Ryan Drese	.20	.06
274 Eric Dubose	.20	.06
275 Barry Zito	.30	.09
276 Mike Crudale	.20	.06
277 Paul Byrd	.20	.06
278 Eric Gagne	.75	.23
279 Aramis Ramirez	.30	.09
280 Ray Durham	.30	.09
281 Tony Graffanino	.20	.06
282 Jeremy Guthrie	.20	.06
283 Erik Bedard	.20	.06
284 Vince Faison	.20	.06
285 Bobby Kielty	.20	.06
286 Francis Beltran	.20	.06
287 Alexis Gomez	.20	.06
288 Vladimir Guerrero	.75	.23
289 Kevin Appier	.30	.09
290 Gil Meche	.20	.06
291 Marquis Grissom	.30	.09
292 John Burkett	.20	.06
293 Vinny Castilla	.30	.09
294 Tyler Walker	.20	.06
295 Shane Halter	.20	.06
296 Geronimo Gil	.20	.06
297 Eric Hinske	.20	.06
298 Adam Dunn	.50	.15
299 Mike Kinkade	.20	.06
300 Mark Prior	.75	.23
301 Corey Koskie	.30	.09
302 David Dellucci	.20	.06
303 Todd Helton	.50	.15
304 Greg Miller	.20	.06
305 Delvin James	.20	.06
306 Humberto Cota	.20	.06
307 Aaron Harang	.20	.06
308 Jeremy Hill	.20	.06
309 Billy Koch	.20	.06
310 Brandon Claussen	.20	.06
311 Matt Ginter	.20	.06
312 Jason Lane	.20	.06
313 Ben Weber	.20	.06
314 Alan Benes	.20	.06
315 Matt Walbeck	.20	.06
316 Danny Graves	.20	.06
317 Jason Johnson	.20	.06
318 Jason Grimsley	.20	.06
319 Steve Kline	.20	.06
320 Johnny Damon	.75	.23
321 Jay Gibbons	.20	.06
322 J.J. Putz	.20	.06
323 Stephen Randolph RC	.40	.12
324 Bobby Higginson	.30	.09
325 Kazuhisa Ishii	.30	.09
326 Carlos Lee	.30	.09
327 J.R. House	.20	.06
328 Mark Loretta	.30	.09
329 Mike Matheny	.30	.09
330 Ben Diggins	.20	.06
331 Seth Etherton	.20	.06
332 Eli Whiteside FY RC	.40	.12
333 Juan Rivera	.20	.06
334 Jeff Conine	.30	.09
335 John McDonald	.20	.06
336 Erik Hiljus	.20	.06
337 David Eckstein	.20	.06
338 Jeff Bagwell	.50	.15
339 Matt Holliday	.20	.06
340 Jeff Liefer	.20	.06
341 Greg Myers	.20	.06
342 Scott Sauerbeck	.20	.06
343 Omar Infante	.20	.06
344 Ryan Langerhans	.20	.06
345 Abraham Nunez	.20	.06
346 Mike MacDougal	.20	.06
347 Travis Phelps	.20	.06
348 Terry Shumpert	.20	.06
349 Alex Rodriguez	1.25	.35
350 Bobby Seay	.20	.06
351 Ichiro Suzuki	1.25	.35
352 Brandon Inge	.20	.06
353 Jack Wilson	.30	.09
354 John Ennis	.20	.06
355 Jamal Strong	.20	.06
356 Jason Jennings	.20	.06
357 Jeff Kent	.30	.09
358 Scott Chiasson	.20	.06
359 Jeremy Griffiths RC	.50	.15
360 Paul Konerko	.30	.09
361 Jeff Austin	.20	.06
362 Todd Van Poppel	.20	.06
363 Sun Woo Kim	.20	.06
364 Jerry Hairston Jr.	.20	.06
365 Tony Torcato	.20	.06
366 Arthur Rhodes	.20	.06
367 Jose Jimenez	.20	.06
368 Matt LeCroy	.20	.06
369 Curtis Leskanic	.20	.06
370 Ramon Vazquez	.20	.06
371 Joe Randa	.20	.06
372 John Franco	.20	.06
373 Bobby Estalella	.20	.06
374 Craig Wilson	.30	.09
375 Michael Young	.50	.15
376 Mark Ellis	.20	.06
377 Joe Mauer	.75	.23
378 Checklist 1	.20	.06
379 Jason Kendall	.30	.09

380 Checklist 2 .20 .06
381 Alex Gonzalez .20 .06
382 Tom Gordon .20 .06
383 John Buck .20 .06
384 Shigetoshi Hasegawa .30 .09
385 Scott Stewart .20 .06
386 Luke Hudson .20 .06
387 Todd Jones .20 .06
388 Fred McGriff .50 .15
389 Mike Sweeney .30 .09
390 Marlon Anderson .20 .06
391 Terry Adams .20 .06
392 Mark DeRosa .20 .06
393 Doug Mientkiewicz .30 .09
394 Miguel Cairo .20 .06
395 Jamie Moyer .30 .09
396 Jose Leon .20 .06
397 Matt Clement .20 .06
398 Bengie Molina .20 .06
399 Marcus Thames .20 .06
400 Nick Bierbrodt .20 .06
401 Tim Kalita .20 .06
402 Corwin Malone .20 .06
403 Jesse Orosco .20 .06
404 Brandon Phillips .20 .06
405 Eric Cyr .20 .06
406 Jason Michaels .20 .06
407 Julio Lugo .20 .06
408 Gabe Kapler .20 .06
409 Mark Mulder .30 .09
410 Adam Eaton .20 .06
411 Ken Harvey .20 .06
412 Jolbert Cabrera .20 .06
413 Eric Milton .20 .06
414 Josh Hall RC .50 .15
415 Bob File .20 .06
416 Brett Evert .20 .06
417 Ron Chiavacci .20 .06
418 Jorge De La Rosa .20 .06
419 Quinton McCracken .20 .06
420 Luther Hackman .20 .06
421 Gary Knotts .20 .06
422 Kevin Brown .30 .09
423 Jeff Cirillo .20 .06
424 Damaso Marte .20 .06
425 Chan Ho Park .30 .09
426 Nathan Haynes .20 .06
427 Matt Lawton .20 .06
428 Mike Stanton .20 .06
429 Bernie Williams .50 .15
430 Kevin Jarvis .20 .06
431 Joe McEwing .20 .06
432 Mark Kotsay .20 .06
433 Juan Cruz .20 .06
434 Russ Ortiz .30 .09
435 Jeff Nelson .20 .06
436 Alan Embree .20 .06
437 Miguel Tejada .30 .09
438 Kirk Saarloos .20 .06
439 Cliff Lee .20 .06
440 Ryan Ludwick .20 .06
441 Derrek Lee .30 .09
442 Bobby Abreu .30 .09
443 Dustan Mohr .20 .06
444 Nook Logan RC .40 .12
445 Seth McClung .20 .06
446 Miguel Olivo .20 .06
447 Henry Blanco .20 .06
448 Seung Song .20 .06
449 Kris Wilson .20 .06
450 Xavier Nady .20 .06
451 Corky Miller .20 .06
452 Jim Thome .75 .23
453 George Lombard .20 .06
454 Rey Ordonez .20 .06
455 Deivis Santos .20 .06
456 Mike Myers .20 .06
457 Edgar Renteria .30 .09
458 Braden Looper .20 .06
459 Guillermo Mota .20 .06
460 Scott Rolen .75 .23
461 Lance Berkman .30 .09
462 Jeff Heaverlo .20 .06
463 Ramon Hernandez .20 .06
464 Jason Simontacchi .20 .06
465 So Taguchi .30 .09
466 Dave Veres .20 .06
467 Shane Loux .20 .06
468 Rodrigo Lopez .20 .06
469 Bubba Trammell .20 .06
470 Scott Sullivan .20 .06
471 Mike Mussina .50 .15
472 Ramon Ortiz .20 .06
473 Lyle Overbay .30 .09
474 Mike Lowell .30 .09
475 Al Martin .20 .06
476 Larry Bigbie .20 .06
477 Rey Sanchez .20 .06
478 Magglio Ordonez .30 .09
479 Rondell White .30 .09
480 Jay Witasick .20 .06
481 Jimmy Rollins .30 .09
482 Mike Maroth .20 .06
483 Alejandro Machado .20 .06
484 Nick Neugebauer .20 .06
485 Victor Zambrano .20 .06
486 Travis Lee .20 .06
487 Bobby Bradley .20 .06
488 Marcus Giles .30 .09
489 Steve Trachsel .20 .06
490 Derek Lowe .30 .09
491 Hideo Nomo .75 .23
492 Brad Hawpe .20 .06
493 Jesus Medrano .20 .06
494 Rick Ankiel .20 .06
495 Pasqual Coco .20 .06
496 Michael Barrett .20 .06
497 Joe Beimel .20 .06
498 Marty Cordova .20 .06
499 Aaron Sele .20 .06
500 Sammy Sosa 1.25 .35
501 Ivan Rodriguez .75 .23
502 Keith Osik .20 .06
503 Hank Blalock .50 .15
504 Hiram Bocachica .20 .06
505 Junior Spivey .20 .06
506 Edgardo Alfonzo .20 .06
507 Alex Graman .20 .06
508 J.J. Davis .20 .06
509 Roger Cedeno .20 .06
510 Joe Roa .20 .06
511 Wily Mo Pena .30 .09
512 Eric Munson .20 .06
513 Arnie Munoz RC .40 .12
514 Albie Lopez .20 .06
515 Andy Pettitte .50 .15
516 Jim Edmonds .30 .09
517 Jeff Davanon .20 .06
518 Aaron Myette .20 .06
519 C.C. Sabathia .30 .09
520 Gerardo Garcia .20 .06
521 Brian Schneider .20 .06
522 Wes Obermueller .20 .06
523 John Mabry .20 .06
524 Casey Fossum .20 .06
525 Toby Hall .20 .06
526 Denny Neagle .20 .06
527 Willie Bloomquist .30 .09
528 A.J. Pierzynski .30 .09
529 Bartolo Colon .30 .09
530 Chad Harville .20 .06
531 Blaine Neal .20 .06
532 Luis Terrero .20 .06
533 Reggie Taylor .20 .06
534 Melvin Mora .30 .09
535 Tino Martinez .50 .15
536 Peter Bergeron .20 .06
537 Jorge Padilla .20 .06
538 Oscar Villarreal RC .40 .12
539 David Weathers .20 .06
540 Mike Lamb .20 .06
541 Greg Norton .20 .06
542 Michael Tucker .20 .06
543 Ben Kozlowski .20 .06
544 Alex Sanchez .20 .06
545 Trey Lunsford .20 .06
546 Abraham Nunez .20 .06
547 Mike Lincoln .20 .06
548 Orlando Hernandez .20 .06
549 Kevin Mench .20 .06
550 Garret Anderson .30 .09
551 Kyle Farnsworth .20 .06
552 Kevin Olsen .20 .06
553 Joel Pineiro .30 .09
554 Jorge Julio .20 .06
555 Jose Mesa .20 .06
556 Jorge Posada .50 .15
557 Jose Ortiz .20 .06
558 Mike Tonis .20 .06
559 Gabe White .20 .06
560 Rafael Furcal .30 .09
561 Matt Franco .20 .06
562 Trey Hodges .20 .06
563 Esteban German .20 .06
564 Josh Fogg .20 .06
565 Fernando Tatis .20 .06
566 Alex Cintron .20 .06
567 Grant Roberts .20 .06
568 Gene Stechschulte .20 .06
569 Rafael Palmeiro .50 .15
570 Mike Hampton .30 .09
571 Ben Davis .20 .06
572 Dean Palmer .30 .09
573 Jerrod Riggan .20 .06
574 Nate Frese .20 .06
575 Josh Phelps .20 .06
576 Freddie Bynum .20 .06
577 Morgan Ensberg .20 .06
578 Juan Rincon .20 .06
579 Kazuhiro Sasaki .30 .09
580 Yorvit Torrealba .20 .06
581 Tim Wakefield .30 .09
582 Sterling Hitchcock .20 .06
583 Craig Paquette .20 .06
584 Kevin Millwood .30 .09
585 Damian Rolls .20 .06
586 Brad Baisley .20 .06
587 Kyle Snyder .20 .06
588 Paul Quantrill .20 .06
589 Trot Nixon .30 .09
590 J.T. Snow .30 .09
591 Kevin Young .20 .06
592 Tomo Ohka .20 .06
593 Brian Boehringer .20 .06
594 Danny Patterson .20 .06
595 Jeff Tam .20 .06
596 Anastacio Martinez .20 .06
597 Rod Barajas .20 .06
598 Octavio Dotel .20 .06
599 Jason Tyner .20 .06
600 Gary Sheffield .30 .09
601 Ruben Quevedo .20 .06
602 Jay Payton .20 .06
603 Mo Vaughn .30 .09
604 Pat Burrell .30 .09
605 Fernando Vina .20 .06
606 Wes Anderson .20 .06
607 Alex Gonzalez .20 .06
608 Ted Lilly .20 .06
609 Nick Punto .20 .06
610 Ryan Madson .20 .06
611 Odalis Perez .20 .06
612 Chris Woodward .20 .06
613 John Olerud .30 .09
614 Brad Cresse .20 .06
615 Chad Zerbe .20 .06
616 Brad Penny .20 .06
617 Barry Larkin .50 .15
618 Brandon Duckworth .20 .06
619 Brad Radke .30 .09
620 Troy Brohawn .20 .06
621 Juan Pierre .30 .09
622 Rick Reed .20 .06
623 Omar Daal .20 .06
624 Jose Hernandez .20 .06
625 Greg Maddux 1.25 .35
626 Henry Mateo .20 .06
627 Kip Wells .20 .06
628 Kevin Cash .20 .06
629 Wil Ledezma FY RC .50 .15
630 Luis Gonzalez .30 .09
631 Jason Conti .20 .06
632 Ricardo Rincon .20 .06
633 Mike Bynum .20 .06
634 Mike Redmond .20 .06
635 Chance Caple .20 .06
636 Chris Widger .20 .06
637 Michael Restovich .20 .06
638 Mark Grudzielanek .20 .06
639 Brandon Larson .20 .06
640 Rocco Baldelli .30 .09
641 Javy Lopez .30 .09
642 Rene Reyes .20 .06
643 Orlando Merced .20 .06
644 Jason Phillips .20 .06
645 Luis Ugueto .20 .06
646 Ron Calloway .20 .06
647 Josh Paul .20 .06
648 Todd Greene .20 .06
649 Joe Girardi .20 .06
650 Todd Ritchie .20 .06
651 Kevin Millar Sox .30 .09
652 Shawn Wooten .20 .06
653 David Riske .20 .06
654 Luis Rivas .20 .06
655 Roy Halladay .20 .06
656 Travis Driskill .20 .06
657 Ricky Ledee .20 .06
658 Timo Perez .20 .06
659 Fernando Rodney .20 .06
660 Trevor Hoffman .30 .09
661 Pat Hentgen .30 .09
662 Bret Boone .30 .09
663 Ryan Jensen .20 .06
664 Ricardo Rodriguez .20 .06
665 Jeremy Lambert .20 .06
666 Troy Percival .30 .09
667 Jon Rauch .20 .06
668 Mariano Rivera .50 .15
669 Jason LaRue .20 .06
670 J.C. Romero .20 .06
671 Cody Ross .20 .06
672 Eric Byrnes .20 .06
673 Paul Lo Duca .30 .09
674 Brad Fullmer .20 .06
675 Cliff Politte .20 .06
676 Justin Miller .20 .06
677 Nic Jackson .20 .06
678 Kris Benson .20 .06
679 Carl Sadler .20 .06
680 Joe Nathan .20 .06
681 Julio Santana .20 .06
682 Wade Miller .20 .06
683 Josh Pearce .20 .06
684 Tony Armas Jr. .20 .06
685 Al Leiter .30 .09
686 Raul Ibanez .20 .06
687 Danny Bautista .20 .06
688 Travis Hafner .30 .09
689 Carlos Zambrano .30 .09
690 Pedro Martinez .75 .23
691 Ramon Santiago .20 .06
692 Felipe Lopez .20 .06
693 David Ross .20 .06
694 Chone Figgins .20 .06
695 Antonio Osuna .20 .06
696 Jay Powell .20 .06
697 Ryan Church .20 .06
698 Alexis Rios .50 .15
699 Tanyon Sturtze .20 .06
700 Turk Wendell .20 .06
701 Richard Hidalgo .20 .06
702 Joe Mays .20 .06
703 Jorge Sosa .20 .06
704 Eric Karros .30 .09
705 Steve Finley .30 .09
706 Sean Smith FY RC .50 .15
707 Jeremy Giambi .20 .06
708 Scott Hodges .20 .06
709 Vicente Padilla .20 .06
710 Erubiel Durazo .20 .06
711 Aaron Rowand .30 .09
712 Dennis Tankersley .20 .06
713 Rick Bauer .20 .06
714 Tim Olson FY RC .50 .15
715 Jeff Urban .20 .06
716 Steve Sparks .20 .06
717 Glendon Rusch .20 .06
718 Ricky Stone .20 .06
719 Benji Gil .20 .06
720 Pete Walker .20 .06
721 Tim Worrell .20 .06
722 Michael Tejera .20 .06
723 David Kelton .20 .06
724 Britt Reames .20 .06
725 John Stephens .20 .06
726 Mark McLemore .20 .06
727 Jeff Zimmerman .20 .06
728 Checklist 3 .20 .06
729 Andres Torres .20 .06
730 Checklist 4 .20 .06
731 Johan Santana .50 .15
732 Dane Sardinha .20 .06
733 Rodrigo Rosario .20 .06
734 Frank Thomas .75 .23
735 Tom Glavine .50 .15
736 Doug Mirabelli .20 .06
737 Juan Uribe .20 .06
738 Ryan Anderson .20 .06
739 Sean Burroughs .30 .09
740 Eric Chavez .30 .09
741 Enrique Wilson .20 .06
742 Elmer Dessens .20 .06
743 Marlon Byrd .20 .06
744 Brendan Donnelly .20 .06
745 Gary Bennett .20 .06
746 Roy Oswalt .30 .09
747 Andy Van Hekken .20 .06
748 Jesus Colome .20 .06
749 Erick Almonte .20 .06
750 Frank Catalanotto .20 .06
751 Kenny Lofton .30 .09
752 Carlos Delgado .30 .09
753 Ryan Franklin .20 .06
754 Wilkin Ruan .20 .06
755 Kelvim Escobar .20 .06
756 Tim Drew .20 .06
757 Jarrod Washburn .20 .06
758 Runelvys Hernandez .20 .06
759 Cory Vance .20 .06
760 Doug Glanville .20 .06
761 Ryan Rupe .20 .06
762 Jermaine Dye .30 .09
763 Mike Cameron .20 .06
764 Scott Erickson .20 .06
765 Richie Sexson .30 .09
766 Jose Vidro .20 .06
767 Brian West .20 .06
768 Shawn Estes .20 .06
769 Brian Tallet .20 .06
770 Larry Walker .50 .15
771 Josh Hamilton .20 .06
772 Orlando Hudson .20 .06
773 Justin Morneau .50 .15
774 Ryan Bukvich .20 .06
775 Mike Gonzalez .20 .06
776 Tsuyoshi Shinjo .30 .09
777 Matt Mantei .20 .06
778 Jimmy Journell .20 .06
779 Brian Lawrence .20 .06
780 Mike Lieberthal .30 .09
781 Scott Mullen .20 .06
782 Zach Day .20 .06
783 John Thomson .20 .06
784 Ben Sheets .30 .09
785 Damon Minor .20 .06
786 Jose Valentin .20 .06
787 Armando Benitez .30 .09
788 Jamie Walker RC .25 .07
789 Preston Wilson .30 .09
790 Josh Wilson .20 .06
791 Phil Nevin .30 .09
792 Roberto Hernandez .20 .06
793 Mike Williams .20 .06
794 Jake Peavy .30 .09
795 Paul Shuey .20 .06
796 Chad Bradford .20 .06
797 Bobby Jenks .20 .06
798 Sean Douglass .20 .06
799 Damian Miller .20 .06
800 Mark Wohlers .20 .06
801 Ty Wigginton .20 .06
802 Alfonso Soriano .50 .15
803 Randy Johnson .75 .23
804 Placido Polanco .20 .06
805 Drew Henson .30 .09
806 Tony Womack .20 .06
807 Pokey Reese .20 .06
808 Albert Pujols 1.50 .45
809 Henri Stanley .20 .06
810 Mike Rivera .20 .06
811 John Lackey .20 .06
812 Brian Wright FY RC .40 .12
813 Eric Good .20 .06
814 Dernell Stenson .20 .06
815 Kirk Rueter .20 .06
816 Todd Zeile .20 .06
817 Brad Thomas .20 .06
818 Shawn Sedlacek .20 .06
819 Garrett Stephenson .20 .06
820 Mark Teixeira .30 .09
821 Tim Hudson .30 .09
822 Mike Koplove .20 .06
823 Chris Reitsma .20 .06
824 Rafael Soriano .20 .06
825 Ugueth Urbina .20 .06
826 Lance Carter .20 .06
827 Colin Young .20 .06
828 Pat Strange .20 .06
829 Juan Pena .20 .06
830 Joe Thurston .20 .06
831 Shawn Green .30 .09
832 Pedro Astacio .20 .06
833 Danny Wright .20 .06
834 Wes O'Brien FY RC .40 .12
835 Luis Lopez .20 .06
836 Randall Simon .20 .06
837 Jaret Wright .20 .06
838 Jayson Werth .20 .06
839 Endy Chavez .20 .06
840 Checklist 5 .20 .06
841 Chad Paronto .20 .06
842 Randy Winn .20 .06
843 Sidney Ponson .20 .06
844 Robin Ventura .30 .09
845 Rich Aurilia .20 .06
846 Joaquin Benoit .20 .06
847 Barry Bonds 2.00 .60
848 Carl Crawford .30 .09
849 Jeromy Burnitz .30 .09
850 Orlando Cabrera .30 .09
851 Luis Vizcaino .20 .06
852 Randy Wolf .20 .06
853 Todd Walker .20 .06
854 Jeremy Affeldt .20 .06
855 Einar Diaz .20 .06
856 Carl Everett .30 .09
857 Wiki Gonzalez .20 .06
858 Mike Paradis .20 .06
859 Travis Harper .20 .06
860 Mike Piazza 1.25 .35
861 Will Ohman .20 .06
862 Eric Young .20 .06
863 Jason Grabowski .20 .06
864 Rett Johnson RC .50 .15
865 Aubrey Huff .30 .09
866 John Smoltz .50 .15
867 Mickey Callaway .20 .06
868 Joe Kennedy .20 .06
869 Tim Redding .20 .06
870 Colby Lewis .20 .06
871 Salomon Torres .20 .06
872 Marco Scutaro .20 .06
873 Tony Batista .20 .06
874 Dmitri Young .30 .09
875 Scott Williamson .20 .06
876 Scott Spiezio .20 .06
877 John Webb .20 .06
878 Jose Acevedo .20 .06
879 Kevin Orie .20 .06
880 Jacque Jones .30 .09
881 Ben Francisco FY RC .50 .15
882 Bobby Basham FY RC .50 .15
883 Corey Shafer FY RC .50 .15
884 J.D. Durbin FY RC .75 .23
885 Chien-Ming Wang FY RC 1.00 .30
886 Adam Stern FY RC .40 .12
887 Wayne Lydon FY RC .40 .12
888 Derell McCall FY RC .40 .12
889 Jon Nelson FY RC .40 .12
890 Willie Eyre FY RC .40 .12
891 R.Nivar-Martinez FY RC .75 .23
892 Adrian Myers FY RC .25 .07
893 Jamie Athas FY RC .40 .12
894 Ismael Castro FY RC .50 .15
895 David Martinez FY RC .40 .12
896 Terry Tiffee FY RC .75 .23
897 Nathan Panther FY RC .75 .23
898 Kyle Roat FY RC .40 .12
899 Kason Gabbard FY RC .40 .12
900 Hanley Ramirez FY RC 2.00 .60
901 Bryan Grace FY RC .40 .12
902 B.J. Barns FY RC .40 .12
903 Greg Bruso FY RC .40 .12
904 Mike Neu FY RC .40 .12
905 Dustin Yount FY RC .50 .15
906 Shane Victorino FY RC .40 .12
907 Brian Burgamy FY RC .40 .12
908 Beau Kemp FY RC .40 .12
909 David Corrente FY RC .40 .12
910 Dexter Cooper FY RC .40 .12
911 Chris Colton FY RC .40 .12
912 David Cash FY RC .40 .12
913 Bernie Castro FY RC .40 .12
914 Luis Hodge FY RC .40 .12
915 Jeff Clark FY RC .40 .12
916 Jason Kubel FY RC 2.00 .60
917 T.J. Bohn FY RC .40 .12
918 Luke Steidlmayer FY RC .40 .12
919 Matthew Peterson FY RC .40 .12
920 Darrell Rasner FY RC .40 .12
921 Scott Tyler FY RC .50 .15
922 G.Schneidmiller FY RC .40 .12
923 Gregor Blanco FY RC .40 .12
924 Ryan Cameron FY RC .40 .12
925 Wilfredo Rodriguez FY .20 .06
926 Rajai Davis FY RC .50 .15
927 E.Bastida-Martinez FY RC .40 .12
928 Chris Duncan FY RC .40 .12
929 Dave Pember FY RC .40 .12
930 Branden Florence FY RC .40 .12
931 Eric Eckenstahler FY .20 .06
932 Hong-Chih Kuo FY RC .75 .23
933 Il Kim FY RC .40 .12
934 Mi. Garciaparra FY RC .75 .23
935 Kip Bouknight FY RC .50 .15
936 Gary Harris FY RC .40 .12
937 Derry Hammond FY RC .40 .12
938 Joey Gomes FY RC .40 .12
939 Donnie Hood FY RC .50 .15
940 Clay Hensley FY RC .40 .12
941 David Pahucki FY RC .40 .12
942 Wilton Reynolds FY RC .40 .12
943 Michael Hinckley FY RC 1.00 .30
944 Josh Willingham FY RC .50 .15
945 Pete LaForest FY RC .50 .15
946 Pete Smart FY RC .40 .12
947 Jay Sitzman FY RC .40 .12
948 Mark Malaska FY RC .40 .12
949 Mike Gallo FY RC .40 .12
950 Matt Diaz FY RC .50 .15
951 Brennan King FY RC .40 .12
952 Ryan Howard FY RC 3.00 .90
953 Daryl Clark FY RC .50 .15
954 Dayton Buller FY RC .40 .12
955 Rylan Reed FY RC .40 .12
956 Chris Booker FY .20 .06
957 Brandon Watson FY RC .40 .12
958 Matt DeMarco FY RC .40 .12
959 Doug Waechter FY RC .50 .15
960 Callix Crabbe FY RC .50 .15
961 Jairo Garcia FY RC .75 .23
962 Jason Perry FY RC .75 .23
963 Eric Riggs FY RC .50 .15
964 Travis Ishikawa FY RC .40 .12
965 Simon Pond FY RC .75 .23
966 Manuel Ramirez FY RC .50 .15
967 Tyler Johnson FY RC .40 .12
968 Jaime Bubela FY RC .40 .12
969 Haj Turay FY RC .50 .15
970 Tyson Graham FY RC .40 .12
971 David DeJesus FY RC .50 .15
972 Franklin Gutierrez FY RC 2.00 .60
973 Craig Brazell FY RC .50 .15
974 Keith Stamler FY RC .40 .12
975 Jemel Spearman FY RC .40 .12
976 Ozzie Chavez FY RC .40 .12
977 Nick Trzesniak FY RC .40 .12
978 Bill Simon FY RC .40 .12
979 Matthew Hagen FY RC .75 .23
980 Chris Kroski FY RC .40 .12
981 Prentice Redman FY RC .40 .12
982 Kevin Randel FY RC .40 .12
983 Tho. Story-Harden FY RC .40 .12
984 Brian Shackelford FY RC .40 .12
985 Mike Adams FY RC .40 .12
986 Brian McCann FY RC .75 .23
987 Mike McNutt FY RC .40 .12
988 Aron Weston FY RC .40 .12
989 Dustin Moseley FY RC .50 .15
990 Bryan Bullington FY RC 1.25 .35

2003 Topps Total Silver

Nm-Mt Ex-Mt
*SILVER: 1X TO 2.5X BASIC
*SILVER RC'S: 1X TO 2.5X BASIC
STATED ODDS 1:1

2003 Topps Total Award Winners

	Nm-Mt	Ex-Mt
COMPLETE SET (30)	40.00	12.00
STATED ODDS 1:12		
AW1 Barry Zito	.75	.23
AW2 Randy Johnson	2.00	.60
AW3 Miguel Tejada	.75	.23
AW4 Barry Bonds	5.00	1.50
AW5 Sammy Sosa	3.00	.90
AW6 Barry Bonds	5.00	1.50
AW7 Mike Piazza	3.00	.90
AW8 Todd Helton	1.25	.35
AW9 Jeff Kent	.75	.23
AW10 Edgar Renteria	.75	.23
AW11 Scott Rolen	2.00	.60
AW12 Vladimir Guerrero	2.00	.60

Card	Nm-Mt	Ex-Mt
AW13 Mike Hampton	.75	.23
AW14 Jason Giambi	.75	.23
AW15 Alfonso Soriano	1.25	.35
AW16 Alex Rodriguez	3.00	.90
AW17 Eric Chavez	.75	.23
AW18 Jorge Posada	1.25	.35
AW19 Bernie Williams	1.25	.35
AW20 Magglio Ordonez	.75	.23
AW21 Garret Anderson	.75	.23
AW22 Manny Ramirez	1.25	.35
AW23 Jason Jennings	.75	.23
AW24 Eric Hinske	.75	.23
AW25 Billy Koch	.75	.23
AW26 John Smoltz	1.25	.35
AW27 Alex Rodriguez	3.00	.90
AW28 Barry Bonds	5.00	1.50
AW29 Tony La Russa MG	.75	.23
AW30 Mike Scioscia MG	.75	.23

2003 Topps Total Production

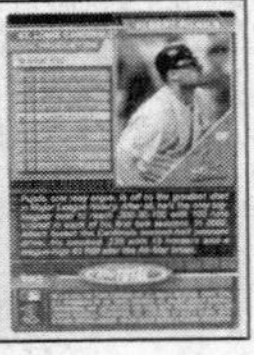

	Nm-Mt	Ex-Mt
COMPLETE SET (10)	15.00	4.50
STATED ODDS 1:18		
TP1 Barry Bonds	5.00	1.50
TP2 Manny Ramirez	1.25	.35
TP3 Albert Pujols	4.00	1.20
TP4 Jason Giambi	.75	.23
TP5 Magglio Ordonez	.75	.23
TP6 Lance Berkman	.75	.23
TP7 Todd Helton	1.25	.35
TP8 Miguel Tejada	.75	.23
TP9 Sammy Sosa	3.00	.90
TP10 Alex Rodriguez	3.00	.90

2003 Topps Total Signatures

	Nm-Mt	Ex-Mt
STATED ODDS 1:176		
TS-BP Brandon Phillips	10.00	3.00
TS-EM Eli Marrero	10.00	3.00
TS-MB Marlon Byrd	10.00	3.00
TS-MT Marcus Thames	10.00	3.00
TS-TT Tony Torcato	10.00	3.00

2003 Topps Total Team Checklists

	Nm-Mt	Ex-Mt
COMPLETE SET (30)	15.00	4.50
RANDOM INSERTS IN PACKS		
1 Troy Glaus	.30	.09
2 Randy Johnson	.75	.23
3 Greg Maddux	1.25	.35
4 Jay Gibbons	.30	.09
5 Nomar Garciaparra	1.25	.35
6 Sammy Sosa	1.25	.35
7 Paul Konerko	.30	.09
8 Ken Griffey Jr.	1.25	.35
9 Omar Vizquel	.50	.15
10 Todd Helton	.50	.15
11 Carlos Pena	.30	.09
12 Mike Lowell	.30	.09
13 Lance Berkman	.30	.09
14 Mike Sweeney	.30	.09
15 Shawn Green	.30	.09
16 Richie Sexson	.30	.09
17 Torii Hunter	.30	.09
18 Vladimir Guerrero	.75	.23
19 Mike Piazza	1.25	.35
20 Jason Giambi	.30	.09
21 Eric Chavez	.30	.09
22 Jim Thome	.75	.23
23 Brian Giles	.30	.09
24 Ryan Klesko	.30	.09
25 Barry Bonds	2.00	.60
26 Ichiro Suzuki	1.25	.35
27 Albert Pujols	1.50	.45
28 Carl Crawford	.30	.09
29 Alex Rodriguez	1.25	.35
30 Carlos Delgado	.30	.09

2003 Topps Total Topps

	Nm-Mt	Ex-Mt
COMPLETE SET (50)	40.00	12.00
STATED ODDS 1:7		
TT1 Ichiro Suzuki	3.00	.90
TT2 Alex Rodriguez	3.00	.90
TT3 Barry Bonds	5.00	1.50
TT4 Jason Giambi	.75	.23
TT5 Troy Glaus	.75	.23
TT6 Greg Maddux	3.00	.90

Card	Nm-Mt	Ex-Mt
TT7 Albert Pujols	4.00	1.20
TT8 Randy Johnson	2.00	.60
TT9 Chipper Jones	2.00	.60
TT10 Magglio Ordonez	.75	.23
TT11 Jim Thome	2.00	.60
TT12 Jeff Kent	.75	.23
TT13 Curt Schilling	.75	.23
TT14 Alfonso Soriano	1.25	.35
TT15 Rafael Palmeiro	1.25	.35
TT16 Carlos Delgado	.75	.23
TT17 Torii Hunter	.75	.23
TT18 Pat Burrell	.75	.23
TT19 Adam Dunn	1.25	.35
TT20 Roberto Alomar	1.25	.35
TT21 Eric Chavez	.75	.23
TT22 Derek Jeter	4.00	1.20
TT23 Nomar Garciaparra	3.00	.90
TT24 Lance Berkman	.75	.23
TT25 Jim Edmonds	.75	.23
TT26 Todd Helton	1.25	.35
TT27 Sammy Sosa	3.00	.90
TT28 Phil Nevin	.75	.23
TT29 Andruw Jones	.75	.23
TT30 Barry Zito	.75	.23
TT31 Richie Sexson	.75	.23
TT32 Ken Griffey Jr.	3.00	.90
TT33 Gary Sheffield	.75	.23
TT34 Shawn Green	.75	.23
TT35 Mike Sweeney	.75	.23
TT36 Mike Lowell	.75	.23
TT37 Larry Walker	.75	.23
TT38 Manny Ramirez	1.25	.35
TT39 Miguel Tejada	.75	.23
TT40 Mike Piazza	3.00	.90
TT41 Scott Rolen	2.00	.60
TT42 Brian Giles	.75	.23
TT43 Garret Anderson	.75	.23
TT44 Vladimir Guerrero	2.00	.60
TT45 Bartolo Colon	.75	.23
TT46 Jorge Posada	1.25	.35
TT47 Ivan Rodriguez	2.00	.60
TT48 Ryan Klesko	.75	.23
TT49 Jose Vidro	.75	.23
TT50 Pedro Martinez	2.00	.60

2004 Topps Total

This 880-card set was released in May, 2004. This set was issued in 10 card packs with an $1 SRP which came 36 packs to box and six boxes to a case. Cards numbered 781 through 875 feature Rookie Cards while cards numbered 876 through 880 are checklists.

	Nm-Mt	Ex-Mt
COMPLETE SET (880)	150.00	45.00
OVERALL PRESS PLATES ODDS 1:159		
PLATES PRINT RUN 1 #'d SET PER COLOR		
PLATES: BLACK, CYAN, MAGENTA & YELLOW		
NO PLATES PRICING DUE TO SCARCITY		
1 Kevin Brown	.30	.09
2 Mike Mordecai	.20	.06
3 Seung Song	.20	.06
4 Mike Maroth	.20	.06
5 Mike Lieberthal	.30	.09
6 Billy Koch	.20	.06
7 Mike Stanton	.20	.06
8 Brad Penny	.30	.09
9 Brooks Kieschnick	.20	.06
10 Carlos Delgado	.30	.09
11 Brady Clark	.20	.06
12 Ramon Martinez	.20	.06
13 Dan Wilson	.20	.06
14 Guillermo Mota	.20	.06
15 Trevor Hoffman	.30	.09
16 Tony Batista	.30	.09
17 Rusty Greer	.30	.09
18 David Weathers	.20	.06
19 Horacio Ramirez	.20	.06
20 Aubrey Huff	.30	.09
21 Casey Blake	.20	.06
22 Ryan Bukvich	.20	.06
23 Garrett Atkins	.20	.06
24 Jose Contreras	.30	.09
25 Chipper Jones	.75	.23
26 Neifi Perez	.20	.06
27 Scott Linebrink	.20	.06
28 Matt Kinney	.20	.06
29 Michael Restovich	.20	.06
30 Scott Rolen	.75	.23
31 John Franco	.30	.09
32 Toby Hall	.20	.06
33 Wily Mo Pena	.30	.09
34 Dennis Tankersley	.20	.06
35 Robb Nen	.30	.09
36 Jose Valverde	.20	.06
37 Chin-Feng Chen	.30	.09
38 Gary Knotts	.20	.06
39 Mark Sweeney	.20	.06
40 Bret Boone	.30	.09
41 Josh Phelps	.20	.06
42 Jason LaRue	.20	.06
43 Tim Redding	.20	.06
44 Greg Myers	.20	.06
45 Darin Erstad	.30	.09
46 Kip Wells	.20	.06
47 Matt Ford	.20	.06
48 Jerome Williams	.30	.09
49 Brian Meadows	.20	.06
50 Albert Pujols	1.50	.45
51 Kirk Saarloos	.20	.06
52 Scott Eyre	.20	.06
53 John Flaherty	.20	.06
54 Rafael Soriano	.20	.06
55 Shea Hillenbrand	.30	.09
56 Kyle Farnsworth	.20	.06
57 Nate Cornejo	.20	.06
58 Julian Tavarez	.20	.06
59 Ryan Vogelsong	.20	.06
60 Ryan Klesko	.30	.09
61 Luke Hudson	.20	.06
62 Justin Morneau	.30	.09
63 Frank Catalanotto	.20	.06
64 Derrick Turnbow	.20	.06
65 Marcus Giles	.30	.09
66 Mark Mulder	.30	.09
67 Matt Anderson	.20	.06
68 Mike Matheny	.30	.09
69 Brian Lawrence	.20	.06
70 Bobby Abreu	.30	.09
71 Damian Moss	.20	.06
72 Richard Hidalgo	.20	.06
73 Mark Kotsay	.20	.06
74 Mike Cameron	.30	.09
75 Troy Glaus	.30	.09
76 Matt Holliday	.20	.06
77 Byung-Hyun Kim	.30	.09
78 Aaron Sele	.20	.06
79 Danny Graves	.20	.06
80 Barry Zito	.30	.09
81 Matt LeCroy	.20	.06
82 Jason Isringhausen	.30	.09
83 Colby Lewis	.20	.06
84 Franklyn German	.20	.06
85 Luis Matos	.20	.06
86 Mike Timlin	.20	.06
87 Miguel Batista	.20	.06
88 John McDonald	.20	.06
89 Joey Eischen	.20	.06
90 Mike Mussina	.50	.15
91 Jack Wilson	.30	.09
92 Aaron Cook	.20	.06
93 John Parrish	.20	.06
94 Jose Valentin	.20	.06
95 Johnny Damon	.75	.23
96 Pat Burrell	.30	.09
97 Brendan Donnelly	.20	.06
98 Lance Carter	.20	.06
99 Omar Daal	.20	.06
100 Ichiro Suzuki	1.25	.35
101 Robin Ventura	.30	.09
102 Brian Shouse	.20	.06
103 Kevin Jarvis	.20	.06
104 Jason Young	.20	.06
105 Moises Alou	.30	.09
106 Wes Obermueller	.20	.06
107 David Segui	.20	.06
108 Mike MacDougal	.20	.06
109 John Buck	.20	.06
110 Gary Sheffield	.30	.09
111 Yorvit Torrealba	.20	.06
112 Matt Kata	.20	.06
113 David Bell	.20	.06
114 Juan Gonzalez	.50	.15
115 Kelvim Escobar	.20	.06
116 Ruben Sierra	.30	.09
117 Todd Wellemeyer	.20	.06
118 Jamie Walker	.20	.06
119 Will Cunnane	.20	.06
120 Cliff Floyd	.30	.09
121 Aramis Ramirez	.30	.09
122 Damaso Marte	.20	.06
123 Juan Castro	.20	.06
124 Chris Woodward	.20	.06
125 Andruw Jones	.30	.09
126 Ben Weber	.20	.06
127 Dee Brown	.20	.06
128 Steve Reed	.20	.06
129 Gabe Kapler	.20	.06
130 Miguel Cabrera	.50	.15
131 Billy McMillon	.20	.06
132 Julio Mateo	.20	.06
133 Preston Wilson	.30	.09
134 Tony Clark	.20	.06
135 Carlos Lee	.30	.09
136 Carlos Baerga	.20	.06
137 Mike Crudale	.20	.06
138 David Ross	.20	.06
139 Josh Fogg	.20	.06
140 Dmitri Young	.30	.09
141 Cliff Lee	.20	.06
142 Mike Lowell	.30	.09
143 Jason Lane	.20	.06
144 Pedro Feliz	.20	.06
145 Ken Griffey Jr.	1.25	.35
146 Dustin Hermanson	.20	.06
147 Scott Hodges	.20	.06
148 Aquilino Lopez	.20	.06
149 Wes Helms	.20	.06
150 Jason Giambi	.30	.09
151 Erasmo Ramirez	.20	.06
152 Sean Burroughs	.30	.09
153 J.T. Snow	.30	.09
154 Eddie Guardado	.20	.06
155 C.C. Sabathia	.30	.09
156 Kyle Lohse	.20	.06
157 Roberto Hernandez	.20	.06
158 Jason Simontacchi	.20	.06
159 Tim Spooneybarger	.20	.06
160 Alfonso Soriano	.50	.15
161 Mike Gonzalez	.20	.06
162 Alex Cora	.20	.06
163 Kevin Gryboski	.20	.06
164 Mike Lincoln	.20	.06
165 Luis Castillo	.20	.06
166 Odalis Perez	.30	.09
167 Alex Sanchez	.20	.06
168 Rob Mackowiak	.20	.06
169 Francisco Rodriguez	.30	.09
170 Roy Oswalt	.30	.09
171 Omar Infante	.20	.06
172 Ryan Jensen	.20	.06
173 Ben Broussard	.20	.06
174 Mark Hendrickson	.20	.06
175 Manny Ramirez	.50	.15
176 Rob Bell	.20	.06
177 Adam Everett	.20	.06
178 Chris George	.20	.06
179 Ronnie Belliard	.20	.06
180 Eric Gagne	.75	.23
181 Scott Schoeneweis	.20	.06
182 Kris Benson	.20	.06
183 Amaury Telemaco	.20	.06
184 John Riedling	.20	.06
185 Juan Pierre	.30	.09
186 Ramon Ortiz	.20	.06
187 Luis Rivas	.20	.06
188 Larry Bigbie	.20	.06
189 Robby Hammock	.20	.06
190 Geoff Jenkins	.30	.09
191 Chad Cordero	.20	.06
192 Mark Ellis	.20	.06
193 Mark Loretta	.30	.09
194 Ryan Drese	.20	.06
195 Lance Berkman	.30	.09
196 Kevin Appier	.30	.09
197 Kiko Calero	.20	.06
198 Mickey Callaway	.20	.06
199 Chase Utley	.30	.09
200 Nomar Garciaparra	1.25	.35
201 Kevin Cash	.20	.06
202 Ramiro Mendoza	.20	.06
203 Shane Reynolds	.20	.06
204 Chris Spurling	.20	.06
205 Aaron Guiel	.20	.06
206 Mark DeRosa	.20	.06
207 Adam Kennedy	.20	.06
208 Andy Pettitte	.50	.15
209 Rafael Palmeiro	.50	.15
210 Luis Gonzalez	.30	.09
211 Ryan Franklin	.20	.06
212 Bob Wickman	.20	.06
213 Ron Calloway	.20	.06
214 Jae Weong Seo	.20	.06
215 Kazuhisa Ishii	.30	.09
216 Sterling Hitchcock	.20	.06
217 Jimmy Gobble	.20	.06
218 Chad Moeller	.20	.06
219 Jake Peavy	.30	.09
220 John Smoltz	.50	.15
221 Donovan Osborne	.20	.06
222 David Wells	.30	.09
223 Brad Lidge	.30	.09
224 Carlos Zambrano	.30	.09
225 Kerry Wood	.75	.23
226 Alex Cintron	.20	.06
227 Javier A. Lopez	.20	.06
228 Jeremy Griffiths	.20	.06
229 Jon Garland	.20	.06
230 Curt Schilling	.75	.23
231 Alex Scott Gonzalez	.20	.06
232 Jay Gibbons	.20	.06
233 Aaron Miles	.30	.09
234 Mike Gallo	.20	.06
235 Johan Santana	.50	.15
236 Jose Guillen	.30	.09
237 Jeff Conine	.30	.09
238 Matt Roney	.20	.06
239 Desi Relaford	.20	.06
240 Frank Thomas	.75	.23
241 Danny Patterson	.20	.06
242 Kevin Mench	.20	.06
243 Mike Redmond	.20	.06
244 Jeff Suppan	.20	.06
245 Carl Everett	.30	.09
246 Jack Cressend	.20	.06
247 Matt Mantei	.20	.06
248 Enrique Wilson	.20	.06
249 Craig Counsell	.20	.06
250 Mark Prior	.75	.23
251 Jared Sandberg	.20	.06
252 Scott Strickland	.20	.06
253 Lew Ford	.30	.09
254 Hee Seop Choi	.20	.06
255 Jason Phillips	.20	.06
256 Jason Jennings	.20	.06
257 Todd Pratt	.20	.06
258 Matt Herges	.20	.06
259 Kerry Ligtenberg	.20	.06
260 Austin Kearns	.30	.09
261 Jay Witasick	.20	.06
262 Tony Armas Jr.	.20	.06
263 Tom Martin	.20	.06
264 Oliver Perez	.30	.09
265 Jorge Posada	.50	.15
266 Jason Boyd	.20	.06
267 Ben Hendrickson	.20	.06
268 Reggie Sanders	.20	.06
269 Julio Lugo	.20	.06
270 Pedro Martinez	.75	.23
271 Kyle Snyder	.20	.06
272 Felipe Lopez	.20	.06
273 Kevin Millar	.30	.09
274 Travis Hafner	.30	.09
275 Magglio Ordonez	.30	.09
276 Marlon Byrd	.20	.06
277 Scott Spiezio	.20	.06
278 Mark Corey	.20	.06
279 Tim Salmon	.50	.15
280 Alex Gonzalez	.20	.06
281 Marquis Grissom	.30	.09
282 Miguel Olivo	.20	.06
283 Orlando Hudson	.20	.06
284 Rondell White	.30	.09
285 Jermaine Dye	.30	.09
286 Paul Shuey	.20	.06
287 Brandon Inge	.20	.06
288 B.J. Surhoff	.30	.09
289 Edgar Gonzalez	.20	.06
290 Angel Berroa	.20	.06
291 Claudio Vargas	.20	.06
292 Cesar Izturis	.20	.06
293 Brandon Phillips	.20	.06
294 Jeff Duncan	.20	.06
295 Randy Wolf	.20	.06
296 Barry Larkin	.50	.15
297 Felix Rodriguez	.20	.06
298 Robb Quinlan	.20	.06
299 Brian Jordan	.30	.09
300 Dontrelle Willis	.30	.09
301 Doug Davis	.20	.06
302 Ricky Stone	.20	.06
303 Travis Harper	.20	.06
304 Jaret Wright	.20	.06
305 Edgardo Alfonzo	.20	.06
306 Quinton McCracken	.20	.06
307 Jason Bay	.30	.09
308 Joe Randa	.20	.06
309 Steve Sparks	.20	.06
310 Roy Halladay	.20	.06
311 Antonio Alfonseca	.20	.06
312 Michael Cuddyer	.20	.06
313 John Patterson	.20	.06
314 Chris Widger	.20	.06
315 Shigetoshi Hasegawa	.30	.09
316 Tim Wakefield	.30	.09
317 Scott Hatteberg	.20	.06
318 Mike Remlinger	.20	.06
319 Jose Vizcaino	.20	.06
320 Rocco Baldelli	.30	.09
321 David Riske	.20	.06
322 Steve Karsay	.20	.06
323 Peter Bergeron	.20	.06
324 Jeff Weaver	.20	.06
325 Larry Walker	.50	.15
326 Jack Cust	.20	.06
327 Bo Hart	.20	.06
328 Rod Beck	.20	.06
329 Jose Acevedo	.20	.06
330 Hank Blalock	.30	.09
331 Tom Gordon	.20	.06
332 Brian Fuentes	.20	.06
333 Tomas Perez	.20	.06
334 Lenny Harris	.20	.06
335 Matt Morris	.30	.09
336 Jeremi Gonzalez	.20	.06
337 David Eckstein	.20	.06
338 Aaron Rowand	.30	.09
339 Rick Bauer	.20	.06
340 Jim Edmonds	.30	.09
341 Joe Borowski	.20	.06
342 Eric DuBose	.20	.06
343 D'Angelo Jimenez	.20	.06
344 Tomo Ohka	.20	.06
345 Victor Zambrano	.20	.06
346 Joe McEwing	.20	.06
347 Jorge Sosa	.20	.06
348 Keith Ginter	.20	.06
349 A.J. Pierzynski	.30	.09
350 Mike Sweeney	.30	.09
351 Shawn Chacon	.20	.06
352 Matt Clement	.20	.06
353 Vance Wilson	.20	.06
354 Benito Santiago	.30	.09
355 Eric Hinske	.20	.06
356 Vladimir Guerrero	.75	.23
357 Kenny Rogers	.30	.09
358 Travis Lee	.20	.06
359 Jay Powell	.20	.06
360 Phil Nevin	.30	.09
361 Willie Harris	.20	.06
362 Ty Wigginton	.20	.06
363 Chad Fox	.20	.06
364 Junior Spivey	.20	.06
365 Brandon Webb	.20	.06
366 Brett Myers	.20	.06
367 Alexis Gomez	.20	.06
368 Dave Roberts	.20	.06
369 LaTroy Hawkins	.20	.06
370 Kevin Millwood	.30	.09
371 Brian Schneider	.20	.06
372 Blaine Neal	.20	.06
373 Jeromy Burnitz	.30	.09
374 Ted Lilly	.20	.06
375 Shawn Green	.30	.09
376 Carlos Pena	.20	.06
377 Gil Meche	.20	.06
378 Jeff Bagwell	.50	.15
379 Alex Escobar	.20	.06
380 Erubiel Durazo	.20	.06
381 Cristian Guzman	.20	.06
382 Rocky Biddle	.20	.06
383 Craig Wilson	.30	.09
384 Rey Sanchez	.20	.06
385 Russ Ortiz	.30	.09
386 Freddy Garcia	.30	.09
387 Luis Vizcaino	.20	.06
388 David Ortiz	.75	.23
389 Jose Molina	.20	.06
390 Edgar Martinez	.50	.15
391 Nate Bump	.20	.06
392 Brent Mayne	.20	.06
393 Ray King	.20	.06
394 Paul Wilson	.20	.06
395 Melvin Mora	.30	.09
396 Morgan Ensberg	.20	.06
397 Ramon Hernandez	.20	.06
398 Juan Rincon	.20	.06
399 Ron Mahay	.20	.06
400 Jeff Kent	.30	.09
401 Cal Eldred	.20	.06
402 Mike Difelice	.20	.06
403 Valerio De Los Santos	.20	.06
404 Steve Finley	.30	.09
405 Trot Nixon	.30	.09
406 Akinori Otsuka RC	.40	.12
407 Ryan Freel	.20	.06
408 Ray Durham	.30	.09
409 Aaron Heilman	.20	.06
410 Edgar Renteria	.30	.09
411 Mike Hampton	.30	.09
412 Kirk Rueter	.20	.06
413 Jim Mecir	.20	.06
414 Brian Roberts	.20	.06
415 Paul Konerko	.30	.09
416 Reed Johnson	.20	.06
417 Roger Clemens	1.50	.45
418 Coco Crisp	.20	.06
419 Carlos Hernandez	.20	.06
420 Scott Podsednik	.30	.09
421 Miguel Cairo	.20	.06
422 Abraham Nunez	.20	.06
423 Endy Chavez	.20	.06
424 Eric Munson	.20	.06
425 Torii Hunter	.30	.09
426 Ben Howard	.20	.06
427 Chris Gomez	.20	.06
428 Francisco Cordero	.20	.06
429 Jeffrey Hammonds	.20	.06
430 Shannon Stewart	.30	.09
431 Einar Diaz	.20	.06
432 Eric Byrnes	.20	.06
433 Marty Cordova	.20	.06
434 Matt Ginter	.20	.06
435 Victor Martinez	.30	.0
436 Geronimo Gil	.20	.0

437 Grant Balfour .20 .06
438 Ramon Vazquez .20 .06
439 Jose Cruz Jr. .20 .06
440 Orlando Cabrera .30 .09
441 Joe Kennedy .20 .06
442 Scott Williamson .20 .06
443 Troy Percival .30 .09
444 Derrek Lee .30 .09
445 Runelvys Hernandez .20 .06
446 Mark Grudzielanek .20 .06
447 Trey Hodges .20 .06
448 Jimmy Haynes .20 .06
449 Eric Milton .30 .09
450 Todd Helton .50 .15
451 Greg Zaun .20 .06
452 Woody Williams .20 .06
453 Todd Walker .20 .06
454 Juan Cruz .20 .06
455 Fernando Vina .20 .06
456 Omar Vizquel .50 .15
457 Roberto Alomar .50 .15
458 Bill Hall .20 .06
459 Juan Rivera .20 .06
460 Tom Glavine .50 .15
461 Ramon Castro .20 .06
462 Cory Vance .20 .06
463 Dan Miceli .20 .06
464 Lyle Overbay .30 .09
465 Craig Biggio .50 .15
466 Ricky Ledee .20 .06
467 Michael Barrett .20 .06
468 Jason Anderson .20 .06
469 Matt Stairs .20 .06
470 Jarrod Washburn .20 .06
471 Todd Hundley .20 .06
472 Grant Roberts .20 .06
473 Randy Winn .20 .06
474 Pat Hentgen .20 .06
475 Jose Vidro .20 .06
476 Tony Torcato .20 .06
477 Jeremy Affeldt .20 .06
478 Carlos Guillen .30 .09
479 Paul Quantrill .20 .06
480 Rafael Furcal .30 .09
481 Adam Melhuse .20 .06
482 Jerry Hairston Jr. .20 .06
483 Adam Bernero .20 .06
484 Terrence Long .30 .09
485 Paul Lo Duca .30 .09
486 Corey Koskie .30 .09
487 John Lackey .20 .06
488 Chad Zerbe .20 .06
489 Vinny Castilla .30 .09
490 Corey Patterson .30 .09
491 John Olerud .30 .09
492 Josh Bard .20 .06
493 Darren Dreifort .20 .06
494 Jason Standridge .20 .06
495 Ben Sheets .30 .09
496 Jose Castillo .20 .06
497 Jay Payton .20 .06
498 Rob Bowen .20 .06
499 Bobby Higginson .30 .09
500 Alex Rodriguez Yanks 1.25 .35
501 Octavio Dotel .20 .06
502 Rheal Cormier .20 .06
503 Felix Heredia .20 .06
504 Dan Wright .20 .06
505 Michael Young .30 .09
506 Wilfredo Ledezma .20 .06
507 Sun Woo Kim .20 .06
508 Michael Tejera .20 .06
509 Herbert Perry .20 .06
510 Esteban Loaiza .20 .06
511 Alan Embree .20 .06
512 Ben Davis .20 .06
513 Greg Colbrunn .20 .06
514 Josh Hall .20 .06
515 Raul Ibanez .20 .06
516 Jason Kershner .20 .06
517 Corky Miller .20 .06
518 Jason Marquis .20 .06
519 Roger Cedeno .20 .06
520 Adam Dunn .50 .15
521 Paul Byrd .20 .06
522 Sandy Alomar Jr. .20 .06
523 Salomon Torres .20 .06
524 John Halama .20 .06
525 Mike Piazza 1.25 .35
526 Buddy Groom .20 .06
527 Adrian Beltre .50 .15
528 Chad Harville .20 .06
529 Javier Vazquez .30 .09
530 Jody Gerut .20 .06
531 Elmer Dessens .20 .06
532 B.J. Ryan .20 .06
533 Chad Durbin .20 .06
534 Doug Mirabelli .20 .06
535 Bernie Williams .50 .15
536 Jeff DaVanon .20 .06
537 Dave Berg .20 .06
538 Geoff Blum .20 .06
539 John Thomson .20 .06
540 Jeremy Bonderman .20 .06
541 Jeff Zimmerman .20 .06
542 Derek Lowe .30 .09
543 Scot Shields .20 .06
544 Michael Tucker .20 .06
545 Tim Hudson .30 .09
546 Ryan Ludwick .20 .06
547 Rick Reed .20 .06
548 Placido Polanco .20 .06
549 Tony Graffanino .20 .06
550 Garret Anderson .30 .09
551 Timo Perez .20 .06
552 Jesus Colome .20 .06
553 R.A. Dickey .20 .06
554 Tim Worrell .20 .06
555 Jason Kendall .30 .09
556 Tom Goodwin .20 .06
557 Joaquin Benoit .20 .06
558 Stephen Randolph .20 .06
559 Miguel Tejada .30 .09
560 A.J. Burnett .20 .06
561 Ben Diggins .20 .06
562 Kent Mercker .20 .06
563 Zach Day .20 .06
564 Antonio Perez .20 .06
565 Jason Schmidt .30 .09
566 Armando Benitez .30 .09
567 Denny Neagle .20 .06
568 Eric Eckenstahler .20 .06
569 Chan Ho Park .30 .09
570 Carlos Beltran .50 .15
571 Brett Tomko .20 .06
572 Henry Mateo .20 .06
573 Ken Harvey .20 .06
574 Matt Lawton .20 .06
575 Mariano Rivera .50 .15
576 Darrell May .20 .06
577 Jamie Moyer .30 .09
578 Paul Bako .20 .06
579 Cory Lidle .20 .06
580 Jacque Jones .30 .09
581 Jolbert Cabrera .20 .06
582 Jason Grimsley .20 .06
583 Danny Kolb .20 .06
584 Billy Wagner .30 .09
585 Rich Aurilia .20 .06
586 Vicente Padilla .20 .06
587 Oscar Villarreal .20 .06
588 Rene Reyes .20 .06
589 Jon Lieber .20 .06
590 Nick Johnson .20 .06
591 Bobby Crosby .50 .15
592 Steve Trachsel .20 .06
593 Brian Boehringer .20 .06
594 Juan Uribe .20 .06
595 Bartolo Colon .30 .09
596 Bobby Hill .20 .06
597 Chris Shelton RC .75 .23
598 Carl Pavano .30 .09
599 Kurt Ainsworth .20 .06
600 Derek Jeter 1.50 .45
601 Doug Mientkiewicz .30 .09
602 Orlando Palmeiro .20 .06
603 J.C. Romero .20 .06
604 Scott Sullivan .20 .06
605 Brad Radke .30 .09
606 Fernando Rodney .20 .06
607 Jim Brower .20 .06
608 Josh Towers .20 .06
609 Brad Fullmer .30 .09
610 Jose Reyes .30 .09
611 Ryan Wagner .20 .06
612 Joe Mays .20 .06
613 Jung Bong .20 .06
614 Curtis Leskanic .20 .06
615 Al Leiter .30 .09
616 Wade Miller .30 .09
617 Keith Foulke Sox .50 .15
618 Casey Fossum .20 .06
619 Craig Monroe .30 .09
620 Hideo Nomo .75 .23
621 Bob File .20 .06
622 Steve Kline .20 .06
623 Bobby Kielty .20 .06
624 Dewon Brazelton .20 .06
625 Eric Chavez .30 .09
626 Chris Carpenter .20 .06
627 Alexis Rios .30 .09
628 Jason Davis .20 .06
629 Jose Jimenez .20 .06
630 Vernon Wells .30 .09
631 Kenny Lofton .30 .09
632 Chad Bradford .20 .06
633 Brad Wilkerson .20 .06
634 Pokey Reese .20 .06
635 Richie Sexson .30 .09
636 Chin-Hui Tsao .30 .09
637 Eli Marrero .20 .06
638 Chris Reitsma .20 .06
639 Daryle Ward .20 .06
640 Mark Teixeira .30 .09
641 Corwin Malone .20 .06
642 Adam Eaton .20 .06
643 Jimmy Rollins .30 .09
644 Brian Anderson .20 .06
645 Bill Mueller .30 .09
646 Jake Westbrook .20 .06
647 Bengie Molina .20 .06
648 Jorge Julio .20 .06
649 Billy Traber .20 .06
650 Randy Johnson .75 .23
651 Javy Lopez .30 .09
652 Doug Glanville .20 .06
653 Jeff Cirillo .20 .06
654 Tino Martinez .50 .15
655 Mark Buehrle .30 .09
656 Jason Michaels .20 .06
657 Damian Rolls .20 .06
658 Rosman Garcia .20 .06
659 Scott Hairston .30 .09
660 Carl Crawford .30 .09
661 Livan Hernandez .20 .06
662 Danny Bautista .20 .06
663 Brad Ausmus .20 .06
664 Juan Acevedo .20 .06
665 Sean Casey .30 .09
666 Josh Beckett .30 .09
667 Milton Bradley .30 .09
668 Braden Looper .20 .06
669 Paul Abbott .20 .06
670 Joel Pineiro .20 .06
671 Luis Terrero .20 .06
672 Rodrigo Lopez .20 .06
673 Joe Crede .20 .06
674 Mike Koplove .20 .06
675 Brian Giles .30 .09
676 Jeff Nelson .20 .06
677 Russell Branyan .20 .06
678 Mike DeJean .20 .06
679 Brian Daubach .20 .06
680 Ellis Burks .30 .09
681 Ryan Dempster .20 .06
682 Cliff Politte .20 .06
683 Brian Reith .20 .06
684 Scott Stewart .20 .06
685 Allan Simpson .20 .06
686 Shawn Estes .20 .06
687 Jason Johnson .20 .06
688 Wil Cordero .20 .06
689 Kelly Stinnett .20 .06
690 Jose Lima .20 .06
691 Gary Bennett .20 .06
692 T.J. Tucker .20 .06
693 Shane Spencer .20 .06
694 Chris Hammond .20 .06
695 Raul Mondesi .30 .09
696 Xavier Nady .20 .06
697 Cody Ransom .20 .06
698 Ron Villone .20 .06
699 Brook Fordyce .20 .06
700 Sammy Sosa 1.25 .35
701 Terry Adams .20 .06
702 Ricardo Rincon .20 .06
703 Tike Redman .20 .06
704 Chris Stynes .20 .06
705 Mark Redman .20 .06
706 Juan Encarnacion .20 .06
707 Jhonny Peralta .30 .09
708 Denny Hocking .20 .06
709 Ivan Rodriguez .75 .23
710 Jose Hernandez .20 .06
711 Brandon Duckworth .20 .06
712 Dave Burba .20 .06
713 Joe Nathan .20 .06
714 Dan Smith .20 .06
715 Karim Garcia .20 .06
716 Arthur Rhodes .20 .06
717 Shawn Wooten .20 .06
718 Ramon Santiago .20 .06
719 Luis Ugueto .20 .06
720 Danys Baez .20 .06
721 Alfredo Amezaga PROS .20 .06
722 Sidney Ponson .20 .06
723 Joe Mauer PROS .50 .15
724 Jesse Foppert PROS .20 .06
725 Todd Greene .20 .06
726 Dan Haren PROS .20 .06
727 Brandon Larson PROS .20 .06
728 Bobby Jenks PROS .20 .06
729 Grady Sizemore PROS .30 .09
730 Ben Grieve .20 .06
731 Khalil Greene PROS .75 .23
732 Chad Gaudin PROS .20 .06
733 Johnny Estrada PROS .20 .06
734 Joe Valentine PROS .20 .06
735 Tim Raines Jr. PROS .20 .06
736 Brandon Claussen PROS .20 .06
737 Sam Marsonek PROS .20 .06
738 Delmon Young PROS .50 .15
739 David Dellucci .20 .06
740 Sergio Mitre PROS .20 .06
741 Nick Neugebauer PROS .20 .06
742 Laynce Nix PROS .30 .09
743 Joe Thurston PROS .20 .06
744 Ryan Langerhans PROS .20 .06
745 Pete LaForest PROS .20 .06
746 Arnie Munoz PROS .20 .06
747 Rickie Weeks PROS .30 .09
748 Neal Cotts PROS .20 .06
749 Jonny Gomes PROS .20 .06
750 Jim Thome .75 .23
751 Jon Rauch PROS .20 .06
752 Edwin Jackson PROS .30 .09
753 Ryan Madson PROS .20 .06
754 Andrew Good PROS .20 .06
755 Eddie Perez .20 .06
756 Joe Borchard PROS .20 .06
757 Jeremy Guthrie PROS .20 .06
758 Jose Mesa .20 .06
759 Doug Waechter PROS .20 .06
760 J.D. Drew .30 .09
761 Adam LaRoche PROS .20 .06
762 Rich Harden PROS .30 .09
763 Justin Speier .20 .06
764 Todd Zeile .20 .06
765 Turk Wendell .20 .06
766 Mark Bellhorn Sox .50 .15
767 Mike Jackson .20 .06
768 Chone Figgins .20 .06
769 Mike Neu .20 .06
770 Greg Maddux 1.25 .35
771 Frank Menechino .20 .06
772 Alec Zumwalt RC .25 .07
773 Eric Young .20 .06
774 Dustan Mohr .20 .06
775 Shane Halter .20 .06
776 Brian Buchanan .20 .06
777 So Taguchi .30 .09
778 Eric Karros .30 .09
779 Ramon Nivar .20 .06
780 Marlon Anderson .20 .06
781 Brayan Pena FY RC .40 .12
782 Chris O'Riordan FY RC .40 .12
783 Dioner Navarro FY RC 1.25 .35
784 Alberto Callaspo FY RC .75 .23
785 Hector Gimenez FY RC .25 .07
786 Yadier Molina FY RC 1.00 .30
787 Kevin Richardson FY RC .25 .07
788 Brian Pilkington FY RC .40 .12
789 Adam Greenberg FY RC .50 .15
790 Ervin Santana FY RC 1.25 .35
791 Brant Colamarino FY RC .75 .23
792 Ben Himes FY RC .25 .07
793 Todd Self FY RC .40 .12
794 Brad Vericker FY RC .40 .12
795 Donald Kelly FY RC .40 .12
796 Brock Jacobsen FY RC .25 .07
797 Brock Peterson FY RC .40 .12
798 Carlos Sosa FY RC .40 .12
799 Chad Chop FY RC .40 .12
800 Matt Moses FY RC 1.00 .30
801 Chris Aguila FY RC .40 .12
802 David Murphy FY RC 1.00 .30
803 Don Sutton FY RC 1.00 .30
804 Jereme Milons FY RC .40 .12
805 Jon Coutlangus FY RC .25 .07
806 Greg Thissen FY RC .40 .12
807 Jose Capellan FY RC 1.50 .45
808 Chad Santos FY RC .40 .12
809 Wardell Starling FY RC .40 .12
810 Kevin Kouzmanoff FY RC .75 .23
811 Kevin Davidson FY RC .25 .07
812 Michael Mooney FY RC .40 .12
813 Rodney Choy Foo FY RC .25 .07
814 Reid Gorecki FY RC .40 .12
815 Rudy Guillen FY RC 1.00 .30
816 Harvey Garcia FY RC .25 .07
817 Warner Madrigal FY RC .75 .23
818 Kenny Perez FY RC .40 .12
819 Joaquin Arias FY RC .40 .12
820 Benji DeQuin FY RC .25 .07
821 Lastings Milledge FY RC 2.00 .60
822 Blake Hawksworth FY RC .50 .15
823 Estee Harris FY RC .40 .12
824 Bobby Brownlie FY RC .75 .23
825 Wanell Severino FY RC .25 .07
826 Bobby Madritsch FY .75 .23
827 Travis Hanson FY RC .40 .12
828 Brandon Medders FY RC .25 .07
829 Kevin Howard FY RC .50 .15
830 Brian Steffek FY RC .25 .07
831 Terry Jones FY RC .50 .15
832 Anthony Acevedo FY RC .40 .12
833 Kory Casto FY RC .40 .12
834 Brooks Conrad FY RC UER .40 .12
Anthony Acevedo Pictured on front
835 Juan Gutierrez FY RC .40 .12
836 Charlie Zink FY RC .25 .07
837 David Aardsma FY RC .40 .12
838 Carl Loadenthal FY RC .50 .15
839 Donald Levinski FY RC .25 .07
840 Dustin Nippert FY RC .40 .12
841 Calvin Hayes FY RC .50 .15
842 Felix Hernandez FY RC 3.00 .90
843 Tyler Davidson FY RC .50 .15
844 George Sherrill FY RC .40 .12
845 Craig Ansman FY RC .40 .12
846 Jeff Allison FY RC .50 .15
847 Tommy Murphy FY RC .40 .12
848 Jerome Gamble FY RC .25 .07
849 Jesse English FY RC .40 .12
850 Alex Romero FY RC .40 .12
851 Joel Zumaya FY RC .75 .23
852 Carlos Quentin FY RC 2.00 .60
853 Jose Valdez FY RC .40 .12
854 J.J. Furmaniak FY RC .75 .23
855 Juan Cedeno FY RC .40 .12
856 Kyle Sleeth FY RC 1.00 .30
857 Josh Labandeira FY RC .40 .12
858 Lee Gwaltney FY RC .25 .07
859 Lincoln Holdzkom FY RC .40 .12
860 Ivan Ochoa FY RC .40 .12
861 Luke Anderson FY RC .25 .07
862 Conor Jackson FY RC 2.00 .60
863 Matt Capps FY RC .40 .12
864 Merkin Valdez FY RC 1.00 .30
865 Paul Bacot FY RC .50 .15
866 Erick Aybar FY RC 1.25 .35
867 Scott Proctor FY RC .50 .15
868 Tim Stauffer FY RC .75 .23
869 Matt Creighton FY RC .40 .12
870 Zach Miner FY RC .50 .15
871 Danny Gonzalez FY RC .25 .07
872 Tom Farmer FY RC .25 .07
873 John Santor FY RC .40 .12
874 Logan Kensing FY RC .40 .12
875 Vito Chiaravalloti FY RC .75 .23
876 Checklist .20 .06
877 Checklist .20 .06
878 Checklist .20 .06
879 Checklist .20 .06
880 Checklist .20 .06

2004 Topps Total Parallel

Nm-Mt Ex-Mt
*PARALLEL: 1X TO 2.5X BASIC
*PARALLEL RC's: 1X TO 2.5X BASIC RC's
ONE PER PACK

2004 Topps Total Award Winners

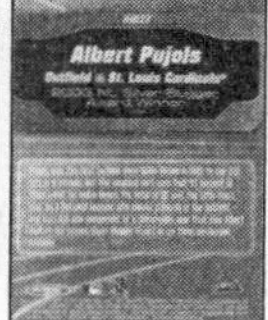

Nm-Mt Ex-Mt
COMPLETE SET (30) 30.00 9.00
STATED ODDS 1:12
OVERALL PRESS PLATES ODDS 1:159
PLATES PRINT RUN 1 #'d SET PER COLOR
PLATES: BLACK, CYAN, MAGENTA & YELLOW
NO PLATES PRICING DUE TO SCARCITY
AW1 Roy Halladay CY .75 .23
AW2 Eric Gagne CY 2.00 .60
AW3 Alex Rodriguez MVP 3.00 .90
AW4 Albert Pujols POY 4.00 1.20
AW5 Alex Rodriguez POY 3.00 .90
AW6 Jorge Posada SS 1.25 .35
AW7 Javy Lopez SS .75 .23
AW8 Carlos Delgado SS .75 .23
AW9 Todd Helton SS 1.25 .35
AW10 Bret Boone SS .75 .23
AW11 Jose Vidro SS .75 .23
AW12 Bill Mueller SS .75 .23
AW13 Mike Lowell SS .75 .23
AW14 Alex Rodriguez SS 3.00 .90
AW15 Edgar Renteria SS .75 .23
AW16 Garret Anderson SS .75 .23
AW17 Albert Pujols SS 4.00 1.20
AW18 Manny Ramirez SS 1.25 .35
AW19 Vernon Wells SS .75 .23
AW20 Gary Sheffield SS .75 .23
AW21 Edgar Martinez SS 1.25 .35
AW22 Mike Hampton SS .75 .23
AW23 Angel Berroa ROY .75 .23
AW24 Dontrelle Willis ROY .75 .23
AW25 Keith Foulke Rolaids .75 .23
AW26 Eric Gagne Rolaids 2.00 .60
AW27 Alex Rodriguez HA 3.00 .90
AW28 Albert Pujols HA 4.00 1.20
AW29 Tony Pena MG .75 .23
AW30 Jack McKeon MG .75 .23

2004 Topps Total Production

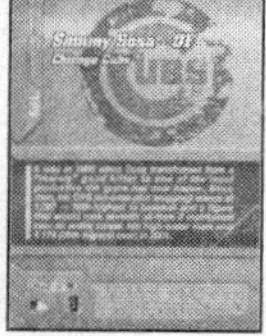

Nm-Mt Ex-Mt
COMPLETE SET (10) 15.00 4.50
STATED ODDS 1:18
OVERALL PRESS PLATES ODDS 1:159
PLATES PRINT RUN 1 #'d SET PER COLOR
PLATES: BLACK, CYAN, MAGENTA & YELLOW
NO PLATES PRICING DUE TO SCARCITY
TP1 Alex Rodriguez 3.00 .90
TP2 Albert Pujols 4.00 1.20
TP3 Sammy Sosa 3.00 .90
TP4 Carlos Delgado .75 .23
TP5 Gary Sheffield .75 .23
TP6 Manny Ramirez 1.25 .35
TP7 Jim Thome 2.00 .60
TP8 Todd Helton 1.25 .35
TP9 Garret Anderson .75 .23
TP10 Nomar Garciaparra 3.00 .90

2004 Topps Total Signatures

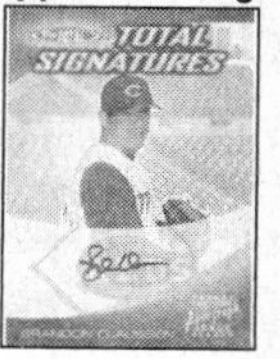

Nm-Mt Ex-Mt
STATED ODDS 1:414
BC Brandon Claussen 10.00 3.00
GB Grant Balfour 10.00 3.00
JJ Jimmy Journell 10.00 3.00
LB Larry Bigbie 15.00 4.50
TB Toby Hall 10.00 3.00

2004 Topps Total Team Checklists

Nm-Mt Ex-Mt
COMPLETE SET (30) 15.00 4.50
STATED ODDS 1:4
OVERALL PRESS PLATES ODDS 1:159
PLATES PRINT RUN 1 #'d SET PER COLOR
PLATES: BLACK, CYAN, MAGENTA & YELLOW
NO PLATES PRICING DUE TO SCARCITY
TTC1 Garret Anderson .30 .09
TTC2 Randy Johnson .75 .23
TTC3 Chipper Jones .75 .23
TTC4 Miguel Tejada .30 .09
TTC5 Nomar Garciaparra 1.25 .35
TTC6 Mark Prior .75 .23
TTC7 Magglio Ordonez .30 .09
TTC8 Ken Griffey Jr. 1.25 .35
TTC9 C.C. Sabathia .30 .09
TTC10 Todd Helton .50 .15
TTC11 Ivan Rodriguez .75 .23
TTC12 Dontrelle Willis .30 .09
TTC13 Roger Clemens 1.50 .45
TTC14 Mike Sweeney .30 .09
TTC15 Shawn Green .30 .09
TTC16 Geoff Jenkins .30 .09
TTC17 Torii Hunter .30 .09
TTC18 Jose Vidro .30 .09
TTC19 Mike Piazza 1.25 .35
TTC20 Alex Rodriguez 2.00 .60
TTC21 Eric Chavez .30 .09
TTC22 Jim Thome .75 .23
TTC23 Jason Kendall .30 .09
TTC24 Brian Giles .30 .09
TTC25 Jason Schmidt .30 .09
TTC26 Ichiro Suzuki 1.25 .35
TTC27 Albert Pujols 1.50 .45
TTC28 Aubrey Huff .30 .09
TTC29 Hank Blalock .30 .09
TTC30 Carlos Delgado .30 .09

2004 Topps Total Topps

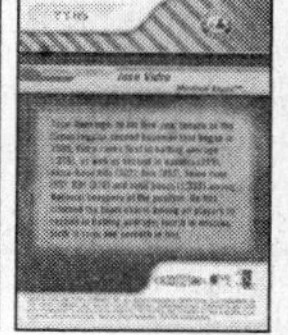

Nm-Mt Ex-Mt
COMPLETE SET (50) 50.00 15.00
STATED ODDS 1:7
OVERALL PRESS PLATES ODDS 1:159
PLATES PRINT RUN 1 SERIAL #'d SET
NO PLATES PRICING DUE TO SCARCITY
TT1 Derek Jeter 4.00 1.20
TT2 Jose Reyes .75 .23
TT3 Miguel Tejada .75 .23
TT4 Larry Walker 1.25 .35
TT5 Frank Thomas 2.00 .60
TT6 Carlos Delgado .75 .23
TT7 Vernon Wells .75 .23
TT8 Jeff Bagwell 1.25 .35
TT9 Jason Giambi .75 .23
TT10 Mike Lowell .75 .23
TT11 Shannon Stewart .75 .23
TT12 Mike Piazza 3.00 .90
TT13 Todd Helton 1.25 .35
TT14 Austin Kearns .75 .23
TT15 Jim Edmonds .75 .23
TT16 Jose Vidro .75 .23

Card	Nm-Mt	Ex-Mt
TT17 Andruw Jones	.75	.23
TT18 Gary Sheffield	.75	.23
TT19 Eric Chavez	.75	.23
TT20 Magglio Ordonez	.75	.23
TT21 Geoff Jenkins	.75	.23
TT22 Ken Griffey Jr.	3.00	.90
TT23 Jeff Kent	.75	.23
TT24 Jorge Posada	1.25	.35
TT25 Albert Pujols	4.00	1.20
TT26 Javy Lopez	.75	.23
TT27 Alfonso Soriano	1.25	.35
TT28 Brian Giles	.75	.23
TT29 Mike Sweeney	.75	.23
TT30 Miguel Cabrera	1.25	.35
TT31 Luis Gonzalez	.75	.23
TT32 Scott Rolen	2.00	.60
TT33 Jim Thome	2.00	.60
TT34 Garret Anderson	.75	.23
TT35 Vladimir Guerrero	2.00	.60
TT36 Shawn Green	.75	.23
TT37 Hank Blalock	.75	.23
TT38 Marcus Giles	.75	.23
TT39 Torii Hunter	.75	.23
TT40 Sammy Sosa	3.00	.90
TT41 Nomar Garciaparra	3.00	.90
TT42 Bobby Abreu	.75	.23
TT43 Richie Sexson	.75	.23
TT44 Manny Ramirez	1.25	.35
TT45 Troy Glaus	.75	.23
TT46 Preston Wilson	.75	.23
TT47 Ivan Rodriguez	2.00	.60
TT48 Ichiro Suzuki	3.00	.90
TT49 Chipper Jones	2.00	.60
TT50 Alex Rodriguez	5.00	1.50

2001 Topps Tribute

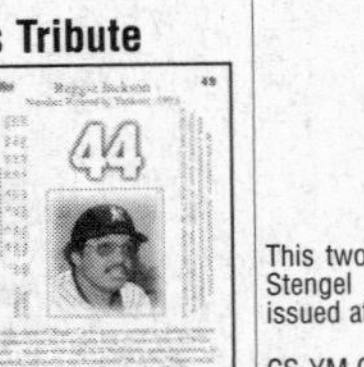

This hobby-only product was released in mid-December 2001, and featured a 90-card base set that honors Hall of Fame caliber players like Babe Ruth and Mickey Mantle. Each pack contained four-cards, and carried a suggested retail price of 40.00.

	Nm-Mt	Ex-Mt
COMPLETE SET (90)	250.00	75.00
1 Pee Wee Reese	6.00	1.80
2 Babe Ruth	20.00	6.00
3 Ralph Kiner	5.00	1.50
4 Brooks Robinson	5.00	1.50
5 Don Sutton	5.00	1.50
6 Carl Yastrzemski	10.00	3.00
7 Roger Maris	6.00	1.80
8 Andre Dawson	5.00	1.50
9 Luis Aparicio	5.00	1.50
10 Wade Boggs	5.00	1.50
11 Johnny Bench	6.00	1.80
12 Ernie Banks	6.00	1.80
13 Thurman Munson	6.00	1.80
14 Harmon Killebrew	6.00	1.80
15 Ted Kluszewski	5.00	1.50
16 Bob Feller	5.00	1.50
17 Mike Schmidt	12.00	3.60
18 Warren Spahn	5.00	1.50
19 Jim Palmer	5.00	1.50
20 Don Mattingly	15.00	4.50
21 Willie Mays	12.00	3.60
22 Gil Hodges	6.00	1.80
23 Juan Marichal	5.00	1.50
24 Robin Yount	10.00	3.00
25 Nolan Ryan Angels	15.00	4.50
26 Dave Winfield	5.00	1.50
27 Hank Greenberg	6.00	1.80
28 Honus Wagner	8.00	2.40
29 Nolan Ryan Rangers	15.00	4.50
30 Phil Niekro	5.00	1.50
31 Robin Roberts	5.00	1.50
32 Casey Stengel Yankees	5.00	1.50
33 Willie McCovey	5.00	1.50
34 Roy Campanella	6.00	1.80
35 Rollie Fingers A's	5.00	1.50
36 Tom Seaver	5.00	1.50
37 Jackie Robinson	6.00	1.80
38 Hank Aaron Braves	12.00	3.60
39 Bob Gibson	5.00	1.50
40 Carlton Fisk Red Sox	5.00	1.50
41 Hank Aaron Brewers	12.00	3.60
42 George Brett	15.00	4.50
43 Orlando Cepeda	5.00	1.50
44 Red Schoendienst	5.00	1.50
45 Don Drysdale	6.00	1.80
46 Mel Ott	6.00	1.80
47 Casey Stengel Mets	6.00	1.80
48 Al Kaline	6.00	1.80
49 Reggie Jackson	6.00	1.80
50 Tony Perez	5.00	1.50
51 Ozzie Smith	10.00	3.00
52 Billy Martin	5.00	1.50
53 Bill Dickey	5.00	1.50
54 Catfish Hunter	5.00	1.50
55 Duke Snider	5.00	1.50
56 Dale Murphy	6.00	1.80
57 Bobby Doerr	5.00	1.50
58 Earl Averill UER	5.00	1.50
Card pictures Earl Averill Jr.		
59 Carlton Fisk White Sox	5.00	1.50
60 Tom Lasorda	5.00	1.50
61 Lou Gehrig	12.00	3.60
62 Enos Slaughter	5.00	1.50
63 Jim Bunning	5.00	1.50
64 Rollie Fingers Brewers	5.00	1.50
65 Frank Robinson Reds	5.00	1.50
66 Earl Weaver	5.00	1.50
67 Eddie Mathews	6.00	1.80
68 Kirby Puckett	6.00	1.80
69 Phil Rizzuto	6.00	1.80
70 Lou Brock	5.00	1.50
71 Walt Alston	5.00	1.50
72 Billy Pierce	5.00	1.50
73 Joe Morgan	5.00	1.50
74 Roberto Clemente	15.00	4.50
75 Whitey Ford	5.00	1.50
76 Richie Ashburn	5.00	1.50
77 Elston Howard	5.00	1.50
78 Gary Carter	5.00	1.50
79 Carl Hubbell	5.00	1.50
80 Yogi Berra	6.00	1.80
81 Ken Boyer	5.00	1.50
82 Nolan Ryan Astros	15.00	4.50
83 Bill Mazeroski	5.00	1.50
84 Dizzy Dean	6.00	1.80
85 Nellie Fox	5.00	1.50
86 Stan Musial	10.00	3.00
87 Steve Carlton	5.00	1.50
88 Willie Stargell	5.00	1.50
89 Hal Newhouser	5.00	1.50
90 Frank Robinson Orioles	5.00	1.50
NNO Mickey Mantle PSA Redemption		
NNO Mickey Mantle Buyback EXCH		
NNO Jackie Robinson Buyback EXCH		
NNO Ted Williams Buyback EXCH		

2001 Topps Tribute Dual Relics

This two-card set features relic cards of Casey Stengel and Frank Robinson. Each card was issued at 1:860 packs.

	Nm-Mt	Ex-Mt
CS-YM Casey Stengel	120.00	36.00
FR-RO Frank Robinson	120.00	36.00

2001 Topps Tribute Franchise Figures Relics

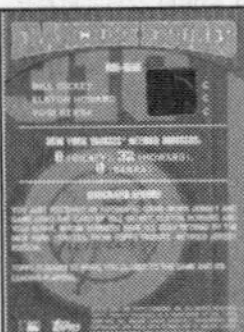

This 19-card set features relic cards of franchise players from teams past. Please note that these cards were broken into two groups: Group A were inserted at a rate of 1:106, while, Group B were inserted at 1:34. Card backs carry a "RM" prefix.

	Nm-Mt	Ex-Mt
AL Walt Alston Jsy Tommy Lasorda Jsy A	80.00	24.00
CD Gary Carter Andre Dawson B	80.00	24.00
FY Carlton Fisk Carl Yastrzemski A	150.00	45.00
JM Reggie Jackson Billy Martin A	200.00	60.00
KG Al Kaline Hank Greenberg A	150.00	45.00
MM Thurman Munson Jsy Don Mattingly Jsy A	250.00	75.00
PK Kirby Puckett Harmon Killebrew A	120.00	36.00
RG Babe Ruth Lou Gehrig A	800.00	240.00
RR Brooks Robinson Bat Frank Robinson Uni A	120.00	36.00
AFF Luis Aparicio Nellie Fox Carlton Fisk A	120.00	36.00
HDB Bill Dickey Jsy Elston Howard Bat Yogi Berra Jsy A	200.00	60.00
HSS Gil Hodges Casey Stengel Tom Seaver A	150.00	45.00
MCS Bill Mazeroski Roberto Clemente Willie Stargell A	250.00	75.00
MMA Dale Murphy Eddie Mathews Hank Aaron A	200.00	60.00
MMC Willie Mays Jsy Willie McCovey Bat Orlando Cepeda Jsy A	200.00	60.00
RSC Pee Wee Reese Duke Snider Roy Campanella A	200.00	60.00
SAC Mike Schmidt Jsy Richie Ashburn Bat Steve Carlton Uni A	150.00	45.00
BPKRM Johnny Bench Tony Perez Ted Kluszewski Frank Robinson Joe Morgan A	150.00	45.00
SBSM Ozzie Smith Lou Brock Red Schoendienst Stan Musial A	150.00	45.00

2001 Topps Tribute Game Bat Relics

This 31-card set features bat relic cards of classic players like George Brett and Hank Aaron.

Please note that these cards were broken into two groups: Group 1 were inserted at a rate of 1:2, while, Group 2 were inserted at 1:35. Card backs carry a "RB" prefix.

	Nm-Mt	Ex-Mt
BAT LOGO AND STENCIL CUT-OUT SAME QTY		
BAT LOGO AND STENCIL CUT-OUT SAME VALUE		
RBAK Al Kaline 1	30.00	9.00
RBBM Billy Martin 1	30.00	9.00
RBBR Babe Ruth 2	200.00	60.00
RBBRO B.Robinson 1	30.00	9.00
RBCFR C.Fisk Red Sox 1	30.00	9.00
RBCFW C.Fisk W.Sox 1	30.00	9.00
RBCS Casey Stengel 1	30.00	9.00
RBCY Carl Yastrzemski 1	40.00	12.00
RBDM Don Mattingly 1	40.00	12.00
RBFRR F.Robinson Reds 1	30.00	9.00
RBGB George Brett 1	40.00	12.00
RBGH Gil Hodges 1	30.00	9.00
RBHA H.Aaron Braves 1	60.00	18.00
RBHAB Hank Aaron Brewers 1	60.00	18.00
RBHG Hank Greenberg 1	60.00	18.00
RBHK Harmon Killebrew 1	30.00	9.00
RBHW Honus Wagner 1	150.00	45.00
RBJR Jackie Robinson 1		
RBKB Ken Boyer 1	20.00	6.00
RBLA Luis Aparicio 1	20.00	6.00
RBLB Lou Brock 1	30.00	9.00
RBLG Lou Gehrig 1	150.00	45.00
RBOS Ozzie Smith 1	30.00	9.00
RBPWR P.W.Reese 1	30.00	9.00
RBRA Richie Ashburn 1	30.00	9.00
RBRC Roy Campanella 1	30.00	9.00
RBRCL R.Clemente 1	100.00	30.00
RBRJ Reggie Jackson 1	30.00	9.00
RBRM Roger Maris 1	60.00	18.00
RBTM T.Munson 1	40.00	12.00
RBWM Willie McCovey 1	20.00	6.00

2001 Topps Tribute Game Patch-Number Relics

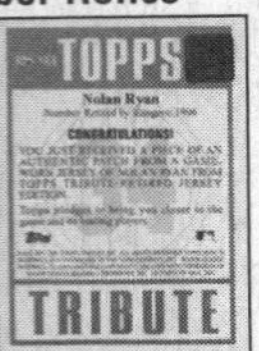

This 23-card set features swatches of actual game-used jersey patches. These cards were issued into packs at 1:61. Card backs carry a "RPN" prefix.

	Nm-Mt	Ex-Mt
RPNBD Bill Dickey	150.00	45.00
RPNBDO Bobby Doerr	150.00	45.00
RPNCY Carl Yastrzemski	250.00	75.00
RPNDM Don Mattingly	300.00	90.00
RPNDW Dave Winfield	150.00	45.00
RPNEM Eddie Mathews	250.00	75.00
RPNGB George Brett	400.00	120.00
RPNHK Harmon Killebrew	250.00	75.00
RPNJB Johnny Bench	250.00	75.00
RPNJM Juan Marichal	150.00	45.00
RPNJP Jim Palmer	150.00	45.00
RPNKB Kirby Puckett	250.00	75.00
RPNLB Lou Brock	150.00	45.00
RPNMS Mike Schmidt	300.00	90.00
RPNNRA N.Ryan Angels	500.00	150.00
RPNNRH N.Ryan Astros	500.00	150.00
RPNNRR Nolan Ryan Rgr	500.00	150.00
RPNRS Red Schoendienst	150.00	45.00
RPNRY Robin Yount	250.00	75.00
RPNTL Tom Lasorda	150.00	45.00
RPNWA Walt Alston	150.00	45.00
RPNWB Wade Boggs	150.00	45.00
RPNYB Yogi Berra	250.00	75.00

2001 Topps Tribute Game Worn Relics

This 39-card set features swatches of actual game-used jerseys. These cards were issued into packs in two different groups: Group 1 (1:282), and Group 2 (1:13) packs. Card backs carry a "RJ" prefix.

	Nm-Mt	Ex-Mt
RJ-BD Bill Dickey 5	30.00	9.00
RJ-BDO Bobby Doerr 2	30.00	9.00
RJ-CS Casey Stengel 5	30.00	9.00
RJ-CY C.Yastrzemski White 3	40.00	12.00
RJ-CYA C.Yastrzemski Gray 3	40.00	12.00
RJ-DD Dizzy Dean Uni 4	50.00	15.00
RJ-DM Don Mattingly 2	40.00	12.00
RJ-DW Dave Winfield 2	20.00	6.00
RJ-EB E.Banks White 2	30.00	9.00
RJ-EM Eddie Mathews 2	30.00	9.00
RJ-EBA E.Banks Gray 2	30.00	9.00
RJ-FR Frank Robinson 2	30.00	9.00
RJ-GB George Brett 2	40.00	12.00
RJ-HK H.Killebrew 2	30.00	9.00
RJ-JB J.Bench White 2	30.00	9.00
RJ-JP Jim Palmer White 2	20.00	6.00
RJ-JR Jackie Robinson 1	250.00	75.00
RJ-JBE Johnny Bench Gray 2	30.00	9.00
RJ-JMG Juan Marichal 2	20.00	6.00
RJ-JPA Jim Palmer Gray 2	20.00	6.00
RJ-KP Kirby Puckett 2	30.00	9.00
RJ-LB Lou Brock 2	30.00	9.00
RJ-MSB M.Schmidt Blue 2	40.00	12.00
RJ-MSW M.Schmidt White 2	40.00	12.00
RJ-NF Nellie Fox 2	30.00	9.00
RJ-NRA N.Ryan Angels 2	60.00	18.00
RJ-NRH N.Ryan Astros 2	60.00	18.00
RJ-NRR N.Ryan Rangers 2	60.00	18.00
RJ-RS R.Schoendienst 2	20.00	6.00
RJ-RY Robin Yount 2	30.00	9.00
RJ-SC Steve Carlton 2	20.00	6.00
RJ-SM Stan Musial 2	50.00	15.00
RJ-TL Tom Lasorda 4	20.00	6.00
RJ-WA Walt Alston 4	20.00	6.00
RJ-WB Wade Boggs 2	30.00	9.00
RJ-WMF W.Mays Gray 2	80.00	24.00
RJ-WMW W.Mays White 2	80.00	24.00
RJ-WST Willie Stargell 2	30.00	9.00
RJ-YB Yogi Berra 2	30.00	9.00

2001 Topps Tribute Tri-Relic

This one-card set features a tri-relic card of Nolan Ryan. This card was issued at 1:1292. Card backs carry a "NR" prefix.

	Nm-Mt	Ex-Mt
NR-AAR Nolan Ryan		

2002 Topps Tribute

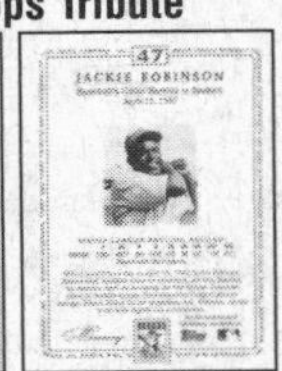

This 90 card set was released in November, 2002. These cards were issued in five card packs which came six packs to a box and four boxes to a case. Each of these packs had an SRP of $50 per pack.

	Nm-Mt	Ex-Mt
COMPLETE SET (90)	120.00	36.00
1 Hank Aaron	10.00	3.00
2 Rogers Hornsby	5.00	1.50
3 Bobby Thomson	4.00	1.20
4 Eddie Collins	4.00	1.20
5 Joe Carter	4.00	1.20
6 Jim Palmer	4.00	1.20
7 Willie Mays	10.00	3.00
8 Willie Stargell	4.00	1.20
9 Vida Blue	4.00	1.20
10 Whitey Ford	4.00	1.20
11 Bob Gibson	4.00	1.20
12 Nellie Fox	5.00	1.50
13 Napoleon Lajoie	5.00	1.50
14 Frankie Frisch	4.00	1.20
15 Nolan Ryan	12.00	3.60
16 Brooks Robinson	4.00	1.20
17 Kirby Puckett	5.00	1.50
18 Fergie Jenkins	4.00	1.20
19 Edd Roush	4.00	1.20
20 Honus Wagner	8.00	2.40
21 Richie Ashburn	4.00	1.20
22 Bob Feller	4.00	1.20
23 Joe Morgan	4.00	1.20
24 Orlando Cepeda	4.00	1.20
25 Steve Garvey	4.00	1.20
26 Hank Greenberg	5.00	1.50
27 Stan Musial	8.00	2.40
28 Sam Crawford	4.00	1.20
29 Jim Rice	4.00	1.20
30 Hack Wilson	4.00	1.20
31 Lou Brock	4.00	1.20
32 Mickey Vernon	4.00	1.20
33 Chuck Klein	4.00	1.20
34 Tony Gwynn	6.00	1.80
35 Duke Snider	4.00	1.20
36 Ryne Sandberg	10.00	3.00
37 Johnny Bench	5.00	1.50
38 Sam Rice	4.00	1.20
39 Lou Gehrig	10.00	3.00
40 Robin Yount	8.00	2.40
41 Don Sutton	4.00	1.20
42 Jim Bottomley	4.00	1.20
43 Billy Herman	4.00	1.20
44 Zach Wheat	4.00	1.20
45 Juan Marichal	4.00	1.20
46 Bert Blyleven	4.00	1.20
47 Jackie Robinson	5.00	1.50
48 Gil Hodges	4.00	1.20
49 Mike Schmidt	12.00	3.60
50 Dale Murphy	5.00	1.50
51 Phil Rizzuto	5.00	1.50
52 Ty Cobb	8.00	2.40
53 Andre Dawson	4.00	1.20
54 Fred Lindstrom	4.00	1.20
55 Roy Campanella	5.00	1.50
56 Don Larsen	4.00	1.20
57 Harry Heilmann	4.00	1.20
58 Catfish Hunter	4.00	1.20
59 Frank Robinson	4.00	1.20
60 Bill Mazeroski	4.00	1.20
61 Roger Maris	5.00	1.50
62 Dave Winfield	4.00	1.20
63 Warren Spahn	4.00	1.20
64 Babe Ruth	15.00	4.50
65 Ernie Banks	5.00	1.50
66 Wade Boggs	4.00	1.20
67 Carl Yastrzemski	8.00	2.40
68 Ron Santo	4.00	1.20
69 Dennis Martinez	4.00	1.20
70 Yogi Berra	5.00	1.50
71 Paul Waner	4.00	1.20
72 George Brett	12.00	3.60
73 Eddie Mathews	5.00	1.50
74 Bill Dickey	4.00	1.20
75 Carlton Fisk	4.00	1.20
76 Thurman Munson	5.00	1.50
77 Reggie Jackson	4.00	1.20
78 Phil Niekro	4.00	1.20
79 Luis Aparicio	4.00	1.20
80 Steve Carlton	4.00	1.20
81 Tris Speaker	4.00	1.20
82 Johnny Mize	4.00	1.20
83 Tom Seaver	4.00	1.20
84 Heinie Manush	4.00	1.20
85 Tommy John	4.00	1.20
86 Joe Cronin	4.00	1.20
87 Don Mattingly	12.00	3.60
88 Kirk Gibson	4.00	1.20
89 Bo Jackson	5.00	1.50
90 Mel Ott	5.00	1.50

2002 Topps Tribute First Impressions

Inserted into packs at a stated rate of one in 16, this is a parallel to the Topps Tribute set. Each of these cards were printed to a stated print run which matched the player's major league debut season. For those players who debuted in 1925 or before, no pricing is provided due to market scarcity.

	Nm-Mt	Ex-Mt
1 Hank Aaron/54	60.00	18.00
2 Rogers Hornsby/15		
3 Bobby Thomson/46	30.00	9.00
4 Eddie Collins/6		
5 Joe Carter/83	15.00	4.50
6 Jim Palmer/65	25.00	7.50
7 Willie Mays/51	60.00	18.00
8 Willie Stargell/62	25.00	7.50
9 Vida Blue/69	20.00	6.00
10 Whitey Ford/50	30.00	9.00
11 Bob Gibson/59	25.00	7.50
12 Nellie Fox/47	50.00	15.00
13 Napoleon Lajoie/96	20.00	6.00
14 Frankie Frisch/19		
15 Nolan Ryan/66	60.00	18.00
16 Brooks Robinson/55	25.00	7.50
17 Kirby Puckett/84	20.00	6.00
18 Fergie Jenkins/65	25.00	7.50
19 Edd Roush/13		
20 Honus Wagner/97	30.00	9.00
21 Richie Ashburn/48	30.00	9.00
22 Bob Feller/36	30.00	9.00
23 Joe Morgan/63	25.00	7.50
24 Orlando Cepeda/58	25.00	7.50
25 Steve Garvey/69	20.00	6.00
26 Hank Greenberg/30	50.00	15.00
27 Stan Musial/41	60.00	18.00
28 Sam Crawford/99	15.00	4.50
29 Jim Rice/74	20.00	6.00
30 Hack Wilson/23		
31 Lou Brock/61	25.00	7.50
32 Mickey Vernon/39	30.00	9.00
33 Chuck Klein/28	40.00	12.00
34 Tony Gwynn/82	25.00	7.50
35 Duke Snider/47	30.00	9.00
36 Ryne Sandberg/81	60.00	18.00
37 Johnny Bench/67	25.00	7.50
38 Sam Rice/15		
39 Lou Gehrig/23		
40 Robin Yount/74	40.00	12.00
41 Don Sutton/66	20.00	6.00
42 Jim Bottomley/22		
43 Billy Herman/31	40.00	12.00
44 Zach Wheat/9		
45 Juan Marichal/60	25.00	7.50
46 Bert Blyleven/70	20.00	6.00
47 Jackie Robinson/47	40.00	12.00
48 Gil Hodges/43	30.00	9.00
49 Mike Schmidt/72	60.00	18.00
50 Dale Murphy/76	50.00	15.00
51 Phil Rizzuto/41	30.00	9.00
52 Ty Cobb/5		
53 Andre Dawson/76	20.00	6.00
54 Fred Lindstrom/24		
55 Roy Campanella/48	40.00	12.00
56 Don Larsen/53	25.00	7.50
57 Harry Heilmann/14		
58 Catfish Hunter/65	25.00	7.50
59 Frank Robinson/56	25.00	7.50
60 Bill Mazeroski/56	25.00	7.50
61 Roger Maris/57	30.00	9.00
62 Dave Winfield/73	20.00	6.00
63 Warren Spahn/42	30.00	9.00
64 Babe Ruth/14		
65 Ernie Banks/53	30.00	9.00
66 Wade Boggs/82	15.00	4.50
67 Carl Yastrzemski/61	50.00	15.00
68 Ron Santo/60	25.00	7.50
69 Dennis Martinez/76	20.00	6.00
70 Yogi Berra/46	40.00	12.00
71 Paul Waner/26	40.00	12.00
72 George Brett/73	60.00	18.00
73 Eddie Mathews/52	50.00	15.00
74 Bill Dickey/28	40.00	12.00
75 Carlton Fisk/69	20.00	6.00
76 Thurman Munson/69	25.00	7.50
77 Reggie Jackson/67	20.00	6.00
78 Phil Niekro/64	25.00	7.50
79 Luis Aparicio/56	25.00	7.50
80 Steve Carlton/65	25.00	7.50
81 Tris Speaker/7		
82 Johnny Mize/36	30.00	9.00
83 Tom Seaver/67	20.00	6.00
84 Heinie Manush/23		
85 Tommy John/63	25.00	7.50
86 Joe Cronin/26	40.00	12.00

87 Don Mattingly/82 .... 50.00 15.00
88 Kirk Gibson/79 .... 20.00 6.00
89 Bo Jackson/86 .... 20.00 6.00
90 Mel Ott/26 .... 50.00 15.00

2002 Topps Tribute Lasting Impressions

Inserted into packs at a stated rate of one in 13, this is a parallel to the Topps Tribute set. Each of these cards were printed to a stated print run which matched the player's major league final season. For those players who retired in 1925 or before (or 2001 or later), no pricing is provided due to market scarcity.

Nm-Mt Ex-Mt
1 Hank Aaron/76 .... 50.00 15.00
2 Rogers Hornsby/37 .... 40.00 12.00
3 Bobby Thomson/60 .... 25.00 7.50
4 Eddie Collins/30 .... 40.00 12.00
5 Joe Carter/98 .... 15.00 4.50
6 Jim Palmer/84 .... 15.00 4.50
7 Willie Mays/73 .... 50.00 15.00
8 Willie Stargell/82 .... 15.00 4.50
9 Vida Blue/86 .... 15.00 4.50
10 Whitey Ford/67 .... 20.00 6.00
11 Bob Gibson/75 .... 20.00 6.00
12 Nellie Fox/65 .... 50.00 15.00
13 Napoleon Lajoie/16 ....
14 Frankie Frisch/37 .... 30.00 9.00
15 Nolan Ryan/93 .... 50.00 15.00
16 Brooks Robinson/77 .... 20.00 6.00
17 Kirby Puckett/95 .... 20.00 6.00
18 Fergie Jenkins/83 .... 15.00 4.50
19 Edd Roush/31 .... 40.00 12.00
20 Honus Wagner/17 ....
21 Richie Ashburn/62 .... 25.00 7.50
22 Bob Feller/56 .... 25.00 7.50
23 Joe Morgan/84 .... 15.00 4.50
24 Orlando Cepeda/74 .... 20.00 6.00
25 Steve Garvey/87 .... 15.00 4.50
26 Hank Greenberg/47 .... 40.00 12.00
27 Stan Musial/63 .... 50.00 15.00
28 Sam Crawford/17 ....
29 Jim Rice/89 .... 15.00 4.50
30 Hack Wilson/34 .... 40.00 12.00
31 Lou Brock/79 .... 20.00 6.00
32 Mickey Vernon/60 .... 25.00 7.50
33 Chuck Klein/44 .... 30.00 9.00
34 Tony Gwynn/1 ....
35 Duke Snider/64 .... 25.00 7.50
36 Ryne Sandberg/97 .... 60.00 18.00
37 Johnny Bench/83 .... 20.00 6.00
38 Sam Rice/34 .... 40.00 12.00
39 Lou Gehrig/39 .... 80.00 24.00
40 Robin Yount/93 .... 40.00 12.00
41 Don Sutton/88 .... 15.00 4.50
42 Jim Bottomley/37 .... 30.00 9.00
43 Billy Herman/47 .... 30.00 9.00
44 Zach Wheat/27 .... 40.00 12.00
45 Juan Marichal/75 .... 20.00 6.00
46 Bert Blyleven/92 .... 15.00 4.50
47 Jackie Robinson/56 .... 30.00 9.00
48 Gil Hodges/63 .... 25.00 7.50
49 Mike Schmidt/89 .... 60.00 18.00
50 Dale Murphy/93 .... 50.00 15.00
51 Phil Rizzuto/56 .... 25.00 7.50
52 Ty Cobb/28 .... 80.00 24.00
53 Andre Dawson/96 .... 15.00 4.50
54 Fred Lindstrom/36 .... 30.00 9.00
55 Roy Campanella/57 .... 30.00 9.00
56 Don Larsen/67 .... 20.00 6.00
57 Harry Heilmann/32 .... 40.00 12.00
58 Catfish Hunter/79 .... 20.00 6.00
59 Frank Robinson/76 .... 20.00 6.00
60 Bill Mazeroski/72 .... 20.00 6.00
61 Roger Maris/68 .... 25.00 7.50
62 Dave Winfield/95 .... 15.00 4.50
63 Warren Spahn/65 .... 25.00 7.50
64 Babe Ruth/35 .... 80.00 24.00
65 Ernie Banks/71 .... 25.00 7.50
66 Wade Boggs/99 .... 15.00 4.50
67 Carl Yastrzemski/83 .... 30.00 9.00
68 Ron Santo/74 .... 20.00 6.00
69 Dennis Martinez/98 .... 15.00 4.50
70 Yogi Berra/65 .... 30.00 9.00
71 Paul Waner/45 .... 30.00 9.00
72 George Brett/93 .... 60.00 18.00
73 Eddie Mathews/68 .... 50.00 15.00
74 Bill Dickey/46 .... 30.00 9.00
75 Carlton Fisk/93 .... 15.00 4.50
76 Thurman Munson/79 .... 25.00 7.50
77 Reggie Jackson/87 .... 15.00 4.50
78 Phil Niekro/87 .... 15.00 4.50
79 Luis Aparicio/73 .... 20.00 6.00
80 Steve Carlton/88 .... 15.00 4.50
81 Tris Speaker/28 .... 40.00 12.00
82 Johnny Mize/53 .... 25.00 7.50
83 Tom Seaver/86 .... 15.00 4.50
84 Heinie Manush/39 .... 30.00 9.00
85 Tommy John/89 .... 15.00 4.50
86 Joe Cronin/45 .... 30.00 9.00
87 Don Mattingly/95 .... 50.00 15.00
88 Kirk Gibson/95 .... 15.00 4.50
89 Bo Jackson/94 .... 20.00 6.00
90 Mel Ott/47 .... 40.00 12.00

2002 Topps Tribute The Catch Dual Relic

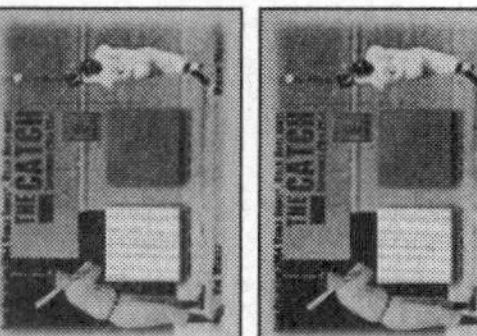

Inserted into packs at a stated rate of one in 1023, this card features relics from players involved in Willie Mays' legendary catch during the 1954 World Series when he ran down a well hit ball by Vic Wertz.

Nm-Mt Ex-Mt
JSY NUMBER ODDS 1:3161 ....
JSY NUMBER PRINT RUN 24 #'d CARDS
NO JSY NUM.PRICING DUE TO SCARCITY
*SEASON: .6X TO 1.2X BASIC DUAL RELIC
SEASON ODDS 1:1391 ....
SEASON PRINT RUN 54 SERIAL #'d CARDS
MW Vic Wertz Bat 300.00 90.00
Willie Mays Glove

2002 Topps Tribute Marks of Excellence Autograph

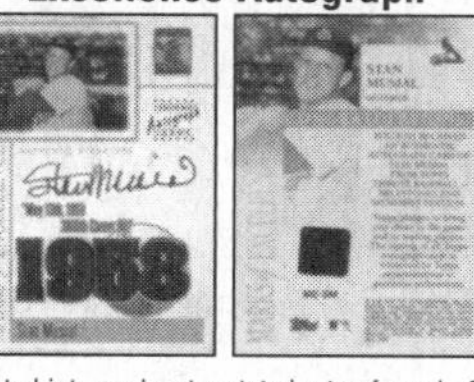

Inserted into packs at a stated rate of one in 61, these six cards feature players who signed cards honoring their signature moment.

Nm-Mt Ex-Mt
DL Don Larsen 50.00 15.00
LB Lou Brock 50.00 15.00
MS Mike Schmidt 120.00 36.00
SC Steve Carlton 50.00 15.00
SM Stan Musial 100.00 30.00
WS Warren Spahn 80.00 24.00

2002 Topps Tribute Marks of Excellence Autograph Relics

Inserted in packs at a stated rate of one in 61, these six cards feature game-used memorabilia pieces honoring players and their signature moment.

Nm-Mt Ex-Mt
BR Brooks Robinson Bat 80.00 24.00
DM Don Mattingly Jsy 150.00 45.00
DS Duke Snider Uni 80.00 24.00
FJ Fergie Jenkins Jsy 50.00 15.00
JP Jim Palmer Uni 50.00 15.00
RY Robin Yount Uni 80.00 24.00

2002 Topps Tribute Matching Marks Dual Relics

Inserted into packs at an overall stated rate of one in 11, these 22 cards feature two players and a game-used memorabilia piece from each of them.

Nm-Mt Ex-Mt
GROUP A ODDS 1:134 ....
GROUP B ODDS 1:368 ....
GROUP C ODDS 1:123 ....
GROUP D ODDS 1:43 ....
GROUP E ODDS 1:105 ....
GROUP F ODDS 1:82 ....
GROUP G ODDS 1:31 ....
AR Hank Aaron Bat 400.00 120.00
Babe Ruth Bat A
BB Wade Boggs Jsy 50.00 15.00
George Brett Jsy C
BF Johnny Bench Bat 60.00 18.00
Carlton Fisk Bat A
BM Vida Blue Jsy 15.00 4.50
Dennis Martinez Jsy G
BMA George Brett Jsy 150.00 45.00
Don Mattingly Jsy A
BS Bert Blyleven Jsy 20.00 6.00
Don Sutton Jsy C
GA Hank Greenberg Bat 120.00 36.00
Richie Ashburn Bat A
GH Steve Garvey Bat 25.00 7.50
Gil Hodges Bat D
JS Fergie Jenkins Jsy 50.00 15.00
Tom Seaver Jsy B
MA Willie Mays Uni 250.00 75.00
Hank Aaron Bat A
NS Phil Niekro Uni 20.00 6.00
Tom Seaver Uni G
PJ Jim Palmer Jsy 25.00 7.50
Tommy John Jsy D
RJ Frank Robinson Uni 60.00 18.00
Reggie Jackson Bat A
RS Nolan Ryan Jsy 150.00 45.00
Tom Seaver Jsy A
SB Tris Speaker Bat 120.00 36.00
George Brett Bat A
SBA Ron Santo Bat 25.00 7.50
Ernie Banks Bat D
SM Duke Snider Bat 100.00 30.00
Willie Mays Uni A
SR Willie Stargell Uni 20.00 6.00
Jim Rice Uni E
WY Dave Winfield Bat 40.00 12.00
Carl Yastrzemski Bat D
WYO Dave Winfield Uni 20.00 6.00
Robin Yount Uni F
YK Carl Yastrzemski Bat 100.00 30.00
Chuck Klein Bat A
YP Robin Yount Uni 80.00 24.00
Kirby Puckett Uni A

2002 Topps Tribute Memorable Materials

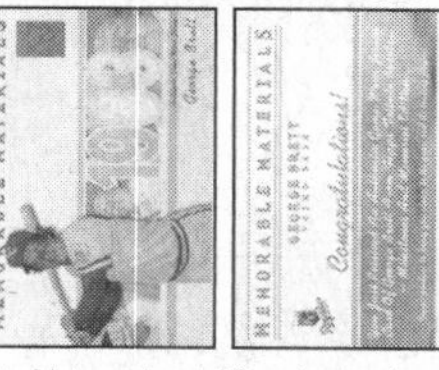

Inserted into packs at different rates depending on what group and game-used memorabilia piece, these 22 cards feature players from the tribute set as well as a memorabilia piece. We have notated next to the player's name what group this memorabilia piece belongs to.

Nm-Mt Ex-Mt
BAT GROUP A ODDS 1:11,592 ....
BAT GROUP B ODDS 1:6 ....
JSY/UNI GROUP A ODDS 1:246 ....
JSY/UNI GROUP B ODDS 1:12 ....
BJ Bo Jackson Jsy B 25.00 7.50
BM Bill Mazeroski Uni B 20.00 6.00
BT Bobby Thomson Bat B 20.00 6.00
CF Carlton Fisk Bat B 25.00 7.50
CK Chuck Klein Bat B 40.00 12.00
CY Carl Yastrzemski Uni B 30.00 9.00
DM Don Mattingly Jsy B 40.00 12.00
GB George Brett Jsy B 40.00 12.00
HA Hank Aaron Bat B 50.00 15.00
HW Hack Wilson Bat B 50.00 15.00
JC Joe Carter Bat B 20.00 6.00
JM Joe Morgan Bat B 20.00 6.00
JR Jackie Robinson Bat B 50.00 15.00
KG Kirk Gibson Bat B 20.00 6.00
KP Kirby Puckett Bat B 40.00 12.00
LG Lou Gehrig Bat A ....
NR Nolan Ryan Jsy A 50.00 15.00
PR Phil Rizzuto Bat B 25.00 7.50
RC Roy Campanella Bat B 40.00 12.00
RJ Reggie Jackson Bat B 25.00 7.50
RM Roger Maris Bat B 80.00 24.00
TM Thurman Munson Bat B 50.00 15.00

2002 Topps Tribute Memorable Materials Jersey Number

Inserted into packs at a different rate depending on whether it is a bat or a uniform piece, this is a parallel to the Memorable Materials insert set. Each of these cards are issued to a stated print run matching the uniform number that the player wore during his career. For cards with less than 40 cards printed, no pricing is provided due to market scarcity.

Nm-Mt Ex-Mt
BAT STATED ODDS 1:208 ....
JSY/UNI STATED ODDS 1:644 ....
BJ Bo Jackson Jsy/16 ....
BM Bill Mazeroski Uni/9 ....
BT Bobby Thomson Bat/23 ....
CF Carlton Fisk Bat/27 ....
CK Chuck Klein Bat/1 ....
CY Carl Yastrzemski Uni/27 UER ....
Yaz jersey number is actually 8
DM Don Mattingly Jsy/23 ....
GB George Brett Jsy/5 ....
HA Hank Aaron Bat/44 .... 120.00 36.00
HW Hack Wilson Bat/1 ....
JC Joe Carter Bat/29 ....
JM Joe Morgan Bat/8 ....
JR Jackie Robinson Bat/42 .... 120.00 36.00
KG Kirk Gibson Bat/23 ....
KP Kirby Puckett Bat/34 ....
LG Lou Gehrig Bat/4 ....
NR Nolan Ryan Jsy/34 ....
PR Phil Rizzuto Bat/10 ....
RC Roy Campanella Bat/39 ....
RJ Reggie Jackson Bat/44 .... 60.00 18.00
RM Roger Maris Bat/9 ....
TM Thurman Munson Bat/15 ....

2002 Topps Tribute Memorable Materials Season

Inserted into packs at a different rate depending on whether it is a bat or a uniform piece, this is a parallel to the Memorable Materials insert set. Each of these cards are issued to a stated print run matching the most memorable season that the player had during his career. For cards with less than 40 cards printed, no pricing is provided due to market scarcity.

Nm-Mt Ex-Mt
BAT STATED ODDS 1:72 ....
JSY/UNI STATED ODDS 1:152 ....
BJ Bo Jackson Jsy/89 .... 80.00 24.00
BM Bill Mazeroski Uni/60 .... 40.00 12.00
BT Bobby Thomson Bat/51 .... 40.00 12.00
CF Carlton Fisk Bat/75 .... 40.00 12.00
CK Chuck Klein Bat/33 ....
CY Carl Yastrzemski Uni/75 UER 50.00 15.00
Card commemorates 1967 season
DM Don Mattingly Jsy/87 .... 60.00 18.00
GB George Brett Jsy/83 .... 80.00 24.00
HA Hank Aaron Bat/74 .... 80.00 24.00
HW Hack Wilson Bat/30 ....
JC Joe Carter Bat/93 .... 30.00 9.00
JM Joe Morgan Bat/76 .... 30.00 9.00
JR Jackie Robinson Bat/47 .... 100.00 30.00
KG Kirk Gibson Bat/88 .... 30.00 9.00
KP Kirby Puckett Bat/91 .... 60.00 18.00
LG Lou Gehrig Bat/39 ....
NR Nolan Ryan Jsy/91 .... 80.00 24.00
PR Phil Rizzuto Bat/50 .... 50.00 15.00
RC Roy Campanella Bat/55 .... 80.00 24.00
RJ Reggie Jackson Bat/77 .... 40.00 12.00
RM Roger Maris Bat/61 .... 150.00 45.00
TM Thurman Munson Bat/76 .... 80.00 24.00

2002 Topps Tribute Milestone Materials

Inserted at different stated odds depending on whether it is a bat or a jersey/uniform piece, these 50 cards feature game-used memorabilia from the feature player's career.

Nm-Mt Ex-Mt
BAT STATED ODDS 1:4 ....
JSY/UNI STATED ODDS 1:5 ....
AD Andre Dawson Jsy 15.00 4.50
BD Bill Dickey Uni 25.00 7.50
BF Bob Feller Bat 25.00 7.50
BG Bob Gibson Uni 20.00 6.00
BH Billy Herman Uni 15.00 4.50
BR Babe Ruth Bat 200.00 60.00
BRO Brooks Robinson Bat 25.00 7.50
CH Catfish Hunter Jsy 20.00 6.00
DM Dale Murphy Jsy 25.00 7.50
DS Duke Snider Uni 20.00 6.00
EB Ernie Banks Uni 25.00 7.50
EC Eddie Collins Bat 40.00 12.00
EM Eddie Mathews Jsy 25.00 7.50
ER Edd Roush Bat 40.00 12.00
FF Frankie Frisch Bat 25.00 7.50
FL Fred Lindstrom Uni 25.00 7.50
FR Frank Robinson Bat 25.00 7.50
HH Harry Heilmann Bat 25.00 7.50
HM Heinie Manush Bat 40.00 12.00
HW Honus Wagner Bat 150.00 45.00
JB Johnny Bench Jsy 25.00 7.50
JBO Jim Bottomley Bat 25.00 7.50
JC Joe Cronin Bat 25.00 7.50
JM Johnny Mize Uni 20.00 6.00
JMA Juan Marichal Jsy 15.00 4.50
JP Jim Palmer Uni 15.00 4.50
LA Luis Aparicio Bat 20.00 6.00
LG Lou Gehrig Bat 150.00 45.00
MO Mel Ott Bat 60.00 18.00
MV Mickey Vernon Bat 20.00 6.00
NF Nellie Fox Uni 25.00 7.50
NL Napoleon Lajoie Bat 80.00 24.00
NR Nolan Ryan Jsy 50.00 15.00
OC Orlando Cepeda Jsy 15.00 4.50
PW Paul Waner Bat 40.00 12.00
RH Rogers Hornsby Bat 60.00 18.00
RJ Reggie Jackson Jsy 20.00 6.00
RS Ryne Sandberg Bat 40.00 12.00
RY Robin Yount Uni 25.00 7.50
SC Sam Crawford Bat 25.00 7.50
SR Sam Rice Bat 25.00 7.50
TC Ty Cobb Bat 150.00 45.00
TS Tom Seaver Jsy 20.00 6.00
TSP Tris Speaker Bat 80.00 24.00
WB Wade Boggs Uni 20.00 6.00
WF Whitey Ford Uni 20.00 6.00
WM Willie Mays Uni 50.00 15.00
WS Willie Stargell Uni 20.00 6.00
YB Yogi Berra Jsy 25.00 7.50
ZW Zach Wheat Bat 40.00 12.00

2002 Topps Tribute Milestone Materials Jersey Number

Inserted into packs at a different rate depending on whether it is a bat or a uniform piece, this is a parallel to the Milestone Materials insert set. Each of these cards are issued to a stated print run matching the uniform number that the player wore during his career. For cards with less than 40 cards printed, no pricing is provided due to market scarcity.

Nm-Mt Ex-Mt
BAT STATED ODDS 1:443 ....
JSY/UNI STATED ODDS 1:148 ....
AD Andre Dawson Jsy/8 ....
BD Bill Dickey Uni/8 ....
BF Bob Feller Bat/19 ....
BG Bob Gibson Uni/45 .... 50.00 15.00
BH Billy Herman Uni/2 ....
BR Babe Ruth Bat/3 ....
BRO Brooks Robinson Bat/5 ....
CH Catfish Hunter Jsy/27 ....
DM Dale Murphy Jsy/3 ....
DS Duke Snider Uni/4 ....
EB Ernie Banks Uni/14 ....
EC Eddie Collins Bat/1 ....
EM Eddie Mathews Jsy/41 .... 60.00 18.00
ER Edd Roush Bat/1 ....
FF Frankie Frisch Bat/3 ....
FL Fred Lindstrom Uni/3 ....
FR Frank Robinson Bat/20 ....
HH Harry Heilmann Bat/1 ....
HM Heinie Manush Bat/3 ....
HW Honus Wagner Bat/33 ....
JB Johnny Bench Jsy/5 ....
JBO Jim Bottomley Bat/4 ....
JC Joe Cronin Bat/4 ....
JM Johnny Mize Uni/36 ....
JMA Juan Marichal Jsy/27 ....
JP Jim Palmer Uni/22 ....
LA Luis Aparicio Bat/11 ....
LG Lou Gehrig Bat/4 ....
MO Mel Ott Bat/4 ....
MV Mickey Vernon Bat/3 ....
NF Nellie Fox Uni/2 ....
NL Napoleon Lajoie Bat/1 ....
NR Nolan Ryan Jsy/34 ....
OC Orlando Cepeda Jsy/30 ....
PW Paul Waner Bat/9 ....
RH Rogers Hornsby Bat/9 ....
RJ Reggie Jackson Jsy/44 .... 50.00 15.00
RS Ryne Sandberg Bat/23 ....
RY Robin Yount Uni/19 ....
SC Sam Crawford Bat/1 ....
SR Sam Rice Bat/1 ....
TC Ty Cobb Bat/1 ....
TS Tom Seaver Jsy/41 .... 50.00 15.00
TSP Tris Speaker Bat/1 ....
WB Wade Boggs Uni/26 ....
WF Whitey Ford Uni/16 ....
WM Willie Mays Uni/24 ....
WS Willie Stargell Uni/8 ....
YB Yogi Berra Jsy/8 ....
ZW Zach Wheat Bat/1 ....

2002 Topps Tribute Milestone Materials Season

Inserted into packs at a different rate depending on whether it is a bat or a uniform piece, this is a parallel to the Memorable Materials insert set. Each of these cards are issued to a stated print run matching the most memorable season that the player had during his career. For cards with less than 40 cards printed, no pricing is provided due to market scarcity.

Nm-Mt Ex-Mt
BAT STATED ODDS 1:73 ....
JSY/UNI STATED ODDS 1:41 ....
AD Andre Dawson Jsy/95 .... 30.00 9.00
BD Bill Dickey Uni/46 .... 60.00 18.00
BF Bob Feller Bat/54 .... 60.00 18.00
BG Bob Gibson Uni/74 .... 40.00 12.00
BH Billy Herman Uni/47 .... 40.00 12.00
BR Babe Ruth Bat/34 ....
BRO Brooks Robinson Bat/74 .... 50.00 15.00
CH Catfish Hunter Jsy/79 .... 40.00 12.00
DM Dale Murphy Jsy/91 .... 50.00 15.00
DS Duke Snider Uni/63 .... 50.00 15.00
EB Ernie Banks Uni/70 .... 50.00 15.00
EC Eddie Collins Bat/25 ....
EM Eddie Mathews Jsy/67 .... 50.00 15.00
ER Edd Roush Bat/31 ....
FF Frankie Frisch Bat/35 ....
FL Fred Lindstrom Uni/36 ....
FR Frank Robinson Bat/71 .... 50.00 15.00
HH Harry Heilmann Bat/32 ....
HM Heinie Manush Bat/39 ....
HW Honus Wagner Bat/14 ....
JB Johnny Bench Jsy/80 .... 50.00 15.00
JBO Jim Bottomley Bat/36 ....
JC Joe Cronin Bat/45 .... 60.00 18.00
JM Johnny Mize Uni/50 .... 50.00 15.00
JMA Juan Marichal Jsy/71 .... 30.00 9.00
JP Jim Palmer Uni/82 .... 30.00 9.00
LA Luis Aparicio Bat/73 .... 40.00 12.00
LG Lou Gehrig Bat/37 ....
MO Mel Ott Bat/45 .... 150.00 45.00
MV Mickey Vernon Bat/56 .... 50.00 15.00
NF Nellie Fox Uni/41 .... 100.00 30.00
NL Napoleon Lajoie Bat/14 ....
NR Nolan Ryan Jsy/89 .... 100.00 30.00
OC Orlando Cepeda Jsy/73 .... 30.00 9.00
PW Paul Waner Bat/42 .... 100.00 30.00
RH Rogers Hornsby Bat/37 ....
RJ Reggie Jackson Jsy/84 .... 40.00 12.00
RS Ryne Sandberg Bat/93 .... 80.00 24.00
RY Robin Yount Uni/92 .... 80.00 24.00
SC Sam Crawford Bat/16 ....
SR Sam Rice Bat/34 ....
TC Ty Cobb Bat/27 ....
TS Tom Seaver Jsy/81 .... 40.00 12.00
TSP Tris Speaker Bat/25 ....
WB Wade Boggs Uni/99 .... 40.00 12.00
WF Whitey Ford Uni/62 .... 50.00 15.00
WM Willie Mays Uni/69 .... 100.00 30.00
WS Willie Stargell Uni/80 .... 40.00 12.00
YB Yogi Berra Jsy/61 .... 60.00 18.00
ZW Zach Wheat Bat/25 ....

2002 Topps Tribute Pastime Patches

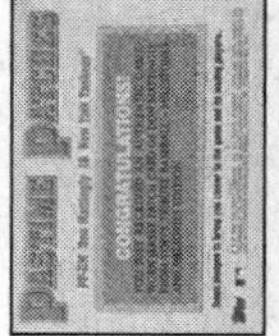

Inserted into packs at a stated overall rate of one in 92, these 12 cards feature game-worn patch relic cards of these baseball legends.

Nm-Mt Ex-Mt
*LOGO PATCHES: 2.5X VALUE ....
GROUP A ODDS 1:184 ....
GROUP B ODDS 1:184 ....
OVERALL ODDS 1:92 ....
BD Bill Dickey B 150.00 45.00
CY Carl Yastrzemski B 200.00 60.00
DM Don Mattingly A 200.00 60.00
DW Dave Winfield A 150.00 45.00
EM Eddie Mathews A 150.00 45.00
GB George Brett A 200.00 60.00
JB Johnny Bench B 150.00 45.00
JP Jim Palmer B 150.00 45.00
KP Kirby Puckett B 150.00 45.00
RY Robin Yount B 150.00 45.00
WB Wade Boggs B 150.00 45.00
NRR Nolan Ryan B 250.00 75.00

2002 Topps Tribute Signature Cuts

Inserted into packs at a stated rate of one in 9936, these four cards feature cut autographs of four of baseball's most legendary figures. According to Topps, each of these cards were issued to a print run of two cards.

Nm-Mt Ex-Mt
BR Babe Ruth
JR Jackie Robinson
LG Lou Gehrig
TC Ty Cobb

2003 Topps Tribute Contemporary

This 110 card set was released in August, 2003. These cards were issued in five card packs with an $50 SRP which came six packs to a box and four boxes to a case. Cards numbered 1-90 feature veterans and cards 91-100 feature rookies. Cards numbered 101 through 110 also feature rookies, but those cards are signed and were issued to a stated print run of 499 serial numbered sets and these cards were inserted at a stated rate of one in seven. Jose Contreras did not return his cards in time for inclusion in this product and those cards could be redeemed until August 31, 2005.

MINT NRMT
COMMON CARD (1-90) 2.00 .90
COMMON CARD (91-100) 2.00 .90
COMMON CARD (101-110) 15.00 6.75
1 Jim Thome 4.00 1.80
2 Edgardo Alfonzo 2.00 .90
3 Edgar Martinez 2.50 1.10
4 Scott Rolen 4.00 1.80
5 Eric Hinske 2.00 .90
6 Mark Mulder 2.00 .90
7 Jason Giambi 2.00 .90
8 Bernie Williams 2.50 1.10
9 Cliff Floyd 2.00 .90
10 Ichiro Suzuki 6.00 2.70
11 Pat Burrell 2.00 .90
12 Garret Anderson 2.00 .90
13 Gary Sheffield 2.00 .90
14 Johnny Damon 4.00 1.80
15 Kerry Wood 4.00 1.80
16 Bartolo Colon 2.00 .90
17 Adam Dunn 2.50 1.10
18 Omar Vizquel 2.50 1.10
19 Todd Helton 2.50 1.10
20 Nomar Garciaparra 6.00 2.70
21 A.J. Burnett 2.00 .90
22 Craig Biggio 2.50 1.10
23 Carlos Beltran 2.50 1.10
24 Kazuhisa Ishii 2.00 .90
25 Vladimir Guerrero 4.00 1.80
26 Roberto Alomar 2.50 1.10
27 Roger Clemens 8.00 3.60
28 Tim Hudson 2.00 .90
29 Brian Giles 2.00 .90
30 Barry Bonds 10.00 4.50
31 Jim Edmonds 2.00 .90
32 Rafael Palmeiro 2.50 1.10
33 Francisco Rodriguez 2.00 .90
34 Andruw Jones 2.00 .90
35 Shea Hillenbrand 2.00 .90
36 Moises Alou 2.00 .90
37 Luis Gonzalez 2.00 .90
38 Darin Erstad 2.00 .90
39 John Smoltz 2.50 1.10
40 Derek Jeter 10.00 4.50
41 Aubrey Huff 2.00 .90
42 Eric Chavez 2.00 .90
43 Doug Mientkiewicz 2.00 .90
44 Lance Berkman 2.00 .90
45 Josh Beckett 2.00 .90
46 Austin Kearns 2.00 .90
47 Frank Thomas 4.00 1.80
48 Pedro Martinez 4.00 1.80
49 Tim Salmon 2.00 .90
50 Alex Rodriguez 6.00 2.70
51 Ryan Klesko 2.00 .90
52 Tom Glavine 2.50 1.10
53 Shawn Green 2.00 .90
54 Jeff Kent 2.00 .90
55 Carlos Pena 2.00 .90
56 Paul Konerko 2.00 .90
57 Troy Glaus 2.00 .90
58 Manny Ramirez 2.50 1.10
59 Jason Jennings 2.00 .90
60 Randy Johnson 4.00 1.80
61 Ivan Rodriguez 4.00 1.80
62 Roy Oswalt 2.00 .90
63 Kevin Brown 2.00 .90
64 Jose Vidro 2.00 .90
65 Jorge Posada 2.50 1.10
66 Mike Piazza 6.00 2.70
67 Bret Boone 2.00 .90
68 Carlos Delgado 2.00 .90
69 Jimmy Rollins 2.00 .90
70 Alfonso Soriano 2.50 1.10
71 Greg Maddux 6.00 2.70
72 Mark Prior 4.00 1.80
73 Jeff Bagwell 2.50 1.10
74 Richie Sexson 2.00 .90
75 Sammy Sosa 6.00 2.70
76 Curt Schilling 2.00 .90
77 Mike Sweeney 2.00 .90
78 Torii Hunter 2.00 .90
79 Larry Walker 2.50 1.10
80 Miguel Tejada 2.00 .90
81 Rich Aurilia 2.00 .90
82 Bobby Abreu 2.00 .90
83 Phil Nevin 2.00 .90
84 Rodrigo Lopez 2.00 .90
85 Chipper Jones 4.00 1.80
86 Ken Griffey Jr. 6.00 2.70
87 Mike Lowell 2.00 .90
88 Magglio Ordonez 2.00 .90
89 Barry Zito 2.00 .90
90 Albert Pujols 8.00 3.60
91 Corey Shafer FY RC 3.00 1.35
92 Dan Haren FY RC 3.00 1.35
93 Jeremy Bonderman FY RC 3.00 1.35
94 Branden Florence FY RC 2.00 .90
95 E.Bastida-Martinez FY RC 2.00 .90
96 Brian Wright FY RC 2.00 .90
97 Elizardo Ramirez FY RC 3.00 1.35
98 Mi.Garciaparra FY RC 3.00 1.35
99 Clay Hensley FY RC 2.00 .90
100 Bobby Basham FY RC 3.00 1.35
101 J.Contreras FY AU RC EXCH 25.00 11.00
102 Br. Bullington FY AU RC 25.00 11.00
103 Joey Gomes FY AU RC 15.00 6.75
104 Craig Brazell FY AU RC 15.00 6.75
105 Andy Marte FY AU RC 80.00 36.00
106 Han. Ramirez FY AU RC 50.00 22.00
107 Ryan Shealy FY AU RC 15.00 6.75
108 Daryl Clark FY AU RC 15.00 6.75
109 Tyler Johnson FY AU RC 15.00 6.75
110 Ben Francisco FY AU RC 15.00 6.75

2003 Topps Tribute Contemporary Gold

MINT NRMT
RANDOM INSERTS IN PACKS
STATED PRINT RUN 25 SERIAL #'d SETS
NO PRICING DUE TO SCARCITY
CONTRERAS EXCH.DEADLINE 08/31/05

2003 Topps Tribute Contemporary Red

MINT NRMT
*RED 1-90: .6X TO 1.5X BASIC CARDS
*RED 91-100: .75X TO 2X BASIC CARDS
1-100 PRINT RUN 225 SERIAL #'d SETS
*RED 101-110: .6X TO 1.5X BASIC
101-110 PRINT RUN 99 SERIAL #'d SETS
RANDOM INSERTS IN PACKS

2003 Topps Tribute Contemporary Bonds Tribute Relics

MINT NRMT
*RED BONDS: .6X TO 1.5X BASIC BONDS
RED BONDS PRINT RUN 50 #'d SETS
GOLD BONDS PRINT RUN 1 #'d SET.
NO GOLD PRICING DUE TO SCARCITY
RANDOM INSERTS IN PACKS
DB Barry Bonds Bat-Jsy 50.00 22.00
SB Barry Bonds Jsy 40.00 18.00
TB Barry Bonds Bat-Cap-Jsy 80.00 36.00

2003 Topps Tribute Contemporary Bonds Tribute 40-40 Club Relics

MINT NRMT
RANDOM INSERTS IN PACKS
NO GOLD PRICING DUE TO SCARCITY
CBR Jose Canseco Uni 80.00 36.00
Barry Bonds Uni
Alex Rodriguez Uni
CBRG Jose Canseco Uni
Barry Bonds Uni
Alex Rodriguez Uni Gold/1
CBRR Jose Canseco Uni 120.00 55.00
Barry Bonds Uni
Alex Rodriguez Uni Red/50

2003 Topps Tribute Contemporary Bonds Tribute 600 HR Club Relics

MINT NRMT
*RED 600: .6X TO 1.5X BASIC
RED 600 PRINT RUN 50 SERIAL #'d SETS
GOLD 600 PRINT RUN 1 SERIAL #'d SET.
NO GOLD PRICING DUE TO SCARCITY
RANDOM INSERTS IN PACKS
BB Barry Bonds Bat 40.00 18.00
BR Babe Ruth Bat 150.00 70.00
HA Hank Aaron Bat 40.00 18.00
WM Willie Mays Uni 50.00 22.00

2003 Topps Tribute Contemporary Bonds Tribute 600 HR Club Double Relics

MINT NRMT
*RED 600 DOUBLE: .6X TO 1.5X BASIC
RED 600 DOUBLE PRINT RUN 50 #'d SETS
GOLD 600 DOUBLE PRINT 1 SERIAL #'d SET
NO GOLD PRICING DUE TO SCARCITY
RANDOM INSERTS IN PACKS
BA Barry Bonds Bat 100.00 45.00
Hank Aaron Bat
BM Barry Bonds Bat 100.00 45.00
Willie Mays Uni
RB Babe Ruth Bat 200.00 90.00
Barry Bonds Bat

2003 Topps Tribute Contemporary Bonds Tribute 600 HR Club Quad Relics

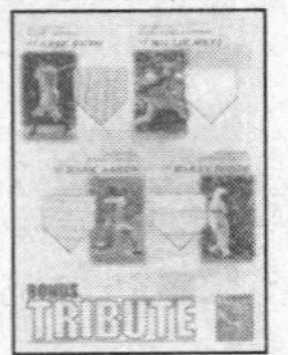

MINT NRMT
RANDOM INSERTS IN PACKS
PRINT RUNS B/WN 1-50 COPIES PER
NO GOLD/RED PRICING DUE TO SCARCITY
HR Babe Ruth Bat 600.00 275.00
Willie Mays Uni
Hank Aaron Bat
Barry Bonds Bat/50
HRG Babe Ruth Bat
Willie Mays Uni
Hank Aaron Bat
Barry Bonds Bat Gold/1
HRR Babe Ruth Bat
Willie Mays Uni
Hank Aaron Bat
Barry Bonds Bat Red/25

2003 Topps Tribute Contemporary Matching Marks Dual Relics

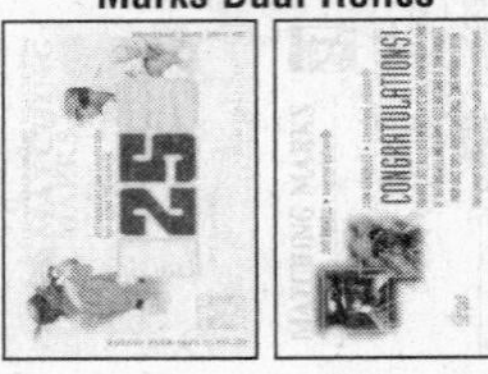

MINT NRMT
*RED MARKS: .6X TO 1.5X BASIC
RED MARKS PRINT RUN 50 SERIAL #'d SETS
GOLD MARKS PRINT RUN 1 SERIAL #'d SET
NO GOLD PRICING DUE TO SCARCITY
RANDOM INSERTS IN PACKS
AP Roberto Alomar Bat 15.00 6.75
Rafael Palmeiro Bat
BG Jeff Bagwell Uni 15.00 6.75
Juan Gonzalez Bat
BP Barry Bonds Bat 40.00 18.00
Rafael Palmeiro Bat
GR Nomar Garciaparra Jsy 25.00 11.00
Alex Rodriguez Jsy
HR Rickey Henderson Bat 15.00 6.75
Manny Ramirez Bat
MG Fred McGriff Bat 15.00 6.75
Juan Gonzalez Bat
MP Fred McGriff Bat 15.00 6.75
Rafael Palmeiro Bat
PA Rafael Palmeiro Bat 15.00 6.75
Roberto Alomar Uni
PH Rafael Palmeiro Bat 15.00 6.75
Rickey Henderson Bat
PS Rafael Palmeiro Uni 25.00 11.00
Sammy Sosa Bat
RP Manny Ramirez Jsy 25.00 11.00
Mike Piazza Uni
SB Sammy Sosa Bat 20.00 9.00
Jeff Bagwell Uni
SG Alfonso Soriano Uni 15.00 6.75
Vladimir Guerrero Bat

2003 Topps Tribute Contemporary Memorable Materials Relics

MINT NRMT
*RED MEM: .6X TO 1.5X BASIC
RED MEM PRINT RUN 50 SERIAL #'d SETS
GOLD MEM PRINT RUN 1 SERIAL #'d SET
NO GOLD PRICING DUE TO SCARCITY
RANDOM INSERTS IN PACKS
AJ Andruw Jones Jsy 10.00 4.50
AP Albert Pujols Jsy 25.00 11.00
AR Alex Rodriguez Jsy 20.00 9.00
AS Alfonso Soriano Uni 15.00 6.75

BB Barry Bonds Jsy 40.00 18.00
CR Cal Ripken Bat 50.00 22.00
GM Greg Maddux Jsy 15.00 6.75
JG Jason Giambi Jsy 10.00 4.50
JG2 Jason Giambi Bat 10.00 4.50
KW Kerry Wood Jsy 15.00 6.75
LG Luis Gonzalez Bat 10.00 4.50
MT Miguel Tejada Bat 10.00 4.50
RH Rickey Henderson Uni 15.00 6.75
SG Shawn Green Jsy 10.00 4.50
SS Sammy Sosa Bat 20.00 9.00
SS2 Sammy Sosa Jsy 20.00 9.00
TG Troy Glaus Uni 10.00 4.50
TH Torii Hunter Jsy 10.00 4.50
VG Vladimir Guerrero Bat 15.00 6.75

2003 Topps Tribute Contemporary Milestone Materials Relics

MINT NRMT
*RED MILE: .6X TO 1.5X BASIC
RED MILE PRINT RUN 50 SERIAL #'d SETS
GOLD PRINT RUN 1 SERIAL #'d SET.
NO GOLD PRICING DUE TO SCARCITY
RANDOM INSERTS IN PACKS
AR Alex Rodriguez Jsy 20.00 9.00
BB1 Barry Bonds 1500 RBI Uni 25.00 11.00
BB2 Barry Bonds 1500 Runs Uni 25.00 11.00
BB3 Barry Bonds 2000 Hits Uni 25.00 11.00
BB4 Barry Bonds 500 2B Uni 25.00 11.00
BB5 Barry Bonds 600 HR Uni 25.00 11.00
CJ Chipper Jones Jsy 15.00 6.75
FM1 Fred McGriff Cubs Bat 10.00 4.50
FM2 Fred McGriff 2000 Hits Bat 10.00 4.50
FM3 Fred McGriff 400 HR Bat 10.00 4.50
FT Frank Thomas Jsy 15.00 6.75
JB1 Jeff Bagwell Jsy 10.00 4.50
JB2 Jeff Bagwell Uni 10.00 4.50
JG1 Juan Gonzalez Indians Bat 10.00 4.50
JG2 Juan Gonzalez Rgr Bat 10.00 4.50
MP1 Mike Piazza Bat 15.00 6.75
MP2 Mike Piazza Uni 15.00 6.75
MR1 Manny Ramirez Bat 10.00 4.50
MR2 Manny Ramirez Jsy 10.00 4.50
NG Nomar Garciaparra Jsy 25.00 11.00
RA Roberto Alomar Uni 15.00 6.75
RH1 R.Henderson Mets Bat 10.00 4.50
RH2 R.Henderson Sox Bat 10.00 4.50
RH3 R.Henderson A's Bat 10.00 4.50
RH4 R.Henderson 3000 Hits Bat 10.00 4.50
RH5 R.Henderson 500 2B Bat 10.00 4.50
RP1 R.Palmeiro 1500 RBI Jsy 10.00 4.50
RP2 R.Palmeiro 2500 Hits Bat 10.00 4.50
RP3 R.Palmeiro 500 HR Uni 10.00 4.50
RP4 R.Palmeiro 500 2B Bat 10.00 4.50
SS1 Sammy Sosa 1250 RBI Jsy 15.00 6.75
SS2 Sammy Sosa 2000 Hits Jsy 15.00 6.75
SS3 Sammy Sosa Bat 15.00 6.75
TH Todd Helton Jsy 15.00 6.75
VG Vladimir Guerrero Bat 15.00 6.75

2003 Topps Tribute Contemporary Modern Marks Autographs

Inserted at a stated rate of one in 19, these nine cards feature authentic autographs from current major leaguers.

MINT NRMT
STATED ODDS 1:19
*RED MARKS: .5X TO 1.2X BASIC
RED MARKS STATED ODDS 1:38
RED MARKS PRINT RUN 99 SERIAL #'d SETS
GOLD MARKS STATED ODDS 1:149
GOLD MARKS PRINT RUN 25 SERIAL #'d SETS
NO GOLD PRICING DUE TO SCARCITY
CF Cliff Floyd 15.00 6.75
EH Eric Hinske 15.00 6.75
LB Lance Berkman 20.00 9.00
MO Magglio Ordonez 20.00 9.00
MS Mike Sweeney 15.00 6.75
PK Paul Konerko 15.00 6.75
PL Paul Lo Duca 15.00 6.75
RC Roger Clemens 150.00 70.00
TH Torii Hunter 15.00 6.75

2003 Topps Tribute Contemporary Perennial All-Star Relics

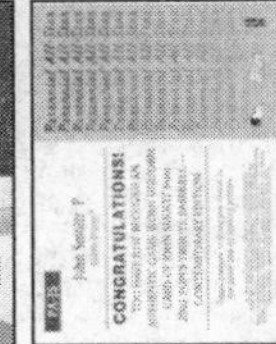

MINT NRMT
*RED AS: .6X TO 1.5X BASIC
RED AS PRINT RUN 50 SERIAL #'d SETS
GOLD AS PRINT RUN 1 SERIAL #'d SET
NO GOLD PRICING DUE TO SCARCITY
RANDOM INSERTS IN PACKS
AR Alex Rodriguez Jsy 20.00 9.00
BB Barry Bonds Uni 25.00 11.00
BS Benito Santiago Bat 10.00 4.50
BW Bernie Williams Bat 15.00 6.75
CB Craig Biggio Uni 15.00 6.75
CJ Chipper Jones Jsy 15.00 6.75
CS Curt Schilling Jsy 10.00 4.50
EM Edgar Martinez Bat 15.00 6.75
FT Frank Thomas Bat 15.00 6.75
GM Greg Maddux Jsy 15.00 6.75
GS Gary Sheffield Bat 10.00 4.50
IR Ivan Rodriguez Bat 15.00 6.75
JS John Smoltz Uni 15.00 6.75
LW Larry Walker Bat 15.00 6.75
MM Mike Mussina Uni 15.00 6.75
MP Mike Piazza Bat 15.00 6.75
MR Manny Ramirez Bat 15.00 6.75
PM Pedro Martinez Jsy 15.00 6.75
RA Roberto Alomar Bat 15.00 6.75
RC Roger Clemens Uni 20.00 9.00
RH Rickey Henderson Bat 15.00 6.75
SS Sammy Sosa Bat 20.00 9.00

2003 Topps Tribute Contemporary Performance Double Relics

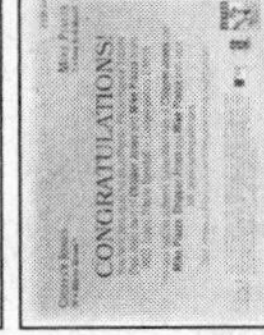

MINT NRMT
*RED DOUBLE: .6X TO 1.5X BASIC
RED DOUBLE PRINT RUN 50 #'d SETS
GOLD DOUBLE PRINT RUN 1 #'d SET
NO GOLD PRICING DUE TO SCARCITY
RANDOM INSERTS IN PACKS
BJ Barry Bonds Uni 25.00 11.00
Chipper Jones Bat
CM Roger Clemens Uni 40.00 18.00
Greg Maddux Jsy
GG Luis Gonzalez Bat 10.00 4.50
Troy Glaus Uni
JP Chipper Jones Bat 20.00 9.00
Mike Piazza Bat
MM Pedro Martinez Jsy 20.00 9.00
Greg Maddux Uni
PR Mike Piazza Uni 20.00 9.00
Ivan Rodriguez Bat
PS Mike Piazza Bat 20.00 9.00
Benito Santiago Bat
PW Albert Pujols Jsy 25.00 11.00
Kerry Wood Jsy
RG Alex Rodriguez Jsy 40.00 18.00
Nomar Garciaparra Jsy
RR Cal Ripken Bat 60.00 27.00
Alex Rodriguez Jsy
RT Alex Rodriguez Jsy 20.00 9.00
Miguel Tejada Bat
SA Alfonso Soriano Uni 15.00 6.75
Roberto Alomar Uni
SG Sammy Sosa Bat 20.00 9.00
Juan Gonzalez Bat
ZJ Barry Zito Uni 15.00 6.75
Randy Johnson Uni

2003 Topps Tribute Contemporary Performance Triple Relics

MINT NRMT
*RED TRIPLE: .6X TO 1.5X BASIC
RED TRIPLE PRINT RUN 50 #'d SETS
GOLD TRIPLE PRINT RUN 1 #'d SET.
NO GOLD PRICING DUE TO SCARCITY
RANDOM INSERTS IN PACKS
BMP Barry Bonds Uni 40.00 18.00
Fred McGriff Bat
Rafael Palmeiro Jsy
CMJ Roger Clemens Uni 40.00 18.00
Greg Maddux Jsy
Randy Johnson Jsy
RPH Manny Ramirez Jsy 40.00 18.00
Mike Piazza Uni

Rickey Henderson Bat
SPM Sammy Sosa Bat............. 30.00 13.50
Rafael Palmeiro Bat
Fred McGriff Bat
STB Sammy Sosa Jsy.............. 30.00 13.50
Frank Thomas Jsy
Jeff Bagwell Jsy

2003 Topps Tribute Contemporary Team Double Relics

MINT NRMT
*RED DOUBLE: .6X TO 1.5X BASIC....
RED DOUBLE PRINT RUN 50 #'d SETS
GOLD DOUBLE PRINT RUN 1 #'d SET
NO GOLD PRICING DUE TO SCARCITY
RANDOM INSERTS IN PACKS ....
BB Craig Biggio Jsy 15.00 6.75
Jeff Bagwell Uni
GR Nomar Garciaparra Jsy 25.00 11.00
Manny Ramirez Jsy
N Kazuhisa Ishii Jsy.............. 40.00 18.00
Hideo Nomo Jsy
MS Greg Maddux Jsy 50.00 22.00
John Smoltz Jsy
RP Alex Rodriguez Jsy............. 20.00 9.00
Rafael Palmeiro Bat
WH Larry Walker Jsy 15.00 6.75
Todd Helton Jsy

2003 Topps Tribute Contemporary Team Triple Relics

MINT NRMT
*RED TRIPLE: .6X TO 1.5X BASIC......
RED TRIPLE PRINT RUN 50 SERIAL #'d SETS
GOLD PRINT RUN 1 SERIAL #'d SET
NO GOLD PRICING DUE TO SCARCITY
RANDOM INSERTS IN PACKS ....
ASP Moises Alou Bat............... 30.00 13.50
Sammy Sosa Jsy
Corey Patterson Bat
BBB Craig Biggio Uni............... 25.00 11.00
Lance Berkman Bat
Jeff Bagwell Uni
CTM Eric Chavez Uni................ 25.00 11.00
Miguel Tejada Jsy
Mark Mulder Uni
GRM Nomar Garciaparra Jsy 40.00 18.00
Manny Ramirez Jsy
Pedro Martinez Jsy
HZM Tim Hudson Uni 25.00 11.00
Barry Zito Uni
Mark Mulder Uni
SJ Andruw Jones Jsy............. 30.00 13.50
Gary Sheffield Bat
Chipper Jones Jsy
MHM Joe Mauer Bat................. 30.00 13.50
Torii Hunter Jsy
Doug Mientkiewicz Bat
MOB Edgar Martinez Jsy.......... 25.00 11.00
John Olerud Bat
Bret Boone Jsy
PER Albert Pujols Bat 40.00 18.00
Jim Edmonds Jsy
Scott Rolen Bat
RBT Alex Rodriguez Bat........... 30.00 13.50
Hank Blalock Bat
Mark Teixeira Bat
RGP Alex Rodriguez Jsy 30.00 13.50
Juan Gonzalez Bat
Rafael Palmeiro Jsy
SGV Alfonso Soriano Bat.......... 25.00 11.00
Jason Giambi Bat
Robin Ventura Bat
TBB Jim Thome Jsy................ 30.00 13.50
Marlon Byrd Jsy
Pat Burrell Jsy
TOK Frank Thomas Jsy............ 30.00 13.50
Magglio Ordonez Jsy
Paul Konerko Jsy

2003 Topps Tribute Contemporary Tribute to the Stars Dual Relics

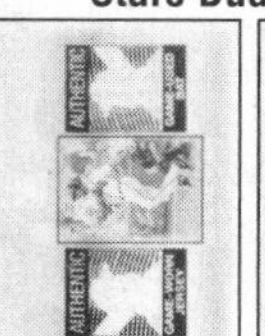

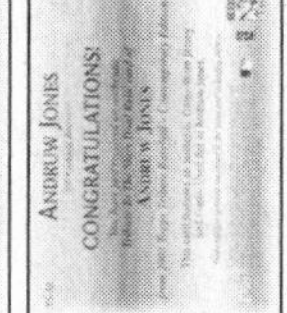

MINT NRMT
*RED DUAL: .6X TO 1.5X BASIC ....
RED DUAL PRINT RUN 50 #'d SETS ..
GOLD DUAL PRINT RUN 1 SERIAL #'d SET
NO GOLD PRICING DUE TO SCARCITY
RANDOM INSERTS IN PACKS ....
AD Adam Dunn Bat-Jsy 15.00 6.75
AJ Andruw Jones Bat-Jsy 15.00 6.75
AP Albert Pujols Bat-Uni 40.00 18.00
AR Alex Rodriguez Bat-Jsy 30.00 13.50
AS Alfonso Soriano Bat-Uni...... 15.00 6.75
BB Barry Bonds Bat-Uni........... 50.00 22.00
CJ Chipper Jones Bat-Jsy 15.00 6.75
EC Eric Chavez Bat-Uni 15.00 6.75
FT Frank Thomas Bat-Jsy 15.00 6.75
GA Garret Anderson Bat-Uni 15.00 6.75
GM Greg Maddux Bat-Jsy 20.00 9.00
JT Jim Thome Bat-Jsy 15.00 6.75
LB Lance Berkman Bat-Jsy 15.00 6.75
LW Larry Walker Bat-Jsy 15.00 6.75
MP Mike Piazza Bat-Uni........... 20.00 9.00
NG Nomar Garciaparra Bat-Jsy . 40.00 18.00
PB Pat Burrell Bat-Jsy............. 15.00 6.75
RA Roberto Alomar Bat-Uni...... 15.00 6.75
RH Rickey Henderson Bat-Uni .. 15.00 6.75
RP Rafael Palmeiro Bat-Jsy 15.00 6.75
SS Sammy Sosa Bat-Jsy 25.00 11.00
TG Troy Glaus Bat-Uni 15.00 6.75
TH Todd Helton Bat-Jsy 15.00 6.75
VG Vladimir Guerrero Bat-Jsy... 15.00 6.75
THU Torii Hunter Bat-Jsy 15.00 6.75

2003 Topps Tribute Contemporary Tribute to the Stars Patchworks Dual Relics

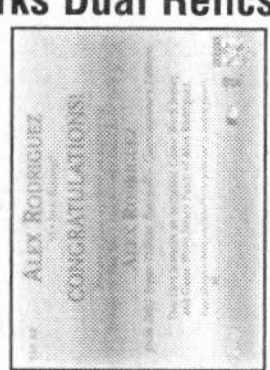

MINT NRMT
STATED ODDS 1:34.......................
STATED PRINT RUN 50 SERIAL #'d SETS
AP Albert Pujols.................. 100.00 45.00
AR Alex Rodriguez................. 60.00 27.00
AR2 Alex Rodriguez Blue 60.00 27.00
BB Barry Bonds 100.00 45.00
CJ Chipper Jones.................. 40.00 18.00
CS Curt Schilling................... 25.00 11.00
FT Frank Thomas 40.00 18.00
GM Greg Maddux................... 50.00 22.00
JB Jeff Bagwell 40.00 18.00
KW Kerry Wood 40.00 18.00
LG Luis Gonzalez 25.00 11.00
MR Manny Ramirez 40.00 18.00
NG Nomar Garciaparra............ 50.00 22.00
PM Pedro Martinez 40.00 18.00
RJ Randy Johnson.................. 40.00 18.00
RP Rafael Palmeiro................. 40.00 18.00
SG Shawn Green.................... 25.00 11.00
SS Sammy Sosa 50.00 22.00
TH Todd Helton 40.00 18.00
THU Torii Hunter..................... 25.00 11.00

2003 Topps Tribute Contemporary World Series Relics

MINT NRMT
*RED WS: .6X TO 1.5X BASIC...........
RED WS PRINT RUN 50 SERIAL #'d SETS
GOLD WS PRINT RUN 1 SERIAL #'d SET
NO GOLD PRICING DUE TO SCARCITY
RANDOM INSERTS IN PACKS ....
MR Mariano Rivera Jsy.......... 15.00 6.75
TG Troy Glaus Uni.................. 10.00 4.50

2003 Topps Tribute Contemporary World Series Double Relics

MINT NRMT
*RED WS DOUBLE: .6X TO 1.5X BASIC
RED WS DOUBLE PRINT RUN 50 #'d SETS
GOLD WS DOUBLE PRINT RUN 1 #'d SET
NO GOLD PRICING DUE TO SCARCITY
RANDOM INSERTS IN PACKS ....
BG Barry Bonds Uni............... 40.00 18.00
Troy Glaus Uni
LP John Lackey Uni 10.00 4.50
Troy Percival Uni
PC Mike Piazza Bat................ 40.00 18.00
Roger Clemens Uni
PP Jorge Posada Bat 25.00 11.00
Andy Pettitte Jsy
SJ Curt Schilling Jsy............... 15.00 6.75
Randy Johnson Jsy
WG Bernie Williams Bat.......... 15.00 6.75
Luis Gonzalez Bat
WO Bernie Williams Bat.......... 15.00 6.75
Paul O'Neill Bat

2003 Topps Tribute Contemporary World Series Triple Relics

MINT NRMT
*RED WS TRIPLE: .6X TO 1.5X BASIC
RED WS TRIPLE PRINT RUN 50 #'d SETS
GOLD WS TRIPLE PRINT RUN 1 #'d SET
NO GOLD PRICING DUE TO SCARCITY
RANDOM INSERTS IN PACKS ....
EGS Darin Erstad Uni............... 25.00 11.00
Troy Glaus Uni
Tim Salmon Uni
LGP John Lackey Uni............... 15.00 6.75
Troy Glaus Bat
Troy Percival Uni

2003 Topps Tribute Perennial All-Star

This 50 card set was released in February, 2003. These cards were issued in five card packs with an $50 SRP. These packs were issued in six pack boxes which came four boxes to a case. These cards honored players who made at least five trips to the All-Star game during their career.

Nm-Mt Ex-Mt
COMPLETE SET (50).............. 100.00 30.00
1 Willie Mays 10.00 3.00
2 Don Mattingly 12.00 3.60
3 Hoyt Wilhelm 4.00 1.20
4 Hank Aaron 10.00 3.00
5 Hank Greenberg 5.00 1.50
6 Johnny Bench 5.00 1.50
7 Duke Snider 4.00 1.20
8 Carl Yastrzemski 8.00 2.40
9 Jim Palmer............................ 4.00 1.20
10 Roberto Clemente 12.00 3.60
11 Mike Schmidt...................... 10.00 3.00
12 Joe Cronin 4.00 1.20
13 Lou Brock 4.00 1.20
14 Orlando Cepeda 4.00 1.20
15 Bill Mazeroski........................ 4.00 1.20
16 Whitey Ford 4.00 1.20
17 Rod Carew 4.00 1.20
18 Joe Morgan............................ 4.00 1.20
19 Luis Aparicio 4.00 1.20
20 Nolan Ryan 12.00 3.60
21 Bobby Doerr.......................... 4.00 1.20
22 Dale Murphy 5.00 1.50
23 Bob Feller.............................. 4.00 1.20
24 Paul Molitor 4.00 1.20
25 Tom Seaver........................... 4.00 1.20
26 Ozzie Smith........................... 8.00 2.40
27 Stan Musial 8.00 2.40
28 Willie McCovey 4.00 1.20
29 Gary Carter 4.00 1.20
30 Reggie Jackson..................... 4.00 1.20
31 Gaylord Perry........................ 4.00 1.20
32 George Brett........................ 12.00 3.60
33 Robin Roberts........................ 4.00 1.20
34 Wade Boggs........................... 4.00 1.20
35 Cal Ripken........................... 15.00 4.50
36 Carlton Fisk........................... 4.00 1.20
37 Al Kaline................................ 5.00 1.50
38 Kirby Puckett 5.00 1.50
39 Phil Rizzuto 4.00 1.20
40 Willie Stargell........................ 4.00 1.20
41 Harmon Killebrew 5.00 1.50
42 Red Schoendienst.................. 4.00 1.20
43 Tony Gwynn 6.00 1.80
44 Ralph Kiner 4.00 1.20
45 Yogi Berra 5.00 1.50
46 Catfish Hunter 4.00 1.20
47 Frank Robinson..................... 4.00 1.20
48 Ernie Banks........................... 5.00 1.50
49 Warren Spahn 4.00 1.20
50 Brooks Robinson 4.00 1.20

2003 Topps Tribute Perennial All-Star Gold

This is a parallel to the Topps Tribute set. These cards were issued at different rates depending on what group the card was issued from. We have notated that information next to the player's name in our checklist.

Nm-Mt Ex-Mt
*GOLD p/r 81-86: 1.5X TO 4X BASIC .
*GOLD p/r 66-80: 2X TO 5X BASIC ...
*GOLD p/r 51-65: 2.5X TO 6X BASIC .
*GOLD p/r 36-50: 3X TO 8X BASIC ....
*GOLD p/r 26-35: 4X TO 10X BASIC ..
GROUP A ODDS 1:106........................
GROUP B ODDS 1:49..........................
GROUP C ODDS 1:38..........................

2003 Topps Tribute Perennial All-Star Relics

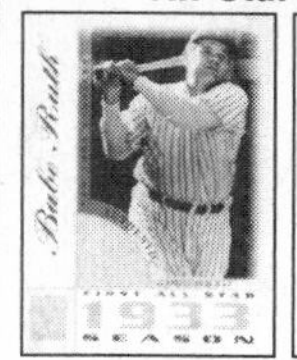

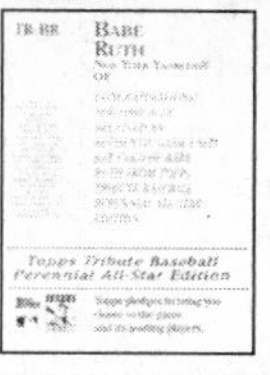

This 65-card insert set was inserted at various odds depending on what type of relic and what group the card belonged to. We have notated the group, the odds for the group as well as the relic in our checklist.

Nm-Mt Ex-Mt
BAT GROUP A ODDS 1:556 ....
BAT GROUP B ODDS 1: ....
BAT GROUP C ODDS 1:276 ....
BAT GROUP D ODDS 1:61 ....
BAT GROUP E ODDS 1:158.................
BAT GROUP F ODDS 1:23...................
BAT GROUP G ODDS 1:111 ....
BAT GROUP H ODDS 1:46...................
BAT GROUP I ODDS 1:85 ....
BAT GROUP J ODDS 1:16....................
BAT GROUP K ODDS 1:18 ....
BAT GROUP L ODDS 1:31....................
BAT GROUP M ODDS 1:50 ....
BAT GROUP N ODDS 1:46 ....
BAT GROUP O ODDS 1:21 ....
BAT GROUP P ODDS 1:37 ....
JSY/UNI GROUP A ODDS 1:368 ....
JSY/UNI GROUP B ODDS 1:148 ....
JSY/UNI GROUP C ODDS 1:92 ....
JSY/UNI GROUP D ODDS 1:185 ....
JSY/UNI GROUP E ODDS 1:69 ....
JSY/UNI GROUP F ODDS 1:55.............
JSY/UNI GROUP G ODDS 1:79 ....
JSY/UNI GROUP H ODDS 1:61 ....
JSY/UNI GROUP I ODDS 1:55 ....
JSY/UNI GROUP J ODDS 1:25..............
JSY/UNI GROUP K ODDS 1:46 ....
JSY/UNI GROUP L ODDS 1:43 ....
JSY/UNI GROUP M ODDS 1:21 ....
JSY/UNI GROUP N ODDS 1:8...............
JSY/UNI GROUP O ODDS 1:29 ....
JSY/UNI GROUP P ODDS 1:10 ....
AD Andre Dawson Bat F............ 20.00 6.00
AK Al Kaline Bat E.................... 30.00 9.00
BD Bobby Doerr Jsy N............. 15.00 4.50
BF Bob Feller Bat I 15.00 4.50
BM Bill Mazeroski Uni C 25.00 7.50
BR Babe Ruth Bat J 180.00 55.00
BRO Brooks Robinson Bat J 20.00 6.00
CF Carlton Fisk Bat J 20.00 6.00
CH Catfish Hunter Jsy B 25.00 7.50
CRB Cal Ripken Bat P 40.00 12.00
CY Carl Yastrzemski Jsy E 40.00 12.00
DD Dizzy Dean Uni E................ 50.00 15.00
DM Dale Murphy Jsy A............. 50.00 15.00
DMA Don Mattingly Jsy L.......... 40.00 12.00
DN Don Newcombe Bat K......... 15.00 4.50
DSN Duke Snider Bat F............ 25.00 7.50
EB Ernie Banks Bat M.............. 20.00 6.00
EM Eddie Mathews Jsy K......... 20.00 6.00
FR Frank Robinson Uni G......... 20.00 6.00
GB George Brett Jsy M 30.00 9.00
GC Gary Carter Jsy I 15.00 4.50
HA Hank Aaron Bat O............... 40.00 12.00
HG Hank Greenberg Bat D 50.00 15.00
HK Harmon Killebrew Jsy J 20.00 6.00
HW Honus Wagner Bat B......... 180.00 55.00
HWI Hoyt Wilhelm Uni N 15.00 4.50
JBE Johnny Bench Uni F.......... 30.00 9.00
JCR Joe Cronin Bat N 15.00 4.50
JF Jimmie Foxx Bat F 50.00 15.00
JMI Johnny Mize Uni D............. 20.00 6.00
JMO Joe Morgan Bat K............. 15.00 4.50
JP Jim Palmer Uni N................ 15.00 4.50
JR Jackie Robinson Bat L 50.00 15.00
KP Kirby Puckett Jsy N 20.00 6.00
LA Luis Aparicio Bat C 20.00 6.00
LB Lou Brock Bat A.................. 30.00 9.00
LBU Lou Brock Uni H................ 20.00 6.00
LG Lou Gehrig Bat F 150.00 45.00
MO Mel Ott Bat D..................... 30.00 9.00
MS Mike Schmidt Uni P............ 20.00 6.00
NL Nap Lajoie Bat D................ 80.00 24.00
NR Nolan Ryan Rangers Uni O . 40.00 12.00
NRA Nolan Ryan Astros Jsy F... 50.00 15.00
OC Orlando Cepeda Jsy C........ 20.00 6.00
OS Ozzie Smith Uni J 20.00 6.00
PM Paul Molitor Bat K 20.00 6.00
PR Phil Rizzuto Bat H 25.00 7.50
RC Roberto Clemente Bat L 60.00 18.00
RCA Roy Campanella Bat F 25.00 7.50
RH Rogers Hornsby Bat G 50.00 15.00
RJ Reggie Jackson Bat O......... 20.00 6.00
ROD Rod Carew Jsy N.............. 20.00 6.00
RS Red Schoendienst Bat H 15.00 4.50
SM Stan Musial Bat J 40.00 12.00
TC Ty Cobb Bat F 120.00 36.00
TG Tony Gwynn Jsy P.............. 15.00 4.50
TM Thurman Munson Jsy M..... 30.00 9.00
TS Tris Speaker Bat A 100.00 30.00
TSE Tom Seaver Jsy A............. 30.00 9.00
WB Wade Boggs Uni C 25.00 7.50
WF Whitey Ford Uni B.............. 25.00 7.50
WM Willie Mays Bat K 40.00 12.00
WMC Willie McCovey Bat J........ 15.00 4.50
WST Willie Stargell Uni B 25.00 7.50
YB Yogi Berra Jsy A 50.00 15.00

2003 Topps Tribute Perennial All-Star Patch Relics

Inserted at a stated rate of one in 123, these 15 cards feature premium relics from prestigious retired talents. These game-worn uniform patch relic cards display a unique design featuring the player, his relic and the site of an All-Star appearance. These cards were issued to a stated print run of 30 serial numbered sets.

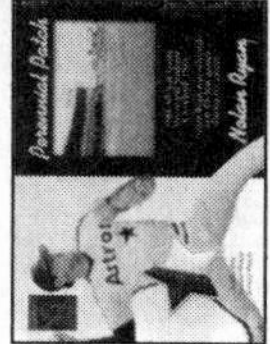

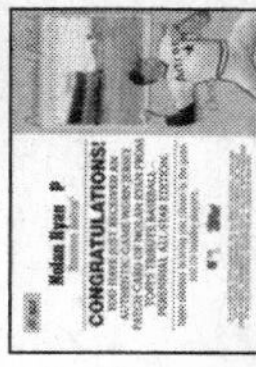

Nm-Mt Ex-Mt
CR Cal Ripken......................... 300.00 90.00
CY Carl Yastrzemski................ 200.00 60.00
DMU Dale Murphy 120.00 36.00
GB George Brett..................... 250.00 75.00
GC Gary Carter......................... 50.00 15.00
HK Harmon Killebrew............. 120.00 36.00
JM Joe Morgan......................... 50.00 15.00
MS Mike Schmidt 250.00 75.00
NR Nolan Ryan Rangers 250.00 75.00
NRA Nolan Ryan Astros.......... 250.00 75.00
OS Ozzie Smith 200.00 60.00
TG Tony Gwynn...................... 150.00 45.00
WB Wade Boggs 80.00 24.00
WM Willie McCovey.................. 50.00 15.00
WS Willie Stargell 80.00 24.00

2003 Topps Tribute Perennial All-Star Signing

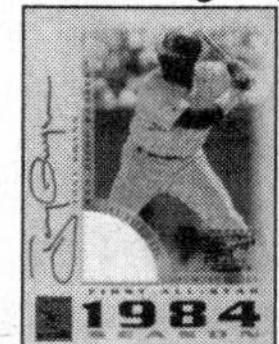

Issued at a stated rate of one in 34, these cards feature not only a game-used relic from the player's career but also an authentic signature of the featured player.

Nm-Mt Ex-Mt
GOLD STATED ODDS 1:201 ....
GOLD PRINT RUN 25 SERIAL #'d SETS
NO GOLD PRICING DUE TO SCARCITY
AD Andre Dawson Bat................ 40.00 12.00
AK Al Kaline Bat 80.00 24.00
DM Dale Murphy Jsy 80.00 24.00
DMA Don Mattingly Jsy 120.00 36.00
DSN Duke Snider Bat................ 80.00 24.00
GC Gary Carter Jsy 40.00 12.00
JP Jim Palmer Uni 40.00 12.00
LB Lou Brock Bat...................... 60.00 18.00
MS Mike Schmidt Uni 120.00 36.00
OC Orlando Cepeda Jsy 40.00 12.00
TG Tony Gwynn Jsy 100.00 30.00

2003 Topps Tribute Perennial All-Star 1st Class Cut Relics

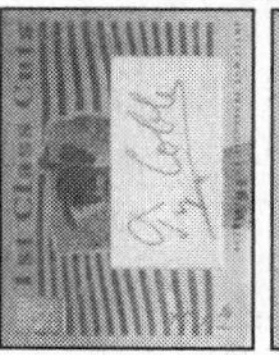

Inserted at a stated rate of one in 7461, these seven cards feature autograph cuts from among the most legendary figures in the game. On back each card is an authentic USPS stamp of the featured player. Each of these cards is a true 1 of 1 and is stamped as such on back.

Nm-Mt Ex-Mt
BR Babe Ruth.......................................
DD Dizzy Dean ....
HW Honus Wagner ....
JR Jackie Robinson ....
LG Lou Gehrig.......................................
TC Ty Cobb...
TS Tris Speaker ....

2003 Topps Tribute Perennial All-Star Memorable Match-Up Relics

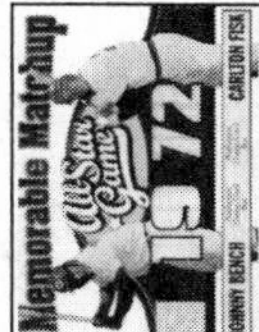

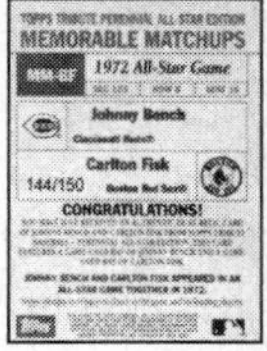

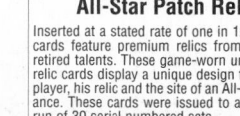

Issued at a stated rate of one in 41, these 10 cards feature two all stars who appeared in the same all-star game along with a game-used relic from each of their career. These cards were issued to a stated print run of 150 serial numbered sets.

Nm-Mt Ex-Mt
GOLD STATED ODDS 1:245 ....
GOLD PRINT RUN 25 SERIAL #'d SETS
NO GOLD PRICING DUE TO SCARCITY
BF Johnny Bench Bat............... 60.00 18.00
Carlton Fisk Bat
BG Wade Boggs Bat................. 60.00 18.00
Tony Gwynn Bat
BS George Brett Jsy................ 120.00 36.00
Mike Schmidt Uni

CM Gary Carter Jsy 80.00 24.00
Don Mattingly Jsy
KA Harmon Killebrew Jsy 120.00 36.00
Hank Aaron Bat
MJ Willie Mays Bat 100.00 30.00
Reggie Jackson Bat
PG Kirby Puckett Bat 60.00 18.00
Tony Gwynn Bat
YB Carl Yastrzemski Jsy 80.00 24.00
Johnny Bench Bat
YBR Carl Yastrzemski Jsy 60.00 18.00
Lou Brock Bat

2003 Topps Tribute World Series

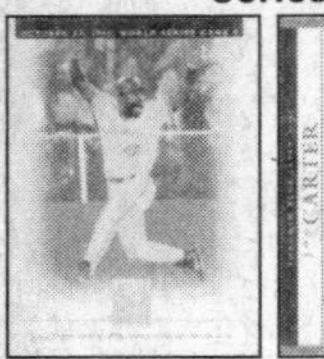

This 150 card set was released in October, 2003. The set was issued in four card packs with an $50 SRP which came six packs to a box and four boxes to a case. Cards numbered 1 through 130 feature players from a year in which their team participated in a World Series while cards 131 through 150 is a Fall Classic sub set featuring key moments in World Series history.

	MINT	NRMT
COMMON CARD (1-130)	4.00	1.80
COMMON CARD (131-150)	4.00	1.80
1 Willie Mays 54	10.00	4.50
2 Gary Carter 86	4.00	1.80
3 Yogi Berra 47	5.00	2.20
4 Dennis Eckersley 88	4.00	1.80
5 Willie McCovey 62	4.00	1.80
6 Willie Stargell 71	4.00	1.80
7 Mike Schmidt 80	10.00	4.50
8 Robin Yount 82	8.00	3.60
9 Bucky Harris 24	4.00	1.80
10 Carl Yastrzemski 67	8.00	3.60
11 Lenny Dykstra 86	4.00	1.80
12 Boog Powell 66	4.00	1.80
13 Bill Lee 75	4.00	1.80
14 Lou Brock 64	4.00	1.80
15 Bob Friend 60	4.00	1.80
16 Hank Greenberg 34	5.00	2.20
17 Maury Wills 59	4.00	1.80
18 Tom Lasorda 77	4.00	1.80
19 Moose Skowron 55	4.00	1.80
20 Frank Robinson 61	4.00	1.80
21 Rollie Fingers 72	4.00	1.80
22 Doug DeCinces 79	4.00	1.80
23 Eric Davis 90	4.00	1.80
24 Johnny Podres 53	4.00	1.80
25 Darrell Evans 84	4.00	1.80
26 Ron Cey 74	4.00	1.80
27 Ray Knight 86	4.00	1.80
28 Don Larsen 55	4.00	1.80
29 Harold Baines 90	4.00	1.80
30 Brooks Robinson 66	4.00	1.80
31 Wade Boggs 86	4.00	1.80
32 Joe Morgan 72	4.00	1.80
33 Kirk Gibson 84	4.00	1.80
34 Tommy John 77	4.00	1.80
35 Monte Irvin 51	4.00	1.80
36 Goose Gossage 78	4.00	1.80
37 Tug McGraw 73	4.00	1.80
38 Walt Weiss 88	4.00	1.80
39 Bill Madlock 79	4.00	1.80
40 Juan Marichal 62	4.00	1.80
41 Willie McGee 82	4.00	1.80
42 Joe Cronin 33	4.00	1.80
43 Paul Blair 66	4.00	1.80
44 Norm Cash 59	4.00	1.80
45 Ken Griffey 75	4.00	1.80
46 Bret Saberhagen 85	4.00	1.80
47 Don Sutton 74	4.00	1.80
48 Kirby Puckett 87	5.00	2.20
49 Keith Hernandez 82	4.00	1.80
50 George Brett 80	12.00	5.50
51 Bobby Richardson 57	4.00	1.80
52 Jose Canseco 88	5.00	2.20
53 Greg Luzinski 80	4.00	1.80
54 Bill Mazeroski 60	4.00	1.80
55 Red Schoendienst 46	4.00	1.80
56 Graig Nettles 76	4.00	1.80
57 Jerry Koosman 69	4.00	1.80
58 Tony Perez 70	4.00	1.80
59 Jim Rice 86	4.00	1.80
60 Duke Snider 49	4.00	1.80
61 David Justice 91	4.00	1.80
62 Johnny Sain 48	4.00	1.80
63 Chuck Klein 35	4.00	1.80
64 Sparky Anderson 70	4.00	1.80
65 Alan Trammell 84	4.00	1.80
66 Willie Wilson 80	4.00	1.80
67 Hoyt Wilhelm 54	4.00	1.80
68 Joe Pepitone 63	4.00	1.80
69 Darren Daulton 93	4.00	1.80
70 Tom Seaver 69	4.00	1.80
71 Catfish Hunter 72	4.00	1.80
72 Tim McCarver 64	4.00	1.80
73 Dave Parker 79	4.00	1.80
74 Earl Weaver 69	4.00	1.80
75 Ted Kluszewski 59	4.00	1.80
76 John Kruk 93	4.00	1.80
77 Dwight Evans 75	4.00	1.80
78 Ron Darling 86	4.00	1.80
79 Tony Oliva 65	4.00	1.80
80 Johnny Bench 70	5.00	2.20
81 Sam Crawford 07	4.00	1.80
82 Steve Yeager 74	4.00	1.80
83 Paul Molitor 82	4.00	1.80
84 Bert Campaneris 72	4.00	1.80
85 Mickey Rivers 76	4.00	1.80
86 Vince Coleman 87	4.00	1.80
87 Kent Tekulve 79	4.00	1.80
88 Dwight Gooden 86	4.00	1.80
89 Whitey Herzog 82	4.00	1.80
90 Whitey Ford 50	4.00	1.80
91 Warren Spahn 48	4.00	1.80
92 Fred Lynn 75	4.00	1.80
93 Joe Tinker 06	4.00	1.80
94 Bill Buckner 74	4.00	1.80
95 Bob Feller 48	4.00	1.80
96 Hank Bauer 49	4.00	1.80
97 Joe Rudi 72	4.00	1.80
98 Steve Sax 81	4.00	1.80
99 Bruce Sutter 82	4.00	1.80
100 Nolan Ryan 69	12.00	5.50
101 Bobby Thomson 51	4.00	1.80
102 Bob Watson 81	4.00	1.80
103 Vida Blue 72	4.00	1.80
104 Robin Roberts 50	4.00	1.80
105 Orlando Cepeda 62	4.00	1.80
106 Jim Bottomley 26	4.00	1.80
107 Heinie Manush 33	4.00	1.80
108 Jim Gilliam 53	4.00	1.80
109 Dave Concepcion 70	4.00	1.80
110 Al Kaline 68	5.00	2.20
111 Howard Johnson 84	4.00	1.80
112 Phil Rizzuto 41	4.00	1.80
113 Steve Garvey 74	4.00	1.80
114 George Foster 72	4.00	1.80
115 Carlton Fisk 75	4.00	1.80
116 Don Newcombe 49	4.00	1.80
117 Lance Parrish 84	4.00	1.80
118 Reggie Jackson 73	4.00	1.80
119 Luis Aparicio 59	4.00	1.80
120 Jim Palmer 66	4.00	1.80
121 Ron Guidry 77	4.00	1.80
122 Frankie Frisch 21	4.00	1.80
123 Chet Lemon 84	4.00	1.80
124 Cecil Cooper 75	4.00	1.80
125 Harmon Killebrew 65	5.00	2.20
126 Luis Tiant 75	4.00	1.80
127 John McGraw 05	4.00	1.80
128 Paul O'Neill 90	4.00	1.80
129 Jack Clark 85	4.00	1.80
130 Stan Musial 42	8.00	3.60
131 Mike Schmidt FC	10.00	4.50
132 Kirby Puckett FC	5.00	2.20
133 Carlton Fisk FC	4.00	1.80
134 Bill Mazeroski FC	4.00	1.80
135 Johnny Podres FC	4.00	1.80
136 Robin Yount FC	8.00	3.60
137 David Justice FC	4.00	1.80
138 Bobby Thomson FC	4.00	1.80
139 Joe Carter FC	4.00	1.80
140 Reggie Jackson FC	4.00	1.80
141 Kirk Gibson FC	4.00	1.80
142 Whitey Ford FC	4.00	1.80
143 Don Larsen FC	4.00	1.80
144 Duke Snider FC	4.00	1.80
145 Carl Yastrzemski FC	8.00	3.60
146 Johnny Bench FC	5.00	2.20
147 Lou Brock FC	4.00	1.80
148 Ted Kluszewski FC	4.00	1.80
149 Jim Palmer FC	4.00	1.80
150 Willie Mays FC	10.00	4.50

2003 Topps Tribute World Series Gold

MINT NRMT
*GOLD 1-130: 1.5X TO 4X BASIC
*GOLD 131-150: 1.5X TO 4X BASIC
RANDOM INSERTS IN PACKS
STATED PRINT RUN 100 SERIAL #'d SETS

2003 Topps Tribute World Series Fall Classic Cuts

MINT NRMT
STATED ODDS 1:3437
STATED PRINT RUN 1 SERIAL #'d SET
NO PRICING DUE TO SCARCITY
BR Babe Ruth
HG Hank Greenberg
HW Honus Wagner
JF Jimmie Foxx
JR Jackie Robinson
LG Lou Gehrig
MO Mel Ott
RM Roger Maris
TC Ty Cobb
TM Thurman Munson

2003 Topps Tribute World Series Memorable Match-Up Relics

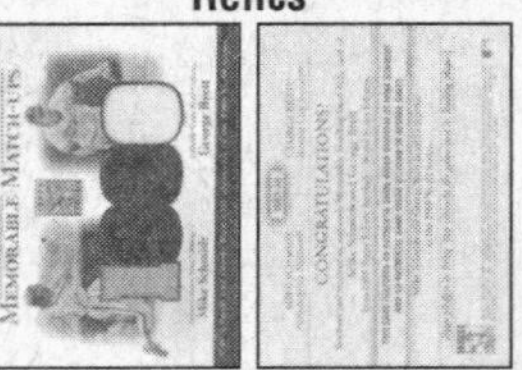

MINT NRMT
STATED ODDS 1:28
PRINT RUNS B/WN 9-88 COPIES PER
NO PRICING ON QTY OF 19 OR LESS
AM Sparky Anderson Uni 25.00 11.00
Billy Martin Uni/76
AS Luis Aparicio Bat 50.00 22.00
Duke Snider Bat/59
CR Eddie Collins Bat
Edd Roush Bat/19
EG Dennis Eckersley Uni 50.00 22.00
Kirk Gibson Bat/88
FS Whitey Ford Uni 80.00 36.00
Duke Snider Bat/52
GF Hank Greenberg Bat 150.00 70.00
Frankie Frisch Bat/34
GK Hank Greenberg Bat 150.00 70.00
Chuck Klein Bat/35
KB Al Kaline Uni 80.00 36.00
Lou Brock Bat/68
MF Bill Mazeroski Jsy 80.00 36.00
Whitey Ford Uni/64
PR Phil Rizzuto Bat 150.00 70.00
Willie Mays Uni/51
RBE Brooks Robinson Bat 80.00 36.00
Johnny Bench Bat/70
RS Frank Robinson Bat 50.00 22.00
Tom Seaver Uni/69
SB Mike Schmidt Uni 100.00 45.00
George Brett Uni/80
SP Willie Stargell Bat 40.00 18.00
Jim Palmer Jsy/79
SRI Mike Schmidt Uni 150.00 70.00
Cal Ripken Uni/83
SY Ozzie Smith Bat 80.00 36.00
Robin Yount Jsy/82
TG Alan Trammell Jsy 80.00 36.00
Tony Gwynn Bat/84
WB Mookie Wilson Bat 50.00 22.00
Bill Buckner Jsy/86
WC Honus Wagner Bat
Ty Cobb Bat/9

2003 Topps Tribute World Series Pastime Patches

MINT NRMT
STATED ODDS 1:146
STATED PRINT RUN 15 SERIAL #'d SETS
NO PRICING DUE TO SCARCITY
AK Al Kaline
AT Alan Trammell
CH Catfish Hunter
CR Cal Ripken
CY Carl Yastrzemski
DE Dennis Eckersley
DP Dave Parker
DS Don Sutton
GB George Brett
JC Jose Canseco
JP Jim Palmer
JR Jim Rice
MS Mike Schmidt
MSK Moose Skowron
RY Robin Yount

2003 Topps Tribute World Series Signature Relics

MINT NRMT
GROUP A ODDS 1:218
GROUP B ODDS 1:94
GROUP C ODDS 1:9
GROUP D ODDS 1:12
GOLD STATED ODDS 1:88
GOLD PRINT RUN 25 SERIAL #'d SETS
NO GOLD PRICING DUE TO SCARCITY
AK Al Kaline Uni C 50.00 22.00
AT Alan Trammell Jsy C 25.00 11.00
BR Brooks Robinson Bat A 80.00 36.00
DJ David Justice Uni B 50.00 22.00
DN Don Newcombe Bat A 50.00 22.00
EW Earl Weaver Jsy D 25.00 11.00
JC Joe Carter Bat C 25.00 11.00
JP Jim Palmer Jsy D 40.00 18.00
KG Kirk Gibson Bat C 40.00 18.00
MS Moose Skowron Bat C 25.00 11.00
MW Maury Wills Jsy D 25.00 11.00
MWI Mookie Wilson Bat B 40.00 18.00
SA Sparky Anderson Uni C 25.00 11.00
SG Steve Garvey Bat C 25.00 11.00
WF Whitey Ford Uni C 60.00 27.00

2003 Topps Tribute World Series Subway Fan Fare Tokens

MINT NRMT
ONE PER BOX
BM Billy Martin 15.00 6.75
DJ David Justice 10.00 4.50
DL Don Larsen 10.00 4.50
DN Don Newcombe 10.00 4.50
DS Duke Snider 15.00 6.75
HB Hank Bauer 10.00 4.50
JP Johnny Podres 10.00 4.50
MS Moose Skowron 10.00 4.50
PO Paul O'Neill 15.00 6.75
PR Phil Rizzuto 15.00 6.75
WF Whitey Ford 15.00 6.75
YB Yogi Berra 20.00 9.00

2003 Topps Tribute World Series Team Tribute Relics

MINT NRMT
GROUP A ODDS 1:436
GROUP B ODDS 1:7
GROUP A PRINT RUN 25 SERIAL #'d SETS
GROUP B PRINT RUN 275 SERIAL #'d SETS
NO GROUP A PRICING DUE TO SCARCITY
CM Orlando Cepeda Bat 30.00 13.50
Juan Marichal Uni B
CPM Dave Concepcion Bat 50.00 22.00
Tony Perez Uni
Joe Morgan Uni B
CYG Ron Cey Bat 30.00 13.50
Steve Yeager Bat
Steve Garvey Bat B
EC Dennis Eckersley Jsy 25.00 11.00
Jose Canseco Jsy B
FB Whitey Ford Uni
Yogi Berra Jsy A
FPG George Foster Bat 40.00 18.00
Tony Perez Uni
Ken Griffey Sr. Bat B
GB Lou Gehrig Bat
Babe Ruth Bat A
GT Kirk Gibson Bat 40.00 18.00
Alan Trammell Jsy B
HCD Keith Hernandez Bat 30.00 13.50
Gary Carter Uni
Lenny Dykstra Bat B
HJ Catfish Hunter Jsy 30.00 13.50
Reggie Jackson Bat B
KCA Al Kaline Uni 40.00 18.00
Norm Cash Bat B
MM Willie Mays Uni 80.00 36.00
Willie McCovey Bat B
OSD Paul O'Neill Bat 40.00 18.00
Chris Sabo Bat
Eric Davis Bat B
SB Bret Saberhagen Jsy 50.00 22.00
George Brett Bat B
SMC Ozzie Smith Uni 60.00 27.00
Willie McGee Bat
Vince Coleman Bat B
SPM Willie Stargell Bat 40.00 18.00
Dave Parker Jsy
Bill Madlock Bat B
SR Moose Skowron Bat
Bobby Richardson Bat A
SRK Tom Seaver Uni 80.00 36.00
Nolan Ryan Bat
Jerry Koosman Jsy B
TA Alan Trammell Jsy 25.00 11.00
Sparky Anderson Uni B
YLK Carl Yastrzemski Jsy 50.00 22.00
Fred Lynn Jsy
Carlton Fisk Bat B
YM Robin Yount Jsy 40.00 18.00
Paul Molitor Bat B

2003 Topps Tribute World Series Tribute Relics

MINT NRMT
GROUP A ODDS 1:41
GROUP B ODDS 1:3
GROUP A PRINT RUN 50 SERIAL #'d SETS
GROUP B PRINT RUN 425 SERIAL #'d SETS
GOLD STATED ODDS 1:25
GOLD PRINT RUN 25 SERIAL #'d SETS
NO GOLD PRICING DUE TO SCARCITY
BH Bucky Harris Bat B 15.00 6.75
BM Bill Mazeroski Uni B 15.00 6.75
BMA Billy Martin Uni B 15.00 6.75
BR Babe Ruth Bat B 150.00 70.00
BT Bobby Thomson Bat B 10.00 4.50
CF Carlton Fisk Bat-Wall B 50.00 22.00
CH Catfish Hunter Jsy B 15.00 6.75
CK Chuck Klein Bat B 15.00 6.75
CR Cal Ripken Uni B 50.00 22.00
CY Carl Yastrzemski Jsy B 40.00 18.00
ER Edd Roush Bat A 50.00 22.00
FF Frankie Frisch Bat B 25.00 11.00
FR Frank Robinson Bat B 15.00 6.75
GB George Brett Uni B 40.00 18.00
HA Hank Aaron Bat A 60.00 27.00
HB Hank Bauer Bat A 50.00 22.00
HG Hank Greenberg Bat A 80.00 36.00
HK Harmon Killebrew Uni B 25.00 11.00
HM Heinie Manush Bat A 50.00 22.00
HW Honus Wagner Bat A 200.00 90.00
JB Jim Bottomley Bat A 50.00 22.00
JBE Johnny Bench Uni B 25.00 11.00
JC Jose Canseco Jsy B 15.00 6.75
JF Jimmie Foxx Bat A 120.00 55.00
JM Juan Marichal Uni B 10.00 4.50
JR Jackie Robinson Bat B 50.00 22.00
JT Joe Tinker Bat B 30.00 13.50
KP Kirby Puckett Bat B 25.00 11.00
LB Lou Brock Bat B 15.00 6.75
LG Lou Gehrig Bat A 250.00 110.00
MS Mike Schmidt Uni B 25.00 11.00
NC Norm Cash Jsy A 50.00 22.00
OC Orlando Cepeda Bat A 50.00 22.00
OS Ozzie Smith Uni B 25.00 11.00
RC Roberto Clemente Bat A 150.00 70.00
RH Rogers Hornsby Bat B 40.00 18.00
RJ Reggie Jackson Bat B 15.00 6.75
RM Roger Maris Bat A 100.00 45.00
RS Red Schoendienst Bat B 15.00 6.75
RY Robin Yount Jsy B 25.00 11.00
SC Sam Crawford Bat A 50.00 22.00
SM Stan Musial Bat B 40.00 18.00
TC Ty Cobb Uni B 120.00 55.00
TG Tony Gwynn Uni B 25.00 11.00
TK Ted Kluszewski Uni B 15.00 6.75
TM Thurman Munson Bat B 30.00 13.50
TS Tom Seaver Uni B 15.00 6.75
TSP Tris Speaker Bat A 120.00 55.00
WB Wade Boggs Bat B 15.00 6.75
WM Willie Mays Uni B 50.00 22.00
WMC Willie McCovey Uni B 10.00 4.50
WS Willie Stargell Uni A 50.00 22.00
YB Yogi Berra Uni B 25.00 11.00

2003 Topps Tribute World Series Tribute Autograph Relics

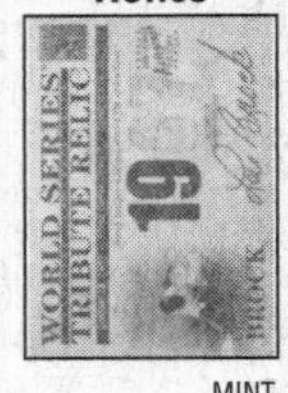

MINT NRMT
STATED ODDS 1:55
GOLD STATED ODDS 1:163
GOLD PRINT RUN 25 SERIAL #'d SETS
NO GOLD PRICING DUE TO SCARCITY
BM Bill Mazeroski Jsy 60.00 27.00
BT Bobby Thomson Bat 40.00 18.00
CF Carlton Fisk Bat-Wall 150.00 70.00
HK Harmon Killebrew Uni 100.00 45.00
JC Jose Canseco Jsy 100.00 45.00
LB Lou Brock Bat 60.00 27.00
MS Mike Schmidt Uni 120.00 55.00
WM Willie Mays Uni 400.00 180.00

2004 UD Diamond All-Star

This 120 card set was released in March, 2004. The set was issued solely through Upper Deck's "retail" outlets. The set was issued in six card packs with an $3 SRP which came 24 packs to a box and 20 boxes to a case. Cards numbered 1-90 feature active veterans which cards numbered 91 through 120 feature rookies. The Rookie Cards were issued at a stated rate of one in six.

	Nm-Mt	Ex-Mt
COMP.SET w/o SP's (90)	25.00	7.50
COMMON CARD (1-90)	.30	.09
COMMON CARD (91-120)	3.00	.90
1 Garret Anderson	.30	.09
2 Darin Erstad	.30	.09
3 Troy Glaus	.30	.09
4 Curt Schilling	.75	.23
5 Brandon Webb	.30	.09
6 Randy Johnson	.75	.23
7 Andruw Jones	.30	.09
8 Chipper Jones	.75	.23
9 Gary Sheffield	.30	.09
10 Jay Gibbons	.30	.09
11 Miguel Tejada	.30	.09
12 Tony Batista	.30	.09
13 Nomar Garciaparra	1.25	.35
14 Manny Ramirez	.50	.15
15 Pedro Martinez	.75	.23
16 Mark Prior	.75	.23
17 Kerry Wood	.75	.23
18 Sammy Sosa	1.25	.35
19 Bartolo Colon	.30	.09
20 Magglio Ordonez	.30	.09
21 Frank Thomas	.75	.23
22 Adam Dunn	.50	.15
23 Austin Kearns	.30	.09
24 Ken Griffey Jr.	1.25	.35
25 Brandon Phillips	.30	.09
26 Milton Bradley	.30	.09
27 Jody Gerut	.30	.09
28 Todd Helton	.50	.15
29 Larry Walker	.50	.15
30 Preston Wilson	.30	.09
31 Jeremy Bonderman	.30	.09
32 Carlos Pena	.30	.09
33 Dmitri Young	.30	.09
34 Dontrelle Willis	.30	.09
35 Miguel Cabrera	.50	.15
36 Mike Lowell	.30	.09
37 Jeff Bagwell	.50	.15
38 Roy Oswalt	.30	.09
39 Lance Berkman	.30	.09
40 Carlos Beltran	.50	.15

	Nm-Mt	Ex-Mt
41 Mike Sweeney	.30	.09
42 Rondell White	.30	.09
43 Hideo Nomo	.75	.23
44 Kevin Brown	.30	.09
45 Shawn Green	.30	.09
46 Ben Sheets	.30	.09
47 Geoff Jenkins	.30	.09
48 Richie Sexson	.30	.09
49 Jacque Jones	.30	.09
50 Johan Santana	.50	.15
51 Torii Hunter	.30	.09
52 Javier Vazquez	.30	.09
53 Jose Vidro	.30	.09
54 Vladimir Guerrero	.75	.23
55 Cliff Floyd	.30	.09
56 Mike Piazza	1.25	.35
57 Jose Reyes	.30	.09
58 Derek Jeter	1.50	.45
59 Jason Giambi	.30	.09
60 Alfonso Soriano	.50	.15
61 Eric Chavez	.30	.09
62 Barry Zito	.30	.09
63 Tim Hudson	.30	.09
64 Bobby Abreu	.30	.09
65 Jim Thome	.75	.23
66 Kevin Millwood	.30	.09
67 Roger Clemens	1.50	.45
68 Jason Kendall	.30	.09
69 Reggie Sanders	.30	.09
70 Phil Nevin	.30	.09
71 Ryan Klesko	.30	.09
72 Brian Giles	.30	.09
73 A.J. Pierzynski	.30	.09
74 Jason Schmidt	.30	.09
75 Sidney Ponson	.30	.09
76 Edgar Martinez	.50	.15
77 Ichiro Suzuki	1.25	.35
78 Bret Boone	.30	.09
79 Albert Pujols	1.50	.45
80 Scott Rolen	.75	.23
81 Jim Edmonds	.30	.09
82 Aubrey Huff	.30	.09
83 Delmon Young	.50	.15
84 Rocco Baldelli	.30	.09
85 Alex Rodriguez	1.25	.35
86 Mark Teixeira	.30	.09
87 Rafael Palmeiro	.50	.15
88 Carlos Delgado	.30	.09
89 Vernon Wells	.30	.09
90 Roy Halladay	.30	.09
91 Brandon Medders FC RC	3.00	.90
92 Colby Miller FC RC	3.00	.90
93 Dave Crouthers FC RC	3.00	.90
94 Dennis Sarfate FC RC	3.00	.90
95 Donald Kelly FC RC	3.00	.90
96 Alec Zumwalt FC RC	3.00	.90
97 Frank Brooks FC RC	3.00	.90
98 Greg Dobbs FC RC	3.00	.90
99 Ian Snell FC RC	4.00	1.20
100 Jake Woods FC RC	3.00	.90
101 Jamie Brown FC RC	3.00	.90
102 Jason Frasor FC RC	3.00	.90
103 Jerome Gamble FC RC	3.00	.90
104 Jesse Harper FC RC	3.00	.90
105 Josh Labandeira FC RC	3.00	.90
106 Justin Hampson FC RC	3.00	.90
107 Justin Huisman FC RC	3.00	.90
108 Justin Leone FC RC	4.00	1.20
109 Chris Aguila FC RC	3.00	.90
110 Lincoln Holdzkom FC RC	3.00	.90
111 Mike Bumatay FC RC	3.00	.90
112 Mike Gosling FC RC	3.00	.90
113 Mike Johnston FC RC	3.00	.90
114 Mike Rouse FC RC	3.00	.90
115 Nick Regilio FC RC	3.00	.90
116 Ryan Meaux FC RC	3.00	.90
117 Scott Dohmann FC RC	3.00	.90
118 Sean Henn FC RC	3.00	.90
119 Tim Bausher FC RC	3.00	.90
120 Tim Bittner FC RC	3.00	.90

2004 UD Diamond All-Star Class of 2004 Autographs

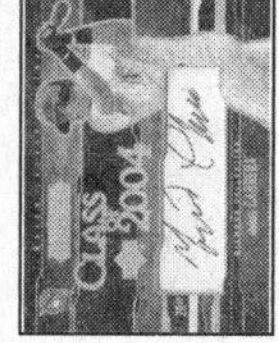

	Nm-Mt	Ex-Mt
STATED ODDS 1:5800		
PRINT RUNS B/WN 50-100 COPIES PER		
BZ Barry Zito/100	25.00	7.50
DW Dontrelle Willis/100	15.00	4.50
HM Hideki Matsui/100	300.00	90.00
JR Jose Reyes/100	15.00	4.50
KG Ken Griffey Jr./100	120.00	36.00
MC Miguel Cabrera/50	30.00	9.00
MP Mark Prior/100	60.00	18.00
RH Rich Harden/100	15.00	4.50
VG Vladimir Guerrero/100	40.00	12.00

2004 UD Diamond All-Star Dean's List Jersey

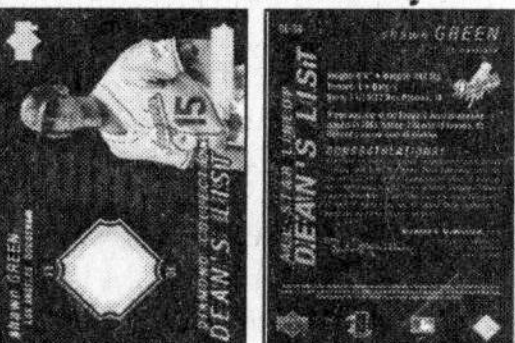

	Nm-Mt	Ex-Mt
STATED ODDS 1:72		
AP Albert Pujols	15.00	4.50
AR Alex Rodriguez	10.00	3.00

	Nm-Mt	Ex-Mt
AS Alfonso Soriano	10.00	3.00
BA Jeff Bagwell	10.00	3.00
CS Curt Schilling	10.00	3.00
DW Dontrelle Willis	8.00	2.40
GL Troy Glaus	8.00	2.40
GM Greg Maddux	10.00	3.00
HB Hank Blalock	8.00	2.40
HM Hideki Matsui	40.00	12.00
HN Hideo Nomo	10.00	3.00
IS Ichiro Suzuki	25.00	7.50
JG Jason Giambi	8.00	2.40
JT Jim Thome	10.00	3.00
KG Ken Griffey Jr.	15.00	4.50
LG Luis Gonzalez	8.00	2.40
MP Mark Prior	10.00	3.00
PI Mike Piazza	10.00	3.00
SG Shawn Green	8.00	2.40
SS Sammy Sosa	10.00	3.00
VG Vladimir Guerrero	10.00	3.00

2004 UD Diamond All-Star Future Gems Jersey

	Nm-Mt	Ex-Mt
STATED ODDS 1:72		
AE Adam Eaton	8.00	2.40
AH Aaron Heilman	8.00	2.40
BA Josh Bard	8.00	2.40
BO Jeremy Bonderman	8.00	2.40
BS Ben Sheets	8.00	2.40
DS David Sanders	8.00	2.40
EM Eric Milton	8.00	2.40
GU Jeremy Guthrie	8.00	2.40
IS Kazuhisa Ishii	8.00	2.40
JB Josh Beckett	8.00	2.40
JJ Jason Jennings	8.00	2.40
JL Jon Leicester	8.00	2.40
JR Jose Reyes	8.00	2.40
KA Matt Kata	8.00	2.40
LF Lew Ford	8.00	2.40
MC Mike Cameron	8.00	2.40
MK Mark Kotsay	8.00	2.40
MT Mark Teixeira	8.00	2.40
PS Phil Seibel	8.00	2.40
RH Roy Halladay	8.00	2.40
RR Rick Roberts	8.00	2.40
SB Sean Burroughs	8.00	2.40
TH Travis Hafner	8.00	2.40
TW Todd Wellemeyer	8.00	2.40
WE Willie Eyre	8.00	2.40
WI Josh Willingham	8.00	2.40

2004 UD Diamond All-Star Premium Stars

	Nm-Mt	Ex-Mt
STATED ODDS 1:4 MASS BLASTER		
AP Albert Pujols		
AR Alex Rodriguez		
AS Alfonso Soriano		
CD Carlos Delgado		
DJ Derek Jeter		
GS Gary Sheffield		
HM Hideki Matsui		
IS Ichiro Suzuki		
JG Jason Giambi		
KG Ken Griffey Jr.		
MP Mike Piazza		
NG Nomar Garciaparra		
SG Shawn Green		
SS Sammy Sosa		
VG Vladimir Guerrero		

2004 UD Diamond All-Star Promo

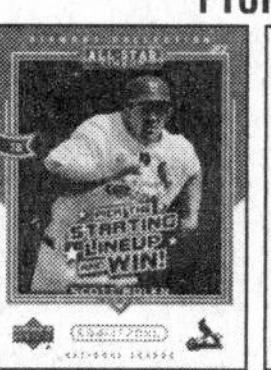

	Nm-Mt	Ex-Mt
ONE PER PACK		
AD Adam Dunn	1.25	.35
AJ Andruw Jones	1.00	.30
AK Austin Kearns	1.00	.30
BA Bobby Abreu	1.00	.30
BC Bartolo Colon	1.00	.30
BE Josh Beckett	1.00	.30
BO Bret Boone	1.00	.30
BZ Barry Zito	1.00	.30
CB Carlos Beltran	1.25	.35
CJ Chipper Jones	2.00	.60
CS Curt Schilling	2.00	.60
DJ Derek Jeter	4.00	1.20
DW Dontrelle Willis	1.00	.30
EC Eric Chavez	1.00	.30
ER Edgar Renteria	1.00	.30
FT Frank Thomas	2.00	.60
GA Garret Anderson	1.00	.30
GS Gary Sheffield	1.00	.30
HB Hank Blalock	1.00	.30
HM Hideki Matsui	3.00	.90
HU Tim Hudson	1.00	.30
IR Ivan Rodriguez	2.00	.60
JB Jeff Bagwell	1.25	.35
JD Johnny Damon	2.00	.60
JE Jim Edmonds	1.00	.30
JG Jason Giambi	1.00	.30
JJ Jacque Jones	1.00	.30
JK Jeff Kent	1.00	.30
JL Javy Lopez	1.00	.30
JP Jorge Posada	1.25	.35
JS Jason Schmidt	1.00	.30
JT Jim Thome	2.00	.60
JV Jason Varitek	1.25	.35
KG Ken Griffey Jr.	3.00	.90
KW Kerry Wood	2.00	.60
MG Marcus Giles	1.00	.30
ML Mike Lowell	1.00	.30
MM Mark Mulder	1.00	.30
MO Magglio Ordonez	1.00	.30
MP Mark Prior	2.00	.60
MR Manny Ramirez	1.25	.35
MS Mike Sweeney	1.00	.30
MT Mark Teixeira	1.00	.30
MU Mike Mussina	1.25	.35
OC Orlando Cabrera	1.00	.30
PI Mike Piazza	3.00	.90
PM Pedro Martinez	2.00	.60
PW Preston Wilson	1.00	.30
RF Rafael Furcal	1.00	.30
RH Roy Halladay	1.00	.30
RJ Randy Johnson	2.00	.60
RP Rafael Palmeiro	1.25	.35
RS Richie Sexson	1.00	.30
SG Shawn Green	1.00	.30
SR Scott Rolen	2.00	.60
TE Miguel Tejada	1.00	.30
TG Troy Glaus	1.00	.30
TH Torii Hunter	1.00	.30
VI Jose Vidro	1.00	.30
VW Vernon Wells	1.00	.30

2004 UD Diamond All-Star Promo e-Card

	Nm-Mt	Ex-Mt
STATED ODDS 1:12		
AP Albert Pujols	5.00	1.50
AR Alex Rodriguez	4.00	1.20
AS Alfonso Soriano	1.50	.45
CD Carlos Delgado	1.50	.45
IS Ichiro Suzuki	4.00	1.20
NG Nomar Garciaparra	4.00	1.20
SS Sammy Sosa	4.00	1.20
TH Todd Helton	1.50	.45
VG Vladimir Guerrero	2.50	.75

2004 UD Diamond Pro Sigs

This 230 card set was released in May, 2004. This set was issued in six card packs with an $3 SRP which came 24 packs to a box and six boxes to a case. Cards numbered 1 through 150 feature veterans while cards numbered 151 through 240 featured players who had signed cards for this product. A few players did not retrun their cards in time so this set is actually 230 cards instead of the projected 240 cards.

	Nm-Mt	Ex-Mt
COMP.SET w/o SP's (90)	15.00	4.50
COMMON CARD (1-90)	.30	.09
COMMON CARD (91-150)	4.00	1.20
91-150 STATED ODDS 1:6		
COMMON CARD (151-240)	10.00	3.00
151-240 STATED ODDS 1:24		
CARDS 160/169/174-175/177 DO NOT EXIST		
CARDS 220/224/226-228 DO NOT EXIST		
INSTANT WIN EXCH.ODDS 1:60,000		
1 Alfonso Soriano	.50	.15
2 Josh Beckett	.30	.09
3 Kerry Wood	.75	.23
4 Brandon Webb	.30	.09
5 Shannon Stewart	.30	.09
6 Larry Walker	.50	.15
7 Tim Hudson	.30	.09
8 Carlos Lee	.30	.09
9 Austin Kearns	.30	.09
10 Vernon Wells	.30	.09
11 Jeff Bagwell	.50	.15
12 Hideo Nomo	.75	.23
13 Jerome Williams	.30	.09
14 Kevin Brown	.30	.09
15 Jose Vidro	.30	.09
16 Rocco Baldelli	.30	.09
17 Frank Thomas	.75	.23
18 Albert Pujols	1.50	.45
19 Bartolo Colon	.30	.09
20 C.C. Sabathia	.30	.09
21 Andruw Jones	.30	.09
22 Reggie Sanders	.30	.09
23 Carlos Beltran	.50	.15
24 Curt Schilling	.75	.23
25 Miguel Tejada	.50	.15
26 Barry Zito	.30	.09
27 Pedro Martinez	.75	.23
28 Sean Burroughs	.30	.09
29 Sammy Sosa	1.25	.35
30 Eric Chavez	.30	.09
31 Roy Halladay	.30	.09
32 Todd Helton	.50	.15
33 Mark Prior	.75	.23
34 Mike Mussina	.50	.15
35 Alex Rodriguez Yanks	1.25	.35
36 Ivan Rodriguez	.75	.23
37 Mike Piazza	1.25	.35
38 Angel Berroa	.30	.09
39 Orlando Cabrera	.30	.09
40 Jim Thome	.75	.23
41 Brian Giles	.30	.09
42 Ichiro Suzuki	1.25	.35
43 Edgar Renteria	.30	.09
44 Eric Gagne	.75	.23
45 Gary Sheffield	.30	.09
46 Torii Hunter	.30	.09
47 Roger Clemens UER Photo on back in Curt Schilling	1.50	.45
48 Scott Rolen	.75	.23
49 Johan Santana	.50	.15
50 Jacque Jones	.30	.09
51 Hank Blalock	.30	.09
52 Rafael Palmeiro	.50	.15
53 Dmitri Young	.30	.09
54 Ryan Klesko	.30	.09
55 Mark Teixeira	.30	.09
56 Nomar Garciaparra	1.25	.35
57 Jose Reyes	.30	.09
58 Vladimir Guerrero	.75	.23
59 Mike Sweeney	.30	.09
60 Jorge Posada	.50	.15
61 Derek Jeter	1.50	.45
62 Milton Bradley	.30	.09
63 Bobby Abreu	.30	.09
64 Greg Maddux	1.25	.35
65 Adam Dunn	.50	.15
66 Troy Glaus	.30	.09
67 Luis Gonzalez	.30	.09
68 Shawn Green	.30	.09
69 Bret Boone	.30	.09
70 Mark Mulder	.30	.09
71 Lance Berkman	.30	.09
72 Preston Wilson	.30	.09
73 Phil Nevin	.30	.09
74 Chipper Jones	.75	.23
75 Garret Anderson	.30	.09
76 Jason Giambi	.30	.09
77 Magglio Ordonez	.30	.09
78 Jeff Kent	.30	.09
79 Richie Sexson	.30	.09
80 Mike Lowell	.30	.09
81 Ben Sheets	.30	.09
82 Randy Johnson	.75	.23
83 Dontrelle Willis	.30	.09
84 Javier Vazquez	.30	.09
85 Geoff Jenkins	.30	.09
86 Manny Ramirez	.50	.15
87 Jim Edmonds	.30	.09
88 Roy Oswalt	.30	.09
89 Edgar Martinez	.50	.15
90 Carlos Delgado	.30	.09
91 Chris Saenz FC RC	4.00	1.20
92 Justin Leone FC RC	5.00	1.50
93 Shawn Hill FC RC	4.00	1.20
94 Chad Bentz FC RC	4.00	1.20
95 Jesse Harper FC RC	4.00	1.20
96 Dave Crouthers FC RC	4.00	1.20
97 Justin Germano FC RC	4.00	1.20
98 Tim Bausher FC RC	4.00	1.20
99 Greg Dobbs FC RC	4.00	1.20
100 Enemencio Pacheco FC RC	4.00	1.20
101 Dennis Sarfate FC RC	4.00	1.20
102 Edwin Moreno FC RC	4.00	1.20
103 Colby Miller FC RC	4.00	1.20
104 Mike Rouse FC RC	4.00	1.20
105 Fernando Nieve FC RC	4.00	1.20
106 Tim Hamulack FC RC	4.00	1.20
107 Jason Frasor FC RC	4.00	1.20
108 Jose Capellan FC RC	6.00	1.80
109 Jamie Brown FC RC	4.00	1.20
110 Mariano Gomez FC RC	4.00	1.20
111 Mike Vento FC RC	5.00	1.50
112 Josh Labandeira FC RC	4.00	1.20
113 Mike Gosling FC RC	4.00	1.20
114 Shingo Takatsu FC RC	5.00	1.50
115 Justin Hampson FC RC	4.00	1.20
116 Tim Bittner FC RC	4.00	1.20
117 Jerry Gil FC RC	4.00	1.20
118 Carlos Vasquez FC RC	5.00	1.50
119 Lincoln Holdzkom FC RC	4.00	1.20
120 Mike Johnston FC RC	4.00	1.20
121 William Bergolla FC RC	4.00	1.20
122 Luis A. Gonzalez FC RC	5.00	1.50
123 Ivan Ochoa FC RC	4.00	1.20
124 Roman Colon FC RC	4.00	1.20
125 Renyel Pinto FC RC	5.00	1.50
126 Donnie Kelly FC RC	4.00	1.20
127 Chris Oxspring FC RC	5.00	1.50
128 Sean Henn FC RC	4.00	1.20
129 Ryan Meaux FC RC	4.00	1.20
130 Shawn Camp FC RC	4.00	1.20
131 Brandon Medders FC RC	4.00	1.20
132 Rusty Tucker FC RC	5.00	1.50
133 Kazuo Matsui FC RC	8.00	2.40
134 Jorge Sequea FC RC	4.00	1.20
135 Hector Gimenez FC RC	4.00	1.20
136 Casey Daigle FC RC	4.00	1.20
137 Ian Snell FC RC	5.00	1.50
138 Scott Dohmann FC RC	4.00	1.20
139 Ronny Cedeno FC RC	4.00	1.20
140 Jorge Vasquez FC RC	4.00	1.20
141 David Aardsma FC RC	4.00	1.20
142 Carlos Hines FC RC	4.00	1.20
143 Scott Proctor FC RC	5.00	1.50
144 Jerome Gamble FC RC	4.00	1.20
145 Jason Bartlett FC RC	5.00	1.50
146 Akinori Otsuka FC RC	4.00	1.20
147 Merkin Valdez FC RC	5.00	1.50
148 Jake Woods FC RC	4.00	1.20
149 Chris Aguila FC RC	4.00	1.20
150 John Gall FC RC	5.00	1.50
151 Aaron Miles AU	15.00	4.50
152 Aquilino Lopez AU	10.00	3.00
153 Bill Hall AU	10.00	3.00
154 Billy Traber AU	10.00	3.00
155 Brad Lidge AU	25.00	7.50
156 Brady Clark AU	10.00	3.00
157 Brandon Duckworth AU	10.00	3.00
158 Brett Tomko AU	10.00	3.00
159 Brian Fuentes AU	10.00	3.00
160 Does Not Exist		
161 Brooks Kieshnick AU	10.00	3.00
162 Carlos Rivera AU	10.00	3.00
163 Chad Cordero AU	10.00	3.00
164 Chad Tracy AU	15.00	4.50
165 Claudio Vargas AU	10.00	3.00
166 D.J. Carrasco AU	10.00	3.00
167 Damian Rolls AU	10.00	3.00
168 David Sanders AU	10.00	3.00
169 Does Not Exist		
170 Derrick Turnbow AU	10.00	3.00
171 Desi Relaford AU	10.00	3.00
172 Doug Davis AU	10.00	3.00
173 Dustan Mohr AU	10.00	3.00
174 Does Not Exist		
175 Does Not Exist		
176 Frank Catalanotto AU	10.00	3.00
177 Does Not Exist		
178 Franklyn German AU	10.00	3.00
179 Ron Belliard AU	10.00	3.00
180 Geoff Geary AU	10.00	3.00
181 Greg Colbrunn AU	10.00	3.00
182 Henry Mateo AU	10.00	3.00
183 Brent Mayne AU	10.00	3.00
184 Horacio Ramirez AU	10.00	3.00
185 J.C. Romero AU	10.00	3.00
186 J.J. Putz AU	10.00	3.00
187 Ferdin Tejada AU	10.00	3.00
188 Jaime Cerda AU	10.00	3.00
189 Jason Michaels AU	10.00	3.00
190 Jason Simontacchi AU	10.00	3.00
191 Jay Witasick AU	10.00	3.00
192 Joe Valentine AU	10.00	3.00
193 Joey Eischen AU	10.00	3.00
194 Johnny Estrada AU	15.00	4.50
195 Jon Garland AU	10.00	3.00
196 Jon Switzer AU	10.00	3.00
197 Jorge Julio AU	10.00	3.00
198 Jorge Sosa AU	10.00	3.00
199 Jose Castillo AU	10.00	3.00
200 Jose Macias AU	10.00	3.00
201 Josh Bard AU	10.00	3.00
202 Juan Cruz AU	10.00	3.00
203 Juan Rivera AU	10.00	3.00
204 Ken Griffey Jr. AU	120.00	36.00
205 Kevin Hooper AU	10.00	3.00
206 Kiko Calero AU	10.00	3.00
207 Chad Gaudin AU	10.00	3.00
208 Luis Rivas AU	10.00	3.00
209 Mark Corey AU	10.00	3.00
210 Matt Ford AU	10.00	3.00
211 Matt Herges AU	10.00	3.00
212 Miguel Cairo AU	10.00	3.00
213 Fernando Cabrera AU	10.00	3.00
214 Mike MacDougal AU	10.00	3.00
215 Mike Neu AU	10.00	3.00
216 Lew Ford AU	15.00	4.50
217 Mike Wood AU	15.00	4.50
218 Nate Robertson AU	15.00	4.50
219 Nick Punto AU	10.00	3.00
220 Does Not Exist		
221 Oscar Villarreal AU	10.00	3.00
222 Ramon Vazquez AU	10.00	3.00
223 Randall Simon AU	10.00	3.00
224 Does Not Exist		
225 Ricky Stone AU	10.00	3.00
226 Does Not Exist		
227 Does Not Exist		
228 Does Not Exist		
229 Ryan Drese AU	10.00	3.00
230 Ryan Ludwick AU	10.00	3.00
231 Scot Shields AU	10.00	3.00
232 Shane Nance AU	10.00	3.00
233 Steve Colyer AU	10.00	3.00
234 Tony Armas Jr. AU	10.00	3.00
235 Robby Hammock AU	10.00	3.00
236 Travis Hafner AU	15.00	4.50
237 Victor Martinez AU	15.00	4.50
238 Wilfredo Ledezma AU	10.00	3.00
239 Willie Bloomquist AU	10.00	3.00
240 Yorvit Torrealba AU	10.00	3.00
NNO Instant Win Exchange		

2004 UD Diamond Pro Sigs Gold

	Nm-Mt	Ex-Mt
*GOLD: 3X TO 8X BASIC		
OVERALL PARALLEL ODDS 1:6		

2004 UD Diamond Pro Sigs Silver

	Nm-Mt	Ex-Mt
*SILVER: 1.5X TO 4X BASIC		
OVERALL PARALLEL ODDS 1:6		

2004 UD Diamond Pro Sigs Signature Blue Ink

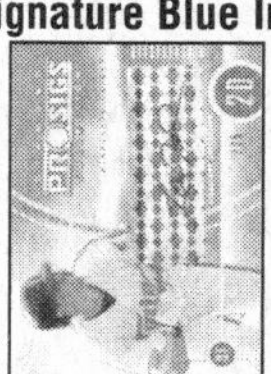

	Nm-Mt	Ex-Mt
STATED PRINT RUN 25 SERIAL #'d SETS		
RED INK PRINT RUN 10 SERIAL #'d SETS		
OVERALL AU ODDS 1:24		
NO PRICING DUE TO SCARCITY		

2004 UD Diamond Pro Sigs Hall of Famers

	Nm-Mt	Ex-Mt
ONE PER SEALED STARTER BOX		
NO PRICING DUE TO LACK OF MARKET INFO		
1 Al Kaline		
2 Billy Williams		
3 Bob Feller		
4 Bob Gibson		
5 Brooks Robinson		
6 Catfish Hunter		
7 Eddie Mathews		
8 Ernie Banks		
9 Ferguson Jenkins		
10 Harmon Killebrew		
11 Joe DiMaggio		
12 Joe Morgan		
13 Juan Marichal		
14 Lou Brock		
15 Mickey Mantle		
16 Mike Schmidt		
17 Nolan Ryan		
18 Pee Wee Reese		
19 Phil Rizzuto		
20 Ralph Kiner		
21 Robin Yount		
22 Rollie Fingers		
23 Stan Musial		
24 Ted Williams		
25 Tom Seaver		
26 Warren Spahn		
27 Whitey Ford		
28 Willie McCovey		
29 Willie Stargell		
30 Yogi Berra		

1999 UD Ionix

This 90-card set (produced by Upper Deck) was distributed in four-card packs with a suggested retail price of $4.99. The set features color action photos of top MLB players printed on super-thick, double-laminated, metalized cards. The set contains a 30-card short-printed subset, Techno (61-90), of which cards were randomly inserted in packs at the rate of one in four. A game-used bat from Hall of Fame slugger Frank Robinson was cut up and incorporated into 370 special 500 Home Run Bat Cards. Robinson signed 20 of these cards. Pack odds for these cards was not officially released, but suffice to say, they're few and far between. Pricing for these bat cards can be referenced under 1999 Upper Deck A Piece of History 500 Club. In addition, a Ken Griffey Jr. sample card was distributed to dealers and hobby media several weeks prior to the product's release. The card can be readily identified by the bold "SAMPLE" text running diagonally across the back.

	Nm-Mt	Ex-Mt
COMPLETE SET (90)	120.00	36.00
COMP.SET w/o SP's (60)	20.00	6.00
COMMON CARD (1-60)	.40	.12
COMMON TECH (61-90)	2.00	.60
1 Troy Glaus	.40	.12
2 Darin Erstad	.40	.12
3 Travis Lee	.40	.12
4 Matt Williams	.40	.12
5 Chipper Jones	1.00	.30
6 Greg Maddux	1.50	.45
7 Andruw Jones	.40	.12
8 Andres Galarraga	.40	.12
9 Tom Glavine	.60	.18
10 Cal Ripken	3.00	.90
11 Ryan Minor	.40	.12
12 Nomar Garciaparra	1.50	.45
13 Mo Vaughn	.40	.12
14 Pedro Martinez	1.00	.30
15 Sammy Sosa	1.50	.45
16 Kerry Wood	1.00	.30
17 Albert Belle	.40	.12
18 Frank Thomas	1.00	.30
19 Sean Casey	.40	.12
20 Kenny Lofton	.40	.12
21 Manny Ramirez	.60	.18
22 Jim Thome	1.00	.30
23 Bartolo Colon	.40	.12
24 Jaret Wright	.40	.12
25 Larry Walker	.60	.18
26 Tony Clark	.40	.12
27 Gabe Kapler	.40	.12
28 Edgar Renteria	.40	.12
29 Randy Johnson	1.00	.30
30 Craig Biggio	.60	.18
31 Jeff Bagwell	.60	.18
32 Moises Alou	.40	.12
33 Johnny Damon	.60	.18
34 Adrian Beltre	.60	.18
35 Jeromy Burnitz	.40	.12
36 Todd Walker	.40	.12
37 Corey Koskie	.40	.12
38 Vladimir Guerrero	1.00	.30
39 Mike Piazza	1.50	.45
40 Hideo Nomo	1.00	.30
41 Derek Jeter	2.50	.75
42 Tino Martinez	.60	.18
43 Orlando Hernandez	.40	.12
44 Ben Grieve	.40	.12
45 Rickey Henderson	1.00	.30
46 Scott Rolen	1.00	.30
47 Curt Schilling	.40	.12
48 Aramis Ramirez	.40	.12
49 Tony Gwynn	1.25	.35
50 Kevin Brown	.40	.12
51 Barry Bonds	2.50	.75
52 Ken Griffey Jr.	1.50	.45
53 Alex Rodriguez	1.50	.45
54 Mark McGwire	2.50	.75
55 J.D. Drew	.40	.12
56 Rolando Arrojo	.40	.12
57 Ivan Rodriguez	1.00	.30
58 Juan Gonzalez	.60	.18
59 Roger Clemens	2.00	.60
60 Jose Cruz Jr.	.40	.12
61 Travis Lee TECH	2.00	.60
62 Andres Galarraga TECH	2.00	.60
63 Andruw Jones TECH	2.00	.60
64 Chipper Jones TECH	4.00	1.20
65 Greg Maddux TECH	6.00	1.80
66 Cal Ripken TECH	12.00	3.60
67 N.Garciaparra TECH	6.00	1.80
68 Mo Vaughn TECH	2.00	.60
69 Sammy Sosa TECH	6.00	1.80
70 Frank Thomas TECH	4.00	1.20
71 Kerry Wood TECH	4.00	1.20
72 Kenny Lofton TECH	2.00	.60
73 Manny Ramirez TECH	2.50	.75
74 Larry Walker TECH	2.50	.75
75 Jeff Bagwell TECH	2.50	.75
76 Randy Johnson TECH	4.00	1.20
77 Paul Molitor TECH	2.50	.75
78 Derek Jeter TECH	10.00	3.00
79 Tino Martinez TECH	2.50	.75
80 Mike Piazza TECH	6.00	1.80
81 Ben Grieve TECH	2.00	.60
82 Scott Rolen TECH	4.00	1.20
83 Mark McGwire TECH	10.00	3.00
84 Tony Gwynn TECH	5.00	1.50
85 Barry Bonds TECH	10.00	3.00
86 Ken Griffey Jr. TECH	6.00	1.80
87 Alex Rodriguez TECH	6.00	1.80
88 Juan Gonzalez TECH	2.50	.75
89 Roger Clemens TECH	8.00	2.40
90 J.D. Drew TECH	2.00	.60
S100 K.Griffey Jr. Sample	2.00	.60

1999 UD Ionix Reciprocal

This 90-card set is a parallel version of the base set and swaps the photos from the backs of the regular cards and places them on the fronts. Only 750 of cards 1-60 were produced and sequentially numbered. Only 100 of the 30-card Techno subset (61-90) were produced and sequentially numbered.

Nm-Mt Ex-Mt

*RECIP.1-60: 4X TO 10X BASIC 1-60
*TECH RECIP: 3X TO 8X BASIC TECH

1999 UD Ionix Cyber

Randomly inserted in packs at the rate of one in 53, this 25-card set features color action photos of some of the current most collectible superstars, hot rookies and crowd-pleasing favorites.

	Nm-Mt	Ex-Mt
C1 Ken Griffey Jr.	25.00	7.50
C2 Cal Ripken	50.00	15.00
C3 Frank Thomas	15.00	4.50
C4 Greg Maddux	25.00	7.50
C5 Mike Piazza	25.00	7.50
C6 Alex Rodriguez	25.00	7.50
C7 Chipper Jones	15.00	4.50
C8 Derek Jeter	40.00	12.00
C9 Mark McGwire	40.00	12.00
C10 Juan Gonzalez	10.00	3.00
C11 Kerry Wood	15.00	4.50
C12 Tony Gwynn	20.00	6.00
C13 Scott Rolen	15.00	4.50
C14 Nomar Garciaparra	25.00	7.50
C15 Roger Clemens	30.00	9.00
C16 Sammy Sosa	25.00	7.50
C17 Travis Lee	6.00	1.80
C18 Ben Grieve	6.00	1.80
C19 Jeff Bagwell	10.00	3.00
C20 Ivan Rodriguez	15.00	4.50
C21 Barry Bonds	40.00	12.00
C22 J.D. Drew	6.00	1.80
C23 Kenny Lofton	6.00	1.80
C24 Andruw Jones	6.00	1.80
C25 Vladimir Guerrero	15.00	4.50

1999 UD Ionix HoloGrFX

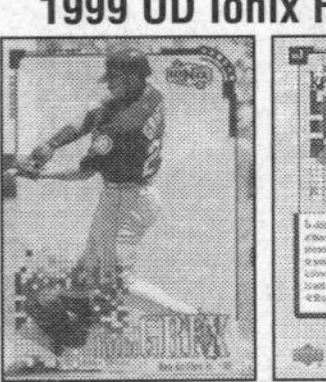

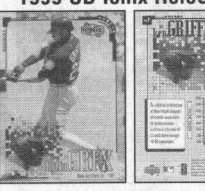

Randomly inserted in packs at the rate of one in 1500, this 10-card set features color action photos of the current best players in the game.

	Nm-Mt	Ex-Mt
HG1 Ken Griffey Jr.	50.00	15.00
HG2 Cal Ripken	100.00	30.00
HG3 Frank Thomas	30.00	9.00
HG4 Greg Maddux	50.00	15.00
HG5 Mike Piazza	50.00	15.00
HG6 Alex Rodriguez	50.00	15.00
HG7 Chipper Jones	30.00	9.00
HG8 Derek Jeter	80.00	24.00
HG9 Mark McGwire	80.00	24.00
HG10 Juan Gonzalez	30.00	9.00

1999 UD Ionix Hyper

Randomly inserted in packs at the rate of one in nine, this 20-card set features color action photos of some of the current great MLB performers.

	Nm-Mt	Ex-Mt
COMPLETE SET (20)	150.00	45.00
H1 Ken Griffey Jr.	8.00	2.40
H2 Cal Ripken	15.00	4.50
H3 Frank Thomas	5.00	1.50
H4 Greg Maddux	8.00	2.40
H5 Mike Piazza	8.00	2.40
H6 Alex Rodriguez	8.00	2.40
H7 Chipper Jones	5.00	1.50
H8 Derek Jeter	12.00	3.60
H9 Mark McGwire	12.00	3.60
H10 Juan Gonzalez	3.00	.90
H11 Kerry Wood	5.00	1.50
H12 Tony Gwynn	6.00	1.80
H13 Scott Rolen	5.00	1.50
H14 Nomar Garciaparra	8.00	2.40
H15 Roger Clemens	10.00	3.00
H16 Sammy Sosa	8.00	2.40
H17 Travis Lee	2.00	.60
H18 Ben Grieve	2.00	.60
H19 Jeff Bagwell	3.00	.90
H20 J.D. Drew	2.00	.60

1999 UD Ionix Nitro

Randomly inserted in packs at the rate of one in 18, this 10-card set features color action photos of the ten most collectible players in the game printed on rainbow foil IONIX cards.

	Nm-Mt	Ex-Mt
COMPLETE SET (10)	80.00	24.00
N1 Ken Griffey Jr.	8.00	2.40
N2 Cal Ripken	15.00	4.50
N3 Frank Thomas	5.00	1.50
N4 Greg Maddux	8.00	2.40
N5 Mike Piazza	8.00	2.40
N6 Alex Rodriguez	8.00	2.40
N7 Chipper Jones	5.00	1.50
N8 Derek Jeter	12.00	3.60
N9 Mark McGwire	12.00	3.60
N10 J.D. Drew	2.00	.60

1999 UD Ionix Warp Zone

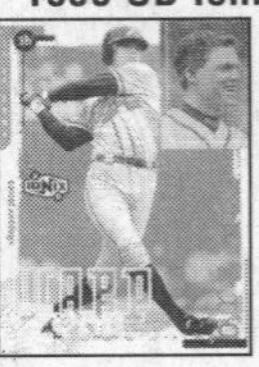

Randomly inserted in packs at the rate of one in 216, this 15-card set features color action player photos with a special holographic foil enhancement.

	Nm-Mt	Ex-Mt
COMPLETE SET (15)	400.00	120.00
WZ1 Ken Griffey Jr.	25.00	7.50
WZ2 Cal Ripken	50.00	15.00
WZ3 Frank Thomas	15.00	4.50
WZ4 Greg Maddux	25.00	7.50
WZ5 Mike Piazza	25.00	7.50
WZ6 Alex Rodriguez	25.00	7.50
WZ7 Chipper Jones	15.00	4.50
WZ8 Derek Jeter	40.00	12.00
WZ9 Mark McGwire	40.00	12.00
WZ10 Juan Gonzalez	10.00	3.00
WZ11 Kerry Wood	15.00	4.50
WZ12 Tony Gwynn	20.00	6.00
WZ13 Scott Rolen	15.00	4.50
WZ14 Nomar Garciaparra	25.00	7.50
WZ15 J.D. Drew	10.00	3.00

2000 UD Ionix

The 90 card standard-size set (produced by Upper Deck) was issued in 24 count boxes and 12 box cases. The packs had an SRP of $3.99 per pack and were issued early in 2000. The final 30 cards in the set feature stars of the future and were inserted at a rate on every four packs. Also, a selection of A Piece of History 3000 Club Roberto Clemente memorabilia cards were randomly seeded into packs. 350 bat cards, four hand-numbered, autograph cut cards and five hand-numbered, combination bat chip and autograph cut cards were produced. Pricing for these memorabilia cards can be referenced under 2000 Upper Deck A Piece of History 3000 Club.

	Nm-Mt	Ex-Mt
COMPLETE SET (90)	80.00	24.00
COMP.SET w/o SP's (60)	25.00	7.50
COMMON CARD (1-60)	.40	.12
COMMON FUT. (61-90)	2.00	.60
1 Mo Vaughn	.40	.12
2 Troy Glaus	.40	.12
3 Jeff Bagwell	.60	.18
4 Craig Biggio	.60	.18
5 Jose Lima	.40	.12
6 Jason Giambi	.40	.12
7 Tim Hudson	.40	.12
8 Shawn Green	.40	.12
9 Carlos Delgado	.40	.12
10 Chipper Jones	1.00	.30
11 Andruw Jones	.40	.12
12 Greg Maddux	1.50	.45
13 Jeromy Burnitz	.40	.12
14 Mark McGwire	2.50	.75
15 J.D. Drew	.40	.12
16 Sammy Sosa	1.50	.45
17 Jose Canseco	1.00	.30
18 Fred McGriff	.60	.18
19 Randy Johnson	1.00	.30
20 Matt Williams	.40	.12
21 Kevin Brown	.60	.18
22 Gary Sheffield	.40	.12
23 Vladimir Guerrero	1.00	.30
24 Barry Bonds	2.50	.75
25 Jim Thome	1.00	.30
26 Manny Ramirez	.60	.18
27 Roberto Alomar	.60	.18
28 Kenny Lofton	.40	.12
29 Ken Griffey Jr.	1.50	.45
30 Alex Rodriguez	1.50	.45
31 Alex Gonzalez	.40	.12
32 Preston Wilson	.40	.12
33 Mike Piazza	1.50	.45
34 Robin Ventura	.60	.18
35 Cal Ripken	3.00	.90
36 Albert Belle	.40	.12
37 Tony Gwynn	1.25	.35
38 Scott Rolen	1.00	.30
39 Curt Schilling	.40	.12
40 Brian Giles	.40	.12
41 Juan Gonzalez	.60	.18
42 Ivan Rodriguez	1.00	.30
43 Rafael Palmeiro	.60	.18
44 Pedro Martinez	1.00	.30
45 Nomar Garciaparra	1.50	.45
46 Sean Casey	.40	.12
47 Aaron Boone	.40	.12
48 Barry Larkin	.60	.18
49 Larry Walker	.60	.18
50 Vinny Castilla	.40	.12
51 Carlos Beltran	.60	.18
52 Gabe Kapler	.40	.12
53 Dean Palmer	.40	.12
54 Eric Milton	.40	.12
55 Corey Koskie	.40	.12
56 Frank Thomas	1.00	.30
57 Magglio Ordonez	.40	.12
58 Roger Clemens	2.00	.60
59 Bernie Williams	.60	.18
60 Derek Jeter	2.50	.75
61 Josh Beckett FUT	2.50	.75
62 Eric Munson FUT	2.00	.60
63 Rick Ankiel FUT	2.00	.60
64 Matt Riley FUT	2.00	.60
65 Rob Ramsay FUT	2.00	.60
66 Vernon Wells FUT	2.00	.60
67 Eric Gagne FUT	6.00	1.80
68 Robert Fick FUT	2.00	.60
69 Mark Quinn FUT	2.00	.60
70 Kip Wells FUT	2.00	.60
71 Peter Bergeron FUT	2.00	.60
72 Ed Yarnall FUT	2.00	.60
73 Jorge Toca FUT	2.00	.60
74 Alfonso Soriano FUT	4.00	1.20
75 Calvin Murray FUT	2.00	.60
76 Ramon Ortiz FUT	2.00	.60
77 Chad Meyers FUT	2.00	.60
78 Jason LaRue FUT	2.00	.60
79 Pat Burrell FUT	2.00	.60
80 Chad Hermansen FUT	2.00	.60
81 Lance Berkman FUT	2.00	.60
82 Erubiel Durazo FUT	2.00	.60
83 Juan Pena FUT	2.00	.60
84 Adam Kennedy FUT	2.00	.60
85 Ben Petrick FUT	2.00	.60
86 Kevin Barker FUT	2.00	.60
87 Bruce Chen FUT	2.00	.60
88 Jerry Hairston Jr. FUT	2.00	.60
89 A.J. Burnett FUT	2.00	.60
90 Gary Matthews Jr. FUT	2.00	.60

2000 UD Ionix Reciprocal

This 90 card set is a parallel to the regular UD Ionix set. They were issued one every four packs for the lower numbers (R1-R60) and one every 11 packs for the future cards (R61-R90).

Nm-Mt Ex-Mt

*STARS 1-60: 1.5X TO 4X BASIC 1-60
*FUTURE 61-90: .6X TO 1.5X BASIC 61-90

2000 UD Ionix Atomic

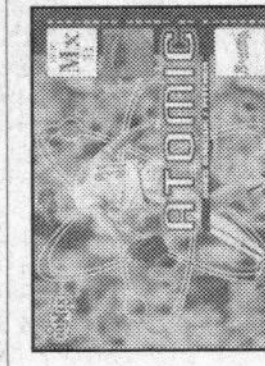

Issued one every eight packs, this set features 15 of the most popular and collectible hitters and pitchers currently active.

	Nm-Mt	Ex-Mt
COMPLETE SET (15)	60.00	18.00
A1 Pedro Martinez	3.00	.90
A2 Mark McGwire	10.00	3.00
A3 Ken Griffey Jr.	8.00	2.40
A4 Jeff Bagwell	3.00	.90
A5 Greg Maddux	6.00	1.80
A6 Derek Jeter	10.00	3.00
A7 Cal Ripken	10.00	3.00
A8 Manny Ramirez	3.00	.90
A9 Randy Johnson	3.00	.90
A10 Nomar Garciaparra	8.00	2.40
A11 Tony Gwynn	5.00	1.50
A12 Bernie Williams	2.50	.75
A13 Mike Piazza	6.00	1.80
A14 Roger Clemens	6.00	1.80
A15 Alex Rodriguez	8.00	2.40

2000 UD Ionix Awesome Powers

These cards, with a design based on 1960's psychedelic art, highlights some of the most prolific power hitters of the current crop of sluggers. These cards were inserted one every 23 packs.

	Nm-Mt	Ex-Mt
COMPLETE SET (15)	120.00	36.00
AP1 Ken Griffey Jr.	6.00	1.80
AP2 Mike Piazza	6.00	1.80
AP3 Carlos Delgado	1.50	.45
AP4 Mark McGwire	10.00	3.00
AP5 Chipper Jones	4.00	1.20
AP6 Scott Rolen	4.00	1.20
AP7 Cal Ripken	12.00	3.60
AP8 Alex Rodriguez	6.00	1.80
AP9 Larry Walker	2.50	.75
AP10 Sammy Sosa	6.00	1.80
AP11 Barry Bonds	10.00	3.00
AP12 Nomar Garciaparra	6.00	1.80
AP13 Jose Canseco	4.00	1.20
AP14 Manny Ramirez	2.50	.75
AP15 Jeff Bagwell	2.50	.75

2000 UD Ionix BIOrhythm

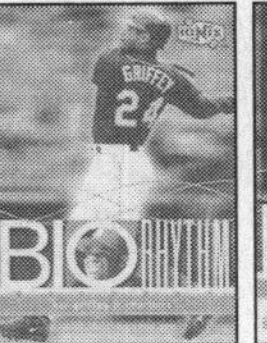

Issued one every 11 packs, this 15-card set features many of the leading players of the game.

	Nm-Mt	Ex-Mt
COMPLETE SET (15)	80.00	24.00
B1 Randy Johnson	3.00	.90
B2 Derek Jeter	8.00	2.40
B3 Sammy Sosa	5.00	1.50
B4 Jose Lima	1.25	.35
B5 Chipper Jones	3.00	.90
B6 Barry Bonds	8.00	2.40
B7 Ken Griffey Jr.	5.00	1.50
B8 Nomar Garciaparra	5.00	1.50
B9 Frank Thomas	3.00	.90
B10 Pedro Martinez	3.00	.90
B11 Larry Walker	2.00	.60
B12 Greg Maddux	5.00	1.50
B13 Alex Rodriguez	5.00	1.50
B14 Mark McGwire	8.00	2.40
B15 Cal Ripken	10.00	3.00

2000 UD Ionix Pyrotechnics

Inserted one every 72 packs, these 15 cards feature baseball's most popular players.

	Nm-Mt	Ex-Mt
COMPLETE SET (15)	350.00	105.00
P1 Roger Clemens	12.00	3.60
P2 Chipper Jones	6.00	1.80
P3 Alex Rodriguez	10.00	3.00
P4 Jeff Bagwell	4.00	1.20
P5 Mark McGwire	15.00	4.50
P6 Pedro Martinez	6.00	1.80
P7 Manny Ramirez	4.00	1.20
P8 Cal Ripken	20.00	6.00
P9 Mike Piazza	10.00	3.00
P10 Derek Jeter	15.00	4.50
P11 Ken Griffey Jr.	10.00	3.00
P12 Frank Thomas	6.00	1.80
P13 Sammy Sosa	10.00	3.00
P14 Nomar Garciaparra	10.00	3.00
P15 Greg Maddux	10.00	3.00

2000 UD Ionix Shockwave

Using a rainbow foil Ionix technology, these 15 cards featuring the most powerful sluggers were inserted into packs at a rate of one every four packs.

	Nm-Mt	Ex-Mt
COMPLETE SET (15)	20.00	6.00
S1 Mark McGwire	3.00	.90
S2 Sammy Sosa	2.00	.60

S3 Manny Ramirez .75 .23
S4 Ken Griffey Jr. 2.00 .60
S5 Vladimir Guerrero 1.25 .35
S6 Barry Bonds 3.00 .90
S7 Albert Belle .50 .15
S8 Ivan Rodriguez 1.25 .35
S9 Chipper Jones 1.25 .35
S10 Mo Vaughn .50 .15
S11 Jose Canseco 1.25 .35
S12 Jeff Bagwell .75 .23
S13 Matt Williams .50 .15
S14 Alex Rodriguez 2.00 .60
S15 Carlos Delgado .50 .15

2000 UD Ionix UD Authentics

Randomly inserted into packs at an overall rate of one in 144, these 13 cards feature signed cards of various major leaguers. Please note that the Ben Davis, Derek Jeter and Manny Ramirez cards were exchange cards with a deadline date of September 20th, 2000.

	Nm-Mt	Ex-Mt
AB Adrian Beltre	25.00	7.50
BD Ben Davis	10.00	3.00
DJ Derek Jeter	120.00	36.00
JC Jose Canseco	40.00	12.00
JR Ken Griffey Jr.	100.00	30.00
MR Manny Ramirez	50.00	15.00
PB Pat Burrell	15.00	4.50
RM Ruben Mateo	10.00	3.00
SC Sean Casey	15.00	4.50
SG Shawn Green	15.00	4.50
SR Scott Rolen	40.00	12.00
VG Vladimir Guerrero	40.00	12.00
CBE Carlos Beltran	40.00	12.00

2000 UD Ionix Warp Zone

The toughest of the UD Ionix inserts, these 15 cards featured on holographic Ionix technology were inserted at a rate of one every 288 packs.

	Nm-Mt	Ex-Mt
WZ1 Cal Ripken	40.00	12.00
WZ2 Barry Bonds	30.00	9.00
WZ3 Ken Griffey Jr.	20.00	6.00
WZ4 Nomar Garciaparra	20.00	6.00
WZ5 Chipper Jones	12.00	3.60
WZ6 Ivan Rodriguez	12.00	3.60
WZ7 Greg Maddux	20.00	6.00
WZ8 Derek Jeter	30.00	9.00
WZ9 Mike Piazza	20.00	6.00
WZ10 Sammy Sosa	20.00	6.00
WZ11 Roger Clemens	25.00	7.50
WZ12 Alex Rodriguez	20.00	6.00
WZ13 Vladimir Guerrero	12.00	3.60
WZ14 Pedro Martinez	12.00	3.60
WZ15 Mark McGwire	30.00	9.00

2004 UD Legends Timeless Teams

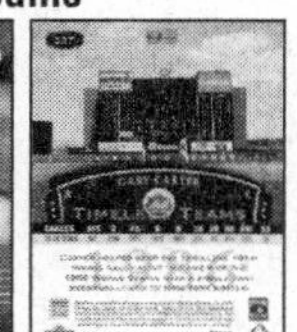

This 300-card set was released in September, 2004. The set was issued in six card packs with an $5 SRP which came 18 packs to a box and 20 boxes to a case.

	Nm-Mt	Ex-Mt
COMPLETE SET (300)	50.00	15.00
1 Bob Gibson 64	1.00	.30
2 Lou Brock MM 64	1.00	.30
3 Ray Washburn 64	.40	.12
4 Tim McCarver 64	.60	.18
5 Harmon Killebrew 65	1.50	.45
6 Jim Kaat 65	.60	.18
7 Jim Perry 65	.40	.12
8 Mudcat Grant 65	.40	.12
9 Boog Powell 66	.60	.18
10 Brooks Robinson 66	1.00	.30
11 Frank Robinson MM 66	.60	.18
12 Jim Palmer 66	.60	.18
13 Carl Yastrzemski MM 67	2.50	.75
14 Jim Lonborg 67	.40	.12
15 George Scott 67	.40	.12
16 Sparky Lyle 67	.40	.12
17 Rico Petrocelli 67	.40	.12
18 Bob Gibson 67	1.00	.30
19 Julian Javier 67	.40	.12
20 Lou Brock 67	1.00	.30
21 Orlando Cepeda 67	.60	.18
22 Ray Washburn 67	.40	.12
23 Steve Carlton 67	.60	.18
24 Tim McCarver 67	.60	.18
25 Al Kaline 68	1.50	.45
26 Bill Freehan 68	.60	.18
27 Denny McLain MM 68	.60	.18
28 Dick McAuliffe 68	.40	.12
29 Jim Northrup 68	.40	.12
30 John Hiller 68	.40	.12
31 Mickey Lolich MM 68	.40	.12
32 Mickey Stanley 68	.40	.12
33 Willie Horton 68	.40	.12
34 Bob Gibson MM 68	1.00	.30
35 Julian Javier 68	.40	.12
36 Lou Brock 68	1.00	.30
37 Orlando Cepeda 68	.60	.18
38 Steve Carlton 68	.60	.18
39 Boog Powell 69	.60	.18
40 Brooks Robinson 69	1.00	.30
41 Davey Johnson 69	.40	.12
42 Merv Rettenmund 69	.40	.12
43 Eddie Watt 69	.40	.12
44 Frank Robinson 69	.60	.18
45 Jim Palmer 69	.60	.18
46 Mike Cuellar 69	.40	.12
47 Paul Blair 69	.40	.12
48 Pete Richert 69	.40	.12
49 Ellie Hendricks 69	.40	.12
50 Billy Williams 69	.60	.18
51 Randy Hundley 69	.40	.12
52 Ernie Banks 69	1.50	.45
53 Fergie Jenkins 69	.60	.18
54 Jim Hickman 69	.40	.12
55 Ken Holtzman 69	.40	.12
56 Ron Santo MM 69	1.00	.30
57 Ed Kranepool 69	.60	.18
58 Jerry Koosman MM 69	.60	.18
59 Nolan Ryan 69	4.00	1.20
60 Tom Seaver 69	1.00	.30
61 Boog Powell 70	.60	.18
62 Brooks Robinson MM 70	1.00	.30
63 Davey Johnson 70	.40	.12
64 Merv Rettenmund 70	.40	.12
65 Eddie Watt 70	.40	.12
66 Frank Robinson 70	.60	.18
67 Jim Palmer 70	.60	.18
68 Mike Cuellar 70	.40	.12
69 Paul Blair 70	.40	.12
70 Pete Richert 70	.40	.12
71 Ellie Hendricks 70	.40	.12
72 Al Kaline 72	1.50	.45
73 Bill Freehan 72	.60	.18
74 Dick McAuliffe 72	.40	.12
75 Jim Northrup 72	.40	.12
76 John Hiller 72	.40	.12
77 Mickey Lolich 72	.40	.12
78 Mickey Stanley 72	.40	.12
79 Willie Horton 72	.40	.12
80 Bert Campaneris 72	.40	.12
81 Blue Moon Odom MM 72	.40	.12
82 Sal Bando 72	.40	.12
83 Joe Rudi 72	.40	.12
84 Ken Holtzman 72	.40	.12
85 Billy North 73	.40	.12
86 Blue Moon Odom 73	.40	.12
87 Gene Tenace 73	.40	.12
88 Manny Trillo 73	.40	.12
89 Dick Green 73	.40	.12
90 Rollie Fingers 73	.60	.18
91 Sal Bando 73	.40	.12
92 Vida Blue 73	.60	.18
93 Bill Buckner 74	.60	.18
94 Davey Lopes 74	.60	.18
95 Don Sutton 74	.60	.18
96 Al Downing MM 74	.40	.12
97 Ron Cey 74	.60	.18
98 Steve Garvey 74	.60	.18
99 Tommy John 74	.60	.18
100 Bert Campaneris 74	.40	.12
101 Billy North 74	.40	.12
102 Joe Rudi MM 74	.40	.12
103 Sal Bando 74	.40	.12
104 Vida Blue 74	.60	.18
105 Carl Yastrzemski 75	2.50	.75
106 Carlton Fisk MM 75	1.00	.30
107 Cecil Cooper 75	.60	.18
108 Dwight Evans 75	.60	.18
109 Fred Lynn 75	.60	.18
110 Jim Rice 75	.60	.18
111 Luis Tiant 75	.60	.18
112 Rick Burleson 75	.40	.12
113 Rico Petrocelli 75	.40	.12
114 Pedro Borbon 75	.40	.12
115 Dave Concepcion 75	.60	.18
116 Don Gullett 75	.40	.12
117 George Foster 75	.60	.18
118 Joe Morgan MM 75	.60	.18
119 Johnny Bench 75	1.50	.45
120 Rawly Eastwick 75	.40	.12
121 Sparky Anderson 75	.60	.18
122 Tony Perez 75	.60	.18
123 Billy Williams 75	.60	.18
124 Gene Tenace 75	.40	.12
125 Jim Perry 75	.40	.12
126 Vida Blue 75	.60	.18
127 Pedro Borbon 76	.40	.12
128 Dave Concepcion 76	.60	.18
129 Don Gullett 76	.40	.12
130 George Foster 76	.60	.18
131 Joe Morgan 76	.60	.18
132 Johnny Bench MM 76	1.50	.45
133 Ken Griffey Sr. 76	.60	.18
134 Rawly Eastwick 76	.40	.12
135 Tony Perez 76	.60	.18
136 Bill Russell 77	.40	.12
137 Burt Hooton 77	.40	.12
138 Davey Lopes 77	.60	.18
139 Don Sutton 77	.60	.18
140 Dusty Baker 77	.60	.18
141 Steve Yeager 77	.40	.12
142 Ron Cey 77	.60	.18
143 Steve Garvey MM 77	.60	.18
144 Tommy John 77	.60	.18
145 Bucky Dent 77	.60	.18
146 Chris Chambliss 77	.60	.18
147 Ed Figueroa 77	.40	.12
148 Graig Nettles 77	.60	.18
149 Lou Piniella 77	.60	.18
150 Roy White 77	.40	.12
151 Don Gullett 77	.40	.12
152 Sparky Lyle 77	.60	.18
153 Brian Doyle 78	.40	.12
154 Bucky Dent MM 78	.60	.18
155 Chris Chambliss 78	.60	.18
156 Ed Figueroa 78	.40	.12
157 Graig Nettles 78	.60	.18
158 Lou Piniella 78	.60	.18
159 Roy White 78	.40	.12
160 Rich Gossage 78	.60	.18
161 Sparky Lyle 78	.60	.18
162 Bobby Grich 79	.60	.18
163 Brian Downing 79	.60	.18
164 Dan Ford 79	.40	.12
165 Nolan Ryan 79	4.00	1.20
166 Dave Concepcion 79	.60	.18
167 George Foster 79	.60	.18
168 Johnny Bench 79	1.50	.45
169 Ray Knight 79	.60	.18
170 Tom Seaver 79	1.00	.30
171 Bert Blyleven 79	.60	.18
172 Bill Madlock 79	.60	.18
173 Dave Parker MM 79	.60	.18
174 Phil Garner 79	.40	.12
175 Bill Russell 80	.40	.12
176 Steve Yeager 80	.40	.12
177 Don Sutton 80	.60	.18
178 Dusty Baker 80	.60	.18
179 Jerry Reuss 80	.40	.12
180 Mickey Hatcher 80	.40	.12
181 Pedro Guerrero 80	.40	.12
182 Ron Cey 80	.60	.18
183 Steve Garvey 80	.60	.18
184 Rudy May 80	.40	.12
185 Brian Doyle 80	.40	.12
186 Bucky Dent 80	.60	.18
187 Jim Kaat 80	.60	.18
188 Lou Piniella 80	.60	.18
189 Luis Tiant 80	.60	.18
190 Tommy John 80	.60	.18
191 Bake McBride 80	.40	.12
192 Bob Boone 80	.60	.18
193 Dickie Noles MM 80	.40	.12
194 Manny Trillo 80	.40	.12
195 Mike Schmidt 80	3.00	.90
196 Sparky Lyle 80	.60	.18
197 Steve Carlton 80	.60	.18
198 Steve Yeager 80	.40	.12
199 Burt Hooton 81	.40	.12
200 Dusty Baker 81	.60	.18
201 Jerry Reuss 81	.40	.12
202 Mike Scioscia 81	.60	.18
203 Pedro Guerrero 81	.60	.18
204 Ron Cey 81	.60	.18
205 Steve Garvey 81	.60	.18
206 Alejandro Pena 81	.40	.12
207 Steve Sax 81	.40	.12
208 Cecil Cooper 81	.60	.18
209 Gorman Thomas 81	.40	.12
210 Paul Molitor 81	1.00	.30
211 Robin Yount 81	2.50	.75
212 Rollie Fingers 81	.60	.18
213 Don Money 81	.40	.12
214 Rudy May 81	.40	.12
215 Bucky Dent 81	.60	.18
216 Dave Winfield 81	.60	.18
217 Lou Piniella 81	.60	.18
218 Rich Gossage 81	.60	.18
219 Tommy John 81	.60	.18
220 Cecil Cooper 82	.60	.18
221 Gorman Thomas 82	.60	.18
222 Paul Molitor MM 82	1.00	.30
223 Robin Yount 82	2.50	.75
224 Don Money 82	.40	.12
225 Cal Ripken MM 83	5.00	1.50
226 Dan Ford 83	.40	.12
227 Jim Palmer 83	.60	.18
228 John Shelby 83	.40	.12
229 Alan Trammell 84	.60	.18
230 Chet Lemon 84	.40	.12
231 Howard Johnson 84	.40	.12
232 Jack Morris MM 84	.60	.18
233 Kirk Gibson 84	.60	.18
234 Lou Whitaker 84	.60	.18
235 Sparky Anderson 84	.60	.18
236 Dave Winfield 85	.60	.18
237 Don Mattingly 85	3.00	.90
238 Ken Griffey Sr. 85	.60	.18
239 Phil Niekro 85	.60	.18
240 Yogi Berra 85	1.00	.30
241 Bill Buckner MM 86	.60	.18
242 Bruce Hurst 86	.40	.12
243 Dave Henderson 86	.40	.12
244 Dwight Evans 86	.60	.18
245 Jim Rice 86	.60	.18
246 Tom Seaver 86	1.00	.30
247 Wade Boggs 86	1.00	.30
248 Bob Boone 86	.60	.18
249 Bobby Grich 86	.60	.18
250 Brian Downing 86	.60	.18
251 Don Sutton 86	.60	.18
252 Terry Forster 86	.40	.12
253 Rick Burleson 86	.40	.12
254 Wally Joyner MM 86	.40	.12
255 Darryl Strawberry 86	.60	.18
256 Dwight Gooden 86	.60	.18
257 Gary Carter 86	.60	.18
258 Jesse Orosco MM 86	.40	.12
259 Keith Hernandez 86	.60	.18
260 Lenny Dykstra 86	.60	.18
261 Mookie Wilson 86	.60	.18
262 Ray Knight 86	.60	.18
263 Wally Backman 86	.40	.12
264 Sid Fernandez 86	.40	.12
265 Alan Trammell 87	.60	.18
266 Dan Petry 87	.40	.12
267 Chet Lemon 87	.40	.12
268 Sparky Anderson 87	.60	.18
269 Jack Morris 87	.60	.18
270 Kirk Gibson 87	.60	.18
271 Lou Whitaker 87	.60	.18
272 Bert Blyleven 87	.60	.18
273 Kent Hrbek MM 87	.60	.18
274 Kirby Puckett 87	1.50	.45
275 Alejandro Pena 88	.40	.12
276 Jesse Orosco 88	.40	.12
277 John Shelby 88	.40	.12
278 Kirk Gibson MM 88	.60	.18
279 Mickey Hatcher 88	.40	.12
280 Mike Scioscia 88	.60	.18
281 Steve Sax 88	.40	.12
282 Darryl Strawberry 88	.60	.18
283 Dwight Gooden 88	.60	.18
284 Gary Carter 88	.60	.18
285 Howard Johnson 88	.40	.12
286 Keith Hernandez 88	.60	.18
287 Lenny Dykstra 88	.60	.18
288 Mookie Wilson 88	.60	.18
289 Wally Backman 88	.40	.12
290 Sid Fernandez 88	.40	.12
291 Jack Morris 91	.60	.18
292 Kent Hrbek 91	.60	.18
293 Kirby Puckett MM 91	1.50	.45
294 Dave Winfield MM 92	.60	.18
295 Jack Morris 92	.60	.18
296 Joe Carter 92	.60	.18
297 Don Mattingly MM 95	3.00	.90
298 Paul O'Neill 95	1.00	.30
299 Jack McDowell 95	.40	.12
300 Wade Boggs 95	1.00	.30

2004 UD Legends Timeless Teams Gold

	Nm-Mt	Ex-Mt
STATED ODDS 1:360		
STATED PRINT RUN 5 SERIAL #'d SETS		
NO PRICING DUE TO SCARCITY		

2004 UD Legends Timeless Teams Autographs

	Nm-Mt	Ex-Mt
OVERALL AU PARALLEL ODDS 1:9		
SP PRINT RUNS B/WN 25-100 COPIES PER		
SP'S ARE NOT SERIAL-NUMBERED		
SP PRINT RUNS PROVIDED BY UD		
EXCHANGE DEADLINE 08/19/07		
ASTERISK ='s SOME LIVE/SOME EXCH		
1 Bob Gibson 64 SP/50	30.00	9.00
2 Lou Brock MM 64 SP/75 *	25.00	7.50
3 Ray Washburn 64	10.00	3.00
4 Tim McCarver 64	15.00	4.50
5 Harmon Killebrew 65	40.00	12.00
6 Jim Kaat 65	15.00	4.50
7 Jim Perry 65	10.00	3.00
8 Mudcat Grant 65	15.00	4.50
9 Boog Powell 66	15.00	4.50
10 Brooks Robinson 66	25.00	7.50
11 F.Robinson MM 66 SP/35	40.00	12.00
12 Jim Palmer 66 SP/50	30.00	9.00
13 C.Yastrzemski MM 67 SP/25	80.00	24.00
14 Jim Lonborg 67	10.00	3.00
15 George Scott 67	10.00	3.00
16 Sparky Lyle 67 *	10.00	3.00
17 Rico Petrocelli 67	10.00	3.00
18 Bob Gibson 67 SP/35	40.00	12.00
19 Julian Javier 67	10.00	3.00
20 Lou Brock 67 SP/60	30.00	9.00
21 Orlando Cepeda 67 SP/50	20.00	6.00
22 Ray Washburn 67	10.00	3.00
23 Steve Carlton 67 SP/25	40.00	12.00
24 Tim McCarver 67	15.00	4.50
25 Al Kaline 68 *	30.00	9.00
26 Bill Freehan 68	15.00	4.50
27 Denny McLain MM 68	15.00	4.50
28 Dick McAuliffe 68	10.00	3.00
29 Jim Northrup 68	15.00	4.50
30 John Hiller 68	10.00	3.00
31 Mickey Lolich MM 68	15.00	4.50
32 Mickey Stanley 68	10.00	3.00
33 Willie Horton 68	10.00	3.00
34 Bob Gibson MM 68 SP/25	40.00	12.00
35 Julian Javier 68	10.00	3.00
36 Lou Brock 68 SP/50	30.00	9.00
37 Orlando Cepeda 68 SP/25	25.00	7.50
38 Steve Carlton 68 SP/35	40.00	12.00
39 Boog Powell 69	15.00	4.50
40 Brooks Robinson 69 SP/100	25.00	7.50
41 Davey Johnson 69	10.00	3.00
42 Merv Rettenmund 69	10.00	3.00
43 Eddie Watt 69	10.00	3.00
44 Frank Robinson 69 SP/25	40.00	12.00
45 Jim Palmer 69 SP/25	40.00	12.00
46 Mike Cuellar 69	10.00	3.00
47 Paul Blair 69	10.00	3.00
48 Pete Richert 69	10.00	3.00
49 Ellie Hendricks 69	10.00	3.00
50 Billy Williams 69 SP/75	25.00	7.50
51 Randy Hundley 69	15.00	4.50
52 Ernie Banks 69 SP/50	50.00	15.00
53 Fergie Jenkins 69	15.00	4.50
54 Jim Hickman 69	15.00	4.50
55 Ken Holtzman 69	15.00	4.50
56 Ron Santo MM 69	30.00	9.00
57 Ed Kranepool 69	10.00	3.00
58 Jerry Koosman MM 69	15.00	4.50
59 Nolan Ryan 69 SP/50		
60 Tom Seaver 69 SP/50	40.00	12.00
61 Boog Powell 70	15.00	4.50
62 B.Robinson MM 70 SP/35	40.00	12.00
63 Davey Johnson 70	10.00	3.00
64 Merv Rettenmund 70	10.00	3.00
65 Eddie Watt 70	10.00	3.00
66 Frank Robinson 70 SP/50	30.00	9.00
67 Jim Palmer 70 SP/75	25.00	7.50
68 Mike Cuellar 70	10.00	3.00
69 Paul Blair 70	10.00	3.00
70 Pete Richert 70	10.00	3.00
71 Ellie Hendricks 70	10.00	3.00
72 Al Kaline 72 *	30.00	9.00
73 Bill Freehan 72	15.00	4.50
74 Dick McAuliffe 72	10.00	3.00
75 Jim Northrup 72	15.00	4.50
76 John Hiller 72	10.00	3.00
77 Mickey Lolich 72	15.00	4.50
78 Mickey Stanley 72	10.00	3.00
79 Willie Horton 72	10.00	3.00
80 Bert Campaneris 72	10.00	3.00
81 Blue Moon Odom MM 72	10.00	3.00
82 Sal Bando 72 EXCH	10.00	3.00
83 Joe Rudi 72	10.00	3.00
84 Ken Holtzman 72	15.00	4.50
85 Billy North 73	10.00	3.00
86 Blue Moon Odom 73	10.00	3.00
87 Gene Tenace 73	10.00	3.00
88 Manny Trillo 73	10.00	3.00
89 Dick Green 73	10.00	3.00
90 Rollie Fingers 73	15.00	4.50
91 Sal Bando 73	10.00	3.00
92 Vida Blue 73	10.00	3.00
93 Bill Buckner 74 *	15.00	4.50
94 Davey Lopes 74	10.00	3.00
95 Don Sutton 74	15.00	4.50
96 Al Downing MM 74	10.00	3.00
97 Ron Cey 74 SP/25	15.00	4.50
98 Steve Garvey 74 SP/25	40.00	12.00
99 Tommy John 74 SP/25	15.00	4.50
100 Bert Campaneris 74	10.00	3.00
101 Billy North 74	10.00	3.00
102 Joe Rudi MM 74	10.00	3.00
103 Sal Bando 74	10.00	3.00
104 Vida Blue 74 SP/100 *	10.00	3.00
105 Carl Yastrzemski 75 SP/50	60.00	18.00
106 Carlton Fisk MM 75 SP/100	25.00	7.50
107 Cecil Cooper 75 SP/75	15.00	4.50
108 Dwight Evans 75 SP/75	15.00	4.50
109 Fred Lynn 75	10.00	3.00
110 Jim Rice 75 SP/100 EXCH	15.00	4.50
111 Luis Tiant 75 EXCH	10.00	3.00
112 Rick Burleson 75	10.00	3.00
113 Rico Petrocelli 75	10.00	3.00
114 Pedro Borbon 75	10.00	3.00
115 Dave Concepcion 75 EXCH	15.00	4.50
116 Don Gullett 75	10.00	3.00
117 George Foster 75 SP/50	12.00	3.60
118 Joe Morgan MM 75 SP/25	25.00	7.50
119 Johnny Bench 75 SP/85	50.00	15.00
120 Rawly Eastwick 75	10.00	3.00
121 Sparky Anderson 75	15.00	4.50
122 Tony Perez 75	25.00	7.50
123 Billy Williams 75 SP/50	30.00	9.00
124 Gene Tenace 75	10.00	3.00
125 Jim Perry 75	10.00	3.00
126 Vida Blue 75 SP/75	10.00	3.00
127 Pedro Borbon 76	10.00	3.00
128 Dave Concepcion 76 EXCH	15.00	4.50
129 Don Gullett 76	10.00	3.00
130 George Foster 76 SP/35	15.00	4.50
131 Joe Morgan 76 SP/50	20.00	6.00
132 J.Bench MM 76 SP/50	60.00	18.00
133 Ken Griffey Sr. 76	15.00	4.50
134 Rawly Eastwick 76	10.00	3.00
135 Tony Perez 76	25.00	7.50
136 Bill Russell 77	10.00	3.00
137 Burt Hooton 77	10.00	3.00
138 Davey Lopes 77	10.00	3.00
139 Don Sutton 77	15.00	4.50
140 Dusty Baker 77 EXCH	15.00	4.50
141 S.Yeager 77 SP/75 EXCH	10.00	3.00
142 Ron Cey 77 SP/35	15.00	4.50
143 Steve Garvey MM 77 SP/35	40.00	12.00
144 Tommy John 77 SP/35	15.00	4.50
145 Bucky Dent 77 SP/75	15.00	4.50
146 Chris Chambliss 77	10.00	3.00
147 Ed Figueroa 77	10.00	3.00
148 Graig Nettles 77	15.00	4.50
149 Lou Piniella 77 SP/25	15.00	4.50
150 Roy White 77	10.00	3.00
151 Don Gullett 77	10.00	3.00
152 Sparky Lyle 77 *	10.00	3.00
153 Brian Doyle 78	10.00	3.00
154 Bucky Dent MM 78 SP/75	15.00	4.50
155 Chris Chambliss 78	10.00	3.00
156 Ed Figueroa 78	10.00	3.00
157 Graig Nettles 78	15.00	4.50
158 Lou Piniella 78 SP/35	15.00	4.50
159 Roy White 78	10.00	3.00
160 Rich Gossage 78	15.00	4.50
161 Sparky Lyle 78 *	10.00	3.00
162 Bobby Grich 79	10.00	3.00
163 Brian Downing 79	10.00	3.00
164 Dan Ford 79	10.00	3.00
165 Nolan Ryan 79 SP/25	150.00	45.00
166 D.Conc 79 SP/75 EXCH	15.00	4.50
167 George Foster 79 SP/25	15.00	4.50
168 Johnny Bench 79 SP/25	80.00	24.00
169 Ray Knight 79	10.00	3.00
170 Tom Seaver 79 SP/35	50.00	15.00
171 Bert Blyleven 79 *	10.00	3.00
172 Bill Madlock 79	15.00	4.50
173 Dave Parker MM 79	15.00	4.50
174 Phil Garner 79	10.00	3.00
175 Bill Russell 80	10.00	3.00
176 Steve Yeager 80	10.00	3.00
177 Don Sutton 80 SP/50	20.00	6.00
178 Dusty Baker 80	15.00	4.50
179 Jerry Reuss 80	10.00	3.00
180 Mickey Hatcher 80	10.00	3.00
181 Pedro Guerrero 80	10.00	3.00
182 Ron Cey 80 SP/50	12.00	3.60
183 Steve Garvey 80 SP/50	30.00	9.00
184 Rudy May 80	10.00	3.00
185 Brian Doyle 80	10.00	3.00
186 Bucky Dent 80 SP/60	20.00	6.00
187 Jim Kaat 80	15.00	4.50
188 Lou Piniella 80 SP/50	12.00	3.60
189 Luis Tiant 80	10.00	3.00
190 Tommy John 80 SP/50	12.00	3.60
191 Bake McBride 80	15.00	4.50
192 Bob Boone 80	15.00	4.50
193 Dickie Noles MM 80	10.00	3.00
194 Manny Trillo 80	10.00	3.00
195 Mike Schmidt 80 SP/50		
196 Sparky Lyle 80	10.00	3.00
197 Steve Carlton 80 SP/50	30.00	9.00
198 Steve Yeager 81	10.00	3.00
199 Burt Hooton 81	10.00	3.00
200 Dusty Baker 81 EXCH	15.00	4.50

201 Jerry Reuss 81 .... 10.00 3.00
202 Mike Scioscia 81.............. 10.00 3.00
203 Pedro Guerrero 81 .... 10.00 3.00
204 Ron Cey 81 SP/75 .... 10.00 3.00
205 Steve Garvey 81 SP/75 .... 25.00 7.50
206 Alejandro Pena 81 .... 10.00 3.00
207 Steve Sax 81 SP/100 .... 10.00 3.00
208 Cecil Cooper 81 SP/85 .... 15.00 4.50
209 Gorman Thomas 81 EXCH. 10.00 3.00
210 Paul Molitor 81 SP/25 .... 50.00 15.00
211 Robin Yount 81 SP/25 ....
212 Rollie Fingers 81 .... 15.00 4.50
213 Don Money 81 .... 10.00 3.00
214 Rudy May 81 .... 10.00 3.00
215 Bucky Dent 81 SP/25.......... 25.00 7.50
216 Dave Winfield 81 SP/50...... 30.00 9.00
217 Lou Piniella 81 SP/75 .... 10.00 3.00
218 Rich Gossage 81 .... 15.00 4.50
219 Tommy John 81 SP/75........ 10.00 3.00
220 Cecil Cooper 82 .... 15.00 4.50
221 Gorman Thomas 82 EXCH. 10.00 3.00
222 Paul Molitor MM 82 SP/50 40.00 12.00
223 Robin Yount 82 SP/50 .... 60.00 18.00
224 Don Money 82 .... 10.00 3.00
225 Cal Ripken MM 83 SP/50. 250.00 75.00
226 Dan Ford 83 .... 10.00 3.00
227 Jim Palmer 83 SP/35......... 40.00 12.00
228 John Shelby 83.................. 10.00 3.00
229 Alan Trammell 84 .... 15.00 4.50
230 Chet Lemon 84 .... 10.00 3.00
231 Howard Johnson 84............ 10.00 3.00
232 Jack Morris MM 84 SP/35. 25.00 7.50
233 Kirk Gibson 84 .... 15.00 4.50
234 Lou Whitaker 84 SP/100.... 15.00 4.50
235 Sparky Anderson 84 * 15.00 4.50
236 Dave Winfield 85 SP/25 ..... 40.00 12.00
237 Don Mattingly 85 SP/50..... 60.00 18.00
238 Ken Griffey Sr. 85.............. 15.00 4.50
239 Phil Niekro 85 .... 15.00 4.50
240 Yogi Berra 85 SP/47 UER .. 60.00 18.00
Front says 1978 instead of 1985
241 Bill Buckner MM 86 .... 15.00 4.50
242 Bruce Hurst 86.................. 15.00 4.50
243 Dave Henderson 86 .... 15.00 4.50
244 Dwight Evans 86 SP/50 ...... 20.00 6.00
245 Jim Rice 86 SP/75 EXCH ... 15.00 4.50
246 Tom Seaver 86 SP/25 .... 50.00 15.00
247 Wade Boggs 86 SP/50........ 40.00 12.00
248 Bob Boone 86 .... 15.00 4.50
249 Bobby Grich 86.................. 10.00 3.00
250 Brian Downing 86 .... 10.00 3.00
251 Don Sutton 86 SP/75.......... 15.00 4.50
252 Terry Forster 86 .... 10.00 3.00
253 Rick Burleson 86 .... 10.00 3.00
254 Wally Joyner MM 86........... 15.00 4.50
255 Darryl Strawberry 86 .... 25.00 7.50
256 Dwight Gooden 86 .... 15.00 4.50
257 Gary Carter 86 SP/75......... 15.00 4.50
258 Jesse Orosco MM 86 .... 10.00 3.00
259 Keith Hernandez 86............ 15.00 4.50
260 Lenny Dykstra 86 .... 15.00 4.50
261 Mookie Wilson 86............... 15.00 4.50
262 Ray Knight 86 .... 10.00 3.00
263 Wally Backman 86 .... 10.00 3.00
264 Sid Fernandez 86 EXCH 10.00 3.00
265 Alan Trammell 87 .... 15.00 4.50
266 Dan Petry 87...................... 10.00 3.00
267 Chet Lemon 87 .... 10.00 3.00
268 Sparky Anderson 87 .... 15.00 4.50
269 Jack Morris 87 SP/25 .... 25.00 7.50
270 Kirk Gibson 87 .... 15.00 4.50
271 Lou Whitaker 87 SP/50....... 20.00 6.00
272 Bert Blyleven 87 * 10.00 3.00
273 Kent Hrbek MM 87............. 15.00 4.50
274 Kirby Puckett 87 SP/25...... 80.00 24.00
275 Alejandro Pena 88............... 10.00 3.00
276 Jesse Orosco 88 .... 10.00 3.00
277 John Shelby 88................... 10.00 3.00
278 Kirk Gibson MM 88 SP/50 . 20.00 6.00
279 Mickey Hatcher 88 .... 10.00 3.00
280 Mike Scioscia 88................. 10.00 3.00
281 Steve Sax 88...................... 10.00 3.00
282 Darryl Strawberry 88 .... 25.00 7.50
283 Dwight Gooden 88 .... 15.00 4.50
284 Gary Carter 88 SP/50.......... 20.00 6.00
285 Howard Johnson 88............. 10.00 3.00
286 Keith Hernandez 88............. 15.00 4.50
287 Lenny Dykstra 88 .... 15.00 4.50
288 Mookie Wilson 88 .... 15.00 4.50
289 Wally Backman 88 .... 10.00 3.00
290 Sid Fernandez 88 EXCH 10.00 3.00
291 Jack Morris 91 SP/50 .... 20.00 6.00
292 Kent Hrbek 91 .... 15.00 4.50
293 Kirby Puckett MM 91 SP/50 60.00 18.00
294 D.Winfield MM 92 SP/35 ... 40.00 12.00
295 Jack Morris 92 SP/75 .... 15.00 4.50
296 Joe Carter 92 SP/100.......... 15.00 4.50
297 Don Mattingly MM 95 SP/25 80.00 24.00
298 Paul O'Neill 95 * 25.00 7.50
299 Jack McDowell 95.............. 10.00 3.00
300 Wade Boggs 95 SP/75....... 30.00 9.00

2004 UD Legends Timeless Teams Legendary Combo Cuts

Nm-Mt Ex-Mt
OVERALL FOLD-OPEN CARD ODDS 1:360
STATED PRINT RUN 1 SERIAL #'d SET
NO PRICING DUE TO SCARCITY ....
DM Joe DiMaggio ....
Mickey Mantle
KJ John F. Kennedy...........................
Thomas Jefferson
LR Abraham Lincoln ....
Jackie Robinson
RW Franklin D. Roosevelt....................
Ted Williams
WR George Washington......................
Babe Ruth

2004 UD Legends Timeless Teams Legendary Combo Signatures

Nm-Mt Ex-Mt
OVERALL FOLD-OPEN CARD ODDS 1:360
STATED PRINT RUN 10 SERIAL #'d SETS
NO PRICING DUE TO SCARCITY ....
AL Brooks Robinson...........................
Carl Yastrzemski
Frank Robinson
Harmon Killebrew
Robin Yount
CY Bob Gibson....................................
Denny McLain
Jim Palmer
Steve Carlton
Tom Seaver
HC Al Kaline ....
Cal Ripken
Lou Brock
Paul Molitor
Wade Boggs
NL Ernie Banks....................................
Joe Morgan
Johnny Bench
Mike Schmidt
Orlando Cepeda
WS Bill Buckner ....
Carlton Fisk
Joe Carter
Kirby Puckett
Kirk Gibson

2004 UD Legends Timeless Teams Legendary Signatures Dual

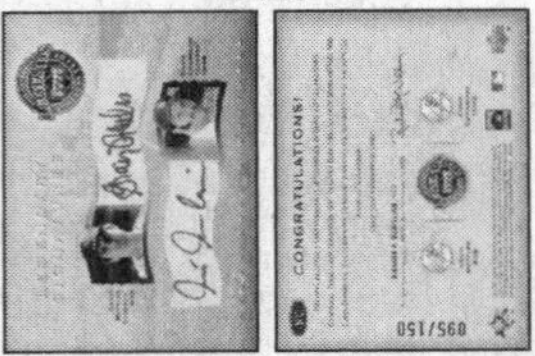

Nm-Mt Ex-Mt
OVERALL DUAL/TRIPLE SIG ODDS 1:90
PRINT RUNS B/WN 25-150 COPIES PER
EXCHANGE DEADLINE 08/19/07........
BC Lou Brock........................ 60.00 18.00
Orlando Cepeda/75
BJ Lou Brock 40.00 12.00
Julian Javier/150
BM Wade Boggs 150.00 45.00
Don Mattingly/50
BO Vida Blue 40.00 12.00
Blue Moon Odom/150
BW Ernie Banks 120.00 36.00
Billy Williams/25
CB Steve Carlton 50.00 15.00
Bob Boone/150
CG Ron Cey........................... 40.00 12.00
Steve Garvey/150
CH Gary Carter 40.00 12.00
Keith Hernandez/150
CM Dave Concepcion 50.00 15.00
Joe Morgan/75 EXCH
CW Joe Carter..
Dave Winfield/25
DD Bucky Dent....................... 40.00 12.00
Brian Doyle/150
FR Fred Lynn.......................... 50.00 15.00
Jim Rice/150
GA Kirk Gibson 40.00 12.00
Sparky Anderson/150
GB Bob Gibson 80.00 24.00
Lou Brock/50
GC Dwight Gooden 40.00 12.00
Gary Carter/150
GL Rich Gossage 40.00 12.00
Sparky Lyle/150 EXCH
GM Bob Gibson....................... 60.00 18.00
Tim McCarver/50
HJ Ken Holtzman 40.00 12.00
Fergie Jenkins/150
HK Keith Hernandez 40.00 12.00
Ray Knight/150
JH Fergie Jenkins.................... 40.00 12.00
Randy Hundley/150
JS Tommy John 40.00 12.00
Don Sutton/150
KH Al Kaline 50.00 15.00
Willie Horton/150
KK Harmon Killebrew 50.00 15.00
Jim Kaat/150
LM Mickey Lolich..................... 50.00 15.00
Denny McLain/75
MB Joe Morgan 100.00 30.00
Johnny Bench/25
MF Denny McLain 40.00 12.00
Bill Freehan/150
NC Graig Nettles 40.00 12.00
Chris Chambliss/150
OM Paul O'Neill..................... 120.00 36.00
Don Mattingly/75
PC Jim Palmer 40.00 12.00
Mike Cuellar/150
PF Tony Perez 50.00 15.00
George Foster/150
PH Kirby Puckett.....................................
Kent Hrbek/50
PN Lou Piniella 40.00 12.00
Graig Nettles/150
PR Jim Palmer 40.00 12.00
Merv Rettenmund/150
RL Bill Russell.......................... 25.00 7.50
Davey Lopes/150
RR Brooks Robinson 80.00 24.00
Frank Robinson/50
RS Nolan Ryan...................... 300.00 90.00
Tom Seaver/25
SD Steve Garvey 40.00 12.00
Davey Lopes/150
SG Darryl Strawberry 50.00 15.00
Dwight Gooden/150
SY Don Sutton 40.00 12.00
Steve Yeager/150
TF Luis Tiant 60.00 18.00
Carlton Fisk/50
TM Gorman Thomas 50.00 15.00
Paul Molitor/150 EXCH
WB Mookie Wilson 40.00 12.00
Bill Buckner/150
WT Lou Whitaker 60.00 18.00
Alan Trammell/75
YM Robin Yount..................... 120.00 36.00
Paul Molitor/50
YP Carl Yastrzemski 80.00 24.00
Rico Petrocelli/50

2004 UD Legends Timeless Teams Legendary Signatures Triple

Nm-Mt Ex-Mt
OVERALL DUAL/TRIPLE AU ODDS 1:90
PRINT RUNS B/WN 25-75 COPIES PER
EXCHANGE DEADLINE 08/19/07........
BCM Johnny Bench 120.00 36.00
Dave Concepcion
Joe Morgan/25 EXCH
BOM Wade Boggs 200.00 60.00
Paul O'Neill
Don Mattingly/50
BRB Sal Bando......................... 50.00 15.00
Joe Rudi
Vida Blue/75
BSW Ernie Banks 175.00 52.50
Ron Santo
Billy Williams/25
CDK Gary Carter..................... 60.00 18.00
Lenny Dykstra
Ray Knight/50
CND Chris Chambliss............... 60.00 18.00
Graig Nettles
Bucky Dent/50
ERL Dwight Evans.................. 175.00 52.50
Jim Rice
Fred Lynn/50
GBC Steve Garvey 80.00 24.00
Dusty Baker
Ron Cey/50
GBM Bob Gibson 100.00 30.00
Lou Brock
Tim McCarver/25
GDR Bobby Grich................... 200.00 60.00
Brian Downing
Nolan Ryan/25
GHS Kirk Gibson 100.00 30.00
Mickey Hatcher
Mike Scioscia/75
GMP Phil Garner 60.00 18.00
Bill Madlock
Dave Parker/50
HHS Jim Hickman..................... 80.00 24.00
Ken Holtzman
Ron Santo/75
HSJ Burt Hooton....................... 60.00 18.00
Don Sutton
Tommy John/50
JHH Fergie Jenkins 60.00 18.00
Randy Hundley
Ken Holtzman/75
KKP Harmon Killebrew.............. 80.00 24.00
Jim Kaat
Jim Perry/50
KPG Jim Kaat 60.00 18.00
Jim Perry
Mudcat Grant/75 EXCH
KSR Jerry Koosman............... 350.00 105.00
Tom Seaver
Nolan Ryan/25
MHP Jack Morris 100.00 30.00
Kent Hrbek
Kirby Puckett/50
MLF Denny McLain 60.00 18.00
Mickey Lolich
Bill Freehan/50
NKH Jim Northrup 80.00 24.00
Al Kaline
Willie Horton/75
PBH Kirby Puckett.................. 100.00 30.00
Bert Blyleven
Kent Hrbek/50
PCR Jim Palmer......................... 50.00 15.00
Mike Cuellar
Pete Richert/75
PPW Jim Palmer 60.00 18.00
Boog Powell
Earl Weaver/75
RPR Frank Robinson............... 100.00 30.00
Boog Powell
Brooks Robinson/50
RWP Cal Ripken..................... 300.00 90.00
Earl Weaver
Jim Palmer/25
SCB Mike Schmidt 175.00 52.50
Steve Carlton
Bob Boone/50
SGS Steve Sax 60.00 18.00
Pedro Guerrero
Mike Scioscia/75
STM Mike Schmidt...................................
Manny Trillo
Bake McBride/50
TWA Alan Trammell 80.00 24.00
Lou Whitaker
Sparky Anderson/50
YCT Robin Yount.................... 120.00 36.00
Cecil Cooper
Gorman Thomas/50 EXCH
YFT Carl Yastrzemski 175.00 52.50
Carlton Fisk
Luis Tiant/25
YMT Robin Yount.................... 150.00 45.00
Paul Molitor
Gorman Thomas/75 EXCH

2004 UD Legends Timeless Teams Team Terrific GU Team Logo

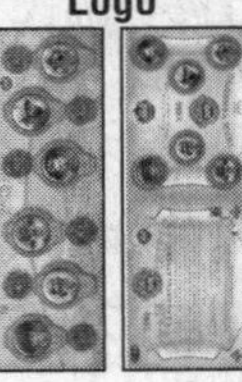
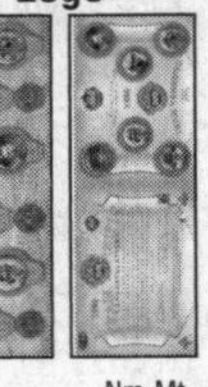

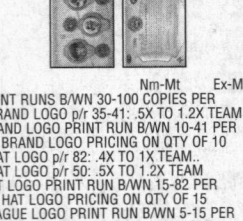

Nm-Mt Ex-Mt
PRINT RUNS B/WN 30-100 COPIES PER
*BRAND LOGO p/r 35-41: .5X TO 1.2X TEAM
BRAND LOGO PRINT RUN B/WN 10-41 PER
NO BRAND LOGO PRICING ON QTY OF 10
*HAT LOGO p/r 82: .4X TO 1X TEAM
*HAT LOGO p/r 50: .5X TO 1.2X TEAM
HAT LOGO PRINT RUN B/WN 15-82 PER
NO HAT LOGO PRICING ON QTY OF 15
LEAGUE LOGO PRINT RUN B/WN 5-15 PER
NO LEAGUE LOGO PRICING AVAILABLE
STATS PRINT RUN B/WN 1-5 COPIES PER
NO STATS PRICING AVAILABLE
OVERALL FOLD-OPEN CARD ODDS 1:360
BO Boog Powell Bat 100.00 30.00
Brooks Robinson Bat
Cal Ripken Bat
Davey Johnson Bat
Frank Robinson Bat
Paul Blair Bat/85
BR Carl Yastrzemski Bat 80.00 24.00
Carlton Fisk Bat
Dwight Evans Bat
Fred Lynn Bat
Jim Rice Bat
Rico Petrocelli Bat/85
CR Dave Concepcion Bat 100.00 30.00
George Foster Bat
Joe Morgan Bat
Johnny Bench Bat
Ken Griffey Sr. Bat
Tony Perez Bat/31
LD Bill Russell Bat 60.00 18.00
Davey Lopes Bat
Dusty Baker Bat
Ron Cey Bat
Steve Garvey Bat
Steve Yeager Bat/42
MB Cecil Cooper Jsy/Pants....... 50.00 15.00
Don Money Bat
Paul Molitor Bat
Robin Yount Bat
Rollie Fingers Jsy
Sal Bando Bat/100
NM Darryl Strawberry Bat......... 50.00 15.00
Gary Carter Bat
Keith Hernandez Bat
Lenny Dykstra Bat
Mookie Wilson Bat
Ray Knight Bat/85
NY Babe Ruth Bat ....
Don Mattingly Bat
Joe DiMaggio Bat
Lou Gehrig Jsy/Pants
Mickey Mantle Bat
Yogi Berra Bat/30
OA Bert Campaneris Bat 40.00 12.00
Billy North Bat
Billy Williams Bat
Gene Tenace Bat
Joe Rudi Jsy
Sal Bando Bat/100
SC Bob Gibson Jsy 80.00 24.00
Lou Brock Bat
Orlando Cepeda Bat
Stan Musial Bat
Steve Carlton Bat
Tim McCarver Bat/100

2001 UD Reserve

The 2001 UD Reserve product was released in late July, 2001 and featured a 210-card base set. The base set was broken into tiers as follows: Base Veterans (1-180), and Prospects (181-210) that are serial numbered to 2500 sets. Each pack contained 5 cards, and carried a suggested retail price of $2.49.

Nm-Mt Ex-Mt
COMP.SET w/o SP's (180) 25.00 7.50
COMMON CARD (1-180) .... .30 .09
COMMON (181-210).................. 4.00 1.20
1 Darin Erstad .... .30 .09
2 Tim Salmon .... .50 .15
3 Bengie Molina .... .30 .09
4 Troy Glaus .... .30 .09
5 Glenallen Hill.......................... .30 .09
6 Garret Anderson...................... .30 .09
7 Jason Giambi .... .30 .09
8 Johnny Damon........................ .50 .15
9 Eric Chavez .... .30 .09
10 Tim Hudson .... .30 .09
11 Miguel Tejada........................ .30 .09
12 Barry Zito .... .50 .15
13 Jose Ortiz............................. .30 .09
14 Tony Batista .... .30 .09
15 Carlos Delgado...................... .30 .09
16 Shannon Stewart .... .30 .09
17 Raul Mondesi .... .30 .09
18 Ben Grieve .... .30 .09
19 Aubrey Huff........................... .30 .09
20 Greg Vaughn .... .30 .09
21 Fred McGriff.......................... .50 .15
22 Gerald Williams...................... .30 .09
23 Bartolo Colon .... .30 .09
24 Roberto Alomar .... .50 .15
25 Jim Thome............................ .75 .23
26 Omar Vizquel .... .50 .15
27 Juan Gonzalez....................... .50 .15
28 Ellis Burks .... .30 .09
29 Edgar Martinez...................... .50 .15
30 Aaron Sele .... .30 .09
31 Jay Buhner............................ .30 .09
32 Mike Cameron....................... .30 .09
33 Kazuhiro Sasaki .... .30 .09
34 John Olerud .... .30 .09
35 Cal Ripken......................... 2.50 .75
36 Brady Anderson .... .30 .09
37 Pat Hentgen .... .30 .09
38 Chris Richard .... .30 .09
39 Jerry Hairston Jr. .... .30 .09
40 Mike Bordick......................... .30 .09
41 Ivan Rodriguez...................... .75 .23
42 Rick Helling.......................... .30 .09
43 Rafael Palmeiro..................... .50 .15
44 Alex Rodriguez.................... 1.25 .35
45 Andres Galarraga .... .30 .09
46 Rusty Greer.......................... .30 .09
47 Ruben Mateo .... .30 .09
48 Ken Caminiti......................... .30 .09
49 Nomar Garciaparra.............. 1.25 .35
50 Pedro Martinez...................... .75 .23
51 Manny Ramirez..................... .50 .15
52 Carl Everett .... .30 .09
53 Dante Bichette...................... .30 .09
54 Hideo Nomo.......................... .75 .23
55 Mike Sweeney .... .30 .09
56 Carlos Beltran .... .50 .15
57 Jeff Suppan.......................... .30 .09
58 Jermaine Dye .... .30 .09
59 Mark Quinn .... .30 .09
60 Joe Randa............................ .30 .09
61 Bobby Higginson .... .30 .09
62 Tony Clark............................ .30 .09
63 Brian Moehler .... .30 .09
64 Dean Palmer .... .30 .09
65 Brandon Inge .... .30 .09
66 Damion Easley .... .30 .09
67 Brad Radke .... .30 .09
68 Corey Koskie........................ .30 .09
69 Cristian Guzman................... .30 .09
70 Eric Milton .... .30 .09
71 Jacque Jones .... .30 .09
72 Matt Lawton......................... .30 .09
73 Frank Thomas .... .75 .23
74 David Wells.......................... .30 .09
75 Magglio Ordonez.................. .30 .09
76 Paul Konerko .... .30 .09
77 Sandy Alomar Jr. .... .30 .09
78 Ray Durham......................... .30 .09
79 Roger Clemens .... 1.50 .45
80 Bernie Williams.................... .50 .15
81 Derek Jeter...................... 2.00 .60
82 David Justice .... .30 .09
83 Paul O'Neill .... .50 .15
84 Mike Mussina....................... .50 .15
85 Jorge Posada .... .50 .15
86 Jeff Bagwell .... .50 .15
87 Richard Hidalgo .... .30 .09
88 Craig Biggio .... .50 .15
89 Scott Elarton .... .30 .09
90 Moises Alou .... .30 .09
91 Greg Maddux .... 1.25 .35
92 Rafael Furcal .... .30 .09
93 Andruw Jones .... .30 .09
94 Tom Glavine .... .50 .15
95 Chipper Jones .... .75 .23
96 Javy Lopez .... .30 .09
97 Richie Sexson .... .30 .09
98 Jeromy Burnitz..................... .30 .09
99 Jeff D'Amico .... .30 .09
100 Jeffrey Hammonds............. .30 .09
101 Geoff Jenkins .... .30 .09
102 Ben Sheets........................ .50 .15
103 Mark McGwire .... 2.00 .60
104 Rick Ankiel .... .30 .09
105 Darryl Kile .... .30 .09
106 Edgar Renteria .... .30 .09
107 Jim Edmonds..................... .30 .09
108 J.D. Drew .... .30 .09
109 Sammy Sosa................... 1.25 .35
110 Corey Patterson .... .30 .09
111 Kerry Wood........................ .75 .23
112 Todd Hundley .... .30 .09
113 Rondell White .... .30 .09
114 Matt Stairs .... .30 .09
115 Randy Johnson................... .75 .23
116 Mark Grace .... .50 .15
117 Steve Finley........................ .30 .09
118 Luis Gonzalez..................... .30 .09
119 Matt Williams...................... .30 .09
120 Curt Schilling .... .30 .09
121 Gary Sheffield .... .30 .09
122 Kevin Brown........................ .30 .09
123 Shawn Green .... .30 .09
124 Eric Karros.......................... .30 .09
125 Chan Ho Park...................... .30 .09
126 Adrian Beltre .... .50 .15
127 Vladimir Guerrero .... .75 .23
128 Fernando Tatis.................... .30 .09
129 Lee Stevens .... .30 .09
130 Jose Vidro........................... .30 .09
131 Peter Bergeron.................... .30 .09
132 Michael Barrett.................... .30 .09
133 Jeff Kent.............................. .30 .09
134 Russ Ortiz .... .30 .09
135 Barry Bonds.................... 2.00 .60
136 J.T. Snow .... .30 .09
137 Livan Hernandez .... .30 .09
138 Rich Aurilia .... .30 .09
139 Preston Wilson .... .30 .09
140 Mike Lowell......................... .30 .09
141 Ryan Dempster .... .30 .09
142 Charles Johnson .... .30 .09
143 Matt Clement .... .30 .09
144 Luis Castillo .... .30 .09
145 Mike Piazza UER .... 1.25 .35
Card lists him as a Dodger
146 Al Leiter .... .30 .09
147 Robin Ventura...................... .30 .09

148 Jay Payton .30 .09
149 Todd Zeile .30 .09
150 Edgardo Alfonzo .30 .09
151 Tony Gwynn 1.00 .30
152 Ryan Klesko .30 .09
153 Phil Nevin .30 .09
154 Mark Kotsay .30 .09
155 Trevor Hoffman .30 .09
156 Damian Jackson .30 .09
157 Scott Rolen .75 .23
158 Mike Lieberthal .30 .09
159 Bruce Chen .30 .09
160 Bobby Abreu .30 .09
161 Pat Burrell .30 .09
162 Travis Lee .30 .09
163 Jason Kendall .30 .09
164 Derek Bell .30 .09
165 Kris Benson .30 .09
166 Kevin Young .30 .09
167 Brian Giles .30 .09
168 Pat Meares .30 .09
169 Sean Casey .30 .09
170 Pokey Reese .30 .09
171 Pete Harnisch .30 .09
172 Barry Larkin .50 .15
173 Ken Griffey Jr. 1.25 .35
174 Dmitri Young .30 .09
175 Mike Hampton .30 .09
176 Todd Helton .50 .15
177 Jeff Cirillo .30 .09
178 Denny Neagle .30 .09
179 Larry Walker .50 .15
180 Todd Hollandsworth .30 .09
181 Ichiro Suzuki SP RC 40.00 12.00
182 Wilson Betemit SP RC 4.00 1.20
183 A. Hernandez SP RC 4.00 1.20
184 Travis Hafner SP RC 10.00 3.00
185 Sean Douglass SP RC 4.00 1.20
186 Juan Diaz SP RC 4.00 1.20
187 H. Ramirez SP RC 5.00 1.50
188 M. Ensberg SP RC 5.00 1.50
189 B. Duckworth SP RC 4.00 1.20
190 Jack Wilson SP RC 8.00 2.40
191 Erick Almonte SP RC 4.00 1.20
192 R. Rodriguez SP RC 4.00 1.20
193 E. Guzman SP RC 4.00 1.20
194 Juan Uribe SP RC 5.00 1.50
195 Ryan Freel SP RC 4.00 1.20
196 C. Parker SP RC 4.00 1.20
197 J. Melian SP RC 4.00 1.20
198 Jose Mieses SP RC 4.00 1.20
199 Andres Torres SP RC 4.00 1.20
200 Jason Smith SP RC 4.00 1.20
201 J. Estrada SP RC 5.00 1.50
202 Cesar Crespo SP RC 4.00 1.20
203 C. Valderrama SP RC 4.00 1.20
204 Albert Pujols SP RC 50.00 15.00
205 Wilkin Ruan SP RC 4.00 1.20
206 Josh Fogg SP RC 4.00 1.20
207 Bert Snow SP RC 4.00 1.20
208 B. Lawrence SP RC 4.00 1.20
209 Esix Snead SP RC 4.00 1.20
210 T. Shinjo SP RC 5.00 1.50

2001 UD Reserve Ball-Base Duos

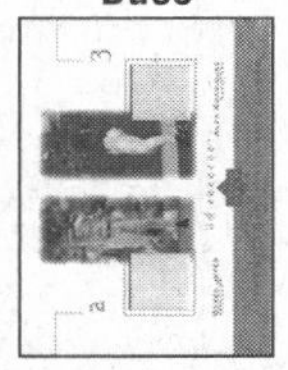

Randomly inserted into packs at one in 240, this 15-card insert set features swatches of both game-used baseball and base. Each of these cards feature two superstar caliber players on the card front. Card backs carry a "B" prefix followed by the players' initials.

Nm-Mt Ex-Mt
B-BH Barry Bonds 40.00 12.00
Todd Helton
B-CR Roger Clemens 30.00 9.00
Alex Rodriguez
B-GD Vladimir Guerrero 20.00 6.00
Carlos Delgado
B-GJ Ken Griffey Jr. 40.00 12.00
Derek Jeter
B-GR Nomar Garciaparra 30.00 9.00
Alex Rodriguez
B-GS Ken Griffey Jr. 25.00 7.50
Sammy Sosa
B-JN Chipper Jones 25.00 7.50
Nomar Garciaparra
B-JP Derek Jeter 40.00 12.00
Mike Piazza
B-JR Derek Jeter 40.00 12.00
Alex Rodriguez
B-MG Mark McGwire 50.00 15.00
Ken Griffey Jr.
B-MJ Mark McGwire 50.00 15.00
Derek Jeter
B-MP Mark McGwire 50.00 15.00
Mike Piazza
B-NJ Nomar Garciaparra 40.00 12.00
Derek Jeter
B-RM Alex Rodriguez 50.00 15.00
Mark McGwire
B-ST Sammy Sosa 25.00 7.50
Frank Thomas

2001 UD Reserve Ball-Base Quads

Randomly inserted into packs, this five card insert set features swatches of both game-used baseball and base. Each of these cards feature four superstar caliber players on the card front. Card backs carry a "B" prefix followed by the players' initials. Please note that there were only 50 serial numbered sets produced.

Nm-Mt Ex-Mt
GBJE Ken Griffey Jr. 100.00 30.00

Barry Bonds
Andruw Jones
Jim Edmonds
GPJG Vladimir Guerrero 80.00 24.00
Mike Piazza
Chipper Jones
Nomar Garciaparra
PMJR Mike Piazza 200.00 60.00
Mark McGwire
Derek Jeter
Alex Rodriguez
SGRM Alex Rodriguez 150.00 45.00
Ken Griffey Jr.
Sammy Sosa
Mark McGwire
THMJ Frank Thomas 120.00 36.00
Todd Helton
Mark McGwire
Derek Jeter

2001 UD Reserve Ball-Base Trios

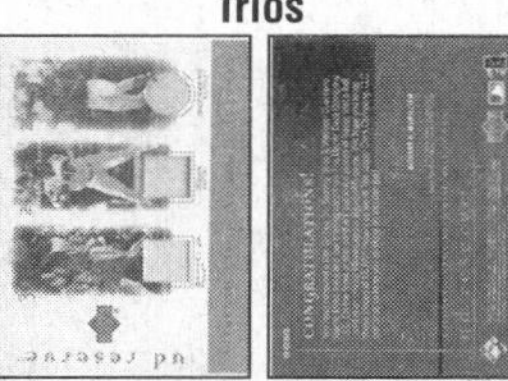

Randomly inserted into packs at one in 480, this 10-card insert set features swatches of both game-used baseball and base. Each of these cards feature three superstar caliber players on the card front. Card backs carry a "B" prefix followed by the players' initials.

Nm-Mt Ex-Mt
BSH Barry Bonds 50.00 15.00
Gary Sheffield
Todd Helton
CMJ Roger Clemens 60.00 18.00
Pedro Martinez
Derek Jeter
GPJ Vladimir Guerrero 40.00 12.00
Mike Piazza
Chipper Jones
GSG Ken Griffey Jr. 40.00 12.00
Sammy Sosa
Vladimir Guerrero
JGS Derek Jeter 60.00 18.00
Ken Griffey Jr.
Sammy Sosa
JRG Derek Jeter 60.00 18.00
Alex Rodriguez
Nomar Garciaparra
MJR Mark McGwire 100.00 30.00
Derek Jeter
Alex Rodriguez
PRS Mike Piazza 60.00 18.00
Alex Rodriguez
Sammy Sosa
SGM Sammy Sosa 100.00 30.00
Ken Griffey Jr.
Mark McGwire
THM Frank Thomas 100.00 30.00
Todd Helton
Mark McGwire

2001 UD Reserve Big Game

Randomly inserted into packs at one in 24, this 10-card insert set features players that usually come up big in clutch situations. Card backs carry a "BG" prefix.

Nm-Mt Ex-Mt
COMPLETE SET (10) 50.00 15.00
BG1 Alex Rodriguez 5.00 1.50
BG2 Ken Griffey Jr. 5.00 1.50
BG3 Mark McGwire 8.00 2.40
BG4 Derek Jeter 8.00 2.40
BG5 Sammy Sosa 5.00 1.50
BG6 Pedro Martinez 3.00 .90
BG7 Jason Giambi 2.00 .60
BG8 Todd Helton 2.00 .60
BG9 Carlos Delgado 2.00 .60
BG10 Mike Piazza 5.00 1.50

2001 UD Reserve Game Jersey Duos

Randomly inserted into packs at one in 240, this 15-card insert set features swatches of game-used jerseys. Each of these cards feature two superstar caliber players on the card front. Card backs carry a "J" prefix followed by the players' initials.

Nm-Mt Ex-Mt
J-BK Barry Bonds 50.00 15.00
Jeff Kent

J-DG Carlos Delgado 25.00 7.50
Jason Giambi
J-GE Troy Glaus 25.00 7.50
Darin Erstad
J-GK Jason Giambi 25.00 7.50
Jeff Kent
J-GW Brian Giles 25.00 7.50
Bernie Williams
J-HE Todd Helton 25.00 7.50
Darin Erstad
J-HG Tim Hudson 25.00 7.50
Jason Giambi
J-JG Chipper Jones 25.00 7.50
Troy Glaus
J-JJ Andruw Jones 25.00 7.50
Chipper Jones
J-JW Randy Johnson 25.00 7.50
David Wells
J-RB Alex Rodriguez 40.00 12.00
Tony Batista
J-SB Gary Sheffield 50.00 15.00
Barry Bonds
J-SG Sammy Sosa 40.00 12.00
Troy Glaus
J-WE Bernie Williams 25.00 7.50
Jim Edmonds
J-WO David Wells 25.00 7.50
Magglio Ordonez

2001 UD Reserve Game Jersey Quads

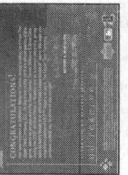

Randomly inserted into packs at one in 480, this five card insert set features swatches of game-used jerseys. Each of these cards feature four superstar caliber players on the card front. Card backs carry a "J" prefix followed by the players' initials.

Nm-Mt Ex-Mt
RGS Carlos Delgado 80.00 24.00
Alex Rodriguez
Troy Glaus
Sammy Sosa
WBG Jason Giambi 60.00 18.00
Bernie Williams
Barry Bonds
Brian Giles
HKEJ Todd Helton 50.00 15.00
Jeff Kent
Jim Edmonds
Chipper Jones
JRSB Andruw Jones 100.00 30.00
Alex Rodriguez
Sammy Sosa
Barry Bonds
SOEB Gary Sheffield 40.00 12.00
Magglio Ordonez
Darin Erstad
Tony Batista

2001 UD Reserve Game Jersey Trios

Randomly inserted into packs at one in 480, this 10-card insert set features swatches of game-used jerseys. Each of these cards feature three superstar caliber players on the card front. Card backs carry a "J" prefix followed by the players' initials.

Nm-Mt Ex-Mt
J-BSH Barry Bonds 60.00 18.00
Gary Sheffield
Todd Helton
J-BWD Tony Batista 40.00 12.00
Bernie Williams
Carlos Delgado
J-EKE Darin Erstad 25.00 7.50
Jeff Kent
Jim Edmonds
J-GGR Jason Giambi 40.00 12.00
Troy Glaus
Alex Rodriguez
J-GHD Jason Giambi 40.00 12.00
Todd Helton
Carlos Delgado
J-HJW Tim Hudson 40.00 12.00
Randy Johnson
David Wells
J-RSS Alex Rodriguez 60.00 18.00
Sammy Sosa
Gary Sheffield
J-SOD Sammy Sosa 50.00 15.00
Magglio Ordonez
Carlos Delgado
J-WEJ Bernie Williams 40.00 12.00
Jim Edmonds
Andruw Jones
J-WSH David Wells 50.00 15.00
Sammy Sosa
Todd Helton

2001 UD Reserve New Order

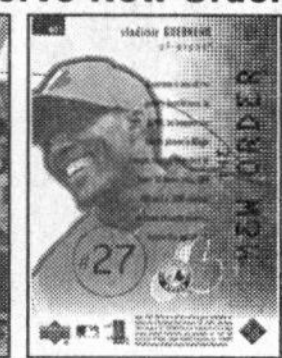

Randomly inserted into packs at one in 24, this 10-card insert set features players that are part of the "new generation" of baseball. Card backs carry a "NO" prefix.

Nm-Mt Ex-Mt
COMPLETE SET (10) 50.00 15.00
NO1 Vladimir Guerrero 3.00 .90
NO2 Andruw Jones 1.25 .35
NO3 Corey Patterson 1.25 .35
NO4 Derek Jeter 8.00 2.40
NO5 Alex Rodriguez 5.00 1.50
NO6 Pat Burrell 1.25 .35
NO7 Ichiro Suzuki 20.00 6.00
NO8 Barry Zito 2.00 .60
NO9 Rafael Furcal 1.25 .35
NO10 Troy Glaus 1.25 .35

2001 UD Reserve Royalty

Randomly inserted into packs at one in 24, this 10-card insert set features players that are among baseball's most elite. Card backs carry a "R" prefix.

Nm-Mt Ex-Mt
COMPLETE SET (10) 50.00 15.00
R1 Ken Griffey Jr. 5.00 1.50
R2 Derek Jeter 8.00 2.40
R3 Alex Rodriguez 5.00 1.50
R4 Sammy Sosa 5.00 1.50
R5 Mark McGwire 8.00 2.40
R6 Mike Piazza 5.00 1.50
R7 Vladimir Guerrero 3.00 .90
R8 Chipper Jones 3.00 .90
R9 Frank Thomas 3.00 .90
R10 Nomar Garciaparra 5.00 1.50

2001 Ultimate Collection

This product was released in mid-January 2002, and featured a 120-card base set that was broken up into tiers as follows: 90 Base Veterans, 10 Prospects numbered to 1000, 10 Prospects numbered to 750, and 10 Prospects numbered to 250. Exchange cards were seeded into packs for signed cards of Mark Prior and Mark Teixiera.

Nm-Mt Ex-Mt
COMMON CARD (1-90) 4.00 1.20
COMMON CARD (91-100) 10.00 3.00
COMMON (101-110) 10.00 3.00
COMMON CARD (111-120) 25.00 7.50
1 Troy Glaus 4.00 1.20
2 Darin Erstad 4.00 1.20
3 Jason Giambi 4.00 1.20
4 Barry Zito 4.00 1.20
5 Tim Hudson 4.00 1.20
6 Miguel Tejada 4.00 1.20
7 Carlos Delgado 4.00 1.20
8 Shannon Stewart 4.00 1.20
9 Greg Vaughn 4.00 1.20
10 Toby Hall 4.00 1.20
11 Roberto Alomar 4.00 1.20
12 Juan Gonzalez 4.00 1.20
13 Jim Thome 6.00 1.80
14 Edgar Martinez 4.00 1.20
15 Freddy Garcia 4.00 1.20
16 Bret Boone 4.00 1.20
17 Kazuhiro Sasaki 4.00 1.20
18 Cal Ripken 20.00 6.00
19 Tim Raines Jr. 4.00 1.20
20 Alex Rodriguez 10.00 3.00
21 Ivan Rodriguez 6.00 1.80
22 Rafael Palmeiro 4.00 1.20
23 Pedro Martinez 6.00 1.80
24 Nomar Garciaparra 10.00 3.00
25 Manny Ramirez 4.00 1.20
26 Hideo Nomo 6.00 1.80
27 Mike Sweeney 4.00 1.20
28 Carlos Beltran 4.00 1.20
29 Tony Clark 4.00 1.20
30 Dean Palmer 4.00 1.20
31 Doug Mientkiewicz 4.00 1.20
32 Cristian Guzman 4.00 1.20
33 Corey Koskie 4.00 1.20
34 Frank Thomas 6.00 1.80
35 Magglio Ordonez 4.00 1.20
36 Jose Canseco 6.00 1.80
37 Roger Clemens 12.00 3.60
38 Derek Jeter 15.00 4.50
39 Bernie Williams 4.00 1.20
40 Mike Mussina 4.00 1.20
41 Tino Martinez 4.00 1.20
42 Jeff Bagwell 4.00 1.20
43 Lance Berkman 4.00 1.20
44 Roy Oswalt 4.00 1.20
45 Chipper Jones 6.00 1.80
46 Greg Maddux 10.00 3.00
47 Andruw Jones 4.00 1.20
48 Tom Glavine 4.00 1.20
49 Richie Sexson 4.00 1.20
50 Jeromy Burnitz 4.00 1.20
51 Ben Sheets 4.00 1.20
52 Mark McGwire 15.00 4.50
53 Matt Morris 4.00 1.20
54 Jim Edmonds 4.00 1.20
55 J.D. Drew 4.00 1.20
56 Sammy Sosa 10.00 3.00
57 Fred McGriff 4.00 1.20
58 Kerry Wood 6.00 1.80
59 Randy Johnson 6.00 1.80
60 Luis Gonzalez 4.00 1.20
61 Curt Schilling 4.00 1.20
62 Shawn Green 4.00 1.20
63 Kevin Brown 4.00 1.20
64 Gary Sheffield 4.00 1.20
65 Vladimir Guerrero 6.00 1.80
66 Barry Bonds 15.00 4.50
67 Jeff Kent 4.00 1.20
68 Rich Aurilia 4.00 1.20
69 Cliff Floyd 4.00 1.20
70 Charles Johnson 4.00 1.20
71 Josh Beckett 4.00 1.20
72 Mike Piazza 10.00 3.00
73 Edgardo Alfonzo 4.00 1.20
74 Robin Ventura 4.00 1.20
75 Tony Gwynn 8.00 2.40
76 Ryan Klesko 4.00 1.20
77 Phil Nevin 4.00 1.20
78 Scott Rolen 6.00 1.80
79 Bobby Abreu 4.00 1.20
80 Jimmy Rollins 4.00 1.20
81 Brian Giles 4.00 1.20
82 Jason Kendall 4.00 1.20
83 Aramis Ramirez 4.00 1.20
84 Ken Griffey Jr. 10.00 3.00
85 Adam Dunn 4.00 1.20
86 Sean Casey 4.00 1.20
87 Barry Larkin 4.00 1.20
88 Larry Walker 4.00 1.20
89 Mike Hampton 4.00 1.20
90 Todd Helton 4.00 1.20
91 Ken Harvey T1 10.00 3.00
92 Bill Ortega T1 RC 10.00 3.00
93 Juan Diaz T1 RC 10.00 3.00
94 Greg Miller T1 RC 10.00 3.00
95 Brandon Berger T1 RC 10.00 3.00
96 Brandon Lyon T1 RC 10.00 3.00
97 Jay Gibbons T1 RC 15.00 4.50
98 Rob Mackowiak T1 RC 15.00 4.50
99 Erick Almonte T1 RC 10.00 3.00
100 J.Middlebrook T1 RC 10.00 3.00
101 Johnny Estrada T2 RC 15.00 4.50
102 Juan Uribe T2 RC 15.00 4.50
103 Travis Hafner T2 RC 25.00 7.50
104 M.Ensberg T2 RC 15.00 4.50
105 Mike Rivera T2 RC 10.00 3.00
106 Josh Towers T2 RC 10.00 3.00
107 A.Hernandez T2 RC 10.00 3.00
108 Rafael Soriano T2 RC 15.00 4.50
109 Jackson Melian T2 RC 10.00 3.00
110 Wilkin Ruan T2 RC 10.00 3.00
111 Albert Pujols T3 RC 300.00 90.00
112 T.Shinjo T3 RC 30.00 9.00
113 B.Duckworth T3 RC 25.00 7.50
114 Juan Cruz T3 RC 25.00 7.50
115 D.Brazelton T3 RC 30.00 9.00
116 Mark Prior T3 AU RC 400.00 120.00
117 Mark Teixeira T3 AU RC 250.00 75.00
118 Wilson Betemit T3 RC 25.00 7.50
119 Bud Smith T3 RC 25.00 7.50
120 I.Suzuki T3 AU RC 800.00 240.00

2001 Ultimate Collection Game Jersey

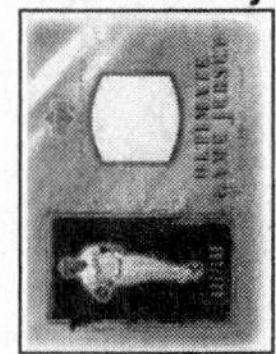

These cards feature swatches of actual game-used jerseys from various major league stars. Game Jersey cards (including Copper, Silver and Gold parallel versions) were cumulatively issued into packs at 1:2. Each card is serial-numbered to 150.

Nm-Mt Ex-Mt
COPPER RANDOM INSERTS IN PACKS
COPPER PRINT RUN 24 SERIAL #'d SETS
NO COPPER PRICING DUE TO SCARCITY
GOLD RANDOM INSERTS IN PACKS
GOLD PRINT RUN 15 SERIAL #'d SETS
NO GOLD PRICING DUE TO SCARCITY
SILVER RANDOM INSERTS IN PACKS
SILVER PRINT RUN 20 SERIAL #'d SETS
NO SILVER PRICING DUE TO SCARCITY
U-AJ Andruw Jones 15.00 4.50
U-AP Albert Pujols 80.00 24.00
U-AR Alex Rodriguez 25.00 7.50
U-BB Barry Bonds 40.00 12.00
U-BW Bernie Williams 25.00 7.50
U-CD Carlos Delgado 15.00 4.50
U-CJ Chipper Jones 25.00 7.50
U-CR Cal Ripken 50.00 15.00

U-DE Darin Erstad 15.00 4.50
U-FT Frank Thomas 25.00 7.50
U-GM Greg Maddux 25.00 7.50
U-GS Gary Sheffield 15.00 4.50
U-IR Ivan Rodriguez 25.00 7.50
U-JAG Jason Giambi 15.00 4.50
U-JB Jeff Bagwell 25.00 7.50
U-JC Jose Canseco 25.00 7.50
U-JG Juan Gonzalez 25.00 7.50
U-KG Ken Griffey Jr. 25.00 7.50
U-LG Luis Gonzalez 15.00 4.50
U-LW Larry Walker 25.00 7.50
U-MO Magglio Ordonez 15.00 4.50
U-MP Mike Piazza 25.00 7.50
U-RA Roberto Alomar 25.00 7.50
U-RC Roger Clemens 25.00 7.50
U-RJ Randy Johnson 25.00 7.50
U-SG Shawn Green 15.00 4.50
U-SR Scott Rolen 25.00 7.50
U-SS Sammy Sosa 25.00 7.50
U-TG Tony Gwynn 25.00 7.50
U-TH Todd Helton 25.00 7.50

2001 Ultimate Collection Ichiro Ball

This five-card insert set features game-used ball cards from the 2001 Rookie of the Year, Ichiro Suzuki. There is a Base, Copper, Silver, Gold and Autographed version. Card backs carry a "BB" prefix. Print runs are listed in our checklist. The signed Ichiro Ball card was available via an exchange card seeded into packs. The redemption date for the exchange card was February, 25th, 2004.

Nm-Mt Ex-Mt
BI Ichiro Suzuki AU/25
IA Ichiro Suzuki SP 80.00 24.00
IG Ichiro Suzuki Gold/25
IH I.Suzuki Copper/150 120.00 36.00
IS I.Suzuki Silver/50 150.00 45.00

2001 Ultimate Collection Ichiro Base

This five-card insert set features game-used base cards from the 2001 Rookie of the Year, Ichiro Suzuki. There is a Base, Copper, Silver, Gold and Autographed version. Card backs carry a "U" preifx. Print runs are listed in our checklist. The autograph card was seeded into packs in the form of an exchange card of which carried a redemption deadline of 02/25/04.

Nm-Mt Ex-Mt
SUI Ichiro Suzuki AU/25
UIA Ichiro Suzuki 40.00 12.00
UIC Ichiro Suzuki Copper/150. 100.00 30.00
UIG Ichiro Suzuki Gold/25
UIS Ichiro Suzuki Silver/50 120.00 36.00

2001 Ultimate Collection Ichiro Bat

This five-card insert set features game-used bat cards from the 2001 Rookie of the Year, Ichiro Suzuki. There is a Base, Copper, Silver, Gold and Autographed version. Card backs carry a "B" prefix.. Print runs are listed in our checklist. The autograph card was seeded into packs in the form of an exchange card of which carried a redemption deadline of 02/25/04.

Nm-Mt Ex-Mt
BIA I.Suzuki Away SP 80.00 24.00
BIC I.Suzuki Home SP 100.00 30.00
BIG I.Suzuki Gold/200 120.00 36.00
BIS I.Suzuki Silver/250 100.00 30.00
SBI Ichiro Suzuki AU/50 800.00 240.00

2001 Ultimate Collection Ichiro Batting Glove

This two-card insert set features game-used batting glove cards from the 2001 Rookie of the Year, Ichiro Suzuki. There are two versions available, Base and Gold. Cards carry a "BG" prefix. Print runs are listed in our checklist.

Nm-Mt Ex-Mt
BGI Ichiro Suzuki/75 200.00 60.00
BGIG Ichiro Suzuki Gold/25

2001 Ultimate Collection Ichiro Fielders Glove

Randomly inserted into Ultimate Collection packs, these two cards feature swatches of Ichiro Suzuki gloves. The cards are printed to different amounts and we have listed those cards in our checklist.

Nm-Mt Ex-Mt
FGI Ichiro Suzuki/75 250.00 75.00
FGIG Ichiro Suzuki Gold/25

2001 Ultimate Collection Ichiro Jersey

This five-card insert set features game-used jersey cards from the 2001 Rookie of the Year, Ichiro Suzuki. There is a Base, Copper, Silver, Gold and Autographed version. Card backs carry a "J" prefix. Print runs listed in our checklist. The autographed card was seeded into packs in the form of an exchange card of which carried a redemption deadline of 02/25/04.

Nm-Mt Ex-Mt
JIA Ichiro Suzuki Away 50.00 15.00
JIG I.Suzuki Gold/200 120.00 36.00
JIH I.Suzuki Home SP 80.00 24.00
JIS I.Suzuki Silver/250 100.00 30.00
SJI Ichiro Suzuki AU/50 800.00 240.00

2001 Ultimate Collection Magic Numbers Game Jersey

These cards feature swatches of actual game-used jerseys from various major league stars. They were issued into packs at 1:2. Card backs carry a "MN" prefix.

Nm-Mt Ex-Mt
GAME JERSEY CUMULATIVE ODDS 1:2
STATED PRINT RUN 150 SERIAL #'d SETS
*RED: .75X TO 2X BASIC MAGIC NUMBERS
RED RANDOM INSERTS IN PACKS
RED PRINT RUN 30 SERIAL #'d SETS
COPPER RANDOM INSERTS IN PACKS
COPPER PRINT RUN 24 SERIAL #'d SETS
NO COPPER PRICING DUE TO SCARCITY
SILVER RANDOM INSERTS IN PACKS
SILVER PRINT RUN 20 SERIAL #'d SETS
NO SILVER PRICING DUE TO SCARCITY
GOLD RANDOM INSERTS IN PACKS
GOLD PRINT RUN 15 SERIAL #'d SETS
NO GOLD PRICING DUE TO SCARCITY
MN-G Tony Gwynn 25.00 7.50
MNAJ Andruw Jones 15.00 4.50
MNAP Albert Pujols 80.00 24.00
MNAR Alex Rodriguez 25.00 7.50
MNBB Barry Bonds 40.00 12.00
MNBW Bernie Williams 25.00 7.50
MNCD Carlos Delgado 15.00 4.50
MNCJ Chipper Jones 25.00 7.50
MNCR Cal Ripken 50.00 15.00
MNDE Darin Erstad 15.00 4.50
MNFT Frank Thomas 25.00 7.50
MNGM Greg Maddux 25.00 7.50
MNGS Gary Sheffield 15.00 4.50
MNIR Ivan Rodriguez 25.00 7.50
MNJAG Jason Giambi 15.00 4.50
MNJB Jeff Bagwell 25.00 7.50
MNJC Jose Canseco 25.00 7.50
MNJG Juan Gonzalez 25.00 7.50
MNKG Ken Griffey Jr. 25.00 7.50
MNLG Luis Gonzalez 15.00 4.50
MNLW Larry Walker 25.00 7.50
MNMO Magglio Ordonez 15.00 4.50
MNMP Mike Piazza 25.00 7.50
MNRA Roberto Alomar 25.00 7.50
MNRC Roger Clemens 25.00 7.50
MNRJ Randy Johnson 25.00 7.50
MNSG Shawn Green 15.00 4.50
MNSR Scott Rolen 25.00 7.50
MNSS Sammy Sosa 25.00 7.50
MNTH Todd Helton 25.00 7.50

2001 Ultimate Collection Signatures

These cards feature authentic autographs from various major league stars. They were issued into packs at 1:4. Card backs carry the player's initials as numbering. Please note that there were only 150 sets produced. The following players cards were seeded into packs as exchange cards with a redemption deadline of 02/25/04: Cal Ripken, Edgar Martinez, Ken Griffey Jr. and Tom Glavine.

Nm-Mt Ex-Mt
*COPPER: .75X TO 1.5X BASIC SIG
COPPER PRINT RUN 70 SERIAL #'d SETS
GOLD PRINT RUN 15 SERIAL #'d SETS
NO GOLD PRICING DUE TO SCARCITY
SILVER PRINT RUN 24 SERIAL #'d SETS
NO SILVER PRICING DUE TO SCARCITY
AR Alex Rodriguez 100.00 30.00
BAB Barry Bonds 250.00 75.00
CD Carlos Delgado 25.00 7.50
CF Carlton Fisk 40.00 12.00
CR Cal Ripken 150.00 45.00
DS Duke Snider 40.00 12.00
EB Ernie Banks 50.00 15.00
EM Edgar Martinez 50.00 15.00
FT Frank Thomas 50.00 15.00
GS Gary Sheffield 40.00 12.00
IR Ivan Rodriguez 50.00 15.00
JAG Jason Giambi 25.00 7.50
JT Jim Thome 50.00 15.00
KG Ken Griffey Jr. 120.00 36.00
KP Kirby Puckett 50.00 15.00
LG Luis Gonzalez 25.00 7.50
RA Roberto Alomar 40.00 12.00
RC Roger Clemens 100.00 30.00
RK Ryan Klesko 25.00 7.50
RY Robin Yount 60.00 18.00
SK Sandy Koufax 300.00 90.00
SS Sammy Sosa 150.00 45.00
TG Tony Gwynn 80.00 24.00
TGL Tom Glavine 50.00 15.00
TP Tony Perez 25.00 7.50
TS Tom Seaver 40.00 12.00

2002 Ultimate Collection

This 120 card set was released in late December, 2002. These cards were issued in five card packs which came four packs to a box and four boxes to a case with an SRP of approximately $100 per pack. Card numbered 61 through 120 featured Rookie Cards with cards numbered 110 through 120 being autographed by the player. The cards between 61 and 110 were issued to a stated print run of 500 serial numbered sets while cards numbered 111 through 113 were issued to a stated print run of 300 serial numbered sets and cards numbered 114 through 120 were issued to a stated print run of 550 serial numbered sets. One hundred Mark McGwire Priority Signing exchange cards were randomly seeded in to packs (at a believed odds of 1:1000 packs). The bearer of the card was allowed to send in one item of his or her choice to Upper Deck for McGwire to sign.

Nm-Mt Ex-Mt
COMMON CARD (1-60) 4.00 1.20
COMMON CARD (61-110) 10.00 3.00
61-110 PRINT RUN 550 SERIAL #'d SETS
COMMON CARD (111-113) 25.00 7.50
COMMON CARD (114-120) 15.00 4.50
1 Troy Glaus 4.00 1.20
2 Luis Gonzalez 4.00 1.20
3 Curt Schilling 4.00 1.20
4 Randy Johnson 6.00 1.80
5 Andruw Jones 4.00 1.20
6 Greg Maddux 10.00 3.00
7 Chipper Jones 6.00 1.80
8 Gary Sheffield 4.00 1.20
9 Cal Ripken 20.00 6.00
10 Manny Ramirez 4.00 1.20
11 Pedro Martinez 6.00 1.80
12 Nomar Garciaparra 10.00 3.00
13 Sammy Sosa 10.00 3.00
14 Kerry Wood 6.00 1.80
15 Mark Prior 10.00 3.00
16 Magglio Ordonez 4.00 1.20
17 Frank Thomas 6.00 1.80
18 Adam Dunn 4.00 1.20
19 Ken Griffey Jr. 10.00 3.00
20 Jim Thome 6.00 1.80
21 Larry Walker 4.00 1.20
22 Todd Helton 4.00 1.20
23 Nolan Ryan 15.00 4.50
24 Jeff Bagwell 4.00 1.20
25 Roy Oswalt 4.00 1.20
26 Lance Berkman 4.00 1.20
27 Mike Sweeney 4.00 1.20
28 Shawn Green 4.00 1.20
29 Hideo Nomo 6.00 1.80
30 Torii Hunter 4.00 1.20
31 Vladimir Guerrero 6.00 1.80
32 Tom Seaver 4.00 1.20
33 Mike Piazza 10.00 3.00
34 Roberto Alomar 4.00 1.20
35 Derek Jeter 15.00 4.50
36 Alfonso Soriano 4.00 1.20
37 Jason Giambi 4.00 1.20
38 Roger Clemens 12.00 3.60
39 Mike Mussina 4.00 1.20
40 Bernie Williams 4.00 1.20
41 Joe DiMaggio 12.00 3.60
42 Mickey Mantle 25.00 7.50
43 Miguel Tejada 4.00 1.20
44 Eric Chavez 4.00 1.20
45 Barry Zito 4.00 1.20
46 Pat Burrell 4.00 1.20
47 Jason Kendall 4.00 1.20
48 Brian Giles 4.00 1.20
49 Barry Bonds 15.00 4.50
50 Ichiro Suzuki 10.00 3.00
51 Stan Musial 10.00 3.00
52 J.D. Drew 4.00 1.20
53 Scott Rolen 6.00 1.80
54 Albert Pujols 12.00 3.60
55 Mark McGwire 15.00 4.50
56 Alex Rodriguez 10.00 3.00
57 Ivan Rodriguez 6.00 1.80
58 Juan Gonzalez 4.00 1.20
59 Rafael Palmeiro 4.00 1.20
60 Carlos Delgado 4.00 1.20
61 Jose Valverde UR RC 15.00 4.50
62 Doug Devore UR RC 10.00 3.00
63 John Ennis UR RC 10.00 3.00
64 Joey Dawley UR RC 10.00 3.00
65 Trey Hodges UR RC 10.00 3.00
66 Mike Mahoney UR 10.00 3.00
67 Aaron Cook UR RC 10.00 3.00
68 Rene Reyes UR RC 10.00 3.00
69 Mark Corey UR RC 10.00 3.00
70 Hansel Izquierdo UR RC 10.00 3.00
71 Brandon Puffer UR RC 10.00 3.00
72 Jeriome Robertson UR RC 10.00 3.00
73 Jose Diaz UR RC 10.00 3.00
74 David Ross UR RC 10.00 3.00
75 Jayson Durocher UR RC 10.00 3.00
76 Eric Good UR RC 10.00 3.00
77 Satoru Komiyama UR RC 10.00 3.00
78 Tyler Yates UR RC 15.00 4.50
79 Eric Junge UR RC 10.00 3.00
80 Anderson Machado UR RC 10.00 3.00
81 Adrian Burnside UR RC 10.00 3.00
82 Ben Howard UR RC 10.00 3.00
83 Clay Condrey UR RC 10.00 3.00
84 Nelson Castro UR RC 10.00 3.00
85 So Taguchi UR RC 15.00 4.50
86 Mike Crudale UR RC 10.00 3.00
87 Scotty Layfield UR RC 10.00 3.00
88 Steve Bechler UR RC 10.00 3.00
89 Travis Driskill UR RC 10.00 3.00
90 Howie Clark UR RC 10.00 3.00
91 Josh Hancock UR RC 10.00 3.00
92 Jorge De La Rosa UR RC 10.00 3.00
93 Anastacio Martinez UR RC 10.00 3.00
94 Brian Tallet UR RC 10.00 3.00
95 Carl Sadler UR RC 10.00 3.00
96 Cliff Lee UR RC 15.00 4.50
97 Josh Bard UR RC 10.00 3.00
98 Wes Obermueller UR RC 10.00 3.00
99 Juan Brito UR RC 10.00 3.00
100 Aaron Guiel UR RC 10.00 3.00
101 Jeremy Hill UR RC 10.00 3.00
102 Kevin Frederick UR RC 10.00 3.00
103 Nate Field UR RC 10.00 3.00
104 Julio Mateo UR RC 10.00 3.00
105 Chris Snelling UR RC 10.00 3.00
106 Felix Escalona UR RC 10.00 3.00
107 Reynaldo Garcia UR RC 10.00 3.00
108 Mike Smith UR RC 10.00 3.00
109 Ken Huckaby UR RC 10.00 3.00
110 Kevin Cash UR RC 10.00 3.00
111 Kazuhisa Ishii UR AU RC 50.00 15.00
112 Fr. Sanchez UR AU RC 25.00 7.50
113 J.Simontacchi UR AU RC 25.00 7.50
114 Jorge Padilla UR AU RC 15.00 4.50
115 Kirk Saarloos UR AU RC 15.00 4.50
116 Ro. Rosario UR AU RC 15.00 4.50
117 Oliver Perez UR AU RC 70.00 21.00
118 Mi. Asencio UR AU RC 15.00 4.50
119 Fr. German UR AU RC 15.00 4.50
120 Jaime Cerda UR AU RC 15.00 4.50
MM M.McGwire AU EXCH/100

2002 Ultimate Collection Double Barrel Action

Randomly inserted into packs, these 18 cards feature two bat "barrell" cards of the featured player. As each of these cards have a stated print run of nine or fewer cards, we have not priced these cards due to market scarcity.

Nm-Mt Ex-Mt
BR Jeff Bagwell
Manny Ramirez/1
DG Joe DiMaggio
Ken Griffey Jr./5
DJ Carlos Delgado
Jason Giambi/2
GH Shawn Green
Todd Helton/2
GI Ken Griffey Jr.
Ichiro Suzuki/3
GJ Luis Gonzalez
Randy Johnson/1
GP Juan Gonzalez
Rafael Palmeiro/3
IM Ichiro Suzuki
Edgar Martinez/1
JJ Chipper Jones
Andruw Jones/2
JM Chipper Jones
Greg Maddux/1
RI Alex Rodriguez
Ivan Rodriguez/5
RM Alex Rodriguez
Miguel Tejada/2
RR Alex Rodriguez
Cal Ripken/9
RS Manny Ramirez
Sammy Sosa/1
SC Sammy Sosa
Fred McGriff/3
SM Sammy Sosa
Mark McGwire/1
TD Jim Thome
Carlos Delgado/3
TO Frank Thomas
Magglio Ordonez/4

2002 Ultimate Collection Game Jersey Tier 1

Randomly inserted into packs, these 21 cards were issued to a stated print run of 99 serial numbered sets. These cards can be differentiated from the other game jersey as they have a "JB" numbering prefix as well as featuring batting images and the swatches are on the right side.

Nm-Mt Ex-Mt
AD Adam Dunn 25.00 7.50
AJ Andruw Jones 15.00 4.50
AR Alex Rodriguez 25.00 7.50
AS Alfonso Soriano 25.00 7.50
CJ Chipper Jones 25.00 7.50
CR Cal Ripken 40.00 12.00
IR Ivan Rodriguez 25.00 7.50
IS Ichiro Suzuki 50.00 15.00
JD Joe DiMaggio 100.00 30.00
JG Jason Giambi 15.00 4.50
KG Ken Griffey Jr. 25.00 7.50
KI Kazuhisa Ishii 25.00 7.50
MC Mark McGwire 80.00 24.00
MM Mickey Mantle 150.00 45.00
MP Mike Piazza 25.00 7.50
MR Manny Ramirez 25.00 7.50
PM Pedro Martinez 25.00 7.50
PR Mark Prior 30.00 9.00
RC Roger Clemens 25.00 7.50
RJ Randy Johnson 25.00 7.50
SS Sammy Sosa 25.00 7.50

2002 Ultimate Collection Game Jersey Tier 1 Gold

Randomly inserted into packs, this is a parallel to the Tier 1 set. These cards have a stated print run of 50 serial numbered sets.

Nm-Mt Ex-Mt
*TIER 1 GOLD: .75X TO 1.5X TIER 1 JSY

2002 Ultimate Collection Game Jersey Tier 2

Randomly inserted into packs, these 21 cards were issued to a stated print run of 99 serial numbered sets. These cards can be differentiated from the other game jersey as they have a "JF" numbering prefix as well as featuring fielding images and the swatches are on the left side.

Nm-Mt Ex-Mt
*TIER 2: .4X TO 1X TIER 1 JSY

2002 Ultimate Collection Game Jersey Tier 2 Gold

Randomly inserted into packs, this is a parallel to the Tier 1 set. These cards have a stated print run of 30 serial numbered sets.

Nm-Mt Ex-Mt
*TIER 2 GOLD: .75X TO 2X TIER JSY

2002 Ultimate Collection Game Jersey Tier 3

Randomly inserted into packs, these 21 cards were issued to a stated print run of 199 serial numbered sets. These cards can be differentiated from the other game jersey as they have a "JP" numbering prefix as well as featuring profile images and the swatches are on the right side.

Nm-Mt Ex-Mt
*TIER 3: .3X TO .8X TIER 1 JSY

2002 Ultimate Collection Game Jersey Tier 4

Randomly inserted into packs, these 21 cards were issued to a stated print run of 199 serial numbered sets. These cards can be differentiated from the other game jersey as they have a "JR" numbering prefix as well as featuring running images and the swatches are on the left side.

Nm-Mt Ex-Mt
*TIER 4: .3X TO .8X TIER 1 JSY

2002 Ultimate Collection Patch Card

Randomly inserted into packs, these 10 cards featue game-used patch swatched of the feature player. Each of these cards were issued to a stated print run of 100 serial numbered sets.

Nm-Mt Ex-Mt
*3-COLOR PATCH: 1X TO 1.5X HI COLUMN
CJ Chipper Jones 50.00 15.00

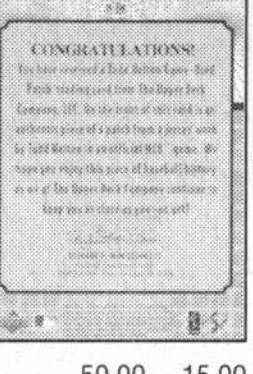

IR Ivan Rodriguez 50.00 15.00
IS Ichiro Suzuki....................... 150.00 45.00
KI Kazuhisa Ishii 60.00 18.00
LG Luis Gonzalez 40.00 12.00
MM Mark McGwire 150.00 45.00
MP Mark Prior 50.00 15.00
SG Shawn Green....................... 40.00 12.00
SS Sammy Sosa 80.00 24.00
TH Todd Helton 50.00 15.00

2002 Ultimate Collection Patch Card Double

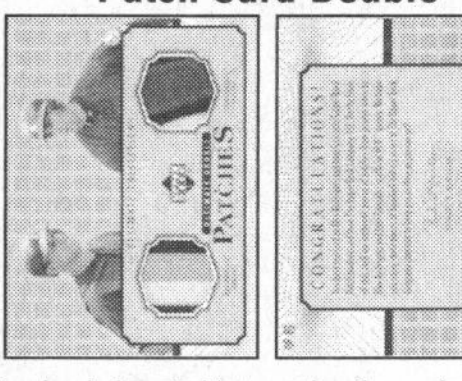
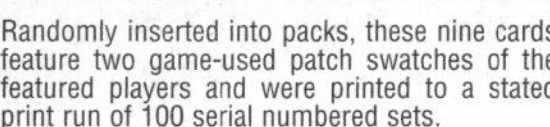

Randomly inserted into packs, these nine cards feature two game-used patch swatches of the featured players and were printed to a stated print run of 100 serial numbered sets.

Nm-Mt Ex-Mt
DE J.D. Drew............................ 50.00 15.00
Jim Edmonds
GC Jason Giambi 100.00 30.00
Roger Clemens
IG Ichiro Suzuki 150.00 45.00
Ken Griffey Jr.
JS Randy Johnson.................... 80.00 24.00
Curt Schilling
MG Greg Maddux..................... 100.00 30.00
Tom Glavine
MS Mark McGwire 200.00 60.00
Sammy Sosa
PA Mike Piazza 100.00 30.00
Roberto Alomar
RG Alex Rodriguez................. 100.00 30.00
Juan Gonzalez
RM Manny Ramirez 80.00 24.00
Pedro Martinez

2002 Ultimate Collection Patch Card Double Gold

Randomly inserted into packs, these cards parallel the Patch Card Double insert set and were issued to a stated print run of 50 serial numbered sets. Please note that a card featuring Mickey Mantle and Joe DiMaggio was issued to a stated print run of 13 serial numbered sets and is not priced due to market scarcity.

Nm-Mt Ex-Mt
*GOLD: .75X TO 1.5X BASIC PATCH ..
MD Mickey Mantle ....
Joe DiMaggio/13

2002 Ultimate Collection Signatures Tier 1

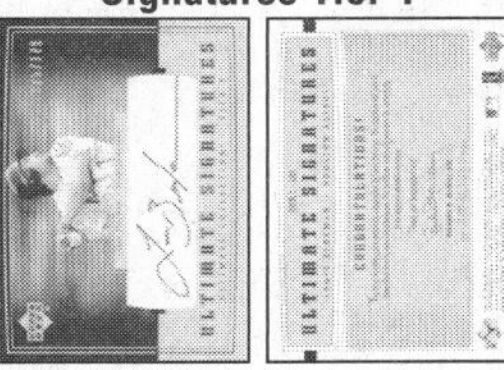

Randomly inserted into packs, these 19 cards feature signatures of some of the leading players in baseball. As the cards are signed to a differing amount of signatures, we have notated that information next to their name in our checklist.

Nm-Mt Ex-Mt
GOLD PRINT RUN 25 SERIAL #'d SETS
NO GOLD PRICING DUE TO SCARCITY
AD1 Adam Dunn/125 .... 50.00 15.00
AR1 Alex Rodriguez/329 .... 120.00 36.00
BG1 Brian Giles/220................. 20.00 6.00
BZ1 Barry Zito/199.................. 30.00 9.00
CD1 Carlos Delgado/95............ 30.00 9.00
CR1 Cal Ripken/75.................. 200.00 60.00
GS1 Gary Sheffield/95 .... 50.00 15.00
JD1 J.D. Drew/220.................. 30.00 9.00
JG1 Jason Giambi/295............ 20.00 6.00
JK1 Jason Kendall/220 .... 20.00 6.00
JT1 Jim Thome/90.................. 60.00 18.00
KG1 Ken Griffey Jr./195 .... 120.00 36.00
LB1 Lance Berkman/179.......... 30.00 9.00
LG1 Luis Gonzalez/199 .... 20.00 6.00
MP1 Mark Prior/160 .... 80.00 24.00
PB1 Pat Burrell/95 .... 30.00 9.00
RA1 Roberto Alomar/155.......... 30.00 9.00
RC1 Roger Clemens/320.......... 100.00 30.00
SR1 Scott Rolen/160 .... 50.00 15.00

2002 Ultimate Collection Signatures Tier 2

Randomly inserted into packs, these 16 cards feature signatures of some of the leading players in baseball. As the cards are signed to a differing amount of signatures, we have notated that information next to their name in our checklist.

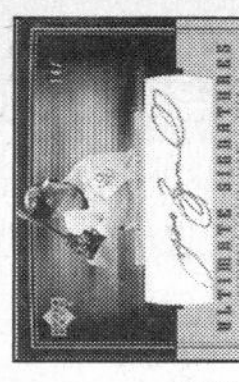

Nm-Mt Ex-Mt
GOLD PRINT RUN 10 SERIAL #'d SETS
NO GOLD PRICING DUE TO SCARCITY
AJ2 Andruw Jones/51 .... 50.00 15.00
AR2 Alex Rodriguez/75 .... 150.00 45.00
BZ2 Barry Zito/70.................... 50.00 15.00
DS2 Duke Snider/51 .... 60.00 18.00
FT2 Frank Thomas/51 .... 80.00 24.00
JB2 Jeff Bagwell/51 .... 80.00 24.00
JG2 Jason Giambi/50............... 50.00 15.00
KG2 Ken Griffey Jr./30 .... 150.00 45.00
KP2 Kirby Puckett/75................ 80.00 24.00
KW2 Kerry Wood/51 .... 80.00 24.00
LB2 Lance Berkman/85............. 50.00 15.00
LG2 Luis Gonzalez/70 .... 30.00 9.00
MP2 Mark Prior/60 .... 120.00 36.00
SR2 Scott Rolen/60 .... 80.00 24.00
TG2 Tony Gwynn/51 .... 100.00 30.00
TH2 Todd Helton/51 .... 60.00 18.00

2002 Ultimate Collection Signed Excellence

Randomly inserted into packs, these 20 cards feature signed cards of Upper Deck Spokespeople. Most of the cards were issued to a stated print run of 100 or fewer cards. Mark McGwire added a 583 HR notation to some of his signatures.

Nm-Mt Ex-Mt
*MCGWIRE 583 HR: 1X TO 1.5X HI COLUMN
I1 Ichiro Suzuki/56.................. 400.00 120.00
I2 Ichiro Suzuki/51.................. 400.00 120.00
I3 Ichiro Suzuki/23...................................
I4 Ichiro Suzuki/12...................................
I5 Ichiro Suzuki Batting.......... 350.00 105.00
I6 Ichiro Suzuki Throwing....... 350.00 105.00
MM1 Mark McGwire/70 .... 400.00 120.00
MM2 Mark McGwire/65 .... 400.00 120.00
MM3 Mark McGwire A's/49 .... 400.00 120.00
MM4 Mark McGwire/25 ....
MM5 Mark McGwire Standing 350.00 105.00
MM6 Mark McGwire Waving .. 350.00 105.00
MM7 Mark McGwire A's Fldg . 350.00 105.00
SS1 Sammy Sosa/66 .... 200.00 60.00
SS2 Sammy Sosa/64 .... 200.00 60.00
SS3 Sammy Sosa/54 .... 200.00 60.00
SS4 Sammy Sosa/21 ....
SS5 Sammy Sosa Running..... 150.00 45.00
SS6 Sammy Sosa Holding Bat 150.00 45.00
SS7 Sammy Sosa Throwing ... 150.00 45.00

2002 Ultimate Collection Signed Excellence Gold

Randomly inserted into packs, these cards partially parallel the Signed Excellence insert set and were printed to a stated print run of 1 serial numbered sets. Due to market scarcity, no pricing is provided for these cards.

Nm-Mt Ex-Mt
I4 Ichiro Suzuki ....
MM4 Mark McGwire ....
SS4 Sammy Sosa ....

2003 Ultimate Collection

This 180 card set was released in very early January, 2004. The set was issued in four card packs with an $100 SRP which came four packs to a box and four boxes to a case. Cards numbered 1-84 feature veterans and were issued to a stated print run of 850 serial numbered sets. Cards 85-117 are Tier 1 Rookie Cards and were issued to a stated print run of 625 serial numbered sets. Cards numbered 118 through 140 are Tier 2 Rookie Cards and were issued to a stated print run of 399 serial numbered sets. Cards numbered 141 through 158 are Tier 3 Rookie Cards and were issued to a stated print run of 250 serial numbered sets. Cards numbered 159 through 168 are Tier 4 Rookie Cards and were issued to a stated print run of 100 serial numbered sets. Cards numbered 169 through 180 were each signed and inserted into packs at slightly different odds.

MINT NRMT
COMMON CARD (1-84) 3.00 1.35
1-84 STATED ODDS TWO PER PACK..
COMMON CARD (85-117) 5.00 2.20
COMMON CARD (118-140) 5.00 2.20
118-140 PRINT RUN 399 SERIAL #'d SETS
COMMON CARD (141-158) 6.00 2.70
COMMON CARD (159-168) 12.00 5.50
159-168 PRINT RUN 100 SERIAL #'d SETS
85-168 STATED ODDS ONE PER PACK
COMMON CARD (169-174) 15.00 6.75
169-174 AND ULT.SIG.OVERALL ODDS 1:4
COMMON CARD (175-180) 15.00 6.75
175-180 AND BUYBACK OVERALL ODDS 1:8
169-180 PRINT RUN 250 SERIAL #'d SETS
MATSUI PART LIVE/ PART EXCH........
EXCHANGE DEADLINE 12/17/06........
1 Ichiro Suzuki.......................... 8.00 3.60
2 Ken Griffey Jr. 8.00 3.60
3 Sammy Sosa............................ 8.00 3.60
4 Jason Giambi 3.00 1.35
5 Mike Piazza 8.00 3.60
6 Derek Jeter.......................... 12.00 5.50
7 Randy Johnson........................ 5.00 2.20
8 Barry Bonds......................... 12.00 5.50
9 Carlos Delgado........................ 3.00 1.35
10 Mark Prior............................. 5.00 2.20
11 Vladimir Guerrero 5.00 2.20
12 Alfonso Soriano 5.00 2.20
13 Jim Thome............................. 5.00 2.20
14 Pedro Martinez....................... 5.00 2.20
15 Nomar Garciaparra................ 8.00 3.60
16 Chipper Jones........................ 5.00 2.20
17 Rocco Baldelli 3.00 1.35
18 Dontrelle Willis...................... 5.00 2.20
19 Garret Anderson.................... 3.00 1.35
20 Jeff Bagwell 5.00 2.20
21 Jim Edmonds......................... 3.00 1.35
22 Rickey Henderson.................. 5.00 2.20
23 Torii Hunter 3.00 1.35
24 Tom Glavine.......................... 5.00 2.20
25 Hideo Nomo.......................... 5.00 2.20
26 Luis Gonzalez........................ 3.00 1.35
27 Alex Rodriguez...................... 8.00 3.60
28 Albert Pujols 10.00 4.50
29 Manny Ramirez...................... 5.00 2.20
30 Rafael Palmeiro...................... 5.00 2.20
31 Bernie Williams...................... 5.00 2.20
32 Curt Schilling 3.00 1.35
33 Roger Clemens 10.00 4.50
34 Andruw Jones........................ 3.00 1.35
35 J.D. Drew.............................. 3.00 1.35
36 Kerry Wood........................... 5.00 2.20
37 Scott Rolen 5.00 2.20
38 Darin Erstad.......................... 3.00 1.35
39 Joe DiMaggio........................ 8.00 3.60
40 Magglio Ordonez................... 3.00 1.35
41 Todd Helton 5.00 2.20
42 Barry Zito.............................. 3.00 1.35
43 Mickey Mantle.................... 15.00 6.75
44 Miguel Tejada........................ 3.00 1.35
45 Troy Glaus............................. 3.00 1.35
46 Kazuhisa Ishii........................ 3.00 1.35
47 Adam Dunn 5.00 2.20
48 Ted Williams 8.00 3.60
49 Mike Mussina........................ 5.00 2.20
50 Ivan Rodriguez...................... 5.00 2.20
51 Jacque Jones 3.00 1.35
52 Stan Musial........................... 8.00 3.60
53 Mariano Rivera...................... 5.00 2.20
54 Larry Walker 5.00 2.20
55 Aaron Boone 3.00 1.35
56 Hank Blalock 5.00 2.20
57 Rich Harden........................... 5.00 2.20
58 Lance Berkman 3.00 1.35
59 Eric Chavez 3.00 1.35
60 Carlos Beltran 5.00 2.20
61 Roy Oswalt............................ 3.00 1.35
62 Moises Alou 3.00 1.35
63 Nolan Ryan 10.00 4.50
64 Jeff Kent................................ 3.00 1.35
65 Roberto Alomar 5.00 2.20
66 Runelvys Hernandez 3.00 1.35
67 Roy Halladay.......................... 3.00 1.35
68 Tim Hudson 3.00 1.35
69 Tom Seaver............................ 5.00 2.20
70 Edgardo Alfonzo..................... 3.00 1.35
71 Andy Pettitte 5.00 2.20
72 Preston Wilson 3.00 1.35
73 Frank Thomas 5.00 2.20
74 Jerome Williams 3.00 1.35
75 Shawn Green 3.00 1.35
76 David Wells............................ 3.00 1.35
77 John Smoltz........................... 5.00 2.20
78 Jorge Posada......................... 5.00 2.20
79 Marlon Byrd........................... 3.00 1.35
80 Austin Kearns........................ 3.00 1.35
81 Bret Boone............................ 3.00 1.35
82 Rafael Furcal 3.00 1.35
83 Jay Gibbons........................... 3.00 1.35
84 Shane Reynolds..................... 3.00 1.35
85 Nate Bland UR T1 RC............ 5.00 2.20
86 Willie Eyre UR T1 RC 5.00 2.20
87 Jeremy Guthrie UR T1 .... 5.00 2.20
88 Jeremy Wedel UR T1 RC 5.00 2.20
89 Jhonny Peralta UR T1 .... 5.00 2.20
90 Luis Ayala UR T1 RC.............. 5.00 2.20
91 Michael Hessman UR T1 RC.. 5.00 2.20
92 Michael Nakamura UR T1 RC 5.00 2.20
93 Nook Logan UR T1 RC........... 5.00 2.20
94 Rett Johnson UR T1 RC......... 8.00 3.60
95 Josh Hall UR T1 RC 8.00 3.60
96 Julio Manon UR T1 RC 5.00 2.20
97 Heath Bell UR T1 RC.............. 5.00 2.20
98 Ian Ferguson UR T1 RC 5.00 2.20
99 Jason Gilfillan UR T1 RC 5.00 2.20
100 Jason Roach UR T1 RC 5.00 2.20
101 Jason Shiell UR T1 RC......... 5.00 2.20
102 Terrmel Sledge UR T1 RC 8.00 3.60
103 Phil Seibel UR T1 RC 5.00 2.20
104 Jeff Duncan UR T1 RC......... 8.00 3.60
105 Mike Neu UR T1 RC............. 5.00 2.20
106 Colin Porter UR T1 RC......... 5.00 2.20
107 David Matranga UR T1 RC... 5.00 2.20
108 Aaron Looper UR T1 RC 5.00 2.20
109 Jeremy Bonderman UR T1 RC 8.00 3.60
110 Miguel Ojeda UR T1 RC 5.00 2.20
111 Chad Cordero UR T1 RC...... 5.00 2.20
112 Shane Bazzell UR T1 RC 5.00 2.20
113 Tim Olson UR T1 RC............ 8.00 3.60
114 Michel Hernandez UR T1 RC 5.00 2.20
115 Chien-Ming Wang UR T1 RC 8.00 3.60
116 Josh Stewart UR T1 RC 5.00 2.20
117 Clint Barmes UR T1 RC 8.00 3.60
118 Craig Brazell UR T2 RC 8.00 3.60
119 Josh Willingham UR T2 RC . 8.00 3.60
120 Brent Hoard UR T2 RC......... 5.00 2.20
121 Francisco Rosario UR T2 RC 5.00 2.20
122 Rick Roberts UR T2 RC 5.00 2.20
123 Geoff Geary UR T2 RC......... 5.00 2.20
124 Edgar Gonzalez UR T2 RC ... 5.00 2.20
125 Kevin Correia UR T2 RC....... 5.00 2.20
126 Ryan Cameron UR T2 RC 5.00 2.20
127 Beau Kemp UR T2 RC.......... 5.00 2.20
128 Tommy Phelps UR T2 .... 5.00 2.20
129 Mark Malaska UR T2 RC...... 5.00 2.20
130 Kevin Ohme UR T2 RC......... 5.00 2.20
131 Humberto Quintero UR T2 RC 5.00 2.20
132 Aquilino Lopez UR T2 RC 5.00 2.20
133 Andrew Brown UR T2 RC 8.00 3.60
134 Wilfredo Ledezma UR T2 RC 8.00 3.60
135 Luis De Los Santos UR T2... 5.00 2.20
136 Garrett Atkins UR T2........... 5.00 2.20
137 Fernando Cabrera UR T2 RC 5.00 2.20
138 D.J. Carrasco UR T2 RC 5.00 2.20
139 Alfredo Gonzalez UR T2 RC . 5.00 2.20
140 Alex Prieto UR T2 RC........... 5.00 2.20
141 Matt Kata UR T3 RC.......... 10.00 4.50
142 Chris Capuano UR T3 RC..... 6.00 2.70
143 Bobby Madritsch UR T3 RC 40.00 18.00
144 Greg Jones UR T3 RC.......... 6.00 2.70
145 Pete Zoccolillo UR T3 RC..... 6.00 2.70
146 Chad Gaudin UR T3 RC 6.00 2.70
147 Rosman Garcia UR T3 RC.... 6.00 2.70
148 Gerald Laird UR T3 .... 6.00 2.70
149 Danny Garcia UR T3 RC....... 6.00 2.70
150 Stephen Randolph UR T3 RC 6.00 2.70
151 Pete LaForest UR T3 RC 10.00 4.50
152 Brian Sweeney UR T3 RC 6.00 2.70
153 Aaron Miles UR T3 RC....... 10.00 4.50
154 Jorge DePaula UR T3 UER... 6.00 2.70
Real name is Julio DePaula
155 Graham Koonce UR T3 RC 15.00 6.75
156 Tom Gregorio UR T3 RC 6.00 2.70
157 Javier Lopez UR T3 RC........ 6.00 2.70
158 Oscar Villarreal UR T3 RC.... 6.00 2.70
159 Prentice Redman UR T4 RC 12.00 5.50
160 Francisco Cruceta UR T4 RC 12.00 5.50
161 Guillermo Quiroz UR T4 RC 20.00 9.00
162 Jeremy Griffiths UR T4 RC 20.00 9.00
163 Lew Ford UR T4 RC........... 25.00 11.00
164 Rob Hammock UR T4 RC .. 20.00 9.00
165 Todd Wellemeyer UR T4 RC 20.00 9.00
166 Ryan Wagner UR T4 RC 20.00 9.00
167 Edwin Jackson UR T4 RC .. 40.00 18.00
168 Dan Haren UR T4 RC 20.00 9.00
169 Hideki Matsui AU RC 300.00 135.00
170 Jose Contreras AU RC 40.00 18.00
171 Delmon Young AU RC...... 200.00 90.00
172 Rickie Weeks AU RC........ 100.00 45.00
173 Brandon Webb AU RC........ 30.00 13.50
174 Bo Hart AU RC.................... 25.00 11.00
175 Rocco Baldelli YS AU......... 25.00 11.00
176 Jose Reyes YS AU 25.00 11.00
177 Dontrelle Willis YS AU 40.00 18.00
178 Bobby Hill YS AU 15.00 6.75
179 Jae Weong Seo YS AU....... 25.00 11.00
180 Jesse Foppert YS AU 25.00 11.00

2003 Ultimate Collection Gold

Nm-Mt Ex-Mt
*GOLD ACTIVE 1-84: 1.25X TO 3X BASIC
*GOLD RETIRED 1-84: 1.5X TO 4X BASIC
1-84 PRINT RUN 50 SERIAL #'d SETS
*GOLD 84-117: 1X TO 2.5X BASIC.....
84-117 PRINT RUN 50 SERIAL #'d SETS
*GOLD 118-140: 1X TO 2.5X BASIC...
118-140 PRINT RUN 35 SERIAL #'d SETS
*GOLD 141-158: 1X TO 2.5X BASIC...
141-158 PRINT RUN 25 SERIAL #'d SETS
159-168 PRINT RUN 10 SERIAL #'d SETS
159-168 NO PRICING DUE TO SCARCITY
169-174 AU PRINT RUN 25 SERIAL #'d SETS
169-174 AU NO PRICING DUE TO SCARCITY
175-180 AU PRINT RUN 25 SERIAL #'d SETS
175-180 AU NO PRICING DUE TO SCARCITY
RANDOM INSERTS IN PACKS ....

2003 Ultimate Collection Buybacks

These 231 cards, which were randomly inserted into packs, feature mainly 2003 cards (with a smattering of earlier year cards) from varying Upper Deck products which UD bought back and had the player signed. Please note that for cards with print runs of 15 or fewer copies pricing is not provided due to scarity of market evidence.

Nm-Mt Ex-Mt
BUYBACKS & YS 175-180 OVERALL ODDS 1:8
1 Rocco Baldelli 03 UDA Blue/10........
2 Rocco Baldelli 03 UDA Red/10 ....
3 Hank Blalock 02-3 SUP/10..............
4 Hank Blalock 02-3 SUP/35..... 40.00 12.00
5 Hank Blalock 03 40M/25........ 50.00 15.00
6 Hank Blalock 03 GF/25........... 50.00 15.00
7 Hank Blalock 03 MVP/10 ....
8 Hank Blalock 03 Patch/25...... 50.00 15.00
9 Hank Blalock 03 SPA/20 .... 50.00 15.00
10 Hank Blalock 03 SPA/25 ...... 50.00 15.00
11 Hank Blalock 03 UD/10.................
12 Hank Blalock 03 VIN/25 .... 50.00 15.00
13 Carlos Delgado 03 40M/10 ....
14 Carlos Delgado 03 40M Flag/2.......
15 Carlos Delgado 03 GF/2 ....
16 Carlos Delgado 03 MVP/3..............
17 Carlos Delgado 03 Patch/2 ....
18 Carlos Delgado 03 PB/5.................
19 Carlos Delgado 03 PB Red/3..........
20 Carlos Delgado 03 SPA/11.............
21 Carlos Delgado 03 UD/1 ....
22 Carlos Delgado 03 UD LS Jsy/4.....
23 Carlos Delgado 03 UDA/5 ....
24 Carlos Delgado 03 VIN/2................
25 Adam Dunn 03 40M Rain/1 ....
26 Adam Dunn 03 40M Rain AS/5......
27 Adam Dunn 03 GF/1 ....
28 Adam Dunn 03 MVP/5 ....
29 Adam Dunn 03 Patch/7..................
30 Adam Dunn 03 PB/9 ....
31 Adam Dunn 03 PB Red/1...............
32 Adam Dunn 03 UD/7.....................
33 Adam Dunn 03 UDA/5...................
34 Adam Dunn 03 VIN/1 ....
35 Adam Dunn 03 VIN 3D/7 ....
36 Nomar Garciaparra 03 40M/2 ....
37 Nomar Garciaparra 03 40M Flag/1.
38 Nomar Garciaparra 03 GF/3 ....
39 Nomar Garciaparra 03 MVP/1 ....
40 Nomar Garciaparra 03 PB/7 ....
41 Nomar Garciaparra 03 PB Red/2....
42 Nomar Garciaparra 03 SPA/1 ....
43 Nomar Garciaparra 03 UD/3..........
44 Nomar Garciaparra 03 UD MP/2 ....
45 Nomar Garciaparra 03 UDA/2 ....
46 Nomar Garciaparra 03 VIN/1..........
47 Tom Glavine 03 40M/1..................
48 Tom Glavine 03 40M Flag/3 ....
49 Tom Glavine 03 GF/3....................
50 Tom Glavine 03 GF w/Vlad/2.........
51 Tom Glavine 03 MVP/1 ....
52 Tom Glavine 03 PB/5 ....
53 Tom Glavine 03 PB Red/3.............
54 Tom Glavine 03 SPA/7 ....
55 Tom Glavine 03 UD/8....................
56 Tom Glavine 03 UD/5....................
57 Tom Glavine 03 UDA/5..................
58 Tom Glavine 03 VIN/7 ....
59 Luis Gonzalez 03 40M/10 ....
60 Luis Gonzalez 03 40M AS/15.........
61 Luis Gonzalez 03 40M HR/25 50.00 15.00
62 Luis Gonzalez 03 40M T40/15 ....
63 Luis Gonzalez 03 40M Flag/5.........
64 Luis Gonzalez 03 GF/15 ....
65 Luis Gonzalez 03 MVP/3...............
66 Luis Gonzalez 03 Patch/17... 50.00 15.00
67 Luis Gonzalez 03 PB/15 ....
68 Luis Gonzalez 03 SPA/25..... 50.00 15.00
69 Luis Gonzalez 03 SWS/15.............
70 Luis Gonzalez 03 UDA/15 ....
71 Luis Gonzalez 03 VIN/25...... 50.00 15.00
72 K.Griffey Jr. 02-3 SUP/75 .. 120.00 36.00
73 K.Griffey 02-3 SUP Spok/50 150.00 45.00
74 K.Griffey Jr. 03 40M/50...... 150.00 45.00
75 K.Griffey 03 40M HR824/50 150.00 45.00
76 K.Griffey 03 40M HR825/50 150.00 45.00
77 K.Griffey 03 40M HR829/50 150.00 45.00
78 K.Griffey Jr. 03 40M T40/50 150.00 45.00
79 K.Griffey Jr. 03 GF/50 .... 150.00 45.00
80 K.Griffey Jr. 03 GF GF/3 ....
81 K.Griffey Jr. 03 GF w/Oswalt/9 ......
82 K.Griffey Jr. 03 HON/50 ..... 150.00 45.00
83 K.Griffey Jr. 03 HON SP/30 150.00 45.00
84 K.Griffey Jr. 03 Patch/75.... 120.00 36.00
85 K.Griffey Jr. 03 PB/75 .... 120.00 36.00
86 K.Griffey Jr. 03 SPA/50 ...... 150.00 45.00
87 K.Griffey Jr. 03 SPA/75 ...... 120.00 36.00
88 K.Griffey Jr. 03 SPx/75 ...... 120.00 36.00
89 K.Griffey Jr. 03 SWS/75..... 120.00 36.00
90 K.Griffey Jr. 03 UD MP2/3 ....
91 K.Griffey Jr. 03 UD MP4/3 ....
92 K.Griffey Jr. 03 UD MP7/3 ....
93 K.Griffey Jr. 03 UD MP26/3 ....
94 K.Griffey Jr. 03 UDA/75...... 120.00 36.00
95 K.Griffey Jr. 03 VIN/50....... 150.00 45.00
96 Torii Hunter 03 40M/18........ 50.00 15.00
97 Torii Hunter 03 40M Flag/7 ....
98 Torii Hunter 03 MVP/1 ....
99 Torii Hunter 03 Patch/25...... 50.00 15.00
100 Torii Hunter 03 PB/50 .... 40.00 12.00
101 Torii Hunter 03 PB Red/5............
102 Torii Hunter 03 SPA/4 ....
103 Torii Hunter 03 UD/10.................
104 Torii Hunter 03 UDA/5.................
105 Torii Hunter 03 VIN/25....... 50.00 15.00
106 Randy Johnson 03 40M/7............
107 Randy Johnson 03 40M Flag/5 ....
108 Randy Johnson 03 GF/10 ....
109 Randy Johnson 03 MVP/1 ....
110 Randy Johnson 03 PB/10 ....
111 Randy Johnson 03 PB Red/5.......
112 Randy Johnson 03 SPA/1 ....
113 Randy Johnson 03 UD/3.............
114 Randy Johnson 03 UDA/5............
115 Randy Johnson 03 VIN/3............
116 Austin Kearns 02-3 SUP/10 ....
117 Austin Kearns 03 40M/8 ....
118 Austin Kearns 03 40M/33 .. 40.00 12.00
119 Austin Kearns 03 40M Flag/10.....
120 Austin Kearns 03 GF/10 ....
121 Austin Kearns 03 MVP/3..............
122 Austin Kearns 03 Patch/10 ....
123 Austin Kearns 03 SPA/9...............
124 Austin Kearns 03 UDA/5 ....
125 Austin Kearns 03 VIN/10.............
126 Matsui 03 40M NR/20 ..... 300.00 90.00
127 H.Mat 03 40M FlagNR/20 300.00 90.00
128 H.Mat 03 GFw/Pedro/18 .. 300.00 90.00
129 Hideki Matsui 03 MVP/12 ....
130 Hideki Matsui 03 PB/17 ... 300.00 90.00
131 Hideki Matsui 03 PB Red/6..........
132 Hideki Matsui 03 UD/25... 300.00 90.00
133 Hideki Matsui 03 UD LS Jsy/4 .....
134 Hideki Matsui 03 UD MP/3 ....
135 Hideki Matsui 03 VIN/25.. 300.00 90.00
136 Stan Musial 99 CL/15 ....
137 Stan Musial 99 HIT/25 ....
138 Stan Musial 00 LG/5 ....
139 Stan Musial 01 HF/10 ....
140 Stan Musial 01 LG/10 ....
141 Stan Musial 01 SPLC/15.............
142 Stan Musial 02 SPLC/1 ....
143 Stan Musial 02 SPLC/30.... 80.00 24.00
144 Stan Musial 02 WSH/25...............
145 Stan Musial 03 PB/50 .... 60.00 18.00
146 Stan Musial 03 PB Red/15...........
147 Stan Musial 03 SWSC/37... 80.00 24.00
148 Stan Musial 03 UD MP/3 ....
149 Stan Musial 03 UDA/9.................
150 Stan Musial 03 VIN/50....... 60.00 18.00
151 Mark Prior 03 40M/1 ....

152 Mark Prior 03 40M Flag/5
153 Mark Prior 03 GF/5
154 Mark Prior 03 GF w/Berkman/7
155 Mark Prior 03 MVP/1
156 Mark Prior 03 Patch/3
157 Mark Prior 03 PB/10
158 Mark Prior 03 PB Red/1
159 Mark Prior 03 UD/7
160 Mark Prior 03 UDA/5
161 Mark Prior 03 VIN/5
162 Scott Rolen 03 40M/5
163 Scott Rolen 03 40M AS/7
164 Scott Rolen 03 40M Flag/1
165 Scott Rolen 03 GF/4
166 Scott Rolen 03 MVP/1
167 Scott Rolen 03 Patch/1
168 Scott Rolen 03 PB/5
169 Scott Rolen 03 PB Red/5
170 Scott Rolen 03 SPA/6
171 Scott Rolen 03 UD/5
172 Scott Rolen 03 UDA/5
173 Scott Rolen 03 VIN/4
174 Curt Schilling 02 SPA/1
175 Curt Schilling 03 40M/1
176 Curt Schilling 03 40M AS/1
177 Curt Schilling 03 GF/2
178 Curt Schilling 03 MVP/1
179 Curt Schilling 03 Patch/1
180 Curt Schilling 03 PB/6
181 Curt Schilling 03 PB Red/1
182 Curt Schilling 03 SPA/6
183 Curt Schilling 03 SWS/1
184 Curt Schilling 03 UDA/1
185 Curt Schilling 03 VIN/3
186 Sammy Sosa 02-3 SUP/25 200.00 60.00
187 Sammy Sosa 03 40M/13
188 Sammy Sosa 03 40M AS/1
189 Sammy Sosa 03 GF/10
190 Sammy Sosa 03 GF GF/10
191 S.Sosa 03 GF w/Mac/17
192 Sammy Sosa 03 MVP/7
193 Sammy Sosa 03 Patch/10
194 Sammy Sosa 03 PB/25 200.00 60.00
195 Sammy Sosa 03 SPA/25 200.00 60.00
196 Sammy Sosa 03 UD/7
197 Sammy Sosa 03 UD LS Jsy/5
198 Sammy Sosa 03 UD MP/3
199 Sammy Sosa 03 UDA/17 200.00 60.00
200 Sammy Sosa 03 UDA Blue/10
201 Sammy Sosa 03 UDA Red/10
202 Sammy Sosa 03 VIN/25 200.00 60.00
203 Mark Teixeira 03 40M/50 40.00 12.00
204 Mark Teixeira 03 40M Rain/15
205 Mark Teixeira 03 Patch/50 40.00 12.00
206 Mark Teixeira 03 SPA RA/25 50.00 15.00
207 Mark Teixeira 03 SWS/23 50.00 15.00
208 Mark Teixeira 03 UD/25 50.00 15.00
209 Mark Teixeira 03 UDA/15
210 Mark Teixeira 03 VIN/25 50.00 15.00
211 Kerry Wood 03 40M Flag/13
212 Kerry Wood 03 GF/7
213 Kerry Wood 03 GF w/Pujols/3
214 Kerry Wood 03 MVP/3
215 Kerry Wood 03 PB/10
216 Kerry Wood 03 PB Red/13
217 Kerry Wood 03 SPA/10
218 Kerry Wood 03 UD/7
219 Kerry Wood 03 UDA/5
220 Kerry Wood 03 VIN/4
221 Barry Zito 03 40M/2
222 Barry Zito 03 40M Flag/2
223 Barry Zito 03 GF/7
224 Barry Zito 03 MVP/2
225 Barry Zito 03 Patch/2
226 Barry Zito 03 PB/1
227 Barry Zito 03 PB Red/2
228 Barry Zito 03 SPA/7
229 Barry Zito 03 SPx/10
230 Barry Zito 03 UD/10
231 Barry Zito 03 UDA/5

2003 Ultimate Collection Double Barrel

Nm-Mt Ex-Mt
RANDOM INSERTS IN PACKS
PRINT RUNS B/WN 1-3 COPIES PER
NO PRICING DUE TO SCARCITY
AB Roberto Alomar
Craig Biggio/3
AC Edgardo Alfonzo
Jose Cruz Jr./2
AE Garrett Anderson
Darin Erstad/3
AJ Bobby Abreu
Chipper Jones/1
BC Bret Boone
Mike Cameron/1
BH Rocco Baldelli
Torii Hunter/1
BK Sean Burroughs
Mark Kotsay/1
BL Kevin Brown
Paul Lo Duca/1
BR Pat Burrell
Jimmy Rollins/1
BS Carlos Beltran
Mike Sweeney/2
DP Carlos Delgado
Albert Pujols/1
DR Johnny Damon
Manny Ramirez/1
DT Adam Dunn
Jim Thome/1
EM Jim Edmonds
Stan Musial/2
FS Rafael Furcal
Gary Sheffield/3
GK Brian Giles
Jason Kendall/2
GM Ken Griffey Jr.
Fred McGriff/2
GS Tom Glavine
Tom Seaver/2
HL Mike Hampton
Javy Lopez/1
HP Rickey Henderson
Juan Pierre/1
HV Shea Hillenbrand
Jose Vidro/1
JB Jeff Bagwell
Barry Larkin/1
KN Ryan Klesko
Phil Nevin/1
KT Paul Konerko
Frank Thomas/1
LO Carlos Lee
Magglio Ordonez/1
LP Mike Lieberthal
Mike Piazza/2
LR Luis Gonzalez
Raul Mondesi/1
LV Al Leiter
Mo Vaughn/1
MN Hideki Matsui
Hideo Nomo/1
MO Edgar Martinez
John Olerud/1
MR Tino Martinez
Scott Rolen/1
PP Corey Patterson
Jay Payton/3
PR Jorge Posada
Mariano Rivera/1
TP Todd Helton
Preston Wilson/1

2003 Ultimate Collection Dual Jersey

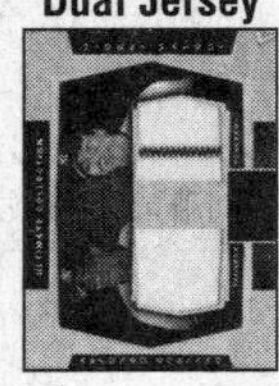

Nm-Mt Ex-Mt
STATED PRINT RUN 50 SERIAL #'d SETS
*GOLD: .75X TO 1.5X BASIC
GOLD PRINT RUN 25 SERIAL #'d SETS
OVERALL GU ODDS 3:4
ALL ARE DUAL JSY UNLESS NOTED
AH Alfonso Soriano Jsy 50.00 15.00
Hideki Matsui Jsy
AI Albert Pujols Jsy 60.00 18.00
Ichiro Suzuki Jsy
BK Jeff Bagwell Jsy 25.00 7.50
Jeff Kent Jsy
CA Chipper Jones Jsy 25.00 7.50
Andruw Jones Jsy
CJ Carlos Delgado Jsy 15.00 4.50
Jason Giambi Jsy
DE J.D. Drew Jsy 15.00 4.50
Jim Edmonds Jsy
DG Carlos Delgado Jsy 25.00 7.50
Vladimir Guerrero Jsy
DM Joe DiMaggio Pants 300.00 90.00
Mickey Mantle Jsy/Pants
DP Carlos Delgado Jsy 25.00 7.50
Rafael Palmeiro Jsy
DW Joe DiMaggio Jsy/Pants 175.00 52.50
Ted Williams Jsy
GB Shawn Green Jsy 15.00 4.50
Kevin Brown Jsy
GD Ken Griffey Jr. Jsy 40.00 12.00
Adam Dunn Jsy
GE Troy Glaus Jsy 15.00 4.50
Darin Erstad Jsy
GP Ken Griffey Jr. Jsy 40.00 12.00
Rafael Palmeiro Jsy
GR Nomar Garciaparra Jsy 40.00 12.00
Alex Rodriguez Jsy
GS Vladimir Guerrero Jsy 25.00 7.50
Sammy Sosa Jsy
HJ Torii Hunter Jsy 15.00 4.50
Jacque Jones Jsy
HZ Roy Halladay Jsy 15.00 4.50
Barry Zito Jsy
IG Ichiro Suzuki Jsy 60.00 18.00
Ken Griffey Jr. Jsy
IN Ichiro Suzuki Jsy 80.00 24.00
Hideo Nomo Jsy
IS Ichiro Suzuki Jsy 60.00 18.00
Sammy Sosa Jsy
JF Andruw Jones Jsy 15.00 4.50
Rafael Furcal Jsy
JM Jorge Posada Jsy 40.00 12.00
Mike Piazza Jsy
MC Greg Maddux Jsy 40.00 12.00
Roger Clemens Jsy
MW Mickey Mantle Jsy/Pants 250.00 75.00
Ted Williams Jsy
NI Hideo Nomo Jsy 40.00 12.00
Kazuhusa Ishii Jsy
NM Hideo Nomo Jsy 60.00 18.00
Hideki Matsui Jsy
PC Pedro Martinez Jsy 40.00 12.00
Roger Clemens Jsy
PM Andy Pettitte Jsy 25.00 7.50
Mike Mussina Jsy
PS Mark Prior Jsy 40.00 12.00
Sammy Sosa Jsy
RM Manny Ramirez Jsy 25.00 7.50
Pedro Martinez Jsy
RP Alex Rodriguez Jsy 25.00 7.50
Rafael Palmeiro Jsy
SA Scott Rolen Jsy 50.00 15.00
Albert Pujols Jsy
SB Alfonso Soriano Jsy 25.00 7.50
Bernie Williams Jsy
SJ Curt Schilling Jsy 25.00 7.50
Randy Johnson Jsy
SM John Smoltz Jsy 40.00 12.00
Greg Maddux Jsy
TB Mark Teixeira Jsy 25.00 7.50
Hank Blalock Jsy
TH Jim Thome Jsy 25.00 7.50
Todd Helton Jsy
TR Miguel Tejada Jsy 25.00 7.50
Alex Rodriguez Jsy
WL Dontrelle Willis Jsy 25.00 7.50
Mike Lowell Jsy
YW Delmon Young Pants 40.00 12.00
Rickie Weeks Jsy

2003 Ultimate Collection Dual Patch

Nm-Mt Ex-Mt
OVERALL GU ODDS 3:4
PRINT RUNS B/WN 14-99 COPIES PER
NO PRICING ON QTY OF 14 OR LESS
AI Albert Pujols 120.00 36.00
Ichiro Suzuki/99
AM Andy Pettitte 50.00 15.00
Mike Mussina/99
BK Jeff Bagwell 50.00 15.00
Jeff Kent/99
CA Chipper Jones 50.00 15.00
Andruw Jones/99
CV Carlos Delgado 50.00 15.00
Vladimir Guerrero/99
DE J.D. Drew 40.00 12.00
Jim Edmonds/99
DG Carlos Delgado 40.00 12.00
Jason Giambi/99
DP Carlos Delgado
Rafael Palmeiro/14
GB Shawn Green 40.00 12.00
Kevin Brown/99
GD Ken Griffey Jr. 60.00 18.00
Adam Dunn/99
GE Troy Glaus 40.00 12.00
Darin Erstad/99
GP Ken Griffey Jr.
Rafael Palmeiro/14
GR Nomar Garciaparra 100.00 30.00
Alex Rodriguez/99
GS Vladimir Guerrero 50.00 15.00
Sammy Sosa/99
HJ Torii Hunter 40.00 12.00
Jacque Jones/83
HZ Roy Halladay 40.00 12.00
Barry Zito/99
IG Ichiro Suzuki 120.00 36.00
Ken Griffey Jr./99
IN Ichiro Suzuki 150.00 45.00
Hideo Nomo/99
IS Ichiro Suzuki 120.00 36.00
Sammy Sosa/99
JF Andruw Jones 40.00 12.00
Rafael Furcal/99
JG John Smoltz 60.00 18.00
Greg Maddux/99
MC Greg Maddux 80.00 24.00
Roger Clemens/75
NI Hideo Nomo 100.00 30.00
Kazuhisa Ishii/63
PM Jorge Posada 60.00 18.00
Mike Piazza/73
PS Mark Prior 60.00 18.00
Sammy Sosa/99
RM Manny Ramirez 50.00 15.00
Pedro Martinez/99
SA Scott Rolen 100.00 30.00
Albert Pujols/99
SB Alfonso Soriano 80.00 24.00
Bernie Williams/21
SJ Curt Schilling 50.00 15.00
Randy Johnson/99
SM Alfonso Soriano 80.00 24.00
Hideki Matsui/99
TB Mark Teixeira 50.00 15.00
Hank Blalock/99
TH Jim Thome 50.00 15.00
Todd Helton/99
TR Miguel Tejada 60.00 18.00
Alex Rodriguez/99
WL Dontrelle Willis 50.00 15.00
Mike Lowell/85
YW Delmon Young 100.00 30.00
Rickie Weeks/28

2003 Ultimate Collection Signatures

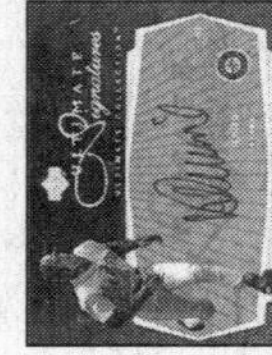

Nm-Mt Ex-Mt
ULT.SIG. & AU RC OVERALL ODDS 1:4
PRINT RUNS B/WN 30-350 COPIES PER
GRIFFEY/MATSUI PART LIVE/ PART EXCH.
EXCHANGE DEADLINE 12/17/06
AP1 Albert Pujols w/Glove/40 200.00 60.00
AP2 Albert Pujols w/Bat/35 200.00 60.00
AR1 Alex Rodriguez/75 EXCH 150.00 45.00
AR2 Alex Rodriguez/60 EXCH 150.00 45.00
BG1 Bob Gibson Arm Up/299 30.00 9.00
BG2 Bob Gibson Stance/199 30.00 9.00
CD1 Carlos Delgado Hitting/150 30.00 9.00
CR1 Cal Ripken w/Helmet/85 150.00 45.00
CR2 Cal Ripken Fielding/85 150.00 45.00
CY1 Carl Yastrzemski w/Bat/199 80.00 24.00
DY1 Delmon Young Run/300 50.00 15.00
DY2 Delmon Young w/Bat/300 50.00 15.00
EG1 Eric Gagne Arm Down/350 50.00 15.00
GC1 Gary Carter Hitting/199 20.00 6.00
GM1 Greg Maddux New Uni/250 80.00 24.00
GM2 G.Maddux Retro Uni/140 100.00 30.00
HM1 H.Matsui w/Glove/250 250.00 75.00
HM2 H.Matsui Throwing/240 250.00 75.00
IS1 I.Suzuki w/Shades/199 300.00 90.00
IS2 Ichiro Suzuki Running/99 350.00 105.00
JG1 Jason Giambi Torso/35 50.00 15.00
JG2 J.Giambi Open Swing/35 50.00 15.00
KG1 Ken Griffey Jr. Hitting/350 100.00 30.00
KG2 Ken Griffey Jr. w/Bat/350 100.00 30.00
KW1 K.Wood Black Glv/170 50.00 15.00
KW2 K.Wood Brown Glv/85 60.00 18.00
MP1 Mark Prior w/Glove/299 60.00 18.00
MP2 Mark Prior Arm Up/225 60.00 18.00
NG1 N.Garciaparra/125 EXCH 120.00 36.00
NG2 N.Garciaparra Hitting/180 120.00 36.00
NR1 Nolan Ryan Blue Uni/85 150.00 45.00
NR2 Nolan Ryan White Uni/75 150.00 45.00
OS1 Ozzie Smith Hitting/199 60.00 18.00
RC1 R.Clemens Glove Out/70 150.00 45.00
RC2 R.Clemens Arm Up/30 175.00 52.50
RJ1 R.Johnson Stripe Uni/75 100.00 30.00
RJ2 R.Johnson Black Uni/50 120.00 36.00
RS1 R.Sandberg Blue Uni/240 60.00 18.00
RS2 R.Sandberg Stripe Uni/200 60.00 18.00
RW1 R.Weeks White Uni/300 40.00 12.00
RW2 R.Weeks Red Uni/300 40.00 12.00
TS1 Tom Seaver Arms Up/75 50.00 15.00
TS2 Tom Seaver Arm Down/60 50.00 15.00
VG1 V.Guerrero Smiling/75 60.00 18.00
VG2 V.Guerrero Hitting/50 80.00 24.00

2003 Ultimate Collection Game Jersey Tier 1

Nm-Mt Ex-Mt
STATED PRINT RUN 99 SERIAL #'d SETS
COPPER PRINT RUN 10 SERIAL #'d SETS
NO COPPER PRICING DUE TO SCARCITY
*GOLD p/r 75: .4X TO 1X BASIC
*GOLD MATSUI p/r 55: .6X TO 1.5X BASIC
*GOLD p/r 51: .6X TO 1.5X BASIC
*GOLD p/r 44-48: .75X TO 2X BASIC
*GOLD p/r 25-35: 1X TO 2.5X BASIC
*GOLD p/r 17-24: 1.25X TO 3X BASIC
GOLD PRINT RUNS B/WN 1-75 COPIES PER
NO GOLD PRICING ON QTY OF 15 OR LESS
OVERALL GU ODDS 3:4
AD Adam Dunn Red Jsy 15.00 4.50
AJ Andruw Jones w/Bat 10.00 3.00
AP Albert Pujols Running 25.00 7.50
AR Alex Rodriguez Throw 20.00 6.00
AS Alfonso Soriano No Glv 15.00 4.50
BW Bernie Williams White Jsy 15.00 4.50
BZ Barry Zito Green Jsy 10.00 3.00
CD Carlos Delgado Blue Jsy 10.00 3.00
CJ Chipper Jones No Bat 15.00 4.50
CS Curt Schilling Arm Up 15.00 4.50
DW Dontrelle Willis Black Jsy 15.00 4.50
DY Delmon Young Throw 15.00 4.50
FT Frank Thomas Black Jsy 15.00 4.50
GM Greg Maddux White Jsy 20.00 6.00
GS Gary Sheffield Throw 10.00 3.00
HM Hideki Matsui Ball Toss 50.00 15.00
HN Hideo Nomo Gray Jsy 25.00 7.50
IS Ichiro Suzuki Gray Jsy 60.00 18.00
JE Jim Edmonds White Jsy 10.00 3.00
JG Jason Giambi No Bat 10.00 3.00
JR Jose Reyes Throw 10.00 3.00
JT Jim Thome Red Jsy 15.00 4.50
KG Ken Griffey Jr. Gray Jsy 25.00 7.50
KI Kazuhisa Ishii Arms Up 10.00 3.00
KW Kerry Wood Pitching 15.00 4.50
MI Mike Piazza Mask On 20.00 6.00
MM Mike Mussina Blue Jsy 15.00 4.50
MP Mark Prior Pitching 15.00 4.50
MR Manny Ramirez Red Jsy 15.00 4.50
MT Miguel Tejada White Jsy 10.00 3.00
PB Pat Burrell Running 10.00 3.00
RB Rocco Baldelli Batting 10.00 3.00
RC Roger Clemens White Jsy 25.00 7.50
RF Rafael Furcal Fielding 10.00 3.00
RJ Randy Johnson White Jsy 15.00 4.50
RW Rickie Weeks Bat Up 15.00 4.50
SG Shawn Green White Jsy 10.00 3.00
SS Sammy Sosa Running 25.00 7.50
TG Tom Glavine Black Jsy 15.00 4.50
TH Torii Hunter Running 10.00 3.00
TR Troy Glaus Dirty Jsy 10.00 3.00
VG Vladimir Guerrero w/Bat 15.00 4.50

2003 Ultimate Collection Game Jersey Tier 2

Nm-Mt Ex-Mt
STATED PRINT RUN 75 SERIAL #'d SETS
COPPER PRINT RUN 10 SERIAL #'d SETS
NO COPPER PRICING DUE TO SCARCITY
*GOLD p/r 75: .4X TO 1X BASIC
*GOLD MATSUI p/r 55: .6X TO 1.5X BASIC
*GOLD p/r 51: .6X TO 1.5X BASIC
*GOLD p/r 44-48: .75X TO 2X BASIC
*GOLD p/r 25-35: 1X TO 2.5X BASIC
*GOLD p/r 17-24: 1.25X TO 3X BASIC
GOLD PRINT RUNS B/WN 1-75 COPIES PER
NO GOLD PRICING ON QTY OF 15 OR LESS
OVERALL GU ODDS 3:4
AD2 Adam Dunn Swing 15.00 4.50
AJ2 Andruw Jones w/Glv 10.00 3.00
AP2 Albert Pujols Batting 25.00 7.50
AR2 Alex Rodriguez Running 20.00 6.00
AS2 Alfonso Soriano w/Glv 15.00 4.50
BW2 Bernie Williams Gray Jsy 15.00 4.50
BZ2 Barry Zito Gray Jsy 10.00 3.00
CD2 Carlos Delgado Gray Jsy 10.00 3.00
CJ2 Chipper Jones w/Bat 15.00 4.50
CS2 Curt Schilling Arm Down 10.00 3.00
DW Dontrelle Willis Gray Jsy 15.00 4.50
DY2 Delmon Young w/Ball 15.00 4.50
FT2 Frank Thomas White Jsy 15.00 4.50
GM2 Greg Maddux Blue Jsy 20.00 6.00
GS2 Gary Sheffield Batting 10.00 3.00
HM2 Hideki Matsui w/Bat 50.00 15.00
HN2 Hideo Nomo Blue Jsy 25.00 7.50
IS2 Ichiro Suzuki w/Bat 60.00 18.00
JE2 Jim Edmonds Gray Jsy 10.00 3.00
JG2 Jason Giambi w/Bat 10.00 3.00
JR2 Jose Reyes Walking 10.00 3.00
JT2 Jim Thome White Jsy 15.00 4.50
KG2 Ken Griffey Jr. Red Jsy 25.00 7.50
KI2 Kazuhisa Ishii Arms Down 10.00 3.00
KW2 Kerry Wood Standing 15.00 4.50
MI2 Mike Piazza w/Bat 20.00 6.00
MM2 Mike Mussina Gray Jsy 15.00 4.50
MP2 Mark Prior Hitting 15.00 4.50
MR2 Manny Ramirez Gray Jsy 15.00 4.50
MT2 Miguel Tejada Green Jsy 10.00 3.00
PB2 Pat Burrell Swinging 10.00 3.00
RB2 Rocco Baldelli Running 10.00 3.00
RC2 Roger Clemens Blue Jsy 25.00 7.50
RF2 Rafael Furcal Running 10.00 3.00
RJ2 Randy Johnson Black Jsy 15.00 4.50
RW2 Rickie Weeks Bat Forward 15.00 4.50
SG2 Shawn Green Gray Jsy 10.00 3.00
SS2 Sammy Sosa Batting 25.00 7.50
TG2 Tom Glavine Orange Jsy 15.00 4.50
TH2 Torii Hunter Swinging 10.00 3.00
TR2 Troy Glaus Clean Jsy 10.00 3.00
VG2 Vladimir Guerrero Point Up 15.00 4.50

2003 Ultimate Collection Game Patch

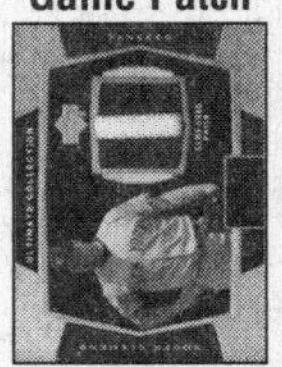

Nm-Mt Ex-Mt
STATED PRINT RUN 99 SERIAL #'d SETS
SORIANO PRINT RUN 42 SERIAL #'d CARDS
*COPPER: .6X TO 1.2X BASIC p/r 99
*COPPER: .6X TO 1.2X BASIC p/r 42
COPPER PRINT RUN 35 SERIAL #'d SETS
*GOLD: .75X TO 1.5X BASIC p/r 99
*GOLD: .75X TO 1.5X BASIC p/r 42
GOLD PRINT RUN 25 SERIAL #'d SETS
OVERALL GU ODDS 3:4
AD Adam Dunn 40.00 12.00
AJ Andruw Jones 25.00 7.50
AP Albert Pujols 60.00 18.00
AR Alex Rodriguez 50.00 15.00
AS Alfonso Soriano/42 40.00 12.00
BW Bernie Williams 40.00 12.00
BZ Barry Zito 25.00 7.50
CD Carlos Delgado 25.00 7.50
CJ Chipper Jones 40.00 12.00
CS Curt Schilling 25.00 7.50
DW Dontrelle Willis 40.00 12.00
DY Delmon Young 40.00 12.00
FT Frank Thomas 40.00 12.00
GM Greg Maddux 50.00 15.00
HM Hideki Matsui 100.00 30.00
HN Hideo Nomo 50.00 15.00
IS Ichiro Suzuki 120.00 36.00
JE Jim Edmonds 25.00 7.50
JG Jason Giambi 25.00 7.50
JR Jose Reyes 25.00 7.50
JT Jim Thome 40.00 12.00
KG Ken Griffey Jr. 60.00 18.00
KI Kazuhisa Ishii 25.00 7.50
KW Kerry Wood 40.00 12.00
MI Mike Piazza 50.00 15.00
MM Mike Mussina 40.00 12.00
MP Mark Prior 40.00 12.00
MR Manny Ramirez 40.00 12.00
MT Miguel Tejada 25.00 7.50
PB Pat Burrell 25.00 7.50
RB Rocco Baldelli 25.00 7.50
RC Roger Clemens 60.00 18.00
RF Rafael Furcal 25.00 7.50
RH Roy Halladay 25.00 7.50
RJ Randy Johnson 40.00 12.00
RW Rickie Weeks 30.00 9.00
SG Shawn Green 25.00 7.50
SS Sammy Sosa 50.00 15.00
TG Tom Glavine 40.00 12.00
TH Torii Hunter 25.00 7.50
TR Troy Glaus 25.00 7.50
VG Vladimir Guerrero 40.00 12.00

1999 Ultimate Victory

The 1999 Upper Deck Ultimate Victory Product was issued late in 1999. The cards were distributed in five card packs with a SRP of $2.99 per pack and each box had 24 packs in it. The set, consisting of 180 cards has 120 cards printed in normal quantites and 60 short prints. The cards from 121 through 150 feature players in their rookie campaign and cards numbered 151 through 180 all feature Mark McGwire in a set entitled "McGwire's Magic". Cards 121-180 were all released at a rate of one in four. Rookie Cards of Rick Ankiel, Josh Beckett, Pat Burrell, Freddy Garcia, Eric Munson, and Alfonso Soriano are all included in this set.

	Nm-Mt	Ex-Mt
COMPLETE SET (180)	200.00	60.00
COMP.SET w/o SP's (120)	25.00	7.50
COMMON CARD (1-120)	.30	.09
COMMON SP (121-150)	2.00	.60
COMMON (151-180)	2.00	.60
1 Troy Glaus	.30	.09
2 Tim Salmon	.50	.15
3 Mo Vaughn	.30	.09
4 Garret Anderson	.30	.09
5 Darin Erstad	.30	.09
6 Randy Johnson	.75	.23
7 Matt Williams	.30	.09
8 Travis Lee	.30	.09
9 Jay Bell	.30	.09
10 Steve Finley	.30	.09
11 Luis Gonzalez	.30	.09
12 Greg Maddux	1.25	.35
13 Chipper Jones	.75	.23
14 Javy Lopez	.30	.09
15 Tom Glavine	.50	.15
16 John Smoltz	.50	.15
17 Cal Ripken	2.50	.75
18 Charles Johnson	.30	.09
19 Albert Belle	.30	.09
20 Mike Mussina	.50	.15
21 Pedro Martinez	.75	.23
22 Nomar Garciaparra	1.25	.35
23 Jose Offerman	.30	.09
24 Sammy Sosa	1.25	.35
25 Mark Grace	.50	.15
26 Kerry Wood	.75	.23
27 Frank Thomas	.75	.23
28 Ray Durham	.30	.09
29 Paul Konerko	.30	.09
30 Pete Harnisch	.30	.09
31 Greg Vaughn	.30	.09
32 Sean Casey	.30	.09
33 Manny Ramirez	.50	.15
34 Jim Thome	.75	.23
35 Sandy Alomar Jr.	.30	.09
36 Roberto Alomar	.50	.15
37 Travis Fryman	.30	.09
38 Kenny Lofton	.30	.09
39 Omar Vizquel	.50	.15
40 Larry Walker	.50	.15
41 Todd Helton	.50	.15
42 Vinny Castilla	.30	.09
43 Tony Clark	.30	.09
44 Juan Encarnacion	.30	.09
45 Dean Palmer	.30	.09
46 Damion Easley	.30	.09
47 Mark Kotsay	.30	.09
48 Cliff Floyd	.30	.09
49 Jeff Bagwell	.50	.15
50 Ken Caminiti	.30	.09
51 Craig Biggio	.50	.15
52 Moises Alou	.30	.09
53 Johnny Damon	.50	.15
54 Larry Sutton	.30	.09
55 Kevin Brown	.50	.15
56 Adrian Beltre	.50	.15
57 Raul Mondesi	.30	.09
58 Gary Sheffield	.30	.09
59 Jeromy Burnitz	.30	.09
60 Sean Berry	.30	.09
61 Jeff Cirillo	.30	.09
62 Brad Radke	.30	.09
63 Todd Walker	.30	.09
64 Matt Lawton	.30	.09
65 Vladimir Guerrero	.75	.23
66 Rondell White	.30	.09
67 Dustin Hermanson	.30	.09
68 Mike Piazza	1.25	.35
69 Rickey Henderson	.75	.23
70 Robin Ventura	.30	.09
71 John Olerud	.30	.09
72 Derek Jeter	2.00	.60
73 Roger Clemens	1.50	.45
74 Orlando Hernandez	.30	.09
75 Paul O'Neill	.50	.15
76 Bernie Williams	.50	.15
77 Chuck Knoblauch	.30	.09
78 Tino Martinez	.50	.15
79 Jason Giambi	.30	.09
80 Ben Grieve	.30	.09
81 Matt Stairs	.30	.09
82 Scott Rolen	.75	.23
83 Ron Gant	.30	.09
84 Bobby Abreu	.30	.09
85 Curt Schilling	.30	.09
86 Brian Giles	.30	.09
87 Jason Kendall	.30	.09
88 Kevin Young	.30	.09
89 Mark McGwire	2.00	.60
90 Fernando Tatis	.30	.09
91 Ray Lankford	.30	.09
92 Eric Davis	.30	.09
93 Tony Gwynn	1.00	.30
94 Reggie Sanders	.30	.09
95 Wally Joyner	.30	.09
96 Trevor Hoffman	.30	.09
97 Robb Nen	.30	.09
98 Barry Bonds	2.00	.60
99 Jeff Kent	.30	.09
100 J.T. Snow	.30	.09
101 Ellis Burks	.30	.09
102 Ken Griffey Jr.	1.25	.35
103 Alex Rodriguez	1.25	.35
104 Jay Buhner	.30	.09
105 Edgar Martinez	.50	.15
106 David Bell	.30	.09
107 Bobby Smith	.30	.09
108 Wade Boggs	.50	.15
109 Fred McGriff	.50	.15
110 Rolando Arrojo	.30	.09
111 Jose Canseco	.75	.23
112 Ivan Rodriguez	.75	.23
113 Juan Gonzalez	.50	.15
114 Rafael Palmeiro	.50	.15
115 Rusty Greer	.30	.09
116 Todd Zeile	.30	.09
117 Jose Cruz Jr.	.30	.09
118 Carlos Delgado	.30	.09
119 Shawn Green	.30	.09
120 David Wells	.30	.09
121 Eric Munson SP RC	5.00	1.50
122 Lance Berkman SP	3.00	.90
123 Ed Yarnall SP	2.00	.60
124 Jacque Jones SP	3.00	.90
125 K.Farnsworth SP RC	3.00	.90
126 Ryan Rupe SP RC	2.00	.60
127 Jeff Weaver SP RC	5.00	1.50
128 Gabe Kapler SP	2.00	.60
129 Alex Gonzalez SP	2.00	.60
130 Randy Wolf SP	2.00	.60
131 Ben Davis SP	2.00	.60
132 Carlos Beltran SP	5.00	1.50
133 Jim Morris SP RC	5.00	1.50
134 J.Zimmerman SP RC	3.00	.90
135 Bruce Aven SP	2.00	.60
136 A.Soriano SP RC	30.00	9.00
137 Tim Hudson SP RC	20.00	6.00
138 Josh Beckett SP RC	40.00	12.00
139 Michael Barrett SP	2.00	.60
140 Eric Chavez SP	3.00	.90
141 Pat Burrell SP RC	12.00	3.60
142 Kris Benson SP	2.00	.60
143 J.D. Drew SP	3.00	.90
144 Matt Clement SP	2.00	.60
145 Rick Ankiel SP RC	25.00	7.50
146 Vernon Wells SP	3.00	.90
147 Ruben Mateo SP UER	2.00	.60
Card is misnumbered		
148 Roy Halladay SP	2.00	.60
149 Joe McEwing SP RC	3.00	.90
150 Freddy Garcia SP RC	8.00	2.40
151 Mark McGwire MM	2.00	.60
152 Mark McGwire MM	2.00	.60
153 Mark McGwire MM	2.00	.60
154 Mark McGwire MM	2.00	.60
155 Mark McGwire MM	2.00	.60
156 Mark McGwire MM	2.00	.60
157 Mark McGwire MM	2.00	.60
158 Mark McGwire MM	2.00	.60
159 Mark McGwire MM	2.00	.60
160 Mark McGwire MM	2.00	.60
161 Mark McGwire MM	2.00	.60
162 Mark McGwire MM	2.00	.60
163 Mark McGwire MM	2.00	.60
164 Mark McGwire MM	2.00	.60
165 Mark McGwire MM	2.00	.60
166 Mark McGwire MM	2.00	.60
167 Mark McGwire MM	2.00	.60
168 Mark McGwire MM	2.00	.60
169 Mark McGwire MM	2.00	.60
170 Mark McGwire MM	2.00	.60
171 Mark McGwire MM	2.00	.60
172 Mark McGwire MM	2.00	.60
173 Mark McGwire MM	2.00	.60
174 Mark McGwire MM	2.00	.60
175 Mark McGwire MM	2.00	.60
176 Mark McGwire MM	2.00	.60
177 Mark McGwire MM	2.00	.60
178 Mark McGwire MM	2.00	.60
179 Mark McGwire MM	2.00	.60
180 Mark McGwire MM	2.00	.60

1999 Ultimate Victory Parallel

Inserted at a rate of one in 12, these card parallel the regular set. They can be differentiated from the regular cards with the addition of linear holographic foil on each card.

Nm-Mt Ex-Mt

*STARS 1-120: 2X TO 5X BASIC CARDS
*PROSPECT 121-150: .6X TO 1.5X BASIC
*PROSPECT RC'S 121-150: .6X TO 1.5X BASIC

1999 Ultimate Victory Parallel 100

Randomly inserted into packs, these cards parallel the regular Ultimate Victory set. They feature silver holographic foil in trippy circular patterns and are sequentially numbered to 100 on the front.

Nm-Mt Ex-Mt

*STARS 1-120: 5X TO 12X BASIC CARDS
*PROSPECT 121-150: 1.5X TO 4X BASIC
*PROSP.RC'S 121-150: 2X TO 4X BASIC
*MCGWIRE 151-180: 3X TO 8X BASIC

1999 Ultimate Victory Bleacher Reachers

Inserted one every 23 packs, these horizontal cards feature 11 players who are among baseball's leading sluggers.

	Nm-Mt	Ex-Mt
COMPLETE SET (11)	50.00	15.00
BR1 Ken Griffey Jr.	4.00	1.20
BR2 Mark McGwire	6.00	1.80
BR3 Sammy Sosa	4.00	1.20
BR4 Barry Bonds	6.00	1.80
BR5 Nomar Garciaparra	4.00	1.20
BR6 Juan Gonzalez	1.50	.45
BR7 Jose Canseco	2.50	.75
BR8 Manny Ramirez	1.50	.45
BR9 Mike Piazza	4.00	1.20
BR10 Jeff Bagwell	1.50	.45
BR11 Alex Rodriguez	4.00	1.20

1999 Ultimate Victory Fame-Used Memorabilia

Randomly inserted into packs, these cards feature pieces of bats used by the four inductees into the Hall of Fame in 1999. Similar to the other bat cards Upper Deck has produced, approximately 350 of each card were made. There was also a special card made with bat pieces of all four of these players. Ninety-nine copies of that combo card were produced.

	Nm-Mt	Ex-Mt
GB George Brett	25.00	7.50
NR Nolan Ryan	40.00	12.00
OC Orlando Cepeda	10.00	3.00
RY Robin Yount	15.00	4.50
HOF Nolan Ryan	150.00	45.00
George Brett		
Robin Yount		
Orlando Cepeda		

1999 Ultimate Victory Frozen Ropes

Inserted one every 23 packs, these 10 cards feature players who consistently are among the best in the majors.

	Nm-Mt	Ex-Mt
COMPLETE SET (10)	50.00	15.00
F1 Ken Griffey Jr.	4.00	1.20
F2 Mark McGwire	6.00	1.80
F3 Sammy Sosa	4.00	1.20
F4 Derek Jeter	6.00	1.80
F5 Tony Gwynn	3.00	.90
F6 Nomar Garciaparra	4.00	1.20
F7 Alex Rodriguez	4.00	1.20
F8 Mike Piazza	4.00	1.20
F9 Mo Vaughn	1.00	.30
F10 Craig Biggio	1.50	.45

1999 Ultimate Victory STATure

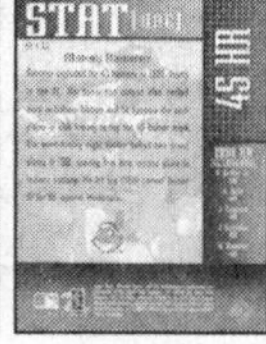

Inserted one every six packs, these fifteen cards featured players who are among the statistical leaders.

	Nm-Mt	Ex-Mt
COMPLETE SET (15)	25.00	7.50
S1 Ken Griffey Jr.	1.25	.35
S2 Mark McGwire	2.00	.60
S3 Sammy Sosa	1.25	.35
S4 Nomar Garciaparra	1.25	.35
S5 Roger Clemens	1.50	.45
S6 Greg Maddux	1.25	.35
S7 Alex Rodriguez	1.25	.35
S8 Derek Jeter	2.00	.60
S9 Juan Gonzalez	.50	.15
S10 Manny Ramirez	.50	.15
S11 Mike Piazza	1.25	.35
S12 Tony Gwynn	1.00	.30
S13 Chipper Jones	.75	.23
S14 Pedro Martinez	.75	.23
S15 Frank Thomas	.75	.23

1999 Ultimate Victory Tribute 1999

Inserted one every 11 packs, this set honors the four inductees into the Hall of Fame in 1999. Card backs carry a "T" prefix.

	Nm-Mt	Ex-Mt
COMPLETE SET (4)	15.00	4.50
T1 Nolan Ryan	6.00	1.80
T2 Robin Yount	4.00	1.20
T3 George Brett	6.00	1.80
T4 Orlando Cepeda	1.50	.45

1999 Ultimate Victory Ultimate Competitors

Inserted one every 23 packs, this 12 card set highlights the players who bring an winning attitude to the ballpark every day.

	Nm-Mt	Ex-Mt
COMPLETE SET (12)	60.00	18.00
U1 Ken Griffey Jr.	5.00	1.50
U2 Roger Clemens	6.00	1.80
U3 Scott Rolen	3.00	.90
U4 Greg Maddux	5.00	1.50
U5 Mark McGwire	8.00	2.40
U6 Derek Jeter	8.00	2.40
U7 Randy Johnson	3.00	.90
U8 Cal Ripken	10.00	3.00
U9 Craig Biggio	2.00	.60
U10 Kevin Brown	2.00	.60
U11 Chipper Jones	3.00	.90
U12 Vladimir Guerrero	3.00	.90

1999 Ultimate Victory Ultimate Hit Men

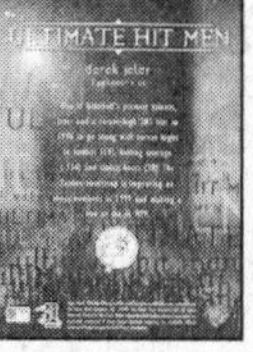

Inserted one every 23 packs, this eight card set features players who were among the leading contenders for the 1999 batting titles in their respective leagues.

	Nm-Mt	Ex-Mt
COMPLETE SET (8)	30.00	9.00
H1 Tony Gwynn	2.50	.75
H2 Cal Ripken	6.00	1.80
H3 Wade Boggs	1.25	.35
H4 Larry Walker	1.25	.35
H5 Alex Rodriguez	3.00	.90
H6 Derek Jeter	5.00	1.50
H7 Ivan Rodriguez	2.00	.60
H8 Ken Griffey Jr.	3.00	.90

2000 Ultimate Victory

The 2000 Upper Deck Ultimate Victory product was released in October, 2000. The set features 120 cards broken into tiers as follows: 90 veterans (1-90), 10 Rookies serial numbered to 3500, 10 Rookies serial numbered to 2500, and 10 Rookies serial numbered to 1000. Each pack contained five cards and carried a suggested retail price of $3.99.

	Nm-Mt	Ex-Mt
COMP.SET w/o SP's (90)	25.00	7.50
COMMON CARD (1-90)	.30	.09
1 Mo Vaughn	.30	.09
2 Darin Erstad	.30	.09
3 Troy Glaus	.30	.09
4 Adam Kennedy	.30	.09
5 Jason Giambi	.30	.09
6 Ben Grieve	.30	.09
7 Terrence Long	.30	.09
8 Tim Hudson	.30	.09
9 David Wells	.30	.09
10 Carlos Delgado	.30	.09
11 Shannon Stewart	.30	.09
12 Greg Vaughn	.30	.09
13 Gerald Williams	.30	.09
14 Manny Ramirez	.50	.15
15 Roberto Alomar	.50	.15
16 Jim Thome	.75	.23
17 Edgar Martinez	.50	.15
18 Alex Rodriguez	1.25	.35
19 Matt Riley	.30	.09
20 Cal Ripken	2.50	.75
21 Mike Mussina	.50	.15
22 Albert Belle	.30	.09
23 Ivan Rodriguez	.75	.23
24 Rafael Palmeiro	.50	.15
25 Nomar Garciaparra	1.25	.35
26 Pedro Martinez	.75	.23
27 Carl Everett	.30	.09
28 Tomokazu Ohka RC	.30	.09
29 Jermaine Dye	.30	.09
30 Johnny Damon	.50	.15
31 Dean Palmer	.30	.09
32 Juan Gonzalez	.50	.15
33 Eric Milton	.30	.09
34 Matt Lawton	.30	.09
35 Frank Thomas	.75	.23
36 Paul Konerko	.30	.09
37 Magglio Ordonez	.30	.09
38 Jon Garland	.30	.09
39 Derek Jeter	2.00	.60
40 Roger Clemens	1.50	.45
41 Bernie Williams	.50	.15
42 Nick Johnson	.30	.09
43 Julio Lugo	.30	.09
44 Jeff Bagwell	.50	.15
45 Richard Hidalgo	.30	.09
46 Chipper Jones	.75	.23
47 Greg Maddux	1.25	.35
48 Andruw Jones	.30	.09
49 Andres Galarraga	.30	.09
50 Rafael Furcal	.30	.09
51 Jeromy Burnitz	.30	.09
52 Geoff Jenkins	.30	.09
53 Mark McGwire	2.00	.60
54 Jim Edmonds	.30	.09
55 Rick Ankiel	.30	.09
56 Sammy Sosa	1.25	.35
57 Julio Zuleta RC	.30	.09
58 Kerry Wood	.75	.23
59 Randy Johnson	.75	.23
60 Matt Williams	.30	.09
61 Steve Finley	.30	.09
62 Gary Sheffield	.30	.09
63 Kevin Brown	.30	.09
64 Shawn Green	.30	.09
65 Milton Bradley	.30	.09
66 Vladimir Guerrero	.75	.23
67 Jose Vidro	.30	.09
68 Barry Bonds	2.00	.60
69 Jeff Kent	.30	.09
70 Preston Wilson	.30	.09
71 Mike Lowell	.30	.09
72 Mike Piazza	1.25	.35
73 Robin Ventura	.30	.09
74 Edgardo Alfonzo	.30	.09
75 Jay Payton	.30	.09
76 Tony Gwynn	1.00	.30
77 Adam Eaton	.30	.09
78 Phil Nevin	.30	.09
79 Scott Rolen	.75	.23
80 Bob Abreu	.30	.09
81 Pat Burrell	.30	.09
82 Brian Giles	.30	.09
83 Jason Kendall	.30	.09
84 Kris Benson	.30	.09
85 Gookie Dawkins	.30	.09
86 Ken Griffey Jr.	1.25	.35
87 Barry Larkin	.50	.15
88 Larry Walker	.50	.15
89 Todd Helton	.50	.15
90 Ben Petrick	.30	.09
91 Alex Cabrera/3500 RC	4.00	1.20
92 M.Wheatland/1000 RC	10.00	3.00
93 Joe Torres/1000 RC	10.00	3.00
94 Xavier Nady/1000 RC	15.00	4.50
95 Kenny Kelly/3500 RC	4.00	1.20
96 Matt Ginter/3500 RC	4.00	1.20
97 Ben Diggins/1000 RC	10.00	3.00
98 Danys Baez/3500 RC	4.00	1.20
99 Daylan Holt/2500 RC	5.00	1.50
100 K.Sasaki/3500 RC	5.00	1.50
101 D.Artman/2500 RC	5.00	1.50
102 Mike Tonis/1000 RC	10.00	3.00
103 Timo Perez/2500 RC	5.00	1.50
104 Barry Zito/2500 RC	10.00	3.00
105 Koyie Hill/2500 RC	5.00	1.50
106 B.Wilkerson/2500 RC	8.00	2.40
107 Juan Pierre/3500 RC	5.00	1.50
108 A.McNeal/3500 RC	4.00	1.20
109 J.Spurgeon/3500 RC	4.00	1.20
110 Sean Burnett/1000 RC	15.00	4.50
111 Luis Matos/3500 RC	4.00	1.20
112 Dave Krynzel/1000 RC	10.00	3.00
113 Scott Heard/1000 RC	10.00	3.00
114 Ben Sheets/2500 RC	10.00	3.00
115 D.Sardinha/1000 RC	10.00	3.00
116 D.Espinosa/1000 RC	10.00	3.00
117 Leo Estrella/3500 RC	4.00	1.20
118 K.Ainsworth/2500 RC	5.00	1.50
119 Jon Rauch/2500 RC	5.00	1.50
120 R.Franklin/2500 RC	5.00	1.50

2000 Ultimate Victory Parallel 25

Randomly inserted into packs, this 120-card insert is a complete parallel of the base set. They can be differentiated from the regular cards with the addition of gold foil on each card. Each card is serial numbered to 25.

Nm-Mt Ex-Mt

*STARS 1-90: 15X TO 40X BASIC 1-90

2000 Ultimate Victory Parallel 100

Randomly inserted into packs, this 120-card insert is a complete parallel of the base set. They can be differentiated from the regular cards with the addition of red foil on each card. Each card is serial numbered to 100.

Nm-Mt Ex-Mt

*STARS 1-90: 8X TO 20X BASIC 1-90
*ROOKIES 1-90: 10X TO 25X BASIC 1-90
*TIER 1 91-120: &&.4X TO 1X BASIC RC 1000
*TIER 2 91-120: .75X TO 2X BASIC 2500
*TIER 3 91-120: 1X TO 2.5X BASIC 3500

2000 Ultimate Victory Parallel 250

Randomly inserted into packs, this 120-card insert is a complete parallel of the base set. They can be differentiated from the regular cards with the addition of silver foil on each card. Each card is serial numbered to 250.

Nm-Mt Ex-Mt

*STARS 1-90: 3X TO 8X BASIC 1-90..
*ROOKIES 1-90: 6X TO 15X BASIC 1-90
*TIER 1 91-120: .2X TO .5X BASIC 1000
*TIER 2 91-120: .4X TO 1X BASIC 2500
*TIER 3 91-120: .6X TO 1.5X BASIC 3500

2000 Ultimate Victory Diamond Dignitaries

Randomly inserted into packs at one in 23, this 10-card insert set features players that are leaders on the playing field. Card backs carry a "D" prefix.

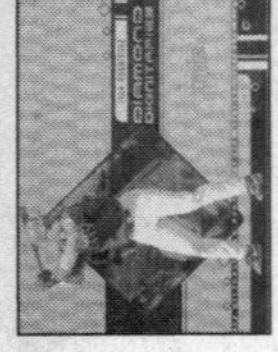

	Nm-Mt	Ex-Mt
COMPLETE SET (10)	60.00	18.00
D1 Ken Griffey Jr.	6.00	1.80
D2 Nomar Garciaparra	6.00	1.80
D3 Chipper Jones	4.00	1.20
D4 Ivan Rodriguez	4.00	1.20
D5 Mark McGwire	10.00	3.00
D6 Cal Ripken	12.00	3.60
D7 Vladimir Guerrero	4.00	1.20
D8 Alex Rodriguez	6.00	1.80
D9 Sammy Sosa	6.00	1.80
D10 Derek Jeter	10.00	3.00

2000 Ultimate Victory Hall of Fame Game Jersey

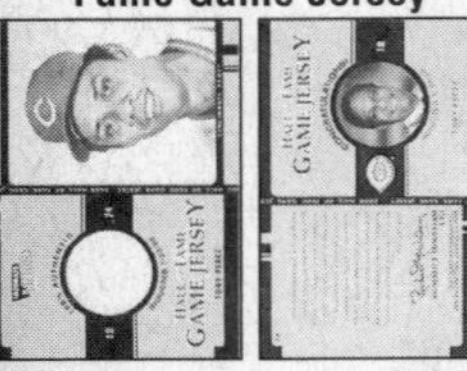

Randomly inserted into packs, this four-card insert set features jersey cards of players that were inducted into the Hall of Fame in 2000. Each card was serial numbered to 500, and the card backs carry the player's initials as numbering. Please note that the combo card of Fisk/Anderson/Perez was serial numbered to 100.

	Nm-Mt	Ex-Mt
CF Carlton Fisk	15.00	4.50
SA Sparky Anderson	15.00	4.50
TP Tony Perez	15.00	4.50
HOF Carlton Fisk Sparky Anderson Tony Perez/100	60.00	18.00

2000 Ultimate Victory Lasting Impressions

Randomly inserted into packs at one in 11, this 10-card insert set features players that leave a lasting impression on those who watch them perform. Card backs carry a "L" prefix.

	Nm-Mt	Ex-Mt
COMPLETE SET (10)	30.00	9.00
L1 Barry Bonds	5.00	1.50
L2 Mike Piazza	3.00	.90
L3 Manny Ramirez	1.25	.35
L4 Pedro Martinez	2.00	.60
L5 Mark McGwire	5.00	1.50
L6 Ken Griffey Jr.	3.00	.90
L7 Ivan Rodriguez	2.00	.60
L8 Jeff Bagwell	1.25	.35
L9 Randy Johnson	2.00	.60
L10 Alex Rodriguez	3.00	.90

2000 Ultimate Victory Starstruck

Randomly inserted into packs at one in 11, this 10-card insert set features players that have been starstruck. Card backs carry a "S" prefix.

	Nm-Mt	Ex-Mt
COMPLETE SET (10)	30.00	9.00
S1 Alex Rodriguez	3.00	.90
S2 Frank Thomas	2.00	.60
S3 Derek Jeter	5.00	1.50
S4 Mark McGwire	5.00	1.50
S5 Nomar Garciaparra	3.00	.90
S6 Chipper Jones	2.00	.60
S7 Cal Ripken	6.00	1.80
S8 Sammy Sosa	3.00	.90
S9 Vladimir Guerrero	2.00	.60
S10 Ken Griffey Jr.	3.00	.90

1991 Ultra

This 400-card standard-size set marked Fleer's first entry into the premium card market. The cards were distributed exclusively in foil-wrapped packs. Fleer claimed in their original press release that there would only be 15 percent the amount of Ultra issued as there was of the regular 1991 Fleer issue. The cards feature full color action photography on the fronts and three full-color photos on the backs. Fleer also issued the sets in their now traditional alphabetical order as well as the teams in alphabetical order. Subsets include Major League Prospects (373-390), Elite Performance (391-396), and Checklists (397-400). Rookie Cards include Eric Karros and Denny Neagle.

	Nm-Mt	Ex-Mt
COMPLETE SET (400)	20.00	6.00
1 Steve Avery	.10	.03
2 Jeff Blauser	.10	.03
3 Francisco Cabrera	.10	.03
4 Ron Gant	.20	.06
5 Tom Glavine	.30	.09
6 Tommy Gregg	.10	.03
7 Dave Justice	.20	.06
8 Oddibe McDowell	.10	.03
9 Greg Olson	.10	.03
10 Terry Pendleton	.20	.06
11 Lonnie Smith	.10	.03
12 John Smoltz	.30	.09
13 Jeff Treadway	.10	.03
14 Glenn Davis	.10	.03
15 Mike Devereaux	.10	.03
16 Leo Gomez	.10	.03
17 Chris Hoiles	.10	.03
18 Dave Johnson	.10	.03
19 Ben McDonald	.10	.03
20 Randy Milligan	.10	.03
21 Gregg Olson	.10	.03
22 Joe Orsulak	.10	.03
23 Bill Ripken	.10	.03
24 Cal Ripken	1.50	.45
25 David Segui	.10	.03
26 Craig Worthington	.10	.03
27 Wade Boggs	.30	.09
28 Tom Bolton	.10	.03
29 Tom Brunansky	.10	.03
30 Ellis Burks	.20	.06
31 Roger Clemens	1.00	.30
32 Mike Greenwell	.10	.03
33 Greg A. Harris	.10	.03
34 Daryl Irvine	.10	.03
35 Mike Marshall UER (1990 in stats is shown as 990)	.10	.03
36 Tim Naehring	.10	.03
37 Tony Pena	.10	.03
38 Phil Plantier RC	.15	.04
39 Carlos Quintana	.10	.03
40 Jeff Reardon	.20	.06
41 Jody Reed	.10	.03
42 Luis Rivera	.10	.03
43 Jim Abbott	.30	.09
44 Chuck Finley	.20	.06
45 Bryan Harvey	.10	.03
46 Donnie Hill	.10	.03
47 Jack Howell	.10	.03
48 Wally Joyner	.20	.06
49 Mark Langston	.10	.03
50 Kirk McCaskill	.10	.03
51 Lance Parrish	.20	.06
52 Dick Schofield	.10	.03
53 Lee Stevens	.10	.03
54 Dave Winfield	.20	.06
55 George Bell	.10	.03
56 Damon Berryhill	.10	.03
57 Mike Bielecki	.10	.03
58 Andre Dawson	.20	.06
59 Shawon Dunston	.10	.03
60 Joe Girardi UER (Bats right, LH hitter shown is Doug Dascenzo)	.10	.03
61 Mark Grace	.30	.09
62 Mike Harkey	.10	.03
63 Les Lancaster	.10	.03
64 Greg Maddux	.75	.23
65 Derrick May	.10	.03
66 Ryne Sandberg	.75	.23
67 Luis Salazar	.10	.03
68 Dwight Smith	.10	.03
69 Hector Villanueva	.10	.03
70 Jerome Walton	.10	.03
71 Mitch Williams	.10	.03
72 Carlton Fisk	.30	.09
73 Scott Fletcher	.10	.03
74 Ozzie Guillen	.10	.03
75 Greg Hibbard	.10	.03
76 Lance Johnson	.10	.03
77 Steve Lyons	.10	.03
78 Jack McDowell	.10	.03
79 Dan Pasqua	.10	.03
80 Melido Perez	.10	.03
81 Tim Raines	.20	.06
82 Sammy Sosa	1.00	.30
83 Cory Snyder	.10	.03
84 Bobby Thigpen	.10	.03
85 Frank Thomas (Card says he is an outfielder)	.50	.15
86 Robin Ventura	.20	.06
87 Todd Benzinger	.10	.03
88 Glenn Braggs	.10	.03
89 Tom Browning UER (Front photo actually Norm Charlton)	.10	.03
90 Norm Charlton	.10	.03
91 Eric Davis	.20	.06
92 Rob Dibble	.20	.06
93 Bill Doran	.10	.03
94 Mariano Duncan UER (Right back photo is Billy Hatcher)	.10	.03
95 Billy Hatcher	.10	.03
96 Barry Larkin	.30	.09
97 Randy Myers	.10	.03
98 Hal Morris	.10	.03
99 Joe Oliver	.10	.03
100 Paul O'Neill	.30	.09
101 Jeff Reed (See also 104)	.10	.03
102 Jose Rijo	.10	.03
103 Chris Sabo (See also 106)	.10	.03
104 Beau Allred UER (Card number is 101)	.10	.03
105 Sandy Alomar Jr.	.10	.03
106 Carlos Baerga UER (Card number is 103)	.10	.03
107 Albert Belle	.20	.06
108 Jerry Browne	.10	.03
109 Tom Candiotti	.10	.03
110 Alex Cole	.10	.03
111 John Farrell (See also 114)	.10	.03
112 Felix Fermin	.10	.03
113 Brook Jacoby	.10	.03
114 Chris James UER (Card number is 111)	.10	.03
115 Doug Jones	.10	.03
116 Steve Olin (See also 119)	.10	.03
117 Greg Swindell	.10	.03
118 Turner Ward RC	.15	.04
119 Mitch Webster UER (Card number is 116)	.10	.03
120 Dave Bergman	.10	.03
121 Cecil Fielder	.20	.06
122 Travis Fryman	.20	.06
123 Mike Henneman	.10	.03
124 Lloyd Moseby	.10	.03
125 Dan Petry	.10	.03
126 Tony Phillips	.10	.03
127 Mark Salas	.10	.03
128 Frank Tanana	.10	.03
129 Alan Trammell	.20	.06
130 Lou Whitaker	.20	.06
131 Eric Anthony	.10	.03
132 Craig Biggio	.30	.09
133 Ken Caminiti	.20	.06
134 Casey Candaele	.10	.03
135 Andujar Cedeno	.10	.03
136 Mark Davidson	.10	.03
137 Jim Deshaies	.10	.03
138 Mark Portugal	.10	.03
139 Rafael Ramirez	.10	.03
140 Mike Scott	.10	.03
141 Eric Yelding	.10	.03
142 Gerald Young	.10	.03
143 Kevin Appier	.20	.06
144 George Brett	1.25	.35
145 Jeff Conine RC	.50	.15
146 Jim Eisenreich	.10	.03
147 Tom Gordon	.10	.03
148 Mark Gubicza	.10	.03
149 Bo Jackson	.50	.15
150 Brent Mayne	.10	.03
151 Mike Macfarlane	.10	.03
152 Brian McRae RC	.40	.12
153 Jeff Montgomery	.10	.03
154 Bret Saberhagen	.20	.06
155 Kevin Seitzer	.10	.03
156 Terry Shumpert	.10	.03
157 Kurt Stillwell	.10	.03
158 Danny Tartabull	.10	.03
159 Tim Belcher	.10	.03
160 Kal Daniels	.10	.03
161 Alfredo Griffin	.10	.03
162 Lenny Harris	.10	.03
163 Jay Howell	.10	.03
164 Ramon Martinez	.10	.03
165 Mike Morgan	.10	.03
166 Eddie Murray	.50	.15
167 Jose Offerman	.10	.03
168 Juan Samuel	.10	.03
169 Mike Scioscia	.10	.03
170 Mike Sharperson	.10	.03
171 Darryl Strawberry	.20	.06
172 Greg Brock	.10	.03
173 Chuck Crim	.10	.03
174 Jim Gantner	.10	.03
175 Ted Higuera	.10	.03
176 Mark Knudson	.10	.03
177 Tim McIntosh	.10	.03
178 Paul Molitor	.30	.09
179 Dan Plesac	.10	.03
180 Gary Sheffield	.20	.06
181 Bill Spiers	.10	.03
182 B.J. Surhoff	.20	.06
183 Greg Vaughn	.10	.03
184 Robin Yount	.75	.23
185 Rick Aguilera	.20	.06
186 Greg Gagne	.10	.03
187 Dan Gladden	.10	.03
188 Brian Harper	.10	.03
189 Kent Hrbek	.20	.06
190 Gene Larkin	.10	.03
191 Shane Mack	.10	.03
192 Pedro Munoz RC	.15	.04
193 Al Newman	.10	.03
194 Junior Ortiz	.10	.03
195 Kirby Puckett	.50	.15
196 Kevin Tapani	.10	.03
197 Dennis Boyd	.10	.03
198 Tim Burke	.10	.03
199 Ivan Calderon	.10	.03
200 Delino DeShields	.20	.06
201 Mike Fitzgerald	.10	.03
202 Steve Frey	.10	.03
203 Andres Galarraga	.20	.06
204 Marquis Grissom	.20	.06
205 Dave Martinez	.10	.03
206 Dennis Martinez	.20	.06
207 Junior Noboa	.10	.03
208 Spike Owen	.10	.03
209 Scott Ruskin	.10	.03
210 Tim Wallach	.10	.03
211 Daryl Boston	.10	.03
212 Vince Coleman	.10	.03
213 David Cone	.20	.06
214 Ron Darling	.10	.03
215 Kevin Elster	.10	.03
216 Sid Fernandez	.10	.03
217 John Franco	.20	.06
218 Dwight Gooden	.20	.06
219 Tom Herr	.10	.03
220 Todd Hundley	.10	.03
221 Gregg Jefferies	.10	.03
222 Howard Johnson	.10	.03
223 Dave Magadan	.10	.03
224 Kevin McReynolds	.10	.03
225 Keith Miller	.10	.03
226 Mackey Sasser	.10	.03
227 Frank Viola	.20	.06
228 Jesse Barfield	.10	.03
229 Greg Cadaret	.10	.03
230 Alvaro Espinoza	.10	.03
231 Bob Geren	.10	.03
232 Lee Guetterman	.10	.03
233 Mel Hall	.10	.03
234 Andy Hawkins UER (Back center photo is not him)	.10	.03
235 Roberto Kelly	.10	.03
236 Tim Leary	.10	.03
237 Jim Leyritz	.10	.03
238 Kevin Maas	.10	.03
239 Don Mattingly	1.25	.35
240 Hensley Meulens	.10	.03
241 Eric Plunk	.10	.03
242 Steve Sax	.10	.03
243 Todd Burns	.10	.03
244 Jose Canseco	.50	.15
245 Dennis Eckersley	.20	.06
246 Mike Gallego	.10	.03
247 Dave Henderson	.10	.03
248 Rickey Henderson	.50	.15
249 Rick Honeycutt	.10	.03
250 Carney Lansford	.20	.06
251 Mark McGwire	1.25	.35
252 Mike Moore	.10	.03
253 Terry Steinbach	.10	.03
254 Dave Stewart	.20	.06
255 Walt Weiss	.10	.03
256 Bob Welch	.10	.03
257 Curt Young	.10	.03
258 Wes Chamberlain RC	.40	.12
259 Pat Combs	.10	.03
260 Darren Daulton	.20	.06
261 Jose DeJesus	.10	.03
262 Len Dykstra	.20	.06
263 Charlie Hayes	.10	.03
264 Von Hayes	.10	.03
265 Ken Howell	.10	.03
266 John Kruk	.20	.06
267 Roger McDowell	.10	.03
268 Mickey Morandini	.10	.03
269 Terry Mulholland	.10	.03
270 Dale Murphy	.50	.15
271 Randy Ready	.10	.03
272 Dickie Thon	.10	.03
273 Stan Belinda	.10	.03
274 Jay Bell	.20	.06
275 Barry Bonds	1.25	.35
276 Bobby Bonilla	.20	.06
277 Doug Drabek	.10	.03
278 Carlos Garcia RC	.15	.04
279 Neal Heaton	.10	.03
280 Jeff King	.10	.03
281 Bill Landrum	.10	.03
282 Mike LaValliere	.10	.03
283 Jose Lind	.10	.03
284 Orlando Merced RC	.15	.04
285 Gary Redus	.10	.03
286 Don Slaught	.10	.03
287 Andy Van Slyke	.20	.06
288 Jose DeLeon	.10	.03
289 Pedro Guerrero	.20	.06
290 Ray Lankford	.10	.03
291 Joe Magrane	.10	.03
292 Jose Oquendo	.10	.03
293 Tom Pagnozzi	.10	.03
294 Bryn Smith	.10	.03
295 Lee Smith	.20	.06
296 Ozzie Smith UER (Born 12-26, 54, should have hyphen)	.75	.23
297 Milt Thompson	.10	.03
298 Craig Wilson	.10	.03
299 Todd Zeile	.10	.03
300 Shawn Abner	.10	.03
301 Andy Benes	.10	.03
302 Paul Faries	.10	.03
303 Tony Gwynn	.60	.18
304 Greg W. Harris	.10	.03
305 Thomas Howard	.10	.03
306 Bruce Hurst	.10	.03
307 Craig Lefferts	.10	.03
308 Fred McGriff	.30	.09
309 Dennis Rasmussen	.10	.03
310 Bip Roberts	.10	.03
311 Benito Santiago	.20	.06
312 Garry Templeton	.10	.03
313 Ed Whitson	.10	.03
314 Dave Anderson	.10	.03
315 Kevin Bass	.10	.03
316 Jeff Brantley	.10	.03
317 John Burkett	.10	.03
318 Will Clark	.50	.15
319 Steve Decker	.10	.03
320 Scott Garrelts	.10	.03
321 Terry Kennedy	.10	.03
322 Mark Leonard	.10	.03
323 Darren Lewis	.10	.03
324 Greg Litton	.10	.03
325 Willie McGee	.20	.06
326 Kevin Mitchell	.10	.03
327 Don Robinson	.10	.03
328 Andres Santana	.10	.03
329 Robby Thompson	.10	.03
330 Jose Uribe	.10	.03
331 Matt Williams	.20	.06
332 Scott Bradley	.10	.03
333 Henry Cotto	.10	.03
334 Alvin Davis	.10	.03
335 Ken Griffey Sr.	.20	.06
336 Ken Griffey Jr.	1.00	.30
337 Erik Hanson	.10	.03
338 Brian Holman	.10	.03
339 Randy Johnson	.60	.18
340 Edgar Martinez UER (Listed as playing SS)	.30	.09
341 Tino Martinez	.30	.09
342 Pete O'Brien	.10	.03
343 Harold Reynolds	.20	.06
344 Dave Valle	.10	.03
345 Omar Vizquel	.30	.09
346 Brad Arnsberg	.10	.03
347 Kevin Brown	.20	.06
348 Julio Franco	.20	.06
349 Jeff Huson	.10	.03
350 Rafael Palmeiro	.30	.09
351 Geno Petralli	.10	.03
352 Gary Pettis	.10	.03
353 Kenny Rogers	.20	.06
354 Jeff Russell	.10	.03
355 Nolan Ryan	2.00	.60
356 Ruben Sierra	.10	.03
357 Bobby Witt	.10	.03
358 Roberto Alomar	.30	.09
359 Pat Borders	.10	.03
360 Joe Carter UER (Reverse negative on back photo)	.20	.06
361 Kelly Gruber	.10	.03
362 Tom Henke	.10	.03
363 Glenallen Hill	.10	.03
364 Jimmy Key	.20	.06
365 Manny Lee	.10	.03
366 Rance Mulliniks	.10	.03
367 John Olerud UER (Throwing left on card; back has throws right; he does throw lefty)	.20	.06
368 Dave Stieb	.10	.03
369 Duane Ward	.10	.03
370 David Wells	.20	.06
371 Mark Whiten	.10	.03
372 Mookie Wilson	.20	.06
373 Willie Banks MLP	.10	.03
374 Steve Carter MLP	.10	.03
375 S.Chiamparino MLP	.10	.03
376 Steve Chitren MLP	.10	.03
377 Darrin Fletcher MLP	.10	.03
378 Rich Garces MLP RC	.15	.04
379 Reggie Jefferson MLP	.10	.03
380 Eric Karros MLP RC	.50	.15
381 Pat Kelly MLP RC	.15	.04
382 C.Knoblauch MLP	.20	.06
383 D.Neagle MLP RC	.40	.12
384 Dan Opperman MLP	.10	.03
385 John Ramos MLP	.10	.03
386 H.Rodriguez MLP RC	.40	.12
387 Mo Vaughn MLP	.20	.06
388 G.Williams MLP RC	.40	.12
389 Mike York MLP	.10	.03
390 Eddie Zosky MLP	.10	.03
391 Barry Bonds EP	.60	.18
392 Cecil Fielder EP	.10	.03
393 Rickey Henderson EP	.30	.09
394 Dave Justice EP	.10	.03
395 Nolan Ryan EP	1.00	.30
396 Bobby Thigpen EP	.10	.03
397 Gregg Jefferies CL	.10	.03
398 Von Hayes CL	.10	.03
399 Terry Kennedy CL	.10	.03
400 Nolan Ryan CL	.50	.15

1991 Ultra Gold

This ten-card standard-size set presents Fleer's 1991 Ultra Team. These cards were randomly inserted into Ultra packs. The set is sequenced in alphabetical order.

	Nm-Mt	Ex-Mt
COMPLETE SET (10)	10.00	3.00
1 Barry Bonds	2.50	.75
2 Will Clark	1.00	.30
3 Doug Drabek	.20	.06
4 Ken Griffey Jr.	2.00	.60
5 Rickey Henderson	1.00	.30
6 Bo Jackson	1.00	.30
7 Ramon Martinez	.20	.06
8 Kirby Puckett UER (Boggs won 1988 batting title, so Puckett didn't win consecutive titles)	1.00	.30
9 Chris Sabo	.20	.06
10 Ryne Sandberg UER (Johnson and Hornsby didn't hit 40 homers in 1990, Fielder did hit 51 in '90)	1.50	.45

1991 Ultra Update

The 120-card set was distributed exclusively in factory set form along with 20 team logo stickers through hobby dealers. The set includes the year's hottest rookies and important veteran players traded after the original Ultra series was produced. Card design is identical to regular issue 1991 cards except for the U-prefixed numbering on back. Cards are ordered alphabetically within and according to teams for each league. Rookie Cards in this set include Jeff Bagwell, Mike Mussina, and Ivan Rodriguez.

	Nm-Mt	Ex-Mt
COMP.FACT.SET (120)	25.00	7.50

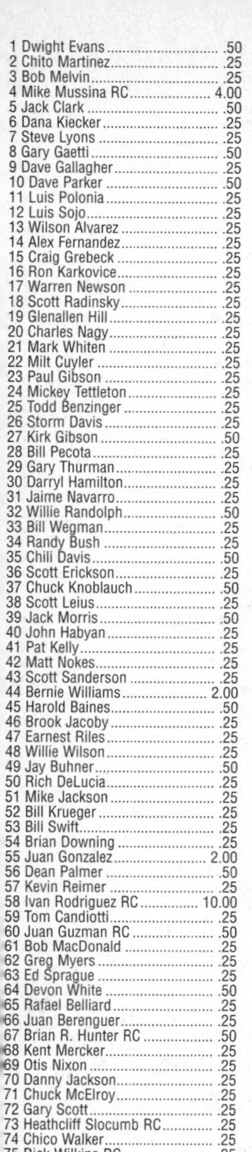

1 Dwight Evans .50 .15
2 Chito Martinez .25 .07
3 Bob Melvin .25 .07
4 Mike Mussina RC 4.00 1.20
5 Jack Clark .50 .15
6 Dana Kiecker .25 .07
7 Steve Lyons .25 .07
8 Gary Gaetti .50 .15
9 Dave Gallagher .25 .07
10 Dave Parker .50 .15
11 Luis Polonia .25 .07
12 Luis Sojo .25 .07
13 Wilson Alvarez .25 .07
14 Alex Fernandez .25 .07
15 Craig Grebeck .25 .07
16 Ron Karkovice .25 .07
17 Warren Newson .25 .07
18 Scott Radinsky .25 .07
19 Glenallen Hill .25 .07
20 Charles Nagy .25 .07
21 Mark Whiten .25 .07
22 Milt Cuyler .25 .07
23 Paul Gibson .25 .07
24 Mickey Tettleton .25 .07
25 Todd Benzinger .25 .07
26 Storm Davis .25 .07
27 Kirk Gibson .50 .15
28 Bill Pecota .25 .07
29 Gary Thurman .25 .07
30 Darryl Hamilton .25 .07
31 Jaime Navarro .25 .07
32 Willie Randolph .50 .15
33 Bill Wegman .25 .07
34 Randy Bush .25 .07
35 Chili Davis .50 .15
36 Scott Erickson .25 .07
37 Chuck Knoblauch .50 .15
38 Scott Leius .25 .07
39 Jack Morris .50 .15
40 John Habyan .25 .07
41 Pat Kelly .25 .07
42 Matt Nokes .25 .07
43 Scott Sanderson .25 .07
44 Bernie Williams 2.00 .60
45 Harold Baines .50 .15
46 Brook Jacoby .25 .07
47 Earnest Riles .25 .07
48 Willie Wilson .25 .07
49 Jay Buhner .50 .15
50 Rich DeLucia .25 .07
51 Mike Jackson .25 .07
52 Bill Krueger .25 .07
53 Bill Swift .25 .07
54 Brian Downing .25 .07
55 Juan Gonzalez 2.00 .60
56 Dean Palmer .50 .15
57 Kevin Reimer .25 .07
58 Ivan Rodriguez RC 10.00 3.00
59 Tom Candiotti .25 .07
60 Juan Guzman RC .50 .15
61 Bob MacDonald .25 .07
62 Greg Myers .25 .07
63 Ed Sprague .25 .07
64 Devon White .50 .15
65 Rafael Belliard .25 .07
66 Juan Berenguer .25 .07
67 Brian R. Hunter RC .50 .15
68 Kent Mercker .25 .07
69 Otis Nixon .25 .07
70 Danny Jackson .25 .07
71 Chuck McElroy .25 .07
72 Gary Scott .25 .07
73 Heathcliff Slocumb RC .25 .07
74 Chico Walker .25 .07
75 Rick Wilkins RC .25 .07
76 Chris Hammond .25 .07
77 Luis Quinones .25 .07
78 Herm Winningham .25 .07
79 Jeff Bagwell RC 8.00 2.40
80 Jim Corsi .25 .07
81 Steve Finley .50 .15
82 Luis Gonzalez RC 1.50 .45
83 Pete Harnisch .50 .15
84 Darryl Kile .50 .15
85 Brett Butler .50 .15
86 Gary Carter .50 .15
87 Tim Crews .25 .07
88 Orel Hershiser .50 .15
89 Bob Ojeda .25 .07
90 Bret Barberie RC** .25 .07
91 Barry Jones .25 .07
92 Gilberto Reyes .25 .07
93 Larry Walker 1.25 .35
94 Hubie Brooks .25 .07
95 Tim Burke .25 .07
96 Rick Cerone .25 .07
97 Jeff Innis .25 .07
98 Wally Backman .25 .07
99 Tommy Greene .25 .07
100 Ricky Jordan .25 .07
101 Mitch Williams .25 .07
102 John Smiley .25 .07
103 Randy Tomlin RC .25 .07
104 Gary Varsho .25 .07
105 Cris Carpenter .25 .07
106 Ken Hill .25 .07
107 Felix Jose .25 .07
108 Omar Olivares RC .25 .07
109 Gerald Perry .25 .07
110 Jerald Clark .25 .07
111 Tony Fernandez .25 .07
112 Darrin Jackson .25 .07
113 Mike Maddux .25 .07
114 Tim Teufel .25 .07
115 Bud Black .25 .07
116 Kelly Downs .25 .07
117 Mike Felder .25 .07
118 Willie McGee .50 .15
119 Trevor Wilson .25 .07
120 Checklist 1-120 .25 .07

1992 Ultra

Consisting of 600 standard-size cards, the 1992 Ultra set was issued in two series of 300 cards each. Cards were distributed exclusively in foil packs. The cards are numbered on the back and ordered below alphabetically within and according to teams for each league with AL preceding NL. Some cards have been found without the

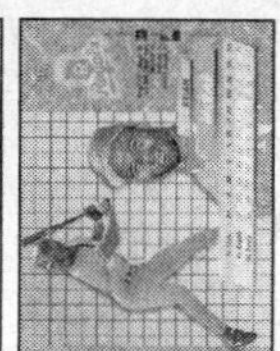

word Fleer on the front.

	Nm-Mt	Ex-Mt
COMPLETE SET (600)	30.00	9.00
COMP. SERIES 1 (300)	20.00	6.00
COMP. SERIES 2 (300)	10.00	3.00

1 Glenn Davis .10 .03
2 Mike Devereaux .10 .03
3 Dwight Evans .20 .06
4 Leo Gomez .10 .03
5 Chris Hoiles .10 .03
6 Sam Horn .10 .03
7 Chito Martinez .10 .03
8 Randy Milligan .10 .03
9 Mike Mussina .50 .15
10 Billy Ripken .10 .03
11 Cal Ripken 1.50 .45
12 Tom Brunansky .10 .03
13 Ellis Burks .20 .06
14 Jack Clark .20 .06
15 Roger Clemens 1.00 .30
16 Mike Greenwell .10 .03
17 Joe Hesketh .10 .03
18 Tony Pena .10 .03
19 Carlos Quintana .10 .03
20 Jeff Reardon .20 .06
21 Jody Reed .10 .03
22 Luis Rivera .10 .03
23 Mo Vaughn .20 .06
24 Gary DiSarcina .10 .03
25 Chuck Finley .20 .06
26 Gary Gaetti .20 .06
27 Bryan Harvey .10 .03
28 Lance Parrish .20 .06
29 Luis Polonia .10 .03
30 Dick Schofield .10 .03
31 Luis Sojo .10 .03
32 Wilson Alvarez .10 .03
33 Carlton Fisk .30 .09
34 Craig Grebeck .10 .03
35 Ozzie Guillen .10 .03
36 Greg Hibbard .10 .03
37 Charlie Hough .20 .06
38 Lance Johnson .10 .03
39 Ron Karkovice .10 .03
40 Jack McDowell .10 .03
41 Donn Pall .10 .03
42 Melido Perez .10 .03
43 Tim Raines .20 .06
44 Frank Thomas .50 .15
45 Sandy Alomar Jr. .10 .03
46 Carlos Baerga .10 .03
47 Albert Belle .20 .06
48 Jerry Browne UER .10 .03
(Reversed negative on card back)
49 Felix Fermin .10 .03
50 Reggie Jefferson UER .10 .03
(Born 1968, not 1966)
51 Mark Lewis .10 .03
52 Carlos Martinez .10 .03
53 Steve Olin .10 .03
54 Jim Thome .50 .15
55 Mark Whiten .10 .03
56 Dave Bergman .10 .03
57 Milt Cuyler .10 .03
58 Rob Deer .10 .03
59 Cecil Fielder .20 .06
60 Travis Fryman .20 .06
61 Scott Livingstone .10 .03
62 Tony Phillips .10 .03
63 Mickey Tettleton .10 .03
64 Alan Trammell .20 .06
65 Lou Whitaker .20 .06
66 Kevin Appier .20 .06
67 Mike Boddicker .10 .03
68 George Brett 1.25 .35
69 Jim Eisenreich .10 .03
70 Mark Gubicza .10 .03
71 David Howard .10 .03
72 Joel Johnson .10 .03
73 Mike Macfarlane .10 .03
74 Brent Mayne .10 .03
75 Brian McRae .10 .03
76 Jeff Montgomery .10 .03
77 Terry Shumpert .10 .03
78 Don August .10 .03
79 Dante Bichette .20 .06
80 Ted Higuera .10 .03
81 Paul Molitor .30 .09
82 Jaime Navarro .10 .03
83 Gary Sheffield .20 .06
84 Bill Spiers .10 .03
85 B.J. Surhoff .20 .06
86 Greg Vaughn .10 .03
87 Robin Yount .75 .23
88 Rick Aguilera .20 .06
89 Chili Davis .20 .06
90 Scott Erickson .10 .03
91 Brian Harper .10 .03
92 Kent Hrbek .20 .06
93 Chuck Knoblauch .20 .06
94 Scott Leius .10 .03
95 Shane Mack .10 .03
96 Mike Pagliarulo .10 .03
97 Kirby Puckett .50 .15
98 Kevin Tapani .10 .03
99 Jesse Barfield .10 .03
100 Alvaro Espinoza .10 .03
101 Mel Hall .10 .03
102 Pat Kelly .10 .03
103 Roberto Kelly .10 .03
104 Kevin Maas .10 .03
105 Don Mattingly 1.25 .35
106 Hensley Meulens .10 .03
107 Matt Nokes .10 .03
108 Steve Sax .10 .03
109 Harold Baines .20 .06
110 Jose Canseco .50 .15
111 Ron Darling .10 .03
112 Mike Gallego .10 .03
113 Dave Henderson .10 .03
114 Rickey Henderson .50 .15
115 Mark McGwire 1.25 .35
116 Terry Steinbach .10 .03
117 Dave Stewart .20 .06
118 Todd Van Poppel .10 .03
119 Bob Welch .10 .03
120 Greg Briley .10 .03
121 Jay Buhner .20 .06
122 Rich DeLucia .10 .03
123 Ken Griffey Jr. .75 .23
124 Erik Hanson .10 .03
125 Randy Johnson .50 .15
126 Edgar Martinez .30 .09
127 Tino Martinez .30 .09
128 Pete O'Brien .10 .03
129 Harold Reynolds .20 .06
130 Dave Valle .10 .03
131 Julio Franco .20 .06
132 Juan Gonzalez .30 .09
133 Jeff Huson .20 .06
(Shows Jose Canseco sliding into second)
134 Mike Jeffcoat .10 .03
135 Terry Mathews .10 .03
136 Rafael Palmeiro .30 .09
137 Dean Palmer .20 .06
138 Geno Petralli .10 .03
139 Ivan Rodriguez .50 .15
140 Jeff Russell .10 .03
141 Nolan Ryan 2.00 .60
142 Ruben Sierra .10 .03
143 Roberto Alomar .30 .09
144 Pat Borders .10 .03
145 Joe Carter .20 .06
146 Kelly Gruber .10 .03
147 Jimmy Key .20 .06
148 Manny Lee .10 .03
149 Rance Mulliniks .10 .03
150 Greg Myers .10 .03
151 John Olerud .20 .06
152 Dave Stieb .10 .03
153 Todd Stottlemyre .10 .03
154 Duane Ward .10 .03
155 Devon White .20 .06
156 Eddie Zosky .10 .03
157 Steve Avery .10 .03
158 Rafael Belliard .10 .03
159 Jeff Blauser .10 .03
160 Sid Bream .10 .03
161 Ron Gant .20 .06
162 Tom Glavine .30 .09
163 Brian Hunter .10 .03
164 Dave Justice .20 .06
165 Mark Lemke .10 .03
166 Greg Olson .10 .03
167 Terry Pendleton .20 .06
168 Lonnie Smith .10 .03
169 John Smoltz .30 .09
170 Mike Stanton .10 .03
171 Jeff Treadway .10 .03
172 Paul Assenmacher .10 .03
173 George Bell .10 .03
174 Shawon Dunston .10 .03
175 Mark Grace .30 .09
176 Danny Jackson .10 .03
177 Les Lancaster .10 .03
178 Greg Maddux .75 .23
179 Luis Salazar .10 .03
180 Rey Sanchez RC .25 .07
181 Ryne Sandberg .75 .23
182 Jose Vizcaino .10 .03
183 Chico Walker .10 .03
184 Jerome Walton .10 .03
185 Glenn Braggs .10 .03
186 Tom Browning .10 .03
187 Rob Dibble .20 .06
188 Bill Doran .10 .03
189 Chris Hammond .10 .03
190 Billy Hatcher .10 .03
191 Barry Larkin .30 .09
192 Hal Morris .10 .03
193 Joe Oliver .10 .03
194 Paul O'Neill .30 .09
195 Jeff Reed .10 .03
196 Jose Rijo .10 .03
197 Chris Sabo .10 .03
198 Jeff Bagwell .50 .15
199 Craig Biggio .30 .09
200 Ken Caminiti .20 .06
201 Andujar Cedeno .10 .03
202 Steve Finley .20 .06
203 Luis Gonzalez .20 .06
204 Pete Harnisch .10 .03
205 Xavier Hernandez .10 .03
206 Darryl Kile .20 .06
207 Al Osuna .10 .03
208 Curt Schilling .30 .09
209 Brett Butler .20 .06
210 Kal Daniels .10 .03
211 Lenny Harris .10 .03
212 Stan Javier .10 .03
213 Ramon Martinez .10 .03
214 Roger McDowell .10 .03
215 Jose Offerman .10 .03
216 Juan Samuel .10 .03
217 Mike Scioscia .10 .03
218 Mike Sharperson .10 .03
219 Darryl Strawberry .20 .06
220 Delino DeShields .20 .06
221 Tom Foley .10 .03
222 Steve Frey .10 .03
223 Dennis Martinez .20 .06
224 Spike Owen .10 .03
225 Gilberto Reyes .10 .03
226 Tim Wallach .10 .03
227 Daryl Boston .10 .03
228 Tim Burke .10 .03
229 Vince Coleman .10 .03
230 David Cone .20 .06
231 Kevin Elster .10 .03
232 Dwight Gooden .20 .06
233 Todd Hundley .10 .03
234 Jeff Innis .10 .03
235 Howard Johnson .10 .03
236 Dave Magadan .10 .03
237 Mackey Sasser .10 .03
238 Anthony Young .10 .03
239 Wes Chamberlain .10 .03
240 Darren Daulton .20 .06
241 Len Dykstra .20 .06
242 Tommy Greene .10 .03
243 Charlie Hayes .10 .03
244 Dave Hollins .10 .03
245 Ricky Jordan .10 .03
246 John Kruk .20 .06
247 Mickey Morandini .10 .03
248 Terry Mulholland .10 .03
249 Dale Murphy .50 .15
250 Jay Bell .20 .06
251 Barry Bonds 1.25 .35
252 Steve Buechele .10 .03
253 Doug Drabek .10 .03
254 Mike LaValliere .10 .03
255 Jose Lind .10 .03
256 Lloyd McClendon .10 .03
257 Orlando Merced .10 .03
258 Don Slaught .10 .03
259 John Smiley .10 .03
260 Zane Smith .10 .03
261 Randy Tomlin .10 .03
262 Andy Van Slyke .20 .06
263 Pedro Guerrero .20 .06
264 Felix Jose .10 .03
265 Ray Lankford .10 .03
266 Omar Olivares .10 .03
267 Jose Oquendo .10 .03
268 Tom Pagnozzi .10 .03
269 Bryn Smith .10 .03
270 Lee Smith UER .20 .06
(1991 record listed as 61-61)
271 Ozzie Smith UER .75 .23
(Comma before year of birth on card back)
272 Milt Thompson .10 .03
273 Todd Zeile .10 .03
274 Andy Benes .10 .03
275 Jerald Clark .10 .03
276 Tony Fernandez .10 .03
277 Tony Gwynn .60 .18
278 Greg W. Harris .10 .03
279 Thomas Howard .10 .03
280 Bruce Hurst .10 .03
281 Mike Maddux .10 .03
282 Fred McGriff .30 .09
283 Benito Santiago .20 .06
284 Kevin Bass .10 .03
285 Jeff Brantley .10 .03
286 John Burkett .10 .03
287 Will Clark .50 .15
288 Royce Clayton .10 .03
289 Steve Decker .10 .03
290 Kelly Downs .10 .03
291 Mike Felder .10 .03
292 Darren Lewis .10 .03
293 Kirt Manwaring .10 .03
294 Willie McGee .20 .06
295 Robby Thompson .10 .03
296 Matt Williams .20 .06
297 Trevor Wilson .10 .03
298 Checklist 1-100 .10 .03
299 Checklist 101-200 .10 .03
300 Checklist 201-300 .10 .03
301 Brady Anderson .20 .06
302 Todd Frohwirth .10 .03
303 Ben McDonald .10 .03
304 Mark McLemore .10 .03
305 Jose Mesa .10 .03
306 Bob Milacki .10 .03
307 Gregg Olson .10 .03
308 David Segui .10 .03
309 Rick Sutcliffe .20 .06
310 Jeff Tackett .10 .03
311 Wade Boggs .30 .09
312 Scott Cooper .10 .03
313 John Flaherty .10 .03
314 Wayne Housie .10 .03
315 Peter Hoy .10 .03
316 John Marzano .10 .03
317 Tim Naehring .10 .03
318 Phil Plantier .10 .03
319 Frank Viola .20 .06
320 Matt Young .10 .03
321 Jim Abbott .30 .09
322 Hubie Brooks .10 .03
323 Chad Curtis RC .25 .07
324 Alvin Davis .10 .03
325 Junior Felix .10 .03
326 Von Hayes .10 .03
327 Mark Langston .10 .03
328 Scott Lewis .10 .03
329 Don Robinson .10 .03
330 Bobby Rose .10 .03
331 Lee Stevens .10 .03
332 George Bell .10 .03
333 Esteban Beltre .10 .03
334 Joey Cora .10 .03
335 Alex Fernandez .10 .03
336 Roberto Hernandez .10 .03
337 Mike Huff .10 .03
338 Kirk McCaskill .10 .03
339 Dan Pasqua .10 .03
340 Scott Radinsky .10 .03
341 Steve Sax .10 .03
342 Bobby Thigpen .10 .03
343 Robin Ventura .20 .06
344 Jack Armstrong .10 .03
345 Alex Cole .10 .03
346 Dennis Cook .10 .03
347 Glenallen Hill .10 .03
348 Thomas Howard .10 .03
349 Brook Jacoby .10 .03
350 Kenny Lofton .30 .09
351 Charles Nagy .10 .03
352 Rod Nichols .10 .03
353 Junior Ortiz .10 .03
354 Dave Otto .10 .03
355 Tony Perezchica .10 .03
356 Scott Scudder .10 .03
357 Paul Sorrento .10 .03
358 Skeeter Barnes .10 .03
359 Mark Carreon .10 .03
360 John Doherty RC .10 .03
361 Dan Gladden .10 .03
362 Bill Gullickson .10 .03
363 Shawn Hare RC .10 .03
364 Mike Henneman .10 .03
365 Chad Kreuter .10 .03
366 Mark Leiter .10 .03
367 Mike Munoz .10 .03
368 Kevin Ritz .10 .03
369 Mark Davis .10 .03
370 Tom Gordon .10 .03
371 Chris Gwynn .10 .03
372 Gregg Jefferies .10 .03
373 Wally Joyner .20 .06
374 Kevin McReynolds .10 .03
375 Keith Miller .10 .03
376 Rico Rossy .10 .03
377 Curtis Wilkerson .10 .03
378 Ricky Bones .10 .03
379 Chris Bosio .10 .03
380 Cal Eldred .10 .03
381 Scott Fletcher .10 .03
382 Jim Gantner .10 .03
383 Darryl Hamilton .10 .03
384 Doug Henry RC .25 .07
385 Pat Listach RC .25 .07
386 Tim McIntosh .10 .03
387 Edwin Nunez .10 .03
388 Dan Plesac .10 .03
389 Kevin Seitzer .10 .03
390 Franklin Stubbs .10 .03
391 William Suero .10 .03
392 Bill Wegman .10 .03
393 Willie Banks .10 .03
394 Jarvis Brown .10 .03
395 Greg Gagne .10 .03
396 Mark Guthrie .10 .03
397 Bill Krueger .10 .03
398 Pat Mahomes RC .25 .07
399 Pedro Munoz .10 .03
400 John Smiley .10 .03
401 Gary Wayne .10 .03
402 Lenny Webster .10 .03
403 Carl Willis .10 .03
404 Greg Cadaret .10 .03
405 Steve Farr .10 .03
406 Mike Gallego .10 .03
407 Charlie Hayes .10 .03
408 Steve Howe .10 .03
409 Dion James .10 .03
410 Jeff Johnson .10 .03
411 Tim Leary .10 .03
412 Jim Leyritz .10 .03
413 Melido Perez .10 .03
414 Scott Sanderson .10 .03
415 Andy Stankiewicz .10 .03
416 Mike Stanley .10 .03
417 Danny Tartabull .10 .03
418 Lance Blankenship .10 .03
419 Mike Bordick .10 .03
420 Scott Brosius RC .40 .12
421 Dennis Eckersley .20 .06
422 Scott Hemond .10 .03
423 Carney Lansford .20 .06
424 Henry Mercedes .10 .03
425 Mike Moore .10 .03
426 Gene Nelson .10 .03
427 Randy Ready .10 .03
428 Bruce Walton .10 .03
429 Willie Wilson .10 .03
430 Rich Amaral .10 .03
431 Dave Cochrane .10 .03
432 Henry Cotto .10 .03
433 Calvin Jones .10 .03
434 Kevin Mitchell .10 .03
435 Clay Parker .10 .03
436 Omar Vizquel .30 .09
437 Floyd Bannister .10 .03
438 Kevin Brown .20 .06
439 John Cangelosi .10 .03
440 Brian Downing .10 .03
441 Monty Fariss .10 .03
442 Jose Guzman .10 .03
443 Donald Harris .10 .03
444 Kevin Reimer .10 .03
445 Kenny Rogers .20 .06
446 Wayne Rosenthal .10 .03
447 Dickie Thon .10 .03
448 Derek Bell .20 .06
449 Juan Guzman .10 .03
450 Tom Henke .10 .03
451 Candy Maldonado .10 .03
452 Jack Morris .20 .06
453 David Wells .20 .06
454 Dave Winfield .20 .06
455 Juan Berenguer .10 .03
456 Damon Berryhill .10 .03
457 Mike Bielecki .10 .03
458 Marvin Freeman .10 .03
459 Charlie Leibrandt .10 .03
460 Kent Mercker .10 .03
461 Otis Nixon .10 .03
462 Alejandro Pena .10 .03
463 Ben Rivera .10 .03
464 Deion Sanders .30 .09
465 Mark Wohlers .10 .03
466 Shawn Boskie .10 .03
467 Frank Castillo .10 .03
468 Andre Dawson .20 .06
469 Joe Girardi .10 .03
470 Chuck McElroy .10 .03
471 Mike Morgan .10 .03
472 Ken Patterson .10 .03
473 Bob Scanlan .10 .03
474 Gary Scott .10 .03
475 Dave Smith .10 .03
476 Sammy Sosa .75 .23
477 Hector Villanueva .10 .03
478 Scott Bankhead .10 .03
479 Tim Belcher .10 .03
480 Freddie Benavides .10 .03
481 Jacob Brumfield .10 .03
482 Norm Charlton .10 .03
483 Dwayne Henry .10 .03
484 Dave Martinez .10 .03
485 Bip Roberts .10 .03
486 Reggie Sanders .10 .03
487 Greg Swindell .10 .03
488 Ryan Bowen .10 .03
489 Casey Candaele .10 .03
490 Juan Guerrero UER .10 .03
(photo on front is Andujar Cedeno
491 Pete Incaviglia .10 .03
492 Jeff Juden .10 .03

493 Rob Murphy .10 .03
494 Mark Portugal .10 .03
495 Rafael Ramirez .10 .03
496 Scott Servais .10 .03
497 Ed Taubensee RC .25 .07
498 Brian Williams RC .10 .03
499 Todd Benzinger .10 .03
500 John Candelaria .10 .03
501 Tom Candiotti .10 .03
502 Tim Crews .10 .03
503 Eric Davis .20 .06
504 Jim Gott .10 .03
505 Dave Hansen .10 .03
506 Carlos Hernandez .10 .03
507 Orel Hershiser .20 .06
508 Eric Karros .20 .06
509 Bob Ojeda .10 .03
510 Steve Wilson .10 .03
511 Moises Alou .20 .06
512 Bret Barberie .10 .03
513 Ivan Calderon .10 .03
514 Gary Carter .20 .06
515 Archi Cianfrocco RC .10 .03
516 Jeff Fassero .10 .03
517 Darrin Fletcher .10 .03
518 Marquis Grissom .20 .06
519 Chris Haney .10 .03
520 Ken Hill .10 .03
521 Chris Nabholz .10 .03
522 Bill Sampen .10 .03
523 John Vander Wal .10 .03
524 Dave Wainhouse .10 .03
525 Larry Walker .30 .09
526 John Wetteland .20 .06
527 Bobby Bonilla .20 .06
528 Sid Fernandez .10 .03
529 John Franco .20 .06
530 Dave Gallagher .10 .03
531 Paul Gibson .10 .03
532 Eddie Murray .50 .15
533 Junior Noboa .10 .03
534 Charlie O'Brien .10 .03
535 Bill Pecota .10 .03
536 Willie Randolph .20 .06
537 Bret Saberhagen .20 .06
538 Dick Schofield .10 .03
539 Pete Schourek .10 .03
540 Ruben Amaro .10 .03
541 Andy Ashby .10 .03
542 Kim Batiste .10 .03
543 Cliff Brantley .10 .03
544 Mariano Duncan .10 .03
545 Jeff Grotewold .10 .03
546 Barry Jones .10 .03
547 Julio Peguero .10 .03
548 Curt Schilling .30 .09
549 Mitch Williams .10 .03
550 Stan Belinda .10 .03
551 Scott Bullett RC .10 .03
552 Cecil Espy .10 .03
553 Jeff King .10 .03
554 Roger Mason .10 .03
555 Paul Miller .10 .03
556 Denny Neagle .20 .06
557 Vicente Palacios .10 .03
558 Bob Patterson .10 .03
559 Tom Prince .10 .03
560 Gary Redus .10 .03
561 Gary Varsho .10 .03
562 Juan Agosto .10 .03
563 Cris Carpenter .10 .03
564 Mark Clark RC .25 .07
565 Jose DeLeon .10 .03
566 Rich Gedman .10 .03
567 Bernard Gilkey .10 .03
568 Rex Hudler .10 .03
569 Tim Jones .10 .03
570 Donovan Osborne .10 .03
571 Mike Perez .10 .03
572 Gerald Perry .10 .03
573 Bob Tewksbury .10 .03
574 Todd Worrell .10 .03
575 Dave Eiland .10 .03
576 Jeremy Hernandez RC .10 .03
577 Craig Lefferts .10 .03
578 Jose Melendez .10 .03
579 Randy Myers .10 .03
580 Gary Pettis .10 .03
581 Rich Rodriguez .10 .03
582 Gary Sheffield .20 .06
583 Craig Shipley .10 .03
584 Kurt Stillwell .10 .03
585 Tim Teufel .10 .03
586 Rod Beck RC .40 .12
587 Dave Burba .10 .03
588 Craig Colbert .10 .03
589 Bryan Hickerson RC .10 .03
590 Mike Jackson .10 .03
591 Mark Leonard .10 .03
592 Jim McNamara .10 .03
593 John Patterson RC .10 .03
594 Dave Righetti .20 .06
595 Cory Snyder .10 .03
596 Bill Swift .10 .03
597 Ted Wood .10 .03
598 Checklist 301-400 .10 .03
599 Checklist 401-500 .10 .03
600 Checklist 501-600 .10 .03

1992 Ultra All-Rookies

Cards from this ten-card standard-size set highlighting a selection of top rookies were randomly inserted in 1992 Ultra II foil packs.

Nm-Mt Ex-Mt
COMPLETE SET (10) 6.00 1.80
1 Eric Karros 1.00 .30
2 Andy Stankiewicz .50 .15
3 Gary DiSarcina .50 .15
4 Archi Cianfrocco .50 .15
5 Jim McNamara .50 .15
6 Chad Curtis 1.25 .35
7 Kenny Lofton 1.50 .45
8 Reggie Sanders .50 .15
9 Pat Mahomes 1.25 .35
10 Donovan Osborne .50 .15

1992 Ultra All-Stars

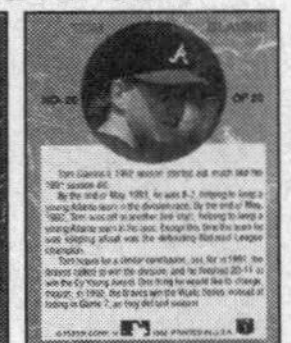

Featuring many of the 1992 season's stars, cards from this 20-card standard-size set were randomly inserted in 1992 Ultra II foil packs.

Nm-Mt Ex-Mt
COMPLETE SET (20) 25.00 7.50
1 Mark McGwire 4.00 1.20
2 Roberto Alomar 1.00 .30
3 Cal Ripken Jr. 5.00 1.50
4 Wade Boggs 1.00 .30
5 Mickey Tettleton .30 .09
6 Ken Griffey Jr. 2.50 .75
7 Roberto Kelly .30 .09
8 Kirby Puckett 1.50 .45
9 Frank Thomas 1.50 .45
10 Jack McDowell .30 .09
11 Will Clark 1.50 .45
12 Ryne Sandberg 2.50 .75
13 Barry Larkin 1.00 .30
14 Gary Sheffield .60 .18
15 Tom Pagnozzi .30 .09
16 Barry Bonds 4.00 1.20
17 Deion Sanders 1.00 .30
18 Darryl Strawberry .60 .18
19 David Cone .60 .18
20 Tom Glavine 1.00 .30

1992 Ultra Award Winners

This 25-card standard-size set features 18 Gold Glove winners, both Cy Young Award winners, both Rookies of the Year, both league MVP's, and the World Series MVP. The cards were randomly inserted in 1992 Fleer Ultra I packs.

Nm-Mt Ex-Mt
COMPLETE SET (25) 40.00 12.00
1 Jack Morris 1.00 .30
2 Chuck Knoblauch 1.00 .30
3 Jeff Bagwell 2.50 .75
4 Terry Pendleton 1.00 .30
5 Cal Ripken 8.00 2.40
6 Roger Clemens 5.00 1.50
7 Tom Glavine 1.50 .45
8 Tom Pagnozzi .50 .15
9 Ozzie Smith 4.00 1.20
10 Andy Van Slyke 1.00 .30
11 Barry Bonds 6.00 1.80
12 Tony Gwynn 3.00 .90
13 Matt Williams 1.00 .30
14 Will Clark 2.50 .75
15 Robin Ventura 1.00 .30
16 Mark Langston .50 .15
17 Tony Pena .50 .15
18 Devon White 1.00 .30
19 Don Mattingly 6.00 1.80
20 Roberto Alomar 1.50 .45
21A Cal Ripken ERR 8.00 2.40
(Reversed negative
on card back)
21B Cal Ripken COR 8.00 2.40
22 Ken Griffey Jr. 4.00 1.20
23 Kirby Puckett 2.50 .75
24 Greg Maddux 4.00 1.20
25 Ryne Sandberg 4.00 1.20

1992 Ultra Gwynn

Tony Gwynn served as a spokesperson for Ultra during 1992 and was the exclusive subject of this 12-card standard-size set. The first ten cards of this set were randomly inserted in 1992 Ultra one packs. More than 2,000 of these cards were personally autographed by Gwynn. These cards are numbered on the back as "X of 10." An additional special two-card subset was available through a mail-in offer for ten 1992 Ultra baseball wrappers plus 1.00 for shipping and handling. This offer was good through October 31st and, according to Fleer, over 100,000 sets were produced. The standard-size cards display action shots of Gwynn framed by green marbled borders. The player's name and the words "Commemorative Series" appear in gold-foil lettering in the bottom border. On a green marbled background, the backs features a color head shot and either a player profile (Special No. 1 on the card back) or Gwynn's comments about other players or the game itself (Special No. 2 on the card back).

Nm-Mt Ex-Mt
COMPLETE SET (10) 10.00 3.00
COMMON GWYNN (1-10) 1.00 .30
COMMON MAIL(S1-S2) 1.00 .30
AU Tony Gwynn AU 80.00 24.00
(Autographed with
certified signature)

1993 Ultra

The 1993 Ultra baseball set was issued in two series and totaled 650 standard-size cards. The cards are numbered on the back, grouped alphabetically within teams, with NL teams preceding AL. The first series closes with checklist cards (298-300). The second series features 83 Ultra Rookies, 51 Rockies and Marlins, traded veteran players, and other major league veterans not included in the first series. The Rookie cards show a gold foil stamped Rookie "flag" as part of the card design. The key Rookie Card in this set is Jim Edmonds.

Nm-Mt Ex-Mt
COMPLETE SET (650) 30.00 9.00
COMP. SERIES 1 (300) 15.00 4.50
COMP. SERIES 2 (350) 15.00 4.50
1 Steve Avery .15 .04
2 Rafael Belliard .15 .04
3 Damon Berryhill .15 .04
4 Sid Bream .15 .04
5 Ron Gant .30 .09
6 Tom Glavine .50 .15
7 Ryan Klesko .30 .09
8 Mark Lemke .15 .04
9 Javier Lopez .50 .15
10 Greg Olson .15 .04
11 Terry Pendleton .30 .09
12 Deion Sanders .50 .15
13 Mike Stanton .15 .04
14 Paul Assenmacher .15 .04
15 Steve Buechele .15 .04
16 Frank Castillo .15 .04
17 Shawon Dunston .15 .04
18 Mark Grace .50 .15
19 Derrick May .15 .04
20 Chuck McElroy .15 .04
21 Mike Morgan .15 .04
22 Bob Scanlan .15 .04
23 Dwight Smith .15 .04
24 Sammy Sosa 1.25 .35
25 Rick Wilkins .15 .04
26 Tim Belcher .15 .04
27 Jeff Branson .15 .04
28 Bill Doran .15 .04
29 Chris Hammond .15 .04
30 Barry Larkin .50 .15
31 Hal Morris .15 .04
32 Joe Oliver .15 .04
33 Jose Rijo .15 .04
34 Bip Roberts .15 .04
35 Chris Sabo .15 .04
36 Reggie Sanders .15 .04
37 Craig Biggio .50 .15
38 Ken Caminiti .30 .09
39 Steve Finley .30 .09
40 Luis Gonzalez .30 .09
41 Juan Guerrero .15 .04
42 Pete Harnisch .15 .04
43 Xavier Hernandez .15 .04
44 Doug Jones .15 .04
45 Al Osuna .15 .04
46 Eddie Taubensee .15 .04
47 Scooter Tucker .15 .04
48 Brian Williams .15 .04
49 Pedro Astacio .15 .04
50 Rafael Bournigal .15 .04
51 Brett Butler .30 .09
52 Tom Candiotti .15 .04
53 Eric Davis .30 .09
54 Lenny Harris .15 .04
55 Orel Hershiser .30 .09
56 Eric Karros .30 .09
57 Pedro Martinez 1.50 .45
58 Roger McDowell .15 .04
59 Jose Offerman .15 .04
60 Mike Piazza 2.00 .60
61 Moises Alou .30 .09
62 Kent Bottenfield .15 .04
63 Archi Cianfrocco .15 .04
64 Greg Colbrunn .15 .04
65 Wil Cordero .15 .04
66 Delino DeShields .15 .04
67 Darrin Fletcher .15 .04
68 Ken Hill .15 .04
69 Chris Nabholz .15 .04
70 Mel Rojas .15 .04
71 Larry Walker .50 .15
72 Sid Fernandez .15 .04
73 John Franco .30 .09
74 Dave Gallagher .15 .04
75 Todd Hundley .15 .04
76 Howard Johnson .15 .04
77 Jeff Kent .75 .23
78 Eddie Murray .75 .23
79 Bret Saberhagen .30 .09
80 Chico Walker .15 .04
81 Anthony Young .15 .04
82 Kyle Abbott .15 .04
83 Ruben Amaro .15 .04
84 Juan Bell .15 .04
85 Wes Chamberlain .15 .04
86 Darren Daulton .30 .09
87 Mariano Duncan .15 .04
88 Dave Hollins .15 .04
89 Ricky Jordan .15 .04
90 John Kruk .30 .09
91 Mickey Morandini .15 .04
92 Terry Mulholland .15 .04
93 Ben Rivera .15 .04
94 Mike Williams .15 .04
95 Stan Belinda .15 .04
96 Jay Bell .30 .09
97 Jeff King .15 .04
98 Mike LaValliere .15 .04
99 Lloyd McClendon .15 .04
100 Orlando Merced .15 .04
101 Zane Smith .15 .04
102 Randy Tomlin .15 .04
103 Andy Van Slyke .30 .09
104 Tim Wakefield .75 .23
105 John Wehner .15 .04
106 Bernard Gilkey .15 .04
107 Brian Jordan .30 .09
108 Ray Lankford .15 .04
109 Donovan Osborne .15 .04
110 Tom Pagnozzi .15 .04
111 Mike Perez .15 .04
112 Lee Smith .30 .09
113 Ozzie Smith 1.25 .35
114 Bob Tewksbury .15 .04
115 Todd Zeile .15 .04
116 Andy Benes .15 .04
117 Greg W. Harris .15 .04
118 Darrin Jackson .15 .04
119 Fred McGriff .50 .15
120 Rich Rodriguez .15 .04
121 Frank Seminara .15 .04
122 Gary Sheffield .30 .09
123 Craig Shipley .15 .04
124 Kurt Stillwell .15 .04
125 Dan Walters .15 .04
126 Rod Beck .15 .04
127 Mike Benjamin .15 .04
128 Jeff Brantley .15 .04
129 John Burkett .15 .04
130 Will Clark .75 .23
131 Royce Clayton .15 .04
132 Steve Hosey .15 .04
133 Mike Jackson .15 .04
134 Darren Lewis .15 .04
135 Kirt Manwaring .15 .04
136 Bill Swift .15 .04
137 Robby Thompson .15 .04
138 Brady Anderson .30 .09
139 Glenn Davis .15 .04
140 Leo Gomez .15 .04
141 Chito Martinez .15 .04
142 Ben McDonald .15 .04
143 Alan Mills .15 .04
144 Mike Mussina .50 .15
145 Gregg Olson .15 .04
146 David Segui .15 .04
147 Jeff Tackett .15 .04
148 Jack Clark .30 .09
149 Scott Cooper .15 .04
150 Danny Darwin .15 .04
151 John Dopson .15 .04
152 Mike Greenwell .15 .04
153 Tim Naehring .15 .04
154 Tony Pena .15 .04
155 Paul Quantrill .15 .04
156 Mo Vaughn .30 .09
157 Frank Viola .30 .09
158 Bob Zupcic .15 .04
159 Chad Curtis .15 .04
160 Gary DiSarcina .15 .04
161 Damion Easley .15 .04
162 Chuck Finley .30 .09
163 Tim Fortugno .15 .04
164 Rene Gonzales .15 .04
165 Joe Grahe .15 .04
166 Mark Langston .15 .04
167 John Orton .15 .04
168 Luis Polonia .15 .04
169 Julio Valera .15 .04
170 Wilson Alvarez .15 .04
171 George Bell .15 .04
172 Joey Cora .15 .04
173 Alex Fernandez .15 .04
174 Lance Johnson .15 .04
175 Ron Karkovice .15 .04
176 Jack McDowell .15 .04
177 Scott Radinsky .15 .04
178 Tim Raines .30 .09
179 Steve Sax .15 .04
180 Bobby Thigpen .15 .04
181 Frank Thomas .75 .23
182 Sandy Alomar Jr. .15 .04
183 Carlos Baerga .15 .04
184 Felix Fermin .15 .04
185 Thomas Howard .15 .04
186 Mark Lewis .15 .04
187 Derek Lilliquist .15 .04
188 Carlos Martinez .15 .04
189 Charles Nagy .15 .04
190 Scott Scudder .15 .04
191 Paul Sorrento .15 .04
192 Jim Thome .75 .23
193 Mark Whiten .15 .04
194 Milt Cuyler UER .15 .04
(Reversed negative
on card front)
195 Rob Deer .15 .04
196 John Doherty .15 .04
197 Travis Fryman .30 .09
198 Dan Gladden .15 .04
199 Mike Henneman .15 .04
200 John Kiely .15 .04
201 Chad Kreuter .15 .04
202 Scott Livingstone .15 .04
203 Tony Phillips .15 .04
204 Alan Trammell .30 .09
205 Mike Boddicker .15 .04
206 George Brett 2.00 .60
207 Tom Gordon .15 .04
208 Mark Gubicza .15 .04
209 Gregg Jefferies .15 .04
210 Wally Joyner .30 .09
211 Kevin Koslofski .15 .04
212 Brent Mayne .15 .04
213 Brian McRae .15 .04
214 Kevin McReynolds .15 .04
215 Rusty Meacham .15 .04
216 Steve Shifflett .15 .04
217 Jim Austin .15 .04
218 Cal Eldred .15 .04
219 Darryl Hamilton .15 .04
220 Doug Henry .15 .04
221 John Jaha .15 .04
222 Dave Nilsson .15 .04
223 Jesse Orosco .15 .04
224 B.J. Surhoff .30 .09
225 Greg Vaughn .15 .04
226 Bill Wegman .15 .04
227 Robin Yount UER 1.25 .35
Born in Illinois,
not in Virginia
228 Rick Aguilera .15 .04
229 J.T. Bruett .15 .04
230 Scott Erickson .15 .04
231 Kent Hrbek .30 .09
232 Terry Jorgensen .15 .04
233 Scott Leius .15 .04
234 Pat Mahomes .15 .04
235 Pedro Munoz .15 .04
236 Kirby Puckett .75 .23
237 Kevin Tapani .15 .04
238 Lenny Webster .15 .04
239 Carl Willis .15 .04
240 Mike Gallego .15 .04
241 John Habyan .15 .04
242 Pat Kelly .15 .04
243 Kevin Maas .15 .04
244 Don Mattingly 2.00 .60
245 Hensley Meulens .15 .04
246 Sam Militello .15 .04
247 Matt Nokes .15 .04
248 Melido Perez .15 .04
249 Andy Stankiewicz .15 .04
250 Randy Velarde .15 .04
251 Bob Wickman .15 .04
252 Bernie Williams .50 .15
253 Lance Blankenship .15 .04
254 Mike Bordick .15 .04
255 Jerry Browne .15 .04
256 Ron Darling .15 .04
257 Dennis Eckersley .30 .09
258 Rickey Henderson .75 .23
259 Vince Horsman .15 .04
260 Troy Neel .15 .04
261 Jeff Parrett .15 .04
262 Terry Steinbach .15 .04
263 Bob Welch .15 .04
264 Bobby Witt .15 .04
265 Rich Amaral .15 .04
266 Bret Boone .50 .15
267 Jay Buhner .30 .09
268 Dave Fleming .15 .04
269 Randy Johnson .75 .23
270 Edgar Martinez .50 .15
271 Mike Schooler .15 .04
272 Russ Swan .15 .04
273 Dave Valle .15 .04
274 Omar Vizquel .50 .15
275 Kerry Woodson .15 .04
276 Kevin Brown .30 .09
277 Julio Franco .30 .09
278 Jeff Frye .15 .04
279 Juan Gonzalez .50 .15
280 Jeff Huson .15 .04
281 Rafael Palmeiro .50 .15
282 Dean Palmer .30 .09
283 Roger Pavlik .15 .04
284 Ivan Rodriguez .75 .23
285 Kenny Rogers .30 .09
286 Derek Bell .15 .04
287 Pat Borders .15 .04
288 Joe Carter .30 .09
289 Bob MacDonald .15 .04
290 Jack Morris .30 .09
291 John Olerud .30 .09
292 Ed Sprague .15 .04
293 Todd Stottlemyre .15 .04
294 Mike Timlin .15 .04
295 Duane Ward .15 .04
296 David Wells .30 .09
297 Devon White .30 .09
298 Ray Lankford CL .15 .04
299 Bobby Witt CL .15 .04
300 Mike Piazza CL .75 .23
301 Steve Bedrosian .15 .04
302 Jeff Blauser .15 .04
303 Francisco Cabrera .15 .04
304 Marvin Freeman .15 .04
305 Brian Hunter .15 .04
306 David Justice .30 .09
307 Greg Maddux 1.25 .35
308 Greg McMichael RC .30 .09
309 Kent Mercker .15 .04
310 Otis Nixon .15 .04
311 Pete Smith .15 .04
312 John Smoltz .50 .15
313 Jose Guzman .15 .04
314 Mike Harkey .15 .04
315 Greg Hibbard .15 .04
316 Candy Maldonado .15 .04
317 Randy Myers .15 .04
318 Dan Plesac .15 .04
319 Rey Sanchez .15 .04
320 Ryne Sandberg 1.25 .35
321 Tommy Shields .15 .04
322 Jose Vizcaino .15 .04
323 Matt Walbeck RC .30 .09
324 Willie Wilson .15 .04
325 Tom Browning .15 .04
326 Tim Costo .15 .04
327 Rob Dibble .30 .09
328 Steve Foster .15 .04
329 Roberto Kelly .15 .04
330 Randy Milligan .15 .04
331 Kevin Mitchell .15 .04
332 Tim Pugh RC .30 .09
333 Jeff Reardon .30 .09
334 John Roper .15 .04
335 Juan Samuel .15 .04
336 John Smiley .15 .04
337 Dan Wilson .30 .09
338 Scott Aldred .15 .04
339 Andy Ashby .15 .04
340 Freddie Benavides .15 .04
341 Dante Bichette .30 .09
342 Willie Blair .15 .04

343 Daryl Boston .15 .04
344 Vinny Castilla .30 .09
345 Jerald Clark .15 .04
346 Alex Cole .15 .04
347 Andres Galarraga .30 .09
348 Joe Girardi .15 .04
349 Ryan Hawblitzel .15 .04
350 Charlie Hayes .15 .04
351 Butch Henry .15 .04
352 Darren Holmes .15 .04
353 Dale Murphy .75 .23
354 David Nied .15 .04
355 Jeff Parrett .15 .04
356 Steve Reed RC .30 .09
357 Bruce Ruffin .15 .04
358 Danny Sheaffer RC .30 .09
359 Bryn Smith .15 .04
360 Jim Tatum RC .30 .09
361 Eric Young .15 .04
362 Gerald Young .15 .04
363 Luis Aquino .15 .04
364 Alex Arias .15 .04
365 Jack Armstrong .15 .04
366 Bret Barberie .15 .04
367 Ryan Bowen .15 .04
368 Greg Briley .15 .04
369 Cris Carpenter .15 .04
370 Chuck Carr .15 .04
371 Jeff Conine .30 .09
372 Steve Decker .15 .04
373 Orestes Destrade .15 .04
374 Monty Fariss .15 .04
375 Junior Felix .15 .04
376 Chris Hammond .15 .04
377 Bryan Harvey .15 .04
378 Trevor Hoffman .30 .09
379 Charlie Hough .30 .09
380 Joe Klink .15 .04
381 Richie Lewis RC .30 .09
382 Dave Magadan .15 .04
383 Bob McClure .15 .04
384 Scott Pose RC .30 .09
385 Rich Renteria .15 .04
386 Benito Santiago .30 .09
387 Walt Weiss .15 .04
388 Nigel Wilson .15 .04
389 Eric Anthony .15 .04
390 Jeff Bagwell .50 .15
391 Andujar Cedeno .15 .04
392 Doug Drabek .15 .04
393 Darryl Kile .30 .09
394 Mark Portugal .15 .04
395 Karl Rhodes .15 .04
396 Scott Servais .15 .04
397 Greg Swindell .15 .04
398 Tom Goodwin .15 .04
399 Kevin Gross .15 .04
400 Carlos Hernandez .15 .04
401 Ramon Martinez .15 .04
402 Raul Mondesi .30 .09
403 Jody Reed .15 .04
404 Mike Sharperson .15 .04
405 Cory Snyder .15 .04
406 Darryl Strawberry .30 .09
407 Rick Trlicek .15 .04
408 Tim Wallach .15 .04
409 Todd Worrell .15 .04
410 Tavo Alvarez .15 .04
411 Sean Berry .15 .04
412 Frank Bolick .15 .04
413 Cliff Floyd .30 .09
414 Mike Gardiner .15 .04
415 Marquis Grissom .30 .09
416 Tim Laker RC .30 .09
417 Mike Lansing RC .50 .15
418 Dennis Martinez .30 .09
419 John Vander Wal .15 .04
420 John Wetteland .30 .09
421 Rondell White .30 .09
422 Bobby Bonilla .30 .09
423 Jeromy Burnitz .30 .09
424 Vince Coleman .15 .04
425 Mike Draper .15 .04
426 Tony Fernandez .15 .04
427 Dwight Gooden .30 .09
428 Jeff Innis .15 .04
429 Bobby Jones .30 .09
430 Mike Maddux .15 .04
431 Charlie O'Brien .15 .04
432 Joe Orsulak .15 .04
433 Pete Schourek .15 .04
434 Frank Tanana .15 .04
435 Ryan Thompson .15 .04
436 Kim Batiste .15 .04
437 Mark Davis .15 .04
438 Jose DeLeon .15 .04
439 Len Dykstra .30 .09
440 Jim Eisenreich .15 .04
441 Tommy Greene .15 .04
442 Pete Incaviglia .15 .04
443 Danny Jackson .15 .04
444 Todd Pratt RC .50 .15
445 Curt Schilling .30 .09
446 Milt Thompson .15 .04
447 David West .15 .04
448 Mitch Williams .15 .04
449 Steve Cooke .15 .04
450 Carlos Garcia .15 .04
451 Al Martin .15 .04
452 Blas Minor .15 .04
453 Dennis Moeller .15 .04
454 Denny Neagle .30 .09
455 Don Slaught .15 .04
456 Lonnie Smith .15 .04
457 Paul Wagner .15 .04
458 Bob Walk .15 .04
459 Kevin Young .30 .09
460 Rene Arocha RC .50 .15
461 Brian Barber .15 .04
462 Rheal Cormier .15 .04
463 Gregg Jefferies .15 .04
464 Joe Magrane .15 .04
465 Omar Olivares .15 .04
466 Geronimo Pena .15 .04
467 Allen Watson .15 .04
468 Mark Whiten .15 .04
469 Derek Bell .15 .04
470 Phil Clark .15 .04
471 Pat Gomez RC .30 .09
472 Tony Gwynn 1.00 .30
473 Jeremy Hernandez .15 .04
474 Bruce Hurst .15 .04
475 Phil Plantier .15 .04
476 Scott Sanders RC .30 .09
477 Tim Scott .15 .04
478 Darrell Sherman RC .30 .09
479 Guillermo Velasquez .15 .04
480 Tim Worrell RC .30 .09
481 Todd Benzinger .15 .04
482 Bud Black .15 .04
483 Barry Bonds 2.00 .60
484 Dave Burba .15 .04
485 Bryan Hickerson .15 .04
486 Dave Martinez .15 .04
487 Willie McGee .30 .09
488 Jeff Reed .15 .04
489 Kevin Rogers .15 .04
490 Matt Williams .30 .09
491 Trevor Wilson .15 .04
492 Harold Baines .30 .09
493 Mike Devereaux .15 .04
494 Todd Frohwirth .15 .04
495 Chris Hoiles .15 .04
496 Luis Mercedes .15 .04
497 Sherman Obando RC .30 .09
498 Brad Pennington .15 .04
499 Harold Reynolds .30 .09
500 Arthur Rhodes .15 .04
501 Cal Ripken 2.50 .75
502 Rick Sutcliffe .30 .09
503 Fernando Valenzuela .30 .09
504 Mark Williamson .15 .04
505 Scott Bankhead .15 .04
506 Greg Blosser .15 .04
507 Ivan Calderon .15 .04
508 Roger Clemens 1.50 .45
509 Andre Dawson .30 .09
510 Scott Fletcher .15 .04
511 Greg A. Harris .15 .04
512 Billy Hatcher .15 .04
513 Bob Melvin .15 .04
514 Carlos Quintana .15 .04
515 Luis Rivera .15 .04
516 Jeff Russell .15 .04
517 Ken Ryan RC .30 .09
518 Chili Davis .30 .09
519 Jim Edmonds RC 5.00 1.50
520 Gary Gaetti .30 .09
521 Torey Lovullo .15 .04
522 Troy Percival .50 .15
523 Tim Salmon .50 .15
524 Scott Sanderson .15 .04
525 J.T. Snow RC .75 .23
526 Jerome Walton .15 .04
527 Jason Bere .15 .04
528 Rod Bolton .15 .04
529 Ellis Burks .30 .09
530 Carlton Fisk .50 .15
531 Craig Grebeck .15 .04
532 Ozzie Guillen .15 .04
533 Roberto Hernandez .15 .04
534 Bo Jackson .75 .23
535 Kirk McCaskill .15 .04
536 Dave Stieb .15 .04
537 Robin Ventura .30 .09
538 Albert Belle .30 .09
539 Mike Bielecki .15 .04
540 Glenallen Hill .15 .04
541 Reggie Jefferson .15 .04
542 Kenny Lofton .30 .09
543 Jeff Mutis .15 .04
544 Junior Ortiz .15 .04
545 Manny Ramirez .75 .23
546 Jeff Treadway .15 .04
547 Kevin Wickander .15 .04
548 Cecil Fielder .30 .09
549 Kirk Gibson .30 .09
550 Greg Gohr .15 .04
551 David Haas .15 .04
552 Bill Krueger .15 .04
553 Mike Moore .15 .04
554 Mickey Tettleton .15 .04
555 Lou Whitaker .30 .09
556 Kevin Appier .30 .09
557 Billy Brewer .15 .04
558 David Cone .30 .09
559 Greg Gagne .15 .04
560 Mark Gardner .15 .04
561 Phil Hiatt .15 .04
562 Felix Jose .15 .04
563 Jose Lind .15 .04
564 Mike Macfarlane .15 .04
565 Keith Miller .15 .04
566 Jeff Montgomery .15 .04
567 Hipolito Pichardo .15 .04
568 Ricky Bones .15 .04
569 Tom Brunansky .15 .04
570 Joe Kmak .15 .04
571 Pat Listach .15 .04
572 Graeme Lloyd RC .50 .15
573 Carlos Maldonado .15 .04
574 Josias Manzanillo .15 .04
575 Matt Mieske .15 .04
576 Kevin Reimer .15 .04
577 Bill Spiers .15 .04
578 Dickie Thon .15 .04
579 Willie Banks .15 .04
580 Jim Deshaies .15 .04
581 Mark Guthrie .15 .04
582 Brian Harper .15 .04
583 Chuck Knoblauch .30 .09
584 Gene Larkin .15 .04
585 Shane Mack .15 .04
586 David McCarty .15 .04
587 Mike Pagliarulo .15 .04
588 Mike Trombley .15 .04
589 Dave Winfield .30 .09
590 Jim Abbott .50 .15
591 Wade Boggs .50 .15
592 Russ Davis RC .30 .09
593 Steve Farr .15 .04
594 Steve Howe .15 .04
595 Mike Humphreys .15 .04
596 Jimmy Key .30 .09
597 Jim Leyritz .15 .04
598 Bobby Munoz .15 .04
599 Paul O'Neill .50 .15
600 Spike Owen .15 .04
601 Mike Stanley .15 .04
602 Danny Tartabull .15 .04
603 Scott Brosius .30 .09
604 Storm Davis .15 .04
605 Eric Fox .15 .04
606 Rich Gossage .30 .09
607 Scott Hemond .15 .04
608 Dave Henderson .15 .04
609 Mark McGwire 2.00 .60
610 Mike Mohler RC .30 .09
611 Edwin Nunez .15 .04
612 Kevin Seitzer .15 .04
613 Ruben Sierra .15 .04
614 Chris Bosio .15 .04
615 Norm Charlton .15 .04
616 Jim Converse RC .30 .09
617 John Cummings RC .30 .09
618 Mike Felder .15 .04
619 Ken Griffey Jr. 1.25 .35
620 Mike Hampton .30 .09
621 Erik Hanson .15 .04
622 Bill Haselman .15 .04
623 Tino Martinez .50 .15
624 Lee Tinsley .15 .04
625 Fernando Vina RC .75 .23
626 David Wainhouse .15 .04
627 Jose Canseco .75 .23
628 Benji Gil .15 .04
629 Tom Henke .15 .04
630 David Hulse RC .30 .09
631 Manuel Lee .15 .04
632 Craig Lefferts .15 .04
633 Robb Nen .30 .09
634 Gary Redus .15 .04
635 Bill Ripken .15 .04
636 Nolan Ryan 3.00 .90
637 Dan Smith .15 .04
638 Matt Whiteside RC .30 .09
639 Roberto Alomar .50 .15
640 Juan Guzman .15 .04
641 Pat Hentgen .15 .04
642 Darrin Jackson .15 .04
643 Randy Knorr .15 .04
644 Domingo Martinez RC .30 .09
645 Paul Molitor .50 .15
646 Dick Schofield .15 .04
647 Dave Stewart .30 .09
648 Rey Sanchez CL .15 .04
649 Jeremy Hernandez CL .15 .04
650 Junior Ortiz CL .15 .04

1993 Ultra All-Rookies

Inserted into series II packs at a rate of one in 18, this ten-card standard-size set features cutout color player action shots that are superposed upon a black background, which carries the player's uniform number, position, team name, and the set's title in multicolored lettering. The set is sequenced in alphabetical order. The key cards in this set are Mike Piazza and Tim Salmon.

	Nm-Mt	Ex-Mt
COMPLETE SET (10)	15.00	4.50
1 Rene Arocha	2.00	.60
2 Jeff Conine	1.25	.35
3 Phil Hiatt	.60	.18
4 Mike Lansing	2.00	.60
5 Al Martin	.60	.18
6 David Nied	.60	.18
7 Mike Piazza	8.00	2.40
8 Tim Salmon	2.00	.60
9 J.T. Snow	3.00	.90
10 Kevin Young	1.25	.35

1993 Ultra All-Stars

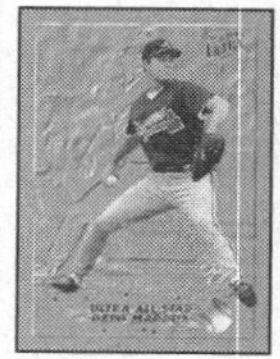
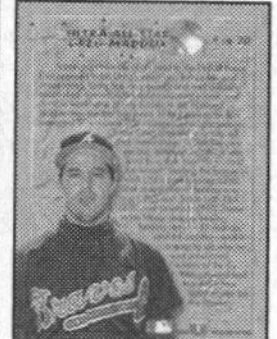

Inserted into series II packs at a rate of one in nine, this 20-card standard-size set features National League (1-10) and American League (11-20) All-Stars.

	Nm-Mt	Ex-Mt
COMPLETE SET (20)	40.00	12.00
1 Darren Daulton	1.25	.35
2 Will Clark	3.00	.90
3 Ryne Sandberg	5.00	1.50
4 Barry Larkin	2.00	.60
5 Gary Sheffield	1.25	.35
6 Barry Bonds	8.00	2.40
7 Ray Lankford	.60	.18
8 Larry Walker	2.00	.60
9 Greg Maddux	5.00	1.50
10 Lee Smith	1.25	.35
11 Ivan Rodriguez	3.00	.90
12 Mark McGwire	8.00	2.40
13 Carlos Baerga	.60	.18
14 Cal Ripken	10.00	3.00
15 Edgar Martinez	2.00	.60
16 Juan Gonzalez	2.00	.60
17 Ken Griffey Jr.	5.00	1.50
18 Kirby Puckett	3.00	.90
19 Frank Thomas	3.00	.90
20 Mike Mussina	2.00	.60

1993 Ultra Award Winners

Randomly inserted in first series packs, this 25-card standard-size insert set of 1993 Ultra Award

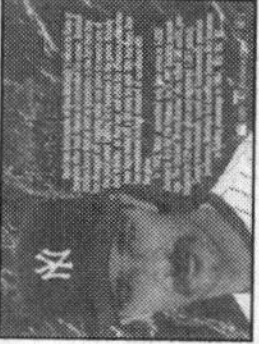

Winners honors the Top Glove for the National (1-9) and American (10-18) Leagues and other major award winners (19-25).

	Nm-Mt	Ex-Mt
COMPLETE SET (25)	40.00	12.00
1 Greg Maddux	5.00	1.50
2 Tom Pagnozzi	.60	.18
3 Mark Grace	2.00	.60
4 Jose Lind	.60	.18
5 Terry Pendleton	1.25	.35
6 Ozzie Smith	5.00	1.50
7 Barry Bonds	8.00	2.40
8 Andy Van Slyke	1.25	.35
9 Larry Walker	2.00	.60
10 Mark Langston	.60	.18
11 Ivan Rodriguez	3.00	.90
12 Don Mattingly	8.00	2.40
13 Roberto Alomar	2.00	.60
14 Robin Ventura	1.25	.35
15 Cal Ripken	10.00	3.00
16 Ken Griffey	5.00	1.50
17 Kirby Puckett	3.00	.90
18 Devon White	1.25	.35
19 Pat Listach	.60	.18
20 Eric Karros	1.25	.35
21 Pat Borders	.60	.18
22 Greg Maddux	5.00	1.50
23 Dennis Eckersley	1.25	.35
24 Barry Bonds	8.00	2.40
25 Gary Sheffield	1.25	.35

1993 Ultra Eckersley

Randomly inserted in first series foil packs, this 10-card (cards 11 and 12 were mail-aways) standard-size set salutes one of baseball's greatest relief pitchers, Dennis Eckersley. Two additional cards (11 and 12) were available through a mail-in offer for ten 1993 Fleer Ultra baseball wrappers plus 1.00 for postage and handling. The expiration for this offer was September 30, 1993. Eckersley personally autographed more than 2,000 of these cards. The cards feature silver foil stamping on both sides.

	Nm-Mt	Ex-Mt
COMPLETE SET (10)	4.00	1.20
COMMON CARD (1-10)	.50	.15
COMMON MAIL (11-12)	1.00	.30
P1 Dennis Eckersley Paul Mullan Promo	4.00	1.20
AU Dennis Eckersley AU (Certified autograph)	50.00	15.00

1993 Ultra Home Run Kings

Randomly inserted into all 1993 Ultra packs, this ten-card standard-size set features the best long ball hitters in baseball.

	Nm-Mt	Ex-Mt
COMPLETE SET (10)	20.00	6.00
1 Juan Gonzalez	2.50	.75
2 Mark McGwire	10.00	3.00
3 Cecil Fielder	1.50	.45
4 Fred McGriff	2.50	.75
5 Albert Belle	1.50	.45
6 Barry Bonds	10.00	3.00
7 Joe Carter	1.50	.45
8 Gary Sheffield	1.50	.45
9 Darren Daulton	1.50	.45
10 Dave Hollins	.75	.23

1993 Ultra Performers

This ten-card standard-size set could only be ordered directly from Fleer by sending in 9.95, five Fleer/Ultra baseball wrappers, and an order blank found in hobby and sports periodicals.

	Nm-Mt	Ex-Mt
COMPLETE SET (10)	20.00	6.00
1 Barry Bonds	5.00	1.50
2 Juan Gonzalez	1.25	.35
3 Ken Griffey Jr.	3.00	.90
4 Eric Karros	.75	.23
5 Pat Listach	.40	.12
6 Greg Maddux	3.00	.90
7 David Nied	.40	.12
8 Gary Sheffield	.75	.23
9 J.T. Snow	2.00	.60
10 Frank Thomas	2.00	.60

1993 Ultra Strikeout Kings

Inserted into series II packs at a rate of one in 37, this five-card standard-size showcases outstanding pitchers from both leagues.

	Nm-Mt	Ex-Mt
COMPLETE SET (5)	25.00	7.50
1 Roger Clemens	10.00	3.00
2 Juan Guzman	1.00	.30
3 Randy Johnson	5.00	1.50
4 Nolan Ryan	20.00	6.00
5 John Smoltz	3.00	.90

1994 Ultra

The 1994 Ultra baseball set consists of 600 standard-size cards that were issued in two series of 300. Each pack contains at least one insert card, while "Hot Packs" have nothing but insert cards in them. The cards are numbered on the back, grouped alphabetically within teams, and checklisted below alphabetically according to teams for each league with AL preceding NL. Rookie Cards include Ray Durham and Chan Ho Park.

	Nm-Mt	Ex-Mt
COMPLETE SET (600)	30.00	9.00
COMP. SERIES 1 (300)	15.00	4.50
COMP. SERIES 2 (300)	15.00	4.50
1 Jeffrey Hammonds	.15	.04
2 Chris Hoiles	.15	.04
3 Ben McDonald	.15	.04
4 Mark McLemore	.15	.04
5 Alan Mills	.15	.04
6 Jamie Moyer	.30	.09
7 Brad Pennington	.15	.04
8 Jim Poole	.15	.04
9 Cal Ripken Jr.	2.50	.75
10 Jack Voigt	.15	.04
11 Roger Clemens	1.50	.45
12 Danny Darwin	.15	.04
13 Andre Dawson	.30	.09
14 Scott Fletcher	.15	.04
15 Greg A. Harris	.15	.04
16 Billy Hatcher	.15	.04
17 Jeff Russell	.15	.04
18 Aaron Sele	.15	.04
19 Mo Vaughn	.30	.09
20 Mike Butcher	.15	.04
21 Rod Correia	.15	.04
22 Steve Frey	.15	.04
23 Phil Leftwich RC	.15	.04
24 Torey Lovullo	.15	.04
25 Ken Patterson	.15	.04
26 Eduardo Perez UER (listed as a Twin instead of Angel)	.15	.04
27 Tim Salmon	.50	.15
28 J.T. Snow	.30	.09
29 Chris Turner	.15	.04
30 Wilson Alvarez	.15	.04
31 Jason Bere	.15	.04
32 Joey Cora	.15	.04
33 Alex Fernandez	.15	.04
34 Roberto Hernandez	.15	.04
35 Lance Johnson	.15	.04
36 Ron Karkovice	.15	.04
37 Kirk McCaskill	.15	.04
38 Jeff Schwarz	.15	.04
39 Frank Thomas	.75	.23
40 Sandy Alomar Jr.	.15	.04
41 Albert Belle	.30	.09
42 Felix Fermin	.15	.04
43 Wayne Kirby	.15	.04
44 Tom Kramer	.15	.04
45 Kenny Lofton	.30	.09
46 Jose Mesa	.15	.04
47 Eric Plunk	.15	.04
48 Paul Sorrento	.15	.04
49 Jim Thome	.75	.23
50 Bill Wertz	.15	.04
51 John Doherty	.15	.04
52 Cecil Fielder	.30	.09
53 Travis Fryman	.30	.09
54 Chris Gomez	.15	.04
55 Mike Henneman	.15	.04
56 Chad Kreuter	.15	.04
57 Bob MacDonald	.15	.04
58 Mike Moore	.15	.04
59 Tony Phillips	.15	.04
60 Lou Whitaker	.30	.09
61 Kevin Appier	.30	.09
62 Greg Gagne	.15	.04
63 Chris Gwynn	.15	.04
64 Bob Hamelin	.15	.04
65 Chris Haney	.15	.04

66 Phil Hiatt .15 .04
67 Felix Jose .15 .04
68 Jose Lind .15 .04
69 Mike Macfarlane .15 .04
70 Jeff Montgomery .15 .04
71 Hipolito Pichardo .15 .04
72 Juan Bell .15 .04
73 Cal Eldred .15 .04
74 Darryl Hamilton .15 .04
75 Doug Henry .15 .04
76 Mike Ignasiak .15 .04
77 John Jaha .15 .04
78 Graeme Lloyd .15 .04
79 Angel Miranda .15 .04
80 Dave Nilsson .15 .04
81 Troy O'Leary .15 .04
82 Kevin Reimer .15 .04
83 Willie Banks .15 .04
84 Larry Casian .15 .04
85 Scott Erickson .15 .04
86 Eddie Guardado .15 .04
87 Kent Hrbek .30 .09
88 Terry Jorgensen .15 .04
89 Chuck Knoblauch .30 .09
90 Pat Meares .15 .04
91 Mike Trombley .15 .04
92 Dave Winfield .30 .09
93 Wade Boggs .50 .15
94 Scott Kamieniecki .15 .04
95 Pat Kelly .15 .04
96 Jimmy Key .30 .09
97 Jim Leyritz .15 .04
98 Bobby Munoz .15 .04
99 Paul O'Neill .50 .15
100 Melido Perez .15 .04
101 Mike Stanley .15 .04
102 Danny Tartabull .15 .04
103 Bernie Williams .50 .15
104 Kurt Abbott RC .40 .12
105 Mike Bordick .15 .04
106 Ron Darling .15 .04
107 Brent Gates .15 .04
108 Miguel Jimenez .15 .04
109 Steve Karsay .15 .04
110 Scott Lydy .15 .04
111 Mark McGwire 2.00 .60
112 Troy Neel .15 .04
113 Craig Paquette .15 .04
114 Bob Welch .15 .04
115 Bobby Witt .15 .04
116 Rich Amaral .15 .04
117 Mike Blowers .15 .04
118 Jay Buhner .30 .09
119 Dave Fleming .15 .04
120 Ken Griffey Jr. 1.25 .35
121 Tino Martinez .50 .15
122 Marc Newfield .15 .04
123 Ted Power .15 .04
124 Mackey Sasser .15 .04
125 Omar Vizquel .50 .15
126 Kevin Brown .30 .09
127 Juan Gonzalez .50 .15
128 Tom Henke .15 .04
129 David Hulse .15 .04
130 Dean Palmer .30 .09
131 Roger Pavlik .15 .04
132 Ivan Rodriguez .75 .23
133 Kenny Rogers .30 .09
134 Doug Strange .15 .04
135 Pat Borders .15 .04
136 Joe Carter .30 .09
137 Darnell Coles .15 .04
138 Pat Hentgen .15 .04
139 Al Leiter .30 .09
140 Paul Molitor .50 .15
141 John Olerud .30 .09
142 Ed Sprague .15 .04
143 Dave Stewart .30 .09
144 Mike Timlin .15 .04
145 Duane Ward .15 .04
146 Devon White .30 .09
147 Steve Avery .15 .04
148 Steve Bedrosian .15 .04
149 Damon Berryhill .15 .04
150 Jeff Blauser .15 .04
151 Tom Glavine .50 .15
152 Chipper Jones .75 .23
153 Mark Lemke .15 .04
154 Fred McGriff .50 .15
155 Greg McMichael .15 .04
156 Deion Sanders .50 .15
157 John Smoltz .50 .15
158 Mark Wohlers .15 .04
159 Jose Bautista .15 .04
160 Steve Buechele .15 .04
161 Mike Harkey .15 .04
162 Greg Hibbard .15 .04
163 Chuck McElroy .15 .04
164 Mike Morgan .15 .04
165 Kevin Roberson .15 .04
166 Ryne Sandberg 1.25 .35
167 Jose Vizcaino .15 .04
168 Rick Wilkins .15 .04
169 Willie Wilson .15 .04
170 Willie Greene .15 .04
171 Roberto Kelly .15 .04
172 Larry Luebbers RC .15 .04
173 Kevin Mitchell .15 .04
174 Joe Oliver .15 .04
175 John Roper .15 .04
176 Johnny Ruffin .15 .04
177 Reggie Sanders .15 .04
178 John Smiley .15 .04
179 Jerry Spradlin RC .15 .04
180 Freddie Benavides .15 .04
181 Dante Bichette .30 .09
182 Willie Blair .15 .04
183 Kent Bottenfield .15 .04
184 Jerald Clark .15 .04
185 Joe Girardi .15 .04
186 Roberto Mejia .15 .04
187 Steve Reed .15 .04
188 Armando Reynoso .15 .04
189 Bruce Ruffin .15 .04
190 Eric Young .15 .04
191 Luis Aquino .15 .04
192 Bret Barberie .15 .04
193 Ryan Bowen .15 .04
194 Chuck Carr .15 .04
195 Orestes Destrade .15 .04
196 Richie Lewis .15 .04
197 Dave Magadan .15 .04
198 Bob Natal .15 .04
199 Gary Sheffield .30 .09
200 Matt Turner .15 .04
201 Darrell Whitmore .15 .04
202 Eric Anthony .15 .04
203 Jeff Bagwell .50 .15
204 Andujar Cedeno .15 .04
205 Luis Gonzalez .30 .09
206 Xavier Hernandez .15 .04
207 Doug Jones .15 .04
208 Darryl Kile .30 .09
209 Scott Servais .15 .04
210 Greg Swindell .15 .04
211 Brian Williams .15 .04
212 Pedro Astacio .15 .04
213 Brett Butler .30 .09
214 Omar Daal .15 .04
215 Jim Gott .15 .04
216 Raul Mondesi .30 .09
217 Jose Offerman .15 .04
218 Mike Piazza 1.50 .45
219 Cory Snyder .15 .04
220 Tim Wallach .15 .04
221 Todd Worrell .15 .04
222 Moises Alou .30 .09
223 Sean Berry .15 .04
224 Wil Cordero .15 .04
225 Jeff Fassero .15 .04
226 Darrin Fletcher .15 .04
227 Cliff Floyd .30 .09
228 Marquis Grissom .30 .09
229 Ken Hill .15 .04
230 Mike Lansing .15 .04
231 Kirk Rueter .30 .09
232 John Wetteland .30 .09
233 Rondell White .30 .09
234 Tim Bogar .15 .04
235 Jeromy Burnitz .30 .09
236 Dwight Gooden .30 .09
237 Todd Hundley .15 .04
238 Jeff Kent .30 .09
239 Josias Manzanillo .15 .04
240 Joe Orsulak .15 .04
241 Ryan Thompson .15 .04
242 Kim Batiste .15 .04
243 Darren Daulton .30 .09
244 Tommy Greene .15 .04
245 Dave Hollins .15 .04
246 Pete Incaviglia .15 .04
247 Danny Jackson .15 .04
248 Ricky Jordan .15 .04
249 John Kruk .30 .09
250 Mickey Morandini .15 .04
251 Terry Mulholland .15 .04
252 Ben Rivera .15 .04
253 Kevin Stocker .15 .04
254 Jay Bell .30 .09
255 Steve Cooke .15 .04
256 Jeff King .15 .04
257 Al Martin .15 .04
258 Danny Miceli .15 .04
259 Blas Minor .15 .04
260 Don Slaught .15 .04
261 Paul Wagner .15 .04
262 Tim Wakefield .30 .09
263 Kevin Young .15 .04
264 Rene Arocha .15 .04
265 Richard Batchelor RC .15 .04
266 Gregg Jefferies .15 .04
267 Brian Jordan .30 .09
268 Jose Oquendo .15 .04
269 Donovan Osborne .15 .04
270 Erik Pappas .15 .04
271 Mike Perez .15 .04
272 Bob Tewksbury .15 .04
273 Mark Whiten .15 .04
274 Todd Zeile .15 .04
275 Andy Ashby .15 .04
276 Brad Ausmus .30 .09
277 Phil Clark .15 .04
278 Jeff Gardner .15 .04
279 Ricky Gutierrez .15 .04
280 Tony Gwynn 1.00 .30
281 Tim Mauser .15 .04
282 Scott Sanders .15 .04
283 Frank Seminara .15 .04
284 Wally Whitehurst .15 .04
285 Rod Beck .15 .04
286 Barry Bonds 2.00 .60
287 Dave Burba .15 .04
288 Mark Carreon .15 .04
289 Royce Clayton .15 .04
290 Mike Jackson .15 .04
291 Darren Lewis .15 .04
292 Kirt Manwaring .15 .04
293 Dave Martinez .15 .04
294 Billy Swift .15 .04
295 Salomon Torres .15 .04
296 Matt Williams .30 .09
297 Checklist 1-75 .15 .04
298 Checklist 76-150 .15 .04
299 Checklist 151-225 .15 .04
300 Checklist 226-300 .15 .04
301 Brady Anderson .30 .09
302 Harold Baines .30 .09
303 Damon Buford .15 .04
304 Mike Devereaux .15 .04
305 Sid Fernandez .15 .04
306 Rick Krivda RC .15 .04
307 Mike Mussina .50 .15
308 Rafael Palmeiro .50 .15
309 Arthur Rhodes .15 .04
310 Chris Sabo .15 .04
311 Lee Smith .30 .09
312 Gregg Zaun RC .15 .04
313 Scott Cooper .15 .04
314 Mike Greenwell .15 .04
315 Tim Naehring .15 .04
316 Otis Nixon .15 .04
317 Paul Quantrill .15 .04
318 John Valentin .15 .04
319 Dave Valle .15 .04
320 Frank Viola .30 .09
321 Brian Anderson RC .40 .12
322 Garret Anderson .75 .23
323 Chad Curtis .15 .04
324 Chili Davis .30 .09
325 Gary DiSarcina .15 .04
326 Damion Easley .15 .04
327 Jim Edmonds .75 .23
328 Chuck Finley .30 .09
329 Joe Grahe .15 .04
330 Bo Jackson .75 .23
331 Mark Langston .15 .04
332 Harold Reynolds .30 .09
333 James Baldwin .15 .04
334 Ray Durham RC .60 .18
335 Julio Franco .30 .09
336 Craig Grebeck .15 .04
337 Ozzie Guillen .15 .04
338 Joe Hall RC .15 .04
339 Darrin Jackson .15 .04
340 Jack McDowell .15 .04
341 Tim Raines .30 .09
342 Robin Ventura .30 .09
343 Carlos Baerga .15 .04
344 Derek Lilliquist .15 .04
345 Dennis Martinez .30 .09
346 Jack Morris .30 .09
347 Eddie Murray .75 .23
348 Chris Nabholz .15 .04
349 Charles Nagy .15 .04
350 Chad Ogea .15 .04
351 Manny Ramirez .50 .15
352 Omar Vizquel .50 .15
353 Tim Belcher .15 .04
354 Eric Davis .30 .09
355 Kirk Gibson .30 .09
356 Rick Greene .15 .04
357 Mickey Tettleton .15 .04
358 Alan Trammell .30 .09
359 David Wells .30 .09
360 Stan Belinda .15 .04
361 Vince Coleman .15 .04
362 David Cone .30 .09
363 Gary Gaetti .30 .09
364 Tom Gordon .15 .04
365 Dave Henderson .15 .04
366 Wally Joyner .30 .09
367 Brent Mayne .15 .04
368 Brian McRae .15 .04
369 Michael Tucker .15 .04
370 Ricky Bones .15 .04
371 Brian Harper .15 .04
372 Tyrone Hill .15 .04
373 Mark Kiefer .15 .04
374 Pat Listach .15 .04
375 Mike Matheny RC 2.00 .60
376 Jose Mercedes RC .15 .04
377 Jody Reed .15 .04
378 Kevin Seitzer .15 .04
379 B.J. Surhoff .30 .09
380 Greg Vaughn .15 .04
381 Turner Ward .15 .04
382 Wes Weger RC .15 .04
383 Bill Wegman .15 .04
384 Rick Aguilera .15 .04
385 Rich Becker .15 .04
386 Alex Cole .15 .04
387 Steve Dunn .15 .04
388 Keith Garagozzo RC .15 .04
389 LaTroy Hawkins RC .60 .18
390 Shane Mack .15 .04
391 David McCarty .15 .04
392 Pedro Munoz .15 .04
393 Derek Parks .15 .04
394 Kirby Puckett .75 .23
395 Kevin Tapani .15 .04
396 Matt Walbeck .15 .04
397 Jim Abbott .50 .15
398 Mike Gallego .15 .04
399 Xavier Hernandez .15 .04
400 Don Mattingly 2.00 .60
401 Terry Mulholland .15 .04
402 Matt Nokes .15 .04
403 Luis Polonia .15 .04
404 Bob Wickman .15 .04
405 Mark Acre RC .15 .04
406 Fausto Cruz RC .15 .04
407 Dennis Eckersley .30 .09
408 Rickey Henderson .75 .23
409 Stan Javier .15 .04
410 Carlos Reyes RC .15 .04
411 Ruben Sierra .15 .04
412 Terry Steinbach .15 .04
413 Bill Taylor RC .15 .04
414 Todd Van Poppel .15 .04
415 Eric Anthony .15 .04
416 Bobby Ayala .15 .04
417 Chris Bosio .15 .04
418 Tim Davis .15 .04
419 Randy Johnson .75 .23
420 Kevin King RC .15 .04
421 Anthony Manahan RC .15 .04
422 Edgar Martinez .50 .15
423 Keith Mitchell .15 .04
424 Roger Salkeld .15 .04
425 Mac Suzuki RC .40 .12
426 Dan Wilson .15 .04
427 Duff Brumley RC .15 .04
428 Jose Canseco .75 .23
429 Will Clark .75 .23
430 Steve Dreyer RC .15 .04
431 Rick Helling .15 .04
432 Chris James .15 .04
433 Matt Whiteside .15 .04
434 Roberto Alomar .50 .15
435 Scott Brow .15 .04
436 Domingo Cedeno .15 .04
437 Carlos Delgado .50 .15
438 Juan Guzman .15 .04
439 Paul Spoljaric .15 .04
440 Todd Stottlemyre .15 .04
441 Woody Williams .15 .04
442 David Justice .30 .09
443 Mike Kelly .15 .04
444 Ryan Klesko .30 .09
445 Javier Lopez .30 .09
446 Greg Maddux 1.25 .35
447 Kent Mercker .15 .04
448 Charlie O'Brien .15 .04
449 Terry Pendleton .30 .09
450 Mike Stanton .15 .04
451 Tony Tarasco .15 .04
452 Terrell Wade RC .15 .04
453 Willie Banks .15 .04
454 Shawon Dunston .15 .04
455 Mark Grace .50 .15
456 Jose Guzman .15 .04
457 Jose Hernandez .15 .04
458 Glenallen Hill .15 .04
459 Blaise Ilsley RC .15 .04
460 Brooks Kieschnick RC .40 .12
461 Derrick May .15 .04
462 Randy Myers .15 .04
463 Karl Rhodes .15 .04
464 Sammy Sosa 1.00 .30
465 Steve Trachsel .15 .04
466 Anthony Young .15 .04
467 Eddie Zambrano RC .15 .04
468 Bret Boone .30 .09
469 Tom Browning .15 .04
470 Hector Carrasco .15 .04
471 Rob Dibble .30 .09
472 Erik Hanson .15 .04
473 Thomas Howard .15 .04
474 Barry Larkin .50 .15
475 Hal Morris .15 .04
476 Jose Rijo .15 .04
477 John Burke .15 .04
478 Ellis Burks .30 .09
479 Marvin Freeman .15 .04
480 Andres Galarraga .30 .09
481 Greg W. Harris .15 .04
482 Charlie Hayes .15 .04
483 Darren Holmes .15 .04
484 Howard Johnson .15 .04
485 Marcus Moore .15 .04
486 David Nied .15 .04
487 Mark Thompson .15 .04
488 Walt Weiss .15 .04
489 Kurt Abbott .30 .09
490 Matias Carrillo RC .15 .04
491 Jeff Conine .30 .09
492 Chris Hammond .15 .04
493 Bryan Harvey .15 .04
494 Charlie Hough .30 .09
495 Yorkis Perez .15 .04
496 Pat Rapp .15 .04
497 Benito Santiago .30 .09
498 David Weathers .15 .04
499 Craig Biggio .50 .15
500 Ken Caminiti .30 .09
501 Doug Drabek .15 .04
502 Tony Eusebio .15 .04
503 Steve Finley .30 .09
504 Pete Harnisch .15 .04
505 Brian L. Hunter .15 .04
506 Domingo Jean .15 .04
507 Todd Jones .15 .04
508 Orlando Miller .15 .04
509 James Mouton .15 .04
510 Roberto Petagine .15 .04
511 Shane Reynolds .15 .04
512 Mitch Williams .15 .04
513 Billy Ashley .15 .04
514 Tom Candiotti .15 .04
515 Delino DeShields .15 .04
516 Kevin Gross .15 .04
517 Orel Hershiser .30 .09
518 Eric Karros .30 .09
519 Ramon Martinez .15 .04
520 Chan Ho Park RC .60 .18
521 Henry Rodriguez .15 .04
522 Joey Eischen .15 .04
523 Rod Henderson .15 .04
524 Pedro Martinez .75 .23
525 Mel Rojas .15 .04
526 Larry Walker .50 .15
527 Gabe White .15 .04
528 Bobby Bonilla .30 .09
529 Jonathan Hurst .15 .04
530 Bobby Jones .15 .04
531 Kevin McReynolds .15 .04
532 Bill Pulsipher .30 .09
533 Bret Saberhagen .30 .09
534 David Segui .15 .04
535 Pete Smith .15 .04
536 Kelly Stinnett RC .40 .12
537 Dave Telgheder .15 .04
538 Quilvio Veras .15 .04
539 Jose Vizcaino .15 .04
540 Pete Walker RC .15 .04
541 Ricky Bottalico RC .40 .12
542 Wes Chamberlain .15 .04
543 Mariano Duncan .15 .04
544 Lenny Dykstra .30 .09
545 Jim Eisenreich .15 .04
546 Phil Geisler RC .15 .04
547 Wayne Gomes RC .40 .12
548 Doug Jones .15 .04
549 Jeff Juden .15 .04
550 Mike Lieberthal .30 .09
551 Tony Longmire .15 .04
552 Tom Marsh .15 .04
553 Bobby Munoz .15 .04
554 Curt Schilling .30 .09
555 Carlos Garcia .15 .04
556 Ravelo Manzanillo RC .15 .04
557 Orlando Merced .15 .04
558 Will Pennyfeather .15 .04
559 Zane Smith .15 .04
560 Andy Van Slyke .30 .09
561 Rick White .15 .04
562 Luis Alicea .15 .04
563 Brian Barber .15 .04
564 Clint Davis RC .15 .04
565 Bernard Gilkey .15 .04
566 Ray Lankford .15 .04
567 Tom Pagnozzi .15 .04
568 Ozzie Smith 1.25 .35
569 Rick Sutcliffe .30 .09
570 Allen Watson .15 .04
571 Dmitri Young .30 .09
572 Derek Bell .15 .04
573 Andy Benes .15 .04
574 Archi Cianfrocco .15 .04
575 Joey Hamilton .30 .09
576 Gene Harris .15 .04
577 Trevor Hoffman .30 .09
578 Tim Hyers RC .15 .04
579 Brian Johnson RC .30 .09
580 Keith Lockhart RC .40 .12
581 Pedro A. Martinez RC .15 .04
582 Ray McDavid .15 .04
583 Phil Plantier .15 .04
584 Bip Roberts .15 .04
585 Dave Staton .15 .04
586 Todd Benzinger .15 .04
587 John Burkett .15 .04
588 Bryan Hickerson .15 .04
589 Willie McGee .30 .09
590 John Patterson .15 .04
591 Mark Portugal .15 .04
592 Kevin Rogers .15 .04
593 Joe Rosselli .15 .04
594 Steve Soderstrom RC .15 .04
595 Robby Thompson .15 .04
596 125th Anniversary .15 .04
597 Jaime Navarro CL .15 .04
598 Andy Van Slyke CL .15 .04
599 Checklist .15 .04
600 Bryan Harvey CL .15 .04
P243 D.Daulton Promo 2.00 .60
P249 John Kruk Promo 2.00 .60

1994 Ultra All-Rookies

This 10-card standard-size set features top rookies of 1994 and were randomly inserted in second series jumbo and foil packs at a rate of one in 10.

	Nm-Mt	Ex-Mt
COMPLETE SET (10)	8.00	2.40
*JUMBOS: .75X TO 2X BASIC CARDS		
ONE JUMBO SET PER 2ND SERIES HOBBY CASE		
1 Kurt Abbott	1.00	.30
2 Carlos Delgado	1.00	.30
3 Cliff Floyd	1.00	.30
4 Jeffrey Hammonds	.50	.15
5 Ryan Klesko	1.00	.30
6 Javier Lopez	1.00	.30
7 Raul Mondesi	1.00	.30
8 James Mouton	.50	.15
9 Chan Ho Park	1.00	.30
10 Dave Staton	.50	.15

1994 Ultra All-Stars

Randomly inserted in second series foil and jumbo packs at a rate of one in three, this 20-card standard-size set contains top major league stars.

	Nm-Mt	Ex-Mt
COMPLETE SET (20)	15.00	4.50
1 Chris Hoiles	.25	.07
2 Frank Thomas	1.25	.35
3 Roberto Alomar	.75	.23
4 Cal Ripken Jr.	4.00	1.20
5 Robin Ventura	.50	.15
6 Albert Belle	.50	.15
7 Juan Gonzalez	.75	.23
8 Ken Griffey Jr.	2.00	.60
9 John Olerud	.50	.15
10 Jack McDowell	.25	.07
11 Mike Piazza	2.50	.75
12 Fred McGriff	.75	.23
13 Ryne Sandberg	2.00	.60
14 Jay Bell	.50	.15
15 Matt Williams	.50	.15
16 Barry Bonds	3.00	.90
17 Lenny Dykstra	.50	.15
18 David Justice	.50	.15
19 Tom Glavine	.75	.23
20 Greg Maddux	2.00	.60

1994 Ultra Award Winners

Randomly inserted in all first series packs at a rate of one in three, this 25-card standard-size set features three MVP's, two Rookies of the Year, and 18 Top Glove defensive standouts. The set is divided into American League Top Gloves (1-9), National League Top Gloves (10-18), and Award Winners (19-25).

	Nm-Mt	Ex-Mt
COMPLETE SET (25)	15.00	4.50
1 Ivan Rodriguez	1.25	.35
2 Don Mattingly	3.00	.90
3 Roberto Alomar	.75	.23
4 Robin Ventura	.50	.15
5 Omar Vizquel	.75	.23
6 Ken Griffey Jr.	2.00	.60
7 Kenny Lofton	.50	.15
8 Devon White	.50	.15
9 Mark Langston	.25	.07
10 Kirt Manwaring	.25	.07
11 Mark Grace	.75	.23
12 Robby Thompson	.25	.07
13 Matt Williams	.50	.15

14 Jay Bell	.50	.15
15 Barry Bonds	3.00	.90
16 Marquis Grissom	.50	.15
17 Larry Walker	.75	.23
18 Greg Maddux	2.00	.60
19 Frank Thomas	1.25	.35
20 Barry Bonds	3.00	.90
21 Paul Molitor	.75	.23
22 Jack McDowell	.25	.07
23 Greg Maddux	2.00	.60
24 Tim Salmon	.75	.23
25 Mike Piazza	2.50	.75

1994 Ultra Career Achievement

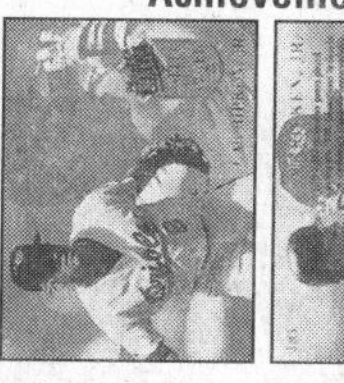

Randomly inserted in all second series packs at a rate of one in 21, this five card standard-size set highlights veteran stars and milestones they have reached during their brilliant careers.

	Nm-Mt	Ex-Mt
COMPLETE SET (5)	10.00	3.00
1 Joe Carter	1.00	.30
2 Paul Molitor	1.50	.45
3 Cal Ripken Jr.	8.00	2.40
4 Ryne Sandberg	4.00	1.20
5 Dave Winfield	1.00	.30

1994 Ultra Firemen

Randomly inserted in all first series packs at a rate of one in 11, this ten-card standard-size set features ten of baseball's top relief pitchers. The set is arranged according to American League (1-5) and National League (6-10) players.

	Nm-Mt	Ex-Mt
COMPLETE SET (10)	5.00	1.50
1 Jeff Montgomery	.50	.15
2 Duane Ward	.50	.15
3 Tom Henke	.50	.15
4 Roberto Hernandez	.50	.15
5 Dennis Eckersley	1.00	.30
6 Randy Myers	.50	.15
7 Rod Beck	.50	.15
8 Bryan Harvey	.50	.15
9 John Wetteland	1.00	.30
10 Mitch Williams	.50	.15

1994 Ultra Hitting Machines

Randomly inserted in all second series packs at a rate of one in five, this 10-card horizontally designed standard-size set features top hitters from 1993.

	Nm-Mt	Ex-Mt
COMPLETE SET (10)	10.00	3.00
1 Roberto Alomar	.75	.23
2 Carlos Baerga	.25	.07
3 Barry Bonds	3.00	.90
4 Andres Galarraga	.50	.15
5 Juan Gonzalez	.75	.23
6 Tony Gwynn	1.50	.45
7 Paul Molitor	.75	.23
8 John Olerud	.50	.15
9 Mike Piazza	2.50	.75
10 Frank Thomas	1.25	.35

1994 Ultra Home Run Kings

Randomly inserted exclusively in first series foil packs at a rate of one in 36, these 12 standard-size cards highlight home run hitters by an etched metalized look. Cards 1-6 feature American League Home Run Kings while cards 7-12 present National League Home Run Kings.

	Nm-Mt	Ex-Mt
COMPLETE SET (12)	60.00	18.00
1 Juan Gonzalez	4.00	1.20
2 Ken Griffey Jr.	10.00	3.00
3 Frank Thomas	6.00	1.80
4 Albert Belle	2.50	.75
5 Rafael Palmeiro	4.00	1.20
6 Joe Carter	2.50	.75
7 Barry Bonds	15.00	4.50
8 David Justice	2.50	.75
9 Matt Williams	2.50	.75
10 Fred McGriff	4.00	1.20
11 Ron Gant	1.25	.35
12 Mike Piazza	12.00	3.60

1994 Ultra League Leaders

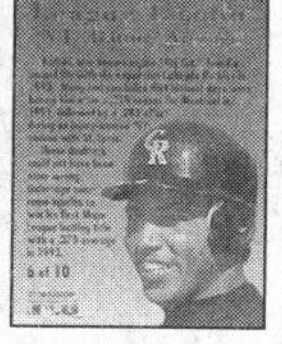

Randomly inserted in all first series packs at a rate of one in 11, this ten-card standard-size set features ten of 1993's leading players. The set is arranged according to American League (1-5) and National League (6-10) players.

	Nm-Mt	Ex-Mt
COMPLETE SET (10)	5.00	1.50
1 John Olerud	.75	.23
2 Rafael Palmeiro	1.25	.35
3 Kenny Lofton	.75	.23
4 Jack McDowell	.40	.12
5 Randy Johnson	2.00	.60
6 Andres Galarraga	.75	.23
7 Lenny Dykstra	.75	.23
8 Chuck Carr	.40	.12
9 Tom Glavine	1.25	.35
10 Jose Rijo	.40	.12

1994 Ultra On-Base Leaders

Randomly inserted in second series jumbo packs at a rate of one in 36, this 12-card standard-size set features those that were among the Major League leaders in on-base percentage.

	Nm-Mt	Ex-Mt
COMPLETE SET (12)	100.00	30.00
1 Roberto Alomar	8.00	2.40
2 Barry Bonds	30.00	9.00
3 Lenny Dykstra	5.00	1.50
4 Andres Galarraga	5.00	1.50
5 Mark Grace	8.00	2.40
6 Ken Griffey Jr.	20.00	6.00
7 Gregg Jefferies	2.50	.75
8 Orlando Merced	2.50	.75
9 Paul Molitor	8.00	2.40
10 John Olerud	5.00	1.50
11 Tony Phillips	2.50	.75
12 Frank Thomas	12.00	3.60

1994 Ultra Phillies Finest

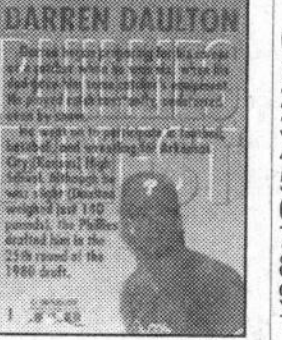

As the "Highlight Series" insert set, this 20-card standard-size set features Darren Daulton and John Kruk of the 1993 National League champion Philadelphia Phillies. The cards were inserted at a rate of one in six first series and one in 10 second series packs. Ten cards spotlight each player's career. Daulton and Kruk each signed more than 1,000 of their cards for random insertion. Moreover, the collector could receive four more cards (two of each player) through a mail-in offer by sending in ten 1994 series I wrappers plus 1.50 for postage and handling. The expiration for this redemption was September 30, 1994.

	Nm-Mt	Ex-Mt
COMPLETE SET (20)	10.00	3.00
COMPLETE SERIES 1 (10)	5.00	1.50
COMPLETE SERIES 2 (10)	5.00	1.50
COMMON (1-5/11-15)	.50	.15
COMMON (6-10/16-20)	.50	.15
COMMON MAIL-IN (M1-M4)	1.00	.30
AU1 Darren Daulton Certified Autograph	60.00	18.00
AU2 John Kruk Certified Autograph	60.00	18.00

1994 Ultra RBI Kings

Randomly inserted in first series jumbo packs at a rate of one in 36, this 12-card standard-size set features RBI leaders. These horizontal, metallized cards have a color player photo on front that superimposes a player image.The backs have a write-up and a small color player photo. Cards 1-6 feature American League RBI Kings while cards 7-12 present National League RBI Kings.

	Nm-Mt	Ex-Mt
COMPLETE SET (12)	60.00	18.00
1 Albert Belle	3.00	.90
2 Frank Thomas	8.00	2.40
3 Joe Carter	3.00	.90
4 Juan Gonzalez	5.00	1.50
5 Cecil Fielder	3.00	.90
6 Carlos Baerga	1.50	.45
7 Barry Bonds	20.00	6.00
8 David Justice	3.00	.90
9 Ron Gant	1.50	.45
10 Mike Piazza	15.00	4.50
11 Matt Williams	3.00	.90
12 Darren Daulton	3.00	.90

1994 Ultra Rising Stars

Randomly inserted in second series foil packs and jumbo packs at a rate of one in 36, this 12-card set spotlights top young major league stars.

	Nm-Mt	Ex-Mt
COMPLETE SET (12)	60.00	18.00
1 Carlos Baerga	2.00	.60
2 Jeff Bagwell	6.00	1.80
3 Albert Belle	4.00	1.20
4 Cliff Floyd	4.00	1.20
5 Travis Fryman	4.00	1.20
6 Marquis Grissom	4.00	1.20
7 Kenny Lofton	4.00	1.20
8 John Olerud	4.00	1.20
9 Mike Piazza	20.00	6.00
10 Kirk Rueter	4.00	1.20
11 Tim Salmon	6.00	1.80
12 Aaron Sele	2.00	.60

1994 Ultra Second Year Standouts

Randomly inserted in all first series packs at a rate of one in 11, this 10-card standard-size set included 10 1993 outstanding rookies who are destined to become future stars. The set is arranged in alphabetical order according to American League (1-5) and National League (6-10) players.

	Nm-Mt	Ex-Mt
COMPLETE SET (10)	10.00	3.00
1 Jason Bere	.60	.18
2 Brent Gates	.60	.18
3 Jeffrey Hammonds	.60	.18
4 Tim Salmon	2.00	.60
5 Aaron Sele	.60	.18
6 Chuck Carr	.60	.18
7 Jeff Conine	1.25	.35
8 Greg McMichael	.60	.18
9 Mike Piazza	6.00	1.80
10 Kevin Stocker	.60	.18

1994 Ultra Strikeout Kings

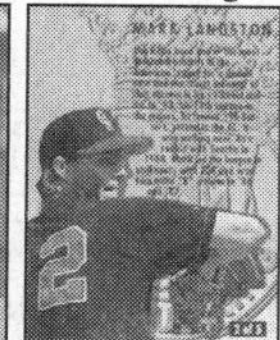

Randomly inserted in all second series packs at a rate of one in seven, this five-card standard-size set features top strikeout artists.

	Nm-Mt	Ex-Mt
COMPLETE SET (5)	4.00	1.20
1 Randy Johnson	1.25	.35
2 Mark Langston	.25	.07
3 Greg Maddux	2.00	.60
4 Jose Rijo	.25	.07
5 John Smoltz	.75	.23

1995 Ultra

This 450-card standard-size set was issued in two series. The first series contained 250 cards while the second series consisted of 200 cards. They were issued in 12-card packs (either hobby or retail) with a suggested retail price of $1.99. Also, 15-card pre-priced packs with a suggested retail of $2.69. Each pack contained two inserts: one is a Gold Medallion parallel while the other is from one of Ultra's many insert sets. "Hot Packs" contained nothing but insert cards. The full-bleed fronts feature the player's photo with the team name and player's name at the bottom. The "95 Fleer Ultra" logo is in the upper right corner. The backs have a two-photo design; one of which is a full-size duotone shot with the other being a full-color action shot. In each series the cards were grouped alphabetically within teams and checklisted alphabetically according to teams for each league with AL preceding NL.

	Nm-Mt	Ex-Mt
COMPLETE SET (450)	30.00	9.00
COMP. SERIES 1 (250)	18.00	5.50
COMP.SERIES 2 (200)	12.00	3.60
1 Brady Anderson	.30	.09
2 Sid Fernandez	.15	.04
3 Jeffrey Hammonds	.15	.04
4 Chris Hoiles	.15	.04
5 Ben McDonald	.15	.04
6 Mike Mussina	.50	.15
7 Rafael Palmeiro	.50	.15
8 Jack Voigt	.15	.04
9 Wes Chamberlain	.15	.04
10 Roger Clemens	1.50	.45
11 Chris Howard	.15	.04
12 Tim Naehring	.15	.04
13 Otis Nixon	.15	.04
14 Rich Rowland	.15	.04
15 Ken Ryan	.15	.04
16 John Valentin	.15	.04
17 Mo Vaughn	.30	.09
18 Brian Anderson	.15	.04
19 Chili Davis	.30	.09
20 Damion Easley	.15	.04
21 Jim Edmonds	.50	.15
22 Mark Langston	.15	.04
23 Tim Salmon	.50	.15
24 J.T. Snow	.30	.09
25 Chris Turner	.15	.04
26 Wilson Alvarez	.15	.04
27 Joey Cora	.15	.04
28 Alex Fernandez	.15	.04
29 Roberto Hernandez	.15	.04
30 Lance Johnson	.15	.04
31 Ron Karkovice	.15	.04
32 Kirk McCaskill	.15	.04
33 Tim Raines	.30	.09
34 Frank Thomas	.75	.23
35 Sandy Alomar Jr.	.15	.04
36 Albert Belle	.30	.09
37 Mark Clark	.15	.04
38 Kenny Lofton	.30	.09
39 Eddie Murray	.75	.23
40 Eric Plunk	.15	.04
41 Manny Ramirez	.50	.15
42 Jim Thome	.75	.23
43 Omar Vizquel	.50	.15
44 Danny Bautista	.15	.04
45 Junior Felix	.15	.04
46 Cecil Fielder	.30	.09
47 Chris Gomez	.15	.04
48 Chad Kreuter	.15	.04
49 Mike Moore	.15	.04
50 Tony Phillips	.15	.04
51 Alan Trammell	.30	.09
52 David Wells	.30	.09
53 Kevin Appier	.30	.09
54 Billy Brewer	.15	.04
55 David Cone	.30	.09
56 Greg Gagne	.15	.04
57 Bob Hamelin	.15	.04
58 Jose Lind	.15	.04
59 Brent Mayne	.15	.04
60 Brian McRae	.15	.04
61 Terry Shumpert	.15	.04
62 Ricky Bones	.15	.04
63 Mike Fetters	.15	.04
64 Darryl Hamilton	.15	.04
65 John Jaha	.15	.04
66 Graeme Lloyd	.15	.04
67 Matt Mieske	.15	.04
68 Kevin Seitzer	.15	.04
69 Jose Valentin	.15	.04
70 Turner Ward	.15	.04
71 Rick Aguilera	.15	.04
72 Rich Becker	.15	.04
73 Alex Cole	.15	.04
74 Scott Leius	.15	.04
75 Pat Meares	.15	.04
76 Kirby Puckett	.75	.23
77 Dave Stevens	.15	.04
78 Kevin Tapani	.15	.04
79 Matt Walbeck	.15	.04
80 Wade Boggs	.50	.15
81 Scott Kamieniecki	.15	.04
82 Pat Kelly	.15	.04
83 Jimmy Key	.30	.09
84 Paul O'Neill	.50	.15
85 Luis Polonia	.15	.04
86 Mike Stanley	.15	.04
87 Danny Tartabull	.15	.04
88 Bob Wickman	.15	.04
89 Mark Acre	.15	.04
90 Geronimo Berroa	.15	.04
91 Mike Bordick	.15	.04
92 Ron Darling	.15	.04
93 Stan Javier	.15	.04
94 Mark McGwire	2.00	.60
95 Troy Neel	.15	.04
96 Ruben Sierra	.15	.04
97 Terry Steinbach	.15	.04
98 Eric Anthony	.15	.04
99 Chris Bosio	.15	.04
100 Dave Fleming	.15	.04
101 Ken Griffey Jr.	1.25	.35
102 Reggie Jefferson	.15	.04
103 Randy Johnson	.75	.23
104 Edgar Martinez	.50	.15
105 Bill Risley	.15	.04
106 Dan Wilson	.15	.04
107 Cris Carpenter	.15	.04
108 Will Clark	.75	.23
109 Juan Gonzalez	.50	.15
110 Rusty Greer	.30	.09
111 David Hulse	.15	.04
112 Roger Pavlik	.15	.04
113 Ivan Rodriguez	.75	.23
114 Doug Strange	.15	.04
115 Matt Whiteside	.15	.04
116 Roberto Alomar	.50	.15
117 Brad Cornett	.15	.04
118 Carlos Delgado	.30	.09
119 Alex Gonzalez	.15	.04
120 Darren Hall	.15	.04
121 Pat Hentgen	.15	.04
122 Paul Molitor	.50	.15
123 Ed Sprague	.15	.04
124 Devon White	.30	.09
125 Tom Glavine	.50	.15
126 David Justice	.30	.09
127 Roberto Kelly	.15	.04
128 Mark Lemke	.15	.04
129 Greg Maddux	1.25	.35
130 Greg McMichael	.15	.04
131 Kent Mercker	.15	.04
132 Charlie O'Brien	.15	.04
133 John Smoltz	.50	.15
134 Willie Banks	.15	.04
135 Steve Buechele	.15	.04
136 Kevin Foster	.15	.04
137 Glenallen Hill	.15	.04
138 Rey Sanchez	.15	.04
139 Sammy Sosa	1.25	.35
140 Steve Trachsel	.15	.04
141 Rick Wilkins	.15	.04
142 Jeff Brantley	.15	.04
143 Hector Carrasco	.15	.04
144 Kevin Jarvis	.15	.04
145 Barry Larkin	.50	.15
146 Chuck McElroy	.15	.04
147 Jose Rijo	.15	.04
148 Johnny Ruffin	.15	.04
149 Deion Sanders	.50	.15
150 Eddie Taubensee	.15	.04
151 Dante Bichette	.30	.09
152 Ellis Burks	.30	.09
153 Joe Girardi	.15	.04
154 Charlie Hayes	.15	.04
155 Mike Kingery	.15	.04
156 Steve Reed	.15	.04
157 Kevin Ritz	.15	.04
158 Bruce Ruffin	.15	.04
159 Eric Young	.15	.04
160 Kurt Abbott	.15	.04
161 Chuck Carr	.15	.04
162 Chris Hammond	.15	.04
163 Bryan Harvey	.15	.04
164 Terry Mathews	.15	.04
165 Yorkis Perez	.15	.04
166 Pat Rapp	.15	.04
167 Gary Sheffield	.30	.09
168 Dave Weathers	.15	.04
169 Jeff Bagwell	.50	.15
170 Ken Caminiti	.30	.09
171 Doug Drabek	.15	.04
172 Steve Finley	.30	.09
173 John Hudek	.15	.04
174 Todd Jones	.15	.04
175 James Mouton	.15	.04
176 Shane Reynolds	.15	.04
177 Scott Servais	.15	.04
178 Tom Candiotti	.15	.04
179 Omar Daal	.15	.04
180 Darren Dreifort	.15	.04
181 Eric Karros	.30	.09
182 Ramon J.Martinez	.15	.04
183 Raul Mondesi	.30	.09
184 Henry Rodriguez	.15	.04
185 Todd Worrell	.15	.04
186 Moises Alou	.30	.09
187 Sean Berry	.15	.04
188 Wil Cordero	.15	.04
189 Jeff Fassero	.15	.04
190 Darrin Fletcher	.15	.04
191 Butch Henry	.15	.04
192 Ken Hill	.15	.04
193 Mel Rojas	.15	.04
194 John Wetteland	.30	.09
195 Bobby Bonilla	.30	.09
196 Rico Brogna	.15	.04
197 Bobby Jones	.15	.04
198 Jeff Kent	.30	.09
199 Josias Manzanillo	.15	.04
200 Kelly Stinnett	.15	.04
201 Ryan Thompson	.15	.04
202 Jose Vizcaino	.15	.04
203 Lenny Dykstra	.30	.09
204 Jim Eisenreich	.15	.04
205 Dave Hollins	.15	.04
206 Mike Lieberthal	.30	.09
207 Mickey Morandini	.15	.04
208 Bobby Munoz	.15	.04
209 Curt Schilling	.30	.09
210 Heathcliff Slocumb	.15	.04
211 David West	.15	.04
212 Dave Clark	.15	.04
213 Steve Cooke	.15	.04
214 Midre Cummings	.15	.04
215 Carlos Garcia	.15	.04
216 Jeff King	.15	.04
217 Jon Lieber	.15	.04
218 Orlando Merced	.15	.04
219 Don Slaught	.15	.04
220 Rick White	.15	.04
221 Rene Arocha	.15	.04
222 Bernard Gilkey	.15	.04
223 Brian Jordan	.30	.09
224 Tom Pagnozzi	.15	.04
225 Vicente Palacios	.15	.04
226 Geronimo Pena	.15	.04
227 Ozzie Smith	1.25	.35
228 Allen Watson	.15	.04
229 Mark Whiten	.15	.04
230 Brad Ausmus	.15	.04
231 Derek Bell	.15	.04
232 Andy Benes	.15	.04
233 Tony Gwynn	1.00	.30
234 Joey Hamilton	.15	.04
235 Luis Lopez	.15	.04
236 Pedro A.Martinez	.15	.04
237 Scott Sanders	.15	.04
238 Eddie Williams	.15	.04
239 Rod Beck	.15	.04

240 Dave Burba .15 .04
241 Darren Lewis .15 .04
242 Kirt Manwaring .15 .04
243 Mark Portugal .15 .04
244 Darryl Strawberry .30 .09
245 Robby Thompson .15 .04
246 Wm.VanLandingham .15 .04
247 Matt Williams .30 .09
248 Checklist .15 .04
249 Checklist .15 .04
250 Checklist .15 .04
251 Harold Baines .30 .09
252 Bret Barberie .15 .04
253 Armando Benitez .30 .09
254 Mike Devereaux .15 .04
255 Leo Gomez .15 .04
256 Jamie Moyer .30 .09
257 Arthur Rhodes .15 .04
258 Cal Ripken 2.50 .75
259 Luis Alicea .15 .04
260 Jose Canseco .75 .23
261 Scott Cooper .15 .04
262 Andre Dawson .30 .09
263 Mike Greenwell .15 .04
264 Aaron Sele .15 .04
265 Garret Anderson .30 .09
266 Chad Curtis .15 .04
267 Gary DiSarcina .15 .04
268 Chuck Finley .30 .09
269 Rex Hudler .15 .04
270 Andrew Lorraine .15 .04
271 Spike Owen .15 .04
272 Lee Smith .30 .09
273 Jason Bere .15 .04
274 Ozzie Guillen .15 .04
275 Norberto Martin .15 .04
276 Scott Ruffcorn .15 .04
277 Robin Ventura .30 .09
278 Carlos Baerga .15 .04
279 Jason Grimsley .15 .04
280 Dennis Martinez .30 .09
281 Charles Nagy .15 .04
282 Paul Sorrento .15 .04
283 Dave Winfield .30 .09
284 John Doherty .15 .04
285 Travis Fryman .30 .09
286 Kirk Gibson .30 .09
287 Lou Whitaker .30 .09
288 Gary Gaetti .30 .09
289 Tom Gordon .15 .04
290 Mark Gubicza .15 .04
291 Wally Joyner .30 .09
292 Mike Macfarlane .15 .04
293 Jeff Montgomery .15 .04
294 Jeff Cirillo .15 .04
295 Cal Eldred .15 .04
296 Pat Listach .15 .04
297 Jose Mercedes .15 .04
298 Dave Nilsson .15 .04
299 Duane Singleton .15 .04
300 Greg Vaughn .15 .04
301 Scott Erickson .15 .04
302 Denny Hocking .15 .04
303 Chuck Knoblauch .30 .09
304 Pat Mahomes .15 .04
305 Pedro Munoz .15 .04
306 Erik Schullstrom .15 .04
307 Jim Abbott .50 .15
308 Tony Fernandez .15 .04
309 Sterling Hitchcock .15 .04
310 Jim Leyritz .15 .04
311 Don Mattingly 2.00 .60
312 Jack McDowell .15 .04
313 Melido Perez .15 .04
314 Bernie Williams .50 .15
315 Scott Brosius .30 .09
316 Dennis Eckersley .30 .09
317 Brent Gates .15 .04
318 Rickey Henderson .75 .23
319 Steve Karsay .15 .04
320 Steve Ontiveros .15 .04
321 Bill Taylor .15 .04
322 Todd Van Poppel .15 .04
323 Bob Welch .15 .04
324 Bobby Ayala .15 .04
325 Mike Blowers .15 .04
326 Jay Buhner .30 .09
327 Felix Fermin .15 .04
328 Tino Martinez .50 .15
329 Marc Newfield .15 .04
330 Greg Pirkl .15 .04
331 Alex Rodriguez 2.00 .60
332 Kevin Brown .30 .09
333 John Burkett .15 .04
334 Jeff Frye .15 .04
335 Kevin Gross .15 .04
336 Dean Palmer .30 .09
337 Joe Carter .30 .09
338 Shawn Green .30 .09
339 Juan Guzman .15 .04
340 Mike Huff .15 .04
341 Al Leiter .30 .09
342 John Olerud .30 .09
343 Dave Stewart .30 .09
344 Todd Stottlemyre .15 .04
345 Steve Avery .15 .04
346 Jeff Blauser .15 .04
347 Chipper Jones .75 .23
348 Mike Kelly .15 .04
349 Ryan Klesko .30 .09
350 Javier Lopez .30 .09
351 Fred McGriff .50 .15
352 Jose Oliva .15 .04
353 Terry Pendleton .30 .09
354 Mike Stanton .15 .04
355 Tony Tarasco .15 .04
356 Mark Wohlers .15 .04
357 Jim Bullinger .15 .04
358 Shawon Dunston .15 .04
359 Mark Grace .50 .15
360 Derrick May .15 .04
361 Randy Myers .15 .04
362 Karl Rhodes .15 .04
363 Bret Boone .30 .09
364 Brian Dorsett .15 .04
365 Ron Gant .30 .09
366 Brian R.Hunter .15 .04
367 Hal Morris .15 .04
368 Jack Morris .30 .09
369 John Roper .15 .04
370 Reggie Sanders .15 .04
371 Pete Schourek .15 .04
372 John Smiley .15 .04
373 Marvin Freeman .15 .04
374 Andres Galarraga .30 .09
375 Mike Munoz .15 .04
376 David Nied .15 .04
377 Walt Weiss .15 .04
378 Greg Colbrunn .15 .04
379 Jeff Conine .30 .09
380 Charles Johnson .30 .09
381 Kurt Miller .15 .04
382 Robb Nen .30 .09
383 Benito Santiago .30 .09
384 Craig Biggio .50 .15
385 Tony Eusebio .15 .04
386 Luis Gonzalez .30 .09
387 Brian L.Hunter .15 .04
388 Darryl Kile .30 .09
389 Orlando Miller .15 .04
390 Phil Plantier .15 .04
391 Greg Swindell .15 .04
392 Billy Ashley .15 .04
393 Pedro Astacio .15 .04
394 Brett Butler .30 .09
395 Delino DeShields .15 .04
396 Orel Hershiser .30 .09
397 Garey Ingram .15 .04
398 Chan Ho Park .30 .09
399 Mike Piazza 1.25 .35
400 Ismael Valdes .15 .04
401 Tim Wallach .15 .04
402 Cliff Floyd .30 .09
403 Marquis Grissom .30 .09
404 Mike Lansing .15 .04
405 Pedro Martinez .75 .23
406 Kirk Rueter .15 .04
407 Tim Scott .15 .04
408 Jeff Shaw .15 .04
409 Larry Walker .50 .15
410 Rondell White .30 .09
411 John Franco .30 .09
412 Todd Hundley .15 .04
413 Jason Jacome .15 .04
414 Joe Orsulak .15 .04
415 Bret Saberhagen .30 .09
416 David Segui .15 .04
417 Darren Daulton .30 .09
418 Mariano Duncan .15 .04
419 Tommy Greene .15 .04
420 Gregg Jefferies .15 .04
421 John Kruk .30 .09
422 Kevin Stocker .15 .04
423 Jay Bell .30 .09
424 Al Martin .15 .04
425 Denny Neagle .30 .09
426 Zane Smith .15 .04
427 Andy Van Slyke .30 .09
428 Paul Wagner .15 .04
429 Tom Henke .15 .04
430 Danny Jackson .15 .04
431 Ray Lankford .15 .04
432 John Mabry .15 .04
433 Bob Tewksbury .15 .04
434 Todd Zeile .15 .04
435 Andy Ashby .15 .04
436 Andujar Cedeno .15 .04
437 Donnie Elliott .15 .04
438 Bryce Florie .15 .04
439 Trevor Hoffman .30 .09
440 Melvin Nieves .15 .04
441 Bip Roberts .15 .04
442 Barry Bonds 2.00 .60
443 Royce Clayton .15 .04
444 Mike Jackson .15 .04
445 John Patterson .15 .04
446 J.R. Phillips .15 .04
447 Bill Swift .15 .04
448 Checklist .15 .04
449 Checklist .15 .04
450 Checklist .15 .04

1995 Ultra Gold Medallion

This 450-card parallels the regular Ultra issue. These cards were issued one per pack and are differentiated from the regular cards by the Ultra logo being replaced by the "Ultra Gold Medallion Edition logo."

Nm-Mt Ex-Mt
COMPLETE SET (450) 110.00 33.00
COMP. SERIES 1 (250) 60.00 18.00
COMP. SERIES 2 (200) 50.00 15.00
*STARS: 1.25X TO 3X BASIC CARDS.

1995 Ultra All-Rookies

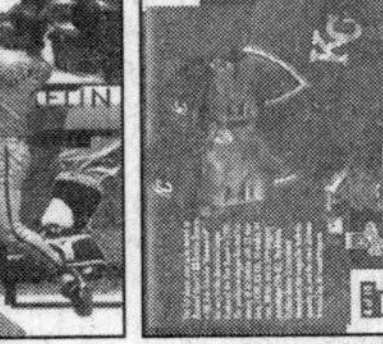

This 10-card standard-size set features rookies who emerged with an impact in 1994. These cards were inserted one in every five second series packs. The cards are numbered in the lower left as "X" of 10 and are sequenced in alphabetical order.

Nm-Mt Ex-Mt
COMPLETE SET (10) 5.00 1.50
*GOLD MEDAL: .75X TO 2X BASIC AR
GM SER.2 STATED ODDS 1:50
1 Cliff Floyd .75 .23
2 Chris Gomez .40 .12
3 Rusty Greer .75 .23
4 Bob Hamelin .40 .12
5 Joey Hamilton .40 .12
6 John Hudek .40 .12
7 Ryan Klesko .75 .23
8 Raul Mondesi .75 .23
9 Manny Ramirez 1.25 .35
10 Steve Trachsel .40 .12

1995 Ultra All-Stars

This 20-card standard-size set feature players who are considered to be the top players in the game. Cards were inserted one in every four second series packs. The fronts feature two photos. The cards are numbered in the bottom left as "X" of 20 and are sequenced in alphabetical order.

Nm-Mt Ex-Mt
COMPLETE SET (20) 15.00 4.50
*GOLD MEDAL: .75X TO 2X BASIC ALL-STARS
GM SER.2 STATED ODDS 1:40
1 Moises Alou .50 .15
2 Albert Belle .50 .15
3 Craig Biggio .75 .23
4 Wade Boggs .75 .23
5 Barry Bonds 3.00 .90
6 David Cone .50 .15
7 Ken Griffey Jr. 2.00 .60
8 Tony Gwynn 1.50 .45
9 Chuck Knoblauch .50 .15
10 Barry Larkin .75 .23
11 Kenny Lofton .50 .15
12 Greg Maddux 2.00 .60
13 Fred McGriff .75 .23
14 Paul O'Neill .75 .23
15 Mike Piazza 2.00 .60
16 Kirby Puckett 1.25 .35
17 Cal Ripken 4.00 1.20
18 Ivan Rodriguez 1.25 .35
19 Frank Thomas 1.25 .35
20 Matt Williams .50 .15

1995 Ultra Award Winners

Featuring players who won major awards in 1994, this 25-card standard-size set was inserted one in every four first series packs. The cards are numbered as "X" of 25.

Nm-Mt Ex-Mt
COMPLETE SET (25) 20.00 6.00
*GOLD MEDAL: .75X TO 2X BASIC BASIC AW
GM SER.1 STATED ODDS 1:40
1 Ivan Rodriguez 1.25 .35
2 Don Mattingly 3.00 .90
3 Roberto Alomar .75 .23
4 Wade Boggs .75 .23
5 Omar Vizquel .75 .23
6 Ken Griffey Jr. 2.00 .60
7 Kenny Lofton .50 .15
8 Devon White .50 .15
9 Mark Langston .25 .07
10 Tom Pagnozzi .25 .07
11 Jeff Bagwell .75 .23
12 Craig Biggio .75 .23
13 Matt Williams .50 .15
14 Barry Larkin .75 .23
15 Barry Bonds 3.00 .90
16 Marquis Grissom .50 .15
17 Darren Lewis .25 .07
18 Greg Maddux 2.00 .60
19 Frank Thomas 1.25 .35
20 Jeff Bagwell .75 .23
21 David Cone .50 .15
22 Greg Maddux 2.00 .60
23 Bob Hamelin .25 .07
24 Raul Mondesi .50 .15
25 Moises Alou .50 .15

1995 Ultra Gold Medallion Rookies

This 20-card standard-size set was available through a mail-in wrapper offer that expired 9/30/95. These players featured were all rookies in 1995 and were not included in the regular Ultra set. The design is essentially the same as the corresponding basic cards save for the medallion in the upper left-hand corner. The cards are numbered with an "M" prefix. The set is sequenced in alphabetical order.

Nm-Mt Ex-Mt
COMPLETE SET (20) 8.00 2.40
M1 Manny Alexander .25 .07
M2 Edgardo Alfonzo .50 .15
M3 Jason Bates .25 .07
M4 Andres Berumen .25 .07
M5 Darren Bragg .25 .07
M6 Jamie Brewington .25 .07
M7 Jason Christiansen .25 .07
M8 Brad Clontz .25 .07
M9 Marty Cordova .25 .07
M10 Johnny Damon .75 .23
M11 Vaughn Eshelman .25 .07
M12 Chad Fonville .25 .07
M13 Curtis Goodwin .25 .07
M14 Tyler Green .25 .07
M15 Bobby Higginson .75 .23
M16 Jason Isringhausen .50 .15
M17 Hideo Nomo 2.50 .75
M18 Jon Nunnally .25 .07
M19 Carlos Perez .50 .15
M20 Julian Tavarez .25 .07

1995 Ultra Golden Prospects

Inserted one every eight first series hobby packs, this 10-card standard-size set features potential impact players. The cards are numbered as "X" of 10 and are sequenced alphabetically.

Nm-Mt Ex-Mt
COMPLETE SET (10) 10.00 3.00
*GOLD MEDAL: .75X TO 2X BASIC PROSPECTS
GM SER.1 STATED ODDS 1:80
1 James Baldwin .50 .15
2 Alan Benes .50 .15
3 Armando Benitez 1.00 .30
4 Ray Durham 1.00 .30
5 LaTroy Hawkins .50 .15
6 Brian L.Hunter .50 .15
7 Derek Jeter 4.00 1.20
8 Charles Johnson 1.00 .30
9 Alex Rodriguez 4.00 1.20
10 Michael Tucker .50 .15

1995 Ultra Hitting Machines

This 10-card standard-size set features some of baseball's leading batters. Inserted one in every eight second-series retail packs, these horizontal cards have the player's photo against a background of the words "Hitting Machine." The cards are numbered as "X" of 10 in the upper right and are sequenced in alphabetical order.

Nm-Mt Ex-Mt
COMPLETE SET (10) 12.00 3.60
*GOLD MEDAL: .75X TO 2X BASIC HIT.MACH.
GM SER.2 STATED ODDS 1:80 RETAIL
1 Jeff Bagwell .75 .23
2 Albert Belle .50 .15
3 Dante Bichette .50 .15
4 Barry Bonds 3.00 .90
5 Jose Canseco 1.25 .35
6 Ken Griffey Jr. 2.00 .60
7 Tony Gwynn 1.50 .45
8 Fred McGriff .75 .23
9 Mike Piazza 2.00 .60
10 Frank Thomas 1.25 .35

1995 Ultra Home Run Kings

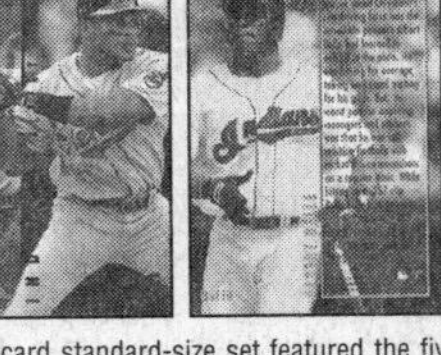

This 10-card standard-size set featured the five leading home run hitters in each league. These cards were issued one every eight first series retail packs. The cards are numbered as "X" of 10 and are sequenced by league according to 1994's home rum standings. A Barry Bonds sample card was issued to dealers to prior to the release of 1995 Ultra.

Nm-Mt Ex-Mt
COMPLETE SET (10) 30.00 9.00
*GOLD MEDAL: .75X TO 2X BASIC HR KINGS
GM SER.1 STATED ODDS 1:80 RETAIL
1 Ken Griffey Jr. 5.00 1.50
2 Frank Thomas 3.00 .90
3 Albert Belle 1.25 .35
4 Jose Canseco 3.00 .90
5 Cecil Fielder 1.25 .35
6 Matt Williams 1.25 .35
7 Jeff Bagwell 2.00 .60
8 Barry Bonds 8.00 2.40
9 Fred McGriff 2.00 .60
10 Andres Galarraga 1.25 .35
S8 Barry Bonds Sample 2.00 .60

1995 Ultra League Leaders

This 10-card standard-size set was inserted one every three first series packs.

Nm-Mt Ex-Mt
COMPLETE SET (10) 6.00 1.80
*GOLD MEDAL: .75X TO 2X BASIC LL
GM SER.1 STATED ODDS 1:30

1 Paul O'Neill .75 .23
2 Kenny Lofton .50 .15
3 Jimmy Key .50 .15
4 Randy Johnson 1.25 .35
5 Lee Smith .50 .15
6 Tony Gwynn 1.50 .45
7 Craig Biggio .75 .23
8 Greg Maddux 2.00 .60
9 Andy Benes .25 .07
10 John Franco .50 .15

1995 Ultra On-Base Leaders

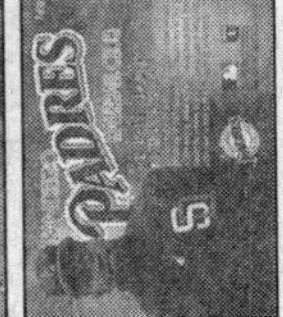

This 10-card standard-size set features ten players who are constantly reaching base safely. These cards were inserted one in every eight pre-priced second series jumbo packs. The cards are numbered in the upper right corner as "X" of 10 and are sequenced in alphabetical order.

Nm-Mt Ex-Mt
COMPLETE SET (10) 40.00 12.00
*GOLD MEDAL: .75X TO 2X BASIC OBL
GM SER.2 STATED ODDS 1:80 JUMBO
1 Jeff Bagwell 3.00 .90
2 Albert Belle 2.00 .60
3 Craig Biggio 3.00 .90
4 Wade Boggs 3.00 .90
5 Barry Bonds 12.00 3.60
6 Will Clark 5.00 1.50
7 Tony Gwynn 6.00 1.80
8 David Justice 2.00 .60
9 Paul O'Neill 3.00 .90
10 Frank Thomas 5.00 1.50

1995 Ultra Power Plus

This six-card standard-size set was inserted one in every 37 first series packs. The six players portrayed are not only sluggers, but also excel at another part of the game. Unlike the 1995 Ultra cards and the other insert sets, these cards are 100 percent foil. The cards are numbered on the bottom right as "X" of 6 and are sequenced in alphabetical order by league.

Nm-Mt Ex-Mt
COMPLETE SET (6) 25.00 7.50
*GOLD MEDAL: .75X TO 2X BASIC PLUS
GM SER.1 STATED ODDS 1:370
1 Albert Belle 1.50 .45
2 Ken Griffey Jr. 6.00 1.80
3 Frank Thomas 4.00 1.20
4 Jeff Bagwell 2.50 .75
5 Barry Bonds 10.00 3.00
6 Matt Williams 1.50 .45

1995 Ultra RBI Kings

This 10-card standard-size set was inserted into series one jumbo packs at a rate of one every 11. The cards are numbered in the upper left as "X" of 10 and are sequenced in order by league.

Nm-Mt Ex-Mt
COMPLETE SET (10) 30.00 9.00
*GOLD MEDAL: .75X TO 2X BASIC RBI KINGS
GM SER.1 STATED ODDS 1:110 JUMBO
1 Kirby Puckett 5.00 1.50
2 Joe Carter 2.00 .60
3 Albert Belle 2.00 .60
4 Frank Thomas 5.00 1.50
5 Julio Franco 1.00 .30
6 Jeff Bagwell 3.00 .90
7 Matt Williams 2.00 .60
8 Dante Bichette 2.00 .60
9 Fred McGriff 3.00 .90
10 Mike Piazza 8.00 2.40

1995 Ultra Rising Stars

This nine-card standard-size set was inserted one every 37 second series packs. The cards are numbered "X" of 9 and are sequenced in alpha

betical order.

Nm-Mt Ex-Mt
COMPLETE SET (9) 40.00 12.00
*GOLD MEDAL: .75X TO 2X BASIC RISING
GM SER.2 STATED ODDS 1:370
1 Moises Alou 3.00 .90
2 Jeff Bagwell 5.00 1.50
3 Albert Belle 3.00 .90
4 Juan Gonzalez 5.00 1.50
5 Chuck Knoblauch 3.00 .90
6 Kenny Lofton 3.00 .90
7 Raul Mondesi 3.00 .90
8 Mike Piazza 12.00 3.60
9 Frank Thomas 8.00 2.40

1995 Ultra Second Year Standouts

This 15-card standard-size set was inserted into first series packs at a rate of not greater than one in six packs. The players in this set were all rookies in 1994 whom big things were expected from in 1995. The cards are numbered in the lower right as "X" of 15 and are sequenced in alphabetical order.

Nm-Mt Ex-Mt
COMPLETE SET (15) 8.00 2.40
*GOLD MEDAL: .75X TO 2X BASIC 2YS
GM SER.1 STATED ODDS 1:60
1 Cliff Floyd 1.25 .35
2 Chris Gomez .60 .18
3 Rusty Greer 1.25 .35
4 Darren Hall .60 .18
5 Bob Hamelin .60 .18
6 Joey Hamilton .60 .18
7 Jeffrey Hammonds .60 .18
8 John Hudek .60 .18
9 Ryan Klesko 1.25 .35
10 Raul Mondesi 1.25 .35
11 Manny Ramirez 2.00 .60
12 Bill Risley .60 .18
13 Steve Trachsel .60 .18
14 W.VanLandingham .60 .18
15 Rondell White 1.25 .35

1995 Ultra Strikeout Kings

This six-card standard-size set was inserted one every five second series packs. The cards are numbered as "X" of 6 and are sequenced in alphabetical order.

Nm-Mt Ex-Mt
COMPLETE SET (6) 5.00 1.50
*GOLD MEDAL: .75X TO 2X BASIC K KINGS
GM SER.2 STATED ODDS 1:50
1 Andy Benes .25 .07
2 Roger Clemens 2.50 .75
3 Randy Johnson 1.25 .35
4 Greg Maddux 2.00 .60
5 Pedro Martinez 1.25 .35
6 Jose Rijo .25 .07

1996 Ultra

The 1996 Ultra set, produced by Fleer, contains 600 standard-size cards. The cards were distributed in packs that included two inserts. One insert is a Gold Medallion parallel while the other insert comes from one of the many Ultra insert sets. The cards are thicker than their 1995 counterparts and the fronts feature the player in an action shot in full-bleed color. The cards are sequenced in alphabetical order within league and team order.

Nm-Mt Ex-Mt
COMPLETE SET (600) 50.00 15.00
COMP.SERIES 1 (300) 25.00 7.50
COMP.SERIES 2 (300) 25.00 7.50
RIPKEN DUST AVAIL.VIA MAIL EXCHANGE
1 Manny Alexander .30 .09
2 Brady Anderson .30 .09
3 Bobby Bonilla .30 .09
4 Scott Erickson .30 .09
5 Curtis Goodwin .30 .09
6 Chris Hoiles .30 .09
7 Doug Jones .30 .09
8 Jeff Manto .30 .09
9 Mike Mussina .50 .15
10 Rafael Palmeiro .50 .15
11 Cal Ripken 2.50 .75
12 Rick Aguilera .30 .09
13 Luis Alicea .30 .09
14 Stan Belinda .30 .09
15 Jose Canseco .75 .23
16 Roger Clemens 1.50 .45
17 Mike Greenwell .30 .09
18 Mike Macfarlane .30 .09
19 Tim Naehring .30 .09
20 Troy O'Leary .30 .09
21 John Valentin .30 .09
22 Mo Vaughn .30 .09
23 Tim Wakefield .30 .09
24 Brian Anderson .30 .09
25 Garret Anderson .30 .09
26 Chili Davis .30 .09
27 Gary DiSarcina .30 .09
28 Jim Edmonds .30 .09
29 Jorge Fabregas .30 .09
30 Chuck Finley .30 .09
31 Mark Langston .30 .09
32 Troy Percival .30 .09
33 Tim Salmon .50 .15
34 Lee Smith .30 .09
35 Wilson Alvarez .30 .09
36 Ray Durham .30 .09
37 Alex Fernandez .30 .09
38 Ozzie Guillen .30 .09
39 Roberto Hernandez .30 .09
40 Lance Johnson .30 .09
41 Ron Karkovice .30 .09
42 Lyle Mouton .30 .09
43 Tim Raines .30 .09
44 Frank Thomas .75 .23
45 Carlos Baerga .30 .09
46 Albert Belle .30 .09
47 Orel Hershiser .30 .09
48 Kenny Lofton .30 .09
49 Dennis Martinez .30 .09
50 Jose Mesa .30 .09
51 Eddie Murray .75 .23
52 Chad Ogea .30 .09
53 Manny Ramirez .50 .15
54 Jim Thome .75 .23
55 Omar Vizquel .50 .15
56 Dave Winfield .30 .09
57 Chad Curtis .30 .09
58 Cecil Fielder .30 .09
59 John Flaherty .30 .09
60 Travis Fryman .30 .09
61 Chris Gomez .30 .09
62 Bob Higginson .30 .09
63 Felipe Lira .30 .09
64 Brian Maxcy .30 .09
65 Alan Trammell .50 .15
66 Lou Whitaker .30 .09
67 Kevin Appier .30 .09
68 Gary Gaetti .30 .09
69 Tom Goodwin .30 .09
70 Tom Gordon .30 .09
71 Jason Jacome .30 .09
72 Wally Joyner .30 .09
73 Brent Mayne .30 .09
74 Jeff Montgomery .30 .09
75 Jon Nunnally .30 .09
76 Joe Vitiello .30 .09
77 Ricky Bones .30 .09
78 Jeff Cirillo .30 .09
79 Mike Fetters .30 .09
80 Darryl Hamilton .30 .09
81 David Hulse .30 .09
82 Dave Nilsson .30 .09
83 Kevin Seitzer .30 .09
84 Steve Sparks .30 .09
85 B.J. Surhoff .30 .09
86 Jose Valentin .30 .09
87 Greg Vaughn .30 .09
88 Marty Cordova .30 .09
89 Chuck Knoblauch .30 .09
90 Pat Meares .30 .09
91 Pedro Munoz .30 .09
92 Kirby Puckett .75 .23
93 Brad Radke .30 .09
94 Scott Stahoviak .30 .09
95 Dave Stevens .30 .09
96 Mike Trombley .30 .09
97 Matt Walbeck .30 .09
98 Wade Boggs .50 .15
99 Russ Davis .30 .09
100 Jim Leyritz .30 .09
101 Don Mattingly 2.00 .60
102 Jack McDowell .30 .09
103 Paul O'Neill .50 .15
104 Andy Pettitte .50 .15
105 Mariano Rivera .50 .15
106 Ruben Sierra .30 .09
107 Darryl Strawberry .30 .09
108 John Wetteland .30 .09
109 Bernie Williams .50 .15
110 Geronimo Berroa .30 .09
111 Scott Brosius .30 .09
112 Dennis Eckersley .30 .09
113 Brent Gates .30 .09
114 Rickey Henderson .75 .23
115 Mark McGwire 2.00 .60
116 Ariel Prieto .30 .09
117 Terry Steinbach .30 .09
118 Todd Stottlemyre .30 .09
119 Todd Van Poppel .30 .09
120 Steve Wojciechowski .30 .09
121 Rich Amaral .30 .09
122 Bobby Ayala .30 .09
123 Mike Blowers .30 .09
124 Chris Bosio .30 .09
125 Joey Cora .30 .09
126 Ken Griffey Jr. 1.25 .35
127 Randy Johnson .75 .23
128 Edgar Martinez .50 .15
129 Tino Martinez .50 .15
130 Alex Rodriguez 1.50 .45
131 Dan Wilson .30 .09
132 Will Clark .75 .23
133 Jeff Frye .30 .09
134 Benji Gil .30 .09
135 Juan Gonzalez .50 .15
136 Rusty Greer .30 .09
137 Mark McLemore .30 .09
138 Roger Pavlik .30 .09
139 Ivan Rodriguez .75 .23
140 Kenny Rogers .30 .09
141 Mickey Tettleton .30 .09
142 Roberto Alomar .50 .15
143 Joe Carter .30 .09
144 Tony Castillo .30 .09
145 Alex Gonzalez .30 .09
146 Shawn Green .30 .09
147 Pat Hentgen .30 .09
148 Sandy Martinez .30 .09
149 Paul Molitor .50 .15
150 John Olerud .30 .09
151 Ed Sprague .30 .09
152 Jeff Blauser .30 .09
153 Brad Clontz .30 .09
154 Tom Glavine .50 .15
155 Marquis Grissom .30 .09
156 Chipper Jones .75 .23
157 David Justice .30 .09
158 Ryan Klesko .30 .09
159 Javier Lopez .30 .09
160 Greg Maddux 1.25 .35
161 John Smoltz .50 .15
162 Mark Wohlers .30 .09
163 Jim Bullinger .30 .09
164 Frank Castillo .30 .09
165 Shawon Dunston .30 .09
166 Kevin Foster .30 .09
167 Luis Gonzalez .30 .09
168 Mark Grace .50 .15
169 Rey Sanchez .30 .09
170 Scott Servais .30 .09
171 Sammy Sosa 1.25 .35
172 Ozzie Timmons .30 .09
173 Steve Trachsel .30 .09
174 Bret Boone .30 .09
175 Jeff Branson .30 .09
176 Jeff Brantley .30 .09
177 Dave Burba .30 .09
178 Ron Gant .30 .09
179 Barry Larkin .50 .15
180 Darren Lewis .30 .09
181 Mark Portugal .30 .09
182 Reggie Sanders .30 .09
183 Pete Schourek .30 .09
184 John Smiley .30 .09
185 Jason Bates .30 .09
186 Dante Bichette .30 .09
187 Ellis Burks .30 .09
188 Vinny Castilla .30 .09
189 Andres Galarraga .30 .09
190 Darren Holmes .30 .09
191 Armando Reynoso .30 .09
192 Kevin Ritz .30 .09
193 Bill Swift .30 .09
194 Larry Walker .50 .15
195 Kurt Abbott .30 .09
196 John Burkett .30 .09
197 Greg Colbrunn .30 .09
198 Jeff Conine .30 .09
199 Andre Dawson .30 .09
200 Chris Hammond .30 .09
201 Charles Johnson .30 .09
202 Robb Nen .30 .09
203 Terry Pendleton .30 .09
204 Quilvio Veras .30 .09
205 Jeff Bagwell .50 .15
206 Derek Bell .30 .09
207 Doug Drabek .30 .09
208 Tony Eusebio .30 .09
209 Mike Hampton .30 .09
210 Brian L. Hunter .30 .09
211 Todd Jones .30 .09
212 Orlando Miller .30 .09
213 James Mouton .30 .09
214 Shane Reynolds .30 .09
215 Dave Veres .30 .09
216 Billy Ashley .30 .09
217 Brett Butler .30 .09
218 Chad Fonville .30 .09
219 Todd Hollandsworth .30 .09
220 Eric Karros .30 .09
221 Ramon Martinez .30 .09
222 Raul Mondesi .30 .09
223 Hideo Nomo .75 .23
224 Mike Piazza 1.25 .35
225 Kevin Tapani .30 .09
226 Ismael Valdes .30 .09
227 Todd Worrell .30 .09
228 Moises Alou .30 .09
229 Wil Cordero .30 .09
230 Jeff Fassero .30 .09
231 Darrin Fletcher .30 .09
232 Mike Lansing .30 .09
233 Pedro Martinez .75 .23
234 Carlos Perez .30 .09
235 Mel Rojas .30 .09
236 David Segui .30 .09
237 Tony Tarasco .30 .09
238 Rondell White .30 .09
239 Edgardo Alfonzo .30 .09
240 Rico Brogna .30 .09
241 Carl Everett .30 .09
242 Todd Hundley .30 .09
243 Butch Huskey .30 .09
244 Jason Isringhausen .30 .09
245 Bobby Jones .30 .09
246 Jeff Kent .30 .09
247 Bill Pulsipher .30 .09
248 Jose Vizcaino .30 .09
249 Ricky Bottalico .30 .09
250 Darren Daulton .30 .09
251 Jim Eisenreich .30 .09
252 Tyler Green .30 .09
253 Charlie Hayes .30 .09
254 Gregg Jefferies .30 .09
255 Tony Longmire .30 .09
256 Michael Mimbs .30 .09
257 Mickey Morandini .30 .09
258 Paul Quantrill .30 .09
259 Heathcliff Slocumb .30 .09
260 Jay Bell .30 .09
261 Jacob Brumfield .30 .09
262 A.Encarnacion RC .30 .09
263 John Ericks .30 .09
264 Mark Johnson .30 .09
265 Esteban Loaiza .30 .09
266 Al Martin .30 .09
267 Orlando Merced .30 .09
268 Dan Miceli .30 .09
269 Denny Neagle .30 .09
270 Brian Barber .30 .09
271 Scott Cooper .30 .09
272 Tripp Cromer .30 .09
273 Bernard Gilkey .30 .09
274 Tom Henke .30 .09
275 Brian Jordan .30 .09
276 John Mabry .30 .09
277 Tom Pagnozzi .30 .09
278 Mark Petkovsek .30 .09
279 Ozzie Smith 1.25 .35
280 Andy Ashby .30 .09
281 Brad Ausmus .30 .09
282 Ken Caminiti .30 .09
283 Glenn Dishman .30 .09
284 Tony Gwynn 1.00 .30
285 Joey Hamilton .30 .09
286 Trevor Hoffman .30 .09
287 Phil Plantier .30 .09
288 Jody Reed .30 .09
289 Eddie Williams .30 .09
290 Barry Bonds 2.00 .60
291 Jamie Brewington RC .30 .09
292 Mark Carreon .30 .09
293 Royce Clayton .30 .09
294 Glenallen Hill .30 .09
295 Mark Leiter .30 .09
296 Kirt Manwaring .30 .09
297 J.R. Phillips .30 .09
298 Deion Sanders .50 .15
299 Wm. VanLandingham .30 .09
300 Matt Williams .30 .09
301 Roberto Alomar .50 .15
302 Armando Benitez .30 .09
303 Mike Devereaux .30 .09
304 Jeffrey Hammonds .30 .09
305 Jimmy Haynes .30 .09
306 Scott McClain .30 .09
307 Kent Mercker .30 .09
308 Randy Myers .30 .09
309 B.J. Surhoff .30 .09
310 Tony Tarasco .30 .09
311 David Wells .30 .09
312 Wil Cordero .30 .09
313 Alex Delgado .30 .09
314 Tom Gordon .30 .09
315 Dwayne Hosey .30 .09
316 Jose Malave .30 .09
317 Kevin Mitchell .30 .09
318 Jamie Moyer .30 .09
319 Aaron Sele .30 .09
320 Heathcliff Slocumb .30 .09
321 Mike Stanley .30 .09
322 Jeff Suppan .30 .09
323 Jim Abbott .50 .15
324 George Arias .30 .09
325 Todd Greene .30 .09
326 Bryan Harvey .30 .09
327 J.T. Snow .30 .09
328 Randy Velarde .30 .09
329 Tim Wallach .30 .09
330 Harold Baines .30 .09
331 Jason Bere .30 .09
332 Darren Lewis .30 .09
333 Norberto Martin .30 .09
334 Tony Phillips .30 .09
335 Bill Simas .30 .09
336 Chris Snopek .30 .09
337 Kevin Tapani .30 .09
338 Danny Tartabull .30 .09
339 Robin Ventura .30 .09
340 Sandy Alomar Jr. .30 .09
341 Julio Franco .30 .09
342 Jack McDowell .30 .09
343 Charles Nagy .30 .09
344 Julian Tavarez .30 .09
345 Kimera Bartee .30 .09
346 Greg Keagle .30 .09
347 Mark Lewis .30 .09
348 Jose Lima .30 .09
349 Melvin Nieves .30 .09
350 Mark Parent .30 .09
351 Eddie Williams .30 .09
352 Johnny Damon .50 .15
353 Sal Fasano .30 .09
354 Mark Gubicza .30 .09
355 Bob Hamelin .30 .09
356 Chris Haney .30 .09
357 Keith Lockhart .30 .09
358 Mike Macfarlane .30 .09
359 Jose Offerman .30 .09
360 Bip Roberts .30 .09
361 Michael Tucker .30 .09
362 Chuck Carr .30 .09
363 Bobby Hughes .30 .09
364 John Jaha .30 .09
365 Mark Loretta .30 .09
366 Mike Matheny .30 .09
367 Ben McDonald .30 .09
368 Matt Mieske .30 .09
369 Angel Miranda .30 .09
370 Fernando Vina .30 .09
371 Rick Aguilera .30 .09
372 Rich Becker .30 .09
373 LaTroy Hawkins .30 .09
374 Dave Hollins .30 .09
375 Roberto Kelly .30 .09
376 Matt Lawton RC .60 .18
377 Paul Molitor .50 .15
378 Dan Naulty .30 .09
379 Rich Robertson .30 .09
380 Frank Rodriguez .30 .09
381 David Cone .30 .09
382 Mariano Duncan .30 .09
383 Andy Fox .30 .09
384 Joe Girardi .30 .09
385 Dwight Gooden .30 .09
386 Derek Jeter 2.00 .60
387 Pat Kelly .30 .09
388 Jimmy Key .30 .09
389 Matt Luke .30 .09
390 Tino Martinez .50 .15
391 Jeff Nelson .30 .09
392 Melido Perez .30 .09
393 Tim Raines .30 .09
394 Ruben Rivera .30 .09
395 Kenny Rogers .30 .09
396 Tony Batista RC .60 .18
397 Allen Battle .30 .09
398 Mike Bordick .30 .09
399 Steve Cox .30 .09
400 Jason Giambi .30 .09
401 Doug Johns .30 .09
402 Pedro Munoz .30 .09
403 Phil Plantier .30 .09
404 Scott Spiezio .30 .09
405 George Williams .30 .09
406 Ernie Young .30 .09
407 Darren Bragg .30 .09
408 Jay Buhner .30 .09
409 Norm Charlton .30 .09
410 Russ Davis .30 .09
411 Sterling Hitchcock .30 .09
412 Edwin Hurtado .30 .09
413 Raul Ibanez RC .60 .18
414 Mike Jackson .30 .09
415 Luis Sojo .30 .09
416 Paul Sorrento .30 .09
417 Bob Wolcott .30 .09
418 Damon Buford .30 .09
419 Kevin Gross .30 .09
420 Darryl Hamilton UER .30 .09
421 Mike Henneman .30 .09
422 Ken Hill .30 .09
423 Dean Palmer .30 .09
424 Bobby Witt .30 .09
425 Tilson Brito RC .30 .09
426 Giovanni Carrara RC .30 .09
427 Domingo Cedeno .30 .09
428 Felipe Crespo .30 .09
429 Carlos Delgado .30 .09
430 Juan Guzman .30 .09
431 Erik Hanson .30 .09
432 Marty Janzen .30 .09
433 Otis Nixon .30 .09
434 Robert Perez .30 .09
435 Paul Quantrill .30 .09
436 Bill Risley .30 .09
437 Steve Avery .30 .09
438 Jermaine Dye .30 .09
439 Mark Lemke .30 .09
440 Marty Malloy RC .30 .09
441 Fred McGriff .50 .15
442 Greg McMichael .30 .09
443 Wonderful Monds RC .30 .09
444 Eddie Perez .30 .09
445 Jason Schmidt .50 .15
446 Terrell Wade .30 .09
447 Terry Adams .30 .09
448 Scott Bullett .30 .09
449 Robin Jennings .30 .09
450 Doug Jones .30 .09
451 Brooks Kieschnick .30 .09
452 Dave Magadan .30 .09
453 Jason Maxwell RC .30 .09
454 Brian McRae .30 .09
455 Rodney Myers RC .30 .09
456 Jaime Navarro .30 .09
457 Ryne Sandberg 1.25 .35
458 Vince Coleman .30 .09
459 Eric Davis .30 .09
460 Steve Gibralter .30 .09
461 Thomas Howard .30 .09
462 Mike Kelly .30 .09
463 Hal Morris .30 .09
464 Eric Owens .30 .09
465 Jose Rijo .30 .09
466 Chris Sabo .30 .09
467 Eddie Taubensee .30 .09
468 Trenidad Hubbard .30 .09
469 Curt Leskanic .30 .09
470 Quinton McCracken .30 .09
471 Jayhawk Owens .30 .09
472 Steve Reed .30 .09
473 Bryan Rekar .30 .09
474 Bruce Ruffin .30 .09
475 Bret Saberhagen .30 .09
476 Walt Weiss .30 .09
477 Eric Young .30 .09
478 Kevin Brown .30 .09
479 Al Leiter .30 .09
480 Pat Rapp .30 .09
481 Gary Sheffield .30 .09
482 Devon White .30 .09
483 Bob Abreu .30 .09
484 Sean Berry .30 .09
485 Craig Biggio .50 .15
486 Jim Dougherty .30 .09
487 Richard Hidalgo .30 .09
488 Darryl Kile .30 .09
489 Derrick May .30 .09
490 Greg Swindell .30 .09
491 Rick Wilkins .30 .09
492 Mike Blowers .30 .09
493 Tom Candiotti .30 .09
494 Roger Cedeno .30 .09
495 Delino DeShields .30 .09
496 Greg Gagne .30 .09
497 Karim Garcia .30 .09
498 Wilton Guerrero RC .40 .12
499 Chan Ho Park .30 .09
500 Israel Alcantara .30 .09
501 Shane Andrews .30 .09
502 Yamil Benitez .30 .09
503 Cliff Floyd .30 .09
504 Mark Grudzielanek .30 .09
505 Ryan McGuire .30 .09
506 Sherman Obando .30 .09
507 Jose Paniagua .30 .09
508 Henry Rodriguez .30 .09
509 Kirk Rueter .30 .09
510 Juan Acevedo .30 .09
511 John Franco .30 .09
512 Bernard Gilkey .30 .09
513 Lance Johnson .30 .09
514 Rey Ordonez .30 .09
515 Robert Person .30 .09
516 Paul Wilson .30 .09
517 Toby Borland .30 .09
518 David Doster RC .30 .09
519 Lenny Dykstra .30 .09
520 Sid Fernandez .30 .09
521 Mike Grace RC .30 .09

522 Rich Hunter .30 .09
523 Benito Santiago .30 .09
524 Gene Schall .30 .09
525 Curt Schilling .30 .09
526 Kevin Sefcik RC .30 .09
527 Lee Tinsley .30 .09
528 David West .30 .09
529 Mark Whiten .30 .09
530 Todd Zeile .30 .09
531 Carlos Garcia .30 .09
532 Charlie Hayes .30 .09
533 Jason Kendall .30 .09
534 Jeff King .30 .09
535 Mike Kingery .30 .09
536 Nelson Liriano .30 .09
537 Dan Plesac .30 .09
538 Paul Wagner .30 .09
539 Luis Alicea .30 .09
540 David Bell .30 .09
541 Alan Benes .30 .09
542 Andy Benes .30 .09
543 Mike Busby RC .30 .09
544 Royce Clayton .30 .09
545 Dennis Eckersley .30 .09
546 Gary Gaetti .30 .09
547 Ron Gant .30 .09
548 Aaron Holbert .30 .09
549 Ray Lankford .30 .09
550 T.J. Mathews .30 .09
551 Willie McGee .30 .09
552 Miguel Mejia .30 .09
553 Todd Stottlemyre .30 .09
554 Sean Bergman .30 .09
555 Willie Blair .30 .09
556 Andujar Cedeno .30 .09
557 Steve Finley .30 .09
558 Rickey Henderson .75 .23
559 Wally Joyner .30 .09
560 Scott Livingstone .30 .09
561 Marc Newfield .30 .09
562 Bob Tewksbury .30 .09
563 Fernando Valenzuela .30 .09
564 Rod Beck .30 .09
565 Doug Creek .30 .09
566 Shawon Dunston .30 .09
567 O.Fernandez RC .30 .09
568 Stan Javier .30 .09
569 Marcus Jensen .30 .09
570 Steve Scarsone .30 .09
571 Robby Thompson .30 .09
572 Allen Watson .30 .09
573 Roberto Alomar STA .30 .09
574 Jeff Bagwell STA .30 .09
575 Albert Belle STA .30 .09
576 Wade Boggs STA .30 .09
577 Barry Bonds STA .75 .23
578 Juan Gonzalez STA .30 .09
579 Ken Griffey Jr. STA .75 .23
580 Tony Gwynn STA .50 .15
581 Randy Johnson STA .50 .15
582 Chipper Jones STA .50 .15
583 Barry Larkin STA .30 .09
584 Kenny Lofton STA .30 .09
585 Greg Maddux STA .75 .23
586 Raul Mondesi STA .30 .09
587 Mike Piazza STA .75 .23
588 Cal Ripken STA 1.25 .35
589 Tim Salmon STA .30 .09
590 Frank Thomas STA .50 .15
591 Mo Vaughn STA .30 .09
592 Matt Williams STA .30 .09
593 Marty Cordova RAW .30 .09
594 Jim Edmonds RAW .30 .09
595 Cliff Floyd RAW .30 .09
596 Chipper Jones RAW .50 .15
597 Ryan Klesko RAW .30 .09
598 Raul Mondesi RAW .30 .09
599 Manny Ramirez RAW .30 .09
600 Ruben Rivera RAW .30 .09
DD1 C. Ripken DD 50.00 15.00
Issued through dealers
Serial numbered to 2131
DD2 Cal Ripken DD 25.00 7.50
Issued through a wrapper redemption

1996 Ultra Gold Medallion

The 1996 Ultra Gold Medallion is a parallel to the regular Ultra issue. The cards were inserted one per pack in both first and second series. The card consists of a full gold foil paper with a full-color player cut out on top. Backs are identical to the regular cards.

Nm-Mt Ex-Mt
COMPLETE SET (600) 200.00 60.00
COMP.SERIES 1 (300) 100.00 30.00
COMP.SERIES 2 (300) 100.00 30.00
*STARS: 1.25X TO 3X BASIC CARDS.
*ROOKIES: 1.25X TO 3X BASIC CARDS

1996 Ultra Call to the Hall

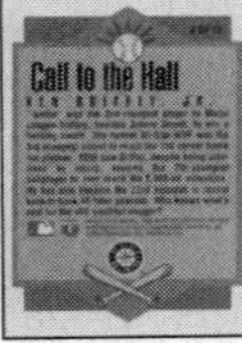

Randomly inserted in second series packs at a rate of one in 24, this ten-card set features original illustrations of possible future Hall of Famers. The backs state why the player is a possible HOF.

Nm-Mt Ex-Mt
COMPLETE SET (10) 60.00 18.00
*GOLD MEDAL: .75X TO 2X BASIC CALL
GM SER.2 STATED ODDS 1:240
1 Barry Bonds 12.00 3.60
2 Ken Griffey Jr. 8.00 2.40
3 Tony Gwynn 6.00 1.80
4 Rickey Henderson 5.00 1.50
5 Greg Maddux 8.00 2.40
6 Eddie Murray 5.00 1.50
7 Cal Ripken 15.00 4.50
8 Ryne Sandberg 8.00 2.40
9 Ozzie Smith 8.00 2.40
10 Frank Thomas 5.00 1.50

1996 Ultra Checklists

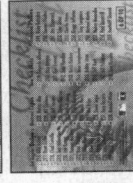

Randomly inserted in packs at a rate of one every four packs, this set of 20 standard-size cards features superstars of the game. Fronts are full-bleed color action photos of players with "Checklist" written in gold foil across the card. The horizontal backs are numbered and show the different card sets that are included in the Ultra line. The cards are sequenced in alphabetical order. A gold medallion parallel version of each card was issued.

Nm-Mt Ex-Mt
COMPLETE SERIES 1 (10) 10.00 3.00
COMPLETE SERIES 2 (10) 8.00 2.40
*GOLD MEDAL: .75X TO 2X BASIC CL
GM STATED ODDS 1:40
A1 Jeff Bagwell .60 .18
A2 Barry Bonds 2.50 .75
A3 Juan Gonzalez .60 .18
A4 Ken Griffey Jr. 1.50 .45
A5 Chipper Jones 1.00 .30
A6 Mike Piazza 1.50 .45
A7 Manny Ramirez .60 .18
A8 Cal Ripken 3.00 .90
A9 Frank Thomas 1.00 .30
A10 Matt Williams .40 .12
B1 Albert Belle .40 .12
B2 Cecil Fielder .40 .12
B3 Ken Griffey Jr. 1.50 .45
B4 Tony Gwynn 1.25 .35
B5 Derek Jeter 2.50 .75
B6 Jason Kendall .40 .12
B7 Ryan Klesko .40 .12
B8 Greg Maddux 1.50 .45
B9 Cal Ripken 3.00 .90
B10 Frank Thomas 1.00 .30

1996 Ultra Diamond Producers

This 12-card standard-size set highlights the achievements of Major League stars. The cards were randomly inserted at a rate of one in 20. The cards are sequenced in alphabetical order and there are also gold medallion versions of these cards.

Nm-Mt Ex-Mt
COMPLETE SET (12) 60.00 18.00
*GOLD MEDAL: .75X TO 2X BASIC DIAMOND
GM SER.1 STATED ODDS 1:200
1 Albert Belle 1.50 .45
2 Barry Bonds 10.00 3.00
3 Ken Griffey Jr. 6.00 1.80
4 Tony Gwynn 5.00 1.50
5 Greg Maddux 6.00 1.80
6 Hideo Nomo 4.00 1.20
7 Mike Piazza 6.00 1.80
8 Kirby Puckett 4.00 1.20
9 Cal Ripken 12.00 3.60
10 Frank Thomas 4.00 1.20
11 Mo Vaughn 1.50 .45
12 Matt Williams 1.50 .45

1996 Ultra Fresh Foundations

Randomly inserted one every three packs, this 10-card standard-size set highlights the play of hot young players. The cards are sequenced in alphabetical order and there are also gold medallion versions of these cards.

Nm-Mt Ex-Mt
COMPLETE SET (10) 3.00 .90
*GOLD MEDAL: .75X TO 2X BASIC FRESH
GM SER.1 STATED ODDS 1:30
1 Garret Anderson .30 .09
2 Marty Cordova .30 .09
3 Jim Edmonds .30 .09
4 Brian L.Hunter .30 .09
5 Chipper Jones .75 .23
6 Ryan Klesko .30 .09
7 Raul Mondesi .30 .09
8 Hideo Nomo .75 .23
9 Manny Ramirez .50 .15
10 Rondell White .30 .09

1996 Ultra Golden Prospects

Randomly inserted at a rate of one in five hobby packs, this 10-card standard-size set features players who are likely to make it as major leaguers. The cards are sequenced in alphabetical order and there are also gold medallion versions of these cards.

Nm-Mt Ex-Mt
COMPLETE SET (10) 5.00 1.50
*GOLD MEDAL: .75X TO 2X BASIC GOLDEN
GM SER.1 STATED ODDS 1:50 HOBBY
1 Yamil Benitez .60 .18
2 Alberto Castillo .60 .18
3 Roger Cedeno .60 .18
4 Johnny Damon 1.00 .30
5 Micah Franklin .60 .18
6 Jason Giambi .60 .18
7 Jose Herrera .60 .18
8 Derek Jeter 4.00 1.20
9 Kevin Jordan .60 .18
10 Ruben Rivera .60 .18

1996 Ultra Golden Prospects Hobby

Randomly inserted in hobby packs only at a rate of one in 72, this 15-card set is printed on crystal card stock and showcases players awaiting their Major League debut. The backs carry some information about their accomplishments in the Minor Leagues. A first year card of Tony Batista is featured within this set.

Nm-Mt Ex-Mt
COMPLETE SET (15) 100.00 30.00
*GOLD MED: .75X TO 2X BASIC GOLD.HOB
GM SER.2 STATED ODDS 1:720 HOBBY
1 Bob Abreu 4.00 1.20
2 Israel Alcantara 4.00 1.20
3 Tony Batista 5.00 1.50
4 Mike Cameron 8.00 2.40
5 Steve Cox 4.00 1.20
6 Jermaine Dye 4.00 1.20
7 Wilton Guerrero 4.00 1.20
8 Richard Hidalgo 4.00 1.20
9 Raul Ibanez 8.00 2.40
10 Marty Janzen 4.00 1.20
11 Robin Jennings 4.00 1.20
12 Jason Maxwell 4.00 1.20
13 Scott McClain 4.00 1.20
14 Wonderful Monds 4.00 1.20
15 Chris Singleton 4.00 1.20

1996 Ultra Hitting Machines

Randomly inserted in second series packs at a rate of one in 288, this 10-card set features players who hit the ball hard and often.

Nm-Mt Ex-Mt
COMPLETE SET (10) 100.00 30.00
*GOLD MEDAL: .75X TO 2X BASIC HIT.MACH.
GM SER.2 STATED ODDS 1:2880
1 Albert Belle 6.00 1.80
2 Barry Bonds 40.00 12.00
3 Juan Gonzalez 10.00 3.00
4 Ken Griffey Jr. 25.00 7.50
5 Edgar Martinez 10.00 3.00
6 Rafael Palmeiro 10.00 3.00
7 Mike Piazza 25.00 7.50
8 Tim Salmon 10.00 3.00
9 Frank Thomas 15.00 4.50
10 Matt Williams 6.00 1.80

1996 Ultra Home Run Kings

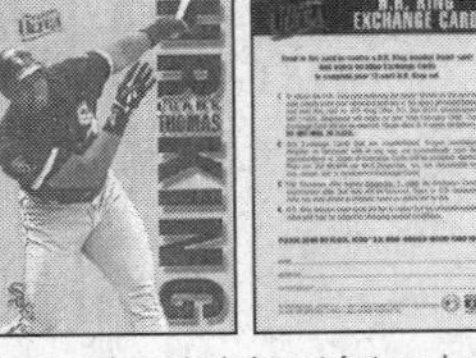

This 12-card standard-size set features leading power hitters. These cards were randomly inserted at a rate of one in 75 packs. The card fronts are thin wood with a color cut out of the player and HR KING printed diagonally in copper foil down the left side. The Fleer company was not happy with the final look of the card because of the transfer of the copper foil. Therefore all cards were made redemption cards. Backs of the cards have information about how to redeem the cards for replacement. The exchange offer expired on December 1, 1996. The cards are sequenced in alphabetical order.

Nm-Mt Ex-Mt
COMPLETE SET (12) 50.00 15.00
*GOLD MEDAL: 4X TO 10X BASIC HR KINGS
GM SER.1 STATED ODDS 1:750
*REDEMPTION: .6X TO 1.5X BASIC HR KINGS
ONE RDMP.CARD VIA MAIL PER HR CARD
1 Albert Belle 2.00 .60
2 Dante Bichette 2.00 .60
3 Barry Bonds 12.00 3.60
4 Jose Canseco 5.00 1.50
5 Juan Gonzalez 3.00 .90
6 Ken Griffey Jr. 8.00 2.40
7 Mark McGwire 12.00 3.60
8 Manny Ramirez 3.00 .90
9 Tim Salmon 3.00 .90
10 Frank Thomas 5.00 1.50
11 Mo Vaughn 2.00 .60
12 Matt Williams 2.00 .60

1996 Ultra On-Base Leaders

Randomly inserted in second series packs at a rate of one in four, this 10-card set features players with consistently high on-base percentage.

Nm-Mt Ex-Mt
COMPLETE SET (10) 5.00 1.50
*GOLD MEDAL: .75X TO 2X BASIC OBL
GM SER.2 STATED ODDS 1:40
1 Wade Boggs .60 .18
2 Barry Bonds 2.50 .75
3 Tony Gwynn 1.25 .35
4 Rickey Henderson 1.00 .30
5 Chuck Knoblauch .40 .12
6 Edgar Martinez .60 .18
7 Mike Piazza 1.50 .45
8 Tim Salmon .60 .18
9 Frank Thomas 1.00 .30
10 Jim Thome 1.00 .30

1996 Ultra Power Plus

Randomly inserted at a rate of one in ten packs, this 12-card standard-size set features top all-around players. The cards are sequenced in alphabetical order and gold medallion versions of these cards were also issued.

Nm-Mt Ex-Mt
COMPLETE SET (12) 25.00 7.50
*GOLD MEDAL: .75X TO 2X BASIC PLUS
GM SER.1 STATED ODDS 1:100
1 Jeff Bagwell 1.50 .45
2 Barry Bonds 6.00 1.80
3 Ken Griffey Jr. 4.00 1.20
4 Raul Mondesi 1.00 .30
5 Rafael Palmeiro 1.50 .45
6 Mike Piazza 4.00 1.20
7 Manny Ramirez 1.50 .45
8 Tim Salmon 1.50 .45
9 Reggie Sanders 1.00 .30
10 Frank Thomas 2.50 .75
11 Larry Walker 1.50 .45
12 Matt Williams 1.00 .30

1996 Ultra Prime Leather

Eighteen outstanding defensive players are featured in this standard-size set which is inserted approximately one in every eight packs. The cards are sequenced in alphabetical order and gold medallion versions of these cards were also issued.

Nm-Mt Ex-Mt
COMPLETE SET (18) 25.00 7.50
*GOLD MEDAL: .75X TO 2X BASIC LEATHER
GM SER.1 STATED ODDS 1:80
1 Ivan Rodriguez 2.50 .75
2 Will Clark 2.50 .75
3 Roberto Alomar 1.50 .45
4 Cal Ripken 8.00 2.40
5 Wade Boggs 1.50 .45
6 Ken Griffey Jr. 4.00 1.20
7 Kenny Lofton 1.00 .30
8 Kirby Puckett 2.50 .75
9 Tim Salmon 1.50 .45
10 Mike Piazza 4.00 1.20
11 Mark Grace 1.50 .45
12 Craig Biggio 1.50 .45
13 Barry Larkin 1.50 .45
14 Matt Williams 1.00 .30
15 Barry Bonds 6.00 1.80
16 Tony Gwynn 3.00 .90
17 Brian McRae 1.00 .30
18 Raul Mondesi 1.00 .30
S4 Cal Ripken Jr Promo 8.00 2.40

1996 Ultra Rawhide

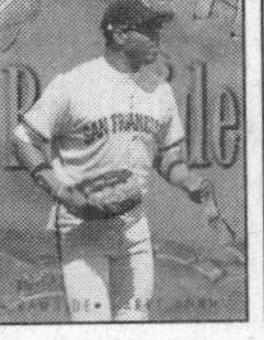

Randomly inserted in second series packs at a rate of one in eight, this 10-card set features leading defensive players.

Nm-Mt Ex-Mt
COMPLETE SET (10) 15.00 4.50
*GOLD MEDAL: .75X TO 2X BASIC RAWHIDE
GM SER.2 STATED ODDS 1:80
1 Roberto Alomar 1.00 .30
2 Barry Bonds 4.00 1.20
3 Mark Grace 1.00 .30
4 Ken Griffey Jr. 2.50 .75
5 Kenny Lofton .60 .18
6 Greg Maddux 2.50 .75
7 Raul Mondesi .60 .18
8 Mike Piazza 2.50 .75
9 Cal Ripken 5.00 1.50
10 Matt Williams .60 .18

1996 Ultra RBI Kings

This 10-card standard-size set was randomly inserted at a rate of one in five retail packs. The cards are sequenced in alphabetical order and gold medallion versions of these cards were also issued.

Nm-Mt Ex-Mt
COMPLETE SET (10) 30.00 9.00
*GOLD MEDAL: .75X TO 2X BASIC RBI KINGS
GM SER.1 STATED ODDS 1:50 RETAIL
1 Derek Bell 2.00 .60
2 Albert Belle 2.00 .60
3 Dante Bichette 2.00 .60
4 Barry Bonds 12.00 3.60
5 Jim Edmonds 2.00 .60
6 Manny Ramirez 3.00 .90
7 Reggie Sanders 2.00 .60
8 Sammy Sosa 8.00 2.40
9 Frank Thomas 5.00 1.50
10 Mo Vaughn 2.00 .60

1996 Ultra Respect

Randomly inserted in second series packs at a rate of one in 18, this 10-card set features players who are well regarded by their peers for both on and off field activies.

Nm-Mt Ex-Mt
COMPLETE SET (10) 50.00 15.00
*GOLD MEDAL: .75X TO 2X BASIC RESPECT
GM SER.2 STATED ODDS 1:180
1 Joe Carter 1.50 .45
2 Ken Griffey Jr. 6.00 1.80
3 Tony Gwynn 5.00 1.50
4 Greg Maddux 6.00 1.80
5 Eddie Murray 4.00 1.20
6 Kirby Puckett 4.00 1.20
7 Cal Ripken 12.00 3.60
8 Ryne Sandberg 6.00 1.80
9 Frank Thomas 4.00 1.20
10 Mo Vaughn 1.50 .45

1996 Ultra Rising Stars

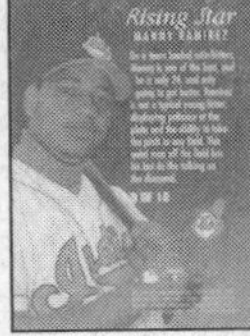

Randomly inserted in second series packs at a rate of one in four, this 10-card set features leading players of tomorrow.

Nm-Mt Ex-Mt
COMPLETE SET (10) 4.00 1.20
*GOLD MEDAL: .75X TO 2X BASIC RISING

GM SER.2 STATED ODDS 1:40
1 Garret Anderson .30 .09
2 Marty Cordova .30 .09
3 Jim Edmonds .30 .09
4 Cliff Floyd .30 .09
5 Brian L.Hunter .30 .09
6 Chipper Jones .75 .23
7 Ryan Klesko .30 .09
8 Hideo Nomo .75 .23
9 Manny Ramirez .50 .15
10 Rondell White .30 .09

1996 Ultra Season Crowns

This set features ten award winners and stat leaders. The cards were randomly inserted at a rate of one in ten. The clear acetate cards feature a full-color player cutout against a background of colored foliage and laurels.

Nm-Mt Ex-Mt
COMPLETE SET (10) 30.00 9.00
*GOLD MEDAL: .75X TO 2X BASIC CROWNS
GM SER.1 STATED ODDS 1:100
1 Barry Bonds 6.00 1.80
2 Tony Gwynn 3.00 .90
3 Randy Johnson 2.50 .75
4 Kenny Lofton 1.00 .30
5 Greg Maddux 4.00 1.20
6 Edgar Martinez 1.50 .45
7 Hideo Nomo 2.50 .75
8 Cal Ripken 8.00 2.40
9 Frank Thomas 2.50 .75
10 Tim Wakefield 1.00 .30

1996 Ultra Thunderclap

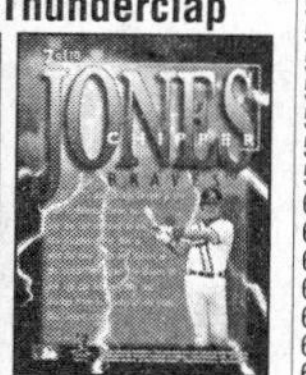

Randomly inserted one in 72 retail packs, these cards feature the leading power hitters.

Nm-Mt Ex-Mt
COMPLETE SET (20) 100.00 30.00
*GOLD MEDAL: .75X TO 2X BASIC THUNDER
GM SER.2 STATED ODDS 1:720 RETAIL
1 Albert Belle 5.00 1.50
2 Barry Bonds 30.00 9.00
3 Bobby Bonilla 5.00 1.50
4 Jose Canseco 12.00 3.60
5 Joe Carter 5.00 1.50
6 Will Clark 12.00 3.60
7 Andre Dawson 5.00 1.50
8 Cecil Fielder 5.00 1.50
9 Andres Galarraga 5.00 1.50
10 Juan Gonzalez 8.00 2.40
11 Ken Griffey Jr. 20.00 6.00
12 Fred McGriff 8.00 2.40
13 Mark McGwire 30.00 9.00
14 Eddie Murray 12.00 3.60
15 Rafael Palmeiro 8.00 2.40
16 Kirby Puckett 12.00 3.60
17 Cal Ripken 40.00 12.00
18 Ryne Sandberg 25.00 7.50
19 Frank Thomas 12.00 3.60
20 Matt Williams 5.00 1.50

1997 Ultra

'he 1997 Ultra was issued in two series totalling 53 cards. The first series consisted of 300 ards with the second containing 253. The 10-ard packs had a suggested retail price of 2.49 ach. Each pack had two insert cards, with one nsert being a gold medallion parallel and the ther insert being from one of several other nsert sets. The fronts features borderless color ction player photos with career statistics on the acks. As in most Fleer produced sets, the cards re arranged in alphabetical order by league, layer and team. Second series retail packs conained only cards 301-450 while second series obby packs contained all cards from 301-553. ookie Cards include Jose Cruz Jr., Brian Giles nd Fernando Tatis.

Nm-Mt Ex-Mt
OMPLETE SET (553) 60.00 18.00
OMP.SERIES 1 (300) 30.00 9.00
OMP.SERIES 2 (253) 30.00 9.00
OMMON CARD (1-553) .30 .09
OMMON RC .40 .12
Roberto Alomar .50 .15
Brady Anderson .30 .09
Rocky Coppinger .30 .09
Jeffrey Hammonds .30 .09
Chris Hoiles .30 .09
Eddie Murray .75 .23
7 Mike Mussina .50 .15
8 Jimmy Myers .30 .09
9 Randy Myers .30 .09
10 Arthur Rhodes .30 .09
11 Cal Ripken 2.50 .75
12 Jose Canseco .75 .23
13 Roger Clemens 1.50 .45
14 Tom Gordon .30 .09
15 Jose Malave .30 .09
16 Tim Naehring .30 .09
17 Troy O'Leary .30 .09
18 Bill Selby .30 .09
19 Heathcliff Slocumb .30 .09
20 Mike Stanley .30 .09
21 Mo Vaughn .30 .09
22 Garret Anderson .30 .09
23 George Arias .30 .09
24 Chili Davis .30 .09
25 Jim Edmonds .30 .09
26 Darin Erstad .30 .09
27 Chuck Finley .30 .09
28 Todd Greene .30 .09
29 Troy Percival .30 .09
30 Tim Salmon .50 .15
31 Jeff Schmidt .30 .09
32 Randy Velarde .30 .09
33 Shad Williams .30 .09
34 Wilson Alvarez .30 .09
35 Harold Baines .30 .09
36 James Baldwin .30 .09
37 Mike Cameron .30 .09
38 Ray Durham .30 .09
39 Ozzie Guillen .30 .09
40 Roberto Hernandez .30 .09
41 Darren Lewis .30 .09
42 Jose Munoz .30 .09
43 Tony Phillips .30 .09
44 Frank Thomas .75 .23
45 Sandy Alomar Jr. .30 .09
46 Albert Belle .30 .09
47 Mark Carreon .30 .09
48 Julio Franco .30 .09
49 Orel Hershiser .30 .09
50 Kenny Lofton .30 .09
51 Jack McDowell .30 .09
52 Jose Mesa .30 .09
53 Charles Nagy .30 .09
54 Manny Ramirez .50 .15
55 Julian Tavarez .30 .09
56 Omar Vizquel .50 .15
57 Raul Casanova .30 .09
58 Tony Clark .30 .09
59 Travis Fryman .30 .09
60 Bob Higginson .30 .09
61 Melvin Nieves .30 .09
62 Curtis Pride .30 .09
63 Justin Thompson .30 .09
64 Alan Trammell .50 .15
65 Kevin Appier .30 .09
66 Johnny Damon .50 .15
67 Keith Lockhart .30 .09
68 Jeff Montgomery .30 .09
69 Jose Offerman .30 .09
70 Bip Roberts .30 .09
71 Jose Rosado .30 .09
72 Chris Stynes .30 .09
73 Mike Sweeney .30 .09
74 Jeff Cirillo .30 .09
75 Jeff D'Amico .30 .09
76 John Jaha .30 .09
77 Scott Karl .30 .09
78 Mike Matheny .30 .09
79 Ben McDonald .30 .09
80 Matt Mieske .30 .09
81 Marc Newfield .30 .09
82 Dave Nilsson .30 .09
83 Jose Valentin .30 .09
84 Fernando Vina .30 .09
85 Rick Aguilera .30 .09
86 Marty Cordova .30 .09
87 Chuck Knoblauch .30 .09
88 Matt Lawton .30 .09
89 Pat Meares .30 .09
90 Paul Molitor .50 .15
91 Greg Myers .30 .09
92 Dan Naulty .30 .09
93 Kirby Puckett .75 .23
94 Frank Rodriguez .30 .09
95 Wade Boggs .50 .15
96 Cecil Fielder .30 .09
97 Joe Girardi .30 .09
98 Dwight Gooden .50 .15
99 Derek Jeter 2.00 .60
100 Tino Martinez .50 .15
101 Ramiro Mendoza RC .30 .09
102 Andy Pettitte .50 .15
103 Mariano Rivera .50 .15
104 Ruben Rivera .30 .09
105 Kenny Rogers .30 .09
106 Darryl Strawberry .50 .15
107 Bernie Williams .50 .15
108 Tony Batista .30 .09
109 Geronimo Berroa .30 .09
110 Bobby Chouinard .30 .09
111 Brent Gates .30 .09
112 Jason Giambi .75 .23
113 Damon Mashore .30 .09
114 Mark McGwire 2.00 .60
115 Scott Spiezio .30 .09
116 John Wasdin .30 .09
117 Steve Wojciechowski .30 .09
118 Ernie Young .30 .09
119 Norm Charlton .30 .09
120 Joey Cora .30 .09
121 Ken Griffey Jr. 1.25 .35
122 Sterling Hitchcock .30 .09
123 Raul Ibanez .30 .09
124 Randy Johnson .75 .23
125 Edgar Martinez .50 .15
126 Alex Rodriguez 1.25 .35
127 Matt Wagner .30 .09
128 Bob Wells .30 .09
129 Dan Wilson .30 .09
130 Will Clark .75 .23
131 Kevin Elster .30 .09
132 Juan Gonzalez .50 .15
133 Rusty Greer .30 .09
134 Darryl Hamilton .30 .09
135 Mike Henneman .30 .09
136 Ken Hill .30 .09
137 Mark McLemore .30 .09
138 Dean Palmer .30 .09
139 Roger Pavlik .30 .09
140 Ivan Rodriguez .75 .23
141 Joe Carter .30 .09
142 Carlos Delgado .30 .09
143 Alex Gonzalez .30 .09
144 Juan Guzman .30 .09
145 Pat Hentgen .30 .09
146 Marty Janzen .30 .09
147 Otis Nixon .30 .09
148 Charlie O'Brien .30 .09
149 John Olerud .30 .09
150 Robert Perez .30 .09
151 Jermaine Dye .30 .09
152 Tom Glavine .50 .15
153 Andruw Jones .30 .09
154 Chipper Jones .75 .23
155 Ryan Klesko .30 .09
156 Javier Lopez .30 .09
157 Greg Maddux 1.25 .35
158 Fred McGriff .50 .15
159 Wonderful Monds .30 .09
160 John Smoltz .50 .15
161 Terrell Wade .30 .09
162 Mark Wohlers .30 .09
163 Brant Brown .30 .09
164 Mark Grace .50 .15
165 Tyler Houston .30 .09
166 Robin Jennings .30 .09
167 Jason Maxwell .30 .09
168 Ryne Sandberg 1.25 .35
169 Sammy Sosa 1.25 .35
170 Amaury Telemaco .30 .09
171 Steve Trachsel .30 .09
172 Pedro Valdes RC .30 .09
173 Tim Belk .30 .09
174 Bret Boone .30 .09
175 Jeff Brantley .30 .09
176 Eric Davis .30 .09
177 Barry Larkin .50 .15
178 Chad Mottola .30 .09
179 Mark Portugal .30 .09
180 Reggie Sanders .30 .09
181 John Smiley .30 .09
182 Eddie Taubensee .30 .09
183 Dante Bichette .30 .09
184 Ellis Burks .30 .09
185 Andres Galarraga .30 .09
186 Curt Leskanic .30 .09
187 Quinton McCracken .30 .09
188 Jeff Reed .30 .09
189 Kevin Ritz .30 .09
190 Walt Weiss .30 .09
191 Jamey Wright .30 .09
192 Eric Young .30 .09
193 Kevin Brown .30 .09
194 Luis Castillo .30 .09
195 Jeff Conine .30 .09
196 Andre Dawson .30 .09
197 Charles Johnson .30 .09
198 Al Leiter .30 .09
199 Ralph Milliard .30 .09
200 Robb Nen .30 .09
201 Edgar Renteria .30 .09
202 Gary Sheffield .30 .09
203 Bob Abreu .30 .09
204 Jeff Bagwell .50 .15
205 Derek Bell .30 .09
206 Sean Berry .30 .09
207 Richard Hidalgo .30 .09
208 Todd Jones .30 .09
209 Darryl Kile .30 .09
210 Orlando Miller .30 .09
211 Shane Reynolds .30 .09
212 Billy Wagner .30 .09
213 Donne Wall .30 .09
214 Roger Cedeno .30 .09
215 Greg Gagne .30 .09
216 Karim Garcia .30 .09
217 Wilton Guerrero .30 .09
218 Todd Hollandsworth .30 .09
219 Ramon Martinez .30 .09
220 Raul Mondesi .30 .09
221 Hideo Nomo .75 .23
222 Chan Ho Park .30 .09
223 Mike Piazza 1.25 .35
224 Ismael Valdes .30 .09
225 Moises Alou .30 .09
226 Derek Aucoin .30 .09
227 Yamil Benitez .30 .09
228 Jeff Fassero .30 .09
229 Darrin Fletcher .30 .09
230 Mark Grudzielanek .30 .09
231 Barry Manuel .30 .09
232 Pedro Martinez .75 .23
233 Henry Rodriguez .30 .09
234 Ugueth Urbina .30 .09
235 Rondell White .30 .09
236 Carlos Baerga .30 .09
237 John Franco .30 .09
238 Bernard Gilkey .30 .09
239 Todd Hundley .30 .09
240 Butch Huskey .30 .09
241 Jason Isringhausen .30 .09
242 Lance Johnson .30 .09
243 Bobby Jones .30 .09
244 Alex Ochoa .30 .09
245 Rey Ordonez .30 .09
246 Paul Wilson .30 .09
247 Ron Blazier .30 .09
248 David Doster .30 .09
249 Jim Eisenreich .30 .09
250 Mike Grace .30 .09
251 Mike Lieberthal .30 .09
252 Wendell Magee .30 .09
253 Mickey Morandini .30 .09
254 Ricky Otero .30 .09
255 Scott Rolen .75 .23
256 Curt Schilling .50 .15
257 Todd Zeile .30 .09
258 Jermaine Allensworth .30 .09
259 Trey Beamon .30 .09
260 Carlos Garcia .30 .09
261 Mark Johnson .30 .09
262 Jason Kendall .30 .09
263 Jeff King .30 .09
264 Al Martin .30 .09
265 Denny Neagle .30 .09
266 Matt Ruebel .30 .09
267 Marc Wilkins .30 .09
268 Alan Benes .30 .09
269 Dennis Eckersley .30 .09
270 Ron Gant .30 .09
271 Aaron Holbert .30 .09
272 Brian Jordan .30 .09
273 Ray Lankford .30 .09
274 John Mabry .30 .09
275 T.J. Mathews .30 .09
276 Ozzie Smith 1.25 .35
277 Todd Stottlemyre .30 .09
278 Mark Sweeney .30 .09
279 Andy Ashby .30 .09
280 Steve Finley .30 .09
281 John Flaherty .30 .09
282 Chris Gomez .30 .09
283 Tony Gwynn 1.00 .30
284 Joey Hamilton .30 .09
285 Rickey Henderson .75 .23
286 Trevor Hoffman .30 .09
287 Jason Thompson .30 .09
288 Fernando Valenzuela .30 .09
289 Greg Vaughn .30 .09
290 Barry Bonds 2.00 .60
291 Jay Canizaro .30 .09
292 Jacob Cruz .30 .09
293 Shawon Dunston .30 .09
294 Shawn Estes .30 .09
295 Mark Gardner .30 .09
296 Marcus Jensen .30 .09
297 Bill Mueller RC 3.00 .90
298 Chris Singleton .30 .09
299 Allen Watson .30 .09
300 Matt Williams .30 .09
301 Rod Beck .30 .09
302 Jay Bell .30 .09
303 Shawon Dunston .30 .09
304 Reggie Jefferson .30 .09
305 Darren Oliver .30 .09
306 Benito Santiago .30 .09
307 Gerald Williams .30 .09
308 Damon Buford .30 .09
309 Jeromy Burnitz .30 .09
310 Sterling Hitchcock .30 .09
311 Dave Hollins .30 .09
312 Mel Rojas .30 .09
313 Robin Ventura .30 .09
314 David Wells .30 .09
315 Cal Eldred .30 .09
316 Gary Gaetti .30 .09
317 John Hudek .30 .09
318 Brian Johnson .30 .09
319 Denny Neagle .30 .09
320 Larry Walker .50 .15
321 Russ Davis .30 .09
322 Delino DeShields .30 .09
323 Charlie Hayes .30 .09
324 Jermaine Dye .30 .09
325 John Ericks .30 .09
326 Jeff Fassero .30 .09
327 Nomar Garciaparra 1.25 .35
328 Willie Greene .30 .09
329 Greg McMichael .30 .09
330 Damion Easley .30 .09
331 Ricky Bones .30 .09
332 John Burkett .30 .09
333 Royce Clayton .30 .09
334 Greg Colbrunn .30 .09
335 Tony Eusebio .30 .09
336 Gregg Jefferies .30 .09
337 Wally Joyner .30 .09
338 Jim Leyritz .30 .09
339 Paul O'Neill .50 .15
340 Bruce Ruffin .30 .09
341 Michael Tucker .30 .09
342 Andy Benes .30 .09
343 Craig Biggio .50 .15
344 Rex Hudler .30 .09
345 Brad Radke .30 .09
346 Deion Sanders .50 .15
347 Moises Alou .30 .09
348 Brad Ausmus .30 .09
349 Armando Benitez .30 .09
350 Mark Gubicza .30 .09
351 Terry Steinbach .30 .09
352 Mark Whiten .30 .09
353 Ricky Bottalico .30 .09
354 Brian Giles RC 1.50 .45
355 Eric Karros .30 .09
356 Jimmy Key .30 .09
357 Carlos Perez .30 .09
358 Alex Fernandez .30 .09
359 J.T. Snow .30 .09
360 Bobby Bonilla .30 .09
361 Scott Brosius .30 .09
362 Greg Swindell .30 .09
363 Jose Vizcaino .30 .09
364 Matt Williams .30 .09
365 Darren Daulton .30 .09
366 Shane Andrews .30 .09
367 Jim Eisenreich .30 .09
368 Ariel Prieto .30 .09
369 Bob Tewksbury .30 .09
370 Mike Bordick .30 .09
371 Rheal Cormier .30 .09
372 Cliff Floyd .30 .09
373 David Justice .30 .09
374 John Wetteland .30 .09
375 Mike Blowers .30 .09
376 Jose Canseco .75 .23
377 Roger Clemens 1.50 .45
378 Kevin Mitchell .30 .09
379 Todd Zeile .30 .09
380 Jim Thome .75 .23
381 Turk Wendell .30 .09
382 Rico Brogna .30 .09
383 Eric Davis .30 .09
384 Mike Lansing .30 .09
385 Devon White .30 .09
386 Marquis Grissom .30 .09
387 Todd Worrell .30 .09
388 Jeff Kent .30 .09
389 Mickey Tettleton .30 .09
390 Steve Avery .30 .09
391 David Cone .30 .09
392 Scott Cooper .30 .09
393 Lee Stevens .30 .09
394 Kevin Elster .30 .09
395 Tom Goodwin .30 .09
396 Shawn Green .30 .09
397 Pete Harnisch .30 .09
398 Eddie Murray .75 .23
399 Joe Randa .30 .09
400 Scott Sanders .30 .09
401 John Valentin .30 .09
402 Todd Jones .30 .09
403 Terry Adams .30 .09
404 Brian Hunter .30 .09
405 Pat Listach .30 .09
406 Kenny Lofton .30 .09
407 Hal Morris .30 .09
408 Ed Sprague .30 .09
409 Rich Becker .30 .09
410 Edgardo Alfonzo .30 .09
411 Albert Belle .30 .09
412 Jeff King .30 .09
413 Kirt Manwaring .30 .09
414 Jason Schmidt .30 .09
415 Allen Watson .30 .09
416 Lee Tinsley .30 .09
417 Brett Butler .30 .09
418 Carlos Garcia .30 .09
419 Mark Lemke .30 .09
420 Jaime Navarro .30 .09
421 David Segui .30 .09
422 Ruben Sierra .30 .09
423 B.J. Surhoff .30 .09
424 Julian Tavarez .30 .09
425 Billy Taylor .30 .09
426 Ken Caminiti .30 .09
427 Chuck Carr .30 .09
428 Benji Gil .30 .09
429 Terry Mulholland .30 .09
430 Mike Stanton .30 .09
431 Wil Cordero .30 .09
432 Chili Davis .30 .09
433 Mariano Duncan .30 .09
434 Orlando Merced .30 .09
435 Kent Mercker .30 .09
436 John Olerud .30 .09
437 Quilvio Veras .30 .09
438 Mike Fetters .30 .09
439 Glenallen Hill .30 .09
440 Bill Swift .30 .09
441 Tim Wakefield .30 .09
442 Pedro Astacio .30 .09
443 Vinny Castilla .30 .09
444 Doug Drabek .30 .09
445 Alan Embree .30 .09
446 Lee Smith .30 .09
447 Darryl Hamilton .30 .09
448 Brian McRae .30 .09
449 Mike Timlin .30 .09
450 Bob Wickman .30 .09
451 Jason Dickson .30 .09
452 Chad Curtis .30 .09
453 Mark Leiter .30 .09
454 Damon Berryhill .30 .09
455 Kevin Orie .30 .09
456 Dave Burba .30 .09
457 Chris Holt .30 .09
458 Ricky Ledee RC .40 .12
459 Mike Devereaux .30 .09
460 Pokey Reese .30 .09
461 Tim Raines .30 .09
462 Ryan Jones .30 .09
463 Shane Mack .30 .09
464 Darren Dreifort .30 .09
465 Mark Parent .30 .09
466 Mark Portugal .30 .09
467 Dante Powell .30 .09
468 Craig Grebeck .30 .09
469 Ron Villone .30 .09
470 Dmitri Young .30 .09
471 Shannon Stewart .30 .09
472 Rick Helling .30 .09
473 Bill Haselman .30 .09
474 Albie Lopez .30 .09
475 Glendon Rusch .30 .09
476 Derrick May .30 .09
477 Chad Ogea .30 .09
478 Kirk Rueter .30 .09
479 Chris Hammond .30 .09
480 Russ Johnson .30 .09
481 James Mouton .30 .09
482 Mike Macfarlane .30 .09
483 Scott Ruffcorn .30 .09
484 Jeff Frye .30 .09
485 Richie Sexson .30 .09
486 Emil Brown RC .40 .12
487 Desi Wilson .30 .09
488 Brent Gates .30 .09
489 Tony Graffanino .30 .09
490 Dan Miceli .30 .09
491 Orlando Cabrera RC 1.50 .60
492 Tony Womack RC .60 .18
493 Jerome Walton .30 .09
494 Mark Thompson .30 .09
495 Jose Guillen .30 .09
496 Willie Blair .30 .09
497 T.J. Staton RC .40 .12
498 Scott Kamieniecki .30 .09
499 Vince Coleman .30 .09
500 Jeff Abbott .30 .09
501 Chris Widger .30 .09
502 Kevin Tapani .30 .09
503 Carlos Castillo RC .40 .12
504 Luis Gonzalez .30 .09
505 Tim Belcher .30 .09
506 Armando Reynoso .30 .09
507 Jamie Moyer .30 .09
508 Randall Simon RC .40 .12
509 Vladimir Guerrero .75 .23
510 Wady Almonte RC .40 .12
511 Dustin Hermanson .30 .09
512 Deivi Cruz RC .40 .12
513 Luis Alicea .30 .09
514 Felix Heredia RC .40 .12
515 Don Slaught .30 .09
516 S.Hasegawa RC 1.00 .30
517 Matt Walbeck .30 .09
518 David Arias-Ortiz RC 20.00 6.00
519 Brady Raggio RC .40 .12
520 Rudy Pemberton .30 .09
521 Wayne Kirby .30 .09
522 Calvin Maduro .30 .09
523 Mark Lewis .30 .09
524 Mike Jackson .30 .09
525 Sid Fernandez .30 .09
526 Mike Bielecki .30 .09

527 Bubba Trammell RC	.40	.12
528 Brent Brede RC	.40	.12
529 Matt Morris	.30	.09
530 Joe Borowski RC	.40	.12
531 Orlando Miller	.30	.09
532 Jim Bullinger	.30	.09
533 Robert Person	.30	.09
534 Doug Glanville	.30	.09
535 Terry Pendleton	.30	.09
536 Jorge Posada	.50	.15
537 Marc Sagmoen RC	.40	.12
538 Fernando Tatis RC	.40	.12
539 Aaron Sele	.30	.09
540 Brian Banks	.30	.09
541 Derrek Lee	.30	.09
542 John Wasdin	.30	.09
543 Justin Towle RC	.40	.12
544 Pat Cline	.30	.09
545 Dave Magadan	.30	.09
546 Jeff Blauser	.30	.09
547 Phil Nevin	.30	.09
548 Todd Walker	.30	.09
549 Eli Marrero	.30	.09
550 Bartolo Colon	.30	.09
551 Jose Cruz Jr. RC	.60	.18
552 Todd Dunwoody	.30	.09
553 Hideki Irabu RC	.40	.12
P11 Cal Ripken Promo Three Card Strip	2.00	.60

1997 Ultra Gold Medallion

This 553-card set is a gold-holofoil-stamped parallel version of the regular Ultra set and was inserted one per pack of both series one and series two cards. Unlike previous Gold Medallion sets, the 1997 edition features different photos than the corresponding regular cards.

	Nm-Mt	Ex-Mt
COMPLETE SET (553)	270.00	80.00
COMP. SERIES 1 (300)	150.00	45.00
COMP. SERIES 2 (253)	120.00	36.00
*STARS: 1.25X TO 3X BASIC CARDS.		
*ROOKIES: .75X TO 2X BASIC		

1997 Ultra Platinum Medallion

This 553-card set is a parallel to the regular Ultra and was inserted one per 100 packs of both series 1 and series 2 cards. Sparkling platinum lettering on front differentiates these cards from their far more common regular issue brethren. No set price is provided due to scarcity. As with the 1997 Gold Medallion set, the Platinum Medallion set features different photos than the corresponding regular cards.

	Nm-Mt	Ex-Mt
*STARS 1-450: 12.5X TO 30X BASIC CARDS		
*STARS 451-553: 10X TO 25X BASIC CARDS		
*ROOKIES 1-450: 8X TO 20X BASIC		
*ROOKIES: 451-553: 5X TO 12X BASIC		
297 Bill Mueller	30.00	9.00

1997 Ultra Autographstix Emeralds

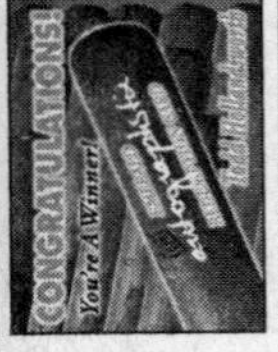

This six-card hobby exclusive Series two insert set consists of individually numbered Redemption cards for autographed bats from the players checklisted below. Only 25 of each card was produced. The deadline to exchange cards was July 1st, 1998. The bat a collector received for these cards was not easily identifiable as a special bat. Prices listed refer to the exchange cards.

	Nm-Mt	Ex-Mt
EXCHANGE DEADLINE: 07/01/98		
1 Alex Ochoa		
2 Todd Walker		
3 Scott Rolen		
4 Darin Erstad		
5 Alex Rodriguez		
6 Todd Hollandsworth		

1997 Ultra Baseball Rules

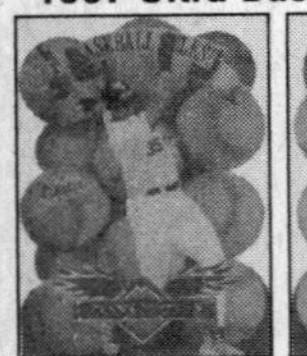
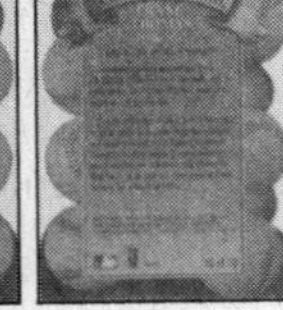

Randomly inserted into first series retail packs of 1997 Ultra at a rate of 1:36, cards from this 10-card set feature a selection of baseball's top performers from the 1996 season. The die cut cards feature a player photo surrounded by a group of baseballs. The back explains some of the rules involved in making various awards.

	Nm-Mt	Ex-Mt
COMPLETE SET (10)	120.00	36.00
1 Barry Bonds	15.00	4.50
2 Ken Griffey Jr.	10.00	3.00
3 Derek Jeter	15.00	4.50
4 Chipper Jones	6.00	1.80
5 Greg Maddux	10.00	3.00
6 Mark McGwire	15.00	4.50
7 Troy Percival	2.50	.75
8 Mike Piazza	10.00	3.00
9 Cal Ripken	20.00	6.00
10 Frank Thomas	6.00	1.80

1997 Ultra Checklists

Randomly inserted in all first and second series packs at a rate of one in four, this 20-card set features borderless player photos on the front along with the word "Checklist", the player's name as well as the "ultra" logo at the bottom. The backs are checklists. The checklists for Series 1 are listed below with an "A" prefix and for Series 2 with a "B" prefix.

	Nm-Mt	Ex-Mt
COMPLETE SERIES 1 (10)	8.00	2.40
COMPLETE SERIES 2 (10)	12.00	3.60
A1 Dante Bichette	.30	.09
A2 Barry Bonds	2.00	.60
A3 Ken Griffey Jr.	1.25	.35
A4 Greg Maddux	1.25	.35
A5 Mark McGwire	2.00	.60
A6 Mike Piazza	1.25	.35
A7 Cal Ripken	2.50	.75
A8 John Smoltz	.50	.15
A9 Sammy Sosa	1.25	.35
A10 Frank Thomas	.75	.23
B1 Andruw Jones	.30	.09
B2 Ken Griffey Jr.	1.25	.35
B3 Frank Thomas	.75	.23
B4 Alex Rodriguez	1.25	.35
B5 Cal Ripken	2.50	.75
B6 Mike Piazza	1.25	.35
B7 Greg Maddux	1.25	.35
B8 Chipper Jones	.75	.23
B9 Derek Jeter	2.00	.60
B10 Juan Gonzalez	.50	.15

1997 Ultra Diamond Producers

Randomly inserted in all first series packs at a rate of one in 288, this 12-card set features "flannel" material mounted on card stock and attempt to look and feel like actual uniforms.

	Nm-Mt	Ex-Mt
COMPLETE SET (12)	250.00	75.00
1 Jeff Bagwell	10.00	3.00
2 Barry Bonds	40.00	12.00
3 Ken Griffey Jr.	25.00	7.50
4 Chipper Jones	15.00	4.50
5 Kenny Lofton	6.00	1.80
6 Greg Maddux	25.00	7.50
7 Mark McGwire	40.00	12.00
8 Mike Piazza	25.00	7.50
9 Cal Ripken	50.00	15.00
10 Alex Rodriguez	25.00	7.50
11 Frank Thomas	15.00	4.50
12 Matt Williams	6.00	1.80

1997 Ultra Double Trouble

Randomly inserted in series one packs at a rate of one in four, this 20-card set features two players from each team. The horizontal cards feature players photos with their names in silver foil on the bottom and the words "double trouble" on the top. The backs feature information on what the players contributed to their team in 1996

	Nm-Mt	Ex-Mt
COMPLETE SET (20)	10.00	3.00
1 Roberto Alomar Cal Ripken	2.50	.75
2 Mo Vaughn Jose Canseco	.30	.09
3 Jim Edmonds Tim Salmon	.30	.09
4 Harold Baines Frank Thomas	.75	.23
5 Albert Belle Kenny Lofton	.30	.09
6 Marty Cordova Chuck Knoblauch	.30	.09
7 Derek Jeter Andy Pettitte	2.00	.60
8 Jason Giambi Mark McGwire	2.00	.60
9 Ken Griffey Jr. Alex Rodriguez	1.25	.35
10 Juan Gonzalez Will Clark	.50	.15
11 Greg Maddux Chipper Jones	1.25	.35
12 Mark Grace Sammy Sosa	1.25	.35
13 Dante Bichette Andres Galarraga	.30	.09
14 Jeff Bagwell Derek Bell	.50	.15
15 Hideo Nomo Mike Piazza	1.25	.35
16 Henry Rodriguez Moises Alou	.30	.09
17 Rey Ordonez Alex Ochoa	.30	.09
18 Ray Lankford Ron Gant	.30	.09
19 Tony Gwynn Rickey Henderson	1.00	.30
20 Barry Bonds Matt Williams	2.00	.60

1997 Ultra Fame Game

Randomly inserted in series two hobby packs only at a rate of one in eight, this 18-card set features color photos of players who have displayed Hall of Fame potential on an elegant card design.

	Nm-Mt	Ex-Mt
COMPLETE SET (18)	60.00	18.00
1 Ken Griffey Jr.	5.00	1.50
2 Frank Thomas	3.00	.90
3 Alex Rodriguez	5.00	1.50
4 Cal Ripken	10.00	3.00
5 Mike Piazza	5.00	1.50
6 Greg Maddux	5.00	1.50
7 Derek Jeter	8.00	2.40
8 Jeff Bagwell	2.00	.60
9 Juan Gonzalez	2.00	.60
10 Albert Belle	1.25	.35
11 Tony Gwynn	4.00	1.20
12 Mark McGwire	8.00	2.40
13 Andy Pettitte	2.00	.60
14 Kenny Lofton	1.25	.35
15 Roberto Alomar	2.00	.60
16 Ryne Sandberg	5.00	1.50
17 Barry Bonds	8.00	2.40
18 Eddie Murray	3.00	.90

1997 Ultra Fielder's Choice

Randomly inserted in series one packs at a rate of one in 144, this 18-card set uses leather and gold foil to honor leading defensive players. The horizontal cards also include a player photo on the front as well as the big bold words "97 Fleer Ultra", "Fielder's Choice" and the player's name. The horizontal backs have another player photo as well as information about their defensive prowess.

	Nm-Mt	Ex-Mt
COMPLETE SET (18)	200.00	60.00
1 Roberto Alomar	8.00	2.40
2 Jeff Bagwell	8.00	2.40
3 Wade Boggs	8.00	2.40
4 Barry Bonds	30.00	9.00
5 Mark Grace	8.00	2.40
6 Ken Griffey Jr.	20.00	6.00
7 Marquis Grissom	5.00	1.50
8 Charles Johnson	5.00	1.50
9 Chuck Knoblauch	5.00	1.50
10 Barry Larkin	8.00	2.40
11 Kenny Lofton	5.00	1.50
12 Greg Maddux	20.00	6.00
13 Raul Mondesi	5.00	1.50
14 Rey Ordonez	5.00	1.50
15 Cal Ripken	40.00	12.00
16 Alex Rodriguez	20.00	6.00
17 Ivan Rodriguez	12.00	3.60
18 Matt Williams	5.00	1.50

1997 Ultra Golden Prospects

Randomly inserted in series two hobby packs only at a rate of one in four, this 10-card set features color action player images on a gold baseball background with commentary on what makes these players so promising..

	Nm-Mt	Ex-Mt
COMPLETE SET (10)	5.00	1.50
1 Andruw Jones	.30	.09
2 Vladimir Guerrero	.75	.23
3 Todd Walker	.30	.09
4 Karim Garcia	.30	.09
5 Kevin Orie	.30	.09
6 Brian Giles	1.50	.45
7 Jason Dickson	.30	.09
8 Jose Guillen	.30	.09
9 Ruben Rivera	.30	.09
10 Derrek Lee	.30	.09

1997 Ultra Hitting Machines

Randomly inserted in series two hobby packs only at a rate of one in 36, this 18-card set features color action player images of the MLB's most productive hitters in "machine-style" die-cut settings.

	Nm-Mt	Ex-Mt
COMPLETE SET (18)	120.00	36.00
1 Andruw Jones	2.50	.75
2 Ken Griffey Jr.	10.00	3.00
3 Frank Thomas	6.00	1.80
4 Alex Rodriguez	10.00	3.00
5 Cal Ripken	20.00	6.00
6 Mike Piazza	10.00	3.00
7 Derek Jeter	15.00	4.50
8 Albert Belle	2.50	.75
9 Tony Gwynn	8.00	2.40
10 Jeff Bagwell	4.00	1.20
11 Mark McGwire	15.00	4.50
12 Kenny Lofton	2.50	.75
13 Manny Ramirez	4.00	1.20
14 Roberto Alomar	4.00	1.20
15 Ryne Sandberg	10.00	3.00
16 Eddie Murray	6.00	1.80
17 Sammy Sosa	10.00	3.00
18 Ken Caminiti	2.50	.75

1997 Ultra Home Run Kings

Randomly inserted in series one hobby packs only at a rate of one in 36, this 12-card set feaures ultra crystal cards with transparent refractive holo-foil technology. The players pictured are all leading power hitters.

	Nm-Mt	Ex-Mt
COMPLETE SET (12)	80.00	24.00
1 Albert Belle	2.50	.75
2 Barry Bonds	15.00	4.50
3 Juan Gonzalez	4.00	1.20
4 Ken Griffey Jr.	10.00	3.00
5 Todd Hundley	2.50	.75
6 Ryan Klesko	2.50	.75
7 Mark McGwire	15.00	4.50
8 Mike Piazza	10.00	3.00
9 Sammy Sosa	10.00	3.00
10 Frank Thomas	6.00	1.80
11 Mo Vaughn	2.50	.75
12 Matt Williams	2.50	.75

1997 Ultra Leather Shop

Randomly inserted in series two hobby packs only at a rate of one in six, this 12-card set features color player images of some of the best fielders in the game highlighted by simulated leather backgrounds.

	Nm-Mt	Ex-Mt
COMPLETE SET (12)	15.00	4.50
1 Ken Griffey Jr.	1.50	.45
2 Alex Rodriguez	1.50	.45
3 Cal Ripken	3.00	.90
4 Derek Jeter	2.50	.75
5 Juan Gonzalez	.60	.18
6 Tony Gwynn	1.25	.35
7 Jeff Bagwell	.60	.18
8 Roberto Alomar	.60	.18
9 Ryne Sandberg	1.50	.45
10 Ken Caminiti	.40	.12
11 Kenny Lofton	.40	.12
12 John Smoltz	.60	.18

1997 Ultra Power Plus

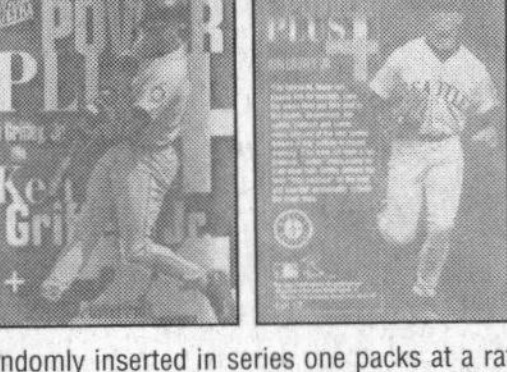

Randomly inserted in series one packs at a rate of one in 24 and Series two hobby only packs at the rate of one in eight, this 12-card set utilizes silver rainbow holo-foil and features players who not only hit with power but also excel at other parts of the game. The cards in the Series one insert set have an "A" prefix while the cards in the Series two insert set carry a "B" prefix in the checklist below.

	Nm-Mt	Ex-Mt
COMPLETE SERIES 1 (12)	80.00	24.00
COMPLETE SERIES 2 (12)	1.50	.45
A1 Jeff Bagwell	2.50	.75
A2 Barry Bonds	10.00	3.00
A3 Juan Gonzalez	2.50	.75
A4 Ken Griffey Jr.	6.00	1.80
A5 Chipper Jones	4.00	1.20
A6 Mark McGwire	10.00	3.00
A7 Mike Piazza	6.00	1.80
A8 Cal Ripken	12.00	3.60
A9 Alex Rodriguez	6.00	1.80
A10 Sammy Sosa	6.00	1.80
A11 Frank Thomas	4.00	1.20
A12 Matt Williams	1.50	.45
B1 Ken Griffey Jr.	2.50	.75
B2 Frank Thomas	1.50	.45
B3 Alex Rodriguez	2.50	.75
B4 Cal Ripken	5.00	1.50
B5 Mike Piazza	2.50	.75
B6 Chipper Jones	1.50	.45
B7 Albert Belle	.60	.18
B8 Juan Gonzalez	1.00	.30
B9 Jeff Bagwell	1.00	.30
B10 Mark McGwire	4.00	1.20
B11 Mo Vaughn	.60	.18
B12 Barry Bonds	4.00	1.20

1997 Ultra RBI Kings

Randomly inserted in series one packs at a rate of one in 18, this 10-card set features 100 percent etched-foil cards. The cards feature players who drive in many runs. The horizontal backs contain player information and another player photo.

	Nm-Mt	Ex-Mt
COMPLETE SET (10)	30.00	9.00
1 Jeff Bagwell	2.50	.75
2 Albert Belle	1.50	.45
3 Dante Bichette	1.50	.45
4 Barry Bonds	10.00	3.00
5 Jay Buhner	1.50	.45
6 Juan Gonzalez	2.50	.75
7 Ken Griffey Jr.	6.00	1.80
8 Sammy Sosa	6.00	1.80
9 Frank Thomas	4.00	1.20
10 Mo Vaughn	1.50	.45

1997 Ultra Rookie Reflections

Randomly inserted in series one packs at a rate of one in four, this 10-card set uses a silver foil design to feature young players. The horizontal backs contain player information as well as another player photo.

	Nm-Mt	Ex-Mt
COMPLETE SET (10)	4.00	1.20
1 James Baldwin	.40	.12
2 Jermaine Dye	.40	.12
3 Darin Erstad	.40	.12
4 Todd Hollandsworth	.40	.12
5 Derek Jeter	2.50	.75
6 Jason Kendall	.40	.12
7 Alex Ochoa	.40	.12
8 Rey Ordonez	.40	.12
9 Edgar Renteria	.40	.12
10 Scott Rolen	1.00	.30

1997 Ultra Season Crowns

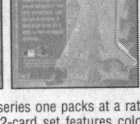

Randomly inserted in series one packs at a rate of one in eight, this 12-card set features color photos of baseball's top stars with etched foil backgrounds.

	Nm-Mt	Ex-Mt
COMPLETE SET (12)	10.00	3.00
1 Albert Belle	.40	.12
2 Dante Bichette	.40	.12
3 Barry Bonds	2.50	.75
4 Kenny Lofton	.40	.12
5 Edgar Martinez	.60	.18
6 Mark McGwire	2.50	.75
7 Andy Pettitte	.60	.18
8 Mike Piazza	1.50	.45
9 Alex Rodriguez	1.50	.45
10 John Smoltz	.60	.18
11 Sammy Sosa	1.50	.45
12 Frank Thomas	1.00	.30

1997 Ultra Starring Role

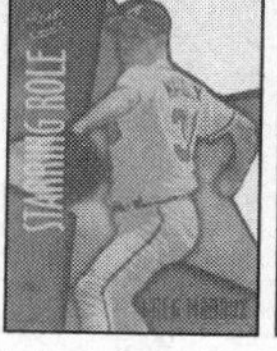

Randomly inserted in series two hobby packs only at a rate of one in 288, this 12-card set features color photos of tried-and-true clutch performers on die-cut plastic cards with foil stamping.

	Nm-Mt	Ex-Mt
COMPLETE SET (12)	250.00	75.00
1 Andruw Jones	6.00	1.80
2 Ken Griffey Jr.	25.00	7.50
3 Frank Thomas	15.00	4.50
4 Alex Rodriguez	25.00	7.50
5 Cal Ripken	50.00	15.00
6 Mike Piazza	25.00	7.50
7 Greg Maddux	25.00	7.50
8 Chipper Jones	15.00	4.50
9 Derek Jeter	40.00	12.00
10 Juan Gonzalez	10.00	3.00
11 Albert Belle	6.00	1.80
12 Tony Gwynn	20.00	6.00

1997 Ultra Thunderclap

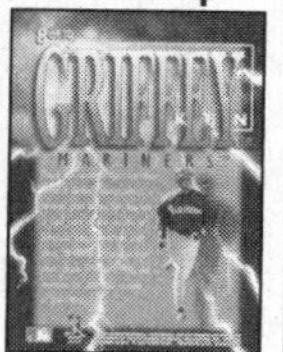

Randomly inserted in series two hobby packs only at a rate of one in 18, this 10-card set features color images of superstars who are feared by opponents for their ability to totally dominate a game on a background displaying lightning from a thunderstorm.

	Nm-Mt	Ex-Mt
COMPLETE SET (10)	60.00	18.00
1 Barry Bonds	10.00	3.00
2 Mo Vaughn	1.50	.45
3 Mark McGwire	10.00	3.00
4 Jeff Bagwell	2.50	.75
5 Juan Gonzalez	2.50	.75
6 Alex Rodriguez	6.00	1.80
7 Chipper Jones	4.00	1.20
8 Ken Griffey Jr.	6.00	1.80
9 Mike Piazza	6.00	1.80
10 Frank Thomas	4.00	1.20

1997 Ultra Top 30

Randomly inserted one in every Ultra series two retail packs only, this 30-card set features color action player images of top stars with a "Top 30" circle in the team-colored background. The backs carry another player image with his team logo the backsground circle.

	Nm-Mt	Ex-Mt
COMPLETE SET (30)	40.00	12.00
*GOLD MED: 2.5X TO 6X BASIC TOP 30		
G.MED SER.2 STATED ODDS 1:18 RETAIL		
1 Andruw Jones	.50	.15
2 Ken Griffey	2.00	.60
3 Frank Thomas	1.25	.35
4 Alex Rodriguez	2.00	.60
5 Cal Ripken	4.00	1.20
6 Mike Piazza	2.00	.60
7 Greg Maddux	2.00	.60
8 Chipper Jones	1.25	.35
9 Derek Jeter	3.00	.90
10 Juan Gonzalez	.75	.23
11 Albert Belle	.50	.15
12 Tony Gwynn	1.50	.45
13 Jeff Bagwell	.75	.23
14 Mark McGwire	3.00	.90
15 Andy Pettitte	.75	.23
16 Mo Vaughn	.50	.15
17 Kenny Lofton	.50	.15
18 Manny Ramirez	.75	.23
19 Roberto Alomar	.75	.23
20 Ryne Sandberg	2.00	.60
21 Hideo Nomo	1.25	.35
22 Barry Bonds	3.00	.90
23 Eddie Murray	1.25	.35
24 Ken Caminiti	.50	.15
25 John Smoltz	.75	.23
26 Pat Hentgen	.50	.15
27 Todd Hollandsworth	.50	.15
28 Matt Williams	.50	.15
29 Bernie Williams	.75	.23
30 Brady Anderson	.50	.15

1998 Ultra

The complete 1998 Ultra set features 501 cards and was distributed in 10-card first and second series packs with a suggested retail price of $2.59. The fronts carry UV coated color action player photos printed on 20 pt. card stock. The backs display another player photo with player information and career statistics. The set contains the following subsets: Season's Crown (211-220) seeded 1:12 packs, Prospects (221-245) seeded 1:4 packs, Checklists (246-250), and Checklists (473-475) seeded 1:4 packs and Pizzazz (476-500) seeded 1:4 packs. Rookie Cards include Kevin Millwood and Magglio Ordonez. Though not confirmed by the manufacturer, it's believed that several cards within the Prospects subset are in shorter supply than others - most notably number 238 Ricky Ledee and number 243 Jorge Velandia. Also, seeded one in every pack, was one of 50 Million Dollar Moment cards which pictured some of the greatest moments in baseball histroy and gave the collector a chance to win a million dollars. As a special last minute promotion, Fleer/SkyBox got Alex Rodriguez to autograph 750 of his 1998 Fleer Promo cards. Each card is serial-numbered by hand on the card front. The signed cards were randomly seeded into Ultra Series two hobby packs.

	Nm-Mt	Ex-Mt
COMPLETE SET (501)	160.00	47.50
COMP.SERIES 1 (250)	100.00	30.00
COMP.SERIES 2 (251)	60.00	18.00
COMP.SER.1 w/o SP's (210)	15.00	4.50
COMP.SER.2 w/o SP's (226)	15.00	4.50
COMMON (1-220/246-250)	.30	.09
COMMON (251-475/501)	.30	.09
COMMON SC (211-220)	2.00	.60
COMMON (221-245)	3.00	.90
COMMON PZ (476-500)	1.00	.30
1 Ken Griffey Jr.	1.25	.35
2 Matt Morris	.30	.09
3 Roger Clemens	1.50	.45
4 Matt Williams	.30	.09
5 Roberto Hernandez	.30	.09
6 Rondell White	.30	.09
7 Tim Salmon	.50	.15
8 Brad Radke	.30	.09
9 Brett Butler	.30	.09
10 Carl Everett	.30	.09
11 Chili Davis	.30	.09
12 Chuck Finley	.30	.09
13 Darryl Kile	.30	.09
14 Deivi Cruz	.30	.09
15 Gary Gaetti	.30	.09
16 Matt Stairs	.30	.09
17 Pat Meares	.30	.09
18 Will Cunnane	.30	.09
19 Steve Woodard	.30	.09
20 Andy Ashby	.30	.09
21 Bobby Higginson	.30	.09
22 Brian Jordan	.30	.09
23 Craig Biggio	.50	.15
24 Jim Edmonds	.30	.09
25 Ryan McGuire	.30	.09
26 Scott Hatteberg	.30	.09
27 Willie Greene	.30	.09
28 Albert Belle	.30	.09
29 Ellis Burks	.30	.09
30 Hideo Nomo	.75	.23
31 Jeff Bagwell	.50	.15
32 Kevin Brown	.50	.15
33 Nomar Garciaparra	1.25	.35
34 Pedro Martinez	.75	.23
35 Raul Mondesi	.30	.09
36 Ricky Bottalico	.30	.09
37 Shawn Estes	.30	.09
38 Otis Nixon	.30	.09
39 Terry Steinbach	.30	.09
40 Tom Glavine	.50	.15
41 Todd Dunwoody	.30	.09
42 Deion Sanders	.50	.15
43 Gary Sheffield	.30	.09
44 Mike Lansing	.30	.09
45 Mike Lieberthal	.30	.09
46 Paul Sorrento	.30	.09
47 Paul O'Neill	.50	.15
48 Tom Goodwin	.30	.09
49 Andruw Jones	.30	.09
50 Barry Bonds	2.00	.60
51 Bernie Williams	.50	.15
52 Jeremi Gonzalez	.30	.09
53 Mike Piazza	1.25	.35
54 Russ Davis	.30	.09
55 Vinny Castilla	.30	.09
56 Rod Beck	.30	.09
57 Andres Galarraga	.30	.09
58 Ben McDonald	.30	.09
59 Billy Wagner	.30	.09
60 Charles Johnson	.30	.09
61 Fred McGriff	.50	.15
62 Dean Palmer	.30	.09
63 Frank Thomas	.75	.23
64 Ismael Valdes	.30	.09
65 Mark Bellhorn	.30	.09
66 Jeff King	.30	.09
67 John Wetteland	.30	.09
68 Mark Grace	.50	.15
69 Mark Kotsay	.30	.09
70 Scott Rolen	.75	.23
71 Todd Hundley	.30	.09
72 Todd Worrell	.30	.09
73 Wilson Alvarez	.30	.09
74 Bobby Jones	.30	.09
75 Jose Canseco	.75	.23
76 Kevin Appier	.30	.09
77 Neifi Perez	.30	.09
78 Paul Molitor	.50	.15
79 Quilvio Veras	.30	.09
80 Randy Johnson	.75	.23
81 Glendon Rusch	.30	.09
82 Curt Schilling	.30	.09
83 Alex Rodriguez	1.25	.35
84 Rey Ordonez	.30	.09
85 Jeff Juden	.30	.09
86 Mike Cameron	.30	.09
87 Ryan Klesko	.30	.09
88 Trevor Hoffman	.30	.09
89 Chuck Knoblauch	.30	.09
90 Larry Walker	.50	.15
91 Mark McLemore	.30	.09
92 B.J. Surhoff	.30	.09
93 Darren Daulton	.30	.09
94 Ray Durham	.30	.09
95 Sammy Sosa	1.25	.35
96 Eric Young	.30	.09
97 Gerald Williams	.30	.09
98 Javy Lopez	.30	.09
99 John Smiley	.30	.09
100 Juan Gonzalez	.50	.15
101 Shawn Green	.30	.09
102 Charles Nagy	.30	.09
103 David Justice	.30	.09
104 Joey Hamilton	.30	.09
105 Pat Hentgen	.30	.09
106 Raul Casanova	.30	.09
107 Tony Phillips	.30	.09
108 Tony Gwynn	1.00	.30
109 Will Clark	.75	.23
110 Jason Giambi	.30	.09
111 Jay Bell	.30	.09
112 Johnny Damon	.50	.15
113 Alan Benes	.30	.09
114 Jeff Suppan	.30	.09
115 Kevin Polcovich	.30	.09
116 Shigetoshi Hasegawa	.30	.09
117 Steve Finley	.30	.09
118 Tony Clark	.30	.09
119 David Cone	.30	.09
120 Jose Guillen	.30	.09
121 Kevin Millwood RC	1.00	.30
122 Greg Maddux	1.25	.35
123 Dave Nilsson	.30	.09
124 Hideki Irabu	.30	.09
125 Jason Kendall	.30	.09
126 Jim Thome	.75	.23
127 Delino DeShields	.30	.09
128 Edgar Renteria	.30	.09
129 Edgardo Alfonzo	.30	.09
130 J.T. Snow	.30	.09
131 Jeff Abbott	.30	.09
132 Jeffrey Hammonds	.30	.09
133 Todd Greene	.30	.09
134 Vladimir Guerrero	.75	.23
135 Jay Buhner	.30	.09
136 Jeff Cirillo	.30	.09
137 Jeromy Burnitz	.30	.09
138 Mickey Morandini	.30	.09
139 Tino Martinez	.50	.15
140 Jeff Shaw	.30	.09
141 Rafael Palmeiro	.50	.15
142 Bobby Bonilla	.30	.09
143 Cal Ripken	2.50	.75
144 Chad Fox RC	.30	.09
145 Dante Bichette	.30	.09
146 Dennis Eckersley	.30	.09
147 Mariano Rivera	.50	.15
148 Mo Vaughn	.30	.09
149 Reggie Sanders	.30	.09
150 Derek Jeter	2.00	.60
151 Rusty Greer	.30	.09
152 Brady Anderson	.30	.09
153 Brett Tomko	.30	.09
154 Jaime Navarro	.30	.09
155 Kevin Orie	.30	.09
156 Roberto Alomar	.50	.15
157 Edgar Martinez	.50	.15
158 John Olerud	.30	.09
159 John Smoltz	.50	.15
160 Ryne Sandberg	1.25	.35
161 Billy Taylor	.30	.09
162 Chris Holt	.30	.09
163 Damion Easley	.30	.09
164 Darin Erstad	.30	.09
165 Joe Carter	.30	.09
166 Kelvim Escobar	.30	.09
167 Ken Caminiti	.30	.09
168 Pokey Reese	.30	.09
169 Ray Lankford	.30	.09
170 Livan Hernandez	.30	.09
171 Steve Kline	.30	.09
172 Tom Gordon	.30	.09
173 Travis Fryman	.30	.09
174 Al Martin	.30	.09
175 Andy Pettitte	.50	.15
176 Jeff Kent	.30	.09
177 Jimmy Key	.30	.09
178 Mark Grudzielanek	.30	.09
179 Tony Saunders	.30	.09
180 Barry Larkin	.50	.15
181 Bubba Trammell	.30	.09
182 Carlos Delgado	.30	.09
183 Carlos Baerga	.30	.09
184 Derek Bell	.30	.09
185 Henry Rodriguez	.30	.09
186 Jason Dickson	.30	.09
187 Ron Gant	.30	.09
188 Tony Womack	.30	.09
189 Justin Thompson	.30	.09
190 Fernando Tatis	.30	.09
191 Mark Wohlers	.30	.09
192 Takashi Kashiwada	.30	.09
193 Garret Anderson	.30	.09
194 Jose Cruz Jr.	.30	.09
195 Ricardo Rincon	.30	.09
196 Tim Naehring	.30	.09
197 Moises Alou	.30	.09
198 Eric Karros	.30	.09
199 John Jaha	.30	.09
200 Marty Cordova	.30	.09
201 Ken Hill	.30	.09
202 Chipper Jones	.75	.23
203 Kenny Lofton	.30	.09
204 Mike Mussina	.50	.15
205 Manny Ramirez	.30	.09
206 Todd Hollandsworth	.30	.09
207 Cecil Fielder	.30	.09
208 Mark McGwire	2.00	.60
209 Jim Leyritz	.30	.09
210 Ivan Rodriguez	.75	.23
211 Jeff Bagwell SC	2.00	.60
212 Barry Bonds SC	8.00	2.40
213 Roger Clemens SC	6.00	1.80
214 N.Garciaparra SC	5.00	1.50
215 Ken Griffey Jr. SC	5.00	1.50
216 Tony Gwynn SC	4.00	1.20
217 Randy Johnson SC	3.00	.90
218 Mark McGwire SC	8.00	2.40
219 Scott Rolen SC	3.00	.90
220 Frank Thomas SC	3.00	.90
221 Matt Perisho PROS	3.00	.90
222 Wes Helms PROS	3.00	.90
223 D.Dellucci PROS RC	3.00	.90
224 Todd Helton PROS	3.00	.90
225 Brian Rose PROS	3.00	.90
226 Aaron Boone PROS	3.00	.90
227 Keith Foulke PROS	3.00	.90
228 Homer Bush PROS	3.00	.90
229 S.Stewart PROS	3.00	.90
230 R.Hidalgo PROS	3.00	.90
231 Russ Johnson PROS	3.00	.90
232 H.Blanco PROS RC	3.00	.90
233 Paul Konerko PROS	3.00	.90
234 A.Williamson PROS	3.00	.90
235 S.Bowers PROS RC	3.00	.90
236 Jose Vidro PROS	3.00	.90
237 Derek Wallace PROS	3.00	.90
238 Ricky Ledee PROS SP	5.00	1.50
239 Ben Grieve PROS	3.00	.90
240 Lou Collier PROS	3.00	.90
241 Derrek Lee PROS	3.00	.90
242 Ruben Rivera PROS	3.00	.90
243 J.Velandia PROS SP	5.00	1.50
244 Andrew Vessel PROS	3.00	.90
245 Chris Carpenter PROS	3.00	.90
246 Ken Griffey Jr. CL	.75	.23
247 Alex Rodriguez CL	.75	.23
248 Diamond Ink CL	.30	.09
249 Frank Thomas CL	.50	.15
250 Cal Ripken CL	1.25	.35
251 Carlos Perez	.30	.09
252 Larry Sutton	.30	.09
253 Gary Sheffield	.30	.09
254 Wally Joyner	.30	.09
255 Todd Stottlemyre	.30	.09
256 Nerio Rodriguez	.30	.09
257 Charles Johnson	.30	.09
258 Pedro Astacio	.30	.09
259 Cal Eldred	.30	.09
260 Chili Davis	.30	.09
261 Freddy Garcia	.30	.09
262 Bobby Witt	.30	.09
263 Michael Coleman	.30	.09
264 Mike Caruso	.30	.09
265 Mike Lansing	.30	.09
266 Dennis Reyes	.30	.09
267 F.P. Santangelo	.30	.09
268 Darryl Hamilton	.30	.09
269 Mike Fetters	.30	.09
270 Charlie Hayes	.30	.09
271 Royce Clayton	.30	.09
272 Doug Drabek	.30	.09
273 James Baldwin	.30	.09
274 Brian Hunter	.30	.09
275 Chan Ho Park	.30	.09
276 John Franco	.30	.09
277 David Wells	.30	.09
278 Eli Marrero	.30	.09
279 Kerry Wood	.75	.23
280 Donnie Sadler	.30	.09
281 Scott Winchester RC	.30	.09
282 Hal Morris	.30	.09
283 Brad Fullmer	.30	.09
284 Bernard Gilkey	.30	.09
285 Ramiro Mendoza	.30	.09
286 Kevin Brown	.50	.15
287 David Segui	.30	.09
288 Willie McGee	.30	.09
289 Darren Oliver	.30	.09
290 Antonio Alfonseca	.30	.09
291 Eric Davis	.30	.09
292 Mickey Morandini	.30	.09
293 Frank Catalanotto RC	.50	.15
294 Derrek Lee	.30	.09
295 Todd Zeile	.30	.09
296 Chuck Knoblauch	.30	.09
297 Wilson Delgado	.30	.09
298 Bobby Bonilla	.30	.09
299 Orel Hershiser	.30	.09
300 Ozzie Guillen	.30	.09
301 Aaron Sele	.30	.09
302 Joe Carter	.30	.09
303 Darryl Kile	.30	.09
304 Shane Reynolds	.30	.09
305 Todd Dunn	.30	.09
306 Bob Abreu	.30	.09
307 Doug Strange	.30	.09
308 Jose Canseco	.75	.23
309 Lance Johnson	.30	.09
310 Harold Baines	.30	.09
311 Todd Pratt	.30	.09
312 Greg Colbrunn	.30	.09
313 Masato Yoshii RC	.50	.15
314 Felix Heredia	.30	.09
315 Dennis Martinez	.30	.09
316 Geronimo Berroa	.30	.09
317 Darren Lewis	.30	.09
318 Bill Ripken	.30	.09
319 Enrique Wilson	.30	.09
320 Alex Ochoa	.30	.09
321 Doug Glanville	.30	.09
322 Mike Stanley	.30	.09
323 Gerald Williams	.30	.09
324 Pedro Martinez	.75	.23
325 Jaret Wright	.30	.09
326 Terry Pendleton	.30	.09
327 LaTroy Hawkins	.30	.09
328 Emil Brown	.30	.09
329 Walt Weiss	.30	.09
330 Omar Vizquel	.50	.15
331 Carl Everett	.30	.09
332 Fernando Vina	.30	.09
333 Mike Blowers	.30	.09
334 Dwight Gooden	.50	.15
335 Mark Lewis	.30	.09
336 Jim Leyritz	.30	.09
337 Kenny Lofton	.30	.09
338 John Halama RC	.30	.09
339 Jose Valentin	.30	.09
340 Desi Relaford	.30	.09
341 Dante Powell	.30	.09
342 Ed Sprague	.30	.09
343 Reggie Jefferson	.30	.09
344 Mike Hampton	.30	.09
345 Marquis Grissom	.30	.09
346 Heathcliff Slocumb	.30	.09
347 Francisco Cordova	.30	.09
348 Ken Cloude	.30	.09
349 Benito Santiago	.30	.09
350 Denny Neagle	.30	.09
351 Sean Casey	.30	.09
352 Robb Nen	.30	.09
353 Orlando Merced	.30	.09
354 Adrian Brown	.30	.09
355 Gregg Jefferies	.30	.09
356 Otis Nixon	.30	.09
357 Michael Tucker	.30	.09
358 Eric Milton	.30	.09
359 Travis Fryman	.30	.09
360 Gary DiSarcina	.30	.09
361 Mario Valdez	.30	.09
362 Craig Counsell	.30	.09
363 Jose Offerman	.30	.09
364 Tony Fernandez	.30	.09
365 Jason McDonald	.30	.09
366 Sterling Hitchcock	.30	.09
367 Donovan Osborne	.30	.09
368 Troy Percival	.30	.09
369 Henry Rodriguez	.30	.09
370 Dmitri Young	.30	.09
371 Jay Powell	.30	.09
372 Jeff Conine	.30	.09
373 Orlando Cabrera	.30	.09
374 Butch Huskey	.30	.09
375 Mike Lowell RC	1.50	.45
376 Kevin Young	.30	.09
377 Jamie Moyer	.30	.09
378 Jeff D'Amico	.30	.09
379 Scott Erickson	.30	.09
380 Magglio Ordonez RC	2.50	.75
381 Melvin Nieves	.30	.09
382 Ramon Martinez	.30	.09
383 A.J. Hinch	.30	.09
384 Jeff Brantley	.30	.09
385 Kevin Elster	.30	.09
386 Allen Watson	.30	.09
387 Moises Alou	.30	.09
388 Jeff Blauser	.30	.09
389 Pete Harnisch	.30	.09
390 Shane Andrews	.30	.09
391 Rico Brogna	.30	.09
392 Stan Javier	.30	.09
393 David Howard	.30	.09
394 Darryl Strawberry	.30	.09
395 Kent Mercker	.30	.09
396 Juan Encarnacion	.30	.09
397 Sandy Alomar Jr.	.30	.09
398 Al Leiter	.30	.09
399 Tony Graffanino	.30	.09
400 Terry Adams	.30	.09
401 Bruce Aven	.30	.09
402 Derrick Gibson	.30	.09
403 Jose Cabrera RC	.30	.09
404 Rich Becker	.30	.09
405 David Ortiz	.75	.23
406 Brian McRae	.30	.09
407 Bobby Estalella	.30	.09
408 Bill Mueller	.30	.09
409 Dennis Eckersley	.30	.09
410 Sandy Martinez	.30	.09
411 Jose Vizcaino	.30	.09
412 Jermaine Allensworth	.30	.09
413 Miguel Tejada	.30	.09
414 Turner Ward	.30	.09
415 Glenallen Hill	.30	.09
416 Lee Stevens	.30	.09
417 Cecil Fielder	.30	.09
418 Ruben Sierra	.30	.09
419 Jon Nunnally	.30	.09
420 Rod Myers	.30	.09
421 Dustin Hermanson	.30	.09
422 James Mouton	.30	.09
423 Dan Wilson	.30	.09
424 Roberto Kelly	.30	.09
425 Antonio Osuna	.30	.09
426 Jacob Cruz	.30	.09
427 Brent Mayne	.30	.09
428 Matt Karchner	.30	.09
429 Damian Jackson	.30	.09
430 Roger Cedeno	.30	.09
431 Rickey Henderson	.75	.23
432 Joe Randa	.30	.09
433 Greg Vaughn	.30	.09
434 Andres Galarraga	.30	.09
435 Rod Beck	.30	.09
436 Curtis Goodwin	.30	.09
437 Brad Ausmus	.30	.09
438 Bob Hamelin	.30	.09
439 Todd Walker	.30	.09
440 Scott Brosius	.30	.09
441 Len Dykstra	.30	.09
442 Abraham Nunez	.30	.09
443 Brian Johnson	.30	.09
444 Randy Myers	.30	.09
445 Bret Boone	.30	.09
446 Oscar Henriquez	.30	.09
447 Mike Sweeney	.30	.09
448 Kenny Rogers	.30	.09
449 Mark Langston	.30	.09
450 Luis Gonzalez	.30	.09
451 John Burkett	.30	.09
452 Bip Roberts	.30	.09
453 Travis Lee	.30	.09
454 Felix Rodriguez	.30	.09
455 Andy Benes	.30	.09
456 Willie Blair	.30	.09
457 Brian Anderson	.30	.09
458 Jay Bell	.30	.09
459 Matt Williams	.30	.09
460 Devon White	.30	.09
461 Karim Garcia	.30	.09
462 Jorge Fabregas	.30	.09
463 Wilson Alvarez	.30	.09
464 Roberto Hernandez	.30	.09
465 Tony Saunders	.30	.09
466 Rolando Arrojo RC	.30	.09
467 Wade Boggs	.75	.23
468 Fred McGriff	.50	.15
469 Paul Sorrento	.30	.09
470 Kevin Stocker	.30	.09
471 Bubba Trammell	.30	.09
472 Quinton McCracken	.30	.09
473 Ken Griffey Jr. CL	.75	.23

474 Cal Ripken CL 1.25 .35
475 Frank Thomas CL .50 .15
476 Ken Griffey Jr. PZ 4.00 1.20
477 Cal Ripken PZ 8.00 2.40
478 Frank Thomas PZ 2.50 .75
479 Alex Rodriguez PZ 4.00 1.20
480 Nomar Garciaparra PZ 4.00 1.20
481 Derek Jeter PZ 6.00 1.80
482 Andruw Jones PZ 1.00 .30
483 Chipper Jones PZ 2.50 .75
484 Greg Maddux PZ 4.00 1.20
485 Mike Piazza PZ 4.00 1.20
486 Juan Gonzalez PZ 1.50 .45
487 Jose Cruz Jr. PZ 1.00 .30
488 Jaret Wright PZ 1.00 .30
489 Hideo Nomo PZ 2.50 .75
490 Scott Rolen PZ 2.50 .75
491 Tony Gwynn PZ 3.00 .90
492 Roger Clemens PZ 5.00 1.50
493 Darin Erstad PZ 1.00 .30
494 Mark McGwire PZ 6.00 1.80
495 Jeff Bagwell PZ 1.50 .45
496 Mo Vaughn PZ 1.00 .30
497 Albert Belle PZ 1.00 .30
498 Kenny Lofton PZ 1.00 .30
499 Ben Grieve PZ 1.00 .30
500 Barry Bonds PZ 6.00 1.80
501 Mike Piazza 1.25 .35
S100 A.Rodriguez AU/750 80.00 24.00

1998 Ultra Gold Medallion

Randomly inserted one in every first and second series hobby pack, this 501-card set is parallel to the base set and features a gold metallic foil background.

Nm-Mt Ex-Mt
COMPLETE SET (501) 300.00 90.00
COMP.SERIES 1 (250) 150.00 45.00
COMP.SERIES 2 (251) 150.00 45.00
*STARS: 1.25X TO 3X BASIC CARDS.
*ROOKIES: .75X TO 2X BASIC CARDS
*SEASON CROWNS: .3X TO .8X BASIC SC
*PROSPECTS: .25X TO .6X BASIC PROS.
*CHECKLISTS: 1.25X TO 3X BASIC CL'S
*PIZZAZZ: .40X TO 1.X BASIC PIZZAZZ

1998 Ultra Platinum Medallion

Randomly inserted in first and second series hobby packs, this 498-card set is parallel to the base set. Only 100 first series sets and 98 second series sets were produced and each card is serially numbered in gold foil on back. Ten Platinum exchange cards good for a complete Platinum series one set were inserted into first series hobby packs. Another ten Platinum exchange cards good for a complete series two set were inserted in second series hobby packs. The three basic-issue checklist cards (473,474 and 475) were never printed in platinum form.

Nm-Mt Ex-Mt
*STARS: 10X TO 25X BASIC CARDS..
*ROOKIES: 10X TO 25X BASIC CARDS
*SEASON CROWNS: 1.5X TO 4X BASIC SC
*PROSPECTS: 2.5X TO 6X BASIC PROSP.
*CHECKLISTS: 12.5X TO 30X BASIC CL'S
*PIZZAZZ: 2X TO 5X BASIC PIZZAZZ.

1998 Ultra Artistic Talents

Randomly inserted in Series one packs at the rate of one in eight, this 18-card set features color pictures of top players on art enhanced cards.

Nm-Mt Ex-Mt
COMPLETE SET (18) 50.00 15.00
1 Ken Griffey Jr. 4.00 1.20
2 Andruw Jones 1.00 .30
3 Alex Rodriguez 4.00 1.20
4 Frank Thomas 2.50 .75
5 Cal Ripken 8.00 2.40
6 Derek Jeter 6.00 1.80
7 Chipper Jones 2.50 .75
8 Greg Maddux 4.00 1.20
9 Mike Piazza 4.00 1.20
10 Albert Belle 1.00 .30
11 Darin Erstad 1.00 .30
12 Juan Gonzalez 1.50 .45
13 Jeff Bagwell 1.50 .45
14 Tony Gwynn 3.00 .90
15 Mark McGwire 6.00 1.80
16 Scott Rolen 2.50 .75
17 Barry Bonds 6.00 1.80
18 Kenny Lofton 1.00 .30

1998 Ultra Back to the Future

Randomly inserted in Series one packs at the rate of one in six, this 15-card set features color photos of top Rookies. The backs carry player information.

Nm-Mt Ex-Mt
COMPLETE SET (15) 12.00 3.60
1 Andruw Jones .50 .15
2 Alex Rodriguez 2.00 .60
3 Derek Jeter 3.00 .90
4 Darin Erstad .50 .15
5 Mike Cameron .50 .15
6 Scott Rolen 1.25 .35
7 Nomar Garciaparra 2.00 .60
8 Hideki Irabu .50 .15
9 Jose Cruz Jr. .50 .15
10 Vladimir Guerrero 1.25 .35
11 Mark Kotsay .50 .15
12 Tony Womack .50 .15
13 Jason Dickson .50 .15
14 Jose Guillen .50 .15
15 Tony Clark .50 .15

1998 Ultra Big Shots

Randomly inserted in Series one packs at the rate of one in four, this 15-card set features color photos of players who hit the longest home runs in the 1997 season.

Nm-Mt Ex-Mt
COMPLETE SET (15) 10.00 3.00
1 Ken Griffey Jr. 1.50 .45
2 Frank Thomas 1.00 .30
3 Chipper Jones 1.00 .30
4 Albert Belle .40 .12
5 Juan Gonzalez .60 .18
6 Jeff Bagwell .60 .18
7 Mark McGwire 2.50 .75
8 Barry Bonds 2.50 .75
9 Manny Ramirez .60 .18
10 Mo Vaughn .40 .12
11 Matt Williams .40 .12
12 Jim Thome 1.00 .30
13 Tino Martinez .60 .18
14 Mike Piazza 1.50 .45
15 Tony Clark .40 .12

1998 Ultra Diamond Immortals

Randomly inserted in packs at a rate of one in 288, this 15-card insert set highlights color action photos of future Hall of Famers on die-cut cards with full silver holofoil backgrounds.

Nm-Mt Ex-Mt
COMPLETE SET (15) 400.00 120.00
1 Ken Griffey Jr. 40.00 12.00
2 Frank Thomas 25.00 7.50
3 Alex Rodriguez 40.00 12.00
4 Cal Ripken 80.00 24.00
5 Mike Piazza 40.00 12.00
6 Mark McGwire 60.00 18.00
7 Greg Maddux 40.00 12.00
8 Andruw Jones 10.00 3.00
9 Chipper Jones 25.00 7.50
10 Derek Jeter 60.00 18.00
11 Tony Gwynn 30.00 9.00
12 Juan Gonzalez 15.00 4.50
13 Jose Cruz Jr. 10.00 3.00
14 Roger Clemens 50.00 15.00
15 Barry Bonds 60.00 18.00

1998 Ultra Diamond Producers

Randomly inserted in Series one packs at the rate of one in 288, this 15-card set features color photos of Major League Baseball's top players.

Nm-Mt Ex-Mt
COMPLETE SET (15) 400.00 120.00
1 Ken Griffey Jr. 30.00 9.00
2 Andruw Jones 8.00 2.40
3 Alex Rodriguez 30.00 9.00
4 Frank Thomas 20.00 6.00
5 Cal Ripken 60.00 18.00
6 Derek Jeter 50.00 15.00
7 Chipper Jones 20.00 6.00
8 Greg Maddux 30.00 9.00
9 Mike Piazza 30.00 9.00
10 Juan Gonzalez 12.00 3.60
11 Jeff Bagwell 12.00 3.60
12 Tony Gwynn 25.00 7.50
13 Mark McGwire 50.00 15.00
14 Barry Bonds 50.00 15.00
15 Jose Cruz Jr. 8.00 2.40

1998 Ultra Double Trouble

Randonly inserted in Series one packs at the rate of one in four, this 20-card set features color photos of two star players per card.

Nm-Mt Ex-Mt
COMPLETE SET (20) 12.00 3.60
1 Ken Griffey Jr. 1.50 .45
Alex Rodriguez
2 Vladimir Guerrero .60 .18
Pedro Martinez
3 Andruw Jones .60 .18
Kenny Lofton
4 Chipper Jones 1.00 .30
Greg Maddux
5 Derek Jeter 1.50 .45
Tino Martinez
6 Frank Thomas .60 .18
Albert Belle
7 Cal Ripken 2.50 .75
Roberto Alomar
8 Mike Piazza 1.25 .35
Hideo Nomo
9 Darin Erstad 20.00 6.00
Jason Dickson
10 Juan Gonzalez .60 .18
Ivan Rodriguez
11 Jeff Bagwell .40 .12
Darryl Kile
UER front Kyle
12 Tony Gwynn 1.25 .35
Steve Finley
13 Mark McGwire 2.00 .60
Ray Lankford
14 Barry Bonds 1.00 .30
Jeff Kent
15 Andy Pettitte .40 .12
Bernie Williams
16 Mo Vaughn 1.25 .35
Nomar Garciaparra
17 Matt Williams .60 .18
Jim Thome
18 Hideki Irabu .60 .18
Mariano Rivera
19 Roger Clemens 2.00 .60
Jose Cruz Jr.
20 Manny Ramirez .40 .12
David Justice

1998 Ultra Fall Classics

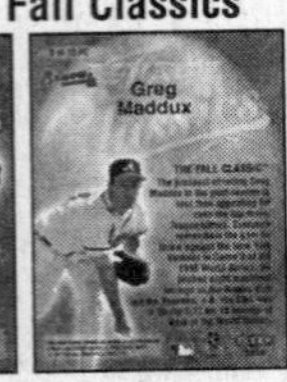

Randomly inserted in Series one packs at the rate of one in 18, this 15-card set features color photos of the top potential postseason heroes. The backs carry player information.

Nm-Mt Ex-Mt
COMPLETE SET (15) 100.00 30.00
1 Ken Griffey Jr. 8.00 2.40
2 Andruw Jones 2.00 .60
3 Alex Rodriguez 8.00 2.40
4 Frank Thomas 5.00 1.50
5 Cal Ripken 15.00 4.50
6 Derek Jeter 12.00 3.60
7 Chipper Jones 5.00 1.50
8 Greg Maddux 8.00 2.40
9 Mike Piazza 8.00 2.40
10 Albert Belle 2.00 .60
11 Juan Gonzalez 3.00 .90
12 Jeff Bagwell 3.00 .90
13 Tony Gwynn 6.00 1.80
14 Mark McGwire 12.00 3.60
15 Barry Bonds 12.00 3.60

1998 Ultra Kid Gloves

Radomly inserted in Series one packs at the rate of one in eight, this 12-card set features color photos of top young defensive players. The backs carry player information.

Nm-Mt Ex-Mt
COMPLETE SET (12) 15.00 4.50
1 Andruw Jones .60 .18
2 Alex Rodriguez 2.50 .75
3 Derek Jeter 4.00 1.20
4 Chipper Jones 1.50 .45
5 Darin Erstad .60 .18
6 Todd Walker .60 .18
7 Scott Rolen 1.50 .45
8 Nomar Garciaparra 2.50 .75
9 Jose Cruz Jr. .60 .18
10 Charles Johnson .60 .18
11 Rey Ordonez .60 .18
12 Vladimir Guerrero 1.50 .45

1998 Ultra Millennium Men

Randomly inserted in hobby only packs at a rate of one in 35, this 15-card insert set features a

player action photo on an irridescent silver foil underlay that opens to reveal a second photo with a personal profile. For an added touch, a foil stamp embossed in the center gives the feel of a wax seal.

Nm-Mt Ex-Mt
COMPLETE SET (15) 120.00 36.00
1 Jose Cruz Jr. 2.50 .75
2 Ken Griffey Jr. 10.00 3.00
3 Cal Ripken 20.00 6.00
4 Derek Jeter 15.00 4.50
5 Andruw Jones 2.50 .75
6 Alex Rodriguez 10.00 3.00
7 Chipper Jones 6.00 1.80
8 Scott Rolen 6.00 1.80
9 Nomar Garciaparra 10.00 3.00
10 Frank Thomas 6.00 1.80
11 Mike Piazza 10.00 3.00
12 Greg Maddux 10.00 3.00
13 Juan Gonzalez 4.00 1.20
14 Ben Grieve 25.00 7.50
15 Jaret Wright 2.50 .75

1998 Ultra Notables

Randomly inserted in packs at a rate of one in four, this 20-card set features a color action player photo on a borderless UV coated front with a design of the American Eagle in the background.

Nm-Mt Ex-Mt
COMPLETE SET (20) 25.00 7.50
1 Frank Thomas 1.25 .35
2 Ken Griffey Jr. 2.00 .60
3 Edgar Renteria .50 .15
4 Albert Belle .50 .15
5 Juan Gonzalez .75 .23
6 Jeff Bagwell .75 .23
7 Mark McGwire 3.00 .90
8 Barry Bonds 3.00 .90
9 Scott Rolen 1.25 .35
10 Mo Vaughn .50 .15
11 Andruw Jones .50 .15
12 Chipper Jones 1.25 .35
13 Tino Martinez .75 .23
14 Mike Piazza 2.00 .60
15 Tony Clark .50 .15
16 Jose Cruz Jr. .50 .15
17 Nomar Garciaparra 2.00 .60
18 Cal Ripken 4.00 1.20
19 Alex Rodriguez 2.00 .60
20 Derek Jeter 3.00 .90

1998 Ultra Power Plus

Randomly inserted in Series one packs at the rate of one in 36, this 10-card set features color action photos of top young and veteran players. The backs carry player information.

Nm-Mt Ex-Mt
COMPLETE SET (10) 60.00 18.00
1 Ken Griffey Jr. 12.00 3.60
2 Andruw Jones 3.00 .90
3 Alex Rodriguez 12.00 3.60
4 Frank Thomas 8.00 2.40
5 Mike Piazza 12.00 3.60
6 Albert Belle 3.00 .90
7 Juan Gonzalez 5.00 1.50
8 Jeff Bagwell 5.00 1.50
9 Barry Bonds 20.00 6.00
10 Jose Cruz Jr. 3.00 .90

1998 Ultra Prime Leather

Randomly inserted in Series one packs at the rate of one in 144, this 18-card set features color photos of young and veteran players considered to be good glove men. The backs carry player information.

Nm-Mt Ex-Mt
1 Ken Griffey Jr. 25.00 7.50
2 Andruw Jones 6.00 1.80
3 Alex Rodriguez 25.00 7.50
4 Frank Thomas 15.00 4.50
5 Cal Ripken 50.00 15.00
6 Derek Jeter 40.00 12.00
7 Chipper Jones 15.00 4.50
8 Greg Maddux 25.00 7.50
9 Mike Piazza 25.00 7.50
10 Albert Belle 6.00 1.80
11 Darin Erstad 6.00 1.80
12 Juan Gonzalez 10.00 3.00
13 Jeff Bagwell 10.00 3.00
14 Tony Gwynn 20.00 6.00
15 Roberto Alomar 10.00 3.00
16 Barry Bonds 40.00 12.00
17 Kenny Lofton 6.00 1.80
18 Jose Cruz Jr. 6.00 1.80

1998 Ultra Rocket to Stardom

Randomly inserted in packs at a rate of one in 20, this 15-card insert set showcases rookies on a sculpted embossed and die-cut card designed to resemble a cloud of smoke.

Nm-Mt Ex-Mt
COMPLETE SET (15) 30.00 9.00
1 Ben Grieve 2.00 .60
2 Magglio Ordonez 8.00 2.40
3 Travis Lee 2.00 .60
4 Mike Caruso 2.00 .60
5 Brian Rose 2.00 .60
6 Brad Fullmer 2.00 .60
7 Michael Coleman 2.00 .60
8 Juan Encarnacion 2.00 .60
9 Karim Garcia 2.00 .60
10 Todd Helton 3.00 .90
11 Richard Hidalgo 2.00 .60
12 Paul Konerko 2.00 .60
13 Rod Myers 2.00 .60
14 Jaret Wright 2.00 .60
15 Miguel Tejada 2.00 .60

1998 Ultra Ticket Studs

Randomly inserted in packs at a rate of one in 144, this 15-card insert set features color action player photos on sculpture embossed ticket-like designed cards. The cards open up to give details on what makes fans so crazy about their favorite players.

Nm-Mt Ex-Mt
COMPLETE SET (15) 250.00 75.00
1 Travis Lee 6.00 1.80
2 Tony Gwynn 20.00 6.00
3 Scott Rolen 15.00 4.50
4 Nomar Garciaparra 25.00 7.50
5 Mike Piazza 25.00 7.50
6 Mark McGwire 40.00 12.00
7 Ken Griffey Jr. 25.00 7.50
8 Juan Gonzalez 10.00 3.00
9 Jose Cruz Jr. 6.00 1.80
10 Frank Thomas 15.00 4.50
11 Derek Jeter 40.00 12.00
12 Chipper Jones 15.00 4.50
13 Cal Ripken 50.00 15.00
14 Andruw Jones 6.00 1.80
15 Alex Rodriguez 25.00 7.50

1998 Ultra Top 30

These cards which feature 30 of the leading baseball players were issued one per retail series two pack.

Nm-Mt Ex-Mt
COMPLETE SET (30) 25.00 7.50
1 Barry Bonds 2.50 .75
2 Ivan Rodriguez 1.00 .30
3 Kenny Lofton .40 .12
4 Albert Belle .40 .12
5 Mo Vaughn .40 .12
6 Jeff Bagwell .60 .18
7 Mark McGwire 2.50 .75
8 Darin Erstad .40 .12
9 Roger Clemens 2.00 .60
10 Tony Gwynn 1.25 .35
11 Scott Rolen 1.00 .30
12 Hideo Nomo 1.00 .30
13 Juan Gonzalez .60 .18
14 Mike Piazza 1.50 .45
15 Greg Maddux 1.50 .45
16 Chipper Jones 1.00 .30

Card	Nm-Mt	Ex-Mt
17 Andruw Jones	.40	.12
18 Derek Jeter	2.50	.75
19 Nomar Garciaparra	1.50	.45
20 Alex Rodriguez	1.50	.45
21 Frank Thomas	1.00	.30
22 Cal Ripken	3.00	.90
23 Ken Griffey Jr.	1.50	.45
24 Jose Cruz Jr.	.40	.12
25 Jaret Wright	.40	.12
26 Travis Lee	.40	.12
27 Wade Boggs	1.00	.30
28 Chuck Knoblauch	.40	.12
29 Joe Carter	.40	.12
30 Ben Grieve	.40	.12

1998 Ultra Win Now

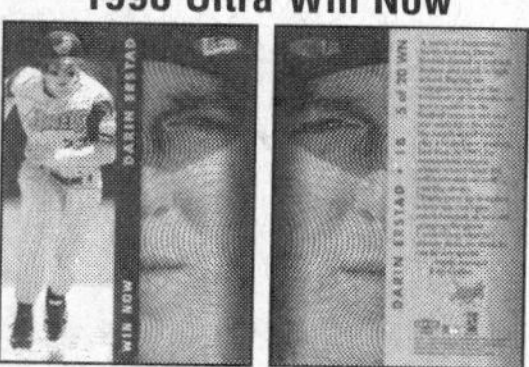

Randomly inserted in packs at a rate of one in 72, this 20-card insert set features color action photos on plastic cards. A transparent section of the front allows you to see the player image in reverse from the back.

Card	Nm-Mt	Ex-Mt
COMPLETE SET (20)	250.00	75.00
1 Alex Rodriguez	20.00	6.00
2 Andruw Jones	5.00	1.50
3 Cal Ripken	40.00	12.00
4 Chipper Jones	12.00	3.60
5 Darin Erstad	5.00	1.50
6 Derek Jeter	30.00	9.00
7 Frank Thomas	12.00	3.60
8 Greg Maddux	20.00	6.00
9 Hideo Nomo	12.00	3.60
10 Jeff Bagwell	8.00	2.40
11 Jose Cruz Jr.	5.00	1.50
12 Juan Gonzalez	8.00	2.40
13 Ken Griffey Jr.	20.00	6.00
14 Mark McGwire	30.00	9.00
15 Mike Piazza	20.00	6.00
16 Mo Vaughn	5.00	1.50
17 Nomar Garciaparra	20.00	6.00
18 Roger Clemens	25.00	7.50
19 Scott Rolen	12.00	3.60
20 Tony Gwynn	15.00	4.50

1999 Ultra

This 250-card single-series set was distributed in 10-card packs with a suggested retail price of $2.69 and features color player photos on the fronts with stats by year in 15 categories and career highlights on the backs for 210 veterans. The set contains the following subsets: Prospects (25 rookie cards seeded 1:4 packs), Season Crowns (10 1998 statistical leaders seeded 1:8) and five checklist cards.

Card	Nm-Mt	Ex-Mt
COMPLETE SET (250)	80.00	24.00
COMP.SET w/o SP's (215)	25.00	7.50
COMMON CARD (1-215)	.30	.09
COMMON SC (216-225)	.75	.23
COMMON (226-250)	2.00	.60
1 Greg Maddux	1.25	.35
2 Greg Vaughn	.30	.09
3 John Wetteland	.30	.09
4 Tino Martinez	.50	.15
5 Todd Walker	.30	.09
6 Troy O'Leary	.30	.09
7 Barry Larkin	.50	.15
8 Mike Lansing	.30	.09
9 Delino DeShields	.30	.09
10 Brett Tomko	.30	.09
11 Carlos Perez	.30	.09
12 Mark Langston	.30	.09
13 Jamie Moyer	.30	.09
14 Jose Guillen	.30	.09
15 Bartolo Colon	.30	.09
16 Brady Anderson	.30	.09
17 Walt Weiss	.30	.09
18 Shane Reynolds	.30	.09
19 David Segui	.30	.09
20 Vladimir Guerrero	.75	.23
21 Freddy Garcia	.30	.09
22 Carl Everett	.30	.09
23 Jose Cruz Jr.	.30	.09
24 David Ortiz	.50	.15
25 Andruw Jones	.30	.09
26 Darren Lewis	.30	.09
27 Ray Lankford	.30	.09
28 Wally Joyner	.30	.09
29 Charles Johnson	.30	.09
30 Derek Jeter	2.00	.60
31 Sean Casey	.30	.09
32 Bobby Bonilla	.30	.09
33 Todd Zeile	.30	.09
34 Todd Helton	.50	.15
35 David Wells	.30	.09
36 Darin Erstad	.30	.09
37 Ivan Rodriguez	.75	.23
38 Antonio Osuna	.30	.09
39 Mickey Morandini	.30	.09
40 Rusty Greer	.30	.09
41 Rod Beck	.30	.09
42 Larry Sutton	.30	.09
43 Edgar Renteria	.30	.09
44 Otis Nixon	.30	.09
45 Eli Marrero	.30	.09
46 Reggie Jefferson	.30	.09
47 Trevor Hoffman	.30	.09
48 Andres Galarraga	.30	.09
49 Scott Brosius	.30	.09
50 Vinny Castilla	.30	.09
51 Bret Boone	.30	.09
52 Masato Yoshii	.30	.09
53 Matt Williams	.30	.09
54 Robin Ventura	.30	.09
55 Jay Powell	.30	.09
56 Dean Palmer	.30	.09
57 Eric Milton	.30	.09
58 Willie McGee	.30	.09
59 Tony Gwynn	1.00	.30
60 Tom Gordon	.30	.09
61 Dante Bichette	.30	.09
62 Jaret Wright	.30	.09
63 Devon White	.30	.09
64 Frank Thomas	.75	.23
65 Mike Piazza	1.25	.35
66 Jose Offerman	.30	.09
67 Pat Meares	.30	.09
68 Brian Meadows	.30	.09
69 Nomar Garciaparra	1.25	.35
70 Mark McGwire	2.00	.60
71 Tony Graffanino	.30	.09
72 Ken Griffey Jr.	1.25	.35
73 Ken Caminiti	.30	.09
74 Todd Jones	.30	.09
75 A.J. Hinch	.30	.09
76 Marquis Grissom	.30	.09
77 Jay Buhner	.30	.09
78 Albert Belle	.30	.09
79 Brian Anderson	.30	.09
80 Quinton McCracken	.30	.09
81 Omar Vizquel	.50	.15
82 Todd Stottlemyre	.30	.09
83 Cal Ripken	2.50	.75
84 Magglio Ordonez	.30	.09
85 John Olerud	.30	.09
86 Hal Morris	.30	.09
87 Derrek Lee	.30	.09
88 Doug Glanville	.30	.09
89 Marty Cordova	.30	.09
90 Kevin Brown	.30	.09
91 Kevin Young	.30	.09
92 Rico Brogna	.30	.09
93 Wilson Alvarez	.30	.09
94 Bob Wickman	.30	.09
95 Jim Thome	.75	.23
96 Mike Mussina	.50	.15
97 Al Leiter	.30	.09
98 Travis Lee	.30	.09
99 Jeff King	.30	.09
100 Kerry Wood	.75	.23
101 Cliff Floyd	.30	.09
102 Jose Valentin	.30	.09
103 Manny Ramirez	.50	.15
104 Butch Huskey	.30	.09
105 Scott Erickson	.30	.09
106 Ray Durham	.30	.09
107 Johnny Damon	.50	.15
108 Craig Counsell	.30	.09
109 Rolando Arrojo	.30	.09
110 Bob Abreu	.30	.09
111 Tony Womack	.30	.09
112 Mike Stanley	.30	.09
113 Kenny Lofton	.30	.09
114 Eric Davis	.30	.09
115 Jeff Conine	.30	.09
116 Carlos Baerga	.30	.09
117 Rondell White	.30	.09
118 Billy Wagner	.30	.09
119 Ed Sprague	.30	.09
120 Jason Schmidt	.30	.09
121 Edgar Martinez	.50	.15
122 Travis Fryman	.30	.09
123 Armando Benitez	.30	.09
124 Matt Stairs	.30	.09
125 Roberto Hernandez	.30	.09
126 Jay Bell	.30	.09
127 Justin Thompson	.30	.09
128 John Jaha	.30	.09
129 Mike Caruso	.30	.09
130 Miguel Tejada	.30	.09
131 Geoff Jenkins	.30	.09
132 Wade Boggs	.50	.15
133 Andy Benes	.30	.09
134 Aaron Sele	.30	.09
135 Bret Saberhagen	.30	.09
136 Mariano Rivera	.50	.15
137 Neifi Perez	.30	.09
138 Paul Konerko	.30	.09
139 Barry Bonds	2.00	.60
140 Garret Anderson	.30	.09
141 Bernie Williams	.50	.15
142 Gary Sheffield	.30	.09
143 Rafael Palmeiro	.50	.15
144 Orel Hershiser	.30	.09
145 Craig Biggio	.50	.15
146 Dmitri Young	.30	.09
147 Damion Easley	.30	.09
148 Henry Rodriguez	.30	.09
149 Brad Radke	.30	.09
150 Pedro Martinez	.75	.23
151 Mike Lieberthal	.30	.09
152 Jim Leyritz	.30	.09
153 Chuck Knoblauch	.30	.09
154 Darryl Kile	.30	.09
155 Brian Jordan	.30	.09
156 Chipper Jones	.75	.23
157 Pete Harnisch	.30	.09
158 Moises Alou	.30	.09
159 Ismael Valdes	.30	.09
160 Stan Javier	.30	.09
161 Mark Grace	.50	.15
162 Jason Giambi	.30	.09
163 Chuck Finley	.30	.09
164 Juan Encarnacion	.30	.09
165 Chan Ho Park	.30	.09
166 Randy Johnson	.75	.23
167 J.T. Snow	.30	.09
168 Tim Salmon	.50	.15
169 Brian L.Hunter	.30	.09
170 Rickey Henderson	.75	.23
171 Cal Eldred	.30	.09
172 Curt Schilling	.30	.09
173 Alex Rodriguez	1.25	.35
174 Dustin Hermanson	.30	.09
175 Mike Hampton	.30	.09
176 Shawn Green	.30	.09
177 Roberto Alomar	.50	.15
178 Sandy Alomar Jr.	.30	.09
179 Larry Walker	.50	.15
180 Mo Vaughn	.30	.09
181 Raul Mondesi	.30	.09
182 Hideki Irabu	.30	.09
183 Jim Edmonds	.30	.09
184 Shawn Estes	.30	.09
185 Tony Clark	.30	.09
186 Dan Wilson	.30	.09
187 Michael Tucker	.30	.09
188 Jeff Shaw	.30	.09
189 Mark Grudzielanek	.30	.09
190 Roger Clemens	1.50	.45
191 Juan Gonzalez	.50	.15
192 Sammy Sosa	1.25	.35
193 Troy Percival	.30	.09
194 Robb Nen	.30	.09
195 Bill Mueller	.30	.09
196 Ben Grieve	.30	.09
197 Luis Gonzalez	.30	.09
198 Will Clark	.75	.23
199 Jeff Cirillo	.30	.09
200 Scott Rolen	.75	.23
201 Reggie Sanders	.30	.09
202 Fred McGriff	.50	.15
203 Denny Neagle	.30	.09
204 Brad Fullmer	.30	.09
205 Royce Clayton	.30	.09
206 Jose Canseco	.75	.23
207 Jeff Bagwell	.50	.15
208 Hideo Nomo	.75	.23
209 Karim Garcia	.30	.09
210 Kenny Rogers	.30	.09
211 Kerry Wood CL	.50	.15
212 Alex Rodriguez CL	.75	.23
213 Cal Ripken CL	1.25	.35
214 Frank Thomas CL	.50	.15
215 Ken Griffey Jr. CL	.75	.23
216 Alex Rodriguez SC	3.00	.90
217 Greg Maddux SC	3.00	.90
218 Juan Gonzalez SC	1.25	.35
219 Ken Griffey Jr. SC	3.00	.90
220 Kerry Wood SC	2.00	.60
221 Mark McGwire SC	5.00	1.50
222 Mike Piazza SC	3.00	.90
223 Rickey Henderson SC	2.00	.60
224 Sammy Sosa SC	3.00	.90
225 Travis Lee SC	.75	.23
226 Gabe Alvarez PROS	2.00	.60
227 Matt Anderson PROS	2.00	.60
228 Adrian Beltre PROS	3.00	.90
229 O.Cabrera PROS	2.00	.60
230 Orl. Hernandez PROS	2.00	.60
231 A.Ramirez PROS	2.00	.60
232 Troy Glaus PROS	2.00	.60
233 Gabe Kapler PROS	2.00	.60
234 Jeremy Giambi PROS	2.00	.60
235 Derrick Gibson PROS	2.00	.60
236 Carlton Loewer PROS	2.00	.60
237 Mike Frank PROS	2.00	.60
238 Carlos Guillen PROS	2.00	.60
239 Alex Gonzalez PROS	2.00	.60
240 Enrique Wilson PROS	2.00	.60
241 J.D. Drew PROS	2.00	.60
242 Bruce Chen PROS	2.00	.60
243 Ryan Minor PROS	2.00	.60
244 Preston Wilson PROS	2.00	.60
245 Josh Booty PROS	2.00	.60
246 Luis Ordaz PROS	2.00	.60
247 G.Lombard PROS	2.00	.60
248 Matt Clement PROS	2.00	.60
249 Eric Chavez PROS	2.00	.60
250 Corey Koskie PROS	2.00	.60

1999 Ultra Gold Medallion

Randomly inserted one in every hobby only pack for regular cards, one in 40 for Prospects, and one in 80 for Season Crowns, this 250-card set is a gold parallel version of the base set.

	Nm-Mt	Ex-Mt
*GOLD: 1.25X TO 3X BASIC CARDS ..		
*GOLD SC: 2X TO 5X BASIC SC		
*GOLD PROS: 1X TO 2.5X BASIC PROS		

1999 Ultra Platinum Medallion

Randomly inserted in hobby packs only, this 250-card set is a parallel version of the base set. Only 99 of the 210 veteran cards were produced and numbered. Only 65 of the Prospects (cards numbered from 226 through 250) subset was produced and serially numbered. Only 50 of the Season Crowns (cards numbered from 216 through 225) subset was produced and serially numbered.

	Nm-Mt	Ex-Mt
*PLAT: 15X TO 40X BASIC CARDS		
*PLAT SC: 12.5X TO 30X BASIC SC		
*PLAT PROS: 2.5X TO 6X BASIC PROS		

1999 Ultra The Book On

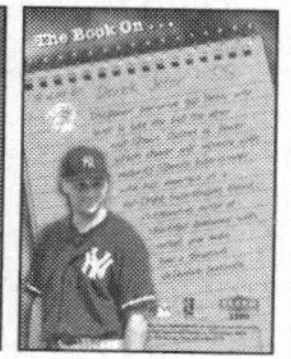

Randomly inserted in packs at the rate of one in six, this 20-card set features action color photos of top players with a detailed analysis of why they are so good printed on the backs.

Card	Nm-Mt	Ex-Mt
COMPLETE SET (20)	50.00	15.00
1 Kerry Wood	2.00	.60
2 Ken Griffey Jr.	3.00	.90
3 Frank Thomas	2.00	.60
4 Albert Belle	.75	.23
5 Juan Gonzalez	1.25	.35
6 Jeff Bagwell	1.25	.35
7 Mark McGwire	5.00	1.50
8 Barry Bonds	5.00	1.50
9 Andruw Jones	.75	.23
10 Mo Vaughn	.75	.23
11 Scott Rolen	2.00	.60
12 Travis Lee	.75	.23
13 Tony Gwynn	2.50	.75
14 Greg Maddux	3.00	.90
15 Mike Piazza	3.00	.90
16 Chipper Jones	2.00	.60
17 Nomar Garciaparra	3.00	.90
18 Cal Ripken	6.00	1.80
19 Derek Jeter	5.00	1.50
20 Alex Rodriguez	3.00	.90

1999 Ultra Damage Inc.

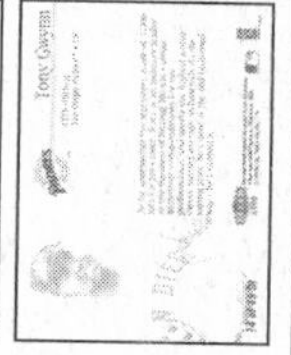

Randomly inserted in packs at the rate of one in 72, this 15-card set features color images of top players printed on a business card design.

Card	Nm-Mt	Ex-Mt
COMPLETE SET (15)	200.00	60.00
1 Alex Rodriguez	15.00	4.50
2 Greg Maddux	15.00	4.50
3 Cal Ripken	30.00	9.00
4 Chipper Jones	10.00	3.00
5 Derek Jeter	25.00	7.50
6 Frank Thomas	10.00	3.00
7 Juan Gonzalez	6.00	1.80
8 Ken Griffey Jr.	15.00	4.50
9 Kerry Wood	10.00	3.00
10 Mark McGwire	25.00	7.50
11 Mike Piazza	15.00	4.50
12 Nomar Garciaparra	15.00	4.50
13 Scott Rolen	10.00	3.00
14 Tony Gwynn	12.00	3.60
15 Travis Lee	4.00	1.20

1999 Ultra Diamond Producers

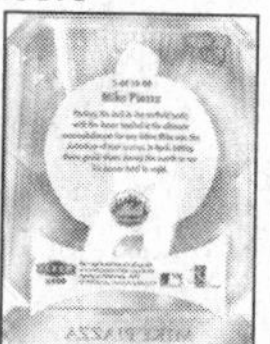

Randomly inserted in packs at the rate of one in 288, this 10-card set features action color player photos printed on full foil plastic die-cut cards with custom embossing.

Card	Nm-Mt	Ex-Mt
COMPLETE SET (10)	300.00	90.00
1 Ken Griffey Jr.	20.00	6.00
2 Frank Thomas	12.00	3.60
3 Alex Rodriguez	20.00	6.00
4 Cal Ripken	40.00	12.00
5 Mike Piazza	20.00	6.00
6 Mark McGwire	30.00	9.00
7 Greg Maddux	20.00	6.00
8 Kerry Wood	12.00	3.60
9 Chipper Jones	12.00	3.60
10 Derek Jeter	30.00	9.00

1999 Ultra RBI Kings

Randomly inserted one in every retail pack only, this 30-card set features action color photos of top run producing players.

Card	Nm-Mt	Ex-Mt
COMPLETE SET (30)	30.00	9.00
1 Rafael Palmeiro	.60	.18
2 Mo Vaughn	.40	.12
3 Ivan Rodriguez	1.00	.30
4 Barry Bonds	2.50	.75
5 Albert Belle	.40	.12
6 Jeff Bagwell	.60	.18
7 Mark McGwire	2.50	.75
8 Darin Erstad	.40	.12
9 Manny Ramirez	.60	.18
10 Chipper Jones	1.00	.30
11 Jim Thome	1.00	.30
12 Scott Rolen	1.00	.30
13 Tony Gwynn	1.25	.35
14 Juan Gonzalez	.60	.18
15 Mike Piazza	1.50	.45
16 Sammy Sosa	1.50	.45
17 Andruw Jones	.40	.12
18 Derek Jeter	2.50	.75
19 Nomar Garciaparra	1.50	.45
20 Alex Rodriguez	1.50	.45
21 Frank Thomas	1.00	.30
22 Cal Ripken	3.00	.90
23 Ken Griffey Jr.	1.50	.45
24 Travis Lee	.40	.12
25 Paul O'Neill	.40	.12
26 Greg Vaughn	.40	.12
27 Andres Galarraga	.40	.12
28 Tino Martinez	.60	.18
29 Jose Canseco	1.00	.30
30 Ben Grieve	.40	.12

1999 Ultra Thunderclap

Randomly inserted in packs at the rate of one in 36, this 15-card set features color player photos printed on embossed cards with silver pattern holofoil.

Card	Nm-Mt	Ex-Mt
COMPLETE SET (15)	100.00	30.00
1 Alex Rodriguez	8.00	2.40
2 Andruw Jones	2.00	.60
3 Cal Ripken	15.00	4.50
4 Chipper Jones	5.00	1.50
5 Darin Erstad	2.00	.60
6 Derek Jeter	12.00	3.60
7 Frank Thomas	5.00	1.50
8 Jeff Bagwell	3.00	.90
9 Juan Gonzalez	3.00	.90
10 Ken Griffey Jr.	8.00	2.40
11 Mark McGwire	12.00	3.60
12 Mike Piazza	8.00	2.40
13 Travis Lee	2.00	.60
14 Nomar Garciaparra	8.00	2.40
15 Scott Rolen	5.00	1.50

1999 Ultra World Premiere

Randomly inserted in packs at the rate of one in 18, this 15-card set features action color photos of top 1998 rookies printed on sculpture embossed silver holofoil cards.

Card	Nm-Mt	Ex-Mt
COMPLETE SET (15)	20.00	6.00
1 Gabe Alvarez	1.25	.35
2 Kerry Wood	5.00	1.50
3 Orlando Hernandez	1.25	.35
4 Mike Caruso	2.00	.60
5 Matt Anderson	1.25	.35
6 Randall Simon	2.00	.60
7 Adrian Beltre	2.00	.60
8 Scott Elarton	2.00	.60
9 Karim Garcia	2.00	.60
10 Mike Frank	1.25	.35
11 Richard Hidalgo	2.00	.60
12 Paul Konerko	2.00	.60
13 Travis Lee	2.00	.60
14 J.D. Drew	2.00	.60
15 Miguel Tejada	2.00	.60

2000 Ultra

This 300 card set was issued late in 1999. The cards were distributed in 10 card packs with an SRP of $2.69. The product was issued in either 8, 12 or 30 box cases. The prospect subset were numbered from 251 through 300 and were printed in shorter quantity than the regular cards and inserted one every four packs. Two separate Alex Rodriguez Promo cards were distributed to dealers and hobby media several weeks prior to the product's release. The first card features identical glossy card front stock as the basic Ultra 2000 product and has the words "PROMOTIONAL SAMPLE" running diagonally across the back of the card. The second, more scarce, card features a lenticular ribbed plastic card front (creating a primitive 3-D effect). Both promos share the same photo of Rodriguez as is used on the basic issue A-Rod 2000 Ultra card.

Card	Nm-Mt	Ex-Mt
COMPLETE SET (300)	100.00	30.00
COMP.SET w/o SP's (250)	25.00	7.50
COMMON CARD (1-250)	.30	.09
COMMON (251-300)	4.00	1.20
1 Alex Rodriguez	1.25	.35
2 Shawn Green	.30	.09
3 Magglio Ordonez	.30	.09
4 Tony Gwynn	1.00	.30
5 Joe McEwing	.30	.09
6 Jose Rosado	.30	.09
7 Sammy Sosa	1.25	.35
8 Gary Sheffield	.30	.09
9 Mickey Morandini	.30	.09
10 Mo Vaughn	.30	.09
11 Todd Hollandsworth	.30	.09
12 Tom Gordon	.30	.09
13 Charles Johnson	.30	.09
14 Derek Bell	.30	.09
15 Kevin Young	.30	.09

16 Jay Buhner .30 .09
17 J.T. Snow .30 .09
18 Jay Bell .30 .09
19 John Rocker .30 .09
20 Ivan Rodriguez .75 .23
21 Pokey Reese .30 .09
22 Paul O'Neill .50 .15
23 Ronnie Belliard .30 .09
24 Ryan Rupe .30 .09
25 Travis Fryman .30 .09
26 Trot Nixon .30 .09
27 Wally Joyner .30 .09
28 Andy Pettitte .50 .15
29 Dan Wilson .30 .09
30 Orlando Hernandez .30 .09
31 Dmitri Young .30 .09
32 Edgar Renteria .30 .09
33 Eric Karros .30 .09
34 Fernando Seguignol .30 .09
35 Jason Kendall .30 .09
36 Jeff Shaw .30 .09
37 Matt Lawton .30 .09
38 Robin Ventura .50 .15
39 Scott Williamson .30 .09
40 Ben Grieve .30 .09
41 Billy Wagner .30 .09
42 Javy Lopez .30 .09
43 Joe Randa .30 .09
44 Neifi Perez .30 .09
45 David Justice .30 .09
46 Ray Durham .30 .09
47 Dustin Hermanson .30 .09
48 Andres Galarraga .30 .09
49 Brad Fullmer .30 .09
50 Nomar Garciaparra 1.25 .35
51 David Cone .30 .09
52 David Nilsson .30 .09
53 David Wells .30 .09
54 Miguel Tejada .30 .09
55 Ismael Valdes .30 .09
56 Jose Lima .30 .09
57 Juan Encarnacion .30 .09
58 Fred McGriff .50 .15
59 Kenny Rogers .30 .09
60 Vladimir Guerrero .75 .23
61 Benito Santiago .30 .09
62 Chris Singleton .30 .09
63 Carlos Lee .30 .09
64 Sean Casey .30 .09
65 Tom Goodwin .30 .09
66 Todd Hundley .30 .09
67 Ellis Burks .30 .09
68 Tim Hudson .30 .09
69 Matt Stairs .30 .09
70 Chipper Jones UER .75 .23
Dodgers logo on the back
71 Craig Biggio .50 .15
72 Brian Rose .30 .09
73 Carlos Delgado .30 .09
74 Eddie Taubensee .30 .09
75 John Smoltz .50 .15
76 Ken Caminiti .30 .09
77 Rafael Palmeiro .50 .15
78 Sidney Ponson .30 .09
79 Todd Helton .50 .15
80 Juan Gonzalez .50 .15
81 Bruce Aven .30 .09
82 Desi Relaford .30 .09
83 Johnny Damon .50 .15
84 Albert Belle .30 .09
85 Mark McGwire 2.00 .60
86 Rico Brogna .30 .09
87 Tom Glavine .50 .15
88 Harold Baines .30 .09
89 Chad Allen .30 .09
90 Barry Bonds 2.00 .60
91 Mark Grace .50 .15
92 Paul Byrd .30 .09
93 Roberto Alomar .50 .15
94 Roberto Hernandez .30 .09
95 Steve Finley .30 .09
96 Bret Boone .30 .09
97 Charles Nagy .30 .09
98 Eric Chavez .30 .09
99 Jamie Moyer .30 .09
100 Ken Griffey Jr. 1.25 .35
101 J.D. Drew .30 .09
102 Todd Stottlemyre .30 .09
103 Tony Fernandez .30 .09
104 Jeromy Burnitz .30 .09
105 Jeremy Giambi .30 .09
106 Livan Hernandez .30 .09
107 Marlon Anderson .30 .09
108 Troy Glaus .30 .09
109 Troy O'Leary .30 .09
110 Scott Rolen .75 .23
111 Bernard Gilkey .30 .09
112 Brady Anderson .30 .09
113 Chuck Knoblauch .30 .09
114 Jeff Weaver .30 .09
115 B.J. Surhoff .30 .09
116 Alex Gonzalez .30 .09
117 Vinny Castilla .30 .09
118 Tim Salmon .50 .15
119 Brian Jordan .30 .09
120 Corey Koskie .30 .09
121 Dean Palmer .30 .09
122 Gabe Kapler .30 .09
123 Jim Edmonds .30 .09
124 John Jaha .30 .09
125 Mark Grudzielanek .30 .09
126 Mike Bordick .30 .09
127 Mike Lieberthal .30 .09
128 Pete Harnisch .30 .09
129 Russ Ortiz .30 .09
130 Kevin Brown .50 .15
131 Troy Percival .30 .09
132 Alex Gonzalez .30 .09
133 Bartolo Colon .30 .09
134 John Valentin .30 .09
135 Jose Hernandez .30 .09
136 Marquis Grissom .30 .09
137 Wade Boggs .50 .15
138 Dante Bichette .30 .09
139 Bobby Higginson .30 .09
140 Frank Thomas .75 .23
141 Geoff Jenkins .30 .09
142 Jason Giambi .30 .09
143 Jeff Cirillo .30 .09
144 Sandy Alomar Jr. .30 .09
145 Luis Gonzalez .30 .09
146 Preston Wilson .30 .09
147 Carlos Beltran .50 .15
148 Greg Vaughn .30 .09
149 Carlos Febles .30 .09
150 Jose Canseco .75 .23
151 Kris Benson .30 .09
152 Chuck Finley .30 .09
153 Michael Barrett .30 .09
154 Rey Ordonez .30 .09
155 Adrian Beltre .50 .15
156 Andruw Jones .30 .09
157 Barry Larkin .50 .15
158 Brian Giles .30 .09
159 Carl Everett .30 .09
160 Manny Ramirez .50 .15
161 Darryl Kile .30 .09
162 Edgar Martinez .50 .15
163 Jeff Kent .30 .09
164 Matt Williams .30 .09
165 Mike Piazza 1.25 .35
166 Pedro Martinez .75 .23
167 Ray Lankford .30 .09
168 Roger Cedeno .30 .09
169 Ron Coomer .30 .09
170 Cal Ripken 2.50 .75
171 Jose Offerman .30 .09
172 Kenny Lofton .30 .09
173 Kent Bottenfield .30 .09
174 Kevin Millwood .30 .09
175 Omar Daal .30 .09
176 Orlando Cabrera .30 .09
177 Pat Hentgen .30 .09
178 Tino Martinez .50 .15
179 Tony Clark .30 .09
180 Roger Clemens 1.50 .45
181 Brad Radke .30 .09
182 Darin Erstad .30 .09
183 Jose Jimenez .30 .09
184 Jim Thome .75 .23
185 John Wetteland .30 .09
186 Justin Thompson .30 .09
187 John Halama .30 .09
188 Lee Stevens .30 .09
189 Miguel Cairo .30 .09
190 Mike Mussina .50 .15
191 Raul Mondesi .30 .09
192 Armando Rios .30 .09
193 Trevor Hoffman .30 .09
194 Tony Batista .30 .09
195 Will Clark .75 .23
196 Brad Ausmus .30 .09
197 Chili Davis .30 .09
198 Cliff Floyd .30 .09
199 Curt Schilling .30 .09
200 Derek Jeter 2.00 .60
201 Henry Rodriguez .30 .09
202 Jose Cruz Jr. .30 .09
203 Omar Vizquel .50 .15
204 Randy Johnson .75 .23
205 Reggie Sanders .30 .09
206 Al Leiter .30 .09
207 Damion Easley .30 .09
208 David Bell .30 .09
209 Fernando Tatis .30 .09
210 Kerry Wood .75 .23
211 Kevin Appier .30 .09
212 Mariano Rivera .50 .15
213 Mike Caruso .30 .09
214 Moises Alou .30 .09
215 Randy Winn .30 .09
216 Roy Halladay .30 .09
217 Shannon Stewart .30 .09
218 Todd Walker .30 .09
219 Jim Parque .30 .09
220 Travis Lee .30 .09
221 Andy Ashby .30 .09
222 Ed Sprague .30 .09
223 Larry Walker .50 .15
224 Rick Helling .30 .09
225 Rusty Greer .30 .09
226 Todd Zeile .30 .09
227 Freddy Garcia .30 .09
228 Hideo Nomo .75 .23
229 Marty Cordova .30 .09
230 Greg Maddux 1.25 .35
231 Rondell White .30 .09
232 Paul Konerko .30 .09
233 Warren Morris .30 .09
234 Bernie Williams .50 .15
235 Bob Abreu .30 .09
236 John Olerud .30 .09
237 Doug Glanville .30 .09
238 Eric Young .30 .09
239 Robb Nen .30 .09
240 Jeff Bagwell .50 .15
241 Sterling Hitchcock .30 .09
242 Todd Greene .30 .09
243 Bill Mueller .30 .09
244 Rickey Henderson .75 .23
245 Chan Ho Park .30 .09
246 Jason Schmidt .30 .09
247 Jeff Zimmerman .30 .09
248 Jermaine Dye .30 .09
249 Randall Simon .30 .09
250 Richie Sexson .30 .09
251 Micah Bowie PROS 4.00 1.20
252 Joe Nathan PROS 4.00 1.20
253 C.Woodward PROS 4.00 1.20
254 Lance Berkman PROS 4.00 1.20
255 Ruben Mateo PROS 4.00 1.20
256 R.Branyan PROS 4.00 1.20
257 Randy Wolf PROS 4.00 1.20
258 A.J. Burnett PROS 4.00 1.20
259 Mark Quinn PROS 4.00 1.20
260 Buddy Carlyle PROS 4.00 1.20
261 Ben Davis PROS 4.00 1.20
262 Yamid Haad PROS 4.00 1.20
263 Mike Colangelo PROS 4.00 1.20
264 Rick Ankiel PROS 4.00 1.20
265 Jacque Jones PROS 4.00 1.20
266 Kelly Dransfeldt PROS 4.00 1.20
267 Matt Riley PROS 4.00 1.20
268 Adam Kennedy PROS 4.00 1.20
269 Octavio Dotel PROS 4.00 1.20
270 F.Cordero PROS 4.00 1.20
271 Wilton Veras PROS 4.00 1.20
272 C.Pickering PROS 4.00 1.20
273 Alex Sanchez PROS 4.00 1.20
274 Tony Armas Jr. PROS 4.00 1.20
275 Pat Burrell PROS 4.00 1.20
276 Chad Meyers PROS 4.00 1.20
277 Ben Petrick PROS 4.00 1.20
278 R.Hernandez PROS 4.00 1.20
279 Ed Yarnall PROS 4.00 1.20
280 Erubiel Durazo PROS 4.00 1.20
281 Vernon Wells PROS 4.00 1.20
282 G.Matthews Jr. PROS 4.00 1.20
283 Kip Wells PROS 4.00 1.20
284 Peter Bergeron PROS 4.00 1.20
285 Travis Dawkins PROS 4.00 1.20
286 Jorge Toca PROS 4.00 1.20
287 Cole Liniak PROS 4.00 1.20
288 C.Hermansen PROS 4.00 1.20
289 Eric Gagne PROS 8.00 2.40
290 C.Hutchinson PROS 4.00 1.20
291 Eric Munson PROS 4.00 1.20
292 Wiki Gonzalez PROS 4.00 1.20
293 A.Soriano PROS 5.00 1.50
294 T.Durrington PROS 4.00 1.20
295 Ben Molina PROS 4.00 1.20
296 Aaron Myette PROS 4.00 1.20
297 Wily Pena PROS 4.00 1.20
298 Kevin Barker PROS 4.00 1.20
299 Geoff Blum PROS 4.00 1.20
300 Josh Beckett PROS 5.00 1.50
P1 Alex Rodriguez Promo 1.50 .45
P2 A.Rodriguez Promo 3-D 5.00 1.50

2000 Ultra Gold Medallion

This set is a parallel to the regular Ultra set. The regular cards from 1 through 250 were issued one per hobby pack and the prospect cards were issued one every 24 hobby packs. These cards have special die-cutting and have gold coating and gold foil stamping.

Nm-Mt Ex-Mt
*GOLD 1-250: 1.25X TO 3X BASIC CARDS
*GOLD PROS: .75X TO 2X BASIC CARDS

2000 Ultra Platinum Medallion

Randomly inserted into hobby packs, these cards parallel the regular Ultra set. These cards are serial numbered to 50 for the veterans and 25 for the prospects (251-300). These die cut cards have silver coating and silver foil. Pricing is unavaiable due to scarcity on cards 251-300.

Nm-Mt Ex-Mt
*PLAT 1-250: 15X TO 40X BASIC CARDS
*PROSPECTS: 4X TO 10X BASIC CARDS
251-300 NO PRICING DUE TO SCARCITY

2000 Ultra Crunch Time

Inserted one every 72 packs, these 15 cards feature players who are among those players known for their clutch performances. The horizontal cards are printed on suede stock and then are gold foil stamped.

Nm-Mt Ex-Mt
COMPLETE SET (15) 200.00 60.00
1 Nomar Garciaparra 12.00 3.60
2 Ken Griffey Jr. 12.00 3.60
3 Mark McGwire 20.00 6.00
4 Alex Rodriguez 12.00 3.60
5 Derek Jeter 20.00 6.00
6 Sammy Sosa 12.00 3.60
7 Mike Piazza 12.00 3.60
8 Cal Ripken 25.00 7.50
9 Frank Thomas 8.00 2.40
10 Juan Gonzalez 5.00 1.50
11 J.D. Drew 3.00 .90
12 Greg Maddux 12.00 3.60
13 Tony Gwynn 10.00 3.00
14 Vladimir Guerrero 8.00 2.40
15 Ben Grieve 3.00 .90

2000 Ultra Diamond Mine

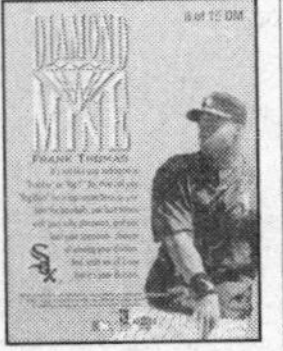

Inserted one every six packs, these 15 cards feature some of the brightest stars of the baseball diamond. The cards are printed on silver metallic ink and have silver foil stamping.

Nm-Mt Ex-Mt
COMPLETE SET (15) 30.00 9.00
1 Greg Maddux 2.00 .60
2 Mark McGwire 3.00 .90
3 Ken Griffey Jr. 2.00 .60
4 Cal Ripken 4.00 1.20
5 Nomar Garciaparra 2.00 .60
6 Mike Piazza 2.00 .60
7 Alex Rodriguez 2.00 .60
8 Frank Thomas 1.25 .35
9 Juan Gonzalez .75 .23
10 Derek Jeter 3.00 .90
11 Tony Gwynn 1.50 .45
12 Chipper Jones 1.25 .35
13 Sammy Sosa 2.00 .60
14 Roger Clemens 2.50 .75
15 Vladimir Guerrero 1.25 .35

2000 Ultra Feel the Game

Inserted at a rate of one in 168, these cards feature pieces of game used memorabilia of some of today's stars. There is a player photo to go with the swatch of clothing used. It is widely believed that the Frank Thomas is the toughest card to find in the set.

Nm-Mt Ex-Mt
1 Alex Rodriguez Jsy 25.00 7.50
2 Chipper Jones Jsy 15.00 4.50
3 Rob Alomar Btg Glv SP 50.00 15.00
4 Greg Maddux Jsy 15.00 4.50
5 Pedro Martinez Jsy 15.00 4.50
6 Cal Ripken Jsy 50.00 15.00
7 Robin Ventura Jsy 10.00 3.00
8 J.D. Drew Jsy 10.00 3.00
9 Randy Johnson Jsy 15.00 4.50
10 Scott Rolen Jsy 15.00 4.50
11 Kevin Millwood Jsy 10.00 3.00
12 Frank Thomas Btg Glv SP 80.00 24.00
13 Tony Gwynn Btg Glv SP 60.00 18.00
14 Curt Schilling Jsy 10.00 3.00
15 Edgar Martinez Btg Glv 15.00 4.50

2000 Ultra Fresh Ink

Randomly inserted into packs, these cards feature signed cards of either young players or veteran stars. One card in this set is a combo signature card of the three players used in the Club 3000 series. After each player name in our checklist is a number indicating how many cards they signed for this promotion.

Nm-Mt Ex-Mt
1 Bob Abreu/200 25.00 7.50
2 Chad Allen/975 10.00 3.00
3 Marlon Anderson/975 10.00 3.00
4 Rick Ankiel/500 15.00 4.50
5 Glen Barker/975 10.00 3.00
6 Michael Barrett/975 10.00 3.00
7 Carlos Beltran/975 40.00 12.00
8 Adrian Beltre/900 25.00 7.50
9 Peter Bergeron/1000 10.00 3.00
10 Wade Boggs/250 40.00 12.00
11 Barry Bonds/250 250.00 75.00
12 Pat Burrell/600 15.00 4.50
13 Roger Cedeno/500 15.00 4.50
14 Eric Chavez/800 15.00 4.50
15 Bruce Chen/600 10.00 3.00
16 Johnny Damon/750 25.00 7.50
17 Ben Davis/1000 10.00 3.00
18 Carlos Delgado/275 25.00 7.50
19 Einar Diaz/975 10.00 3.00
20 Octavio Dotel/950 10.00 3.00
21 J.D. Drew/600 25.00 7.50
22 Scott Elarton/1000 10.00 3.00
23 Freddy Garcia/500 15.00 4.50
24 Jeremy Giambi/975 10.00 3.00
25 Troy Glaus/500 15.00 4.50
26 Shawn Green/350 25.00 7.50
27 Tony Gwynn/250 60.00 18.00
28 Richard Hidalgo/500 10.00 3.00
29 Bobby Higginson/975 10.00 3.00
30 Tim Hudson/975 25.00 7.50
31 Norm Hutchins/1000 10.00 3.00
32 Derek Jeter/95 250.00 75.00
33 Randy Johnson/240 80.00 24.00
34 Gabe Kapler/725 10.00 3.00
35 Jason Kendall/375 25.00 7.50
36 Paul Konerko/500 15.00 4.50
37 Matt Lawton/1000 10.00 3.00
38 Carlos Lee/900 15.00 4.50
39 Jose Macias/1000 10.00 3.00
40 Greg Maddux/225 120.00 36.00
41 Kevin Millwood/500 15.00 4.50
42 Warren Morris/1000 10.00 3.00
43 Eric Munson/900 10.00 3.00
44 Heath Murray/925 10.00 3.00
45 Joe Nathan/1000 15.00 4.50
46 Magglio Ordonez/335 25.00 7.50
47 Angel Pena/1000 10.00 3.00
48 Cal Ripken/350 150.00 45.00
49 Alex Rodriguez/350 120.00 36.00
50 Scott Rolen/250 50.00 15.00
51 Ryan Rupe/1000 10.00 3.00
52 Curt Schilling/375 50.00 15.00
53 Randall Simon/1000 10.00 3.00
54 Alfonso Soriano/975 40.00 12.00
55 Shannon Stewart/275 25.00 7.50
56 Miguel Tejada/1000 15.00 4.50
57 Frank Thomas/150 100.00 30.00
58 Jeff Weaver/1000 15.00 4.50
59 Randy Wolf/1000 15.00 4.50
60 Ed Yarnall/1000 10.00 3.00
61 Kevin Young/1000 10.00 3.00
62 Wade Boggs 500.00 150.00
Tony Gwynn
Nolan Ryan 100

2000 Ultra Swing Kings

Inserted one every 24 packs, these 10 cards feature some of the leading power hitters in baseball. These cards are made of contemporary

plastice with glittering silver foil highlights.

Nm-Mt Ex-Mt
COMPLETE SET (10) 50.00 15.00
1 Cal Ripken 8.00 2.40
2 Nomar Garciaparra 4.00 1.20
3 Frank Thomas 2.50 .75
4 Tony Gwynn 3.00 .90
5 Ken Griffey Jr. 4.00 1.20
6 Chipper Jones 2.50 .75
7 Mark McGwire 6.00 1.80
8 Sammy Sosa 4.00 1.20
9 Derek Jeter 6.00 1.80
10 Alex Rodriguez 4.00 1.20

2000 Ultra Talented

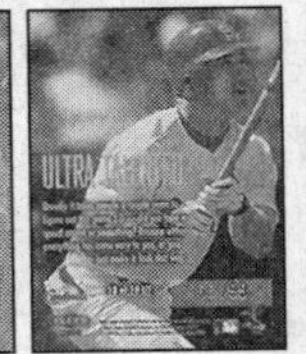

Randomly inserted into hobby packs, these 10 cards feature multi-talented players. These cards feature metallic ink on holofoil background with gold fil stamped accents.

Nm-Mt Ex-Mt
1 Sammy Sosa 50.00 15.00
2 Derek Jeter 80.00 24.00
3 Alex Rodriguez 50.00 15.00
4 Mike Piazza 50.00 15.00
5 Ken Griffey Jr. 50.00 15.00
6 Nomar Garciaparra 50.00 15.00
7 Mark McGwire 80.00 24.00
8 Cal Ripken 100.00 30.00
9 Frank Thomas 30.00 9.00
10 J.D. Drew 12.00 3.60

2000 Ultra World Premiere

Inserted one every 12 packs, these 10 cards feature 12 of the leading prospects in baseball. The die cut cards are printed with etched foil.

Nm-Mt Ex-Mt
COMPLETE SET (10) 12.00 3.60
1 Ruben Mateo 1.00 .30
2 Lance Berkman 1.25 .35
3 Octavio Dotel 1.00 .30
4 Ben Davis 1.00 .30
5 Warren Morris 1.00 .30
6 Carlos Beltran 2.00 .60
7 Rick Ankiel 1.25 .35
8 Adam Kennedy 1.00 .30
9 Tim Hudson 1.25 .35
10 Jorge Toca 1.00 .30

2001 Ultra

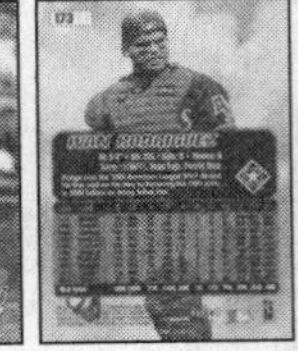

The 2001 Ultra product was released in December, 2000 and features a 275-card base set. The base set is broken into tiers as follows: 250 Base Veterans, and 25 Prospects (1:4). Each pack contained 10-cards, and carried a suggested retail price of $2.99.

Nm-Mt Ex-Mt
COMPLETE SET (275) 120.00 36.00
COMP.SET w/o SP's (250) 25.00 7.50
COMMON CARD (1-250) .30 .09
COMMON (251-275) 3.00 .90
COMMON (276-280) 5.00 1.50
1 Pedro Martinez .75 .23
2 Derek Jeter 2.00 .60
3 Cal Ripken 2.50 .75
4 Alex Rodriguez 1.25 .35
5 Vladimir Guerrero .75 .23
6 Troy Glaus .30 .09
7 Sammy Sosa 1.25 .35
8 Mike Piazza 1.25 .35
9 Tony Gwynn 1.00 .30
10 Tim Hudson .30 .09
11 John Flaherty .30 .09
12 Jeff Cirillo .30 .09
13 Ellis Burks .30 .09
14 Carlos Lee .30 .09
15 Carlos Beltran .50 .15
16 Ruben Rivera .30 .09

17 Richard Hidalgo .30 .09
18 Omar Vizquel .50 .15
19 Michael Barrett .30 .09
20 Jose Canseco .75 .23
21 Jason Giambi .30 .09
22 Greg Maddux 1.25 .35
23 Charles Johnson .30 .09
24 Sandy Alomar Jr. .30 .09
25 Rick Ankiel .30 .09
26 Richie Sexson .30 .09
27 Matt Williams .30 .09
28 Joe Girardi .30 .09
29 Jason Kendall .30 .09
30 Brad Fullmer .30 .09
31 Alex Gonzalez .30 .09
32 Rick Helling .30 .09
33 Mike Mussina .50 .15
34 Joe Randa .30 .09
35 J.T. Snow .30 .09
36 Edgardo Alfonzo .30 .09
37 Dante Bichette .30 .09
38 Brad Ausmus .30 .09
39 Bobby Abreu .30 .09
40 Warren Morris .30 .09
41 Tony Womack .30 .09
42 Russell Branyan .30 .09
43 Mike Lowell .30 .09
44 Mark Grace .50 .15
45 Jeromy Burnitz .30 .09
46 J.D. Drew .30 .09
47 David Justice .30 .09
48 Alex Gonzalez .30 .09
49 Tino Martinez .50 .15
50 Raul Mondesi .30 .09
51 Rafael Furcal .30 .09
52 Marquis Grissom .30 .09
53 Kevin Young .30 .09
54 Jon Lieber .30 .09
55 Henry Rodriguez .30 .09
56 Dave Burba .30 .09
57 Shannon Stewart .30 .09
58 Preston Wilson .30 .09
59 Paul O'Neill .50 .15
60 Jimmy Haynes .30 .09
61 Darryl Kile .30 .09
62 Bret Boone .30 .09
63 Bartolo Colon .30 .09
64 Andres Galarraga .30 .09
65 Trot Nixon .30 .09
66 Steve Finley .30 .09
67 Shawn Green .30 .09
68 Robert Person .30 .09
69 Kenny Rogers .30 .09
70 Bobby Higginson .30 .09
71 Barry Larkin .50 .15
72 Al Martin .30 .09
73 Tom Glavine .50 .15
74 Rondell White .30 .09
75 Ray Lankford .30 .09
76 Moises Alou .30 .09
77 Matt Clement .30 .09
78 Geoff Jenkins .30 .09
79 David Wells .30 .09
80 Chuck Finley .30 .09
81 Andy Pettitte .50 .15
82 Travis Fryman .30 .09
83 Ron Coomer .30 .09
84 Mark McGwire 2.00 .60
85 Kerry Wood .75 .23
86 Jorge Posada .50 .15
87 Jeff Bagwell .50 .15
88 Andruw Jones .30 .09
89 Ryan Klesko .30 .09
90 Mariano Rivera .50 .15
91 Lance Berkman .30 .09
92 Kenny Lofton .30 .09
93 Jacque Jones .30 .09
94 Eric Young .30 .09
95 Edgar Renteria .30 .09
96 Chipper Jones .75 .23
97 Todd Helton .50 .15
98 Shawn Estes .30 .09
99 Mark Mulder .30 .09
100 Lee Stevens .30 .09
101 Jermaine Dye .30 .09
102 Greg Vaughn .30 .09
103 Chris Singleton .30 .09
104 Brady Anderson .30 .09
105 Terrence Long .30 .09
106 Quilvio Veras .30 .09
107 Magglio Ordonez .30 .09
108 Johnny Damon .50 .15
109 Jeffrey Hammonds .30 .09
110 Fred McGriff .50 .15
111 Carl Pavano .30 .09
112 Bobby Estalella .30 .09
113 Todd Hundley .30 .09
114 Scott Rolen .75 .23
115 Robin Ventura .50 .15
116 Pokey Reese .30 .09
117 Luis Gonzalez .30 .09
118 Jose Offerman .30 .09
119 Edgar Martinez .50 .15
120 Dean Palmer .30 .09
121 David Segui .30 .09
122 Troy O'Leary .30 .09
123 Tony Batista .30 .09
124 Todd Zeile .30 .09
125 Randy Johnson .75 .23
126 Luis Castillo .30 .09
127 Kris Benson .30 .09
128 John Olerud .30 .09
129 Eric Karros .30 .09
130 Eddie Taubensee .30 .09
131 Neifi Perez .30 .09
132 Matt Stairs .30 .09
133 Luis Alicea .30 .09
134 Jeff Kent .30 .09
135 Javier Vazquez .30 .09
136 Garret Anderson .30 .09
137 Frank Thomas .75 .23
138 Carlos Febles .30 .09
139 Albert Belle .30 .09
140 Tony Clark .30 .09
141 Pat Burrell .30 .09
142 Mike Sweeney .30 .09
143 Jay Buhner .30 .09
144 Gabe Kapler .30 .09
145 Derek Bell .30 .09
146 B.J. Surhoff .30 .09
147 Adam Kennedy .30 .09
148 Aaron Boone .30 .09
149 Todd Stottlemyre .30 .09
150 Roberto Alomar .50 .15
151 Orlando Hernandez .30 .09
152 Jason Varitek .50 .15
153 Gary Sheffield .30 .09
154 Cliff Floyd .30 .09
155 Chad Hermansen .30 .09
156 Carlos Delgado .30 .09
157 Aaron Sele .30 .09
158 Sean Casey .30 .09
159 Ruben Mateo .30 .09
160 Mike Bordick .30 .09
161 Mike Cameron .30 .09
162 Doug Glanville .30 .09
163 Damion Easley .30 .09
164 Carl Everett .30 .09
165 Bengie Molina .30 .09
166 Adrian Beltre .50 .15
167 Tom Goodwin .30 .09
168 Rickey Henderson .75 .23
169 Mo Vaughn .30 .09
170 Mike Lieberthal .30 .09
171 Ken Griffey Jr. 1.25 .35
172 Juan Gonzalez .50 .15
173 Ivan Rodriguez .75 .23
174 Al Leiter .30 .09
175 Vinny Castilla .30 .09
176 Peter Bergeron .30 .09
177 Pedro Astacio .30 .09
178 Paul Konerko .30 .09
179 Mitch Meluskey .30 .09
180 Kevin Millwood .30 .09
181 Ben Grieve .30 .09
182 Barry Bonds 2.00 .60
183 Rusty Greer .30 .09
184 Miguel Tejada .30 .09
185 Mark Quinn .30 .09
186 Larry Walker .50 .15
187 Jose Valentin .30 .09
188 Jose Vidro .30 .09
189 Delino DeShields .30 .09
190 Darin Erstad .30 .09
191 Bill Mueller .30 .09
192 Ray Durham .30 .09
193 Ken Caminiti .30 .09
194 Jim Thome .75 .23
195 Javy Lopez .30 .09
196 Fernando Vina .30 .09
197 Eric Chavez .30 .09
198 Eric Owens .30 .09
199 Brad Radke .30 .09
200 Travis Lee .30 .09
201 Tim Salmon .50 .15
202 Rafael Palmeiro .50 .15
203 Nomar Garciaparra 1.25 .35
204 Mike Hampton .30 .09
205 Kevin Brown .30 .09
206 Juan Encarnacion .30 .09
207 Danny Graves .30 .09
208 Carlos Guillen .30 .09
209 Phil Nevin .30 .09
210 Matt Lawton .30 .09
211 Manny Ramirez .50 .15
212 James Baldwin .30 .09
213 Fernando Tatis .30 .09
214 Craig Biggio .50 .15
215 Brian Jordan .30 .09
216 Bernie Williams .50 .15
217 Ryan Dempster .30 .09
218 Roger Clemens 1.50 .45
219 Jose Cruz Jr. .30 .09
220 John Valentin .30 .09
221 Dmitri Young .30 .09
222 Curt Schilling .30 .09
223 Jim Edmonds .30 .09
224 Chan Ho Park .30 .09
225 Brian Giles .30 .09
226 Jimmy Anderson .30 .09
Tike Redman
227 Adam Piatt .30 .09
Jose Ortiz
228 Kenny Kelly .30 .09
Aubrey Huff
229 Randy Choate .30 .09
Craig Dingman
230 Eric Cammack .30 .09
Grant Roberts
231 Yovanny Lara .30 .09
Andy Tracy
232 Wayne Franklin .30 .09
Scott Linebrink
233 Cameron Cairncross .30 .09
Chan Perry
234 J.C. Romero .30 .09
Matt LeCroy
235 Geraldo Guzman .30 .09
Jason Conti
236 Morgan Burkhart .30 .09
Paxton Crawford
237 Pasqual Coco .30 .09
Leo Estrella
238 John Parrish .30 .09
Fernando Lunar
239 Keith McDonald .30 .09
Justin Brunette
240 Carlos Casimiro .30 .09
Ivanon Coffie
241 Daniel Garibay .30 .09
Ruben Quevedo
242 Sang-Hoon Lee .30 .09
Tomo Ohka
243 Hector Ortiz .30 .09
Jeff D'Amico
244 Jeff Sparks .30 .09
Travis Harper
245 Jason Boyd .30 .09
David Coggin
246 Mark Buehrle .30 .09
Lorenzo Barcelo
247 Adam Melhuse .30 .09
Ben Petrick
248 Kane Davis .30 .09
Paul Rigdon
249 Mike Darr .30 .09
Kory DeHaan
250 Vicente Padilla 3.00 .90
Mark Brownson
251 Barry Zito PROS 5.00 1.50
252 Tim Drew PROS 3.00 .90
253 Luis Matos PROS 3.00 .90
254 Alex Cabrera PROS 3.00 .90
255 Jon Garland PROS 3.00 .90
256 Milton Bradley PROS 3.00 .90
257 Juan Pierre PROS 3.00 .90
258 Ismael Villegas PROS 3.00 .90
259 Eric Munson PROS 3.00 .90
260 T.De la Rosa PROS 3.00 .90
261 Chris Richard PROS 3.00 .90
262 Jason Tyner PROS 3.00 .90
263 B.J. Waszgis PROS 3.00 .90
264 Jason Marquis PROS 3.00 .90
265 Dusty Allen PROS 3.00 .90
266 C.Patterson PROS 3.00 .90
267 Eric Byrnes PROS 3.00 .90
268 Xavier Nady PROS 3.00 .90
269 G.Lombard PROS 3.00 .90
270 Timo Perez PROS 3.00 .90
271 G.Matthews Jr. PROS 3.00 .90
272 Chad Durbin PROS 3.00 .90
273 Tony Armas Jr. PROS 3.00 .90
274 F.Cordero PROS 3.00 .90
275 A.Soriano PROS 5.00 1.50
276 Junior Spivey RC 8.00 2.40
Juan Uribe RC
277 Albert Pujols RC 50.00 15.00
Bud Smith RC
278 Ichiro Suzuki RC 30.00 9.00
Tsuyoshi Shinjo RC
279 Drew Henson RC 5.00 1.50
Jackson Melian RC
280 Matt White RC 5.00 1.50
Adrian Hernandez RC

2001 Ultra Gold Medallion

Inserted into packs at a rate of one per pack (251-275 were inserted at 1:24), this 275-card set is a complete parallel of the Ultra base set. Please note that these cards were produced with gold coating and gold foil stamping.

Nm-Mt Ex-Mt
*STARS 1-225: 1.25X TO 3X BASIC CARDS
*PROSPECTS 226-250: 1.25X TO 3X BASIC
*PROSPECTS 251-275: .75X TO 2X BASIC

2001 Ultra Platinum Medallion

Randomly inserted into packs, this 275-card set is a complete parallel of the Ultra base set. Cards 1-250 were individually serial numbered to 50, and cards 251-275 were individually serial numbered to 25. Please note that these cards were produced with a silver coating and silver foil stamping.

Nm-Mt Ex-Mt
*PLATINUM 1-225: 15X TO 40X BASIC
*PLATINUM 251-275: 3X TO 8X BASIC

2001 Ultra Decade of Dominance

Randomly inserted into packs at one in eight, this 15-card insert set features players that dominated Major League Baseball in the 1990's. Card backs carry a "DD" prefix.

Nm-Mt Ex-Mt
COMPLETE SET (15) 30.00 9.00
PLATINUM RANDOM INSERTS IN PACKS
PLATINUM PRINT RUN 10 SERIAL #'d SETS
PLATINUM NO PRICING DUE TO SCARCITY
DD1 Barry Bonds 4.00 1.20
DD2 Mark McGwire 4.00 1.20
DD3 Sammy Sosa 2.50 .75
DD4 Ken Griffey Jr. 2.50 .75
DD5 Cal Ripken 5.00 1.50
DD6 Tony Gwynn 2.00 .60
DD7 Albert Belle .75 .23
DD8 Frank Thomas 1.50 .45
DD9 Randy Johnson 1.50 .45
DD10 Juan Gonzalez 1.00 .30
DD11 Greg Maddux 2.50 .75
DD12 Craig Biggio 1.00 .30
DD13 Edgar Martinez 1.00 .30
DD14 Roger Clemens 3.00 .90
DD15 Andres Galarraga .75 .23

2001 Ultra Fall Classics

Inserted into packs at one in 20, this 37-card insert set features some of the most legendary players of all time. Card backs carry a "FC" prefix.

Nm-Mt Ex-Mt
FC1 Jackie Robinson 5.00 1.50
FC2 Enos Slaughter 3.00 .90
FC3 Mariano Rivera 3.00 .90
FC4 Hank Bauer 3.00 .90
FC5 Cal Ripken 15.00 4.50
FC6 Babe Ruth 15.00 4.50
FC7 Thurman Munson 5.00 1.50
FC8 Tom Glavine 3.00 .90
FC9 Fred Lynn 3.00 .90
FC10 Johnny Bench 5.00 1.50
FC11 Tony Lazzeri 3.00 .90
FC12 Al Kaline 5.00 1.50
FC13 Reggie Jackson 3.00 .90
FC14 Derek Jeter 12.00 3.60
FC15 Willie Stargell 3.00 .90
FC16 Roy Campanella 5.00 1.50
FC17 Phil Rizzuto 5.00 1.50
FC18 Roberto Clemente 15.00 4.50
FC19 Carlton Fisk 3.00 .90
FC20 Duke Snider 3.00 .90
FC21 Ted Williams 12.00 3.60
FC22 Bill Skowron 3.00 .90
FC23 Bucky Dent 3.00 .90
FC24 Mike Schmidt 10.00 3.00
FC25 Lou Brock 3.00 .90
FC26 Whitey Ford 3.00 .90
FC27 Brooks Robinson 3.00 .90
FC28 Roberto Alomar 3.00 .90
FC29 Yogi Berra 5.00 1.50
FC30 Joe Carter 3.00 .90
FC31 Bill Mazeroski 3.00 .90
FC32 Bob Gibson 3.00 .90
FC33 Hank Greenberg 6.00 1.80
FC34 Andruw Jones 3.00 .90
FC35 Bernie Williams 3.00 .90
FC36 Don Larsen 3.00 .90
FC37 Billy Martin 5.00 1.50

2001 Ultra Fall Classics Memorabilia

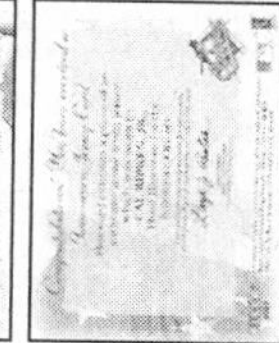

Randomly inserted into packs, this 26-card insert features game-used memorabilia from players like Derek Jeter, Al Kaline, and Cal Ripken. Please note that the cards a checklisted below in alphabetical order for convience.

Nm-Mt Ex-Mt
1 Hank Bauer Bat 15.00 4.50
2 Johnny Bench Jsy 25.00 7.50
3 Lou Brock Jsy 25.00 7.50
4 Roy Campanella Bat 50.00 15.00
5 Roberto Clemente Bat 100.00 30.00
6 Bucky Dent Bat 15.00 4.50
7 Carlton Fisk Jsy 25.00 7.50
8 Tom Glavine Jsy 25.00 7.50
9 Reggie Jackson Jsy 25.00 7.50
10 Derek Jeter Jsy 40.00 12.00
11 Al Kaline Jsy 25.00 7.50
12 Tony Lazzeri Bat 15.00 4.50
13 Fred Lynn Bat 15.00 4.50
14 Thurman Munson Bat 40.00 12.00
15 Cal Ripken Jsy 40.00 12.00
16 Mariano Rivera Jsy 25.00 7.50
17 Phil Rizzuto Bat 25.00 7.50
18 Brooks Robinson Bat 25.00 7.50
19 Jackie Robinson Pants 60.00 18.00
20 Babe Ruth Bat 200.00 60.00
21 Mike Schmidt Jsy 25.00 7.50
22 Bill Skowron Bat 15.00 4.50
23 Enos Slaughter Bat 15.00 4.50
24 Duke Snider Bat 25.00 7.50
25 Willie Stargell Bat 25.00 7.50
26 Ted Williams Bat 100.00 30.00

2001 Ultra Fall Classics Memorabilia Autograph

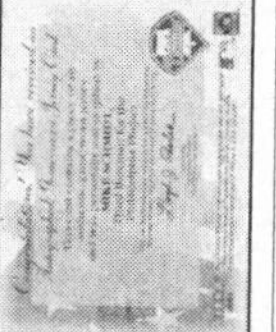

Randomly inserted into packs, this nine-card insert features game-used memorabilia and autographs of legendary players. Due to market scarcity, not all cards are priced. All are listed for checklisting purposes. Please note that the Al Kaline jersey/autograph card contained an error, Kaline actually wore jersey number 6. However, Fleer produced seven of these cards. Reggie Jackson's card was distributed as an exchange card in packs. The exchange deadline was January 2nd, 2002.

Nm-Mt Ex-Mt
1 Lou Brock Jsy AU/20
2 Carlton Fisk Jsy AU/27
3 Reggie Jackson 120.00 36.00
Bat-Jsy/44
4 Derek Jeter Jsy AU/2
5 Al Kaline Jsy AU/7 UER
Kaline wore Jersey number 6
6 Cal Ripken Jsy AU/8
7 Mike Schmidt Jsy AU/20
8 Enos Slaughter Jsy AU/9
9 Willie Stargell Jsy AU/8

2001 Ultra Greatest Hits

Randomly inserted into packs at one in 12, this 10-card insert set features players that dominante the Major Leagues. Card backs carry a "GH" prefix.

Nm-Mt Ex-Mt
COMPLETE SET (10) 25.00 7.50
PLATINUM RANDOM INSERTS IN PACKS
PLATINUM PRINT RUN 10 SERIAL #'d SETS
PLATINUM NO PRICING DUE TO SCARCITY
GH1 Mark McGwire 4.00 1.20
GH2 Alex Rodriguez 2.50 .75

GH3 Ken Griffey Jr. 2.50 .75
GH4 Ivan Rodriguez 1.50 .45
GH5 Cal Ripken 5.00 1.50
GH6 Todd Helton 1.00 .30
GH7 Derek Jeter 4.00 1.20
GH8 Pedro Martinez 1.50 .45
GH9 Tony Gwynn 2.00 .60
GH10 Jim Edmonds 1.00 .30

2001 Ultra Power Plus

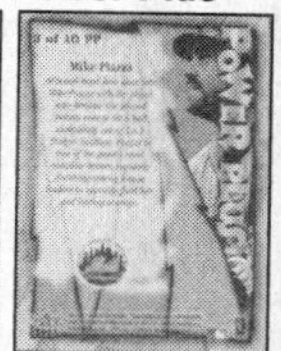

Randomly inserted into packs at one in 24, this 10-card insert set features players that are among the league leaders in homeruns every year. Card backs carry a "PP" prefix.

Nm-Mt Ex-Mt
COMPLETE SET (10) 40.00 12.00
PLATINUM RANDOM INSERTS IN PACKS
PLATINUM PRINT RUN 10 SERIAL #'d SETS
PLATINUM NO PRICING DUE TO SCARCITY
PP1 Vladimir Guerrero 2.50 .75
PP2 Mark McGwire 6.00 1.80
PP3 Mike Piazza 4.00 1.20
PP4 Derek Jeter 6.00 1.80
PP5 Chipper Jones 2.50 .75
PP6 Carlos Delgado 1.50 .45
PP7 Sammy Sosa 4.00 1.20
PP8 Ken Griffey Jr. 4.00 1.20
PP9 Nomar Garciaparra 4.00 1.20
PP10 Alex Rodriguez 4.00 1.20

2001 Ultra Tomorrow's Legends

Randomly inserted into packs at one in 4, this 15-card insert set features players that will most likely make the Hall of Fame when their careers are through. Card backs carry a "TL" prefix.

Nm-Mt Ex-Mt
COMPLETE SET (15) 15.00 4.50
PLATINUM RANDOM INSERTS IN PACKS
PLATINUM PRINT RUN 10 SERIAL #'d SETS
PLATINUM NO PRICING DUE TO SCARCITY
TL1 Rick Ankiel .50 .15
TL2 J.D. Drew .50 .15
TL3 Carlos Delgado .50 .15
TL4 Todd Helton .75 .23
TL5 Andruw Jones .50 .15
TL6 Troy Glaus .50 .15
TL7 Jermaine Dye .50 .15
TL8 Vladimir Guerrero 1.25 .35
TL9 Brian Giles .50 .15
TL10 Scott Rolen 1.25 .35
TL11 Darin Erstad .50 .15
TL12 Derek Jeter 3.00 .90
TL13 Alex Rodriguez 2.00 .60
TL14 Pat Burrell .50 .15
TL15 Nomar Garciaparra 2.00 .60

2002 Ultra

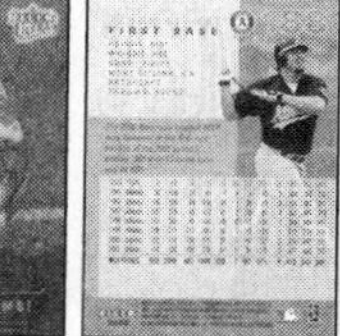

This 285 card set was issued in November, 2001. The following subsets were issued for this set: All-Stars (cards numbered 201-220), Teammates (a veteran and prospect from each team, numbered 221-250), and Prospects (cards numbered 251-285). All three of these subsets were issued at a rate of one in four packs.

Nm-Mt Ex-Mt
COMPLETE SET (285) 200.00 60.00
COMP.SET w/o SP's (200) 25.00 7.50
COMMON CARD (1-200) .30 .09
COMMON (201-220) 1.00 .30
COMMON (221-250) 1.00 .30
COMMON (251-285) 3.00 .90
1 Jeff Bagwell .50 .15
2 Derek Jeter 2.00 .60
3 Alex Rodriguez 1.25 .35
4 Eric Chavez .30 .09

5 Tsuyoshi Shinjo .30 .09
6 Chris Stynes .30 .09
7 Ivan Rodriguez .75 .23
8 Cal Ripken 2.50 .75
9 Freddy Garcia .30 .09
10 Chipper Jones .75 .23
11 Hideo Nomo .75 .23
12 Rafael Furcal .30 .09
13 Preston Wilson .30 .09
14 Jimmy Rollins .30 .09
15 Cristian Guzman .30 .09
16 Garret Anderson .30 .09
17 Todd Helton .50 .15
18 Moises Alou .30 .09
19 Tony Gwynn 1.00 .30
20 Jorge Posada .50 .15
21 Sean Casey .30 .09
22 Kazuhiro Sasaki .30 .09
23 Ray Lankford .30 .09
24 Manny Ramirez .50 .15
25 Barry Bonds 2.00 .60
26 Fred McGriff .50 .15
27 Vladimir Guerrero .75 .23
28 Jermaine Dye .30 .09
29 Adrian Beltre .50 .15
30 Ken Griffey Jr. 1.25 .35
31 Ramon Hernandez .30 .09
32 Kerry Wood .75 .23
33 Greg Maddux 1.25 .35
34 Rondell White .30 .09
35 Mike Mussina .50 .15
36 Jim Edmonds .30 .09
37 Scott Rolen .75 .23
38 Mike Lowell .30 .09
39 Al Leiter .30 .09
40 Tony Clark .30 .09
41 Joe Mays .30 .09
42 Mo Vaughn .30 .09
43 Geoff Jenkins .30 .09
44 Curt Schilling .30 .09
45 Pedro Martinez .75 .23
46 Andy Pettitte .50 .15
47 Tim Salmon .50 .15
48 Carl Everett .30 .09
49 Lance Berkman .30 .09
50 Troy Glaus .30 .09
51 Ichiro Suzuki 1.25 .35
52 Alfonso Soriano .50 .15
53 Tomo Ohka .30 .09
54 Dean Palmer .30 .09
55 Kevin Brown .30 .09
56 Albert Pujols 1.50 .45
57 Homer Bush .30 .09
58 Tim Hudson .30 .09
59 Frank Thomas .75 .23
60 Joe Randa .30 .09
61 Chan Ho Park .30 .09
62 Bobby Higginson .30 .09
63 Bartolo Colon .30 .09
64 Aramis Ramirez .30 .09
65 Jeff Cirillo .30 .09
66 Roberto Alomar .50 .15
67 Mark Kotsay .30 .09
68 Mike Cameron .30 .09
69 Mike Hampton .30 .09
70 Trot Nixon .30 .09
71 Juan Gonzalez .50 .15
72 Damian Rolls .30 .09
73 Brad Fullmer .50 .15
74 David Ortiz .50 .15
75 Brandon Inge .30 .09
76 Orlando Hernandez .30 .09
77 Matt Stairs .30 .09
78 Jay Gibbons .30 .09
79 Greg Vaughn .30 .09
80 Brady Anderson .30 .09
81 Jim Thome .75 .23
82 Ben Sheets .30 .09
83 Rafael Palmeiro .50 .15
84 Edgar Renteria .30 .09
85 Doug Mientkiewicz .30 .09
86 Raul Mondesi .30 .09
87 Shane Reynolds .30 .09
88 Steve Finley .30 .09
89 Jose Cruz Jr. .30 .09
90 Edgardo Alfonzo .30 .09
91 Jose Valentin .30 .09
92 Mark McGwire 2.00 .60
93 Mark Grace .50 .15
94 Mike Lieberthal .30 .09
95 Barry Larkin .50 .15
96 Chuck Knoblauch .30 .09
97 Deivi Cruz .30 .09
98 Jeromy Burnitz .30 .09
99 Shannon Stewart .30 .09
100 David Wells .30 .09
101 Brook Fordyce .30 .09
102 Rusty Greer .30 .09
103 Andruw Jones .30 .09
104 Jason Kendall .30 .09
105 Nomar Garciaparra 1.25 .35
106 Shawn Green .30 .09
107 Craig Biggio .50 .15
108 Masato Yoshii .30 .09
109 Ben Petrick .30 .09
110 Gary Sheffield .30 .09
111 Travis Lee .30 .09
112 Matt Williams .30 .09
113 Billy Wagner .30 .09
114 Robin Ventura .30 .09
115 Jerry Hairston .30 .09
116 Paul LoDuca .30 .09
117 Darin Erstad .30 .09
118 Ruben Sierra .30 .09
119 Ricky Gutierrez .30 .09
120 Bret Boone .30 .09
121 John Rocker .30 .09
122 Roger Clemens 1.50 .45
123 Eric Karros .30 .09
124 J.D. Drew .30 .09
125 Carlos Delgado .30 .09
126 Jeffrey Hammonds .30 .09
127 Jeff Kent .30 .09
128 David Justice .30 .09
129 Cliff Floyd .30 .09
130 Omar Vizquel .50 .15
131 Matt Morris .30 .09
132 Rich Aurilia .30 .09
133 Larry Walker .50 .15
134 Miguel Tejada .30 .09
135 Eric Young .30 .09
136 Aaron Sele .30 .09
137 Eric Milton .30 .09
138 Travis Fryman .30 .09
139 Maggio Ordonez .30 .09
140 Sammy Sosa 1.25 .35
141 Pokey Reese .30 .09
142 Adam Eaton .30 .09
143 Adam Kennedy .30 .09
144 Mike Piazza 1.25 .35
145 Larry Barnes .30 .09
146 Darryl Kile .30 .09
147 Tom Glavine .50 .15
148 Ryan Klesko .30 .09
149 Jose Vidro .30 .09
150 Joe Kennedy .30 .09
151 Bernie Williams .50 .15
152 C.C. Sabathia .30 .09
153 Alex Ochoa .30 .09
154 A.J. Pierzynski .30 .09
155 Johnny Damon .50 .15
156 Omar Daal .30 .09
157 A.J. Burnett .30 .09
158 Eric Munson .30 .09
159 Fernando Vina .30 .09
160 Chris Singleton .30 .09
161 Juan Pierre .30 .09
162 John Olerud .30 .09
163 Randy Johnson .75 .23
164 Paul Konerko .30 .09
165 Tino Martinez .50 .15
166 Richard Hidalgo .30 .09
167 Luis Gonzalez .30 .09
168 Ben Grieve .30 .09
169 Matt Lawton .30 .09
170 Gabe Kapler .30 .09
171 Mariano Rivera .50 .15
172 Kenny Lofton .30 .09
173 Brian Jordan .30 .09
174 Brian Giles .30 .09
175 Mark Quinn .30 .09
176 Neifi Perez .30 .09
177 Ellis Burks .30 .09
178 Bobby Abreu .30 .09
179 Jeff Weaver .30 .09
180 Andres Galarraga .30 .09
181 Javy Lopez .30 .09
182 Todd Walker .30 .09
183 Fernando Tatis .30 .09
184 Charles Johnson .30 .09
185 Pat Burrell .30 .09
186 Jay Bell .30 .09
187 Aaron Boone .30 .09
188 Jason Giambi .30 .09
189 Jay Payton .30 .09
190 Carlos Lee .30 .09
191 Phil Nevin .30 .09
192 Mike Sweeney .30 .09
193 J.T. Snow .30 .09
194 Dmitri Young .30 .09
195 Richie Sexson .30 .09
196 Derrek Lee .30 .09
197 Corey Koskie .30 .09
198 Edgar Martinez .50 .15
199 Wade Miller .30 .09
200 Tony Batista .30 .09
201 John Olerud AS 1.00 .30
202 Bret Boone AS 1.00 .30
203 Cal Ripken AS 5.00 1.50
204 Alex Rodriguez AS 2.50 .75
205 Ichiro Suzuki AS 2.50 .75
206 Manny Ramirez AS .50 .15
207 Juan Gonzalez AS 1.50 .45
208 Ivan Rodriguez AS 1.50 .45
209 Roger Clemens AS 3.00 .90
210 Edgar Martinez AS 1.50 .45
211 Todd Helton AS 1.50 .45
212 Jeff Kent AS 1.00 .30
213 Chipper Jones AS 1.50 .45
214 Rich Aurilia AS 1.00 .30
215 Barry Bonds AS 4.00 1.20
216 Sammy Sosa AS 2.50 .75
217 Luis Gonzalez AS 1.00 .30
218 Mike Piazza AS 2.50 .75
219 Randy Johnson AS 1.50 .45
220 Larry Walker AS 1.50 .45
221 Todd Helton 1.00 .30
Juan Uribe
222 Pat Burrell 1.00 .30
Eric Valent
223 Edgar Martinez 2.50 .75
Ichiro Suzuki
224 Ben Grieve 1.00 .30
Jason Tyner
225 Mark Quinn 1.00 .30
Dee Brown
226 Cal Ripken 5.00 1.50
Brian Roberts
227 Cliff Floyd 1.00 .30
Abraham Nunez
228 Jeff Bagwell 1.00 .30
Adam Everett
229 Mark McGwire 4.00 1.20
Albert Pujols
230 Doug Mientkewicz 1.00 .30
Luis Rivas
231 Juan Gonzalez 1.00 .30
Danny Peoples
232 Kevin Brown 1.00 .30
Luke Prokopec
233 Richie Sexson 1.00 .30
Ben Sheets
234 Jason Giambi 1.00 .30
Jason Hart
235 Barry Bonds 4.00 1.20
Carlos Valderrama
236 Tony Gwynn 2.00 .60
Cesar Crespo
237 Ken Griffey Jr. 2.50 .75
Adam Dunn
238 Frank Thomas .75 .23
Joe Crede
239 Derek Jeter 4.00 1.20
Drew Henson
240 Chipper Jones 1.50 .45
Wilson Betemit
241 Luis Gonzalez 1.00 .30
Junior Spivey
242 Bobby Higginson 1.00 .30
Andres Torres
243 Carlos Delgado 1.00 .30
Vernon Wells
244 Sammy Sosa 2.50 .75
Corey Patterson
245 Nomar Garciaparra 2.50 .75
Shea Hillenbrand
246 Alex Rodriguez 2.50 .75
Jason Romano
247 Troy Glaus 1.00 .30
David Eckstein
248 Mike Piazza 2.50 .75
Alex Escobar
249 Brian Giles 1.00 .30
Jack Wilson
250 Vladimir Guerrero 1.50 .45
Scott Hodges
251 Bud Smith PROS 3.00 .90
252 Juan Diaz PROS 3.00 .90
253 Wilkin Ruan PROS 3.00 .90
254 C. Spurling PROS RC 3.00 .90
255 Toby Hall PROS 3.00 .90
256 Jason Jennings PROS 3.00 .90
257 George Perez PROS 3.00 .90
258 D. Jimenez PROS 3.00 .90
259 Jose Acevedo PROS 3.00 .90
260 Josue Perez PROS 3.00 .90
261 Brian Rogers PROS 3.00 .90
262 C. Maldonado PROS RC 3.00 .90
263 Travis Phelps PROS 3.00 .90
264 R. Mackowiak PROS 3.00 .90
265 Ryan Drese PROS 3.00 .90
266 Carlos Garcia PROS 3.00 .90
267 Alexis Gomez PROS 3.00 .90
268 Jeremy Affeldt PROS 3.00 .90
269 S. Podsednik PROS .50 .15
270 Adam Johnson PROS 3.00 .90
271 Pedro Santana PROS 3.00 .90
272 Les Walrond PROS 3.00 .90
273 Jackson Melian PROS 3.00 .90
274 C. Hernandez PROS 3.00 .90
275 M. Nussbeck PROS RC 3.00 .90
276 Cory Aldridge PROS 3.00 .90
277 Troy Mattes PROS 3.00 .90
278 B. Abernathy PROS 3.00 .90
279 J.J. Davis PROS 3.00 .90
280 B. Duckworth PROS 3.00 .90
281 Kyle Lohse PROS 3.00 .90
282 Justin Kaye PROS 3.00 .90
283 Cody Ransom PROS 3.00 .90
284 Dave Williams PROS 3.00 .90
285 Luis Lopez PROS 3.00 .90

2002 Ultra Gold Medallion

Issued at packs at different rates, this is a parallel to the Ultra set. Cards numbered 1-200 were issued at a rate of one per pack, cards numbered 201-250 were issued at a rate of one in 24 packs and cards numbered 251-285 were randomly inserted in packs. Cards numbered 251-285 were issued to 100 serial numbered sets.

Nm-Mt Ex-Mt
COMP.SET w/o SP's (200) 150.00 45.00
*GOLD 1-200: 1.25X TO 3X BASIC
*GOLD 201-220: .75X TO 2X BASIC
*GOLD 221-250: 1X TO 2.5X BASIC
*GOLD 251-285: 3X TO 8X BASIC

2002 Ultra Fall Classic

Issued at a rate of one in 20 hobby packs, these 36 cards feature players who participated in the World Series.

Nm-Mt Ex-Mt
COMPLETE SET (36) 200.00 60.00
1 Ty Cobb 10.00 3.00
2 Lou Gehrig 10.00 3.00
3 Babe Ruth 20.00 6.00
4 Stan Musial 10.00 3.00
5 Ted Williams 12.00 3.60
6 Dizzy Dean 8.00 2.40
7 Mickey Cochrane 5.00 1.50
8 Jimmie Foxx 8.00 2.40
9 Mel Ott 8.00 2.40
10 Rogers Hornsby 8.00 2.40
12 Clete Boyer 5.00 1.50
13 George Brett 15.00 4.50
14 Bob Gibson 8.00 2.40
15 Carlton Fisk 8.00 2.40
16 Johnny Bench 8.00 2.40
18 Willie McCovey 5.00 1.50
19 Paul Molitor 8.00 2.40
20 Jim Palmer 5.00 1.50
21 Frank Robinson 8.00 2.40
22 Derek Jeter 12.00 3.60
23 Earl Weaver 5.00 1.50
24 Lefty Grove 5.00 1.50
25 Tony Perez 5.00 1.50
26 Reggie Jackson 8.00 2.40
27 Sparky Anderson 5.00 1.50
28 Casey Stengel 5.00 1.50
29 Roy Campanella 8.00 2.40
31 Don Drysdale 8.00 2.40
32 Joe Morgan 5.00 1.50
33 Eddie Murray 8.00 2.40
34 Nolan Ryan 15.00 4.50
35 Tom Seaver 8.00 2.40
36 Bill Mazeroski 5.00 1.50
37 Jackie Robinson 8.00 2.40
38 Kirk Gibson 5.00 1.50
39 Robin Yount 10.00 3.00

2002 Ultra Fall Classic Autographs

This partial parallel to the Fall Classic set features authentic autographs from the featured players. Almost all of the players except for Sparky Anderson and Earl Weaver were exchange cards. A few players were produced in lower quantities and those have been notated with SP's in our checklist.

Nm-Mt Ex-Mt
1 Sparky Anderson 15.00 4.50
2 Johnny Bench SP 50.00 15.00
3 George Brett SP 100.00 30.00
4 Carlton Fisk 25.00 7.50
5 Bob Gibson 25.00 7.50
6 Kirk Gibson 25.00 7.50
7 Reggie Jackson SP 50.00 15.00
8 Derek Jeter SP
9 Bill Mazeroski 25.00 7.50
10 Willie McCovey SP 40.00 12.00
11 Joe Morgan 15.00 4.50
12 Eddie Murray SP 50.00 15.00
13 Stan Musial SP
14 Jim Palmer 15.00 4.50
15 Tony Perez 15.00 4.50
16 Frank Robinson 25.00 7.50
17 Nolan Ryan SP 250.00 75.00
18 Tom Seaver SP 40.00 12.00
19 Earl Weaver 15.00 4.50
20 Robin Yount SP 60.00 18.00

2002 Ultra Fall Classic Memorabilia

Inserted at a rate of one in 113, these 37 cards feature memorabila from players who participated in World Series. A few cards were printed in lesser quantities and those have been notated with print runs as provided by Fleer.

Nm-Mt Ex-Mt
1 Sparky Anderson Pants 10.00 3.00
2 Johnny Bench Pants 15.00 4.50
3 Johnny Bench Jsy 15.00 4.50
4 George Brett White Jsy 25.00 7.50
5 George Brett Bat 25.00 7.50
6 George Brett Blue Jsy/65
7 Roy Campanella Bat/21
8 Carlton Fisk Jsy 15.00 4.50
9 Carlton Fisk Bat/42 50.00 15.00
10 Jimmie Foxx Bat 50.00 15.00
11 Bob Gibson Jsy 15.00 4.50
12 Kirk Gibson Bat 10.00 3.00
13 Reggie Jackson Bat 15.00 4.50
14 Reggie Jackson Bat
15 Reggie Jackson Jsy/73
16 Derek Jeter Pants 40.00 12.00
17 Willie McCovey Jsy 10.00 3.00
18 Paul Molitor Bat 15.00 4.50
19 Paul Molitor Jsy
20 Joe Morgan Bat 10.00 3.00
21 Joe Morgan Jsy
22 Eddie Murray Bat 15.00 4.50
23 Eddie Murray Jsy/91 50.00 15.00
24 Jim Palmer White Jsy 10.00 3.00
25 J.Palmer Gray Jsy/85 40.00 12.00
26 Tony Perez Bat 10.00 3.00
27 Frank Robinson Bat/40 40.00 12.00
28 Jackie Robinson Pants 60.00 18.00
29 Babe Ruth Bat/44 200.00 60.00
30 Nolan Ryan Pants 50.00 15.00
31 Tom Seaver Jsy 15.00 4.50
32 Earl Weaver Jsy 10.00 3.00
33 Ted Williams Jsy 100.00 30.00
34 Ted Williams Bat/30
35 Robin Yount Gray Jsy
36 Robin Yount White Jsy/30
37 Robin Yount Bat 15.00 4.50

2002 Ultra Glove Works

Inserted at a rate of one in 20, these 15 cards feature some of the leading fielders in the game.

Nm-Mt Ex-Mt
COMPLETE SET (15) 50.00 15.00
1 Andruw Jones 3.00 .90
2 Derek Jeter 8.00 2.40
3 Cal Ripken 10.00 3.00
4 Larry Walker 3.00 .90
5 Chipper Jones 4.00 1.20
6 Barry Bonds 8.00 2.40
7 Scott Rolen 4.00 1.20
8 Jim Edmonds 3.00 .90
9 Robin Ventura 3.00 .90
10 Darin Erstad 3.00 .90
11 Barry Larkin 3.00 .90
12 Raul Mondesi 3.00 .90
13 Mark Grace 3.00 .90
14 Bernie Williams 3.00 .90
15 Ivan Rodriguez 4.00 1.20

2002 Ultra Glove Works Memorabilia

This 11-card insert set features game-used fielding mitts and batting gloves incorporated into the actual card. Each card is serial numbered to 450 copies - except for Barry Larkin (375 cards), Andruw Jones (100 cards) and Chipper Jones (100 cards). The first 75 serial numbered copies of the Cal Ripken, Barry Bonds and Ivan

Rodriguez cards feature batting glove patches and cards serial numbered 76-450 for these players feature fielding mitt patches. The short-printed Andruw and Chipper Jones cards feature batting glove patches.

Nm-Mt Ex-Mt
PLATINUM RANDOM INSERTS IN PACKS
PLATINUM PRINT RUN 25 SERIAL #'d SETS
PLATINUM NO PRICING DUE TO SCARCITY
1 Derek Jeter 40.00 12.00
2 Andruw Jones SP/100
3 Cal Ripken 60.00 18.00
5 Chipper Jones SP/100
6 Barry Bonds 40.00 12.00
8 Robin Ventura 15.00 4.50
9 Barry Larkin SP/375 15.00 4.50
10 Raul Mondesi 15.00 4.50
11 Ivan Rodriguez 20.00 6.00

2002 Ultra Hitting Machines

Inserted at a rate of one in 20 retail packs, these 25 cards feature some of baseball's leading hitters.

Nm-Mt Ex-Mt
COMPLETE SET (25) 120.00 36.00
1 Frank Thomas 5.00 1.50
2 Derek Jeter 12.00 3.60
3 Vladimir Guerrero 5.00 1.50
4 Jim Edmonds 2.50 .75
5 Mike Piazza 8.00 2.40
6 Ivan Rodriguez 5.00 1.50
7 Chipper Jones 5.00 1.50
8 Tony Gwynn 6.00 1.80
9 Manny Ramirez 3.00 .90
10 Andruw Jones 2.50 .75
11 Carlos Delgado 2.50 .75
12 Bernie Williams 3.00 .90
13 Larry Walker 3.00 .90
14 Juan Gonzalez 3.00 .90
15 Ichiro Suzuki 8.00 2.40
16 Albert Pujols 10.00 3.00
17 Barry Bonds 12.00 3.60
18 Cal Ripken 15.00 4.50
19 Edgar Martinez 3.00 .90
20 Luis Gonzalez 2.50 .75
21 Moises Alou 2.50 .75
22 Roberto Alomar 3.00 .90
23 Todd Helton 3.00 .90
24 Rafael Palmeiro 3.00 .90
25 Bobby Abreu 2.50 .75

2002 Ultra Hitting Machines Game Bat

Issued at a rate of one in 81 packs, these cards feature not only some of the leading hitters but also a slice of a game-used bat.

Nm-Mt Ex-Mt
PLATINUM RANDOM INSERTS IN PACKS
PLATINUM PRINT RUN 25 SERIAL #'d SETS
PLATINUM: NO PRICING DUE TO SCARCITY
1 Bobby Abreu 10.00 3.00
2 Roberto Alomar 15.00 4.50
3 Moises Alou 10.00 3.00
4 Barry Bonds 30.00 9.00
5 Carlos Delgado 10.00 3.00
6 Jim Edmonds 10.00 3.00
7 Juan Gonzalez 15.00 4.50
8 Luis Gonzalez 10.00 3.00
9 Tony Gwynn 15.00 4.50
10 Todd Helton 15.00 4.50
11 Derek Jeter 30.00 9.00
12 Andruw Jones 10.00 3.00
13 Chipper Jones 15.00 4.50
14 Edgar Martinez 15.00 4.50
15 Rafael Palmeiro 15.00 4.50
16 Mike Piazza 15.00 4.50
17 Albert Pujols 40.00 12.00
18 Manny Ramirez 15.00 4.50
19 Cal Ripken 50.00 15.00
20 Ivan Rodriguez 15.00 4.50
21 Frank Thomas 15.00 4.50
22 Larry Walker 15.00 4.50
23 Bernie Williams 15.00 4.50

2002 Ultra On the Road Game Jersey

Inserted at a rate of one in 93, these 14 cards feature swatches of away uniforms used by the featured players.

Nm-Mt Ex-Mt
PLATINUM RANDOM INSERTS IN PACKS
PLATINUM PRINT RUN 25 SERIAL #'d SETS
PLATINUM: NO PRICING DUE TO SCARCITY
1 Derek Jeter 40.00 12.00
2 Ivan Rodriguez 20.00 6.00
3 Carlos Delgado 15.00 4.50
4 Larry Walker 20.00 6.00
5 Roberto Alomar 20.00 6.00
6 Tony Gwynn 20.00 6.00
7 Greg Maddux 20.00 6.00
8 Barry Bonds 40.00 12.00
9 Todd Helton 20.00 6.00
10 Kazuhiro Sasaki 15.00 4.50
11 Jeff Bagwell 20.00 6.00
12 Omar Vizquel 20.00 6.00
13 Chan Ho Park 15.00 4.50
14 Tom Glavine 20.00 6.00

2002 Ultra Rising Stars

Issued at a rate of one in 12 packs, these 15 cards feature some of the leading young players in baseball.

Nm-Mt Ex-Mt
COMPLETE SET (15) 30.00 9.00
1 Ichiro Suzuki 4.00 1.20
2 Derek Jeter 6.00 1.80
3 Albert Pujols 5.00 1.50
4 Jimmy Rollins 2.00 .60
5 Adam Dunn 2.00 .60
6 Sean Casey 2.00 .60
7 Kerry Wood 2.50 .75
8 Tsuyoshi Shinjo 2.00 .60
9 Shea Hillenbrand 2.00 .60
10 Pat Burrell 2.00 .60
11 Ben Sheets 2.00 .60
12 Alfonso Soriano 2.00 .60
13 J.D. Drew 2.00 .60
14 Kazuhiro Sasaki 2.00 .60
15 Corey Patterson 2.00 .60

2002 Ultra Rising Stars Game Hat

Randomly inserted in packs, these six cards feature not only some of the best young players in baseball but also a sliver of a cap they wore while playing.

Nm-Mt Ex-Mt
PLATINUM RANDOM IN HOBBY PACKS
PLATINUM PRINT RUN 25 SERIAL #'d SETS
PLATINUM NO PRICING DUE TO SCARCITY
1 Derek Jeter 80.00 24.00
2 Albert Pujols 50.00 15.00
3 Tsuyoshi Shinjo 40.00 12.00
4 Alfonso Soriano 40.00 12.00
5 J.D. Drew 40.00 12.00
6 Kazuhiro Sasaki 40.00 12.00

2003 Ultra

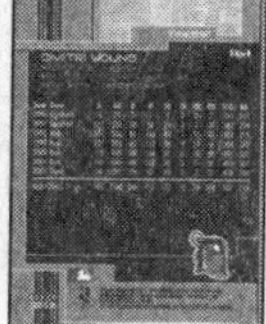

This 265-card set was issued in two separate series. The primary Ultra product - containing the first 250 cards from the basic set - was released in November, 2002. It was issued in 10 card packs which were packed 24 packs to a box and 16 boxes to a case. Cards numbered 1 through 200 featured veterans while cards numbered 201 through 220 featured All-Stars, cards numbered 221 through 240 featured rookies of 2002 and cards numbered 241 through 250 featured rookies of 2003. Cards numbered 201 through 220 were inserted at a stated rate of one in four while cards numbered 221 through 250 were inserted at a stated rate of one in two. Cards 251-265 were randomly seeded within Fleer Rookies and Greats packs of which was distributed in December, 2003. Each of these 15 update cards features a top prospect and is serial numbered to 1,500 copies.

Nm-Mt Ex-Mt
COMP.LO SET (250) 100.00 30.00
COMP.LO SET w/o SP's (200) 25.00 7.50
COMMON CARD (201-220) 1.50 .45
COMMON CARD (221-250) 2.00 .60
COMMON CARD (251-265) 3.00 .90
1 Barry Bonds 2.00 .60
2 Derek Jeter 2.00 .60
3 Ichiro Suzuki 1.25 .35
4 Mike Lowell .30 .09
5 Hideo Nomo .75 .23
6 Javier Vazquez .30 .09
7 Jeremy Giambi .30 .09
8 Jamie Moyer .30 .09
9 Rafael Palmeiro .50 .15
10 Magglio Ordonez .30 .09
11 Trot Nixon .30 .09
12 Luis Castillo .30 .09
13 Paul Byrd .30 .09
14 Adam Kennedy .30 .09
15 Trevor Hoffman .30 .09
16 Matt Morris .30 .09
17 Nomar Garciaparra 1.25 .35
18 Matt Lawton .30 .09
19 Carlos Beltran .50 .15
20 Jason Giambi .30 .09
21 Brian Giles .30 .09
22 Jim Edmonds .30 .09
23 Garret Anderson .30 .09
24 Tony Batista .30 .09
25 Aaron Boone .30 .09
26 Mike Hampton .30 .09
27 Billy Wagner .30 .09
28 Kazuhisa Ishii .30 .09
29 Al Leiter .30 .09
30 Pat Burrell .30 .09
31 Jeff Kent .30 .09
32 Randy Johnson .75 .23
33 Ray Durham .30 .09
34 Josh Beckett .30 .09
35 Cristian Guzman .30 .09
36 Roger Clemens 1.50 .45
37 Freddy Garcia .30 .09
38 Roy Halladay .30 .09
39 David Eckstein .30 .09
40 Jerry Hairston .30 .09
41 Barry Larkin .50 .15
42 Larry Walker .50 .15
43 Craig Biggio .50 .15
44 Edgardo Alfonzo .30 .09
45 Marlon Byrd .30 .09
46 J.T. Snow .30 .09
47 Juan Gonzalez .50 .15
48 Ramon Ortiz .30 .09
49 Jay Gibbons .30 .09
50 Adam Dunn .50 .15
51 Juan Pierre .30 .09
52 Jeff Bagwell .50 .15
53 Kevin Brown .30 .09
54 Pedro Astacio .30 .09
55 Mike Lieberthal .30 .09
56 Johnny Damon .75 .23
57 Tim Salmon .50 .15
58 Mike Bordick .30 .09
59 Ken Griffey Jr. 1.25 .35
60 Jason Jennings .30 .09
61 Lance Berkman .30 .09
62 Jeromy Burnitz .30 .09
63 Jimmy Rollins .30 .09
64 Tsuyoshi Shinjo .30 .09
65 Alex Rodriguez 1.25 .35
66 Greg Maddux 1.25 .35
67 Mark Prior .75 .23
68 Mike Maroth .30 .09
69 Geoff Jenkins .30 .09
70 Tony Armas Jr. .30 .09
71 Jermaine Dye .30 .09
72 Albert Pujols 1.50 .45
73 Shannon Stewart .30 .09
74 Troy Glaus .30 .09
75 Brook Fordyce .30 .09
76 Juan Encarnacion .30 .09
77 Todd Hollandsworth .30 .09
78 Roy Oswalt .30 .09
79 Paul Lo Duca .30 .09
80 Mike Piazza 1.25 .35
81 Bobby Abreu .30 .09
82 Sean Burroughs .30 .09
83 Randy Winn .30 .09
84 Curt Schilling .30 .09
85 Chris Singleton .30 .09
86 Sean Casey .30 .09
87 Todd Zeile .30 .09
88 Richard Hidalgo .30 .09
89 Roberto Alomar .50 .15
90 Tim Hudson .30 .09
91 Ryan Klesko .30 .09
92 Greg Vaughn .30 .09
93 Tony Womack .30 .09
94 Fred McGriff .50 .15
95 Tom Glavine .50 .15
96 Todd Walker .30 .09
97 Travis Fryman .30 .09
98 Shane Reynolds .30 .09
99 Shawn Green .30 .09
100 Mo Vaughn .30 .09
101 Adam Piatt .30 .09
102 Deivi Cruz .30 .09
103 Steve Cox .30 .09
104 Luis Gonzalez .30 .09
105 Russell Branyan .30 .09
106 Daryle Ward .30 .09
107 Mariano Rivera .50 .15
108 Phil Nevin .30 .09
109 Ben Grieve .30 .09
110 Moises Alou .30 .09
111 Omar Vizquel .50 .15
112 Joe Randa .30 .09
113 Jorge Posada .50 .15
114 Mark Kotsay .30 .09
115 Ryan Rupe .30 .09
116 Javy Lopez .30 .09
117 Corey Patterson .30 .09
118 Bobby Higginson .30 .09
119 Jose Vidro .30 .09
120 Barry Zito .30 .09
121 Scott Rolen .75 .23
122 Gary Sheffield .30 .09
123 Kerry Wood .75 .23
124 Brandon Inge .30 .09
125 Jose Hernandez .30 .09
126 Michael Barrett .30 .09
127 Miguel Tejada .30 .09
128 Edgar Renteria .30 .09
129 Junior Spivey .30 .09
130 Jose Valentin .30 .09
131 Derrek Lee .30 .09
132 A.J. Pierzynski .30 .09
133 Mike Mussina .50 .15
134 Bret Boone .30 .09
135 Chan Ho Park .30 .09
136 Steve Finley .30 .09
137 Mark Buehrle .30 .09
138 A.J. Burnett .30 .09
139 Ben Sheets .30 .09
140 David Ortiz .50 .15
141 Nick Johnson .30 .09
142 Randall Simon .30 .09
143 Carlos Delgado .30 .09
144 Darin Erstad .30 .09
145 Shea Hillenbrand .30 .09
146 Todd Helton .50 .15
147 Preston Wilson .30 .09
148 Eric Gagne .75 .23
149 Vladimir Guerrero .75 .23
150 Brandon Duckworth .30 .09
151 Rich Aurilia .30 .09
152 Ivan Rodriguez .75 .23
153 Andruw Jones .30 .09
154 Carlos Lee .30 .09
155 Robert Fick .30 .09
156 Jacque Jones .30 .09
157 Bernie Williams .50 .15
158 John Olerud .30 .09
159 Eric Hinske .30 .09
160 Matt Clement .30 .09
161 Dmitri Young .30 .09
162 Torii Hunter .30 .09
163 Carlos Pena .30 .09
164 Mike Cameron .30 .09
165 Raul Mondesi .30 .09
166 Pedro Martinez .75 .23
167 Bob Wickman .30 .09
168 Mike Sweeney .30 .09
169 David Wells .30 .09
170 Jason Kendall .30 .09
171 Tino Martinez .50 .15
172 Matt Williams .50 .15
173 Frank Thomas .75 .23
174 Cliff Floyd .30 .09
175 Corey Koskie .30 .09
176 Orlando Hernandez .30 .09
177 Edgar Martinez .50 .15
178 Richie Sexson .30 .09
179 Manny Ramirez .50 .15
180 Jim Thome .75 .23
181 Andy Pettitte .50 .15
182 Aramis Ramirez .30 .09
183 J.D. Drew .30 .09
184 Brian Jordan .30 .09
185 Sammy Sosa 1.25 .35
186 Jeff Weaver .30 .09
187 Jeffrey Hammonds .30 .09
188 Eric Milton .30 .09
189 Eric Chavez .30 .09
190 Kazuhiro Sasaki .30 .09
191 Jose Cruz Jr. .30 .09
192 Derek Lowe .30 .09
193 C.C. Sabathia .30 .09
194 Adrian Beltre .50 .15
195 Alfonso Soriano .50 .15
196 Jack Wilson .30 .09
197 Fernando Vina .30 .09
198 Chipper Jones .75 .23
199 Paul Konerko .30 .09
200 Rusty Greer .30 .09
201 Jason Giambi AS 1.50 .45
202 Alfonso Soriano AS 1.50 .45
203 Shea Hillenbrand AS 1.50 .45
204 Alex Rodriguez AS 2.50 .75
205 Jorge Posada AS 1.50 .45
206 Ichiro Suzuki AS 2.50 .75
207 Manny Ramirez AS 1.50 .45
208 Torii Hunter AS 1.50 .45
209 Todd Helton AS 1.50 .45
210 Jose Vidro AS 1.50 .45
211 Scott Rolen AS 1.50 .45
212 Jimmy Rollins AS 1.50 .45
213 Mike Piazza AS 2.50 .75
214 Barry Bonds AS 4.00 1.20
215 Sammy Sosa AS 2.50 .75
216 Vladimir Guerrero AS 1.50 .45
217 Lance Berkman AS 1.50 .45
218 Derek Jeter AS 4.00 1.20
219 Nomar Garciaparra AS 2.50 .75
220 Luis Gonzalez AS 1.50 .45
221 Kazuhisa Ishii 02R 2.00 .60
222 Satoru Komiyama 02R 2.00 .60
223 So Taguchi 02R 2.00 .60
224 Jorge Padilla 02R 2.00 .60
225 Ben Howard 02R 2.00 .60
226 Jason Simontacchi 02R 2.00 .60
227 Barry Wesson 02R 2.00 .60
228 Howie Clark 02R 2.00 .60
229 Aaron Guiel 02R 2.00 .60
230 Oliver Perez 02R 2.00 .60
231 David Ross 02R 2.00 .60
232 Julius Matos 02R 2.00 .60
233 Chris Snelling 02R 2.00 .60
234 Rodrigo Lopez 02R 2.00 .60
235 Will Nieves 02R 2.00 .60
236 Joe Borchard 02R 2.00 .60
237 Aaron Cook 02R 2.00 .60
238 Anderson Machado 02R 2.00 .60
239 Corey Thurman 02R 2.00 .60
240 Tyler Yates 02R 2.00 .60
241 Coco Crisp 03R 2.00 .60
242 Andy Van Hekken 03R 2.00 .60
243 Jim Rushford 03R 2.00 .60
244 Jeriome Robertson 03R 2.00 .60
245 Shane Nance 03R 2.00 .60
246 Kevin Cash 03R 2.00 .60
247 Kirk Saarloos 03R 2.00 .60
248 Josh Bard 03R 2.00 .60
249 Dave Pember 03R RC 2.00 .60
250 Freddy Sanchez 03R 2.00 .60
251 Chien-Ming Wang PROS RC 4.00 1.20
252 Rickie Weeks PROS RC 6.00 1.80
253 Brandon Webb PROS RC 4.00 1.20
254 Hideki Matsui PROS RC 10.00 3.00
255 Michael Hessman PROS RC 3.00 .90
256 Ryan Wagner PROS RC 4.00 1.20
257 Matt Kata PROS RC 4.00 1.20
258 Edwin Jackson PROS RC 6.00 1.80
259 Jose Contreras PROS RC 3.00 .90
260 Delmon Young PROS RC 8.00 2.40
261 Bo Hart PROS RC 4.00 1.20
262 Jeff Duncan PROS RC 4.00 1.20
263 Robby Hammock PROS RC 4.00 1.20
264 Jeremy Bonderman PROS RC 4.00 1.20
265 Clint Barmes PROS RC 4.00 1.20

2003 Ultra Gold Medallion

This 250 card set is a parallel to the 2003 Ultra set. The first 200 cards were inserted at a stated rate of one per pack while cards numbered 221 through 250 were issued at a stated rate of one per 24 packs.

Nm-Mt Ex-Mt
*GOLD MED 1-200: 1.25X TO 3X BASIC
*GOLD MED 201-220: 1X TO 2.5X BASIC
*GOLD MED 221-250: 1X TO 2.5X BASIC

2003 Ultra Back 2 Back

Randomly inserted into packs, these 17 cards feature some of the leading players in baseball. Each of these cards were printed to a stated print run of 1000 serial numbered sets.

Nm-Mt Ex-Mt
1 Derek Jeter 15.00 4.50
2 Barry Bonds 15.00 4.50
3 Mike Piazza 10.00 3.00
4 Alex Rodriguez 10.00 3.00
5 Todd Helton 6.00 1.80
6 Edgar Martinez 6.00 1.80
7 Chipper Jones 6.00 1.80
8 Shawn Green 6.00 1.80
9 Chan Ho Park 6.00 1.80
10 Preston Wilson 6.00 1.80
11 Manny Ramirez 6.00 1.80
12 Aramis Ramirez 6.00 1.80
13 Pedro Martinez 6.00 1.80
14 Ivan Rodriguez 6.00 1.80
15 Ichiro Suzuki 10.00 3.00
16 Sammy Sosa 10.00 3.00
17 Jason Giambi 6.00 1.80

2003 Ultra Back 2 Back Memorabilia

Randomly inserted into packs, this is a parallel of the Ultra Back 2 Back insert set. Each of these cards feature a game-used memorabilia piece of the featured player and is issued to a stated print run of 500 serial numbered sets.

Nm-Mt Ex-Mt
*GOLD: 1.25X TO 3X BASIC B2B MEMORABILIA
GOLD PRINT RUN 50 SERIAL #'d SETS
1 Derek Jeter Jsy 25.00 7.50
2 Barry Bonds Bat 25.00 7.50
3 Mike Piazza Jsy 15.00 4.50
4 Alex Rodriguez Jsy 20.00 6.00
5 Todd Helton Jsy 15.00 4.50
6 Edgar Martinez Jsy 15.00 4.50
7 Chipper Jones Jsy 15.00 4.50
8 Shawn Green Jsy 10.00 3.00
9 Chan Ho Park Bat 10.00 3.00
10 Preston Wilson Jsy 10.00 3.00
11 Manny Ramirez Jsy 15.00 4.50
12 Aramis Ramirez Pants 10.00 3.00
13 Pedro Martinez Jsy 15.00 4.50
14 Ivan Rodriguez Jsy 15.00 4.50
15 Ichiro Suzuki Base 20.00 6.00
16 Sammy Sosa Base 15.00 4.50
17 Jason Giambi Base 10.00 3.00

2003 Ultra Double Up

Inserted into packs at a stated rate of one in eight, each of these 16 cards feature two players with something in common. Among the common threads are teammates, nationality and position played.

Nm-Mt Ex-Mt
COMPLETE SET (16) 40.00 12.00
1 Derek Jeter 6.00 1.80
Mike Piazza
2 Alex Rodriguez 4.00 1.20
Rafael Palmeiro
3 Chipper Jones 2.50 .75
Andruw Jones
4 Derek Jeter 6.00 1.80
Alex Rodriguez
5 Nomar Garciaparra 6.00 1.80
Derek Jeter
6 Barry Bonds 6.00 1.80
Jason Giambi
7 Ichiro Suzuki 4.00 1.20
Hideo Nomo
8 Randy Johnson 2.50 .75
Curt Schilling
9 Pedro Martinez 4.00 1.20
Nomar Garciaparra
10 Roger Clemens 5.00 1.50
Kevin Brown
11 Nomar Garciaparra 4.00 1.20
Manny Ramirez
12 Kazuhiro Sasaki 2.50 .75
Hideo Nomo
13 Mike Piazza 4.00 1.20
Ivan Rodriguez
14 Ichiro Suzuki 4.00 1.20
Ken Griffey Jr.
15 Barry Bonds 6.00 1.80
Sammy Sosa
16 Alfonso Soriano 2.50 .75
Roberto Alomar

2003 Ultra Double Up Memorabilia

Randomly inserted into packs, this is a parallel to the Double Up insert set. Each of these cards feature a piece of memorabilia from each of the players featured.

Nm-Mt Ex-Mt
1 Derek Jeter Jsy 60.00 18.00
Mike Piazza Jsy
2 Alex Rodriguez Jsy 40.00 12.00
Rafael Palmeiro Jsy
3 Chipper Jones Bat 25.00 7.50
Andruw Jones Jsy
4 Derek Jeter Jsy 60.00 18.00
Alex Rodriguez Jsy
5 Nomar Garciaparra Jsy 60.00 18.00
Derek Jeter Jsy
6 Barry Bonds Bat 40.00 12.00
Jason Giambi Base
7 Ichiro Suzuki Base 120.00 36.00
Hideo Nomo Jsy
8 Randy Johnson Jsy 25.00 7.50
Curt Schilling Jsy
9 Pedro Martinez Jsy 40.00 12.00
Nomar Garciaparra Jsy
10 Roger Clemens Jsy 40.00 12.00
Kevin Brown Jsy
11 Nomar Garciaparra Jsy 40.00 12.00
Manny Ramirez Jsy
12 Kazuhiro Sasaki Jsy 60.00 18.00
Hideo Nomo Jsy
13 Mike Piazza Jsy 40.00 12.00
Ivan Rodriguez Jsy
14 Ichiro Suzuki Base 80.00 24.00
Ken Griffey Jr. Base
15 Barry Bonds Bat 60.00 18.00
Sammy Sosa Base
16 Alfonso Soriano Pants 25.00 7.50
Roberto Alomar Jsy

2003 Ultra Moonshots

Inserted into packs at a stated rate of one in 12, these 20 cards feature some of the leading power hitters in baseball.

Nm-Mt Ex-Mt
1 Mike Piazza 4.00 1.20
2 Alex Rodriguez 4.00 1.20
3 Manny Ramirez 2.00 .60
4 Ivan Rodriguez 2.50 .75
5 Luis Gonzalez 2.00 .60
6 Shawn Green 2.00 .60
7 Barry Bonds 6.00 1.80
8 Jason Giambi 2.00 .60
9 Nomar Garciaparra 4.00 1.20
10 Edgar Martinez 2.00 .60
11 Mo Vaughn 2.00 .60
12 Chipper Jones 2.50 .75
13 Todd Helton 2.00 .60
14 Raul Mondesi 2.00 .60
15 Preston Wilson 2.00 .60
16 Rafael Palmeiro 2.00 .60
17 Jim Edmonds 2.00 .60
18 Bernie Williams 2.00 .60
19 Vladimir Guerrero 2.50 .75
20 Alfonso Soriano 2.00 .60

2003 Ultra Moonshots Memorabilia

Inserted into packs at a stated rate of one in 20, this set parallels the Moonshot insert set except a game-used memorabilia piece is used on each of these cards.

Nm-Mt Ex-Mt
1 Mike Piazza Jsy 15.00 4.50
2 Alex Rodriguez Jsy 15.00 4.50
3 Manny Ramirez Jsy 10.00 3.00

4 Ivan Rodriguez Jsy 10.00 3.00
5 Luis Gonzalez Jsy 8.00 2.40
6 Shawn Green Jsy 8.00 2.40
7 Barry Bonds Jsy 15.00 4.50
8 Jason Giambi Base 8.00 2.40
9 Nomar Garciaparra Jsy 15.00 4.50
10 Edgar Martinez Jsy 10.00 3.00
11 Mo Vaughn Jsy 8.00 2.40
12 Chipper Jones Jsy 10.00 3.00
13 Todd Helton Jsy 10.00 3.00
14 Raul Mondesi Jsy 8.00 2.40
15 Preston Wilson Jsy 8.00 2.40
16 Rafael Palmeiro Jsy 10.00 3.00
17 Jim Edmonds Jsy 8.00 2.40
18 Bernie Williams Jsy 10.00 3.00
19 Vladimir Guerrero Base 10.00 3.00
20 Alfonso Soriano Pants 10.00 3.00

2003 Ultra Photo Effex

Inserted into packs at a stated rate of one in 12, these 20 cards feature intriguing photos of some of the leading players in the game.

Nm-Mt Ex-Mt
GOLD RANDOM INSERTS IN PACKS..
GOLD PRINT RUN 25 SERIAL #'d SETS
GOLD NO PRICING DUE TO SCARCITY
1 Derek Jeter 6.00 1.80
2 Barry Bonds 6.00 1.80
3 Sammy Sosa 4.00 1.20
4 Troy Glaus .... 2.00 .60
5 Albert Pujols 5.00 1.50
6 Alex Rodriguez 4.00 1.20
7 Ichiro Suzuki 4.00 1.20
8 Greg Maddux 4.00 1.20
9 Nomar Garciaparra 4.00 1.20
10 Jeff Bagwell .... 2.00 .60
11 Chipper Jones .... 2.50 .75
12 Mike Piazza 4.00 1.20
13 Randy Johnson .... 2.50 .75
14 Vladimir Guerrero .... 2.50 .75
15 Alfonso Soriano .... 2.00 .60
16 Lance Berkman .... 2.00 .60
17 Todd Helton .... 2.00 .60
18 Mike Lowell .... 2.00 .60
19 Carlos Delgado .... 2.00 .60
20 Jason Giambi .... 2.00 .60

2003 Ultra When It Was A Game

Inserted into packs at a stated rate of one in 20, these 40 cards basically feature retired stars from baseball's past. Other than Derek Jeter and Barry Bonds, all the players in this set were retired at the time of issue.

Nm-Mt Ex-Mt
1 Derek Jeter 12.00 3.60
2 Barry Bonds 12.00 3.60
3 Luis Aparicio 5.00 1.50
4 Richie Ashburn 8.00 2.40
5 Ernie Banks 8.00 2.40
6 Enos Slaughter 5.00 1.50
7 Yogi Berra 8.00 2.40
8 Lou Boudreau 5.00 1.50
9 Lou Brock 8.00 2.40
10 Jim Bunning 5.00 1.50
11 Rod Carew 8.00 2.40
12 Orlando Cepeda 5.00 1.50
13 Larry Doby 5.00 1.50
14 Bobby Doerr 5.00 1.50
15 Bob Feller 5.00 1.50
16 Brooks Robinson 8.00 2.40
17 Rollie Fingers 5.00 1.50
18 Whitey Ford 8.00 2.40
19 Bob Gibson 8.00 2.40
20 Catfish Hunter 8.00 2.40
21 Nolan Ryan 15.00 4.50
22 Reggie Jackson 8.00 2.40
23 Fergie Jenkins 5.00 1.50
24 Al Kaline 8.00 2.40
25 Mike Schmidt 15.00 4.50
26 Harmon Killebrew 8.00 2.40
27 Ralph Kiner 5.00 1.50
28 Willie Stargell 8.00 2.40
29 Billy Williams 5.00 1.50
30 Tom Seaver 8.00 2.40
31 Juan Marichal 5.00 1.50
32 Eddie Mathews 8.00 2.40
33 Willie McCovey 5.00 1.50
34 Joe Morgan 5.00 1.50
35 Stan Musial 10.00 3.00
36 Robin Roberts 5.00 1.50
37 Robin Yount 10.00 3.00
38 Jim Palmer 5.00 1.50
39 Phil Rizzuto 8.00 2.40
40 Pee Wee Reese 8.00 2.40

2003 Ultra When It Was A Game Used

Randomly inserted into packs, these 12 cards form a partial parallel to the When it was a Game Insert set. Since several different print runs were used, we have notated that print run information next to the player's name in our checklist.

Nm-Mt Ex-Mt
1 Yogi Berra Bat/100 .... 50.00 15.00
2 Barry Bonds Bat/200 .... 40.00 12.00
3 Larry Doby Bat/150 .... 20.00 6.00
4 Catfish Hunter Jsy/200 .... 20.00 6.00
5 Reggie Jackson Bat/300 .... 20.00 6.00
6 Derek Jeter Jsy/200 .... 40.00 12.00
7 Juan Marichal Jsy/300 .... 15.00 4.50
8 Eddie Mathews Bat/300 .... 25.00 7.50
9 Willie McCovey Jsy/150 .... 20.00 6.00
10 Joe Morgan Pants/200 .... 15.00 4.50
11 Jim Palmer Pants/300 .... 15.00 4.50
12 Tom Seaver Pants/100 .... 25.00 7.50

2004 Ultra

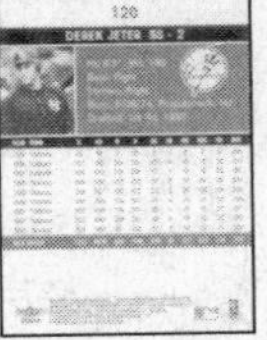

This 220-card set was released in November, 2003. This set was issued in eight-card packs with an $2.99 SRP which came 24 packs to a box and 16 boxes to a case. Please note that cards 201-220 feature leading prospects and were randomly inserted into packs. An 170-card update set was released in October, 2004. The set was issued in five card hobby packs with an $6 SRP which came 12 packs to a box and 16 boxes to a case and in eight-card retail packs with an $3 SRP which came 24 packs to a box and 20 boxes to a case. Cards numbered 221 through 295 feature players who switched teams in the off-season while cards numbered 296 through 382 featured Rookie Cards. Cards numbered 383 through 395 feature 13 of the Leading rookies and the reason they are the lucky 13 is that they are the final 13 cards in the set and the platinum parallel of these cards were printed to a stated print run of 13 serial numbered sets.

MINT NRMT
COMPLETE SERIES 1 (220) 60.00 27.00
COMP.SERIES 1 w/o SP's (200) 25.00 11.00
COMP.SERIES 2 w/o SP's (75) . 25.00 11.00
COMP.SERIES 2 w/o L13 (162) 100.00 45.00
COMMON CARD (1-200) .... .30 .14
COMMON CARD (201-220) .... 1.25 .55
201-220 APPROXIMATE ODDS 1:2 HOBBY
201-220 RANDOM IN RETAIL PACKS.
COMMON CARD (296-382) .... 2.00 .90
296-382 ODDS TWO PER HOBBY/RETAIL
COMMON CARD (383-395) 20.00 9.00
383-395 ODDS 1:28 HOBBY, 1:2000 RETAIL
383-395 PRINT RUN 500 SERIAL #'d SETS
1 Magglio Ordonez .30 .14
2 Bobby Abreu .30 .14
3 Eric Munson .30 .14
4 Eric Byrnes .30 .14
5 Bartolo Colon .30 .14
6 Juan Encarnacion .30 .14
7 Jody Gerut .30 .14
8 Eddie Guardado .30 .14
9 Shea Hillenbrand .30 .14
10 Andruw Jones .30 .14
11 Carlos Lee .30 .14
12 Pedro Martinez .75 .35
13 Barry Larkin .50 .23
14 Angel Berroa .30 .14
15 Edgar Martinez .50 .23
16 Sidney Ponson .30 .14
17 Mariano Rivera .50 .23
18 Richie Sexson .30 .14
19 Frank Thomas .75 .35
20 Jerome Williams .30 .14
21 Barry Zito .30 .14
22 Roberto Alomar .50 .23
23 Rocky Biddle .30 .14
24 Orlando Cabrera .30 .14
25 Placido Polanco .30 .14
26 Morgan Ensberg .30 .14
27 Jason Giambi .30 .14
28 Jim Thome .75 .35
29 Vladimir Guerrero .75 .35
30 Tim Hudson .30 .14
31 Jacque Jones .30 .14
32 Derrek Lee .30 .14
33 Rafael Palmeiro .50 .23
34 Mike Mussina .50 .23
35 Corey Patterson .30 .14
36 Mike Cameron .30 .14
37 Ivan Rodriguez .75 .35
38 Ben Sheets .30 .14
39 Woody Williams .30 .14
40 Ichiro Suzuki 1.25 .55
41 Moises Alou .30 .14
42 Craig Biggio .50 .23
43 Jorge Posada .50 .23
44 Craig Monroe .30 .14
45 Darin Erstad .30 .14
46 Jay Gibbons .30 .14
47 Aaron Guiel .30 .14
48 Travis Lee .30 .14
49 Jorge Julio .30 .14
50 Torii Hunter .30 .14
51 Luis Matos .30 .14
52 Brett Myers .30 .14
53 Sean Casey .30 .14
54 Mark Prior .75 .35
55 Alex Rodriguez 1.25 .55
56 Gary Sheffield .30 .14
57 Jason Varitek .50 .23
58 Dontrelle Willis .30 .14
59 Garret Anderson .30 .14
60 Casey Blake .30 .14
61 Jay Payton .30 .14
62 Carl Crawford .30 .14
63 Carl Everett .30 .14
64 Marcus Giles .30 .14
65 Jose Guillen .30 .14
66 Eric Karros .30 .14
67 Mike Lieberthal .30 .14
68 Hideki Matsui 1.25 .55
69 Xavier Nady .30 .14
70 Hank Blalock .30 .14
71 Albert Pujols 1.50 .70
72 Jose Cruz Jr. .30 .14
73 Randall Simon .30 .14
74 Javier Vazquez .30 .14
75 Preston Wilson .30 .14
76 Danys Baez .30 .14
77 Alex Cintron .30 .14
78 Jake Peavy .30 .14
79 Scott Rolen .75 .35
80 Robert Fick .30 .14
81 Brian Giles .30 .14
82 Roy Halladay .30 .14
83 Kazuhisa Ishii .30 .14
84 Austin Kearns .30 .14
85 Paul Lo Duca .30 .14
86 Darrell May .30 .14
87 Phil Nevin .30 .14
88 Carlos Pena .30 .14
89 Manny Ramirez .50 .23
90 C.C. Sabathia .30 .14
91 John Smoltz .50 .23
92 Jose Vidro .30 .14
93 Randy Wolf .30 .14
94 Jeff Bagwell .50 .23
95 Barry Bonds 2.00 .90
96 Frank Catalanotto .30 .14
97 Zach Day .30 .14
98 David Ortiz .75 .35
99 Troy Glaus .30 .14
100 Bo Hart .30 .14
101 Geoff Jenkins .30 .14
102 Jason Kendall .30 .14
103 Esteban Loaiza .30 .14
104 Doug Mientkiewicz .30 .14
105 Trot Nixon .30 .14
106 Troy Percival .30 .14
107 Aramis Ramirez .30 .14
108 Alex Sanchez .30 .14
109 Alfonso Soriano .50 .23
110 Omar Vizquel .50 .23
111 Kerry Wood .75 .35
112 Rocco Baldelli .30 .14
113 Bret Boone .30 .14
114 Shawn Chacon .30 .14
115 Carlos Delgado .30 .14
116 Shawn Green .30 .14
117 Tim Worrell .30 .14
118 Tom Glavine .50 .23
119 Shigetoshi Hasegawa .30 .14
120 Derek Jeter 1.50 .70
121 Jeff Kent .30 .14
122 Braden Looper .30 .14
123 Kevin Millwood .30 .14
124 Hideo Nomo .75 .35
125 Jason Phillips .30 .14
126 Tim Redding .30 .14
127 Reggie Sanders .30 .14
128 Sammy Sosa 1.25 .55
129 Billy Wagner .30 .14
130 Miguel Batista .30 .14
131 Milton Bradley .30 .14
132 Eric Chavez .30 .14
133 J.D. Drew .30 .14
134 Keith Foulke .30 .14
135 Luis Gonzalez .30 .14
136 LaTroy Hawkins .30 .14
137 Randy Johnson .75 .35
138 Byung-Hyun Kim .30 .14
139 Javy Lopez .30 .14
140 Melvin Mora .30 .14
141 Aubrey Huff .30 .14
142 Mike Piazza 1.25 .55
143 Mark Redman .30 .14
144 Kazuhiro Sasaki .30 .14
145 Shannon Stewart .30 .14
146 Larry Walker .50 .23
147 Dmitri Young .30 .14
148 Josh Beckett .30 .14
149 Jae Weong Seo .30 .14
150 Hee Seop Choi .30 .14
151 Adam Dunn .50 .23
152 Rafael Furcal .30 .14
153 Juan Gonzalez .50 .23
154 Todd Helton .50 .23
155 Carlos Zambrano .30 .14
156 Ryan Klesko .30 .14
157 Mike Lowell .30 .14
158 Jamie Moyer .30 .14
159 Russ Ortiz .30 .14
160 Juan Pierre .30 .14
161 Edgar Renteria .30 .14
162 Curt Schilling .30 .14
163 Mike Sweeney .30 .14
164 Brandon Webb .30 .14
165 Michael Young .30 .14
166 Carlos Beltran .50 .23
167 Sean Burroughs .30 .14
168 Luis Castillo .30 .14
169 David Eckstein .30 .14
170 Eric Gagne .75 .35
171 Chipper Jones .75 .35
172 Livan Hernandez .30 .14
173 Nick Johnson .30 .14
174 Corey Koskie .30 .14
175 Jason Schmidt .30 .14
176 Bill Mueller .30 .14
177 Steve Finley .30 .14
178 A.J. Pierzynski .30 .14
179 Rene Reyes .30 .14
180 Jason Johnson .30 .14
181 Mark Teixeira .30 .14
182 Kip Wells .30 .14
183 Mike MacDougal .30 .14
184 Lance Berkman .30 .14
185 Victor Zambrano .30 .14
186 Roger Clemens 1.50 .70
187 Jim Edmonds .30 .14
188 Nomar Garciaparra 1.25 .55
189 Ken Griffey Jr. 1.25 .55
190 Richard Hidalgo .30 .14
191 Cliff Floyd .30 .14
192 Greg Maddux 1.25 .55
193 Mark Mulder .30 .14
194 Roy Oswalt .30 .14
195 Marlon Byrd .30 .14
196 Jose Reyes .30 .14
197 Kevin Brown .30 .14
198 Miguel Tejada .30 .14
199 Vernon Wells .30 .14
200 Joel Pineiro .30 .14
201 Rickie Weeks AR 2.00 .90
202 Chad Gaudin AR 1.25 .55
203 Ryan Wagner AR 1.25 .55
204 Chris Bootcheck AR 1.25 .55
205 Koyie Hill AR 1.25 .55
206 Jeff Duncan AR 1.25 .55
207 Rich Harden AR 2.00 .90
208 Edwin Jackson AR 2.00 .90
209 Robby Hammock AR 1.25 .55
210 Khalil Greene AR 3.00 1.35
211 Chien-Ming Wang AR 2.00 .90
212 Prentice Redman AR 1.25 .55
213 Todd Wellemeyer AR 1.25 .55
214 Clint Barmes AR 1.25 .55
215 Matt Kata AR 1.25 .55
216 Jon Leicester AR 1.25 .55
217 Jeremy Guthrie AR 1.25 .55
218 Chin-Hui Tsao AR 2.00 .90
219 Dan Haren AR 1.25 .55
220 Delmon Young AR 3.00 1.35
221 Vladimir Guerrero 1.25 .55
222 Andy Pettitte .75 .35
223 Gary Sheffield .50 .23
224 Javier Vazquez .50 .23
225 Alex Rodriguez 2.00 .90
226 Billy Wagner .50 .23
227 Miguel Tejada .50 .23
228 Greg Maddux 2.00 .90
229 Ivan Rodriguez 1.25 .55
230 Roger Clemens 2.50 1.10
231 Alfonso Soriano .75 .35
232 Miguel Cabrera .75 .35
233 Javy Lopez .50 .23
234 David Wells .50 .23
235 Eric Milton .50 .23
236 Armando Benitez .50 .23
237 Mike Cameron .50 .23
238 J.D. Drew .50 .23
239 Carlos Beltran .75 .35
240 Bartolo Colon .50 .23
241 Jose Guillen .50 .23
242 Kevin Brown .50 .23
243 Carlos Guillen .50 .23
244 Kenny Lofton .50 .23
245 Pokey Reese .50 .23
246 Rafael Palmeiro .75 .35
247 Nomar Garciaparra 2.00 .90
248 Hee Seop Choi .50 .23
249 Juan Uribe .50 .23
250 Nick Johnson .50 .23
251 Scott Podsednik .50 .23
252 Richie Sexson .50 .23
253 Keith Foulke Sox .75 .35
254 Jaret Wright .50 .23
255 Johnny Estrada .50 .23
256 Michael Barrett .50 .23
257 Bernie Williams .75 .35
258 Octavio Dotel .50 .23
259 Jeromy Burnitz .50 .23
260 Kevin Youkilis .50 .23
261 Derrek Lee .50 .23
262 Jack Wilson .50 .23
263 Craig Wilson .50 .23
264 Richard Hidalgo .50 .23
265 Royce Clayton .50 .23
266 Curt Schilling 1.25 .55
267 Joe Mauer .75 .35
268 Bobby Crosby .50 .23
269 Zack Greinke .50 .23
270 Victor Martinez .50 .23
271 Pedro Feliz .50 .23
272 Tony Batista .50 .23
273 Casey Kotchman .50 .23
274 Freddy Garcia .50 .23
275 Adam Everett .50 .23
276 Alexis Rios .50 .23
277 Lew Ford .50 .23
278 Adam LaRoche .50 .23
279 Lyle Overbay .50 .23
280 Juan Gonzalez .75 .35
281 A.J. Pierzynski .50 .23
282 Scott Hairston .50 .23
283 Danny Bautista .50 .23
284 Brad Penny .50 .23
285 Paul Konerko .50 .23
286 Matt Lawton .50 .23
287 Carl Pavano .50 .23
288 Pat Burrell .50 .23
289 Kenny Rogers .50 .23
290 Laynce Nix .50 .23
291 Johnny Damon 1.25 .55
292 Paul Wilson .50 .23
293 Vinny Castilla .50 .23
294 Aaron Miles .50 .23
295 Ken Harvey .50 .23
296 Onil Joseph RC 2.00 .90
297 Kazuhito Tadano RC 3.00 1.35
298 Jeff Bennett RC 2.00 .90
299 Chad Bentz RC 2.00 .90
300 Akinori Otsuka RC 2.00 .90
301 Jon Knott RC 2.00 .90
302 Ian Snell RC 3.00 1.35
303 Fernando Nieve RC 2.00 .90
304 Mike Rouse RC 2.00 .90
305 Dennis Sarfate RC 2.00 .90
306 Josh Labandeira RC 2.00 .90
307 Chris Oxspring RC 3.00 1.35
308 Alfredo Simon RC 2.00 .90
309 Rusty Tucker RC 3.00 1.35
310 Lincoln Holdzkom RC 2.00 .90
311 Justin Leone RC 3.00 1.35
312 Jorge Sequea RC 2.00 .90
313 Brian Dallimore RC 2.00 .90
314 Tim Bittner RC 2.00 .90
315 Ronny Cedeno RC 2.00 .90
316 Justin Hampson RC 2.00 .90
317 Ryan Wing RC 2.00 .90
318 Mariano Gomez RC 2.00 .90
319 Carlos Vasquez RC 3.00 1.35
320 Casey Daigle RC 2.00 .90
321 Renyel Pinto RC 3.00 1.35
322 Chris Shelton RC 3.00 1.35
323 Mike Gosling RC 2.00 .90
324 Aarom Baldiris RC 3.00 1.35
325 Ramon Ramirez RC 2.00 .90
326 Roberto Novoa RC 3.00 1.35
327 Sean Henn RC 2.00 .90
328 Nick Regilio RC 2.00 .90
329 Dave Crouthers RC 2.00 .90
330 Greg Dobbs RC 2.00 .90
331 Angel Chavez RC 2.00 .90
332 Luis A. Gonzalez RC 2.00 .90
333 Justin Knoedler RC 2.00 .90
334 Jason Frasor RC 2.00 .90
335 Jerry Gil RC 2.00 .90
336 Carlos Hines RC 2.00 .90
337 Ivan Ochoa RC 2.00 .90
338 Jose Capellan RC 3.00 1.35
339 Hector Gimenez RC 2.00 .90
340 Shawn Hill RC 2.00 .90
341 Freddy Guzman RC 2.00 .90
342 Scott Proctor RC 3.00 1.35
343 Frank Francisco RC 2.00 .90
344 Brandon Medders RC 2.00 .90
345 Andy Green RC 2.00 .90
346 Eddy Rodriguez RC 3.00 1.35
347 Tim Hamulack RC 2.00 .90
348 Michael Wuertz RC 3.00 1.35
349 Arnie Munoz 2.00 .90
350 Enemencio Pacheco RC 2.00 .90
351 Dusty Bergman RC 2.00 .90
352 Charles Thomas RC 3.00 1.35
353 William Bergolla RC 2.00 .90
354 Ramon Castro RC 2.00 .90
355 Justin Lehr RC 2.00 .90
356 Lino Urdaneta RC 2.00 .90
357 Donnie Kelly RC 2.00 .90
358 Kevin Cave RC 3.00 1.35
359 Franklyn Gracesqui RC 2.00 .90
360 Chris Aguila RC 2.00 .90
361 Jorge Vasquez RC 2.00 .90
362 Andres Blanco RC 2.00 .90
363 Orlando Rodriguez RC 2.00 .90
364 Colby Miller RC 2.00 .90
365 Shawn Camp RC 2.00 .90
366 Jake Woods RC 2.00 .90
367 George Sherrill RC 2.00 .90
368 Justin Huisman RC 2.00 .90
369 Jimmy Serrano RC 2.00 .90
370 Mike Johnston RC 2.00 .90
371 Ryan Meaux RC 2.00 .90
372 Scott Dohmann RC 2.00 .90
373 Brad Halsey RC 3.00 1.35
374 Joey Gathright RC 3.00 1.35
375 Yadier Molina RC 4.00 1.80
376 Travis Blackley RC 3.00 1.35
377 Steve Andrade RC 2.00 .90
378 Phil Stockman RC 2.00 .90
379 Roman Colon RC 2.00 .90
380 Jesse Crain RC 3.00 1.35
381 Edwardo Sierra RC 3.00 1.35
382 Justin Germano RC 2.00 .90
383 Kaz Matsui L13 RC 25.00 11.00
384 Shingo Takatsu L13 RC 25.00 11.00
385 John Gall L13 RC 20.00 9.00
386 Chris Saenz L13 RC 20.00 9.00
387 Merkin Valdez L13 RC 25.00 11.00
388 Jamie Brown L13 RC 20.00 9.00
389 Jason Bartlett L13 RC 20.00 9.00
390 David Aardsma L13 RC 20.00 9.00
391 Scott Kazmir L13 RC 30.00 13.50
392 David Wright L13 40.00 18.00
393 Dioner Navarro L13 RC 25.00 11.00
394 B.J. Upton L13 25.00 11.00
395 Gavin Floyd L13 25.00 11.00

2004 Ultra Gold Medallion

MINT NRMT
*GOLD 1-200: 1.25X TO 3X BASIC.....
1-200 SERIES 1 ODDS 1:1
*GOLD 201-220: 1X TO 2.5X BASIC...
201-220 SERIES 1 ODDS 1:8
*GOLD 221-295: .75X TO 2X BASIC...
221-295 SERIES 2 ODDS 1:1 H, 1:3 R
*GOLD 296-382: .6X TO 1.5X BASIC..
*GOLD 383-395: .15X TO .4X BASIC..
296-395 SERIES 2 ODDS 1:4 H, 1:12 R
391 Scott Kazmir L13 15.00 6.75
392 David Wright L13 30.00 13.50

2004 Ultra Platinum Medallion

MINT NRMT
*PLATINUM 1-200: 8X TO 20X BASIC
*PLATINUM 201-220: 3X TO 8X BASIC
1-220 SERIES 1 ODDS 1:36 ....
1-220 PRINT RUN 66 SERIAL #'d SETS
*PLATINUM 221-295: 4X TO 10X BASIC
*PLATINUM 296-382: 1.5X TO 4X BASIC
221-382 PRINT RUN 100 SERIAL #'d SETS
383-395 PRINT RUN 13 SERIAL #'d SETS
383-395 NO PRICING DUE TO SCARCITY
221-395 SER.2 ODDS 1:12 HOB, 1:145 RET

2004 Ultra Season Crowns Autograph

Rickie Weeks did not return his autographs in time for pack-out, thus those cards were issued

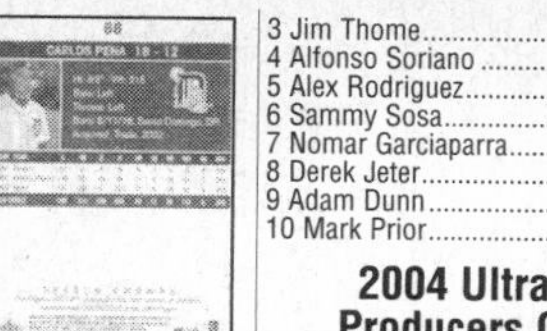

as exchange cards. There is no expiration date for those redemptions.

MINT NRMT
STATED PRINT RUN 150 SERIAL #'d SETS
GOLD PRINT RUN 25 SERIAL #'d SETS
NO GOLD PRICING DUE TO SCARCITY
SERIES 1 AUTO PARALLEL ODDS 1:192
EXCHANGE DEADLINE INDEFINITE ....
35 Corey Patterson 20.00 9.00
58 Dontrelle Willis 20.00 9.00
70 Hank Blalock 20.00 9.00
79 Scott Rolen 40.00 18.00
84 Austin Kearns 20.00 9.00
88 Carlos Pena 12.00 5.50
100 Bo Hart 12.00 5.50
112 Rocco Baldelli 20.00 9.00
141 Aubrey Huff 20.00 9.00
151 Mike Lowell 20.00 9.00
164 Brandon Webb 12.00 5.50
171 Chipper Jones 60.00 27.00
196 Jose Reyes 20.00 9.00
198 Miguel Tejada 20.00 9.00
201 Rickie Weeks EXCH 25.00 11.00

2004 Ultra Season Crowns Game Used

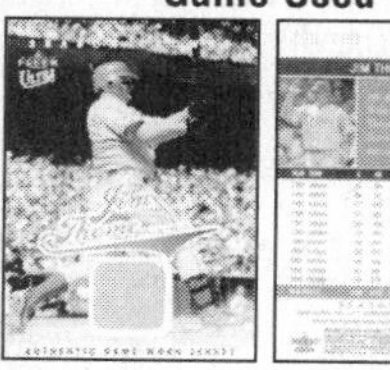

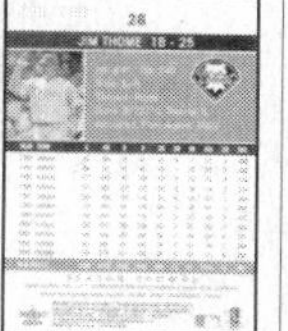

MINT NRMT
STATED PRINT RUN 399 SERIAL #'d SETS
*GOLD: .5X TO 1.2X BASIC ....
GOLD PRINT RUN 99 SERIAL #'d SETS
*PLATINUM: .75X TO 2X BASIC ....
PLATINUM PRINT RUN 25 SERIAL #'d SETS
SERIES 1 GU PARALLEL ODDS 1:24..
10 Andruw Jones Bat 8.00 3.60
12 Pedro Martinez Jsy 10.00 4.50
14 Angel Berroa Jsy 8.00 3.60
19 Frank Thomas Jsy 10.00 4.50
22 Roberto Alomar Bat 10.00 4.50
27 Jason Giambi Jsy 8.00 3.60
28 Jim Thome Jsy 10.00 4.50
29 Vladimir Guerrero Jsy 10.00 4.50
30 Tim Hudson Jsy 8.00 3.60
40 Ichiro Suzuki Base 25.00 11.00
50 Torii Hunter Bat 8.00 3.60
53 Sean Casey Bat 8.00 3.60
55 Alex Rodriguez Jsy 15.00 6.75
56 Gary Sheffield Bat 8.00 3.60
58 Dontrelle Willis Jsy 8.00 3.60
68 Hideki Matsui Base 25.00 11.00
70 Hank Blalock Bat 8.00 3.60
71 Albert Pujols Jsy 20.00 9.00
79 Scott Rolen Bat 10.00 4.50
84 Austin Kearns Bat 8.00 3.60
88 Carlos Pena Bat 8.00 3.60
89 Manny Ramirez Jsy 10.00 4.50
94 Jeff Bagwell Pants 10.00 4.50
95 Barry Bonds Base 20.00 9.00
99 Troy Glaus Jsy 8.00 3.60
102 Jason Kendall Jsy 8.00 3.60
109 Alfonso Soriano Bat 10.00 4.50
110 Omar Vizquel Jsy 10.00 4.50
112 Rocco Baldelli Jsy 8.00 3.60
115 Carlos Delgado Jsy 8.00 3.60
116 Shawn Green Jsy 8.00 3.60
118 Tom Glavine Bat 10.00 4.50
120 Derek Jeter Jsy 25.00 11.00
124 Hideo Nomo Jsy 10.00 4.50
128 Sammy Sosa Jsy 15.00 6.75
137 Randy Johnson Jsy 10.00 4.50
142 Mike Piazza Bat 15.00 6.75
144 Kazuhiro Sasaki Jsy 8.00 3.60
146 Larry Walker Jsy 10.00 4.50
151 Adam Dunn Bat 10.00 4.50
154 Todd Helton Jsy 10.00 4.50
164 Brandon Webb Jsy 8.00 3.60
166 Carlos Beltran Jsy 10.00 4.50
167 Sean Burroughs Jsy 8.00 3.60
171 Chipper Jones Jsy 10.00 4.50
184 Lance Berkman Bat 8.00 3.60
186 Roger Clemens Jsy 15.00 6.75
192 Greg Maddux Jsy 15.00 6.75
193 Mark Mulder Jsy 8.00 3.60
196 Jose Reyes Jsy 8.00 3.60

2004 Ultra Diamond Producers

MINT NRMT
SERIES 1 STATED ODDS 1:144 ....
1 Greg Maddux 20.00 9.00
2 Dontrelle Willis 20.00 9.00
3 Jim Thome 20.00 9.00
4 Alfonso Soriano 20.00 9.00
5 Alex Rodriguez 20.00 9.00
6 Sammy Sosa 20.00 9.00
7 Nomar Garciaparra 20.00 9.00
8 Derek Jeter 25.00 11.00
9 Adam Dunn 20.00 9.00
10 Mark Prior 20.00 9.00

2004 Ultra Diamond Producers Game Used

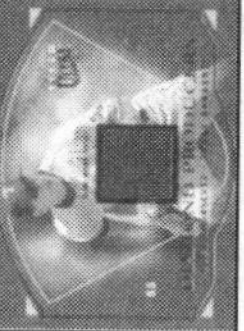

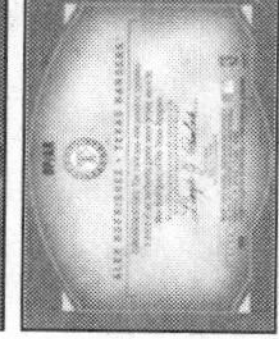

MINT NRMT
SERIES 1 GU INSERT ODDS 1:12....
STATED PRINT RUN 1000 SERIAL #'d SETS
1 Greg Maddux Jsy 10.00 4.50
2 Dontrelle Willis Jsy 8.00 3.60
3 Jim Thome Jsy 10.00 4.50
4 Alfonso Soriano Bat 10.00 4.50
5 Alex Rodriguez Jsy 15.00 6.75
6 Sammy Sosa Jsy 15.00 6.75
7 Nomar Garciaparra Jsy 15.00 6.75
8 Derek Jeter Jsy 25.00 11.00
9 Adam Dunn Bat 10.00 4.50
10 Mark Prior Jsy 10.00 4.50

2004 Ultra Hitting Machines

Nm-Mt Ex-Mt
SERIES 2 ODDS 1:12 HOBBY, 1:24 RETAIL
*DIE CUT: .75X TO 2X BASIC ....
DC RANDOM IN SER.2 VINTAGE/MVP RETAIL
1 Albert Pujols 6.00 1.80
2 Ken Griffey Jr. 5.00 1.50
3 Vladimir Guerrero 3.00 .90
4 Mike Piazza 5.00 1.50
5 Ichiro Suzuki 5.00 1.50
6 Miguel Cabrera 2.00 .60
7 Hideki Matsui 5.00 1.50
8 Nomar Garciaparra 5.00 1.50
9 Derek Jeter 6.00 1.80
10 Chipper Jones 3.00 .90

2004 Ultra Hitting Machines Jersey Silver

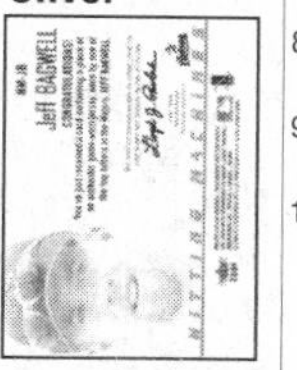

Nm-Mt Ex-Mt
*GOLD: 1.25X TO 3X SILVER ....
GOLD PRINT RUN 50 SERIAL #'d SETS
PLATINUM PRINT RUN 10 SERIAL #'d SETS
NO PLATINUM PRICING DUE TO SCARCITY
SER.2 OVERALL GU ODDS 1:6 H, 1:48 R
AD Adam Dunn 8.00 2.40
AP Albert Pujols 15.00 4.50
CJ Chipper Jones 8.00 2.40
FT Frank Thomas 8.00 2.40
HM Hideki Matsui 20.00 6.00
JB Jeff Bagwell 8.00 2.40
MC Miguel Cabrera 8.00 2.40
MP Mike Piazza 10.00 3.00
TH Todd Helton 8.00 2.40
VG Vladimir Guerrero 8.00 2.40

2004 Ultra HR Kings

MINT NRMT
SERIES 1 HR/K/RBI KING ODDS 1:12
*GOLD: 2X TO 5X BASIC ....
GOLD SER.1 HR/K/RBI KING ODDS 1:350
GOLD PRINT RUN 50 SERIAL #'d SETS
1 Barry Bonds 6.00 2.70
2 Albert Pujols 5.00 2.20
3 Jason Giambi 2.50 1.10
4 Jeff Bagwell 2.50 1.10
5 Ken Griffey Jr. 4.00 1.80
6 Alex Rodriguez 4.00 1.80
7 Sammy Sosa 4.00 1.80
8 Alfonso Soriano 2.50 1.10
9 Chipper Jones 2.50 1.10
10 Mike Piazza 4.00 1.80

2004 Ultra K Kings

MINT NRMT
SERIES 1 HR/K/RBI KING ODDS 1:12
*GOLD: 2X TO 5X BASIC ....
GOLD SER.1 HR/K/RBI KING ODDS 1:350
GOLD PRINT RUN 50 SERIAL #'d SETS
1 Randy Johnson 2.50 1.10
2 Pedro Martinez 2.50 1.10
3 Curt Schilling 2.50 1.10
4 Roger Clemens 5.00 2.20
5 Mike Mussina 2.50 1.10
6 Roy Halladay 2.50 1.10
7 Kerry Wood 2.50 1.10
8 Dontrelle Willis 2.50 1.10
9 Greg Maddux 4.00 1.80
10 Mark Prior 2.50 1.10

2004 Ultra Kings Triple Swatch

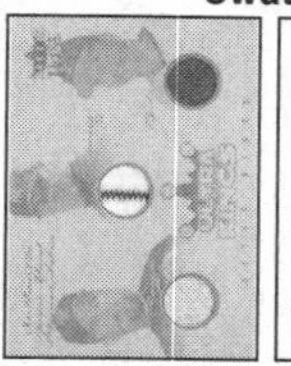

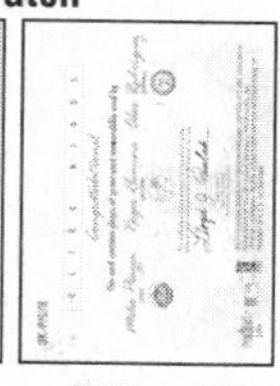

MINT NRMT
SERIES 1 GU INSERT ODDS 1:12....
STATED PRINT RUN 33 SERIAL #'d SETS
NO PRICING DUE TO SCARCITY ....
1 Mike Piazza Bat
Roger Clemens Jsy
Alex Rodriguez Jsy
2 Albert Pujols Jsy
Mark Prior Jsy
Todd Helton Jsy
3 Alfonso Soriano Bat
Dontrelle Willis Jsy
Albert Pujols Jsy
4 Pedro Martinez Jsy
Sammy Sosa Jsy
Albert Pujols Jsy
5 Greg Maddux Jsy
Chipper Jones Jsy
Vladimir Guerrero Jsy
6 Randy Johnson Jsy
Albert Pujols Jsy
Todd Helton Jsy
7 Dontrelle Willis Jsy
Chipper Jones Jsy
Albert Pujols Jsy
8 Kerry Wood Jsy
Sammy Sosa Jsy
Nomar Garciaparra Jsy
9 Dontrelle Willis Jsy
Jeff Bagwell Pants
Jim Thome Jsy
10 Greg Maddux Jsy
Jason Giambi Jsy
Manny Ramirez Jsy

2004 Ultra Legendary 13 Collection Game Used

Nm-Mt Ex-Mt
STATED PRINT RUN 13 SERIAL #'d SETS
KEY PLAYER HAS OVERSIZED SWATCH
AUTO MASTERPIECE PRINT RUN 1 #'d SET
AUTO MP KEY PLAYER HAS AUTOGRAPH
SER.2 OVERALL LGD 13 ODDS 1:192 HOBBY
EACH CARD FEATURES 13 JSY SWATCHES
NO PRICING DUE TO SCARCITY ....
AP Albert Pujols Oversized Jsy ....
Nolan Ryan Jsy
Roger Clemens Jsy
Cal Ripken Jsy
Mike Schmidt Jsy
Carlton Fisk Jsy
Carl Yastrzemski Jsy
Ted Williams Jsy
Stan Musial Jsy
Mark Prior Jsy
Yogi Berra Jsy
Johnny Bench Jsy
Don Mattingly Jsy
CF Carlton Fisk Oversized Jsy ....
Carl Yastrzemski Jsy
Ted Williams Jsy
Stan Musial Jsy
Mark Prior Jsy
Yogi Berra Jsy
Johnny Bench Jsy
Don Mattingly Jsy
Albert Pujols Jsy
Nolan Ryan Jsy
Roger Clemens Jsy
Cal Ripken Jsy
Mike Schmidt Jsy
CR Cal Ripken Oversized Jsy ....
Mike Schmidt Jsy
Carlton Fisk Jsy
Carl Yastrzemski Jsy
Ted Williams Jsy
Stan Musial Jsy
Mark Prior Jsy
Yogi Berra Jsy
Johnny Bench Jsy
Don Mattingly Jsy
Albert Pujols Jsy
Nolan Ryan Jsy
Roger Clemens Jsy
CY Carl Yastrzemski Oversized Jsy ....
Ted Williams Jsy
Stan Musial Jsy
Mark Prior Jsy
Yogi Berra Jsy
Johnny Bench Jsy
Don Mattingly Jsy
Albert Pujols Jsy
Nolan Ryan Jsy
Roger Clemens Jsy
Cal Ripken Jsy
Mike Schmidt Jsy
Carlton Fisk Jsy
DM Don Mattingly Oversized Jsy ....
Albert Pujols Jsy
Nolan Ryan Jsy
Roger Clemens Jsy
Cal Ripken Jsy
Mike Schmidt Jsy
Carlton Fisk Jsy
Carl Yastrzemski Jsy
Ted Williams Jsy
Stan Musial Jsy
Mark Prior Jsy
Yogi Berra Jsy
Johnny Bench Jsy
JB Johnny Bench Oversized Jsy ....
Don Mattingly Jsy
Albert Pujols Jsy
Nolan Ryan Jsy
Roger Clemens Jsy
Cal Ripken Jsy
Mike Schmidt Jsy
Carlton Fisk Jsy
Carl Yastrzemski Jsy
Ted Williams Jsy
Stan Musial Jsy
Mark Prior Jsy
Yogi Berra Jsy
MP Mark Prior Oversized Jsy ....
Yogi Berra Jsy
Johnny Bench Jsy
Don Mattingly Jsy
Albert Pujols Jsy
Nolan Ryan Jsy
Roger Clemens Jsy
Cal Ripken Jsy
Mike Schmidt Jsy
Carlton Fisk Jsy
Carl Yastrzemski Jsy
Ted Williams Jsy
Stan Musial Jsy
MS Mike Schmidt Oversized Jsy ....
Carlton Fisk Jsy
Carl Yastrzemski Jsy
Ted Williams Jsy
Stan Musial Jsy
Mark Prior Jsy
Yogi Berra Jsy
Johnny Bench Jsy
Don Mattingly Jsy
Albert Pujols Jsy
Nolan Ryan Jsy
Roger Clemens Jsy
Cal Ripken Jsy
NR Nolan Ryan Oversized Jsy ....
Roger Clemens Jsy
Cal Ripken Jsy
Mike Schmidt Jsy
Carlton Fisk Jsy
Carl Yastrzemski Jsy
Ted Williams Jsy
Stan Musial Jsy
Mark Prior Jsy
Yogi Berra Jsy
Johnny Bench Jsy
Don Mattingly Jsy
Albert Pujols Jsy
RC Roger Clemens Oversized Jsy ....
Cal Ripken Jsy
Mike Schmidt Jsy
Carlton Fisk Jsy
Carl Yastrzemski Jsy
Ted Williams Jsy
Stan Musial Jsy
Mark Prior Jsy
Yogi Berra Jsy
Johnny Bench Jsy
Don Mattingly Jsy
Albert Pujols Jsy
Nolan Ryan Jsy
SM Stan Musial Oversized Jsy ....
Mark Prior Jsy
Yogi Berra Jsy
Johnny Bench Jsy
Don Mattingly Jsy
Albert Pujols Jsy
Nolan Ryan Jsy
Roger Clemens Jsy
Cal Ripken Jsy
Mike Schmidt Jsy
Carlton Fisk Jsy
Carl Yastrzemski Jsy
Ted Williams Jsy
TW Ted Williams Oversized Jsy ....
Stan Musial Jsy
Mark Prior Jsy
Yogi Berra Jsy
Johnny Bench Jsy
Don Mattingly Jsy
Albert Pujols Jsy
Nolan Ryan Jsy
Roger Clemens Jsy
Cal Ripken Jsy
Mike Schmidt Jsy
Carlton Fisk Jsy
Carl Yastrzemski Jsy
YB Yogi Berra Oversized Jsy ....
Johnny Bench Jsy
Don Mattingly Jsy
Albert Pujols Jsy
Nolan Ryan Jsy
Roger Clemens Jsy
Cal Ripken Jsy
Mike Schmidt Jsy
Carlton Fisk Jsy
Carl Yastrzemski Jsy
Ted Williams Jsy
Stan Musial Jsy
Mark Prior Jsy

2004 Ultra Legendary 13 Dual Game Used Gold

Nm-Mt Ex-Mt
STATED PRINT RUN 22 SERIAL #'d SETS
MASTERPIECE PRINT RUN 1 #'d SET
NO M'PIECE PRICING DUE TO SCARCITY
PLATINUM PRINT RUN 10 #'d SETS..
NO PLATINUM PRICING DUE TO SCARCITY
SER.2 OVERALL LGD 13 ODDS 1:192 HOBBY
APCF Albert Pujols Patch ....
Carlton Fisk Patch
APCY Albert Pujols Patch ....
Carl Yastrzemski Jsy
CFMP Carlton Fisk Patch ....
Mark Prior Patch
CRMS Cal Ripken Patch ....
Mike Schmidt Patch
CYTW Carl Yastrzemski Jsy ....
Ted Williams Bat
DMAP Don Mattingly Patch ....
Albert Pujols Patch
DMCR Don Mattingly Patch ....
Cal Ripken Patch
MSSM Mike Schmidt Patch ....
Stan Musial Jsy
NRMP Nolan Ryan Patch ....
Mark Prior Patch
NRRC Nolan Ryan Jsy ....
Roger Clemens Patch
RCMP Roger Clemens Patch ....
Mark Prior Patch
YBDM Yogi Berra Bat ....
Don Mattingly Patch
YBJB Yogi Berra Bat ....
Johnny Bench Patch

2004 Ultra Legendary 13 Dual Game Used Autograph Platinum

Nm-Mt Ex-Mt
STATED PRINT RUN 3 SERIAL #'d SETS
MASTERPIECE PRINT RUN 1 #'d SET
SER.2 OVERALL LGD 13 ODDS 1:192 HOBBY
NO PRICING DUE TO SCARCITY ....

2004 Ultra Legendary 13 Single Game Used Gold

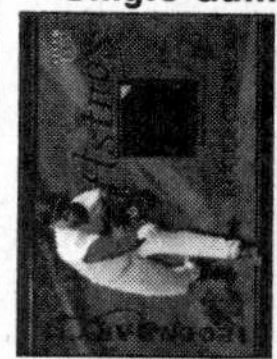

Nm-Mt Ex-Mt
PRINT RUNS B/WN 5-72 COPIES PER
NO PRICING ON QTY OF 9 OR LESS..
MASTERPIECE PRINT RUN 1 #'d SET
NO M'PIECE PRICING DUE TO SCARCITY
SER.2 OVERALL LGD 13 ODDS 1:192 HOBBY
AP Albert Pujols Patch/5 ....
CF Carlton Fisk Jsy/72 15.00 4.50
CR Cal Ripken Patch/8 ....
CY Carl Yastrzemski Jsy/8 ....
DM Don Mattingly Patch/23 80.00 24.00
JB Johnny Bench Patch/5 ....
MP Mark Prior Patch/22 40.00 12.00
MS Mike Schmidt Patch/20 100.00 30.00
NR Nolan Ryan Jsy/34 40.00 12.00
RC Roger Clemens Patch/22 50.00 15.00
SM Stan Musial Jsy/6 ....
TW Ted Williams Bat/9 ....
YB Yogi Berra Bat/8 ....

2004 Ultra Legendary 13 Single Game Used Autograph Platinum

Nm-Mt Ex-Mt
STATED PRINT RUN 5 SERIAL #'d SETS

MASTERPIECE PRINT RUN 1 #'d SET
SER.2 OVERALL LGD 13 ODDS 1:192 HOBBY
NO PRICING DUE TO SCARCITY

2004 Ultra Performers

MINT NRMT
COMPLETE SET (15) 25.00 11.00
SERIES 1 STATED ODDS 1:6
1 Ichiro Suzuki 3.00 1.35
2 Albert Pujols 4.00 1.80
3 Barry Bonds 5.00 2.20
4 Hideki Matsui 3.00 1.35
5 Randy Johnson 2.00 .90
6 Jason Giambi 2.00 .90
7 Pedro Martinez 2.00 .90
8 Hank Blalock 2.00 .90
9 Chipper Jones 2.00 .90
10 Mike Piazza 3.00 1.35
11 Derek Jeter 4.00 1.80
12 Vladimir Guerrero 2.00 .90
13 Barry Zito 2.00 .90
14 Rocco Baldelli 2.00 .90
15 Hideo Nomo 2.00 .90

2004 Ultra Performers Game Used

MINT NRMT
SERIES 1 GU INSERT ODDS 1:12
STATED PRINT RUN 500 SERIAL #'d SETS
1 Albert Pujols Jsy 20.00 9.00
2 Barry Bonds Base 20.00 9.00
3 Randy Johnson Jsy 10.00 4.50
4 Jason Giambi Jsy 8.00 3.60
5 Pedro Martinez Jsy 10.00 4.50
6 Hank Blalock Bat 8.00 3.60
7 Chipper Jones Jsy 10.00 4.50
8 Mike Piazza Bat 10.00 4.50
9 Derek Jeter Jsy 25.00 11.00
10 Vladimir Guerrero Jsy 10.00 4.50
11 Rocco Baldelli Jsy 8.00 3.60
12 Hideo Nomo Jsy 10.00 4.50

2004 Ultra RBI Kings

MINT NRMT
OVERALL HR/K/RBI KING ODDS 1:12
*GOLD: 2X TO 5X BASIC
GOLD SER.1 HR/K/RBI KING ODDS 1:350
GOLD PRINT RUN 50 SERIAL #'d SETS
1 Hideki Matsui 4.00 1.80
2 Albert Pujols 5.00 2.20
3 Todd Helton 2.50 1.10
4 Jim Thome 2.50 1.10
5 Carlos Delgado 2.50 1.10
6 Alex Rodriguez 4.00 1.80
7 Barry Bonds 6.00 2.70
8 Manny Ramirez 2.50 1.10
9 Vladimir Guerrero 2.50 1.10
10 Nomar Garciaparra 4.00 1.80

2004 Ultra Turn Back the Clock

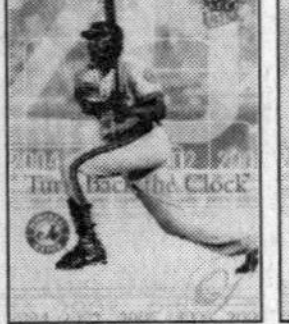

Nm-Mt Ex-Mt
SERIES 2 ODDS 1:6 HOBBY, 1:12 RETAIL
1 Roger Clemens Sox 6.00 1.80
2 Alex Rodriguez Rgr 5.00 1.50
3 Randy Johnson M's 3.00 .90
4 Pedro Martinez Expos 3.00 .90
5 Alfonso Soriano Yanks 2.00 .60
6 Curt Schilling Phils 2.00 .60
7 Miguel Tejada A's 2.00 .60
8 Scott Rolen Phils 3.00 .90
9 Jim Thome Indians 3.00 .90
10 Manny Ramirez Indians 2.00 .60
11 Vladimir Guerrero Expos 3.00 .90
12 Tom Glavine Braves 2.00 .60
13 Andy Pettitte Yanks 2.00 .60
14 Ivan Rodriguez Marlins 3.00 .90
15 Jason Giambi A's 2.00 .60
16 Rafael Palmeiro Rgr 2.00 .60
17 Greg Maddux Braves 5.00 1.50
18 Hideo Nomo Sox 3.00 .90
19 Mike Mussina O's 2.00 .60
20 Sammy Sosa Sox 5.00 1.50

2004 Ultra Turn Back the Clock Jersey Copper

Nm-Mt Ex-Mt
STATED PRINT RUN 399 SERIAL #'d SETS
*GOLD: .6X TO 1.5X COPPER
GOLD PRINT RUN 99 SERIAL #'d SETS
*SILVER: .5X TO 1.2X COPPER
SILVER PRINT RUN 199 SERIAL #'d SETS
*PATCH PLAT: 1.5X TO 4X COPPER
PATCH PLATINUM PRINT RUN 29 #'d SETS
SER.2 OVERALL GU ODDS 1:6 H, 1:48 R
AP Andy Pettitte Yanks 10.00 3.00
AR Alex Rodriguez Rgr 12.00 3.60
AS Alfonso Soriano Yanks 10.00 3.00
CS Curt Schilling Phils 8.00 2.40
GM Greg Maddux Braves 12.00 3.60
HM Hideo Nomo Sox 10.00 3.00
IR Ivan Rodriguez Marlins 10.00 3.00
JG Jason Giambi A's 8.00 2.40
JT Jim Thome Indians 10.00 3.00
MM Mike Mussina O's 10.00 3.00
MR Manny Ramirez Indians 10.00 3.00
MT Miguel Tejada A's 8.00 2.40
PR Pedro Martinez Expos 10.00 3.00
RC Roger Clemens Sox 12.00 3.60
RJ Randy Johnson M's 10.00 3.00
RP Rafael Palmeiro Rgr 10.00 3.00
SR Scott Rolen Phils 10.00 3.00
SS Sammy Sosa Sox 12.00 3.60
TG Tom Glavine Braves 10.00 3.00
VG Vladimir Guerrero Expos 10.00 3.00

2005 Ultra

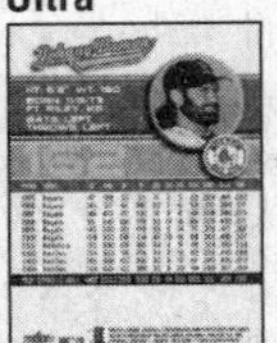

This 220-card set, the first of the 2005 sets to hit the market, was released in November, 2004. Both the eight-card hobby and retail packs were issued with an $3 SRP although the insert ratios were far different between the two classes of packs. The hobby packs were issued 24 packs to a box and 16 boxes to a case while the hobby packs were issued 24 packs to a box and 20 boxes to a case. The first 200 cards of the set featured veterans while cards 201 through 220, which were issued at a stated rate of one in four hobby and one in five retail, feature leading prospects.

Nm-Mt Ex-Mt
COMPLETE SET (220) 100.00 30.00
COMP.SET w/o SP's (200) 40.00 12.00
COMMON CARD (1-200) .30 .09
COMMON CARD (201-220) 2.00 .60
201-220 ODDS 1:4 HOBBY, 1:5 RETAIL
1 Andy Pettitte .50 .15
2 Jose Cruz Jr. .30 .09
3 Cliff Floyd .30 .09
4 Paul Konerko .30 .09
5 Joe Mauer .50 .15
6 Scott Spiezio .30 .09
7 Ben Sheets .30 .09
8 Kerry Wood .75 .23
9 Carl Pavano .30 .09
10 Matt Morris .30 .09
11 Kaz Matsui .30 .09
12 Ivan Rodriguez .75 .23
13 Victor Martinez .30 .09
14 Justin Morneau .30 .09
15 Adam Everett .30 .09
16 Carl Crawford .30 .09
17 David Ortiz .75 .23
18 Jason Giambi .30 .09
19 Derrek Lee .30 .09
20 Magglio Ordonez .30 .09
21 Bobby Abreu .30 .09
22 Milton Bradley .30 .09
23 Jeff Bagwell .50 .15
24 Jim Edmonds .30 .09
25 Garret Anderson .30 .09
26 Jacque Jones .30 .09
27 Ted Lilly .30 .09
28 Greg Maddux 1.25 .35
29 Jermaine Dye .30 .09
30 Bill Mueller .30 .09
31 Roy Oswalt .30 .09
32 Tony Womack .30 .09
33 Andruw Jones .30 .09
34 Tom Glavine .50 .15
35 Mariano Rivera .50 .15
36 Sean Casey .30 .09
37 Edgardo Alfonzo .30 .09
38 Brad Penny .30 .09
39 Johan Santana .50 .15
40 Mark Teixeira .30 .09
41 Manny Ramirez .50 .15
42 Gary Sheffield .30 .09
43 Matt Lawton .30 .09
44 Troy Percival .30 .09
45 Rocco Baldelli .30 .09
46 Doug Mientkiewicz .30 .09
47 Corey Patterson .30 .09
48 Austin Kearns .30 .09
49 Edgar Martinez .50 .15
50 Brad Radke .30 .09
51 Barry Larkin .50 .15
52 Chone Figgins .30 .09
53 Alexis Rios .30 .09
54 Alex Rodriguez 1.25 .35
55 Vinny Castilla .30 .09
56 Javier Vazquez .30 .09
57 Javy Lopez .30 .09
58 Mike Cameron .30 .09
59 Brian Giles .30 .09
60 Dontrelle Willis .30 .09
61 Rafael Furcal .30 .09
62 Trot Nixon .30 .09
63 Mark Mulder .30 .09
64 Josh Beckett .30 .09
65 J.D. Drew .30 .09
66 Brandon Webb .30 .09
67 Wade Miller .30 .09
68 Lyle Overbay .30 .09
69 Pedro Martinez .75 .23
70 Rich Harden .30 .09
71 Al Leiter .30 .09
72 Adam Eaton .30 .09
73 Mike Sweeney .30 .09
74 Steve Finley .30 .09
75 Kris Benson .30 .09
76 Jim Thome .75 .23
77 Juan Pierre .30 .09
78 Bartolo Colon .30 .09
79 Carlos Delgado .30 .09
80 Jack Wilson .30 .09
81 Ken Harvey .30 .09
82 Nomar Garciaparra 1.25 .35
83 Paul Lo Duca .30 .09
84 Cesar Izturis .30 .09
85 Adrian Beltre .50 .15
86 Brian Roberts .30 .09
87 David Eckstein .30 .09
88 Jimmy Rollins .30 .09
89 Roger Clemens 1.50 .45
90 Randy Johnson .75 .23
91 Orlando Hudson .30 .09
92 Tim Hudson .30 .09
93 Dmitri Young .30 .09
94 Chipper Jones .75 .23
95 John Smoltz .50 .15
96 Billy Wagner .30 .09
97 Hideo Nomo .75 .23
98 Sammy Sosa 1.25 .35
99 Darin Erstad .30 .09
100 Todd Helton .50 .15
101 Aubrey Huff .30 .09
102 Alfonso Soriano .50 .15
103 Jose Vidro .30 .09
104 Carlos Lee .30 .09
105 Corey Koskie .30 .09
106 Bret Boone .30 .09
107 Torii Hunter .30 .09
108 Aramis Ramirez .30 .09
109 Chase Utley .30 .09
110 Reggie Sanders .30 .09
111 Livan Hernandez .30 .09
112 Jeromy Burnitz .30 .09
113 Carlos Zambrano .30 .09
114 Hank Blalock .30 .09
115 Sidney Ponson .30 .09
116 Zack Greinke .30 .09
117 Trevor Hoffman .30 .09
118 Jeff Kent .30 .09
119 Richie Sexson .30 .09
120 Melvin Mora .30 .09
121 Eric Chavez .30 .09
122 Miguel Cabrera .50 .15
123 Ryan Freel .30 .09
124 Russ Ortiz .30 .09
125 Craig Wilson .30 .09
126 Craig Biggio .50 .15
127 Curt Schilling .75 .23
128 Kaz Ishii .30 .09
129 Marquis Grissom .30 .09
130 Bernie Williams .50 .15
131 Travis Hafner .30 .09
132 Hee Seop Choi .30 .09
133 Scott Rolen .50 .15
134 Tony Batista .30 .09
135 Frank Thomas .75 .23
136 Jason Varitek .50 .15
137 Ichiro Suzuki 1.25 .35
138 Junior Spivey .30 .09
139 Adam Dunn .50 .15
140 Jorge Posada .50 .15
141 Edgar Renteria .30 .09
142 Hideki Matsui 1.25 .35
143 Carlos Guillen .30 .09
144 Jody Gerut .30 .09
145 Wily Mo Pena .30 .09
146 Derek Jeter 1.50 .45
147 C.C. Sabathia .30 .09
148 Geoff Jenkins .30 .09
149 Albert Pujols 1.50 .45
150 Eric Munson .30 .09
151 Moises Alou .30 .09
152 Jerry Hairston .30 .09
153 Ray Durham .30 .09
154 Mike Piazza 1.25 .35
155 Omar Vizquel .30 .09
156 A.J. Pierzynski .30 .09
157 Michael Young .30 .09
158 Jason Bay .30 .09
159 Mark Loretta .30 .09
160 Shawn Green .30 .09
161 Luis Gonzalez .30 .09
162 Johnny Damon .75 .23
163 Eric Milton .30 .09
164 Mike Lowell .30 .09
165 Jose Guillen .30 .09
166 Eric Hinske .30 .09
167 Jason Kendall .30 .09
168 Carlos Beltran .50 .15
169 Johnny Estrada .30 .09
170 Scott Hatteberg .30 .09
171 Laynce Nix .30 .09
172 Eric Gagne .75 .23
173 Richard Hidalgo .30 .09
174 Bobby Crosby .30 .09
175 Woody Williams .30 .09
176 Justin Leone .30 .09
177 Orlando Cabrera .30 .09
178 Mark Prior .75 .23
179 Jorge Julio .30 .09
180 Jamie Moyer .30 .09
181 Jose Reyes .30 .09
182 Ken Griffey Jr. 1.25 .35
183 Mike Lieberthal .30 .09
184 Kenny Rogers .30 .09
185 Mike Mussina .50 .15
186 Preston Wilson .30 .09
187 Khalil Greene .75 .23
188 Angel Berroa .30 .09
189 Miguel Tejada .30 .09
190 Freddy Garcia .30 .09
191 Pat Burrell .30 .09
192 Luis Castillo .30 .09
193 Vladimir Guerrero .75 .23
194 Roy Halladay .30 .09
195 Barry Zito .30 .09
196 Lance Berkman .30 .09
197 Rafael Palmeiro .50 .15
198 Nate Robertson .30 .09
199 Jason Schmidt .30 .09
200 Scott Podsednik .30 .09
201 Casey Kotchman AR 3.00 .90
202 Scott Kazmir AR 5.00 1.50
203 Bucky Jacobsen AR 3.00 .90
204 Jeff Keppinger AR 2.00 .60
205 Dave Bush AR 3.00 .90
206 Gavin Floyd AR 3.00 .90
207 David Wright AR 8.00 2.40
208 B.J. Upton AR 5.00 1.50
209 David Aardsma AR 2.00 .60
210 Jason Bartlett AR 2.00 .60
211 Dioner Navarro AR 3.00 .90
212 Jason Kubel AR 3.00 .90
213 Ryan Howard AR 3.00 .90
214 Charles Thomas AR 2.00 .60
215 Freddy Guzman AR 2.00 .60
216 Brad Halsey AR 2.00 .60
217 Joey Gathright AR 3.00 .90
218 Jeff Francis AR 3.00 .90
219 Terry Tiffee AR 2.00 .60
220 Nick Swisher AR 5.00 .90

2005 Ultra Gold Medallion

Nm-Mt Ex-Mt
*GOLD 1-200: 1.25X TO 3X BASIC
*GOLD 201-220: .6X TO 1.5X BASIC
STATED ODDS 1:1 HOBBY, 1:3 RETAIL

2005 Ultra Platinum Medallion

Nm-Mt Ex-Mt
*PLATINUM 1-200: 8X TO 20X BASIC
*PLATINUM 201-220: 2X TO 5X BASIC
RANDOM INSERTS IN HOBBY PACKS
STATED PRINT RUN 50 SERIAL #'d SETS

2005 Ultra Season Crown Autographs Copper

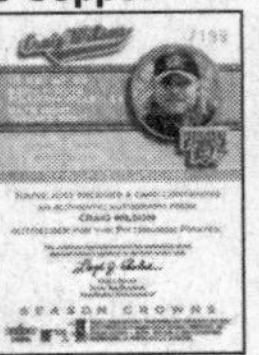

Nm-Mt Ex-Mt
OVERALL SC AU ODDS 1:192 HOBBY
STATED PRINT RUN 199 SERIAL #'d SETS
UER'S #'d OF 199 BUT 22-199 PER MADE
ACTUAL UER QTY PROVIDED BY FLEER
31 Roy Oswalt/50 UER 25.00 7.50
80 Jack Wilson/199 20.00 6.00
125 Craig Wilson/130 UER 20.00 6.00
157 Michael Young/150 UER 20.00 6.00
200 Scott Podsednik/22 UER 30.00 9.00

2005 Ultra Season Crown Autographs Gold

Nm-Mt Ex-Mt
OVERALL SC AU ODDS 1:192 HOBBY
STATED PRINT RUN 99 SERIAL #'d SETS
UER'S ARE #'d OF 99 BUT 13-99 PER MADE
ACTUAL UER QTY PROVIDED BY FLEER
NO PRICING ON QTY OF 13 OR LESS
20 Magglio Ordonez/13 UER
31 Roy Oswalt/99 20.00 6.00
40 Mark Teixeira/25 UER 50.00 15.00
50 Brad Radke/89 UER 20.00 6.00
51 Barry Larkin/99 30.00 9.00
62 Trot Nixon/37 UER 25.00 7.50
70 Rich Harden/41 UER 25.00 7.50
80 Jack Wilson/99 20.00 6.00
88 Jimmy Rollins/45 UER 25.00 7.50
121 Eric Chavez/69 UER 20.00 6.00
125 Craig Wilson/99 20.00 6.00
157 Michael Young/99 20.00 6.00
200 Scott Podsednik/99 20.00 6.00
201 Casey Kotchman AR/21 UER 30.00 9.00

2005 Ultra Season Crown Autographs Masterpiece

Nm-Mt Ex-Mt
OVERALL SC AU ODDS 1:192 HOBBY
STATED PRINT RUN 1 SERIAL #'d SET
NO PRICING DUE TO SCARCITY

2005 Ultra Season Crown Autographs Platinum

Nm-Mt Ex-Mt
OVERALL SC AU ODDS 1:192 HOBBY
STATED PRINT RUN 50 SERIAL #'d SETS
UER'S ARE #'d OF 50 BUT 7-50 PER MADE
ACTUAL UER QTY PROVIDED BY FLEER
NO PRICING ON QTY OF 10 OR LESS
8 Kerry Wood/7 UER
12 Ivan Rodriguez/25 UER 60.00 18.00
20 Magglio Ordonez/50 25.00 7.50
25 Garret Anderson/50 25.00 7.50
31 Roy Oswalt/50 25.00 7.50
35 Mariano Rivera/25 UER 60.00 18.00
40 Mark Teixeira/50 40.00 12.00
41 Manny Ramirez/25 UER 60.00 18.00
50 Brad Radke/50 25.00 7.50
51 Barry Larkin/50 40.00 12.00
62 Trot Nixon/50 25.00 7.50
65 J.D. Drew/19 UER 60.00 18.00
70 Rich Harden/50 25.00 7.50
80 Jack Wilson/50 25.00 7.50
87 David Eckstein/45 UER 25.00 7.50
88 Jimmy Rollins/50 25.00 7.50
90 Randy Johnson/10 UER
94 Chipper Jones/19 UER 80.00 24.00
95 John Smoltz/23 UER 60.00 18.00
96 Billy Wagner/50 40.00 12.00
116 Zack Greinke/49 UER 25.00 7.50
121 Eric Chavez/50 25.00 7.50
125 Craig Wilson/50 25.00 7.50
130 Bernie Williams/15 UER 80.00 24.00
136 Jason Varitek/19 UER 60.00 18.00
149 Albett Pujols/10 UER
154 Mike Piazza/10 UER
157 Michael Young/50 25.00 7.50
161 Luis Gonzalez/50 25.00 7.50
185 Mike Mussina/50 40.00 12.00
195 Barry Zito/50 25.00 7.50
199 Jason Schmidt/50 40.00 12.00
200 Scott Podsednik/50 25.00 7.50
201 Casey Kotchman AR/50 25.00 7.50

2005 Ultra Season Crowns Game Used Copper

Nm-Mt Ex-Mt
STATED PRINT RUN 399 SERIAL #'d SETS
*GOLD: .5X TO 1.2X COPPER
GOLD PRINT RUN 99 SERIAL #'d SETS
*PLATINUM: .75X TO 2X COPPER
*PLATINUM PATCH: ADD 100% PREMIUM
PLATINUM PRINT RUN 25 SERIAL #'d SETS
OVERALL SC GU 1:24 HOBBY
1 Andy Pettitte Jsy 10.00 3.00
3 Cliff Floyd Jsy 8.00 2.40
7 Ben Sheets Jsy 8.00 2.40
8 Kerry Wood Jsy 10.00 3.00
11 Kaz Matsui Bat 15.00 4.50
13 Victor Martinez Jsy 8.00 2.40
17 David Ortiz Jsy 10.00 3.00
20 Magglio Ordonez Bat 8.00 2.40
21 Bobby Abreu Bat 8.00 2.40
24 Jim Edmonds Jsy 8.00 2.40
31 Roy Oswalt Jsy 8.00 2.40
33 Andruw Jones Jsy 8.00 2.40
34 Tom Glavine Bat 10.00 3.00
36 Sean Casey Jsy 8.00 2.40
37 Edgardo Alfonzo Bat 8.00 2.40
41 Manny Ramirez Bat 10.00 3.00
42 Gary Sheffield Bat 8.00 2.40
45 Rocco Baldelli Jsy 8.00 2.40
48 Austin Kearns Jsy 8.00 2.40
49 Edgar Martinez Jsy 10.00 3.00
60 Dontrelle Willis Jsy 8.00 2.40
65 J.D. Drew Jsy 8.00 2.40
70 Rich Harden Jsy 8.00 2.40
71 Al Leiter Jsy 8.00 2.40
80 Jack Wilson Bat 8.00 2.40
93 Dmitri Young Bat 8.00 2.40
94 Chipper Jones Bat 10.00 3.00
97 Hideo Nomo Jsy 10.00 3.00
98 Sammy Sosa Bat 15.00 4.50
100 Todd Helton Bat 10.00 3.00
102 Alfonso Soriano Bat 10.00 3.00
107 Torii Hunter Jsy 8.00 2.40
114 Hank Blalock Bat 8.00 2.40

119 Richie Sexson Jsy 8.00 2.40
121 Eric Chavez Jsy 8.00 2.40
130 Bernie Williams Bat 10.00 3.00
135 Frank Thomas Bat 10.00 3.00
139 Adam Dunn Bat 10.00 3.00
142 Hideki Matsui Bat 25.00 7.50
144 Jody Gerut Bat 8.00 2.40
154 Mike Piazza Bat 15.00 4.50
158 Jason Bay Bat 8.00 2.40
162 Johnny Damon Jsy 10.00 3.00
168 Carlos Beltran Bat 10.00 3.00
173 Richard Hidalgo Jsy 8.00 2.40
181 Jose Reyes Bat 8.00 2.40
187 Khalil Greene Jsy 15.00 4.50
191 Pat Burrell Bat 8.00 2.40
193 Vladimir Guerrero Bat 10.00 3.00
197 Rafael Palmeiro Jsy 10.00 3.00

2005 Ultra 3 Kings Jersey Triple Swatch

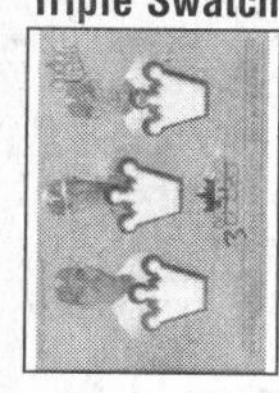

Nm-Mt Ex-Mt
BCB Jeff Bagwell 50.00 15.00
Roger Clemens
Lance Berkman
BCR Josh Beckett 40.00 12.00
Miguel Cabrera
Ivan Rodriguez
JMM Randy Johnson 40.00 12.00
Greg Maddux
Pedro Martinez
MPW Greg Maddux 50.00 15.00
Mark Prior
Kerry Wood
PDC Albert Pujols 50.00 15.00
Adam Dunn
Miguel Cabrera
RJB Scott Rolen 40.00 12.00
Chipper Jones
Adrian Beltre
SMP Gary Sheffield 50.00 15.00
Hideki Matsui
Mike Piazza
SMR Curt Schilling 60.00 18.00
Pedro Martinez
Manny Ramirez
TBS Mark Teixeira 40.00 12.00
Hank Blalock
Alfonso Soriano
TBW Jim Thome 50.00 15.00
Pat Burrell
Billy Wagner

2005 Ultra Follow the Leader

Nm-Mt Ex-Mt
:OMPLETE SET (15) 25.00 7.50
STATED ODDS 1:6 HOBBY, 1:8 RETAIL
DIE CUT: .6X TO 1.5X BASIC
IE CUT RANDOM IN EXCEL/MVP RETAIL
Roger Clemens 4.00 1.20
Albert Pujols 4.00 1.20
Sammy Sosa 3.00 .90
Manny Ramirez 2.00 .60
Vladimir Guerrero 2.00 .60
Ivan Rodriguez 2.00 .60
Mike Piazza 3.00 .90
Scott Rolen 2.00 .60
Ichiro Suzuki 3.00 .90
0 Randy Johnson 2.00 .60
1 Mark Prior 2.00 .60
2 Jim Thome 2.00 .60
3 Greg Maddux 3.00 .90
4 Pedro Martinez 2.00 .60
5 Miguel Cabrera 2.00 .60

2005 Ultra Follow the Leader Jersey Copper

Nm-Mt Ex-Mt
OPPER ISSUED ONLY IN HOBBY PACKS
OLD: .4X TO 1X COPPER
OLD PRINT RUN 250 SERIAL #'d SETS
LATINUM: .5X TO 1.2X COPPER
LATINUM PATCH: ADD 100% PREMIUM
LATINUM PRINT RUN 99 SERIAL #'d SETS
LATINUM ISSUED ONLY IN HOBBY PACKS
RED: .4X TO 1X COPPER
ED STATED ODDS 1:48 RETAIL
ED RANDOM IN HOBBY HOT PACKS
LTRA p/r 45-51: .75X TO 2X COPPER
LTRA p/r 21-31: 1X TO 2.5X COPPER

ULTRA PRINT RUNS B/WN 5-51 PER.
NO ULTRA PRICING ON QTY OF 7 OR LESS
OVERALL GU ODDS 1:12 HOB, 1:48 RET
AP Albert Pujols 15.00 4.50
GM Greg Maddux 15.00 4.50
IR Ivan Rodriguez 10.00 3.00
JT Jim Thome 10.00 3.00
MC Miguel Cabrera 10.00 3.00
MPI Mike Piazza 15.00 4.50
MPR Mark Prior 10.00 3.00
MR Manny Ramirez 10.00 3.00
PM Pedro Martinez 10.00 3.00
RC Roger Clemens 15.00 4.50
RJ Randy Johnson 10.00 3.00
SR Scott Rolen 10.00 3.00
SS Sammy Sosa 15.00 4.50
VG Vladimir Guerrero 10.00 3.00

2005 Ultra Kings

Nm-Mt Ex-Mt
OVERALL KINGS ODDS 1:12 HOB, 1:24 RET
K PERCEIVED 3X TOUGHER THAN HR-RBI
*GOLD: 2X TO 5X BASIC HR-RBI
*GOLD: 1.25X TO 3X BASIC K
GOLD RANDOM INSERTS IN HOBBY PACKS
GOLD PRINT RUN 50 SERIAL #'d SETS
H1 Jim Thome HR 2.50 .75
H2 David Ortiz HR 2.50 .75
H3 Adam Dunn HR 2.50 .75
H4 Albert Pujols HR 5.00 1.50
H5 Manny Ramirez HR 2.50 .75
H6 Vladimir Guerrero HR 2.50 .75
H7 Miguel Tejada HR 2.50 .75
H8 Rafael Palmeiro HR 2.50 .75
H9 Mark Teixeira HR 2.50 .75
H10 Sammy Sosa HR 4.00 1.20
H11 Frank Thomas HR 2.50 .75
H12 Pat Burrell HR 2.50 .75
H13 Adrian Beltre HR 2.50 .75
H14 Miguel Cabrera HR 2.50 .75
H15 Gary Sheffield HR 2.50 .75
K1 Pedro Martinez K 4.00 1.20
K2 Randy Johnson K 4.00 1.20
K3 Mark Mulder K 4.00 1.20
K4 Barry Zito K 4.00 1.20
K5 Roger Clemens K 8.00 2.40
K6 Mark Prior K 4.00 1.20
K7 Ben Sheets K 4.00 1.20
K8 Curt Schilling K 4.00 1.20
K9 Billy Wagner K 4.00 1.20
K10 Eric Gagne K 4.00 1.20
K11 Josh Beckett K 4.00 1.20
K12 Kerry Wood K 4.00 1.20
K13 Jason Schmidt K 4.00 1.20
K14 Roy Halladay K 4.00 1.20
K15 Greg Maddux K 6.00 1.80
R1 Sean Casey RBI 2.50 .75
R2 Ivan Rodriguez RBI 2.50 .75
R3 Mike Piazza RBI 4.00 1.20
R4 Todd Helton RBI 2.50 .75
R5 Scott Rolen RBI 2.50 .75
R6 Hideki Matsui RBI 4.00 1.20
R7 Gary Sheffield RBI 2.50 .75
R8 Alfonso Soriano RBI 2.50 .75
R9 Bobby Abreu RBI 2.50 .75
R10 Lance Berkman RBI 2.50 .75
R11 Miguel Tejada RBI 2.50 .75
R12 Travis Hafner RBI 2.50 .75
R13 Hank Blalock RBI 2.50 .75
R14 Jeff Bagwell RBI 2.50 .75
R15 Chipper Jones RBI 2.50 .75

2005 Ultra Kings Jersey Gold

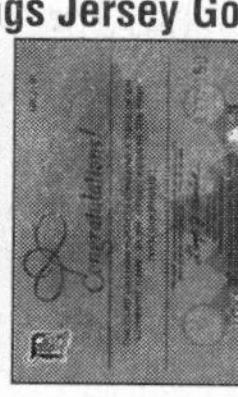

Nm-Mt Ex-Mt
STATED PRINT RUN 150 SERIAL #'d SETS
*ULTRA p/r 75: .5X TO 1.2X GOLD
*ULTRA p/r 38-55: .6X TO 1.5X GOLD
*ULTRA p/r 20-34: .75X TO 2X GOLD
*ULTRA p/r 15-17: 1X TO 2.5X GOLD
ULTRA PRINT RUN B/WN 5-75 #'d PER
NO ULTRA PRICING ON QTY 13 OR LESS
*PLATINUM: .6X TO 1.5X COPPER
*PLATINUM PATCH: ADD 100% PREMIUM
PLATINUM PRINT RUN 25 SERIAL #'d SETS
PLATINUM ISSUED ONLY IN HOBBY PACKS
OVERALL GU ODDS 1:12 HOB, 1:48 RET
AB Adrian Beltre HR 12.00 3.60
AD Adam Dunn HR 12.00 3.60
AP Albert Pujols HR 20.00 6.00
AS Alfonso Soriano RBI 12.00 3.60
BA Bobby Abreu RBI 10.00 3.00
BS Ben Sheets K 10.00 3.00
BW Billy Wagner K 10.00 3.00
BZ Barry Zito K 10.00 3.00
CJ Chipper Jones RBI 12.00 3.60
CS Curt Schilling K 12.00 3.60
DO David Ortiz HR 12.00 3.60
EG Eric Gagne K 12.00 3.60
FT Frank Thomas HR 12.00 3.60
GM Greg Maddux K 20.00 6.00
GSH Gary Sheffield HR 10.00 3.00
GSR Gary Sheffield RBI 10.00 3.00
HB Hank Blalock RBI 10.00 3.00
HM Hideki Matsui RBI 30.00 9.00
IR Ivan Rodriguez RBI 12.00 3.60
JBA Jeff Bagwell RBI 12.00 3.60
JBE Josh Beckett K 10.00 3.00
JS Jason Schmidt K 10.00 3.00
JT Jim Thome HR 12.00 3.60
KW Kerry Wood K 12.00 3.60
LB Lance Berkman RBI 10.00 3.00
MC Miguel Cabrera HR 12.00 3.60
MM Mark Mulder K 10.00 3.00
MPI Mike Piazza RBI 20.00 6.00
MPR Mark Prior K 12.00 3.60
MR Manny Ramirez HR 12.00 3.60
MTH Miguel Tejada HR 10.00 3.00
MTR Miguel Tejada RBI 10.00 3.00
MTX Mark Teixeira HR 10.00 3.00
PB Pat Burrell HR 10.00 3.00
PM Pedro Martinez K 12.00 3.60
RC Roger Clemens K 20.00 6.00
RH Roy Halladay K 10.00 3.00
RJ Randy Johnson K 12.00 3.60
RP Rafael Palmeiro HR 12.00 3.60
SC Sean Casey RBI 10.00 3.00
SR Scott Rolen RBI 12.00 3.60
SS Sammy Sosa HR 20.00 6.00
THA Travis Hafner RBI 10.00 3.00
THE Todd Helton RBI 12.00 3.60
VG Vladimir Guerrero HR 12.00 3.60

1989 Upper Deck

This attractive 800-card standard-size set was introduced in 1989 as the premier issue by the then-fledgling Upper Deck company. Unlike other 1989 releases, this set was issued in two separate series - a low series numbered 1-700 and a high series numbered 701-800. Cards were primarily issued in fin-wrapped low and high series foil packs, complete 800-card factory sets and 100-card high series factory sets. High series packs contained a mixture of both low and high series cards. Collectors should also note that many dealers consider that Upper Deck's "planned" production of 1,000,000 of each player was increased (perhaps even doubled) later in the year due to the explosion in popularity of the product. The cards feature slick paper stock, full color on both the front and the back and carry a hologram on the reverse to protect against counterfeiting. Subsets include Rookie Stars (1-26) and Collector's Choice art cards (668-693). The more significant variations involving changed photos or changed type are listed below. According to the company, the Murphy and Sheridan cards were corrected very early, after only two percent of the cards had been produced. Similarly, the Sheffield was corrected after 15 percent had been printed; Varsho, Gallego, and Schroeder were corrected after 20 percent; and Holton, Manrique, and Winningham were corrected 30 percent of the way through. Rookie Cards in the set include Jim Abbott, Sandy Alomar Jr., Dante Bichette, Craig Biggio, Steve Finley, Ken Griffey Jr., Randy Johnson, Gary Sheffield, John Smoltz and Todd Zeile. Cards with missing or duplicate holograms appear to be relatively common and are generally considered to be flawed copies that sell for substantial discounts.

Nm-Mt Ex-Mt
COMPLETE SET (800) 80.00 32.00
COMP.FACT.SET (800) 100.00 40.00
COMP.HI FACT.SET (100) 10.00 4.00
1 Ken Griffey Jr. RC 50.00 20.00
2 Luis Medina RC .25 .10
3 Tony Chance RC .25 .10
4 Dave Otto .25 .10
5 S.Alomar Jr. RC UER 1.00 .40
Born 6/16/66, should be 6/18/66
6 Rolando Roomes RC .25 .10
7 Dave West RC .25 .10
8 Cris Carpenter RC .25 .10
9 Gregg Jefferies .25 .10
10 Doug Dascenzo RC .25 .10
11 Ron Jones RC .25 .10
12 Luis DeLosSantos RC .25 .10
13 Gary Sheffield COR RC 6.00 2.40
13A G.Sheffield ERR RC 6.00 2.40
SS upside down on card front
14 Mike Harkey RC .25 .10
15 Lance Blankenship RC .25 .10
16 William Brennan RC .25 .10
17 John Smoltz RC 4.00 1.60
18 Ramon Martinez RC .50 .20
19 Mark Lemke RC 1.00 .40
20 Juan Bell RC .25 .10
21 Rey Palacios RC .25 .10
22 Felix Jose RC .25 .10
23 Van Snider RC .25 .10
24 Dante Bichette RC 1.00 .40
25 Randy Johnson RC 15.00 6.00
26 Carlos Quintana RC .25 .10
27 Star Rookie CL .25 .10
28 Mike Schooler .25 .10
29 Randy St.Claire .25 .10
30 Jerald Clark RC .25 .10
31 Kevin Gross .25 .10
32 Dan Firova .25 .10
33 Jeff Calhoun .25 .10
34 Tommy Hinzo .25 .10
35 Ricky Jordan RC .50 .20
36 Larry Parrish .25 .10
37 Bret Saberhagen UER .40 .16
Hit total 931, should be 1031
38 Mike Smithson .25 .10
39 Dave Dravecky .25 .10
40 Ed Romero .25 .10
41 Jeff Musselman .25 .10
42 Ed Hearn .25 .10
43 Rance Mulliniks .25 .10
44 Jim Eisenreich .25 .10
45 Sil Campusano .25 .10
46 Mike Krukow .25 .10
47 Paul Gibson .25 .10
48 Mark LaCoss .25 .10
49 Larry Herndon .25 .10
50 Scott Garrelts .25 .10
51 Dwayne Henry .25 .10
52 Jim Acker .25 .10
53 Steve Sax .25 .10
54 Pete O'Brien .25 .10
55 Paul Runge .25 .10
56 Rick Rhoden .25 .10
57 John Dopson .25 .10
58 Casey Candaele UER .25 .10
(No stats for Astros for '88 season)
59 Dave Righetti .40 .16
60 Joe Hesketh .25 .10
61 Frank DiPino .25 .10
62 Tim Laudner .25 .10
63 Jamie Moyer .40 .16
64 Fred Toliver .25 .10
65 Mitch Webster .25 .10
66 John Tudor .40 .16
67 John Cangelosi .25 .10
68 Mike Devereaux .25 .10
69 Brian Fisher .25 .10
70 Mike Marshall .25 .10
71 Zane Smith .25 .10
72A Brian Holton ERR 1.00 .40
(Photo actually Shawn Hillegas)
72B Brian Holton COR .40 .16
73 Jose Guzman .25 .10
74 Rick Mahler .25 .10
75 John Shelby .25 .10
76 Jim Deshaies .25 .10
77 Bobby Meacham .25 .10
78 Bryn Smith .25 .10
79 Joaquin Andujar .40 .16
80 Richard Dotson .25 .10
81 Charlie Lea .25 .10
82 Calvin Schiraldi .25 .10
83 Les Straker .25 .10
84 Les Lancaster .25 .10
85 Allan Anderson .25 .10
86 Junior Ortiz .25 .10
87 Jesse Orosco .25 .10
88 Felix Fermin .25 .10
89 Dave Anderson .25 .10
90 Rafael Belliard UER .25 .10
(Born '61, not '51)
91 Franklin Stubbs .25 .10
92 Cecil Espy .25 .10
93 Albert Hall .25 .10
94 Tim Leary .25 .10
95 Mitch Williams .25 .10
96 Tracy Jones .25 .10
97 Danny Darwin .25 .10
98 Gary Ward .25 .10
99 Neal Heaton .25 .10
100 Jim Pankovits .25 .10
101 Bill Doran .25 .10
102 Tim Wallach .25 .10
103 Joe Magrane .25 .10
104 Ozzie Virgil .25 .10
105 Alvin Davis .25 .10
106 Tom Brookens .25 .10
107 Shawon Dunston .25 .10
108 Tracy Woodson .25 .10
109 Nelson Liriano .25 .10
110 Devon White UER .40 .16
(Doubles total 46, should be 56)
111 Steve Balboni .25 .10
112 Buddy Bell .40 .16
113 German Jimenez .25 .10
114 Ken Dayley .25 .10
115 Andres Galarraga .40 .16
116 Mike Scioscia .40 .16
117 Gary Pettis .25 .10
118 Ernie Whitt .25 .10
119 Bob Boone .40 .16
120 Ryne Sandberg 1.50 .60
121 Bruce Benedict .25 .10
122 Hubie Brooks .25 .10
123 Mike Moore .25 .10
124 Wallace Johnson .25 .10
125 Bob Horner .40 .16
126 Chili Davis .40 .16
127 Manny Trillo .25 .10
128 Chet Lemon .40 .16
129 John Cerutti .25 .10
130 Orel Hershiser .40 .16
131 Terry Pendleton .40 .16
132 Jeff Blauser .25 .10
133 Mike Fitzgerald .25 .10
134 Henry Cotto .25 .10
135 Gerald Young .25 .10
136 Luis Salazar .25 .10
137 Alejandro Pena .25 .10
138 Jack Howell .25 .10
139 Tony Fernandez .25 .10
140 Mark Grace 1.00 .40
141 Ken Caminiti .40 .16
142 Mike Jackson .25 .10
143 Larry McWilliams .25 .10
144 Andres Thomas .25 .10
145 Nolan Ryan 3X 4.00 1.60
146 Mike Davis .25 .10
147 DeWayne Buice .25 .10
148 Jody Davis .25 .10
149 Jesse Barfield .40 .16
150 Matt Nokes .25 .10
151 Jerry Reuss .25 .10
152 Rick Cerone .25 .10
153 Storm Davis .25 .10
154 Marvell Wynne .25 .10
155 Will Clark 1.00 .40
156 Luis Aguayo .25 .10
157 Willie Upshaw .25 .10
158 Randy Bush .25 .10
159 Ron Darling .25 .10
160 Kal Daniels .25 .10
161 Spike Owen .25 .10
162 Luis Polonia .25 .10
163 Kevin Mitchell UER .40 .16
('88/total HR's 18/52, should be 19/53)
164 Dave Gallagher .25 .10
165 Benito Santiago .40 .16
166 Greg Gagne .25 .10
167 Ken Phelps .25 .10
168 Sid Fernandez .25 .10
169 Bo Diaz .25 .10
170 Cory Snyder .25 .10
171 Eric Show .25 .10
172 Robby Thompson .25 .10
173 Marty Barrett .25 .10
174 Dave Henderson .25 .10
175 Ozzie Guillen .25 .10
176 Barry Lyons .25 .10
177 Kelvin Torve .25 .10
178 Don Slaught .25 .10
179 Steve Lombardozzi .25 .10
180 Chris Sabo RC 1.00 .40
181 Jose Uribe .25 .10
182 Shane Mack .25 .10
183 Ron Karkovice .25 .10
184 Todd Benzinger .25 .10
185 Dave Stewart .40 .16
186 Julio Franco .40 .16
187 Ron Robinson .25 .10
188 Wally Backman .25 .10
189 Randy Velarde .25 .10
190 Joe Carter .40 .16
191 Bob Welch .40 .16
192 Kelly Paris .25 .10
193 Chris Brown .25 .10
194 Rick Reuschel .40 .16
195 Roger Clemens 2.00 .80
196 Dave Concepcion .40 .16
197 Al Newman .25 .10
198 Brook Jacoby .25 .10
199 Mookie Wilson .40 .16
200 Don Mattingly 2.50 1.00
201 Dick Schofield .25 .10
202 Mark Gubicza .25 .10
203 Gary Gaetti .40 .16
204 Dan Pasqua .25 .10
205 Andre Dawson .40 .16
206 Chris Speier .25 .10
207 Kent Tekulve .25 .10
208 Rod Scurry .25 .10
209 Scott Bailes .25 .10
210 R.Henderson UER 1.00 .40
Throws Right
211 Harold Baines .40 .16
212 Tony Armas .40 .16
213 Kent Hrbek .40 .16
214 Darrin Jackson .25 .10
215 George Brett 2.50 1.00
216 Rafael Santana .25 .10
217 Andy Allanson .25 .10
218 Brett Butler .40 .16
219 Steve Jeltz .25 .10
220 Jay Buhner .40 .16
221 Bo Jackson 1.00 .40
222 Angel Salazar .25 .10
223 Kirk McCaskill .25 .10
224 Steve Lyons .25 .10
225 Bert Blyleven .40 .16
226 Scott Bradley .25 .10
227 Bob Melvin .25 .10
228 Ron Kittle .25 .10
229 Phil Bradley .25 .10
230 Tommy John .40 .16
231 Greg Walker .25 .10
232 Juan Berenguer .25 .10
233 Pat Tabler .25 .10
234 Terry Clark .25 .10
235 Rafael Palmeiro 1.00 .40
236 Paul Zuvella .25 .10
237 Willie Randolph .40 .16
238 Bruce Fields .25 .10
239 Mike Aldrete .25 .10
240 Lance Parrish .40 .16
241 Greg Maddux 2.50 1.00
242 John Moses .25 .10
243 Melido Perez .25 .10
244 Willie Wilson .40 .16
245 Mark McLemore .40 .16
246 Von Hayes .25 .10
247 Matt Williams 1.00 .40
248 John Candelaria UER .25 .10
Listed as Yankee for part of '87, should be Mets
249 Harold Reynolds .40 .16
250 Greg Swindell .25 .10
251 Juan Agosto .25 .10
252 Mike Felder .25 .10
253 Vince Coleman .25 .10
254 Larry Sheets .25 .10
255 George Bell .40 .16
256 Terry Steinbach .40 .16
257 Jack Armstrong RC .50 .20
258 Dickie Thon .25 .10
259 Ray Knight .40 .16
260 Darryl Strawberry .40 .16
261 Doug Sisk .25 .10
262 Alex Trevino .25 .10
263 Jeffrey Leonard .25 .10
264 Tom Henke .25 .10
265 Ozzie Smith 1.50 .60
266 Dave Bergman .25 .10
267 Tony Phillips .25 .10
268 Mark Davis .25 .10
269 Kevin Elster .25 .10
270 Barry Larkin .60 .24
271 Manny Lee .25 .10
272 Tom Brunansky .25 .10
273 Craig Biggio RC 3.00 1.20
274 Jim Gantner .25 .10
275 Eddie Murray 1.00 .40
276 Jeff Reed .25 .10
277 Tim Teufel .25 .10
278 Rick Honeycutt .25 .10
279 Guillermo Hernandez .25 .10
280 John Kruk .40 .16
281 Luis Alicea RC .50 .20
282 Jim Clancy .25 .10
283 Billy Ripken .25 .10
284 Craig Reynolds .25 .10

285 Robin Yount 1.50 .60
286 Jimmy Jones .25 .10
287 Ron Oester .25 .10
288 Terry Leach .25 .10
289 Dennis Eckersley .60 .24
290 Alan Trammell .40 .16
291 Jimmy Key .40 .16
292 Chris Bosio .25 .10
293 Jose DeLeon .25 .10
294 Jim Traber .25 .10
295 Mike Scott .40 .16
296 Roger McDowell .25 .10
297 Garry Templeton .40 .16
298 Doyle Alexander .25 .10
299 Nick Esasky .25 .10
300 Mark McGwire UER 5.00 2.00
(Doubles total 52,
should be 51)
301 Darryl Hamilton RC .50 .20
302 Dave Smith .25 .10
303 Rick Sutcliffe .40 .16
304 Dave Stapleton .25 .10
305 Alan Ashby .25 .10
306 Pedro Guerrero .40 .16
307 Ron Guidry .40 .16
308 Steve Farr .25 .10
309 Curt Ford .25 .10
310 Claudell Washington .25 .10
311 Tom Prince .25 .10
312 Chad Kreuter RC .50 .20
313 Ken Oberkfell .25 .10
314 Jerry Browne .25 .10
315 R.J. Reynolds .25 .10
316 Scott Bankhead .25 .10
317 Milt Thompson .25 .10
318 Mario Diaz .25 .10
319 Bruce Ruffin .25 .10
320 Dave Valle .25 .10
321A Gary Varsho ERR 2.00 .80
(Back photo actually
Mike Bielecki bunting)
321B Gary Varsho COR .25 .10
(In road uniform)
322 Paul Mirabella .25 .10
323 Chuck Jackson .25 .10
324 Drew Hall .25 .10
325 Don August .25 .10
326 Israel Sanchez .25 .10
327 Denny Walling .25 .10
328 Joel Skinner .25 .10
329 Danny Tartabull .25 .10
330 Tony Pena .25 .10
331 Jim Sundberg .40 .16
332 Jeff D. Robinson .25 .10
333 Oddibe McDowell .25 .10
334 Jose Lind .25 .10
335 Paul Kilgus .25 .10
336 Juan Samuel .25 .10
337 Mike Campbell .25 .10
338 Mike Maddux .25 .10
339 Darnell Coles .25 .10
340 Bob Dernier .25 .10
341 Rafael Ramirez .25 .10
342 Scott Sanderson .25 .10
343 B.J. Surhoff .40 .16
344 Billy Hatcher .25 .10
345 Pat Perry .25 .10
346 Jack Clark .40 .16
347 Gary Thurman .25 .10
348 Tim Jones .25 .10
349 Dave Winfield .40 .16
350 Frank White .40 .16
351 Dave Collins .25 .10
352 Jack Morris .40 .16
353 Eric Plunk .25 .10
354 Leon Durham .25 .10
355 Ivan DeJesus .25 .10
356 Brian Holman RC .25 .10
357A Dale Murphy ERR 30.00 12.00
(Front has
reverse negative)
357B Dale Murphy COR .60 .24
358 Mark Portugal .25 .10
359 Andy McGaffigan .25 .10
360 Tom Glavine 1.00 .40
361 Keith Moreland .25 .10
362 Todd Stottlemyre .25 .10
363 Dave Leiper .25 .10
364 Cecil Fielder .40 .16
365 Carmelo Martinez .25 .10
366 Dwight Evans .40 .16
367 Kevin McReynolds .25 .10
368 Rich Gedman .25 .10
369 Len Dykstra .40 .16
370 Jody Reed .25 .10
371 Jose Canseco UER 1.00 .40
(Strikeout total 391,
should be 491)
372 Rob Murphy .25 .10
373 Mike Henneman .25 .10
374 Walt Weiss .25 .10
375 Rob Dibble RC 1.50 .60
376 Kirby Puckett 1.00 .40
(Mark McGwire
in background)
377 Dennis Martinez .40 .16
378 Ron Gant .40 .16
379 Brian Harper .25 .10
380 Nelson Santovenia .25 .10
381 Lloyd Moseby .25 .10
382 Lance McCullers .25 .10
383 Dave Stieb .40 .16
384 Tony Gwynn 1.25 .50
385 Mike Flanagan .25 .10
386 Bob Ojeda .25 .10
387 Bruce Hurst .25 .10
388 Dave Magadan .25 .10
389 Wade Boggs .60 .24
390 Gary Carter .40 .16
391 Frank Tanana .40 .16
392 Curt Young .25 .10
393 Jeff Treadway .25 .10
394 Darrell Evans .40 .16
395 Glenn Hubbard .25 .10
396 Chuck Cary .25 .10
397 Frank Viola .40 .16
398 Jeff Parrett .25 .10
399 Terry Blocker .25 .10
400 Dan Gladden .25 .10
401 Louie Meadows .25 .10
402 Tim Raines .40 .16
403 Joey Meyer .25 .10
404 Larry Andersen .25 .10
405 Rex Hudler .25 .10
406 Mike Schmidt 2.00 .80
407 John Franco .40 .16
408 Brady Anderson RC 1.00 .40
409 Don Carman .25 .10
410 Eric Davis .40 .16
411 Bob Stanley .25 .10
412 Pete Smith .25 .10
413 Jim Rice .40 .16
414 Bruce Sutter .40 .16
415 Oil Can Boyd .25 .10
416 Ruben Sierra .25 .10
417 Mike LaValliere .25 .10
418 Steve Buechele .25 .10
419 Gary Redus .25 .10
420 Scott Fletcher .25 .10
421 Dale Sveum .25 .10
422 Bob Knepper .25 .10
423 Luis Rivera .25 .10
424 Ted Higuera .25 .10
425 Kevin Bass .25 .10
426 Ken Gerhart .25 .10
427 Shane Rawley .25 .10
428 Paul O'Neill .60 .24
429 Joe Orsulak .25 .10
430 Jackie Gutierrez .25 .10
431 Gerald Perry .25 .10
432 Mike Greenwell .25 .10
433 Jerry Royster .25 .10
434 Ellis Burks .40 .16
435 Ed Olwine .25 .10
436 Dave Rucker .25 .10
437 Charlie Hough .40 .16
438 Bob Walk .25 .10
439 Bob Brower .25 .10
440 Barry Bonds 5.00 2.00
441 Tom Foley .25 .10
442 Rob Deer .25 .10
443 Glenn Davis .25 .10
444 Dave Martinez .25 .10
445 Bill Wegman .25 .10
446 Lloyd McClendon .25 .10
447 Dave Schmidt .25 .10
448 Darren Daulton .40 .16
449 Frank Williams .25 .10
450 Don Aase .25 .10
451 Lou Whitaker .40 .16
452 Rich Gossage .40 .16
453 Ed Whitson .25 .10
454 Jim Walewander .25 .10
455 Damon Berryhill .25 .10
456 Tim Burke .25 .10
457 Barry Jones .25 .10
458 Joel Youngblood .25 .10
459 Floyd Youmans .25 .10
460 Mark Salas .25 .10
461 Jeff Russell .25 .10
462 Darrell Miller .25 .10
463 Jeff Kunkel .25 .10
464 Sherman Corbett .25 .10
465 Curtis Wilkerson .25 .10
466 Bud Black .25 .10
467 Cal Ripken 3.00 1.20
468 John Farrell .25 .10
469 Terry Kennedy .25 .10
470 Tom Candiotti .25 .10
471 Roberto Alomar 1.00 .40
472 Jeff M. Robinson .25 .10
473 Vance Law .25 .10
474 Randy Ready UER .25 .10
(Strikeout total 136,
should be 115)
475 Walt Terrell .25 .10
476 Kelly Downs .25 .10
477 Johnny Paredes .25 .10
478 Shawn Hillegas .25 .10
479 Bob Brenly .25 .10
480 Otis Nixon .25 .10
481 Johnny Ray .25 .10
482 Geno Petralli .25 .10
483 Stu Cliburn .25 .10
484 Pete Incaviglia .25 .10
485 Brian Downing .40 .16
486 Jeff Stone .25 .10
487 Carmen Castillo .25 .10
488 Tom Niedenfuer .25 .10
489 Jay Bell .40 .16
490 Rick Schu .25 .10
491 Jeff Pico .25 .10
492 Mark Parent .25 .10
493 Eric King .25 .10
494 Al Nipper .25 .10
495 Andy Hawkins .25 .10
496 Daryl Boston .25 .10
497 Ernie Riles .25 .10
498 Pascual Perez .25 .10
499 Bill Long UER .25 .10
(Games started total
70, should be 44)
500 Kirt Manwaring .25 .10
501 Chuck Crim .25 .10
502 Candy Maldonado .25 .10
503 Dennis Lamp .25 .10
504 Glenn Braggs .25 .10
505 Joe Price .25 .10
506 Ken Williams .25 .10
507 Bill Pecota .25 .10
508 Rey Quinones .25 .10
509 Jeff Bittiger .25 .10
510 Kevin Seitzer .25 .10
511 Steve Bedrosian .25 .10
512 Todd Worrell .25 .10
513 Chris James .25 .10
514 Jose Oquendo .25 .10
515 David Palmer .25 .10
516 John Smiley .25 .10
517 Dave Clark .25 .10
518 Mike Dunne .25 .10
519 Ron Washington .25 .10
520 Bob Kipper .25 .10
521 Lee Smith .40 .16
522 Juan Castillo .25 .10
523 Don Robinson .25 .10
524 Kevin Romine .25 .10
525 Paul Molitor .60 .24
526 Mark Langston .25 .10
527 Donnie Hill .25 .10
528 Larry Owen .25 .10
529 Jerry Reed .25 .10
530 Jack McDowell .40 .16
531 Greg Mathews .25 .10
532 John Russell .25 .10
533 Dan Quisenberry .25 .10
534 Greg Gross .25 .10
535 Danny Cox .25 .10
536 Terry Francona .40 .16
537 Andy Van Slyke .40 .16
538 Mel Hall .25 .10
539 Jim Gott .25 .10
540 Doug Jones .25 .10
541 Craig Lefferts .25 .10
542 Mike Boddicker .25 .10
543 Greg Brock .25 .10
544 Atlee Hammaker .25 .10
545 Tom Bolton .25 .10
546 Mike Macfarlane RC .50 .20
547 Rich Renteria .25 .10
548 John Davis .25 .10
549 Floyd Bannister .25 .10
550 Mickey Brantley .25 .10
551 Duane Ward .25 .10
552 Dan Petry .25 .10
553 Mickey Tettleton UER .25 .10
(Walks total 175,
should be 136)
554 Rick Leach .25 .10
555 Mike Witt .25 .10
556 Sid Bream .25 .10
557 Bobby Witt .25 .10
558 Tommy Herr .25 .10
559 Randy Milligan .25 .10
560 Jose Cecena .25 .10
561 Mackey Sasser .25 .10
562 Carney Lansford .40 .16
563 Rick Aguilera .25 .10
564 Ron Hassey .25 .10
565 Dwight Gooden .40 .16
566 Paul Assenmacher .25 .10
567 Neil Allen .25 .10
568 Jim Morrison .25 .10
569 Mike Pagliarulo .25 .10
570 Ted Simmons .40 .16
571 Mark Thurmond .25 .10
572 Fred McGriff .60 .24
573 Wally Joyner .40 .16
574 Jose Bautista RC .25 .10
575 Kelly Gruber .25 .10
576 Cecilio Guante .25 .10
577 Mark Davidson .25 .10
578 Bobby Bonilla UER .40 .16
(Total steals 2 in '87,
should be 3)
579 Mike Stanley .25 .10
580 Gene Larkin .25 .10
581 Stan Javier .25 .10
582 Howard Johnson .40 .16
583A Mike Gallego ERR 1.00 .40
(Front reversed
negative)
583B Mike Gallego COR 1.00 .40
584 David Cone .40 .16
585 Doug Jennings .25 .10
586 Charles Hudson .25 .10
587 Dion James .25 .10
588 Al Leiter 1.00 .40
589 Charlie Puleo .25 .10
590 Roberto Kelly .25 .10
591 Thad Bosley .25 .10
592 Pete Stanicek .25 .10
593 Pat Borders RC .50 .20
594 Bryan Harvey RC .50 .20
595 Jeff Ballard .25 .10
596 Jeff Reardon .40 .16
597 Doug Drabek .25 .10
598 Edwin Correa .25 .10
599 Keith Atherton .25 .10
600 Dave LaPoint .25 .10
601 Don Baylor .40 .16
602 Tom Pagnozzi .25 .10
603 Tim Flannery .25 .10
604 Gene Walter .25 .10
605 Dave Parker .40 .16
606 Mike Diaz .25 .10
607 Chris Gwynn .25 .10
608 Odell Jones .25 .10
609 Carlton Fisk .60 .24
610 Jay Howell .25 .10
611 Tim Crews .25 .10
612 Keith Hernandez .40 .16
613 Willie Fraser .25 .10
614 Jim Eppard .25 .10
615 Jeff Hamilton .25 .10
616 Kurt Stillwell .25 .10
617 Tom Browning .25 .10
618 Jeff Montgomery .25 .10
619 Jose Rijo .40 .16
620 Jamie Quirk .25 .10
621 Willie McGee .40 .16
622 Mark Grant UER .25 .10
(Glove on wrong hand)
623 Bill Swift .25 .10
624 Orlando Mercado .25 .10
625 John Costello .25 .10
626 Jose Gonzalez .25 .10
627A Bill Schroeder ERR .60 .24
(Back photo actually
Ronn Reynolds buckling
shin guards)
627B Bill Schroeder COR .60 .24
628A Fred Manrique ERR .60 .24
(Back photo actually
Ozzie Guillen throwing)
628B Fred Manrique COR .25 .10
(Swinging bat on back)
629 Ricky Horton .25 .10
630 Dan Plesac .25 .10
631 Alfredo Griffin .25 .10
632 Chuck Finley .40 .16
633 Kirk Gibson .40 .16
634 Randy Myers .40 .16
635 Greg Minton .25 .10
636A Herm Winningham 1.00 .40
ERR (W1nningham
on back)
636B H.Winningham COR .25 .10
637 Charlie Leibrandt .25 .10
638 Tim Birtsas .25 .10
639 Bill Buckner .40 .16
640 Danny Jackson .25 .10
641 Greg Booker .25 .10
642 Jim Presley .25 .10
643 Gene Nelson .25 .10
644 Rod Booker .25 .10
645 Dennis Rasmussen .25 .10
646 Juan Nieves .25 .10
647 Bobby Thigpen .25 .10
648 Tim Belcher .25 .10
649 Mike Young .25 .10
650 Ivan Calderon .25 .10
651 Oswald Peraza .25 .10
652A Pat Sheridan ERR 15.00 6.00
(No position on front)
652B Pat Sheridan COR .25 .10
653 Mike Morgan .25 .10
654 Mike Heath .25 .10
655 Jay Tibbs .25 .10
656 Fernando Valenzuela .40 .16
657 Lee Mazzilli .40 .16
658 Frank Viola AL CY .25 .10
659A J.Canseco AL MVP .60 .24
Eagle logo in black
659B J.Canseco AL MVP .60 .24
Eagle logo in blue
660 Walt Weiss AL ROY .25 .10
661 Orel Hershiser NL CY .25 .10
662 Kirk Gibson NL MVP .40 .16
663 Chris Sabo NL ROY .40 .16
664 Dennis Eckersley .40 .16
ALCS MVP
665 Orel Hershiser .40 .16
NLCS MVP
666 Kirk Gibson WS 1.00 .40
667 O.Hershiser WS MVP .25 .10
668 Wally Joyner TC .25 .10
669 Nolan Ryan TC 1.25 .50
670 Jose Canseco TC .60 .24
671 Fred McGriff TC .40 .16
672 Dale Murphy TC .40 .16
673 Paul Molitor TC .40 .16
674 Ozzie Smith TC 1.00 .40
675 Ryne Sandberg TC 1.00 .40
676 Kirk Gibson TC .25 .10
677 Andres Galarraga TC .25 .10
678 Will Clark TC .40 .16
679 Cory Snyder TC .25 .10
680 Alvin Davis TC .25 .10
681 Darryl Strawberry TC .25 .10
682 Cal Ripken TC 1.00 .40
683 Tony Gwynn TC .60 .24
684 Mike Schmidt TC 1.00 .40
685 A.Van Slyke TC UER .25 .10
96 Junior Ortiz
686 Ruben Sierra TC .25 .10
687 Wade Boggs TC .40 .16
688 Eric Davis TC .25 .10
689 George Brett TC 1.00 .40
690 Alan Trammell TC .25 .10
691 Frank Viola TC .25 .10
692 Harold Baines TC .25 .10
693 Don Mattingly TC 1.00 .40
694 Checklist 1-100 .25 .10
695 Checklist 101-200 .25 .10
696 Checklist 201-300 .25 .10
697 Checklist 301-400 .25 .10
698 CL 401-500 UER .25 .10
467 Cal Ripkin Jr.
699 CL 501-600 UER .25 .10
543 Greg Booker
700 Checklist 601-700 .25 .10
701 Checklist 701-800 .25 .10
702 Jesse Barfield .40 .16
703 Walt Terrell .25 .10
704 Dickie Thon .25 .10
705 Al Leiter 1.00 .40
706 Dave LaPoint .25 .10
707 Charlie Hayes RC .50 .20
708 Andy Hawkins .25 .10
709 Mickey Hatcher .25 .10
710 Lance McCullers .25 .10
711 Ron Kittle .25 .10
712 Bert Blyleven .40 .16
713 Rick Dempsey .25 .10
714 Ken Williams .25 .10
715 Steve Rosenberg .25 .10
716 Joe Skalski .25 .10
717 Spike Owen .25 .10
718 Todd Burns .25 .10
719 Kevin Gross .25 .10
720 Tommy Herr .25 .10
721 Rob Ducey .25 .10
722 Gary Green .25 .10
723 Gregg Olson RC .50 .20
724 Greg W. Harris RC .25 .10
725 Craig Worthington .25 .10
726 Tom Howard RC .25 .10
727 Dale Mohorcic .25 .10
728 Rich Yett .25 .10
729 Mel Hall .25 .10
730 Floyd Youmans .25 .10
731 Lonnie Smith .25 .10
732 Wally Backman .25 .10
733 Trevor Wilson RC .25 .10
734 Jose Alvarez RC .25 .10
735 Bob Milacki .25 .10
736 Tom Gordon RC 1.00 .40
737 Wally Whitehurst RC .25 .10
738 Mike Aldrete .25 .10
739 Keith Miller .25 .10
740 Randy Milligan .25 .10
741 Jeff Parrett .25 .10
742 Steve Finley RC 1.50 .60
743 Junior Felix RC .25 .10
744 Pete Harnisch RC .50 .20
745 Bill Spiers RC .50 .20
746 Hensley Meulens RC .25 .10
747 Juan Bell RC .25 .10
748 Steve Sax .25 .10
749 Phil Bradley .25 .10
750 Rey Quinones .25 .10
751 Tommy Gregg .25 .10
752 Kevin Brown 1.00 .40
753 Derek Lilliquist RC .25 .10
754 Todd Zeile RC 1.00 .40
755 Jim Abbott RC 1.50 .60
Triple exposure
756 Ozzie Canseco .25 .10
757 Nick Esasky .25 .10
758 Mike Moore .25 .10
759 Rob Murphy .25 .10
760 Rick Mahler .25 .10
761 Fred Lynn .40 .16
762 Kevin Blankenship .25 .10
763 Eddie Murray 1.00 .40
764 Steve Searcy .25 .10
765 Jerome Walton RC .50 .20
766 Erik Hanson RC .50 .20
767 Bob Boone .40 .16
768 Edgar Martinez 1.00 .40
769 Jose DeJesus .25 .10
770 Greg Briley .25 .10
771 Steve Peters .25 .10
772 Rafael Palmeiro 1.00 .40
773 Jack Clark .40 .16
774 Nolan Ryan 4.00 1.60
(Throwing football)
775 Lance Parrish .40 .16
776 Joe Girardi RC 1.00 .40
777 Willie Randolph .40 .16
778 Mitch Williams .25 .10
779 Dennis Cook RC .50 .20
780 Dwight Smith RC .50 .20
781 Lenny Harris RC .50 .20
782 Torey Lovullo RC .25 .10
783 Norm Charlton RC .50 .20
784 Chris Brown .25 .10
785 Todd Benzinger .25 .10
786 Shane Rawley .25 .10
787 Omar Vizquel RC 2.00 .80
788 LaVel Freeman .25 .10
789 Jeffrey Leonard .25 .10
790 Eddie Williams .25 .10
791 Jamie Moyer .40 .16
792 Bruce Hurst UER .25 .10
(Workd Series)
793 Julio Franco .40 .16
794 Claudell Washington .25 .10
795 Jody Davis .25 .10
796 Oddibe McDowell .25 .10
797 Paul Kilgus .25 .10
798 Tracy Jones .25 .10
799 Steve Wilson .25 .10
800 Pete O'Brien .25 .10

1990 Upper Deck

The 1990 Upper Deck set contains 800 standard-size cards issued in two series, low numbers (1-700) and high numbers (701-800). Cards were distributed in fin-wrapped low and high series foil packs, complete 800-card factory sets and 100-card high series factory sets. High series foil packs contained a mixture of low and high series cards. The front and back borders are white, and both sides feature full-color photos. The horizontally oriented backs have recent stats and anti-counterfeiting holograms. Team checklist cards are mixed in with the first 100 cards of the set. Rookie Cards in the set include Juan Gonzalez, David Justice, Ray Lankford, Dean Palmer, Sammy Sosa and Larry Walker. The high series contains a Nolan Ryan variation; all cards produced before August 12th only discuss Ryan's sixth no-hitter while the later-issue cards include a stripe honoring Ryan's 300th victory. Card 702 (Rookie Threats) was originally scheduled to be Mike Witt. A few Witt cards with 702 on back and checklist cards showing Witt as 702 escaped into early packs; they are characterized by a black rectangle covering much of the card's back.

	Nm-Mt	Ex-Mt
COMPLETE SET (800)	25.00	7.50
COMP.FACT.SET (800)	25.00	7.50
COMPLETE LO SET (700)	25.00	7.50
COMPLETE HI SET (100)	5.00	1.50
COMP.HI FACT.SET (100)	4.00	1.20

1 Star Rookie Checklist .10 .03
2 Randy Nosek .10 .03
3 Tom Drees UER .10 .03
(11th line, hulred,
should be hurled
4 Curt Young .10 .03
5 Devon White TC .10 .03
6 Luis Salazar .10 .03
7 Von Hayes TC .10 .03
8 Jose Bautista .10 .03
9 Marquis Grissom RC .50 .15
10 Orel Hershiser TC .10 .03
11 Rick Aguilera .20 .06
12 Benito Santiago TC .10 .03
13 Deion Sanders .50 .15
14 Marvell Wynne .10 .03
15 Dave West .10 .03
16 Bobby Bonilla TC .10 .03
17 Sammy Sosa RC 5.00 1.50
18 Steve Sax TC .10 .03
19 Jack Howell .10 .03
20 Mike Schmidt Special 1.00 .30
UER (Suprising,
should be surprising)
21 Robin Ventura UER .50 .15
(Samta Maria)
22 Brian Meyer .10 .03
23 Blaine Beatty .10 .03
24 Ken Griffey Jr. TC .60 .18
25 Greg Vaughn UER .10 .03
(Association misspelled
as assiocation)
26 Xavier Hernandez RC .10 .03
27 Jason Grimsley RC .10 .03
28 Eric Anthony RC UER .10 .03
(Ashville, should
be Asheville)
29 Tim Raines TC UER .10 .03
(Wallach listed before Walker)

30 David Wells .20 .06
31 Hal Morris .10 .03
32 Bo Jackson TC .20 .06
33 Kelly Mann .10 .03
34 Nolan Ryan Special 1.00 .30
35 Scott Service UER .10 .03
(Born Cincinnati on
7/27/67, should be
Cincinnati 2/27)
36 Mark McGwire TC .60 .18
37 Tino Martinez .50 .15
38 Chili Davis .20 .06
39 Scott Sanderson .10 .03
40 Kevin Mitchell TC .10 .03
41 Lou Whitaker TC .10 .03
42 Scott Coolbaugh UER .10 .03
(Definately) RC
43 Jose Cano UER .10 .03
(Born 9/7/62, should
be 3/7/62)
44 Jose Vizcaino RC .25 .07
45 Bob Hamelin RC .25 .07
46 Jose Offerman RC UER .25 .07
(Posesses)
47 Kevin Blankenship .10 .03
48 Kirby Puckett TC .30 .09
49 Tommy Greene RC UER .10 .03
(Livest, should be
liveliest)
50 Will Clark Special .20 .06
UER (Perenial, should
be perennial)
51 Rob Nelson .10 .03
52 C.Hammond RC UER .10 .03
Chatanooga
53 Joe Carter TC .10 .03
54A B.McDonald RC ERR 2.00 .60
No Rookie designation
on card front
54B B.McDonald COR RC .25 .07
55 Andy Benes UER .20 .06
(Whichita)
56 John Olerud RC .75 .23
57 Roger Clemens TC .50 .15
58 Tony Armas .10 .03
59 George Canale .10 .03
60A Mickey Tettleton TC 2.00 .60
ERR (683 Jamie Weston)
60B Mickey Tettleton TC .10 .03
COR (683 Mickey Weston)
61 Mike Stanton RC .25 .07
62 Dwight Gooden TC .10 .03
63 Kent Mercker RC UER .25 .07
(Albuguerque)
64 Francisco Cabrera .10 .03
65 Steve Avery UER .10 .03
(Born NJ, should be MI,
Merker should be Mercker
66 Jose Canseco .50 .15
67 Matt Merullo .10 .03
68 Vince Coleman TC UER .10 .03
(Guerrero)
69 Ron Karkovice .10 .03
70 Kevin Maas RC .25 .07
71 Dennis Cook UER .10 .03
(Shown with righty
glove on card back)
72 Juan Gonzalez RC UER 2.50 .75
(135 games for Tulsa
in '89, should be 133)
73 Andre Dawson TC .10 .03
74 Dean Palmer RC UER .25 .07
(Permanent misspelled
as perminant)
75 Bo Jackson Special .20 .06
UER (Monsterous,
should be monstrous)
76 Rob Richie .10 .03
77 Bobby Rose UER .10 .03
(Pickin, should
be pick in)
78 Brian DuBois UER .10 .03
(Commiting)
79 Ozzie Guillen TC .10 .03
80 Gene Nelson .10 .03
81 Bob McClure .10 .03
82 Julio Franco TC .10 .03
83 Greg Minton .10 .03
84 John Smoltz TC UER .30 .09
(Oddibe not Odibbe)
85 Willie Fraser .10 .03
86 Neal Heaton .10 .03
87 Kevin Tapani RC UER .25 .07
(24th line has excpet,
should be except)
88 Mike Scott TC .10 .03
89A Jim Gott ERR 2.00 .60
(Photo actually
Rick Reed)
89B Jim Gott COR .10 .03
90 Lance Johnson .10 .03
91 Robin Yount TC UER .50 .15
(Checklist on back has
178 Rob Deer and
176 Mike Felder)
92 Jeff Parrett .10 .03
93 Julio Machado UER .10 .03
(Valenzuelan, should
be Venezuelan)
94 Ron Jones .10 .03
95 George Bell TC .10 .03
96 Jerry Reuss .10 .03
97 Brian Fisher .10 .03
98 Kevin Ritz UER .10 .03
(Amercian)
99 Barry Larkin TC .20 .06
100 Checklist 1-100 .10 .03
101 Gerald Perry .10 .03
102 Kevin Appier .20 .06
103 Julio Franco .20 .06
104 Craig Biggio .30 .09
105 Bo Jackson UER .50 .15
('89 BA wrong,
should be .256)
106 Junior Felix .10 .03
107 Mike Harkey .10 .03
108 Fred McGriff .50 .15
109 Rick Sutcliffe .20 .06
110 Pete O'Brien .10 .03
111 Kelly Gruber .10 .03
112 Dwight Evans .20 .06
113 Pat Borders .10 .03
114 Dwight Gooden .20 .06
115 Kevin Batiste .10 .03
116 Eric Davis .20 .06
117 Kevin Mitchell UER .10 .03
(Career HR total 99,
should be 100)
118 Ron Oester .10 .03
119 Brett Butler .20 .06
120 Danny Jackson .10 .03
121 Tommy Gregg .10 .03
122 Ken Caminiti .20 .06
123 Kevin Brown .20 .06
124 George Brett UER 1.25 .35
(133 runs, should
be 1300)
125 Mike Scott .10 .03
126 Cory Snyder .10 .03
127 George Bell .10 .03
128 Mark Grace .30 .09
129 Devon White .20 .06
130 Tony Fernandez .10 .03
131 Don Aase .10 .03
132 Rance Mulliniks .10 .03
133 Marty Barrett .10 .03
134 Nelson Liriano .10 .03
135 Mark Carreon .10 .03
136 Candy Maldonado .10 .03
137 Tim Birtsas .10 .03
138 Tom Brookens .10 .03
139 John Franco .20 .06
140 Mike LaCoss .10 .03
141 Jeff Treadway .10 .03
142 Pat Tabler .10 .03
143 Darrell Evans .20 .06
144 Rafael Ramirez .10 .03
145 O.McDowell UER .10 .03
Misspelled Odibbe
146 Brian Downing .10 .03
147 Curt Wilkerson .10 .03
148 Ernie Whitt .10 .03
149 Bill Schroeder .10 .03
150 Domingo Ramos UER .10 .03
(Says throws right,
but shows him
throwing lefty)
151 Rick Honeycutt .10 .03
152 Don Slaught .10 .03
153 Mitch Webster .10 .03
154 Tony Phillips .10 .03
155 Paul Kilgus .10 .03
156 Ken Griffey Jr. UER 1.50 .45
(Simultaniously)
157 Gary Sheffield .50 .15
158 Wally Backman .10 .03
159 B.J. Surhoff .20 .06
160 Louie Meadows .10 .03
161 Paul O'Neill .30 .09
162 Jeff McKnight .10 .03
163 Alvaro Espinoza .10 .03
164 Scott Scudder .10 .03
165 Jeff Reed .10 .03
166 Gregg Jefferies .20 .06
167 Barry Larkin .30 .09
168 Gary Carter .20 .06
169 Robby Thompson .10 .03
170 Rolando Roomes .10 .03
171 Mark McGwire UER 1.25 .35
(Total games 427 and
hits 479, should be
467 and 427)
172 Steve Sax .10 .03
173 Mark Williamson .10 .03
174 Mitch Williams .10 .03
175 Brian Holton .10 .03
176 Rob Deer .10 .03
177 Tim Raines .20 .06
178 Mike Felder .10 .03
179 Harold Reynolds .20 .06
180 Terry Francona .20 .06
181 Chris Sabo .10 .03
182 Darryl Strawberry .20 .06
183 Willie Randolph .20 .06
184 Bill Ripken .10 .03
185 Mackey Sasser .10 .03
186 Todd Benzinger .10 .03
187 Kevin Elster UER .10 .03
(16 homers in 1989,
should be 10)
188 Jose Uribe .10 .03
189 Tom Browning .10 .03
190 Keith Miller .10 .03
191 Don Mattingly 1.25 .35
192 Dave Parker .20 .06
193 Roberto Kelly UER .10 .03
(96 RBI, should be 62)
194 Phil Bradley .10 .03
195 Ron Hassey .10 .03
196 Gerald Young .10 .03
197 Hubie Brooks .10 .03
198 Bill Doran .10 .03
199 Al Newman .10 .03
200 Checklist 101-200 .10 .03
201 Terry Puhl .10 .03
202 Frank DiPino .10 .03
203 Jim Clancy .10 .03
204 Bob Ojeda .10 .03
205 Alex Trevino .10 .03
206 Dave Henderson .10 .03
207 Henry Cotto .10 .03
208 Rafael Belliard UER .10 .03
(Born 1961, not 1951)
209 Stan Javier .10 .03
210 Jerry Reed .10 .03
211 Doug Dascenzo .10 .03
212 Andres Thomas .10 .03
213 Greg Maddux .75 .23
214 Mike Schooler .10 .03
215 Lonnie Smith .10 .03
216 Jose Rijo .10 .03
217 Greg Gagne .10 .03
218 Jim Gantner .10 .03
219 Allan Anderson .10 .03
220 Rick Mahler .10 .03
221 Jim Deshaies .10 .03
222 Keith Hernandez .20 .06
223 Vince Coleman .10 .03
224 David Cone .20 .06
225 Ozzie Smith .75 .23
226 Matt Nokes .10 .03
227 Barry Bonds 1.25 .35
228 Felix Jose .10 .03
229 Dennis Powell .10 .03
230 Mike Gallego .10 .03
231 Shawon Dunston UER .10 .03
('89 stats are
Andre Dawson's)
232 Ron Gant .20 .06
233 Omar Vizquel .50 .15
234 Derek Lilliquist .10 .03
235 Erik Hanson .10 .03
236 Kirby Puckett UER .50 .15
(824 games, should
be 924)
237 Bill Spiers .10 .03
238 Dan Gladden .10 .03
239 Bryan Clutterbuck .10 .03
240 John Moses .10 .03
241 Ron Darling .10 .03
242 Joe Magrane .10 .03
243 Dave Magadan .10 .03
244 Pedro Guerrero UER .10 .03
(Misspelled Guerero)
245 Glenn Davis .10 .03
246 Terry Steinbach .10 .03
247 Fred Lynn .10 .03
248 Gary Redus .10 .03
249 Ken Williams .10 .03
250 Sid Bream .10 .03
251 Bob Welch UER .10 .03
(2587 career strike-
outs, should be 1587)
252 Bill Buckner .10 .03
253 Carney Lansford .20 .06
254 Paul Molitor .30 .09
255 Jose DeJesus .10 .03
256 Orel Hershiser .20 .06
257 Tom Brunansky .10 .03
258 Mike Davis .10 .03
259 Jeff Ballard .10 .03
260 Scott Terry .10 .03
261 Sid Fernandez .10 .03
262 Mike Marshall .10 .03
263 Howard Johnson UER .10 .03
(192 SO, should be 592)
264 Kirk Gibson UER .20 .06
(659 runs, should
be 669)
265 Kevin McReynolds .10 .03
266 Cal Ripken 1.50 .45
267 Ozzie Guillen UER .10 .03
(Career triples 27,
should be 29)
268 Jim Traber .10 .03
269 Bobby Thigpen UER .10 .03
(31 saves in 1989,
should be 34)
270 Joe Orsulak .10 .03
271 Bob Boone .20 .06
272 Dave Stewart UER .20 .06
(Totals wrong due to
omission of '86 stats)
273 Tim Wallach .10 .03
274 Luis Aquino UER .10 .03
(Says throws lefty,
but shows him
throwing righty)
275 Mike Moore .10 .03
276 Tony Pena .10 .03
277 Eddie Murray UER .50 .15
(Several typos in
career total stats)
278 Milt Thompson .10 .03
279 Alejandro Pena .10 .03
280 Ken Dayley .10 .03
281 Carmelo Castillo .10 .03
282 Tom Henke .10 .03
283 Mickey Hatcher .10 .03
284 Roy Smith .10 .03
285 Manny Lee .10 .03
286 Dan Pasqua .10 .03
287 Larry Sheets .10 .03
288 Garry Templeton .10 .03
289 Eddie Williams .10 .03
290 Brady Anderson UER .20 .06
(Home: Silver Springs,
not Siver Springs)
291 Spike Owen .10 .03
292 Storm Davis .10 .03
293 Chris Bosio .10 .03
294 Jim Eisenreich .10 .03
295 Don August .10 .03
296 Jeff Hamilton .10 .03
297 Mickey Tettleton .10 .03
298 Mike Scioscia .10 .03
299 Kevin Hickey .10 .03
300 Checklist 201-300 .10 .03
301 Shawn Abner .10 .03
302 Kevin Bass .10 .03
303 Bip Roberts .10 .03
304 Joe Girardi .30 .09
305 Danny Darwin .10 .03
306 Mike Heath .10 .03
307 Mike Macfarlane .10 .03
308 Ed Whitson .10 .03
309 Tracy Jones .10 .03
310 Scott Fletcher .10 .03
311 Darnell Coles .10 .03
312 Mike Brumley .10 .03
313 Bill Swift .10 .03
314 Charlie Hough .20 .06
315 Jim Presley .10 .03
316 Luis Polonia .10 .03
317 Mike Morgan .10 .03
318 Lee Guetterman .10 .03
319 Jose Oquendo .10 .03
320 Wayne Tolleson .10 .03
321 Jody Reed .10 .03
322 Damon Berryhill .10 .03
323 Roger Clemens 1.00 .30
324 Ryne Sandberg .75 .23
325 Benito Santiago UER .20 .06
(Misspelled Santago
on card back)
326 Bret Saberhagen UER .20 .06
(1140 hits, should be
1240; 56 CG, should
be 52)
327 Lou Whitaker .20 .06
328 Dave Gallagher .10 .03
329 Mike Pagliarulo .10 .03
330 Doyle Alexander .10 .03
331 Jeffrey Leonard .10 .03
332 Torey Lovullo .10 .03
333 Pete Incaviglia .10 .03
334 Rickey Henderson .50 .15
335 Rafael Palmeiro .30 .09
336 Ken Hill .20 .06
337 Dave Winfield UER .20 .06
(1418 RBI, should
be 1438)
338 Alfredo Griffin .10 .03
339 Andy Hawkins .10 .03
340 Ted Power .10 .03
341 Steve Wilson .10 .03
342 Jack Clark UER .20 .06
(916 BB, should be
1006; 1142 SO,
should be 1130)
343 Ellis Burks .30 .09
344 Tony Gwynn UER .60 .18
(Doubles stats on
card back are wrong)
345 Jerome Walton UER .10 .03
(Total At Bats 476,
should be 475)
346 Roberto Alomar UER .30 .09
(61 doubles, should
be 51)
347 Carlos Martinez UER .10 .03
(Born 8/11/64, should
be 8/11/65)
348 Chet Lemon .10 .03
349 Willie Wilson .10 .03
350 Greg Walker .10 .03
351 Tom Bolton .10 .03
352 German Gonzalez .10 .03
353 Harold Baines .20 .06
354 Mike Greenwell .10 .03
355 Ruben Sierra .10 .03
356 Andres Galarraga .20 .06
357 Andre Dawson .20 .06
358 Jeff Brantley .10 .03
359 Mike Bielecki .10 .03
360 Ken Oberkfell .10 .03
361 Kurt Stillwell .10 .03
362 Brian Holman .10 .03
363 Kevin Seitzer UER .10 .03
(Career triples total
does not add up)
364 Alvin Davis .10 .03
365 Tom Gordon .20 .06
366 Bobby Bonilla UER .20 .06
(Two steals in 1987,
should be 3)
367 Carlton Fisk .30 .09
368 Steve Carter UER .10 .03
(Charlotesville)
369 Joel Skinner .10 .03
370 John Cangelosi .10 .03
371 Cecil Espy .10 .03
372 Gary Wayne .10 .03
373 Jim Rice .20 .06
374 Mike Dyer RC .10 .03
375 Joe Carter .20 .06
376 Dwight Smith .10 .03
377 John Wetteland .50 .15
378 Earnie Riles .10 .03
379 Otis Nixon .10 .03
380 Vance Law .10 .03
381 Dave Bergman .10 .03
382 Frank White .20 .06
383 Scott Bradley .10 .03
384 Israel Sanchez UER .10 .03
(Totals don't in-
clude '89 stats)
385 Gary Pettis .10 .03
386 Donn Pall .10 .03
387 John Smiley .10 .03
388 Tom Candiotti .10 .03
389 Junior Ortiz .10 .03
390 Steve Lyons .10 .03
391 Brian Harper .10 .03
392 Fred Manrique .10 .03
393 Lee Smith .20 .06
394 Jeff Kunkel .10 .03
395 Claudell Washington .10 .03
396 John Tudor .10 .03
397 Terry Kennedy UER .10 .03
(Career totals all
wrong)
398 Lloyd McClendon .10 .03
399 Craig Lefferts .10 .03
400 Checklist 301-400 .10 .03
401 Keith Moreland .10 .03
402 Rich Gedman .10 .03
403 Jeff D. Robinson .10 .03
404 Randy Ready .10 .03
405 Rick Cerone .10 .03
406 Jeff Blauser .10 .03
407 Larry Andersen .10 .03
408 Joe Boever .10 .03
409 Felix Fermin .10 .03
410 Glenn Wilson .10 .03
411 Rex Hudler .10 .03
412 Mark Grant .10 .03
413 Dennis Martinez .20 .06
414 Darrin Jackson .10 .03
415 Mike Aldrete .10 .03
416 Roger McDowell .10 .03
417 Jeff Reardon .20 .06
418 Darren Daulton .20 .06
419 Tim Laudner .10 .03
420 Don Carman .10 .03
421 Lloyd Moseby .10 .03
422 Doug Drabek .10 .03
423 Lenny Harris UER .10 .03
(Walks 2 in '89,
should be 20)
424 Jose Lind .10 .03
425 Dave Johnson (P) .10 .03
426 Jerry Browne .10 .03
427 Eric Yelding .10 .03
428 Brad Komminsk .10 .03
429 Jody Davis .10 .03
430 Mariano Duncan .10 .03
431 Mark Davis .10 .03
432 Nelson Santovenia .10 .03
433 Bruce Hurst .10 .03
434 Jeff Huson RC .10 .03
435 Chris James .10 .03
436 Mark Guthrie .10 .03
437 Charlie Hayes .10 .03
438 Shane Rawley .10 .03
439 Dickie Thon .10 .03
440 Juan Berenguer .10 .03
441 Kevin Romine .10 .03
442 Bill Landrum .10 .03
443 Todd Frohwirth .10 .03
444 Craig Worthington .10 .03
445 Fernando Valenzuela .20 .06
446 Joey Belle .50 .15
447 Ed Whited UER .10 .03
(Ashville, should
be Asheville)
448 Dave Smith .10 .03
449 Dave Clark .10 .03
450 Juan Agosto .10 .03
451 Dave Valle .10 .03
452 Kent Hrbek .20 .06
453 Von Hayes .10 .03
454 Gary Gaetti .20 .06
455 Greg Briley .10 .03
456 Glenn Braggs .10 .03
457 Kirt Manwaring .10 .03
458 Mel Hall .10 .03
459 Brook Jacoby .10 .03
460 Pat Sheridan .10 .03
461 Rob Murphy .10 .03
462 Jimmy Key .20 .06
463 Nick Esasky .10 .03
464 Rob Ducey .10 .03
465 Carlos Quintana UER .10 .03
(Internatinoal)
466 Larry Walker RC 1.50 .45
467 Todd Worrell .10 .03
468 Kevin Gross .10 .03
469 Terry Pendleton .20 .06
470 Dave Martinez .10 .03
471 Gene Larkin .10 .03
472 Len Dykstra UER .20 .06
('89 and total runs
understated by 10)
473 Barry Lyons .10 .03
474 Terry Mulholland .10 .03
475 Chip Hale .10 .03
476 Jesse Barfield .10 .03
477 Dan Plesac .10 .03
478A Scott Garrelts ERR 2.00 .60
(Photo actually
Bill Bathe)
478B Scott Garrelts COR .10 .03
479 Dave Righetti .10 .03
480 Gus Polidor UER .10 .03
Wearing 14 on front,
but 10 on back
481 Mookie Wilson .20 .06
482 Luis Rivera .10 .03
483 Mike Flanagan .10 .03
484 Dennis Boyd .10 .03
485 John Cerutti .10 .03
486 John Costello .10 .03
487 Pascual Perez .10 .03
488 Tommy Herr .10 .03
489 Tom Foley .10 .03
490 Curt Ford .10 .03
491 Steve Lake .10 .03
492 Tim Teufel .10 .03
493 Randy Bush .10 .03
494 Mike Jackson .10 .03
495 Steve Jeltz .10 .03
496 Paul Gibson .10 .03
497 Steve Balboni .10 .03
498 Bud Black .10 .03
499 Dale Sveum .10 .03
500 Checklist 401-500 .10 .03
501 Tim Jones .10 .03
502 Mark Portugal .10 .03
503 Ivan Calderon .10 .03
504 Rick Rhoden .10 .03
505 Willie McGee .20 .06
506 Kirk McCaskill .10 .03
507 Dave LaPoint .10 .03
508 Jay Howell .10 .03
509 Johnny Ray .10 .03
510 Dave Anderson .10 .03
511 Chuck Crim .10 .03
512 Joe Hesketh .10 .03
513 Dennis Eckersley .20 .06
514 Greg Brock .10 .03
515 Tim Burke .10 .03
516 Frank Tanana .10 .03
517 Jay Bell .20 .06
518 Guillermo Hernandez .10 .03
519 Randy Kramer UER .10 .03
(Codiroli misspelled
as Codoroli)
520 Charles Hudson .10 .03
521 Jim Corsi .10 .03
Word "originally" is
misspelled on back
522 Steve Rosenberg .10 .03
523 Cris Carpenter .10 .03
524 Matt Winters .10 .03
525 Melido Perez .10 .03
526 Chris Gwynn UER .10 .03
(Albeguergue)
527 Bert Blyleven UER .20 .06
(Games career total is
wrong, should be 644)
528 Chuck Cary .10 .03
529 Daryl Boston .10 .03
530 Dale Mohorcic .10 .03
531 Geronimo Berroa .10 .03
532 Edgar Martinez .30 .09
533 Dale Murphy .50 .15
534 Jay Buhner .20 .06
535 John Smoltz UER .50 .15
(HEA Stadium)
536 Andy Van Slyke .20 .06
537 Mike Henneman .10 .03
538 Miguel Garcia .10 .03
539 Frank Williams .10 .03
540 R.J. Reynolds .10 .03
541 Shawn Hillegas .10 .03
542 Walt Weiss .10 .03
543 Greg Hibbard RC .10 .03
544 Nolan Ryan 2.00 .60
545 Todd Zeile .20 .06

546 Hensley Meulens .10 .03
547 Tim Belcher .10 .03
548 Mike Witt .10 .03
549 Greg Cadaret UER .10 .03
(Aquiring, should be Acquiring)
550 Franklin Stubbs .10 .03
551 Tony Castillo .10 .03
552 Jeff M. Robinson .10 .03
553 Steve Olin RC .25 .07
554 Alan Trammell .20 .06
555 Wade Boggs 4X .30 .09
(Bo Jackson in background)
556 Will Clark .50 .15
557 Jeff King .10 .03
558 Mike Fitzgerald .10 .03
559 Ken Howell .10 .03
560 Bob Kipper .10 .03
561 Scott Bankhead .10 .03
562A Jeff Innis ERR 2.00 .60
(Photo actually David West)
562B Jeff Innis COR .10 .03
563 Randy Johnson 1.00 .23
564 Wally Whitehurst .10 .03
565 Gene Harris .10 .03
566 Norm Charlton .10 .03
567 Robin Yount UER .75 .23
(7602 career hits, should be 2606)
568 Joe Oliver UER .10 .03
(Fl.orida)
569 Mark Parent .10 .03
570 John Farrell UER .10 .03
(Loss total added wrong)
571 Tom Glavine .30 .09
572 Rod Nichols .10 .03
573 Jack Morris .20 .06
574 Greg Swindell .10 .03
575 Steve Searcy .10 .03
576 Ricky Jordan .10 .03
577 Matt Williams .20 .06
578 Mike LaValliere .10 .03
579 Bryn Smith .10 .03
580 Bruce Ruffin .10 .03
581 Randy Myers .20 .06
582 Rick Wrona .10 .03
583 Juan Samuel .10 .03
584 Les Lancaster .10 .03
585 Jeff Musselman .10 .03
586 Rob Dibble .20 .06
587 Eric Show .10 .03
588 Jesse Orosco .10 .03
589 Herm Winningham .10 .03
590 Andy Allanson .10 .03
591 Dion James .10 .03
592 Carmelo Martinez .10 .03
593 Luis Quinones .10 .03
594 Dennis Rasmussen .10 .03
595 Rich Yett .10 .03
596 Bob Walk .10 .03
597A A.McGaffigan ERR 2.00 .60
Photo actually Rich Thompson
597B A.McGaffigan COR .10 .03
598 Billy Hatcher .10 .03
599 Bob Knepper .10 .03
600 CL 501-600 UER .10 .03
599 Bob Kneppers
601 Joey Cora .20 .06
602 Steve Finley .20 .06
603 Kal Daniels UER .10 .03
(12 hits in '87, should be 123; 335 runs, should be 235)
604 Gregg Olson .20 .06
605 Dave Stieb .20 .06
606 Kenny Rogers .20 .06
(Shown catching football)
607 Zane Smith .10 .03
608 Bob Geren UER .10 .03
(Origionally)
609 Chad Kreuter .10 .03
610 Mike Smithson .10 .03
611 Jeff Wetherby .10 .03
612 Gary Mielke .10 .03
613 Pete Smith .10 .03
614 Jack Daugherty UER .10 .03
(Born 7/30/60, should be 7/3/60)
615 Lance McCullers .10 .03
616 Don Robinson .10 .03
617 Jose Guzman .10 .03
618 Steve Bedrosian .10 .03
619 Jamie Moyer .20 .06
620 Atlee Hammaker .10 .03
621 Rick Luecken UER .10 .03
(Innings pitched wrong)
622 Greg W. Harris .10 .03
623 Pete Harnisch .10 .03
624 Jerald Clark .10 .03
625 Jack McDowell UER .10 .03
(Career totals for Games and GS don't include 1987 season)
626 Frank Viola .10 .03
627 Teddy Higuera .10 .03
628 Marty Pevey .10 .03
629 Bill Wegman .10 .03
630 Eric Plunk .10 .03
631 Drew Hall .10 .03
632 Doug Jones .10 .03
633 Geno Petralli UER .10 .03
(Sacremento)
634 Jose Alvarez .10 .03
635 Bob Milacki .10 .03
636 Bobby Witt .10 .03
637 Trevor Wilson .10 .03
638 Jeff Russell UER .10 .03
(Shutout stats wrong)
639 Mike Krukow .10 .03
640 Rick Leach .10 .03
641 Dave Schmidt .10 .03
642 Terry Leach .10 .03
643 Calvin Schiraldi .10 .03
644 Bob Melvin .10 .03
645 Jim Abbott .30 .09
646 Jaime Navarro .10 .03
647 Mark Langston UER .10 .03
(Several errors in stats totals)
648 Juan Nieves .10 .03
649 Damaso Garcia .10 .03
650 Charlie O'Brien .10 .03
651 Eric King .10 .03
652 Mike Boddicker .10 .03
653 Duane Ward .10 .03
654 Bob Stanley .10 .03
655 Sandy Alomar Jr. .20 .06
656 Danny Tartabull UER .10 .03
(395 BB, should be 295)
657 Randy McCament .10 .03
658 Charlie Leibrandt .10 .03
659 Dan Quisenberry .10 .03
660 Paul Assenmacher .10 .03
661 Walt Terrell .10 .03
662 Tim Leary .10 .03
663 Randy Milligan .10 .03
664 Bo Diaz .10 .03
665 Mark Lemke UER .10 .03
(Richmond misspelled as Richomond)
666 Jose Gonzalez .10 .03
667 Chuck Finley UER .20 .06
(Born 11/16/62, should be 11/26/62)
668 John Kruk .20 .06
669 Dick Schofield .10 .03
670 Tim Crews .10 .03
671 John Dopson .10 .03
672 John Orton RC .10 .03
673 Eric Hetzel .10 .03
674 Lance Parrish .10 .03
675 Ramon Martinez .10 .03
676 Mark Gubicza .10 .03
677 Greg Litton .10 .03
678 Greg Mathews .10 .03
679 Dave Dravecky .20 .06
680 Steve Farr .10 .03
681 Mike Devereaux .10 .03
682 Ken Griffey Sr. .20 .06
683A Mickey Weston ERR 2.00 .60
(Listed as Jamie on card)
683B Mickey Weston COR .10 .03
(Technically still an error as birthdate is listed as 3/26/81)
684 Jack Armstrong .10 .03
685 Steve Buechele .10 .03
686 Bryan Harvey .10 .03
687 Lance Blankenship .10 .03
688 Dante Bichette .50 .15
689 Todd Burns .10 .03
690 Dan Petry .10 .03
691 Kent Anderson .10 .03
692 Todd Stottlemyre .20 .06
693 Wally Joyner UER .20 .06
(Several stats errors)
694 Mike Rochford .10 .03
695 Floyd Bannister .10 .03
696 Rick Reuschel .10 .03
697 Jose DeLeon .10 .03
698 Jeff Montgomery .20 .06
699 Kelly Downs .10 .03
700A Checklist 601-700 2.00 .60
(683 Jamie Weston)
700B Checklist 601-700 .10 .03
(683 Mickey Weston)
701 Jim Gott .10 .03
702 Delino DeShields .50 .15
Marquis Grissom
Larry Walker
702A Mike Witt 10.00 3.00
Black rectangle covers much of back
703 Alejandro Pena .10 .03
704 Willie Randolph .20 .06
705 Tim Leary .10 .03
706 Chuck McElroy RC .10 .03
707 Gerald Perry .10 .03
708 Tom Brunansky .10 .03
709 John Franco .20 .06
710 Mark Davis .10 .03
711 David Justice RC .75 .23
712 Storm Davis .10 .03
713 Scott Ruskin .10 .03
714 Glenn Braggs .10 .03
715 Kevin Bearse .10 .03
716 Jose Nunez .10 .03
717 Tim Layana .10 .03
718 Greg Myers .10 .03
719 Pete O'Brien .10 .03
720 John Candelaria .10 .03
721 Craig Grebeck RC .10 .03
722 Shawn Boskie RC .10 .03
723 Jim Leyritz RC .25 .07
724 Bill Sampen .10 .03
725 Scott Radinsky RC .10 .03
726 Todd Hundley RC .25 .07
727 Scott Hemond RC .10 .03
728 Lenny Webster RC .10 .03
729 Jeff Reardon .20 .06
730 Mitch Webster .10 .03
731 Brian Bohanon RC .10 .03
732 Rick Parker .10 .03
733 Terry Shumpert .10 .03
734A Nolan Ryan 3.00 .90
6th No-Hitter
(No stripe on front)
734B Nolan Ryan 1.00 .30
6th No-Hitter
(stripe added on card front for 300th win)
735 John Burkett .10 .03
736 Derrick May RC .10 .03
737 Carlos Baerga RC .25 .07
738 Greg Smith .10 .03
739 Scott Sanderson .10 .03
740 Joe Kraemer .10 .03
741 Hector Villanueva RC .10 .03
742 Mike Fetters RC .25 .07
743 Mark Gardner RC .10 .03
744 Matt Nokes .10 .03
745 Dave Winfield .20 .06
746 Delino DeShields RC .25 .07
747 Dann Howitt .10 .03
748 Tony Pena .10 .03
749 Oil Can Boyd .10 .03
750 Mike Benjamin .10 .03
751 Alex Cole RC .10 .03
752 Eric Gunderson .10 .03
753 Howard Farmer .10 .03
754 Joe Carter .20 .06
755 Ray Lankford RC .25 .07
756 Sandy Alomar Jr. .20 .06
757 Alex Sanchez .10 .03
758 Nick Esasky .10 .03
759 Stan Belinda RC .10 .03
760 Jim Presley .10 .03
761 Gary DiSarcina RC .25 .07
762 Wayne Edwards .10 .03
763 Pat Combs .10 .03
764 Mickey Pina .10 .03
765 Wilson Alvarez RC .25 .07
766 Dave Parker .20 .06
767 Mike Blowers RC .10 .03
768 Tony Phillips .10 .03
769 Pascual Perez .10 .03
770 Gary Pettis .10 .03
771 Fred Lynn .10 .03
772 Mel Rojas RC .10 .03
773 David Segui RC .25 .07
774 Gary Carter .20 .06
775 Rafael Valdez .10 .03
776 Glenallen Hill .10 .03
777 Keith Hernandez .20 .06
778 Billy Hatcher .10 .03
779 Marty Clary .10 .03
780 Candy Maldonado .10 .03
781 Mike Marshall .10 .03
782 Billy Joe Robidoux .10 .03
783 Mark Langston .10 .03
784 Paul Sorrento RC .25 .07
785 Dave Hollins RC .25 .07
786 Cecil Fielder .20 .06
787 Matt Young .10 .03
788 Jeff Huson .10 .03
789 Lloyd Moseby .10 .03
790 Ron Kittle .10 .03
791 Hubie Brooks .10 .03
792 Craig Lefferts .10 .03
793 Kevin Bass .10 .03
794 Bryn Smith .10 .03
795 Juan Samuel .10 .03
796 Sam Horn .10 .03
797 Randy Myers .20 .06
798 Chris James .10 .03
799 Bill Gullickson .10 .03
800 Checklist 701-800 .10 .03

1990 Upper Deck Jackson Heroes

This ten-card standard-size set was issued as an insert in 1990 Upper Deck High Number packs as part of the Upper Deck promotional giveaway of 2,500 officially signed and personally numbered Reggie Jackson cards. Signed cards ending with 00 have the words "Mr. October" added to the autograph. These cards cover Jackson's major league career. The complete set price refers only to the unautographed card set of ten. One-card packs of over-sized (3 1/2" by 5") versions of these cards were later inserted into retail blister repacks containing one foil pack each of 1993 Upper Deck Series I and II. These cards were later inserted into various forms of repackaging. The larger cards are also distinguishable by the Upper Deck Fifth Anniversary logo and "1993 Hall of Fame Inductee" logo on the front of the card. These over-sized cards were a limited edition of 10,000 numbered cards and have no extra value than the basic cards.

Nm-Mt Ex-Mt
COMPLETE SET (10) 15.00 4.50
COMMON REGGIE (1-9) 1.50 .45
NNO Reggie Jackson 3.00 .90
Header Card
AU1 Reggie Jackson AU 150.00 45.00
(Signed and Numbered out of 2500)

1991 Upper Deck

This set marked the third year Upper Deck issued a 800-card standard-size set in two separate series of 700 and 100 cards respectively. Cards were distributed in low and high series foil packs and factory sets. The 100-card extended or high-number series was issued by Upper Deck several months after the release of their first series. For the first time in Upper Deck's three-year history, they did not issue a factory Extended set. The basic cards are made on the typical Upper Deck slick, white card stock and features full-color photos on both the front and the back. Subsets include Star Rookies (1-26), Team Cards (28-34, 43-49, 77-82, 95-99) and Top Prospects (50-76). Several other special achievement cards are seeded throughout the set. The team checklist (TC) cards in the set feature an attractive Vernon Wells drawing of a featured player for that particular team. Rookie Cards in this set include Jeff Bagwell, Luis Gonzalez, Chipper Jones, Eric Karros, and Mike Mussina. A special Michael Jordan card (numbered SP1) was randomly included in packs on a somewhat limited basis. The Hank Aaron hologram card was randomly inserted in the 1991 Upper Deck high number foil packs. Neither card is included in the price of the regular issue set though both are listed at the end of our checklist.

Nm-Mt Ex-Mt
COMPLETE SET (800) 15.00 4.50
COMP.FACT.SET (800) 20.00 6.00
COMPLETE LO SET (700) 15.00 4.50
COMPLETE HI SET (100) 5.00 1.50
1 Star Rookie Checklist .05 .02
2 Phil Plantier RC .10 .03
3 D.J. Dozier .05 .02
4 Dave Hansen .05 .02
5 Maurice Vaughn .10 .03
6 Leo Gomez .05 .02
7 Scott Aldred .05 .02
8 Scott Chiamparino .05 .02
9 Lance Dickson RC .10 .03
10 Sean Berry RC .10 .03
11 Bernie Williams .25 .07
12 Brian Barnes UER .10 .03
(Photo either not him or in wrong jersey)
13 Narciso Elvira .05 .02
14 Mike Gardiner .05 .02
15 Greg Colbrunn RC .25 .07
16 Bernard Gilkey .05 .02
17 Mark Lewis .05 .02
18 Mickey Morandini .05 .02
19 Charles Nagy .05 .02
20 Geronimo Pena .05 .02
21 Henry Rodriguez RC .25 .07
22 Scott Cooper .05 .02
23 Andujar Cedeno UER .05 .02
(Shown batting left, back says right)
24 Eric Karros RC .40 .12
25 Steve Decker UER .05 .02
Lewis-Clark State College, not Lewis and Clark
26 Kevin Belcher .05 .02
27 Jeff Conine RC .40 .12
28 Dave Stewart TC .05 .02
29 Carlton Fisk TC .10 .03
30 Rafael Palmeiro TC .10 .03
31 Chuck Finley TC .05 .02
32 Harold Reynolds TC .05 .02
33 Bret Saberhagen TC .05 .02
34 Gary Gaetti TC .05 .02
35 Scott Leius .05 .02
36 Neal Heaton .05 .02
37 Terry Lee .05 .02
38 Gary Redus .05 .02
39 Barry Jones .05 .02
40 Chuck Knoblauch .10 .03
41 Larry Andersen .05 .02
42 Darryl Hamilton .05 .02
43 Mike Greenwell TC .05 .02
44 Kelly Gruber TC .05 .02
45 Jack Morris TC .05 .02
46 Sandy Alomar Jr. TC .05 .02
47 Gregg Olson TC .05 .02
48 Dave Parker TC .05 .02
49 Roberto Kelly TC .05 .02
50 Top Prospect Checklist .05 .02
51 Kyle Abbott .05 .02
52 Jeff Juden .05 .02
53 T.Van Poppel UER RC .25 .07
Born Arlington and attended John Martin HS, should say Hinsdale and James Martin HS
54 Steve Karsay RC .25 .07
55 Chipper Jones RC 4.00 1.20
56 Chris Johnson RC UER .10 .03
(Called Tim on back)
57 John Ericks .05 .02
58 Gary Scott .05 .02
59 Kiki Jones .05 .02
60 Wil Cordero RC .10 .03
61 Royce Clayton .05 .02
62 Tim Costo RC .10 .03
63 Roger Salkeld .05 .02
64 Brook Fordyce RC .25 .07
65 Mike Mussina RC 1.25 .35
66 Dave Staton RC .10 .03
67 Mike Lieberthal RC .40 .12
68 Kurt Miller RC .05 .02
69 Dan Peltier RC .10 .03
70 Greg Blosser .05 .02
71 Reggie Sanders RC .40 .12
72 Brent Mayne .05 .02
73 Rico Brogna .05 .02
74 Willie Banks .05 .02
75 Len Brutcher .05 .02
76 Pat Kelly RC .10 .03
77 Chris Sabo TC .05 .02
78 Ramon Martinez TC .05 .02
79 Matt Williams TC .05 .02
80 Roberto Alomar TC .10 .03
81 Glenn Davis TC .05 .02
82 Ron Gant TC .05 .02
83 Cecil Fielder FEAT .05 .02
84 Orlando Merced RC .10 .03
85 Domingo Ramos .05 .02
86 Tom Bolton .05 .02
87 Andres Santana .05 .02
88 John Dopson .05 .02
89 Kenny Williams .05 .02
90 Marty Barrett .05 .02
91 Tom Pagnozzi .05 .02
92 Carmelo Martinez .05 .02
93 Bobby Thigpen SAVE .05 .02
94 Barry Bonds TC .30 .09
95 Gregg Jefferies TC .05 .02
96 Tim Wallach TC .05 .02
97 Len Dykstra TC .05 .02
98 Pedro Guerrero TC .05 .02
99 Mark Grace TC .10 .03
100 Checklist 1-100 .05 .02
101 Kevin Elster .05 .02
102 Tom Brookens .05 .02
103 Mackey Sasser .05 .02
104 Felix Fermin .05 .02
105 Kevin McReynolds .05 .02
106 Dave Stieb .05 .02
107 Jeffrey Leonard .05 .02
108 Dave Henderson .05 .02
109 Sid Bream .05 .02
110 Henry Cotto .05 .02
111 Shawon Dunston .05 .02
112 Mariano Duncan .05 .02
113 Joe Girardi .05 .02
114 Billy Hatcher .05 .02
115 Greg Maddux .40 .12
116 Jerry Browne .05 .02
117 Juan Samuel .05 .02
118 Steve Olin .05 .02
119 Alfredo Griffin .05 .02
120 Mitch Webster .05 .02
121 Joel Skinner .05 .02
122 Frank Viola .10 .03
123 Cory Snyder .05 .02
124 Howard Johnson .05 .02
125 Carlos Baerga .05 .02
126 Tony Fernandez .05 .02
127 Dave Stewart .10 .03
128 Jay Buhner .10 .03
129 Mike LaValliere .05 .02
130 Scott Bradley .05 .02
131 Tony Phillips .05 .02
132 Ryne Sandberg .40 .12
133 Paul O'Neill .15 .04
134 Mark Grace .15 .04
135 Chris Sabo .05 .02
136 Ramon Martinez .05 .02
137 Brook Jacoby .05 .02
138 Candy Maldonado .05 .02
139 Mike Scioscia .05 .02
140 Chris James .05 .02
141 Craig Worthington .05 .02
142 Manny Lee .05 .02
143 Tim Raines .10 .03
144 Sandy Alomar Jr. .05 .02
145 John Olerud .10 .03
146 Ozzie Canseco .10 .03
(With Jose)
147 Pat Borders .05 .02
148 Harold Reynolds .10 .03
149 Tom Henke .05 .02
150 R.J. Reynolds .05 .02
151 Mike Gallego .05 .02
152 Bobby Bonilla .10 .03
153 Terry Steinbach .05 .02
154 Barry Bonds .60 .18
155 Jose Canseco .25 .07
156 Gregg Jefferies .05 .02
157 Matt Williams .10 .03
158 Craig Biggio .15 .04
159 Daryl Boston .05 .02
160 Ricky Jordan .05 .02
161 Stan Belinda .05 .02
162 Ozzie Smith .40 .12
163 Tom Brunansky .05 .02
164 Todd Zeile .05 .02
165 Mike Greenwell .05 .02
166 Kal Daniels .05 .02
167 Kent Hrbek .10 .03
168 Franklin Stubbs .05 .02
169 Dick Schofield .05 .02
170 Junior Ortiz .05 .02
171 Hector Villanueva .05 .02
172 Dennis Eckersley .10 .03
173 Mitch Williams .05 .02
174 Mark McGwire .60 .18
175 F.Valenzuela 3X .10 .03
176 Gary Carter .10 .03
177 Dave Magadan .05 .02
178 Robby Thompson .05 .02
179 Bob Ojeda .05 .02
180 Ken Caminiti .10 .03
181 Don Slaught .05 .02
182 Luis Rivera .05 .02
183 Jay Bell .10 .03
184 Jody Reed .05 .02
185 Wally Backman .05 .02
186 Dave Martinez .05 .02
187 Luis Polonia .05 .02
188 Shane Mack .05 .02
189 Spike Owen .05 .02
190 Scott Bailes .05 .02
191 John Russell .05 .02
192 Walt Weiss .05 .02
193 Jose Oquendo .05 .02
194 Carney Lansford .10 .03
195 Jeff Huson .05 .02
196 Keith Miller .05 .02
197 Eric Yelding .05 .02
198 Ron Darling .05 .02
199 John Kruk .10 .03
200 Checklist 101-200 .05 .02
201 John Shelby .05 .02
202 Bob Geren .05 .02
203 Lance McCullers .05 .02
204 Alvaro Espinoza .05 .02
205 Mark Salas .05 .02
206 Mike Pagliarulo .05 .02
207 Jose Uribe .05 .02
208 Jim Deshaies .05 .02
209 Ron Karkovice .05 .02
210 Rafael Ramirez .05 .02
211 Donnie Hill .05 .02
212 Brian Harper .05 .02
213 Jack Howell .05 .02
214 Wes Gardner .05 .02
215 Tim Burke .05 .02
216 Doug Jones .05 .02
217 Hubie Brooks .05 .02
218 Tom Candiotti .05 .02
219 Gerald Perry .05 .02
220 Jose DeLeon .05 .02
221 Wally Whitehurst .05 .02
222 Alan Mills .05 .02
223 Alan Trammell .10 .03
224 Dwight Gooden .10 .03
225 Travis Fryman .10 .03
226 Joe Carter .10 .03
227 Julio Franco .10 .03
228 Craig Lefferts .05 .02
229 Gary Pettis .05 .02
230 Dennis Rasmussen .05 .02
231A Brian Downing ERR .05 .02
(No position on front)
231B Brian Downing COR .25 .07

(DH on front)
232 Carlos Quintana .05 .02
233 Gary Gaetti .10 .03
234 Mark Langston .05 .02
235 Tim Wallach .05 .02
236 Greg Swindell .05 .02
237 Eddie Murray .25 .07
238 Jeff Manto .05 .02
239 Lenny Harris .05 .02
240 Jesse Orosco .05 .02
241 Scott Lusader .05 .02
242 Sid Fernandez .05 .02
243 Jim Leyritz .05 .02
244 Cecil Fielder .10 .03
245 Darryl Strawberry .10 .03
246 Frank Thomas UER .25 .07
(Comiskey Park
misspelled Comisky)
247 Kevin Mitchell .05 .02
248 Lance Johnson .05 .02
249 Rick Reuschel .05 .02
250 Mark Portugal .05 .02
251 Derek Lilliquist .05 .02
252 Brian Holman .05 .02
253 Rafael Valdez UER .05 .02
(Born 4/17/68,
should be 12/17/67)
254 B.J. Surhoff .10 .03
255 Tony Gwynn .30 .09
256 Andy Van Slyke .10 .03
257 Todd Stottlemyre .05 .02
258 Jose Lind .05 .02
259 Greg Myers .05 .02
260 Jeff Ballard .05 .02
261 Bobby Thigpen .05 .02
262 Jimmy Kremers .05 .02
263 Robin Ventura .10 .03
264 John Smoltz .15 .04
265 Sammy Sosa .50 .15
266 Gary Sheffield .10 .03
267 Len Dykstra .10 .03
268 Bill Spiers .05 .02
269 Charlie Hayes .05 .02
270 Brett Butler .10 .03
271 Bip Roberts .05 .02
272 Rob Deer .05 .02
273 Fred Lynn .05 .02
274 Dave Parker .10 .03
275 Andy Benes .05 .02
276 Glenallen Hill .05 .02
277 Steve Howard .05 .02
278 Doug Drabek .05 .02
279 Joe Oliver .05 .02
280 Todd Benzinger .05 .02
281 Eric King .05 .02
282 Jim Presley .05 .02
283 Ken Patterson .05 .02
284 Jack Daugherty .05 .02
285 Ivan Calderon .05 .02
286 Edgar Diaz .05 .02
287 Kevin Bass .05 .02
288 Don Carman .05 .02
289 Greg Brock .05 .02
290 John Franco .10 .03
291 Joey Cora .05 .02
292 Bill Wegman .05 .02
293 Eric Show .05 .02
294 Scott Bankhead .05 .02
295 Garry Templeton .05 .02
296 Mickey Tettleton .05 .02
297 Luis Sojo .05 .02
298 Jose Rijo .05 .02
299 Dave Johnson .05 .02
300 Checklist 201-300 .05 .02
301 Mark Grant .05 .02
302 Pete Harnisch .05 .02
303 Greg Olson .05 .02
304 Anthony Telford .05 .02
305 Lonnie Smith .05 .02
306 Chris Hoiles .05 .02
307 Bryn Smith .05 .02
308 Mike Devereaux .05 .02
309A Milt Thompson ERR .25 .07
(Under yr information
has print dot)
309B Milt Thompson COR .05 .02
(Under yr information
says 86)
310 Bob Melvin .05 .02
311 Luis Salazar .05 .02
312 Ed Whitson .05 .02
313 Charlie Hough .10 .03
314 Dave Clark .05 .02
315 Eric Gunderson .05 .02
316 Dan Petry .05 .02
317 Dante Bichette UER .10 .03
(Assists misspelled
as assissts)
318 Mike Heath .05 .02
319 Damon Berryhill .05 .02
320 Walt Terrell .05 .02
321 Scott Fletcher .05 .02
322 Dan Plesac .05 .02
323 Jack McDowell .05 .02
324 Paul Molitor .15 .04
325 Ozzie Guillen .05 .02
326 Gregg Olson .05 .02
327 Pedro Guerrero .10 .03
328 Bob Milacki .05 .02
329 John Tudor UER .05 .02
('90 Cardinals,
should be '90 Dodgers)
330 Steve Finley UER .10 .03
(Born 3/12/65,
should be 5/12)
331 Jack Clark .10 .03
332 Jerome Walton .05 .02
333 Andy Hawkins .05 .02
334 Derrick May .05 .02
335 Roberto Alomar .15 .04
336 Jack Morris .10 .03
337 Dave Winfield .10 .03
338 Steve Searcy .05 .02
339 Chili Davis .10 .03
340 Larry Sheets .05 .02
341 Ted Higuera .05 .02
342 David Segui .05 .02
343 Greg Cadaret .05 .02
344 Robin Yount .40 .12
345 Nolan Ryan 1.00 .30
346 Ray Lankford .05 .02
347 Cal Ripken .75 .23
348 Lee Smith .10 .03
349 Brady Anderson .10 .03
350 Frank DiPino .05 .02
351 Hal Morris .05 .02
352 Deion Sanders .15 .04
353 Barry Larkin .15 .04
354 Don Mattingly .60 .18
355 Eric Davis .10 .03
356 Jose Offerman .05 .02
357 Mel Rojas .05 .02
358 Rudy Seanez .05 .02
359 Oil Can Boyd .05 .02
360 Nelson Liriano .05 .02
361 Ron Gant .10 .03
362 Howard Farmer .05 .02
363 David Justice .10 .03
364 Delino DeShields .10 .03
365 Steve Avery .05 .02
366 David Cone .10 .03
367 Lou Whitaker .10 .03
368 Von Hayes .05 .02
369 Frank Tanana .05 .02
370 Tim Teufel .05 .02
371 Randy Myers .05 .02
372 Roberto Kelly .05 .02
373 Jack Armstrong .05 .02
374 Kelly Gruber .05 .02
375 Kevin Maas .05 .02
376 Randy Johnson .30 .09
377 David West .05 .02
378 Brent Knackert .05 .02
379 Rick Honeycutt .05 .02
380 Kevin Gross .05 .02
381 Tom Foley .05 .02
382 Jeff Blauser .05 .02
383 Scott Ruskin .05 .02
384 Andres Thomas .05 .02
385 Dennis Martinez .10 .03
386 Mike Henneman .05 .02
387 Felix Jose .05 .02
388 Alejandro Pena .05 .02
389 Chet Lemon .05 .02
390 Craig Wilson .05 .02
391 Chuck Crim .05 .02
392 Mel Hall .05 .02
393 Mark Knudson .05 .02
394 Norm Charlton .05 .02
395 Mike Felder .05 .02
396 Tim Layana .05 .02
397 Steve Frey .05 .02
398 Bill Doran .05 .02
399 Dion James .05 .02
400 Checklist 301-400 .05 .02
401 Ron Hassey .05 .02
402 Don Robinson .05 .02
403 Gene Nelson .05 .02
404 Terry Kennedy .05 .02
405 Todd Burns .05 .02
406 Roger McDowell .05 .02
407 Bob Kipper .05 .02
408 Darren Daulton .10 .03
409 Chuck Cary .05 .02
410 Bruce Ruffin .05 .02
411 Juan Berenguer .05 .02
412 Gary Ward .05 .02
413 Al Newman .05 .02
414 Danny Jackson .05 .02
415 Greg Gagne .05 .02
416 Tom Herr .05 .02
417 Jeff Parrett .05 .02
418 Jeff Reardon .10 .03
419 Mark Lemke .05 .02
420 Charlie O'Brien .05 .02
421 Willie Randolph .10 .03
422 Steve Bedrosian .05 .02
423 Mike Moore .05 .02
424 Jeff Brantley .05 .02
425 Bob Welch .05 .02
426 Terry Mulholland .05 .02
427 Willie Blair .05 .02
428 Darrin Fletcher .05 .02
429 Mike Witt .05 .02
430 Joe Boever .05 .02
431 Tom Gordon .05 .02
432 Pedro Munoz RC .10 .03
433 Kevin Seitzer .05 .02
434 Kevin Tapani .05 .02
435 Bret Saberhagen .10 .03
436 Ellis Burks .10 .03
437 Chuck Finley .10 .03
438 Mike Boddicker .05 .02
439 Francisco Cabrera .05 .02
440 Todd Hundley .05 .02
441 Kelly Downs .05 .02
442 Dann Howitt .05 .02
443 Scott Garrelts .05 .02
444 Rickey Henderson 3X .25 .07
445 Will Clark .25 .07
446 Ben McDonald .05 .02
447 Dale Murphy .25 .07
448 Dave Righetti .10 .03
449 Dickie Thon .05 .02
450 Ted Power .05 .02
451 Scott Coolbaugh .05 .02
452 Dwight Smith .05 .02
453 Pete Incaviglia .05 .02
454 Andre Dawson .10 .03
455 Ruben Sierra .05 .02
456 Andres Galarraga .10 .03
457 Alvin Davis .05 .02
458 Tony Castillo .05 .02
459 Pete O'Brien .05 .02
460 Charlie Leibrandt .05 .02
461 Vince Coleman .05 .02
462 Steve Sax .05 .02
463 Omar Olivares RC .10 .03
464 Oscar Azocar .05 .02
465 Joe Magrane .05 .02
466 Karl Rhodes .05 .02
467 Benito Santiago .10 .03
468 Joe Klink .05 .02
469 Sil Campusano .05 .02
470 Mark Parent .05 .02
471 Shawn Boskie UER .05 .02
(Depleted misspelled
as depleated)
472 Kevin Brown .10 .03
473 Rick Sutcliffe .10 .03
474 Rafael Palmeiro .15 .04
475 Mike Harkey .05 .02
476 Jaime Navarro .05 .02
477 Marquis Grissom UER .10 .03
(DeShields misspelled
as DeSheilds)
478 Marty Clary .05 .02
479 Greg Briley .05 .02
480 Tom Glavine .15 .04
481 Lee Guetterman .05 .02
482 Rex Hudler .05 .02
483 Dave LaPoint .05 .02
484 Terry Pendleton .10 .03
485 Jesse Barfield .05 .02
486 Jose DeJesus .05 .02
487 Paul Abbott RC .25 .07
488 Ken Howell .05 .02
489 Greg W. Harris .05 .02
490 Roy Smith .05 .02
491 Paul Assenmacher .05 .02
492 Geno Petralli .05 .02
493 Steve Wilson .05 .02
494 Kevin Reimer .05 .02
495 Bill Long .05 .02
496 Mike Jackson .05 .02
497 Oddibe McDowell .05 .02
498 Bill Swift .05 .02
499 Jeff Treadway .05 .02
500 Checklist 401-500 .05 .02
501 Gene Larkin .05 .02
502 Bob Boone .10 .03
503 Allan Anderson .05 .02
504 Luis Aquino .05 .02
505 Mark Guthrie .05 .02
506 Joe Orsulak .05 .02
507 Dana Kiecker .05 .02
508 Dave Gallagher .05 .02
509 Greg A. Harris .05 .02
510 Mark Williamson .05 .02
511 Casey Candaele .05 .02
512 Mookie Wilson .10 .03
513 Dave Smith .05 .02
514 Chuck Carr .05 .02
515 Glenn Wilson .05 .02
516 Mike Fitzgerald .05 .02
517 Devon White .10 .03
518 Dave Hollins .05 .02
519 Mark Eichhorn .05 .02
520 Otis Nixon .05 .02
521 Terry Shumpert .05 .02
522 Scott Erickson .05 .02
523 Danny Tartabull .05 .02
524 Orel Hershiser .10 .03
525 George Brett .60 .18
526 Greg Vaughn .05 .02
527 Tim Naehring .05 .02
528 Curt Schilling .25 .07
529 Chris Bosio .05 .02
530 Sam Horn .05 .02
531 Mike Scott .05 .02
532 George Bell .05 .02
533 Eric Anthony .05 .02
534 Julio Valera .05 .02
535 Glenn Davis .05 .02
536 Larry Walker UER .25 .07
(Should have comma
after Expos in text)
537 Pat Combs .05 .02
538 Chris Nabholz .05 .02
539 Kirk McCaskill .05 .02
540 Randy Ready .05 .02
541 Mark Gubicza .05 .02
542 Rick Aguilera .10 .03
543 Brian McRae RC .25 .07
544 Kirby Puckett .25 .07
545 Bo Jackson .25 .07
546 Wade Boggs .15 .04
547 Tim McIntosh .05 .02
548 Randy Milligan .05 .02
549 Dwight Evans .10 .03
550 Billy Ripken .05 .02
551 Erik Hanson .05 .02
552 Lance Parrish .10 .03
553 Tino Martinez .15 .04
554 Jim Abbott .15 .04
555 Ken Griffey Jr. UER .50 .15
(Second most votes for
1991 All-Star Game)
556 Milt Cuyler .05 .02
557 Mark Leonard .05 .02
558 Jay Howell .05 .02
559 Lloyd Moseby .05 .02
560 Chris Gwynn .05 .02
561 Mark Whiten .05 .02
562 Harold Baines .10 .03
563 Junior Felix .05 .02
564 Darren Lewis .05 .02
565 Fred McGriff .15 .04
566 Kevin Appier .10 .03
567 Luis Gonzalez RC .50 .15
568 Frank White .10 .03
569 Juan Agosto .05 .02
570 Mike Macfarlane .05 .02
571 Bert Blyleven .10 .03
572 Ken Griffey Sr. .25 .07
Ken Griffey Jr.
573 Lee Stevens .05 .02
574 Edgar Martinez .15 .04
575 Wally Joyner .10 .03
576 Tim Belcher .05 .02
577 John Burkett .05 .02
578 Mike Morgan .05 .02
579 Paul Gibson .05 .02
580 Jose Vizcaino .05 .02
581 Duane Ward .05 .02
582 Scott Sanderson .05 .02
583 David Wells .10 .03
584 Willie McGee .10 .03
585 John Cerutti .05 .02
586 Danny Darwin .05 .02
587 Kurt Stillwell .05 .02
588 Rich Gedman .05 .02
589 Mark Davis .05 .02
590 Bill Gullickson .05 .02
591 Matt Young .05 .02
592 Bryan Harvey .05 .02
593 Omar Vizquel .15 .04
594 Scott Lewis RC .10 .03
595 Dave Valle .05 .02
596 Tim Crews .05 .02
597 Mike Bielecki .05 .02
598 Mike Sharperson .05 .02
599 Dave Bergman .05 .02
600 Checklist 501-600 .05 .02
601 Steve Lyons .05 .02
602 Bruce Hurst .05 .02
603 Donn Pall .05 .02
604 Jim Vatcher .05 .02
605 Dan Pasqua .05 .02
606 Kenny Rogers .10 .03
607 Jeff Schulz .05 .02
608 Brad Arnsberg .05 .02
609 Willie Wilson .05 .02
610 Jamie Moyer .10 .03
611 Ron Oester .05 .02
612 Dennis Cook .05 .02
613 Rick Mahler .05 .02
614 Bill Landrum .05 .02
615 Scott Scudder .05 .02
616 Tom Edens .05 .02
617 1917 Revisited .10 .03
(White Sox vintage uniforms)
618 Jim Gantner .05 .02
619 Darrel Akerfelds .05 .02
620 Ron Robinson .05 .02
621 Scott Radinsky .05 .02
622 Pete Smith .05 .02
623 Melido Perez .05 .02
624 Jerald Clark .05 .02
625 Carlos Martinez .05 .02
626 Wes Chamberlain RC .25 .07
627 Bobby Witt .05 .02
628 Ken Dayley .05 .02
629 John Barfield .05 .02
630 Bob Tewksbury .05 .02
631 Glenn Braggs .05 .02
632 Jim Neidlinger .05 .02
633 Tom Browning .05 .02
634 Kirk Gibson .10 .03
635 Rob Dibble .10 .03
636 Rickey Henderson SB .25 .07
Lou Brock
May 1, 1991 on front
636A R.Henderson SB .25 .07
Lou Brock
no date on card
637 Jeff Montgomery .05 .02
638 Mike Schooler .05 .02
639 Storm Davis .05 .02
640 Rich Rodriguez .05 .02
641 Phil Bradley .05 .02
642 Kent Mercker .05 .02
643 Carlton Fisk .15 .04
644 Mike Bell .05 .02
645 Alex Fernandez .05 .02
646 Juan Gonzalez .15 .04
647 Ken Hill .05 .02
648 Jeff Russell .05 .02
649 Chuck Malone .05 .02
650 Steve Buechele .05 .02
651 Mike Benjamin .05 .02
652 Tony Pena .05 .02
653 Trevor Wilson .05 .02
654 Alex Cole .05 .02
655 Roger Clemens .50 .15
656 Mark McGwire BASH .30 .09
657 Joe Grahe RC .10 .03
658 Jim Eisenreich .05 .02
659 Dan Gladden .05 .02
660 Steve Farr .05 .02
661 Bill Sampen .05 .02
662 Dave Rohde .05 .02
663 Mark Gardner .05 .02
664 Mike Simms .05 .02
665 Moises Alou .10 .03
666 Mickey Hatcher .05 .02
667 Jimmy Key .10 .03
668 John Wetteland .10 .03
669 John Smiley .05 .02
670 Jim Acker .05 .02
671 Pascual Perez .05 .02
672 Reggie Harris UER .05 .02
(Opportunity misspelled
as oppurtinity)
673 Matt Nokes .05 .02
674 Rafael Novoa .05 .02
675 Hensley Meulens .05 .02
676 Jeff M. Robinson .05 .02
677 Ground Breaking .10 .03
(New Comiskey Park;
Carlton Fisk and
Robin Ventura)
678 Johnny Ray .05 .02
679 Greg Hibbard .05 .02
680 Paul Sorrento .05 .02
681 Mike Marshall .05 .02
682 Jim Clancy .05 .02
683 Rob Murphy .05 .02
684 Dave Schmidt .05 .02
685 Jeff Gray .05 .02
686 Mike Hartley .05 .02
687 Jeff King .05 .02
688 Stan Javier .05 .02
689 Bob Walk .05 .02
690 Jim Gott .05 .02
691 Mike LaCoss .05 .02
692 John Farrell .05 .02
693 Tim Leary .05 .02
694 Mike Walker .05 .02
695 Eric Plunk .05 .02
696 Mike Fetters .05 .02
697 Wayne Edwards .05 .02
698 Tim Drummond .05 .02
699 Willie Fraser .05 .02
700 Checklist 601-700 .05 .02
701 Mike Heath .05 .02
702 Luis Gonzalez 1.00 .30
Karl Rhodes
Jeff Bagwell
703 Jose Mesa .05 .02
704 Dave Smith .05 .02
705 Danny Darwin .05 .02
706 Rafael Belliard .05 .02
707 Rob Murphy .05 .02
708 Terry Pendleton .10 .03
709 Mike Pagliarulo .05 .02
710 Sid Bream .05 .02
711 Junior Felix .05 .02
712 Dante Bichette .10 .03
713 Kevin Gross .05 .02
714 Luis Sojo .05 .02
715 Bob Ojeda .05 .02
716 Julio Machado .05 .02
717 Steve Farr .05 .02
718 Franklin Stubbs .05 .02
719 Mike Boddicker .05 .02
720 Willie Randolph .10 .03
721 Willie McGee .10 .03
722 Chili Davis .10 .03
723 Danny Jackson .05 .02
724 Cory Snyder .05 .02
725 Andre Dawson .25 .07
George Bell
Ryne Sandberg
726 Rob Deer .05 .02
727 Rich DeLucia .05 .02
728 Mike Perez RC .10 .03
729 Mickey Tettleton .05 .02
730 Mike Blowers .05 .02
731 Gary Gaetti .10 .03
732 Brett Butler .10 .03
733 Dave Parker .10 .03
734 Eddie Zosky .05 .02
735 Jack Clark .10 .03
736 Jack Morris .10 .03
737 Kirk Gibson .10 .03
738 Steve Bedrosian .05 .02
739 Candy Maldonado .05 .02
740 Matt Young .05 .02
741 Rich Garces RC .10 .03
742 George Bell .05 .02
743 Deion Sanders .15 .04
744 Bo Jackson .25 .07
745 Luis Mercedes RC .10 .03
746 Reggie Jefferson UER .05 .02
(Throwing left on card;
back has throws right)
747 Pete Incaviglia .05 .02
748 Chris Hammond .05 .02
749 Mike Stanton .05 .02
750 Scott Sanderson .05 .02
751 Paul Faries .05 .02
752 Al Osuna RC .05 .02
753 Steve Chitren .05 .02
754 Tony Fernandez .05 .02
755 Jeff Bagwell RC UER 1.50 .45
(Strikeout and walk
totals reversed)
756 K.Dressendorfer RC .10 .03
757 Glenn Davis .05 .02
758 Gary Carter .10 .03
759 Zane Smith .05 .02
760 Vance Law .05 .02
761 Denis Boucher RC .10 .03
762 Turner Ward RC .10 .03
763 Roberto Alomar .15 .04
764 Albert Belle .10 .03
765 Joe Carter .10 .03
766 Pete Schourek RC .10 .03
767 H.Slocumb RC .10 .03
768 Vince Coleman .05 .02
769 Mitch Williams .05 .02
770 Brian Downing .05 .02
771 Dana Allison .05 .02
772 Pete Harnisch .05 .02
773 Tim Raines .10 .03
774 Darryl Kile .10 .03
775 Fred McGriff .15 .04
776 Dwight Evans .10 .03
777 Joe Slusarski .05 .02
778 Dave Righetti .10 .03
779 Jeff Hamilton .05 .02
780 Ernest Riles .05 .02
781 Ken Dayley .05 .02
782 Eric King .05 .02
783 Devon White .10 .03
784 Beau Allred .05 .02
785 Mike Timlin RC .40 .12
786 Ivan Calderon .05 .02
787 Hubie Brooks .05 .02
788 Juan Agosto .05 .02
789 Barry Jones .05 .02
790 Wally Backman .05 .02
791 Jim Presley .05 .02
792 Charlie Hough .10 .03
793 Larry Andersen .05 .02
794 Steve Finley .10 .03
795 Shawn Abner .05 .02
796 Jeff M. Robinson .05 .02
797 Joe Bitker .05 .02
798 Eric Show .05 .02
799 Bud Black .05 .02
800 Checklist 701-800 .05 .02
HH1 H.Aaron Hologram 1.50 .45
SP1 Michael Jordan SP 8.00 2.40
(Shown batting in
White Sox uniform)
SP2 Rickey Henderson 2.00 .60
Nolan Ryan
May 1, 1991 Records

1991 Upper Deck Aaron Heroes

These standard-size cards were issued in honor of Hall of Famer Hank Aaron and inserted in Upper Deck high number wax packs. Aaron autographed 2,500 of card number 27, which featured his portrait by noted sports artist Vernon Wells. The cards are numbered on the back in continuation of the Baseball Heroes set.

	Nm-Mt	Ex-Mt
COMPLETE SET (10)	5.00	1.50
COMMON AARON (19-27)	.50	.15
NNO Title/Header card SP	1.00	.30
AU3 Hank Aaron AU (Signed and Numbered out of 2500)	150.00	45.00

1991 Upper Deck Heroes of Baseball

These standard-size cards were randomly inserted in Upper Deck Baseball Heroes wax packs. The fourth card features a color portrait of the three players by noted sports artist Vernon Wells. Each of the features heroes also signed 3,000 of each card for inclusion in this product.

	Nm-Mt	Ex-Mt
COMPLETE SET (4)	25.00	7.50
H1 Harmon Killebrew	8.00	2.40
H2 Gaylord Perry	5.00	1.50
H3 Ferguson Jenkins	5.00	1.50
H4 Harmon Killebrew ART	8.00	2.40
Ferguson Jenkins		
Gaylord Perry		
AU1 Harmon Killebrew AU	40.00	12.00
3000		
AU2 Gaylord Perry AU	25.00	7.50
3000		
AU3 Fergie Jenkins AU	25.00	7.50
3000		

1991 Upper Deck Ryan Heroes

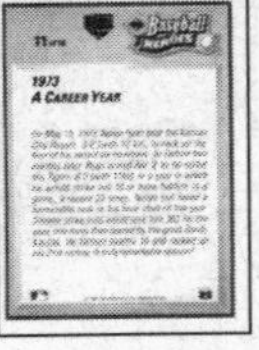

This nine-card standard-size set was included in first series 1991 Upper Deck packs. The set which honors Nolan Ryan and is numbered as a continuation of the Baseball Heroes set which began with Reggie Jackson in 1990. This set honors Ryan's long career and his place in Baseball History. Card number 18 features the artwork of Vernon Wells while the other cards are photos. The complete set price below does not include the signed Ryan card of which only 2500 were made. Signed cards ending with 00 have the expression "Strikeout King" added. These Ryan cards were apparently issued on 100-card sheets with the following configuration: ten each of the nine Ryan Baseball Heroes cards, five Michael Jordan cards and five Baseball Heroes header cards. The Baseball Heroes header card is a standard size card which explains the continuation of the Baseball Heroes series on the back while the front just says Baseball Heroes.

	Nm-Mt	Ex-Mt
COMPLETE SET (10)	5.00	1.50
COMMON RYAN (10-18)	.50	.15
NNO Baseball Heroes SP	1.00	.30
(Header card)		
AU2 Nolan Ryan AU	200.00	60.00
(Signed and Numbered out of 2500)		

1991 Upper Deck Silver Sluggers

The Upper Deck Silver Slugger set features nine players from each league, representing the nine batting positions on the team. The cards were issued one per 1991 Upper Deck jumbo pack. The cards measure the standard size. The cards are numbered on the back with an "SS" prefix.

	Nm-Mt	Ex-Mt
COMPLETE SET (18)	15.00	4.50
SS1 Julio Franco	.75	.23
SS2 Alan Trammell	.75	.23
SS3 Rickey Henderson	2.00	.60
SS4 Jose Canseco	2.00	.60
SS5 Barry Bonds	5.00	1.50
SS6 Eddie Murray	2.00	.60
SS7 Kelly Gruber	.40	.12
SS8 Ryne Sandberg	3.00	.90
SS9 Darryl Strawberry	.75	.23
SS10 Ellis Burks	.75	.23
SS11 Lance Parrish	.75	.23
SS12 Cecil Fielder	.75	.23
SS13 Matt Williams	.75	.23
SS14 Dave Parker	.75	.23
SS15 Bobby Bonilla	.75	.23
SS16 Don Robinson	.40	.12
SS17 Benito Santiago	.75	.23
SS18 Barry Larkin	1.25	.35

1991 Upper Deck Final Edition

The 1991 Upper Deck Final Edition boxed set contains 100 standard-size cards and showcas

es players who made major contributions during their team's late-season pennant drive. In addition to the late season traded and impact rookie cards (22-78), the set includes two special subsets: Diamond Skills cards (1-21), depicting the best Minor League prospects, and All-Star cards (80-99). Six assorted team logo hologram cards were issued with each set. The cards are numbered on the back with an F suffix. Among the outstanding Rookie Cards in this set are Ryan Klesko, Kenny Lofton, Pedro Martinez, Ivan Rodriguez, Jim Thome, Rondell White, and Dmitri Young.

	Nm-Mt	Ex-Mt
COMP.FACT.SET (100)	10.00	3.00
1F Ryan Klesko CL	.10	.03
Reggie Sanders		
2F Pedro Martinez RC	5.00	1.50
3F Lance Dickson	.05	.02
4F Royce Clayton	.05	.02
5F Scott Bryant	.05	.02
6F Dan Wilson RC	.25	.07
7F Dmitri Young RC	.40	.12
8F Ryan Klesko RC	.50	.15
9F Tom Goodwin	.05	.02
10F Rondell White RC	.40	.12
11F Reggie Sanders	.15	.04
12F Todd Van Poppel	.05	.02
13F Arthur Rhodes RC	.25	.07
14F Eddie Zosky	.05	.02
15F Gerald Williams RC	.25	.07
16F Robert Eenhoorn RC	.10	.03
17F Jim Thome RC	2.50	.75
18F Marc Newfield RC	.10	.03
19F Kerwin Moore RC	.10	.03
20F Jeff McNeely RC	.10	.03
21F Frankie Rodriguez RC	.10	.03
22F Andy Mota	.05	.02
23F Chris Haney RC	.10	.03
24F Kenny Lofton RC	.50	.15
25F Dave Nilsson RC	.25	.07
26F Derek Bell	.10	.03
27F Frank Castillo RC	.25	.07
28F Candy Maldonado	.05	.02
29F Chuck McElroy	.05	.02
30F Chito Martinez	.05	.02
31F Steve Howe	.05	.02
32F Freddie Benavides	.05	.02
33F Scott Kamieniecki RC	.10	.03
34F Denny Neagle RC	.25	.07
35F Mike Humphreys RC	.10	.03
36F Mike Remlinger	.05	.02
37F Scott Coolbaugh	.05	.02
38F Darren Lewis	.05	.02
39F Thomas Howard	.05	.02
40F John Candelaria	.05	.02
41F Todd Benzinger	.05	.02
42F Wilson Alvarez	.05	.02
43F Patrick Lennon RC	.10	.03
44F Rusty Meacham RC	.10	.03
45F Ryan Bowen RC	.10	.03
46F Rick Wilkins RC	.10	.03
47F Ed Sprague	.05	.02
48F Bob Scanlan	.05	.02
49F Tom Candiotti	.05	.02
50F Dennis Martinez	.10	.03
(Perfecto)		
51F Oil Can Boyd	.05	.02
52F Glenallen Hill	.05	.02
53F Scott Livingstone RC	.10	.03
54F Brian R. Hunter RC	.25	.07
55F Ivan Rodriguez RC	1.50	.45
56F Keith Mitchell RC	.10	.03
57F Roger McDowell	.05	.02
58F Otis Nixon	.05	.02
59F Juan Bell	.05	.02
60F Bill Krueger	.05	.02
61F Chris Donnels	.05	.02
62F Tommy Greene	.05	.02
63F Doug Simons	.05	.02
64F Andy Ashby RC	.25	.07
65F Anthony Young RC	.10	.03
66F Kevin Morton	.05	.02
67F Bret Barberie RC**	.10	.03
68F Scott Servais RC	.25	.07
69F Ron Darling	.05	.02
70F Tim Burke	.05	.02
71F Vicente Palacios	.05	.02
72F Gerald Alexander	.05	.02
73F Reggie Jefferson	.05	.02
74F Dean Palmer	.10	.03
75F Mark Whiten	.05	.02
76F Randy Tomlin RC	.10	.03
77F Mark Wohlers RC	.25	.07
78F Brook Jacoby	.05	.02
79F Ken Griffey Jr. CL	.40	.12
Ryne Sandberg		
80F Jack Morris AS	.05	.02
81F Sandy Alomar Jr. AS	.05	.02
82F Cecil Fielder AS	.05	.02
83F Roberto Alomar AS	.10	.03
84F Wade Boggs AS	.10	.03
85F Cal Ripken AS	.40	.12
86F Rickey Henderson AS	.15	.04
87F Ken Griffey Jr. AS	.25	.07
88F Dave Henderson AS	.05	.02
89F Danny Tartabull AS	.05	.02
90F Tom Glavine AS	.10	.03
91F Benito Santiago AS	.05	.02
92F Will Clark AS	.10	.03
93F Ryne Sandberg AS	.25	.07
94F Chris Sabo AS	.05	.02
95F Ozzie Smith AS	.25	.07
96F Ivan Calderon AS	.05	.02
97F Tony Gwynn AS	.15	.04
98F Andre Dawson AS	.05	.02
99F Bobby Bonilla AS	.05	.02
100F Checklist 1-100	.05	.02

1992 Upper Deck

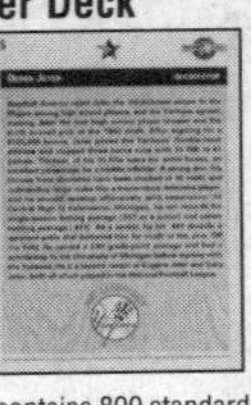

The 1992 Upper Deck set contains 800 standard-size cards issued in two separate series of 700 and 100 cards respectively. The cards were distributed in low and high series foil packs in addition to factory sets. Factory sets feature a unique gold-foil hologram on the card backs (in contrast to the silver hologram on foil pack cards). Special subsets included in the set are Star Rookies (1-27), Team Checklists (29-40/86-99), with player portraits by Vernon Wells Sr.; Top Prospects (52-77); Bloodlines (79-85), Diamond Skills (640-650/711-721) and Diamond Debuts (771-780). Rookie Cards in the set include Shawn Green, Brian Jordan and Manny Ramirez. A special card picturing Tom Selleck and Frank Thomas, commemorating the forgettable movie "Mr. Baseball", was randomly inserted into high series packs. A standard-size Ted Williams hologram card was randomly inserted into low series packs. By mailing in 15 low series foil wrappers, a completed order form, and a handling fee, the collector could receive an 8 1/2" by 11" numbered, black and white lithograph picturing Ted Williams in his batting swing.

	Nm-Mt	Ex-Mt
COMPLETE SET (800)	25.00	7.50
COMPLETE LO SET (700)	20.00	6.00
COMPLETE HI SET (100)	5.00	1.50
1 Ryan Klesko CL	.25	.07
Jim Thome		
2 Royce Clayton SR	.05	.02
3 Brian Jordan SR RC	.40	.12
4 Dave Fleming SR	.05	.02
5 Jim Thome SR	.25	.07
6 Jeff Juden SR	.05	.02
7 Roberto Hernandez SR	.05	.02
8 Kyle Abbott SR	.05	.02
9 Chris George SR	.05	.02
10 Rob Maurer SR	.05	.02
11 Donald Harris SR	.05	.02
12 Ted Wood SR	.05	.02
13 Patrick Lennon SR	.05	.02
14 Willie Banks SR	.05	.02
15 Roger Salkeld SR UER	.05	.02
(Bill was his grand-father, not his father)		
16 Wil Cordero SR	.05	.02
17 Arthur Rhodes SR	.05	.02
18 Pedro Martinez SR	1.00	.30
19 Andy Ashby SR	.05	.02
20 Tom Goodwin SR	.05	.02
21 Braulio Castillo SR	.05	.02
22 Todd Van Poppel SR	.05	.02
23 Brian Williams SR RC	.05	.02
24 Ryan Klesko SR	.10	.03
25 Kenny Lofton SR	.15	.04
26 Derek Bell SR	.10	.03
27 Reggie Sanders SR	.05	.02
28 Dave Winfield's 400th	.05	.02
29 David Justice TC	.05	.02
30 Rob Dibble TC	.05	.02
31 Craig Biggio TC	.10	.03
32 Eddie Murray TC	.15	.04
33 Fred McGriff TC	.10	.03
34 Willie McGee TC	.05	.02
35 Shawon Dunston TC	.05	.02
36 Delino DeShields TC	.05	.02
37 Howard Johnson TC	.05	.02
38 John Kruk TC	.05	.02
39 Doug Drabek TC	.05	.02
40 Todd Zeile TC	.05	.02
41 Steve Avery	.05	.02
Playoff Perfection		
42 Jeremy Hernandez RC	.05	.02
43 Doug Henry RC	.10	.03
44 Chris Donnels	.05	.02
45 Mo Sanford	.05	.02
46 Scott Kamieniecki	.05	.02
47 Mark Lemke	.05	.02
48 Steve Farr	.05	.02
49 Francisco Oliveras	.05	.02
50 Ced Landrum	.05	.02
51 Rondell White CL	.10	.03
Mark Newfield		
52 Eduardo Perez TP RC	.25	.07
53 Tom Nevers TP	.05	.02
54 David Zancanaro TP	.05	.02
55 Shawn Green TP RC	1.50	.45
56 Mark Wohlers TP	.05	.02
57 Dave Nilsson TP	.05	.02
58 Dmitri Young TP	.10	.03
59 Ryan Hawblitzel TP RC	.10	.03
60 Raul Mondesi TP	.10	.03
61 Rondell White TP	.10	.03
62 Steve Hosey TP	.05	.02
63 Manny Ramirez TP RC	2.50	.75
64 Marc Newfield TP	.05	.02
65 Jeromy Burnitz TP	.10	.03
66 Mark Smith TP RC	.10	.03
67 Joey Hamilton TP RC	.25	.07
68 Tyler Green TP RC	.10	.03
69 Jon Farrell TP RC	.10	.03
70 Kurt Miller TP	.05	.02
71 Jeff Plympton TP	.05	.02
72 Dan Wilson TP	.05	.02
73 Joe Vitiello TP RC	.10	.03
74 Rico Brogna TP	.05	.02
75 David McCarty TP RC	.25	.07
76 Bob Wickman TP	.05	.02
77 Carlos Rodriguez TP	.05	.02
78 Jim Abbott	.10	.03
Stay In School		
79 Ramon Martinez	.25	.07
Pedro Martinez		
80 Kevin Mitchell	.05	.02
Keith Mitchell		
81 Sandy Alomar Jr.	.10	.03
Roberto Alomar		
82 Cal Ripken	.50	.15
Billy Ripken		
83 Tony Gwynn	.15	.04
Chris Gwynn		
84 Dwight Gooden	.10	.03
Gary Sheffield		
85 Ken Griffey Sr.	.25	.07
Ken Griffey Jr.		
Craig Griffey		
86 Jim Abbott TC	.10	.03
87 Frank Thomas TC	.15	.04
88 Danny Tartabull TC	.05	.02
89 Scott Erickson TC	.05	.02
90 Rickey Henderson TC	.15	.04
91 Edgar Martinez TC	.10	.03
92 Nolan Ryan TC	.50	.15
93 Ben McDonald TC	.05	.02
94 Ellis Burks TC	.05	.02
95 Greg Swindell TC	.05	.02
96 Cecil Fielder TC	.05	.02
97 Greg Vaughn TC	.05	.02
98 Kevin Maas TC	.05	.02
99 Dave Stieb TC	.05	.02
100 Checklist 1-100	.05	.02
101 Joe Oliver	.05	.02
102 Hector Villanueva	.05	.02
103 Ed Whitson	.05	.02
104 Danny Jackson	.05	.02
105 Chris Hammond	.05	.02
106 Ricky Jordan	.05	.02
107 Kevin Bass	.05	.02
108 Darrin Fletcher	.05	.02
109 Junior Ortiz	.05	.02
110 Tom Bolton	.05	.02
111 Jeff King	.05	.02
112 Dave Magadan	.05	.02
113 Mike LaValliere	.05	.02
114 Hubie Brooks	.05	.02
115 Jay Bell	.10	.03
116 David Wells	.10	.03
117 Jim Leyritz	.05	.02
118 Manuel Lee	.05	.02
119 Alvaro Espinoza	.05	.02
120 B.J. Surhoff	.10	.03
121 Hal Morris	.05	.02
122 Shawon Dawson	.05	.02
123 Chris Sabo	.05	.02
124 Andre Dawson	.10	.03
125 Eric Davis	.10	.03
126 Chili Davis	.10	.03
127 Dale Murphy	.25	.07
128 Kirk McCaskill	.05	.02
129 Terry Mulholland	.05	.02
130 Rick Aguilera	.10	.03
131 Vince Coleman	.05	.02
132 Andy Van Slyke	.10	.03
133 Gregg Jefferies	.05	.02
134 Barry Bonds	.60	.18
135 Dwight Gooden	.10	.03
136 Dave Stieb	.05	.02
137 Albert Belle	.10	.03
138 Teddy Higuera	.05	.02
139 Jesse Barfield	.05	.02
140 Pat Borders	.05	.02
141 Bip Roberts	.05	.02
142 Rob Dibble	.10	.03
143 Mark Grace	.15	.04
144 Barry Larkin	.15	.04
145 Ryne Sandberg	.40	.12
146 Scott Erickson	.05	.02
147 Luis Polonia	.05	.02
148 John Burkett	.05	.02
149 Luis Sojo	.05	.02
150 Dickie Thon	.05	.02
151 Walt Weiss	.05	.02
152 Mike Scioscia	.05	.02
153 Mark McGwire	.60	.18
154 Matt Williams	.10	.03
155 Rickey Henderson	.25	.07
156 Sandy Alomar Jr.	.05	.02
157 Brian McRae	.05	.02
158 Harold Baines	.10	.03
159 Kevin Appier	.10	.03
160 Felix Fermin	.05	.02
161 Leo Gomez	.05	.02
162 Craig Biggio	.15	.04
163 Ben McDonald	.05	.02
164 Randy Johnson	.25	.07
165 Cal Ripken	.75	.23
166 Frank Thomas	.25	.07
167 Delino DeShields	.05	.02
168 Greg Gagne	.05	.02
169 Ron Karkovice	.05	.02
170 Charlie Leibrandt	.05	.02
171 Dave Righetti	.10	.03
172 Dave Henderson	.05	.02
173 Steve Decker	.05	.02
174 Darryl Strawberry	.10	.03
175 Will Clark	.25	.07
176 Ruben Sierra	.05	.02
177 Ozzie Smith	.40	.12
178 Charles Nagy	.05	.02
179 Gary Pettis	.05	.02
180 Kirk Gibson	.10	.03
181 Randy Milligan	.05	.02
182 Dave Valle	.05	.02
183 Chris Hoiles	.05	.02
184 Tony Phillips	.05	.02
185 Brady Anderson	.10	.03
186 Scott Fletcher	.05	.02
187 Gene Larkin	.05	.02
188 Lance Johnson	.05	.02
189 Greg Olson	.05	.02
190 Melido Perez	.05	.02
191 Lenny Harris	.05	.02
192 Terry Kennedy	.05	.02
193 Mike Gallego	.05	.02
194 Willie McGee	.10	.03
195 Juan Samuel	.05	.02
196 Jeff Huson	.10	.03
(Shows Jose Canseco sliding into second)		
197 Alex Cole	.05	.02
198 Ron Robinson	.05	.02
199 Joel Skinner	.05	.02
200 Checklist 101-200	.05	.02
201 Kevin Reimer	.05	.02
202 Stan Belinda	.05	.02
203 Pat Tabler	.05	.02
204 Jose Guzman	.05	.02
205 Jose Lind	.05	.02
206 Spike Owen	.05	.02
207 Joe Orsulak	.05	.02
208 Charlie Hayes	.05	.02
209 Mike Devereaux	.05	.02
210 Mike Fitzgerald	.05	.02
211 Willie Randolph	.10	.03
212 Rod Nichols	.05	.02
213 Mike Boddicker	.05	.02
214 Bill Spiers	.05	.02
215 Steve Olin	.05	.02
216 David Howard	.05	.02
217 Gary Varsho	.05	.02
218 Mike Harkey	.05	.02
219 Luis Aquino	.05	.02
220 Chuck McElroy	.05	.02
221 Doug Drabek	.05	.02
222 Dave Winfield	.10	.03
223 Rafael Palmeiro	.15	.04
224 Joe Carter	.10	.03
225 Bobby Bonilla	.10	.03
226 Ivan Calderon	.05	.02
227 Gregg Olson	.05	.02
228 Tim Wallach	.05	.02
229 Terry Pendleton	.10	.03
230 Gilberto Reyes	.05	.02
231 Carlos Baerga	.05	.02
232 Greg Vaughn	.05	.02
233 Bret Saberhagen	.10	.03
234 Gary Sheffield	.10	.03
235 Mark Lewis	.05	.02
236 George Bell	.05	.02
237 Danny Tartabull	.05	.02
238 Willie Wilson	.05	.02
239 Doug Dascenzo	.05	.02
240 Bill Pecota	.05	.02
241 Julio Franco	.10	.03
242 Ed Sprague	.05	.02
243 Juan Gonzalez	.15	.04
244 Chuck Finley	.10	.03
245 Ivan Rodriguez	.25	.07
246 Len Dykstra	.10	.03
247 Deion Sanders	.15	.04
248 Dwight Evans	.10	.03
249 Larry Walker	.15	.04
250 Billy Ripken	.05	.02
251 Mickey Tettleton	.05	.02
252 Tony Pena	.05	.02
253 Benito Santiago	.10	.03
254 Kirby Puckett	.25	.07
255 Cecil Fielder	.10	.03
256 Howard Johnson	.05	.02
257 Andujar Cedeno	.05	.02
258 Jose Rijo	.05	.02
259 Al Osuna	.05	.02
260 Todd Hundley	.05	.02
261 Orel Hershiser	.10	.03
262 Ray Lankford	.05	.02
263 Robin Ventura	.10	.03
264 Felix Jose	.05	.02
265 Eddie Murray	.25	.07
266 Kevin Mitchell	.05	.02
267 Gary Carter	.10	.03
268 Mike Benjamin	.05	.02
269 Dick Schofield	.05	.02
270 Jose Uribe	.05	.02
271 Pete Incaviglia	.05	.02
272 Tony Fernandez	.05	.02
273 Alan Trammell	.10	.03
274 Tony Gwynn	.30	.09
275 Mike Greenwell	.05	.02
276 Jeff Bagwell	.25	.07
277 Frank Viola	.10	.03
278 Randy Myers	.05	.02
279 Ken Caminiti	.10	.03
280 Bill Doran	.05	.02
281 Dan Pasqua	.05	.02
282 Alfredo Griffin	.05	.02
283 Jose Oquendo	.05	.02
284 Kal Daniels	.05	.02
285 Bobby Thigpen	.05	.02
286 Robby Thompson	.05	.02
287 Mark Eichhorn	.05	.02
288 Mike Felder	.05	.02
289 Dave Gallagher	.05	.02
290 Dave Anderson	.05	.02
291 Mel Hall	.05	.02
292 Jerald Clark	.05	.02
293 Al Newman	.05	.02
294 Rob Deer	.05	.02
295 Matt Nokes	.05	.02
296 Jack Armstrong	.05	.02
297 Jim Deshaies	.05	.02
298 Jeff Innis	.05	.02
299 Jeff Reed	.05	.02
300 Checklist 201-300	.05	.02
301 Lonnie Smith	.05	.02
302 Jimmy Key	.10	.03
303 Junior Felix	.05	.02
304 Mike Heath	.05	.02
305 Mark Langston	.05	.02
306 Greg W. Harris	.05	.02
307 Brett Butler	.10	.03
308 Luis Rivera	.05	.02
309 Bruce Ruffin	.05	.02
310 Paul Faries	.05	.02
311 Terry Leach	.05	.02
312 Scott Brosius RC	.40	.12
313 Scott Leius	.05	.02
314 Harold Reynolds	.10	.03
315 Jack Morris	.10	.03
316 David Segui	.05	.02
317 Bill Gullickson	.05	.02
318 Todd Frohwirth	.05	.02
319 Mark Leiter	.05	.02
320 Jeff M. Robinson	.05	.02
321 Gary Gaetti	.10	.03
322 John Smoltz	.15	.04
323 Andy Benes	.05	.02
324 Kelly Gruber	.05	.02
325 Jim Abbott	.15	.04
326 John Kruk	.10	.03
327 Kevin Seitzer	.05	.02
328 Darrin Jackson	.05	.02
329 Kurt Stillwell	.05	.02
330 Mike Maddux	.05	.02
331 Dennis Eckersley	.10	.03

332 Dan Gladden .05 .02
333 Jose Canseco .25 .07
334 Kent Hrbek .10 .03
335 Ken Griffey Sr. .10 .03
336 Greg Swindell .05 .02
337 Trevor Wilson .05 .02
338 Sam Horn .05 .02
339 Mike Henneman .05 .02
340 Jerry Browne .05 .02
341 Glenn Braggs .05 .02
342 Tom Glavine .15 .04
343 Wally Joyner .10 .03
344 Fred McGriff .15 .04
345 Ron Gant .10 .03
346 Ramon Martinez .05 .02
347 Wes Chamberlain .05 .02
348 Terry Shumpert .05 .02
349 Tim Teufel .05 .02
350 Wally Backman .05 .02
351 Joe Girardi .05 .02
352 Devon White .10 .03
353 Greg Maddux .40 .12
354 Ryan Bowen .05 .02
355 Roberto Alomar .15 .04
356 Don Mattingly .60 .18
357 Pedro Guerrero .10 .03
358 Steve Sax .05 .02
359 Joey Cora .05 .02
360 Jim Gantner .05 .02
361 Brian Barnes .05 .02
362 Kevin McReynolds .05 .02
363 Bret Barberie .05 .02
364 David Cone .10 .03
365 Dennis Martinez .10 .03
366 Brian Hunter .05 .02
367 Edgar Martinez .15 .04
368 Steve Finley .10 .03
369 Greg Briley .05 .02
370 Jeff Blauser .05 .02
371 Todd Stottlemyre .05 .02
372 Luis Gonzalez .10 .03
373 Rick Wilkins .05 .02
374 Darryl Kile .10 .03
375 John Olerud .10 .03
376 Lee Smith .10 .03
377 Kevin Maas .05 .02
378 Dante Bichette .10 .03
379 Tom Pagnozzi .05 .02
380 Mike Flanagan .05 .02
381 Charlie O'Brien .05 .02
382 Dave Martinez .05 .02
383 Keith Miller .05 .02
384 Scott Ruskin .05 .02
385 Kevin Elster .05 .02
386 Alvin Davis .05 .02
387 Casey Candaele .05 .02
388 Pete O'Brien .05 .02
389 Jeff Treadway .05 .02
390 Scott Bradley .05 .02
391 Mookie Wilson .10 .03
392 Jimmy Jones .05 .02
393 Candy Maldonado .05 .02
394 Eric Yelding .05 .02
395 Tom Henke .05 .02
396 Franklin Stubbs .05 .02
397 Milt Thompson .05 .02
398 Mark Carreon .05 .02
399 Randy Velarde .05 .02
400 Checklist 301-400 .05 .02
401 Omar Vizquel .15 .04
402 Joe Boever .05 .02
403 Bill Krueger .05 .02
404 Jody Reed .05 .02
405 Mike Schooler .05 .02
406 Jason Grimsley .05 .02
407 Greg Myers .05 .02
408 Randy Ready .05 .02
409 Mike Timlin .05 .02
410 Mitch Williams .05 .02
411 Garry Templeton .05 .02
412 Greg Cadaret .05 .02
413 Donnie Hill .05 .02
414 Wally Whitehurst .05 .02
415 Scott Sanderson .05 .02
416 Thomas Howard .05 .02
417 Neal Heaton .05 .02
418 Charlie Hough .10 .03
419 Jack Howell .05 .02
420 Greg Hibbard .05 .02
421 Carlos Quintana .05 .02
422 Kim Batiste .05 .02
423 Paul Molitor .15 .04
424 Ken Griffey Jr. .40 .12
425 Phil Plantier .05 .02
426 Denny Neagle .10 .03
427 Von Hayes .05 .02
428 Shane Mack .05 .02
429 Darren Daulton .10 .03
430 Dwayne Henry .05 .02
431 Lance Parrish .10 .03
432 Mike Humphreys .05 .02
433 Tim Burke .05 .02
434 Bryan Harvey .05 .02
435 Pat Kelly .05 .02
436 Ozzie Guillen .05 .02
437 Bruce Hurst .05 .02
438 Sammy Sosa .40 .12
439 Dennis Rasmussen .05 .02
440 Ken Patterson .05 .02
441 Jay Buhner .10 .03
442 Pat Combs .05 .02
443 Wade Boggs .15 .04
444 George Brett .60 .18
445 Mo Vaughn .10 .03
446 Chuck Knoblauch .10 .03
447 Tom Candiotti .05 .02
448 Mark Portugal .05 .02
449 Mickey Morandini .05 .02
450 Duane Ward .05 .02
451 Otis Nixon .05 .02
452 Bob Welch .05 .02
453 Rusty Meacham .05 .02
454 Keith Mitchell .05 .02
455 Marquis Grissom .10 .03
456 Robin Yount .40 .12
457 Harvey Pulliam .05 .02
458 Jose DeLeon .05 .02
459 Mark Gubicza .05 .02
460 Darryl Hamilton .05 .02
461 Tom Browning .05 .02
462 Monty Fariss .05 .02
463 Jerome Walton .05 .02
464 Paul O'Neill .15 .04
465 Dean Palmer .10 .03
466 Travis Fryman .10 .03
467 John Smiley .05 .02
468 Lloyd Moseby .05 .02
469 John Wehner .05 .02
470 Skeeter Barnes .05 .02
471 Steve Chitren .05 .02
472 Kent Mercker .05 .02
473 Terry Steinbach .05 .02
474 Andres Galarraga .10 .03
475 Steve Avery .05 .02
476 Tom Gordon .05 .02
477 Cal Eldred .05 .02
478 Omar Olivares .05 .02
479 Julio Machado .05 .02
480 Bob Milacki .05 .02
481 Les Lancaster .05 .02
482 John Candelaria .05 .02
483 Brian Downing .05 .02
484 Roger McDowell .05 .02
485 Scott Scudder .05 .02
486 Zane Smith .05 .02
487 John Cerutti .05 .02
488 Steve Buechele .05 .02
489 Paul Gibson .05 .02
490 Curtis Wilkerson .05 .02
491 Marvin Freeman .05 .02
492 Tom Foley .05 .02
493 Juan Berenguer .05 .02
494 Ernest Riles .05 .02
495 Sid Bream .05 .02
496 Chuck Crim .05 .02
497 Mike Macfarlane .05 .02
498 Dale Sveum .05 .02
499 Storm Davis .05 .02
500 Checklist 401-500 .05 .02
501 Jeff Reardon .10 .03
502 Shawn Abner .05 .02
503 Tony Fossas .05 .02
504 Cory Snyder .05 .02
505 Matt Young .05 .02
506 Allan Anderson .05 .02
507 Mark Lee .05 .02
508 Gene Nelson .05 .02
509 Mike Pagliarulo .05 .02
510 Rafael Belliard .05 .02
511 Jay Howell .05 .02
512 Bob Tewksbury .05 .02
513 Mike Morgan .05 .02
514 John Franco .10 .03
515 Kevin Gross .05 .02
516 Lou Whitaker .10 .03
517 Orlando Merced .05 .02
518 Todd Benzinger .05 .02
519 Gary Redus .05 .02
520 Walt Terrell .05 .02
521 Jack Clark .10 .03
522 Dave Parker .10 .03
523 Tim Naehring .05 .02
524 Mark Whiten .05 .02
525 Ellis Burks .10 .03
526 Frank Castillo .05 .02
527 Brian Harper .05 .02
528 Brook Jacoby .05 .02
529 Rick Sutcliffe .10 .03
530 Joe Klink .05 .02
531 Terry Bross .05 .02
532 Jose Offerman .05 .02
533 Todd Zeile .05 .02
534 Eric Karros .10 .03
535 Anthony Young .05 .02
536 Milt Cuyler .05 .02
537 Randy Tomlin .05 .02
538 Scott Livingstone .05 .02
539 Jim Eisenreich .05 .02
540 Don Slaught .05 .02
541 Scott Cooper .05 .02
542 Joe Grahe .05 .02
543 Tom Brunansky .05 .02
544 Eddie Zosky .05 .02
545 Roger Clemens .50 .15
546 David Justice .10 .03
547 Dave Stewart .10 .03
548 David West .05 .02
549 Dave Smith .05 .02
550 Dan Plesac .05 .02
551 Alex Fernandez .05 .02
552 Bernard Gilkey .05 .02
553 Jack McDowell .05 .02
554 Tino Martinez .15 .04
555 Bo Jackson .25 .07
556 Bernie Williams .15 .04
557 Mark Gardner .05 .02
558 Glenallen Hill .05 .02
559 Oil Can Boyd .05 .02
560 Chris James .05 .02
561 Scott Servais .05 .02
562 Rey Sanchez RC .25 .07
563 Paul McClellan .05 .02
564 Andy Mota .05 .02
565 Darren Lewis .05 .02
566 Jose Melendez .05 .02
567 Tommy Greene .05 .02
568 Rich Rodriguez .05 .02
569 Heathcliff Slocumb .05 .02
570 Joe Hesketh .05 .02
571 Carlton Fisk .15 .04
572 Erik Hanson .05 .02
573 Wilson Alvarez .05 .02
574 Rheal Cormier .05 .02
575 Tim Raines .10 .03
576 Bobby Witt .05 .02
577 Roberto Kelly .05 .02
578 Kevin Brown .10 .03
579 Chris Nabholz .05 .02
580 Jesse Orosco .05 .02
581 Jeff Brantley .05 .02
582 Rafael Ramirez .05 .02
583 Kelly Downs .05 .02
584 Mike Simms .05 .02
585 Mike Remlinger .05 .02
586 Dave Hollins .05 .02
587 Larry Andersen .05 .02
588 Mike Gardiner .05 .02
589 Craig Lefferts .05 .02
590 Paul Assenmacher .05 .02
591 Bryn Smith .05 .02
592 Donn Pall .05 .02
593 Mike Jackson .05 .02
594 Scott Radinsky .05 .02
595 Brian Holman .05 .02
596 Geronimo Pena .05 .02
597 Mike Jeffcoat .05 .02
598 Carlos Martinez .05 .02
599 Geno Petralli .05 .02
600 Checklist 501-600 .05 .02
601 Jerry Don Gleaton .05 .02
602 Adam Peterson .05 .02
603 Craig Grebeck .05 .02
604 Mark Guthrie .05 .02
605 Frank Tanana .05 .02
606 Hensley Meulens .05 .02
607 Mark Davis .05 .02
608 Eric Plunk .05 .02
609 Mark Williamson .05 .02
610 Lee Guetterman .05 .02
611 Bobby Rose .05 .02
612 Bill Wegman .05 .02
613 Mike Hartley .05 .02
614 Chris Beasley .05 .02
615 Chris Bosio .05 .02
616 Henry Cotto .05 .02
617 Chico Walker .05 .02
618 Russ Swan .05 .02
619 Bob Walk .05 .02
620 Bill Swift .05 .02
621 Warren Newson .05 .02
622 Steve Bedrosian .05 .02
623 Ricky Bones .05 .02
624 Kevin Tapani .05 .02
625 Juan Guzman .05 .02
626 Jeff Johnson .05 .02
627 Jeff Montgomery .05 .02
628 Ken Hill .05 .02
629 Gary Thurman .05 .02
630 Steve Howe .05 .02
631 Jose DeJesus .05 .02
632 Kirk Dressendorfer .05 .02
633 Jaime Navarro .05 .02
634 Lee Stevens .05 .02
635 Pete Harnisch .05 .02
636 Bill Landrum .05 .02
637 Rich DeLucia .05 .02
638 Luis Salazar .05 .02
639 Rob Murphy .05 .02
640 Jose Canseco CL .15 .04
Rickey Henderson
641 Roger Clemens DS .25 .07
642 Jim Abbott DS .10 .03
643 Travis Fryman DS .05 .02
644 Jesse Barfield DS .05 .02
645 Cal Ripken DS .40 .12
646 Wade Boggs DS .10 .03
647 Cecil Fielder DS .05 .02
648 Rickey Henderson DS .15 .04
649 Jose Canseco DS .10 .03
650 Ken Griffey Jr. DS .25 .07
651 Kenny Rogers .10 .03
652 Luis Mercedes .05 .02
653 Mike Stanton .05 .02
654 Glenn Davis .05 .02
655 Nolan Ryan 1.00 .30
656 Reggie Jefferson .05 .02
657 Javier Ortiz .05 .02
658 Greg A. Harris .05 .02
659 Mariano Duncan .05 .02
660 Jeff Shaw .05 .02
661 Mike Moore .05 .02
662 Chris Haney .05 .02
663 Joe Slusarski .05 .02
664 Wayne Housie .05 .02
665 Carlos Garcia .05 .02
666 Bob Ojeda .05 .02
667 Bryan Hickerson RC .10 .03
668 Tim Belcher .05 .02
669 Ron Darling .05 .02
670 Rex Hudler .05 .02
671 Sid Fernandez .05 .02
672 Chito Martinez .05 .02
673 Pete Schourek .05 .02
674 Armando Reynoso RC .25 .07
675 Mike Mussina .25 .07
676 Kevin Morton .05 .02
677 Norm Charlton .05 .02
678 Danny Darwin .05 .02
679 Eric King .05 .02
680 Ted Power .05 .02
681 Barry Jones .05 .02
682 Carney Lansford .10 .03
683 Mel Rojas .05 .02
684 Rick Honeycutt .05 .02
685 Jeff Fassero .05 .02
686 Cris Carpenter .05 .02
687 Tim Crews .05 .02
688 Scott Terry .05 .02
689 Chris Gwynn .05 .02
690 Gerald Perry .05 .02
691 John Barfield .05 .02
692 Bob Melvin .05 .02
693 Juan Agosto .05 .02
694 Alejandro Pena .05 .02
695 Jeff Russell .05 .02
696 Carmelo Martinez .05 .02
697 Bud Black .05 .02
698 Dave Otto .05 .02
699 Billy Hatcher .05 .02
700 Checklist 601-700 .05 .02
701 Clemente Nunez RC .05 .02
702 Mark Clark .05 .02
Donovan Osborne
Brian Jordan
703 Mike Morgan .05 .02
704 Keith Miller .05 .02
705 Kurt Stillwell .05 .02
706 Damon Berryhill .05 .02
707 Von Hayes .05 .02
708 Rick Sutcliffe .10 .03
709 Hubie Brooks .05 .02
710 Ryan Turner RC .10 .03
711 Barry Bonds CL .30 .09
Andy Van Slyke
712 Jose Rijo DS .05 .02
713 Tom Glavine DS .10 .03
714 Shawon Dunston DS .05 .02
715 Andy Van Slyke DS .05 .02
716 Ozzie Smith DS .25 .07
717 Tony Gwynn DS .15 .04
718 Will Clark DS .10 .03
719 Marquis Grissom DS .05 .02
720 Howard Johnson DS .05 .02
721 Barry Bonds DS .30 .09
722 Kirk McCaskill .05 .02
723 Sammy Sosa .75 .23
724 George Bell .05 .02
725 Gregg Jefferies .05 .02
726 Gary DiSarcina .05 .02
727 Mike Bordick .05 .02
728 Eddie Murray 400 HR .15 .04
729 Rene Gonzales .05 .02
730 Mike Bielecki .05 .02
731 Calvin Jones .05 .02
732 Jack Morris .10 .03
733 Frank Viola .10 .03
734 Dave Winfield .10 .03
735 Kevin Mitchell .05 .02
736 Bill Swift .05 .02
737 Dan Gladden .05 .02
738 Mike Jackson .05 .02
739 Mark Carreon .05 .02
740 Kirt Manwaring .05 .02
741 Randy Myers .05 .02
742 Kevin McReynolds .05 .02
743 Steve Sax .05 .02
744 Wally Joyner .10 .03
745 Gary Sheffield .10 .03
746 Danny Tartabull .05 .02
747 Julio Valera .05 .02
748 Denny Neagle .10 .03
749 Lance Blankenship .05 .02
750 Mike Gallego .05 .02
751 Bret Saberhagen .10 .03
752 Ruben Amaro .05 .02
753 Eddie Murray .25 .07
754 Kyle Abbott .05 .02
755 Bobby Bonilla .10 .03
756 Eric Davis .10 .03
757 Eddie Taubensee RC .25 .07
758 Andres Galarraga .10 .03
759 Pete Incaviglia .05 .02
760 Tom Candiotti .05 .02
761 Tim Belcher .05 .02
762 Ricky Bones .05 .02
763 Bip Roberts .05 .02
764 Pedro Munoz .05 .02
765 Greg Swindell .05 .02
766 Kenny Lofton .15 .04
767 Gary Carter .10 .03
768 Charlie Hayes .05 .02
769 Dickie Thon .05 .02
770 D. Osborne DD CL .05 .02
771 Bret Boone DD .25 .07
772 A. Cianfrocco DD RC .10 .03
773 Mark Clark DD RC .10 .03
774 Chad Curtis DD RC .25 .07
775 Pat Listach DD RC .25 .07
776 Pat Mahomes DD RC .25 .07
777 Donovan Osborne DD .05 .02
778 John Patterson DD RC .10 .03
779 Andy Stankiewicz DD .05 .02
780 Turk Wendell DD RC .25 .07
781 Bill Krueger .05 .02
782 Rickey Henderson 1000 .15 .04
783 Kevin Seitzer .05 .02
784 Dave Martinez .05 .02
785 John Smiley .05 .02
786 Matt Stairs RC .25 .07
787 Scott Scudder .05 .02
788 John Wetteland .10 .03
789 Jack Armstrong .05 .02
790 Ken Hill .05 .02
791 Dick Schofield .05 .02
792 Mariano Duncan .05 .02
793 Bill Pecota .05 .02
794 Mike Kelly RC .10 .03
795 Willie Randolph .10 .03
796 Butch Henry .05 .02
797 Carlos Hernandez .05 .02
798 Doug Jones .05 .02
799 Melido Perez .05 .02
800 Checklist 701-800 .05 .02
HH2 T.Williams Hologram 2.00 .60
Top left corner says
91 Upper Deck 92
SP3 Deion Sanders FB/BB 1.00 .30
SP4 Tom Selleck 1.00 .30
Frank Thomas SP
(Mr. Baseball)

1992 Upper Deck Gold Hologram

All cards issued in 1992 Upper Deck factory sets have a gold hologram on the back.

	Nm-Mt	Ex-Mt
COMP.FACT.SET (800)	25.00	7.50
*STARS: .4X TO 1X BASIC CARDS		
*ROOKIES: .4X TO 1X BASIC		

1992 Upper Deck Bench/Morgan Heroes

This standard size 10-card set was randomly inserted in 1992 Upper Deck high number packs. Both Bench and Morgan autographed 2,500 of card number 45, which displays a portrait by sports artist Vernon Wells. The fronts feature color photos of Bench (37-39), Morgan (40-42), or both (43-44) at various stages of their baseball careers.

	Nm-Mt	Ex-Mt
COMPLETE SET (10)	15.00	4.50
COMMON CARD (37-45)	1.50	.45
NNO Baseball Heroes SP (Header card)	2.50	.75
AU5 Johnny Bench and Joe Morgan AU	120.00	36.00

(Signed and Numbered of 2500)

1992 Upper Deck College POY Holograms

This three-card standard-size set was randomly inserted in 1992 Upper Deck high series foil packs. This set features College Player of the Year winners for 1989 through 1991. The cards are numbered on the back with the prefix "CP".

	Nm-Mt	Ex-Mt
COMPLETE SET (3)	2.00	.60
CP1 David McCarty	1.00	.30
CP2 Mike Kelly	1.00	.30
CP3 Ben McDonald	1.00	.30

1992 Upper Deck Heroes of Baseball

Continuing a popular insert set introduced the previous year, Upper Deck produced four new commemorative cards, including three player cards and one portrait card by sports artist Vernon Wells. These cards were randomly inserted in 1992 Upper Deck baseball low number foil packs. Three thousand of each card were personally numbered and autographed by each player.

	Nm-Mt	Ex-Mt
H5 Vida Blue	2.00	.60
H6 Lou Brock	2.00	.60
H7 Rollie Fingers	2.00	.60
H8 Vida Blue ART Lou Brock Rollie Fingers	2.00	.60
AU5 Vida Blue AU/3000	15.00	4.50
AU6 Lou Brock AU/3000	25.00	7.50
AU7 R.Fingers AU/3000	15.00	4.50

1992 Upper Deck Home Run Heroes

This 26-card standard-size set was inserted one per pack into 1992 Upper Deck low series jumbo packs. The set spotlights the 1991 home run leaders from each of the 26 Major League teams.

	Nm-Mt	Ex-Mt
COMPLETE SET (26)	12.00	3.60
HR1 Jose Canseco	.75	.23
HR2 Cecil Fielder	.30	.09
HR3 Howard Johnson	.15	.04
HR4 Cal Ripken	2.50	.75
HR5 Matt Williams	.30	.09
HR6 Joe Carter	.30	.09
HR7 Ron Gant	.30	.09
HR8 Frank Thomas	.75	.23
HR9 Andre Dawson	.30	.09
HR10 Fred McGriff	.50	.15
HR11 Danny Tartabull	.15	.04
HR12 Chili Davis	.30	.09
HR13 Albert Belle	.30	.09
HR14 Jack Clark	.30	.09
HR15 Paul O'Neill	.50	.15
HR16 Darryl Strawberry	.30	.09
HR17 Dave Winfield	.30	.09
HR18 Jay Buhner	.30	.09
HR19 Juan Gonzalez	.50	.15
HR20 Greg Vaughn	.15	.04
HR21 Barry Bonds	2.00	.60
HR22 Matt Nokes	.15	.04
HR23 John Kruk	.30	.09
HR24 Ivan Calderon	.15	.04
HR25 Jeff Bagwell	.75	.23
HR26 Todd Zeile	.15	.04

1992 Upper Deck Scouting Report

Inserted one per high series jumbo pack, cards from this 25-card standard-size set feature outstanding prospects in baseball. Please note these cards are highly condition sensitive and are priced below in NmMt condition. Mint copies trade for premiums.

	Nm-Mt	Ex-Mt
COMPLETE SET (25)	20.00	6.00
SR1 Andy Ashby	1.00	.30
SR2 Willie Banks	1.00	.30
SR3 Kim Batiste	1.00	.30
SR4 Derek Bell	1.00	.30
SR5 Archi Cianfrocco	1.00	.30
SR6 Royce Clayton	1.00	.30
SR7 Gary DiSarcina	1.00	.30
SR8 Dave Fleming	1.00	.30
SR9 Butch Henry	1.00	.30
SR10 Todd Hundley	1.00	.30
SR11 Brian Jordan	1.00	.30
SR12 Eric Karros	1.00	.30
SR13 Pat Listach	1.00	.30
SR14 Scott Livingstone	1.00	.30
SR15 Kenny Lofton	1.00	.30
SR16 Pat Mahomes	1.00	.30
SR17 Denny Neagle	1.00	.30
SR18 Dave Nilsson	1.00	.30
SR19 Donovan Osborne	1.00	.30
SR20 Reggie Sanders	1.00	.30
SR21 Andy Stankiewicz	1.00	.30
SR22 Jim Thome	2.00	.60
SR23 Julio Valera	1.00	.30
SR24 Mark Wohlers	1.00	.30
SR25 Anthony Young	1.00	.30

1992 Upper Deck Williams Best

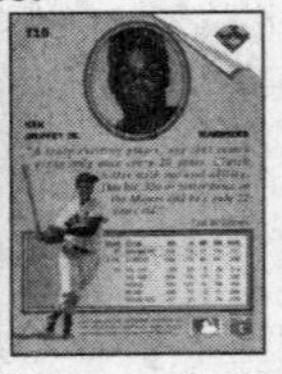

This 20-card standard-size set contains Ted Williams' choices of best current and future hitters in the game. The cards were randomly inserted in Upper Deck high number foil packs. These cards are condition sensitive and priced below in NmMt condition. True mint condition copies do sell for more than these listed prices.

	Nm-Mt	Ex-Mt
COMPLETE SET (20)	20.00	6.00
T1 Wade Boggs	.75	.23
T2 Barry Bonds	3.00	.90
T3 Jose Canseco	1.25	.35
T4 Will Clark	1.25	.35
T5 Cecil Fielder	.50	.15
T6 Tony Gwynn	1.50	.45
T7 Rickey Henderson	1.25	.35
T8 Fred McGriff	.75	.23
T9 Kirby Puckett	1.25	.35
T10 Ruben Sierra	.25	.07
T11 Roberto Alomar	.75	.23
T12 Jeff Bagwell	1.25	.35
T13 Albert Belle	.50	.15
T14 Juan Gonzalez	.75	.23
T15 Ken Griffey Jr.	2.00	.60
T16 Chris Hoiles	.25	.07
T17 David Justice	.50	.15
T18 Phil Plantier	.25	.07
T19 Frank Thomas	1.25	.35
T20 Robin Ventura	.50	.15

1992 Upper Deck Williams Heroes

This standard-size ten-card set was randomly inserted in 1992 Upper Deck low number foil packs. Williams autographed 2,500 of card 36, which displays his portrait by sports artist Vernon Wells. The cards are numbered on the back in continuation of the Upper Deck heroes series.

	Nm-Mt	Ex-Mt
COMPLETE SET (10)	6.00	1.80
COMMON (28-36)	.50	.15
NNO Baseball Heroes SP (Header card)	2.00	.60
AU4 Ted Williams (Signed and Numbered of 2500)	500.00	150.00

1992 Upper Deck FanFest

As a title sponsor of the 1992 All-Star FanFest in San Diego, Upper Deck produced this 54-card standard size set to commemorate past, present, and future All-Stars Heroes of Major League Baseball. Sixty sets were packaged in a case, and each case had at least one gold foil set. Cards 1-10 feature ten Future Heroes that are, in Upper Deck's opinion, sure bets to make an upcoming team; cards 11-44 present active All-Star alumni; and cards 45-54 salute All-Star Heroes of the past with ten fan favorites.

	Nm-Mt	Ex-Mt
COMP.FACT SET (54)	10.00	3.00
*GOLD: 10X VALUE		
1 Steve Avery	.10	.03
2 Ivan Rodriguez	.75	.23
3 Jeff Bagwell	.75	.23
4 Delino DeShields	.20	.06
5 Royce Clayton	.10	.03
6 Robin Ventura	.50	.15
7 Phil Plantier	.10	.03
8 Ray Lankford	.20	.06
9 Juan Gonzalez	.75	.23
10 Frank Thomas	1.00	.30
11 Roberto Alomar	.50	.15
12 Sandy Alomar Jr.	.20	.06
13 Wade Boggs	.75	.23
14 Barry Bonds	1.50	.45
15 Bobby Bonilla	.10	.03
16 George Brett	1.50	.45
17 Jose Canseco	.60	.18
18 Will Clark	.50	.15
19 Roger Clemens	1.50	.45
20 Eric Davis	.20	.06
21 Rob Dibble	.10	.03
22 Cecil Fielder	.20	.06
23 Dwight Gooden	.20	.06
24 Ken Griffey Jr.	2.00	.60
25 Tony Gwynn	1.50	.45
26 Bryan Harvey	.10	.03
27 Rickey Henderson	1.00	.30
28 Howard Johnson	.10	.03
29 Wally Joyner	.20	.06
30 Barry Larkin	.50	.15
31 Don Mattingly	1.50	.45
32 Mark McGwire	2.50	.75
33 Dale Murphy	.50	.15
34 Rafael Palmeiro	.50	.15
35 Kirby Puckett	.75	.23
36 Cal Ripken	3.00	.90
37 Nolan Ryan	3.00	.90
38 Chris Sabo	.10	.03
39 Ryne Sandberg	1.50	.45
40 Benito Santiago	.20	.06
41 Ruben Sierra	.20	.06
42 Ozzie Smith	1.50	.45
43 Darryl Strawberry	.20	.06
44 Robin Yount	.75	.23
45 Rollie Fingers	.20	.06
46 Reggie Jackson	.50	.15
47 Billy Williams	.20	.06
48 Lou Brock	.50	.15
49 Gaylord Perry	.20	.06
50 Ted Williams	3.00	.90
51 Brooks Robinson	.50	.15
52 Bob Gibson	.50	.15
53 Bobby Bonds	.20	.06
54 Robin Roberts	.20	.06

1993 Upper Deck

The 1993 Upper Deck set consists of two series of 420 standard-size cards. Special subsets featured include Star Rookies (1-29), Community Heroes (30-40), and American League Teammates (41-55), Top Prospects (421-449), Inside the Numbers (450-470), Team Stars (471-485), Award Winners (486-499), and Diamond Debuts (500-510). Derek Jeter is the only notable Rookie Card in this set. A special card (SP5) was randomly inserted in first series packs to commemorate the 3,000th hit of George Brett and Robin Yount. A special card (SP6) commemorating Nolan Ryan's last season was randomly inserted into second series packs. Both SP cards were inserted at a rate of one every 72 packs

	Nm-Mt	Ex-Mt
COMPLETE SET (840)	40.00	12.00
COMP.FACT.SET (840)	50.00	15.00
COMP. SERIES 1 (420)	15.00	4.50
COMP. SERIES 2 (420)	25.00	7.50
1 Tim Salmon CL	.20	.06
2 Mike Piazza SR	1.50	.45
3 Rene Arocha SR RC	.50	.15
4 Willie Greene SR	.10	.03
5 Manny Alexander	.10	.03
6 Dan Wilson	.20	.06
7 Dan Smith	.10	.03
8 Kevin Rogers	.10	.03
9 Kurt Miller SR	.10	.03
10 Joe Vitko	.10	.03
11 Tim Costo	.10	.03
12 Alan Embree SR	.50	.15
13 Jim Tatum SR RC	.15	.04
14 Cris Colon	.10	.03
15 Steve Hosey	.10	.03
16 S. Hitchcock SR RC	.50	.15
17 Dave Mlicki	.10	.03
18 Jessie Hollins	.10	.03
19 Bobby Jones SR	.20	.06
20 Kurt Miller	.10	.03
21 Melvin Nieves SR	.10	.03
22 Billy Ashley SR	.10	.03
23 J.T. Snow SR RC	.75	.23
24 Chipper Jones SR	.50	.15
25 Tim Salmon SR	.30	.09
26 Tim Pugh SR RC	.15	.04
27 David Nied SR	.10	.03
28 Mike Trombley	.10	.03
29 Javier Lopez SR	.30	.09
30 Jim Abbott CH CL	.20	.06
31 Jim Abbott CH	.10	.03
32 Dale Murphy CH	.30	.09
33 Tony Pena CH	.10	.03
34 Kirby Puckett CH	.30	.09
35 Harold Reynolds CH	.10	.03
36 Cal Ripken CH	.75	.23
37 Nolan Ryan CH	1.00	.30
38 Ryne Sandberg CH	.50	.15
39 Dave Stewart CH	.10	.03
40 Dave Winfield CH	.10	.03
41 Joe Carter CL	.50	.15
Mark McGwire		
42 Joe Carter	.20	.06
Roberto Alomar		
43 Paul Molitor	.50	.15
Pat Listach		
Robin Yount		
44 Cal Ripken	.50	.15
Brady Anderson		
45 Albert Belle	.30	.09
Sandy Alomar Jr.		
Jim Thome		
Carlos Baerga		
Kenny Lofton		
46 Cecil Fielder	.10	.03
Mickey Tettleton		
47 Roberto Kelly	.60	.18
Don Mattingly		
48 Frank Viola	.50	.15
Roger Clemens		
49 Ruben Sierra	.50	.15
Mark McGwire		
50 Kent Hrbek	.30	.09
Kirby Puckett		
51 Robin Ventura	.30	.09
Frank Thomas		
52 Juan Gonzalez	.50	.15
Jose Canseco		
Ivan Rodriguez		
Rafael Palmeiro		
53 Mark Langston	.20	.06
Jim Abbott		
Chuck Finley		
54 Wally Joyner	.50	.15
Gregg Jefferies		
George Brett		
55 Kevin Mitchell	.50	.15
Ken Griffey Jr.		
Jay Buhner		
56 George Brett	1.25	.35
57 Scott Cooper	.10	.03
58 Mike Maddux	.10	.03
59 Rusty Meacham	.10	.03
60 Wil Cordero	.10	.03
61 Tim Teufel	.10	.03
62 Jeff Montgomery	.10	.03
63 Scott Livingstone	.10	.03
64 Doug Dascenzo	.10	.03
65 Bret Boone	.30	.09
66 Tim Wakefield	.50	.15
67 Curt Schilling	.20	.06
68 Frank Tanana	.10	.03
69 Len Dykstra	.20	.06
70 Derek Lilliquist	.10	.03
71 Anthony Young	.10	.03
72 Hipolito Pichardo	.10	.03
73 Rod Beck	.10	.03
74 Kent Hrbek	.20	.06
75 Tom Glavine	.30	.09
76 Kevin Brown	.20	.06
77 Chuck Finley	.20	.06
78 Bob Walk	.10	.03
79 Rheal Cormier UER (Born in New Brunswick, not British Columbia)	.10	.03
80 Rick Sutcliffe	.20	.06
81 Harold Baines	.20	.06
82 Lee Smith	.20	.06
83 Geno Petralli	.10	.03
84 Jose Oquendo	.10	.03
85 Mark Gubicza	.10	.03
86 Mickey Tettleton	.10	.03
87 Bobby Witt	.10	.03
88 Mark Lewis	.10	.03
89 Kevin Appier	.20	.06
90 Mike Stanton	.10	.03
91 Rafael Belliard	.10	.03
92 Kenny Rogers	.20	.06
93 Randy Velarde	.10	.03
94 Luis Sojo	.10	.03
95 Mark Leiter	.10	.03
96 Jody Reed	.10	.03
97 Pete Harnisch	.10	.03
98 Tom Candiotti	.10	.03
99 Mark Portugal	.10	.03
100 Dave Valle	.10	.03
101 Shawon Dunston	.10	.03
102 B.J. Surhoff	.20	.06
103 Jay Bell	.20	.06
104 Sid Bream	.10	.03
105 Frank Thomas CL	.30	.09
106 Mike Morgan	.10	.03
107 Bill Doran	.10	.03
108 Lance Blankenship	.10	.03
109 Mark Lemke	.10	.03
110 Brian Harper	.10	.03
111 Brady Anderson	.20	.06
112 Bip Roberts	.10	.03
113 Mitch Williams	.10	.03
114 Craig Biggio	.30	.09
115 Eddie Murray	.50	.15
116 Matt Nokes	.10	.03
117 Lance Parrish	.20	.06
118 Bill Swift	.10	.03
119 Jeff Innis	.10	.03
120 Mike LaValliere	.10	.03
121 Hal Morris	.10	.03
122 Walt Weiss	.10	.03
123 Ivan Rodriguez	.50	.15
124 Andy Van Slyke	.20	.06
125 Roberto Alomar	.30	.09
126 Robby Thompson	.10	.03
127 Sammy Sosa	.75	.23
128 Mark Langston	.10	.03
129 Jerry Browne	.10	.03
130 Chuck McElroy	.10	.03
131 Frank Viola	.20	.06
132 Leo Gomez	.10	.03
133 Ramon Martinez	.10	.03
134 Don Mattingly	1.25	.35
135 Roger Clemens	1.00	.30
136 Rickey Henderson	.50	.15
137 Darren Daulton	.20	.06
138 Ken Hill	.10	.03
139 Ozzie Guillen	.10	.03
140 Jerald Clark	.10	.03
141 Dave Fleming	.10	.03
142 Delino DeShields	.10	.03
143 Matt Williams	.20	.06
144 Larry Walker	.30	.09
145 Ruben Sierra	.10	.03
146 Ozzie Smith	.75	.23
147 Chris Sabo	.10	.03
148 Carlos Hernandez	.10	.03
149 Pat Borders	.10	.03
150 Orlando Merced	.10	.03
151 Royce Clayton	.10	.03
152 Kurt Stillwell	.10	.03
153 Dave Hollins	.10	.03
154 Mike Greenwell	.10	.03
155 Nolan Ryan	2.00	.60
156 Felix Jose	.10	.03
157 Junior Felix	.10	.03
158 Derek Bell	.10	.03
159 Steve Buechele	.10	.03
160 John Burkett	.10	.03
161 Pat Howell	.10	.03
162 Milt Cuyler	.10	.03
163 Terry Pendleton	.20	.06
164 Jack Morris	.20	.06
165 Tony Gwynn	.60	.18
166 Deion Sanders	.30	.09
167 Mike Devereaux	.10	.03
168 Ron Darling	.10	.03
169 Orel Hershiser	.20	.06
170 Mike Jackson	.10	.03
171 Doug Jones	.10	.03
172 Dan Walters	.10	.03
173 Darren Lewis	.10	.03
174 Carlos Baerga	.10	.03
175 Ryne Sandberg	.75	.23
176 Gregg Jefferies	.10	.03
177 John Jaha	.10	.03
178 Luis Polonia	.10	.03
179 Kirt Manwaring	.10	.03
180 Mike Magnante	.10	.03
181 Billy Ripken	.10	.03
182 Mike Moore	.10	.03
183 Eric Anthony	.10	.03
184 Lenny Harris	.10	.03
185 Tony Pena	.10	.03
186 Mike Felder	.10	.03
187 Greg Olson	.10	.03
188 Rene Gonzales	.10	.03
189 Mike Bordick	.10	.03
190 Mel Rojas	.10	.03
191 Todd Frohwirth	.10	.03
192 Darryl Hamilton	.10	.03
193 Mike Fetters	.10	.03
194 Omar Olivares	.10	.03
195 Tony Phillips	.10	.03
196 Paul Sorrento	.10	.03
197 Trevor Wilson	.10	.03
198 Kevin Gross	.10	.03
199 Ron Karkovice	.10	.03
200 Brook Jacoby	.10	.03
201 Mariano Duncan	.10	.03
202 Dennis Cook	.10	.03
203 Daryl Boston	.10	.03
204 Mike Perez	.10	.03
205 Manuel Lee	.10	.03
206 Steve Olin	.10	.03
207 Charlie Hough	.20	.06
208 Scott Scudder	.10	.03
209 Charlie O'Brien	.10	.03
210 Barry Bonds CL	.60	.18
211 Jose Vizcaino	.10	.03
212 Scott Leius	.10	.03
213 Kevin Mitchell	.10	.03
214 Brian Barnes	.10	.03
215 Pat Kelly	.10	.03
216 Chris Hammond	.10	.03
217 Rob Deer	.10	.03
218 Cory Snyder	.10	.03
219 Gary Carter	.20	.06
220 Danny Darwin	.10	.03
221 Tom Gordon	.10	.03
222 Gary Sheffield	.20	.06
223 Joe Carter	.20	.06
224 Jay Buhner	.20	.06
225 Jose Offerman	.10	.03
226 Jose Rijo	.10	.03
227 Mark Whiten	.10	.03
228 Randy Milligan	.10	.03
229 Bud Black	.10	.03
230 Gary DiSarcina	.10	.03
231 Steve Finley	.20	.06
232 Dennis Martinez	.20	.06
233 Mike Mussina	.30	.09
234 Joe Oliver	.10	.03
235 Chad Curtis	.10	.03
236 Shane Mack	.10	.03
237 Jaime Navarro	.10	.03
238 Brian McRae	.10	.03
239 Chili Davis	.20	.06
240 Jeff King	.10	.03
241 Dean Palmer	.20	.06
242 Danny Tartabull	.10	.03
243 Charles Nagy	.10	.03
244 Ray Lankford	.10	.03
245 Barry Larkin	.30	.09
246 Steve Avery	.10	.03
247 John Kruk	.20	.06
248 Derrick May	.10	.03
249 Stan Javier	.10	.03
250 Roger McDowell	.10	.03
251 Dan Gladden	.10	.03
252 Wally Joyner	.20	.06
253 Pat Listach	.10	.03
254 Chuck Knoblauch	.20	.06
255 Sandy Alomar Jr.	.10	.03
256 Jeff Bagwell	.30	.09
257 Andy Stankiewicz	.10	.03
258 Darrin Jackson	.10	.03
259 Brett Butler	.20	.06
260 Joe Orsulak	.10	.03
261 Andy Benes	.10	.03
262 Kenny Lofton	.20	.06
263 Robin Ventura	.20	.06
264 Ron Gant	.20	.06
265 Ellis Burks	.20	.06
266 Juan Guzman	.10	.03
267 Wes Chamberlain	.10	.03
268 John Smiley	.10	.03
269 Franklin Stubbs	.10	.03
270 Tom Browning	.10	.03
271 Dennis Eckersley	.20	.06
272 Carlton Fisk	.30	.09
273 Lou Whitaker	.20	.06
274 Phil Plantier	.10	.03
275 Bobby Bonilla	.20	.06
276 Ben McDonald	.10	.03
277 Bob Zupcic	.10	.03
278 Terry Steinbach	.10	.03
279 Terry Mulholland	.10	.03
280 Lance Johnson	.10	.03
281 Willie McGee	.20	.06
282 Bret Saberhagen	.20	.06
283 Randy Myers	.10	.03
284 Randy Tomlin	.10	.03
285 Mickey Morandini	.10	.03
286 Brian Williams	.10	.03
287 Tino Martinez	.30	.09
288 Jose Melendez	.10	.03
289 Jeff Huson	.10	.03
290 Joe Grahe	.10	.03
291 Mel Hall	.10	.03
292 Otis Nixon	.10	.03
293 Todd Hundley	.10	.03
294 Casey Candaele	.10	.03
295 Kevin Seitzer	.10	.03
296 Eddie Taubensee	.10	.03
297 Moises Alou	.20	.06
298 Scott Radinsky	.10	.03
299 Thomas Howard	.10	.03
300 Kyle Abbott	.10	.03
301 Omar Vizquel	.30	.09
302 Keith Miller	.10	.03
303 Rick Aguilera	.10	.03
304 Bruce Hurst	.10	.03
305 Ken Caminiti	.20	.06
306 Mike Pagliarulo	.10	.03
307 Frank Seminara	.10	.03
308 Andre Dawson	.20	.06
309 Jose Lind	.10	.03
310 Joe Boever	.10	.03
311 Jeff Parrett	.10	.03
312 Alan Mills	.10	.03
313 Kevin Tapani	.10	.03
314 Darryl Kile	.20	.06
315 Will Clark CL	.20	.06
316 Mike Sharperson	.10	.03
317 John Orton	.10	.03
318 Bob Tewksbury	.10	.03
319 Xavier Hernandez	.10	.03
320 Paul Assenmacher	.10	.03
321 John Franco	.20	.06
322 Mike Timlin	.10	.03
323 Jose Guzman	.10	.03
324 Pedro Martinez	1.00	.30
325 Bill Spiers	.10	.03
326 Melido Perez	.10	.03
327 Mike Macfarlane	.10	.03
328 Ricky Bones	.10	.03
329 Scott Bankhead	.10	.03
330 Rich Rodriguez	.10	.03
331 Geronimo Pena	.10	.03
332 Bernie Williams	.30	.09
333 Paul Molitor	.30	.09
334 Carlos Garcia	.10	.03
335 David Cone	.20	.06
336 Randy Johnson	.50	.15
337 Pat Mahomes	.10	.03
338 Erik Hanson	.10	.03
339 Duane Ward	.10	.03
340 Al Martin	.10	.03
341 Pedro Munoz	.10	.03
342 Greg Colbrunn	.10	.03
343 Julio Valera	.10	.03
344 John Olerud	.20	.06
345 George Bell	.10	.03
346 Devon White	.20	.06
347 Donovan Osborne	.10	.03
348 Mark Gardner	.10	.03
349 Zane Smith	.10	.03
350 Wilson Alvarez	.10	.03
351 Kevin Koslofski	.10	.03
352 Roberto Hernandez	.10	.03
353 Glenn Davis	.10	.03
354 Reggie Sanders	.10	.03
355 Ken Griffey Jr.	.75	.23
356 Marquis Grissom	.20	.06
357 Jack McDowell	.10	.03
358 Jimmy Key	.20	.06
359 Stan Belinda	.10	.03
360 Gerald Williams	.10	.03
361 Sid Fernandez	.10	.03
362 Alex Fernandez	.10	.03
363 John Smoltz	.30	.09
364 Travis Fryman	.20	.06
365 Jose Canseco	.50	.15
366 David Justice	.20	.06
367 Pedro Astacio	.10	.03
368 Tim Belcher	.10	.03
369 Steve Sax	.10	.03
370 Gary Gaetti	.20	.06
371 Jeff Frye	.10	.03
372 Bob Wickman	.10	.03
373 Ryan Thompson	.10	.03
374 David Hulse RC	.15	.04
375 Cal Eldred	.10	.03
376 Ryan Klesko	.20	.06
377 Damion Easley	.10	.03
378 John Kiely	.10	.03
379 Jim Bullinger	.10	.03
380 Brian Bohanon	.10	.03
381 Rod Brewer	.10	.03
382 Fernando Ramsey RC	.15	.04
383 Sam Militello	.10	.03
384 Arthur Rhodes	.10	.03
385 Eric Karros	.20	.06
386 Rico Brogna	.10	.03
387 John Valentin	.10	.03
388 Kerry Woodson	.10	.03
389 Ben Rivera	.10	.03
390 Matt Whiteside RC	.15	.04
391 Henry Rodriguez	.10	.03
392 John Wetteland	.20	.06
393 Kent Mercker	.10	.03
394 Bernard Gilkey	.10	.03

395 Doug Henry .10 .03
396 Mo Vaughn .20 .06
397 Scott Erickson .10 .03
398 Bill Gullickson .10 .03
399 Mark Guthrie .10 .03
400 Dave Martinez .10 .03
401 Jeff Kent .50 .15
402 Chris Hoiles .10 .03
403 Mike Henneman .10 .03
404 Chris Nabholz .10 .03
405 Tom Pagnozzi .10 .03
406 Kelly Gruber .10 .03
407 Bob Welch .10 .03
408 Frank Castillo .10 .03
409 John Dopson .10 .03
410 Steve Farr .10 .03
411 Henry Cotto .10 .03
412 Bob Patterson .10 .03
413 Todd Stottlemyre .10 .03
414 Greg A. Harris .10 .03
415 Denny Neagle .20 .06
416 Bill Wegman .10 .03
417 Willie Wilson .10 .03
418 Terry Leach .10 .03
419 Willie Randolph .20 .06
420 Mark McGwire CL .30 .09
421 Calvin Murray CL .10 .03
422 Pete Janicki TP RC .15 .04
423 Todd Jones TP .10 .03
424 Mike Neill TP .10 .03
425 Carlos Delgado TP .50 .15
426 Jose Oliva TP .10 .03
427 Tyrone Hill TP .10 .03
428 Dmitri Young TP .20 .06
429 Derek Wallace TP RC .15 .04
430 Michael Moore TP RC .15 .04
431 Cliff Floyd TP .20 .06
432 Calvin Murray TP .10 .03
433 Manny Ramirez TP .50 .15
434 Marc Newfield TP .10 .03
435 Charles Johnson TP .20 .06
436 Butch Huskey TP .10 .03
437 Brad Pennington TP .10 .03
438 Ray McDavid TP RC .15 .04
439 Chad McConnell TP .10 .03
440 M.Cummings TP RC .15 .04
441 Benji Gil TP .10 .03
442 Frankie Rodriguez TP .10 .03
443 Chad Mottola TP RC .15 .04
444 John Burke TP RC .15 .04
445 Michael Tucker TP .20 .06
446 Rick Greene TP .10 .03
447 Rich Becker TP .10 .03
448 Mike Robertson TP .10 .03
449 Derek Jeter TP RC 10.00 3.00
450 Ivan Rodriguez CL .30 .09
David McCarty
451 Jim Abbott IN .20 .06
452 Jeff Bagwell IN .20 .06
453 Jason Bere IN .10 .03
454 Delino DeShields IN .10 .03
455 Travis Fryman IN .10 .03
456 Alex Gonzalez IN .10 .03
457 Phil Hiatt IN .10 .03
458 Dave Hollins IN .10 .03
459 Chipper Jones IN .30 .09
460 David Justice IN .10 .03
461 Ray Lankford IN .10 .03
462 David McCarty IN .10 .03
463 Mike Mussina IN .20 .06
464 Jose Offerman IN .10 .03
465 Dean Palmer IN .10 .03
466 Geronimo Pena IN .10 .03
467 Eduardo Perez IN .10 .03
468 Ivan Rodriguez IN .30 .09
469 Reggie Sanders IN .10 .03
470 Bernie Williams IN .20 .06
471 Barry Bonds CL .50 .15
Matt Williams
Will Clark
472 Greg Maddux .50 .15
Steve Avery
John Smoltz
Tom Glavine
473 Jose Rijo .20 .06
Rob Dibble
Roberto Kelly
Reggie Sanders
Barry Larkin
474 Gary Sheffield .20 .06
Phil Plantier
Tony Gwynn
Fred McGriff
475 Doug Drabek .20 .06
Craig Biggio
Jeff Bagwell
476 Will Clark .50 .15
Barry Bonds
Matt Williams
477 Eric Davis .20 .06
Darryl Strawberry
478 Dante Bichette .20 .06
David Nied
Andres Galarraga
479 Dave Magadan .10 .03
Orestes Destrade
Bret Barberie
Jeff Conine
480 Tim Wakefield .20 .06
Andy Van Slyke
Jay Bell
481 Marquis Grissom .20 .06
Delino DeShields
Dennis Martinez
Larry Walker
482 Geronimo Pena .50 .15
Ray Lankford
Ozzie Smith
Bernard Gilkey
483 Randy Myers .50 .15
Ryne Sandberg
Mark Grace
484 Eddie Murray .30 .09
Howard Johnson
Bobby Bonilla
485 John Kruk .10 .03
Dave Hollins
Darren Daulton
Len Dykstra
486 Barry Bonds AW .60 .18
487 Dennis Eckersley AW .20 .06
488 Greg Maddux AW .50 .15
489 Dennis Eckersley AW .20 .06
490 Eric Karros AW .10 .03
491 Pat Listach AW .10 .03
492 Gary Sheffield AW .10 .03
493 Mark McGwire AW .60 .18
494 Gary Sheffield AW .10 .03
495 Edgar Martinez AW .20 .06
496 Fred McGriff AW .20 .06
497 Juan Gonzalez AW .20 .06
498 Darren Daulton AW .10 .03
499 Cecil Fielder AW .10 .03
500 Brent Gates CL .10 .03
501 Tavo Alvarez DD .10 .03
502 Rod Bolton .10 .03
503 J.Cummings DD RC .15 .04
504 Brent Gates DD .10 .03
505 Tyler Green .10 .03
506 Jose Martinez DD RC .15 .04
507 Troy Percival .30 .09
508 Kevin Stocker DD .10 .03
509 Matt Walbeck DD RC .15 .04
510 Rondell White DD .20 .06
511 Billy Ripken .10 .03
512 Mike Moore .10 .03
513 Jose Lind .10 .03
514 Chito Martinez .10 .03
515 Jose Guzman .10 .03
516 Kim Batiste .10 .03
517 Jeff Tackett .10 .03
518 Charlie Hough .20 .06
519 Marvin Freeman .10 .03
520 Carlos Martinez .10 .03
521 Eric Young .10 .03
522 Pete Incaviglia .10 .03
523 Scott Fletcher .10 .03
524 Orestes Destrade .10 .03
525 Ken Griffey Jr. CL .50 .15
526 Ellis Burks .20 .06
527 Juan Samuel .10 .03
528 Dave Magadan .10 .03
529 Jeff Parrett .10 .03
530 Bill Krueger .10 .03
531 Frank Bolick .10 .03
532 Alan Trammell .20 .06
533 Walt Weiss .10 .03
534 David Cone .20 .06
535 Greg Maddux .75 .23
536 Kevin Young .20 .06
537 Dave Hansen .10 .03
538 Alex Cole .10 .03
539 Greg Hibbard .10 .03
540 Gene Larkin .10 .03
541 Jeff Reardon .20 .06
542 Felix Jose .10 .03
543 Jimmy Key .20 .06
544 Reggie Jefferson .10 .03
545 Gregg Jefferies .10 .03
546 Dave Stewart .20 .06
547 Tim Wallach .10 .03
548 Spike Owen .10 .03
549 Tommy Greene .10 .03
550 Fernando Valenzuela .20 .06
551 Rich Amaral .10 .03
552 Bret Barberie .10 .03
553 Edgar Martinez .30 .09
554 Jim Abbott .30 .09
555 Frank Thomas .50 .15
556 Wade Boggs .30 .09
557 Tom Henke .10 .03
558 Milt Thompson .10 .03
559 Lloyd McClendon .10 .03
560 Vinny Castilla .20 .06
561 Ricky Jordan .10 .03
562 Andujar Cedeno .10 .03
563 Greg Vaughn .10 .03
564 Cecil Fielder .20 .06
565 Kirby Puckett .50 .15
566 Mark McGwire 1.25 .35
567 Barry Bonds 1.25 .35
568 Jody Reed .10 .03
569 Todd Zeile .10 .03
570 Mark Carreon .10 .03
571 Joe Girardi .10 .03
572 Luis Gonzalez .20 .06
573 Mark Grace .30 .09
574 Rafael Palmeiro .30 .09
575 Darryl Strawberry .20 .06
576 Will Clark .50 .15
577 Fred McGriff .30 .09
578 Kevin Reimer .10 .03
579 Dave Righetti .20 .06
580 Juan Bell .10 .03
581 Jeff Brantley .10 .03
582 Brian Hunter .10 .03
583 Tim Naehring .10 .03
584 Glenallen Hill .10 .03
585 Cal Ripken 1.50 .45
586 Albert Belle .20 .06
587 Robin Yount .75 .23
588 Chris Bosio .10 .03
589 Pete Smith .10 .03
590 Chuck Carr .10 .03
591 Jeff Blauser .10 .03
592 Kevin McReynolds .10 .03
593 Andres Galarraga .20 .06
594 Kevin Maas .10 .03
595 Eric Davis .20 .06
596 Brian Jordan .20 .06
597 Tim Raines .20 .06
598 Rick Wilkins .10 .03
599 Steve Cooke .10 .03
600 Mike Gallego .10 .03
601 Mike Munoz .10 .03
602 Luis Rivera .10 .03
603 Junior Ortiz .10 .03
604 Brent Mayne .10 .03
605 Luis Alicea .10 .03
606 Damon Berryhill .10 .03
607 Dave Henderson .10 .03
608 Kirk McCaskill .10 .03
609 Jeff Fassero .10 .03
610 Mike Harkey .10 .03
611 Francisco Cabrera .10 .03
612 Rey Sanchez .10 .03
613 Scott Servais .10 .03
614 Darrin Fletcher .10 .03
615 Felix Fermin .10 .03
616 Kevin Seitzer .10 .03
617 Bob Scanlan .10 .03
618 Billy Hatcher .10 .03
619 John Vander Wal .10 .03
620 Joe Hesketh .10 .03
621 Hector Villanueva .10 .03
622 Randy Milligan .10 .03
623 Tony Tarasco RC .15 .04
624 Russ Swan .10 .03
625 Willie Wilson .10 .03
626 Frank Tanana .10 .03
627 Pete O'Brien .10 .03
628 Lenny Webster .10 .03
629 Mark Clark .10 .03
630 Roger Clemens CL .50 .15
631 Alex Arias .10 .03
632 Chris Gwynn .10 .03
633 Tom Bolton .10 .03
634 Greg Briley .10 .03
635 Kent Bottenfield .10 .03
636 Kelly Downs .10 .03
637 Manuel Lee .10 .03
638 Al Leiter .20 .06
639 Jeff Gardner .10 .03
640 Mike Gardiner .10 .03
641 Mark Gardner .10 .03
642 Jeff Branson .10 .03
643 Paul Wagner .10 .03
644 Sean Berry .10 .03
645 Phil Hiatt .10 .03
646 Kevin Mitchell .10 .03
647 Charlie Hayes .10 .03
648 Jim Deshaies .10 .03
649 Dan Pasqua .10 .03
650 Mike Maddux .10 .03
651 Domingo Martinez RC .15 .04
652 Greg McMichael RC .15 .04
653 Eric Wedge RC .50 .15
654 Mark Whiten .10 .03
655 Roberto Kelly .10 .03
656 Julio Franco .20 .06
657 Gene Harris .10 .03
658 Pete Schourek .10 .03
659 Mike Bielecki .10 .03
660 Ricky Gutierrez .10 .03
661 Chris Hammond .10 .03
662 Tim Scott .10 .03
663 Norm Charlton .10 .03
664 Doug Drabek .10 .03
665 Dwight Gooden .20 .06
666 Jim Gott .10 .03
667 Randy Myers .10 .03
668 Darren Holmes .10 .03
669 Tim Spehr .10 .03
670 Bruce Ruffin .10 .03
671 Bobby Thigpen .10 .03
672 Tony Fernandez .10 .03
673 Darrin Jackson .10 .03
674 Gregg Olson .10 .03
675 Rob Dibble .20 .06
676 Howard Johnson .10 .03
677 Mike Lansing RC .50 .15
678 Charlie Leibrandt .10 .03
679 Kevin Bass .10 .03
680 Hubie Brooks .10 .03
681 Scott Brosius .20 .06
682 Randy Knorr .10 .03
683 Dante Bichette .20 .06
684 Bryan Harvey .10 .03
685 Greg Gohr .10 .03
686 Willie Banks .10 .03
687 Robb Nen .20 .06
688 Mike Scioscia .10 .03
689 John Farrell .10 .03
690 John Candelaria .10 .03
691 Damon Buford .10 .03
692 Todd Worrell .10 .03
693 Pat Hentgen .10 .03
694 John Smiley .10 .03
695 Greg Swindell .10 .03
696 Derek Bell .10 .03
697 Terry Jorgensen .10 .03
698 Jimmy Jones .10 .03
699 David Wells .20 .06
700 Dave Martinez .10 .03
701 Steve Bedrosian .10 .03
702 Jeff Russell .10 .03
703 Joe Magrane .10 .03
704 Matt Mieske .10 .03
705 Paul Molitor .30 .09
706 Dale Murphy .50 .15
707 Steve Howe .10 .03
708 Greg Gagne .10 .03
709 Dave Eiland .10 .03
710 David West .10 .03
711 Luis Aquino .10 .03
712 Joe Orsulak .10 .03
713 Eric Plunk .10 .03
714 Mike Felder .10 .03
715 Joe Klink .10 .03
716 Lonnie Smith .10 .03
717 Monty Fariss .10 .03
718 Craig Lefferts .10 .03
719 John Habyan .10 .03
720 Willie Blair .10 .03
721 Darnell Coles .10 .03
722 Mark Williamson .10 .03
723 Bryn Smith .10 .03
724 Greg W. Harris .10 .03
725 Graeme Lloyd RC .50 .15
726 Cris Carpenter .10 .03
727 Chico Walker .10 .03
728 Tracy Woodson .10 .03
729 Jose Uribe .10 .03
730 Stan Javier .10 .03
731 Jay Howell .10 .03
732 Freddie Benavides .10 .03
733 Jeff Reboulet .10 .03
734 Scott Sanderson .10 .03
735 Ryne Sandberg CL .50 .15
736 Archi Cianfrocco .10 .03
737 Daryl Boston .10 .03
738 Craig Grebeck .10 .03
739 Doug Dascenzo .10 .03
740 Gerald Young .10 .03
741 Candy Maldonado .10 .03
742 Joey Cora .10 .03
743 Don Slaught .10 .03
744 Steve Decker .10 .03
745 Blas Minor .10 .03
746 Storm Davis .10 .03
747 Carlos Quintana .10 .03
748 Vince Coleman .10 .03
749 Todd Burns .10 .03
750 Steve Frey .10 .03
751 Ivan Calderon .10 .03
752 Steve Reed RC .15 .04
753 Danny Jackson .10 .03
754 Jeff Conine .20 .06
755 Juan Gonzalez .30 .09
756 Mike Kelly .10 .03
757 John Doherty .10 .03
758 Jack Armstrong .10 .03
759 John Wehner .10 .03
760 Scott Bankhead .10 .03
761 Jim Tatum .10 .03
762 Scott Pose RC .15 .04
763 Andy Ashby .10 .03
764 Ed Sprague .10 .03
765 Harold Baines .20 .06
766 Kirk Gibson .20 .06
767 Troy Neel .10 .03
768 Dick Schofield .10 .03
769 Dickie Thon .10 .03
770 Butch Henry .10 .03
771 Junior Felix .10 .03
772 Ken Ryan RC .15 .04
773 Trevor Hoffman .20 .06
774 Phil Plantier .10 .03
775 Bo Jackson .50 .15
776 Benito Santiago .20 .06
777 Andre Dawson .20 .06
778 Bryan Hickerson .10 .03
779 Dennis Moeller .10 .03
780 Ryan Bowen .10 .03
781 Eric Fox .10 .03
782 Joe Kmak .10 .03
783 Mike Hampton .20 .06
784 Darrell Sherman RC .15 .04
785 J.T. Snow .30 .09
786 Dave Winfield .20 .06
787 Jim Austin .10 .03
788 Craig Shipley .10 .03
789 Greg Myers .10 .03
790 Todd Benzinger .10 .03
791 Cory Snyder .10 .03
792 David Segui .10 .03
793 Armando Reynoso .10 .03
794 Chili Davis .20 .06
795 Dave Nilsson .10 .03
796 Paul O'Neill .30 .09
797 Jerald Clark .10 .03
798 Jose Mesa .10 .03
799 Brain Holman .10 .03
800 Jim Eisenreich .10 .03
801 Mark McLemore .10 .03
802 Luis Sojo .10 .03
803 Harold Reynolds .20 .06
804 Dan Plesac .10 .03
805 Dave Stieb .10 .03
806 Tom Brunansky .10 .03
807 Kelly Gruber .10 .03
808 Bob Ojeda .10 .03
809 Dave Burba .10 .03
810 Joe Boever .10 .03
811 Jeremy Hernandez .10 .03
812 Tim Salmon TC .20 .06
813 Jeff Bagwell TC .20 .06
814 Dennis Eckersley TC .20 .06
815 Roberto Alomar TC .20 .06
816 Steve Avery TC .10 .03
817 Pat Listach TC .10 .03
818 Gregg Jefferies TC .10 .03
819 Sammy Sosa TC .50 .15
820 Darryl Strawberry TC .10 .03
821 Dennis Martinez TC .10 .03
822 Robby Thompson TC .10 .03
823 Albert Belle TC .20 .06
824 Randy Johnson TC .30 .09
825 Nigel Wilson TC .10 .03
826 Bobby Bonilla TC .10 .03
827 Glenn Davis TC .10 .03
828 Gary Sheffield TC .10 .03
829 Darren Daulton TC .10 .03
830 Jay Bell TC .10 .03
831 Juan Gonzalez TC .20 .06
832 Andre Dawson TC .10 .03
833 Hal Morris TC .10 .03
834 David Nied TC .10 .03
835 Felix Jose TC .10 .03
836 Travis Fryman TC .10 .03
837 Shane Mack TC .10 .03
838 Robin Ventura TC .10 .03
839 Danny Tartabull TC .10 .03
840 Roberto Alomar CL .20 .06
SP5 George Brett 1.00 .30
Robin Yount
SP6 Nolan Ryan 2.00 .60

1993 Upper Deck Gold Hologram

These gold parallel cards were made available exclusively in factory set form. One set in every 15 ct. case of factory sets featured cards with gold foil holograms on the card backs, rather than the traditional silver foil holograms. The factory boxes for the basic sets and the much scarcer Gold Hologram sets are identical, thus all Gold Hologram sets offered for sale are for opened factory sets. Please refer to the multipliers provided below for values on single cards.

	Nm-Mt	Ex-Mt
COMP.FACT.SET (840)	150.00	45.00

*STARS: 3X TO 8X BASIC CARDS
*ROOKIES: 3X TO 8X BASIC CARDS

1993 Upper Deck Clutch Performers

These 20 standard-size cards were inserted one every nine series II retail foil packs, as well as inserted one per series II retail jumbo packs. The cards are numbered on the back with an "R" prefix and appear in alphabetical order. These 20 cards represent Reggie Jackson's selection of players who have come through under pressure. Please note these cards are condition sensitive and trade for premium values if found in Mint.

	Nm-Mt	Ex-Mt
COMPLETE SET (20)	20.00	6.00
R1 Roberto Alomar	.75	.23
R2 Wade Boggs	.75	.23
R3 Barry Bonds	3.00	.90
R4 Jose Canseco	1.25	.35
R5 Joe Carter	.50	.15
R6 Will Clark	1.25	.35
R7 Roger Clemens	2.50	.75
R8 Dennis Eckersley	.50	.15
R9 Cecil Fielder	.50	.15
R10 Juan Gonzalez	.75	.23
R11 Ken Griffey Jr.	2.00	.60
R12 Rickey Henderson	1.25	.35
R13 Barry Larkin	.75	.23
R14 Don Mattingly	3.00	.90
R15 Fred McGriff	.75	.23
R16 Terry Pendleton	.50	.15
R17 Kirby Puckett	1.25	.35
R18 Ryne Sandberg	2.00	.60
R19 John Smoltz	.75	.23
R20 Frank Thomas	1.25	.35

1993 Upper Deck Fifth Anniversary

This 15-card standard-size set celebrates Upper Deck's five years in the sports card business.The cards are essentially reprinted versions of some of Upper Deck's most popular cards in the last five years. These cards were inserted one every nine second series hobby packs. The black-bordered fronts feature player photos that previously appeared on an Upper Deck card. The cards are numbered on the back with an "A" prefix. These cards are condition sensitive and trade for premium values in Mint.

	Nm-Mt	Ex-Mt
COMPLETE SET (15)	15.00	4.50
A1 Ken Griffey Jr.	2.00	.60
A2 Gary Sheffield	.50	.15
A3 Roberto Alomar	.75	.23
A4 Jim Abbott	.75	.23
A5 Nolan Ryan	5.00	1.50
A6 Juan Gonzalez	.75	.23
A7 David Justice	.50	.15
A8 Carlos Baerga	.25	.07
A9 Reggie Jackson	.75	.23
A10 Eric Karros	.50	.15
A11 Chipper Jones	1.25	.35
A12 Ivan Rodriguez	1.25	.35
A13 Pat Listach	.25	.07
A14 Frank Thomas	1.25	.35
A15 Tim Salmon	.75	.23

1993 Upper Deck Future Heroes

Inserted in second series foil packs at a rate of one every nine pack; this set continues the Heroes insert set begun in the 1990 Upper Deck high-number set, this ten-card standard-size set features eight different "Future Heroes" along with a checklist and header card.

	Nm-Mt	Ex-Mt
COMPLETE SET (10)	12.00	3.60
55 Roberto Alomar	.75	.23
56 Barry Bonds	3.00	.90
57 Roger Clemens	2.50	.75
58 Juan Gonzalez	.75	.23
59 Ken Griffey Jr.	2.00	.60
60 Mark McGwire	3.00	.90
61 Kirby Puckett	1.25	.35
62 Frank Thomas	1.25	.35
63 Checklist	.50	.15
NNO Header Card SP	.25	.07

1993 Upper Deck Home Run Heroes

This 28-card standard-size set features the home run leader from each Major League team. Each 1993 first series 27-card jumbo pack contained one of these cards. The cards are numbered on the back with an "HR" prefix and the set is arranged in descending order according to the number of home runs.

	Nm-Mt	Ex-Mt
COMPLETE SET (28)	15.00	4.50
HR1 Juan Gonzalez	.75	.23
HR2 Mark McGwire	3.00	.90
HR3 Cecil Fielder	.50	.15
HR4 Fred McGriff	.75	.23
HR5 Albert Belle	.50	.15
HR6 Barry Bonds	3.00	.90
HR7 Joe Carter	.50	.15
HR8 Darren Daulton	.50	.15
HR9 Ken Griffey Jr.	2.00	.60
HR10 Dave Hollins	.25	.07
HR11 Ryne Sandberg	2.00	.60
HR12 George Bell	.25	.07
HR13 Danny Tartabull	.25	.07
HR14 Mike Devereaux	.25	.07
HR15 Greg Vaughn	.25	.07
HR16 Larry Walker	.75	.23
HR17 David Justice	.50	.15
HR18 Terry Pendleton	.50	.15
HR19 Eric Karros	.50	.15
HR20 Ray Lankford	.25	.07
HR21 Matt Williams	.50	.15
HR22 Eric Anthony	.25	.07
HR23 Bobby Bonilla	.50	.15
HR24 Kirby Puckett	1.25	.35
HR25 Mike Macfarlane	.25	.07
HR26 Tom Brunansky	.25	.07
HR27 Paul O'Neill	.75	.23
HR28 Gary Gaetti	.50	.15

1993 Upper Deck Iooss Collection

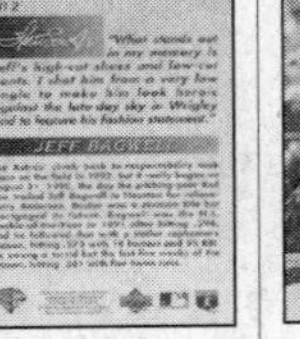

This 27-card standard-size set spotlights the work of famous sports photographer Walter Iooss Jr. by presenting 26 of the game's current greats in a candid photo set. The cards were inserted in series I retail foil packs at a rate of one every nine packs. They were also in retail jumbo packs at a rate of one in five packs. The cards are numbered on the back with a "WI" prefix. Please note these cards are condition sensitive and trade for premium values in Mint.

	Nm-Mt	Ex-Mt
COMPLETE SET (27)	30.00	9.00
WI1 Tim Salmon	1.00	.30
WI2 Jeff Bagwell	1.00	.30
WI3 Mark McGwire	4.00	1.20
WI4 Roberto Alomar	1.00	.30
WI5 Steve Avery	.30	.09
WI6 Paul Molitor	1.00	.30
WI7 Ozzie Smith	2.50	.75
WI8 Mark Grace	1.00	.30
WI9 Eric Karros	.60	.18
WI10 Delino DeShields	.30	.09
WI11 Will Clark	1.50	.45
WI12 Albert Belle	.60	.18
WI13 Ken Griffey Jr.	2.50	.75
WI14 Howard Johnson	.30	.09
WI15 Cal Ripken Jr.	5.00	1.50
WI16 Fred McGriff	1.00	.30
WI17 Darren Daulton	.60	.18
WI18 Andy Van Slyke	.60	.18
WI19 Nolan Ryan	6.00	1.80
WI20 Wade Boggs	1.00	.30
WI21 Barry Larkin	1.00	.30
WI22 George Brett	4.00	1.20
WI23 Cecil Fielder	.60	.18
WI24 Kirby Puckett	1.50	.45
WI25 Frank Thomas	1.50	.45
WI26 Don Mattingly	4.00	1.20
NNO Title Card Iooss Header	.30	.09

1993 Upper Deck Mays Heroes

This standard-size ten-card set was randomly inserted in 1993 Upper Deck first series foil packs. The fronts feature color photos of Mays at various stages of his career that are partially contained within a black bordered circle. The cards are numbered in continuation of Upper Deck's Heroes series.

	Nm-Mt	Ex-Mt
COMPLETE SET (10)	3.00	.90
COMMON (46-54/HDR)	.50	.15

1993 Upper Deck On Deck

Inserted one per series II jumbo packs, these 25 standard-size cards profile baseball's top players. The cards are numbered on the back with a "D" prefix in alphabetical order by name.

	Nm-Mt	Ex-Mt
COMPLETE SET (25)	20.00	6.00
D1 Jim Abbott	.75	.23
D2 Roberto Alomar	.75	.23
D3 Carlos Baerga	.25	.07
D4 Albert Belle	.50	.15
D5 Wade Boggs	.75	.23
D6 George Brett	3.00	.90
D7 Jose Canseco	1.25	.35
D8 Will Clark	1.25	.35
D9 Roger Clemens	2.50	.75
D10 Dennis Eckersley	.50	.15
D11 Cecil Fielder	.50	.15
D12 Juan Gonzalez	.75	.23
D13 Ken Griffey Jr.	2.00	.60
D14 Tony Gwynn	1.50	.45
D15 Bo Jackson	1.25	.35
D16 Chipper Jones	1.25	.35
D17 Eric Karros	.50	.15
D18 Mark McGwire	3.00	.90
D19 Kirby Puckett	1.25	.35
D20 Nolan Ryan	5.00	1.50
D21 Tim Salmon	.75	.23
D22 Ryne Sandberg	2.00	.60
D23 Darryl Strawberry	.50	.15
D24 Frank Thomas	1.25	.35
D25 Andy Van Slyke	.50	.15

1993 Upper Deck Season Highlights

This 20-card standard-size insert set captures great moments of the 1992 Major League Baseball season. The cards were exclusively distributed in specially marked cases that were available only at Upper Deck Heroes of Baseball Card Shows and through the purchase of a specified quantity of second series cases. In these packs, the cards were inserted at a rate of one every nine. The cards are numbered on the back with an "HI" prefix in alphabetical order by player's name.

	Nm-Mt	Ex-Mt
COMPLETE SET (20)	120.00	36.00
HI1 Roberto Alomar	5.00	1.50
HI2 Steve Avery	1.50	.45
HI3 Harold Baines	3.00	.90
HI4 Damon Berryhill	1.50	.45
HI5 Barry Bonds	20.00	6.00
HI6 Bret Boone	5.00	1.50
HI7 George Brett	20.00	6.00
HI8 Francisco Cabrera	1.50	.45
HI9 Ken Griffey Jr.	12.00	3.60
HI10 Rickey Henderson	8.00	2.40
HI11 Kenny Lofton	3.00	.90
HI12 Mickey Morandini	1.50	.45
HI13 Eddie Murray	8.00	2.40
HI14 David Nied	1.50	.45
HI15 Jeff Reardon	3.00	.90
HI16 Bip Roberts	1.50	.45
HI17 Nolan Ryan	30.00	9.00
HI18 Ed Sprague	1.50	.45
HI19 Dave Winfield	3.00	.90
HI20 Robin Yount	12.00	3.60

1993 Upper Deck Then And Now

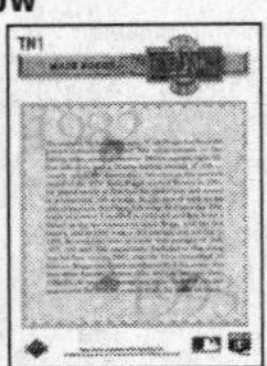

This 18-card, standard-size hologram set highlights veteran stars in their rookie year and today, reflecting on how they and the game have changed. Cards 1-9 were randomly inserted in series I foil packs; cards 10-18 were randomly inserted in series II foil packs. In either series, the cards were inserted one every 27 packs. The nine lithogram cards in the second series feature one card each of Hall of Famers Reggie Jackson, Mickey Mantle, and Willie Mays, as well as six active players. The cards are numbered on the back with a "TN" prefix and arranged alphabetically within subgroup according to player's last name.

	Nm-Mt	Ex-Mt
COMPLETE SET (18)	40.00	12.00
COMPLETE SERIES 1 (9)	15.00	4.50
COMPLETE SERIES 2 (9)	25.00	7.50
TN1 Wade Boggs	1.25	.35
TN2 George Brett	5.00	1.50
TN3 Rickey Henderson	2.00	.60
TN4 Cal Ripken	6.00	1.80
TN5 Nolan Ryan	8.00	2.40
TN6 Ryne Sandberg	3.00	.90
TN7 Ozzie Smith	3.00	.90
TN8 Darryl Strawberry	.75	.23
TN9 Dave Winfield	.75	.23
TN10 Dennis Eckersley	.75	.23
TN11 Tony Gwynn	2.50	.75
TN12 Howard Johnson	.40	.12
TN13 Don Mattingly	5.00	1.50
TN14 Eddie Murray	2.00	.60
TN15 Robin Yount	3.00	.90
TN16 Reggie Jackson	2.50	.75
TN17 Mickey Mantle	12.00	3.60
TN18 Willie Mays	6.00	1.80

1993 Upper Deck Triple Crown

This ten-card, standard-size insert set highlights ten players who were selected by Upper Deck as having the best shot at winning Major League Baseball's Triple Crown. The cards were randomly inserted in series I hobby foil packs at a rate of one in 15. The cards are numbered on the back with a "TC" prefix and arranged alphabetically by player's last name.

	Nm-Mt	Ex-Mt
COMPLETE SET (10)	12.00	3.60
TC1 Barry Bonds	3.00	.90
TC2 Jose Canseco	1.25	.35
TC3 Will Clark	1.25	.35
TC4 Ken Griffey Jr.	2.00	.60
TC5 Fred McGriff	.75	.23
TC6 Kirby Puckett	1.25	.35
TC7 Cal Ripken Jr.	4.00	1.20
TC8 Gary Sheffield	.50	.15
TC9 Frank Thomas	1.25	.35
TC10 Larry Walker	.75	.23

1994 Upper Deck

The 1994 Upper Deck set was issued in two series of 280 and 270 standard-size cards for a total of 550. There are number of topical subsets including Star Rookies (1-30), Fantasy Team (31-40), The Future is Now (41-55), Home Field Advantage (267-294), Upper Deck Classic Alumni (295-299), Diamond Debuts (511-522) and Top Prospects (523-550). Three autograph cards were randomly inserted into first series retail packs. They are Ken Griffey Jr. (KG), Mickey Mantle (MM) and a combo card with Griffey and Mantle (GM). An Alex Rodriguez (298A) autograph card was randomly inserted into second series retail packs. Rookie Cards include Michael Jordan (as an baseball player), Chan Ho Park, Alex Rodriguez and Billy Wagner. Many cards have been found with a significant variation on the back. The player's name, the horizontal bar containing the biographical information and the vertical bar containing the stats header are normally printed in copper-gold color. On the variation cards, these areas are printed in silver. It is not known exactly how many of the 550 cards have silver versions, nor has any premium been established for them. Also, all of the American League Home Field Advantage subset cards (numbers 281-294) are minor uncorrected errors because the Upper Deck logos on the front are missing the year "1994".

	Nm-Mt	Ex-Mt
COMPLETE SET (550)	50.00	15.00
COMP. SERIES 1 (280)	30.00	9.00
COMP. SERIES 2 (270)	20.00	6.00
1 Brian Anderson RC	.40	.12
2 Shane Andrews	.15	.04
3 James Baldwin	.15	.04
4 Rich Becker	.15	.04
5 Greg Blosser	.15	.04
6 Ricky Bottalico RC	.40	.12
7 Midre Cummings	.15	.04
8 Carlos Delgado	.50	.15
9 Steve Dreyer RC	.15	.04
10 Joey Eischen	.15	.04
11 Carl Everett	.30	.09
12 Cliff Floyd UER (text indicates he throws left; should be right)	.30	.09
13 Alex Gonzalez	.15	.04
14 Jeff Granger	.15	.04
15 Shawn Green	.75	.23
16 Brian L. Hunter	.15	.04
17 Butch Huskey	.15	.04
18 Mark Hutton	.15	.04
19 Michael Jordan RC	8.00	2.40
20 Steve Karsay	.15	.04
21 Jeff McNeely	.15	.04
22 Marc Newfield	.15	.04
23 Manny Ramirez	.50	.15
24 Alex Rodriguez RC	15.00	4.50
25 Scott Ruffcorn UER (photo on back is Robert Ellis)	.15	.04
26 Paul Spoljaric UER (Expos logo on back)	.15	.04
27 Salomon Torres	.15	.04
28 Steve Trachsel	.15	.04
29 Chris Turner	.15	.04
30 Gabe White	.15	.04
31 Randy Johnson FT	.50	.15
32 John Wetteland FT	.15	.04
33 Mike Piazza FT	.75	.23
34 Rafael Palmeiro FT	.30	.09
35 Roberto Alomar FT	.30	.09
36 Matt Williams FT	.15	.04
37 Travis Fryman FT	.15	.04
38 Barry Bonds FT	1.00	.30
39 Marquis Grissom FT	.15	.04
40 Albert Belle FT	.30	.09
41 Steve Avery FUT	.15	.04
42 Jason Bere FUT	.15	.04
43 Alex Fernandez FUT	.15	.04
44 Mike Mussina FUT	.30	.09
45 Aaron Sele FUT	.15	.04
46 Rod Beck FUT	.15	.04
47 Mike Piazza FUT	.75	.23
48 John Olerud FUT	.15	.04
49 Carlos Baerga FUT	.15	.04
50 Gary Sheffield FUT	.15	.04
51 Travis Fryman FUT	.15	.04
52 Juan Gonzalez FUT	.30	.09
53 Ken Griffey Jr. FUT	.75	.23
54 Tim Salmon FUT	.30	.09
55 Frank Thomas FUT	.50	.15
56 Tony Phillips	.15	.04
57 Julio Franco	.30	.09
58 Kevin Mitchell	.15	.04
59 Raul Mondesi	.30	.09
60 Rickey Henderson	.75	.23
61 Jay Buhner	.30	.09
62 Bill Swift	.15	.04
63 Brady Anderson	.30	.09
64 Ryan Klesko	.30	.09
65 Darren Daulton	.30	.09
66 Damion Easley	.15	.04
67 Mark McGwire	2.00	.60
68 John Roper	.15	.04
69 Dave Telgheder	.15	.04
70 David Nied	.15	.04
71 Mo Vaughn	.30	.09
72 Tyler Green	.15	.04
73 Dave Magadan	.15	.04
74 Chili Davis	.30	.09
75 Archi Cianfrocco	.15	.04
76 Joe Girardi	.15	.04
77 Chris Hoiles	.15	.04
78 Ryan Bowen	.15	.04
79 Greg Gagne	.15	.04
80 Aaron Sele	.15	.04
81 Dave Winfield	.30	.09
82 Chad Curtis	.15	.04
83 Andy Van Slyke	.30	.09
84 Kevin Stocker	.15	.04
85 Deion Sanders	.50	.15
86 Bernie Williams	.50	.15
87 John Smoltz	.50	.15
88 Ruben Santana	.15	.04
89 Dave Stewart	.30	.09
90 Don Mattingly	2.00	.60
91 Joe Carter	.30	.09
92 Ryne Sandberg	1.25	.35
93 Chris Gomez	.15	.04
94 Tino Martinez	.50	.15
95 Terry Pendleton	.30	.09
96 Andre Dawson	.30	.09
97 Wil Cordero	.15	.04
98 Kent Hrbek	.30	.09
99 John Olerud	.30	.09
100 Kirt Manwaring	.15	.04
101 Tim Bogar	.15	.04
102 Mike Mussina	.50	.15
103 Nigel Wilson	.15	.04
104 Ricky Gutierrez	.15	.04
105 Roberto Mejia	.15	.04
106 Tom Pagnozzi	.15	.04
107 Mike Macfarlane	.15	.04
108 Jose Bautista	.15	.04
109 Luis Ortiz	.15	.04
110 Brent Gates	.15	.04
111 Tim Salmon	.50	.15
112 Wade Boggs	.50	.15
113 Tripp Cromer	.15	.04
114 Denny Hocking	.15	.04
115 Carlos Baerga	.15	.04
116 J.R. Phillips	.15	.04
117 Bo Jackson	.75	.23
118 Lance Johnson	.15	.04
119 Bobby Jones	.15	.04
120 Bobby Witt	.15	.04
121 Ron Karkovice	.15	.04
122 Jose Vizcaino	.15	.04
123 Danny Darwin	.15	.04
124 Eduardo Perez	.15	.04
125 Brian Looney RC	.15	.04
126 Pat Hentgen	.15	.04
127 Frank Viola	.30	.09
128 Darren Holmes	.15	.04
129 Wally Whitehurst	.15	.04
130 Matt Walbeck	.15	.04
131 Albert Belle	.30	.09
132 Steve Cooke	.15	.04
133 Kevin Appier	.30	.09
134 Joe Oliver	.15	.04
135 Benji Gil	.15	.04
136 Steve Buechele	.15	.04
137 Devon White	.30	.09
138 S.Hitchcock UER two losses for career; should be four	.15	.04
139 Phil Leftwich RC	.15	.04
140 Jose Canseco	.75	.23
141 Rick Aguilera	.15	.04
142 Rod Beck	.15	.04
143 Jose Rijo	.15	.04
144 Tom Glavine	.50	.15
145 Phil Plantier	.15	.04
146 Jason Bere	.15	.04
147 Jamie Moyer	.30	.09
148 Wes Chamberlain	.15	.04
149 Glenallen Hill	.15	.04
150 Mark Whiten	.15	.04
151 Bret Barberie	.15	.04
152 Chuck Knoblauch	.30	.09
153 Trevor Hoffman	.30	.09
154 Rick Wilkins	.15	.04
155 Juan Gonzalez	.50	.15
156 Ozzie Guillen	.15	.04
157 Jim Eisenreich	.15	.04
158 Pedro Astacio	.15	.04
159 Joe Magrane	.15	.04
160 Ryan Thompson	.15	.04
161 Jose Lind	.15	.04
162 Jeff Conine	.30	.09
163 Todd Benzinger	.15	.04
164 Roger Salkeld	.15	.04
165 Gary DiSarcina	.15	.04
166 Kevin Gross	.15	.04
167 Charlie Hayes	.15	.04
168 Tim Costo	.15	.04
169 Wally Joyner	.30	.09
170 Johnny Ruffin	.15	.04
171 Kirk Rueter	.30	.09
172 Lenny Dykstra	.30	.09
173 Ken Hill	.15	.04
174 Mike Bordick	.15	.04
175 Billy Hall	.15	.04
176 Rob Butler	.15	.04
177 Jay Bell	.30	.09
178 Jeff Kent	.30	.09
179 David Wells	.30	.09
180 Dean Palmer	.30	.09
181 Mariano Duncan	.15	.04
182 Orlando Merced	.15	.04
183 Brett Butler	.30	.09
184 Milt Thompson	.15	.04
185 Chipper Jones	.75	.23
186 Paul O'Neill	.50	.15
187 Mike Greenwell	.15	.04
188 Harold Baines	.30	.09
189 Todd Stottlemyre	.15	.04
190 Jeromy Burnitz	.30	.09
191 Rene Arocha	.15	.04
192 Jeff Fassero	.15	.04
193 Robby Thompson	.15	.04
194 Greg W. Harris	.15	.04
195 Todd Van Poppel	.15	.04
196 Jose Guzman	.15	.04
197 Shane Mack	.15	.04
198 Carlos Garcia	.15	.04
199 Kevin Roberson	.15	.04
200 David McCarty	.15	.04
201 Alan Trammell	.30	.09
202 Chuck Carr	.15	.04
203 Tommy Greene	.15	.04
204 Wilson Alvarez	.15	.04
205 Dwight Gooden	.30	.09
206 Tony Tarasco	.15	.04
207 Darren Lewis	.15	.04
208 Eric Karros	.30	.09
209 Chris Hammond	.15	.04
210 Jeffrey Hammonds	.15	.04
211 Rich Amaral	.15	.04
212 Danny Tartabull	.15	.04
213 Jeff Russell	.15	.04
214 Dave Staton	.15	.04
215 Kenny Lofton	.30	.09
216 Manuel Lee	.15	.04
217 Brian Koelling	.15	.04
218 Scott Lydy	.15	.04
219 Tony Gwynn	1.00	.30
220 Cecil Fielder	.30	.09
221 Royce Clayton	.15	.04
222 Reggie Sanders	.15	.04
223 Brian Jordan	.30	.09
224 Ken Griffey Jr.	1.25	.35
225 Fred McGriff	.50	.15
226 Felix Jose	.15	.04
227 Brad Pennington	.15	.04
228 Chris Bosio	.15	.04
229 Mike Stanley	.15	.04
230 Willie Greene	.15	.04
231 Alex Fernandez	.15	.04
232 Brad Ausmus	.15	.04
233 Darrell Whitmore	.15	.04
234 Marcus Moore	.15	.04
235 Allen Watson	.15	.04
236 Jose Offerman	.15	.04
237 Rondell White	.30	.09
238 Jeff King	.15	.04
239 Luis Alicea	.15	.04
240 Dan Wilson	.15	.04
241 Ed Sprague	.15	.04
242 Todd Hundley	.15	.04
243 Al Martin	.15	.04
244 Mike Lansing	.15	.04
245 Ivan Rodriguez	.75	.23
246 Dave Fleming	.15	.04
247 John Doherty	.15	.04
248 Mark McLemore	.15	.04
249 Bob Hamelin	.15	.04
250 Curtis Pride RC	.40	.12
251 Zane Smith	.15	.04
252 Eric Young	.15	.04
253 Brian McRae	.15	.04
254 Tim Raines	.30	.09
255 Javier Lopez	.30	.09
256 Melvin Nieves	.15	.04
257 Randy Myers	.15	.04
258 Willie McGee	.30	.09
259 Jimmy Key UER (birthdate missing on back)	.30	.09
260 Tom Candiotti	.15	.04
261 Eric Davis	.30	.09
262 Craig Paquette	.15	.04
263 Robin Ventura	.30	.09
264 Pat Kelly	.15	.04
265 Gregg Jefferies	.15	.04
266 Cory Snyder	.15	.04
267 David Justice HFA	.15	.04
268 Sammy Sosa HFA	.75	.23
269 Barry Larkin HFA	.30	.09
270 Andres Galarraga HFA	.15	.04
271 Gary Sheffield HFA	.15	.04
272 Jeff Bagwell HFA	.30	.09
273 Mike Piazza HFA	.75	.23
274 Larry Walker HFA	.15	.04
275 Bobby Bonilla HFA	.15	.04
276 John Kruk HFA	.15	.04
277 Jay Bell HFA	.15	.04
278 Ozzie Smith HFA	.75	.23
279 Tony Gwynn HFA	.50	.15
280 Barry Bonds HFA	1.00	.30
281 Cal Ripken Jr. HFA	1.25	.35
282 Mo Vaughn HFA	.15	.04
283 Tim Salmon HFA	.30	.09
284 Frank Thomas HFA	.50	.15
285 Albert Belle HFA	.30	.09
286 Cecil Fielder HFA	.15	.04
287 Wally Joyner HFA	.15	.04
288 Greg Vaughn HFA	.15	.04
289 Kirby Puckett HFA	.50	.15
290 Don Mattingly HFA	1.00	.30

291 Terry Steinbach HFA .15 .04
292 Ken Griffey Jr. HFA .75 .23
293 Juan Gonzalez HFA .30 .09
294 Paul Molitor HFA .30 .09
295 Tavo Alvarez UDC .15 .04
296 Matt Brunson UDC .15 .04
297 Shawn Green UDC .30 .09
298 Alex Rodriguez UDC 5.00 1.50
299 S.Stewart UDC .75 .23
300 Frank Thomas .75 .23
301 Mickey Tettleton .15 .04
302 Pedro Munoz .15 .04
303 Jose Valentin .15 .04
304 Orestes Destrade .15 .04
305 Pat Listach .15 .04
306 Scott Brosius .30 .09
307 Kurt Miller .15 .04
308 Rob Dibble .30 .09
309 Mike Blowers .15 .04
310 Jim Abbott .50 .15
311 Mike Jackson .15 .04
312 Craig Biggio .50 .15
313 Kurt Abbott RC .40 .12
314 Chuck Finley .30 .09
315 Andres Galarraga .30 .09
316 Mike Moore .15 .04
317 Doug Strange .15 .04
318 Pedro Martinez .75 .23
319 Kevin McReynolds .15 .04
320 Greg Maddux 1.25 .35
321 Mike Henneman .15 .04
322 Scott Leius .15 .04
323 John Franco .30 .09
324 Jeff Blauser .15 .04
325 Kirby Puckett .75 .23
326 Darryl Hamilton .15 .04
327 John Smiley .15 .04
328 Derrick May .15 .04
329 Jose Vizcaino .15 .04
330 Randy Johnson .75 .23
331 Jack Morris .30 .09
332 Graeme Lloyd .15 .04
333 Dave Valle .15 .04
334 Greg Myers .15 .04
335 John Wetteland .30 .09
336 Jim Gott .15 .04
337 Tim Naehring .15 .04
338 Mike Kelly .15 .04
339 Jeff Montgomery .15 .04
340 Rafael Palmeiro .50 .15
341 Eddie Murray .75 .23
342 Xavier Hernandez .15 .04
343 Bobby Munoz .15 .04
344 Bobby Bonilla .30 .09
345 Travis Fryman .30 .09
346 Steve Finley .30 .09
347 Chris Sabo .15 .04
348 Armando Reynoso .15 .04
349 Ramon Martinez .15 .04
350 Will Clark .75 .23
351 Moises Alou .30 .09
352 Jim Thome .75 .23
353 Bob Tewksbury .15 .04
354 Andujar Cedeno .15 .04
355 Orel Hershiser .30 .09
356 Mike Devereaux .15 .04
357 Mike Perez .15 .04
358 Dennis Martinez .30 .09
359 Dave Nilsson .15 .04
360 Ozzie Smith 1.25 .35
361 Eric Anthony .15 .04
362 Scott Sanders .15 .04
363 Paul Sorrento .15 .04
364 Tim Belcher .15 .04
365 Dennis Eckersley .30 .09
366 Mel Rojas .15 .04
367 Tom Henke .15 .04
368 Randy Tomlin .15 .04
369 B.J. Surhoff .30 .09
370 Larry Walker .50 .15
371 Joey Cora .15 .04
372 Mike Harkey .15 .04
373 John Valentin .15 .04
374 Doug Jones .15 .04
375 David Justice .30 .09
376 Vince Coleman .15 .04
377 David Hulse .15 .04
378 Kevin Seitzer .15 .04
379 Pete Harnisch .15 .04
380 Ruben Sierra .15 .04
381 Mark Lewis .15 .04
382 Bip Roberts .15 .04
383 Paul Wagner .15 .04
384 Stan Javier .15 .04
385 Barry Larkin .50 .15
386 Mark Portugal .15 .04
387 Roberto Kelly .15 .04
388 Andy Benes .15 .04
389 Felix Fermin .15 .04
390 Marquis Grissom .30 .09
391 Troy Neel .15 .04
392 Chad Kreuter .15 .04
393 Gregg Olson .15 .04
394 Charles Nagy .15 .04
395 Jack McDowell .15 .04
396 Luis Gonzalez .30 .09
397 Benito Santiago .30 .09
398 Chris James .15 .04
399 Terry Mulholland .15 .04
400 Barry Bonds 2.00 .60
401 Joe Grahe .15 .04
402 Duane Ward .15 .04
403 John Burkett .15 .04
404 Scott Servais .15 .04
405 Bryan Harvey .15 .04
406 Bernard Gilkey .15 .04
407 Greg McMichael .15 .04
408 Tim Wallach .15 .04
409 Ken Caminiti .30 .09
410 John Kruk .30 .09
411 Darrin Jackson .15 .04
412 Mike Gallego .15 .04
413 David Cone .30 .09
414 Lou Whitaker .30 .09
415 Sandy Alomar Jr. .15 .04
416 Bill Wegman .15 .04
417 Pat Borders .15 .04
418 Roger Pavlik .15 .04
419 Pete Smith .15 .04
420 Steve Avery .15 .04
421 David Segui .15 .04
422 Rheal Cormier .15 .04
423 Harold Reynolds .30 .09
424 Edgar Martinez .50 .15
425 Cal Ripken Jr. 2.50 .75
426 Jaime Navarro .15 .04
427 Sean Berry .15 .04
428 Bret Saberhagen .30 .09
429 Bob Welch .15 .04
430 Juan Guzman .15 .04
431 Cal Eldred .15 .04
432 Dave Hollins .15 .04
433 Sid Fernandez .15 .04
434 Willie Banks .15 .04
435 Darryl Kile .30 .09
436 Henry Rodriguez .15 .04
437 Tony Fernandez .15 .04
438 Walt Weiss .15 .04
439 Kevin Tapani .15 .04
440 Mark Grace .50 .15
441 Brian Harper .15 .04
442 Kent Mercker .15 .04
443 Anthony Young .15 .04
444 Todd Zeile .15 .04
445 Greg Vaughn .15 .04
446 Ray Lankford .15 .04
447 Dave Weathers .15 .04
448 Bret Boone .30 .09
449 Charlie Hough .30 .09
450 Roger Clemens 1.50 .45
451 Mike Morgan .15 .04
452 Doug Drabek .15 .04
453 Danny Jackson .15 .04
454 Dante Bichette .30 .09
455 Roberto Alomar .50 .15
456 Ben McDonald .15 .04
457 Kenny Rogers .30 .09
458 Bill Gullickson .15 .04
459 Darrin Fletcher .15 .04
460 Curt Schilling .30 .09
461 Billy Hatcher .15 .04
462 Howard Johnson .15 .04
463 Mickey Morandini .15 .04
464 Frank Castillo .15 .04
465 Delino DeShields .15 .04
466 Gary Gaetti .30 .09
467 Steve Farr .15 .04
468 Roberto Hernandez .15 .04
469 Jack Armstrong .15 .04
470 Paul Molitor .50 .15
471 Melido Perez .15 .04
472 Greg Hibbard .15 .04
473 Jody Reed .15 .04
474 Tom Gordon .15 .04
475 Gary Sheffield .30 .09
476 John Jaha .15 .04
477 Shawon Dunston .15 .04
478 Reggie Jefferson .15 .04
479 Don Slaught .15 .04
480 Jeff Bagwell .50 .15
481 Tim Pugh .15 .04
482 Kevin Young .15 .04
483 Ellis Burks .30 .09
484 Greg Swindell .15 .04
485 Mark Langston .15 .04
486 Omar Vizquel .50 .15
487 Kevin Brown .30 .09
488 Terry Steinbach .15 .04
489 Mark Lemke .15 .04
490 Matt Williams .30 .09
491 Pete Incaviglia .15 .04
492 Karl Rhodes .15 .04
493 Shawn Green .75 .23
494 Hal Morris .15 .04
495 Derek Bell .15 .04
496 Luis Polonia .15 .04
497 Otis Nixon .15 .04
498 Ron Darling .15 .04
499 Mitch Williams .15 .04
500 Mike Piazza 1.50 .45
501 Pat Meares .15 .04
502 Scott Cooper .15 .04
503 Scott Erickson .15 .04
504 Jeff Juden .15 .04
505 Lee Smith .30 .09
506 Bobby Ayala .15 .04
507 Dave Henderson .15 .04
508 Erik Hanson .15 .04
509 Bob Wickman .15 .04
510 Sammy Sosa 1.25 .35
511 Hector Carrasco .15 .04
512 Tim Davis .15 .04
513 Joey Hamilton .15 .04
514 Robert Eenhoorn .15 .04
515 Jorge Fabregas .15 .04
516 Tim Hyers RC .15 .04
517 John Hudek RC .15 .04
518 James Mouton .15 .04
519 Herbert Perry RC .40 .12
520 Chan Ho Park RC .60 .18
521 W.Va Landingham RC .15 .04
522 Paul Shuey .15 .04
523 Ryan Hancock RC .15 .04
524 Billy Wagner RC 1.00 .30
525 Jason Giambi .75 .23
526 Jose Silva RC .15 .04
527 Terrell Wade RC .15 .04
528 Todd Dunn .15 .04
529 Alan Benes RC .40 .12
530 B.Kieschnick RC .40 .12
531 T.Hollandsworth .15 .04
532 Brad Fullmer RC .60 .18
533 S.Soderstrom RC .15 .04
534 Daron Kirkreit .15 .04
535 Arquimedez Pozo RC .15 .04
536 Charles Johnson .30 .09
537 Preston Wilson .30 .09
538 Alex Ochoa .15 .04
539 Derrek Lee RC 1.00 .30
540 Wayne Gomes RC .15 .04
541 J.Allensworth RC .15 .04
542 Mike Bell RC .15 .04
543 Trot Nixon RC 1.00 .30
544 Pokey Reese .15 .04
545 Neifi Perez RC .40 .12
546 Johnny Damon .75 .23
547 Matt Brunson RC .15 .04
548 L.Hawkins RC .60 .18
549 Eddie Pearson RC .15 .04
550 Derek Jeter 2.50 .75
A298 Alex Rodriguez AU 300.00 90.00
P224 K.Griffey Jr. Promo 2.00 .60
GM1 Ken Griffey Jr. AU 1200.00 350.00
Mickey Mantle AU/1000
KG1 K.Griffey Jr. AU/1000 200.00 60.00
MM1 M.Mantle AU/1000 500.00 150.00

1994 Upper Deck Electric Diamond

This 550-card set is a parallel issue to the basic 1994 Upper Deck cards. The cards were issued one per foil pack and two per mini jumbo. The only differences between these and the basic cards is the "Electric Diamond" in silver foil toward the bottom and the player's name is also in silver foil.

Nm-Mt Ex-Mt
COMPLETE SET (550) 100.00 30.00
COMP.SERIES 1 (280) 60.00 18.00
COMP.SERIES 2 (270) 40.00 12.00
*STARS: .75X TO 2X BASIC CARDS...
*ROOKIES: .6X TO 1.5X BASIC CARDS

1994 Upper Deck Diamond Collection

This 30-card standard-size set was inserted regionally in first series hobby packs at a rate of one in 18. The three regions are Central (C1-C10), East (E1-E10) and West (W1-W10). While each card has the same horizontal format, the color scheme differs by region. The Central cards have a blue background, the East green and the West a deep shade of red. Color player photos are superimposed over the backgrounds. Each card has, "The Upper Deck Diamond Collection" as part of the background. The backs have a small photo and career highlights.

Nm-Mt Ex-Mt
COMPLETE SET (30) 180.00 55.00
COMPLETE CENTRAL (10) 80.00 24.00
COMPLETE EAST (10) 40.00 12.00
COMPLETE WEST (10) 60.00 18.00
C1 Jeff Bagwell 4.00 1.20
C2 Michael Jordan 15.00 4.50
C3 Barry Larkin 4.00 1.20
C4 Kirby Puckett 6.00 1.80
C5 Manny Ramirez 4.00 1.20
C6 Ryne Sandberg 10.00 3.00
C7 Ozzie Smith 10.00 3.00
C8 Frank Thomas 6.00 1.80
C9 Andy Van Slyke 2.50 .75
C10 Robin Yount 6.00 1.80
E1 Roberto Alomar 4.00 1.20
E2 Roger Clemens 12.00 3.60
E3 Lenny Dykstra 2.50 .75
E4 Cecil Fielder 2.50 .75
E5 Cliff Floyd 2.50 .75
E6 Dwight Gooden 2.50 .75
E7 David Justice 2.50 .75
E8 Don Mattingly 15.00 4.50
E9 Cal Ripken Jr. 20.00 6.00
E10 Gary Sheffield 2.50 .75
W1 Barry Bonds 15.00 4.50
W2 Andres Galarraga 2.50 .75
W3 Juan Gonzalez 4.00 1.20
W4 Ken Griffey Jr. 10.00 3.00
W5 Tony Gwynn 8.00 2.40
W6 Rickey Henderson 6.00 1.80
W7 Bo Jackson 6.00 1.80
W8 Mark McGwire 15.00 4.50
W9 Mike Piazza 12.00 3.60
W10 Tim Salmon 4.00 1.20

1994 Upper Deck Mantle Heroes

Randomly inserted in second series packs at a rate of one in 35, this 10-card standard-size set looks at various moments from The Mick's career. Metallic fronts feature a vintage photo with the card title at the bottom. The backs contain career highlights with a small scrapbook like photo. The numbering (64-72) is a continuation from previous Heroes sets.

Nm-Mt Ex-Mt
COMPLETE SET (10) 80.00 24.00
COMMON (64-72/HDR) 10.00 3.00

1994 Upper Deck Mantle's Long Shots

Randomly inserted in first series retail packs at a rate of one in 18, this 21-card silver foil standard-size set features top longball hitters as selected by Mickey Mantle. The cards are numbered on the back with a "MM" prefix and sequenced in alphabetical order. Two trade cards, were also random inserts and were redeemable (expiration: December 31, 1994) for either the basic silver foil set version (Silver Trade card) or the Electric Diamond version (blue Trade card).

Nm-Mt Ex-Mt
COMPLETE SET (21) 40.00 12.00
*ED: .5X TO 1.2X BASIC MANTLE LS.
ONE ED SET VIA MAIL PER BLUE TRADE CARD
MANTLE TRADES: RANDOM IN SER.1 HOB
MM1 Jeff Bagwell 1.50 .45
MM2 Albert Belle 1.00 .30
MM3 Barry Bonds 6.00 1.80
MM4 Jose Canseco 2.50 .75
MM5 Joe Carter 1.00 .30
MM6 Carlos Delgado 1.50 .45
MM7 Cecil Fielder 1.00 .30
MM8 Cliff Floyd 1.00 .30
MM9 Juan Gonzalez 1.50 .45
MM10 Ken Griffey Jr. 4.00 1.20
MM11 David Justice 1.00 .30
MM12 Fred McGriff 1.50 .45
MM13 Mark McGwire 6.00 1.80
MM14 Dean Palmer 1.00 .30
MM15 Mike Piazza 5.00 1.50
MM16 Manny Ramirez 1.50 .45
MM17 Tim Salmon 1.50 .45
MM18 Frank Thomas 2.50 .75
MM19 Mo Vaughn 1.00 .30
MM20 Matt Williams 1.00 .30
MM21 Mickey Mantle 15.00 4.50
NNO Mickey Mantle 6.00 1.80
Silver Trade
NNO Mickey Mantle 15.00 4.50
Blue ED Trade

1994 Upper Deck Next Generation

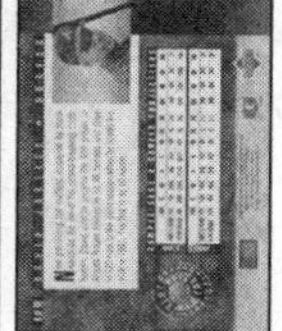

Randomly inserted in second series retail packs at a rate of one in 20, this 18-card standard-size set spotlights young established stars and promising prospects. The set is sequenced in alphabetical order. A Next Generation Electric Diamond Trade Card and a Next Generation Trade Card were seeded randomly in second series hobby packs. Each card could be redeemed for that set. Expiration date for redemption was October 31, 1994.

Nm-Mt Ex-Mt
COMPLETE SET (18) 120.00 36.00
1 Roberto Alomar 3.00 .90
2 Carlos Delgado 3.00 .90
3 Cliff Floyd 2.00 .60
4 Alex Gonzalez 1.00 .30
5 Juan Gonzalez 3.00 .90
6 Ken Griffey Jr. 8.00 2.40
7 Jeffrey Hammonds 1.00 .30
8 Michael Jordan 15.00 4.50
9 David Justice 2.00 .60
10 Ryan Klesko 2.00 .60
11 Javier Lopez 2.00 .60
12 Raul Mondesi 2.00 .60
13 Mike Piazza 10.00 3.00
14 Kirby Puckett 5.00 1.50
15 Manny Ramirez 3.00 .90
16 Alex Rodriguez 40.00 12.00
17 Tim Salmon 3.00 .90
18 Gary Sheffield 2.00 .60
NNO Exp. NG Trade Card 1.00 .30

1994 Upper Deck Next Generation Electric Diamond

This 18 card set parallels the regular Next Generation insert set. The cards are differentiated by an "Electric Diamond" logo on the bottom. These cards were sent if a collector received a ED trade card in a pack.

Nm-Mt Ex-Mt
*ELEC.DIAM: .5X TO 1.2X BASIC NEXT.GEN.
8 Michael Jordan 25.00 7.50
16 Alex Rodriguez 60.00 18.00

1994 Upper Deck All-Time Heroes

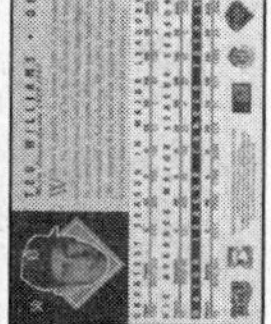

This set consists of 225 standard-size cards. According to Upper Deck, production was limited to 4,015 numbered cases. Special subsets featured are Off The Wire (1-18), All-Time Heroes (101-125), Diamond Legends (151-177), and Heroes of Baseball (208-224). Mickey Mantle and three other superstars (Reggie Jackson, Tom Seaver, and George Brett) each autographed 1,000 cards that were randomly inserted into packs. (Nolan Ryan had been expected to sign cards for this product but did not. Instead, Brett signed an additional 1,000 cards). According to Upper Deck, a signed card would be found in one of every 385 packs. A Reggie Jackson Promo card was distributed to dealers and hobby media to preview the set.

Nm-Mt Ex-Mt
COMPLETE SET (225) 15.00 4.50
1 Ted Williams OW .50 .15
2 J. Vander Meer OW .10 .03
3 Lou Brock OW .30 .09
4 Lou Gehrig OW .50 .15
5 Hank Aaron OW .50 .15
6 Tommie Agee OW .10 .03
7 Mickey Mantle OW 1.00 .30
8 Bill Mazeroski OW .20 .06
9 Reggie Jackson OW .30 .09
10 Willie Mays 1.00 .30
Mickey Mantle
11 Roy Campanella OW .20 .06
12 Harvey Haddix OW .10 .03
13 Jimmy Piersall OW .10 .03
14 Enos Slaughter OW .10 .03
15 Nolan Ryan OW .75 .23
16 Bobby Thomson OW .10 .03
17 Willie Mays OW .50 .15
18 Bucky Dent OW .10 .03
19 Joe Garagiola .20 .06
20 George Brett 1.25 .35
21 Cecil Cooper .20 .06
22 Ray Boone .10 .03
23 King Kelly .20 .06
24 Willie Mays 1.00 .30
25 Napoleon Lajoie .30 .09
26 Gil McDougald .20 .06
27 Nelson Briles .10 .03
28 Bucky Dent .20 .06
29 Manny Sanguillen .10 .03
30 Ty Cobb .75 .23
31 Jim Grant .10 .03
32 Del Ennis .10 .03
33 Ron Hunt .10 .03
34 Nolan Ryan 1.50 .45
35 Christy Mathewson .30 .09
36 Robin Roberts .20 .06
37 Frank Crosetti .10 .03
38 Johnny Vander Meer .10 .03
39 Virgil Trucks .10 .03
40 Lou Gehrig 1.00 .30
41 Luke Appling .20 .06
42 Rico Petrocelli .10 .03
43 Harry Walker .10 .03
44 Reggie Jackson .30 .09
45 Mel Ott .30 .09
46 Phil Cavarretta .20 .06
47 Larry Doby .20 .06
48 Johnny Mize .20 .06
49 Ralph Kiner .30 .09
50 Ted Williams 1.00 .30
51 Bobby Thomson .20 .06
52 Joe Black .20 .06
53 Monte Irvin .20 .06
54 Bill Virdon .20 .06
55 Honus Wagner .50 .15
56 Herb Score .20 .06
57 Jerry Coleman .10 .03
58 Jimmie Foxx .30 .09
59 Roy Face .10 .03
60 Babe Ruth 1.50 .45
61 Jimmy Piersall .20 .06
62 Ed Charles .10 .03
63 Johnny Podres .20 .06
64 Charlie Neal .10 .03
65 Bill White .20 .06
66 Bill Skowron .30 .09
67 Al Rosen .20 .06
68 Eddie Lopat .10 .03
69 Bud Harrelson .20 .06
70 Steve Carlton .20 .06
71 Vida Blue .10 .03
72 Don Newcombe .20 .06
73 Al Bumbry .10 .03
74 Bill Madlock .20 .06
75 Hank Aaron CL .30 .09
76 Bill Mazeroski .30 .09
77 Ron Cey .20 .06
78 Tommy John .20 .06
79 Lou Brock .30 .09
80 Walter Johnson .50 .15
81 Harvey Haddix .20 .06
82 Al Oliver .20 .06
83 Johnny Logan .20 .06
84 Dave Dravecky .20 .06
85 Tony Oliva .20 .06
86 Dave Kingman .20 .06
87 Luis Tiant .20 .06
88 Sal Bando .20 .06
89 Cesar Cedeno .20 .06
90 Warren Spahn .30 .09
91 Mickey Lolich .10 .03
92 Lew Burdette .20 .06
93 Hank Bauer .20 .06
94 Marv Throneberry .10 .03
95 Willie Stargell .30 .09
96 George Kell .30 .09
97 Ferguson Jenkins .20 .06
98 Al Kaline .50 .15
99 Billy Martin .30 .09
100 Mickey Mantle 2.00 .60
101 1869 Red Stockings ATH .10 .03
102 King Kelly ATH .10 .03
103 Nap Lajoie ATH .20 .06
104 C. Mathewson ATH .20 .06
105 Cy Young ATH .20 .06
106 Ty Cobb ATH .50 .15
107 Reggie Jackson CL .20 .06
108 Rogers Hornsby ATH .20 .06
109 Walter Johnson ATH .20 .06
110 Babe Ruth ATH .75 .23
111 Hack Wilson ATH .20 .06
112 Lou Gehrig ATH .50 .15
113 Ted Williams ATH .50 .15
114 Yogi Berra ATH .30 .09
115 Bobby Thomson ATH .10 .03
116 Mickey Mantle ATH 1.00 .30
117 Willie Mays ATH .50 .15
118 Bill Mazeroski ATH .20 .06
119 Bob Gibson ATH .20 .06
120 Nolan Ryan .50 .15

Card	Nm-Mt	Ex-Mt
Tom Seaver Tommie Agee		
121 Hank Aaron ATH	.50	.15
122 Reggie Jackson ATH	.30	.09
123 George Brett ATH	.60	.18
124 Steve Carlton ATH	.10	.03
125 Nolan Ryan ATH	.75	.23
126 Frank Thomas	.20	.06
127 Sam McDowell	.20	.06
128 Jim Lonborg	.10	.03
129 Bert Campaneris	.10	.03
130 Bob Gibson	.30	.09
131 Bobby Richardson	.20	.06
132 Bobby Grich	.20	.06
133 Billy Pierce	.20	.06
134 Enos Slaughter	.20	.06
135 Honus Wagner CL	.20	.06
136 Orlando Cepeda	.20	.06
137 Rennie Stennett	.10	.03
138 Gene Alley	.10	.03
139 Manny Mota	.10	.03
140 Rogers Hornsby	.30	.09
141 Joe Charboneau	.10	.03
142 Rick Ferrell	.20	.06
143 Toby Harrah	.10	.03
144 Hank Aaron	1.00	.30
145 Yogi Berra	.50	.15
146 Whitey Ford	.30	.09
147 Roy Campanella	.50	.15
148 Graig Nettles	.20	.06
149 Bobby Brown	.10	.03
150 Willie Mays CL	.30	.09
151 Cy Young LGD	.20	.06
152 Walter Johnson LGD	.20	.06
153 C. Mathewson LGD	.20	.06
154 Warren Spahn LGD	.30	.09
155 Steve Carlton LGD	.10	.03
156 Bob Gibson LGD	.20	.06
157 Whitey Ford LGD	.20	.06
158 Yogi Berra LGD	.30	.09
159 Roy Campanella LGD	.20	.06
160 Lou Gehrig LGD	.50	.15
161 Johnny Mize LGD	.10	.03
162 Rogers Hornsby LGD	.20	.06
163 Honus Wagner LGD	.20	.06
164 Hank Aaron LGD	.50	.15
165 Babe Ruth LGD	.75	.23
166 Willie Mays LGD	.50	.15
167 Reggie Jackson LGD	.30	.09
168 Mickey Mantle LGD	1.00	.30
169 Jimmie Foxx LGD	.20	.06
170 Ted Williams LGD	.50	.15
171 Mel Ott LGD	.20	.06
172 Willie Stargell LGD	.20	.06
173 Al Kaline LGD	.20	.06
174 Ty Cobb LGD	.50	.15
175 Nap Lajoie LGD	.20	.06
176 Lou Brock LGD	.30	.09
177 Tom Seaver LGD	.20	.06
178 Mark Fidrych	.20	.06
179 Don Baylor	.20	.06
180 Tom Seaver	.30	.09
181 Jerry Grote	.10	.03
182 George Foster	.10	.03
183 Buddy Bell	.20	.06
184 Ralph Garr	.20	.06
185 Steve Garvey	.20	.06
186 Joe Torre	.20	.06
187 Carl Erskine	.30	.09
188 Tommy Davis	.10	.03
189 Bill Buckner	.20	.06
190 Hack Wilson	.30	.09
191 Steve Blass	.10	.03
192 Ken Brett	.10	.03
193 Lee May	.10	.03
194 Bob Horner	.20	.06
195 Boog Powell	.20	.06
196 Darrell Evans	.20	.06
197 Paul Blair	.10	.03
198 Johnny Callison	.20	.06
199 Jimmie Reese	.10	.03
200 Cy Young	.50	.15
201 Ron Santo	.20	.06
202 Rico Carty	.10	.03
203 Ron Necciai	.10	.03
204 Lou Boudreau	.20	.06
205 Minnie Minoso	.20	.06
206 Eddie Yost	.10	.03
207 Tommie Agee	.10	.03
208 Dave Kingman HB	.10	.03
209 Tony Oliva HB	.20	.06
210 Reggie Jackson HB	.30	.09
211 Paul Blair HB	.10	.03
212 Ferguson Jenkins HB	.10	.03
213 Steve Garvey HB	.20	.06
214 Bert Campaneris HB	.10	.03
215 Orlando Cepeda HB	.20	.06
216 Bill Madlock HB	.10	.03
217 Rennie Stennett HB	.10	.03
218 Frank Thomas HB	.10	.03
219 Bob Gibson HB	.20	.06
220 Lou Brock HB	.30	.09
221 Rico Carty HB	.10	.03
222 Mickey Mantle HB	1.00	.30
223 Robin Roberts HB	.20	.06
224 Manny Sanguillen HB	.10	.03
225 Mickey Mantle CL	.50	.15
P44 R.Jackson Promo	3.00	.90

1994 Upper Deck All-Time Heroes 125th

This 225-card standard-size set is identical to the regular issue 1994 Upper Deck All-Time Heroes of Baseball series, except that each card has on its front "Major League Baseball" and "125th Anniversary" stamped in bronze foil along the right edge. Every pack contained one 125th Anniversary gold card.

	Nm-Mt	Ex-Mt
COMPLETE SET (225)	50.00	15.00
*STARS: 1.5X TO 4X BASIC CARDS...		

1994 Upper Deck All-Time Heroes 1954 Archives

Measuring the standard-size, these three chase cards were randomly inserted in the foil packs at a ratio of one card per 30 ten-card foil packs.

Cards numbered 1 and 250 of Ted Williams, which are similar in design to the two that were originally issued by Topps in 1954, were not included in that company's 1954 Archives edition due to the terms of his contract with Upper Deck. Like Williams, Mickey Mantle had an exclusive agreement with Upper Deck that precluded his appearance in the 1954 Topps Archives set. Mantle didn't even appear in the original 1954 Topps set due to his then exclusive contract with Bowman. This "card that never was" is similar to the original 1954 set design.

	Nm-Mt	Ex-Mt
1 Ted Williams	50.00	15.00
250 Ted Williams	50.00	15.00
259 Mickey Mantle	100.00	30.00

1994 Upper Deck All-Time Heroes Autographs

These four autograph cards were inserted one every 385 packs into the All-Time Heroes packs. Three players signed 1,000 cards while George Brett signed 2,000 cards since Nolan Ryan did not sign the 1,000 cards he had been expected to sign for this product. Each card came with a certification of authenticity on the back and could be registered with Upper Deck upon receipt.

	Nm-Mt	Ex-Mt
1 George Brett	60.00	18.00
2 Reggie Jackson	40.00	12.00
3 Mickey Mantle	500.00	150.00
4 Tom Seaver	40.00	12.00

1994 Upper Deck All-Time Heroes Next In Line

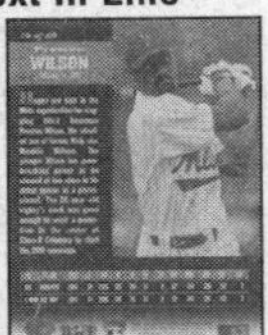

Capturing up and coming Minor League stars, this 20-card standard-size set was randomly inserted at a ratio of one in every 39 packs. Production was limited to 2,500 of each card. The fronts have a metallic finish with a color player cutout on the left, silhouetted by a blue-foil line. A black border on the right features the words "Next In Line," a color player headshot, and the player's name. The backs carry another color player photo, player information, and 1993 statistics. The cards are numbered on the back as "X of 20".

	Nm-Mt	Ex-Mt
COMPLETE SET (20)	50.00	15.00
1 Mike Bell	2.00	.60
2 Alan Benes	2.00	.60
3 D.J. Boston	2.00	.60
4 Johnny Damon	5.00	1.50
5 Brad Fullmer	5.00	1.50
6 LaTroy Hawkins	5.00	1.50
7 Derek Jeter	20.00	6.00
8 Daron Kirkreit	2.00	.60
9 Trot Nixon	5.00	1.50
10 Alex Ochoa	2.00	.60
11 Kirk Presley	2.00	.60
12 Jose Silva	2.00	.60
13 Terrell Wade	2.00	.60
14 Billy Wagner	3.00	.90
15 Glenn Williams	2.00	.60
16 Preston Wilson	3.00	.90
17 Wayne Gomes	2.00	.60
18 Ben Grieve	3.00	.90
19 Dustin Hermanson	3.00	.90
20 Paul Wilson	3.00	.90

1995 Upper Deck

The 1995 Upper Deck baseball set was issued in two series of 225 cards for a total of 450. The cards were distributed in 12-card packs (36 per box) with a suggested retail price of $1.99. Subsets include Top Prospect (1-15, 251-265), 90's Midpoint (101-110), Star Rookie (211-240), and Diamond Debuts (241-250). Rookie Cards in this set include Hideo Nomo. Five randomly inserted Trade Cards were each redeemable for nine updated cards of new rookies or players who changed teams, comprising a 45-card Trade Redemption set. The Trade cards expired Feb 1, 1996. Autographed jumbo cards (Roger Clemens for series one, Alex Rodriguez for either series) were available through a wrapper redemption offer.

	Nm-Mt	Ex-Mt
COMP.MASTER SET (495)	110.00	33.00
COMPLETE SET (450)	50.00	15.00
COMP. SERIES 1 (225)	25.00	7.50
COMP. SERIES 2 (225)	25.00	7.50
COMMON CARD (1-450)	.15	.04
COMP.TRADE SET (45)	60.00	18.00
COMMON (451T-495T)	1.00	.30
1 Ruben Rivera	.15	.04
2 Bill Pulsipher	.15	.04
3 Ben Grieve	.30	.09
4 Curtis Goodwin	.15	.04
5 Damon Hollins	.15	.04
6 Todd Greene	.15	.04
7 Glenn Williams	.15	.04
8 Bret Wagner	.15	.04
9 Karim Garcia RC	.40	.12
10 Nomar Garciaparra	2.00	.60
11 Raul Casanova RC	.15	.04
12 Matt Smith	.15	.04
13 Paul Wilson	.15	.04
14 Jason Isringhausen	.30	.09
15 Reid Ryan	.30	.09
16 Lee Smith	.30	.09
17 Chili Davis	.30	.09
18 Brian Anderson	.15	.04
19 Gary DiSarcina	.15	.04
20 Bo Jackson	.75	.23
21 Chuck Finley	.30	.09
22 Darryl Kile	.30	.09
23 Shane Reynolds	.15	.04
24 Tony Eusebio	.15	.04
25 Craig Biggio	.50	.15
26 Doug Drabek	.15	.04
27 Brian L. Hunter	.15	.04
28 James Mouton	.15	.04
29 Geronimo Berroa	.15	.04
30 Rickey Henderson	.75	.23
31 Steve Karsay	.15	.04
32 Steve Ontiveros	.15	.04
33 Ernie Young	.15	.04
34 Dennis Eckersley	.30	.09
35 Mark McGwire	2.00	.60
36 Dave Stewart	.30	.09
37 Pat Hentgen	.15	.04
38 Carlos Delgado	.30	.09
39 Joe Carter	.30	.09
40 Roberto Alomar	.50	.15
41 John Olerud	.30	.09
42 Devon White	.30	.09
43 Roberto Kelly	.15	.04
44 Jeff Blauser	.15	.04
45 Fred McGriff	.50	.15
46 Tom Glavine	.50	.15
47 Mike Kelly	.15	.04
48 Javier Lopez	.30	.09
49 Greg Maddux	1.25	.35
50 Matt Mieske	.15	.04
51 Troy O'Leary	.15	.04
52 Jeff Cirillo	.15	.04
53 Cal Eldred	.15	.04
54 Pat Listach	.15	.04
55 Jose Valentin	.15	.04
56 John Mabry	.15	.04
57 Bob Tewksbury	.15	.04
58 Brian Jordan	.30	.09
59 Gregg Jefferies	.15	.04
60 Ozzie Smith	1.25	.35
61 Geronimo Pena	.15	.04
62 Mark Whiten	.15	.04
63 Rey Sanchez	.15	.04
64 Willie Banks	.15	.04
65 Mark Grace	.50	.15
66 Randy Myers	.15	.04
67 Steve Trachsel	.15	.04
68 Derrick May	.15	.04
69 Brett Butler	.30	.09
70 Eric Karros	.30	.09
71 Tim Wallach	.15	.04
72 Delino DeShields	.15	.04
73 Darren Dreifort	.15	.04
74 Orel Hershiser	.30	.09
75 Billy Ashley	.15	.04
76 Sean Berry	.15	.04
77 Ken Hill	.15	.04
78 John Wetteland	.30	.09
79 Moises Alou	.30	.09
80 Cliff Floyd	.30	.09
81 Marquis Grissom	.30	.09
82 Larry Walker	.50	.15
83 Rondell White	.30	.09
84 W.VanLandingham	.15	.04
85 Matt Williams	.30	.09
86 Rod Beck	.15	.04
87 Darren Lewis	.15	.04
88 Robby Thompson	.15	.04
89 Darryl Strawberry	.30	.09
90 Kenny Lofton	.30	.09
91 Charles Nagy	.15	.04
92 Sandy Alomar Jr.	.15	.04
93 Mark Clark	.15	.04
94 Dennis Martinez	.30	.09
95 Dave Winfield	.30	.09
96 Jim Thome	.75	.23
97 Manny Ramirez	.50	.15
98 Goose Gossage	.30	.09
99 Tino Martinez	.50	.15
100 Ken Griffey Jr.	1.25	.35
101 Greg Maddux ANA	.75	.23
102 Randy Johnson ANA	.50	.15
103 Barry Bonds ANA	1.00	.30
104 Juan Gonzalez ANA	.30	.09
105 Frank Thomas ANA	.50	.15
106 Matt Williams ANA	.15	.04
107 Paul Molitor ANA	.30	.09
108 Fred McGriff ANA	.30	.09
109 Carlos Baerga ANA	.15	.04
110 Ken Griffey Jr. ANA	.75	.23
111 Reggie Jefferson	.15	.04
112 Randy Johnson	.75	.23
113 Marc Newfield	.15	.04
114 Robb Nen	.30	.09
115 Jeff Conine	.30	.09
116 Kurt Abbott	.15	.04
117 Charlie Hough	.30	.09
118 Dave Weathers	.15	.04
119 Juan Castillo	.15	.04
120 Bret Saberhagen	.30	.09
121 Rico Brogna	.15	.04
122 John Franco	.30	.09
123 Todd Hundley	.15	.04
124 Jason Jacome	.15	.04
125 Bobby Jones	.15	.04
126 Bret Barberie	.15	.04
127 Ben McDonald	.15	.04
128 Harold Baines	.30	.09
129 Jeffrey Hammonds	.15	.04
130 Mike Mussina	.50	.15
131 Chris Hoiles	.15	.04
132 Brady Anderson	.30	.09
133 Eddie Williams	.15	.04
134 Andy Benes	.15	.04
135 Tony Gwynn	1.00	.30
136 Bip Roberts	.15	.04
137 Joey Hamilton	.15	.04
138 Luis Lopez	.15	.04
139 Ray McDavid	.15	.04
140 Lenny Dykstra	.30	.09
141 Mariano Duncan	.15	.04
142 Fernando Valenzuela	.30	.09
143 Bobby Munoz	.15	.04
144 Kevin Stocker	.15	.04
145 John Kruk	.30	.09
146 Jon Lieber	.15	.04
147 Zane Smith	.15	.04
148 Steve Cooke	.15	.04
149 Andy Van Slyke	.30	.09
150 Jay Bell	.30	.09
151 Carlos Garcia	.15	.04
152 John Dettmer	.15	.04
153 Darren Oliver	.15	.04
154 Dean Palmer	.30	.09
155 Otis Nixon	.15	.04
156 Rusty Greer	.30	.09
157 Rick Helling	.15	.04
158 Jose Canseco	.75	.23
159 Roger Clemens	1.50	.45
160 Andre Dawson	.30	.09
161 Mo Vaughn	.30	.09
162 Aaron Sele	.15	.04
163 John Valentin	.15	.04
164 Brian R. Hunter	.15	.04
165 Bret Boone	.30	.09
166 Hector Carrasco	.15	.04
167 Pete Schourek	.15	.04
168 Willie Greene	.15	.04
169 Kevin Mitchell	.15	.04
170 Deion Sanders	.50	.15
171 John Roper	.15	.04
172 Charlie Hayes	.15	.04
173 David Nied	.15	.04
174 Ellis Burks	.30	.09
175 Dante Bichette	.30	.09
176 Marvin Freeman	.15	.04
177 Eric Young	.15	.04
178 David Cone	.30	.09
179 Greg Gagne	.15	.04
180 Bob Hamelin	.15	.04
181 Wally Joyner	.30	.09
182 Jeff Montgomery	.15	.04
183 Jose Lind	.15	.04
184 Chris Gomez	.15	.04
185 Travis Fryman	.30	.09
186 Kirk Gibson	.30	.09
187 Mike Moore	.15	.04
188 Lou Whitaker	.30	.09
189 Sean Bergman	.15	.04
190 Shane Mack	.15	.04
191 Rick Aguilera	.15	.04
192 Denny Hocking	.15	.04
193 Chuck Knoblauch	.30	.09
194 Kevin Tapani	.15	.04
195 Kent Hrbek	.30	.09
196 Ozzie Guillen	.15	.04
197 Wilson Alvarez	.15	.04
198 Tim Raines	.30	.09
199 Scott Ruffcorn	.15	.04
200 Michael Jordan	2.50	.75
201 Robin Ventura	.30	.09
202 Jason Bere	.15	.04
203 Darrin Jackson	.15	.04
204 Russ Davis	.15	.04
205 Jimmy Key	.30	.09
206 Jack McDowell	.15	.04
207 Jim Abbott	.50	.15
208 Paul O'Neill	.50	.15
209 Bernie Williams	.50	.15
210 Don Mattingly	2.00	.60
211 Orlando Miller	.15	.04
212 Alex Gonzalez	.15	.04
213 Terrell Wade	.15	.04
214 Jose Oliva	.15	.04
215 Alex Rodriguez	2.00	.60
216 Garret Anderson	.30	.09
217 Alan Benes	.15	.04
218 Armando Benitez	.30	.09
219 Dustin Hermanson	.30	.09
220 Charles Johnson	.30	.09
221 Julian Tavarez	.15	.04
222 Jason Giambi	.50	.15
223 LaTroy Hawkins	.15	.04
224 Todd Hollandsworth	.15	.04
225 Derek Jeter	2.00	.60
226 Hideo Nomo RC	2.00	.60
227 Tony Clark	.15	.04
228 Roger Cedeno	.15	.04
229 Scott Stahoviak	.15	.04
230 Michael Tucker	.15	.04
231 Joe Rosselli	.15	.04
232 Antonio Osuna	.15	.04
233 Bobby Higginson RC	.75	.23
234 Mark Grudzielanek RC	.40	.12
235 Ray Durham	.30	.09
236 Frank Rodriguez	.15	.04
237 Quilvio Veras	.15	.04
238 Darren Bragg	.15	.04
239 Ugueth Urbina	.15	.04
240 Jason Bates	.15	.04
241 David Bell	.15	.04
242 Ron Villone	.15	.04
243 Joe Randa	.15	.04
244 Carlos Perez RC	.40	.12
245 Brad Clontz	.15	.04
246 Steve Rodriguez	.15	.04
247 Joe Vitiello	.15	.04
248 Ozzie Timmons	.15	.04
249 Rudy Pemberton	.15	.04
250 Marty Cordova	.15	.04
251 Tony Graffanino	.15	.04
252 Mark Johnson RC	.40	.12
253 Tomas Perez RC	.15	.04
254 Jimmy Hurst	.15	.04
255 Edgardo Alfonzo	.30	.09
256 Jose Malave	.15	.04
257 Brad Radke RC	.75	.23
258 Jon Nunnally	.15	.04
259 Dilson Torres RC	.15	.04
260 Esteban Loaiza	.15	.04
261 Freddy Adrian Garcia RC	.15	.04
262 Don Wengert	.15	.04
263 Robert Person RC	.40	.12
264 Tim Unroe RC	.15	.04
265 Juan Acevedo RC	.15	.04
266 Eduardo Perez	.15	.04
267 Tony Phillips	.15	.04
268 Jim Edmonds	.50	.15
269 Jorge Fabregas	.15	.04
270 Tim Salmon	.50	.15
271 Mark Langston	.15	.04
272 J.T. Snow	.30	.09
273 Phil Plantier	.15	.04
274 Derek Bell	.15	.04
275 Jeff Bagwell	.50	.15
276 Luis Gonzalez	.30	.09
277 John Hudek	.15	.04
278 Todd Stottlemyre	.15	.04
279 Mark Acre	.15	.04
280 Ruben Sierra	.15	.04
281 Mike Bordick	.15	.04
282 Ron Darling	.15	.04
283 Brent Gates	.15	.04
284 Todd Van Poppel	.15	.04
285 Paul Molitor	.50	.15
286 Ed Sprague	.15	.04
287 Juan Guzman	.15	.04
288 David Cone	.30	.09
289 Shawn Green	.30	.09
290 Marquis Grissom	.30	.09
291 Kent Mercker	.15	.04
292 Steve Avery	.15	.04
293 Chipper Jones	.75	.23
294 John Smoltz	.50	.15
295 David Justice	.30	.09
296 Ryan Klesko	.30	.09
297 Joe Oliver	.15	.04
298 Ricky Bones	.15	.04
299 John Jaha	.15	.04
300 Greg Vaughn	.15	.04
301 Dave Nilsson	.15	.04
302 Kevin Seitzer	.15	.04
303 Bernard Gilkey	.15	.04
304 Allen Battle	.15	.04
305 Ray Lankford	.15	.04
306 Tom Pagnozzi	.15	.04
307 Allen Watson	.15	.04
308 Danny Jackson	.15	.04
309 Ken Hill	.15	.04
310 Todd Zeile	.15	.04
311 Kevin Roberson	.15	.04
312 Steve Buechele	.15	.04
313 Rick Wilkins	.15	.04
314 Kevin Foster	.15	.04
315 Sammy Sosa	1.25	.35
316 Howard Johnson	.15	.04
317 Greg Hansell	.15	.04
318 Pedro Astacio	.15	.04
319 Rafael Bournigal	.15	.04
320 Mike Piazza	1.25	.35
321 Ramon Martinez	.15	.04
322 Raul Mondesi	.30	.09
323 Ismael Valdes	.15	.04
324 Wil Cordero	.15	.04
325 Tony Tarasco	.15	.04
326 Roberto Kelly	.15	.04
327 Jeff Fassero	.15	.04
328 Mike Lansing	.15	.04
329 Pedro Martinez	.75	.23
330 Kirk Rueter	.15	.04
331 Glenallen Hill	.15	.04
332 Kirt Manwaring	.15	.04
333 Royce Clayton	.15	.04
334 J.R. Phillips	.15	.04
335 Barry Bonds	2.00	.60
336 Mark Portugal	.15	.04
337 Terry Mulholland	.15	.04
338 Omar Vizquel	.50	.15
339 Carlos Baerga	.15	.04
340 Albert Belle	.30	.09
341 Eddie Murray	.75	.23
342 Wayne Kirby	.15	.04
343 Chad Ogea	.15	.04
344 Tim Davis	.15	.04
345 Jay Buhner	.30	.09
346 Bobby Ayala	.15	.04
347 Mike Blowers	.15	.04
348 Dave Fleming	.15	.04
349 Edgar Martinez	.50	.15
350 Andre Dawson	.30	.09
351 Darrell Whitmore	.15	.04
352 Chuck Carr	.15	.04
353 John Burkett	.15	.04
354 Chris Hammond	.15	.04
355 Gary Sheffield	.30	.09
356 Pat Rapp	.15	.04
357 Greg Colbrunn	.15	.04
358 David Segui	.15	.04
359 Jeff Kent	.30	.09
360 Bobby Bonilla	.30	.09
361 Pete Harnisch	.15	.04
362 Ryan Thompson	.15	.04
363 Jose Vizcaino	.15	.04
364 Brett Butler	.30	.09
365 Cal Ripken Jr.	2.50	.75
366 Rafael Palmeiro	.50	.15
367 Leo Gomez	.15	.04
368 Andy Van Slyke	.30	.09
369 Arthur Rhodes	.15	.04
370 Ken Caminiti	.30	.09

371 Steve Finley .30 .09
372 Melvin Nieves .15 .04
373 Andujar Cedeno .15 .04
374 Trevor Hoffman .30 .09
375 Fernando Valenzuela .30 .09
376 Ricky Bottalico .15 .04
377 Dave Hollins .15 .04
378 Charlie Hayes .15 .04
379 Tommy Greene .15 .04
380 Darren Daulton .30 .09
381 Curt Schilling .30 .09
382 Midre Cummings .15 .04
383 Al Martin .15 .04
384 Jeff King .15 .04
385 Orlando Merced .15 .04
386 Denny Neagle .30 .09
387 Don Slaught .15 .04
388 Dave Clark .15 .04
389 Kevin Gross .15 .04
390 Will Clark .75 .23
391 Ivan Rodriguez .75 .23
392 Benji Gil .15 .04
393 Jeff Frye .15 .04
394 Kenny Rogers .30 .09
395 Juan Gonzalez .50 .15
396 Mike Macfarlane .15 .04
397 Lee Tinsley .15 .04
398 Tim Naehring .15 .04
399 Tim Vanegmond .15 .04
400 Mike Greenwell .15 .04
401 Ken Ryan .15 .04
402 John Smiley .15 .04
403 Tim Pugh .15 .04
404 Reggie Sanders .15 .04
405 Barry Larkin .50 .15
406 Hal Morris .15 .04
407 Jose Rijo .15 .04
408 Lance Painter .15 .04
409 Joe Girardi .15 .04
410 Andres Galarraga .30 .09
411 Mike Kingery .15 .04
412 Roberto Mejia .15 .04
413 Walt Weiss .15 .04
414 Bill Swift .15 .04
415 Larry Walker .50 .15
416 Billy Brewer .15 .04
417 Pat Borders .15 .04
418 Tom Gordon .15 .04
419 Kevin Appier .30 .09
420 Gary Gaetti .30 .09
421 Greg Gohr .15 .04
422 Felipe Lira .15 .04
423 John Doherty .15 .04
424 Chad Curtis .15 .04
425 Cecil Fielder .30 .09
426 Alan Trammell .30 .09
427 David McCarty .15 .04
428 Scott Erickson .15 .04
429 Pat Mahomes .15 .04
430 Kirby Puckett .75 .23
431 Dave Stevens .15 .04
432 Pedro Munoz .15 .04
433 Chris Sabo .15 .04
434 Alex Fernandez .15 .04
435 Frank Thomas .75 .23
436 Roberto Hernandez .15 .04
437 Lance Johnson .15 .04
438 Jim Abbott .50 .15
439 John Wetteland .30 .09
440 Melido Perez .15 .04
441 Tony Fernandez .15 .04
442 Pat Kelly .15 .04
443 Mike Stanley .15 .04
444 Danny Tartabull .15 .04
445 Wade Boggs .50 .15
446 Robin Yount 1.25 .35
447 Ryne Sandberg 1.25 .35
448 Nolan Ryan 3.00 .90
449 George Brett 2.00 .60
450 Mike Schmidt 1.25 .35
451 Jim Abbott TRADE 2.00 .60
452 D.Tartabull TRADE 1.00 .30
453 Ariel Prieto TRADE 1.00 .30
454 Scott Cooper TRADE 1.00 .30
455 Tom Henke TRADE 1.00 .30
456 Todd Zeile TRADE 1.00 .30
457 Brian McRae TRADE 1.00 .30
458 Luis Gonzalez TRADE 1.50 .45
459 Jaime Navarro TRADE 1.00 .30
460 Todd Worrell TRADE 1.00 .30
461 Roberto Kelly TRADE 1.00 .30
462 Chad Fonville TRADE 1.00 .30
463 S.Andrews TRADE 1.00 .30
464 David Segui TRADE 1.00 .30
465 Deion Sanders TRADE 2.00 .60
466 Orel Hershiser TRADE 1.50 .45
467 Ken Hill TRADE 1.00 .30
468 Andy Benes TRADE 1.00 .30
469 T.Pendleton TRADE 1.50 .45
470 Bobby Bonilla TRADE 1.50 .45
471 Scott Erickson TRADE 1.00 .30
472 Kevin Brown TRADE 1.50 .45
473 G.Dishman TRADE 1.00 .30
474 Phil Plantier TRADE 1.00 .30
475 G.Jefferies TRADE 1.00 .30
476 Tyler Green TRADE 1.00 .30
477 H. Slocumb TRADE 1.00 .30
478 Mark Whiten TRADE 1.00 .30
479 M.Tettleton TRADE 1.00 .30
480 Tim Wakefield TRADE 1.50 .45
481 V. Eshelman TRADE 1.00 .30
482 Rick Aguilera TRADE 1.00 .30
483 Erik Hanson TRADE 1.00 .30
484 Willie McGee TRADE 1.50 .45
485 Troy O'Leary TRADE 1.00 .30
486 B.Santiago TRADE 1.50 .45
487 Darren Lewis TRADE 1.00 .30
488 Dave Burba TRADE 1.00 .30
489 Ron Gant TRADE 1.50 .45
490 B.Saberhagen TRADE 1.50 .45
491 Vinny Castilla TRADE 1.50 .45
492 F.Rodriguez TRADE 1.00 .30
493 Andy Pettitte TRADE 2.00 .60
494 Ruben Sierra TRADE 1.00 .30
495 David Cone TRADE 1.50 .45
59 R. Clemens Jumbo AU 80.00 24.00
215 A. Rodriguez Jumbo AU 80.00 24.00
00 K.Griffey Jr. Promo 2.00 .60

1995 Upper Deck Electric Diamond

This 450-card parallel set was inserted one per retail pack or two per mini-jumbo pack. These cards are distinguished from their regular issue counterparts in that they are printed on a heavier cardstock and use a special foil treatment.

	Nm-Mt	Ex-Mt
COMPLETE SET (450)	100.00	30.00
COMP. SERIES 1 (225)	50.00	15.00
COMP. SERIES 2 (225)	60.00	18.00

*STARS: 1.25X to 3X BASIC CARDS ..
*ROOKIES: 1X TO 2.5X BASIC CARDS

1995 Upper Deck Electric Diamond Gold

Cards from this 450-card parallel standard-size set were randomly inserted at a rate of 1:35 retail packs. They were also randomly seeded into mini-jumbo packs. These cards are identical to the Electric Diamond series except for the special gold foil treatment on the ED logo.

Nm-Mt Ex-Mt
*STARS: 8X TO 20X BASIC CARDS....
*ROOKIES: 10X TO 25X BASIC CARDS

1995 Upper Deck Autographs

Trade cards to redeem these autographed issues were randomly seeded into second series packs. The actual signed cards share the same front design as the basic issue 1995 Upper Deck cards. The cards were issued along with a card signed in fascimile by Brain Burr of Upper Deck along with instructions on how to register these cards.

	Nm-Mt	Ex-Mt
AC1 Reggie Jackson	40.00	12.00
AC2 Willie Mays	100.00	30.00
AC3 Frank Robinson	40.00	12.00
AC4 Roger Clemens	80.00	24.00
AC5 Raul Mondesi	25.00	7.50

1995 Upper Deck Checklists

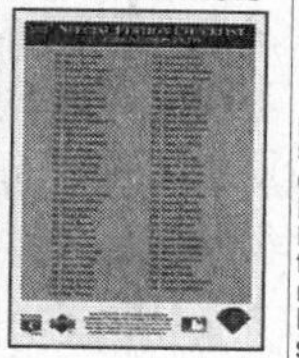

Each of these 10 cards features a star player(s) on the front and a checklist on the back. The cards were randomly inserted in hobby and retail packs at a rate of one in 17. The horizontal fronts feature a player photo along with a sentence about the 1994 highlight. The cards are numbered as "X" of 5 in the upper left.

	Nm-Mt	Ex-Mt
COMPLETE SET (5)	12.00	3.60
COMPLETE SERIES 1 (5)	4.00	1.20
COMPLETE SERIES 2 (5)	8.00	2.40
1A Montreal Expos	.30	.09
2A Fred McGriff	1.00	.30
3A John Valentin	.30	.09
4A Kenny Rogers	.60	.18
5A Greg Maddux	2.50	.75
1B Cecil Fielder	.60	.18
2B Tony Gwynn	2.00	.60
3B Greg Maddux	2.50	.75
4B Randy Johnson	1.50	.45
5B Mike Schmidt	2.50	.75

1995 Upper Deck Predictor Award Winners

Cards from this set were inserted in hobby packs at a rate of approximately one in 30. This 40-card standard-size set features nine players and a Long Shot in each league for each of two categories -- MVP and Rookie of the Year. If the player pictured on the card won his category, the card was redeemable for a special foil version of all 20 Hobby Predictor cards. Winning cards are marked with a "W" in the checklist below. Both MVP winners for the season (Barry Larkin in the NL and Mo Vaughn in the AL) were not featured on their own Predictor cards and thus the Longshot card became the winner. Fronts are full-color player action photos. Backs include the rules of the contest. These cards were redeemable until December 31, 1995.

	Nm-Mt	Ex-Mt
COMPLETE SERIES 1 (20)	40.00	12.00
COMPLETE SERIES 2 (20)	40.00	12.00

*AW EXCH: .4X TO 1X BASIC PRED.AW
ONE EXCH.SET VIA MAIL PER PRED.WINNER

H1 Albert Belle MVP	1.25	.35
H2 Juan Gonzalez MVP	2.00	.60
H3 Ken Griffey Jr. MVP	5.00	1.50
H4 Kirby Puckett MVP	3.00	.90
H5 Frank Thomas MVP	3.00	.90
H6 Jeff Bagwell MVP	2.00	.60
H7 Barry Bonds MVP	8.00	2.40
H8 Mike Piazza MVP	5.00	1.50
H9 Matt Williams MVP	1.25	.35
H10 MVP Wild Card W	.60	.18
Mo Vaughn, Barry Larkin		
H11 A.Benitez ROY	1.25	.35
H12 Alex Gonzalez ROY	.60	.18
H13 Shawn Green ROY	1.25	.35
H14 Derek Jeter ROY	8.00	2.40
H15 Alex Rodriguez ROY	8.00	2.40
H16 Alan Benes ROY	.60	.18
H17 Brian L.Hunter ROY	.60	.18
H18 Charles Johnson ROY	1.25	.35
H19 Jose Oliva ROY	.60	.18
H20 ROY Wild Card	.60	.18
H21 Cal Ripken MVP	10.00	3.00
H22 Don Mattingly MVP	8.00	2.40
H23 Roberto Alomar MVP	2.00	.60
H24 Kenny Lofton MVP	1.25	.35
H25 Will Clark MVP	3.00	.90
H26 Mark McGwire MVP	8.00	2.40
H27 Greg Maddux MVP	5.00	1.50
H28 Fred McGriff MVP	2.00	.60
H29 A.Galarraga MVP	1.25	.35
H30 Jose Canseco MVP	3.00	.90
H31 Ray Durham ROY	1.25	.35
H32 M.Grudzielanek ROY	1.50	.45
H33 Scott Ruffcorn ROY	.60	.18
H34 Michael Tucker ROY	.60	.18
H35 Garret Anderson ROY	1.25	.35
H36 Darren Bragg ROY	.60	.18
H37 Quilvio Veras ROY	.60	.18
H38 Hideo Nomo ROY W	8.00	2.40
H39 Chipper Jones ROY	3.00	.90
H40 M.Cordova ROY W	.60	.18

1995 Upper Deck Predictor League Leaders

Cards from this 60-card standard size set were seeded exclusively in first and second series retail packs at a rate of 1:30 and ANCO packs at 1:17. Cards 1-30 were distributed in series one packs and cards 31-60 in series two packs. The set includes nine players and a Long Shot in each league for each of three categories -- Batting Average Leader, Home Run Leader and Runs Batted In Leader. If the player pictured on the card won his category, the card was redeemable for a special foil version of 30 Retail Predictor cards (based upon the first or second series that it was associated with). These cards were redeemable until December 31, 1995. Card fronts are full-color action photos of the player emerging from a marble diamond. Backs list the rules of the game. Winning cards are designated with a W in our listings and are in noticeably shorter supply than other cards from this set as the bulk of them were mailed in to Upper Deck (and destroyed) in exchange for the parallel card prizes.

	Nm-Mt	Ex-Mt
COMPLETE SERIES 1 (30)	60.00	18.00
COMPLETE SERIES 2 (30)	40.00	12.00

*EXCH: .5X TO 1.2X BASIC PREDICTOR LL
ONE EXCH.SET VIA MAIL PER PRED.WINNER

R1 Albert Belle HR W	1.25	.35
R2 Jose Canseco HR	3.00	.90
R3 Juan Gonzalez HR	2.00	.60
R4 Ken Griffey Jr. HR	5.00	1.50
R5 Frank Thomas HR	3.00	.90
R6 Jeff Bagwell HR	2.00	.60
R7 Barry Bonds HR	8.00	2.40
R8 Fred McGriff HR	2.00	.60
R9 Matt Williams HR	1.25	.35
R10 HR Wild Card W	.60	.18
Dante Bichette		
R11 Albert Belle RBI W	1.25	.35
R12 Joe Carter RBI	1.25	.35
R13 Cecil Fielder RBI	1.25	.35
R14 Kirby Puckett RBI	3.00	.90
R15 Frank Thomas RBI	3.00	.90
R16 Jeff Bagwell RBI	2.00	.60
R17 Barry Bonds RBI	8.00	2.40
R18 Mike Piazza RBI	5.00	1.50
R19 Matt Williams RBI	1.25	.35
R20 RBI Wild Card W	.60	.18
Mo Vaughn		
R21 Wade Boggs BAT	2.00	.60
R22 Kenny Lofton BAT	1.25	.35
R23 Paul Molitor BAT	2.00	.60
R24 Paul O'Neill BAT	2.00	.60
R25 Frank Thomas BAT	3.00	.90
R26 Jeff Bagwell BAT	2.00	.60
R27 Tony Gwynn BAT W	4.00	1.20
R28 Gregg Jefferies BAT	.60	.18
R29 Hal Morris BAT	.60	.18
R30 Batting WC W	.60	.18
Edgar Martinez		
R31 Joe Carter HR	1.25	.35
R32 Cecil Fielder HR	1.25	.35
R33 Rafael Palmeiro HR	2.00	.60
R34 Larry Walker HR	2.00	.60
R35 Manny Ramirez HR	2.00	.60
R36 Tim Salmon HR	2.00	.60
R37 Mike Piazza HR	5.00	1.50
R38 Andres Galarraga HR	1.25	.35
R39 David Justice HR	1.25	.35
R40 Gary Sheffield HR	1.25	.35
R41 Juan Gonzalez RBI	2.00	.60
R42 Jose Canseco RBI	3.00	.90
R43 Will Clark RBI	3.00	.90
R44 Rafael Palmeiro RBI	2.00	.60
R45 Ken Griffey Jr. RBI	5.00	1.50
R46 Ruben Sierra RBI	.60	.18
R47 Larry Walker RBI	2.00	.60
R48 Fred McGriff RBI	2.00	.60
R49 Dante Bichette RBI W	1.25	.35
R50 Darren Daulton RBI	1.25	.35
R51 Will Clark BAT	3.00	.90
R52 Ken Griffey Jr. BAT	5.00	1.50
R53 Don Mattingly BAT	8.00	2.40
R54 John Olerud BAT	1.25	.35
R55 Kirby Puckett BAT	3.00	.90
R56 Raul Mondesi BAT	1.25	.35
R57 Moises Alou BAT	1.25	.35
R58 Bret Boone BAT	1.25	.35
R59 Albert Belle BAT	1.25	.35
R60 Mike Piazza BAT	5.00	1.50

1995 Upper Deck Ruth Heroes

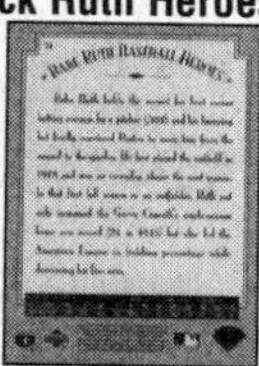

Randomly inserted in second series hobby and retail packs at a rate of 1:34, this set of 10 standard-size cards celebrates the achievements of one of baseball's all-time greats. The set was issued on the Centennial of Ruth's birth. The numbering (73-81) is a continuation from previous Heroes sets.

	Nm-Mt	Ex-Mt
COMPLETE SET (10)	100.00	30.00
COMMON (73-81/HDR)	15.00	4.50

1995 Upper Deck Special Edition

Inserted at a rate of one per pack, this 270 standard-size card set features full color action shots of players on a silver foil background. The back highlights the player's previous performance, including 1994 and career statistics. Another player photo is also featured on the back.

	Nm-Mt	Ex-Mt
COMPLETE SET (270)	100.00	30.00
COMP. SERIES 1 (135)	50.00	15.00
COMP. SERIES 2 (135)	50.00	15.00

*SE GOLD: 2.5X TO 6X BASIC SE
*SE GOLD RC's: 2.5X TO 6X BASIC SE
SE GOLD ODDS 1:35 HOBBY

1 Cliff Floyd	.75	.23
2 Wil Cordero	.40	.12
3 Pedro Martinez	2.00	.60
4 Larry Walker	1.25	.35
5 Derek Jeter	5.00	1.50
6 Mike Stanley	.40	.12
7 Melido Perez	.40	.12
8 Jim Leyritz	.40	.12
9 Danny Tartabull	.40	.12
10 Wade Boggs	1.25	.35
11 Ryan Klesko	.75	.23
12 Steve Avery	.40	.12
13 Damon Hollins	.40	.12
14 Chipper Jones	2.00	.60
15 David Justice	.75	.23
16 Glenn Williams	.40	.12
17 Jose Oliva	.40	.12
18 Terrell Wade	.40	.12
19 Alex Fernandez	.40	.12
20 Frank Thomas	2.00	.60
21 Ozzie Guillen	.40	.12
22 Roberto Hernandez	.40	.12
23 Albie Lopez	.40	.12
24 Eddie Murray	2.00	.60
25 Albert Belle	.75	.23
26 Omar Vizquel	1.25	.35
27 Carlos Baerga	.40	.12
28 Jose Rijo	.40	.12
29 Hal Morris	.40	.12
30 Reggie Sanders	.40	.12
31 Jack Morris	.75	.23
32 Raul Mondesi	.75	.23
33 Karim Garcia	.75	.23
34 Todd Hollandsworth	.40	.12
35 Mike Piazza	3.00	.90
36 Chan Ho Park	.75	.23
37 Ramon Martinez	.40	.12
38 Kenny Rogers	.75	.23
39 Will Clark	2.00	.60
40 Juan Gonzalez	1.25	.35
41 Ivan Rodriguez	2.00	.60
42 Orlando Miller	.40	.12
43 John Hudek	.40	.12
44 Luis Gonzalez	.75	.23
45 Jeff Bagwell	1.25	.35
46 Cal Ripken	6.00	1.80
47 Mike Oquist	.40	.12
48 Armando Benitez	.75	.23
49 Ben McDonald	.40	.12
50 Rafael Palmeiro	1.25	.35
51 Curtis Goodwin	.40	.12
52 Vince Coleman	.40	.12
53 Tom Gordon	.40	.12
54 Mike Macfarlane	.40	.12
55 Brian McRae	.40	.12
56 Matt Smith	.40	.12
57 David Segui	.40	.12
58 Paul Wilson	.40	.12
59 Bill Pulsipher	.40	.12
60 Bobby Bonilla	.75	.23
61 Jeff Kent	.75	.23
62 Ryan Thompson	.40	.12
63 Jason Isringhausen	.75	.23
64 Ed Sprague	.40	.12
65 Paul Molitor	1.25	.35
66 Juan Guzman	.40	.12
67 Alex Gonzalez	.40	.12
68 Shawn Green	.75	.23
69 Mark Portugal	.40	.12
70 Barry Bonds	5.00	1.50
71 Robby Thompson	.40	.12
72 Royce Clayton	.40	.12
73 Ricky Bottalico	.40	.12
74 Doug Jones	.40	.12
75 Darren Daulton	.75	.23
76 Gregg Jefferies	.40	.12
77 Scott Cooper	.40	.12
78 Nomar Garciaparra	5.00	1.50
79 Ken Ryan	.40	.12
80 Mike Greenwell	.40	.12
81 LaTroy Hawkins	.40	.12
82 Rich Becker	.40	.12
83 Scott Erickson	.40	.12
84 Pedro Munoz	.40	.12
85 Kirby Puckett	2.00	.60
86 Orlando Merced	.40	.12
87 Jeff King	.40	.12
88 Midre Cummings	.40	.12
89 Bernard Gilkey	.40	.12
90 Ray Lankford	.40	.12
91 Todd Zeile	.40	.12
92 Alan Benes	.40	.12
93 Bret Wagner	.40	.12
94 Rene Arocha	.40	.12
95 Cecil Fielder	.75	.23
96 Alan Trammell	.75	.23
97 Tony Phillips	.40	.12
98 Junior Felix	.40	.12
99 Brian Harper	.40	.12
100 Greg Vaughn	.40	.12
101 Ricky Bones	.40	.12
102 Walt Weiss	.40	.12
103 Lance Painter	.40	.12
104 Roberto Mejia	.40	.12
105 Andres Galarraga	.75	.23
106 Todd Van Poppel	.40	.12
107 Ben Grieve	.75	.23
108 Brent Gates	.40	.12
109 Jason Giambi	1.25	.35
110 Ruben Sierra	.40	.12
111 Terry Steinbach	.40	.12
112 Chris Hammond	.40	.12
113 Charles Johnson	.75	.23
114 Jesus Tavarez	.40	.12
115 Gary Sheffield	.75	.23
116 Chuck Carr	.40	.12
117 Bobby Ayala	.40	.12
118 Randy Johnson	2.00	.60
119 Edgar Martinez	1.25	.35
120 Alex Rodriguez	5.00	1.50
121 Kevin Foster	.40	.12
122 Kevin Roberson	.40	.12
123 Sammy Sosa	3.00	.90
124 Steve Trachsel	.40	.12
125 Eduardo Perez	.40	.12
126 Tim Salmon	1.25	.35
127 Todd Greene	.40	.12
128 Jorge Fabregas	.40	.12
129 Mark Langston	.40	.12
130 Mitch Williams	.40	.12
131 Raul Casanova	.40	.12
132 Mel Nieves	.40	.12
133 Andy Benes	.40	.12
134 Dustin Hermanson	.40	.12
135 Trevor Hoffman	.75	.23
136 Mark Grudzielanek	.75	.23
137 Ugueth Urbina	.40	.12
138 Moises Alou	.75	.23
139 Roberto Kelly	.40	.12
140 Rondell White	.75	.23
141 Paul O'Neill	1.25	.35
142 Jimmy Key	.75	.23
143 Jack McDowell	.40	.12
144 Ruben Rivera	.40	.12
145 Don Mattingly	5.00	1.50
146 John Wetteland	.75	.23
147 Tom Glavine	1.25	.35
148 Marquis Grissom	.75	.23
149 Javier Lopez	.75	.23
150 Fred McGriff	1.25	.35
151 Greg Maddux	3.00	.90
152 Chris Sabo	.40	.12
153 Ray Durham	.75	.23
154 Robin Ventura	.75	.23
155 Jim Abbott	1.25	.35
156 Jimmy Hurst	.40	.12
157 Tim Raines	.75	.23
158 Dennis Martinez	.75	.23
159 Kenny Lofton	.75	.23
160 Dave Winfield	.75	.23
161 Manny Ramirez	1.25	.35
162 Jim Thome	2.00	.60
163 Barry Larkin	1.25	.35
164 Bret Boone	.75	.23
165 Deion Sanders	1.25	.35
166 Ron Gant	.75	.23
167 Benito Santiago	.75	.23
168 Hideo Nomo	5.00	1.50
169 Billy Ashley	.40	.12
170 Roger Cedeno	.40	.12
171 Ismael Valdes	.40	.12
172 Eric Karros	.75	.23
173 Rusty Greer	.75	.23
174 Rick Helling	.40	.12
175 Nolan Ryan	8.00	2.40
176 Dean Palmer	.75	.23
177 Phil Plantier	.40	.12
178 Darryl Kile	.75	.23
179 Derek Bell	.40	.12
180 Doug Drabek	.40	.12
181 Craig Biggio	1.25	.35
182 Kevin Brown	.75	.23
183 Harold Baines	.75	.23
184 Jeffrey Hammonds	.40	.12
185 Chris Hoiles	.40	.12
186 Mike Mussina	1.25	.35
187 Bob Hamelin	.40	.12
188 Jeff Montgomery	.40	.12
189 Michael Tucker	.40	.12

Card	Nm-Mt	Ex-Mt
190 George Brett	5.00	1.50
191 Edgardo Alfonzo	.75	.23
192 Brett Butler	.75	.23
193 Bobby Jones	.40	.12
194 Todd Hundley	.40	.12
195 Bret Saberhagen	.75	.23
196 Pat Hentgen	.40	.12
197 Roberto Alomar	1.25	.35
198 David Cone	.75	.23
199 Carlos Delgado	.75	.23
200 Joe Carter	.75	.23
201 Wm. VanLandingham	.40	.12
202 Rod Beck	.40	.12
203 J.R. Phillips	.40	.12
204 Darren Lewis	.40	.12
205 Matt Williams	.75	.23
206 Lenny Dykstra	.75	.23
207 Dave Hollins	.40	.12
208 Mike Schmidt	3.00	.90
209 Charlie Hayes	.40	.12
210 Mo Vaughn	.75	.23
211 Jose Malave	.40	.12
212 Roger Clemens	4.00	1.20
213 Jose Canseco	2.00	.60
214 Mark Whiten	.40	.12
215 Marty Cordova	.40	.12
216 Rick Aguilera	.40	.12
217 Kevin Tapani	.40	.12
218 Chuck Knoblauch	.75	.23
219 Al Martin	.40	.12
220 Jay Bell	.75	.23
221 Carlos Garcia	.40	.12
222 Freddy Adrian Garcia	.40	.12
223 Jon Lieber	.40	.12
224 Danny Jackson	.40	.12
225 Ozzie Smith	3.00	.90
226 Brian Jordan	.75	.23
227 Ken Hill	.40	.12
228 Scott Cooper	.40	.12
229 Chad Curtis	.40	.12
230 Lou Whitaker	.75	.23
231 Kirk Gibson	.75	.23
232 Travis Fryman	.75	.23
233 Jose Valentin	.40	.12
234 Dave Nilsson	.40	.12
235 Cal Eldred	.40	.12
236 Matt Mieske	.40	.12
237 Bill Swift	.40	.12
238 Marvin Freeman	.40	.12
239 Jason Bates	.40	.12
240 Larry Walker	1.25	.35
241 Dave Nied	.40	.12
242 Dante Bichette	.75	.23
243 Dennis Eckersley	.75	.23
244 Todd Stottlemyre	.40	.12
245 Rickey Henderson	2.00	.60
246 Geronimo Berroa	.40	.12
247 Mark McGwire	5.00	1.50
248 Quilvio Veras	.40	.12
249 Terry Pendleton	.75	.23
250 Andre Dawson	.75	.23
251 Jeff Conine	.75	.23
252 Kurt Abbott	.40	.12
253 Jay Buhner	.75	.23
254 Darren Bragg	.40	.12
255 Ken Griffey Jr.	3.00	.90
256 Tino Martinez	1.25	.35
257 Mark Grace	1.25	.35
258 Ryne Sandberg	3.00	.90
259 Randy Myers	.40	.12
260 Howard Johnson	.40	.12
261 Lee Smith	.75	.23
262 J.T. Snow	.75	.23
263 Chili Davis	.75	.23
264 Chuck Finley	.75	.23
265 Eddie Williams	.40	.12
266 Joey Hamilton	.40	.12
267 Ken Caminiti	.75	.23
268 Andujar Cedeno	.40	.12
269 Steve Finley	.75	.23
270 Tony Gwynn	2.50	.75

1995 Upper Deck Steal of a Deal

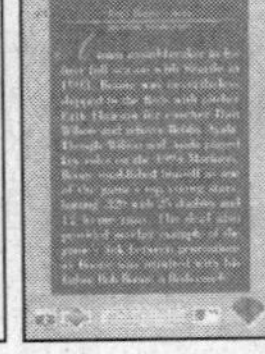

This set was inserted in hobby and retail packs at a rate of approximately one in 34. This 15-card standard-size set focuses on players who were acquired through, according to Upper Deck, "astute trades" or low round draft picks. The cards are numbered in the upper left with an "SD" prefix.

Card	Nm-Mt	Ex-Mt
COMPLETE SET (15)	80.00	24.00
SD1 Mike Piazza	12.00	3.60
SD2 Fred McGriff	5.00	1.50
SD3 Kenny Lofton	3.00	.90
SD4 Jose Oliva	1.50	.45
SD5 Jeff Bagwell	5.00	1.50
SD6 Roberto Alomar Joe Carter	5.00	1.50
SD7 Steve Karsay	1.50	.45
SD8 Ozzie Smith	12.00	3.60
SD9 Dennis Eckersley	3.00	.90
SD10 Jose Canseco	8.00	2.40
SD11 Carlos Baerga	1.50	.45
SD12 Cecil Fielder	3.00	.90
SD13 Don Mattingly	20.00	6.00
SD14 Bret Boone	3.00	.90
SD15 Michael Jordan	25.00	7.50

1995 Upper Deck Trade Exchange

These five cards were randomly inserted into second series Upper Deck packs. A collector could send in these cards and receive nine cards

from the trade set for the base 1995 Upper Deck set (numbers 451-495). These cards were redeemable until February 1, 1996.

Card	Nm-Mt	Ex-Mt
COMPLETE SET (5)	5.00	1.50
TC1 Orel Hershiser	1.50	.45
TC2 Terry Pendleton	1.00	.30
TC3 Benito Santiago	1.50	.45
TC4 Kevin Brown	2.00	.60
TC5 Gregg Jefferies	1.00	.30

1996 Upper Deck

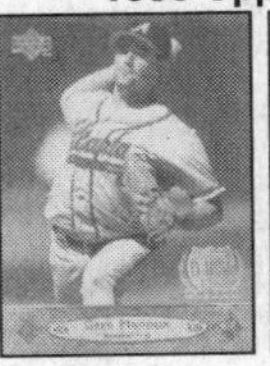

The 1996 Upper Deck set was issued in two series of 240 cards, and a 30 card update set, for a total of 510 cards. The cards were distributed in 10-card packs with a suggested retail price of $1.99, and 28 packs were contained in each box. Upper Deck issued 15,000 factory sets (containing all 510 cards) at season's end. In addition to being included in factory sets, the 30-card Update sets (U481-U510) were also available via mail through a wrapper exchange program. The attractive fronts of each basic card feature a full-bleed photo above a bronze foil bar that includes the player's name, team and position in a white oval. Subsets include Young at Heart (100-117), Beat the Odds (145-153), Postseason Checklist (218-222), Best of a Generation (370-387), Strange But True (415-423) and Managerial Salute Checklists (476-480). The only Rookie Card of note is Livan Hernandez.

Card	Nm-Mt	Ex-Mt
COMPLETE SET (480)	50.00	15.00
COMP.FACT.SET (510)	100.00	30.00
COMP. SERIES 1 (240)	25.00	7.50
COMP. SERIES 2 (240)	25.00	7.50
COMMON CARD (1-480)	.30	.09
COMP.UPDATE SET (30)	20.00	6.00
COMMON (481U-510U)	.50	.15
1 Cal Ripken 2131	4.00	1.20
2 Eddie Murray 3000 Hits	.50	.15
3 Mark Wohlers	.30	.09
4 David Justice	.30	.09
5 Chipper Jones	.75	.23
6 Javier Lopez	.30	.09
7 Mark Lemke	.30	.09
8 Marquis Grissom	.30	.09
9 Tom Glavine	.50	.15
10 Greg Maddux	1.25	.35
11 Manny Alexander	.30	.09
12 Curtis Goodwin	.30	.09
13 Scott Erickson	.30	.09
14 Chris Hoiles	.30	.09
15 Rafael Palmeiro	.50	.15
16 Rick Krivda	.30	.09
17 Jeff Manto	.30	.09
18 Mo Vaughn	.30	.09
19 Tim Wakefield	.30	.09
20 Roger Clemens	1.50	.45
21 Tim Naehring	.30	.09
22 Troy O'Leary	.30	.09
23 Mike Greenwell	.30	.09
24 Stan Belinda	.30	.09
25 John Valentin	.30	.09
26 J.T. Snow	.30	.09
27 Gary DiSarcina	.30	.09
28 Mark Langston	.30	.09
29 Brian Anderson	.30	.09
30 Jim Edmonds	.30	.09
31 Garret Anderson	.30	.09
32 Orlando Palmeiro	.30	.09
33 Brian McRae	.30	.09
34 Kevin Foster	.30	.09
35 Sammy Sosa	1.25	.35
36 Todd Zeile	.30	.09
37 Jim Bullinger	.30	.09
38 Luis Gonzalez	.30	.09
39 Lyle Mouton	.30	.09
40 Ray Durham	.30	.09
41 Ozzie Guillen	.30	.09
42 Alex Fernandez	.30	.09
43 Brian Keyser	.30	.09
44 Robin Ventura	.30	.09
45 Reggie Sanders	.30	.09
46 Pete Schourek	.30	.09
47 John Smiley	.30	.09
48 Jeff Brantley	.30	.09
49 Thomas Howard	.30	.09
50 Bret Boone	.30	.09
51 Kevin Jarvis	.30	.09
52 Jeff Branson	.30	.09
53 Carlos Baerga	.30	.09
54 Jim Thome	.75	.23
55 Manny Ramirez	.50	.15
56 Omar Vizquel	.50	.15
57 Jose Mesa	.30	.09
58 Julian Tavarez UER	.30	.09
59 Orel Hershiser	.30	.09
60 Larry Walker	.50	.15
61 Bret Saberhagen	.30	.09
62 Vinny Castilla	.30	.09
63 Eric Young	.30	.09
64 Bryan Rekar	.30	.09
65 Andres Galarraga	.30	.09
66 Steve Reed	.30	.09
67 Chad Curtis	.30	.09
68 Bobby Higginson	.30	.09
69 Phil Nevin	.30	.09
70 Cecil Fielder	.30	.09
71 Felipe Lira	.30	.09
72 Chris Gomez	.30	.09
73 Charles Johnson	.30	.09
74 Quilvio Veras	.30	.09
75 Jeff Conine	.30	.09
76 John Burkett	.30	.09
77 Greg Colbrunn	.30	.09
78 Terry Pendleton	.30	.09
79 Shane Reynolds	.30	.09
80 Jeff Bagwell	.50	.15
81 Orlando Miller	.30	.09
82 Mike Hampton	.30	.09
83 James Mouton	.30	.09
84 Brian L. Hunter	.30	.09
85 Derek Bell	.30	.09
86 Kevin Appier	.30	.09
87 Joe Vitiello	.30	.09
88 Wally Joyner	.30	.09
89 Michael Tucker	.30	.09
90 Johnny Damon	.50	.65
91 Jon Nunnally	.30	.09
92 Jason Jacome	.30	.09
93 Chad Fonville	.30	.09
94 Chan Ho Park	.30	.09
95 Hideo Nomo	.75	.23
96 Ismael Valdes	.30	.09
97 Greg Gagne	.30	.09
98 Arizona Diamondbacks Tampa Bay Devil Rays	.75	.23
99 Raul Mondesi	.30	.09
100 Dave Winfield YH	.30	.09
101 Dennis Eckersley YH	.30	.09
102 Andre Dawson YH	.30	.09
103 Dennis Martinez YH	.30	.09
104 Lance Parrish YH	.30	.09
105 Eddie Murray YH	.50	.15
106 Alan Trammell YH	.30	.09
107 Lou Whitaker YH	.30	.09
108 Ozzie Smith YH	.75	.23
109 Paul Molitor YH	.30	.09
110 Rickey Henderson YH	.50	.15
111 Tim Raines YH	.30	.09
112 Harold Baines YH	.30	.09
113 Lee Smith YH	.30	.09
114 F.Valenzuela YH	.30	.09
115 Cal Ripken YH	1.25	.35
116 Tony Gwynn YH	.50	.15
117 Wade Boggs	.50	.15
118 Todd Hollandsworth	.30	.09
119 Dave Nilsson	.30	.09
120 Jose Valentin	.30	.09
121 Steve Sparks	.30	.09
122 Chuck Carr	.30	.09
123 John Jaha	.30	.09
124 Scott Karl	.30	.09
125 Chuck Knoblauch	.30	.09
126 Brad Radke	.30	.09
127 Pat Meares	.30	.09
128 Ron Coomer	.30	.09
129 Pedro Munoz	.30	.09
130 Kirby Puckett	.75	.23
131 David Segui	.30	.09
132 Mark Grudzielanek	.30	.09
133 Mike Lansing	.30	.09
134 Sean Berry	.30	.09
135 Rondell White	.30	.09
136 Pedro Martinez	.75	.23
137 Carl Everett	.30	.09
138 Dave Mlicki	.30	.09
139 Bill Pulsipher	.30	.09
140 Jason Isringhausen	.30	.09
141 Rico Brogna	.30	.09
142 Edgardo Alfonzo	.30	.09
143 Jeff Kent	.30	.09
144 Andy Pettitte	.50	.15
145 Mike Piazza BO	.75	.23
146 Cliff Floyd BO	.30	.09
147 J.Isringhausen BO	.30	.09
148 Tim Wakefield BO	.30	.09
149 Chipper Jones BO	.50	.15
150 Hideo Nomo BO	.50	.15
151 Mark McGwire BO	1.00	.30
152 Ron Gant BO	.30	.09
153 Gary Gaetti BO	.30	.09
154 Don Mattingly	2.00	.60
155 Paul O'Neill	.50	.15
156 Derek Jeter	2.00	.60
157 Joe Girardi	.30	.09
158 Ruben Sierra	.30	.09
159 Jorge Posada	.50	.15
160 Geronimo Berroa	.30	.09
161 Steve Ontiveros	.30	.09
162 George Williams	.30	.09
163 Doug Johns	.30	.09
164 Ariel Prieto	.30	.09
165 Scott Brosius	.30	.09
166 Mike Bordick	.30	.09
167 Tyler Green	.30	.09
168 Mickey Morandini	.30	.09
169 Darren Daulton	.30	.09
170 Gregg Jefferies	.30	.09
171 Jim Eisenreich	.30	.09
172 Heathcliff Slocumb	.30	.09
173 Kevin Stocker	.30	.09
174 Esteban Loaiza	.30	.09
175 Jeff King	.30	.09
176 Mark Johnson	.30	.09
177 Denny Neagle	.30	.09
178 Orlando Merced	.30	.09
179 Carlos Garcia	.30	.09
180 Brian Jordan	.30	.09
181 Mike Morgan	.30	.09
182 Mark Petkovsek	.30	.09
183 Bernard Gilkey	.30	.09
184 John Mabry	.30	.09
185 Tom Henke	.30	.09
186 Glenn Dishman	.30	.09
187 Andy Ashby	.30	.09
188 Bip Roberts	.30	.09
189 Melvin Nieves	.30	.09
190 Ken Caminiti	.30	.09
191 Brad Ausmus	.30	.09
192 Deion Sanders	.50	.15
193 Jamie Brewington RC	.30	.09
194 Glenallen Hill	.30	.09
195 Barry Bonds	2.00	.60
196 Wm. Van Landingham	.30	.09
197 Mark Carreon	.30	.09
198 Royce Clayton	.30	.09
199 Joey Cora	.30	.09
200 Ken Griffey Jr.	1.25	.35
201 Jay Buhner	.30	.09
202 Alex Rodriguez	1.50	.45
203 Norm Charlton	.30	.09
204 Andy Benes	.30	.09
205 Edgar Martinez	.50	.15
206 Juan Gonzalez	.50	.15
207 Will Clark	.75	.23
208 Kevin Gross	.30	.09
209 Roger Pavlik	.30	.09
210 Ivan Rodriguez	.75	.23
211 Rusty Greer	.30	.09
212 Angel Martinez	.30	.09
213 Tomas Perez	.30	.09
214 Alex Gonzalez	.30	.09
215 Joe Carter	.30	.09
216 Shawn Green	.30	.09
217 Edwin Hurtado	.30	.09
218 Edgar Martinez Tony Pena CL	.30	.09
219 Chipper Jones Barry Larkin CL	.50	.15
220 Orel Hershiser CL	.30	.09
221 Mike Devereaux CL	.30	.09
222 Tom Glavine CL	.30	.09
223 Karim Garcia	.30	.09
224 Arquimedez Pozo	.30	.09
225 Billy Wagner	.30	.09
226 John Wasdin	.30	.09
227 Jeff Suppan	.30	.09
228 Steve Gibralter	.30	.09
229 Jimmy Haynes	.30	.09
230 Ruben Rivera	.30	.09
231 Chris Snopek	.30	.09
232 Alex Ochoa	.30	.09
233 Shannon Stewart	.30	.09
234 Quinton McCracken	.30	.09
235 Trey Beamon	.30	.09
236 Billy McMillon	.30	.09
237 Steve Cox	.30	.09
238 George Arias	.30	.09
239 Yamil Benitez	.30	.09
240 Todd Greene	.30	.09
241 Jason Kendall	.30	.09
242 Brooks Kieschnick	.30	.09
243 O. Fernandez RC	.30	.09
244 Livan Hernandez RC	.75	.23
245 Rey Ordonez	.30	.09
246 Mike Grace RC	.30	.09
247 Jay Canizaro	.30	.09
248 Bob Wolcott	.30	.09
249 Jermaine Dye	.30	.09
250 Jason Schmidt	.50	.15
251 Mike Sweeney RC	1.50	.45
252 Marcus Jensen	.30	.09
253 Mendy Lopez	.30	.09
254 Wilton Guerrero RC	.50	.15
255 Paul Wilson	.30	.09
256 Edgar Renteria	.30	.09
257 Richard Hidalgo	.30	.09
258 Bob Abreu	.30	.09
259 Robert Smith RC	.30	.09
260 Sal Fasano	.30	.09
261 Enrique Wilson	.30	.09
262 Rich Hunter RC	.30	.09
263 Sergio Nunez	.30	.09
264 Dan Serafini	.30	.09
265 David Doster	.30	.09
266 Ryan McGuire	.30	.09
267 Scott Spiezio	.30	.09
268 Rafael Orellano	.30	.09
269 Steve Avery	.30	.09
270 Fred McGriff	.50	.15
271 John Smoltz	.50	.15
272 Ryan Klesko	.30	.09
273 Jeff Blauser	.30	.09
274 Brad Clontz	.30	.09
275 Roberto Alomar	.50	.15
276 B.J. Surhoff	.30	.09
277 Jeffrey Hammonds	.30	.09
278 Brady Anderson	.30	.09
279 Bobby Bonilla	.30	.09
280 Cal Ripken	2.50	.75
281 Mike Mussina	.50	.15
282 Wil Cordero	.30	.09
283 Mike Stanley	.30	.09
284 Aaron Sele	.30	.09
285 Jose Canseco	.75	.23
286 Tom Gordon	.30	.09
287 Heathcliff Slocumb	.30	.09
288 Lee Smith	.30	.09
289 Troy Percival	.30	.09
290 Tim Salmon	.50	.15
291 Chuck Finley	.30	.09
292 Jim Abbott	.50	.15
293 Chili Davis	.30	.09
294 Steve Trachsel	.30	.09
295 Mark Grace	.50	.15
296 Rey Sanchez	.30	.09
297 Scott Servais	.30	.09
298 Jaime Navarro	.30	.09
299 Frank Castillo	.30	.09
300 Frank Thomas	.75	.23
301 Jason Bere	.30	.09
302 Danny Tartabull	.30	.09
303 Darren Lewis	.30	.09
304 Roberto Hernandez	.30	.09
305 Tony Phillips	.30	.09
306 Wilson Alvarez	.30	.09
307 Jose Rijo	.30	.09
308 Hal Morris	.30	.09
309 Mark Portugal	.30	.09
310 Barry Larkin	.50	.15
311 Dave Burba	.30	.09
312 Eddie Taubensee	.30	.09
313 Sandy Alomar Jr.	.30	.09
314 Dennis Martinez	.30	.09
315 Albert Belle	.30	.09
316 Eddie Murray	.75	.23
317 Charles Nagy	.30	.09
318 Chad Ogea	.30	.09
319 Kenny Lofton	.30	.09
320 Dante Bichette	.30	.09
321 Armando Reynoso	.30	.09
322 Walt Weiss	.30	.09
323 Ellis Burks	.30	.09
324 Kevin Ritz	.30	.09
325 Bill Swift	.30	.09
326 Jason Bates	.30	.09
327 Tony Clark	.30	.09
328 Travis Fryman	.30	.09
329 Mark Parent	.30	.09
330 Alan Trammell	.30	.09
331 C.J. Nitkowski	.30	.09
332 Jose Lima	.30	.09
333 Phil Plantier	.30	.09
334 Kurt Abbott	.30	.09
335 Andre Dawson	.30	.09
336 Chris Hammond	.30	.09
337 Robb Nen	.30	.09
338 Pat Rapp	.30	.09
339 Al Leiter	.30	.09
340 Gary Sheffield UER (HR total says 17	.30	.09
341 Todd Jones	.30	.09
342 Doug Drabek	.30	.09
343 Greg Swindell	.30	.09
344 Tony Eusebio	.30	.09
345 Craig Biggio	.50	.15
346 Darryl Kile	.30	.09
347 Mike Macfarlane	.30	.09
348 Jeff Montgomery	.30	.09
349 Chris Haney	.30	.09
350 Bip Roberts	.30	.09
351 Tom Goodwin	.30	.09
352 Mark Gubicza	.30	.09
353 Joe Randa	.30	.09
354 Ramon Martinez	.30	.09
355 Eric Karros	.30	.09
356 Delino DeShields	.30	.09
357 Brett Butler	.30	.09
358 Todd Worrell	.30	.09
359 Mike Blowers	.30	.09
360 Mike Piazza	1.25	.35
361 Ben McDonald	.30	.09
362 Ricky Bones	.30	.09
363 Greg Vaughn	.30	.09
364 Matt Mieske	.30	.09
365 Kevin Seitzer	.30	.09
366 Jeff Cirillo	.30	.09
367 LaTroy Hawkins	.30	.09
368 Frank Rodriguez	.30	.09
369 Rick Aguilera	.30	.09
370 Roberto Alomar BG	.30	.09
371 Albert Belle BG	.30	.09
372 Wade Boggs BG	.30	.09
373 Barry Bonds BG	.75	.23
374 Roger Clemens BG	.75	.23
375 Dennis Eckersley BG	.30	.09
376 Ken Griffey Jr. BG	.75	.23
377 Tony Gwynn BG	.50	.15
378 Rickey Henderson BG	.50	.15
379 Greg Maddux BG	.75	.23
380 Fred McGriff BG	.30	.09
381 Paul Molitor BG	.30	.09
382 Eddie Murray BG	.50	.15
383 Mike Piazza BG	.75	.23
384 Kirby Puckett BG	.50	.15
385 Cal Ripken BG	1.25	.35
386 Ozzie Smith BG	.75	.23
387 Frank Thomas BG	.50	.15
388 Matt Walbeck	.30	.09
389 Dave Stevens	.30	.09
390 Marty Cordova	.30	.09
391 Darrin Fletcher	.30	.09
392 Cliff Floyd	.30	.09
393 Mel Rojas	.30	.09
394 Shane Andrews	.30	.09
395 Moises Alou	.30	.09
396 Carlos Perez	.30	.09
397 Jeff Fassero	.30	.09
398 Bobby Jones	.30	.09
399 Todd Hundley	.30	.09
400 John Franco	.30	.09
401 Jose Vizcaino	.30	.09
402 Bernard Gilkey	.30	.09
403 Pete Harnisch	.30	.09
404 Pat Kelly	.30	.09
405 David Cone	.30	.09
406 Bernie Williams	.50	.15
407 John Wetteland	.30	.09
408 Scott Kamieniecki	.30	.09
409 Tim Raines	.30	.09
410 Wade Boggs	.50	.15
411 Terry Steinbach	.30	.09
412 Jason Giambi	.30	.09
413 Todd Van Poppel	.30	.09
414 Pedro Munoz	.30	.09
415 Eddie Murray SBT	.50	.15
416 Dennis Eckersley SBT	.30	.09
417 Bip Roberts SBT	.30	.09
418 Glenallen Hill SBT	.30	.09
419 John Hudek SBT	.30	.09
420 Derek Bell SBT	.30	.09
421 Larry Walker SBT	.30	.09
422 Greg Maddux SBT	.75	.23
423 Ken Caminiti SBT	.30	.09
424 Brent Gates	.30	.09
425 Mark McGwire	2.00	.60
426 Mark Whiten	.30	.09
427 Sid Fernandez	.30	.09
428 Ricky Bottalico	.30	.09
429 Mike Mimbs	.30	.09
430 Lenny Dykstra	.30	.09
431 Todd Zeile	.30	.09
432 Benito Santiago	.30	.09
433 Danny Miceli	.30	.09
434 Al Martin	.30	.09
435 Jay Bell	.30	.09
436 Charlie Hayes	.30	.09
437 Mike Kingery	.30	.09
438 Paul Wagner	.30	.09
439 Tom Pagnozzi	.30	.09
440 Ozzie Smith	1.25	.35
441 Ray Lankford	.30	.09
442 Dennis Eckersley	.30	.09
443 Ron Gant	.30	.09
444 Alan Benes	.30	.09
445 Rickey Henderson	.75	.23
446 Jody Reed	.30	.09
447 Trevor Hoffman	.30	.09
448 Andujar Cedeno	.30	.09
449 Steve Finley	.30	.09
450 Tony Gwynn	1.00	.30
451 Joey Hamilton	.30	.09

452 Mark Leiter .30 .09
453 Rod Beck .30 .09
454 Kirt Manwaring .30 .09
455 Matt Williams .30 .09
456 Robby Thompson .30 .09
457 Shawon Dunston .30 .09
458 Russ Davis .30 .09
459 Paul Sorrento .30 .09
460 Randy Johnson .75 .23
461 Chris Bosio .30 .09
462 Luis Sojo .30 .09
463 Sterling Hitchcock .30 .09
464 Benji Gil .30 .09
465 Mickey Tettleton .30 .09
466 Mark McLemore .30 .09
467 Darryl Hamilton .30 .09
468 Ken Hill .30 .09
469 Dean Palmer .30 .09
470 Carlos Delgado .30 .09
471 Ed Sprague .30 .09
472 Otis Nixon .30 .09
473 Pat Hentgen .30 .09
474 Juan Guzman .30 .09
475 John Olerud .30 .09
476 Buck Showalter CL .30 .09
477 Bobby Cox CL .30 .09
478 Tommy Lasorda CL .30 .09
479 Buck Showalter CL .30 .09
480 Sparky Anderson CL .30 .09
481U Randy Myers .50 .15
482U Kent Mercker .50 .15
483U David Wells .75 .23
484U Kevin Mitchell .50 .15
485U Randy Velarde .50 .15
486U Ryne Sandberg 4.00 1.20
487U Doug Jones .50 .15
488U Terry Adams .50 .15
489U Kevin Tapani .50 .15
490U Harold Baines .75 .23
491U Eric Davis .75 .23
492U Julio Franco .75 .23
493U Jack McDowell .50 .15
494U Devon White .75 .23
495U Kevin Brown .75 .23
496U Rick Wilkins .50 .15
497U Sean Berry .50 .15
498U Keith Lockhart .50 .15
499U Mark Loretta .75 .23
500U Paul Molitor 1.25 .35
501U Roberto Kelly .50 .15
502U Lance Johnson .50 .15
503U Tino Martinez 1.25 .35
504U Kenny Rogers .75 .23
505U Todd Stottlemyre .50 .15
506U Gary Gaetti .75 .23
507U Royce Clayton .50 .15
508U Andy Benes .50 .15
509U Wally Joyner .75 .23
510U Erik Hanson .50 .15
100 Ken Griffey Jr Promo 3.00 .90

1996 Upper Deck Blue Chip Prospects

andomly inserted in first series retail packs at a te of one in 72, this 20-card set, diecut on the o and bottom, features some of the best young ars in the majors against a bluish background.

Nm-Mt Ex-Mt
MPLETE SET (20) 100.00 30.00
1 Hideo Nomo 10.00 3.00
2 Johnny Damon 6.00 1.80
3 Jason Isringhausen 4.00 1.20
4 Bill Pulsipher 4.00 1.20
5 Marty Cordova 4.00 1.20
6 Michael Tucker 4.00 1.20
7 John Wasdin 4.00 1.20
8 Karim Garcia 4.00 1.20
9 Ruben Rivera 4.00 1.20
10 Chipper Jones 10.00 3.00
11 Billy Wagner 4.00 1.20
12 Brooks Kieschnick 4.00 1.20
13 Alan Benes 4.00 1.20
14 Roger Cedeno 4.00 1.20
15 Alex Rodriguez 20.00 6.00
16 Jason Schmidt 6.00 1.80
17 Derek Jeter 25.00 7.50
18 Brian L.Hunter 4.00 1.20
19 Garret Anderson 4.00 1.20
20 Manny Ramirez 6.00 1.80

1996 Upper Deck Diamond Destiny

ued one per Wal Mart pack, these 40 cards ture leading players of baseball. The cards ve two photos on the front with the player's e listed on the bottom. The backs have other photo along with biographical informa- n.

Nm-Mt Ex-Mt
MPLETE SET (40) 80.00 24.00
OLD: 5X TO 12 X BASIC DESTINY
LD ODDS 1:143 UD TECH RETAIL PACKS
*SILVER: 1.5X TO 4X BASIC DESTINY
SILVER ODDS 1:35 UD TECH RETAIL PACKS
DD1 Chipper Jones 2.50 .75
DD2 Fred McGriff 1.50 .45
DD3 John Smoltz 1.50 .45
DD4 Ryan Klesko 1.00 .30
DD5 Greg Maddux 4.00 1.20
DD6 Cal Ripken 8.00 2.40
DD7 Roberto Alomar 1.50 .45
DD8 Eddie Murray 2.50 .75
DD9 Brady Anderson 1.00 .30
DD10 Mo Vaughn 1.00 .30
DD11 Roger Clemens 5.00 1.50
DD12 Darin Erstad 2.00 .60
DD13 Sammy Sosa 4.00 1.20
DD14 Frank Thomas 2.50 .75
DD15 Barry Larkin 1.50 .45
DD16 Albert Belle 1.00 .30
DD17 Manny Ramirez 1.50 .45
DD18 Kenny Lofton 1.00 .30
DD19 Dante Bichette 1.00 .30
DD20 Gary Sheffield 1.00 .30
DD21 Jeff Bagwell 1.50 .45
DD22 Hideo Nomo 2.50 .75
DD23 Mike Piazza 4.00 1.20
DD24 Kirby Puckett 2.50 .75
DD25 Paul Molitor 4.00 1.20
DD26 Chuck Knoblauch 1.00 .30
DD27 Wade Boggs 1.50 .45
DD28 Derek Jeter 6.00 1.80
DD29 Rey Ordonez 1.00 .30
DD30 Mark McGwire 6.00 1.80
DD31 Ozzie Smith 4.00 1.20
DD32 Tony Gwynn 3.00 .90
DD33 Barry Bonds 6.00 1.80
DD34 Matt Williams 1.00 .30
DD35 Ken Griffey Jr. 4.00 1.20
DD36 Jay Buhner 1.00 .30
DD37 Randy Johnson 2.50 .75
DD38 Alex Rodriguez 5.00 1.50
DD39 Juan Gonzalez 1.50 .45
DD40 Joe Carter 1.00 .30

1996 Upper Deck Future Stock Prospects

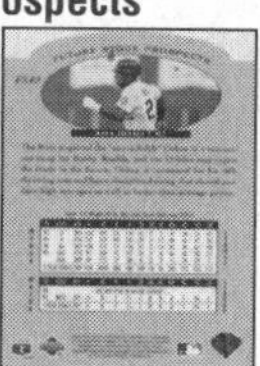

Randomly inserted in packs at a rate of one in 6, this 20-card set highlights the top prospects who made their major league debuts in 1995. The cards are diecut at the top and feature a purple border surrounding the player's picture.

Nm-Mt Ex-Mt
COMPLETE SET (20) 8.00 2.40
FS1 George Arias 1.00 .30
FS2 Brian Barber 1.00 .30
FS3 Trey Beamon 1.00 .30
FS4 Yamil Benitez 1.00 .30
FS5 Jamie Brewington 1.00 .30
FS6 Tony Clark 1.00 .30
FS7 Steve Cox 1.00 .30
FS8 Carlos Delgado 1.00 .30
FS9 Chad Fonville 1.00 .30
FS10 Alex Ochoa 1.00 .30
FS11 Curtis Goodwin 1.00 .30
FS12 Todd Greene 1.00 .30
FS13 Jimmy Haynes 1.00 .30
FS14 Quinton McCracken 1.00 .30
FS15 Billy McMillon 1.00 .30
FS16 Chan Ho Park 1.00 .30
FS17 Arquimedez Pozo 1.00 .30
FS18 Chris Snopek 1.00 .30
FS19 Shannon Stewart 1.00 .30
FS20 Jeff Suppan 1.00 .30

1996 Upper Deck Gameface

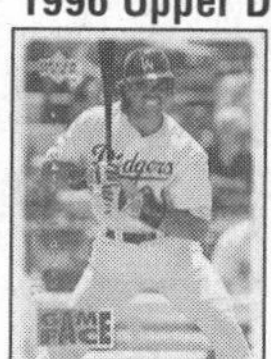

These Gameface cards were seeded at a rate of one per Upper Deck and Collector's Choice Wal Mart retail pack. The Upper Deck packs contained eight cards and the Collector's Choice packs contained sixteen cards. Both packs carried a suggested retail price of $1.50. The card fronts feature the player's photo surrounded by a "cloudy" white border along with a Gameface logo at the bottom.

Nm-Mt Ex-Mt
COMPLETE SET (10) 12.00 3.60
GF1 Ken Griffey Jr. 1.25 .35
GF2 Frank Thomas .75 .23
GF3 Barry Bonds 2.00 .60
GF4 Albert Belle .30 .09
GF5 Cal Ripken 2.50 .75
GF6 Mike Piazza 1.25 .35
GF7 Chipper Jones .75 .23
GF8 Matt Williams .30 .09
GF9 Hideo Nomo .75 .23
GF10 Greg Maddux 1.25 .35

1996 Upper Deck Hot Commodities

Cards from this 20 card set double die-cut set were randomly inserted into series two Upper Deck packs at a rate of one in 37. The set features some of baseball's most popular players.

Nm-Mt Ex-Mt
COMPLETE SET (20) 150.00 45.00
HC1 Ken Griffey Jr. 12.00 3.60
HC2 Hideo Nomo 8.00 2.40
HC3 Roberto Alomar 5.00 1.50
HC4 Paul Wilson 3.00 .90
HC5 Albert Belle 3.00 .90
HC6 Manny Ramirez 5.00 1.50
HC7 Kirby Puckett 8.00 2.40
HC8 Johnny Damon 5.00 1.50
HC9 Randy Johnson 8.00 2.40
HC10 Greg Maddux 12.00 3.60
HC11 Chipper Jones 8.00 2.40
HC12 Barry Bonds 20.00 6.00
HC13 Mo Vaughn 3.00 .90
HC14 Mike Piazza 12.00 3.60
HC15 Cal Ripken 25.00 7.50
HC16 Tim Salmon 5.00 1.50
HC17 Sammy Sosa 12.00 3.60
HC18 Kenny Lofton 3.00 .90
HC19 Tony Gwynn 10.00 3.00
HC20 Frank Thomas 8.00 2.40

1996 Upper Deck V.J. Lovero Showcase

Upper Deck utilized photos from the files of V.J. Lovero to produce this set. The cards feature the photos along with a story of how Lovero took the photos. The cards are numbered with a "VJ" prefix. These cards were inserted at a rate of one every six packs.

Nm-Mt Ex-Mt
COMPLETE SET (19) 25.00 7.50
VJ1 Jim Abbott 1.25 .35
VJ2 Hideo Nomo 2.00 .60
VJ3 Derek Jeter 5.00 1.50
VJ4 Barry Bonds 5.00 1.50
VJ5 Greg Maddux 3.00 .90
VJ6 Mark McGwire 5.00 1.50
VJ7 Jose Canseco 2.00 .60
VJ8 Ken Caminiti .75 .23
VJ9 Raul Mondesi .75 .23
VJ10 Ken Griffey Jr. 3.00 .90
VJ11 Jay Buhner .75 .23
VJ12 Randy Johnson 2.00 .60
VJ13 Roger Clemens 4.00 1.20
VJ14 Brady Anderson .75 .23
VJ15 Frank Thomas 2.00 .60
VJ16 Garret Anderson .75 .23
Jim Edmonds
Tim Salmon
VJ17 Mike Piazza 3.00 .90
VJ18 Dante Bichette .75 .23
VJ19 Tony Gwynn 2.50 .75

1996 Upper Deck Nomo Highlights

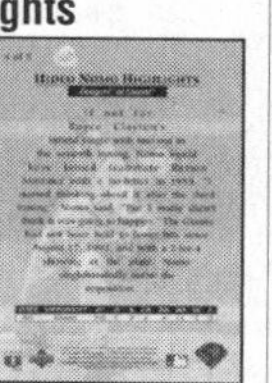

Los Angeles Dodgers star pitcher and Upper Deck spokesperson Hideo Nomo was featured in this special five card set. The cards were randomly seeded into second series packs at a rate of one in 24 and feature game action as well as descriptions of some of Nomo's key 1995 games.

Nm-Mt Ex-Mt
COMPLETE SET (5) 20.00 6.00
COMMON CARD (1-5) 5.00 1.50

1996 Upper Deck Power Driven

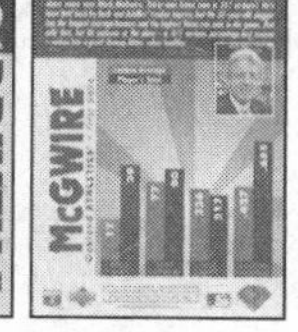

Randomly inserted in first series packs at a rate of one in 36, this 20-card set consists of embossed rainbow foil inserts of baseball's top power hitters.

Nm-Mt Ex-Mt
COMPLETE SET (20) 120.00 36.00
PD1 Albert Belle 3.00 .90
PD2 Barry Bonds 20.00 6.00
PD3 Jay Buhner 3.00 .90
PD4 Jose Canseco 8.00 2.40
PD5 Cecil Fielder 3.00 .90
PD6 Juan Gonzalez 5.00 1.50
PD7 Ken Griffey Jr. 12.00 3.60
PD8 Eric Karros 3.00 .90
PD9 Fred McGriff 5.00 1.50
PD10 Mark McGwire 20.00 6.00
PD11 Rafael Palmeiro 5.00 1.50
PD12 Mike Piazza 12.00 3.60
PD13 Manny Ramirez 5.00 1.50
PD14 Tim Salmon 5.00 1.50
PD15 Reggie Sanders 3.00 .90
PD16 Sammy Sosa 12.00 3.60
PD17 Frank Thomas 8.00 2.40
PD18 Mo Vaughn 3.00 .90
PD19 Larry Walker 5.00 1.50
PD20 Matt Williams 3.00 .35

1996 Upper Deck Predictor Hobby

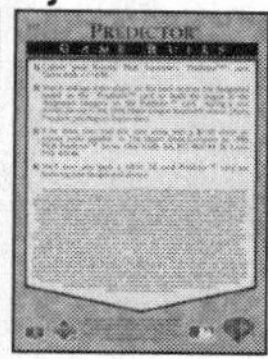

Randomly inserted in both series hobby packs at a rate of one in 12, this 60-card predictor set offered six different 10-card parallel exchange sets for prizes as featured players competed for monthly milestones and awards. The fronts feature a cutout player photo against a pinstriped background surrounded by a gray marble border. Card backs feature game rules and guidelines. Winner cards are signified with a W in our listings and are in noticeably shorter supply since they had to be mailed in to Upper Deck (where they were destroyed) to claim your exchange cards. The deadline to mail in winning cards was November 18th, 1996.

Nm-Mt Ex-Mt
COMPLETE SERIES 1 (30) 30.00 9.00
COMPLETE SERIES 2 (30) 30.00 9.00
*EXCHANGE: .4X TO 1X BASIC PREDICTOR
ONE EXCH.SET VIA MAIL PER PRED.WINNER
H1 Albert Belle .60 .18
H2 Kenny Lofton .60 .18
H3 Rafael Palmeiro 1.00 .30
H4 Ken Griffey Jr. 2.50 .75
H5 Tim Salmon 1.00 .30
H6 Cal Ripken 5.00 1.50
H7 Mark McGwire W 4.00 1.20
H8 Frank Thomas W 1.50 .45
H9 Mo Vaughn W .60 .18
H10 Player of Month LS W .60 .18
H11 Roger Clemens 3.00 .90
H12 David Cone .60 .18
H13 Jose Mesa .60 .18
H14 Randy Johnson 1.50 .45
H15 Chuck Finley .60 .18
H16 Mike Mussina 1.00 .30
H17 Kevin Appier .60 .18
H18 Kenny Rogers 1.50 .45
H19 Lee Smith .60 .18
H20 Pitcher of Month LS W .60 .18
H21 George Arias .60 .18
H22 Jose Herrera .60 .18
H23 Tony Clark .60 .18
H24 Todd Greene .60 .18
H25 Derek Jeter W 4.00 1.20
H26 Arquimedez Pozo .60 .18
H27 Matt Lawton .60 .18
H28 Shannon Stewart .60 .18
H29 Chris Snopek .60 .18
H30 Most Rookie Hits LS .60 .18
H31 Jeff Bagwell W 1.00 .30
H32 Dante Bichette .60 .18
H33 Barry Bonds W 4.00 1.20
H34 Tony Gwynn 2.00 .60
H35 Chipper Jones 1.50 .45
H36 Eric Karros .60 .18
H37 Barry Larkin 1.00 .30
H38 Mike Piazza 2.50 .75
H39 Matt Williams .60 .18
H40 Long Shot Card .60 .18
H41 Osvaldo Fernandez .60 .18
H42 Tom Glavine 1.00 .30
H43 Jason Isringhausen .60 .18
H44 Greg Maddux 2.50 .75
H45 Pedro Martinez 1.50 .45
H46 Hideo Nomo 1.50 .45
H47 Pete Schourek .60 .18
H48 Paul Wilson .60 .18
H49 Mark Wohlers .60 .18
H50 Long Shot Card .60 .18
H51 Bob Abreu .60 .18
H52 Trey Beamon .60 .18
H53 Yamil Benitez .60 .18
H54 Roger Cedeno .60 .18
H55 Todd Hollandsworth .60 .18
H56 Marvin Benard .60 .18
H57 Jason Kendall .60 .18
H58 Brooks Kieschnick .60 .18
H59 Rey Ordonez W .60 .18
H60 Long Shot Card .60 .18

1996 Upper Deck Predictor Retail

Randomly inserted in both series retail packs at a rate of one in 12, this 60-card Predictor set offered six different 10-card parallel exchange sets as featured players competed for "monthly milestones and awards." The fronts feature a "cutout" player photo against a pinstriped background surrounded by a gray marble border. Card backs feature game rules and guidelines. Winner cards are signified with a W in our listings and are in noticeably shorter supply since

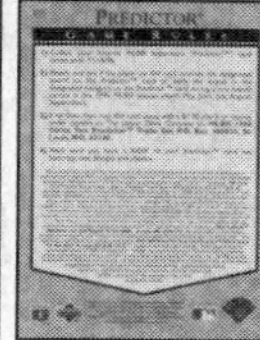

they had to be mailed in to Upper Deck (where they were destroyed) to claim your exchange cards. The expiration date to send in cards was November 18th, 1996.

Nm-Mt Ex-Mt
COMPLETE SERIES 1 (30) 40.00 12.00
COMPLETE SERIES 2 (30) 40.00 12.00
*EXCHANGE: .4X TO 1X BASIC PREDICTOR
ONE EXCH.SET VIA MAIL PER PRED.WINNER
R1 Albert Belle W .60 .18
R2 Jay Buhner W .60 .18
R3 Juan Gonzalez 1.00 .30
R4 Ken Griffey Jr. 2.50 .75
R5 Mark McGwire W 4.00 1.20
R6 Rafael Palmeiro 1.00 .30
R7 Tim Salmon 1.00 .30
R8 Frank Thomas 1.50 .45
R9 Mo Vaughn W .60 .18
R10 Monthly HR Ldr LS W .60 .18
R11 Albert Belle W .60 .18
R12 Jay Buhner .60 .18
R13 Jim Edmonds .60 .18
R14 Cecil Fielder .60 .18
R15 Ken Griffey Jr. 2.50 .75
R16 Edgar Martinez 1.00 .30
R17 Manny Ramirez 1.00 .30
R18 Frank Thomas 1.50 .45
R19 Mo Vaughn W .60 .18
R20 Monthly RBI Ldr LS W .60 .18
R21 Roberto Alomar W 1.00 .30
R22 Carlos Baerga .60 .18
R23 Wade Boggs 1.00 .30
R24 Ken Griffey Jr. 2.50 .75
R25 Chuck Knoblauch .60 .18
R26 Kenny Lofton .60 .18
R27 Edgar Martinez 1.00 .30
R28 Tim Salmon 1.00 .30
R29 Frank Thomas 1.50 .45
R30 Monthly Hits Ldr Longshot W .60 .18
R31 Dante Bichette .60 .18
R32 Barry Bonds W 4.00 1.20
R33 Ron Gant .60 .18
R34 Chipper Jones 1.50 .45
R35 Fred McGriff 1.00 .30
R36 Mike Piazza 2.50 .75
R37 Sammy Sosa 2.50 .75
R38 Larry Walker 1.00 .30
R39 Matt Williams .60 .18
R40 Long Shot Card .60 .18
R41 Jeff Bagwell W 1.00 .30
R42 Dante Bichette .60 .18
R43 Barry Bonds W 4.00 1.20
R44 Jeff Conine .60 .18
R45 Andres Galarraga .60 .18
R46 Mike Piazza 2.50 .75
R47 Reggie Sanders .60 .18
R48 Sammy Sosa 2.50 .75
R49 Matt Williams .60 .18
R50 Long Shot Card .60 .18
R51 Jeff Bagwell 1.00 .30
R52 Derek Bell .60 .18
R53 Dante Bichette .60 .18
R54 Craig Biggio 1.00 .30
R55 Barry Bonds 4.00 1.20
R56 Bret Boone .60 .18
R57 Tony Gwynn 2.00 .60
R58 Barry Larkin 1.00 .30
R59 Mike Piazza W 2.50 .75
R60 Long Shot Card .60 .18

1996 Upper Deck Ripken Collection

This 23 card set was issued across all the various Upper Deck brands. The cards were issued to commemorate Cal Ripken's career, which had been capped the previous season by the breaking of the consecutive game streak long held by Lou Gehrig. The cards were inserted at the following ratios: Cards 1-4 were in Collector Choice first series packs at a rate of one in 12. Cards 5-8 were inserted into Upper Deck series one packs at a rate of one in 24. Cards 9-12 were placed into second series Collector Choice packs at a rate of one in 12. Cards 13-17 were in second series Upper Deck packs at a rate of one in 24. And Cards 18-22 were in SP Packs at a rate of one in 45. The header card (number 23) was also inserted into only Collector Choice packs.

Nm-Mt Ex-Mt
COMMON COLC (1-4/9-12) 3.00 .90
COMMON UD (5-8/13-17) 6.00 1.80
COMMON SP (18-22) 15.00 4.50
NNO C.Ripken Header COLC 3.00 .90

1996 Upper Deck Run Producers

This 20 card set was randomly inserted into series two packs at a rate of one every 71 packs. The cards are thermographically printed, which gives the card a rubber surface texture. The cards are double die-cut and are foil stamped. These cards are highly condition sensitive, often

found with noticable chipping on the edges.

	Nm-Mt	Ex-Mt
COMPLETE SET (20)	150.00	45.00
RP1 Albert Belle	4.00	1.20
RP2 Dante Bichette	4.00	1.20
RP3 Barry Bonds	25.00	7.50
RP4 Jay Buhner	4.00	1.20
RP5 Jose Canseco	10.00	3.00
RP6 Juan Gonzalez	6.00	1.80
RP7 Ken Griffey Jr.	15.00	4.50
RP8 Tony Gwynn	12.00	3.60
RP9 Kenny Lofton	4.00	1.20
RP10 Edgar Martinez	6.00	1.80
RP11 Fred McGriff	6.00	1.80
RP12 Mark McGwire	25.00	7.50
RP13 Rafael Palmeiro	6.00	1.80
RP14 Mike Piazza	15.00	4.50
RP15 Manny Ramirez	6.00	1.80
RP16 Tim Salmon	6.00	1.80
RP17 Sammy Sosa	15.00	4.50
RP18 Frank Thomas	10.00	3.00
RP19 Mo Vaughn	4.00	1.20
RP20 Matt Williams	4.00	1.20

1996 Upper Deck All-Stars Jumbos

This 18-card set measures approximately 3 1/2" by 5" with a suggested retail price of $19.95 a set. The fronts feature borderless color player photos and are foil stamped with the official 1996 Major League Baseball All-Star game logo. The backs carry another player photo with player information and statistics. The cards are checklisted below in alphabetical order.

	Nm-Mt	Ex-Mt
1 Roberto Alomar	.75	.23
2 Sandy Alomar Jr.	.40	.12
3 Jeff Bagwell	1.00	.30
4 Albert Belle	.40	.12
5 Dante Bichette	.40	.12
6 Craig Biggio	.60	.18
7 Wade Boggs	1.00	.30
8 Barry Bonds	2.00	.60
9 Ken Griffey Jr.	2.50	.75
10 Tony Gwynn	2.00	.60
11 Barry Larkin	.75	.23
12 Kenny Lofton	.60	.18
13 Charles Nagy	.20	.06
14 Mike Piazza	3.00	.90
15 Cal Ripken Jr.	4.00	1.20
16 John Smoltz	.40	.12
17 Frank Thomas	1.00	.30
18 Matt Williams	.60	.18

1997 Upper Deck

The 1997 Upper Deck set was issued in two series (series one 1-240, series two 271-520). The 12-card packs retailed for $2.49 each. Many cards have dates on the front to identify when, and when possible, what significant event is pictured. The backs include a player photo, stats and a brief blurb to go with vital statistics. Subsets include Jackie Robinson Tribute (1-9), Strike Force (64-72), Defensive Gems (136-153), Global Impact (181-207), Season Highlight Checklists (214-222/316-324), Star Rookies (223-240/271-288), Capture the Flag (370-387), Griffey's Hot List (415-424) and Diamond Debuts (470-483). It's critical to note that the Griffey's Hot List subset cards (in an unannounced move by the manufacturer) were shortprinted (about 1:7 packs) in relation to other cards in the series two set. The comparatively low print run on these cards created a dramatic surge in demand amongst set collectors and the cards soared in value on the secondary market. A 30-card first series Update set (numbered 241-270) was available to collectors that mailed in 10 series one wrappers along with $3 for postage and handling. The Series One Update set is composed primarily of 1996 post-season highlights. An additional 30-card series two Trade set (numbered 521-550) was also released around the end of the season. It too was available to collectors that mailed in ten series two wrappers along with $3 for postage and handling. The Series Two Trade set is composed primarily of traded players pictured in their new uniforms and a selection of rookies and prospects highlighted by the inclusion of Jose Cruz Jr. and Hideki Irabu.

	Nm-Mt	Ex-Mt
COMP.MASTER SET (550)	200.00	60.00
COMPLETE SET (490)	100.00	30.00
COMP. SERIES 1 (240)	40.00	12.00
COMP. SERIES 2 (250)	60.00	18.00
COMP.SER.2 w/o GHL (240)	25.00	7.50
COMMON (1-240/271-520)	.30	.09
COMP.UPDATE SET (30)	80.00	24.00
COMMON (241-270)	1.00	.30
ONE UPD.SET VIA MAIL PER 10 SER.1 WRAPPERS		
COMMON GHL (415-424)	1.50	.45
COMP.TRADE SET (30)	20.00	6.00
COMMON (521-550)	.50	.15
1 Jackie Robinson The Beginnings	.50	.15
2 Jackie Robinson Breaking the Barrier	.50	.15
3 Jackie Robinson The MVP Season, 1949	.50	.15
4 Jackie Robinson 1951 season	.50	.15
5 Jackie Robinson 1952 and 1953 seasons	.50	.15
6 Jackie Robinson 1954 season	.50	.15
7 Jackie Robinson 1955 season	.50	.15
8 Jackie Robinson 1956 season	.50	.15
9 Jackie Robinson HOF	.50	.15
10 Chipper Jones	.75	.23
11 Marquis Grissom	.30	.09
12 Jermaine Dye	.30	.09
13 Mark Lemke	.30	.09
14 Terrell Wade	.30	.09
15 Fred McGriff	.50	.15
16 Tom Glavine	.50	.15
17 Mark Wohlers	.30	.09
18 Randy Myers	.30	.09
19 Roberto Alomar	.50	.15
20 Cal Ripken	2.50	.75
21 Rafael Palmeiro	.50	.15
22 Mike Mussina	.50	.15
23 Brady Anderson	.30	.09
24 Jose Canseco	.75	.23
25 Mo Vaughn	.30	.09
26 Roger Clemens	1.50	.45
27 Tim Naehring	.30	.09
28 Jeff Suppan	.30	.09
29 Troy Percival	.30	.09
30 Sammy Sosa	1.25	.35
31 Amaury Telemaco	.30	.09
32 Rey Sanchez	.30	.09
33 Scott Servais	.30	.09
34 Steve Trachsel	.30	.09
35 Mark Grace	.50	.15
36 Wilson Alvarez	.30	.09
37 Harold Baines	.30	.09
38 Tony Phillips	.30	.09
39 James Baldwin	.30	.09
40 Frank Thomas UER Bio information is Ken Griffey Jr.'s	.75	.23
41 Lyle Mouton	.30	.09
42 Chris Snopek	.30	.09
43 Hal Morris	.30	.09
44 Eric Davis	.30	.09
45 Barry Larkin	.50	.15
46 Reggie Sanders	.30	.09
47 Pete Schourek	.30	.09
48 Lee Smith	.30	.09
49 Charles Nagy	.30	.09
50 Albert Belle	.30	.09
51 Julio Franco	.30	.09
52 Kenny Lofton	.30	.09
53 Orel Hershiser	.30	.09
54 Omar Vizquel	.50	.15
55 Eric Young	.30	.09
56 Curtis Leskanic	.30	.09
57 Quinton McCracken	.30	.09
58 Kevin Ritz	.30	.09
59 Walt Weiss	.30	.09
60 Dante Bichette	.30	.09
61 Mark Lewis	.30	.09
62 Tony Clark	.30	.09
63 Travis Fryman	.30	.09
64 John Smoltz SF	.30	.09
65 Greg Maddux SF	.75	.23
66 Tom Glavine SF	.30	.09
67 Mike Mussina SF	.30	.09
68 Andy Pettitte SF	.30	.09
69 Mariano Rivera SF	.30	.09
70 Hideo Nomo SF	.30	.09
71 Kevin Brown SF	.30	.09
72 Randy Johnson SF	.50	.15
73 Felipe Lira	.30	.09
74 Kimera Bartee	.30	.09
75 Alan Trammell	.30	.09
76 Kevin Brown	.30	.09
77 Edgar Renteria	.30	.09
78 Al Leiter	.30	.09
79 Charles Johnson	.30	.09
80 Andre Dawson	.30	.09
81 Billy Wagner	.30	.09
82 Donne Wall	.30	.09
83 Jeff Bagwell	.50	.15
84 Keith Lockhart	.30	.09
85 Jeff Montgomery	.30	.09
86 Tom Goodwin	.30	.09
87 Tim Belcher	.30	.09
88 Mike Macfarlane	.30	.09
89 Joe Randa	.30	.09
90 Brett Butler	.30	.09
91 Todd Worrell	.30	.09
92 Todd Hollandsworth	.30	.09
93 Ismael Valdes	.30	.09
94 Hideo Nomo	.75	.23
95 Mike Piazza	1.25	.35
96 Jeff Cirillo	.30	.09
97 Ricky Bones	.30	.09
98 Fernando Vina	.30	.09
99 Ben McDonald	.30	.09
100 John Jaha	.30	.09
101 Mark Loretta	.30	.09
102 Paul Molitor	.50	.15
103 Rick Aguilera	.30	.09
104 Marty Cordova	.30	.09
105 Kirby Puckett	.75	.23
106 Dan Naulty	.30	.09
107 Frank Rodriguez	.30	.09
108 Shane Andrews	.30	.09
109 Henry Rodriguez	.30	.09
110 Mark Grudzielanek	.30	.09
111 Pedro Martinez	.75	.23
112 Ugueth Urbina	.30	.09
113 David Segui	.30	.09
114 Rey Ordonez	.30	.09
115 Bernard Gilkey	.30	.09
116 Butch Huskey	.30	.09
117 Paul Wilson	.30	.09
118 Alex Ochoa	.30	.09
119 John Franco	.30	.09
120 Dwight Gooden	.30	.09
121 Ruben Rivera	.30	.09
122 Andy Pettitte	.50	.15
123 Tino Martinez	.50	.15
124 Bernie Williams	.50	.15
125 Wade Boggs	.50	.15
126 Paul O'Neill	.50	.15
127 Scott Brosius	.30	.09
128 Ernie Young	.30	.09
129 Doug Johns	.30	.09
130 Geronimo Berroa	.30	.09
131 Jason Giambi	.30	.09
132 John Wasdin	.30	.09
133 Jim Eisenreich	.30	.09
134 Ricky Otero	.30	.09
135 Ricky Bottalico	.30	.09
136 Mark Langston DG	.30	.09
137 Greg Maddux DG	.75	.23
138 Ivan Rodriguez DG	.50	.15
139 Charles Johnson DG	.30	.09
140 J.T. Snow DG	.30	.09
141 Mark Grace DG	.30	.09
142 Roberto Alomar DG	.30	.09
143 Craig Biggio DG	.30	.09
144 Ken Caminiti DG	.30	.09
145 Matt Williams DG	.30	.09
146 Omar Vizquel DG	.30	.09
147 Cal Ripken DG	1.25	.35
148 Ozzie Smith DG	.75	.23
149 Rey Ordonez DG	.30	.09
150 Ken Griffey Jr. DG	.75	.23
151 Devon White DG	.30	.09
152 Barry Bonds DG	.75	.23
153 Kenny Lofton DG	.30	.09
154 Mickey Morandini	.30	.09
155 Gregg Jefferies	.30	.09
156 Curt Schilling	.30	.09
157 Jason Kendall	.30	.09
158 Francisco Cordova	.30	.09
159 Dennis Eckersley	.30	.09
160 Ron Gant	.30	.09
161 Ozzie Smith	1.25	.35
162 Brian Jordan	.30	.09
163 John Mabry	.30	.09
164 Andy Ashby	.30	.09
165 Steve Finley	.30	.09
166 Fernando Valenzuela	.30	.09
167 Archi Cianfrocco	.30	.09
168 Wally Joyner	.30	.09
169 Greg Vaughn	.30	.09
170 Barry Bonds	2.00	.60
171 W.VanLandingham	.30	.09
172 Marvin Benard	.30	.09
173 Rich Aurilia	.30	.09
174 Jay Canizaro	.30	.09
175 Ken Griffey Jr.	1.25	.35
176 Bob Wells	.30	.09
177 Jay Buhner	.30	.09
178 Sterling Hitchcock	.30	.09
179 Edgar Martinez	.50	.15
180 Rusty Greer	.30	.09
181 Dave Nilsson GI	.30	.09
182 Larry Walker GI	.30	.09
183 Edgar Renteria GI	.30	.09
184 Rey Ordonez GI	.30	.09
185 Rafael Palmeiro GI	.30	.09
186 Osvaldo Fernandez GI	.30	.09
187 Raul Mondesi GI	.30	.09
188 Manny Ramirez GI	.30	.09
189 Sammy Sosa GI UER The flag pictured is wrong	.75	.23
190 Robert Eenhoorn GI	.30	.09
191 Devon White GI	.30	.09
192 Hideo Nomo GI	.30	.09
193 Mac Suzuki GI	.30	.09
194 Chan Ho Park GI	.30	.09
195 F.Valenzuela GI	.30	.09
196 Andruw Jones GI	.30	.09
197 Vinny Castilla GI	.30	.09
198 Dennis Martinez GI	.30	.09
199 Ruben Rivera GI	.30	.09
200 Juan Gonzalez GI	.30	.09
201 Roberto Alomar GI	.30	.09
202 Edgar Martinez GI	.30	.09
203 Ivan Rodriguez GI	.50	.15
204 Carlos Delgado GI	.30	.09
205 Andres Galarraga GI	.30	.09
206 Ozzie Guillen GI	.30	.09
207 Midre Cummings GI	.30	.09
208 Roger Pavlik	.30	.09
209 Darren Oliver	.30	.09
210 Dean Palmer	.30	.09
211 Ivan Rodriguez	.75	.23
212 Otis Nixon	.30	.09
213 Pat Hentgen	.30	.09
214 Ozzie Smith Andre Dawson Kirby Pucket HL CL	.50	.15
215 Barry Bonds Gary Sheffield Brady Anderson HL CL	.75	.23
216 Ken Caminiti SH CL	.30	.09
217 John Smoltz SH CL	.30	.09
218 Eric Young SH CL	.30	.09
219 Juan Gonzalez SH CL	.30	.09
220 Eddie Murray SH CL	.50	.15
221 T. Lasorda SH CL	.30	.09
222 Paul Molitor SH CL	.30	.09
223 Luis Castillo	.30	.09
224 Justin Thompson	.30	.09
225 Rocky Coppinger	.30	.09
226 Jermaine Allensworth	.30	.09
227 Jeff D'Amico	.30	.09
228 Jamey Wright	.30	.09
229 Scott Rolen	.75	.23
230 Darin Erstad	.30	.09
231 Marty Janzen	.30	.09
232 Jacob Cruz	.30	.09
233 Raul Ibanez	.30	.09
234 Nomar Garciaparra	1.25	.35
235 Todd Walker	.30	.09
236 Brian Giles RC	1.25	.35
237 Matt Beech	.30	.09
238 Mike Cameron	.30	.09
239 Jose Paniagua	.30	.09
240 Andruw Jones	.30	.09
241 Brant Brown UPD	1.00	.30
242 Robin Jennings UPD	1.00	.30
243 Willie Adams UPD	1.00	.30
244 Ken Caminiti UPD	1.50	.45
245 Brian Jordan UPD	1.50	.45
246 Chipper Jones UPD	4.00	1.20
247 Juan Gonzalez UPD	2.50	.75
248 Bernie Williams UPD	2.50	.75
249 Roberto Alomar UPD	2.50	.75
250 Bernie Williams UPD	2.50	.75
251 David Wells UPD	1.50	.45
252 Cecil Fielder UPD	1.50	.45
253 D.Strawberry UPD	1.50	.45
254 Andy Pettitte UPD	2.50	.75
255 Javier Lopez UPD	1.50	.45
256 Gary Gaetti UPD	1.50	.45
257 Ron Gant UPD	1.50	.45
258 Brian Jordan UPD	1.50	.45
259 John Smoltz UPD	2.50	.75
260 Greg Maddux UPD	8.00	2.40
261 Tom Glavine UPD	2.50	.75
262 Andruw Jones UPD	1.50	.45
263 Greg Maddux UPD	8.00	2.40
264 David Cone UPD	1.50	.45
265 Jim Leyritz UPD	1.00	.30
266 Andy Pettitte UPD	2.50	.75
267 John Wetteland UPD	1.50	.45
268 Dario Veras UPD	1.00	.30
269 Neifi Perez UPD	1.00	.30
270 Bill Mueller UPD	8.00	2.40
271 Vladimir Guerrero	.75	.23
272 Dmitri Young	.30	.09
273 Nerio Rodriguez RC	.30	.09
274 Kevin Orie	.30	.09
275 Felipe Crespo	.30	.09
276 Danny Graves	.30	.09
277 Rod Myers	.30	.09
278 Felix Heredia RC	.30	.09
279 Ralph Milliard	.30	.09
280 Greg Norton	.30	.09
281 Derek Wallace	.30	.09
282 Trot Nixon	.30	.09
283 Bobby Chouinard	.30	.09
284 Jay Witasick	.30	.09
285 Travis Miller	.30	.09
286 Brian Bevil RC	.30	.09
287 Bobby Estalella	.30	.09
288 Steve Soderstrom	.30	.09
289 Mark Langston	.30	.09
290 Tim Salmon	.50	.15
291 Jim Edmonds	.30	.09
292 Garret Anderson	.30	.09
293 George Arias	.30	.09
294 Gary DiSarcina	.30	.09
295 Chuck Finley	.30	.09
296 Todd Greene	.30	.09
297 Randy Velarde	.30	.09
298 David Justice	.30	.09
299 Ryan Klesko	.30	.09
300 John Smoltz	.50	.15
301 Javier Lopez	.30	.09
302 Greg Maddux	1.25	.35
303 Denny Neagle	.30	.09
304 B.J. Surhoff	.30	.09
305 Chris Hoiles	.30	.09
306 Eric Davis	.30	.09
307 Scott Erickson	.30	.09
308 Mike Bordick	.30	.09
309 John Valentin	.30	.09
310 Heathcliff Slocumb	.30	.09
311 Tom Gordon	.30	.09
312 Mike Stanley	.30	.09
313 Reggie Jefferson	.30	.09
314 Darren Bragg	.30	.09
315 Troy O'Leary	.30	.09
316 John Mabry SH CL	.30	.09
317 Mark Whiten SH CL	.30	.09
318 Edgar Martinez SH CL	.30	.09
319 Alex Rodriguez SH CL	.75	.23
320 Mark McGwire SH CL	1.00	.30
321 Hideo Nomo SH CL	.30	.09
322 Todd Hundley SH CL	.30	.09
323 Barry Bonds SH CL	.75	.23
324 Andruw Jones SH CL	.30	.09
325 Ryne Sandberg	1.25	.35
326 Brian McRae	.30	.09
327 Frank Castillo	.30	.09
328 Shawon Dunston	.30	.09
329 Ray Durham	.30	.09
330 Robin Ventura	.30	.09
331 Ozzie Guillen	.30	.09
332 Roberto Hernandez	.30	.09
333 Albert Belle	.30	.09
334 Dave Martinez	.30	.09
335 Willie Greene	.30	.09
336 Jeff Brantley	.30	.09
337 Kevin Jarvis	.30	.09
338 John Smiley	.30	.09
339 Eddie Taubensee	.30	.09
340 Bret Boone	.30	.09
341 Kevin Seitzer	.30	.09
342 Jack McDowell	.30	.09
343 Sandy Alomar Jr.	.30	.09
344 Chad Curtis	.30	.09
345 Manny Ramirez	.50	.15
346 Chad Ogea	.30	.09
347 Jim Thome	.75	.23
348 Mark Thompson	.30	.09
349 Ellis Burks	.30	.09
350 Andres Galarraga	.30	.09
351 Vinny Castilla	.30	.09
352 Kirt Manwaring	.30	.09
353 Larry Walker	.50	.15
354 Omar Olivares	.30	.09
355 Bobby Higginson	.30	.09
356 Melvin Nieves	.30	.09
357 Brian Johnson	.30	.09
358 Devon White	.30	.09
359 Jeff Conine	.30	.09
360 Gary Sheffield	.30	.09
361 Robb Nen	.30	.09
362 Mike Hampton	.30	.09
363 Bob Abreu	.30	.09
364 Luis Gonzalez	.30	.09
365 Derek Bell	.30	.09
366 Sean Berry	.30	.09
367 Craig Biggio	.50	.15
368 Darryl Kile	.30	.09
369 Shane Reynolds	.30	.09
370 Jeff Bagwell CF	.30	.09
371 Ron Gant CF	.30	.09
372 Andy Benes CF	.30	.09
373 Gary Gaetti CF	.30	.09
374 Ramon Martinez CF	.30	.09
375 Raul Mondesi CF	.30	.09
376 Steve Finley CF	.30	.09
377 Ken Caminiti CF	.30	.09
378 Tony Gwynn CF	.50	.15
379 Dario Veras RC	.30	.09
380 Andy Pettitte CF	.30	.09
381 Ruben Rivera CF	.30	.09
382 David Cone CF	.30	.09
383 Roberto Alomar CF	.30	.09
384 Edgar Martinez CF	.30	.09
385 Ken Griffey Jr. CF	.75	.23
386 Mark McGwire CF	1.00	.30
387 Rusty Greer CF	.30	.09
388 Jose Rosado	.30	.09
389 Kevin Appier	.30	.09
390 Johnny Damon	.50	.15
391 Jose Offerman	.30	.09
392 Michael Tucker	.30	.09
393 Craig Paquette	.30	.09
394 Bip Roberts	.30	.09
395 Ramon Martinez	.30	.09
396 Greg Gagne	.30	.09
397 Chan Ho Park	.30	.09
398 Karim Garcia	.30	.09
399 Wilton Guerrero	.30	.09
400 Eric Karros	.30	.09
401 Raul Mondesi	.30	.09
402 Matt Mieske	.30	.09
403 Mike Fetters	.30	.09
404 Dave Nilsson	.30	.09
405 Jose Valentin	.30	.09
406 Scott Karl	.30	.09
407 Marc Newfield	.30	.09
408 Cal Eldred	.30	.09
409 Rich Becker	.30	.09
410 Terry Steinbach	.30	.09
411 Chuck Knoblauch	.30	.09
412 Pat Meares	.30	.09
413 Brad Radke	.30	.09
414 Kirby Puckett UER Card numbered 415	.75	.23
415 A.Jones GHL SP	1.50	.45
416 C.Jones GHL SP	2.50	.75
417 Mo Vaughn GHL SP	1.50	.45
418 F.Thomas GHL SP	2.50	.75
419 Albert Belle GHL SP	1.50	.45
420 M.McGwire GHL SP	8.00	2.40
421 Derek Jeter GHL SP	8.00	2.40
422 A.Rodriguez GHL SP	5.00	1.50
423 J.Gonzalez GHL SP	1.50	.45
424 K.Griffey Jr. GHL SP	5.00	1.50
425 Rondell White	.30	.09
426 Darrin Fletcher	.30	.09
427 Cliff Floyd	.30	.09
428 Mike Lansing	.30	.09
429 F.P. Santangelo	.30	.09
430 Todd Hundley	.30	.09
431 Mark Clark	.30	.09
432 Pete Harnisch	.30	.09
433 Jason Isringhausen	.30	.09
434 Bobby Jones	.30	.09
435 Lance Johnson	.30	.09
436 Carlos Baerga	.30	.09
437 Mariano Duncan	.30	.09
438 David Cone	.30	.09
439 Mariano Rivera	.50	.15
440 Derek Jeter	2.00	.60
441 Joe Girardi	.30	.09
442 Charlie Hayes	.30	.09
443 Tim Raines	.30	.09
444 Darryl Strawberry	.30	.09
445 Cecil Fielder	.30	.09
446 Ariel Prieto	.30	.09
447 Tony Batista	.30	.09
448 Brent Gates	.30	.09
449 Scott Spiezio	.30	.09
450 Mark McGwire	2.00	.60
451 Don Wengert	.30	.09
452 Mike Lieberthal	.30	.09
453 Lenny Dykstra	.30	.09
454 Rex Hudler	.30	.09
455 Darren Daulton	.30	.09
456 Kevin Stocker	.30	.09
457 Trey Beamon	.30	.09
458 Midre Cummings	.30	.09
459 Mark Johnson	.30	.09
460 Al Martin	.30	.09
461 Kevin Elster	.30	.09
462 Jon Lieber	.30	.09
463 Jason Schmidt	.30	.09
464 Paul Wagner	.30	.09
465 Andy Benes	.30	.09
466 Alan Benes	.30	.09
467 Royce Clayton	.30	.09
468 Gary Gaetti	.30	.09
469 Curt Lyons RC	.30	.09
470 Eugene Kingsale DD	.30	.09
471 Damian Jackson DD	.30	.09
472 Wendell Magee DD	.30	.09
473 Kevin L. Brown DD	.30	.09
474 Raul Casanova DD	.30	.09
475 R.Mendoza DD RC	.30	.09
476 Todd Dunn DD	.30	.09
477 Chad Mottola DD	.30	.09
478 Andy Larkin DD	.30	.09
479 Jaime Bluma DD	.30	.09
480 Mac Suzuki DD	.30	.09
481 Brian Banks DD	.30	.09
482 Desi Wilson DD	.30	.09
483 Einar Diaz DD	.30	.09
484 Tom Pagnozzi	.30	.09
485 Ray Lankford	.30	.09
486 Todd Stottlemyre	.30	.09
487 Donovan Osborne	.30	.09
488 Trevor Hoffman	.30	.09
489 Chris Gomez	.30	.09
490 Ken Caminiti	.30	.09
491 John Flaherty	.30	.09

492 Tony Gwynn 1.00 .30
493 Joey Hamilton .30 .09
494 Rickey Henderson .75 .23
495 Glenallen Hill .30 .09
496 Rod Beck .30 .09
497 Osvaldo Fernandez .30 .09
498 Rick Wilkins .30 .09
499 Joey Cora .30 .09
500 Alex Rodriguez 1.25 .35
501 Randy Johnson .75 .23
502 Paul Sorrento .30 .09
503 Dan Wilson .30 .09
504 Jamie Moyer .30 .09
505 Will Clark .75 .23
506 Mickey Tettleton .30 .09
507 John Burkett .30 .09
508 Ken Hill .30 .09
509 Mark McLemore .30 .09
510 Juan Gonzalez .50 .15
511 Bobby Witt .30 .09
512 Carlos Delgado .30 .09
513 Alex Gonzalez .30 .09
514 Shawn Green .30 .09
515 Joe Carter .30 .09
516 Juan Guzman .30 .09
517 Charlie O'Brien .30 .09
518 Ed Sprague .30 .09
519 Mike Timlin .30 .09
520 Roger Clemens 1.50 .45
521 Eddie Murray TRADE 2.00 .60
522 Jason Dickson TRADE .50 .15
523 Jim Leyritz TRADE .50 .15
524 M.Tucker TRADE .50 .15
525 Kenny Lofton TRADE .75 .23
526 Jimmy Key TRADE .75 .23
527 Mel Rojas TRADE .50 .15
528 Deion Sanders TRADE 1.25 .35
529 Bartolo Colon TRADE .75 .23
530 Matt Williams TRADE .75 .23
531 M.Grissom TRADE .75 .23
532 David Justice TRADE .75 .23
533 B.Trammell TRADE .75 .23
534 Moises Alou TRADE .75 .23
535 Bobby Bonilla TRADE .75 .23
536 A.Fernandez TRADE .50 .15
537 Jay Bell TRADE .75 .23
538 Chili Davis TRADE .75 .23
539 Jeff King TRADE .50 .15
540 Todd Zeile TRADE .50 .15
541 John Olerud TRADE .75 .23
542 Jose Guillen TRADE .75 .23
543 Derrek Lee TRADE .75 .23
544 Dante Powell TRADE .50 .15
545 J.T. Snow TRADE .75 .23
546 Jeff Kent TRADE .75 .23
547 Jose Cruz Jr. TRADE 1.25 .35
548 J.Wetteland TRADE .75 .23
549 O.Merced TRADE .50 .15
550 Hideki Irabu TRADE .75 .23

1997 Upper Deck Amazing Greats

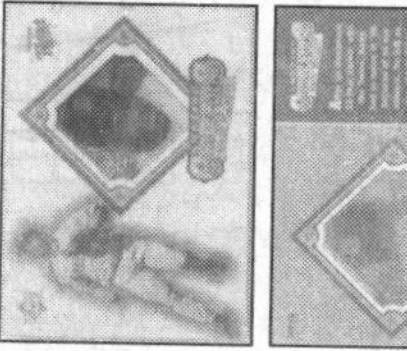
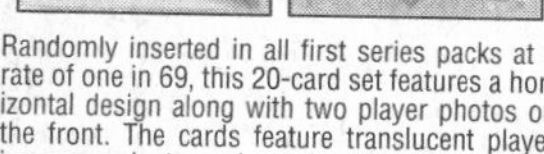

Randomly inserted in all first series packs at a rate of one in 69, this 20-card set features a horizontal design along with two player photos on the front. The cards feature translucent player images against a real wood grain stock.

Nm-Mt Ex-Mt
COMPLETE SET (20) 300.00 90.00
AG1 Ken Griffey Jr. 20.00 6.00
AG2 Roberto Alomar 8.00 2.40
AG3 Alex Rodriguez 20.00 6.00
AG4 Paul Molitor 8.00 2.40
AG5 Chipper Jones 12.00 3.60
AG6 Tony Gwynn 15.00 4.50
AG7 Kenny Lofton 5.00 1.50
AG8 Albert Belle 5.00 1.50
AG9 Matt Williams 5.00 1.50
AG10 Frank Thomas 12.00 3.60
AG11 Greg Maddux 20.00 6.00
AG12 Sammy Sosa 20.00 6.00
AG13 Kirby Puckett 12.00 3.60
AG14 Jeff Bagwell 8.00 2.40
AG15 Cal Ripken 40.00 12.00
AG16 Manny Ramirez 8.00 2.40
AG17 Barry Bonds 30.00 9.00
AG18 Mo Vaughn 5.00 1.50
AG19 Eddie Murray 12.00 3.60
AG20 Mike Piazza 20.00 6.00

1997 Upper Deck Blue Chip Prospects

This rare 20-card set, randomly inserted into series two packs, features color photos of high expectation prospects who are likely to have a big impact on Major League Baseball. Only 500 of this crash numbered, limited edition set was produced.

Nm-Mt Ex-Mt
BC1 Andruw Jones 10.00 3.00
BC2 Derek Jeter 60.00 18.00
BC3 Scott Rolen 25.00 7.50
BC4 Manny Ramirez 15.00 4.50
BC5 Todd Walker 10.00 3.00
BC6 Rocky Coppinger 10.00 3.00
BC7 Nomar Garciaparra 40.00 12.00
BC8 Darin Erstad 10.00 3.00
BC9 Jermaine Dye 10.00 3.00
BC10 Vladimir Guerrero 25.00 7.50
BC11 Edgar Renteria 10.00 3.00
BC12 Bob Abreu 10.00 3.00
BC13 Karim Garcia 10.00 3.00
BC14 Jeff D'Amico 10.00 3.00
BC15 Chipper Jones 25.00 7.50
BC16 Todd Hollandsworth 10.00 3.00
BC17 Andy Pettitte 15.00 4.50
BC18 Ruben Rivera 10.00 3.00
BC19 Jason Kendall 10.00 3.00
BC20 Alex Rodriguez 40.00 12.00

1997 Upper Deck Game Jersey

Randomly inserted in all first series packs at a rate of one in 800, this three-card set feaures swatches of real game-worn jerseys cut up and placed on the cards. These cards represent the first memorabilia insert cards to hit the baseball card market and thus carry a significant impact in the development of the hobby in the late 1990's.

Nm-Mt Ex-Mt
GJ1 Ken Griffey Jr. 150.00 45.00
GJ2 Tony Gwynn 60.00 18.00
GJ3 Rey Ordonez 25.00 7.50

1997 Upper Deck Hot Commodities

Randomly inserted in series two packs at a rate of one in 13, this 20-card set features color player images on a flame background in a black border. The backs carry a player head photo, statistics, and a commentary by ESPN sportscaster Dan Patrick.

Nm-Mt Ex-Mt
COMPLETE SET (20) 60.00 18.00
HC1 Alex Rodriguez 4.00 1.20
HC2 Andruw Jones 1.00 .30
HC3 Derek Jeter 6.00 1.80
HC4 Frank Thomas 2.50 .75
HC5 Ken Griffey Jr. 4.00 1.20
HC6 Chipper Jones 2.50 .75
HC7 Juan Gonzalez 1.50 .45
HC8 Cal Ripken 8.00 2.40
HC9 John Smoltz 1.50 .45
HC10 Mark McGwire 6.00 1.80
HC11 Barry Bonds 6.00 1.80
HC12 Albert Belle 1.00 .30
HC13 Mike Piazza 4.00 1.20
HC14 Manny Ramirez 1.50 .45
HC15 Mo Vaughn 1.00 .30
HC16 Tony Gwynn 3.00 .90
HC17 Vladimir Guerrero 2.50 .75
HC18 Hideo Nomo 2.50 .75
HC19 Greg Maddux 4.00 1.20
HC20 Kirby Puckett 2.50 .75

1997 Upper Deck Long Distance Connection

Randomly inserted in series two packs at a rate of one in 35, this 20-card set features color player images of some of the League's top power hitters on backgrounds utilizing Light/FX technology. The backs carry the pictured player's statistics.

Nm-Mt Ex-Mt
COMPLETE SET (20) 150.00 45.00
LD1 Mark McGwire 15.00 4.50
LD2 Brady Anderson 2.50 .75
LD3 Ken Griffey Jr. 10.00 3.00
LD4 Albert Belle 2.50 .75
LD5 Juan Gonzalez 4.00 1.20
LD6 Andres Galarraga 2.50 .75
LD7 Jay Buhner 2.50 .75
LD8 Mo Vaughn 2.50 .75
LD9 Barry Bonds 15.00 4.50
LD10 Gary Sheffield 2.50 .75
LD11 Todd Hundley 2.50 .75
LD12 Frank Thomas 6.00 1.80
LD13 Sammy Sosa 10.00 3.00
LD14 Rafael Palmeiro 4.00 1.20
LD15 Alex Rodriguez 10.00 3.00
LD16 Mike Piazza 10.00 3.00
LD17 Ken Caminiti 2.50 .75
LD18 Chipper Jones 6.00 1.80
LD19 Manny Ramirez 4.00 1.20
LD20 Andruw Jones 2.50 .75

1997 Upper Deck Memorable Moments

Cards from these sets were distributed exclusively in six-card retail Collector's Choice series one and two packs. Each pack contained one of ten different Memorable Moments inserts. Each set features a selection of top stars captured in highlights of season's gone by. Each card features wave-like die cut top and bottom borders wth gold foil.

Nm-Mt Ex-Mt
COMPLETE SERIES 1 (10) 12.00 3.60
COMPLETE SERIES 2 (10) 12.00 3.60
A1 Andruw Jones .30 .09
A2 Chipper Jones .75 .23
A3 Cal Ripken 2.50 .75
A4 Frank Thomas .75 .23
A5 Manny Ramirez .50 .15
A6 Mike Piazza 1.25 .35
A7 Mark McGwire 2.00 .60
A8 Barry Bonds 2.00 .60
A9 Ken Griffey Jr. 1.25 .35
A10 Alex Rodriguez 1.25 .35
B1 Ken Griffey Jr. 1.25 .35
B2 Albert Belle .30 .09
B3 Derek Jeter 2.00 .60
B4 Greg Maddux 1.25 .35
B5 Tony Gwynn 1.00 .30
B6 Ryne Sandberg 1.25 .35
B7 Juan Gonzalez .50 .15
B8 Roger Clemens 1.50 .45
B9 Jose Cruz Jr. .50 .15
B10 Mo Vaughn .30 .09

1997 Upper Deck Power Package

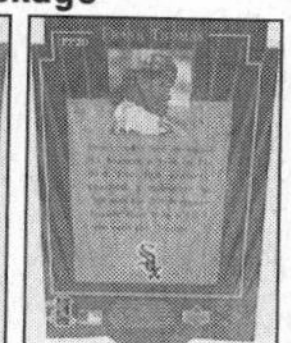

Randomly inserted in all first series packs at a rate of one in 24, this 20-card set feaures some of the best longball hitters. The die cut cards feature some of baseball's leading power hitters.

Nm-Mt Ex-Mt
COMPLETE SET (20) 80.00 24.00
*JUMBOS: .2X TO .5X BASIC PP
JUMBOS ONE PER RETAIL JUMBO PACK
PP1 Ken Griffey Jr. 8.00 2.40
PP2 Joe Carter 2.00 .60
PP3 Rafael Palmeiro 3.00 .90
PP4 Jay Buhner 2.00 .60
PP5 Sammy Sosa 8.00 2.40
PP6 Fred McGriff 3.00 .90
PP7 Jeff Bagwell 3.00 .90
PP8 Albert Belle 2.00 .60
PP9 Matt Williams 2.00 .60
PP10 Mark McGwire 12.00 3.60
PP11 Gary Sheffield 2.00 .60
PP12 Tim Salmon 3.00 .90
PP13 Ryan Klesko 2.00 .60
PP14 Manny Ramirez 3.00 .90
PP15 Mike Piazza 8.00 2.40
PP16 Barry Bonds 12.00 3.60
PP17 Mo Vaughn 2.00 .60
PP18 Jose Canseco 5.00 1.50
PP19 Juan Gonzalez 3.00 .90
PP20 Frank Thomas 5.00 1.50

1997 Upper Deck Predictor

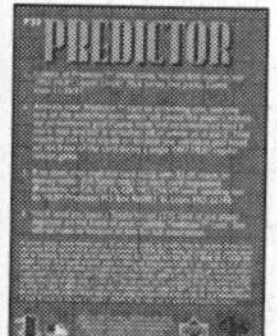

Randomly inserted in series two packs at a rate of one in five, this 30-card set featues a color player photo alongside a series of bats. The collector could activate the card by scratching off one of the bats to predict the performance of the pictured player during a single game. If the player matches or exceeds the predicted performance, the card could be mailed in with $2 to receive a Totally Virtual high-tech cel-card of the player pictured on the front. The backs carry the rules of the game. The deadline to redeem these cards was November 22nd, 1997. Winners and Losers are specified in our checklist with a "W" or a "L" after the player's name.

Nm-Mt Ex-Mt
COMPLETE SET (30) 30.00 9.00
*SCRATCH LOSER: .25X TO .6X UNSCRATCH
*EXCH.WIN: 1X TO 2.5X BASIC PREDICTOR
SER.2 STATED ODDS 1:5
1 Andruw Jones L .40 .12
2 Chipper Jones L 1.00 .30
3 Greg Maddux W 1.50 .45
Complete Game Shutout
4 Fred McGriff W .60 .18
4 Hits/2HR/3B
5 John Smoltz W .60 .18
Complete Game Shutout
6 Brady Anderson W .40 .12
Leadoff HR
7 Cal Ripken W 3.00 .90
Grand Slam
8 Mo Vaughn W .40 .12
3HR/6RBI
9 Sammy Sosa L 1.50 .45
10 Albert Belle W .40 .12
Grand Slam/9th HR
11 Frank Thomas L 1.00 .30
12 Kenny Lofton W .40 .12
5 Hits
13 Jim Thome L 1.00 .30
14 Dante Bichette W .40 .12
6RBI's
15 Andres Galarraga L .40 .12
16 Gary Sheffield L .40 .12
17 Hideo Nomo W 1.00 .30
Base Hit
18 Mike Piazza W 1.50 .45
Steal/9th HR
19 Derek Jeter W 2.50 .75
2HR
20 Bernie Williams L .60 .18
21 Mark McGwire W 2.50 .75
Grand Slam/4HR
22 Ken Caminiti W .40 .12
5RBI's
23 Tony Gwynn W 1.25 .35
2 2B/3RBI
24 Barry Bonds W 2.50 .75
5RBI's
25 Jay Buhner W .40 .12
5RBI's
26 Ken Griffey Jr. W 1.50 .45
3HR's
27 Alex Rodriguez W 1.50 .45
Cycle
28 Juan Gonzalez W .60 .18
5RBI's/4 Hits
29 Dean Palmer W .40 .12
2HR's/5RBI's
30 Roger Clemens W 2.00 .60
Complete Game Shutout

1997 Upper Deck Rock Solid Foundation

Randomly inserted in all first series packs at a rate of one in seven, this 20-card set features players 25 and under who have made an impact in the majors. The fronts feature a player photo against a "silver" type background. The backs give player information as well as another player photo and are numbered with a "RS" prefix.

Nm-Mt Ex-Mt
COMPLETE SET (20) 40.00 12.00
RS1 Alex Rodriguez 6.00 1.80
RS2 Rey Ordonez 1.50 .45
RS3 Derek Jeter 10.00 3.00
RS4 Darin Erstad 1.50 .45
RS5 Chipper Jones 4.00 1.20
RS6 Johnny Damon 2.50 .75
RS7 Ryan Klesko 1.50 .45
RS8 Charles Johnson 1.50 .45
RS9 Andy Pettitte 2.50 .75
RS10 Manny Ramirez 2.50 .75
RS11 Ivan Rodriguez 4.00 1.20
RS12 Jason Kendall 1.50 .45
RS13 Rondell White 1.50 .45
RS14 Alex Ochoa 1.50 .45
RS15 Javier Lopez 1.50 .45
RS16 Pedro Martinez 4.00 1.20
RS17 Carlos Delgado 1.50 .45
RS18 Paul Wilson 1.50 .45
RS19 Alan Benes 1.50 .45
RS20 Raul Mondesi 1.50 .45

1997 Upper Deck Run Producers

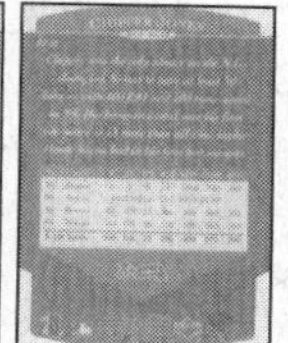

Randomly inserted in series two packs at a rate of one in 69, this 24-card set features color player images on die-cut cards that actually look and feel like home plate. The backs carry player information and career statistics.

Nm-Mt Ex-Mt
COMPLETE SET (24) 150.00 45.00
RP1 Ken Griffey Jr. 15.00 4.50
RP2 Barry Bonds 25.00 7.50
RP3 Albert Belle 4.00 1.20
RP4 Mark McGwire 25.00 7.50
RP5 Frank Thomas 10.00 3.00
RP6 Juan Gonzalez 6.00 1.80
RP7 Brady Anderson 4.00 1.20
RP8 Andres Galarraga 4.00 1.20
RP9 Rafael Palmeiro 6.00 1.80
RP10 Alex Rodriguez 15.00 4.50
RP11 Jay Buhner 4.00 1.20
RP12 Gary Sheffield 4.00 1.20
RP13 Sammy Sosa 15.00 4.50
RP14 Dante Bichette 4.00 1.20
RP15 Mike Piazza 15.00 4.50
RP16 Manny Ramirez 6.00 1.80
RP17 Kenny Lofton 4.00 1.20
RP18 Mo Vaughn 4.00 1.20
RP19 Tim Salmon 6.00 1.80
RP20 Chipper Jones 10.00 3.00
RP21 Jim Thome 10.00 3.00
RP22 Ken Caminiti 4.00 1.20
RP23 Jeff Bagwell 6.00 1.80
RP24 Paul Molitor 6.00 1.80

1997 Upper Deck Star Attractions

These 20 cards were issued one per pack in special Upper Deck Memorabilia Madness packs. The Memorabilia Madness packs included various redemptions for signed 8 by 10 photos with the grand prize being a grouping of Ken Griffey Jr. signed jersey, baseball and 8 by 10 photo. The die cut cards feature the words "Star Attraction" on the top with the player and team identification on the sides. The backs have a photo and a brief blurb on the player. Cards numbered 1-10 were inserted in Upper Deck packs while cards numbered 11-20 were in Collectors Choice packs.

Nm-Mt Ex-Mt
COMPLETE SET (20) 25.00 7.50
*GOLD: 2X TO 5X BASE STAR ATT. 1.00 .30
GOLD INSERTS IN UD/CC MADNESS RETAIL
1 Ken Griffey Jr. 1.50 .45
2 Barry Bonds 2.50 .75
3 Jeff Bagwell .60 .18
4 Nomar Garciaparra 1.50 .45
5 Tony Gwynn 1.25 .35
6 Roger Clemens 2.00 .60
7 Chipper Jones 1.00 .30
8 Tino Martinez .60 .18
9 Albert Belle .40 .12
10 Kenny Lofton .40 .12
11 Alex Rodriguez 1.50 .45
12 Mark McGwire 2.50 .75
13 Cal Ripken 3.00 .90
14 Larry Walker .60 .18
15 Mike Piazza 1.50 .45
16 Frank Thomas 1.00 .30
17 Juan Gonzalez .60 .18
18 Greg Maddux 1.50 .45
19 Jose Cruz Jr. 1.00 .30
20 Mo Vaughn .40 .12

1997 Upper Deck Ticket To Stardom

Randomly inserted in all first series packs at a rate of one in 34, this 20-card set is designed in the form of a ticket and are designed to be matched. The horizontal fronts feature two player photos as well as using "light f/x technology and embossed player images.

Nm-Mt Ex-Mt
TS1 Chipper Jones 6.00 1.80
TS2 Jermaine Dye 2.50 .75
TS3 Rey Ordonez 2.50 .75
TS4 Alex Ochoa 2.50 .75
TS5 Derek Jeter 15.00 4.50
TS6 Ruben Rivera 2.50 .75
TS7 Billy Wagner 2.50 .75
TS8 Jason Kendall 2.50 .75
TS9 Darin Erstad 2.50 .75
TS10 Alex Rodriguez 10.00 3.00
TS11 Bob Abreu 2.50 .75
TS12 Richard Hidalgo 6.00 1.80
TS13 Karim Garcia 2.50 .75
TS14 Andruw Jones 2.50 .75
TS15 Carlos Delgado 2.50 .75
TS16 Rocky Coppinger 2.50 .75
TS17 Jeff D'Amico 2.50 .75
TS18 Johnny Damon 4.00 1.20
TS19 John Wasdin 2.50 .75
TS20 Manny Ramirez 4.00 1.20

1998 Upper Deck

The 1998 Upper Deck set was issued in three series consisting of a 270-card first series, a 270-card second series and a 211-card third series. Each series was distributed in 12-card packs which carried a suggested retail price of $2.49. Card fronts feature game dated photographs of some of the season's most memorable moments. The following subsets are contained within the set: History in the Making (1-8/361-369), Griffey's Hot List (9-18), Define the Game (136-153), Season Highlights (244-252/532-540/748-750), Star Rookies (253-288/541-600), Postseason Headliners (415-432), Upper Echelon (451-459) and Eminent Prestige (601-630). The Eminent Prestige subset cards were slightly shortprinted (approximately 1:4 packs) and Upper Deck offered a free service to collectors trying to finish their Series three sets whereby Eminent Prestige cards were mailed to collectors who sent in proof of purchase of one-and-a-half boxes or more. The print run for Mike Piazza card number 681 was split exactly in half creating two shortprints: card number 681 (picturing Piazza as a New York Met) and card number 681A (picturing Piazza as a Florida Marlin). Both cards are exactly two times tougher to pull from packs than other regular issue Series three cards. The series three set is considered complete with both versions at 251 total cards. Notable Rookie Cards include Gabe Kapler and Magglio Ordonez.

Nm-Mt Ex-Mt
COMPLETE SET (751) 200.00 60.00
COMP.SERIES 1 (270) 40.00 12.00
COMP.SERIES 2 (270) 40.00 12.00
COMP.SERIES 3 (211) 120.00 36.00
COMMON (1-600/631-750) .30 .09
COMMON EP (601-630) 2.00 .60
EP SER.2 ODDS APPROXIMATELY 1:4
1 Tino Martinez HIST .30 .09
2 Jimmy Key HIST .30 .09
3 Jay Buhner HIST .30 .09
4 Mark Gardner HIST .30 .09
5 Greg Maddux HIST .75 .23
6 Pedro Martinez HIST .50 .15
7 Hideo Nomo HIST .50 .15
8 Sammy Sosa HIST .75 .23
9 Mark McGwire GHL 1.00 .30
10 Ken Griffey Jr. GHL .75 .23
11 Larry Walker GHL .30 .09
12 Tino Martinez GHL .30 .09
13 Mike Piazza GHL .75 .23
14 Jose Cruz Jr. GHL .30 .09
15 Tony Gwynn GHL .50 .15
16 Greg Maddux GHL .75 .23
17 Roger Clemens GHL .75 .23
18 Alex Rodriguez GHL .75 .23
19 Shigetoshi Hasegawa .30 .09
20 Eddie Murray .75 .23
21 Jason Dickson .30 .09
22 Darin Erstad .30 .09
23 Chuck Finley .30 .09
24 Dave Hollins .30 .09
25 Garret Anderson .30 .09
26 Michael Tucker .30 .09
27 Kenny Lofton .30 .09
28 Javier Lopez .30 .09
29 Fred McGriff .50 .15
30 Greg Maddux 1.25 .35
31 Jeff Blauser .30 .09
32 John Smoltz .50 .15
33 Mark Wohlers .30 .09
34 Scott Erickson .30 .09
35 Jimmy Key .30 .09
36 Harold Baines .30 .09
37 Randy Myers .30 .09
38 B.J. Surhoff .30 .09
39 Eric Davis .30 .09
40 Rafael Palmeiro .50 .15
41 Jeffrey Hammonds .30 .09
42 Mo Vaughn .30 .09
43 Tom Gordon .30 .09
44 Tim Naehring .30 .09
45 Darren Bragg .30 .09
46 Aaron Sele .30 .09
47 Troy O'Leary .30 .09
48 John Valentin .30 .09
49 Doug Glanville .30 .09
50 Ryne Sandberg 1.25 .35
51 Steve Trachsel .30 .09
52 Mark Grace .50 .15
53 Kevin Foster .30 .09
54 Kevin Tapani .30 .09
55 Kevin Orie .30 .09
56 Lyle Mouton .30 .09
57 Ray Durham .30 .09
58 Jaime Navarro .30 .09
59 Mike Cameron .30 .09
60 Albert Belle .30 .09
61 Doug Drabek .30 .09
62 Chris Snopek .30 .09
63 Eddie Taubensee .30 .09
64 Terry Pendleton .30 .09
65 Barry Larkin .50 .15
66 Willie Greene .30 .09
67 Deion Sanders .50 .15
68 Pokey Reese .30 .09
69 Jeff Shaw .30 .09
70 Jim Thome .75 .23
71 Orel Hershiser .30 .09
72 Omar Vizquel .50 .15
73 Brian Giles .30 .09
74 David Justice .30 .09
75 Bartolo Colon .30 .09
76 Sandy Alomar Jr. .30 .09
77 Neifi Perez .30 .09
78 Dante Bichette .30 .09
79 Vinny Castilla .30 .09
80 Eric Young .30 .09
81 Quinton McCracken .30 .09
82 Jamey Wright .30 .09
83 John Thomson .30 .09
84 Damion Easley .30 .09
85 Justin Thompson .30 .09
86 Willie Blair .30 .09
87 Raul Casanova .30 .09
88 Bobby Higginson .30 .09
89 Bubba Trammell .30 .09
90 Tony Clark .30 .09
91 Livan Hernandez .30 .09
92 Charles Johnson .30 .09
93 Edgar Renteria .30 .09
94 Alex Fernandez .30 .09
95 Gary Sheffield .30 .09
96 Moises Alou .30 .09
97 Tony Saunders .30 .09
98 Robb Nen .30 .09
99 Darryl Kile .30 .09
100 Craig Biggio .50 .15
101 Chris Holt .30 .09
102 Bob Abreu .30 .09
103 Luis Gonzalez .30 .09
104 Billy Wagner .30 .09
105 Brad Ausmus .30 .09
106 Chili Davis .30 .09
107 Tim Belcher .30 .09
108 Dean Palmer .30 .09
109 Jeff King .30 .09
110 Jose Rosado .30 .09
111 Mike Macfarlane .30 .09
112 Jay Bell .30 .09
113 Todd Worrell .30 .09
114 Chan Ho Park .30 .09
115 Raul Mondesi .30 .09
116 Brett Butler .30 .09
117 Greg Gagne .30 .09
118 Hideo Nomo .75 .23
119 Todd Zeile .30 .09
120 Eric Karros .30 .09
121 Cal Eldred .30 .09
122 Jeff D'Amico .30 .09
123 Antone Williamson .30 .09
124 Doug Jones .30 .09
125 Dave Nilsson .30 .09
126 Gerald Williams .30 .09
127 Fernando Vina .30 .09
128 Ron Coomer .30 .09
129 Matt Lawton .30 .09
130 Paul Molitor .50 .15
131 Todd Walker .30 .09
132 Rick Aguilera .30 .09
133 Brad Radke .30 .09
134 Bob Tewksbury .30 .09
135 Vladimir Guerrero .75 .23
136 Tony Gwynn DG .50 .15
137 Roger Clemens DG .75 .23
138 Dennis Eckersley DG .30 .09
139 Brady Anderson DG .30 .09
140 Ken Griffey Jr. DG .75 .23
141 Derek Jeter DG 1.00 .30
142 Ken Caminiti DG .30 .09
143 Frank Thomas DG .50 .15
144 Barry Bonds DG .75 .23
145 Cal Ripken DG 1.25 .35
146 Alex Rodriguez DG .75 .23
147 Greg Maddux DG .75 .23
148 Kenny Lofton DG .30 .09
149 Mike Piazza DG .75 .23
150 Mark McGwire DG 1.00 .30
151 Andruw Jones DG .30 .09
152 Rusty Greer DG .30 .09
153 F.P. Santangelo DG .30 .09
154 Mike Lansing .30 .09
155 Lee Smith .30 .09
156 Carlos Perez .30 .09
157 Pedro Martinez .75 .23
158 Ryan McGuire .30 .09
159 F.P. Santangelo .30 .09
160 Rondell White .30 .09
161 T.Kashiwada RC .40 .12
162 Butch Huskey .30 .09
163 Edgardo Alfonzo .30 .09
164 John Franco .30 .09
165 Todd Hundley .30 .09
166 Rey Ordonez .30 .09
167 Armando Reynoso .30 .09
168 John Olerud .30 .09
169 Bernie Williams .50 .15
170 Andy Pettitte .50 .15
171 Wade Boggs .50 .15
172 Paul O'Neill .50 .15
173 Cecil Fielder .30 .09
174 Charlie Hayes .30 .09
175 David Cone .30 .09
176 Hideki Irabu .30 .09
177 Mark Bellhorn .30 .09
178 Steve Karsay .30 .09
179 Damon Mashore .30 .09
180 Jason McDonald .30 .09
181 Scott Spiezio .30 .09
182 Ariel Prieto .30 .09
183 Jason Giambi .30 .09
184 Wendell Magee .30 .09
185 Rico Brogna .30 .09
186 Garrett Stephenson .30 .09
187 Wayne Gomes .30 .09
188 Ricky Bottalico .30 .09
189 Mickey Morandini .30 .09
190 Mike Lieberthal .30 .09
191 Kevin Polcovich .30 .09
192 Francisco Cordova .30 .09
193 Kevin Young .30 .09
194 Jon Lieber .30 .09
195 Kevin Elster .30 .09
196 Tony Womack .30 .09
197 Lou Collier .30 .09
198 Mike Difelice RC .40 .12
199 Gary Gaetti .30 .09
200 Dennis Eckersley .30 .09
201 Alan Benes .30 .09
202 Willie McGee .30 .09
203 Ron Gant .30 .09
204 Fernando Valenzuela .30 .09
205 Mark McGwire 2.00 .60
206 Archi Cianfrocco .30 .09
207 Andy Ashby .30 .09
208 Steve Finley .30 .09
209 Quilvio Veras .30 .09
210 Ken Caminiti .30 .09
211 Rickey Henderson .75 .23
212 Joey Hamilton .30 .09
213 Derrek Lee .30 .09
214 Bill Mueller .30 .09
215 Shawn Estes .30 .09
216 J.T. Snow .30 .09
217 Mark Gardner .30 .09
218 Terry Mulholland .30 .09
219 Dante Powell .30 .09
220 Jeff Kent .30 .09
221 Jamie Moyer .30 .09
222 Joey Cora .30 .09
223 Jeff Fassero .30 .09
224 Dennis Martinez .30 .09
225 Ken Griffey Jr. 1.25 .35
226 Edgar Martinez .50 .15
227 Russ Davis .30 .09
228 Dan Wilson .30 .09
229 Will Clark .75 .23
230 Ivan Rodriguez .75 .23
231 Benji Gil .30 .09
232 Lee Stevens .30 .09
233 Mickey Tettleton .30 .09
234 Julio Santana .30 .09
235 Rusty Greer .30 .09
236 Bobby Witt .30 .09
237 Ed Sprague .30 .09
238 Pat Hentgen .30 .09
239 Kelvim Escobar .30 .09
240 Joe Carter .30 .09
241 Carlos Delgado .30 .09
242 Shannon Stewart .30 .09
243 Benito Santiago .30 .09
244 Tino Martinez SH .30 .09
245 Ken Griffey Jr. SH .75 .23
246 Kevin Brown SH .30 .09
247 Ryne Sandberg SH .50 .15
248 Mo Vaughn SH .30 .09
249 Darryl Hamilton SH .30 .09
250 Randy Johnson SH .50 .15
251 Steve Finley SH .30 .09
252 Bobby Higginson SH .30 .09
253 Brett Tomko .30 .09
254 Mark Kotsay .30 .09
255 Jose Guillen .30 .09
256 Eli Marrero .30 .09
257 Dennis Reyes .30 .09
258 Richie Sexson .30 .09
259 Pat Cline .30 .09
260 Todd Helton .50 .15
261 Juan Melo .30 .09
262 Matt Morris .30 .09
263 Jeremi Gonzalez .30 .09
264 Jeff Abbott .30 .09
265 Aaron Boone .30 .09
266 Todd Dunwoody .30 .09
267 Jaret Wright .30 .09
268 Derrick Gibson .30 .09
269 Mario Valdez .30 .09
270 Fernando Tatis .30 .09
271 Craig Counsell .30 .09
272 Brad Rigby .30 .09
273 Danny Clyburn .30 .09
274 Brian Rose .30 .09
275 Miguel Tejada .75 .23
276 Jason Varitek .75 .23
277 Dave Dellucci RC .60 .18
278 Michael Coleman .30 .09
279 Adam Riggs .30 .09
280 Ben Grieve .30 .09
281 Brad Fullmer .30 .09
282 Ken Cloude .30 .09
283 Tom Evans .30 .09
284 Kevin Millwood RC 1.00 .30
285 Paul Konerko .30 .09
286 Juan Encarnacion .30 .09
287 Chris Carpenter .30 .09
288 Tom Fordham .30 .09
289 Gary DiSarcina .30 .09
290 Tim Salmon .50 .15
291 Troy Percival .30 .09
292 Todd Greene .30 .09
293 Ken Hill .30 .09
294 Dennis Springer .30 .09
295 Jim Edmonds .30 .09
296 Allen Watson .30 .09
297 Brian Anderson .30 .09
298 Keith Lockhart .30 .09
299 Tom Glavine .50 .15
300 Chipper Jones .75 .23
301 Randall Simon .30 .09
302 Mark Lemke .30 .09
303 Ryan Klesko .30 .09
304 Denny Neagle .30 .09
305 Andruw Jones .30 .09
306 Mike Mussina .50 .15
307 Brady Anderson .30 .09
308 Chris Hoiles .30 .09
309 Mike Bordick .30 .09
310 Cal Ripken 2.50 .75
311 Geronimo Berroa .30 .09
312 Armando Benitez .30 .09
313 Roberto Alomar .50 .15
314 Tim Wakefield .30 .09
315 Reggie Jefferson .30 .09
316 Jeff Frye .30 .09
317 Scott Hatteberg .30 .09
318 Steve Avery .30 .09
319 Robinson Checo .30 .09
320 Nomar Garciaparra 1.25 .35
321 Lance Johnson .30 .09
322 Tyler Houston .30 .09
323 Mark Clark .30 .09
324 Terry Adams .30 .09
325 Sammy Sosa 1.25 .35
326 Scott Servais .30 .09
327 Manny Alexander .30 .09
328 Norberto Martin .30 .09
329 Scott Eyre .30 .09
330 Frank Thomas .75 .23
331 Robin Ventura .30 .09
332 Matt Karchner .30 .09
333 Keith Foulke .30 .09
334 James Baldwin .30 .09
335 Chris Stynes .30 .09
336 Bret Boone .30 .09
337 Jon Nunnally .30 .09
338 Dave Burba .30 .09
339 Eduardo Perez .30 .09
340 Reggie Sanders .30 .09
341 Mike Remlinger .30 .09
342 Pat Watkins .30 .09
343 Chad Ogea .30 .09
344 John Smiley .30 .09
345 Kenny Lofton .30 .09
346 Jose Mesa .30 .09
347 Charles Nagy .30 .09
348 Enrique Wilson .30 .09
349 Bruce Aven .30 .09
350 Manny Ramirez .50 .15
351 Jerry DiPoto .30 .09
352 Ellis Burks .30 .09
353 Kirt Manwaring .30 .09
354 Vinny Castilla .30 .09
355 Larry Walker .50 .15
356 Kevin Ritz .30 .09
357 Pedro Astacio .30 .09
358 Scott Sanders .30 .09
359 Deivi Cruz .30 .09
360 Brian L. Hunter .30 .09
361 Pedro Martinez HM .50 .15
362 Tom Glavine HM .30 .09
363 Willie McGee HM .30 .09
364 J.T. Snow HM .30 .09
365 Rusty Greer HM .30 .09
366 Mike Grace HM .30 .09
367 Tony Clark HM .30 .09
368 Ben Grieve HM .30 .09
369 Gary Sheffield HM .30 .09
370 Joe Oliver .30 .09
371 Todd Jones .30 .09
372 Frank Catalanotto RC .60 .18
373 Brian Moehler .30 .09
374 Cliff Floyd .30 .09
375 Bobby Bonilla .30 .09
376 Al Leiter .30 .09
377 Josh Booty .30 .09
378 Darren Daulton .30 .09
379 Jay Powell .30 .09
380 Felix Heredia .30 .09
381 Jim Eisenreich .30 .09
382 Richard Hidalgo .30 .09
383 Mike Hampton .30 .09
384 Shane Reynolds .30 .09
385 Jeff Bagwell .50 .15
386 Derek Bell .30 .09
387 Ricky Gutierrez .30 .09
388 Bill Spiers .30 .09
389 Jose Offerman .30 .09
390 Johnny Damon .50 .15
391 Jermaine Dye .30 .09
392 Jeff Montgomery .30 .09
393 Glendon Rusch .30 .09
394 Mike Sweeney .30 .09
395 Kevin Appier .30 .09
396 Joe Vitiello .30 .09
397 Ramon Martinez .30 .09
398 Darren Dreifort .30 .09
399 Wilton Guerrero .30 .09
400 Mike Piazza 1.25 .35
401 Eddie Murray .75 .23
402 Ismael Valdes .30 .09
403 Todd Hollandsworth .30 .09
404 Mark Loretta .30 .09
405 Jeromy Burnitz .30 .09
406 Jeff Cirillo .30 .09
407 Scott Karl .30 .09
408 Mike Matheny .30 .09
409 Jose Valentin .30 .09
410 John Jaha .30 .09
411 Terry Steinbach .30 .09
412 Torii Hunter .30 .09
413 Pat Meares .30 .09
414 Marty Cordova .30 .09
415 Jaret Wright PH .30 .09
416 Mike Mussina PH .30 .09
417 John Smoltz PH .30 .09
418 Devon White PH .30 .09
419 Denny Neagle PH .30 .09
420 Livan Hernandez PH .30 .09
421 Kevin Brown PH .30 .09
422 Marquis Grissom PH .30 .09
423 Mike Mussina PH .30 .09
424 Eric Davis PH .30 .09
425 Tony Fernandez PH .30 .09
426 Moises Alou PH .30 .09
427 Sandy Alomar Jr. PH .30 .09
428 Gary Sheffield PH .30 .09
429 Jaret Wright PH .30 .09
430 Livan Hernandez PH .30 .09
431 Chad Ogea PH .30 .09
432 Edgar Renteria PH .30 .09
433 LaTroy Hawkins .30 .09
434 Rich Robertson .30 .09
435 Chuck Knoblauch .30 .09
436 Jose Vidro .30 .09
437 Dustin Hermanson .30 .09
438 Jim Bullinger .30 .09
439 Orlando Cabrera .30 .09
440 Vladimir Guerrero .75 .23
441 Ugueth Urbina .30 .09
442 Brian McRae .30 .09
443 Matt Franco .30 .09
444 Bobby Jones .30 .09
445 Bernard Gilkey .30 .09
446 Dave Mlicki .30 .09
447 Brian Bohanon .30 .09
448 Mel Rojas .30 .09
449 Tim Raines .30 .09
450 Derek Jeter 2.00 .60
451 Roger Clemens UE .75 .23
452 N.Garciaparra UE .75 .23
453 Mike Piazza UE .75 .23
454 Mark McGwire UE 1.00 .30
455 Ken Griffey Jr. UE .75 .23
456 Larry Walker UE .30 .09
457 Alex Rodriguez UE .75 .23
458 Tony Gwynn UE .50 .15
459 Frank Thomas UE .50 .15
460 Tino Martinez .50 .15
461 Chad Curtis .30 .09
462 Ramiro Mendoza .30 .09
463 Joe Girardi .30 .09
464 David Wells .30 .09
465 Mariano Rivera .50 .15
466 Willie Adams .30 .09
467 George Williams .30 .09
468 Dave Telgheder .30 .09
469 Dave Magadan .30 .09
470 Matt Stairs .30 .09
471 Bill Taylor .30 .09
472 Jimmy Haynes .30 .09
473 Gregg Jefferies .30 .09
474 Midre Cummings .30 .09
475 Curt Schilling .30 .09
476 Mike Grace .30 .09
477 Mark Leiter .30 .09
478 Matt Beech .30 .09
479 Scott Rolen .75 .23
480 Jason Kendall .30 .09
481 Esteban Loaiza .30 .09
482 Jermaine Allensworth .30 .09
483 Mark Smith .30 .09
484 Jason Schmidt .30 .09
485 Jose Guillen .30 .09
486 Al Martin .30 .09
487 Delino DeShields .30 .09
488 Todd Stottlemyre .30 .09
489 Brian Jordan .30 .09
490 Ray Lankford .30 .09
491 Matt Morris .30 .09
492 Royce Clayton .30 .09
493 John Mabry .30 .09
494 Wally Joyner .30 .09
495 Trevor Hoffman .30 .09
496 Chris Gomez .30 .09
497 Sterling Hitchcock .30 .09
498 Pete Smith .30 .09
499 Greg Vaughn .30 .09
500 Tony Gwynn 1.00 .30
501 Will Cunnane .30 .09
502 Darryl Hamilton .30 .09
503 Brian Johnson .30 .09
504 Kirk Rueter .30 .09
505 Barry Bonds 2.00 .60
506 Osvaldo Fernandez .30 .09
507 Stan Javier .30 .09
508 Julian Tavarez .30 .09
509 Rich Aurilia .30 .09
510 Alex Rodriguez 1.25 .35
511 David Segui .30 .09
512 Rich Amaral .30 .09
513 Raul Ibanez .30 .09
514 Jay Buhner .30 .09
515 Randy Johnson .75 .23
516 Heathcliff Slocumb .30 .09
517 Tony Saunders .30 .09
518 Kevin Elster .30 .09
519 John Burkett .30 .09
520 Juan Gonzalez .50 .15
521 John Wetteland .30 .09
522 Domingo Cedeno .30 .09
523 Darren Oliver .30 .09
524 Roger Pavlik .30 .09
525 Jose Cruz Jr. .30 .09
526 Woody Williams .30 .09
527 Alex Gonzalez .30 .09
528 Robert Person .30 .09
529 Juan Guzman .30 .09
530 Roger Clemens 1.50 .45
531 Shawn Green .30 .09
532 Francisco Cordova SH .30 .09
Ricardo Rincon
Mark Smith
533 N.Garciaparra SH .75 .23
534 Roger Clemens SH .75 .23
535 Mark McGwire SH 1.00 .30
536 Larry Walker SH .30 .09
537 Mike Piazza SH .75 .23
538 Curt Schilling SH .30 .09
539 Tony Gwynn SH .50 .15
540 Ken Griffey Jr. SH .75 .23
541 Carl Pavano .50 .15
542 Shane Monahan .30 .09
543 Gabe Kapler RC .60 .18
544 Eric Milton .30 .09
545 Gary Matthews Jr. RC .40 .12
546 Mike Kinkade RC .30 .09
547 Ryan Christenson RC .30 .09
548 Corey Koskie RC 1.00 .30
549 Norm Hutchins .30 .09
550 Russell Branyan .30 .09
551 Masato Yoshii RC .60 .18
552 Jesus Sanchez RC .30 .09
553 Anthony Sanders .30 .09
554 Edwin Diaz .30 .09
555 Gabe Alvarez .30 .09
556 Carlos Lee RC 1.00 .30
557 Mike Darr .30 .09
558 Kerry Wood .75 .23
559 Carlos Guillen .30 .09
560 Sean Casey .30 .09
561 Manny Aybar RC .30 .09
562 Octavio Dotel .30 .09
563 Jarrod Washburn .30 .09
564 Mark L. Johnson .30 .09
565 Ramon Hernandez .30 .09
566 Rich Butler RC .30 .09
567 Mike Caruso .30 .09
568 Cliff Politte .30 .09
569 Scott Elarton .30 .09
570 Magglio Ordonez RC 3.00 .90
571 Adam Butler RC .30 .09
572 Marlon Anderson .30 .09
573 Julio Ramirez RC .30 .09
574 Darron Ingram RC .30 .09
575 Bruce Chen .30 .09
576 Steve Woodard .30 .09
577 Hiram Bocachica .30 .09
578 Kevin Witt .30 .09
579 Javier Vazquez .30 .09
580 Alex Gonzalez .30 .09
581 Brian Powell .30 .09
582 Wes Helms .30 .09
583 Ron Wright .30 .09
584 Rafael Medina .30 .09
585 Daryle Ward .30 .09
586 Geoff Jenkins .30 .09
587 Preston Wilson .30 .09
588 Jim Chamblee RC .30 .09
589 Mike Lowell RC 2.00 .60
590 A.J. Hinch .30 .09
591 Francisco Cordero RC .30 .09
592 Rolando Arrojo RC .40 .12
593 Braden Looper .30 .09
594 Sidney Ponson .30 .09
595 Matt Clement .30 .09
596 Carlton Loewer .30 .09
597 Brian Meadows .30 .09
598 Danny Klassen .30 .09
599 Larry Sutton .30 .09
600 Travis Lee .30 .09
601 Randy Johnson EP 2.50 .75
602 Greg Maddux EP 4.00 1.20
603 Roger Clemens EP 5.00 1.50
604 Jaret Wright EP 2.00 .60
605 Mike Piazza EP 4.00 1.20
606 Tino Martinez EP 2.00 .60
607 Frank Thomas EP 2.50 .75
608 Mo Vaughn EP 2.00 .60
609 Todd Helton EP 2.00 .60

610 Mark McGwire EP 6.00 1.80
611 Jeff Bagwell EP 2.00 .60
612 Travis Lee EP 2.00 .60
613 Scott Rolen EP 2.50 .75
614 Cal Ripken EP 8.00 2.40
615 Chipper Jones EP 2.50 .75
616 Nomar Garciaparra EP 4.00 1.20
617 Alex Rodriguez EP 4.00 1.20
618 Derek Jeter EP 6.00 1.80
619 Tony Gwynn EP 3.00 .90
620 Ken Griffey Jr. EP 4.00 1.20
621 Kenny Lofton EP 2.00 .60
622 Juan Gonzalez EP 2.00 .60
623 Jose Cruz Jr. EP 2.00 .60
624 Larry Walker EP 2.00 .60
625 Barry Bonds EP 6.00 1.80
626 Ben Grieve EP 2.00 .60
627 Andruw Jones EP 2.00 .60
628 Vladimir Guerrero EP 2.50 .75
629 Paul Konerko EP 2.00 .60
630 Paul Molitor EP 2.00 .60
631 Cecil Fielder .30 .09
632 Jack McDowell .30 .09
633 Mike James .30 .09
634 Brian Anderson .30 .09
635 Jay Bell .30 .09
636 Devon White .30 .09
637 Andy Stankiewicz .30 .09
638 Tony Batista .30 .09
639 Omar Daal .30 .09
640 Matt Williams .30 .09
641 Brent Brede .30 .09
642 Jorge Fabregas .30 .09
643 Karim Garcia .30 .09
644 Felix Rodriguez .30 .09
645 Andy Benes .30 .09
646 Willie Blair .30 .09
647 Jeff Suppan .30 .09
648 Yamil Benitez .30 .09
649 Walt Weiss .30 .09
650 Andres Galarraga .30 .09
651 Doug Drabek .30 .09
652 Ozzie Guillen .30 .09
653 Joe Carter .30 .09
654 Dennis Eckersley .30 .09
655 Pedro Martinez .75 .23
656 Jim Leyritz .30 .09
657 Henry Rodriguez .30 .09
658 Rod Beck .30 .09
659 Mickey Morandini .30 .09
660 Jeff Blauser .30 .09
661 Ruben Sierra .30 .09
662 Mike Sirotka .30 .09
663 Pete Harnisch .30 .09
664 Damian Jackson .30 .09
665 Dmitri Young .30 .09
666 Steve Cooke .30 .09
667 Geronimo Berroa .30 .09
668 Shawon Dunston .30 .09
669 Mike Jackson .30 .09
670 Travis Fryman .30 .09
671 Dwight Gooden .30 .09
672 Paul Assenmacher .30 .09
673 Eric Plunk .30 .09
674 Mike Lansing .30 .09
675 Darryl Kile .30 .09
676 Luis Gonzalez .30 .09
677 Frank Castillo .30 .09
678 Joe Randa .30 .09
679 Bip Roberts .30 .09
680 Derrek Lee .30 .09
681 Mike Piazza SP 3.00 .90
New York Mets
681A Mike Piazza SP 3.00 .90
Florida Marlins
682 Sean Berry .30 .09
683 Ramon Garcia .30 .09
684 Carl Everett .30 .09
685 Moises Alou .30 .09
686 Hal Morris .30 .09
687 Jeff Conine .30 .09
688 Gary Sheffield .30 .09
689 Jose Vizcaino .30 .09
690 Charles Johnson .30 .09
691 Bobby Bonilla .30 .09
692 Marquis Grissom .30 .09
693 Alex Ochoa .30 .09
694 Mike Morgan .30 .09
695 Orlando Merced .30 .09
696 David Ortiz .75 .23
697 Brent Gates .30 .09
698 Otis Nixon .30 .09
699 Trey Moore .30 .09
700 Derrick May .30 .09
701 Rich Becker .30 .09
702 Al Leiter .30 .09
703 Chili Davis .30 .09
704 Scott Brosius .30 .09
705 Chuck Knoblauch .30 .09
706 Kenny Rogers .30 .09
707 Mike Blowers .30 .09
708 Mike Fetters .30 .09
709 Tom Candiotti .30 .09
710 Rickey Henderson .75 .23
711 Bob Abreu .30 .09
712 Mark Lewis .30 .09
713 Doug Glanville .30 .09
714 Desi Relaford .30 .09
715 Kent Mercker .30 .09
716 Kevin Brown .50 .15
717 James Mouton .30 .09
718 Mark Langston .30 .09
719 Greg Myers .30 .09
720 Orel Hershiser .30 .09
721 Charlie Hayes .30 .09
722 Robb Nen .30 .09
723 Glenallen Hill .30 .09
724 Tony Saunders .30 .09
725 Wade Boggs .50 .15
726 Kevin Stocker .30 .09
727 Wilson Alvarez .30 .09
728 Albie Lopez .30 .09
729 Dave Martinez .30 .09
730 Fred McGriff .50 .15
731 Quinton McCracken .30 .09
732 Bryan Rekar .30 .09
733 Paul Sorrento .30 .09
734 Roberto Hernandez .30 .09
735 Bubba Trammell .30 .09
736 Miguel Cairo .30 .09
737 John Flaherty .30 .09
738 Terrell Wade .30 .09
739 Roberto Kelly .30 .09
740 Mark McLemore .30 .09
741 Danny Patterson .30 .09
742 Aaron Sele .30 .09
743 Tony Fernandez .30 .09
744 Randy Myers .30 .09
745 Jose Canseco .75 .23
746 Darrin Fletcher .30 .09
747 Mike Stanley .30 .09
748 M.Grissom SH CL .30 .09
749 Fred McGriff SH CL .30 .09
750 Travis Lee SH CL .30 .09

1998 Upper Deck 10th Anniversary Preview

Randomly inserted in Series one packs at the rate of one in five, this 60-card set features color player photos in a design similar to the inaugural 1989 Upper Deck series. The backs carry a photo of that player's previous Upper Deck card. A 10th Anniversary Ballot Card was inserted one in four packs which allowed the collector to vote for the players they wanted to see in the 1999 Upper Deck tenth anniversary series.

Nm-Mt Ex-Mt
COMPLETE SET (60) 120.00 36.00
*RETAIL: .4X TO .1X BASIC 10TH ANN
RETAIL DISTRIBUTED AS FACTORY SET
1 Greg Maddux 5.00 1.50
2 Mike Mussina 2.00 .60
3 Roger Clemens 6.00 1.80
4 Hideo Nomo 3.00 .90
5 David Cone 1.25 .35
6 Tom Glavine 2.00 .60
7 Andy Pettitte 2.00 .60
8 Jimmy Key 1.25 .35
9 Randy Johnson 3.00 .90
10 Dennis Eckersley 1.25 .35
11 Lee Smith 1.25 .35
12 John Franco 1.25 .35
13 Randy Myers 1.25 .35
14 Mike Piazza 5.00 1.50
15 Ivan Rodriguez 3.00 .90
16 Todd Hundley 1.25 .35
17 Sandy Alomar Jr. 1.25 .35
18 Frank Thomas 3.00 .90
19 Rafael Palmeiro 2.00 .60
20 Mark McGwire 8.00 2.40
21 Mo Vaughn 1.25 .35
22 Fred McGriff 2.00 .60
23 Andres Galarraga 1.25 .35
24 Mark Grace 2.00 .60
25 Jeff Bagwell 2.00 .60
26 Roberto Alomar 2.00 .60
27 Chuck Knoblauch 1.25 .35
28 Ryne Sandberg 5.00 1.50
29 Eric Young 1.25 .35
30 Craig Biggio 2.00 .60
31 Carlos Baerga 1.25 .35
32 Robin Ventura 1.25 .35
33 Matt Williams 1.25 .35
34 Wade Boggs 2.00 .60
35 Dean Palmer 1.25 .35
36 Chipper Jones 3.00 .90
37 Vinny Castilla 1.25 .35
38 Ken Caminiti 1.25 .35
39 Omar Vizquel 2.00 .60
40 Cal Ripken 10.00 3.00
41 Derek Jeter 8.00 2.40
42 Alex Rodriguez 5.00 1.50
43 Barry Larkin 2.00 .60
44 Mark Grudzielanek 1.25 .35
45 Albert Belle 1.25 .35
46 Manny Ramirez 2.00 .60
47 Jose Canseco 3.00 .90
48 Ken Griffey Jr. 5.00 1.50
49 Juan Gonzalez 2.00 .60
50 Kenny Lofton 1.25 .35
51 Sammy Sosa 5.00 1.50
52 Larry Walker 2.00 .60
53 Gary Sheffield 1.25 .35
54 Rickey Henderson 3.00 .90
55 Tony Gwynn 4.00 1.20
56 Barry Bonds 8.00 2.40
57 Paul Molitor 2.00 .60
58 Edgar Martinez 2.00 .60
59 Chili Davis 1.25 .35
60 Eddie Murray 3.00 .90

1998 Upper Deck A Piece of the Action 1

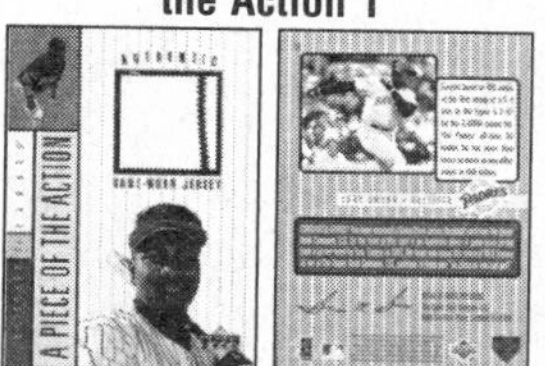

Randomly inserted in first series packs at the rate of one in 2,500, cards from this set feature color photos of top players with pieces of actual game worn jerseys and/or game used bats embedded in the cards.

Nm-Mt Ex-Mt
1 Jay Buhner Bat 25.00 7.50
2 Tony Gwynn Bat 50.00 15.00
3 Tony Gwynn Jersey 50.00 15.00
4 Todd Hollandsworth Bat 15.00 4.50
5 T.Hollandsworth Jersey 15.00 4.50
6 Greg Maddux Jersey 60.00 18.00
7 Alex Rodriguez Bat 60.00 18.00
8 Alex Rodriguez Jersey 60.00 18.00
9 Gary Sheffield Bat 25.00 7.50
10 Gary Sheffield Jersey 25.00 7.50

1998 Upper Deck A Piece of the Action 2

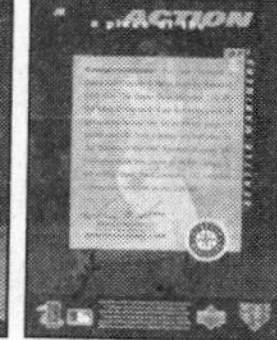

Randomly seeded into second series packs at a rate of 1:2500, each of these four different cards features pieces of both game-used bats and jerseys incorporated into the design of the card. According to information provided on the media release, only 225 of each card was produced. The cards are numbered by the player's initials.

Nm-Mt Ex-Mt
AJ Andruw Jones 40.00 12.00
GS Gary Sheffield 40.00 12.00
JB Jay Buhner 40.00 12.00
RA Roberto Alomar 60.00 18.00

1998 Upper Deck A Piece of the Action 3

Randomly seeded into third series packs, each of these cards featured a jersey swatch embedded on the card. The portion of the bat which was in series two is now just a design element. Ken Griffey, Jr. signed 24 of these cards and they were inserted into the packs as well.

Nm-Mt Ex-Mt
GRIFFEY AU PRINT RUN 24 #'d CARDS
NO GRIFFEY AU PRICE DUE TO SCARCITY
BG Ben Grieve/200 25.00 7.50
JC Jose Cruz Jr./200 25.00 7.50
KG Ken Griffey Jr./300 120.00 36.00
TL Travis Lee/200 25.00 7.50
KGS Ken Griffey Jr. AU/24

1998 Upper Deck All-Star Credentials

Randomly inserted in packs at a rate of one in nine, this 30-card insert set features players who have the best chance of appearing in future All-Star games.

Nm-Mt Ex-Mt
COMPLETE SET (30) 100.00 30.00
AS1 Ken Griffey Jr. 5.00 1.50
AS2 Travis Lee 1.25 .35
AS3 Ben Grieve 1.25 .35
AS4 Jose Cruz Jr. 1.25 .35
AS5 Andruw Jones 1.25 .35
AS6 Craig Biggio 2.00 .60
AS7 Hideo Nomo 3.00 .90
AS8 Cal Ripken 10.00 3.00
AS9 Jaret Wright 1.25 .35
AS10 Mark McGwire 8.00 2.40
AS11 Derek Jeter 8.00 2.40
AS12 Scott Rolen 3.00 .90
AS13 Jeff Bagwell 2.00 .60
AS14 Manny Ramirez 2.00 .60
AS15 Alex Rodriguez 5.00 1.50
AS16 Chipper Jones 3.00 .90
AS17 Larry Walker 2.00 .60
AS18 Barry Bonds 8.00 2.40
AS19 Tony Gwynn 4.00 1.20
AS20 Mike Piazza 5.00 1.50
AS21 Roger Clemens 6.00 1.80
AS22 Greg Maddux 5.00 1.50
AS23 Jim Thome 3.00 .90
AS24 Tino Martinez 2.00 .60
AS25 Nomar Garciaparra 5.00 1.50
AS26 Juan Gonzalez 2.00 .60
AS27 Kenny Lofton 1.25 .35
AS28 Randy Johnson 3.00 .90
AS29 Todd Helton 2.00 .60
AS30 Frank Thomas 3.00 .90

1998 Upper Deck Amazing Greats

Randomly inserted in Series one packs, this 30-card set features color photos of amazing players printed on a hi-tech plastic card. Only 2000 of this set were produced and are sequentially numbered.

Nm-Mt Ex-Mt
COMPLETE SET (30) 400.00 120.00
*DIE CUTS: 1X TO 2.5X BASIC AMAZING
DIE CUT PRINT RUN 250 SERIAL #'d SETS
RANDOM INSERTS IN SER.1 PACKS
AG1 Ken Griffey Jr. 12.00 3.60
AG2 Derek Jeter 20.00 6.00
AG3 Alex Rodriguez 12.00 3.60
AG4 Paul Molitor 5.00 1.50
AG5 Jeff Bagwell 5.00 1.50
AG6 Larry Walker 5.00 1.50
AG7 Kenny Lofton 3.00 .90
AG8 Cal Ripken 25.00 7.50
AG9 Juan Gonzalez 5.00 1.50
AG10 Chipper Jones 8.00 2.40
AG11 Greg Maddux 12.00 3.60
AG12 Roberto Alomar 5.00 1.50
AG13 Mike Piazza 12.00 3.60
AG14 Andres Galarraga 3.00 .90
AG15 Barry Bonds 20.00 6.00
AG16 Andy Pettitte 5.00 1.50
AG17 Nomar Garciaparra 12.00 3.60
AG18 Tino Martinez 5.00 1.50
AG19 Tony Gwynn 10.00 3.00
AG20 Frank Thomas 8.00 2.40
AG21 Roger Clemens 15.00 4.50
AG22 Sammy Sosa 12.00 3.60
AG23 Jose Cruz Jr. 3.00 .90
AG24 Manny Ramirez 5.00 1.50
AG25 Mark McGwire 20.00 6.00
AG26 Randy Johnson 8.00 2.40
AG27 Mo Vaughn 3.00 .90
AG28 Gary Sheffield 3.00 .90
AG29 Andruw Jones 3.00 .90
AG30 Albert Belle 3.00 .90

1998 Upper Deck Blue Chip Prospects

Randomly inserted in Series two packs, this 30-card set features color photos of some of the league's most impressive prospects printed on die-cut acetate cards. Only 2,000 of each card were produced.

Nm-Mt Ex-Mt
COMPLETE SET (30) 250.00 75.00
BC1 Nomar Garciaparra 25.00 7.50
BC2 Scott Rolen 15.00 4.50
BC3 Jason Dickson 4.00 1.20
BC4 Darin Erstad 6.00 1.80
BC5 Brad Fullmer 4.00 1.20
BC6 Jaret Wright 4.00 1.20
BC7 Justin Thompson 4.00 1.20
BC8 Matt Morris 6.00 1.80
BC9 Fernando Tatis 4.00 1.20
BC10 Alex Rodriguez 25.00 7.50
BC11 Todd Helton 10.00 3.00
BC12 Andy Pettitte 10.00 3.00
BC13 Jose Cruz Jr. 4.00 1.20
BC14 Mark Kotsay 4.00 1.20
BC15 Derek Jeter 40.00 12.00
BC16 Paul Konerko 6.00 1.80
BC17 Todd Dunwoody 4.00 1.20
BC18 Vladimir Guerrero 15.00 4.50
BC19 Miguel Tejada 6.00 1.80
BC20 Chipper Jones 15.00 4.50
BC21 Kevin Orie 4.00 1.20
BC22 Juan Encarnacion 4.00 1.20
BC23 Brian Rose 4.00 1.20
BC24 Livan Hernandez 4.00 1.20
BC25 Andruw Jones 6.00 1.80
BC26 Brian Giles 6.00 1.80
BC27 Brett Tomko 4.00 1.20
BC28 Jose Guillen 6.00 1.80
BC29 Aaron Boone 6.00 1.80
BC30 Ben Grieve 4.00 1.20

1998 Upper Deck Clearly Dominant

Randomly inserted in Series two packs, this 30-card set features color head photos of top players with a black-and-white action shot in the background printed on Light F/X plastic stock. Only 250 sequentially numbered sets were produced.

Nm-Mt Ex-Mt
CD1 Mark McGwire 40.00 12.00
CD2 Derek Jeter 40.00 12.00
CD3 Alex Rodriguez 25.00 7.50
CD4 Paul Molitor 10.00 3.00
CD5 Jeff Bagwell 10.00 3.00
CD6 Ivan Rodriguez 15.00 4.50
CD7 Kenny Lofton 6.00 1.80
CD8 Cal Ripken 50.00 15.00
CD9 Albert Belle 6.00 1.80
CD10 Chipper Jones 15.00 4.50
CD11 Gary Sheffield 6.00 1.80
CD12 Roberto Alomar 10.00 3.00
CD13 Mo Vaughn 6.00 1.80
CD14 Andres Galarraga 6.00 1.80
CD15 Nomar Garciaparra 25.00 7.50
CD16 Randy Johnson 15.00 4.50
CD17 Mike Mussina 10.00 3.00
CD18 Greg Maddux 25.00 7.50
CD19 Tony Gwynn 20.00 6.00
CD20 Frank Thomas 15.00 4.50
CD21 Roger Clemens 30.00 9.00
CD22 Dennis Eckersley 6.00 1.80
CD23 Juan Gonzalez 10.00 3.00
CD24 Tino Martinez 10.00 3.00
CD25 Andruw Jones 6.00 1.80
CD26 Larry Walker 10.00 3.00
CD27 Ken Caminiti 6.00 1.80
CD28 Mike Piazza 25.00 7.50
CD29 Barry Bonds 40.00 12.00
CD30 Ken Griffey Jr. 25.00 7.50

1998 Upper Deck Destination Stardom

Randomly inserted in packs at a rate of one in five, this 60-card insert set features color action photos of today's star potential placed in a diamond-cut center with four colored corners. The cards are foil enhanced and die-cut.

Nm-Mt Ex-Mt
COMPLETE SET (60) 100.00 30.00
DS1 Travis Lee 1.00 .30
DS2 Nomar Garciaparra 6.00 1.80
DS3 Alex Gonzalez 1.00 .30
DS4 Richard Hidalgo 1.00 .30
DS5 Jaret Wright 1.00 .30
DS6 Mike Kinkade 4.00 1.20
DS7 Matt Morris 1.50 .45
DS8 Gary Matthews Jr. 4.00 1.20
DS9 Brett Tomko 1.00 .30
DS10 Todd Helton 2.50 .75
DS11 Scott Elarton 1.00 .30
DS12 Scott Rolen 4.00 1.20
DS13 Jose Cruz Jr. 1.00 .30
DS14 Jarrod Washburn 1.00 .30
DS15 Sean Casey 1.50 .45
DS16 Magglio Ordonez 8.00 2.40
DS17 Gabe Alvarez 1.00 .30
DS18 Todd Dunwoody 1.00 .30
DS19 Kevin Witt 1.00 .30
DS20 Ben Grieve 1.00 .30
DS21 Daryle Ward 1.00 .30
DS22 Matt Clement 1.00 .30
DS23 Carlton Loewer 1.00 .30
DS24 Javier Vazquez 1.50 .45
DS25 Paul Konerko 1.50 .45
DS26 Preston Wilson 1.50 .45
DS27 Wes Helms 1.00 .30
DS28 Derek Jeter 10.00 3.00
DS29 Corey Koskie 4.00 1.20
DS30 Russell Branyan 1.00 .30
DS31 Vladimir Guerrero 4.00 1.20
DS32 Ryan Christenson 1.50 .45
DS33 Carlos Lee 4.00 1.20
DS34 Dave Dellucci 2.50 .75
DS35 Bruce Chen 1.00 .30
DS36 Ricky Ledee 1.00 .30
DS37 Ron Wright 1.00 .30
DS38 Derrek Lee 1.50 .45
DS39 Miguel Tejada 1.50 .45
DS40 Brad Fullmer 1.00 .30
DS41 Rich Butler 1.00 .30
DS42 Chris Carpenter 1.00 .30
DS43 Alex Rodriguez 6.00 1.80
DS44 Darron Ingram 1.50 .45
DS45 Kerry Wood 4.00 1.20
DS46 Jason Varitek 4.00 1.20
DS47 Ramon Hernandez 1.00 .30
DS48 Aaron Boone 1.50 .45
DS49 Juan Encarnacion 1.00 .30
DS50 A.J. Hinch 1.00 .30
DS51 Mike Lowell 6.00 1.80
DS52 Fernando Tatis 1.00 .30
DS53 Jose Guillen 1.50 .45
DS54 Mike Caruso 1.00 .30
DS55 Carl Pavano 2.50 .45
DS56 Chris Clemons 1.00 .30
DS57 Mark L. Johnson 1.00 .30
DS58 Ken Cloude 1.00 .30
DS59 Rolando Arrojo 4.00 1.20
DS60 Mark Kotsay 1.00 .30

1998 Upper Deck Griffey Home Run Chronicles

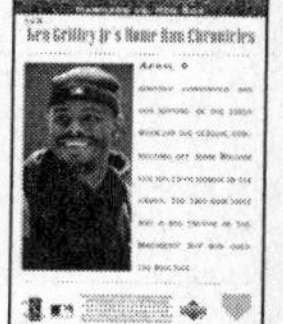

Randomly inserted in first and second series packs at the rate of one in nine, this 56-card set features color photos of Ken Griffey Jr.'s 56

home runs of the 1997 season. The fronts of the Series one inserts have photos and a brief headline of each homer. The backs all have the same photo and more details about each homer. The cards are notated on the back with what date each homer was hit. Series two inserts feature game-dated photos from the actual games in which the homers were hit.

	Nm-Mt	Ex-Mt
COMPLETE SET (56)	100.00	30.00
COMMON GRIFFEY (1-56)	2.00	.60

1998 Upper Deck National Pride

Randomly inserted in Series one packs at the rate of one in 23, this 42-card set features color photos of some of the league's great players from countries other than the United States printed on die-cut rainbow foil cards. The backs carry player information.

	Nm-Mt	Ex-Mt
NP1 Dave Nilsson	5.00	1.50
NP2 Larry Walker	8.00	2.40
NP3 Edgar Renteria	5.00	1.50
NP4 Jose Canseco	12.00	3.60
NP5 Rey Ordonez	5.00	1.50
NP6 Rafael Palmeiro	8.00	2.40
NP7 Livan Hernandez	5.00	1.50
NP8 Andruw Jones	5.00	1.50
NP9 Manny Ramirez	8.00	2.40
NP10 Sammy Sosa	20.00	6.00
NP11 Raul Mondesi	5.00	1.50
NP12 Moises Alou	5.00	1.50
NP13 Pedro Martinez	12.00	3.60
NP14 Vladimir Guerrero	12.00	3.60
NP15 Chili Davis	5.00	1.50
NP16 Hideo Nomo	12.00	3.60
NP17 Hideki Irabu	5.00	1.50
NP18 S.Hasegawa	5.00	1.50
NP19 Takashi Kashiwada	6.00	1.80
NP20 Chan Ho Park	5.00	1.50
NP21 Fernando Valenzuela	5.00	1.50
NP22 Vinny Castilla	5.00	1.50
NP23 Armando Reynoso	5.00	1.50
NP24 Karim Garcia	5.00	1.50
NP25 Marvin Benard	5.00	1.50
NP26 Mariano Rivera	8.00	2.40
NP27 Juan Gonzalez	8.00	2.40
NP28 Roberto Alomar	8.00	2.40
NP29 Ivan Rodriguez	12.00	3.60
NP30 Carlos Delgado	5.00	1.50
NP31 Bernie Williams	8.00	2.40
NP32 Edgar Martinez	8.00	2.40
NP33 Frank Thomas	12.00	3.60
NP34 Barry Bonds	30.00	9.00
NP35 Mike Piazza	20.00	6.00
NP36 Chipper Jones	12.00	3.60
NP37 Cal Ripken	40.00	12.00
NP38 Alex Rodriguez	20.00	6.00
NP39 Ken Griffey Jr.	20.00	6.00
NP40 Andres Galarraga	5.00	1.50
NP41 Omar Vizquel	8.00	2.40
NP42 Ozzie Guillen	5.00	1.50

1998 Upper Deck Power Deck Audio Griffey

In an effort to premier their new Power Deck Audio technology, Upper Deck created three special Ken Griffey Jr. cards (blue, green and silver backgrounds), each of which contained the same five minute interview with the Mariner's superstar. These cards were randomly seeded exclusively into test packs comprising only 10 percent of the total first series 1998 Upper Deck print run. The seeding ratios are as follows: blue 1:8, green 1:100 and silver 1:2400. Each test issue box contained a clear CD disc for which the card could be placed upon for playing on any common CD player. To play the card, the center hole had to be punched out. Prices below are for Mint unpunched cards. Punched out cards trade at twenty-five percent of the listed values.

	Nm-Mt	Ex-Mt
1 Ken Griffey Jr. Blue	2.00	.60
2 Ken Griffey Jr. Green	12.00	3.60
3 Ken Griffey Jr. Silver	40.00	12.00

1998 Upper Deck Prime Nine

Randomly inserted in Series two packs at the rate of one in five, this 60-card set features color photos of the current most popular players printed on premium silver card stock.

	Nm-Mt	Ex-Mt
COMPLETE SET (60)	100.00	30.00
COMMON GRIFFEY (1-7)	2.00	.60
COMMON PIAZZA (8-14)	2.00	.60
COMMON THOMAS (15-21)	1.25	.35
COMMON MCGWIRE (22-28)	3.00	.90
COMMON RIPKEN (29-35)	4.00	1.20
COMMON GONZALEZ (36-42)	.75	.23
COMMON GWYNN (43-49)	2.00	.60
COMMON BONDS (50-55)	3.00	.90
COMMON MADDUX (56-60)	2.00	.60

1998 Upper Deck Retrospectives

Randomly inserted in series three packs at a rate of one in 24, this 30-card insert set takes a look back at the unforgettable careers of some of baseball's most valuable contributors. The fronts feature a color action photo from each player's rookie season.

	Nm-Mt	Ex-Mt
1 Dennis Eckersley	3.00	.90
2 Rickey Henderson	8.00	2.40
3 Harold Baines	3.00	.90
4 Cal Ripken	25.00	7.50
5 Tony Gwynn	10.00	3.00
6 Wade Boggs	5.00	1.50
7 Orel Hershiser	3.00	.90
8 Joe Carter	3.00	.90
9 Roger Clemens	15.00	4.50
10 Barry Bonds	20.00	6.00
11 Mark McGwire	20.00	6.00
12 Greg Maddux	12.00	3.60
13 Fred McGriff	5.00	1.50
14 Rafael Palmeiro	5.00	1.50
15 Craig Biggio	5.00	1.50
16 Brady Anderson	3.00	.90
17 Randy Johnson	8.00	2.40
18 Gary Sheffield	3.00	.90
19 Albert Belle	3.00	.90
20 Ken Griffey Jr.	12.00	3.60
21 Juan Gonzalez	5.00	1.50
22 Larry Walker	5.00	1.50
23 Tino Martinez	5.00	1.50
24 Frank Thomas	8.00	2.40
25 Jeff Bagwell	5.00	1.50
26 Kenny Lofton	3.00	.90
27 Mo Vaughn	3.00	.90
28 Mike Piazza	12.00	3.60
29 Alex Rodriguez	12.00	3.60
30 Chipper Jones	8.00	2.40

1998 Upper Deck Rookie Edition Preview

Randomly inserted in Upper Deck Series two packs at an approximate rate of one in six, this 10-card set features color photos of players who were top rookies. The backs carry player information.

	Nm-Mt	Ex-Mt
COMPLETE SET (10)	6.00	1.80
1 Nomar Garciaparra	2.00	.60
2 Scott Rolen	1.25	.35
3 Mark Kotsay	.50	.15
4 Todd Helton	.75	.23
5 Paul Konerko	.50	.15
6 Juan Encarnacion	.50	.15
7 Brad Fullmer	.50	.15
8 Miguel Tejada	.50	.15
9 Richard Hidalgo	.50	.15
10 Ben Grieve	.50	.15

1998 Upper Deck Tape Measure Titans

Randomly inserted in Series two packs at the rate of one in 23, this 30-card set features color photos of the league's most productive long-ball hitters printed on unique retro cards.

	Nm-Mt	Ex-Mt
COMPLETE SET (30)	150.00	45.00
*GOLD: .4X TO 1X BASIC TITAN		
GOLD: RANDOM IN RETAIL PACKS		
GOLD PRINT RUN 2667 SERIAL #'d SETS		
1 Mark McGwire	20.00	6.00
2 Andres Galarraga	3.00	.90
3 Jeff Bagwell	5.00	1.50
4 Larry Walker	5.00	1.50
5 Frank Thomas	8.00	2.40
6 Rafael Palmeiro	5.00	1.50
7 Nomar Garciaparra	12.00	3.60
8 Mo Vaughn	3.00	.90
9 Albert Belle	3.00	.90
10 Ken Griffey Jr.	12.00	3.60
11 Manny Ramirez	5.00	1.50
12 Jim Thome	8.00	2.40
13 Tony Clark	3.00	.90
14 Juan Gonzalez	5.00	1.50
15 Mike Piazza	12.00	3.60
16 Jose Canseco	8.00	2.40
17 Jay Buhner	3.00	.90
18 Alex Rodriguez	12.00	3.60
19 Jose Cruz Jr.	3.00	.90
20 Tino Martinez	5.00	1.50
21 Carlos Delgado	3.00	.90
22 Andruw Jones	3.00	.90
23 Chipper Jones	8.00	2.40
24 Fred McGriff	5.00	1.50
25 Matt Williams	3.00	.90
26 Sammy Sosa	12.00	3.60
27 Vinny Castilla	3.00	.90
28 Tim Salmon	5.00	1.50
29 Ken Caminiti	3.00	.90
30 Barry Bonds	20.00	6.00

1998 Upper Deck Unparalleled

Randomly inserted in series three hobby packs only at a rate of one in 72, this 20-card insert set features color action photos on a high-tech designed card.

	Nm-Mt	Ex-Mt
COMPLETE SET (20)	250.00	75.00
1 Ken Griffey Jr.	15.00	4.50
2 Travis Lee	4.00	1.20
3 Ben Grieve	4.00	1.20
4 Jose Cruz Jr.	4.00	1.20
5 Nomar Garciaparra	15.00	4.50
6 Hideo Nomo	10.00	3.00
7 Kenny Lofton	4.00	1.20
8 Cal Ripken	30.00	9.00
9 Roger Clemens	20.00	6.00
10 Mike Piazza	15.00	4.50
11 Jeff Bagwell	6.00	1.80
12 Chipper Jones	10.00	3.00
13 Greg Maddux	15.00	4.50
14 Randy Johnson	10.00	3.00
15 Alex Rodriguez	15.00	4.50
16 Barry Bonds	25.00	7.50
17 Frank Thomas	10.00	3.00
18 Juan Gonzalez	6.00	1.80
19 Tony Gwynn	12.00	3.60
20 Mark McGwire	25.00	7.50

1999 Upper Deck

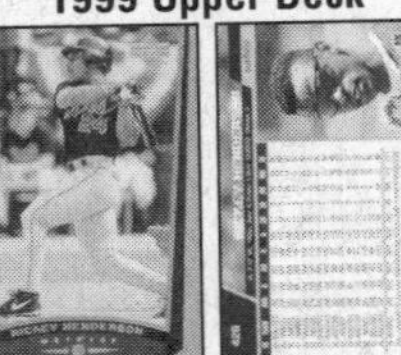

This 525-card set was distributed in two separate series. Series one packs contained cards 1-255 and series two contained 266-535. Cards 256-265 were never created. Subsets are as follows: Star Rookies (1-18, 266-292), Foreign Focus (229-246), Season Highlights Checklists (247-255, 527-535), and Arms Race '99 (518-526). The product was distributed in 10-card packs with a suggested retail price of $2.99. Though not confirmed by Upper Deck, it's widely believed by dealers that broke a good deal of product that these subset cards were slightly short-printed in comparison to other cards in the set. Notable Rookie Cards include Pat Burrell. 100 signed 1989 Upper Deck Ken Griffey Jr. RC's were randomly seeded into series one packs. These signed cards are real 89 RC's and they contain an additional diamond shaped hologram on back signifying that UD has verified Griffey's signature. Approximately 350 Babe Ruth A Piece of History cards were randomly seeded into all series one packs at a rate of one in 15,000. 50 Babe Ruth A Piece of History 500 Club bat cards were randomly seeded into second series packs. Pricing for these bat cards can be referenced under 1999 Upper Deck A Piece of History 500 Club.

	Nm-Mt	Ex-Mt
COMPLETE SET (525)	100.00	30.00
COMP. SERIES 1 (255)	60.00	18.00
COMP. SERIES 2 (270)	40.00	12.00
COMMON (19-255/293-535)	.30	.09
COMMON SER.1 SR (1-18)	.50	.15
COMMON (266-292)	.50	.15
1 Troy Glaus SR	.50	.15
2 Adrian Beltre SR	.75	.23
3 Matt Anderson SR	.50	.15
4 Eric Chavez SR	.50	.15
5 Jin Ho Cho SR	.50	.15
6 Robert Smith SR	.50	.15
7 George Lombard SR	.50	.15
8 Mike Kinkade SR	.50	.15
9 Seth Greisinger SR	.50	.15
10 J.D. Drew SR	.50	.15
11 Aramis Ramirez SR	.50	.15
12 Carlos Guillen SR	.50	.15
13 Justin Baughman SR	.50	.15
14 Jim Parque SR	.50	.15
15 Ryan Jackson SR	.50	.15
16 Ramon E.Martinez SR RC	.50	.15
17 Orlando Hernandez SR	.50	.15
18 Jeremy Giambi SR	.50	.15
19 Gary DiSarcina	.30	.09
20 Darin Erstad	.30	.09
21 Troy Glaus	.30	.09
22 Chuck Finley	.30	.09
23 Dave Hollins	.30	.09
24 Troy Percival	.30	.09
25 Tim Salmon	.50	.15
26 Brian Anderson	.30	.09
27 Jay Bell	.30	.09
28 Andy Benes	.30	.09
29 Brent Brede	.30	.09
30 David Dellucci	.30	.09
31 Karim Garcia	.30	.09
32 Travis Lee	.30	.09
33 Andres Galarraga	.30	.09
34 Ryan Klesko	.30	.09
35 Keith Lockhart	.30	.09
36 Kevin Millwood	.30	.09
37 Denny Neagle	.30	.09
38 John Smoltz	.50	.15
39 Michael Tucker	.30	.09
40 Walt Weiss	.30	.09
41 Dennis Martinez	.30	.09
42 Javy Lopez	.30	.09
43 Brady Anderson	.30	.09
44 Harold Baines	.30	.09
45 Mike Bordick	.30	.09
46 Roberto Alomar	.50	.15
47 Scott Erickson	.30	.09
48 Mike Mussina	.50	.15
49 Cal Ripken	2.50	.75
50 Darren Bragg	.30	.09
51 Dennis Eckersley	.30	.09
52 Nomar Garciaparra	1.25	.35
53 Scott Hatteberg	.30	.09
54 Troy O'Leary	.30	.09
55 Bret Saberhagen	.30	.09
56 John Valentin	.30	.09
57 Rod Beck	.30	.09
58 Jeff Blauser	.30	.09
59 Brant Brown	.30	.09
60 Mark Clark	.30	.09
61 Mark Grace	.50	.15
62 Kevin Tapani	.30	.09
63 Henry Rodriguez	.30	.09
64 Mike Cameron	.30	.09
65 Mike Caruso	.30	.09
66 Ray Durham	.30	.09
67 Jaime Navarro	.30	.09
68 Magglio Ordonez	.30	.09
69 Mike Sirotka	.30	.09
70 Sean Casey	.30	.09
71 Barry Larkin	.50	.15
72 Jon Nunnally	.30	.09
73 Paul Konerko	.30	.09
74 Chris Stynes	.30	.09
75 Brett Tomko	.30	.09
76 Dmitri Young	.30	.09
77 Sandy Alomar Jr.	.30	.09
78 Bartolo Colon	.30	.09
79 Travis Fryman	.30	.09
80 Brian Giles	.30	.09
81 David Justice	.30	.09
82 Omar Vizquel	.50	.15
83 Jaret Wright	.30	.09
84 Jim Thome	.75	.23
85 Charles Nagy	.30	.09
86 Pedro Astacio	.30	.09
87 Todd Helton	.50	.15
88 Darryl Kile	.30	.09
89 Mike Lansing	.30	.09
90 Neifi Perez	.30	.09
91 John Thomson	.30	.09
92 Larry Walker	.50	.15
93 Tony Clark	.30	.09
94 Deivi Cruz	.30	.09
95 Damion Easley	.30	.09
96 Brian L.Hunter	.30	.09
97 Todd Jones	.30	.09
98 Brian Moehler	.30	.09
99 Gabe Alvarez	.30	.09
100 Craig Counsell	.30	.09
101 Cliff Floyd	.30	.09
102 Livan Hernandez	.30	.09
103 Andy Larkin	.30	.09
104 Derrek Lee	.30	.09
105 Brian Meadows	.30	.09
106 Moises Alou	.30	.09
107 Sean Berry	.30	.09
108 Craig Biggio	.50	.15
109 Ricky Gutierrez	.30	.09
110 Mike Hampton	.30	.09
111 Jose Lima	.30	.09
112 Billy Wagner	.30	.09
113 Hal Morris	.30	.09
114 Johnny Damon	.50	.15
115 Jeff King	.30	.09
116 Jeff Montgomery	.30	.09
117 Glendon Rusch	.30	.09
118 Larry Sutton	.30	.09
119 Bobby Bonilla	.30	.09
120 Jim Eisenreich	.30	.09
121 Eric Karros	.30	.09
122 Matt Luke	.30	.09
123 Ramon Martinez	.30	.09
124 Gary Sheffield	.30	.09
125 Eric Young	.30	.09
126 Charles Johnson	.30	.09
127 Jeff Cirillo	.30	.09
128 Marquis Grissom	.30	.09
129 Jeromy Burnitz	.30	.09
130 Bob Wickman	.30	.09
131 Scott Karl	.30	.09
132 Mark Loretta	.30	.09
133 Fernando Vina	.30	.09
134 Matt Lawton	.30	.09
135 Pat Meares	.30	.09
136 Eric Milton	.30	.09
137 Paul Molitor	.50	.15
138 David Ortiz	.50	.15
139 Todd Walker	.30	.09
140 Shane Andrews	.30	.09
141 Brad Fullmer	.30	.09
142 Vladimir Guerrero	.75	.23
143 Dustin Hermanson	.30	.09
144 Ryan McGuire	.30	.09
145 Ugueth Urbina	.30	.09
146 John Franco	.30	.09
147 Butch Huskey	.30	.09
148 Bobby Jones	.30	.09
149 John Olerud	.30	.09
150 Rey Ordonez	.30	.09
151 Mike Piazza	1.25	.35
152 Hideo Nomo	.75	.23
153 Masato Yoshii	.30	.09
154 Derek Jeter	2.00	.60
155 Chuck Knoblauch	.30	.09
156 Paul O'Neill	.50	.15
157 Andy Pettitte	.50	.15
158 Mariano Rivera	.50	.15
159 Darryl Strawberry	.30	.09
160 David Wells	.30	.09
161 Jorge Posada	.50	.15
162 Ramiro Mendoza	.30	.09
163 Miguel Tejada	.30	.09
164 Ryan Christenson	.30	.09
165 Rickey Henderson	.75	.23
166 A.J. Hinch	.30	.09
167 Ben Grieve	.30	.09
168 Kenny Rogers	.30	.09
169 Matt Stairs	.30	.09
170 Bob Abreu	.30	.09
171 Rico Brogna	.30	.09
172 Doug Glanville	.30	.09
173 Mike Grace	.30	.09
174 Desi Relaford	.30	.09
175 Scott Rolen	.75	.23
176 Jose Guillen	.30	.09
177 Francisco Cordova	.30	.09
178 Al Martin	.30	.09
179 Jason Schmidt	.30	.09
180 Turner Ward	.30	.09
181 Kevin Young	.30	.09
182 Mark McGwire	2.00	.60
183 Delino DeShields	.30	.09
184 Eli Marrero	.30	.09
185 Tom Lampkin	.30	.09
186 Ray Lankford	.30	.09
187 Willie McGee	.30	.09
188 Matt Morris UER	.30	.09
Career strikeout totals are wrong		
189 Andy Ashby	.30	.09
190 Kevin Brown	.50	.15
191 Ken Caminiti	.30	.09
192 Trevor Hoffman	.30	.09
193 Wally Joyner	.30	.09
194 Greg Vaughn	.30	.09
195 Danny Darwin	.30	.09
196 Shawn Estes	.30	.09
197 Orel Hershiser	.30	.09
198 Jeff Kent	.30	.09
199 Bill Mueller	.30	.09
200 Robb Nen	.30	.09
201 J.T. Snow	.30	.09
202 Ken Cloude	.30	.09
203 Russ Davis	.30	.09
204 Jeff Fassero	.30	.09
205 Ken Griffey Jr.	1.25	.35
206 Shane Monahan	.30	.09
207 David Segui	.30	.09
208 Dan Wilson	.30	.09
209 Wilson Alvarez	.30	.09
210 Wade Boggs	.50	.15
211 Miguel Cairo	.30	.09
212 Bubba Trammell	.30	.09
213 Quinton McCracken	.30	.09
214 Paul Sorrento	.30	.09
215 Kevin Stocker	.30	.09
216 Will Clark	.75	.23
217 Rusty Greer	.30	.09
218 Rick Helling	.30	.09
219 Mark McLemore	.30	.09
220 Ivan Rodriguez	.75	.23
221 John Wetteland	.30	.09
222 Jose Canseco	.75	.23
223 Roger Clemens	1.50	.45
224 Carlos Delgado	.30	.09
225 Darrin Fletcher	.30	.09
226 Alex Gonzalez	.30	.09
227 Jose Cruz Jr.	.30	.09
228 Shannon Stewart	.30	.09
229 Rolando Arrojo FF	.30	.09
230 Livan Hernandez FF	.30	.09
231 Orlando Hernandez FF	.30	.09
232 Raul Mondesi FF	.30	.09
233 Moises Alou FF	.30	.09
234 Pedro Martinez FF	.75	.23
235 Sammy Sosa FF	1.25	.35
236 Vladimir Guerrero FF	.75	.23
237 Bartolo Colon FF	.30	.09
238 Miguel Tejada FF	.30	.09
239 Ismael Valdes FF	.30	.09
240 Mariano Rivera FF	.50	.15
241 Jose Cruz Jr. FF	.30	.09
242 Juan Gonzalez FF	.50	.15
243 Ivan Rodriguez FF	.75	.23
244 Sandy Alomar Jr. FF	.30	.09
245 Roberto Alomar FF	.50	.15
246 Magglio Ordonez FF	.30	.09
247 Kerry Wood SH CL	.50	.15
248 Mark McGwire SH CL	2.00	.60
249 David Wells SH CL	.30	.09
250 Rolando Arrojo SH CL	.30	.09
251 Ken Griffey Jr. SH CL	1.25	.35
252 T.Hoffman SH CL	.30	.09
253 Travis Lee SH CL	.30	.09
254 R.Alomar SH CL	.30	.09
255 Sammy Sosa SH CL	1.25	.35
266 Pat Burrell SR RC	1.50	.45
267 S.Hillenbrand SR RC	1.00	.30
268 Robert Fick SR	.50	.15
269 Roy Halladay SR	.50	.15
270 Ruben Mateo SR	.50	.15
271 Bruce Chen SR	.50	.15
272 Angel Pena SR	.50	.15
273 Michael Barrett SR	.50	.15
274 Kevin Witt SR	.50	.15
275 Damon Minor SR	.50	.15
276 Ryan Minor SR	.50	.15
277 A.J. Pierzynski SR	.50	.15
278 A.J. Burnett SR RC	1.00	.30
279 Dermal Brown SR	.50	.15
280 Joe Lawrence SR	.50	.15
281 Derrick Gibson SR	.50	.15
282 Carlos Febles SR	.50	.15
283 Chris Haas SR	.50	.15
284 Cesar King SR	.50	.15
285 Calvin Pickering SR	.50	.15
286 Mitch Meluskey SR	.50	.15
287 Carlos Beltran SR	.75	.23
288 Ron Belliard SR	.50	.15
289 Jerry Hairston Jr. SR	.50	.15
290 F.Seguignol SR	.50	.15
291 Kris Benson SR	.50	.15
292 C.Hutchinson SR RC	.50	.15
293 Jarrod Washburn	.30	.09
294 Jason Dickson	.30	.09

295 Mo Vaughn .30 .09
296 Garret Anderson .30 .09
297 Jim Edmonds .30 .09
298 Ken Hill .30 .09
299 Shigetoshi Hasegawa .30 .09
300 Todd Stottlemyre .30 .09
301 Randy Johnson .75 .23
302 Omar Daal .30 .09
303 Steve Finley .30 .09
304 Matt Williams .30 .09
305 Danny Klassen .30 .09
306 Tony Batista .30 .09
307 Brian Jordan .30 .09
308 Greg Maddux 1.25 .35
309 Chipper Jones .75 .23
310 Bret Boone .30 .09
311 Ozzie Guillen .30 .09
312 John Rocker .30 .09
313 Tom Glavine .50 .15
314 Andruw Jones .30 .09
315 Albert Belle .30 .09
316 Charles Johnson .30 .09
317 Will Clark .75 .23
318 B.J. Surhoff .30 .09
319 Delino DeShields .30 .09
320 Heathcliff Slocumb .30 .09
321 Sidney Ponson .30 .09
322 Juan Guzman .30 .09
323 Reggie Jefferson .30 .09
324 Mark Portugal .30 .09
325 Tim Wakefield .30 .09
326 Jason Varitek .50 .15
327 Jose Offerman .30 .09
328 Pedro Martinez .75 .23
329 Trot Nixon .30 .09
330 Kerry Wood .75 .23
331 Sammy Sosa 1.25 .35
332 Glenallen Hill .30 .09
333 Gary Gaetti .30 .09
334 Mickey Morandini .30 .09
335 Benito Santiago .30 .09
336 Jeff Blauser .30 .09
337 Frank Thomas .75 .23
338 Paul Konerko .30 .09
339 Jaime Navarro .30 .09
340 Carlos Lee .30 .09
341 Brian Simmons .30 .09
342 Mark Johnson .30 .09
343 Jeff Abbott .30 .09
344 Steve Avery .30 .09
345 Mike Cameron .30 .09
346 Michael Tucker .30 .09
347 Greg Vaughn .30 .09
348 Hal Morris .30 .09
349 Pete Harnisch .30 .09
350 Denny Neagle .30 .09
351 Manny Ramirez .50 .15
352 Roberto Alomar .50 .15
353 Dwight Gooden .30 .09
354 Kenny Lofton .30 .09
355 Mike Jackson .30 .09
356 Charles Nagy .30 .09
357 Enrique Wilson .30 .09
358 Russ Branyan .30 .09
359 Richie Sexson .30 .09
360 Vinny Castilla .30 .09
361 Dante Bichette .30 .09
362 Kirt Manwaring .30 .09
363 Darryl Hamilton .30 .09
364 Jamey Wright .30 .09
365 Curtis Leskanic .30 .09
366 Jeff Reed .30 .09
367 Bobby Higginson .30 .09
368 Justin Thompson .30 .09
369 Brad Ausmus .30 .09
370 Dean Palmer .30 .09
371 Gabe Kapler .30 .09
372 Juan Encarnacion .30 .09
373 Karim Garcia .30 .09
374 Alex Gonzalez .30 .09
375 Braden Looper .30 .09
376 Preston Wilson .30 .09
377 Todd Dunwoody .30 .09
378 Alex Fernandez .30 .09
379 Mark Kotsay .30 .09
380 Matt Mantei .30 .09
381 Ken Caminiti .30 .09
382 Scott Elarton .30 .09
383 Jeff Bagwell .50 .15
384 Derek Bell .30 .09
385 Ricky Gutierrez .30 .09
386 Richard Hidalgo .30 .09
387 Shane Reynolds .30 .09
388 Carl Everett .30 .09
389 Scott Service .30 .09
390 Jeff Suppan .30 .09
391 Joe Randa .30 .09
392 Kevin Appier .30 .09
393 Shane Halter .30 .09
394 Chad Kreuter .30 .09
395 Mike Sweeney .30 .09
396 Kevin Brown .50 .15
397 Devon White .30 .09
398 Todd Hollandsworth .30 .09
399 Todd Hundley .30 .09
400 Chan Ho Park .30 .09
401 Mark Grudzielanek .30 .09
402 Raul Mondesi .30 .09
403 Ismael Valdes .30 .09
404 Rafael Roque RC .30 .09
405 Sean Berry .30 .09
406 Kevin Barker .30 .09
407 Dave Nilsson .30 .09
408 Geoff Jenkins .30 .09
409 Jim Abbott .50 .15
410 Bobby Hughes .30 .09
411 Corey Koskie .30 .09
412 Rick Aguilera .30 .09
413 LaTroy Hawkins .30 .09
414 Ron Coomer .30 .09
415 Denny Hocking .30 .09
416 Marty Cordova .30 .09
417 Terry Steinbach .30 .09
418 Rondell White .30 .09
419 Wilton Guerrero .30 .09
420 Shane Andrews .30 .09
421 Orlando Cabrera .30 .09
422 Carl Pavano .30 .09
423 Javier Vazquez .30 .09
424 Chris Widger .30 .09
425 Robin Ventura .30 .09
426 Rickey Henderson .75 .23
427 Al Leiter .30 .09
428 Bobby Jones .30 .09
429 Brian McRae .30 .09
430 Roger Cedeno .30 .09
431 Bobby Bonilla .30 .09
432 Edgardo Alfonzo .30 .09
433 Bernie Williams .50 .15
434 Ricky Ledee .30 .09
435 Chili Davis .30 .09
436 Tino Martinez .50 .15
437 Scott Brosius .30 .09
438 David Cone .30 .09
439 Joe Girardi .30 .09
440 Roger Clemens 1.50 .45
441 Chad Curtis .30 .09
442 Hideki Irabu .30 .09
443 Jason Giambi .30 .09
444 Scott Spiezio .30 .09
445 Tony Phillips .30 .09
446 Ramon Hernandez .30 .09
447 Mike Macfarlane .30 .09
448 Tom Candiotti .30 .09
449 Billy Taylor .30 .09
450 Bobby Estalella .30 .09
451 Curt Schilling .30 .09
452 Carlton Loewer .30 .09
453 Marlon Anderson .30 .09
454 Kevin Jordan .30 .09
455 Ron Gant .30 .09
456 Chad Ogea .30 .09
457 Abraham Nunez .30 .09
458 Jason Kendall .30 .09
459 Pat Meares .30 .09
460 Brant Brown .30 .09
461 Brian Giles .30 .09
462 Chad Hermansen .30 .09
463 Freddy Adrian Garcia .30 .09
464 Edgar Renteria .30 .09
465 Fernando Tatis .30 .09
466 Eric Davis .30 .09
467 Darren Bragg .30 .09
468 Donovan Osborne .30 .09
469 Manny Aybar .30 .09
470 Jose Jimenez .30 .09
471 Kent Mercker .30 .09
472 Reggie Sanders .30 .09
473 Ruben Rivera .30 .09
474 Tony Gwynn 1.00 .30
475 Jim Leyritz .30 .09
476 Chris Gomez .30 .09
477 Matt Clement .30 .09
478 Carlos Hernandez .30 .09
479 Sterling Hitchcock .30 .09
480 Ellis Burks .30 .09
481 Barry Bonds 2.00 .60
482 Marvin Benard .30 .09
483 Kirk Rueter .30 .09
484 F.P. Santangelo .30 .09
485 Stan Javier .30 .09
486 Jeff Kent .30 .09
487 Alex Rodriguez 1.25 .35
488 Tom Lampkin .30 .09
489 Jose Mesa .30 .09
490 Jay Buhner .30 .09
491 Edgar Martinez .50 .15
492 Butch Huskey .30 .09
493 John Mabry .30 .09
494 Jamie Moyer .30 .09
495 Roberto Hernandez .30 .09
496 Tony Saunders .30 .09
497 Fred McGriff .50 .15
498 Dave Martinez .30 .09
499 Jose Canseco .75 .23
500 Rolando Arrojo .30 .09
501 Esteban Yan .30 .09
502 Juan Gonzalez .50 .15
503 Rafael Palmeiro .50 .15
504 Aaron Sele .30 .09
505 Royce Clayton .30 .09
506 Todd Zeile .30 .09
507 Tom Goodwin .30 .09
508 Lee Stevens .30 .09
509 Esteban Loaiza .30 .09
510 Joey Hamilton .30 .09
511 Homer Bush .30 .09
512 Willie Greene .30 .09
513 Shawn Green .30 .09
514 David Wells .30 .09
515 Kelvim Escobar .30 .09
516 Tony Fernandez .30 .09
517 Pat Hentgen .30 .09
518 Mark McGwire AR 1.00 .30
519 Ken Griffey Jr. AR .75 .23
520 Sammy Sosa AR .75 .23
521 Juan Gonzalez AR .30 .09
522 J.D. Drew AR .30 .09
523 Chipper Jones AR .50 .15
524 Alex Rodriguez AR .75 .23
525 Mike Piazza AR .75 .23
526 N.Garciaparra AR .75 .23
527 Mark McGwire SH CL 1.00 .30
528 Sammy Sosa SH CL .75 .23
529 Scott Brosius SH CL .30 .09
530 Cal Ripken SH CL 1.25 .35
531 Barry Bonds SH CL .75 .23
532 Roger Clemens SH CL .75 .23
533 Ken Griffey Jr. SH CL .75 .23
534 Alex Rodriguez SH CL .75 .23
535 Curt Schilling SH CL .30 .09
NNO Ken Griffey Jr. 800.00 240.00
1989 AU/100

1999 Upper Deck Exclusives Level 1

This 525-card set is a hobby only parallel version of the base set. Each card is sequentially numbered to 100 on back. In addition, Bronze foil fronts make them easy to differentiate from their silver foiled basic issue brethren. As is the case with the basic set, cards 256-265 were never printed due to a numbering error at the manufacturer.

Nm-Mt Ex-Mt
*STARS: 10X TO 25X BASIC CARDS..
*SER.1 STAR ROOK: 4X TO 10X BASIC SR
*SER.2 STAR ROOK: 6X TO 15X BASIC SR

1999 Upper Deck 10th Anniversary Team

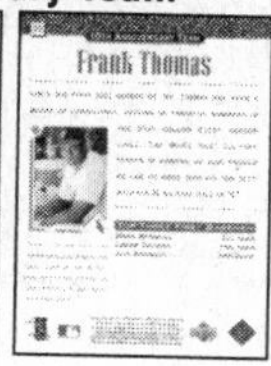

Randomly inserted in first series packs at the rate of one in four, this 30-card set features color photos of collectors' favorite players selected for this special All-Star team.

Nm-Mt Ex-Mt
COMPLETE SET (30) 50.00 15.00
*DOUBLES: 1.25X TO 3X BASIC 10TH ANN.
DOUBLES RANDOM INSERTS IN SER.1 PACKS
DOUBLES PRINT RUN 4000 SERIAL #'d SETS
*TRIPLES: 8X TO 20X BASIC 10TH ANN
TRIPLES RANDOM INSERTS IN SER.1 PACKS
TRIPLES PRINT RUN 100 SERIAL #'d SETS
HR'S RANDOM INSERTS IN SER.1 PACKS
HOME RUN PRINT RUN 1 SERIAL #'d SET
HR'S NOT PRICED DUE TO SCARCITY
X1 Mike Piazza 2.50 .75
X2 Mark McGwire 4.00 1.20
X3 Roberto Alomar 1.00 .30
X4 Chipper Jones 1.50 .45
X5 Cal Ripken 5.00 1.50
X6 Ken Griffey Jr. 2.50 .75
X7 Barry Bonds 4.00 1.20
X8 Tony Gwynn 2.00 .60
X9 Nolan Ryan 6.00 1.80
X10 Randy Johnson 1.50 .45
X11 Dennis Eckersley .60 .18
X12 Ivan Rodriguez 1.50 .45
X13 Frank Thomas 1.50 .45
X14 Craig Biggio 1.00 .30
X15 Wade Boggs 1.00 .30
X16 Alex Rodriguez 2.50 .75
X17 Albert Belle .60 .18
X18 Juan Gonzalez 1.00 .30
X19 Rickey Henderson 1.50 .45
X20 Greg Maddux 2.50 .75
X21 Tom Glavine 1.00 .30
X22 Randy Myers .60 .18
X23 Sandy Alomar Jr. .60 .18
X24 Jeff Bagwell 1.00 .30
X25 Derek Jeter 4.00 1.20
X26 Matt Williams .60 .18
X27 Kenny Lofton .60 .18
X28 Sammy Sosa 2.50 .75
X29 Larry Walker 1.00 .30
X30 Roger Clemens 3.00 .90

1999 Upper Deck A Piece of History

This limited edition set features photos of Babe Ruth along with a bat chip from an actual game-used Louisville Slugger swung by him during the late 20's. Approximately 350 cards were made and seeded into packs at a rate of 1:15,000. Another insert card incorporates both a "cut" signature of Ruth along with a piece of his game-used bat. Only three of these cards were produced.

Nm-Mt Ex-Mt
B.RUTH AU RANDOM IN SER.1 PACKS
B.RUTH AU PRINT RUN 3 #'d CARDS
PHLC Babe Ruth AU/3
PH Babe Ruth 600.00 180.00

1999 Upper Deck A Piece of History 500 Club

During the 1999 season, Upper Deck inserted into various products these cards which are cut up bats from all except one of the members of the 500 homer club. Mark McGwire asked that one of his bats not be included in this set, thus there was no Mark McGwire card in this grouping (until 2003 when McGwire signed a deal with Upper Deck). With the exception of Babe Ruth, approximately 350 of each card was produced. Only 50 Babe Ruth's were made. The cards were released in the following products: 1999 SP Authentic: Ernie Banks; 1999 SP Signature: Mel Ott; 1999 SPx: Willie Mays, 1999 UD Choice: Eddie Murray; 1999 UD Ionix: Frank Robinson; 1999 Upper Deck 2: Babe Ruth; 1999 Upper Deck Century Legends: Jimmie Foxx; 1999 Upper Deck Challengers for 70: Harmon Killebrew; 1999 Upper Deck HoloGrFx: Eddie Mathews and Willie McCovey; 1999 Upper Deck MVP: Mike Schmidt; 1999 Upper Deck Ovation: Mickey Mantle: 1999 Upper Deck Retro: Ted Williams; 2000 Black Diamond: Reggie Jackson; 2000 Upper Deck 1: Hank Aaron.

Nm-Mt Ex-Mt
BR Babe Ruth/50
EB Ernie Banks 150.00 45.00
EM Eddie Mathews 150.00 45.00
EM Eddie Murray 150.00 45.00
FR Frank Robinson 120.00 36.00
HA Hank Aaron 250.00 75.00
HK Harmon Killebrew 150.00 45.00
JF Jimmie Foxx 200.00 60.00
MM Mickey Mantle 500.00 150.00
MO Mel Ott 150.00 45.00
MS Mike Schmidt 150.00 45.00
RJ Reggie Jackson 120.00 36.00
TW Ted Williams 250.00 75.00
WM Willie Mays 250.00 75.00
WM Willie McCovey 100.00 30.00
XX Instant Winner Card

1999 Upper Deck A Piece of History 500 Club Autographs

As part of the Upper Deck A Piece of History 500 Club Autograph promotion, Upper Deck had most of the living members of the 500 homer club sign a number of cards which matched their uniform number. On some of the players, the cards are not priced due to scarcity. Each card is serial numbered on the front.

Nm-Mt Ex-Mt
EBAU Ernie Banks/14
EMAU Eddie Mathews/41 800.00 240.00
FRAU Frank Robinson/20
HAAU Hank Aaron/44 1200.00 350.00
HKAU Harmon Killebrew/3
MSAU Mike Schmidt/20
RJAU Reggie Jackson/44 600.00 180.00
TWAU Ted Williams/9
WMAU Willie Mays/24
WMAU Willie McCovey/44 800.00 240.00

1999 Upper Deck Crowning Glory

Randomly inserted in first series packs at the rate of one in 23, this three-card set features color photos of players who reached major milestones during the '98 MLB season and printed on double sided cards.

Nm-Mt Ex-Mt
COMPLETE SET (3) 60.00 18.00
*DOUBLES: .6X TO 1.5X BASIC CROWN
DOUBLES RANDOM INSERTS IN SER.1 PACKS
DOUBLES PRINT RUN 1000 SERIAL #'d SETS
*TRIPLES: 4X TO 10X BASIC CROWN
TRIPLES RANDOM INSERTS IN SER.1 PACKS
TRIPLES PRINT RUN 25 SERIAL #'d SETS
HR'S RANDOM INSERTS IN SER.1 PACKS
HOME RUNS PRINT RUN 1 SERIAL #'d SET
HOME RUNS NOT PRICED DUE TO SCARCITY
CG1 Roger Clemens 15.00 4.50
Kerry Wood
CG2 Mark McGwire 20.00 6.00
Barry Bonds
CG3 Ken Griffey Jr. 15.00 4.50
Mark McGwire

1999 Upper Deck Forte

Randomly inserted in series two packs at the rate of one in 23, this 30-card set features color photos of the most collectible superstars captured on super premium cards with extensive rainbow foil coverage. Three limited parallel sets were also produced and randomly inserted into Series two packs. Forte Doubles was serially numbered to 2000; Forte Triples, to 100; and Forte Quadruples, to 10.

Nm-Mt Ex-Mt
COMPLETE SET (30) 200.00 60.00
*DOUBLES: .6X TO 1.5X BASIC FORTE
DOUBLES RANDOM INSERTS IN SER.2 PACKS
DOUBLES PRINT RUN 2000 SERIAL #'d SETS
*TRIPLES: 2X TO 5X BASIC FORTE
TRIPLES RANDOM INSERTS IN SER.2 PACKS
TRIPLES PRINT RUN 100 SERIAL #'d SETS
QUADS RANDOM INSERTS IN SER.2 PACKS
QUADRUPLES NOT PRICED DUE TO SCARCITY
F1 Darin Erstad 2.50 .75
F2 Troy Glaus 2.50 .75
F3 Mo Vaughn 2.50 .75
F4 Greg Maddux 10.00 3.00
F5 Andres Galarraga 2.50 .75
F6 Chipper Jones 6.00 1.80
F7 Cal Ripken 20.00 6.00
F8 Albert Belle 2.50 .75
F9 Nomar Garciaparra 10.00 3.00
F10 Sammy Sosa 10.00 3.00
F11 Kerry Wood 6.00 1.80
F12 Frank Thomas 6.00 1.80
F13 Jim Thome 6.00 1.80
F14 Jeff Bagwell 4.00 1.20
F15 Vladimir Guerrero 6.00 1.80
F16 Mike Piazza 10.00 3.00
F17 Derek Jeter 15.00 4.50
F18 Ben Grieve 2.50 .75
F19 Eric Chavez 1.25 .35
F20 Scott Rolen 6.00 1.80
F21 Mark McGwire 15.00 4.50
F22 J.D. Drew 1.25 .35
F23 Tony Gwynn 8.00 2.40
F24 Barry Bonds 15.00 4.50
F25 Alex Rodriguez 10.00 3.00
F26 Ken Griffey Jr. 10.00 3.00
F27 Ivan Rodriguez 6.00 1.80
F28 Juan Gonzalez 4.00 1.20
F29 Roger Clemens 12.00 3.60
F30 Andruw Jones 2.50 .75

1999 Upper Deck Game Jersey

This set consists of 23 cards inserted in first and second series packs. Hobby packs contained Game Jersey hobby cards (signified in the listings with an H after the player's name) at a rate of 1:288. Hobby and retail packs contained much scarcer Game Jersey hobby/retail cards (signified with an H/R after the player's name in the listings below) at a rate of 1:2500. Each card features a piece of an actual game worn jersey. Five additional cards were signed by the athlete and serial numbered by hand to the player's respective jersey number. These rare signed Game Jersey cards are priced below but not considered part of the complete set.

Nm-Mt Ex-Mt
AB Adrian Beltre H1 40.00 12.00
AR Alex Rodriguez HR1 50.00 15.00
BF Brad Fullmer H2 15.00 4.50
BG Ben Grieve H1 15.00 4.50
BT Bubba Trammell H2 15.00 4.50
CJ Charles Johnson HR1 25.00 7.50
CJ Chipper Jones H2 40.00 12.00
DE Darin Erstad H1 25.00 7.50
EC Eric Chavez H2 25.00 7.50
FT Frank Thomas HR2 40.00 12.00
GM Greg Maddux HR2 50.00 15.00
IR Ivan Rodriguez H1 40.00 12.00
JD J.D. Drew H2 25.00 7.50
JG Juan Gonzalez HR1 40.00 12.00
JR K.Griffey Jr. HR2 50.00 15.00
KG K.Griffey Jr. H1 50.00 15.00
KW Kerry Wood HR1 40.00 12.00
MP Mike Piazza HR1 50.00 15.00
MR Manny Ramirez H2 40.00 12.00
NRA Nolan Ryan 80.00 24.00
Astros H2
NRB Nolan Ryan 80.00 24.00
Rangers HR2
SS Sammy Sosa H2 50.00 15.00
TH Todd Helton H2 40.00 12.00
TGW Tony Gwynn H2 40.00 12.00
TL Travis Lee H1 15.00 4.50
JDS J.Drew AU/8 H2
JRS Ken Griffey Jr. AU/24 HR2
KGAU Ken Griffey Jr. AU/24 H1
KWAU Kerry Wood AU/34 300.00 90.00
HR1
NRAS Nolan Ryan Astros 800.00 240.00
AU/34, H2

1999 Upper Deck Immaculate Perception

Randomly inserted in Series one packs at the rate of one in 23, this 27-card set features top player photos printed on unique, foil-enhanced cards.

Nm-Mt Ex-Mt
COMPLETE SET (27) 250.00 75.00
*DOUBLES: .75X TO 2X BASIC IMM.PERC.
DOUBLES RANDOM INSERTS IN SER.1 PACKS
DOUBLES PRINT RUN 1000 SERIAL #'d SETS
*TRIPLES: 5X TO 12X BASIC IMM.PERC.
TRIPLES RANDOM INSERTS IN SER.1 PACKS
TRIPLES PRINT RUN 25 SERIAL #'d SETS
HR'S RANDOM INSERTS IN SER.1 PACKS
HOME RUNS PRINT RUN 1 SERIAL #'d SET
HOME RUNS NOT PRICED DUE TO SCARCITY
I1 Jeff Bagwell 5.00 1.50
I2 Craig Biggio 5.00 1.50
I3 Barry Bonds 20.00 6.00
I4 Roger Clemens 15.00 4.50
I5 Jose Cruz Jr. 3.00 .90
I6 Nomar Garciaparra 12.00 3.60
I7 Tony Clark 3.00 .90
I8 Ben Grieve 3.00 .90
I9 Ken Griffey Jr. 12.00 3.60
I10 Tony Gwynn 10.00 3.00
I11 Randy Johnson 8.00 2.40
I12 Chipper Jones 8.00 2.40
I13 Travis Lee 3.00 .90
I14 Kenny Lofton 3.00 .90
I15 Greg Maddux 12.00 3.60
I16 Mark McGwire 20.00 6.00
I17 Hideo Nomo 8.00 2.40
I18 Mike Piazza 12.00 3.60
I19 Manny Ramirez 5.00 1.50
I20 Cal Ripken 25.00 7.50
I21 Alex Rodriguez 12.00 3.60
I22 Scott Rolen 8.00 2.40
I23 Frank Thomas 8.00 2.40
I24 Kerry Wood 8.00 2.40
I25 Larry Walker 5.00 1.50
I26 Vinny Castilla 3.00 .90
I27 Derek Jeter 20.00 6.00

1999 Upper Deck Textbook Excellence

Inserted one every 23 second series packs, these cards offer information on the skills of some of the game's most fundamentally sound performers.

Nm-Mt Ex-Mt
COMPLETE SET (30) 50.00 15.00
*DOUBLES: 1.5X TO 4X BASIC TEXTBOOK
DOUBLES RANDOM INSERTS IN SER.2 PACKS
DOUBLES PRINT RUN 2000 SERIAL #'d SETS
*TRIPLES: 6X TO 15X BASIC TEXTBOOK
TRIPLES RANDOM INSERTS IN SER.2 PACKS
TRIPLES PRINT RUN 100 SERIAL #'d SETS
QUADS RANDOM INSERTS IN SER.2 PACKS
QUADRUPLES PRINT RUN 10 SERIAL #'d SETS
QUADRUPLES NOT PRICED DUE TO SCARCITY
T1 Mo Vaughn .75 .23
T2 Greg Maddux 3.00 .90
T3 Chipper Jones 2.00 .60
T4 Andruw Jones .75 .23
T5 Cal Ripken 6.00 1.80
T6 Albert Belle .75 .23
T7 Roberto Alomar 1.25 .35
T8 Nomar Garciaparra 3.00 .90
T9 Kerry Wood 2.00 .60
T10 Sammy Sosa 3.00 .90
T11 Greg Vaughn .75 .23
T12 Jeff Bagwell 1.25 .35
T13 Kevin Brown 1.25 .35
T14 Vladimir Guerrero 2.00 .60
T15 Mike Piazza 3.00 .90
T16 Bernie Williams 1.25 .35
T17 Derek Jeter 5.00 1.50
T18 Ben Grieve .75 .23
T19 Eric Chavez .40 .12
T20 Scott Rolen 2.00 .60
T21 Mark McGwire 5.00 1.50
T22 David Wells .75 .23
T23 J.D. Drew .40 .12
T24 Tony Gwynn 2.50 .75
T25 Barry Bonds 5.00 1.50
T26 Alex Rodriguez 3.00 .90
T27 Ken Griffey Jr. 3.00 .90
T28 Juan Gonzalez 1.25 .35
T29 Ivan Rodriguez 2.00 .60
T30 Roger Clemens 4.00 1.20

1999 Upper Deck View to a Thrill

These cards, inserted one every seven second series packs feature special die-cuts and embossing and takes a new look at 30 of the best overall athletes in baseball.

Nm-Mt Ex-Mt
COMPLETE SET (30) 100.00 30.00
*DOUBLES: 1X TO 2.5X BASIC VIEW
DOUBLES RANDOM INSERTS IN SER.2 PACKS
DOUBLES PRINT RUN 2000 SERIAL #'d SETS
*TRIPLES: 4X TO 10X BASIC VIEW
TRIPLES RANDOM INSERTS IN SER.2 PACKS
TRIPLES PRINT RUN 100 SERIAL #'d SETS
QUADS RANDOM INSERTS IN SER.2 PACKS
QUADRUPLES PRINT RUN 10 SERIAL #'d SETS
QUADRUPLES NOT PRICED DUE TO SCARCITY
V1 Mo Vaughn 1.25 .35
V2 Darin Erstad 1.25 .35
V3 Travis Lee 1.25 .35
V4 Chipper Jones 3.00 .90
V5 Greg Maddux 5.00 1.50
V6 Gabe Kapler 1.25 .35
V7 Cal Ripken 10.00 3.00
V8 Nomar Garciaparra 5.00 1.50
V9 Kerry Wood 3.00 .90
V10 Frank Thomas 3.00 .90
V11 Manny Ramirez 2.00 .60
V12 Larry Walker 2.00 .60
V13 Tony Clark 1.25 .35
V14 Jeff Bagwell 2.00 .60
V15 Craig Biggio 2.00 .60
V16 Vladimir Guerrero 3.00 .90
V17 Mike Piazza 5.00 1.50
V18 Bernie Williams 2.00 .60
V19 Derek Jeter 8.00 2.40
V20 Ben Grieve 1.25 .35
V21 Eric Chavez .60 .18
V22 Scott Rolen 3.00 .90
V23 Mark McGwire 8.00 2.40
V24 Tony Gwynn 4.00 1.20
V25 Barry Bonds 8.00 2.40
V26 Ken Griffey Jr. 5.00 1.50
V27 Alex Rodriguez 5.00 1.50
V28 J.D. Drew .60 .18
V29 Juan Gonzalez 2.00 .60
V30 Roger Clemens 6.00 1.80

1999 Upper Deck Wonder Years

Randomly inserted in Series one packs at the rate of one in seven, this 30-card set features color photos of top stars.

Nm-Mt Ex-Mt
COMPLETE SET (30) 80.00 24.00
*DOUBLES: 1X TO 2.5X BASIC WONDER
DOUBLES RANDOM INSERTS IN SER.1 PACKS
DOUBLES PRINT RUN 2000 SERIAL #'d SETS
*TRIPLES: 8X TO 20X BASIC WONDER
TRIPLES RANDOM INSERTS IN SER.1 PACKS
TRIPLES PRINT RUN 50 SERIAL #'d SETS
HR'S RANDOM INSERTS IN SER.1 PACKS
HOME RUNS PRINT RUN 1 SERIAL #'d SET
HOME RUNS NOT PRICED DUE TO SCARCITY
W1 Kerry Wood 3.00 .90
W2 Travis Lee 1.25 .35
W3 Jeff Bagwell 2.00 .60
W4 Barry Bonds 8.00 2.40
W5 Roger Clemens 6.00 1.80
W6 Jose Cruz Jr. 1.25 .35
W7 Andres Galarraga 1.25 .35
W8 Nomar Garciaparra 5.00 1.50
W9 Juan Gonzalez 2.00 .60
W10 Ken Griffey Jr. 5.00 1.50
W11 Tony Gwynn 4.00 1.20
W12 Derek Jeter 8.00 2.40
W13 Randy Johnson 3.00 .90
W14 Andruw Jones 1.25 .35
W15 Chipper Jones 3.00 .90
W16 Kenny Lofton 1.25 .35
W17 Greg Maddux 5.00 1.50
W18 Tino Martinez 2.00 .60
W19 Mark McGwire 8.00 2.40
W20 Paul Molitor 2.00 .60
W21 Mike Piazza 5.00 1.50
W22 Manny Ramirez 2.00 .60
W23 Cal Ripken 10.00 3.00
W24 Alex Rodriguez 5.00 1.50
W25 Sammy Sosa 5.00 1.50
W26 Frank Thomas 3.00 .90
W27 Mo Vaughn 1.25 .35
W28 Larry Walker 2.00 .60
W29 Scott Rolen 3.00 .90
W30 Ben Grieve 1.25 .35

2000 Upper Deck

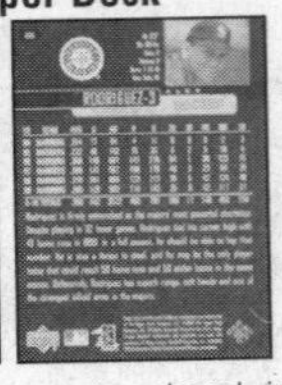

Upper Deck Series one was released in December, 1999 and offered 270 standard-size cards. The first series was distributed in 10 card packs with a SRP of $2.99 per pack. The second series was released in July, 2000 and offered 270 standard-size cards. The cards were issued in 24 pack boxes. Cards numbered 1-28 and 271-297 are Star Rookie subsets while cards numbered 262-270 and 532-540 feature 1999 season highlights and have checklists on back. Cards 523-531 feature the All-UD Team subset - a collection of top stars as selected by Upper Deck. Notable Rookie Cards include Kazuhiro Sasaki. Also, 350 1999 A Piece of History 500 Club Hank Aaron bat cards were randomly seeded into first series packs. In addition, Aaron signed and numbered 44 copies. Pricing for these bat cards can be referenced under 1999 Upper Deck A Piece of History 500 Club. Also, a selection of A Piece of History 3000 Club Hank Aaron memorabilia cards were randomly seeded into second series packs. 350 bat cards, 350 jersey cards, 100 hand-numbered, combination bat-jersey cards and forty-four hand-numbered, autographed, combination bat-jersey cards were produced. Pricing for these memorabilia cards can be referenced under 2000 Upper Deck A Piece of History 3000 Club.

Nm-Mt Ex-Mt
COMPLETE SET (540) 100.00 30.00
COMP. SERIES 1 (270) 50.00 15.00
COMP. SERIES 2 (270) 50.00 15.00
COMMON (28-270/298-540) .30 .09
COMMON (1-28/271-297) .50 .15
1 Rick Ankiel SR .75 .23
2 Vernon Wells SR .75 .23
3 Ryan Anderson SR .50 .15
4 Ed Yarnall SR .50 .15
5 Brian McNichol SR .50 .15
6 Ben Petrick SR .50 .15
7 Kip Wells SR .50 .15
8 Eric Munson SR .50 .15
9 Matt Riley SR .50 .15
10 Peter Bergeron SR .50 .15
11 Eric Gagne SR 3.00 .90
12 Ramon Ortiz SR .50 .15
13 Josh Beckett SR 1.25 .35
14 Alfonso Soriano SR 2.00 .60
15 Jorge Toca SR .50 .15
16 Buddy Carlyle SR .50 .15
17 Chad Hermansen SR .50 .15
18 Matt Perisho SR .50 .15
19 Tomokazu Ohka SR RC .75 .23
20 Jacque Jones SR .75 .23
21 Josh Paul SR .50 .15
22 Dermal Brown SR .50 .15
23 Adam Kennedy SR .50 .15
24 Chad Harville SR .50 .15
25 Calvin Murray SR .50 .15
26 Chad Meyers SR .50 .15
27 Brian Cooper SR .50 .15
28 Troy Glaus .30 .09
29 Ben Molina .30 .09
30 Troy Percival .30 .09
31 Ken Hill .30 .09
32 Chuck Finley .30 .09
33 Todd Greene .30 .09
34 Tim Salmon .50 .15
35 Gary DiSarcina .30 .09
36 Luis Gonzalez .30 .09
37 Tony Womack .30 .09
38 Omar Daal .30 .09
39 Randy Johnson .75 .23
40 Erubiel Durazo .30 .09
41 Jay Bell .30 .09
42 Steve Finley .30 .09
43 Travis Lee .30 .09
44 Greg Maddux 1.25 .35
45 Bret Boone .30 .09
46 Brian Jordan .30 .09
47 Kevin Millwood .30 .09
48 Odalis Perez .30 .09
49 Javy Lopez .30 .09
50 John Smoltz .50 .15
51 Bruce Chen .30 .09
52 Albert Belle .30 .09
53 Jerry Hairston Jr. .30 .09
54 Will Clark .75 .23
55 Sidney Ponson .30 .09
56 Charles Johnson .30 .09
57 Cal Ripken 2.50 .75
58 Ryan Minor .30 .09
59 Mike Mussina .50 .15
60 Tom Gordon .30 .09
61 Jose Offerman .30 .09
62 Trot Nixon .30 .09
63 Pedro Martinez .75 .23
64 John Valentin .30 .09
65 Jason Varitek .50 .15
66 Juan Pena .30 .09
67 Troy O'Leary .30 .09
68 Sammy Sosa 1.25 .35
69 Henry Rodriguez .30 .09
70 Kyle Farnsworth .30 .09
71 Glenallen Hill .30 .09
72 Lance Johnson .30 .09
73 Mickey Morandini .30 .09
74 Jon Lieber .30 .09
75 Kevin Tapani .30 .09
76 Carlos Lee .30 .09
77 Ray Durham .30 .09
78 Jim Parque .30 .09
79 Bob Howry .30 .09
80 Magglio Ordonez .30 .09
81 Paul Konerko .30 .09
82 Mike Caruso .30 .09
83 Chris Singleton .30 .09
84 Sean Casey .30 .09
85 Barry Larkin .50 .15
86 Pokey Reese .30 .09
87 Eddie Taubensee .30 .09
88 Scott Williamson .30 .09
89 Jason LaRue .30 .09
90 Aaron Boone .30 .09
91 Jeffrey Hammonds .30 .09
92 Omar Vizquel .50 .15
93 Manny Ramirez .50 .15
94 Kenny Lofton .30 .09
95 Jaret Wright .30 .09
96 Einar Diaz .30 .09
97 Charles Nagy .30 .09
98 David Justice .30 .09
99 Richie Sexson .30 .09
100 Steve Karsay .30 .09
101 Todd Helton .50 .15
102 Dante Bichette .30 .09
103 Larry Walker .50 .15
104 Pedro Astacio .30 .09
105 Neifi Perez .30 .09
106 Brian Bohanon .30 .09
107 Edgard Clemente .30 .09
108 Dave Veres .30 .09
109 Gabe Kapler .30 .09
110 Juan Encarnacion .30 .09
111 Jeff Weaver .30 .09
112 Damion Easley .30 .09
113 Justin Thompson .30 .09
114 Brad Ausmus .30 .09
115 Frank Catalanotto .30 .09
116 Todd Jones .30 .09
117 Preston Wilson .30 .09
118 Cliff Floyd .30 .09
119 Mike Lowell .30 .09
120 Antonio Alfonseca .30 .09
121 Alex Gonzalez .30 .09
122 Braden Looper .30 .09
123 Bruce Aven .30 .09
124 Richard Hidalgo .30 .09
125 Mitch Meluskey .30 .09
126 Jeff Bagwell .50 .15
127 Jose Lima .30 .09
128 Derek Bell .30 .09
129 Billy Wagner .30 .09
130 Shane Reynolds .30 .09
131 Moises Alou .30 .09
132 Carlos Beltran .50 .15
133 Carlos Febles .30 .09
134 Jermaine Dye .30 .09
135 Jeremy Giambi .30 .09
136 Joe Randa .30 .09
137 Jose Rosado .30 .09
138 Chad Kreuter .30 .09
139 Jose Vizcaino .30 .09
140 Adrian Beltre .50 .15
141 Kevin Brown .50 .15
142 Ismael Valdes .30 .09
143 Angel Pena .30 .09
144 Chan Ho Park .30 .09
145 Mark Grudzielanek .30 .09
146 Jeff Shaw .30 .09
147 Geoff Jenkins .30 .09
148 Jeromy Burnitz .30 .09
149 Hideo Nomo .75 .23
150 Ron Belliard .30 .09
151 Sean Berry .30 .09
152 Mark Loretta .30 .09
153 Steve Woodard .30 .09
154 Joe Mays .30 .09
155 Eric Milton .30 .09
156 Corey Koskie .30 .09
157 Ron Coomer .30 .09
158 Brad Radke .30 .09
159 Terry Steinbach .30 .09
160 Cristian Guzman .30 .09
161 Vladimir Guerrero .75 .23
162 Wilton Guerrero .30 .09
163 Michael Barrett .30 .09
164 Chris Widger .30 .09
165 Fernando Seguignol .30 .09
166 Ugueth Urbina .30 .09
167 Dustin Hermanson .30 .09
168 Kenny Rogers .30 .09
169 Edgardo Alfonzo .30 .09
170 Orel Hershiser .30 .09
171 Robin Ventura .30 .09
172 Octavio Dotel .30 .09
173 Rickey Henderson .75 .23
174 Roger Cedeno .30 .09
175 John Olerud .30 .09
176 Derek Jeter 2.00 .60
177 Tino Martinez .50 .15
178 Orlando Hernandez .30 .09
179 Chuck Knoblauch .30 .09
180 Bernie Williams .50 .15
181 Chili Davis .30 .09
182 David Cone .30 .09
183 Ricky Ledee .30 .09
184 Paul O'Neill .50 .15
185 Jason Giambi .30 .09
186 Eric Chavez .30 .09
187 Matt Stairs .30 .09
188 Miguel Tejada .30 .09
189 Olmedo Saenz .30 .09
190 Tim Hudson .30 .09
191 John Jaha .30 .09
192 Randy Velarde .30 .09
193 Rico Brogna .30 .09
194 Mike Lieberthal .30 .09
195 Marlon Anderson .30 .09
196 Bob Abreu .30 .09
197 Ron Gant .30 .09
198 Randy Wolf .30 .09
199 Desi Relaford .30 .09
200 Doug Glanville .30 .09
201 Warren Morris .30 .09
202 Kris Benson .30 .09
203 Kevin Young .30 .09
204 Brian Giles .30 .09
205 Jason Schmidt .30 .09
206 Ed Sprague .30 .09
207 Francisco Cordova .30 .09
208 Mark McGwire 2.00 .60
209 Jose Jimenez .30 .09
210 Fernando Tatis .30 .09
211 Kent Bottenfield .30 .09
212 Eli Marrero .30 .09
213 Edgar Renteria .30 .09
214 Joe McEwing .30 .09
215 J.D. Drew .30 .09
216 Tony Gwynn 1.00 .30
217 Gary Matthews Jr. .30 .09
218 Eric Owens .30 .09
219 Damian Jackson .30 .09
220 Reggie Sanders .30 .09
221 Trevor Hoffman .30 .09
222 Ben Davis .30 .09
223 Shawn Estes .30 .09
224 F.P. Santangelo .30 .09
225 Livan Hernandez .30 .09
226 Ellis Burks .30 .09
227 J.T. Snow .30 .09
228 Jeff Kent .30 .09
229 Robb Nen .30 .09
230 Marvin Benard .30 .09
231 Ken Griffey Jr. 1.25 .35
232 John Halama .30 .09
233 Gil Meche .30 .09
234 David Bell .30 .09
235 Brian Hunter .30 .09
236 Jay Buhner .30 .09
237 Edgar Martinez .50 .15
238 Jose Mesa .30 .09
239 Wilson Alvarez .30 .09
240 Wade Boggs .50 .15
241 Fred McGriff .50 .15
242 Jose Canseco .75 .23
243 Kevin Stocker .30 .09
244 Roberto Hernandez .30 .09
245 Bubba Trammell .30 .09
246 John Flaherty .30 .09
247 Ivan Rodriguez .75 .23
248 Rusty Greer .30 .09
249 Rafael Palmeiro .50 .15
250 Jeff Zimmerman .30 .09
251 Royce Clayton .30 .09
252 Todd Zeile .30 .09
253 John Wetteland .30 .09
254 Ruben Mateo .30 .09
255 Kelvim Escobar .30 .09
256 David Wells .30 .09
257 Shawn Green .30 .09
258 Homer Bush .30 .09
259 Shannon Stewart .30 .09
260 Carlos Delgado .30 .09
261 Roy Halladay .30 .09
262 Fernando Tatis SH CL .30 .09
263 Jose Jimenez SH CL .30 .09
264 Tony Gwynn SH CL .50 .15
265 Wade Boggs SH CL .30 .09
266 Cal Ripken SH CL 1.25 .35
267 David Cone SH CL .30 .09
268 Mark McGwire SH CL 1.25 .35
269 Pedro Martinez SH CL .50 .15
270 N. Garciaparra SH CL .75 .23
271 Nick Johnson SR .50 .15
272 Mark Quinn SR .50 .15
273 Roosevelt Brown SR .50 .15
274 Terrence Long SR .50 .15
275 Jason Marquis SR .50 .15
276 K.Sasaki SR RC 2.00 .60
277 Aaron Myette SR .50 .15
278 Danys Baez SR RC .75 .23
279 Travis Dawkins SR .50 .15
280 Mark Mulder SR .75 .23
281 Chris Haas SR .50 .15
282 Milton Bradley SR .75 .23
283 Brad Penny SR .50 .15
284 Rafael Furcal SR .75 .23
285 Luis Matos SR RC .75 .23
286 Victor Santos SR RC .75 .23
287 R.Washington SR RC .50 .15
288 Rob Bell SR .50 .15
289 Joe Crede SR .50 .15
290 Pablo Ozuna SR .50 .15
291 W.Serrano SR RC .50 .15
292 S-H. Lee SR RC .50 .15
293 C.Wakeland SR RC .50 .15
294 Luis Rivera SR RC .50 .15
295 Mike Lamb SR RC .75 .23
296 Wily Mo Pena SR .75 .23
297 Mike Meyers SR RC .75 .23
298 Mo Vaughn .30 .09
299 Darin Erstad .30 .09
300 Garret Anderson .30 .09
301 Tim Belcher .30 .09
302 Scott Spiezio .30 .09
303 Kent Bottenfield .30 .09
304 Orlando Palmeiro .30 .09
305 Jason Dickson .30 .09
306 Matt Williams .30 .09
307 Brian Anderson .30 .09
308 Hanley Frias .30 .09
309 Todd Stottlemyre .30 .09
310 Matt Mantei .30 .09
311 David Dellucci .30 .09
312 Armando Reynoso .30 .09
313 Bernard Gilkey .30 .09
314 Chipper Jones .75 .23
315 Tom Glavine .50 .15
316 Quilvio Veras .30 .09
317 Andruw Jones .30 .09
318 Bobby Bonilla .30 .09
319 Reggie Sanders .30 .09
320 Andres Galarraga .30 .09
321 George Lombard .30 .09
322 John Rocker .30 .09
323 Wally Joyner .30 .09
324 B.J. Surhoff .30 .09
325 Scott Erickson .30 .09
326 Delino DeShields .30 .09
327 Jeff Conine .30 .09
328 Mike Timlin .30 .09
329 Brady Anderson .30 .09
330 Mike Bordick .30 .09
331 Harold Baines .30 .09
332 Nomar Garciaparra 1.25 .35
333 Bret Saberhagen .30 .09
334 Ramon Martinez .30 .09
335 Donnie Sadler .30 .09
336 Wilton Veras .30 .09
337 Mike Stanley .30 .09
338 Brian Rose .30 .09
339 Carl Everett .30 .09
340 Tim Wakefield .30 .09
341 Mark Grace .50 .15
342 Kerry Wood .75 .23
343 Eric Young .30 .09
344 Jose Nieves .30 .09
345 Ismael Valdes .30 .09
346 Joe Girardi .30 .09
347 Damon Buford .30 .09
348 Ricky Gutierrez .30 .09
349 Frank Thomas .75 .23
350 Brian Simmons .30 .09
351 James Baldwin .30 .09
352 Brook Fordyce .30 .09
353 Jose Valentin .30 .09
354 Mike Sirotka .30 .09
355 Greg Norton .30 .09
356 Dante Bichette .30 .09
357 Deion Sanders .50 .15
358 Ken Griffey Jr. 1.25 .35
359 Denny Neagle .30 .09
360 Dmitri Young .30 .09
361 Pete Harnisch .30 .09
362 Michael Tucker .30 .09
363 Roberto Alomar .50 .15
364 Dave Roberts .30 .09
365 Jim Thome .75 .23
366 Bartolo Colon .30 .09
367 Travis Fryman .30 .09
368 Chuck Finley .30 .09
369 Russell Branyan .30 .09
370 Alex Ramirez .30 .09
371 Jeff Cirillo .30 .09
372 Jeffrey Hammonds .30 .09
373 Scott Karl .30 .09
374 Brent Mayne .30 .09
375 Tom Goodwin .30 .09
376 Jose Jimenez .30 .09
377 Rolando Arrojo .30 .09
378 Terry Shumpert .30 .09
379 Juan Gonzalez .50 .15
380 Bobby Higginson .30 .09
381 Tony Clark .30 .09
382 Dave Mlicki .30 .09
383 Deivi Cruz .30 .09
384 Brian Moehler .30 .09
385 Dean Palmer .30 .09
386 Luis Castillo .30 .09
387 Mike Redmond .30 .09
388 Alex Fernandez .30 .09
389 Brant Brown .30 .09
390 Dave Berg .30 .09
391 A.J. Burnett .30 .09
392 Mark Kotsay .30 .09
393 Craig Biggio .50 .15
394 Daryle Ward .30 .09
395 Lance Berkman .30 .09
396 Roger Cedeno .30 .09
397 Scott Elarton .30 .09
398 Octavio Dotel .30 .09
399 Ken Caminiti .30 .09
400 Johnny Damon .50 .15
401 Mike Sweeney .30 .09
402 Jeff Suppan .30 .09
403 Rey Sanchez .30 .09
404 Blake Stein .30 .09
405 Ricky Bottalico .30 .09
406 Jay Witasick .30 .09
407 Shawn Green .30 .09
408 Orel Hershiser .30 .09
409 Gary Sheffield .30 .09
410 Todd Hollandsworth .30 .09
411 Terry Adams .30 .09
412 Todd Hundley .30 .09
413 Eric Karros .30 .09
414 F.P. Santangelo .30 .09
415 Alex Cora .30 .09
416 Marquis Grissom .30 .09
417 Henry Blanco .30 .09
418 Jose Hernandez .30 .09
419 Kyle Peterson .30 .09
420 John Snyder RC .30 .09
421 Bob Wickman .30 .09
422 Jamey Wright .30 .09
423 Chad Allen .30 .09
424 Todd Walker .30 .09
425 J.C. Romero RC .30 .09
426 Butch Huskey .30 .09
427 Jacque Jones .30 .09
428 Matt Lawton .30 .09
429 Rondell White .30 .09
430 Jose Vidro .30 .09
431 Hideki Irabu .30 .09
432 Javier Vazquez .30 .09
433 Lee Stevens .30 .09
434 Mike Thurman .30 .09
435 Geoff Blum .30 .09
436 Mike Hampton .30 .09
437 Mike Piazza 1.25 .35
438 Al Leiter .30 .09
439 Derek Bell .30 .09
440 Armando Benitez .30 .09
441 Rey Ordonez .30 .09
442 Todd Zeile .30 .09
443 Roger Clemens 1.50 .45
444 Ramiro Mendoza .30 .09
445 Andy Pettitte .50 .15
446 Scott Brosius .30 .09

447 Mariano Rivera .50 .15
448 Jim Leyritz .30 .09
449 Jorge Posada .50 .15
450 Omar Olivares .30 .09
451 Ben Grieve .30 .09
452 A.J. Hinch .30 .09
453 Gil Heredia .30 .09
454 Kevin Appier .30 .09
455 Ryan Christenson .30 .09
456 Ramon Hernandez .30 .09
457 Scott Rolen .75 .23
458 Alex Arias .30 .09
459 Andy Ashby .30 .09
460 K.Jordan UER 474 .30 .09
461 Robert Person .30 .09
462 Paul Byrd .30 .09
463 Curt Schilling .30 .09
464 Mike Jackson .30 .09
465 Jason Kendall .30 .09
466 Pat Meares .30 .09
467 Bruce Aven .30 .09
468 Todd Ritchie .30 .09
469 Wil Cordero .30 .09
470 Aramis Ramirez .30 .09
471 Andy Benes .30 .09
472 Ray Lankford .30 .09
473 Fernando Vina .30 .09
474 Jim Edmonds .30 .09
475 Craig Paquette .30 .09
476 Pat Hentgen .30 .09
477 Darryl Kile .30 .09
478 Sterling Hitchcock .30 .09
479 Ruben Rivera .30 .09
480 Ryan Klesko .30 .09
481 Phil Nevin .30 .09
482 Woody Williams .30 .09
483 Carlos Hernandez .30 .09
484 Brian Meadows .30 .09
485 Bret Boone .30 .09
486 Barry Bonds 2.00 .60
487 Russ Ortiz .30 .09
488 Bobby Estalella .30 .09
489 Rich Aurilia .30 .09
490 Bill Mueller .30 .09
491 Joe Nathan .30 .09
492 Russ Davis .30 .09
493 John Olerud .30 .09
494 Alex Rodriguez 1.25 .35
495 Freddy Garcia .30 .09
496 Carlos Guillen .30 .09
497 Aaron Sele .30 .09
498 Brett Tomko .30 .09
499 Jamie Moyer .30 .09
500 Mike Cameron .30 .09
501 Vinny Castilla .30 .09
502 Gerald Williams .30 .09
503 Mike DiFelice .30 .09
504 Ryan Rupe .30 .09
505 Greg Vaughn .30 .09
506 Miguel Cairo .30 .09
507 Juan Guzman .30 .09
508 Jose Guillen .30 .09
509 Gabe Kapler .30 .09
510 Rick Helling .30 .09
511 David Segui .30 .09
512 Doug Davis .30 .09
513 Justin Thompson .30 .09
514 Chad Curtis .30 .09
515 Tony Batista .30 .09
516 Billy Koch .30 .09
517 Raul Mondesi .30 .09
518 Joey Hamilton .30 .09
519 Darrin Fletcher .30 .09
520 Brad Fullmer .30 .09
521 Jose Cruz Jr. .30 .09
522 Kevin Witt .30 .09
523 Mark McGwire AUT 1.00 .30
524 Roberto Alomar AUT .30 .09
525 Chipper Jones AUT .50 .15
526 Derek Jeter AUT 1.00 .30
527 Ken Griffey Jr. AUT .75 .23
528 Sammy Sosa AUT .75 .23
529 Manny Ramirez AUT .50 .15
530 Ivan Rodriguez AUT .50 .15
531 Pedro Martinez AUT .50 .15
532 Mariano Rivera CL .50 .15
533 Sammy Sosa CL .75 .23
534 Cal Ripken CL 1.25 .35
535 Vladimir Guerrero CL .50 .15
536 Tony Gwynn CL .50 .15
537 Mark McGwire CL 1.00 .30
538 Bernie Williams CL .30 .09
539 Pedro Martinez CL .50 .15
540 Ken Griffey Jr. CL .75 .23

2000 Upper Deck Exclusives Silver

This set parallels the regular Upper Deck set and cards were randomly seeded into packs. The cards feature coral and red borders and utilize silver foil stamping on front (instead of blue borders and bronze foil in the base set). In addition, each Exclusive Silver parallel is machine serial numbered to 100 on front.

Nm-Mt Ex-Mt
*STARS: 8X TO 20X BASIC CARDS
*SR NON-RC'S: 2.5X TO 6X BASIC SR
*SR RC'S: 4X TO 10X BASIC SR

2000 Upper Deck 2K Plus

Inserted one every 23 first series packs, these 12 cards feature some players who are expected to be stars in the beginning of the 21st century.

Nm-Mt Ex-Mt
COMPLETE SET (12) 60.00 18.00
*DIE CUTS: 2.5X TO 6X BASIC 2K PLUS
DIE CUTS RANDOM INSERTS IN SER.1 HOBBY
DIE CUTS PRINT RUN 100 SERIAL #'d SETS
GOLD DIE CUTS RANDOM IN SER.1 HOBBY
GOLD DIE CUT PRINT RUN 1 SERIAL #'d SET
GOLD DC NOT PRICED DUE TO SCARCITY
2K1 Ken Griffey Jr. 6.00 1.80
2K2 J.D. Drew 1.50 .45
2K3 Derek Jeter 10.00 3.00
2K4 Nomar Garciaparra 6.00 1.80
2K5 Pat Burrell 10.00 3.00
2K6 Ruben Mateo 1.50 .45
2K7 Carlos Beltran 2.50 .75
2K8 Vladimir Guerrero 4.00 1.20
2K9 Scott Rolen 4.00 1.20
2K10 Chipper Jones 4.00 1.20
2K11 Alex Rodriguez 6.00 1.80
2K12 Magglio Ordonez 1.50 .45

2000 Upper Deck A Piece of History 3000 Club

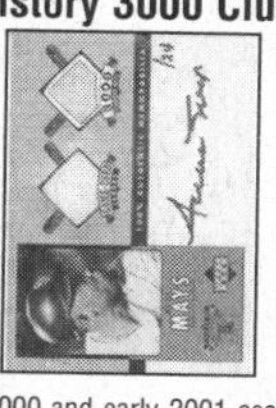

During the 2000 and early 2001 season, Upper Deck inserted a selection of memorabilia cards celebrating members of the 3000 hit club. Approximately 350 of each bat or jersey card was produced. In addition, a wide array of scarce, hand-numbered, autographed cards and combination memorabilia cards were made available. Complete print run information for these cards is provided in our checklist. The cards were released in the following products: 2000 SP Authentic: Tris Speaker and Paul Waner; 2000 SPx: Ty Cobb; 2000 UD Ionix: Roberto Clemente; 2000 Upper Deck 2: Hank Aaron; 2000 Upper Deck Gold Reserve: Al Kaline; 2000 Upper Deck Hitter's Club: Wade Boggs and Tony Gwynn; 2000 Upper Deck HoloGrFx: George Brett and Robin Yount; 2000 Upper Deck Legends: Paul Molitor and Carl Yastrzemski; 2000 Upper Deck MVP: Stan Musial; 2000 Upper Deck Ovation: Willie Mays; 2000 Upper Deck Pros and Prospects: Lou Brock and Rod Carew; 2000 Upper Deck Yankees Legends: Dave Winfield; 2001 Upper Deck: Eddie Murray and Cal Ripken. Exchange cards were seeded into packs for the following cards: Al Kaline Bat AU, Eddie Murray Bat AU, Cal Ripken Bat and Cal Ripken Bat-Jsy. The deadline to exchange the Kaline card was April 10th, 2001 and the Murray/Ripken cards was August 22nd, 2001.

Nm-Mt Ex-Mt
AK-B Al Kaline Bat/400 40.00 12.00
AK-BS Al Kaline Bat AU/6 EXCH
BG-B Wade Boggs 150.00 45.00
Tony Gwynn Bat/99
BY-B George Brett 200.00 60.00
Robin Yount
Bat/99
BY-BS George Brett
Robin Yount
Bat AU/10
BY-J George Brett 200.00 60.00
Robin Yount
Jersey/99
BY-JS George Brett
Robin Yount
Jersey AU/10
CR-B Cal Ripken 60.00 18.00
Bat/350 EXCH
CR-J Cal Ripken 60.00 18.00
Jersey/350
CR-JB Cal Ripken 200.00 60.00
Bat-Jsy/100
CR-JBS Cal Ripken
Bat-Jsy AU/8
CY-B Carl Yaz 40.00 12.00
Bat/350
CY-J Carl Yaz 50.00 15.00
Jersey/350
CY-JB Carl Yaz 120.00 36.00
Bat-Jsy/100
CY-JBS Carl Yaz
Bat-Jsy AU/8
DW-B Dave Winf. 15.00 4.50
Bat/350
DW-J Dave Winf 15.00 4.50
Jersey/350
DW-JB Dave Winf. 40.00 12.00
Bat-Jsy/100
DW-JBS Dave Winfield
Bat-Jsy AU/31
EM-B Eddie Murray 40.00 12.00
Bat/350
EM-J Eddie Murray 40.00 12.00
Jersey/350
EM-JB Eddie Murray 100.00 30.00
Bat-Jsy/100
EM-JBS Eddie Murray
Bat-Jsy AU/33 EXCH
GB-B George Brett 40.00 12.00
Bat/350
GB-J George Brett 40.00 12.00
Jersey/350
HA-B Hank Aaron 60.00 18.00
Bat/350
HA-BS Hank Aaron 1000.00 300.00
Bat-Jsy AU/44
HA-J Hank Aaron 80.00 24.00
Jersey/350
HA-JB Hank Aaron 200.00 60.00
Bat-Jsy/100
LB-B Lou Brock 25.00 7.50
Bat/350
LB-J Lou Brock 25.00 7.50
Jsy/350
LB-JB Lou Brock 60.00 18.00
Bat-Jsy/100
LB-JBS Lou Brock
Bat-Jsy AU/20
PM-B Paul Molitor 25.00 7.50
Bat/350
PW-B Paul Waner 50.00 15.00
Bat/350
PW-BC Paul Waner
Bat-Cut AU/5
RCA-B Rod Carew 25.00 7.50
Bat/350
RCA-J Rod Carew 25.00 7.50
Jsy/350
RCA-BJ Rod Carew 60.00 18.00
Bat-Jsy/100
RCA-JS Rod Carew
Bat-Jsy AU/30
RCL-B Roberto Clemente 120.00 36.00
Bat/350
RCL-C Roberto Clemente
Cut AU/4
RCL-BC Roberto Clemente
Bat-Cut AU/5
RY-B Robin Yount 25.00 7.50
Bat/350
RY-J Robin Yount 25.00 7.50
Jersey/350
SM-B Stan Musial 50.00 15.00
Bat/350
SM-J Stan Musial 60.00 18.00
Jersey/350
SM-JB Stan Musial 150.00 45.00
Bat-Jsy/100
SM-JBS Stan Musial
Bat-Jsy AU/6
TC-B Ty Cobb 150.00 45.00
Bat/350
TC-BC Ty Cobb
Bat-Cut AU/1
TC-C Ty Cobb
Cut AU/3
TG-B Tony Gwynn 40.00 12.00
Bat/350
TG-BC Tony Gwynn 150.00 45.00
Bat-Cap/50
TG-BS Tony Gwynn
Bat AU/19
TS-B Tris Speaker 100.00 30.00
Bat/350
TS-BC Tris Speaker
Bat-Cut AU/5
WB-B Wade Boggs 25.00 7.50
Bat/350
WB-BC Wade Boggs 100.00 30.00
Bat-Cap/50
WB-BS Wade Boggs
Bat AU/12
WM-B Willie Mays 60.00 18.00
Bat/300
WM-J Willie Mays 80.00 24.00
Jersey/350
WM-JB Willie Mays 250.00 75.00
Bat-Jsy/50
WM-JBS Willie Mays
Bat-Jsy AU/24

2000 Upper Deck Cooperstown Calling

Randomly inserted into Upper Deck Series two packs at one in 23, this 15-card insert features players that will be going to Cooperstown after they retire from baseball. Card backs carry a "CC" prefix.

Nm-Mt Ex-Mt
COMPLETE SET (15) 100.00 30.00
CC1 Roger Clemens 8.00 2.40
CC2 Cal Ripken 12.00 3.60
CC3 Ken Griffey Jr. 6.00 1.80
CC4 Mike Piazza 6.00 1.80
CC5 Tony Gwynn 5.00 1.50
CC6 Sammy Sosa 6.00 1.80
CC7 Jose Canseco 4.00 1.20
CC8 Larry Walker 2.50 .75
CC9 Barry Bonds 10.00 3.00
CC10 Greg Maddux 6.00 1.80
CC11 Derek Jeter 10.00 3.00
CC12 Mark McGwire 10.00 3.00
CC13 Randy Johnson 4.00 1.20
CC14 Frank Thomas 4.00 1.20
CC15 Jeff Bagwell 2.50 .75

2000 Upper Deck e-Card

Inserted as a two-pack box-topper in Upper Deck Series two, this six-card insert features cards that can be viewed over the Upper Deck website. Cards feature a serial number that is to be typed in a the Upper Deck website to reveal that card. Card backs carry an "E" prefix.

Nm-Mt Ex-Mt
COMPLETE SET (6) 8.00 2.40
E1 Ken Griffey Jr. 1.50 .45
E2 Alex Rodriguez 1.50 .45
E3 Cal Ripken Jr. 3.00 .90
E4 Jeff Bagwell .60 .18
E5 Barry Bonds 2.50 .75
E6 Manny Ramirez .60 .18

2000 Upper Deck eVolve Autograph

Lucky participants in Upper Deck's E-Card program received special upgraded E-Cards available by checking the UD website (www.upperdeck.com) and entering their basic E-Card serial code (printed on the front of each basic E-Card). When viewed on the Upper Deck website, if an autographed card of the depicted player appeared, the bearer of the base card could then exchange their basic E-Card and receive the signed upgrade via mail. Only 200 serial numbered E-Card Autograph sets were produced. Signed E-Cards all have an ES prefix on the card numbers.

Nm-Mt Ex-Mt
ES-1 Ken Griffey Jr. 100.00 30.00
ES-2 Alex Rodriguez 120.00 36.00
ES-3 Cal Ripken 150.00 45.00
ES-4 Jeff Bagwell 50.00 15.00
ES-5 Barry Bonds 250.00 75.00
ES-6 Manny Ramirez 50.00 15.00

2000 Upper Deck eVolve Game Jersey

Lucky participants in Upper Deck's E-Card program received special upgraded E-Cards available by checking the UD website (www.upperdeck.com) and entering their basic E-Card serial code (printed on the front of each basic E-Card). When viewed on the Upper Deck website, if a jersey card of the depicted player appeared, the bearer of the base card could then exchange their basic E-Card and receive the Game Jersey upgrade via mail. The cards closely parallel basic 2000 Game Jerseys that were distributed in first and second series packs except for the gold foil "e-volve" logo on front. Only 300 serial numbered E-Card Jersey sets were produced with each card being serial - numbered by hand in blue ink sharpie at the bottom right front corner. Unsigned E-Card Game Jerseys all have an EJ prefix on the card numbers.

Nm-Mt Ex-Mt
EJ-1 Ken Griffey Jr. 40.00 12.00
EJ-2 Alex Rodriguez 40.00 12.00
EJ-3 Cal Ripken 60.00 18.00
EJ-4 Jeff Bagwell 25.00 7.50
EJ-5 Barry Bonds 50.00 15.00
EJ-6 Manny Ramirez 25.00 7.50

2000 Upper Deck eVolve Game Jersey Autograph

Lucky participants in Upper Deck's E-Card program received special upgraded E-Cards available by checking the UD website (www.upperdeck.com) and entering their basic E-Card serial code (printed on the front of each basic E-Card). When viewed on the Upper Deck website, if an autographed card of the depicted player appeared, the bearer of the base card could then exchange their basic E-Card and receive the signed jersey upgrade via mail. A mere 50 serial numbered sets were produced. Signed jersey E-Cards all have an ESJ prefix on the card numbers.

Nm-Mt Ex-Mt
ESJ-1 Ken Griffey Jr. 120.00 36.00
ESJ-2 Alex Rodriguez 200.00 60.00
ESJ-3 Cal Ripken 250.00 75.00
ESJ-4 Jeff Bagwell 100.00 30.00
ESJ-5 Barry Bonds 400.00 120.00
ESJ-6 Manny Ramirez 100.00 30.00

2000 Upper Deck Faces of the Game

Inserted one every 11 first series packs, these 20 cards feature leading players captured by exceptional photography.

Nm-Mt Ex-Mt
COMPLETE SET (20) 80.00 24.00
*DIE CUTS: 3X TO 8X BASIC FACES 3.00 .90
DIE CUTS RANDOM INSERTS IN SER.1 HOBBY
DIE CUTS PRINT RUN 100 SERIAL #'d SETS
GOLD DIE CUTS RANDOM IN SER.1 HOBBY
GOLD DIE CUT PRINT RUN 1 SERIAL #'d SET
GOLD DC NOT PRICED DUE TO SCARCITY
F1 Ken Griffey Jr. 5.00 1.50
F2 Mark McGwire 8.00 2.40
F3 Sammy Sosa 5.00 1.50
F4 Alex Rodriguez 5.00 1.50
F5 Manny Ramirez 2.00 .60
F6 Derek Jeter 8.00 2.40
F7 Jeff Bagwell 2.00 .60
F8 Roger Clemens 6.00 1.80
F9 Scott Rolen 3.00 .90
F10 Tony Gwynn 4.00 1.20
F11 Nomar Garciaparra 5.00 1.50
F12 Randy Johnson 3.00 .90
F13 Greg Maddux 5.00 1.50
F14 Mike Piazza 5.00 1.50
F15 Frank Thomas 3.00 .90
F16 Cal Ripken 10.00 3.00
F17 Ivan Rodriguez 3.00 .90
F18 Mo Vaughn 1.25 .35
F19 Chipper Jones 3.00 .90
F20 Sean Casey 1.25 .35

2000 Upper Deck Five-Tool Talents

Randomly inserted into packs at one in 11, this 15-card insert features players that possess all of the tools needed to succeed in the Major Leagues. Card backs carry a "FT" prefix.

Nm-Mt Ex-Mt
COMPLETE SET (15) 30.00 9.00
FT1 Vladimir Guerrero 2.00 .60
FT2 Barry Bonds 5.00 1.50
FT3 Jason Kendall .75 .23
FT4 Derek Jeter 5.00 1.50
FT5 Ken Griffey Jr. 3.00 .90
FT6 Andruw Jones .75 .23
FT7 Bernie Williams 1.25 .35
FT8 Jose Canseco 2.00 .60
FT9 Scott Rolen 2.00 .60
FT10 Shawn Green .75 .23
FT11 Nomar Garciaparra 3.00 .90
FT12 Jeff Bagwell 1.25 .35
FT13 Larry Walker 1.25 .35
FT14 Chipper Jones 2.00 .60
FT15 Alex Rodriguez 3.00 .90

2000 Upper Deck Game Ball

Randomly inserted into packs at one in 287, this 10-card insert features game-used baseballs from the depicted players. Card backs carry a "B" prefix.

Nm-Mt Ex-Mt
B-AJ Andruw Jones 10.00 3.00
B-AR Alex Rodriguez 15.00 4.50
B-BW Bernie Williams 10.00 3.00
B-DJ Derek Jeter 25.00 7.50
B-JB Jeff Bagwell 10.00 3.00
B-KG Ken Griffey Jr. 15.00 4.50
B-MM Mark McGwire 40.00 12.00
B-RC Roger Clemens 15.00 4.50
B-TG Tony Gwynn 15.00 4.50
B-VG Vladimir Guerrero 10.00 3.00

2000 Upper Deck Game Jersey

These cards feature swatches of jerseys of various major league stars. The cards with an "H" after the player names are available only in hobby packs at a rate of one every 288 first series and 1:287 second series. The cards which have an "HR" after the player names are available in either hobby or retail packs at a rate of one every 2500 packs.

Nm-Mt Ex-Mt
AJ Andruw Jones HR2 15.00 4.50
AR Alex Rodriguez H1 50.00 15.00
AR Alex Rodriguez HR2 50.00 15.00
BG Ben Grieve HR2 15.00 4.50
CJ Chipper Jones HR1 40.00 12.00
CR Cal Ripken HR1 60.00 18.00
CY Tom Glavine H1 25.00 7.50
DC David Cone HR2 15.00 4.50
DJ Derek Jeter H1 60.00 18.00
EC Eric Chavez HR2 15.00 4.50

EM Edgar Martinez HR2 .... 25.00 7.50
FT Frank Thomas H1 .... 40.00 12.00
FT Frank Thomas HR2 .... 40.00 12.00
GK Gabe Kapler HR1 .... 15.00 4.50
GM Greg Maddux HR1 .... 50.00 15.00
GM Greg Maddux HR2 .... 50.00 15.00
GV Greg Vaughn HR1 .... 15.00 4.50
JB Jeff Bagwell H1 .... 25.00 7.50
JC Jose Canseco HR1 .... 40.00 12.00
JR Ken Griffey Jr. H1 .... 50.00 15.00
KG K.Griffey Jr. Reds HR2 .... 50.00 15.00
KM Kevin Millwood HR2 .... 15.00 4.50
MH Mike Hampton HR2 .... 15.00 4.50
MP Mike Piazza H1 .... 50.00 15.00
MR Manny Ramirez HR1 .... 25.00 7.50
MV Mo Vaughn HR2 .... 15.00 4.50
MW Matt Williams HR2 .... 15.00 4.50
PM Pedro Martinez H1 .... 40.00 12.00
RJ Randy Johnson HR2 .... 40.00 12.00
RV Robin Ventura HR2 .... 15.00 4.50
SA Sandy Alomar Jr. HR2 .... 15.00 4.50
TG Tony Gwynn HR2 .... 40.00 12.00
TH Todd Helton HR1 .... 25.00 7.50
TH Todd Helton HR2 .... 25.00 7.50
VG Vladimir Guerrero HR1 .... 40.00 12.00
TGL Tom Glavine HR2 .... 25.00 7.50
TRG Troy Glaus H1 .... 15.00 4.50
TRG Troy Glaus HR2 .... 15.00 4.50

2000 Upper Deck Game Jersey Autograph

Randomly inserted into Upper Deck Series two hobby packs, this insert set features autographed game-used jersey cards from some of the hottest players in major league baseball. Card backs carry an "H" prefix. A few autographs were not available in packs and had to be exchanged for signed cards. These cards had to be returned to Upper Deck by March 6th, 2001.

Nm-Mt Ex-Mt
HAR A.Rodriguez EXCH 150.00 45.00
HBB Barry Bonds 350.00 105.00
HCR Cal Ripken 150.00 45.00
HDJ Derek Jeter 200.00 60.00
HIR I.Rodriguez AU H2 .... 60.00 18.00
HJB Jeff Bagwell 60.00 18.00
HJC Jose Canseco 60.00 18.00
HJK Jason Kendall 40.00 12.00
HKG K.Griffey Jr. Reds EXCH 150.00 45.00
HMR M.Ramirez EXCH 60.00 18.00
HPO Paul O'Neill 50.00 15.00
HSR Scott Rolen 60.00 18.00
HVG Vladimir Guerrero 60.00 18.00

2000 Upper Deck Game Jersey Autograph Numbered

Randomly inserted into Upper Deck hobby packs, this insert set features autographed game-used jersey cards of the hottest players in baseball. Please note that these cards are hand-numbered on front in blue ink sharpie pen to the depicted players jersey number. Due to scarcity, some of these cards are not priced. A few cards were available via exchange: Series one exchange cards had to be redeemed by July 15th, 2000 while series two exchange cards were to be redeemed by March 6th, 2001. Cards tagged with an H1 or H2 suffix in the description were distributed exclusively in first and second series hobby packs. Cards tagged with an HR1 or HR2 suffix were distributed in hobby and retail packs. The "hobby-only" cards carry an "HN" prefix for the numbering on the back of each card (i.e. Scott Rolen is HN-SR). In addition, each of these cards features features a congratulations from UD President Richard McWilliams with the reference to the card being "crash numbered". These two differences make these scarce numbered inserts easy to legitimize against possible fakes whereby unscrupulous parties may have numbered the cards themselves on front (not very tough to do given the cards were hand-numbered by UD). Unfortunately, the hobby-retail cards do not carry these key differences in design. It's believed that these Numbered inserts feature a gold hologram on back (lower left corner) rather than the silver hologram featured on the more common non-Numbered Game Jersey Autograph cards. Nonetheless, buyers are encouraged to exercise extreme caution for fakes when purchasing the hobby-retail versions of these cards.

Nm-Mt Ex-Mt
AJ Andruw Jones/25 H2 ....
AR Alex Rodriguez/3 HR1 ....
BB Barry Bonds/25 H2 ....
BG Ben Grieve /14 HR2 ....
CR Cal Ripken/8 H2 ....
DJ Derek Jeter/2 HR1 ....
EM Edgar Martinez /11 HR2 ....
FT Frank Thomas/35 HR2 .... 200.00 60.00
GM Greg Maddux/31 HR2 .... 300.00 90.00
IR Ivan Rodriguez/7 H2 ....
JB Jeff Bagwell/5 H2 ....
JC Jose Canseco/33 H2 .... 250.00 75.00
JK Jason Kendall/18 H2 ....
JR K.Griffey Jr./24 H1 EX ....
KG K.Griffey Jr. Reds/30 H2 .... 250.00 75.00
MH Mike Hampton/10 HR2 ....
MR Manny Ramirez/24 H1 ....
MR M.Ramirez/24 H2 EX ....
MV Mo Vaughn/42 HR2 .... 80.00 24.00
MW Matt Williams/9 HR2 ....
PO Paul O'Neill/21 H2 ....
RJ R.Johnson/51 HR2 .... 200.00 60.00
SR Scott Rolen/17 H2 ....
TG Tony Gwynn/19 HR2 ....
VG V.Guerrero/27 H2 .... 300.00 90.00
TGl Tom Glavine/47 HR2 .... 150.00 45.00
TRG Troy Glaus/14 HR2 ....

2000 Upper Deck Game Jersey Patch

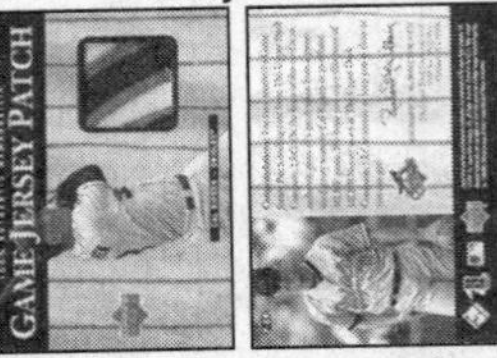

Randomly inserted into series one packs at one in 10,000 and series two packs at a rate of 1:7500, these cards feature game-worn uniform patches.

Nm-Mt Ex-Mt
1 OF 1 PATCH RANDOM IN ALL PACKS
1 OF 1 PATCH PRINT RUN 1 SERIAL #'d SET
NO 1 OF 1 PATCH PRICING AVAILABLE
P-AJ Andruw Jones 2 .... 50.00 15.00
P-AR Alex Rodriguez 1 .... 120.00 36.00
P-AR Alex Rodriguez 2 .... 120.00 36.00
P-BB Barry Bonds 2 .... 200.00 60.00
P-BG Ben Grieve 2 .... 50.00 15.00
P-CJ Chipper Jones 1 .... 100.00 30.00
P-CR Cal Ripken 1 .... 200.00 60.00
P-CR Cal Ripken 2 .... 200.00 60.00
P-CY Tom Glavine 1 .... 80.00 24.00
P-DC David Cone 50.00 15.00
P-DJ Derek Jeter 1 .... 150.00 45.00
P-DJ Derek Jeter 2 .... 150.00 45.00
P-EC Eric Chavez 1 .... 50.00 15.00
P-FT Frank Thomas 1 .... 100.00 30.00
P-GK Gabe Kapler 1 .... 50.00 15.00
P-GM Greg Maddux 1 .... 120.00 36.00
P-GM Greg Maddux 2 .... 120.00 36.00
P-GV Greg Vaughn 1 .... 50.00 15.00
P-IR Ivan Rodriguez 2 .... 100.00 30.00
P-JB Jeff Bagwell 1 .... 80.00 24.00
P-JC Jose Canseco 1 .... 100.00 30.00
P-JR Ken Griffey Jr. 1 .... 120.00 36.00
P-KG K.Griffey Jr. Reds 2 .... 120.00 36.00
P-MP Mike Piazza 1 .... 120.00 36.00
P-MR Manny Ramirez 1 .... 80.00 24.00
P-MR Manny Ramirez 2 .... 80.00 24.00
P-MV Mo Vaughn 2 .... 50.00 15.00
P-MW Matt Williams 2 .... 50.00 15.00
P-PM Pedro Martinez 1 .... 100.00 30.00
P-RJ Randy Johnson 2 .... 100.00 30.00
P-SR Scott Rolen 2 .... 100.00 30.00
P-TG Tony Gwynn 2 .... 120.00 36.00
P-TH Todd Helton 1 .... 80.00 24.00
P-TRG Troy Glaus 1 .... 50.00 15.00
P-TRG Troy Glaus 2 .... 50.00 15.00
P-VG Vladimir Guerrero 1 .... 100.00 30.00
P-VG Vladimir Guerrero 2 .... 100.00 30.00

2000 Upper Deck Hit Brigade

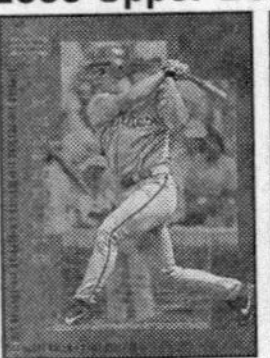

Inserted into first series packs at a rate of one in eight, these 15 cards feature some of the best hitters. These cards are printed in etched foil.

Nm-Mt Ex-Mt
COMPLETE SET (15) 30.00 9.00
*DIE CUTS: 6X TO 15X BASIC HIT BRIGADE
DIE CUTS RANDOM INSERTS IN SER.1 PACKS
DIE CUTS PRINT RUN 100 SERIAL #'d SETS
GOLD DIE CUTS RANDOM IN SER.1 PACKS
GOLD DIE CUT PRINT RUN 1 SERIAL #'d SET
GOLD DC NOT PRICED DUE TO SCARCITY
H1 Ken Griffey Jr. .... 2.50 .75
H2 Tony Gwynn .... 2.00 .60
H3 Alex Rodriguez .... 2.50 .75
H4 Derek Jeter 4.00 1.20
H5 Mike Piazza .... 2.50 .75
H6 Sammy Sosa .... 2.50 .75
H7 Juan Gonzalez .... 1.00 .30
H8 Scott Rolen .... 1.50 .45
H9 Nomar Garciaparra .... 2.50 .75
H10 Barry Bonds 4.00 1.20
H11 Craig Biggio .... 1.00 .30
H12 Chipper Jones .... 1.50 .45
H13 Frank Thomas .... 1.50 .45
H14 Larry Walker .... 1.00 .30
H15 Mark McGwire 4.00 1.20

2000 Upper Deck Hot Properties

Randomly inserted into Upper Deck series two packs at one in 11, this 15-card insert features the major league's top prospects. Card backs carry a "HP" prefix.

Nm-Mt Ex-Mt
COMPLETE SET (15) 12.00 3.60
HP1 Carlos Beltran .... 1.25 .35
HP2 Rick Ankiel .... 1.25 .35
HP3 Sean Casey .... .75 .23
HP4 Preston Wilson .... .75 .23
HP5 Vernon Wells .... 1.25 .35
HP6 Pat Burrell .... .50 .15
HP7 Eric Chavez .... .75 .23
HP8 J.D. Drew .... .75 .23
HP9 Alfonso Soriano .... 3.00 .90
HP10 Gabe Kapler .... .75 .23
HP11 Rafael Furcal .... 1.25 .35
HP12 Ruben Mateo .... .75 .23
HP13 Corey Koskie .... .50 .15
HP14 Kip Wells .... .75 .23
HP15 Ramon Ortiz .... .75 .23

2000 Upper Deck Legendary Cuts

Randomly inserted into Upper Deck series two packs, this eight-card insert features cut-signatures from some of the all-time great players of the 20th Century. Please note that only one set was produced of this insert.

Nm-Mt Ex-Mt
1 Cap Anson ....
2 Roberto Clemente ....
3 Ty Cobb ....
4 Eddie Collins ....
5 Nap Lajoie ....
6 Tris Speaker ....
7 Honus Wagner ....
8 Paul Waner ....

2000 Upper Deck Pennant Driven

Randomly inserted into packs at one in four, this 10-card insert features players that are driven to win the pennant. Card backs carry a "PD" prefix.

Nm-Mt Ex-Mt
COMPLETE SET (10) 10.00 3.00
PD1 Derek Jeter .... 2.00 .60
PD2 Roberto Alomar .... .50 .15
PD3 Chipper Jones .... .75 .23
PD4 Jeff Bagwell .... .50 .15
PD5 Roger Clemens .... 1.50 .45
PD6 Nomar Garciaparra .... 1.25 .35
PD7 Manny Ramirez .... .50 .15
PD8 Mike Piazza .... 1.25 .35
PD9 Ivan Rodriguez .... .75 .23
PD10 Randy Johnson .... .75 .23

2000 Upper Deck People's Choice

Randomly inserted into second series packs at one in 23, this 15-card set features players that people have voted as their favorites to watch. Card backs carry a "PC" prefix.

Nm-Mt Ex-Mt
COMPLETE SET (15) 100.00 30.00
PC1 Mark McGwire 10.00 3.00
PC2 Nomar Garciaparra 6.00 1.80
PC3 Derek Jeter 10.00 3.00
PC4 Shawn Green .... 1.50 .45
PC5 Manny Ramirez .... 2.50 .75
PC6 Pedro Martinez 4.00 1.20
PC7 Ivan Rodriguez 4.00 1.20
PC8 Alex Rodriguez 6.00 1.80
PC9 Juan Gonzalez .... 2.50 .75
PC10 Ken Griffey Jr. 6.00 1.80
PC11 Sammy Sosa 6.00 1.80
PC12 Jeff Bagwell .... 2.50 .75
PC13 Chipper Jones 4.00 1.20
PC14 Cal Ripken 12.00 3.60
PC15 Mike Piazza 6.00 1.80

2000 Upper Deck Power MARK

Inserted one every 23 first series packs, these 10 cards all feature Mark McGwire.

Nm-Mt Ex-Mt
COMPLETE SET (10) 50.00 15.00
COMMON (MC1-MC10) 6.00 1.80
*DIE CUTS: 3X TO 8X BASIC POWER MARK
DIE CUTS RANDOM INSERTS IN SER.1 HOBBY
DIE CUTS PRINT RUN 100 SERIAL #'d SETS
GOLD DIE CUTS RANDOM IN SER.1 HOBBY
GOLD DIE CUT PRINT RUN 1 SERIAL #'d SET
GOLD DC NOT PRICED DUE TO SCARCITY

2000 Upper Deck Power Rally

Inserted one every 11 first series packs, these 15 cards feature baseball's leading power hitters.

Nm-Mt Ex-Mt
COMPLETE SET (15) 40.00 12.00
*DIE CUTS: 5X TO 12X BASIC POWER RALLY
DIE CUTS RANDOM INSERTS IN SER.1 PACKS
DIE CUTS PRINT RUN 100 SERIAL #'d SETS
GOLD DIE CUTS RANDOM IN SER.1 PACKS
GOLD DIE CUT PRINT RUN 1 SERIAL #'d SET
GOLD DC NOT PRICED DUE TO SCARCITY
P1 Ken Griffey Jr. .... 3.00 .90
P2 Mark McGwire 5.00 1.50
P3 Sammy Sosa .... 3.00 .90
P4 Jose Canseco .... 2.00 .60
P5 Juan Gonzalez .... 1.25 .35
P6 Bernie Williams .... 1.25 .35
P7 Jeff Bagwell .... 1.25 .35
P8 Chipper Jones .... 2.00 .60
P9 Vladimir Guerrero .... 2.00 .60
P10 Mo Vaughn .... .75 .23
P11 Derek Jeter 5.00 1.50
P12 Mike Piazza .... 3.00 .90
P13 Barry Bonds 5.00 1.50
P14 Alex Rodriguez .... 3.00 .90
P15 Nomar Garciaparra .... 3.00 .90

2000 Upper Deck PowerDeck Inserts

These CD's were inserted into packs at two different rates. PD1 through PD 8 were inserted at a rate of one every 23 packs while PD9 through PD 11 were inserted at a rate of one every 287 packs. Due to problems at the manufacturer, the Alex Rodriguez CD was not inserted into the first series packs so a collector could acquire one of those by sending in a UPC code on the bottom of the 2000 Upper Deck first series boxes. Also, some of the 1999 Upper Deck PowerDeck CD's were mistakenly inserted into this product. Those CD's are priced under the 1999 Upper Deck PowerDeck listings. Finally, Ken Griffey Jr., Reggie Jackson and Mark McGwire have all been confirmed as short prints by representatives at Upper Deck.

Nm-Mt Ex-Mt
COMPLETE SET (11) 120.00 36.00
PD1 Ken Griffey Jr. 6.00 1.80
PD2 Cal Ripken 12.00 3.60
PD3 Mark McGwire 10.00 3.00
PD4 Tony Gwynn 5.00 1.50
PD5 Roger Clemens 8.00 2.40
PD6 Alex Rodriguez EXCH 8.00 2.40
PD7 Sammy Sosa 6.00 1.80
PD8 Derek Jeter 10.00 3.00
PD9 Ken Griffey Jr. SP 15.00 4.50
PD10 Mark McGwire SP 25.00 7.50
PD11 Reggie Jackson SP 15.00 4.50

2000 Upper Deck Prime Performers

Randomly inserted into series two packs at one in eight, this 10-card insert features players that are prime performers. Card backs carry a "PP" prefix.

Nm-Mt Ex-Mt
COMPLETE SET (10) 12.00 3.60
PP1 Manny Ramirez .... .60 .18
PP2 Pedro Martinez .... 1.00 .30
PP3 Carlos Delgado .... .40 .12
PP4 Ken Griffey Jr. .... 1.50 .45
PP5 Derek Jeter .... 2.50 .75
PP6 Chipper Jones .... 1.00 .30
PP7 Sean Casey .... .40 .12
PP8 Shawn Green .... .40 .12
PP9 Sammy Sosa .... 1.50 .45
PP10 Alex Rodriguez .... 1.50 .45

2000 Upper Deck Statitude

Inserted one every four packs, these 30 cards feature some of the most statistically dominant players in baseball.

Nm-Mt Ex-Mt
COMPLETE SET (30) 40.00 12.00
*DIE CUTS: 6X TO 15X BASIC STATITUDE
DIE CUTS RANDOM INSERTS IN SER.1 RETAIL
DIE CUTS PRINT RUN 100 SERIAL #'d SETS
GOLD DIE CUTS RANDOM IN SER.1 RETAIL
GOLD DIE CUT PRINT RUN 1 SERIAL #'d SET
GOLD DC NOT PRICED DUE TO SCARCITY
S1 Mo Vaughn .... .60 .18
S2 Matt Williams .... .60 .18
S3 Travis Lee .... .60 .18
S4 Chipper Jones .... 1.50 .45
S5 Greg Maddux .... 2.50 .75
S6 Gabe Kapler .... .60 .18
S7 Cal Ripken 5.00 1.50
S8 Nomar Garciaparra .... 2.50 .75
S9 Sammy Sosa .... 2.50 .75
S10 Frank Thomas .... 1.50 .45
S11 Manny Ramirez .... 1.00 .30
S12 Larry Walker .... 1.00 .30
S13 Ivan Rodriguez .... 1.50 .45
S14 Jeff Bagwell .... 1.00 .30
S15 Craig Biggio .... 1.00 .30
S16 Vladimir Guerrero .... 1.50 .45
S17 Mike Piazza .... 2.50 .75
S18 Bernie Williams .... 1.00 .30
S19 Derek Jeter 4.00 1.20
S20 Jose Canseco .... 1.50 .45
S21 Eric Chavez .... .60 .18
S22 Scott Rolen .... 1.50 .45
S23 Mark McGwire 4.00 1.20
S24 Tony Gwynn .... 2.00 .60
S25 Barry Bonds 4.00 1.20
S26 Ken Griffey Jr. .... 2.50 .75
S27 Alex Rodriguez .... 2.50 .75
S28 J.D. Drew .... .60 .18
S29 Juan Gonzalez .... 1.00 .30
S30 Roger Clemens .... 3.00 .90

2001 Upper Deck

The 2001 Upper Deck Series one product was released in November, 2000 and featured a 270-card base set. Series two (entitled Mid-Summer Classic) was released in June, 2001 and featured a 180-card base set. The complete set is broken into subsets as follows: Star Rookies (1-45/271-300), basic cards (46-261/301-444), and Season Highlight checklists (262-270/445-450). Each pack contained 10-cards and carried a suggested retail price of $1.99. Key Rookie Cards in the set include Albert Pujols and Ichiro Suzuki. Also, a selection of A Piece of History 3000 Club Eddie Murray and Cal Ripken memorabilia cards were randomly seeded into series one packs. 350 bat cards, 350 jersey cards and 100 hand-numbered, combination bat-jersey cards were produced for each player. In addition, thirty-three autographed, hand-numbered, combination bat-jersey Eddie Murray cards and eight autographed, hand-numbered, combination bat-jersey Cal Ripken cards were produced. The Ripken Bat, Ripken Bat-Jsy Combo and Murray Bat-Jsy Combo Autograph were all exchange cards. The deadline to send in the exchange cards was August 22nd, 2001. Pricing for these memorabilia cards can be referenced under 2000 Upper Deck A Piece of History 3000 Club.

Nm-Mt Ex-Mt
COMPLETE SET (450) 100.00 30.00
COMP. SERIES 1 (270) 40.00 12.00
COMP. SERIES 2 (180) 60.00 18.00
COMMON (46-270/300-450) .... .30 .09
COMMON SR (1-45) .... .50 .15
1 Jeff DaVanon SR .... .50 .15
2 Aubrey Huff SR .... .50 .15
3 Pasqual Coco SR .... .50 .15
4 Barry Zito SR .... .60 .18
5 Augie Ojeda SR .... .50 .15
6 Chris Richard SR .... .50 .15
7 Josh Phelps SR .... .50 .15
8 Kevin Nicholson SR .... .50 .15
9 Juan Guzman SR .... .50 .15
10 Brandon Kolb SR .... .50 .15
11 Johan Santana SR 5.00 1.50
12 Josh Kalinowski SR .... .50 .15
13 Tike Redman SR .... .50 .15
14 Ivanon Coffie SR .... .50 .15
15 Chad Durbin SR .... .50 .15
16 Derrick Turnbow SR .... .50 .15
17 Scott Downs SR .... .50 .15
18 Jason Grilli SR .... .50 .15
19 Mark Buehrle SR .... .50 .15
20 Paxton Crawford SR .... .50 .15
21 Bronson Arroyo SR .... 1.00 .30
22 Tomas De la Rosa SR .... .50 .15
23 Paul Rigdon SR .... .50 .15
24 Rob Ramsay SR .... .50 .15
25 Damian Rolls SR .... .50 .15
26 Jason Conti SR .... .50 .15
27 John Parrish SR .... .50 .15
28 Geraldo Guzman SR .... .50 .15
29 Tony Mota SR .... .50 .15
30 Luis Rivas SR .... .50 .15
31 Brian Tollberg SR .... .50 .15
32 Adam Bernero SR .... .50 .15
33 Michael Cuddyer SR .... .50 .15
34 Josue Espada SR .... .50 .15
35 Joe Lawrence SR .... .50 .15
36 Chad Moeller SR .... .50 .15
37 Nick Bierbrodt SR .... .50 .15
38 DeWayne Wise SR .... .50 .15
39 Javier Cardona SR .... .50 .15
40 Hiram Bocachica SR .... .50 .15
41 G.Chiaramonte SR .... .50 .15
42 Alex Cabrera SR .... .50 .15
43 Jimmy Rollins SR .... .50 .15
44 Pat Flury SR RC .... .50 .15
45 Leo Estrella SR .... .50 .15
46 Darin Erstad .... .30 .09
47 Seth Etherton .... .30 .09

48 Troy Glaus .30 .09
49 Brian Cooper .30 .09
50 Tim Salmon .50 .15
51 Adam Kennedy .30 .09
52 Bengie Molina .30 .09
53 Jason Giambi .30 .09
54 Miguel Tejada .30 .09
55 Tim Hudson .30 .09
56 Eric Chavez .30 .09
57 Terrence Long .30 .09
58 Jason Isringhausen .30 .09
59 Ramon Hernandez .30 .09
60 Raul Mondesi .30 .09
61 David Wells .30 .09
62 Shannon Stewart .30 .09
63 Tony Batista .30 .09
64 Brad Fullmer .30 .09
65 Chris Carpenter .30 .09
66 Homer Bush .30 .09
67 Gerald Williams .30 .09
68 Miguel Cairo .30 .09
69 Ryan Rupe .30 .09
70 Greg Vaughn .30 .09
71 John Flaherty .30 .09
72 Dan Wheeler .30 .09
73 Fred McGriff .50 .15
74 Roberto Alomar .50 .15
75 Bartolo Colon .30 .09
76 Kenny Lofton .30 .09
77 David Segui .30 .09
78 Omar Vizquel .50 .15
79 Russ Branyan .30 .09
80 Chuck Finley .30 .09
81 Manny Ramirez UER .50 .15
Back photo is of David Segui
82 Alex Rodriguez 1.25 .35
83 John Halama .30 .09
84 Mike Cameron .30 .09
85 David Bell .30 .09
86 Jay Buhner .30 .09
87 Aaron Sele .30 .09
88 Rickey Henderson .75 .23
89 Brook Fordyce .30 .09
90 Cal Ripken 2.50 .75
91 Mike Mussina .50 .15
92 Delino DeShields .30 .09
93 Melvin Mora .30 .09
94 Sidney Ponson .30 .09
95 Brady Anderson .30 .09
96 Ivan Rodriguez .75 .23
97 Ricky Ledee .30 .09
98 Rick Helling .30 .09
99 Ruben Mateo .30 .09
100 Luis Alicea .30 .09
101 John Wetteland .30 .09
102 Mike Lamb .30 .09
103 Carl Everett .30 .09
104 Troy O'Leary .30 .09
105 Wilton Veras .30 .09
106 Pedro Martinez .75 .23
107 Rolando Arrojo .30 .09
108 Scott Hatteberg .30 .09
109 Jason Varitek .50 .15
110 Jose Offerman .30 .09
111 Carlos Beltran .50 .15
112 Johnny Damon .50 .15
113 Mark Quinn .30 .09
114 Rey Sanchez .30 .09
115 Mac Suzuki .30 .09
116 Jermaine Dye .30 .09
117 Chris Fussell .30 .09
118 Jeff Weaver .30 .09
119 Dean Palmer .30 .09
120 Robert Fick .30 .09
121 Brian Moehler .30 .09
122 Damion Easley .30 .09
123 Juan Encarnacion .30 .09
124 Tony Clark .30 .09
125 Cristian Guzman .30 .09
126 Matt LeCroy .30 .09
127 Eric Milton .30 .09
128 Jay Canizaro .30 .09
129 David Ortiz .50 .15
130 Brad Radke .30 .09
131 Jacque Jones .30 .09
132 Magglio Ordonez .30 .09
133 Carlos Lee .30 .09
134 Mike Sirotka .30 .09
135 Ray Durham .30 .09
136 Paul Konerko .30 .09
137 Charles Johnson .30 .09
138 James Baldwin .30 .09
139 Jeff Abbott .30 .09
140 Roger Clemens 1.50 .45
141 Derek Jeter 2.00 .60
142 David Justice .30 .09
143 Ramiro Mendoza .30 .09
144 Chuck Knoblauch .30 .09
145 Orlando Hernandez .30 .09
146 Alfonso Soriano .50 .15
147 Jeff Bagwell .50 .15
148 Julio Lugo .30 .09
149 Mitch Meluskey .30 .09
150 Jose Lima .30 .09
151 Richard Hidalgo .30 .09
152 Moises Alou .30 .09
153 Scott Elarton .30 .09
154 Andruw Jones .30 .09
155 Quilvio Veras .30 .09
156 Greg Maddux 1.25 .35
157 Brian Jordan .30 .09
158 Andres Galarraga .30 .09
159 Kevin Millwood .30 .09
160 Rafael Furcal .30 .09
161 Jeromy Burnitz .30 .09
162 Jimmy Haynes .30 .09
163 Mark Loretta .30 .09
164 Ron Belliard .30 .09
165 Richie Sexson .30 .09
166 Kevin Barker .30 .09
167 Jeff D'Amico .30 .09
168 Rick Ankiel .30 .09
169 Mark McGwire 2.00 .60
170 J.D. Drew .30 .09
171 Eli Marrero .30 .09
172 Darryl Kile .30 .09
173 Edgar Renteria .30 .09
174 Will Clark .75 .23
175 Eric Young .30 .09
176 Mark Grace .50 .15
177 Jon Lieber .30 .09
178 Damon Buford .30 .09
179 Kerry Wood .75 .23
180 Rondell White .30 .09
181 Joe Girardi .30 .09
182 Curt Schilling .30 .09
183 Randy Johnson .75 .23
184 Steve Finley .30 .09
185 Kelly Stinnett .30 .09
186 Jay Bell .30 .09
187 Matt Mantei .30 .09
188 Luis Gonzalez .30 .09
189 Shawn Green .30 .09
190 Todd Hundley .30 .09
191 Chan Ho Park .30 .09
192 Adrian Beltre .50 .15
193 Mark Grudzielanek .30 .09
194 Gary Sheffield .30 .09
195 Tom Goodwin .30 .09
196 Lee Stevens .30 .09
197 Javier Vazquez .30 .09
198 Milton Bradley .30 .09
199 Vladimir Guerrero .75 .23
200 Carl Pavano .30 .09
201 Orlando Cabrera .30 .09
202 Tony Armas Jr. .30 .09
203 Jeff Kent .30 .09
204 Calvin Murray .30 .09
205 Ellis Burks .30 .09
206 Barry Bonds 2.00 .60
207 Russ Ortiz .30 .09
208 Marvin Benard .30 .09
209 Joe Nathan .30 .09
210 Preston Wilson .30 .09
211 Cliff Floyd .30 .09
212 Mike Lowell .30 .09
213 Ryan Dempster .30 .09
214 Brad Penny .30 .09
215 Mike Redmond .30 .09
216 Luis Castillo .30 .09
217 Derek Bell .30 .09
218 Mike Hampton .30 .09
219 Todd Zeile .30 .09
220 Robin Ventura .30 .09
221 Mike Piazza 1.25 .35
222 Al Leiter .30 .09
223 Edgardo Alfonzo .30 .09
224 Mike Bordick .30 .09
225 Phil Nevin .30 .09
226 Ryan Klesko .30 .09
227 Adam Eaton .30 .09
228 Eric Owens .30 .09
229 Tony Gwynn 1.00 .30
230 Matt Clement .30 .09
231 Wiki Gonzalez .30 .09
232 Robert Person .30 .09
233 Doug Glanville .30 .09
234 Scott Rolen .75 .23
235 Mike Lieberthal .30 .09
236 Randy Wolf .30 .09
237 Bob Abreu .30 .09
238 Pat Burrell .30 .09
239 Bruce Chen .30 .09
240 Kevin Young .30 .09
241 Todd Ritchie .30 .09
242 Adrian Brown .30 .09
243 Chad Hermansen .30 .09
244 Warren Morris .30 .09
245 Kris Benson .30 .09
246 Jason Kendall .30 .09
247 Pokey Reese .30 .09
248 Rob Bell .30 .09
249 Ken Griffey Jr. 1.25 .35
250 Sean Casey .30 .09
251 Aaron Boone .30 .09
252 Pete Harnisch .30 .09
253 Barry Larkin .50 .15
254 Dmitri Young .30 .09
255 Todd Hollandsworth .30 .09
256 Pedro Astacio .30 .09
257 Todd Helton .50 .15
258 Terry Shumpert .30 .09
259 Neifi Perez .30 .09
260 Jeffrey Hammonds .30 .09
261 Ben Petrick .30 .09
262 Mark McGwire SH 1.00 .30
263 Derek Jeter SH 1.00 .30
264 Sammy Sosa SH .75 .23
265 Cal Ripken SH 1.25 .35
266 Pedro Martinez SH .50 .15
267 Barry Bonds SH .75 .23
268 Fred McGriff SH .30 .09
269 Randy Johnson SH .50 .15
270 Darin Erstad SH .30 .09
271 Ichiro Suzuki SR RC 15.00 4.50
272 W. Betemit SR RC .50 .15
273 Corey Patterson SR .50 .15
274 Sean Douglass SR RC .50 .15
275 Mike Penney SR RC .50 .15
276 Nate Teut SR RC .50 .15
277 R. Rodriguez SR RC .50 .15
278 B. Duckworth SR RC .50 .15
279 Rafael Soriano SR RC .60 .18
280 Juan Diaz SR RC .50 .15
281 H. Ramirez SR RC .60 .18
282 T. Shinjo SR RC .60 .18
283 Keith Ginter SR .50 .15
284 Esix Snead SR RC .50 .15
285 Erick Almonte SR RC .50 .15
286 Travis Hafner SR RC 2.50 .75
287 Jason Smith SR RC .50 .15
288 J. Melian SR RC .50 .15
289 Tyler Walker SR RC .50 .15
290 Jason Standridge SR .50 .15
291 Juan Uribe SR RC .60 .18
292 A. Hernandez SR RC .50 .15
293 J. Michaels SR RC .50 .15
294 Jason Hart SR .50 .15
295 Albert Pujols SR RC 40.00 12.00
296 M. Ensberg SR RC 1.00 .30
297 Brandon Inge SR .50 .15
298 Jesus Colome SR .50 .15
299 K. Kessel SR RC UER .50 .15
L Missing from MLB experience
300 Timo Perez SR .50 .15
301 Mo Vaughn .30 .09
302 Ismael Valdes .30 .09
303 Glenallen Hill .30 .09
304 Garret Anderson .30 .09
305 Johnny Damon .50 .15
306 Jose Ortiz .30 .09
307 Mark Mulder .30 .09
308 Adam Piatt .30 .09
309 Gil Heredia .30 .09
310 Mike Sirotka .30 .09
311 Carlos Delgado .30 .09
312 Alex Gonzalez .30 .09
313 Jose Cruz Jr. .30 .09
314 Darrin Fletcher .30 .09
315 Ben Grieve .30 .09
316 Vinny Castilla .30 .09
317 Wilson Alvarez .30 .09
318 Brent Abernathy .30 .09
319 Ellis Burks .30 .09
320 Jim Thome .75 .23
321 Juan Gonzalez .50 .15
322 Ed Taubensee .30 .09
323 Travis Fryman .30 .09
324 John Olerud .30 .09
325 Edgar Martinez .50 .15
326 Freddy Garcia .30 .09
327 Bret Boone .50 .15
328 Kazuhiro Sasaki .30 .09
329 Albert Belle .30 .09
330 Mike Bordick .30 .09
331 David Segui .30 .09
332 Pat Hentgen .30 .09
333 Alex Rodriguez 1.25 .35
334 Andres Galarraga .30 .09
335 Gabe Kapler .30 .09
336 Ken Caminiti .30 .09
337 Rafael Palmeiro .50 .15
338 Manny Ramirez .50 .15
339 David Cone .30 .09
340 Nomar Garciaparra 1.25 .35
341 Trot Nixon .30 .09
342 Derek Lowe .30 .09
343 Roberto Hernandez .30 .09
344 Mike Sweeney .30 .09
345 Carlos Febles .30 .09
346 Jeff Suppan .30 .09
347 Roger Cedeno .30 .09
348 Bobby Higginson .30 .09
349 Deivi Cruz .30 .09
350 Mitch Meluskey .30 .09
351 Matt Lawton .30 .09
352 Mark Redman .30 .09
353 Jay Canizaro .30 .09
354 Corey Koskie .30 .09
355 Matt Kinney .30 .09
356 Frank Thomas .75 .23
357 Sandy Alomar Jr. .30 .09
358 David Wells .30 .09
359 Jim Parque .30 .09
360 Chris Singleton .30 .09
361 Tino Martinez .50 .15
362 Paul O'Neill .50 .15
363 Mike Mussina .50 .15
364 Bernie Williams .50 .15
365 Andy Pettite .50 .15
366 Mariano Rivera .50 .15
367 Brad Ausmus .30 .09
368 Craig Biggio .50 .15
369 Lance Berkman .30 .09
370 Shane Reynolds .30 .09
371 Chipper Jones .75 .23
372 Tom Glavine .50 .15
373 B.J. Surhoff .30 .09
374 John Smoltz .50 .15
375 Rico Brogna .30 .09
376 Geoff Jenkins .30 .09
377 Jose Hernandez .30 .09
378 Tyler Houston .30 .09
379 Henry Blanco .30 .09
380 Jeffrey Hammonds .30 .09
381 Jim Edmonds .30 .09
382 Fernando Vina .30 .09
383 Andy Benes .30 .09
384 Ray Lankford .30 .09
385 Dustin Hermanson .30 .09
386 Todd Hundley .30 .09
387 Sammy Sosa 1.25 .35
388 Tom Gordon .30 .09
389 Bill Mueller .30 .09
390 Ron Coomer .30 .09
391 Matt Stairs .30 .09
392 Mark Grace .50 .15
393 Matt Williams .30 .09
394 Todd Stottlemyre .30 .09
395 Tony Womack .30 .09
396 Erubiel Durazo .30 .09
397 Reggie Sanders .30 .09
398 Andy Ashby .30 .09
399 Eric Karros .30 .09
400 Kevin Brown .30 .09
401 Darren Dreifort .30 .09
402 Fernando Tatis .30 .09
403 Jose Vidro .30 .09
404 Peter Bergeron .30 .09
405 Geoff Blum .30 .09
406 J.T. Snow .30 .09
407 Livan Hernandez .30 .09
408 Robb Nen .30 .09
409 Bobby Estalella .30 .09
410 Rich Aurilia .30 .09
411 Eric Davis .30 .09
412 Charles Johnson .30 .09
413 Alex Gonzalez .30 .09
414 A.J. Burnett .30 .09
415 Antonio Alfonseca .30 .09
416 Derek Lee .30 .09
417 Jay Payton .30 .09
418 Kevin Appier .30 .09
419 Steve Trachsel .30 .09
420 Rey Ordonez .30 .09
421 Darryl Hamilton .30 .09
422 Ben Davis .30 .09
423 Damian Jackson .30 .09
424 Mark Kotsay .30 .09
425 Trevor Hoffman .30 .09
426 Travis Lee .30 .09
427 Omar Daal .30 .09
428 Paul Byrd .30 .09
429 Reggie Taylor .30 .09
430 Brian Giles .30 .09
431 Derek Bell .30 .09
432 Francisco Cordova .30 .09
433 Pat Meares .30 .09
434 Scott Williamson .30 .09
435 Jason LaRue .30 .09
436 Michael Tucker .30 .09
437 Wilton Guerrero .30 .09
438 Mike Hampton .30 .09
439 Ron Gant .30 .09
440 Jeff Cirillo .30 .09
441 Denny Neagle .30 .09
442 Larry Walker .50 .15
443 Juan Pierre .30 .09
444 Todd Walker .30 .09
445 Jason Giambi SH CL .30 .09
446 Jeff Kent SH CL .30 .09
447 Mariano Rivera SH CL .30 .09
448 Edgar Martinez SH CL .30 .09
449 Troy Glaus SH CL .30 .09
450 Alex Rodriguez SH CL .75 .23

2001 Upper Deck Exclusives Gold

Randomly inserted into series one packs, this 270-card set is a complete parallel of the 2001 Upper Deck series one base set. Please note that these cards were produced with gold lettering on the front and are individually serial numbered to 25. The words "Gold UD Exclusives" also run down the left side of each card front.

Nm-Mt Ex-Mt
*STARS: 40X TO 80X BASIC CARDS..
*SR STARS: 20X TO 40X BASIC SR...
*SR ROOKIES: 20X TO 40X BASIC SR
11 Johan Santana SR 50.00 15.00

2001 Upper Deck Exclusives Silver

Randomly inserted into series one packs, this 270-card set is a complete parallel of the 2001 Upper Deck series one base set. Please note that these cards were produced with silver lettering on the front and are individually serial numbered to 100. The words "UD Exclusives" also run down the left side of each card front.

Nm-Mt Ex-Mt
STARS: 12.5X TO 30X BASIC CARDS.
*SR YNG.STARS: 6X TO 15X BASIC..
*SR RC's: 6X TO 15X BASIC SR ....
11 Johan Santana SR 25.00 7.50

2001 Upper Deck 1971 All-Star Game Salute

Inserted in second series packs at a rate of one in 288, these 12 memorabilia cards feature players who participated in the 1971 All-Star Game which was highlighted by Reggie Jackson's home run off the light tower at Tiger Stadium.

	Nm-Mt	Ex-Mt
AS-BR B. Robinson Bat	20.00	6.00
AS-FR Frank Robinson Jsy	15.00	4.50
AS-HA Hank Aaron Bat	40.00	12.00
AS-HA Hank Aaron Jsy	50.00	15.00
AS-JB Johnny Bench Bat	20.00	6.00
AS-JB Johnny Bench Jsy	20.00	6.00
AS-LA Luis Aparicio Jsy	15.00	4.50
AS-LB Lou Brock Bat	20.00	6.00
AS-RC R. Clemente Jsy	100.00	30.00
AS-RJ Reggie Jackson Jsy	20.00	6.00
AS-TM T. Munson Jsy	40.00	12.00
AS-TS Tom Seaver Jsy	20.00	6.00

2001 Upper Deck All-Star Heroes

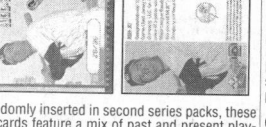

Randomly inserted in second series packs, these 14 cards feature a mix of past and present players who have starred in All-Star Games. Since each player was issued to a different amount, we have notated that information in our checklist.

	Nm-Mt	Ex-Mt
ASH-AR Alex Rodriguez Bat/1998	15.00	4.50
ASH-BR Babe Ruth Bat/1933	150.00	45.00
ASH-CR Cal Ripken Bat/1991	40.00	12.00
ASH-DJ Derek Jeter Base/2000	25.00	7.50
ASH-JD Joe DiMaggio Jsy/36		
ASH-KG Ken Griffey Jr. Bat/1992	15.00	4.50
ASH-MM Mickey Mantle Jsy/54	350.00	105.00
ASH-MP Mike Piazza Base/1996	15.00	4.50
ASH-RC Roger Clemens Jsy/1986	15.00	4.50
ASH-RJ Randy Johnson Jsy/1993	15.00	4.50
ASH-SS Sammy Sosa Jsy/2000	15.00	4.50
ASH-TG Tony Gwynn Jsy/1994	15.00	4.50
ASH-TP Tony Perez Bat 1967	10.00	3.00
ASH-ROC R.Clemente Bat/1961	100.00	30.00

2001 Upper Deck Big League Beat

Randomly inserted into packs at one in three, this 20-card insert features some of the most prolific players in the Major Leagues. Card backs carry a "BB" prefix.

	Nm-Mt	Ex-Mt
COMPLETE SET (20)	20.00	6.00
BB1 Barry Bonds	2.00	.60
BB2 Nomar Garciaparra	1.25	.35
BB3 Mark McGwire	2.00	.60
BB4 Roger Clemens	1.50	.45
BB5 Chipper Jones	.75	.23
BB6 Jeff Bagwell	.50	.15
BB7 Sammy Sosa	1.25	.35
BB8 Cal Ripken	2.50	.75
BB9 Randy Johnson	.75	.23
BB10 Carlos Delgado	.50	.15
BB11 Manny Ramirez	.50	.15
BB12 Derek Jeter	2.00	.60
BB13 Tony Gwynn	1.00	.30
BB14 Pedro Martinez	.75	.23
BB15 Jose Canseco	.75	.23
BB16 Frank Thomas	.75	.23
BB17 Alex Rodriguez	1.25	.35
BB18 Bernie Williams	.50	.15
BB19 Greg Maddux	1.25	.35
BB20 Rafael Palmeiro	.50	.15

2001 Upper Deck Big League Challenge Game Jerseys

Issued at a rate of one in 288 second series packs, these 11 cards feature jersey pieces from participants in the 2001 Big League Challenge home run hitting contest.

	Nm-Mt	Ex-Mt
BLC-BB Barry Bonds	40.00	12.00
BLC-FT Frank Thomas	20.00	6.00
BLC-GS Gary Sheffield	15.00	4.50
BLC-JC Jose Canseco	20.00	6.00
BLC-JE Jim Edmonds	15.00	4.50
BLC-MP Mike Piazza	25.00	7.50
BLC-RH Richard Hidalgo	15.00	4.50
BLC-RP Rafael Palmeiro	20.00	6.00
BLC-SF Steve Finley	15.00	4.50
BLC-TG Troy Glaus	15.00	4.50
BLC-TH Todd Helton	20.00	6.00

2001 Upper Deck e-Card

Inserted as a two-pack box-topper, this six-card insert features cards that can be viewed over the Upper Deck website. Cards feature a serial number that is to be typed in a the Upper Deck website to reveal that card. Card backs carry an "E" prefix.

	Nm-Mt	Ex-Mt
COMPLETE SET (12)	15.00	4.50
COMPLETE SERIES 1 (6)	6.00	1.80
COMPLETE SERIES 2 (6)	10.00	3.00
E1 Andruw Jones	1.00	.30
E2 Alex Rodriguez	1.50	.45
E3 Frank Thomas	1.00	.30
E4 Todd Helton	1.00	.30
E5 Troy Glaus	1.00	.30
E6 Barry Bonds	2.50	.75
E7 Alex Rodriguez	1.50	.45
E8 Ken Griffey Jr.	1.50	.45
E9 Sammy Sosa	1.50	.45
E10 Gary Sheffield	1.00	.30
E11 Barry Bonds	2.50	.75
E12 Andruw Jones	1.00	.30

2001 Upper Deck eVolve Autograph

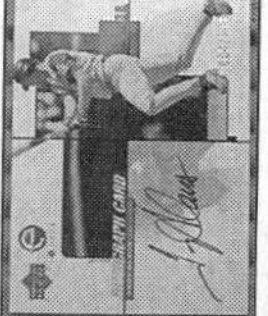

Lucky participants in Upper Deck's E-Card program received special upgraded E-Cards available by checking the UD website (www.upperdeck.com) and entering their basic E-Card serial code (printed on the front of each basic E-Card). When viewed on the Upper Deck website, if an autographed card of the depicted player appeared, the bearer of the base card could then exchange their basic E-Card and receive the signed upgrade via mail. Only 200 serial numbered E-Card Autograph sets were produced. Signed E-Cards all have an ES prefix on the card numbers.

	Nm-Mt	Ex-Mt
ES-AJ Andruw Jones S1	30.00	9.00
ES-AJ Andruw Jones S2	30.00	9.00
ES-AR Alex Rodriguez S1	100.00	30.00
ES-AR Alex Rodriguez S2	100.00	30.00
ES-BB Barry Bonds S1	250.00	75.00
ES-BB Barry Bonds S2	250.00	75.00
ES-FT Frank Thomas S1	60.00	18.00
ES-GS Gary Sheffield S2	50.00	15.00
ES-KG Ken Griffey Jr. S2	100.00	30.00
ES-SS Sammy Sosa S2	150.00	45.00
ES-TG Troy Glaus S1	30.00	9.00
ES-TH Todd Helton S1	50.00	15.00

2001 Upper Deck eVolve Game Jersey

Lucky participants in Upper Deck's E-Card program received special upgraded E-Cards available by checking the UD website (www.upperdeck.com) and entering their basic E-Card serial code (printed on the front of each basic E-Card). When viewed on the Upper Deck website, if a jersey card of the depicted player appeared, the bearer of the base card could then exchange their basic E-Card and receive the Game Jersey upgrade via mail. The cards closely parallel basic 2000 Game Jerseys that were distributed in first and second series packs except for the gold foil "e-volve" logo on front. Only 300 serial numbered E-Card Jersey sets were produced with each card being serial -numbered by hand in blue ink sharpie at the bottom right front corner. Unsigned E-Card Game Jerseys all have an EJ prefix on the card numbers.

	Nm-Mt	Ex-Mt
EJ-AJ Andruw Jones S1	10.00	3.00
EJ-AJ Andruw Jones S2	10.00	3.00
EJ-AR Alex Rodriguez S1	20.00	6.00
EJ-AR Alex Rodriguez S2	20.00	6.00
EJ-BB Barry Bonds S1	30.00	9.00
EJ-BB Barry Bonds S2	30.00	9.00
EJ-FT Frank Thomas S1	15.00	4.50
EJ-GS Gary Sheffield S2	10.00	3.00
EJ-KG Ken Griffey Jr. S2	25.00	7.50
EJ-SS Sammy Sosa S2	25.00	7.50
EJ-TG Troy Glaus S1	10.00	3.00
EJ-TH Todd Helton S1	15.00	4.50

2001 Upper Deck eVolve Game Jersey Autograph

Lucky participants in Upper Deck's E-Card program received special upgraded E-Cards available by checking the UD website (www.upperdeck.com) and entering their basic E-Card serial code (printed on the front of each basic E-Card). When viewed on the Upper Deck website, if an autographed card of the depicted player appeared, the bearer of the base card could then exchange their basic E-Card and receive the signed jersey upgrade via mail. A mere 50 serial numbered sets were produced. Signed jersey E-Cards all have an ESJ prefix on the card numbers.

	Nm-Mt	Ex-Mt
ESJ-AJ Andruw Jones S1	40.00	12.00
ESJ-AJ Andruw Jones S2	40.00	12.00
ESJ-AR Alex Rodriguez S1	150.00	45.00
ESJ-AR Alex Rodriguez S2	150.00	45.00
ESJ-BB Barry Bonds S1	300.00	90.00
ESJ-BB Barry Bonds S2	300.00	90.00
ESJ-FT Frank Thomas S1	80.00	24.00
ESJ-GS Gary Sheffield S2	60.00	18.00
ESJ-KG Ken Griffey Jr. S2	120.00	36.00
ESJ-SS Sammy Sosa S2	200.00	60.00
ESJ-TG Troy Glaus S1	40.00	12.00
ESJ-TH Todd Helton S1	60.00	18.00

2001 Upper Deck Franchise

Inserted at a rate of one in 36 second series packs, these 10 cards feature players who are considered the money players for their franchise.

	Nm-Mt	Ex-Mt
COMPLETE SET (10)	60.00	18.00
F1 Frank Thomas	4.00	1.20
F2 Mark McGwire	10.00	3.00
F3 Ken Griffey Jr.	6.00	1.80
F4 Manny Ramirez	4.00	1.20
F5 Alex Rodriguez	6.00	1.80

	Nm-Mt	Ex-Mt
F6 Greg Maddux	6.00	1.80
F7 Sammy Sosa	6.00	1.80
F8 Derek Jeter	10.00	3.00
F9 Mike Piazza	6.00	1.80
F10 Vladimir Guerrero	4.00	1.20

2001 Upper Deck Game Ball 1

Randomly inserted into packs, this 18-card insert features game-used baseballs from the depicted players. Card backs carry a "B" prefix. Please note that only 100 serial numbered sets were produced.

	Nm-Mt	Ex-Mt
B-AJ Andruw Jones	25.00	7.50
B-AR A.Rodriguez Mariners	60.00	18.00
B-BB Barry Bonds	80.00	24.00
B-DJ Derek Jeter	80.00	24.00
B-IR Ivan Rodriguez	40.00	12.00
B-JG Jason Giambi	25.00	7.50
B-JG Jeff Bagwell	40.00	12.00
B-KG Ken Griffey Jr.	50.00	15.00
B-MM Mark McGwire	100.00	30.00
B-MP Mike Piazza	60.00	18.00
B-RA Rick Ankiel	25.00	7.50
B-RJ Randy Johnson	40.00	12.00
B-SG Shawn Green	25.00	7.50
B-SS Sammy Sosa	50.00	15.00
B-TH Todd Helton	40.00	12.00
B-TOG Tony Gwynn	40.00	12.00
B-TRG Troy Glaus	25.00	7.50
B-VG Vladimir Guerrero	40.00	12.00

2001 Upper Deck Game Ball 2

Inserted into second series packs at a rate of one in 288 , this 18-card insert features game-used baseballs from the depicted players. Card backs carry a "B" prefix. The Nomar Garciaparra card was short printed and has been notated as such in our checklist.

	Nm-Mt	Ex-Mt
B-AJ Andruw Jones	10.00	3.00
B-AR A.Rodriguez Rangers	25.00	7.50
B-BB Barry Bonds	40.00	12.00
B-BW Bernie Williams	15.00	4.50
B-CJ Chipper Jones	15.00	4.50
B-CR Cal Ripken	40.00	12.00
B-DJ Derek Jeter	40.00	12.00
B-GS Gary Sheffield	10.00	3.00
B-JB Jeff Bagwell	15.00	4.50
B-JK Jeff Kent	10.00	3.00
B-KG Ken Griffey Jr.	25.00	7.50
B-MM Mark McGwire	50.00	15.00
B-MP Mike Piazza	25.00	7.50
B-MR Mariano Rivera	15.00	4.50
B-NG N.Garciaparra SP	40.00	12.00
B-RC Roger Clemens	25.00	7.50
B-SS Sammy Sosa	25.00	7.50
B-VG Vladimir Guerrero	15.00	4.50

2001 Upper Deck Game Ball Gold Autograph

Randomly inserted into packs, this nine-card insert set features autographs and game-used baseball swatches from the depicted players below. Card backs carry a "SB" prefix. Please note that only 25 serial numbered sets were produced. The following cards packed out as exchange cards with a redmption deadline of August 7th, 2001: Alex Rodriguez, Jeff Bagwell, Ken Griffey Jr. and Rick Ankiel.

	Nm-Mt	Ex-Mt
SB-AR Alex Rodriguez		
SB-BB Barry Bonds		
SB-JB Jeff Bagwell		
SB-JG Jason Giambi		
SB-KG Ken Griffey Jr.		
SB-RA Rick Ankiel		
SB-RJ Randy Johnson		
SB-SG Shawn Green		
SB-TH Todd Helton		

2001 Upper Deck Game Jersey

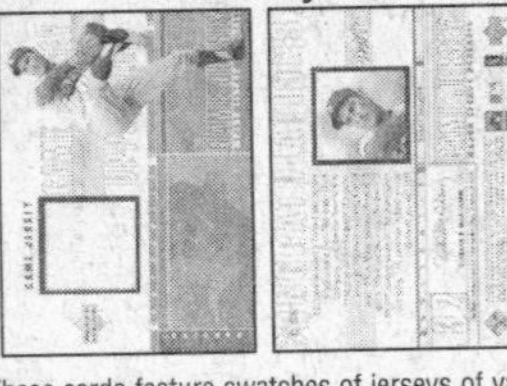

These cards feature swatches of jerseys of various major league stars. These cards were available in either series one hobby or retail packs at a rate of one every 288 packs. Card backs carry a "C" prefix.

	Nm-Mt	Ex-Mt
C-AJ A.Jones HR1	15.00	4.50
C-AR Alex Rodriguez	25.00	7.50
C-BW B.Williams HR1	25.00	7.50
C-CR Cal Ripken	50.00	15.00
C-DJ Derek Jeter	50.00	15.00
C-FT Fernando Tatis	15.00	4.50
C-IR Ivan Rodriguez	25.00	7.50
C-KG Ken Griffey Jr.	40.00	12.00
C-MR M.Ramirez HR1	25.00	7.50
C-MW Matt Williams	15.00	4.50
C-NRA Nolan Ryan Astros HR1	50.00	15.00
C-NRR Nolan Ryan Rangers HR1	50.00	15.00
C-PO Paul O'Neill	25.00	7.50
C-RV Robin Ventura	15.00	4.50
C-SK Sandy Koufax	150.00	45.00
C-TG Tony Gwynn	25.00	7.50
C-TH Todd Helton	25.00	7.50
C-TIH Tim Hudson	15.00	4.50

2001 Upper Deck Game Jersey Autograph 1

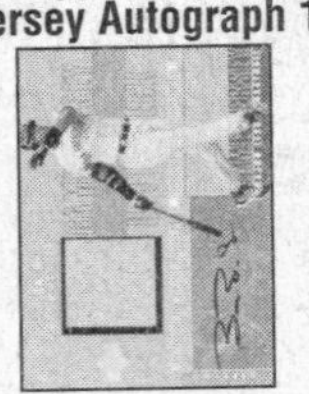

These cards feature both autographs and swatches of jerseys from various major league stars. The cards which have an "H1" after the player names are available in series one hobby packs at a rate of one in every 288 packs. Card backs carry a "H" prefix. The following cards were distributed in packs as exchange cards: Alex Rodriguez, Jeff Bagwell, Ken Griffey Jr., Mike Hampton and Rick Ankiel. The deadline to exchange these cards was August 7th, 2001.

	Nm-Mt	Ex-Mt
H-AR A.Rodriguez H1	150.00	45.00
H-BB Barry Bonds	350.00	105.00
H-FT Frank Thomas	60.00	18.00
H-GM Greg Maddux	150.00	45.00
H-JB J.Bagwell H1	60.00	18.00
H-JC Jose Canseco	60.00	18.00
H-JD J.D. Drew	50.00	15.00
H-JG Jason Giambi	40.00	12.00
H-JL Javy Lopez	40.00	12.00
H-KG K.Griffey Jr. H1	120.00	36.00
H-MH M.Hampton H1	40.00	12.00
H-NRA Nolan Ryan Angels	200.00	60.00
H-NRM Nolan Ryan Mets	200.00	60.00
H-RA R.Ankiel H1	25.00	7.50
H-RJ Randy Johnson	100.00	30.00
H-RP Rafael Palmeiro	60.00	18.00
H-SC Sean Casey	40.00	12.00
H-SG Shawn Green	40.00	12.00

2001 Upper Deck Game Jersey Autograph 2

These cards feature both autographs and swatches of jerseys from various major league stars. The cards which have an "H2" after the player names are available in series one hobby packs at a rate of one in every 288 packs. Card backs carry a "H" prefix. Please note a few of the players were issued in lesser quantites and we have notated those as SP's. The following players packed out as exchange cards: Alex Rodriguez and Ken Griffey Jr. The deadline for exchange is June 26th, 2006.

	Nm-Mt	Ex-Mt
AJ Andruw Jones	40.00	12.00
AR Alex Rodriguez EXCH	150.00	45.00
BB Barry Bonds	350.00	105.00
CJ Chipper Jones	60.00	18.00
CR Cal Ripken SP	200.00	60.00
GS Gary Sheffield	50.00	15.00
IR Ivan Rodriguez SP	100.00	30.00
JB Johnny Bench	60.00	18.00
JC Jose Canseco	60.00	18.00
KG Ken Griffey Jr. EXCH	120.00	36.00
NR Nolan Ryan	200.00	60.00
RC Roger Clemens	150.00	45.00
SS Sammy Sosa SP	200.00	60.00
TG Troy Glaus	40.00	12.00

2001 Upper Deck Game Jersey Autograph Numbered

These cards feature both autographs and swatches of jerseys from various major league stars. The cards which have an "H" after the player names were only available in series one hobby packs, while the cards with a "C" can be found in either series one hobby or retail packs. Hobby cards feature gold backgrounds and say "Signed Game Jersey" on front. Hobby/Retail cards feature white backgrounds and simply say "Game Jersey" on front. These cards are individually serial numbered to the depicted player's jersey number. The following players packed out as exchange cards: Alex Rodriguez, Ken Griffey Jr., Jeff Bagwell, Mike Hampton and Rick Ankiel. The exchange deadline was August 7th, 2001.

	Nm-Mt	Ex-Mt
C-AJ Andruw Jones/25		
C-AR Alex Rodriguez/3		
C-FT Fernando Tatis/23		
C-IR Ivan Rodriguez/7		
C-JL Javy Lopez/8		
C-KG Ken Griffey Jr./30 HR1	250.00	75.00
C-MW Matt Williams/9		
C-NRA Nolan Ryan Astros/34 HR1	400.00	120.00
C-NRR Nolan Ryan Rangers 34 HR1	400.00	120.00
C-PO Paul O'Neill/21		
C-RV Robin Ventura/4		
C-SK Sandy Koufax 32 HR1	1200.00	350.00
C-TG Tony Gwynn/19		
C-TH Todd Helton/17		
C-TIH Tim Hudson/15		
H-AR Alex Rodriguez/3		
H-BB Barry Bonds/25		
H-FT Frank Thomas/35	150.00	45.00
H-GM Greg Maddux/31	300.00	90.00
H-JB Jeff Bagwell/5		
H-JC Jose Canseco/33	150.00	45.00
H-JD J.D. Drew/7		
H-JG Jason Giambi/16		
H-KG Ken Griffey Jr. 30 H1	250.00	75.00
H-MH Mike Hampton/32	40.00	12.00
H-NRA Nolan Ryan 30/Angels H1	400.00	120.00
H-NRM Nolan Ryan 30/Mets H1	500.00	150.00
H-RA Rick Ankiel 66 H1	40.00	12.00
H-RJ Randy Johnson 51 H1	150.00	45.00
H-RP Rafael Palmeiro 25 H1		
H-SC Sean Casey/21		
H-SG Shawn Green/15		

2001 Upper Deck Game Jersey Combo

Randomly inserted into series one packs, these 13 cards feature dual player game-worn uniform patches. Card backs carry both players initials as numbering. Please note that there were only 50 serial numbered sets produced.

	Nm-Mt	Ex-Mt
AJKG Andruw Jones Ken Griffey Jr.	80.00	24.00
BBJC Barry Bonds Jose Canseco	100.00	30.00
BBKG Barry Bonds Ken Griffey Jr.	100.00	30.00
DJAR Derek Jeter Alex Rodriguez	100.00	30.00
FTJB Frank Thomas Jeff Bagwell	50.00	15.00
IRRP Ivan Rodriguez Rafael Palmeiro	50.00	15.00
JDRA J.D. Drew Rick Ankiel	40.00	12.00
MMKG Mickey Mantle Ken Griffey Jr.		
NRAR Nolan Rya Astros-Rangers	120.00	36.00
NRMA Nolan Ryan Mets-Angels	120.00	36.00
RATH Rick Ankiel Tim Hudson	40.00	12.00
RJGM Randy Johnson Greg Maddux	60.00	18.00
TGCR Tony Gwynn Cal Ripken	100.00	30.00
VGMR Vladimir Guerrero Manny Ramirez	50.00	15.00

2001 Upper Deck Game Jersey Combo Autograph

Randomly inserted into series one hobby packs, these seven cards feature autographed dual player game-worn uniform patches. Card backs carry both players initials as numbering with a "S" prefix. Please note that there were only 10 serial numbered sets produced. Cards SAJ-KG and SJD-RA both packed out as exchange cards with a redemption deadline of 8/07/01. Due to market scarcity, no pricing is provided.

	Nm-Mt	Ex-Mt
SAJ-KG Andruw Jones Ken Griffey Jr. EXCH		
SBB-JC Barry Bonds Jose Canseco		
SBB-KG Barry Bonds Ken Griffey Jr.		
SDJ-AR Derek Jeter Alex Rodriguez		
SJD-RA J.D. Drew Rick Ankiel		
SNR-AR Nolan Ryan Astros-Rangers		
SNR-MA Nolan Ryan Mets-Angels		

2001 Upper Deck Game Jersey Patch

Randomly inserted into series one packs at one in 7500 and series 2 packs at 1:5000, these cards feature game-worn uniform patches. Card backs carry a "P" prefix.

	Nm-Mt	Ex-Mt
P-AR Alex Rodriguez S1	120.00	36.00
P-AR Alex Rodriguez S2	120.00	36.00
P-BB Barry Bonds S1	150.00	45.00
P-BB Barry Bonds S2	150.00	45.00
P-CJ Chipper Jones S2	80.00	24.00
P-CR Cal Ripken S1	150.00	45.00
P-CR Cal Ripken S2	150.00	45.00
P-DJ Derek Jeter S1	150.00	45.00
P-FT Frank Thomas S1	80.00	24.00
P-IR Ivan Rodriguez S1	80.00	24.00
P-IR Ivan Rodriguez S2	80.00	24.00
P-JB Johnny Bench S2	80.00	24.00
P-JB Jeff Bagwell S1	80.00	24.00
P-JC Jose Canseco S1	80.00	24.00
P-JG Jason Giambi S1	50.00	15.00
P-KG Ken Griffey Jr. S1	100.00	30.00
P-KG Ken Griffey Jr. S2	100.00	30.00
P-NRA Nolan Ryan Astros	150.00	45.00
P-NRR N.Ryan Rangers S1	150.00	45.00
P-NRR N.Ryan Rangers S2	150.00	45.00
P-RA Rick Ankiel S1	50.00	15.00
P-RP Rafael Palmeiro S1	80.00	24.00
P-SS Sammy Sosa S2	120.00	36.00
P-TG Tony Gwynn S1	100.00	30.00

2001 Upper Deck Game Jersey Patch Autograph Numbered

Randomly inserted into series one hobby packs, these cards feature both autographs and game-worn uniform patches. Card backs carry a "SP" prefix. Please note that these cards are hand-numbered to the depicted players jersey number. All of these cards packed out as exchange cards with a redemption deadline of 8/07/01.

	Nm-Mt	Ex-Mt
SP-AR Alex Rodriguez/3		
SP-KG K.Griffey Jr./30	500.00	150.00
SP-RA Rick Ankiel/66	60.00	18.00

2001 Upper Deck Home Run Derby Heroes

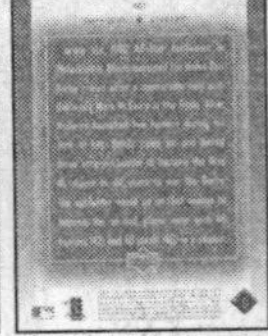

Inserted in second series packs at a rate of one in 36, these 10 cards features a look back at some of the most explosive performances from past Home Run Derby competitions.

	Nm-Mt	Ex-Mt
COMPLETE SET (10)	50.00	15.00
HD1 Mark McGwire 99	10.00	3.00
HD2 Sammy Sosa 00	6.00	1.80
HD3 Frank Thomas 96	4.00	1.20
HD4 Cal Ripken 91	12.00	3.60
HD5 Tino Martinez 97	2.50	.75
HD6 Ken Griffey Jr. 99	6.00	1.80
HD7 Barry Bonds 96	10.00	3.00
HD8 Albert Belle 95	2.00	.60
HD9 Mark McGwire 92	10.00	3.00
HD10 Juan Gonzalez 93	2.50	.75

2001 Upper Deck Home Run Explosion

Randomly inserted into series one packs at one in 12, this 15-card insert features players that are among the league leaders in homeruns every year. Card backs carry a "HR" prefix.

	Nm-Mt	Ex-Mt
COMPLETE SET (15)	40.00	12.00
HR1 Mark McGwire	5.00	1.50
HR2 Chipper Jones	2.00	.60
HR3 Jeff Bagwell	1.25	.35
HR4 Carlos Delgado	1.00	.30
HR5 Barry Bonds	5.00	1.50
HR6 Troy Glaus	1.00	.30
HR7 Sammy Sosa	3.00	.90
HR8 Alex Rodriguez	3.00	.90
HR9 Mike Piazza	3.00	.90
HR10 Vladimir Guerrero	2.00	.60
HR11 Ken Griffey Jr.	3.00	.90
HR12 Frank Thomas	2.00	.60
HR13 Ivan Rodriguez	2.00	.60
HR14 Jason Giambi	1.00	.30
HR15 Carl Everett	1.00	.30

2001 Upper Deck Midseason Superstar Summit

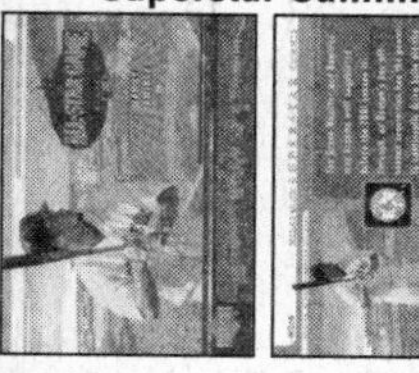

nserted in series two packs at a rate of one in 4, these 15 cards feature some of the most lominant players of the 2000 season.

	Nm-Mt	Ex-Mt
OMPLETE SET (15)	60.00	18.00
MS1 Derek Jeter	10.00	3.00
MS2 Sammy Sosa	6.00	1.80
MS3 Jeff Bagwell	2.50	.75
MS4 Tony Gwynn	5.00	1.50
MS5 Alex Rodriguez	6.00	1.80
MS6 Greg Maddux	6.00	1.80
MS7 Jason Giambi	2.00	.60
MS8 Mark McGwire	10.00	3.00
MS9 Barry Bonds	10.00	3.00
MS10 Ken Griffey Jr.	6.00	1.80
MS11 Carlos Delgado	2.00	.60
MS12 Troy Glaus	2.00	.60
MS13 Todd Helton	2.50	.75
MS14 Manny Ramirez	2.50	.75
MS15 Jeff Kent	2.00	.60

2001 Upper Deck Midsummer Classic Moments

serted in series two packs at a rate of one in 2, these 20 cards feature some of the most emorable moments from All Star Game histo-

	Nm-Mt	Ex-Mt
OMPLETE SET (20)	40.00	12.00
M1 Joe DiMaggio 36	3.00	.90
M2 Joe DiMaggio 51	3.00	.90
M3 Mickey Mantle 52	6.00	1.80
M4 Mickey Mantle 68	6.00	1.80
M5 Roger Clemens 86	4.00	1.20
M6 Mark McGwire 87	5.00	1.50
M7 Cal Ripken 91	6.00	1.80
M8 Ken Griffey Jr. 92	3.00	.90
M9 Randy Johnson 93	2.00	.60
M10 Tony Gwynn 94	2.50	.75
M11 Fred McGriff 94	1.25	.35
M12 Hideo Nomo 95	2.00	.60
M13 Jeff Conine 95	1.00	.30
M14 Mike Piazza 96	3.00	.90
M15 Sandy Alomar Jr.	1.00	.30
M16 Alex Rodriguez 98	2.50	.75
M17 Roberto Alomar 98	1.25	.35
M18 Pedro Martinez 99	2.00	.60
M19 Andres Galarraga	1.00	.30
M20 Derek Jeter 00	4.00	1.20

2001 Upper Deck People's Choice

serted one per 24 series two packs, these 15 rds feature the players who fans want to see most.

	Nm-Mt	Ex-Mt
MPLETE SET (15)	80.00	24.00
1 Alex Rodriguez	6.00	1.80
2 Ken Griffey Jr.	6.00	1.80
3 Mark McGwire	10.00	3.00
4 Todd Helton	2.50	.75
5 Manny Ramirez	2.50	.75
6 Mike Piazza	6.00	1.80
7 Vladimir Guerrero	4.00	1.20
8 Randy Johnson	4.00	1.20
9 Cal Ripken	12.00	3.60
10 Andruw Jones	2.50	.75
11 Sammy Sosa	6.00	1.80
12 Derek Jeter	10.00	3.00

PC13 Pedro Martinez	4.00	1.20
PC14 Frank Thomas	4.00	1.20
PC15 Nomar Garciaparra	6.00	1.80

2001 Upper Deck Rookie Roundup

Randomly inserted into series one packs at one in six, this 10-card insert features some of the younger players in Major League baseball. Card backs carry a "RR" prefix.

	Nm-Mt	Ex-Mt
COMPLETE SET (10)	5.00	1.50
RR1 Rick Ankiel	.50	.15
RR2 Adam Kennedy	.50	.15
RR3 Mike Lamb	.50	.15
RR4 Adam Eaton	.50	.15
RR5 Rafael Furcal	.75	.23
RR6 Pat Burrell	.75	.23
RR7 Adam Piatt	.50	.15
RR8 Eric Munson	.50	.15
RR9 Brad Penny	.50	.15
RR10 Mark Mulder	.75	.23

2001 Upper Deck Subway Series Game Jerseys

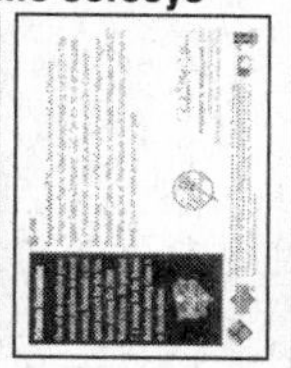

While the set name seemed to indicate that these cards were from jerseys worn during the 2000 World series, they were actually swatches from regular-season game jerseys.

	Nm-Mt	Ex-Mt
SS-AL Al Leiter	10.00	3.00
SS-AP Andy Pettitte	25.00	7.50
SS-BW Bernie Williams	25.00	7.50
SS-EA Edgardo Alfonzo	8.00	2.40
SS-JF John Franco	10.00	3.00
SS-JP Jay Payton	8.00	2.40
SS-OH Orlando Hernandez	15.00	4.50
SS-PO Paul O'Neill	25.00	7.50
SS-RC Roger Clemens	40.00	12.00
SS-TP Timo Perez	8.00	2.40

2001 Upper Deck Superstar Summit

Randomly inserted into packs at one in 12, this 15-card insert features the Major League's top superstar caliber players. Card backs carry a "SS" prefix.

	Nm-Mt	Ex-Mt
COMPLETE SET (15)	50.00	15.00
SS1 Derek Jeter	5.00	1.50
SS2 Randy Johnson	2.00	.60
SS3 Barry Bonds	5.00	1.50
SS4 Frank Thomas	2.00	.60
SS5 Cal Ripken	6.00	1.80
SS6 Pedro Martinez	2.00	.60
SS7 Ivan Rodriguez	2.00	.60
SS8 Mike Piazza	3.00	.90
SS9 Mark McGwire	5.00	1.50
SS10 Manny Ramirez	2.00	.60
SS11 Ken Griffey Jr.	3.00	.90
SS12 Sammy Sosa	3.00	.90
SS13 Alex Rodriguez	3.00	.90
SS14 Chipper Jones	2.00	.60
SS15 Nomar Garciaparra	3.00	.90

2001 Upper Deck UD's Most Wanted

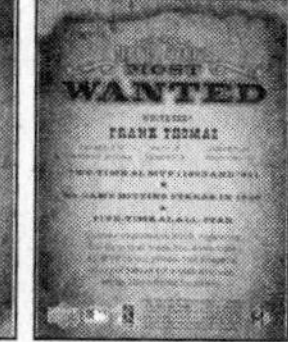

Randomly inserted into packs at one in 14, this 15-card insert features players that are in high demand on the collectibles market. Card backs carry a "MW" prefix.

	Nm-Mt	Ex-Mt
COMPLETE SET (15)	60.00	18.00
MW1 Mark McGwire	6.00	1.80
MW2 Cal Ripken	8.00	2.40
MW3 Ivan Rodriguez	2.50	.75
MW4 Pedro Martinez	2.50	.75
MW5 Sammy Sosa	4.00	1.20
MW6 Tony Gwynn	3.00	.90
MW7 Vladimir Guerrero	2.50	.75
MW8 Derek Jeter	6.00	1.80
MW9 Mike Piazza	4.00	1.20
MW10 Chipper Jones	2.50	.75
MW11 Alex Rodriguez	4.00	1.20
MW12 Barry Bonds	6.00	1.80
MW13 Jeff Bagwell	2.50	.75
MW14 Frank Thomas	2.50	.75
MW15 Nomar Garciaparra	4.00	1.20

2001 Upper Deck Pinstripe Exclusives DiMaggio

This 56-card set features a wide selection of cards focusing on Yankees legend Joe DiMaggio. The cards were distributed in special three-card foil wrapped packs, exclusively seeded into 2001 SP Game Bat Milestone, SP Game-Used, SPx, Upper Deck Decade 1970's, Upper Deck Gold Glove, Upper Deck Legends, Upper Deck Ovation and Upper Deck Sweet Spot hobby boxes at a rate of one pack per sealed box.

	Nm-Mt	Ex-Mt
COMPLETE SET (56)	60.00	18.00
COMMON (JD1-JD56)	1.50	.45

2001 Upper Deck Pinstripe Exclusives DiMaggio Memorabilia

Randomly seeded into special three-card Pinstripe Exclusives DiMaggio foil packs (of which were distributed exclusively in 2001 SP Game Bat Milestone, SP Game-Used, SPx, Upper Deck Decade 1970's, Upper Deck Gold Glove, Upper Deck Legends, Upper Deck Ovation and Upper Deck Sweet Spot Sweet Spot hobby boxes) were a selection of scarce game-used memorabilia and autograph cut cards featuring Joe DiMaggio. Each card is serial-numbered and features either a game-used bat chip, jersey swatch or autograph cut.

	Nm-Mt	Ex-Mt
COMMON BAT (B1-B9)	80.00	24.00
COMMON JERSEY (J1-J9)	80.00	24.00

SUFFIX 1 CARDS DIST.IN SWEET SPOT
SUFFIX 2 CARDS DIST.IN OVATION....
SUFFIX 3 CARDS DIST.IN SPX..........
SUFFIX 4 CARDS DIST.IN SP GAME USED
SUFFIX 5 CARDS DIST.IN LEGENDS...
SUFFIX 6 CARDS DIST. IN DECADE 1970
SUFFIX 7 CARDS DIST.IN SP BAT MILE
SUFFIX 8 CARDS DIST.IN UD GOLD GLOVE
BAT 1-9 PRINT RUN 100 SERIAL #'d SETS
BAT-CUT 1-7 PRINT RUN 5 SERIAL #'d SETS
COMBO 1-6 PRINT RUN 50 SERIAL #'D SETS
CUT 1-8 PRINT RUN 5 SERIAL #'d SETS
JERSEY 1-8 PRINT RUN 100 SERIAL #'d SETS

CJ1 Joe DiMaggio Jsy	600.00	180.00
Lou Gehrig Pants/50		
CJ2 Joe DiMaggio Jsy	400.00	120.00
Mickey Mantle Jsy/50		
CJ3 Joe DiMaggio Jsy	200.00	60.00
Ken Griffey Jr. Jsy/50		
CJ4 Joe DiMaggio Jsy	250.00	75.00
Dom DiMaggio Jsy/50		
CJ5 Joe DiMaggio Jsy	400.00	120.00
Mickey Mantle Jsy/50		
CJ6 Joe DiMaggio Jsy	400.00	120.00
Mickey Mantle Jsy/50		

2001 Upper Deck Pinstripe Exclusives Mantle

This 56-card set features a wide selection of cards focusing on Yankees legend Mickey Mantle. The cards were distributed in special three-card foil wrapped packs, seeded into 2001 Upper Deck Series 2, Upper Deck Hall of Famers, Upper Deck MVP and Upper Deck Vintage hobby boxes at a rate of one pack per 24 ct. box.

	Nm-Mt	Ex-Mt
COMPLETE SET (56)	100.00	30.00
COMMON (MM1-MM56)	2.50	.75

2001 Upper Deck Pinstripe Exclusives Mantle Memorabilia

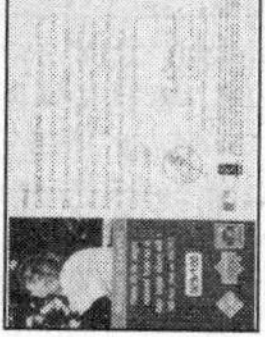

Randomly seeded into special three-card Pinstripe Exclusives Mantle foil packs (of which were distributed in hobby boxes of 2001 SP Authentic, 2001 SP Game Bat Milestone, 2001 Upper Deck series 2, 2001 Upper Deck Hall of Famers, 2001 Upper Deck Legends of New York, 2001 Upper Deck MVP and 2001 Upper Deck Vintage) were a selection of scarce game-used memorabilia and autograph cut cards featuring Mickey Mantle. Each card is serial-numbered and features either a game-used bat chip, jersey swatch or autograph cut.

	Nm-Mt	Ex-Mt
COMMON BAT (B1-B4)	150.00	45.00
COMMON JERSEY (J1-J7)	150.00	45.00
COMMON BAT CUT (BC1-BC4)		
COMMON CUT (C1-C4)		

SUFFIX 1 CARDS DIST.IN UD VINTAGE
SUFFIX 2 CARDS DIST.IN UD HOF'ers
SUFFIX 3 CARDS DIST.IN UD MVP.....
SUFFIX 4 CARDS DIST.IN UD SER.2....
SUFFIX 5 CARDS DIST. IN SP AUTH ..
SUFFIX 6 CARDS DIST. IN SP GAME BAT MILE
SUFFIX 7 CARDS DIST. IN UD LEG OF NY
BAT 1-9 PRINT RUN 100 SERIAL #'d SETS
BAT-CUT 1-4 PRINT RUN 7 SERIAL #'d SETS
COMBO 1-6 PRINT RUN 50 SERIAL #'d SETS
CUT 1-4 PRINT RUN 7 SERIAL #'D SETS
JERSEY 1-7 PRINT RUN 100 SERIAL #'d SETS

CJ1 Mickey Mantle	400.00	120.00
Roger Maris Jsy/50		
CJ2 Mickey Mantle	300.00	90.00
Joe DiMag Jsy/50		
CJ3 Mickey Mantle	200.00	60.00
Ken Griffey Jsy/50		
CJ4 Mickey Mantle	400.00	120.00
Roger Maris Jsy/50		
CJ5 Mickey Mantle	300.00	90.00
Joe DiMaggio Jsy/50		
CJ6 Mickey Mantle	300.00	90.00
Joe DiMaggio Jsy/50		
CJ7 Mickey Mantle	300.00	90.00
Joe DiMaggio Jsy 50		

2002 Upper Deck

The 500 card first series set was issued in November, 2001. The 245-card second series set was issued in May, 2002. The cards were issued in eight card packs with 24 packs to a box. Subsets include Star Rookies (cards numbered 1-50, 501-545), World Stage (cards numbered 461-480), Griffey Gallery (481-490) and Checklists (491-500, 736-745) and Year of the Record (726-735). Star Rookies were inserted at a rate of one per pack into second series packs, making them 1.75X times tougher to pull than veteran second series cards.

	Nm-Mt	Ex-Mt
COMPLETE SET (745)	160.00	47.50
COMPLETE SERIES 1 (500)	110.00	33.00
COMPLETE SERIES 2 (245)	50.00	15.00
COMMON (51-500/546-745)	.30	.09
COMMON SR (1-50/501-545)	1.00	.30
1 Mark Prior SR	4.00	1.20
2 Mark Teixeira SR	1.50	.45
3 Brian Roberts SR	1.00	.30
4 Jason Romano SR	1.00	.30
5 Dennis Stark SR	1.00	.30
6 Oscar Salazar SR	1.00	.30
7 John Patterson SR	1.00	.30
8 Shane Loux SR	1.00	.30
9 Marcus Giles SR	1.00	.30
10 Juan Cruz SR	1.00	.30
11 Jorge Julio SR	1.00	.30
12 Adam Dunn SR	1.50	.45
13 Delvin James SR	1.00	.30
14 Jeremy Affeldt SR	1.00	.30
15 Tim Raines Jr. SR	1.00	.30
16 Luke Hudson SR	1.00	.30
17 Todd Sears SR	1.00	.30
18 George Perez SR	1.00	.30
19 Wilmy Caceres SR	1.00	.30
20 Abraham Nunez SR	1.00	.30
21 Mike Amrhein SR RC	1.00	.30
22 Carlos Hernandez SR	1.00	.30
23 Scott Hodges SR	1.00	.30
24 Brandon Knight SR	1.00	.30
25 Geoff Goetz SR	1.00	.30
26 Carlos Garcia SR	1.00	.30
27 Luis Pineda SR	1.00	.30
28 Chris Gissell SR	1.00	.30
29 Jae Weong Seo SR	1.00	.30
30 Paul Phillips SR	1.00	.30
31 Cory Aldridge SR	1.00	.30
32 Aaron Cook SR RC	1.00	.30
33 Rendy Espina SR RC	1.00	.30
34 Jason Phillips SR	1.00	.30
35 Carlos Silva SR	1.00	.30
36 Ryan Mills SR	1.00	.30
37 Pedro Santana SR	1.00	.30
38 John Grabow SR	1.00	.30
39 Cody Ransom SR	1.00	.30
40 Orlando Woodards SR	1.00	.30
41 Bud Smith SR	1.00	.30
42 Junior Guerrero SR	1.00	.30
43 David Brous SR	1.00	.30
44 Steve Green SR	1.00	.30
45 Brian Rogers SR	1.00	.30
46 Juan Figueroa SR RC	1.00	.30
47 Nick Punto SR	1.00	.30
48 Junior Herndon SR	1.00	.30
49 Justin Kaye SR	1.00	.30
50 Jason Karnuth SR	1.00	.30
51 Troy Glaus	.30	.09
52 Bengie Molina	.30	.09
53 Ramon Ortiz	.30	.09
54 Adam Kennedy	.30	.09
55 Jarrod Washburn	.30	.09
56 Troy Percival	.30	.09
57 David Eckstein	.30	.09
58 Ben Weber	.30	.09
59 Larry Barnes	.30	.09
60 Ismael Valdes	.30	.09
61 Benji Gil	.30	.09
62 Scott Schoeneweis	.30	.09
63 Pat Rapp	.30	.09
64 Jason Giambi	.30	.09
65 Mark Mulder	.30	.09
66 Ron Gant	.30	.09
67 Johnny Damon	.50	.15
68 Adam Piatt	.30	.09
69 Jermaine Dye	.30	.09
70 Jason Hart	.30	.09
71 Eric Chavez	.30	.09
72 Jim Mecir	.30	.09
73 Barry Zito	.30	.09
74 Jason Isringhausen	.30	.09
75 Jeremy Giambi	.30	.09
76 Olmedo Saenz	.30	.09
77 Terrence Long	.30	.09
78 Ramon Hernandez	.30	.09
79 Chris Carpenter	.30	.09
80 Raul Mondesi	.30	.09
81 Carlos Delgado	.30	.09
82 Billy Koch	.30	.09
83 Vernon Wells	.30	.09
84 Darrin Fletcher	.30	.09
85 Homer Bush	.30	.09
86 Pasqual Coco	.30	.09
87 Shannon Stewart	.30	.09
88 Chris Woodward	.30	.09
89 Joe Lawrence	.30	.09
90 Esteban Loaiza	.30	.09
91 Cesar Izturis	.30	.09
92 Kelvim Escobar	.30	.09
93 Greg Vaughn	.30	.09
94 Brent Abernathy	.30	.09
95 Tanyon Sturtze	.30	.09
96 Steve Cox	.30	.09
97 Aubrey Huff	.30	.09
98 Jesus Colome	.30	.09
99 Ben Grieve	.30	.09
100 Esteban Yan	.30	.09
101 Joe Kennedy	.30	.09
102 Felix Martinez	.30	.09
103 Nick Bierbrodt	.30	.09
104 Damian Rolls	.30	.09
105 Russ Johnson	.30	.09
106 Toby Hall	.30	.09
107 Roberto Alomar	.50	.15
108 Bartolo Colon	.30	.09
109 John Rocker	.30	.09
110 Juan Gonzalez	.50	.15
111 Einar Diaz	.30	.09
112 Chuck Finley	.30	.09
113 Kenny Lofton	.30	.09
114 Danys Baez	.30	.09
115 Travis Fryman	.30	.09
116 C.C. Sabathia	.30	.09
117 Paul Shuey	.30	.09
118 Marty Cordova	.30	.09
119 Ellis Burks	.30	.09
120 Bob Wickman	.30	.09
121 Edgar Martinez	.50	.15
122 Freddy Garcia	.30	.09
123 Ichiro Suzuki	1.25	.35
124 John Olerud	.30	.09
125 Gil Meche	.30	.09
126 Dan Wilson	.30	.09
127 Aaron Sele	.30	.09
128 Kazuhiro Sasaki	.30	.09
129 Mark McLemore	.30	.09
130 Carlos Guillen	.30	.09
131 Al Martin	.30	.09
132 David Bell	.30	.09
133 Jay Buhner	.30	.09
134 Stan Javier	.30	.09
135 Tony Batista	.30	.09
136 Jason Johnson	.30	.09
137 Brook Fordyce	.30	.09
138 Mike Kinkade	.30	.09
139 Willis Roberts	.30	.09
140 David Segui	.30	.09
141 Josh Towers	.30	.09
142 Jeff Conine	.30	.09
143 Chris Richard	.30	.09
144 Pat Hentgen	.30	.09
145 Melvin Mora	.30	.09
146 Jerry Hairston Jr.	.30	.09
147 Calvin Maduro	.30	.09
148 Brady Anderson	.30	.09
149 Alex Rodriguez	1.25	.35
150 Kenny Rogers	.30	.09
151 Chad Curtis	.30	.09
152 Ricky Ledee	.30	.09
153 Rafael Palmeiro	.50	.15
154 Rob Bell	.30	.09
155 Rick Helling	.30	.09
156 Doug Davis	.30	.09
157 Mike Lamb	.30	.09
158 Gabe Kapler	.30	.09
159 Jeff Zimmerman	.30	.09
160 Bill Haselman	.30	.09
161 Tim Crabtree	.30	.09
162 Carlos Pena	.30	.09
163 Nomar Garciaparra	1.25	.35
164 Shea Hillenbrand	.30	.09
165 Hideo Nomo	.75	.23
166 Manny Ramirez	.50	.15

Card	Nm-Mt	Ex-Mt
167 Jose Offerman	.30	.09
168 Scott Hatteberg	.30	.09
169 Trot Nixon	.30	.09
170 Darren Lewis	.30	.09
171 Derek Lowe	.30	.09
172 Troy O'Leary	.30	.09
173 Tim Wakefield	.30	.09
174 Chris Stynes	.30	.09
175 John Valentin	.30	.09
176 David Cone	.30	.09
177 Neifi Perez	.30	.09
178 Brent Mayne	.30	.09
179 Dan Reichert	.30	.09
180 A.J. Hinch	.30	.09
181 Chris George	.30	.09
182 Mike Sweeney	.30	.09
183 Jeff Suppan	.30	.09
184 Roberto Hernandez	.30	.09
185 Joe Randa	.30	.09
186 Paul Byrd	.30	.09
187 Luis Ordaz	.30	.09
188 Kris Wilson	.30	.09
189 Dee Brown	.30	.09
190 Tony Clark	.30	.09
191 Matt Anderson	.30	.09
192 Robert Fick	.30	.09
193 Juan Encarnacion	.30	.09
194 Dean Palmer	.30	.09
195 Victor Santos	.30	.09
196 Damion Easley	.30	.09
197 Jose Lima	.30	.09
198 Deivi Cruz	.30	.09
199 Roger Cedeno	.30	.09
200 Jose Macias	.30	.09
201 Jeff Weaver	.30	.09
202 Brandon Inge	.30	.09
203 Brian Moehler	.30	.09
204 Brad Radke	.30	.09
205 Doug Mientkiewicz	.30	.09
206 Cristian Guzman	.30	.09
207 Corey Koskie	.30	.09
208 LaTroy Hawkins	.30	.09
209 J.C. Romero	.30	.09
210 Chad Allen	.30	.09
211 Torii Hunter	.30	.09
212 Travis Miller	.30	.09
213 Joe Mays	.30	.09
214 Todd Jones	.30	.09
215 David Ortiz	.50	.15
216 Brian Buchanan	.30	.09
217 A.J. Pierzynski	.30	.09
218 Carlos Lee	.30	.09
219 Gary Glover	.30	.09
220 Jose Valentin	.30	.09
221 Aaron Rowand	.30	.09
222 Sandy Alomar Jr.	.30	.09
223 Herbert Perry	.30	.09
224 Jon Garland	.30	.09
225 Mark Buehrle	.30	.09
226 Chris Singleton	.30	.09
227 Kip Wells	.30	.09
228 Ray Durham	.30	.09
229 Joe Crede	.30	.09
230 Keith Foulke	.30	.09
231 Royce Clayton	.30	.09
232 Andy Pettitte	.50	.15
233 Derek Jeter	2.00	.60
234 Jorge Posada	.50	.15
235 Roger Clemens	1.50	.45
236 Paul O'Neill	.50	.15
237 Nick Johnson	.30	.09
238 Gerald Williams	.30	.09
239 Mariano Rivera	.50	.15
240 Alfonso Soriano	.50	.15
241 Ramiro Mendoza	.30	.09
242 Mike Mussina	.50	.15
243 Luis Sojo	.30	.09
244 Scott Brosius	.30	.09
245 David Justice	.30	.09
246 Wade Miller	.30	.09
247 Brad Ausmus	.30	.09
248 Jeff Bagwell	.50	.15
249 Daryle Ward	.30	.09
250 Shane Reynolds	.30	.09
251 Chris Truby	.30	.09
252 Billy Wagner	.30	.09
253 Craig Biggio	.50	.15
254 Moises Alou	.30	.09
255 Vinny Castilla	.30	.09
256 Tim Redding	.30	.09
257 Roy Oswalt	.30	.09
258 Julio Lugo	.30	.09
259 Chipper Jones	.75	.23
260 Greg Maddux	1.25	.35
261 Ken Caminiti	.30	.09
262 Kevin Millwood	.30	.09
263 Keith Lockhart	.30	.09
264 Rey Sanchez	.30	.09
265 Jason Marquis	.30	.09
266 Brian Jordan	.30	.09
267 Steve Karsay	.30	.09
268 Wes Helms	.30	.09
269 B.J. Surhoff	.30	.09
270 Wilson Betemit	.30	.09
271 John Smoltz	.50	.15
272 Rafael Furcal	.30	.09
273 Jeromy Burnitz	.30	.09
274 Jimmy Haynes	.30	.09
275 Mark Loretta	.30	.09
276 Jose Hernandez	.30	.09
277 Paul Rigdon	.30	.09
278 Alex Sanchez	.30	.09
279 Chad Fox	.30	.09
280 Devon White	.30	.09
281 Tyler Houston	.30	.09
282 Ronnie Belliard	.30	.09
283 Luis Lopez	.30	.09
284 Ben Sheets	.30	.09
285 Curtis Leskanic	.30	.09
286 Henry Blanco	.30	.09
287 Mark McGwire	2.00	.60
288 Edgar Renteria	.30	.09
289 Matt Morris	.30	.09
290 Gene Stechschulte	.30	.09
291 Dustin Hermanson	.30	.09
292 Eli Marrero	.30	.09
293 Albert Pujols	1.50	.45
294 Luis Saturria	.30	.09
295 Bobby Bonilla	.30	.09
296 Garrett Stephenson	.30	.09
297 Jim Edmonds	.30	.09
298 Rick Ankiel	.30	.09
299 Placido Polanco	.30	.09
300 Dave Veres	.30	.09
301 Sammy Sosa	1.25	.35
302 Eric Young	.30	.09
303 Kerry Wood	.75	.23
304 Jon Lieber	.30	.09
305 Joe Girardi	.30	.09
306 Fred McGriff	.50	.15
307 Jeff Fassero	.30	.09
308 Julio Zuleta	.30	.09
309 Kevin Tapani	.30	.09
310 Rondell White	.30	.09
311 Julian Tavarez	.30	.09
312 Tom Gordon	.30	.09
313 Corey Patterson	.30	.09
314 Bill Mueller	.30	.09
315 Randy Johnson	.75	.23
316 Chad Moeller	.30	.09
317 Tony Womack	.30	.09
318 Erubiel Durazo	.30	.09
319 Luis Gonzalez	.30	.09
320 Brian Anderson	.30	.09
321 Reggie Sanders	.30	.09
322 Greg Colbrunn	.30	.09
323 Robert Ellis	.30	.09
324 Jack Cust	.30	.09
325 Bret Prinz	.30	.09
326 Steve Finley	.30	.09
327 Byung-Hyun Kim	.30	.09
328 Albie Lopez	.30	.09
329 Gary Sheffield	.30	.09
330 Mark Grudzielanek	.30	.09
331 Paul LoDuca	.30	.09
332 Tom Goodwin	.30	.09
333 Andy Ashby	.30	.09
334 Hiram Bocachica	.30	.09
335 Dave Hansen	.30	.09
336 Kevin Brown	.30	.09
337 Marquis Grissom	.30	.09
338 Terry Adams	.30	.09
339 Chan Ho Park	.30	.09
340 Adrian Beltre	.50	.15
341 Luke Prokopec	.30	.09
342 Jeff Shaw	.30	.09
343 Vladimir Guerrero	.75	.23
344 Orlando Cabrera	.30	.09
345 Tony Armas Jr.	.30	.09
346 Michael Barrett	.30	.09
347 Geoff Blum	.30	.09
348 Ryan Minor	.30	.09
349 Peter Bergeron	.30	.09
350 Graeme Lloyd	.30	.09
351 Jose Vidro	.30	.09
352 Javier Vazquez	.30	.09
353 Matt Blank	.30	.09
354 Masato Yoshii	.30	.09
355 Carl Pavano	.30	.09
356 Barry Bonds	2.00	.60
357 Shawon Dunston	.30	.09
358 Livan Hernandez	.30	.09
359 Felix Rodriguez	.30	.09
360 Pedro Feliz	.30	.09
361 Calvin Murray	.30	.09
362 Robb Nen	.30	.09
363 Marvin Benard	.30	.09
364 Russ Ortiz	.30	.09
365 Jason Schmidt	.30	.09
366 Rich Aurilia	.30	.09
367 John Vander Wal	.30	.09
368 Benito Santiago	.30	.09
369 Ryan Dempster	.30	.09
370 Charles Johnson	.30	.09
371 Alex Gonzalez	.30	.09
372 Luis Castillo	.30	.09
373 Mike Lowell	.30	.09
374 Antonio Alfonseca	.30	.09
375 A.J. Burnett	.30	.09
376 Brad Penny	.30	.09
377 Jason Grilli	.30	.09
378 Derrek Lee	.30	.09
379 Matt Clement	.30	.09
380 Eric Owens	.30	.09
381 Vladimir Nunez	.30	.09
382 Cliff Floyd	.30	.09
383 Mike Piazza	1.25	.35
384 Lenny Harris	.30	.09
385 Glendon Rusch	.30	.09
386 Todd Zeile	.30	.09
387 Al Leiter	.30	.09
388 Armando Benitez	.30	.09
389 Alex Escobar	.30	.09
390 Kevin Appier	.30	.09
391 Matt Lawton	.30	.09
392 Bruce Chen	.30	.09
393 John Franco	.30	.09
394 Tsuyoshi Shinjo	.30	.09
395 Rey Ordonez	.30	.09
396 Joe McEwing	.30	.09
397 Ryan Klesko	.30	.09
398 Brian Lawrence	.30	.09
399 Kevin Walker	.30	.09
400 Phil Nevin	.30	.09
401 Bubba Trammell	.30	.09
402 Wiki Gonzalez	.30	.09
403 D'Angelo Jimenez	.30	.09
404 Rickey Henderson	.75	.23
405 Mike Darr	.30	.09
406 Trevor Hoffman	.30	.09
407 Damian Jackson	.30	.09
408 Santiago Perez	.30	.09
409 Cesar Crespo	.30	.09
410 Robert Person	.30	.09
411 Travis Lee	.30	.09
412 Scott Rolen	.75	.23
413 Turk Wendell	.30	.09
414 Randy Wolf	.30	.09
415 Kevin Jordan	.30	.09
416 Jose Mesa	.30	.09
417 Mike Lieberthal	.30	.09
418 Bobby Abreu	.30	.09
419 Tomas Perez	.30	.09
420 Doug Glanville	.30	.09
421 Reggie Taylor	.30	.09
422 Jimmy Rollins	.30	.09
423 Brian Giles	.30	.09
424 Rob Mackowiak	.30	.09
425 Bronson Arroyo	.30	.09
426 Kevin Young	.30	.09
427 Jack Wilson	.30	.09
428 Adrian Brown	.30	.09
429 Chad Hermansen	.30	.09
430 Jimmy Anderson	.30	.09
431 Aramis Ramirez	.30	.09
432 Todd Ritchie	.30	.09
433 Pat Meares	.30	.09
434 Warren Morris	.30	.09
435 Derek Bell	.30	.09
436 Ken Griffey Jr.	1.25	.35
437 Elmer Dessens	.30	.09
438 Ruben Rivera	.30	.09
439 Jason LaRue	.30	.09
440 Sean Casey	.30	.09
441 Pete Harnisch	.30	.09
442 Danny Graves	.30	.09
443 Aaron Boone	.30	.09
444 Dmitri Young	.30	.09
445 Brandon Larson	.30	.09
446 Pokey Reese	.30	.09
447 Todd Walker	.30	.09
448 Juan Castro	.30	.09
449 Todd Helton	.50	.15
450 Ben Petrick	.30	.09
451 Juan Pierre	.30	.09
452 Jeff Cirillo	.30	.09
453 Juan Uribe	.30	.09
454 Brian Bohanon	.30	.09
455 Terry Shumpert	.30	.09
456 Mike Hampton	.30	.09
457 Shawn Chacon	.30	.09
458 Adam Melhuse	.30	.09
459 Greg Norton	.30	.09
460 Gabe White	.30	.09
461 Ichiro Suzuki WS	.75	.23
462 Carlos Delgado WS	.30	.09
463 Manny Ramirez WS	.30	.09
464 Miguel Tejada WS	.30	.09
465 Tsuyoshi Shinjo WS	.30	.09
466 Bernie Williams WS	.30	.09
467 Juan Gonzalez WS	.30	.09
468 Andruw Jones WS	.30	.09
469 Ivan Rodriguez WS	.50	.15
470 Larry Walker WS	.50	.15
471 Hideo Nomo WS	.50	.15
472 Albert Pujols WS	.75	.23
473 Pedro Martinez WS	.50	.15
474 Vladimir Guerrero WS	.50	.15
475 Tony Batista WS	.30	.09
476 Kazuhiro Sasaki WS	.30	.09
477 Richard Hidalgo WS	.30	.09
478 Carlos Lee WS	.30	.09
479 Roberto Alomar WS	.30	.09
480 Rafael Palmeiro WS	.30	.09
481 Ken Griffey Jr. GG	.75	.23
482 Ken Griffey Jr. GG	.75	.23
483 Ken Griffey Jr. GG	.75	.23
484 Ken Griffey Jr. GG	.75	.23
485 Ken Griffey Jr. GG	.75	.23
486 Ken Griffey Jr. GG	.75	.23
487 Ken Griffey Jr. GG	.75	.23
488 Ken Griffey Jr. GG	.75	.23
489 Ken Griffey Jr. GG	.75	.23
490 Ken Griffey Jr. GG	.75	.23
491 Barry Bonds CL	.75	.23
492 Hideo Nomo CL	.30	.09
493 Ichiro Suzuki CL	.75	.23
494 Cal Ripken CL	1.25	.35
495 Tony Gwynn CL	.50	.15
496 Randy Johnson CL	.50	.15
497 A.J. Burnett CL	.30	.09
498 Rickey Henderson CL	.50	.15
499 Albert Pujols CL	.75	.23
500 Luis Gonzalez CL	.30	.09
501 Brandon Puffer SR RC	1.00	.30
502 Rodrigo Rosario SR RC	1.00	.30
503 Tom Shearn SR RC	1.00	.30
504 Reed Johnson SR RC	1.50	.45
505 Chris Baker SR RC	1.00	.30
506 John Ennis SR RC	1.00	.30
507 Luis Martinez SR RC	1.00	.30
508 So Taguchi SR RC	1.50	.45
509 Scotty Layfield SR RC	1.00	.30
510 Francis Beltran SR RC	1.00	.30
511 Brandon Backe SR RC	1.50	.45
512 Doug Devore SR RC	1.00	.30
513 Jeremy Ward SR RC	1.00	.30
514 Jose Valverde SR RC	1.50	.45
515 P.J. Bevis SR RC	1.00	.30
516 Victor Alvarez SR RC	1.00	.30
517 Kazuhisa Ishii SR RC	2.50	.75
518 Jorge Nunez SR RC	1.00	.30
519 Eric Good SR RC	1.00	.30
520 Ron Calloway SR RC	1.00	.30
521 Val Pascucci SR	1.00	.30
522 Nelson Castro SR RC	1.00	.30
523 Deivis Santos SR	1.00	.30
524 Luis Ugueto SR RC	1.00	.30
525 Matt Thornton SR RC	1.00	.30
526 Hansel Izquierdo SR RC	1.00	.30
527 Tyler Yates SR RC	1.50	.45
528 Mark Corey SR RC	1.00	.30
529 Jaime Cerda SR RC	1.00	.30
530 Satoru Komiyama SR RC	1.00	.30
531 Steve Bechler SR RC	1.00	.30
532 Ben Howard SR RC	1.00	.30
533 An. Machado SR RC	1.00	.30
534 Jorge Padilla SR RC	1.00	.30
535 Eric Junge SR RC	1.00	.30
536 Adrian Burnside SR RC	1.00	.30
537 Mike Gonzalez SR RC	1.00	.30
538 Josh Hancock SR RC	1.00	.30
539 Colin Young SR RC	1.00	.30
540 Rene Reyes SR RC	1.00	.30
541 Cam Esslinger SR RC	1.00	.30
542 Tim Kalita SR RC	1.00	.30
543 Kevin Frederick SR RC	1.00	.30
544 Kyle Kane SR RC	1.00	.30
545 Edwin Almonte SR RC	1.00	.30
546 Aaron Sele	.30	.09
547 Garret Anderson	.30	.09
548 Darin Erstad	.30	.09
549 Brad Fullmer	.30	.09
550 Kevin Appier	.30	.09
551 Tim Salmon	.50	.15
552 David Justice	.30	.09
553 Billy Koch	.30	.09
554 Scott Hatteberg	.30	.09
555 Tim Hudson	.30	.09
556 Miguel Tejada	.30	.09
557 Carlos Pena	.30	.09
558 Mike Sirotka	.30	.09
559 Jose Cruz Jr.	.30	.09
560 Josh Phelps	.30	.09
561 Brandon Lyon	.30	.09
562 Luke Prokopec	.30	.09
563 Felipe Lopez	.30	.09
564 Jason Standridge	.30	.09
565 Chris Gomez	.30	.09
566 John Flaherty	.30	.09
567 Jason Tyner	.30	.09
568 Bobby Smith	.30	.09
569 Wilson Alvarez	.30	.09
570 Matt Lawton	.30	.09
571 Omar Vizquel	.50	.15
572 Jim Thome	.75	.23
573 Brady Anderson	.30	.09
574 Alex Escobar	.30	.09
575 Russell Branyan	.30	.09
576 Bret Boone	.30	.09
577 Ben Davis	.30	.09
578 Mike Cameron	.30	.09
579 Jamie Moyer	.30	.09
580 Ruben Sierra	.30	.09
581 Jeff Cirillo	.30	.09
582 Marty Cordova	.30	.09
583 Mike Bordick	.30	.09
584 Brian Roberts	.30	.09
585 Luis Matos	.30	.09
586 Geronimo Gil	.30	.09
587 Jay Gibbons	.30	.09
588 Carl Everett	.30	.09
589 Ivan Rodriguez	.75	.23
590 Chan Ho Park	.30	.09
591 Juan Gonzalez	.50	.15
592 Hank Blalock	.75	.23
593 Todd Van Poppel	.30	.09
594 Pedro Martinez	.75	.23
595 Jason Varitek	.50	.15
596 Tony Clark	.30	.09
597 Johnny Damon Sox	.75	.23
598 Dustin Hermanson	.30	.09
599 John Burkett	.30	.09
600 Carlos Beltran	.50	.15
601 Mark Quinn	.30	.09
602 Chuck Knoblauch	.30	.09
603 Michael Tucker	.30	.09
604 Carlos Febles	.30	.09
605 Jose Rosado	.30	.09
606 Dmitri Young	.30	.09
607 Bobby Higginson	.30	.09
608 Craig Paquette	.30	.09
609 Mitch Meluskey	.30	.09
610 Wendell Magee	.30	.09
611 Mike Rivera	.30	.09
612 Jacque Jones	.30	.09
613 Luis Rivas	.30	.09
614 Eric Milton	.30	.09
615 Eddie Guardado	.30	.09
616 Matt LeCroy	.30	.09
617 Mike Jackson	.30	.09
618 Magglio Ordonez	.30	.09
619 Frank Thomas	.75	.23
620 Rocky Biddle	.30	.09
621 Paul Konerko	.30	.09
622 Todd Ritchie	.30	.09
623 Jon Rauch	.30	.09
624 John Vander Wal	.30	.09
625 Rondell White	.30	.09
626 Jason Giambi	.30	.09
627 Robin Ventura	.30	.09
628 David Wells	.30	.09
629 Bernie Williams	.50	.15
630 Lance Berkman	.30	.09
631 Richard Hidalgo	.30	.09
632 Greg Zaun	.30	.09
633 Jose Vizcaino	.30	.09
634 Octavio Dotel	.30	.09
635 Morgan Ensberg	.30	.09
636 Andruw Jones	.30	.09
637 Tom Glavine	.50	.15
638 Gary Sheffield	.30	.09
639 Vinny Castilla	.30	.09
640 Javy Lopez	.30	.09
641 Albie Lopez	.30	.09
642 Geoff Jenkins	.30	.09
643 Jeffrey Hammonds	.30	.09
644 Alex Ochoa	.30	.09
645 Richie Sexson	.30	.09
646 Eric Young	.30	.09
647 Glendon Rusch	.30	.09
648 Tino Martinez	.50	.15
649 Fernando Vina	.30	.09
650 J.D. Drew	.30	.09
651 Woody Williams	.30	.09
652 Darryl Kile	.30	.09
653 Jason Isringhausen	.30	.09
654 Moises Alou	.30	.09
655 Alex Gonzalez	.30	.09
656 Delino DeShields	.30	.09
657 Todd Hundley	.30	.09
658 Chris Stynes	.30	.09
659 Jason Bere	.30	.09
660 Curt Schilling	.30	.09
661 Craig Counsell	.30	.09
662 Mark Grace	.50	.15
663 Matt Williams	.30	.09
664 Jay Bell	.30	.09
665 Rick Helling	.30	.09
666 Shawn Green	.30	.09
667 Eric Karros	.30	.09
668 Hideo Nomo	.75	.23
669 Omar Daal	.30	.09
670 Brian Jordan	.30	.09
671 Cesar Izturis	.30	.09
672 Fernando Tatis	.30	.09
673 Lee Stevens	.30	.09
674 Tomo Ohka	.30	.09
675 Brian Schneider	.30	.09
676 Brad Wilkerson	.30	.09
677 Bruce Chen	.30	.09
678 Tsuyoshi Shinjo	.30	.09
679 Jeff Kent	.30	.09
680 Kirk Rueter	.30	.09
681 J.T. Snow	.30	.09
682 David Bell	.30	.09
683 Reggie Sanders	.30	.09
684 Preston Wilson	.30	.09
685 Vic Darensbourg	.30	.09
686 Josh Beckett	.30	.09
687 Pablo Ozuna	.30	.09
688 Mike Redmond	.30	.09
689 Scott Strickland	.30	.09
690 Mo Vaughn	.30	.09
691 Roberto Alomar	.50	.15
692 Edgardo Alfonzo	.30	.09
693 Shawn Estes	.30	.09
694 Roger Cedeno	.30	.09
695 Jeromy Burnitz	.30	.09
696 Ray Lankford	.30	.09
697 Mark Kotsay	.30	.09
698 Kevin Jarvis	.30	.09
699 Bobby Jones	.30	.09
700 Sean Burroughs	.30	.09
701 Ramon Vazquez	.30	.09
702 Pat Burrell	.30	.09
703 Marlon Byrd	.30	.09
704 Brandon Duckworth	.30	.09
705 Marlon Anderson	.30	.09
706 Vicente Padilla	.30	.09
707 Kip Wells	.30	.09
708 Jason Kendall	.30	.09
709 Pokey Reese	.30	.09
710 Pat Meares	.30	.09
711 Kris Benson	.30	.09
712 Armando Rios	.30	.09
713 Mike Williams	.30	.09
714 Barry Larkin	.50	.15
715 Adam Dunn	.50	.15
716 Juan Encarnacion	.30	.09
717 Scott Williamson	.30	.09
718 Wilton Guerrero	.30	.09
719 Chris Reitsma	.30	.09
720 Larry Walker	.50	.15
721 Denny Neagle	.30	.09
722 Todd Zeile	.30	.09
723 Jose Ortiz	.30	.09
724 Jason Jennings	.30	.09
725 Tony Eusebio	.30	.09
726 Ichiro Suzuki YR	.75	.23
727 Barry Bonds YR	.75	.23
728 Randy Johnson YR	.50	.15
729 Albert Pujols YR	.75	.23
730 Roger Clemens YR	.75	.23
731 Sammy Sosa YR	.75	.23
732 Alex Rodriguez YR	.75	.23
733 Chipper Jones YR	.50	.15
734 Rickey Henderson YR	.50	.15
735 Ichiro Suzuki YR	.75	.23
736 Luis Gonzalez SH CL	.30	.09
737 Derek Jeter SH CL	1.00	.30
738 Ichiro Suzuki SH CL	.75	.23
739 Barry Bonds SH CL	.75	.23
740 Curt Schilling SH CL	.30	.09
741 Shawn Green SH CL	.30	.09
742 Jason Giambi SH CL	.30	.09
743 Roberto Alomar SH CL	.30	.09
744 Larry Walker SH CL	.30	.09
745 Mark McGwire SH CL	1.00	.30

2002 Upper Deck 2001 Greatest Hits

Issued into first series packs at a rate of one i 14, these 10 cards feature some of the leadin hitters during the 2001 season.

	Nm-Mt	Ex-Mt
COMPLETE SET (10)	40.00	12.00
GH1 Barry Bonds	6.00	1.80
GH2 Ichiro Suzuki	4.00	1.20
GH3 Albert Pujols	5.00	1.50
GH4 Mike Piazza	4.00	1.20
GH5 Alex Rodriguez	4.00	1.20
GH6 Mark McGwire	6.00	1.80
GH7 Manny Ramirez	2.50	.75
GH8 Ken Griffey Jr.	4.00	1.20
GH9 Sammy Sosa	4.00	1.20
GH10 Derek Jeter	6.00	1.80

2002 Upper Deck A Piece of History 500 Club

Randomly inserted in 2002 Upper Deck secon series packs, this card features a bat slice fror Mark McGwire and continues the Upper Deck A Piece of History set begun in 1999. This car was printed to a stated print run of 350 seria numbered sets.

	Nm-Mt	Ex-Mt
MMC Mark McGwire	400.00	120.00

2002 Upper Deck A Piece of History 500 Club Autograph

Randomly inserted in 2002 Upper Deck secon series packs, this card features a bat slice fror Mark McGwire and an authentic autograph an continues the Upper Deck A Piece of History se begun in 1999. This card was printed to a state print run of 25 serial numbered sets.

	Nm-Mt	Ex-Mt
S-MMC Mark McGwire/25		

2002 Upper Deck AL Centennial Memorabilia

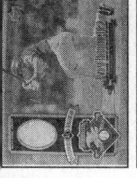

ıserted into first series packs at a rate of one in 44, these 10 cards feature memorabilia from ome of the leading players in American League istory. The bat jersey cards were produced in maller quantites than the jersey cards and we ave notated those cards with SP's in our checkst.

	Nm-Mt	Ex-Mt
LB-BR Babe Ruth Bat SP	150.00	45.00
LB-JD Joe DiMaggio Bat SP	100.00	30.00
LB-MM M. Mantle Bat SP	150.00	45.00
LJ-AR A. Rodriguez Jsy	15.00	4.50
LJ-CR Cal Ripken Jsy	40.00	12.00
LJ-FT Frank Thomas Jsy	15.00	4.50
LJ-IR Ivan Rodriguez Jsy	15.00	4.50
LJ-NR Nolan Ryan Jsy	40.00	12.00
LJ-PM P. Martinez Jsy	15.00	4.50
LJ-RA R. Alomar Jsy	15.00	4.50

2002 Upper Deck AL Centennial Memorabilia Autograph

andomly inserted into first series packs, these our cards featured autographs of players whose nemorabilia is featured in the Centennial Memorabilia set. These cards are serial numbered to 25. Due to market scarcity, no pricing is provided.

	Nm-Mt	Ex-Mt
AL-CR Cal Ripken Jsy		
AL-IR Ivan Rodriguez Jsy		
AL-NR Nolan Ryan Jsy		
AL-PM Pedro Martinez Jsy		

2002 Upper Deck All-Star Home Run Derby Game Jersey

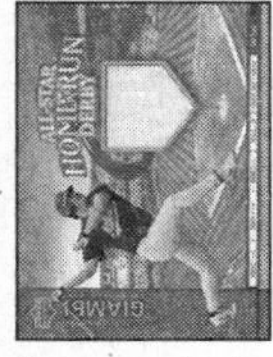

ıserted into first series packs at a rate of one in 88, these seven cards feature jersey swatches om these players who participated in the Home un Derby. A couple of the jerseys were from egular use and we have notated that information our checklist.

	Nm-Mt	Ex-Mt
OLD RANDOM INSERTS IN PACKS..		
OLD PRINT RUN 25 SERIAL #'d SETS		
O GOLD PRICING DUE TO SCARCITY		
S-AR Alex Rodriguez	25.00	7.50
S-BB Bret Boone	15.00	4.50
S-JG1 Jason Giambi	15.00	4.50
S-JG2 Jason Giambi A's	15.00	4.50
S-SS1 Sammy Sosa	30.00	9.00
S-SS2 S. Sosa Cubs	30.00	9.00
S-TH Todd Helton	15.00	4.50

2002 Upper Deck All-Star Salute Game Jersey

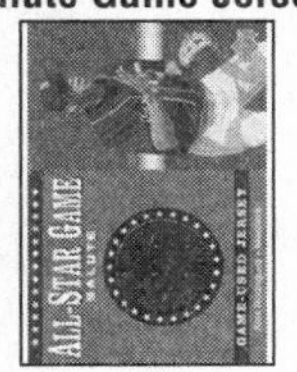

ıserted into first series packs at a rate of one in 88, these nine cards feature game jersey watches of some of the most exciting All-Star erformers.

	Nm-Mt	Ex-Mt
OLD RANDOM INSERTS IN PACKS..		
OLD PRINT RUN 25 SERIAL #'d SETS		
O GOLD PRICING DUE TO SCARCITY		
JAR1 A.Rodriguez Mariners	25.00	7.50
JAR2 A.Rodriguez Rangers	25.00	7.50
JDE Dennis Eckersley	15.00	4.50
JDS Don Sutton	15.00	4.50
JIS Ichiro Suzuki	50.00	15.00
JKG Ken Griffey Jr.	30.00	9.00
JLB Lou Boudreau	15.00	4.50
JNF Nellie Fox	15.00	4.50
JSA Sparky Anderson	15.00	4.50

2002 Upper Deck Authentic McGwire

andomly inserted in second series packs, these wo cards feature authentic memorabilia from Mark McGwire's career. These cards have a stated print run of 70 serial numbered sets.

	Nm-Mt	Ex-Mt
AM-B Mark McGwire Bat	100.00	30.00
AM-J Mark McGwire Jsy	100.00	30.00

2002 Upper Deck Big Fly Zone

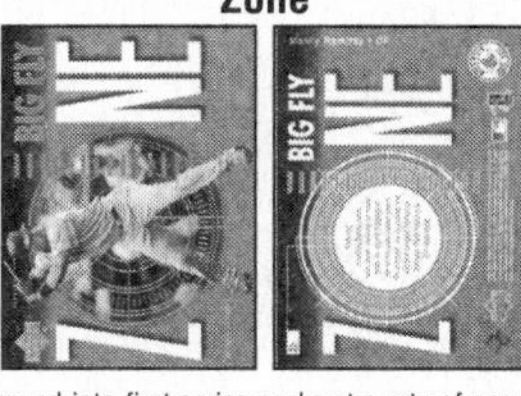

Issued into first series packs at a rate of one in 14, these 10 cards feature some of the leading power hitters in the game.

	Nm-Mt	Ex-Mt
COMPLETE SET (10)	30.00	9.00
Z1 Mark McGwire	6.00	1.80
Z2 Ken Griffey Jr.	4.00	1.20
Z3 Manny Ramirez	1.50	.45
Z4 Sammy Sosa	4.00	1.20
Z5 Todd Helton	1.50	.45
Z6 Barry Bonds	6.00	1.80
Z7 Luis Gonzalez	1.50	.45
Z8 Alex Rodriguez	4.00	1.20
Z9 Carlos Delgado	1.50	.45
Z10 Chipper Jones	2.50	.75

2002 Upper Deck Breakout Performers

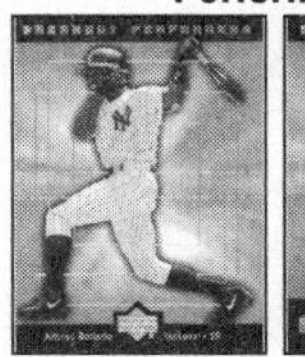

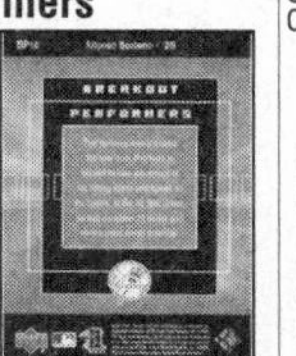

Issued into first series packs at a rate of one in 14, these 10 cards feature players who had breakout seasons in 2001.

	Nm-Mt	Ex-Mt
COMPLETE SET (10)	25.00	7.50
BP1 Ichiro Suzuki	4.00	1.20
BP2 Albert Pujols	5.00	1.50
BP3 Doug Mientkiewicz	1.50	.45
BP4 Lance Berkman	1.50	.45
BP5 Tsuyoshi Shinjo	1.50	.45
BP6 Ben Sheets	1.50	.45
BP7 Jimmy Rollins	1.50	.45
BP8 J.D. Drew	1.50	.45
BP9 Bret Boone	1.50	.45
BP10 Alfonso Soriano	1.50	.45

2002 Upper Deck Championship Caliber

Inserted into first series packs at a rate of one in 23, these six cards feature players who have all earned World Series rings.

	Nm-Mt	Ex-Mt
COMPLETE SET (6)	20.00	6.00
CC1 Derek Jeter	6.00	1.80
CC2 Roberto Alomar	1.50	.45
CC3 Chipper Jones	2.50	.75
CC4 Gary Sheffield	1.50	.45
CC5 Roger Clemens	5.00	1.50
CC6 Greg Maddux	4.00	1.20

2002 Upper Deck Championship Caliber Swatch

Inserted in second series packs at a stated rate of one in 288, these 14 cards feature not only players who have been on World Champions but also a game-worn swatch. A few players were issued in shorter supply and we have notated that information in our checklist.

	Nm-Mt	Ex-Mt
AP Andy Pettitte	15.00	4.50
BL Barry Larkin	15.00	4.50
BW Bernie Williams	15.00	4.50
CF Cliff Floyd	10.00	3.00
CHJ Charles Johnson	10.00	3.00
CJO Chipper Jones SP		
CS Curt Schilling	10.00	3.00
GM Greg Maddux SP		
JO John Olerud	10.00	3.00
JP Jorge Posada	15.00	4.50
KB Kevin Brown SP	15.00	4.50
RA Roberto Alomar SP		
RJ Randy Johnson	15.00	4.50
TM Tino Martinez	15.00	4.50

2002 Upper Deck Chasing History

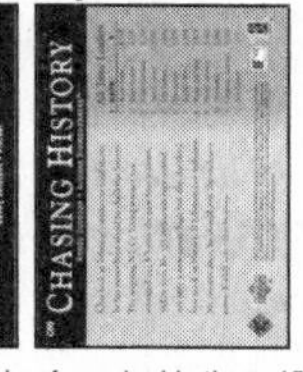

Inserted at stated odds of one in 11, these 15 cards feature players who are moving up in the record books.

	Nm-Mt	Ex-Mt
COMPLETE SET (15)	40.00	12.00
CH1 Sammy Sosa	5.00	1.50
CH2 Ken Griffey Jr.	5.00	1.50
CH3 Roger Clemens	6.00	1.80
CH4 Barry Bonds	8.00	2.40
CH5 Rafael Palmeiro	2.00	.60
CH6 Andres Galarraga	2.00	.60
CH7 Juan Gonzalez	2.00	.60
CH8 Roberto Alomar	2.00	.60
CH9 Randy Johnson	3.00	.90
CH10 Jeff Bagwell	2.00	.60
CH11 Fred McGriff	2.00	.60
CH12 Matt Williams	2.00	.60
CH13 Greg Maddux	5.00	1.50
CH14 Robb Nen	2.00	.60
CH15 Kenny Lofton	2.00	.60

2002 Upper Deck Combo Memorabilia

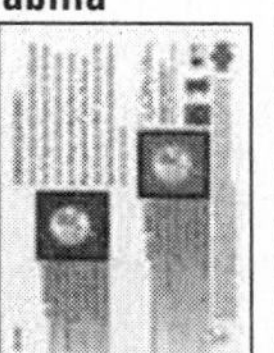

Issued into first series packs at a rate of one in 288, these seven cards feature two pieces of game-used memorabilia from players who have something in common.

	Nm-Mt	Ex-Mt
GOLD RANDOM INSERTS IN PACKS..		
GOLD PRINT RUN 25 SERIAL #'d SETS		
NO GOLD PRICING DUE TO SCARCITY		
B-DM Joe DiMaggio Mickey Mantle Bat	200.00	60.00
B-RG Alex Rodriguez Ken Griffey Jr. Bat	40.00	12.00
J-BS Barry Bonds Sammy Sosa Jsy	50.00	15.00
J-HK S. Hasegawa Byung-Hyun Kim Jsy	15.00	4.50
J-RC Nolan Ryan Roger Clemens Jsy	60.00	18.00
J-RM Nolan Ryan Pedro Martinez Jsy	50.00	15.00
J-RS Alex Rodriguez Sammy Sosa Jsy	40.00	12.00

2002 Upper Deck Double Game Worn Gems

Randomly inserted in second series retail packs, these 12 cards feature two teammates along with pieces of game used memorabilia. These cards have a stated print run of 450 serial numbered sets.

	Nm-Mt	Ex-Mt
DG-AP Roberto Alomar Mike Piazza	25.00	7.50
DG-DF Carlos Delgado Shannon Stewart	15.00	4.50
DG-DH Jermaine Dye Tim Hudson	15.00	4.50
DG-GS Luis Gonzalez Curt Schilling	15.00	4.50
DG-KG Jason Kendall Brian Giles	15.00	4.50
DG-MI Edgar Martinez Ichiro Suzuki SP/150		
DG-MM Kevin Millwood Greg Maddux	25.00	7.50
DG-NK Phil Nevin Ryan Klesko	15.00	4.50
DG-PL Robert Person Mike Lieberthal	15.00	4.50
DG-PN Chan Ho Park Hideo Nomo	50.00	15.00
DG-TO Frank Thomas Magglio Ordonez	20.00	6.00
DG-VB Omar Vizquel Russell Branyan	15.00	4.50

2002 Upper Deck Double Game Worn Gems Gold

Randomly inserted in second series retail packs, these cards parallel the Double Game Worn Gem insert set. These cards have a stated print run of 100 serial numbered sets.

	Nm-Mt	Ex-Mt
DG-AP Roberto Alomar Mike Piazza	50.00	15.00
DG-DF Carlos Delgado Shannon Stewart	30.00	9.00
DG-DH Jermaine Dye Tim Hudson	30.00	9.00
DG-GS Luis Gonzalez Curt Schilling	30.00	9.00
DG-KG Jason Kendall Brian Giles	30.00	9.00
DG-MI Edgar Martinez Ichiro Suzuki SP/40	100.00	30.00
DG-MM Kevin Millwood Greg Maddux	50.00	15.00
DG-NK Phil Nevin Ryan Klesko	30.00	9.00
DG-PL Robert Person Mike Lieberthal	30.00	9.00
DG-PN Chan Ho Park Hideo Nomo	100.00	30.00
DG-TO Frank Thomas Magglio Ordonez	40.00	12.00
DG-VB Omar Vizquel Russell Branyan	30.00	9.00

2002 Upper Deck First Timers Game Jersey

Inserted into first series hobby packs at a rate of one in 288 hobby packs, these nine cards feature players who have never been featured on a Upper Deck game jersey card before.

	Nm-Mt	Ex-Mt
FT-AP Albert Pujols	50.00	15.00
FT-CP Corey Patterson	10.00	3.00
FT-EM Eric Milton	10.00	3.00
FT-FG Freddy Garcia	10.00	3.00
FT-JM Joe Mays	10.00	3.00
FT-ML Matt Lawton	10.00	3.00
FT-OD Omar Daal	10.00	3.00
FT-RB Russell Branyan	10.00	3.00
FT-SS Shannon Stewart	10.00	3.00

2002 Upper Deck First Timers Game Jersey Autograph

This parallel to the First Timers Game Jersey set features the players signing 25 copies of these cards. These cards were distributed exclusively in first series hobby packs. Freddy Garcia did not return his cards in time for packout and thus was available only in exchange format with a redemption deadline of 11/19/04. Due to market scarcity, no pricing is provided.

	Nm-Mt	Ex-Mt
SFT-AP Albert Pujols		
SFT-CP Corey Patterson		
SFT-FG Freddy Garcia		
SFT-JM Joe Mays		
SFT-SS Shannon Stewart		

2002 Upper Deck Game Base

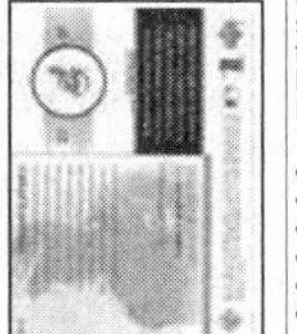

Inserted into first series packs at a rate of one in 288, these 22 cards feature authentic pieces of bases used in official Major League games.

	Nm-Mt	Ex-Mt
B-AJ Andruw Jones	10.00	3.00
B-AR Alex Rodriguez	20.00	6.00
B-BB Barry Bonds	30.00	9.00
B-CD Carlos Delgado	10.00	3.00
B-CJ Chipper Jones	15.00	4.50
B-CR Cal Ripken	40.00	12.00
B-DJ Derek Jeter	30.00	9.00
B-IR Ivan Rodriguez	15.00	4.50
B-IS Ichiro Suzuki	50.00	15.00
B-JG Jason Giambi	10.00	3.00
B-JG Juan Gonzalez	15.00	4.50
B-KG Ken Griffey Jr.	20.00	6.00
B-KS Kazuhiro Sasaki	10.00	3.00
B-LG Luis Gonzalez	10.00	3.00
B-MM Mark McGwire	50.00	15.00
B-MP Mike Piazza	15.00	4.50
B-RC Roger Clemens	25.00	7.50
B-SG Shawn Green	10.00	3.00
B-SS Sammy Sosa	20.00	6.00
B-TG Troy Glaus	10.00	3.00
CB-MJ Mark McGwire Derek Jeter	60.00	18.00
CB-RG Alex Rodriguez Ken Griffey Jr.	40.00	12.00

2002 Upper Deck Game Base Autograph

Randomly inserted into first series packs, Ken Griffey Jr. signed 25 cards for inclusion in this set. However, Griffey did not return his cards in time for inclusion in the packs and therefore these cards could be redeemed until November 5, 2004. Due to market scarcity, no pricing is provided.

	Nm-Mt	Ex-Mt
SB-KG Ken Griffey Jr.		

2002 Upper Deck Game Jersey

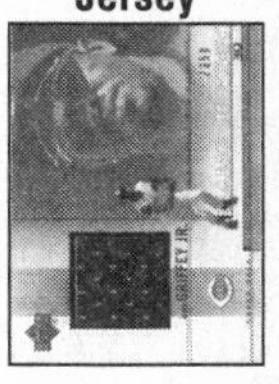

Randomly inserted in packs, these 11 cards feature some of today's star players along with a game-worn swatch of the featured player.

	Nm-Mt	Ex-Mt
AB Adrian Beltre	15.00	4.50
CS Curt Schilling	10.00	3.00
FT Frank Thomas	15.00	4.50
JC Jeff Cirillo Pants	10.00	3.00
KG Ken Griffey Jr.	25.00	7.50
MP Mike Piazza Pants	15.00	4.50
PW Preston Wilson	10.00	3.00
SR Scott Rolen	15.00	4.50
SS Sammy Sosa	25.00	7.50
TB Tony Batista	10.00	3.00
TH Tim Hudson	10.00	3.00

2002 Upper Deck Game Jersey Gold

Randomly inserted in second series hobby packs, these cards parallel the Game Jersey insert set. These cards are printed to a stated print run of 100 serial numbered sets.

	Nm-Mt	Ex-Mt
*GOLD: .75X TO 2X BASIC GAME JSY		

2002 Upper Deck Game Jersey Autograph

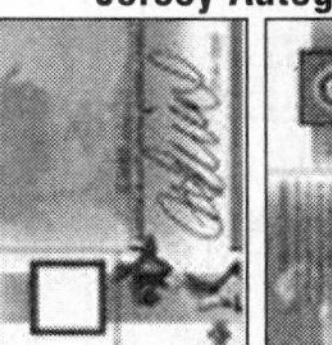

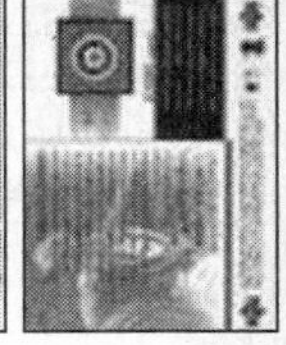

Randomly inserted into first series hobby packs, these 12 cards feature not only a game jersey swatch but also an authentic autograph of the player featured. These cards are serial numbered to 200. The following players did not return their signed cards in time for release in the packs and those cards had an exchange deadline of November 19, 2004: Andruw Jones, Albert Pujols and Ken Griffey Jr.

	Nm-Mt	Ex-Mt
J-AJ Andruw Jones	25.00	7.50
J-AP Albert Pujols	150.00	45.00
J-BB Barry Bonds	350.00	105.00
J-CD Carlos Delgado	25.00	7.50
J-CR Cal Ripken	200.00	60.00
J-GS Gary Sheffield	40.00	12.00
J-IS Ichiro Suzuki UER Word Close repeated in ninth line of text	400.00	120.00
J-JGI Jason Giambi	25.00	7.50
J-KG Ken Griffey Jr.	120.00	36.00
J-NR Nolan Ryan	150.00	45.00
J-PW Preston Wilson	25.00	7.50
J-RF Rafael Furcal	25.00	7.50

2002 Upper Deck Game Jersey Patch

Inserted at a rate of one in 2,500 first series packs, these cards feature a jersey patch from the star players featured.

	Nm-Mt	Ex-Mt
PL-AR Alex Rodriguez L	120.00	36.00
PL-BB Barry Bonds L	150.00	45.00
PL-CR Cal Ripken L	150.00	45.00
PL-JG Jason Giambi L	50.00	15.00
PL-KG Ken Griffey Jr. L	100.00	30.00
PL-PM Pedro Martinez L	80.00	24.00
PL-SS Sammy Sosa L	100.00	30.00
PN-AR Alex Rodriguez N	120.00	36.00
PN-BB Barry Bonds N	150.00	45.00
PN-CR Cal Ripken N	150.00	45.00
PN-JG Jason Giambi N	50.00	15.00
PN-KG Ken Griffey Jr. N	100.00	30.00
PN-PM Pedro Martinez N	80.00	24.00
PN-SS Sammy Sosa N	100.00	30.00
PS-AR Alex Rodriguez S	120.00	36.00
PS-BB Barry Bonds S	150.00	45.00
PS-CR Cal Ripken S	150.00	45.00
PS-JG Jason Giambi S	50.00	15.00
PS-KG Ken Griffey Jr. S	100.00	30.00
PS-PM Pedro Martinez S	80.00	24.00
PS-SS Sammy Sosa S	100.00	30.00

2002 Upper Deck Game Jersey Patch Autograph

Randomly inserted into first series packs, these six cards feature not only a game jersey patch swatch but also an authentic autograph of the player featured. These cards are serial numbered to 25. Ken Griffey Jr. did not return his cards in time for pack out and those cards were issued as exchange cards with a redemption deadline of 11/5/04. Due to market scarcity, no pricing is provided.

	Nm-Mt	Ex-Mt
SPNBB Barry Bonds N		
SPNCR Cal Ripken N		
SPNKG Ken Griffey Jr. N		
SPNSS Sammy Sosa N		
SPSBB Barry Bonds S		
SPSCR Cal Ripken S		

2002 Upper Deck Game Worn Gems

Inserted in second series retail packs at a stated rate of one in 48 retail packs, these 31 cards feature leading stars along a game-used memorabilia piece. A few cards were issued in shorter supply and those cards are notated in our checklist with an SP. Cards notated with an SP are not priced due to market scarcity.

	Nm-Mt	Ex-Mt
G-AS Aaron Sele	10.00	3.00
G-CD Carlos Delgado	10.00	3.00
G-CJ Chipper Jones	15.00	4.50
G-CR Cal Ripken	50.00	15.00
G-CS Curt Schilling	10.00	3.00
G-DE Darin Erstad SP		
G-EC Eric Chavez	10.00	3.00
G-EM Edgar Martinez	15.00	4.50
G-EM Eric Milton	10.00	3.00
G-FG Freddy Garcia SP		
G-FT Frank Thomas	15.00	4.50
G-GM Greg Maddux	15.00	4.50
G-GS Gary Sheffield SP		
G-HN Hideo Nomo SP		
G-IR Ivan Rodriguez	15.00	4.50
G-JG Juan Gonzalez	15.00	4.50
G-JK Jason Kendall	10.00	3.00
G-JM Joe Mays	10.00	3.00
G-JO John Olerud SP		
G-LG Luis Gonzalez SP		
G-MH Mike Hampton SP		
G-OV Omar Vizquel SP		
G-PM Pedro Martinez SP		
G-PN Phil Nevin	10.00	3.00
G-RA Roberto Alomar	15.00	4.50
G-RK Ryan Klesko SP		
G-RP Robert Person	10.00	3.00
G-RY Robin Yount	15.00	4.50
G-SR Scott Rolen	15.00	4.50
G-TG Tom Glavine	15.00	4.50
G-TM Tino Martinez	15.00	4.50

2002 Upper Deck Game Worn Gems Gold

Randomly inserted in second series retail packs, these cards parallel the Game Worn Gems insert set. These cards are printed to a stated print run of 100 serial numbered sets. Specific pricing is provided for those cards which were short printed in the regular Game Worn Gems insert set.

	Nm-Mt	Ex-Mt
*GOLD: .75X TO 2X BASIC		
G-DE Darin Erstad	20.00	6.00
G-FG Freddy Garcia	20.00	6.00
G-GS Gary Sheffield	20.00	6.00
G-HN Hideo Nomo	80.00	24.00
G-JO John Olerud	20.00	6.00
G-LG Luis Gonzalez	20.00	6.00
G-MH Mike Hampton	20.00	6.00
G-OV Omar Vizquel	30.00	9.00
G-PM Pedro Martinez	40.00	12.00
G-RK Ryan Klesko	20.00	6.00

2002 Upper Deck Global Swatch Game Jersey

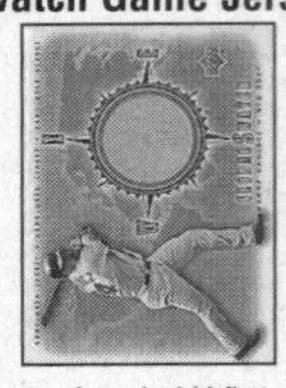

Issued at a rate of one in 144 first series packs, these 10 cards feature swatches of game jerseys worn by players who were born outside the continental United States.

	Nm-Mt	Ex-Mt
GSBK Byung-Hyun Kim	10.00	3.00
GSCD Carlos Delgado	10.00	3.00
GSCP Chan Ho Park	10.00	3.00
GSHN Hideo Nomo	40.00	12.00
GSIS Ichiro Suzuki	60.00	18.00
GSKS Kazuhiro Sasaki	10.00	3.00
GSMR Manny Ramirez	15.00	4.50
GSMY Masato Yoshii	10.00	3.00
GSSH S. Hasegawa	10.00	3.00
GSTS Tsuyoshi Shinjo	10.00	3.00

2002 Upper Deck Global Swatch Game Jersey Autograph

Randomly inserted into first series packs, these five cards feature not only a game-jersey swatch but also authentic autographs from the players. These cards are serial numbered to 25. Due to market scarcity, no pricing is provided.

	Nm-Mt	Ex-Mt
SGSBK Byung-Hyun Kim		
SGSCD Carlos Delgado		
SGSCP Chan Ho Park		
SGSHN Hideo Nomo		
SGSTS Tsuyoshi Shinjo		

2002 Upper Deck McGwire Combo Jersey

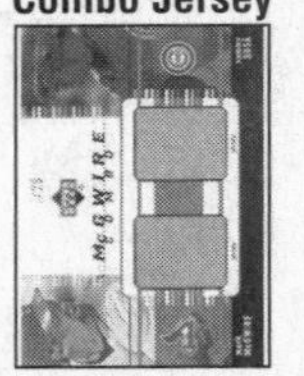

Randomly inserted in second series packs, these three cards feature swatches of both Mark McGwire and a player with which he says something in common. These cards were printed to a stated print run of 25 serial numbered sets and no pricing is available due to market scarcity.

	Nm-Mt	Ex-Mt
MMJG Mark McGwire Jason Giambi		
MMKG Mark McGwire Ken Griffey Jr.		
MMSS Mark McGwire Sammy Sosa		

2002 Upper Deck Peoples Choice Game Jersey

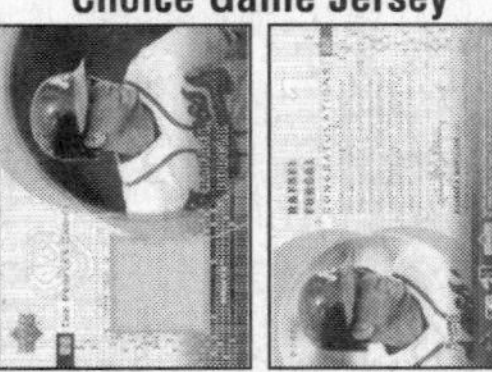

Inserted in second series hobby packs at a stated rate of one in 24, these 39 cards feature some of the most popular player in baseball along with a game-worn memorablia swatch. A few cards were in lesser quantity and we have notated those cards with an SP in our checklist.

	Nm-Mt	Ex-Mt
PJ-AG Andres Galarraga SP	15.00	4.50
PJ-AP Andy Pettitte	15.00	4.50
PJ-AR Alex Rodriguez	15.00	4.50
PJ-BG Brian Giles	10.00	3.00
PJ-BW Bernie Williams	15.00	4.50
PJ-CD Carlos Delgado	10.00	3.00
PJ-CJ Charles Johnson	10.00	3.00
PJ-CS Curt Schilling	10.00	3.00
PJ-DL Derek Lowe	10.00	3.00
PJ-DW David Wells	10.00	3.00
PJ-EB Ellis Burks SP	15.00	4.50
PJ-FT Frank Thomas	15.00	4.50
PJ-GM Greg Maddux	15.00	4.50
PJ-HI Hideki Irabu	10.00	3.00
PJ-JG Juan Gonzalez	15.00	4.50
PJ-JN Jeff Nelson	10.00	3.00
PJ-JS J.T. Snow	10.00	3.00
PJ-JBA Jeff Bagwell	15.00	4.50
PJ-JBU Jeromy Burnitz	10.00	3.00
PJ-KG Ken Griffey Jr.	20.00	6.00
PJ-MP Mike Piazza	15.00	4.50
PJ-MS Mike Stanton	10.00	3.00
PJ-MW Matt Williams SP	15.00	4.50
PJ-MRA Manny Ramirez	15.00	4.50
PJ-MRI Mariano Rivera	15.00	4.50
PJ-OD Omar Daal	10.00	3.00
PJ-OV Omar Vizquel	15.00	4.50
PJ-RF Rafael Furcal	10.00	3.00
PJ-RO Rey Ordonez	10.00	3.00
PJ-RP Rafael Palmeiro SP	25.00	7.50
PJ-RP Robert Person SP	15.00	4.50
PJ-RV Robin Ventura	10.00	3.00
PJ-SH Sterling Hitchcock	10.00	3.00
PJ-SS Sammy Sosa	20.00	6.00
PJ-TG Tony Gwynn	15.00	4.50
PJ-TM Tino Martinez	15.00	4.50
PJ-TR Tim Raines Sr.	10.00	3.00
PJ-TS Tim Salmon	15.00	4.50
PJ-TSh Tsuyoshi Shinjo	10.00	3.00

2002 Upper Deck Peoples Choice Game Jersey Gold

Randomly inserted in second series hobby packs, these cards parallel the People's Choice Game Jersey insert set. These cards are printed to a stated print run of 100 serial numbered sets.

	Nm-Mt	Ex-Mt
*GOLD: .75X TO 2X BASIC PC GAME JSY		
*GOLD SP: .5X TO 1.2X BASIC GAME JSY SP		

2002 Upper Deck Return of the Ace

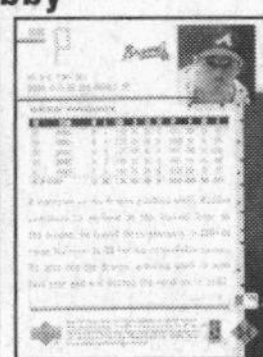

Inserted into second series packs at a stated rate of one in 11 packs, these 15 cards feature some of today's leading pitchers.

	Nm-Mt	Ex-Mt
COMPLETE SET (15)	30.00	9.00
RA1 Randy Johnson	3.00	.90
RA2 Greg Maddux	5.00	1.50
RA3 Pedro Martinez	3.00	.90
RA4 Freddy Garcia	2.00	.60
RA5 Matt Morris	2.00	.60
RA6 Mark Mulder	2.00	.60
RA7 Wade Miller	2.00	.60
RA8 Kevin Brown	2.00	.60
RA9 Roger Clemens	6.00	1.80
RA10 Jon Lieber	2.00	.60
RA11 C.C. Sabathia	2.00	.60
RA12 Tim Hudson	2.00	.60
RA13 Curt Schilling	2.00	.60
RA14 Al Leiter	2.00	.60
RA15 Mike Mussina	2.00	.60

2002 Upper Deck Sons of Summer Game Jersey

Inserted at a stated rate of one in 288 second series packs, these eight cards feature some of the best players in the game along with a game jersey swatch. According to Upper Deck, the Pedro Martinez card was issued in shorter supply.

	Nm-Mt	Ex-Mt
SS-AR Alex Rodriguez	20.00	6.00
SS-GM Greg Maddux	20.00	6.00
SS-JB Jeff Bagwell	20.00	6.00
SS-JG Juan Gonzalez	20.00	6.00
SS-MP Mike Piazza	20.00	6.00
SS-PM Pedro Martinez SP	25.00	7.50
SS-RA Roberto Alomar	20.00	6.00
SS-RC Roger Clemens	30.00	9.00

2002 Upper Deck Superstar Summit I

Inserted into first series packs at a rate of one in 23, these six cards feature the most popular players in the game.

	Nm-Mt	Ex-Mt
COMPLETE SET (6)	25.00	7.50
SS1 Sammy Sosa	4.00	1.20
SS2 Alex Rodriguez	4.00	1.20
SS3 Mark McGwire	6.00	1.80
SS4 Barry Bonds	6.00	1.80
SS5 Mike Piazza	4.00	1.20
SS6 Ken Griffey Jr.	4.00	1.20

2002 Upper Deck Superstar Summit II

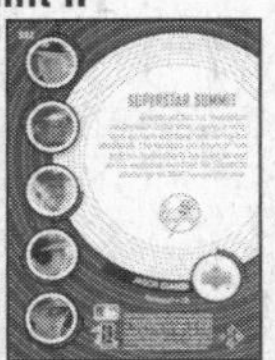

Inserted into second series packs at a rate of one in 11, these fifteen cards feature the most popular players in the game.

	Nm-Mt	Ex-Mt
COMPLETE SET (15)	60.00	18.00
SS1 Alex Rodriguez	5.00	1.50
SS2 Jason Giambi	3.00	.90
SS3 Vladimir Guerrero	3.00	.90
SS4 Randy Johnson	3.00	.90
SS5 Chipper Jones	3.00	.90
SS6 Ichiro Suzuki	5.00	1.50
SS7 Sammy Sosa	5.00	1.50
SS8 Greg Maddux	5.00	1.50
SS9 Ken Griffey Jr.	5.00	1.50
SS10 Todd Helton	3.00	.90
SS11 Barry Bonds	8.00	2.40
SS12 Derek Jeter	8.00	2.40
SS13 Mike Piazza	5.00	1.50
SS14 Ivan Rodriguez	3.00	.90
SS15 Frank Thomas	3.00	.90

2002 Upper Deck UD Plus Hobby

Issued as a two-card box topper in second series Upper Deck packs, these 100 cards could be exchanged for Joe DiMaggio or Mickey Mantle jersey cards if a collector finished the entire set. These cards were numbered to a stated print run of 1125 serial numbered sets. Hobby cards feature silver foil accents on front (unlike the Retail UD Plus cards - of which feature bronze fronts and backs). These cards could be exchanged until May 16, 2003.

	Nm-Mt	Ex-Mt
UD1 Darin Erstad	5.00	1.50
UD2 Troy Glaus	5.00	1.50
UD3 Tim Hudson	5.00	1.50
UD4 Jermaine Dye	5.00	1.50
UD5 Barry Zito	5.00	1.50
UD6 Carlos Delgado	5.00	1.50
UD7 Shannon Stewart	5.00	1.50
UD8 Greg Vaughn	5.00	1.50
UD9 Jim Thome	6.00	1.80
UD10 C.C. Sabathia	5.00	1.50
UD11 Ichiro Suzuki	10.00	3.00
UD12 Edgar Martinez	5.00	1.50
UD13 Bret Boone	5.00	1.50
UD14 Freddy Garcia	5.00	1.50
UD15 Matt Thornton	5.00	1.50
UD16 Jeff Conine	5.00	1.50
UD17 Steve Bechler	5.00	1.50
UD18 Rafael Palmeiro	5.00	1.50
UD19 Juan Gonzalez	5.00	1.50
UD20 Alex Rodriguez	10.00	3.00
UD21 Ivan Rodriguez	6.00	1.80
UD22 Carl Everett	5.00	1.50
UD23 Manny Ramirez	5.00	1.50
UD24 Nomar Garciaparra	10.00	3.00
UD25 Pedro Martinez	6.00	1.80
UD26 Mike Sweeney	5.00	1.50
UD27 Chuck Knoblauch	5.00	1.50
UD28 Dmitri Young	5.00	1.50
UD29 Bobby Higginson	5.00	1.50
UD30 Dean Palmer	5.00	1.50
UD31 Doug Mientkiewicz	5.00	1.50
UD32 Corey Koskie	5.00	1.50
UD33 Brad Radke	5.00	1.50
UD34 Cristian Guzman	5.00	1.50
UD35 Frank Thomas	6.00	1.80
UD36 Magglio Ordonez	5.00	1.50
UD37 Carlos Lee	5.00	1.50
UD38 Roger Clemens	12.00	3.60
UD39 Bernie Williams	5.00	1.50
UD40 Derek Jeter	15.00	4.50
UD41 Jason Giambi	5.00	1.50
UD42 Mike Mussina	5.00	1.50
UD43 Jeff Bagwell	5.00	1.50
UD44 Lance Berkman	5.00	1.50
UD45 Wade Miller	5.00	1.50
UD46 Greg Maddux	10.00	3.00
UD47 Chipper Jones	6.00	1.80
UD48 Andruw Jones	5.00	1.50
UD49 Gary Sheffield	5.00	1.50
UD50 Richie Sexson	5.00	1.50
UD51 Albert Pujols	12.00	3.60
UD52 J.D. Drew	5.00	1.50
UD53 Matt Morris	5.00	1.50
UD54 Jim Edmonds	5.00	1.50
UD55 So Taguchi	5.00	1.50
UD56 Sammy Sosa	10.00	3.00
UD57 Fred McGriff	5.00	1.50
UD58 Kerry Wood	6.00	1.80
UD59 Moises Alou	5.00	1.50
UD60 Randy Johnson	6.00	1.80
UD61 Luis Gonzalez	5.00	1.50
UD62 Mark Grace	5.00	1.50
UD63 Curt Schilling	5.00	1.50
UD64 Matt Williams	5.00	1.50
UD65 Kevin Brown	5.00	1.50
UD66 Brian Jordan	5.00	1.50
UD67 Shawn Green	5.00	1.50
UD68 Hideo Nomo	12.00	3.60
UD69 Kazuhisa Ishii	10.00	3.00
UD70 Vladimir Guerrero	6.00	1.80
UD71 Jose Vidro	5.00	1.50
UD72 Eric Good	5.00	1.50
UD73 Barry Bonds	15.00	4.50
UD74 Jeff Kent	5.00	1.50
UD75 Rich Aurilia	5.00	1.50
UD76 Deivis Santos	5.00	1.50
UD77 Preston Wilson	5.00	1.50
UD78 Cliff Floyd	5.00	1.50
UD79 Josh Beckett	5.00	1.50
UD80 Hansel Izquierdo	5.00	1.50
UD81 Mike Piazza	10.00	3.00
UD82 Roberto Alomar	5.00	1.50
UD83 Mo Vaughn	5.00	1.50
UD84 Jeromy Burnitz	5.00	1.50
UD85 Phil Nevin	5.00	1.50
UD86 Ryan Klesko	5.00	1.50
UD87 Bobby Abreu	5.00	1.50
UD88 Scott Rolen	6.00	1.80
UD89 Jimmy Rollins	5.00	1.50
UD90 Jason Kendall	5.00	1.50
UD91 Brian Giles	5.00	1.50
UD92 Aramis Ramirez	5.00	1.50
UD93 Ken Griffey Jr.	10.00	3.00
UD94 Sean Casey	5.00	1.50
UD95 Barry Larkin	5.00	1.50
UD96 Adam Dunn	5.00	1.50
UD97 Todd Helton	5.00	1.50
UD98 Larry Walker	5.00	1.50
UD99 Mike Hampton	5.00	1.50
UD100 Rene Reyes	5.00	1.50

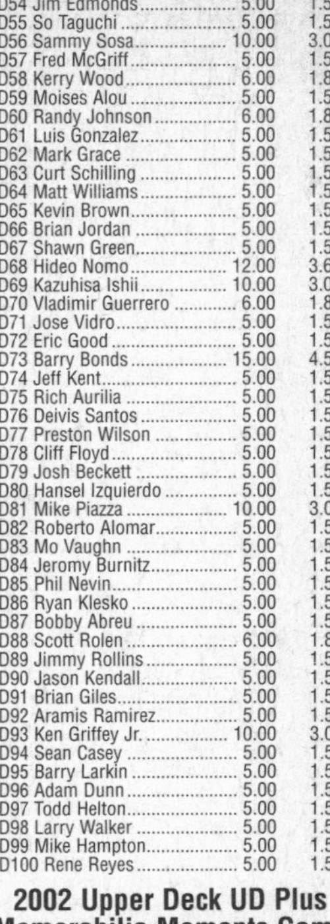

2002 Upper Deck UD Plus Memorabilia Moments Game Uniform

These cards were available only through a mail exchange. Collectors who finished the UD Plus set earliest had an opportunity to receive cards with game-used jersey swatches of either Mickey Mantle or Joe DiMaggio. These cards were issued to a stated print run of 25 serial numbred sets. The deadline to redeem these cards was 5/16/03. Due to market scarcity, no pricing will be provided for these cards.

	Nm-Mt	Ex-Mt
COMMON DIMAGGIO (1-5)	150.00	45.00
COMMON MANTLE (1-5)	300.00	90.00
AVAILABLE VIA MAIL EXCHANGE		
STATED PRINT RUN 25 SERIAL #'d SETS		

2002 Upper Deck World Series Heroes Memorabilia

Issued into first series packs at a rate of one in 288 hobby packs, these eight cards feature memorabilia from players who had star moments in the World Series.

	Nm-Mt	Ex-Mt
B-DJ Derek Jeter Base SP	40.00	12.00
B-ES E.Slaughter Bat	15.00	4.50
B-JD Joe DiMaggio Bat SP	100.00	30.00
B-KP Kirby Puckett Bat	25.00	7.50
B-MM M.Mantle Bat	120.00	36.00
S-BM B.Mazeroski Jsy	20.00	6.00
S-CF Carlton Fisk Jsy	20.00	6.00
S-DL Don Larsen Jsy	20.00	6.00
S-JC Joe Carter Jsy	15.00	4.50

2002 Upper Deck World Series Heroes Memorabilia Autograph

Randomly inserted in first series hobby packs, these four cards feature not only a piece of memorabilia from a World Series hero but also were signed by the featured player. A stated print run of twenty-five serial numbered cards were produced. Due to market scarcity, no pricing is provided for these cards.

Nm-Mt Ex-Mt
S-BM Bill Mazeroski Jsy
S-CF Carlton Fisk Jsy
S-DL Don Larsen Jsy
S-JC Joe Carter Jsy

2002 Upper Deck Yankee Dynasty Memorabilia

Issued into first series packs at a rate of one in 144, these 13 cards feature two pieces of game-worn memorabilia from various members of the Yankees Dynasty.

	Nm-Mt	Ex-Mt
YBCJ Roger Clemens Derek Jeter Bat SP	150.00	45.00
YBJW Derek Jeter Bernie Williams Bat	100.00	30.00
YJBJ Scott Brosius David Justice Jsy	25.00	7.50
YJBT Wade Boggs Joe Torre Jsy	25.00	7.50
YJCP Roger Clemens Jorge Posada Jsy	50.00	15.00
YJDM Joe DiMaggio Mickey Mantle Jsy	300.00	90.00
YJGC Joe Girardi David Cone Jsy	25.00	7.50
YJKR Chuck Knoblauch Tim Raines J	25.00	7.50
YJOM Paul O'Neill Tino Martinez Jsy	25.00	7.50
YJPR Andy Pettitte Mariano Rivera Jsy	25.00	7.50
YJRK Willie Randolph Chuck Knoblauch Jsy	25.00	7.50
YJWG David Wells Dwight Gooden Jsy	25.00	7.50
YJWO Bernie Williams Paul O'Neill Jsy	25.00	7.50

2003 Upper Deck

The 270 card first series was released in November, 2002. The 270 card second series was released in June, 2003. The final 60 cards were released as part of an special boxed insert in the 2004 Upper Deck Series one product. The first tw series cards were issued in eight card packs which came 24 packs to a box and 12 boxes to a case with an SRP of $3 per pack. Cards numbered from 1 through 30 featured leading rookie prospects while cards numbered from 261 through 270 featured checklist cards honoring the leading events of the 2002 season. In the second series the following subsets were issued: Cards numbered 501 through 530 feature Star Rookies while cards numbered 531 through 540 feature Season Highlight fronts and checklist backs. Due to an error in printing, card 19 was originally intended to feature Marcos Scutaro but the card was erroneously numbered as card 96. Thus, the set features two card 96's (Scutaro and Nomar Garciaparra) and no card number 19.

	Nm-Mt	Ex-Mt
COMPLETE SERIES 1 (270)	50.00	15.00
COMPLETE SERIES 2 (270)	50.00	15.00
COMP.UPDATE SET (60)	20.00	6.00
COMMON (31-500/531-600)	.30	.09
COMMON (1-30/501-530)	1.00	.30
COMMON RC (541-600)	.50	.15

SR 1-30/501-530 ARE NOT SHORT PRINTS
CARD 19 DOES NOT EXIST
SCUTARO/NOMAR ARE BOTH CARD 96
541-600 ISSUED IN 04 UD1 HOBBY BOXES
UPDATE SET EXCH 1:240 '04 UD1 RETAIL
UPDATE SET EXCH.DEADLINE 11/10/06

	Nm-Mt	Ex-Mt
1 John Lackey SR	1.00	.30
2 Alex Cintron SR	1.00	.30
3 Jose Leon SR	1.00	.30
4 Bobby Hill SR	1.00	.30
5 Brandon Larson SR	1.00	.30
6 Raul Gonzalez SR	1.00	.30
7 Ben Broussard SR	1.00	.30
8 Earl Snyder SR	1.00	.30
9 Ramon Santiago SR	1.00	.30
10 Jason Lane SR	1.00	.30
11 Keith Ginter SR	1.00	.30
12 Kirk Saarloos SR	1.00	.30
13 Juan Brito SR	1.00	.30
14 Runelvys Hernandez SR	1.00	.30
15 Shawn Sedlacek SR	1.00	.30
16 Jayson Durocher SR	1.00	.30
17 Kevin Frederick SR	1.00	.30
18 Zach Day SR	1.00	.30
19 Marcos Scutaro SR UER Card number 96 on back	1.00	.30
20 Marcus Thames SR	1.00	.30
21 Esteban German SR	1.00	.30
22 Brett Myers SR	1.00	.30
23 Oliver Perez SR	1.00	.30
24 Dennis Tankersley SR	1.00	.30
25 Julius Matos SR	1.00	.30
26 Jake Peavy SR	1.00	.30
27 Eric Cyr SR	1.00	.30
28 Mike Crudale SR	1.00	.30
29 Josh Pearce SR	1.00	.30
30 Carl Crawford SR	1.00	.30
31 Tim Salmon	.50	.15
32 Troy Glaus	.30	.09
33 Adam Kennedy	.30	.09
34 David Eckstein	.30	.09
35 Ben Molina	.30	.09
36 Jarrod Washburn	.30	.09
37 Ramon Ortiz	.30	.09
38 Eric Chavez	.30	.09
39 Miguel Tejada	.30	.09
40 Adam Piatt	.30	.09
41 Jermaine Dye	.30	.09
42 Olmedo Saenz	.30	.09
43 Tim Hudson	.30	.09
44 Barry Zito	.30	.09
45 Billy Koch	.30	.09
46 Shannon Stewart	.30	.09
47 Kelvim Escobar	.30	.09
48 Jose Cruz Jr.	.30	.09
49 Vernon Wells	.30	.09
50 Roy Halladay	.30	.09
51 Esteban Loaiza	.30	.09
52 Eric Hinske	.30	.09
53 Steve Cox	.30	.09
54 Brent Abernathy	.30	.09
55 Ben Grieve	.30	.09
56 Aubrey Huff	.30	.09
57 Jared Sandberg	.30	.09
58 Paul Wilson	.30	.09
59 Tanyon Sturtze	.30	.09
60 Jim Thome	.75	.23
61 Omar Vizquel	.50	.15
62 C.C. Sabathia	.30	.09
63 Chris Magruder	.30	.09
64 Ricky Gutierrez	.30	.09
65 Einar Diaz	.30	.09
66 Danys Baez	.30	.09
67 Ichiro Suzuki	1.25	.35
68 Ruben Sierra	.30	.09
69 Carlos Guillen	.30	.09
70 Mark McLemore	.30	.09
71 Dan Wilson	.30	.09
72 Jamie Moyer	.30	.09
73 Joel Pineiro	.30	.09
74 Edgar Martinez	.50	.15
75 Tony Batista	.30	.09
76 Jay Gibbons	.30	.09
77 Chris Singleton	.30	.09
78 Melvin Mora	.30	.09
79 Geronimo Gil	.30	.09
80 Rodrigo Lopez	.30	.09
81 Jorge Julio	.30	.09
82 Rafael Palmeiro	.50	.15
83 Juan Gonzalez	.50	.15
84 Mike Young	.50	.15
85 Hideki Irabu	.30	.09
86 Chan Ho Park	.30	.09
87 Kevin Mench	.30	.09
88 Doug Davis	.30	.09
89 Pedro Martinez	.75	.23
90 Shea Hillenbrand	.30	.09
91 Derek Lowe	.30	.09
92 Jason Varitek	.50	.15
93 Tony Clark	.30	.09
94 John Burkett	.30	.09
95 Frank Castillo	.30	.09
96 Nomar Garciaparra	1.25	.35
97 Rickey Henderson	.75	.23
98 Mike Sweeney	.30	.09
99 Carlos Febles	.30	.09
100 Mark Quinn	.30	.09
101 Raul Ibanez	.30	.09
102 A.J. Hinch	.30	.09
103 Paul Byrd	.30	.09
104 Chuck Knoblauch	.30	.09
105 Dmitri Young	.30	.09
106 Randall Simon	.30	.09
107 Brandon Inge	.30	.09
108 Damion Easley	.30	.09
109 Carlos Pena	.30	.09
110 George Lombard	.30	.09
111 Juan Acevedo	.30	.09
112 Torii Hunter	.30	.09
113 Doug Mientkiewicz	.30	.09
114 David Ortiz	.50	.15
115 Eric Milton	.30	.09
116 Eddie Guardado	.30	.09
117 Cristian Guzman	.30	.09
118 Corey Koskie	.30	.09
119 Magglio Ordonez	.30	.09
120 Mark Buehrle	.30	.09
121 Todd Ritchie	.30	.09
122 Jose Valentin	.30	.09
123 Paul Konerko	.30	.09
124 Carlos Lee	.30	.09
125 Jon Garland	.30	.09
126 Jason Giambi	.30	.09
127 Derek Jeter	2.00	.60
128 Roger Clemens	1.50	.45
129 Raul Mondesi	.30	.09
130 Jorge Posada	.50	.15
131 Rondell White	.30	.09
132 Robin Ventura	.30	.09
133 Mike Mussina	.50	.15
134 Jeff Bagwell	.50	.15
135 Craig Biggio	.50	.15
136 Morgan Ensberg	.30	.09
137 Richard Hidalgo	.30	.09
138 Brad Ausmus	.30	.09
139 Roy Oswalt	.30	.09
140 Carlos Hernandez	.30	.09
141 Shane Reynolds	.30	.09
142 Gary Sheffield	.30	.09
143 Andruw Jones	.30	.09
144 Tom Glavine	.50	.15
145 Rafael Furcal	.30	.09
146 Javy Lopez	.30	.09
147 Vinny Castilla	.30	.09
148 Marcus Giles	.30	.09
149 Kevin Millwood	.30	.09
150 Jason Marquis	.30	.09
151 Ruben Quevedo	.30	.09
152 Ben Sheets	.30	.09
153 Geoff Jenkins	.30	.09
154 Jose Hernandez	.30	.09
155 Glendon Rusch	.30	.09
156 Jeffrey Hammonds	.30	.09
157 Alex Sanchez	.30	.09
158 Jim Edmonds	.30	.09
159 Tino Martinez	.50	.15
160 Albert Pujols	1.50	.45
161 Eli Marrero	.30	.09
162 Woody Williams	.30	.09
163 Fernando Vina	.30	.09
164 Jason Isringhausen	.30	.09
165 Jason Simontacchi	.30	.09
166 Kerry Robinson	.30	.09
167 Sammy Sosa	1.25	.35
168 Juan Cruz	.30	.09
169 Fred McGriff	.50	.15
170 Antonio Alfonseca	.30	.09
171 Jon Lieber	.30	.09
172 Mark Prior	.75	.23
173 Moises Alou	.30	.09
174 Matt Clement	.30	.09
175 Mark Bellhorn	.30	.09
176 Randy Johnson	.75	.23
177 Luis Gonzalez	.30	.09
178 Tony Womack	.30	.09
179 Mark Grace	.50	.15
180 Junior Spivey	.30	.09
181 Byung Hyun Kim	.30	.09
182 Danny Bautista	.30	.09
183 Brian Anderson	.30	.09
184 Shawn Green	.30	.09
185 Brian Jordan	.30	.09
186 Eric Karros	.30	.09
187 Andy Ashby	.30	.09
188 Cesar Izturis	.30	.09
189 Dave Roberts	.30	.09
190 Eric Gagne	.75	.23
191 Kazuhisa Ishii	.30	.09
192 Adrian Beltre	.50	.15
193 Vladimir Guerrero	.75	.23
194 Tony Armas Jr.	.30	.09
195 Bartolo Colon	.30	.09
196 Troy O'Leary	.30	.09
197 Tomo Ohka	.30	.09
198 Brad Wilkerson	.30	.09
199 Orlando Cabrera	.30	.09
200 Barry Bonds	2.00	.60
201 David Bell	.30	.09
202 Tsuyoshi Shinjo	.30	.09
203 Benito Santiago	.30	.09
204 Livan Hernandez	.30	.09
205 Jason Schmidt	.30	.09
206 Kirk Rueter	.30	.09
207 Ramon E. Martinez	.30	.09
208 Mike Lowell	.30	.09
209 Luis Castillo	.30	.09
210 Derrek Lee	.30	.09
211 Andy Fox	.30	.09
212 Eric Owens	.30	.09
213 Charles Johnson	.30	.09
214 Brad Penny	.30	.09
215 A.J. Burnett	.30	.09
216 Edgardo Alfonzo	.30	.09
217 Roberto Alomar	.50	.15
218 Rey Ordonez	.30	.09
219 Al Leiter	.30	.09
220 Roger Cedeno	.30	.09
221 Timo Perez	.30	.09
222 Jeromy Burnitz	.30	.09
223 Pedro Astacio	.30	.09
224 Joe McEwing	.30	.09
225 Ryan Klesko	.30	.09
226 Ramon Vazquez	.30	.09
227 Mark Kotsay	.30	.09
228 Bubba Trammell	.30	.09
229 Wiki Gonzalez	.30	.09
230 Trevor Hoffman	.30	.09
231 Ron Gant	.30	.09
232 Bob Abreu	.30	.09
233 Marlon Anderson	.30	.09
234 Jeremy Giambi	.30	.09
235 Jimmy Rollins	.30	.09
236 Mike Lieberthal	.30	.09
237 Vicente Padilla	.30	.09
238 Randy Wolf	.30	.09
239 Pokey Reese	.30	.09
240 Brian Giles	.30	.09
241 Jack Wilson	.30	.09
242 Mike Williams	.30	.09
243 Kip Wells	.30	.09
244 Rob Mackowiak	.30	.09
245 Craig Wilson	.30	.09
246 Adam Dunn	.50	.15
247 Sean Casey	.30	.09
248 Todd Walker	.30	.09
249 Corky Miller	.30	.09
250 Ryan Dempster	.30	.09
251 Reggie Taylor	.30	.09
252 Aaron Boone	.30	.09
253 Larry Walker	.50	.15
254 Jose Ortiz	.30	.09
255 Todd Zeile	.30	.09
256 Bobby Estalella	.30	.09
257 Juan Pierre	.30	.09
258 Terry Shumpert	.30	.09
259 Mike Hampton	.30	.09
260 Denny Stark	.30	.09
261 Shawn Green SH CL	.30	.09
262 Derek Lowe SH CL	.30	.09
263 Barry Bonds SH CL	.75	.23
264 Mike Cameron SH CL	.30	.09
265 Luis Castillo SH CL	.30	.09
266 Vladimir Guerrero SH CL	.50	.15
267 Jason Giambi SH CL	.30	.09
268 Eric Gagne SH CL	.50	.15
269 Magglio Ordonez SH CL	.30	.09
270 Jim Thome SH CL	.50	.15
271 Garret Anderson	.30	.09
272 Troy Percival	.30	.09
273 Brad Fullmer	.30	.09
274 Scott Spiezio	.30	.09
275 Darin Erstad	.30	.09
276 Francisco Rodriguez	.30	.09
277 Kevin Appier	.30	.09
278 Shawn Wooten	.30	.09
279 Eric Owens	.30	.09
280 Scott Hatteberg	.30	.09
281 Terrence Long	.30	.09
282 Mark Mulder	.30	.09
283 Ramon Hernandez	.30	.09
284 Ted Lilly	.30	.09
285 Erubiel Durazo	.30	.09
286 Mark Ellis	.30	.09
287 Carlos Delgado	.30	.09
288 Orlando Hudson	.30	.09
289 Chris Woodward	.30	.09
290 Mark Hendrickson	.30	.09
291 Josh Phelps	.30	.09
292 Ken Huckaby	.30	.09
293 Justin Miller	.30	.09
294 Travis Lee	.30	.09
295 Jorge Sosa	.30	.09
296 Joe Kennedy	.30	.09
297 Carl Crawford	.30	.09
298 Toby Hall	.30	.09
299 Rey Ordonez	.30	.09
300 Brandon Phillips	.30	.09
301 Matt Lawton	.30	.09
302 Ellis Burks	.30	.09
303 Bill Selby	.30	.09
304 Travis Hafner	.30	.09
305 Milton Bradley	.30	.09
306 Karim Garcia	.30	.09
307 Cliff Lee	.30	.09
308 Jeff Cirillo	.30	.09
309 John Olerud	.30	.09
310 Kazuhiro Sasaki	.30	.09
311 Freddy Garcia	.30	.09
312 Bret Boone	.30	.09
313 Mike Cameron	.30	.09
314 Ben Davis	.30	.09
315 Randy Winn	.30	.09
316 Gary Matthews Jr.	.30	.09
317 Jeff Conine	.30	.09
318 Sidney Ponson	.30	.09
319 Jerry Hairston	.30	.09
320 David Segui	.30	.09
321 Scott Erickson	.30	.09
322 Marty Cordova	.30	.09
323 Hank Blalock	.50	.15
324 Herbert Perry	.30	.09
325 Alex Rodriguez	1.25	.35
326 Carl Everett	.30	.09
327 Einar Diaz	.30	.09
328 Ugueth Urbina	.30	.09
329 Mark Teixeira	.30	.09
330 Manny Ramirez	.50	.15
331 Johnny Damon	.75	.23
332 Trot Nixon	.30	.09
333 Tim Wakefield	.30	.09
334 Casey Fossum	.30	.09
335 Todd Walker	.30	.09
336 Jeremy Giambi	.30	.09
337 Bill Mueller	.30	.09
338 Ramiro Mendoza	.30	.09
339 Carlos Beltran	.50	.15
340 Jason Grimsley	.30	.09
341 Brent Mayne	.30	.09
342 Angel Berroa	.30	.09
343 Albie Lopez	.30	.09
344 Michael Tucker	.30	.09
345 Bobby Higginson	.30	.09
346 Shane Halter	.30	.09
347 Jeremy Bonderman RC	.75	.23
348 Eric Munson	.30	.09
349 Andy Van Hekken	.30	.09
350 Matt Anderson	.30	.09
351 Jacque Jones	.30	.09
352 A.J. Pierzynski	.30	.09
353 Joe Mays	.30	.09
354 Brad Radke	.30	.09
355 Dustan Mohr	.30	.09
356 Bobby Kielty	.30	.09
357 Michael Cuddyer	.30	.09
358 Luis Rivas	.30	.09
359 Frank Thomas	.75	.23
360 Joe Borchard	.30	.09
361 D'Angelo Jimenez	.30	.09
362 Bartolo Colon	.30	.09
363 Joe Crede	.30	.09
364 Miguel Olivo	.30	.09
365 Billy Koch	.30	.09
366 Bernie Williams	.50	.15
367 Nick Johnson	.30	.09
368 Andy Pettitte	.50	.15
369 Mariano Rivera	.50	.15
370 Alfonso Soriano	.50	.15
371 David Wells	.30	.09
372 Drew Henson	.30	.09
373 Juan Rivera	.30	.09
374 Steve Karsay	.30	.09
375 Jeff Kent	.30	.09
376 Lance Berkman	.30	.09
377 Octavio Dotel	.30	.09
378 Julio Lugo	.30	.09
379 Jason Lane	.30	.09
380 Wade Miller	.30	.09
381 Billy Wagner	.30	.09
382 Brad Ausmus	.30	.09
383 Mike Hampton	.30	.09
384 Chipper Jones	.75	.23
385 John Smoltz	.50	.15
386 Greg Maddux	1.25	.35
387 Javy Lopez	.30	.09
388 Robert Fick	.30	.09
389 Mark DeRosa	.30	.09
390 Russ Ortiz	.30	.09
391 Julio Franco	.30	.09
392 Richie Sexson	.30	.09
393 Eric Young	.30	.09
394 Robert Machado	.30	.09
395 Mike DeJean	.30	.09
396 Todd Ritchie	.30	.09
397 Royce Clayton	.30	.09
398 Nick Neugebauer	.30	.09
399 J.D. Drew	.30	.09
400 Edgar Renteria	.30	.09
401 Scott Rolen	.75	.23
402 Matt Morris	.30	.09
403 Garrett Stephenson	.30	.09
404 Eduardo Perez	.30	.09
405 Mike Matheny	.30	.09
406 Miguel Cairo	.30	.09
407 Brett Tomko	.30	.09
408 Bobby Hill	.30	.09
409 Troy O'Leary	.30	.09
410 Corey Patterson	.30	.09
411 Kerry Wood	.75	.23
412 Eric Karros	.30	.09
413 Hee Seop Choi	.30	.09
414 Alex Gonzalez	.30	.09
415 Matt Clement	.30	.09
416 Mark Grudzielanek	.30	.09
417 Curt Schilling	.30	.09
418 Steve Finley	.30	.09
419 Craig Counsell	.30	.09
420 Matt Williams	.30	.09
421 Quinton McCracken	.30	.09
422 Chad Moeller	.30	.09
423 Lyle Overbay	.30	.09
424 Miguel Batista	.30	.09
425 Paul Lo Duca	.30	.09
426 Kevin Brown	.30	.09
427 Hideo Nomo	.75	.23
428 Fred McGriff	.50	.15
429 Joe Thurston	.30	.09
430 Odalis Perez	.30	.09
431 Darren Dreifort	.30	.09
432 Todd Hundley	.30	.09
433 Dave Roberts	.30	.09
434 Jose Vidro	.30	.09
435 Javier Vazquez	.30	.09
436 Michael Barrett	.30	.09
437 Fernando Tatis	.30	.09
438 Peter Bergeron	.30	.09
439 Endy Chavez	.30	.09
440 Orlando Hernandez	.30	.09
441 Marvin Benard	.30	.09
442 Rich Aurilia	.30	.09
443 Pedro Feliz	.30	.09
444 Robb Nen	.30	.09
445 Ray Durham	.30	.09
446 Marquis Grissom	.30	.09
447 Damian Moss	.30	.09
448 Edgardo Alfonzo	.30	.09
449 Juan Pierre	.30	.09
450 Braden Looper	.30	.09
451 Alex Gonzalez	.30	.09
452 Justin Wayne	.30	.09
453 Josh Beckett	.30	.09
454 Juan Encarnacion	.30	.09
455 Ivan Rodriguez	.75	.23
456 Todd Hollandsworth	.30	.09
457 Cliff Floyd	.30	.09
458 Rey Sanchez	.30	.09
459 Mike Piazza	1.25	.35
460 Mo Vaughn	.30	.09
461 Armando Benitez	.30	.09
462 Tsuyoshi Shinjo	.30	.09
463 Tom Glavine	.50	.15
464 David Cone	.30	.09
465 Phil Nevin	.30	.09
466 Sean Burroughs	.30	.09
467 Jake Peavy	.30	.09
468 Brian Lawrence	.30	.09
469 Mark Loretta	.30	.09
470 Dennis Tankersley	.30	.09
471 Jesse Orosco	.30	.09
472 Jim Thome	.75	.23
473 Kevin Millwood	.30	.09
474 David Bell	.30	.09
475 Pat Burrell	.30	.09
476 Brandon Duckworth	.30	.09
477 Jose Mesa	.30	.09
478 Marlon Byrd	.30	.09
479 Reggie Sanders	.30	.09
480 Jason Kendall	.30	.09
481 Aramis Ramirez	.30	.09
482 Kris Benson	.30	.09
483 Matt Stairs	.30	.09
484 Kevin Young	.30	.09
485 Kenny Lofton	.30	.09
486 Austin Kearns	.30	.09
487 Barry Larkin	.50	.15
488 Jason LaRue	.30	.09
489 Ken Griffey Jr.	1.25	.35
490 Danny Graves	.30	.09
491 Russell Branyan	.30	.09
492 Reggie Taylor	.30	.09
493 Jimmy Haynes	.30	.09
494 Charles Johnson	.30	.09
495 Todd Helton	.50	.15
496 Juan Uribe	.30	.09
497 Preston Wilson	.30	.09
498 Chris Stynes	.30	.09
499 Jason Jennings	.30	.09
500 Jay Payton	.30	.09
501 Hideki Matsui SR RC	5.00	1.50
502 Jose Contreras SR RC	2.00	.60
503 Brandon Webb SR RC	2.00	.60
504 Robby Hammock SR RC	1.50	.45
505 Matt Kata SR RC	1.50	.45
506 Tim Olson SR RC	1.50	.45
507 Michael Hessman SR RC	1.00	.30
508 Jon Leicester SR RC	1.00	.30
509 Todd Wellemeyer SR RC	1.50	.45
510 David Sanders SR RC	1.00	.30
511 Josh Stewart SR RC	1.00	.30
512 Luis Ayala SR RC	1.00	.30
513 Clint Barmes SR RC	1.50	.45
514 Josh Willingham SR RC	1.50	.45
515 Al. Machado SR RC	1.00	.30
516 Felix Sanchez SR RC	1.00	.30
517 Willie Eyre SR RC	1.00	.30
518 Brent Hoard SR RC	1.00	.30
519 Lew Ford SR RC	2.50	.75
520 Terrmel Sledge SR RC	1.50	.45
521 Jeremy Griffiths SR RC	1.50	.45
522 Phil Seibel SR RC	1.00	.30
523 Craig Brazell SR RC	1.50	.45
524 Prentice Redman SR RC	1.00	.30
525 Jeff Duncan SR RC	1.50	.45
526 Shane Bazzell SR RC	1.00	.30
527 Bernie Castro SR RC	1.00	.30
528 Rett Johnson SR RC	1.50	.45
529 Bobby Madritsch SR RC	4.00	1.20
530 Rocco Baldelli SR	1.00	.30
531 Alex Rodriguez SH CL	.75	.23
532 Eric Chavez SH CL	.30	.09
533 Miguel Tejada SH CL	.30	.09
534 Ichiro Suzuki SH CL	.75	.23
535 Sammy Sosa SH CL	.75	.23
536 Barry Zito SH CL	.30	.09
537 Darin Erstad SH CL	.30	.09
538 Alfonso Soriano SH CL	.30	.09
539 Troy Glaus SH CL	.30	.09

540 N.Garciaparra SH CL	.75	.23
541 Bo Hart RC	.50	.15
542 Dan Haren RC	.75	.23
543 Ryan Wagner RC	.50	.15
544 Rich Harden	.50	.15
545 Dontrelle Willis	.50	.15
546 Jerome Williams	.30	.09
547 Bobby Crosby	.50	.15
548 Greg Jones RC	.50	.15
549 Todd Linden	.30	.09
550 Byung-Hyun Kim	.30	.09
551 Rickie Weeks RC	2.50	.75
552 Jason Roach RC	.50	.15
553 Oscar Villarreal RC	.50	.15
554 Justin Duchscherer	.30	.09
555 Chris Capuano RC	.50	.15
556 Josh Hall RC	.50	.15
557 Luis Matos	.30	.09
558 Miguel Ojeda RC	.50	.15
559 Kevin Ohme RC	.50	.15
560 Julio Manon RC	.50	.15
561 Kevin Correia RC	.50	.15
562 Delmon Young RC	4.00	1.20
563 Aaron Boone	.30	.09
564 Aaron Looper RC	.50	.15
565 Mike Neu RC	.50	.15
566 Aquilino Lopez RC	.50	.15
567 Jhonny Peralta	.50	.15
568 Duaner Sanchez	.30	.09
569 Stephen Randolph RC	.50	.15
570 Nate Bland RC	.50	.15
571 Chin-Hui Tsao	.30	.09
572 Michel Hernandez RC	.50	.15
573 Rocco Baldelli	.30	.09
574 Robb Quinlan	.30	.09
575 Aaron Heilman	.30	.09
576 Jae Weong Seo	.30	.09
577 Joe Borowski	.30	.09
578 Chris Bootcheck	.30	.09
579 Michael Ryan RC	.50	.15
580 Mark Malaska RC	.50	.15
581 Jose Guillen	.30	.09
582 Josh Towers	.30	.09
583 Tom Gregorio RC	.50	.15
584 Edwin Jackson RC	2.50	.75
585 Jason Anderson	.30	.09
586 Jose Reyes	.30	.09
587 Miguel Cabrera	.75	.23
588 Nate Bump	.30	.09
589 Jeromy Burnitz	.30	.09
590 David Ross	.30	.09
591 Chase Utley	.30	.09
592 Brandon Webb	.75	.23
593 Masao Kida	.30	.09
594 Jimmy Journell	.30	.09
595 Eric Young	.30	.09
596 Tony Womack	.30	.09
597 Amaury Telemaco	.30	.09
598 Rickey Henderson	.75	.23
599 Esteban Loaiza	.30	.09
600 Sidney Ponson	.30	.09
NNO Update Set Exchange Card		

2003 Upper Deck Gold

	MINT	NRMT
COMP.FACT.SET (60)	40.00	18.00
*GOLD: 2X TO 5X BASIC		
*GOLD: 1.25X TO 3X BASIC RC'S		
ONE GOLD SET PER 12 CT HOBBY CASE		

2003 Upper Deck A Piece of History 500 Club

This card, which continues the Upper Deck A Piece of History 500 club set which began in 1999, was randomly inserted into second series packs. These cards were issued to a stated print run of 350 cards.

	Nm-Mt	Ex-Mt
SS Sammy Sosa	200.00	60.00

2003 Upper Deck A Piece of History 500 Club Autograph

Randomly inserted into packs, this is a parallel to the Piece of History insert card of Sammy Sosa. Sosa signed 21 copies of this card but did not return them in time for pack-out. Please note that the exchange date for these cards are June 9th, 2006 and since only 21 cards were created there is no pricing due to market scarcity.

	Nm-Mt	Ex-Mt
RANDOM INSERT IN SERIES 2 PACKS		
STATED PRINT RUN 21 SERIAL #'d CARDS		
NO PRICING DUE TO SCARCITY		
EXCHANGE DEADLINE 06/09/06		
SSAU Sammy Sosa AU/21 EXCH		

2003 Upper Deck AL All-Star Swatches

Inserted into first series retail packs at a stated rate of one in 144, these 13 cards feature game-used uniform swatches of players who had made the AL All-Star game during their career.

	Nm-Mt	Ex-Mt
AP Andy Pettitte	15.00	4.50
AS Aaron Sele	10.00	3.00
CE Carl Everett	10.00	3.00
CF Chuck Finley	10.00	3.00
JG Juan Gonzalez	15.00	4.50
JM Joe Mays	10.00	3.00
JP Jorge Posada	15.00	4.50
MC Mike Cameron	10.00	3.00
MO Magglio Ordonez	10.00	3.00
MR Mariano Rivera	15.00	4.50
MS Mike Sweeney	10.00	3.00
RD Ray Durham	10.00	3.00
TF Travis Fryman	10.00	3.00

2003 Upper Deck Big League Breakdowns

Inserted into series one packs at a stated rate of one in eight, these 15 cards feature some of the leading hitters in the game.

	Nm-Mt	Ex-Mt
COMPLETE SET (15)	40.00	12.00
BL1 Troy Glaus	2.00	.60
BL2 Miguel Tejada	2.00	.60
BL3 Chipper Jones	2.50	.75
BL4 Torii Hunter	2.00	.60
BL5 Nomar Garciaparra	4.00	1.20
BL6 Sammy Sosa	4.00	1.20
BL7 Todd Helton	2.00	.60
BL8 Lance Berkman	2.00	.60
BL9 Shawn Green	2.00	.60
BL10 Vladimir Guerrero	2.50	.75
BL11 Jason Giambi	2.00	.60
BL12 Derek Jeter	6.00	1.80
BL13 Barry Bonds	6.00	1.80
BL14 Ichiro Suzuki	4.00	1.20
BL15 Alex Rodriguez	4.00	1.20

2003 Upper Deck Chase for 755

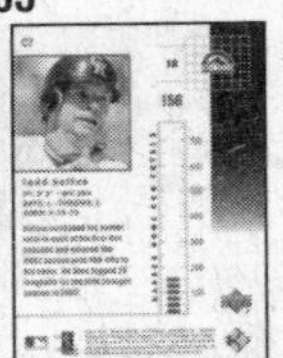

Inserted into first series packs at a stated rate of one in eight, these 15 cards feature players who are considered to have some chance of surpassing Hank Aaron's career home run total.

	Nm-Mt	Ex-Mt
COMPLETE SET (15)	30.00	9.00
C1 Troy Glaus	2.00	.60
C2 Andruw Jones	2.00	.60
C3 Manny Ramirez	2.00	.60
C4 Sammy Sosa	4.00	1.20
C5 Ken Griffey Jr.	4.00	1.20
C6 Adam Dunn	2.00	.60
C7 Todd Helton	2.00	.60
C8 Lance Berkman	2.00	.60
C9 Jeff Bagwell	2.00	.60
C10 Shawn Green	2.00	.60
C11 Vladimir Guerrero	2.50	.75
C12 Barry Bonds	6.00	1.80
C13 Alex Rodriguez	4.00	1.20
C14 Juan Gonzalez	2.00	.60
C15 Carlos Delgado	2.00	.60

2003 Upper Deck Game Swatches

Inserted into first series packs at a stated rate of one in 72, these 25 cards feature game-used memorabilia swatches. A few cards were printed to a lesser quantity and we have notated those cards in our checklist.

	Nm-Mt	Ex-Mt
HJ-AR Alex Rodriguez	15.00	4.50
HJ-BW Bernie Williams	10.00	3.00
HJ-CC C.C. Sabathia	8.00	2.40
HJ-CD Carlos Delgado SP	15.00	4.50
HJ-CP Carlos Pena	8.00	2.40
HJ-CS Curt Schilling SP/100	15.00	4.50
HJ-GM Greg Maddux	10.00	3.00
HJ-MM Mike Mussina	10.00	3.00
HJ-MO Magglio Ordonez	8.00	2.40
HJ-MP Mike Piazza SP	25.00	7.50
HJ-SB Sean Burroughs SP	15.00	4.50
HJ-SS Sammy Sosa	15.00	4.50
RJ-AD Adam Dunn	10.00	3.00
RJ-DE Darin Erstad	8.00	2.40
RJ-EM Edgar Martinez	10.00	3.00
RJ-FT Frank Thomas	10.00	3.00
RJ-IR Ivan Rodriguez	10.00	3.00
RJ-JD J.D. Drew	8.00	2.40
RJ-JE Jim Edmonds	8.00	2.40
RJ-JG Jason Giambi	8.00	2.40
RJ-JK Jeff Kent	8.00	2.40
RJ-KG Ken Griffey Jr.	15.00	4.50
RJ-RC Roger Clemens	20.00	6.00
RJ-RJ Randy Johnson	10.00	3.00
RJ-TH Tim Hudson	8.00	2.40

2003 Upper Deck Leading Swatches

	Nm-Mt	Ex-Mt
SERIES 2 STATED ODDS 1:24 HOB/1:48 RET		
SP INFO PROVIDED BY UPPER DECK		
SP'S ARE NOT SERIAL-NUMBERED...		
*GOLD: .75X TO 2X BASIC SWATCHES		
*GOLD: .6X TO 1.5X BASIC SP SWATCHES		
*GOLD MATSUI HR: .75X TO 1.5X BASIC HR		
*GOLD MATSUI RBI: .6X TO 1.2X BASIC RBI		
GOLD RANDOM INSERTS IN SER.2 PACKS		
GOLD PRINT RUN 100 SERIAL #'d SETS		
AB Adrian Beltre GM	10.00	3.00
AD Adam Dunn RUN	10.00	3.00
AD1 Adam Dunn BB SP	15.00	4.50
AJ Andruw Jones HR	8.00	2.40
AJ1 Andruw Jones AB SP	10.00	3.00
AP Andy Pettitte WIN SP	15.00	4.50
AR Alex Rodriguez HR	15.00	4.50
AR1 Alex Rodriguez RBI	15.00	4.50
AS Alfonso Soriano SB	10.00	3.00
AS1 Alfonso Soriano RUN	10.00	3.00
AS2 Aaron Sele WIN	8.00	2.40
BA Bobby Abreu 2B	8.00	2.40
BG Brian Giles HR	8.00	2.40
BG1 Brian Giles OBP	8.00	2.40
BW Bernie Williams 333 AVG	10.00	3.00
BW1 Bernie Williams 339 AVG	10.00	3.00
BZ Barry Zito WIN	8.00	2.40
CD Carlos Delgado RBI	8.00	2.40
CJ Chipper Jones AVG-RBI	10.00	3.00
CP Corey Patterson HR	8.00	2.40
CS Curt Schilling WIN	8.00	2.40
EC Eric Chavez HR	8.00	2.40
GA Garret Anderson RBI	8.00	2.40
GM Greg Maddux 2.62 ERA	10.00	3.00
GM1 Greg Maddux 1.56 ERA SP	15.00	4.50
GO Juan Gonzalez RBI	10.00	3.00
HM Hideki Matsui HR	40.00	12.00
HM1 Hideki Matsui RBI SP	50.00	15.00
HN Hideo Nomo WIN	15.00	4.50
IR Ivan Rodriguez AVG	10.00	3.00
IS Ichiro Suzuki HIT	30.00	9.00
IS1 Ichiro Suzuki SB SP	40.00	12.00
JB Jeff Bagwell RBI	10.00	3.00
JB1 Jeff Bagwell SLG SP	15.00	4.50
JD J.D. Drew RBI	8.00	2.40
JE Jim Edmonds RUN	8.00	2.40
JG Jason Giambi HR	8.00	2.40
JG1 Jason Giambi SLG	8.00	2.40
JL Javy Lopez NLCS	8.00	2.40
JP Jay Payton 3B	8.00	2.40
JS J.T. Snow GLV	8.00	2.40
JT Jim Thome HR	10.00	3.00
JT1 Jim Thome SLG	10.00	3.00
KE Jason Kendall RUN	8.00	2.40
KG Ken Griffey Jr. 40 HR	15.00	4.50
KG1 Ken Griffey Jr. 56 HR SP	20.00	6.00
KI Kazuhisa Ishii K	8.00	2.40
KS Kazuhiro Sasaki SV	8.00	2.40
KW Kerry Wood K	10.00	3.00
LB Lance Berkman HR	8.00	2.40
LG Luis Gonzalez RUN	8.00	2.40
LW Larry Walker AVG	10.00	3.00
MP Mike Piazza HR	15.00	4.50
MP1 Mike Piazza SLG	15.00	4.50
MR Manny Ramirez AVG	10.00	3.00
MSL Mike Sweeney AVG	8.00	2.40
MSW Mike Stanton Pants GM	8.00	2.40
MT Miguel Tejada RBI	8.00	2.40
MT1 Miguel Tejada GM SP	10.00	3.00
OV Omar Vizquel SAC	10.00	3.00
PB Pat Burrell HR	8.00	2.40
PB1 Pat Burrell RBI	8.00	2.40
PM Pedro Martinez K	10.00	3.00
RC Roger Clemens K	15.00	4.50
RC1 Roger Clemens ERA	15.00	4.50
RJ Randy Johnson K	10.00	3.00
RJ1 Randy Johnson ERA	10.00	3.00
RO Roy Oswalt WIN	8.00	2.40
RO1 Roy Oswalt PCT SP	10.00	3.00
RP Rafael Palmeiro HR	10.00	3.00
RP1 Rafael Palmeiro 2B	10.00	3.00
SG Shawn Green HR	8.00	2.40
SG1 Shawn Green TB	8.00	2.40
SR Scott Rolen HR	10.00	3.00
SS Sammy Sosa 49 HR	15.00	4.50
SS1 Sammy Sosa 50 HR SP/170	20.00	6.00
TB Tony Batista HR	8.00	2.40
TG Troy Glaus HR	8.00	2.40
THE Todd Helton RBI	10.00	3.00
THU Tim Hudson IP	8.00	2.40
THU1 Tim Hudson GM SP	10.00	3.00
TP Troy Percival SV	8.00	2.40
VG Vladimir Guerrero HIT	10.00	3.00

2003 Upper Deck Lineup Time Jerseys

Inserted into first series hobby packs at a stated rate of one in 96, these 10 cards feature game-used uniform swatches from some of the leading players in the game. A couple of cards were printed to a smaller quantity and we have notated those cards with an SP in our checklist.

	Nm-Mt	Ex-Mt
BW Bernie Williams	10.00	3.00
CD Carlos Delgado	8.00	2.40
GM Greg Maddux	10.00	3.00
IS Ichiro Suzuki	40.00	12.00
JD J.D. Drew	8.00	2.40
JT Jim Thome	10.00	3.00
RC Roger Clemens SP	25.00	7.50
RJ Randy Johnson SP	20.00	6.00
SG Shawn Green	8.00	2.40
TH Todd Helton	10.00	3.00

2003 Upper Deck Magical Performances

	Nm-Mt	Ex-Mt
*GOLD: 1X TO 2.5X BASIC MAGIC		
GOLD RANDOM INSERTS IN SER.2 PACKS		
GOLD PRINT RUN 50 SERIAL #'d SETS		
DUPE STARS EQUALLY VALUED		
MP1 Hideki Matsui	20.00	6.00
MP2 Ken Griffey Jr.	20.00	6.00
MP3 Ichiro Suzuki	20.00	6.00
MP4 Ken Griffey Jr.	20.00	6.00
MP5 Hideo Nomo	15.00	4.50
MP6 Mickey Mantle	50.00	15.00
MP7 Ken Griffey Jr.	20.00	6.00
MP8 Barry Bonds	25.00	7.50
MP9 Mickey Mantle	50.00	15.00
MP10 Tom Seaver	15.00	4.50
MP11 Mike Piazza	20.00	6.00
MP12 Roger Clemens	20.00	6.00
MP13 Nolan Ryan	40.00	12.00
MP14 Nomar Garciaparra	20.00	6.00
MP15 Ernie Banks	15.00	4.50
MP16 Stan Musial	25.00	7.50
MP17 Mickey Mantle	50.00	15.00
MP18 Nolan Ryan	40.00	12.00
MP19 Nolan Ryan	40.00	12.00
MP20 Mickey Mantle	50.00	15.00
MP21 Ichiro Suzuki	20.00	6.00
MP22 Nolan Ryan	40.00	12.00
MP23 Tom Seaver	15.00	4.50
MP24 Ken Griffey Jr.	20.00	6.00
MP25 Hideo Nomo	15.00	4.50
MP26 Ken Griffey Jr.	20.00	6.00
MP27 Mark McGwire	25.00	7.50
MP28 Barry Bonds	25.00	7.50
MP29 Alex Rodriguez	20.00	6.00
MP30 Nolan Ryan	40.00	12.00
MP31 Mark McGwire	25.00	7.50
MP32 Nolan Ryan	40.00	12.00
MP33 Sammy Sosa	20.00	6.00
MP34 Ichiro Suzuki	20.00	6.00
MP35 Barry Bonds	25.00	7.50
MP36 Derek Jeter	25.00	7.50
MP37 Roger Clemens	20.00	6.00
MP38 Jason Giambi	15.00	4.50
MP39 Mickey Mantle	50.00	15.00
MP40 Ted Williams	30.00	9.00
MP41 Ted Williams	30.00	9.00
MP42 Ted Williams	30.00	9.00

2003 Upper Deck Mark of Greatness Autograph Jerseys

Randomly inserted into first series packs, these three cards feature authentically signed Mark McGwire cards. There are three different versions of this card, which were all signed to a different print run, and we have notated that information in our checklist.

	Nm-Mt	Ex-Mt
MOG M.McGwire/400	400.00	120.00
MOGG M.McGwire Gold/25		
MOGS M.McGwire Silver/70	500.00	150.00

2003 Upper Deck Masters with the Leather

	Nm-Mt	Ex-Mt
COMPLETE SET (12)	25.00	7.50
L1 Darin Erstad	2.00	.60
L2 Andruw Jones	2.00	.60
L3 Greg Maddux	4.00	1.20
L4 Nomar Garciaparra	4.00	1.20
L5 Torii Hunter	2.00	.60
L6 Roberto Alomar	2.00	.60
L7 Derek Jeter	6.00	1.80
L8 Eric Chavez	2.00	.60
L9 Ichiro Suzuki	4.00	1.20
L10 Jim Edmonds	2.00	.60
L11 Scott Rolen	2.50	.75
L12 Alex Rodriguez	4.00	1.20

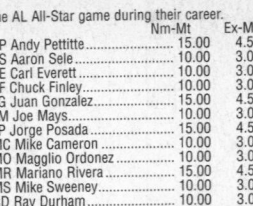

2003 Upper Deck Mid-Summer Stars Swatches

Inserted into first series packs at a stated rate of one in 72, these 23 cards feature a mix of players who shine all during the season. A few cards do not feature jersey swatches and we have notated that information in our checklist. In addition, a few cards were issued to a smaller quantity and we have notated those cards with an SP in our checklist.

	Nm-Mt	Ex-Mt
AJ Andruw Jones	8.00	2.40
AR Alex Rodriguez	15.00	4.50
BZ Barry Zito	8.00	2.40
CD Carlos Delgado	8.00	2.40
CS Curt Schilling	8.00	2.40
DE Darin Erstad	8.00	2.40
DW David Wells	8.00	2.40
EM Edgar Martinez	10.00	3.00
FG Freddy Garcia	8.00	2.40
FT Frank Thomas	10.00	3.00
HN Hideo Nomo	20.00	6.00
IS Ichiro Suzuki Turtleneck SP	50.00	15.00
JE Jim Edmonds SP *	10.00	3.00
JG Juan Gonzalez Pants	10.00	3.00
KS Kazuhiro Sasaki	8.00	2.40
MP Mike Piazza	15.00	4.50
MR Manny Ramirez	10.00	3.00
RC Roger Clemens	15.00	4.50
RJ Randy Johnson Shirt	10.00	3.00
RV Robin Ventura	10.00	3.00
SG Shawn Green SP	10.00	3.00
SS Sammy Sosa	15.00	4.50
TG Tom Glavine	10.00	3.00

2003 Upper Deck NL All-Star Swatches

Inserted into first series hobby packs at a stated rate of one in 72, these 12 cards feature game-used memorabilia swatch of players who had participated in the All-Star game for the National League.

	Nm-Mt	Ex-Mt
AL Al Leiter	8.00	2.40
CF Cliff Floyd	8.00	2.40
CS Curt Schilling	8.00	2.40
FM Fred McGriff	10.00	3.00
JV Jose Vidro	8.00	2.40
MH Mike Hampton	8.00	2.40
MM Matt Morris	8.00	2.40
RK Ryan Klesko	8.00	2.40
SC Sean Casey	8.00	2.40
TG Tom Glavine	10.00	3.00
TG Tony Gwynn	15.00	4.50
TH Trevor Hoffman	8.00	2.40

2003 Upper Deck National Pride Memorabilia

	Nm-Mt	Ex-Mt
SERIES 2 ODDS 1:24 HOBBY/1:48 RETAIL		
SP PRINT RUNS PROVIDED BY UPPER DECK		
SP'S ARE NOT SERIAL-NUMBERED...		
ALL FEATURE PANTS UNLESS NOTED		
AA Abe Alvarez	8.00	2.40
AH Aaron Hill	8.00	2.40
AJ A.J. Hinch Jsy	8.00	2.40
AK A.Kearns Right Jsy	8.00	2.40
AK1 A.Kearns Left Jsy SP/250	15.00	4.50
BH Bobby Hill Field Jsy	8.00	2.40
BH1 Bobby Hill Run Jsy SP/100	20.00	6.00
BS Brad Sullivan Wind Up	8.00	2.40
BS1 Brad Sullivan Throw SP/250	15.00	4.50
BZ Bob Zimmermann	5.00	1.50
CC Chad Cordero	5.00	1.50
CJ Conor Jackson	10.00	3.00
CQ Carlos Quentin	10.00	3.00

CS Clint Sammons ... 5.00 1.50
DP Dustin Pedroia ... 10.00 3.00
EM Eric Milton White Jsy ... 8.00 2.40
EM1 Eric Milton Blue Jsy SP/50 20.00 6.00
EP Eric Patterson ... 8.00 2.40
GJ Grant Johnson ... 5.00 1.50
HS Huston Street ... 8.00 2.40
JJO J.Jones White Jsy ... 8.00 2.40
JJ1 J.Jones Blue Jsy SP/250 ... 15.00 4.50
JJE Jason Jennings Jsy ... 8.00 2.40
KB Kyle Bakker ... 5.00 1.50
KSA K.Saarloos Red Jsy ... 8.00 2.40
KSL Kyle Sleeth ... 8.00 2.40
KSA1 K.Saarloos Grey Jsy SP/250 15.00 4.50
LP Landon Powell ... 8.00 2.40
MA Michael Aubrey ... 10.00 3.00
MJ Mark Jurich ... 5.00 1.50
MP Mark Prior Pinstripes Jsy ... 10.00 3.00
MP1 Mark Prior Grey Jsy SP/100 25.00 7.50
PH Philip Humber ... 8.00 2.40
RF Robert Fick Jsy ... 8.00 2.40
RO R.Oswalt Behind Jsy ... 8.00 2.40
RO1 R.Oswalt Beside Jsy SP/100 20.00 6.00
RW R.Weeks Glove-Chest ... 15.00 4.50
RW1 R.Weeks Glove-Head SP/250 ...
SB Sean Burroughs ... 8.00 2.40
SC Shane Costa ... 8.00 2.40
SF Sam Fuld ... 5.00 1.50
WL Wes Littleton ... 8.00 2.40

2003 Upper Deck Piece of the Action Game Ball

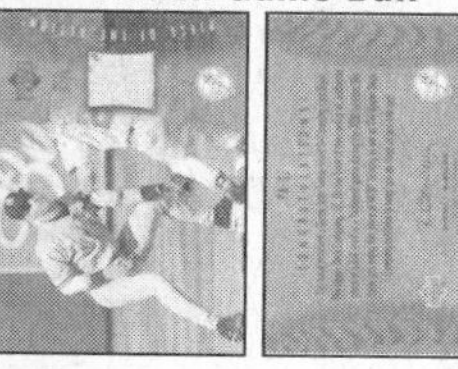
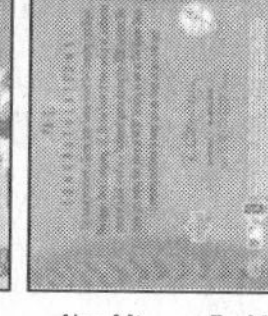

Nm-Mt Ex-Mt
SERIES 2 ODDS 1:288 HOBBY/1:576 RETAIL
PRINT RUNS B/WN 10-175 COPIES PER
PRINT RUNS PROVIDED BY UPPER DECK
CARDS ARE NOT SERIAL-NUMBERED
NO PRICING ON QTY OF 25 OR LESS
AB Adrian Beltre/100 ... 15.00 4.50
ARA Aramis Ramirez/100 ... 10.00 3.00
ARO Alex Rodriguez/100 ... 25.00 7.50
BA Bobby Abreu/125 ... 10.00 3.00
BB Barry Bonds/125 ... 40.00 12.00
BG Brian Giles/100 ... 10.00 3.00
BW Bernie Williams/125 ... 15.00 4.50
CJ Chipper Jones/62 ... 25.00 7.50
CS Curt Schilling/100 ... 10.00 3.00
DE Darin Erstad/125 ... 10.00 3.00
DJ Derek Jeter/65 ... 60.00 18.00
EM Edgar Martinez/125 ... 15.00 4.50
FG Freddy Garcia/100 ... 10.00 3.00
FT Frank Thomas/150 ... 15.00 4.50
GA Garret Anderson/150 ... 10.00 3.00
GS Gary Sheffield/100 ... 10.00 3.00
HN Hideo Nomo/100 ... 40.00 12.00
IR Ivan Rodriguez/10 ...
IS Ichiro Suzuki/25 ...
JG Juan Gonzalez/100 ... 15.00 4.50
JK Jason Kendall/100 ... 10.00 3.00
JT Jim Thome/125 ... 15.00 4.50
JV Jose Vidro/100 ... 10.00 3.00
KB Kevin Brown/100 ... 10.00 3.00
KE Jeff Kent/150 ... 10.00 3.00
KS Kazuhiro Sasaki/100 ... 10.00 3.00
LG Luis Gonzalez/100 ... 10.00 3.00
LW Larry Walker/150 ... 15.00 4.50
MP Mike Piazza/150 ... 25.00 7.50
PB Pat Burrell/150 ... 10.00 3.00
PM Pedro Martinez/150 ... 15.00 4.50
PN Phil Nevin/75 ... 15.00 4.50
RJ Randy Johnson/100 ... 15.00 4.50
RK Ryan Klesko/75 ... 15.00 4.50
RP Rafael Palmeiro/150 ... 15.00 4.50
RS Richie Sexson/160 ... 10.00 3.00
SG Shawn Green/175 ... 10.00 3.00
SS Sammy Sosa/85 ... 40.00 12.00
TG Troy Glaus/150 ... 10.00 3.00
THE Todd Helton/100 ... 15.00 4.50
THO Trevor Hoffman/150 ... 10.00 3.00
VG Vladimir Guerrero/50 ... 25.00 7.50

2003 Upper Deck Piece of the Action Game Ball Gold

Nm-Mt Ex-Mt
GOLD: 1X TO 2.5X GAME BALL p/r 150-175
GOLD: 1X TO 2.5X GAME BALL p/r 100-125
GOLD: .6X TO 1.5X GAME BALL p/r 50-85
RANDOM INSERTS IN SERIES 2 PACKS
STATED PRINT RUN 50 SERIAL #'d SETS
IR Ivan Rodriguez ... 40.00 12.00
IS Ichiro Suzuki ...

2003 Upper Deck Signed Game Jerseys

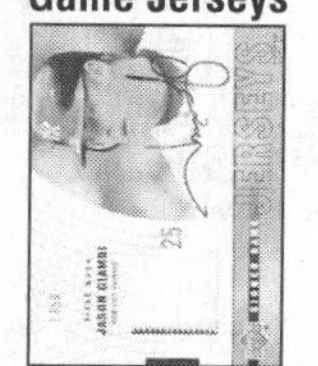

Randomly inserted into first series packs, these seven cards feature not only game-used memorabilia swatches but also an authentic autograph of the player. We have notated the print run for each card next to the player's name. In addition, Ken Griffey Jr. did not sign cards in time for inclusion into packs and those cards could be redeemed until February 11, 2006.
Nm-Mt Ex-Mt
RANDOM INSERTS IN SERIES 1 PACKS
PRINT RUNS B/WN 150-350 COPIES PER
EXCHANGE DEADLINE 02/11/06 ...
AR Alex Rodriguez/350 ... 150.00 45.00
CR Cal Ripken/350 ... 150.00 45.00
JG Jason Giambi/350 ... 50.00 15.00
KG Ken Griffey Jr./350 EXCH .. 120.00 36.00
MM Mark McGwire/150 ... 400.00 120.00
RC Roger Clemens/350 ... 150.00 45.00
SS Sammy Sosa/150 ... 200.00 60.00

2003 Upper Deck Signed Game Jerseys Gold

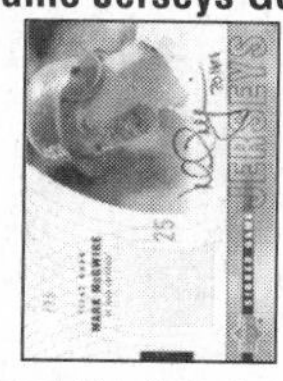

Randomly inserted into first series packs, this is a partial parallel to the Signed Game Jersey insert set. These three cards were issued to a stated print run of 25 serial numbered sets and no pricing is provided due to market scarcity. Please note that Ken Griffey Jr. did not return his cards in time for inclusion in packs and those cards could be redeemed until February 11, 2006.
Nm-Mt Ex-Mt
KG Ken Griffey Jr. EXCH ...
MM Mark McGwire ...
SS Sammy Sosa ...

2003 Upper Deck Signed Game Jerseys Silver

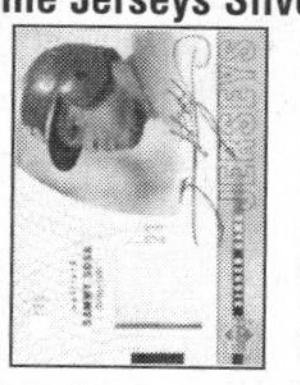

Randomly inserted into first series packs, this is a partial parallel to the Signed Game Jersey insert set. These five cards were issued to a stated print run of 75 serial numbered sets. Please note that Ken Griffey Jr. did not return his cards in time for inclusion in packs and those cards could be redeemed until February 11, 2006.
Nm-Mt Ex-Mt
RANDOM INSERTS IN SER.1 HOBBY PACKS
STATED PRINT RUN 75 SERIAL #'d SETS
AR Alex Rodriguez ...
JG Jason Giambi ... 60.00 18.00
KG Ken Griffey Jr. EXCH ...
MM Mark McGwire ...
SS Sammy Sosa ...

2003 Upper Deck Slammin Sammy Autograph Jerseys

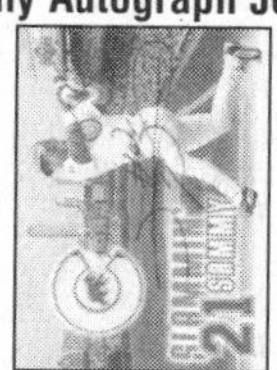

Randomly inserted into first series packs, these three cards feature authenitically signed Sammy Sosa cards. Each of these cards also have a game-worn uniform swatch on them. There are three different versions of this card, which were all signed to a different print run, and we have notated that information in our checklist.
Nm-Mt Ex-Mt
RANDOM INSERTS IN SERIES 1 PACKS
PRINT RUNS B/WN 25-384 COPIES PER
NO PRICING ON QTY OF 25 OR LESS
SST Sammy Sosa/384 ... 250.00 75.00
SSTG Sammy Sosa Gold/25 ...
SSTS Sammy Sosa Silver/66 .. 300.00 90.00

2003 Upper Deck Star-Spangled Swatches

Inserted into first series packs at a stated rate of one in 72, these 16 cards feature game-worn uniform swatches of players who were on the USA National Team.
Nm-Mt Ex-Mt
AH Aaron Hill H ... 8.00 2.40
BS Brad Sullivan H ... 8.00 2.40
CC Chad Cordero H ... 5.00 1.50
CJ Conor Jackson Pants R ... 10.00 3.00
CQ Carlos Quentin H ... 10.00 3.00
DP Dustin Pedroia R ... 10.00 3.00
EP Eric Patterson H ... 8.00 2.40
GJ Grant Johnson H ... 5.00 1.50
HS Huston Street R ... 8.00 2.40
KB Kyle Bakker R ... 5.00 1.50
KS Kyle Sleeth R ... 8.00 2.40
LP Landon Powell R ... 8.00 2.40
MA Michael Aubrey H ... 10.00 3.00
PH Philip Humber R ... 8.00 2.40
RW Rickie Weeks H ... 15.00 4.50
SC Shane Costa R ... 8.00 2.40

2003 Upper Deck Superior Sluggers

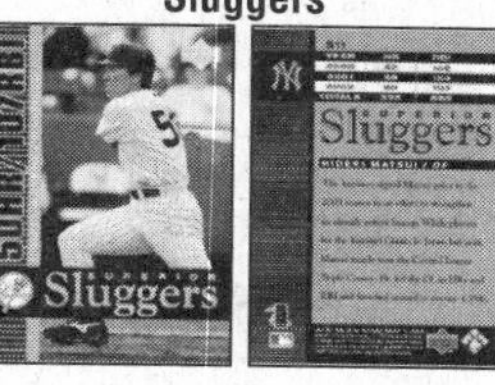

Inserted into second series packs at a stated rate of one in eight, these cards feature a mix of active and retired players known for their extra base power while batting.
Nm-Mt Ex-Mt
COMPLETE SET (18) ... 40.00 12.00
S1 Troy Glaus ... 2.00 .60
S2 Chipper Jones ... 2.50 .75
S3 Manny Ramirez ... 2.00 .60
S4 Ken Griffey Jr. ... 4.00 1.20
S5 Jim Thome ... 2.50 .75
S6 Todd Helton ... 2.00 .60
S7 Lance Berkman ... 2.00 .60
S8 Derek Jeter ... 6.00 1.80
S9 Vladimir Guerrero ... 2.50 .75
S10 Mike Piazza ... 4.00 1.20
S11 Hideki Matsui ... 5.00 1.50
S12 Barry Bonds ... 6.00 1.80
S13 Mickey Mantle ... 10.00 3.00
S14 Alex Rodriguez ... 4.00 1.20
S15 Ted Williams ... 6.00 1.80
S16 Carlos Delgado ... 2.00 .60
S17 Frank Thomas ... 2.50 .75
S18 Adam Dunn ... 2.00 .60

2003 Upper Deck Superstar Scrapbooks

Randomly inserted into series one packs, these seven cards feature game-worn jersey swatches of some of baseball's major superstars. Each of these cards was issued to a stated print run of 24 serial numbered sets and there is no pricing due to market scarcity.
Nm-Mt Ex-Mt
AR Alex Rodriguez ...
IS Ichiro Suzuki ...
JG Jason Giambi ...
KG Ken Griffey Jr. ...
MP Mike Piazza ...
RC Roger Clemens ...
SS Sammy Sosa ...

2003 Upper Deck Superstar Scrapbooks Gold

Randomly inserted into series one packs, these seven cards are a parallel ot the Superstar Scrapbook set. Each of these cards feature game-worn jersey swatches of some of baseball's major superstars. Each of these cards was issued to a stated print run of one serial numbered set and there is no pricing due to market scarcity.
Nm-Mt Ex-Mt
RANDOM INSERTS IN SERIES 1 PACKS
STATED PRINT RUN 1 SERIAL #'d SET
NO PRICING DUE TO SCARCITY ...
IS Ichiro Suzuki ...
KG Ken Griffey Jr. ...
SS Sammy Sosa ...

2003 Upper Deck Superstar Scrapbooks Silver

Randomly inserted into series one packs, these seven cards are a parallel ot the Superstar Scrapbook set. Each of these cards feature game-worn jersey swatches of some of baseball's major superstars. Each of these cards was issued to a stated print run of six serial numbered set and there is no pricing due to market scarcity.
Nm-Mt Ex-Mt
RANDOM INSERTS IN SERIES 1 PACKS
STATED PRINT RUN 6 SERIALS #'d SETS
NO PRICING DUE TO SCARCITY ...
AR Alex Rodriguez ...
IS Ichiro Suzuki ...
JG Jason Giambi ...
KG Ken Griffey Jr. ...
SS Sammy Sosa ...

2003 Upper Deck Triple Game Jersey

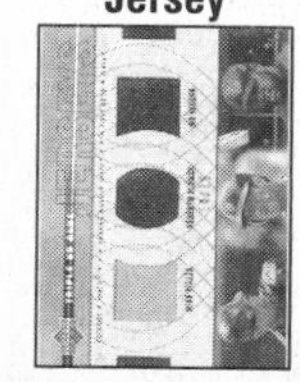

Randomly inserted into first series packs, these nine cards feature three game-worn uniform swatches of teammates. These cards were issued to a stated print run of anywhere from 25 to 150 serial numbered sets depending on which group the card belongs to. Please note the cards from group C are not priced due to market scarcity.
Nm-Mt Ex-Mt
GROUP A 150 SERIAL #'d SETS ...
GROUP B 75 SERIAL #'d SETS ...
GROUP C 25 SERIAL #'d SETS ...
ARZ Randy Johnson ... 50.00 15.00
Curt Schilling
Luis Gonzalez A
ATL Chipper Jones ... 80.00 24.00
Greg Maddux
Gary Sheffield B
CHC Sammy Sosa ... 60.00 18.00
Moises Alou
Kerry Wood B
CIN Ken Griffey Jr. ... 40.00 12.00
Sean Casey
Adam Dunn A
HOU Jeff Bagwell ... 50.00 15.00
Lance Berkman
Craig Biggio A
NYM Mike Piazza Pants ... 50.00 15.00
Roberto Alomar
Mo Vaughn B
NYY Roger Clemens ...
Jason Giambi
Bernie Williams C
SEA Ichiro Suzuki ... 120.00 36.00
Freddy Garcia
Bret Boone B
TEX Rafael Palmeiro ... 50.00 15.00
Alex Rodriguez
Juan Gonzalez A

2003 Upper Deck Triple Game Jersey Gold

Randomly inserted in packs, this is a parallel to the Triple Game Jersey insert set. Depending on the group, each card is printed to a stated print run of between 10 and 50 serial numbered sets. Those cards in group B and C are not priced due to market scarcity.
Nm-Mt Ex-Mt
GROUP A 50 SERIAL #'d SETS ...
GROUP B 25 SERIAL #'d SETS ...
GROUP C 10 SERIAL #'d SETS ...

2003 Upper Deck UD Bonus

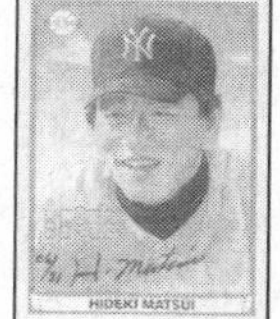
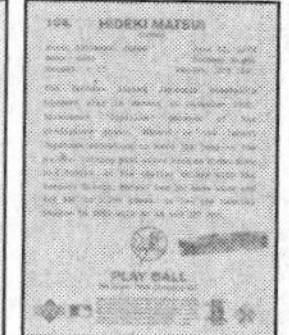

Inserted into second series packs at a stated rate of one in 288, these are copies of various recent year Upper Deck cards which were repurchased for insertion in 2003 Upper Deck 2nd series. Please note that these cards were all stamped with a "UD Bonus" logo. Each of these cards were issued to differening print runs and we have notated the print runs next to the player's name in our checklist.
Nm-Mt Ex-Mt
1 Jeff Bagwell 01 GG Glv/6 ...
2 Josh Beckett 01 TP AU/55 ... 30.00 9.00
3 C.Beltran 00 SPA AU/118 ... 40.00 12.00
4 Barry Bonds 01 UD Ball/34 ...
5 Barry Bonds 01 GG Glv/5 ...
6 Barry Bonds 01 P/P Jsy/117 .. 25.00 7.50
7 Lou Brock 00 LGD AU/198 ... 25.00 7.50
8 Gary Carter 00 LGD AU/63 ... 20.00 6.00
9 Sean Casey 00 SPA AU/11 ...
10 Roger Clemens 00 HFX Base/12 ...
11 Roger Clemens 00 LGD Jsy/12 ...
12 Roger Clemens 01 P/P Jsy/117 15.00 4.50
13 A.Dawson 00 LGD AU/140 ... 15.00 4.50
14 J.D. Drew 00 SPA AU/55 ... 30.00 9.00
15 Rollie Fingers 00 LGD AU/116 15.00 4.50
16 Rafael Furcal 00 SPA AU/87. 15.00 4.50
17 Rafael Furcal 00 SPA AU/39 ...
18 Jason Giambi 00 SPA AU/106 15.00 4.50
19 Jason Giambi 01 UD Ball/35 ...
20 Jason Giambi 01 P/P Jsy/97 10.00 3.00
21 Troy Glaus 00 SPA AU/110 .. 15.00 4.50
22 Shawn Green 01 UD Ball/10 ...
23 Ken Griffey Jr. 01 UD Ball/28 ...
24 Ken Griffey Jr. 01 GG Glv/2 ...
25 Vladimir Guerrero 00 SPA AU/8 ...
26 Vladimir Guerrero 00 LGD AU/26 ..
27 Vladimir Guerrero 00 OV Bat/16 ...
28 Brandon Inge 01 TP AU/113 10.00 3.00
29 Derek Jeter 01 UD Ball/17 ...
30 Randy Johnson 01 UD Ball/37 ...
31 Andruw Jones 01 UD Ball/38 ...
32 Chipper Jones 00 HFX AU/5 ...
33 Chipper Jones 00 OV Bat/19 ...
34 Harmon Killebrew 00 LGD AU/31 ..
35 Roger Maris 00 YL Jsy/11 ...
36 Eddie Mathews 00 LGD Jsy/12 ...
37 Hideki Matsui 03 PB AU/31 ...
38 Hideki Matsui 03 PB Red AU/20 ...
39 Don Mattingly 00 YL Jsy/26 ...
40 Don Mattingly 01 LGD NY Bat/20 ..
41 Joe Mays 00 SPA AU/30 ...
42 Mark McGwire 01 UD Ball/19 ...
43 D.Mientkiewicz 00 BD Jsy/57 10.00 3.00
44 Dale Murphy 00 LGD AU/91 40.00 12.00
45 Stan Musial 00 LGD AU/5 ...
46 Jim Palmer 00 LGD AU/121. 15.00 4.50
47 P.Reese 01 HOF Jsy/46 ... 15.00 4.50
48 Phil Rizzuto 00 YL Jsy/19 ...
49 Ivan Rodriguez 00 SPA AU/27 ...
50 Ivan Rodriguez 01 GG Glv/4 ...
51 Nolan Ryan 01 HOF Bat/37 ...
52 Nolan Ryan 01 HOF Jsy/76 ...
53 C.C. Sabathia 01 TP AU/64 .. 20.00 6.00
54 Tim Salmon 01 GG Glv/12 ...
55 Tom Seaver 00 LGD Jsy/18 ...
56 Ben Sheets 01 TP AU/60 ... 20.00 6.00
57 Ozzie Smith 00 LGD Jsy/14 ...
58 Alf Soriano 00 SPA AU/80 ... 40.00 12.00
59 Sammy Sosa 01 P/P Jsy/77 15.00 4.50
60 Larry Walker 01 GG Glv/10 ...
61 Bernie Williams 01 GG Glv/10 ...
62 Maury Wills 00 LGD Jsy/22 ...
63 Dave Winfield 00 YL Bat/53. 10.00 3.00
64 Bernie Williams ... 50.00 15.00
Ichiro Suzuki 01 P/P Bat/87
65 Sammy Sosa ... 15.00 4.50
Luis Gonzalez 01 P/P Bat/61

2003 Upper Deck UD Patch Logos

Inserted into first series packs at a stated rate of one in 7500, these eight cards feature game-used patch pieces. Each card has a print run between 41 and 54 and we have notated that print run information next to the player's name in our checklist.
Nm-Mt Ex-Mt
BW Bernie Williams/42 ...
CJ Chipper Jones/52 ... 120.00 36.00
FT Frank Thomas/52 ... 120.00 36.00
GM Greg Maddux/50 ... 150.00 45.00
JB Jeff Bagwell/41 ...
KI Kazuhisa Ishii/54 ... 100.00 30.00
RJ Randy Johnson/50 ... 120.00 36.00
TH Todd Helton/41 ...

2003 Upper Deck UD Patch Logos Exclusives

Inserted into first series packs at a stated rate of one in 7500, these ten cards feature game-used patch pieces. Each card has a print run between nine and 61 and we have notated that print run information next to the player's name in our checklist. The cards with a print run of 25 or fewer are not priced due to market scarcity.
Nm-Mt Ex-Mt
AR Alex Rodriguez/34 ...
IS Ichiro Suzuki/46 ...
JD Joe DiMaggio/9 ...
JG Jason Giambi/34 ...
KG Ken Griffey Jr./50 ... 120.00 36.00
MG Mark McGwire/43 ...
MM Mickey Mantle/10 ...
MP Mike Piazza/61 ... 150.00 45.00
RC Roger Clemens/34 ...
SS Sammy Sosa/60 ... 120.00 36.00

2003 Upper Deck UD Patch Numbers

Inserted into first series packs at a stated rate of one in 7500, these six cards feature game-used patch number pieces. Each card has a print run between 27 and 90 and we have notated that print run information next to the player's name in our checklist.
Nm-Mt Ex-Mt
BW Bernie Williams/66 ... 80.00 24.00
CJ Chipper Jones/44 ...
FT Frank Thomas/91 ... 80.00 24.00
KI Kazuhisa Ishii/63 ... 60.00 18.00
RJ Randy Johnson/90 ... 80.00 24.00
TH Todd Helton/27 ...

2003 Upper Deck UD Patch Numbers Exclusives

Inserted into first series packs at a stated rate of one in 7500, these six cards feature game-used patch number pieces. Each card has a print run between 56 and 100 and we have notated that print run information next to the player's name in our checklist.
Nm-Mt Ex-Mt
AR Alex Rodriguez/56 ... 120.00 36.00
JG Jason Giambi/68 ... 60.00 18.00
KG Ken Griffey Jr./97 ... 80.00 24.00
MG Mark McGwire/60 ... 250.00 75.00
SS Sammy Sosa/100 ... 100.00 30.00

2003 Upper Deck UD Patch Stripes

Inserted into first series packs at a stated rate of one in 7500, these seven cards feature game-used patch striped pieces. Each card has a print run between 43 and 73 and we have notated that print run information next to the player's name in our checklist.

	Nm-Mt	Ex-Mt
BW Bernie Williams/58	80.00	24.00
CJ Chipper Jones/58	80.00	24.00
FT Frank Thomas/58	80.00	24.00
JB Jeff Bagwell/73	80.00	24.00
KI Kazuhisa Ishii/58	60.00	18.00
RJ Randy Johnson/58	80.00	24.00
TH Todd Helton/43		

2003 Upper Deck UD Patch Stripes Exclusives

Inserted into first series packs at a stated rate of one in 7500, these seven cards feature game-used patch striped pieces. Each card has a print run between 63 and 66 and we have notated that print run information next to the player's name in our checklist.

	Nm-Mt	Ex-Mt
AR Alex Rodriguez/63	100.00	30.00
IS Ichiro Suzuki/63	300.00	90.00
JG Jason Giambi/66	60.00	18.00
KG Ken Griffey Jr./63	100.00	30.00
MG Mark McGwire/63	250.00	75.00
SS Sammy Sosa/63	120.00	36.00

2003 Upper Deck UD Super Patch Logos

	Nm-Mt	Ex-Mt
AJ Andruw Jones/92	50.00	15.00
AR Alex Rodriguez/45		
AS Alfonso Soriano/15		
GM Greg Maddux/95	150.00	45.00
HM Hideki Matsui/8		
IS Ichiro Suzuki/20		
KG Ken Griffey Jr./22		
MP Mike Piazza/30		
MR Manny Ramirez/22		
SS Sammy Sosa/21		

2003 Upper Deck UD Super Patch Numbers

	Nm-Mt	Ex-Mt
AP Albert Pujols/8		
AR Alex Rodriguez/13		
CJ Chipper Jones/11		
CS Curt Schilling/18		
IR Ivan Rodriguez/10		
IS Ichiro Suzuki/14		
JB Jeff Bagwell/8		
JG Jason Giambi/40		
RC Roger Clemens/12		

2003 Upper Deck UD Super Patch Stripes

	Nm-Mt	Ex-Mt
AD Adam Dunn/70	80.00	24.00
AS Alfonso Soriano/16		
JG Jason Giambi/50	50.00	15.00
KG Ken Griffey Jr./12		
LB Lance Berkman/30		
MP Mike Piazza/10		
RJ Randy Johnson/73	100.00	30.00
SS Sammy Sosa/70	120.00	36.00
TH Todd Helton/50	80.00	24.00
VG Vladimir Guerrero/75	100.00	30.00

2003 Upper Deck UD Superstar Slam Jerseys

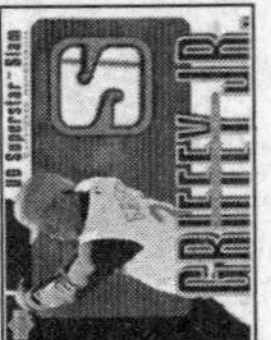

Inserted into first series hobby packs at a stated rate of one in 48, these 10 cards feature game-used jersey pieces of the featured players.

	Nm-Mt	Ex-Mt
AR Alex Rodriguez	15.00	4.50
CJ Chipper Jones	10.00	3.00
FT Frank Thomas	10.00	3.00
JB Jeff Bagwell	10.00	3.00
JG Jason Giambi	8.00	2.40
KG Ken Griffey Jr.	15.00	4.50
LG Luis Gonzalez	8.00	2.40
MP Mike Piazza	15.00	4.50
SS Sammy Sosa	15.00	4.50
JGO Juan Gonzalez	10.00	3.00

2004 Upper Deck

The 270-card first series was released in November, 2003. The cards were issued in eight-card hobby packs with an $3 SRP which came 24 packs to a box and 12 boxes to a case. These cards were also issued in nine-card retail packs also with a $3 SRP which came 24 packs to a box and 12 boxes to a case. Please note that insert cards were much more prevalent in the

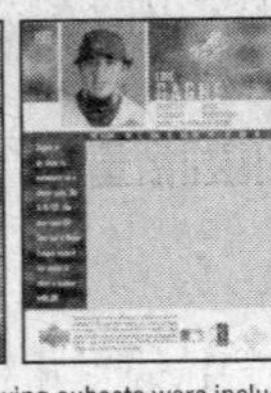

hobby packs. The following subsets were included in the first series: Super Rookies (1-30); Season Highlights Checklists (261-270). In addition, please note that the Super Rookie cards were not short printed.

	MINT	NRMT
COMPLETE SERIES 1 (270)	50.00	22.00
COMPLETE SERIES 2 (270)	50.00	22.00
COMP.UPDATE SET (50)	15.00	6.75
COMMON (31-480/541-565)	.30	.14
COMMON (1-30/481-540)	1.00	.45
COMMON CARD (566-590)	.50	.23
541-590 ONE SET PER '05 UD1 HOBBY BOX		
UPDATE SET EXCH 1:480 '05 UD1 RETAIL		
UPDATE SET EXCH.DEADLINE TBD		
1 Dontrelle Willis SR	1.00	.45
2 Edgar Gonzalez SR	1.00	.45
3 Jose Reyes SR	1.00	.45
4 Jae Weong Seo SR	1.00	.45
5 Miguel Cabrera SR	1.50	.70
6 Jesse Foppert SR	1.00	.45
7 Mike Neu SR	1.00	.45
8 Michael Nakamura SR	1.00	.45
9 Luis Ayala SR	1.00	.45
10 Jared Sandberg SR	1.00	.45
11 Jhonny Peralta SR	1.00	.45
12 Wil Ledezma SR	1.00	.45
13 Jason Roach SR	1.00	.45
14 Kirk Saarloos SR	1.00	.45
15 Cliff Lee SR	1.00	.45
16 Bobby Hill SR	1.00	.45
17 Lyle Overbay SR	1.00	.45
18 Josh Hall SR	1.00	.45
19 Joe Thurston SR	1.00	.45
20 Matt Kata SR	1.00	.45
21 Jeremy Bonderman SR	1.00	.45
22 Julio Manon SR	1.00	.45
23 Rodrigo Rosario SR	1.00	.45
24 Robby Hammock SR	1.00	.45
25 David Sanders SR	1.00	.45
26 Miguel Ojeda SR	1.00	.45
27 Mark Teixeira SR	1.00	.45
28 Franklyn German SR	1.00	.45
29 Ken Harvey SR	1.00	.45
30 Xavier Nady SR	1.00	.45
31 Tim Salmon	.50	.23
32 Troy Glaus	.30	.14
33 Adam Kennedy	.30	.14
34 David Eckstein	.30	.14
35 Ben Molina	.30	.14
36 Jarrod Washburn	.30	.14
37 Ramon Ortiz	.30	.14
38 Eric Chavez	.30	.14
39 Miguel Tejada	.30	.14
40 Chris Singleton	.30	.14
41 Jermaine Dye	.30	.14
42 John Halama	.30	.14
43 Tim Hudson	.30	.14
44 Barry Zito	.30	.14
45 Ted Lilly	.30	.14
46 Bobby Kielty	.30	.14
47 Kelvim Escobar	.30	.14
48 Josh Phelps	.30	.14
49 Vernon Wells	.30	.14
50 Roy Halladay	.30	.14
51 Orlando Hudson	.30	.14
52 Eric Hinske	.30	.14
53 Brandon Backe	.30	.14
54 Dewon Brazelton	.30	.14
55 Ben Grieve	.30	.14
56 Aubrey Huff	.30	.14
57 Toby Hall	.30	.14
58 Rocco Baldelli	.30	.14
59 Al Martin	.30	.14
60 Brandon Phillips	.30	.14
61 Omar Vizquel	.50	.23
62 C.C. Sabathia	.30	.14
63 Milton Bradley	.30	.14
64 Ricky Gutierrez	.30	.14
65 Matt Lawton	.30	.14
66 Danys Baez	.30	.14
67 Ichiro Suzuki	1.25	.55
68 Randy Winn	.30	.14
69 Carlos Guillen	.30	.14
70 Mark McLemore	.30	.14
71 Dan Wilson	.30	.14
72 Jamie Moyer	.30	.14
73 Joel Pineiro	.30	.14
74 Edgar Martinez	.50	.23
75 Tony Batista	.30	.14
76 Jay Gibbons	.30	.14
77 Jeff Conine	.30	.14
78 Melvin Mora	.30	.14
79 Geronimo Gil	.30	.14
80 Rodrigo Lopez	.30	.14
81 Jorge Julio	.30	.14
82 Rafael Palmeiro	.50	.23
83 Juan Gonzalez	.50	.23
84 Mike Young	.30	.14
85 Alex Rodriguez	1.25	.55
86 Einar Diaz	.30	.14
87 Kevin Mench	.30	.14
88 Hank Blalock	.30	.14
89 Pedro Martinez	.75	.35
90 Byung-Hyun Kim	.30	.14
91 Derek Lowe	.30	.14
92 Jason Varitek	.50	.23
93 Manny Ramirez	.50	.23
94 John Burkett	.30	.14
95 Todd Walker	.30	.14
96 Nomar Garciaparra	1.25	.55
97 Trot Nixon	.30	.14
98 Mike Sweeney	.30	.14
99 Carlos Febles	.30	.14
100 Mike MacDougal	.30	.14
101 Raul Ibanez	.30	.14
102 Jason Grimsley	.30	.14
103 Chris George	.30	.14
104 Brent Mayne	.30	.14
105 Dmitri Young	.30	.14
106 Eric Munson	.30	.14
107 A.J. Hinch	.30	.14
108 Andres Torres	.30	.14
109 Bobby Higginson	.30	.14
110 Shane Halter	.30	.14
111 Matt Walbeck	.30	.14
112 Torii Hunter	.30	.14
113 Doug Mientkiewicz	.30	.14
114 Lew Ford	.30	.14
115 Eric Milton	.30	.14
116 Eddie Guardado	.30	.14
117 Cristian Guzman	.30	.14
118 Corey Koskie	.30	.14
119 Magglio Ordonez	.30	.14
120 Mark Buehrle	.30	.14
121 Billy Koch	.30	.14
122 Jose Valentin	.30	.14
123 Paul Konerko	.30	.14
124 Carlos Lee	.30	.14
125 Jon Garland	.30	.14
126 Jason Giambi	.30	.14
127 Derek Jeter	1.50	.70
128 Roger Clemens	1.50	.70
129 Andy Pettitte	.50	.23
130 Jorge Posada	.50	.23
131 David Wells	.30	.14
132 Hideki Matsui	1.25	.55
133 Mike Mussina	.50	.23
134 Jeff Bagwell	.50	.23
135 Craig Biggio	.50	.23
136 Morgan Ensberg	.30	.14
137 Richard Hidalgo	.30	.14
138 Brad Ausmus	.30	.14
139 Roy Oswalt	.30	.14
140 Billy Wagner	.30	.14
141 Octavio Dotel	.30	.14
142 Gary Sheffield	.30	.14
143 Andruw Jones	.30	.14
144 John Smoltz	.50	.23
145 Rafael Furcal	.30	.14
146 Javy Lopez	.30	.14
147 Shane Reynolds	.30	.14
148 Horacio Ramirez	.30	.14
149 Mike Hampton	.30	.14
150 Jung Bong	.30	.14
151 Ruben Quevedo	.30	.14
152 Ben Sheets	.30	.14
153 Geoff Jenkins	.30	.14
154 Royce Clayton	.30	.14
155 Glendon Rusch	.30	.14
156 John Vander Wal	.30	.14
157 Scott Podsednik	.30	.14
158 Jim Edmonds	.30	.14
159 Tino Martinez	.50	.23
160 Albert Pujols	1.50	.70
161 Matt Morris	.30	.14
162 Woody Williams	.30	.14
163 Edgar Renteria	.30	.14
164 Jason Isringhausen	.30	.14
165 Jason Simontacchi	.30	.14
166 Kerry Robinson	.30	.14
167 Sammy Sosa	1.25	.55
168 Joe Borowski	.30	.14
169 Tony Womack	.30	.14
170 Antonio Alfonseca	.30	.14
171 Corey Patterson	.30	.14
172 Mark Prior	.75	.35
173 Moises Alou	.30	.14
174 Matt Clement	.30	.14
175 Randall Simon	.30	.14
176 Randy Johnson	.75	.35
177 Luis Gonzalez	.30	.14
178 Craig Counsell	.30	.14
179 Miguel Batista	.30	.14
180 Steve Finley	.30	.14
181 Brandon Webb	.30	.14
182 Danny Bautista	.30	.14
183 Oscar Villarreal	.30	.14
184 Shawn Green	.30	.14
185 Brian Jordan	.30	.14
186 Fred McGriff	.50	.23
187 Andy Ashby	.30	.14
188 Rickey Henderson	.75	.35
189 Dave Roberts	.30	.14
190 Eric Gagne	.75	.35
191 Kazuhisa Ishii	.30	.14
192 Adrian Beltre	.50	.23
193 Vladimir Guerrero	.75	.35
194 Livan Hernandez	.30	.14
195 Ron Calloway	.30	.14
196 Sun Woo Kim	.30	.14
197 Wil Cordero	.30	.14
198 Brad Wilkerson	.30	.14
199 Orlando Cabrera	.30	.14
200 Barry Bonds	2.00	.90
201 Ray Durham	.30	.14
202 Andres Galarraga	.30	.14
203 Benito Santiago	.30	.14
204 Jose Cruz Jr.	.30	.14
205 Jason Schmidt	.30	.14
206 Kirk Rueter	.30	.14
207 Felix Rodriguez	.30	.14
208 Mike Lowell	.30	.14
209 Luis Castillo	.30	.14
210 Derrek Lee	.30	.14
211 Andy Fox	.30	.14
212 Tommy Phelps	.30	.14
213 Todd Hollandsworth	.30	.14
214 Brad Penny	.30	.14
215 Juan Pierre	.30	.14
216 Mike Piazza	1.25	.55
217 Jae Weong Seo	.30	.14
218 Ty Wigginton	.30	.14
219 Al Leiter	.30	.14
220 Roger Cedeno	.30	.14
221 Timo Perez	.30	.14
222 Aaron Heilman	.30	.14
223 Pedro Astacio	.30	.14
224 Joe McEwing	.30	.14
225 Ryan Klesko	.30	.14
226 Brian Giles	.30	.14
227 Mark Kotsay	.30	.14
228 Brian Lawrence	.30	.14
229 Rod Beck	.30	.14
230 Trevor Hoffman	.30	.14
231 Sean Burroughs	.30	.14
232 Bob Abreu	.30	.14
233 Jim Thome	.75	.35
234 David Bell	.30	.14
235 Jimmy Rollins	.30	.14
236 Mike Lieberthal	.30	.14
237 Vicente Padilla	.30	.14
238 Randy Wolf	.30	.14
239 Reggie Sanders	.30	.14
240 Jason Kendall	.30	.14
241 Jack Wilson	.30	.14
242 Jose Hernandez	.30	.14
243 Kip Wells	.30	.14
244 Carlos Rivera	.30	.14
245 Craig Wilson	.30	.14
246 Adam Dunn	.50	.23
247 Sean Casey	.30	.14
248 Danny Graves	.30	.14
249 Ryan Dempster	.30	.14
250 Barry Larkin	.50	.23
251 Reggie Taylor	.30	.14
252 Wily Mo Pena	.30	.14
253 Larry Walker	.50	.23
254 Mark Sweeney	.30	.14
255 Preston Wilson	.30	.14
256 Jason Jennings	.30	.14
257 Charles Johnson	.30	.14
258 Jay Payton	.30	.14
259 Chris Stynes	.30	.14
260 Juan Uribe	.30	.14
261 Hideki Matsui SH CL	.75	.35
262 Barry Bonds SH CL	1.00	.45
263 Dontrelle Willis SH CL	.30	.14
264 Kevin Millwood SH CL	.30	.14
265 Billy Wagner SH CL	.30	.14
266 Rocco Baldelli SH CL	.30	.14
267 Roger Clemens SH CL	.75	.35
268 Rafael Palmeiro SH CL	.30	.14
269 Miguel Cabrera SH CL	.50	.23
270 Jose Contreras SH CL	.30	.14
271 Aaron Sele	.30	.14
272 Bartolo Colon	.30	.14
273 Darin Erstad	.30	.14
274 Francisco Rodriguez	.30	.14
275 Garret Anderson	.30	.14
276 Jose Guillen	.30	.14
277 Troy Percival	.30	.14
278 Alex Cintron	.30	.14
279 Casey Fossum	.30	.14
280 Elmer Dessens	.30	.14
281 Jose Valverde	.30	.14
282 Matt Mantei	.30	.14
283 Richie Sexson	.30	.14
284 Roberto Alomar	.50	.23
285 Shea Hillenbrand	.30	.14
286 Chipper Jones	.75	.35
287 Greg Maddux	1.25	.55
288 J.D. Drew	.30	.14
289 Marcus Giles	.30	.14
290 Mike Hessman	.30	.14
291 John Thomson	.30	.14
292 Russ Ortiz	.30	.14
293 Adam Loewen	.30	.14
294 Jack Cust	.30	.14
295 Jerry Hairston Jr.	.30	.14
296 Kurt Ainsworth	.30	.14
297 Luis Matos	.30	.14
298 Marty Cordova	.30	.14
299 Sidney Ponson	.30	.14
300 Bill Mueller	.30	.14
301 Curt Schilling	.50	.23
302 David Ortiz	.75	.35
303 Johnny Damon	.75	.35
304 Keith Foulke Sox	.50	.23
305 Pokey Reese	.30	.14
306 Scott Williamson	.30	.14
307 Tim Wakefield	.30	.14
308 Alex Gonzalez	.30	.14
309 Aramis Ramirez	.30	.14
310 Carlos Zambrano	.30	.14
311 Juan Cruz	.30	.14
312 Kerry Wood	.75	.35
313 Kyle Farnsworth	.30	.14
314 Aaron Rowand	.30	.14
315 Esteban Loaiza	.30	.14
316 Frank Thomas	.75	.35
317 Joe Borchard	.30	.14
318 Joe Crede	.30	.14
319 Miguel Olivo	.30	.14
320 Willie Harris	.30	.14
321 Aaron Harang	.30	.14
322 Austin Kearns	.30	.14
323 Brandon Claussen	.30	.14
324 Brandon Larson	.30	.14
325 Ryan Freel	.30	.14
326 Ken Griffey Jr.	1.25	.55
327 Ryan Wagner	.30	.14
328 Alex Escobar	.30	.14
329 Coco Crisp	.30	.14
330 David Riske	.30	.14
331 Jody Gerut	.30	.14
332 Josh Bard	.30	.14
333 Travis Hafner	.30	.14
334 Chin-Hui Tsao	.30	.14
335 Denny Stark	.30	.14
336 Jeromy Burnitz	.30	.14
337 Shawn Chacon	.30	.14
338 Todd Helton	.50	.23
339 Vinny Castilla	.30	.14
340 Alex Sanchez	.30	.14
341 Carlos Pena	.30	.14
342 Fernando Vina	.30	.14
343 Jason Johnson	.30	.14
344 Matt Anderson	.30	.14
345 Mike Maroth	.30	.14
346 Rondell White	.30	.14
347 A.J. Burnett	.30	.14
348 Alex Gonzalez	.30	.14
349 Armando Benitez	.30	.14
350 Carl Pavano	.30	.14
351 Hee Seop Choi	.30	.14
352 Ivan Rodriguez	.75	.35
353 Josh Beckett	.30	.14
354 Josh Willingham	.30	.14
355 Adam Everett	.30	.14
356 Brandon Duckworth	.30	.14
357 Jason Lane	.30	.14
358 Jeff Kent	.30	.14
359 Jeriome Robertson	.30	.14
360 Lance Berkman	.30	.14
361 Wade Miller	.30	.14
362 Aaron Guiel	.30	.14
363 Angel Berroa	.30	.14
364 Carlos Beltran	.50	.23
365 David DeJesus	.30	.14
366 Desi Relaford	.30	.14
367 Joe Randa	.30	.14
368 Runelvys Hernandez	.30	.14
369 Edwin Jackson	.30	.14
370 Hideo Nomo	.75	.35
371 Jeff Weaver	.30	.14
372 Juan Encarnacion	.30	.14
373 Odalis Perez	.30	.14
374 Paul Lo Duca	.30	.14
375 Robin Ventura	.30	.14
376 Bill Hall	.30	.14
377 Chad Moeller	.30	.14
378 Chris Capuano	.30	.14
379 Junior Spivey	.30	.14
380 Rickie Weeks	.30	.14
381 Wes Helms	.30	.14
382 Brad Radke	.30	.14
383 Jacque Jones	.30	.14
384 Joe Mays	.30	.14
385 Joe Nathan	.30	.14
386 Johan Santana	.50	.23
387 Nick Punto	.30	.14
388 Shannon Stewart	.30	.14
389 Carl Everett	.30	.14
390 Claudio Vargas	.30	.14
391 Jose Vidro	.30	.14
392 Nick Johnson	.30	.14
393 Rocky Biddle	.30	.14
394 Tony Armas Jr.	.30	.14
395 Braden Looper	.30	.14
396 Cliff Floyd	.30	.14
397 Jason Phillips	.30	.14
398 Mike Cameron	.30	.14
399 Tom Glavine	.50	.23
400 Kenny Lofton	.30	.14
401 Alfonso Soriano	.50	.23
402 Bernie Williams	.50	.23
403 Javier Vazquez	.30	.14
404 Jon Lieber	.30	.14
405 Jose Contreras	.30	.14
406 Kevin Brown	.30	.14
407 Mariano Rivera	.50	.23
408 Arthur Rhodes	.30	.14
409 Eric Byrnes	.30	.14
410 Erubiel Durazo	.30	.14
411 Graham Koonce	.30	.14
412 Marco Scutaro	.30	.14
413 Mark Mulder	.30	.14
414 Mark Redman	.30	.14
415 Rich Harden	.30	.14
416 Brett Myers	.30	.14
417 Chase Utley	.30	.14
418 Kevin Millwood	.30	.14
419 Marlon Byrd	.30	.14
420 Pat Burrell	.30	.14
421 Placido Polanco	.30	.14
422 Tim Worrell	.30	.14
423 Jason Bay	.30	.14
424 Josh Fogg	.30	.14
425 Kris Benson	.30	.14
426 Mike Gonzalez	.30	.14
427 Oliver Perez	.30	.14
428 Tike Redman	.30	.14
429 Adam Eaton	.30	.14
430 Ismael Valdes	.30	.14
431 Jake Peavy	.30	.14
432 Khalil Greene	.75	.35
433 Mark Loretta	.30	.14
434 Phil Nevin	.30	.14
435 Ramon Hernandez	.30	.14
436 A.J. Pierzynski	.30	.14
437 Edgardo Alfonzo	.30	.14
438 J.T. Snow	.30	.14
439 Jerome Williams	.30	.14
440 Marquis Grissom	.30	.14
441 Robb Nen	.30	.14
442 Bret Boone	.30	.14
443 Freddy Garcia	.30	.14
444 Gil Meche	.30	.14
445 John Olerud	.30	.14
446 Rich Aurilia	.30	.14
447 Shigetoshi Hasegawa	.30	.14
448 Bo Hart	.30	.14
449 Danny Haren	.30	.14
450 Jason Marquis	.30	.14
451 Marlon Anderson	.30	.14
452 Scott Rolen	.75	.35
453 So Taguchi	.30	.14
454 Carl Crawford	.30	.14
455 Delmon Young	.50	.23
456 Geoff Blum	.30	.14
457 Jesus Colome	.30	.14
458 Jonny Gomes	.30	.14
459 Lance Carter	.30	.14
460 Robert Fick	.30	.14
461 Chan Ho Park	.30	.14
462 Francisco Cordero	.30	.14
463 Jeff Nelson	.30	.14
464 Jeff Zimmerman	.30	.14
465 Kenny Rogers	.30	.14
466 Aquilino Lopez	.30	.14
467 Carlos Delgado	.30	.14
468 Frank Catalanotto	.30	.14
469 Reed Johnson	.30	.14
470 Pat Hentgen	.30	.14
471 Curt Schilling SH CL	.30	.14
472 Gary Sheffield SH CL	.30	.14
473 Javier Vazquez SH CL	.30	.14
474 Kazuo Matsui SH CL	1.50	.70
475 Kevin Brown SH CL	.30	.14
476 Rafael Palmeiro SH CL	.30	.14
477 Richie Sexson SH CL	.30	.14
478 Roger Clemens SH CL	.75	.35
479 Vladimir Guerrero SH CL	.50	.23
480 Alex Rodriguez SH CL	.75	.35
481 Jake Woods SR RC	1.00	.45
482 Tim Bittner SR RC	1.00	.45
483 Brandon Medders SR RC	1.00	.45
484 Casey Daigle SR RC	1.00	.45
485 Jerry Gil SR RC	1.00	.45
486 Mike Gosling SR RC	1.00	.45
487 Jose Capellan SR RC	2.50	1.10
488 Onil Joseph SR RC	1.00	.45
489 Roman Colon SR RC	1.00	.45
490 Dave Crouthers SR RC	1.00	.45
491 Eddy Rodriguez SR RC	1.50	.70
492 Franklyn Gracesqui SR RC	1.00	.45

493 Jamie Brown SR RC 1.00 .45
494 Jerome Gamble SR RC 1.00 .45
495 Tim Hamulack SR RC 1.00 .45
496 Carlos Vasquez SR RC 1.50 .70
497 Renyel Pinto SR RC 1.50 .70
498 Ronny Cedeno SR RC 1.00 .45
499 Enemencio Pacheco SR RC 1.00 .45
500 Ryan Meaux SR RC 1.00 .45
501 Ryan Wing SR RC 1.00 .45
502 Shingo Takatsu SR RC 2.00 .90
503 William Bergolla SR RC 1.00 .45
504 Ivan Ochoa SR RC 1.00 .45
505 Mariano Gomez SR RC 1.00 .45
506 Justin Hampson SR RC 1.00 .45
507 Justin Huisman SR RC 1.00 .45
508 Scott Dohmann SR RC 1.00 .45
509 Donnie Kelly SR RC 1.00 .45
510 Chris Aguila SR RC 1.00 .45
511 Lincoln Holdzkom SR RC 1.00 .45
512 Freddy Guzman SR RC 1.00 .45
513 Hector Gimenez SR RC 1.00 .45
514 Jorge Vasquez SR RC 1.00 .45
515 Jason Frasor SR RC 1.00 .45
516 Chris Saenz SR RC 1.00 .45
517 Dennis Sarfate SR RC 1.00 .45
518 Colby Miller SR RC 1.00 .45
519 Jason Bartlett SR RC 1.50 .70
520 Chad Bentz SR RC 1.00 .45
521 Josh Labandeira SR RC 1.00 .45
522 Shawn Hill SR RC 1.00 .45
523 Kazuo Matsui SR RC 3.00 1.35
524 Carlos Hines SR RC 1.00 .45
525 Mike Vento SR RC 1.50 .70
526 Scott Proctor SR RC 1.50 .70
527 Sean Henn SR RC 1.00 .45
528 David Aardsma SR RC 1.00 .45
529 Ian Snell SR RC 1.50 .70
530 Mike Johnston SR RC 1.00 .45
531 Akinori Otsuka SR RC 1.00 .45
532 Rusty Tucker SR RC 1.50 .70
533 Justin Knoedler SR RC 1.00 .45
534 Merkin Valdez SR RC 2.00 .90
535 Greg Dobbs SR RC 1.00 .45
536 Justin Leone SR RC 1.50 .70
537 Shawn Camp SR RC 1.00 .45
538 Edwin Moreno SR RC 1.00 .45
539 Angel Chavez SR RC 1.00 .45
540 Jesse Harper SR RC 1.00 .45
541 Alex Rodriguez 1.25 .55
542 Roger Clemens 1.50 .70
543 Andy Pettitte .50 .23
544 Vladimir Guerrero .75 .35
545 David Wells .30 .14
546 Derrek Lee .30 .14
547 Carlos Beltran .50 .23
548 Orlando Cabrera Sox .50 .23
549 Paul Lo Duca .30 .14
550 Dave Roberts .30 .14
551 Guillermo Mota .30 .14
552 Steve Finley .30 .14
553 Juan Encarnacion .30 .14
554 Larry Walker .50 .23
555 Ty Wigginton .30 .14
556 Doug Mientkiewicz .30 .14
557 Roberto Alomar .50 .23
558 B.J. Upton .50 .23
559 Brad Penny .30 .14
560 Hee Seop Choi .30 .14
561 David Wright 3.00 1.35
562 Nomar Garciaparra 1.25 .55
563 Felix Rodriguez .30 .14
564 Victor Zambrano .30 .14
565 Kris Benson .30 .14
566 Aarom Baldiris SR RC .50 .23
567 Joey Gathright SR RC 1.00 .45
568 Charles Thomas SR RC .50 .23
569 Brian Dallimore SR RC .50 .23
570 Chris Oxspring SR RC .50 .23
571 Chris Shelton SR RC .75 .35
572 Dioner Navarro SR RC 1.00 .45
573 Edwardo Sierra SR RC .50 .23
574 Fernando Nieve SR RC .50 .23
575 Frank Francisco SR RC .50 .23
576 Jeff Bennett SR RC .50 .23
577 Justin Lehr SR RC .50 .23
578 John Gall SR RC .50 .23
579 Jorge Sequea SR RC .50 .23
580 Justin Germano SR RC .50 .23
581 Kazuhito Tadano SR RC .50 .23
582 Kevin Cave SR RC .50 .23
583 Jesse Crain SR RC .75 .35
584 Luis A. Gonzalez SR RC .50 .23
585 Michael Wuertz SR RC .50 .23
586 Orlando Rodriguez SR RC .50 .23
587 Phil Stockman SR RC .50 .23
588 Ramon Ramirez SR RC .50 .23
589 Roberto Novoa SR RC .50 .23
590 Scott Kazmir SR RC 3.00 1.35
NNO Update Set Exchange Card

2004 Upper Deck Glossy

Nm-Mt Ex-Mt
COMP.FACT.SET (590) 100.00 30.00
*GLOSSY: .75X TO 2X BASIC
ISSUED ONLY IN FACTORY SET FORM

2004 Upper Deck A Piece of History 500 Club

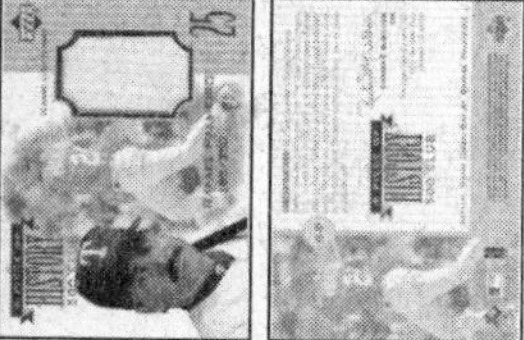

MINT NRMT
SERIES 1 STATED ODDS 1:8700
STATED PRINT RUN 350 SERIAL #'D CARDS
504HR Rafael Palmeiro 200.00 90.00

2004 Upper Deck A Piece of History 500 Club Autograph

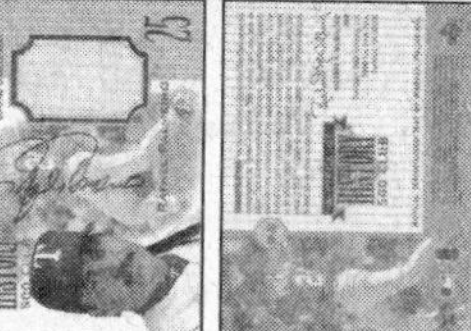

MINT NRMT
RANDOM INSERT IN SERIES 1 PACKS
STATED PRINT RUN 25 SERIAL #'d CARDS
NO PRICING DUE TO SCARCITY
RPAU0 Rafael Palmeiro AU/25

2004 Upper Deck Authentic Stars Jersey

MINT NRMT
SERIES 1 ODDS 1:48 HOBBY, 1:96 RETAIL
*GOLD: .75X TO 2X BASIC AS JSY
GOLD RANDOM INSERTS IN SERIES 1 PACKS
GOLD PRINT RUN 100 SERIAL #'d SETS
AJ Andruw Jones 8.00 3.60
AP Albert Pujols 15.00 6.75
AR Alex Rodriguez 10.00 4.50
AS Alfonso Soriano 10.00 4.50
BA Bob Abreu 8.00 3.60
BW Bernie Williams 10.00 4.50
BZ Barry Zito 8.00 3.60
CD Carlos Delgado 8.00 3.60
CJ Chipper Jones 10.00 4.50
CS Curt Schilling 8.00 3.60
DE Darin Erstad 8.00 3.60
EC Eric Chavez 8.00 3.60
FT Frank Thomas 10.00 4.50
GM Greg Maddux 10.00 4.50
HB Hank Blalock 8.00 3.60
HM Hideki Matsui 40.00 18.00
IR Ivan Rodriguez 10.00 4.50
IS Ichiro Suzuki 25.00 11.00
JB Jeff Bagwell 10.00 4.50
JD J.D. Drew 8.00 3.60
JG Jason Giambi 8.00 3.60
JH Josh Beckett 8.00 3.60
JK Jeff Kent 8.00 3.60
KG Ken Griffey Jr. 15.00 6.75
LW Larry Walker 10.00 4.50
MI Mike Piazza 10.00 4.50
MP Mark Prior 10.00 4.50
MT Mark Teixeira 8.00 3.60
PM Pedro Martinez 10.00 4.50
PN Phil Nevin 8.00 3.60
RB Rocco Baldelli 8.00 3.60
RC Roger Clemens 15.00 6.75
RJ Randy Johnson 10.00 4.50
RO Roberto Alomar 10.00 4.50
SG Shawn Green 8.00 3.60
SS Sammy Sosa 15.00 6.75
TG Troy Glaus 8.00 3.60
TH Todd Helton 10.00 4.50
TL Tom Glavine 10.00 4.50
TM Tino Martinez 10.00 4.50
TO Torii Hunter 8.00 3.60
VG Vladimir Guerrero 10.00 4.50

2004 Upper Deck Authentic Stars Jersey Update

Nm-Mt Ex-Mt
UPDATE GU ODDS 1:12 '04 UPDATE SETS
STATED PRINT RUN 75 SERIAL #'d SETS
AK Austin Kearns 10.00 3.00
CB Carlos Beltran 15.00 4.50
DJ Derek Jeter 40.00 12.00
HA Roy Halladay 10.00 3.00
HN Hideo Nomo 25.00 7.50
HU Tim Hudson 10.00 3.00
JE Jim Edmonds 10.00 3.00
JR Jose Reyes 10.00 3.00
JT Jim Thome 15.00 4.50
KW Kerry Wood 15.00 4.50
LB Lance Berkman 10.00 3.00
MO Magglio Ordonez 10.00 3.00
MR Manny Ramirez 15.00 4.50
OS Roy Oswalt 10.00 3.00
PW Preston Wilson 10.00 3.00
RF Rafael Furcal 10.00 3.00
RH Rich Harden 10.00 3.00
RP Rafael Palmeiro 15.00 4.50
SR Scott Rolen 15.00 4.50
TE Miguel Tejada 10.00 3.00
VW Vernon Wells 10.00 3.00
WE Brandon Webb 10.00 3.00

2004 Upper Deck Awesome Honors

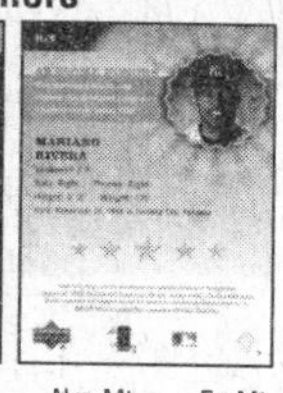

Nm-Mt Ex-Mt
COMPLETE SET (10) 20.00 6.00
SERIES 2 STATED ODDS 1:12 H/R
1 Albert Pujols 5.00 1.50
2 Alex Rodriguez 4.00 1.20
3 Angel Berroa 2.00 .60
4 Dontrelle Willis 2.00 .60
5 Eric Gagne 2.50 .75
6 Garret Anderson 2.00 .60
7 Ivan Rodriguez 2.50 .75
8 Josh Beckett 2.00 .60
9 Mariano Rivera 2.00 .60
10 Roy Halladay 2.00 .60

2004 Upper Deck Awesome Honors Jersey

Nm-Mt Ex-Mt
*GOLD: .6X TO 1.5X BASIC
GOLD PRINT RUN 165 SERIAL #'d SETS
OVERALL SER.2 GU ODDS 1:12 H, 1:24 R
AJ Andruw Jones GG 5.00 1.50
AP Albert Pujols PC 15.00 4.50
AP1 Albert Pujols HA 15.00 4.50
AP2 Albert Pujols POM 15.00 4.50
AR Alex Rodriguez MVP 12.00 3.60
AR1 Alex Rodriguez GG 12.00 3.60
AR2 Alex Rodriguez HA 12.00 3.60
AR3 Alex Rodriguez POM 12.00 3.60
AS Alfonso Soriano POM 8.00 2.40
BB Bret Boone GG 5.00 1.50
BM Ben Molina GG 5.00 1.50
DL Derrek Lee GG 5.00 1.50
DW Dontrelle Willis ROY 5.00 1.50
EC Eric Chavez GG 5.00 1.50
EG Eric Gagne CY 8.00 2.40
EG1 Eric Gagne RA 8.00 2.40
EM Edgar Martinez POM 8.00 2.40
GA Garret Anderson AS MVP 5.00 1.50
HU Torii Hunter GG 5.00 1.50
IR Ivan Rodriguez NLCS MVP 8.00 2.40
IS Ichiro Suzuki GG 25.00 7.50
JB Josh Beckett WS MVP 5.00 1.50
JE Jim Edmonds GG 5.00 1.50
JG Jason Giambi POM 5.00 1.50
JM Jamie Moyer MAN 5.00 1.50
JO John Olerud GG 5.00 1.50
JS John Smoltz MAN 8.00 2.40
JT Jim Thome POM 8.00 2.40
LC Luis Castillo GG 5.00 1.50
MC Mike Cameron GG 5.00 1.50
MH Mike Hampton GG 5.00 1.50
MO Magglio Ordonez POM 5.00 1.50
MR Mariano Rivera ALCS MVP 8.00 2.40
MU Mike Mussina GG 8.00 2.40
RH Roy Halladay CY 5.00 1.50
SR Scott Rolen GG 8.00 2.40
TH Todd Helton POM 8.00 2.40
VG Vladimir Guerrero POM 8.00 2.40

2004 Upper Deck Awesome Honors Jersey Update

Nm-Mt Ex-Mt
UPDATE GU ODDS 1:12 '04 UPDATE SETS
AB Angel Berroa 10.00 3.00
AP Albert Pujols 25.00 7.50
AS Alfonso Soriano 15.00 4.50
BE Adrian Beltre 15.00 4.50
BG Brian Giles 10.00 3.00
DL Derrek Lee 10.00 3.00
EG Eric Gagne 15.00 4.50
GS Gary Sheffield 10.00 3.00
IR Ivan Rodriguez 15.00 4.50
JM Joe Mauer 15.00 4.50
KB Kevin Brown 10.00 3.00
KM Kazuo Matsui 25.00 7.50
MC Miguel Cabrera 15.00 4.50
PE Andy Pettitte 15.00 4.50
RC Roger Clemens 25.00 7.50
RS Richie Sexson 10.00 3.00
SC Curt Schilling 15.00 4.50
SP Scott Podsednik 10.00 3.00
VA Javier Vazquez 10.00 3.00

2004 Upper Deck First Pitch Inserts

MINT NRMT
SERIES 1 STATED ODDS 1:72
CARD SP9 DOES NOT EXIST
SP7 LeBron James 15.00 6.75
SP8 Gordie Howe 10.00 4.50
SP9 Does Not Exist
SP10 Ernie Banks 10.00 4.50
SP11 General Tommy Franks 5.00 2.20
SP12 Ben Affleck 10.00 4.50
SP13 Halle Berry UER 10.00 4.50
Last name misspelled Barry
SP14 George H.W. Bush 5.00 2.20
SP15 George W. Bush 10.00 4.50

2004 Upper Deck Game Winners Bat

Nm-Mt Ex-Mt
*GOLD: .6X TO 1.5X BASIC
GOLD PRINT RUN 50 SERIAL #'d SETS
OVERALL SER.2 GU ODDS 1:12 H, 1:24 R
AG Alex Gonzalez 8.00 2.40
AJ Andruw Jones 8.00 2.40
AP Albert Pujols 20.00 6.00
AS Alfonso Soriano 10.00 3.00
BA Bobby Abreu 8.00 2.40
BW Bernie Williams 10.00 3.00
CJ Chipper Jones 10.00 3.00
CP Corey Patterson 8.00 2.40
DE Darin Erstad 8.00 2.40
DJ Derek Jeter 25.00 7.50
GA Garret Anderson
GS Gary Sheffield 8.00 2.40
HB Hank Blalock 8.00 2.40
HM Hideki Matsui 30.00 9.00
HU Torii Hunter 8.00 2.40
IR Ivan Rodriguez 10.00 3.00
JB Jeff Bagwell 10.00 3.00
JE Jim Edmonds 8.00 2.40
JG Jason Giambi 8.00 2.40
JL Javy Lopez
JP Jorge Posada 10.00 3.00
JT Jim Thome 10.00 3.00
KG Ken Griffey Jr.
MC Miguel Cabrera 10.00 3.00
ML Mike Lowell 8.00 2.40
MO Magglio Ordonez 8.00 2.40
MP Mike Piazza 15.00 4.50
MT Mark Teixeira 8.00 2.40
RF Rafael Furcal 8.00 2.40
RH Ramon Hernandez 8.00 2.40
RK Ryan Klesko 8.00 2.40
SG Shawn Green 8.00 2.40
SR Scott Rolen 10.00 3.00
TE Miguel Tejada 8.00 2.40
TG Troy Glaus 8.00 2.40
TH Todd Helton 10.00 3.00
TN Trot Nixon 8.00 2.40
VG Vladimir Guerrero 10.00 3.00

2004 Upper Deck Going Deep Bat

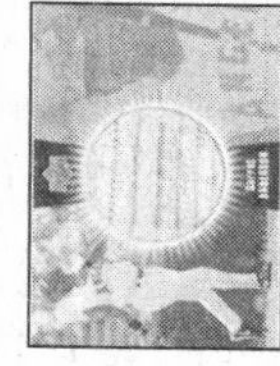

MINT NRMT
SERIES 1 ODDS 1:288 HOB, 1:576 RET
SP PRINT RUNS B/WN 12-123 COPIES PER
SP PRINT RUNS PROVIDED BY UPPER DECK
NO PRICING ON QTY OF 41 OR LESS
GOLD RANDOM INSERTS IN PACKS
GOLD PRINT RUN 50 SERIAL #'d SETS
NO GOLD PRICING DUE TO SCARCITY
AJ Andruw Jones SP/12
AP Albert Pujols 25.00 11.00
AS Alfonso Soriano SP/53 15.00 6.75
BA Bob Abreu SP/110 10.00 4.50
BW Bernie Williams SP/56 15.00 6.75
CB Craig Biggio SP/89 15.00 6.75
CJ Chipper Jones SP/69 15.00 6.75
CP Corey Patterson SP/41
CS Curt Schilling SP/57 10.00 4.50
DE Darin Erstad 10.00 4.50
DM Doug Mientkiewicz SP/123 10.00 4.50
GA Garret Anderson 10.00 4.50
HM Hideki Matsui SP/70 40.00 18.00
HN Hideo Nomo 15.00 6.75
JB Jeff Bagwell SP/92 15.00 6.75
JE Jim Edmonds SP 10.00 4.50
JL Javy Lopez SP/77 10.00 4.50
JPA Jorge Posada 15.00 6.75
JPO Jay Payton SP/100 10.00 4.50
JT Jim Thome 15.00 6.75
KG Ken Griffey Jr. SP 40.00 18.00
KW Kerry Wood SP/108 15.00 6.75
MO Magglio Ordonez 10.00 4.50
MP Mike Piazza 15.00 6.75
MT Miguel Tejada SP/23
OV Omar Vizquel SP/115 15.00 6.75
RA Rich Aurilia SP/102 10.00 4.50
RB Rocco Baldelli SP/77 10.00 4.50
RF Rafael Furcal SP 10.00 4.50
RH Rickey Henderson SP/77 15.00 6.75
RO Roberto Alomar 15.00 6.75
SC Sandy Alomar Jr. SP/95 10.00 4.50
SG Shawn Green SP/100 10.00 4.50
SR Scott Rolen SP/77 15.00 6.75
TG Troy Glaus SP/113 10.00 4.50
TH Torii Hunter SP/115 10.00 4.50

2004 Upper Deck Headliners Jersey

MINT NRMT
SERIES 1 ODDS 1:48 HOBBY, 1:96 RETAIL
SP PRINT RUNS B/WN 97-153 COPIES PER
SP PRINT RUNS PROVIDED BY UPPER DECK
*GOLD: .75X TO 2X BASIC
GOLD RANDOM INSERTS IN SERIES 1 PACKS
GOLD PRINT RUN 100 SERIAL #'d SETS
AD Adam Dunn 10.00 4.50
BK Byung-Hyun Kim AS 8.00 3.60
BS Benito Santiago AS 8.00 3.60
CS Curt Schilling 8.00 3.60
GM Greg Maddux 10.00 4.50
HM Hideki Matsui 40.00 18.00
IS Ichiro Suzuki SP/153 40.00 18.00
JB Josh Beckett 8.00 3.60
JD Joe DiMaggio SP/153 100.00 45.00
JE Jim Edmonds 8.00 3.60
JH Jose Hernandez AS 8.00 3.60
JR Jimmy Rollins AS 8.00 3.60
JS Junior Spivey AS 8.00 3.60
JT Jim Thome 10.00 4.50
JV Jose Vidro AS 8.00 3.60
KG Ken Griffey Jr. 15.00 6.75
LB Lance Berkman 8.00 3.60
LC Luis Castillo AS 8.00 3.60
LG Luis Gonzalez 8.00 3.60
MA Mariano Rivera 10.00 4.50
MB Mark Buehrle AS 8.00 3.60
ML Mike Lowell AS 8.00 3.60
MM Mickey Mantle SP/97 150.00 70.00
MO Magglio Ordonez 8.00 3.60
MR Manny Ramirez 10.00 4.50
MS Matt Morris AS 8.00 3.60
MT Miguel Tejada 8.00 3.60
MU Mike Mussina 10.00 4.50
MY Mike Sweeney AS 8.00 3.60
PK Paul Konerko AS 8.00 3.60
PM Pedro Martinez 10.00 4.50
RF Robert Fick AS 8.00 3.60
RH Roy Halladay AS 8.00 3.60
RK Ryan Klesko 8.00 3.60
RO Roy Oswalt 8.00 3.60
SG Shawn Green 8.00 3.60
TB Tony Batista AS 8.00 3.60
TG Tom Glavine 10.00 4.50
TH Trevor Hoffman AS 8.00 3.60
TW Ted Williams SP/153 80.00 36.00
VG Vladimir Guerrero SP/153 15.00 6.75

2004 Upper Deck Derek Jeter Bonus

Nm-Mt Ex-Mt
COMMON CARD (1-25) 5.00 1.50
1-25 THREE PER JETER BONUS PACK
COMMON JSY (26-32) 40.00 12.00
26-32 JSY PRINT RUN 99 #'d SETS
COMMON AU (33-37)
33-37 AU PRINT RUN 50 #'d SETS
38-42 AU JSY PRINT RUN 10 #'d SETS
AU JSY NO PRICING DUE TO SCARCITY
26-42 RANDOM IN JETER BONUS PACKS
ONE JETER BONUS PACK PER FACT.SET

2004 Upper Deck Magical Performances

MINT NRMT
SERIES 1 STATED ODDS 1:96 HOBBY
GOLD RANDOM INSERTS IN SER.1 HOBBY
GOLD STATED ODDS 1:1300 RETAIL
GOLD PRINT RUN 50 SERIAL #'d SETS
NO GOLD PRICING DUE TO SCARCITY
1 Mickey Mantle USC HR 50.00 22.00
2 Mickey Mantle 56 Triple Crown 50.00 22.00
3 Joe DiMaggio 56th Game 25.00 11.00
4 Joe DiMaggio Slides Home 25.00 11.00
5 Derek Jeter The Flip 25.00 11.00
6 Derek Jeter 00 AS/MVP 25.00 11.00
7 R.Clemens 300 Win/4000 K 25.00 11.00
8 Roger Clemens 20-1 25.00 11.00
9 Alfonso Soriano Walkoff 20.00 9.00

10 Andy Pettitte 96 20.00 9.00
11 Hideki Matsui Grand Slam 25.00 11.00
12 Mike Mussina 1-Hitter 20.00 9.00
13 Jorge Posada ALDS HR 20.00 9.00
14 Jason Giambi Grand Slam 15.00 6.75
15 David Wells Perfect 15.00 6.75
16 Mariano Rivera 99 WS MVP 20.00 9.00
17 Yogi Berra 12 K's 20.00 9.00
18 Phil Rizzuto 50 MVP 20.00 9.00
19 Whitey Ford 61 CY 20.00 9.00
20 Jose Contreras 1st Win 15.00 6.75
21 Catfish Hunter Free Agent 20.00 9.00
22 Mickey Mantle Cycle 50.00 22.00
23 M.Mantle HR's Both Sides 50.00 22.00
24 Joe DiMaggio 3-Time MVP 25.00 11.00
25 Joe DiMaggio Cycle 25.00 11.00
26 Derek Jeter 7 Seasons 25.00 11.00
27 Derek Jeter Mr. November 25.00 11.00
28 Roger Clemens 1-Hitter 25.00 11.00
29 Roger Clemens 01 CY 25.00 11.00
30 Alfonso Soriano HR Record 20.00 9.00
31 Andy Pettitte ALCS 20.00 9.00
32 Hideki Matsui 4 Hits 25.00 11.00
33 Mike Mussina 1st Postseason 20.00 9.00
34 Jorge Posada 40 Doubles 20.00 9.00
35 Jason Giambi 200th HR 15.00 6.75
36 David Wells 3-Hitter 15.00 6.75
37 Mariano Rivera Saves 3 20.00 9.00
38 Yogi Berra 3-Time MVP 20.00 9.00
39 Phil Rizzuto Broadcasting 20.00 9.00
40 Whitey Ford 10 WS Wins 20.00 9.00
41 Jose Contreras 2 Hits 15.00 6.75
42 Catfish Hunter 200th Win 20.00 9.00

2004 Upper Deck Matsui Chronicles

MINT NRMT
COMPLETE SET (60) 60.00 27.00
COMMON CARD (HM1-HM60) 2.00 .90
ONE PER SERIES 1 RETAIL PACK

2004 Upper Deck National Pride

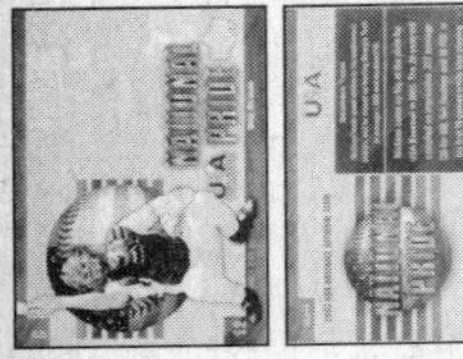

MINT NRMT
SERIES 1 STATED ODDS 1:6
1 Justin Orenduff 1.50 .70
2 Micah Owings 1.50 .70
3 Steven Register 1.50 .70
4 Huston Street 1.50 .70
5 Justin Verlander 2.50 1.10
6 Jered Weaver 2.50 1.10
7 Matt Campbell 1.50 .70
8 Stephen Head 1.50 .70
9 Mark Romanczuk 1.50 .70
10 Jeff Clement 2.50 1.10
11 Mike Nickeas 1.50 .70
12 Tyler Greene 1.50 .70
13 Paul Janish 1.50 .70
14 Jeff Larish 1.50 .70
15 Eric Patterson 1.50 .70
16 Dustin Pedroia 2.00 .90
17 Michael Griffin 1.50 .70
18 Brent Lillibridge 1.50 .70
19 Danny Putnam 1.50 .70
20 Seth Smith 2.00 .90

2004 Upper Deck National Pride Jersey 1

MINT NRMT
SERIES 1 ODDS 1:24 HOBBY, 1:48 RETAIL
1 Justin Orenduff 5.00 2.20
2 Micah Owings 5.00 2.20
3 Steven Register 5.00 2.20
4 Huston Street 5.00 2.20
5 Justin Verlander 10.00 4.50
6 Jered Weaver 10.00 4.50
7 Matt Campbell 5.00 2.20
8 Stephen Head 5.00 2.20
9 Mark Romanczuk 5.00 2.20
10 Jeff Clement 8.00 3.60
11 Mike Nickeas 5.00 2.20
12 Tyler Greene 5.00 2.20
13 Paul Janish 5.00 2.20
14 Jeff Larish 5.00 2.20
15 Eric Patterson 5.00 2.20
16 Dustin Pedroia 8.00 3.60
17 Michael Griffin 5.00 2.20
18 Brent Lillibridge 5.00 2.20
19 Danny Putnam 5.00 2.20
20 Seth Smith 8.00 3.60
21 Justin Orenduff SP 8.00 3.60
22 Micah Owings SP 8.00 3.60
23 Steven Register SP 8.00 3.60
24 Huston Street SP 8.00 3.60
25 Justin Verlander SP 12.00 5.50
26 Jered Weaver SP 12.00 5.50
27 Matt Campbell SP 8.00 3.60
28 Stephen Head SP 8.00 3.60
29 Mark Romanczuk SP 8.00 3.60
30 Jeff Clement SP 10.00 4.50
31 Mike Nickeas SP 8.00 3.60
32 Tyler Greene SP 8.00 3.60
33 Paul Janish SP 8.00 3.60
34 Jeff Larish SP 8.00 3.60
35 Eric Patterson SP 8.00 3.60
36 Dustin Pedroia SP 10.00 4.50
37 Michael Griffin SP 8.00 3.60
38 Brent Lillibridge SP 8.00 3.60
39 Danny Putnam SP 8.00 3.60
40 Seth Smith SP 10.00 4.50
41 Delmon Young SP 15.00 6.75
42 Rickie Weeks SP 10.00 4.50

2004 Upper Deck National Pride Memorabilia 2

Nm-Mt Ex-Mt
OVERALL SER.2 GU ODDS 1:12 H, 1:24 R
BBJ Brian Bruney Jsy 5.00 1.50
CBJ Chris Burke Jsy 5.00 1.50
CBP Chris Burke Pants 5.00 1.50
DUJ Justin Duchscherer Jsy 5.00 1.50
DUP Justin Duchscherer Pants 5.00 1.50
ERJ Eddie Rodriguez CO Jsy 5.00 1.50
ERP Eddie Rodriguez CO Pants 5.00 1.50
EYJ Ernie Young Jsy 5.00 1.50
GGJ Gabe Gross Jsy 5.00 1.50
GKJ Graham Koonce Jsy 5.00 1.50
GKP Graham Koonce Pants 5.00 1.50
GLJ Gerald Laird Jsy 5.00 1.50
GSJ Grady Sizemore Jsy 5.00 1.50
GSP Grady Sizemore Pants 5.00 1.50
HRJ Horacio Ramirez Jsy 5.00 1.50
HRP Horacio Ramirez Pants 5.00 1.50
JBJ John Van Benschoten Jsy 5.00 1.50
JBP John Van Benschoten Pants 5.00 1.50
JCJ Jesse Crain Jsy 8.00 2.40
JCP Jesse Crain Pants 8.00 2.40
JDJ J.D. Durbin Jsy 5.00 1.50
JGJ John Grabow Jsy 5.00 1.50
JHJ J.J. Hardy Jsy 5.00 1.50
JLJ Justin Leone Jsy 8.00 2.40
JLP Justin Leone Pants 8.00 2.40
JMJ Joe Mauer Jsy 15.00 4.50
JMP Joe Mauer Pants 15.00 4.50
JRJ Jeremy Reed Jsy 10.00 3.00
JSJ Jason Stanford Jsy 5.00 1.50
JSP Jason Stanford Pants 5.00 1.50
MLJ Mike Lamb Jsy 5.00 1.50
MRJ Mike Rouse Jsy 5.00 1.50
MRP Mike Rouse Pants 5.00 1.50
RMP Ryan Madson Pants 5.00 1.50
RRJ Royce Ring Jsy 5.00 1.50
RRP Royce Ring Pants 5.00 1.50
TBJ Thad Bosley CO Jsy 5.00 1.50
TWJ Todd Williams Jsy 5.00 1.50

2004 Upper Deck Peak Performers Jersey

Nm-Mt Ex-Mt
*GOLD: .6X TO 1.5X BASIC
GOLD PRINT RUN 165 SERIAL #'d SETS
OVERALL SER.2 GU ODDS 1:12 H, 1:24 R
AP Albert Pujols 15.00 4.50
AS Alfonso Soriano 8.00 2.40
BE Josh Beckett 5.00 1.50
BP Brandon Phillips 5.00 1.50
CB Craig Biggio 8.00 2.40
CD Carlos Delgado 5.00 1.50
CS Curt Schilling 8.00 2.40
EG Eric Gagne 8.00 2.40
FT Frank Thomas 8.00 2.40
HB Hank Blalock 5.00 1.50
HM Hideki Matsui 25.00 7.50
HN Hideo Nomo 8.00 2.40
IR Ivan Rodriguez 8.00 2.40
IS Ichiro Suzuki 25.00 7.50
JB Jeff Bagwell 8.00 2.40
JR Jose Reyes 5.00 1.50
JT Jim Thome 8.00 2.40
KG Ken Griffey Jr. 15.00 4.50
KW Kerry Wood 8.00 2.40
LB Lance Berkman 5.00 1.50
LC Luis Castillo 5.00 1.50
MM Mike Mussina 8.00 2.40
MO Magglio Ordonez 5.00 1.50
MP Mark Prior 8.00 2.40
MT Miguel Tejada 5.00 1.50
OV Omar Vizquel 8.00 2.40
PB Pat Burrell 5.00 1.50
PE Andy Pettitte 8.00 2.40
PL Paul Lo Duca 5.00 1.50
PM Pedro Martinez 8.00 2.40
RF Rafael Furcal 5.00 1.50
RP Rafael Palmeiro 8.00 2.40
SA C.C. Sabathia 5.00 1.50
SG Shawn Green 5.00 1.50
SR Scott Rolen 8.00 2.40
TH Todd Helton 8.00 2.40
VG Vladimir Guerrero 8.00 2.40
VW Vernon Wells 5.00 1.50

2004 Upper Deck Famous Quotes

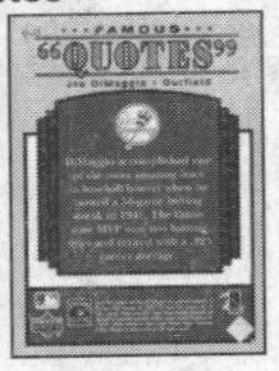

Nm-Mt Ex-Mt
COMPLETE SET (20) 40.00 12.00
SERIES 2 STATED ODDS 1:6 H/R
1 Al Lopez 2.00 .60
2 Bob Feller 2.00 .60
3 Bob Gibson 2.00 .60
4 Brooks Robinson 2.00 .60
5 Cal Ripken 8.00 2.40
6 Carl Yastrzemski 4.00 1.20
7 Earl Weaver 2.00 .60
8 Eddie Mathews 2.50 .75
9 Ernie Banks 2.50 .75
10 Greg Maddux 4.00 1.20
11 Joe DiMaggio 5.00 1.50
12 Mickey Mantle 8.00 2.40
13 Nolan Ryan 6.00 1.80
14 Stan Musial 4.00 1.20
15 Ted Williams 6.00 1.80
16 Tom Seaver 2.00 .60
17 Tommy Lasorda 2.00 .60
18 Warren Spahn 2.00 .60
19 Whitey Ford 2.00 .60
20 Yogi Berra 2.50 .75

2004 Upper Deck Signature Stars Black Ink 1

Please note that Roger Clemens did not return his cards in time for pack-out and those cards could be redeemed until November 10, 2006.

MINT NRMT
SER.1 ODDS 1:288 H,1:24 UPD BOX, 1:1800 R
PRINT RUNS B/WN 18-479 COPIES PER
NO PRICING ON QTY OF 25 OR LESS
EXCHANGE DEADLINE 11/10/06
AG Andres Galarraga/248 15.00 6.75
AH Aaron Heilman/49 25.00 11.00
BG Bob Gibson/19
BK Billy Koch/429 10.00 4.50
CR Cal Ripken/69 200.00 90.00
DR1 Dave Roberts/278 10.00 4.50
HM Hideki Matsui/25
IS1 Ichiro Suzuki/19
JRA Joe Randa/271 10.00 4.50
KI Kazuhisa Ishii/58 25.00 11.00
MO Magglio Ordonez/377 15.00 6.75
MU Mike Mussina/68 40.00 18.00
NG Nomar Garciaparra/69 150.00 70.00
NR1 Nolan Ryan/69 150.00 70.00
RA Rich Aurilia/479 10.00 4.50
RC Roger Clemens/19 EXCH
RH1 Rich Harden/163 15.00 6.75
RP Rafael Palmeiro/18
TH Torii Hunter/374 15.00 6.75
VG Vladimir Guerrero/68 60.00 27.00

2004 Upper Deck Signature Stars Black Ink 2

Nm-Mt Ex-Mt
OVERALL SER.2 SIG ODDS 1:288 H, 1:1500 R
PRINT RUNS B/WN 43-450 COPIES PER
BB Bret Boone/43 40.00 12.00
BW Brandon Webb/60 15.00 4.50
DB Dewon Brazelton/96 10.00 3.00
DR2 Dave Roberts/450 10.00 3.00
DS Darryl Strawberry/160 25.00 7.50
DW Dontrelle Willis/160 15.00 4.50
EC Eric Chavez/60 25.00 7.50
EG Eric Gagne/160 40.00 12.00
JC Jose Canseco/160 40.00 12.00
JV Javier Vazquez/60 25.00 7.50
KG Ken Griffey Jr./450 100.00 30.00
MT Mark Teixeira/200 25.00 7.50
NR2 Nolan Ryan/95 150.00 45.00
RH2 Rich Harden/65 25.00 7.50
RW Rickie Weeks/65 25.00 7.50

2004 Upper Deck Signature Stars Blue Ink 1

MINT NRMT
SER.1 ODDS 1:288 H,1:24 UPD BOX, 1:1800 R
STATED PRINT RUN 25 SERIAL #'d SETS
MATSUI PRINT RUN 324 SERIAL #'d CARDS
NO PRICING ON QTY OF 25 OR LESS
EXCHANGE DEADLINE 11/10/06
HM Hideki Matsui/324 250.00 110.00

2004 Upper Deck Signature Stars Blue Ink 2

Nm-Mt Ex-Mt
OVERALL SER.2 SIG ODDS 1:288 H, 1:1500 R
PRINT RUNS B/WN 20-25 COPIES PER
NO PRICING DUE TO SCARCITY

2004 Upper Deck Signature Stars Red Ink 1

MINT NRMT
SER.1 ODDS 1:288 H,1:24 UPD BOX, 1:1800 R
STATED PRINT RUN 10 SERIAL #'d SETS
NO PRICING DUE TO SCARCITY
EXCHANGE DEADLINE 11/10/06

2004 Upper Deck Signature Stars Red Ink 2

Nm-Mt Ex-Mt
OVERALL SER.2 SIG ODDS 1:288 H, 1:1500 R
PRINT RUNS B/WN 5-10 COPIES PER
NO PRICING DUE TO SCARCITY

2004 Upper Deck Signature Stars Gold

MINT NRMT
SER.1 ODDS 1:288 H, 1:24 MINI, 1:1800 R
STATED PRINT RUN 99 SERIAL #'d SETS
ALL EXCEPT MATSUI FEATURE BLUE INK
NO PRICING DUE TO SCARCITY
EXCHANGE DEADLINE 11/10/06

2004 Upper Deck Super Patch Logos 2

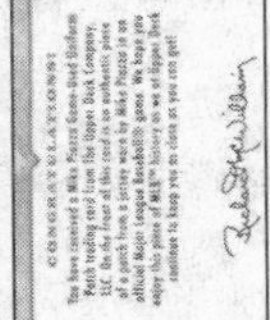

Nm-Mt Ex-Mt
OVERALL SERIES 2 ODDS 1:2500 H/R
PRINT RUNS B/WN 8-34 COPIES PER
PRINT RUNS PROVIDED BY UPPER DECK
CARDS ARE NOT SERIAL-NUMBERED
NO PRICING DUE TO SCARCITY
HU Torii Hunter/32
MP Mike Piazza/22
PM Pedro Martinez/10
RJ Randy Johnson/20
RP Rafael Palmeiro/8
RS Richie Sexson/9
SS Sammy Sosa/16
TH Todd Helton/29
VG Vladimir Guerrero/34
VW Vernon Wells/13

2004 Upper Deck Super Patches Logos 1

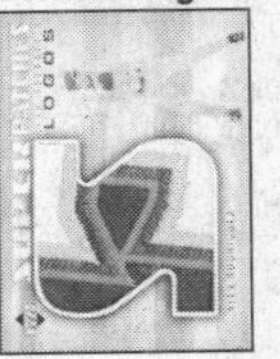

MINT NRMT
OVERALL PATCH SERIES 1 ODDS 1:7500
PRINT RUNS B/WN 8-25 COPIES PER
PRINT RUNS PROVIDED BY UPPER DECK
NO PRICING DUE TO SCARCITY
AD Adam Dunn/8
AJ Andruw Jones/25
AP Albert Pujols/20
AR Alex Rodriguez/20
AS Alfonso Soriano/10
CJ Chipper Jones/25
CS Curt Schilling/20
GM Greg Maddux/25
HM Hideki Matsui /10
IS Ichiro Suzuki/20

2004 Upper Deck Super Patch Numbers 2

MINT Ex-Mt
OVERALL SERIES 2 ODDS 1:2500 H/R
PRINT RUNS B/WN 2-45 COPIES PER
PRINT RUNS PROVIDED BY UPPER DECK
CARDS ARE NOT SERIAL-NUMBERED
NO PRICING DUE TO SCARCITY
BE Josh Beckett/17
IR Ivan Rodriguez/2
JB Jeff Bagwell/14
JK Jeff Kent/2
JT Jim Thome/21
KG Ken Griffey Jr./45
LB Lance Berkman/12
MR Manny Ramirez/10

2004 Upper Deck Super Patches Numbers 1

MINT NRMT
OVERALL PATCH SERIES 1 ODDS 1:7500
PRINT RUNS B/WN 10-25 COPIES PER
PRINT RUNS PROVIDED BY UPPER DECK
NO PRICING DUE TO SCARCITY
IR Ivan Rodriguez/14
JB Jeff Bagwell/16
JG Jason Giambi/10
JK Jeff Kent/20
JT Jim Thome/25
KG Ken Griffey Jr./15
LB Lance Berkman/10
MP Mark Prior/20
MR Manny Ramirez/18
SS Sammy Sosa/15

2004 Upper Deck Super Patch Stripes 2

Nm-Mt Ex-Mt
OVERALL SERIES 2 ODDS 1:2500 H/R
PRINT RUNS B/WN 6-65 COPIES PER
PRINT RUNS PROVIDED BY UPPER DECK
CARDS ARE NOT SERIAL-NUMBERED
NO PRICING DUE TO SCARCITY
AJ Andruw Jones/52

AP Albert Pujols/37
AR Alex Rodriguez/65
AS Alfonso Soriano/6
CJ Chipper Jones/37
CS Curt Schilling/14
GM Greg Maddux/19
HN Hideo Nomo/27
IS Ichiro Suzuki/29

2004 Upper Deck Super Patches Stripes 1

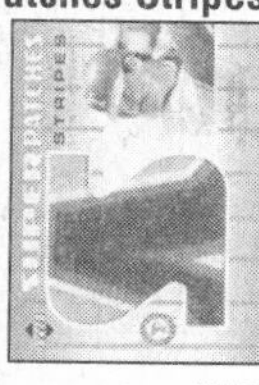

MINT NRMT
OVERALL PATCH SERIES 1 ODDS 1:7500
PRINT RUNS B/WN 25-40 COPIES PER
PRINT RUNS PROVIDED BY UPPER DECK
NO PRICING DUE TO SCARCITY
MP Mike Piazza/30
PM Pedro Martinez/25
RB Rocco Baldelli/30
RC Roger Clemens/30
RJ Randy Johnson/30
RP Rafael Palmeiro/40
SS Sammy Sosa/30
TH Todd Helton/30
TH Torii Hunter/30
VG Vladimir Guerrero/40

2004 Upper Deck Super Sluggers

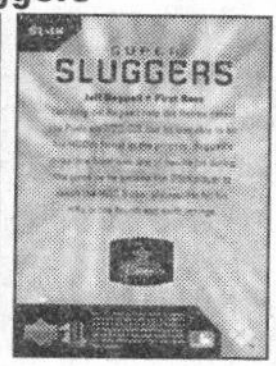

Nm-Mt Ex-Mt
COMPLETE SET (30) 25.00 7.50
ONE PER SERIES 2 RETAIL PACK
1 Albert Pujols 2.50 .75
2 Alex Rodriguez 2.00 .60
3 Alfonso Soriano 1.00 .30
4 Andruw Jones 1.00 .30
5 Bret Boone 1.00 .30
6 Carlos Delgado 1.00 .30
7 Edgar Renteria 1.00 .30
8 Eric Chavez 1.00 .30
9 Frank Thomas 1.25 .35
10 Garret Anderson 1.00 .30
11 Gary Sheffield 1.00 .30
12 Jason Giambi 1.00 .30
13 Javy Lopez 1.00 .30
14 Jeff Bagwell 1.00 .30
15 Jim Edmonds 1.00 .30
16 Jim Thome 1.25 .35
17 Jorge Posada 1.00 .30
18 Lance Berkman 1.00 .30
19 Magglio Ordonez 1.00 .30
20 Manny Ramirez 1.00 .30
21 Mike Lowell 1.00 .30
22 Nomar Garciaparra 2.00 .60
23 Preston Wilson 1.00 .30
24 Rafael Palmeiro 1.00 .30
25 Richie Sexson 1.00 .30
26 Sammy Sosa 2.00 .60
27 Shawn Green 1.00 .30
28 Todd Helton 1.00 .30
29 Vernon Wells 1.00 .30
30 Vladimir Guerrero 1.25 .35

2004 Upper Deck Twenty-Five Salute

MINT NRMT
COMPLETE SET (10) 20.00 9.00
SERIES 1 STATED ODDS 1:12
1 Barry Bonds 6.00 2.70
2 Troy Glaus 2.00 .90
3 Andruw Jones 2.00 .90
4 Jay Gibbons 2.00 .90
5 Jeremy Giambi 2.00 .90
6 Jason Giambi 2.00 .90
7 Jim Thome 2.50 1.10
8 Rafael Palmeiro 2.00 .90
9 Carlos Delgado 2.00 .90
10 Dmitri Young 2.00 .90

2005 Upper Deck

Nm-Mt Ex-Mt
COMPLETE SERIES 1 (300) 50.00 15.00
COMMON (1-210) .30 .09
COMMON CARD (211-250) 1.00 .30
OVERALL PLATES SER.1 ODDS 1:1080 H
PLATES PRINT RUN 1 #'d SET PER COLOR
BLACK-CYAN-MAGENTA-YELLOW ISSUED
NO PLATES PRICING DUE TO SCARCITY

1 Casey Kotchman .50 .15
2 Chone Figgins .30 .09
3 David Eckstein .30 .09
4 Jarrod Washburn .30 .09
5 Robb Quinlan .30 .09
6 Troy Glaus .30 .09
7 Vladimir Guerrero .75 .23
8 Brandon Webb .30 .09
9 Danny Bautista .30 .09
10 Luis Gonzalez .30 .09
11 Matt Kata .30 .09
12 Randy Johnson .75 .23
13 Robby Hammock .30 .09
14 Shea Hillenbrand .30 .09
15 Adam LaRoche .30 .09
16 Andruw Jones .30 .09
17 Horacio Ramirez .30 .09
18 John Smoltz .50 .15
19 Johnny Estrada .30 .09
20 Mike Hampton .30 .09
21 Rafael Furcal .30 .09
22 Brian Roberts .30 .09
23 Javy Lopez .30 .09
24 Jay Gibbons .30 .09
25 Jorge Julio .30 .09
26 Melvin Mora .30 .09
27 Miguel Tejada .30 .09
28 Rafael Palmeiro .50 .15
29 Derek Lowe .30 .09
30 Jason Varitek .50 .15
31 Kevin Youkilis .30 .09
32 Manny Ramirez .50 .15
33 Curt Schilling .75 .23
34 Pedro Martinez .75 .23
35 Trot Nixon .30 .09
36 Corey Patterson .30 .09
37 Derrek Lee .30 .09
38 LaTroy Hawkins .30 .09
39 Mark Prior .75 .23
40 Matt Clement .30 .09
41 Moises Alou .30 .09
42 Sammy Sosa 1.25 .35
43 Aaron Rowand .30 .09
44 Carlos Lee .30 .09
45 Jose Valentin .30 .09
46 Juan Uribe .30 .09
47 Magglio Ordonez .30 .09
48 Mark Buehrle .30 .09
49 Paul Konerko .30 .09
50 Adam Dunn .50 .15
51 Barry Larkin .50 .15
52 D'Angelo Jimenez .30 .09
53 Danny Graves .30 .09
54 Paul Wilson .30 .09
55 Sean Casey .30 .09
56 Wily Mo Pena .30 .09
57 Ben Broussard .30 .09
58 C.C. Sabathia .30 .09
59 Casey Blake .30 .09
60 Cliff Lee .30 .09
61 Matt Lawton .30 .09
62 Omar Vizquel .30 .09
63 Victor Martinez .30 .09
64 Charles Johnson .30 .09
65 Joe Kennedy .30 .09
66 Jeromy Burnitz .30 .09
67 Matt Holliday .30 .09
68 Preston Wilson .30 .09
69 Royce Clayton .30 .09
70 Shawn Estes .30 .09
71 Bobby Higginson .30 .09
72 Brandon Inge .30 .09
73 Carlos Guillen .30 .09
74 Dmitri Young .30 .09
75 Eric Munson .30 .09
76 Jeremy Bonderman .30 .09
77 Ugueth Urbina .30 .09
78 Josh Beckett .30 .09
79 Dontrelle Willis .30 .09
80 Jeff Conine .30 .09
81 Juan Pierre .30 .09
82 Luis Castillo .30 .09
83 Miguel Cabrera .50 .15
84 Mike Lowell .30 .09
85 Andy Pettitte .50 .15
86 Brad Lidge .30 .09
87 Carlos Beltran .50 .15
88 Craig Biggio .50 .15
89 Jeff Bagwell .50 .15
90 Roger Clemens 1.50 .45
91 Roy Oswalt .30 .09
92 Benito Santiago .30 .09
93 Jeremy Affeldt .30 .09
94 Juan Gonzalez .50 .15
95 Ken Harvey .30 .09
96 Mike MacDougal .30 .09
97 Mike Sweeney .30 .09
98 Zach Greinke .30 .09
99 Adrian Beltre .50 .15
100 Alex Cora .30 .09
101 Cesar Izturis .30 .09
102 Eric Gagne .75 .23
103 Kazuhisa Ishii .30 .09
104 Milton Bradley .30 .09
105 Shawn Green .30 .09
106 Danny Kolb .30 .09
107 Ben Sheets .30 .09
108 Brooks Kieschnick .30 .09
109 Craig Counsell .30 .09
110 Geoff Jenkins .30 .09
111 Lyle Overbay .30 .09
112 Scott Podsednik .30 .09
113 Corey Koskie .30 .09
114 Johan Santana .50 .15
115 Joe Mauer .50 .15
116 Justin Morneau .30 .09
117 Lew Ford .30 .09
118 Matt LeCroy .30 .09
119 Torii Hunter .30 .09
120 Brad Wilkerson .30 .09
121 Chad Cordero .30 .09
122 Livan Hernandez .30 .09
123 Jose Vidro .30 .09
124 Termel Sledge .30 .09
125 Tony Batista .30 .09
126 Zach Day .30 .09
127 Al Leiter .30 .09
128 Jae Weong Seo .30 .09
129 Jose Reyes .30 .09
130 Kazuo Matsui .30 .09
131 Mike Piazza 1.25 .35
132 Todd Zeile .30 .09
133 Cliff Floyd .30 .09
134 Alex Rodriguez 1.25 .35
135 Derek Jeter 1.50 .45
136 Gary Sheffield .30 .09
137 Hideki Matsui 1.25 .35
138 Jason Giambi .30 .09
139 Jorge Posada .50 .15
140 Mike Mussina .50 .15
141 Barry Zito .30 .09
142 Bobby Crosby .30 .09
143 Octavio Dotel .30 .09
144 Eric Chavez .30 .09
145 Jermaine Dye .30 .09
146 Mark Kotsay .30 .09
147 Tim Hudson .30 .09
148 Billy Wagner .30 .09
149 Bobby Abreu .30 .09
150 David Bell .30 .09
151 Jim Thome .75 .23
152 Jimmy Rollins .30 .09
153 Mike Lieberthal .30 .09
154 Randy Wolf .30 .09
155 Craig Wilson .30 .09
156 Daryle Ward .30 .09
157 Jack Wilson .30 .09
158 Jason Kendall .30 .09
159 Kip Wells .30 .09
160 Oliver Perez .30 .09
161 Rob Mackowiak .30 .09
162 Brian Giles .30 .09
163 Brian Lawrence .30 .09
164 David Wells .30 .09
165 Jay Payton .30 .09
166 Ryan Klesko .30 .09
167 Sean Burroughs .30 .09
168 Trevor Hoffman .30 .09
169 Brett Tomko .30 .09
170 J.T. Snow .30 .09
171 Jason Schmidt .30 .09
172 Kirk Rueter .30 .09
173 A.J. Pierzynski .30 .09
174 Pedro Feliz .30 .09
175 Ray Durham .30 .09
176 Eddie Guardado .30 .09
177 Edgar Martinez .50 .15
178 Ichiro Suzuki 1.25 .35
179 Jamie Moyer .30 .09
180 Joel Pineiro .30 .09
181 Randy Winn .30 .09
182 Raul Ibanez .30 .09
183 Albert Pujols 1.50 .45
184 Edgar Renteria .30 .09
185 Jason Isringhausen .30 .09
186 Jim Edmonds .30 .09
187 Matt Morris .30 .09
188 Reggie Sanders .30 .09
189 Tony Womack .30 .09
190 Aubrey Huff .30 .09
191 Danys Baez .30 .09
192 Carl Crawford .30 .09
193 Jose Cruz Jr. .30 .09
194 Rocco Baldelli .30 .09
195 Tino Martinez .50 .15
196 Dewon Brazelton .30 .09
197 Alfonso Soriano .50 .15
198 Brad Fullmer .30 .09
199 Gerald Laird .30 .09
200 Hank Blalock .30 .09
201 Laynce Nix .30 .09
202 Mark Teixeira .30 .09
203 Michael Young .30 .09
204 Alexis Rios .30 .09
205 Eric Hinske .30 .09
206 Miguel Batista .30 .09
207 Orlando Hudson .30 .09
208 Roy Halladay .30 .09
209 Ted Lilly .30 .09
210 Vernon Wells .30 .09
211 Aarom Baldiris SR 1.00 .30
212 B.J. Upton SR 1.50 .45
213 Dallas McPherson SR 1.50 .45
214 Brian Dallimore SR 1.00 .30
215 Chris Oxspring SR 1.00 .30
216 Chris Shelton SR 1.00 .30
217 David Wright SR 2.00 .60
218 Edwardo Sierra SR 1.00 .30
219 Fernando Nieve SR 1.00 .30
220 Frank Francisco SR 1.00 .30
221 Jeff Bennett SR 1.00 .30
222 Justin Lehr SR 1.00 .30
223 John Gall SR 1.00 .30
224 Jorge Sequea SR 1.00 .30
225 Justin Germano SR 1.00 .30
226 Kazuhito Tadano SR 1.00 .30
227 Kevin Cave SR 1.00 .30
228 Joe Blanton SR 1.00 .30
229 Luis A. Gonzalez SR 1.00 .30
230 Michael Wuertz SR 1.00 .30
231 Mike Rouse SR 1.00 .30
232 Nick Regilio SR 1.00 .30
233 Orlando Rodriguez SR 1.00 .30
234 Phil Stockman SR 1.00 .30
235 Ramon Ramirez SR 1.00 .30
236 Roberto Novoa SR 1.00 .30
237 Dioner Navarro SR 1.00 .30
238 Tim Bausher SR 1.00 .30
239 Logan Kensing SR 1.00 .30
240 Andy Green SR 1.00 .30
241 Brad Halsey SR 1.00 .30
242 Charles Thomas SR 1.00 .30
243 George Sherrill SR 1.00 .30
244 Jesse Crain SR 1.00 .30
245 Jimmy Serrano SR 1.00 .30
246 Joe Horgan SR 1.00 .30
247 Chris Young SR 1.00 .30
248 Joey Gathright SR 1.00 .30
249 Gavin Floyd SR 1.00 .30
250 Ryan Howard SR 1.00 .30
251 Lance Cormier SR 1.00 .30
252 Matt Treanor SR 1.00 .30
253 Jeff Francis SR 1.00 .30
254 Nick Swisher SR 1.50 .30
255 Scott Atchison SR 1.00 .30
256 Travis Blackley SR 1.00 .30
257 Travis Smith SR 1.00 .30
258 Yadier Molina SR 1.00 .30
259 Jeff Keppinger SR 1.00 .30
260 Scott Kazmir SR 1.50 .45
261 Garret Anderson .50 .15
Vladimir Guerrero TL
262 Luis Gonzalez .50 .15
Randy Johnson TL
263 Andruw Jones .50 .15
Chipper Jones TL
264 Miguel Tejada .30 .09
Rafael Palmeiro TL
265 Curt Schilling .75 .23
Manny Ramirez TL
266 Mark Prior .75 .23
Sammy Sosa TL
267 Frank Thomas .50 .15
Magglio Ordonez TL
268 Barry Larkin .75 .23
Ken Griffey Jr. TL
269 C.C. Sabathia .30 .09
Victor Martinez TL
270 Jeromy Burnitz .30 .09
Todd Helton TL
271 Dmitri Young .50 .15
Ivan Rodriguez TL
272 Josh Beckett .30 .09
Miguel Cabrera TL
273 Jeff Bagwell .75 .23
Roger Clemens TL
274 Ken Harvey .30 .09
Mike Sweeney TL
275 Adrian Beltre .30 .09
Eric Gagne TL
276 Ben Sheets .30 .09
Geoff Jenkins TL
277 Joe Mauer .30 .09
Torii Hunter TL
278 Jose Vidro .30 .09
Livan Hernandez TL
279 Kazuo Matsui .75 .23
Mike Piazza TL
280 Alex Rodriguez 1.50 .45
Derek Jeter TL
281 Eric Chavez .30 .09
Tim Hudson TL
282 Bobby Abreu .50 .15
Jim Thome TL
283 Craig Wilson .30 .09
Jason Kendall TL
284 Brian Giles .30 .09
Phil Nevin TL
285 A.J. Pierzynski .30 .09
Jason Schmidt TL
286 Bret Boone .75 .23
Ichiro Suzuki TL
287 Albert Pujols .75 .23
Scott Rolen TL
288 Aubrey Huff .30 .09
Tino Martinez TL
289 Hank Blalock .30 .09
Mark Teixeira TL
290 Carlos Delgado .30 .09
Roy Halladay TL
291 Vladimir Guerrero PR .50 .15
292 Curt Schilling PR .50 .15
293 Mark Prior PR .50 .15
294 Josh Beckett PR .30 .09
295 Roger Clemens PR .75 .23
296 Derek Jeter PR .75 .23
297 Eric Chavez PR .30 .09
298 Jim Thome PR .50 .15
299 Albert Pujols PR .75 .23
300 Hank Blalock PR .30 .09

2005 Upper Deck American Flag

Nm-Mt Ex-Mt
SERIES 1 STATED ODDS 1:220 HOBBY
STATED PRINT RUN 15 SERIAL #'d SETS
NO PRICING DUE TO SCARCITY
OVERALL PLATES SER.1 ODDS 1:1080 H
PLATES PRINT RUN 1 #'d SET PER COLOR
BLACK-CYAN-MAGENTA-YELLOW ISSUED
NO PLATES PRICING DUE TO SCARCITY

2005 Upper Deck Retro

Nm-Mt Ex-Mt
*RETRO: 1.25X TO 3X BASIC
ONE RETRO BOX PER SER.1 HOBBY CASE
SER.1 HOBBY CASES CONTAIN 12 BOXES
OVERALL PLATES SER.1 ODDS 1:1080 H
PLATES PRINT RUN 1 #'d SET PER COLOR
BLACK-CYAN-MAGENTA-YELLOW ISSUED
NO PLATES PRICING DUE TO SCARCITY

2005 Upper Deck 4000 Strikeout

Nm-Mt Ex-Mt
RANDOM INSERTS IN SERIES 1 PACKS
STATED PRINT RUN 4000 SERIAL #'d SETS
CRCJ Steve Carlton 15.00 4.50
Nolan Ryan
Roger Clemens
Randy Johnson/4000

2005 Upper Deck 4000 Strikeout Autographs

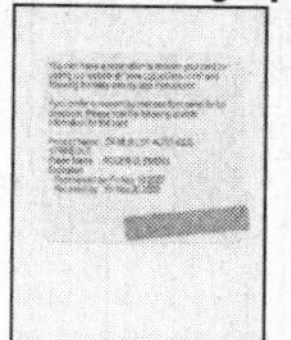

Nm-Mt Ex-Mt
RANDOM INSERTS IN SERIES 1 PACKS
STATED PRINT RUN 50 SERIAL #'d SETS
QUAD PRINT RUN 10 SERIAL #'d CARDS
NO QUAD PRICING DUE TO SCARCITY
ALL ARE EXCHANGE CARDS
EXCHANGE DEADLINE 11/16/07
NR Nolan Ryan AU/50
Steve Carlton
Roger Clemens
Randy Johnson
RC Roger Clemens AU/50
Steve Carlton
Nolan Ryan
Randy Johnson
RJ Randy Johnson AU/50
Steve Carlton
Nolan Ryan
Roger Clemens
SC Steve Carlton AU/50
Nolan Ryan
Roger Clemens
Randy Johnson
CRCJ Steve Carlton AU
Nolan Ryan AU
Roger Clemens AU
Randy Johnson AU/10

2005 Upper Deck Baseball Heroes Jeter

Nm-Mt Ex-Mt
COMPLETE SET (9) 30.00 9.00
COMMON CARD (91-99) 4.00 1.20
SERIES 1 STATED ODDS 1:6 H/R

2005 Upper Deck Baseball Heroes Jeter Jersey

Nm-Mt Ex-Mt
COMMON CARD (1-9)
SERIES 1 STATED ODDS 1:3500 H/R
STATED PRINT RUN 75 SERIAL #'d SETS

2005 Upper Deck Baseball Heroes Jeter Signature

Nm-Mt Ex-Mt
SERIES 1 STATED ODDS 1:1,200,000 H/R
STATED PRINT RUN 2 SERIAL #'d SETS
NO PRICING DUE TO SCARCITY

2005 Upper Deck Hall of Fame Plaques

Nm-Mt Ex-Mt
SERIES 1 STATED ODDS 1:36 H/R
16 Ernie Banks 8.00 2.40
17 Yogi Berra 8.00 2.40
18 Whitey Ford 8.00 2.40
19 Bob Gibson 8.00 2.40
20 Willie McCovey 8.00 2.40
21 Stan Musial 10.00 3.00
22 Nolan Ryan 15.00 4.50
23 Mike Schmidt 10.00 3.00
24 Tom Seaver 8.00 2.40
25 Robin Yount 10.00 3.00

2005 Upper Deck Marquee Attractions Jersey

Nm-Mt Ex-Mt
SER.1 OVERALL GU ODDS 1:12 H
AD Adam Dunn 10.00 3.00
AJ Andruw Jones 8.00 2.40

AP Albert Pujols 15.00 4.50
BE Josh Beckett 8.00 2.40
BG Brian Giles 8.00 2.40
BW Billy Wagner 8.00 2.40
CD Carlos Delgado 8.00 2.40
CJ Chipper Jones 10.00 3.00
CS Curt Schilling 10.00 3.00
DJ Derek Jeter 20.00 6.00
DW Dontrelle Willis 8.00 2.40
EG Eric Gagne 10.00 3.00
GM Greg Maddux 12.00 3.60
HM Hideki Matsui 25.00 7.50
HN Hideo Nomo 10.00 3.00
HO Trevor Hoffman 8.00 2.40
IR Ivan Rodriguez 10.00 3.00
IS Ichiro Suzuki 25.00 7.50
JB Jeff Bagwell 10.00 3.00
JG Jason Giambi 8.00 2.40
JM Joe Mauer 10.00 3.00
JS Jason Schmidt 8.00 2.40
JT Jim Thome 10.00 3.00
KB Kevin Brown 8.00 2.40
KM Kazuo Matsui 8.00 2.40
KW Kerry Wood 10.00 3.00
MC Miguel Cabrera 10.00 3.00
MP Mark Prior 10.00 3.00
MT Miguel Tejada 8.00 2.40
PE Andy Pettitte 10.00 3.00
PI Mike Piazza 12.00 3.60
PM Pedro Martinez 10.00 3.00
PW Preston Wilson 8.00 2.40
RC Roger Clemens 12.00 3.60
RJ Randy Johnson 10.00 3.00
SG Shawn Green 8.00 2.40
SS Sammy Sosa 12.00 3.60
TH Todd Helton 10.00 3.00
VG Vladimir Guerrero 10.00 3.00

2005 Upper Deck Marquee Attractions Jersey Gold

Nm-Mt Ex-Mt
*GOLD: .6X TO 1.5X BASIC
SER.1 OVERALL GU ODDS 1:12 H
GA Garret Anderson 12.00 3.60
KG Ken Griffey Jr.
RO Roy Oswalt 12.00 3.60

2005 Upper Deck Matinee Idols Jersey

Nm-Mt Ex-Mt
SER.1 OVERALL GU ODDS 1:12 H, 1:24 R
SP INFO PROVIDED BY UPPER DECK
BB Bret Boone SP 10.00 3.00
BE Josh Beckett 8.00 2.40
BW Billy Wagner 8.00 2.40
BZ Barry Zito 8.00 2.40
CD Carlos Delgado 8.00 2.40
CJ Chipper Jones 10.00 3.00
CR Cal Ripken 40.00 12.00
CS Curt Schilling 10.00 3.00
DJ Derek Jeter 20.00 6.00
DW Dontrelle Willis 8.00 2.40
EC Eric Chavez 8.00 2.40
GS Gary Sheffield 8.00 2.40
HB Hank Blalock 8.00 2.40
HU Torii Hunter 8.00 2.40
JB Jeff Bagwell 10.00 3.00
JE Jim Edmonds 8.00 2.40
JG Jason Giambi 8.00 2.40
JT Jim Thome 10.00 3.00
KG Ken Griffey Jr. 15.00 4.50
KW Kerry Wood 10.00 3.00
ML Mike Lowell 10.00 3.00
MM Mike Mussina 10.00 3.00
MP Mark Prior 10.00 3.00
MT Mark Teixeira 8.00 2.40
NR Nolan Ryan 40.00 12.00
PB Pat Burrell 8.00 2.40
PI Mike Piazza 12.00 3.60
RB Rocco Baldelli 8.00 2.40
RC Roger Clemens 12.00 3.60
RH Roy Halladay 8.00 2.40
RJ Randy Johnson 10.00 3.00
RW Rickie Weeks 8.00 2.40
SG Shawn Green 8.00 2.40
SR Scott Rolen 10.00 3.00
SS Sammy Sosa 12.00 3.60
TG Troy Glaus 8.00 2.40
TH Todd Helton 10.00 3.00
TS Tom Seaver 15.00 4.50
VG Vladimir Guerrero 10.00 3.00
VW Vernon Wells 8.00 2.40

2005 Upper Deck Origins Jersey

Nm-Mt Ex-Mt
SER.1 OVERALL GU ODDS 1:12 H, 1:24 R
AB Adrian Beltre 10.00 3.00
AJ Andruw Jones 8.00 2.40
AP Albert Pujols 15.00 4.50
AS Alfonso Soriano 10.00 3.00

BG Brian Giles 8.00 2.40
BU B.J. Upton 10.00 3.00
CB Carlos Beltran 10.00 3.00
EG Eric Gagne 10.00 3.00
GA Garret Anderson 8.00 2.40
GM Greg Maddux 12.00 3.60
HM Hideki Matsui 25.00 7.50
HN Hideo Nomo 10.00 3.00
IR Ivan Rodriguez 10.00 3.00
IS Ichiro Suzuki 25.00 7.50
JG Juan Gonzalez 10.00 3.00
JK Jeff Kent 8.00 2.40
JL Javy Lopez 8.00 2.40
JP Jorge Posada 10.00 3.00
JR Jose Reyes 8.00 2.40
JS Jason Schmidt 8.00 2.40
JV Javier Vazquez 8.00 2.40
KM Kazuo Matsui 8.00 2.40
LB Lance Berkman 8.00 2.40
LG Luis Gonzalez
MC Miguel Cabrera 10.00 3.00
MM Mark Mulder 8.00 2.40
MO Magglio Ordonez 8.00 2.40
MR Manny Ramirez 10.00 3.00
MT Miguel Tejada 8.00 2.40
PE Jake Peavy 8.00 2.40
PM Pedro Martinez 10.00 3.00
PW Preston Wilson 8.00 2.40
RF Rafael Furcal 8.00 2.40
RP Rafael Palmeiro 10.00 3.00
RS Richie Sexson 8.00 2.40
SS Sammy Sosa 12.00 3.60
TH Tim Hudson 8.00 2.40
VG Vladimir Guerrero 10.00 3.00

2005 Upper Deck Signature Stars Hobby

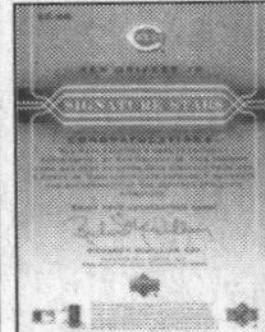

Nm-Mt Ex-Mt
SERIES 1 STATED ODDS 1:288 HOBBY
SP INFO PROVIDED BY UPPER DECK
BB Bret Boone
BC Bobby Crosby 25.00 7.50
BS Ben Sheets 15.00 4.50
BZ Barry Zito
CB Carlos Beltran SP
CR Cal Ripken SP 200.00 60.00
DW Dontrelle Willis 15.00 4.50
DY Delmon Young 25.00 7.50
HB Hank Blalock 25.00 7.50
JB Josh Beckett SP
JL Javy Lopez 15.00 4.50
JM Joe Mauer 25.00 7.50
KG Ken Griffey Jr. 100.00 30.00
KW Kerry Wood 40.00 12.00
LB Lance Berkman SP
LF Lew Ford 15.00 4.50
MC Miguel Cabrera 25.00 7.50
MO Magglio Ordonez SP
MP Mark Prior
MT Mark Teixeira SP
NG Nomar Garciaparra SP
OP Odalis Perez
RO Roy Oswalt SP
RW Rickie Weeks SP

2005 Upper Deck Signature Stars Retail

Nm-Mt Ex-Mt
SERIES 1 STATED ODDS 1:480 RETAIL
SP INFO PROVIDED BY UPPER DECK
BB1 Bret Boone
CB1 Carlos Beltran
JB1 Josh Beckett SP
KG1 Ken Griffey Jr.
KW1 Kerry Wood
MC1 Miguel Cabrera
MO1 Magglio Ordonez
MP1 Mark Prior SP
NG1 Nomar Garciaparra

2005 Upper Deck Super Patch Logos

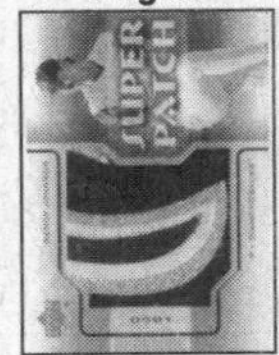

Nm-Mt Ex-Mt
SER.1 OVERALL GU ODDS 1:12 H, 1:24 R
PRINT RUNS B/WN 8-34 COPIES PER
CARDS ARE NOT SERIAL-NUMBERED
PRINT RUNS PROVIDED BY UPPER DECK
AP Albert Pujols/34 *
BZ Barry Zito/26 *
JT Jim Thome/28 *
KW Kerry Wood/24 *
MP Mike Piazza/24 *
MR Manny Ramirez/8 *
MT Miguel Tejada/24 *
RH Roy Halladay/24 *
RJ Randy Johnson/24 *
SG Shawn Green/24 *

2005 Upper Deck Super Patch Names

Nm-Mt Ex-Mt
SER.1 OVERALL GU ODDS 1:12 H, 1:24 R
PRINT RUNS B/WN 10-78 COPIES PER
CARDS ARE NOT SERIAL-NUMBERED
PRINT RUNS PROVIDED BY UPPER DECK
CB Carlos Beltran/10 *
JR Jose Reyes/16 *
KG Ken Griffey Jr./78 *
MC Miguel Cabrera/27 *
RC Roger Clemens/31 *
RS Richie Sexson/23 *
SS Sammy Sosa/25 *
VG Vladimir Guerrero/27 *

2005 Upper Deck Super Patch Numbers

Nm-Mt Ex-Mt
SER.1 OVERALL GU ODDS 1:12 H, 1:24 R
PRINT RUNS B/WN 8-34 COPIES PER
CARDS ARE NOT SERIAL-NUMBERED
PRINT RUNS PROVIDED BY UPPER DECK
BE Josh Beckett/24 *
CD Carlos Delgado/30 *
EC Eric Chavez/24 *
HN Hideo Nomo/29 *
IS Ichiro Suzuki/10 *
JB Jeff Bagwell/20 *
KM Kazuo Matsui/24 *
MP Mark Prior/24 *
MT Mark Teixeira/24 *
PM Pedro Martinez/31 *

2005 Upper Deck Wingfield Collection

Nm-Mt Ex-Mt
COMPLETE SET (20) 60.00 18.00
SERIES 1 STATED ODDS 1:9 H/R
1 Eddie Mathews 3.00 .90
2 Ernie Banks 3.00 .90
3 Joe DiMaggio 4.00 1.20
4 Mickey Mantle 10.00 3.00
5 Pee Wee Reese 3.00 .90
6 Phil Rizzuto 3.00 .90
7 Stan Musial 4.00 1.20
8 Ted Williams 5.00 1.50
9 Bob Feller 3.00 .90
10 Whitey Ford 3.00 .90
11 Willie Stargell 3.00 .90
12 Yogi Berra 3.00 .90
13 Roy Campanella 3.00 .90
14 Franklin D. Roosevelt 3.00 .90
15 Harry Truman 3.00 .90
16 Dwight D. Eisenhower 3.00 .90
17 John F. Kennedy 5.00 1.50
18 Lyndon Johnson 3.00 .90
19 Richard Nixon 3.00 .90
20 Thurman Munson 3.00 .90

2005 Upper Deck World Series Heroes

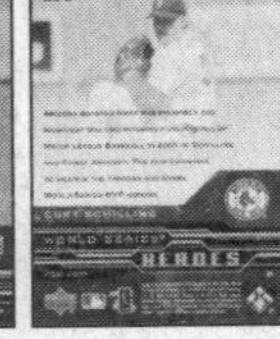

Nm-Mt Ex-Mt
COMPLETE SET (45) 25.00 7.50
SERIES 1 STATED ODDS 1:1 RETAIL
1 Garret Anderson .50 .15
2 Troy Glaus .50 .15
3 Vladimir Guerrero 1.00 .30
4 Andruw Jones .50 .15
5 Chipper Jones 1.00 .30
6 Curt Schilling 1.00 .30
7 Keith Foulke .75 .23
8 Manny Ramirez .75 .23
9 Nomar Garciaparra 1.50 .45
10 Pedro Martinez 1.00 .30
11 Kerry Wood 1.00 .30
12 Mark Prior 1.00 .30
13 Sammy Sosa 1.50 .45
14 Frank Thomas 1.00 .30
15 Magglio Ordonez .50 .15
16 Dontrelle Willis .50 .15
17 Josh Beckett .50 .15
18 Miguel Cabrera .75 .23
19 Jeff Bagwell .75 .23
20 Lance Berkman .50 .15
21 Roger Clemens 2.00 .60
22 Eric Gagne 1.00 .30
23 Torii Hunter .50 .15
24 Mike Piazza 1.50 .45
25 Alex Rodriguez 1.50 .45
26 Derek Jeter 2.00 .60
27 Gary Sheffield .50 .15
28 Hideki Matsui 1.50 .45
29 Jason Giambi .50 .15
30 Jorge Posada .75 .23
31 Kevin Brown .50 .15
32 Mariano Rivera .75 .23
33 Mike Mussina .75 .23
34 Eric Chavez .50 .15
35 Mark Mulder .50 .15
36 Tim Hudson .50 .15
37 Billy Wagner .50 .15
38 Jim Thome 1.00 .30
39 Brian Giles .50 .15
40 Jason Schmidt .50 .15
41 Albert Pujols 2.00 .60
42 Scott Rolen 1.00 .30
43 Alfonso Soriano .75 .23
44 Hank Blalock .50 .15
45 Mark Teixeira .50 .15

2002 Upper Deck 40-Man

This overwhelming 1182 card set was released in July, 2002. The set was issued in 10-card packs with an $3 SRP that were issued 24 packs to a box and 14 boxes to a case. These cards, feature just about every player on the 40 man rosters of the major league teams except for those players who had served as replacement players during the 1994-95 strike.

Nm-Mt Ex-Mt
COMPLETE SET (1182) 200.00 60.00
1 Darin Erstad .40 .12
2 Kevin Appier .40 .12
3 Scott Schoeneweis .40 .12
4 Ben Molina .40 .12
5 Troy Glaus .40 .12
6 Adam Kennedy .40 .12
7 Aaron Sele .40 .12
8 Garret Anderson .40 .12
9 Ramon Ortiz .40 .12
10 Dennis Cook .40 .12
11 Scott Spiezio .40 .12
12 Orlando Palmeiro .40 .12
13 Troy Percival .40 .12
14 David Eckstein .40 .12
15 Jarrod Washburn .40 .12
16 Nathan Haynes .40 .12
17 Benji Gil .40 .12
18 Alfredo Amezaga .40 .12
19 Ben Weber .40 .12
20 Al Levine .40 .12
21 Brad Fullmer .40 .12
22 Elpidio Guzman .40 .12
23 Tim Salmon .60 .18
24 Jose Nieves .40 .12
25 Shawn Wooten .40 .12
26 Lou Pote .40 .12
27 Mickey Callaway .40 .12
28 Steve Green .40 .12
29 John Lackey .40 .12
30 Mark Lukasiewicz .40 .12
31 Jorge Fabregas .40 .12
32 Jeff DaVanon .40 .12
33 Elvin Nina .40 .12
34 Donne Wall .40 .12
35 Eric Chavez .40 .12
36 Jermaine Dye .40 .12
37 Scott Hatteberg .40 .12
38 Mark Mulder .40 .12
39 Ramon Hernandez .40 .12
40 Jim Mecir .40 .12
41 Barry Zito .40 .12
42 Greg Myers .40 .12
43 David Justice .40 .12
44 Mike Magnante .40 .12
45 Terrence Long .40 .12
46 Tim Hudson .40 .12
47 Olmedo Saenz .40 .12
48 Billy Koch .40 .12
49 Carlos Pena .40 .12
50 Mike Venafro .40 .12
51 Mark Ellis .40 .12
52 Randy Velarde .40 .12
53 Jeremy Giambi .40 .12
54 Mike Colangelo .40 .12
55 Mike Holtz .40 .12
56 Chad Bradford .40 .12
57 Miguel Tejada .40 .12
58 Mike Fyhrie .40 .12
59 Erik Hiljus .40 .12
60 Juan Pena .40 .12
61 Mario Valdez .40 .12
62 Franklyn German RC .60 .18
63 Carlos Delgado .40 .12
64 Orlando Hudson .40 .12
65 Chris Carpenter .40 .12
66 Kelvim Escobar .40 .12
67 Felipe Lopez .40 .12
68 Brandon Lyon .40 .12
69 Jose Cruz Jr. .40 .12
70 Luke Prokopec .40 .12
71 Darrin Fletcher .40 .12
72 Bob File .40 .12
73 Felix Heredia .40 .12
74 Mike Sirotka .40 .12
75 Shannon Stewart .40 .12
76 Joe Lawrence .40 .12
77 Chris Woodward .40 .12
78 Dan Plesac .40 .12
79 Pedro Borbon .40 .12
80 Roy Halladay .40 .12
81 Raul Mondesi .40 .12
82 Steve Parris .40 .12
83 Homer Bush .40 .12
84 Esteban Loaiza .40 .12
85 Vernon Wells .40 .12
86 Justin Miller .40 .12
87 Scott Eyre .40 .12
88 Dave Berg .40 .12
89 Gustavo Chacin RC 1.00 .30
90 Joe Orloski RC .60 .18
91 Corey Thurman RC .60 .18
92 Tom Wilson RC .60 .18
93 Eric Hinske .40 .12
94 Chris Baker RC .60 .18
95 Reed Johnson RC 1.00 .30
96 Greg Vaughn .40 .12
97 Toby Hall .40 .12
98 Brent Abernathy .40 .12
99 Bobby Smith .40 .12
100 Tanyon Sturtze .40 .12
101 Chris Gomez .40 .12
102 Joe Kennedy .40 .12
103 Ben Grieve .40 .12
104 Aubrey Huff .40 .12
105 Jesus Colome .40 .12
106 Felix Escalona RC .60 .18
107 Paul Wilson .40 .12
108 Ryan Rupe .40 .12
109 Jason Tyner .40 .12
110 Esteban Yan .40 .12
111 Russ Johnson .40 .12
112 Randy Winn .40 .12
113 Wilson Alvarez .40 .12
114 Wilmy Caceres .40 .12
115 Steve Cox .40 .12
116 Dewon Brazelton .40 .12
117 Doug Creek .40 .12
118 Jason Conti .40 .12
119 John Flaherty .40 .12
120 Delvin James .40 .12
121 Steve Kent .40 .12
122 Kevin McGlinchy .40 .12
123 Travis Phelps .40 .12
124 Bobby Seay .40 .12
125 Travis Harper .40 .12
126 Victor Zambrano .40 .12
127 Jace Brewer .40 .12
128 Jason Smith .40 .12
129 Ramon Soler .40 .12
130 Brandon Backe RC 1.50 .45
131 Jorge Sosa RC .60 .18
132 Jim Thome 1.00 .30
133 Brady Anderson .40 .12
134 C.C. Sabathia .40 .12
135 Einar Diaz .40 .12
136 Ricky Gutierrez .40 .12
137 Danys Baez .40 .12
138 Bob Wickman .40 .12
139 Milton Bradley .40 .12
140 Bartolo Colon .40 .12
141 Jolbert Cabrera .40 .12
142 Eddie Taubensee .40 .12
143 Ellis Burks .40 .12
144 Omar Vizquel .60 .18
145 Eddie Perez .40 .12
146 Jaret Wright .40 .12
147 Chuck Finley .40 .12
148 Paul Shuey .40 .12
149 Travis Fryman .40 .12
150 Wil Cordero .40 .12
151 Ricardo Rincon .40 .12
152 Victor Martinez 1.00 .30
153 Charles Nagy .40 .12
154 Alex Escobar .40 .12
155 Russell Branyan .40 .12
156 Matt Lawton .40 .12
157 Ryan Drese .40 .12
158 Jerrod Riggan .40 .12
159 David Riske .40 .12
160 Jake Westbrook .40 .12
161 Mark Wohlers .40 .12
162 John McDonald .40 .12
163 Ichiro Suzuki 1.50 .45
164 Freddy Garcia .40 .12
165 Edgar Martinez .60 .18
166 Ben Davis .40 .12
167 Shigetoshi Hasegawa .40 .12
168 Carlos Guillen .40 .12
169 Ruben Sierra .40 .12
170 Joel Pineiro .40 .12
171 Norm Charlton .40 .12
172 Bret Boone .40 .12
173 Jamie Moyer .40 .12
174 Jeff Nelson .40 .12
175 Kazuhiro Sasaki .40 .12
176 Jeff Cirillo .40 .12
177 Mark McLemore .40 .12
178 Paul Abbott .40 .12
179 Mike Cameron .40 .12
180 Dan Wilson .40 .12
181 John Olerud .40 .12
182 Arthur Rhodes .40 .12
183 Desi Relaford .40 .12
184 John Halama .40 .12
185 Antonio Perez .40 .12
186 Ryan Anderson .40 .12
187 James Baldwin .40 .12
188 Ryan Franklin .40 .12
189 Justin Kaye .40 .12
190 J.J. Putz RC .60 .18
191 Allan Simpson RC .40 .12
192 Matt Thornton RC .60 .18
193 Luis Ugueto RC .60 .18
194 Chris Richard .40 .12
195 Sidney Ponson .40 .12
196 Brook Fordyce .40 .12
197 Luis Matos .40 .12
198 Josh Towers .40 .12
199 David Segui .40 .12
200 Chris Brock RC .40 .12
201 Tony Batista .40 .12
202 Erik Bedard .40 .12

203 Marty Cordova .40 .12
204 Jerry Hairston Jr. .40 .12
205 Jason Johnson .40 .12
206 Buddy Groom .40 .12
207 Mike Bordick .40 .12
208 Melvin Mora .40 .12
209 Calvin Maduro .40 .12
210 Jeff Conine .40 .12
211 Luis Rivera .40 .12
212 Jay Gibbons .40 .12
213 B.J. Ryan .40 .12
214 Sean Douglass .40 .12
215 Rodrigo Lopez .40 .12
216 Rick Bauer .40 .12
217 Scott Erickson .40 .12
218 Jorge Julio .40 .12
219 Willis Roberts .40 .12
220 John Stephens .40 .12
221 Geronimo Gil .40 .12
222 Chris Singleton .40 .12
223 Mike Paradis .40 .12
224 John Parrish .40 .12
225 Steve Bechler RC .60 .18
226 Mike Moriarty RC .40 .12
227 Luis Garcia RC .60 .18
228 Alex Rodriguez 1.50 .45
229 Mark Teixeira 1.00 .30
230 Chan Ho Park .40 .12
231 Todd Van Poppel .40 .12
232 Mike Young 1.00 .30
233 Kenny Rogers .40 .12
234 Rusty Greer .40 .12
235 Rafael Palmeiro .60 .18
236 Francisco Cordero .40 .12
237 John Rocker .40 .12
238 Dave Burba .40 .12
239 Travis Hafner .40 .12
240 Kevin Mench .40 .12
241 Carl Everett .40 .12
242 Ivan Rodriguez 1.00 .30
243 Jeff Zimmerman .40 .12
244 Juan Gonzalez .60 .18
245 Herbert Perry .40 .12
246 Rob Bell .40 .12
247 Doug Davis .40 .12
248 Frank Catalanotto .40 .12
249 Jay Powell .40 .12
250 Gabe Kapler .40 .12
251 Joaquin Benoit .40 .12
252 Jovanny Cedeno .40 .12
253 Hideki Irabu .40 .12
254 Dan Miceli .40 .12
255 Danny Kolb .40 .12
256 Colby Lewis .40 .12
257 Rich Rodriguez .40 .12
258 Ismael Valdes .40 .12
259 Bill Haselman .40 .12
260 Jason Hart .40 .12
261 Rudy Seanez .40 .12
262 Travis Hughes RC .60 .18
263 Hank Blalock 1.50 .45
264 Steve Woodard .40 .12
265 Nomar Garciaparra 1.50 .45
266 Pedro Martinez 1.00 .30
267 Frank Castillo .40 .12
268 Johnny Damon Sox 1.00 .30
269 Doug Mirabelli .40 .12
270 Derek Lowe .40 .12
271 Shea Hillenbrand .40 .12
272 Paxton Crawford .40 .12
273 Tony Clark .40 .12
274 Dustin Hermanson .40 .12
275 Trot Nixon .40 .12
276 John Burkett .40 .12
277 Rich Garces .40 .12
278 Josh Hancock RC .60 .18
279 Michael Coleman .40 .12
280 Darren Oliver .40 .12
281 Jason Varitek .60 .18
282 Jose Offerman .40 .12
283 Tim Wakefield .40 .12
284 Rolando Arrojo .40 .12
285 Rickey Henderson 1.00 .30
286 Ugueth Urbina .40 .12
287 Casey Fossum .40 .12
288 Manny Ramirez .60 .18
289 Sun-Woo Kim .40 .12
290 Juan Diaz .40 .12
291 Willie Banks .40 .12
292 Jorge De La Rosa RC .60 .18
293 Juan Pena .40 .12
294 Jeff Wallace .40 .12
295 Calvin Pickering .40 .12
296 Anastacio Martinez RC .60 .18
297 Carlos Baerga .40 .12
298 Rey Sanchez .40 .12
299 Mike Sweeney .40 .12
300 Jeff Suppan .40 .12
301 Brent Mayne .40 .12
302 Chad Durbin .40 .12
303 Dan Reichert .40 .12
304 Raul Ibanez .40 .12
305 Joe Randa .40 .12
306 Chris George .40 .12
307 Michael Tucker .40 .12
308 Paul Byrd .40 .12
309 Kris Wilson .40 .12
310 Luis Alicea .40 .12
311 Neifi Perez .40 .12
312 Brian Shouse .40 .12
313 Chuck Knoblauch .40 .12
314 Dave McCarty .40 .12
315 Blake Stein .40 .12
316 Alexis Gomez .40 .12
317 Mark Quinn .40 .12
318 A.J. Hinch .40 .12
319 Carlos Febles .40 .12
320 Roberto Hernandez .40 .12
321 Brandon Berger .40 .12
322 Jeff Austin RC .60 .18
323 Cory Bailey .40 .12
324 Tony Cogan .40 .12
325 Nate Field RC .60 .18
326 Jason Grimsley .40 .12
327 Darrell May RC .40 .12
328 Donnie Sadler .40 .12
329 Carlos Beltran .60 .18
330 Miguel Asencio RC .60 .18
331 Jeff Weaver .40 .12
332 Bobby Higginson .40 .12
333 Mike Rivera .40 .12
334 Matt Anderson .40 .12
335 Craig Paquette .40 .12
336 Jose Lima .40 .12
337 Juan Acevedo .40 .12
338 Danny Patterson .40 .12
339 Andres Torres .40 .12
340 Dean Palmer .40 .12
341 Randall Simon .40 .12
342 Craig Monroe .40 .12
343 Damion Easley .40 .12
344 Robert Fick .40 .12
345 Steve Sparks .40 .12
346 Dmitri Young .40 .12
347 Nate Cornejo .40 .12
348 Matt Miller .40 .12
349 Wendell Magee .40 .12
350 Shane Halter .40 .12
351 Brian Moehler .40 .12
352 Mitch Meluskey .40 .12
353 Jose Macias .40 .12
354 Mark Redman .40 .12
355 Jeff Farnsworth .40 .12
356 Kris Keller .40 .12
357 Adam Pettyjohn .40 .12
358 Fernando Rodney .40 .12
359 Andy Van Hekken .40 .12
360 Damian Jackson .40 .12
361 Jose Paniagua .40 .12
362 Jacob Cruz .40 .12
363 Doug Mientkiewicz .40 .12
364 Torii Hunter .40 .12
365 Brad Radke .40 .12
366 Denny Hocking .40 .12
367 Mike Jackson .40 .12
368 Eddie Guardado .40 .12
369 Jacque Jones .40 .12
370 Joe Mays .40 .12
371 Matt Kinney .40 .12
372 Kyle Lohse .40 .12
373 David Ortiz .60 .18
374 Luis Rivas .40 .12
375 Jay Canizaro .40 .12
376 Dustan Mohr .40 .12
377 LaTroy Hawkins .40 .12
378 Warren Morris .40 .12
379 A.J. Pierzynski .40 .12
380 Eric Milton .40 .12
381 Bob Wells .40 .12
382 Cristian Guzman .40 .12
383 Brian Buchanan .40 .12
384 Bobby Kielty .40 .12
385 Corey Koskie .40 .12
386 J.C. Romero .40 .12
387 Jack Cressend .40 .12
388 Mike Duvall .40 .12
389 Tony Fiore .40 .12
390 Tom Prince .40 .12
391 Todd Sears .40 .12
392 Kevin Frederick RC .60 .18
393 Frank Thomas 1.00 .30
394 Mark Buehrle .40 .12
395 Jon Garland .40 .12
396 Jeff Liefer .40 .12
397 Magglio Ordonez .40 .12
398 Rocky Biddle .40 .12
399 Lorenzo Barcelo .40 .12
400 Ray Durham .40 .12
401 Bob Howry .40 .12
402 Aaron Rowand .40 .12
403 Keith Foulke .40 .12
404 Paul Konerko .40 .12
405 Sandy Alomar Jr. .40 .12
406 Mark Johnson .40 .12
407 Carlos Lee .40 .12
408 Jose Valentin .40 .12
409 Jon Rauch .40 .12
410 Royce Clayton .40 .12
411 Kenny Lofton .40 .12
412 Tony Graffanino .40 .12
413 Todd Ritchie .40 .12
414 Antonio Osuna .40 .12
415 Gary Glover .40 .12
416 Mike Porzio .40 .12
417 Danny Wright .40 .12
418 Kelly Wunsch .40 .12
419 Miguel Olivo .40 .12
420 Edwin Almonte RC .60 .18
421 Kyle Kane RC .40 .12
422 Mitch Wylie RC .60 .18
423 Derek Jeter 2.50 .75
424 Jason Giambi .40 .12
425 Roger Clemens 2.00 .60
426 Enrique Wilson .40 .12
427 David Wells .40 .12
428 Mike Mussina .60 .18
429 Bernie Williams .60 .18
430 Mike Stanton .40 .12
431 Sterling Hitchcock .40 .12
432 Alex Graman .40 .12
433 Robin Ventura .40 .12
434 Mariano Rivera .60 .18
435 Jay Tessmer .40 .12
436 Andy Pettitte .60 .18
437 John Vander Wal .40 .12
438 Adrian Hernandez .40 .12
439 Alberto Castillo .40 .12
440 Steve Karsay .40 .12
441 Alfonso Soriano .60 .18
442 Rondell White .40 .12
443 Nick Johnson .40 .12
444 Jorge Posada .60 .18
445 Ramiro Mendoza .40 .12
446 Gerald Williams .40 .12
447 Orlando Hernandez .40 .12
448 Randy Choate .40 .12
449 Randy Keisler .40 .12
450 Ted Lilly .40 .12
451 Christian Parker .40 .12
452 Ron Coomer .40 .12
453 Marcus Thames .40 .12
454 Drew Henson .60 .18
455 Jeff Bagwell .60 .18
456 Wade Miller .40 .12
457 Lance Berkman .40 .12
458 Julio Lugo .40 .12
459 Roy Oswalt .40 .12
460 Nelson Cruz .40 .12
461 Morgan Ensberg .40 .12
462 Geoff Blum .40 .12
463 Ryan Jamison .40 .12
464 Billy Wagner .40 .12
465 Dave Mlicki .40 .12
466 Brad Ausmus .40 .12
467 Jose Vizcaino .40 .12
468 Craig Biggio .60 .18
469 Shane Reynolds .40 .12
470 Greg Zaun .40 .12
471 Octavio Dotel .40 .12
472 Carlos Hernandez .40 .12
473 Richard Hidalgo .40 .12
474 Daryle Ward .40 .12
475 Orlando Merced .40 .12
476 John Buck .40 .12
477 Adam Everett .40 .12
478 Doug Brocail .40 .12
479 Brad Lidge .40 .12
480 Scott Linebrink .40 .12
481 T.J. Mathews .40 .12
482 Greg Miller .40 .12
483 Hipolito Pichardo .40 .12
484 Brandon Puffer RC .60 .18
485 Ricky Stone RC .40 .12
486 Jason Lane .40 .12
487 Brian L. Hunter .40 .12
488 Rodrigo Rosario RC .60 .18
489 Tom Shearn RC .60 .18
490 Gary Sheffield .40 .12
491 Tom Glavine .60 .18
492 Mike Remlinger .40 .12
493 Henry Blanco .40 .12
494 Vinny Castilla .40 .12
495 Chris Hammond .40 .12
496 Kevin Millwood .40 .12
497 Darren Holmes .40 .12
498 Cory Aldridge .40 .12
499 Tim Spooneybarger .40 .12
500 Rafael Furcal .40 .12
501 Albie Lopez .40 .12
502 Javy Lopez .40 .12
503 Greg Maddux 1.50 .45
504 Andruw Jones .40 .12
505 Steve Torrealba .40 .12
506 George Lombard .40 .12
507 B.J. Surhoff .40 .12
508 Marcus Giles .40 .12
509 Derrick Lewis .40 .12
510 Wes Helms .40 .12
511 John Smoltz .60 .18
512 Chipper Jones 1.00 .30
513 Jason Marquis .40 .12
514 Mark DeRosa .40 .12
515 Jung Bong .40 .12
516 Kevin Gryboski RC .40 .12
517 Damian Moss .40 .12
518 Horacio Ramirez .40 .12
519 Scott Sobkowiak .40 .12
520 Billy Sylvester .40 .12
521 Nick Green .40 .12
522 Travis Wilson UER .40 .12
Mistakenly numbered as 617
523 Ryan Langerhans .40 .12
524 John Ennis RC .60 .18
525 John Foster RC .60 .18
526 Keith Lockhart .40 .12
527 Julio Franco .40 .12
528 Richie Sexson .40 .12
529 Jeffrey Hammonds .40 .12
530 Ben Sheets .40 .12
531 Mike DeJean .40 .12
532 Mark Loretta .40 .12
533 Alex Ochoa .40 .12
534 Jamey Wright .40 .12
535 Jose Hernandez .40 .12
536 Glendon Rusch .40 .12
537 Geoff Jenkins .40 .12
538 Luis Lopez .40 .12
539 Curtis Leskanic .40 .12
540 Chad Fox .40 .12
541 Tyler Houston .40 .12
542 Nick Neugebauer .40 .12
543 Matt Stairs .40 .12
544 Paul Rigdon .40 .12
545 Bill Hall .40 .12
546 Luis Vizcaino .40 .12
547 Lenny Harris .40 .12
548 Alex Sanchez .40 .12
549 Raul Casanova .40 .12
550 Eric Young .40 .12
551 Jeff Deardorff .40 .12
552 Nelson Figueroa .40 .12
553 Ron Belliard .40 .12
554 Mike Buddie .40 .12
555 Jose Cabrera .40 .12
556 J.M. Gold .40 .12
557 Ray King .40 .12
558 Jose Mieses .40 .12
559 Takahito Nomura RC .60 .18
560 Ruben Quevedo .40 .12
561 Jackson Melian .40 .12
562 Cristian Guerrero .40 .12
563 Paul Bako .40 .12
564 Luis Martinez RC .60 .18
565 Brian Mallette RC .40 .12
566 Matt Morris .40 .12
567 Tino Martinez .60 .18
568 Fernando Vina .40 .12
569 Gene Stechschulte .40 .12
570 Andy Benes .40 .12
571 Placido Polanco .40 .12
572 Luis Garcia .40 .12
573 Jim Edmonds .40 .12
574 Bud Smith .40 .12
575 Mike Matheny .40 .12
576 Garrett Stephenson .40 .12
577 Mike Cairo .40 .12
578 Darryl Kile .40 .12
579 Mike Timlin .40 .12
580 Rick Ankiel .40 .12
581 Jason Isringhausen .40 .12
582 Albert Pujols UER 2.00 .60
He is credited with a 13 yr career on the back
583 Eli Marrero .40 .12
584 Steve Kline .40 .12
585 J.D. Drew .40 .12
586 Mike DiFelice .40 .12
587 Dave Veres .40 .12
588 Kerry Robinson .40 .12
589 Edgar Renteria .40 .12
590 Woody Williams .40 .12
591 Chance Caple .40 .12
592 Mike Crudale RC .60 .18
593 Luther Hackman .40 .12
594 Josh Pearce .40 .12
595 Kevin Joseph .40 .12
596 Jim Journell .40 .12
597 Jeremy Lambert RC .60 .18
598 Mike Matthews .40 .12
599 Les Walrond .40 .12
600 Keith McDonald .40 .12
601 William Ortega .40 .12
602 Scotty Layfield RC .60 .18
603 So Taguchi RC 1.00 .30
604 Eduardo Perez .40 .12
605 Sammy Sosa 1.50 .45
606 Kerry Wood 1.00 .30
607 Kyle Farnsworth .40 .12
608 Alex Gonzalez .40 .12
609 Tom Gordon .40 .12
610 Carlos Zambrano .40 .12
611 Roosevelt Brown .40 .12
612 Bill Mueller .40 .12
613 Mark Prior 2.50 .75
614 Darren Lewis .40 .12
615 Joe Girardi .40 .12
616 Fred McGriff .60 .18
617 Jon Lieber .40 .12
618 Robert Machado .40 .12
619 Corey Patterson .40 .12
620 Joe Borowski .40 .12
621 Todd Hundley .40 .12
622 Jason Bere .40 .12
623 Moises Alou .40 .12
624 Jeff Fassero .40 .12
625 Jesus Sanchez .40 .12
626 Chris Stynes .40 .12
627 Delino Deshields .40 .12
628 Augie Ojeda .40 .12
629 Juan Cruz .40 .12
630 Ben Christensen .40 .12
631 Mike Meyers .40 .12
632 Will Ohman .40 .12
633 Steve Smyth .40 .12
634 Mark Bellhorn .40 .12
635 Nate Frese .40 .12
636 David Kelton .40 .12
637 Francis Beltran RC .60 .18
638 Antonio Alfonseca .40 .12
639 Donovan Osborne .40 .12
640 Shawn Sonnier .40 .12
641 Matt Clement .40 .12
642 Luis Gonzalez .40 .12
643 Brian Anderson .40 .12
644 Randy Johnson 1.00 .30
645 Mark Grace .60 .18
646 Danny Bautista .40 .12
647 Junior Spivey .40 .12
648 Jay Bell .40 .12
649 Miguel Batista .40 .12
650 Tony Womack .40 .12
651 Byung-Hyun Kim .40 .12
652 Steve Finley .40 .12
653 Rick Helling .40 .12
654 Curt Schilling .40 .12
655 Erubiel Durazo .40 .12
656 Chris Donnels .40 .12
657 Greg Colbrunn .40 .12
658 Mike Morgan .40 .12
659 Jose Guillen .40 .12
660 Matt Williams .40 .12
661 Craig Counsell .40 .12
662 Greg Swindell .40 .12
663 Rod Barajas .40 .12
664 David Dellucci .40 .12
665 Todd Stottlemyre .40 .12
666 P.J. Bevis RC .60 .18
667 Mike Koplove .40 .12
668 Mike Myers .40 .12
669 John Patterson .40 .12
670 Bret Prinz .40 .12
671 Jeremy Ward RC .60 .18
672 Danny Klassen .40 .12
673 Luis Terrero .40 .12
674 Jose Valverde RC 1.00 .30
675 Doug Devore RC .60 .18
676 Quinton McCracken .40 .12
677 Paul LoDuca .40 .12
678 Mark Grudzielanek .40 .12
679 Kevin Brown .40 .12
680 Paul Quantrill .40 .12
681 Shawn Green .40 .12
682 Hideo Nomo 1.00 .30
683 Eric Gagne 1.00 .30
684 Giovanni Carrara .40 .12
685 Marquis Grissom .40 .12
686 Hiram Bocachica .40 .12
687 Guillermo Mota .40 .12
688 Alex Cora .40 .12
689 Odalis Perez .40 .12
690 Brian Jordan .40 .12
691 Andy Ashby .40 .12
692 Eric Karros .40 .12
693 Chad Kreuter .40 .12
694 Dave Roberts .40 .12
695 Omar Daal .40 .12
696 Dave Hansen .40 .12
697 Adrian Beltre .60 .18
698 Terry Mulholland .40 .12
699 Cesar Izturis .40 .12
700 Steve Colyer .40 .12
701 Carlos Garcia .40 .12
702 Ricardo Rodriguez .40 .12
703 Darren Dreifort .40 .12
704 Jeff Reboulet .40 .12
705 Victor Alvarez RC .60 .18
706 Kazuhisa Ishii RC 2.50 .75
707 Jose Vidro .40 .12
708 Henry Mateo .40 .12
709 Tony Armas Jr. .40 .12
710 Carl Pavano .40 .12
711 Peter Bergeron .40 .12
712 Bruce Chen .40 .12
713 Orlando Cabrera .40 .12
714 Britt Reames .40 .12
715 Masato Yoshii .40 .12
716 Fernando Tatis .40 .12
717 Graeme Lloyd .40 .12
718 Scott Stewart .40 .12
719 Lou Collier .40 .12
720 Michael Barrett .40 .12
721 Vladimir Guerrero 1.00 .30
722 Troy Mattes .40 .12
723 Brian Schneider .40 .12
724 Lee Stevens .40 .12
725 Javier Vazquez .40 .12
726 Brad Wilkerson .40 .12
727 Zach Day .40 .12
728 Ed Vosberg .40 .12
729 Tomo Ohka .40 .12
730 Mike Mordecai .40 .12
731 Donnie Bridges .40 .12
732 Ron Chiavacci .40 .12
733 T.J. Tucker .40 .12
734 Scott Hodges .40 .12
735 Valentino Pascucci .40 .12
736 Andres Galarraga .40 .12
737 Scott Downs .40 .12
738 Eric Good RC .60 .18
739 Ron Calloway RC .60 .18
740 Jorge Nunez RC .60 .18
741 Henry Rodriguez .40 .12
742 Jeff Kent .40 .12
743 Russ Ortiz .40 .12
744 Felix Rodriguez .40 .12
745 Benito Santiago .40 .12
746 Tsuyoshi Shinjo .40 .12
747 Tim Worrell .40 .12
748 Marvin Benard .40 .12
749 Kurt Ainsworth .40 .12
750 Edwards Guzman .40 .12
751 J.T. Snow .40 .12
752 Jason Christiansen .40 .12
753 Robb Nen .40 .12
754 Barry Bonds 2.50 .75
755 Shawon Dunston .40 .12
756 Chad Zerbe .40 .12
757 Ramon E. Martinez .40 .12
758 Calvin Murray .40 .12
759 Pedro Feliz .40 .12
760 Jason Schmidt .40 .12
761 Damon Minor .40 .12
762 Reggie Sanders .40 .12
763 Rich Aurilia .40 .12
764 Kirk Rueter .40 .12
765 David Bell .40 .12
766 Yorvit Torrealba .40 .12
767 Livan Hernandez .40 .12
768 Felix Diaz .40 .12
769 Aaron Fultz .40 .12
770 Ryan Jensen .40 .12
771 Arturo McDowell .40 .12
772 Carlos Valderrama .40 .12
773 Nelson Castro RC .60 .18
774 Jay Witasick .40 .12
775 Deivis Santos .40 .12
776 Josh Beckett .40 .12
777 Charles Johnson .40 .12
778 Derrek Lee .40 .12
779 A.J. Burnett .40 .12
780 Vic Darensbourg .40 .12
781 Cliff Floyd .40 .12
782 Jose Cueto .40 .12
783 Nate Teut .40 .12
784 Alex Gonzalez .40 .12
785 Brad Penny .40 .12
786 Kevin Olsen .40 .12
787 Mike Lowell .40 .12
788 Mike Redmond .40 .12
789 Braden Looper .40 .12
790 Eric Owens .40 .12
791 Andy Fox .40 .12
792 Vladimir Nunez .40 .12
793 Luis Castillo .40 .12
794 Ryan Dempster .40 .12
795 Armando Almanza .40 .12
796 Preston Wilson .40 .12
797 Pablo Ozuna .40 .12
798 Gary Knotts .40 .12
799 Ramon Castro .40 .12
800 Benito Baez .40 .12
801 Michael Tejera .40 .12
802 Claudio Vargas .40 .12
803 Chip Ambres .40 .12
804 Hansel Izquierdo RC .60 .18
805 Tim Raines Sr. .40 .12
806 Marty Malloy .40 .12
807 Julian Tavarez .40 .12
808 Roberto Alomar .60 .18
809 Al Leiter .40 .12
810 Jeromy Burnitz .40 .12
811 John Franco .40 .12
812 Edgardo Alfonzo .40 .12
813 Mike Piazza 1.50 .45
814 Shawn Estes .40 .12
815 Joe McEwing .40 .12
816 David Weathers .40 .12
817 Pedro Astacio .40 .12
818 Timo Perez .40 .12
819 Grant Roberts .40 .12
820 Rey Ordonez .40 .12
821 Steve Trachsel .40 .12
822 Roger Cedeno .40 .12
823 Mark Johnson .40 .12
824 Armando Benitez .40 .12
825 Vance Wilson .40 .12
826 Jay Payton .40 .12
827 Mo Vaughn .40 .12
828 Scott Strickland .40 .12
829 Mark Guthrie .40 .12
830 Jeff D'Amico .40 .12
831 Mark Corey RC .60 .18
832 Kane Davis .40 .12
833 Jae Weong Seo .40 .12
834 Pat Strange .40 .12
835 Adam Walker RC .60 .18
836 Tyler Walker RC .40 .12
837 Gary Matthews Jr. .40 .12
838 Jaime Cerda RC .60 .18
839 Satoru Komiyama RC .60 .18
840 Tyler Yates RC 1.00 .30
841 John Valentin .40 .12
842 Ryan Klesko .40 .12
843 Wiki Gonzalez .40 .12
844 Trevor Hoffman .40 .12
845 Sean Burroughs .60 .18
846 Alan Embree .40 .12
847 Dennis Tankersley .40 .12
848 D'Angelo Jimenez .40 .12
849 Kevin Jarvis .40 .12

850 Mark Kotsay .40 .12
851 Phil Nevin .40 .12
852 Jeremy Fikac .40 .12
853 Brett Tomko .40 .12
854 Brian Lawrence .40 .12
855 Steve Reed .40 .12
856 Bubba Trammell .40 .12
857 Tom Davey .40 .12
858 Ramon Vazquez .40 .12
859 Tom Lampkin .40 .12
860 Bobby Jones .40 .12
861 Ray Lankford .40 .12
862 Mark Sweeney .40 .12
863 Adam Eaton .40 .12
864 Trenidad Hubbard .40 .12
865 Jason Boyd .40 .12
866 Javier Cardona .40 .12
867 Cliff Bartosh RC .60 .18
868 Mike Bynum .40 .12
869 Eric Cyr .40 .12
870 Jose Nunez .40 .12
871 Ron Gant .40 .12
872 Deivi Cruz .40 .12
873 Ben Howard RC .60 .18
874 Todd Donovan RC .60 .18
875 Andy Shibilo RC .60 .18
876 Scott Rolen 1.00 .30
877 Jose Mesa .40 .12
878 Rheal Cormier .40 .12
879 Travis Lee .40 .12
880 Mike Lieberthal .40 .12
881 Brandon Duckworth .40 .12
882 David Coggin .40 .12
883 Bob Abreu .40 .12
884 Turk Wendell .40 .12
885 Marlon Byrd .40 .12
886 Jason Michaels .40 .12
887 Robert Person .40 .12
888 Tomas Perez .40 .12
889 Jimmy Rollins .40 .12
890 Vicente Padilla .40 .12
891 Pat Burrell .40 .12
892 Dave Hollins .40 .12
893 Randy Wolf .40 .12
894 Jose Santiago .40 .12
895 Doug Glanville .40 .12
896 Cliff Politte .40 .12
897 Marlon Anderson .40 .12
898 Ricky Bottalico .40 .12
899 Terry Adams .40 .12
900 Brad Baisley .40 .12
901 Hector Mercado .40 .12
902 Elio Serrano RC .60 .18
903 Todd Pratt .40 .12
904 Pete Zamora RC .60 .18
905 Nick Punto .40 .12
906 Ricky Ledee .40 .12
907 Eric Junge RC .60 .18
908 Anderson Machado RC .60 .18
909 Jorge Padilla RC .60 .18
910 John Mabry .40 .12
911 Brian Giles .40 .12
912 Jason Kendall .40 .12
913 Jack Wilson .40 .12
914 Kris Benson .40 .12
915 Aramis Ramirez .40 .12
916 Mike Fetters .40 .12
917 Adrian Brown .40 .12
918 Pokey Reese .40 .12
919 Dave Williams .40 .12
920 Mike Benjamin .40 .12
921 Kip Wells .40 .12
922 Mike Williams .40 .12
923 Pat Meares .40 .12
924 Ron Villone .40 .12
925 Armando Rios .40 .12
926 Jimmy Anderson .40 .12
927 Rob Mackowiak .40 .12
928 Kevin Young .40 .12
929 Brian Boehringer .40 .12
930 Joe Beimel .40 .12
931 Chad Hermansen .40 .12
932 Scott Sauerbeck .40 .12
933 Josh Fogg .40 .12
934 Mike Gonzalez RC .60 .18
935 Mike Lincoln .40 .12
936 Sean Lowe .40 .12
937 Matt Guerrier .40 .12
938 Ryan Vogelsong .40 .12
939 J.R. House .40 .12
940 Craig Wilson .40 .12
941 Tony Alvarez .40 .12
942 J.J. Davis .40 .12
943 Abraham Nunez .40 .12
944 Adrian Burnside RC .60 .18
945 Ken Griffey Jr. 1.50 .45
946 Jimmy Haynes .40 .12
947 Juan Castro .40 .12
948 Jose Rijo .40 .12
949 Corky Miller .40 .12
950 Elmer Dessens .40 .12
951 Aaron Boone .40 .12
952 Juan Encarnacion .40 .12
953 Chris Reitsma .40 .12
954 Wilton Guerrero .40 .12
955 Danny Graves .40 .12
956 Jim Brower .40 .12
957 Barry Larkin .60 .18
958 Todd Walker .40 .12
959 Gabe White .40 .12
960 Adam Dunn .60 .18
961 Jason LaRue .40 .12
962 Reggie Taylor .40 .12
963 Sean Casey .40 .12
964 Scott Williamson .40 .12
965 Austin Kearns .60 .18
966 Kelly Stinnett .40 .12
967 Jose Acevedo .40 .12
968 Gookie Dawkins .40 .12
969 Brady Clark .40 .12
970 Scott Sullivan .40 .12
971 Ricardo Aramboles .40 .12
972 Lance Davis .40 .12
973 Seth Etherton .40 .12
974 Luke Hudson .40 .12
975 Joey Hamilton .40 .12
976 Luis Pineda .40 .12
977 John Riedling .40 .12
978 Jose Silva .40 .12
979 Dane Sardinha .40 .12
980 Ben Broussard .40 .12
981 David Espinosa .40 .12
982 Ruben Mateo .40 .12
983 Larry Walker .60 .18
984 Juan Uribe .40 .12
985 Mike Hampton .40 .12
986 Aaron Cook RC .60 .18
987 Jose Ortiz .40 .12
988 Todd Jones .40 .12
989 Todd Helton .60 .18
990 Shawn Chacon .40 .12
991 Jason Jennings .40 .12
992 Todd Zeile .40 .12
993 Ben Petrick .40 .12
994 Denny Neagle .40 .12
995 Jose Jimenez .40 .12
996 Juan Pierre .40 .12
997 Todd Hollandsworth .40 .12
998 Kent Mercker .40 .12
999 Greg Norton .40 .12
1000 Terry Shumpert .40 .12
1001 Mark Little .40 .12
1002 Gary Bennett .40 .12
1003 Dennis Reyes .40 .12
1004 Justin Speier .40 .12
1005 John Thomson .40 .12
1006 Rick White .40 .12
1007 Colin Young RC .60 .18
1008 Cam Esslinger RC .60 .18
1009 Rene Reyes RC .60 .18
1010 Mike James .40 .12
1011 Morgan Ensberg NR .40 .12
1012 Adam Everett NR .40 .12
1013 Rodrigo Rosario NR .40 .12
1014 Carlos Pena NR .40 .12
1015 Eric Hinske NR .40 .12
1016 Orlando Hudson NR .40 .12
1017 Reed Johnson NR .50 .15
1018 Jung Bong NR .40 .12
1019 Bill Hall NR .40 .12
1020 Mark Prior NR 1.25 .35
1021 Francis Beltran NR .40 .12
1022 David Kelton NR .40 .12
1023 Felix Escalona NR .40 .12
1024 Jorge Sosa NR .40 .12
1025 Dewon Brazelton NR .40 .12
1026 Jose Valverde NR .40 .12
1027 Luis Terrero NR .40 .12
1028 Kazuhisa Ishii NR 1.25 .35
1029 Cesar Izturis NR .40 .12
1030 Ryan Jensen NR .40 .12
1031 Matt Thornton NR .40 .12
1032 Hansel Izquierdo NR .40 .12
1033 Jaime Cerda NR .40 .12
1034 Erik Bedard NR .40 .12
1035 Sean Burroughs NR .40 .12
1036 Ben Howard NR .40 .12
1037 Ramon Vazquez NR .40 .12
1038 Marlon Byrd NR .40 .12
1039 Josh Fogg NR .40 .12
1040 Hank Blalock NR .75 .23
1041 Mark Teixeira NR .50 .15
1042 Kevin Mench NR .40 .12
1043 Dane Sardinha NR .40 .12
1044 Austin Kearns NR .40 .12
1045 Rene Reyes NR .40 .12
1046 Eric Munson NR .40 .12
1047 Jon Rauch NR .40 .12
1048 Nick Johnson NR .40 .12
1049 Alex Graman NR .40 .12
1050 Drew Henson NR .40 .12
1051 Darin Erstad HM .40 .12
1052 Garret Anderson HM .40 .12
1053 Craig Biggio HM .40 .12
1054 Lance Berkman HM .40 .12
1055 Jeff Bagwell HM .40 .12
1056 Shannon Stewart HM .40 .12
1057 Chipper Jones HM .60 .18
1058 J.D. Drew HM .40 .12
1059 Moises Alou HM .40 .12
1060 Mark Grace HM .40 .12
1061 Jose Vidro HM .40 .12
1062 Vladimir Guerrero HM .60 .18
1063 Matt Lawton HM .40 .12
1064 Ichiro Suzuki HM 1.00 .30
1065 Edgar Martinez HM .40 .12
1066 John Olerud HM .40 .12
1067 Jeff Cirillo HM .40 .12
1068 Mike Lowell HM .40 .12
1069 Mike Piazza HM 1.00 .30
1070 Roberto Alomar HM .40 .12
1071 Bob Abreu HM .40 .12
1072 Jason Kendall HM .40 .12
1073 Brian Giles HM .40 .12
1074 Rafael Palmeiro HM .40 .12
1075 Ivan Rodriguez HM .60 .18
1076 Alex Rodriguez HM 1.00 .30
1077 Juan Gonzalez HM .40 .12
1078 Nomar Garciaparra HM 1.00 .30
1079 Manny Ramirez HM .40 .12
1080 Sean Casey HM .40 .12
1081 Barry Larkin HM .40 .12
1082 Larry Walker HM .40 .12
1083 Carlos Beltran HM .60 .18
1084 Corey Koskie HM .40 .12
1085 Maggio Ordonez HM .40 .12
1086 Frank Thomas HM 1.00 .30
1087 Kenny Lofton HM .40 .12
1088 Derek Jeter HM 1.25 .35
1089 Bernie Williams HM .40 .12
1090 Jason Giambi HM .60 .18
1091 Troy Glaus PC .40 .12
1092 Jeff Bagwell PC .40 .12
1093 Lance Berkman PC .40 .12
1094 David Justice PC .40 .12
1095 Eric Chavez PC .40 .12
1096 Carlos Delgado PC .40 .12
1097 Gary Sheffield PC .40 .12
1098 Chipper Jones PC .60 .18
1099 Andruw Jones PC .40 .12
1100 Richie Sexson PC .40 .12
1101 Albert Pujols PC 1.00 .30
1102 Sammy Sosa PC 1.00 .30
1103 Fred McGriff PC .40 .12
1104 Greg Vaughn PC .40 .12
1105 Matt Williams PC .40 .12
1106 Luis Gonzalez PC .40 .12
1107 Shawn Green PC .40 .12
1108 Andres Galarraga PC .40 .12
1109 Vladimir Guerrero PC .60 .18
1110 Barry Bonds PC 1.25 .35
1111 Rich Aurilia PC .40 .12
1112 Ellis Burks PC .40 .12
1113 Jim Thome PC .60 .18
1114 Bret Boone PC .40 .12
1115 Cliff Floyd PC .40 .12
1116 Mike Piazza PC 1.00 .30
1117 Jeromy Burnitz PC .40 .12
1118 Phil Nevin PC .40 .12
1119 Brian Giles PC .40 .12
1120 Rafael Palmeiro PC .40 .12
1121 Juan Gonzalez PC .40 .12
1122 Alex Rodriguez PC 1.00 .30
1123 Manny Ramirez PC .40 .12
1124 Ken Griffey Jr. PC 1.00 .30
1125 Larry Walker PC .40 .12
1126 Todd Helton PC .40 .12
1127 Mike Sweeney PC .40 .12
1128 Frank Thomas PC 1.00 .30
1129 Paul Konerko PC .40 .12
1130 Jason Giambi PC .40 .12
1131 Aaron Sele RT .40 .12
1132 Roy Oswalt RT .40 .12
1133 Wade Miller RT .40 .12
1134 Tim Hudson RT .40 .12
1135 Barry Zito RT .40 .12
1136 Mark Mulder RT .40 .12
1137 Greg Maddux RT 1.00 .30
1138 Tom Glavine RT .40 .12
1139 Ben Sheets RT .40 .12
1140 Darryl Kile RT .40 .12
1141 Matt Morris RT .40 .12
1142 Kerry Wood RT .60 .18
1143 Jon Lieber RT .40 .12
1144 Juan Cruz RT .40 .12
1145 Randy Johnson RT .60 .18
1146 Curt Schilling RT .40 .12
1147 Kevin Brown RT .40 .12
1148 Javier Vazquez RT .40 .12
1149 Russ Ortiz RT .40 .12
1150 C.C. Sabathia RT .40 .12
1151 Bartolo Colon RT .40 .12
1152 Freddy Garcia RT .40 .12
1153 Jamie Moyer RT .40 .12
1154 Josh Beckett RT .40 .12
1155 Brad Penny RT .40 .12
1156 Al Leiter RT .40 .12
1157 Brandon Duckworth RT .40 .12
1158 Robert Person RT .40 .12
1159 Kris Benson RT .40 .12
1160 Chan Ho Park RT .40 .12
1161 Pedro Martinez RT .60 .18
1162 Mike Hampton RT .40 .12
1163 Jeff Weaver RT .40 .12
1164 Joe Mays RT .40 .12
1165 Brad Radke RT .40 .12
1166 Eric Milton RT .40 .12
1167 Roger Clemens RT 1.00 .30
1168 Mike Mussina RT .40 .12
1169 Andy Pettitte RT .40 .12
1170 David Wells RT .40 .12
1171 Ken Griffey Jr. CL 1.00 .30
1172 Ichiro Suzuki CL 1.00 .30
1173 Jason Giambi CL .40 .12
1174 Alex Rodriguez CL 1.00 .30
1175 Sammy Sosa CL 1.00 .30
1176 Nomar Garciaparra CL 1.00 .30
1177 Barry Bonds CL 1.25 .35
1178 Mike Piazza CL 1.00 .30
1179 Derek Jeter CL 1.25 .35
1180 Randy Johnson CL .60 .18
1181 Jeff Bagwell CL .40 .12
1182 Albert Pujols CL 1.00 .30

2002 Upper Deck 40-Man Electric

Inserted in packs at stated odds of one in four, this is a complete parallel of the 40-man set. These cards all have a silver printing to them.

Nm-Mt Ex-Mt
*ELECTRIC: 1.25X TO 3X BASIC
*ELECTRIC RC'S: .75X TO 2X BASIC
*ELECTRIC 1011-1050: 1.25X TO 3X BASIC
*ELECTRIC 1011-1050 RC's: .75X TO 2X BASIC

2002 Upper Deck 40-Man Electric Rainbow

Randomly inserted in packs, this is a complete parallel of the 40-man set. These cards all have a gold printing to them and all are serial numbered to 40 copies.

Nm-Mt Ex-Mt
*ELEC.RAIN: 10X TO 25X BASIC
*ELEC.RAIN RC'S: 5X TO 12X
*ELEC.RAIN 1011-1050: 10X TO 25X.
*ELEC.RAIN 1011-1050 RC's: 5X TO 12X

2002 Upper Deck 40-Man Gargantuan Gear

Inserted at stated odds of one in 48 retail packs, these 30 cards feature big jersey swatches from some of the biggest names in baseball. Some of the players were produced in shorter quantity and we have provided that information next to their names in our checklist.

Nm-Mt Ex-Mt
G-AJ Andruw Jones 10.00 3.00
G-AP Andy Pettitte 15.00 4.50
G-AR Alex Rodriguez 15.00 4.50
G-AS Aaron Sele 10.00 3.00
G-BC Bruce Chen 10.00 3.00
G-BG Ben Grieve 10.00 3.00
G-BR Brad Radke 10.00 3.00
G-BW Bernie Williams 15.00 4.50
G-BZ Barry Zito 10.00 3.00
G-CS Curt Schilling 10.00 3.00
G-DY Dmitri Young 10.00 3.00
G-IS Ichiro Suzuki SP 50.00 15.00
G-JB James Baldwin 10.00 3.00
G-JB Jeromy Burnitz 10.00 3.00
G-JD Jermaine Dye SP 15.00 4.50
G-JG Juan Gonzalez 15.00 4.50
G-JK Jeff Kent 10.00 3.00
G-JO John Olerud 10.00 3.00
G-JP Jorge Posada 15.00 4.50
G-KG Ken Griffey Jr. 20.00 6.00
G-LG Luis Gonzalez 10.00 3.00
G-ML Mike Lieberthal 10.00 3.00
G-MO Maggio Ordonez 10.00 3.00
G-MP Mike Piazza SP 25.00 7.50
G-PM Pedro Martinez 15.00 4.50
G-SR Scott Rolen 15.00 4.50
G-SS Sammy Sosa 20.00 6.00
G-TH Tim Hudson SP 15.00 4.50
G-TM Tino Martinez 15.00 4.50
G-TZ Todd Zeile 10.00 3.00

2002 Upper Deck 40-Man Gargantuan Gear Gold

Randomly inserted in packs, this is a parallel to the Gargantuan Gear insert set. These cards are printed with some gold apparent on them and have a stated print run of 100 serial numbered sets.

Nm-Mt Ex-Mt
*GEAR GOLD: .75X TO 2X BASIC GEAR
*GEAR GOLD: .6X TO 1.5X BASIC GEAR SP's

2002 Upper Deck 40-Man Looming Large Jerseys

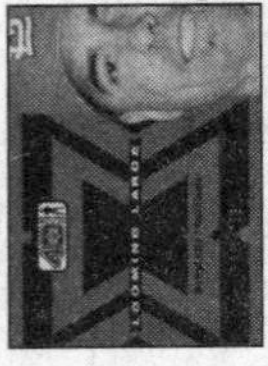

Randomly inserted into packs, this 41 card set features swatches of game-worn jerseys from some of the leading players of the game. These cards were printed to a stated print run of 250 serial numbered sets.

Nm-Mt Ex-Mt
L-AL Al Leiter 10.00 3.00
L-AR Alex Rodriguez 15.00 4.50
L-BG Brian Giles 10.00 3.00
L-BZ Barry Zito 10.00 3.00
L-CE Carl Everett 10.00 3.00
L-CF Chuck Finley 10.00 3.00
L-CS Curt Schilling 10.00 3.00
L-DK Darryl Kile 10.00 3.00
L-EM Edgar Martinez 15.00 4.50
L-FM Fred McGriff 15.00 4.50
L-FT Frank Thomas 15.00 4.50
L-GM Greg Maddux 15.00 4.50
L-HN Hideo Nomo 60.00 18.00
L-IV Ismael Valdes 10.00 3.00
L-JBA Jeff Bagwell 15.00 4.50
L-JBU John Burkett 10.00 3.00
L-JC Jeff Cirillo 10.00 3.00
L-JD J.D. Drew 10.00 3.00
L-JGI Jason Giambi 10.00 3.00
L-JGO Juan Gonzalez 15.00 4.50
L-JP Jorge Posada 15.00 4.50
L-JR Jimmy Rollins 10.00 3.00
L-JS J.T. Snow 10.00 3.00
L-KG Ken Griffey Jr. 25.00 7.50
L-KL Kenny Lofton 10.00 3.00
L-KS Kazuhiro Sasaki 10.00 3.00
L-LB Lance Berkman 10.00 3.00
L-ML Mike Lieberthal 10.00 3.00
L-MO Maggio Ordonez 10.00 3.00
L-RC Roger Clemens 25.00 7.50
L-RJ Randy Johnson 15.00 4.50
L-RP Rafael Palmeiro 15.00 4.50
L-RV Ron Villone 10.00 3.00
L-RV Randy Velarde 10.00 3.00
L-SC Sean Casey 10.00 3.00
L-SR Shane Reynolds 10.00 3.00
L-SS Sammy Sosa 25.00 7.50
L-TC Tony Clark 10.00 3.00
L-TF Travis Fryman 10.00 3.00
L-TG Tom Glavine 15.00 4.50
L-TH Todd Helton 15.00 4.50

2002 Upper Deck 40-Man Looming Large Jerseys Gold

Randomly inserted into packs, this 41 card set is a parallel of the Looming Large insert set and features swatches of game-worn jerseys from some of the leading players of the game. These cards were printed to a stated print run of 40 serial numbered sets.

Nm-Mt Ex-Mt
*GOLD: 1X TO 2.5X BASIC LOOMING

2002 Upper Deck 40-Man Lumber Yard

Issued at stated odds of one in 168, this 18 card set features game-used bat pieces of leading hitters.

Nm-Mt Ex-Mt
COMPLETE SET (18) 400.00 120.00
LY1 Chipper Jones 15.00 4.50
LY2 Joe DiMaggio 40.00 12.00
LY3 Albert Pujols 25.00 7.50
LY4 Mark McGwire 40.00 12.00
LY5 Sammy Sosa 20.00 6.00
LY6 Vladimir Guerrero 15.00 4.50
LY7 Barry Bonds 30.00 9.00
LY8 Mickey Mantle 60.00 18.00
LY9 Mike Piazza 15.00 4.50
LY10 Alex Rodriguez 20.00 6.00
LY11 Nomar Garciaparra 20.00 6.00
LY12 Ken Griffey Jr. 20.00 6.00
LY13 Frank Thomas 15.00 4.50
LY14 Jason Giambi 15.00 4.50
LY15 Derek Jeter 30.00 9.00
LY16 Luis Gonzalez 15.00 4.50
LY17 Jeff Bagwell 15.00 4.50
LY18 Todd Helton 15.00 4.50

2002 Upper Deck 40-Man Mark McGwire Autograph Buybacks

Randomly inserted into packs, these 44 cards feature original Mark McGwire Upper Deck cards which were bought in the secondary market and then were authentically autographed by McGwire. Since there were only 250 cards signed in totality for this product and no more than six of any one card, we have not priced these cards due to market scarcity.

Nm-Mt Ex-Mt
1 Mark McGwire 89/6
2 Mark McGwire 90/6
3 Mark McGwire 90 TC/6
4 Mark McGwire 91/6
5 Mark McGwire 91 BASH/6
6 Mark McGwire 92/6
7 Mark McGwire 93/6
8 Mark McGwire 93 AW/6
9 Mark McGwire 94/6
10 Mark McGwire 95/3
11 Mark McGwire 96/6
12 Mark McGwire 96 BO/6
13 Mark McGwire 97/3
14 Mark McGwire 97 CF/6
15 Mark McGwire 97 GHL/2
16 Mark McGwire 97 SH CL/6
17 Mark McGwire 98/6
18 Mark McGwire 98 DG/4
19 Mark McGwire 98 GHL/4
20 Mark McGwire 98 SH/2
21 Mark McGwire 98 UE/2
22 Mark McGwire 99/6
23 Mark McGwire 99 AR/6
24 Mark McGwire 99 SH CL1/6
25 Mark McGwire 99 SH CL2/6
26 Mark McGwire 99 CEN/6
27 Mark McGwire 99 CEN MEM/6
28 Mark McGwire 99 ENC/6
29 Mark McGwire 99 ENC HO/1
30 Mark McGwire 99 ENC SG/6
31 Mark McGwire 00/6
32 Mark McGwire 00 AUT/2
33 Mark McGwire 00 CL/6
34 Mark McGwire 00 SH CL/6
35 Mark McGwire 00 GR/6
36 Mark McGwire 00 GR CL/6
37 Mark McGwire 00 LGD/6
38 Mark McGwire 00 LGD 20C/5
39 Mark McGwire 01/6
40 Mark McGwire 01 SH/5
41 Mark McGwire 01 LGD/6
42 Mark McGwire 02/4
43 Mark McGwire 02 BFZ/1
44 Mark McGwire 02 SS2/1

2002 Upper Deck 40-Man Mark McGwire Flashbacks

Issued in packs at stated odds of one in 24, these 40 cards go through and feature the highlights of Mark McGwire's career which ended after the 2001 season.

Nm-Mt Ex-Mt
COMPLETE SET (40) 200.00 60.00
COMMON CARD (MM1-MM40) 8.00 2.40
MM1 Mark McGwire USA 10.00 3.00

2002 Upper Deck 40-Man Super Swatch

Randomly inserted into packs, this 42 card set features swatches of game-worn jerseys from some of the leading players of the game. These cards were printed to a stated print run of 250 serial numbered sets.

Nm-Mt Ex-Mt
S-AR Alex Rodriguez 25.00 7.50
S-BS Ben Sheets 10.00 3.00
S-CD Carlos Delgado 10.00 3.00
S-CJ Chipper Jones 15.00 4.50

S-CS Curt Schilling 10.00 3.00
S-DE Darin Erstad 10.00 3.00
S-DJ David Justice 10.00 3.00
S-DW David Wells 10.00 3.00
S-EA Edgardo Alfonzo 10.00 3.00
S-EB Ellis Burks 10.00 3.00
S-EM Eric Milton 10.00 3.00
S-FT Frank Thomas 15.00 4.50
S-GV Greg Vaughn 10.00 3.00
S-HN Hideo Nomo 60.00 18.00
S-IR Ivan Rodriguez 15.00 4.50
S-IS Ichiro Suzuki 50.00 15.00
S-JB Jeff Bagwell 15.00 4.50
S-JG Juan Gonzalez Standing 15.00 4.50
S-JGO Juan Gonzalez Batting 15.00 4.50
S-JM Joe Mays 10.00 3.00
S-JP Jorge Posada 15.00 4.50
S-JV Jose Vidro 10.00 3.00
S-KG Ken Griffey Jr. Batting 25.00 7.50
S-KG Ken Griffey Jr. Fielding 25.00 7.50
S-KL Kenny Lofton 10.00 3.00
S-KS Kazuhiro Sasaki 10.00 3.00
S-LB Lance Berkman 10.00 3.00
S-MG Mark Grace 15.00 4.50
S-MH Mike Hampton 10.00 3.00
S-MM Matt Morris 10.00 3.00
S-MR Manny Ramirez 15.00 4.50
S-MR Mariano Rivera 15.00 4.50
S-MS Mike Sweeney 10.00 3.00
S-MY Masato Yoshii 10.00 3.00
S-RA Rich Aurilia 10.00 3.00
S-RC Roger Cedeno 10.00 3.00
S-RD Ray Durham 10.00 3.00
S-SC Sean Casey 10.00 3.00
S-SG Shawn Green 10.00 3.00
S-SS Sammy Sosa 25.00 7.50
S-TG Tony Gwynn 15.00 4.50
S-TH Trevor Hoffman 10.00 3.00

2003 Upper Deck 40-Man

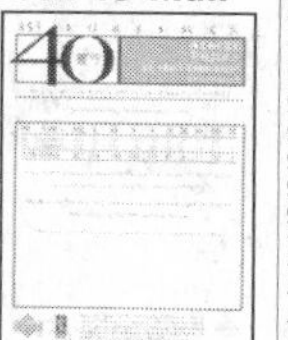

This 990 card set was released in July, 2003. These cards were issued in 10 card packs which came 36 packs to a box and 14 boxes to a case. The first 759 card feature most of the veterans on major league rosters. Cards numbered 760 through 820 feature the players from the 2002 All-Star game. Cards numbered 821 through 829 feature players who have won the Home Run Derby. Cards numbered 830 through 836 feature highlights from the 2002 World Series. Cards numbered 837 through 876 feature Upper Deck's selection as the leading 40 players in the game. Cards 877 through 960 feature a mix of rookies and prospects. Then Cards 961 through 990 feature a team checklist set in which one player or two players from each team is featured. A sample card of Ken Griffey Jr was issued several weeks before this product became live to give dealers and hobby media an idea of what these cards looked like.

	MINT	NRMT
COMPLETE SET (990)	200.00	90.00
COMMON CARD (1-990)	.40	.18
COMMON NR (877-960)	.40	.18
COMMON NR RC (877-960)	.40	.18

1 Troy Glaus .40 .18
2 Darin Erstad .40 .18
3 Garret Anderson .40 .18
4 Aaron Sele .40 .18
5 Adam Kennedy .40 .18
6 Scott Spiezio .40 .18
7 Troy Percival .40 .18
8 David Eckstein .40 .18
9 Ramon Ortiz .40 .18
10 Bengie Molina .40 .18
11 Tim Salmon .60 .25
12 John Lackey .40 .18
13 Brad Fullmer .40 .18
14 Jarrod Washburn .40 .18
15 Shawn Wooten .40 .18
16 Kevin Appier .40 .18
17 Ben Weber .40 .18
18 Eric Owens .40 .18
19 Matt Wise .40 .18
20 Francisco Rodriguez .40 .18
21 Scot Shields .40 .18
22 Jose Molina .40 .18
23 Scott Schoeneweis .40 .18
24 Derrick Turnbow .40 .18
25 Benji Gil .40 .18
26 Julio Ramirez .40 .18
27 Mickey Callaway .40 .18
28 Barry Zito .40 .18
29 Tim Hudson .40 .18
30 Mark Mulder .40 .18
31 Eric Chavez .40 .18
32 Miguel Tejada .40 .18
33 Terrence Long .40 .18
34 Jermaine Dye .40 .18
35 Erubiel Durazo .40 .18
36 Scott Hatteberg .40 .18
37 Chris Singleton .40 .18
38 Keith Foulke .40 .18
39 John Halama .40 .18
40 Mark Ellis .40 .18
41 Ted Lilly .40 .18
42 Jim Mecir .40 .18
43 Adam Piatt .40 .18
44 Freddie Bynum .40 .18
45 Adam Morrissey .40 .18
46 Jeremy Fikac .40 .18
47 Ricardo Rincon .40 .18
48 Ramon Hernandez .40 .18
49 Micah Bowie .40 .18
50 Chad Bradford .40 .18
51 Eric Byrnes .40 .18
52 Ron Gant .40 .18
53 Jose Flores .40 .18
54 Mark Johnson .40 .18
55 Carlos Delgado .40 .18
56 Orlando Hudson .40 .18
57 Kelvim Escobar .40 .18
58 Eric Hinske .40 .18
59 Doug Creek .40 .18
60 Josh Phelps .40 .18
61 Shannon Stewart .40 .18
62 Roy Halladay .40 .18
63 Vernon Wells .40 .18
64 Mark Hendrickson .40 .18
65 Mike Bordick .40 .18
66 Jayson Werth .40 .18
67 Chris Woodward .40 .18
68 Ken Huckaby .40 .18
69 Frank Catalanotto .40 .18
70 Jason Kershner .40 .18
71 Greg Myers .40 .18
72 Tanyon Sturtze .40 .18
73 Trever Miller .40 .18
74 Pete Walker .40 .18
75 Alexis Rios .60 .25
76 Tom Wilson .40 .18
77 Dave Berg .40 .18
78 Doug Linton .40 .18
79 Cliff Politte UER .40 .18
Career IP total is wrong
80 Damion Easley .40 .18
81 Toby Hall .40 .18
82 George Lombard .40 .18
83 Ben Grieve .40 .18
84 Aubrey Huff .40 .18
85 Jesus Colome .40 .18
86 Dewon Brazelton .40 .18
87 Rey Ordonez .40 .18
88 Al Martin .40 .18
89 Carl Crawford .40 .18
90 Travis Lee .40 .18
91 Marlon Anderson .40 .18
92 Javier Valentin .40 .18
93 Joe Kennedy .40 .18
94 Jorge Sosa .40 .18
95 Travis Harper .40 .18
96 Bobby Seay .40 .18
97 Seth McClung .40 .18
98 Delvin James .40 .18
99 Victor Zambrano .40 .18
100 Terry Shumpert .40 .18
101 Josh Hamilton .40 .18
102 Jared Sandberg .40 .18
103 Steve Parris .40 .18
104 C.C. Sabathia .40 .18
105 Omar Vizquel .60 .25
106 Milton Bradley .40 .18
107 Ellis Burks .40 .18
108 Danys Baez .40 .18
109 Jason Davis .40 .18
110 Terry Mulholland .40 .18
111 Matt Lawton .40 .18
112 Alex Escobar .40 .18
113 Mark Wohlers .40 .18
114 Josh Bard .40 .18
115 Bill Selby .40 .18
116 Brandon Phillips .40 .18
117 Jason Bere .40 .18
118 Casey Blake .40 .18
119 Travis Hafner .40 .18
120 Brian Anderson .40 .18
121 David Riske .40 .18
122 Karim Garcia .40 .18
123 Ricardo Rodriguez .40 .18
124 Carl Sadler .40 .18
125 Jose Santiago .40 .18
126 Tim Laker .40 .18
127 John McDonald .40 .18
128 Jake Westbrook .40 .18
129 Ichiro Suzuki 1.50 .70
130 Freddy Garcia .40 .18
131 Edgar Martinez .60 .25
132 Ben Davis .40 .18
133 Shigetoshi Hasegawa .40 .18
134 Carlos Guillen .40 .18
135 Randy Winn .40 .18
136 John Mabry .40 .18
137 Matt Thornton .40 .18
138 Bret Boone .40 .18
139 Jamie Moyer .40 .18
140 Giovanni Carrara .40 .18
141 Kazuhiro Sasaki .40 .18
142 Jeff Cirillo .40 .18
143 Mark McLemore .40 .18
144 Pat Borders .40 .18
145 Mike Cameron .40 .18
146 Dan Wilson .40 .18
147 John Olerud .40 .18
148 Arthur Rhodes .40 .18
149 Rafael Soriano .40 .18
150 Greg Colbrunn .40 .18
151 Ryan Franklin .40 .18
152 Joel Pineiro .40 .18
153 Jeff Nelson .40 .18
154 Jerry Hairston Jr. .40 .18
155 Rick Helling .40 .18
156 Gary Matthews Jr. .40 .18
157 Jeff Conine .40 .18
158 Sidney Ponson .40 .18
159 Tony Batista .40 .18
160 Jay Gibbons .40 .18
161 Marty Cordova .40 .18
162 Geronimo Gil .40 .18
163 Deivi Cruz .40 .18
164 B.J. Ryan .40 .18
165 Jason Johnson .40 .18
166 Buddy Groom .40 .18
167 Pat Hentgen .40 .18
168 Omar Daal .40 .18
169 Willis Roberts .40 .18
170 Scott Erickson .40 .18
171 David Segui .40 .18
172 Brook Fordyce .40 .18
173 Rodrigo Lopez .40 .18
174 Jose Leon .40 .18
175 Jose Morban .40 .18
176 Melvin Mora .40 .18
177 B.J. Surhoff .40 .18
178 Jorge Julio .40 .18
179 Alex Rodriguez 1.50 .70
180 Mark Teixeira .40 .18
181 Chan Ho Park .40 .18
182 Todd Van Poppel .40 .18
183 Todd Greene .40 .18
184 Ismael Valdes .40 .18
185 Rusty Greer .40 .18
186 Rafael Palmeiro .60 .25
187 Francisco Cordero .40 .18
188 Einar Diaz .40 .18
189 Doug Glanville .40 .18
190 Michael Young .60 .25
191 Kevin Mench .40 .18
192 Carl Everett .40 .18
193 Herbert Perry .40 .18
194 Jeff Zimmerman .40 .18
195 Juan Gonzalez .60 .25
196 Ugueth Urbina .40 .18
197 Jermaine Clark .40 .18
198 John Thomson .40 .18
199 Hank Blalock .60 .25
200 Jay Powell .40 .18
201 Mike Lamb .40 .18
202 Aaron Fultz .40 .18
203 Esteban Yan .40 .18
204 Nomar Garciaparra 1.50 .70
205 Pedro Martinez 1.00 .45
206 John Burkett .40 .18
207 Johnny Damon 1.00 .45
208 Doug Mirabelli .40 .18
209 Derek Lowe .40 .18
210 Shea Hillenbrand .40 .18
211 Brandon Lyon .40 .18
212 Trot Nixon .40 .18
213 Jason Varitek .60 .25
214 Tim Wakefield .40 .18
215 Manny Ramirez .60 .25
216 Todd Walker .40 .18
217 Jeremy Giambi .40 .18
218 Ramiro Mendoza .40 .18
219 Bill Mueller .40 .18
220 David Ortiz .60 .25
221 Mike Timlin .40 .18
222 Alan Embree .40 .18
223 Bob Howry .40 .18
224 Chad Fox .40 .18
225 Damian Jackson .40 .18
226 Casey Fossum .40 .18
227 Steve Woodard .40 .18
228 Freddy Sanchez .40 .18
229 Mike Sweeney .40 .18
230 Desi Relaford .40 .18
231 Brent Mayne .40 .18
232 Angel Berroa .40 .18
233 Albie Lopez .40 .18
234 Raul Ibanez .40 .18
235 Joe Randa .40 .18
236 Chris George .40 .18
237 Michael Tucker .40 .18
238 Mendy Lopez .40 .18
239 Kris Wilson .40 .18
240 Jason Grimsley .40 .18
241 Carlos Febles .40 .18
242 Runelvys Hernandez .40 .18
243 Mike MacDougal .40 .18
244 Carlos Beltran .60 .25
245 Brandon Berger .40 .18
246 Darrell May .40 .18
247 Miguel Asencio .40 .18
248 Ryan Bukvich .40 .18
249 Dee Brown .40 .18
250 Jeremy Hill .40 .18
251 Jeremy Affeldt .40 .18
252 Ken Harvey .40 .18
253 Bobby Higginson .40 .18
254 Matt Anderson .40 .18
255 Dmitri Young .40 .18
256 Gene Kingsale .40 .18
257 Craig Paquette .40 .18
258 Adam Bernero .40 .18
259 Andres Torres .40 .18
260 Carlos Pena .40 .18
261 Dean Palmer .40 .18
262 Eric Munson .40 .18
263 Omar Infante .40 .18
264 Shane Halter .40 .18
265 Jeremy Bonderman RC 1.50 .70
266 Steve Sparks .40 .18
267 Gary Knotts .40 .18
268 Mike Maroth .40 .18
269 Nate Cornejo .40 .18
270 Matt Roney .40 .18
271 Franklyn German .40 .18
272 Matt Walbeck .40 .18
273 Brandon Inge .40 .18
274 Hiram Bocachica .40 .18
275 Chris Spurling .40 .18
276 Craig Monroe .40 .18
277 Ramon Santiago .40 .18
278 Doug Mientkiewicz .40 .18
279 Torii Hunter .40 .18
280 Brad Radke .40 .18
281 Denny Hocking .40 .18
282 Tom Prince .40 .18
283 Eddie Guardado .40 .18
284 Jacque Jones .40 .18
285 Joe Mays .40 .18
286 Mike Fetters .40 .18
287 LaTroy Hawkins .40 .18
288 A.J. Pierzynski .40 .18
289 Eric Milton .40 .18
290 Cristian Guzman .40 .18
291 Bobby Kielty .40 .18
292 Corey Koskie .40 .18
293 J.C. Romero .40 .18
294 Mike Cuddyer .40 .18
295 Luis Rivas .40 .18
296 Matt LeCroy .40 .18
297 Tony Fiore .40 .18
298 Dustan Mohr .40 .18
299 Chris Gomez .40 .18
300 Johan Santana .60 .25
301 Kyle Lohse .40 .18
302 Frank Thomas 1.00 .45
303 Mark Buehrle .40 .18
304 Jon Garland .40 .18
305 Magglio Ordonez .40 .18
306 Paul Konerko .40 .18
307 Sandy Alomar Jr. .40 .18
308 Carlos Lee .40 .18
309 Jon Rauch .40 .18
310 Esteban Loaiza .40 .18
311 Danny Wright .40 .18
312 Kelly Wunsch .40 .18
313 Tony Graffanino .40 .18
314 Aaron Rowand .40 .18
315 Armando Rios .40 .18
316 Jose Valentin .40 .18
317 D'Angelo Jimenez .40 .18
318 Joe Crede .40 .18
319 Miguel Olivo .40 .18
320 Rick White .40 .18
321 Billy Koch .40 .18
322 Tom Gordon .40 .18
323 Bartolo Colon .40 .18
324 Josh Paul .40 .18
325 Joe Borchard .40 .18
326 Damaso Marte .40 .18
327 Derek Jeter 2.50 1.10
328 Jason Giambi .40 .18
329 Roger Clemens 2.00 .90
330 Enrique Wilson .40 .18
331 David Wells .40 .18
332 Mike Mussina .60 .25
333 Bernie Williams .60 .25
334 Todd Zeile .40 .18
335 Sterling Hitchcock .40 .18
336 Juan Acevedo .40 .18
337 Robin Ventura .40 .18
338 Mariano Rivera .60 .25
339 John Flaherty .40 .18
340 Andy Pettitte .60 .25
341 Antonio Osuna .40 .18
342 Erick Almonte .40 .18
343 Chris Hammond .40 .18
344 Steve Karsay .40 .18
345 Alfonso Soriano .60 .25
346 Bubba Trammell .40 .18
347 Nick Johnson .40 .18
348 Jorge Posada .60 .25
349 Jeff Weaver .40 .18
350 Raul Mondesi .60 .25
351 Randy Choate .40 .18
352 Drew Henson .40 .18
353 Jeff Bagwell .60 .25
354 Wade Miller .40 .18
355 Lance Berkman .40 .18
356 Julio Lugo .40 .18
357 Roy Oswalt .40 .18
358 Bruce Chen .40 .18
359 Morgan Ensberg .40 .18
360 Geoff Blum .40 .18
361 Brian Moehler .40 .18
362 Billy Wagner .40 .18
363 Pete Munro .40 .18
364 Brad Ausmus .40 .18
365 Jose Vizcaino .40 .18
366 Craig Biggio .60 .25
367 Tim Redding .40 .18
368 Gregg Zaun .40 .18
369 Octavio Dotel .40 .18
370 Carlos Hernandez .40 .18
371 Richard Hidalgo .40 .18
372 Jeriome Robertson .40 .18
373 Orlando Merced .40 .18
374 John Buck .40 .18
375 Adam Everett .40 .18
376 Raul Chavez .40 .18
377 Brad Lidge .40 .18
378 Jeff Kent .40 .18
379 Scott Linebrink .40 .18
380 Greg Miller .40 .18
381 Kirk Saarloos .40 .18
382 Brandon Puffer .40 .18
383 Ricky Stone .40 .18
384 Jason Lane .40 .18
385 Brian L. Hunter .40 .18
386 Rodrigo Rosario .40 .18
387 Horacio Ramirez .40 .18
388 Gary Sheffield .40 .18
389 Mike Hampton .40 .18
390 Robert Fick .40 .18
391 Henry Blanco .40 .18
392 Vinny Castilla .40 .18
393 Joe Dawley .40 .18
394 Jung Bong .40 .18
395 Rafael Furcal .40 .18
396 Javy Lopez .40 .18
397 Greg Maddux 1.50 .70
398 Andruw Jones .40 .18
399 John Smoltz .60 .25
400 Chipper Jones 1.00 .45
401 Mark DeRosa .40 .18
402 Shane Reynolds .40 .18
403 Kevin Gryboski .40 .18
404 Russ Ortiz .40 .18
405 Roberto Hernandez .40 .18
406 Ray King .40 .18
407 Matt Franco .40 .18
408 Marcus Giles .40 .18
409 Trey Hodges .40 .18
410 Darren Holmes .40 .18
411 Julio Franco .40 .18
412 Darren Bragg .40 .18
413 Richie Sexson .40 .18
414 Jeffrey Hammonds .40 .18
415 Ben Sheets .40 .18
416 Mike DeJean .40 .18
417 Royce Clayton .40 .18
418 Wes Helms .40 .18
419 Valerio de Los Santos .40 .18
420 Brady Clark .40 .18
421 Glendon Rusch .40 .18
422 Geoff Jenkins .40 .18
423 John Foster .40 .18
424 Curtis Leskanic .40 .18
425 Todd Ritchie .40 .18
426 Enrique Cruz .40 .18
427 Wayne Franklin .40 .18
428 Matt Ford .40 .18
429 Matt Kinney .40 .18
430 Scott Podsednik .40 .18
431 Luis Vizcaino .40 .18
432 Shane Nance .40 .18
433 Alex Sanchez .40 .18
434 John Vander Wal .40 .18
435 Eric Young .40 .18
436 Eddie Perez .40 .18
437 Jason Conti .40 .18
438 Matt Morris .40 .18
439 Tino Martinez .60 .25
440 Fernando Vina .40 .18
441 Kiko Calero RC .60 .25
442 Cal Eldred .40 .18
443 Jimmy Journell .40 .18
444 Jim Edmonds .40 .18
445 Jeff Fassero .40 .18
446 Mike Matheny .40 .18
447 Garrett Stephenson .40 .18
448 Brett Tomko .40 .18
449 So Taguchi .40 .18
450 Eduardo Perez .40 .18
451 Lance Painter .40 .18
452 Jason Isringhausen .40 .18
453 Albert Pujols 2.00 .90
454 Eli Marrero .40 .18
455 Jason Simontacchi .40 .18
456 J.D. Drew .40 .18
457 Scott Rolen 1.00 .45
458 Orlando Palmeiro .40 .18
459 Dustin Hermanson .40 .18
460 Edgar Renteria .40 .18
461 Woody Williams .40 .18
462 Chris Carpenter .40 .18
463 Sammy Sosa 1.50 .70
464 Kerry Wood 1.00 .45
465 Kyle Farnsworth .40 .18
466 Alex Gonzalez .40 .18
467 Eric Karros .40 .18
468 Troy O'Leary .40 .18
469 Mark Grudzielanek .40 .18
470 Alan Benes .40 .18
471 Mark Prior 1.00 .45
472 Paul Bako .40 .18
473 Shawn Estes .40 .18
474 Matt Clement .40 .18
475 Ramon E. Martinez .40 .18
476 Tom Goodwin .40 .18
477 Corey Patterson .40 .18
478 Moises Alou .40 .18
479 Juan Cruz .40 .18
480 Bobby Hill .40 .18
481 Mark Bellhorn .40 .18
482 Mark Guthrie .40 .18
483 Mike Remlinger .40 .18
484 Lenny Harris .40 .18
485 Antonio Alfonseca .40 .18
486 Dave Veres .40 .18
487 Hee Seop Choi .40 .18
488 Luis Gonzalez .40 .18
489 Lyle Overbay .40 .18
490 Randy Johnson 1.00 .45
491 Mark Grace .60 .25
492 Danny Bautista .40 .18
493 Junior Spivey .40 .18
494 Matt Williams .40 .18
495 Miguel Batista .40 .18
496 Tony Womack .40 .18
497 Byung-Hyun Kim .40 .18
498 Steve Finley .40 .18
499 Craig Counsell .40 .18
500 Curt Schilling .40 .18
501 Elmer Dessens .40 .18
502 Rod Barajas .40 .18
503 David Dellucci .40 .18
504 Mike Koplove .40 .18
505 Mike Myers .40 .18
506 Matt Mantei .40 .18
507 Stephen Randolph RC .60 .25
508 Chad Moeller .40 .18
509 Carlos Baerga .40 .18
510 Andrew Good .40 .18
511 Quinton McCracken .40 .18
512 Jason Romano .40 .18
513 Jolbert Cabrera .40 .18
514 Darren Dreifort .40 .18
515 Kevin Brown .40 .18
516 Paul Quantrill .40 .18
517 Shawn Green .40 .18
518 Hideo Nomo 1.00 .45
519 Eric Gagne 1.00 .45
520 Troy Brohawn .40 .18
521 Kazuhisa Ishii .40 .18
522 Guillermo Mota .40 .18
523 Alex Cora .40 .18
524 Odalis Perez .40 .18
525 Brian Jordan .40 .18
526 Andy Ashby .40 .18
527 Fred McGriff .60 .25
528 Adrian Beltre .60 .25
529 Daryle Ward .40 .18
530 Todd Hundley .40 .18
531 David Ross .40 .18
532 Paul Shuey .40 .18
533 Paul Lo Duca .40 .18
534 Dave Roberts .40 .18
535 Mike Kinkade .40 .18
536 Cesar Izturis .40 .18
537 Ron Coomer .40 .18
538 Jose Vidro .40 .18
539 Henry Mateo .40 .18
540 Tony Armas Jr. .40 .18
541 Joey Eischen .40 .18
542 Orlando Cabrera .40 .18
543 Jose Macias .40 .18
544 Fernando Tatis .40 .18
545 Jeff Liefer .40 .18
546 Michael Barrett .40 .18
547 Vladimir Guerrero 1.00 .45
548 Javier Vazquez .40 .18
549 Brad Wilkerson .40 .18
550 Zach Day .40 .18
551 Tomo Ohka .40 .18
552 Livan Hernandez .40 .18
553 Endy Chavez .40 .18
554 Dan Smith .40 .18
555 Scott Stewart .40 .18
556 T.J. Tucker .40 .18
557 Jamey Carroll .40 .18
558 Ron Calloway .40 .18

559 Brian Schneider .40 .18
560 Orlando Hernandez .40 .18
561 Wil Cordero .40 .18
562 Rocky Biddle .40 .18
563 Edgardo Alfonzo .40 .18
564 Andres Galaragga .40 .18
565 Felix Rodriguez .40 .18
566 Benito Santiago .40 .18
567 Jose Cruz Jr. .40 .18
568 Tim Worrell .40 .18
569 Marvin Benard .40 .18
570 Kurt Ainsworth .40 .18
571 Jim Brower .40 .18
572 J.T. Snow .40 .18
573 Scott Eyre .40 .18
574 Robb Nen .40 .18
575 Barry Bonds 2.50 1.10
576 Ray Durham .40 .18
577 Marquis Grissom .40 .18
578 Pedro Feliz .40 .18
579 Jason Schmidt .40 .18
580 Rich Aurilia .40 .18
581 Kirk Rueter .40 .18
582 Chad Zerbe .40 .18
583 Damian Moss .40 .18
584 Neifi Perez .40 .18
585 Joe Nathan .40 .18
586 Ruben Rivera .40 .18
587 Yorvit Torrealba .40 .18
588 Josh Beckett .40 .18
589 Todd Hollandsworth .40 .18
590 Derrek Lee .40 .18
591 A.J. Burnett .40 .18
592 Juan Pierre .40 .18
593 Mark Redman .40 .18
594 Blaine Neal .40 .18
595 Mike Mordecai .40 .18
596 Alex Gonzalez .40 .18
597 Brad Penny .40 .18
598 Tim Spooneybarger .40 .18
599 Mike Lowell .40 .18
600 Mike Redmond .40 .18
601 Braden Looper .40 .18
602 Ivan Rodriguez 1.00 .45
603 Andy Fox .40 .18
604 Vladimir Nunez .40 .18
605 Luis Castillo .40 .18
606 Juan Encarnacion .40 .18
607 Armando Almanza .40 .18
608 Gerald Williams .40 .18
609 Carl Pavano .40 .18
610 Michael Tejera .40 .18
611 Ramon Castro .40 .18
612 Brian Banks .40 .18
613 Roberto Alomar .60 .25
614 Al Leiter .40 .18
615 Jeromy Burnitz .40 .18
616 John Franco .40 .18
617 Tom Glavine .60 .25
618 Mike Piazza 1.50 .70
619 Cliff Floyd .40 .18
620 Joe McEwing .40 .18
621 David Weathers .40 .18
622 Pedro Astacio .40 .18
623 Timo Perez .40 .18
624 Jason Phillips .40 .18
625 Ty Wigginton .40 .18
626 Steve Trachsel UER .40 .18
Career IP total is wrong
627 Roger Cedeno .40 .18
628 Tsuyoshi Shinjo .40 .18
629 Armando Benitez .40 .18
630 Vance Wilson .40 .18
631 Mike Stanton .40 .18
632 Mo Vaughn .40 .18
633 Scott Strickland .40 .18
634 Rey Sanchez .40 .18
635 Jay Bell .40 .18
636 David Cone .40 .18
637 Jae Weong Seo .40 .18
638 Ryan Klesko .40 .18
639 Wiki Gonzalez .40 .18
640 Trevor Hoffman .40 .18
641 Sean Burroughs .40 .18
642 Mike Bynum .40 .18
643 Clay Condrey .40 .18
644 Gary Bennett .40 .18
645 Kevin Jarvis .40 .18
646 Mark Kotsay .40 .18
647 Phil Nevin .40 .18
648 Dave Hansen .40 .18
649 Keith Lockhart .40 .18
650 Brian Lawrence .40 .18
651 Jay Witasick .40 .18
652 Rondell White .40 .18
653 Jaret Wright .40 .18
654 Luther Hackman .40 .18
655 Jake Peavy .40 .18
656 Brian Buchanan .40 .18
657 Mark Loretta .40 .18
658 Oliver Perez .40 .18
659 Adam Eaton .40 .18
660 Xavier Nady .40 .18
661 Jesse Orosco .40 .18
662 Ramon Vazquez .40 .18
663 Jim Thome 1.00 .45
664 Jose Mesa .40 .18
665 Rheal Cormier .40 .18
666 David Bell .40 .18
667 Mike Lieberthal .40 .18
668 Brandon Duckworth .40 .18
669 David Coggin .40 .18
670 Bobby Abreu .40 .18
671 Turk Wendell .40 .18
672 Marlon Byrd .40 .18
673 Jason Michaels .40 .18
674 Kevin Millwood .40 .18
675 Tomas Perez .40 .18
676 Jimmy Rollins .40 .18
677 Vicente Padilla .40 .18
678 Pat Burrell .40 .18
679 Tyler Houston .40 .18
680 Hector Mercado .40 .18
681 Carlos Silva .40 .18
682 Nick Punto .40 .18
683 Ricky Ledee .40 .18
684 Randy Wolf .40 .18
685 Todd Pratt .40 .18
686 Placido Polanco .40 .18
687 Chase Utley .40 .18
688 Brian Giles .40 .18
689 Jason Kendall .40 .18
690 Matt Stairs .40 .18
691 Kris Benson .40 .18
692 Julian Tavarez .40 .18
693 Reggie Sanders .40 .18
694 Jeff D'Amico .40 .18
695 Pokey Reese .40 .18
696 Kenny Lofton .40 .18
697 Mike Williams .40 .18
698 David Williams .40 .18
699 Kevin Young .40 .18
700 Brian Boehringer .40 .18
701 Scott Sauerbeck .40 .18
702 Josh Fogg .40 .18
703 Joe Beimel .40 .18
704 Dennis Reyes .40 .18
705 Jeff Suppan .40 .18
706 Salomon Torres .40 .18
707 Kip Wells .40 .18
708 Craig Wilson .40 .18
709 Jack Wilson .40 .18
710 Rob Mackowiak .40 .18
711 Abraham Nunez .40 .18
712 Randall Simon .40 .18
713 Josias Manzanillo .40 .18
714 Ken Griffey Jr. 1.50 .70
715 Jimmy Haynes .40 .18
716 Felipe Lopez .40 .18
717 Jimmy Anderson .40 .18
718 Ryan Dempster .40 .18
719 Russell Branyan .40 .18
720 Aaron Boone .40 .18
721 Luke Prokopec .40 .18
722 Felix Heredia .40 .18
723 Scott Sullivan .40 .18
724 Danny Graves .40 .18
725 Kent Mercker .40 .18
726 Barry Larkin .60 .25
727 Jason LaRue .40 .18
728 Gabe White .40 .18
729 Adam Dunn .60 .25
730 Brandon Larson .40 .18
731 Reggie Taylor .40 .18
732 Sean Casey .40 .18
733 Scott Williamson .40 .18
734 Austin Kearns .40 .18
735 Kelly Stinnett .40 .18
736 Ruben Mateo .40 .18
737 Wily Mo Pena .40 .18
738 Larry Walker .60 .25
739 Juan Uribe .40 .18
740 Denny Neagle .40 .18
741 Darren Oliver .40 .18
742 Charles Johnson .40 .18
743 Todd Jones .40 .18
744 Todd Helton .60 .25
745 Shawn Chacon .40 .18
746 Jason Jennings .40 .18
747 Preston Wilson .40 .18
748 Chris Richard .40 .18
749 Chris Stynes .40 .18
750 Jose Jimenez .40 .18
751 Gabe Kapler .40 .18
752 Jay Payton .40 .18
753 Aaron Cook .40 .18
754 Greg Norton .40 .18
755 Scott Elarton .40 .18
756 Brian Fuentes .40 .18
757 Jose Hernandez .40 .18
758 Nelson Cruz .40 .18
759 Justin Speier .40 .18
760 Javier A. Lopez RC .60 .25
761 Garret Anderson AS .40 .18
762 Tony Batista AS .40 .18
763 Mark Buehrle AS .40 .18
764 Johnny Damon AS .60 .25
765 Freddy Garcia AS .40 .18
766 Nomar Garciaparra AS 1.00 .45
767 Jason Giambi AS .40 .18
768 Roy Halladay AS .40 .18
769 Shea Hillenbrand AS .40 .18
770 Torii Hunter AS .40 .18
771 Derek Jeter AS 1.25 .55
772 Paul Konerko AS .40 .18
773 Derek Lowe AS .40 .18
774 Pedro Martinez AS .60 .25
775 A.J. Pierzynski AS .40 .18
776 Jorge Posada AS .40 .18
777 Manny Ramirez AS .40 .18
778 Mariano Rivera AS .40 .18
779 Alex Rodriguez AS 1.00 .45
780 Kazuhiro Sasaki AS .40 .18
781 Alfonso Soriano AS .40 .18
782 Ichiro Suzuki AS 1.00 .45
783 Mike Sweeney AS .40 .18
784 Miguel Tejada AS .40 .18
785 Ugueth Urbina AS .40 .18
786 Robin Ventura AS .40 .18
787 Omar Vizquel AS .40 .18
788 Randy Winn AS .40 .18
789 Barry Zito AS .40 .18
790 Lance Berkman AS .40 .18
791 Barry Bonds AS 1.25 .55
792 Adam Dunn AS .40 .18
793 Tom Glavine AS .40 .18
794 Luis Gonzalez AS .40 .18
795 Shawn Green AS .40 .18
796 Vladimir Guerrero AS .60 .25
797 Todd Helton AS .40 .18
798 Trevor Hoffman AS .40 .18
799 Randy Johnson AS .60 .25
800 Andruw Jones AS .40 .18
801 Byung-Hyun Kim AS .40 .18
802 Mike Lowell AS .40 .18
803 Eric Gagne AS .60 .25
804 Matt Morris AS .40 .18
805 Robb Nen AS .40 .18
806 Vicente Padilla AS .40 .18
807 Odalis Perez AS .40 .18
808 Mike Piazza AS 1.00 .45
809 Mike Remlinger AS .40 .18
810 Scott Rolen AS .60 .25
811 Jimmy Rollins AS .40 .18
812 Benito Santiago AS .40 .18
813 Curt Schilling AS .40 .18
814 Richie Sexson AS .40 .18
815 John Smoltz AS .40 .18
816 Sammy Sosa AS 1.00 .45
817 Junior Spivey AS .40 .18
818 Jose Vidro AS .40 .18
819 Mike Williams AS .40 .18
820 Luis Castillo AS .40 .18
821 Jason Giambi HR Derby .40 .18
822 Luis Gonzalez HR Derby .40 .18
823 Sammy Sosa HR Derby 1.00 .45
824 Ken Griffey Jr. HR Derby 1.00 .45
825 Ken Griffey Jr. HR Derby 1.00 .45
826 Tino Martinez HR Derby .40 .18
827 Barry Bonds HR Derby 1.25 .55
828 Frank Thomas HR Derby .60 .25
829 Ken Griffey Jr. HR Derby 1.00 .45
830 Barry Bonds 02 WS 1.25 .55
831 Tim Salmon 02 WS .40 .18
832 Troy Glaus 02 WS .40 .18
833 Robb Nen 02 WS .40 .18
834 Jeff Kent 02 WS .40 .18
835 Scott Spiezio 02 WS .40 .18
836 Darin Erstad 02 WS .40 .18
837 Randy Johnson T40 .60 .25
838 Chipper Jones T40 .60 .25
839 Greg Maddux T40 1.00 .45
840 Nomar Garciaparra T40 1.00 .45
841 Manny Ramirez T40 .40 .18
842 Pedro Martinez T40 .60 .25
843 Sammy Sosa T40 1.00 .45
844 Ken Griffey Jr. T40 1.00 .45
845 Jim Thome T40 .60 .25
846 Vladimir Guerrero T40 .60 .25
847 Mike Piazza T40 1.00 .45
848 Derek Jeter T40 1.25 .55
849 Jason Giambi T40 .40 .18
850 Roger Clemens T40 1.00 .45
851 Alfonso Soriano T40 .40 .18
852 Hideki Matsui T40 4.00 1.80
853 Barry Bonds T40 1.25 .55
854 Ichiro Suzuki T40 1.00 .45
855 Albert Pujols T40 1.00 .45
856 Alex Rodriguez T40 1.00 .45
857 Darin Erstad T40 .40 .18
858 Troy Glaus T40 .40 .18
859 Curt Schilling T40 .40 .18
860 Luis Gonzalez T40 .40 .18
861 Tom Glavine T40 .40 .18
862 Andruw Jones T40 .40 .18
863 Gary Sheffield T40 .40 .18
864 Frank Thomas T40 .60 .25
865 Mark Prior T40 .60 .25
866 Ivan Rodriguez T40 .60 .25
867 Jeff Bagwell T40 .40 .18
868 Lance Berkman T40 .40 .18
869 Shawn Green T40 .40 .18
870 Hideo Nomo T40 .60 .25
871 Torii Hunter T40 .40 .18
872 Bernie Williams T40 .40 .18
873 Barry Zito T40 .40 .18
874 Pat Burrell T40 .60 .25
875 Carlos Delgado T40 .40 .18
876 Miguel Tejada T40 .40 .18
877 Hideki Matsui NR RC 8.00 3.60
878 Jose Contreras NR RC 2.00 .90
879 Jason Anderson NR .40 .18
880 Jason Shiell NR RC .60 .25
881 Kevin Tolar NR RC .60 .25
882 Michel Hernandez NR RC .60 .25
883 Arnie Munoz NR RC .60 .25
884 David Sanders NR RC .60 .25
885 Willie Eyre NR RC .60 .25
886 Brent Hoard NR RC .60 .25
887 Lew Ford NR RC 2.50 1.10
888 Beau Kemp NR RC .60 .25
889 Jon Pridie NR RC .60 .25
890 Mike Ryan NR RC 1.00 .45
891 Richard Fischer NR RC .60 .25
892 Luis Ayala NR RC .60 .25
893 Mike Neu NR RC .60 .25
894 Joe Valentine NR RC .60 .25
895 Nate Bland NR RC .60 .25
896 Shane Bazzell NR RC .60 .25
897 Aquilino Lopez NR RC .60 .25
898 D.Markwell NR RC .60 .25
899 Francisco Rosario NR RC .60 .25
900 Guillermo Quiroz NR RC 1.50 .70
901 Luis De Los Santos NR .40 .18
902 Fern.Cabrera NR RC .60 .25
903 Francisco Cruceta NR RC .60 .25
904 Jhonny Peralta NR .60 .25
905 Rett Johnson NR RC 1.00 .45
906 Aaron Looper NR RC .60 .25
907 Bobby Madritsch NR RC 4.00 1.80
908 Luis Matos NR .40 .18
909 Jose Castillo NR .40 .18
910 Chris Waters NR RC .60 .25
911 Jeremy Guthrie NR .40 .18
912 Pedro Liriano NR .40 .18
913 Joe Borowski NR .40 .18
914 Felix Sanchez NR RC .60 .25
915 Jon Leicester NR RC .60 .25
916 Todd Wellemeyer NR RC 1.00 .45
917 Matt Bruback NR RC .40 .18
918 Chris Capuano NR RC .60 .25
919 Oscar Villarreal NR RC .60 .25
920 Matt Kata NR RC 1.50 .70
921 Robby Hammock NR RC 1.00 .45
922 Gerald Laird NR .40 .18
923 Brandon Webb NR RC 2.00 .90
924 Tommy Whiteman NR .40 .18
925 Andrew Brown NR RC 1.00 .45
926 Alfredo Gonzalez NR RC .60 .25
927 Carlos Rivera NR .40 .18
928 Rick Roberts NR RC .60 .25
929 Terrmel Sledge NR RC 1.00 .45
930 Josh Willingham NR RC 1.00 .45
931 Prentice Redman NR RC .60 .25
932 Jeff Duncan NR RC 1.00 .45
933 Craig Brazell NR RC 1.00 .45
934 Jeremy Griffiths NR RC 1.00 .45
935 Phil Seibel NR RC .60 .25
936 Heath Bell NR RC .60 .25
937 Bernie Castro NR RC .60 .25
938 Mike Nicolas NR RC .60 .25
939 Cory Stewart NR RC .60 .25
940 Shane Victorino NR RC .60 .25
941 Brandon Villafuerte NR .40 .18
942 Jeremy Wedel NR RC .60 .25
943 Tommy Phelps NR .40 .18
944 Josh Hall NR RC 1.00 .45
945 Ryan Cameron NR RC .60 .25
946 Garrett Atkins NR .40 .18
947 Clint Barmes NR RC 1.00 .45
948 Mike Hessman NR RC .60 .25
949 Brian Stokes NR RC .60 .25
950 Rocco Baldelli NR .40 .18
951 Hector Luna NR RC .60 .25
952 Jaime Cerda NR .40 .18
953 D.J. Carrasco NR RC .60 .25
954 Ian Ferguson NR RC .60 .25
955 Tim Olson NR RC 1.00 .45
956 Al. Machado NR RC .60 .25
957 Jorge Cordova NR RC .60 .25
958 Wilfredo Ledezma NR RC 1.00 .45
959 Nate Robertson NR RC 3.00 1.35
960 Nook Logan NR RC .60 .25
961 Troy Glaus TC .40 .18
962 Jay Gibbons TC .40 .18
963 Nomar Garciaparra TC .40 .18
964 Paul Konerko TC .40 .18
965 Ellis Burks TC .40 .18
966 Bobby Higginson TC .40 .18
967 Mike Sweeney TC .40 .18
968 Torii Hunter .40 .18
Doug Mientkiewicz TC
969 Jorge Posada TC .40 .18
970 Miguel Tejada TC .40 .18
971 Ichiro Suzuki TC .40 .18
972 Toby Hall TC .40 .18
973 Alex Rodriguez .40 .18
Juan Gonzalez TC
974 Shannon Stewart TC .40 .18
975 Luis Gonzalez .40 .18
Mark Grace TC
976 Andruw Jones TC .40 .18
977 Antonio Alfonseca TC .40 .18
978 Aaron Boone TC .40 .18
979 Todd Helton TC .40 .18
980 Ivan Rodriguez TC .40 .18
981 Craig Biggio TC .40 .18
982 Shawn Green TC .40 .18
983 Richie Sexson TC .40 .18
984 Vladimir Guerrero TC .40 .18
985 Roberto Alomar TC .40 .18
986 Jim Thome TC .40 .18
987 Humberto Cota TC .40 .18
988 Ryan Klesko TC .40 .18
989 Barry Bonds .40 .18
Benito Santiago TC
990 Albert Pujols .40 .18
J.D. Drew TC
KG Ken Griffey Jr. Sample 1.00 .45

2003 Upper Deck 40-Man Rainbow

MINT NRMT
*RAINBOW: 10X TO 25X BASIC
*RAINBOW RC'S: 4X TO 10X BASIC
*RAINBOW NR: 10X TO 25X BASIC
*RAINBOW NR RC'S: 4X TO 10X BASIC
RANDOM INSERTS IN PACKS
STATED PRINT RUN 40 SERIAL #'d SETS

2003 Upper Deck 40-Man Red White and Blue

MINT NRMT
*RWB: 1.5X TO 4X BASIC
*RWB NR: 1.5X TO 4X BASIC
1-752 STATED ODDS 1:6
877-960 STATED ODDS 1:36

2003 Upper Deck 40-Man Endorsements Signatures

Inserted in packs at a stated rate of one in 500, these 33 cards feature authentic autographs from the player. Many of these cards were signed to print runs of 50 or fewer and we have put the stated print run next to the player's name in our checklist. Please note that if a card was signed to a print run of 25 or fewer copies there is no pricing due to market scarcity.

MINT NRMT
AGO Alex Graman/50
AV Andy Van Hekken/50
BC Brad Cresse/35
BD Ben Diggins 15.00 6.75
BH Ben Howard/25
BP Brandon Phillips/25
BR Brandon Claussen/35
CM Corwin Malone/50
CS C.C. Sabathia/10
DBO Dewon Brazelton/50
DH Drew Henson/25
DK David Kelton/50
HI Hansel Izquierdo/50
JA Jay Gibbons/24
JB John Buck/25
JD Johnny Damon/23
JG Jason Giambi/10
JJ Jimmy Journell/30
JL Jon Lieber 15.00 6.75
JU Justin Wayne/25
JW Jerome Williams/50
JYO Jayson Werth/50
KG Ken Griffey Jr./33
KGS Ken Griffey Sr. 15.00 6.75
KL Kenny Lofton/25
MA Mark Buehrle/23
MB Milton Bradley/50
MT Matt Thornton/50
MX Mark Teixeira/25
RA Rick Ankiel 25.00 11.00
SR Scott Rolen/10
TG Tony Gwynn/20
TO Tomo Ohka 40.00 18.00

2000 Upper Deck Brooklyn Dodgers Master Collection

The 2000 Upper Deck Brooklyn Dodgers Master Collection was released in November, 2000 and included a 15-card base set, an 11-card Legends of Flatbush insert set, and one mystery pack card. Please note that only 250 Master Collections exist.

Nm-Mt Ex-Mt
COMPLETE SET (15) 300.00 90.00
BD1 Jackie Robinson 40.00 12.00
BD2 Duke Snider 25.00 7.50
BD3 Pee Wee Reese 40.00 12.00
BD4 Gil Hodges 40.00 12.00
BD5 Carl Furillo 15.00 4.50
BD6 Don Newcombe 15.00 4.50
BD7 Sandy Koufax 100.00 30.00
BD8 Roy Campanella 40.00 12.00
BD9 Jim Gilliam 15.00 4.50
BD10 Don Drysdale 40.00 12.00
BD11 Sandy Amoros 15.00 4.50
BD12 Joe Black 15.00 4.50
BD13 Carl Erskine 15.00 4.50
BD14 Johnny Podres 15.00 4.50
BD15 Zack Wheat 25.00 7.50
NNO Mini Bat Mail Out/750 5.00 1.50

2000 Upper Deck Brooklyn Dodgers Master Collection Legends of Flatbush

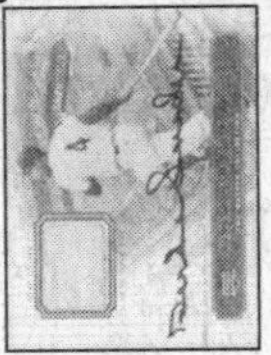

This insert set was issued in the 2000 Brooklyn Dodgers Master Collection. The set features game-used memorabilia cards from Dodger greats like Sandy Koufax and Duke Snider. Please note that Don Newcombe, Duke Snider, and Sandy Koufax autographed all of their cards.

Nm-Mt Ex-Mt
LOF1 Gil Hodges Bat 60.00 18.00
LOF2 Jackie Robinson Bat 100.00 30.00
LOF3 Pee Wee Reese Bat 50.00 15.00
LOF4 Jim Gilliam Bat 40.00 12.00
LOF5 Roy Campanella Bat 60.00 18.00
LOF6 Zach Wheat Bat 60.00 18.00
LOF7 Carl Furillo Bat 40.00 12.00
LOF8 D.Newcombe Bat AU 60.00 18.00
LOF9 Duke Snider Bat AU 100.00 30.00
LOF10 Don Drysdale Jsy 60.00 18.00
LOF11 S.Koufax Jsy AU 800.00 240.00

2000 Upper Deck Brooklyn Dodgers Master Collection Mystery Pack Inserts

Inserted into Brooklyn Dodgers Master Collection's at one per set, this 10-card insert features game-used memorablia and autographs of many Dodger greats. Please note that these cards came in a special mystery package that was inserted into every Brooklyn Dodgers Master Collection.

Nm-Mt Ex-Mt
DN-CF Don Newcombe
Carl Furillo Bat/35
DS-DN Duke Snider AU
Don Newcombe AU
GH-BC1-3 Gil Hodges Bat-Cut AU/3
JR-BC1-5 Jackie Robinson Bat-Cut AU/5
JR-DS Jackie Robinson
Duke Snider Bat/35
JR-GH Jackie Robinson
Gil Hodges
JR-PW Jackie Robinson
Pee Wee Reese Bat
JR-RC Jackie Robinson
Roy Campanella Bat
PW-BC1-8 Pee Wee Reese Bat-Cut AU/8
SK-DD Sandy Koufax Jsy
Don Drysdale Jsy/35

1999 Upper Deck Century Legends

This set was released in June, 1999 and was distributed in five card packs with an SRP of $4.99 per pack. The packs came 24 to a box. The first 47 card of the set feature an assortment of players honored from the Sporting News of 100 Greatest Players. The next 50 cards feature Upper Deck's choices of the best active players. The final cards are utilized for the following subsets: 21 CP (Cards numbered 101 through 120) and Memorablue Shots (Cards numbered 122 through 135.) Cards 11, 25, 26 and 126 do not exist. Due to contractual problems, Upper Deck had to pull the player's originally intended to be featured on these cards. Thus, though the set is numbered 1-135, it is complete at only 131 cards. A game-used bat from legendary slugger Jimmie Foxx was cut into approximately 350 pieces, incorporated into special A Piece of History 500 Club cards and randomly seeded into packs. Pricing for these scarce Foxx bat cards can be referenced under 1999 Upper Deck A Piece of History 500 Club. A Babe Ruth sample card was distributed to dealers and media several weeks prior to the product's national release. The card parallels Ruth's regular issue card except for the word "SAMPLE" running in red text diagonally across the card back.

	Nm-Mt	Ex-Mt
COMPLETE SET (131)	50.00	15.00
1 Babe Ruth	2.50	.75
2 Willie Mays	1.50	.45
3 Ty Cobb	1.25	.35
4 Walter Johnson	.75	.23
5 Hank Aaron	1.50	.45
6 Lou Gehrig	1.50	.45
7 Christy Mathewson	.75	.23
8 Ted Williams	1.50	.45
9 Rogers Hornsby	.75	.23
10 Stan Musial	1.25	.35
12 Grover Alexander	.75	.23
13 Honus Wagner	.75	.23
14 Cy Young	.75	.23
15 Jimmie Foxx	.75	.23
16 Johnny Bench	.75	.23
17 Mickey Mantle	3.00	.90
18 Josh Gibson	.75	.23
19 Satchel Paige	.75	.23
20 Roberto Clemente	1.50	.45
21 Warren Spahn	.50	.15
22 Frank Robinson	.50	.15
23 Lefty Grove	.75	.23
24 Eddie Collins	.50	.15
27 Tris Speaker	.75	.23
28 Mike Schmidt	1.50	.45
29 Napoleon Lajoie	.75	.23
30 Steve Carlton	.40	.12
31 Bob Gibson	.50	.15
32 Tom Seaver	.50	.15
33 George Sisler	.40	.12
34 Barry Bonds	2.00	.60
35 Joe Jackson NNO UER	1.00	.30
36 Bob Feller	.40	.12
37 Hank Greenberg	.75	.23
38 Ernie Banks	.75	.23
39 Greg Maddux	1.25	.35
40 Yogi Berra	.75	.23
41 Nolan Ryan	2.00	.60
42 Mel Ott	.75	.23
43 Al Simmons	.40	.12
44 Jackie Robinson	.75	.23
45 Carl Hubbell	.50	.15
46 Charley Gehringer	.40	.12
47 Buck Leonard	.40	.12
48 Reggie Jackson	.50	.15
49 Tony Gwynn	1.00	.30
50 Roy Campanella	.75	.23
51 Ken Griffey Jr.	1.25	.35
52 Barry Bonds	2.00	.60
53 Roger Clemens	1.50	.45
54 Tony Gwynn	1.00	.30
55 Cal Ripken	2.50	.75
56 Greg Maddux	1.25	.35
57 Frank Thomas	.75	.23
58 Mark McGwire	2.00	.60
59 Mike Piazza	1.25	.35
60 Wade Boggs	.50	.15
61 Alex Rodriguez	1.25	.35
62 Juan Gonzalez	.50	.15
63 Mo Vaughn	.40	.12
64 Albert Belle	.40	.12
65 Sammy Sosa	1.25	.35
66 Nomar Garciaparra	1.25	.35
67 Derek Jeter	2.00	.60
68 Kevin Brown	.50	.15
69 Jose Canseco	.75	.23
70 Randy Johnson	.75	.23
71 Tom Glavine	.50	.15
72 Barry Larkin	.50	.15
73 Curt Schilling	.40	.12
74 Moises Alou	.40	.12
75 Fred McGriff	.50	.15
76 Pedro Martinez	.75	.23
77 Andres Galarraga	.40	.12
78 Will Clark	.75	.23
79 Larry Walker	.50	.15
80 Ivan Rodriguez	.75	.23
81 Chipper Jones	.75	.23
82 Jeff Bagwell	.50	.15
83 Craig Biggio	.50	.15
84 Kerry Wood	.75	.23
85 Roberto Alomar	.50	.15
86 Vinny Castilla	.40	.12
87 Kenny Lofton	.40	.12
88 Rafael Palmeiro	.50	.15
89 Manny Ramirez	.50	.15
90 David Wells	.40	.12
91 Mark Grace	.50	.15
92 Bernie Williams	.50	.15
93 David Cone	.40	.12
94 John Olerud	.40	.12
95 John Smoltz	.50	.15
96 Tino Martinez	.50	.15
97 Raul Mondesi	.40	.12
98 Gary Sheffield	.40	.12
99 Orel Hershiser	.40	.12
100 Rickey Henderson	.75	.23
101 J.D. Drew 21CP	.40	.12
102 Troy Glaus 21CP	.40	.12
103 N.Garciaparra 21CP	1.25	.35
104 Scott Rolen 21CP	.50	.15
105 Ryan Minor 21CP	.30	.09
106 Travis Lee 21CP	.30	.09
107 Roy Halladay 21CP	.30	.09
108 Carlos Beltran 21CP	.50	.15
109 Alex Rodriguez 21CP	1.25	.35
110 Eric Chavez 21CP	.40	.12
111 V.Guerrero 21CP	.75	.23
112 Ben Grieve 21CP	.30	.09
113 Kerry Wood 21CP	.75	.23
114 Alex Gonzalez 21CP	.30	.09
115 Darin Erstad 21CP	.40	.12
116 Derek Jeter 21CP	2.00	.60
117 Jaret Wright 21CP	.30	.09
118 Jose Cruz Jr. 21CP	.30	.09
119 Chipper Jones 21CP	.75	.23
120 Gabe Kapler 21CP	.30	.09
121 Satchel Paige MEM	.75	.23
122 Willie Mays MEM	1.50	.45
123 R.Clemente MEM	1.50	.45
124 Lou Gehrig MEM	1.50	.45
125 Mark McGwire MEM	2.00	.60
127 Bob Gibson MEM	.50	.15
128 J.VanderMeer MEM	.30	.09
129 Walter Johnson MEM	.75	.23
130 Ty Cobb MEM	1.25	.35
131 Don Larsen MEM	.40	.12
132 Jackie Robinson MEM	.75	.23
133 Tom Seaver MEM	.40	.12
134 Johnny Bench MEM	.50	.15
135 Frank Robinson MEM	.50	.15
S1 Babe Ruth Sample	2.00	.60

1999 Upper Deck Century Legends Century Collection

Randomly inserted into hobby packs only, this 131-card set is a die-cut parallel version of the base set and is sequentially numbered to 100. Cards 11, 25, 26, and 126 do not exist.

Nm-Mt Ex-Mt

*ACTIVE STARS: 8X TO 20X BASIC...
*POST-WAR STARS: 12.5X TO 30X BASIC
*PRE-WAR STARS: 6X TO 15X BASIC
*21ST CENT: 8X TO 20X BASIC..........

1999 Upper Deck Century Legends All-Century Team

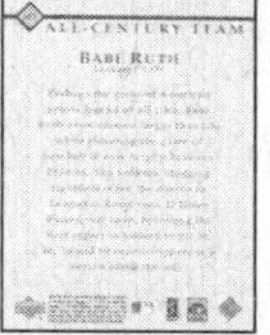

Randomly inserted in packs at the rate of one in 23, this 10-card set features photos of Upper Deck's All-Time All-Star Team.

	Nm-Mt	Ex-Mt
COMPLETE SET (10)	60.00	18.00
AC1 Babe Ruth	12.00	3.60
AC2 Ty Cobb	6.00	1.80
AC3 Willie Mays	8.00	2.40
AC4 Lou Gehrig	8.00	2.40
AC5 Jackie Robinson	4.00	1.20
AC6 Mike Schmidt	8.00	2.40
AC7 Ernie Banks	4.00	1.20
AC8 Johnny Bench	4.00	1.20
AC9 Cy Young	4.00	1.20
AC10 Lineup Sheet	1.50	.45

1999 Upper Deck Century Legends Artifacts

Randomly inserted in packs, this nine-card set features redemption cards for memorabilia from some of the top players of the century. Only one of each card was produced. No pricing is available due to the scarcity of these cards.

Nm-Mt Ex-Mt

1900 Ty Cobb Framed Cut
1910 Babe Ruth Framed Cut
1920 Rogers Hornsby Framed Cut
1930 Satchel Paige Framed Cut
1950 Hank Aaron
Willie Mays
Mickey Mantle AU Balls
1960 Ernie Banks
Bob Gibson
Johnny Bench AU Balls
1970 Tom Seaver
Mike Schmidt
Steve Carlton AU Balls
1980 Nolan Ryan
Ken Griffey Jr. AU Balls
1990 Ken Griffey Jr. AU Jersey

1999 Upper Deck Century Legends Epic Milestones

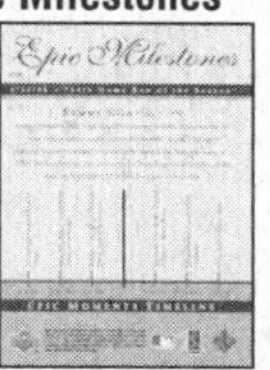

Randomly inserted into packs at the rate of one in 12, this nine-card set features color photos of players with the most impressive milestones in MLB history. Card EM1 does not exist.

	Nm-Mt	Ex-Mt
COMPLETE SET (9)	40.00	12.00
EM2 Jackie Robinson	2.50	.75
EM3 Nolan Ryan	6.00	1.80
EM4 Mark McGwire	6.00	1.80
EM5 Roger Clemens	5.00	1.50
EM6 Sammy Sosa	4.00	1.20
EM7 Cal Ripken	8.00	2.40
EM8 Rickey Henderson	2.50	.75
EM9 Hank Aaron	5.00	1.50
EM10 Barry Bonds	6.00	1.80

1999 Upper Deck Century Legends Epic Signatures

Randomly inserted into packs at the rate of one in 24, this 30-card set features autographed

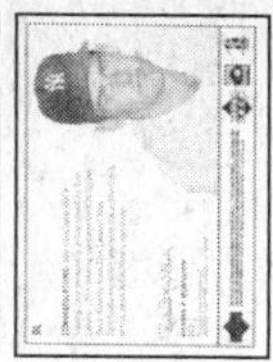

photos of retired stars and current players. Stickered exchange cards for Johnny Bench, Yogi Berra, Carlton Fisk and Willie McCovey were seeded into packs. The deadline to exchange those cards was December 31, 1999.

	Nm-Mt	Ex-Mt
AR Alex Rodriguez	150.00	45.00
BB Barry Bonds	250.00	75.00
BD Bucky Dent	15.00	4.50
BF Bob Feller	25.00	7.50
BG Bob Gibson	25.00	7.50
BM Bill Mazeroski	25.00	7.50
BT Bobby Thomson	15.00	4.50
CF Carlton Fisk	25.00	7.50
CFX Carlton Fisk EXCH	6.00	1.80
DL Don Larsen	25.00	7.50
EB Ernie Banks	50.00	15.00
EMA Eddie Mathews	60.00	18.00
FR Frank Robinson	40.00	12.00
FT Frank Thomas	80.00	24.00
GM Greg Maddux	100.00	30.00
HK Harmon Killebrew	40.00	12.00
JB Johnny Bench	50.00	15.00
JBX Johnny Bench EXCH	6.00	1.80
JG Juan Gonzalez	25.00	7.50
JR Ken Griffey Jr.	100.00	30.00
MS Mike Schmidt	60.00	18.00
NR Nolan Ryan	150.00	45.00
RJ Reggie Jackson	60.00	18.00
SC Steve Carlton	25.00	7.50
SM Stan Musial	60.00	18.00
SR Ken Griffey Sr.	15.00	4.50
TG Tony Gwynn	50.00	15.00
TS Tom Seaver	40.00	12.00
VG Vladimir Guerrero	40.00	12.00
WMC Willie McCovey	25.00	7.50
WMCX W.McCovey EXCH	4.00	1.20
WS Warren Spahn	50.00	15.00
YB Yogi Berra	50.00	15.00
YBX Yogi Berra EXCH	5.00	1.50

1999 Upper Deck Century Legends Epic Signatures Century

Randomly inserted in packs, this 32-card set features autographed color photos of past and present players with gold-foil stamping. Each card is hand-numbered to 100.

	Nm-Mt	Ex-Mt
AR Alex Rodriguez	250.00	75.00
BB Barry Bonds	300.00	90.00
BD Bucky Dent	25.00	7.50
BF Bob Feller	50.00	15.00
BG Bob Gibson	50.00	15.00
BM Bill Mazeroski	50.00	15.00
BT Bobby Thomson	25.00	7.50
CF Carlton Fisk	50.00	15.00
CFX Carlton Fisk EXCH	12.00	3.60
DL Don Larsen	50.00	15.00
EB Ernie Banks	100.00	30.00
EMA Eddie Mathews	100.00	30.00
FR Frank Robinson	80.00	24.00
FT Frank Thomas	150.00	45.00
GM Greg Maddux	150.00	45.00
HK Harmon Killebrew	80.00	24.00
JB Johnny Bench	100.00	30.00
JBX Johnny Bench EXCH	15.00	4.50
JG Juan Gonzalez	50.00	15.00
JR Ken Griffey Jr.	150.00	45.00
MS Mike Schmidt	120.00	36.00
NR Nolan Ryan	250.00	75.00
RJ Reggie Jackson	80.00	24.00
SC Steve Carlton	50.00	15.00
SM Stan Musial	120.00	36.00
SR Ken Griffey Sr.	25.00	7.50
TG Tony Gwynn	100.00	30.00
TS Tom Seaver	80.00	24.00
TW Ted Williams	1000.00	300.00
VG Vladimir Guerrero	80.00	24.00
WM Willie Mays	300.00	90.00
WMC Willie McCovey	50.00	15.00
WMCX W.McCovey EXCH	6.00	1.80
WS Warren Spahn	100.00	30.00
YB Yogi Berra	100.00	30.00
YBX Yogi Berra EXCH	15.00	4.50

1999 Upper Deck Century Legends Jerseys of the Century

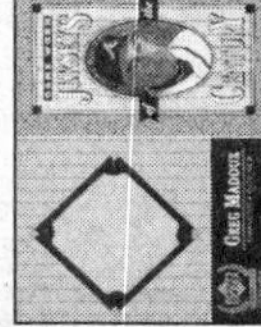
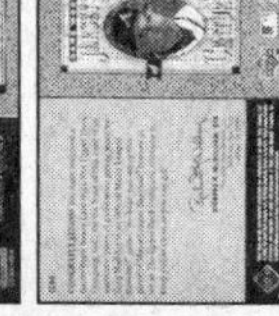

Randomly inserted in packs at the rate of one in 418, this nine-card set features color photos of top current and retired players with pieces of their actual game-worn jerseys embedded in the cards.

	Nm-Mt	Ex-Mt
DW Dave Winfield	15.00	4.50
EM Eddie Murray	25.00	7.50
GB George Brett	40.00	12.00
GM Greg Maddux	25.00	7.50
MS Mike Schmidt	40.00	12.00
NR Nolan Ryan	100.00	30.00
OZ Ozzie Smith	25.00	7.50
RC Roger Clemens	40.00	12.00
TG Tony Gwynn	30.00	9.00

1999 Upper Deck Century Legends Legendary Cuts

Randomly inserted into packs, this nine-card set features actual signature cuts from some of baseball's greatest players. Only one of each of these cards was produced.

Nm-Mt Ex-Mt

BR Babe Ruth
CY Cy Young
LG Lefty Grove
MO Mel Ott
RC Roy Campanella
SP Satchel Paige
TY Ty Cobb
WJ Walter Johnson
XX Jimmie Foxx

1999 Upper Deck Century Legends Memorable Shots

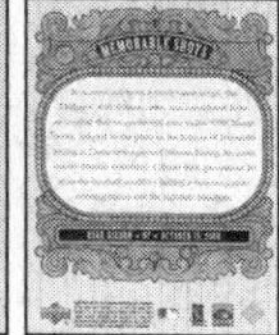

Randomly inserted into packs at the rate of one in 12, this 10-card set features photos of the most memorable home runs launched during this century.

	Nm-Mt	Ex-Mt
COMPLETE SET (10)	30.00	9.00
HR1 Babe Ruth	10.00	3.00
HR2 Bobby Thomson	1.00	.30
HR3 Kirk Gibson	1.00	.30
HR4 Carlton Fisk	1.00	.30
HR5 Bill Mazeroski	1.00	.30
HR6 Bucky Dent	1.00	.30
HR7 Mark McGwire	5.00	1.50
HR8 Mickey Mantle	10.00	3.00
HR9 Joe Carter	1.00	.30
HR10 Mark McGwire	5.00	1.50

1999 Upper Deck Century Legends MVPs

Randomly inserted in packs, this 100-card set features color action photos of Upper Deck's 1999 MVP players printed with rainbow-foil. Only one of each card was produced. Pricing for stars is unavailable due to scarcity. A checklist has been provided for cataloging purposes.

Nm-Mt Ex-Mt

C1 Mo Vaughn
C2 Troy Glaus
C3 Darin Erstad
C4 Randy Johnson
C5 Travis Lee
C6 Chipper Jones
C7 Greg Maddux
C8 Tom Glavine
C9 John Smoltz
C10 Cal Ripken
C11 Charles Johnson
C12 Albert Belle
C13 Nomar Garciaparra
C14 Pedro Martinez
C15 Kerry Wood
C16 Sammy Sosa
C17 Mark Grace
C18 Frank Thomas
C19 Paul Konerko
C20 Ray Durham
C21 Denny Neagle
C22 Sean Casey
C23 Barry Larkin
C24 Roberto Alomar
C25 Kenny Lofton
C26 Travis Fryman
C27 Jim Thome
C28 Manny Ramirez
C29 Vinny Castilla
C30 Todd Helton
C31 Dante Bichette
C32 Larry Walker
C33 Gabe Kapler
C34 Dean Palmer
C35 Tony Clark
C36 Juan Encarnacion
C37 Alex Gonzalez
C38 Preston Wilson
C39 Derrek Lee
C40 Ken Caminiti
C41 Jeff Bagwell
C42 Moises Alou
C43 Craig Biggio
C44 Carlos Beltran
C45 Jeremy Giambi
C46 Johnny Damon
C47 Kevin Brown
C48 Chan Ho Park
C49 Raul Mondesi
C50 Gary Sheffield
C51 Sean Berry
C52 Jeromy Burnitz
C53 Brad Radke
C54 Eric Milton
C55 Todd Walker
C56 Vladimir Guerrero
C57 Rondell White
C58 Mike Piazza
C59 Rickey Henderson
C60 Rey Ordonez
C61 Derek Jeter
C62 Bernie Williams
C63 Paul O'Neill
C64 Scott Brosius
C65 Tino Martinez
C66 Roger Clemens
C67 Orlando Hernandez
C68 Ben Grieve
C69 Eric Chavez
C70 Jason Giambi
C71 Curt Schilling
C72 Scott Rolen
C73 Pat Burrell
C74 Jason Kendall
C75 Aramis Ramirez
C76 Mark McGwire
C77 J.D. Drew
C78 Edgar Renteria
C79 Tony Gwynn
C80 Sterling Hitchcock
C81 Ruben Rivera
C82 Trevor Hoffman
C83 Barry Bonds
C84 Ellis Burks
C85 Robb Nen
C86 Ken Griffey Jr.
C87 Alex Rodriguez
C88 Carlos Guillen
C89 Edgar Martinez
C90 Jose Canseco
C91 Rolando Arrojo
C92 Wade Boggs
C93 Fred McGriff
C94 Juan Gonzalez
C95 Ivan Rodriguez
C96 Rafael Palmeiro
C97 David Wells
C98 Roy Halladay
C99 Carlos Delgado
C100 Jose Cruz Jr.

1999 Upper Deck Challengers for 70 Swinging for the Fences Autograph

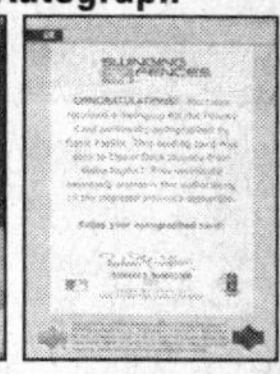

Randomly inserted in packs, this six-card set features autographed versions of some of the regular Swinging for the Fences insert cards. Only 2700 total cards were signed but not all players signed in equal quantities. Please note, a redemption card was seeded into packs for Alex Rodriguez.

	Nm-Mt	Ex-Mt
AR Alex Rodriguez	120.00	36.00
GK Gabe Kapler	15.00	4.50
JR Ken Griffey Jr.	120.00	36.00
TH Todd Helton	25.00	7.50
TL Travis Lee	15.00	4.50
VG Vladimir Guerrero	40.00	12.00

2001 Upper Deck Decade 1970's

This 180 card set was issued in five card packs with an SRP of $2.99 per pack. Some topical subsets included: Rookie Flashback (91-110), Decade Dateline (111-140), Award Winners (141-170) and World Series Highlights (171-180).

	Nm-Mt	Ex-Mt
COMPLETE SET (180)	40.00	12.00
1 Nolan Ryan	4.00	1.20

2 Don Baylor .60 .18
3 Bobby Grich .60 .18
4 Reggie Jackson 1.00 .30
5 Catfish Hunter 1.00 .30
6 Gene Tenace .60 .18
7 Rollie Fingers .60 .18
8 Sal Bando .60 .18
9 Bert Campaneris .60 .18
10 John Mayberry .40 .12
11 Rico Carty .40 .12
12 Gaylord Perry .60 .18
13 Andre Thornton .40 .12
14 Buddy Bell .60 .18
15 Dennis Eckersley .60 .18
16 Ruppert Jones .40 .12
17 Brooks Robinson 1.00 .30
18 Tommy Davis .40 .12
19 Eddie Murray 1.50 .45
20 Boog Powell 1.00 .30
21 Al Oliver .60 .18
22 Jeff Burroughs .40 .12
23 Mike Hargrove .60 .18
24 Dwight Evans .60 .18
25 Fred Lynn .60 .18
26 Rico Petrocelli .40 .12
27 Carlton Fisk 1.00 .30
28 Luis Aparicio .60 .18
29 Amos Otis .40 .12
30 Hal McRae .60 .18
31 Jason Thompson .40 .12
32 Al Kaline 1.50 .45
33 Jim Perry .60 .18
34 Bert Blyleven .60 .18
35 Harmon Killebrew 1.50 .45
36 Wilbur Wood .60 .18
37 Jim Kaat .60 .18
38 Ron Guidry .60 .18
39 Thurman Munson 1.50 .45
40 Graig Nettles .60 .18
41 Bobby Murcer .60 .18
42 Chris Chambliss .60 .18
43 Roy White .40 .12
44 J.R. Richard .60 .18
45 Jose Cruz .60 .18
46 Hank Aaron 3.00 .90
47 Phil Niekro .60 .18
48 Bob Horner .40 .12
49 Darrell Evans .60 .18
50 Gorman Thomas .60 .18
51 Don Money .40 .12
52 Robin Yount 2.50 .75
53 Joe Torre .60 .18
54 Tim McCarver .60 .18
55 Lou Brock 1.00 .30
56 Keith Hernandez .60 .18
57 Bill Madlock .60 .18
58 Ron Santo 1.00 .30
59 Billy Williams .60 .18
60 Ferguson Jenkins .60 .18
61 Steve Garvey .60 .18
62 Bill Russell UER .60 .18
Trivia question has several wrong answers
63 Maury Wills .60 .18
64 Ron Cey .60 .18
65 Manny Mota .40 .12
66 Ron Fairly .40 .12
67 Steve Rogers .40 .12
68 Gary Carter .60 .18
69 Andre Dawson .60 .18
70 Bobby Bonds .60 .18
71 Jack Clark .60 .18
72 Willie McCovey .60 .18
73 Tom Seaver 1.00 .30
74 Bud Harrelson .60 .18
75 Dave Kingman .60 .18
76 Jerry Koosman .60 .18
77 Jon Matlack .40 .12
78 Randy Jones .40 .12
79 Ozzie Smith 2.50 .75
80 Garry Maddox .40 .12
81 Mike Schmidt 3.00 .90
82 Greg Luzinski .60 .18
83 Tug McGraw .60 .18
84 Willie Stargell 1.00 .30
85 Dave Parker .60 .18
86 Roberto Clemente 4.00 1.20
87 Johnny Bench 1.50 .45
88 Joe Morgan .60 .18
89 George Foster .60 .18
90 Ken Griffey Sr. .60 .18
91 Carlton Fisk RF 1.00 .30
92 Andre Dawson RF .60 .18
93 Fred Lynn RF .60 .18
94 Eddie Murray RF 1.50 .45
95 Bob Horner RF .40 .12
96 Jon Matlack RF .40 .12
97 Mike Hargrove RF .60 .18
98 Robin Yount RF 2.50 .75
99 Mike Schmidt RF 1.50 .45
100 Gary Carter RF .60 .18
101 Ozzie Smith RF 1.50 .45
102 Paul Molitor RF 1.00 .30
103 Dennis Eckersley RF .60 .18
104 Dale Murphy RF 1.50 .45
105 Bert Blyleven RF .60 .18
106 Thurman Munson RF 1.50 .45
107 Dave Parker RF .60 .18
108 Jack Clark RF .60 .18
109 Keith Hernandez RF .60 .18
110 Ron Cey RF .60 .18
111 Billy Williams DD .40 .12
112 Tom Seaver DD .60 .18
113 Reggie Jackson DD .60 .18
114 Bobby Bonds DD .40 .12
115 Willie Stargell DD .60 .18
116 Harmon Killebrew DD 1.50 .45
117 Roberto Clemente DD 2.00 .60
118 Wilbur Wood DD .40 .12
119 Billy Williams DD .40 .12
120 Nolan Ryan DD 2.00 .60
121 Ron Blomberg DD .40 .12
122 Hank Aaron DD 1.50 .45
123 Lou Brock DD .60 .18
124 Al Kaline DD UER 1.00 .30
Kaline got his 3,000 hit in 1974, not 1964
125 Brooks Robinson DD .60 .18
126 Bill Madlock DD .40 .12
127 Rennie Stennett DD .40 .12
128 Carlton Fisk DD .60 .18
129 Chris Chambliss DD .40 .12
130 Ruppert Jones DD .40 .12
131 Ron Fairly DD .40 .12
132 George Foster DD .40 .12
133 Reggie Jackson DD .60 .18
134 Ron Guidry DD .40 .12
135 Gaylord Perry DD .40 .12
136 Bucky Dent DD .40 .12
137 Dave Kingman DD .40 .12
138 Lou Brock DD .60 .18
139 Thurman Munson DD 1.00 .30
140 Willie Stargell DD .60 .18
141 Johnny Bench AW 1.00 .30
142 Boog Powell AW .60 .18
143 Jim Perry AW .40 .12
144 Joe Torre AW .40 .12
145 Chris Chambliss AW .40 .12
146 Ferguson Jenkins AW .40 .12
147 Carlton Fisk AW .60 .18
148 Gaylord Perry AW .60 .18
149 Johnny Bench AW 1.00 .30
150 Reggie Jackson AW .60 .18
151 Tom Seaver AW .60 .18
152 Thurman Munson AW 1.00 .30
153 Steve Garvey AW .40 .12
154 Catfish Hunter AW .60 .18
155 Mike Hargrove AW .40 .12
156 Joe Morgan AW .40 .12
157 Fred Lynn AW .40 .12
158 Tom Seaver AW .60 .18
159 Thurman Munson AW 1.00 .30
160 Randy Jones AW .40 .12
161 Joe Morgan AW .40 .12
162 George Foster AW .40 .12
163 Eddie Murray AW 1.00 .30
164 Andre Dawson AW .40 .12
165 Gaylord Perry AW .40 .12
166 Ron Guidry AW .40 .12
167 Dave Parker AW .40 .12
168 Don Baylor AW .40 .12
169 Bruce Sutter AW .40 .12
170 Willie Stargell AW .60 .18
171 Brooks Robinson WS .60 .18
172 Roberto Clemente WS 2.00 .60
173 Gene Tenace WS .40 .12
174 Reggie Jackson WS .60 .18
175 Rollie Fingers WS .40 .12
176 Carlton Fisk WS .60 .18
177 Johnny Bench WS 1.00 .30
178 Reggie Jackson WS .60 .18
179 Bucky Dent WS .40 .12
180 Willie Stargell WS .60 .18

2001 Upper Deck Decade 1970's Arms Race

Issued at a rate of one in 14, these 10 cards pay homage to the great pitchers of yesteryear.

Nm-Mt Ex-Mt
COMPLETE SET (10) 25.00 7.50
AR1 Nolan Ryan 8.00 2.40
AR2 Ferguson Jenkins 1.25 .35
AR3 Jim Hunter 2.00 .60
AR4 Tom Seaver 2.00 .60
AR5 Randy Jones 1.25 .35
AR6 J.R. Richard 1.25 .35
AR7 Rollie Fingers 1.25 .35
AR8 Gaylord Perry 1.25 .35
AR9 Ron Guidry 1.25 .35
AR10 Phil Niekro 1.25 .35

2001 Upper Deck Decade 1970's Bellbottomed Bashers

Issued at a rate of one in 14, these 10 cards feature some of the 1970's most powerful sluggers.

Nm-Mt Ex-Mt
COMPLETE SET (10) 25.00 7.50
BB1 Reggie Jackson 2.00 .60
BB2 Gorman Thomas 1.25 .35
BB3 Willie McCovey 1.25 .35
BB4 Willie Stargell 2.00 .60
BB5 Mike Schmidt 6.00 1.80
BB6 George Foster 1.25 .35
BB7 Johnny Bench 3.00 .90
BB8 Dave Kingman 1.25 .35
BB9 Graig Nettles 1.25 .35
BB10 Steve Garvey 1.25 .35

2001 Upper Deck Decade 1970's Disco Era Dandies

Issued at a rate of one in 23, these six cards feature some of the best players of the "disco" era.

Nm-Mt Ex-Mt
COMPLETE SET (6) 20.00 6.00
DE1 Mike Schmidt 6.00 1.80
DE2 Johnny Bench 3.00 .90
DE3 Lou Brock 2.00 .60
DE4 Reggie Jackson 2.00 .60
DE5 Willie Stargell 2.00 .60
DE6 Tom Seaver 2.00 .60

2001 Upper Deck Decade 1970's Dynasties

Issued at a rate of one in 14, these 10 cards feature stars from 10 of baseball's best teams during the 1970's.

Nm-Mt Ex-Mt
COMPLETE SET (10) 25.00 7.50
D1 Boog Powell 1.25 .35
D2 Johnny Bench 3.00 .90
D3 Willie Stargell 2.00 .60
D4 Jim Hunter 2.00 .60
D5 Steve Garvey 1.25 .35
D6 Carlton Fisk 2.00 .60
D7 Mike Schmidt 6.00 1.80
D8 Hal McRae 1.25 .35
D9 Tom Seaver 2.00 .60
D10 Reggie Jackson 2.00 .60

2001 Upper Deck Decade 1970's Game Bat

Issued at a rate of one in 24 hobby and one in 48 retail, these 48 cards featuure game-used pat pieces from various stars of the 1970's. A few players were printed in lesser quantites and we have notated them in our checklist with an SP along with print run information supplied by Upper Deck.

Nm-Mt Ex-Mt
B-AD Andre Dawson 10.00 3.00
B-AO Al Oliver 10.00 3.00
B-BB Bobby Bonds 10.00 3.00
B-BG Bobby Grich 10.00 3.00
B-BH B.Harrelson SP/290 10.00 3.00
B-BIM Bill Madlock 10.00 3.00
B-BOM Bobby Murcer 40.00 12.00
B-BP Boog Powell 15.00 4.50
B-BR Bill Russell 10.00 3.00
B-CF Carlton Fisk 15.00 4.50
B-DAE Darrell Evans 10.00 3.00
B-DB Don Baylor 10.00 3.00
B-DC Dave Concepcion 10.00 3.00
B-DP Dave Parker 10.00 3.00
B-DW Dave Winfield 10.00 3.00
B-DWE Dwight Evans 10.00 3.00
B-EM Eddie Murray 15.00 4.50
B-FL Fred Lynn 10.00 3.00
B-GC Gary Carter 10.00 3.00
B-GF George Foster 10.00 3.00
B-GL Greg Luzinski 10.00 3.00
B-GM Garry Maddox 10.00 3.00
B-GN Graig Nettles SP/219
B-HA Hank Aaron 50.00 15.00
B-HM Hal McRae 10.00 3.00
B-JAC Jack Clark 10.00 3.00
B-JM Joe Morgan 10.00 3.00
B-JOC Jose Cruz 10.00 3.00
B-KG Ken Griffey Sr. 10.00 3.00
B-KH K.Hernandez SP/243 25.00 7.50
B-MM Manny Mota 10.00 3.00
B-MW Maury Wills 10.00 3.00
B-NR Nolan Ryan 40.00 12.00
B-OS Ozzie Smith 15.00 4.50
B-RAJ Randy Jones 10.00 3.00
B-RC R.Clemente SP/243 100.00 30.00
B-REJ Reggie Jackson 15.00 4.50
B-RH Ron Hunt 10.00 3.00
B-RM Rick Monday 10.00 3.00
B-RS Ron Santo 15.00 4.50
B-RW Roy White 10.00 3.00
B-SG Steve Garvey 10.00 3.00
B-TD Tommy Davis 10.00 3.00
B-TIM Tim McCarver 10.00 3.00
B-TOS T.Seaver SP/121 40.00 12.00
B-TUM Tug McGraw SP/97
B-WM Willie Montanez 10.00 3.00
B-WR Willie Randolph 10.00 3.00

2001 Upper Deck Decade 1970's Game Bat Combos

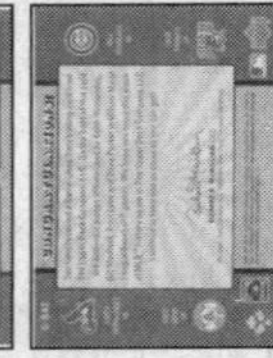

Issued at a rate of one in 336, these 19 cards feature game-used bat pieces from four different players. A handful of cards were announced as short-prints by Upper Deck with specific print runs revealed. That information is detailed in our checklist.

Nm-Mt Ex-Mt
LA Steve Garvey 25.00 7.50
Ron Cey
Bill Russell
Rick Monday
RD George Foster 25.00 7.50
Joe Morgan
Ron Cey
Bill Russell
RY Chris Chambliss 80.00 24.00
Reggie Jackson
Roy White
Hal McRae
WS72 Reggie Jackson 80.00 24.00
Bert Campaneris
Dave Concepcion
Johnny Bench SP/97
WS73 Reggie Jackson 40.00 12.00
Bert Campaneris
Tom Seaver
Bud Harrelson
WS74 Reggie Jackson 40.00 12.00
Bert Campaneris
Steve Garvey
Ron Cey
WS75 Carlton Fisk 40.00 12.00
Fred Lynn
George Foster
Joe Morgan
WS76 Chris Chambliss 80.00 24.00
Graig Nettles
Johnny Bench
Ken Griffey Sr.
WS77 Reggie Jackson 40.00 12.00
Graig Nettles
Steve Garvey
Ron Cey
WS78 Graig Nettles 60.00 18.00
Chris Chambliss
Bill Russell
Ron Cey
BAT Keith Hernandez 25.00 7.50
Bill Madlock
Fred Lynn
Dave Parker
CIN Johnny Bench 50.00 15.00
George Foster
Ken Griffey Sr.
Joe Morgan
GGA Carlton Fisk 40.00 12.00
Graig Nettles
Bobby Grich
Fred Lynn
GGN Johnny Bench 100.00 30.00
Roberto Clemente
Dave Concepcion
Garry Maddox
NYM Tom Seaver 40.00 12.00
Bud Harrelson
Ron Hunt
Tug McGraw
NYY Reggie Jackson 50.00 15.00
Graig Nettles
Chris Chambliss
Roy White
ROY Andre Dawson 50.00 15.00
Fred Lynn
Carlton Fisk
Eddie Murray
ASMV Bill Madlock 25.00 7.50
Joe Morgan
Steve Garvey
Dave Parker
MVPN Johnny Bench 50.00 15.00
Steve Garvey
Willie Stargell
George Foster

2001 Upper Deck Decade 1970's Game Jersey

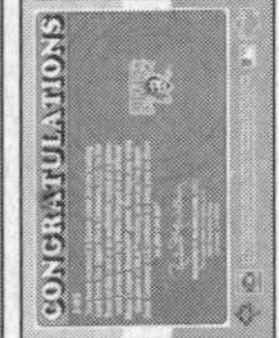

Issued at a rate of one on 168, these 27 cards feature swatches of their game-used uniforms. A few players were issued in shorter supply; we have notated them with an SP in our checklist along with print run information supplied by Upper Deck.

Nm-Mt Ex-Mt
J-BH Burt Hooton 10.00 3.00
J-BM Bobby Murcer 40.00 12.00
J-BM Bill Madlock 10.00 3.00
J-CF Carlton Fisk 15.00 4.50
J-CH Catfish Hunter 15.00 4.50
J-HA Hank Aaron 50.00 15.00
J-JB Johnny Bench 15.00 4.50
J-JKA Jim Kaat 10.00 3.00
J-JKO Jerry Koosman 10.00 3.00
J-JM Jon Matlack 10.00 3.00
J-JP Jim Perry 10.00 3.00
J-KG Ken Griffey Sr. SP/15
J-LA Luis Aparicio 10.00 3.00
J-LP Lou Piniella 10.00 3.00
J-MW Maury Wills 10.00 3.00
J-NR Nolan Ryan SP/50 60.00 18.00
J-RC Roberto Clemente 100.00 30.00
J-RF Rollie Fingers 10.00 3.00
J-RG Ron Guidry 10.00 3.00
J-RJ Reggie Jackson
J-RP Rico Petrocelli SP/15
J-SB Sal Bando SP/15
J-TM Tug McGraw 10.00 3.00
J-TS Tom Seaver 15.00 4.50
J-WD Willie Davis 10.00 3.00
J-WR Willie Randolph 10.00 3.00
J-WS Willie Stargell 15.00 4.50

2001 Upper Deck Decade 1970's Game Jersey Autograph

Issued at a rate of one in 168 hobby and one in 480 retail, these 18 cards have not only a game-used jersey piece but also an authentic autograph of the featured player. Some of the cards were released in lesser quantites and we have notated that information in our checklist with an SP along with print run information provided by Upper Deck.

Nm-Mt Ex-Mt
SJ-BH Burt Hooton 25.00 7.50
SJ-BM Bobby Murcer 60.00 18.00
SJ-BM Bill Madlock 25.00 7.50
SJ-CF Carlton Fisk SP/243 40.00 12.00
SJ-HA Hank Aaron SP/97 200.00 60.00
SJ-JB Johnny Bench 100.00 30.00
SJ-JKA Jim Kaat 25.00 7.50
SJ-JKO Jerry Koosman
SJ-KG Ken Griffey Sr. 25.00 7.50
SJ-LA Luis Aparicio 25.00 7.50
SJ-MW Maury Wills 25.00 7.50
SJ-NR Nolan Ryan SP/291 150.00 45.00
SJ-RF Rollie Fingers 25.00 7.50
SJ-RG Ron Guidry 40.00 12.00
SJ-RJ R.Jackson SP/291 100.00 30.00
SJ-RP Rico Petrocelli 25.00 7.50
SJ-SB Sal Bando 25.00 7.50
SJ-TM Tug McGraw 50.00 15.00

2001 Upper Deck Decade 1970's Game Jersey Patch

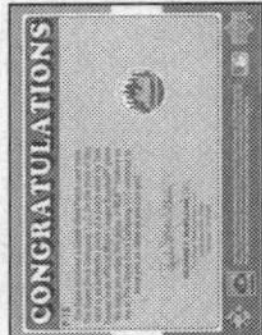

Issued at a rate of one in 7.500, these 26 cards features pieces of game-used uniform patches. Due to scarcity, no pricing is provided for these cards.

Nm-Mt Ex-Mt
P-BH Burt Hooton
P-BM Bill Madlock
P-BM Bobby Murcer
P-CH Jim Hunter
P-HA Hank Aaron
P-JB Johnny Bench
P-JKA Jim Kaat
P-JKO Jerry Koosman
P-JM Jon Matlack
P-JP Jim Perry
P-KG Ken Griffey Sr.
P-LA Luis Aparicio
P-LP Lou Piniella
P-MW Maury Wills
P-NR Nolan Ryan
P-RC Roberto Clemente
P-RF Rollie Fingers
P-RG Ron Guidry
P-RJ Reggie Jackson
P-RP Rico Petrocelli
P-SB Sal Bando
P-TM Tug McGraw
P-TS Tom Seaver
P-WD Willie Davis
P-WR Willie Randolph
P-WS Willie Stargell

2001 Upper Deck Decade 1970's Super Powers

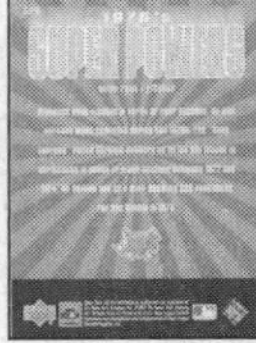

Inserted at a rate of one in 23, these six cards feature the players who carried the most clout during the 1970's.

Nm-Mt Ex-Mt
COMPLETE SET (6) 20.00 6.00
SP1 Reggie Jackson 2.00 .60
SP2 Joe Morgan 2.00 .60
SP3 Willie Stargell 2.00 .60
SP4 Willie McCovey 2.00 .60
SP5 Mike Schmidt 6.00 1.80
SP6 Nolan Ryan 8.00 2.40

2004 Upper Deck Etchings

This 150-card set was released in August, 2004. The set was issued in five card packs with an $5

RP which were packed 12 packs to a box and
5 boxes to a case. Cards numbered 1-90 fea-
re veterans while cards numbered 91-120 fea-
re unsigned Rookie Cards which were issued
a stated print run of 2004 serial numbered
ts and were issued at stated odds of one in six.
ard numbered 121-150 were issued to a stated
int run of 700 serial numbered sets. Autograph
rds in this product were inserted at a stated
te of one in four.

Nm-Mt Ex-Mt
OMP.SET w/o SP's (90).......... 25.00 7.50
OMMON CARD (1-90) .... .50 .15
OMMON CARD (91-120) 4.00 1.20
-120 STATED ODDS 1:6 ....
-120 PRINT RUN 2004 SERIAL #'d SETS
OMMON AUTO (121-150)......... 8.00 2.40
21-150 OVERALL AU ODDS 1:4 ....
21-150 PRINT RUN 700 SERIAL #'d SETS
Albert Pujols .... 2.50 .75
Torii Hunter .... .50 .15
Jim Edmonds............................. .50 .15
Alex Rodriguez....................... 2.00 .60
Rafael Palmeiro.......................... .75 .23
Ken Griffey Jr. .... 2.00 .60
Adam Dunn................................ .75 .23
Andruw Jones............................ .50 .15
Carlos Lee................................. .50 .15
0 Mike Piazza .... 2.00 .60
1 Jeff Bagwell .... .75 .23
2 Hideki Matsui .... 2.00 .60
3 Gary Sheffield .... .50 .15
4 Edgar Renteria .... .50 .15
5 Shawn Green .... .50 .15
6 Kerry Wood............................ 1.25 .35
7 Ivan Rodriguez........................ 1.25 .35
8 Josh Beckett .... .50 .15
9 Scott Rolen .... 1.25 .35
0 Brian Giles .... .50 .15
1 Derrek Lee .... .50 .15
2 Mike Lowell............................... .50 .15
3 Mike Mussina............................ .75 .23
4 Sammy Sosa.......................... 2.00 .60
5 Brandon Webb .... .50 .15
6 Jacque Jones .... .50 .15
7 Randy Johnson...................... 1.25 .35
8 Luis Gonzalez............................ .50 .15
9 Eric Chavez .... .50 .15
0 Carlos Delgado.......................... .50 .15
1 Phil Nevin.................................. .50 .15
2 Ichiro Suzuki .... 2.00 .60
3 Roy Oswalt................................ .50 .15
4 Tim Hudson .... .50 .15
5 Juan Gonzalez............................ .75 .23
6 Frank Thomas .... 1.25 .35
7 Mark Mulder .... .50 .15
8 Mark Teixeira............................. .50 .15
9 Miguel Tejada............................ .50 .15
0 Jeff Kent.................................... .50 .15
1 Andy Pettitte .... .75 .23
2 Barry Zito .... .50 .15
3 Roy Halladay .... .50 .15
4 Rocco Baldelli .... .50 .15
5 Derek Jeter........................... 2.50 .75
6 Corey Patterson .... .50 .15
7 Javy Lopez .... .50 .15
8 A.J. Burnett................................ .50 .15
9 Chipper Jones........................ 1.25 .35
0 Curt Schilling .... 1.25 .35
1 Todd Helton .... .75 .23
2 Pedro Martinez...................... 1.25 .35
3 Hideo Nomo.......................... 1.25 .35
4 Jose Reyes................................. .50 .15
5 Vernon Wells.............................. .50 .15
6 Geoff Jenkins .... .50 .15
7 Troy Glaus................................. .50 .15
8 Greg Maddux .... 2.00 .60
9 Jason Schmidt .... .50 .15
0 Preston Wilson .... .50 .15
1 Miguel Cabrera.......................... .75 .23
2 Hank Blalock .... .50 .15
3 Rafael Furcal .... .50 .15
4 Vladimir Guerrero .... 1.25 .35
5 Lance Berkman .... .50 .15
6 Javier Vazquez .... .50 .15
7 Bret Boone .... .50 .15
8 Mark Prior............................ 1.25 .35
9 Magglio Ordonez....................... .50 .15
0 Dontrelle Willis.......................... .50 .15
1 Richie Sexson .... .50 .15
2 Alfonso Soriano .... .75 .23
3 Edwin Jackson .... .50 .15
4 Jose Vidro.................................. .50 .15
5 Jason Giambi .... .50 .15
6 Kevin Brown.............................. .50 .15
7 Orlando Cabrera........................ .50 .15
8 Nomar Garciaparra.............. 2.00 .60
9 Bobby Abreu .... .50 .15
0 Manny Ramirez......................... .75 .23
1 J.D. Drew .... .50 .15
2 Roger Clemens .... 2.50 .75
3 Pat Burrell................................. .50 .15
4 Ryan Klesko .... .50 .15
5 Garret Anderson........................ .50 .15
6 Johan Santana .... .75 .23
7 Kevin Millwood .... .50 .15
8 Austin Kearns............................ .50 .15
9 Jim Thome............................ 1.25 .35
0 Carlos Beltran .... .75 .23
1 Kazuo Matsui FE RC.............. 8.00 2.40
2 Jamie Brown FE RC 4.00 1.20
3 Brandon Medders FE RC........ 4.00 1.20
4 Carlos Vasquez FE RC........... 5.00 1.50
5 Chris Aguila FE RC................. 4.00 1.20
6 David Aardsma FE RC............ 4.00 1.20
7 Justin Leone FE RC................ 5.00 1.50
8 Mike Johnston FE RC............. 4.00 1.20
99 Tim Bittner FE RC 4.00 1.20
100 Mike Rouse FE RC............... 4.00 1.20
101 Dennis Sarfate FE RC.......... 4.00 1.20
102 Jason Frasor FE RC 4.00 1.20
103 Jorge Vasquez FE RC.......... 4.00 1.20
104 Mike Gosling FE RC............. 4.00 1.20
105 Jake Woods FE RC.............. 4.00 1.20
106 Akinori Otsuka FE RC.......... 4.00 1.20
107 Lincoln Holdzkom FE RC 4.00 1.20
108 Jesse Harper FE RC 4.00 1.20
109 Edwin Moreno FE RC........... 4.00 1.20
110 Shingo Takatsu FE RC......... 5.00 1.50
111 Ryan Meaux FE RC.............. 4.00 1.20
112 Donnie Kelly FE RC.............. 4.00 1.20
113 Jerome Gamble FE RC......... 4.00 1.20
114 Josh Labandeira FE RC........ 4.00 1.20
115 Ian Snell FE RC 5.00 1.50
116 Michael Wuertz FE RC 5.00 1.50
117 Greg Dobbs FE RC............... 4.00 1.20
118 Sean Henn FE RC................. 4.00 1.20
119 Dave Crouthers FE RC 4.00 1.20
120 Hector Gimenez FE RC......... 4.00 1.20
121 Renyel Pinto FE AU RC 10.00 3.00
122 Tim Hamulack FE AU RC....... 8.00 2.40
123 Chris Saenz FE AU RC......... 8.00 2.40
124 Carlos Hines FE AU RC........ 8.00 2.40
125 Justin Knoedler FE AU RC ... 8.00 2.40
126 Onil Joseph FE AU RC 8.00 2.40
127 Ryan Wing FE AU RC 8.00 2.40
128 Scott Proctor FE AU RC...... 10.00 3.00
129 Rusty Tucker FE AU RC...... 10.00 3.00
130 Fernando Nieve FE AU RC.... 8.00 2.40
131 Chad Bentz FE AU RC.......... 8.00 2.40
132 Jerry Gil FE AU RC............... 8.00 2.40
133 Mariano Gomez FE AU RC ... 8.00 2.40
134 Justin Germano FE AU RC ... 8.00 2.40
135 Jason Bartlett FE AU RC 10.00 3.00
136 Ronald Belisario FE AU RC .. 8.00 2.40
137 E.Pacheco FE AU RC 8.00 2.40
138 Justin Hampson FE AU RC ... 8.00 2.40
139 Mike Vento FE AU RC 10.00 3.00
140 Merkin Valdez FE AU RC..... 10.00 3.00
141 Casey Daigle FE AU RC........ 8.00 2.40
142 Eddy Rodriguez FE AU RC . 10.00 3.00
143 William Bergolla FE AU RC .. 8.00 2.40
144 Jose Capellan FE AU RC ... 20.00 6.00
145 Ronny Cedeno FE AU RC...... 8.00 2.40
146 F.Gracesqui FE AU RC.......... 8.00 2.40
147 Roman Colon FE AU RC........ 8.00 2.40
148 Roberto Novoa FE AU RC .. 10.00 3.00
149 Ivan Ochoa FE AU RC........... 8.00 2.40
150 Shawn Hill FE AU RC............ 8.00 2.40

2004 Upper Deck Etchings Blue Ink

Nm-Mt Ex-Mt
*BLUE INK: .6X TO 1.5X BLACK INK..
OVERALL AU ODDS 1:4......................
STATED PRINT RUN 200 SERIAL #'d SETS

2004 Upper Deck Etchings A Piece of History 500 Club

Nm-Mt Ex-Mt
RANDOM INSERTS IN PACKS ....
STATED PRINT RUN 350 CARDS........
KG Ken Griffey Jr. 175.00 52.50

2004 Upper Deck Etchings A Piece of History 500 Club Autograph

Nm-Mt Ex-Mt
RANDOM INSERTS IN PACKS ....
STATED PRINT RUN 25 SERIAL #'d CARDS
KG Ken Griffey Jr./25 ....

2004 Upper Deck Etchings Combo Etching Autograph Copper Foil

Nm-Mt Ex-Mt
OVERALL AU ODDS 1:4......................
PRINT RUNS B/WN 5-115 COPIES PER
NO PRICING ON QTY OF 10 OR LESS
EXCHANGE DEADLINE 08/06/07.........
AR A.Rod w/Glasses/15.......... 250.00 75.00
AR1 A.Rod Smile w/o Glass/15 250.00 75.00
AR2 A.Rod Smile w/Glass/115 150.00 45.00

CD C.Delgado Face Right/15..... 50.00 15.00
CD1 C.Delgado Face Left/15 ..... 50.00 15.00
CR Cal Ripken Smile/15.......... 300.00 90.00
CR1 Cal Ripken No Smile/15 .. 300.00 90.00
DJ Derek Jeter Look Ahead/15 300.00 90.00
DJ1 Derek Jeter Look Left/25 . 250.00 75.00
IS Ichiro Look Right/15........... 600.00 180.00
IS1 Ichiro Look Left/15 .... 600.00 180.00
IS2 Ichiro Look Right Smile/5.............
JB Josh Beckett/25 .... 50.00 15.00
KG Ken Griffey Jr./100 .... 100.00 30.00
KG1 K.Grif Jr. Look Right/90 .. 100.00 30.00
KG2 K.Grif Jr. Look Left/90..... 100.00 30.00
KG3 Ken Griffey Jr./10 ....
KW Kerry Wood Face Right/20 . 80.00 24.00
KW1 K.Wood Face Right Smile/20 80.00 24.00
KW2 K.Wood Look Ahead/30.... 80.00 24.00
MC Miguel Cabrera Smile/23 .... 50.00 15.00
MC1 M.Cabrera No Smile/22 .... 50.00 15.00
MP Mark Prior Face Right/15 . 150.00 45.00
MP1 Mark Prior Face Left/5 ....
MP2 M.Prior Face Ahead/15 ... 150.00 45.00
MR M.Ram Mouth Open/60 EX 80.00 24.00
MR1 M.Ram Mouth Close/60 EX 80.00 24.00
MT Miguel Tejada Smile/25....... 40.00 12.00
MT1 M.Tejada Mouth Open/10............
PI Mike Piazza Black Cap/15 ... 200.00 60.00
PI1 Mike Piazza Blue Cap/15... 200.00 60.00
VG Vladimir Guerrero/60........... 80.00 24.00

2004 Upper Deck Etchings Combo Etching Autograph Gold Foil

Nm-Mt Ex-Mt
*GOLD p/r 50: .6X TO 1.2X CPR p/r 100
*GOLD p/r 15: .75X TO 1.5X CPR p/r 90
*GOLD p/r 15: .6X TO 1.2X CPR p/r 60
*GOLD p/r 15: .6X TO 1.2X CPR p/r 22-23
OVERALL AU ODDS 1:4......................
PRINT RUNS B/WN 1-50 COPIES PER
NO PRICING ON QTY OF 10 OR LESS
EXCHANGE DEADLINE 08/06/07.........
MP1 Mark Prior Face Left/15.. 150.00 45.00
MT1 M.Tejada Mouth Open/25.. 50.00 15.00

2004 Upper Deck Etchings Combo Etching Autograph Silver Foil

Nm-Mt Ex-Mt
*SILVER p/r 50: .6X TO 1.2X CPR p/r 100
*SILVER p/r 25: .6X TO 1.2X CPR p/r 90-115
*SILVER p/r 25: .5X TO 1X CPR p/r 60
*SILVER p/r 25: .5X TO 1X CPR p/r 22-23
*SILVER p/r 15: .6X TO 1.2X CPR p/r 30
*SILVER p/r 15: .6X TO 1.2X CPR p/r 25
OVERALL AU ODDS 1:4......................
PRINT RUNS B/WN 4-50 COPIES PER
NO PRICING ON QTY OF 10 OR LESS
EXCHANGE DEADLINE 08/06/07.........
IS2 Ichiro Look Right Smile/15 600.00 180.00
MT1 M.Tejada Mouth Open/15.. 50.00 15.00

2004 Upper Deck Etchings Etched in Time Autograph Black

Nm-Mt Ex-Mt
OVERALL AU ODDS 1:4......................
PRINT RUNS B/WN 100-1625 COPIES PER
EXCHANGE DEADLINE 08/06/07.........
AA Alfredo Amezaga/375 .... 10.00 3.00
AB Angel Berroa/1325................ 8.00 2.40
AC Alex Cintron/375.................. 10.00 3.00
AD Andre Dawson/375.............. 15.00 4.50
AE Adam Everett/1325 .... 8.00 2.40
AG Adrian Gonzalez/1325 .... 12.00 3.60
AH Aaron Harang/375............... 15.00 4.50
AK Adam Kennedy/375 .... 10.00 3.00
AL Adam Loewen/375............... 10.00 3.00
AT Alan Trammell/375............... 15.00 4.50
BA Dusty Baker/150.................. 15.00 4.50
BB Bert Blyleven/375 .... 10.00 3.00
BC Bobby Crosby/1325............. 20.00 6.00
BD Brandon Duckworth/375 ..... 10.00 3.00
BE Carlos Beltran/150.............. 40.00 12.00
BG Brian Giles/375.................... 15.00 4.50
BK Bobby Kielty/1325 .... 8.00 2.40
BP Brad Penny/375.................. 15.00 4.50
BR Brooks Robinson/375 .... 20.00 6.00
BS Ben Sheets/375 .... 15.00 4.50
CA Chris Capuano/375............. 10.00 3.00
CB Chris Bootcheck/375 .... 10.00 3.00
CC Chad Cordero/375 .... 10.00 3.00
CG Chad Gaudin/375................ 10.00 3.00
CL Brandon Claussen/375......... 10.00 3.00
CP Corey Patterson/375........... 15.00 4.50
CR Cal Ripken/100.................. 150.00 45.00
CS Carlos Lee/325 .... 15.00 4.50
CU Chase Utley/375 .... 25.00 7.50
CZ Carlos Zambrano/375 .... 25.00 7.50
DB Dewon Brazelton/375 .... 10.00 3.00
DE Dwight Evans/375 .... 15.00 4.50
DG Dwight Gooden/375 .... 15.00 4.50
DJ Derek Jeter/100 .... 150.00 45.00
DK Dave Kingman/375............. 15.00 4.50
DM Don Mattingly/150............. 60.00 18.00
DS Darryl Strawberry/150......... 15.00 4.50
DY Delmon Young/375 .... 25.00 7.50
EB Eric Byrnes/375 EXCH 15.00 4.50
EC Eric Chavez/375.................. 15.00 4.50
EJ Edwin Jackson/325 .... 15.00 4.50
GB Geoff Blum/375................... 10.00 3.00
GK Graham Koonce/375 .... 10.00 3.00
GO Jonny Gomes/325............... 10.00 3.00
GR Ken Griffey Sr./375............. 15.00 4.50
HA Rich Harden/1325 .... 12.00 3.60
HB Hank Blalock/375 .... 15.00 4.50
HE Ramon Hernandez/325........ 10.00 3.00
HK Harmon Killebrew/150 EXCH 40.00 12.00
JB Jason Bay/375 .... 15.00 4.50
JF Josh Fogg/325 .... 10.00 3.00
JI Jim Rice/375......................... 15.00 4.50
JJ Jacque Jones/375 .... 15.00 4.50
JM Justin Miller/325 .... 10.00 3.00
JP Jason Phillips/375 .... 10.00 3.00
JR Jose Reyes/325 .... 15.00 4.50
JW Jerome Williams/1325........ 12.00 3.60
KA Al Kaline/375 .... 25.00 7.50
KF Kyle Farnsworth/1325............ 8.00 2.40
KG Ken Griffey Jr./1625 .... 60.00 18.00
KW Kerry Wood/150.................. 40.00 12.00
LA Adam LaRoche/1325 .... 8.00 2.40
LE Cliff Lee/1325........................ 8.00 2.40
LF Lew Ford/375 .... 15.00 4.50
LM Luis Matos/325.................... 10.00 3.00
LN Laynce Nix/375 EXCH.......... 15.00 4.50
LO Lyle Overbay/1325............... 12.00 3.60
LP Lou Piniella/150................... 15.00 4.50
LT Luis Tiant/375 .... 10.00 3.00
MA Joe Mauer/375 .... 25.00 7.50
MB Marlon Byrd/1025.................. 8.00 2.40
MC Miguel Cabrera/1025 .... 20.00 6.00
ME Morgan Ensberg/1325 .... 8.00 2.40
MG Marcus Giles/325 .... 15.00 4.50
MK Matt Kata/325..................... 10.00 3.00
ML Mike Lowell/375 .... 15.00 4.50
MM Mark Mulder/375............... 15.00 4.50
MN Mike Neu/325..................... 10.00 3.00
MO Jack Morris/375 .... 15.00 4.50
MP Mark Prior/150 .... 60.00 18.00
MS Mike Scioscia/375 .... 15.00 4.50
MT Mark Teixeira/325 .... 25.00 7.50
MU Dale Murphy/375................ 20.00 6.00
MY Michael Young/1325........... 20.00 6.00
NG Nomar Garciaparra/100..... 100.00 30.00
PA Jim Palmer/375 .... 20.00 6.00
PF Pedro Feliz/325 .... 10.00 3.00
PO Boog Powell/375 .... 15.00 4.50
RA Randy Winn/375 .... 10.00 3.00
RF Rollie Fingers/375............... 15.00 4.50
RH Rob Hammock/325............. 10.00 3.00
RI Raul Ibanez/325 .... 10.00 3.00
RO Roy Oswalt/375.................. 15.00 4.50
RS Ryne Sandberg/150............. 60.00 18.00
RW Ryan Wagner/1325 .... 8.00 2.40
SA Sparky Anderson/375.......... 15.00 4.50
SH Scott Hairston/375 .... 10.00 3.00
SO Ron Santo/375 .... 20.00 6.00
SS Steve Sax/375 .... 10.00 3.00
TA Tony Armas Jr./325............. 10.00 3.00
TG Tony Gwynn/150 .... 50.00 15.00
TL Ted Lilly/325 .... 10.00 3.00
TS Terrmel Sledge/325............. 10.00 3.00
WC Will Clark/150.................... 40.00 12.00
WE Willie Eyre/375 .... 10.00 3.00
WI Josh Willingham/1325........... 8.00 2.40
WK Rickie Weeks/375 EXCH..... 15.00 4.50

2004 Upper Deck Etchings Etched in Time Autograph Blue

Nm-Mt Ex-Mt
*BLUE p/r 150-250: .5X TO 1.2X p/r 1025-1625
*BLUE p/r 150-250: .4X TO 1X p/r 325-375
*BLUE p/r 100: .4X TO 1X p/r 325-375
*BLUE p/r 50: .5X TO 1.2X p/r 150.....
*BLUE p/r 50: .5X TO 1.2X p/r 100.....
OVERALL AU ODDS 1:4......................
PRINT RUNS B/WN 50-250 COPIES PER
EXCHANGE DEADLINE 08/06/07.........
VG Vladimir Guerrero/50........... 50.00 15.00

2004 Upper Deck Etchings Etched in Time Autograph Red

Nm-Mt Ex-Mt
*RED: 1X TO 2.5X BLACK p/r 1025-1625
*RED: .75X TO 2X BLACK p/r 325-375
*RED: .6X TO 1.5X BLACK p/r 150.....
*RED: .75X TO 1.5X BLACK p/r 100...
OVERLL AU ODDS 1:4......................
STATED PRINT RUN 25 SERIAL #'d SETS
EXCHANGE DEADLINE 08/06/07.........
VG Vladimir Guerrero................ 60.00 18.00

2004 Upper Deck Etchings Game Bat Dual

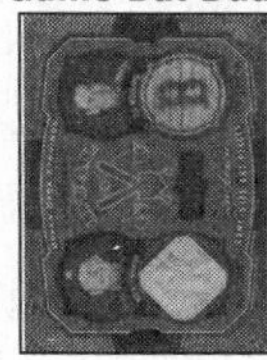

Nm-Mt Ex-Mt
OVERALL GU ODDS 1:4......................
STATED PRINT RUN 150 SERIAL #'d SETS
MM Hideki Matsui...................... 40.00 12.00
Kazuo Matsui
MW Mickey Mantle 200.00 60.00
Ted Williams
PG Albert Pujols........................ 40.00 12.00
Vladimir Guerrero
RJ Alex Rodriguez...................... 80.00 24.00
Derek Jeter
RP Jose Reyes........................... 25.00 7.50
Mike Piazza
WP Kerry Wood 40.00 12.00
Mark Prior

2004 Upper Deck Etchings Game Bat Triple

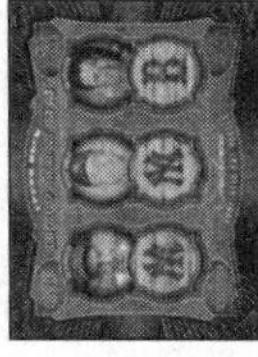

Nm-Mt Ex-Mt
OVERALL GU ODDS 1:4......................
STATED PRINT RUN 50 SERIAL #'d SETS
DMW Joe DiMaggio................ 500.00 150.00
Mickey Mantle
Ted Williams
PER Albert Pujols.................... 100.00 30.00
Jim Edmonds
Scott Rolen
RJM Alex Rodriguez 120.00 36.00
Derek Jeter
Hideki Matsui
SBT Alfonso Soriano................. 40.00 12.00
Hank Blalock
Mark Teixeira
SRG Curt Schilling 50.00 15.00
Manny Ramirez
Nomar Garciaparra
WPS Kerry Wood....................... 50.00 15.00
Mark Prior
Sammy Sosa

2004 Upper Deck Etchings Master Etchings Autograph

Nm-Mt Ex-Mt
OVERALL MASTER ODDS 1:30,000....
STATED PRINT RUN 1 SERIAL #'d SET
NO PRICING DUE TO SCARCITY ....
BWRC Josh Beckett............................
Kerry Wood
Nolan Ryan
Roger Clemens
DCSG Carlos Delgado ....
Eric Chavez
Ichiro Suzuki
Vladimir Guerrero
RJTG Alex Rodriguez ....
Derek Jeter
Miguel Tejada
Nomar Garciaparra
YRTW Delmon Young ....

Jose Reyes
Mark Teixeira
Rickie Weeks

2004 Upper Deck Etchings Master Etchings Game Bat

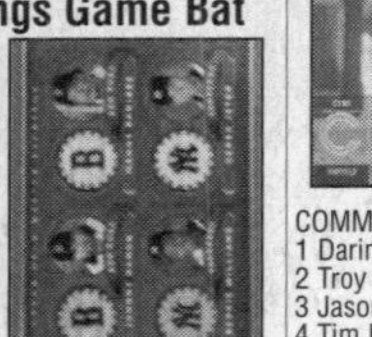

Nm-Mt Ex-Mt
OVERALL MASTER ODDS 1:30,000
STATED PRINT RUN 1 SERIAL #'d SET
NO PRICING DUE TO SCARCITY
AL Alex Rodriguez
Alfonso Soriano
Carlos Delgado
Garret Anderson
Hideki Matsui
Ichiro Suzuki
Jorge Posada
Troy Glaus
BN Johnny Damon
Manny Ramirez
Nomar Garciaparra
Ted Williams
Bernie Williams
Derek Jeter
Hideki Matsui
Mickey Mantle
CF Corey Patterson
Kerry Wood
Mark Prior
Sammy Sosa
Ivan Rodriguez
Josh Beckett
Miguel Cabrera
Mike Lowell
NYY Alex Rodriguez
Bernie Williams
Derek Jeter
Gary Sheffield
Hideki Matsui
Jason Giambi
Joe DiMaggio
Mickey Mantle

2004 Upper Deck Etchings Star Etchings Autograph

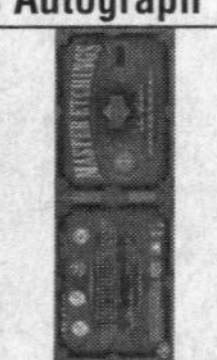

Nm-Mt Ex-Mt
STATED ODDS 1:192
PRINT RUNS B/WN 10-50 COPIES PER
NO PRICING ON QTY OF 10 OR LESS
EXCHANGE DEADLINE 08/06/07
AD Adam Dunn/50 40.00 12.00
BA Bobby Abreu/50
BB Bret Boone/50 25.00 7.50
BG Brian Giles/50
BW Brandon Webb/50 15.00 4.50
CB Carlos Beltran/50 50.00 15.00
DJ Derek Jeter/10
DL Derrek Lee/50 25.00 7.50
DW Dontrelle Willis/50 25.00 7.50
EC Eric Chavez/50 25.00 7.50
FT Frank Thomas/15 80.00 24.00
GA Garret Anderson/50 25.00 7.50
GJ Geoff Jenkins/50 25.00 7.50
HB Hank Blalock/50 25.00 7.50
HE Todd Helton/15 60.00 18.00
IR Ivan Rodriguez/15 80.00 24.00
JB Josh Beckett/50 40.00 12.00
JD J.D. Drew/50 40.00 12.00
JL Javy Lopez/50 EXCH 25.00 7.50
JS Jason Schmidt/50 25.00 7.50
KG K.Grif Jr. w/Glasses/50 100.00 30.00
KG1 K.Grif Jr.w/o Glasses/50 100.00 30.00
KW Kerry Wood/50 50.00 15.00
LB Lance Berkman/15 40.00 12.00
MC Miguel Cabrera/50 40.00 12.00
ML Mike Lowell/50 EXCH 25.00 7.50
MM Mike Mussina/15 60.00 18.00
MO Magglio Ordonez/50 25.00 7.50
MP Mike Piazza/10
MR Manny Ramirez/15 80.00 24.00
MT Mark Teixeira/50 40.00 12.00
MU Mark Mulder/50 25.00 7.50
NG Nomar Garciaparra/15 150.00 45.00
PR Mark Prior/50 80.00 24.00
RH Roy Halladay/50
RO Roy Oswalt/50 25.00 7.50
TE Miguel Tejada/15 40.00 12.00
TH Tim Hudson/50 40.00 12.00
VG Vladimir Guerrero/15 80.00 24.00
VW Vernon Wells/50

2001 Upper Deck Evolution

The 2001 Upper Deck Evolution product released in October, 2001 and featured a 120-card base set. Each pack contained 5 cards, and carried a suggested retail price of $2.99 per pack. The set was broken into two tiers, Base Cards (1-90) and Prospects (91-120). The Prospects cards were serial numbered to 2250.

Nm-Mt Ex-Mt
COMP.SET w/o SP's (90) 15.00 4.50
COMMON CARD (1-90) .30 .09

COMMON CARD (91-120) 4.00 1.20
1 Darin Erstad .30 .09
2 Troy Glaus .30 .09
3 Jason Giambi .30 .09
4 Tim Hudson .30 .09
5 Jermaine Dye .30 .09
6 Barry Zito .50 .15
7 Carlos Delgado .30 .09
8 Shannon Stewart .30 .09
9 Jose Cruz Jr. .30 .09
10 Greg Vaughn .30 .09
11 Juan Gonzalez .50 .15
12 Roberto Alomar .50 .15
13 Omar Vizquel .50 .15
14 Jim Thome .75 .23
15 Edgar Martinez .50 .15
16 John Olerud .30 .09
17 Kazuhiro Sasaki .30 .09
18 Cal Ripken 2.50 .75
19 Alex Rodriguez 1.25 .35
20 Ivan Rodriguez .75 .23
21 Rafael Palmeiro .50 .15
22 Pedro Martinez .75 .23
23 Nomar Garciaparra 1.25 .35
24 Manny Ramirez .50 .15
25 Carl Everett .30 .09
26 Mark Quinn .30 .09
27 Mike Sweeney .30 .09
28 Neifi Perez .30 .09
29 Tony Clark .30 .09
30 Doug Mientkiewicz .30 .09
31 Eric Milton .30 .09
32 Corey Koskie .30 .09
33 Frank Thomas .75 .23
34 David Wells .30 .09
35 Magglio Ordonez .30 .09
36 Derek Jeter 2.00 .60
37 Mike Mussina .50 .15
38 Bernie Williams .50 .15
39 Roger Clemens 1.50 .45
40 David Justice .30 .09
41 Jeff Bagwell .50 .15
42 Richard Hidalgo .30 .09
43 Wade Miller .30 .09
44 Chipper Jones .75 .23
45 Greg Maddux 1.25 .35
46 Andruw Jones .30 .09
47 Rafael Furcal .30 .09
48 Geoff Jenkins .30 .09
49 Jeromy Burnitz .30 .09
50 Ben Sheets .50 .15
51 Richie Sexson .30 .09
52 Mark McGwire 2.00 .60
53 Jim Edmonds .30 .09
54 Darryl Kile .30 .09
55 J.D. Drew .30 .09
56 Sammy Sosa 1.25 .35
57 Kerry Wood .75 .23
58 Randy Johnson .75 .23
59 Luis Gonzalez .30 .09
60 Matt Williams .30 .09
61 Kevin Brown .30 .09
62 Gary Sheffield .30 .09
63 Shawn Green .30 .09
64 Chan Ho Park .30 .09
65 Vladimir Guerrero .75 .23
66 Jose Vidro .30 .09
67 Fernando Tatis .30 .09
68 Barry Bonds 2.00 .60
69 Jeff Kent .30 .09
70 Russ Ortiz .30 .09
71 Preston Wilson .30 .09
72 Ryan Dempster .30 .09
73 Charles Johnson .30 .09
74 Mike Piazza 1.25 .35
75 Edgardo Alfonzo .30 .09
76 Robin Ventura .30 .09
77 Jay Payton .30 .09
78 Tony Gwynn 1.00 .30
79 Phil Nevin .30 .09
80 Pat Burrell .30 .09
81 Scott Rolen .75 .23
82 Bob Abreu .30 .09
83 Brian Giles .30 .09
84 Jason Kendall .30 .09
85 Ken Griffey Jr. 1.25 .35
86 Barry Larkin .50 .15
87 Sean Casey .30 .09
88 Todd Helton .50 .15
89 Larry Walker .50 .15
90 Mike Hampton .30 .09
91 Ichiro Suzuki PROS RC 25.00 7.50
92 Albert Pujols PROS RC 40.00 12.00
93 W.Betemit PROS RC 4.00 1.20
94 Jay Gibbons PROS RC 5.00 1.50
95 Juan Uribe PROS RC 5.00 1.50
96 M. Ensberg PROS RC 5.00 1.50
97 C. Parker PROS RC 4.00 1.20
98 T. Shinjo PROS RC 5.00 1.50
99 Jack Wilson PROS RC 8.00 2.40
100 D. Mendez PROS RC 4.00 1.20
101 Ryan Freel PROS RC 4.00 1.20
102 Juan Diaz PROS RC 4.00 1.20
103 H. Ramirez PROS RC 5.00 1.50
104 R. Rodriguez PROS RC 4.00 1.20
105 E. Almonte PROS RC 4.00 1.20
106 J. Towers PROS RC 4.00 1.20
107 A.Hernandez PROS RC 4.00 1.20
108 B.Duckworth PROS RC 4.00 1.20
109 T. Hafner PROS RC 10.00 3.00
110 M. Vargas PROS RC 4.00 1.20
111 Kris Keller PROS RC 4.00 1.20
112 B. Lawrence PROS RC 4.00 1.20
113 Esix Snead PROS RC 4.00 1.20
114 Wilkin Ruan PROS RC 4.00 1.20
115 J. Mieses PROS RC 4.00 1.20
116 J. Estrada PROS RC 5.00 1.50
117 E. Guzman PROS RC 4.00 1.20
118 S. Douglass PROS RC 4.00 1.20
119 B. Sylvester PROS RC 4.00 1.20
120 Bret Prinz PROS RC 4.00 1.20

2001 Upper Deck Evolution e-Card Classics

Randomly inserted at one in , this six-card insert features cards that can be viewed over the Upper Deck website. Cards feature a serial number that is to be typed in a the Upper Deck website to reveal that card. Card backs carry an "E" prefix.

Nm-Mt Ex-Mt
COMPLETE SET (15) 40.00 12.00
EC1 Ken Griffey Jr. 89 5.00 1.50
EC2 Gary Sheffield 89 1.00 .30
EC3 Randy Johnson 89 2.50 .75
EC4 Sammy Sosa 90 4.00 1.20
EC5 Carlos Delgado 93 1.00 .30
EC6 Ichiro Suzuki 01 15.00 4.50
EC7 Andruw Jones 97 1.00 .30
EC8 Chipper Jones 91 2.50 .75
EC9 Kazuhiro Sasaki 00 1.00 .30
EC10 Shawn Green 92 1.00 .30
EC11 Alex Rodriguez 94 4.00 1.20
EC12 Brian Giles 97 1.00 .30
EC13 J.D. Drew 99 1.00 .30
EC14 Pat Burrell 99 1.00 .30
EC15 Ivan Rodriguez 91 2.50 .75

2001 Upper Deck Evolution e-Card Game Bat

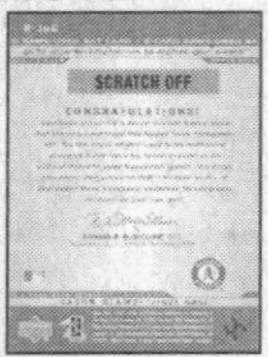

Randomly inserted into packs at one in 120, these 10-card set features a piece of game-used bat. The card backs have a scratch off box that reveals a number that can be entered at Upper Deck's website. Winning bat cards evolve in bat-jersey autograph cards. Card backs carry a "B" prefix.

Nm-Mt Ex-Mt
B-AJ Andruw Jones 10.00 3.00
B-AR Alex Rodriguez 25.00 7.50
B-CD Carlos Delgado 10.00 3.00
B-GS Gary Sheffield 10.00 3.00
B-JaG Jason Giambi 10.00 3.00
B-JD J.D. Drew 10.00 3.00
B-JK Jason Kendall 10.00 3.00
B-KG Ken Griffey Jr. 20.00 6.00
B-PB Pat Burrell 10.00 3.00
B-RB Russell Branyan 10.00 3.00

2001 Upper Deck Evolution e-Card Game Bat-Jersey Autograph

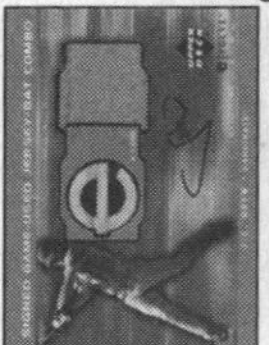
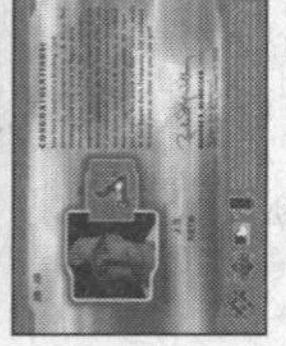

Issued at a rate of one in 480 Evolved upgrades, these cards have not only a game-used piece but also an autograph of the featured player.

Nm-Mt Ex-Mt
STATED ODDS 1:480 EVOLVE UPGRADES
STATED PRINT RUN 5 SERIAL #'d SETS

2001 Upper Deck Evolution Game Jersey

Randomly inserted into packs at one in 120, this 15-card set features game-used jersey cards of the players. Cards are numbered using the players intials with a "J" prefix.

Nm-Mt Ex-Mt
J-JaG Jason Giambi 10.00 3.00
J-AJ Andruw Jones 10.00 3.00
J-AR Alex Rodriguez 25.00 7.50
J-BG Brian Giles 10.00 3.00
J-CJ Chipper Jones 15.00 4.50
J-CR Cal Ripken 40.00 12.00
J-GS Gary Sheffield 10.00 3.00
J-JD J.D. Drew 10.00 3.00
J-JK Jason Kendall 10.00 3.00
J-KG Ken Griffey Jr. 20.00 6.00
J-PB Pat Burrell 10.00 3.00
J-RB Russell Branyan 10.00 3.00
J-SG Shawn Green 10.00 3.00
J-SS Sammy Sosa 20.00 6.00
J-TG Troy Glaus 10.00 3.00

2001 Upper Deck Evolution Ichiro Suzuki All-Star Game

Randomly inserted into packs, this card was originally intended to be distributed at the All-Star Game Fanfest in Seattle. The card comes in three versions, bronze, silver and gold. The silver and gold versions are serial numbered. Approximately 10 percent of the gold cards have been discovered without the serial numbering. We are continuing to evaluate more about that specific card and see if it is more than just a printing flaw.

Nm-Mt Ex-Mt
51B Ichiro Suzuki 10.00 3.00
Bronze
51G Ichiro Suzuki 150.00 45.00
Gold/51
51S Ichiro Suzuki 25.00 7.50
Silver/2001

2003 Upper Deck Finite

This 380-card set was released in December, 2003. This set was issued in three-card packs with an $9.99 SRP which came 11 packs to a box and 12 boxes to a case. This set is split into many different subsets: Cards numbered 1-100 feature veterans and those cards were issued to a stated print run of 1999 serial numbered sets. Cards numbered 101-150 are a Major Factors subset and they cards were issued to a stated print run of 1599 serial numbered sets. Cards numbered 151 through 180 were Prominent Powers subset and they were issued to a stated print run of 499 serial numbered sets. Cards numbered 181 through 200 were the First Class cards and they were issued to a stated print run of 199 serial numbered sets. Cards numbered 201 through 380 featured Rookies and those cards were issued in varying tiers. Cards numbered 201-300 were issued to a stated print run of 1299 serial numbered sets. Cards numbered 301-330 were issued to a stated print run of 599 serial numbered sets. Cards numbered 331 through 360 were issued to a stated print run of 299 serial numbered sets and cards numbered 361-380 were issued to a stated print run of 150 serial numbered sets. In addition, update cards for the following Upper Deck products: SP Authentic, SPX, Upper Deck Game Face and UD Authentics) were randomly inserted into these packs.

MINT NRMT
COMMON CARD (1-100) 2.00 .90
COMMON CARD (101-150) 2.50 1.10
COMMON CARD (151-180) 4.00 1.80
COMMON CARD (181-200) 5.00 2.20
1-200 STATED ODDS TWO PER PACK
COMMON CARD (201-300) 3.00 1.35
COMMON CARD (301-330) 5.00 2.20
301-330 PRINT RUN 599 SERIAL #'d SETS
COMMON CARD (331-360) 10.00 4.50
331-360 PRINT RUN 299 SERIAL #'d SETS
COMMON CARD (361-380) 15.00 6.75
361-380 PRINT RUN 150 SERIAL #'d SETS
201-380/STARS 'N STRIPES ODDS 1:1
1 Darin Erstad 2.00 .90
2 Garret Anderson 2.00 .90
3 Tim Salmon 2.50 1.10
4 Troy Glaus 2.00 .90
5 Luis Gonzalez 2.00 .90
6 Randy Johnson 2.50 1.10
7 Curt Schilling 2.00 .90
8 Andruw Jones 2.00 .90
9 Gary Sheffield 2.00 .90
10 Rafael Furcal 2.00 .90
11 Greg Maddux 4.00 1.80
12 Chipper Jones 2.50 1.10
13 Tony Batista 2.00 .90
14 Jay Gibbons 2.00 .90
15 Johnny Damon 2.50 1.10
16 Derek Lowe 2.00 .90
17 Nomar Garciaparra 4.00 1.80
18 Pedro Martinez 2.50 1.10
19 Manny Ramirez 2.50 1.10
20 Mark Prior 2.50 1.10
21 Kerry Wood 2.50 1.10
22 Corey Patterson 2.00 .90
23 Sammy Sosa 4.00 1.80
24 Moises Alou 2.00 .90
25 Magglio Ordonez 2.00 .90
26 Frank Thomas 2.50 1.10
27 Paul Konerko 2.00 .90
28 Bartolo Colon 2.00 .90
29 Adam Dunn 2.50 1.10
30 Austin Kearns 2.00 .90
31 Aaron Boone 2.00 .90
32 Ken Griffey Jr. 4.00 1.80
33 Omar Vizquel 2.50 1.10
34 C.C. Sabathia 2.00 .90
35 Brandon Phillips 2.00 .90
36 Larry Walker 2.50 1.10
37 Preston Wilson 2.00 .90
38 Todd Helton 2.50 1.10
39 Eric Munson 2.00 .90
40 Ivan Rodriguez 2.50 1.10
41 Josh Beckett 2.00 .90
42 Roy Oswalt 2.00 .90
43 Craig Biggio 2.50 1.10
44 Jeff Bagwell 2.50 1.10
45 Dontrelle Willis 2.50 1.10
46 Carlos Beltran 2.50 1.10
47 Brent Mayne 2.00 .90
48 Hideo Nomo 2.50 1.10
49 Rickey Henderson 2.50 1.10
50 Adrian Beltre 2.50 1.10
51 Miguel Cabrera 2.50 1.10
52 Kazuhisa Ishii 2.00 .90
53 Richie Sexson 2.00 .90
54 Torii Hunter 2.00 .90
55 Jacque Jones 2.00 .90
56 A.J. Pierzynski 2.00 .90
57 Jose Vidro 2.00 .90
58 Vladimir Guerrero 2.50 1.10
59 Tom Glavine 2.50 1.10
60 Jose Reyes 2.00 .90
61 Mike Piazza 4.00 1.80
62 Jorge Posada 2.50 1.10
63 Mike Mussina 2.50 1.10
64 Robin Ventura 2.00 .90
65 Mariano Rivera 2.50 1.10
66 Roger Clemens 5.00 2.20
67 Jason Giambi 2.00 .90
68 Bernie Williams 2.50 1.10
69 Alfonso Soriano 2.50 1.10
70 Derek Jeter 6.00 2.70
71 Miguel Tejada 2.00 .90
72 Eric Chavez 2.00 .90
73 Tim Hudson 2.00 .90
74 Barry Zito 2.00 .90
75 Pat Burrell 2.00 .90
76 Jim Thome 2.50 1.10
77 Bobby Abreu 2.00 .90
78 Brian Giles 2.00 .90
79 Reggie Sanders 2.00 .90
80 Ryan Klesko 2.00 .90
81 Edgardo Alfonzo 2.00 .90
82 Rich Aurilia 2.00 .90
83 Barry Bonds 6.00 2.70
84 Mike Cameron 2.00 .90
85 Kazuhiro Sasaki 2.00 .90
86 Bret Boone 2.00 .90
87 Ichiro Suzuki 4.00 1.80
88 J.D. Drew 2.00 .90
89 Jim Edmonds 2.00 .90
90 Scott Rolen 2.50 1.10
91 Matt Morris 2.00 .90
92 Tino Martinez 2.50 1.10
93 Albert Pujols 5.00 2.20
94 Rocco Baldelli 2.00 .90
95 Hank Blalock 2.50 1.10
96 Alex Rodriguez 4.00 1.80
97 Rafael Palmeiro 2.50 1.10
98 Eric Hinske 2.00 .90
99 Orlando Hudson 2.00 .90
100 Carlos Delgado 2.00 .90
101 Albert Pujols MF 6.00 2.70
102 Alex Rodriguez MF 5.00 2.20
103 Alfonso Soriano MF 3.00 1.35
104 Andruw Jones MF 2.50 1.10
105 Barry Zito MF 2.50 1.10
106 Bernie Williams MF 3.00 1.35
107 Carlos Delgado MF 2.50 1.10
108 Chipper Jones MF 3.00 1.35
109 Curt Schilling MF 2.50 1.10
110 Doug Mientkiewicz MF 2.50 1.10
111 Frank Thomas MF 3.00 1.35
112 Garret Anderson MF 2.50 1.10
113 Gary Sheffield MF 2.50 1.10
114 Greg Maddux MF 5.00 2.20
115 Hank Blalock MF 3.00 1.35
116 Hideki Matsui MF 6.00 2.70
117 Hideo Nomo MF 3.00 1.35
118 Ichiro Suzuki MF 5.00 2.20
119 Ivan Rodriguez MF 3.00 1.35
120 Jason Giambi MF 2.50 1.10
121 Jeff Bagwell MF 3.00 1.35
122 Jeff Kent MF 2.50 1.10
123 Jerome Williams MF 2.50 1.10
124 Jeromy Burnitz MF 2.50 1.10
125 Jim Thome MF 3.00 1.35
126 Jose Cruz Jr. MF 2.50 1.10
127 Ken Griffey Jr. MF 5.00 2.20
128 Kerry Wood MF 3.00 1.35
129 Lance Berkman MF 2.50 1.10
130 Luis Gonzalez MF 2.50 1.10
131 Manny Ramirez MF 3.00 1.35
132 Mark Prior MF 3.00 1.35
133 Miguel Cabrera MF 3.00 1.35
134 Miguel Tejada MF 2.50 1.10
135 Mike Piazza MF 5.00 2.20
136 Pat Burrell MF 2.50 1.10
137 Pedro Martinez MF 3.00 1.35
138 Rafael Furcal MF 2.50 1.10
139 Randy Johnson MF 3.00 1.35
140 Rich Harden MF 3.00 1.35
141 Rickey Henderson MF 3.00 1.35
142 Roberto Alomar MF 3.00 1.35
143 Roger Clemens MF 6.00 2.70
144 Sammy Sosa MF 5.00 2.20
145 Shawn Green MF 2.50 1.10
146 Todd Helton MF 3.00 1.35
147 Tom Glavine MF 3.00 1.35
148 Torii Hunter MF 2.50 1.10
149 Troy Glaus MF 2.50 1.10
150 Vladimir Guerrero MF 3.00 1.35
151 Adam Dunn PP 5.00 2.20
152 Albert Pujols PP 10.00 4.50
153 Alex Rodriguez PP 8.00 3.60
154 Alfonso Soriano PP 5.00 2.20
155 Andruw Jones PP 4.00 1.80
156 Barry Bonds PP 12.00 5.50
157 Carlos Delgado PP 4.00 1.80
158 Chipper Jones PP 5.00 2.20

Derek Jeter PP 12.00 5.50
Gary Sheffield PP 4.00 1.80
Hank Blalock PP 5.00 2.20
Hideki Matsui PP 10.00 4.50
Ichiro Suzuki PP 8.00 3.60
J.D. Drew PP 4.00 1.80
Jason Giambi PP 4.00 1.80
Jeff Bagwell PP 5.00 2.20
Jeff Kent PP 4.00 1.80
Jim Edmonds PP 4.00 1.80
Jim Thome PP 5.00 2.20
Ken Griffey Jr. PP 8.00 3.60
Luis Gonzalez PP 4.00 1.80
Magglio Ordonez PP 4.00 1.80
Manny Ramirez PP 5.00 2.20
Mike Lowell PP 4.00 1.80
Mike Piazza PP 8.00 3.60
Nomar Garciaparra PP 8.00 3.60
Rafael Palmeiro PP 5.00 2.20
Shawn Green PP 4.00 1.80
Troy Glaus PP 4.00 1.80
Vladimir Guerrero PP 5.00 2.20
Albert Pujols FC 12.00 5.50
Alex Rodriguez FC 10.00 4.50
Alfonso Soriano FC 6.00 2.70
Bernie Williams FC 6.00 2.70
Chipper Jones FC 6.00 2.70
Derek Jeter FC 15.00 6.75
Hideki Matsui FC 12.00 5.50
Ichiro Suzuki FC 10.00 4.50
Jim Thome FC 6.00 2.70
Joe DiMaggio FC 10.00 4.50
Ken Griffey Jr. FC 10.00 4.50
Mickey Mantle FC 20.00 9.00
Mike Piazza FC 10.00 4.50
Pedro Martinez FC 6.00 2.70
Randy Johnson FC 6.00 2.70
Roger Clemens FC 12.00 5.50
Sammy Sosa FC 10.00 4.50
Ted Williams FC 10.00 4.50
Troy Glaus FC 5.00 2.20
Vladimir Guerrero FC 6.00 2.70
Aaron Looper T1 RC 3.00 1.35
Alejandro Machado T1 RC 3.00 1.35
Alfredo Gonzalez T1 RC 3.00 1.35
Andrew Brown T1 RC 5.00 2.20
Anthony Ferrari T1 RC 3.00 1.35
Aquilino Lopez T1 RC 3.00 1.35
Beau Kemp T1 RC 3.00 1.35
Bernie Castro T1 RC 3.00 1.35
Bobby Madritsch T1 RC 15.00 6.75
Brandon Villafuerte T1 3.00 1.35
Brent Hoard T1 RC 3.00 1.35
Brian Stokes T1 RC 3.00 1.35
Carlos Mendez T1 RC 3.00 1.35
Chris Capuano T1 RC 3.00 1.35
Chris Waters T1 RC 3.00 1.35
Clint Barmes T1 RC 5.00 2.20
Colin Porter T1 RC 3.00 1.35
Cory Stewart T1 RC 3.00 1.35
Craig Brazell T1 RC 5.00 2.20
D.J. Carrasco T1 RC 3.00 1.35
Daniel Cabrera T1 RC 6.00 2.70
David Matranga T1 RC 3.00 1.35
David Sanders T1 RC 3.00 1.35
Diegomar Markwell T1 RC 3.00 1.35
Edgar Gonzalez T1 RC 3.00 1.35
Felix Sanchez T1 RC 3.00 1.35
Fernando Cabrera T1 RC 3.00 1.35
Francisco Cruceta T1 RC 3.00 1.35
Francisco Rosario T1 RC 3.00 1.35
Garrett Atkins T1 3.00 1.35
Gerald Laird T1 3.00 1.35
Guillermo Quiroz T1 RC 5.00 2.20
Heath Bell T1 RC 3.00 1.35
Delmon Young T1 RC 10.00 4.50
Jason Shiell T1 RC 3.00 1.35
Jeremy Bonderman T1 RC 5.00 2.20
Jeremy Griffiths T1 RC 5.00 2.20
Jeremy Guthrie T1 3.00 1.35
Jeremy Wedel T1 RC 3.00 1.35
Carlos Rivera T1 3.00 1.35
Joe Valentine T1 RC 3.00 1.35
Jon Leicester T1 RC 3.00 1.35
Jon Pridie T1 RC 3.00 1.35
Jorge Cordova T1 RC 3.00 1.35
Jose Castillo T1 3.00 1.35
Josh Hall T1 RC 5.00 2.20
Josh Stewart T1 RC 3.00 1.35
Josh Willingham T1 RC 5.00 2.20
Julio Manon T1 RC 3.00 1.35
Kevin Correia T1 RC 3.00 1.35
Kevin Ohme T1 RC 3.00 1.35
Kevin Tolar T1 RC 3.00 1.35
Luis De Los Santos T1 3.00 1.35
Jermaine Clark T1 3.00 1.35
Mark Malaska T1 RC 3.00 1.35
Juan Dominguez T1 3.00 1.35
Michael Hessman T1 RC 3.00 1.35
Michael Nakamura T1 RC 3.00 1.35
Miguel Ojeda T1 RC 3.00 1.35
Mike Gallo T1 RC 3.00 1.35
Edwin Jackson T1 RC 8.00 3.60
Mike Ryan T1 RC 5.00 2.20
Nate Bland T1 RC 3.00 1.35
Nate Robertson T1 RC 8.00 3.60
Nook Logan T1 RC 3.00 1.35
Phil Seibel T1 RC 3.00 1.35
Prentice Redman T1 RC 3.00 1.35
Rafael Betancourt T1 RC 5.00 2.20
Rett Johnson T1 RC 5.00 2.20
Richard Fischer T1 RC 3.00 1.35
Rick Roberts T1 RC 3.00 1.35
Roger Deago T1 RC 3.00 1.35
Ryan Cameron T1 RC 3.00 1.35
Shane Bazzell T1 RC 3.00 1.35
Erasmo Ramirez T1 3.00 1.35
Termel Sledge T1 RC 5.00 2.20
Tim Olson T1 RC 5.00 2.20
Tommy Phelps T1 3.00 1.35
Tommy Whiteman T1 3.00 1.35
Willie Eyre T1 RC 3.00 1.35
Alex Prieto T1 RC 3.00 1.35
Michel Hernandez T1 RC 3.00 1.35
Greg Jones T1 RC 3.00 1.35
Victor Martinez T1 5.00 2.20
Tom Gregorio T1 RC 3.00 1.35
Marcus Thames T1 3.00 1.35
Jorge DePaula T1 3.00 1.35
Aaron Miles T1 RC 5.00 2.20

289 Reynaldo Garcia T1 3.00 1.35
290 Brian Sweeney T1 RC 3.00 1.35
291 Pete LaForest T1 RC 5.00 2.20
292 Pete Zoccolillo T1 RC 3.00 1.35
293 Danny Garcia T1 RC 3.00 1.35
294 Jonny Gomes T1 3.00 1.35
295 Rosman Garcia T1 RC 3.00 1.35
296 Mike Edwards T1 3.00 1.35
297 Marlon Byrd T1 3.00 1.35
298 Khalil Greene T1 10.00 4.50
299 Jose Valverde T1 3.00 1.35
300 Drew Henson T1 3.00 1.35
301 Chris Bootcheck T2 5.00 2.20
302 Matt Belisle T2 5.00 2.20
303 Kevin Gregg T2 5.00 2.20
304 Bobby Jenks T2 5.00 2.20
305 Jason Young T2 5.00 2.20
306 Laynce Nix T2 5.00 2.20
307 Robb Quinlan T2 5.00 2.20
308 Chase Utley T2 5.00 2.20
309 Humberto Quintero T2 RC 5.00 2.20
310 Tim Raines Jr. T2 5.00 2.20
311 Stephen Smitherman T2 5.00 2.20
312 Jason Anderson T2 5.00 2.20
313 Joe Dawley T2 5.00 2.20
314 Chad Cordero T2 RC 5.00 2.20
315 Victor Alvarez T2 5.00 2.20
316 Jimmy Gobble T2 5.00 2.20
317 Jared Fernandez T2 5.00 2.20
318 Eric Bruntlett T2 5.00 2.20
319 Neal Cotts T2 5.00 2.20
320 Ryan Madson T2 5.00 2.20
321 Rocco Baldelli T2 5.00 2.20
322 Graham Koonce T2 RC 8.00 3.60
323 Bobby Crosby T2 8.00 3.60
324 Mike Wood T2 5.00 2.20
325 Jesse Garcia T2 5.00 2.20
326 Noah Lowry T2 8.00 3.60
327 Edwin Almonte T2 5.00 2.20
328 Justin Morneau T2 8.00 3.60
329 Steve Colyer T2 5.00 2.20
330 Vinnie Chulk T2 5.00 2.20
331 Brian Schmack T3 RC 10.00 4.50
332 Stephen Randolph T3 RC 10.00 4.50
333 Pedro Feliciano T3 RC 15.00 6.75
334 Koyie Hill T3 10.00 4.50
335 Geoff Geary T3 RC 10.00 4.50
336 Jon Switzer T3 10.00 4.50
337 Xavier Nady T3 10.00 4.50
338 Rich Harden T3 15.00 6.75
339 Dontrelle Willis T3 15.00 6.75
340 Angel Berroa T3 10.00 4.50
341 Jerome Williams T3 10.00 4.50
342 Brandon Claussen T3 10.00 4.50
343 Kurt Ainsworth T3 10.00 4.50
344 Horacio Ramirez T3 10.00 4.50
345 Hee Seop Choi T3 10.00 4.50
346 Billy Traber T3 10.00 4.50
347 Brandon Phillips T3 10.00 4.50
348 Jody Gerut T3 10.00 4.50
349 Mark Teixeira T3 10.00 4.50
350 Javier Lopez T3 RC 10.00 4.50
351 Miguel Cabrera T3 15.00 6.75
352 Brad Lidge T3 10.00 4.50
353 Mike MacDougal T3 10.00 4.50
354 Ken Harvey T3 10.00 4.50
355 Chien-Ming Wang T3 RC 25.00 11.00
356 Aaron Heilman T3 10.00 4.50
357 Jason Phillips T3 10.00 4.50
358 Jason Bay T3 10.00 4.50
359 Arnie Munoz T3 RC 10.00 4.50
360 Ian Ferguson T3 RC 10.00 4.50
361 Ryan Wagner T4 RC 20.00 9.00
362 Rickie Weeks T4 RC 50.00 22.00
363 Chad Gaudin T4 RC 15.00 6.75
364 Jason Gilfillan T4 RC 15.00 6.75
365 Jason Roach T4 RC 15.00 6.75
366 Jhonny Peralta T4 15.00 6.75
367 Mike Neu T4 RC 15.00 6.75
368 Jose Contreras T4 RC 20.00 9.00
369 Wilfredo Ledezma T4 RC 20.00 9.00
370 Lew Ford T4 RC 20.00 9.00
371 Luis Ayala T4 RC 15.00 6.75
372 Bo Hart T4 RC 20.00 9.00
373 Brandon Webb T4 RC 20.00 9.00
374 Dan Haren T4 RC 20.00 9.00
375 Hideki Matsui T4 RC 40.00 18.00
376 Jeff Duncan T4 RC 20.00 9.00
377 Matt Kata T4 RC 20.00 9.00
378 Oscar Villarreal T4 RC 15.00 6.75
379 Rob Hammock T4 RC 20.00 9.00
380 Todd Wellemeyer T4 RC 20.00 9.00

2003 Upper Deck Finite Gold

MINT NRMT

*GOLD 1-100: .75X TO 2X BASIC
*GOLD 101-150: .6X TO 1.5X BASIC
*GOLD 151-180: .4X TO 1X BASIC
1-180 PRINT RUN 199 SERIAL #'d SETS
*GOLD 181-200 ACTIVE: .6X TO 1.5X BASIC
*GOLD 181-200 RETIRED: 1X TO 2.5X BASIC
181-200 PRINT RUN 99 SERIAL #'d SETS
RANDOM INSERTS IN PACKS

2003 Upper Deck Finite Elements Game Jersey

MINT NRMT

OVERALL GU ODDS 1:3
SP INFO PROVIDED BY UPPER DECK
AD Adam Dunn 10.00 4.50
AL Albert Pujols 15.00 6.75
AP Andy Pettitte 10.00 4.50
AR Alex Rodriguez 10.00 4.50
AS Alfonso Soriano 10.00 4.50
CJ Chipper Jones 10.00 4.50
CP Corey Patterson 8.00 3.60
DW Dontrelle Willis 10.00 4.50
DY Delmon Young SP/100 25.00 11.00
GM Greg Maddux 10.00 4.50
HB Hank Blalock 10.00 4.50
HC Hee Seop Choi 8.00 3.60
HM Hideki Matsui 15.00 6.75
IS Ichiro Suzuki 25.00 11.00
JB Jeff Bagwell 10.00 4.50
JD J.D. Drew 8.00 3.60
JE Jim Edmonds 8.00 3.60
JK Jeff Kent 8.00 3.60
JT Jim Thome 10.00 4.50
KG Ken Griffey Jr. SP 25.00 11.00
KW Kerry Wood 10.00 4.50
MI Mike Piazza 10.00 4.50
ML Mike Lowell 8.00 3.60
MM Matt Morris 8.00 3.60
MP Mark Prior 10.00 4.50
RB Rocco Baldelli 8.00 3.60
RO Roy Oswalt 8.00 3.60
RW Rickie Weeks SP/100 20.00 9.00
SG Shawn Green 8.00 3.60
TH Torii Hunter 8.00 3.60

2003 Upper Deck Finite Elements Game Patch

MINT NRMT

RANDOM INSERTS IN PACKS
STATED PRINT RUN 25 SERIAL #'d SETS
NO PRICING DUE TO SCARCITY

2003 Upper Deck Finite First Class Game Jersey

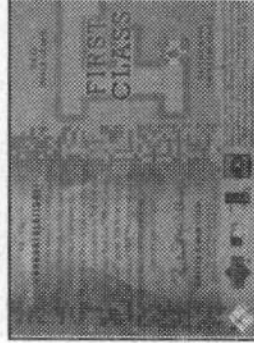

MINT NRMT

OVERALL GU ODDS 1:3
SP INFO PROVIDED BY UPPER DECK
AP Albert Pujols 15.00 6.75
AR Alex Rodriguez 10.00 4.50
AS Alfonso Soriano 10.00 4.50
BW Bernie Williams 10.00 4.50
CJ Chipper Jones 10.00 4.50
HM Hideki Matsui 15.00 6.75
IS Ichiro Suzuki 25.00 11.00
JDO J.DiMaggio Pants SP/200 80.00 36.00
JT Jim Thome 10.00 4.50
KG Ken Griffey Jr. 15.00 6.75
LG Luis Gonzalez 8.00 3.60
MMO M.Mantle Pants SP/100 120.00 55.00
MP Mike Piazza 10.00 4.50
PM Pedro Martinez 10.00 4.50
RC Roger Clemens 15.00 6.75
RJ Randy Johnson 10.00 4.50
SS Sammy Sosa 15.00 6.75
TG Troy Glaus 8.00 3.60
TWO T.Williams Pants SP/100 80.00 36.00
VG Vladimir Guerrero 10.00 4.50

2003 Upper Deck Finite Signatures

MINT NRMT

STATED ODDS 1:120
PRINT RUNS B/WN 25-355 COPIES PER
NO PRICING ON QTY OF 25 OR LESS
BH Bo Hart/150 15.00 6.75
BW Brandon Webb/150 20.00 9.00
CS C.C. Sabathia/50 25.00 11.00
DS David Sanders/150 10.00 4.50
DW Dontrelle Willis/50 40.00 18.00
DY Delmon Young/50 125.00 55.00
EA Erick Almonte/355 10.00 4.50
HM Hideki Matsui/99 250.00 110.00
IS Ichiro Suzuki/25
JR Jose Reyes/100 25.00 11.00
JW Jerome Williams/150 15.00 6.75
MC Miguel Cabrera/100 50.00 22.00
MP Mark Prior/75 60.00 27.00
MT Mark Teixeira/200 25.00 11.00
NG Nomar Garciaparra/50 250.00 110.00
PS Phil Seibel/200 10.00 4.50
RC Roger Clemens/50 175.00 80.00
RK Rob Hammock/200 15.00 6.75
RN Rich Harden/150 25.00 11.00
RW Rickie Weeks/25
SR Scott Rolen/100 50.00 22.00
SZ Shane Bazzell/250 10.00 4.50
WE Willie Eyre/200 10.00 4.50

2003 Upper Deck Finite Stars and Stripes

MINT NRMT

STRIPES/FINITE RC OVERALL ODDS 1:1
STATED PRINT RUN 299 SERIAL #'d SETS
1 Justin Orenduff 8.00 3.60
2 Micah Owings 8.00 3.60
3 Steven Register 8.00 3.60
4 Huston Street 8.00 3.60
5 Justin Verlander 15.00 6.75
6 Jered Weaver 15.00 6.75
7 Matt Campbell 8.00 3.60

8 Stephen Head 8.00 3.60
9 Mark Romanczuk 5.00 2.20
10 Jeff Clement 12.00 5.50
11 Mike Nickeas 8.00 3.60
12 Tyler Greene 8.00 3.60
13 Paul Janish 8.00 3.60
14 Jeff Larish 10.00 4.50
15 Eric Patterson 8.00 3.60
16 Dustin Pedroia 10.00 4.50
17 Michael Griffin 5.00 2.20
18 Brent Lillibridge 5.00 2.20
19 Danny Putnam 8.00 3.60
20 Seth Smith 10.00 4.50

2003 Upper Deck Finite Stars and Stripes Game Jersey

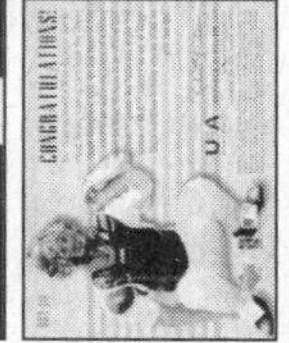

MINT NRMT

OVERALL GU ODDS 1:3
J1 Justin Orenduff 8.00 3.60
J2 Micah Owings 8.00 3.60
J3 Steven Register 8.00 3.60
J4 Huston Street 8.00 3.60
J5 Justin Verlander 12.00 5.50
J6 Jered Weaver 12.00 5.50
J7 Matt Campbell 8.00 3.60
J8 Stephen Head 8.00 3.60
J9 Mark Romanczuk 5.00 2.20
J10 Jeff Clement 10.00 4.50
J11 Mike Nickeas 8.00 3.60
J12 Tyler Greene 8.00 3.60
J13 Paul Janish 8.00 3.60
J14 Jeff Larish 8.00 3.60
J15 Eric Patterson 8.00 3.60
J16 Dustin Pedroia 10.00 4.50
J17 Michael Griffin 5.00 2.20
J18 Brent Lillibridge 5.00 2.20
J19 Danny Putnam 8.00 3.60
J20 Seth Smith 10.00 4.50

2003 Upper Deck First Pitch

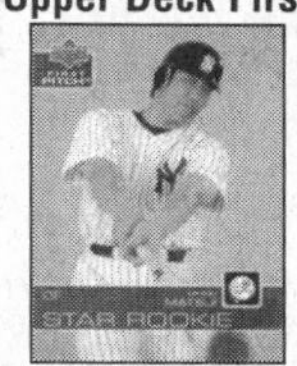

This 300-card set was released in April, 2003. These cards were issued in five card packs with an 99 cent SRP which came 36 packs to a box and 20 boxes to a case. This set parallels the 2003 Upper Deck first series however, there is a rookie and prospect subset added (271-283) and a traded/free agent subset (284-300). Those cards (271-300) were issued at a stated rate of one in four.

Nm-Mt Ex-Mt

COMP.SET w/o SP's (270) 50.00 15.00
*FIRST PITCH 1-270: .4X TO 1X BASIC UD
COMMON CARD (271-283) 1.00 .30
COMMON CARD (284-300) 3.00 .90
271 Hideki Matsui SP RC 15.00 4.50
272 Jose Contreras SP RC 4.00 1.20
273 Robert Madritsch SP RC 10.00 3.00
274 Shane Bazzell SP RC 1.00 .30
275 Felix Sanchez SP RC 1.00 .30
276 Todd Wellemeyer SP RC 4.00 1.20
277 Lew Ford SP RC 4.00 1.20
278 Jeremy Griffiths SP RC 4.00 1.20
279 Oscar Villarreal SP RC 1.00 .30
280 Brandon Webb SP RC 4.00 1.20
281 Delvis Lantigua SP RC 1.00 .30
282 Josh Willingham SP RC 4.00 1.20
283 Mike Nicolas SP RC 1.00 .30
284 Mike Hampton SP
285 Jim Thome SP 4.00 1.20
286 Bartolo Colon SP
287 Orlando Hernandez SP 3.00 .90
288 Jeremy Giambi SP 3.00 .90
289 Jeff Kent SP
290 Tom Glavine SP 3.00 .90
291 Cliff Floyd SP
292 Tsuyoshi Shinjo SP
293 Jose Cruz Jr. SP 3.00 .90
294 Edgardo Alfonzo SP 3.00 .90
295 Andres Galarraga SP
296 Troy O'Leary SP 3.00 .90
297 Eric Karros SP
298 Ivan Rodriguez SP 4.00 1.20
299 Fred McGriff SP 3.00 .90
300 Preston Wilson SP

2003 Upper Deck First Pitch Signature Stars

Randomly inserted into packs, these six cards feature authentic player signatures. We have

noted the stated print run for each player next to their name in our checklist. Please note that Ken Griffey Jr did not return his card in time for inclusion in packs and collectors could redeem exchange cards for his autograph until April 11, 2006.

Nm-Mt Ex-Mt

IS Ichiro Suzuki/50
JG Jason Giambi/100
KG Ken Griffey Jr./100 EXCH
KGS Ken Griffey Sr./800
NM Nomar Garciaparra/100
SS Sammy Sosa/50

2004 Upper Deck First Pitch

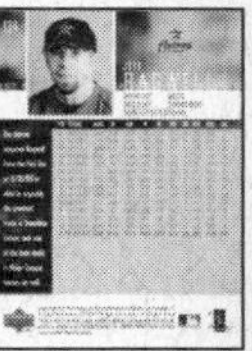

This 300 card set was released in February, 2004. The set was issued in five-card packs which came 36 packs to a box and 20 boxes to a case. The first 270 cards are issued in the same quantity while the final 30 cards which featture leading prospects of 2004 were issued at a stated rate of one in four.

Nm-Mt Ex-Mt

COMP.SET w/o SP'S (270) 50.00 15.00
*FIRST PITCH 1-270: .4X TO 1X BASIC UD
COMMON CARD (271-300) 1.00 .30
271-300 STATED ODDS 1:4
271 Rickie Weeks SP 1.00 .30
272 Delmon Young SP 4.00 1.20
273 Chien-Ming Wang SP 1.00 .30
274 Rich Harden SP 1.00 .30
275 Edwin Jackson SP 1.00 .30
276 Dan Haren SP 1.00 .30
277 Todd Wellemeyer SP 1.00 .30
278 Prentice Redman SP 1.00 .30
279 Ryan Wagner SP 1.00 .30
280 Aaron Looper SP 1.00 .30
281 Rick Roberts SP 1.00 .30
282 Josh Willingham SP 1.00 .30
283 Dave Crouthers SP RC 1.00 .30
284 Chris Capuano SP 1.00 .30
285 Mike Gosling SP RC 1.00 .30
286 Brian Sweeney SP 1.00 .30
287 Donald Kelly SP RC 1.00 .30
288 Ryan Meaux SP RC 1.00 .30
289 Colin Porter SP 1.00 .30
290 Jerome Gamble SP RC 1.00 .30
291 Colby Miller SP RC 1.00 .30
292 Ian Ferguson SP 1.00 .30
293 Tim Bittner SP RC 1.00 .30
294 Jason Frasor SP RC 1.00 .30
295 Brandon Medders SP RC 1.00 .30
296 Mike Johnston SP RC 1.00 .30
297 Tim Bausher SP RC 1.00 .30
298 Justin Leone SP RC 4.00 1.20
299 Sean Henn SP RC 1.00 .30
300 Michel Hernandez SP 1.00 .30

2004 Upper Deck First Pitch First and Foremost Jumbos

Nm-Mt Ex-Mt

BW Brandon Webb 5.00 1.50
DH Dan Haren 5.00 1.50
DW Dontrelle Willis 5.00 1.50
EB Ernie Banks 8.00 2.40
GH George H.W. Bush 10.00 3.00
GW George W. Bush 15.00 4.50
HR Horacio Ramirez 5.00 1.50
JC Jose Contreras 5.00 1.50
JW Jerome Williams 5.00 1.50
LT Luis Tiant 5.00 1.50
MS Mike Schmidt 10.00 3.00
RH Rich Harden 5.00 1.50
RW Ryan Wagner 5.00 1.50
WF Whitey Ford 8.00 2.40

2001 Upper Deck Gold Glove

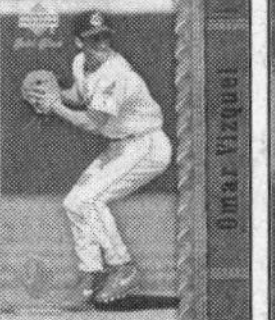

Issued in November 2001, this 135 card set featured many of the best defensive players in the majors. Cards numbered 91-135 were short printed and featured all Rookie Cards. Cards numbered 91-129 were serial numbered to 1000 and cards numbered 130-135 were serial numbered to 500.

	Nm-Mt	Ex-Mt
COMP.SET w/o SP'S (90)	15.00	4.50
COMMON CARD (1-90)	.60	.18
COMMON CARD (91-129)	5.00	1.50
COMMON (130-135)	10.00	3.00
1 Troy Glaus	.60	.18
2 Darin Erstad	.60	.18
3 Jason Giambi	.60	.18
4 Tim Hudson	.60	.18
5 Jermaine Dye	.60	.18
6 Raul Mondesi	.60	.18
7 Carlos Delgado	.60	.18
8 Shannon Stewart	.60	.18
9 Greg Vaughn	.60	.18
10 Aubrey Huff	.60	.18
11 Juan Gonzalez	1.00	.30
12 Roberto Alomar	1.00	.30
13 Omar Vizquel	1.00	.30
14 Jim Thome	1.50	.45
15 John Olerud	.60	.18
16 Edgar Martinez	1.00	.30
17 Kazuhiro Sasaki	.60	.18
18 Aaron Sele	.60	.18
19 Cal Ripken	5.00	1.50
20 Chris Richard	.60	.18
21 Ivan Rodriguez	1.50	.45
22 Rafael Palmeiro	1.00	.30
23 Alex Rodriguez	2.50	.75
24 Pedro Martinez	1.50	.45
25 Nomar Garciaparra	2.50	.75
26 Manny Ramirez	1.00	.30
27 Neifi Perez	.60	.18
28 Mike Sweeney	.60	.18
29 Bobby Higginson	.60	.18
30 Dean Palmer	.60	.18
31 Tony Clark	.60	.18
32 Doug Mientkiewicz	.60	.18
33 Brad Radke	.60	.18
34 Joe Mays	.60	.18
35 Frank Thomas	1.50	.45
36 Magglio Ordonez	.60	.18
37 Carlos Lee	.60	.18
38 Bernie Williams	1.00	.30
39 Mike Mussina	1.00	.30
40 Derek Jeter	4.00	1.20
41 Roger Clemens	3.00	.90
42 Craig Biggio	1.00	.30
43 Jeff Bagwell	1.00	.30
44 Lance Berkman	.60	.18
45 Andruw Jones	.60	.18
46 Greg Maddux	2.50	.75
47 Chipper Jones	1.50	.45
48 Geoff Jenkins	.60	.18
49 Ben Sheets	1.00	.30
50 Jeromy Burnitz	.60	.18
51 Jim Edmonds	.60	.18
52 Mark McGwire	4.00	1.20
53 Mike Matheny	.60	.18
54 J.D. Drew	.60	.18
55 Sammy Sosa	2.50	.75
56 Kerry Wood	1.50	.45
57 Fred McGriff	1.00	.30
58 Randy Johnson	1.50	.45
59 Steve Finley	.60	.18
60 Mark Grace	1.00	.30
61 Matt Williams	.60	.18
62 Luis Gonzalez	.60	.18
63 Shawn Green	.60	.18
64 Kevin Brown	.60	.18
65 Gary Sheffield	.60	.18
66 Vladimir Guerrero	1.50	.45
67 Tony Armas Jr.	.60	.18
68 Barry Bonds	4.00	1.20
69 J.T. Snow	.60	.18
70 Jeff Kent	.60	.18
71 Charles Johnson	.60	.18
72 Preston Wilson	.60	.18
73 Cliff Floyd	.60	.18
74 Robin Ventura	.60	.18
75 Mike Piazza	2.50	.75
76 Edgardo Alfonzo	.60	.18
77 Tony Gwynn	2.00	.60
78 Ryan Klesko	.60	.18
79 Scott Rolen	1.50	.45
80 Mike Lieberthal	.60	.18
81 Pat Burrell	.60	.18
82 Jason Kendall	.60	.18
83 Brian Giles	.60	.18
84 Ken Griffey Jr.	2.50	.75
85 Barry Larkin	1.00	.30
86 Pokey Reese	.60	.18
87 Larry Walker	1.00	.30
88 Mike Hampton	.60	.18
89 Juan Pierre	.60	.18
90 Todd Helton	1.00	.30
91 Mike Penney GD RC	5.00	1.50
92 Wilkin Ruan GD RC	5.00	1.50
93 Greg Miller GD RC	5.00	1.50
94 Johnny Estrada GD RC	8.00	2.40
95 Tsuyoshi Shinjo GD RC	8.00	2.40
96 Josh Towers GD RC	5.00	1.50
97 H. Ramirez GD RC	8.00	2.40
98 Ryan Freel GD RC	5.00	1.50
99 M. Ensberg GD RC	8.00	2.40
100 A. Hernandez GD RC	5.00	1.50
101 Juan Uribe GD RC	8.00	2.40
102 Jose Mieses GD RC	5.00	1.50
103 Jack Wilson GD RC	8.00	2.40
104 Cesar Crespo GD RC	5.00	1.50
105 Bud Smith GD RC	5.00	1.50
106 Erick Almonte GD RC	5.00	1.50
107 E. Guzman GD RC	5.00	1.50
108 B. Duckworth GD RC	5.00	1.50
109 Juan Diaz GD RC	5.00	1.50
110 Kris Keller GD RC	5.00	1.50
111 J. Michaels GD RC	5.00	1.50
112 Bret Prinz GD RC	5.00	1.50
113 Henry Mateo GD RC	5.00	1.50
114 R. Rodriguez GD RC	5.00	1.50
115 Travis Hafner GD RC	10.00	3.00
116 Nate Teut GD RC	5.00	1.50
117 Alexis Gomez GD RC	5.00	1.50
118 Billy Sylvester GD RC	5.00	1.50
119 A. Pettyjohn GD RC	5.00	1.50
120 Josh Fogg GD RC	5.00	1.50
121 Juan Cruz GD RC	5.00	1.50
122 C. Valderrama GD RC	5.00	1.50
123 Jay Gibbons GD RC	8.00	2.40
124 D. Mendez GD RC	5.00	1.50
125 Bill Ortega GD RC	5.00	1.50
126 Sean Douglass GD RC	5.00	1.50
127 C. Parker GD RC	5.00	1.50
128 Grant Balfour GD RC	5.00	1.50
129 Joe Kennedy GD RC	8.00	2.40
130 Albert Pujols GD RC	80.00	24.00
131 W. Betemit GD RC	10.00	3.00
132 Mark Teixeira GD RC	30.00	9.00
133 Mark Prior GD RC	50.00	15.00
134 D. Brazelton GD RC	15.00	4.50
135 Ichiro Suzuki GD RC	50.00	15.00

2001 Upper Deck Gold Glove Finite

This parallel to the basic Gold Glove set was randomly inserted in packs. The veterans are valued as a multiple of the basic cards while the rookies are serial numbered to 25.

Nm-Mt Ex-Mt

*STARS 1-90: 15X TO 40X BASIC CARDS

2001 Upper Deck Gold Glove Limited

Randomly inserted in packs, this is a parallel to the basic Gold Glove set. These cards are serial numbered to 100 and are valued as a multiple of the basic cards.

Nm-Mt Ex-Mt

*STARS 1-90: 5X TO 12X BASIC CARDS
*DEBUT 91-129: .6X TO 1.5X BASIC..
*DEBUT 130-135: .6X TO 1.5X BASIC

2001 Upper Deck Gold Glove Game Jersey

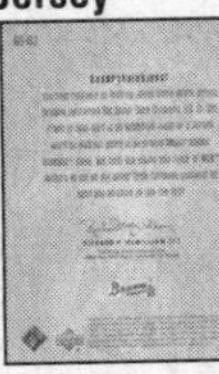

Issued at a rate of one in 20, these 27 cards feature game-used jerseys of defensive stars of the past and present. A few cards were issued in lesser quantities. Those cards are notated in our checklist with an SP along with specific print information provided by Upper Deck.

	Nm-Mt	Ex-Mt
STATED ODDS 1:20		
SP PRINT RUNS PROVIDED BY UPPER DECK		
SP'S ARE NOT SERIAL NUMBERED...		
GOLD RANDOM INSERTS IN PACKS..		
GOLD PRINT RUN 25 SERIAL #'d SETS		
GOLD NO PRICING DUE TO SCARCITY		
GG-AJ Andruw Jones	10.00	3.00
GG-BB Barry Bonds	25.00	7.50
GG-BR B.Richardson SP/274	25.00	7.50
GG-BW Bernie Williams	15.00	4.50
GG-CC Cesar Cedeno	10.00	3.00
GG-CF Carlton Fisk	15.00	4.50
GG-CR Cal Ripken	40.00	12.00
GG-DE Darin Erstad	10.00	3.00
GG-DM Don Mattingly	25.00	7.50
GG-GC Gary Carter	10.00	3.00
GG-GM Greg Maddux	15.00	4.50
GG-IR Ivan Rodriguez	15.00	4.50
GG-IS Ichiro Suzuki	80.00	24.00
GG-JB Jeff Bagwell	15.00	4.50
GG-JK Jim Kaat	10.00	3.00
GG-KG Ken Griffey Jr.	15.00	4.50
GG-LA Luis Aparicio	10.00	3.00
GG-MG Mark Grace	15.00	4.50
GG-MMA M. Mantle SP/264	200.00	60.00
GG-MMU Mike Mussina	15.00	4.50
GG-OS Ozzie Smith	15.00	4.50
GG-OV Omar Vizquel	15.00	4.50
GG-RG Ron Guidry	10.00	3.00
GG-RM R. Maris SP/265	80.00	24.00
GG-RP Rafael Palmeiro	15.00	4.50
GG-SG Shawn Green	10.00	3.00
GG-TM T. Munson SP/204	80.00	24.00

2001 Upper Deck Gold Glove Leather Bound

Inserted at a rate of one in 60, these 60 cards showcase the fielding talents of some of the best fielders in the game. It was originally reported by the manufacturer that a handful of cards were short-printed to a quantity of 100 copies each. Upon further investigation in 2003, Beckett price guide staff worked with representatives at Upper Deck to get final print run quantities on all cards. It was ultimately verified by the manufacturer, though they lack serial-numbering every card in the set was produced to a quantity of 100 copies each.

	Nm-Mt	Ex-Mt
GOLD RANDOM INSERTS IN PACKS..		
GOLD PRINT RUN 25 SERIAL #'d SETS		
NO GOLD PRICING DUE TO SCARCITY		
LB-AF Alex Fernandez		
LB-AG Alex Gonzalez	15.00	4.50
LB-AR Alex Rodriguez	40.00	12.00
LB-AS Aaron Sele	15.00	4.50
LB-BB Barry Bonds	60.00	18.00
LB-BG Ben Grieve	15.00	4.50
LB-CB Craig Biggio	25.00	7.50
LB-CF Cliff Floyd	15.00	4.50
LB-CJ Chipper Jones	25.00	7.50
LB-CL Carlos Lee	15.00	4.50
LB-CP Chan Ho Park	15.00	4.50
LB-DE Dock Ellis	15.00	4.50
LB-DW Dave Winfield	15.00	4.50
LB-EM Edgar Martinez	25.00	7.50
LB-FR Frank Robinson		
LB-FT Frank Thomas		
LB-GA Garret Anderson		
LB-GC Gary Carter	15.00	4.50
LB-GL Greg Luzinski	15.00	4.50
LB-GS Gary Sheffield	15.00	4.50
LB-HI Hideki Irabu	15.00	4.50
LB-HK Harvey Kuenn	15.00	4.50
LB-I Ichiro Suzuki	250.00	75.00
LB-IR Ivan Rodriguez	25.00	7.50
LB-JD Johnny Damon	25.00	7.50
LB-JE Jim Edmonds	15.00	4.50
LB-JI Jason Isringhausen		
LB-JL Javy Lopez	15.00	4.50
LB-JM Jose Mesa		
LB-JO John Olerud	15.00	4.50
LB-JBL Johnny Blanchard	15.00	4.50
LB-JBU Jay Buhner		
LB-JKA Jim Kaat	15.00	4.50
LB-JKE Jason Kendall	15.00	4.50
LB-KC Ken Caminiti	15.00	4.50
LB-KG Ken Griffey Jr.	40.00	12.00
LB-KL Kenny Lofton	15.00	4.50
LB-LD Leon Day		
LB-LG Lefty Grove	120.00	36.00
LB-MG Marquis Grissom	15.00	4.50
LB-MP Mike Piazza	40.00	12.00
LB-MR Manny Ramirez	25.00	7.50
LB-MY Masato Yoshii		
LB-NF Nellie Fox	25.00	7.50
LB-OD Octavio Dotel	15.00	4.50
LB-OH Orlando Hernandez	15.00	4.50
LB-OS Ozzie Smith	50.00	15.00
LB-OV Omar Vizquel	25.00	7.50
LB-PM Pedro Martinez	25.00	7.50
LB-PO Paul O'Neill	25.00	7.50
LB-RF Rafael Furcal	15.00	4.50
LB-RJ Reggie Jackson	25.00	7.50
LB-RK Ryan Klesko	15.00	4.50
LB-RP Rafael Palmeiro	25.00	7.50
LB-RCA Roy Campanella	100.00	30.00
LB-RCE Roger Cedeno		
LB-SS Sammy Sosa	40.00	12.00
LB-TS Tim Salmon	25.00	7.50
LB-THE Todd Helton	25.00	7.50
LB-THO T. Hollandsworth	15.00	4.50

2001 Upper Deck Gold Glove Leather Bound Autograph

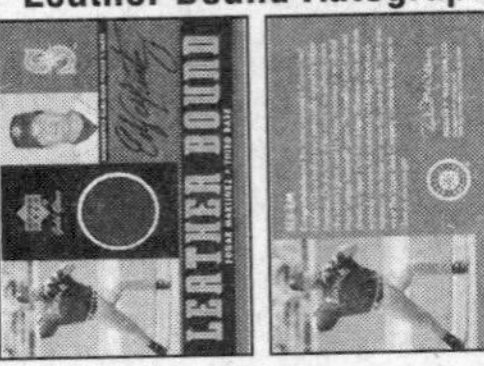

Issued at a rate of one in 240, these 31 cards feature not only information about the defensive star but also are signed by the player on the card. In 2003, more than two years after the product's initial release, the Beckett price guide staff managed to obtain specific print runs for short prints within this set (of which are detailed in our checklist) and finally settled lingering questions about the possible existence of cards featuring Aaron Sele, Barry Bonds, Chipper Jones, Gary Sheffield, Jim Edmonds, Mike Piazza, Pedro Martinez, Rafael Palmeiro, Sammy Sosa and Todd Helton. None of these cards had been seen in the secondary market but all were originally detailed on press release materials. In 2003, however, UD officially verified that none of the cards were created.

	Nm-Mt	Ex-Mt
STATED ODDS 1:240		
SP PRINT RUNS B/WN 29-68 COPIES PER		
SP'S ARE NOT SERIAL-NUMBERED...		
SP PRINT RUNS PROVIDED BY UPPER DECK		
SP'S NOT PRICED DUE TO SCARCITY		
SLB-I Ichiro Suzuki SP/50		
SLB-AR Alex Rodriguez SP/29		
SLB-CF Cliff Floyd	25.00	7.50
SLB-DW Dave Winfield	60.00	18.00
SLB-EM Edgar Martinez	80.00	24.00
SLB-FR Frank Robinson	60.00	18.00
SLB-FT Frank Thomas	80.00	24.00
SLB-GL Greg Luzinski	25.00	7.50
SLB-IR Ivan Rodriguez	80.00	24.00
SLB-JD Johnny Damon	60.00	18.00
SLB-JK Jim Kaat	25.00	7.50
SLB-JK Jason Kendall	25.00	7.50
SLB-JL Javy Lopez	25.00	7.50
SLB-JO John Olerud	25.00	7.50
SLB-KG Ken Griffey Jr. SP/49		
SLB-KL Kenny Lofton	60.00	18.00
SLB-OS Ozzie Smith	100.00	30.00
SLB-PO Paul O'Neill	60.00	18.00
SLB-RF Rafael Furcal	25.00	7.50
SLB-RJ Reggie Jackson SP/68		
SLB-RK Ryan Klesko	25.00	7.50

2001 Upper Deck Gold Glove Official Issue Game Ball

Inserted at a rate of one in 20, these 57 cards feature two players along with pieces of game-used memorabilia. A few cards were printed in lesser quantities and those have been noted as SP's in our checklist. We have also provided print run information provided by Upper Deck for these cards.

	Nm-Mt	Ex-Mt
OI-AG Roberto Alomar Juan Gonzalez	15.00	4.50
OI-BA Pat Burrell Bobby Abreu	10.00	3.00
OI-BB Jeff Bagwell Lance Berkman	15.00	4.50
OI-BH Lance Berkman Richard Hidalgo	10.00	3.00
OI-BK Barry Bonds Jeff Kent	30.00	9.00
OI-BS Jeromy Burnitz Richie Sexson	10.00	3.00
OI-CJ Roger Clemens Derek Jeter SP/17		
OI-DM Carlos Delgado Raul Mondesi	10.00	3.00
OI-DP J.D.Drew Albert Pujols	50.00	15.00
OI-EA Darin Erstad Garrett Anderson	10.00	3.00
OI-FJ Cliff Floyd Charles Johnson	10.00	3.00
OI-GB Shawn Green Adrian Beltre	15.00	4.50
OI-GC Ken Griffey Jr. Sean Casey	20.00	6.00
OI-GE Troy Glaus Darin Erstad	10.00	3.00
OI-GG Luis Gonzalez Mark Grace	15.00	4.50
OI-GJ Cristian Guzman Jacque Jones SP/194	15.00	4.50
OI-GK Tony Gwynn Ryan Klesko	20.00	6.00
OI-GR Brian Giles Aramis Ramirez	10.00	3.00
OI-GT Jason Giambi Miguel Tejada	10.00	3.00
OI-GV Vladimir Guerrero Jose Vidro	15.00	4.50
OI-HC Bobby Higginson Tony Clark SP/160	15.00	4.50
OI-HH Mike Hampton Todd Helton	15.00	4.50
OI-HW Todd Helton Larry Walker	15.00	4.50
OI-IO Ichiro Suzuki John Olerud	40.00	12.00
OI-JB Geoff Jenkins Jeromy Burnitz	10.00	3.00
OI-JF Andruw Jones Rafael Furcal	10.00	3.00
OI-JG Randy Johnson Luis Gonzalez	15.00	4.50
OI-JJ Chipper Jones Andruw Jones	15.00	4.50
OI-JW Deter Jeter Bernie Williams SP/17		
OI-KA Jeff Kent Rich Aurilia	10.00	3.00
OI-KG Jason Kendall Brian Giles	10.00	3.00
OI-LG Barry Larkin Ken Griffey Jr.	20.00	6.00
OI-MG Doug Mientkiewicz Cristian Guzman SP/194	15.00	4.50
OI-MJ Greg Maddux Chipper Jones	20.00	6.00
OI-MO Edgar Martinez John Olerud SP/160	25.00	7.50
OI-MP Mark McGwire Albert Pujols	100.00	30.00
OI-NK Phil Nevin Ryan Klesko	10.00	3.00
OI-PE Albert Pujols Jim Edmonds	50.00	15.00
OI-PR Rafael Palmeiro Alex Rodriguez	25.00	7.50
OI-PS Mike Piazza Tsuyoshi Shinjo	15.00	4.50
OI-RB Cal Ripken Tony Batista	40.00	12.00
OI-RE Manny Ramirez Carl Everett	15.00	4.50
OI-RP Ivan Rodriguez Rafael Palmeiro	15.00	4.50
OI-RR Alex Rodriguez Ivan Rodriguez	25.00	7.50
OI-RBU Scott Rolen Pat Burrell	15.00	4.50
OI-SB Mike Sweeney Carlos Beltran	15.00	4.50
OI-SG Gary Sheffield Shawn Green	10.00	3.00
OI-SV Tsuyoshi Shinjo Robin Ventura	15.00	4.50
OI-SW Sammy Sosa Rondell White	20.00	6.00
OI-TC Miguel Tejada Eric Chavez	10.00	3.00
OI-TO Frank Thomas Magglio Ordonez SP/160	25.00	7.50
OI-VM Greg Vaughn Fred McGriff SP/170	25.00	7.50
OI-VP Robin Ventura Mike Piazza	20.00	6.00
OI-WF Preston Wilson Cliff Floyd	10.00	3.00
OI-WP Larry Walker Juan Pierre	15.00	4.50
OI-WS Kerry Wood Sammy Sosa	20.00	6.00
OI-WPO Bernie Williams Jorge Posada SP/17		

2001 Upper Deck Gold Glove Slugger's Choice

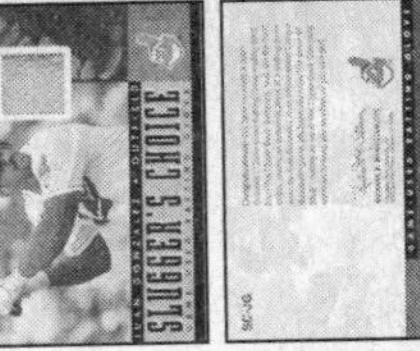

Issued at a rate of one in 20, these 26 cards feature authentic pieces of game-used batting gloves of baseball's top hitters. A few cards were short printed compared to the other cards. We have notated these cards with an SP and print run information provided by Upper Deck in our checklist.

	Nm-Mt	Ex-Mt
GOLD RANDOM INSERTS IN PACKS..		
GOLD PRINT RUN 25 SERIAL #'d SETS		
NO GOLD PRICING DUE TO SCARCITY		
SC-AG Andres Galarraga	10.00	3.00
SC-ARM A.Rodriguez Mariners	15.00	4.50
SC-ARR A.Rodriguez Rangers	15.00	4.50
SC-BA Bobby Abreu	10.00	3.00
SC-BA Brady Anderson	10.00	3.00
SC-BB Barry Bonds	25.00	7.50
SC-CJ Chipper Jones	15.00	4.50
SC-EM Edgar Martinez	15.00	4.50
SC-FT F.Tatis SP/147	10.00	3.00
SC-GS G.Sheffield SP/201	10.00	3.00
SC-HR H.Rodriguez SP/185	10.00	3.00
SC-IR Ivan Rodriguez	15.00	4.50
SC-JC J.Cruz Jr. SP/191	10.00	3.00
SC-JG Juan Gonzalez	15.00	4.50
SC-JI Jason Isringhausen	10.00	3.00
SC-KGM K.Griffey Jr. Mariners	15.00	4.50
SC-KGR K.Griffey Jr. Reds	15.00	4.50
SC-MC Marty Cordova	10.00	3.00
SC-MR Manny Ramirez	15.00	4.50
SC-MT Miguel Tejada	10.00	3.00
SC-NP Neifi Perez	10.00	3.00
SC-PO Paul O'Neill	15.00	4.50
SC-RF Rafael Furcal	10.00	3.00
SC-RP Rafael Palmeiro	15.00	4.50
SC-SS Sammy Sosa	15.00	4.50
SC-TB Tony Batista	10.00	3.00

2001 Upper Deck Hall of Famers

The 2001 Upper Deck Hall of Famers product was released in early April, 2001 and features a 90-card base set that is broken into tiers as follows: Base Veterans (1-50), Origins of the Game (51-60), National Pastime (61-80), and finally Hall of Records (81-90). Each pack contained 5 cards and carried a suggested retail price of $3.99.

	Nm-Mt	Ex-Mt
COMPLETE SET (90)	20.00	6.00
1 Reggie Jackson	.40	.12
2 Hank Aaron	1.25	.35
3 Eddie Mathews	.60	.18
4 Warren Spahn	.40	.12
5 Robin Yount	1.00	.30
6 Lou Brock	.40	.12
7 Dizzy Dean	.60	.18
8 Bob Gibson	.40	.12
9 Stan Musial	1.00	.30
10 Enos Slaughter	.25	.07
11 Rogers Hornsby	.60	.18
12 Ernie Banks	.60	.18
13 Fergie Jenkins	.25	.07
14 Roy Campanella	.60	.18
15 Pee Wee Reese	.60	.18
16 Jackie Robinson	.60	.18
17 Juan Marichal	.25	.07
18 Christy Mathewson	.60	.18
19 Willie Mays	1.25	.35
20 Hoyt Wilhelm	.25	.07
21 Buck Leonard	.25	.07
22 Bob Feller	.25	.07
23 Cy Young	.60	.18
24 Satchel Paige	.60	.18
25 Tom Seaver	.40	.12
26 Brooks Robinson	.40	.12
27 Mike Schmidt	1.25	.35
28 Roberto Clemente	1.50	.45
29 Ralph Kiner	.25	.07
30 Willie Stargell	.40	.12
31 Honus Wagner	.75	.23
32 Josh Gibson	.60	.18
33 Nolan Ryan	1.50	.45
34 Carlton Fisk	.40	.12
35 Jimmie Foxx	.60	.18
36 Johnny Bench	.60	.18
37 Joe Morgan	.25	.07
38 George Brett	1.50	.45
39 Walter Johnson	.60	.18
40 Cool Papa Bell	.25	.07
41 Ty Cobb	1.00	.30
42 Al Kaline	.60	.18
43 Harmon Killebrew	.60	.18
44 Luis Aparicio	.25	.07
45 Yogi Berra	.60	.18
46 Joe DiMaggio	1.25	.35
47 Whitey Ford	.40	.12
48 Lou Gehrig	1.25	.35
49 Mickey Mantle	2.50	.75
50 Babe Ruth	2.00	.60

51 Josh Gibson OG .40 .12
52 Honus Wagner OG .60 .18
53 Hoyt Wilhelm OG .25 .07
54 Cy Young OG .40 .12
55 Walter Johnson OG .40 .12
56 Satchel Paige OG .40 .12
57 Rogers Hornsby OG .40 .12
58 Christy Mathewson OG .40 .12
59 Tris Speaker OG .40 .12
60 Nap Lajoie OG .60 .18
61 Mickey Mantle NP 1.25 .35
62 Jackie Robinson NP .40 .12
63 Nolan Ryan NP 1.00 .30
64 Josh Gibson NP .40 .12
65 Yogi Berra NP .40 .12
66 Brooks Robinson NP .25 .07
67 Stan Musial NP .60 .18
68 Mike Schmidt NP .60 .18
69 Joe DiMaggio NP .60 .18
70 Ernie Banks NP .40 .12
71 Willie Stargell NP .25 .07
72 Johnny Bench NP .40 .12
73 Willie Mays NP .60 .18
74 Satchel Paige NP .40 .12
75 Bob Gibson NP .25 .07
76 Harmon Killebrew NP .60 .18
77 Al Kaline NP .40 .12
78 Carlton Fisk NP .25 .07
79 Tom Seaver NP .25 .07
80 Reggie Jackson NP .25 .07
81 Bob Gibson HR .25 .07
82 Nolan Ryan HR 1.00 .30
83 Walter Johnson HR .40 .12
84 Stan Musial HR .60 .18
85 Josh Gibson HR .40 .12
86 Cy Young HR .40 .12
87 Joe DiMaggio HR .60 .18
88 Hoyt Wilhelm HR .25 .07
89 Lou Brock HR .25 .07
90 Mickey Mantle HR 1.25 .35

2001 Upper Deck Hall of Famers 20th Century Showcase

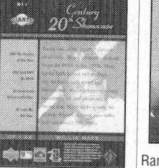

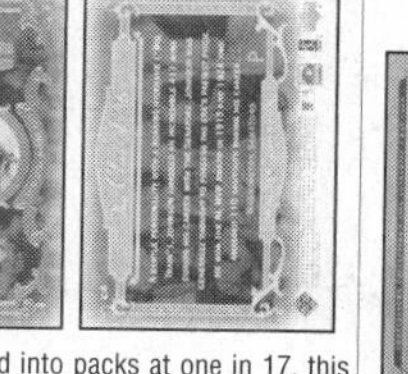

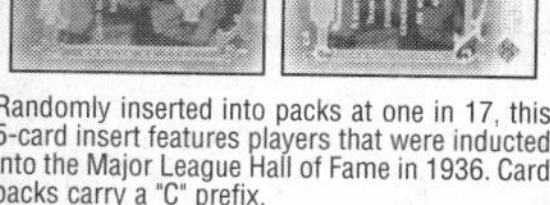

Randomly inserted into packs at one in eight, this 11-card insert set features some of the Major League's top players throughout the 20th Century. Card backs carry an "S" prefix.

	Nm-Mt	Ex-Mt
COMPLETE SET (11)	30.00	9.00
S1 Cy Young	2.00	.60
S2 Joe DiMaggio	4.00	1.20
S3 Harmon Killebrew	2.00	.60
S4 Stan Musial	3.00	.90
S5 Mickey Mantle	8.00	2.40
S6 Satchel Paige	2.00	.60
S7 Nolan Ryan	5.00	1.50
S8 Bob Gibson	1.50	.45
S9 Ernie Banks	2.00	.60
S10 Mike Schmidt	4.00	1.20
S11 Willie Mays	4.00	1.20

2001 Upper Deck Hall of Famers Class of '36

Randomly inserted into packs at one in 17, this 5-card insert set features players that were inducted into the Major League Hall of Fame in 1936. Card backs carry a "C" prefix.

	Nm-Mt	Ex-Mt
COMPLETE SET (5)	15.00	4.50
C1 Ty Cobb	3.00	.90
C2 Babe Ruth	6.00	1.80
C3 Christy Mathewson	2.00	.60
C4 Walter Johnson	2.00	.60
C5 Honus Wagner	2.50	.75

2001 Upper Deck Hall of Famers Cut Signatures

Randomly inserted into packs, this five-card insert set features cut-signatures from deceased Major League Ballplayers. Card backs carry a "C" prefix followed by the player's initials. A total of only eleven cards were produced for this set.

	Nm-Mt	Ex-Mt
LC1 Honus Wagner		
Ty Cobb		
Babe Ruth		
Christy Mathewson		
Walter Johnson/1		
C-BR Babe Ruth/2		
C-CM Christy Mathewson/1		
C-HW Honus Wagner/1		
C-TC Ty Cobb/2		
C-WJ Walter Johnson/5		

2001 Upper Deck Hall of Famers Endless Summer

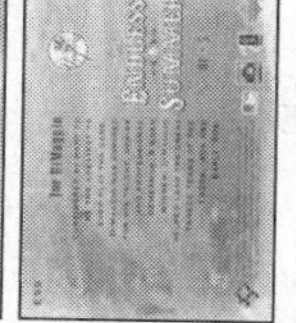

Randomly inserted into packs at one in eight, this 11-card insert set features classic players that had amazing careers in Major League Baseball. Card backs carry an "ES" prefix.

	Nm-Mt	Ex-Mt
COMPLETE SET (11)	30.00	9.00
ES1 Mickey Mantle	8.00	2.40
ES2 Yogi Berra	2.00	.60
ES3 Mike Schmidt	4.00	1.20
ES4 Jackie Robinson	2.00	.60
ES5 Johnny Bench	2.00	.60
ES6 Tom Seaver	2.00	.60
ES7 Ernie Banks	2.00	.60
ES8 Harmon Killebrew	2.00	.60
ES9 Joe DiMaggio	4.00	1.20
ES10 Willie Mays	4.00	1.20
ES11 Brooks Robinson	2.00	.60

2001 Upper Deck Hall of Famers Gallery

Randomly inserted into packs at one in six, this 15-card insert set features Major League Ballplayers that have been inducted into the Hall of Fame. Card backs carry a "G" prefix.

	Nm-Mt	Ex-Mt
COMPLETE SET (15)	40.00	12.00
G1 Reggie Jackson	1.25	.35
G2 Tom Seaver	1.25	.35
G3 Bob Gibson	1.25	.35
G4 Jackie Robinson	2.00	.60
G5 Joe DiMaggio	4.00	1.20
G6 Ernie Banks	2.00	.60
G7 Mickey Mantle	8.00	2.40
G8 Willie Mays	4.00	1.20
G9 Cy Young	2.00	.60
G10 Nolan Ryan	5.00	1.50
G11 Johnny Bench	2.00	.60
G12 Yogi Berra	2.00	.60
G13 Satchel Paige	2.00	.60
G14 George Brett	5.00	1.50
G15 Stan Musial	3.00	.90

2001 Upper Deck Hall of Famers Game Bat

Randomly inserted into packs at one in 24 (about one a box), this 40-card insert features slivers of actual game-used bats. Card backs carry a "B" prefix followed by the players initials. Though they lack any actual form of serial-numbering, Upper Deck announced specific print runs for several short prints within this set. That information is detailed within our checklist. In addition, based upon extensive market research by our analysts, several cards are tagged with an asterisk within our checklist to indicate a perceived larger supply.

	Nm-Mt	Ex-Mt
B-BR Babe Ruth	200.00	60.00
B-BRO Brooks Robinson	15.00	4.50
B-BW Billy Williams	10.00	3.00
B-CF Carlton Fisk *	15.00	4.50
B-DD Don Drysdale	15.00	4.50
B-DS Duke Snider	15.00	4.50
B-EB Ernie Banks	15.00	4.50
B-ES Enos Slaughter	10.00	3.00
B-EW Early Wynn	15.00	4.50
B-FR Frank Robinson	15.00	4.50
B-GB George Brett *	15.00	4.50
B-GK George Kell	15.00	4.50
B-HA Hank Aaron *	40.00	12.00
B-HG Hank Greenberg	50.00	15.00
B-JB Johnny Bench *	15.00	4.50
B-JBO Jim Bottomley	15.00	4.50
B-JD Joe DiMaggio	100.00	30.00
B-JF Jimmie Foxx	60.00	18.00
B-JM Johnny Mize	15.00	4.50
B-JMO Joe Morgan *	10.00	3.00
B-JP Jim Palmer SP/372	50.00	15.00
B-JR J.Robinson SP/371	150.00	45.00
B-LA Luis Aparicio	10.00	3.00
B-MM Mickey Mantle	150.00	45.00
B-MO Mel Ott	60.00	18.00
B-NF Nellie Fox	15.00	4.50
B-NR Nolan Ryan	40.00	12.00
B-OC Orlando Cepeda	10.00	3.00
B-RC R.Clemente SP/409	120.00	36.00
B-RCA Roy Campanella	40.00	12.00
B-RF Rollie Fingers	10.00	3.00
B-RH Rogers Hornsby	100.00	30.00
B-RJ Reggie Jackson *	15.00	4.50
B-RK Ralph Kiner	15.00	4.50
B-RS Red Schoendienst	15.00	4.50
B-RY Robin Yount *	15.00	4.50
B-TP Tony Perez	10.00	3.00
B-WM Willie Mays *	40.00	12.00
B-WS Willie Stargell	15.00	4.50
B-YB Yogi Berra	15.00	4.50

2001 Upper Deck Hall of Famers Game Jersey

Randomly inserted into packs at one in 168, this 18-card insert features swatches of actual game-used jerseys. Card backs carry a "J" prefix followed by the players initials. Though they lack actual serial-numbering, Upper Deck announced specific print runs for several short-prints within this set. That information is detailed within our checklist. In addition, based upon extensive market research by our analysts, several cards are tagged with an asterisk within our checklist to indicate a perceived larger supply.

	Nm-Mt	Ex-Mt
J-BR Brooks Robinson	25.00	7.50
J-DD Don Drysdale SP/49		
J-DS Duke Snider SP/267	80.00	24.00
J-DSU Don Sutton	15.00	4.50
J-FR Frank Robinson	25.00	7.50
J-JD Joe DiMaggio	120.00	36.00
J-JM Joe Morgan	15.00	4.50
J-LA Luis Aparicio	15.00	4.50
J-LG L.Gehrig Pants SP/194	300.00	90.00
J-MM M.Mantle SP/216	300.00	90.00
J-NR Nolan Ryan *	40.00	12.00
J-OC Orlando Cepeda	15.00	4.50
J-PW Pee Wee Reese	25.00	7.50
J-RC Roberto Clemente	120.00	36.00
J-TP Tony Perez	15.00	4.50
J-TS Tom Seaver	25.00	7.50
J-WM Willie Mays	100.00	30.00
J-WS Willie Stargell	25.00	7.50

2001 Upper Deck Hall of Famers Game Jersey Autograph

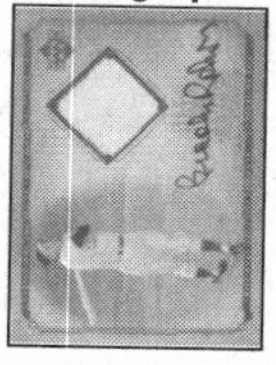

Randomly inserted into packs at one in 504, this 14-card insert features swatches of actual game-used jerseys, as well as, an authentic autograph from the depicted player. Card backs carry a "SJ" prefix followed by the players initials. Willie Stargell was supposed to sign cards for this set but he passed away on April 9th, 2001 . . . before any of the exchange cards were produced.

	Nm-Mt	Ex-Mt
SJ-BR Brooks Robinson	80.00	24.00
SJ-DS Duke Snider	80.00	24.00
SJ-DSU Don Sutton	60.00	18.00
SJ-EB Ernie Banks	100.00	30.00
SJ-FR Frank Robinson	80.00	24.00
SJ-GB George Brett	150.00	45.00
SJ-JM Joe Morgan	60.00	18.00
SJ-LA Luis Aparicio	60.00	18.00
SJ-NR Nolan Ryan	175.00	52.50
SJ-OC Orlando Cepeda	60.00	18.00
SJ-RJ Reggie Jackson	100.00	30.00
SJ-TP Tony Perez	60.00	18.00
SJ-TS Tom Seaver	80.00	24.00
SJ-WS Willie Stargell EXCH	5.00	1.50

2000 Upper Deck Legends

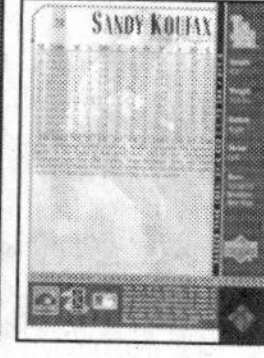

The 2000 Upper Deck Legends product was released in late August, 2000 and featured a 135-card base set that was broken into tiers as follows: (90) Base Veterans (1-90), (15) Y2K Subset cards (91-105) (1:9), and (30) 20th Century Legends Subset cards (106-135) (1:5). Each pack contained five cards and carried a suggested retail price of $4.99. Also, a selection of A Piece of History 3000 Club Paul Molitor and Carl Yastrzemski memorabilia cards were randomly seeded into packs. 350 bat cards for each player were produced. Also for Carl Yatsrzemski only, 350 jersey cards, 100 hand-numbered bat-jersey combination cards and eight autographed, hand-numbered, combination bat-jersey cards were produced. Pricing for these memorabilia cards can be referenced under 2000 Upper Deck A Piece of History 3000 Club.

	Nm-Mt	Ex-Mt
COMPLETE SET (135)	80.00	24.00
COMP.SET w/o SP'S (90)	20.00	6.00
COMMON CARD (1-90)	.30	.09
COMMON CARD (91-105)	2.00	.60
COMMON (106-135)	2.00	.60
1 Darin Erstad	.30	.09
2 Troy Glaus	.30	.09
3 Mo Vaughn	.30	.09
4 Craig Biggio	.50	.15
5 Jeff Bagwell	.50	.15
6 Reggie Jackson	.50	.15
7 Tim Hudson	.30	.09
8 Jason Giambi	.30	.09
9 Hank Aaron	1.50	.45
10 Greg Maddux	1.25	.35
11 Chipper Jones	.75	.23
12 Andres Galarraga	.30	.09
13 Robin Yount	1.25	.35
14 Jeromy Burnitz	.30	.09
15 Paul Molitor	.50	.15
16 David Wells	.30	.09
17 Carlos Delgado	.30	.09
18 Ernie Banks	.75	.23
19 Sammy Sosa	1.25	.35
20 Kerry Wood	.75	.23
21 Stan Musial	1.25	.35
22 Bob Gibson	.50	.15
23 Mark McGwire	2.00	.60
24 Fernando Tatis	.30	.09
25 Randy Johnson	.75	.23
26 Matt Williams	.30	.09
27 Jackie Robinson	.75	.23
28 Sandy Koufax	2.00	.60
29 Shawn Green	.30	.09
30 Kevin Brown	.50	.15
31 Gary Sheffield	.30	.09
32 Greg Vaughn	.30	.09
33 Jose Canseco	.75	.23
34 Gary Carter	.30	.09
35 Vladimir Guerrero	.75	.23
36 Willie Mays	1.50	.45
37 Barry Bonds	2.00	.60
38 Jeff Kent	.30	.09
39 Bob Feller	.30	.09
40 Roberto Alomar	.50	.15
41 Jim Thome	.75	.23
42 Manny Ramirez	.50	.15
43 Alex Rodriguez	1.25	.35
44 Preston Wilson	.30	.09
45 Tom Seaver	.50	.15
46 Robin Ventura	.30	.09
47 Mike Piazza	1.25	.35
48 Mike Hampton	.30	.09
49 Brooks Robinson	.50	.15
50 Frank Robinson	.50	.15
51 Cal Ripken	2.50	.75
52 Albert Belle	.30	.09
53 Eddie Murray	.75	.23
54 Tony Gwynn	1.00	.30
55 Roberto Clemente	1.50	.45
56 Willie Stargell	.50	.15
57 Brian Giles	.30	.09
58 Jason Kendall	.30	.09
59 Mike Schmidt	1.50	.45
60 Bob Abreu	.30	.09
61 Scott Rolen	.75	.23
62 Curt Schilling	.30	.09
63 Johnny Bench	.75	.23
64 Sean Casey	.30	.09
65 Barry Larkin	.50	.15
66 Ken Griffey Jr.	1.25	.35
67 George Brett	2.00	.60
68 Carlos Beltran	.50	.15
69 Nolan Ryan	2.50	.75
70 Ivan Rodriguez	.75	.23
71 Rafael Palmeiro	.50	.15
72 Larry Walker	.50	.15
73 Todd Helton	.50	.15
74 Jeff Cirillo	.30	.09
75 Carl Everett	.30	.09
76 Nomar Garciaparra	1.25	.35
77 Pedro Martinez	.75	.23
78 Harmon Killebrew	.75	.23
79 Corey Koskie	.30	.09
80 Ty Cobb	1.25	.35
81 Dean Palmer	.30	.09
82 Juan Gonzalez	.50	.15
83 Carlton Fisk	.50	.15
84 Frank Thomas	.75	.23
85 Magglio Ordonez	.30	.09
86 Lou Gehrig	1.50	.45
87 Babe Ruth	2.50	.75
88 Derek Jeter	2.00	.60
89 Roger Clemens	1.50	.45
90 Bernie Williams	.50	.15
91 Rick Ankiel Y2K	2.00	.60
92 Kip Wells Y2K	2.00	.60
93 Pat Burrell Y2K	2.00	.60
94 Mark Quinn Y2K	2.00	.60
95 Ruben Mateo Y2K	2.00	.60
96 Adam Kennedy Y2K	2.00	.60
97 Brad Penny Y2K	2.00	.60
98 K.Sasaki Y2K RC	3.00	.90
99 Peter Bergeron Y2K	2.00	.60
100 Rafael Furcal Y2K	2.00	.60
101 Eric Munson Y2K	2.00	.60
102 Nick Johnson Y2K	2.00	.60
103 Rob Bell Y2K	2.00	.60
104 Vernon Wells Y2K	2.00	.60
105 Ben Petrick Y2K	2.00	.60
106 Babe Ruth 20C	8.00	2.40
107 Mark McGwire 20C	5.00	1.50
108 Nolan Ryan 20C	6.00	1.80
109 Hank Aaron 20C	4.00	1.20
110 Barry Bonds 20C	5.00	1.50
111 N.Garciaparra 20C	3.00	.90
112 Roger Clemens 20C	4.00	1.20
113 Johnny Bench 20C	2.00	.60
114 Alex Rodriguez 20C	3.00	.90
115 Cal Ripken 20C	6.00	1.80
116 Willie Mays 20C	4.00	1.20
117 Mike Piazza 20C	3.00	.90
118 Reggie Jackson 20C	2.00	.60
119 Tony Gwynn 20C	2.50	.75
120 Cy Young 20C	2.00	.60
121 George Brett 20C	4.00	1.20
122 Greg Maddux 20C	3.00	.90
123 Yogi Berra 20C	2.00	.60
124 Sammy Sosa 20C	3.00	.90
125 Randy Johnson 20C	2.00	.60
126 Bob Gibson 20C	2.00	.60
127 Lou Gehrig 20C	5.00	1.50
128 Ken Griffey Jr. 20C	3.00	.90
129 Derek Jeter 20C	5.00	1.50
130 Mike Schmidt 20C	4.00	1.20
131 Pedro Martinez 20C	2.00	.60
132 Jackie Robinson 20C	2.00	.60
133 Jose Canseco 20C	2.00	.60
134 Ty Cobb 20C	3.00	.90
135 Stan Musial 20C	3.00	.90

2000 Upper Deck Legends Commemorative Collection

Randomly inserted into packs, this 135-card insert is a complete parallel of the Upper Deck Legends base set. Each card in this set is individually serial numbered to 100.

Nm-Mt Ex-Mt

*ACTIVE STARS 1-90: 8X TO 20X BASIC
*POST-WAR STARS 1-90: 10X TO 25X BASIC
*PRE-WAR STARS 1-90: 6X TO 15X BASIC
*Y2K: 2X TO 5X BASIC Y2K
*ACTIVE 20C: 3X TO 8X BASIC 20C
*POST-WAR 20C: 5X TO 12X BASIC 20C
*PRE-WAR 20C: 2.5X TO 6X BASIC 20C

2000 Upper Deck Legends Defining Moments

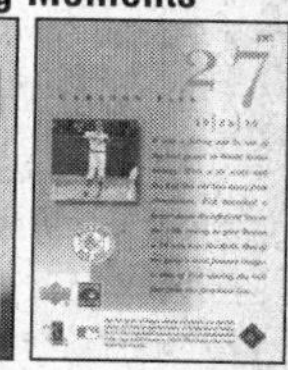

Randomly inserted into packs at one in 12, this 10-card insert focuses on some of Major League baseball's most defining moments Card backs carry a "DM" prefix.

	Nm-Mt	Ex-Mt
COMPLETE SET (10)	50.00	15.00
DM1 Reggie Jackson	1.50	.45
DM2 Hank Aaron	5.00	1.50
DM3 Babe Ruth	8.00	2.40
DM4 Cal Ripken	8.00	2.40
DM5 Carlton Fisk	1.50	.45
DM6 Ken Griffey Jr.	4.00	1.20
DM7 Nolan Ryan	8.00	2.40
DM8 Roger Clemens	5.00	1.50
DM9 Willie Mays	5.00	1.50
DM10 Mark McGwire	6.00	1.80

2000 Upper Deck Legends Eternal Glory

Randomly inserted into packs at one in 24, this six-card insert features players whose greatness will live on in the minds of many. Please note that card number 3 does not exist. Card backs carry an "EG" prefix.

	Nm-Mt	Ex-Mt
COMPLETE SET (6)	40.00	12.00
EG1 Nolan Ryan	10.00	3.00
EG2 Ken Griffey Jr.	5.00	1.50
EG3 Does Not Exist		
EG4 Sammy Sosa	5.00	1.50
EG5 Derek Jeter	8.00	2.40
EG6 Willie Mays	6.00	1.80
EG7 Roger Clemens	6.00	1.80

2000 Upper Deck Legends Legendary Game Jerseys

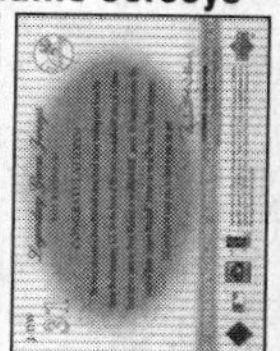

Randomly inserted into packs at one in 48, this 50-card insert set features game-used jersey cards of past and present Major League stars. Cards are numbered using the player's initials with a "J" prefix.

	Nm-Mt	Ex-Mt
SP'S ARE NOT SERIAL-NUMBERED		
SP INFO PROVIDED BY UPPER DECK		
J-AR Alex Rodriguez	25.00	7.50
J-BAB Barry Bonds	40.00	12.00
J-BG Bob Gibson Pants	15.00	4.50
J-BM Bill Mazeroski	10.00	3.00
J-BOB Bobby Bonds	10.00	3.00
J-BR Brooks Robinson	15.00	4.50

J-CJ Chipper Jones 15.00 4.50
J-CR Cal Ripken 40.00 12.00
J-DC Dave Concepcion 10.00 3.00
J-DD Don Drysdale 15.00 4.50
J-DJ Derek Jeter 40.00 12.00
J-DM Dale Murphy 15.00 4.50
J-DW Dave Winfield 10.00 3.00
J-EM Eddie Mathews 15.00 4.50
J-EW Earl Weaver 10.00 3.00
J-FR Frank Robinson 15.00 4.50
J-FT Frank Thomas 15.00 4.50
J-GB George Brett 25.00 7.50
J-GM Greg Maddux 25.00 7.50
J-GP Gaylord Perry 10.00 3.00
J-HA Hank Aaron 60.00 18.00
J-JB Jeff Bagwell 15.00 4.50
J-JB Johnny Bench 15.00 4.50
J-JC Jose Canseco 15.00 4.50
J-JP Jim Palmer 10.00 3.00
J-JT Joe Torre 15.00 4.50
J-KG Ken Griffey Jr. 25.00 7.50
J-LB Lou Brock 15.00 4.50
J-LG Lou Gehrig Pants 250.00 75.00
J-MM Mickey Mantle 200.00 60.00
J-MR Manny Ramirez 15.00 4.50
J-MS Mike Schmidt 25.00 7.50
J-MW Matt Williams 10.00 3.00
J-MW Maury Wills 10.00 3.00
J-NR Nolan Ryan 40.00 12.00
J-OS Ozzie Smith 15.00 4.50
J-RAJ Randy Johnson 15.00 4.50
J-RC Roger Clemens 25.00 7.50
J-RF Rollie Fingers 10.00 3.00
J-RJ Reggie Jackson 15.00 4.50
J-RM Roger Maris Pants 80.00 24.00
J-SK Sandy Koufax SP/95 400.00 120.00
J-SM Stan Musial SP/28
J-TG Tony Gwynn 15.00 4.50
J-TM Thurman Munson 50.00 15.00
J-TS Tom Seaver 15.00 4.50
J-WB Wade Boggs 15.00 4.50
J-WM Willie Mays SP/29
J-WMC Willie McCovey 10.00 3.00
J-WS Willie Stargell 15.00 4.50
S-JSK Sandy Koufax AU/32

2000 Upper Deck Legends Legendary Signatures

Randomly inserted into packs at one in 24, this 39-card insert features autographed cards of past and present superstars. Card backs are numbered using the player's initials and an "S" prefix. Though print run numbers were not initially released, Upper Deck did confirm to Beckett Publications that Hank Aaron, Derek Jeter and Manny Ramirez signed less cards than other players in the set. Specific quantities for each of these players is detailed in the checklist below. Finally, Dave Concepcion, Frank Thomas, Ken Griffey Jr., Manny Ramirez, Mo Vaughn, Ozzie Smith and Willie Stargell cards were inserted in packs as stickered exchange cards. The deadline for this exchange was April 22nd, 2001. In addition to the exchange cards, real autographed cards did make their into packs for the following players: Willie Stargell, Ozzie Smith and Dave Concepcion.

	Nm-Mt	Ex-Mt
S-AD Andre Dawson	15.00	4.50
S-AR Alex Rodriguez	120.00	36.00
S-AT Alan Trammell	15.00	4.50
S-BB Bobby Bonds	25.00	7.50
S-CJ Chipper Jones	40.00	12.00
S-CR Cal Ripken	150.00	45.00
S-DC D.Concepcion EXCH*	15.00	4.50
S-DJ Derek Jeter SP/61	600.00	180.00
S-DM Dale Murphy	40.00	12.00
S-FL Fred Lynn	15.00	4.50
S-FT Frank Thomas	40.00	12.00
S-GB George Brett	80.00	24.00
S-GC Gary Carter	15.00	4.50
S-HA Hank Aaron SP/94	300.00	90.00
S-HK Harmon Killebrew	40.00	12.00
S-IR Ivan Rodriguez	40.00	12.00
S-JB Johnny Bench	40.00	12.00
S-JC Jose Canseco	40.00	12.00
S-JP Jim Palmer	15.00	4.50
S-KG Ken Griffey Jr.	100.00	30.00
S-LB Lou Brock	25.00	7.50
S-MP Mike Piazza	200.00	60.00
S-MR Manny Ramirez SP/141	60.00	18.00
S-MS Mike Schmidt	60.00	18.00
S-MV Mo Vaughn	15.00	4.50
S-MW Matt Williams	15.00	4.50
S-NR Nolan Ryan	120.00	36.00
S-OS Ozzie Smith	40.00	12.00
S-PN Phil Niekro	15.00	4.50
S-RC Roger Clemens	100.00	30.00
S-RF Rollie Fingers	15.00	4.50
S-RJ Reggie Jackson	40.00	12.00
S-SC Sean Casey	15.00	4.50
S-SM Stan Musial	60.00	18.00
S-TG Tony Gwynn	40.00	12.00
S-TS Tom Seaver	25.00	7.50
S-VG Vladimir Guerrero	40.00	12.00
S-WS Willie Stargell EXCH*	60.00	18.00
SRAJ Randy Johnson	80.00	24.00

2000 Upper Deck Legends Legendary Signatures Gold

Randomly inserted into packs, this set is a parallel of the Legendary Signatures insert. Each card features gold colored fronts (instead of silver for the basic cards) and is individually serial

numbered to 50 on front in blue ink sharpie. Each card is numbered on the back using the player's initials and an "S" prefix. Also, Dave Concepcion, Frank Thomas, Ken Griffey Jr., Manny Ramirez, Mo Vaughn, Ozzie Smith and Willie Stargell cards were inserted in packs as stickered exchange cards. The deadline for this exchange was April 22nd, 2001. In addition to the exchange cards, real autographed cards did make their into packs for the following players: Willie Stargell, Ozzie Smith and Dave Concepcion. Please note, that Derek Jeter did not sign any Gold cards. The Yankees star shortstop signed only 61 cards for this entire product - all of which were basic Legendary Signatures.

	Nm-Mt	Ex-Mt
S-AD Andre Dawson	40.00	12.00
S-AR Alex Rodriguez	200.00	60.00
S-AT Alan Trammell	40.00	12.00
S-BB Bobby Bonds	50.00	15.00
S-CJ Chipper Jones	80.00	24.00
S-CR Cal Ripken	250.00	75.00
S-DC D.Concepcion EXCH*	40.00	12.00
S-DM Dale Murphy	80.00	24.00
S-FL Fred Lynn	40.00	12.00
S-FT Frank Thomas	80.00	24.00
S-GB George Brett	150.00	45.00
S-GC Gary Carter	40.00	12.00
S-HA Hank Aaron	250.00	75.00
S-HK Harmon Killebrew	80.00	24.00
S-IR Ivan Rodriguez	80.00	24.00
S-JB Johnny Bench	80.00	24.00
S-JC Jose Canseco	80.00	24.00
S-JP Jim Palmer	40.00	12.00
S-KG Ken Griffey Jr.	120.00	36.00
S-LB Lou Brock	50.00	15.00
S-MP Mike Piazza	250.00	75.00
S-MR M.Ramirez EXCH	80.00	24.00
S-MS Mike Schmidt	150.00	45.00
S-MV Mo Vaughn	40.00	12.00
S-MW Matt Williams	40.00	12.00
S-NR Nolan Ryan	200.00	60.00
S-OS Ozzie Smith	100.00	30.00
S-PN Phil Niekro	40.00	12.00
S-RC Roger Clemens	200.00	60.00
S-RF Rollie Fingers	40.00	12.00
S-RJ Reggie Jackson	80.00	24.00
S-SC Sean Casey	40.00	12.00
S-SM Stan Musial	100.00	30.00
S-TG Tony Gwynn	100.00	30.00
S-TS Tom Seaver	50.00	15.00
S-VG Vladimir Guerrero	80.00	24.00
S-WS W.Stargell EXCH*	80.00	24.00
SRAJ Randy Johnson	150.00	45.00

2000 Upper Deck Legends Millennium Team

Randomly inserted into packs at one in four, this nine-card insert features the most famous players of the 20th Century. Please note that card number 6 does not exist. Card backs carry a "UD" prefix.

	Nm-Mt	Ex-Mt
COMPLETE SET (9)	10.00	3.00
UD1 Mark McGwire	2.00	.60
UD2 Jackie Robinson	.75	.23
UD3 Mike Schmidt	1.50	.45
UD4 Cal Ripken	2.50	.75
UD5 Babe Ruth	2.50	.75
UD6 Does Not Exist		
UD7 Willie Mays	1.50	.45
UD8 Johnny Bench	.75	.23
UD9 Nolan Ryan	2.50	.75
UD10 Ken Griffey Jr.	1.25	.35

2000 Upper Deck Legends Ones for the Ages

Randomly inserted into packs at one in 24, this seven-card insert features Major League Baseball's most legendary players. Card backs carry an "O" prefix.

	Nm-Mt	Ex-Mt
COMPLETE SET (7)	25.00	7.50
O1 Ty Cobb	5.00	1.50
O2 Cal Ripken	10.00	3.00
O3 Babe Ruth	10.00	3.00
O4 Jackie Robinson	3.00	.90
O5 Mark McGwire	8.00	2.40
O6 Alex Rodriguez	5.00	1.50
O7 Mike Piazza	5.00	1.50

2000 Upper Deck Legends Reflections in Time

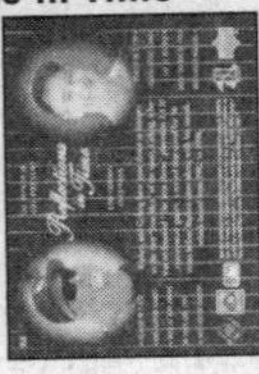

Randomly inserted into packs at one in 12, this 10-card insert features dual-player cards of players that have had very similar major league careers. Card backs carry a "R" prefix.

	Nm-Mt	Ex-Mt
COMPLETE SET (10)	40.00	12.00
R1 Ken Griffey Jr. / Hank Aaron	4.00	1.20
R2 Sammy Sosa / Roberto Clemente	4.00	1.20
R3 Roger Clemens / Nolan Ryan	5.00	1.50
R4 Ivan Rodriguez / Johnny Bench	2.50	.75
R5 Alex Rodriguez / Ernie Banks	4.00	1.20
R6 Tony Gwynn / Stan Musial	4.00	1.20
R7 Barry Bonds / Willie Mays	5.00	1.50
R8 Cal Ripken / Lou Gehrig	5.00	1.50
R9 Chipper Jones / Mike Schmidt	5.00	1.50
R10 Mark McGwire / Babe Ruth	8.00	2.40

2001 Upper Deck Legends

This 90 card set was released in July, 2001. The cards were issued in five card packs with an SRP of $4.99 per pack and these packs were issued 24 to a box. The set has a mixture of past and present superstars.

	Nm-Mt	Ex-Mt
COMPLETE SET (90)	20.00	6.00
1 Darin Erstad	.30	.09
2 Troy Glaus	.30	.09
3 Nolan Ryan	2.00	.60
4 Reggie Jackson	.50	.15
5 Catfish Hunter	.50	.15
6 Jason Giambi	.30	.09
7 Tim Hudson	.30	.09
8 Miguel Tejada	.30	.09
9 Carlos Delgado	.30	.09
10 Shannon Stewart	.30	.09
11 Greg Vaughn	.30	.09
12 Larry Doby	.30	.09
13 Jim Thome	.75	.23
14 Juan Gonzalez	.50	.15
15 Roberto Alomar	.50	.15
16 Edgar Martinez	.50	.15
17 John Olerud	.30	.09
18 Eddie Murray	.75	.23
19 Cal Ripken	2.50	.75
20 Alex Rodriguez	1.25	.35
21 Ivan Rodriguez	.75	.23
22 Rafael Palmeiro	.50	.15
23 Jimmie Foxx	.75	.23
24 Cy Young	.75	.23
25 Manny Ramirez	.50	.15
26 Pedro Martinez	.75	.23
27 Nomar Garciaparra	1.25	.35
28 George Brett	2.00	.60
29 Mike Sweeney	.30	.09
30 Jermaine Dye	.30	.09
31 Ty Cobb	1.25	.35
32 Dean Palmer	.30	.09
33 Harmon Killebrew	.75	.23
34 Matt Lawton	.30	.09
35 Luis Aparicio	.30	.09
36 Frank Thomas	.75	.23
37 Magglio Ordonez	.30	.09
38 David Wells	.30	.09
39 Mickey Mantle	3.00	.90
40 Joe DiMaggio	1.50	.45
41 Roger Maris	.75	.23
42 Babe Ruth	2.50	.75
43 Derek Jeter	2.00	.60
44 Roger Clemens	1.50	.45
45 Bernie Williams	.50	.15
46 Jeff Bagwell	.50	.15
47 Richard Hidalgo	.30	.09
48 Warren Spahn	.50	.15
49 Greg Maddux	1.25	.35
50 Chipper Jones	.75	.23
51 Andruw Jones	.30	.09
52 Robin Yount	1.25	.35
53 Jeromy Burnitz	.30	.09
54 Jeffrey Hammonds	.30	.09
55 Ozzie Smith	1.25	.35
56 Stan Musial	1.25	.35
57 Mark McGwire	2.00	.60
58 Jim Edmonds	.30	.09
59 Sammy Sosa	1.25	.35
60 Ernie Banks	.75	.23
61 Kerry Wood	.75	.23
62 Randy Johnson	.75	.23
63 Luis Gonzalez	.30	.09
64 Don Drysdale	.75	.23
65 Jackie Robinson	.75	.23
66 Gary Sheffield	.30	.09
67 Kevin Brown	.30	.09
68 Vladimir Guerrero	.75	.23
69 Willie Mays	1.50	.45
70 Mel Ott	.75	.23
71 Jeff Kent	.30	.09
72 Barry Bonds	2.00	.60
73 Preston Wilson	.30	.09
74 Ryan Dempster	.30	.09
75 Tom Seaver	.50	.15
76 Mike Piazza	1.25	.35
77 Robin Ventura	.30	.09
78 Dave Winfield	.30	.09
79 Tony Gwynn	1.00	.30
80 Bob Abreu	.30	.09
81 Scott Rolen	.75	.23
82 Mike Schmidt	1.50	.45
83 Roberto Clemente	2.00	.60
84 Brian Giles	.30	.09
85 Ken Griffey Jr.	1.25	.35
86 Frank Robinson	.50	.15
87 Johnny Bench	.75	.23
88 Todd Helton	.50	.15
89 Larry Walker	.50	.15
90 Mike Hampton	.30	.09

2001 Upper Deck Legends Fiorentino Collection

Inserted in packs at a rate of one in 12, these 14 cards feature the original artwork of James Fiorentino. The cards have a "F" prefix.

	Nm-Mt	Ex-Mt
COMPLETE SET (14)	40.00	12.00
F1 Babe Ruth	8.00	2.40
F2 Satchel Paige	2.50	.75
F3 Joe DiMaggio	5.00	1.50
F4 Willie Mays	5.00	1.50
F5 Ty Cobb	4.00	1.20
F6 Nolan Ryan	8.00	2.40
F7 Lou Gehrig	5.00	1.50
F8 Jackie Robinson	2.50	.75
F9 Hank Aaron	5.00	1.50
F10 Roberto Clemente	5.00	1.50
F11 Stan Musial	3.00	.90
F12 Johnny Bench	2.50	.75
F13 Honus Wagner	2.50	.75
F14 Reggie Jackson	2.50	.75

2001 Upper Deck Legends Legendary Cuts

Randomly inserted in packs, these six cards feature cut signatures from the five original members of the Hall of Fame. Due to scarcity, no pricing is provided.

	Nm-Mt	Ex-Mt
C-1 Ty Cobb / Babe Ruth / Christy Mathewson / Walter Johnson / Honus Wagner/1		
C-BR Babe Ruth/3		
C-CM Christy Mathewson/1		
C-HW Honus Wagner/2		
C-TC Ty Cobb/3		
C-WJ Walter Johnson/3		

2001 Upper Deck Legends Legendary Game Jersey

Issued at a rate of one in 24, these 33 cards feature authentic game jersey pieces from past and current players. A few players are perceived to be produced in larger quantites, we have notated those players with asterisks in our checklist. In addition, a few players were printed in shorter supply. We have notated those players with an SP as well as print run information provided by Upper Deck.

	Nm-Mt	Ex-Mt
GOLD RANDOM INSERTS IN PACKS..		
GOLD PRINT RUN 25 SERIAL #'d SETS		
NO GOLD PRICING DUE TO SCARCITY		
J-AR Alex Rodriguez	15.00	4.50
J-BB Barry Bonds	25.00	7.50
J-CJ Chipper Jones	15.00	4.50
J-CR Cal Ripken *	40.00	12.00
J-DW Dave Winfield	10.00	3.00
J-EB Ernie Banks Uniform	15.00	4.50
J-GM Greg Maddux	15.00	4.50
J-GS Gary Sheffield	10.00	3.00
J-HA Hank Aaron	60.00	18.00
J-IR Ivan Rodriguez *	15.00	4.50
J-JB Jeff Bagwell	15.00	4.50
J-JC Jose Canseco	15.00	4.50
J-JD Joe DiMaggio Uniform SP/245	150.00	45.00
J-KG Ken Griffey Jr.	15.00	4.50
J-KS Kazuhiro Sasaki	10.00	3.00
J-MM Mickey Mantle Uniform SP/245	250.00	75.00
J-MP Mike Piazza	15.00	4.50
J-MR Manny Ramirez	15.00	4.50
J-NR Nolan Ryan	40.00	12.00
J-OS Ozzie Smith *	15.00	4.50
J-PM Pedro Martinez	15.00	4.50
J-RCL Roger Clemens	15.00	4.50
J-RJA R.Jackson Uniform	15.00	4.50
J-RJO Randy Johnson *	15.00	4.50
J-RM Roger Maris SP/343	100.00	30.00
J-ROC R.Clemente SP/195	120.00	36.00
J-RY Robin Yount	15.00	4.50
J-SM Stan Musial Uniform SP/490	50.00	15.00
J-SS Sammy Sosa	15.00	4.50
J-TG T.Gwynn Uniform *	15.00	4.50
J-TS Tom Seaver	15.00	4.50
J-WM Willie Mays	50.00	15.00
J-YB Yogi Berra Uniform	15.00	4.50

2001 Upper Deck Legends Legendary Game Jersey Autographs

Issued at a rate of one in 288, these cards feature not only a game jersey piece but an authentic autograph of the player pictured. Ken Griffey Jr. did not return his cards in time for packout; those cards could be redeemed until July 9, 2004. In addition, a few cards were produced in lesser quantites. Those cards are notated in our checklist with an SP and print run information provided by Upper Deck.

	Nm-Mt	Ex-Mt
GOLD RANDOM INSERTS IN PACKS..		
GOLD PRINT RUN 25 SERIAL #'d SETS		
NO GOLD PRICING DUE TO SCARCITY		
SJ-AR Alex Rodriguez	150.00	45.00
SJ-EB Ernie Banks	80.00	24.00
SJ-KG K.Griffey Jr. EXCH	120.00	36.00
SJ-NR Nolan Ryan	150.00	45.00
SJ-OS Ozzie Smith	80.00	24.00
SJ-RC R.Clemens SP/211	150.00	45.00
SJ-RJ R.Jackson SP/224	100.00	30.00
SJ-SM S.Musial SP/266	120.00	36.00
SJ-SS Sammy Sosa SP/91	300.00	90.00
SJ-TS Tom Seaver	60.00	18.00

2001 Upper Deck Legends Legendary Lumber

Inserted in packs at a rate of one in 24, these 32 cards feature authentic game bat pieces from past and current players. A few cards are available in larger supply and we have notated those with asterisks in our checklist. In addition, certain cards were short printed. We have notated those with an SP as well as print run information provided by Upper Deck.

	Nm-Mt	Ex-Mt
GOLD RANDOM INSERTS IN PACKS..		
GOLD PRINT RUN 25 SERIAL #'d SETS		
NO GOLD PRICING DUE TO SCARCITY		
L-AJ Andruw Jones	10.00	3.00
L-AP Albert Pujols	60.00	18.00
L-AR Alex Rodriguez	15.00	4.50
L-BB Barry Bonds *	25.00	7.50
L-CJ Chipper Jones	15.00	4.50
L-CR Cal Ripken	40.00	12.00
L-EB Ernie Banks SP/80	60.00	18.00
L-EM Eddie Murray	15.00	4.50
L-FR Frank Robinson	15.00	4.50
L-GS Gary Sheffield *	10.00	3.00
L-HA Hank Aaron	40.00	12.00
L-IR Ivan Rodriguez *	15.00	4.50
L-JB Johnny Bench	15.00	4.50
L-JC Jose Canseco	15.00	4.50
L-JD Joe DiMaggio	100.00	30.00
L-JF Jimmie Foxx SP/351	60.00	18.00
L-KG Ken Griffey Jr.	15.00	4.50
L-LA Luis Aparicio	10.00	3.00
L-MM Mickey Mantle	200.00	60.00
L-MO Mel Ott SP/355	50.00	15.00
L-MP Mike Piazza	15.00	4.50
L-MR Manny Ramirez	15.00	4.50
L-OS Ozzie Smith	15.00	4.50
L-RCA R.Campanella SP/335	60.00	18.00
L-RCL Roger Clemens	15.00	4.50
L-RJ Reggie Jackson	15.00	4.50
L-RJ Randy Johnson	15.00	4.50
L-RM Roger Maris	50.00	15.00
L-ROC R.Clemente SP/170	120.00	36.00
L-SS Sammy Sosa *	15.00	4.50
L-TG Tony Gwynn	15.00	4.50
L-WM Willie Mays *	40.00	12.00

2001 Upper Deck Legends Legendary Lumber Autographs

This partial parallel to the Legendary Lumber insert set features authentic autographs from the player on the card. Ken Griffey Jr. did not return his cards in time for inclusion in packs. These cards were redeemable until July 9, 2004. In addition, a few cards were signed in lesser quantites. We have notated those cards with an SP

and print run information provided by Upper Deck.

Nm-Mt Ex-Mt
GOLD RANDOM INSERTS IN PACKS..
GOLD PRINT RUN 25 SERIAL #'d SETS
NO GOLD PRICNG DUE TO SCARCITY
SL-AR Alex Rodriguez 150.00 45.00
SL-EB Ernie Banks 80.00 24.00
SL-EM Eddie Murray 60.00 18.00
SL-KG K.Griffey Jr. EXCH 120.00 36.00
SL-LA Luis Aparicio 50.00 15.00
SL-RC R.Clemens SP/227 120.00 36.00
SL-RJ R.Jackson SP/211 80.00 24.00
SL-SS S.Sosa SP/66 250.00 75.00
SL-TG Tony Gwynn 80.00 24.00

2001 Upper Deck Legends Reflections in Time

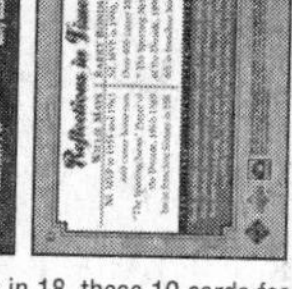

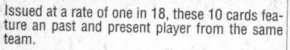

Issued at a rate of one in 18, these 10 cards feature an past and present player from the same team.

Nm-Mt Ex-Mt
COMPLETE SET (10) 30.00 9.00
R1 Bernie Williams 10.00 3.00
Mickey Mantle
R2 Pedro Martinez 2.50 .75
Cy Young
R3 Barry Bonds 8.00 2.40
Willie Mays
R4 Scott Rolen 5.00 1.50
Mike Schmidt
R5 Mark McGwire 6.00 1.80
Stan Musial
R6 Ken Griffey Jr. 4.00 1.20
Frank Robinson
R7 Sammy Sosa 4.00 1.20
Andre Dawson
R8 Kevin Brown 2.50 .75
Don Drysdale
R9 Jason Giambi 1.50 .45
Reggie Jackson
R10 Tim Hudson 1.50 .45
Jim "Catfish" Hunter

2001 Upper Deck Legends of NY

This product was released in late December, 2001. The 200-card base set features baseball greats like Babe Ruth and Mickey Mantle. Each pack contained five cards and carried a suggested retail price of $2.99

Nm-Mt Ex-Mt
COMPLETE SET (200) 50.00 15.00
1 Billy Herman .50 .15
2 Carl Erskine .50 .15
3 Burleigh Grimes .50 .15
4 Don Newcombe .50 .15
5 Gil Hodges 1.25 .35
6 Pee Wee Reese 1.25 .35
7 Jackie Robinson 1.25 .35
8 Duke Snider .75 .23
9 Jim Gilliam .50 .15
10 Roy Campanella 1.25 .35
11 Carl Furillo .50 .15
12 Casey Stengel .75 .23
13 Casey Stengel DB .50 .15
14 Billy Herman DB .40 .12
15 Jackie Robinson DB .75 .23
16 Jackie Robinson DB .75 .23
17 Gil Hodges DB 1.25 .35
18 Carl Furillo DB .40 .12
19 Roy Campanella DB .75 .23
20 Don Newcombe DB .40 .12
21 Duke Snider DB .50 .15
22 Casey Stengel BNS .50 .15
23 Burleigh Grimes BNS .40 .12
24 Pee Wee Reese BNS .75 .23
25 Jackie Robinson BNS .75 .23
26 Jackie Robinson BNS .75 .23
27 Carl Erskine BNS .40 .12
28 Roy Campanella BNS .75 .23
29 Duke Snider BNS .50 .15
30 Rube Marquard .50 .15
31 Ross Youngs .50 .15
32 Bobby Thomson .50 .15
33 Christy Mathewson 1.25 .35
34 Carl Hubbell 1.25 .35
35 Hoyt Wilhelm .50 .15
36 Johnny Mize .50 .15
37 John McGraw .75 .23
38 Monte Irvin .50 .15
39 Travis Jackson .50 .15
40 Mel Ott 1.25 .35
41 Dusty Rhodes .40 .12
42 Leo Durocher .50 .15
43 John McGraw BG .50 .15
44 Christy Mathewson BG .75 .23
45 The Polo Grounds BG .40 .12
46 Travis Jackson BG .40 .12
47 Mel Ott BG .75 .23
48 Johnny Mize BG .40 .12
49 Leo Durocher BG .40 .12
50 Bobby Thomson BG .40 .12
51 Monte Irvin BG .40 .12
52 Bobby Thomson BG .40 .12
53 Christy Mathewson BNS .75 .23
54 Christy Mathewson BNS .75 .23
55 Christy Mathewson BNS .75 .23
56 John McGraw BNS .50 .15
57 John McGraw BNS .50 .15
58 John McGraw BNS .50 .15
59 Travis Jackson BNS .40 .12
60 Mel Ott BNS .75 .23
61 Mel Ott BNS .75 .23
62 Carl Hubbell BNS .50 .15
63 Bobby Thomson BNS .40 .12
64 Monte Irvin BNS .40 .12
65 Al Weis .40 .12
66 Donn Clendenon .40 .12
67 Ed Kranepool .50 .15
68 Gary Carter .50 .15
69 Tommie Agee .40 .12
70 Jon Matlack .40 .12
71 Ken Boswell .40 .12
72 Len Dykstra .50 .15
73 Nolan Ryan 3.00 .90
74 Ray Sadecki .40 .12
75 Ron Darling .50 .15
76 Ron Swoboda .50 .15
77 Dwight Gooden .50 .15
78 Tom Seaver .75 .23
79 Wayne Garrett .40 .12
80 Casey Stengel MM .50 .15
81 Tom Seaver MM .50 .15
82 Tommie Agee MM .40 .12
83 Tom Seaver MM .50 .15
84 Yogi Berra MM .75 .23
85 Yogi Berra MM .75 .23
86 Tom Seaver MM .50 .15
87 Dwight Gooden MM .50 .15
88 Gary Carter MM .40 .12
89 Ron Darling MM .40 .12
90 Tommie Agee BNS .40 .12
91 Tom Seaver BNS .50 .15
92 Gary Carter BNS .50 .15
93 Len Dykstra BNS .40 .12
94 Babe Ruth 4.00 1.20
95 Bill Dickey .75 .23
96 Rich Gossage .50 .15
97 Casey Stengel UER .50 .15
Card has a Dodger logo on the back
98 Catfish Hunter .75 .23
99 Charlie Keller .40 .12
100 Chris Chambliss .50 .15
101 Don Larsen .50 .15
102 Dave Winfield .50 .15
103 Don Mattingly 3.00 .90
104 Elston Howard .75 .23
105 Frankie Crosetti .50 .15
106 Hank Bauer .50 .15
107 Joe DiMaggio 2.50 .75
108 Graig Nettles .50 .15
109 Lefty Gomez .75 .23
110 Phil Rizzuto 1.25 .35
111 Lou Gehrig 2.50 .75
112 Lou Piniella .50 .15
113 Mickey Mantle 5.00 1.50
114 Red Rolfe .50 .15
115 Reggie Jackson .75 .23
116 Roger Maris 1.25 .35
117 Roy White .40 .12
118 Thurman Munson 1.25 .35
119 Tom Tresh .50 .15
120 Tommy Henrich .50 .15
121 Waite Hoyt .50 .15
122 Willie Randolph .50 .15
123 Whitey Ford .75 .23
124 Yogi Berra 1.25 .35
125 Babe Ruth BT 2.00 .60
126 Babe Ruth BT 2.00 .60
127 Lou Gehrig BT 1.25 .35
128 Babe Ruth BT 2.00 .60
129 Joe DiMaggio BT 1.25 .35
130 Joe DiMaggio BT 1.25 .35
131 Mickey Mantle BT 2.50 .75
132 Roger Maris BT .75 .23
133 Mickey Mantle BT 2.50 .75
134 Reggie Jackson BT .50 .15
135 Babe Ruth BNS 2.00 .60
136 Babe Ruth BNS 2.00 .60
137 Babe Ruth BNS 2.00 .60
138 Lefty Gomez BNS .50 .15
139 Lou Gehrig BNS 1.25 .35
140 Lou Gehrig BNS 1.25 .35
141 Joe DiMaggio BNS 1.25 .35
142 Joe DiMaggio BNS 1.25 .35
143 Casey Stengel BNS .50 .15
144 Mickey Mantle BNS 2.50 .75
145 Yogi Berra BNS .75 .23
146 Mickey Mantle BNS 2.50 .75
147 Elston Howard BNS .50 .15
148 Whitey Ford BNS .50 .15
149 Reggie Jackson BNS .50 .15
150 Reggie Jackson BNS .50 .15
151 John McGraw 2.00 .60
Babe Ruth
152 Babe Ruth 2.00 .60
John McGraw
153 Lou Gehrig 1.25 .35
Mel Ott
154 Joe DiMaggio 1.25 .35
Mel Ott
155 Joe DiMaggio 1.25 .35
Billy Herman
156 Joe DiMaggio 1.25 .35
Jackie Robinson
157 Mickey Mantle 2.50 .75
Bobby Thomson
158 Yogi Berra .75 .23
Pee Wee Reese
159 Roy Campanella 2.50 .75
Mickey Mantle
160 Don Larsen .50 .15
Duke Snider
161 Christy Mathewson TT .75 .23
162 Christy Mathewson TT .75 .23
163 Rube Marquard TT .40 .12
164 Christy Mathewson TT .75 .23
165 John McGraw TT .50 .15
166 Burleigh Grimes TT .40 .12
167 Babe Ruth TT 2.00 .60
168 Burleigh Grimes TT .40 .12
169 Babe Ruth TT 2.00 .60
170 John McGraw TT .50 .15
171 Lou Gehrig TT 1.25 .35
172 Babe Ruth TT 2.00 .60
173 Babe Ruth TT 2.00 .60
174 Carl Hubbell TT .50 .15
175 Joe DiMaggio TT 1.25 .35
176 Lou Gehrig TT 1.25 .35
177 Leo Durocher TT .40 .12
178 Mel Ott TT .75 .23
179 Joe DiMaggio TT 1.25 .35
180 Jackie Robinson TT .75 .23
181 Babe Ruth TT 2.00 .60
182 Bobby Thomson TT .40 .12
183 Joe DiMaggio TT 1.25 .35
184 Mickey Mantle TT 2.50 .75
185 Monte Irvin TT .40 .12
186 Roy Campanella TT .75 .23
187 Duke Snider TT .75 .23
188 Dusty Rhodes TT .40 .12
189 Yogi Berra TT .75 .23
190 Mickey Mantle TT 2.50 .75
191 Mickey Mantle TT 2.50 .75
192 Casey Stengel TT .50 .15
193 Tom Seaver TT .50 .15
194 Mickey Mantle TT UER 2.50 .75
Text has Mantle retiring in 1939
195 Tommie Agee TT .40 .12
196 Tom Seaver TT .50 .15
197 Chris Chambliss TT .40 .12
198 Reggie Jackson TT .50 .15
199 Reggie Jackson TT .50 .15
200 Gary Carter TT .40 .12

2001 Upper Deck Legends of NY Combo Autographs

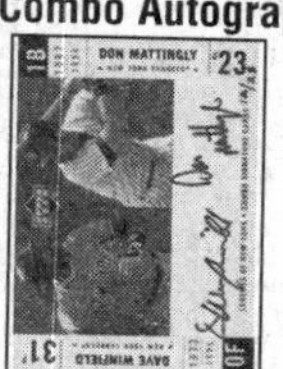

Randomly inserted into packs, this nine-card insert set features dual-autographs from Hall of Famers like Nolan Ryan and Tom Seaver. Each card is individually serial numbered to 25. Due to market scarcity, no pricing is provided.

Nm-Mt Ex-Mt
SCN Chris Chambliss
Graig Nettles
SGJ Ron Guidry
Tommy John
SLB Don Larsen
Yogi Berra
SNP Don Newcombe
Johnny Podres
SRD Willie Randolph
Bucky Dent
SRS Nolan Ryan
Tom Seaver
SRW Mickey Rivers
Roy White
SWJ Dave Winfield
Reggie Jackson
SWM Dave Winfield
Don Mattingly

2001 Upper Deck Legends of NY Cut Signatures

This five-card insert set features authentic cut signatures from deceased greats like Babe Ruth and Jackie Robinson. There were a total of 49 cut cards issued in this set. Specific print runs are listed in our checklist.

Nm-Mt Ex-Mt
LC-BR Babe Ruth/5
LC-GH Gil Hodges/1
LC-JD Joe DiMaggio/38
LC-JR Jackie Robinson/3
LC-MO Mel Ott/2

2001 Upper Deck Legends of NY Game Base

This two card set features game-used base cards of Jackie Robinson and Tom Seaver. Each card is individually serial numbered to 100.

Nm-Mt Ex-Mt
GOLD RANDOM INSERTS IN PACKS..
GOLD PRINT RUN 25 SERIAL #'d SETS
NO GOLD PRICING DUE TO SCARCITY
SILVER RANDOM INSERTS IN PACKS
SILVER PRINT RUN 50 SERIAL #'d SETS
SILVER NO PRICING DUE TO SCARCITY
EF-JR Jackie Robinson
SS-TS Tom Seaver

2001 Upper Deck Legends of NY Game Bat

This 33-card insert set features authentic game-used bat chips. Collectors received either on bat or jersey card per box. A few cards were produced in lesser quantites, those print runs are provided in our checklist.

Nm-Mt Ex-Mt
LDB-BH Billy Herman 10.00 3.00
LDB-DN Don Newcombe SP/67
LDB-JG Jim Gilliam 10.00 3.00
LGB-BTH Bobby Thomson 10.00 3.00
LMB-AW Al Weis 10.00 3.00
LMB-DC Donn Clendenon SP/60
LMB-EK Ed Kranepool 10.00 3.00
LMB-GC Gary Carter 10.00 3.00
LMB-JM J.C. Martin 10.00 3.00
LMB-KB Ken Boswell 10.00 3.00
LMB-LD Len Dykstra 10.00 3.00
LMB-NR Nolan Ryan 40.00 12.00
LMB-RS Ron Swoboda 10.00 3.00
LMB-TS Tom Seaver 15.00 4.50
LMB-WG Wayne Garrett 10.00 3.00
LYB-BD Bill Dickey 15.00 4.50
LYB-BR Babe Ruth SP/107
LYB-CC Chris Chambliss SP/130
LYB-CK Charlie Keller 10.00 3.00
LYB-DM Don Mattingly 25.00 7.50
LYB-DW Dave Winfield UER 10.00 3.00
Playing career has the wrong years
LYB-EH Elston Howard 15.00 4.50
LYB-HB Hank Bauer 10.00 3.00
LYB-JD Joe DiMaggio SP/43
LYB-LP Lou Piniella 10.00 3.00
LYB-MM Mickey Mantle SP/134
LYB-MR Mickey Rivers 10.00 3.00
LYB-RJ Reggie Jackson 15.00 4.50
LYB-RM Roger Maris SP/60 120.00 36.00
LYB-TH Tommy Henrich 10.00 3.00
LYB-TM Thurman Munson 30.00 9.00
LYB-TT Tom Tresh 10.00 3.00
LYB-YB Yogi Berra 15.00 4.50

2001 Upper Deck Legends of NY Game Bat Autograph

This insert set is a partial parallel to the 2001 Upper Deck Legends of NY Game Bat insert. Each of these cards were signed, and issued into packs at 1:336. A few cards were printed in lesser quantities, those print runs are provided in our checklist.

Nm-Mt Ex-Mt
SDB-DN Don Newcombe 40.00 12.00
SMB-DC Donn Clendenon 30.00 9.00
SMB-GC Gary Carter 40.00 12.00
SMB-NR N.Ryan SP/129 200.00 60.00
SMB-RS Ron Swoboda
SMB-TS Tom Seaver SP/89
SYB-CC Chris Chambliss 40.00 12.00
SYB-DM Don Mattingly 100.00 30.00
SYB-DW Dave Winfield SP/167
SYB-MR Mickey Rivers 40.00 12.00
SYB-RJ Reggie Jackson SP/123
SYB-RW Roy White 30.00 9.00
SYB-YB Yogi Berra 80.00 24.00

2001 Upper Deck Legends of NY Game Jersey

This 36-card insert set features authentic game-used jersey swatches. Collectors received either on bat or jersey card per box. A few cards were printed in small quantities, those print runs are provided in our checklist.

Nm-Mt Ex-Mt
LYJ-BT Bob Turley 10.00 3.00
LYJ-CD Chuck Dressen 10.00 3.00
LYJ-CE Carl Erskine 10.00 3.00
LYJ-CH Catfish Hunter 15.00 4.50
LYJ-CM C.Mathewson SP/63 400.00 120.00
LYJ-CS Casey Stengel 15.00 4.50
LYJ-DM Duke Maas 10.00 3.00
LYJ-DW Dave Winfield 10.00 3.00
LYJ-EH Elston Howard 15.00 4.50
LYJ-FC Frank Crosetti 10.00 3.00
LYJ-GN Graig Nettles 10.00 3.00
LYJ-HB Hank Behrman 10.00 3.00
LYJ-HB Hank Bauer 10.00 3.00
LYJ-JD Joe DiMaggio SP/63
LYJ-JM Jon Matlack 10.00 3.00
LYJ-JP Joe Pepitone 10.00 3.00
LYJ-JR J.Robinson Pants SP/126 150.0045.00
LYJ-JT Joe Torre 15.00 4.50
LYJ-LM Lindy McDaniel 10.00 3.00
LYJ-MM Mickey Mantle SP/63
LYJ-PN Phil Niekro 10.00 3.00
LYJ-RD Ron Darling 10.00 3.00
LYJ-RM Roger Maris SP/63
LYJ-RR Red Rolfe 10.00 3.00
LYJ-RS Ray Sadecki 10.00 3.00
LYJ-SJ Spider Jorgensen 10.00 3.00
LYJ-TH Tommy Henrich 10.00 3.00
LYJ-TM Thurman Munson 40.00 12.00
LYJ-TS Tom Seaver 15.00 4.50
LYJ-WR Willie Randolph 10.00 3.00

2001 Upper Deck Legends of NY Game Jersey Autograph

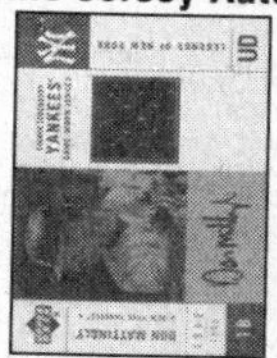

This 22-card insert is a partial parallel to the 2001 Upper Deck Legends of NY Game Jersey insert set. Each of these cards were signed, and issued into packs at 1:336. A few cards were printed in lesser quantity and those cards are notated in our checklist as SP's along with print run information provided by Upper Deck.

Nm-Mt Ex-Mt
SDJ-CE Carl Erskine 50.00 15.00
SDJ-JG Jim Gilliam SP/49
SDJ-JP J. Podres SP/193 60.00 18.00
SMJ-CS Craig Swan 50.00 15.00
SMJ-GF G.Foster SP/196 50.00 15.00
SMJ-NR Nolan Ryan SP/47
SMJ-TS Tom Seaver SP/60
SYJ-BD Bucky Dent 50.00 15.00
SYJ-DL Don Larsen 60.00 18.00
SYJ-DM Don Mattingly SP/72 150.00 45.00
SYJ-DR Dave Righetti 50.00 15.00
SYJ-GN Graig Nettles 50.00 15.00
SYJ-HL H.Lopez SP/195 50.00 15.00
SYJ-JP Joe Pepitone 50.00 15.00
SYJ-PN P.Niekro SP/195 60.00 18.00
SYJ-RG Ron Guidry 60.00 18.00
SYJ-RG R.Gossage SP/145 50.00 15.00
SYJ-RJ Reggie Jackson SP/47
SYJ-SL Sparky Lyle 50.00 15.00
SYJ-TJ Tommy John 50.00 15.00
SYJ-WR Willie Randolph 50.00 15.00
SYJ-YB Yogi Berra SP/73

2001 Upper Deck Legends of NY Game Jersey Gold

This 24-card insert is a partial parallel set to the 2001 Upper Deck Legends of NY Game Jersey set, and features game-used jersey cards on a gold-foil based card. Print runs, of which vary between 125 and 500 numbered copies, are listed for each card in our checklist.

Nm-Mt Ex-Mt
LDJ-CD C.Dressen/400 12.00 3.60
LDJ-CE Carl Erskine/400 12.00 3.60
LDJ-HB H.Behrman/500 12.00 3.60
LDJ-SJ S.Jorgensen/500 12.00 3.60
LMJ-JM Jon Matlack/400 12.00 3.60
LMJ-JT Joe Torre/250 25.00 7.50
LMJ-RD Ron Darling/400 12.00 3.60
LMJ-RS Ray Sadecki/400 12.00 3.60
LMJ-TS Tom Seaver/400 20.00 6.00
LYJ-BT Bob Turley/400 12.00 3.60
LYJ-CH C.Hunter/500 20.00 6.00
LYJ-DM Duke Maas/400 12.00 3.60
LYJ-DW D.Winfield/250 15.00 4.50
LYJ-EH E.Howard/400 20.00 6.00
LYJ-FC Frank Crosetti/400 12.00 3.60
LYJ-GN Graig Nettles/250 15.00 4.50
LYJ-HB Hank Bauer/400 12.00 3.60
LYJ-JP Joe Pepitone/250 15.00 4.50
LYJ-LM L.McDaniel/400 12.00 3.60
LYJ-PN Phil Niekro/125 20.00 6.00
LYJ-RR Red Rolfe/400 12.00 3.60
LYJ-TH T.Henrich/400 12.00 3.60
LYJ-TM T.Munson/400 50.00 15.00
LYJ-WR W.Randolph/125 20.00 6.00

2001 Upper Deck Legends of NY Stadium Seat

This two card set features stadium seat cards of Jackie Robinson and Mickey Mantle. Each card is individually serial numbered to 100.

Nm-Mt Ex-Mt
GOLD RANDOM INSERTS IN PACKS..
GOLD PRINT RUN 25 SERIAL #'d SETS
GOLD NO PRICING DUE TO SCARCITY
SILVER RANDOM INSERTS IN PACKS
SILVER PRINT RUN 50 SERIAL #'d SETS
SILVER NO PRICING DUE TO SCARCITY
EFS-JR Jackie Robinson 40.00 12.00
YS-MM Mickey Mantle 120.00 36.00

2001 Upper Deck Legends of NY Tri-Combo Autographs

Randomly inserted into packs, this seven-card insert set features tri-combo autographs from greats like Ryan/Seaver/Swoboda. Each card is individually serial numbered to 25. Each card carries a "S" prefix. Due to market scarcity, no pricing is provided.

Nm-Mt Ex-Mt
CND Chris Chambliss ....
Graig Nettles
Bucky Dent
GJG Ron Guidry ....
Tommy John
Goose Gossage
LBP Don Larsen ....
Yogi Berra
Joe Pepitone
LRG Sparky Lyle ....
Dave Righetti
Goose Gossage
NPE Don Newcombe ....
Johnny Podres
Carl Erskine
RSS Nolan Ryan ....
Tom Seaver
Ron Swoboda
WMN Dave Winfield ....
Don Mattingly
Graig Nettles

2001 Upper Deck Legends of NY United We Stand

This 15-card insert set honors the FDNY/PDNY for their relief work in the Sept. 11, 2001 terrorist attacks in New York. Card backs carry a "USA" prefix. This insert was issued at a rate of 1:12 packs.

Nm-Mt Ex-Mt
COMPLETE SET (15) 60.00 18.00
COMMON CARD (1-15) 5.00 1.50

1999 Upper Deck MVP

This 220 card set was distributed in 10 cards packs with an SRP of $1.59 per pack. Cards numbered from 218 through 220 are checklist subsets. Approximately 350 Mike Schmidt A Piece of History 500 Home Run Game-Used bat cards were distributed in this product. In addition, 20 hand serial numbered versions of this card personally signed by Schmidt himself were also randomly seeded into packs. Pricing for these bat cards can be referenced under 1999 Upper Deck A Piece of History 500 Club. A Ken Griffey Jr. Sample card was distributed to dealers and hobby media several weeks prior to the product's national release. Unlike most Upper Deck promotional cards, this card does not have the word "SAMPLE" pasted across the back of the card. The card, however, is numbered "S3". It's believed that cards S1 and S2 were Upper Deck MVP football and basketball promo cards.

Nm-Mt Ex-Mt
COMPLETE SET (220) 25.00 7.50
1 Mo Vaughn .... .20 .06
2 Tim Belcher .... .20 .06
3 Jack McDowell .... .20 .06
4 Troy Glaus .... .20 .06
5 Darin Erstad .... .20 .06
6 Tim Salmon .... .30 .09
7 Jim Edmonds .... .20 .06
8 Randy Johnson .... .50 .15
9 Steve Finley .... .20 .06
10 Travis Lee .... .20 .06
11 Matt Williams .... .20 .06
12 Todd Stottlemyre .... .20 .06
13 Jay Bell .... .20 .06
14 David Dellucci .... .20 .06
15 Chipper Jones .... .50 .15
16 Andruw Jones .... .20 .06
17 Greg Maddux .... .75 .23
18 Tom Glavine .... .30 .09
19 Javy Lopez .... .20 .06
20 Brian Jordan .... .20 .06
21 George Lombard .... .20 .06
22 John Smoltz .... .30 .09
23 Cal Ripken .... 1.50 .45
24 Charles Johnson .... .20 .06
25 Albert Belle .... .20 .06
26 Brady Anderson .... .20 .06
27 Mike Mussina .... .30 .09
28 Calvin Pickering .... .20 .06
29 Ryan Minor .... .20 .06
30 Jerry Hairston Jr. .... .20 .06
31 Nomar Garciaparra .... .75 .23
32 Pedro Martinez .... .50 .15
33 Jason Varitek .... .30 .09
34 Troy O'Leary .... .20 .06
35 Donnie Sadler .... .20 .06
36 Mark Portugal .... .20 .06
37 John Valentin .... .20 .06
38 Kerry Wood .... .50 .15
39 Sammy Sosa .... .75 .23
40 Mark Grace .... .30 .09
41 Henry Rodriguez .... .20 .06
42 Rod Beck .... .20 .06
43 Benito Santiago .... .20 .06
44 Kevin Tapani .... .20 .06
45 Frank Thomas .... .50 .15
46 Mike Caruso .... .20 .06
47 Magglio Ordonez .... .20 .06
48 Paul Konerko .... .20 .06
49 Ray Durham .... .20 .06
50 Jim Parque .... .20 .06
51 Carlos Lee .... .20 .06
52 Denny Neagle .... .20 .06
53 Pete Harnisch .... .20 .06
54 Michael Tucker .... .20 .06
55 Sean Casey .... .20 .06
56 Eddie Taubensee .... .20 .06
57 Barry Larkin .... .30 .09
58 Pokey Reese .... .20 .06
59 Sandy Alomar Jr. .... .20 .06
60 Roberto Alomar .... .30 .09
61 Bartolo Colon .... .20 .06
62 Kenny Lofton .... .20 .06
63 Omar Vizquel .... .30 .09
64 Travis Fryman .... .20 .06
65 Jim Thome .... .50 .15
66 Manny Ramirez .... .30 .09
67 Jaret Wright .... .20 .06
68 Darryl Kile .... .20 .06
69 Kirt Manwaring .... .20 .06
70 Vinny Castilla .... .20 .06
71 Todd Helton .... .30 .09
72 Dante Bichette .... .20 .06
73 Larry Walker .... .30 .09
74 Derrick Gibson .... .20 .06
75 Gabe Kapler .... .20 .06
76 Dean Palmer .... .20 .06
77 Matt Anderson .... .20 .06
78 Bobby Higginson .... .20 .06
79 Damion Easley .... .20 .06
80 Tony Clark .... .20 .06
81 Juan Encarnacion .... .20 .06
82 Livan Hernandez .... .20 .06
83 Alex Gonzalez .... .20 .06
84 Preston Wilson .... .20 .06
85 Derrek Lee .... .20 .06
86 Mark Kotsay .... .20 .06
87 Todd Dunwoody .... .20 .06
88 Cliff Floyd .... .20 .06
89 Ken Caminiti .... .20 .06
90 Jeff Bagwell .... .30 .09
91 Moises Alou .... .20 .06
92 Craig Biggio .... .30 .09
93 Billy Wagner .... .20 .06
94 Richard Hidalgo .... .20 .06
95 Derek Bell .... .20 .06
96 Hipolito Pichardo .... .20 .06
97 Jeff King .... .20 .06
98 Carlos Beltran .... .30 .09
99 Jeremy Giambi .... .20 .06
100 Larry Sutton .... .20 .06
101 Johnny Damon .... .30 .09
102 Dee Brown .... .20 .06
103 Kevin Brown .... .30 .09
104 Chan Ho Park .... .20 .06
105 Raul Mondesi .... .20 .06
106 Eric Karros .... .20 .06
107 Adrian Beltre .... .30 .09
108 Devon White .... .20 .06
109 Gary Sheffield .... .20 .06
110 Sean Berry .... .20 .06
111 Alex Ochoa .... .20 .06
112 Marquis Grissom .... .20 .06
113 Fernando Vina .... .20 .06
114 Jeff Cirillo .... .20 .06
115 Geoff Jenkins .... .20 .06
116 Jeromy Burnitz .... .20 .06
117 Brad Radke .... .20 .06
118 Eric Milton .... .20 .06
119 A.J. Pierzynski .... .20 .06
120 Todd Walker .... .20 .06
121 David Ortiz .... .30 .09
122 Corey Koskie .... .20 .06
123 Vladimir Guerrero .... .50 .15
124 Rondell White .... .20 .06
125 Brad Fullmer .... .20 .06
126 Ugueth Urbina .... .20 .06
127 Dustin Hermanson .... .20 .06
128 Michael Barrett .... .20 .06
129 Fernando Seguignol .... .20 .06
130 Mike Piazza .... .75 .23
131 Rickey Henderson .... .50 .15
132 Rey Ordonez .... .20 .06
133 John Olerud .... .20 .06
134 Robin Ventura .... .20 .06
135 Hideo Nomo .... .50 .15
136 Mike Kinkade .... .20 .06
137 Al Leiter .... .20 .06
138 Brian McRae .... .20 .06
139 Derek Jeter .... 1.25 .35
140 Bernie Williams .... .30 .09
141 Paul O'Neill .... .30 .09
142 Scott Brosius .... .20 .06
143 Tino Martinez .... .30 .09
144 Roger Clemens .... 1.00 .30
145 Orlando Hernandez .... .20 .06
146 Mariano Rivera .... .30 .09
147 Ricky Ledee .... .20 .06
148 A.J. Hinch .... .20 .06
149 Ben Grieve .... .20 .06
150 Eric Chavez .... .20 .06
151 Miguel Tejada .... .20 .06
152 Matt Stairs .... .20 .06
153 Ryan Christenson .... .20 .06
154 Jason Giambi .... .20 .06
155 Curt Schilling .... .20 .06
156 Scott Rolen .... .50 .15
157 Pat Burrell RC .... .75 .23
158 Doug Glanville .... .20 .06
159 Bobby Abreu .... .20 .06
160 Rico Brogna .... .20 .06
161 Ron Gant .... .20 .06
162 Jason Kendall .... .20 .06
163 Aramis Ramirez .... .20 .06
164 Jose Guillen .... .20 .06
165 Emil Brown .... .20 .06
166 Pat Meares .... .20 .06
167 Kevin Young .... .20 .06
168 Brian Giles .... .20 .06
169 Mark McGwire .... 1.25 .35
170 J.D. Drew .... .20 .06
171 Edgar Renteria .... .20 .06
172 Fernando Tatis .... .20 .06
173 Matt Morris .... .20 .06
174 Eli Marrero .... .20 .06
175 Ray Lankford .... .20 .06
176 Tony Gwynn .... .60 .18
177 Sterling Hitchcock .... .20 .06
178 Ruben Rivera .... .20 .06
179 Wally Joyner .... .20 .06
180 Trevor Hoffman .... .20 .06
181 Jim Leyritz .... .20 .06
182 Carlos Hernandez .... .20 .06
183 Barry Bonds UER .... 1.25 .35
Uniform number 24 on front, 25 on back
184 Ellis Burks .... .20 .06
185 F.P. Santangelo .... .20 .06
186 J.T. Snow .... .20 .06
187 Ramon E.Martinez RC .... .20 .06
188 Jeff Kent .... .20 .06
189 Robb Nen .... .20 .06
190 Ken Griffey Jr. .... .75 .23
191 Alex Rodriguez .... .75 .23
192 Shane Monahan .... .20 .06
193 Carlos Guillen .... .20 .06
194 Edgar Martinez .... .30 .09
195 David Segui .... .20 .06
196 Jose Mesa .... .20 .06
197 Jose Canseco .... .50 .15
198 Rolando Arrojo .... .20 .06
199 Wade Boggs .... .30 .09
200 Fred McGriff .... .30 .09
201 Quinton McCracken .... .20 .06
202 Bobby Smith .... .20 .06
203 Bubba Trammell .... .20 .06
204 Juan Gonzalez .... .30 .09
205 Ivan Rodriguez .... .50 .15
206 Rafael Palmeiro .... .30 .09
207 Royce Clayton .... .20 .06
208 Rick Helling .... .20 .06
209 Todd Zeile .... .20 .06
210 Rusty Greer .... .20 .06
211 David Wells .... .20 .06
212 Roy Halladay .... .20 .06
213 Carlos Delgado .... .20 .06
214 Darrin Fletcher .... .20 .06
215 Shawn Green .... .20 .06
216 Kevin Witt .... .20 .06
217 Jose Cruz Jr. .... .20 .06
218 Ken Griffey Jr. CL .... .50 .15
219 Sammy Sosa CL .... .50 .15
220 Mark McGwire CL .... .60 .18
S3 Ken Griffey Jr. Sample .... 1.00 .30

1999 Upper Deck MVP Gold Script

Randomly inserted into hobby packs, these parallel cards of the regular Upper Deck MVP set are serial numbered to 100 and have a gold foil fascimile signature on the front of the card.

Nm-Mt Ex-Mt
*STARS: 12.5X TO 30X BASIC CARDS
*ROOKIES: 12.5X TO 30X BASIC CARDS

1999 Upper Deck MVP Silver Script

These parallels were seeded at a rate of one in every two packs. Unlike basic MVP cards, each Silver Script parallel features the player's facsimile autograph in silver foil on the front of the card. A Ken Griffey Jr. sample card was distributed to dealers and hobby media several weeks prior to the product's national release. The card is numbered "S3" on back.

Nm-Mt Ex-Mt
COMPLETE SET (220) 150.00 45.00
*STARS: 1.5X TO 4X BASIC CARDS...
*ROOKIES: 1.5X TO 4X BASIC CARDS
S3 Ken Griffey Jr. Sample 4.00 1.20

1999 Upper Deck MVP Super Script

This parallel set of the Upper Deck MVP set is serial numbered to 25. The fascimile signatures on these cards are printed in a special holo-foil format.

Nm-Mt Ex-Mt
*STARS: 30X TO 80X BASIC CARDS..

1999 Upper Deck MVP Dynamics

Inserted one every 28 packs, these cards feature the most collectible stars in basebll. The front of the card has a player photo, the word "Dynamics" in black ink on the bottom and lots of fancy graphics.

Nm-Mt Ex-Mt
COMPLETE SET (15) 100.00 30.00
D1 Ken Griffey Jr. 6.00 1.80
D2 Alex Rodriguez 6.00 1.80
D3 Nomar Garciaparra 6.00 1.80
D4 Mike Piazza 6.00 1.80

D5 Mark McGwire 10.00 3.00
D6 Sammy Sosa 6.00 1.80
D7 Chipper Jones 4.00 1.20
D8 Mo Vaughn .... 1.50 .45
D9 Tony Gwynn 5.00 1.50
D10 Vladimir Guerrero 4.00 1.20
D11 Derek Jeter 10.00 3.00
D12 Jeff Bagwell .... 2.50 .75
D13 Cal Ripken 12.00 3.60
D14 Juan Gonzalez .... 2.50 .75
D15 J.D. Drew .... 1.50 .45

1999 Upper Deck MVP Game Used Souvenirs

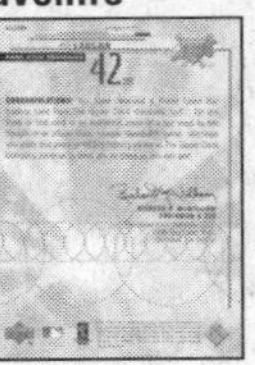

These 11 cards were randomly inserted into packs at a rate of one in 144. Each card features a chip of actual game-used bat from the player featured.

Nm-Mt Ex-Mt
GUBB Barry Bonds 40.00 12.00
GUCJ Chipper Jones 20.00 6.00
GUCR Cal Ripken 50.00 15.00
GUJB Jeff Bagwell 15.00 4.50
GUJD J.D. Drew 10.00 3.00
GUKG Ken Griffey Jr. 25.00 7.50
GUMP Mike Piazza 30.00 9.00
GUMV Mo Vaughn 10.00 3.00
GUSR Scott Rolen 20.00 6.00
GAKG K. Griffey Jr. AU/24 ....
GACJ Chipper Jones AU/10 ....

1999 Upper Deck MVP Power Surge

These cards were inserted one every nine packs. The horizontal cards feature some of the leading sluggers in baseball and are printed on rainbow foil.

Nm-Mt Ex-Mt
COMPLETE SET (15) 25.00 7.50
P1 Mark McGwire .... 3.00 .90
P2 Sammy Sosa .... 2.00 .60
P3 Ken Griffey Jr. .... 2.00 .60
P4 Alex Rodriguez .... 2.00 .60
P5 Juan Gonzalez .... .75 .23
P6 Nomar Garciaparra .... 2.00 .60
P7 Vladimir Guerrero .... 1.25 .35
P8 Chipper Jones .... 1.25 .35
P9 Albert Belle .... .50 .15
P10 Frank Thomas .... 1.25 .35
P11 Mike Piazza .... 2.00 .60
P12 Jeff Bagwell .... .75 .23
P13 Manny Ramirez .... .75 .23
P14 Mo Vaughn .... .50 .15
P15 Barry Bonds .... 3.00 .90

1999 Upper Deck MVP ProSign

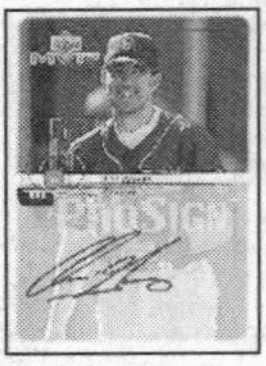

Inserted as a rate of one every 216 retail packs, these cards feature autographs from various baseball players. It's believed that the veteran stars in this set are in much shorter supply than the various young prospects.Some of these star cards have rarely been seen in the secondary market and no pricing is yet available for those cards.

Nm-Mt Ex-Mt
AG Alex Gonzalez 10.00 3.00
AN Abraham Nunez 10.00 3.00
BC Bruce Chen 10.00 3.00
BF Brad Fullmer 10.00 3.00
BG Ben Grieve 10.00 3.00
CB Carlos Beltran 40.00 12.00
CG Chris Gomez 10.00 3.00
CJ Chipper Jones SP 100.00 30.00
CK Corey Koskie 15.00 4.50
CP Calvin Pickering 10.00 3.00
DG Derrick Gibson 10.00 3.00
EC Eric Chavez 15.00 4.50
GK Gabe Kapler 10.00 3.00
GL George Lombard 10.00 3.00
IR Ivan Rodriguez SP 100.00 30.00
JG Jeremy Giambi 10.00 3.00
JP Jim Parque 10.00 3.00
JR Ken Griffey Jr. SP 120.00 36.00
KW Kevin Witt 10.00 3.00
MA Matt Anderson 10.00 3.00
ML Mike Lincoln 10.00 3.00
NG Nomar Garciaparra SP 150.00 45.00
RB Russ Branyan 10.00 3.00
RH Richard Hidalgo 10.00 3.00
RL Ricky Ledee 10.00 3.00
RM Ryan Minor 10.00 3.00
RR Ruben Rivera 10.00 3.00
SH Shea Hillenbrand 15.00 4.50
SK Scott Karl 10.00 3.00
SM Shane Monahan 10.00 3.00
JRA Jason Rakers 10.00 3.00
MLO Mike Lowell 15.00 4.50

1999 Upper Deck MVP Scout's Choice

Inserted one every nine packs, these cards feature the best young stars and rookies captured on Light F/X packs.

Nm-Mt Ex-Mt
COMPLETE SET (15) 12.00 3.60
SC1 J.D. Drew .... .60 .18
SC2 Ben Grieve .... .60 .18
SC3 Troy Glaus .... .60 .18
SC4 Gabe Kapler .... .60 .18
SC5 Carlos Beltran .... 1.00 .30
SC6 Aramis Ramirez .... .60 .18
SC7 Pat Burrell .... 1.00 .30
SC8 Kerry Wood .... 1.50 .45
SC9 Ryan Minor .... .60 .18
SC10 Todd Helton .... 1.00 .30
SC11 Eric Chavez .... .60 .18
SC12 Russ Branyan .... .60 .18
SC13 Travis Lee .... .60 .18
SC14 Ruben Mateo .... .60 .18
SC15 Roy Halladay .... .60 .18

1999 Upper Deck MVP Super Tools

Issued one every 14 packs, these cards focus on big leaguers who posess various tools of greatness.

Nm-Mt Ex-Mt
COMPLETE SET (15) 50.00 15.00
T1 Ken Griffey Jr. 4.00 1.20
T2 Alex Rodriguez 4.00 1.20
T3 Sammy Sosa 4.00 1.20
T4 Derek Jeter 6.00 1.80
T5 Vladimir Guerrero .... 2.50 .75
T6 Ben Grieve .... 1.00 .30
T7 Mike Piazza 4.00 1.20
T8 Kenny Lofton .... 1.00 .30
T9 Barry Bonds 6.00 1.80
T10 Darin Erstad .... 1.00 .30
T11 Nomar Garciaparra 4.00 1.20
T12 Cal Ripken 8.00 2.40
T13 J.D. Drew .... 1.00 .30
T14 Larry Walker .... 1.50 .45
T15 Chipper Jones .... 2.50 .75

1999 Upper Deck MVP Swing Time

Issued one every six packs, these cards focus on players who have swings considered to be among the sweetest in the game.

Nm-Mt Ex-Mt
COMPLETE SET (12) 20.00 6.00
S1 Ken Griffey Jr. .... 1.50 .45
S2 Mark McGwire .... 2.50 .75
S3 Sammy Sosa .... 1.50 .45
S4 Tony Gwynn .... 1.25 .35
S5 Alex Rodriguez .... 1.50 .45
S6 Nomar Garciaparra .... 1.50 .45
S7 Barry Bonds .... 2.50 .75
S8 Frank Thomas .... 1.00 .30
S9 Chipper Jones .... 1.00 .30
S10 Ivan Rodriguez .... 1.00 .30
S11 Mike Piazza .... 1.50 .45
S12 Derek Jeter .... 2.50 .75

1999 Upper Deck MVP FanFest

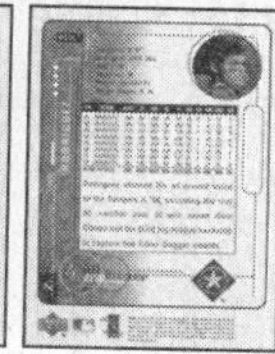

This 30 card standard-size set was issued by Upper Deck during the annual FanFest celebration. The cards were issued in three-card packs with 15,000 packs produced and distributed during the show. The cards have a silver All-Star Game logo on the lower right corner of the card and they are all numbered with an "AS" prefix. Ten of the cards were printed in smaller quantities then the other 20 cards, those cards are notated with an SP in the listings below

Nm-Mt Ex-Mt
COMPLETE SET 60.00 18.00
COMMON (AS1-AS30) .30 .09
COMMON SP 2.00 .60
AS1 Mo Vaughn SP 2.00 .60
AS2 Randy Johnson .75 .23
AS3 Chipper Jones 1.50 .45
AS4 Greg Maddux SP 6.00 1.80
AS5 Cal Ripken 3.00 .90
AS6 Albert Belle .30 .09
AS7 N.Garciaparra SP 6.00 1.80
AS8 Pedro Martinez .75 .23
AS9 Sammy Sosa 1.50 .45
AS10 Frank Thomas .75 .23
AS11 Sean Casey .30 .09
AS12 Roberto Alomar .60 .18
AS13 Manny Ramirez .75 .23
AS14 Larry Walker .30 .09
AS15 Jeff Bagwell SP 3.00 .90
AS16 Craig Biggio .60 .18
AS17 Raul Mondesi .30 .09
AS18 Vladimir Guerrero .75 .23
AS19 Mike Piazza SP 8.00 2.40
AS20 Derek Jeter SP 12.00 3.60
AS21 Roger Clemens SP 6.00 1.80
AS22 Scott Rolen .60 .18
AS23 Mark McGwire SP 10.00 3.00
AS24 Tony Gwynn 1.50 .45
AS25 Barry Bonds 1.50 .45
AS26 Ken Griffey Jr SP 8.00 2.40
AS27 Alex Rodriguez 1.50 .45
AS28 Jose Canseco .75 .23
AS29 Juan Gonzalez .75 .23
AS30 Ivan Rodriguez .75 .23

2000 Upper Deck MVP

he 2000 Upper Deck MVP product was released June, 2000 as a 220-card set. Each pack contained 10 cards and carried a suggested retail rice of $1.59. Please note that cards 218-220 re player/checklist cards. Also, a selection of A iece of History 3000 Club Stan Musial memorabilia cards were randomly seeded into packs. 50 bat cards, 350 jersey cards, 100 hand-numbered combination bat-jersey cards and six autographed, hand-numbered, combination bat-jersey cards were produced. Pricing for these memorabilia cards can be referenced under 000 Upper Deck A Piece of History 3000 Club.

Nm-Mt Ex-Mt
OMPLETE SET (220) 15.00 4.50
Garret Anderson .20 .06
Mo Vaughn .20 .06
Tim Salmon .30 .09
Ramon Ortiz .20 .06
Darin Erstad .20 .06
Troy Glaus .20 .06
Troy Percival .20 .06
Jeff Bagwell .30 .09
Ken Caminiti .20 .06
Daryle Ward .20 .06
Craig Biggio .30 .09
Jose Lima .20 .06
Moises Alou .20 .06
Octavio Dotel .20 .06
Ben Grieve .20 .06
Jason Giambi .20 .06
Tim Hudson .20 .06
Eric Chavez .20 .06
Matt Stairs .20 .06
Miguel Tejada .20 .06
John Jaha .20 .06
Chipper Jones .50 .15
Kevin Millwood .20 .06
Brian Jordan .20 .06
Andruw Jones .20 .06
Andres Galarraga .20 .06
Greg Maddux .75 .23
Reggie Sanders .20 .06
Javy Lopez .20 .06
Jeromy Burnitz .20 .06
Kevin Barker .20 .06
Jose Hernandez .20 .06
Ron Belliard .20 .06
Henry Blanco .20 .06
Marquis Grissom .20 .06
Geoff Jenkins .20 .06
Carlos Delgado .20 .06
Raul Mondesi .20 .06
Roy Halladay .20 .06
Tony Batista .20 .06
41 David Wells .20 .06
42 Shannon Stewart .20 .06
43 Vernon Wells .20 .06
44 Sammy Sosa .75 .23
45 Ismael Valdes .20 .06
46 Joe Girardi .20 .06
47 Mark Grace .30 .09
48 Henry Rodriguez .20 .06
49 Kerry Wood .50 .15
50 Eric Young .20 .06
51 Mark McGwire 1.25 .35
52 Darryl Kile .20 .06
53 Fernando Vina .20 .06
54 Ray Lankford .20 .06
55 J.D. Drew .20 .06
56 Fernando Tatis .20 .06
57 Rick Ankiel .20 .06
58 Matt Williams .20 .06
59 Erubiel Durazo .20 .06
60 Tony Womack .20 .06
61 Jay Bell .20 .06
62 Randy Johnson .50 .15
63 Steve Finley .20 .06
64 Matt Mantei .20 .06
65 Luis Gonzalez .20 .06
66 Gary Sheffield .20 .06
67 Eric Gagne .75 .23
68 Adrian Beltre .30 .09
69 Mark Grudzielanek .20 .06
70 Kevin Brown .20 .06
71 Chan Ho Park .20 .06
72 Shawn Green .20 .06
73 Vinny Castilla .20 .06
74 Fred McGriff .30 .09
75 Wilson Alvarez .20 .06
76 Greg Vaughn .20 .06
77 Gerald Williams .20 .06
78 Ryan Rupe .20 .06
79 Jose Canseco .50 .15
80 Vladimir Guerrero .50 .15
81 Dustin Hermanson .20 .06
82 Michael Barrett .20 .06
83 Rondell White .20 .06
84 Tony Armas Jr. .20 .06
85 Wilton Guerrero .20 .06
86 Jose Vidro .20 .06
87 Barry Bonds 1.25 .35
88 Russ Ortiz .20 .06
89 Ellis Burks .20 .06
90 Jeff Kent .20 .06
91 Russ Davis .20 .06
92 J.T. Snow .20 .06
93 Roberto Alomar .30 .09
94 Manny Ramirez .30 .09
95 Chuck Finley .20 .06
96 Kenny Lofton .20 .06
97 Jim Thome .50 .15
98 Bartolo Colon .20 .06
99 Omar Vizquel .30 .09
100 Richie Sexson .20 .06
101 Mike Cameron .20 .06
102 Brett Tomko .20 .06
103 Edgar Martinez .30 .09
104 Alex Rodriguez .75 .23
105 John Olerud .20 .06
106 Freddy Garcia .20 .06
107 Kazuhiro Sasaki RC .50 .15
108 Preston Wilson .20 .06
109 Luis Castillo .20 .06
110 A.J. Burnett .20 .06
111 Mike Lowell .20 .06
112 Cliff Floyd .20 .06
113 Brad Penny .20 .06
114 Alex Gonzalez .20 .06
115 Mike Piazza .75 .23
116 Derek Bell .20 .06
117 Edgardo Alfonzo .20 .06
118 Rickey Henderson .50 .15
119 Todd Zeile .20 .06
120 Mike Hampton .20 .06
121 Al Leiter .20 .06
122 Robin Ventura .20 .06
123 Cal Ripken 1.50 .45
124 Mike Mussina .30 .09
125 B.J. Surhoff .20 .06
126 Jerry Hairston Jr. .20 .06
127 Brady Anderson .20 .06
128 Albert Belle .20 .06
129 Sidney Ponson .20 .06
130 Tony Gwynn .60 .18
131 Ryan Klesko .20 .06
132 Sterling Hitchcock .20 .06
133 Eric Owens .20 .06
134 Trevor Hoffman .20 .06
135 Al Martin .20 .06
136 Bret Boone .20 .06
137 Brian Giles .20 .06
138 Chad Hermansen .20 .06
139 Kevin Young .20 .06
140 Kris Benson .20 .06
141 Warren Morris .20 .06
142 Jason Kendall .20 .06
143 Wil Cordero .20 .06
144 Scott Rolen .50 .15
145 Curt Schilling .20 .06
146 Doug Glanville .20 .06
147 Mike Lieberthal .20 .06
148 Mike Jackson .20 .06
149 Rico Brogna .20 .06
150 Andy Ashby .20 .06
151 Bob Abreu .20 .06
152 Sean Casey .20 .06
153 Pete Harnisch .20 .06
154 Dante Bichette .20 .06
155 Pokey Reese .20 .06
156 Aaron Boone .20 .06
157 Ken Griffey Jr. .75 .23
158 Barry Larkin .30 .09
159 Scott Williamson .20 .06
160 Carlos Beltran .30 .09
161 Jermaine Dye .20 .06
162 Jose Rosado .20 .06
163 Joe Randa .20 .06
164 Johnny Damon .30 .09
165 Mike Sweeney .20 .06
166 Mark Quinn .20 .06
167 Ivan Rodriguez .50 .15
168 Rusty Greer .20 .06
169 Ruben Mateo .20 .06
170 Doug Davis .20 .06
171 Gabe Kapler .20 .06
172 Justin Thompson .20 .06
173 Rafael Palmeiro .30 .09
174 Larry Walker .30 .09
175 Neifi Perez .20 .06
176 Rolando Arrojo .20 .06
177 Jeffrey Hammonds .20 .06
178 Todd Helton .30 .09
179 Pedro Astacio .20 .06
180 Jeff Cirillo .20 .06
181 Pedro Martinez .50 .15
182 Carl Everett .20 .06
183 Troy O'Leary .20 .06
184 Nomar Garciaparra .75 .23
185 Jose Offerman .20 .06
186 Bret Saberhagen .20 .06
187 Trot Nixon .20 .06
188 Jason Varitek .30 .09
189 Todd Walker .20 .06
190 Eric Milton .20 .06
191 Chad Allen .20 .06
192 Jacque Jones .20 .06
193 Brad Radke .20 .06
194 Corey Koskie .20 .06
195 Joe Mays .20 .06
196 Juan Gonzalez .30 .09
197 Jeff Weaver .20 .06
198 Juan Encarnacion .20 .06
199 Deivi Cruz .20 .06
200 Damion Easley .20 .06
201 Tony Clark .20 .06
202 Dean Palmer .20 .06
203 Frank Thomas .50 .15
204 Carlos Lee .20 .06
205 Mike Sirotka .20 .06
206 Kip Wells .20 .06
207 Magglio Ordonez .20 .06
208 Paul Konerko .20 .06
209 Chris Singleton .20 .06
210 Derek Jeter 1.25 .35
211 Tino Martinez .30 .09
212 Mariano Rivera .30 .09
213 Roger Clemens 1.00 .30
214 Nick Johnson .20 .06
215 Paul O'Neill .30 .09
216 Bernie Williams .30 .09
217 David Cone .20 .06
218 Ken Griffey Jr. CL .50 .15
219 Sammy Sosa CL .50 .15
220 Mark McGwire CL .60 .18

2000 Upper Deck MVP Gold Script

Randomly inserted into packs, this 220-card insert is a complete parallel of the Upper Deck MVP base set. Each card in the set is individually serial numbered to 50. Please note that each card features a gold foiled facsimile autograph on the front of the card.

Nm-Mt Ex-Mt
*STARS: 25X TO 60X BASIC CARDS
*ROOKIES: 20X TO 50X BASIC CARDS

2000 Upper Deck MVP Silver Script

Randomly inserted into packs at one in two, this 220-card insert is a complete parallel of the Upper Deck MVP base set. Please note that each card features a silver foiled facsimile autograph on the front of the card.

Nm-Mt Ex-Mt
COMPLETE SET (220) 150.00 45.00
*STARS: 1.25X TO 3X BASIC CARDS
*ROOKIES: 1.25X TO 3X BASIC CARDS

2000 Upper Deck MVP All Star Game

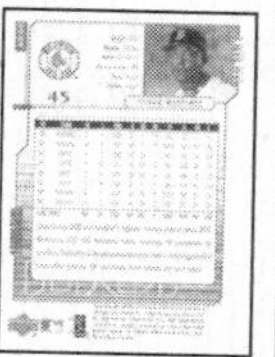

This 30-card insert set was released in three-card packs at the All-Star Fan Fest in Atlanta in July, 2000.

Nm-Mt Ex-Mt
COMPLETE SET (30) 40.00 12.00
AS1 Mo Vaughn .40 .12
AS2 Jeff Bagwell 1.00 .30
AS3 Jason Giambi 1.00 .30
AS4 Chipper Jones 1.50 .45
AS5 Greg Maddux 2.00 .60
AS6 Tony Batista .25 .07
AS7 Sammy Sosa 2.00 .60
AS8 Mark McGwire 3.00 .90
AS9 Randy Johnson 1.00 .30
AS10 Shawn Green .75 .23
AS11 Greg Vaughn .40 .12
AS12 Vladimir Guerrero 1.00 .30
AS13 Barry Bonds 2.00 .60
AS14 Manny Ramirez 1.00 .30
AS15 Alex Rodriguez 2.00 .60
AS16 Preston Wilson .40 .12
AS17 Mike Piazza 2.50 .75
AS18 Cal Ripken Jr. 4.00 1.20
AS19 Tony Gwynn 2.00 .60
AS20 Scott Rolen .75 .23
AS21 Ken Griffey Jr. 2.50 .75
AS22 Carlos Beltran .60 .18
AS23 Ivan Rodriguez 1.00 .30
AS24 Larry Walker .40 .12
AS25 Nomar Garciaparra 2.00 .60
AS26 Pedro Martinez 1.00 .30
AS27 Juan Gonzalez 1.00 .30
AS28 Frank Thomas 1.50 .45
AS29 Derek Jeter 4.00 1.20
AS30 Bernie Williams .75 .23

2000 Upper Deck MVP Draw Your Own Card

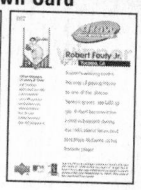

Randomly inserted into packs at one in six, this 31-card insert features player drawings from the 2000 Draw Your Own Card winners. Card backs carry a "DT" prefix.

Nm-Mt Ex-Mt
COMPLETE SET (31) 50.00 15.00
DT1 Frank Thomas 1.00 .30
DT2 Joe DiMaggio 2.00 .60
DT3 Barry Bonds 2.50 .75
DT4 Mark McGwire 2.50 .75
DT5 Ken Griffey Jr. 1.50 .45
DT6 Mark McGwire 2.50 .75
DT7 Mike Stanley .40 .12
DT8 Nomar Garciaparra 1.50 .45
DT9 Mickey Mantle 4.00 1.20
DT10 Randy Johnson 1.00 .30
DT11 Nolan Ryan 2.50 .75
DT12 Chipper Jones 1.00 .30
DT13 Ken Griffey Jr. 1.50 .45
DT14 Troy Glaus .40 .12
DT15 Manny Ramirez .60 .18
DT16 Mark McGwire 2.50 .75
DT17 Ivan Rodriguez 1.00 .30
DT18 Mike Piazza 1.50 .45
DT19 Sammy Sosa 1.50 .45
DT20 Ken Griffey Jr. 1.50 .45
DT21 Jeff Bagwell .60 .18
DT22 Ken Griffey Jr. 1.50 .45
DT23 Kerry Wood 1.00 .30
DT24 Mark McGwire 2.50 .75
DT25 Greg Maddux 1.50 .45
DT26 Sandy Alomar Jr. .40 .12
DT27 Albert Belle .40 .12
DT28 Sammy Sosa 1.50 .45
DT29 Alexandra Brunet .40 .12
DT30 Mark McGwire 2.50 .75
DT31 Nomar Garciaparra 1.50 .45

2000 Upper Deck MVP Drawing Power

Randomly inserted into packs at one in 28, this seven-card insert features players that bring fans to the ballpark. Card backs carry a "DP" prefix.

Nm-Mt Ex-Mt
COMPLETE SET (7) 30.00 9.00
DP1 Mark McGwire 6.00 1.80
DP2 Ken Griffey Jr. 4.00 1.20
DP3 Mike Piazza 4.00 1.20
DP4 Chipper Jones 2.50 .75
DP5 Nomar Garciaparra 4.00 1.20
DP6 Sammy Sosa 4.00 1.20
DP7 Jose Canseco 2.50 .75

2000 Upper Deck MVP Game Used Souvenirs

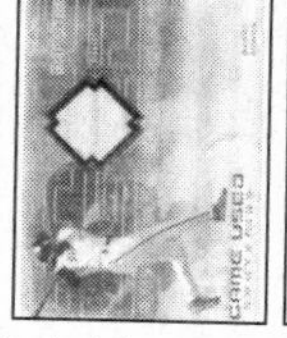
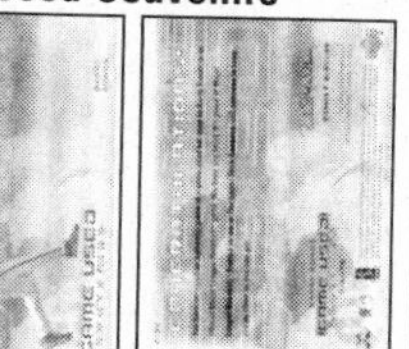

Randomly inserted into packs at one in 130, this 30-card insert features game-used bat and game used glove cards from players such as Chipper Jones and Ken Griffey Jr.

Nm-Mt Ex-Mt
AB-G Albert Belle Glove 20.00 6.00
AF-G Alex Fernandez Glove 15.00 4.50
AG-G Alex Gonzalez Glove 15.00 4.50
AR-B Alex Rodriguez Bat 15.00 4.50
AR-G Alex Rodriguez Glove 50.00 15.00
BB-B Barry Bonds Bat 25.00 7.50
BB-G Barry Bonds Glove 80.00 24.00
BG-G Ben Grieve Glove 15.00 4.50
BW-G Bernie Williams Glove 30.00 9.00
CR-G Cal Ripken Glove 80.00 24.00
IR-B Ivan Rodriguez Bat 15.00 4.50
IR-G Ivan Rodriguez Glove 30.00 9.00
JB-G Jeff Bagwell Glove 30.00 9.00
JC-B Jose Canseco Bat 15.00 4.50
KG-B Ken Griffey Jr. Bat 20.00 6.00
KG-G Ken Griffey Jr. Glove 50.00 15.00
KL-G Kenny Lofton Glove 20.00 6.00
LW-G Larry Walker Glove 30.00 9.00
MR-B Manny Ramirez Bat 15.00 4.50
NR-G Nolan Ryan Glove 80.00 24.00
PO-G Paul O'Neill Glove 30.00 9.00
RA-G Roberto Alomar Glove 30.00 9.00
RM-G Raul Mondesi Glove 20.00 6.00
RP-G Rafael Palmeiro Glove 50.00 15.00
TG-B Tony Gwynn Bat 20.00 6.00
TG-G Tony Gwynn Glove 40.00 12.00
TS-G Tim Salmon Glove 30.00 9.00
WC-G Will Clark Glove 30.00 9.00

2000 Upper Deck MVP Game Used Souvenirs Signed

Randomly inserted into packs, this autographed insert features game-used bat and game-used glove cards from players such as Chipper Jones and Ken Griffey Jr. Each card was individually serial numbered to 25 on front. Stickered exchange cards were placed into packs for Ken Griffey Jr. The exchange deadline for these stickered redemption cards was February 2nd, 2001. Due to market scarcity, no pricing is provided for these cards.

Nm-Mt Ex-Mt
ABSG Albert Belle Glove
BBSB Barry Bonds Bat
BBSG Barry Bonds Glove
CJSB Chipper Jones Bat
JCSB Jose Canseco Bat
KGSB Ken Griffey Jr. Bat
KGSG Ken Griffey Jr. Glove EX
KLSG Kenny Lofton Glove
NRSG Nolan Ryan Glove
RASG Roberto Alomar Glove
RPSG Rafael Palmeiro Glove
TGSB Tony Gwynn Bat
TGSG Tony Gwynn Glove

2000 Upper Deck MVP Prolifics

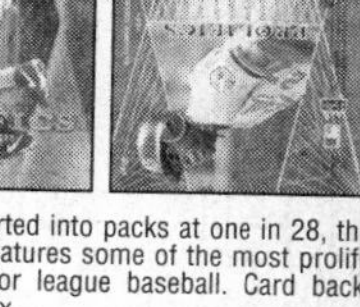

Randomly inserted into packs at one in 28, this 7-card insert features some of the most prolific players in major league baseball. Card backs carry a "P" prefix.

Nm-Mt Ex-Mt
COMPLETE SET (7) 25.00 7.50
P1 Manny Ramirez 1.50 .45
P2 Vladimir Guerrero 2.50 .75
P3 Derek Jeter 6.00 1.80
P4 Pedro Martinez 2.50 .75
P5 Shawn Green 1.00 .30
P6 Alex Rodriguez 4.00 1.20
P7 Cal Ripken 8.00 2.40

2000 Upper Deck MVP ProSign

Randomly inserted into retail packs only at one in 143, this 18-card insert features autographs of players such as Mike Sweeney, Rick Ankiel, and Tim Hudson. Card backs are numbered using the players initials.

Nm-Mt Ex-Mt
LIMITED RANDOM IN PACKS
LIMITED PRINT RUN 25 SERIAL #'d SETS
NO LTD PRICING DUE TO SCARCITY
BP Ben Petrick 10.00 3.00
BT Bubba Trammell 10.00 3.00
DD Doug Davis 10.00 3.00
EY Ed Yarnall 10.00 3.00
JM Jim Morris 25.00 7.50
JV Jose Vidro 10.00 3.00
JZ Jeff Zimmerman 10.00 3.00
KW Kevin Witt 10.00 3.00
MB Michael Barrett 10.00 3.00
MM Mike Meyers 15.00 4.50
MQ Mark Quinn 10.00 3.00
MS Mike Sweeney 15.00 4.50
PW Preston Wilson 15.00 4.50
RA Rick Ankiel 15.00 4.50
SW Scott Williamson 10.00 3.00
TH Tim Hudson 25.00 7.50
TN Trot Nixon 15.00 4.50
WM Warren Morris 10.00 3.00

2000 Upper Deck MVP Pure Grit

Randomly inserted into packs at one in six, this 10-card insert features players that constantly

give their best day in, day out. Card backs carry a "G" prefix.

	Nm-Mt	Ex-Mt
COMPLETE SET (10)	15.00	4.50
G1 Derek Jeter	3.00	.90
G2 Kevin Brown	.50	.15
G3 Craig Biggio	.75	.23
G4 Ivan Rodriguez	1.25	.35
G5 Scott Rolen	1.25	.35
G6 Carlos Beltran	.75	.23
G7 Ken Griffey Jr.	2.00	.60
G8 Cal Ripken	4.00	1.20
G9 Nomar Garciaparra	2.00	.60
G10 Randy Johnson	1.25	.35

2000 Upper Deck MVP Scout's Choice

Randomly inserted into packs at one in 14, this 10-card insert features players that major league scouts believe will be future stars in the major leagues. Card backs carry a "SC" prefix.

	Nm-Mt	Ex-Mt
COMPLETE SET (10)	10.00	3.00
SC1 Rick Ankiel	1.00	.30
SC2 Vernon Wells	1.00	.30
SC3 Pat Burrell	1.00	.30
SC4 Travis Dawkins	1.00	.30
SC5 Eric Munson	1.00	.30
SC6 Nick Johnson	1.00	.30
SC7 Dermal Brown	1.00	.30
SC8 Alfonso Soriano	1.50	.45
SC9 Ben Petrick	1.00	.30
SC10 Adam Everett	1.00	.30

2000 Upper Deck MVP Second Season Standouts

Randomly inserted into packs at one in six, this 10-card insert features players that had outstanding sophomore years in the major leagues. Card backs carry a "SS" prefix.

	Nm-Mt	Ex-Mt
COMPLETE SET (10)	10.00	3.00
SS1 Pedro Martinez	1.25	.35
SS2 Mariano Rivera	.75	.23
SS3 Orlando Hernandez	.50	.15
SS4 Ken Caminiti	.50	.15
SS5 Bernie Williams	.75	.23
SS6 Jim Thome	1.25	.35
SS7 Nomar Garciaparra	2.00	.60
SS8 Edgardo Alfonzo	.50	.15
SS9 Derek Jeter	3.00	.90
SS10 Kevin Millwood	.50	.15

2001 Upper Deck MVP

This 330-card set was released in May, 2001. These cards were issued in eight card packs with an SRP of $1.99. These packs were issued 24 packs to a box.

	Nm-Mt	Ex-Mt
COMPLETE SET (330)	40.00	12.00
1 Mo Vaughn	.20	.06
2 Troy Percival	.20	.06
3 Adam Kennedy	.20	.06
4 Darin Erstad	.20	.06
5 Tim Salmon	.30	.09
6 Bengie Molina	.20	.06
7 Troy Glaus	.20	.06
8 Garret Anderson	.20	.06
9 Ismael Valdes	.20	.06
10 Glenallen Hill	.20	.06
11 Tim Hudson	.20	.06
12 Eric Chavez	.20	.06
13 Johnny Damon	.30	.09
14 Barry Zito	.30	.09
15 Jason Giambi	.20	.06
16 Terrence Long	.20	.06
17 Jason Hart	.20	.06
18 Jose Ortiz	.20	.06
19 Miguel Tejada	.20	.06
20 Jason Isringhausen	.20	.06
21 Adam Piatt	.20	.06
22 Jeremy Giambi	.20	.06
23 Tony Batista	.20	.06
24 Darrin Fletcher	.20	.06
25 Mike Sirotka	.20	.06
26 Carlos Delgado	.20	.06
27 Billy Koch	.20	.06
28 Shannon Stewart	.20	.06
29 Raul Mondesi	.20	.06
30 Brad Fullmer	.20	.06
31 Jose Cruz Jr.	.20	.06
32 Kelvim Escobar	.20	.06
33 Greg Vaughn	.20	.06
34 Aubrey Huff	.20	.06
35 Albie Lopez	.20	.06
36 Gerald Williams	.20	.06
37 Ben Grieve	.20	.06
38 John Flaherty	.20	.06
39 Fred McGriff	.30	.09
40 Ryan Rupe	.20	.06
41 Travis Harper	.20	.06
42 Steve Cox	.20	.06
43 Roberto Alomar	.30	.09
44 Jim Thome	.50	.15
45 Russell Branyan	.20	.06
46 Bartolo Colon	.20	.06
47 Omar Vizquel	.30	.09
48 Travis Fryman	.20	.06
49 Kenny Lofton	.20	.06
50 Chuck Finley	.20	.06
51 Ellis Burks	.20	.06
52 Eddie Taubensee	.20	.06
53 Juan Gonzalez	.30	.09
54 Edgar Martinez	.30	.09
55 Aaron Sele	.20	.06
56 John Olerud	.20	.06
57 Jay Buhner	.20	.06
58 Mike Cameron	.20	.06
59 John Halama	.20	.06
60 Ichiro Suzuki RC	10.00	3.00
61 David Bell	.20	.06
62 Freddy Garcia	.20	.06
63 Carlos Guillen	.20	.06
64 Bret Boone	.20	.06
65 Al Martin	.20	.06
66 Cal Ripken	1.50	.45
67 Delino DeShields	.20	.06
68 Chris Richard	.20	.06
69 Sean Douglass RC	.50	.15
70 Melvin Mora	.20	.06
71 Luis Matos	.20	.06
72 Sidney Ponson	.20	.06
73 Mike Bordick	.20	.06
74 Brady Anderson	.20	.06
75 David Segui	.20	.06
76 Jeff Conine	.20	.06
77 Alex Rodriguez	.75	.23
78 Gabe Kapler	.20	.06
79 Ivan Rodriguez	.50	.15
80 Rick Helling	.20	.06
81 Kenny Rogers	.20	.06
82 Andres Galarraga	.20	.06
83 Rusty Greer	.20	.06
84 Justin Thompson	.20	.06
85 Ken Caminiti	.20	.06
86 Rafael Palmeiro	.30	.09
87 Ruben Mateo	.20	.06
88 Travis Hafner RC	1.50	.45
89 Manny Ramirez	.30	.09
90 Pedro Martinez	.50	.15
91 Carl Everett	.20	.06
92 Dante Bichette	.20	.06
93 Derek Lowe	.20	.06
94 Jason Varitek	.30	.09
95 Nomar Garciaparra	.75	.23
96 David Cone	.20	.06
97 Tomokazu Ohka	.20	.06
98 Troy O'Leary	.20	.06
99 Trot Nixon	.20	.06
100 Jermaine Dye	.20	.06
101 Joe Randa	.20	.06
102 Jeff Suppan	.20	.06
103 Roberto Hernandez	.20	.06
104 Mike Sweeney	.20	.06
105 Mac Suzuki	.20	.06
106 Carlos Febles	.20	.06
107 Jose Rosado	.20	.06
108 Mark Quinn	.20	.06
109 Carlos Beltran	.30	.09
110 Dean Palmer	.20	.06
111 Mitch Meluskey	.20	.06
112 Bobby Higginson	.20	.06
113 Brandon Inge	.20	.06
114 Tony Clark	.20	.06
115 Brian Moehler	.20	.06
116 Juan Encarnacion	.20	.06
117 Damion Easley	.20	.06
118 Roger Cedeno	.20	.06
119 Jeff Weaver	.20	.06
120 Matt Lawton	.20	.06
121 Jay Canizaro	.20	.06
122 Eric Milton	.20	.06
123 Corey Koskie	.20	.06
124 Mark Redman	.20	.06
125 Jacque Jones	.20	.06
126 Brad Radke	.20	.06
127 Cristian Guzman	.20	.06
128 Joe Mays	.20	.06
129 Denny Hocking	.20	.06
130 Frank Thomas	.50	.15
131 David Wells	.20	.06
132 Ray Durham	.20	.06
133 Paul Konerko	.20	.06
134 Joe Crede	.20	.06
135 Jim Parque	.20	.06
136 Carlos Lee	.20	.06
137 Magglio Ordonez	.20	.06
138 Sandy Alomar Jr.	.20	.06
139 Chris Singleton	.20	.06
140 Jose Valentin	.20	.06
141 Roger Clemens	1.00	.30
142 Derek Jeter	1.25	.35
143 Orlando Hernandez	.20	.06
144 Tino Martinez	.30	.09
145 Bernie Williams	.30	.09
146 Jorge Posada	.30	.09
147 Mariano Rivera	.30	.09
148 David Justice	.20	.06
149 Paul O'Neill	.30	.09
150 Mike Mussina	.30	.09
151 Christian Parker RC	.50	.15
152 Andy Pettitte	.30	.09
153 Alfonso Soriano	.30	.09
154 Jeff Bagwell	.30	.09
155 Morgan Ensberg RC	.75	.23
156 Daryle Ward	.20	.06
157 Craig Biggio	.30	.09
158 Richard Hidalgo	.20	.06
159 Shane Reynolds	.20	.06
160 Scott Elarton	.20	.06
161 Julio Lugo	.20	.06
162 Moises Alou	.20	.06
163 Lance Berkman	.20	.06
164 Chipper Jones	.50	.15
165 Greg Maddux	.75	.23
166 Javy Lopez	.20	.06
167 Andruw Jones	.20	.06
168 Rafael Furcal	.20	.06
169 Brian Jordan	.20	.06
170 Wes Helms	.20	.06
171 Tom Glavine	.30	.09
172 B.J. Surhoff	.20	.06
173 John Smoltz	.30	.09
174 Quilvio Veras	.20	.06
175 Rico Brogna	.20	.06
176 Jeromy Burnitz	.20	.06
177 Jeff D'Amico	.20	.06
178 Geoff Jenkins	.20	.06
179 Henry Blanco	.20	.06
180 Mark Loretta	.20	.06
181 Richie Sexson	.20	.06
182 Jimmy Haynes	.20	.06
183 Jeffrey Hammonds	.20	.06
184 Ron Belliard	.20	.06
185 Tyler Houston	.20	.06
186 Mark McGwire	1.25	.35
187 Rick Ankiel	.20	.06
188 Darryl Kile	.20	.06
189 Jim Edmonds	.20	.06
190 Mike Matheny	.20	.06
191 Edgar Renteria	.20	.06
192 Ray Lankford	.20	.06
193 Garrett Stephenson	.20	.06
194 J.D. Drew	.20	.06
195 Fernando Vina	.20	.06
196 Dustin Hermanson	.20	.06
197 Sammy Sosa	.75	.23
198 Corey Patterson	.20	.06
199 Jon Lieber	.20	.06
200 Kerry Wood	.50	.15
201 Todd Hundley	.20	.06
202 Kevin Tapani	.20	.06
203 Rondell White	.20	.06
204 Eric Young	.20	.06
205 Matt Stairs	.20	.06
206 Bill Mueller	.20	.06
207 Randy Johnson	.50	.15
208 Mark Grace	.30	.09
209 Jay Bell	.20	.06
210 Curt Schilling	.20	.06
211 Erubiel Durazo	.20	.06
212 Luis Gonzalez	.20	.06
213 Steve Finley	.20	.06
214 Matt Williams	.20	.06
215 Reggie Sanders	.20	.06
216 Tony Womack	.20	.06
217 Gary Sheffield	.20	.06
218 Kevin Brown	.20	.06
219 Adrian Beltre	.30	.09
220 Shawn Green	.20	.06
221 Darren Dreifort	.20	.06
222 Chan Ho Park	.20	.06
223 Eric Karros	.20	.06
224 Alex Cora	.20	.06
225 Mark Grudzielanek	.20	.06
226 Andy Ashby	.20	.06
227 Vladimir Guerrero	.50	.15
228 Tony Armas Jr.	.20	.06
229 Fernando Tatis	.20	.06
230 Jose Vidro	.20	.06
231 Javier Vazquez	.20	.06
232 Lee Stevens	.20	.06
233 Milton Bradley	.20	.06
234 Carl Pavano	.20	.06
235 Peter Bergeron	.20	.06
236 Wilton Guerrero	.20	.06
237 Ugueth Urbina	.20	.06
238 Barry Bonds	1.25	.35
239 Livan Hernandez	.20	.06
240 Jeff Kent	.20	.06
241 Pedro Feliz	.20	.06
242 Bobby Estalella	.20	.06
243 J.T. Snow	.20	.06
244 Shawn Estes	.20	.06
245 Robb Nen	.20	.06
246 Rich Aurilia	.20	.06
247 Russ Ortiz	.20	.06
248 Preston Wilson	.20	.06
249 Brad Penny	.20	.06
250 Cliff Floyd	.20	.06
251 A.J. Burnett	.20	.06
252 Mike Lowell	.20	.06
253 Luis Castillo	.20	.06
254 Ryan Dempster	.20	.06
255 Derrek Lee	.20	.06
256 Charles Johnson	.20	.06
257 Pablo Ozuna	.20	.06
258 Antonio Alfonseca	.20	.06
259 Mike Piazza	.75	.23
260 Robin Ventura	.20	.06
261 Al Leiter	.20	.06
262 Timo Perez	.20	.06
263 Edgardo Alfonzo	.20	.06
264 Jay Payton	.20	.06
265 Tsuyoshi Shinjo RC	.50	.15
266 Todd Zeile	.20	.06
267 Armando Benitez	.20	.06
268 Glendon Rusch	.20	.06
269 Rey Ordonez	.20	.06
270 Kevin Appier	.20	.06
271 Tony Gwynn	.60	.18
272 Phil Nevin	.20	.06
273 Mark Kotsay	.20	.06
274 Ryan Klesko	.20	.06
275 Adam Eaton	.20	.06
276 Mike Darr	.20	.06
277 Damian Jackson	.20	.06
278 Woody Williams	.20	.06
279 Chris Gomez	.20	.06
280 Trevor Hoffman	.20	.06
281 Xavier Nady	.20	.06
282 Scott Rolen	.50	.15
283 Bruce Chen	.20	.06
284 Pat Burrell	.20	.06
285 Mike Lieberthal	.20	.06
286 B. Duckworth RC	.50	.15
287 Travis Lee	.20	.06
288 Bobby Abreu	.20	.06
289 Jimmy Rollins	.20	.06
290 Robert Person	.20	.06
291 Randy Wolf	.20	.06
292 Jason Kendall	.20	.06
293 Derek Bell	.20	.06
294 Brian Giles	.20	.06
295 Kris Benson	.20	.06
296 John VanderWal	.20	.06
297 Todd Ritchie	.20	.06
298 Warren Morris	.20	.06
299 Kevin Young	.20	.06
300 Francisco Cordova	.20	.06
301 Aramis Ramirez	.20	.06
302 Ken Griffey Jr.	.75	.23
303 Pete Harnisch	.20	.06
304 Aaron Boone	.20	.06
305 Sean Casey	.20	.06
306 Jackson Melian RC	.50	.15
307 Rob Bell	.20	.06
308 Barry Larkin	.30	.09
309 Dmitri Young	.20	.06
310 Danny Graves	.20	.06
311 Pokey Reese	.20	.06
312 Leo Estrella	.20	.06
313 Todd Helton	.30	.09
314 Mike Hampton	.20	.06
315 Juan Pierre	.20	.06
316 Brent Mayne	.20	.06
317 Larry Walker	.30	.09
318 Denny Neagle	.20	.06
319 Jeff Cirillo	.20	.06
320 Pedro Astacio	.20	.06
321 Todd Hollandsworth	.20	.06
322 Neifi Perez	.20	.06
323 Ron Gant	.20	.06
324 Todd Walker	.20	.06
325 Alex Rodriguez CL	.50	.15
326 Ken Griffey Jr. CL	.50	.15
327 Mark McGwire CL	.60	.18
328 Pedro Martinez CL	.30	.09
329 Derek Jeter CL	.60	.18
330 Mike Piazza CL	.50	.15

2001 Upper Deck MVP Authentic Griffey

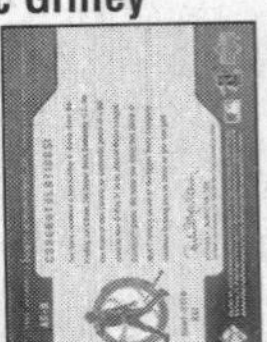

Inserted in packs at a rate of one in 288, these 12 cards feature memorabilia relating to the career of Ken Griffey Jr. A few cards were printed to a stated print run of 30 (Griffey's uniform number with the Reds), and we have notated those cards in our checklist. Griffey did not return his autographs in time for inclusion in the product and those cards could be redeemed until January 15th, 2002.

	Nm-Mt	Ex-Mt
B Ken Griffey Jr. Bat	15.00	4.50
C Ken Griffey Jr. Cap	40.00	12.00
J Ken Griffey Jr. Jsy	15.00	4.50
S K.Griffey Jr. AU EXCH*	100.00	30.00
U K.Griffey Jr. Uni	15.00	4.50
GB Ken Griffey Jr. Gold Bat/30	100.00	30.00
GC Ken Griffey Jr. Gold Cap/30	100.00	30.00
GJ Ken Griffey Jr. Gold Jsy/30	100.00	30.00
GS Ken Griffey Jr. Gold AU/30 EXCH	200.00	60.00
CGR Ken Griffey Jr. Alex Rodriguez	80.00	24.00
CGS Ken Griffey Jr. Sammy Sosa	80.00	24.00
CGT Ken Griffey Jr. Frank Thomas Jsy/100	60.00	18.00

2001 Upper Deck MVP Drawing Power

Inserted in packs at a rate of one in 12, these 10 cards feature the players who help to draw the most fans to ballparks.

	Nm-Mt	Ex-Mt
COMPLETE SET (10)	25.00	7.50
DP1 Mark McGwire	6.00	1.80
DP2 Vladimir Guerrero	2.50	.75
DP3 Manny Ramirez	2.50	.75
DP4 Frank Thomas	2.50	.75
DP5 Ken Griffey Jr.	4.00	1.20
DP6 Alex Rodriguez	4.00	1.20
DP7 Mike Piazza	4.00	1.20
DP8 Derek Jeter	6.00	1.80
DP9 Sammy Sosa	4.00	1.20
DP10 Todd Helton	2.50	.75

2001 Upper Deck MVP Game Souvenirs Bat Duos

Inserted one in 144, these 14 cards feature two pieces of game-used bats on the same card.

	Nm-Mt	Ex-Mt
B-3K Tony Gwynn Cal Ripken	50.00	15.00
B-DV Carlos Delgado Jose Vidro	15.00	4.50
B-GS Ken Griffey Jr. Sammy Sosa	40.00	12.00
B-HR Jose Canseco Ken Griffey Jr.	30.00	9.00
B-JF Chipper Jones Rafael Furcal	25.00	7.50
B-JJ Andruw Jones Chipper Jones	25.00	7.50
B-OW Paul O'Neill Bernie Williams	25.00	7.50
B-RM Alex Rodriguez Edgar Martinez	30.00	9.00
B-RP Ivan Rodriguez Rafael Palmeiro	25.00	7.50
B-RR Alex Rodriguez Ivan Rodriguez	40.00	12.00
B-TG Jim Thome Ken Griffey Jr.	30.00	9.00
B-TO Frank Thomas Magglio Ordonez	25.00	7.50
B-TS Frank Thomas Sammy Sosa	30.00	9.00
B-WA Kerry Wood Rick Ankiel	25.00	7.50

2001 Upper Deck MVP Game Souvenirs Bat Trios

Randomly inserted in packs, these six cards feature three pieces of game-used bats. These cards are serial numbered to 25. Due to market scarcity, no pricing is provided.

	Nm-Mt	Ex-Mt
B-BGJ Barry Bonds Ken Griffey Jr. Andruw Jones		
B-CBG Jose Canseco Barry Bonds Ken Griffey Jr.		
B-JEG Andruw Jones Jim Edmonds Ken Griffey Jr.		
B-JGC Chipper Jones Troy Glaus Eric Chavez		
B-JWO David Justice Bernie Williams Paul O'Neill		
B-SGR Sammy Sosa Ken Griffey Jr. Alex Rodriguez		

2001 Upper Deck MVP Game Souvenirs Batting Glove

Inserted one per 96 hobby packs, these 18 cards feature a swatch of game-used batting glove of various major leaguers. A couple of players were issued in lesser quantities. We have notated those cards as SP's as well as print run information (as provided by Upper Deck) in our checklist.

	Nm-Mt	Ex-Mt
G-AR Alex Rodriguez	25.00	7.50
G-BB Barry Bonds	50.00	15.00
G-CJ Chipper Jones	15.00	4.50
G-CR Cal Ripken	60.00	18.00
G-EM Edgar Martinez	15.00	4.50
G-FM Fred McGriff	15.00	4.50
G-FT Frank Thomas	15.00	4.50
G-GM Greg Maddux SP/95	80.00	24.00
G-IR Ivan Rodriguez	15.00	4.50
G-JG Juan Gonzalez	15.00	4.50
G-JL Javy Lopez	10.00	3.00
G-KG Ken Griffey Jr.	25.00	7.50
G-MT Miguel Tejada	10.00	3.00
G-MV Mo Vaughn	10.00	3.00
G-RP Rafael Palmeiro	15.00	4.50
G-SS Sammy Sosa	25.00	7.50

G-TOG T.Gwynn SP/200 40.00 12.00
G-TRG Troy Glaus 10.00 3.00

2001 Upper Deck MVP Game Souvenirs Batting Glove Autograph

Randomly inserted in packs, these nine cards feature not only a swatch of a game-used batting glove but also an authentic autograph of the player. These cards have a stated print run of 25 sets. Troy Glaus did not return his cards in time for inclusion in the packs and these cards were only available as redemptions. Due to market scarcity, no pricing is provided.

Nm-Mt Ex-Mt
SG-AR Alex Rodriguez
SG-CJ Chipper Jones
SG-CR Cal Ripken
SG-FT Frank Thomas
SG-IR Ivan Rodriguez
SG-KG Ken Griffey Jr.
SG-SS Sammy Sosa
SG-TOG Tony Gwynn
SG-TRG Troy Glaus

2001 Upper Deck MVP Super Tools

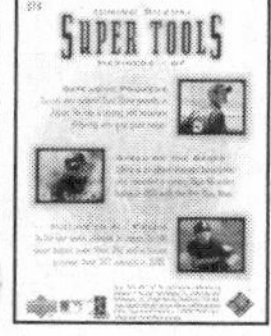

Inserted one per six packs, these 20 cards feature players whose tools seem to be far above the other players.

Nm-Mt Ex-Mt
COMPLETE SET (20) 40.00 12.00
ST1 Ken Griffey Jr. 4.00 1.20
ST2 Carlos Delgado 1.00 .30
ST3 Alex Rodriguez 4.00 1.20
ST4 Troy Glaus 1.00 .30
ST5 Jeff Bagwell 1.50 .45
ST6 Ichiro Suzuki 10.00 3.00
ST7 Derek Jeter 6.00 1.80
ST8 Jim Edmonds 1.00 .30
ST9 Vladimir Guerrero 2.50 .75
ST10 Jason Giambi 1.00 .30
ST11 Todd Helton 1.50 .45
ST12 Cal Ripken 8.00 2.40
ST13 Barry Bonds 6.00 1.80
ST14 N.Garciaparra UER 4.00 1.20
Spelled Garicaparra on the front
ST15 Randy Johnson 2.50 .75
ST16 Jermaine Dye 1.00 .30
ST17 Andruw Jones 1.00 .30
ST18 Ivan Rodriguez 2.50 .75
ST19 Sammy Sosa 4.00 1.20
ST20 Pedro Martinez 2.50 .75

2002 Upper Deck MVP

This 300 card set was issued in May, 2002. These cards were issued in eight card packs which came 24 packs to a box and 12 boxes to a case. Cards number 295-300 feature players on the front and checklisting information on the back. Card 301, featuring Kazuhisa Ishii, was added to the product at the last minute. According to representatives at Upper Deck, the card was seeded only into very late boxes of MVP.

Nm-Mt Ex-Mt
COMPLETE SET (301) 40.00 12.00
1 Darin Erstad .20 .06
2 Ramon Ortiz .20 .06
3 Garret Anderson .20 .06
4 Jarrod Washburn .20 .06
5 Troy Glaus .20 .06
6 Brendan Donnelly RC .50 .15
7 Troy Percival .20 .06
8 Tim Salmon .30 .09
9 Aaron Sele .20 .06
10 Brad Fullmer .20 .06
11 Scott Hatteberg .20 .06
12 Barry Zito .20 .06
13 Tim Hudson .20 .06
14 Miguel Tejada .20 .06
15 Jermaine Dye .20 .06
16 Mark Mulder .20 .06
17 Eric Chavez .20 .06
18 Terrence Long .20 .06
19 Carlos Pena .20 .06
20 David Justice .20 .06
21 Jeremy Giambi .20 .06
22 Shannon Stewart .20 .06
23 Raul Mondesi .20 .06
24 Chris Carpenter .20 .06
25 Carlos Delgado .20 .06
26 Mike Sirotka .20 .06
27 Reed Johnson RC .50 .15
28 Darrin Fletcher .20 .06
29 Jose Cruz Jr. .20 .06
30 Vernon Wells .20 .06
31 Tanyon Sturtze .20 .06
32 Toby Hall .20 .06
33 Brent Abernathy .20 .06
34 Ben Grieve .20 .06
35 Joe Kennedy .20 .06
36 Dewon Brazelton .20 .06
37 Aubrey Huff .20 .06
38 Steve Cox .20 .06
39 Greg Vaughn .20 .06
40 Brady Anderson .20 .06
41 Chuck Finley .20 .06
42 Jim Thome .50 .15
43 Russell Branyan .20 .06
44 C.C. Sabathia .20 .06
45 Matt Lawton .20 .06
46 Omar Vizquel .30 .09
47 Bartolo Colon .20 .06
48 Alex Escobar .20 .06
49 Ellis Burks .20 .06
50 Bret Boone .20 .06
51 John Olerud .20 .06
52 Jeff Cirillo .20 .06
53 Ichiro Suzuki .75 .23
54 Kazuhiro Sasaki .20 .06
55 Freddy Garcia .20 .06
56 Edgar Martinez .30 .09
57 Matt Thornton RC .50 .15
58 Mike Cameron .20 .06
59 Carlos Guillen .20 .06
60 Jeff Conine .20 .06
61 Tony Batista .20 .06
62 Jason Johnson .20 .06
63 Melvin Mora .20 .06
64 Brian Roberts .20 .06
65 Josh Towers .20 .06
66 Steve Bechler RC .50 .15
67 Jerry Hairston Jr. .20 .06
68 Chris Richard .20 .06
69 Alex Rodriguez .75 .23
70 Chan Ho Park .20 .06
71 Ivan Rodriguez .50 .15
72 Jeff Zimmerman .20 .06
73 Mark Teixeira .30 .09
74 Gabe Kapler .20 .06
75 Frank Catalanotto .20 .06
76 Rafael Palmeiro .30 .09
77 Doug Davis .20 .06
78 Carl Everett .20 .06
79 Pedro Martinez .50 .15
80 Nomar Garciaparra .75 .23
81 Tony Clark .20 .06
82 Trot Nixon .20 .06
83 Manny Ramirez .30 .09
84 Josh Hancock RC .50 .15
85 Johnny Damon Sox .50 .15
86 Jose Offerman .20 .06
87 Rich Garces .20 .06
88 Shea Hillenbrand .20 .06
89 Carlos Beltran .30 .09
90 Mike Sweeney .20 .06
91 Jeff Suppan .20 .06
92 Joe Randa .20 .06
93 Chuck Knoblauch .20 .06
94 Mark Quinn .20 .06
95 Neifi Perez .20 .06
96 Carlos Febles .20 .06
97 Miguel Asencio RC .50 .15
98 Michael Tucker .20 .06
99 Dean Palmer .20 .06
100 Jose Lima .20 .06
101 Craig Paquette .20 .06
102 Dmitri Young .20 .06
103 Bobby Higginson .20 .06
104 Jeff Weaver .20 .06
105 Matt Anderson .20 .06
106 Damion Easley .20 .06
107 Eric Milton .20 .06
108 Doug Mientkiewicz .20 .06
109 Cristian Guzman .20 .06
110 Brad Radke .20 .06
111 Torii Hunter .20 .06
112 Corey Koskie .20 .06
113 Joe Mays .20 .06
114 Jacque Jones .20 .06
115 David Ortiz .30 .09
116 Kevin Frederick RC .50 .15
117 Magglio Ordonez .20 .06
118 Ray Durham .20 .06
119 Mark Buehrle .20 .06
120 Jon Garland .20 .06
121 Paul Konerko .20 .06
122 Todd Ritchie .20 .06
123 Frank Thomas .50 .15
124 Edwin Almonte RC .50 .15
125 Carlos Lee .20 .06
126 Kenny Lofton .20 .06
127 Roger Clemens 1.00 .30
128 Derek Jeter 1.25 .35
129 Jorge Posada .30 .09
130 Bernie Williams .30 .09
131 Mike Mussina .30 .09
132 Alfonso Soriano .30 .09
133 Robin Ventura .20 .06
134 John Vander Wal .20 .06
135 Jason Giambi Yankees .20 .06
136 Mariano Rivera .30 .09
137 Rondell White .20 .06
138 Jeff Bagwell .30 .09
139 Wade Miller .20 .06
140 Richard Hidalgo .20 .06
141 Julio Lugo .20 .06
142 Roy Oswalt .20 .06
143 Rodrigo Rosario RC .50 .15
144 Lance Berkman .20 .06
145 Craig Biggio .30 .09
146 Shane Reynolds .20 .06
147 John Smoltz .30 .09
148 Chipper Jones .50 .15
149 Gary Sheffield .20 .06
150 Rafael Furcal .20 .06
151 Greg Maddux .75 .23
152 Tom Glavine .30 .09
153 Andruw Jones .20 .06
154 John Ennis RC .50 .15
155 Vinny Castilla .20 .06
156 Marcus Giles .20 .06
157 Javy Lopez .20 .06
158 Richie Sexson .20 .06
159 Geoff Jenkins .20 .06
160 Jeffrey Hammonds .20 .06
161 Alex Ochoa .20 .06
162 Ben Sheets .20 .06
163 Jose Hernandez .20 .06
164 Eric Young .20 .06
165 Luis Martinez RC .50 .15
166 Albert Pujols 1.00 .30
167 Darryl Kile .20 .06
168 So Taguchi RC .50 .15
169 Jim Edmonds .20 .06
170 Fernando Vina .20 .06
171 Matt Morris .20 .06
172 J.D. Drew .20 .06
173 Bud Smith .20 .06
174 Edgar Renteria .20 .06
175 Placido Polanco .20 .06
176 Tino Martinez .30 .09
177 Sammy Sosa .75 .23
178 Moises Alou .20 .06
179 Kerry Wood .50 .15
180 Delino DeShields .20 .06
181 Alex Gonzalez .20 .06
182 Jon Lieber .20 .06
183 Fred McGriff .30 .09
184 Corey Patterson .20 .06
185 Mark Prior .75 .23
186 Tom Gordon .20 .06
187 Francis Beltran RC .50 .15
188 Randy Johnson .50 .15
189 Luis Gonzalez .20 .06
190 Matt Williams .20 .06
191 Mark Grace .30 .09
192 Curt Schilling .20 .06
193 Doug Devore RC .50 .15
194 Erubiel Durazo .20 .06
195 Steve Finley .20 .06
196 Craig Counsell .20 .06
197 Shawn Green .20 .06
198 Kevin Brown .20 .06
199 Paul LoDuca .20 .06
200 Brian Jordan .20 .06
201 Andy Ashby .20 .06
202 Darren Dreifort .20 .06
203 Adrian Beltre .30 .09
204 Victor Alvarez RC .50 .15
205 Eric Karros .20 .06
206 Hideo Nomo .50 .15
207 Vladimir Guerrero .50 .15
208 Javier Vazquez .20 .06
209 Michael Barrett .20 .06
210 Jose Vidro .20 .06
211 Brad Wilkerson .20 .06
212 Tony Armas Jr. .20 .06
213 Eric Good RC .50 .15
214 Orlando Cabrera .20 .06
215 Lee Stevens .20 .06
216 Jeff Kent .20 .06
217 Rich Aurilia .20 .06
218 Robb Nen .20 .06
219 Calvin Murray .20 .06
220 Russ Ortiz .20 .06
221 Deivis Santos .20 .06
222 Marvin Benard .20 .06
223 Jason Schmidt .20 .06
224 Reggie Sanders .20 .06
225 Barry Bonds 1.25 .35
226 Brad Penny .20 .06
227 Cliff Floyd .20 .06
228 Mike Lowell .20 .06
229 Derrek Lee .20 .06
230 Ryan Dempster .20 .06
231 Josh Beckett .20 .06
232 Hansel Izquierdo RC .50 .15
233 Preston Wilson .20 .06
234 A.J. Burnett .20 .06
235 Charles Johnson .20 .06
236 Mike Piazza .75 .23
237 Al Leiter .20 .06
238 Jay Payton .20 .06
239 Roger Cedeno .20 .06
240 Jeromy Burnitz .20 .06
241 Roberto Alomar .30 .09
242 Mo Vaughn .20 .06
243 Shawn Estes .20 .06
244 Armando Benitez .20 .06
245 Tyler Yates RC .50 .15
246 Phil Nevin .20 .06
247 D'Angelo Jimenez .20 .06
248 Ramon Vazquez .20 .06
249 Bubba Trammell .20 .06
250 Trevor Hoffman .20 .06
251 Ben Howard RC .50 .15
252 Mark Kotsay .20 .06
253 Ray Lankford .20 .06
254 Ryan Klesko .20 .06
255 Scott Rolen .50 .15
256 Robert Person .20 .06
257 Jimmy Rollins .20 .06
258 Pat Burrell .20 .06
259 Anderson Machado RC .50 .15
260 Randy Wolf .20 .06
261 Travis Lee .20 .06
262 Mike Lieberthal .20 .06
263 Doug Glanville .20 .06
264 Bobby Abreu .20 .06
265 Brian Giles .20 .06
266 Kris Benson .20 .06
267 Aramis Ramirez .20 .06
268 Kevin Young .20 .06
269 Jack Wilson .20 .06
270 Mike Williams .20 .06
271 Jimmy Anderson .20 .06
272 Jason Kendall .20 .06
273 Pokey Reese .20 .06
274 Rob Mackowiak .20 .06
275 Sean Casey .20 .06
276 Juan Encarnacion .20 .06
277 Austin Kearns .20 .06
278 Danny Graves .20 .06
279 Ken Griffey Jr. .75 .23
280 Barry Larkin .30 .09
281 Todd Walker .20 .06
282 Elmer Dessens .20 .06
283 Aaron Boone .20 .06
284 Adam Dunn .30 .09
285 Larry Walker .30 .09
286 Rene Reyes RC .50 .15
287 Juan Uribe .20 .06
288 Mike Hampton .20 .06
289 Todd Helton .30 .09
290 Juan Pierre .20 .06
291 Denny Neagle .20 .06
292 Jose Ortiz .20 .06
293 Todd Zeile .20 .06
294 Ben Petrick .20 .06
295 Ken Griffey Jr. CL .50 .15
296 Derek Jeter CL .60 .18
297 Sammy Sosa CL .50 .15
298 Ichiro Suzuki CL .50 .15
299 Barry Bonds CL .50 .15
300 Alex Rodriguez CL .50 .15
301 Kazuhisa Ishii RC 3.00 .90

2002 Upper Deck MVP Silver

Inserted randomly into hobby and retail packs, these cards parallel the regular MVP set and have a stated print run of 100 serial numbered sets.

Nm-Mt Ex-Mt
*SILVER STARS: 12.5X TO 30X BASIC CARDS
*SILVER ROOKIES: 6X TO 15X BASIC

2002 Upper Deck MVP Game Souvenirs Bat

Issued exclusively in hobby packs at stated odds of one in 144, these 27 cards feature bat chips from the featured players. A few players were issued to lesser quantities and we have notated that stated print run information in our checklist.

Nm-Mt Ex-Mt
B-AR Alex Rodriguez 25.00 7.50
B-BG Brian Giles 15.00 4.50
B-BW Bernie Williams 20.00 6.00
B-CD Carlos Delgado
B-DJ David Justice
B-DM Doug Mientkiewicz 15.00 4.50
B-EM Edgar Martinez 20.00 6.00
B-FT Frank Thomas SP/97
B-GM Greg Maddux
B-GS Gary Sheffield
B-GV Greg Vaughn 15.00 4.50
B-IR Ivan Rodriguez 20.00 6.00
B-JK Jeff Kent 15.00 4.50
B-JT Jim Thome 20.00 6.00
B-KG Ken Griffey Jr. 25.00 7.50
B-LG Luis Gonzalez 15.00 4.50
B-LW Larry Walker 20.00 6.00
B-MO Magglio Ordonez 15.00 4.50
B-MP Mike Piazza SP/97
B-MS Mike Sweeney
B-RA Roberto Alomar
B-RK Ryan Klesko 15.00 4.50
B-RP Rafael Palmeiro SP/97
B-SG Shawn Green 15.00 4.50
B-SR Scott Rolen
B-SS Sammy Sosa 25.00 7.50
B-TH Todd Helton

2002 Upper Deck MVP Game Souvenirs Bat Jersey Combos

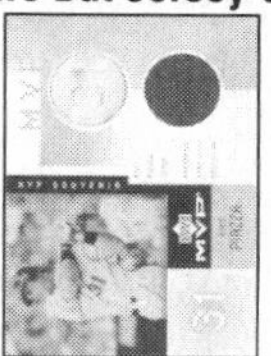

Inserted exclusively in hobby packs at stated odds of one in 144, these 28 cards feature both a bat chip and a jersey swatch from the featured player. A few players were issued in smaller quantities and we have notated that information with the stated print run in our checklist.

Nm-Mt Ex-Mt
GOLD RANDOM INSERTS IN PACKS
GOLD PRINT RUN 25 SERIAL #'d SETS
NO GOLD PRICING DUE TO SCARCITY
C-AB Adrian Beltre 25.00 7.50
C-AR Alex Rodriguez 50.00 15.00
C-BG Brian Giles 20.00 6.00
C-BW Bernie Williams SP/97
C-CD Carlos Delgado w/Pants 20.00 6.00
C-CJ Chipper Jones 40.00 12.00
C-DE Darin Erstad 20.00 6.00
C-EA Edgardo Alfonzo 20.00 6.00
C-IR Ivan Rodriguez 40.00 12.00
C-JB Jeff Bagwell w/Pants
C-JG Jason Giambi 20.00 6.00
C-JK Jeff Kent 20.00 6.00
C-JT Jim Thome 40.00 12.00
C-KG Ken Griffey Jr. 50.00 15.00
C-LG Luis Gonzalez 20.00 6.00
C-MO Magglio Ordonez 20.00 6.00
C-MP Mike Piazza 50.00 15.00
C-OV Omar Vizquel w/Pants SP/97
C-PB Pat Burrell SP/97
C-RA Roberto Alomar w/Pants
C-RJ Randy Johnson 40.00 12.00
C-RP Rafael Palmeiro 25.00 7.50
C-RV Robin Ventura 20.00 6.00
C-SG Shawn Green 20.00 6.00
C-SR Scott Rolen 40.00 12.00
C-SS Sammy Sosa 50.00 15.00
C-TH Todd Helton 25.00 7.50
C-TZ Todd Zeile 20.00 6.00

2002 Upper Deck MVP Game Souvenirs Jersey

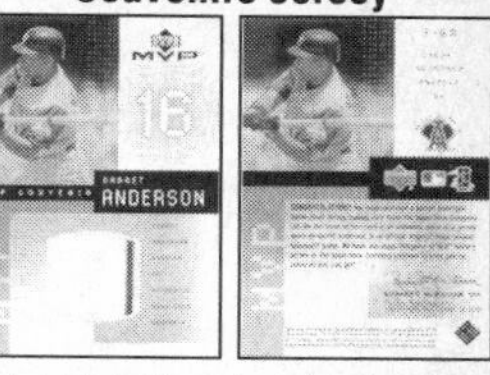

Inserted into hobby and retail packs at stated odds of one in 48, these 29 cards feature jersey swatches from the featured player. A few cards were printed in smaller quantity and we have notated those with an SP in our checklist. In addition, a few players appeared to be in larger supply and we have notated that information with an asterisk in our checklist.

Nm-Mt Ex-Mt
J-AB Adrian Beltre 15.00 4.50
J-AR Alex Rodriguez 15.00 4.50
J-CD Carlos Delgado Pants 10.00 3.00
J-DE Darin Erstad 10.00 3.00
J-EM Edgar Martinez 15.00 4.50
J-FT Frank Thomas 15.00 4.50
J-GA Garret Anderson 10.00 3.00
J-IR Ivan Rodriguez 15.00 4.50
J-JB Jeff Bagwell Pants 15.00 4.50
J-JB Jeromy Burnitz 10.00 3.00
J-JG Juan Gonzalez 15.00 4.50
J-JK Jeff Kent 10.00 3.00
J-JP Jay Payton SP 15.00 4.50
J-JT Jim Thome SP 25.00 7.50
J-KL Kenny Lofton 10.00 3.00
J-MK Mark Kotsay 10.00 3.00
J-MP Mike Piazza 15.00 4.50
J-OV Omar Vizquel Pants * 15.00 4.50
J-PK Paul Konerko SP 15.00 4.50
J-PW Preston Wilson 10.00 3.00
J-RA Roberto Alomar Pants 15.00 4.50
J-RC Roger Clemens 25.00 7.50
J-RF Rafael Furcal 10.00 3.00
J-RV Robin Ventura 10.00 3.00
J-SR Scott Rolen 15.00 4.50
J-THO Trevor Hoffman 10.00 3.00
J-THU Tim Hudson 10.00 3.00
J-TS Tim Salmon 15.00 4.50
J-TZ Todd Zeile 10.00 3.00

2002 Upper Deck MVP Ichiro A Season to Remember

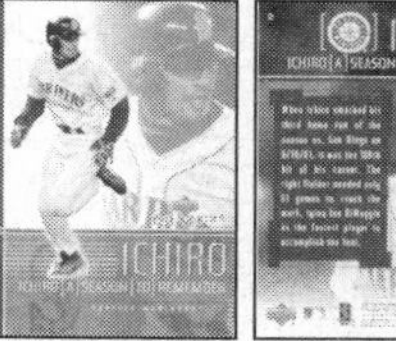

Inserted in hobby and retail packs at stated odds of one in 12, these 10 cards feature highlights from Ichiro's rookie season.

Nm-Mt Ex-Mt
COMPLETE SET (10) 30.00 9.00
COMMON CARD (I1-I10) 3.00 .90

2002 Upper Deck MVP Ichiro A Season to Remember Memorabilia

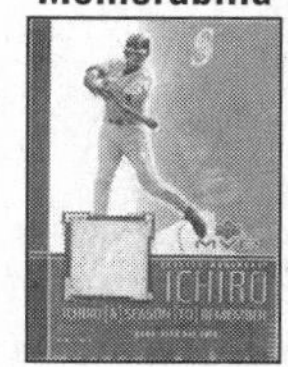

Randomly inserted in hobby and retail packs, these cards feature memorabilia pieces from Ichiro's rookie season. These cards are serial numbered to 25 and no pricing is available due to market scarcity.

Nm-Mt Ex-Mt
I-B Ichiro Suzuki Bat
I-J Ichiro Suzuki Jsy

2003 Upper Deck MVP

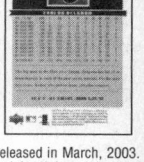

This 220 card set was released in March, 2003. These cards were issued in eight card packs which came 24 packs to a box and 12 boxes to a case. Cards numbered 219 and 220 are checklists featuring Upper Deck spokespeople. Cards numbered 221 through 330 were issued in special factory "tin" sets.

Nm-Mt Ex-Mt
COMP.FACT.SET (330) 40.00 12.00
COMPLETE LO SET (220) 25.00 7.50
COMMON CARD (1-330) .20 .06
1 Troy Glaus .20 .06
2 Darin Erstad .20 .06
3 Jarrod Washburn .20 .06
4 Francisco Rodriguez .20 .06
5 Garret Anderson .20 .06
6 Tim Salmon .30 .09
7 Adam Kennedy .20 .06
8 Randy Johnson .50 .15
9 Luis Gonzalez .20 .06
10 Curt Schilling .20 .06
11 Junior Spivey .20 .06
12 Craig Counsell .20 .06
13 Mark Grace .30 .09
14 Steve Finley .20 .06
15 Javy Lopez .20 .06
16 Rafael Furcal .20 .06
17 John Smoltz .30 .09
18 Greg Maddux .75 .23
19 Chipper Jones .50 .15
20 Gary Sheffield .20 .06
21 Andruw Jones .20 .06
22 Tony Batista .20 .06
23 Geronimo Gil .20 .06
24 Jay Gibbons .20 .06
25 Rodrigo Lopez .20 .06
26 Chris Singleton .20 .06
27 Melvin Mora .20 .06
28 Jeff Conine .20 .06
29 Nomar Garciaparra .75 .23
30 Pedro Martinez .50 .15
31 Manny Ramirez .30 .09
32 Shea Hillenbrand .20 .06
33 Johnny Damon .50 .15
34 Jason Varitek .30 .09
35 Derek Lowe .20 .06
36 Trot Nixon .20 .06
37 Sammy Sosa .75 .23
38 Kerry Wood .50 .15
39 Mark Prior .50 .15
40 Moises Alou .20 .06
41 Corey Patterson .20 .06
42 Hee Seop Choi .20 .06
43 Mark Bellhorn .20 .06
44 Frank Thomas .50 .15
45 Mark Buehrle .20 .06
46 Magglio Ordonez .20 .06
47 Carlos Lee .20 .06
48 Paul Konerko .20 .06
49 Joe Borchard .20 .06
50 Joe Crede .20 .06
51 Ken Griffey Jr. .75 .23
52 Adam Dunn .30 .09
53 Austin Kearns .20 .06
54 Aaron Boone .20 .06
55 Sean Casey .20 .06
56 Danny Graves .20 .06
57 Russell Branyan .20 .06
58 Matt Lawton .20 .06
59 C.C. Sabathia .20 .06
60 Omar Vizquel .30 .09
61 Brandon Phillips .20 .06
62 Karim Garcia .20 .06
63 Ellis Burks .20 .06
64 Cliff Lee .20 .06
65 Todd Helton .30 .09
66 Larry Walker .30 .09
67 Jay Payton .20 .06
68 Brent Butler .20 .06
69 Juan Uribe .20 .06
70 Jason Jennings .20 .06
71 Denny Stark .20 .06
72 Dmitri Young .20 .06
73 Carlos Pena .20 .06
74 Andres Torres .20 .06
75 Andy Van Hekken .20 .06
76 George Lombard .20 .06
77 Eric Munson .20 .06
78 Bobby Higginson .20 .06
79 Luis Castillo .20 .06
80 A.J. Burnett .20 .06
81 Juan Encarnacion .20 .06
82 Ivan Rodriguez .50 .15
83 Mike Lowell .20 .06
84 Josh Beckett .20 .06
85 Brad Penny .20 .06
86 Craig Biggio .30 .09
87 Jeff Kent .20 .06
88 Morgan Ensberg .20 .06
89 Daryle Ward .20 .06
90 Jeff Bagwell .30 .09
91 Roy Oswalt .20 .06
92 Lance Berkman .20 .06
93 Mike Sweeney .20 .06
94 Carlos Beltran .30 .09
95 Raul Ibanez .20 .06
96 Carlos Febles .20 .06
97 Joe Randa .20 .06
98 Shawn Green .20 .06
99 Kevin Brown .20 .06
100 Paul Lo Duca .20 .06
101 Adrian Beltre .30 .09
102 Eric Gagne .50 .15
103 Kazuhisa Ishii .20 .06
104 Odalis Perez .20 .06
105 Brian Jordan .20 .06
106 Geoff Jenkins .20 .06
107 Richie Sexson .20 .06
108 Ben Sheets .20 .06
109 Alex Sanchez .20 .06
110 Eric Young .20 .06
111 Jose Hernandez .20 .06
112 Torii Hunter .20 .06
113 Eric Milton .20 .06
114 Corey Koskie .20 .06
115 Doug Mientkiewicz .20 .06
116 A.J. Pierzynski .20 .06
117 Jacque Jones .20 .06
118 Cristian Guzman .20 .06
119 Bartolo Colon .20 .06
120 Brad Wilkerson .20 .06
121 Michael Barrett .20 .06
122 Vladimir Guerrero .50 .15
123 Jose Vidro .20 .06
124 Javier Vazquez .20 .06
125 Endy Chavez .20 .06
126 Roberto Alomar .30 .09
127 Mike Piazza .75 .23
128 Jeromy Burnitz .20 .06
129 Mo Vaughn .20 .06
130 Tom Glavine .30 .09
131 Al Leiter .20 .06
132 Armando Benitez .20 .06
133 Timo Perez .20 .06
134 Roger Clemens 1.00 .30
135 Derek Jeter 1.25 .35
136 Jason Giambi .20 .06
137 Alfonso Soriano .20 .06
138 Bernie Williams .30 .09
139 Mike Mussina .30 .09
140 Jorge Posada .30 .09
141 Hideki Matsui RC 4.00 1.20
142 Robin Ventura .20 .06
143 David Wells .20 .06
144 Nick Johnson .20 .06
145 Tim Hudson .20 .06
146 Eric Chavez .20 .06
147 Barry Zito .20 .06
148 Miguel Tejada .20 .06
149 Jermaine Dye .20 .06
150 Mark Mulder .20 .06
151 Terrence Long .20 .06
152 Scott Hatteberg .20 .06
153 Marlon Byrd .20 .06
154 Jim Thome .50 .15
155 Marlon Anderson .20 .06
156 Vicente Padilla .20 .06
157 Bobby Abreu .20 .06
158 Jimmy Rollins .20 .06
159 Pat Burrell .20 .06
160 Brian Giles .20 .06
161 Aramis Ramirez .20 .06
162 Jason Kendall .20 .06
163 Josh Fogg .20 .06
164 Kip Wells .20 .06
165 Pokey Reese .20 .06
166 Kris Benson .20 .06
167 Ryan Klesko .20 .06
168 Brian Lawrence .20 .06
169 Mark Kotsay .20 .06
170 Jake Peavy .20 .06
171 Phil Nevin .20 .06
172 Sean Burroughs .20 .06
173 Trevor Hoffman .20 .06
174 Jason Schmidt .20 .06
175 Kirk Rueter .20 .06
176 Barry Bonds 1.25 .35
177 Pedro Feliz .20 .06
178 Rich Aurilia .20 .06
179 Benito Santiago .20 .06
180 J.T. Snow .20 .06
181 Robb Nen .20 .06
182 Ichiro Suzuki .75 .23
183 Edgar Martinez .30 .09
184 Bret Boone .20 .06
185 Freddy Garcia .20 .06
186 John Olerud .20 .06
187 Mike Cameron .20 .06
188 Joel Piniero .20 .06
189 Albert Pujols 1.00 .30
190 Matt Morris .30 .09
191 J.D. Drew .20 .06
192 Scott Rolen .50 .15
193 Tino Martinez .30 .09
194 Jim Edmonds .20 .06
195 Edgar Renteria .20 .06
196 Fernando Vina .20 .06
197 Jason Isringhausen .20 .06
198 Ben Grieve .20 .06
199 Carl Crawford .20 .06
200 Dewon Brazelton .20 .06
201 Aubrey Huff .20 .06
202 Jared Sandberg .20 .06
203 Steve Cox .20 .06
204 Carl Everett .20 .06
205 Kevin Mench .20 .06
206 Alex Rodriguez .75 .23
207 Rafael Palmeiro .30 .09
208 Michael Young .30 .09
209 Hank Blalock .30 .09
210 Juan Gonzalez .30 .09
211 Carlos Delgado .20 .06
212 Eric Hinske .20 .06
213 Josh Phelps .20 .06
214 Mark Hendrickson .20 .06
215 Roy Halladay .20 .06
216 Orlando Hudson .20 .06
217 Shannon Stewart .20 .06
218 Vernon Wells .20 .06
219 Ichiro Suzuki CL .50 .15
220 Jason Giambi CL .20 .06
221 Scott Spiezio .20 .06
222 Rich Fischer RC .40 .12
223 Bengie Molina .20 .06
224 David Eckstein .20 .06
225 Brandon Webb RC 1.00 .30
226 Oscar Villarreal RC .40 .12
227 Rob Hammock RC .50 .15
228 Matt Kata RC .75 .23
229 Lyle Overbay .20 .06
230 Chris Capuano RC .40 .12
231 Horacio Ramirez .20 .06
232 Shane Reynolds .20 .06
233 Russ Ortiz .20 .06
234 Mike Hampton .20 .06
235 Mike Hessman RC .40 .12
236 Byung-Hyun Kim .20 .06
237 Freddy Sanchez .20 .06
238 Jason Shiell RC .40 .12
239 Ryan Cameron RC .40 .12
240 Todd Wellemeyer RC .50 .15
241 Joe Borowski .20 .06
242 Alex Gonzalez .20 .06
243 Jon Leicester RC .40 .12
244 David Sanders RC .40 .12
245 Roberto Alomar .20 .06
246 Barry Larkin .30 .09
247 Jhonny Peralta .20 .06
248 Zach Sorensen .20 .06
249 Jason Davis .20 .06
250 Coco Crisp .20 .06
251 Greg Vaughn .20 .06
252 Preston Wilson .20 .06
253 Denny Neagle .20 .06
254 Clint Barmes RC .50 .15
255 Jeremy Bonderman RC .75 .23
256 Wilfredo Ledezma RC .50 .15
257 Dontrelle Willis .30 .09
258 Alex Gonzalez .20 .06
259 Tommy Phelps .20 .06
260 Kirk Saarloos .20 .06
261 Colin Porter RC .40 .12
262 Nate Bland RC .40 .12
263 Jason Gilfillan RC .40 .12
264 Mike MacDougal .20 .06
265 Ken Harvey .20 .06
266 Brent Mayne .20 .06
267 Miguel Cabrera .50 .15
268 Hideo Nomo .50 .15
269 Dave Roberts .20 .06
270 Fred McGriff .30 .09
271 Joe Thurston .20 .06
272 Royce Clayton .20 .06
273 Michael Nakamura RC .40 .12
274 Brad Radke .20 .06
275 Joe Mays .20 .06
276 Lew Ford RC 1.25 .35
277 Michael Cuddyer .20 .06
278 Luis Ayala RC .40 .12
279 Julio Manon RC .25 .07
280 Anthony Ferrari RC .40 .12
281 Livan Hernandez .20 .06
282 Jae Weong Seo .20 .06
283 Jose Reyes .20 .06
284 Tony Clark .20 .06
285 Ty Wigginton .20 .06
286 Cliff Floyd .20 .06
287 Jeremy Griffiths RC .50 .15
288 Jason Roach RC .40 .12
289 Jeff Duncan RC .50 .15
290 Phil Seibel RC .40 .12
291 Prentice Redman RC .40 .12
292 Jose Contreras RC 1.00 .30
293 Ruben Sierra .20 .06
294 Andy Pettitte .30 .09
295 Aaron Boone .20 .06
296 Mariano Rivera .30 .09
297 Michel Hernandez RC .40 .12
298 Mike Neu RC .40 .12
299 Erubiel Durazo .20 .06
300 Billy McMillon .20 .06
301 Rich Harden .30 .09
302 David Bell .20 .06
303 Kevin Millwood .20 .06
304 Mike Lieberthal .20 .06
305 Jeremy Wedel RC .40 .12
306 Kenny Lofton .20 .06
307 Reggie Sanders .20 .06
308 Randall Simon .20 .06
309 Xavier Nady .20 .06
310 Rod Beck .20 .06
311 Miguel Ojeda RC .40 .12
312 Mark Loretta .20 .06
313 Edgardo Alfonzo .20 .06
314 Andres Galarraga .20 .06
315 Jose Cruz Jr. .20 .06
316 Jesse Foppert .20 .06
317 Kurt Ainsworth .20 .06
318 Dan Wilson .20 .06
319 Ben Davis .20 .06
320 Rocco Baldelli .20 .06
321 Al Martin .20 .06
322 Runelvys Hernandez .20 .06
323 Dan Haren RC .75 .23
324 Bo Hart RC .50 .15
325 Einar Diaz .20 .06
326 Mike Lamb .20 .06
327 Aquilino Lopez RC .40 .12
328 Reed Johnson .20 .06
329 Diegomar Markwell RC .40 .12
330 Hideki Matsui CL 1.50 .45

2003 Upper Deck MVP Black

Randomly inserted in packs, this is a parallel to the Upper Deck MVP low number set. These cards were issued to a stated print run of 50 serial numbered sets.

Nm-Mt Ex-Mt
*BLACK: 15X TO 40X BASIC

2003 Upper Deck MVP Gold

Randomly inserted in packs, this is a parallel to the MVP low number set. These cards were issued to a stated print run of 125 serial numbered sets.

Nm-Mt Ex-Mt
*GOLD: 10X TO 25X BASIC
*GOLD RC'S: 2.5X TO 6X BASIC

2003 Upper Deck MVP Silver

These cards, which parallel the MVP low number set, were actually inserted at a stated rate of one in 12. This is different from the stated wrapper odds which said these cards were inserted at a rate of one in two.

Nm-Mt Ex-Mt
*SILVER: 3X TO 8X BASIC
*SILVER RC'S: .75X TO 2X BASIC

2003 Upper Deck MVP Base-to-Base

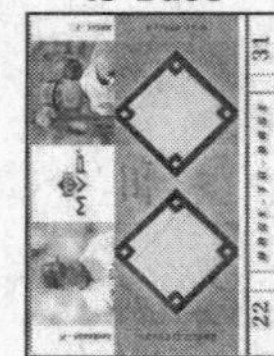

Issued at a stated rate of one in 488, these six cards feature two players as well as bases used in one of their games.

Nm-Mt Ex-Mt
CP Roger Clemens 25.00 7.50
Mike Piazza
IG Ichiro Suzuki 40.00 12.00
Ken Griffey Jr.
IJ Ichiro Suzuki 50.00 15.00
Derek Jeter
JW Derek Jeter 25.00 7.50
Bernie Williams
MB Mark McGwire 60.00 18.00
Barry Bonds
RJ Alex Rodriguez 40.00 12.00
Derek Jeter

2003 Upper Deck MVP Celebration

Randomly inserted into packs, these 90 cards honor various players leading achievements in baseball. Each of these cards were issued to a stated print run of between 1955 and 2002 cards and we have notated the print run information next to the player's name in our checklist.

Nm-Mt Ex-Mt
*GOLD: 1.25X TO 3X BASIC
GOLD PRINT RUN 75 SERIAL #'d SETS
1 Yogi Berra MVP/1955 4.00 1.20
2 Mickey Mantle MVP/1956 15.00 4.50
3 Mickey Mantle MVP/1957 15.00 4.50
4 Mickey Mantle MVP/1962 15.00 4.50
5 Roger Clemens MVP/1986 8.00 2.40
6 Rickey Henderson MVP/1990 4.00 1.20
7 Frank Thomas MVP/1993 4.00 1.20
8 Mo Vaughn MVP/1995 3.00 .90
9 Juan Gonzalez MVP/1996 3.00 .90
10 Ken Griffey Jr. MVP/1997 6.00 1.80
11 Juan Gonzalez MVP/1998 3.00 .90
12 Ivan Rodriguez MVP/1998 4.00 1.20
13 Jason Giambi MVP/2000 3.00 .90
14 Ichiro Suzuki MVP/2001 6.00 1.80
15 Miguel Tejada MVP/2002 3.00 .90
16 Barry Bonds MVP/1990 10.00 3.00
17 Barry Bonds MVP/1992 10.00 3.00
18 Barry Bonds MVP/1993 10.00 3.00
19 Jeff Bagwell MVP/1994 3.00 .90
20 Barry Larkin MVP/1995 3.00 .90
21 Larry Walker MVP/1997 3.00 .90
22 Sammy Sosa MVP/1998 6.00 1.80
23 Chipper Jones MVP/1999 4.00 1.20
24 Jeff Kent MVP/2000 3.00 .90
25 Barry Bonds MVP/2001 10.00 3.00
26 Barry Bonds MVP/2002 10.00 3.00
27 Ken Griffey Sr. AS/1980 3.00 .90
28 Roger Clemens AS/1986 8.00 2.40
29 Ken Griffey Jr. AS/1992 6.00 1.80
30 Fred McGriff AS/1994 3.00 .90
31 Jeff Conine AS/1995 3.00 .90
32 Mike Piazza AS/1996 6.00 1.80
33 Sandy Alomar Jr. AS/1997 3.00 .90
34 Roberto Alomar AS/1998 3.00 .90
35 Pedro Martinez AS/1999 4.00 1.20
36 Derek Jeter AS/2000 10.00 3.00
37 Rickey Henderson ALCS/1989 4.00 1.20
38 Roberto Alomar ALCS/1992 3.00 .90
39 Bernie Williams ALCS/1996 3.00 .90
40 Marquis Grissom ALCS/1997 3.00 .90
41 David Wells ALCS/1998 3.00 .90
42 Orlando Hernandez ALCS/1999 3.00 .90
43 David Justice ALCS/2000 3.00 .90
44 Andy Pettitte ALCS/2001 3.00 .90
45 Adam Kennedy ALCS/2002 3.00 .90
46 John Smoltz NLCS/1992 3.00 .90
47 Curt Schilling NLCS/1993 3.00 .90
48 Javy Lopez NLCS/1996 3.00 .90
49 Livan Hernandez NLCS/1997 3.00 .90
50 Sterling Hitchcock NLCS/1998 3.00 .90
51 Mike Hampton NLCS/2000 3.00 .90
52 Craig Counsell NLCS/2001 3.00 .90
53 Benito Santiago NLCS/2002 3.00 .90
54 Tom Glavine WS/1995 3.00 .90
55 Livan Hernandez WS/1997 3.00 .90
56 Mariano Rivera WS/1999 3.00 .90
57 Derek Jeter WS/2000 10.00 3.00
58 Randy Johnson WS/2001 4.00 1.20
59 Curt Schilling WS/2001 3.00 .90
60 Troy Glaus WS/2002 3.00 .90
61 Yogi Berra MM/1951 4.00 1.20
62 Yogi Berra MM/1955 4.00 1.20
63 Mickey Mantle MM/1956 15.00 4.50
64 Mickey Mantle MM/1957 15.00 4.50
65 Ken Griffey Sr. MM/1980 3.00 .90
66 Rickey Henderson MM/1989 4.00 1.20
67 Roberto Alomar MM/1992 3.00 .90
68 Bernie Williams MM/1996 3.00 .90
69 Livan Hernandez MM/1997 3.00 .90
70 Sammy Sosa MM/1998 6.00 1.80
71 Sterling Hitchcock MM/1998 3.00 .90
72 David Wells MM/1998 3.00 .90
73 Mariano Rivera MM/1999 3.00 .90
74 Chipper Jones MM/1999 4.00 1.20
75 Ivan Rodriguez MM/1999 4.00 1.20
76 Derek Jeter MM/2000 10.00 3.00
77 Jason Giambi MM/2000 3.00 .90
78 Jeff Kent MM/2000 3.00 .90
79 Mike Hampton MM/2000 3.00 .90
80 Randy Johnson MM/2001 4.00 1.20
81 Curt Schilling MM/2001 3.00 .90
82 Barry Bonds MM/2001 10.00 3.00
83 Ichiro Suzuki MM/2001 6.00 1.80
84 Ichiro Suzuki MM/2001 6.00 1.80
85 Adam Kennedy MM/2002 3.00 .90
86 Benito Santiago MM/2002 3.00 .90
87 Troy Glaus MM/2002 3.00 .90
88 Troy Glaus MM/2002 3.00 .90
89 Miguel Tejada MM/2002 3.00 .90
90 Barry Bonds MM/2002 10.00 3.00

2003 Upper Deck MVP Covering the Bases

Issued at a stated rate of one in 125, these 15 cards feature game-used bases from the featured player's career.

Nm-Mt Ex-Mt
AR Alex Rodriguez 15.00 4.50
BB Barry Bonds 20.00 6.00
CD Carlos Delgado 8.00 2.40
DE Darin Erstad 8.00 2.40
DJ Derek Jeter 20.00 6.00
FT Frank Thomas 10.00 3.00
IR Ivan Rodriguez 10.00 3.00
IS Ichiro Suzuki 20.00 6.00
JD J.D. Drew 8.00 2.40
JT Jim Thome 10.00 3.00
LG Luis Gonzalez 8.00 2.40
MP Mike Piazza 15.00 4.50
MT Miguel Tejada 8.00 2.40
SG Shawn Green 8.00 2.40
TG Troy Glaus 8.00 2.40

2003 Upper Deck MVP Covering the Plate Game Bat

Issued at a stated rate of one in 160, these six cards feature game-used bat pieces from the featured player.

Nm-Mt Ex-Mt
FM Fred McGriff 15.00 4.50
JT Jim Thome 15.00 4.50
MG Mark McGwire 60.00 18.00
RA Roberto Alomar 15.00 4.50
RF Rafael Furcal 10.00 3.00
VG Vladimir Guerrero 15.00 4.50

2003 Upper Deck MVP Dual Aces Game Base

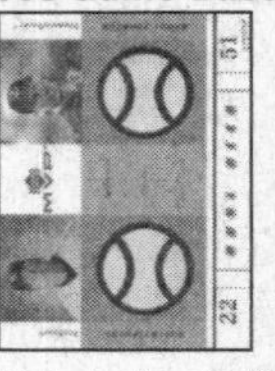

Issued at a stated rate of one in 488, these six cards feature bases used in games featuring two key pitchers.

Nm-Mt Ex-Mt
BS Kevin Brown 10.00 3.00
Curt Schilling
CJ Roger Clemens 20.00 6.00
Randy Johnson
CL Roger Clemens 15.00 4.50
Al Leiter
ML Matt Morris 10.00 3.00
Al Leiter
SJ Curt Schilling 10.00 3.00
Randy Johnson
SP Curt Schilling 10.00 3.00
Andy Pettitte

2003 Upper Deck MVP Express Delivery

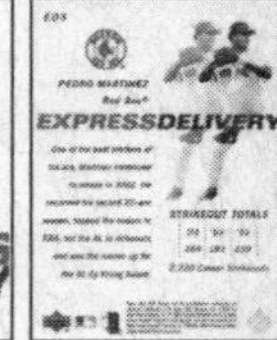

Inserted at a stated rate of one in 12, these 15 cards feature players who are among the leading pitchers in baseball.

Nm-Mt Ex-Mt
ED1 Randy Johnson 2.00 .60
ED2 Curt Schilling 1.50 .45
ED3 Pedro Martinez 2.00 .60
ED4 Kerry Wood 2.00 .60
ED5 Mark Prior 2.00 .60
ED6 A.J. Burnett 1.50 .45
ED7 Josh Beckett 1.50 .45
ED8 Roy Oswalt 1.50 .45
ED9 Hideo Nomo 2.00 .60
ED10 Ben Sheets 1.50 .45
ED11 Bartolo Colon 1.50 .45
ED12 Roger Clemens 4.00 1.20
ED13 Mike Mussina 1.50 .45
ED14 Tim Hudson 1.50 .45
ED15 Matt Morris 1.50 .45

2003 Upper Deck MVP Pro Sign

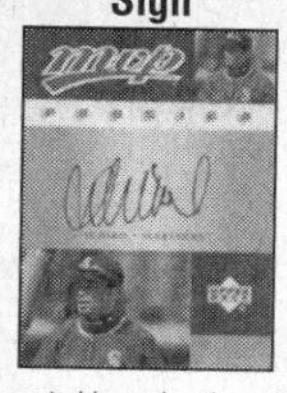

Randomly inserted in packs, these 23 cards feature authentic autographs from the featured players. Each of these cards are printed to a stated print run of 25 serial numbered sets and no pricing is provided due to market scarcity.

	Nm-Mt	Ex-Mt
AD Adam Dunn		
AK Austin Kearns		
BG Brian Giles		
BZ Barry Zito		
CD Carlos Delgado		
DH Drew Henson		
DM Doug Mientkiewicz		
FG Freddy Garcia		
GI Jay Gibbons		
HB Hank Blalock		
IS Ichiro Suzuki		
JD Johnny Damon		
JG Jason Giambi		
KG Ken Griffey Jr.		
LB Lance Berkman		
MM Mark McGwire		
MP Mark Prior		
MS Mike Sweeney		
RS Richie Sexson		
SB Sean Burroughs		
SS Sammy Sosa		
TG Tony Gwynn		
TH Tim Hudson		

2003 Upper Deck MVP Pro View

Issued as a two-card box topper pack, these 45 cards are a special hologram set.

	Nm-Mt	Ex-Mt
*GOLD: .75X TO 2X BASIC PRO VIEW		
ONE 2-CARD PACK PER 6 SEALED BOXES		
PV1 Troy Glaus	3.00	.90
PV2 Darin Erstad	3.00	.90
PV3 Randy Johnson	4.00	1.20
PV4 Curt Schilling	3.00	.90
PV5 Luis Gonzalez	3.00	.90
PV6 Chipper Jones	4.00	1.20
PV7 Andruw Jones	3.00	.90
PV8 Greg Maddux	6.00	1.80
PV9 Pedro Martinez	4.00	1.20
PV10 Manny Ramirez	3.00	.90
PV11 Sammy Sosa	6.00	1.80
PV12 Mark Prior	4.00	1.20
PV13 Magglio Ordonez	3.00	.90
PV14 Frank Thomas	4.00	1.20
PV15 Ken Griffey Jr.	6.00	1.80
PV16 Adam Dunn	3.00	.90
PV17 Jim Thome	4.00	1.20
PV18 Todd Helton	3.00	.90
PV19 Jeff Bagwell	3.00	.90
PV20 Lance Berkman	3.00	.90
PV21 Shawn Green	3.00	.90
PV22 Hideo Nomo	4.00	1.20
PV23 Vladimir Guerrero	4.00	1.20
PV24 Roberto Alomar	3.00	.90
PV25 Mike Piazza	6.00	1.80
PV26 Jason Giambi	3.00	.90
PV27 Roger Clemens	8.00	2.40
PV28 Alfonso Soriano	3.00	.90
PV29 Derek Jeter	10.00	3.00
PV30 Miguel Tejada	3.00	.90
PV31 Eric Chavez	3.00	.90
PV32 Barry Zito	3.00	.90
PV33 Pat Burrell	3.00	.90
PV34 Brian Giles	3.00	.90
PV35 Barry Bonds	10.00	3.00
PV36 Ichiro Suzuki	6.00	1.80
PV37 Albert Pujols	8.00	2.40
PV38 Scott Rolen	4.00	1.20
PV39 J.D. Drew	3.00	.90
PV40 Mark McGwire	10.00	3.00
PV41 Alex Rodriguez	6.00	1.80
PV42 Rafael Palmeiro	3.00	.90
PV43 Juan Gonzalez	3.00	.90
PV44 Eric Hinske	3.00	.90
PV45 Carlos Delgado	3.00	.90

2003 Upper Deck MVP SportsNut

Inserted at a stated rate of one in three, this 90 card insert set could be used as interactive game cards. The contest could be entered on either a season or a weekly basis.

	Nm-Mt	Ex-Mt
SN1 Troy Glaus	1.00	.30
SN2 Darin Erstad	1.00	.30
SN3 Luis Gonzalez	1.00	.30
SN4 Andruw Jones	1.00	.30
SN5 Chipper Jones	2.50	.75
SN6 Gary Sheffield	1.00	.30
SN7 Jay Gibbons	1.00	.30
SN8 Manny Ramirez	1.50	.45
SN9 Shea Hillenbrand	1.00	.30
SN10 Johnny Damon	2.50	.75
SN11 Nomar Garciaparra	4.00	1.20
SN12 Sammy Sosa	4.00	1.20
SN13 Magglio Ordonez	1.00	.30
SN14 Frank Thomas	2.50	.75
SN15 Ken Griffey Jr.	4.00	1.20
SN16 Adam Dunn	1.50	.45
SN17 Matt Lawton	1.00	.30
SN18 Larry Walker	1.50	.45
SN19 Todd Helton	1.50	.45
SN20 Carlos Pena	1.00	.30
SN21 Mike Lowell	1.00	.30
SN22 Jeff Bagwell	1.50	.45
SN23 Lance Berkman	1.00	.30
SN24 Mike Sweeney	1.00	.30
SN25 Carlos Beltran	1.50	.45
SN26 Shawn Green	1.00	.30
SN27 Richie Sexson	1.00	.30
SN28 Torii Hunter	1.00	.30
SN29 Jacque Jones	1.00	.30
SN30 Vladimir Guerrero	2.50	.75
SN31 Jose Vidro	1.00	.30
SN32 Roberto Alomar	1.50	.45
SN33 Mike Piazza	4.00	1.20
SN34 Alfonso Soriano	1.50	.45
SN35 Derek Jeter	6.00	1.80
SN36 Jason Giambi	1.00	.30
SN37 Bernie Williams	1.50	.45
SN38 Eric Chavez	1.00	.30
SN39 Miguel Tejada	1.00	.30
SN40 Jim Thome	2.50	.75
SN41 Pat Burrell	1.00	.30
SN42 Bobby Abreu	1.00	.30
SN43 Brian Giles	1.00	.30
SN44 Jason Kendall	1.00	.30
SN45 Ryan Klesko	1.00	.30
SN46 Phil Nevin	1.00	.30
SN47 Barry Bonds	6.00	1.80
SN48 Rich Aurilia	1.00	.30
SN49 Ichiro Suzuki	4.00	1.20
SN50 Bret Boone	1.00	.30
SN51 J.D. Drew	1.00	.30
SN52 Jim Edmonds	1.00	.30
SN53 Albert Pujols	5.00	1.50
SN54 Scott Rolen	2.50	.75
SN55 Ben Grieve	1.00	.30
SN56 Alex Rodriguez	4.00	1.20
SN57 Rafael Palmeiro	1.50	.45
SN58 Juan Gonzalez	1.50	.45
SN59 Carlos Delgado	1.00	.30
SN60 Josh Phelps	1.00	.30
SN61 Jarrod Washburn	1.00	.30
SN62 Randy Johnson	2.50	.75
SN63 Curt Schilling	1.00	.30
SN64 Greg Maddux	4.00	1.20
SN65 Mike Hampton	1.00	.30
SN66 Rodrigo Lopez	1.00	.30
SN67 Pedro Martinez	2.50	.75
SN68 Derek Lowe	1.00	.30
SN69 Mark Prior	2.50	.75
SN70 Kerry Wood	2.50	.75
SN71 Mark Buehrle	1.00	.30
SN72 Roy Oswalt	1.00	.30
SN73 Wade Miller	1.00	.30
SN74 Odalis Perez	1.00	.30
SN75 Hideo Nomo	2.50	.75
SN76 Ben Sheets	1.00	.30
SN77 Eric Milton	1.00	.30
SN78 Bartolo Colon	1.00	.30
SN79 Tom Glavine	1.50	.45
SN80 Al Leiter	1.00	.30
SN81 Roger Clemens	5.00	1.50
SN82 Mike Mussina	1.50	.45
SN83 Tim Hudson	1.00	.30
SN84 Barry Zito	1.00	.30
SN85 Mark Mulder	1.00	.30
SN86 Vicente Padilla	1.00	.30
SN87 Jason Schmidt	1.00	.30
SN88 Freddy Garcia	1.00	.30
SN89 Matt Morris	1.00	.30
SN90 Roy Halladay	1.00	.30

2003 Upper Deck MVP Talk of the Town

Inserted at a stated rate of one in 12, this 15 card set features some of the most talked about players in baseball.

	Nm-Mt	Ex-Mt
TT1 Hideki Matsui	5.00	1.50
TT2 Chipper Jones	2.00	.60
TT3 Manny Ramirez	1.50	.45
TT4 Sammy Sosa	3.00	.90
TT5 Ken Griffey Jr.	3.00	.90
TT6 Lance Berkman	1.50	.45
TT7 Shawn Green	1.50	.45
TT8 Vladimir Guerrero	2.00	.60
TT9 Mike Piazza	3.00	.90
TT10 Jason Giambi	1.50	.45
TT11 Alfonso Soriano	1.50	.45
TT12 Ichiro Suzuki	3.00	.90
TT13 Albert Pujols	4.00	1.20
TT14 Alex Rodriguez	3.00	.90
TT15 Eric Hinske	1.50	.45

2003 Upper Deck MVP Three Bagger Game Base

Inserted at a stated rate of one in 488, this six-card set features base pieces involving three players on each card.

	Nm-Mt	Ex-Mt
BMP Barry Bonds Mark McGwire Mike Piazza	100.00	30.00
GIB Ken Griffey Jr. Ichiro Suzuki Barry Bonds	80.00	24.00
GTD Troy Glaus Frank Thomas Carlos Delgado	15.00	4.50
IBJ Ichiro Suzuki Barry Bonds Derek Jeter	100.00	30.00
JWP Derek Jeter Bernie Williams Jorge Posada	40.00	12.00
SCB Curt Schilling Roger Clemens Kevin Brown	25.00	7.50

2003 Upper Deck MVP Total Bases

Randomly inserted into packs, this is an insert set featuring one base piece on each card. Each card was issued to a stated print run of 150 serial numbered sets.

	Nm-Mt	Ex-Mt
AR Alex Rodriguez	25.00	7.50
BB Barry Bonds	40.00	12.00
DJ Derek Jeter	40.00	12.00
IS Ichiro Suzuki	40.00	12.00
KG Ken Griffey Jr.	25.00	7.50
MM Mark McGwire	50.00	15.00
MP Mike Piazza	25.00	7.50
RC Roger Clemens	25.00	7.50
TG Troy Glaus	10.00	3.00

2003 Upper Deck Play Ball

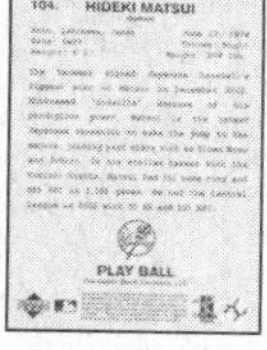

This 104 card set was released in February, 2004. The set was issued in five card packs with an $4 SRP. The packs were issued in 24 pack boxes which came 14 boxes to a case. The following subsets were included as part of the set: Summer of 1941 (74-88); Ted Williams Tribute (89-103). Cards numbered 74-103 were issued at stated rate of one in 24. In addition, one of the earliest cards of New York Yankee rookie Hideki Matsui was issued as card number 104. Shortly before the product debuted, an sample card of Mark McGwire was issued to preview what the set would look like.

	Nm-Mt	Ex-Mt
COMP.SET w/o SP's (74)	40.00	12.00
COMMON ACTIVE (1-73/104)	.30	.09
COMMON RETIRED (1-73/104)	.40	.12
COMMON CARD (74-88)	8.00	2.40
COMMON T.WILLIAMS (89-103)	10.00	3.00
1 Troy Glaus	.30	.09
2 Darin Erstad	.30	.09
3 Randy Johnson	.75	.23
4 Luis Gonzalez	.30	.09
5 Curt Schilling	.30	.09
6 Tom Glavine	.50	.15
7 Chipper Jones	.75	.23
8 Greg Maddux	1.25	.35
9 Andruw Jones	.30	.09
10 Pedro Martinez	.75	.23
11 Manny Ramirez	.50	.15
12 Nomar Garciaparra	1.25	.35
13 Billy Williams	.40	.12
14 Sammy Sosa	1.25	.35
15 Kerry Wood	.75	.23
16 Mark Prior	.75	.23
17 Ernie Banks	1.00	.30
18 Frank Thomas	.75	.23
19 Joe Morgan	.40	.12
20 Ken Griffey Jr.	1.25	.35
21 Adam Dunn	.50	.15
22 Jim Thome	.75	.23
23 Todd Helton	.50	.15
24 Larry Walker	.50	.15
25 Lance Berkman	.30	.09
26 Roy Oswalt	.30	.09
27 Jeff Bagwell	.50	.15
28 Nolan Ryan	2.50	.75
29 Mike Sweeney	.30	.09
30 Shawn Green	.30	.09
31 Hideo Nomo	.75	.23
32 Kazuhisa Ishii	.30	.09
33 Richie Sexson	.30	.09
34 Robin Yount	1.50	.45
35 Harmon Killebrew	1.00	.30
36 Torii Hunter	.30	.09
37 Vladimir Guerrero	.75	.23
38 Roberto Alomar	.50	.15
39 Mike Piazza	1.25	.35
40 Tom Seaver	.60	.18
41 Phil Rizzuto	.60	.18
42 Yogi Berra	1.00	.30
43 Mike Mussina	.50	.15
44 Roger Clemens	1.50	.45
45 Derek Jeter	2.00	.60
46 Jason Giambi	.30	.09
47 Bernie Williams	.50	.15
48 Alfonso Soriano	.50	.15
49 Catfish Hunter	.60	.18
50 Barry Zito	.30	.09
51 Eric Chavez	.30	.09
52 Tim Hudson	.30	.09
53 Rollie Fingers	.40	.12
54 Miguel Tejada	.30	.09
55 Pat Burrell	.30	.09
56 Brian Giles	.30	.09
57 Willie Stargell	.60	.18
58 Phil Nevin	.30	.09
59 Orlando Cepeda	.40	.12
60 Barry Bonds	2.00	.60
61 Jeff Kent	.30	.09
62 Willie McCovey	.40	.12
63 Ichiro Suzuki	1.25	.35
64 Stan Musial	1.50	.45
65 Albert Pujols	1.50	.45
66 J.D. Drew	.30	.09
67 Scott Rolen	.75	.23
68 Mark McGwire	1.50	.45
69 Alex Rodriguez	1.25	.35
70 Juan Gonzalez	.50	.15
71 Ivan Rodriguez	.75	.23
72 Rafael Palmeiro	.50	.15
73 Carlos Delgado	.30	.09
74 Ted Williams S41	12.00	3.60
75 Hank Greenberg S41	10.00	3.00
76 Joe DiMaggio S41	15.00	4.50
77 Lefty Gomez S41	10.00	3.00
78 Tommy Henrich S41	8.00	2.40
79 Pee Wee Reese S41	10.00	3.00
80 Mel Ott S41	10.00	3.00
81 Carl Hubbell S41	10.00	3.00
82 Jimmie Foxx S41	10.00	3.00
83 Joe Cronin S41	8.00	2.40
84 Charlie Gehringer S41	8.00	2.40
85 Frank Hayes S41	8.00	2.40
86 Babe Dahlgren S41	8.00	2.40
87 Dolph Camilli S41	8.00	2.40
88 Johnny Vandermeer S41	8.00	2.40
89 Ted Williams TRIB	10.00	3.00
90 Ted Williams TRIB	10.00	3.00
91 Ted Williams TRIB	10.00	3.00
92 Ted Williams TRIB	10.00	3.00
93 Ted Williams TRIB	10.00	3.00
94 Ted Williams TRIB	10.00	3.00
95 Ted Williams TRIB	10.00	3.00
96 Ted Williams TRIB	10.00	3.00
97 Ted Williams TRIB	10.00	3.00
98 Ted Williams TRIB	10.00	3.00
99 Ted Williams TRIB	10.00	3.00
100 Ted Williams TRIB	10.00	3.00
101 Ted Williams TRIB	10.00	3.00
102 Ted Williams TRIB	10.00	3.00
103 Ted Williams TRIB	10.00	3.00
104 Hideki Matsui RC	5.00	1.50
MM1 Mark McGwire Sample	2.00	.60

2003 Upper Deck Play Ball 1941 Series

Issued at a stated rate of one in two, this is a partial parallel to the Play Ball set. These cards are issued to the size of the original 1941 Play Ball cards.

	Nm-Mt	Ex-Mt
*1941 ACTIVE: 1.25X TO 3X BASIC		
*1941 RETIRED: 1.25X TO 3X BASIC		

2003 Upper Deck Play Ball Red Backs

Issued at a stated rate of one per pack for cards 1-73 and 104 and one in 96 for 74-103; this is a complete parallel to the Red Backs set. These cards can be identified as all the text on the card is in red ink.

	Nm-Mt	Ex-Mt
*RED BACK ACTIVE 1-73: .75X TO 2X BASIC		
*RED BACK RETIRED 1-73: .75X TO 2X BASIC		
*RED BACK 74-88: .6X TO 1.5X BASIC		
*RED BACK 89-103: .6X TO 1.5X BASIC		
*RED BACK 104: .75X TO 2X BASIC		

2003 Upper Deck Play Ball 1941 Reprints

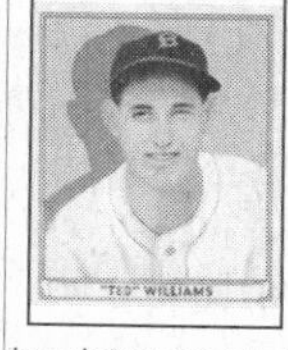

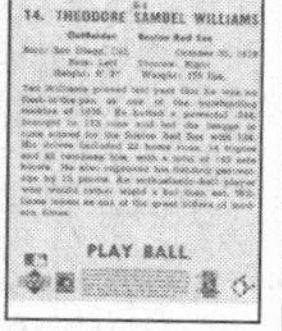

Issued at a stated rate of one in two, this 25 card insert set features cards reprinted from their 1941 originals.

	Nm-Mt	Ex-Mt
COMPLETE SET (25)	30.00	9.00
R1 Ted Williams	8.00	2.40
R2 Hank Greenberg	3.00	.90
R3 Joe DiMaggio	8.00	2.40
R4 Lefty Gomez	3.00	.90
R5 Tommy Henrich	2.00	.60
R6 Pee Wee Reese	3.00	.90
R7 Mel Ott	3.00	.90
R8 Carl Hubbell	3.00	.90
R9 Jimmie Foxx	3.00	.90
R10 Joe Cronin	2.00	.60
R11 Charley Gehringer	2.00	.60
R12 Frank Hayes	2.00	.60
R13 Babe Dahlgren	2.00	.60
R14 Dolph Camilli	2.00	.60
R15 Johnny Vandermeer	2.00	.60
R16 Bucky Walters	2.00	.60
R17 Red Ruffing	2.00	.60
R18 Charlie Keller	2.00	.60
R19 Indian Bob Johnson	2.00	.60
R20 Dutch Leonard	2.00	.60
R21 Barney McCosky	2.00	.60
R22 Soupy Campbell	2.00	.60
R23 Stormy Weatherly	2.00	.60
R24 Bobby Doerr	2.00	.60
R25 Bill Dickey	3.00	.90

2003 Upper Deck Play Ball Game Used Memorabilia Tier 1

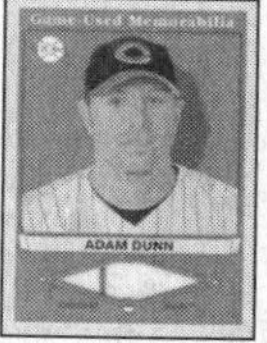

Inserted at a stated rate of one in 82, these 21 cards feature game-used memorabilia of the featured players. Interestingly, the only retired player with a memorabilia piece in this set is Tommy Henrich.

	Nm-Mt	Ex-Mt
GOLD RANDOM INSERTS IN PACKS		
GOLD PRINT RUN 25 SERIAL #'d SETS		
NO GOLD PRICING DUE TO SCARCITY		
AD1 Adam Dunn Jsy	10.00	3.00
AS1 Alfonso Soriano Jsy	10.00	3.00
BW1 Bernie Williams Jsy	10.00	3.00
CD1 Carlos Delgado Jsy	8.00	2.40
CJ1 Chipper Jones Jsy	10.00	3.00
CS1 Curt Schilling Jsy	8.00	2.40
DR1 J.D. Drew Jsy	8.00	2.40
IR1 Ivan Rodriguez Jsy	10.00	3.00
IS1 Ichiro Suzuki Jsy	40.00	12.00
JG1 Jason Giambi Jsy	8.00	2.40
KG1 Ken Griffey Jr. Jsy	25.00	7.50
KI1 Kazuhisa Ishii Jsy	8.00	2.40
LG1 Luis Gonzalez Jsy	8.00	2.40
MM1 Mark McGwire Jsy	60.00	18.00
MP1 Mike Piazza Jsy	15.00	4.50
MS1 Mike Sweeney Jsy	8.00	2.40
PR1 Mark Prior Jsy	10.00	3.00
RC1 Roger Clemens Jsy	20.00	6.00
RP1 Rafael Palmeiro Jsy	10.00	3.00
SS1 Sammy Sosa Jsy	20.00	6.00
TH1 Tommy Henrich Pants	8.00	2.40

2003 Upper Deck Play Ball Game Used Memorabilia Tier 2

Randomly inserted in packs, these 21 cards feature game-used memorabilia of the featured players. These cards were issued to a stated print run of 150 serial numbered sets.

	Nm-Mt	Ex-Mt
AJ2 Andruw Jones Jsy	10.00	3.00
AR2 Alex Rodriguez Jsy	25.00	7.50
CJ2 Chipper Jones Jsy	20.00	6.00
CS2 Curt Schilling Jsy	10.00	3.00
DE2 Darin Erstad Jsy	10.00	3.00
GM2 Greg Maddux Jsy	15.00	4.50
IS2 Ichiro Suzuki Jsy	80.00	24.00
JB2 Jeff Bagwell Jsy	15.00	4.50
JD2 Joe DiMaggio Jsy	120.00	36.00
JG2 Jason Giambi Jsy	10.00	3.00
JT2 Jim Thome Jsy	20.00	6.00
KG2 Ken Griffey Jr. Jsy	25.00	7.50
KW2 Kerry Wood Jsy	20.00	6.00
LB2 Lance Berkman Jsy	10.00	3.00
MM2 Mark McGwire Jsy	80.00	24.00
MP2 Mike Piazza Jsy	15.00	4.50
MR2 Manny Ramirez Jsy	15.00	4.50
PM2 Pedro Martinez Jsy	20.00	6.00
RJ2 Randy Johnson Jsy	20.00	6.00
SG2 Shawn Green Jsy	10.00	3.00
SS2 Sammy Sosa Jsy	25.00	7.50

2003 Upper Deck Play Ball Game Used Memorabilia Tier 2 Signatures

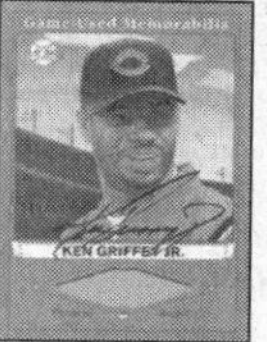

Randomly isnerted in packs, these cards parallel the Game Used Memorabilia Tier 2 insert set. With the exception of the Alex Rodriguez card, these cards were issued to a stated print run of 50 serial numbered sets. The Alex Rodriguez card was issued to a stated print run of 285 sets. Please note that Mark McGwire signed all his cards with an "all century" notation.

Nm-Mt Ex-Mt
AJ2 Andruw Jones Jsy 80.00 24.00
AR2 Alex Rodriguez Jsy/285 150.00 45.00
CS2 Curt Schilling Jsy 100.00 30.00
DE2 Darin Erstad Jsy 80.00 24.00
IS2 Ichiro Suzuki Jsy 400.00 120.00
JB2 Jeff Bagwell Jsy 120.00 36.00
JG2 Jason Giambi Jsy 80.00 24.00
JT2 Jim Thome Jsy 100.00 30.00
KG2 Ken Griffey Jr. Jsy 150.00 45.00
KW2 Kerry Wood Jsy 100.00 30.00
LB2 Lance Berkman Jsy 100.00 30.00
MM2 Mark McGwire Jsy 400.00 120.00
SS2 Sammy Sosa Jsy 250.00 75.00

2003 Upper Deck Play Ball Yankee Clipper 1941 Streak

Inserted at a stated rate of one in 12 for cards 1-41 and one in 24 for cards numbered 42-56, this is a 56 card set honoring Joe DiMaggio's 56-game consecutive game hitting streak in 1941. Each card features a box score from the matching game during the streak.

Nm-Mt Ex-Mt
COMMON CARD (1-41) 8.00 2.40
COMMON CARD (42-56) 8.00 2.40

2004 Upper Deck Play Ball

The initial 183-card Play Ball set was released in April, 2004. The set was issued in five-card packs with an $4 SRP which came 24 packs to a box and 14 boxes to a case. Cards numbered 1-132 feature a mix of today's leading stars as well as all-time greats. Card numbered 133-162 feature a mix of leading rookies and prospects. Those cards were inserted at a stated rate of one in 16 and were issued to a stated print run of 2004 serial numbered sets. Cards numbered 163 through 183 feature multi-player "classic combo" cards and those were inserted at a stated rate of one in 24 and were issued to a stated print run of 1999 serial numbered sets. A 50-card Update set (containing cards 183-232) was issued in factory set form and distributed randomly into one in every four hobby boxes of 2004 Upper Deck series 2 baseball in June 2004.

Nm-Mt Ex-Mt
COMP.SET w/o SP's (132) 25.00 7.50
COMP.UPDATE SET (50) 20.00 6.00
COMMON ACTIVE (1-132) .30 .09
COMMON RETIRED (1-132) .40 .12
COMMON CARD (133-162) 4.00 1.20
COMMON CARD (163-183) 4.00 1.20
163-183 STATED ODDS 1:24
163-183 PRINT RUN 1999 SERIAL #'d SETS
COMMON CARD (183-232) .40 .12
ONE UPDATE SET PER 4 UD2 HOBBY BOXES
1 Hideo Nomo .75 .23
2 Curt Schilling .75 .23
3 Barry Zito .30 .09
4 Nomar Garciaparra 1.25 .35
5 Yogi Berra 1.00 .30
6 Randy Johnson .75 .23
7 Jason Giambi .30 .09
8 Sammy Sosa 1.25 .35
9 David Ortiz .75 .23
10 Derek Jeter 1.50 .45
11 Warren Spahn .60 .18
12 Mark Prior .75 .23
13 Roger Clemens 1.50 .45
14 Mike Piazza 1.25 .35
15 Nolan Ryan 2.50 .75
16 Joe DiMaggio 2.00 .60
17 Alfonso Soriano .50 .15
18 Brandon Webb .30 .09
19 Shawn Green .30 .09
20 Bob Feller .40 .12
21 Mike Schmidt 2.00 .60
22 Mark Teixeira .30 .09
23 Pedro Martinez .75 .23
24 Vladimir Guerrero .75 .23
25 Rafael Furcal .30 .09
26 Derrek Lee .30 .09
27 Carlos Delgado .30 .09
28 Mickey Mantle 5.00 1.50
29 Dontrelle Willis .30 .09
30 Ted Williams 2.50 .75
31 Vernon Wells .30 .09
32 Alex Rodriguez Yanks 1.25 .35
33 Brooks Robinson .60 .18
34 Tom Seaver .60 .18
35 Ernie Banks 1.00 .30
36 Bob Gibson .60 .18
37 Jim Thome .75 .23
38 Mike Mussina .50 .15
39 Eric Chavez .30 .09
40 Roy Halladay .30 .09
41 Eric Gagne .75 .23
42 Jose Reyes .30 .09
43 Jeff Bagwell .50 .15
44 Rich Harden .30 .09
45 Jeff Kent .30 .09
46 Lance Berkman .30 .09
47 Adam Dunn .50 .15
48 Richie Sexson .30 .09
49 Andruw Jones .30 .09
50 Ichiro Suzuki 1.25 .35
51 Edgar Renteria .30 .09
52 Rocco Baldelli .30 .09
53 Jim Edmonds .30 .09
54 Maggio Ordonez .30 .09
55 Austin Kearns .30 .09
56 Garret Anderson .30 .09
57 Manny Ramirez .50 .15
58 Roy Oswalt .30 .09
59 Gary Sheffield .30 .09
60 Mark Mulder .30 .09
61 Ben Sheets .30 .09
62 Scott Rolen .75 .23
63 Greg Maddux 1.25 .35
64 Jose Contreras .30 .09
65 Miguel Cabrera .50 .15
66 Hank Blalock .30 .09
67 Miguel Tejada .30 .09
68 Albert Pujols 1.50 .45
69 Hideki Matsui 1.25 .35
70 Mike Lowell .30 .09
71 Tim Hudson .30 .09
72 Bret Boone .30 .09
73 Ivan Rodriguez .75 .23
74 Josh Beckett .30 .09
75 Todd Helton .50 .15
76 Brian Giles .30 .09
77 Orlando Cabrera .30 .09
78 Carlos Beltran .50 .15
79 Jason Schmidt .30 .09
80 Kerry Wood .75 .23
81 Preston Wilson .30 .09
82 Troy Glaus .30 .09
83 Kevin Brown .30 .09
84 Rafael Palmeiro .50 .15
85 Chipper Jones .75 .23
86 Reggie Sanders .30 .09
87 Cliff Floyd .30 .09
88 Corey Patterson .30 .09
89 Kevin Millwood .30 .09
90 Aaron Boone .30 .09
91 Darin Erstad .30 .09
92 Richard Hidalgo .30 .09
93 Dmitri Young .30 .09
94 Jeremy Bonderman .30 .09
95 Larry Walker .50 .15
96 Edgar Martinez .50 .15
97 Jerome Williams .30 .09
98 Luis Gonzalez .30 .09
99 Roberto Alomar .50 .15
100 Jerry Hairston Jr. .30 .09
101 Luis Matos .30 .09
102 Andy Pettitte .50 .15
103 Frank Thomas .75 .23
104 Rondell White .30 .09
105 Jody Gerut .30 .09
106 Bartolo Colon .30 .09
107 Johnny Damon .75 .23
108 Ryan Klesko .30 .09
109 Geoff Jenkins .30 .09
110 Jorge Posada .50 .15
111 Melvin Mora .30 .09
112 Bernie Williams .50 .15
113 Shannon Stewart .30 .09
114 Bobby Abreu .30 .09
115 Jose Guillen .30 .09
116 Brandon Phillips .30 .09
117 Jose Vidro .30 .09
118 Mike Sweeney .30 .09
119 Jacque Jones .30 .09
120 Josh Phelps .30 .09
121 Milton Bradley .30 .09
122 Torii Hunter .30 .09
123 Carl Crawford .30 .09
124 Javier Vazquez .30 .09
125 Juan Gonzalez .50 .15
126 Travis Hafner .30 .09
127 Ken Griffey Jr. 1.25 .35
128 Phil Nevin .30 .09
129 Trot Nixon .30 .09
130 Carlos Lee .30 .09
131 Javy Lopez .30 .09
132 Jay Gibbons .30 .09
133 Brandon Medders RP RC 4.00 1.20
134 Colby Miller RP RC 4.00 1.20
135 Dave Crouthers RP RC 4.00 1.20
136 Dennis Sarfate RP RC 4.00 1.20
137 Donald Kelly RP RC 4.00 1.20
138 Frank Brooks RP RC 4.00 1.20
139 Chris Aguila RP RC 4.00 1.20
140 Greg Dobbs RP RC 4.00 1.20
141 Ian Snell RP RC 5.00 1.50
142 Jake Woods RP RC 4.00 1.20
143 Jamie Brown RP RC 4.00 1.20
144 Jason Frasor RP RC 4.00 1.20
145 Jerome Gamble RP RC 4.00 1.20
146 Jesse Harper RP RC 4.00 1.20
147 Josh Labandeira RP RC 4.00 1.20
148 Justin Hampson RP RC 4.00 1.20
149 Justin Huisman RP RC 4.00 1.20
150 Justin Leone RP RC 5.00 1.50
151 Lincoln Holdzkom RP RC 4.00 1.20
152 Mike Bumatay RP RC 4.00 1.20
153 Mike Gosling RP RC 4.00 1.20
154 Mike Johnston RP RC 4.00 1.20
155 Mike Rouse RP RC 4.00 1.20
156 Nick Regilio RP RC 4.00 1.20
157 Ryan Meaux RP RC 4.00 1.20
158 Scott Dohmann RP RC 4.00 1.20
159 Sean Henn RP RC 4.00 1.20
160 Tim Bausher RP RC 4.00 1.20
161 Tim Bittner RP RC 4.00 1.20
162 Alec Zumwalt RP RC 4.00 1.20
163 Aaron Boone 5.00 1.50
Bret Boone
Geoff Jenkins
Mark Prior
Barry Zito CC
164 Albert Pujols 5.00 1.50
Edgar Renteria
Alex Rodriguez CC
165 Alfonso Soriano 5.00 1.50
Sammy Sosa CC
166 Bobby Abreu 5.00 1.50
Jim Thome CC
167 Bret Boone 5.00 1.50
John Olerud
Ichiro Suzuki CC
168 Derek Jeter 8.00 2.40
Alfonso Soriano CC
169 Eric Chavez 4.00 1.20
Miguel Tejada CC
170 Garret Anderson 4.00 1.20
Jim Edmonds
Troy Glaus CC
171 Hank Blalock 5.00 1.50
Alex Rodriguez CC
172 Alex Rodriguez 5.00 1.50
Mark Teixeira
Michael Young
Rafael Palmeiro CC
173 Ivan Rodriguez 5.00 1.50
Dontrelle Willis CC
174 Jason Giambi 8.00 2.40
Derek Jeter CC
175 Joe DiMaggio 10.00 3.00
Mickey Mantle CC
176 Joe DiMaggio 10.00 3.00
Mickey Mantle
Ted Williams CC
177 Joe DiMaggio 10.00 3.00
Ted Williams CC
178 Nomar Garciaparra 5.00 1.50
Alfonso Soriano CC
179 Nomar Garciaparra 5.00 1.50
Jason Giambi CC
180 Paul LoDuca 5.00 1.50
Hideo Nomo CC
181 Rafael Palmeiro 5.00 1.50
Alex Rodriguez
Michael Young CC
182 Ralph Kiner 8.00 2.40
Ted Williams CC
183 Aaron Boone 8.00 2.40
Derek Jeter CC
183 Kazuo Matsui RC 4.00 1.20
184 Jerry Gil RC .60 .18
185 Jose Capellan RC 3.00 .90
186 Tim Hamulack RC .40 .12
187 Renyel Pinto RC 1.00 .30
188 Carlos Vasquez RC .60 .18
189 Enemencio Pacheco RC .60 .18
190 Ronny Cedeno RC .60 .18
191 Mariano Gomez RC 1.00 .30
192 Carlos Hines RC .60 .18
193 Mike Vento RC 1.00 .30
194 David Aardsma RC .60 .18
195 Hector Gimenez RC .40 .12
196 Fernando Nieve RC .60 .18
197 Chris Saenz RC .40 .12
198 Shawn Hill RC .60 .18
199 Angel Chavez RC .60 .18
200 Scott Proctor RC 1.00 .30
201 William Bergolla RC .60 .18
202 Justin Germano RC .60 .18
203 Onil Joseph RC .60 .18
204 Rusty Tucker RC 1.00 .30
205 Justin Knoedler RC .60 .18
206 Casey Daigle RC .60 .18
207 Edwin Moreno RC .60 .18
208 Chad Bentz RC .60 .18
209 Ryan Wing RC .60 .18
210 Shawn Camp RC .40 .12
211 Eddy Rodriguez RC 1.00 .30
212 Roman Colon RC .60 .18
213 Jason Bartlett RC 1.00 .30
214 Jorge Vasquez RC .60 .18
215 Ivan Ochoa RC .60 .18
216 Akinori Otsuka RC .60 .18
217 Merkin Valdez RC 2.50 .75
218 Shingo Takatsu RC 2.50 .75
219 Chris Oxspring RC 1.00 .30
220 Kevin Cave RC 1.00 .30
221 Ramon Ramirez RC .60 .18
222 Orlando Rodriguez RC .60 .18
223 Lino Urdaneta RC .60 .18
224 Franklyn Gracesqui RC .40 .12
225 Michael Wuertz RC 1.00 .30
226 Jorge Sequea RC .60 .18
227 Luis A. Gonzalez RC 1.00 .30
228 Jason Szuminski RC .40 .12
229 John Gall RC 1.00 .30
230 Freddy Guzman RC .60 .18
231 Jeff Bennett RC .60 .18
232 Roberto Novoa RC 1.00 .30

2004 Upper Deck Play Ball Blue

Nm-Mt Ex-Mt
*BLUE ACTIVE: 1.5X TO 4X BASIC
*BLUE RETIRED: 2X TO 5X BASIC
STATED ODDS 1:6

2004 Upper Deck Play Ball Green

Nm-Mt Ex-Mt
RANDOM INSERTS IN PACKS
STATED PRINT RUN 15 SERIAL #'d SETS
NO PRICING DUE TO SCARCITY

2004 Upper Deck Play Ball Parallel 175

Nm-Mt Ex-Mt
*PAR.175 ACTIVE: 2.5X TO 6X BASIC
*PAR.175 RETIRED: 3X TO 8X BASIC
RANDOM INSERTS IN PACKS
STATED PRINT RUN 175 SERIAL #'d SETS
1-42 FEATURE THICK RED BORDERS
43-132 FEATURE DIE-CUT SILVER BORDERS

2004 Upper Deck Play Ball Purple

Nm-Mt Ex-Mt
RANDOM INSERTS IN PACKS
STATED PRINT RUN 1 SERIAL #'d SET
NO PRICING DUE TO SCARCITY

2004 Upper Deck Play Ball Apparel Collection

Nm-Mt Ex-Mt
STATED ODDS 1:24

SP INFO PROVIDED BY UPPER DECK
AD Adam Dunn 10.00 3.00
AP Albert Pujols 15.00 4.50
AR Alex Rodriguez SP 15.00 4.50
AS Alfonso Soriano 10.00 3.00
BE Josh Beckett 8.00 2.40
BH Bo Hart 8.00 2.40
BW Bernie Williams 10.00 3.00
BZ Barry Zito SP 10.00 3.00
CD Carlos Delgado 8.00 2.40
CJ Chipper Jones 10.00 3.00
CS Curt Schilling 8.00 2.40
DJ Derek Jeter 20.00 6.00
DW Dontrelle Willis 8.00 2.40
HA Roy Halladay 8.00 2.40
HM Hideki Matsui 25.00 7.50
HN Hideo Nomo 10.00 3.00
IS Ichiro Suzuki 25.00 7.50
JB Jeff Bagwell 10.00 3.00
JD Joe DiMaggio SP/150 100.00 30.00
JG Jason Giambi 8.00 2.40
JP Jorge Posada 10.00 3.00
JT Jim Thome 10.00 3.00
KG Ken Griffey Jr. 15.00 4.50
KW Kerry Wood 10.00 3.00
LB Lance Berkman 8.00 2.40
ML Mike Lowell SP 10.00 3.00
MM Mickey Mantle SP/150 120.00 36.00
MP Mark Prior 10.00 3.00
MR Manny Ramirez 10.00 3.00
MU Mike Mussina 10.00 3.00
PI Mike Piazza 10.00 3.00
PM Pedro Martinez SP 15.00 4.50
RB Rocco Baldelli 8.00 2.40
RF Rafael Furcal 8.00 2.40
RH Rich Harden SP 10.00 3.00
RJ Randy Johnson 10.00 3.00
RO Roy Oswalt 8.00 2.40
RP Rafael Palmeiro 10.00 3.00
SS Sammy Sosa 10.00 3.00
TG Troy Glaus 8.00 2.40
TH Torii Hunter 8.00 2.40
TW Ted Williams SP/150 60.00 18.00

2004 Upper Deck Play Ball Artist's Touch Jersey

Nm-Mt Ex-Mt
STATED PRINT RUN 250 SERIAL #'d SETS
*JERSEY 50: .6X TO 1.5X BASIC
JERSEY 50 PRINT 50 SERIAL #'d SETS
RANDOM INSERTS IN PACKS
AP Albert Pujols 15.00 4.50
AR Alex Rodriguez 10.00 3.00
AS Alfonso Soriano 10.00 3.00
BH Bo Hart 8.00 2.40
BW Bernie Williams 10.00 3.00
BZ Barry Zito 8.00 2.40
CD Carlos Delgado 8.00 2.40
CJ Chipper Jones 10.00 3.00
DJ Derek Jeter 20.00 6.00
DW Dontrelle Willis 8.00 2.40
HA Roy Halladay 8.00 2.40
HM Hideki Matsui 25.00 7.50
HN Hideo Nomo 10.00 3.00
IS Ichiro Suzuki 25.00 7.50
JB Josh Beckett 8.00 2.40
JG Jason Giambi 8.00 2.40
JP Jorge Posada 10.00 3.00
JT Jim Thome 10.00 3.00
KG Ken Griffey Jr. 15.00 4.50
KW Kerry Wood 10.00 3.00
LB Lance Berkman 8.00 2.40
MM Mike Mussina 10.00 3.00
MP Mark Prior 10.00 3.00
MR Manny Ramirez 10.00 3.00
PI Mike Piazza 12.00 3.60
PM Pedro Martinez 10.00 3.00
RB Rocco Baldelli 8.00 2.40
RF Rafael Furcal 8.00 2.40
RJ Randy Johnson 10.00 3.00
RO Roy Oswalt 8.00 2.40
RP Rafael Palmeiro 10.00 3.00
SS Sammy Sosa 12.00 3.60
TG Troy Glaus 8.00 2.40
TH Torii Hunter 8.00 2.40

2004 Upper Deck Play Ball Home Run Heroics

Nm-Mt Ex-Mt
STATED ODDS 1:24
AB Aaron Boone Walk-Off 5.00 1.50
AR Alex Rodriguez M's 40th 8.00 2.40
AR1 Alex Rodriguez Rgr 57th 8.00 2.40
AS Alfonso Soriano 13th Lead 8.00 2.40
BM Bill Mueller 2 Slams 5.00 1.50
CD Carlos Delgado 4 HR's 5.00 1.50
CR Cal Ripken 15.00 4.50
2,131th consecutive game
CR1 Cal Ripken 15.00 4.50
2130th consecutive game
EB Ernie Banks 500th 8.00 2.40
EM Eddie Mathews 500th 8.00 2.40
FR Frank Robinson AS 5.00 1.50
HB Hank Blalock AS 5.00 1.50
HK Harmon Killebrew 500th 8.00 2.40
HM Hideki Matsui 8.00 2.40
1st career homer
HM1 Hideki Matsui 8.00 2.40
World Series homer
JD Joe DiMaggio 10.00 3.00
Final career homer
JD1 Joe DiMaggio 10.00 3.00
1st homer
JG Jason Giambi Slam 5.00 1.50
KG Ken Griffey Jr. M's 8.00 2.40
1st career homer
KG1 Ken Griffey Jr. M's 8.00 2.40
8 homers in 8 straight games
MC Miguel Cabrera Walk-Off 8.00 2.40
MM Mickey Mantle 25.00 7.50
1st career homer
MM1 Mickey Mantle 25.00 7.50
16th World Series Homer
MM2 Mickey Mantle 25.00 7.50
500th career homer
MS Mike Schmidt 500th 10.00 3.00
RH Rickey Henderson 81st Lead 8.00 2.40
RJ Randy Johnson 1st 8.00 2.40
RP Rafael Palmeiro 500th 8.00 2.40
RS Red Schoendienst 14th Inn 5.00 1.50
SG Shawn Green 7 HR's 5.00 1.50
SM Stan Musial Walk-Off 10.00 3.00
SS Sammy Sosa Rgr 1st 8.00 2.40
SS1 Sammy Sosa Cubs 8.00 2.40
20th homer in June, 1998
SS2 Sammy Sosa Cubs 8.00 2.40
66th homer of the 1998 season
SS3 Sammy Sosa Cubs 8.00 2.40
500th career homer
TW Ted Williams 12.00 3.60
1941 All-Star Game homer
TW1 Ted Williams 12.00 3.60
500th career homer
TW2 Ted Williams 12.00 3.60
Homer in final time at bat
TW3 Ted Williams 12.00 3.60
1st career homer
WM Willie McCovey 500th 5.00 1.50

2004 Upper Deck Play Ball Rookie Portfolio Signature

Nm-Mt Ex-Mt
STATED ODDS 1:30
AZ Alec Zumwalt 8.00 2.40
BI Tim Bittner 8.00 2.40
BM Brandon Medders 8.00 2.40
CA Chris Aguila 8.00 2.40
CM Colby Miller 8.00 2.40
DC Dave Crouthers 8.00 2.40
DK Donald Kelly 8.00 2.40
DS Dennis Sarfate 8.00 2.40
FB Frank Brooks 8.00 2.40
GD Greg Dobbs 8.00 2.40
HA Justin Hampson 8.00 2.40
HU Justin Huisman 8.00 2.40
IS Ian Snell 10.00 3.00
JB Jamie Brown 8.00 2.40
JF Jason Frasor 8.00 2.40
JG Jerome Gamble 8.00 2.40
JH Jesse Harper 8.00 2.40
JL Josh Labandeira 8.00 2.40
JW Jake Woods 8.00 2.40
LE Justin Leone 10.00 3.00
LH Lincoln Holdzkom 8.00 2.40
MB Mike Bumatay 8.00 2.40
MG Mike Gosling 8.00 2.40
MJ Mike Johnston 8.00 2.40
MR Mike Rouse 8.00 2.40
NR Nick Regilio 8.00 2.40
RM Ryan Meaux 8.00 2.40
SD Scott Dohmann 8.00 2.40
SH Sean Henn 8.00 2.40
TB Tim Bausher 8.00 2.40

2004 Upper Deck Play Ball Signature Portfolio Black 100

Nm-Mt Ex-Mt
STATED PRINT RUN 100 SERIAL #'d SETS
BLACK 10 PRINT RUN 10 SERIAL #'d SETS
NO BLACK 10 PRICING DUE TO SCARCITY

BLUE 25 PRINT RUN 25 SERIAL #'d SETS
NO BLUE 25 PRICING DUE TO SCARCITY
BLUE 5 PRINT RUN 5 SERIAL #'d SETS
NO BLUE 5 PRICING DUE TO SCARCITY
RED 10 PRINT RUN 10 SERIAL #'d SETS
NO RED 10 PRICING DUE TO SCARCITY
RED 1 PRINT RUN 1 SERIAL #'d SET
NO RED 1 PRICING DUE TO SCARCITY
RANDOM INSERTS IN PACKS
BZ Barry Zito 30.00 9.00
CR Cal Ripken 150.00 45.00
CZ Carl Yastrzemski 80.00 24.00
HM Hideki Matsui 250.00 75.00
KG Ken Griffey Jr. 100.00 30.00
TS Tom Seaver 50.00 15.00

2004 Upper Deck Play Ball Tools of the Stars Bat

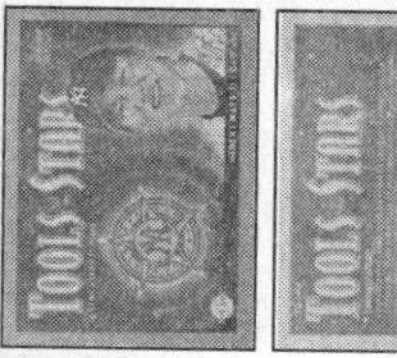
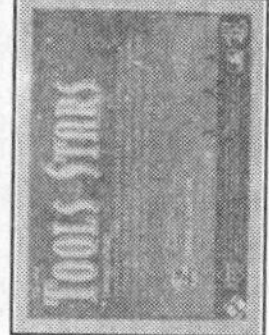

Nm-Mt Ex-Mt
STATED ODDS 1:48
TOOLS 25 RANDOM INSERTS IN PACKS
TOOLS 25 PRINT RUN 25 SERIAL #'d SETS
NO TOOLS 25 PRICING DUE TO SCARCITY
*TOOLS 250: .4X TO 1X BASIC
TOOLS 250 RANDOM INSERTS IN PACKS
TOOLS 250 PRINT RUN 250 SERIAL #'d SETS
AP Albert Pujols 15.00 4.50
AR Alex Rodriguez 10.00 3.00
AS Alfonso Soriano 10.00 3.00
CD Carlos Delgado 8.00 2.40
CJ Chipper Jones 10.00 3.00
DJ Derek Jeter 20.00 6.00
HM Hideki Matsui 25.00 7.50
HN Hideo Nomo 10.00 3.00
IS Ichiro Suzuki 25.00 7.50
JB Josh Beckett 8.00 2.40
JT Jim Thome 10.00 3.00
KG Ken Griffey Jr. 15.00 4.50
KW Kerry Wood 10.00 3.00
PI Mike Piazza 10.00 3.00

2004 Upper Deck Power Up

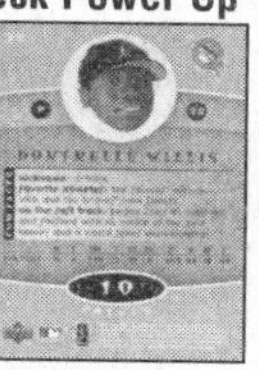

This 100-card set was released in April, 2004. These cards were issued in nine-card packs with an $2 SRP which came 24 packs to a box and 20 boxes to a case.

Nm-Mt Ex-Mt
COMPLETE SET (100) 25.00 7.50
BASIC CARDS WORTH 10 POINTS EACH
1 Austin Kearns .25 .07
2 Rafael Furcal .25 .07
3 Larry Walker .40 .12
4 Jeremy Bonderman .25 .07
5 Scott Rolen .60 .18
6 Nomar Garciaparra 1.00 .30
7 Jody Gerut .25 .07
8 Troy Glaus .25 .07
9 Roy Halladay .25 .07
10 Barry Zito .25 .07
11 Gary Sheffield .25 .07
12 Ichiro Suzuki 1.00 .30
13 Juan Gonzalez .40 .12
14 Jim Edmonds .25 .07
15 Hank Blalock .25 .07
16 Roy Oswalt .25 .07
17 Magglio Ordonez .25 .07
18 Garret Anderson .25 .07
19 Mark Teixeira .25 .07
20 Mike Sweeney .25 .07
21 Reggie Sanders .25 .07
22 Rafael Palmeiro .40 .12
23 Orlando Cabrera .25 .07
24 Edgar Renteria .25 .07
25 Ryan Klesko .25 .07
26 Torii Hunter .25 .07
27 Bret Boone .25 .07
28 Roberto Alomar .40 .12
29 Frank Thomas .60 .18
30 Chipper Jones .60 .18
31 Eric Chavez .25 .07
32 Miguel Tejada .25 .07
33 Carlos Beltran .40 .12
34 Geoff Jenkins .25 .07
35 Hideki Matsui 1.00 .30
36 Jason Kendall .25 .07
37 Adam Dunn .40 .12
38 Jay Gibbons .25 .07
39 Ivan Rodriguez .60 .18
40 Sidney Ponson .25 .07
41 Albert Pujols 1.25 .35
42 Bartolo Colon .25 .07
43 Lance Berkman .40 .12
44 Brandon Webb .25 .07
45 Shannon Stewart .25 .07
46 Josh Beckett .25 .07
47 Jason Schmidt .25 .07
48 Luis Gonzalez .25 .07
49 Jacque Jones .25 .07
50 Andruw Jones .25 .07
51 Todd Helton .40 .12
52 Javier Vazquez .25 .07
53 Alfonso Soriano .40 .12
54 Manny Ramirez .40 .12
55 Bobby Abreu .25 .07
56 Rocco Baldelli .25 .07
57 Kerry Wood .60 .18
58 Derek Jeter 1.25 .35
59 Phil Nevin .25 .07
60 Jeff Bagwell .40 .12
61 Sammy Sosa 1.00 .30
62 Tom Glavine .40 .12
63 Miguel Cabrera .40 .12
64 Shawn Green .25 .07
65 Mark Prior .60 .18
66 Jose Reyes .25 .07
67 Curt Schilling .25 .07
68 Hideo Nomo .60 .18
69 Mike Lowell .25 .07
70 Randy Johnson .60 .18
71 Edgar Martinez .40 .12
72 Dontrelle Willis .25 .07
73 Milton Bradley .25 .07
74 Preston Wilson .25 .07
75 Mike Piazza 1.00 .30
76 Mike Mussina .40 .12
77 Darin Erstad .25 .07
78 Greg Maddux 1.00 .30
79 Tim Hudson .25 .07
80 Kevin Millwood .25 .07
81 Dmitri Young .25 .07
82 Ben Sheets .25 .07
83 Alex Rodriguez 1.00 .30
84 Johan Santana .40 .12
85 Jeff Kent .25 .07
86 Pedro Martinez .60 .18
87 Carlos Delgado .25 .07
88 Jim Thome .60 .18
89 Aubrey Huff .25 .07
90 Ken Griffey Jr. 1.00 .30
91 Kevin Brown .25 .07
92 Tony Batista .25 .07
93 Richie Sexson .25 .07
94 Cliff Floyd .25 .07
95 Jose Vidro .25 .07
96 Brian Giles .25 .07
97 Jorge Posada .40 .12
98 Vernon Wells .25 .07
99 Vladimir Guerrero .60 .18
100 Jason Giambi .25 .07

2004 Upper Deck Power Up Blue

Nm-Mt Ex-Mt
STATED ODDS 1:240
BLUE WORTH 1000 POINTS EACH
ALSO REFERRED TO AS MEGA RARE
NO PRICING DUE TO SCARCITY

2004 Upper Deck Power Up Lavender

Nm-Mt Ex-Mt
*LAVENDER: 6X TO 15X BASIC
STATED ODDS 1:96
LAVENDER WORTH 500 POINTS EACH
ALSO REFERRED TO AS SUPER RARE

2004 Upper Deck Power Up Orange

Nm-Mt Ex-Mt
*ORANGE: 2.5X TO 6X BASIC
STATED ODDS 1:6
ORANGE WORTH 100 POINTS EACH
ALSO REFERRED TO AS RARE

2004 Upper Deck Power Up Purple

Nm-Mt Ex-Mt
*PURPLE: 4X TO 10X BASIC
STATED ODDS 1:24
PURPLE WORTH 250 POINTS EACH
ALSO REFERRED TO AS ULTRA RARE

2004 Upper Deck Power Up Shining Through

Nm-Mt Ex-Mt
STATED ODDS 1:1
SHINING WORTH 50 POINTS EACH
1 Hideo Nomo 2.00 .60
2 Mark Prior 2.00 .60
3 Scott Rolen 2.00 .60
4 Luis Gonzalez .75 .23
5 Miguel Tejada .75 .23
6 Richie Sexson .75 .23
7 Jim Edmonds .75 .23
8 Carlos Beltran 1.25 .35
9 Manny Ramirez 1.25 .35
10 Torii Hunter .75 .23
11 Garret Anderson .75 .23
12 Eric Chavez .75 .23
13 Juan Gonzalez 1.25 .35
14 Albert Pujols 4.00 1.20
15 Tim Hudson .75 .23
16 Roy Halladay .75 .23
17 Roy Oswalt .75 .23
18 Andruw Jones .75 .23
19 Gary Sheffield .75 .23
20 Magglio Ordonez .75 .23
21 Jason Giambi .75 .23
22 Brian Giles .75 .23
23 Barry Zito .75 .23
24 Todd Helton 1.25 .35
25 Randy Johnson 2.00 .60
26 Pedro Martinez 2.00 .60
27 Vernon Wells .75 .23
28 Lance Berkman .75 .23
29 Mike Mussina 1.25 .35
30 Carlos Delgado .75 .23
31 Ivan Rodriguez 2.00 .60
32 Kevin Brown .75 .23
33 Kerry Wood 2.00 .60
34 Mark Teixeira .75 .23
35 Hideki Matsui 3.00 .90
36 Troy Glaus .75 .23
37 Mike Piazza 3.00 .90
38 Nomar Garciaparra 3.00 .90
39 Vladimir Guerrero 2.00 .60
40 Derek Jeter 4.00 1.20
41 Jason Schmidt .75 .23
42 Alex Rodriguez Yanks 4.00 1.20
43 Jeff Bagwell 1.25 .35
44 Shawn Green .75 .23
45 Sammy Sosa 3.00 .90
46 Josh Beckett .75 .23
47 Bret Boone .75 .23
48 Ichiro Suzuki 3.00 .90
49 Jeff Kent .75 .23
50 Rafael Palmeiro 1.25 .35
51 Curt Schilling .75 .23
52 Greg Maddux 3.00 .90
53 Mike Lowell .75 .23
54 Dontrelle Willis .75 .23
55 Alfonso Soriano 1.25 .35
56 Preston Wilson .75 .23
57 Jorge Posada 1.25 .35
58 Frank Thomas 2.00 .60
59 Jim Thome 2.00 .60
60 Ken Griffey Jr. 3.00 .90
61 Rocco Baldelli .75 .23
62 Jose Vidro .75 .23
63 Austin Kearns .75 .23
64 Cliff Floyd .75 .23
65 Phil Nevin .75 .23
66 Darin Erstad .75 .23
67 Johan Santana .75 .23
68 Chipper Jones 2.00 .60
69 Brandon Webb .75 .23
70 Hank Blalock .75 .23
71 Adam Dunn 1.25 .35
72 Javier Vazquez .75 .23
73 Jacque Jones .75 .23
74 Bobby Abreu .75 .23
75 Edgar Renteria .75 .23
76 Roger Clemens 4.00 1.20
77 Rafael Furcal .75 .23
78 Mike Sweeney .75 .23
79 Geoff Jenkins .75 .23
80 Orlando Cabrera .75 .23
81 Ben Sheets .75 .23
82 Shannon Stewart .75 .23
83 Ryan Klesko .75 .23
84 Edgar Martinez 1.25 .35
85 Kevin Millwood .75 .23
86 Bartolo Colon .75 .23
87 Larry Walker 1.25 .35
88 Tom Glavine 1.25 .35
89 Miguel Cabrera 1.25 .35
90 Jose Reyes .75 .23

2004 Upper Deck Power Up Stickers

Nm-Mt Ex-Mt
STATED ODDS 1:6
1 Hideo Nomo 4.00 1.20
2 Mark Prior 4.00 1.20
3 Scott Rolen 4.00 1.20
4 Luis Gonzalez 1.50 .45
5 Miguel Tejada 1.50 .45
6 Richie Sexson 1.50 .45
7 Jim Edmonds 1.50 .45
8 Carlos Beltran 2.50 .75
9 Manny Ramirez 2.50 .75
10 Torii Hunter 1.50 .45
11 Garret Anderson 1.50 .45
12 Eric Chavez 1.50 .45
13 Juan Gonzalez 2.50 .75
14 Albert Pujols 8.00 2.40
15 Tim Hudson 1.50 .45
16 Roy Halladay 1.50 .45
17 Roy Oswalt 1.50 .45
18 Andruw Jones 1.50 .45
19 Gary Sheffield 1.50 .45
20 Magglio Ordonez 1.50 .45
21 Jason Giambi 1.50 .45
22 Brian Giles 1.50 .45
23 Barry Zito 1.50 .45
24 Todd Helton 2.50 .75
25 Randy Johnson 4.00 1.20
26 Pedro Martinez 4.00 1.20
27 Vernon Wells 1.50 .45
28 Lance Berkman 1.50 .45
29 Mike Mussina 2.50 .75
30 Carlos Delgado 1.50 .45
31 Ivan Rodriguez 4.00 1.20
32 Kevin Brown 1.50 .45
33 Kerry Wood 4.00 1.20
34 Mark Teixeira 1.50 .45
35 Hideki Matsui 6.00 1.80
36 Troy Glaus 1.50 .45
37 Mike Piazza 6.00 1.80
38 Nomar Garciaparra 6.00 1.80
39 Vladimir Guerrero 4.00 1.20
40 Derek Jeter 8.00 2.40
41 Jason Schmidt 1.50 .45
42 Alex Rodriguez 6.00 1.80
43 Jeff Bagwell 2.50 .75
44 Shawn Green 1.50 .45
45 Sammy Sosa 6.00 1.80
46 Josh Beckett 1.50 .45
47 Bret Boone 1.50 .45
48 Ichiro Suzuki 6.00 1.80
49 Jeff Kent 1.50 .45
50 Rafael Palmeiro 2.50 .75
51 Curt Schilling 1.50 .45
52 Greg Maddux 6.00 1.80
53 Mike Lowell 1.50 .45
54 Dontrelle Willis 1.50 .45
55 Alfonso Soriano 2.50 .75
56 Preston Wilson 1.50 .45
57 Jorge Posada 2.50 .75
58 Frank Thomas 4.00 1.20
59 Jim Thome 4.00 1.20
60 Ken Griffey Jr. 6.00 1.80
61 Rocco Baldelli 1.50 .45
62 Jose Vidro 1.50 .45
63 Austin Kearns 1.50 .45
64 Phil Nevin 1.50 .45
65 Darin Erstad 1.50 .45
66 Johan Santana 2.50 .75
67 Chipper Jones 4.00 1.20
68 Brandon Webb 1.50 .45
69 Hank Blalock 1.50 .45
70 Adam Dunn 2.50 .75
71 Javier Vazquez 1.50 .45
72 Jacque Jones 1.50 .45
73 Bobby Abreu 1.50 .45
74 Edgar Renteria 1.50 .45
75 Rafael Furcal 1.50 .45
76 Mike Sweeney 1.50 .45
77 Geoff Jenkins 1.50 .45
78 Shannon Stewart 1.50 .45
79 Ryan Klesko 1.50 .45
80 Edgar Martinez 2.50 .75
81 Kevin Millwood 1.50 .45
82 Bartolo Colon 1.50 .45
83 Tom Glavine 2.50 .75
84 Miguel Cabrera 2.50 .75
85 Jose Reyes 1.50 .45
86 San Diego Padres 1.50 .45
Houston Astros
Oakland A's
Anaheim Angels
Chicago Cubs
Tampa Bay Devil Rays
87 Pittsburgh Pirates 1.50 .45
Seattle Mariners
Montreal Expos
Minnesota Twins
Cincinnati Reds
Philadelphia Phillies
88 Kansas City Royals 1.50 .45
Baltimore Orioles
Chicago White Sox
Los Angeles Dodgers
Florida Marlins
New York Yankees
89 San Francisco Giants 1.50 .45
New York Mets
St. Louis Cardinals
Cleveland Indians
Atlanta Braves
Texas Rangers
90 Detroit Tigers 1.50 .45
Boston Red Sox
Colorado Rockies
Arizona Diamondbacks
Milwaukee Brewers
Toronto Blue Jays

2000 Upper Deck PowerDeck Magical Moments Autographs

Randomly inserted into hobby packs, this two-card set is a complete parallel of the Magical Moments insert. This parallel features autographed cards of Ken Griffey Jr. and Cal Ripken. Please note that each card is individually serial numbered to 50, and are numbered on the back using the player's initials.

Nm-Mt Ex-Mt
CR Cal Ripken 400.00 120.00
KG Ken Griffey Jr. 200.00 60.00

2000 Upper Deck Pros and Prospects

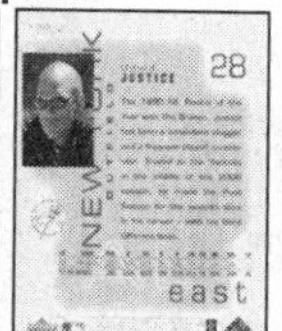

The 2000 Upper Deck Pros and Prospects product was initially released in early October as a 132-card basic set that was broken into tiers as follows: 90 Veterans (1-90), 30 Prospective Superstars (91-120) each serial numbered to 1350, and 12 Pro Fame cards (121-132) each serial numbered to 1000. Each pack contained five cards and carried a suggested retail price of $4.99. In late December, 2000, Upper Deck released their Rookie Update brand which carried a selection of new cards to extend the 2000 SP Authentic, SPx and UD Pros and Prospects brands. The new Pros and Prospects cards featured an extension of the Prospective Superstars subset (cards 133-162) with each card serial numbered to 1,600 and a selection of veterans (cards 163-192) composed of player's either initially not included in the basic set or traded to new teams. Notable Rookie Cards include Barry Zito (his first licensed MLB card), Xavier Nady, Jon Rauch and Ben Sheets. Also, a selection of A Piece of History 3000 Club Lou Brock and Rod Carew memorabilia cards were randomly seeded into packs. 350 bat cards, 350 jersey cards and 100 hand-numbered combination bat-jersey cards were produced for each player. In addition, twenty autographed, hand-numbered, combination bat-jersey Lou Brock cards and twenty nine autographed, hand-numbered, combination bat-jersey Rod Carew cards were produced. Pricing for these memorabilia cards can be referenced under 2000 Upper Deck A Piece of History 3000 Club.

Nm-Mt Ex-Mt
COMP.BASIC w/o SP's (90) 20.00 6.00
COMP.UPDATE w/o SP'S (30) 10.00 3.00
COMMON CARD (1-90) .40 .12
COMMON PS (91-120) 5.00 1.50
COMMON PF (121-132) 4.00 1.20
COMMON PS (133-162) 5.00 1.50
COMMON (163-192) .60 .18
1 Darin Erstad .40 .12
2 Troy Glaus .40 .12
3 Mo Vaughn .40 .12
4 Jason Giambi .40 .12
5 Tim Hudson .40 .12
6 Ben Grieve .40 .12
7 Eric Chavez .40 .12
8 Shannon Stewart .40 .12
9 Raul Mondesi .40 .12
10 Carlos Delgado .40 .12
11 Jose Canseco 1.00 .30
12 Fred McGriff .60 .18
13 Greg Vaughn .40 .12
14 Manny Ramirez .60 .18
15 Roberto Alomar .60 .18
16 Jim Thome 1.00 .30
17 Alex Rodriguez 1.50 .45
18 Freddy Garcia .40 .12
19 John Olerud .40 .12
20 Cal Ripken 3.00 .90
21 Albert Belle .40 .12
22 Mike Mussina .60 .18
23 Ivan Rodriguez 1.00 .30
24 Rafael Palmeiro .60 .18
25 Ruben Mateo .40 .12
26 Gabe Kapler .40 .12
27 Pedro Martinez 1.00 .30
28 Nomar Garciaparra 1.50 .45
29 Carl Everett .40 .12
30 Carlos Beltran .60 .18
31 Jermaine Dye .40 .12
32 Johnny Damon UER .60 .18
Picture on front is Joe Randa
33 Juan Gonzalez .60 .18
34 Juan Encarnacion .40 .12
35 Dean Palmer .40 .12
36 Jacque Jones .40 .12
37 Matt Lawton .40 .12
38 Frank Thomas 1.00 .30
39 Paul Konerko .40 .12
40 Magglio Ordonez .40 .12
41 Derek Jeter 2.50 .75
42 Bernie Williams .60 .18
43 Mariano Rivera .60 .18
44 Roger Clemens 2.00 .60
45 Jeff Bagwell .60 .18
46 Craig Biggio .60 .18
47 Richard Hidalgo .40 .12
48 Chipper Jones 1.00 .30
49 Andres Galarraga .40 .12
50 Andruw Jones .40 .12
51 Greg Maddux 1.50 .45
52 Jeromy Burnitz .40 .12
53 Geoff Jenkins .40 .12
54 Mark McGwire 2.50 .75
55 Jim Edmonds .40 .12
56 Fernando Tatis .40 .12
57 J.D. Drew .40 .12
58 Sammy Sosa 1.50 .45
59 Kerry Wood 1.00 .30
60 Randy Johnson 1.00 .30
61 Matt Williams .40 .12
62 Erubiel Durazo .40 .12
63 Shawn Green .40 .12
64 Kevin Brown .40 .12
65 Gary Sheffield .40 .12
66 Adrian Beltre .60 .18
67 Vladimir Guerrero 1.00 .30
68 Jose Vidro .40 .12
69 Barry Bonds 2.50 .75
70 Jeff Kent .40 .12
71 Preston Wilson .40 .12
72 Ryan Dempster .40 .12
73 Mike Lowell .40 .12
74 Mike Piazza 1.50 .45
75 Robin Ventura .40 .12
76 Edgardo Alfonzo .40 .12
77 Derek Bell .40 .12
78 Tony Gwynn 1.25 .35
79 Matt Clement .40 .12
80 Scott Rolen 1.00 .30
81 Bobby Abreu .40 .12
82 Curt Schilling .40 .12
83 Brian Giles .40 .12
84 Jason Kendall .40 .12
85 Kris Benson .40 .12
86 Ken Griffey Jr. 1.50 .45
87 Sean Casey .40 .12
88 Pokey Reese .40 .12
89 Larry Walker .60 .18
90 Todd Helton .60 .18
91 Rick Ankiel PS 5.00 1.50
92 Milton Bradley PS 5.00 1.50
93 Vernon Wells PS 5.00 1.50
94 Rafael Furcal PS 5.00 1.50
95 Kazuhiro Sasaki PS RC 8.00 2.40
96 Joe Torres PS RC 5.00 1.50
97 Adam Kennedy PS 5.00 1.50
98 Adam Piatt PS 5.00 1.50
99 Matt Wheatland PS RC 5.00 1.50
100 Alex Cabrera PS RC 5.00 1.50
101 Barry Zito PS RC 12.00 3.60
102 Mike Lamb PS RC 5.00 1.50
103 Scott Heard PS RC 5.00 1.50
104 Danys Baez PS RC 5.00 1.50
105 Matt Riley PS 5.00 1.50
106 Mark Mulder PS 5.00 1.50
107 W.Rodriguez PS RC 5.00 1.50

108 Luis Matos PS RC 5.00 1.50
109 Alfonso Soriano PS 8.00 2.40
110 Pat Burrell PS 5.00 1.50
111 Mike Tonis PS RC 5.00 1.50
112 Aaron McNeal PS RC 5.00 1.50
113 Dave Krynzel PS RC 5.00 1.50
114 Josh Beckett PS 8.00 2.40
115 Sean Burnett PS RC 8.00 2.40
116 Eric Munson PS 5.00 1.50
117 Scott Downs PS RC 5.00 1.50
118 Brian Tollberg PS RC 5.00 1.50
119 Nick Johnson PS 5.00 1.50
120 Leo Estrella PS RC 5.00 1.50
121 Ken Griffey Jr. PF 10.00 3.00
122 Frank Thomas PF 6.00 1.80
123 Cal Ripken PF 20.00 6.00
124 Ivan Rodriguez PF 6.00 1.80
125 Derek Jeter PF 15.00 4.50
126 Mark McGwire PF 15.00 4.50
127 Pedro Martinez PF 6.00 1.80
128 Chipper Jones PF 6.00 1.80
129 Sammy Sosa PF 10.00 3.00
130 Alex Rodriguez PF 10.00 3.00
131 Vladimir Guerrero PF 6.00 1.80
132 Jeff Bagwell PF 6.00 1.80
133 Dane Artman PS RC 5.00 1.50
134 Juan Pierre PS RC 8.00 2.40
135 Jace Brewer PS RC 5.00 1.50
136 Sun Woo Kim PS RC 5.00 1.50
137 Jon Rauch PS RC 5.00 1.50
138 Juan Guzman PS RC 5.00 1.50
139 Daylan Holt PS RC 5.00 1.50
140 R.Washington PS RC 5.00 1.50
141 Ben Diggins PS RC 5.00 1.50
142 Mike Meyers PS RC 5.00 1.50
143 C.Wakeland PS RC 5.00 1.50
144 Cory Vance PS RC 5.00 1.50
145 Keith Ginter PS RC 5.00 1.50
146 Koyie Hill PS RC 5.00 1.50
147 Julio Zuleta PS RC 5.00 1.50
148 G.Guzman PS RC 5.00 1.50
149 Jay Spurgeon PS RC 5.00 1.50
150 Ross Gload PS RC 5.00 1.50
151 Ben Sheets PS RC 12.00 3.60
152 J.Kalinowski PS RC 5.00 1.50
153 Kurt Ainsworth PS RC 5.00 1.50
154 P.Crawford PS RC 5.00 1.50
155 Xavier Nady PS RC 8.00 2.40
156 B.Wilkerson PS RC 8.00 2.40
157 Kris Wilson PS RC 5.00 1.50
158 Paul Rigdon PS RC 5.00 1.50
159 R.Kohlmeier PS RC 5.00 1.50
160 Dane Sardinha PS RC 5.00 1.50
161 Javier Cardona PS RC 5.00 1.50
162 Brad Cresse PS RC 5.00 1.50
163 Ron Gant .60 .18
164 Mark Mulder .60 .18
165 David Wells .60 .18
166 Jason Tyner .60 .18
167 David Segui .60 .18
168 Al Martin .60 .18
169 Melvin Mora .60 .18
170 Ricky Ledee .60 .18
171 Rolando Arrojo .60 .18
172 Mike Sweeney .60 .18
173 Bobby Higginson .60 .18
174 Eric Milton .60 .18
175 Charles Johnson .60 .18
176 David Justice .60 .18
177 Moises Alou .60 .18
178 Andy Ashby .60 .18
179 Richie Sexson .60 .18
180 Will Clark 1.50 .45
181 Rondell White .60 .18
182 Curt Schilling .60 .18
183 Tom Goodwin .60 .18
184 Lee Stevens .60 .18
185 Ellis Burks .60 .18
186 Henry Rodriguez .60 .18
187 Mike Bordick .60 .18
188 Ryan Klesko .60 .18
189 Travis Lee .60 .18
190 Kevin Young .60 .18
191 Barry Larkin 1.00 .30
192 Jeff Cirillo .60 .18

2000 Upper Deck Pros and Prospects Best in the Bigs

Randomly inserted into packs at one in 12, this 10-card insert features the best players in Major League Baseball. Card backs carry a "B" prefix.

	Nm-Mt	Ex-Mt
COMPLETE SET (10)	40.00	12.00
B1 Sammy Sosa	4.00	1.20
B2 Tony Gwynn	3.00	.90
B3 Pedro Martinez	2.50	.75
B4 Mark McGwire	6.00	1.80
B5 Chipper Jones	2.50	.75
B6 Derek Jeter	6.00	1.80
B7 Ken Griffey Jr.	4.00	1.20
B8 Cal Ripken	8.00	2.40
B9 Greg Maddux	4.00	1.20
B10 Ivan Rodriguez	2.50	.75

2000 Upper Deck Pros and Prospects Future Forces

Randomly inserted into packs at one in six, this 10-card insert features Major League prospects that hope to play a major role on their teams. Card backs carry a "F" prefix.

	Nm-Mt	Ex-Mt
COMPLETE SET (10)	10.00	3.00
F1 Pat Burrell	1.00	.30
F2 Brad Penny	1.00	.30
F3 Rick Ankiel	1.00	.30

F4 Adam Kennedy	1.00	.30
F5 Eric Munson	1.00	.30
F6 Rafael Furcal	1.00	.30
F7 Mark Mulder	1.00	.30
F8 Vernon Wells	1.00	.30
F9 Matt Riley	1.00	.30
F10 Nick Johnson	1.00	.30

2000 Upper Deck Pros and Prospects Game Jersey Autograph

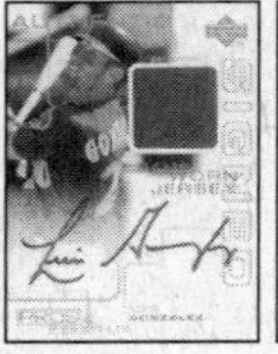

Randomly inserted into packs at an approximate rate of one in 96, this 21-card insert features autographs of many of the Major Leagues elite players. Card backs are numbered using the players initials. The following players packed out as stickered exchange cards: Cal Ripken, Ivan Rodriguez, Jose Canseco, Ken Griffey Jr., Mo Vaughn and Tom Glavine. Please note that Jose Canseco and Tom Glavine both only signed partial quantities of their cards, thus half packed out as proper autos and the other half packed out as exchange cards. Due to problems with the players, UD was not able to get the athletes to sign their remaining cards and were forced to redeem the exchange cards with signed Mo Vaughn cards instead. The deadline to redeem exchange cards was July 5th, 2001. Representatives at Upper Deck have confirmed that the Derek Jeter card was produced in shorter supply than other cards from this set. This set also contains the first-ever certified autograph of Luis Gonzalez.

	Nm-Mt	Ex-Mt
AR Alex Rodriguez	175.00	52.50
BB Barry Bonds	300.00	90.00
CJ Chipper Jones	60.00	18.00
CR Cal Ripken	175.00	52.50
DJ Derek Jeter SP	500.00	150.00
FT Frank Thomas	60.00	18.00
GS Gary Sheffield	50.00	15.00
IR Ivan Rodriguez	50.00	15.00
JC Jose Canseco EXCH NO AU	10.00	3.00
JC Jose Canseco	50.00	15.00
JD J.D. Drew	50.00	15.00
KG Ken Griffey Jr.	150.00	45.00
KL Kenny Lofton	50.00	15.00
LG Luis Gonzalez	40.00	12.00
MV Mo Vaughn	40.00	12.00
MW Matt Williams	40.00	12.00
PW Preston Wilson	40.00	12.00
RJ Randy Johnson	100.00	30.00
RV Robin Ventura	40.00	12.00
SR Scott Rolen	40.00	12.00
TGL Tom Glavine EXCH NO AU	10.00	3.00
TGL Tom Glavine	50.00	15.00
TGW Tony Gwynn	60.00	18.00

2000 Upper Deck Pros and Prospects Game Jersey Autograph Gold

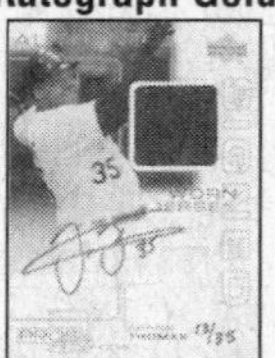

Randomly inserted into packs, this 21-card insert is a complete parallel of the 2000 Pros and Prospects Game Jerseys. Each card is serial numbered to the player's jersey number, and are numbered on the back using the player's initials. Please note that Upper Deck has announced the exchange cards of Jose Canseco and Tom Glavine will be redeemed with Mo Vaughn. Some cards are not priced due to market scarcity. The following cards packed out as exchange cards with a redemption deadline of 07/05/01: Cal Ripken, Ivan Rodriguez, Ken Griffey Jr. and Mo Vaughn.

	Nm-Mt	Ex-Mt
AR Alex Rodriguez/3		
BB Barry Bonds/25		
CJ Chipper Jones/10		
CR Cal Ripken/8		
DJ Derek Jeter/2		
FT Frank Thomas/35	150.00	45.00
GS Gary Sheffield/10		
IR Ivan Rodriguez/7		
JC Jose Canseco/33		
JD J.D. Drew/7		
KG Ken Griffey Jr. 30 EXCH	250.00	75.00
KL Kenny Lofton/7		
LG Luis Gonzalez/20		
MV Mo Vaughn/42	60.00	18.00
MW Matt Williams/9		
PW Preston Wilson/44	40.00	12.00
RJ Randy Johnson/51	250.00	75.00
RV Robin Ventura/4		
SR Scott Rolen/17		
TGL Tom Glavine/47	120.00	36.00
TGW Tony Gwynn/19		

2000 Upper Deck Pros and Prospects ProMotion

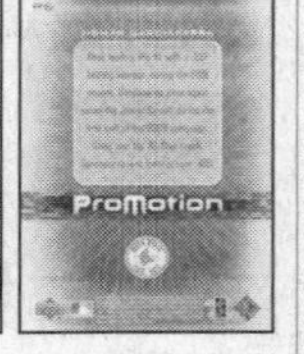

Randomly inserted into packs at one in six, this 10-card insert features baseball's greatest all-around players. Card backs carry a "P" prefix.

	Nm-Mt	Ex-Mt
COMPLETE SET (10)	25.00	7.50
P1 Derek Jeter	4.00	1.20
P2 Mike Piazza	2.50	.75
P3 Mark McGwire	4.00	1.20
P4 Ivan Rodriguez	1.50	.45
P5 Kerry Wood	1.50	.45
P6 Nomar Garciaparra	2.50	.75
P7 Sammy Sosa	2.50	.75
P8 Alex Rodriguez	2.50	.75
P9 Ken Griffey Jr.	2.50	.75
P10 Vladimir Guerrero	1.50	.45

2000 Upper Deck Pros and Prospects Rare Breed

Randomly inserted into packs at one in 12, this 12-card insert features players that have rare talents. Card backs carry a "R" prefix.

	Nm-Mt	Ex-Mt
COMPLETE SET (12)	40.00	12.00
R1 Mark McGwire	6.00	1.80
R2 Frank Thomas	2.50	.75
R3 Mike Piazza	4.00	1.20
R4 Barry Bonds	6.00	1.80
R5 Manny Ramirez	1.50	.45
R6 Ken Griffey Jr.	4.00	1.20
R7 Nomar Garciaparra	4.00	1.20
R8 Randy Johnson	2.50	.75
R9 Vladimir Guerrero	2.50	.75
R10 Jeff Bagwell	1.50	.45
R11 Rick Ankiel	12.00	3.60
R12 Alex Rodriguez	4.00	1.20

2001 Upper Deck Pros and Prospects

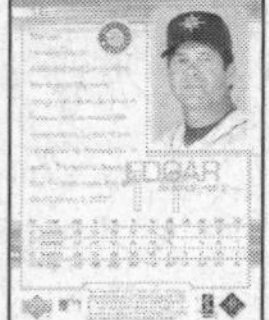

This 135 card set was issued in five card packs. Cards numbered 91-141 were shorter printed than the other cards. Cards numbered 91-135 had a print run of 1,250 serial numbered sets while cards numbered 136-141 had a print run of 500 sets.

	Nm-Mt	Ex-Mt
COMP.SET w/o SP's (90)	15.00	4.50
COMMON CARD (1-90)	.40	.12
COMMON CARD (91-135)	5.00	1.50
COMMON (136-141)	20.00	6.00
1 Troy Glaus	.40	.12
2 Darin Erstad	.40	.12
3 Tim Hudson	.40	.12
4 Jason Giambi	.40	.12
5 Jermaine Dye	.40	.12
6 Barry Zito	.60	.18
7 Carlos Delgado	.40	.12
8 Shannon Stewart	.40	.12
9 Raul Mondesi	.40	.12
10 Greg Vaughn	.40	.12
11 Ben Grieve	.40	.12
12 Roberto Alomar	.60	.18
13 Juan Gonzalez	.60	.18
14 Jim Thome	1.00	.30
15 C.C. Sabathia	.40	.12
16 Edgar Martinez	.60	.18
17 Kazuhiro Sasaki	.40	.12
18 Aaron Sele	.40	.12
19 John Olerud	.40	.12
20 Cal Ripken	3.00	.90
21 Rafael Palmeiro	.60	.18
22 Ivan Rodriguez	1.00	.30
23 Alex Rodriguez	1.50	.45
24 Manny Ramirez	.60	.18
25 Pedro Martinez	1.00	.30
26 Carl Everett	.40	.12
27 Nomar Garciaparra	1.50	.45
28 Neifi Perez	.40	.12
29 Mike Sweeney	.40	.12
30 Bobby Higginson	.40	.12
31 Tony Clark	.40	.12
32 Doug Mientkiewicz	.40	.12
33 Cristian Guzman	.40	.12
34 Brad Radke	.40	.12
35 Magglio Ordonez	.40	.12
36 Carlos Lee	.40	.12
37 Frank Thomas	1.00	.30
38 Roger Clemens	2.00	.60
39 Bernie Williams	.60	.18
40 Derek Jeter	2.50	.75
41 Tino Martinez	.60	.18
42 Wade Miller	.40	.12
43 Jeff Bagwell	.60	.18
44 Lance Berkman	.40	.12
45 Richard Hidalgo	.40	.12
46 Greg Maddux	1.50	.45
47 Andruw Jones	.40	.12
48 Chipper Jones	1.00	.30
49 Rafael Furcal	.40	.12
50 Jeromy Burnitz	.40	.12
51 Geoff Jenkins	.40	.12
52 Ben Sheets	.60	.18
53 Mark McGwire	2.50	.75
54 Jim Edmonds	.40	.12
55 J.D. Drew	.40	.12
56 Fred McGriff	.60	.18
57 Sammy Sosa	1.50	.45
58 Kerry Wood	1.00	.30
59 Randy Johnson	1.00	.30
60 Luis Gonzalez	.40	.12
61 Curt Schilling	.40	.12
62 Kevin Brown	.40	.12
63 Shawn Green	.40	.12
64 Gary Sheffield	.40	.12
65 Vladimir Guerrero	1.00	.30
66 Jose Vidro	.40	.12
67 Barry Bonds	2.50	.75
68 Jeff Kent	.40	.12
69 Rich Aurilia	.40	.12
70 Preston Wilson	.40	.12
71 Charles Johnson	.40	.12
72 Cliff Floyd	.40	.12
73 Mike Piazza	1.50	.45
74 Al Leiter	.40	.12
75 Matt Lawton	.40	.12
76 Tony Gwynn	1.25	.35
77 Ryan Klesko	.40	.12
78 Phil Nevin	.40	.12
79 Scott Rolen	1.00	.30
80 Pat Burrell	.40	.12
81 Jimmy Rollins	.40	.12
82 Jason Kendall	.40	.12
83 Brian Giles	.40	.12
84 Aramis Ramirez	.40	.12
85 Ken Griffey Jr.	1.50	.45
86 Barry Larkin	.60	.18
87 Sean Casey	.40	.12
88 Larry Walker	.60	.18
89 Todd Helton	.60	.18
90 Mike Hampton	.40	.12
91 Juan Cruz PS RC	5.00	1.50
92 Brian Lawrence PS RC	5.00	1.50
93 Brandon Lyon PS RC	5.00	1.50
94 A.Hernandez PS RC	5.00	1.50
95 Jose Mieses PS RC	5.00	1.50
96 Juan Uribe PS RC	8.00	2.40
97 M.Ensberg PS RC	8.00	2.40
98 Wilson Betemit PS RC	5.00	1.50
99 Ryan Freel PS RC	5.00	1.50
100 Jack Wilson PS RC	10.00	3.00
101 Cesar Crespo PS RC	5.00	1.50
102 Bret Prinz PS RC	5.00	1.50
103 H.Ramirez PS RC	8.00	2.40
104 E. Guzman PS RC	5.00	1.50
105 Josh Towers PS RC	5.00	1.50
106 B. Duckworth PS RC	5.00	1.50
107 Esix Snead PS RC	5.00	1.50
108 Billy Sylvester PS RC	5.00	1.50
109 Alexis Gomez PS RC	5.00	1.50
110 J. Estrada PS RC	8.00	2.40
111 Joe Kennedy PS RC	8.00	2.40
112 Travis Hafner PS RC	12.00	3.60
113 Martin Vargas PS RC	5.00	1.50
114 Jay Gibbons PS RC	8.00	2.40
115 Andres Torres PS RC	5.00	1.50
116 Sean Douglass PS RC	5.00	1.50
117 Juan Diaz PS RC	5.00	1.50
118 Greg Miller PS RC	5.00	1.50
119 C. Valderrama PS RC	5.00	1.50
120 Bill Ortega PS RC	5.00	1.50
121 Josh Fogg PS RC	5.00	1.50
122 Wilken Ruan PS RC	5.00	1.50
123 Kris Keller PS RC	5.00	1.50
124 Erick Almonte PS RC	5.00	1.50
125 R. Rodriguez PS RC	5.00	1.50
126 Grant Balfour PS RC	5.00	1.50
127 Nick Maness PS RC	5.00	1.50
128 Jeremy Owens PS RC	5.00	1.50
129 Doug Nickle PS RC	5.00	1.50
130 Bert Snow PS RC	5.00	1.50
131 Jason Smith PS RC	5.00	1.50
132 Henry Mateo PS RC	5.00	1.50
133 Mike Penney PS RC	5.00	1.50
134 Bud Smith PS RC	5.00	1.50
135 Junior Spivey PS RC	8.00	2.40
136 Ichiro Suzuki JSY RC	100.00	30.00
137 Albert Pujols JSY RC	150.00	45.00
138 Mark Teixeira JSY RC	100.00	30.00
139 D. Brazelton JSY RC	20.00	6.00
140 Mark Prior JSY RC	100.00	30.00
141 T. Shinjo JSY RC	20.00	6.00

2001 Upper Deck Pros and Prospects Franchise Building Blocks

Issued at a rate of one in six, these 30 cards feature leading player as well as the leading prospect or rookie from each major league franchise.

	Nm-Mt	Ex-Mt
COMPLETE SET (30)	50.00	15.00
F1 Darin Erstad / Elpidio Guzman	1.00	.30
F2 Jason Giambi / Jason Hart	1.00	.30
F3 Carlos Delgado / Vernon Wells	1.00	.30
F4 Greg Vaughn / Aubrey Huff	1.00	.30
F5 Jim Thome / C.C. Sabathia	1.50	.45
F6 Edgar Martinez / Ichiro Suzuki	5.00	1.50
F7 Cal Ripken Jr. / Josh Towers	5.00	1.50
F8 Ivan Rodriguez / Carlos Pena	1.50	.45
F9 Nomar Garciaparra / Dernell Stenson	2.50	.75
F10 Mike Sweeney / Dee Brown	1.00	.30
F11 Bobby Higginson / Brandon Inge	1.00	.30
F12 Brad Radke / Adam Johnson	1.00	.30
F13 Frank Thomas / Joe Crede	1.50	.45
F14 Derek Jeter / Nick Johnson	4.00	1.20
F15 Jeff Bagwell / Morgan Ensberg	1.50	.45
F16 Chipper Jones / Wilson Betemit	1.50	.45
F17 Jeromy Burnitz / Ben Sheets	1.00	.30
F18 Mark McGwire / Albert Pujols	10.00	3.00
F19 Sammy Sosa / Corey Patterson	2.50	.75
F20 Luis Gonzalez / Jack Cust	1.00	.30
F21 Kevin Brown / Luke Prokopec	1.00	.30
F22 Vladimir Guerrero / Wilkin Ruan	1.50	.45
F23 Barry Bonds / Carlos Valderrama	4.00	1.20
F24 Preston Wilson / Abraham Nunez	1.00	.30
F25 Mike Piazza / Alex Escobar	2.50	.75
F26 Tony Gwynn / Xavier Nady	2.00	.60
F27 Scott Rolen / Jimmy Rollins	1.50	.45
F28 Jason Kendall / Jack Wilson	2.00	.60
F29 Ken Griffey Jr. / Adam Dunn	2.50	.75
F30 Todd Helton / Juan Uribe	1.00	.30

2001 Upper Deck Pros and Prospects Game Bat

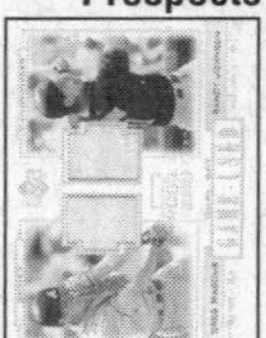

Issued at a rate of one in 24, these 13 cards feature two bat pieces on each card.

GOLD RANDOM INSERTS IN PACKS..
GOLD PRINT RUN 25 SERIAL #'d SETS
NO GOLD PRICING DUE TO SCARCITY

	Nm-Mt	Ex-Mt
PPBT Jeff Bagwell / Frank Thomas	15.00	4.50
PPGBO Ken Griffey Jr. / Barry Bonds	40.00	12.00
PPGBU Shawn Green / Jeromy Burnitz	10.00	3.00
PPJL Andruw Jones / Kenny Lofton	10.00	3.00
PPJP Chipper Jones / Albert Pujols	50.00	15.00
PPKA Jeff Kent / Roberto Alomar	15.00	4.50
PPMJ Greg Maddux / Randy Johnson	15.00	4.50
PPPT Rafael Palmeiro / Jim Thome	15.00	4.50
PPRF Alex Rodriguez / Rafael Furcal	15.00	4.50
PPRG Manny Ramirez / Juan Gonzalez	15.00	4.50
PPRP Ivan Rodriguez / Mike Piazza	15.00	4.50
PPSG Sammy Sosa / Luis Gonzalez	15.00	4.50
PPWI Bernie Williams / Ichiro Suzuki	40.00	12.00

2001 Upper Deck Pros and Prospects Ichiro World Tour

Issued one per 12 packs, these 15 cards feature Ichrio Suzuki and information about various ballparks he played in.

	Nm-Mt	Ex-Mt
COMPLETE SET (15)	100.00	30.00
COMMON CARD (WT1-WT15)	8.00	2.40

2001 Upper Deck Pros and Prospects Legends Game Bat

Issued one per 216 packs, these six cards feature two bat pieces from players whose careers are related to each other.

	Nm-Mt	Ex-Mt
GOLD RANDOM INSERTS IN PACKS..		
GOLD PRINT RUN 25 SERIAL #'d SETS		
NO GOLD PRICING DUE TO SCARCITY		
PL-BY Jeromy Burnitz	25.00	7.50
Robin Yount		
PL-GM Ken Griffey Jr.		
Joe Morgan		
PL-RF Manny Ramirez	25.00	7.50
Carlton Fisk		
PL-RG Cal Ripken Jr.	50.00	15.00
Tony Gwynn		
PL-SB Sammy Sosa		
Ernie Banks		
PL-WJ Bernie Williams	25.00	7.50
Reggie Jackson		

2001 Upper Deck Pros and Prospects Specialty Game Jersey

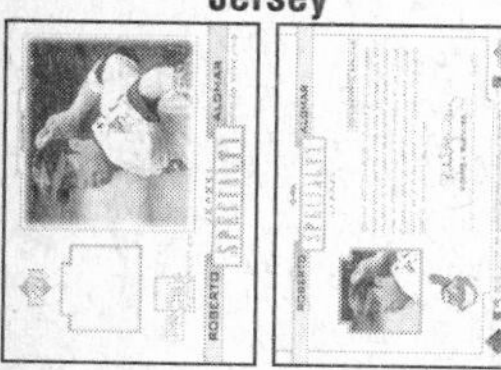

Inserted one per 24 packs, these cards feature a piece of a jersey worn by the featured player in a special event.

	Nm-Mt	Ex-Mt
GOLD RANDOM INSERTS IN PACKS..		
GOLD PRINT RUN 25 SERIAL #'d SETS		
NO GOLD PRICING DUE TO SCARCITY		
S-I Ichiro Suzuki	50.00	15.00
S-AR Alex Rodriguez	15.00	4.50
S-BB Barry Bonds	25.00	7.50
S-CR Cal Ripken	40.00	12.00
S-JE Jim Edmonds	8.00	2.40
S-JG Juan Gonzalez	10.00	3.00
S-JT Jim Thome	10.00	3.00
S-LW Larry Walker	10.00	3.00
S-RA Roberto Alomar	10.00	3.00
S-RJ Randy Johnson	10.00	3.00
S-SG Shawn Green	8.00	2.40
S-SR Scott Rolen	10.00	3.00
S-SS Sammy Sosa	15.00	4.50
S-TG Tony Gwynn	15.00	4.50

2001 Upper Deck Pros and Prospects Then and Now Game Jersey

Issued at a rate of one in 24, these 25 cards feature a retrospective look at the showcased player's career by including a jersey swatch from both his past team and his current team. Nolan Ryan is featured with three different swatches.

	Nm-Mt	Ex-Mt
GOLD RANDOM INSERTS IN PACKS..		
GOLD PRINT RUN 25 SERIAL #'d SETS		
NO GOLD PRICING DUE TO SCARCITY		
TN-AR Alex Rodriguez	25.00	7.50
TN-B Barry Bonds	40.00	12.00
TN-CS Curt Schilling	10.00	3.00
TN-FG Freddy Garcia	10.00	3.00
TN-GM Greg Maddux	15.00	4.50
TN-GS Gary Sheffield	10.00	3.00
TN-JE Jim Edmonds	10.00	3.00
TN-JG Jason Giambi	10.00	3.00
TN-JG Juan Gonzalez	15.00	4.50
TN-KB Kevin Brown	10.00	3.00
TN-KG Ken Griffey Jr.	20.00	6.00
TN-MP Mike Piazza	15.00	4.50
TN-MR Manny Ramirez	15.00	4.50
TN-NR Nolan Ryan	120.00	36.00
TN-PM Pedro Martinez	15.00	4.50
TN-PN Phil Nevin	10.00	3.00
TN-RA Rick Ankiel	10.00	3.00
TN-RC Roger Clemens	30.00	9.00
TN-RJ Randy Johnson	15.00	4.50
TN-RV Robin Ventura	10.00	3.00
TN-XN Xavier Nady	10.00	3.00

2001 Upper Deck Prospect Premieres

The 2001 Upper Deck Prospect Premieres was released in October 2001 and features a 102-card set. The first 90 cards are regular and the last 12 are autographed cards numbered to 1000 randomly inserted into packs. The packs contain four cards and have a SRP of $2.99 per pack. There were 18 packs per box.

	Nm-Mt	Ex-Mt
COMP.SET w/o SP's (90)	25.00	7.50
COMMON CARD (1-90)	.40	.12
COMMON AUTO (91-102)	15.00	4.50
1 Jeff Mathis XRC	1.50	.45
2 Jake Woods XRC	.40	.12
3 Dallas McPherson XRC	6.00	1.80
4 Steven Shell XRC	.40	.12
5 Ryan Budde XRC	.40	.12
6 Kirk Saarloos XRC	.40	.12
7 Ryan Stegall XRC	.40	.12
8 Bobby Crosby XRC	4.00	1.20
9 J.T. Stotts XRC	.40	.12
10 Neal Cotts XRC	1.00	.30
11 J.Bonderman XRC	.75	.23
12 Brandon League XRC	.40	.12
13 Tyrell Godwin XRC	.40	.12
14 Gabe Gross XRC	.50	.15
15 Chris Neylan XRC	.40	.12
16 Macay McBride XRC	.40	.12
17 Josh Burrus XRC	.40	.12
18 Adam Stern XRC	.40	.12
19 Richard Lewis XRC	1.00	.30
20 Cole Barthel XRC	.40	.12
21 Mike Jones XRC	.50	.15
22 J.J. Hardy XRC	2.00	.60
23 Jon Steitz XRC	.40	.12
24 Brad Nelson XRC	1.25	.35
25 Justin Pope XRC	.40	.12
26 Dan Haren XRC UER	.75	.23
Blurb incorrectly lists him as a lefty		
27 Andy Sisco XRC	1.00	.30
28 Ryan Theriot XRC	.40	.12
29 Ricky Nolasco XRC	.40	.12
30 Jon Switzer XRC	.40	.12
31 Justin Wechsler XRC	.40	.12
32 Mike Gosling XRC	.40	.12
33 Scott Hairston XRC	1.50	.45
34 Brian Pilkington XRC	.40	.12
35 Kole Strayhorn XRC	.40	.12
36 David Taylor XRC	.40	.12
37 Donald Levinski XRC	.40	.12
38 Mike Hinckley XRC	1.00	.30
39 Nick Long XRC	.40	.12
40 Brad Hennessey XRC	.75	.23
41 Noah Lowry XRC	2.00	.60
42 Josh Cram XRC	.40	.12
43 Jesse Foppert XRC	1.00	.30
44 Julian Benavidez XRC	.40	.12
45 Dan Denham XRC	.40	.12
46 Travis Foley XRC	.40	.12
47 Mike Conroy XRC	.40	.12
48 Jake Dittler XRC	.75	.23
49 Rene Rivera XRC	.40	.12
50 John Cole XRC	.40	.12
51 Lazaro Abreu XRC	.40	.12
52 David Wright XRC	12.00	3.60
53 Aaron Heilman XRC	.40	.12
54 Len DiNardo XRC	.40	.12
55 Alhaji Turay XRC	.50	.15
56 Chris Smith XRC	.40	.12
57 Rommie Lewis XRC	.40	.12
58 Bryan Bass XRC	.40	.12
59 David Crouthers XRC	.40	.12
60 Josh Barfield XRC	1.50	.45
61 Jake Peavy XRC	2.00	.60
62 Ryan Howard XRC	4.00	1.20
63 Gavin Floyd XRC	2.50	.75
64 Michael Floyd XRC	.40	.12
65 Stefan Bailie XRC	.40	.12
66 Jon DeVries XRC	.40	.12
67 Steve Kelly XRC	.40	.12
68 Alan Moye XRC	.40	.12
69 Justin Gillman XRC	.40	.12
70 Jayson Nix XRC	.75	.23
71 John Draper XRC	.40	.12
72 Kenny Baugh XRC	.40	.12
73 Michael Woods XRC	.40	.12
74 Preston Larrison XRC	.50	.15
75 Matt Coenen XRC	.40	.12
76 Scott Tyler XRC	.50	.15
77 Jose Morales XRC	.40	.12
78 Corwin Malone XRC	.40	.12
79 Dennis Ulacia XRC	.50	.15
80 Andy Gonzalez XRC	.40	.12
81 Kris Honel XRC	1.50	.45
82 Wyatt Allen XRC	.40	.12
83 Ryan Wing XRC	.40	.12
84 Sean Henn XRC	.40	.12
85 John-Ford Griffin XRC	.40	.12
86 Bronson Sardinha XRC	.75	.23
87 Jon Skaggs XRC	.40	.12
88 Shelley Duncan XRC	.40	.12
89 Jason Arnold XRC	.75	.23
90 Aaron Rifkin XRC	.50	.15
91 Colt Griffin AU XRC	25.00	7.50
92 J.D. Martin AU XRC	15.00	4.50
93 Justin Wayne AU XRC	15.00	4.50
94 J.VanBenschoten AU XRC	30.00	9.00
95 Chris Burke AU XRC	25.00	7.50
96 C. Kotchman AU XRC	70.00	21.00
97 M. Garciaparra AU XRC	25.00	7.50
98 Jake Gautreau AU XRC	15.00	4.50
99 J. Williams AU XRC	40.00	12.00
100 Toe Nash AU XRC	15.00	4.50
101 Joe Borchard AU XRC	25.00	7.50
102 Mark Prior AU XRC	150.00	45.00

2001 Upper Deck Prospect Premieres Heroes of Baseball Game Bat

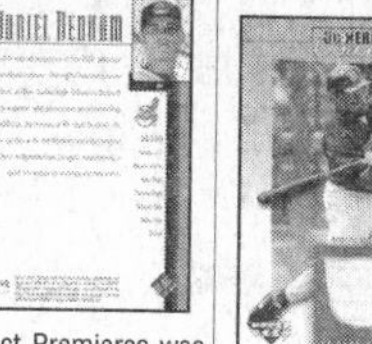

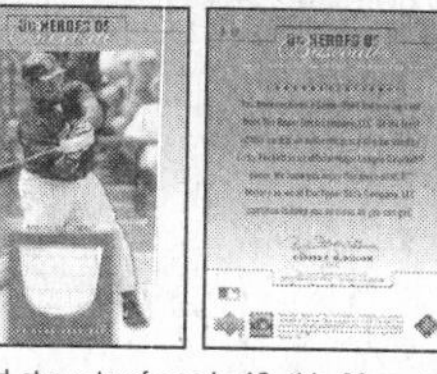

Inserted at a rate of one in 18, this 23-card set features bat pieces of retired players. The cards carry a 'B' prefix.

	Nm-Mt	Ex-Mt
B-AO Al Oliver	10.00	3.00
B-BB Bill Buckner	10.00	3.00
B-BM Bill Madlock	10.00	3.00
B-DB Don Baylor	10.00	3.00
B-DE Dwight Evans	10.00	3.00
B-DL Davey Lopes	10.00	3.00
B-DP Dave Parker	10.00	3.00
B-DW Dave Winfield	10.00	3.00
B-EM Eddie Murray	15.00	4.50
B-FL Fred Lynn	10.00	3.00
B-GC Gary Carter	10.00	3.00
B-GM Gary Matthews	10.00	3.00
B-JM Joe Morgan	10.00	3.00
B-KEG Ken Griffey Sr.	10.00	3.00
B-KIG Kirk Gibson	10.00	3.00
B-KP Kirby Puckett	15.00	4.50
B-MM Manny Mota	10.00	3.00
B-OS Ozzie Smith	15.00	4.50
B-RJ Reggie Jackson	15.00	4.50
B-SG Steve Garvey	10.00	3.00
B-TM Tim McCarver	10.00	3.00
B-TP Tony Perez	10.00	3.00
B-WB Wade Boggs	15.00	4.50

2001 Upper Deck Prospect Premieres Heroes of Baseball Game Jersey Duos

Inserted at a rate of one in 144, this seven card set featured dual game jerseys of both current and retired players. The cards carry a 'J' prefix.

	Nm-Mt	Ex-Mt
J-BH Bryan Bass	10.00	3.00
J.J. Hardy		
J-DG Shelley Duncan	8.00	2.40
Tyrell Godwin		
J-GS Steve Garvey	8.00	2.40
Reggie Smith		
J-HB Aaron Heilman	10.00	3.00
Jeremy Bonderman		
J-JJ Michael Jordan	100.00	30.00
Michael Jordan		
J-SG Jon Switzer	8.00	2.40
Mike Gosling		
J-WP Dave Winfield	25.00	7.50
Kirby Puckett		

2001 Upper Deck Prospect Premieres Heroes of Baseball Game Jersey Duos Autograph

Randomly inserted into packs, this six card set featured dual game jerseys with autographs of both current and retired players. The cards were serial numbered to 25.The cards carry a 'SJ' prefix. Due to scarcity, no pricing is provided.

	Nm-Mt	Ex-Mt
SJBH Bryan Bass		
J.J. Hardy		
SJGS Steve Garvey		
Reggie Smith		
SJHB Aaron Heilman		
Jeremy Bonderman		
SJJJ Michael Jordan		
Michael Jordan		
SJMG Joe Morgan		
Ken Griffey Sr		
SJWP Dave Winfield		
Kirby Puckett		

2001 Upper Deck Prospect Premieres Heroes of Baseball Game Jersey Trios

Inserted in packs at a rate of one in 144, these nine cards feature three swatches of game-worn jerseys on a card. Representatives at Upper Deck have confirmed that the Maris-Mantle-DiMaggio card is in noticeably short supply. In addition, the following cards did not packout and were available via exchange cards that were seeded

into packs in their place: Crosby/Garciaparra/Sardinha, Gautreau/Godwin/Heilman, Gross/Kotchman/Baugh, Griffin/Martin/Switzer and VanBenSchoten/Prior/Jones. The deadline to mail in these exchange cards was October 22nd, 2004.

	Nm-Mt	Ex-Mt
BBC Chris Burke	15.00	4.50
Bryan Bass		
Bobby Crosby UER		
CGS Bobby Crosby UER	15.00	4.50
Michael Garciaparra		
Bronson Sardinha		
GGH Jake Gautreau	8.00	2.40
Tyrell Godwin		
Aaron Heilman		
GKB Gabe Gross	15.00	4.50
Casey Kotchmann		
Kenny Baugh		
GMS Colt Griffin	10.00	3.00
J.D. Martin		
Jon Switzer		
JMD Michael Jordan	400.00	120.00
Mickey Mantle		
Joe DiMaggio		
JPW Michael Jordan	80.00	24.00
Kirby Puckett		
Dave Winfield		
MMD Roger Maris	400.00	120.00
Mickey Mantle		
Joe DiMaggio SP		
VPJ Jon VanBenSchoten	25.00	7.50
Mark Prior		
Mike Jones		

2001 Upper Deck Prospect Premieres Heroes of Baseball Game Jersey Trios Autograph

Randomly inserted in packs, these cards feature not only three swatches of game-worn jerseys but also autographs of the featured players. These cards are serial numbered to 25. Due to scarcity, no pricing is provided.

	Nm-Mt	Ex-Mt
SJ-BBC Chris Burke		
Bryan Bass		
Bobby Crosby UER		
SJ-JPW Michael Jordan		
Kirby Puckett		
Dave Winfield		
SJ-MGP Joe Morgan		
Ken Griffey Sr.		
Tony Perez		

2001 Upper Deck Prospect Premieres MJ Grandslam Game Bat

Randomly inserted in packs, these five cards feature bat cards from basketball legend turned baseball prospect. Card number "MJ5" was printed in lesser quantities and is notated in our checklist as an SP.

	Nm-Mt	Ex-Mt
COMMON CARD (MJ1-MJ4)	30.00	9.00
MJ5 Michael Jordan SP	60.00	18.00

2001 Upper Deck Prospect Premieres Tribute to 42

Issued at a rate of one in 750, these seven cards honor the memory of the integration trail blazer and all time great.

	Nm-Mt	Ex-Mt
B Jackie Robinson Bat	50.00	15.00
C Jackie Robinson Cut AU		
J Jackie Robinson Pants	50.00	15.00
BC Jackie Robinson Bat-Cut AU		
GB Jackie Robinson	80.00	24.00
Gold Bat/42		
GJ J.Robinson Pants Gold/42	80.00	24.00
JC Jackie Robinson Pants-Cut AU		

2002 Upper Deck Prospect Premieres

This 109 card set was released in November, 2002. It was issued in four count packs which

came 24 packs to a box and 20 boxes to a case with an SRP of $3 per pack. Cards number 61 through 85 feature game-worn jersey pieces and were inserted at a stated rate of one in 18 packs. Cards numbered 86 through 97 feature player's autographs and were issued at a stated rate of one in 18 packs. Cards numbered 98 through 109 feature tribute cards to recently retired superstars Cal Ripken and Mark McGwire along with Yankee great Joe DiMaggio. Matt Pender's basic XRC erroneously packed out picturing Curtis Granderson. A corrected version of the card was made available to collectors a few months after the product went live via a mail exchange program directly from Upper Deck.

	Nm-Mt	Ex-Mt
COMP.SET w/o SP's (72)	25.00	7.50
COMMON CARD (1-60)	.40	.12
COMMON CARD (61-85)	5.00	1.50
COMMON CARD (86-97)	10.00	3.00
COMMON RIPKEN (98-99)	2.00	.60
COMMON MCGWIRE (100-105)	2.00	.60
COMMON DIMAGGIO (106-109)	1.50	.45
PENDER COR AVAIL.VIA MAIL EXCHANGE		
1 Josh Rupe XRC	.40	.12
2 Blair Johnson XRC	.40	.12
3 Jason Pridie XRC	.75	.23
4 Tim Gilhooly XRC	.40	.12
5 Kennard Jones XRC	.40	.12
6 Darrell Rasner XRC	.40	.12
7 Adam Donachie XRC	.40	.12
8 Josh Murray XRC	.40	.12
9 Brian Dopirak XRC	2.50	.75
10 Jason Cooper XRC	.50	.15
11 Zach Hammes XRC	.40	.12
12 Jon Lester XRC	.40	.12
13 Kevin Jepsen XRC	1.00	.30
14 Curtis Granderson XRC	1.25	.35
15 David Bush XRC	.75	.23
16 Joel Guzman	.50	.15
17A Matt Pender UER XRC	.75	.23
Pictures Curtis Granderson		
17B Matt Pender COR		
18 Derick Grigsby XRC	.40	.12
19 Jeremy Reed XRC	2.50	.75
20 Jonathan Broxton XRC	.75	.23
21 Jesse Crain XRC	.75	.23
22 Justin Jones XRC	1.00	.30
23 Brian Slocum XRC	.40	.12
24 Brian McCann XRC	.75	.23
25 Francisco Liriano XRC	.50	.15
26 Fred Lewis XRC	.40	.12
27 Steve Stanley XRC	.40	.12
28 Chris Snyder XRC	.75	.23
29 Dan Cevette XRC	.40	.12
30 Kiel Fisher XRC	.50	.15
31 Brandon Weeden XRC	.40	.12
32 Pat Osborn XRC	.40	.12
33 Taber Lee XRC	.40	.12
34 Dan Ortmeier XRC	.75	.23
35 Josh Johnson XRC	.40	.12
36 Val Majewski XRC	1.00	.30
37 Larry Broadway XRC	.75	.23
38 Joey Gomes XRC	.40	.12
39 Eric Thomas XRC	.40	.12
40 James Loney XRC	1.50	.45
41 Charlie Morton XRC	.40	.12
42 Mark McLemore XRC	.40	.12
43 Matt Craig XRC	.50	.15
44 Ryan Rodriguez XRC	.40	.12
45 Rich Hill XRC	.40	.12
46 Bob Malek XRC	.40	.12
47 Justin Maureau XRC	.40	.12
48 Randy Braun XRC	.40	.12
49 Brian Grant XRC	.40	.12
50 Tyler Davidson XRC	.50	.15
51 Travis Hanson XRC	.40	.12
52 Kyle Boyer XRC	.40	.12
53 James Holcomb XRC	.40	.12
54 Ryan Williams XRC	.40	.12
55 Ben Crockett XRC	.40	.12
56 Adam Greenberg XRC	.50	.15
57 John Baker XRC	.40	.12
58 Matt Carson XRC	.40	.12
59 Jonathan George XRC	.40	.12
60 David Jensen XRC	.40	.12
61 Nick Swisher JSY XRC	15.00	4.50
62 Br.Clevlen JSY XRC UER	8.00	2.40
Name mispelled as Cleven		
63 Royce Ring JSY XRC	8.00	2.40
64 Mike Nixon JSY XRC	5.00	1.50
65 Ricky Barrett JSY XRC	5.00	1.50
66 Russ Adams JSY XRC	8.00	2.40
67 Joe Mauer JSY XRC	20.00	6.00
68 Jeff Francoeur JSY XRC	20.00	6.00
69 Joseph Blanton JSY XRC	8.00	2.40
70 Micah Schilling JSY XRC	5.00	1.50
71 John McCurdy JSY XRC	5.00	1.50
72 Sergio Santos JSY XRC	10.00	3.00
73 Josh Womack JSY XRC	5.00	1.50
74 Jared Doyle JSY XRC	5.00	1.50
75 Ben Fritz JSY XRC	5.00	1.50
76 Greg Miller JSY XRC	10.00	3.00
77 Luke Hagerty JSY XRC	5.00	1.50
78 Matt Whitney JSY XRC	8.00	2.40
79 Dan Meyer JSY XRC	8.00	2.40
80 Bill Murphy JSY XRC	8.00	2.40
81 Zach Segovia JSY XRC	8.00	2.40
82 St. Obenchain JSY XRC	5.00	1.50
83 Matt Clanton JSY XRC	5.00	1.50
84 Mark Teahen JSY XRC	10.00	3.00
85 Kyle Pawelczyk JSY XRC	5.00	1.50
86 Khalil Greene AU XRC	70.00	21.00
87 Joe Saunders AU XRC	10.00	3.00
88 Jeremy Hermida AU XRC	25.00	7.50
89 Drew Meyer AU XRC	10.00	3.00
90 Jeff Francis AU XRC	25.00	7.50

91 Scott Moore AU XRC 10.00 3.00
92 Prince Fielder AU XRC 70.00 21.00
93 Zack Greinke AU XRC 40.00 12.00
94 Chris Gruler AU XRC 10.00 3.00
95 Scott Kazmir AU XRC 70.00 21.00
96 B.J. Upton AU XRC 70.00 21.00
97 Clint Everts AU XRC 20.00 6.00
98 Cal Ripken TRIB 2.00 .60
99 Cal Ripken TRIB 2.00 .60
100 Mark McGwire TRIB 2.00 .60
101 Mark McGwire TRIB 2.00 .60
102 Mark McGwire TRIB 2.00 .60
103 Mark McGwire TRIB 2.00 .60
104 Mark McGwire TRIB 2.00 .60
105 Joe DiMaggio TRIB 1.50 .45
106 Joe DiMaggio TRIB 1.50 .45
107 Joe DiMaggio TRIB 1.50 .45
108 Joe DiMaggio TRIB 1.50 .45
109 Joe DiMaggio TRIB 1.50 .45

2002 Upper Deck Prospect Premieres Future Gems Quads

Inserted one per sealed box, these 33 cards feature four different cards in a panel and were issued to a stated print run of 600 serial numbered sets.

Nm-Mt Ex-Mt
1 David Bush 8.00 2.40
Matt Craig
Josh Johnson
Brian McCann
2 Jason Cooper 8.00 2.40
Jonathan George
Larry Broadway
Joel Guzman
3 Matt Craig 8.00 2.40
Josh Murray
Brian McCann
Jason Pridie
4 Jesse Crain 8.00 2.40
Brian Grant
Curtis Granderson
Joey Gomes
5 Tyler Davidson 8.00 2.40
Val Majewski
Justin Jones
Daniel Cevette
6 Joe DiMaggio 8.00 2.40
Jon Lester
Mark McGwire
Mark McLemore
7 Jonathan George 8.00 2.40
Jeremy Reed
Adam Donachie
Matt Carson
8 Jonathan George 8.00 2.40
Eric Thomas
Joel Guzman
Kiel Fisher
9 Tim Gilhooly 8.00 2.40
Brandon Weeden
Brian Slocum
Brian Dopirak
10 Brian Grant 8.00 2.40
Rich Hill
Joey Gomes
Joe DiMaggio
11 Derick Grigsby 8.00 2.40
Bob Malek
James Loney
Fred Lewis
12 Zach Hammes 8.00 2.40
James Holcomb
Cal Ripken
Kennard Jones
13 Rich Hill 8.00 2.40
Mark McGwire
Brian Grant
Matt Carson
14 James Holcomb 8.00 2.40
David Jensen
Kennard Jones
Ryan Williams
15 David Jensen 8.00 2.40
Francisco Liriano
Ryan Williams
Travis Hanson
16 Josh Johnson 8.00 2.40
Jesse Crain
Adam Greenberg
Curtis Granderson
17 Jon Lester 8.00 2.40
Jonathan George
Mark McLemore
Adam Donachie
18 Francisco Liriano 8.00 2.40
Mark McGwire
Travis Hanson
Taber Lee
19 Val Majewski 8.00 2.40
Charlie Morton
Daniel Cevette
Joey Gomes
20 Bob Malek 8.00 2.40
Zach Hammes
Fred Lewis
Cal Ripken
21 Justin Maureau 8.00 2.40
Joe DiMaggio
Chris Snyder
Mark McGwire
22 Mark McGwire 8.00 2.40
Bob Malek
Joe DiMaggio
Kyle Boyer
23 Charlie Morton 8.00 2.40
David Bush#Joey Gomes
Josh Johnson
24 Josh Murray 8.00 2.40
Mark McGwire
Jason Pridie
Joe DiMaggio
25 Matt Pender UER 8.00 2.40
Mark McGwire
Mark McLemore
Ryan Rodriguez
26 Jason Pridie 8.00 2.40
Josh Murray
Matt Craig
Brian McCann
27 Jeremy Reed 8.00 2.40
Josh Johnson
Matt Carson
Adam Greenberg
28 Cal Ripken 8.00 2.40
Jason Cooper
Matt Carson
Larry Broadway
29 Ryan Rodriguez 8.00 2.40
Eric Thomas
Pat Osborn
Randy Braun
30 Josh Rupe 8.00 2.40
Tyler Davidson
John Baker
Justin Jones
31 Eric Thomas 8.00 2.40
Derick Grigsby
Randy Braun
James Loney
32 Eric Thomas 8.00 2.40
Matt Pender UER
Kiel Fisher
Mark McLemore
33 Brandon Weeden 8.00 2.40
Rich Hill
Brian Dopirak
Brian Grant

2002 Upper Deck Prospect Premieres Heroes of Baseball

Inserted at stated odds of one per pack, these 90 cards feature 10 cards each of various baseball legends. Each player featured has nine regular cards and one header card.

Nm-Mt Ex-Mt
COMP.RIPKEN SET (10) 20.00 6.00
COMMON RIPKEN (CR1-HDR) 2.50 .75
COMP.DIMAGGIO SET (10) 10.00 3.00
COMMON DIMAGGIO (JD1-HDR) 1.25 .35
COMP.MORGAN SET (10) 5.00 1.50
COMMON MORGAN (JM1-HDR) .75 .23
COMP.MCGWIRE SET (10) 20.00 6.00
COMMON MCGWIRE (MC1-HDR) 2.50 .75
COMP.MANTLE SET (10) 25.00 7.50
COMMON MANTLE (MM1-HDR) 3.00 .90
COMP.OZZIE SET (10) 15.00 4.50
COMMON OZZIE (OS1-HDR) 2.00 .60
COMP.GWYNN SET (10) 15.00 4.50
COMMON GWYNN (TG1-HDR) 2.00 .60
COMP.SEAVER SET (10) 10.00 3.00
COMMON SEAVER (TS1-HDR) 1.25 .35
COMP.STARGELL SET (10) 5.00 1.50
COMMON STARGELL (WS1-HDR) .75 .23

2002 Upper Deck Prospect Premieres Heroes of Baseball 85 Quads

Randomly inserted as boxtoppers, these eight panels feature a mix of four cards of the players featured in the Heroes of Baseball insert set. Each of these cards are issued to a stated print run of 85 serial numbered sets.

Nm-Mt Ex-Mt
1 Joe DiMaggio 15.00 4.50
Tony Gwynn
Tony Gwynn
Joe DiMaggio
2 Joe DiMaggio 25.00 7.50
Tony Gwynn
Cal Ripken
Cal Ripken
3 Joe DiMaggio Hdr 25.00 7.50
Mickey Mantle
Willie Stargell Hdr
Mickey Mantle
4 Tony Gwynn 15.00 4.50
Tony Gwynn
Ozzie Smith
Willie Stargell
5 Tony Gwynn 15.00 4.50
Willie Stargell
Joe DiMaggio
Joe Morgan
6 Tony Gwynn 15.00 4.50
Willie Stargell
Cal Ripken
Ozzie Smith
7 Mickey Mantle 25.00 7.50
Mark McGwire
Joe Morgan
Tom Seaver
8 Mickey Mantle 25.00 7.50
Tom Seaver
Mickey Mantle
Tom Seaver
9 Mark McGwire 25.00 7.50
Joe Morgan
Mark McGwire
Joe Morgan
10 Mark McGwire Hdr 25.00 7.50
Cal Ripken
Tony Gwynn
Joe DiMaggio
11 Mark McGwire 15.00 4.50
Tom Seaver
Joe Morgan
Ozzie Smith
12 Joe Morgan 15.00 4.50
Tony Gwynn
Joe Morgan
Tony Gwynn
13 Joe Morgan 25.00 7.50
Joe DiMaggio
Mickey Mantle
Cal Ripken
14 Joe Morgan 15.00 4.50
Joe DiMaggio
Willie Stargell
Tony Gwynn
15 Ozzie Smith 15.00 4.50
Joe DiMaggio
Ozzie Smith
Willie Stargell
16 Ozzie Smith 15.00 4.50
Mark McGwire
Willie Stargell
Tony Gwynn
17 Ozzie Smith 15.00 4.50
Tom Seaver
Tom Seaver
Mark McGwire
18 Cal Ripken 25.00 7.50
Mickey Mantle
Joe DiMaggio
Joe Morgan
19 Cal Ripken 25.00 7.50
Mark McGwire
Cal Ripken
Mark McGwire
20 Tom Seaver 15.00 4.50
Joe DiMaggio
Tom Seaver
Joe DiMaggio
21 Tom Seaver 15.00 4.50
Joe Morgan
Ozzie Smith
Willie Stargell
22 Tom Seaver 25.00 7.50
Cal Ripken
Mark McGwire
Mickey Mantle
23 Willie Stargell 15.00 4.50
Ozzie Smith
Ozzie Smith
Willie Stargell
24 Willie Stargell 15.00 4.50
Ozzie Smith
Tom Seaver
Joe Morgan

2003 Upper Deck Prospect Premieres

For the third consecutive year, Upper Deck produced a set consisting solely of players who had been taken during that season's amateur draft. This was a 90-card standard-size set which was released in December, 2003. This set was issued in four-card packs with an $2.99 SRP which came 16 packs to a box and 18 boxes to a case.

MINT NRMT
COMPLETE SET (90) 40.00 18.00
1 Bryan Opdyke XRC .40 .18
2 Gabriel Sosa XRC .40 .18
3 Tila Reynolds XRC .40 .18
4 Aaron Hill XRC .75 .35
5 Aaron Marsden XRC .50 .23
6 Abe Alvarez XRC .50 .23
7 Adam Jones XRC .60 .25
8 Adam Miller XRC 1.25 .55
9 Andre Ethier XRC .60 .25
10 Anthony Gwynn XRC 1.00 .45
11 Brad Snyder XRC .75 .35
12 Brad Sullivan XRC .50 .23
13 Brian Anderson XRC 1.50 .70
14 Brian Buscher XRC .40 .18
15 Brian Snyder XRC .50 .23
16 Carlos Quentin XRC 2.00 .90
17 Chad Billingsley XRC 1.00 .45
18 Fraser Dizard XRC .40 .18
19 Chris Durbin XRC .40 .18
20 Chris Ray XRC .50 .23
21 Conor Jackson XRC 2.00 .90
22 Kory Casto XRC .40 .18
23 Craig Whitaker XRC .50 .23
24 Daniel Moore XRC .40 .18
25 Daric Barton XRC 2.00 .90
26 Darin Downs XRC .50 .23
27 David Murphy XRC .75 .35
28 Dustin Majewski XRC .50 .23
29 Edgardo Baez XRC .50 .23
30 Jake Fox XRC .40 .18
31 Jake Stevens XRC 1.00 .45
32 Jamie D'Antona XRC 1.00 .45
33 James Houser XRC .50 .23
34 Jar. Saltalamacchia XRC .60 .25
35 Jason Hirsh XRC .40 .18
36 Javi Herrera XRC .50 .23
37 Jeff Allison XRC .50 .23
38 John Hudgins XRC .40 .18
39 Jo Jo Reyes XRC .50 .23
40 Justin James XRC .40 .18
41 Kurt Isenberg XRC .40 .18
42 Kyle Boyer XRC .40 .18
43 Lastings Milledge XRC 2.00 .90
44 Luis Atilano XRC .40 .18
45 Matt Murton XRC .40 .18
46 Matt Moses XRC .75 .35
47 Matt Harrison XRC .60 .25
48 Michael Bourn XRC .40 .18
49 Miguel Vega XRC .40 .18
50 Mitch Maier XRC .60 .25
51 Omar Quintanilla XRC .60 .25
52 Ryan Sweeney XRC 1.00 .45
53 Scott Baker XRC .40 .18
54 Sean Rodriguez XRC 1.00 .45
55 Steve Lerud XRC .60 .25
56 Thomas Pauly XRC .40 .18
57 Tom Gorzelanny XRC .60 .25
58 Tim Moss XRC .40 .18
59 Robbie Wooley XRC .50 .23
60 Trey Webb XRC .40 .18
61 Wes Littleton XRC .50 .23
62 Beau Vaughan XRC .50 .23
63 Willy Jo Ronda XRC .50 .23
64 Chris Lubanski XRC 1.25 .55
65 Ian Stewart XRC 3.00 1.35
66 John Danks XRC 1.25 .55
67 Kyle Sleeth XRC .75 .35
68 Michael Aubrey XRC 1.50 .70
69 Kevin Kouzmanoff XRC .60 .25
70 Ryan Harvey XRC 1.25 .55
71 Tim Stauffer XRC .60 .25
72 Tony Richie XRC .40 .18
73 Brandon Wood XRC .75 .35
74 David Aardsma XRC .40 .18
75 David Shinskie XRC .40 .18
76 Dennis Dove XRC .50 .23
77 Eric Sultemeier XRC .40 .18
78 Jay Sborz XRC .40 .18
79 Jimmy Barthmaier XRC .40 .18
80 Josh Whitesell XRC .40 .18
81 Josh Anderson XRC .75 .35
82 Kenny Lewis XRC .50 .23
83 Mateo Miramontes XRC .40 .18
84 Nick Markakis XRC .75 .35
85 Paul Bacot XRC .50 .23
86 Peter Stonard XRC .40 .18
87 Reggie Willits XRC .40 .18
88 Shane Costa XRC .50 .23
89 Billy Sadler XRC .40 .18
90 Delmon Young XRC 2.50 1.10

2003 Upper Deck Prospect Premieres Autographs

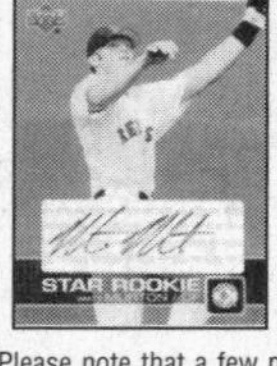

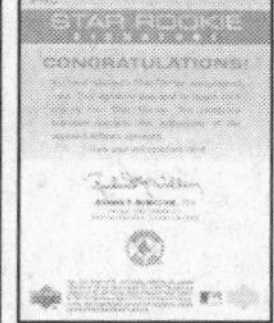

Please note that a few players who were anticipated to have cards in this set do not exist. Those card numbers are P18, P28, P47, P54, P59 and P69.

MINT NRMT
STATED ODDS 1:9
P1 Bryan Opdyke 10.00 4.50
P2 Gabriel Sosa 10.00 4.50
P3 Tila Reynolds 10.00 4.50
P4 Aaron Hill 15.00 6.75
P5 Aaron Marsden 15.00 6.75
P6 Abe Alvarez 15.00 6.75
P7 Adam Jones 15.00 6.75
P8 Adam Miller 25.00 11.00
P9 Andre Ethier 15.00 6.75
P10 Anthony Gwynn 20.00 9.00
P11 Brad Snyder 15.00 6.75
P12 Brad Sullivan 15.00 6.75
P13 Brian Anderson 30.00 13.50
P14 Brian Buscher 10.00 4.50
P15 Brian Snyder 15.00 6.75
P16 Carlos Quentin 40.00 18.00
P17 Chad Billingsley 20.00 9.00
P19 Chris Durbin 10.00 4.50
P20 Chris Ray 15.00 6.75
P21 Conor Jackson 40.00 18.00
P22 Kory Casto 10.00 4.50
P23 Craig Whitaker 15.00 6.75
P24 Daniel Moore 10.00 4.50
P25 Daric Barton 40.00 18.00
P26 Darin Downs 15.00 6.75
P27 David Murphy 15.00 6.75
P29 Edgardo Baez 15.00 6.75
P30 Jake Fox 10.00 4.50
P31 Jake Stevens 20.00 9.00
P32 Jamie D'Antona 20.00 9.00
P33 James Houser 15.00 6.75
P34 Jarrod Saltalamacchia 15.00 6.75
P35 Jason Hirsh 10.00 4.50
P36 Javi Herrera 15.00 6.75
P37 Jeff Allison 15.00 6.75
P38 John Hudgins 10.00 4.50
P39 Jo Jo Reyes 15.00 6.75
P40 Justin James 10.00 4.50
P41 Kurt Isenberg 10.00 4.50
P42 Kyle Boyer 10.00 4.50
P43 Lastings Milledge 50.00 22.00
P44 Luis Atilano 10.00 4.50
P45 Matt Murton 10.00 4.50
P46 Matt Moses 15.00 6.75
P48 Michael Bourn 10.00 4.50
P49 Miguel Vega 10.00 4.50
P50 Mitch Maier 15.00 6.75
P51 Omar Quintanilla 15.00 6.75
P52 Ryan Sweeney 25.00 11.00
P53 Scott Baker 10.00 4.50
P55 Steve Lerud 15.00 6.75
P56 Thomas Pauly 10.00 4.50
P57 Tom Gorzelanny 15.00 6.75
P58 Tim Moss 10.00 4.50
P60 Trey Webb 10.00 4.50
P61 Wes Littleton 15.00 6.75
P62 Beau Vaughan 15.00 6.75
P63 Willy Jo Ronda 15.00 6.75
P64 Chris Lubanski 25.00 11.00
P65 Ian Stewart 70.00 32.00
P66 John Danks 25.00 11.00
P67 Kyle Sleeth 20.00 9.00
P68 Michael Aubrey 40.00 18.00
P70 Ryan Harvey 25.00 11.00
P71 Tim Stauffer 15.00 6.75

2003 Upper Deck Prospect Premieres Game Jersey

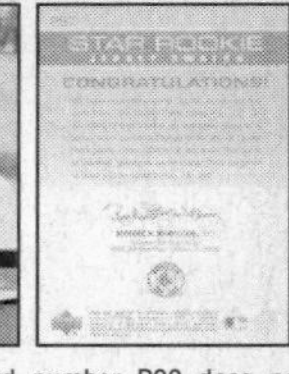

Please note that card number P90 does not exist.

MINT NRMT
STATED ODDS 1:18
P72 Tony Richie 5.00 2.20
P73 Brandon Wood 8.00 3.60
P74 David Aardsma 5.00 2.20
P75 David Shinskie 5.00 2.20
P76 Dennis Dove 8.00 3.60
P77 Eric Sultimeier 5.00 2.20
P78 Jay Sborz 5.00 2.20
P79 Jimmy Barthmaier 5.00 2.20
P80 Josh Whitesell 5.00 2.20
P81 Josh Anderson 10.00 4.50
P82 Kenny Lewis 8.00 3.60
P83 Mateo Miramontes 5.00 2.20
P84 Nick Markakis 10.00 4.50
P85 Paul Bacot 8.00 3.60
P86 Peter Stonard 5.00 2.20
P87 Reggie Willits 5.00 2.20
P88 Shane Costa 8.00 3.60
P89 Billy Sadler 5.00 2.20
P91 Kyle Sleeth 8.00 3.60
P92 Ian Stewart 20.00 9.00
P93 Fraser Dizard 5.00 2.20
P94 Abe Alvarez 8.00 3.60
P95 Adam Jones 8.00 3.60
P96 Brian Anderson 10.00 4.50
P97 Chris Durbin 5.00 2.20
P98 Craig Whitaker 8.00 3.60
P99 Jake Fox 5.00 2.20
P100 Kurt Isenberg 5.00 2.20
P101 Luis Atilano 5.00 2.20
P102 Miguel Vega 5.00 2.20
P103 Mitch Maier 8.00 3.60
P104 Ryan Sweeney 10.00 4.50
P105 Scott Baker 5.00 2.20
P106 Sean Rodriguez 10.00 4.50
P108 Trey Webb 5.00 2.20
P109 Willy Jo Ronda 8.00 3.60
P110 John Danks 10.00 4.50
P111 Michael Aubrey 10.00 4.50
P112 Lastings Milledge 15.00 6.75
P113 Chris Lubanski 10.00 4.50

2004 Upper Deck r-class

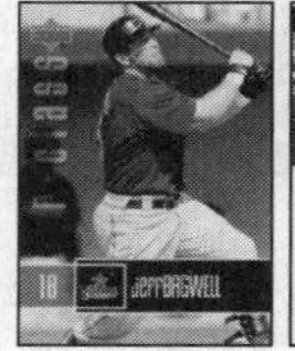

Nm-Mt Ex-Mt
COMPLETE SET (180) 100.00 30.00
COMP.SET w/o SP'S (90) 20.00 6.00
COMMON CARD (1-90) .30 .09
COMMON CARD (91-180) 1.00 .30
91-180 STATED ODDS 1:2
1 Adam Dunn .50 .15
2 Jose Vidro .30 .09
3 Vladimir Guerrero .75 .23
4 Hideo Nomo .75 .23
5 Eric Chavez .30 .09
6 Carlos Delgado .30 .09
7 Javy Lopez .30 .09
8 Javier Vazquez .30 .09
9 Miguel Cabrera .50 .15
10 Manny Ramirez .50 .15
11 Scott Rolen .75 .23
12 Rafael Furcal .30 .09
13 Jim Thome .75 .23
14 Edgar Renteria .30 .09
15 Jason Kendall .30 .09
16 Alfonso Soriano .50 .15
17 Troy Glaus .30 .09
18 Vernon Wells .30 .09
19 Todd Helton .50 .15
20 Mark Mulder .30 .09
21 Albert Pujols 1.50 .45
22 Andy Pettitte .50 .15
23 Kevin Millwood .30 .09
24 Bret Boone .30 .09
25 Ken Griffey Jr. 1.25 .35
26 Kevin Brown .30 .09
27 J.D. Drew .30 .09
28 Corey Patterson .30 .09
29 Jason Giambi .30 .09
30 Jason Schmidt .30 .09
31 Jose Reyes .30 .09

32 Torii Hunter .30 .09
33 Brian Giles .30 .09
34 Garret Anderson .30 .09
35 Mark Teixeira .30 .09
36 Sammy Sosa 1.25 .35
37 Rocco Baldelli .30 .09
38 Jeff Bagwell .50 .15
39 Rafael Palmeiro .50 .15
40 Derrek Lee .30 .09
41 Randy Johnson .75 .23
42 Roger Clemens 1.50 .45
43 Austin Kearns .30 .09
44 Dontrelle Willis .30 .09
45 Lance Berkman .30 .09
46 Juan Gonzalez .50 .15
47 Ichiro Suzuki 1.25 .35
48 Pat Burrell .30 .09
49 Miguel Tejada .30 .09
50 Mike Piazza 1.25 .35
51 Mark Prior .75 .23
52 C.C. Sabathia .30 .09
53 Jacque Jones .30 .09
54 Carlos Beltran .50 .15
55 Mike Mussina .50 .15
56 Mike Lowell .30 .09
57 Phil Nevin .30 .09
58 Andruw Jones .30 .09
59 Barry Zito .30 .09
60 Magglio Ordonez .30 .09
61 Carlos Lee .30 .09
62 Nomar Garciaparra 1.25 .35
63 Kerry Wood .75 .23
64 Luis Gonzalez .30 .09
65 Derek Jeter 1.50 .45
66 Preston Wilson .30 .09
67 Greg Maddux 1.25 .35
68 Pedro Martinez .75 .23
69 Richie Sexson .30 .09
70 Hank Blalock .30 .09
71 Chipper Jones .75 .23
72 Ivan Rodriguez .75 .23
73 Roy Halladay .30 .09
74 Tim Hudson .30 .09
75 Ryan Klesko .30 .09
76 Hideki Matsui 1.25 .35
77 Josh Beckett .30 .09
78 Brandon Webb .30 .09
79 Alex Rodriguez 1.25 .35
80 Jim Edmonds .30 .09
81 Jeff Kent .30 .09
82 Bobby Abreu .30 .09
83 Curt Schilling .75 .23
84 Roy Oswalt .30 .09
85 Orlando Cabrera .30 .09
86 Johan Santana .50 .15
87 Geoff Jenkins .30 .09
88 Gary Sheffield .30 .09
89 Shawn Green .30 .09
90 Frank Thomas .75 .23
91 Tim Hamulack TC RC 1.00 .30
92 Shingo Takatsu TC RC 2.50 .75
93 Justin Huisman TC RC 1.00 .30
94 Sean Henn TC RC 1.00 .30
95 Jamie Brown TC RC 1.00 .30
96 Dennis Sarfate TC RC 1.00 .30
97 Lincoln Holdzkom TC RC 1.00 .30
98 Roman Colon TC RC 1.00 .30
99 Scott Dohmann TC RC 1.00 .30
100 Ivan Ochoa TC RC 1.00 .30
101 Akinori Otsuka TC RC 1.00 .30
102 Fernando Nieve TC RC 1.00 .30
103 Mike Johnston TC RC 1.00 .30
104 Mariano Gomez TC RC 1.00 .30
105 Justin Leone TC RC 1.50 .45
106 Evan Rust TC RC 1.00 .30
107 Mike Rouse TC RC 1.00 .30
108 Ian Snell TC RC 2.00 .60
109 Jason Bartlett TC RC 1.50 .45
110 Ryan Wing TC RC 1.00 .30
111 Nick Regilio TC RC 1.00 .30
112 Merkin Valdez TC RC 2.50 .75
113 Josh Labandeira TC RC 1.00 .30
114 David Aardsma TC RC 1.00 .30
115 Justin Knoedler TC RC 1.00 .30
116 Shawn Hill TC RC 1.00 .30
117 Casey Daigle TC RC 1.00 .30
118 Donnie Kelly TC RC 1.00 .30
119 Justin Germano TC RC 1.00 .30
120 Eddy Rodriguez TC RC 1.50 .45
121 Onil Joseph TC RC 1.00 .30
122 Michael Wuertz TC RC 1.50 .45
123 Roberto Novoa TC RC 1.50 .45
124 Jerome Gamble TC RC 1.00 .30
125 Justin Hampson TC RC 1.00 .30
126 Ronald Belisario TC RC 1.00 .30
127 Tim Bausher TC RC 1.00 .30
128 Chris Saenz TC RC 1.00 .30
129 Hector Gimenez TC RC 1.00 .30
130 Ronny Cedeno TC RC 1.00 .30
131 Jason Frasor TC RC 1.00 .30
132 Kazuo Matsui TC RC 4.00 1.20
133 Mike Gosling TC RC 1.00 .30
134 Jerry Gil TC RC 1.00 .30
135 Orlando Rodriguez TC RC 1.00 .30
136 Jorge Vasquez TC RC 1.00 .30
137 Chris Aguila TC RC 1.00 .30
138 Tim Bittner TC RC 1.00 .30
139 Jake Woods TC RC 1.00 .30
140 Enemencio Pacheco TC RC 1.00 .30
141 Dave Crouthers TC RC 1.00 .30
142 Jose Capellan TC RC 4.00 1.20
143 Chad Bentz TC RC 1.00 .30
144 Mike Vento TC RC 1.50 .45
145 Scott Proctor TC RC 1.50 .45
146 Edwin Moreno TC RC 1.50 .45
147 Brandon Medders TC RC 1.00 .30
148 Renyel Pinto TC RC 1.50 .45
149 Rusty Tucker TC RC 1.50 .45
150 Ryan Meaux TC RC 1.00 .30
151 William Bergolla TC RC 1.00 .30
152 Angel Chavez TC RC 1.00 .30
153 Colby Miller TC RC 1.00 .30
154 John Gall TC RC 1.50 .45
155 Carlos Hines TC RC 1.00 .30
156 Carlos Vasquez TC RC 1.50 .45
157 Justin Lehr TC RC 1.00 .30
158 Kevin Cave TC RC 1.50 .45
159 Jeff Bennett TC RC 1.00 .30
160 Greg Dobbs TC RC 1.00 .30
161 Jorge Sequea TC RC 1.00 .30
162 Chris Oxspring TC RC 1.50 .45
163 Franklyn Gracesqui TC RC 1.00 .30
164 Shawn Camp TC RC 1.00 .30
165 Lino Urdaneta TC RC 1.00 .30
166 Luis A. Gonzalez TC RC 1.00 .30
167 Ramon Ramirez TC RC 1.00 .30
168 Freddy Guzman TC RC 1.00 .30
169 Chris Shelton TC RC 2.00 .60
170 Andres Blanco TC RC 1.00 .30
171 Aarom Baldiris TC RC 1.50 .45
172 Kazuhito Tadano TC RC 1.50 .45
173 Brian Dallimore TC RC 1.00 .30
174 Eduardo Villacis TC RC 1.00 .30
175 Frank Francisco TC RC 1.00 .30
176 Edwin Jackson TC 1.00 .30
177 Bobby Crosby TC 1.50 .45
178 Joe Mauer TC 1.50 .45
179 Rickie Weeks TC 1.00 .30
180 Delmon Young TC 1.50 .45

2004 Upper Deck r-class First Class Autograph Black

Nm-Mt Ex-Mt
STATED ODDS 1:2880
BLUE RANDOM IN BLISTER BOXES
BLUE PRINT RUN 3 SERIAL #'d SETS
NO BLUE PRICING DUE TO SCARCITY
BL Barry Larkin 50.00 15.00
CD Carlos Delgado 40.00 12.00
DW Dontrelle Willis 40.00 12.00
EG Eric Gagne 60.00 18.00
EM Edgar Martinez 50.00 15.00
HR Horacio Ramirez 25.00 7.50
KG Ken Griffey Jr. 100.00 30.00
MC Miguel Cabrera 50.00 15.00
MP Mark Prior 60.00 18.00
PB Pat Burrell 40.00 12.00
PL Paul LoDuca 40.00 12.00
SA Sandy Alomar 25.00 7.50
TH Trevor Hoffman 40.00 12.00

2004 Upper Deck r-class Jersey

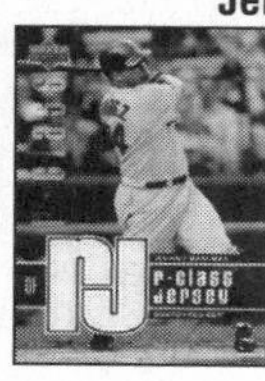

Nm-Mt Ex-Mt
STATED ODDS 1:12
AJ Andruw Jones 5.00 1.50
AP Albert Pujols 15.00 4.50
AS Alfonso Soriano 8.00 2.40
BA Jeff Bagwell 8.00 2.40
BB Bret Boone 5.00 1.50
BW Bernie Williams 8.00 2.40
CD Carlos Delgado 5.00 1.50
CJ Chipper Jones 10.00 3.00
CS Curt Schilling 10.00 3.00
DJ Derek Jeter 20.00 6.00
DW Dontrelle Willis 5.00 1.50
EC Eric Chavez 5.00 1.50
EM Edgar Martinez 8.00 2.40
GL Troy Glaus 5.00 1.50
GS Gary Sheffield 5.00 1.50
HB Hank Blalock 5.00 1.50
HM Hideki Matsui 25.00 7.50
HN Hideo Nomo 10.00 3.00
HU Torii Hunter 5.00 1.50
IR Ivan Rodriguez 10.00 3.00
IS Ichiro Suzuki 25.00 7.50
JB Josh Beckett 5.00 1.50
JG Jason Giambi 5.00 1.50
KB Kevin Brown 5.00 1.50
KG Ken Griffey Jr. 12.00 3.60
KM Kazuo Matsui 15.00 4.50
KW Kerry Wood 10.00 3.00
MP Mark Prior 10.00 3.00
MR Manny Ramirez 8.00 2.40
MT Miguel Tejada 5.00 1.50
PI Mike Piazza 12.00 3.60
PM Pedro Martinez 10.00 3.00
RA Roberto Alomar 8.00 2.40
RB Rocco Baldelli 5.00 1.50
RC Roger Clemens 12.00 3.60
RI Mariano Rivera 8.00 2.40
RJ Randy Johnson 10.00 3.00
SR Scott Rolen 10.00 3.00
SS Sammy Sosa 12.00 3.60
TG Tom Glavine 8.00 2.40
TH Todd Helton 8.00 2.40
VG Vladimir Guerrero 10.00 3.00

2004 Upper Deck r-class Taking Over!

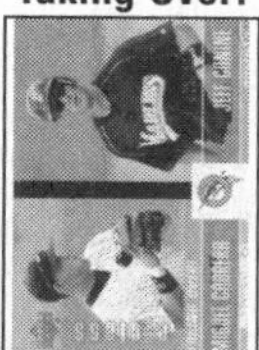

Nm-Mt Ex-Mt
21-30 PRINT RUN 150 SERIAL #'d SETS
RANDOM INSERTS IN BLISTER BOXES
1 Lyle Overbay 4.00 1.20
Richie Sexson
2 Jason Phillips 8.00 2.40
Mike Piazza
3 William Bergolla 5.00 1.50
Barry Larkin
4 Jason DuBois 4.00 1.20
Moises Alou
5 Nook Logan 4.00 1.20
Alex Sanchez
6 Merkin Valdez 5.00 1.50
Robb Nen
7 Francisco Rodriguez 4.00 1.20
Troy Percival
8 David DeJesus 5.00 1.50
Carlos Beltran
9 Michael Young 8.00 2.40
Alex Rodriguez
10 Alexis Rios 4.00 1.20
Vernon Wells
11 Grady Sizemore 4.00 1.20
Matt Lawton
12 Ryan Wagner 4.00 1.20
Danny Graves
13 Miguel Cabrera 5.00 1.50
Jeff Conine
14 Josh Willingham 4.00 1.20
Ramon Castro
15 Rickie Weeks 4.00 1.20
Junior Spivey
16 Guillermo Quiroz 4.00 1.20
Greg Myers
17 Graham Koonce 4.00 1.20
Scott Hatteberg
18 Rene Reyes 5.00 1.50
Larry Walker
19 Khalil Greene 5.00 1.50
Ramon Vazquez
20 Octavio Dotel 4.00 1.20
Billy Wagner
21 Joe Mauer 10.00 3.00
A.J. Pierzynski
22 Javier Vazquez 15.00 4.50
Roger Clemens
23 Brandon Webb 8.00 2.40
Curt Schilling
24 Delmon Young 10.00 3.00
Jose Cruz Jr.
25 Vladimir Guerrero 10.00 3.00
Tim Salmon
26 J.D. Drew 8.00 2.40
Gary Sheffield
27 Bobby Crosby 10.00 3.00
Miguel Tejada
28 Edwin Jackson 8.00 2.40
Kevin Brown
29 Kazuo Matsui 15.00 4.50
Jose Reyes
30 Wily Mo Pena 15.00 4.50
Ken Griffey Jr.

1998 Upper Deck Retro

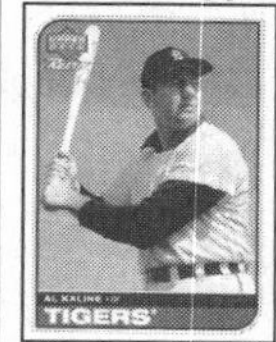

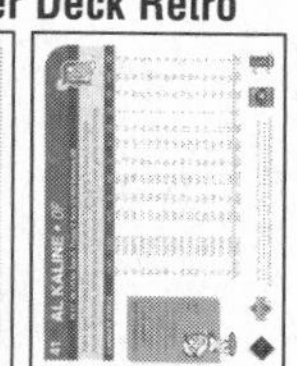

The 1998 Upper Deck Retro set contains 129 standard size cards. The six-card packs retailed for $4.99 each. The set contains the subset: Futurama (101-130). The fronts feature current superstars as well as some retired legends surrounded by a four-sided white border and printed on super-thick, uncoated 24-pt stock card. The featured player's name lines the bottom border of the card. Card number 82 (originally slated to be Stan Musial) does not exist. Rookie Cards include Troy Glaus.

Nm-Mt Ex-Mt
COMPLETE SET (129) 40.00 12.00
1 Jim Edmonds .40 .12
2 Darin Erstad .40 .12
3 Tim Salmon .60 .18
4 Jay Bell .40 .12
5 Matt Williams .40 .12
6 Andres Galarraga .40 .12
7 Andruw Jones .40 .12
8 Chipper J w4fones 1.00
.30
9 Greg Maddux 1.50 .45
10 Rafael Palmeiro .60 .18
11 Cal Ripken 3.00 .90
12 Brooks Robinson .60 .18
13 Nomar Garciaparra 1.50 .45
14 Pedro Martinez 1.00 .30
15 Mo Vaughn .40 .12
16 Ernie Banks 1.00 .30
17 Mark Grace .60 .18
18 Gary Matthews Sr. .40 .12
19 Sammy Sosa 1.50 .45
20 Albert Belle .40 .12
21 Carlton Fisk .60 .18
22 Frank Thomas 1.00 .30
23 Ken Griffey Sr. .40 .12
24 Paul Konerko .40 .12
25 Barry Larkin .60 .18
26 Sean Casey .40 .12
27 Tony Perez .40 .12
28 Bob Feller .40 .12
29 Kenny Lofton .40 .12
30 Manny Ramirez .60 .18
31 Jim Thome 1.00 .30
32 Omar Vizquel .60 .18
33 Dante Bichette .40 .12
34 Larry Walker .60 .18
35 Tony Clark .40 .12
36 Damion Easley .40 .12
37 Cliff Floyd .40 .12
38 Livan Hernandez .40 .12
39 Jeff Bagwell .60 .18
40 Craig Biggio .60 .18
41 Al Kaline 1.00 .30
42 Johnny Damon .60 .18
43 Dean Palmer .40 .12
44 Charles Johnson .40 .12
45 Eric Karros .40 .12
46 Gaylord Perry .40 .12
47 Raul Mondesi .40 .12
48 Gary Sheffield .40 .12
49 Eddie Mathews 1.00 .30
50 Warren Spahn .60 .18
51 Jeromy Burnitz .40 .12
52 Jeff Cirillo .40 .12
53 Marquis Grissom .40 .12
54 Paul Molitor .60 .18
55 Kirby Puckett 1.00 .30
56 Brad Radke .40 .12
57 Todd Walker .40 .12
58 Vladimir Guerrero 1.00 .30
59 Brad Fullmer .40 .12
60 Rondell White .40 .12
61 Bobby Jones .40 .12
62 Hideo Nomo 1.00 .30
63 Mike Piazza 1.50 .45
64 Tom Seaver .60 .18
65 Frank Thomas .40 .12
66 Yogi Berra 1.00 .30
67 Derek Jeter 2.50 .75
68 Tino Martinez .60 .18
69 Paul O'Neill .60 .18
70 Andy Pettitte .60 .18
71 Rollie Fingers .40 .12
72 Rickey Henderson 1.00 .30
73 Matt Stairs .40 .12
74 Scott Rolen 1.00 .30
75 Curt Schilling .40 .12
76 Jose Guillen .40 .12
77 Jason Kendall .40 .12
78 Lou Brock .60 .18
79 Bob Gibson .60 .18
80 Ray Lankford .40 .12
81 Mark McGwire 2.50 .75
83 Kevin Brown .60 .18
84 Ken Caminiti .40 .12
85 Tony Gwynn 1.25 .35
86 Greg Vaughn .40 .12
87 Barry Bonds 2.50 .75
88 Willie Stargell .60 .18
89 Willie McCovey .40 .12
90 Ken Griffey Jr. 1.50 .45
91 Randy Johnson 1.00 .30
92 Alex Rodriguez 1.50 .45
93 Quinton McCracken .40 .12
94 Fred McGriff .60 .18
95 Juan Gonzalez .60 .18
96 Ivan Rodriguez 1.00 .30
97 Nolan Ryan 2.50 .75
98 Jose Canseco 1.00 .30
99 Roger Clemens 2.00 .60
100 Jose Cruz Jr. .40 .12
101 J.Baughman FUT RC .40 .12
102 Dave Dellucci FUT RC .75 .23
103 Travis Lee FUT .40 .12
104 Troy Glaus FUT RC 2.00 .60
105 Kerry Wood FUT 1.00 .30
106 Mike Caruso FUT .40 .12
107 Jim Parque FUT RC .40 .12
108 Brett Tomko FUT .40 .12
109 Russell Branyan FUT .40 .12
110 Jaret Wright FUT .40 .12
111 Todd Helton FUT .60 .18
112 Gabe Alvarez FUT .40 .12
113 M.Anderson FUT RC .40 .12
114 Alex Gonzalez FUT .40 .12
115 Mark Kotsay FUT .40 .12
116 Derrek Lee FUT .40 .12
117 Richard Hidalgo FUT .40 .12
118 Adrian Beltre FUT 1.00 .30
119 Geoff Jenkins FUT .40 .12
120 Eric Milton FUT .40 .12
121 Brad Fullmer FUT .40 .12
122 V.Guerrero FUT 1.00 .30
123 Carl Pavano FUT .40 .12
124 O.Hernandez FUT RC 1.25 .35
125 Ben Grieve FUT .40 .12
126 A.J. Hinch FUT .40 .12
127 Matt Clement FUT .40 .12
128 G.Matthews Jr. FUT RC .50 .15
129 Aramis Ramirez FUT .40 .12
130 R.Arrojo FUT RC .50 .15

1998 Upper Deck Retro Big Boppers

Randomly inserted in packs, this 30-card set is an insert to the Upper Deck Retro base set. The set is serially numbered to 500. The fronts feature today's most powerful hitters on a nostalgic four-sided white bordered card. The featured player's name runs vertically along the left side border.

Nm-Mt Ex-Mt
COMPLETE SET (30) 400.00 120.00
BB1 Darin Erstad 4.00 1.20
BB2 Rafael Palmeiro 6.00 1.80
BB3 Cal Ripken 30.00 9.00
BB4 Nomar Garciaparra 15.00 4.50
BB5 Mo Vaughn 4.00 1.20
BB6 Frank Thomas 10.00 3.00
BB7 Albert Belle 4.00 1.20
BB8 Jim Thome 10.00 3.00
BB9 Manny Ramirez 6.00 1.80
BB10 Tony Clark 4.00 1.20
BB11 Tino Martinez 6.00 1.80
BB12 Ben Grieve 4.00 1.20
BB13 Ken Griffey Jr. 15.00 4.50
BB14 Alex Rodriguez 15.00 4.50
BB15 Jay Buhner 4.00 1.20
BB16 Juan Gonzalez 6.00 1.80
BB17 Jose Cruz Jr. 4.00 1.20
BB18 Jose Canseco 10.00 3.00
BB19 Travis Lee 4.00 1.20
BB20 Chipper Jones 10.00 3.00
BB21 Andres Galarraga 4.00 1.20
BB22 Andruw Jones 4.00 1.20
BB23 Sammy Sosa 15.00 4.50
BB24 Vinny Castilla 4.00 1.20
BB25 Larry Walker 6.00 1.80
BB26 Jeff Bagwell 6.00 1.80
BB27 Gary Sheffield 4.00 1.20
BB28 Mike Piazza 15.00 4.50
BB29 Mark McGwire 25.00 7.50
BB30 Barry Bonds 25.00 7.50

1998 Upper Deck Retro Groovy Kind of Glove

Randomly inserted in packs at a rate of one in seven, this 30-card set is an insert to the Upper Deck Retro base set. The fronts feature today's top defensive players surrounded by a four-sided white border and flourescent inks.

Nm-Mt Ex-Mt
COMPLETE SET (30) 120.00 36.00
G1 Roberto Alomar 5.00 1.50
G2 Cal Ripken 15.00 4.50
G3 Nomar Garciaparra 8.00 2.40
G4 Frank Thomas 5.00 1.50
G5 Robin Ventura 2.00 .60
G6 Omar Vizquel 3.00 .90
G7 Kenny Lofton 2.00 .60
G8 Ben Grieve 2.00 .60
G9 Alex Rodriguez 8.00 2.40
G10 Ken Griffey Jr. 8.00 2.40
G11 Ivan Rodriguez 5.00 1.50
G12 Travis Lee 2.00 .60
G13 Matt Williams 2.00 .60
G14 Greg Maddux 8.00 2.40
G15 Andres Galarraga 2.00 .60
G16 Andruw Jones 2.00 .60
G17 Kerry Wood 5.00 1.50
G18 Mark Grace 3.00 .90
G19 Craig Biggio 3.00 .90
G20 Charles Johnson 2.00 .60
G21 Raul Mondesi 2.00 .60
G22 Mike Piazza 8.00 2.40
G23 Rey Ordonez 2.00 .60
G24 Derek Jeter 12.00 3.60
G25 Scott Rolen 5.00 1.50
G26 Mark McGwire 12.00 3.60
G27 Ken Caminiti 2.00 .60
G28 Tony Gwynn 6.00 1.80
G29 J.T. Snow 2.00 .60
G30 Barry Bonds 12.00 3.60

1998 Upper Deck Retro Legendary Cuts

The three copies produced of this card were randomly inserted into 1998 Upper Deck Retro packs. Upper Deck acquired an autograph album including Babe Ruth signatures and carefully cut out the Ruth's to create these cards. Due to extreme scarcity these cards are not priced.

Nm-Mt Ex-Mt
LC Babe Ruth/3

1998 Upper Deck Retro Lunchboxes

This set features six top Baseball stars pictured on collectible lunchboxes. The lunchboxes themselves doubled as packaging for the 24 packs of Retro trading cards inside and a collectible item in it's own right.

Nm-Mt Ex-Mt
COMPLETE SET (6) 40.00 12.00
1 Nomar Garciaparra 8.00 2.40
2 Ken Griffey Jr. 8.00 2.40
3 Chipper Jones 5.00 1.50
4 Travis Lee 2.00 .60
5 Mark McGwire 12.00 3.60
6 Cal Ripken 15.00 4.50

1998 Upper Deck Retro New Frontier

Randomly inserted in packs, this limited edition 30-card set features color player photos sequentially numbered to 1,000. A first year card of Troy Glaus is featured in this set.

	Nm-Mt	Ex-Mt
COMPLETE SET (30)	100.00	30.00
NF1 Justin Baughman	3.00	.90
NF2 David Dellucci	5.00	1.50
NF3 Travis Lee	3.00	.90
NF4 Troy Glaus	10.00	3.00
NF5 Mike Caruso	3.00	.90
NF6 Jim Parque	3.00	.90
NF7 Kerry Wood	8.00	2.40
NF8 Brett Tomko	3.00	.90
NF9 Russell Branyan	3.00	.90
NF10 Jaret Wright	3.00	.90
NF11 Todd Helton	5.00	1.50
NF12 Gabe Alvarez	3.00	.90
NF13 Matt Anderson	3.00	.90
NF14 Alex Gonzalez	3.00	.90
NF15 Mark Kotsay	3.00	.90
NF16 Derrek Lee	3.00	.90
NF17 Richard Hidalgo	3.00	.90
NF18 Adrian Beltre	8.00	2.40
NF19 Geoff Jenkins	3.00	.90
NF20 Eric Milton	3.00	.90
NF21 Brad Fullmer	3.00	.90
NF22 Vladimir Guerrero	8.00	2.40
NF23 Carl Pavano	5.00	.90
NF24 Orlando Hernandez	8.00	2.40
NF25 Ben Grieve	3.00	.90
NF26 A.J. Hinch	3.00	.90
NF27 Matt Clement	3.00	.90
NF28 Gary Matthews Jr.	3.00	.90
NF29 Aramis Ramirez	3.00	.90
NF30 Rolando Arrojo	3.00	.90

1998 Upper Deck Retro Quantum Leap

Randomly inserted in packs, this scarce 30-card die cut set features a selection of the leagues top players. Only 50 sets were printed and each card is serial numbered. The fronts feature color action photos surrounded by a computer chip design background that highlights the technology of today.

	Nm-Mt	Ex-Mt
Q1 Darin Erstad	20.00	6.00
Q2 Cal Ripken	150.00	45.00
Q3 Nomar Garciaparra	80.00	24.00
Q4 Frank Thomas	50.00	15.00
Q5 Kenny Lofton	20.00	6.00
Q6 Ben Grieve	20.00	6.00
Q7 Ken Griffey Jr.	80.00	24.00
Q8 Alex Rodriguez	80.00	24.00
Q9 Juan Gonzalez	30.00	9.00
Q10 Jose Cruz Jr.	20.00	6.00
Q11 Roger Clemens	100.00	30.00
Q12 Travis Lee	20.00	6.00
Q13 Chipper Jones	50.00	15.00
Q14 Greg Maddux	80.00	24.00
Q15 Kerry Wood	50.00	15.00
Q16 Jeff Bagwell	30.00	9.00
Q17 Mike Piazza	80.00	24.00
Q18 Scott Rolen	50.00	15.00
Q19 Mark McGwire	120.00	36.00
Q20 Tony Gwynn	80.00	24.00
Q21 Larry Walker	30.00	9.00
Q22 Derek Jeter	120.00	36.00
Q23 Sammy Sosa	80.00	24.00
Q24 Barry Bonds	120.00	36.00
Q25 Mo Vaughn	20.00	6.00
Q26 Roberto Alomar	30.00	9.00
Q27 Todd Helton	30.00	9.00
Q28 Ivan Rodriguez	50.00	15.00
Q29 Vladimir Guerrero	50.00	15.00
Q30 Albert Belle	20.00	6.00

1998 Upper Deck Retro Sign of the Times

Randomly inserted in packs at a rate of one in 36, this 31-card set is an insert to the Upper Deck Retro base set. The fronts feature retro style autographs from retired baseball legends and some of today's players surrounded by a four-sided white border. The featured player's name lines the bottom border.

	Nm-Mt	Ex-Mt
PRINT RUNS B/WN 100-1000 COPIES PER		
AK Al Kaline/600	40.00	12.00
BF Bob Feller/600	25.00	7.50
BGI Bob Gibson/300	40.00	12.00
BGR Ben Grieve/300	10.00	3.00
BR Brooks Robinson/300	40.00	12.00
CF Carlton Fisk/600	40.00	12.00
EB Ernie Banks/300	40.00	12.00
EM Eddie Mathews/600	60.00	18.00
FT Frank Thomas/600	15.00	4.50
GMJ G.Matthews Jr./750	10.00	3.00
GMS G.Matthews Sr./600	15.00	4.50
GP Gaylord Perry/1000	15.00	4.50
JC Jose Cruz Jr./300	15.00	4.50
KGJ Ken Griffey Jr./100	150.00	45.00
KGS Ken Griffey Sr./600	15.00	4.50
KP Kirby Puckett/450	50.00	15.00
KW Kerry Wood/200	50.00	15.00
LB Lou Brock/300	40.00	12.00
NR Nolan Ryan/500	100.00	30.00
PK Paul Konerko/750	15.00	4.50
RB Russell Branyan/750	10.00	3.00
RF Rollie Fingers/600	15.00	4.50
SR Scott Rolen/300	40.00	12.00
TG Tony Gwynn/200	50.00	15.00
TLE Travis Lee/300	10.00	3.00
TP Tony Perez/600	25.00	7.50
TS Tom Seaver/300	40.00	12.00
WIS Willie Stargell/600	60.00	18.00
WM Willie McCovey/600	40.00	12.00
WS Warren Spahn/600	50.00	15.00
YB Yogi Berra/150	80.00	24.00

1998 Upper Deck Retro Time Capsule

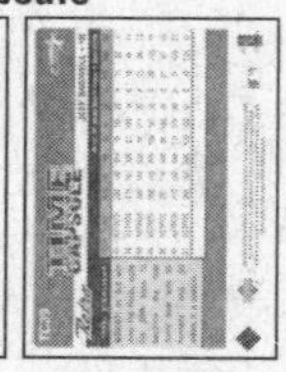

Randomly inserted in packs at the rate of one in two, this 50-card set features color photos of current stars who are destined to earn a place in baseball history.

	Nm-Mt	Ex-Mt
COMPLETE SET (50)	120.00	36.00
TC1 Mike Mussina	3.00	.90
TC2 Rafael Palmeiro	2.00	.60
TC3 Cal Ripken	10.00	3.00
TC4 Nomar Garciaparra	5.00	1.50
TC5 Pedro Martinez	3.00	.90
TC6 Mo Vaughn	1.25	.35
TC7 Albert Belle	1.25	.35
TC8 Frank Thomas	3.00	.90
TC9 David Justice	1.25	.35
TC10 Kenny Lofton	1.25	.35
TC11 Manny Ramirez	2.00	.60
TC12 Jim Thome	3.00	.90
TC13 Derek Jeter	8.00	2.40
TC14 Tino Martinez	2.00	.60
TC15 Ben Grieve	3.00	.90
TC16 Rickey Henderson	3.00	.90
TC17 Ken Griffey Jr.	5.00	1.50
TC18 Randy Johnson	3.00	.90
TC19 Alex Rodriguez	5.00	1.50
TC20 Wade Boggs	3.00	.90
TC21 Fred McGriff	2.00	.60
TC22 Juan Gonzalez	2.00	.60
TC23 Ivan Rodriguez	3.00	.90
TC24 Nolan Ryan	8.00	2.40
TC25 Jose Canseco	3.00	.90
TC26 Roger Clemens	6.00	1.80
TC27 Jose Cruz Jr.	1.25	.35
TC28 Travis Lee	1.25	.35
TC29 Matt Williams	1.25	.35
TC30 Andres Galarraga	1.25	.35
TC31 Andruw Jones	1.25	.35
TC32 Chipper Jones	3.00	.90
TC33 Greg Maddux	5.00	1.50
TC34 Kerry Wood	3.00	.90
TC35 Barry Larkin	2.00	.60
TC36 Dante Bichette	1.25	.35
TC37 Larry Walker	2.00	.60
TC38 Livan Hernandez	1.25	.35
TC39 Jeff Bagwell	2.00	.60
TC40 Craig Biggio	2.00	.60
TC41 Charles Johnson	1.25	.35
TC42 Gary Sheffield	1.25	.35
TC43 Marquis Grissom	1.25	.35
TC44 Mike Piazza	5.00	1.50
TC45 Scott Rolen	3.00	.90
TC46 Curt Schilling	1.25	.35
TC47 Mark McGwire	8.00	2.40
TC48 Ken Caminiti	1.25	.35
TC49 Tony Gwynn	4.00	1.20
TC50 Barry Bonds	8.00	2.40

1999 Upper Deck Retro

This 110 card set features a mix of active stars and retired superstars. Similar to the 1998 Upper Deck Retro set, these cards were issued in special "Luncboxes" which were designed to give the packaging a vintage. The lunchboxes had six cards per pack, 24 packs per box and 12 boxes per case at a SRP of $4.99 each. 350 Ted Williams A Piece of History 500 Club bat cards were randomly seeded into packs. In addition, Williams signed and numbered nine copies. Pricing for these bat cards can be referenced under 1999 Upper Deck A Piece of History 500 Club.

	Nm-Mt	Ex-Mt
COMPLETE SET (110)	25.00	7.50
1 Mo Vaughn	.30	.09
2 Troy Glaus	.30	.09
3 Tim Salmon	.50	.15
4 Randy Johnson	.75	.23
5 Travis Lee	.30	.09
6 Matt Williams	.30	.09
7 Greg Maddux	1.25	.35
8 Chipper Jones	.75	.23
9 Andruw Jones	.30	.09
10 Tom Glavine	.50	.15
11 Javy Lopez	.30	.09
12 Albert Belle	.30	.09
13 Cal Ripken	2.50	.75
14 Brady Anderson	.30	.09
15 Nomar Garciaparra	1.25	.35
16 Pedro Martinez	.75	.23
17 Sammy Sosa	1.25	.35
18 Mark Grace	.50	.15
19 Frank Thomas	.75	.23
20 Ray Durham	.30	.09
21 Sean Casey	.30	.09
22 Greg Vaughn	.30	.09
23 Barry Larkin	.50	.15
24 Manny Ramirez	.50	.15
25 Jim Thome	.75	.23
26 Jaret Wright	.30	.09
27 Kenny Lofton	.30	.09
28 Larry Walker	.50	.15
29 Todd Helton	.50	.15
30 Vinny Castilla	.30	.09
31 Tony Clark	.30	.09
32 Juan Encarnacion	.30	.09
33 Dean Palmer	.30	.09
34 Mark Kotsay	.30	.09
35 Alex Gonzalez	.30	.09
36 Shane Reynolds	.30	.09
37 Ken Caminiti	.30	.09
38 Jeff Bagwell	.50	.15
39 Craig Biggio	.50	.15
40 Carlos Febles	.30	.09
41 Carlos Beltran	.50	.15
42 Jeremy Giambi	.30	.09
43 Raul Mondesi	.30	.09
44 Adrian Beltre	.50	.15
45 Kevin Brown	.50	.15
46 Jeromy Burnitz	.30	.09
47 Jeff Cirillo	.30	.09
48 Corey Koskie	.30	.09
49 Todd Walker	.30	.09
50 Vladimir Guerrero	.75	.23
51 Michael Barrett	.30	.09
52 Mike Piazza	1.25	.35
53 Robin Ventura	.30	.09
54 Edgardo Alfonzo	.30	.09
55 Derek Jeter	2.00	.60
56 Roger Clemens	1.50	.45
57 Tino Martinez	.50	.15
58 Orlando Hernandez	.30	.09
59 Chuck Knoblauch	.30	.09
60 Bernie Williams	.50	.15
61 Eric Chavez	.30	.09
62 Ben Grieve	.30	.09
63 Jason Giambi	.30	.09
64 Scott Rolen	.75	.23
65 Curt Schilling	.30	.09
66 Bobby Abreu	.30	.09
67 Jason Kendall	.30	.09
68 Kevin Young	.30	.09
69 Mark McGwire	2.00	.60
70 J.D. Drew	.30	.09
71 Eric Davis	.30	.09
72 Tony Gwynn	1.00	.30
73 Trevor Hoffman	.30	.09
74 Barry Bonds	2.00	.60
75 Robb Nen	.30	.09
76 Ken Griffey Jr.	1.25	.35
77 Alex Rodriguez	1.25	.35
78 Jay Buhner	.30	.09
79 Carlos Guillen	.30	.09
80 Jose Canseco	.75	.23
81 Bobby Smith	.30	.09
82 Juan Gonzalez	.50	.15
83 Ivan Rodriguez	.75	.23
84 Rafael Palmeiro	.50	.15
85 Rick Helling	.30	.09
86 Jose Cruz Jr.	.30	.09
87 David Wells	.30	.09
88 Carlos Delgado	.30	.09
89 Nolan Ryan	3.00	.90
90 George Brett	2.00	.60
91 Robin Yount	1.25	.35
92 Paul Molitor	.50	.15
93 Dave Winfield	.30	.09
94 Steve Garvey	.30	.09
95 Ozzie Smith	1.25	.35
96 Ted Williams	2.00	.60
97 Don Mattingly	2.00	.60
98 Mickey Mantle	3.00	.90
99 Harmon Killebrew	.75	.23
100 Rollie Fingers	.30	.09
101 Kirk Gibson	.30	.09
102 Bucky Dent	.30	.09
103 Willie Mays	1.50	.45
104 Babe Ruth	2.50	.75
105 Gary Carter	.30	.09
106 Reggie Jackson	.50	.15
107 Frank Robinson	.50	.15
108 Ernie Banks	.75	.23
109 Eddie Murray	.75	.23
110 Mike Schmidt	1.50	.45

1999 Upper Deck Retro Gold

Randomly inserted into packs, these cards parallel the regular Retro set and are serial numbered to 250. These cards can be differentiated by the gold foil borders on them.

Nm-Mt Ex-Mt

*ACTIVE STARS 1-88: 6X TO 15X BASIC
*RETIRED STARS 89-110: 10X TO 25X BASIC

1999 Upper Deck Retro Distant Replay

These cards which were issued one every eight packs, featured the most memorable plays from 15 of the most memorable players active in baseball.

	Nm-Mt	Ex-Mt
COMPLETE SET (15)	60.00	18.00

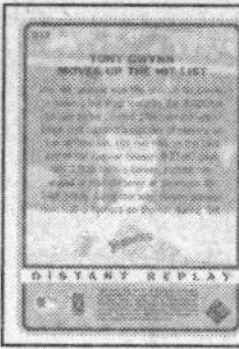

*LEVEL 2: 2.5X TO 6X BASIC DIST.REPLAY
LEVEL 2 RANDOM INSERTS IN PACKS
LEVEL 2 PRINT RUN 100 SERIAL #'d SETS

	Nm-Mt	Ex-Mt
D1 Ken Griffey Jr.	4.00	1.20
D2 Mark McGwire	6.00	1.80
D3 Cal Ripken	8.00	2.40
D4 Greg Maddux	4.00	1.20
D5 Nomar Garciaparra	4.00	1.20
D6 Roger Clemens	5.00	1.50
D7 Alex Rodriguez	4.00	1.20
D8 Frank Thomas	2.50	.75
D9 Mike Piazza	4.00	1.20
D10 Chipper Jones	2.50	.75
D11 Juan Gonzalez	1.50	.45
D12 Tony Gwynn	3.00	.90
D13 Barry Bonds	6.00	1.80
D14 Ivan Rodriguez	2.50	.75
D15 Derek Jeter	6.00	1.80

1999 Upper Deck Retro Inkredible

Inserted one every 24 packs, these cards feature autographs from both active and retired players.The horizontal cards are designed so the primary focus on most of the card is actually the autograph. Eddie Murray and Sean Casey did not return their cards when this set was packed out so their autographs were available via redemption. The deadline for this redemption was April 15th, 2000.

	Nm-Mt	Ex-Mt
AP Angel Pena	10.00	3.00
BD Bucky Dent	15.00	4.50
BW Bernie Williams	80.00	24.00
CBE Carlos Beltran	40.00	12.00
CJ Chipper Jones	40.00	12.00
DE Darin Erstad	15.00	4.50
DM Don Mattingly	60.00	18.00
DW Dave Winfield	25.00	7.50
EM Eddie Murray SP	80.00	24.00
FL Fred Lynn	15.00	4.50
GB George Brett SP	120.00	36.00
GK Gabe Kapler	10.00	3.00
HK Harmon Killebrew	40.00	12.00
IR Ivan Rodriguez	40.00	12.00
JR Ken Griffey Jr.	120.00	36.00
KG Kirk Gibson	15.00	4.50
MR Manny Ramirez	40.00	12.00
NR Nolan Ryan	200.00	60.00
OZ Ozzie Smith	40.00	12.00
PB Pat Burrell	20.00	6.00
PM Paul Molitor	25.00	7.50
PO Paul O'Neill	25.00	7.50
RF Rollie Fingers	15.00	4.50
RG Rusty Greer	15.00	4.50
RY Robin Yount	40.00	12.00
SC Sean Casey	15.00	4.50
SG Steve Garvey	15.00	4.50
TC Tony Clark	10.00	3.00
TG Tony Gwynn	40.00	12.00

1999 Upper Deck Retro Inkredible Level 2

Randomly inserted into packs, these cards parallel the regular Inkredible inserts. The difference is that these cards are serial numbered to the featured player's jersey number. No pricing is available on some of these cards due to their scarcity.

	Nm-Mt	Ex-Mt
AP Angel Pena/36	25.00	7.50
BD Bucky Dent/20		
BW Bernie Williams/51	100.00	30.00
CBE Carlos Beltran/36	100.00	30.00
CJ Chipper Jones/10		
DE Darin Erstad/17		
DM Don Mattingly/23		
DW Dave Winfield/31	60.00	18.00
EM Eddie Murray/33	150.00	45.00
FL Fred Lynn/19		
GB George Brett/5		
GK Gabe Kapler/23		
HK Harmon Killebrew/3		
IR Ivan Rodriguez/7		
JR Ken Griffey Jr./24		
KG Kirk Gibson/23		
MR Manny Ramirez/24		
NR Nolan Ryan/34	400.00	120.00
OZ Ozzie Smith/1		
PB Pat Burrell/76	60.00	18.00
PM Paul Molitor/4		
PO Paul O'Neill/21		
RF Rollie Fingers/34	40.00	12.00
RG Rusty Greer/29	40.00	12.00
RY Robin Yount/19		
SC Sean Casey/21		
SG Steve Garvey/6		
TC Tony Clark/17		
TG Tony Gwynn/19		

1999 Upper Deck Retro Lunchboxes

These 17 "Lunchboxes" feature a mix of active and retired players on them. In 1999, there were also some dual pairings of players on the boxes. The dual player boxes were issued one per 12 box case and are therefore in shorter supply than the regular player lunchboxes.

	Nm-Mt	Ex-Mt
1 Roger Clemens	12.00	3.60
2 Ken Griffey Jr.	25.00	7.50
3 Mickey Mantle	25.00	7.50
4 Mark McGwire	25.00	7.50
5 Mike Piazza	15.00	4.50
6 Alex Rodriguez	15.00	4.50
7 Babe Ruth	25.00	7.50
8 Sammy Sosa	12.00	3.60
9 Ted Williams	20.00	6.00
10 Ken Griffey Jr. / Mickey Mantle	15.00	4.50
11 Ken Griffey Jr. / Mark McGwire	15.00	4.50
12 K.Griffey Jr. / Babe Ruth	15.00	4.50
13 Ken Griffey Jr. / Ted Williams	15.00	4.50
14 Mickey Mantle / Babe Ruth	15.00	4.50
15 Mark McGwire / Mickey Mantle	15.00	4.50
16 Mark McGwire / Babe Ruth	15.00	4.50
17 Marlk McGwire / Ted Williams	15.00	4.50

1999 Upper Deck Retro Old School/New School

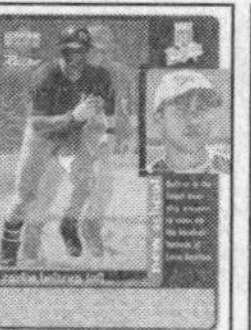

Sequentially numbered to 1000, these cards feature active players broken into "Old School" or veteran and "New School" or youngsters in two different designs.

	Nm-Mt	Ex-Mt
COMPLETE SET (30)	200.00	60.00

*LEVEL 2 STARS: 1.25X TO 3X BASIC SCHOOL
*LEVEL 2 ROOKIES: .75X TO 2X BASIC OLD/NEW SCHOOL
STATED PRINT RUN 50 SERIAL #'d SETS
RANDOM INSERTS IN PACKS

	Nm-Mt	Ex-Mt
S1 Ken Griffey Jr.	10.00	3.00
S2 Alex Rodriguez	10.00	3.00
S3 Frank Thomas	6.00	1.80
S4 Cal Ripken	20.00	6.00
S5 Chipper Jones	6.00	1.80
S6 Craig Biggio	4.00	1.20
S7 Greg Maddux	10.00	3.00
S8 Jeff Bagwell	4.00	1.20
S9 Juan Gonzalez	4.00	1.20
S10 Mark McGwire	15.00	4.50
S11 Mike Piazza	10.00	3.00
S12 Mo Vaughn	2.50	.75
S13 Roger Clemens	12.00	3.60
S14 Sammy Sosa	10.00	3.00
S15 Tony Gwynn	8.00	2.40
S16 Gabe Kapler	2.50	.75
S17 J.D. Drew	2.50	.75
S18 Pat Burrell	5.00	1.50
S19 Roy Halladay	2.50	.75
S20 Jeff Weaver	4.00	1.20
S21 Troy Glaus	2.50	.75
S22 Vladimir Guerrero	6.00	1.80
S23 Michael Barrett	2.50	.75
S24 Carlos Beltran	4.00	1.20
S25 Scott Rolen	6.00	1.80
S26 Nomar Garciaparra	10.00	3.00
S27 Warren Morris	2.50	.75
S28 Alex Gonzalez	2.50	.75
S29 Kyle Farnsworth	2.50	.75
S30 Derek Jeter	15.00	4.50

1999 Upper Deck Retro Throwback Attack

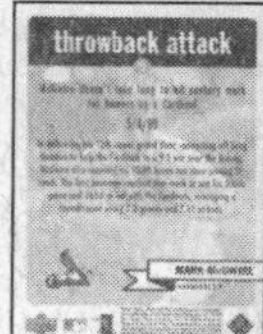

Using a design reminiscent of the 1959 Topps set, these cards were inserted one every five packs. The players featured are among the leading players in the game and this insert set is designed to show how cards of these players would have looked many years ago.

	Nm-Mt	Ex-Mt
COMPLETE SET (15)	40.00	12.00

*LEVEL 2: 1.25X TO 3X BASIC THROWBACK
LEVEL 2 RANDOM INSERTS IN PACKS

T1 Ken Griffey Jr.	3.00	.90
T2 Mark McGwire	5.00	1.50
T3 Sammy Sosa	3.00	.90
T4 Roger Clemens	4.00	1.20
T5 J.D. Drew	.75	.23
T6 Alex Rodriguez	3.00	.90
T7 Greg Maddux	3.00	.90
T8 Mike Piazza	3.00	.90
T9 Juan Gonzalez	1.25	.35
T10 Mo Vaughn	.75	.23
T11 Cal Ripken	6.00	1.80
T12 Frank Thomas	2.00	.60
T13 Nomar Garciaparra	3.00	.90
T14 Vladimir Guerrero	2.00	.60
T15 Tony Gwynn	2.50	.75

2002 Upper Deck Rookie Debut Climbing the Ladder

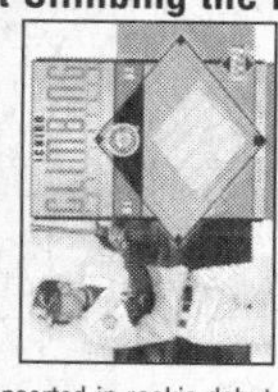

Randomly inserted in rookie debut packs, these cards were issued to a stated print run of 25 serial numbered sets. Due to market scarcity no pricing is provided for these cards.

	Nm-Mt	Ex-Mt
AR Alex Rodriguez		
GM Greg Maddux		
GO Juan Gonzalez		
IS Ichiro Suzuki		
JG Jason Giambi		
JT Jim Thome		
KG Ken Griffey Jr.		
LW Larry Walker		
MM Mark McGwire		
RP Rafael Palmeiro		
SG Shawn Green		
SS Sammy Sosa		

2002 Upper Deck Rookie Debut Elite Company

Randomly inserted into packs, these two cards feature the leading sluggers of 1998 and each of these cards was issued to a stated print run of 25 serial numbered sets. Due to market scarcity, no pricing is provided for these cards.

	Nm-Mt	Ex-Mt
MM Mark McGwire		
SS Sammy Sosa		

2002 Upper Deck Rookie Debut Making Their Marks

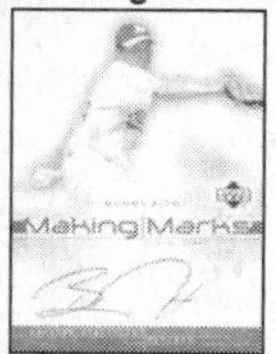

Randomly inserted into packs, these two cards feature some of the leading young players in baseball. Each of these cards was issued to a stated print run of 25 serial numbered sets. Due to market scarcity, no pricing is provided for these cards.

	Nm-Mt	Ex-Mt
BG Brian Giles		
BZ Barry Zito		
DM Doug Mientkiewicz		
HB Hank Blalock		
LB Lance Berkman		
MB Mark Buehrle		
MP Mark Prior		
MS Mike Sweeney		
RS Richie Sexson		
SB Sean Burroughs		
TO Tomo Ohka		
TR Tim Redding		

2002 Upper Deck Rookie Debut Solid Contact

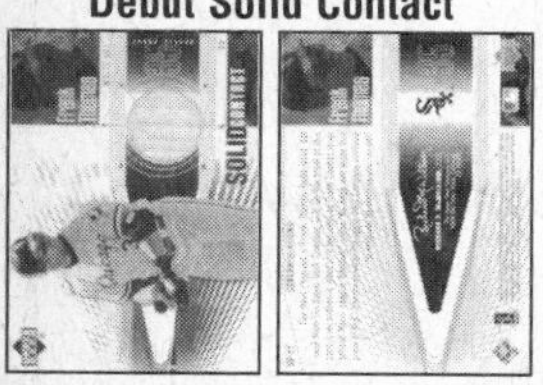

Inserted at a stated rate of one in 24, these 30 cards feature leading hitters in baseball.

	Nm-Mt	Ex-Mt
AR Alex Rodriguez	15.00	4.50
BA Bobby Abreu	10.00	3.00
BG Brian Giles	10.00	3.00
BL Barry Larkin	15.00	4.50
BW Bernie Williams	15.00	4.50
CD Carlos Delgado SP	15.00	4.50
CE Carl Everett	10.00	3.00
DM Doug Mientkiewicz	15.00	4.50
EA Edgardo Alfonzo	10.00	3.00
EM Edgar Martinez	15.00	4.50
FM Fred McGriff	15.00	4.50
FT Frank Thomas	15.00	4.50
GS Gary Sheffield	10.00	3.00
IR Ivan Rodriguez	15.00	4.50
JC Jose Cruz Jr.	10.00	3.00
JE Jim Edmonds	10.00	3.00
JG Jason Giambi SP/50	15.00	4.50
JK Jason Kendall	10.00	3.00
JO John Olerud	10.00	3.00
JP Jorge Posada	15.00	4.50
JT Jim Thome	15.00	4.50
KG Ken Griffey Jr.	20.00	6.00
MA Moises Alou	10.00	3.00
MO Magglio Ordonez	10.00	3.00
MW Matt Williams	10.00	3.00
OV Omar Vizquel	15.00	4.50
RA Roberto Alomar	15.00	4.50
SS Sammy Sosa	20.00	6.00
TA Fernando Tatis	10.00	3.00
TH Todd Helton	15.00	4.50

2001 Upper Deck Rookie Update Ichiro Rookie BuyBacks

As a last minute addition to their Rookie Update brand, Upper Deck added a total of 50 Ichiro Suzuki Rookie Cards into packs. The 50 cards are an assortion from SP Authentic, SPx, Sweet Spot and UD Reserve. Each of the SPx, SP Authentic and Sweet Spot cards have their original serial-numbering, as well as an additional hand numbering by Upper Deck coupled with a serial-numbered hologram on back and an accompanying 2 1/2" by 3" certificate of authenticity of which carries a matching hologram number. Unlike the other cards from this set, the UD Reserve cards were not repurchased from the secondary market and do not carry any type of serial-numbered hologram. Though the original UD Reserve Ichiro cards were serial numbered to 2,500 these BuyBacks, do not carry any factory serial-numbering at all. Collectors who pulled an unnumbered UD Reserve BuyBack Ichiro card were instructed to send it back to Upper Deck for a numbered version. Though the cards are serial numbered cumulatively to 50, representatives at Upper Deck did release actual quantities of each card used for this promotion. They are as follows: SP Authentic - 16, SPx - 3, Sweet Spot - 4 and UD Reserve - 27.

	Nm-Mt	Ex-Mt
1 Ichiro Suzuki SP Authentic/16		
2 Ichiro Suzuki SPx/3		
3 Ichiro Suzuki Sweet Spot/4		
4 Ichiro Suzuki UD Reserve/27		

2001 Upper Deck Rookie Update Ichiro Tribute

This 51-card set was distributed in special three-card Ichiro Tribute mini packs seeded exclusively into 2001 Upper Deck Rookie Update boxes at a rate of one pack per 24-ct box. The set commemorates Ichiro's amazing 2001 MLB campaign. The set is broken down as follows: Basic Cards (1-30), Five Tool Star (31-35), Salute to Ichiro (36-50) and Checklist Card (51).

	Nm-Mt	Ex-Mt
COMPLETE SET (51)	60.00	18.00
COMMON CARD (1-51)	2.00	.60

*GOLD: 5X TO 12X BASIC ICHIRO TRIB.
GOLD PRINT RUN 100 SERIAL #'d SETS
*PLATINUM: 12.5X TO 30X BASIC TRIB
PLATINUM PRINT RUN 25 SERIAL #'d SETS

2001 Upper Deck Rookie Update Ichiro Tribute Game Bat

Randomly inserted into 2001 Ichiro Tribute packs, this 20-card insert features game-used bat cards from the 2001 American Rookie of the Year, Ichiro Suzuki. Card backs carry a "B" prefix. Cards numbered 1 through 12 are serial numbered to 100, cards numbered 13 through 17 are serial numbered to 50, cards numbered 18 and 19 are serial numbered to 25 and card number 20 is serial numbered to 1.

	Nm-Mt	Ex-Mt
COMMON (B-I1-B-I12)	50.00	15.00
COMMON (B-I13-B-I17)	80.00	24.00
COMMON (B-I18-B-I19)	150.00	45.00

2001 Upper Deck Rookie Update Ichiro Tribute Game Pants

Randomly inserted into 2001 Ichiro Tribute packs, this 20-card insert features game-used pants cards from the 2001 American Rookie of the Year, Ichiro Suzuki. Card backs carry a "J" prefix. Cards numbered 1 through 12 are serial numbered to 100, cards numbered 13 through 17 are serial numbered to 50, cards numbered 18 and 19 are serial numbered to 25 and card number 20 is serial numbered to 1.

	Nm-Mt	Ex-Mt
COMMON (J-I1-J-I12)	50.00	15.00
COMMON (J-I13-J-I17)	80.00	24.00
COMMON (J-I18-J-I19)	150.00	45.00

2001 Upper Deck Rookie Update USA Touch of Gold Autographs

Randomly inserted into packs, this 24-card insert features authentic autographs from members of the 2000 U.S.A. Olympic Team. Each card is individually serial numbered to 500.

	Nm-Mt	Ex-Mt
AE Adam Everett	10.00	3.00
AS Anthony Sanders	10.00	3.00
BA Brent Abernathy	10.00	3.00
BW Brad Wilkerson	10.00	3.00
CG Chris George	10.00	3.00
DM Doug Mientkiewicz	15.00	4.50
EY Ernie Young	10.00	3.00
JC John Cotton	10.00	3.00
JR Jon Rauch	10.00	3.00
KU Kurt Ainsworth	10.00	3.00
MJ Marcus Jensen	10.00	3.00
MK Mike Kinkade	10.00	3.00
MN Mike Neill	10.00	3.00
PB Pat Borders	10.00	3.00
RF Ryan Franklin	10.00	3.00
RK Rick Krivda	10.00	3.00
RO Roy Oswalt	25.00	7.50
SB Sean Burroughs	15.00	4.50
SH Shane Heams	10.00	3.00
TD Gookie Dawkins	10.00	3.00
TW Todd Williams	10.00	3.00
TY Tim Young	10.00	3.00
BSE Bobby Seay	10.00	3.00
BSH Ben Sheets	25.00	7.50

2002 Upper Deck Rookie Update Star Tributes

Issued at a stated rate of one in 15, these 29 cards feature some of the leading players in baseball. A few players were issued in smaller quantities and we have notated those players with an SP in our checklist along with print runs when known.

	Nm-Mt	Ex-Mt
AD Adam Dunn	10.00	3.00
AR Alex Rodriguez	15.00	4.50
AS Alfonso Soriano	10.00	3.00
CD Carlos Delgado	8.00	2.40
CJ Chipper Jones	10.00	3.00
CS Curt Schilling	8.00	2.40
FT Frank Thomas	10.00	3.00
IR Ivan Rodriguez	10.00	3.00
IS Ichiro Suzuki SP/19		
JB Josh Beckett	8.00	2.40
JD Joe DiMaggio SP	100.00	30.00
JG Jason Giambi	8.00	2.40
KG Ken Griffey Jr.	15.00	4.50
KI Kazuhisa Ishii	15.00	4.50
KS Kazuhiro Sasaki	8.00	2.40
LB Lance Berkman	8.00	2.40
LG Luis Gonzalez SP	10.00	3.00
MM Mark McGwire SP	60.00	18.00
MPI Mike Piazza	12.00	3.60
MPR Mark Prior	12.00	3.60
MS Mike Sweeney	8.00	2.40
PM Pedro Martinez	10.00	3.00
RC Roger Clemens	15.00	4.50
RJ Randy Johnson	10.00	3.00
RP Rafael Palmeiro	10.00	3.00
SG Shawn Green	8.00	2.40
SS Sammy Sosa	15.00	4.50
TG Tom Glavine	10.00	3.00
TS Tsuyoshi Shinjo	8.00	2.40

2002 Upper Deck Rookie Update Star Tributes Signatures

Randomly inserted into packs, this is a partial parallel to the Star Tributes insert set. These cards were signed by the player and were issued to a stated print run of 50 serial numbered sets.

	Nm-Mt	Ex-Mt

COPPER PRINT RUN 25 SERIAL #'d SETS
NO COPPER PRICING DUE TO SCARCITY
GOLD PRINT RUN 5 SERIAL #'d SETS
SILVER PRINT RUN 25 SERIAL #'d SETS
NO GOLD PRICING DUE TO SCARCITY
NO SILVER PRICING DUE TO SCARCITY

AR Alex Rodriguez		
JG Jason Giambi		
KG Ken Griffey Jr.		
MM Mark McGwire		

2002 Upper Deck Rookie Update USA Future Watch Swatches

Inserted at a stated rate of one in 15, these 22 cards feature game-used jersey swatches of players from the 2002 USA National team.

	Nm-Mt	Ex-Mt

COPPER PRINT RUN 25 SERIAL #'d SETS
NO COPPER PRICING DUE TO SCARCITY
GOLD PRINT RUN 5 SERIAL #'d SETS
NO GOLD PRICING DUE TO SCARCITY
RED PRINT RUN 50 SERIAL #'d SETS
NO RED PRICING DUE TO LACK OF INFO
SILVER PRINT RUN 25 SERIAL #'d SETS
NO SILVER PRICING DUE TO SCARCITY

AA Abe Alvarez	8.00	2.40
AH Aaron Hill	8.00	2.40
BS Brad Sullivan	8.00	2.40
BZ Bob Zimmermann	5.00	1.50
CC Chad Cordero	5.00	1.50
CJ Conor Jackson	10.00	3.00
CQ Carlos Quentin	10.00	3.00
CS Clint Sammons	5.00	1.50
DP Dustin Pedroia	10.00	3.00
EP Eric Patterson	8.00	2.40
GJ Grant Johnson	5.00	1.50
HS Huston Street	8.00	2.40
KB Kyle Bakker	5.00	1.50
KS Kyle Sleeth	8.00	2.40
LP Landon Powell	8.00	2.40
MA Michael Aubrey	10.00	3.00
MJ Mark Jurich	5.00	1.50
PH Philip Humber	8.00	2.40
RW Rickie Weeks	15.00	4.50
SC Shane Costa	8.00	2.40
SF Sam Fuld	5.00	1.50
WL Wes Littleton	8.00	2.40

2003 Upper Deck Standing O

This 126 card set was released in May, 2003. The set was issued in 13 card packs with a $2 SRP which came 24 packs to a box and 20 boxes to a case. Cards numbered 1 through 84 featured veterans while cards 85 through 126 feature rookies and those cards were seeded into packs at a stated rate of one in four.

	Nm-Mt	Ex-Mt
COMP.SET w/o SP's (84)	15.00	4.50
COMMON CARD (1-84)	.30	.09
COMMON CARD (85-126)	2.00	.60
1 Darin Erstad	.30	.09
2 Troy Glaus	.30	.09
3 Tim Salmon	.50	.15
4 Luis Gonzalez	.30	.09
5 Randy Johnson	.75	.23
6 Curt Schilling	.30	.09
7 Andruw Jones	.30	.09
8 Greg Maddux	1.25	.35
9 Chipper Jones	.75	.23
10 Gary Sheffield	.30	.09
11 Rodrigo Lopez	.30	.09
12 Geronimo Gil	.30	.09
13 Nomar Garciaparra	1.25	.35
14 Pedro Martinez	.75	.23
15 Manny Ramirez	.50	.15
16 Mark Prior	.75	.23
17 Kerry Wood	.75	.23
18 Sammy Sosa	1.25	.35
19 Magglio Ordonez	.30	.09
20 Frank Thomas	.75	.23
21 Adam Dunn	.50	.15
22 Ken Griffey Jr.	1.25	.35
23 Sean Casey	.30	.09
24 Omar Vizquel	.50	.15
25 C.C. Sabathia	.30	.09
26 Larry Walker	.50	.15
27 Todd Helton	.50	.15
28 Ivan Rodriguez	.75	.23
29 Josh Beckett	.30	.09
30 Roy Oswalt	.30	.09
31 Jeff Kent	.30	.09
32 Jeff Bagwell	.50	.15
33 Lance Berkman	.30	.09
34 Mike Sweeney	.30	.09
35 Carlos Beltran	.50	.15
36 Hideo Nomo	.75	.23
37 Shawn Green	.30	.09
38 Kazuhisa Ishii	.30	.09
39 Geoff Jenkins	.30	.09
40 Richie Sexson	.30	.09
41 Torii Hunter	.30	.09
42 Jacque Jones	.30	.09
43 Jose Vidro	.30	.09
44 Vladimir Guerrero	.75	.23
45 Cliff Floyd	.30	.09
46 Al Leiter	.30	.09
47 Mike Piazza	1.25	.35
48 Tom Glavine	.50	.15
49 Roberto Alomar	.50	.15
50 Roger Clemens	1.50	.45
51 Jason Giambi	.30	.09
52 Bernie Williams	.50	.15
53 Alfonso Soriano	.50	.15
54 Derek Jeter	2.00	.60
55 Miguel Tejada	.30	.09
56 Eric Chavez	.30	.09
57 Barry Zito	.30	.09
58 Pat Burrell	.30	.09
59 Jim Thome	.75	.23
60 Brian Giles	.30	.09
61 Jason Kendall	.30	.09
62 Ryan Klesko	.30	.09
63 Phil Nevin	.30	.09
64 Sean Burroughs	.30	.09
65 Jason Schmidt	.30	.09
66 Rich Aurilia	.30	.09
67 Barry Bonds	2.00	.60
68 Randy Winn	.30	.09
69 Freddy Garcia	.30	.09
70 Ichiro Suzuki	1.25	.35
71 J.D. Drew	.30	.09
72 Jim Edmonds	.30	.09
73 Scott Rolen	.75	.23
74 Matt Morris	.30	.09
75 Albert Pujols	1.50	.45
76 Tino Martinez	.50	.15
77 Rey Ordonez	.30	.09
78 Carl Crawford	.30	.09
79 Rafael Palmeiro	.50	.15
80 Kevin Mench	.30	.09
81 Alex Rodriguez	1.25	.35
82 Juan Gonzalez	.50	.15
83 Carlos Delgado	.30	.09
84 Eric Hinske	.30	.09
85 Rich Fischer WP RC	2.00	.60
86 Brandon Webb WP RC	3.00	.90
87 Rob Hammock WP RC	3.00	.90
88 Matt Kata WP RC	3.00	.90
89 Tim Olson WP RC	3.00	.90
90 Oscar Villarreal WP RC	2.00	.60
91 Michael Hessman WP RC	2.00	.60
92 Daniel Cabrera WP RC	4.00	1.20
93 Jon Leicester WP RC	2.00	.60
94 Todd Wellemeyer WP RC	3.00	.90
95 Felix Sanchez WP RC	2.00	.60
96 David Sanders WP RC	2.00	.60
97 Josh Stewart WP RC	2.00	.60
98 Arnie Munoz WP RC	2.00	.60
99 Ryan Cameron WP RC	2.00	.60
100 Clint Barmes WP RC	3.00	.90
101 Josh Willingham WP RC	3.00	.90
102 Chris Waters WP RC	2.00	.60
103 Willie Eyre WP RC	2.00	.60
104 Brent Hoard WP RC	2.00	.60
105 Terrmel Sledge WP RC	3.00	.90
106 Phil Seibel WP RC	2.00	.60
107 Craig Brazell WP RC	3.00	.90
108 Jeff Duncan WP RC	3.00	.90
109 Bernie Castro WP RC	2.00	.60
110 Bernie Castro WP RC	2.00	.60
111 Mike Nicolas WP RC	2.00	.60
112 Rett Johnson WP RC	3.00	.90
113 Bobby Madritsch WP RC	8.00	2.40
114 Luis Ayala WP RC	2.00	.60
115 Hideki Matsui WP RC	10.00	3.00
116 Jose Contreras WP RC	3.00	.90
117 Lew Ford WP RC	3.00	.90
118 Jeremy Griffiths WP RC	3.00	.90
119 Guillermo Quiroz WP RC	3.00	.90
120 Al. Machado WP RC	2.00	.60
121 Fran. Cruceta WP RC	2.00	.60
122 Prentice Redman WP RC	2.00	.60
123 Shane Bazzell WP RC	2.00	.60
124 Jason Anderson WP	2.00	.60
125 Ian Ferguson WP RC	2.00	.60
126 Nook Logan WP RC	2.00	.60

2003 Upper Deck Standing O Die Cuts

	Nm-Mt	Ex-Mt

*DIE CUTS 1-84: 1.25X TO 3X BASIC
*DIE CUTS 85-126: .75X TO 2X BASIC

2003 Upper Deck Standing O Starring Role Game Jersey

Collectors who pulled an exchange card for a game-used jersey card from this set were not given any assurances as to what card they would receive from Upper Deck. Those random exchange cards had an expiration date of May 20, 2006.

	Nm-Mt	Ex-Mt
AR Alex Rodriguez		
GO Juan Gonzalez		
HN Hideo Nomo Dodgers		
HN2 Hideo Nomo Red Sox SP/66		
JG Jason Giambi SP		
KG Ken Griffey Jr. SP/35		
LG Luis Gonzalez		
MC Mark McGwire SP		
MCA Mike Cameron		
MM Mickey Mantle SP/100		
MP Mike Piazza		
MT Miguel Tejada		
RC Roger Clemens		
RJ Randy Johnson		
SG Shawn Green		
XX Random Player EXCH		

1999 Upper Deck Victory

This 470 standard-size set was issued in 12 card packs with 39 packs per box and 12 boxes per case. The SRP on these packs was only 99 cents and no insert cards were made for this product. The Subsets include 50 cards featuring 1999 rookies, 20 Rookie Flashback cards (451-470), 15 Power Trip cards, 10 History in the Making cards, 30 Team Checklist cards and 30 Mark McGwire Magic cards (421-450). Unless noted the subset cards are interspersed throughout the set. Also, through an internet-oriented contest, 10 autographed Ken Griffey Jr. jerseys were available through a contest which was entered through the Upper Deck website.

	Nm-Mt	Ex-Mt
COMPLETE SET (470)	75.00	22.00
COMMON CARD (1-470)	.20	.06
COMMON (421-450)	.75	.23
1 Anaheim Angels TC	.20	.06
2 Mark Harriger RC	.20	.06
3 Mo Vaughn PT	.20	.06
4 Darin Erstad BP	.20	.06
5 Troy Glaus	.20	.06
6 Tim Salmon	.30	.09
7 Mo Vaughn	.20	.06
8 Darin Erstad	.20	.06
9 Garret Anderson	.20	.06
10 Todd Greene	.20	.06
11 Troy Percival	.20	.06
12 Chuck Finley	.20	.06
13 Jason Dickson	.20	.06
14 Jim Edmonds	.20	.06
15 Ariz. Diamondbacks TC	.20	.06
16 Randy Johnson	.50	.15
17 Matt Williams	.20	.06
18 Travis Lee	.20	.06
19 Jay Bell	.20	.06
20 Tony Womack	.20	.06
21 Steve Finley	.20	.06
22 Bernard Gilkey	.20	.06
23 Tony Batista	.20	.06
24 Todd Stottlemyre	.20	.06
25 Omar Daal	.20	.06
26 Atlanta Braves TC	.20	.06
27 Bruce Chen	.20	.06
28 George Lombard	.20	.06
29 Chipper Jones PT	.30	.09
30 Chipper Jones BP	.30	.09
31 Greg Maddux	.75	.23
32 Chipper Jones	.50	.15
33 Javy Lopez	.20	.06
34 Tom Glavine	.30	.09
35 John Smoltz	.30	.09
36 Andruw Jones	.20	.06
37 Brian Jordan	.20	.06
38 Walt Weiss	.20	.06
39 Bret Boone	.20	.06
40 Andres Galarraga	.20	.06
41 Baltimore Orioles TC	.20	.06
42 Ryan Minor	.20	.06
43 Jerry Hairston Jr.	.20	.06
44 Calvin Pickering	.20	.06
45 Cal Ripken HM	.75	.23
46 Cal Ripken	1.50	.45
47 Charles Johnson	.20	.06
48 Albert Belle	.20	.06
49 Delino DeShields	.20	.06
50 Mike Mussina	.30	.09
51 Scott Erickson	.20	.06
52 Brady Anderson	.20	.06
53 B.J. Surhoff	.20	.06
54 Harold Baines	.20	.06
55 Will Clark	.50	.15
56 Boston Red Sox TC	.20	.06
57 Shea Hillenbrand RC	.75	.23
58 Trot Nixon	.20	.06
59 Jin Ho Cho	.20	.06
60 Nomar Garciaparra PT	.50	.15
61 Nomar Garciaparra BP	.50	.15
62 Pedro Martinez	.50	.15
63 Nomar Garciaparra	.75	.23
64 Jose Offerman	.20	.06
65 Jason Varitek	.30	.09
66 Darren Lewis	.20	.06
67 Troy O'Leary	.20	.06
68 Donnie Sadler	.20	.06
69 John Valentin	.20	.06
70 Tim Wakefield	.20	.06
71 Bret Saberhagen	.20	.06
72 Chicago Cubs TC	.20	.06
73 Kyle Farnsworth RC	.30	.09
74 Sammy Sosa PT	.50	.15
75 Sammy Sosa BP	.50	.15
76 Sammy Sosa HM	.50	.15
77 Kerry Wood HM	.30	.09
78 Sammy Sosa	.75	.23
79 Mark Grace	.30	.09
80 Kerry Wood	.50	.15
81 Kevin Tapani	.20	.06
82 Benito Santiago	.20	.06
83 Gary Gaetti	.20	.06
84 Mickey Morandini	.20	.06
85 Glenallen Hill	.20	.06
86 Henry Rodriguez	.20	.06
87 Rod Beck	.20	.06
88 Chicago White Sox TC	.20	.06
89 Carlos Lee	.20	.06
90 Mark Johnson	.20	.06
91 Frank Thomas PT	.30	.09
92 Frank Thomas	.50	.15
93 Jim Parque	.20	.06
94 Mike Sirotka	.20	.06
95 Mike Caruso	.20	.06
96 Ray Durham	.20	.06
97 Magglio Ordonez	.20	.06
98 Paul Konerko	.20	.06
99 Bob Howry	.20	.06
100 Brian Simmons	.20	.06
101 Jaime Navarro	.20	.06
102 Cincinnati Reds TC	.20	.06
103 Denny Neagle	.20	.06
104 Pete Harnisch	.20	.06
105 Greg Vaughn	.20	.06
106 Brett Tomko	.20	.06
107 Mike Cameron	.20	.06
108 Sean Casey	.20	.06
109 Aaron Boone	.20	.06
110 Michael Tucker	.20	.06
111 Dmitri Young	.20	.06
112 Barry Larkin	.30	.09
113 Cleveland Indians TC	.20	.06
114 Russ Branyan	.20	.06
115 Jim Thome PT	.30	.09
116 Manny Ramirez PT	.20	.06
117 Manny Ramirez	.30	.09
118 Jim Thome	.50	.15
119 David Justice	.20	.06
120 Sandy Alomar Jr.	.20	.06
121 Roberto Alomar	.30	.09
122 Jaret Wright	.20	.06
123 Bartolo Colon	.20	.06
124 Travis Fryman	.20	.06
125 Kenny Lofton	.20	.06
126 Omar Vizquel	.30	.09
127 Colorado Rockies TC	.20	.06
128 Derrick Gibson	.20	.06
129 Larry Walker BP	.30	.09
130 Larry Walker	.30	.09
131 Dante Bichette	.20	.06
132 Todd Helton	.30	.09
133 Neifi Perez	.20	.06
134 Vinny Castilla	.20	.06
135 Darryl Kile	.20	.06
136 Pedro Astacio	.20	.06
137 Darryl Hamilton	.20	.06
138 Mike Lansing	.20	.06
139 Kirt Manwaring	.20	.06
140 Detroit Tigers TC	.20	.06
141 Jeff Weaver RC	.50	.15
142 Gabe Kapler	.20	.06
143 Tony Clark PT	.20	.06
144 Tony Clark	.20	.06
145 Juan Encarnacion	.20	.06
146 Dean Palmer	.20	.06
147 Damion Easley	.20	.06
148 Bobby Higginson	.20	.06
149 Karim Garcia	.20	.06
150 Justin Thompson	.20	.06
151 Matt Anderson	.20	.06
152 Willie Blair	.20	.06
153 Brian Hunter	.20	.06
154 Florida Marlins TC	.20	.06
155 Alex Gonzalez	.20	.06
156 Mark Kotsay	.20	.06
157 Livan Hernandez	.20	.06
158 Cliff Floyd	.20	.06
159 Todd Dunwoody	.20	.06
160 Alex Fernandez	.20	.06
161 Matt Mantei	.20	.06
162 Derrek Lee	.20	.06
163 Kevin Orie	.20	.06
164 Craig Counsell	.20	.06
165 Rafael Medina	.20	.06
166 Houston Astros TC	.20	.06
167 Daryle Ward	.20	.06
168 Mitch Meluskey	.20	.06
169 Jeff Bagwell PT	.20	.06
170 Jeff Bagwell	.30	.09
171 Ken Caminiti	.20	.06
172 Craig Biggio	.30	.09
173 Derek Bell	.20	.06
174 Moises Alou	.20	.06
175 Billy Wagner	.20	.06
176 Shane Reynolds	.20	.06
177 Carl Everett	.20	.06
178 Scott Elarton	.20	.06
179 Richard Hidalgo	.20	.06
180 K.C Royals TC	.20	.06
181 Carlos Beltran	.30	.09
182 Carlos Febles	.20	.06
183 Jeremy Giambi	.20	.06
184 Johnny Damon	.30	.09
185 Joe Randa	.20	.06
186 Jeff King	.20	.06
187 Hipolito Pichardo	.20	.06
188 Kevin Appier	.20	.06
189 Chad Kreuter	.20	.06
190 Rey Sanchez	.20	.06
191 Larry Sutton	.20	.06
192 Jeff Montgomery	.20	.06
193 Jermaine Dye	.20	.06
194 L.A. Dodgers TC	.20	.06
195 Adam Riggs	.20	.06
196 Angel Pena	.20	.06
197 Todd Hundley	.20	.06
198 Kevin Brown	.30	.09
199 Ismael Valdes	.20	.06
200 Chan Ho Park	.20	.06
201 Adrian Beltre	.30	.09
202 Mark Grudzielanek	.20	.06
203 Raul Mondesi	.20	.06
204 Gary Sheffield	.20	.06
205 Eric Karros	.20	.06
206 Devon White	.20	.06
207 Milw. Brewers TC	.20	.06
208 Ron Belliard	.20	.06
209 Rafael Roque RC	.20	.06
210 Jeromy Burnitz	.20	.06
211 Fernando Vina	.20	.06
212 Scott Karl	.20	.06
213 Jim Abbott	.30	.09
214 Sean Berry	.20	.06
215 Marquis Grissom	.20	.06
216 Geoff Jenkins	.20	.06
217 Jeff Cirillo	.20	.06
218 Dave Nilsson	.20	.06
219 Jose Valentin	.20	.06
220 Minnesota Twins TC	.20	.06
221 Corey Koskie	.20	.06
222 Cristian Guzman	.20	.06
223 A.J. Pierzynski	.20	.06
224 David Ortiz	.30	.09
225 Brad Radke	.20	.06
226 Todd Walker	.20	.06
227 Matt Lawton	.20	.06
228 Rick Aguilera	.20	.06
229 Eric Milton	.20	.06
230 Marty Cordova	.20	.06
231 Torii Hunter	.20	.06
232 Ron Coomer	.20	.06
233 LaTroy Hawkins	.20	.06
234 Montreal Expos TC	.20	.06
235 Fernando Seguignol	.20	.06
236 Michael Barrett	.20	.06
237 Vladimir Guerrero BP	.30	.09
238 Vladimir Guerrero	.50	.15
239 Brad Fullmer	.20	.06
240 Rondell White	.20	.06
241 Ugueth Urbina	.20	.06
242 Dustin Hermanson	.20	.06
243 Orlando Cabrera	.20	.06
244 Wilton Guerrero	.20	.06
245 Carl Pavano	.20	.06
246 Javier Vazquez	.20	.06
247 Chris Widger	.20	.06
248 New York Mets TC	.20	.06
249 Mike Kinkade	.20	.06
250 Octavio Dotel	.20	.06
251 Mike Piazza PT	.50	.15
252 Mike Piazza	.75	.23
253 Rickey Henderson	.50	.15
254 Edgardo Alfonzo	.20	.06
255 Robin Ventura	.20	.06
256 Al Leiter	.20	.06
257 Brian McRae	.20	.06
258 Rey Ordonez	.20	.06
259 Bobby Bonilla	.20	.06
260 Orel Hershiser	.20	.06
261 John Olerud	.20	.06
262 New York Yankees TC	.20	.06
263 Ricky Ledee	.20	.06
264 Bernie Williams BP	.20	.06
265 Derek Jeter BP	.60	.18
266 Scott Brosius HM	.20	.06
267 Derek Jeter	1.25	.35
268 Roger Clemens	1.00	.30
269 Orlando Hernandez	.20	.06
270 Scott Brosius	.20	.06
271 Paul O'Neill	.30	.09
272 Bernie Williams	.30	.09
273 Chuck Knoblauch	.20	.06
274 Tino Martinez	.30	.09
275 Mariano Rivera	.30	.09
276 Jorge Posada	.30	.09
277 Oakland Athletics TC	.20	.06
278 Eric Chavez	.20	.06
279 Ben Grieve HM	.20	.06
280 Jason Giambi	.20	.06
281 John Jaha	.20	.06
282 Miguel Tejada	.20	.06
283 Ben Grieve	.20	.06
284 Matt Stairs	.20	.06
285 Ryan Christenson	.20	.06
286 A.J. Hinch	.20	.06
287 Kenny Rogers	.20	.06
288 Tom Candiotti	.20	.06
289 Scott Spiezio	.20	.06
290 Phi. Phillies TC	.20	.06
291 Pat Burrell RC	1.25	.35
292 Marlon Anderson	.20	.06
293 Scott Rolen BP	.30	.09
294 Scott Rolen	.50	.15
295 Doug Glanville	.20	.06
296 Rico Brogna	.20	.06
297 Ron Gant	.20	.06
298 Bobby Abreu	.20	.06
299 Desi Relaford	.20	.06
300 Curt Schilling	.30	.09
301 Chad Ogea	.20	.06
302 Kevin Jordan	.20	.06
303 Carlton Loewer	.20	.06
304 Pittsburgh Pirates TC	.20	.06
305 Kris Benson	.20	.06
306 Brian Giles	.20	.06
307 Jason Kendall	.20	.06
308 Jose Guillen	.20	.06
309 Pat Meares	.20	.06
310 Brant Brown	.20	.06
311 Kevin Young	.20	.06
312 Ed Sprague	.20	.06
313 Francisco Cordova	.20	.06
314 Aramis Ramirez	.30	.09
315 Freddy Adrian Garcia	.20	.06
316 St. Louis Cardinals TC	.20	.06
317 J.D. Drew	.20	.06
318 Chad Hutchinson RC	.30	.09
319 Mark McGwire PT	.60	.18
320 J.D. Drew PT	.20	.06
321 Mark McGwire BP	.60	.18
322 Mark McGwire HM	.60	.18
323 Mark McGwire	1.25	.35
324 Fernando Tatis	.20	.06
325 Edgar Renteria	.20	.06
326 Ray Lankford	.20	.06
327 Willie McGee	.20	.06
328 Ricky Bottalico	.20	.06
329 Eli Marrero	.20	.06
330 Matt Morris	.20	.06
331 Eric Davis	.20	.06
332 Darren Bragg	.20	.06
333 San Diego Padres TC	.20	.06
334 Matt Clement	.20	.06
335 Ben Davis	.20	.06
336 Gary Matthews Jr.	.20	.06
337 Tony Gwynn BP	.30	.09
338 Tony Gwynn HM	.30	.09
339 Tony Gwynn	.60	.18
340 Reggie Sanders	.20	.06
341 Ruben Rivera	.20	.06
342 Wally Joyner	.20	.06
343 Sterling Hitchcock	.20	.06
344 Carlos Hernandez	.20	.06
345 Andy Ashby	.20	.06
346 Trevor Hoffman	.20	.06
347 Chris Gomez	.20	.06
348 Jim Leyritz	.20	.06
349 S.F. Giants TC	.20	.06
350 Armando Rios	.20	.06
351 Barry Bonds PT	.50	.15
352 Barry Bonds BP	.50	.15
353 Barry Bonds HM	.50	.15
354 Robb Nen	.20	.06
355 Bill Mueller	.20	.06
356 Barry Bonds	1.25	.35
357 Jeff Kent	.20	.06
358 J.T. Snow	.20	.06
359 Ellis Burks	.20	.06
360 F.P. Santangelo	.20	.06
361 Marvin Benard	.20	.06
362 Stan Javier	.20	.06
363 Shawn Estes	.20	.06
364 Seattle Mariners TC	.20	.06
365 Carlos Guillen	.20	.06
366 Ken Griffey Jr. PT	.50	.15
367 Alex Rodriguez PT	.50	.15
368 Ken Griffey Jr. BP	.50	.15
369 Alex Rodriguez BP	.50	.15
370 Ken Griffey Jr. HM	.50	.15
371 Alex Rodriguez HM	.50	.15
372 Ken Griffey Jr.	.75	.23
373 Alex Rodriguez	.75	.23
374 Jay Buhner	.20	.06
375 Edgar Martinez	.30	.09
376 Jeff Fassero	.20	.06
377 David Bell	.20	.06
378 David Segui	.20	.06
379 Russ Davis	.20	.06
380 Dan Wilson	.20	.06
381 Jamie Moyer	.20	.06
382 T.B. Devil Rays TC	.20	.06
383 Roberto Hernandez	.20	.06
384 Bobby Smith	.20	.06
385 Wade Boggs	.30	.09
386 Fred McGriff	.30	.09
387 Rolando Arrojo	.20	.06
388 Jose Canseco	.50	.15
389 Wilson Alvarez	.20	.06
390 Kevin Stocker	.20	.06
391 Miguel Cairo	.20	.06
392 Quinton McCracken	.20	.06
393 Texas Rangers TC	.20	.06
394 Ruben Mateo	.20	.06
395 Cesar King	.20	.06
396 Juan Gonzalez PT	.20	.06
397 Juan Gonzalez BP	.20	.06
398 Ivan Rodriguez	.50	.15
399 Juan Gonzalez	.30	.09
400 Rafael Palmeiro	.30	.09
401 Rick Helling	.20	.06
402 Aaron Sele	.20	.06
403 John Wetteland	.20	.06
404 Rusty Greer	.20	.06
405 Todd Zeile	.20	.06
406 Royce Clayton	.20	.06
407 Tom Goodwin	.20	.06
408 Toronto Blue Jays TC	.20	.06
409 Kevin Witt	.20	.06
410 Roy Halladay	.20	.06
411 Jose Cruz Jr.	.20	.06
412 Carlos Delgado	.20	.06
413 Willie Greene	.20	.06
414 Shawn Green	.20	.06
415 Homer Bush	.20	.06
416 Shannon Stewart	.20	.06
417 David Wells	.20	.06
418 Kelvim Escobar	.20	.06
419 Joey Hamilton	.20	.06
420 Alex Gonzalez	.20	.06
421 Mark McGwire MM	.75	.23
422 Mark McGwire MM	.75	.23
423 Mark McGwire MM	.75	.23
424 Mark McGwire MM	.75	.23
425 Mark McGwire MM	.75	.23
426 Mark McGwire MM	.75	.23
427 Mark McGwire MM	.75	.23
428 Mark McGwire MM	.75	.23
429 Mark McGwire MM	.75	.23
430 Mark McGwire MM	.75	.23
431 Mark McGwire MM	.75	.23
432 Mark McGwire MM	.75	.23
433 Mark McGwire MM	.75	.23
434 Mark McGwire MM	.75	.23
435 Mark McGwire MM	.75	.23
436 Mark McGwire MM	.75	.23
437 Mark McGwire MM	.75	.23
438 Mark McGwire MM	.75	.23
439 Mark McGwire MM	.75	.23
440 Mark McGwire MM	.75	.23
441 Mark McGwire MM	.75	.23
442 Mark McGwire MM	.75	.23
443 Mark McGwire MM	.75	.23
444 Mark McGwire MM	.75	.23
445 Mark McGwire MM	.75	.23
446 Mark McGwire MM	.75	.23
447 Mark McGwire MM	.75	.23
448 Mark McGwire MM	.75	.23
449 Mark McGwire MM	.75	.23
450 Mark McGwire MM	.75	.23
451 Chipper Jones RF	.30	.09
452 Cal Ripken RF	.75	.23
453 Roger Clemens RF	.50	.15
454 Wade Boggs RF	.20	.06
455 Greg Maddux RF	.50	.15
456 Frank Thomas RF	.30	.09
457 Jeff Bagwell RF	.20	.06
458 Mike Piazza RF	.50	.15
459 Randy Johnson RF	.30	.09
460 Mo Vaughn RF	.20	.06
461 Mark McGwire RF	.60	.18
462 Rickey Henderson RF	.30	.09
463 Barry Bonds RF	.50	.15
464 Tony Gwynn RF	.30	.09
465 Ken Griffey Jr. RF	.50	.15
466 Alex Rodriguez RF	.50	.15
467 Sammy Sosa RF	.50	.15
468 Juan Gonzalez RF	.20	.06
469 Kevin Brown RF	.20	.06
470 Fred McGriff RF	.20	.06

2000 Upper Deck Victory

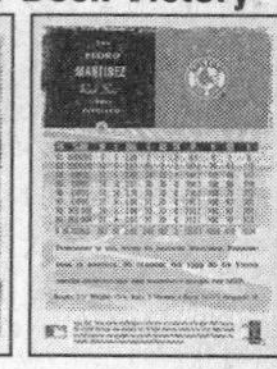

The Upper Deck Victory set was initially released in March, 2000 as a 440-card set that featured 300 player cards, 40 Rookie Subset cards, 20 Big Play Makers, 30 Team Checklists, and 50 Junior Circuit subset cards. Each pack contained 12 cards and carried a suggested retail price of ninety-nine cents. A 466-card factory set was released in December, 2000 containing an exclusive 26-card Team USA subset (cards 441-466) featuring the team that won the Olympic gold medal in Sydney, Australia in September 2000. Finally, special packs were issued in April 2000 for the season-opening Mets/Cubs series in Japan. These packs contained three regular issue Victory cards featuring either Cubs or Mets and two Japanese header cards. One of those cards featured a checklist of the 21 players in the packs and the other one provided set information. Notable rookies in the set include Jon Rauch and Ben Sheets.

	Nm-Mt	Ex-Mt
COMPLETE SET (440)	15.00	4.50
COMP.FACT.SET (466)	20.00	6.00
COMMON CARD (1-390)	.20	.06
COMMON (391-440)	.50	.15
COMMON USA (441-466)	.30	.09
1 Mo Vaughn	.20	.06
2 Garret Anderson	.20	.06
3 Tim Salmon	.30	.09
4 Troy Percival	.20	.06
5 Orlando Palmeiro	.20	.06
6 Darin Erstad	.20	.06
7 Ramon Ortiz	.20	.06
8 Ben Molina	.20	.06
9 Troy Glaus	.20	.06
10 Jim Edmonds	.20	.06
11 Mo Vaughn Troy Percival CL	.20	.06
12 Craig Biggio	.30	.09
13 Roger Cedeno	.20	.06
14 Shane Reynolds	.20	.06
15 Jeff Bagwell	.30	.09
16 Octavio Dotel	.20	.06
17 Moises Alou	.20	.06
18 Jose Lima	.20	.06
19 Ken Caminiti	.20	.06
20 Richard Hidalgo	.20	.06
21 Billy Wagner	.20	.06
22 Lance Berkman	.20	.06
23 Jeff Bagwell Jose Lima CL	.20	.06
24 Jason Giambi	.20	.06
25 Randy Velarde	.20	.06
26 Miguel Tejada	.20	.06
27 Matt Stairs	.20	.06
28 A.J. Hinch	.20	.06
29 Olmedo Saenz	.20	.06
30 Ben Grieve	.20	.06
31 Ryan Christenson	.20	.06
32 Eric Chavez	.20	.06
33 Tim Hudson	.20	.06
34 John Jaha	.20	.06
35 Jason Giambi Matt Stairs CL	.20	.06
36 Raul Mondesi	.20	.06
37 Tony Batista	.20	.06
38 David Wells	.20	.06
39 Homer Bush	.20	.06
40 Carlos Delgado	.20	.06
41 Billy Koch	.20	.06
42 Darrin Fletcher	.20	.06
43 Tony Fernandez	.20	.06
44 Shannon Stewart	.20	.06
45 Roy Halladay	.20	.06
46 Chris Carpenter	.20	.06
47 Carlos Delgado David Wells CL	.20	.06
48 Chipper Jones	.50	.15
49 Greg Maddux	.75	.23
50 Andruw Jones	.20	.06
51 Andres Galarraga	.20	.06
52 Tom Glavine	.30	.09
53 Brian Jordan	.20	.06
54 John Smoltz	.30	.09
55 John Rocker	.20	.06
56 Javy Lopez	.20	.06
57 Eddie Perez	.20	.06
58 Kevin Millwood	.20	.06
59 Chipper Jones Greg Maddux CL	.30	.09
60 Jeromy Burnitz	.20	.06
61 Steve Woodard	.20	.06
62 Ron Belliard	.20	.06

63 Geoff Jenkins .20 .06
64 Bob Wickman .20 .06
65 Marquis Grissom .20 .06
66 Henry Blanco .20 .06
67 Mark Loretta .20 .06
68 Alex Ochoa .20 .06
69 Marquis Grissom .20 .06
Jeromy Burnitz CL
70 Mark McGwire 1.25 .35
71 Edgar Renteria .20 .06
72 Dave Veres .20 .06
73 Eli Marrero .20 .06
74 Fernando Tatis .20 .06
75 J.D. Drew .20 .06
76 Ray Lankford .20 .06
77 Darryl Kile .20 .06
78 Kent Bottenfield .20 .06
79 Joe McEwing .20 .06
80 Mark McGwire .60 .18
Ray Lankford CL
81 Sammy Sosa .75 .23
82 Jose Nieves .20 .06
83 Jon Lieber .20 .06
84 Henry Rodriguez .20 .06
85 Mark Grace .30 .09
86 Eric Young .20 .06
87 Kerry Wood .50 .15
88 Ismael Valdes .20 .06
89 Glenallen Hill .20 .06
90 Sammy Sosa .30 .09
Mark Grace CL
91 Greg Vaughn .20 .06
92 Fred McGriff .30 .09
93 Ryan Rupe .20 .06
94 Bubba Trammell .20 .06
95 Miguel Cairo .20 .06
96 Roberto Hernandez .20 .06
97 Jose Canseco .50 .15
98 Wilson Alvarez .20 .06
99 John Flaherty .20 .06
100 Vinny Castilla .20 .06
101 Jose Canseco .20 .06
Ramon Hernandez CL
102 Randy Johnson .50 .15
103 Matt Williams .20 .06
104 Matt Mantei .20 .06
105 Steve Finley .20 .06
106 Luis Gonzalez .20 .06
107 Travis Lee .20 .06
108 Omar Daal .20 .06
109 Jay Bell .20 .06
110 Erubiel Durazo .20 .06
111 Tony Womack .20 .06
112 Todd Stottlemyre .20 .06
113 Randy Johnson .20 .06
Matt Williams CL
114 Gary Sheffield .20 .06
115 Adrian Beltre .30 .09
116 Kevin Brown .30 .09
117 Todd Hundley .20 .06
118 Eric Karros .20 .06
119 Shawn Green .20 .06
120 Chan Ho Park .20 .06
121 Mark Grudzielanek .20 .06
122 Todd Hollandsworth .20 .06
123 Jeff Shaw .20 .06
124 Darren Dreifort .20 .06
125 Gary Sheffield .20 .06
Kevin Brown CL
126 Vladimir Guerrero .50 .15
127 Michael Barrett .20 .06
128 Dustin Hermanson .20 .06
129 Jose Vidro .20 .06
130 Chris Widger .20 .06
131 Mike Thurman .20 .06
132 Wilton Guerrero .20 .06
133 Brad Fullmer .20 .06
134 Rondell White .20 .06
135 Ugueth Urbina .20 .06
136 Vladimir Guerrero .20 .06
Rondell White CL
137 Barry Bonds 1.25 .35
138 Russ Ortiz .20 .06
139 J.T. Snow .20 .06
140 Joe Nathan .20 .06
141 Rich Aurilia .20 .06
142 Jeff Kent .20 .06
143 Armando Rios .20 .06
144 Ellis Burks .20 .06
145 Robb Nen .20 .06
146 Marvin Benard .20 .06
147 Barry Bonds .50 .15
Russ Ortiz CL
148 Manny Ramirez .30 .09
149 Bartolo Colon .20 .06
150 Kenny Lofton .20 .06
151 Sandy Alomar Jr. .20 .06
152 Travis Fryman .20 .06
153 Omar Vizquel .30 .09
154 Roberto Alomar .30 .09
155 Richie Sexson .20 .06
156 David Justice .20 .06
157 Jim Thome .50 .15
158 Manny Ramirez .20 .06
Roberto Alomar CL
159 Ken Griffey Jr. .75 .23
160 Edgar Martinez .30 .09
161 Freddy Garcia .20 .06
162 Alex Rodriguez .75 .23
163 John Halama .20 .06
164 Russ Davis .20 .06
165 David Bell .20 .06
166 Gil Meche .20 .06
167 Jamie Moyer .20 .06
168 John Olerud .20 .06
169 Ken Griffey Jr. .50 .15
Freddy Garcia CL
170 Preston Wilson .20 .06
171 Antonio Alfonseca .20 .06
172 A.J. Burnett .20 .06
173 Luis Castillo .20 .06
174 Mike Lowell .20 .06
175 Alex Fernandez .20 .06
176 Mike Redmond .20 .06
177 Alex Gonzalez .20 .06
178 Vladimir Nunez .20 .06
179 Mark Kotsay .20 .06
180 Preston Wilson .20 .06
Luis Castillo CL
181 Mike Piazza .75 .23
182 Darryl Hamilton .20 .06
183 Al Leiter .20 .06
184 Robin Ventura .30 .09
185 Rickey Henderson .50 .15
186 Rey Ordonez .20 .06
187 Edgardo Alfonzo .20 .06
188 Derek Bell .20 .06
189 Mike Hampton .20 .06
190 Armando Benitez .20 .06
191 Mike Piazza .30 .09
Rickey Henderson CL
192 Cal Ripken 1.50 .45
193 B.J. Surhoff .20 .06
194 Mike Mussina .30 .09
195 Albert Belle .20 .06
196 Jerry Hairston Jr. .20 .06
197 Will Clark .50 .15
198 Sidney Ponson .20 .06
199 Brady Anderson .20 .06
200 Scott Erickson .20 .06
201 Ryan Minor .20 .06
202 Cal Ripken .75 .23
Albert Belle CL
203 Tony Gwynn .60 .18
204 Bret Boone .20 .06
205 Ryan Klesko .20 .06
206 Ben Davis .20 .06
207 Matt Clement .20 .06
208 Eric Owens .20 .06
209 Trevor Hoffman .20 .06
210 Sterling Hitchcock .20 .06
211 Phil Nevin .20 .06
212 Tony Gwynn .30 .09
Trevor Hoffman CL
213 Scott Rolen .50 .15
214 Bob Abreu .20 .06
215 Curt Schilling .20 .06
216 Rico Brogna .20 .06
217 Robert Person .20 .06
218 Doug Glanville .20 .06
219 Mike Lieberthal .20 .06
220 Andy Ashby .20 .06
221 Randy Wolf .20 .06
222 Bob Abreu .20 .06
Curt Schilling CL
223 Brian Giles .20 .06
224 Jason Kendall .20 .06
225 Kris Benson .20 .06
226 Warren Morris .20 .06
227 Kevin Young .20 .06
228 Al Martin .20 .06
229 Wil Cordero .20 .06
230 Bruce Aven .20 .06
231 Todd Ritchie .20 .06
232 Jason Kendall .20 .06
Brian Giles CL
233 Ivan Rodriguez .50 .15
234 Rusty Greer .20 .06
235 Ruben Mateo .20 .06
236 Justin Thompson .20 .06
237 Rafael Palmeiro .30 .09
238 Chad Curtis .20 .06
239 Royce Clayton UER .20 .06
Mark McLemore pictured on back
240 Gabe Kapler .20 .06
241 Jeff Zimmerman .20 .06
242 John Wetteland .20 .06
243 Ivan Rodriguez .30 .09
Rafael Palmeiro CL
244 Nomar Garciaparra .75 .23
245 Pedro Martinez .50 .15
246 Jose Offerman .20 .06
247 Jason Varitek .30 .09
248 Troy O'Leary .20 .06
249 John Valentin .20 .06
250 Trot Nixon .20 .06
251 Carl Everett .20 .06
252 Wilton Veras .20 .06
253 Bret Saberhagen .20 .06
254 Nomar Garciaparra .50 .15
Pedro Martinez CL
255 Sean Casey .20 .06
256 Barry Larkin .30 .09
257 Pokey Reese .20 .06
258 Pete Harnisch .20 .06
259 Aaron Boone .20 .06
260 Dante Bichette .20 .06
261 Scott Williamson .20 .06
262 Steve Parris .20 .06
263 Dmitri Young .20 .06
264 Mike Cameron .20 .06
265 Sean Casey .20 .06
Scott Williamson CL
266 Larry Walker .30 .09
267 Rolando Arrojo .20 .06
268 Pedro Astacio .20 .06
269 Todd Helton .30 .09
270 Jeff Cirillo .20 .06
271 Neifi Perez .20 .06
272 Brian Bohanon .20 .06
273 Jeffrey Hammonds .20 .06
274 Tom Goodwin .20 .06
275 Larry Walker .20 .06
Todd Helton CL
276 Carlos Beltran .30 .09
277 Jermaine Dye .20 .06
278 Mike Sweeney .20 .06
279 Joe Randa .20 .06
280 Jose Rosado .20 .06
281 Carlos Febles .20 .06
282 Jeff Suppan .20 .06
283 Johnny Damon .30 .09
284 Jeremy Giambi .20 .06
285 Mike Sweeney .20 .06
Carlos Beltran CL
286 Tony Clark .20 .06
287 Damion Easley .20 .06
288 Jeff Weaver .20 .06
289 Dean Palmer .20 .06
290 Juan Gonzalez .30 .09
291 Juan Encarnacion .20 .06
292 Todd Jones .20 .06
293 Karim Garcia .20 .06
294 Deivi Cruz .20 .06
295 Dean Palmer .20 .06
Juan Encarnacion CL
296 Corey Koskie .20 .06
297 Brad Radke .20 .06
298 Doug Mientkiewicz .20 .06
299 Ron Coomer .20 .06
300 Joe Mays .20 .06
301 Eric Milton .20 .06
302 Jacque Jones .20 .06
303 Chad Allen .20 .06
304 Cristian Guzman .20 .06
305 Jason Ryan .20 .06
306 Todd Walker .20 .06
307 Corey Koskie .20 .06
Eric Milton CL
308 Frank Thomas .50 .15
309 Paul Konerko .20 .06
310 Mike Sirotka .20 .06
311 Jim Parque .20 .06
312 Magglio Ordonez .20 .06
313 Bob Howry .20 .06
314 Carlos Lee .20 .06
315 Ray Durham .20 .06
316 Chris Singleton .20 .06
317 Brook Fordyce .20 .06
318 Frank Thomas .30 .09
Magglio Ordonez CL
319 Derek Jeter 1.25 .35
320 Roger Clemens 1.00 .30
321 Paul O'Neill .30 .09
322 Bernie Williams .30 .09
323 Mariano Rivera .30 .09
324 Tino Martinez .30 .09
325 David Cone .20 .06
326 Chuck Knoblauch .20 .06
327 Darryl Strawberry .20 .06
328 Orlando Hernandez .20 .06
329 Ricky Ledee .20 .06
330 Derek Jeter .60 .18
Bernie Williams CL
331 Pat Burrell .20 .06
332 Alfonso Soriano .50 .15
333 Josh Beckett .30 .09
334 Matt Riley .20 .06
335 Brian Cooper .20 .06
336 Eric Munson .20 .06
337 Vernon Wells .20 .06
338 Juan Pena .20 .06
339 Mark DeRosa .20 .06
340 Kip Wells .20 .06
341 Roosevelt Brown .20 .06
342 Jason LaRue .20 .06
343 Ben Petrick .20 .06
344 Mark Quinn .20 .06
345 Julio Ramirez .20 .06
346 Rod Barajas .20 .06
347 Robert Fick .20 .06
348 David Newhan .20 .06
349 Eric Gagne .75 .23
350 Jorge Toca .20 .06
351 Mitch Meluskey .20 .06
352 Ed Yarnall .20 .06
353 Chad Hermansen .20 .06
354 Peter Bergeron .20 .06
355 Dermal Brown .20 .06
356 Adam Kennedy .20 .06
357 Kevin Barker .20 .06
358 Francisco Cordero .20 .06
359 Travis Dawkins .20 .06
360 Jeff Williams RC .20 .06
361 Chad Hutchinson .20 .06
362 D'Angelo Jimenez .20 .06
363 Derrick Gibson .20 .06
364 Calvin Murray .20 .06
365 Doug Davis .20 .06
366 Rob Ramsay .20 .06
367 Mark Redman .20 .06
368 Rick Ankiel .20 .06
369 Domingo Guzman RC .20 .06
370 Eugene Kingsale .20 .06
371 N.Garciaparra BPM .50 .15
372 Ken Griffey Jr. BPM .50 .15
373 Randy Johnson BPM .30 .09
374 Jeff Bagwell BPM .30 .09
375 Ivan Rodriguez BPM .30 .09
376 Derek Jeter BPM .60 .18
377 Carlos Beltran BPM .30 .09
378 V.Guerrero BPM .30 .09
379 Sammy Sosa BPM .50 .15
380 Barry Bonds BPM .50 .15
381 Pedro Martinez BPM .30 .09
382 Chipper Jones BPM .30 .09
383 Mo Vaughn BPM .20 .06
384 Mike Piazza BPM .50 .15
385 Alex Rodriguez BPM .50 .15
386 Manny Ramirez BPM .20 .06
387 Mark McGwire BPM .60 .18
388 Tony Gwynn BPM .30 .09
389 Sean Casey BPM .20 .06
390 Cal Ripken BPM .75 .23
391 Ken Griffey Jr. JC .50 .15
392 Ken Griffey Jr. JC .50 .15
393 Ken Griffey Jr. JC .50 .15
394 Ken Griffey Jr. JC .50 .15
395 Ken Griffey Jr. JC .50 .15
396 Ken Griffey Jr. JC .50 .15
397 Ken Griffey Jr. JC .50 .15
398 Ken Griffey Jr. JC .50 .15
399 Ken Griffey Jr. JC .50 .15
400 Ken Griffey Jr. JC .50 .15
401 Ken Griffey Jr. JC .50 .15
402 Ken Griffey Jr. JC .50 .15
403 Ken Griffey Jr. JC .50 .15
404 Ken Griffey Jr. JC .50 .15
405 Ken Griffey Jr. JC .50 .15
406 Ken Griffey Jr. JC .50 .15
407 Ken Griffey Jr. JC .50 .15
408 Ken Griffey Jr. JC .50 .15
409 Ken Griffey Jr. JC .50 .15
410 Ken Griffey Jr. JC .50 .15
411 Ken Griffey Jr. JC .50 .15
412 Ken Griffey Jr. JC .50 .15
413 Ken Griffey Jr. JC .50 .15
414 Ken Griffey Jr. JC .50 .15
415 Ken Griffey Jr. JC .50 .15
416 Ken Griffey Jr. JC .50 .15
417 Ken Griffey Jr. JC .50 .15
418 Ken Griffey Jr. JC .50 .15
419 Ken Griffey Jr. JC .50 .15
420 Ken Griffey Jr. JC .50 .15
421 Ken Griffey Jr. JC .50 .15
422 Ken Griffey Jr. JC .50 .15
423 Ken Griffey Jr. JC .50 .15
424 Ken Griffey Jr. JC .50 .15
425 Ken Griffey Jr. JC .50 .15
426 Ken Griffey Jr. JC .50 .15
427 Ken Griffey Jr. JC .50 .15
428 Ken Griffey Jr. JC .50 .15
429 Ken Griffey Jr. JC .50 .15
430 Ken Griffey Jr. JC .50 .15
431 Ken Griffey Jr. JC .50 .15
432 Ken Griffey Jr. JC .50 .15
433 Ken Griffey Jr. JC .50 .15
434 Ken Griffey Jr. JC .50 .15
435 Ken Griffey Jr. JC .50 .15
436 Ken Griffey Jr. JC .50 .15
437 Ken Griffey Jr. JC .50 .15
438 Ken Griffey Jr. JC .50 .15
439 Ken Griffey Jr. JC .50 .15
440 Ken Griffey Jr. JC .50 .15
441 T.Lasorda USA MG .30 .09
442 Sean Burroughs USA .20 .06
443 Rick Krivda USA .30 .09
444 Ben Sheets USA RC 3.00 .90
445 Pat Borders USA .30 .09
446 B.Abernathy USA RC .30 .09
447 Tim Young USA .30 .09
448 Adam Everett USA .30 .09
449 Anthony Sanders USA .30 .09
450 Ernie Young USA .30 .09
451 B.Wilkerson USA RC .60 .18
452 K.Ainsworth USA RC .30 .09
453 Ryan Franklin USA RC .30 .09
454 Todd Williams USA .30 .09
455 Jon Rauch USA RC .30 .09
456 Roy Oswalt USA RC 4.00 1.20
457 S.Heams USA RC .30 .09
458 Chris George USA .30 .09
459 Bobby Seay USA .30 .09
460 Mike Kinkade USA .30 .09
461 Marcus Jensen USA .30 .09
462 Travis Dawkins USA .30 .09
463 D.Mientkiewicz USA .30 .09
464 John Cotton USA RC .30 .09
465 Mike Neill USA .30 .09
466 Team Photo USA 1.00 .30

2001 Upper Deck Victory

The 2001 Upper Deck Victory product was released in late February, 2001 and features a 660-card base set. The base set is broken into tiers as follows: 550 Veterans (1-550), (40) Prospects (551-590), (20) Big Play Makers (591-610), and (50) Victory Best cards (611-660). Each pack contains 13 cards and carries a suggested retail price of $1.99.

Nm-Mt Ex-Mt
COMPLETE SET (660) 50.00 15.00
1 Troy Glaus .20 .06
2 Scott Spiezio .20 .06
3 Gary DiSarcina .20 .06
4 Darin Erstad .20 .06
5 Tim Salmon .30 .09
6 Troy Percival .20 .06
7 Ramon Ortiz .20 .06
8 Orlando Palmeiro .20 .06
9 Tim Belcher .20 .06
10 Mo Vaughn .20 .06
11 Bengie Molina .20 .06
12 Benji Gil .20 .06
13 Scott Schoeneweis .20 .06
14 Garret Anderson .20 .06
15 Matt Wise .20 .06
16 Adam Kennedy .20 .06
17 Jarrod Washburn .20 .06
18 Darin Erstad .20 .06
Troy Percival CL
19 Jason Giambi .20 .06
20 Tim Hudson .20 .06
21 Ramon Hernandez .20 .06
22 Eric Chavez .20 .06
23 Gil Heredia .20 .06
24 Jason Isringhausen .20 .06
25 Jeremy Giambi .20 .06
26 Miguel Tejada .20 .06
27 Barry Zito .30 .09
28 Terrence Long .20 .06
29 Ryan Christenson .20 .06
30 Mark Mulder .20 .06
31 Olmedo Saenz .20 .06
32 Adam Piatt .20 .06
33 Ben Grieve .20 .06
34 Omar Olivares .20 .06
35 John Jaha .20 .06
36 Jason Giambi .20 .06
Tim Hudson CL
37 Carlos Delgado .20 .06
38 Esteban Loaiza .20 .06
39 Brad Fullmer .20 .06
40 David Wells .20 .06
41 Chris Woodward .20 .06
42 Billy Koch .20 .06
43 Shannon Stewart .20 .06
44 Chris Carpenter .20 .06
45 Steve Parris .20 .06
46 Darrin Fletcher .20 .06
47 Joey Hamilton .20 .06
48 Jose Cruz Jr. .20 .06
49 Vernon Wells .20 .06
50 Raul Mondesi .20 .06
51 Kelvim Escobar .20 .06
52 Tony Batista .20 .06
53 Alex Gonzalez .20 .06
54 Carlos Delgado .20 .06
David Wells CL
55 Greg Vaughn .20 .06
56 Albie Lopez .20 .06
57 Randy Winn .20 .06
58 Ryan Rupe .20 .06
59 Steve Cox .20 .06
60 Vinny Castilla .20 .06
61 Jose Guillen .20 .06
62 Wilson Alvarez .20 .06
63 Bryan Rekar .20 .06
64 Gerald Williams .20 .06
65 Esteban Yan .20 .06
66 Felix Martinez .20 .06
67 Fred McGriff .30 .09
68 John Flaherty .20 .06
69 Jason Tyner .20 .06
70 Russ Johnson .20 .06
71 Roberto Hernandez .20 .06
72 Greg Vaughn .20 .06
Albie Lopez CL
73 Eddie Taubensee .20 .06
74 Bob Wickman .20 .06
75 Ellis Burks .20 .06
76 Kenny Lofton .20 .06
77 Einar Diaz .20 .06
78 Travis Fryman .20 .06
79 Omar Vizquel .30 .09
80 Jason Bere .20 .06
81 Bartolo Colon .20 .06
82 Jim Thome .50 .15
83 Roberto Alomar .30 .09
84 Chuck Finley .20 .06
85 Steve Woodard .20 .06
86 Russ Branyan .20 .06
87 Dave Burba .20 .06
88 Jaret Wright .20 .06
89 Jacob Cruz .20 .06
90 Steve Karsay .20 .06
91 Manny Ramirez .20 .06
Bartolo Colon CL
92 Raul Ibanez .20 .06
93 Freddy Garcia .20 .06
94 Edgar Martinez .30 .09
95 Jay Buhner .20 .06
96 Jamie Moyer .20 .06
97 John Olerud .20 .06
98 Aaron Sele .20 .06
99 Kazuhiro Sasaki .20 .06
100 Mike Cameron .20 .06
101 John Halama .20 .06
102 David Bell .20 .06
103 Gil Meche .20 .06
104 Carlos Guillen .20 .06
105 Mark McLemore .20 .06
106 Stan Javier .20 .06
107 Al Martin .20 .06
108 Dan Wilson .20 .06
109 Alex Rodriguez .50 .15
Kazuhiro Sasaki CL
110 Cal Ripken 1.50 .45
111 Delino DeShields .20 .06
112 Sidney Ponson .20 .06
113 Albert Belle .20 .06
114 Jose Mercedes .20 .06
115 Scott Erickson .20 .06
116 Jerry Hairston Jr. .20 .06
117 Brook Fordyce .20 .06
118 Luis Matos .20 .06
119 Eugene Kingsale .20 .06
120 Jeff Conine .20 .06
121 Chris Richard .20 .06
122 Fernando Lunar .20 .06
123 John Parrish .20 .06
124 Brady Anderson .20 .06
125 Ryan Kohlmeier .20 .06
126 Melvin Mora .20 .06
127 Albert Belle .20 .06
Jose Mercedes CL
128 Ivan Rodriguez .50 .15
129 Justin Thompson .20 .06
130 Kenny Rogers .20 .06
131 Rafael Palmeiro .30 .09
132 Rusty Greer .20 .06
133 Gabe Kapler .20 .06
134 John Wetteland .20 .06
135 Mike Lamb .20 .06
136 Doug Davis .20 .06
137 Ruben Mateo .20 .06
138 A. Rodriguez Rangers 1.50 .45
139 Chad Curtis .20 .06
140 Rick Helling .20 .06
141 Ryan Glynn .20 .06
142 Andres Galarraga .20 .06
143 Ricky Ledee .20 .06
144 Frank Catalanotto .20 .06
145 Rafael Palmeiro .20 .06
Rick Helling CL
146 Pedro Martinez .50 .15
147 Wilton Veras .20 .06
148 M. Ramirez Red Sox .30 .09
149 Rolando Arrojo .20 .06
150 Nomar Garciaparra .75 .23
151 Darren Lewis .20 .06
152 Troy O'Leary .20 .06
153 Tomokazu Ohka .20 .06
154 Carl Everett .20 .06
155 Jason Varitek .30 .09
156 Frank Castillo .20 .06
157 Pete Schourek .20 .06
158 Jose Offerman .20 .06
159 Derek Lowe .20 .06
160 John Valentin .20 .06
161 Dante Bichette .20 .06
162 Trot Nixon .20 .06
163 Nomar Garciaparra .50 .15
Pedro Martinez CL
164 Jermaine Dye .20 .06
165 Dave McCarty .20 .06
166 Jose Rosado .20 .06
167 Mike Sweeney .20 .06
168 Rey Sanchez .20 .06
169 Jeff Suppan .20 .06
170 Chad Durbin .20 .06
171 Carlos Beltran .30 .09
172 Brian Meadows .20 .06
173 Todd Dunwoody .20 .06
174 Johnny Damon .30 .09
175 Blake Stein .20 .06
176 Carlos Febles .20 .06
177 Joe Randa .20 .06
178 Mac Suzuki .20 .06
179 Mark Quinn .20 .06
180 Gregg Zaun .20 .06
181 Mike Sweeney .20 .06
Jeff Suppan
182 Juan Gonzalez .30 .09
183 Dean Palmer .20 .06
184 Wendell Magee .20 .06
185 Todd Jones .20 .06

186 Bobby Higginson .20 .06
187 Brian Moehler .20 .06
188 Juan Encarnacion .20 .06
189 Tony Clark .20 .06
190 Rich Becker .20 .06
191 Roger Cedeno .20 .06
192 Mitch Meluskey .20 .06
193 Shane Halter .20 .06
194 Jeff Weaver .20 .06
195 Deivi Cruz .20 .06
196 Damion Easley .20 .06
197 Robert Fick .20 .06
198 Matt Anderson .20 .06
199 Bobby Higginson .20 .06
Brian Moehler
200 Brad Radke .20 .06
201 Mark Redman .20 .06
202 Corey Koskie .20 .06
203 Matt Lawton .20 .06
204 Eric Milton .20 .06
205 Chad Moeller .20 .06
206 Jacque Jones .20 .06
207 Matt Kinney .20 .06
208 Jay Canizaro .20 .06
209 Torii Hunter .20 .06
210 Ron Coomer .20 .06
211 Chad Allen .20 .06
212 Denny Hocking .20 .06
213 Cristian Guzman .20 .06
214 LaTroy Hawkins .20 .06
215 Joe Mays .20 .06
216 David Ortiz .30 .09
217 Matt Lawton .20 .06
Eric Milton CL
218 Frank Thomas .50 .15
219 Jose Valentin .20 .06
220 Mike Sirotka .20 .06
221 Kip Wells .20 .06
222 Magglio Ordonez .20 .06
223 Herbert Perry .20 .06
224 James Baldwin .20 .06
225 Jon Garland .20 .06
226 Sandy Alomar Jr. .20 .06
227 Chris Singleton .20 .06
228 Keith Foulke .20 .06
229 Paul Konerko .20 .06
230 Jim Parque .20 .06
231 Greg Norton .20 .06
232 Carlos Lee .20 .06
233 Cal Eldred .20 .06
234 Ray Durham .20 .06
235 Jeff Abbott .20 .06
236 Frank Thomas .30 .09
Mike Sirotka CL
237 Derek Jeter 1.25 .35
238 Glenallen Hill .20 .06
239 Roger Clemens 1.00 .30
240 Bernie Williams .30 .09
241 David Justice .20 .06
242 Luis Sojo .20 .06
243 Orlando Hernandez .20 .06
244 Mike Mussina .30 .09
245 Jorge Posada .30 .09
246 Andy Pettitte .30 .09
247 Paul O'Neill .30 .09
248 Scott Brosius .20 .06
249 Alfonso Soriano .30 .09
250 Mariano Rivera .30 .09
251 Chuck Knoblauch .20 .06
252 Ramiro Mendoza .20 .06
253 Tino Martinez .30 .09
254 David Cone .20 .06
255 Derek Jeter .60 .18
Andy Pettite CL
256 Jeff Bagwell .30 .09
257 Lance Berkman .20 .06
258 Craig Biggio .30 .09
259 Scott Elarton .20 .06
260 Bill Spiers .20 .06
261 Moises Alou .20 .06
262 Billy Wagner .20 .06
263 Shane Reynolds .20 .06
264 Tony Eusebio .20 .06
265 Julio Lugo .20 .06
266 Jose Lima .20 .06
267 Octavio Dotel .20 .06
268 Brad Ausmus .20 .06
269 Daryle Ward .20 .06
270 Glen Barker .20 .06
271 Wade Miller .20 .06
272 Richard Hidalgo .20 .06
273 Chris Truby .20 .06
274 Jeff Bagwell .20 .06
Scott Elarton CL
275 Greg Maddux .75 .23
276 Chipper Jones .50 .15
277 Tom Glavine .30 .09
278 Brian Jordan .20 .06
279 Andruw Jones .20 .06
280 Kevin Millwood .20 .06
281 Rico Brogna .20 .06
282 George Lombard .20 .06
283 Reggie Sanders .20 .06
284 John Rocker .20 .06
285 Rafael Furcal .20 .06
286 John Smoltz .30 .09
287 Javy Lopez .20 .06
288 Walt Weiss .20 .06
289 Quilvio Veras .20 .06
290 Eddie Perez .20 .06
291 B.J. Surhoff .20 .06
292 Chipper Jones .30 .09
Tom Glavine CL
293 Jeromy Burnitz .20 .06
294 Charlie Hayes .20 .06
295 Jeff D'Amico .20 .06
296 Jose Hernandez .20 .06
297 Richie Sexson .20 .06
298 Tyler Houston .20 .06
299 Paul Rigdon .20 .06
300 Jamey Wright .20 .06
301 Mark Loretta .20 .06
302 Geoff Jenkins .20 .06
303 Luis Lopez .20 .06
304 John Snyder .20 .06
305 Henry Blanco .20 .06
306 Curtis Leskanic .20 .06
307 Ron Belliard .20 .06
308 Jimmy Haynes .20 .06
309 Marquis Grissom .20 .06
310 Geoff Jenkins .20 .06
Jeff D'Amico CL
311 Mark McGwire 1.25 .35
312 Rick Ankiel .20 .06
313 Dave Veres .20 .06
314 Carlos Hernandez .20 .06
315 Jim Edmonds .20 .06
316 Andy Benes .20 .06
317 Garrett Stephenson .20 .06
318 Ray Lankford .20 .06
319 Dustin Hermanson .20 .06
320 Steve Kline .20 .06
321 Mike Matheny .20 .06
322 Edgar Renteria .20 .06
323 J.D. Drew .20 .06
324 Craig Paquette .20 .06
325 Darryl Kile .20 .06
326 Fernando Vina .20 .06
327 Eric Davis .20 .06
328 Placido Polanco .20 .06
329 Jim Edmonds .20 .06
Darryl Kile CL
330 Sammy Sosa .75 .23
331 Rick Aguilera .20 .06
332 Willie Greene .20 .06
333 Kerry Wood .50 .15
334 Todd Hundley .20 .06
335 Rondell White .20 .06
336 Julio Zuleta .20 .06
337 Jon Lieber .20 .06
338 Joe Girardi .20 .06
339 Damon Buford .20 .06
340 Kevin Tapani .20 .06
341 Ricky Gutierrez .20 .06
342 Bill Mueller .20 .06
343 Ruben Quevedo .20 .06
344 Eric Young .20 .06
345 Gary Matthews Jr. .20 .06
346 Daniel Garibay .20 .06
347 Sammy Sosa .30 .09
Jon Lieber CL
348 Randy Johnson .50 .15
349 Matt Williams .20 .06
350 Kelly Stinnett .20 .06
351 Brian Anderson .20 .06
352 Steve Finley .20 .06
353 Curt Schilling .20 .06
354 Erubiel Durazo .20 .06
355 Todd Stottlemyre .20 .06
356 Mark Grace .30 .09
357 Luis Gonzalez .20 .06
358 Danny Bautista .20 .06
359 Matt Mantei .20 .06
360 Tony Womack .20 .06
361 Armando Reynoso .20 .06
362 Greg Colbrunn .20 .06
363 Jay Bell .20 .06
364 Byung-Hyun Kim .20 .06
365 Luis Gonzalez .30 .09
Randy Johnson CL
366 Gary Sheffield .20 .06
367 Eric Karros .20 .06
368 Jeff Shaw .20 .06
369 Jim Leyritz .20 .06
370 Kevin Brown .20 .06
371 Alex Cora .20 .06
372 Andy Ashby .20 .06
373 Eric Gagne .50 .15
374 Chan Ho Park .20 .06
375 Shawn Green .20 .06
376 Kevin Elster .20 .06
377 Mark Grudzielanek .20 .06
378 Darren Dreifort .20 .06
379 Dave Hansen .20 .06
380 Bruce Aven .20 .06
381 Adrian Beltre .30 .09
382 Tom Goodwin .20 .06
383 Gary Sheffield .20 .06
Chan Ho Park CL
384 Vladimir Guerrero .50 .15
385 Ugueth Urbina .20 .06
386 Michael Barrett .20 .06
387 Geoff Blum .20 .06
388 Fernando Tatis .20 .06
389 Carl Pavano .20 .06
390 Jose Vidro .20 .06
391 Orlando Cabrera .20 .06
392 Terry Jones .20 .06
393 Mike Thurman .20 .06
394 Lee Stevens .20 .06
395 Tony Armas Jr. .20 .06
396 Wilton Guerrero .20 .06
397 Peter Bergeron .20 .06
398 Milton Bradley .20 .06
399 Javier Vazquez .20 .06
400 Fernando Seguignol .20 .06
401 Vladimir Guerrero .30 .09
Dustin Hermanson CL
402 Barry Bonds 1.25 .35
403 Russ Ortiz .20 .06
404 Calvin Murray .20 .06
405 Armando Rios .20 .06
406 Livan Hernandez .20 .06
407 Jeff Kent .20 .06
408 Bobby Estalella .20 .06
409 Felipe Crespo .20 .06
410 Shawn Estes .20 .06
411 J.T. Snow .20 .06
412 Marvin Benard .20 .06
413 Joe Nathan .20 .06
414 Robb Nen .20 .06
415 Shawon Dunston .20 .06
416 Mark Gardner .20 .06
417 Kirk Rueter .20 .06
418 Rich Aurilia .20 .06
419 Doug Mirabelli .20 .06
420 Russ Davis .20 .06
421 Barry Bonds .60 .18
Livan Hernandez CL
422 Cliff Floyd .20 .06
423 Luis Castillo .20 .06
424 Antonio Alfonseca .20 .06
425 Preston Wilson .20 .06
426 Ryan Dempster .20 .06
427 Jesus Sanchez .20 .06
428 Derrek Lee .20 .06
429 Brad Penny .20 .06
430 Mark Kotsay .20 .06
431 Alex Fernandez .20 .06
432 Mike Lowell .20 .06
433 Chuck Smith .20 .06
434 Alex Gonzalez .20 .06
435 Dave Berg .20 .06
436 A.J. Burnett .20 .06
437 Charles Johnson .20 .06
438 Reid Cornelius .20 .06
439 Mike Redmond .20 .06
440 Preston Wilson .20 .06
Ryan Dempster CL
441 Mike Piazza .75 .23
442 Kevin Appier .20 .06
443 Jay Payton .20 .06
444 Steve Trachsel .20 .06
445 Al Leiter .20 .06
446 Joe McEwing .20 .06
447 Armando Benitez .20 .06
448 Edgardo Alfonzo .20 .06
449 Glendon Rusch .20 .06
450 Mike Bordick .20 .06
451 Lenny Harris .20 .06
452 Matt Franco .20 .06
453 Darryl Hamilton .20 .06
454 Bobby Jones .20 .06
455 Robin Ventura .20 .06
456 Todd Zeile .20 .06
457 John Franco .20 .06
458 Mike Piazza .50 .15
Al Leiter CL
459 Tony Gwynn .60 .18
460 John Mabry .20 .06
461 Trevor Hoffman .20 .06
462 Phil Nevin .20 .06
463 Ryan Klesko .20 .06
464 Wiki Gonzalez .20 .06
465 Matt Clement .20 .06
466 Alex Arias .20 .06
467 Woody Williams .20 .06
468 Ruben Rivera .20 .06
469 Sterling Hitchcock .20 .06
470 Ben Davis .20 .06
471 Bubba Trammell .20 .06
472 Jay Witasick .20 .06
473 Eric Owens .20 .06
474 Damian Jackson .20 .06
475 Adam Eaton .20 .06
476 Mike Darr .20 .06
477 Phil Nevin .20 .06
Trevor Hoffman CL
478 Scott Rolen .50 .15
479 Robert Person .20 .06
480 Mike Lieberthal .20 .06
481 Reggie Taylor .20 .06
482 Paul Byrd .20 .06
483 Bruce Chen .20 .06
484 Pat Burrell .20 .06
485 Kevin Jordan .20 .06
486 Bobby Abreu .20 .06
487 Randy Wolf .20 .06
488 Kevin Sefcik .20 .06
489 Brian Hunter .20 .06
490 Doug Glanville .20 .06
491 Kent Bottenfield .20 .06
492 Travis Lee .20 .06
493 Jeff Brantley .20 .06
494 Omar Daal .20 .06
495 Bobby Abreu .20 .06
Randy Wolf CL
496 Jason Kendall .20 .06
497 Adrian Brown .20 .06
498 Warren Morris .20 .06
499 Brian Giles .20 .06
500 Jimmy Anderson .20 .06
501 John VanderWal .20 .06
502 Mike Williams .20 .06
503 Aramis Ramirez .20 .06
504 Pat Meares .30 .09
505 Jason Schmidt .20 .06
506 Todd Ritchie .20 .06
507 Abraham Nunez .20 .06
508 Jose Silva .20 .06
509 Francisco Cordova .20 .06
510 Kevin Young .20 .06
511 Derek Bell .20 .06
512 Kris Benson .20 .06
513 Brian Giles .20 .06
Jose Silva CL
514 Ken Griffey Jr. .75 .23
515 Scott Williamson .20 .06
516 Dmitri Young .20 .06
517 Sean Casey .20 .06
518 Barry Larkin .30 .09
519 Juan Castro .20 .06
520 Danny Graves .20 .06
521 Aaron Boone .20 .06
522 Pokey Reese .20 .06
523 Elmer Dessens .20 .06
524 Michael Tucker .20 .06
525 Benito Santiago .20 .06
526 Pete Harnisch .20 .06
527 Alex Ochoa .20 .06
528 Gookie Dawkins .20 .06
529 Seth Etherton .20 .06
530 Rob Bell .20 .06
531 Ken Griffey Jr. .50 .15
Steve Parris CL
532 Todd Helton .30 .09
533 Jose Jimenez .20 .06
534 Todd Walker .20 .06
535 Ron Gant .20 .06
536 Neifi Perez .20 .06
537 Butch Huskey .20 .06
538 Pedro Astacio .20 .06
539 Juan Pierre .20 .06
540 Jeff Cirillo .20 .06
541 Ben Petrick .20 .06
542 Brian Bohanon .20 .06
543 Larry Walker .30 .09
544 Masato Yoshii .20 .06
545 Denny Neagle .20 .06
546 Brent Mayne .20 .06
547 Mike Hampton .20 .06
548 Todd Hollandsworth .20 .06
549 Brian Rose .20 .06
550 Todd Helton .20 .06
Pedro Astacio CL
551 Jason Hart .20 .06
552 Joe Crede .20 .06
553 Timo Perez .20 .06
554 Brady Clark .20 .06
555 Adam Pettyjohn RC .20 .06
556 Jason Grilli .20 .06
557 Paxton Crawford .20 .06
558 Jay Spurgeon .20 .06
559 Hector Ortiz .20 .06
560 Vernon Wells .20 .06
561 Aubrey Huff .20 .06
562 Xavier Nady .20 .06
563 Billy McMillon .20 .06
564 Ichiro Suzuki RC 8.00 2.40
565 Tomas De la Rosa .20 .06
566 Matt Ginter .20 .06
567 Sun Woo Kim .20 .06
568 Nick Johnson .20 .06
569 Pablo Ozuna .20 .06
570 Tike Redman .20 .06
571 Brian Cole .20 .06
572 Ross Gload .20 .06
573 Dee Brown .20 .06
574 Tony McKnight .20 .06
575 Allen Levrault .20 .06
576 Lesli Brea .20 .06
577 Adam Bernero .20 .06
578 Tom Davey .20 .06
579 Morgan Burkhart .20 .06
580 Britt Reames .20 .06
581 Dave Coggin .20 .06
582 Trey Moore .20 .06
583 Matt Kinney .20 .06
584 Pedro Feliz .20 .06
585 Brandon Inge .20 .06
586 Alex Hernandez .20 .06
587 Toby Hall .20 .06
588 Grant Roberts .20 .06
589 Brian Sikorski .20 .06
590 Aaron Myette .20 .06
591 Derek Jeter PM 1.25 .35
592 Ivan Rodriguez PM .30 .09
593 Alex Rodriguez PM .75 .23
594 Carlos Delgado PM .20 .06
595 Mark McGwire PM 1.25 .35
596 Troy Glaus PM .20 .06
597 Sammy Sosa PM .75 .23
598 Vladimir Guerrero PM .50 .15
599 Manny Ramirez PM .20 .06
600 Pedro Martinez PM .30 .09
601 Chipper Jones PM .30 .09
602 Jason Giambi PM .20 .06
603 Frank Thomas PM .30 .09
604 Ken Griffey Jr. PM .75 .23
605 Nomar Garciaparra PM .75 .23
606 Randy Johnson PM .30 .09
607 Mike Piazza PM .75 .23
608 Barry Bonds PM 1.25 .35
609 Todd Helton PM .20 .06
610 Jeff Bagwell PM .20 .06
611 Ken Griffey Jr. VB .75 .23
612 Carlos Delgado VB .20 .06
613 Jeff Bagwell VB .20 .06
614 Jason Giambi VB .20 .06
615 Cal Ripken VB 1.50 .45
616 Brian Giles VB .20 .06
617 Bernie Williams VB .20 .06
618 Greg Maddux VB .75 .23
619 Troy Glaus VB .20 .06
620 Greg Vaughn VB .20 .06
621 Sammy Sosa VB .75 .23
622 Pat Burrell VB .20 .06
623 Ivan Rodriguez VB .30 .09
624 Chipper Jones VB .30 .09
625 Barry Bonds VB 1.25 .35
626 Roger Clemens VB 1.00 .30
627 Jim Edmonds VB .20 .06
628 Nomar Garciaparra VB .75 .23
629 Frank Thomas VB .30 .09
630 Mike Piazza VB .75 .23
631 Randy Johnson VB .30 .09
632 Andruw Jones VB .20 .06
633 David Wells VB .20 .06
634 Manny Ramirez VB .20 .06
635 Preston Wilson VB .20 .06
636 Todd Helton VB .20 .06
637 Kerry Wood VB .30 .09
638 Albert Belle VB .20 .06
639 Juan Gonzalez VB .20 .06
640 Vladimir Guerrero VB .50 .15
641 Gary Sheffield VB .20 .06
642 Larry Walker VB .30 .09
643 Magglio Ordonez VB .20 .06
644 Jermaine Dye VB .20 .06
645 Scott Rolen VB .30 .09
646 Tony Gwynn VB .60 .18
647 Shawn Green VB .20 .06
648 Roberto Alomar VB .20 .06
649 Eric Milton VB .20 .06
650 Mark McGwire VB 1.25 .35
651 Tim Hudson VB .20 .06
652 Jose Canseco VB .20 .06
653 Tom Glavine VB .20 .06
654 Derek Jeter VB 1.25 .35
655 Alex Rodriguez VB .75 .23
656 Darin Erstad VB .20 .06
657 Jason Kendall VB .20 .06
658 Pedro Martinez VB .30 .09
659 Richie Sexson VB .20 .06
660 Rafael Palmeiro VB .20 .06

2002 Upper Deck Victory

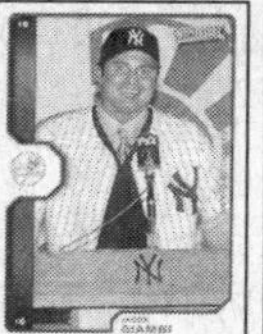

This 660 card set was issued in two separate products. The basic Victory brand, containing cards 1-550, was released in February 2002. These cards were issued in ten count packs which were issued 24 packs to a box and twelve boxes to a case. The following subsets were also included in this product: Cards numbered 491-530 feature rookie prospects and cards numbered 531-550 were Big Play Makers. Cards 551-660 were distributed within retail-only packs of Upper Deck Rookie Debut in mic December 2002. The 110-card update set fea tures traded veterans in their new uniforms an a wide array of prospects and rookies. The card were issued at a rate of approximately two pe pack.

	Nm-Mt	Ex-Mt
COMPLETE SET (660)	75.00	22.00
COMP.LOW SET (550)	50.00	15.00
COMP.UPDATE SET (110)	25.00	7.50
COMMON (1-490/531-550)	.20	.06
COMMON CARD (491-530)	.25	.07
COMMON CARD (551-605)	.40	.12
COMMON CARD (606-660)	.40	.12

1 Troy Glaus .20 .06
2 Tim Salmon .30 .09
3 Troy Percival .20 .06
4 Darin Erstad .20 .06
5 Adam Kennedy .20 .06
6 Scott Spiezio .20 .06
7 Ramon Ortiz .20 .06
8 Ismael Valdes .20 .06
9 Jarrod Washburn .20 .06
10 Garrett Anderson .20 .06
11 David Eckstein .20 .06
12 Mo Vaughn .20 .06
13 Benji Gil .20 .06
14 Bengie Molina .20 .06
15 Scott Schoeneweis .20 .06
16 Troy Glaus .20 .06
Ramon Ortiz
17 David Justice .20 .06
18 Jermaine Dye .20 .06
19 Eric Chavez .20 .06
20 Jeremy Giambi .20 .06
21 Terrence Long .20 .06
22 Miguel Tejada .20 .06
23 Johnny Damon .30 .09
24 Jason Hart .20 .06
25 Adam Piatt .20 .06
26 Billy Koch .20 .06
27 Ramon Hernandez .20 .06
28 Eric Byrnes .20 .06
29 Olmedo Saenz .20 .06
30 Barry Zito .20 .06
31 Tim Hudson .20 .06
32 Mark Mulder .20 .06
33 Jason Giambi .20 .06
Mark Mulder
34 Carlos Delgado .20 .06
35 Shannon Stewart .20 .06
36 Vernon Wells .20 .06
37 Homer Bush .20 .06
38 Brad Fullmer .20 .06
39 Jose Cruz Jr. .20 .06
40 Felipe Lopez .20 .06
41 Raul Mondesi .20 .06
42 Esteban Loaiza .20 .06
43 Darrin Fletcher .20 .06
44 Mike Sirotka .20 .06
45 Luke Prokopec .20 .06
46 Chris Carpenter .20 .06
47 Roy Halladay .20 .06
48 Kelvim Escobar .20 .06
49 Carlos Delgado .20 .06
Billy Koch
50 Nick Bierbrodt .20 .06
51 Greg Vaughn .20 .06
52 Ben Grieve .20 .06
53 Damian Rolls .20 .06
54 Russ Johnson .20 .06
55 Brent Abernathy .20 .06
56 Steve Cox .20 .06
57 Aubrey Huff .20 .06
58 Randy Winn .20 .06
59 Jason Tyner .20 .06
60 Tanyon Sturtze .20 .06
61 Joe Kennedy .20 .06
62 Jared Sandberg .20 .06
63 Esteban Yan .20 .06
64 Ryan Rupe .20 .06
65 Toby Hall .20 .06
66 Greg Vaughn .20 .06
Tanyon Sturtze
67 Matt Lawton .20 .06
68 Juan Gonzalez .30 .09
69 Jim Thome .50 .15
70 Einar Diaz .20 .06
71 Ellis Burks .20 .06
72 Kenny Lofton .20 .06
73 Omar Vizquel .30 .09
74 Russell Branyan .20 .06
75 Brady Anderson .20 .06
76 John Rocker .20 .06
77 Travis Fryman .20 .06
78 Wil Cordero .20 .06
79 Chuck Finley .20 .06
80 C.C. Sabathia .20 .06
81 Bartolo Colon .20 .06
82 Bob Wickman .20 .06
83 Roberto Alomar .20 .06
C.C. Sabathia
84 Ichiro Suzuki .75 .23
85 Edgar Martinez .30 .09
86 Aaron Sele .20 .06
87 Carlos Guillen .20 .06
88 Bret Boone .20 .06
89 John Olerud .20 .06
90 Jamie Moyer .20 .06
91 Ben Davis .20 .06
92 Dan Wilson .20 .06
93 Jeff Cirillo .20 .06
94 John Halama .20 .06
95 Freddy Garcia .20 .06
96 Kazuhiro Sasaki .20 .06
97 Mike Cameron .20 .06
98 Paul Abbott .20 .06
99 Mark McLemore .20 .06
100 Ichiro Suzuki .50 .15
Freddy Garcia
101 Jeff Conine .20 .06
102 David Segui .20 .06
103 Marty Cordova .20 .06
104 Tony Batista .20 .06
105 Chris Richard .20 .06
106 Willis Roberts .20 .06
107 Melvin Mora .20 .06
108 Mike Bordick .20 .06
109 Jay Gibbons .20 .06
110 Mike Kinkade .20 .06

111 Brian Roberts .20 .06
112 Jerry Hairston Jr. .20 .06
113 Jason Johnson .20 .06
114 Josh Towers .20 .06
115 Calvin Maduro .20 .06
116 Sidney Ponson .20 .06
117 Jeff Conine .20 .06
Jason Johnson
118 Alex Rodriguez .75 .23
119 Ivan Rodriguez .50 .15
120 Frank Catalanotto .20 .06
121 Mike Lamb .20 .06
122 Ruben Sierra .20 .06
123 Rusty Greer .20 .06
124 Rafael Palmeiro .30 .09
125 Gabe Kapler .20 .06
126 Aaron Myette .20 .06
127 Kenny Rogers .20 .06
128 Carl Everett .20 .06
129 Rick Helling .20 .06
130 Ricky Ledee .20 .06
131 Michael Young .50 .15
132 Doug Davis .20 .06
133 Jeff Zimmerman .20 .06
134 Alex Rodriguez .50 .15
Rick Helling
135 Manny Ramirez .30 .09
136 Nomar Garciaparra .75 .23
137 Jason Varitek .30 .09
138 Dante Bichette .20 .06
139 Tony Clark .20 .06
140 Scott Hatteberg .20 .06
141 Trot Nixon .20 .06
142 Hideo Nomo .50 .15
143 Dustin Hermanson .20 .06
144 Chris Stynes .20 .06
145 Jose Offerman .20 .06
146 Pedro Martinez .50 .15
147 Shea Hillenbrand .20 .06
148 Tim Wakefield .20 .06
149 Troy O'Leary .20 .06
150 Ugueth Urbina .20 .06
151 Manny Ramirez .30 .09
Hideo Nomo
152 Carlos Beltran .30 .09
153 Dee Brown .20 .06
154 Mike Sweeney .20 .06
155 Luis Alicea .20 .06
156 Raul Ibanez .20 .06
157 Mark Quinn .20 .06
158 Joe Randa .20 .06
159 Roberto Hernandez .20 .06
160 Neifi Perez .20 .06
161 Carlos Febles .20 .06
162 Jeff Suppan .20 .06
163 Dave McCarty .20 .06
164 Blake Stein .20 .06
165 Chad Durbin .20 .06
166 Paul Byrd .20 .06
167 Carlos Beltran .30 .09
Jeff Suppan
168 Craig Paquette .20 .06
169 Dean Palmer .20 .06
170 Shane Halter .20 .06
171 Bobby Higginson .20 .06
172 Robert Fick .20 .06
173 Jose Macias .20 .06
174 Deivi Cruz .20 .06
175 Damion Easley .20 .06
176 Brandon Inge .20 .06
177 Mark Redman .20 .06
178 Dmitri Young .20 .06
179 Steve Sparks .20 .06
180 Jeff Weaver .20 .06
181 Victor Santos .20 .06
182 Jose Lima .20 .06
183 Matt Anderson .20 .06
184 Roger Cedeno .20 .06
Steve Sparks
185 Doug Mientkiewicz .20 .06
186 Cristian Guzman .20 .06
187 Torii Hunter .20 .06
188 Matt LeCroy .20 .06
189 Corey Koskie .20 .06
190 Jacque Jones .20 .06
191 Luis Rivas .20 .06
192 David Ortiz .30 .09
193 A.J. Pierzynski .20 .06
194 Brian Buchanan .20 .06
195 Joe Mays .20 .06
196 Brad Radke .20 .06
197 Denny Hocking .20 .06
198 Eric Milton .20 .06
199 LaTroy Hawkins .20 .06
200 Doug Mientkiewicz .20 .06
Joe Mays
201 Magglio Ordonez .20 .06
202 Jose Valentin .20 .06
203 Chris Singleton .20 .06
204 Aaron Rowand .20 .06
205 Paul Konerko .20 .06
206 Carlos Lee .20 .06
207 Ray Durham .20 .06
208 Keith Foulke .20 .06
209 Todd Ritchie .20 .06
210 Royce Clayton .20 .06
211 Jose Canseco .50 .15
212 Frank Thomas .50 .15
213 David Wells .20 .06
214 Mark Buehrle .20 .06
215 Jon Garland .20 .06
216 Magglio Ordonez .20 .06
Mark Buehrle
217 Derek Jeter 1.25 .35
218 Bernie Williams .30 .09
219 Rondell White .20 .06
220 Jorge Posada .30 .09
221 Alfonso Soriano .30 .09
222 Ramiro Mendoza .20 .06
223 Jason Giambi Yankees 1.25 .35
224 John Vander Wal .20 .06
225 Steve Karsay .20 .06
226 Nick Johnson .20 .06
227 Mariano Rivera .30 .09
228 Orlando Hernandez .20 .06
229 Andy Pettitte .30 .09
230 Robin Ventura .20 .06
231 Roger Clemens 1.00 .30
232 Mike Mussina .30 .09
233 Derek Jeter .60 .18
Roger Clemens
234 Moises Alou .20 .06
235 Lance Berkman .20 .06
236 Craig Biggio .30 .09
237 Octavio Dotel .20 .06
238 Jeff Bagwell .30 .09
239 Richard Hidalgo .20 .06
240 Morgan Ensberg .20 .06
241 Julio Lugo .20 .06
242 Daryle Ward .20 .06
243 Roy Oswalt .20 .06
244 Billy Wagner .20 .06
245 Brad Ausmus .20 .06
246 Jose Vizcaino .20 .06
247 Wade Miller .20 .06
248 Shane Reynolds .20 .06
249 Jeff Bagwell .20 .06
Wade Miller
250 Chipper Jones .50 .15
251 Brian Jordan .20 .06
252 B.J. Surhoff .20 .06
253 Rafael Furcal .20 .06
254 Julio Franco .20 .06
255 Javy Lopez .20 .06
256 John Burkett .20 .06
257 Andruw Jones .20 .06
258 Marcus Giles .20 .06
259 Wes Helms .20 .06
260 Greg Maddux .75 .23
261 John Smoltz .30 .09
262 Tom Glavine .30 .09
263 Vinny Castilla .20 .06
264 Kevin Millwood .20 .06
265 Jason Marquis .20 .06
266 Chipper Jones .30 .09
Greg Maddux
267 Tyler Houston .20 .06
268 Mark Loretta .20 .06
269 Richie Sexson .20 .06
270 Jeromy Burnitz .20 .06
271 Jimmy Haynes .20 .06
272 Geoff Jenkins .20 .06
273 Ron Belliard .20 .06
274 Jose Hernandez .20 .06
275 Jeffrey Hammonds .20 .06
276 Curtis Leskanic .20 .06
277 Devon White .20 .06
278 Ben Sheets .20 .06
279 Henry Blanco .20 .06
280 Jamey Wright .20 .06
281 Allen Levrault .20 .06
282 Jeff D'Amico .20 .06
283 Richie Sexson .20 .06
Jimmy Haynes
284 Albert Pujols 1.00 .30
285 Jason Isringhausen .20 .06
286 J.D. Drew .20 .06
287 Placido Polanco .20 .06
288 Jim Edmonds .20 .06
289 Fernando Vina .20 .06
290 Edgar Renteria .20 .06
291 Mike Matheny .20 .06
292 Bud Smith .20 .06
293 Mike DiFelice .20 .06
294 Woody Williams .20 .06
295 Eli Marrero .20 .06
296 Matt Morris .20 .06
297 Darryl Kile .20 .06
298 Kerry Robinson .20 .06
299 Luis Saturria .20 .06
300 Albert Pujols .50 .15
Matt Morris
301 Sammy Sosa .75 .23
302 Michael Tucker .20 .06
303 Bill Mueller .20 .06
304 Ricky Gutierrez .20 .06
305 Fred McGriff .30 .09
306 Eric Young .20 .06
307 Corey Patterson .20 .06
308 Alex Gonzalez .20 .06
309 Ron Coomer .20 .06
310 Kerry Wood .50 .15
311 Delino DeShields .20 .06
312 Jon Lieber .20 .06
313 Tom Gordon .20 .06
314 Todd Hundley .20 .06
315 Jason Bere .20 .06
316 Kevin Tapani .20 .06
317 Sammy Sosa .30 .09
Jon Lieber
318 Steve Finley .20 .06
319 Luis Gonzalez .20 .06
320 Mark Grace .30 .09
321 Craig Counsell .20 .06
322 Matt Williams .20 .06
323 Tony Womack .20 .06
324 Junior Spivey .20 .06
325 David Dellucci .20 .06
326 Jay Bell .20 .06
327 Curt Schilling .20 .06
328 Randy Johnson .50 .15
329 Danny Bautista .20 .06
330 Miguel Batista .20 .06
331 Erubiel Durazo .20 .06
332 Brian Anderson .20 .06
333 Byung-Hyun Kim .20 .06
334 Luis Gonzalez .20 .06
Curt Schilling
335 Paul LoDuca .20 .06
336 Gary Sheffield .20 .06
337 Shawn Green .20 .06
338 Adrian Beltre .30 .09
339 Darren Dreifort .20 .06
340 Mark Grudzielanek .20 .06
341 Eric Karros .20 .06
342 Cesar Izturis .20 .06
343 Tom Goodwin .20 .06
344 Marquis Grissom .20 .06
345 Kevin Brown .20 .06
346 James Baldwin .20 .06
347 Terry Adams .20 .06
348 Alex Cora .20 .06
349 Andy Ashby .20 .06
350 Chan Ho Park .20 .06
351 Shawn Green .20 .06
Chan Ho Park
352 Jose Vidro .20 .06
353 Vladimir Guerrero .50 .15
354 Orlando Cabrera .20 .06
355 Fernando Tatis .20 .06
356 Michael Barrett .20 .06
357 Lee Stevens .20 .06
358 Geoff Blum .20 .06
359 Brad Wilkerson .20 .06
360 Peter Bergeron .20 .06
361 Javier Vazquez .20 .06
362 Tony Armas Jr. .20 .06
363 Tomo Ohka .20 .06
364 Scott Strickland .20 .06
365 Vladimir Guerrero .20 .06
Javier Vazquez
366 Barry Bonds 1.25 .35
367 Rich Aurilia .20 .06
368 Jeff Kent .20 .06
369 Andres Galarraga .20 .06
370 Desi Relaford .20 .06
371 Shawon Dunston .20 .06
372 Benito Santiago .20 .06
373 Tsuyoshi Shinjo .20 .06
374 Calvin Murray .20 .06
375 Marvin Benard .20 .06
376 J.T. Snow .20 .06
377 Livan Hernandez .20 .06
378 Russ Ortiz .20 .06
379 Robb Nen .20 .06
380 Jason Schmidt .20 .06
381 Barry Bonds .50 .15
Russ Ortiz
382 Cliff Floyd .20 .06
383 Antonio Alfonseca .20 .06
384 Mike Redmond .20 .06
385 Mike Lowell .20 .06
386 Derrek Lee .20 .06
387 Preston Wilson .20 .06
388 Luis Castillo .20 .06
389 Charles Johnson .20 .06
390 Eric Owens .20 .06
391 Alex Gonzalez .20 .06
392 Josh Beckett .20 .06
393 Brad Penny .20 .06
394 Ryan Dempster .20 .06
395 Matt Clement .20 .06
396 A.J. Burnett .20 .06
397 Cliff Floyd .20 .06
Ryan Dempster
398 Mike Piazza .75 .23
399 Joe McEwing .20 .06
400 Todd Zeile .20 .06
401 Jay Payton .20 .06
402 Roger Cedeno .20 .06
403 Rey Ordonez .20 .06
404 Edgardo Alfonzo .20 .06
405 Roberto Alomar .30 .09
406 Glendon Rusch .20 .06
407 Timo Perez .20 .06
408 Al Leiter .20 .06
409 Lenny Harris .20 .06
410 Shawn Estes .20 .06
411 Armando Benitez .20 .06
412 Kevin Appier .20 .06
413 Bruce Chen .20 .06
414 Mike Piazza .30 .09
Al Leiter
415 Phil Nevin .20 .06
416 Ryan Klesko .20 .06
417 Mark Kotsay .20 .06
418 Ray Lankford .20 .06
419 Mike Darr .20 .06
420 D'Angelo Jimenez .20 .06
421 Bubba Trammell .20 .06
422 Adam Eaton .20 .06
423 Ramon Vazquez .20 .06
424 Cesar Crespo .20 .06
425 Trevor Hoffman .20 .06
426 Kevin Jarvis .20 .06
427 Wiki Gonzalez .20 .06
428 Damian Jackson .20 .06
429 Brian Lawrence .20 .06
430 Phil Nevin .20 .06
Trevor Hoffman
431 Scott Rolen .50 .15
432 Marlon Anderson .20 .06
433 Bobby Abreu .20 .06
434 Jimmy Rollins .20 .06
435 Doug Glanville .20 .06
436 Travis Lee .20 .06
437 Brandon Duckworth .20 .06
438 Pat Burrell .20 .06
439 Kevin Jordan .20 .06
440 Robert Person .20 .06
441 Johnny Estrada .20 .06
442 Randy Wolf .20 .06
443 Jose Mesa .20 .06
444 Mike Lieberthal .20 .06
445 Bobby Abreu .20 .06
Robert Person
446 Brian Giles .20 .06
447 Jason Kendall .20 .06
448 Aramis Ramirez .20 .06
449 Rob Mackowiak .20 .06
450 Abraham Nunez .20 .06
451 Pat Meares .20 .06
452 Craig Wilson .20 .06
453 Jack Wilson .20 .06
454 Gary Matthews Jr. .20 .06
455 Kevin Young .20 .06
456 Derek Bell .20 .06
457 Kip Wells .20 .06
458 Jimmy Anderson .20 .06
459 Kris Benson .20 .06
460 Brian Giles .20 .06
Todd Ritchie
461 Sean Casey .20 .06
462 Wilton Guerrero .20 .06
463 Jason LaRue .20 .06
464 Juan Encarnacion .20 .06
465 Todd Walker .20 .06
466 Aaron Boone .20 .06
467 Pete Harnisch .20 .06
468 Ken Griffey Jr. .75 .23
469 Adam Dunn .30 .09
470 Barry Larkin .30 .09
471 Kelly Stinnett .20 .06
472 Pokey Reese .20 .06
473 Brady Clark .20 .06
474 Scott Williamson .20 .06
475 Danny Graves .20 .06
476 Ken Griffey Jr. .50 .15
Elmer Dessens
477 Larry Walker .30 .09
478 Todd Helton .30 .09
479 Juan Pierre .20 .06
480 Juan Uribe .20 .06
481 Mario Encarnacion .20 .06
482 Jose Ortiz .20 .06
483 Todd Hollandsworth .20 .06
484 Alex Ochoa .20 .06
485 Mike Hampton .20 .06
486 Terry Shumpert .20 .06
487 Denny Neagle .20 .06
488 Jose Jimenez .20 .06
489 Jason Jennings .20 .06
490 Todd Helton .20 .06
Mike Hampton
491 Tim Redding ROO .25 .07
492 Mark Teixeira ROO .60 .18
493 Alex Cintron ROO .25 .07
494 Tim Raines Jr. ROO .25 .07
495 Juan Cruz ROO .25 .07
496 Joe Crede ROO .25 .07
497 Steve Green ROO .25 .07
498 Mike Rivera ROO .25 .07
499 Mark Prior ROO 3.00 .90
500 Ken Harvey ROO .25 .07
501 Tim Spooneybarger ROO .25 .07
502 Adam Everett ROO .25 .07
503 Jason Standridge ROO .25 .07
504 Nick Neugebauer ROO .25 .07
505 Adam Johnson ROO .25 .07
506 Sean Douglass ROO .25 .07
507 Brandon Berger ROO .25 .07
508 Alex Escobar ROO .25 .07
509 Doug Nickle ROO .25 .07
510 Jason Middlebrook ROO .25 .07
511 Dewon Brazelton ROO .25 .07
512 Yorvit Torrealba ROO .25 .07
513 Henry Mateo ROO .25 .07
514 Dennis Tankersley ROO .25 .07
515 Marlon Byrd ROO .25 .07
516 Andy Barkett ROO .25 .07
517 Orlando Hudson ROO .25 .07
518 Josh Fogg ROO .25 .07
519 Ryan Drese ROO .25 .07
520 Mike MacDougal ROO .25 .07
521 Luis Pineda ROO .25 .07
522 Jack Cust ROO .25 .07
523 Kurt Ainsworth ROO .25 .07
524 Bart Miadich ROO .25 .07
525 Dernell Stenson ROO .40 .12
526 Carlos Zambrano ROO .40 .12
527 Austin Kearns ROO .40 .12
528 Larry Barnes ROO .25 .07
529 Mike Cuddyer ROO .25 .07
530 Carlos Pena ROO .25 .07
531 Derek Jeter BPM .60 .18
532 Ken Griffey Jr. BPM .50 .15
533 Manny Ramirez BPM .20 .06
534 Luis Gonzalez BPM .20 .06
535 Sammy Sosa BPM .50 .15
536 Roger Clemens BPM .50 .15
537 Phil Nevin BPM .20 .06
538 Mike Piazza BPM .50 .15
539 Alex Rodriguez BPM .50 .15
540 Jason Giambi Yankees BPM .60 .18
541 Randy Johnson BPM .30 .09
542 Albert Pujols BPM .50 .15
543 Jeff Bagwell BPM .20 .06
544 Shawn Green BPM .20 .06
545 Carlos Delgado BPM .20 .06
546 Pedro Martinez BPM .30 .09
547 Todd Helton BPM .20 .06
548 Roberto Alomar BPM .20 .06
549 Barry Bonds BPM .50 .15
550 Ichiro Suzuki BPM .50 .15
551 John Lackey .40 .12
552 Francisco Rodriguez .20 .06
553 Cliff Floyd .40 .12
554 Derek Lowe .40 .12
555 Mark Bellhorn .40 .12
556 Matt Clement .40 .12
557 Hee Seop Choi .40 .12
558 Joe Borchard .40 .12
559 Ryan Dempster .40 .12
560 Russell Branyan .40 .12
561 Brandon Larson .40 .12
562 Coco Crisp .40 .12
563 Karim Garcia .40 .12
564 Brandon Phillips .40 .12
565 Jay Payton .40 .12
566 Gabe Kapler .40 .12
567 Carlos Pena .40 .12
568 George Lombard .40 .12
569 Andy Van Hekken .40 .12
570 Andres Torres .40 .12
571 Justin Wayne .40 .12
572 Juan Encarnacion .40 .12
573 Abraham Nunez .40 .12
574 Peter Munro .40 .12
575 Jason Lane .40 .12
576 Dave Roberts .40 .12
577 Eric Gagne .75 .23
578 Alex Sanchez .40 .12
579 Jim Rushford RC .40 .12
580 Ben Diggins .40 .12
581 Eddie Guardado .40 .12
582 Bartolo Colon .40 .12
583 Endy Chavez .40 .12
584 Raul Mondesi .40 .12
585 Jeff Weaver .40 .12
586 Marcus Thames .40 .12
587 Ted Lilly .40 .12
588 Ray Durham .40 .12
589 Jeremy Giambi .40 .12
590 Vicente Padilla .40 .12
591 Brett Myers .40 .12
592 Josh Fogg .40 .12
593 Tony Alvarez .40 .12
594 Jake Peavy .40 .12
595 Dennis Tankersley .40 .12
596 Sean Burroughs .40 .12
597 Kenny Lofton .40 .12
598 Scott Rolen .75 .23
599 Chuck Finley .40 .12
600 Carl Crawford .40 .12
601 Kevin Mench .40 .12
602 Juan Gonzalez .50 .15
603 Jayson Werth .40 .12
604 Eric Hinske .40 .12
605 Josh Phelps .40 .12
606 Jose Valverde ROO RC .50 .15
607 John Ennis ROO RC .40 .12
608 Trey Hodges ROO RC .40 .12
609 Kevin Gryboski ROO RC .40 .12
610 Travis Driskill ROO RC .40 .12
611 Howie Clark ROO RC .40 .12
612 Freddy Sanchez ROO RC .40 .12
613 Josh Hancock ROO RC .40 .12
614 Jorge De La Rosa ROO RC .40 .12
615 Mike Mahoney ROO .40 .12
616 Jason Davis ROO RC .75 .23
617 Josh Bard ROO RC .40 .12
618 Jason Beverlin ROO RC .40 .12
619 Carl Sadler ROO RC .40 .12
620 Earl Snyder ROO RC .50 .15
621 Aaron Cook ROO RC .40 .12
622 Eric Eckenstahler ROO RC .40 .12
623 Franklyn German ROO RC .40 .12
624 Kirk Saarloos ROO RC .40 .12
625 Rodrigo Rosario ROO RC .40 .12
626 Jeriome Robertson ROO RC .40 .12
627 Brandon Puffer ROO RC .40 .12
628 Miguel Asencio ROO RC .40 .12
629 Aaron Guiel ROO RC .40 .12
630 Ryan Bukvich ROO RC .40 .12
631 Jeremy Hill ROO RC .40 .12
632 Kazuhisa Ishii ROO RC 1.50 .45
633 Jayson Durocher ROO RC .40 .12
634 Shane Nance ROO RC .40 .12
635 Eric Good ROO RC .40 .12
636 Jamey Carroll ROO RC .40 .12
637 Jaime Cerda ROO RC .40 .12
638 Nate Field ROO RC .40 .12
639 Cody McKay ROO RC .40 .12
640 Jose Flores ROO RC .40 .12
641 Jorge Padilla ROO RC .40 .12
642 Anderson Machado ROO RC .40 .12
643 Eric Junge ROO RC .40 .12
644 Oliver Perez ROO RC 3.00 .90
645 Julius Matos ROO RC .40 .12
646 Ben Howard ROO RC .40 .12
647 Julio Mateo ROO RC .40 .12
648 Matt Thornton ROO RC .40 .12
649 Chris Snelling ROO RC .40 .12
650 Jason Simontacchi ROO RC .40 .12
651 So Taguchi ROO RC .50 .15
652 Mike Crudale ROO RC .40 .12
653 Mike Coolbaugh ROO RC .40 .12
654 Felix Escalona ROO RC .40 .12
655 Jorge Sosa ROO RC .40 .12
656 Lance Carter ROO RC .40 .12
657 Reynaldo Garcia ROO RC .40 .12
658 Kevin Cash ROO RC .40 .12
659 Ken Huckaby ROO RC .40 .12
660 Scott Wiggins ROO RC .40 .12

2002 Upper Deck Victory Gold

This set parallels the regular 2002 Upper Deck Victory set and were issued at stated odds of one in two packs.

	Nm-Mt	Ex-Mt
COMMON CARD (1-550)	1.00	.30
*GOLD 1-490/531-550: 4X TO 10X BASIC		
*GOLD 491-530: 3X TO 8X BASIC		

2003 Upper Deck Victory

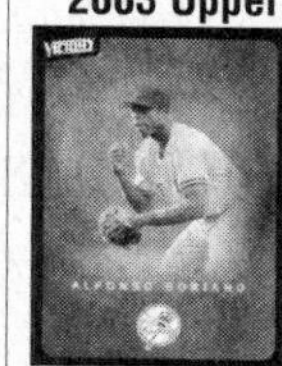

This 200 card set was issued in Feburary, 2003. This set was issued in six card packs with an $1 SRP. The packs were issued 36 to a box and 20 boxes to a case. Cards number 1 through 100 comprise the base set while cards numbered 101 through 200 were produced in smaller quantity. The following subsets were produced: Solid Hits (101-128) were issued at a stated rate of one in four; Clutch Players (129-148) and Laying it on the Line (149-168) were issued at a stated rate of one in five; True Gamers (169-178) and Run Producers (179-188) were issued at a stated rate of one in 10; Difference Makers (189-194) and Winning Formula (195-200) were issued at a stated rate of one in 20.

	Nm-Mt	Ex-Mt
COMPLETE SET (200)	80.00	24.00
COMP.SET w/o SP's (100)	25.00	7.50
COMMON CARD (101-200)	.75	.23
101-128 STATED ODDS 1:4		
129-168 STATED ODDS 1:5		
169-188 STATED ODDS 1:10		
189-200 STATED ODDS 1:20		

1 Troy Glaus .30 .09
2 Garret Anderson .30 .09
3 Tim Salmon .50 .15
4 Darin Erstad .30 .09
5 Luis Gonzalez .30 .09
6 Curt Schilling .30 .09
7 Randy Johnson .75 .23
8 Junior Spivey .30 .09
9 Andruw Jones .30 .09
10 Greg Maddux 1.25 .35
11 Chipper Jones .75 .23
12 Gary Sheffield .30 .09
13 John Smoltz .50 .15
14 Geronimo Gil .30 .09
15 Tony Batista .30 .09
16 Trot Nixon .30 .09
17 Manny Ramirez .50 .15
18 Pedro Martinez .75 .23
19 Nomar Garciaparra 1.25 .35
20 Derek Lowe .30 .09
21 Shea Hillenbrand .30 .09
22 Sammy Sosa 1.25 .35
23 Kerry Wood .75 .23
24 Mark Prior .75 .23
25 Magglio Ordonez .30 .09
26 Frank Thomas .75 .23
27 Mark Buehrle .30 .09
28 Paul Konerko .30 .09

29 Adam Dunn .50 .15
30 Ken Griffey Jr. 1.25 .35
31 Austin Kearns .30 .09
32 Matt Lawton .30 .09
33 Larry Walker .50 .15
34 Todd Helton .50 .15
35 Jeff Bagwell .50 .15
36 Roy Oswalt .30 .09
37 Lance Berkman .30 .09
38 Mike Sweeney .30 .09
39 Carlos Beltran .50 .15
40 Kazuhisa Ishii .30 .09
41 Shawn Green .30 .09
42 Hideo Nomo .75 .23
43 Adrian Beltre .50 .15
44 Richie Sexson .30 .09
45 Ben Sheets .30 .09
46 Torii Hunter .30 .09
47 Jacque Jones .30 .09
48 Corey Koskie .30 .09
49 Vladimir Guerrero .75 .23
50 Jose Vidro .30 .09
51 Mo Vaughn .30 .09
52 Mike Piazza 1.25 .35
53 Roberto Alomar .50 .15
54 Derek Jeter 2.00 .60
55 Alfonso Soriano .50 .15
56 Jason Giambi .30 .09
57 Roger Clemens 1.50 .45
58 Mike Mussina .30 .09
59 Bernie Williams .50 .15
60 Jorge Posada .50 .15
61 Nick Johnson .30 .09
62 Hideki Matsui RC 4.00 1.20
63 Eric Chavez .30 .09
64 Barry Zito .30 .09
65 Miguel Tejada .30 .09
66 Tim Hudson .30 .09
67 Pat Burrell .30 .09
68 Bobby Abreu .30 .09
69 Jimmy Rollins .30 .09
70 Brett Myers .30 .09
71 Jim Thome .75 .23
72 Jason Kendall .30 .09
73 Brian Giles .30 .09
74 Aramis Ramirez .30 .09
75 Sean Burroughs .30 .09
76 Ryan Klesko .30 .09
77 Phil Nevin .30 .09
78 Barry Bonds 2.00 .60
79 J.T.Snow .30 .09
80 Rich Aurilia .30 .09
81 Ichiro Suzuki 1.25 .35
82 Edgar Martinez .50 .15
83 Freddy Garcia .30 .09
84 Jim Edmonds .30 .09
85 J.D. Drew .30 .09
86 Scott Rolen .75 .23
87 Albert Pujols 1.50 .45
88 Mark McGwire 2.00 .60
89 Matt Morris .30 .09
90 Ben Grieve .30 .09
91 Carl Crawford .30 .09
92 Alex Rodriguez 1.25 .35
93 Carl Everett .30 .09
94 Juan Gonzalez .50 .15
95 Rafael Palmeiro .50 .15
96 Hank Blalock .50 .15
97 Carlos Delgado .30 .09
98 Josh Phelps .30 .09
99 Eric Hinske .30 .09
100 Shannon Stewart .30 .09
101 Albert Pujols SH 3.00 .90
102 Alex Rodriguez SH 2.50 .75
103 Alfonso Soriano SH 1.00 .30
104 Barry Bonds SH 4.00 1.20
105 Bernie Williams SH 1.00 .30
106 Brian Giles SH .75 .23
107 Chipper Jones SH 1.50 .45
108 Darin Erstad SH .75 .23
109 Derek Jeter SH 4.00 1.20
110 Eric Chavez SH .75 .23
111 Miguel Tejada SH .75 .23
112 Ichiro Suzuki SH 2.50 .75
113 Rafael Palmeiro SH 1.00 .30
114 Jason Giambi SH .30 .09
115 Jeff Bagwell SH 1.00 .30
116 Jim Thome SH 1.50 .45
117 Ken Griffey Jr. SH 2.50 .75
118 Lance Berkman SH .75 .23
119 Luis Gonzalez SH .75 .23
120 Manny Ramirez SH 1.00 .30
121 Mike Piazza SH 2.50 .75
122 J.D. Drew SH .75 .23
123 Sammy Sosa SH 2.50 .75
124 Scott Rolen SH 1.00 .30
125 Shawn Green SH .75 .23
126 Todd Helton SH 1.00 .30
127 Troy Glaus SH .75 .23
128 Vladimir Guerrero SH 1.50 .45
129 Albert Pujols CP 3.00 .90
130 Brian Giles CP .75 .23
131 Carlos Delgado CP .75 .23
132 Curt Schilling CP .75 .23
133 Derek Jeter CP 4.00 1.20
134 Frank Thomas CP 1.50 .45
135 Greg Maddux CP 2.50 .75
136 Jeff Bagwell CP 1.00 .30
137 Jim Thome CP 1.50 .45
138 Jorge Posada CP 1.00 .30
139 Kazuhisa Ishii CP .75 .23
140 Larry Walker CP 1.00 .30
141 Luis Gonzalez CP .75 .23
142 Miguel Tejada CP .75 .23
143 Pat Burrell CP .75 .23
144 Pedro Martinez CP 1.50 .45
145 Rafael Palmeiro CP 1.00 .30
146 Roger Clemens CP 3.00 .90
147 Tim Hudson CP .75 .23
148 Troy Glaus CP .75 .23
149 Alfonso Soriano LL 1.00 .30
150 Andruw Jones LL .75 .23
151 Barry Zito LL .75 .23
152 Darin Erstad LL .75 .23
153 Eric Chavez LL .75 .23
154 Alex Rodriguez LL 2.50 .75
155 J.D. Drew LL .75 .23
156 Jason Giambi LL .30 .09
157 Jason Kendall LL .75 .23
158 Ken Griffey Jr. LL 2.50 .75
159 Lance Berkman LL .75 .23
160 Mike Mussina LL 1.00 .30
161 Mike Piazza LL 2.50 .75
162 Nomar Garciaparra LL 2.50 .75
163 Randy Johnson LL 1.50 .45
164 Roberto Alomar LL 1.00 .30
165 Scott Rolen LL 1.00 .30
166 Shawn Green LL .75 .23
167 Torii Hunter LL .75 .23
168 Vladimir Guerrero LL 1.50 .45
169 Alex Rodriguez TG 2.50 .75
170 Andruw Jones TG .75 .23
171 Bernie Williams TG 1.00 .30
172 Ichiro Suzuki TG 2.50 .75
173 Miguel Tejada TG .75 .23
174 Nomar Garciaparra TG 2.50 .75
175 Pedro Martinez TG 1.50 .45
176 Randy Johnson TG 1.50 .45
177 Todd Helton TG 1.00 .30
178 Vladimir Guerrero TG 1.50 .45
179 Barry Bonds RP 4.00 1.20
180 Carlos Delgado RP .75 .23
181 Chipper Jones RP 1.50 .45
182 Frank Thomas RP 1.50 .45
183 Lance Berkman RP .75 .23
184 Larry Walker RP 1.00 .30
185 Manny Ramirez RP 1.00 .30
186 Mike Piazza RP 2.50 .75
187 Sammy Sosa RP 2.50 .75
188 Shawn Green RP .75 .23
189 Chipper Jones DM 1.50 .45
190 Curt Schilling DM .75 .23
191 Derek Jeter DM 4.00 1.20
192 Ken Griffey Jr. DM 2.50 .75
193 Sammy Sosa DM 2.50 .75
194 Vladimir Guerrero DM 1.50 .45
195 Alex Rodriguez WF 2.50 .75
196 Barry Bonds WF 4.00 1.20
197 Greg Maddux WF 2.50 .75
198 Ichiro Suzuki WF 2.50 .75
199 Jason Giambi WF .30 .09
200 Mike Piazza WF 2.50 .75

2003 Upper Deck Victory Tier 1 Green

Issued at a stated rate of one per pack, this a parallel to the first 100 cards of the Victory set. These cards can be identified by their green borders.

Nm-Mt Ex-Mt
COMPLETE SET (100) 50.00 15.00
*GREEN: 1X TO 2.5X BASIC
*GREEN MATSUI: .6X TO 1.5X BASIC

2003 Upper Deck Victory Tier 2 Orange

Issued at a stated rate of one per eight packs, this a parallel to the first 100 cards of the Victory set. These cards can be identified by their orange borders.

Nm-Mt Ex-Mt
COMPLETE SET (100) 80.00 24.00
*ORANGE: 2X TO 5X BASIC
*ORANGE MATSUI: 1X TO 2.5X BASIC

2003 Upper Deck Victory Tier 3 Blue

Randomly inserted in packs, this a parallel to the first 100 cards of the basic Victory set. These cards can be identified by their blue borders. These cards were issued to a stated print run of 650 serial numbered sets.

Nm-Mt Ex-Mt
*BLUE: 4X TO 10X BASIC

2003 Upper Deck Victory Tier 4 Purple

Randomly inserted in packs, this a parallel to the first 100 cards of the basic Victory set. These cards can be identified by their purple borders. These cards were issued to a stated print run of 50 serial numbered sets.

Nm-Mt Ex-Mt
*PURPLE: 12.5X TO 30X BASIC

2003 Upper Deck Victory Tier 5 Red

Randomly inserted in packs, this a parallel to the first 100 cards of the basic Victory set. These cards can be identified by their red borders. These cards were issued to a stated print run of 25 serial numbered sets. No pricing is available on these cards due to market scarcity.

Nm-Mt Ex-Mt
NO PRICING DUE TO SCARCITY

2001 Upper Deck Vintage

The 2001 Upper Deck Vintage product released in late January,2001 and featured a 400-card base set. Each pack contained 10 cards, and carried a suggested retail price of $2.99 per pack. The set was broken into tiers as follows: Base Veterans (1-340), Prospects (341-370), Series Highlights (371-390) and League Leaders (391-400). A Sample card featuring Ken Griffey Jr. was distributed to dealers and hobby media several weeks prior to the product's release national release date. The card can be readily identified by the bold "SAMPLE" text running diagonally across the back.

Nm-Mt Ex-Mt
COMPLETE SET (400) 50.00 15.00
COMMON (1-340/371-400) .30 .09
COMMON (341-370) .50 .15
1 Darin Erstad .30 .09
2 Seth Etherton .30 .09
3 Troy Glaus .30 .09
4 Bengie Molina .30 .09
5 Mo Vaughn .30 .09
6 Tim Salmon .50 .15
7 Ramon Ortiz .30 .09
8 Adam Kennedy .30 .09
9 Garret Anderson .30 .09
10 Troy Percival .30 .09
11 Tim Salmon .30 .09
Bengie Molina
MoVaughn
Adam Kennedy
Troy Glaus
Kevin Stocker
Darin Erstad
Garret Anderson
Ron Gant CL
12 Jason Giambi .30 .09
13 Tim Hudson .30 .09
14 Adam Piatt .30 .09
15 Miguel Tejada .30 .09
16 Mark Mulder .30 .09
17 Eric Chavez .30 .09
18 Ramon Hernandez .30 .09
19 Terrence Long .30 .09
20 Jason Isringhausen .30 .09
21 Barry Zito .50 .15
22 Ben Grieve .30 .09
23 Olmedo Saenz .30 .09
Ramon Hernandez
Jason Giambi
Randy Velarde
Eric Chavez
Miguel Tejada
Ben Grieve
Terrence Long
Adam Piatt CL
24 David Wells .30 .09
25 Raul Mondesi .30 .09
26 Darrin Fletcher .30 .09
27 Shannon Stewart .30 .09
28 Kelvim Escobar .30 .09
29 Tony Batista .30 .09
30 Carlos Delgado .30 .09
31 Brad Fullmer .30 .09
32 Billy Koch .30 .09
33 Jose Cruz Jr. .30 .09
34 Brad Fullmer .30 .09
Darrin Fletcher
Carlos Delgado
Homer Bush
Tony Batista
Alex Gonzalez
Shannon Stewart
Jose Cruz Jr.
Raul Mondesi CL
35 Greg Vaughn .30 .09
36 Roberto Hernandez .30 .09
37 Vinny Castilla .30 .09
38 Gerald Williams .30 .09
39 Aubrey Huff .30 .09
40 Bryan Rekar .30 .09
41 Albie Lopez .30 .09
42 Fred McGriff .50 .15
43 Miguel Cairo .30 .09
44 Ryan Rupe .30 .09
45 Greg Vaughn .30 .09
John Flaherty
Fred McGriff
Miguel Cairo
Vinny Castilla
Felix Martinez
Gerald Williams
Jose Guillen
Steve Cox CL
46 Jim Thome .75 .23
47 Roberto Alomar .50 .15
48 Bartolo Colon .30 .09
49 Omar Vizquel .50 .15
50 Travis Fryman .30 .09
51 Manny Ramirez UER .50 .15
Picture is of David Segui
52 Dave Burba .30 .09
53 Chuck Finley .30 .09
54 Russ Branyan .30 .09
55 Kenny Lofton .30 .09
56 Russell Branyan .30 .09
Sandy Alomar Jr.
Jim Thome
Roberto Alomar
Travis Fryman
Omar Vizquel
Wil Cordero
Kenny Lofton
Manny Ramirez
Picture is off David Segui CL UER
57 Alex Rodriguez 1.25 .35
58 Jay Buhner .30 .09
59 Aaron Sele .30 .09
60 Kazuhiro Sasaki .30 .09
61 Edgar Martinez .50 .15
62 John Halama .30 .09
63 Mike Cameron .30 .09
64 Freddy Garcia .30 .09
65 John Olerud .25 .09
66 Jamie Moyer .30 .09
67 Gil Meche .30 .09
68 Edgar Martinez .30 .09
Joe Oliver
John Olerud
David Bell
Carlos Guillen
Alex Rodriguez
Jay Buhner
Mike Cameron
Al Martin CL
69 Cal Ripken 2.50 .75
70 Sidney Ponson .30 .09
71 Chris Richard .30 .09
72 Jose Mercedes .30 .09
73 Albert Belle .30 .09
74 Mike Mussina .50 .15
75 Brady Anderson .30 .09
76 Delino DeShields .30 .09
77 Melvin Mora .30 .09
78 Luis Matos .30 .09
79 Brook Fordyce .30 .09
80 Jeff Conine .30 .09
Brook Fordyce
Chris Richard
Delino DeShields
Cal Ripken
Melvin Mora
Luis Matos
Brady Anderson
Albert Belle CL
81 Rafael Palmeiro .50 .15
82 Rick Helling .30 .09
83 Ruben Mateo .30 .09
84 Rusty Greer .30 .09
85 Ivan Rodriguez .75 .23
86 Doug Davis .30 .09
87 Gabe Kapler .30 .09
88 Mike Lamb .30 .09
89 A.Rodriguez Rangers 3.00 .90
90 Kenny Rogers .30 .09
91 David Segui .50 .15
Ivan Rodriguez
Rafael Palmeiro
Frank Catalanotto
Mike Lamb
Royce Clayton
Ruben Mateo
Gabe Kapler
Rusty Greer CL
92 Nomar Garciaparra 1.25 .35
93 Trot Nixon .30 .09
94 Tomokazu Ohka .30 .09
95 Pedro Martinez .75 .23
96 Dante Bichette .30 .09
97 Jason Varitek .50 .15
98 Rolando Arrojo .30 .09
99 Carl Everett .30 .09
100 Derek Lowe .30 .09
101 Troy O'Leary .30 .09
102 Tim Wakefield .30 .09
103 Troy O'Leary .30 .09
Jason Varitek
Jose Offerman
Mike Lansing
Wilton Veras
Nomar Garciaparra
Carl Everett
Trot Nixon
Dante Bichette CL
104 Mike Sweeney .30 .09
105 Carlos Febles .30 .09
106 Joe Randa .30 .09
107 Jeff Suppan .30 .09
108 Mac Suzuki .30 .09
109 Jermaine Dye .30 .09
110 Carlos Beltran .50 .15
111 Mark Quinn .30 .09
112 Johnny Damon .50 .15
113 Mark Quinn .30 .09
Gregg Zaun
Mike Sweeney
Carlos Febles
Joe Randa
Rey Sanchez
Carlos Beltran
Johnny Damon
Jermaine Dye CL
114 Tony Clark .30 .09
115 Dean Palmer .30 .09
116 Brian Moehler .30 .09
117 Brad Ausmus .30 .09
118 Juan Gonzalez .50 .15
119 Juan Encarnacion .30 .09
120 Jeff Weaver .30 .09
121 Bobby Higginson .30 .09
122 Todd Jones .30 .09
123 Deivi Cruz .30 .09
124 Juan Gonzalez .30 .09
Brad Ausmus
Tony Clark
Damion Easley
Dean Palmer
Deivi Cruz
Bobby Higginson
Juan Encarnacion
Rich Becker CL
125 Corey Koskie .30 .09
126 Matt Lawton .30 .09
127 Mark Redman .30 .09
128 David Ortiz .50 .15
129 Jay Canizaro .30 .09
130 Eric Milton .30 .09
131 Jacque Jones .30 .09
132 J.C. Romero .30 .09
133 Ron Coomer .30 .09
134 Brad Radke .30 .09
135 David Ortiz .50 .15
Matt LeCroy
Ron Coomer
Jay Canizaro
Corey Koskie
Cristian Guzman
Jacque Jones
Matt Lawton
Torii Hunter CL
136 Carlos Lee .30 .09
137 Frank Thomas .75 .23
138 Mike Sirotka .30 .09
139 Charles Johnson .30 .09
140 James Baldwin .30 .09
141 Magglio Ordonez .30 .09
142 Jon Garland .30 .09
143 Paul Konerko .30 .09
144 Ray Durham .30 .09
145 Keith Foulke .30 .09
146 Chris Singleton .30 .09
147 Frank Thomas .50 .15
Charles Johnson
Paul Konerko
Ray Durham
Herbert Perry
Jose Valentin
Carlos Lee
Magglio Ordonez
Chris Singleton CL
148 Bernie Williams .50 .15
149 Orlando Hernandez .30 .09
150 David Justice .30 .09
151 Andy Pettitte .50 .15
152 Mariano Rivera .50 .15
153 Derek Jeter 2.00 .60
154 Jorge Posada .50 .15
155 Jose Canseco .75 .23
156 Glenallen Hill .30 .09
157 Paul O'Neill .50 .15
158 Denny Neagle .30 .09
159 Chuck Knoblauch .30 .09
160 Roger Clemens 1.50 .45
161 Glenallen Hill .75 .23
Jorge Posada
Tino Martinez
Chuck Knoblauch
Scott Brosius
Derek Jeter
Paul O'Neill
Bernie Williams
David Justice CL
162 Jeff Bagwell .50 .15
163 Moises Alou .30 .09
164 Lance Berkman .30 .09
165 Shane Reynolds .30 .09
166 Ken Caminiti .30 .09
167 Craig Biggio .50 .15
168 Jose Lima .30 .09
169 Octavio Dotel .30 .09
170 Richard Hidalgo .30 .09
171 Scott Elarton .30 .09
172 Scott Elarton .50 .15
Mitch Meluskey
Jeff Bagwell
Craig Biggio
Bill Spiers
Julio Lugo
Moises Alou
Richard Hidalgo
Lance Berkman CL
173 Rafael Furcal .30 .09
174 Greg Maddux 1.25 .35
175 Quilvio Veras .30 .09
176 Chipper Jones .75 .23
177 Andres Galarraga .30 .09
178 Brian Jordan .30 .09
179 Tom Glavine .50 .15
180 Kevin Millwood .30 .09
181 Javier Lopez .30 .09
182 B.J. Surhoff .30 .09
183 Andruw Jones .30 .09
184 Andy Ashby .30 .09
185 Tom Glavine .30 .09
Javy Lopez
Andres Galarraga
Quilvio Veras
Chipper Jones
Rafael Furcal
Reggie Sanders
Brian Jordan
Andruw Jones CL
186 Richie Sexson .30 .09
187 Jeff D'Amico .30 .09
188 Ron Belliard .30 .09
189 Jeromy Burnitz .30 .09
190 Jimmy Haynes .30 .09
191 Marquis Grissom .30 .09
192 Jose Hernandez .30 .09
193 Geoff Jenkins .30 .09
194 Jamey Wright .30 .09
195 Mark Loretta .30 .09
196 Jeff D'Amico .30 .09
Henry Blanco
Richie Sexson
Ron Belliard
Tyler Houston
Mark Loretta
Jeromy Burnitz
Marquis Grissom
Geoff Jenkins CL
197 Rick Ankiel .30 .09
198 Mark McGwire 2.00 .60
199 Fernando Vina .30 .09
200 Edgar Renteria .30 .09
201 Darryl Kile .30 .09
202 Jim Edmonds .30 .09
203 Ray Lankford .30 .09
204 Garrett Stephenson .30 .09
205 Fernando Tatis .30 .09
206 Will Clark .75 .23
207 J.D. Drew .30 .09
208 Darryl Kile .30 .09
Mike Matheny
Mark McGwire
Fernando Vina
Fernando Tatis
Edgar Renteria
Ray Lankford
Jim Edmonds
J.D. Drew CL
209 Mark Grace .50 .15
210 Eric Young .30 .09
211 Sammy Sosa 1.25 .35
212 Jon Lieber .30 .09
213 Joe Girardi .30 .09
214 Kevin Tapani .30 .09
215 Ricky Gutierrez .30 .09
216 Kerry Wood .75 .23
217 Rondell White .30 .09
218 Damon Buford .30 .09
219 Jon Lieber .30 .09
Joe Girardi
Mark Grace
Eric Young
Willie Greene
Ricky Gutierrez
Sammy Sosa
Damon Bufford
Rondell White CL
220 Luis Gonzalez .30 .09
221 Randy Johnson .75 .23
222 Jay Bell .30 .09
223 Erubiel Durazo .30 .09
224 Matt Williams .30 .09
225 Steve Finley .30 .09
226 Curt Schilling .30 .09
227 Todd Stottlemyre .30 .09
228 Tony Womack .30 .09
229 Brian Anderson .30 .09
230 Randy Johnson .30 .09
Kelly Stinnett
Greg Colbrunn

Jay Bell
Matt Williams
Tony Womack
Luis Gonzalez
Steve Finley
Danny Bautista CL
231 Gary Sheffield .30 .09
232 Adrian Beltre .50 .15
233 Todd Hundley .30 .09
234 Chan Ho Park .30 .09
235 Shawn Green .30 .09
236 Kevin Brown .30 .09
237 Tom Goodwin .30 .09
238 Mark Grudzielanek .30 .09
239 Ismael Valdes .30 .09
240 Eric Karros .30 .09
241 Kevin Brown .30 .09
Todd Hundley
Eric Karros
Mark Grudzielanek
Adrian Beltre
Alex Cora
Gary Sheffield
Shawn Green
Tom Goodwin CL
242 Jose Vidro .30 .09
243 Javier Vazquez .30 .09
244 Orlando Cabrera .30 .09
245 Peter Bergeron .30 .09
246 Vladimir Guerrero .75 .23
247 Dustin Hermanson .30 .09
248 Tony Armas Jr. .30 .09
249 Lee Stevens .30 .09
250 Milton Bradley .30 .09
251 Carl Pavano .30 .09
252 Dustin Hermanson .30 .09
Michael Barrett
Lee Stevens
Jose Vidro
Geoff Jenkins
Orlando Cabrera
Vladimir Guerrero
Peter Bergeron
Milton Bradley CL
253 Ellis Burks .30 .09
254 Robb Nen .30 .09
255 J.T. Snow .30 .09
256 Barry Bonds 2.00 .60
257 Shawn Estes .30 .09
258 Jeff Kent .30 .09
259 Kirk Rueter .30 .09
260 Bill Mueller .30 .09
261 Livan Hernandez .30 .09
262 Rich Aurilia .30 .09
263 Livan Hernadez .30 .09
Bobby Estalella
J.T. Snow
Jeff Kent
Bill Mueller
Rich Aurilia
Barry Bonds
Marvin Benard
Ellis Burks CL
264 Ryan Dempster .30 .09
265 Cliff Floyd .30 .09
266 Mike Lowell .30 .09
267 A.J. Burnett .30 .09
268 Preston Wilson .30 .09
269 Luis Castillo .30 .09
270 Henry Rodriguez .30 .09
271 Antonio Alfonseca .30 .09
272 Derrek Lee .30 .09
273 Mark Kotsay .30 .09
274 Brad Penny .30 .09
275 Ryan Dempster .30 .09
Mike Redmond
Derrek Lee
Luis Castillo
Mike Lowell
Alex Gonzalez
Cliff Floyd
Mark Kotsay
Preston Wilson CL
276 Mike Piazza 1.25 .35
277 Jay Payton .30 .09
278 Al Leiter .30 .09
279 Mike Bordick .30 .09
280 Armando Benitez .30 .09
281 Todd Zeile .30 .09
282 Mike Hampton .30 .09
283 Edgardo Alfonzo .30 .09
284 Derek Bell .30 .09
285 Robin Ventura .30 .09
286 Mike Hampton .30 .09
Mike Piazza
Todd Zeile
Edgardo Alfonzo
Robin Ventura
Mike Bordick
Derek Bell
Jay Payton
Timo Perez CL
287 Tony Gwynn 1.00 .30
288 Trevor Hoffman .30 .09
289 Ryan Klesko .30 .09
290 Phil Nevin .30 .09
291 Matt Clement .30 .09
292 Ben Davis .30 .09
293 Ruben Rivera .30 .09
294 Bret Boone .30 .09
295 Adam Eaton .30 .09
296 Eric Owens .30 .09
297 Matt Clement .30 .09
Ben Davis
Ryan Klesko
Bret Boone
Phil Nevin
Damian Jackson
Ruben Rivera
Eric Owens
Tony Gwynn CL
298 Bob Abreu .30 .09
299 Mike Lieberthal .30 .09
300 Robert Person .30 .09
301 Scott Rolen .75 .23
302 Randy Wolf .30 .09
303 Bruce Chen .30 .09
304 Travis Lee .30 .09
305 Kent Bottenfield .30 .09
306 Pat Burrell .30 .09
307 Doug Glanville .30 .09
308 Robert Person .30 .09
Mike Lieberthal
Pat Burrell
Kevin Jordan
Scott Rolen
Alex Arias
Bob Abreu
Doug Glanville
Travis Lee CL
309 Brian Giles .30 .09
310 Todd Ritchie .30 .09
311 Warren Morris .30 .09
312 John VanderWal .30 .09
313 Kris Benson .30 .09
314 Jason Kendall .30 .09
315 Kevin Young .30 .09
316 Francisco Cordova .30 .09
317 Jimmy Anderson .30 .09
318 Kris Benson .30 .09
Jason Kendall
Kevin Young
Warren Morris
Mike Benjamin
Pat Meares
John VanderWal
Brian Giles
Adrian Brown CL
319 Ken Griffey Jr. 1.25 .35
320 Pokey Reese .30 .09
321 Chris Stynes .30 .09
322 Barry Larkin .50 .15
323 Steve Parris .30 .09
324 Michael Tucker .30 .09
325 Dmitri Young .30 .09
326 Pete Harnisch .30 .09
327 Danny Graves .30 .09
328 Aaron Boone .30 .09
329 Sean Casey .30 .09
330 Steve Parris .30 .09
Ed Taubensee
Sean Casey
Pokey Reese
Aaron Boone
Barry Larkin
Ken Griffey Jr.
Dmitri Young
Michael Tucker CL
331 Todd Helton .50 .15
332 Pedro Astacio .30 .09
333 Larry Walker .50 .15
334 Ben Petrick .30 .09
335 Brian Bohanon .30 .09
336 Juan Pierre .30 .09
337 Jeffrey Hammonds .30 .09
338 Jeff Cirillo .30 .09
339 Todd Hollandsworth .30 .09
340 Pedro Astacio .30 .09
Brent Mayne
Todd Helton
Todd Walker
Jeff Cirillo
Neifi Perez
Larry Walker
Jeffrey Hammonds
Juan Pierre CL
341 Matt Wise .50 .15
Keith Luuola
Derrick Turnbow
342 Jason Hart .50 .15
Jose Ortiz
Mario Encarnacion
343 Vernon Wells .50 .15
Pasqual Coco
Josh Phelps
344 Travis Harper .50 .15
Kenny Kelley
Toby Hall
345 Danys Baez .50 .15
Tim Drew
Martin Vargas
346 Ichiro Suzuki 15.00 4.50
Ryan Franklin
Ryan Christianson
347 Jay Spurgeon .50 .15
Lesli Brea
Carlos Casimiro
348 B.J. Waszgis .50 .15
Brian Sikorski
Joaquin Benoit
349 Sun-Woo Kim .50 .15
Paxton Crawford
Steve Lomasney
350 Kris Wilson .50 .15
Orber Moreno
Dee Brown
351 Mark Johnson .50 .15
Brandon Inge
Adam Bernero
352 Danny Ardoin .50 .15
Matt Kinney
Jason Ryan
353 Rocky Biddle .50 .15
Joe Crede
Josh Paul
354 Nick Johnson .50 .15
D'Angelo Jimenez
Wily Mo Pena
355 Tony McKnight .50 .15
Aaron McNeal
Keith Ginter
356 Mark DeRosa .30 .09
Jason Marquis
Wes Helms UER
Photos do not match the players ID'd
357 Allen Levrault .50 .15
Horacio Estrada
Santiago Perez
358 Luis Saturria .50 .15
Gene Stechschulte
Britt Reames
359 Joey Nation .50 .15
Corey Patterson
Cole Liniak
360 Alex Cabrera .50 .15
Geraldo Guzman
Nelson Figuero
361 Hiram Bocachica .50 .15
Mike Judd
Luke Prokopec
362 Tomas de la Rosa .50 .15
Yohanny Valera
Talmadge Nunnari
363 Ryan Vogelsong .50 .15
Juan Melo
Chad Zerbe
364 Jason Grilli .50 .15
Pablo Ozuna
Ramon Castro
365 Timo Perez .50 .15
Grant Roberts
Brian Cole
366 Tom Davey .50 .15
Xavier Nady
Dave Maurer
367 Jimmy Rollins .50 .15
Mark Brownson
Reggie Taylor
368 Alex Hernandez .50 .15
Adam Hyzdu
Tike Redman
369 Brady Clark .50 .15
John Riedling
Mike Bell
370 Giovanni Carrara .50 .15
Josh Kalinowski
Craig House
371 Jim Edmonds SH .30 .09
372 Edgar Martinez SH .30 .09
373 Rickey Henderson SH .75 .23
374 Barry Zito SH .50 .15
375 Tino Martinez SH .50 .15
376 J.T. Snow SH .30 .09
377 Bobby Jones SH .30 .09
378 Alex Rodriguez SH .75 .23
379 Mike Hampton SH .30 .09
380 Roger Clemens SH .75 .23
381 Jay Payton SH .30 .09
382 John Olerud SH .30 .09
383 David Justice SH .30 .09
384 Mike Hampton SH .30 .09
385 New York Yankees SH .75 .23
386 Jose Vizcaino SH .30 .09
387 Roger Clemens SH .75 .23
388 Todd Zeile SH .30 .09
389 Derek Jeter SH 1.00 .30
390 New York Yankees SH .75 .23
391 Nomar Garciaparra .75 .23
Darin Erstad
Manny Ramirez
Derek Jeter
Carlos Delgado LL
392 Todd Helton .50 .15
Luis Castillo
Jeffrey Hammonds
Vladimir Guerrero
Moises Alou LL
393 Troy Glaus .75 .23
Frank Thomas
Alex Rodriguez
Jason Giambi
David Justice LL
394 Sammy Sosa .50 .15
Jeff Bagwell
Barry Bonds
Vladimir Guerrero
Richard Hidalgo LL
395 Edgar Martinez .30 .09
Mike Sweeney
Frank Thomas
Carlos Delgado
Jason Giambi LL
396 Todd Helton .30 .09
Jeff Kent
Brian Giles
Sammy Sosa
Jeff Bagwell LL
397 Pedro Martinez .50 .15
Roger Clemens
Mike Mussina
Bartolo Colon
Mike Sirotka LL
398 Kevin Brown .30 .09
Randy Johnson
Jeff D'Amico
Greg Maddux
Mike Hampton LL
399 Tim Hudson .30 .09
David Wells
Aaron Sele
Andy Pettitte
Pedro Martinez LL
400 Tom Glavine .50 .15
Darryl Kile
Randy Johnson
Chan Ho Park
Greg Maddux LL
S30 K.Griffey Jr. Sample 1.25 .35

2001 Upper Deck Vintage All-Star Tributes

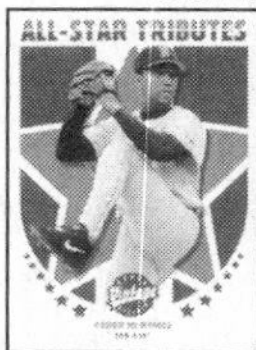

Randomly inserted into packs at one in 23, this 10-card insert features players that make the All-Star team on a consistent basis. Card backs carry an "AS" prefix.

	Nm-Mt	Ex-Mt
COMPLETE SET (10)	40.00	12.00
AS1 Derek Jeter	6.00	1.80
AS2 Mike Piazza	4.00	1.20
AS3 Carlos Delgado	1.50	.45
AS4 Pedro Martinez	2.50	.75
AS5 Vladimir Guerrero	2.50	.75
AS6 Mark McGwire	6.00	1.80
AS7 Alex Rodriguez	4.00	1.20
AS8 Barry Bonds	6.00	1.80
AS9 Chipper Jones	2.50	.75
AS10 Sammy Sosa	4.00	1.20

2001 Upper Deck Vintage Glory Days

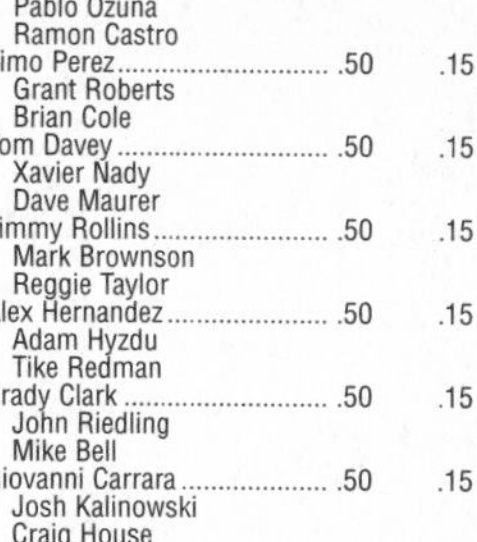

Randomly inserted into packs at one in 15, this 15-card insert features players that remind us of baseball's glory days of the past. Card backs carry a "G" prefix.

	Nm-Mt	Ex-Mt
COMPLETE SET (15)	40.00	12.00
G1 Jermaine Dye	1.50	.45
G2 Chipper Jones	2.50	.75
G3 Todd Helton	1.50	.45
G4 Maggio Ordonez	1.50	.45
G5 Tony Gwynn	3.00	.90
G6 Jim Edmonds	1.50	.45
G7 Rafael Palmeiro	1.50	.45
G8 Barry Bonds	6.00	1.80
G9 Carl Everett	1.50	.45
G10 Mike Piazza	4.00	1.20
G11 Brian Giles	1.50	.45
G12 Tony Batista	1.50	.45
G13 Jeff Bagwell	1.50	.45
G14 Ken Griffey Jr.	4.00	1.20
G15 Troy Glaus	1.50	.45

2001 Upper Deck Vintage Matinee Idols

Randomly inserted into packs at one in four, this 20-card insert features players that are idolized by every young baseball player in America. Card backs carry a "M" prefix.

	Nm-Mt	Ex-Mt
COMPLETE SET (20)	25.00	7.50
M1 Ken Griffey Jr.	2.00	.60
M2 Derek Jeter	3.00	.90
M3 Barry Bonds	3.00	.90
M4 Chipper Jones	1.25	.35
M5 Mike Piazza	2.00	.60
M6 Todd Helton	.75	.23
M7 Randy Johnson	1.25	.35
M8 Alex Rodriguez	2.00	.60
M9 Sammy Sosa	2.00	.60
M10 Cal Ripken	4.00	1.20
M11 Nomar Garciaparra	2.00	.60
M12 Carlos Delgado	.75	.23
M13 Jason Giambi	.75	.23
M14 Ivan Rodriguez	1.25	.35
M15 Vladimir Guerrero	1.25	.35
M16 Gary Sheffield	.75	.23
M17 Frank Thomas	1.25	.35
M18 Jeff Bagwell	.75	.23
M19 Pedro Martinez	1.25	.35
M20 Mark McGwire	3.00	.90

2001 Upper Deck Vintage Retro Rules

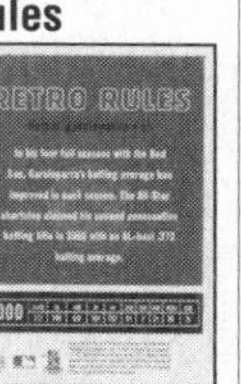

Randomly inserted into packs at one in 15, this 15-card insert features players whose performances remind us of baseball's good ol' days. Card backs carry a "R" prefix.

	Nm-Mt	Ex-Mt
COMPLETE SET (15)	40.00	12.00
R1 Nomar Garciaparra	4.00	1.20
R2 Frank Thomas	2.50	.75
R3 Jeff Bagwell	1.50	.45
R4 Sammy Sosa	4.00	1.20
R5 Derek Jeter	6.00	1.80
R6 David Wells	1.50	.45
R7 Vladimir Guerrero	2.50	.75
R8 Jim Thome	2.50	.75
R9 Mark McGwire	6.00	1.80
R10 Todd Helton	1.50	.45
R11 Tony Gwynn	3.00	.90
R12 Bernie Williams	1.50	.45
R13 Cal Ripken	8.00	2.40
R14 Brian Giles	1.50	.45
R15 Jason Giambi	1.50	.45

2001 Upper Deck Vintage Timeless Teams

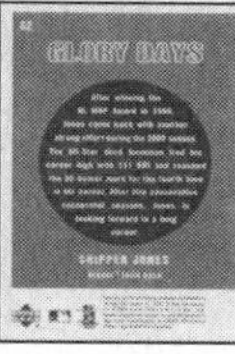

Randomly inserted into packs at one in 72 (Bats) and one in 288 (Jerseys), this 39-card insert features swatches of game-used memorabilia from powerhouse clubs of the past. Card backs carry the team initials/player's initials as numbering.

	Nm-Mt	Ex-Mt
CI2JB Johnny Bench Bat	25.00	7.50
CI2JM Joe Morgan Bat	15.00	4.50
CI2KG Ken Griffey Sr. Bat	25.00	7.50
CI2TP Tony Perez Bat	15.00	4.50
BABP Boog Powell Bat	25.00	7.50
BABR B. Robinson Bat	25.00	7.50
BAFR Frank Robinson Bat	25.00	7.50
BAMB Mark Belanger Bat	15.00	4.50
BKDN Don Newcombe Bat	25.00	7.50
BKGH Gil Hodges Bat	25.00	7.50
BKJR Jackie Robinson Bat	80.00	24.00
BKRC Roy Campanella Bat	50.00	15.00
CIDC D. Concepcion Jsy	15.00	4.50
CIJM Joe Morgan Jsy	15.00	4.50
CIKG Ken Griffey Sr. Jsy	25.00	7.50
CITP Tony Perez Jsy	15.00	4.50
LABR Bill Russell Bat	15.00	4.50
LADB Dusty Baker Bat	15.00	4.50
LARC Ron Cey Bat	15.00	4.50
LASG Steve Garvey Bat	15.00	4.50
NYMEK Ed Kranepool Bat	15.00	4.50
NYMNR Nolan Ryan Bat	40.00	12.00
NYMRS Ron Swoboda Bat	15.00	4.50
NYMTA Tommie Agee Bat	15.00	4.50
NYYBD Bill Dickey Bat	25.00	7.50
NYYBR B. Richardson Jsy	15.00	4.50
NYYCK Charlie Keller Bat	15.00	4.50
NYYJD Joe DiMaggio Bat	100.00	30.00
NYYMM M. Mantle Jsy	200.00	60.00
NYYRM Roger Maris Jsy	60.00	18.00
NYYTH T. Henrich Bat	15.00	4.50
OAGT Gene Tenace Bat	15.00	4.50
OAJR Joe Rudi Bat	15.00	4.50
OARJ Reggie Jackson Bat	25.00	7.50
OASB Sal Bando Bat	15.00	4.50
PIAO Al Oliver Bat	15.00	4.50
PIMS M. Sanguillen Bat	15.00	4.50
PIRC R. Clemente Bat	100.00	30.00
PIWS Willie Stargell Bat	25.00	7.50

2001 Upper Deck Vintage Timeless Teams Combos

Randomly inserted into packs, this 11-card insert features swatches of game-used memorabilia from powerhouse clubs of the past. Please note that these cards feature dual players, and are individually serial numbered to 100. Card backs carry the team initials/year as numbering. Unlike the other cards in this set, only twenty-five serial-numbered copies of the "Fantasy Outfield" card featuring DiMaggio, Mantle and Griffey Jr. were created.

	Nm-Mt	Ex-Mt
LA81 Steve Garvey	50.00	15.00
Ron Cey		
Dusty Baker		
Bill Russell Bat		
BAL70 Brooks Robinson	80.00	24.00
Frank Robinson		
Mark Belanger		
Boog Powell Bat		
BKN55 Jackie Robinson	200.00	60.00
Roy Campanella		
Gil Hodges		
Don Newcombe Bat		
CIN75B Johnny Bench	80.00	24.00
Tony Perez		
Joe Morgan		
Ken Griffey Sr. Bat		
CIN75J Dave Concepcion	50.00	15.00
Tony Perez		
Ken Griffey Sr. Jsy		
NYM69 Nolan Ryan	150.00	45.00
Ron Swoboda		
Ed Kranepool		
Tommie Agee Bat		
NYY41 Joe DiMaggio	200.00	60.00
Tommy Henrich		
Bill Dickey		
Charlie Keller Bat		
NYY61 Mickey Mantle	250.00	75.00
Roger Maris		
Bobby Richardson Jsy		
OAK72 Reggie Jackson	80.00	24.00
Sal Bando		
Gene Tenace		
Joe Rudi Bat		
PIT71 Roberto Clemente	150.00	45.00
Willie Stargell		
Manny Sanguillen		
Al Oliver Bat UER		
Card back says it is a Bill Mazeroski piece		
Manny Sanguillen replaced Mazeroski on card		
FO-CJ Joe DiMaggio		
Mickey Mantle		
Ken Griffey Jr. Jsy/25		

2002 Upper Deck Vintage

Released In January, 2002 this 300 card set features Upper Deck honoring the popular 1971 Topps design for this set. Subsets include Team Checklists, Vintage Rookies (both seeded throughout the set), League Leaders (271-280) and Postseason Scrapbook (281-300). Please note that card number 274 has a variation. A few cards issued very early in the printing cycle featured the players listed as AL Home Run Leaders and no names listed for the players. It is believed this card was corrected very early in the printing cycle.

Nm-Mt Ex-Mt
COMPLETE SET (300) 60.00 18.00
1 Darin Erstad .40 .12
2 Mo Vaughn .40 .12
3 Ramon Ortiz .40 .12
4 Garret Anderson .40 .12
5 Troy Glaus .40 .12
6 Troy Percival .40 .12
7 Tim Salmon .50 .15
8 Wilmy Caceres .40 .12
Elpidio Guzman
9 Ramon Ortiz TC .40 .12
10 Jason Giambi .40 .12
11 Mark Mulder .40 .12
12 Jermaine Dye .40 .12
13 Miguel Tejada .40 .12
14 Tim Hudson .40 .12
15 Eric Chavez .40 .12
16 Barry Zito .40 .12
17 Oscar Salazar .40 .12
Juan Pena
18 Miguel Tejada .40 .12
Jason Giambi TC
19 Carlos Delgado .40 .12
20 Raul Mondesi .40 .12
21 Chris Carpenter .40 .12
22 Jose Cruz Jr. .40 .12
23 Alex Gonzalez .40 .12
24 Brad Fullmer .40 .12
25 Shannon Stewart .40 .12
26 Brandon Lyon .40 .12
Vernon Wells
27 Carlos Delgado TC .40 .12
28 Greg Vaughn .40 .12
29 Toby Hall .40 .12
30 Ben Grieve .40 .12
31 Aubrey Huff .40 .12
32 Tanyon Sturtze .40 .12
33 Brent Abernathy .40 .12
34 Dewon Brazelton .40 .12
Delvin James
35 Greg Vaughn .40 .12
Fred McGriff TC
36 Roberto Alomar .50 .15
37 Juan Gonzalez .50 .15
38 Bartolo Colon .40 .12
39 C.C. Sabathia .40 .12
40 Jim Thome .75 .23
41 Omar Vizquel .50 .15
42 Russell Branyan .40 .12
43 Ryan Drese .40 .12
Roy Smith
44 C.C. Sabathia TC .40 .12
45 Edgar Martinez .50 .15
46 Bret Boone .40 .12
47 Freddy Garcia .40 .12
48 John Olerud .40 .12
49 Kazuhiro Sasaki .40 .12
50 Ichiro Suzuki 1.25 .35
51 Mike Cameron .40 .12
52 Rafael Soriano .40 .12
Dennis Stark
53 Jamie Moyer TC .40 .12
54 Tony Batista .40 .12
55 Jeff Conine .40 .12
56 Jason Johnson .40 .12
57 Jay Gibbons .40 .12
58 Chris Richard .40 .12
59 Josh Towers .40 .12
60 Jerry Hairston Jr. .40 .12
61 Sean Douglass .40 .12
Tim Raines Jr.
62 Cal Ripken TC 1.25 .35
63 Alex Rodriguez 1.25 .35
64 Ruben Sierra .40 .12
65 Ivan Rodriguez .75 .23
66 Gabe Kapler .40 .12
67 Rafael Palmeiro .50 .15
68 Frank Catalanotto .40 .12
69 Mark Teixeira .60 .18
Carlos Pena
70 Alex Rodriguez TC .75 .23
71 Nomar Garciaparra 1.25 .35
72 Pedro Martinez .75 .23
73 Trot Nixon .40 .12
74 Dante Bichette .40 .12
75 Manny Ramirez .50 .15
76 Carl Everett .40 .12
77 Hideo Nomo .75 .23
78 Dernell Stenson .40 .12
Juan Diaz
79 Manny Ramirez TC .40 .12
80 Mike Sweeney .40 .12
81 Carlos Febles .40 .12
82 Dee Brown .40 .12
83 Neifi Perez .40 .12
84 Mark Quinn .40 .12
85 Carlos Beltran .50 .15
86 Joe Randa .40 .12
87 Ken Harvey .40 .12
Mike MacDougal
88 Mike Sweeney TC .40 .12
89 Dean Palmer .40 .12
90 Jeff Weaver .40 .12
91 Jose Lima .40 .12
92 Tony Clark .40 .12
93 Damion Easley .40 .12
94 Bobby Higginson .40 .12
95 Robert Fick .40 .12
96 Pedro Santana .40 .12
Mike Rivera
97 Juan Encarnacion .40 .12
Roger Cedeno TC
98 Doug Mientkiewicz .40 .12
99 David Ortiz .50 .15
100 Joe Mays .40 .12
101 Corey Koskie .40 .12
102 Eric Milton .40 .12
103 Cristian Guzman .40 .12
104 Brad Radke .40 .12
105 Adam Johnson .40 .12
Juan Rincon
106 Corey Koskie TC .40 .12
107 Frank Thomas .75 .23
108 Carlos Lee .40 .12
109 Mark Buehrle .40 .12
110 Jose Canseco .75 .23
111 Magglio Ordonez .40 .12
112 Jon Garland .40 .12
113 Ray Durham .40 .12
114 Joe Crede .40 .12
Josh Fogg
115 Carlos Lee TC .40 .12
116 Derek Jeter 2.00 .60
117 Roger Clemens 1.50 .45
118 Alfonso Soriano .50 .15
119 Paul O'Neill .50 .15
120 Jorge Posada .50 .15
121 Bernie Williams .50 .15
122 Mariano Rivera .50 .15
123 Tino Martinez .50 .15
124 Mike Mussina .50 .15
125 Nick Johnson .40 .12
Erick Almonte
126 Jorge Posada .75 .23
David Justice
Scott Brosius TC
127 Jeff Bagwell .50 .15
128 Wade Miller .40 .12
129 Lance Berkman .40 .12
130 Moises Alou .40 .12
131 Craig Biggio .50 .15
132 Roy Oswalt .40 .12
133 Richard Hidalgo .40 .12
134 Morgan Ensberg .40 .12
Tim Redding
135 Lance Berkman .40 .12
Richard Hidalgo TC
136 Greg Maddux 1.25 .35
137 Chipper Jones .75 .23
138 Brian Jordan .40 .12
139 Marcus Giles .40 .12
140 Andruw Jones .40 .12
141 Tom Glavine .50 .15
142 Rafael Furcal .40 .12
143 Wilson Betemit .40 .12
Horacio Ramirez
144 Chipper Jones .50 .15
Brian Jordan TC
145 Jeromy Burnitz .40 .12
146 Ben Sheets .40 .12
147 Geoff Jenkins .40 .12
148 Devon White .40 .12
149 Jimmy Haynes .40 .12
150 Richie Sexson .40 .12
151 Jose Hernandez .40 .12
152 Jose Mieses .40 .12
Alex Sanchez
153 Richie Sexson TC .40 .12
154 Mark McGwire 2.00 .60
155 Albert Pujols 1.50 .45
156 Matt Morris .40 .12
157 J.D. Drew .40 .12
158 Jim Edmonds .40 .12
159 Bud Smith .40 .12
160 Darryl Kile .40 .12
161 Bill Ortega .40 .12
Luis Saturria
162 Albert Pujols 1.50 .45
Mark McGwire TC
163 Sammy Sosa 1.25 .35
164 Jon Lieber .40 .12
165 Eric Young .40 .12
166 Kerry Wood .75 .23
167 Fred McGriff .50 .15
168 Corey Patterson .40 .12
169 Rondell White .40 .12
170 Juan Cruz 2.00 .60
Mark Prior
171 Sammy Sosa TC .75 .23
172 Luis Gonzalez .40 .12
173 Randy Johnson .75 .23
174 Matt Williams .40 .12
175 Mark Grace .50 .15
176 Steve Finley .40 .12
177 Reggie Sanders .40 .12
178 Curt Schilling .40 .12
179 Alex Cintron .40 .12
Jack Cust
180 Arizona Diamondbacks TC .75 .23
181 Gary Sheffield .40 .12
182 Paul LoDuca .40 .12
183 Chan Ho Park .40 .12
184 Shawn Green .40 .12
185 Eric Karros .40 .12
186 Adrian Beltre .50 .15
187 Kevin Brown .40 .12
188 Ricardo Rodriguez .40 .12
Carlos Garcia
189 Shawn Green .40 .12
Gary Sheffield TC
190 Vladimir Guerrero .75 .23
191 Javier Vazquez .40 .12
192 Jose Vidro .40 .12
193 Fernando Tatis .40 .12
194 Orlando Cabrera .40 .12
195 Lee Stevens .40 .12
196 Tony Armas Jr. .40 .12
197 Donnie Bridges .40 .12
Henry Mateo
198 Vladimir Guerrero .50 .15
Jose Vidro TC
199 Barry Bonds 2.00 .60
200 Rich Aurilia .40 .12
201 Russ Ortiz .40 .12
202 Jeff Kent .40 .12
203 Jason Schmidt .40 .12
204 John Vander Wal .40 .12
205 Robb Nen .40 .12
206 Yorvit Torrealba .40 .12
Kurt Ainsworth
207 Barry Bonds TC .75 .23
208 Preston Wilson .40 .12
209 Brad Penny .40 .12
210 Cliff Floyd .40 .12
211 Luis Castillo .40 .12
212 Ryan Dempster .40 .12
213 Charles Johnson .40 .12
214 A.J. Burnett .40 .12
215 Abraham Nunez .40 .12
Josh Beckett
216 Cliff Floyd TC .40 .12
217 Mike Piazza 1.25 .35
218 Al Leiter .40 .12
219 Edgardo Alfonzo .40 .12
220 Tsuyoshi Shinjo .40 .12
221 Matt Lawton .40 .12
222 Robin Ventura .40 .12
223 Jay Payton .40 .12
224 Alex Escobar .40 .12
Jae Weong Seo
225 Mike Piazza .75 .23
Robin Ventura TC
226 Ryan Klesko .40 .12
227 D'Angelo Jimenez .40 .12
228 Trevor Hoffman .40 .12
229 Phil Nevin .40 .12
230 Mark Kotsay .40 .12
231 Brian Lawrence .40 .12
232 Bubba Trammell .40 .12
233 Jason Middlebrook .40 .12
Xavier Nady
234 Tony Gwynn TC .50 .15
235 Scott Rolen .75 .23
236 Jimmy Rollins .40 .12
237 Mike Lieberthal .40 .12
238 Bobby Abreu .40 .12
239 Brandon Duckworth .40 .12
240 Robert Person .40 .12
241 Pat Burrell .40 .12
242 Nick Punto .40 .12
Carlos Silva
243 Mike Lieberthal TC .40 .12
244 Brian Giles .40 .12
245 Jack Wilson .40 .12
246 Kris Benson .40 .12
247 Jason Kendall .40 .12
248 Aramis Ramirez .40 .12
249 Todd Ritchie .40 .12
250 Rob Mackowiak .40 .12
251 John Grabow .40 .12
Humberto Cota
252 Brian Giles TC .40 .12
253 Ken Griffey Jr. 1.25 .35
254 Barry Larkin .50 .15
255 Sean Casey .40 .12
256 Aaron Boone .40 .12
257 Dmitri Young .40 .12
258 Pokey Reese .40 .12
259 Adam Dunn .50 .15
260 David Espinosa .40 .12
Dane Sardinha
261 Ken Griffey TC .75 .23
262 Todd Helton .50 .15
263 Mike Hampton .40 .12
264 Juan Pierre .40 .12
265 Larry Walker .50 .15
266 Juan Uribe .40 .12
267 Jose Ortiz .40 .12
268 Jeff Cirillo .40 .12
269 Jason Jennings .40 .12
Luke Hudson
270 Larry Walker TC .40 .12
271 Ichiro Suzuki .75 .23
Jason Giambi
Roberto Alomar LL
272 Larry Walker .40 .12
Todd Helton
Moises Alou LL
273 Alex Rodriguez .50 .15
Jim Thome
Rafael Palmeiro LL
274 Barry Bonds 1.00 .30
Sammy Sosa
Luis Gonzalez LL
274A Barry Bonds 15.00 4.50
Sammy Sosa
Luis Gonzalez LL ERR
Card has AL Home Run Leaders
No player names on cards
275 Mark Mulder .50 .15
Roger Clemens
Jamie Moyer LL
276 Curt Schilling .50 .15
Matt Morris
Randy Johnson LL
277 Freddy Garcia .40 .12
Mike Mussina
Joe Mays LL
278 Randy Johnson .50 .15
Curt Schilling
John Burkett LL
279 Mariano Rivera .40 .12
Kazuhiro Sasaki
Keith Foulke LL
280 Robb Nen .50 .15
Armando Benitez
Trevor Hoffman LL
281 Jason Giambi PS .40 .12
282 Jorge Posada PS .40 .12
283 Jim Thome .50 .15
Juan Gonzalez PS
284 Edgar Martinez PS .40 .12
285 Andruw Jones PS .40 .12
286 Chipper Jones PS .50 .15
287 Matt Williams PS .40 .12
288 Curt Schilling PS .40 .12
289 Derek Jeter PS 1.00 .30
290 Mike Mussina PS .40 .12
291 Bret Boone PS .40 .12
292 Alfonso Soriano PS UER .40 .12
Alfonso is spelled incorrectly
293 Randy Johnson PS .50 .15
294 Tom Glavine PS .50 .15
295 Curt Schilling PS .40 .12
296 Randy Johnson PS .50 .15
297 Derek Jeter PS 1.00 .30
298 Tino Martinez PS .40 .12
299 Curt Schilling PS .40 .12
300 Luis Gonzalez PS .40 .12

2002 Upper Deck Vintage Aces Game Jersey

Inserted into packs at stated odds of one in 144 hobby and one in 210 retail, these 14 cards feature a mix of active and retired pitchers along with a game jersey swatch. Roger Clemens was produced in shorter quantity than the other players and we have notated that with an SP in our checklist.

Nm-Mt Ex-Mt
A-FJ Ferguson Jenkins 15.00 4.50
A-GM Greg Maddux 25.00 7.50
A-HN Hideo Nomo 40.00 12.00
A-JD John Denny 10.00 3.00
A-JM Juan Marichal 15.00 4.50
A-JS Johnny Sain 25.00 7.50
A-MMA Mike Marshall 15.00 4.50
A-MMU Mike Mussina 25.00 7.50
A-MT Mike Torrez 10.00 3.00
A-NR Nolan Ryan 120.00 36.00
A-PM Pedro Martinez 25.00 7.50
A-RC Roger Clemens SP
A-RJ Randy Johnson 25.00 7.50
A-TH Tim Hudson 15.00 4.50

2002 Upper Deck Vintage Day At The Park

Inserted into packs at stated odds of one in 23, these six cards feature active players in a design dedicated to capturing the nostalgia of Baseball.

Nm-Mt Ex-Mt
COMPLETE SET (6) 20.00 6.00
DP1 Ichiro Suzuki 4.00 1.20
DP2 Derek Jeter 6.00 1.80
DP3 Alex Rodriguez 4.00 1.20
DP4 Mark McGwire 6.00 1.80
DP5 Barry Bonds 6.00 1.80
DP6 Sammy Sosa 4.00 1.20

2002 Upper Deck Vintage Night Gamers

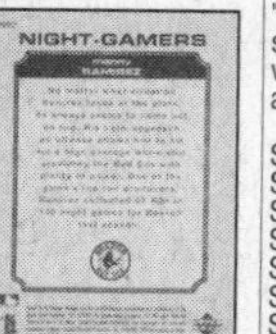

Inserted into packs at stated odds of one in 11, these 12 cards features a salute to primetime games with some of the leading players.

Nm-Mt Ex-Mt
COMPLETE SET (12) 15.00 4.50
NG1 Todd Helton 1.00 .30
NG2 Manny Ramirez 1.00 .30
NG3 Ivan Rodriguez 1.50 .45
NG4 Albert Pujols 3.00 .90
NG5 Greg Maddux 2.50 .75
NG6 Carlos Delgado 1.00 .30
NG7 Frank Thomas 1.50 .45
NG8 Derek Jeter 4.00 1.20
NG9 Troy Glaus 1.00 .30
NG10 Jeff Bagwell 1.00 .30
NG11 Juan Gonzalez 1.00 .30
NG12 Randy Johnson 1.50 .45

2002 Upper Deck Vintage Sandlot Stars

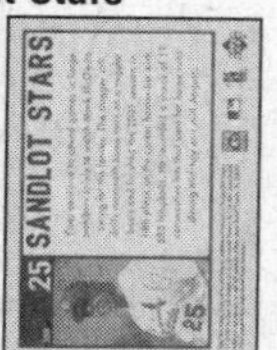

Inserted in packs at stated odds of one in 11, these 12 cards feature some of today's stars in a playful salute to the old days where many players were "discovered" while playing sandlot ball.

Nm-Mt Ex-Mt
COMPLETE SET (12) 20.00 6.00
SS1 Ken Griffey Jr. 2.50 .75
SS2 Derek Jeter 4.00 1.20
SS3 Ichiro Suzuki 2.50 .75
SS4 Nomar Garciaparra 2.50 .75
SS5 Sammy Sosa 2.50 .75
SS6 Chipper Jones 1.50 .45
SS7 Jason Giambi 1.50 .45
SS8 Alex Rodriguez 2.50 .75
SS9 Mark McGwire 4.00 1.20
SS10 Barry Bonds 4.00 1.20
SS11 Mike Piazza 2.50 .75
SS12 Vladimir Guerrero 1.50 .45

2002 Upper Deck Vintage Signature Combos

Randomly inserted in packs, these nine cards feature two signatures of various baseball stars on each card. These cards all have a stated print run of 100 copies.

Nm-Mt Ex-Mt
VS-AT Roberto Alomar 100.00 30.00
Jim Thome
VS-BB Yogi Berra 150.00 45.00
Johnny Bench
VS-BR Sal Bando 50.00 15.00
Joe Rudi
VS-EL Dwight Evans 80.00 24.00
Fred Lynn
VS-FB Carlton Fisk 120.00 36.00
Johnny Bench
VS-GR Ken Griffey Jr. 400.00 120.00
Alex Rodriguez
VS-JM Reggie Jackson 120.00 36.00
Willie McCovey
VS-JO Edgar Martinez 80.00 24.00
John Olerud
VS-SD Ryne Sandberg 150.00 45.00
Andre Dawson

2002 Upper Deck Vintage Special Collection Game Jersey

Issued in packs at stated odds of one in 14 hobby and one in 210 retail, these 15 cards feature past and present stars along with a memorabilia swatch. A few players were produced in smaller quantities and we have notated those players with an SP in our checklist. These cards honored players from the famed Oakland A's "Mustache Gang" which won three straight world series in the 1970's and various Cubs stars who were still looking for their first World Series appearance since 1945.

Nm-Mt Ex-Mt
S-AD Andre Dawson Pants 15.00 4.50
S-BC Bert Campaneris Jsy 15.00 4.50
S-BW Billy Williams Jsy 15.00 4.50
S-CH Catfish Hunter Jsy SP
S-FJ Fergie Jenkins Pants SP 15.00 4.50
S-JR Joe Rudi Jsy 15.00 4.50
S-MG Mark Grace Jsy 20.00 6.00
S-MH Mike Hegan Jsy 10.00 3.00
S-PL Paul Lindblad Jsy 10.00 3.00
S-RF Rollie Fingers Jsy 15.00 4.50
S-RJ Reggie Jackson Jsy SP 20.00 6.00
S-RS Ryne Sandberg Jsy 50.00 15.00
S-SAB Sal Bando Jsy 15.00 4.50
S-SS Sammy Sosa Jsy 30.00 9.00
S-STB Stan Bahnsen Jsy 10.00 3.00

2002 Upper Deck Vintage Timeless Teams Game Bat Quads

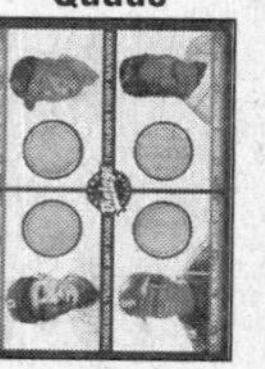

Issued in packs at stated odds of one in 288 hobby and one in 480 retail, these eight cards feature either teammates or position mates along with a bat chip from each of these players career.

Nm-Mt Ex-Mt
B Hank Greenberg 40.00 12.00
Willie McCovey
Frank Thomas
Eddie Murray
OF2 Ken Griffey Jr. 60.00 18.00
Barry Bonds
Rickey Henderson
Tony Gwynn
ATL Tom Glavine 50.00 15.00
Greg Maddux
Chipper Jones
Andruw Jones
CLE Juan Gonzalez 40.00 12.00
Jim Thome
Roberto Alomar
Kenny Lofton
NYY Mariano Rivera 50.00 15.00
Bernie Williams
Paul O'Neill
Jorge Posada
OAK Dave Parker 40.00 12.00
Jose Canseco
Rickey Henderson
Don Baylor
SEA Ichiro Suzuki 80.00 24.00
Edgar Martinez
John Olerud
Bret Boone
OFNY Mickey Mantle
Joe DiMaggio
Reggie Jackson
Babe Ruth SP

2002 Upper Deck Vintage Timeless Teams Game Jersey

Issued in packs at stated odds of one in 144 hobby and one in 210 retail, these 14 cards feature players from a great team of the past or present along with a jersey swatch. Some players were produced in shorter quantities and we

have notated those players with an SP in our checklist.

Nm-Mt Ex-Mt
J-AJ Andruw Jones Jsy 15.00 4.50
J-CH Catfish Hunter Jsy 20.00 6.00
J-CJ Chipper Jones Jsy 20.00 6.00
J-DE Dwight Evans Jsy 20.00 6.00
J-EMA Edgar Martinez Jsy 20.00 6.00
J-EMU Eddie Murray Jsy 25.00 7.50
J-FL Fred Lynn Jsy 20.00 6.00
J-GM Greg Maddux Jsy SP
J-IS Ichiro Suzuki Pants SP
J-JB Johnny Bench Jsy 25.00 7.50
J-KS Kazuhiro Sasaki Jsy 15.00 4.50
J-RF Rollie Fingers Jsy 20.00 6.00
J-RJ Reggie Jackson Jsy 20.00 6.00
J-WM Willie McCovey Pants 20.00 6.00

2002 Upper Deck Vintage Timeless Teams Game Jersey Combos

Issued in hobby packs at stated odds one in 288, these four cards feature either teammates or players with something in common along with a jersey swatch of all three players featured. The card featuring the three Hall of Famers was produced in smaller quantites than the other cards and we have notated that with an SP in our checklist.

Nm-Mt Ex-Mt
ATL Greg Maddux 60.00 18.00
Chipper Jones
Andruw Jones
HOF Ty Cobb
Babe Ruth
Honus Wagner SP
NYY Roger Clemens 60.00 18.00
Mariano Rivera
Bernie Williams
OAK Rollie Fingers 50.00 15.00
Catfish Hunter
Reggie Jackson

2003 Upper Deck Vintage

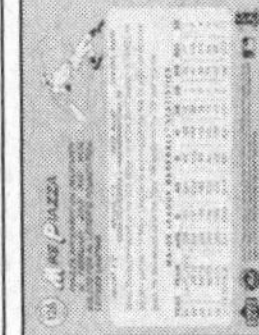

This 280 card set, designed to resemble the 1965 Topps set, was released in January 2003. This set was issued in eight card packs which came 24 packs to a box and 12 boxes to a case. These packs had an SRP of $2. Cards numbered from 223 through 232 feature a pair of prospects from an organiztion. Cards numbered from 233 through 247 are titled Stellar Stat Men. Cards from 248 through 277 were produced in a style reminscent of the Kellogs 3-D cards of the 1970's. Those 3D cards were seeded at a rate of one in 48. In addition, there were other short print cards scattered throughout the set. Those cards which we have noted as either SP, TR1 SP or TR2 SP were inserted at a rate between one in 20 and one in 40. Please note, Eddie Mathews is listed below as card 37 (as was the manufacturer's original intent), but the card is mistakenly numbered as 376. Jason Jennings who was supposed to be card number 178 was mistakenly numbered as 28. In addition, cards number 281 through 341 were later issued at a stated rate of one per Upper Deck 40-man pack.

Nm-Mt Ex-Mt
COMP.SET w/o SP's (200) 50.00 15.00
COMP.UPDATE SET (60) 15.00 4.50
COMMON ACTIVE (1-280) .30 .09
COMMON RETIRED .60 .18
COMMON SP (1-220) 5.00 1.50
COMMON TR1 SP 5.00 1.50
COMMON TR2 SP 5.00 1.50
COMMON CARD (223-232) 2.00 .60
COMMON CARD (233-247) 2.00 .60
COMMON CARD (248-277) 10.00 3.00
COMMON CARD (281-341) .40 .12
COMMON RC (281-341) .40 .12
281-341 ONE PER 2003 UD 40-MAN PACK
1 Troy Glaus .30 .09
2 Darin Erstad .30 .09
3 Garret Anderson .30 .09
4 Jarrod Washburn .30 .09
5 Nolan Ryan 4.00 1.20
6 Tim Salmon .50 .15
7 Troy Percival .30 .09
8 Alex Ochoa TR1 SP 5.00 1.50
9 Daryle Ward .30 .09
10 Jeff Bagwell .50 .15
11 Roy Oswalt .30 .09
12 Lance Berkman .30 .09
13 Craig Biggio .50 .15
14 Richard Hidalgo .30 .09
15 Tim Hudson .30 .09
16 Eric Chavez .30 .09
17 Barry Zito .30 .09
18 Miguel Tejada .30 .09
19 Mark Mulder .30 .09
20 Rollie Fingers .60 .18
21 Catfish Hunter 1.00 .30
22 Jermaine Dye .30 .09
23 Ray Durham TR2 SP 5.00 1.50
24 Carlos Delgado .30 .09
25 Eric Hinske .30 .09
26 Josh Phelps .30 .09
27 Shannon Stewart .30 .09
28 Vernon Wells .30 .09
29 John Smoltz .50 .15
30 Greg Maddux 1.25 .35
31 Chipper Jones .75 .23
32 Gary Sheffield .30 .09
33 Andruw Jones .30 .09
34 Tom Glavine .50 .15
35 Rafael Furcal .30 .09
36 Phil Niekro .60 .18
37 Eddie Mathews UER 376 1.50 .45
38 Robin Yount 2.50 .75
39 Richie Sexson .30 .09
40 Ben Sheets .30 .09
41 Geoff Jenkins .30 .09
42 Alex Sanchez .30 .09
43 Jason Isringhausen .30 .09
44 Albert Pujols 1.50 .45
45 Matt Morris .30 .09
46 J.D. Drew .30 .09
47 Jim Edmonds .30 .09
48 Stan Musial 2.50 .75
49 Red Schoendienst .60 .18
50 Edgar Renteria .30 .09
51 Mark McGwire SP 12.00 3.60
52 Scott Rolen TR2 SP 8.00 2.40
53 Mark Bellhorn .30 .09
54 Kerry Wood .75 .23
55 Mark Prior .75 .23
56 Moises Alou .30 .09
57 Corey Patterson .30 .09
58 Ernie Banks 1.50 .45
59 Hee Seop Choi .30 .09
60 Billy Williams .60 .18
61 Sammy Sosa SP 10.00 3.00
62 Ben Grieve .30 .09
63 Jared Sandberg .30 .09
64 Carl Crawford .30 .09
65 Randy Johnson .75 .23
66 Luis Gonzalez .30 .09
67 Steve Finley .30 .09
68 Junior Spivey .30 .09
69 Erubiel Durazo .30 .09
70 Curt Schilling SP 5.00 1.50
71 Al Lopez .60 .18
72 Pee Wee Reese 1.00 .30
73 Eric Gagne .75 .23
74 Shawn Green .30 .09
75 Kevin Brown .30 .09
76 Paul Lo Duca .30 .09
77 Adrian Beltre .50 .15
78 Hideo Nomo .75 .23
79 Eric Karros .30 .09
80 Odalis Perez .30 .09
81 Kazuhisa Ishii SP 5.00 1.50
82 Tommy Lasorda .60 .18
83 Fernando Tatis .30 .09
84 Vladimir Guerrero .75 .23
85 Jose Vidro .30 .09
86 Javier Vazquez .30 .09
87 Brad Wilkerson .30 .09
88 Bartolo Colon TR1 SP 5.00 1.50
89 Monte Irvin .60 .18
90 Robb Nen .30 .09
91 Reggie Sanders .30 .09
92 Jeff Kent .30 .09
93 Rich Aurilia .30 .09
94 Orlando Cepeda .60 .18
95 Juan Marichal .60 .18
96 Willie McCovey .60 .18
97 David Bell .30 .09
98 Barry Bonds SP 12.00 3.60
99 Kenny Lofton TR2 SP 5.00 1.50
100 Jim Thome .75 .23
101 C.C. Sabathia .30 .09
102 Omar Vizquel .50 .15
103 Lou Boudreau .60 .18
104 Larry Doby .60 .18
105 Bob Lemon .60 .18
106 John Olerud .30 .09
107 Edgar Martinez .50 .15
108 Bret Boone .30 .09
109 Freddy Garcia .30 .09
110 Mike Cameron .30 .09
111 Kazuhiro Sasaki .30 .09
112 Ichiro Suzuki SP 10.00 3.00
113 Mike Lowell .30 .09
114 Josh Beckett .30 .09
115 A.J. Burnett .30 .09
116 Juan Pierre .30 .09
117 Derrek Lee .30 .09
118 Luis Castillo .30 .09
119 Juan Encarnacion TR1 SP 5.00 1.50
120 Roberto Alomar .50 .15
121 Edgardo Alfonzo .30 .09
122 Jeromy Burnitz .30 .09
123 Mo Vaughn .30 .09
124 Tom Seaver 1.00 .30
125 Al Leiter .30 .09
126 Mike Piazza SP 10.00 3.00
127 Tony Batista .30 .09
128 Geronimo Gil .30 .09
129 Chris Singleton .30 .09
130 Rodrigo Lopez .30 .09
131 Jay Gibbons .30 .09
132 Melvin Mora .30 .09
133 Earl Weaver .60 .18
134 Trevor Hoffman .30 .09
135 Phil Nevin .30 .09
136 Sean Burroughs .30 .09
137 Ryan Klesko .30 .09
138 Mark Kotsay .30 .09
139 Mike Lieberthal .30 .09
140 Bobby Abreu .30 .09
141 Jimmy Rollins .30 .09
142 Pat Burrell .30 .09
143 Vicente Padilla .30 .09
144 Richie Ashburn 1.00 .30
145 Jeremy Giambi TR1 SP 5.00 1.50
146 Josh Fogg .30 .09
147 Brian Giles .30 .09
148 Aramis Ramirez .30 .09
149 Jason Kendall .30 .09
150 Ralph Kiner .60 .18
151 Willie Stargell 1.00 .30
152 Kevin Mench .30 .09
153 Rafael Palmeiro .50 .15
154 Ivan Rodriguez .75 .23
155 Hank Blalock .50 .15
156 Juan Gonzalez .50 .15
157 Carl Everett .30 .09
158 Alex Rodriguez SP 10.00 3.00
159 Nomar Garciaparra 1.25 .35
160 Derek Lowe .30 .09
161 Manny Ramirez .50 .15
162 Shea Hillenbrand .30 .09
163 Bobby Doerr .60 .18
164 Johnny Damon .75 .23
165 Jason Varitek .50 .15
166 Pedro Martinez SP 8.00 2.40
167 Cliff Floyd TR2 SP 5.00 1.50
168 Ken Griffey Jr. 1.25 .35
169 Adam Dunn .50 .15
170 Austin Kearns .30 .09
171 Aaron Boone .30 .09
172 Joe Morgan .60 .18
173 Sean Casey .30 .09
174 Todd Walker .30 .09
175 Ryan Dempster TR1 SP 5.00 1.50
176 Shawn Estes TR1 SP 5.00 1.50
177 Gabe Kapler TR1 SP 5.00 1.50
178 Jason Jennings UER .30 .09
Card numbered as 28
179 Todd Helton .50 .15
180 Larry Walker .50 .15
181 Preston Wilson .30 .09
182 Jay Payton TR1 SP 5.00 1.50
183 Mike Sweeney .30 .09
184 Carlos Beltran .50 .15
185 Paul Byrd .30 .09
186 Raul Ibanez .30 .09
187 Rick Ferrell .60 .18
188 Early Wynn .60 .18
189 Dmitri Young .30 .09
190 Jim Bunning 1.00 .30
191 George Kell .60 .18
192 Hal Newhouser .60 .18
193 Bobby Higginson .30 .09
194 Carlos Pena TR1 SP 5.00 1.50
195 Sparky Anderson .60 .18
196 Torii Hunter .30 .09
197 Eric Milton .30 .09
198 Corey Koskie .30 .09
199 Jacque Jones .30 .09
200 Harmon Killebrew 1.50 .45
201 Doug Mientkiewicz .30 .09
202 Frank Thomas .75 .23
203 Mark Buehrle .30 .09
204 Magglio Ordonez .30 .09
205 Paul Konerko .30 .09
206 Joe Borchard .30 .09
207 Hoyt Wilhelm .60 .18
208 Carlos Lee .30 .09
209 Roger Clemens 1.50 .45
210 Nick Johnson .30 .09
211 Jason Giambi .30 .09
212 Alfonso Soriano .50 .15
213 Bernie Williams .50 .15
214 Robin Ventura .30 .09
215 Jorge Posada .50 .15
216 Mike Mussina .50 .15
217 Yogi Berra 1.50 .45
218 Phil Rizzuto 1.00 .30
219 Mariano Rivera .50 .15
220 Derek Jeter SP 12.00 3.60
221 Jeff Weaver TR1 SP 5.00 1.50
222 Raul Mondesi TR2 SP 5.00 1.50
223 Freddy Sanchez 2.00 .60
Josh Hancock
224 Joe Borchard 2.00 .60
Miguel Olivo
225 Brandon Phillips 2.00 .60
Josh Bard
226 Andy Van Hekken 2.00 .60
Andres Torres
227 Jason Lane 2.00 .60
Jeriome Robertson
228 Chin-Feng Chen 2.00 .60
Joe Thurston
229 Endy Chavez 2.00 .60
Jamey Carroll
230 Drew Henson 2.00 .60
Alex Graman
231 Dewon Brazelton 2.00 .60
Lance Carter
232 Jayson Werth 2.00 .60
Kevin Cash
233 Randy Johnson 3.00 .90
Curt Schilling
Barry Zito
234 Pedro Martinez 3.00 .90
Randy Johnson
Derek Lowe
235 Randy Johnson 3.00 .90
Curt Schilling
Pedro Martinez
236 John Smoltz 3.00 .90
Eric Gagne
Mike Williams
237 Randy Johnson 3.00 .90
Bartolo Colon
A.J. Burnett
238 Alfonso Soriano 4.00 1.20
Ichiro Suzuki
Vladimir Guerrero
239 Alex Rodriguez 4.00 1.20
Jim Thome
Sammy Sosa
240 Barry Bonds 4.00 1.20
Manny Ramirez
Mike Sweeney
241 Alfonso Soriano 4.00 1.20
Alex Rodriguez
Derek Jeter
242 Alex Rodriguez 4.00 1.20
Magglio Ordonez
Miguel Tejada
243 Luis Castillo 2.00 .60
Juan Pierre
Dave Roberts
244 Nomar Garciaparra 4.00 1.20
Garrett Anderson
Alfonso Soriano
245 Johnny Damon 4.00 1.20
Jimmy Rollins
Kenny Lofton
246 Barry Bonds 4.00 1.20
Jim Thome
Manny Ramirez
247 Barry Bonds 4.00 1.20
Brian Giles
Manny Ramirez
248 Troy Glaus 3D 10.00 3.00
249 Luis Gonzalez 3D 10.00 3.00
250 Chipper Jones 3D 15.00 4.50
251 Nomar Garciaparra 3D 15.00 4.50
252 Manny Ramirez 3D 15.00 4.50
253 Sammy Sosa 3D 15.00 4.50
254 Frank Thomas 3D 15.00 4.50
255 Magglio Ordonez 3D 10.00 3.00
256 Adam Dunn 3D 15.00 4.50
257 Ken Griffey Jr. 3D 15.00 4.50
258 Jim Thome 3D 15.00 4.50
259 Todd Helton 3D 15.00 4.50
260 Larry Walker 3D 15.00 4.50
261 Lance Berkman 3D 10.00 3.00
262 Jeff Bagwell 3D 15.00 4.50
263 Mike Sweeney 3D 10.00 3.00
264 Shawn Green 3D 10.00 3.00
265 Vladimir Guerrero 3D 15.00 4.50
266 Mike Piazza 3D 15.00 4.50
267 Jason Giambi 3D 10.00 3.00
268 Pat Burrell 3D 10.00 3.00
269 Barry Bonds 3D 25.00 7.50
270 Mark McGwire 3D 25.00 7.50
271 Alex Rodriguez 3D 20.00 6.00
272 Carlos Delgado 3D 10.00 3.00
273 Richie Sexson 3D 10.00 3.00
274 Andruw Jones 3D 10.00 3.00
275 Derek Jeter 3D 25.00 7.50
276 Juan Gonzalez 3D 15.00 4.50
277 Albert Pujols 3D 20.00 6.00
278 Jason Giambi CL .30 .09
279 Sammy Sosa CL .75 .23
280 Ichiro Suzuki CL .75 .23
281 Tom Glavine .60 .18
282 Josh Stewart RC .40 .12
283 Aquilino Lopez RC .40 .12
284 Horacio Ramirez .40 .12
285 Brandon Phillips .40 .12
286 Kirk Saarloos .40 .12
287 Runelvys Hernandez .40 .12
288 Hideki Matsui RC 4.00 1.20
289 Jeremy Bonderman RC .75 .23
290 Russ Ortiz .40 .12
291 Ken Harvey .40 .12
292 Edgardo Alfonzo .40 .12
293 Oscar Villareal RC .40 .12
294 Marlon Byrd .40 .12
295 Josh Bard .40 .12
296 David Cone .40 .12
297 Mike Neu RC .40 .12
298 Cliff Floyd .40 .12
299 Travis Lee .40 .12
300 Jeff Kent .40 .12
301 Ron Calloway .40 .12
302 Bartolo Colon .40 .12
303 Jose Contreras RC 1.25 .35
304 Mark Teixeira .40 .12
305 Ivan Rodriguez 1.00 .30
306 Jim Thome 1.00 .30
307 Shane Reynolds .40 .12
308 Luis Ayala RC .40 .12
309 Lyle Overbay .40 .12
310 Travis Hafner .40 .12
311 Wilfredo Ledezma RC .60 .18
312 Rocco Baldelli .40 .12
313 Jason Anderson .40 .12
314 Kenny Lofton .40 .12
315 Brandon Larson .40 .12
316 Ty Wigginton .40 .12
317 Fred McGriff .60 .18
318 Antonio Osuna .40 .12
319 Corey Patterson .40 .12
320 Erubiel Durazo .40 .12
321 Mike MacDougal .40 .12
322 Sammy Sosa 1.50 .45
323 Mike Hampton .40 .12
324 Ramiro Mendoza .40 .12
325 Kevin Millwood .40 .12
326 Dave Roberts .40 .12
327 Todd Zeile .40 .12
328 Reggie Sanders .40 .12
329 Billy Koch .40 .12
330 Mike Stanton .40 .12
331 Orlando Hernandez .40 .12
332 Tony Clark .40 .12
333 Chris Hammond .40 .12
334 Michael Cuddyer .40 .12
335 Sandy Alomar Jr. .40 .12
336 Jose Cruz Jr. .40 .12
337 Omar Daal .40 .12
338 Robert Fick .40 .12
339 Daryle Ward .40 .12
340 David Bell .40 .12
341 Checklist .40 .12

2003 Upper Deck Vintage All Caps

Randomly inserted into packs, these 15 cards feature swatches of game-used caps. Each of these cards have a stated print run of 250 serial numbered sets.

Nm-Mt Ex-Mt
CP Chan Ho Park 15.00 4.50
DE Darin Erstad 15.00 4.50
GM Greg Maddux 40.00 12.00
JB Jeff Bagwell 20.00 6.00
JG Juan Gonzalez 20.00 6.00
KS Kazuhiro Sasaki 15.00 4.50
LB Lance Berkman 15.00 4.50
LG Luis Gonzalez 15.00 4.50
MP Mike Piazza 40.00 12.00
MV Mo Vaughn 15.00 4.50
RF Rafael Furcal 15.00 4.50
RP Rafael Palmeiro 20.00 6.00
RV Robin Ventura 15.00 4.50
TG Tony Gwynn 25.00 7.50
TH Tim Hudson 15.00 4.50

2003 Upper Deck Vintage Capping the Action

Randomly inserted into packs, these 15 cards feature pieces of game-worn caps embedded into the card. Each of these cards were issued to a stated print run of between 91 and 125 copies.

Nm-Mt Ex-Mt
AR Alex Rodriguez/101 40.00 12.00
AS Alfonso Soriano/109 25.00 7.50
CD Carlos Delgado/91 20.00 6.00
HM Hideo Nomo/117 60.00 18.00
IR Ivan Rodriguez/125 25.00 7.50
JG Juan Gonzalez/99 25.00 7.50
KG Ken Griffey Jr./102 40.00 12.00
MM Mike Mussina/109 50.00 15.00
PM Pedro Martinez/125 25.00 7.50
RA Roberto Alomar/101 25.00 7.50
RP Rafael Palmeiro/125 25.00 7.50
SG Shawn Green/125 20.00 6.00
SR Scott Rolen/109 25.00 7.50
SS Sammy Sosa/125 40.00 12.00
TH Todd Helton/99 25.00 7.50

2003 Upper Deck Vintage Cracking the Lumber

Randomly inserted into packs, these two cards feature authentic game-used bat chips of either Ichiro Suzuki or Jason Giambi. These cards were issued to a stated print run of 25 serial numbered sets. Due to marrket scarcity, no pricing is provided.

Nm-Mt Ex-Mt
GOLD PRINT RUN 5 SERIAL #'d SETS
RANDOM INSERTS IN PACKS
NO PRICING DUE TO SCARCITY
IS Ichiro Suzuki
JG Jason Giambi

2003 Upper Deck Vintage Crowning Glory

Randomly inserted into packs, these 15 cards feature pieces of game-worn caps attached to the card front. These cards were issued to a stated print run of 25 serial numbered sets. Due to market scarcity, no pricing is provided for these cards.

Nm-Mt Ex-Mt
AJ Andruw Jones
AR Alex Rodriguez
CJ Chipper Jones
GM Greg Maddux
IR Ivan Rodriguez
IS Ichiro Suzuki
JG Jason Giambi
KG Ken Griffey Jr.
LG Luis Gonzalez
MP Mike Piazza
MR Manny Ramirez
PM Pedro Martinez
SC Sean Casey
SG Shawn Green
SS Sammy Sosa

2003 Upper Deck Vintage Dropping the Hammer

Inserted into packs at a stated rate of one in 130, these cards feature game-used bat pieces.

Nm-Mt Ex-Mt
*GOLD: .75X TO 2X BASIC HAMMER.
GOLD RANDOM INSERTS IN PACKS..
GOLD PRINT RUN 100 SERIAL #'d SETS
AJ Andruw Jones 10.00 3.00
AR Alex Rodriguez 20.00 6.00
BA Bobby Abreu 10.00 3.00
DJ David Justice 10.00 3.00
FM Fred McGriff 15.00 4.50
FT Frank Thomas 15.00 4.50
JG Jason Giambi 10.00 3.00
JT Jim Thome 15.00 4.50
KG Ken Griffey Jr. 20.00 6.00
KL Kenny Lofton 10.00 3.00
LB Lance Berkman 10.00 3.00
LW Larry Walker 15.00 4.50
MO Magglio Ordonez 10.00 3.00
MP Mike Piazza 25.00 7.50
MT Miguel Tejada 10.00 3.00
OV Omar Vizquel 15.00 4.50
PW Preston Wilson 10.00 3.00
RA Roberto Alomar 15.00 4.50
RF Rafael Furcal 10.00 3.00
RP Rafael Palmeiro 15.00 4.50
RV Robin Ventura 10.00 3.00
SG Shawn Green 10.00 3.00
SS Sammy Sosa 25.00 7.50
TA Fernando Tatis 10.00 3.00
TH Todd Helton 15.00 4.50

2003 Upper Deck Vintage Hitmen

Randomly inserted into packs, these four cards feature game-used bat pieces from Upper Deck spokespeople. Each of these cards was issued to a stated print run of 150 serial numbered sets.

Nm-Mt Ex-Mt
GOLD PRINT RUN 10 SERIAL #'d SETS
NO GOLD PRICING DUE TO SCARCITY
IS Ichiro Suzuki 80.00 24.00
JG Jason Giambi 15.00 4.50
KG Ken Griffey Jr. 40.00 12.00
MM Mark McGwire 80.00 24.00

2003 Upper Deck Vintage Hitmen Double Signed

Randomly inserted into packs, this card features not only game-used bat chips but authentic signatures from the two leading homer hitters in the summer of 1998. This card was issued to a stated print run of 75 serial numbered sets.

Nm-Mt Ex-Mt
GOLD PRINT RUN 5 SERIAL #'d CARDS
NO GOLD PRICING DUE TO SCARCITY
MS Mark McGwire 700.00 210.00
Sammy Sosa

2003 Upper Deck Vintage Men with Hats

Inserted at a stated rate of one in 285, these 15 cards feature leading players with pieces of game-worn caps embedded in them.

Nm-Mt Ex-Mt
MH-AD Adam Dunn 20.00 6.00
MH-AJ Andruw Jones 15.00 4.50
MH-AR Alex Rodriguez 25.00 7.50
MH-BW Bernie Williams 20.00 6.00
MH-EC Eric Chavez 15.00 4.50
MH-FT Frank Thomas 20.00 6.00
MH-HU Tim Hudson 15.00 4.50
MH-JD Johnny Damon 20.00 6.00
MH-JG Jason Giambi 15.00 4.50
MH-JK Jason Kendall 15.00 4.50
MH-KL Kenny Lofton 15.00 4.50
MH-MT Miguel Tejada 15.00 4.50
MH-TH Todd Helton 20.00 6.00
MH-TW Todd Walker 15.00 4.50
MH-VC Vinny Castilla 15.00 4.50

2003 Upper Deck Vintage Slugfest

Randomly inserted into packs, this 10 card set feature pieces of game-used bat chips honoring some of the leading sluggers in baseball. These cards were issued to a stated print run of 200 serial numbered sets.

Nm-Mt Ex-Mt
*GOLD: .75X TO 2X BASIC SLUGFEST
GOLD PRINT RUN 50 SERIAL #'d SETS
S-AJ Andruw Jones 10.00 3.00
S-AR Alex Rodriguez 25.00 7.50
S-BW Bernie Williams 15.00 4.50
S-CD Carlos Delgado 10.00 3.00
S-FT Frank Thomas 15.00 4.50
S-JT Jim Thome 15.00 4.50
S-LW Larry Walker 15.00 4.50
S-MP Mike Piazza 30.00 9.00
S-RP Rafael Palmeiro 15.00 4.50
S-SG Shawn Green 10.00 3.00

2003 Upper Deck Vintage Timeless Teams Bat Quads

Randomly inserted into packs, this is a set featuring four bat pieces from teammates. These cards were issued to a stated print run of 175 serial numbered sets.

Nm-Mt Ex-Mt
BLAR Pat Burrell 25.00 7.50
Mike Lieberthal
Bobby Abreu
Jimmy Rollins
CTDJ Eric Chavez 25.00 7.50
Miguel Tejada
Jermaine Dye
David Justice
DEMR J.D. Drew 40.00 12.00
Jim Edmonds
Tino Martinez
Scott Rolen
DGCL Adam Dunn 40.00 12.00
Ken Griffey Jr.
Sean Casey
Barry Larkin
GNBL Shawn Green 50.00 15.00
Hideo Nomo
Adrian Beltre
Paul Lo Duca
GPMS Jason Giambi 40.00 12.00
Jorge Posada
Raul Mondesi
Alfonso Soriano
GWVS Jason Giambi 40.00 12.00
Bernie Williams
Robin Ventura
Alfonso Soriano
HWPZ Todd Helton 40.00 12.00
Larry Walker
Juan Pierre
Todd Zeile
IMBC Ichiro Suzuki 100.00 30.00
Edgar Martinez
Bret Boone
Mike Cameron
JGSW Randy Johnson 40.00 12.00
Luis Gonzalez
Curt Schilling
Matt Williams
JJSF Chipper Jones 40.00 12.00
Andruw Jones
Gary Sheffield
Rafael Furcal
KNKB Ryan Klesko 25.00 7.50
Phil Nevin
Mark Kotsay
Sean Burroughs
MGLJ Greg Maddux 60.00 18.00
Tom Glavine
Javy Lopez
Chipper Jones
OTLK Magglio Ordonez 40.00 12.00
Frank Thomas
Carlos Lee
Paul Konerko
PVAA Mike Piazza 60.00 18.00
Mo Vaughn
Roberto Alomar
Edgardo Alfonzo
RGRP Alex Rodriguez 50.00 15.00
Juan Gonzalez
Ivan Rodriguez
Rafael Palmeiro
RMHN Manny Ramirez 40.00 12.00
Pedro Martinez
Shea Hillenbrand
Trot Nixon
SMAP Sammy Sosa 50.00 15.00
Fred McGriff
Moises Alou
Corey Patterson

2003 Upper Deck Vintage UD Giants

Inserted as a sealed box-topper, these 42 cards, which were designed in the style of the 1964 Topps Giant set, feature most of the leading players in baseball.

Nm-Mt Ex-Mt
AD Adam Dunn 3.00 .90
AJ Andruw Jones 3.00 .90
AP Albert Pujols 8.00 2.40
AR Alex Rodriguez 6.00 1.80
BB Barry Bonds 10.00 3.00
BG Brian Giles 3.00 .90
BW Bernie Williams 3.00 .90
CD Carlos Delgado 3.00 .90
CJ Chipper Jones 4.00 1.20
CS Curt Schilling 3.00 .90
FT Frank Thomas 4.00 1.20
GM Greg Maddux 6.00 1.80
GO Juan Gonzalez 3.00 .90
HN Hideo Nomo 4.00 1.20
IR Ivan Rodriguez 4.00 1.20
IS Ichiro Suzuki 6.00 1.80
JB Jeff Bagwell 3.00 .90
JD J.D. Drew 3.00 .90
JG Jason Giambi 3.00 .90
JT Jim Thome 4.00 1.20
KG Ken Griffey Jr. 6.00 1.80
KI Kazuhisa Ishii 3.00 .90
KW Kerry Wood 4.00 1.20
LB Lance Berkman 3.00 .90
LG Luis Gonzalez 3.00 .90
MM Mike Mussina 3.00 .90
MO Magglio Ordonez 3.00 .90
MP Mike Piazza 6.00 1.80
MR Manny Ramirez 3.00 .90
NG Nomar Garciaparra 6.00 1.80
PB Pat Burrell 3.00 .90
PM Pedro Martinez 4.00 1.20
PR Mark Prior 4.00 1.20
RA Roberto Alomar 3.00 .90
RC Roger Clemens 8.00 2.40
RJ Randy Johnson 4.00 1.20
RP Rafael Palmeiro 3.00 .90
SG Shawn Green 3.00 .90
SR Scott Rolen 4.00 1.20
SS Sammy Sosa 6.00 1.80
TH Todd Helton 3.00 .90
VG Vladimir Guerrero 4.00 1.20

2004 Upper Deck Vintage

The initial 450-card set was released in January, 2004. The set was issued in eight card packs with an $2.99 SRP which came 24 packs to a box and 12 boxes to a case. Cards numbered from 1 through 300 were printed in heavier quantity than the rest of the set. In that group of 300 the final three cards feature checklists. Cards numbered 301 through 315 are Play Ball Preview Cards while cards numbered 316 through 325 are World Series Highlight Cards. Cards numbered 326 through 335 were players who were traded during the 2003 season. A few leading 2003 rookies were issued as Short Prints between cards 335 and 350. Those cards were issued in two different tiers which we have notated in our checklist. Similar to the 2003 set, many cards (351-440) were issued with lenticular technology and feature 90 of the majors leading sluggers. The set concludes with 10 cards made in the style of the 19th century Old Judge cards. Those cards were issued in "Old Judge Packs" which were issued as one per box "boxtoppers". A 50-card Update set (containing cards 451-500) was issued in factory set format and distributed into one in every 1.5 hobby boxes of 2004 Upper Deck Series 2 baseball in June, 2004.

Nm-Mt Ex-Mt
COMP.SET w/o SP's (300) 60.00 18.00
COMP.UPDATE SET (50) 15.00 4.50
COMMON CARD (1-300) .30 .09
301-315 STATED ODDS 1:5
COMMON CARD (316-325) 2.00 .60
316-325 STATED ODDS 1:7
COMMON CARD (326-350) 4.00 1.20
326-350 STATED ODDS 1:5
COMMON CARD (351-440) 10.00 3.00
351-440 STATED ODDS 1:12
COMMON CARD (441-450) 4.00 1.20
COMMON CARD (451-465) .30 .09
COMMON CARD (466-500) .30 .09
ONE UPDATE SET PER 1.5 UD2 HOB.BOXES
1 Albert Pujols 1.50 .45
2 Carlos Delgado .30 .09
3 Todd Helton .50 .15
4 Nomar Garciaparra 1.25 .35
5 Vladimir Guerrero .75 .23
6 Alfonso Soriano .50 .15
7 Alex Rodriguez 1.25 .35
8 Jason Giambi .30 .09
9 Derek Jeter 1.50 .45
10 Pedro Martinez .75 .23
11 Ivan Rodriguez .75 .23
12 Mark Prior .75 .23
13 Marquis Grissom .30 .09
14 Barry Zito .30 .09
15 Alex Cintron .30 .09
16 Wade Miller .30 .09
17 Eric Chavez .30 .09
18 Matt Clement .30 .09
19 Orlando Cabrera .30 .09
20 Odalis Perez .30 .09
21 Lance Berkman .30 .09
22 Keith Foulke .30 .09
23 Shawn Green .30 .09
24 Byung-Hyun Kim .30 .09
25 Geoff Jenkins .30 .09
26 Torii Hunter .30 .09
27 Richard Hidalgo .30 .09
28 Edgar Martinez .50 .15
29 Placido Polanco .30 .09
30 Brad Lidge .30 .09
31 Alex Escobar .30 .09
32 Garret Anderson .30 .09
33 Larry Walker .50 .15
34 Ken Griffey Jr. 1.25 .35
35 Junior Spivey .30 .09
36 Carlos Beltran .50 .15
37 Bartolo Colon .30 .09
38 Ichiro Suzuki 1.25 .35
39 Ramon Ortiz .30 .09
40 Roy Oswalt .30 .09
41 Mike Piazza 1.25 .35
42 Benito Santiago .30 .09
43 Mike Mussina .50 .15
44 Jeff Kent .30 .09
45 Curt Schilling .30 .09
46 Adam Dunn .50 .15
47 Mike Sweeney .30 .09
48 Chipper Jones .75 .23
49 Frank Thomas .75 .23
50 Kerry Wood .75 .23
51 Rod Beck .30 .09
52 Brian Giles .30 .09
53 Hank Blalock .30 .09
54 Andruw Jones .30 .09
55 Dmitri Young .30 .09
56 Juan Pierre .30 .09
57 Jacque Jones .30 .09
58 Phil Nevin .30 .09
59 Rocco Baldelli .30 .09
60 Greg Maddux 1.25 .35
61 Eric Gagne .75 .23
62 Tim Hudson .30 .09
63 Brian Lawrence .30 .09
64 Sammy Sosa 1.25 .35
65 Corey Koskie .30 .09
66 Bobby Abreu .30 .09
67 Preston Wilson .30 .09
68 Jay Gibbons .30 .09
69 Dontrelle Willis .30 .09
70 Richie Sexson .30 .09
71 Kevin Millwood .30 .09
72 Randy Johnson .75 .23
73 Jack Cust .30 .09
74 Randy Wolf .30 .09
75 Johan Santana .50 .15
76 Magglio Ordonez .30 .09
77 Sean Casey .30 .09
78 Billy Wagner .30 .09
79 Javier Vazquez .30 .09
80 Jorge Posada .50 .15
81 Jason Schmidt .30 .09
82 Bret Boone .30 .09
83 Jeff Bagwell .50 .15
84 Rickie Weeks .30 .09
85 Troy Percival .30 .09
86 Jose Vidro .30 .09
87 Freddy Garcia .30 .09
88 Manny Ramirez .50 .15
89 John Smoltz .50 .15
90 Moises Alou .30 .09
91 Ugueth Urbina .30 .09
92 Bobby Hill .30 .09
93 Marcus Giles .30 .09
94 Aramis Ramirez .30 .09
95 Brad Wilkerson .30 .09
96 Ray Durham .30 .09
97 David Wells .30 .09
98 Paul Lo Duca .30 .09
99 Danny Graves .30 .09
100 Jason Kendall .30 .09
101 Carlos Lee .30 .09
102 Rafael Furcal .30 .09
103 Mike Lowell .30 .09
104 Kevin Brown .30 .09
105 Vicente Padilla .30 .09
106 Miguel Tejada .30 .09
107 Bernie Williams .50 .15
108 Octavio Dotel .30 .09
109 Steve Finley .30 .09
110 Lyle Overbay .30 .09
111 Delmon Young .50 .15
112 Bo Hart .30 .09
113 Jason Lane .30 .09
114 Matt Roney .30 .09
115 Brian Roberts .30 .09
116 Tom Glavine .50 .15
117 Rich Aurilia .30 .09
118 Adam Kennedy .30 .09
119 Hee Seop Choi .30 .09
120 Trot Nixon .30 .09
121 Gary Sheffield .30 .09
122 Jay Payton .30 .09
123 Brad Penny .30 .09
124 Garrett Atkins .30 .09
125 Aubrey Huff .30 .09
126 Juan Gonzalez .50 .15
127 Jason Jennings .30 .09
128 Luis Gonzalez .30 .09
129 Vinny Castilla .30 .09
130 Esteban Loaiza .30 .09
131 Erubiel Durazo .30 .09
132 Eric Hinske .30 .09
133 Scott Rolen .75 .23
134 Craig Biggio .50 .15
135 Tim Wakefield .30 .09
136 Darin Erstad .30 .09
137 Denny Stark .30 .09
138 Ben Sheets .30 .09
139 Hideo Nomo .75 .23
140 Derrek Lee .30 .09
141 Matt Mantei .30 .09
142 Reggie Sanders .30 .09
143 Jose Guillen .30 .09
144 Joe Mays .30 .09
145 Jimmy Rollins .30 .09
146 Juan Encarnacion .30 .09
147 Joe Crede .30 .09
148 Aaron Guiel .30 .09
149 Mark Mulder .30 .09
150 Travis Lee .30 .09
151 Josh Phelps .30 .09
152 Michael Young .30 .09
153 Paul Konerko .30 .09
154 John Lackey .30 .09
155 Damian Moss .30 .09
156 Javy Lopez .30 .09
157 Joe Borowski .30 .09
158 Jose Cruz Jr. .30 .09
159 Ramon Hernandez .30 .09
160 Raul Ibanez .30 .09
161 Adrian Beltre .50 .15
162 Bobby Higginson .30 .09
163 Jorge Julio .30 .09
164 Miguel Batista .30 .09
165 Luis Castillo .30 .09
166 Aaron Harang .30 .09
167 Ken Harvey .30 .09
168 Rocky Biddle .30 .09
169 Mariano Rivera .50 .15
170 Matt Morris .30 .09
171 Laynce Nix .30 .09
172 Mike Maroth .30 .09
173 Francisco Rodriguez .30 .09
174 Livan Hernandez .30 .09
175 Aaron Heilman .30 .09
176 Nick Johnson .30 .09
177 Woody Williams .30 .09
178 Joe Kennedy .30 .09
179 Jesse Foppert .30 .09
180 Ryan Franklin .30 .09
181 Endy Chavez .30 .09
182 Chin-Hui Tsao .30 .09
183 Todd Walker .30 .09
184 Edgardo Alfonzo .30 .09
185 Edgar Renteria .30 .09
186 Matt LeCroy .30 .09
187 Carl Everett .30 .09
188 Jeff Conine .30 .09
189 Jason Varitek .50 .15
190 Russ Ortiz .30 .09
191 Melvin Mora .30 .09
192 Mark Buehrle .30 .09
193 Bill Mueller .30 .09
194 Miguel Cabrera .50 .15
195 Carlos Zambrano .30 .09
196 Jose Valverde .30 .09
197 Danys Baez .30 .09
198 Mike MacDougal .30 .09
199 Zach Day .30 .09
200 Roy Halladay .30 .09
201 Jerome Williams .30 .09
202 Josh Fogg .30 .09
203 Mark Kotsay .30 .09
204 Pat Burrell .30 .09
205 A.J. Pierzynski .30 .09
206 Fred McGriff .50 .15
207 Brandon Larson .30 .09
208 Robb Quinlan .30 .09
209 David Ortiz .75 .23
210 A.J. Burnett .30 .09
211 John Vander Wal .30 .09
212 Jim Thome .75 .23
213 Matt Kata .30 .09
214 Kip Wells .30 .09
215 Scott Podsednik .30 .09
216 Rickey Henderson .75 .23
217 Travis Hafner .30 .09
218 Tony Batista .30 .09
219 Robert Fick .30 .09
220 Derek Lowe .30 .09
221 Ryan Klesko .30 .09
222 Joe Beimel .30 .09
223 Doug Mientkiewicz .30 .09
224 Angel Berroa .30 .09
225 Adam Eaton .30 .09
226 C.C. Sabathia .30 .09
227 Wilfredo Ledezma .30 .09
228 Jason Johnson .30 .09
229 Ryan Wagner .30 .09
230 Al Leiter .30 .09
231 Joel Pineiro .30 .09
232 Jason Isringhausen .30 .09
233 John Olerud .30 .09
234 Ron Calloway .30 .09
235 Jose Reyes .30 .09
236 J.D. Drew .30 .09
237 Jared Sandberg .30 .09
238 Gil Meche .30 .09
239 Jose Contreras .30 .09
240 Eric Milton .30 .09
241 Jason Phillips .30 .09
242 Luis Ayala .30 .09
243 Bobby Kielty .30 .09
244 Jose Lima .30 .09
245 Brooks Kieschnick .30 .09
246 Xavier Nady .30 .09
247 Danny Haren .30 .09
248 Victor Zambrano .30 .09
249 Kelvim Escobar .30 .09
250 Oliver Perez .30 .09
251 Jamie Moyer .30 .09
252 Orlando Hudson .30 .09
253 Danny Kolb .30 .09
254 Jake Peavy .30 .09
255 Kris Benson .30 .09
256 Roger Clemens 1.50 .45
257 Jim Edmonds .30 .09
258 Rafael Palmeiro .50 .15
259 Jae Weong Seo .30 .09
260 Chase Utley .30 .09
261 Rich Harden .30 .09
262 Mark Teixeira .30 .09
263 Johnny Damon .75 .23
264 Luis Matos .30 .09
265 Shigetoshi Hasegawa .30 .09
266 Alfredo Amezaga .30 .09
267 Tim Worrell .30 .09
268 Kazuhisa Ishii .30 .09
269 Miguel Ojeda .30 .09
270 Kazuhiro Sasaki .30 .09
271 Hideki Matsui 1.25 .35
272 Troy Glaus .30 .09
273 Michael Tucker .30 .09
274 Lew Ford .30 .09
275 Brian Jordan .30 .09
276 David Eckstein .30 .09
277 Robby Hammock .30 .09
278 Corey Patterson .30 .09
279 Wes Helms .30 .09
280 Jermaine Dye .30 .09
281 Cliff Floyd .30 .09
282 Dustan Mohr .30 .09
283 Kevin Mench .30 .09
284 Ellis Burks .30 .09
285 Jerry Hairston Jr. .30 .09
286 Tim Salmon .50 .15
287 Omar Vizquel .50 .15
288 Andy Pettitte .50 .15
289 Guillermo Mota .30 .09
290 Tino Martinez .50 .15
291 Lance Carter .30 .09
292 Francisco Cordero .30 .09

293 Robb Nen .30 .09
294 Mike Cameron .30 .09
295 Jhonny Peralta .30 .09
296 Braden Looper .30 .09
297 Jarrod Washburn .30 .09
298 Mark Prior CL .50 .15
299 Alfonso Soriano CL .30 .09
300 Rocco Baldelli CL .30 .09
301 Pedro Martinez PBP 2.50 .75
302 Mark Prior PBP 2.50 .75
303 Barry Zito PBP 2.00 .60
304 Roger Clemens PBP 5.00 1.50
305 Randy Johnson PBP 2.50 .75
306 Roy Halladay PBP 2.00 .60
307 Hideo Nomo PBP 2.50 .75
308 Roy Oswalt PBP 2.00 .60
309 Kerry Wood PBP 2.50 .75
310 Dontrelle Willis PBP 2.00 .60
311 Mark Mulder PBP 2.00 .60
312 Brandon Webb PBP 2.00 .60
313 Mike Mussina PBP 2.00 .60
314 Curt Schilling PBP 2.00 .60
315 Tim Hudson PBP 2.00 .60
316 Dontrelle Willis WSH 2.00 .60
317 Juan Pierre WSH 2.00 .60
318 Hideki Matsui WSH 4.00 1.20
319 Andy Pettitte WSH 2.00 .60
320 Mike Mussina WSH 2.00 .60
321 Roger Clemens WSH 5.00 1.50
322 Alex Gonzalez WSH 2.00 .60
323 Brad Penny WSH 2.00 .60
324 Ivan Rodriguez WSH 2.50 .75
325 Josh Beckett WSH 2.00 .60
326 Aaron Boone TR 4.00 1.20
327 Jeff Suppan TR 4.00 1.20
328 Shea Hillenbrand TR 4.00 1.20
329 Jeromy Burnitz TR 4.00 1.20
330 Sidney Ponson TR 4.00 1.20
331 Rondell White TR 4.00 1.20
332 Shannon Stewart TR 4.00 1.20
333 Armando Benitez TR 4.00 1.20
334 Roberto Alomar TR 4.00 1.20
335 Raul Mondesi TR 4.00 1.20
336 Morgan Ensberg SP1 4.00 1.20
337 Milton Bradley SP1 4.00 1.20
338 Brandon Webb SP1 4.00 1.20
339 Marlon Byrd SP1 4.00 1.20
340 Carlos Pena SP1 4.00 1.20
341 Brandon Phillips SP1 4.00 1.20
342 Josh Beckett SP1 4.00 1.20
343 Eric Munson SP1 4.00 1.20
344 Brett Myers SP1 4.00 1.20
345 Austin Kearns SP1 4.00 1.20
346 Jody Gerut SP2 4.00 1.20
347 Vernon Wells SP2 4.00 1.20
348 Jeff Duncan SP2 4.00 1.20
349 Sean Burroughs SP2 4.00 1.20
350 Jeremy Bonderman SP2 4.00 1.20
351 Hideki Matsui 3D 15.00 4.50
352 Jason Giambi 3D 10.00 3.00
353 Alfonso Soriano 3D 10.00 3.00
354 Derek Jeter 3D 20.00 6.00
355 Aaron Boone 3D 10.00 3.00
356 Jorge Posada 3D 10.00 3.00
357 Bernie Williams 3D 10.00 3.00
358 Manny Ramirez 3D 10.00 3.00
359 Nomar Garciaparra 3D 15.00 4.50
360 Johnny Damon 3D 15.00 4.50
361 Jason Varitek 3D 10.00 3.00
362 Carlos Delgado 3D 10.00 3.00
363 Vernon Wells 3D 10.00 3.00
364 Jay Gibbons 3D 10.00 3.00
365 Tony Batista 3D 10.00 3.00
366 Rocco Baldelli 3D 10.00 3.00
367 Aubrey Huff 3D 10.00 3.00
368 Carlos Beltran 3D 10.00 3.00
369 Mike Sweeney 3D 10.00 3.00
370 Magglio Ordonez 3D 10.00 3.00
371 Frank Thomas 3D 15.00 4.50
372 Carlos Lee 3D 10.00 3.00
373 Roberto Alomar 3D 10.00 3.00
374 Jacque Jones 3D 10.00 3.00
375 Torii Hunter 3D 10.00 3.00
376 Milton Bradley 3D 10.00 3.00
377 Travis Hafner 3D 10.00 3.00
378 Jody Gerut 3D 10.00 3.00
379 Dmitri Young 3D 10.00 3.00
380 Carlos Pena 3D 10.00 3.00
381 Ichiro Suzuki 3D 15.00 4.50
382 Bret Boone 3D 10.00 3.00
383 Edgar Martinez 3D 10.00 3.00
384 Eric Chavez 3D 10.00 3.00
385 Miguel Tejada 3D 10.00 3.00
386 Erubiel Durazo 3D 10.00 3.00
387 Jose Guillen 3D 10.00 3.00
388 Garret Anderson 3D 10.00 3.00
389 Troy Glaus 3D 10.00 3.00
390 Alex Rodriguez 3D 15.00 4.50
391 Rafael Palmeiro 3D 10.00 3.00
392 Hank Blalock 3D 10.00 3.00
393 Mark Teixeira 3D 10.00 3.00
394 Gary Sheffield 3D 10.00 3.00
395 Andruw Jones 3D 10.00 3.00
396 Chipper Jones 3D 15.00 4.50
397 Javy Lopez 3D 10.00 3.00
398 Marcus Giles 3D 10.00 3.00
399 Rafael Furcal 3D 10.00 3.00
400 Jim Thome 3D 15.00 4.50
401 Bobby Abreu 3D 10.00 3.00
402 Pat Burrell 3D 10.00 3.00
403 Mike Lowell 3D 10.00 3.00
404 Ivan Rodriguez 3D 15.00 4.50
405 Derrek Lee 3D 10.00 3.00
406 Miguel Cabrera 3D 10.00 3.00
407 Vladimir Guerrero 3D 15.00 4.50
408 Orlando Cabrera 3D 10.00 3.00
409 Jose Vidro 3D 10.00 3.00
410 Mike Piazza 3D 15.00 4.50
411 Cliff Floyd 3D 10.00 3.00
412 Albert Pujols 3D 20.00 6.00
413 Scott Rolen 3D 15.00 4.50
414 Jim Edmonds 3D 10.00 3.00
415 Edgar Renteria 3D 10.00 3.00
416 Lance Berkman 3D 10.00 3.00
417 Jeff Bagwell 3D 10.00 3.00
418 Jeff Kent 3D 10.00 3.00
419 Richard Hidalgo 3D 10.00 3.00
420 Morgan Ensberg 3D 10.00 3.00
421 Sammy Sosa 3D 15.00 4.50
422 Moises Alou 3D 10.00 3.00
423 Ken Griffey Jr. 3D 15.00 4.50
424 Adam Dunn 3D 10.00 3.00
425 Austin Kearns 3D 10.00 3.00
426 Richie Sexson 3D 10.00 3.00
427 Geoff Jenkins 3D 10.00 3.00
428 Brian Giles 3D 10.00 3.00
429 Reggie Sanders 3D 10.00 3.00
430 Rich Aurilia 3D 10.00 3.00
431 Jose Cruz Jr. 3D 10.00 3.00
432 Shawn Green 3D 10.00 3.00
433 Jeromy Burnitz 3D 10.00 3.00
434 Luis Gonzalez 3D 10.00 3.00
435 Todd Helton 3D 10.00 3.00
436 Preston Wilson 3D 10.00 3.00
437 Larry Walker 3D 10.00 3.00
438 Ryan Klesko 3D 10.00 3.00
439 Phil Nevin 3D 10.00 3.00
440 Sean Burroughs 3D 10.00 3.00
441 Sammy Sosa OJ 8.00 2.40
442 Albert Pujols OJ 10.00 3.00
443 Magglio Ordonez OJ 4.00 1.20
444 Vladimir Guerrero OJ 5.00 1.50
445 Todd Helton OJ 4.00 1.20
446 Jason Giambi OJ 4.00 1.20
447 Ichiro Suzuki OJ 8.00 2.40
448 Alex Rodriguez OJ 8.00 2.40
449 Carlos Delgado OJ 4.00 1.20
450 Manny Ramirez OJ 4.00 1.20
451 Alex Rodriguez 2.00 .60
452 Javy Lopez .30 .09
453 Alfonso Soriano .30 .09
454 Vladimir Guerrero .75 .23
455 Rafael Palmeiro .50 .15
456 Gary Sheffield .30 .09
457 Curt Schilling .30 .09
458 Miguel Tejada .30 .09
459 Kevin Brown .30 .09
460 Richie Sexson .30 .09
461 Roger Clemens 1.50 .45
462 Javier Vazquez .30 .09
463 Bartolo Colon .30 .09
464 Ivan Rodriguez .75 .23
465 Greg Maddux 1.25 .35
466 Jamie Brown RC .30 .09
467 Dave Crouthers RC .30 .09
468 Jason Frasor RC .50 .15
469 Greg Dobbs RC 1.25 .35
470 Jesse Harper RC .50 .15
471 Nick Regilio RC .50 .15
472 Ryan Wing RC .50 .15
473 Akinori Otsuka RC .50 .15
474 Shingo Takatsu RC 1.50 .45
475 Kazuo Matsui RC 2.50 .75
476 Mike Vento RC .75 .23
477 Mike Gosling RC .30 .09
478 Justin Huisman RC .50 .15
479 Justin Hampson RC .50 .15
480 Dennis Sarfate RC .50 .15
481 Ian Snell RC 1.25 .35
482 Tim Bausher RC .50 .15
483 Donnie Kelly RC .50 .15
484 Jerome Gamble RC .30 .09
485 Mike Rouse RC .50 .15
486 Merkin Valdez RC 2.00 .60
487 Lincoln Holdzkom RC .50 .15
488 Justin Leone RC .75 .23
489 Sean Henn RC .50 .15
490 Brandon Medders RC .30 .09
491 Mike Johnston RC .50 .15
492 Tim Bittner RC .50 .15
493 Michael Wuertz RC .75 .23
494 Chad Bentz RC .50 .15
495 Ryan Meaux RC .50 .15
496 Chris Aguila RC .50 .15
497 Jake Woods RC .50 .15
498 Scott Dohmann RC .30 .09
499 Colby Miller RC .50 .15
500 Josh Labandeira RC .50 .15

2004 Upper Deck Vintage Black and White

These cards, pictured in black and white, are a complete parallel of the first 350 cards in the Vintage set.

Nm-Mt Ex-Mt
*B/W 1-300: 3X TO 8X BASIC
1-300 STATED ODDS 1:6
*B/W 301-315: .6X TO 1.5X BASIC
301-315 STATED ODDS 1:24
*B/W 316-325: .6X TO 1.5X BASIC
316-325 STATED ODDS 1:24
*B/W 326-350: .4X TO 1X BASIC
326-350 STATED ODDS 1:20

2004 Upper Deck Vintage Black and White Color Variation

Issued at stated odds of one in 48, these skip-numbered cards are a variation to the black and white parallel cards.

Nm-Mt Ex-Mt
*B/W COLOR: 5X TO 12X BASIC

2004 Upper Deck Vintage Old Judge Subset Blue Back

Nm-Mt Ex-Mt
*OJ BLUE BACK 441-450: .6X TO 1.5X BASIC
STATED ODD 1:4 OJ HOBBY PACKS
ONE 3-CARD OJ PACK PER HOBBY BOX

2004 Upper Deck Vintage Old Judge Subset Red Back

Nm-Mt Ex-Mt
*OJ RED BACK 441-450: fX TO 2.5X BASIC OJ
STATED ODDS 1:12 OJ HOBBY PACKS
ONE 3-CARD OJ PACK PER HOBBY BOX

2004 Upper Deck Vintage Old Judge

Nm-Mt Ex-Mt
DISTRIBUTED IN OLD JUDGE HOBBY PACKS
ONE 3-CARD OJ PACK PER HOBBY BOX
*OJ BLUE BACK 11-30: .6X TO 1.5X BASIC

OJ BLUE BACK ODDS 1:4 OJ HOBBY PACKS
*OJ RED BACK 11-30: 1X TO 2.5X BASIC
OJ RED BACK ODDS 1:12 OJ HOBBY PACKS
11 Randy Johnson 5.00 1.50
12 Pedro Martinez 5.00 1.50
13 Mark Prior 5.00 1.50
14 Barry Zito 4.00 1.20
15 Roy Oswalt 4.00 1.20
16 Roy Halladay 4.00 1.20
17 Curt Schilling 4.00 1.20
18 Mike Mussina 4.00 1.20
19 Kevin Brown 4.00 1.20
20 Roger Clemens 10.00 3.00
21 Eric Gagne 5.00 1.50
22 Mariano Rivera 4.00 1.20
23 Mike Piazza 8.00 2.40
24 Jorge Posada 4.00 1.20
25 Jeff Kent 4.00 1.20
26 Alfonso Soriano 4.00 1.20
27 Scott Rolen 5.00 1.50
28 Eric Chavez 4.00 1.20
29 Edgar Renteria 4.00 1.20
30 Hideki Matsui 8.00 2.40

2004 Upper Deck Vintage Stellar Signatures

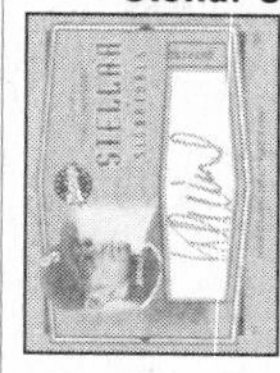
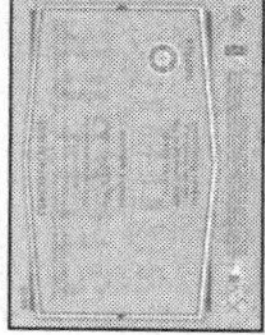

Nm-Mt Ex-Mt
STATED ODDS 1:600
STATED PRINT RUN 150 SERIAL #'d SETS
EXCHANGE DEADLINE 01/27/07
AR Alex Rodriguez EXCH 120.00 36.00
BZ Barry Zito 40.00 12.00
CY Carl Yastrzemski 60.00 18.00
HM Hideki Matsui 300.00 90.00
IS Ichiro Suzuki 300.00 90.00
MP Mike Piazza 200.00 60.00
TS Tom Seaver 40.00 12.00

2004 Upper Deck Vintage Stellar Stat Men Jerseys

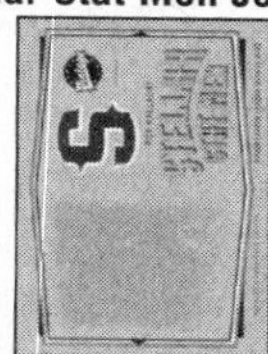

Nm-Mt Ex-Mt
STATED ODDS 1:24
SP PRINT RUNS PROVIDED BY UPPER DECK
SP'S ARE NOT SERIAL-NUMBERED
1 Jose Reyes 8.00 2.40
2 Bo Hart 8.00 2.40
3 Hideki Matsui Pants 25.00 7.50
4 Dontrelle Willis 8.00 2.40
5 Rocco Baldelli 8.00 2.40
6 Ichiro Suzuki 30.00 9.00
7 Mike Lowell 8.00 2.40
8 Derek Jeter 30.00 9.00
9 Ken Griffey Jr. 15.00 4.50
10 Sammy Sosa 15.00 4.50
11 Kerry Wood 10.00 3.00
12 Chipper Jones 10.00 3.00
13 Alfonso Soriano 10.00 3.00
14 Khalil Greene 10.00 3.00
15 Jim Thome 10.00 3.00
16 Rafael Furcal 8.00 2.40
17 Andrew Brown 8.00 2.40
18 Mark Prior 10.00 3.00
19 Barry Zito 8.00 2.40
20 Al Leiter 8.00 2.40
21 Carlos Delgado 8.00 2.40
22 Pedro Martinez 10.00 3.00
23 Alex Rodriguez 15.00 4.50
24 Lance Berkman 8.00 2.40
25 Jeff Bagwell 10.00 3.00
26 Bernie Williams 10.00 3.00
27 Hideo Nomo 15.00 4.50
28 Randy Johnson 10.00 3.00
29 Curt Schilling 8.00 2.40
30 Mike Piazza 15.00 4.50
31 Albert Pujols 15.00 4.50
32 Joe DiMaggio Pants SP/300
33 Ted Williams Pants SP/300 60.00 18.00
34 Mickey Mantle Pants SP/300 150.00 45.00
35 Mike Mussina 10.00 3.00
36 Rich Harden 8.00 2.40
37 Roy Oswalt 8.00 2.40
38 Torii Hunter 8.00 2.40
39 Jorge Posada 10.00 3.00
40 Troy Glaus 8.00 2.40
41 Manny Ramirez 10.00 3.00
42 Roy Halladay 8.00 2.40

2004 Upper Deck Vintage Timeless Teams Quad Bats

Nm-Mt Ex-Mt
STATED ODDS 1:400
STATED PRINT RUN 175 SERIAL #'d SETS
CARD NUMBER 3 DOES NOT EXIST
TT1 Alfonso Soriano 120.00 36.00
Derek Jeter
Hideki Matsui
Jason Giambi
TT2 Luis Gonzalez 40.00 12.00
Curt Schilling
Randy Johnson
Steve Finley
TT4 Manny Ramirez 50.00 15.00
Nomar Garciaparra
Trot Nixon
Johnny Damon
TT5 Alex Rodriguez 40.00 12.00
Rafael Palmeiro
Mark Teixeira
Hank Blalock
TT6 Magglio Ordonez 40.00 12.00
Frank Thomas
Roberto Alomar
Carl Everett
TT7 Jacque Jones 25.00 7.50
Torii Hunter
Doug Mientkiewicz
Shannon Stewart
TT8 Jim Edmonds 50.00 15.00
Scott Rolen
J.D. Drew
Albert Pujols
TT9 Ichiro Suzuki 80.00 24.00
John Olerud
Bret Boone
Mike Cameron
TT10 Jeff Kent 40.00 12.00
Jeff Bagwell
Craig Biggio
Lance Berkman
TT11 Troy Glaus 40.00 12.00
Darin Erstad
Garret Anderson
Tim Salmon
TT12 Bernie Williams 80.00 24.00
Jorge Posada
Hideki Matsui
Alfonso Soriano
TT13 Michael Tucker 40.00 12.00
Carlos Beltran
Mike Sweeney
Brent Mayne
TT14 Jim Thome 40.00 12.00
Marlon Byrd
Mike Lieberthal
Bobby Abreu
TT15 Miguel Cabrera 40.00 12.00
Ivan Rodriguez
Juan Encarnacion
Mike Lowell
TT16 Sammy Sosa 50.00 15.00
Corey Patterson
Moises Alou
Kerry Wood
TT17 Jose Cruz Jr. 25.00 7.50
Edgardo Alfonzo
Rich Aurilia
Andres Galarraga
TT18 Alfonso Soriano 120.00 36.00
Derek Jeter
Hideki Matsui
Bernie Williams

2002 Upper Deck World Series Heroes

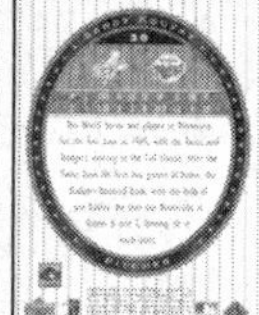

This 180 card set was released in September, 2002. The five card packs were issued in 24 pack boxes which came 20 boxes to a case with an $3 SRP per pack. Cards numbered 1-90 featured a mix of active and retired players who had played in the World Series. Cards numbered 91 through 135 feature Rookie Cards while cards numbered 136 through 180 feature active players who had yet to participate in a World Series. Cards numbered 91 through 180 were all issued at a stated rate of one in 10.

Nm-Mt Ex-Mt
COMP.SET w/o SP's (90) 20.00 6.00
COMMON CARD (1-90) .30 .09
COMMON CARD (91-135) 3.00 .90
COMMON CARD (136-180) 4.00 1.20
1 Catfish Hunter .50 .15
2 Jimmie Foxx .75 .23
3 Mark McGwire 2.00 .60
4 Rollie Fingers .30 .09
5 Rickey Henderson .75 .23
6 Joe Carter .30 .09
7 John Olerud .30 .09
8 Roberto Alomar .50 .15
9 Pat Hentgen .30 .09
10 Devon White .30 .09
11 Eddie Mathews .75 .23
12 Greg Maddux 1.25 .35
13 Chipper Jones .75 .23
14 Tom Glavine .50 .15
15 Andruw Jones .30 .09
16 Dave Justice .30 .09
17 Fred McGriff .50 .15
18 Ryan Klesko .30 .09
19 John Smoltz .50 .15
20 Javy Lopez .30 .09
21 Marquis Grissom .30 .09
22 Robin Yount 1.25 .35
23 Ozzie Smith 1.25 .35
24 Frankie Frisch .50 .15
25 Stan Musial 1.25 .35
26 Randy Johnson .75 .23
27 Luis Gonzalez .30 .09
28 Matt Williams .30 .09
29 Steve Finley .30 .09
30 Sandy Koufax 2.00 .60
31 Duke Snider .50 .15
32 Kirk Gibson .30 .09
33 Steve Garvey .30 .09
34 Jackie Robinson .75 .23
35 Don Drysdale .75 .23
36 Juan Marichal .30 .09
37 Mel Ott .75 .23
38 Orlando Cepeda .30 .09
39 Jim Thome .75 .23
40 Manny Ramirez .50 .15
41 Omar Vizquel .50 .15
42 Lou Boudreau .30 .09
43 Gary Sheffield .30 .09
44 Moises Alou .30 .09
45 Livan Hernandez .30 .09
46 Edgar Renteria .30 .09
47 Al Leiter .30 .09
48 Tom Seaver .50 .15
49 Gary Carter .30 .09
50 Mike Piazza 1.25 .35
51 Nolan Ryan 2.00 .60
52 Robin Ventura .30 .09
53 Mike Hampton .30 .09
54 Jesse Orosco .30 .09
55 Cal Ripken 2.50 .75
56 Brooks Robinson .50 .15
57 Tony Gwynn 1.00 .30
58 Kevin Brown .30 .09
59 Curt Schilling .30 .09
60 Cy Young .75 .23
61 Honus Wagner 1.25 .35
62 Willie Stargell .50 .15
63 Wade Boggs .50 .15
64 Carlton Fisk .50 .15
65 Ken Griffey Sr. .30 .09
66 Joe Morgan .30 .09
67 Johnny Bench .75 .23
68 Barry Larkin .50 .15
69 Jose Rijo .30 .09
70 Ty Cobb 1.25 .35
71 Kirby Puckett .75 .23
72 Chuck Knoblauch .30 .09
73 Harmon Killebrew .75 .23
74 Mickey Mantle 3.00 .90
75 Joe DiMaggio 1.50 .45
76 Don Larsen .30 .09
77 Thurman Munson .75 .23
78 Roger Maris .75 .23
79 Phil Rizzuto .50 .15
80 Babe Ruth 2.50 .75
81 Lou Gehrig 1.50 .45
82 Billy Martin .50 .15
83 Derek Jeter 2.00 .60
84 Roger Clemens 1.50 .45
85 Tino Martinez .50 .15
86 Bernie Williams .50 .15
87 Mariano Rivera .50 .15
88 Andy Pettitte .50 .15
89 David Wells .30 .09
90 Jorge Posada .50 .15
91 Rodrigo Rosario PH RC 3.00 .90
92 Brandon Puffer PH RC 3.00 .90
93 Franklyn German PH RC 3.00 .90
94 Reed Johnson PH RC 5.00 1.50
95 Chris Baker PH RC 3.00 .90
96 John Ennis PH RC 3.00 .90
97 Luis Martinez PH RC 3.00 .90
98 Takaki Nomura PH RC 3.00 .90
99 So Taguchi PH RC 5.00 1.50
100 Michael Crudale PH RC 3.00 .90
101 Francis Beltran PH RC 3.00 .90
102 Steve Kent PH RC 3.00 .90
103 Jorge Sosa PH RC 3.00 .90
104 Felix Escalona PH RC 3.00 .90
105 Jose Valverde PH RC 5.00 1.50
106 Doug Devore PH RC 3.00 .90
107 Kazuhisa Ishii PH RC 6.00 1.80
108 Victor Alvarez PH RC 3.00 .90
109 Eric Good PH RC 3.00 .90
110 Jorge Nunez PH RC 3.00 .90
111 Ron Calloway PH RC 3.00 .90
112 Nelson Castro PH RC 3.00 .90
113 Matt Thornton PH RC 3.00 .90
114 Luis Ugueto PH RC 3.00 .90
115 Hansel Izquierdo PH RC 3.00 .90
116 Jaime Cerda PH RC 3.00 .90
117 Mark Corey PH RC 3.00 .90
118 Tyler Yates PH RC 5.00 1.50
119 Satoru Komiyama PH RC 3.00 .90
120 Steve Bechler PH RC 3.00 .90
121 Ben Howard PH RC 3.00 .90
122 Anderson Machado PH RC 3.00 .90
123 Jorge Padilla PH RC 3.00 .90
124 Eric Junge PH RC 3.00 .90
125 Adrian Burnside PH RC 3.00 .90
126 Mike Gonzalez PH RC 3.00 .90
127 Anastacio Martinez PH RC 3.00 .90
128 Josh Hancock PH RC 3.00 .90
129 Rene Reyes PH RC 3.00 .90
130 Aaron Cook PH RC 3.00 .90
131 Cam Esslinger PH RC 3.00 .90
132 Juan Brito PH RC 3.00 .90
133 Miguel Asencio PH RC 3.00 .90
134 Kevin Frederick PH RC 3.00 .90
135 Edwin Almonte PH RC 3.00 .90
136 Troy Glaus FWS 4.00 1.20
137 Darin Erstad FWS 4.00 1.20
138 Jeff Bagwell FWS 4.00 1.20
139 Lance Berkman FWS 4.00 1.20

140 Tim Hudson FWS	4.00	1.20
141 Eric Chavez FWS	4.00	1.20
142 Barry Zito FWS	4.00	1.20
143 Carlos Delgado FWS	4.00	1.20
144 Richie Sexson FWS	4.00	1.20
145 Albert Pujols FWS	12.00	3.60
146 Sammy Sosa FWS	10.00	3.00
147 Kerry Wood FWS	6.00	1.80
148 Greg Vaughn FWS	4.00	1.20
149 Shawn Green FWS	4.00	1.20
150 Vladimir Guerrero FWS	6.00	1.80
151 Barry Bonds FWS	15.00	4.50
152 C.C. Sabathia FWS	4.00	1.20
153 Ichiro Suzuki FWS	10.00	3.00
154 Freddy Garcia FWS	4.00	1.20
155 Edgar Martinez FWS	4.00	1.20
156 Josh Beckett FWS	4.00	1.20
157 Cliff Floyd FWS	4.00	1.20
158 Mo Vaughn FWS	4.00	1.20
159 Jeromy Burnitz FWS	4.00	1.20
160 Sean Burroughs FWS	4.00	1.20
161 Phil Nevin FWS	4.00	1.20
162 Scott Rolen FWS	6.00	1.80
163 Brian Giles FWS	4.00	1.20
164 Alex Rodriguez FWS	10.00	3.00
165 Ivan Rodriguez FWS	6.00	1.80
166 Juan Gonzalez FWS	4.00	1.20
167 Rafael Palmeiro FWS	4.00	1.20
168 Nomar Garciaparra FWS	10.00	3.00
169 Pedro Martinez FWS	6.00	1.80
170 Ken Griffey Jr. FWS	10.00	3.00
171 Adam Dunn FWS	4.00	1.20
172 Todd Helton FWS	4.00	1.20
173 Mike Sweeney FWS	4.00	1.20
174 Carlos Beltran FWS	4.00	1.20
175 Dmitri Young FWS	4.00	1.20
176 Doug Mientkiewicz FWS	4.00	1.20
177 Torii Hunter FWS	4.00	1.20
178 Frank Thomas FWS	6.00	1.80
179 Magglio Ordonez FWS	4.00	1.20
180 Jason Giambi FWS	4.00	1.20

2002 Upper Deck World Series Heroes Classic Match-Ups Memorabilia

Issued at a stated rate of one in 24, these cards feature two player along with a piece of memorabilia from the player listed first in our checklist. A few cards were produced in lesser quantity and we have notated tha information next to their name in our checklist.

	Nm-Mt	Ex-Mt
MU Mike Piazza Jersey / Roger Clemens	15.00	4.50
MUa Andy Pettitte Pants / Mike Piazza	15.00	4.50
MUb Al Leiter Jersey / Derek Jeter	10.00	3.00
MUc Robin Ventura Jersey / Roger Clemens	10.00	3.00
MUd Edgardo Alfonzo Jersey / Mariano Rivera	10.00	3.00
MUe John Franco Jersey / Derek Jeter	10.00	3.00
MU1 Mariano Rivera Jersey / Luis Gonzalez	15.00	4.50
MU1a Paul O'Neill Pants / Curt Schilling	15.00	4.50
MU1b Bernie Williams / Randy Johnson	10.00	3.00
MU1c David Justice Jersey / Curt Schilling	10.00	3.00
MU1d Randy Johnson Jersey / Bernie Williams	15.00	4.50
MU1e Curt Schilling Jersey / Tino Martinez	10.00	3.00
MU1f Roger Clemens Jersey / Luis Gonzalez	15.00	4.50
MU1g Paul O'Neill Pants / Byung-Hyun Kim	15.00	4.50
MU1h Luis Gonzalez Jersey / Mariano Rivera SP/97	15.00	4.50
MU3 Honus Wagner Pants / Cy Young	100.00	30.00
MU9 Ty Cobb Pants / Honus Wagner SP	120.00	36.00
MU30 Jimmie Foxx Pants / Frankie Frisch	50.00	15.00
MU36 Joe DiMaggio Pants / Mel Ott SP	100.00	30.00
MU49 Duke Snider Jersey / Joe DiMaggio	25.00	7.50
MU53 Jackie Robinson Pants / Billy Martin	50.00	15.00
MU55 Mickey Mantle Pants / Jackie Robinson	150.00	45.00
MU56 Don Larsen Pants / Duke Snider	25.00	7.50
MU56a Don Larsen Pants / Jackie Robinson	25.00	7.50
MU57 Eddie Mathews Jersey / Yogi Berra	25.00	7.50
MU58 Yogi Berra Jersey / Eddie Mathews	25.00	7.50
MU62 Roger Maris Pants / Juan Marichal	60.00	18.00
MU63 Sandy Koufax Jersey / Mickey Mantle	100.00	30.00
MU66 Don Drysdale Jersey / Brooks Robinson SP	50.00	15.00
MU69 Nolan Ryan Jersey / Brooks Robinson	50.00	15.00
MU72 Joe Morgan Jersey / Catfish Hunter	10.00	3.00
MU72a Rollie Fingers Jersey / Johnny Bench	10.00	3.00
MU73 Tom Seaver Pants / Catfish Hunter	15.00	4.50
MU74 Catfish Hunter Jersey / Steve Garvey	15.00	4.50
MU74a Davey Lopes Jersey / Catfish Hunter	10.00	3.00
MU76 Ken Griffey Sr. Jersey / Thurman Munson	10.00	3.00
MU76a Thurman Munson Pants / Johnny Bench	25.00	7.50
MU78 Thurman Munson Pants / Steve Garvey	25.00	7.50
MU78a Bill Russell Jersey / Thurman Munson	10.00	3.00
MU81 Steve Garvey Jersey / Dave Winfield	10.00	3.00
MU82 Robin Yount Jersey / Ozzie Smith	15.00	4.50
MU83 Cal Ripken Pants / Joe Morgan	30.00	9.00
MU84 Jack Morris Jersey / Tony Gwynn	10.00	3.00
MU86 Jesse Orosco Jersey / Roger Clemens	10.00	3.00
MU87 Ozzie Smith Jersey / Kirby Puckett	15.00	4.50
MU88 Mark McGwire Jersey / Kirk Gibson SP	80.00	24.00
MU90 Barry Larkin Jersey / Mark McGwire SP	20.00	6.00
MU91 Tom Glavine Jersey / Kirby Puckett	15.00	4.50
MU93 Joe Carter Jersey / Curt Schilling	10.00	3.00
MU95 Dennis Martinez Jersey / David Justice	10.00	3.00
MU95a Kenny Lofton Jersey / John Smoltz	15.00	4.50
MU96 Andruw Jones Jersey / Andy Pettitte	10.00	3.00
MU96a Tim Raines Pants / Tom Glavine	10.00	3.00
MU96b Kenny Rogers Jersey / Chipper Jones	10.00	3.00
MU97 Jim Thome Jersey / Kevin Brown	15.00	4.50
MU98 Tony Gwynn Pants / Bernie Williams	15.00	4.50
MU98a Trevor Hoffman Jersey / Bernie Williams SP	15.00	4.50
MU99 Jorge Posada Jersey / Greg Maddux	15.00	4.50
MU99a Greg Maddux Jersey / Derek Jeter	15.00	4.50
MU99b Paul O'Neill Pants / John Smoltz	15.00	4.50
MU99c Chipper Jones Jersey / Mariano Rivera	15.00	4.50

2002 Upper Deck World Series Heroes Patch Collection

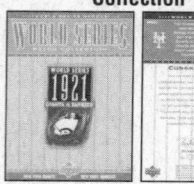

Inserted one per jumbo pack, these 98 "oversized" cards feature patches from each of the previously played World Series. These cards were issued to a stated print run of 298 sets. Exchange cards for a randomly selected patch were seeded into retail packs at a rate of 1:24. The deadline for this redemption was May 17th, 2005.

	Nm-Mt	Ex-Mt
COMMON PATCH	20.00	6.00
WS3 1903 World Series	25.00	7.50
WS12 1912 World Series	25.00	7.50
WS18 1918 World Series	25.00	7.50
WS19 1919 World Series	30.00	9.00
WS27 1927 World Series	30.00	9.00
WS32 1932 World Series	25.00	7.50
WS34 1934 World Series	25.00	7.50
WS55 1955 World Series	40.00	12.00
WS56 1956 World Series	25.00	7.50
WS60 1960 World Series	25.00	7.50
WS61 1961 World Series	40.00	12.00
WS69 1969 World Series	40.00	12.00
WS75 1975 World Series	30.00	9.00
WS77 1977 World Series	25.00	7.50
WS88 1988 World Series	25.00	7.50
WS96 1996 World Series	25.00	7.50
WS2000 2000 World Series	25.00	7.50
NNO Random Patch EXCH	20.00	6.00

2002 Upper Deck World Series Heroes Patch Collection Signatures

Inserted at a stated rate of one in 24 jumbo packs, these 16 cards feature player's signatures on a Patch Card.

	Nm-Mt	Ex-Mt
WS55 Duke Snider	120.00	36.00
WS56 Don Larsen	60.00	18.00
WS65 Sandy Koufax	250.00	75.00
WS69 Nolan Ryan	200.00	60.00
WS70 Brooks Robinson	60.00	18.00
WS73 Tom Seaver	60.00	18.00
WS74 Rollie Fingers	40.00	12.00
WS75 Carlton Fisk	120.00	36.00
WS76 Joe Morgan	40.00	12.00
WS81 Steve Garvey	60.00	18.00
WS82 Ozzie Smith	100.00	30.00
WS83 Cal Ripken	250.00	75.00
WS89 Mark McGwire	300.00	90.00
WS91 Kirby Puckett	80.00	24.00
WS93 Joe Carter	40.00	12.00
WS99 Roger Clemens	100.00	30.00

2000 Upper Deck Yankees Legends

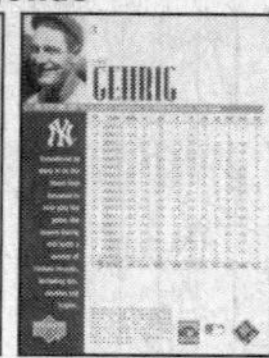

The 2000 Upper Deck Yankee Legends product was released in October, 2000. The product featured a 90-card base set. Please note that a Mickey Mantle promo was issued to dealers and members of the hobby media prior to the release of the product. Each pack contained five cards, and carried a suggested retail price of $2.99. Also, a selection of A Piece of History 3000 Club Dave Winfield memorabilia cards were randomly seeded into packs. 350 bat cards, 350 jersey cards, 100 hand-numbered combination bat-jersey cards and thrity-one autographed, hand-numbered, combination bat-jersey cards were produced. Pricing for these memorabilia cards can be referenced under 2000 Upper Deck A Piece of History 3000 Club.

	Nm-Mt	Ex-Mt
COMPLETE SET (90)	25.00	7.50
1 Babe Ruth	3.00	.90
2 Mickey Mantle	4.00	1.20
3 Lou Gehrig	2.00	.60
4 Joe DiMaggio	2.00	.60
5 Yogi Berra	1.00	.30
6 Don Mattingly	2.50	.75
7 Reggie Jackson	.60	.18
8 Dave Winfield	.40	.12
9 Bill Skowron	.40	.12
10 Willie Randolph	.40	.12
11 Phil Rizzuto	1.00	.30
12 Tony Kubek	.60	.18
13 Thurman Munson	1.00	.30
14 Roger Maris	1.00	.30
15 Billy Martin	1.00	.30
16 Elston Howard	.60	.18
17 Graig Nettles	.40	.12
18 Whitey Ford	.60	.18
19 Earle Combs	.40	.12
20 Tony Lazzeri	.40	.12
21 Bob Meusel	.40	.12
22 Joe Gordon	.40	.12
23 Jerry Coleman	.40	.12
24 Joe Torre	1.00	.30
25 Bucky Dent	.40	.12
26 Don Larsen	.40	.12
27 Bobby Richardson	.40	.12
28 Ron Guidry	.40	.12
29 Bobby Murcer	.40	.12
30 Tommy Henrich	.40	.12
31 Hank Bauer	.40	.12
32 Joe Pepitone	.40	.12
33 Clete Boyer	.40	.12
34 Chris Chambliss	.40	.12
35 Tommy John	.40	.12
36 Goose Gossage	.40	.12
37 Red Ruffing	.40	.12
38 Charlie Keller	.40	.12
39 Billy Gardner	.40	.12
40 Hector Lopez	.40	.12
41 Cliff Johnson	.40	.12
42 Oscar Gamble	.40	.12
43 Allie Reynolds	.40	.12
44 Mickey Rivers	.40	.12
45 Bill Dickey	.60	.18
46 Dave Righetti	.40	.12
47 Mel Stottlemyre	.40	.12
48 Waite Hoyt	.40	.12
49 Lefty Gomez	.60	.18
50 Wade Boggs	.60	.18
51 Billy Martin MN	.60	.18
52 Babe Ruth MN	1.50	.45
53 Lou Gehrig MN	1.00	.30
54 Joe DiMaggio MN	1.00	.30
55 Mickey Mantle MN	2.00	.60
56 Yogi Berra MN	.60	.18
57 Bill Dickey MN	.40	.12
58 Roger Maris MN	.60	.18
59 Phil Rizzuto MN	.60	.18
60 Thurman Munson MN	.60	.18
61 Whitey Ford MN	.40	.12
62 Don Mattingly MN	1.25	.35
63 Elston Howard MN	.40	.12
64 Casey Stengel MN	.60	.18
65 Reggie Jackson MN	.40	.12
66 Babe Ruth '23 TCY	1.50	.45
67 Lou Gehrig '27 TCY	1.00	.30
68 Tony Lazzeri '28 TCY	.40	.12
69 Babe Ruth '32 TCY	1.50	.45
70 Lou Gehrig '36 TCY	1.00	.30
71 Lefty Gomez '37 TCY	.60	.18
72 Bill Dickey '38 TCY	.40	.12
73 T.Henrich '39 TCY	.40	.12
74 Joe DiMaggio '41 TCY	1.00	.30
75 Spud Chandler '43 TCY	.40	.12
76 T.Henrich '47 TCY	.40	.12
77 Phil Rizzuto '49 TCY	.60	.18
78 Whitey Ford '50 TCY	.60	.18
79 Yogi Berra '51 TCY	.60	.18
80 Casey Stengel '52 TCY	.60	.18
81 Billy Martin '53 TCY	.60	.18
82 Don Larsen '56 TCY	.40	.12
83 Elston Howard '58 TCY	.60	.18
84 Roger Maris '61 TCY	.60	.18
85 Mickey Mantle '62 TCY	2.00	.60
86 R.Jackson '77 TCY	.40	.12
87 Bucky Dent '78 TCY	.40	.12
88 Wade Boggs '96 TCY	.40	.12
89 Joe Torre '98 TCY	.60	.18
90 Joe Torre '99 TCY	.60	.18
NNO M.Mantle Promo	3.00	.90

2000 Upper Deck Yankees Legends DiMaggio Memorabilia

Randomly inserted into packs, this three-card set features game-used memorabilia cards from Yankee great Joe DiMaggio. Cards in the set include game-used bat, bat-cut signature, and a bat card numbered to 56. Card backs carry a "YLG" prefix.

	Nm-Mt	Ex-Mt
BAT-AUTO CUT PRICING NOT AVAILABLE		
GOLD BAT PRINT RUN 56 #'d CARDS		
YLBJD Joe DiMaggio Bat	150.00	45.00
YLCJD1 Joe DiMaggio Bat-Cut AU/5		
YLGJD Joe DiMaggio Gold Bat/56	250.00	75.00

2000 Upper Deck Yankees Legends Golden Years

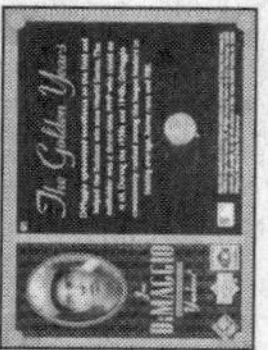

Randomly inserted into packs at one in 11, this 10-card insert set features players that played for the Yankees during their golden years. Card backs carry a "GY" prefix.

	Nm-Mt	Ex-Mt
COMPLETE SET (10)	25.00	7.50
GY1 Joe DiMaggio	5.00	1.50
GY2 Phil Rizzuto	2.50	.75
GY3 Yogi Berra	2.50	.75
GY4 Billy Martin	2.50	.75
GY5 Whitey Ford	1.50	.45
GY6 Roger Maris	2.50	.75
GY7 Mickey Mantle	10.00	3.00
GY8 Elston Howard	1.50	.45
GY9 Tommy Henrich	1.00	.30
GY10 Joe Gordon	1.00	.30

2000 Upper Deck Yankees Legends Legendary Lumber

Randomly inserted into packs at one in 23, this 30-card insert set features game-used bat cards from Yankee greats. Card backs carry a "LL" suffix. Please note that the hologram on the back of these cards is silver and the Bat Chip features a wood "NY".

	Nm-Mt	Ex-Mt
BD-LL Bucky Dent	10.00	3.00
BG-LL Billy Gardner	10.00	3.00
BM-LL Bobby Murcer	40.00	12.00
BR-LL Babe Ruth	200.00	60.00
CB-LL Clete Boyer	10.00	3.00
CC-LL Chris Chambliss	10.00	3.00
CJ-LL Cliff Johnson	10.00	3.00
CK-LL Charlie Keller	10.00	3.00
DM-LL Don Mattingly	40.00	12.00
DW-LL Dave Winfield	10.00	3.00
EH-LL Elston Howard	10.00	3.00
GN-LL Graig Nettles	10.00	3.00
HB-LL Hank Bauer	10.00	3.00
HL-LL Hector Lopez	10.00	3.00
JC-LL Joe Collins	10.00	3.00
JP-LL Joe Pepitone	10.00	3.00
MM-LL Mickey Mantle	150.00	45.00
MR-LL Mickey Rivers	10.00	3.00
MS-LL Moose Skowron	10.00	3.00
OG-LL Oscar Gamble	10.00	3.00
PB-LL Paul Blair	10.00	3.00
RH-LL Ralph Houk	10.00	3.00
RJ-LL Reggie Jackson	15.00	4.50
RM-LL Roger Maris	80.00	24.00
TH-LL Tommy Henrich	10.00	3.00
TJ-LL Tommy John	10.00	3.00
TK-LL Tony Kubek	15.00	4.50
TM-LL Thurman Munson	50.00	15.00
WR-LL Willie Randolph	10.00	3.00
YB-LL Yogi Berra	25.00	7.50

2000 Upper Deck Yankees Legends Legendary Lumber Signature Cut

Randomly inserted into packs, this six card insert features cut-signatures from some of the Yankee's greatest players of all time. Card backs carry a "LC" suffix.

	Nm-Mt	Ex-Mt
BM-LC Billy Martin/1		
BR-LC Babe Ruth/3		
MM-LC Mickey Mantle/7		
RM-LC Roger Maris/9		
TM-LC Thurman Munson/15		

2000 Upper Deck Yankees Legends Legendary Pinstripes

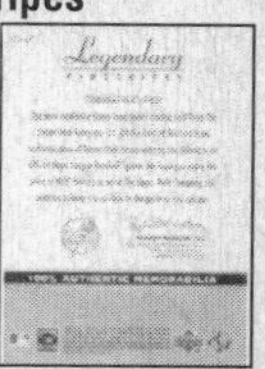

Randomly inserted into packs at one in 144, this 20-card insert set features game-used jersey cards from Yankee greats. Card backs carry a "LP" suffix.

	Nm-Mt	Ex-Mt
AR-LP Allie Reynolds	50.00	15.00
BD-LP Bucky Dent	15.00	4.50
BM-LP Billy Martin	40.00	12.00
BR-LP Bobby Richardson	15.00	4.50
DM-LP Don Mattingly	60.00	18.00
DW-LP Dave Winfield	15.00	4.50
EH-LP Elston Howard	25.00	7.50
GG-LP Goose Gossage	15.00	4.50
GM-LP Gil McDougald	15.00	4.50
HL-LP Hector Lopez	15.00	4.50
JP-LP Joe Pepitone	15.00	4.50
LG-LP Lou Gehrig Pants	300.00	90.00
MM-LP Mickey Mantle	250.00	75.00
PR-LP Phil Rizzuto	25.00	7.50
RG-LP Ron Guidry	15.00	4.50
RJ-LP Reggie Jackson	25.00	7.50
RM-LP Roger Maris	100.00	30.00
TH-LP Tommy Henrich	15.00	4.50
TM-LP Thurman Munson	80.00	24.00
WF-LP Whitey Ford	25.00	7.50

2000 Upper Deck Yankees Legends Legendary Pinstripes Autograph

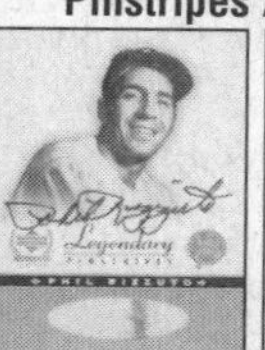

Randomly inserted into packs at one in 287, this 10-card insert set features autographed game-used jersey cards from Yankee greats. Card backs carry an "A" suffix. Please note that Ron Guidry packed out as exchange card with a deadline to redeem no later than July 18th, 2001.

	Nm-Mt	Ex-Mt
BD-A Bucky Dent	40.00	12.00
DM-A Don Mattingly	100.00	30.00
DW-A Dave Winfield	50.00	15.00
GG-A Goose Gossage	40.00	12.00
GM-A Gil McDougald	40.00	12.00
JP-A Joe Pepitone	40.00	12.00
PR-A Phil Rizzuto	50.00	15.00
RG-A Ron Guidry	50.00	15.00
TH-A Tommy Henrich	40.00	12.00
WF-A Whitey Ford	50.00	15.00

2000 Upper Deck Yankees Legends Monument Park

Randomly inserted into packs at one in 23, this six-card set features all-time Yankee greats. Card backs carry a "MP" suffix.

	Nm-Mt	Ex-Mt
COMPLETE SET (6)	25.00	7.50
MP1 Lou Gehrig	6.00	1.80
MP2 Babe Ruth	10.00	3.00
MP3 Mickey Mantle	12.00	3.60
MP4 Joe DiMaggio	6.00	1.80
MP5 Thurman Munson	3.00	.90
MP6 Elston Howard	2.00	.60

2000 Upper Deck Yankees Legends Murderer's Row

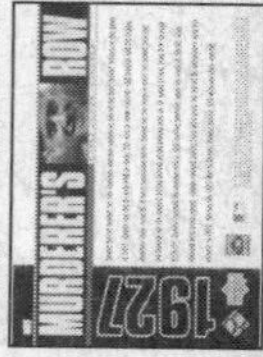

Randomly inserted into packs at one in 11, this 10-card insert set features some of the most dominating New York Yankee players of all-time. Card backs carry a "MR" suffix.

	Nm-Mt	Ex-Mt
COMPLETE SET (10)	20.00	6.00
MR1 Tony Lazzeri	1.00	.30

MR2 Babe Ruth 8.00 2.40
MR3 Bob Meusel 1.00 .30
MR4 Lou Gehrig 5.00 1.50
MR5 Joe Dugan 1.00 .30
MR6 Bill Dickey 1.50 .45
MR7 Waite Hoyt 1.00 .30
MR8 Red Ruffing 1.00 .30
MR9 Earle Combs 1.00 .30
MR10 Lefty Gomez 1.50 .45

2000 Upper Deck Yankees Legends New Dynasty

Randomly inserted into packs at one in 11, this 10-card insert set features New York greats from the last twenty years. Card backs carry a "ND" suffix.

Nm-Mt Ex-Mt
COMPLETE SET (10) 15.00 4.50
ND1 Reggie Jackson 1.50 .45
ND2 Graig Nettles 1.00 .30
ND3 Don Mattingly 6.00 1.80
ND4 Goose Gossage 1.00 .30
ND5 Dave Winfield 1.00 .30
ND6 Chris Chambliss 1.00 .30
ND7 Thurman Munson 2.50 .75
ND8 Willie Randolph 1.00 .30
ND9 Ron Guidry 1.00 .30
ND10 Bucky Dent 1.00 .30

2000 Upper Deck Yankees Legends Pride of the Pinstripes

Randomly inserted into packs at one in 23, this six-card insert set features legendary Yankee greats. Card backs carry a "PP" suffix.

Nm-Mt Ex-Mt
COMPLETE SET (6) 25.00 7.50
PP1 Babe Ruth 10.00 3.00
PP2 Mickey Mantle 12.00 3.60
PP3 Joe DiMaggio 6.00 1.80
PP4 Lou Gehrig 6.00 1.80
PP5 Reggie Jackson 2.00 .60
PP6 Yogi Berra 3.00 .90

2000 Upper Deck Yankees Master Collection

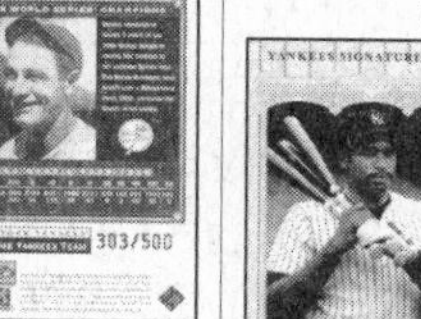

The 2000 Upper Deck Yankees Master Collection was released in early June, 2000. Each box set contains 37 cards. The box set includes a 25-card base set that is individually serial numbered to 500, an 11-card game-used bat set that includes players such a Mickey Mantle, and Babe Ruth, and a one card mystery pack that includes various memorabilia and autographed cards. Card backs carry a "NYY" prefix.

Nm-Mt Ex-Mt
COMPLETE SET (25) 500.00 150.00
NYY1 Babe Ruth 23 50.00 15.00
NYY2 Lou Gehrig 27 30.00 9.00
NYY3 Tony Lazzeri 28 10.00 3.00
NYY4 Babe Ruth 32 50.00 15.00
NYY5 Lou Gehrig 36 30.00 9.00
NYY6 Lefty Gomez 37 10.00 3.00
NYY7 Bill Dickey 38 10.00 3.00
NYY8 Bill Dickey 39 10.00 3.00
NYY9 Tommy Henrich 41 10.00 3.00
NYY10 Spud Chandler 43 10.00 3.00
NYY11 T.Henrich 47 10.00 3.00
NYY12 Phil Rizzuto 49 15.00 4.50
NYY13 Whitey Ford 50 10.00 3.00
NYY14 Yogi Berra 51 15.00 4.50
NYY15 Casey Stengel 52 10.00 3.00
NYY16 Billy Martin 53 10.00 3.00
NYY17 Don Larsen 56 10.00 3.00
NYY18 Elston Howard 58 10.00 3.00
NYY19 Roger Maris 61 15.00 4.50
NYY20 Mickey Mantle 62 60.00 18.00
NYY21 Reggie Jackson 77 10.00 3.00
NYY22 Bucky Dent 78 10.00 3.00
NYY23 Derek Jeter 96 30.00 9.00
NYY24 Derek Jeter 98 30.00 9.00
NYY25 Derek Jeter 99 30.00 9.00

2000 Upper Deck Yankees Master Collection All-Time Yankees Game Bats

One complete 11-card set of All-Time Yankees Game Bats was inserted into each sealed Yankees Master Collection box. Only 500 sets were produced and each card carries serial-numbering. This 11-card game-used bat card set features some of the greatest New York Yankee players of all time. Card backs carry an "ATY" prefix. Please note that card number eleven of Lou Gehrig is a special commemorative card that does not included a piece of game-used bat.

Nm-Mt Ex-Mt
ATY1 Babe Ruth 150.00 45.00
ATY2 Mickey Mantle 150.00 45.00
ATY3 Reggie Jackson 25.00 7.50
ATY4 Don Mattingly 80.00 24.00
ATY5 Billy Martin 25.00 7.50
ATY6 Graig Nettles 15.00 4.50
ATY7 Derek Jeter 80.00 24.00
ATY8 Yogi Berra 25.00 7.50
ATY9 Thurman Munson 80.00 24.00
ATY10 Whitey Ford 25.00 7.50
ATY11 Lou Gehrig COMM 25.00 7.50

2000 Upper Deck Yankees Master Collection Mystery Pack Inserts

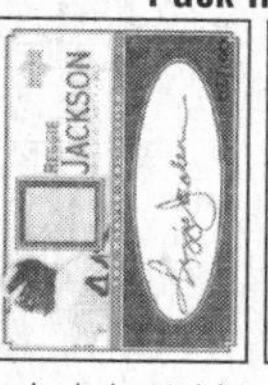

Randomly inserted into each Yankees Master Collection at one per box, this one card mystery pack includes various game-used memorabilia and autographed insert cards.

Nm-Mt Ex-Mt
BM1-2 Billy Martin Bat-Cut AU/2
BR1-3 Babe Ruth Bat-Cut AU/3
MM1-7 Mickey Mantle Bat-Cut AU/7
BRC1-3 Babe Ruth Cut AU/3
LGC1-3 Lou Gehrig Cut AU/3
TMC1-2 Thurman Munson Cut AU/2
DJ-B Derek Jeter Bat 500.00 150.00
AU/100
DJ-J Derek Jeter Jsy 500.00 150.00
AU/100
RJ-B Reggie Jackson 150.00 45.00
Bat AU/100
WF-J Whitey Ford 150.00 45.00
Bat AU/100
YB-B Yogi Berra 150.00 45.00
Bat AU/80

2003 Upper Deck Yankees Signature

This 90 card set was released in April, 2003. These cards were issued in three card packs with an $30 SRP. These packs came 10 packs to a box and eight boxes to a case. In an interesting note this set is sequenced by the first name of the player.

Nm-Mt Ex-Mt
COMPLETE SET (90) 100.00 30.00
1 Al Downing 1.00 .30
2 Al Gettel 1.00 .30
3 Art Ditmar 1.00 .30
4 Babe Ruth 15.00 4.50
5 Bill Virdon MG 1.00 .30
6 Billy Martin 3.00 .90
7 Bob Cerv 1.00 .30
8 Bob Turley 1.00 .30
9 Bobby Cox 2.00 .60
10 Bobby Richardson 2.00 .60
11 Bobby Shantz 1.00 .30
12 Bucky Dent 2.00 .60
13 Bud Metheny XRC 1.00 .30
14 Casey Stengel 3.00 .90
15 Charlie Hayes 1.00 .30
16 Charlie Silvera 1.00 .30
17 Chris Chambliss 2.00 .60
18 Danny Cater 1.00 .30
19 Dave Kingman 2.00 .60
20 Dave Righetti 2.00 .60
21 Dave Winfield 2.00 .60
22 David Cone 2.00 .60
23 Dick Tidrow 1.00 .30
24 Doc Medich 1.00 .30
25 Dock Ellis 2.00 .60
26 Don Gullett 2.00 .60
27 Don Mattingly 15.00 4.50
28 Dwight Gooden 2.00 .60
29 Eddie Robinson 1.00 .30
30 Felipe Alou 2.00 .60
31 Fred Sanford 1.00 .30
32 Fred Stanley 1.00 .30
33 Gene Michael 1.00 .30
34 Hank Bauer 2.00 .60
35 Hector Lopez 1.00 .30
36 Horace Clarke 1.00 .30
37 Jake Gibbs 1.00 .30
38 Jerry Coleman 1.00 .30
39 Jerry Lumpe 1.00 .30
40 Jim Bouton 2.00 .60
41 Jim Kaat 2.00 .60
42 Jim Mason 1.00 .30
43 Jimmy Key 2.00 .60
44 Joe DiMaggio 10.00 3.00
45 Joe Torre 5.00 1.50
46 John Montefusco 2.00 .60
47 Johnny Blanchard 1.00 .30
48 Johnny Callison 2.00 .60
49 Lew Burdette 2.00 .60
50 Johnny Kucks 1.00 .30
51 Steve Balboni 1.00 .30
52 Ken Singleton ANC 2.00 .60
53 Lee Mazzilli 2.00 .60
54 Lou Gehrig 10.00 3.00
55 Lou Piniella 2.00 .60
56 Luis Tiant 2.00 .60
57 Marius Russo XRC 1.00 .30
58 Mel Stottlemyre 2.00 .60
59 Mickey Mantle 15.00 4.50
60 Mike Pagliarulo 1.00 .30
61 Mike Torrez 1.00 .30
62 Miller Huggins MG 1.00 .30
63 Norm Siebern 1.00 .30
64 Paul O'Neill 3.00 .90
65 Phil Niekro 2.00 .60
66 Phil Rizzuto 3.00 .90
67 Ralph Branca 2.00 .60
68 Ralph Houk 2.00 .60
69 Ralph Terry 2.00 .60
70 Randy Gumpert 1.00 .30
71 Roger Maris 5.00 1.50
72 Ron Blomberg 1.00 .30
73 Ron Guidry 2.00 .60
74 Ruben Amaro 1.00 .30
75 Ryne Duren 1.00 .30
76 Sam McDowell 2.00 .60
77 Sparky Lyle 2.00 .60
78 Thurman Munson 5.00 1.50
79 Tom Sturdivant 1.00 .30
80 Tom Tresh 2.00 .60
81 Tommy Byrne 1.00 .30
82 Tommy Henrich 2.00 .60
83 Tommy John 2.00 .60
84 Tony Kubek 3.00 .90
85 Tony Lazzeri 2.00 .60
86 Virgil Trucks 1.00 .30
87 Wade Boggs 3.00 .90
88 Whitey Ford 3.00 .90
89 Willie Randolph 2.00 .60
90 Yogi Berra 5.00 1.50

2003 Upper Deck Yankees Signature Monumental Cuts

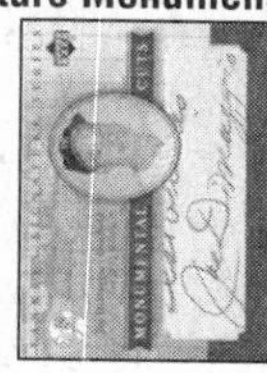

Randomly inserted into packs, these 30 combined cards feature autographs of Yankee Legends who have passed on. We have notated the print run next to the player's name in our checklist.

Nm-Mt Ex-Mt
RANDOM INSERTS IN PACKS
B/WN 1-9 COPIES OF EACH CARD
NO PRICING DUE TO SCARCITY
BM Billy Martin/9
BR Babe Ruth/1
CS Casey Stengel/3
JD Joe DiMaggio/4
LG Lou Gehrig/1
MH Miller Huggins/2
MM Mickey Mantle/1
RM Roger Maris/6
TL Tony Lazzeri/2
TM Thurman Munson/1

2003 Upper Deck Yankees Signature Pinstripe Excellence Autographs

Randomly inserted in packs, these cards feature two autographs on each card. These cards were issued to a stated print run of 125 serial numbered sets.

Nm-Mt Ex-Mt
AA Felipe Alou 80.00 24.00
Ruben Amaro
BA Hank Bauer 80.00 24.00
Felipe Alou
BP Wade Boggs 100.00 30.00
Mike Pagliarulo
BR1 Hank Bauer 100.00 30.00
Phil Rizzuto
BR2 Tommy Byrne 50.00 15.00
Marius Russo
BT Jim Bouton 80.00 24.00
Ralph Terry
CK Chris Chambliss 100.00 30.00
Dave Kingman
DC Bucky Dent 80.00 24.00
Chris Chambliss
DR Bucky Dent 100.00 30.00
Willie Randolph
DS Ryne Duren 50.00 15.00
Tom Sturdivant
FB Whitey Ford 200.00 60.00
Yogi Berra
GB Jake Gibbs 50.00 15.00
Johnny Blanchard
GM Ron Guidry 100.00 30.00
John Montefusco
GR Ron Guidry 100.00 30.00
Willie Randolph
JK Tommy John 80.00 24.00
Jim Kaat
LG Sparky Lyle 100.00 30.00
Ron Guidry
LM Jerry Lumpe 50.00 15.00
Jim Mason
MC John Montefusco 80.00 24.00
Chris Chambliss
MK Gene Michael 100.00 30.00
Tony Kubek
ML Sam McDowell 80.00 24.00
Sparky Lyle
MR Don Mattingly 200.00 60.00
Dave Righetti
NT Phil Niekro 100.00 30.00
Luis Tiant
RB Bobby Richardson 100.00 30.00
Hank Bauer
RC Bobby Richardson 100.00 30.00
Jerry Coleman
SC Ken Singleton 80.00 24.00
Jerry Coleman
ST Tom Sturdivant 50.00 15.00
Bob Turley
TK Luis Tiant 80.00 24.00
Jim Kaat
TM Mike Torrez 80.00 24.00
Lee Mazzilli

2003 Upper Deck Yankees Signature Pride of New York Autographs

Inserted at a stated rate of one per pack, these 88 cards feature authentic autographs from either retired Yankee players or people associated with the franchise in some way. This set included the first certified autographed sports cards for figures such as Yankee GM Brian Cashman, actors John Goodman and Jason Alexander. Bud Metheny was supposed to sign cards for this product but he passed away before he could sign his cards. In addition a few players did not return their cards in time for inclusion in this product and we have notated that information with an EXCH in our checklist. Collectors could redeem those cards until March 27, 2006. David Cone signed some of his cards in time for inclusion and others were available as an exchange card. Upper Deck announced some shorter print runs and we have put that stated print run information next to the player's name in our checklist.

Nm-Mt Ex-Mt
EXCH * = PART LIVE/PART REDEMPTION
AD Al Downing 10.00 3.00
AG Al Gettel 10.00 3.00
BD Brian Doyle 10.00 3.00
BL Johnny Blanchard 10.00 3.00
BR Bobby Richardson 15.00 4.50
BS Bobby Shantz 10.00 3.00
BT Bob Turley 10.00 3.00
BV Bill Virdon MG 10.00 3.00
CA1 Johnny Callison 10.00 3.00
CA2 Brian Cashman/100 EX 400.00 120.00
CC Chris Chambliss 10.00 3.00
CE Bob Cerv 10.00 3.00
CH Charlie Hayes 10.00 3.00
CO David Cone EXCH * 25.00 7.50
CS Charlie Silvera 10.00 3.00
CX Bobby Cox 10.00 3.00
DC Danny Cater 10.00 3.00
DE Bucky Dent 10.00 3.00
DG Don Gullett 10.00 3.00
DI Art Ditmar 10.00 3.00
DK Dave Kingman 10.00 3.00
DM Doc Medich 10.00 3.00
DR Dave Righetti 10.00 3.00
DT Dick Tidrow 10.00 3.00
DW Dave Winfield/350 60.00 18.00
DZ Don Zimmer 60.00 18.00
EL Dock Ellis 10.00 3.00
ER Eddie Robinson 10.00 3.00
FA Felipe Alou 10.00 3.00
FS Fred Sanford 10.00 3.00
GM Gene Michael 10.00 3.00
GO Dwight Gooden EXCH 10.00 3.00
HB Hank Bauer 10.00 3.00
HC Horace Clarke 10.00 3.00
HL Hector Lopez 10.00 3.00
HR Hal Reniff 10.00 3.00
JA Jason Alexander/50 800.00 240.00
JB Jim Bouton 10.00 3.00
JC Jerry Coleman 10.00 3.00
JG1 Jake Gibbs 10.00 3.00
JG2 John Goodman/100 EX 500.00 150.00
JK Jim Kaat 10.00 3.00
JL Jerry Lumpe 10.00 3.00
JM Jim Mason 10.00 3.00
JT Joe Torre 40.00 12.00
JW Jim Wynn 10.00 3.00
KE Jimmy Key 15.00 4.50
KS Ken Singleton ANC 10.00 3.00
KU Johnny Kucks 10.00 3.00
LB Lew Burdette 10.00 3.00
LM Lee Mazzilli 10.00 3.00
LP Lou Piniella/542 15.00 4.50
LT Luis Tiant 10.00 3.00
MA Don Mattingly 100.00 30.00
MO John Montefusco 10.00 3.00
MP Mike Pagliarulo 10.00 3.00
MR Marius Russo 10.00 3.00
MS Mel Stottlemyre 10.00 3.00
MT Mike Torrez 10.00 3.00
NS Norm Siebern 10.00 3.00
PN Phil Niekro 25.00 7.50
PO Paul O'Neill/500 25.00 7.50
PR Phil Rizzuto 50.00 15.00
RA Ruben Amaro 10.00 3.00
RB1 Ron Blomberg 10.00 3.00
RB2 Ralph Branca 10.00 3.00
RD Ryne Duren 10.00 3.00
RG1 Ron Guidry 25.00 7.50
RG2 Randy Gumpert 10.00 3.00
RH Ralph Houk 10.00 3.00
RT Ralph Terry 10.00 3.00
SB Steve Balboni 10.00 3.00
SL Sparky Lyle 10.00 3.00
SM Sam McDowell 10.00 3.00
ST Fred Stanley 10.00 3.00
TB Tommy Byrne 10.00 3.00
TC Tom Carroll 10.00 3.00
TH Tommy Henrich 40.00 12.00
TJ Tommy John 10.00 3.00
TK Tony Kubek 40.00 12.00
TS Tom Sturdivant 10.00 3.00
TT Tom Tresh 15.00 4.50
VT Virgil Trucks 10.00 3.00
WB Wade Boggs 50.00 15.00
WF Whitey Ford 80.00 24.00
WR Willie Randolph/283 15.00 4.50
YB Yogi Berra EXCH 80.00 24.00

2003 Upper Deck Yankees Signature Yankees Forever Autographs

Randomly inserted in packs, these cards feature three Yankee players (usually with something in common) all signing the same card. These cards were issued to a stated print run of 50 serial numbered sets. A few cards were issued as exchange cards and those cards could be redeemed until March 27, 2006.

Nm-Mt Ex-Mt
RANDOM INSERTS IN PACKS
STATED PRINT RUN 50 SERIAL #'d SETS
EXCHANGE DEADLINE 03/27/06
ALB Felipe Alou 150.00 45.00
Hector Lopez
Hank Bauer
AOM Felipe Alou 200.00 60.00
Paul O'Neill
Lee Mazzilli
BSB Yogi Berra 250.00 75.00
Bobby Shantz
Hank Bauer
DFB Al Downing 300.00 90.00
Whitey Ford
Yogi Berra
DRC Bucky Dent 150.00 45.00
Willie Randolph
Chris Chambliss
EMG Dock Ellis 150.00 45.00
Doc Medich
Don Gullett
FKB Whitey Ford 200.00 60.00
Johnny Kucks
Jim Bouton
GCK Dwight Gooden 200.00 60.00
David Cone
Jimmy Key EXCH
GRJ Ron Guidry 200.00 60.00
Dave Righetti
Tommy John EXCH
HMC Ralph Houk 150.00 45.00
Gene Michael
Bobby Cox
HRB Tommy Henrich 200.00 60.00
Phil Rizzuto
Ralph Branca
JKL Tommy John 150.00 45.00
Jim Kaat
Sparky Lyle
KCC Dave Kingman 150.00 45.00
Chris Chambliss
Danny Cater
KGT Jim Kaat 150.00 45.00
Don Gullet
Mike Torrez
KJB Jim Kaat 150.00 45.00
Tommy John
Jim Bouton
MTT John Montefusco 150.00 45.00
Mike Torrez
Dick Tidrow EXCH
OBK Paul O'Neill 200.00 60.00
Wade Boggs
Jimmy Key
PTV Lou Piniella 200.00 60.00
Joe Torre
Bill Virdon
RBC Phil Rizzuto 300.00 90.00
Yogi Berra
Jerry Coleman
RKD Phil Rizzuto 200.00 60.00
Tony Kubek
Bucky Dent
RRC Bobby Richardson 200.00 60.00
Willie Randolph
Jerry Coleman
RSB Marius Russo 150.00 45.00
Tom Sturdivant
Tommy Byrne
SSB Fred Stanley 150.00 45.00
Charlie Silvera
Johnny Blanchard
STE Mel Stottlemyre 150.00 45.00
Luis Tiant
Dock Ellis
TCO Joe Torre 200.00 60.00
David Cone
Paul O'Neill EXCH
TLN Luis Tiant 150.00 45.00
Sparky Lyle
Phil Niekro
TMT Luis Tiant 150.00 45.00
Sam McDowell
Ralph Terry
WHM Dave Winfield 200.00 60.00
Tommy Henrich
Lee Mazzilli
WMG Dave Winfield 400.00 120.00
Don Mattingly
Ron Guidry EXCH
WPC Dave Winfield 150.00 45.00
Lou Piniella
Chris Chambliss EXCH

Index

Acknowledgements

Each year we refine the process of developing the most accurate and up-to-date information for this book. We believe this year's Price Guide is our best yet. Thanks again to all the contributors nationwide (listed below) as well as our staff here in Dallas.

Those who have worked closely with us on this and many other books have again proven themselves invaluable: Frank and Vivian Barning, Pat Blandford, Levi Bleam and Jim Fleck (707 Sportscards), T. Scott Brandon, Peter Brennan, Ray Bright, Card Collectors Co., Dwight Chapin, Theo Chen, Barry Colla, Mike Cramer, Dick DeCourcey, Bill and Diane Dodge, Brett Domue, Dan Even, David Festberg, Donruss/Playoff (Ben Ecklar, Steven Judd, David Porter and Len Shelton), Fleer/SkyBox, Steve Freedman, Gervise Ford, Larry and Jeff Fritsch, Tony Galovich, Dick Gilkeson, Steve Gold (AU Sports), Bill Goodwin (St. Louis Baseball Cards), Mike and Howard Gordon, George Grauer, Steve Green (STB Sports), Greg's Cards, Bill Henderson, Jerry and Etta Hersh, Mike Hersh, Neil Hoppenworth, Mike Jaspersen, Jay and Mary Kasper, Frank and Rose Katen, Jerry Katz, Pete Kennedy, David Kohler (SportsCards Plus), Tom Layberger, Tom Leon, Lew Lipset, Mike Livingston, Mark Macrae, Bill Madden, Bill Mastro, Michael McDonald, Mid-Atlantic Sports Cards (Bill Bossert), Gary Mills, Ernie Montella, Brian Morris, Mike Mosier (Columbia City Collectibles Co.), B.A. Murry, Ralph Nozaki, Oldies and Goodies (Nigel Spill), Jack Pollard, Jeff Prillaman, Pat Quinn, Jerald Reichstein (Fabulous Cardboard), Gavin Riley, Clifton Rouse, John Rumierz, Kevin Savage (Sports Gallery), Gary Sawatski, Mike Schechter, Bill and Darlene Shafer, Barry Sloate, John E. Spalding, Phil Spector, Lee Temanson, Topps (Sy Berger and Clay Luraschi), Ed Twombly, Upper Deck (Steve Ryan), Wayne Varner, Rob Veres, (Burbank Sportscards), Bill Vizas, Bill Wesslund (Portland Sports Card Co.), Kit Young and Bob Ivanjack (Kit Young Cards), Rick Young, Ted Zanidakis, Robert Zanze (Z-Cards and Sports), Bill Zimpleman and Dean Zindler. Finally we give a special acknowledgment to the late Dennis W. Eckes, "Mr. Sport Americana." The success of the Beckett Price Guides has always been the result of a team effort.

It is very difficult to be "accurate" -- one can only do one's best. But this job is especially difficult since we're shooting at a moving target: Prices are fluctuating all the time. Having several full-time pricing experts has definitely proven to be better than just one, and we thank all of them for working together to provide you, our readers, with the most accurate prices possible.

Many people have provided price input, illustrative material, checklist verifications, errata, and/or background information. We should like to individually thank AbD Cards (Dale Wesolewski), Action Card Sales, Jerry Adamic, Johnny and Sandy Adams, Mehdi Ahlei, Alex's MVP Cards & Comics, Doug Allen (Round Tripper Sportscards), Will Allison, Scott Alpaugh, Dennis Anderson, Ed Anderson, Ellis Anmuth, Alan Applegate, Ric Apter, Randy Archer, Burl Armstrong, Ara Arzoumanian, Carlos Ayala, B and J Sportscards, Jeremy Bachman, Ball Four Cards (Frank and Steve Pemper), Bob Bartosz, Bubba Bennett, Carl Berg, Mike Berkus, David Berman, Beulah Sports (Jeff Blatt), B.J. Sportscollectables, David Boedicker (The Wild Pitch Inc.), Bob Boffa, Louis Bollman, Tim Bond (Tim's Cards & Comics),Andrew Bosarge,Terry Boyd, Dan Brandenberry, Jeff Breitenfield, John Brigandi, John Broggi, D. Bruce Brown, Virgil Burns, Greg Bussineau, David Byer, California Card Co., Capital Cards, Danny Cariseo, Carl Carlson (C.T.S.), Jim Carr, Ira Cetron, Ric Chandgie, Ray Cherry, Bigg Wayne Christian, Michael and Abe Citron, Dr. Jeffrey Clair, Mike Clark, Don Coe, Michael Cohen, Jay Conti, Lou Costanzo (Champion Sports), Mike Coyne, Tony Craig (T.C. Card Co.), Solomon Cramer, Allen Custer, Dave Dame, Scott Dantio, Art Day II, Dee's Baseball Cards (Dee Robinson), Joe Delgrippo, Mike DeLuca, Ken Dinerman (California Cruizers), Cliff Dolgins, Discount Dorothy, Richard Dolloff (Dolloff Coin Center), Joe Donato, Jerry Dong, Pat Dorsey, Double Play Baseball Cards, Joe Drelich, Richard Duglin (Baseball Cards-N-More), The Dugout, Ken Edick (Home Plate of Utah), Brad Englehardt, Terry Falkner, Linda Ferrigno and Mark Mezzardi, Jay Finglass, Bob Flitter, Fremont Fong, Perry Fong, Paul Franzetti, Ron Frasier, Tom Freeman, Bill Fusaro, Chris Gala, Richard Galasso, Georgetown Card Exchange, David Giove, Dick Goddard, Brian Goldner, Jeff Goldstein, Ron Gomez, Rich Gove, Mike Grimm, Jay and Jan Grigsby, Bob Grissett, Neil Gubitz (What-A-Card), Gerry Guenther, Hall's Nostalgia, Gregg Hara, Todd Harrell, Steve Hart, Floyd Haynes (H and H Baseball Cards), Kevin Heffner, Joel Hellman, Hit and Run Cards (Jon, David, and Kirk Peterson), Johnny Hustle Card Co., John Inouye, Marshall Jackson, Mike Jardina, Paul Jastrzembski, Jeff's Sports Cards, Donn Jennings Cards, George Johnson, Craig Jones, Chuck and Mary Juliana, Robert Just, Nick Kardoulias, Scott Kashner, Kris Keppler, Kevin's Kards, John Klassnik, Steve Kluback, Don Knutsen, Steven Koenigsberg, Mike Kohlhas, Gregg Kohn, Bob & Bryan Kornfield, Matthew Lancaster (MC's Card and Hobby), Howard Lau, Richard S. Lawrence, William Lawrence, Brent Lee, Morley Leeking, Irv Lerner, Larry and Sally Levine, Larry Loeschen (A and J Sportscards), Neil Lopez, Kendall Loyd (Orlando Sportscards South), Steve Lowe, Jim Macie, Peter Maltin, Paul Marchant, Brian Marcy, Scott Martinez, Dr. William McAvoy, McDag Productions Inc., Bob McDonald, Steve McHenry, Tony McLaughlin, Mendal Mearkle, Ken Melanson, Blake Meyer (Lone Star Sportscards), Tim Meyer, Joe Michalowicz, Cary S. Miller, Wayne Miller, Dick Millerd, Frank Mineo, Mitchell's Baseball Cards, John Morales, William Munn, Mark Murphy, Robert Nappe, National Sportscard Exchange, Roger Neufeldt, Steve Novella, Bud Obermeyer, John O'Hara, Glenn Olson, Scott Olson, Ron Oser, Luther Owen, Earle Parrish, Clay Pasternack, Mickey Payne, Michael Perrotta, Tom Pfirrmann, Don Phlong, Loran Pulver, Bob Ragonese, Bryan Rappaport, Don and Tom Ras, Robert M. Ray, Phil Regli, Carson Ritchey, Craig Roehrig, Mike Sablow, Terry Sack, Thomas Salem, Jennifer Salems, Barry Sanders, Tony Scarpa, John Schad, Dave Schau (Baseball Cards), Kent Sessions, Masa Shinohara, Eddie Silard, Mike Slepcevic, Sam Sliheet, Art Smith, Cary Smith, Lynn and Todd Solt, Sports Card Fan-Attic, The Sport Hobbyist, Norm Stapleton, Lisa Stellato, Andy Stoltz, Bill Stone, Tim Strandberg (East Texas Sports Cards), Ted Straka, Edward Strauss, Strike Three, Richard Strobino, Superior Sport Card, Dr. Richard Swales, George Tahinos, Ian Taylor, Brent Thornton, Jim and Sally Thurtell, Bud Tompkins (Minnesota Connection), Philip J. Tremont, Ralph Triplette, Umpire's Choice Inc., Eric Unglaub, Hoyt Vanderpool, Tom Wall, Gary A. Walter, Brian and Mike Wentz, Richard West, Mike Wheat, Louise and Richard Wiercinski, Rich Wojtasick, Jay Wolt (Cavalcade of Sports), Eric Wu, Joe Yanello, Wes Young, Tom Zocco, Mark Zubrensky and Tim Zwick.

Every year we make active solicitations for expert input. We are particularly appreciative of help (however extensive or cursory) provided for this volume. We receive many inquiries, comments and questions regarding material within this book. In fact, each and every one is read and digested. Time constraints, however, prevent us from personally replying. But keep sharing your knowledge. Your letters, e-mails and other input are part of the "big picture" of hobby information we can pass along to readers in our books and magazines. Even though we cannot respond to each letter or email, you are making significant contributions to the hobby through your interest and comments.

The effort to continually refine and improve this book also involves a growing number of people and types of expertise on our home team.

Our baseball analysts played a major part in compiling this year's book, traveling thousands of miles during the past year to attend sports card shows and visit card shops around the United States and Canada. The Beckett baseball specialists are Brian Fleischer, Gabe Haro, Rich Klein, and Grant Sandground (Senior Price Guide Editor). Their pricing analysis and careful proofreading were key contributions to the accuracy of this annual.

Grant Sandground's coordination and reconciling of prices as Beckett Baseball Card Monthly Price Guide Editor helped immeasurably. Rich Klein, as research analyst, contributed detailed pricing analysis and hours of proofing. t. They were ably assisted by Beverly Melian (who entered a record number of sets into our data base this year).

The price gathering and analytical talents of this fine group of hobbyists have helped make our Beckett team stronger, while making this guide and its companion monthly Price Guide more widely recognized as the hobby's most reliable and relied upon sources of pricing information.

The Beckett Interactive Department, led by Andrew Taylor's efforts played a crucial role in technology. They spent countless hours programming, testing, and implementing it to simplify the handling of thousands of prices that must be checked and updated for each edition.

In the Production Department, Gean Paul Figari responsible for the typesetting and for the card photos you see throughout the book. He helps to make this volume look as attractive as it is.